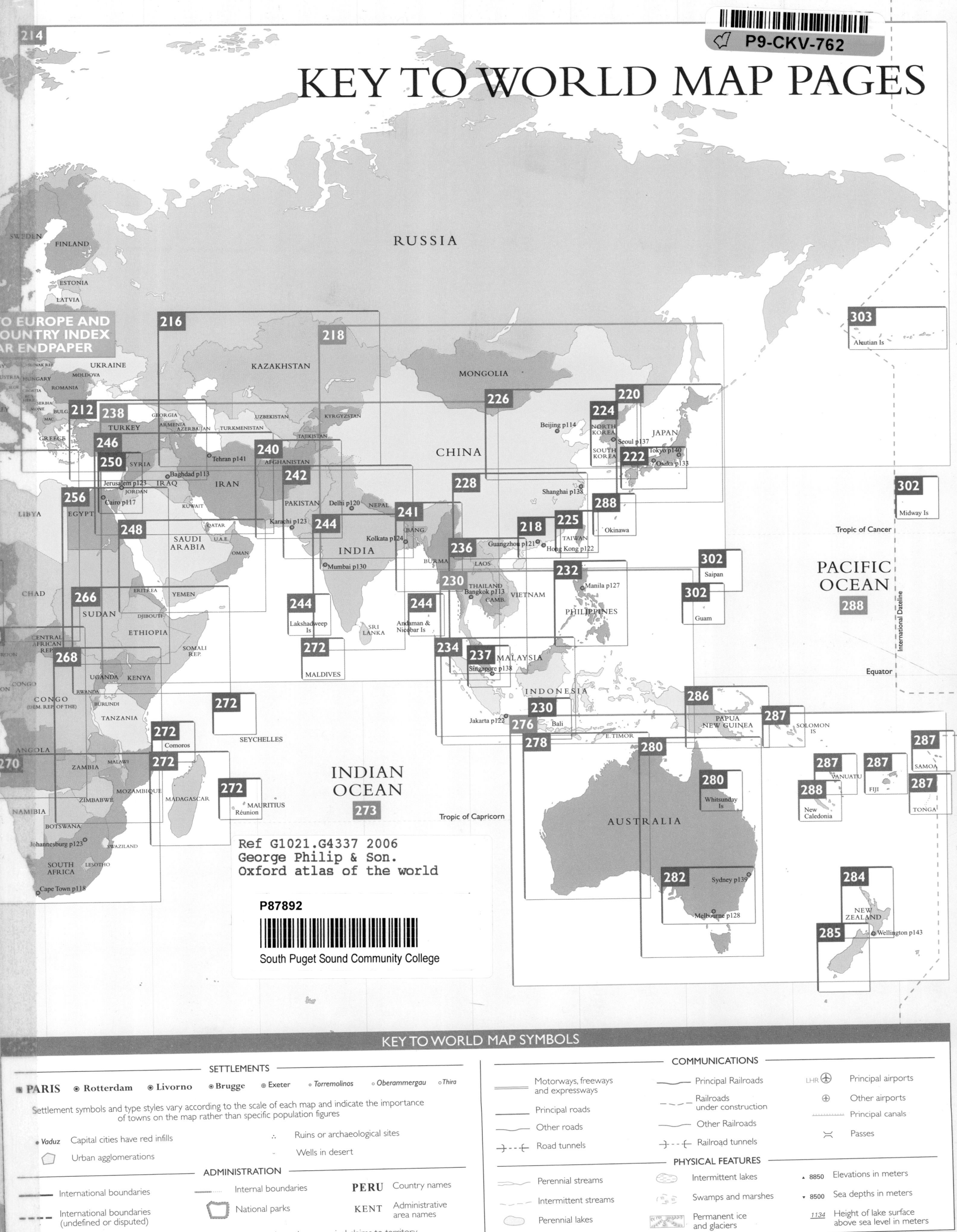

KEY TO WORLD MAP PAGES

P9-CKV-762

Ref G1021.G4337 2006
George Philip & Son.
Oxford atlas of the world

P87892

KEY TO WORLD MAP SYMBOLS

SETTLEMENTS

■ **PARIS**   ◉ Rotterdam   ⊙ Livorno   ⊚ Brugge   ⊛ Exeter   • Torremolinos   ○ Oberammergau   ° Thira

Settlement symbols and type styles vary according to the scale of each map and indicate the importance
of towns on the map rather than specific population figures

▪ *Vaduz*   Capital cities have red infills
⬠   Urban agglomerations

∴   Ruins or archaeological sites
∴   Wells in desert

ADMINISTRATION

——   International boundaries
- - -   Internal boundaries
PERU   Country names

- - -   International boundaries
(undefined or disputed)
⬠   National parks
KENT   Administrative
area names

International boundaries show the *de facto* situation where there are rival claims to territory

COMMUNICATIONS

——   Motorways, freeways
and expressways
——   Principal Railroads
LHR ⊕   Principal airports

——   Principal roads
- - -   Railroads
under construction
⊕   Other airports

——   Other roads
- - -   Other Railroads
········   Principal canals

⊢–·–⊣   Road tunnels
⊢–·–⊣   Railroad tunnels
⋈   Passes

PHYSICAL FEATURES

≈   Perennial streams
⬡   Intermittent lakes
▲ 8850   Elevations in meters

≈   Intermittent streams
⬡   Swamps and marshes
▾ 8500   Sea depths in meters

⬡   Perennial lakes
⬡   Permanent ice
and glaciers
1134   Height of lake surface
above sea level in meters

OXFORD
ATLAS
OF THE
WORLD

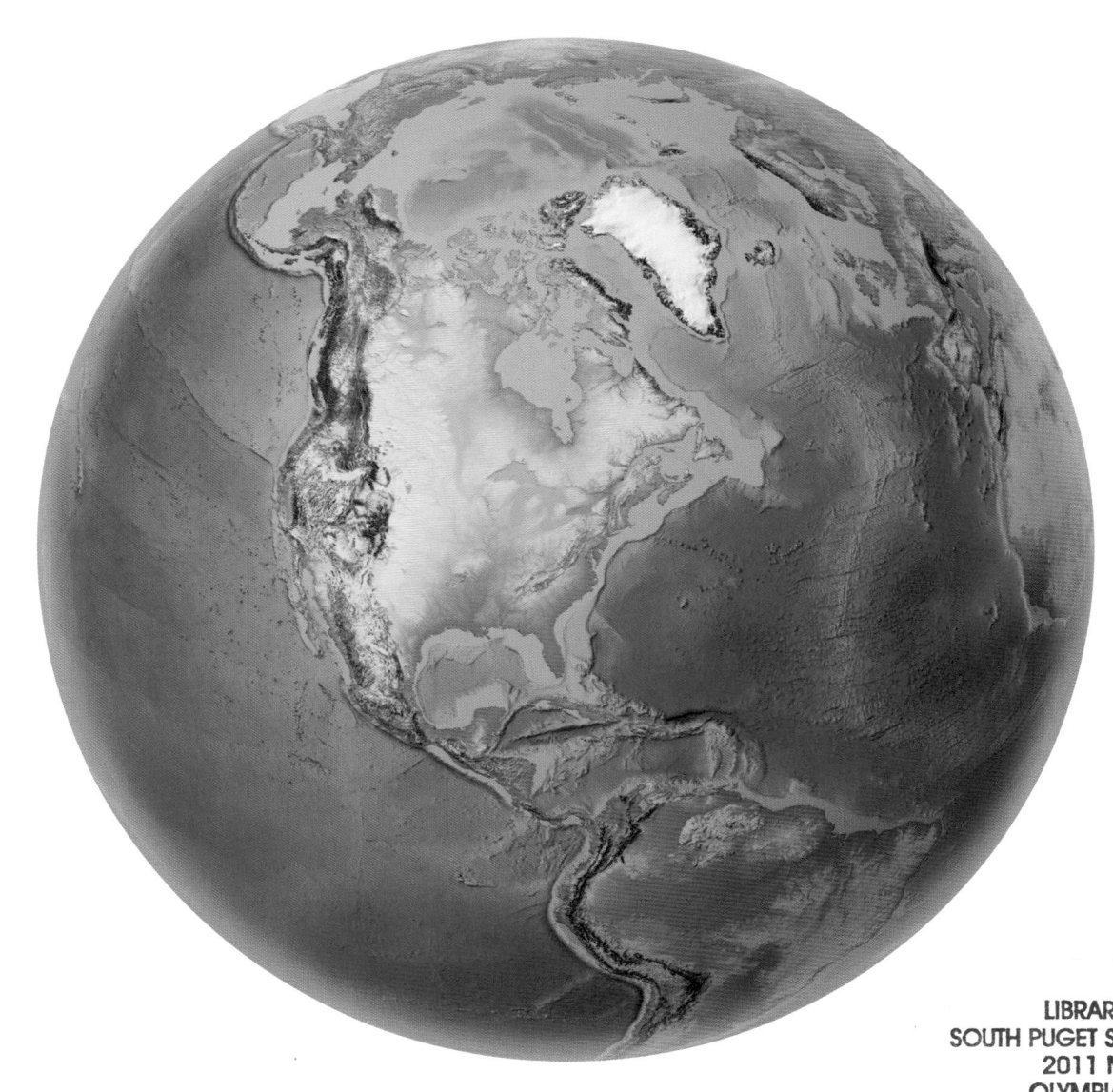

THIRTEENTH EDITION

THE EDITORS would like to thank **Richard Chiles** and the staff at NPA Group, Edenbridge, Kent, UK (www.satmaps.com) for their invaluable assistance in sourcing and processing the satellite imagery that appears in the atlas.

GAZETTEER OF NATIONS
TEXT Keith Lye

PHOTOGRAPHIC ACKNOWLEDGEMENTS
Alamy /*Peter Bowater* 98
Corbis /*Jay Dickman* 109 (bottom left),
/*Marc Garanger* 103, /*Royalty-Free* 89, 94, 97,
/*Vince Streano* 101, /*Liba Taylor* 104, /*David Turnley*
109 (bottom right)
Javier Méndez (ING)/Nik Szymanek (Univ. Herts) 64
NASA/GSFC 84 (bottom left and right), /*Cathy
Clerbaux, NCAR Atmospheric Chemistry Division*
83 (bottom right)
NPA Group 10–27, 28–29, 62–63, 73, 75, 80,
110–111, 144–145, 156–157, 208–209, 252–253,
274–275, 290–291, 324–325 /*Image provided by the
USGS EROS Data Center Satellite Systems Branch* 85
Science Photo Library /*Earth Satellite Corporation* 82

STAR CHARTS
Wil Tirion

CARTOGRAPHY BY PHILIP'S

WORLD CITIES
PAGE 120, DUBLIN: The town plan of Dublin is based on Ordnance Survey Ireland by permission of the Government Permit Number 8097. © Ordnance Survey Ireland and Government of Ireland.

Ordnance Survey® PAGE 121, EDINBURGH, and PAGE 125, LONDON:
This product includes mapping data licensed from Ordnance Survey® with the permission of the Controller of Her Majesty's Stationery Office. © Crown copyright 2006. All rights reserved. Licence number 100011710.

VECTOR DATA: Courtesy of Gräfe and Unser Verlag GmbH, München, Germany (city-center maps of Bangkok, Beijing, Cape Town, Jerusalem, Mexico City, Moscow, Singapore, Sydney, Tokyo and Washington).

The following city maps utilize base data supplied courtesy of MapQuest.com, Inc. (© MapQuest): Las Vegas, New Orleans, Orlando

FOREWORD

AN AUTHORITATIVE AND SERIOUS REFERENCE WORK, the Oxford *Atlas of the World* is one of the finest atlases available anywhere in the world. The atlas incorporates computer-derived maps which have been produced using the very latest in digital cartographic techniques.

The Oxford *Atlas of the World* has been devised with the help of a panel of specialist geography consultants from the United Kingdom and the United States, whose specialties range from the history of cartography, urban and social geography, epidemiology, and the European Union to biogeography and applied geomorphology. The result of their valuable input can be seen in the wealth of maps and data contained in the "World Geography" section of this atlas.

Country names are shown in conventional English form and are those that are in common usage. They are the forms used by publications such as *Newsweek* and *The Washington Post,* and by the BBC and the British Foreign Office. Alternative country names appear in brackets on the maps where space permits — for example, Burma (Myanmar) — and are cross-referenced in the index, for example, Côte d'Ivoire = Ivory Coast.

HOW TO USE THE ATLAS
The atlas is divided into a number of sections which are explained below.

WORLD STATISTICS AND IMAGES OF EARTH
World statistics on topics such as area and population for every country in the world, and physical dimensions — including the largest islands, lakes and seas, the highest mountains and the longest rivers, by continent. Also included in this section is a listing of the world's largest cities by population, arranged in country alphabetical order. This section is followed by a beautifully illustrated satellite section showing 16 of the world's major regions and cities in the Americas, Europe, Africa, Asia, and Australasia.

GAZETTEER OF NATIONS
A comprehensive A–Z reference providing concise profiles of every country's geography, climate, history, politics, and economy, together with ready-reference tables, and illustrated with flags and locator maps.

WORLD GEOGRAPHY
A richly informative section comprising 48 pages of maps, charts, graphs, and diagrams that explain key themes about the world in which we live. The topics covered include the Solar System, oceans, climate, the environment, energy, and trade. Explanatory text on each spread describes the patterns shown by the data.

CITY MAPS
A detailed selection of maps for 69 urban areas around the world. These are useful for planning trips abroad as well as for comparative studies of cities worldwide.

WORLD MAPS
An outstanding collection of 179 pages of distinctive Philip's cartography. The highly acclaimed physical world maps combine relief shading with layer-colored contours to give a striking visual picture of the Earth's surface. Roads, railroads, canals, and airports are accurately depicted on the maps, and towns and cities are clearly marked. More information on the key features employed in the construction and presentation of the maps is given on the facing page.

GEOGRAPHICAL GLOSSARY, REGIONS IN THE NEWS, AND INDEX
The 80,000-name index to the world maps includes geographical features as well as towns and cities, with both latitude/longitude and letter/figure grid references. Preceding the index is a list of geographical terms from various foreign languages that may be found in the place names on the maps and also in the index, together with their meanings. Finally, completing the Atlas is a selection of detailed, up-to-date maps highlighting regions around the world that are currently in the news, such as Iraq, the Near East, Sudan, Kashmir and Afghanistan.

SPECIALIST GEOGRAPHY CONSULTANTS

THE EDITORS are grateful to the following for acting as specialist geography consultants on the "*Introduction to World Geography*" front section:
Professor D. Brunsden Kings College, University of London, UK
Dr C. Clarke Oxford University, UK
Professor P. Haggett University of Bristol, UK
Professor M-L. Hsu University of Minnesota, Minnesota, USA
Professor K. McLachlan Geopolitical and International Boundaries Research Centre, School of Oriental and African Studies, University of London, UK

Professor M. Monmonier Syracuse University, New York, USA
Professor M. J. Tooley University of St Andrews, UK
Dr T. Unwin Royal Holloway, University of London, UK

THE EDITORS would also like to thank:
Keith Lye
Robin Scagell
Dr I. S. Evans Durham University, UK
Dr Andrew Tatham The Royal Geographical Society

USER GUIDE

The reference maps which form the main body of this atlas have been prepared in accordance with the highest standards of international cartography to provide an accurate and detailed representation of the Earth. The scales and projections used have been carefully chosen to give balanced coverage of the world, while emphasizing the most densely populated and economically significant regions. A hallmark of Philip's mapping is the use of hill shading and relief coloring to create a graphic impression of landforms: this makes the maps exceptionally easy to read. However, knowledge of the key features employed in the construction and presentation of the maps will enable the reader to derive the fullest benefit from the atlas.

MAP SEQUENCE

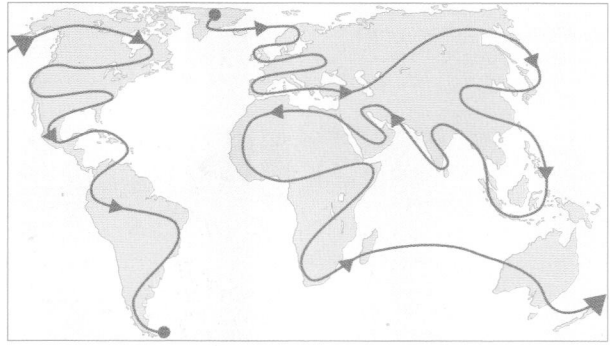

The atlas covers the Earth continent by continent: first Europe; then its land neighbor Asia (mapped north before south, in a clockwise sequence), then Africa, Australia and Oceania, North America, and South America. This is the classic arrangement adopted by most cartographers since the 16th century. For each continent, there are maps at a variety of scales. First, physical relief and political maps of the whole continent; then a series of larger-scale maps of the regions within the continent, each followed, where required, by still larger-scale maps of the most important or densely populated areas. The governing principle is that by turning the pages of the atlas, the reader moves steadily from north to south through each continent, with each map overlapping its neighbors.

MAP PRESENTATION

With very few exceptions (for example, for the Arctic and Antarctic), the maps are drawn with north at the top, regardless of whether they are presented upright or sideways on the page. In the borders will be found the map title; a locator diagram showing the area covered; continuation arrows showing the page numbers for maps of adjacent areas; the scale; the projection used; the degrees of latitude and longitude; and the letters and figures used in the index for locating place names and geographical features. Physical relief maps also have a height reference panel identifying the colors used for each layer of contouring.

MAP SYMBOLS

Each map contains a vast amount of detail which can only be conveyed clearly and accurately by the use of symbols. Points and circles of varying sizes locate and identify the relative importance of towns and cities; different styles of type are employed for administrative, geographical, and regional place names to aid identification. A variety of pictorial symbols denote landforms such as glaciers, marshes and coral reefs, and man-made structures including roads, railroads, airports, and canals. International borders are shown by red lines. Where neighboring countries are in dispute, for example in parts of the Middle East, the maps show the *de facto* boundary between nations, regardless of the legal or historical situation.

The symbols are explained on the front endpapers of the atlas.

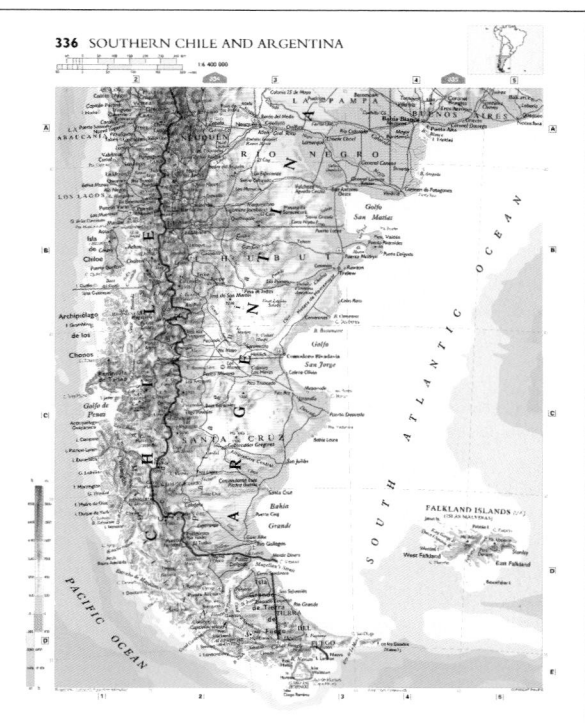

MAP SCALES

1:16 000 000
1 inch = 252 statute miles

The scale of each map is given in the numerical form known as the "representative fraction." The first figure is always one, signifying one unit of distance on the map; the second figure, usually in millions, is the number by which the map unit must be multiplied to give the equivalent distance on the Earth's surface. Calculations can easily be made in centimeters and kilometers, by dividing the Earth units figure by 100 000 (i.e. deleting the last five 0s). Thus 1:1 000 000 means 1 cm = 10 km. The calculation for inches and miles is more laborious, but 1 000 000 divided by 63 360 (the number of inches in a mile) shows that 1:1 000 000 means approximately 1 inch = 16 miles. The table below provides distance equivalents for scales down to 1:50 000 000.

LARGE SCALE		
1:1 000 000	1 cm = 10 km	1 inch = 16 miles
1:2 500 000	1 cm = 25 km	1 inch = 39.5 miles
1:5 000 000	1 cm = 50 km	1 inch = 79 miles
1:6 000 000	1 cm = 60 km	1 inch = 95 miles
1:8 000 000	1 cm = 80 km	1 inch = 126 miles
1:10 000 000	1 cm = 100 km	1 inch = 158 miles
1:15 000 000	1 cm = 150 km	1 inch = 237 miles
1:20 000 000	1 cm = 200 km	1 inch = 316 miles
1:50 000 000	1 cm = 500 km	1 inch = 790 miles
SMALL SCALE		

MEASURING DISTANCES

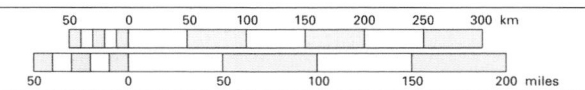

Although each map is accompanied by a scale bar, distances cannot always be measured with confidence because of the distortions involved in portraying the curved surface of the Earth on a flat page. As a general rule, the larger the map scale, the more accurate and reliable will be the distance measured. On small-scale maps such as those of the world and of entire continents, measurement may only be accurate along the "standard parallels," or central axes, and should not be attempted without considering the map projection.

MAP PROJECTIONS

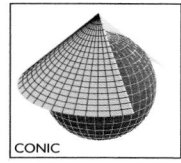 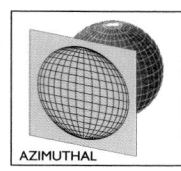 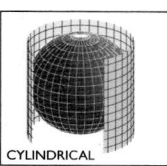

Unlike a globe, no flat map can give a true scale representation of the world in terms of area, shape, and position of every region. Each of the numerous systems that have been devised for projecting the curved surface of the Earth on to a flat page involves the sacrifice of accuracy in one or more of these elements. The variations in shape and position of land masses such as Alaska, Greenland, and Australia, for example, can be quite dramatic when different projections are compared.

For this atlas, the guiding principle has been to select projections that involve the least distortion of size and distance. The projection used for each map is noted in the border. Most fall into one of three categories – conic, azimuthal, or cylindrical – whose basic concepts are shown above. Each involves plotting the forms of the Earth's surface on a grid of latitude and longitude lines, which may be shown as parallels, curves, or radiating spokes.

LATITUDE AND LONGITUDE

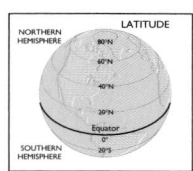 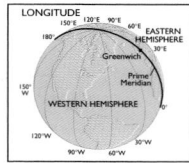 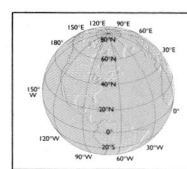

Accurate positioning of individual points on the Earth's surface is made possible by reference to the geometrical system of latitude and longitude. Latitude *parallels* are drawn west–east around the Earth and numbered by degrees north and south of the Equator, which is designated 0° of latitude. Longitude *meridians* are drawn north–south and numbered by degrees east and west of the *prime meridian*, 0° of longitude, which passes through Greenwich in England. By referring to these co-ordinates and their subdivisions of minutes (1/60th of a degree) and seconds (1/60th of a minute), any place on Earth can be located to within a few hundred meters. Latitude and longitude are indicated by blue lines on the maps; they are straight or curved according to the projection employed. Reference to these lines is the easiest way of determining the relative positions of places on different maps, and for plotting compass directions.

NAME FORMS

For ease of reference, both English and local name forms appear in the atlas. Oceans, seas, and countries are shown in English throughout the atlas; country names may be abbreviated to their commonly accepted form (for example, Germany, not The Federal Republic of Germany). Conventional English forms are also used for place names on the smaller-scale maps of the continents. However, local name forms are used on all large-scale and regional maps, with the English form given in brackets only for important cities – the large-scale map of Russia and Northern Asia thus shows Moskva (Moscow). For countries which do not use a Roman script, place names have been transcribed according to the systems adopted by the British and US Geographic Names Authorities. For China, the Pin Yin system has been used, with some more widely known forms appearing in brackets, as with Beijing (Peking). Both English and local names appear in the index, the English form being cross-referenced to the local form.

CONTENTS

WORLD STATISTICS

COUNTRIES	6
CITIES	7
PHYSICAL DIMENSIONS	8
CLIMATE	9

IMAGES OF EARTH

LONDON, UK	12
MOUNT ETNA, SICILY	13
DANUBE DELTA, ROMANIA	14
TOKYO, JAPAN	15
GLACIERS, BHUTAN	16
UPPER BRAHMAPUTRA, INDIA	17
CAIRO, EGYPT	18
CAPE PENINSULA, SOUTH AFRICA	19
NGORONGORO CRATER, TANZANIA	20
SYDNEY, AUSTRALIA	21
MOUNT TARANAKI, NZ	22
VANCOUVER, CANADA	23
NEW YORK, USA	24
NEW ORLEANS, USA	25
MANAUS, BRAZIL	26
SANTIAGO, CHILE	27

GAZETTEER OF NATIONS

AN A–Z GAZETTEER OF COUNTRIES	30–61

WORLD GEOGRAPHY

THE UNIVERSE	64–65
THE SOLAR SYSTEM	66–67
TIME AND MOTION	68–69
GEOLOGY OF THE EARTH	70–71
LANDFORMS	72–73
OCEANS	74–75
THE ATMOSPHERE	76–77
CLIMATE	78–79
WATER AND VEGETATION	80–81
THE NATURAL ENVIRONMENT	82–83
PEOPLE AND THE ENVIRONMENT	84–85
POPULATION	86–87
CITIES	88–89
THE HUMAN FAMILY	90–91
CONFLICT AND COOPERATION	92–93
AGRICULTURE	94–95
ENERGY	96–97
MINERALS	98–99
EMPLOYMENT AND INDUSTRY	100–101
TRADE	102–103
HEALTH	104–105
WEALTH	106–107
STANDARDS OF LIVING	108–109

WORLD CITIES

AMSTERDAM	112
ATHENS	112
ATLANTA	113
BAGHDAD	113
BANGKOK	113
BARCELONA	114
BEIJING	114
BERLIN	115
BOSTON	116
BRUSSELS	116
BUDAPEST	117
BUENOS AIRES	117
CAIRO	117
CAPE TOWN	118
COPENHAGEN	118
CHICAGO	119
DELHI	120
DUBLIN	120
EDINBURGH	121
GUANGZHOU (CANTON)	121
HELSINKI	121
HONG KONG	122
ISTANBUL	122
JAKARTA	122
JERUSALEM	123
JOHANNESBURG	123
KARACHI	123
KOLKATA (CALCUTTA)	124
LAGOS	124
LAS VEGAS	124
LIMA	124
LONDON	125
LISBON	126
LOS ANGELES	126
MADRID	127
MANILA	127
MELBOURNE	128
MEXICO CITY	128
MIAMI	128
MILAN	129
MOSCOW	129
MONTREAL	130
MUMBAI	130
MUNICH	131
NEW ORLEANS	131
NEW YORK	132
ORLANDO	133
OSAKA	133
OSLO	133
PARIS	134
PRAGUE	135
RIO DE JANEIRO	135
ROME	136
SAN FRANCISCO	136
ST PETERSBURG	137
SANTIAGO	137
SÃO PAULO	137
SEOUL	137
SHANGHAI	138
SINGAPORE	138
STOCKHOLM	139
SYDNEY	139
TOKYO	140
TEHRAN	141
TORONTO	141
VIENNA	142
WARSAW	142
WASHINGTON	143
WELLINGTON	143

WORLD MAPS

THE WORLD

MAP SYMBOLS	FRONT ENDPAPER
THE WORLD: PHYSICAL 1:76 000 000	146–147
THE WORLD: POLITICAL 1:76 000 000	148–149
ARCTIC OCEAN 1:28 000 000	150
ANTARCTICA 1:28 000 000	151
ATLANTIC OCEAN 1:41 000 000	152
ISLANDS OF THE ATLANTIC	153
BERMUDA 1:400 000	
NEW PROVIDENCE ISLAND 1:400 000	
MADEIRA 1:800 000	
AZORES 1:1 600 000	
CANARY ISLANDS 1:1 600 000	
FALKLAND ISLANDS 1:6 400 000	
ASCENSION ISLAND 1:400 000	
ST HELENA 1:400 000	
CAPE VERDE ISLANDS 1:8 000 000	
GREENLAND 1:10 000 000	154
ICELAND 1:2 000 000	155

EUROPE

EUROPE: PHYSICAL 1:16 000 000	158
EUROPE: POLITICAL 1:16 000 000	159
SCANDINAVIA 1:4 800 000	160–161
ICELAND 1:4 800 000	
FÆROE ISLANDS 1:4 800 000	
DENMARK AND SOUTHERN SWEDEN 1:2 000 000	162–163
SOUTHERN NORWAY 1:2 000 000	164
BRITISH ISLES 1:4 000 000	165
IRELAND 1:1 600 000	166
SCOTLAND 1:1 600 000	167
ENGLAND AND WALES 1:1 600 000	168–169
NETHERLANDS, BELGIUM AND LUXEMBOURG 1:2 000 000	170
FRANCE 1:4 000 000	171
NORTHERN FRANCE 1:2 000 000	172–173
SOUTHERN FRANCE 1:2 000 000	174–175
CENTRAL EUROPE 1:4 000 000	176–177
GERMANY AND SWITZERLAND 1:2 000 000	178–179
AUSTRIA, CZECH REPUBLIC AND SLOVAK REPUBLIC 1:2 000 000	180–181
HUNGARY, ROMANIA AND THE LOWER DANUBE 1:2 000 000	182–183
POLAND AND THE SOUTHERN BALTIC 1:2 000 000	184–185
EASTERN EUROPE 1:8 000 000	186–187
BALTIC STATES, BELARUS AND UKRAINE 1:4 000 000	188–189
THE VOLGA BASIN AND THE CAUCASUS 1:4 000 000	190–191
SOUTHERN EUROPE 1:8 000 000	192–193
WESTERN SPAIN AND PORTUGAL 1:2 000 000	194–195
EASTERN SPAIN 1:2 000 000	196–197
NORTHERN ITALY, SLOVENIA AND CROATIA 1:2 000 000	198–199
SOUTHERN ITALY 1:2 000 000	200–201
THE BALKANS 1:2 000 000	202–203
SOUTHERN GREECE AND WESTERN TURKEY 1:2 000 000	204–205
MEDITERRANEAN ISLANDS	206–207
IBIZA, MAJORCA, MINORCA 1:800 000	
MALTA 1:400 000	
CORFU 1:800 000	
RHODES 1:800 000	
LEVKAS, ZANTE, CEPHALONIA 1:800 000	
CRETE 1:1 000 000	
CYPRUS 1:1 000 000	

ASIA

ASIA: PHYSICAL 1:40 000 000	210
ASIA: POLITICAL 1:40 000 000	211
TURKEY AND TRANSCAUCASIA 1:4 000 000	212–213

CONTENTS

RUSSIA AND
NORTHERN ASIA   214–215
1:16 000 000

KAZAKHSTAN
AND CENTRAL ASIA   216–127
1:8 000 000

CHINA
AND THE FAR EAST   218–219
1:12 000 000

HONG KONG AND MACAU 1:800 000

JAPAN   220–221
1:4 000 000

RYUKYU ISLANDS 1:4 000 000

SOUTHERN JAPAN   222–223
1:2 000 000

KOREA   224
1:3 100 000

TAIWAN   225
1:1 400 000

NORTHERN CHINA
AND KOREA   226–227
1:4 800 000

SOUTHERN CHINA   228–229
1:4 800 000

SOUTHEAST ASIA   230–231
1:10 000 000

JAVA AND MADURA 1:6 000 000

BALI 1:1 600 000

PHILIPPINES   232–233
1:3 200 000

WESTERN INDONESIA   234–235
1:5 600 000

MAINLAND SOUTHEAST
ASIA   236–237
1:4 800 000

KO PHUKET 1:800 000

KO SAMUI 1:800 000

PINANG 1:800 000

SINGAPORE 1:800 000

SOUTHERN ASIA AND
THE MIDDLE EAST   238–239
1:14 000 000

AFGHANISTAN
AND PAKISTAN   240
1:5 600 000

BANGLADESH,
NORTHEASTERN INDIA
AND BURMA   241
1:4 800 000

NORTHERN INDIA,
PAKISTAN AND
NEPAL   242–243
1:4 800 000

SOUTHERN INDIA AND
SRI LANKA   244–245
1:4 800 000

LAKSHADWEEP ISLANDS 1:4 800 000

ANDAMAN AND
NICOBAR ISLANDS 1:4 800 000

THE MIDDLE EAST   246–247
1:5 600 000

SOUTHERN ARABIAN
PENINSULA   248–249
1:5 600 000

EASTERN
MEDITERRANEAN   250–251
1:2 000 000

AFRICA

AFRICA: PHYSICAL   254
1:33 600 000

AFRICA: POLITICAL   255
1:33 600 000

THE NILE VALLEY   256–257
1:6 400 000

THE NILE DELTA 1:3 200 000

CENTRAL NORTH
AFRICA   258–259
1:6 400 000

NORTHWEST AFRICA   260–261
1:6 400 000

WEST AFRICA   262–263
1:6 400 000

CENTRAL AFRICA   264–265
1:6 400 000

SÃO TOMÉ AND PRÍNCIPE 1:6 400 000

ETHIOPIA AND THE
HORN OF AFRICA   266–267
1:6 400 000

EAST AFRICA   268–269
1:6 400 000

SOUTHERN AFRICA   270–271
1:6 400 000

MADAGASCAR   272
1:6 400 000

COMOROS 1:2 000 000

MAYOTTE 1:800 000

SEYCHELLES 1:2 000 000

RÉUNION 1:800 000

MAURITIUS 1:800 000

MALDIVES 1:6 400 000

INDIAN OCEAN   273
1:40 000 000

AUSTRALIA
AND OCEANIA

AUSTRALIA AND OCEANIA:
PHYSICAL
AND POLITICAL   276–277
1:16 000 000

WESTERN AUSTRALIA   278–279
1:6 400 000

EASTERN AUSTRALIA   280–281
1:6 400 000

WHITSUNDAY GROUP 1:2 000 000

TASMANIA 1:6 400 000

SOUTHEAST
AUSTRALIA   282–283
1:3 200 000

NEW ZEALAND –
NORTH ISLAND   284
1:2 800 000

NEW ZEALAND –
SOUTH ISLAND   285
1:2 800 000

CHATHAM ISLANDS 1:2 800 000

PAPUA NEW GUINEA   286
1:5 200 000

ISLANDS OF THE
SOUTHWEST PACIFIC   287
FIJI 1:4 000 000
VANUATU 1:4 000 000
SOLOMON ISLANDS 1:4 000 000
TONGA 1:4 000 000
YAP 1:830 000
CHUUK 1:830 000
SAMOAN ISLANDS 1:4 000 000

PACIFIC OCEAN   288–289
1:43 200 000
OKINAWA 1:1 550 000
IWO JIMA 1:200 000
PALAU 1:1 550 000
NEW CALEDONIA 1:5 750 000
TAHITI 1:1 150 000
FRENCH POLYNESIA 1:26 000 000
NIUE 1:830 000
RAROTONGA 1:415 000

NORTH
AMERICA

NORTH AMERICA:
PHYSICAL   292
1:28 000 000

NORTH AMERICA:
POLITICAL   293
1:28 000 000

CANADA   294–295
1:12 000 000

WESTERN CANADA   296–297
1:5 600 000

EASTERN CANADA   298–299
1:5 600 000

UNITED STATES   300–301
1:9 600 000

ALASKA 1:24 000 000

HAWAI'I 1:8 000 000

HAWAI'I   302
1:2 500 000
OAHU 1:500 000
NORTHERN MARIANAS 1:12 800 000
WAKE ISLAND 1:200 000
MIDWAY ISLANDS 1:200 000
GUAM 1:800 000
SAIPAN AND TINIAN 1:800 000
TUTUILA 1:640 000
MANUA 1:640 000

ALASKA   303
1:8 000 000

UNITED STATES –
WEST   304–305
1:5 360 000

CENTRAL AND SOUTHERN
CALIFORNIA AND WESTERN
WASHINGTON   306–307
1:2 000 000

UNITED STATES – MIDWEST
AND NORTHEAST   308–309
1:5 360 000

CHICAGO AND
THE MIDWEST   310–311
1:2 000 000

NORTHEASTERN
UNITED STATES   312–313
1:2 000 000

UNITED STATES –
SOUTH   314–315
1:5 360 000

SOUTHEASTERN
UNITED STATES   316–317
1:2 000 000

MEXICO   318–319
1:6 400 000

CENTRAL AMERICA AND
THE WEST INDIES   320–321
1:6 400 000

PUERTO RICO AND THE
VIRGIN ISLANDS 1:1 600 000

JAMAICA 1:1 600 000

LESSER ANTILLES   322–323
NORTHERN LEEWARDS 1:600 000
ANTIGUA AND BARBUDA 1:600 000
ST KITTS AND NEVIS 1:600 000
GUADELOUPE 1:600 000
ARUBA 1:600 000
NETHERLANDS ANTILLES 1:600 000
MARTINIQUE 1:600 000
DOMINICA 1:600 000
ST LUCIA 1:600 000
ST VINCENT AND
THE GRENADINES 1:600 000
MONTSERRAT 1:600 000
GRENADA 1:600 000
BARBADOS 1:600 000
TRINIDAD AND TOBAGO 1:600 000

SOUTH
AMERICA

SOUTH AMERICA:
PHYSICAL   326
1:28 000 000

SOUTH AMERICA:
POLITICAL   327
1:28 000 000

SOUTH AMERICA –
NORTHWEST   328–329
1:6 400 000

SOUTH AMERICA –
WEST   330–331
1:6 400 000

GALAPAGOS ISLANDS 1:3 200 000

EASTER ISLAND 1:400 000

EASTERN BRAZIL   332–333
1:6 400 000

CENTRAL
SOUTH AMERICA   334–335
1:6 400 000

SOUTHERN CHILE AND
ARGENTINA   336
1:6 400 000

GEOGRAPHICAL
GLOSSARY   337–338

INDEX TO
WORLD MAPS   339–448

WORLD: REGIONS
IN THE NEWS   449

This alphabetical list includes the principal countries and territories of the world. If a territory is not completely independent, the country it is associated with is named. The area figures give the total area of land, inland water, and ice. The population figures are 2005 estimates where available. The annual income is the Gross Domestic Product per capita in US dollars. The figures are the latest available, usually 2005 estimates.

Country/Territory	Area km² Thousands	Area miles² Thousands	Population Thousands	Capital	Annual Income US $
Afghanistan	652	252	29,929	Kabul	800
Albania	28.7	11.1	3,563	Tirana	4,900
Algeria	2,382	920	32,532	Algiers	7,300
American Samoa (US)	0.20	0.08	58	Pago Pago	8,000
Andorra	0.47	0.18	71	Andorra La Vella	26,800
Angola	1,247	481	11,191	Luanda	2,500
Anguilla (UK)	0.10	0.04	13	The Valley	7,500
Antigua & Barbuda	0.44	0.17	69	St John's	11,000
Argentina	2,780	1,074	39,538	Buenos Aires	13,600
Armenia	29.8	11.5	2,983	Yerevan	5,100
Aruba (Netherlands)	0.19	0.07	72	Oranjestad	28,000
Australia	7,741	2,989	20,090	Canberra	32,000
Austria	83.9	32.4	8,185	Vienna	32,900
Azerbaijan	86.6	33.4	7,912	Baku	4,600
Azores (Portugal)	2.2	0.86	236	Ponta Delgada	15,000
Bahamas	13.9	5.4	302	Nassau	18,800
Bahrain	0.69	0.27	688	Manama	20,500
Bangladesh	144	55.6	144,320	Dhaka	2,100
Barbados	0.43	0.17	279	Bridgetown	17,300
Belarus	208	80.2	10,300	Minsk	7,600
Belgium	30.5	11.8	10,364	Brussels	31,800
Belize	23.0	8.9	279	Belmopan	6,800
Benin	113	43.5	7,460	Porto-Novo	1,200
Bermuda (UK)	0.05	0.02	65	Hamilton	36,000
Bhutan	47.0	18.1	2,232	Thimphu	1,400
Bolivia	1,099	424	8,858	La Paz/Sucre	2,700
Bosnia-Herzegovina	51.2	19.8	4,025	Sarajevo	6,800
Botswana	582	225	1,640	Gaborone	10,100
Brazil	8,514	3,287	186,113	Brasília	8,500
Brunei	5.8	2.2	372	Bandar Seri Begawan	23,600
Bulgaria	111	42.8	7,450	Sofia	9,000
Burkina Faso	274	106	13,925	Ouagadougou	1,200
Burma (= Myanmar)	677	261	42,909	Rangoon/Pyinmana	1,800
Burundi	27.8	10.7	6,371	Bujumbura	700
Cambodia	181	69.9	13,607	Phnom Penh	2,100
Cameroon	475	184	16,380	Yaoundé	2,000
Canada	9,971	3,850	32,805	Ottawa	32,800
Canary Is. (Spain)	7.2	2.8	1,682	Las Palmas/Santa Cruz	19,900
Cape Verde Is.	4.0	1.6	418	Praia	6,200
Cayman Is. (UK)	0.26	0.10	44	George Town	32,300
Central African Republic	623	241	3,800	Bangui	1,200
Chad	1,284	496	9,826	Ndjaména	1,900
Chile	757	292	15,981	Santiago	11,300
China	9,597	3,705	1,306,314	Beijing	6,200
Colombia	1,139	440	42,954	Bogotá	7,100
Comoros	2.2	0.86	671	Moroni	600
Congo	342	132	3,039	Brazzaville	800
Congo (Dem. Rep. of the)	2,345	905	60,086	Kinshasa	800
Cook Is. (NZ)	0.24	0.09	21	Avarua	5,000
Costa Rica	51.1	19.7	4,016	San José	10,000
Croatia	56.5	21.8	4,496	Zagreb	11,600
Cuba	111	42.8	11,347	Havana	3,300
Cyprus	9.3	3.6	780	Nicosia	21,600
Czech Republic	78.9	30.5	10,241	Prague	18,100
Denmark	43.1	16.6	5,432	Copenhagen	33,500
Djibouti	23.2	9.0	477	Djibouti	1,300
Dominica	0.75	0.29	69	Roseau	5,500
Dominican Republic	48.5	18.7	8,950	Santo Domingo	6,500
East Timor	14.9	5.7	1,041	Dili	400
Ecuador	284	109	13,364	Quito	3,900
Egypt	1,001	387	77,506	Cairo	4,400
El Salvador	21.0	8.1	6,705	San Salvador	5,100
Equatorial Guinea	28.1	10.8	536	Malabo	2,700
Eritrea	118	45.4	4,562	Asmara	1,000
Estonia	45.1	17.4	1,333	Tallinn	16,400
Ethiopia	1,104	426	73,053	Addis Ababa	800
Faroe Is. (Denmark)	1.4	0.54	47	Tórshavn	22,000
Fiji	18.3	7.1	893	Suva	6,000
Finland	338	131	5,223	Helsinki	30,300
France	552	213	60,656	Paris	29,900
French Guiana (France)	90.0	34.7	196	Cayenne	8,300
French Polynesia (France)	4.0	1.5	270	Papeete	17,500
Gabon	268	103	1,389	Libreville	5,800
Gambia, The	11.3	4.4	1,593	Banjul	1,900
Gaza Strip	0.36	0.14	1,376	–	600
Georgia	69.7	26.9	4,677	Tbilisi	3,400
Germany	357	138	82,431	Berlin	29,700
Ghana	239	92.1	21,030	Accra	2,500
Gibraltar (UK)	0.006	0.002	28	Gibraltar Town	27,900
Greece	132	50.9	10,668	Athens	22,800
Greenland (Denmark)	2,176	840	56	Nuuk (Godthåb)	20,000
Grenada	0.34	0.13	90	St George's	5,000
Guadeloupe (France)	1.7	0.66	449	Basse-Terre	7,900
Guam (US)	0.55	0.21	169	Agana	21,000
Guatemala	109	42.0	14,655	Guatemala City	4,300
Guinea	246	94.9	9,468	Conakry	2,200
Guinea-Bissau	36.1	13.9	1,416	Bissau	800
Guyana	215	83.0	765	Georgetown	3,900
Haiti	27.8	10.7	8,122	Port-au-Prince	1,600
Honduras	112	43.3	6,975	Tegucigalpa	2,900
Hong Kong (China)	1.1	0.42	6,899	–	36,800
Hungary	93.0	35.9	10,007	Budapest	15,900
Iceland	103	39.8	297	Reykjavik	34,600
India	3,287	1,269	1,080,264	New Delhi	3,400
Indonesia	1,905	735	241,974	Jakarta	3,700
Iran	1,648	636	68,018	Tehran	8,100
Iraq	438	169	26,075	Baghdad	3,400
Ireland	70.3	27.1	4,016	Dublin	34,100
Israel	20.6	8.0	6,277	Jerusalem	22,200
Italy	301	116	58,103	Rome	28,300
Ivory Coast (= Côte d'Ivoire)	322	125	17,298	Yamoussoukro	1,400
Jamaica	11.0	4.2	2,732	Kingston	4,300
Japan	378	146	127,417	Tokyo	30,400
Jordan	89.3	34.5	5,760	Amman	4,800
Kazakhstan	2,725	1,052	15,186	Astana	8,700
Kenya	580	224	33,830	Nairobi	1,200
Kiribati	0.73	0.28	103	Tarawa	800
Korea, North	121	46.5	22,912	Pyŏngyang	1,800
Korea, South	99.3	38.3	48,423	Seoul	20,300
Kuwait	17.8	6.9	2,336	Kuwait City	22,100
Kyrgyzstan	200	77.2	5,146	Bishkek	1,800
Laos	237	91.4	6,217	Vientiane	1,900
Latvia	64.6	24.9	2,290	Riga	12,800
Lebanon	10.4	4.0	3,826	Beirut	5,100
Lesotho	30.4	11.7	1,867	Maseru	3,300
Liberia	111	43.0	3,482	Monrovia	700
Libya	1,760	679	5,766	Tripoli	8,400
Liechtenstein	0.16	0.06	34	Vaduz	25,000
Lithuania	65.2	25.2	3,597	Vilnius	13,700
Luxembourg	2.6	1.0	469	Luxembourg	62,700
Macau (China)	0.02	0.007	449	–	19,400
Macedonia (FYROM)	25.7	9.9	2,045	Skopje	7,400
Madagascar	587	227	18,040	Antananarivo	900
Madeira (Portugal)	0.78	0.30	241	Funchal	22,700
Malawi	118	45.7	12,159	Lilongwe	600
Malaysia	330	127	23,953	Kuala Lumpur/Putrajaya	10,400
Maldives	0.30	0.12	349	Malé	3,900
Mali	1,240	479	12,292	Bamako	1,000
Malta	0.32	0.12	399	Valletta	18,800
Marshall Is.	0.18	0.07	59	Majuro	1,600
Martinique (France)	1.1	0.43	433	Fort-de-France	14,400
Mauritania	1,026	396	3,087	Nouakchott	2,000
Mauritius	2.0	0.79	1,231	Port Louis	13,300
Mayotte (France)	0.37	0.14	194	Mamoundzou	2,600
Mexico	1,958	756	106,203	Mexico City	10,000
Micronesia, Fed. States of	0.70	0.27	108	Palikir	2,000
Moldova	33.9	13.1	4,455	Chişinău	2,100
Monaco	0.001	0.0004	32	Monaco	27,000
Mongolia	1,567	605	2,791	Ulan Bator	2,200
Montserrat (UK)	0.10	0.04	9	Plymouth	3,400
Morocco	447	172	32,726	Rabat	4,300
Mozambique	802	309	19,407	Maputo	1,300
Namibia	824	318	2,031	Windhoek	7,800
Nauru	0.02	0.008	13	Yaren District	5,000
Nepal	147	56.8	27,677	Katmandu	1,500
Netherlands	41.5	16.0	16,407	Amsterdam/The Hague	30,500
Netherlands Antilles (Neths)	0.80	0.31	220	Willemstad	11,400
New Caledonia (France)	18.6	7.2	216	Nouméa	15,000
New Zealand	271	104	4,035	Wellington	24,100
Nicaragua	130	50.2	5,465	Managua	2,800
Niger	1,267	489	11,665	Niamey	900
Nigeria	924	357	128,772	Abuja	1,000
Northern Mariana Is. (US)	0.46	0.18	80	Saipan	12,500
Norway	324	125	4,593	Oslo	42,400
Oman	310	119	3,002	Muscat	13,400
Pakistan	796	307	162,420	Islamabad	2,400
Palau	0.46	0.18	20	Koror	9,000
Panama	75.5	29.2	3,039	Panamá	7,300
Papua New Guinea	463	179	5,545	Port Moresby	2,400
Paraguay	407	157	6,348	Asunción	4,900
Peru	1,285	496	27,926	Lima	6,000
Philippines	300	116	87,857	Manila	5,100
Poland	323	125	38,635	Warsaw	12,700
Portugal	88.8	34.3	10,566	Lisbon	18,400
Puerto Rico (US)	8.9	3.4	3,917	San Juan	18,500
Qatar	11.0	4.2	863	Doha	26,000
Réunion (France)	2.5	0.97	777	St-Denis	6,200
Romania	238	92.0	22,330	Bucharest	8,300
Russia	17,075	6,593	143,420	Moscow	10,700
Rwanda	26.3	10.2	8,441	Kigali	1,300
St Kitts & Nevis	0.26	0.10	39	Basseterre	8,800
St Lucia	0.54	0.21	166	Castries	5,400
St Vincent & Grenadines	0.39	0.15	118	Kingstown	2,900
Samoa	2.8	1.1	177	Apia	5,600
San Marino	0.06	0.02	29	San Marino	34,600
São Tomé & Príncipe	0.96	0.37	187	São Tomé	1,200
Saudi Arabia	2,150	830	26,418	Riyadh	12,900
Senegal	197	76.0	11,127	Dakar	1,800
Serbia & Montenegro†	102	39.4	10,829	Belgrade	2,600
Seychelles	0.46	0.18	81	Victoria	7,800
Sierra Leone	71.7	27.7	6,018	Freetown	800
Singapore	0.68	0.26	4,426	Singapore City	29,700
Slovak Republic	49.0	18.9	5,431	Bratislava	15,700
Slovenia	20.3	7.8	2,011	Ljubljana	20,900
Solomon Is.	28.9	11.2	538	Honiara	1,700
Somalia	638	246	8,592	Mogadishu	600
South Africa	1,221	471	44,344	Cape Town/Pretoria	11,900
Spain	498	192	40,341	Madrid	25,100
Sri Lanka	65.6	25.3	20,065	Colombo	4,300
Sudan	2,506	967	40,187	Khartoum	2,100
Suriname	163	63.0	438	Paramaribo	4,700
Swaziland	17.4	6.7	1,174	Mbabane	5,300
Sweden	450	174	9,002	Stockholm	29,600
Switzerland	41.3	15.9	7,489	Bern	35,000
Syria	185	71.5	18,449	Damascus	3,500
Taiwan	36.0	13.9	22,894	Taipei	26,700
Tajikistan	143	55.3	7,164	Dushanbe	1,200
Tanzania	945	365	36,766	Dodoma	700
Thailand	513	198	65,444	Bangkok	8,300
Togo	56.8	21.9	5,682	Lomé	1,600
Tonga	0.65	0.25	112	Nuku'alofa	2,300
Trinidad & Tobago	5.1	2.0	1,089	Port of Spain	12,700
Tunisia	164	63.2	10,075	Tunis	7,600
Turkey	775	299	69,661	Ankara	7,900
Turkmenistan	488	188	4,952	Ashkhabad	5,900
Turks & Caicos Is. (UK)	0.43	0.17	21	Cockburn Town	11,500
Tuvalu	0.03	0.01	12	Fongafale	1,100
Uganda	241	93.1	27,269	Kampala	1,700
Ukraine	604	233	47,425	Kiev	6,800
United Arab Emirates	83.6	32.3	2,563	Abu Dhabi	29,100
United Kingdom	242	93.4	60,441	London	30,900
United States of America	9,629	3,718	295,734	Washington, DC	41,800
Uruguay	175	67.6	3,416	Montevideo	10,000
Uzbekistan	447	173	26,851	Tashkent	1,900
Vanuatu	12.2	4.7	206	Port-Vila	2,900
Vatican City	0.0004	0.0002	1	Vatican City	N/A
Venezuela	912	352	25,375	Caracas	6,400
Vietnam	332	128	83,536	Hanoi	3,000
Virgin Is. (UK)	0.15	0.06	23	Road Town	38,500
Virgin Is. (US)	0.35	0.13	109	Charlotte Amalie	17,200
Wallis & Futuna Is. (France)	0.20	0.08	16	Mata-Utu	3,800
West Bank (OPT)*	5.9	2.3	2,386	–	1,100
Western Sahara	266	103	273	El Aaiún	N/A
Yemen	528	204	20,727	Sana'	800
Zambia	753	291	11,262	Lusaka	900
Zimbabwe	391	151	12,747	Harare	1,900

*OPT = Occupied Palestinian Territory N/A = Not available

† In June 2006, Serbia and Montenegro formally declared their independence and are now separate sovereign states

This list shows the principal cities with more than 750,000 inhabitants. The figures are taken from the most recent census or estimate available, usually 2005, and as far as possible are the population of the metropolitan area or urban agglomeration (for example, greater New York, Mexico, or Paris). All the figures are in thousands. Local name forms have been used for the smaller cities (for example, Thessaloniki).

AFGHANISTAN
Kabul 3,288
ALGERIA
Algiers 3,260
ANGOLA
Luanda 2,839
ARGENTINA
Buenos Aires 13,349
Córdoba 1,592
Rosario 1,312
Mendoza 1,072
San Miguel de Tucumán 837
ARMENIA
Yerevan 1,066
AUSTRALIA
Sydney 4,388
Melbourne 3,663
Brisbane 1,769
Perth 1,484
Adelaide 1,137
AUSTRIA
Vienna 2,190
AZERBAIJAN
Baku 1,830
BANGLADESH
Dhaka 12,560
Chittagong 4,171
Khulna 1,497
Rajshahi 1,035
BELARUS
Minsk 1,709
BELGIUM
Brussels 964
BOLIVIA
La Paz 1,533
Santa Cruz 1,352
Cochabamba 797
BRAZIL
São Paulo 18,333
Rio de Janeiro 11,469
Belo Horizonte 5,304
Pôrto Alegre 3,795
Recife 3,527
Brasília 3,341
Salvador 3,331
Fortaleza 3,261
Curitiba 2,871
Campinas 2,640
Belém 2,097
Goiânia 1,878
Manaus 1,673
Santos 1,634
Vitória 1,602
Maceió 1,137
Natal 1,049
São Luís 982
São José dos Campos 972
João Pessoa 931
Teresina 895
Campo Grande 821
BULGARIA
Sofia 1,045
BURKINA FASO
Ouagadougou 870
BURMA (MYANMAR)
Rangoon 4,082
Mandalay 927
CAMBODIA
Phnom Penh 1,174
CAMEROON
Douala 1,980
Yaoundé 1,727
CANADA
Toronto 5,060
Montréal 3,511
Vancouver 2,125
Ottawa 1,120
Calgary 1,074
Edmonton 1,005
CHILE
Santiago 5,623
CHINA
Shanghai 12,665
Beijing 10,849
Tianjin 9,346
Hong Kong 7,182
Wuhan 6,003
Chongqing 4,975
Shenyang 4,916
Guangzhou 3,881
Chengdu 3,478
Xi'an 3,256
Changchun 3,092
Harbin 2,898
Nanjing 2,806
Zibo 2,775
Dalian 2,709
Jinan 2,654
Taiyuan 2,516
Guiyang 2,467
Qingdao 2,431
Zhengzhou 2,250
Zaozhuang 2,189
Handan 2,120
Liupanshui 1,118
Changsha 2,051
Linyi 2,035
Lu'an 2,015
Wanxian 1,963
Hangzhou 1,955
Tianmen 1,948
Jinxi 1,850
Heze 1,847
Lanzhou 1,788
Tangshan 1,773
Xiantao 1,758
Kunming 1,748
Nanchang 1,742
Shijiazhuang 1,733
Yantai 1,707
Yulin 1,691
Yancheng 1,678
Xuzhou 1,662
Luoyang 1,594
Xinghua 1,587
Pingxiang 1,562
Ürümqi 1,562
Zhanjiang 1,562
Tai'an 1,550
Suining, Sichuan 1,520
Yiyang 1,510
Jilin 1,496
Changde 1,483
Wenzhou 1,475
Anshan 1,459
Qiqihar 1,452
Neijiang 1,449
Fushun 1,425
Huainan 1,422
Fuzhou 1,398
Nanning 1,395
Baotou 1,367
Weifang 1,360
Shantou 1,356
Xintai 1,334
Hefei 1,320
Huaian 1,297
Yueyang 1,286
Shenzhen 1,285
Tianshui 1,269
Suqian 1,258
Jingmen 1,228
Yuzhou 1,226
Zaoyang 1,210
Suzhou 1,201
Wuxi 1,192
Ningbo 1,188
Yongzhou 1,182
Mianyang 1,174
Leshan 1,172
Dongguan 1,150
Chifeng 1,140
Xiaoshan 1,130
Yixing 1,129
Zigong 1,123
Daqing 1,117
Datong 1,113
Huzhou 1,102
Jining, Shandong 1,101
Nanchong 1,072
Fuyu 1,068
Liuzhou 1,031
Xinyi, Jiangsu 1,022
Jixi 1,012
Linqing 1,009
Jiamusi 1,006
Hohhot 998
Xianyang 988
Changzhou 976
Zhangjiakou 973
Benxi 967
Xiangxiang 936
Zhangjiagang 936
Xinyu 932
Yichun, Heilongjiang 916
Yichun, Jiangxi 890
Jinzhou 888
Zhaotong 879
Yuyao 876
Anshun 864
Hengyang 853
Xuanzhou 851
Tongliao 847
Huaibei 830
Mudanjiang 827
Jiaxing 817
Kaifeng 810
Fuxin 807
Hunjiang 798
COLOMBIA
Bogotá 7,594
Medellín 3,236
Cali 2,583
Barranquilla 1,918
Bucaramanga 1,069
Cartagena 1,002
Cúcuta 883
CONGO
Brazzaville 1,153
CONGO (DEM. REP.)
Kinshasa 5,717
Lubumbashi 1,102
Mbuji-Mayi 806
COSTA RICA
San José 1,145
CROATIA
Zagreb 1,067
CUBA
Havana 2,192
CZECH REPUBLIC
Prague 1,164
DENMARK
Copenhagen 1,091
DOMINICAN REPUBLIC
Santo Domingo 2,563
Santiago de los Caballeros 804
ECUADOR
Guayaquil 2,387
Quito 1,514
EGYPT
Cairo 11,146
Alexandria 3,760
Shubrâ el Kheima 937
EL SALVADOR
San Salvador 1,472
ETHIOPIA
Addis Ababa 2,899
FINLAND
Helsinki 937
FRANCE
Paris 9,630
Lyons 1,353
Marseilles 1,290
Lille 991
Nice 889
Toulouse 761
Bordeaux 754
GEORGIA
Tbilisi 1,406
GERMANY
Berlin 3,387
Hamburg 1,705
Munich 1,195
Cologne 963
GHANA
Accra 1,970
Kumasi 862
GREECE
Athens 3,238
Thessaloniki 824
GUATEMALA
Guatemala City 3,242
GUINEA
Conakry 1,465
HAITI
Port-au-Prince 2,090
HONDURAS
Tegucigalpa 1,061
HUNGARY
Budapest 1,670
INDIA
Mumbai 18,336
Delhi 15,334
Kolkata 14,299
Chennai 6,915
Bangalore 6,532
Hyderabad 6,145
Ahmedabad 5,171
Pune 4,485
Surat 3,671
Kanpur 3,040
Jaipur 2,796
Lucknow 2,589
Nagpur 2,359
Patna 2,066
Indore 1,941
Vadodara 1,686
Bhopal 1,656
Coimbatore 1,628
Ludhiana 1,583
Agra 1,526
Visakhapatnam 1,468
Cochin 1,461
Nashik 1,408
Meerut 1,340
Faridabad 1,330
Varanasi 1,300
Ghaziabad 1,277
Asansol 1,272
Jamshedpur 1,246
Madurai 1,245
Jabalpur 1,234
Rajkot 1,205
Dhanbad 1,195
Amritsar 1,162
Allahabad 1,153
Vijayawada 1,093
Srinagar 1,093
Aurangabad 1,065
Bhilainagar-Durg 1,051
Solapur 1,012
Ranchi 999
Jodhpur 954
Guwahati 941
Gwalior 939
Trivandrum 918
Calicut 917
Tiruchchirapalli 913
Chandigarh 896
Hubli-Dharwad 854
Mysore 851
INDONESIA
Jakarta 13,194
Bandung 4,020
Surabaya 2,735
Medan 2,109
Palembang 1,675
Ujung Pandang 1,205
Bandar Lampung 915
Malang 898
Tegal 898
Semarang 816
Bogor 761
IRAN
Tehran 7,352
Mashhad 2,147
Esfahan 1,547
Tabriz 1,396
Karaj 1,235
Shiraz 1,230
Qom 1,045
Ahvaz 967
Bakhtaran 771
IRAQ
Baghdad 5,910
Mosul 1,236
Basra 1,187
Irbil 840
IRELAND
Dublin 985
ISRAEL
Tel Aviv-Yafo 3,025
Haifa 948
ITALY
Rome 2,649
Milan 1,183
Naples 993
Turin 857
Genoa 803
IVORY COAST
Abidjan 3,516
JAPAN
Tokyo 12,064
Yokohama 6,427
Osaka 2,599
Nagoya 2,172
Sapporo 1,922
Kobe 1,493
Kyoto 1,468
Fukuoka 1,341
Kawasaki 1,250
Hiroshima 1,126
Kitakyushu 1,011
Sendai 1,008
Chiba 887
Sakai 792
JORDAN
Amman 1,292
KAZAKHSTAN
Almaty 1,103
KENYA
Nairobi 2,818
KOREA, NORTH
Pyŏngyang 3,124
Hamhung 821
KOREA, SOUTH
Seoul 9,888
Pusan 3,830
Inch'on 2,884
Taegu 2,675
Taejŏn 1,522
Kwangju 1,379
Sŏngnam 1,353
Ulsan 1,340
Ansan 984
Puch'on 900
Suwŏn 876
P'ohang 790
KUWAIT
Kuwait City 879
KYRGYZSTAN
Bishkek 828
LATVIA
Riga 719
LEBANON
Beirut 2,070
LIBYA
Tripoli 1,733
Benghazi 829
MADAGASCAR
Antananarivo 1,808
MALAYSIA
Kuala Lumpur 1,392
MALI
Bamako 1,379
MEXICO
Mexico City 19,013
Guadalajara 3,905
Monterrey 3,517
Toluca 1,987
Puebla 1,880
Tijuana 1,570
Ciudad Juárez 1,469
León 1,438
Torreón 1,057
San Luis Potosí 927
Mérida 919
Querétaro 913
Mexicali 840
Culiacán 799
MONGOLIA
Ulan Bator 842
MOROCCO
Casablanca 3,743
Rabat 1,859
Fès 1,032
Marrakesh 951
MOZAMBIQUE
Maputo 1,316
NEPAL
Katmandu 1,176
NETHERLANDS
Amsterdam 1,157
Rotterdam 1,112
NEW ZEALAND
Auckland 1,152
NICARAGUA
Managua 1,159
NIGER
Niamey 997
NIGERIA
Lagos 11,135
Kano 2,884
Ibadan 2,375
Kaduna 1,329
Benin City 1,022
Ogbomosho 959
Port Harcourt 942
NORWAY
Oslo 808
PAKISTAN
Karachi 11,819
Lahore 6,373
Faisalabad 2,533
Rawalpindi 1,794
Gujranwala 1,466
Multan 1,459
Hyderabad 1,392
Peshawar 1,255
Islamabad 791
PANAMA
Panamá 1,173
PARAGUAY
Asunción 1,750
PERU
Lima 8,180
PHILIPPINES
Manila 10,677
Davao 1,326
POLAND
Warsaw 1,626
Lódz 815
PORTUGAL
Lisbon 1,977
Porto 1,303
PUERTO RICO
San Juan 2,357
ROMANIA
Bucharest 1,764
RUSSIA
Moscow 10,672
Saint Petersburg 5,315
Novosibirsk 1,425
Nizhniy Novgorod 1,288
Yekaterinburg 1,281
Samara 1,140
Omsk 1,132
Kazan 1,108
Rostov 1,081
Chelyabinsk 1,067
Ufa 1,035
Volgograd 1,016
Perm 1,014
Voronezh 918
Saratov 881
Simbirsk 864
Krasnoyarsk 840
Togliatti 771
SAUDI ARABIA
Riyadh 5,514
Jedda 3,807
Mecca 1,529
Medina 1,044
Dammam 920
SENEGAL
Dakar 2,313
SERBIA AND MONTENEGRO
Belgrade 1,116
SIERRA LEONE
Freetown 1,007
SINGAPORE
Singapore City 4,372
SOMALIA
Mogadishu 1,257
SOUTH AFRICA
Johannesburg 2,950
Cape Town 2,930
Durban/eThekwini 2,391
Pretoria/Tshwane 1,590
Port Elizabeth 1,006
SPAIN
Madrid 3,017
Barcelona 1,527
SUDAN
Khartoum 2,742
SWEDEN
Stockholm 1,729
Gothenburg 829
SWITZERLAND
Zürich 984
SYRIA
Aleppo 2,505
Damascus 2,317
Homs 915
TAIWAN
Taipei 2,473
Kaohsiung 1,506
T'aichung 1,066
TANZANIA
Dar es Salaam 2,683
THAILAND
Bangkok 6,604
TUNISIA
Tunis 2,063
TURKEY
Istanbul 8,953
Ankara 3,203
Izmir 2,250
Bursa 1,184
Adana 1,133
Gaziantep 862
Konya 761
UGANDA
Kampala 1,345
Kiev 2,621
Kharkov 1,521
Dnepropetrovsk 1,122
Donetsk 1,065
Odessa 1,027
Zaporozhye 863
Lvov 794
UNITED ARAB EMIRATES
Abu Dhabi 928
Dubai 886
UNITED KINGDOM
London 8,089
Birmingham 2,373
Manchester 2,353
Liverpool 852
Glasgow 832
UNITED STATES OF AMERICA
New York 17,800
Los Angeles 11,789
Chicago 8,308
Philadelphia 5,149
Miami 4,919
Dallas–Fort Worth 4,146
Boston 4,032
Washington 3,934
Detroit 3,903
Houston 3,823
Atlanta 3,500
San Francisco 3,229
Phoenix 2,907
Seattle 2,712
San Diego 2,674
Minneapolis–St Paul 2,389
St Louis 2,078
Baltimore 2,076
Tampa–St Petersburg 2,062
Denver 1,985
Cleveland 1,787
Pittsburgh 1,753
Portland 1,583
San Jose 1,538
San Bernardino 1,507
Cincinnati 1,503
Norfolk–Virginia Beach 1,394
Sacramento 1,393
Kansas City 1,362
San Antonio 1,328
Las Vegas 1,314
Milwaukee 1,309
Indianapolis 1,219
Providence 1,175
Orlando 1,157
Columbus 1,133
New Orleans 1,009
Buffalo 977
Memphis 972
Austin 902
Stamford 889
Salt Lake City 888
Jacksonville 882
Louisville 864
Hartford 852
Richmond 819
Charlotte 759
URUGUAY
Montevideo 1,353
UZBEKISTAN
Tashkent 2,160
VENEZUELA
Caracas 3,276
Valencia 2,330
Maracaibo 2,182
Maracay 1,138
Ciudad Guayana 966
Barquisimeto 923
VIETNAM
Ho Chi Minh City 5,030
Hanoi 4,147
Haiphong 1,817
YEMEN
Sana' 1,621
ZAMBIA
Lusaka 1,450
ZIMBABWE
Harare 1,527
Bulawayo 824

UKRAINE

Each topic list is divided into continents and within a continent the items are listed in order of size. The bottom part of many of the lists is selective in order to give examples from as many different countries as possible. The order of the continents is the same as in the atlas, beginning with Europe and ending with South America. The figures are rounded as appropriate.

World, Continents, Oceans

	km²	miles²	%
The World	509,450,000	196,672,000	–
Land	149,450,000	57,688,000	29.3
Water	360,000,000	138,984,000	70.7
Asia	44,500,000	17,177,000	29.8
Africa	30,302,000	11,697,000	20.3
North America	24,241,000	9,357,000	16.2
South America	17,793,000	6,868,000	11.9
Antarctica	14,100,000	5,443,000	9.4
Europe	9,957,000	3,843,000	6.7
Australia & Oceania	8,557,000	3,303,000	5.7
Pacific Ocean	155,557,000	60,061,000	46.4
Atlantic Ocean	76,762,000	29,638,000	22.9
Indian Ocean	68,556,000	26,470,000	20.4
Southern Ocean	20,327,000	7,848,000	6.1
Arctic Ocean	14,056,000	5,427,000	4.2

Ocean Depths

Atlantic Ocean

	m	ft
Puerto Rico (Milwaukee) Deep	9,220	30,249
Cayman Trench	7,680	25,197
Gulf of Mexico	5,203	17,070
Mediterranean Sea	5,121	16,801
Black Sea	2,211	7,254
North Sea	660	2,165

Indian Ocean

	m	ft
Java Trench	7,450	24,442
Red Sea	2,635	8,454

Pacific Ocean

	m	ft
Mariana Trench	11,022	36,161
Tonga Trench	10,882	35,702
Japan Trench	10,554	34,626
Kuril Trench	10,542	34,587

Arctic Ocean

	m	ft
Molloy Deep	5,608	18,399

Southern Ocean

	m	ft
South Sandwich Trench	7,235	23,737

Mountains

Europe

		m	ft
Elbrus	Russia	5,642	18,510
Mont Blanc	France/Italy	4,807	15,771
Monte Rosa	Italy/Switzerland	4,634	15,203
Dom	Switzerland	4,545	14,911
Liskamm	Switzerland	4,527	14,852
Weisshorn	Switzerland	4,505	14,780
Taschorn	Switzerland	4,490	14,730
Matterhorn/Cervino	Italy/Switzerland	4,478	14,691
Mont Maudit	France/Italy	4,465	14,649
Dent Blanche	Switzerland	4,356	14,291
Nadelhorn	Switzerland	4,327	14,196
Grandes Jorasses	France/Italy	4,208	13,806
Jungfrau	Switzerland	4,158	13,642
Grossglockner	Austria	3,797	12,457
Mulhacén	Spain	3,478	11,411
Zugspitze	Germany	2,962	9,718
Olympus	Greece	2,917	9,570
Triglav	Slovenia	2,863	9,393
Gerlachovsky	Slovak Republic	2,655	8,711
Galdhøpiggen	Norway	2,469	8,100
Kebnekaise	Sweden	2,117	6,946
Ben Nevis	UK	1,342	4,403

Asia

		m	ft
Everest	China/Nepal	8,850	29,035
K2 (Godwin Austen)	China/Kashmir	8,611	28,251
Kanchenjunga	India/Nepal	8,598	28,208
Lhotse	China/Nepal	8,516	27,939
Makalu	China/Nepal	8,481	27,824
Cho Oyu	China/Nepal	8,201	26,906
Dhaulagiri	Nepal	8,172	26,811
Manaslu	Nepal	8,156	26,758
Nanga Parbat	Kashmir	8,126	26,660
Annapurna	Nepal	8,078	26,502
Gasherbrum	China/Kashmir	8,068	26,469
Xixabangma	China	8,012	26,286
Kangbachen	Nepal	7,858	25,781
Trivor	Pakistan	7,720	25,328
Pik Imeni Ismail Samani	Tajikistan	7,495	24,590
Demavend	Iran	5,604	18,386
Ararat	Turkey	5,165	16,945
Gunong Kinabalu	Malaysia (Borneo)	4,101	13,455
Fuji-San	Japan	3,776	12,388

Africa

		m	ft
Kilimanjaro	Tanzania	5,895	19,340
Mt Kenya	Kenya	5,199	17,057
Ruwenzori (Margherita)	Ug./Congo (D.R.)	5,109	16,762
Ras Dashen	Ethiopia	4,620	15,157
Meru	Tanzania	4,565	14,977
Karisimbi	Rwanda/Congo (D.R.)	4,507	14,787
Mt Elgon	Kenya/Uganda	4,321	14,176
Batu	Ethiopia	4,307	14,130
Toubkal	Morocco	4,165	13,665
Mt Cameroun	Cameroon	4,070	13,353

Oceania

		m	ft
Puncak Jaya	Indonesia	5,029	16,499
Puncak Trikora	Indonesia	4,730	15,518
Puncak Mandala	Indonesia	4,702	15,427
Mt Wilhelm	Papua New Guinea	4,508	14,790
Mauna Kea	USA (Hawai'i)	4,205	13,796
Mauna Loa	USA (Hawai'i)	4,169	13,681
Aoraki Mt Cook	New Zealand	3,753	12,313
Mt Kosciuszko	Australia	2,230	7,316

North America

		m	ft
Mt McKinley (Denali)	USA (Alaska)	6,194	20,321
Mt Logan	Canada	5,959	19,551
Pico de Orizaba	Mexico	5,610	18,405
Mt St Elias	USA/Canada	5,489	18,008
Popocatépetl	Mexico	5,452	17,887
Mt Foraker	USA (Alaska)	5,304	17,401
Iztaccíhuatl	Mexico	5,286	17,342
Lucania	Canada	5,226	17,146
Mt Steele	Canada	5,073	16,644
Mt Bona	USA (Alaska)	5,005	16,420
Mt Whitney	USA	4,418	14,495
Tajumulco	Guatemala	4,220	13,845
Chirripó Grande	Costa Rica	3,837	12,589
Pico Duarte	Dominican Rep.	3,175	10,417

South America

		m	ft
Aconcagua	Argentina	6,962	22,841
Bonete	Argentina	6,872	22,546
Ojos del Salado	Argentina/Chile	6,863	22,516
Pissis	Argentina	6,779	22,241
Mercedario	Argentina/Chile	6,770	22,211
Huascarán	Peru	6,768	22,204
Llullaillaco	Argentina/Chile	6,723	22,057
Nudo de Cachi	Argentina	6,720	22,047
Yerupaja	Peru	6,632	21,758
Sajama	Bolivia	6,520	21,391
Chimborazo	Ecuador	6,267	20,561
Pico Cristóbal Colón	Colombia	5,800	19,029
Pico Bolívar	Venezuela	5,007	16,427

Antarctica

		m	ft
Vinson Massif		4,897	16,066
Mt Kirkpatrick		4,528	14,855

Rivers

Europe

		km	miles
Volga	Caspian Sea	3,700	2,300
Danube	Black Sea	2,850	1,770
Ural	Caspian Sea	2,535	1,575
Dnepr (Dnipro)	Black Sea	2,285	1,420
Kama	Volga	2,030	1,260
Don	Black Sea	1,990	1,240
Petchora	Arctic Ocean	1,790	1,110
Oka	Volga	1,480	920
Dnister (Dniester)	Black Sea	1,400	870
Vyatka	Kama	1,370	850
Rhine	North Sea	1,320	820
N. Dvina	Arctic Ocean	1,290	800
Elbe	North Sea	1,145	710

Asia

		km	miles
Yangtze	Pacific Ocean	6,380	3,960
Yenisey–Angara	Arctic Ocean	5,550	3,445
Huang He	Pacific Ocean	5,464	3,395
Ob–Irtysh	Arctic Ocean	5,410	3,360
Mekong	Pacific Ocean	4,500	2,795
Amur	Pacific Ocean	4,442	2,760
Lena	Arctic Ocean	4,402	2,735
Irtysh	Ob	4,250	2,640
Yenisey	Arctic Ocean	4,090	2,540
Ob	Arctic Ocean	3,680	2,285
Indus	Indian Ocean	3,100	1,925
Brahmaputra	Indian Ocean	2,900	1,800
Syrdarya	Aral Sea	2,860	1,775
Salween	Indian Ocean	2,800	1,740
Euphrates	Indian Ocean	2,700	1,675
Amudarya	Aral Sea	2,540	1,575

Africa

		km	miles
Nile	Mediterranean	6,670	4,140
Congo	Atlantic Ocean	4,670	2,900
Niger	Atlantic Ocean	4,180	2,595
Zambezi	Indian Ocean	3,540	2,200
Oubangi/Uele	Congo (D.R.)	2,250	1,400
Kasai	Congo (D.R.)	1,950	1,210
Shaballe	Indian Ocean	1,930	1,200
Orange	Atlantic Ocean	1,860	1,155
Cubango	Okavango Delta	1,800	1,120
Limpopo	Indian Ocean	1,770	1,100
Senegal	Atlantic Ocean	1,640	1,020

Australia

		km	miles
Murray–Darling	Southern Ocean	3,750	2,330
Darling	Murray	3,070	1,905
Murray	Southern Ocean	2,575	1,600
Murrumbidgee	Murray	1,690	1,050

North America

		km	miles
Mississippi–Missouri	Gulf of Mexico	5,971	3,710
Mackenzie	Arctic Ocean	4,240	2,630
Missouri	Mississippi	4,088	2,540
Mississippi	Gulf of Mexico	3,782	2,350
Yukon	Pacific Ocean	3,185	1,980
Rio Grande	Gulf of Mexico	3,030	1,880
Arkansas	Mississippi	2,340	1,450
Colorado	Pacific Ocean	2,330	1,445
Red	Mississippi	2,040	1,270
Columbia	Pacific Ocean	1,950	1,210
Saskatchewan	Lake Winnipeg	1,940	1,205

South America

		km	miles
Amazon	Atlantic Ocean	6,450	4,010
Paraná–Plate	Atlantic Ocean	4,500	2,800
Purus	Amazon	3,350	2,080
Madeira	Amazon	3,200	1,990
São Francisco	Atlantic Ocean	2,900	1,800
Paraná	Plate	2,800	1,740
Tocantins	Atlantic Ocean	2,750	1,710
Orinoco	Atlantic Ocean	2,740	1,700
Paraguay	Paraná	2,550	1,580
Pilcomayo	Paraná	2,500	1,550
Araguaia	Tocantins	2,250	1,400

Lakes

Europe

		km²	miles²
Lake Ladoga	Russia	17,700	6,800
Lake Onega	Russia	9,700	3,700
Saimaa system	Finland	8,000	3,100
Vänern	Sweden	5,500	2,100

Asia

		km²	miles²
Caspian Sea	Asia	371,000	143,000
Lake Baikal	Russia	30,500	11,780
Tonlé Sap	Cambodia	20,000	7,700
Lake Balqash	Kazakhstan	18,500	7,100
Aral Sea	Kazakhstan/Uzbekistan	17,160	6,625

Africa

		km²	miles²
Lake Victoria	East Africa	68,000	26,000
Lake Tanganyika	Central Africa	33,000	13,000
Lake Malawi/Nyasa	East Africa	29,600	11,430
Lake Chad	Central Africa	25,000	9,700
Lake Turkana	Ethiopia/Kenya	8,500	3,290
Lake Volta	Ghana	8,480	3,270

Australia

		km²	miles²
Lake Eyre	Australia	8,900	3,400
Lake Torrens	Australia	5,800	2,200
Lake Gairdner	Australia	4,800	1,900

North America

		km²	miles²
Lake Superior	Canada/USA	82,350	31,800
Lake Huron	Canada/USA	59,600	23,010
Lake Michigan	USA	58,000	22,400
Great Bear Lake	Canada	31,800	12,280
Great Slave Lake	Canada	28,500	11,000
Lake Erie	Canada/USA	25,700	9,900
Lake Winnipeg	Canada	24,400	9,400
Lake Ontario	Canada/USA	19,500	7,500
Lake Nicaragua	Nicaragua	8,200	3,200

South America

		km²	miles²
Lake Titicaca	Bolivia/Peru	8,300	3,200
Lake Poopo	Bolivia	2,800	1,100

Islands

Europe

		km²	miles²
Great Britain	UK	229,880	88,700
Iceland	Atlantic Ocean	103,000	39,800
Ireland	Ireland/UK	84,400	32,600
Novaya Zemlya (N.)	Russia	48,200	18,600
Sicily	Italy	25,500	9,800
Corsica	France	8,700	3,400

Asia

		km²	miles²
Borneo	Southeast Asia	744,360	287,400
Sumatra	Indonesia	473,600	182,860
Honshu	Japan	230,500	88,980
Sulawesi (Celebes)	Indonesia	189,000	73,000
Java	Indonesia	126,700	48,900
Luzon	Philippines	104,700	40,400
Hokkaido	Japan	78,400	30,300

Africa

		km²	miles²
Madagascar	Indian Ocean	587,040	226,660
Socotra	Indian Ocean	3,600	1,400
Réunion	Indian Ocean	2,500	965

Oceania

		km²	miles²
New Guinea	Indonesia/Papua NG	821,030	317,000
New Zealand (S.)	Pacific Ocean	150,500	58,100
New Zealand (N.)	Pacific Ocean	114,700	44,300
Tasmania	Australia	67,800	26,200
Hawai'i	Pacific Ocean	10,450	4,000

North America

		km²	miles²
Greenland	Atlantic Ocean	2,175,600	839,800
Baffin Is.	Canada	508,000	196,100
Victoria Is.	Canada	212,200	81,900
Ellesmere Is.	Canada	212,000	81,800
Cuba	Caribbean Sea	110,860	42,800
Hispaniola	Dominican Rep./Haiti	76,200	29,400
Jamaica	Caribbean Sea	11,400	4,400
Puerto Rico	Atlantic Ocean	8,900	3,400

South America

		km²	miles²
Tierra del Fuego	Argentina/Chile	47,000	18,100
Falkland Is. (E.)	Atlantic Ocean	6,800	2,600

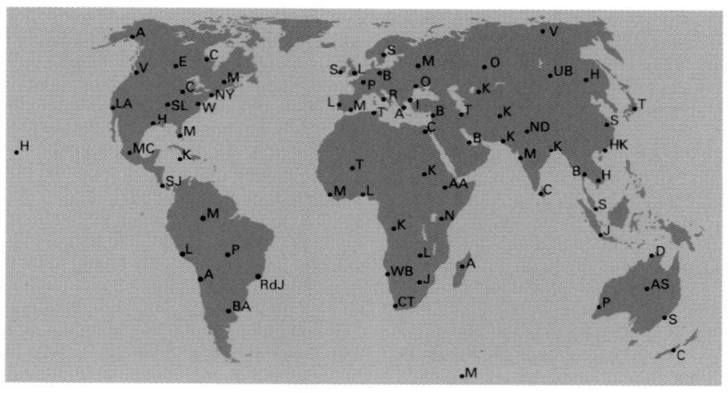

Rainfall and temperature figures are provided for more than 70 cities around the world. As climate is affected by altitude, the height of each city is shown in metres beneath its name. For each location, the top row of figures shows the total rainfall or snow in millimetres, and the bottom row the average temperature in degrees Celsius; the total annual rainfall and average annual temperature are at the end of the rows.

Europe	Jan.	Feb.	Mar.	Apr.	May	June	July	Aug.	Sept.	Oct.	Nov.	Dec.	Year
Athens, Greece	62	37	37	23	23	14	6	7	15	51	56	71	402
107 m	10	10	12	16	20	25	28	28	24	20	15	11	18
Berlin, Germany	46	40	33	42	49	65	73	69	48	49	46	43	603
55 m	–1	0	4	9	14	17	19	18	15	9	5	1	9
Istanbul, Turkey	109	92	72	46	38	34	34	30	58	81	103	119	816
14 m	5	6	7	11	16	20	23	23	20	16	12	8	14
Lisbon, Portugal	111	76	109	54	44	16	3	4	33	62	93	103	708
77 m	11	12	14	16	17	20	22	23	21	18	14	12	17
London, UK	54	40	37	37	46	45	57	59	49	57	64	48	593
5 m	4	5	7	9	12	16	18	17	15	11	8	5	11
Málaga, Spain	61	51	62	46	26	5	1	3	29	64	64	62	474
33 m	12	13	16	17	19	29	25	26	23	20	16	13	18
Moscow, Russia	39	38	36	37	53	58	88	71	58	45	47	54	624
156 m	–13	–10	–4	6	13	16	18	17	12	6	–1	–7	4
Odesa, Ukraine	57	62	30	21	34	34	42	37	37	13	35	71	473
64 m	–3	–1	2	9	15	20	22	22	18	12	9	1	10
Paris, France	56	46	35	42	57	54	59	64	55	50	51	50	619
75 m	3	4	8	11	15	18	20	19	17	12	7	4	12
Rome, Italy	71	62	57	51	46	37	15	21	63	99	129	93	744
17 m	8	9	11	14	18	22	25	25	22	17	13	10	16
Shannon, Irish Republic	94	67	56	53	61	57	77	79	86	86	96	117	929
2 m	5	5	7	9	12	14	16	16	14	11	8	6	10
Stockholm, Sweden	43	30	25	31	34	45	61	76	60	48	53	48	554
44 m	–3	–3	–1	5	10	15	18	17	12	7	3	0	7
Asia													
Bahrain	8	18	13	8	<3	0	0	0	0	0	18	18	81
5 m	17	18	21	25	29	32	33	34	31	28	24	19	26
Bangkok, Thailand	8	20	36	58	198	160	160	175	305	206	66	5	1,397
2 m	26	28	29	30	29	29	28	28	28	28	26	25	28
Beirut, Lebanon	191	158	94	53	18	3	<3	<3	5	51	132	185	892
34 m	14	14	16	18	22	24	27	28	26	24	19	16	21
Colombo, Sri Lanka	89	69	147	231	371	224	135	109	160	348	315	147	2,365
7 m	26	26	27	28	28	27	27	27	27	27	26	26	27
Harbin, China	6	5	10	23	43	94	112	104	46	33	8	5	488
160 m	–18	–15	–5	6	13	19	22	21	14	4	–6	–16	3
Ho Chi Minh, Vietnam	15	3	13	43	221	330	315	269	335	269	114	56	1,984
9 m	26	27	29	30	29	28	28	28	27	27	27	26	28
Hong Kong, China	33	46	74	137	292	394	381	361	257	114	43	31	2,162
33 m	16	15	18	22	26	28	28	28	27	25	21	18	23
Jakarta, Indonesia	300	300	211	147	114	97	64	43	66	112	142	203	1,798
8 m	26	26	27	27	27	27	27	27	27	27	27	26	27
Kabul, Afghanistan	31	36	94	102	20	5	3	3	<3	15	20	10	338
1,815 m	–3	–1	6	13	18	22	25	24	20	14	7	3	12
Karachi, Pakistan	13	10	8	3	3	18	81	41	13	<3	3	5	196
4 m	19	20	24	28	30	31	30	29	28	28	24	20	26
Kazalinsk, Kazakhstan	10	10	13	13	15	5	5	8	8	10	13	15	125
63 m	–12	–11	–3	6	18	23	25	23	16	8	–1	–7	7
Kolkata (Calcutta), India	10	31	36	43	140	297	325	328	252	114	20	5	1,600
6 m	20	22	27	30	30	30	29	29	29	28	23	19	26
Mumbai (Bombay), India	3	3	3	<3	18	485	617	340	264	64	13	3	1,809
11 m	24	24	26	28	30	29	27	27	27	28	27	26	27
New Delhi, India	23	18	13	8	13	74	180	172	117	10	3	10	640
218 m	14	17	23	28	33	34	31	30	29	26	20	15	25
Omsk, Russia	15	8	8	13	31	51	51	51	28	25	18	20	318
85 m	–22	–19	–12	–1	10	16	18	16	10	1	–11	–18	–1
Shanghai, China	48	58	84	94	94	180	147	142	130	71	51	36	1,135
7 m	4	5	9	14	20	24	28	28	23	19	12	7	16
Singapore	252	173	193	188	173	173	170	196	178	208	254	257	2,413
10 m	26	27	28	28	28	28	28	27	27	27	27	27	27
Tehran, Iran	46	38	46	36	13	3	3	3	3	8	20	31	246
1,220 m	2	5	9	16	21	26	30	29	25	18	12	6	17
Tokyo, Japan	48	74	107	135	147	165	142	152	234	208	97	56	1,565
6 m	3	4	7	13	17	21	25	26	23	17	11	6	14
Ulan Bator, Mongolia	<3	<3	3	5	10	28	76	51	23	5	5	3	208
1,325 m	–26	–21	–13	–1	6	14	16	14	8	–1	–13	–22	–3
Verkhoyansk, Russia	5	5	3	5	8	23	28	25	13	8	8	5	134
100 m	–50	–45	–32	–15	0	12	14	9	2	–15	–38	–48	–17
Africa													
Addis Ababa, Ethiopia	<3	3	25	135	213	201	206	239	102	28	<3	0	1,151
2,450 m	19	20	20	20	19	18	18	19	21	22	21	20	20
Antananarivo, Madagas.	300	279	178	53	18	8	8	10	18	61	135	287	1,356
1,372 m	21	21	21	19	18	15	14	15	17	19	21	21	19
Cairo, Egypt	5	5	5	3	3	<3	0	0	<3	<3	3	5	28
116 m	13	15	18	21	25	28	28	28	26	24	20	15	22
Cape Town, S. Africa	15	8	18	48	79	84	89	66	43	31	18	10	508
17 m	21	21	20	17	14	13	12	13	14	16	18	19	17
Johannesburg, S. Africa	114	109	89	38	25	8	8	8	23	56	107	125	709
1,665 m	20	20	18	16	13	10	11	13	16	18	19	20	16

	Jan.	Feb.	Mar.	Apr.	May	June	July	Aug.	Sept.	Oct.	Nov.	Dec.	Year
Khartoum, Sudan	<3	<3	<3	<3	3	8	53	71	18	5	<3	0	158
390 m	24	25	28	31	33	34	32	31	32	32	28	25	29
Kinshasa, Congo (D.R.)	135	145	196	196	158	8	3	3	31	119	221	142	1,354
325 m	26	26	27	27	26	24	23	24	25	26	26	26	25
Lagos, Nigeria	28	46	102	150	269	460	279	64	140	206	69	25	1,836
3 m	27	28	29	28	28	26	26	25	26	26	28	28	27
Lusaka, Zambia	231	191	142	18	3	<3	<3	0	<3	10	91	150	836
1,277 m	21	22	21	21	19	16	16	18	22	24	23	22	21
Monrovia, Liberia	31	56	97	216	516	973	996	373	744	772	236	130	5,138
23 m	26	26	27	27	26	25	24	25	25	25	26	26	26
Nairobi, Kenya	38	64	125	211	158	46	15	23	31	53	109	86	958
1,820 m	19	19	19	19	18	16	16	16	18	19	18	18	18
Timbuktu, Mali	<3	<3	3	<3	5	23	79	81	38	3	<3	<3	231
301 m	22	24	28	32	34	35	32	30	32	31	28	23	29
Tunis, Tunisia	64	51	41	36	18	8	3	8	33	51	48	61	419
66 m	10	11	13	16	19	23	26	27	25	20	16	11	18
Walvis Bay, Namibia	<3	5	8	3	3	<3	<3	3	<3	<3	<3	<3	23
7 m	19	19	19	18	17	16	15	14	14	15	17	18	18
Australia, New Zealand and Antarctica													
Alice Springs, Australia	43	33	28	10	15	13	8	8	8	18	31	38	252
579 m	29	28	25	20	15	12	12	14	18	23	26	28	21
Christchurch, N. Zealand	56	43	48	48	66	66	69	48	46	43	48	56	638
10 m	16	16	14	12	9	6	6	7	9	12	14	16	11
Darwin, Australia	386	312	254	97	15	3	<3	3	13	51	119	239	1,491
30 m	29	29	29	29	28	26	25	26	28	29	30	29	28
Mawson, Antarctica	11	30	20	10	44	180	4	40	3	20	0	0	362
14 m	0	–5	–10	–14	–15	–16	–18	–18	–19	–13	–5	–1	–11
Perth, Australia	8	10	20	43	130	180	170	149	86	56	20	13	881
60 m	23	23	22	19	16	14	13	13	15	16	19	22	18
Sydney, Australia	89	102	127	135	127	117	117	76	73	71	73	73	1,181
42 m	22	22	21	18	15	13	12	13	15	18	19	21	17
North America													
Anchorage, Alaska, USA	20	18	15	10	13	18	41	66	66	56	25	23	371
40 m	–11	–8	–5	2	7	12	14	13	9	2	–5	–11	2
Chicago, Illinois, USA	51	51	66	71	86	89	84	81	79	66	61	51	836
251 m	–4	–3	2	9	14	20	23	22	19	12	5	–1	10
Churchill, Man., Canada	15	13	18	23	32	44	46	58	51	43	39	21	402
13 m	–28	–26	–20	–10	–2	6	12	11	5	–2	–12	–22	–7
Edmonton, Alta., Canada	25	19	19	22	43	77	89	78	39	17	16	25	466
676 m	–15	–10	–5	4	11	15	17	16	11	6	–4	–10	3
Honolulu, Hawai'i, USA	104	66	79	48	25	18	23	28	36	48	64	104	643
12 m	23	18	19	20	22	24	25	26	26	24	22	19	22
Houston, Texas, USA	89	76	84	91	119	117	99	99	104	94	89	109	1,171
12 m	12	13	17	21	24	27	28	29	26	22	16	12	21
Kingston, Jamaica	23	15	23	31	102	89	38	91	99	180	74	36	800
34 m	25	25	25	26	26	28	28	28	27	27	26	26	26
Los Angeles, Calif., USA	79	76	71	25	10	3	<3	<3	5	15	31	66	381
95 m	13	14	14	16	17	19	21	22	21	18	16	14	17
Mexico City, Mexico	13	5	10	20	53	119	170	152	130	51	18	8	747
2,309 m	12	13	16	18	19	19	17	18	18	16	14	13	16
Miami, Florida, USA	71	53	64	81	173	178	155	160	203	234	71	51	1,516
8 m	20	20	22	23	25	27	28	28	27	25	22	21	24
Montréal, Que., Canada	72	65	74	74	66	82	90	92	88	76	81	87	946
57 m	–10	–9	–3	–6	13	18	21	20	15	9	2	–7	6
New York City, NY, USA	94	97	91	81	81	84	107	109	86	89	76	91	1,092
96 m	–1	–1	3	10	16	20	23	23	21	15	7	2	11
St Louis, Mo., USA	58	64	89	97	114	114	89	86	81	74	71	64	1,001
173 m	0	1	7	13	19	24	26	26	22	15	8	2	14
San José, Costa Rica	15	5	20	46	229	241	211	241	305	300	145	41	1,798
1,146 m	19	19	21	21	22	21	21	21	21	20	20	19	20
Vancouver, BC, Canada	154	115	101	60	52	45	32	41	67	114	150	182	1,113
14 m	3	5	6	9	12	15	17	17	14	10	6	4	10
Washington, DC, USA	86	76	91	84	94	99	112	109	94	74	66	79	1,064
22 m	1	2	7	12	18	23	25	24	20	14	8	3	13
SOUTH AMERICA													
Antofagasta, Chile	0	0	0	<3	<3	3	5	3	<3	3	<3	0	13
94 m	21	21	20	18	16	15	14	14	15	16	18	19	17
Buenos Aires, Argentina	79	71	109	89	76	61	56	61	79	86	84	99	950
27 m	23	23	21	17	13	9	10	11	13	15	19	22	16
Lima, Peru	3	<3	<3	<3	5	5	8	8	8	3	3	<3	41
120 m	23	24	24	22	19	17	17	16	17	18	19	21	20
Manaus, Brazil	249	231	262	221	170	84	58	38	46	107	142	203	1,811
44 m	28	28	28	27	28	28	28	28	29	29	29	28	28
Paraná, Brazil	287	236	239	102	13	<3	3	5	28	127	231	310	1,582
260 m	23	23	23	23	23	21	21	22	24	24	24	23	23
Rio de Janeiro, Brazil	125	122	130	107	79	53	41	43	66	79	104	137	1,082
61 m	26	26	25	24	22	21	21	21	21	22	23	25	23

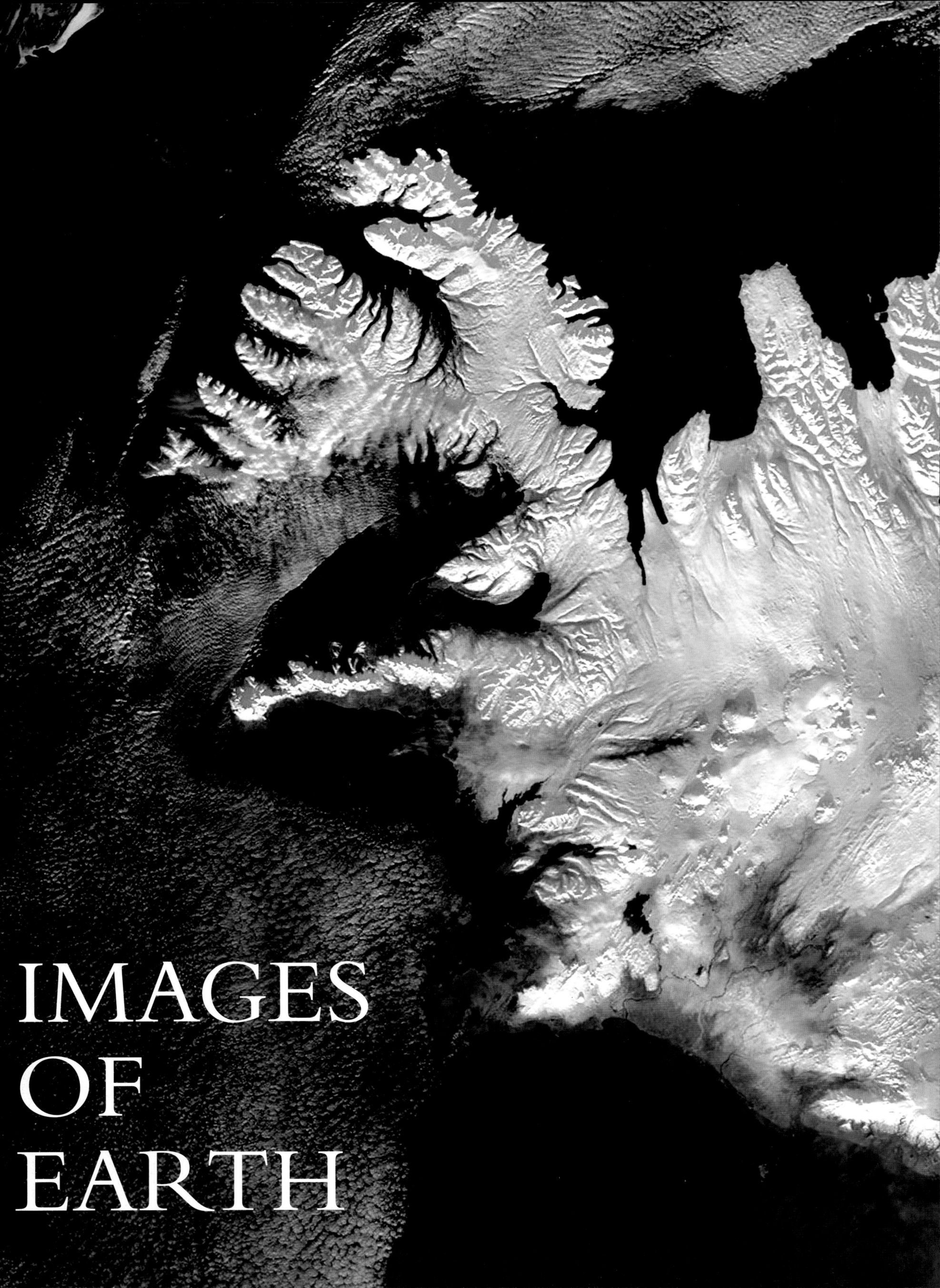

IMAGES
OF
EARTH

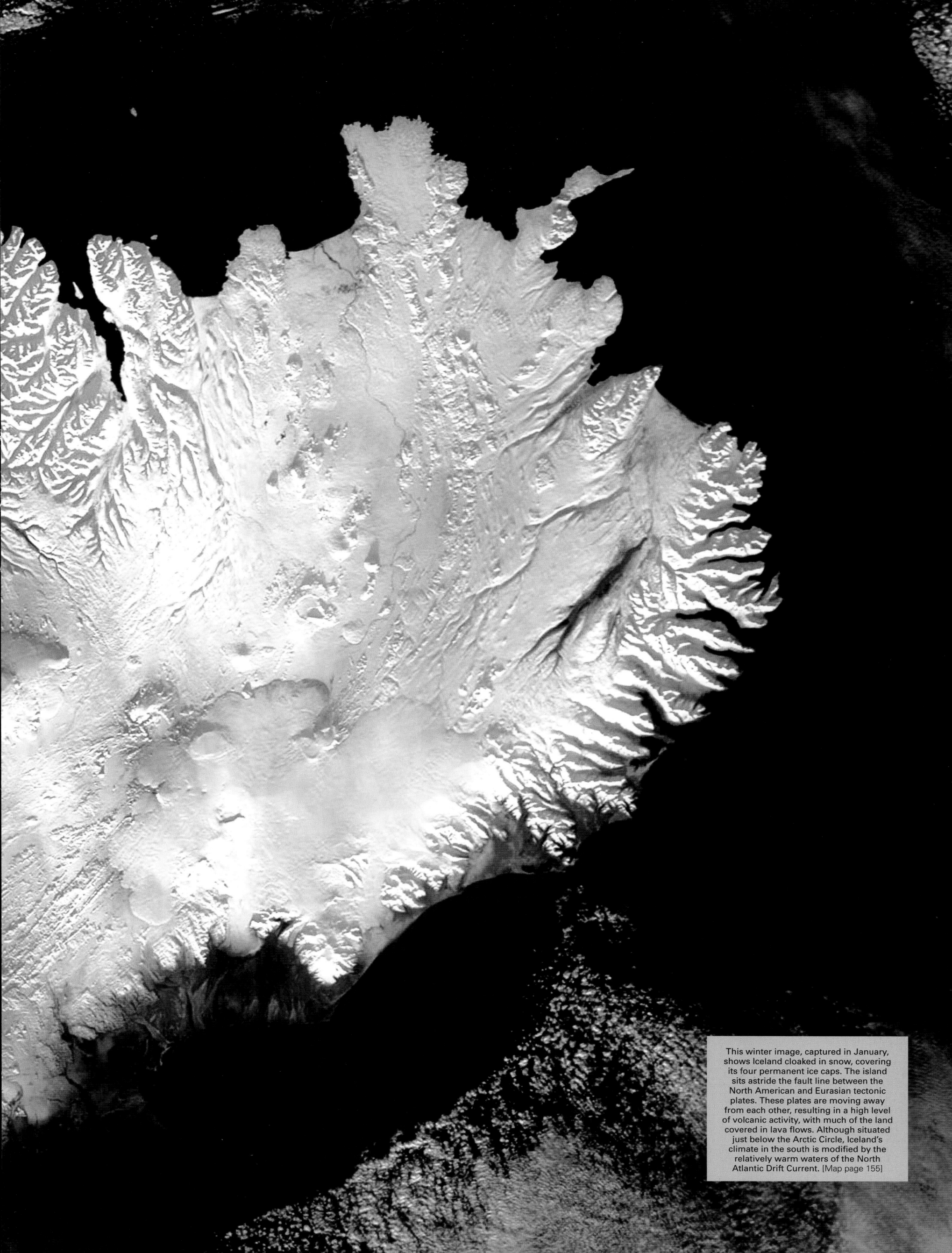

This winter image, captured in January, shows Iceland cloaked in snow, covering its four permanent ice caps. The island sits astride the fault line between the North American and Eurasian tectonic plates. These plates are moving away from each other, resulting in a high level of volcanic activity, with much of the land covered in lava flows. Although situated just below the Arctic Circle, Iceland's climate in the south is modified by the relatively warm waters of the North Atlantic Drift Current. [Map page 155]

The River Thames, flowing from west to east, stands out in this image, as do the former London docks and the extensive reservoirs in the River Lea valley to the north-east. The settlement developed over 1,900 years ago at the river's lowest bridging point, on the main Roman supply route to and from the south coast. Despite having a population in excess of 8 million people, there are still many parks and open spaces around the city centre. Some, such as Regents, Hyde and St James's Parks, are over 300 years old, having previously been royal hunting grounds. [Map page 169]

The most active volcano in Europe, Mount Etna is shown here during the 2002–3 eruption, its plume of ash and smoke spreading southwards over the Mediterranean. As with many other volcanoes, the volcanic debris has weathered to produce fertile soils and there are highly productive vineyards, citrus groves and banana plantations around its base. This area of southern Italy has several other volcanoes, including Vesuvius and Stromboli, as it lies near the junction of the African and Eurasian tectonic plates. [Map page 201]

14 DANUBE DELTA, ROMANIA

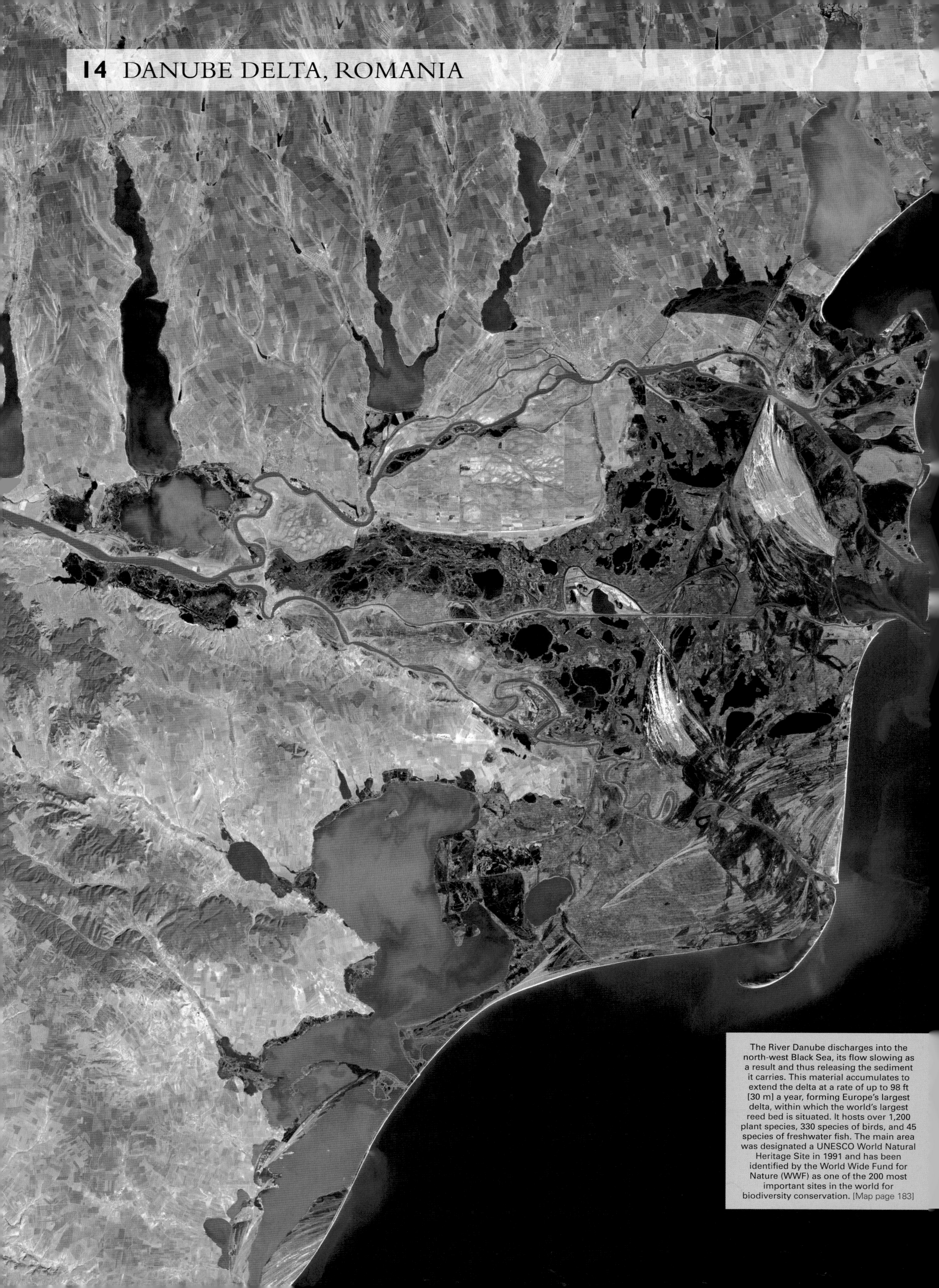

The River Danube discharges into the north-west Black Sea, its flow slowing as a result and thus releasing the sediment it carries. This material accumulates to extend the delta at a rate of up to 98 ft [30 m] a year, forming Europe's largest delta, within which the world's largest reed bed is situated. It hosts over 1,200 plant species, 330 species of birds, and 45 species of freshwater fish. The main area was designated a UNESCO World Natural Heritage Site in 1991 and has been identified by the World Wide Fund for Nature (WWF) as one of the 200 most important sites in the world for biodiversity conservation. [Map page 183]

At the head of Tokyo Bay, the city, with its satellites of Kawasaki and Yokohama, forms one of the world's most densely populated areas with nearly 20 million people. Owing to the shortage of space, much development has taken place on areas reclaimed from the sea. One of these is Haneda International Airport, whose runway pattern is clearly visible at the mouth of the Tama River. The Tokyo Bay bridge/tunnel projects into the Bay from the eastern shore. [Map page 223]

This image shows glaciers flowing from the snow-covered Himalayas on the northern Bhutan border. Glaciers are an important indicator of temperature change. By comparing imagery, researchers have found a strong correlation between increasing temperatures and glacial retreat, as well as volumes of melt water and the size and number of lakes forming on the surface of the glaciers. About 70% of the world's fresh water is frozen in glaciers and the largest concentration of these outside the polar regions is in the Himalayas. It is believed that 67% of these glaciers are retreating. [Map page 241]

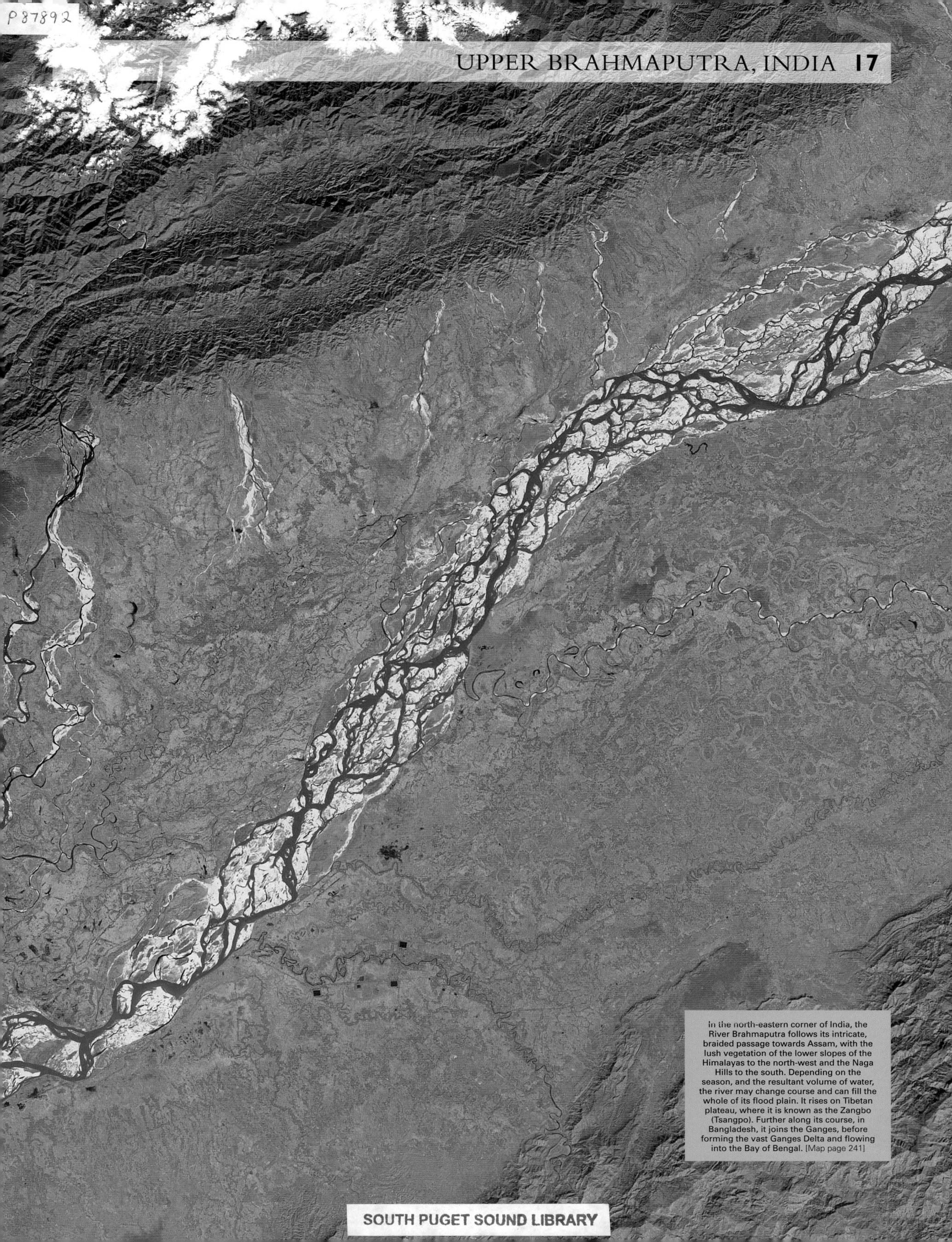

In the north-eastern corner of India, the River Brahmaputra follows its intricate, braided passage towards Assam, with the lush vegetation of the lower slopes of the Himalayas to the north-west and the Naga Hills to the south. Depending on the season, and the resultant volume of water, the river may change course and can fill the whole of its flood plain. It rises on Tibetan plateau, where it is known as the Zangbo (Tsangpo). Further along its course, in Bangladesh, it joins the Ganges, before forming the vast Ganges Delta and flowing into the Bay of Bengal. [Map page 241]

The largest city in Africa, with almost 10 million inhabitants, Cairo evolved on the eastern bank of the River Nile, near its delta. This image clearly shows the differences between the arid desert areas to the south-east and south-west, the fertile lands of the Nile flood plain, and the urban area itself. The shadows of the Pyramids on the Giza Plateau can be seen on the left-hand edge of the cultivated area, below where the road, approaching from the bottom left-hand side, crosses it.

[Map page 256]

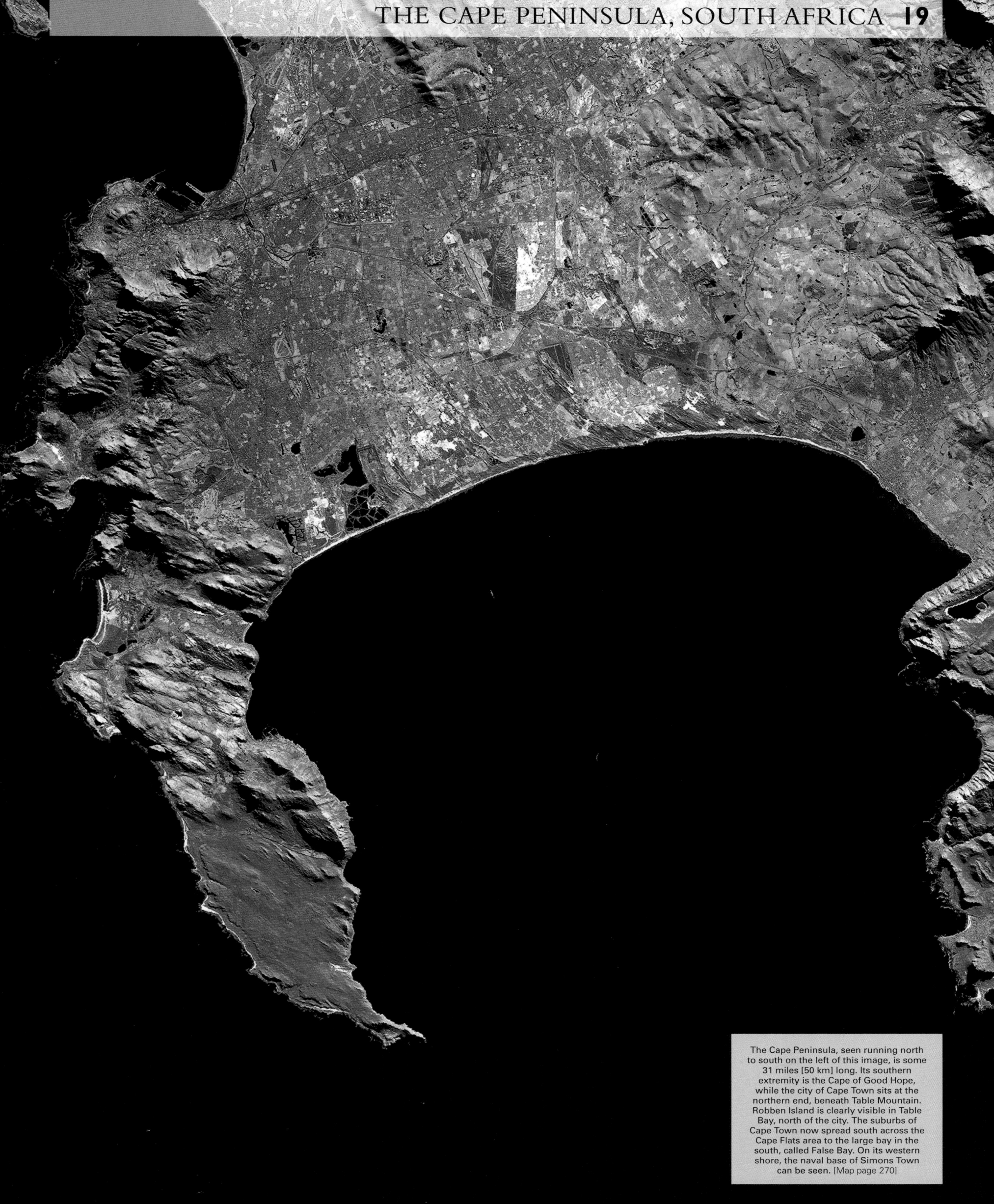

The Cape Peninsula, seen running north to south on the left of this image, is some 31 miles [50 km] long. Its southern extremity is the Cape of Good Hope, while the city of Cape Town sits at the northern end, beneath Table Mountain. Robben Island is clearly visible in Table Bay, north of the city. The suburbs of Cape Town now spread south across the Cape Flats area to the large bay in the south, called False Bay. On its western shore, the naval base of Simons Town can be seen. [Map page 270]

Situated within the Great Rift Valley in northern Tanzania, the crater is the largest complete collapsed volcanic cone, or caldera, in the world. The whole area was one of intense geological activity as can be seen from the surrounding craters, but currently only one, in the north-east, is active. Ngorongoro is the crater in the south of the image, with Lake Magadi within it. The steep sides of the crater limit normal animal migration and within it there is a unique ecosystem supporting a wide range of birds and animals. The two lakes in the south are Lake Eyasi (to the west) and Lake Manyara (to the east). [Map page 268]

Sydney, the largest city in Australia and capital of New South Wales, was founded at the end of the 18th century on the north shore of Botany Bay, the southern of the two enclosed bays shown here. The runways of the international airport project into this, and to the north, on the south shore of the irregularly shaped Sydney Harbour, the shadows of the skyscrapers in the central business district can be seen. The Sydney Harbour Bridge beyond connects it to North Sydney. [Map page 283]

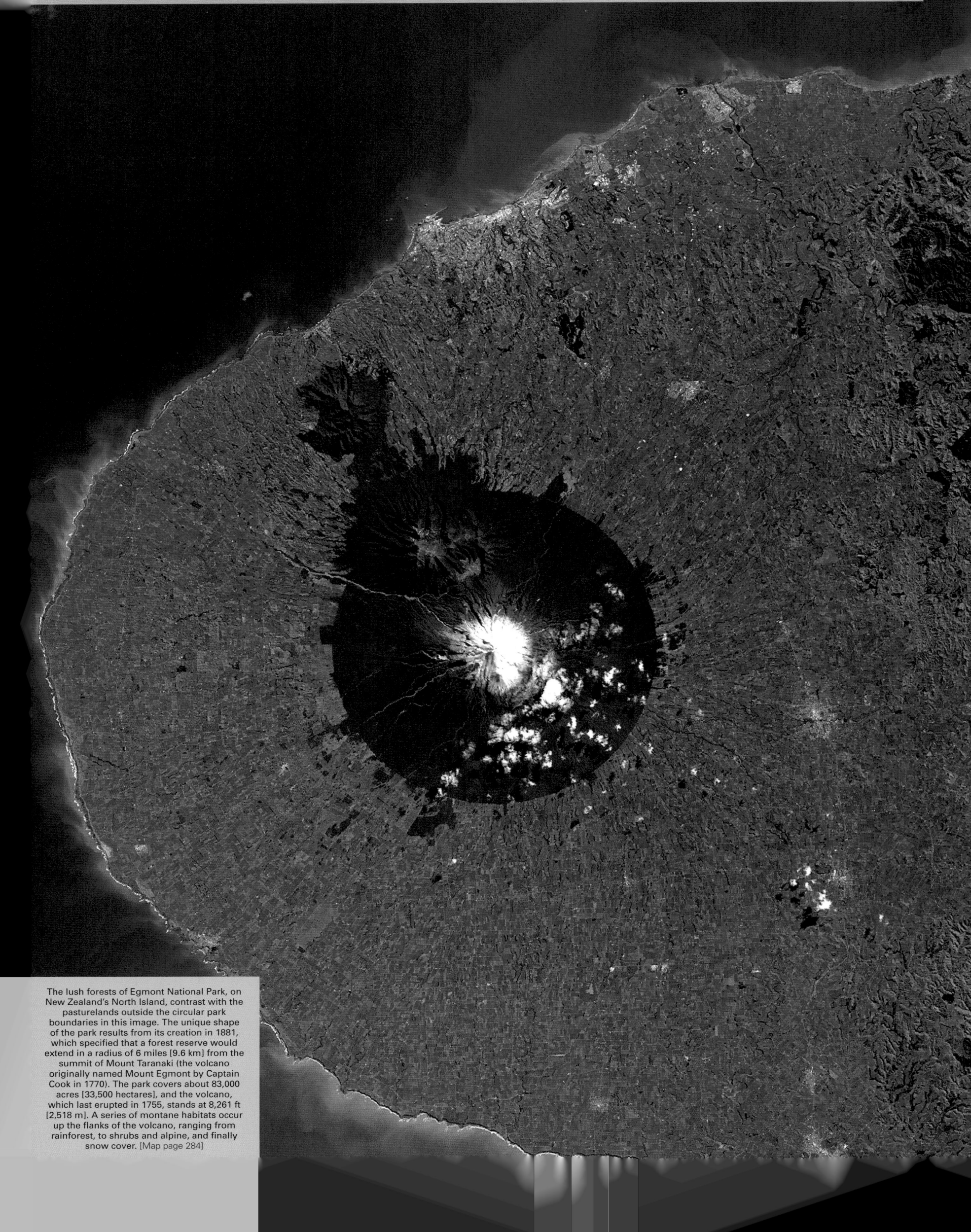

The lush forests of Egmont National Park, on New Zealand's North Island, contrast with the pasturelands outside the circular park boundaries in this image. The unique shape of the park results from its creation in 1881, which specified that a forest reserve would extend in a radius of 6 miles [9.6 km] from the summit of Mount Taranaki (the volcano originally named Mount Egmont by Captain Cook in 1770). The park covers about 83,000 acres [33,500 hectares], and the volcano, which last erupted in 1755, stands at 8,261 ft [2,518 m]. A series of montane habitats occur up the flanks of the volcano, ranging from rainforest, to shrubs and alpine, and finally snow cover. [Map page 284]

The city of Vancouver grew up around its fine, natural harbour on the north side of the Fraser River delta, developing as the western railhead of the Canadian Pacific Railroad. Just to the south of the delta runs the 49th parallel, the boundary between Canada and the USA. To the north of the city lie the snow-capped Coast Mountains, and to the south-west, across the Strait of Georgia, part of Vancouver Island with the town of Victoria, the capital of British Columbia, can be seen. [Map page 296]

This image covers most of the largest urban area in the United States, which has a population of over 17 million people. Flowing from the north, the Hudson River divides the two cities of New York (to the east) and Jersey City (to the west). Towards its mouth on the east bank lies Manhattan Island, with the rectangular Central Park clearly visible. Below this is the end of Long Island, which is connected by bridge to Staten Island, to the west. [Map page 312]

Sometimes called 'The Crescent City', the settlement is situated between the south bank of Lake Pontchartrain (the largest in this view) and the Mississippi River. The latter can be seen meandering to the south of the city on its way to the delta, which lies to the south-east. In August 2005 the flood-control system, which was constructed in the early 20th century, failed in the face of the category 5 Hurricane Katrina, which breached two dams and flooded and destroyed parts of the city, making many homeless. The wetlands to the south are themselves being eroded since less silt is being deposited at the mouth to reinforce the delta. [Map page 315]

The town, with a population of almost 1.5 million, is the light area to the north of the confluence of the Rio Negro, or Black River (to the north), with the Amazon (to the south), some 1,000 miles [1,600 km] from its mouth. The main branch of the river to the south, sometimes also called the Solimões, is carrying a heavy load of sediment from the Andes, hence the marked colour difference. For all of its length across Brazil the river is over 100 ft [30 m] deep and ocean-going vessels can navigate this far upstream, and indeed continue a further 1,300 miles [2,100 km] up the Amazon to Iquitos, in northern Peru.

[Map page 329]

Santiago, the capital city of Chile, lies in a fertile valley at the foot of the Andes, some 37 miles [60 km] south-east of the main port of Valparaíso. To the east the mountains rise to over 20,000 ft [6,000 m]. At top right of the image, the boundary with Argentina runs along the watershed. The city expanded rapidly to its current population of over 5 million inhabitants and this resulted in air pollution problems in the 1980s, though measures have since been taken to deal with this.

[Map page 334]

GAZETTEER
OF
NATIONS

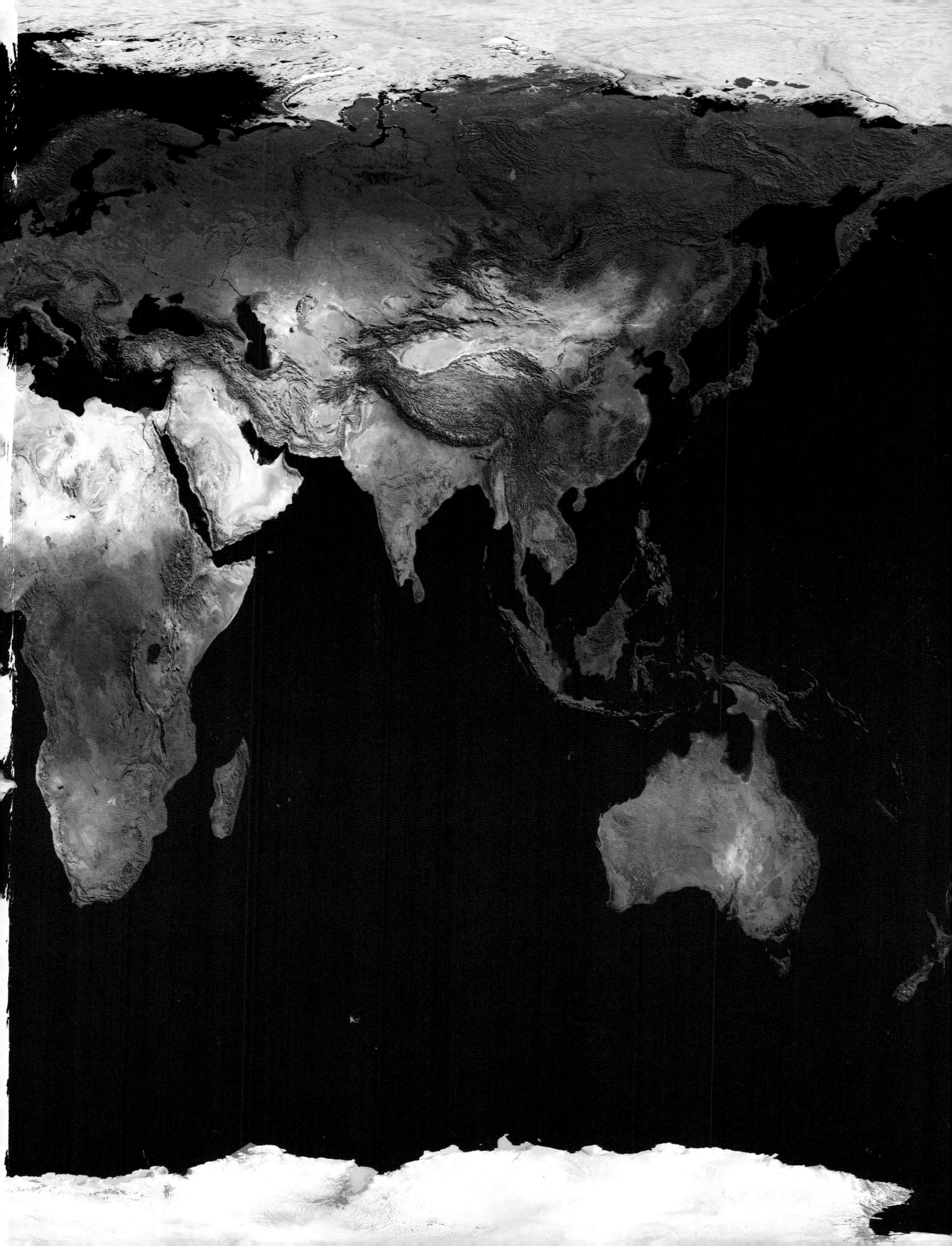

AFGHANISTAN

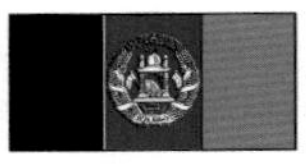

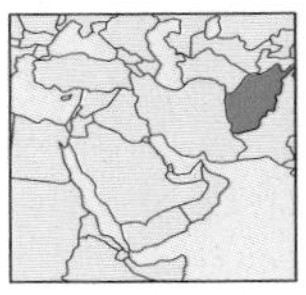

GEOGRAPHY The Republic of Afghanistan is a landlocked, mountainous country in southern Asia. The central highlands reach a height of more than 22,966 ft [7,000 m] in the east and make up nearly three-quarters of Afghanistan. The main range is the Hindu Kush, which is cut by deep, fertile valleys.

In winter, northerly winds bring cold, snowy weather to the mountains, but summers are hot and dry.

POLITICS & ECONOMY The modern history of Afghanistan began in 1747, when the various tribes in the area united for the first time. In the 19th century, Russia and Britain struggled for control of the country. Following Britain's withdrawal in 1919, Afghanistan became fully independent. Soviet troops invaded in 1979 to support a socialist regime in Kabul, but they withdrew in 1989. By 2001, a group called the Taliban ("Islamic students") controlled 90% of the country. In 2001, following the refusal of the Taliban to hand over the terrorist leader Osama bin Laden, an international force invaded Afghanistan. In 2002, a coalition government was set up under Hamid Karzai, who was elected president in 2004 under a new constitution. Despite ongoing conflict, parliamentary elections were held in 2005.

Afghanistan is a poor country and more then 60% of its people are farmers or nomadic herders. Natural gas is produced, together with some coal, copper, gold, precious stones, and salt.

AREA 251,772 sq mi [652,090 sq km] **POPULATION** 29,929,000 **CAPITAL (POPULATION)** Kabul (1,565,000) **GOVERNMENT** Transitional **ETHNIC GROUPS** Pashtun (Pathan) 44%, Tajik 25%, Hazara 10%, Uzbek 8%, others 13% **LANGUAGES** Pashtu, Dari/Persian (both official), Uzbek **RELIGIONS** Islam (Sunni Muslim 84%, Shi'ite Muslim 15%), others 1% **CURRENCY** Afghani = 100 puls

ALBANIA

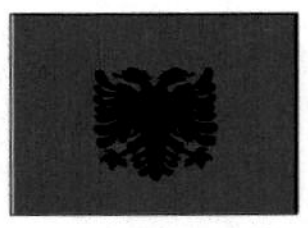

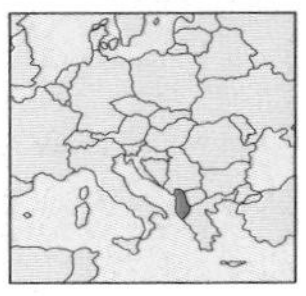

GEOGRAPHY The Republic of Albania lies in the Balkan peninsula, facing the Adriatic Sea. About 70% of the land is mountainous, but most Albanians live in the west on the coastal lowlands.

The coastal areas of Albania experience a typical Mediterranean climate, with fairly dry, sunny summers and cool, moist winters. The mountains have a severe climate, with heavy winter snowfalls.

POLITICS & ECONOMY Albania is one of Europe's poorest nations. A former Communist country, Albania adopted a multi-party system in the early 1990s. The change proved difficult. But after elections in 1997, a socialist government committed to a market system took office. The transition to democracy has been difficult. The 2005 elections, when the center-right Democratic Party defeated the Socialists, were considered to fall short of international standards.

In 2001, agriculture employed more than 60% of the people. Since 1991, private ownership of land has been encouraged, replacing the former state farm and collective system. Albania has some minerals. Chromite, copper, and nickel are exported.

AREA 11,100 sq mi [28,748 sq km] **POPULATION** 3,563,000 **CAPITAL (POPULATION)** Tirana (300,000) **GOVERNMENT** Multiparty republic **ETHNIC GROUPS** Albanian 95%, Greek 3%, Macedonian, Vlachs, Gypsy **LANGUAGES** Albanian (official) **RELIGIONS** Many people say they are non-believers; of the believers, 70% follow Islam and 30% follow Christianity (Orthodox 20%, Roman Catholic 10%) **CURRENCY** Lek = 100 qindars

ALGERIA

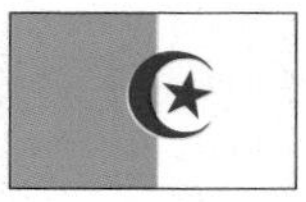

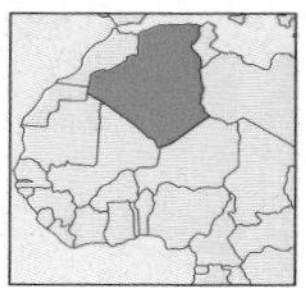

GEOGRAPHY The People's Democratic Republic of Algeria is Africa's second largest country after Sudan. Most Algerians live in the north, on the fertile coastal plains and hill country bordering the Mediterranean Sea. Four-fifths of Algeria is in the Sahara. The coast has a Mediterranean climate, but the arid Sahara is hot by day and cool at night.

POLITICS & ECONOMY France ruled Algeria from 1830 until 1962, when the socialist FLN (National Liberation Front) formed a one-party government. Following the recognition of opposition parties in 1989, a Muslim group, the FIS (Islamic Salvation Front), won an election in 1991. The FLN canceled the elections and civil conflict broke out. About 100,000 people were killed in the 1990s. In 1999, Abdelaziz Bouteflika was elected president. The scale of violence was reduced and Bouteflika was re-elected in 2004. In 2005, the government agreed to accept demands made by the Berber minority and, in 2006, it began releasing Islamic militants under an amnesty.

Algeria is a developing country, whose chief resources are oil and natural gas, which were discovered in the Sahara in 1956. The natural gas reserves are among the world's largest, and gas and oil account for 90% of Algeria's exports. Cement, iron and steel, textiles, and vehicles are manufactured. Barley, citrus fruits, dates, potatoes, and wheat are the major crops.

AREA 919,590 sq mi [2,381,741 sq km] **POPULATION** 32,532,000 **CAPITAL (POPULATION)** Algiers (1,722,000) **GOVERNMENT** Socialist republic **ETHNIC GROUPS** Arab-Berber 99% **LANGUAGES** Arabic and Berber (official), French **RELIGIONS** Sunni Muslim 99% **CURRENCY** Algerian dinar = 100 centimes

AMERICAN SAMOA

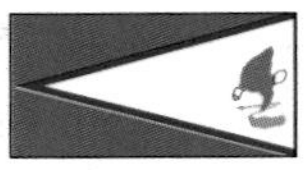

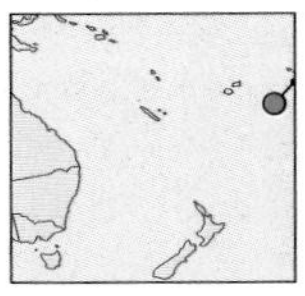

An "unincorporated territory" of the United States, American Samoa lies in the south-central Pacific Ocean.

AREA 77 sq mi [199 sq km] **POPULATION** 58,000 **CAPITAL** Pago Pago

ANDORRA

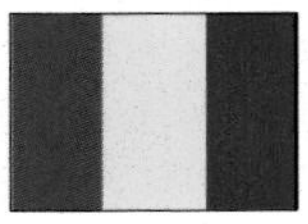

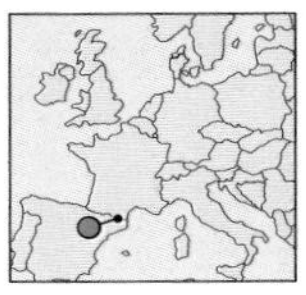

A mini-state situated in the Pyrenees Mountains, Andorra is a co-principality whose main activity is tourism. Most Andorrans live in the six valleys (the Valls) that drain into the River Valira.

AREA 181 sq mi [468 sq km] **POPULATION** 71,000 **CAPITAL** Andorra La Vella

ANGOLA

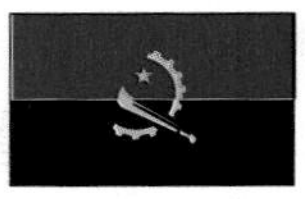

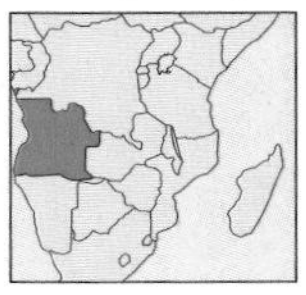

GEOGRAPHY The Republic of Angola is a large country in southwestern Africa. Much of the country is part of the plateau that forms most of southern Africa, with a narrow coastal plain in the west.

Angola has a tropical climate, with temperatures of over 68°F [20°C] throughout the year, though the highest areas are cooler. The coast is dry, but the rainfall increases to the north and east.

POLITICS & ECONOMY Bantu-speaking people settled in Angola in the 13th century and later founded large kingdoms, such as the Kongo and Mbundu. Portugal controlled the coastal slave trade from the 17th century and extended their control inland in the 19th century. Angola became independent from Portugal in 1975, after which rival nationalist groups struggled for power. Despite a ceasefire in the mid-1990s, conflict finally ended in 2002, when the rebel leader, Jonas Savimbi, was killed. Since the war, Angola has faced severe economic problems, despite its mineral wealth.

Angola is a developing country, where 70% of the people are poor farmers. The main food crops are cassava and maize. Coffee is exported. Angola has important oil reserves and oil is exported. Angola also produces diamonds and has reserves of copper, manganese, and phosphates.

AREA 481,351 sq mi [1,246,700 sq km] **POPULATION** 11,191,000 **CAPITAL (POPULATION)** Luanda (2,500,000) **GOVERNMENT** Multiparty republic **ETHNIC GROUPS** Ovimbundu 37%, Kimbundu 25%, Bakongo 13%, others 25% **LANGUAGES** Portuguese (official), many others **RELIGIONS** Traditional beliefs 47%, Roman Catholic 38%, Protestant 15% **CURRENCY** Kwanza = 100 lwei

ANGUILLA

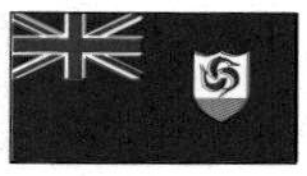

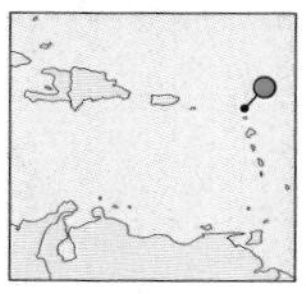

Formerly part of St Kitts and Nevis, Anguilla, the most northerly of the Leeward Islands, became a British dependency (now a British overseas territory) in 1980. The main source of revenue is now tourism, although lobster still accounts for half the island's exports.

AREA 37 sq mi [96 sq km] **POPULATION** 13,000 **CAPITAL** The Valley

ANTIGUA & BARBUDA

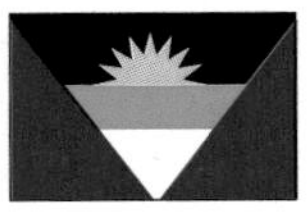

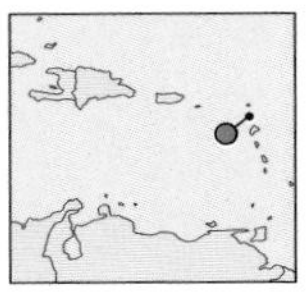

A former British dependency in the Caribbean, Antigua and Barbuda became independent in 1981. Tourism is the main industry, though sugar is an important product.

AREA 171 sq mi [442 sq km] **POPULATION** 69,000 **CAPITAL** St John's

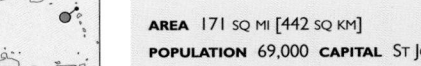

ARGENTINA

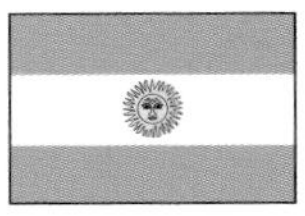

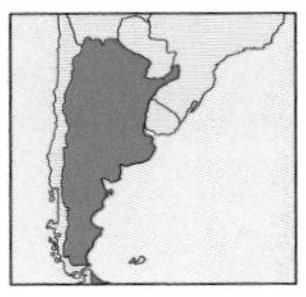

GEOGRAPHY The Argentine Republic is South America's second largest and the world's eighth largest country. The high Andes range in the west contains Mount Aconcagua, the highest peak in the Americas. In southern Argentina, the Andes Mountains overlook Patagonia, a plateau region. In east-central Argentina lies a fertile plain called the pampas.

The climate varies from subtropical in the north to temperate in the south. Rainfall is abundant in the north-east but lower to the west and south. Patagonia is largely desert.

POLITICS & ECONOMY The earliest people were American Indians, but 86% of the people are now of European ancestry. Spain took control in the 16th century and ruled until 1816. Argentina later suffered from instability and periods of military rule. In 1982, Argentina's military regime invaded the Falkland (Malvinas) Islands, but Britain regained the islands later that year. Argentina restored civilian rule in 1983 and adopted a new constitution in 1994.

The World Bank classifies Argentina as an "upper-middle-income" developing country. About 90% of the people live in urban areas. Manufactures include food products, cars, electrical equipment, and textiles. Oil is the chief natural resource and the chief farm products are beef, maize, and wheat. Oil is exported, together with meat, wheat, maize, vegetable oils, hides and skins, and wool. In 1991, Argentina, Brazil, Paraguay, and Uruguay set up an alliance, Mercosur, aimed at creating a common market. However, in late 2001, a severe economic crisis threatened anarchy. The government worked to restore confidence and the economy continued to strengthen between 2003 and 2006.

AREA 1,073,512 sq mi [2,780,400 sq km] **POPULATION** 39,538,000 **CAPITAL (POPULATION)** Buenos Aires (2,965,000) **GOVERNMENT** Federal republic **ETHNIC GROUPS** European 97%, Mestizo, Amerindian **LANGUAGES** Spanish (official) **RELIGIONS** Roman Catholic 92%, Protestant 2%, Jewish 2%, others **CURRENCY** Argentine peso = 10,000 australs

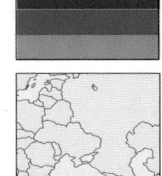

ARMENIA

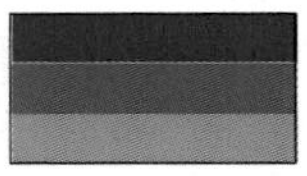

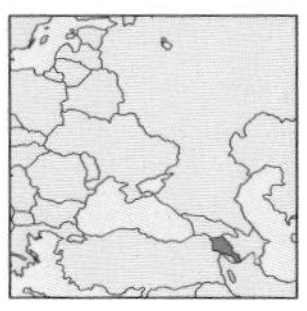

GEOGRAPHY The Republic of Armenia is a landlocked country in southwestern Asia. Most of Armenia consists of a rugged plateau, crisscrossed by long faults (cracks). Movements along the faults cause earthquakes. The highest point is Mount Aragats, at 13,419 ft [4,090 m] above sea level.

The height of the land, which averages 4,920 ft [1,500 m] above sea level gives rise to severe winters and cool summers. The highest peaks are snow-capped, but the total yearly rainfall is generally low.

POLITICS & ECONOMY In 1920, Armenia became a Communist republic and, in 1922, it became, with Azerbaijan and Georgia, part of the Transcaucasian Republic within the Soviet Union. But the three territories became separate Soviet Socialist Republics in 1936. After the breakup of the Soviet Union in 1991, Armenia became an independent republic. Fighting broke out over Nagorno-Karabakh, an area enclosed by Azerbaijan where most people are Armenians. In 1992, Armenia occupied the land between it and Nagorno-Karabakh. A ceasefire in 1994 left Armenia in control of about 20% of Azerbaijan's land area. By 2005, with Azerbaijan and Turkey blocking its borders, Armenia became increasingly dependent on Iran and Georgia for access to the outside world. Talks with Azerbaijan in 2006 again ended in failure.

Armenia has a "lower-middle-income" economy. The government has encouraged free enterprise, selling farmland and state-owned businesses.

AREA 11,506 sq mi [29,800 sq km] **POPULATION** 2,983,000 **CAPITAL (POPULATION)** Yerevan (1,249,000) **GOVERNMENT** Multiparty republic **ETHNIC GROUPS** Armenian 93%, Russian 2%, Azeri 1%, others (mostly Kurds) 4% **LANGUAGES** Armenian (official) **RELIGIONS** Armenian Apostolic 94% **CURRENCY** Dram = 100 couma

NOTE: This alphabetical list includes the principal countries and territories of the world. The area figures give the total area of land, inland water, and ice. The population figures are 2005 estimates where available. The capital city population is for the "city proper" (rather than its urban agglomeration) where available, using the latest census or estimate.

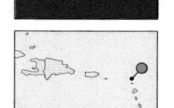

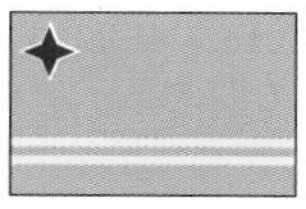
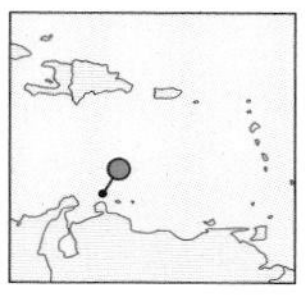

ARUBA

Formerly part of the Netherlands Antilles, Aruba (the most western of the Lesser Antilles) became a separate self-governing Dutch territory in 1986.

AREA 75 sq mi [193 sq km]
POPULATION 72,000 **CAPITAL** Oranjestad

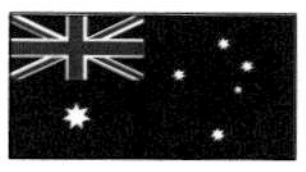
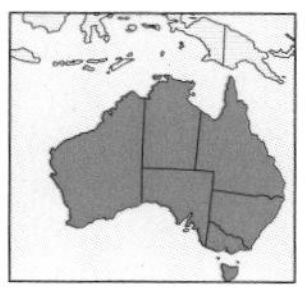

AUSTRALIA

GEOGRAPHY The Commonwealth of Australia, the world's sixth largest country, is also a continent. Australia is the flattest of the continents and the main highland area is in the east. Here the Great Dividing Range separates the eastern coastal plains from the Central Plains. This range extends from the Cape York Peninsula to Victoria in the far south. The longest rivers, the Murray and Darling, drain the southeastern part of the Central Plains. The Western Plateau makes up two-thirds of Australia. A few mountain ranges break the monotony of the generally flat landscape.

Only 10% of Australia has an average yearly rainfall of more than 39 inches [1,000 mm]. These areas include the tropical north, where Darwin is situated, the northeast coast, and the southeast, where Sydney is located. The interior is dry, and water is quickly evaporated in the heat.

POLITICS & ECONOMY The Aboriginal people of Australia entered the continent from Southeast Asia more than 50,000 years ago. The first European explorers were Dutch in the 17th century, but they did not settle. In 1770, the British Captain Cook explored the east coast and, in 1788, the first British settlement was established for convicts on the site of what is now Sydney. Australia has strong ties with the British Isles. But in the last 50 years, people from other parts of Europe and, most recently, from Asia have settled in Australia. Ties with Britain were also weakened by Britain's membership of the European Union. Many Australians believe that they should become more involved with the nations of eastern Asia and the Americas rather than with Europe. In 1999, a majority of Australians voted to retain the country's status as a monarchy. In 2003, Australian troops joined the coalition forces in invading Iraq. In 2004, the conservative prime minister John Howard won a fourth successive general election victory.

Australia is a prosperous country. Crops can be grown on only 6% of the land, but dry pasture covers another 58%. Yet the country remains a major producer and exporter of farm products, particularly cattle, wheat, and wool. Grapes grown for wine-making are also important. The country is a major producer of minerals, including bauxite, coal, copper, diamonds, gold, iron ore, manganese, nickel, silver, tin, tungsten, and zinc. Australia also produces oil and natural gas. Metals, minerals, and farm products account for the bulk of exports. Australia's imports are mostly manufactured goods, especially machinery, though industry is now important, especially the manufacture of consumer goods.

AREA 2,988,885 sq mi [7,741,220 sq km] **POPULATION** 20,090,000 **CAPITAL (POPULATION)** Canberra (309,000) **GOVERNMENT** Federal constitutional monarchy **ETHNIC GROUPS** Caucasian 92%, Asian 7%, Aboriginal 1% **LANGUAGES** English (official) **RELIGIONS** Roman Catholic 26%, Anglican 26%, other Christian 24%, non-Christian 24% **CURRENCY** Australian dollar = 100 cents

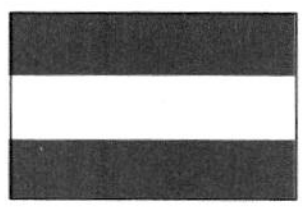
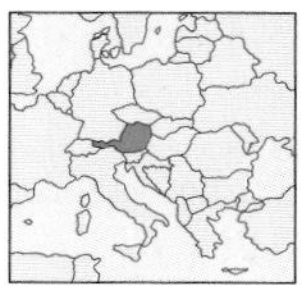

AUSTRIA

GEOGRAPHY Austria is a landlocked country in Europe. Northern Austria contains the valley of the River Danube, which flows from Germany to the Black Sea, and the Vienna basin. Southern Austria contains ranges of the Alps, their highest point at Grossglockner, 12,457 ft [3,797 m] above sea level.

The climate is influenced by westerly and easterly winds. Moist westerly winds bring rain and snow, and moderate temperatures. Dry easterly winds bring cold weather in winter and hot weather in summer.

POLITICS & ECONOMY Formerly part of the monarchy of Austria-Hungary, which collapsed in 1918, Austria was annexed by Germany in 1938. After World War II, the Allies partitioned and occupied the country. In 1955, Austria became a neutral federal republic. It joined the European Union on January 1, 1995, but was a focus of controversy when, in 2000, a coalition government was formed by the right-wing People's Party and the extreme right-wing Freedom Party, which lost much of its support in 2002. The Social Democrat Dr Heinz Fischer was elected president in 2004.

Austria has a highly developed economy, with plenty of hydroelectric power and some oil, gas, and coal reserves. The country's leading economic activity is manufacturing metals and metal products. Crops are grown on 18% of the land, and another 24% is pasture. Dairy and livestock farming are the leading activities. Major crops include barley, potatoes, rye, sugar beet, and wheat. Tourism is a major activity in this scenic country.

AREA 32,378 sq mi [83,859 sq km] **POPULATION** 8,185,000 **CAPITAL (POPULATION)** Vienna (1,560,000) **GOVERNMENT** Federal republic **ETHNIC GROUPS** Austrian 90%, Croatian, Slovene, others **LANGUAGES** German (official) **RELIGIONS** Roman Catholic 78%, Protestant 5%, Islam and others 17% **CURRENCY** Euro = 100 cents

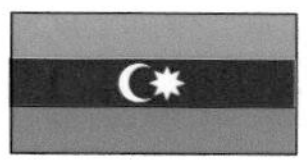
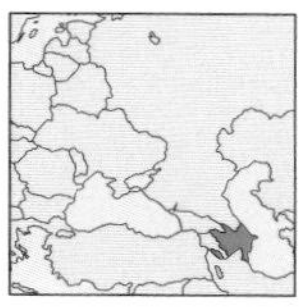

AZERBAIJAN

GEOGRAPHY The Azerbaijani Republic is a country in the southwest of Asia, facing the Caspian Sea to the east. It includes an area called the Naxçivan Autonomous Republic, which is completely cut off from the rest of Azerbaijan by Armenian territory. The Caucasus Mountains border Russia in the north.

Azerbaijan has hot summers and cool winters. The plains are fairly dry, but the mountains are rainy.

POLITICS & ECONOMY After the Russian Revolution of 1917, attempts were made to form a Transcaucasian Federation made up of Armenia, Azerbaijan, and Georgia. When this failed, Azerbaijanis set up an independent state. But Russian forces occupied the area in 1920. In 1922, the Communists set up a Transcaucasian Republic consisting of Armenia, Azerbaijan, and Georgia under Russian control. In 1936, the three areas became separate Soviet Socialist Republics within the Soviet Union. In 1991, following the breakup of the Soviet Union, Azerbaijan became an independent nation. After independence, the country's economic progress was slow, partly because of the conflict with Armenia over the enclave of Nagorno-Karabakh, a region in Azerbaijan where the majority of people are Armenians. A ceasefire in 1994 left Armenia in control of about 20% of Azerbaijan's area, including Nagorno-Karabakh. Talks with Armenia in 2006 again failed to break the deadlock.

In the mid-1990s, the World Bank classified Azerbaijan as a "lower-middle-income" economy. Yet by the late 1990s, the enormous oil reserves in the Baku area on the Caspian Sea, and in the sea itself, held out great promise for the future. Oil extraction and manufacturing, including oil refining and the production of chemicals, machinery, and textiles, are now the most valuable activities.

AREA 33,436 sq mi [86,600 sq km] **POPULATION** 7,912,000 **CAPITAL (POPULATION)** Baku (1,792,000) **GOVERNMENT** Federal multiparty republic **ETHNIC GROUPS** Azeri 90%, Dagestani 3%, Russian, Armenian, others **LANGUAGES** Azerbaijani (official), Russian, Armenian **RELIGIONS** Islam 93%, Russian Orthodox 2%, Armenian Orthodox 2% **CURRENCY** Azerbaijani manat = 100 gopik

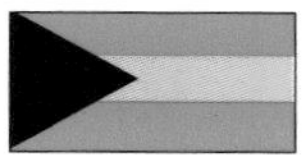
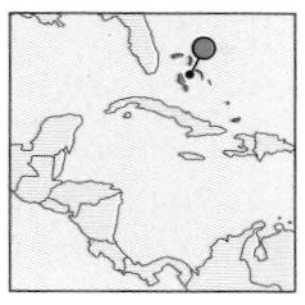

BAHAMAS

A coral-limestone archipelago off the coast of Florida, the Bahamas became independent from Britain in 1973, and has since developed strong ties with the United States. Tourism and banking are major activities.

AREA 5,358 sq mi [13,878 sq km]
POPULATION 302,000 **CAPITAL** Nassau

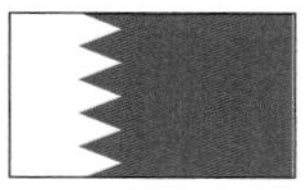
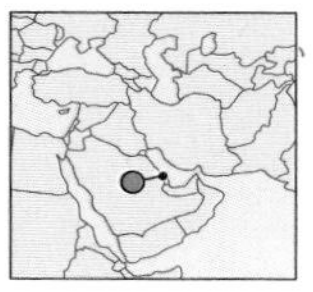

BAHRAIN

The Kingdom of Bahrain, an island nation in the Persian Gulf, became independent from the UK in 1971. Oil accounts for 80% of its exports.

AREA 268 sq mi [694 sq km]
POPULATION 688,000 **CAPITAL** Manama

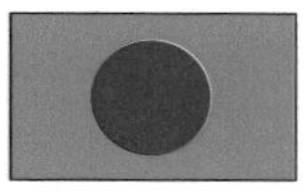
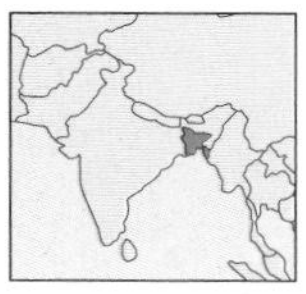

BANGLADESH

GEOGRAPHY The People's Republic of Bangladesh is one of the world's most densely populated countries. Apart from hilly regions in the far northeast and southeast, most of the land is flat and covered by fertile alluvium spread over the land by the Ganges, Brahmaputra, and Meghna rivers. These rivers overflow when they are swollen by the annual monsoon rains. Floods also occur along the coast, 357 mi [575 km] long, when cyclones (hurricanes) drive seawater inland. Bangladesh has a tropical monsoon climate. Dry northerly winds blow in winter, but moist southerly winds bring heavy rain in summer.

POLITICS & ECONOMY In 1947, British India was partitioned between the mainly Hindu India and the Muslim Pakistan. Pakistan consisted of two parts, West and East Pakistan, which were separated by about 1,000 mi [1,600 km] of Indian territory. Differences developed between West and East Pakistan. In 1971, the East Pakistanis rebelled. After a nine-month civil war, they declared East Pakistan to be a new nation named Bangladesh. A famine in 1974 and a coup in 1975 were followed by political upheavals. An Islamic militant group, Jamaat-ul-Mujahideen, launched a bombing campaign in 2005, causing great concern.

Bangladesh is one of the world's poorest countries. Its economy depends mainly on agriculture, which employs over half the population. Bangladesh is the world's fourth largest producer of rice.

AREA 55,598 sq mi [143,998 sq km] **POPULATION** 144,320,000 **CAPITAL (POPULATION)** Dhaka (3,839,000) **GOVERNMENT** Multiparty republic **ETHNIC GROUPS** Bengali 98%, tribal groups **LANGUAGES** Bengali (official), English **RELIGIONS** Islam 83%, Hinduism 16% **CURRENCY** Taka = 100 paisas

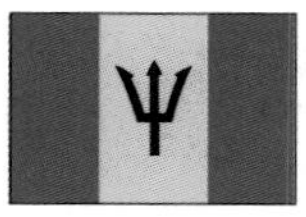
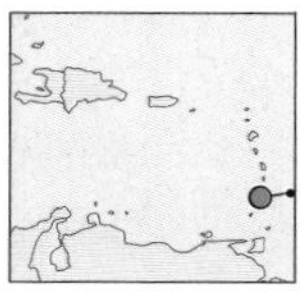

BARBADOS

The most easterly Caribbean country, Barbados became independent from the UK in 1960. A densely populated island, Barbados is prosperous by comparison with most Caribbean countries.

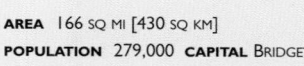

AREA 166 sq mi [430 sq km]
POPULATION 279,000 **CAPITAL** Bridgetown

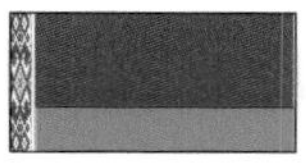
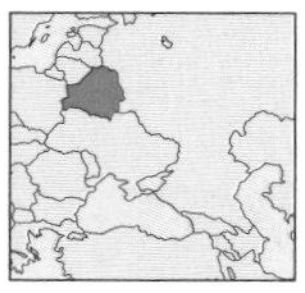

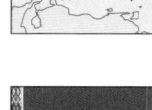

BELARUS

GEOGRAPHY The Republic of Belarus is a landlocked country in Eastern Europe. The land is low-lying and mostly flat. In the south, much of the land is marshy and this area contains Europe's largest marsh and peat bog, the Pripet Marshes. The climate is affected by both the moderating influence of the Baltic Sea and continental conditions to the east. The winters are cold and the summers warm.

POLITICS & ECONOMY In 1918, Belarus (White Russia) became an independent republic, but Russia invaded the country and, in 1919, a Communist state was set up. In 1922, Belarus became a founder republic of the Soviet Union. In 1991, Belarus again became an independent republic, and although Belarus continued to support reunification with Russia, any surrender of sovereignty was not expected. President Alexander Lukashenko, who was elected in flawed elections in 1994, 2001, and 2006, has been criticized for his autocratic rule. His government's poor record on human rights and suppression of freedom of speech has provoked mounting international criticism.

According to the World Bank, Belarus has an "upper-middle-income" economy. Most economic activities remain under government control and, in the 1990s, the economy declined. Mining and manufacturing are the most valuable activities.

AREA 80,154 sq mi [207,600 sq km] **POPULATION** 10,300,000 **CAPITAL (POPULATION)** Minsk (1,677,000) **GOVERNMENT** Multiparty republic **ETHNIC GROUPS** Belarusian 81%, Russian 11%, Polish, Ukrainian, others **LANGUAGES** Belarusian, Russian (both official) **RELIGIONS** Eastern Orthodox 80%, others 20% **CURRENCY** Belarusian rouble = 100 kopecks

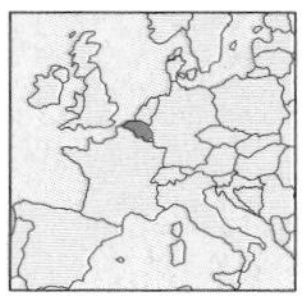

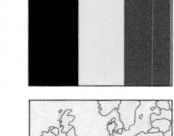

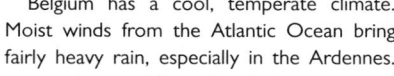

BELGIUM

GEOGRAPHY The Kingdom of Belgium is a densely populated country in western Europe. Behind the coastline on the North Sea, which is 39 mi [63 km] long, lie its coastal plains. Central Belgium consists of low plateaux and the only highland region is the Ardennes in the southeast.

Belgium has a cool, temperate climate. Moist winds from the Atlantic Ocean bring fairly heavy rain, especially in the Ardennes. In January and February much snow falls on the Ardennes.

POLITICS & ECONOMY In 1815, Belgium and the Netherlands united as the "low countries," but Belgium became independent in 1830. Belgium's economy was weakened by the two World

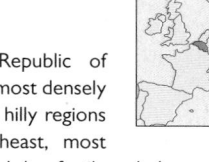

Wars, but, from 1945, the country recovered quickly, first through collaboration with the Netherlands and Luxembourg, which formed a customs union called Benelux, and later through its membership of the European Union.

A central political problem in Belgium has been the tension between the Dutch-speaking Flemings and the French-speaking Walloons. In the 1970s, the government divided the country into three economic regions: Dutch-speaking Flanders, French-speaking Wallonia, and bilingual Brussels. In 1993, Belgium adopted a federal constitution, with each region having its own parliament. Elections under this system were held in 1995, 1999, and 2003.

Belgium is a major trading nation, with a highly developed economy. Most of the materials needed for manufacturing are imported. Its main products include chemicals, processed food, and steel. The textile industry is important. It has existed since medieval times in the Belgian province of Flanders. In 2002, the parliament voted to phase out the use of nuclear energy by 2025.

Agriculture employs less than 1% of the people, but Belgian farmers produce most of the food needed by the people. Barley and wheat are the chief crops, followed by flax, hops, potatoes, and sugar beet, but the most valuable activities are dairy farming and livestock rearing.

AREA 11,787 SQ MI [30,528 SQ KM]
POPULATION 10,364,000
CAPITAL (POPULATION) BRUSSELS (136,000)
GOVERNMENT FEDERAL CONSTITUTIONAL MONARCHY
ETHNIC GROUPS BELGIAN 89% (FLEMING 58%, WALLOON 31%), OTHERS 11% **LANGUAGES** DUTCH, FRENCH, GERMAN (ALL OFFICIAL)
RELIGIONS ROMAN CATHOLIC 75%, OTHERS 25%
CURRENCY EURO = 100 CENTS

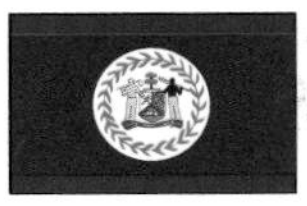
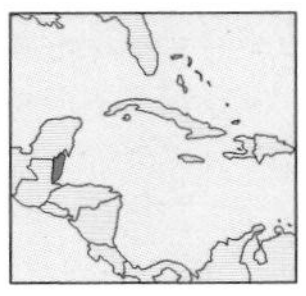

BELIZE

GEOGRAPHY Behind the southern coastal plain, the land rises to the Maya Mountains, which reach 3,674 ft [1,120 m] at Victoria Peak. The north is mostly low-lying and swampy. Temperatures are high all year round, while the average annual rainfall ranges from 51 inches [1,300 mm] in the north to over 150 inches [3,800 mm] in the south. Hurricanes caused much damage in the 1990s and 2000s, but tourist numbers have continued to increase.

POLITICS & ECONOMY From 1862, Belize (then called British Honduras) was a British colony. Full independence was achieved in 1981, but Guatemala, which had claimed the area since the early 19th century, opposed Belize's independence and British troops remained to prevent a possible invasion. In 1983, Guatemala reduced its claim to the southern fifth of Belize. Improved relations in the early 1990s led Guatemala to recognize Belize's independence and, in 1992, Britain agreed to withdraw its troops from the country.

The World Bank classifies Belize as a "lower-middle-income" developing country. Its economy is based on agriculture and sugarcane is the chief commercial crop and export. Other crops include bananas, beans, citrus fruits, maize, and rice. Forestry, fishing, and tourism are other important activities.

AREA 8,867 SQ MI [22,966 SQ KM] **POPULATION** 279,000
CAPITAL (POPULATION) BELMOPAN (8,000)
GOVERNMENT CONSTITUTIONAL MONARCHY **ETHNIC GROUPS** MESTIZO 49%, CREOLE 25%, MAYAN INDIAN 11%, GARIFUNA 6%, OTHERS 9%
LANGUAGES ENGLISH (OFFICIAL), SPANISH, CREOLE
RELIGIONS ROMAN CATHOLIC 50%, PROTESTANT 27%, OTHERS
CURRENCY BELIZEAN DOLLAR = 100 CENTS

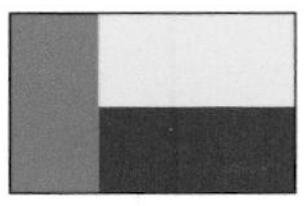
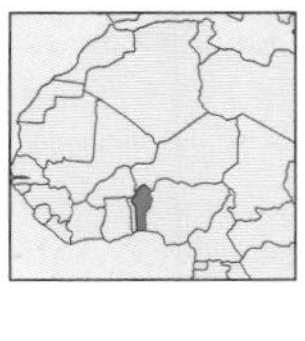

BENIN

GEOGRAPHY The Republic of Benin is one of Africa's smallest countries. It extends north–south for about 390 mi [620 km]. Lagoons line the short coastline, and the country has no natural harbors.

Benin has a hot, wet climate. The average annual temperature on the coast is about 77°F [25°C], and the average rainfall is about 52 inches [1,330 mm]. The inland plains are wetter than the coast.

POLITICS & ECONOMY After slavery was ended in the 19th century, the French began to gain influence in the area. Benin became self-governing in 1958 and fully independent in 1960. After much instability and many changes of government, a military group took over in 1972. The country, renamed Benin in 1975, became a one-party socialist state. Socialism was abandoned in 1989. Former coup leader, Mathieu Kérékou, was defeated in presidential elections in 1991, but served as president from 1996 until 2006.

Benin is a poor developing country. About half of the people live by farming, mainly at subsistence level. Exports include cotton, petroleum, and palm products. Cocoa, coffee, groundnuts (peanuts), tobacco, and shea nuts are also grown for export.

AREA 43,483 SQ MI [112,622 SQ KM] **POPULATION** 7,460,000
CAPITAL (POPULATION) PORTO-NOVO (233,000)
GOVERNMENT MULTIPARTY REPUBLIC **ETHNIC GROUPS** FON, ADJA, BARIBA, YORUBA, FULANI **LANGUAGES** FRENCH (OFFICIAL), FON, ADJA, YORUBA
RELIGIONS TRADITIONAL BELIEFS 50%, CHRISTIANITY 30%, ISLAM 20%
CURRENCY CFA FRANC = 100 CENTIMES

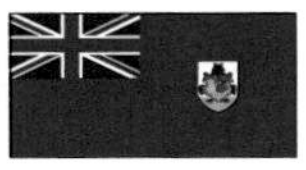
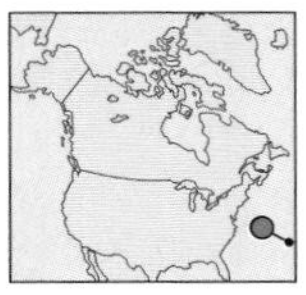

BERMUDA

A group of about 150 small islands situated 570 mi [920 km] east of the USA. Bermuda remains Britain's oldest overseas territory, but it has a long tradition of self-government.

AREA 21 SQ MI [53 SQ KM]
POPULATION 65,000 **CAPITAL** HAMILTON

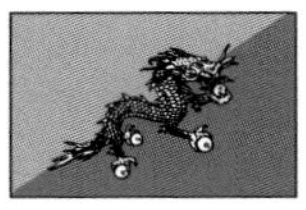
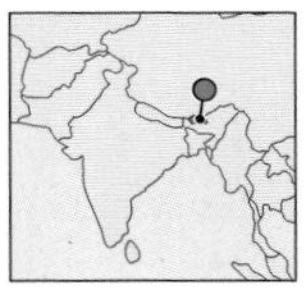

BHUTAN

GEOGRAPHY A mountainous, isolated Himalayan country located between India and Tibet. The climate is similar to that of Nepal, being dependent on altitude and affected by monsoonal winds.

POLITICS & ECONOMY The monarch of Bhutan is head of both state and government and this predominantly Buddhist country remains, even in the Asian context, both conservative and poor. Farming is the main activity. In 2005, the King said he would step down in favor of the Crown Prince in 2008, when the first-ever democratic elections would be held.

AREA 18,147 SQ MI [47,000 SQ KM] **POPULATION** 2,232,000
CAPITAL (POPULATION) THIMPHU (35,000)
GOVERNMENT CONSTITUTIONAL MONARCHY **ETHNIC GROUPS** BHUTANESE 50%, NEPALESE 35% **LANGUAGES** DZONGKHA (OFFICIAL) **RELIGIONS** BUDDHISM 75%, HINDUISM 25% **CURRENCY** NGULTRUM = 100 CHETRUM

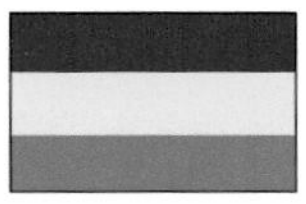
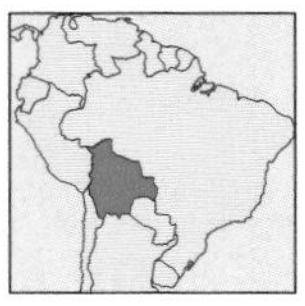

BOLIVIA

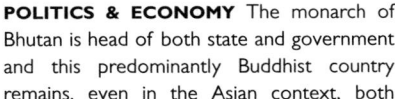

GEOGRAPHY The Republic of Bolivia is a landlocked country which straddles the Andes Mountains in central South America. The Andes rise to a height of 21,391 ft [6,520 m] at Nevado Sajama in the west.

About 40% of Bolivians live on a high plateau called the Altiplano in the Andean region, while the sparsely populated east is essentially a vast lowland plain.

The Bolivian climate is greatly affected by altitude, with the Andean peaks permanently snow-covered, and the eastern plains remaining hot and humid.

POLITICS & ECONOMY American Indians have lived in Bolivia for at least 10,000 years. The main groups today are the Aymara and Quechua people.

In the last 50 years, Bolivia, an independent country since 1825, has been ruled by a succession of civilian and military governments, which violated human rights. Democracy was restored in 1982. Economic problems led a widening of the gap between rich and poor and, in 2005, Evo Morales, a left-wing Aymara farmer, was elected president. He supported the growing of coca, on which many peasant farmers depended, but opposed the trafficking of cocaine.

Bolivia is one of South America's poorest countries. Its resources include natural gas, silver, tin, and zinc, but the main activity is agriculture which employs more than 40% of the people. Soybeans and soybean products are major exports.

AREA 424,162 SQ MI [1,098,581 SQ KM] **POPULATION** 8,858,000
CAPITAL (POPULATION) LA PAZ (SEAT OF GOVERNMENT, 940,000); SUCRE (LEGAL CAPITAL/SEAT OF JUDICIARY, 177,000)
GOVERNMENT MULTIPARTY REPUBLIC **ETHNIC GROUPS** MESTIZO 30%, QUECHUA 30%, AYMARA 25%, WHITE 15% **LANGUAGES** SPANISH, AYMARA, QUECHUA (ALL OFFICIAL) **RELIGIONS** ROMAN CATHOLIC 95%
CURRENCY BOLIVIANO = 100 CENTAVOS

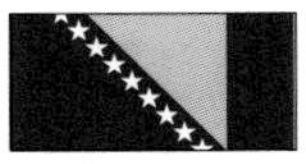
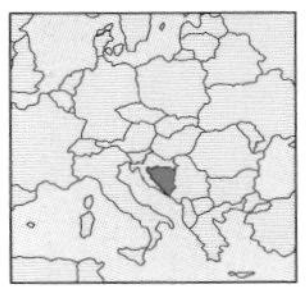

BOSNIA-HERZEGOVINA

GEOGRAPHY The Republic of Bosnia-Herzegovina is one of the five republics to emerge from the former Federal People's Republic of Yugoslavia. Much of the country is mountainous or hilly, with an arid limestone plateau in the southwest. The River Sava, which forms most of the northern border with Croatia, is a tributary of the River Danube. Because of the country's odd shape, the coastline is limited to a short stretch of 13 mi [20 km] on the Adriatic coast.

A Mediterranean climate, with dry, sunny summers and moist, mild winters, prevails only near the coast. Inland, the weather is more severe, with hot, dry summers and bitterly cold, snowy winters.

POLITICS & ECONOMY In 1918, Bosnia-Herzegovina became part of the Kingdom of the Serbs, Croats, and Slovenes, which was renamed Yugoslavia in 1929. Germany occupied the area during World War II (1939–45). From 1945, Communist governments ruled Yugoslavia as a federation containing six republics, one of which was Bosnia-Herzegovina. In the 1980s, the country faced problems as Communist policies proved unsuccessful and differences arose between ethnic groups.

In 1990, free elections were held in Bosnia-Herzegovina and the non-Communists won a majority. A Muslim, Alija Izetbegovic, was elected president. In 1991, Croatia and Slovenia, other parts of the former Yugoslavia, declared themselves independent. In 1992, Bosnia-Herzegovina held a vote on independence. Most Bosnian Serbs boycotted the vote, while the Muslims and Bosnian Croats voted in favor. Many Bosnian Serbs, opposed to independence, started a war against the non-Serbs. They soon occupied more than two-thirds of the land. The Bosnian Serbs were accused of "ethnic cleansing" – that is, the killing or expulsion of other ethnic groups from Serb-occupied areas. The war was later extended when Croat forces seized other parts of the country.

In 1995, the conflict was resolved. Under an agreement, the country's boundaries were maintained, but the territory was divided into two self-governing provinces, one Bosnian-Serb and the other Muslim-Croat, under a central government. Stability was restored with the help of NATO. Government reforms in 2005 paved the way to entry into the European Union and NATO.

The economy of Bosnia-Herzegovina, the least developed of the six republics of the former Yugoslavia apart from Macedonia, was shattered by the war in the early 1990s. Before the war, manufactures were the main exports, including electrical, machinery and transport equipment, and textiles. Farm products include fruits, maize, tobacco, vegetables, and wheat, but food has to be imported.

AREA 19,767 SQ MI [51,197 SQ KM] **POPULATION** 4,025,000
CAPITAL (POPULATION) SARAJEVO (529,000)
GOVERNMENT FEDERAL REPUBLIC **ETHNIC GROUPS** BOSNIAN 48%, SERB 37%, CROAT 14% **LANGUAGES** BOSNIAN, SERBIAN, CROATIAN
RELIGIONS ISLAM 40%, SERBIAN ORTHODOX 31%, ROMAN CATHOLIC 15%, OTHERS 14% **CURRENCY** CONVERTIBLE MARKA = 100 CONVERTIBLE PFENNIGA

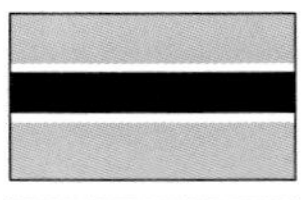
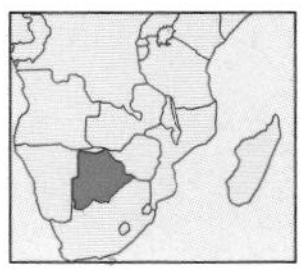

BOTSWANA

GEOGRAPHY The Republic of Botswana is a landlocked country in southern Africa. The Kalahari, a semidesert area covered mostly by grasses and thorn scrub, covers much of the country. Most of the south has no permanent streams. But large depressions in the north are inland drainage basins. In one of them, the Okavango River, which rises in Angola, forms a large, swampy delta.

Temperatures are high in the summer months (October to April), but the winter months are much cooler. In winter, night-time temperatures sometimes drop below freezing point. The average annual rainfall ranges from over 16 inches [400 mm] in the east to less than 8 inches [200 mm] in the southwest.

POLITICS & ECONOMY The earliest inhabitants of the region were the San, who are also called Bushmen. They had a nomadic way of life, hunting wild animals and collecting wild plant foods.

Britain ruled the area as the Bechuanaland Protectorate between 1885 and 1966. When the country became independent, it was renamed Botswana. Since then, the country has been a stable, multiparty democracy. However, a major setback occurred in the early 21st century, when health officials announced that around 25% of the people were infected with HIV/AIDS. In 1966, Botswana was extremely poor, depending on meat and live cattle for its exports. But the discovery of minerals, including coal, cobalt, copper, diamonds, and nickel, has boosted the economy. About 17% of the people now depend on agriculture, raising cattle, and growing crops. Industries include the processing of farm products.

AREA 224,606 sq mi [581,730 sq km] **POPULATION** 1,640,000
CAPITAL (POPULATION) Gaborone (186,000)
GOVERNMENT Multiparty republic **ETHNIC GROUPS** Tswana (or Setswana) 79%, Kalanga 11%, Basarwa 3%, others
LANGUAGES English (official), Setswana **RELIGIONS** Traditional beliefs 85%, Christianity 15% **CURRENCY** Pula = 100 thebe

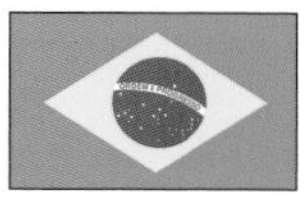

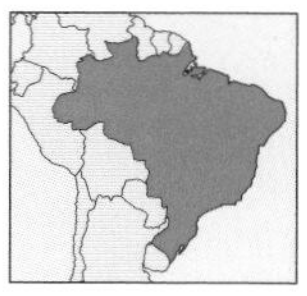

BRAZIL

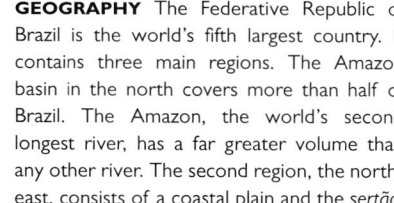

GEOGRAPHY The Federative Republic of Brazil is the world's fifth largest country. It contains three main regions. The Amazon basin in the north covers more than half of Brazil. The Amazon, the world's second longest river, has a far greater volume than any other river. The second region, the north-east, consists of a coastal plain and the *sertão*, which is the name for the inland plateaux and hill country. The main river in this region is the São Francisco.

The third region is made up of the plateaux in the southeast. This region, which covers about a quarter of the country, is the most developed and densely populated part of Brazil. Its main river is the Paraná, which flows south through Argentina.

Manaus has high temperatures all through the year. The rainfall is heavy, though the period from June to September is drier than the rest of the year. The capital, Brasília, and the city Rio de Janeiro also have tropical climates, with much more marked dry seasons than Manaus. The far south has a temperate climate. The north-eastern interior is the driest region, with an average annual rainfall of only 10 inches [250 mm] in places. The rainfall is also unreliable and severe droughts are common in this region.

POLITICS & ECONOMY The Portuguese explorer Pedro Alvarez Cabral claimed Brazil for Portugal in 1500. With Spain occupied in western South America, the Portuguese began to develop their colony, which was more than 90 times as big as Portugal. To do this, they enslaved many local Amerindian people and introduced about 4 million African slaves. Brazil declared itself an independent empire in 1822 and a republic in 1889. From the 1930s, Brazil faced periods of military rule and widespread corruption. Civilian rule was restored in 1985. Brazil adopted a new constitution in 1988.

The United Nations has described Brazil as a "Rapidly Industrializing Country," or RIC. Its total volume of production is one of the largest in the world. But many people, including poor farmers and residents of the *favelas* (city slums), do not share in the country's fast economic growth. Poverty, inflation and unemployment led to the election as president of Luiz Inácio Lula da Silva (popularly called "Lula") in 2002. In office, he worked to create economic stability, but corruption charges in 2005 (not involving the president) caused problems.

Industry is the most important economic sector. Brazil is among the world's top producers of bauxite, chrome, diamonds, gold, iron ore, manganese, and tin. It is also a major manufacturing country. Its products include aircraft, cars, chemicals, processed food, including raw sugar, iron and steel, paper, and textiles.

Brazil is one of the world's leading farming countries and agriculture employs 16% of the people. Coffee is a major export. Other leading products include bananas, citrus fruits, cocoa, maize, rice, soybeans, and sugarcane. Brazil is also the top producer of eggs, meat, and milk in South America.

Forestry is a major industry, though many people fear that the exploitation of the rain forests, with 1.5% to 4% of Brazil's forest being destroyed every year, is a disaster for the entire world.

AREA 3,287,338 sq mi [8,514,215 sq km] **POPULATION** 186,113,000
CAPITAL (POPULATION) Brasília (2,016,000)
GOVERNMENT Federal republic
ETHNIC GROUPS White 55%, Mulatto 38%, Black 6%, others 1% **LANGUAGES** Portuguese (official)
RELIGIONS Roman Catholic 80%
CURRENCY Real = 100 centavos

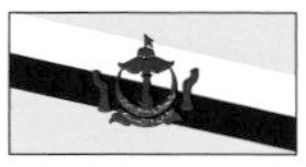

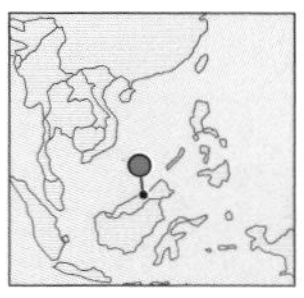

BRUNEI

The Islamic Sultanate of Brunei, a British protectorate until 1984, lies on the north coast of Borneo. The climate is tropical and rain forests cover large areas. Brunei is a prosperous country because of its oil and natural gas production, and the Sultan is said to be among the world's richest men.

AREA 2,226 sq mi [5,765 sq km] **POPULATION** 372,000
CAPITAL (POPULATION) Bandar Seri Begawan (50,000)

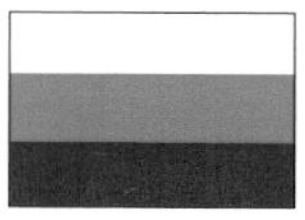

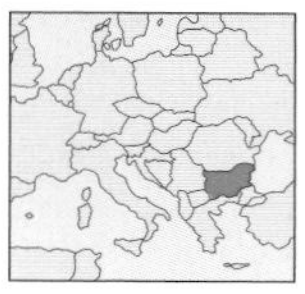

BULGARIA

GEOGRAPHY The Republic of Bulgaria is a country in the Balkan peninsula, facing the Black Sea in the east. The heart of Bulgaria is mountainous. The main ranges are the Balkan Mountains in the center and the Rhodope (or Rhodopi) Mountains in the south.

Summers are hot and winters are cold, though seldom severe. The rainfall is moderate.

POLITICS & ECONOMY Ottoman Turks ruled Bulgaria from 1396 and ethnic Turks still form a sizable minority in the country. In 1879, Bulgaria became a monarchy, and in 1908 it became fully independent. Bulgaria was an ally of Germany in World War I (1914–18) and again in World War II (1939–45). In 1944, Soviet troops invaded Bulgaria and, after the war, the monarchy was abolished and the country became a Communist ally of the Soviet Union. In the late 1980s, reforms in the Soviet Union led Bulgaria's government to introduce a multiparty system in 1990. A non-Communist government was elected in 1991, the first free elections in 44 years. Throughout the 1990s, Bulgaria faced many problems. In 2001, a coalition led by the former King Siméon, who had left Bulgaria in 1948, won the elections. Siméon served as prime minister until 2005. Bulgaria became a member of NATO in 2004. It was expected to join the European Union in 2007 provided it met certain conditions.

Bulgaria has a "lower-middle economy." It has some mineral deposits, including brown coal, manganese, and iron ore. But manufacturing is the leading activity, though, in the early 1990s, much of its industrial plant was out of date. Leading products include chemicals, processed foods, metal products, machinery, and textiles. Manufactures are the leading exports.

AREA 42,823 sq mi [110,912 sq km] **POPULATION** 7,450,000
CAPITAL (POPULATION) Sofia (1,139,000) **GOVERNMENT** Multiparty republic **ETHNIC GROUPS** Bulgarian 84%, Turkish 9%, Gypsy 5%, Macedonian, Armenian, others **LANGUAGES** Bulgarian (official), Turkish **RELIGIONS** Bulgarian Orthodox 83%, Islam 12%, Roman Catholic 2%, others **CURRENCY** Lev = 100 stotinki

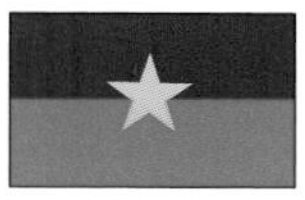

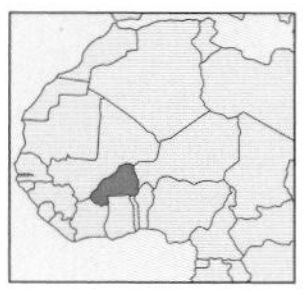

BURKINA FASO

GEOGRAPHY The Democratic People's Republic of Burkina Faso is a landlocked country, a little larger than the United Kingdom, in West Africa. But Burkina Faso has only one-sixth of the population of the UK. The country consists of a plateau, between about 650 ft and 2,300 ft [300 m to 700 m] above sea level. The plateau is cut by several rivers.

The capital city, Ouagadougou, in central Burkina Faso, has high temperatures throughout the year. Most of the rain falls between May and September, but the rainfall is erratic and droughts are common.

POLITICS & ECONOMY The people of Burkina Faso are divided into two main groups. The Voltaic group includes the Mossi, who form the largest single group, and the Bobo. The French conquered the Mossi capital of Ouagadougou in 1897 and they made the area a protectorate. In 1919, the area became a French colony called Upper Volta. After independence in 1960, Upper Volta became a one-party state. But it was unstable – military groups seized power several times and political killings took place. In 1984, the country's name was changed to Burkina Faso. In 1991, 1998, and 2005, the former coup leader, Captain Blaise Compaoré, was elected president. The military continued to influence government.

Burkina Faso is one of the world's 20 poorest countries and has become very dependent on foreign aid. Most of Burkina Faso is dry with thin soils. The country's main food crops are beans, maize, millet, rice, and sorghum. Cotton, groundnuts, and shea nuts, whose seeds produce a fat used to make cooking oil and soap, are grown for sale abroad. Livestock are also an important export.

The country has few resources and manufacturing is on a small scale. There are some deposits of manganese, zinc, lead, and nickel in the north of the country, but there is not yet a good enough transport system there. Many young men seek jobs abroad in Ghana and Ivory Coast. The money they send home to their families is important to the country's economy.

AREA 105,791 sq mi [274,000 sq km] **POPULATION** 13,925,000
CAPITAL (POPULATION) Ouagadougou (637,000)
GOVERNMENT Multiparty republic **ETHNIC GROUPS** Mossi 40%, Gurunsi, Senufo, Lobi, Bobo, Mande, Fulani **LANGUAGES** French (official), Mossi, Fulani **RELIGIONS** Islam 50%, traditional beliefs 40%, Christianity 10% **CURRENCY** CFA franc = 100 centimes

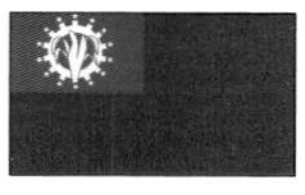

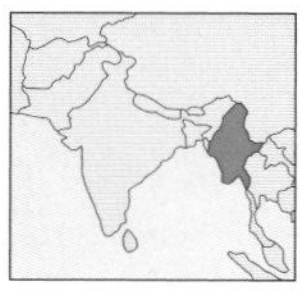

BURMA (MYANMAR)

GEOGRAPHY The Union of Burma is now officially known as the Union of Myanmar; its name was changed in 1989. Mountains border the country in the east and west, with the highest mountains in the north. Burma's highest mountain is Hkakabo Razi, which is 19,294 ft [5,881 m] high. Between these ranges is central Burma, which contains the fertile valleys of the Irrawaddy and Sittang rivers. The Irrawaddy delta on the Bay of Bengal is one of the world's leading rice-growing areas. Burma also includes the long Tenasserim coast in the southeast.

Burma has a tropical monsoon climate. There are three seasons. The rainy season runs from late May to mid-October. A cool, dry season follows, between late October and the middle part of February. The hot season lasts from late February to mid-May, though temperatures remain high during the humid rainy season.

POLITICS & ECONOMY Many groups settled in Burma in ancient times. Some, called the hill peoples, live in remote mountain areas where they have retained their own cultures. The ancestors of the country's main ethnic group today, the Burmese, arrived in the 9th century AD.

Britain conquered Burma in the 19th century and made it a province of British India. But, in 1937, the British granted Burma limited self-government. Japan conquered Burma in 1942, but the Japanese were driven out in 1945. Burma became a fully independent country in 1948.

Revolts by Communists and various hill people led to instability in the 1950s. In 1962, Burma became a military dictatorship and, in 1974, a one-party state. Attempts to control minority liberation movements and the opium trade led to repressive rule. The National League for Democracy led by Aung San Suu Kyi won the elections in 1990, but the military continued their repressive rule throughout the 1990s, earning Burma the reputation for having one of the world's worst human rights record. In 2004, a United Nations report criticized the regime for holding more than 1,800 political detainees and for its failure to release opposition leader Aung San Suu Kyi from house arrest. In 2005, the government announced that Pyinmana, in the highland interior, had become the country's new administrative capital.

Agriculture is the main activity, employing 66% of the people. The chief crop is rice. Maize, pulses, oilseeds, and sugarcane are other major products. Forestry is important. Teak and rice together make up about two-thirds of the total value of the exports. Burma has many mineral resources, though they are mostly undeveloped, but the country is famous for its precious stones, especially rubies. Manufacturing is mostly on a small sca

AREA 261,227 sq mi [676,578 sq km] **POPULATION** 42,909,000
CAPITAL (POPULATION) Rangoon (Yangon, 2,513,000); Pyinmana (administrative capital) **GOVERNMENT** Military regime
ETHNIC GROUPS Burman 68%, Shan 9%, Karen 7%, Rakhine 4%, Chinese, Indian, Mon **LANGUAGES** Burmese (official); minority ethnic groups have their own languages **RELIGIONS** Buddhism 89%, Christianity, Islam **CURRENCY** Kyat = 100 pyas

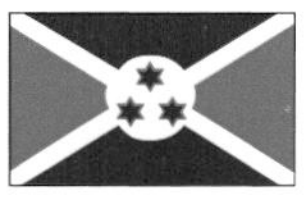

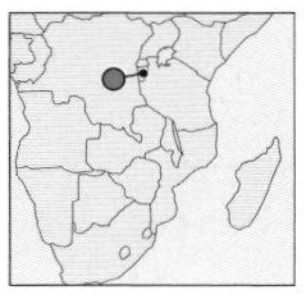

BURUNDI

GEOGRAPHY The Republic of Burundi is the fifth smallest country in mainland Africa. It is also the second most densely populated after its northern neighbor, Rwanda. Part of the Great African Rift Valley, which runs throughout eastern Africa into southwestern Asia, lies in western Burundi. It includes part of Lake Tanganyika. Bujumbura, the capital city, lies on the shore of Lake Tanganyika and has a warm climate. A dry season occurs from June to September, but the other months are fairly rainy. The mountains and plateaux to the east are cooler and wetter, but the rainfall generally decreases to the east.

POLITICS & ECONOMY The Twa, a pygmy people, were the first known inhabitants of Burundi. About 1,000 years ago, the Hutu, a people who speak a Bantu language, gradually began to settle the area, pushing the Twa into remote areas.

From the 15th century, the Tutsi, a cattle-owning people from the northeast, gradually took over the country. The Hutu, though greatly outnumbering the Tutsi, were forced to serve the Tutsi overlords.

Germany conquered the area that is now Burundi and Rwanda in the late 1890s. The area, called Ruanda-Urundi, was taken by Belgium during World War I (1914–18). In 1961, the people of Urundi voted to become a monarchy, while the people of Ruanda voted to become a republic. The two territories became fully independent as Burundi and Rwanda in 1962. After 1962, the rivalries between the Hutu and Tutsi led to periodic outbreaks of

fighting. The Tutsi monarchy was ended in 1966 and Burundi became a republic. Instability continued with coups and massacres as Tutsis and Hutus fought against each other. A power-sharing agreement was reached in 2001, though conflict continued in some areas. Parliamentary and presidential elections were held in 2005 under a new constitution.

Burundi is one of the world's poorest countries. About 93% of the people live by farming, mostly at subsistence level. Food crops include beans, cassava, maize, and sweet potatoes. Livestock are raised and fishing is important. But Burundi has to import food.

AREA 10,747 SQ MI [27,834 SQ KM] **POPULATION** 6,371,000 **CAPITAL (POPULATION)** BUJUMBURA (235,000) **GOVERNMENT** REPUBLIC **ETHNIC GROUPS** HUTU 85%, TUTSI 14%, TWA (PYGMY) 1% **LANGUAGES** FRENCH AND KIRUNDI (BOTH OFFICIAL) **RELIGIONS** ROMAN CATHOLIC 62%, TRADITIONAL BELIEFS 23%, ISLAM 10%, PROTESTANT 5% **CURRENCY** BURUNDI FRANC = 100 CENTIMES

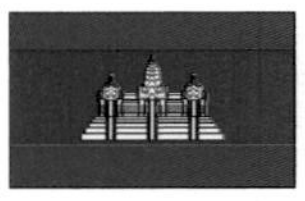

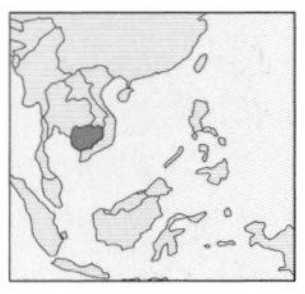

CAMBODIA

GEOGRAPHY The Kingdom of Cambodia is a country in Southeast Asia. Low mountains border the country except in the southeast. But most of Cambodia consists of plains drained by the River Mekong, which enters Cambodia from Laos in the north and exits through Vietnam in the southeast. The northwest contains Tonlé Sap (or Great Lake). In the dry season, this lake drains into the River Mekong. But in the wet season, the level of the Mekong rises and water flows in the opposite direction from the river into Tonlé Sap – the lake then becomes the largest freshwater lake in Asia.

Cambodia has a tropical monsoon climate, with high temperatures throughout the year. The dry season, when winds blow from the north or northeast, runs from November to April. During the rainy season (May to October), moist winds blow from the south or southeast. The high humidity and heat often make conditions unpleasant. Rainfall is heaviest near the coast, and rather lower inland.

POLITICS & ECONOMY From 802 to 1432, the Khmer people ruled a great empire, which reached its peak in the 12th century. The Khmer capital was at Angkor. The Hindu stone temples built there and at nearby Angkor Wat form the world's largest group of religious buildings. France ruled the country between 1863 and 1954, when the country became an independent monarchy. But the monarchy was abolished in 1970 and Cambodia became a republic.

In 1970, US and South Vietnamese troops entered Cambodia but left after destroying North Vietnamese Communist camps in the east. The country became involved in the Vietnamese War, and then in a civil war as Cambodian Communists of the Khmer Rouge organization fought for power. The Khmer Rouge took over Cambodia in 1975 and launched a reign of terror in which between 1 million and 2.5 million people were killed. In 1979, Vietnamese and Cambodian troops overthrew the Khmer Rouge government. But fighting continued between factions. Vietnam withdrew in 1989, and in 1991 Prince Sihanouk was recognized as head of state. Elections were held in May 1993, and in September 1993 the monarchy was restored. Elections were held in 1998 and 2003. In 2001, the government set up courts to try leaders of the Khmer Rouge. In 2004, King Sihanouk abdicated because of ill health and his son, Prince Norodom Sihamoni, became king.

Cambodia is a poor country whose economy has been wrecked by war. Until the 1970s, the country's farmers produced most of the food needed by the people. But by 1986, it was only able to supply 80% of its needs. Farming is the main activity and rice, rubber, and maize are major products. Manufacturing is almost non-existent, apart from rubber processing and a few factories producing items for sale in Cambodia.

AREA 69,898 SQ MI [181,035 SQ KM] **POPULATION** 13,607,000 **CAPITAL (POPULATION)** PHNOM PENH (1,000,000) **GOVERNMENT** CONSTITUTIONAL MONARCHY **ETHNIC GROUPS** KHMER 90%, VIETNAMESE 5%, CHINESE 1%, OTHERS **LANGUAGES** KHMER (OFFICIAL), FRENCH, ENGLISH **RELIGIONS** BUDDHISM 95%, OTHERS 5% **CURRENCY** RIEL = 100 SEN

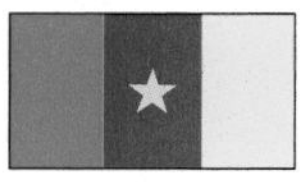

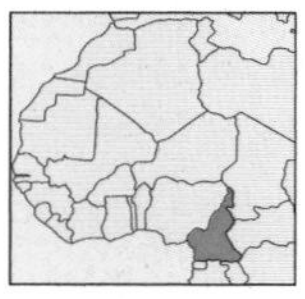

CAMEROON

GEOGRAPHY The Republic of Cameroon in West Africa derived its name from the Portuguese word *camarões*, or prawns. This name was used by Portuguese explorers who fished for prawns along the coast. Behind the narrow coastal plains on the Gulf of Guinea, the land rises to a series of plateaux, with a mountainous region in the southwest where the volcano Mount Cameroun is situated. In the north, the land slopes down toward the Lake Chad basin.

The rainfall is heavy, especially in the highlands. The rainiest months near the coast are June to September. The rainfall decreases to the north and the far north has a hot, dry climate. Temperatures are high on the coast, whereas the inland plateaux are cooler.

POLITICS & ECONOMY Germany lost Cameroon during World War I (1914–18). The country was then divided into two parts, one ruled by Britain and the other by France. In 1960, French Cameroon became the independent Cameroon Republic. In 1961, after a vote in British Cameroon, part of the territory joined the Cameroon Republic to become the Federal Republic of Cameroon – the other part joined Nigeria. In 1972, Cameroon became a unitary state called the United Republic of Cameroon. It adopted the name Republic of Cameroon in 1984, but the country had two official languages. In 1995, partly to placate the English-speaking people, Cameroon became the 52nd member of the Commonwealth.

Like most countries in tropical Africa, Cameroon's economy is based on agriculture, which employs 74% of the people. The chief food crops include cassava, maize, millet, sweet potatoes, and yams. The country also has plantations to produce such crops as cocoa and coffee for export. Cameroon exports oil and bauxite. In 2002, its claim over the oil-rich Bakassi peninsula was upheld by the International Court of Justice, though Nigeria failed to meet the deadline for the handover in 2004. Further talks failed in 2005. Cameroon has few manufacturing industries, but its self-sufficiency in food makes it one of Africa's better-off countries.

AREA 183,568 SQ MI [475,442 SQ KM] **POPULATION** 16,380,000 **CAPITAL (POPULATION)** YAOUNDÉ (649,000) **GOVERNMENT** MULTIPARTY REPUBLIC **ETHNIC GROUPS** CAMEROON HIGHLANDERS 31%, BANTU 27%, KIRDI 11%, FULANI 10%, OTHERS **LANGUAGES** FRENCH AND ENGLISH (BOTH OFFICIAL) **RELIGIONS** CHRISTIANITY 40%, TRADITIONAL BELIEFS 40%, ISLAM 20% **CURRENCY** CFA FRANC = 100 CENTIMES

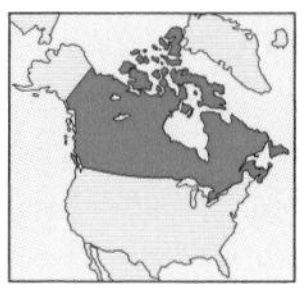

CANADA

GEOGRAPHY Canada is the world's second largest country after Russia. It is thinly populated, however, with much of the land too cold or too mountainous for human settlement. Most Canadians live within 186 mi [300 km] of the southern border.

Western Canada is rugged. It includes the Pacific ranges and the mighty Rocky Mountains. East of the Rockies are the interior plains. In the north lie the bleak Arctic islands, while to the south lie the densely populated lowlands around lakes Erie and Ontario and in the St Lawrence River valley.

Canada has a cold climate. In winter, temperatures fall below freezing point throughout most of Canada. But the southwestern coast has a relatively mild climate. Along the Arctic Circle, mean temperatures are below freezing for seven months a year. The west and southeast have high rainfall, but the prairies are dry with 10 inches to 20 inches [250 mm to 500 mm] of rain every year.

POLITICS & ECONOMY Canada's first people, the ancestors of the Native Americans, or Indians, arrived in North America from Asia around 40,000 years ago. Later arrivals were the Inuit (Eskimos), who also came from Asia. Europeans reached the Canadian coast in 1497 and a race began between Britain and France for control of the territory.

France gained an initial advantage, and the French founded Québec in 1608. But the British later occupied eastern Canada. In 1867, Britain passed the British North America Act, which set up the Dominion of Canada, which was made up of Québec, Ontario, Nova Scotia, and New Brunswick. Other areas were added, the last being Newfoundland in 1949. Canada fought alongside Britain in both World Wars and many Canadians feel close ties with Britain. Canada is a constitutional monarchy, and the British monarch is Canada's head of state.

Rivalries between French- and English-speaking Canadians continue. In 1995, Québeckers voted against a move to make Québec a sovereign state by a majority of less than 1%, but in 2003, the separatist Parti Québecois was defeated in provincial elections, ending nine years in government. The rights of Aboriginal minorities are also important. In 1999, Canada created the territory of Nunavut for the Inuit people. Nunavut covers about 64% of what was formerly the eastern part of the Northwest Territories. In 2006, the Conservative Party was returned to power in national elections, ending 12 years of Liberal Party rule.

Canada is a highly developed and prosperous country. Although farmland covers only 8% of the country, Canadian farms are highly productive. Canada is one of the world's leading producers of barley, wheat, meat, and milk. Forestry and fishing are other important industries. It is rich in natural resources, especially oil and natural gas, and is a major exporter of minerals. The country also produces copper, gold, iron ore, uranium, and zinc. Manufacturing is highly developed, especially in the cities where 80% of the people live. Canada has many factories that process farm and mineral products. It also produces cars, chemicals, electronic goods, machinery, paper, and timber products.

AREA 3,849,653 SQ MI [9,970,610 SQ KM] **POPULATION** 32,805,000 **CAPITAL (POPULATION)** OTTAWA (774,000) **GOVERNMENT** FEDERAL MULTIPARTY CONSTITUTIONAL MONARCHY **ETHNIC GROUPS** BRITISH ORIGIN 28%, FRENCH ORIGIN 23%, OTHER EUROPEAN 15%, AMERINDIAN/INUIT 2%, OTHERS **LANGUAGES** ENGLISH AND FRENCH (BOTH OFFICIAL) **RELIGIONS** ROMAN CATHOLIC 46%, PROTESTANT 36%, JUDAISM, ISLAM, HINDUISM **CURRENCY** CANADIAN DOLLAR = 100 CENTS

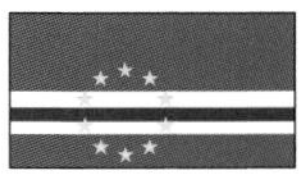

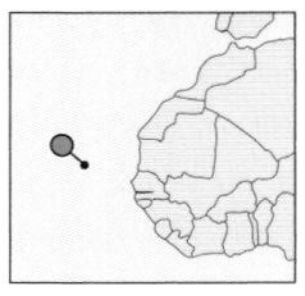

CAPE VERDE

Cape Verde consists of ten large and five small islands, and is situated 350 mi [560 km] west of Dakar in Senegal. The islands have a tropical climate, with high temperatures all year round. Cape Verde became independent from Portugal in 1975 and is rated as a "low-income" developing country by the World Bank.

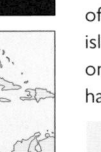

AREA 1,557 SQ MI [4,033 SQ KM] **POPULATION** 418,000 **CAPITAL** PRAIA

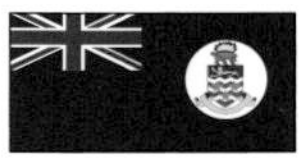

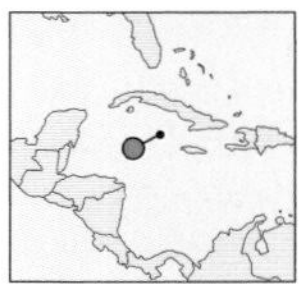

CAYMAN ISLANDS

The Cayman Islands are an overseas territory of the UK, consisting of three low-lying islands. Financial services are the main economic activity and the islands offer a secret tax haven to many companies and banks.

AREA 102 SQ MI [264 SQ KM] **POPULATION** 44,000 **CAPITAL** GEORGE TOWN

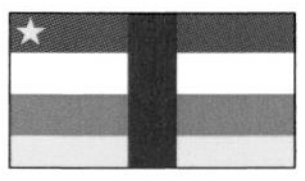

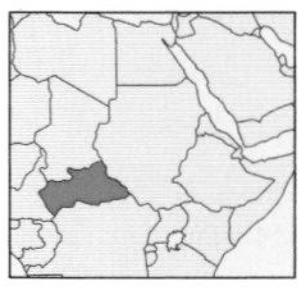

CENTRAL AFRICAN REPUBLIC

GEOGRAPHY The Central African Republic is a remote, landlocked country in the heart of Africa. It consists mostly of a plateau lying between 1,970 ft and 2,620 ft [600 m to 800 m] above sea level. The Ubangi drains the south, while the Chari (or Shari) River flows from the north to the Lake Chad basin. The climate is warm throughout the year, while the annual average rainfall in the capital Bangui totals 62 inches [1,574 mm]. The north is drier, with an average annual rainfall of about 31 inches [800 mm].

POLITICS & ECONOMY France set up an outpost at Bangui in 1899 and ruled the country as a colony from 1894. Known as Ubangi-Shari, the country was ruled by France as part of French Equatorial Africa until it gained independence in 1960.

Central African Republic became a one-party state in 1962, but army officers seized power in 1966. The head of the army, Jean-Bedel Bokassa, made himself emperor in 1976. The country was renamed the Central African Empire, but after a brutal reign, the tyrannical Bokassa was overthrown in a military coup in 1979. The country again became a republic.

The country adopted a new, multiparty constitution in 1991. Elections were held in 1993 and 1998. An army uprising in 2002 culminated in the overthrow of the government in 2003. General François Bozize took power. Bozize was elected president in 2005, but rebel activities caused instability in 2006.

The World Bank classifies Central African Republic as a "low-income" developing country. Over 80% of the people are farmers, and most of them produce little more than they need to feed their families. The main crops are bananas, maize, manioc, millet, and yams. Coffee, cotton, timber, and tobacco are produced for export, mainly on commercial plantations. The country's development has been impeded by its remote position, its poor transport system, and its untrained work force. The country depends heavily on aid, especially from France.

AREA 240,534 SQ MI [622,984 SQ KM] **POPULATION** 3,800,000 **CAPITAL (POPULATION)** BANGUI (553,000) **GOVERNMENT** MULTIPARTY REPUBLIC **ETHNIC GROUPS** BAYA 33%, BANDA 27%, MANDJIA 13%, SARA 10%, MBOUM 7%, MBAKA 4%, OTHERS **LANGUAGES** FRENCH (OFFICIAL), SANGHO **RELIGIONS** TRADITIONAL BELIEFS 35%, PROTESTANT 25%, ROMAN CATHOLIC 25%, ISLAM 15% **CURRENCY** CFA FRANC = 100 CENTIMES

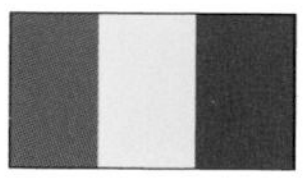
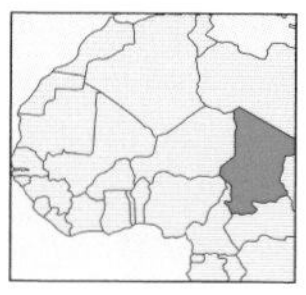

CHAD

GEOGRAPHY The Republic of Chad is a landlocked country in north-central Africa. It is Africa's fifth largest country and is over twice the size of France, the country which once ruled it as a colony.

Ndjamena in central Chad has a hot, tropical climate, with a marked dry season from November to April. The south of the country is wetter, with an average yearly rainfall of around 39 inches [1,000 mm]. The burning-hot desert in the north has an average yearly rainfall of less than 5 inches [130 mm].

POLITICS & ECONOMY Chad straddles two worlds. The north is populated by Muslim Arab and Berber peoples, while black Africans, who follow traditional beliefs or who have converted to Christianity, live in the south. French explorers were active in the area in the late 19th century. France made Chad a colony in 1902.

Chad became independent in 1960, but the 1970s were marked by ethnic conflict that led to civil wars, coups, and conflict with Libya, which supported rebel factions. Chad and Libya agreed a truce in 1987 and, in 1994, the International Court of Justice ruled against Libya's claim on the Aozou Strip. From 2004, Chad forces clashed with pro-Sudanese militias as the conflict in Sudan's Darfur province spilled over the border. In 2006, an attempt to overthrow the government failed.

Chad is one of the world's poorest countries. Farming and fishing employ 83% of the people. Food crops include groundnuts, millet, rice, and sorghum, but cotton is the chief export crop. Chad has few manufacturing industries, but its oil reserves hold out hope for development. Oil production began in 2003.

AREA 495,752 sq mi [1,284,000 sq km] **POPULATION** 9,826,000 **CAPITAL (POPULATION)** Ndjamena (530,000) **GOVERNMENT** Multiparty republic **ETHNIC GROUPS** 200 distinct groups: mostly Muslim in the north and center; mostly Christian or animist in the south **LANGUAGES** French and Arabic (both official), many others **RELIGIONS** Islam 51%, Christianity 35%, animist 7% **CURRENCY** CFA franc = 100 centimes

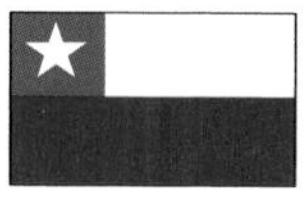
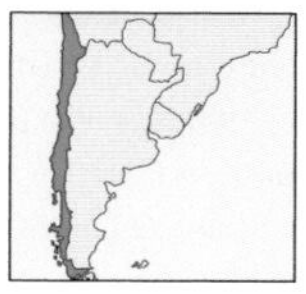

CHILE

GEOGRAPHY The Republic of Chile stretches about 2,650 mi [4,260 km] from north to south, although the maximum east–west distance is only about 267 mi [430 km]. The high Andes Mountains form Chile's eastern borders with Argentina and Bolivia. To the west are basins and valleys, with coastal uplands overlooking the shore. Most people live in the central valley, where Santiago is situated.

Santiago has a Mediterranean climate, with hot, dry summers from November to March and mild, moist winters from April to October. The Atacama Desert in the north is one of the world's driest places, while southern Chile is cold and stormy.

POLITICS & ECONOMY Amerindian people reached the southern tip of South America 8,000 years ago. In 1520, Portuguese navigator Ferdinand Magellan was the first European to sight Chile. The country became a Spanish colony in the 1540s. Chile became independent in 1818. During a war (1879–83), it gained mineral-rich areas from Peru and Bolivia.

In 1970, Salvador Allende became the first Communist leader to be elected democratically. He was overthrown in 1973 by army officers, who were supported by the CIA. General Augusto Pinochet then ruled as a dictator. A new constitution was introduced in 1981. Pinochet remained in power until 1989. Attempts to prosecute Pinochet continued in the 1990s and 2000s, though he seemed unlikely to be brought to trial, partly because of his age and ill-health. In 2006, the center-left, former torture victim Michelle Bachelet was elected president of Chile.

According to the World Bank, Chile has a "lower-middle-income" economy. Mining, especially copper, is important and minerals dominate the exports. But manufacturing is the most valuable activity. Products include processed foods, metals, iron and steel, transport equipment, and textiles. The chief crop is wheat, while beans, fruits, maize, and livestock products are also important. Chile's fishing industry is one of the world's largest.

AREA 292,133 sq mi [756,626 sq km] **POPULATION** 15,981,000 **CAPITAL (POPULATION)** Santiago (4,789,000) **GOVERNMENT** Multiparty republic **ETHNIC GROUPS** Mestizo 95%, Amerindian 3% **LANGUAGES** Spanish (official) **RELIGIONS** Roman Catholic 89%, Protestant 11% **CURRENCY** Chilean peso = 100 centavos

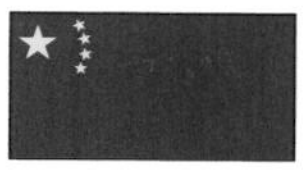
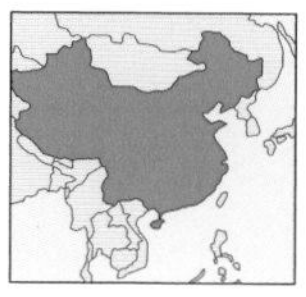

CHINA

GEOGRAPHY The People's Republic of China is the world's third largest country. Most people live in the east – on the coastal plains or in the fertile valleys of the Huang He (Hwang Ho or Yellow River), the Chang Jiang (Yangtze Kiang), which is Asia's longest river at 3,960 mi [6,380 km], and the Xi Jiang (Si Kiang). Western China is thinly populated. It includes the bleak Tibetan plateau which is bounded by the Himalaya, the world's highest mountain range. Other ranges include the Kunlun Shan, the Altun Shan, and the Tian Shan. Deserts include the Gobi Desert along the Mongolian border and the Taklimakan Desert in the far west.

Beijing has cold winters and warm summers with moderate rainfall. To the south, Shanghai has milder winters and more rain. The southeast has a wet, subtropical climate, but the west has a severe climate. Lhasa has very cold winters and a low rainfall.

POLITICS & ECONOMY China is one of the world's oldest civilizations, going back 3,500 years. Under the Han dynasty (202 BC to AD 220), the Chinese empire was as large as the Roman empire. Mongols conquered China in the 13th century, but Chinese rule was restored in 1368. The Manchu people of Mongolia ruled the country from 1644 to 1912, when the country became a republic.

War with Japan (1937–45) was followed by civil war between the nationalists and the Communists. The Communists triumphed in 1949, setting up the People's Republic of China. In the 1980s, following the death of the revolutionary leader Mao Zedong (Mao Tse-tung) in 1976, China encouraged formerly forbidden policies, namely private enterprise and foreign investment. But the Communist leaders have not permitted political freedom. Opponents are still harshly treated, while attempts to negotiate some degree of autonomy for Tibet have been rejected.

China's economy has expanded greatly since the 1970s, with many Communist policies being abandoned. Foreign investors have help to set up many new industries in the east. Between 1989 and 2004, the economy grew by an average of more than 9% per year. By 2005, China's economy ranked sixth in the world, though, as a major producer of consumer goods, it seemed likely to rise to fourth position before long. China benefited from the return of Hong Kong in 1997 and its admission to the World Trade Organization in 2001. China would like to regain the island of Taiwan, which it regards as a renegade province. This seems unlikely in the near future, although Taiwan's economy is closely tied to that of the mainland. In 2005, the 56-year ban on passenger flights from Taiwan to mainland China was lifted.

Despite its recent success, overall China remains a poor country. In 2002, agriculture employed more than 40% of the people, although only 10% of the land is farmed. Products include rice, sweet potatoes, tea, and wheat, and many fruits and vegetables. Livestock farming, especially pig rearing, is important. Resources include coal, iron ore, and other metals. Manufactures include cement, chemicals, fertilizers, machinery, telecommunications and recording equipment, and textiles. China is now a major producer of consumer goods, including air-conditioners, cameras, hard-disk drives and computer monitors, refrigerators, television sets, and washing machines.

AREA 3,705,387 sq mi [9,596,961 sq km] **POPULATION** 1,306,314,000 **CAPITAL (POPULATION)** Beijing (7,362,000) **GOVERNMENT** Single-party Communist republic **ETHNIC GROUPS** Han Chinese 92%, many others **LANGUAGES** Mandarin Chinese (official) **RELIGIONS** Atheist (official) **CURRENCY** Renminbi yuan = 10 jiao = 100 fen

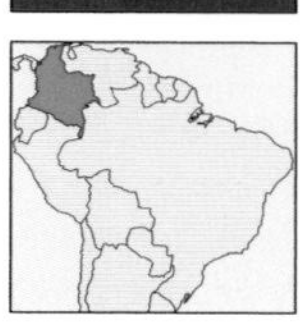

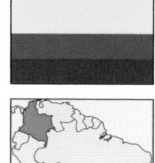

COLOMBIA

GEOGRAPHY The Republic of Colombia, in northeastern South America, is the only country in the continent to have coastlines on both the Pacific and the Caribbean Sea. Colombia also contains the northernmost ranges of the Andes Mountains.

There is a tropical climate in the lowlands, but the altitude greatly affects the climate of the Andes. The capital, Bogotá, which stands on a plateau in the eastern Andes at about 9,200 ft [2,800 m] above sea level, has mild temperatures throughout the year. The rainfall is heavy, especially on the Pacific coast.

POLITICS & ECONOMY Amerindian people have lived in Colombia for thousands of years. But today, only a small proportion of the people are of unmixed Amerindian ancestry. Mestizos (people of mixed white and Amerindian ancestry) form the largest group, followed by whites and mulattos (people of mixed European and African ancestry). Spaniards opened up the area in the early 16th century. They set up a territory known as the Vice-royalty of the New Kingdom of Granada, including Colombia, Ecuador, Panama, and Venezuela. In 1819, the area became independent, but Ecuador and Venezuela soon split away, followed by Panama in 1903.

Instability has marked its recent history. Colombia faces economic and security problems, notably combating left-wing guerrillas and right-wing paramilitaries, while controlling the illicit drug industry. Andrés Pastrana, president between 1998 and 2002, tried to end the guerrilla war, but peace talks collapsed in 2002 and conflict resumed. His successor, Alvaro Uribe, elected in 2002 and 2006, pursued a tough line against the rebels.

Colombia has a "lower-middle-income" economy. It exports oil, coffee, and chemicals.

AREA 439,735 sq mi [1,138,914 sq km] **POPULATION** 42,954,000 **CAPITAL (POPULATION)** Bogotá (6,545,000) **GOVERNMENT** Multiparty republic **ETHNIC GROUPS** Mestizo 58%, White 20%, Mulatto 14%, Black 4% **LANGUAGES** Spanish (official) **RELIGIONS** Roman Catholic 90% **CURRENCY** Colombian peso = 100 centavos

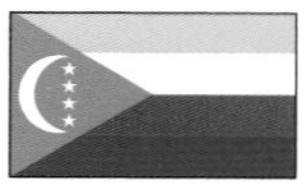
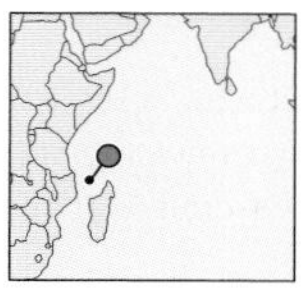

COMOROS

The Union des Isles Comores, as the Comoros is officially called, consists of three large volcanic islands and some smaller ones, lying at the north end of the Mozambique Channel in the Indian Ocean. France took over one of the islands, Mayotte, in 1843, and, in 1886, the other islands came under French protection.

The Comoros became independent in 1974, but Mayotte opted to remain French. In the late 1990s, the islands of Anjouan and Mohéli sought to secede, but, in 2004, the large islands were granted autonomy, with their own presidents and legislatures. Subsistence farming is the main economic activity. Exports include cloves, perfume oils, and vanilla.

AREA 863 sq mi [2,235 sq km] **POPULATION** 671,000 **CAPITAL** Moroni

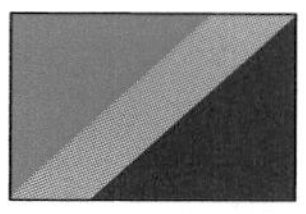
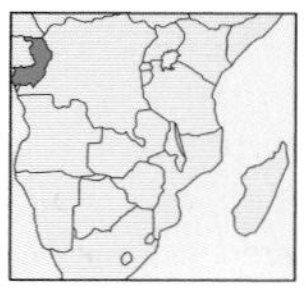

CONGO

GEOGRAPHY The Republic of Congo is a country on the River Congo in west-central Africa. The Equator runs through the center of the country. Congo has a narrow coastal plain on which its main port, Pointe Noire, stands. Behind the plain are uplands through which the River Niari has carved a fertile valley. Central Congo consists of high plains. The north contains large swampy areas in the valleys of the tributaries of the River Congo.

Congo has a hot, wet equatorial climate. Brazzaville has a dry season between June and September. The coast is drier and cooler than the rest of Congo, because of the cold offshore Benguela ocean current.

POLITICS & ECONOMY Part of the huge Kongo kingdom between the 15th and 18th centuries, the coast of the Congo later became a center of the European slave trade. The area came under French protection in 1880. It was later governed as part of a larger region called French Equatorial Africa. The country remained under French control until 1960.

Congo became a one-party state in 1964 and a military group took over the government in 1968. In 1970, Congo declared itself a Communist country, though it continued to seek aid from Western countries. The government officially abandoned its Communist policies in 1990. Multiparty elections were held in 1992, but the elected president, Pascal Lissouba, was overthrown in 1997 by former president Denis Sassou-Nguesso. Civil war again occurred in January 1999, but peace was restored. In 2002, Sassou-Nguesso was elected president.

The World Bank classifies Congo as a "lower-middle-income" developing country. Agriculture is the most important activity, employing about 60% of the people. But many farmers produce little more than they need to feed their families. Major food crops include bananas, cassava, maize, and rice, while the leading cash crops are coffee and cocoa. Congo's main exports are oil (which makes up 90% of the total) and timber. Manufacturing is relatively unimportant at the moment, still hampered by poor transport links, but it is gradually being developed.

AREA 132,046 sq mi [342,000 sq km] **POPULATION** 3,039,000 **CAPITAL (POPULATION)** Brazzaville (938,000) **GOVERNMENT** Military regime **ETHNIC GROUPS** Kongo 48%, Sangha 20%, Teke 17%, M'bochi 12% **LANGUAGES** French (official), many others **RELIGIONS** Christianity 50%, animist 48%, Islam 2% **CURRENCY** CFA franc = 100 centimes

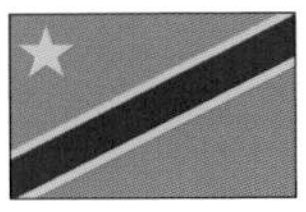

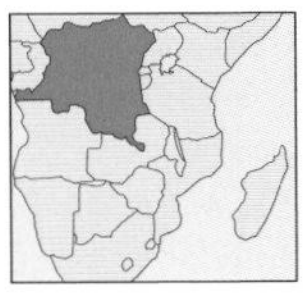

CONGO (DEM. REP. OF THE)

GEOGRAPHY The Democratic Republic of the Congo, formerly known as Zaïre, is the world's 12th largest country. Much of the country lies within the drainage basin of the huge River Congo. The river reaches the sea along the country's coastline, which is 25 mi [40 km] long. Mountains rise in the east, where the country's borders run through lakes Tanganyika, Kivu, Edward, and Albert. The equatorial region has high temperatures and heavy rainfall throughout the year.

POLITICS & ECONOMY Pygmies were the first inhabitants of the region, with Portuguese navigators not reaching the coast until 1482, but the interior was not explored until the late 19th century. In 1885, the country, called Congo Free State, became the personal property of King Léopold II of Belgium. In 1908, the country became a Belgian colony.

The Belgian Congo became independent in 1960 and was renamed Zaïre in 1971. Ethnic rivalries caused instability until 1965, when the country became a one-party state, ruled by President Mobutu. The government allowed the formation of political parties in 1990, but elections were repeatedly postponed. In 1996, fighting broke out in eastern Zaïre, as the Tutsi–Hutu conflict in Burundi and Rwanda spilled over. The rebel leader Laurent Kabila took power in 1997, ousting Mobutu and renaming the country. A rebellion against Kabila broke out in 1998. Rwanda and Uganda supported the rebels, while Angola, Chad, Namibia and Zimbabwe assisted Kabila. A peace treaty was signed in 1999, but fighting continued. Kabila was assassinated in 2001. His son, Major-General Joseph Kabila, became president. A new constitution was adopted in 2005, but continuing sporadic conflict in the east threatened the planned elections in 2006.

The World Bank classifies the Democratic Republic of the Congo as a "low-income" developing country, despite its reserves of copper, the main export, and other minerals. Agriculture, mainly at subsistence level, employs 62% of the people.

AREA 905,350 SQ MI [2,344,858 SQ KM] **POPULATION** 60,086,000
CAPITAL (POPULATION) KINSHASA (4,665,000)
GOVERNMENT SINGLE-PARTY REPUBLIC
ETHNIC GROUPS OVER 200; THE LARGEST ARE MONGO, LUBA, KONGO, MANGBETU-AZANDE
LANGUAGES FRENCH (OFFICIAL), TRIBAL LANGUAGES
RELIGIONS ROMAN CATHOLIC 50%, PROTESTANT 20%, ISLAM 10%, OTHERS
CURRENCY CONGOLESE FRANC = 100 CENTIMES

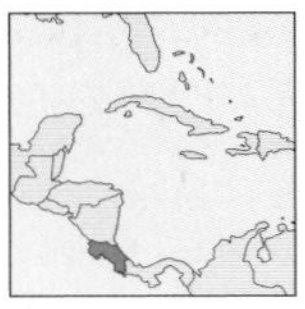

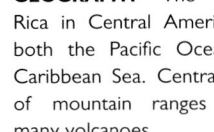

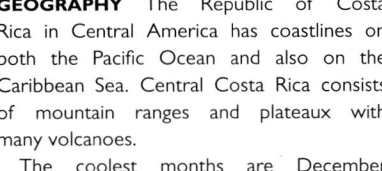

COSTA RICA

GEOGRAPHY The Republic of Costa Rica in Central America has coastlines on both the Pacific Ocean and also on the Caribbean Sea. Central Costa Rica consists of mountain ranges and plateaux with many volcanoes.

The coolest months are December and January. The northeast trade winds bring heavy rain to the Caribbean coast. There is less rainfall in the highlands and on the Pacific coastlands.

POLITICS & ECONOMY Christopher Columbus reached the Caribbean coast in 1502 and rumors of treasure soon attracted many Spaniards to settle in the country. Spain ruled the country until 1821, when Spain's Central American colonies broke away to join Mexico in 1822. In 1823, the Central American states broke with Mexico and set up the Central American Federation. Later, this large union broke up and Costa Rica became fully independent in 1838.

From the late 19th century, Costa Rica experienced a number of revolutions, with periods of dictatorship and periods of democracy. In 1948, following a revolt, the armed forces were abolished. Since 1948, Costa Rica has enjoyed a long period of stable democracy. In 2006, Nobel Peace Prize winner Oscar Arias was elected president.

Costa Rica is classified by the World Bank as a "lower-middle-income" developing country and one of the most prosperous countries in Central America. There are high educational standards and a high average life expectancy (about 74 years for men and 79 years for women). Agriculture employs 15% of the people. Costa Rica's natural resources include its forests, but it lacks minerals apart from some bauxite and manganese. Manufacturing is increasing. The United States is Costa Rica's main trading partner. Tourism is a fast-growing industry.

AREA 19,730 SQ MI [51,100 SQ KM] **POPULATION** 4,016,000 **CAPITAL (POPULATION)** SAN JOSÉ (337,000) **GOVERNMENT** MULTIPARTY REPUBLIC **ETHNIC GROUPS** WHITE (INCLUDING MESTIZO) 94%, BLACK 3%, AMERINDIAN 1%, CHINESE 1%, OTHERS **LANGUAGES** SPANISH (OFFICIAL), ENGLISH **RELIGIONS** ROMAN CATHOLIC 76%, EVANGELICAL 14% **CURRENCY** COSTA RICAN COLÓN = 100 CÉNTIMOS

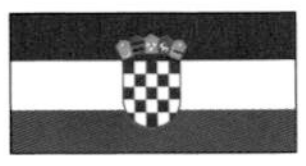

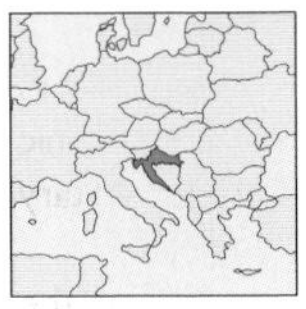

CROATIA

GEOGRAPHY The Republic of Croatia was one of the six republics that made up the former Communist country of Yugoslavia until it became independent in 1991. The region bordering the Adriatic Sea is called Dalmatia. It includes the coastal ranges, which contain large areas of bare limestone. Most of the rest of the country consists of the fertile Pannonian plains.

The coastal area has a typical Mediterranean climate, with hot, dry summers and mild, moist winters. Inland, the climate becomes more continental. Winters are cold, while temperatures often soar to 100°F [38°C] in the summer months.

POLITICS & ECONOMY Slav people settled in the area around 1,400 years ago. In 803, Croatia became part of the Holy Roman empire and the Croats soon adopted Christianity. Croatia was an independent kingdom in the 10th and 11th centuries. In 1102, the king of Hungary also became king of Croatia, creating a union that lasted 800 years. In 1526, part of Croatia came under the Turkish Ottoman empire, while the rest came under the Austrian Habsburgs.

After Austria–Hungary was defeated in World War I (1914–18), Croatia became part of the new Kingdom of the Serbs, Croats, and Slovenes. This kingdom was renamed Yugoslavia in 1929. Germany occupied Yugoslavia during World War II (1939–45). Croatia was proclaimed independent, but it was really ruled by the invaders.

After the war, Communists took power with Josip Broz Tito as the country's leader. Despite ethnic differences between the people, Tito held Yugoslavia together until his death in 1980. In the 1980s, economic and ethnic problems, including a deterioration in relations with Serbia, threatened stability. In the 1990s, Yugoslavia split into five nations, one of which was Croatia, which declared itself independent in 1991.

After Serbia supplied arms to Serbs living in Croatia, war broke out between the two republics, causing great damage. Croatia lost more than 30% of its territory. But in 1992, the United Nations sent a peacekeeping force to Croatia, which effectively ended the war with Serbia.

In 1992, when war broke out in Bosnia-Herzegovina, Bosnian Croats occupied parts of the country. But in 1994, Croatia helped to end Croat–Muslim conflict in Bosnia-Herzegovina and, in 1995, after retaking some areas occupied by Serbs, it helped to draw up the Dayton Peace Accord, ending the civil war. The wars in the early 1990s disrupted the economy. But in the early 21st century, stability, which is so vital to the valuable tourist industry, seemed to be returning. In 2005, the European Union began accession talks with Croatia, though many problems were anticipated. Croatia's main exports are manufactures.

AREA 21,829 SQ MI [56,538 SQ KM] **POPULATION** 4,496,000 **CAPITAL (POPULATION)** ZAGREB (779,000) **GOVERNMENT** MULTIPARTY REPUBLIC **ETHNIC GROUPS** CROAT 90%, SERB 5%, OTHERS **LANGUAGES** CROATIAN 96% **RELIGIONS** ROMAN CATHOLIC 88%, ORTHODOX 4%, ISLAM 1%, OTHERS **CURRENCY** KUNA = 100 LIPAS

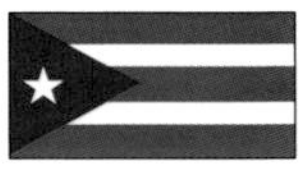

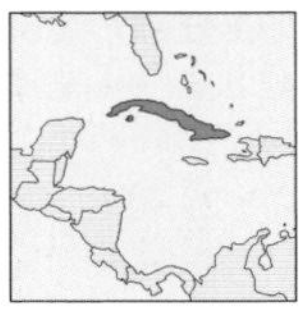

CUBA

GEOGRAPHY The Republic of Cuba is the largest island country in the Caribbean Sea. It consists of one large island, Cuba, the Isle of Youth (Isla de la Juventud) and about 1,600 small islets. Mountains and hills cover about a quarter of Cuba. The highest mountain range, the Sierra Maestra in the southeast, reaches 6,562 ft [2,000 m] above sea level. The rest of the land consists of gently rolling country or coastal plains, crossed by fertile valleys carved by the short, mostly shallow and narrow rivers.

Cuba lies in the tropics. But sea breezes moderate the temperature, warming the land in winter and cooling it in summer.

POLITICS & ECONOMY Christopher Columbus discovered the island in 1492 and Spaniards began to settle there from 1511. Spanish rule ended in 1898, when the United States defeated Spain in the Spanish–American War. American influence in Cuba remained strong until 1959, when revolutionary forces under Fidel Castro overthrew the dictatorial government of Fulgencio Batista.

The United States opposed Castro's policies, when he turned to the Soviet Union for assistance. In 1961, Cuban exiles attempting an invasion were defeated. In 1962, the US learned that nuclear missile bases armed by the Soviet Union had been established in Cuba. The US ordered the Soviet Union to remove the missiles and bases and, after a few days, when many people feared that a world war might break out, the Soviet Union agreed to the American demands.

Cuba's relations with the Soviet Union remained strong until 1991, when the Soviet Union was broken up. The loss of Soviet aid greatly damaged Cuba's economy, but Castro maintained his left-wing policies. In 2004, following a United States crackdown on currency and travel, Cuba declared that US dollars would no longer be accepted as payments for goods and services.

The government runs Cuba's economy and owns 70% of the farmland. Agriculture is important and sugar is the chief export, followed by refined nickel ore. Other exports include cigars, citrus fruits, fish, medical products, and rum.

Before 1959, US companies owned most of Cuba's manufacturing industries. But under Fidel Castro, they became government property. After the collapse of Communist governments in the Soviet Union and its allies, Cuba worked to increase its trade with Latin America and China.

AREA 42,803 SQ MI [110,861 SQ KM] **POPULATION** 11,347,000
CAPITAL (POPULATION) HAVANA (2,192,000)
GOVERNMENT SOCIALIST REPUBLIC
ETHNIC GROUPS MULATTO 51%, WHITE 37%, BLACK 11%
LANGUAGES SPANISH (OFFICIAL) **RELIGIONS** CHRISTIANITY
CURRENCY CUBAN PESO = 100 CENTAVOS

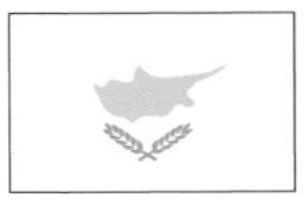

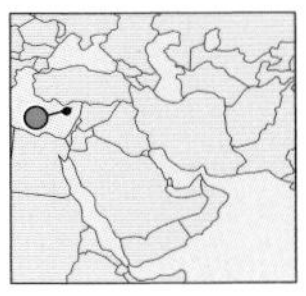

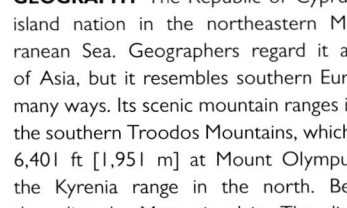

CYPRUS

GEOGRAPHY The Republic of Cyprus is an island nation in the northeastern Mediterranean Sea. Geographers regard it as part of Asia, but it resembles southern Europe in many ways. Its scenic mountain ranges include the southern Troodos Mountains, which reach 6,401 ft [1,951 m] at Mount Olympus, and the Kyrenia range in the north. Between them lies the Mesaoria plain. The climate is Mediterranean, with typically hot, dry summers and mild, moist winters. But the island's proximity to southwestern Asia gives it a hotter climate than places in the western Mediterranean.

POLITICS & ECONOMY Greeks settled on Cyprus around 3,200 years ago. From AD 330, the island was part of the Byzantine empire. In the 1570s, Cyprus became part of the Turkish Ottoman empire. Turkish rule continued until 1878 when Cyprus was leased to Britain. Britain annexed the island in 1914 and proclaimed it a colony in 1925.

In the 1950s, Greek Cypriots, who made up four-fifths of the population, began a campaign for *enosis* (union) with Greece. Their leader was the Greek Orthodox Archbishop Makarios. A secret guerrilla force called EOKA attacked the British, who exiled Makarios. Cyprus became an independent country in 1960, although Britain retained two military bases. Independent Cyprus had a constitution which provided for power-sharing between the Greek and Turkish Cypriots. But the constitution proved unworkable and fighting broke out between the two communities. In 1964, the United Nations sent in a peacekeeping force, but communal clashes recurred in 1967.

In 1974, Cypriot forces led by Greek officers overthrew Makarios. This led Turkey to invade northern Cyprus, a territory occupying about 40% of the island. Many Greek Cypriots fled from the north, which, in 1979, was proclaimed the Turkish Republic of Northern Cyprus. The only country to recognize this state was Turkey. The United Nations regarded Cyprus as a single unit under the Greek-Cypriot government in the south. In 2002, the European Union invited Cyprus to become a member in 2004. In April 2004, the people voted on a UN plan to reunify the island. The Turkish-Cypriots voted in favor, but the Greek-Cypriots voted against. Hence, only the south was admitted to EU membership on May 1, 2004.

Cyprus got its name from the Greek word *kypros*, meaning copper. But little copper remains and the chief minerals today are asbestos and chromium. However, the most valuable activity in Cyprus is tourism. Manufactures include cement, clothes, footwear, tiles, and wine.

In the early 1990s. the United Nations reclassified Cyprus as a developed rather than a developing country, reflecting the rapid economic progress in the south. But the north lagged far behind the prosperous Greek-Cypriot south.

AREA 3,572 sq mi [9,251 sq km] **POPULATION** 780,000
CAPITAL (POPULATION) Nicosia (198,000)
GOVERNMENT Multiparty republic **ETHNIC GROUPS** Greek Cypriot 77%, Turkish Cypriot 18%, others **LANGUAGES** Greek and Turkish (both official), English **RELIGIONS** Greek Orthodox 78%, Islam 18%
CURRENCY Cypriot pound = 100 cents

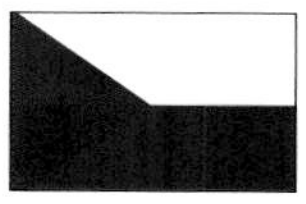
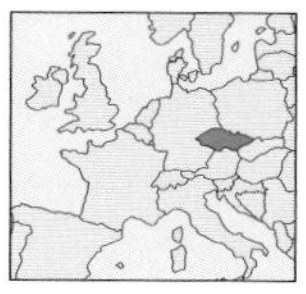

CZECH REPUBLIC

GEOGRAPHY The Czech Republic is the western three-fifths of the former country of Czechoslovakia. It contains two regions: Bohemia in the west and Moravia in the east. Mountains border much of the country in the west. The Bohemian basin in the north-center is a fertile lowland region, with Prague, the capital city, as its main center. Highlands cover much of the center of the country, with lowlands in the southeast.

The climate is influenced by its landlocked position in east-central Europe. Prague has warm, sunny summers and cold winters. The average rainfall is moderate, with 20 inches to 30 inches [500 mm to 750 mm] every year in lowland areas.

POLITICS & ECONOMY After World War I (1914–18), Czechoslovakia was created. Germany seized the country in World War II (1939–45). In 1948, Communist leaders took power and Czechoslovakia was allied to the Soviet Union. When democratic reforms were introduced in the Soviet Union in the late 1980s, the Czechs also demanded reforms. Free elections were held in 1990, but differences between the Czechs and Slovaks led to the partitioning of the country on January 1, 1993. The Czech Republic became a member of NATO in 1999. In 2003, 77% of Czechs voted in favor of their country becoming a member of the European Union. This took place on May 1, 2004.

Under Communist rule the Czech Republic became one of the most industrialized parts of Eastern Europe. The country has deposits of coal, uranium, iron ore, magnesite, tin, and zinc. Manufacturing employs about 25% of the Czech Republic's entire work force. Farming is also important. Under Communism, the government owned the land, but private ownership is now being restored. The country was admitted into the OECD in 1995.

AREA 30,450 sq mi [78,866 sq km] **POPULATION** 10,241,000
CAPITAL (POPULATION) Prague (1,193,000)
GOVERNMENT Multiparty republic **ETHNIC GROUPS** Czech 81%, Moravian 13%, Slovak 3%, Polish, German, Silesian, Gypsy, Hungarian, Ukrainian **LANGUAGES** Czech (official) **RELIGIONS** Atheist 40%, Roman Catholic 39%, Protestant 4%, Orthodox 3%, others
CURRENCY Czech koruna = 100 haler

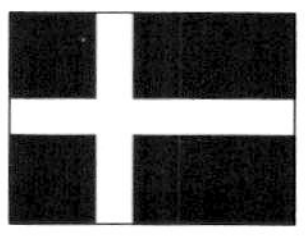
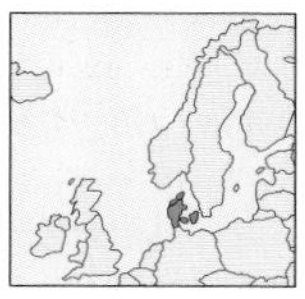

DENMARK

GEOGRAPHY The Kingdom of Denmark is the smallest country in Scandinavia. It consists of a peninsula, called Jutland (or Jylland), which is joined to Germany, and more than 400 islands, 89 of which are inhabited. The land is flat and mostly covered by rocks dropped there by huge ice sheets during the last Ice Age. The highest point in Denmark is on Jutland. It is only 568 ft [173 m] above sea level. Denmark has a mild, moist climate, except during cold spells in winter when The Sound between Sjælland and Sweden may freeze over.

POLITICS & ECONOMY Danish Vikings terrorized much of Western Europe for about 300 years after AD 800. In the late 14th century, Denmark formed a union with Norway and Sweden (which included Finland). Sweden broke away in 1523, while Denmark lost Norway to Sweden in 1814. After 1945, Denmark became a member of the North Atlantic Treaty Organization. It joined the European Union in 1973, though it did not adopt the euro in 2000. The Danes enjoy a high standard of living, but the country's welfare programs are extremely costly.

Denmark has some oil and gas and the economy is highly developed. Manufacturing employs about 15% of the people. Products include furniture, processed food, machinery, television sets, and textiles. Farms cover about three-quarters of the land. Farming employs only 3% of the people, but it is highly scientific. Meat and dairy farming are the chief activities.

AREA 16,639 sq mi [43,094 sq km] **POPULATION** 5,432,000
CAPITAL (POPULATION) Copenhagen (499,000) **GOVERNMENT** Parliamentary monarchy **ETHNIC GROUPS** Scandinavian, Inuit, Færoese **LANGUAGES** Danish (official), English, Færoese **RELIGIONS** Evangelical Lutheran 95% **CURRENCY** Danish krone = 100 øre

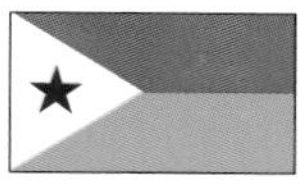
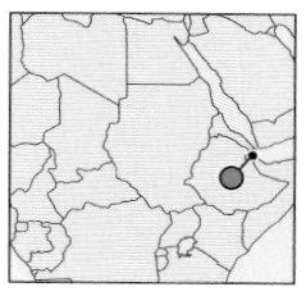

DJIBOUTI

GEOGRAPHY The Republic of Djibouti in eastern Africa occupies a strategic position where the Red Sea meets the Gulf of Aden. Djibouti has one of the world's hottest and driest climates.

POLITICS & ECONOMY France set up a territory called French Somaliland in 1888. Its capital, Djibouti, became important when a railroad was built to Addis Ababa and Djibouti became the main outlet for Ethiopian trade. In 1967, France renamed the dependency the French Territory of the Afars and Issas, but it was renamed Djibouti on independence in 1977. It became a one-party state in 1981, but a new constitution (1992) permitted four parties which had to maintain a balance between the country's ethnic groups. In the 2000s, the United States used Djibouti as a military base to counter terrorism in the region.

Djibouti is a poor country. Its economy is based largely on the revenue it gets from its port and the railroad to Addis Ababa.

AREA 8,958 sq mi [23,200 sq km] **POPULATION** 477,000
CAPITAL (POPULATION) Djibouti (317,000) **GOVERNMENT** Multiparty republic **ETHNIC GROUPS** Somali 60%, Afar 35% **LANGUAGES** Arabic and French (both official) **RELIGIONS** Islam 94%, Christianity 6%
CURRENCY Djiboutian franc = 100 centimes

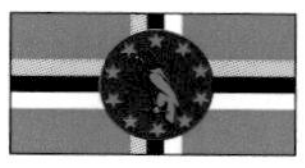
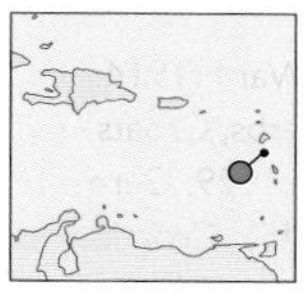

DOMINICA

The Commonwealth of Dominica, a former British colony, became independent in 1978. The island has a mountainous spine and less than 10% of the land is cultivated. But agriculture employs 18% of the people. The manufacture of coconut-based soap is important, while tourism and mining are other economic activities.

AREA 290 sq mi [751 sq km] **POPULATION** 69,000 **CAPITAL** Roseau

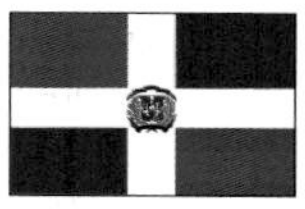
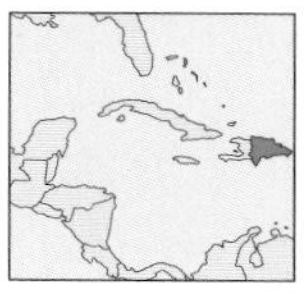

DOMINICAN REPUBLIC

GEOGRAPHY Second largest of the Caribbean nations in both area and population, the Dominican Republic shares the island of Hispaniola with Haiti, with the Dominican Republic occupying the eastern two-thirds. The country is mountainous, and the generally hot and humid climate eases with altitude.

POLITICS & ECONOMY In 1492, Christopher Columbus landed on Hispaniola and Spaniards soon settled the island, followed by the French who occupied the western third of the island (which is now Haiti). The island was held by Haitians from 1822 until 1844, when the Dominican Republic was established. Civil war broke out in 1966 but US intervention ended the conflict. Since 1966, the young democracy has survived violent elections under the watchful eye of the United States.

The Dominican Republic is a developing country and agriculture is the chief activity. Sugarcane, rice, bananas, and cocoa are leading crops. Food processing is also important and some ferronickel is produced.

AREA 18,730 sq mi [48,511 sq km] **POPULATION** 8,950,000
CAPITAL (POPULATION) Santo Domingo (2,061,000)
GOVERNMENT Multiparty republic **ETHNIC GROUPS** Mulatto 73%, White 16%, Black 11% **LANGUAGES** Spanish (official) **RELIGIONS** Roman Catholic 95% **CURRENCY** Dominican peso = 100 centavos

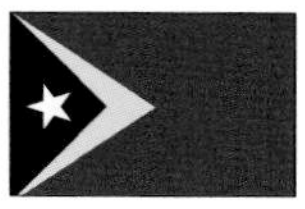
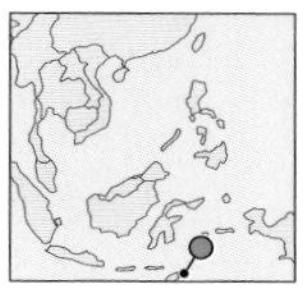

EAST TIMOR

The Republic of East Timor became fully independent and the world's newest country on May 20, 2002. The land is mainly rugged. Temperatures are generally high and the rainfall is moderate. Portugal ruled the area from the late 19th century, when it was called Portuguese Timor. Portugal withdrew in 1975 and Indonesia seized the area. Guerrilla activity mounted under Indonesian rule and, in 1999, the people voted for independence. Agriculture is the main activity and East Timor is the poorest country in Southeast Asia. But, in 2006, East Timor and Australia signed a deal to share the revenue from the oil and natural gas deposits under the Timor Sea.

AREA 5,743 sq mi [14,874 sq km] **POPULATION** 1,041,000 **CAPITAL** Dili

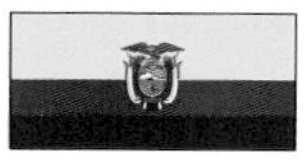
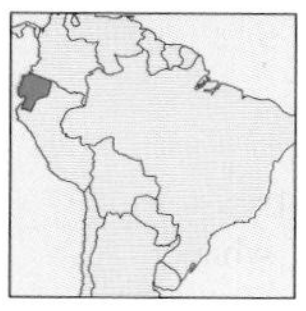

ECUADOR

GEOGRAPHY The Republic of Ecuador straddles the Equator on the west coast of South America. Three ranges of the high Andes Mountains form the backbone of the country. Between the towering, snow-capped peaks of the mountains, some of which are volcanoes, lie a series of high plateaux, or basins. Nearly half of Ecuador's population lives on these plateaux. The coast has a warm tropical climate, despite the cold offshore Peruvian Current. Inland, the altitude gives the plateaux spring-like weather throughout the year.

POLITICS & ECONOMY The Inca people of Peru conquered much of what is now Ecuador in the late 15th century. They introduced their language, Quechua, which is widely spoken today. Spanish forces defeated the Incas in 1533 and took control of Ecuador. The country became independent in 1822, following the defeat of a Spanish force in a battle near Quito.

In the 19th and 20th centuries, Ecuador suffered from political instability, while successive governments failed to tackle the country's social and economic problems. A war with Peru in 1941 led to a loss of territory. Disputes continued until 1995, but a border agreement was signed in January 1998. Economic crises in the early 21st century led to the adoption of the US dollar as the official currency. Political instability marred progress. A coup in 2000 was led by Colonel Lucio Gutiérrez, who was elected president in 2002. However, after he fired Supreme Court judges in 2004, massive protests led to his overthrow in 2005. He was succeeded by former vice-president Alfredo Palacio.

The World Bank classifies Ecuador as a "lower-middle-income" developing country. Agriculture employs 10% of the people and bananas, cocoa, and coffee are all important crops. Fishing, forestry, mining, and manufacturing are other activities.

AREA 109,483 sq mi [283,561 sq km] **POPULATION** 13,364,000
CAPITAL (POPULATION) Quito (1,616,000)
GOVERNMENT Multiparty republic
ETHNIC GROUPS Mestizo (mixed White/Amerindian) 65%, Amerindian 25%, White 7%, Black 3%
LANGUAGES Spanish (official), Quechua
RELIGIONS Roman Catholic 95%
CURRENCY US dollar = 100 cents

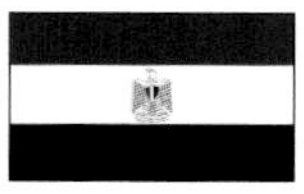
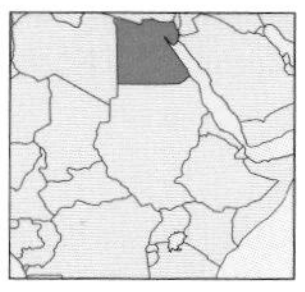

EGYPT

GEOGRAPHY The Arab Republic of Egypt is Africa's second largest country by population after Nigeria, though it ranks 13th in area. Most of Egypt is desert. Almost all the people live either in the Nile Valley and its fertile delta or along the Suez Canal, the artificial waterway between the Mediterranean and Red seas. This canal shortens the sea journey between the United Kingdom and India by 6,027 mi [9,700 km]. Recent attempts have been made to irrigate parts of the western desert and thus redistribute the rapidly growing Egyptian population into previously uninhabited regions.

Apart from the Nile Valley, Egypt has three other main regions. The Western and Eastern deserts are parts of the Sahara. The Sinai peninsula (Es Sina), to the east of the Suez Canal, is a mountainous desert region, geographically within Asia. It contains Egypt's highest peak, Gebel Katherina (8,650 ft [2,637 m]); few people live in this area.

Egypt is a dry country. The low rainfall occurs, if at all, in winter and the country is one of the sunniest places on Earth.

POLITICS & ECONOMY Ancient Egypt, which was founded about 5,000 years ago, was one of the great early civilizations. Throughout the country, pyramids, temples, and richly decorated tombs are memorials to its great achievements.

After Ancient Egypt declined, the country came under successive foreign rulers. Arabs occupied Egypt in AD 639–42. They introduced the Arabic language and Islam. Their influence was so great that most Egyptians now regard themselves as Arabs.

Egypt came under British rule in 1882, but it gained partial independence in 1922, becoming a monarchy. The monarchy was abolished in 1952, when Egypt became a republic. The creation of Israel in 1948 led Egypt into a series of wars in 1948–9, 1956, 1967, and 1973. Since the late 1970s, Egypt has sought for peace. In 1979, Egypt signed a peace treaty with Israel and regained the Sinai region which it had lost in a war in 1967. Extremists opposed contacts with Israel and, in 1981, President Sadat, who had signed the treaty, was assassinated.

While Egypt plays a major part in Arab affairs, most of its people are poor. Some Islamic fundamentalists, who dislike Western influences on their way of life, have resorted to violence. In the

1990s, attacks on foreign visitors caused a decline in the valuable tourist industry, as also did the events of September 11, 2001, and the subsequent "war against terrorism." Hosni Mubarak, president since 1981, was re-elected in 2005, though supporters of the banned Muslim Brotherhood made gains in parliamentary elections.

Egypt is Africa's second most industrialized country after South Africa, but most people are poor. Oil and textiles are the country's main exports.

AREA 386,659 SQ MI [1,001,449 SQ KM] **POPULATION** 77,506,000
CAPITAL (POPULATION) CAIRO (6,801,000)
GOVERNMENT REPUBLIC
ETHNIC GROUPS EGYPTIANS/BEDOUINS/BERBERS 99%
LANGUAGES ARABIC (OFFICIAL), FRENCH, ENGLISH
RELIGIONS ISLAM (MAINLY SUNNI MUSLIM) 94%, CHRISTIANITY (MAINLY COPTIC CHRISTIAN) AND OTHERS 6%
CURRENCY EGYPTIAN POUND = 100 PIASTRES

EL SALVADOR

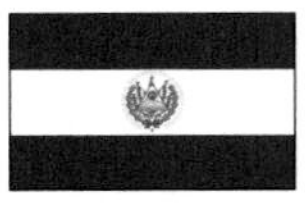
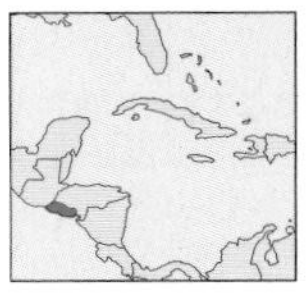

GEOGRAPHY The Republic of El Salvador is the only country in Central America which does not have a coast on the Caribbean Sea. El Salvador has a narrow coastal plain along the Pacific Ocean. Behind the coastal plain, the coastal range is a zone of rugged mountains, including volcanoes, which overlooks a densely populated inland plateau. Beyond the plateau, the land rises to the sparsely populated interior highlands. The coast has a hot, tropical climate. Inland the climate is moderated by the altitude. Rain falls on practically every afternoon between May and October.

POLITICS & ECONOMY Amerindians have lived in El Salvador for thousands of years. The ruins of Mayan pyramids built between AD 100 and 1000 are still found in the western part of the country. Spanish soldiers conquered the area in 1524 and 1525, and Spain ruled until 1821. In 1823, all the Central American countries, except for Panama, set up a Central American Federation. But El Salvador withdrew in 1840 and declared its independence in 1841. El Salvador suffered from instability throughout the 19th century. The 20th century saw a more stable government, but from 1931 military dictatorships alternated with elected governments.

The country remained poor. In the 1970s, protesters demanded that the government introduce reforms to help the poor. Kidnappings and murders committed by left- and right-wing groups caused instability. A civil war broke out in 1979 between the US-backed government forces and left-wing guerrillas. In 12 years, more than 750,000 people died and many were made homeless. A ceasefire was agreed in 1992 and democratic elections were held in 1993, 1999, and 2003. By 2003, the economy had shown signs of recovery, but the World Bank still classifies El Salvador as a "lower-middle-income" economy.

About three-quarters of the country is farmed. Coffee, grown in the highlands, is the main export, followed by sugar and cotton, which grow on the coastal lowlands. Fishing for lobsters and shrimps is important, but manufacturing is on a small scale.

AREA 8,124 SQ MI [21,041 SQ KM] **POPULATION** 6,705,000
CAPITAL (POPULATION) SAN SALVADOR (473,000)
GOVERNMENT REPUBLIC **ETHNIC GROUPS** MESTIZO (MIXED WHITE AND AMERINDIAN) 90%, WHITE 9%, AMERINDIAN 1%
LANGUAGES SPANISH (OFFICIAL) **RELIGIONS** ROMAN CATHOLIC 83%
CURRENCY US DOLLAR = 100 CENTS

EQUATORIAL GUINEA

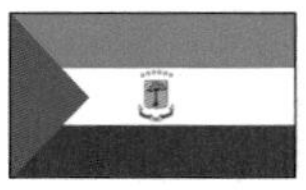
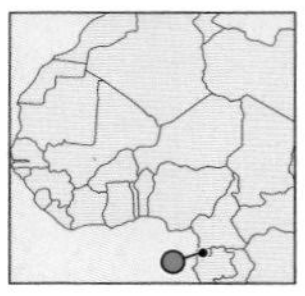

GEOGRAPHY The Republic of Equatorial Guinea is a small republic in west-central Africa. It consists of a mainland territory which makes up 90% of the land area, called Rio Muni, between Cameroon and Gabon, and five offshore islands in the Bight of Bonny, the largest of which is Bioko. The island of Annobon lies 350 mi [560 km] southwest of Rio Muni. Rio Muni consists mainly of hills and plateaux behind the coastal plains.

The climate is hot and humid. Bioko is mountainous, with the land rising to 9,869 ft [3,008 m], and hence it is particularly rainy. However, there is a marked dry season between the months of December and February. Mainland Rio Muni has a similar climate, though the rainfall diminishes inland.

POLITICS & ECONOMY Portuguese navigators reached the area in 1471. In 1778, Portugal granted Bioko, together with rights over Rio Muni, to Spain.

In 1959, Spain made Bioko and Rio Muni provinces of overseas Spain and, in 1963, it gave the provinces a degree of self-government. Equatorial Guinea became independent in 1968.

The first president of Equatorial Guinea, Francisco Macias Nguema, proved to be a tyrant. He was overthrown in 1979 and a group of officers, led by Lieutenant-Colonel Teodoro Obiang Nguema Mbasogo, set up a Supreme Military Council to rule the country. In 1991, the people voted to set up a multiparty democracy. Elections were held, but accusations of human rights abuses continued. In 2004, a coup attempt by mercenaries was foiled and its leaders were arrested.

Agriculture employs more than half of the people. The most valuable crop is coffee. Oil, which has been produced since 1966, accounts for most of the export revenue.

AREA 10,830 SQ MI [28,051 SQ KM] **POPULATION** 536,000
CAPITAL (POPULATION) MALABO (30,000) **GOVERNMENT** MULTIPARTY REPUBLIC (TRANSITIONAL) **ETHNIC GROUPS** BUBI (ON BIOKO), FANG (IN RIO MUNI) **LANGUAGES** SPANISH AND FRENCH (BOTH OFFICIAL)
RELIGIONS CHRISTIANITY **CURRENCY** CFA FRANC = 100 CENTIMES

ERITREA

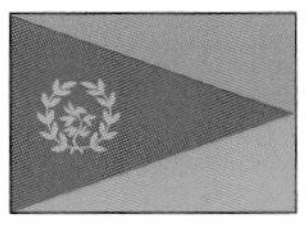
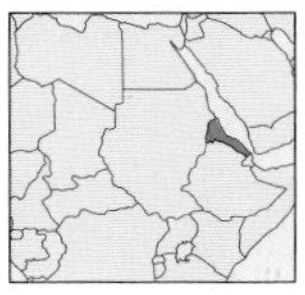

GEOGRAPHY The State of Eritrea consists of a hot, dry coastal plain facing the Red Sea, with a fairly mountainous area in the center. Most people live in the cooler highland area.

POLITICS & ECONOMY From the 1st century AD, Eritrea was part of the ancient Kingdom of Axum, which adopted Christianity in the 4th century AD. It began to decline in the 7th century. The Ottoman Turks took over the area in the 16th century and it became an Italian colony in the 1880s. The Italians were driven out in 1941 and, in 1952, it became part of Ethiopia.

A guerrilla struggle launched in 1961 ended in 1993, when Eritrea became independent. Economic recovery was hampered by conflict with Yemen over three islands in the Red Sea. In 1988–9, clashes occurred along the border with Ethiopia. A peace agreement was signed in 2000, but arguments persisted and, in 2005–6, tensions between the two countries again mounted.

The main economic activities are farming and livestock rearing. The few manufacturing industries are based mainly in Asmara.

AREA 45,405 SQ MI [117,600 SQ KM] **POPULATION** 4,562,000
CAPITAL (POPULATION) ASMARA (358,000) **GOVERNMENT** TRANSITIONAL GOVERNMENT **ETHNIC GROUPS** TIGRINYA 50%, TIGRE AND KUNAMA 40%, AFAR 4%, SAHO 3%, OTHERS **LANGUAGES** AFAR, ARABIC, TIGRE AND KUNAMA, TIGRINYA **RELIGIONS** ISLAM, COPTIC CHRISTIAN, ROMAN CATHOLIC **CURRENCY** NAKFA = 100 CENTS

ESTONIA

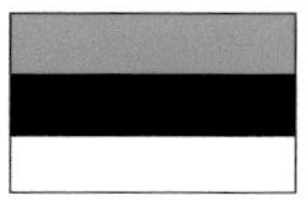
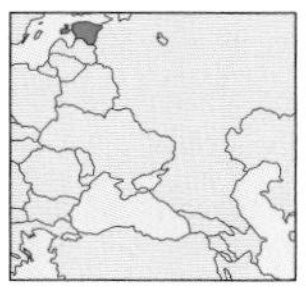

GEOGRAPHY The Republic of Estonia is the smallest of the three states on the Baltic Sea, which were formerly part of the Soviet Union, but which became independent in the early 1990s. Estonia consists of a generally flat plain which was covered by ice sheets during the Ice Age. The land is strewn with moraine (rocks deposited by the ice).

The country is dotted with more than 1,500 small lakes. The large Lake Peipus (Chudskoye Ozero) and the River Narva together make up much of Estonia's eastern border with Russia. Estonia also has more than 800 islands, which together make up about a tenth of the country. The largest island is Saaremaa (Sarema). Despite its northerly position, Estonia has a fairly mild climate because of the moderating effects of the sea.

POLITICS & ECONOMY The ancestors of the Estonians, who are related to the Finns, settled in the area several thousand years ago. German crusaders, known as the Teutonic Knights, introduced Christianity in the early 13th century. By the 16th century, German noblemen owned much of the land in Estonia. In 1561, Sweden took the northern part of the country and Poland the south. From 1625, Sweden controlled the entire country until Sweden handed it over to Russia in 1721.

Estonian nationalists campaigned for their independence from around the mid-19th century. Finally, Estonia was proclaimed independent in 1918. In 1919, the government began to break up the large estates and distribute land among the peasants.

In 1939, Germany and the Soviet Union agreed to take over parts of Eastern Europe. In 1940, Soviet forces occupied Estonia, but they were driven out by the Germans in 1941. Soviet troops returned in 1944 and Estonia became one of the 15 Soviet Socialist Republics of the Soviet Union. The Estonians strongly opposed Soviet rule. Many of them were deported to Siberia.

Political changes in the Soviet Union in the late 1980s led to renewed demands for freedom. In 1990, the Estonian government declared the country independent and, finally, the Soviet Union recognized this act in September 1991, shortly before the Soviet Union was dissolved. Estonia adopted a new constitution in 1992, when multiparty elections were held for a new national assembly. In 1993, Estonia negotiated an agreement with Russia to withdraw its troops.

Under Soviet rule, Estonia was the most prosperous of the three Baltic states. Since 1988, Estonia has worked to restructure its economy. Turning increasingly to the West, it became a member of both the North Atlantic Treaty Organization and the European Union in 2004. Estonia's resources include oil shale and its forests. Industries produce fertilizers, processed food, machinery, petrochemical products, wood products, and textiles. Agriculture and fishing are also important activities.

AREA 17,413 SQ MI [45,100 SQ KM] **POPULATION** 1,333,000
CAPITAL (POPULATION) TALLINN (418,000) **GOVERNMENT** MULTIPARTY REPUBLIC **ETHNIC GROUPS** ESTONIAN 65%, RUSSIAN 28%, UKRAINIAN 3%, BELARUSIAN 2%, FINNISH 1% **LANGUAGES** ESTONIAN (OFFICIAL), RUSSIAN
RELIGIONS LUTHERAN, RUSSIAN AND ESTONIAN ORTHODOX, METHODIST, BAPTIST, ROMAN CATHOLIC **CURRENCY** ESTONIAN KROON = 100 SENTI

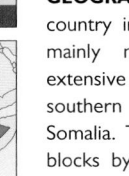

ETHIOPIA

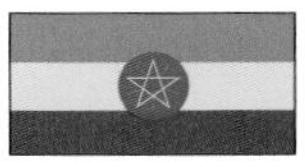
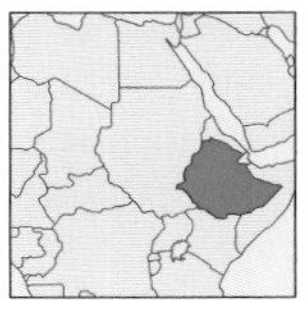

GEOGRAPHY Ethiopia is a landlocked country in northeastern Africa. The land is mainly mountainous, though there are extensive plains in the east, bordering southern Eritrea, and in the south, bordering Somalia. The highlands are divided into two blocks by an arm of the Great Rift Valley which runs throughout eastern Africa. North of the Rift Valley, the land is especially rugged, rising to 15,157 ft [4,620 m] at Ras Dashen. Southeast of Ras Dashen is Lake Tana, source of the River Abay (Blue Nile).

The climate in Ethiopia is greatly affected by the altitude. Addis Ababa, at 8,000 ft [2,450 m], has an average yearly temperature of 68°F [20°C]. The rainfall is generally more than 39 inches [1,000 mm]. But the lowlands bordering the Eritrean coast are hot and arid.

POLITICS & ECONOMY Ethiopia was the home of an ancient monarchy, which became Christian in the 4th century. In the 7th century, Muslims gained control of the lowlands, but Christianity survived in the highlands. Ethiopia resisted attempts to colonize it, but Italy invaded the country in 1935. The Italians were driven out in 1941 during World War II.

In 1952, Eritrea, on the Red Sea coast, was federated with Ethiopia. But in 1961, Eritrean nationalists demanded their freedom and began a struggle that ended in their independence in 1993. In 1995, because of Ethiopia's great ethnic diversity, the country was divided into nine provinces, each with its own regional assembly. In 1998, boundary disputes with Eritrea led to conflict. A peace agreement was reached in 2001, but tensions mounted in 2005–6 when Ethiopia failed to accept an international ruling over the border settlement of Badme.

Ethiopia is one of the world's poorest countries and it is heavily dependent on aid. In 2004, a UN report stated that Ethiopia remained on the brink of disaster, with spiraling population growth, slow economic growth, and environmental degradation. Agriculture remains the main activity.

AREA 426,370 SQ MI [1,104,300 SQ KM] **POPULATION** 73,053,000
CAPITAL (POPULATION) ADDIS ABABA (2,424,000) **GOVERNMENT** FEDERATION OF NINE PROVINCES **ETHNIC GROUPS** OROMO 40%, AMHARA AND TIGRE 32%, SIDAMO 9%, SHANKELLA 6%, SOMALI 6%, OTHERS
LANGUAGES AMHARIC (OFFICIAL), MANY OTHERS **RELIGIONS** ISLAM 47%, ETHIOPIAN ORTHODOX 40%, TRADITIONAL BELIEFS 12%
CURRENCY BIRR = 100 CENTS

FALKLAND ISLANDS

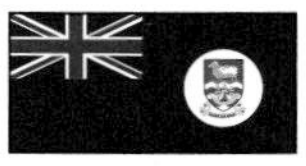
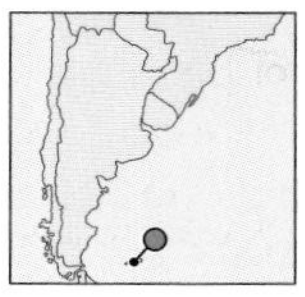

Comprising two main islands and over 200 small islands, the Falkland Islands (or the Islas Malvinas, as they are called in Argentina) lie 300 mi [480 km] from South America. Sheep farming is the main activity, though the search for oil and diamonds holds out hope for the future of this harsh and virtually treeless environment.

AREA 4,700 SQ MI [12,173 SQ KM] **POPULATION** 3,000
CAPITAL (POPULATION) STANLEY (1,600)

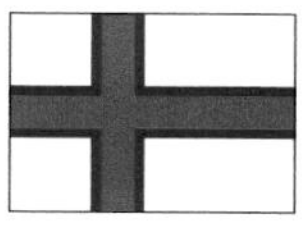

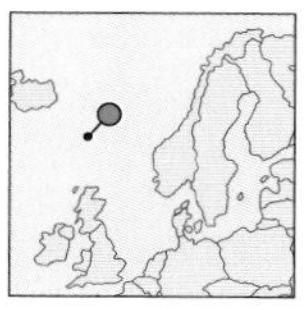

FÆROE ISLANDS

The Færoe Islands are a group of 18 volcanic islands and some reefs in the North Atlantic Ocean. The islands have been Danish since the 1380s, but they became largely self-governing in 1948. In 1998, the government of the Færoes announced its intention to become independent of Denmark.

AREA 540 sq mi [1,399 sq km]
POPULATION 47,000 **CAPITAL** Tórshavn

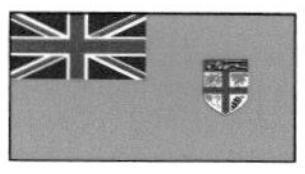

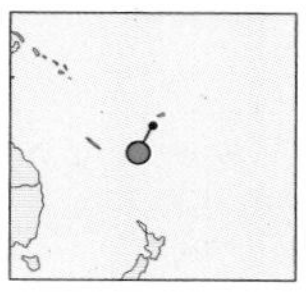

FIJI ISLANDS

The Fiji Islands (the official name of Fiji since 1998) is a republic consisting of more than 800 Melanesian islands, the biggest being Viti Levu and Vanua Levu. The climate is tropical. A former British colony, Fiji became independent in 1970. Its recent history has been marred by efforts by ethnic Fijians to impose their rule, stopping members of the ethnic Indian community from holding senior cabinet posts. This action provoked international criticism.

AREA 7,056 sq mi [18,274 sq km] **POPULATION** 893,000 **CAPITAL** Suva

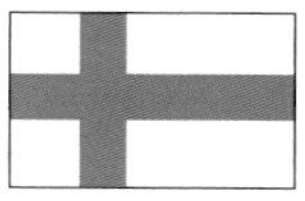

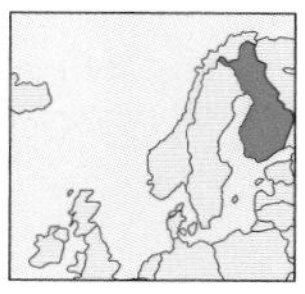

FINLAND

GEOGRAPHY The Republic of Finland is a beautiful country in northern Europe. In the south, behind the coastal lowlands where most Finns live, lies a region of sparkling lakes worn out by ice sheets in the Ice Age. The thinly populated northern uplands cover about two-fifths of the country.

Helsinki, the capital city, has warm summers, but the average temperatures between the months of December and March are below freezing point. Snow covers the land in winter. The north has less precipitation than the south, but it is much colder.

POLITICS & ECONOMY Between 1150 and 1809, Finland was under Swedish rule. The close links between the countries continue today. Swedish remains an official language in Finland and many towns have Swedish as well as Finnish names.

In 1809, Finland became a grand duchy of the Russian empire. It finally declared itself independent in 1917, after the Russian Revolution and the collapse of the Russian empire. But during World War II (1939–45), the Soviet Union declared war on Finland and took part of Finland's territory. Finland allied itself with Germany, but it lost more land to the Soviet Union at the end of the war.

After World War II, Finland became a neutral country and negotiated peace treaties with the Soviet Union. Finland also strengthened its relations with other northern European countries and became an associate member of the European Free Trade Association (EFTA) in 1961. Finland became a full member of EFTA in 1986, but it became a member of the European Union on January 1, 1995. In 2002, Finland adopted the euro as its sole unit of currency. Finland has also discussed joining NATO, but the re-election of the center-left Tarja Halonen in 2006 suggested that NATO membership was unlikely during her six-year term.

Forests are the chief resource and wood, wood products, and paper once dominated the economy. They still make up about a quarter of the exports, but, since World War II, Finland has set up many new industries, producing machinery and transport equipment. The economy has expanded quickly and machinery and apparatus now account for more than a third of the exports.

AREA 130,558 sq mi [338,145 sq km] **POPULATION** 5,223,000
CAPITAL (POPULATION) Helsinki (549,000)
GOVERNMENT Multiparty republic **ETHNIC GROUPS** Finnish 93%, Swedish 6% **LANGUAGES** Finnish and Swedish (both official)
RELIGIONS Evangelical Lutheran 89% **CURRENCY** Euro = 100 cents

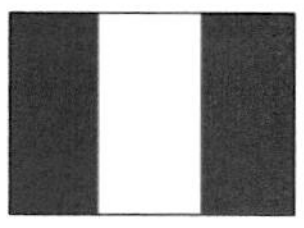

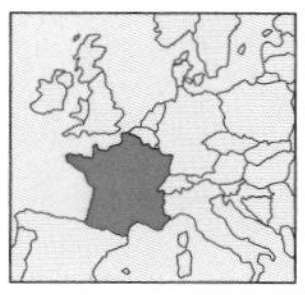

FRANCE

GEOGRAPHY The Republic of France is the largest country in Western Europe. The scenery is extremely varied. The Vosges Mountains overlook the Rhine valley in the northeast, the Jura Mountains and the Alps form the borders with Switzerland and Italy in the southeast, while the Pyrenees straddle France's border with Spain. The only large highland area entirely within France is the Massif Central between the Rhône-Saône valley and the basin of Aquitaine in southern France.

Brittany (Bretagne) and Normandy (Normande) form a scenic hill region. Fertile lowlands cover most of northern France, including the densely populated Paris basin. Another major lowland area, the Aquitanian basin, is in the southwest, while the Rhône-Saône valley and the Mediterranean lowlands are in the southeast.

The climate of France varies from west to east and from north to south. The west comes under the moderating influence of the Atlantic Ocean, giving generally mild weather. To the east, summers are warmer and winters colder. The climate also becomes warmer as one travels from north to south. The Mediterranean Sea coast has hot, dry summers and mild, moist winters. The Alps, Jura, and Pyrenees mountains have snowy winters. Winter sports centers are found in all three areas. Large glaciers occupy high valleys in the Alps.

POLITICS & ECONOMY The Romans conquered France (then called Gaul) in the 50s BC. Roman rule began to decline in the fifth century AD and, in 486, the Frankish realm (as France was called) became independent under a Christian king, Clovis. In 800, Charlemagne, who had been king since 768, became emperor of the Romans. He extended France's boundaries, but, in 843, his empire was divided into three parts and the area of France contracted. After the Norman invasion of England in 1066, large areas of France came under English rule, but this was finally ended in 1453.

France later became a powerful monarchy. But the French Revolution (1789–99) ended absolute rule by French kings. In 1799, Napoleon Bonaparte took power and fought a series of brilliant military campaigns before his final defeat in 1815. The monarchy was restored until 1848, when the Second Republic was founded. In 1852, Napoleon's nephew became Napoleon III, but the Third Republic was established in 1875. France was the scene of much fighting during World War I (1914–18) and World War II (1939–45), causing great loss of life and much damage to the economy.

In 1946, France adopted a new constitution, establishing the Fourth Republic. But political instability and costly colonial wars slowed France's post-war recovery. In 1958, Charles de Gaulle was elected president and he introduced a new constitution, giving the president extra powers and inaugurating the Fifth Republic.

Since the 1960s, France has made rapid economic progress, becoming one of the most prosperous nations in the European Union. But France's government faced a number of problems, including unemployment, pollution and the growing number of elderly people, who find it difficult to live when inflation rates are high. One social problem concerns the presence in France of large numbers of immigrants from Africa and southern Europe, many of whom live in poor areas.

In 2002, the euro became France's sole unit of currency, replacing the franc. In 2005, the people voted against a proposed constitution for the European Union in a national referendum. Raffarin, who had supported the proposal, resigned and was succeeded as prime minister by Dominique de Villepin. Later in 2005, France was rocked by inter-ethnic urban violence.

France is one of the world's most developed countries. Its natural resources include its fertile soil, together with deposits of bauxite, coal, iron ore, oil and natural gas, and potash. France is also one of the world's top manufacturing nations, and it has often innovated in bold and imaginative ways. The TGV and hypermarkets are typical examples. Paris is a world center of fashion industries, but France has many other industrial towns and cities. Major manufactures include aircraft, cars, chemicals, electronic and metal products, machinery, processed food, steel, and textiles.

Agriculture employs about 2% of the people, but France is the largest producer of farm products in Western Europe, producing most of the food it needs. Wheat is the leading crop and livestock farming is of major importance. Fishing and forestry are leading industries, while tourism is a major activity.

AREA 212,934 sq mi [551,500 sq km] **POPULATION** 60,656,000
CAPITAL (POPULATION) Paris (2,152,000) **GOVERNMENT** Multiparty republic **ETHNIC GROUPS** Celtic, Latin, Arab, Teutonic, Slavic
LANGUAGES French (official) **RELIGIONS** Roman Catholic 85%, Islam 8%, others **CURRENCY** Euro = 100 cents

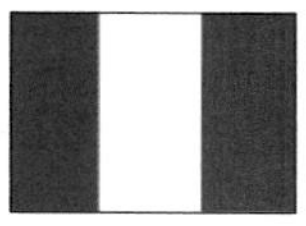

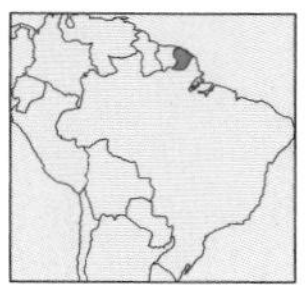

FRENCH GUIANA

GEOGRAPHY French Guiana is the smallest country in mainland South America. The coastal plain is swampy in places, but some dry areas are cultivated. Inland lies a plateau, with the low Tumachumac Mountains in the south. Most of the rivers run north toward the Atlantic Ocean.

French Guiana has a hot, equatorial climate, with high temperatures throughout the year. The rainfall is heavy, especially between December and June, but it is dry between August and October. The northeast trade winds blow constantly across the country.

POLITICS & ECONOMY The first people to live in what is now French Guiana were Amerindians. Today, only a few of them survive in the interior. The first Europeans to explore the coast arrived in 1500, and they were followed by adventurers seeking El Dorado, the mythical city of gold. Cayenne was founded in 1637 by a group of French merchants. The area became a French colony in the late 17th century.

France used the colony as a penal settlement for political prisoners from the times of the French Revolution in the 1790s. From the 1850s to 1945, the country became notorious as a place where prisoners were harshly treated. Many of them died, unable to survive in the tropical conditions.

In 1946, French Guiana became an overseas department of France, and in 1974 it also became an administrative region. An independence movement developed in the 1980s, but most people want to retain their links with France and continue to obtain financial aid to develop their territory.

Although it has rich forest and mineral resources, such as bauxite (aluminum ore), French Guiana is a developing country. It depends greatly on France for money to run its services and the government is the country's biggest employer. Since 1968, Kourou in French Guiana, the European Space Agency's rocket-launching site, has earned money for France by sending communications satellites into space.

AREA 34,749 sq mi [90,000 sq km] **POPULATION** 196,000
CAPITAL (POPULATION) Cayenne (51,000) **GOVERNMENT** Overseas department of France **ETHNIC GROUPS** Black or Mulatto 66%, East Indian/Chinese and Amerindian 12%, White 12%, others 10%
LANGUAGES French (official) **RELIGIONS** Roman Catholic
CURRENCY Euro = 100 cents

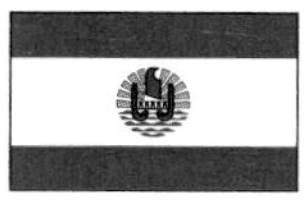

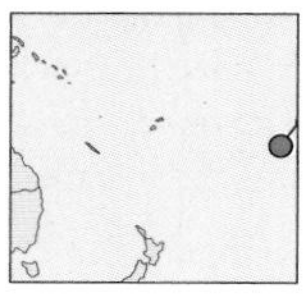

FRENCH POLYNESIA

French Polynesia consists of 130 islands, scattered over 1 million sq mi [2.5 million sq km] of the Pacific Ocean. Tribal chiefs in the area agreed to a French protectorate in 1843. They gained increased autonomy in 1984, but the links with France ensure a high standard of living.

AREA 1,544 sq mi [4,000 sq km]
POPULATION 270,000 **CAPITAL** Papeete

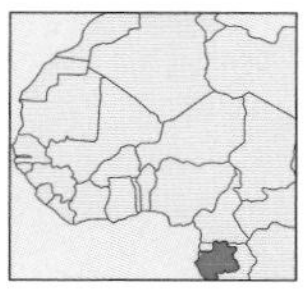

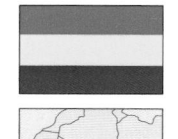

GABON

GEOGRAPHY The Gabonese Republic lies on the Equator in west-central Africa. In area, it is a little larger than the United Kingdom, with a coastline 500 mi [800 km] long. Behind the narrow, partly lagoon-lined coastal plain, the land rises to hills, plateaux and mountains divided by deep valleys carved by the River Ogooué and its tributaries.

Most of Gabon has an equatorial climate, with high temperatures and humidity throughout the year. The rainfall is heavy and the skies are often cloudy.

POLITICS & ECONOMY Gabon became a French colony in the 1880s, but it achieved full independence in 1960. In 1964, an attempted coup was put down when French troops intervened and crushed the revolt. In 1967, Bernard-Albert Bongo, who later renamed himself El Hadj Omar Bongo, became president. He declared Gabon a one-party state in 1968. Opposition parties were legalized in 1991, but Bongo was re-elected president in 1993. In 2003, constitutional changes enabled Bongo to stand again in 2005, when he was re-elected.

Gabon's natural resources include its forests, oil and gas deposits, manganese, and uranium. Its mineral deposits make it one of Africa's better-off countries. But agriculture still employs more than a third of the people and many farmers produce little more than they need to support their families.

AREA 103,347 sq mi [267,668 sq km] **POPULATION** 1,389,000
CAPITAL (POPULATION) Libreville (362,000)
GOVERNMENT Multiparty republic
ETHNIC GROUPS Four major Bantu tribes: Fang, Bapounou, Nzebi and Obamba **LANGUAGES** French (official), Fang, Myene, Nzebi, Bapounou/Eschira, Bandjabi
RELIGIONS Christianity 75%, animist, Islam
CURRENCY CFA franc = 100 centimes

GAMBIA, THE

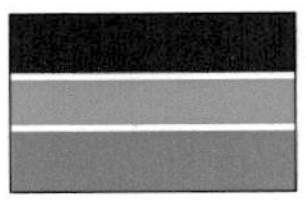

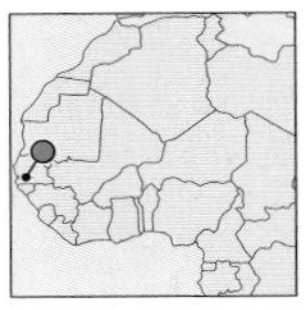

GEOGRAPHY The Republic of The Gambia is the smallest country in mainland Africa. It consists of a narrow strip of land bordering the River Gambia. The Gambia is almost entirely enclosed by Senegal, except along the short Atlantic coastline.

The Gambia has hot and humid summers, but the winter temperatures (November to May) drop to around 61°F [16°C]. In the summer, moist southwesterlies bring rain, which is heaviest on the coast.

POLITICS & ECONOMY English traders bought rights to trade on the River Gambia in 1588, and in 1664 the English established a settlement on an island in the river estuary. In 1765, the British founded Senegambia, which included parts of The Gambia and Senegal. In 1783, Britain handed this colony over to France. In the 19th century, Britain and France discussed the exchange of The Gambia for some other French territory, but an agreement was reached and Britain made The Gambia a British colony in 1888.

The Gambia achieved independence in 1965 and it became a republic in 1970. Relations between the English-speaking Gambians and the French-speaking Senegalese are a major political issue. In 1981, an attempted coup in The Gambia was put down with the help of Senegalese troops. In 1982, The Gambia and Senegal set up a defense alliance, called the Confederation of Senegambia. But this alliance was dissolved in 1989. In 1994, a military group overthrew the president, Sir Dawda Jawara, who fled into exile. Captain Yahya Jammeh, who took power, was elected president in 1996 and re-elected in 2001.

Agriculture is the chief activity. Food crops include cassava, millet, and sorghum, but groundnuts and groundnut products are the main exports. Tourism is growing and, in 2004, the government announced the discovery of offshore oilfields.

AREA 4,361 sq mi [11,295 sq km] **POPULATION** 1,593,000
CAPITAL (POPULATION) Banjul (42,000)
GOVERNMENT Military regime
ETHNIC GROUPS Mandinka 42%, Fula 18%, Wolof 16%, Jola 10%, Serahuli 9%, others
LANGUAGES English (official), Mandinka, Wolof, Fula
RELIGIONS Islam 90%, Christianity 9%, traditional beliefs 1%
CURRENCY Dalasi = 100 butut

GEORGIA

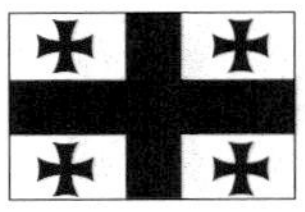

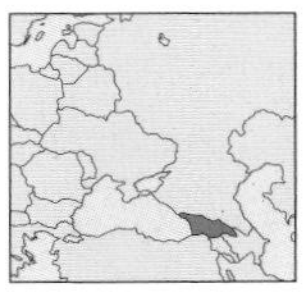

GEOGRAPHY Georgia is a country on the borders of Europe and Asia, facing the Black Sea. The land is rugged with the Caucasus Mountains forming its northern border. The highest mountain in this range, Mount Elbrus (18,510 ft [5,642 m]), lies over the border in Russia.

The Black Sea plains have hot summers and mild winters. The rainfall is heavy, though inland areas are drier.

POLITICS & ECONOMY The first Georgian state was set up nearly 2,500 years ago. But for much of its history, the area was ruled by various conquerors. Christianity was introduced in AD 330. Georgia freed itself of foreign rule in the 11th and 12th centuries, but Mongol armies attacked in the 13th century. From the 16th to the 18th centuries, Iran and the Turkish Ottoman empire struggled for control of the area, and in the late 18th century Georgia sought the protection of Russia and, by the early 19th century, Georgia was part of the Russian empire. After the Russian Revolution of 1917, Georgia declared its independence, but Russia invaded, making the country part of the Soviet regime. Georgia declared itself independent in 1991. It became a separate country when the Soviet Union was dissolved in December 1991.

Georgia contains three regions containing minority peoples: Abkhazia in the northwest, South Ossetia in north-central Georgia, and Adjaria (also spelled Adzharia) in the southwest. Civil war broke out in South Ossetia in the early 1990s, while fierce fighting continued in Abkhazia until the late 1990s. In 2000, Georgia agreed to recognize Adjaria's autonomy in the country's constitution. In 2002, Russian and Georgian troops attacked Chechen rebels in Pankisi Gorge in northeastern Georgia. In 2003, the pro-Western Mikhail Saakashvili was elected president following the "Rose Revolution," which had forced President Eduard Shevardnadze from power. But Georgia still faced disruption caused by the activities of the various secessionist groups.

Georgia is a developing country. Agriculture, food processing, and perfume-making are important activities. Products include barley, citrus fruits, grapes for wine-making, maize, tea, tobacco, and vegetables. Sheep and cattle are reared.

AREA 26,911 sq mi [69,700 sq km] **POPULATION** 4,677,000
CAPITAL (POPULATION) Tbilisi (1,268,000)
GOVERNMENT Multiparty republic **ETHNIC GROUPS** Georgian 70%, Armenian 8%, Russian 6%, Azeri 6%, Ossetian 3%, Greek 2%, Abkhaz 2%, others 3% **LANGUAGES** Georgian (official), Russian
RELIGIONS Georgian Orthodox 65%, Islam 11%, Russian Orthodox 10%, Armenian Apostolic 8%
CURRENCY Lari = 100 tetri

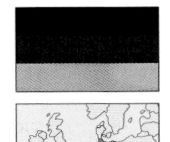

GERMANY

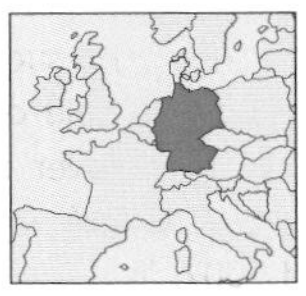

GEOGRAPHY The Federal Republic of Germany is the fourth largest country in Western Europe, after France, Spain and Sweden. The North German plain borders the North Sea in the northwest and the Baltic Sea in the northeast. Major rivers draining the plain include the Weser, Elbe, and Oder.

The central highlands include the Harz Mountains, the Thuringian Forest (Thüringer Wald), the Ore Mountains (Erzgebirge), and the Bohemian Forest (Böhmerwald) on the Czech border. The Bavarian Alps in the south contain Germany's highest peak, Zugspitze, at 9,718 ft [2,962 m] above sea level. The Black Forest (Schwarzwald) in the southwest overlooks the River Rhine. Northwestern Germany has a mild climate, but the Baltic coasts are cooler. To the south, the climate becomes more continental, especially in the highlands. The precipitation is greatest on the uplands, with snow in winter.

POLITICS & ECONOMY Germany and its allies were defeated in World War I (1914–18) and the country became a republic. Adolf Hitler came to power in 1933 and ruled as a dictator. His order to invade Poland led to the start of World War II (1939–45), which ended with Germany in ruins.

In 1945, Germany was divided into four military zones. In 1949, the American, British and French zones were amalgamated to form the Federal Republic of Germany (West Germany), while the Soviet zone became the German Democratic Republic (East Germany), a Communist state. Berlin, which had also been partitioned, became a divided city. West Berlin was part of West Germany, while East Berlin became the capital of East Germany. Bonn was the capital of West Germany.

Tension between East and West mounted during the Cold War, but West Germany rebuilt its economy quickly. In East Germany, the recovery was less rapid. In the late 1980s, reforms in the Soviet Union led to unrest in East Germany. Free elections were held in East Germany in 1990 and, on October 3, 1990, Germany was reunited.

The united Germany adopted West Germany's official name, the Federal Republic of Germany. In the 1990s, the government faced many problems, especially those arising from reunification. In 1999, the parliament moved from Bonn to a reconstructed Reichstag building in Berlin. In 2005, Angela Merkel became Germany's first female Chancellor, when she led the Christian Democratic Union to a narrow victory over the Social Democrats.

West Germany's "economic miracle" after World War II was greatly helped by foreign aid. Today, Germany is one of the world's top economic powers. Manufacturing is the mainstay of the economy and manufactured goods are the chief exports. Cars and other vehicles, cement, chemicals, computers, electrical equipment, processed food, machinery, scientific instruments, ships, steel, textiles, and tools are manufactured. Germany has some coal, potash, and rock salt deposits, but it imports many industrial raw materials. Germany also imports food. Leading products include fruits, grapes for wine-making, potatoes, sugar beet, and vegetables. Livestock include beef and dairy cattle.

AREA 137,846 sq mi [357,022 sq km] **POPULATION** 82,431,000
CAPITAL (POPULATION) Berlin (3,387,000)
GOVERNMENT Federal multiparty republic **ETHNIC GROUPS** German 92%, Turkish 3%, Serbo-Croatian, Italian, Greek, Polish, Spanish
LANGUAGES German (official) **RELIGIONS** Protestant (mainly Lutheran) 34%, Roman Catholic 34%, Islam 4%, others
CURRENCY Euro = 100 cents

GHANA

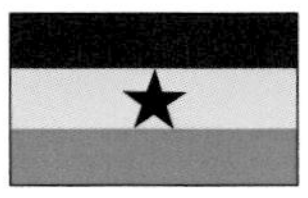

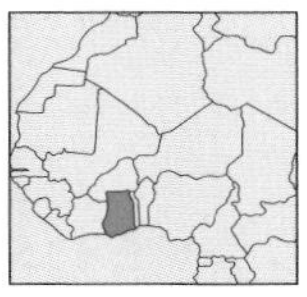

GEOGRAPHY The Republic of Ghana faces the Gulf of Guinea in West Africa. This hot country, just north of the Equator, was formerly called the Gold Coast. Behind the thickly populated southern coastal plains, which are lined with lagoons, lies a plateau region in the southwest.

Accra has a hot, tropical climate. Rain occurs all through the year, though Accra is drier than areas inland.

POLITICS & ECONOMY Portuguese explorers reached the area in 1471 and named it the Gold Coast. The area became a center of the slave trade in the 17th century. The slave trade was ended in the 1860s and, gradually, the British took control of the area. After independence in 1957, attempts were made to develop the economy by creating large state-owned manufacturing industries. But debt and corruption, together with falls in the price of cocoa, the chief export, caused economic problems. This led to instability and frequent coups. In 1981, power was invested in a Provisional National Defense Council, led by Flight-Lieutenant Jerry Rawlings.

The government steadied the economy and introduced several new policies, including the relaxation of government controls. In 1992, the government introduced a new constitution, which allowed for multiparty elections. Rawlings was elected president in 1992 and 1996, but he retired in 2002. He was succeeded as president by John Ageykum Kufuor. The World Bank classifies Ghana as a "low-income" developing country. Most people are poor and farming employs 55% of the population.

AREA 92,098 sq mi [238,533 sq km] **POPULATION** 21,030,000
CAPITAL (POPULATION) Accra (949,000) **GOVERNMENT** Republic
ETHNIC GROUPS Akan 44%, Moshi-Dagomba 16%, Ewe 13%, Ga 8%, Gurma 3%, Yoruba 1% **LANGUAGES** English (official), Akan, Moshi-Dagomba, Ewe, Ga **RELIGIONS** Christianity 63%, traditional beliefs 21%, Islam 16% **CURRENCY** Cedi = 100 pesewas

GIBRALTAR

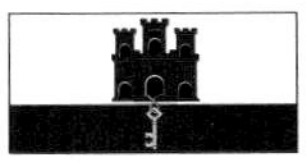

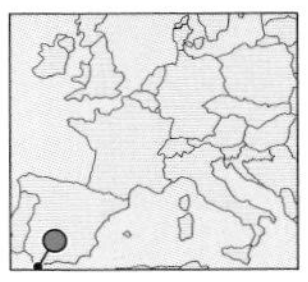

Gibraltar occupies a strategic position on the south coast of Spain where the Mediterranean meets the Atlantic. It was recognized as a British possession in 1713 and, despite Spanish claims, its population has consistently voted to retain its contacts with Britain.

AREA 2.3 sq mi [6 sq km]
POPULATION 28,000 **CAPITAL** Gibraltar Town

GREECE

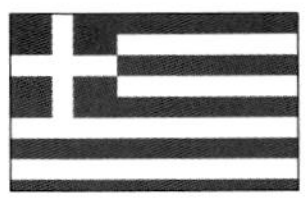

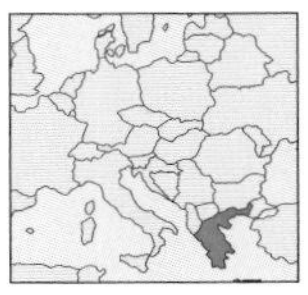

GEOGRAPHY The Hellenic Republic, as Greece is officially called, is a rugged country situated at the southern end of the Balkan peninsula. Olympus, at 9,570 ft [2,917 m] is the highest peak. Islands make up about a fifth of the land.

Low-lying areas in Greece have mild, moist winters and hot, dry summers. The east coast has more than 2,700 hours of sunshine a year and only about half of the rainfall of the west. The mountains have a much more severe climate, with snow on the higher slopes in winter.

POLITICS & ECONOMY Around 2,500 years ago, Greece became the birthplace of Western civilization and Ancient Greek ruins and art still attract millions of tourists to the country. The first civilization, the Minoan, was centered on Crete. It flourished between about 3000 and 1400 BC. Following the end of the related Mycenaean period on the mainland (1580–1100 BC), a "dark age" lasted until about 800 BC. But from 750 BC, Greeks became rich traders and the city-state of Athens reached its peak in 461–431 BC. Greece became a Roman province in 146 BC and, in AD 365, it became part of the Byzantine Empire.

The Byzantine empire fell to the Turks in 1453. But Greece became an independent monarchy in 1830. After World War II (1939–45), when Germany ruled Greece, a civil war broke out between Greek Communists and nationalists. It ended in 1949 and a military dictatorship seized power in 1967. The monarchy was abolished in 1973 and democracy was restored in 1974. Greece joined the European Community (now the European Union) in 1981 and, on January 1, 2002, the euro became the sole unit of currency in Greece.

Greece is one of the EU's less economically developed members. Manufactured products include processed food, cement, chemicals, metal products, textiles, and tobacco. Greece also mines lignite (brown coal), bauxite, and chromite. Farmland covers about a third of the country and grazing land another 40%. Crops include barley, grapes for wine-making, dried fruits, olives, potatoes, sugar beet, and wheat. Livestock farming is also important. Greece's beaches and ancient ruins make the country a major tourist destination.

AREA 50,949 sq mi [131,957 sq km] **POPULATION** 10,668,000
CAPITAL (POPULATION) Athens (772,000)
GOVERNMENT Multiparty republic **ETHNIC GROUPS** Greek 98%
LANGUAGES Greek (official) **RELIGIONS** Greek Orthodox 98%
CURRENCY Euro = 100 cents

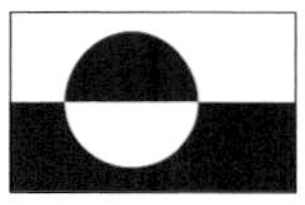

GREENLAND

Greenland is the world's largest island. Settlements are confined to the coast, because an ice sheet covers four-fifths of the land. Greenland became a Danish possession in 1380. Full internal self-government was granted in 1981 and, in 1997, Danish place names were superseded by Inuit forms. However, Greenland remains heavily dependent on Danish subsidies.

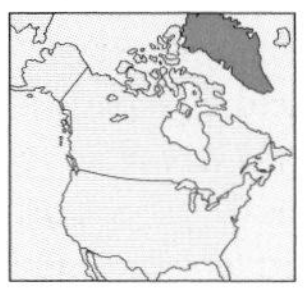

AREA 838,999 sq mi [2,175,600 sq km] **POPULATION** 56,000
CAPITAL (POPULATION) Nuuk (Godthåb) (14,000)

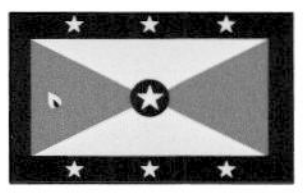

GRENADA

The most southerly of the Windward Islands in the Caribbean Sea, Grenada became independent from the UK in 1974. A military group seized power in 1983, when the prime minister was killed. US troops intervened and restored order and constitutional government.

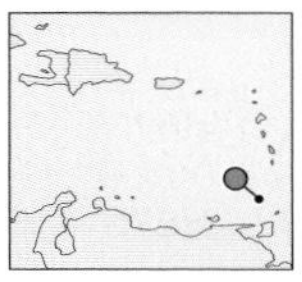

AREA 133 sq mi [344 sq km]
POPULATION 90,000 **CAPITAL** St George's

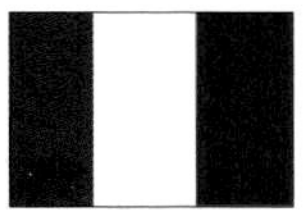

GUADELOUPE

Guadeloupe is a French overseas department which includes seven Caribbean islands, the largest of which is Basse-Terre. French aid has helped to mantain a reasonable standard of living for the people.

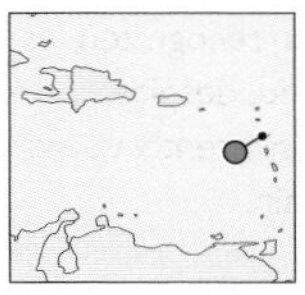

AREA 658 sq mi [1,705 sq km]
POPULATION 449,000 **CAPITAL** Basse-Terre

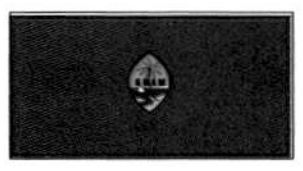

GUAM

Guam, a strategically important "unincorporated territory" of the USA, is the largest of the Mariana Islands in the Pacific Ocean. It is composed of a coralline limestone plateau.

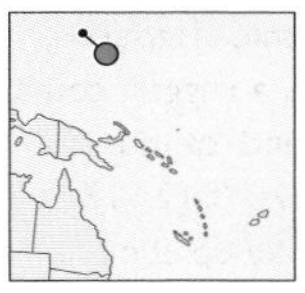

AREA 212 sq mi [549 sq km]
POPULATION 169,000 **CAPITAL** Agana

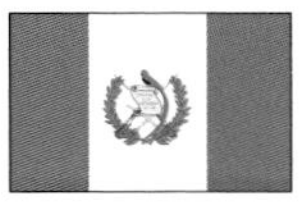

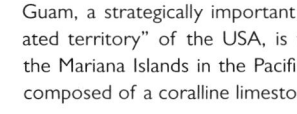

GUATEMALA

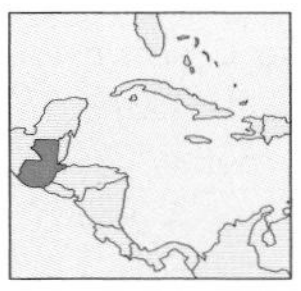

GEOGRAPHY The Republic of Guatemala in Central America contains a thickly populated mountain region, with fertile soils. The mountains, which run in an east–west direction, contain many volcanoes, some of which are active. Volcanic eruptions and earthquakes are common in the highlands. South of the mountains lie the thinly populated Pacific coastlands, while a large inland plain occupies the north.

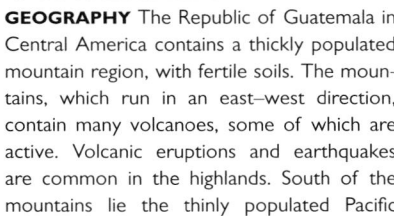

The lowlands of Guatemala are hot and rainy, but the central highlands are cooler and drier. Guatemala City has a pleasant. warm climate with a dry season between November and April.

POLITICS & ECONOMY Much of what is now Guatemala was part of the Maya empire which thrived between AD 300 and 900. Spain ruled the area from the 1520s until 1821. In 1823, Guatemala joined the Central American Federation. But it became fully independent in 1839. Instability and periodic violence have marred its progress. Guatemala has a long-standing claim over Belize, but this was reduced in 1983 to the southern fifth of the country. Between 1960 and 1996, civil war occurred between left-wing groups, including many Amerindians, and government forces. The war claimed perhaps 200,000 lives. In 2004, the government paid US$3.5 million to victims of state-sponsored oppression. In 2004 and 2005, hurricanes caused great damage.

Guatemala is ranked as a "lower-middle-income" economy. Agriculture employs 38% of the population. Coffee, sugar, bananas, and beef are exported, and the spice cardamom and cotton are also important. Maize is the main food crop.

AREA 42,042 sq mi [108,889 sq km] **POPULATION** 14,655,000
CAPITAL (POPULATION) Guatemala City (1,007,000)
GOVERNMENT Republic **ETHNIC GROUPS** Ladino (mixed Hispanic and Amerindian) 55%, Amerindian 43%, others 2%
LANGUAGES Spanish (official), Amerindian languages
RELIGIONS Christianity, indigenous Mayan beliefs
CURRENCY US dollar; Quetzal = 100 centavos

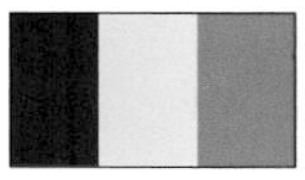

GUINEA

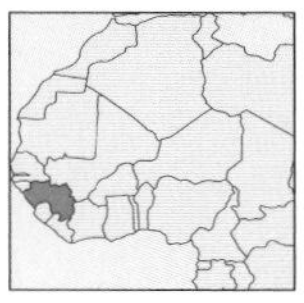

GEOGRAPHY The Republic of Guinea faces the Atlantic Ocean in West Africa. A flat, swampy plain borders the coast. Behind this plain, the land rises to a plateau region called Fouta Djalon. The Upper Niger plains, named after one of Africa's longest rivers, the Niger, which rises there, are in the northeast.

Guinea has a tropical climate and Conakry, on the coast, has heavy rains between May and November. This is also the coolest period in the year. During the dry season, hot, dry harmattan winds blow southwestward from the Sahara Desert.

POLITICS & ECONOMY Guinea came under the influence of several medieval African states, including Ancient Ghana and Ancient Mali. France began to control the area in the late 19th century. Guinea became independent in 1958. Its leaders pursued socialist policies but resorted to repressive measures to hold on to power. A military regime under Lansana Conté took over in 1984, but a multiparty system was restored in 1992. Conté was elected president in 1993 and again in 1998 and 2002. In the late 1990s, Guinea was drawn into civil conflicts in Liberia and Sierra Leone. In 2005, Conté survived an assassination attempt.

Guinea is a "low-income" developing country. Its resources include bauxite (aluminum ore), diamonds, gold, iron ore, and uranium. Bauxite and alumina (processed bauxite) account for more than half of the exports. Agriculture employs more than 70% of the people, but most farmers are poor. Manufactures include alumina, processed food, and textiles.

AREA 94,925 sq mi [245,857 sq km] **POPULATION** 9,468,000
CAPITAL (POPULATION) Conakry (1,232,000)
GOVERNMENT Multiparty republic
ETHNIC GROUPS Peuhl 40%, Malinke 30%, Soussou 20%, others 10% **LANGUAGES** French (official)
RELIGIONS Islam 85%, Christianity 8%, traditional beliefs 7%
CURRENCY Guinean franc = 100 cauris

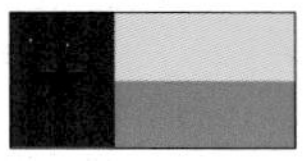

GUINEA-BISSAU

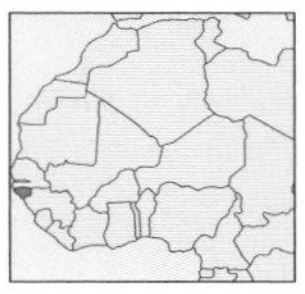

GEOGRAPHY The Republic of Guinea-Bissau, formerly known as Portuguese Guinea, is a small country in West Africa. The land is mostly low-lying, with a broad, swampy coastal plain and many flat offshore islands, including the Bijagós Archipelago.

The country has a tropical climate, with one dry season (December to May) and a rainy season from June to November.

POLITICS & ECONOMY Portuguese explorers reached Guinea-Bissau in 1446 and the area became a center of the slave trade. From 1836, Portugal administered Guinea-Bissau with the Cape Verde Islands but, in 1879, the territories were separated. Guinea-Bissau became a separate colony called Portuguese Guinea. But economic development in the colony was slow.

In 1956, African nationalists in Portuguese Guinea and Cape Verde founded the African Party for the Independence of Guinea and Cape Verde (PAIGC). Because Portugal seemed determined to hang on to its overseas territories, the PAIGC began a guerrilla war in 1963. By 1968, it held two-thirds of the country. In 1972, a rebel National Assembly, elected by the people in the PAIGC-controlled area, voted to make the country independent as Guinea-Bissau.

In 1974, newly independent Guinea-Bissau faced many problems arising from its underdeveloped economy and its lack of trained people to work in the administration. One objective of the leaders of Guinea-Bissau was to unite their country with Cape Verde. But, in 1980, army leaders overthrew Guinea-Bissau's government. The Revolutionary Council, which took over, opposed unification with Cape Verde. Guinea-Bissau ceased to be a one-party state in 1991 and multiparty elections were held in 1994. Civil war broke out in 1998 and a military coup occurred in 1999. Elections were held in 2000. Another coup occurred in 2003, but civilian government was restored in 2004. In 2005, a former military leader, Joao Bernardo Viera, was elected president.

Agriculture, mainly at subsistence level, employs 76% of the people. Crops include coconuts, groundnuts, maize, and rice.

AREA 13,948 sq mi [36,125 sq km] **POPULATION** 1,416,000
CAPITAL (POPULATION) Bissau (200,000)
GOVERNMENT "Interim" government
ETHNIC GROUPS Balanta 30%, Fula 20%, Manjaca 14%, Mandinga 13%, Papel 7% **LANGUAGES** Portuguese (official), Crioulo
RELIGIONS Traditional beliefs 50%, Islam 45%, Christianity 5%
CURRENCY CFA franc = 100 centimes

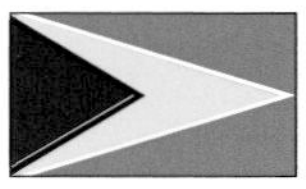

GUYANA

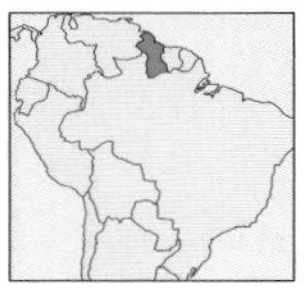

GEOGRAPHY The Cooperative Republic of Guyana is a country facing the Atlantic Ocean in northeastern South America. The coastal plain is flat and much of it is below sea level.

The climate is hot and humid, though the interior highlands are cooler than the coast. The rainfall is heavy, occurring on more than 200 days a year.

POLITICS & ECONOMY Britain gained control of the area in 1814 and ruled British Guiana until it became independent as Guyana in 1966. A black lawyer, Forbes Burnham, was the first prime minister. Under a new constitution adopted in 1980, the president's powers were increased. Burnham became president and served in this post until he died in 1985. He was succeeded by Hugh Desmond Hoyte, who was defeated in 1993 by an ethnic Indian, Cheddi Jagan. Jagan died in 1997 and was succeeded by his wife, Janet. In 1999, Bharrat Jagdeo was elected president. He was re-elected in 2001.

Guyana is a poor country. Its resources include gold, bauxite (aluminum ore) and other minerals, forests, and fertile soils. Sugarcane and rice are leading crops. Guyana has potential for producing hydroelectricity from its many rivers.

AREA 83,000 sq mi [214,969 sq km] **POPULATION** 765,000
CAPITAL (POPULATION) Georgetown (150,000)
GOVERNMENT Multiparty republic
ETHNIC GROUPS East Indian 50%, Black 36%, Amerindian 7%, others **LANGUAGES** English (official), Creole, Hindi, Urdu
RELIGIONS Christianity 50%, Hinduism 35%, Islam 10%, others
CURRENCY Guyanese dollar = 100 cents

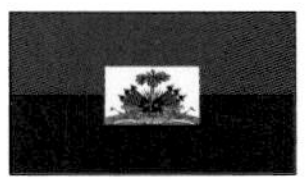

HAITI

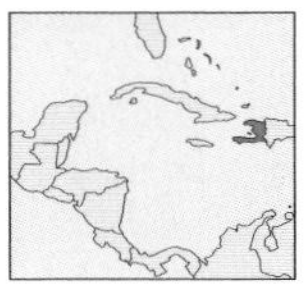

GEOGRAPHY The Republic of Haiti occupies the western third of Hispaniola in the Caribbean. The land is mainly mountainous. The climate is hot and humid, though the northern highlands, with about 79 inches [200 mm], have more than twice as much rainfall as the southern coast.

POLITICS & ECONOMY Visited by Christopher Columbus in 1492, Haiti was later developed by the French. The African slaves revolted in 1791 and the country became independent in 1804. Haiti subsequently suffered from instability, violence, and dictatorial rule. Elections in 1990 returned Jean-Bertrand Aristide as president, but he was overthrown in 1991. In 1995, René Préval was elected president, but Aristide was again elected president in 2000. In 2004, rebel activity forced Aristide to flee the country. A US-backed government was set up to restore order and, in 2006, René Préval was re-elected president in national elections. Haiti suffered much hurricane damage in 2004 and 2005.

AREA 10,714 sq mi [27,750 sq km] **POPULATION** 8,122,000
CAPITAL (POPULATION) Port-au-Prince (917,000)
GOVERNMENT Multiparty republic **ETHNIC GROUPS** Black 95%, Mulatto/White 5% **LANGUAGES** French and Creole (both official)
RELIGIONS Roman Catholic 80%, Voodoo
CURRENCY Gourde = 100 centimes

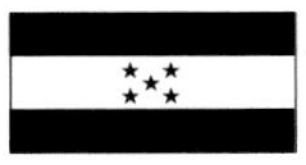

HONDURAS

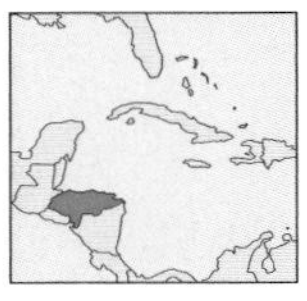

GEOGRAPHY The Republic of Honduras is the second largest country in Central America. The northern coast on the Caribbean Sea extends more than 373 mi [600 km], but the Pacific coast in the southeast is only about 50 mi [80 km] long. Honduras has a tropical climate, but the highlands are cooler. The rainiest months are between May and November. Hurricanes often hit the north coast. Hurricane Mitch in 1998 caused the worst destruction in modern times.

POLITICS & ECONOMY Western Honduras was part of the Maya empire which flourished between AD 300 and 900. Christopher Columbus claimed the area for Spain in 1502 and Spain ruled from 1625 until 1821. Honduras became part of the Central American Federation but withdrew in 1838.

In the 1890s, American companies developed plantations to grow bananas. They soon became the country's chief source of income and Honduras became known as a "banana republic." But instability slowed economic progress. In 1969, Honduras fought a short "Soccer War" with El Salvador. The war was sparked off by the treatment of fans in a World Cup soccer series, though the real reason was that Salvadoreans in Honduras had been forced to give

up land. Since 1980, civilian governments have ruled Honduras, but the military remain influential.

Honduras is a developing country. Its few resources include silver, lead, and zinc. Agriculture is the main activity. Bananas and coffee are exported and maize is the chief food crop. Honduras is one of Central America's least industrialized countries. Products include processed food, textiles, and wood products.

AREA 43,277 SQ MI [112,088 SQ KM] **POPULATION** 6,975,000
CAPITAL (POPULATION) TEGUCIGALPA (850,000)
GOVERNMENT REPUBLIC **ETHNIC GROUPS** MESTIZO 90%, AMERINDIAN 7%, BLACK (INCLUDING BLACK CARIB) 2%, WHITE 1% **LANGUAGES** SPANISH (OFFICIAL), AMERINDIAN DIALECTS **RELIGIONS** ROMAN CATHOLIC 97%
CURRENCY HONDURAN LEMPIRA = 100 CENTAVOS

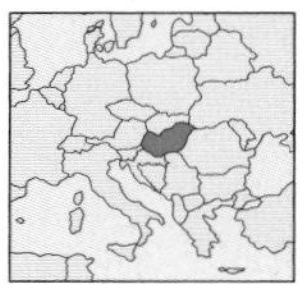

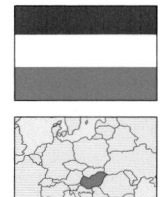

HUNGARY

GEOGRAPHY The Hungarian Republic is a landlocked country in central Europe. The land is mostly low-lying and drained by the Danube (Duna) and its tributary, the Tisza. Most of the land east of the Danube belongs to a region called the Great Plain (Nagyalföld), which covers about half of Hungary.

Hungary lies far from the moderating influence of the sea. As a result, summers are warmer and sunnier, and the winters colder than in Western Europe.

POLITICS & ECONOMY Hungary entered World War II (1939–45) in 1941, as an ally of Germany, but the Germans occupied the country in 1944. The Soviet Union invaded Hungary in 1944 and, in 1946, the country became a republic. The Communists gradually took over the government, taking complete control in 1949. From 1949, Hungary was an ally of the Soviet Union. In 1956, Soviet troops crushed an anti-Communist revolt. But in the 1980s, reforms in the Soviet Union led to the growth of anti-Communist groups in Hungary. In 1989, Hungary adopted a new constitution making it a multiparty state. Elections held in 1990 led to a victory for the non-Communist Democratic Forum. In 2002, the Hungarian Socialist Party, in alliance with the liberal Free Democrats, won a majority in parliament. In 2004, Hungary became a member of both the North Atlantic Treaty Organization and the European Union.

Before World War II, Hungary's economy was based mainly on agriculture. But the Communists set up many manufacturing industries. The new factories were owned by the government, as also was most of the land. However, from the late 1980s, the government has worked to increase private ownership. This change of policy caused many problems, including inflation and high rates of unemployment. Manufacturing is the chief activity. Major products include aluminum, chemicals, and electrical and electronic goods.

AREA 35,920 SQ MI [93,032 SQ KM] **POPULATION** 10,007,000
CAPITAL (POPULATION) BUDAPEST (1,819,000)
GOVERNMENT MULTIPARTY REPUBLIC
ETHNIC GROUPS MAGYAR 90%, GYPSY, GERMAN, SERB, ROMANIAN, SLOVAK **LANGUAGES** HUNGARIAN (OFFICIAL)
RELIGIONS ROMAN CATHOLIC 68%, CALVINIST 20%, LUTHERAN 5%, OTHERS **CURRENCY** FORINT = 100 FILLÉR

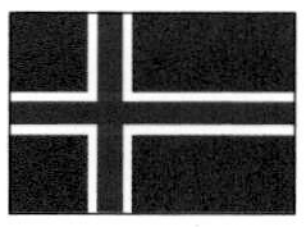
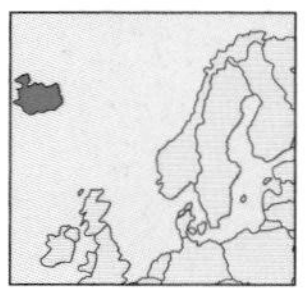

ICELAND

GEOGRAPHY The Republic of Iceland, in the North Atlantic Ocean, is closer to Greenland than Scotland. Iceland sits astride the Mid-Atlantic Ridge. It is slowly getting wider as the ocean is being stretched apart by continental drift.

Iceland has around 200 volcanoes, and eruptions are frequent. An eruption under the Vatnajökull ice cap in 1996 created a subglacial lake which subsequently burst, causing severe flooding. Geysers and hot springs are other common volcanic features. Ice caps and glaciers cover about an eighth of the land. The only habitable regions are the coastal lowlands.

Although it lies far to the north, Iceland's climate is moderated by the warm waters of the Gulf Stream. The port of Reykjavik is ice-free all the year round.

POLITICS & ECONOMY Norwegian Vikings colonized Iceland in AD 874, and in 930 the settlers founded the world's oldest parliament, the Althing.

Iceland united with Norway in 1262. But when Norway united with Denmark in 1380, Iceland came under Danish rule. Iceland became a self-governing kingdom, united with Denmark, in 1918. It became a fully independent republic in 1944, following a referendum in which 97% of the people voted to break their country's ties with Denmark. Iceland has played a leading part in European affairs and is a member of the North Atlantic Treaty Organization. But it has been involved in fishing disputes. In 1992, it left the International Whaling Commission because of its alleged anti-whaling policy. It rejoined in 2002, but, in 2003, it undertook its first whale hunt for 15 years, stating that its aim was to study the impact of whales on fish stocks.

Iceland has few resources besides its fishing grounds. Fishing and fish processing dominate Iceland's overseas trade, but it is one of Europe's richest countries. Barely 1% of the land is used to grow crops, but 23% of the country can be used for grazing sheep and cattle. Vegetables and fruit are grown in greenhouses, heated by water from hot springs.

AREA 39,768 SQ MI [103,000 SQ KM] **POPULATION** 297,000
CAPITAL (POPULATION) REYKJAVIK (108,000)
GOVERNMENT MULTIPARTY REPUBLIC
ETHNIC GROUPS ICELANDIC 97%, DANISH 1%
LANGUAGES ICELANDIC (OFFICIAL) **RELIGIONS** EVANGELICAL LUTHERAN 87%, OTHER PROTESTANT 4%, ROMAN CATHOLIC 2%, OTHERS
CURRENCY ICELANDIC KRÓNA = 100 AURAR

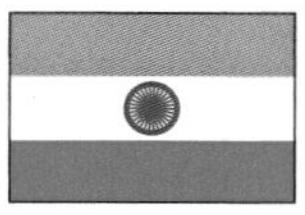
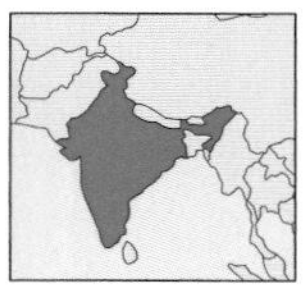

INDIA

GEOGRAPHY The Republic of India is the world's seventh largest country. In population, it ranks second only to China. The north is mountainous, with mountains and foothills of the Himalayan range. Rivers, such as the Brahmaputra and Ganges (Ganga), rise in the Himalaya and flow across the fertile northern plains. Southern India consists of a large plateau, called the Deccan. The Deccan is bordered by two mountain ranges, the Western Ghats and the Eastern Ghats.

India has three main seasons. The cool season runs from October to February. The hot season runs from March to June. The rainy monsoon season starts in the middle of June and continues into September. Delhi has a moderate rainfall, with about 25 inches [640 mm] a year. The southwestern coast and the northeast have far more rain. Darjeeling in the northeast has an average annual rainfall of 120 inches [3,040 mm]. But parts of the Thar Desert in the northwest have only 2 inches [50 mm] of rain per year.

POLITICS & ECONOMY In southern India, most of the people are descendants of the dark-skinned Dravidians, who were among India's earliest people. Most northerners are descendants of lighter-skinned Aryans who arrived around 3,500 years ago.

India was the birthplace of several major religions, including Hinduism, Buddhism and Sikhism. Islam was introduced from about AD 1000. The Muslim Mughal empire was founded in 1526. From the 17th century, Britain began to gain influence. From 1858 to 1947, India was ruled as part of the British empire. An independence movement began after the Sepoy Rebellion (1857–9) and, in 1885, the Indian National Congress was formed. In 1920, Mohandas K. Gandhi became its leader and it soon became a mass movement. When independence was finally achieved in 1947, British India was divided into modern India and Muslim Pakistan. Partition was marred by mass slaughter as Hindus and Sikhs fled from Pakistan, and Indian Muslims poured into Pakistan. In the ensuing disputes, some 1 million people were killed.

Although India has 15 major languages and hundreds of minor ones, together with many religions, the country remains the world's largest democracy. It has faced many problems, especially with Pakistan, over the disputed territory of Jammu and Kashmir. Two wars in 1965 and 1972 failed to alter greatly the 1948 ceasefire lines. In the late 1980s, Kashmiri nationalists in the Indian-controlled area waged a campaign, demanding either integration into Pakistan or independence. India sent in troops and accused Pakistan of intervention. In the 1990s, Pakistani-backed guerrillas fought to break India's hold on the Srinigar valley, Kashmir's most populous region. The tense situation was further aggravated by the testing of nuclear devices by both India and Pakistan in 1998. In 2003–5, India and Pakistan launched a series of peace moves, raising hopes of an agreement, despite continuing intermittent conflict on the ground.

The World Bank classifies India as a "low-income" developing country. To boost the economy, the right-wing coalition government, led by the Hindu Bharatiya Janata Party, introduced free-enterprise policies. However, in 2004, the left-wing United Progressive Alliance was victorious at elections. Manmohan Singh became prime minister.

Agriculture employs 64% of the people. Crops include rice, wheat, millet, sorghum, peas, and beans. India has more cattle than any other country. Milk is produced, but Hindus do not eat beef. Resources include coal, iron ore, and oil. Manufacturing has expanded greatly since 1947. Iron and steel, machinery, refined petroleum, textiles, and transport equipment are major products.

AREA 1,269,212 SQ MI [3,287,263 SQ KM] **POPULATION** 1,080,264,000
CAPITAL (POPULATION) NEW DELHI (295,000)
GOVERNMENT MULTIPARTY FEDERAL REPUBLIC
ETHNIC GROUPS INDO-ARYAN (CAUCASOID) 72%, DRAVIDIAN (ABORIGINAL) 25%, OTHERS (MAINLY MONGOLOID) 3%
LANGUAGES HINDI, ENGLISH, TELUGU, BENGALI, MARATHI, TAMIL, URDU, GUJARATI, MALAYALAM, KANNADA, ORIYA, PUNJABI, ASSAMESE, KASHMIRI, SINDHI AND SANSKRIT ARE ALL OFFICIAL LANGUAGES
RELIGIONS HINDUISM 82%, ISLAM 12%, CHRISTIANITY 2%, SIKHISM 2%, BUDDHISM AND OTHERS **CURRENCY** INDIAN RUPEE = 100 PAISA

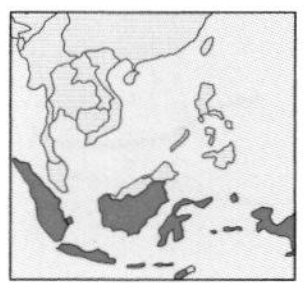

INDONESIA

GEOGRAPHY The Republic of Indonesia is an island nation in Southeast Asia. In all, Indonesia contains about 13,600 islands, less than 6,000 of which are inhabited. Three-quarters of the country is made up of five main areas: the islands of Sumatra, Java, and Sulawesi (Celebes), together with Kalimantan (southern Borneo) and Irian Jaya (western New Guinea). The islands are generally mountainous and volcanic. The larger islands have extensive coastal lowlands. The climate is hot and humid, with a high rainfall. Only Java and the Sunda Islands have relatively dry seasons.

POLITICS & ECONOMY Indonesia is the world's most populous Muslim nation, though Islam was introduced as recently as the 15th century. The Dutch became active in the area in the early 17th century and Indonesia became a Dutch colony in 1799. After a long struggle, the Netherlands recognized Indonesia's independence in 1949. The economy has expanded, but ethnic and religious conflict have slowed down economic progress.

In the early 21st century, Indonesia was facing many problems, arising from widespread corruption in the government and the army. Separatists were operating in Aceh province in northern Sumatra and in West Papua (formerly Irian Jaya), Christian-Muslim clashes led to loss of life in the Moluccas, and East (formerly Portuguese) Timor became an independent country. Terrorist incidents occurred in the early 21st century. In December 2004, a tsunami killed more than 100,000 people. Worst hit was Aceh, but the tragedy was followed by a negotiated peace with local separatists in 2005. A severe earthquake hit Java in 2006. Indonesia is a developing country with a growing industrial sector. It exports oil and natural gas, and also mines tin and other minerals. Timber, textiles, rubber, coffee, and tea are also exported. Rice is the main food crop.

AREA 735,354 SQ MI [1,904,569 SQ KM] **POPULATION** 241,974,000
CAPITAL (POPULATION) JAKARTA (9,374,000)
GOVERNMENT MULTIPARTY REPUBLIC
ETHNIC GROUPS JAVANESE 45%, SUNDANESE 14%, MADURESE 7%, COASTAL MALAYS 7%, APPROXIMATELY 300 OTHERS
LANGUAGES BAHASA INDONESIAN (OFFICIAL), MANY OTHERS
RELIGIONS ISLAM 88%, ROMAN CATHOLIC 3%, HINDUISM 2%, BUDDHISM 1%
CURRENCY INDONESIAN RUPIAH = 100 SEN

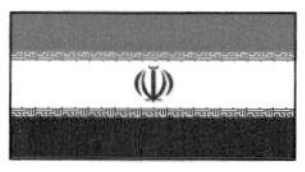
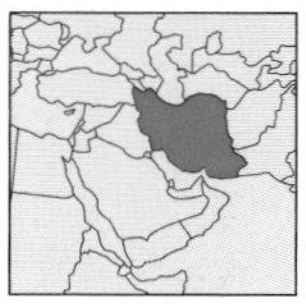

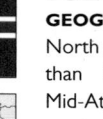

IRAN

GEOGRAPHY The Republic of Iran contains a barren central plateau which covers about half of the country. It includes the Dasht-e-Kavir (Great Salt Desert) and the Dasht-e-Lut (Great Sand Desert). The Elburz Mountains north of the plateau contain Iran's highest peak, Damavand, while narrow lowlands lie between the mountains and the Caspian Sea. West of the plateau are the Zagros Mountains, beyond which the land descends to the plains bordering the Persian Gulf.

Much of Iran has a severe, dry climate, with hot summers and cold winters. In Tehran, rain falls on only about 30 days in the year and the annual temperature range is more than 45°F [25°C]. The climate in the lowlands, however, is generally milder.

POLITICS & ECONOMY Iran was called Persia until 1935. The empire of Ancient Persia flourished between 550 and 350 BC, when it fell to Alexander the Great. Islam was introduced in AD 641.

Britain and Russia competed for influence in the area in the 19th century, and in the early 20th century the British began to develop the country's oil resources. In 1925, the Pahlavi family took power.

Reza Khan became shah (king) and worked to modernize the country. The Pahlavi dynasty was ended in 1979 when a religious leader, Ayatollah Ruhollah Khomeini, made Iran an Islamic republic. In 1980–8, Iran and Iraq fought a war over disputed borders. Khomeini died in 1989, but his fundamentalist views and anti-Western attitudes continued to dominate politics. In 1997, Mohammad Khatami, a liberal, was elected president, but clerics made reform difficult. In the 2000s, Iran was accused of developing nuclear weapons, a charge it denied. In 2005, a hardliner, Mahmoud Ahmadinejad, was elected president.

Iran's prosperity is based on its oil production and oil accounts for 95% of the country's exports. However, the economy was severely damaged by the Iran–Iraq war in the 1980s. Oil revenues have been used to develop a growing manufacturing sector. Agriculture is important even though farms cover only a tenth of the land. The main crops are wheat and barley. Livestock farming and fishing are other important activities, although Iran has to import much of the food it needs.

AREA 636,368 sq mi [1,648,195 sq km] **POPULATION** 68,018,000
CAPITAL (POPULATION) Tehran (7,723,000)
GOVERNMENT Islamic republic **ETHNIC GROUPS** Persian 51%, Azeri 24%, Gilaki and Mazandarani 8%, Kurd 7%, Arab 3%, Lur 2%, Baluchi 2%, Turkmen 2% **LANGUAGES** Persian 58%, Turkic 26%, Kurdish **RELIGIONS** Islam (Shi'ite Muslim 89%)
CURRENCY Iranian rial = 100 dinars

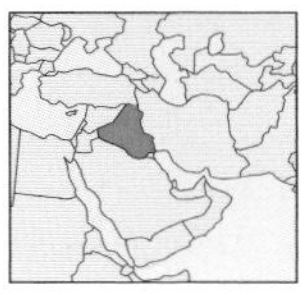

IRAQ

GEOGRAPHY The Republic of Iraq is a southwest Asian country at the head of the Persian Gulf. Rolling deserts cover western and southwestern Iraq, with part of the Zagros Mountains in the northeast, where farming can be practiced without irrigation. The northern plains, across which flow the rivers Euphrates (Nahr al Furat) and Tigris (Nahr Dijlah), are dry. But the southern plains, including Mesopotamia, and the delta of the Shatt al Arab, the river formed south of Al Qurnah by the combined Euphrates and Tigris, contain irrigated farmland, together with marshes.

The climate of Iraq ranges from temperate in the north to subtropical in the south. Baghdad, in central Iraq, has cool winters, with occasional frosts, and hot summers. The rainfall is generally low.

POLITICS & ECONOMY Mesopotamia was the home of several great civilizations, including Sumer, Babylon, and Assyria. It later became part of the Persian empire. Islam was introduced in AD 637 and Baghdad became the brilliant capital of the powerful Arab empire. But Mesopotamia declined after the Mongols invaded it in 1258. From 1534, Mesopotamia became part of the Turkish Ottoman empire. Britain invaded the area in 1916. In 1921, Britain renamed the country Iraq and set up an Arab monarchy. Iraq finally became independent in 1932.

By the 1950s, oil dominated Iraq's economy. In 1952, Iraq agreed to take 50% of the profits of the foreign oil companies. This revenue enabled the government to pay for welfare services and development projects. But many Iraqis felt that they should benefit more from their oil. Since 1958, when army officers killed the king and made Iraq a republic, Iraq has undergone turbulent times. In the 1960s, the Kurds, who live in northern Iraq and also in Iran, Turkey, Syria, and Armenia, asked for self-rule. The government rejected their demands and war broke out. A peace treaty was signed in 1975, but conflict has continued.

In 1979, Saddam Hussein became Iraq's president. Under his leadership, Iraq invaded Iran in 1980, starting an eight-year war. Iraqi Kurds supported Iran and the Iraqi government attacked Kurdish villages with poison gas. In 1990, Iraqi troops occupied Kuwait, but an international force drove them out in 1991. Since 1991, Iraqi troops have attacked Shi'ite Marsh Arabs and Kurds. In 1998, Iraq's failure to permit UN inspectors, charged with disposing of Iraq's deadliest weapons, access to suspect sites led to the Western bombardment of Iraqi military sites. Another major offensive occurred in 2001. In 2002–3, pressure mounted on Iraq to dispose of its alleged weapons of mass destruction. In March–April 2003, a coalition force headed by the United States invaded Iraq. It rapidly achieved its main objectives, but sporadic violence continued. Elections were held in 2005, despite a boycott by the Sunni Arabs, who make up about a fifth of the population.

Civil war, war damage in 1991 and 2003, UN sanctions and mismanagement have all contributed to economic chaos. Oil remains Iraq's main resource, but a UN trade embargo in 1990 halted oil exports. Farmland, including pasture, covers about a fifth of the land. Products include barley, cotton, dates, fruit, livestock, wheat, and wool, but Iraq still has to import food. Industries include oil refining and the manufacture of petrochemicals and consumer goods.

AREA 169,234 sq mi [438,317 sq km] **POPULATION** 26,075,000
CAPITAL (POPULATION) Baghdad (4,865,000)
GOVERNMENT Republic **ETHNIC GROUPS** Arab 77%, Kurdish 19%, Assyrian and others **LANGUAGES** Arabic (official), Kurdish (official in Kurdish areas), Assyrian, Armenian **RELIGIONS** Islam 97%, Christianity and others **CURRENCY** New Iraqi dinar

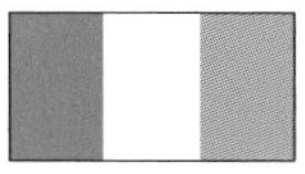

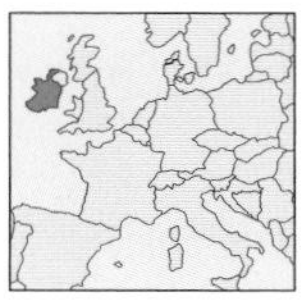

IRELAND

GEOGRAPHY The Republic of Ireland occupies five-sixths of the island of Ireland. The country consists of a large lowland region surrounded by a broken rim of low mountains. The uplands include the Mountains of Kerry where Carrauntoohill, Ireland's highest peak at 3,415 ft [1,041 m], is situated. The River Shannon is the longest in the British Isles. It flows through three large lakes, loughs Allen, Ree, and Derg.

Ireland has a mild, rainy climate influenced by the warm Gulf Stream current, whose effects are greatest in the west. However, Dublin in the east is cooler than places on the west coast.

POLITICS & ECONOMY In 1801, the Act of Union created the United Kingdom of Great Britain and Ireland. But Irish discontent intensified in the 1840s when a potato blight caused a famine in which a million people died and nearly a million emigrated. Britain was blamed for not having done enough to help. In 1916, an uprising in Dublin was crushed, but between 1919 and 1922 civil war occurred. In 1922, the Irish Free State was created as a Dominion in the British Commonwealth. But Northern Ireland remained part of the UK.

Ireland became a republic in 1949. In 1973, Ireland became a member of the European Community (now the European Union) and, since then, the country has prospered economically. In 1998, Ireland took part in the negotiations to produce a constitutional settlement in Northern Ireland. As part of the agreement, Ireland agreed to give up its constitutional claim on Northern Ireland. But the agreement proved difficult to implement.

Major farm products in Ireland include barley, cattle and dairy products, pigs, potatoes, poultry, sheep, sugar beet, and wheat, while fishing provides another valuable source of food. Farming is now profitable, aided by European Union grants, but manufacturing is the leading economic sector. Many factories produce food and beverages. Chemicals and pharmaceuticals, electronic equipment, machinery, paper, and textiles are also important.

AREA 27,132 sq mi [70,273 sq km] **POPULATION** 4,016,000
CAPITAL (POPULATION) Dublin (482,000)
GOVERNMENT Multiparty republic **ETHNIC GROUPS** Irish 94%
LANGUAGES Irish (Gaelic) and English (both official)
RELIGIONS Roman Catholic 92%, Protestant 3%
CURRENCY Euro = 100 cents

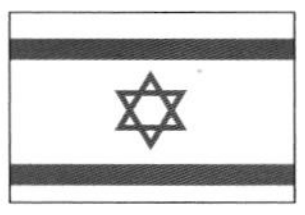

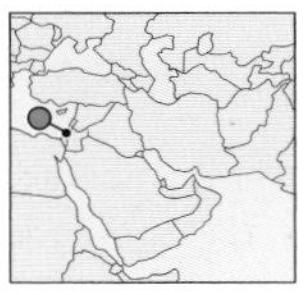

ISRAEL

GEOGRAPHY The State of Israel is a small country in the eastern Mediterranean. It includes a fertile coastal plain, where Israel's main industrial cities, Haifa (Hefa) and Tel Aviv-Jaffa are situated. Inland lie the Judaeo-Galilean highlands, which run from northern Israel to the northern tip of the Negev Desert. To the east lies part of the Great Rift Valley which contains the River Jordan, the Sea of Galilee and the Dead Sea. Summers are hot and dry. Winters on the coast are mild and moist, but the rainfall decreases from west to east and from north to south.

POLITICS & ECONOMY Israel is part of a region called Palestine. Some Jews have always lived in the area, though most modern Israelis are descendants of immigrants who began to settle there from the 1880s. Britain ruled Palestine from 1917. Large numbers of Jews escaping Nazi persecution arrived in the 1930s, provoking an Arab uprising against British rule. In 1947, the UN agreed to partition Palestine into an Arab and a Jewish state. Fighting broke out after Arabs rejected the plan. The State of Israel came into being in May 1948, but fighting continued into 1949. Other Arab-Israeli wars in 1956, 1967, and 1973 led to land gains for Israel.

In 1978, Israel signed a treaty with Egypt which led to the return of the occupied Sinai peninsula to Egypt in 1979. But conflict continued between Israel and the PLO (Palestine Liberation Organization). In 1993, the PLO and Israel agreed to establish Palestinian self-rule in two areas: the occupied Gaza Strip, and in the town of Jericho in the occupied West Bank. The agreement was extended in 1995 to include more than 30% of the West Bank. Israel's prime minister, Yitzhak Rabin, was assassinated in 1995. In 1996, Benjamin Netanyahu was elected prime minister. The peace process stalled until Ehud Barak defeated Netanyahu in 1999. After more violence, Barak resigned and, in 2001, Ariel Sharon succeeded him. In 2005, Sharon ordered the withdrawal of Israeli forces and the handing over of the Gaza Strip, which came under the Palestinian Authority. Sharon formed a new political party, Kadima. After he suffered a stroke, Ehud Olmert became its leader. Kadima won most seats in elections in 2006 and Olmert became prime minister, heading a coalition government.

Israel's most valuable activity is manufacturing and the country's products include chemicals, electronic equipment, fertilizers, military equipment, plastics, processed food, scientific instruments, and textiles. Fruits and vegetables are leading exports.

AREA 7,954 sq mi [20,600 sq km] **POPULATION** 6,277,000
CAPITAL (POPULATION) Jerusalem (685,000)
GOVERNMENT Multiparty republic **ETHNIC GROUPS** Jewish 80%, Arab and others 20% **LANGUAGES** Hebrew and Arabic (both official)
RELIGIONS Judaism 80%, Islam (mostly Sunni) 14%, Christianity 2%, Druze and others 2% **CURRENCY** New Israeli shekel = 100 agorat

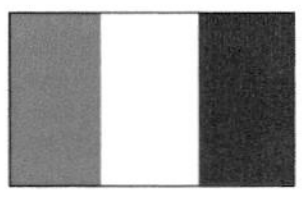

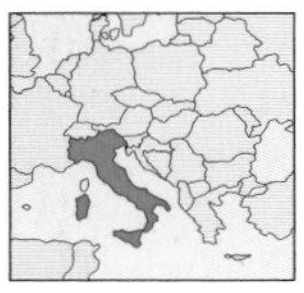

ITALY

GEOGRAPHY The Republic of Italy is famous for its history and traditions, its art and culture, and its beautiful scenery. Northern Italy is bordered in the north by the high Alps, with their many climbing and skiing resorts. The Alps overlook the northern plains – Italy's most fertile and densely populated region – drained by the River Po. The rugged Apennines form the backbone of southern Italy. Bordering the range are scenic hilly areas and coastal plains. Southern Italy contains a string of volcanoes, stretching from Vesuvius, through the Lipari Islands, to Etna on Sicily, the largest Mediterranean island. Northern Italy has cold, often snowy, winters, but the summer months are warm and sunny, with brief summer thunderstorms. Rainfall is abundant. The south has mild, moist winters and warm, dry summers.

POLITICS & ECONOMY Magnificent ruins throughout Italy testify to the glories of the ancient Roman Empire, which was founded, according to legend, in 753 BC. It reached its peak in the AD 100s. It finally collapsed in the 400s, although the Eastern Roman empire, also called the Byzantine empire, survived for another 1,000 years.

In the Middle Ages, Italy was split into many tiny states. These states made a great contribution to the revival of art and learning, called the Renaissance, in the 14th to 16th centuries. Beautiful cities, such as Florence (Firenze) and Venice (Venézia), testify to the artistic achievements of this period.

Italy finally became a united kingdom in 1861, although the Papal Territories (a large area ruled by the Roman Catholic Church) was not added until 1870. The Pope and his successors disputed the takeover of the Papal Territories. The dispute was finally resolved in 1929, when the Vatican City was set up in Rome as a fully independent state.

Italy fought in World War I (1914–18) alongside the Allies – Britain, France and Russia. In 1922, the dictator Benito Mussolini, leader of the Fascist Party, took power. Under Mussolini, Italy conquered Ethiopia. During World War II (1939–45), Italy at first fought on Germany's side against the Allies. But in late 1943, Italy declared war on Germany. Italy became a republic in 1946. It has played an important part in European affairs. It was a founder member of the North Atlantic Treaty Organization (NATO) in 1949 and also of what has now become the European Union in 1958.

After the setting up of the European Union, Italy's economy developed quickly. But the country faced many problems. For example, much of the economic development was in the north. This forced many people to leave the poor south to find jobs in the north or abroad. Social problems, corruption at high levels of society, and a succession of weak coalition governments all contributed to instability. Elections in 1996 were won by the left-wing Olive Tree Alliance led by Romano Prodi. However, in 2001, a center-right coalition led by media tycoon Silvio Berlusconi was elected with a large majority. But, in 2006, a center-left coalition, led by Romano Prodi, defeated Berlusconi's center-right House of Liberties by a narrow majority.

Only 50 years ago, Italy was a mainly agricultural society. But today it is a leading industrial power. It lacks mineral resources, and imports most of the raw materials used in industry. Manufactures include textiles and clothing, processed food, machinery, cars, and chemicals. The chief industrial region is in the northwest.

Farmland covers around 42% of the land, pasture 17%, and forest and woodland 22%. Major crops include citrus fruits, grapes which are used to make wine, olive oil, sugar beet, and vegetables. Livestock farming is important, though meat is imported.

AREA 116,339 sq mi [301,318 sq km] **POPULATION** 58,103,000
CAPITAL (POPULATION) Rome (2,460,000)
GOVERNMENT Multiparty republic **ETHNIC GROUPS** Italian 94%, German, French, Albanian, Slovene, Greek **LANGUAGES** Italian (official), German, French, Slovene **RELIGIONS** Predominantly Roman Catholic **CURRENCY** Euro = 100 cents

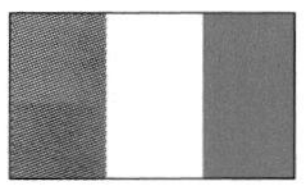

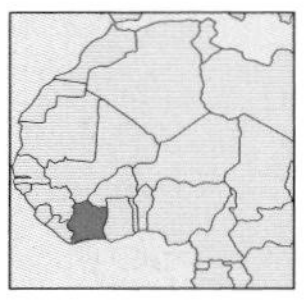

IVORY COAST

GEOGRAPHY The Republic of the Ivory Coast, in West Africa, is officially known as Côte d'Ivoire. The southeast coast is bordered by sand bars that enclose lagoons. The southwest coast is lined by rocky cliffs.

Ivory Coast has a hot and humid tropical climate, with high temperatures all year. The south has two rainy seasons: between May and July, and from October to November. Inland, the rainfall decreases and the north has one dry and one rainy season.

POLITICS & ECONOMY From 1895, Ivory Coast was governed as part of French West Africa, which also included what are now Benin, Burkina Faso, Guinea, Mali, Mauritania, Niger, and Senegal. In 1946, Ivory Coast became a territory in the French Union.

Ivory Coast became fully independent in 1960. Its first president, Félix Houphouët-Boigny, became the longest serving head of state in Africa with an uninterrupted period in office which ended with his death in 1993. Houphouët-Boigny, a pro-Western leader, made Ivory Coast a one-party state. In 1983, the National Assembly voted to make Yamoussoukro, the president's birthplace, the new capital. In 1999, a military coup occurred, but civilian rule was restored in 2000, when Laurent Gbagbo was elected president. An army rebellion began in September 2002. By 2004, the country was divided into the government-held south and the mainly Muslim north, held by rebels who called themselves the New Forces.

Agriculture employs about half of the people, and farm products make up nearly half the value of the exports. Manufacturing has grown in importance since 1960; products include fertilizers, processed food, refined oil, textiles, and timber.

AREA 124,503 sq mi [322,463 sq km] **POPULATION** 17,298,000
CAPITAL (POPULATION) Yamoussoukro (107,000)
GOVERNMENT Multiparty republic **ETHNIC GROUPS** Akan 42%, Voltaiques 18%, Northern Mandes 16%, Krous 11%, Southern Mandes 10% **LANGUAGES** French (official), many native dialects
RELIGIONS Islam 40%, Christianity 30%, traditional beliefs 30%
CURRENCY CFA franc = 100 centimes

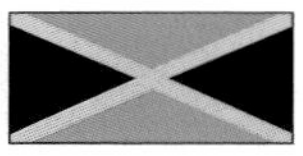

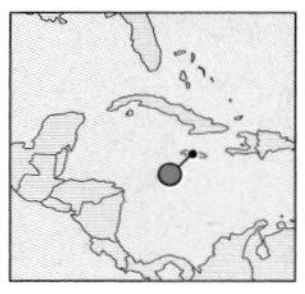

JAMAICA

GEOGRAPHY Third largest of the Caribbean islands, half of Jamaica lies above 1,000 ft [300 m] and moist southeast trade winds bring rain to the central mountain range.

The "cockpit country" in the northwest of the island is an inaccessible limestone area of steep broken ridges and isolated basins.

POLITICS & ECONOMY Britain took Jamaica from Spain in the 17th century, and the island did not gain its independence until 1962. Power has alternated between the People's National Party (PNP) and Jamaica Labor Party. In 2006, Portia Simpson Miller became leader of the PNP and succeeded Percival Patterson as prime minister. Jamaica has a large tourist industry. Farming is important and sugarcane is the main crop. Alumina and bauxite make up 60% of the exports.

AREA 4,244 sq mi [10,991 sq km] **POPULATION** 2,732,000
CAPITAL (POPULATION) Kingston (104,000)
GOVERNMENT Constitutional monarchy
ETHNIC GROUPS Black 91%, Mixed 7%, East Indian 1%
LANGUAGES English (official), patois English
RELIGIONS Protestant 61%, Roman Catholic 4%
CURRENCY Jamaican dollar = 100 cents

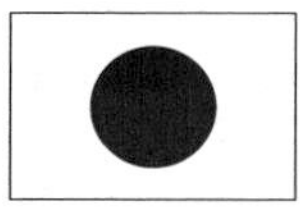

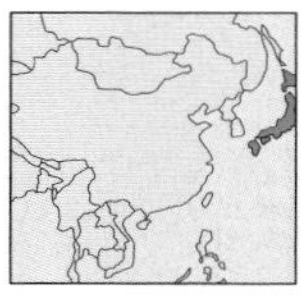

JAPAN

GEOGRAPHY Japan's four largest islands – Honshu, Hokkaido, Kyushu, and Shikoku – make up 98% of the country. But Japan contains thousands of small islands. The four largest islands are mainly mountainous, while many of the small islands are the tips of volcanoes. Japan has more than 150 volcanoes, about 60 of which are active. Volcanic eruptions, earthquakes, and tsunamis (destructive sea waves triggered by underwater earthquakes and eruptions) are common because the islands lie in an unstable part of our planet, where continental plates are always on the move. One powerful recent earthquake killed more than 5,000 people in Kobe in 1995.

The climate of Japan varies greatly from north to south. Hokkaido in the north has cold, snowy winters. At Sapporo, temperatures below 4°F [–20°C] have been recorded between December and March. But summers are warm, with temperatures sometimes exceeding 86°F [30°C]. Rain falls throughout the year, though Hokkaido is one of the driest parts of Japan. Tokyo has higher rainfall and temperatures, while the southern islands of Shikoku and Kyushu have warm temperate climates. Summers are long and hot. Winters are cold.

POLITICS & ECONOMY In the late 19th century, Japan began a program of modernization. Under its new imperial leaders, it began to look for lands to conquer. In 1894–5, it fought a war with China and, in 1904–5, it defeated Russia. Soon its overseas empire included Korea and Taiwan. In 1930, Japan invaded Manchuria (northeast China) and, in 1937, it began a war against China. In 1941, Japan launched an attack on the US base at Pearl Harbor in Hawai'i. This drew both Japan and the United States into World War II.

Japan surrendered in 1945 when the Americans dropped atomic bombs on two cities, Hiroshima and Nagasaki. The United States occupied Japan until 1952. During this period, Japan adopted a democratic constitution. The emperor, who had previously been regarded as a god, became a constitutional monarch. Power was vested in the prime minister and cabinet, who are chosen from the Diet (elected parliament).

From the 1960s, Japan experienced many changes as the country rapidly built up new industries. By the early 1990s, Japan had become the world's second richest economic power after the US. But economic success has brought problems. For example, the rapid growth of cities has led to housing shortages and pollution. Another problem is that the proportion of people over 65 years of age is steadily increasing.

Japan has the world's second highest gross domestic product (GDP) after the United States. [The GDP is the total value of all goods and services produced in a country in one year.] The most important sector of the economy is industry. Yet Japan has to import most of the raw materials and fuels it needs for its industries. Its success is based on its use of the latest technology, its skilled and hard-working labor force, its vigorous export policies and its comparatively small government spending on defense. Manufactures dominate its exports, which include machinery, electrical and electronic equipment, vehicles and transport equipment, iron and steel, chemicals, textiles, and ships. Japan experienced an economic slowdown in the 1990s, which developed into a recession. Signs of recovery appeared in 2005–6.

Japan is one of the world's top fishing nations and fish is an important source of protein. Because the land is so rugged, only 15% of the country can be farmed. Yet Japan produces about 70% of the food it needs. Rice is the chief crop, taking up about half of the total farmland. Other major products include fruits, sugar beet, tea, and vegetables. Livestock farming has increased since the 1950s.

AREA 145,880 sq mi [377,829 sq km] **POPULATION** 127,417,000
CAPITAL (POPULATION) Tokyo (8,130,000)
GOVERNMENT Constitutional monarchy
ETHNIC GROUPS Japanese 99%, Chinese, Korean, Brazilian, and others
LANGUAGES Japanese (official) **RELIGIONS** Shintoism and Buddhism 84% (most Japanese consider themselves to be both Shinto and Buddhist), others **CURRENCY** Yen = 100 sen

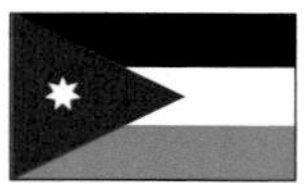

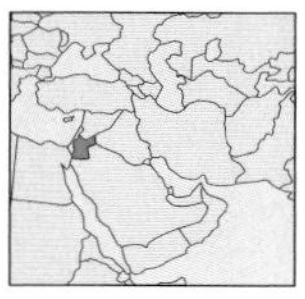

JORDAN

GEOGRAPHY The Hashemite Kingdom of Jordan is an Arab country in southwestern Asia. The Great Rift Valley in the west contains the River Jordan and the Dead Sea, which Jordan shares with Israel. East of the Rift Valley is the Transjordan plateau, where most Jordanians live. To the east and south lie vast areas of desert.

Amman has a much lower rainfall and longer dry season than the Mediterranean lands to the west. The Transjordan plateau, on which Amman stands, is a transition zone between the Mediterranean climate zone and the desert climate to the east.

POLITICS & ECONOMY In 1921, Britain created a territory called Transjordan east of the River Jordan. In 1923, Transjordan became self-governing, but Britain retained control of its defenses, finances, and foreign affairs. This territory became fully independent as Jordan in 1946. Jordan has suffered from instability arising from the Arab–Israeli conflict since the creation of the State of Israel in 1948. After the first Arab–Israeli War in 1948–9, Jordan acquired East Jerusalem and a fertile area called the West Bank. In 1967, Israel occupied this area. In Jordan, the presence of Palestinian refugees led to civil war in 1970–1.

In 1974, Arab leaders declared that the PLO (Palestine Liberation Organization) was the sole representative of the Palestinian people. In 1988, King Hussein of Jordan renounced Jordan's claims to the West Bank and passed responsibility for it to the PLO. Opposition parties were legalized in 1991 and elections were held in 1993. In October 1994, Jordan and Israel signed a peace treaty, ending a state of war that had lasted more than 40 years. Jordan's King Hussein commanded respect for his role in Middle Eastern affairs until his death in 1999. He was succeeded by his eldest son, who became Abdullah II. Jordan supported the US-led war on terrorism. But its reputation as one of the safest countries in the Middle East was damaged in 2005 by suicide bombings on hotels in Amman. An Islamic group based in Iraq but led by a Jordanian-born militant claimed responsibility.

Jordan has a "lower-middle-income" economy. It lacks natural resources, apart from phosphates and potash, and depends on substantial aid. Less than 6% of the land is farmed or used as pasture. Jordan has an oil refinery and manufactures include cement, pharmaceuticals, processed food, fertilizers, and textiles.

AREA 34,495 sq mi [89,342 sq km] **POPULATION** 5,760,000
CAPITAL (POPULATION) Amman (1,148,000)
GOVERNMENT Constitutional monarchy **ETHNIC GROUPS** Arab 98%, of which Palestinians make up roughly half **LANGUAGES** Arabic (official) **RELIGIONS** Islam (mostly Sunni) 94%, Christianity (mostly Greek Orthodox) 6% **CURRENCY** Jordanian dinar = 1,000 fils

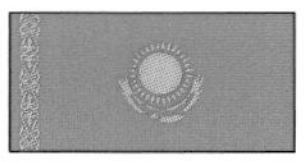

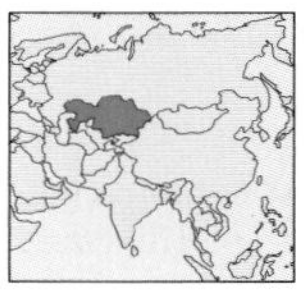

KAZAKHSTAN

GEOGRAPHY Kazakhstan is a large country in west-central Asia. In the west, the Caspian Sea lowlands include the Karagiye depression, which reaches 433 ft [132 m] below sea level. The lowlands extend eastward through the Aral Sea area. The north contains high plains, but the highest land is along the eastern and southern borders. These areas include parts of the Altai and Tian Shan mountain ranges. Eastern Kazakhstan contains several freshwater lakes, the largest of which is Lake Balkhash. The water in the rivers has been used for irrigation, causing ecological problems. For example, the Aral Sea, deprived of water, shrank from 25,830 sq mi [66,900 sq km] in 1960 to 12,989 sq mi [33,642 sq km] in 1993. Large areas are now barren desert.

Kazakhstan lies far from the moderating influence of the oceans and it has an extreme climate. Winters are cold and snow covers the land for about 100 days at Almaty. The rainfall is generally low.

POLITICS & ECONOMY After the Russian Revolution of 1917, many Kazakhs wanted to make their country independent. But the Communists prevailed and in 1936 Kazakhstan became a republic of the Soviet Union, called the Kazakh Soviet Socialist Republic. During World War II and also after the war, the Soviet government moved many people from the west into Kazakhstan. From the 1950s, people were encouraged to work on a "Virgin Lands" project, which involved bringing large areas of grassland under cultivation.

Reforms in the Soviet Union in the 1980s led to its breakup in December 1991. Kazakhstan maintained contacts with Russia through the Commonwealth of Independent States (CIS). In 1997, the government moved its capital from Almaty to Aqmola (later renamed Astana), a town in the north. By the mid-2000s, the economy was in better shape than the other ex-Soviet republics in Central Asia. But President Nursultan Nazarbaev was criticized for his authoritarian rule, and the elections in 2004, won by his Ocan Party, were described as flawed. In 2006, his opponents accused his government of operating death squads.

The World Bank classifies Kazakhstan as a "lower-middle-income" developing country. Livestock farming, especially sheep and cattle, is an important activity, and major crops include barley, cotton, rice, and wheat. The country is rich in mineral resources, including coal and oil reserves, together with bauxite, copper, lead, tungsten, and zinc. Manufactures include chemicals, food products, machinery, and textiles. Oil is exported via a pipeline through Russia; however, to reduce dependence on Russia, Kazakhstan signed an agreement in 1997 to build a new pipeline to China. Other exports include metals, chemicals, grain, wool, and meat.

AREA 1,052,084 sq mi [2,724,900 sq km] **POPULATION** 15,186,000
CAPITAL (POPULATION) Astana (322,000) **GOVERNMENT** Multiparty republic **ETHNIC GROUPS** Kazakh 53%, Russian 30%, Ukrainian 4%, German 2%, Uzbek 2% **LANGUAGES** Kazakh (official); Russian, the former official language, is widely spoken **RELIGIONS** Islam 47%, Russian Orthodox 44% **CURRENCY** Tenge = 100 tiyn

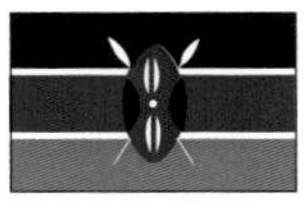

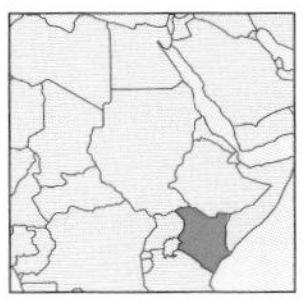

KENYA

GEOGRAPHY The Republic of Kenya is a country in East Africa which straddles the Equator. Behind the narrow coastal plain on the Indian Ocean, the land rises to high plains and highlands, broken by volcanic mountains, including Mount Kenya, the country's highest peak at 17,057 ft [5,199 m]. Crossing the country is an arm of the Great Rift Valley, on the floor of which are several lakes, including Baringo, Magadi, Naivasha, Nakuru and, on the northern frontier, Lake Turkana (formerly Lake Rudolf).

Mombasa on the coast is hot and humid. But inland, the climate is moderated by the height of the land. As a result, Nairobi, in the thickly populated southwestern highlands, has summer temperatures which are 18°F [10°C] lower than Mombasa. Nights can be cool, but temperatures do not fall below freezing. Nairobi's main rainy season is from April to May, with "little rains" in November and December. However, only about 15% of the country has a reliable rainfall of 31 inches [800 mm].

POLITICS & ECONOMY The Kenyan coast has been a trading center for more than 2,000 years. Britain took over the coast in 1895 and soon extended its influence inland. In the 1950s, a secret movement, called Mau Mau, launched an armed struggle against British rule. Although Mau Mau was eventually defeated, Kenya became independent in 1963.

Many Kenyans felt that Kenya should have a strong central government, and Kenya was a one-party state for much of the time since 1963. Democracy was restored in 1992. In 2002, Mwai Kibaki was elected president, promising to combat corruption and make Kenya more democratic. But, in 2005 and 2006, Kenya was hit by a severe drought and Kibaki's government was widely criticized for its failure to halt corruption. Voters also rejected a draft constitution proposed by the government. Many believed that it conferred too many powers on the president.

Kenya remains a "low-income" developing country. Many Kenyans are subsistence farmers. The chief food crop is maize. The main cash crops and the leading exports are coffee and tea. Manufactures include chemicals, leather and footwear, processed food, petroleum products, and textiles.

AREA 224,080 sq mi [580,367 sq km] **POPULATION** 33,830,000
CAPITAL (POPULATION) Nairobi (2,143,000)
GOVERNMENT Multiparty republic **ETHNIC GROUPS** Kikuyu 22%, Luhya 14%, Luo 13%, Kalenjin 12%, Kamba 11%, others
LANGUAGES Kiswahili and English (both official)
RELIGIONS Protestant 45%, Roman Catholic 33%, traditional beliefs 10%, Islam 10% **CURRENCY** Kenyan shilling = 100 cents

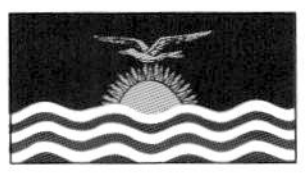

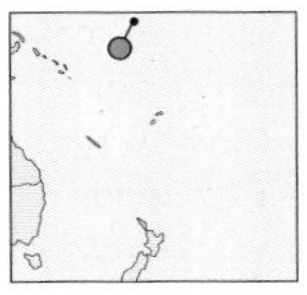

KIRIBATI

The Republic of Kiribati comprises three groups of corall atolls scattered over about 2 million sq mi [5 million sq km]. Kiribati straddles the equator and temperatures are high and the rainfall is abundant.

Formerly part of the British Gilbert and Ellice Islands, Kiribati became independent in 1979. The main export is copra and the country depends heavily on foreign aid.

AREA 280 sq mi [726 sq km] **POPULATION** 103,000 **CAPITAL** Tarawa

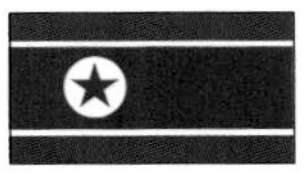

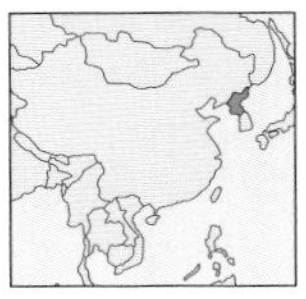

KOREA, NORTH

GEOGRAPHY The Democratic People's Republic of Korea occupies the northern part of the Korean peninsula which extends south from northeastern China. Mountains form the heart of the country, with the highest peak, Paektu-san, reaching 9,003 ft [2,744 m] on the northern border.

North Korea has a fairly severe climate, with bitterly cold winters when winds blow from across central Asia, bringing snow and freezing conditions. In summer, moist winds from the oceans bring rain.

POLITICS & ECONOMY North Korea was created in 1945, when the peninsula, which had been a Japanese colony since 1910, was divided into two parts. Soviet forces occupied the north, with US forces in the south. Soviet occupation led to a Communist government being established in 1948 under the leadership of Kim Il Sung. He initiated a Stalinist regime in which he assumed the role of dictator, and a personality cult developed around him. He was to become the world's most durable Communist leader.

The Korean War began in June 1950 when North Korean troops invaded the south. North Korea, aided by China and the Soviet Union, fought with South Korea, which was supported by troops from the United States and other UN members. The war ended in July 1953. An armistice was signed but no permanent peace treaty was agreed. The end of the Cold War in the late 1990s eased the situation. North and South Korea joined the United Nations in 1991 and they made several agreements, including one in which they agreed not to use force against each other. However, North Korea remained as isolated as ever.

In 1993, North Korea began a new international crisis by announcing that it was withdrawing from the Nuclear Non-Proliferation Treaty. This led to suspicions that North Korea, which had signed the Treaty in 1985, was developing nuclear weapons. Kim Il Sung, who had ruled as a dictator from 1948, died in 1994 and was succeeded by his son, Kim Jong Il. In the early 2000s, attempts were made to reconcile the two Koreas. But, from 2003, relations with the United States deteriorated when the US accused North Korea of having a secret nuclear weapons program. In 2005, North Korea withdrew from international talks, stating that it had already produced nuclear weapons.

North Korea's resources include coal, copper, iron ore, lead, tin, tungsten, and zinc. Under Communism, the country developed heavy, state-owned industries. Manufactures include chemicals, iron and steel, machinery, processed food, and textiles. Agriculture employs 32% of the people and rice is the chief crop. Economic mismanagement and successive floods in 1995 and 1996, and a drought in 1997, caused severe famine.

AREA 46,540 sq mi [120,538 sq km] **POPULATION** 22,912,000
CAPITAL (POPULATION) Pyŏngyang (2,725,000)
GOVERNMENT Single-party people's republic
ETHNIC GROUPS Korean 99%
LANGUAGES Korean (official)
RELIGIONS Buddhism and Confucianism
CURRENCY North Korean won = 100 chon

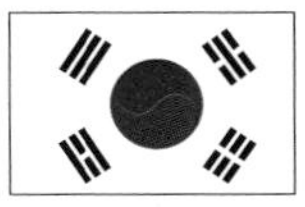

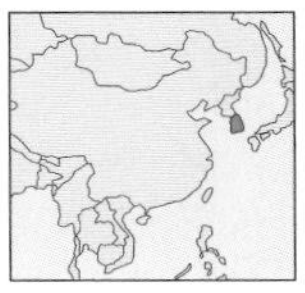

KOREA, SOUTH

GEOGRAPHY The Republic of Korea, as South Korea is officially known, occupies the southern part of the Korean peninsula. Mountains cover much of the country. The southern and western coasts are major farming regions. Many islands are found along the west and south coasts. The largest of these is Cheju-do, which contains South Korea's highest peak, Halla-San, which rises to 6,398 ft [1,950 m].

Like North Korea, South Korea is chilled in winter by cold, dry winds blowing from central Asia. Snow often covers the mountains in the east. The summers are hot and wet, especially in July and August.

POLITICS & ECONOMY After Japan's defeat in World War II (1939–45), North Korea was occupied by troops from the Soviet Union, while South Korea was occupied by United States forces. Attempts to reunify Korea failed and, in 1948, a National Assembly was elected in South Korea. This Assembly created the Republic of Korea, while North Korea became a Communist state. North Korean troops invaded the South in June 1950, sparking off the Korean War (1950–3).

In the 1950s, South Korea had a weak economy, which had been further damaged by the destruction caused by the Korean War. From the 1960s to the 1980s, South Korean governments worked to industrialize the economy. The governments were dominated by military leaders, who often used authoritarian methods and flouted human rights. In 1987, a new constitution was approved, enabling presidential elections to be held every five years. In 1991, South and North Korea became members of the United Nations and they signed agreements, including one in which they agreed not to use force against each other. In the 2000s, South Korea worked to engage the North in closer relations, while the United States threatened sanctions against North Korea if it did not abandon its nuclear ambitions.

The World Bank classifies South Korea as an "upper-middle-income" developing country. It is also one of the world's fastest growing industrial economies. The country's resources include coal and tungsten, and its main manufactures are processed food and textiles. Since partition, heavy industries have been built up, making chemicals, fertilizers, iron and steel, and ships. South Korea has also developed the production of such things as computers, cars, and television sets. But, in late 1997, the expansion of the economy was halted by a market crash which affected many of the booming economies of eastern Asia. However, South Korea recovered faster than any other country in the region.

Farming remains important in South Korea. Rice is the chief crop, together with fruits, grains and vegetables, while fishing provides a major source of protein.

AREA 38,327 sq mi [99,268 sq km] **POPULATION** 48,423,000
CAPITAL (POPULATION) Seoul (9,888,000)
GOVERNMENT Multiparty republic **ETHNIC GROUPS** Korean 99%
LANGUAGES Korean (official) **RELIGIONS** No affiliation 46%, Christianity 26%, Buddhism 26%, Confucianism 1%
CURRENCY South Korean won = 100 chon

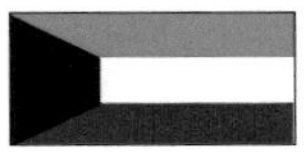

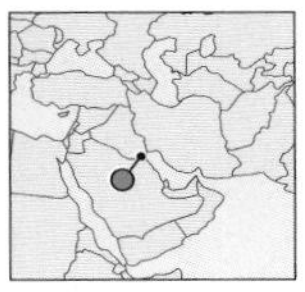

KUWAIT

The State of Kuwait at the north end of the Persian Gulf is an emirate (ruled by an emir or amir). The land is low-lying and largely desert. Summer temperatures are high but winters are cooler. The rainfall is low.

POLITICS & ECONOMY British influence began in 1775 and, in 1899, the local ruler concluded a treaty with Britain, agreeing to support British interests in return for British protection. Kuwait became independent in 1961. Its revenue from its oil exports made it highly prosperous. Iraq invaded Kuwait in 1990 and much damage was inflicted in 1991 when Kuwait was liberated by a coalition force. In the 1990s, reforms were introduced to make the country more democratic and raise the status of women. In 2004, the government announced draft legislation for women to vote and stand for parliament.

AREA 6,880 sq mi [17,818 sq km] **POPULATION** 2,336,000
CAPITAL (POPULATION) Kuwait City (29,000)

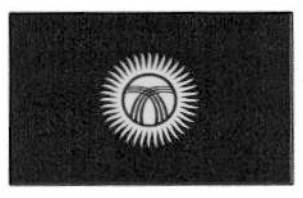

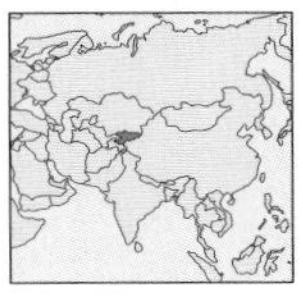

KYRGYZSTAN

GEOGRAPHY The Republic of Kyrgyzstan is a landlocked country between China, Tajikistan, Uzbekistan and Kazakhstan. The country is mountainous, with spectacular scenery. The highest mountain, Pik Pobedy in the Tian Shan range, reaches 24,406 ft [7,439 m] in the east. The lowlands have warm summers and cold winters. But January temperatures in the mountains plummet to –18°F [–28°C]. Kyrgyzstan has a low annual rainfall.

POLITICS & ECONOMY In 1876, Kyrgyzstan became a province of Russia and Russian settlement in the area began. In 1916, Russia crushed a rebellion among the Kyrgyz, and many subsequently fled to China. In 1922, the area became an autonomous oblast (self-governing region) of the newly formed Soviet Union but, in 1936, it became one of the Soviet Socialist Republics. Under Communist rule, local customs and religious worship were suppressed, but education and health services were greatly improved.

In 1991, Kyrgyzstan became an independent country following the breakup of the Soviet Union. The Communist Party was dissolved, but the country maintained ties with Russia through an organization called the Commonwealth of Independent States. Elections were held under a new constitution adopted in 1994. However, massive protests followed flawed parliamentary elections in 2005. Askar Akayev, who had been president since 1990, but who had monopolized power, fled into exile. He was succeeded by Kurmanbek Bakiyev.

In the early 1990s, when Kyrgyzstan was working to reform its economy, the World Bank classified it as a "lower-middle-income" developing country. Agriculture, especially livestock rearing, is the chief activity. The chief products include cotton, eggs, fruits, grain, tobacco, vegetables, and wool. But food must be imported. Industries are mainly concentrated around the capital Bishkek.

AREA 77,181 sq mi [199,900 sq km] **POPULATION** 5,146,000
CAPITAL (POPULATION) Bishkek (753,000) **GOVERNMENT** Multiparty republic **ETHNIC GROUPS** Kyrgyz 65%, Russian 13%, Uzbek 13%
LANGUAGES Kyrgyz and Russian (both official) **RELIGIONS** Islam 75%, Russian Orthodox 20% **CURRENCY** Kyrgyzstani som = 100 tyiyn

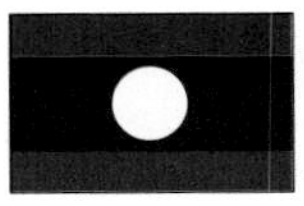

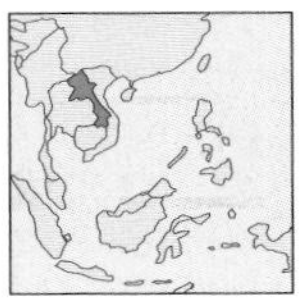

LAOS

GEOGRAPHY The Lao People's Democratic Republic is a landlocked country in Southeast Asia. Mountains and plateaux cover much of the country. Most people live on the plains bordering the River Mekong and its tributaries. This river, one of Asia's longest, forms much of the country's northwestern and southwestern borders.

Laos has a tropical monsoon climate.

Winters are dry and sunny, with winds blowing in from the northeast. The temperatures rise until April, when the wind directions are reversed and moist southwesterly winds reach Laos, heralding the start of the wet monsoon season.

POLITICS & ECONOMY France made Laos a protectorate in the late 19th century and ruled it as part of French Indochina, a region which also included Cambodia and Vietnam. Laos became a member of the French Union in 1948 and an independent kingdom in 1954.

After independence, Laos suffered from instability caused by a long power struggle between royalist government forces and a pro-Communist group called the Pathet Lao. A civil war broke out in 1960 and continued into the 1970s. The Pathet Lao took control in 1975 and the king abdicated. Laos then came under the influence of Communist Vietnam, which had used Laos as a supply base during the Vietnam War (1957–75). From the early 1980s, the economy deteriorated and opposition appeared when bombings occurred in Vientiane in 2000. Some experts attributed them to the minority Hmong people who had been engaged in a low-level rebellion since 1975.

Laos is one of the world's poorest countries. Agriculture employs about 76% of the people, compared with 7% in industry and 17% in services. Rice is the main crop, and timber and coffee are both exported. But the most valuable export is electricity, which is produced at hydroelectric power stations on the River Mekong and is exported to Thailand. Laos also produces opium.

AREA 91,428 sq mi [236,800 sq km] **POPULATION** 6,217,000
CAPITAL (POPULATION) Vientiane (528,000)
GOVERNMENT Single-party republic
ETHNIC GROUPS Lao Loum 68%, Lao Theung 22%, Lao Soung 9%
LANGUAGES Lao (official), French, English **RELIGIONS** Buddhism 60%, traditional beliefs and others 40% **CURRENCY** Kip = 100 at

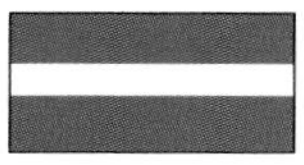

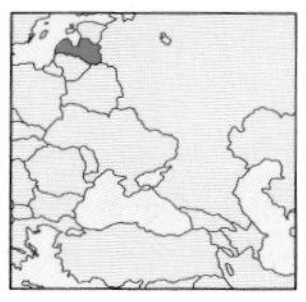

LATVIA

GEOGRAPHY The Republic of Latvia is one of three states on the southeastern corner of the Baltic Sea which were ruled as parts of the Soviet Union between 1940 and 1991. Latvia consists mainly of flat plains separated by low hills, composed of moraine (ice-worn rocks).

Riga has warm summers, but the winter months (from December to March) are subzero. In the winter, the sea often freezes over. The rainfall is moderate and it occurs throughout the year, with light snow in winter.

POLITICS & ECONOMY In 1800, Russia was in control of Latvia, but Latvians declared their independence after World War I. In 1940, under a German-Soviet pact, Soviet troops occupied Latvia, but they were driven out by the Germans in 1941. Soviet troops returned in 1944 and Latvia became part of the Soviet Union. Under Soviet rule, many Russian immigrants settled in Latvia and many Latvians feared that the Russians would become the dominant ethnic group.

In the late 1980s, when reforms were being introduced in the Soviet Union, Latvia's government ended absolute Communist rule and made Latvian the official language. In 1990, it declared the country to be independent, an act which was finally recognized by the Soviet Union in September 1991.

Latvia held its first free elections to its parliament (the Saeima) in 1993. Voting was limited only to citizens of Latvia on June 17, 1940, and their descendants. This meant that about 34% of Latvian residents were unable to vote. In 1994, Latvia restricted the naturalization of non-Latvians, including many Russian settlers, who were not allowed to vote or own land. However, in 1998, the government agreed that all children born since independence should have automatic citizenship. Its cultivation of closer ties to the West was realized in 2004 when Latvia was admitted to membership of both the North Atlantic Treaty Organization and the European Union.

The World Bank classifies Latvia as a "lower-middle-income" country and, in the 1990s, it faced many problems in turning its economy into a free-market system. Products include electronic goods, farm machinery, fertilizers, processed food, plastics, radios, and vehicles. Latvia produces only about a tenth of the electricity it needs. It imports the rest from Belarus, Russia, and Ukraine.

AREA 24,942 sq mi [64,600 sq km] **POPULATION** 2,290,000
CAPITAL (POPULATION) Riga (793,000)
GOVERNMENT Multiparty republic
ETHNIC GROUPS Latvian 58%, Russian 30%, Belarusian, Ukrainian, Polish, Lithuanian **LANGUAGES** Latvian (official), Lithuanian, Russian **RELIGIONS** Lutheran, Roman Catholic, Russian Orthodox
CURRENCY Latvian lat = 10 santimi

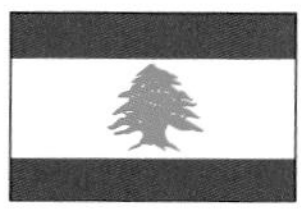

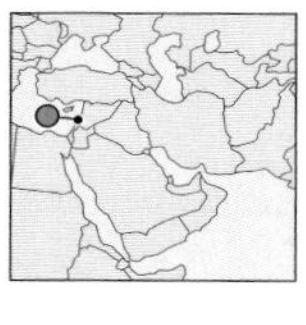

LEBANON

GEOGRAPHY The Republic of Lebanon is a country on the eastern shores of the Mediterranean Sea. Behind the coastal plain are the rugged Lebanon Mountains (Jabal Lubnan), which rise to 10,131 ft [3,088 m]. Another range, the Anti-Lebanon Mountains (Al Jabal Ash Sharqi), form the eastern border with Syria. Between the two ranges is the Bekaa (Beqaa) Valley, a fertile farming region.

The Lebanese coast has the hot, dry summers and mild, wet winters that are typical of many Mediterranean lands. Inland, onshore winds bring heavy rain to the western slopes of the mountains in the winter months, with snow at the higher altitudes.

POLITICS & ECONOMY Lebanon was ruled by Turkey from 1516 until World War I. France ruled the country from 1923, but Lebanon became independent in 1946. After independence, the Muslims and Christians agreed to share power, and Lebanon made rapid economic progress. But from the late 1950s, development was slowed by periodic conflict between Sunni and Shia Muslims, Druze and Christians. The situation was further complicated by the presence of Palestinian refugees who used bases in Lebanon to attack Israel.

In 1975, civil war broke out as private armies representing the many factions struggled for power. This led to intervention by Israel in the south and Syria in the north. UN peacekeeping forces arrived in 1978, but bombings, assassinations, and kidnappings were common in the 1980s. Peace was restored in the 1990s, but the assassination in 2005 of Rafik Hariri, former prime minister, who had helped to rebuild his shattered country, was blamed by many on Syria, which had a military force in Lebanon. Syria withdrew its forces in April 2005.

Lebanon's civil war almost destroyed valuable trade and financial services that had been Lebanon's chief source of income, together with tourism. Manufacturing, formerly a major activity, was badly hit.

AREA 4,015 sq mi [10,400 sq km] **POPULATION** 3,826,000
CAPITAL (POPULATION) Beirut (1,148,000)
GOVERNMENT Multiparty republic **ETHNIC GROUPS** Arab 95%, Armenian 4%, others **LANGUAGES** Arabic (official), French, English, Armenian **RELIGIONS** Islam 70%, Christianity 30%
CURRENCY Lebanese pound = 100 piastres

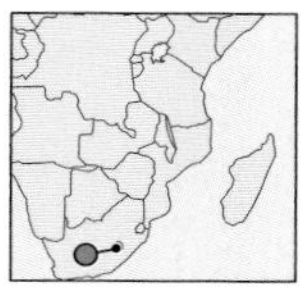

LESOTHO

GEOGRAPHY The Kingdom of Lesotho is a landlocked country, completely enclosed by South Africa. The land is mountainous, rising to 11,424 ft [3,482 m] on the northeastern border. The Drakensberg range covers most of the country.

The climate of Lesotho is greatly affected by the altitude, because most of the country lies above 4,920 ft [1,500 m]. Summers are warm but winters are cold. The rainfall averages about 28 inches [700 mm].

POLITICS & ECONOMY The Basotho nation was founded in the 1820s by King Moshoeshoe I, who united various groups fleeing from tribal wars in southern Africa. Britain made the area a protectorate in 1868 and, in 1871, placed it under the British Cape Colony in South Africa. But in 1884, Basutoland, as the area was called, was reconstituted as a British protectorate, where whites were not allowed to own land.

The country finally became independent in 1966 as the Kingdom of Lesotho, with Moshoeshoe II, great-grandson of Moshoeshoe I, as its king. Since independence, Lesotho has suffered instability. The military seized power in 1986 and stripped Moshoeshoe II of his powers in 1990, installing his son, Letsie III, as monarch. After elections in 1993, Moshoeshoe II was restored to office in 1995. But after his death in a car crash in 1996, Letsie III again became king. In 1998, an army revolt, following an election in which the ruling party won 79 out of the 80 seats, caused much damage to the economy. Lesotho has faced many problems, including drought, while 25% of the people have been infected by the HIV virus. In 2005, the government offered HIV tests to all citizens.

Lesotho lacks natural resources, and the UN has stated that 40% of the people are "ultra-poor." One-third of the people live by farming, mostly at subsistence level. Remittances sent home by Basotho working abroad are important to the economy.

AREA 11,720 sq mi [30,355 sq km] **POPULATION** 1,867,000
CAPITAL (POPULATION) Maseru (109,000)
GOVERNMENT Constitutional monarchy
ETHNIC GROUPS Sotho 99% **LANGUAGES** Sesotho and English (both official) **RELIGIONS** Christianity 80%, traditional beliefs 20%
CURRENCY Loti = 100 lisente

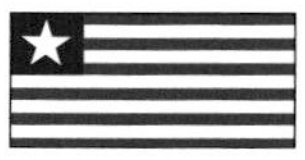

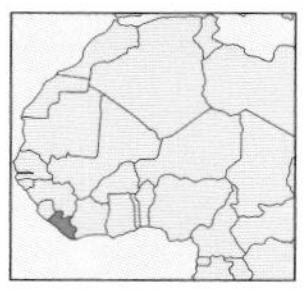

LIBERIA

GEOGRAPHY The Republic of Liberia is a country in West Africa. Behind the coastline, 311 mi [500 km] long, lies a narrow coastal plain. Beyond, the land rises to a plateau region, with the highest land along the border with Guinea. Liberia has a tropical climate with high temperatures and high humidity all through the year. The rainfall is abundant all year round, but there is a particularly wet period from June to November. The rainfall generally increases from east to west.

POLITICS & ECONOMY In the late 18th century, some white Americans in the United States wanted to help freed black slaves to return to Africa. In 1816, they set up the American Colonization Society, which bought land in what is now Liberia.

In 1822, the Society landed former slaves at a settlement on the coast which they named Monrovia. In 1847, Liberia became a fully independent republic with a constitution much like that of the United States. For many years, the Americo-Liberians controlled the country's government. US influence remained strong and the American Firestone Company, which ran Liberia's rubber plantations, was especially influential. Foreign companies were also involved in exploiting Liberia's mineral resources, including its huge iron-ore deposits.

In 1980, a military group composed of people from the local population killed the Americo-Liberian president, William R. Tolbert. An army sergeant, Samuel K. Doe, was made president of Liberia. Elections held in 1985 resulted in victory for Doe. From 1989, the country was plunged into civil war between various ethnic groups. Doe was assassinated in 1990 and the struggle with rebel groups continued. West African peacekeeping forces arrived in Liberia and, in 1995, a ceasefire was agreed. A council of state, composed of former warlords, was set up in 1997 and Charles Taylor became president. Taylor fled the country in 2003 and, in 2006, he was extradited and charged with war crimes. Following elections in 2005, Ellen Sirleaf-Johnson was elected president. She became Africa's first woman president.

Liberia's civil war devastated the economy. Agriculture employs about 67% of the people, though most live at subsistence level. Food crops include cassava, rice, and sugarcane, while rubber, cocoa, and coffee are exported. The most valuable export is iron ore.

Liberia also obtains revenue from its "flag of convenience," which is used by about one-sixth of the world's commercial shipping, exploiting low taxes.

AREA 43,000 sq mi [111,369 sq km] **POPULATION** 3,482,000
CAPITAL (POPULATION) Monrovia (421,000)
GOVERNMENT Multiparty republic **ETHNIC GROUPS** Indigenous African tribes 95% (including Kpelle, Bassa, Grebo, Gio, Kru, Mano)
LANGUAGES English (official), ethnic languages
RELIGIONS Christianity 40%, Islam 20%, traditional beliefs and others 40% **CURRENCY** Liberian dollar = 100 cents

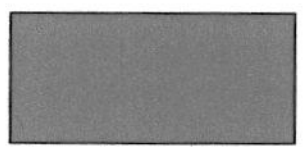

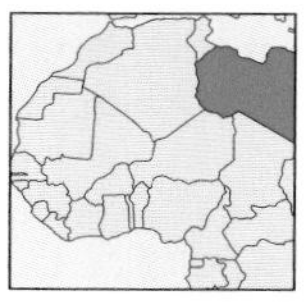

LIBYA

GEOGRAPHY The Socialist People's Libyan Arab Jamahiriya, as Libya is officially called, is a large country in North Africa. Most people live on the coastal plains in the northeast and northwest. The Sahara, the world's largest desert which occupies 95% of Libya, reaches the Mediterranean coast along the Gulf of Sidra (Khalij Surt).

The coastal plains in the northeast and northwest have Mediterranean climates, with hot, dry summers and mild, sometimes wet winters. Inland, the average yearly rainfall drops to 4 inches [100 mm] or less.

POLITICS & ECONOMY Italy took over Libya in 1911, but lost it during World War II. Britain and France jointly ruled Libya until 1951, when the country became an independent kingdom.

In 1969, a military group headed by Colonel Muammar Gaddafi deposed the king and set up a military government. Under Gaddafi, the government took control of the economy and used money from oil exports to finance welfare services and development projects. Gaddafi was criticized for supporting terrorist groups around the world, and Libya became isolated from the mid-1980s. In 1998, he tried to restore Libya's reputation by surrendering for trial two Libyans suspected of planting a bomb on a PanAm plane which exploded over the Scottish town of Lockerbie in 1988. In 2001, one of the Libyans was found guilty and the other acquitted of the bombing. In 2003, Libya announced that it would pay compensation to victims of the bombing. In 2004, relations with the West improved and, in 2006, France and Libya signed an agreement for the peaceful use of nuclear energy. In 2006, the United States restored full diplomatic ties with Libya.

The discovery of oil and natural gas in 1959 led to a transformation of Libya's economy. This formerly poor country soon became Africa's richest in terms of its per capita income. But it remains a developing country, because oil accounts for nearly all its export revenues. Agriculture is important, although Libya imports food. Crops include barley, citrus fruits, dates, olives, potatoes, and wheat, while cattle, sheep, and poultry are raised. Libya has oil refineries and petrochemical plants. Other manufactures include cement and steel.

AREA 679,358 sq mi [1,759,540 sq km] **POPULATION** 5,766,000 **CAPITAL (POPULATION)** Tripoli (1,500,000) **GOVERNMENT** Single-party socialist state **ETHNIC GROUPS** Libyan Arab and Berber 97% **LANGUAGES** Arabic (official), Berber **RELIGIONS** Islam (Sunni Muslim) 97% **CURRENCY** Libyan dinar = 1,000 dirhams

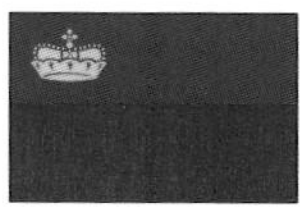

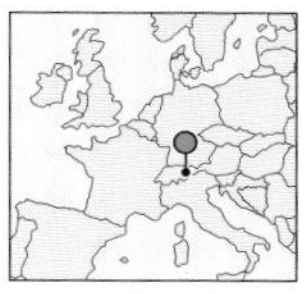

LIECHTENSTEIN

The tiny Principality of Liechtenstein is sandwiched between Switzerland and Austria. The River Rhine flows along its western border, while Alpine peaks rise in the east and south. The climate is relatively mild. Since 1924, Liechtenstein has been in a customs union with Switzerland. Taxation is low and the country is a haven for foreign companies. In 2003, the people voted to give their head of state, Prince Hans Adam II, sovereign powers. However, he later announced his retirement from politics. In 2004, he handed over the running of the country to his son, Prince Alois, although he remained the titular head of state.

AREA 62 sq mi [160 sq km] **POPULATION** 34,000 **CAPITAL** Vaduz

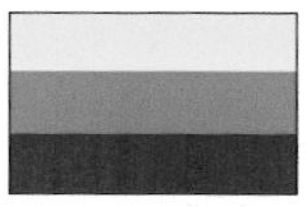

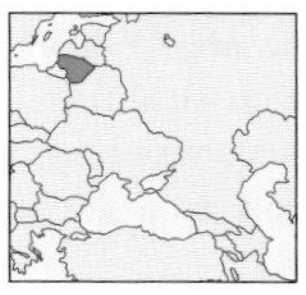

LITHUANIA

GEOGRAPHY The Republic of Lithuania is the southernmost of the three Baltic states which were ruled as part of the Soviet Union between 1940 and 1991. Much of the land is flat or gently rolling, with the highest land in the southeast.

Winters are cold and summers warm. The annual rainfall in the west is about 25 inches [630 mm]. Eastern areas are drier.

POLITICS & ECONOMY The Lithuanian people were united into a single nation in the 12th century, and later joined a union with Poland. In 1795, Lithuania came under Russian rule. After World War I (1914–18), Lithuania declared itself independent, and in 1920 it signed a peace treaty with the Russians, though Poland held Vilnius until 1939. In 1940, the Soviet Union occupied Lithuania, but the Germans invaded in 1941. Soviet forces returned in 1944, and Lithuania was integrated into the Soviet Union. In 1988, when the Soviet Union was introducing reforms, the Lithuanians demanded independence. Their language is one of the oldest in the world, and the country was always the most homogenous of the Baltic states, staunchly Catholic and resistant of attempts to suppress their culture. Pro-independence groups won the national elections in 1990 and, in 1991, the Soviet Union recognized Lithuania's independence.

Since 1991, Lithuania has sought to reform its economy and introduce a private enterprise system. Lithuania has also drawn closer to the West and, in 2004, it became a member of both the North Atlantic Treaty Organization and the European Union.

The World Bank classifies Lithuania as a "lower-middle-income" developing country. Lithuania lacks natural resources, but manufacturing, based on imported materials, is the most valuable activity.

AREA 25,174 sq mi [65,200 sq km] **POPULATION** 3,597,000
CAPITAL (POPULATION) Vilnius (578,000)
GOVERNMENT Multiparty republic
ETHNIC GROUPS Lithuanian 80%, Russian 9%, Polish 7%, Belarusian 2% **LANGUAGES** Lithuanian (official), Russian, Polish
RELIGIONS Mainly Roman Catholic **CURRENCY** Litas = 100 centai

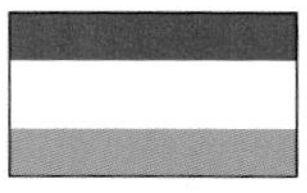

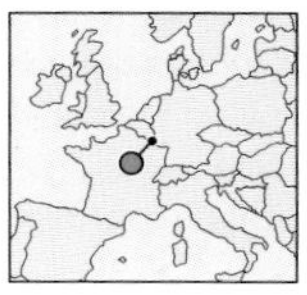

LUXEMBOURG

GEOGRAPHY The Grand Duchy of Luxembourg is one of the smallest and oldest countries in Europe. The north belongs to an upland region which includes the Ardenne in Belgium and Luxembourg, and the Eifel highlands in Germany.

Luxembourg has a temperate climate. The south has warm summers and falls, when grapes ripen in sheltered southeastern valleys. Winters are sometimes severe, especially in upland areas.

POLITICS & ECONOMY Germany occupied Luxembourg in World Wars I and II. In 1944–5, northern Luxembourg was the scene of the famous Battle of the Bulge. In 1948, Luxembourg joined Belgium and the Netherlands in a union called Benelux and, in the 1950s, it was one of the six founders of what is now the European Union. Luxembourg has played a major role in Europe. Its capital contains the headquarters of several international agencies, including the European Coal and Steel Community and the European Court of Justice. The city is also a major financial center.

Luxembourg has iron-ore reserves and is a major steel producer. It also has many high-technology industries, producing electronic goods and computers. Steel and other manufactures, including chemicals, rubber products, glass, and aluminum, dominate the country's exports. Other major activities include tourism and financial services.

AREA 998 sq mi [2,586 sq km] **POPULATION** 469,000
CAPITAL (POPULATION) Luxembourg (77,000)
GOVERNMENT Constitutional monarchy (Grand Duchy)
ETHNIC GROUPS Luxembourger 71%, Portuguese, Italian, French, Belgian, Slavs **LANGUAGES** Luxembourgish (official), French, German **RELIGIONS** Roman Catholic 87%, others 13%
CURRENCY Euro = 100 cents

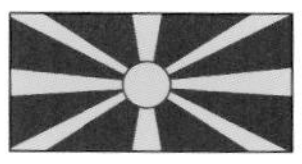

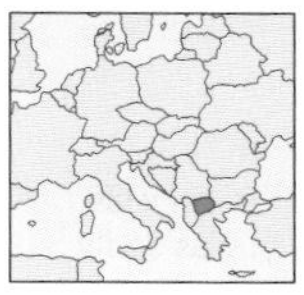

MACEDONIA (FYROM)

GEOGRAPHY The Republic of Macedonia is a country in southeastern Europe, which was once one of the six republics that made up the former Federal People's Republic of Yugoslavia. This landlocked country is largely mountainous or hilly. Macedonia has hot summers, though highland areas are cooler. Winters are cold and snowfalls are often heavy. The climate is fairly continental in character and rain occurs throughout the year.

POLITICS & ECONOMY Until the 20th century, Macedonia's history was closely tied to a larger area, also called Macedonia, which included parts of northern Greece and southwestern Bulgaria. This region reached its peak in power at the time of Philip II (382–336 BC) and his son Alexander the Great (336–323 BC). After Alexander's death, his empire was split up and it gradually declined. The area became a Roman province in the 140s BC and part of the Byzantine Empire from AD 395. In the 6th century, Slavs from eastern Europe settled in the area, followed by the Bulgars from central Asia in the 9th century. The Byzantine Empire regained control in 1018, but Serbia took Macedonia in the early 14th century. In 1371, the Ottoman Turks conquered the area and ruled it for more than 500 years. In 1913, at the end of the Balkan Wars, the area was divided between Serbia, Bulgaria and Greece. At the end of World War I, Serbian Macedonia became part of the Kingdom of the Serbs, Croats, and Slovenes, which was renamed Yugoslavia in 1929. After World War II, Yugoslavia became a Communist country under ex-partisan leader Josip Broz Tito.

Tito died in 1980 and, in the early 1990s, the country broke up into five separate republics. Macedonia declared its independence in September 1991. Greece objected to this territory using the name Macedonia, which it considered to be a Greek name. It also objected to a symbol on Macedonia's flag and a reference in the constitution to the desire to reunite the three parts of the old Macedonia.

Macedonia adopted a new clause in its constitution rejecting any Macedonian claims on Greek territory and, in 1993, the United Nations accepted the new republic as a member under the name of The Former Yugoslav Republic of Macedonia (FYROM). By the end of 1993, all the countries of the EU, except Greece, were establishing diplomatic relations with the FYROM. In 1995, Greece lifted its trade ban, when Macedonia agreed to redesign its flag and remove territorial claims from its constitution. In 2001, fighting along the Kosovo border was attributed to people who wanted to create a Greater Albania. The uprising ended when Macedonia granted its Albanian-speakers increased rights. In 2004, the USA recognized the name Republic of Macedonia instead of FYROM. Despite Greek objections, other nations were expected to follow this lead.

The World Bank describes Macedonia as a "lower-middle-income" economy. Manufactures dominate the country's exports. Coal is mined, but oil and natural gas are imported. The country is self-sufficient in its basic food needs.

AREA 9,928 sq mi [25,713 sq km] **POPULATION** 2,045,000
CAPITAL (POPULATION) Skopje (430,000) **GOVERNMENT** Multiparty republic **ETHNIC GROUPS** Macedonian 64%, Albanian 25%, Turkish 4%, Romanian 3%, Serb 2% **LANGUAGES** Macedonian and Albanian (official) **RELIGIONS** Macedonian Orthodox 70%, Islam 29%
CURRENCY Macedonian denar = 100 paras

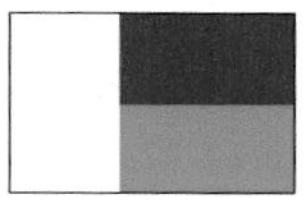

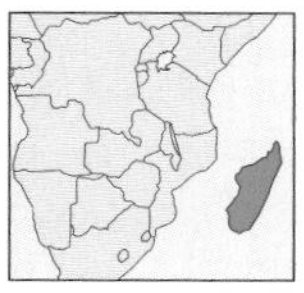

MADAGASCAR

GEOGRAPHY The Democratic Republic of Madagascar, in southeastern Africa, is an island nation, which has a larger area than France. Behind the narrow coastal plains in the east lies a highland zone, mostly between 2,000 ft and 4,000 ft [610 m to 1,220 m] above sea level. Broad plains border the Mozambique Channel in the west.

Temperatures in the highlands are moderated by the altitude. The winters (from April to September) are dry, but heavy rains occur in summer. The eastern coastlands are warm and humid. The west is drier and the south and southwest are hot and dry.

POLITICS & ECONOMY People from Southeast Asia began to settle on Madagascar around 2,000 years ago. Subsequent influxes from Africa and Arabia added to the island's diverse heritage, culture and language.

French troops defeated a Malagasy army in 1895 and Madagascar became a French colony. In 1960, it achieved full independence as the Malagasy Republic. In 1972, army officers seized control and, in 1975, under the leadership of Lieutenant-Commander Didier Ratsiraka, the country was renamed Madagascar. Parliamentary elections were held in 1977, but Ratsiraka remained president of a one-party socialist state. In 2002, the country came close to civil war when Ratsiraka and his opponent, Marc Ravalomanana, both claimed victory in presidential elections. Ravalomanana was finally recognized as president. He has introduced free-market reforms, attracting increased aid and debt cancelation.

Madagascar is a poor country. Poverty and population growth impose pressure on the dwindling forests and the unique wildlife, as well as causing severe soil erosion. Farming, fishing, and forestry employ more than 80% of the people. Food crops include bananas, cassava, rice, and sweet potatoes. Coffee is exported.

AREA 226,657 sq mi [587,041 sq km] **POPULATION** 18,040,000
CAPITAL (POPULATION) Antananarivo (1,250,000)
GOVERNMENT Republic **ETHNIC GROUPS** Merina, Betsimisaraka, Betsileo, Tsimihety, Sakalava, and others
LANGUAGES Malagasy and French (both official)
RELIGIONS Traditional beliefs 52%, Christianity 41%, Islam 7%
CURRENCY Malagasy franc = 100 centimes

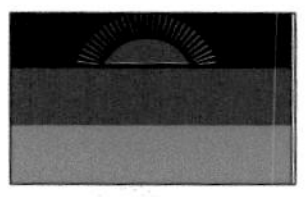

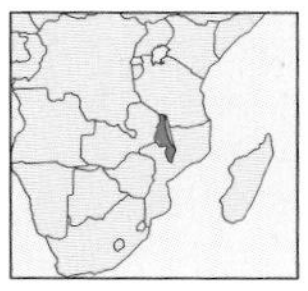

MALAWI

GEOGRAPHY The Republic of Malawi includes part of Lake Malawi, which is drained by the River Shire, a tributary of the River Zambezi. The land is mostly mountainous. The highest peak, Mulanje, reaches 9,843 ft [3,000 m] in the southeast.

While the low-lying areas of Malawi are hot and humid all year round, the uplands have a pleasant climate. Lilongwe, at about 3,609 ft [1,100 m] above sea level, has a warm and sunny climate. Frosts sometimes occur in July and August, in the middle of the long dry season.

POLITICS & ECONOMY Malawi, then called Nyasaland, became a British protectorate in 1891. In 1953, Britain established the Federation of Rhodesia and Nyasaland, which also included what are now Zambia and Zimbabwe. Black African opposition, led in Nyasaland by Dr Hastings Kamuzu Banda, led to the dissolution of the federation in 1963. In 1964, Nyasaland became independent as Malawi, with Banda as prime minister. Banda became president when the country became a republic in 1966 and, in 1971, he was made president for life. Banda was an autocrat, ruling through the only party, the Malawi Congress Party. But a multiparty system was restored in 1993. Bakili Muluzi became president and, in 2004, he was succeeded by Bingu wa Mutharika, leader of the United Democratic Front (UDF). In 2005, he resigned from the UDF and set up a new Democratic Progressive Party.

Malawi is one of the world's poorest countries. More than 80% of the people are farmers, but many grow little more than they need to feed their families.

AREA 45,747 sq mi [118,484 sq km] **POPULATION** 12,159,000
CAPITAL (POPULATION) Lilongwe (440,000)
GOVERNMENT Multiparty republic
ETHNIC GROUPS Chewa, Nyanja, Tonga, Tumbuka, Lomwe, Yao, Ngoni, and others
LANGUAGES Chichewa and English (both official)
RELIGIONS Protestant 55%, Roman Catholic 20%, Islam 20%
CURRENCY Malawian kwacha = 100 tambala

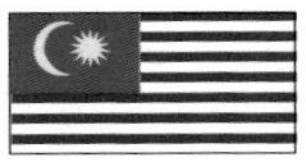

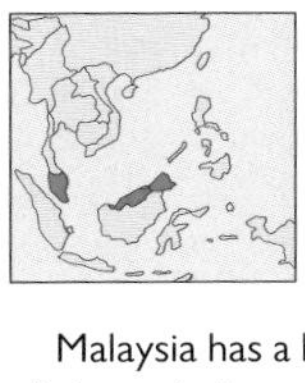

MALAYSIA

GEOGRAPHY The Federation of Malaysia consists of two main parts. Peninsular Malaysia, which is joined to mainland Asia, contains about 80% of the population. The other main regions, Sabah and Sarawak, are in northern Borneo, an island which Malaysia shares with Indonesia. Behind the coastal lowlands, the interior is mountainous.

Malaysia has a hot equatorial climate. The temperatures are high all through the year, though the mountains are much cooler than the lowland areas. The rainfall is heavy throughout the year.

POLITICS & ECONOMY Around 1,200 years ago, Indian traders introduced Hinduism and Buddhism into the Malay peninsula, while Arabs introduced Islam in the 15th century. Portuguese traders reached Melaka in 1509, but the Dutch took over in 1641. Britain became established in the area in 1786.

Japan occupied the area during World War II (1939–45), but the area reverted to British rule in 1945. In the 1940s and 1950s, Communist guerrillas battled unsuccessfully for power. Malaya (Peninsular Malaysia) became independent in 1957. Malaysia was created in 1963, when Malaya, Singapore, Sabah, and Sarawak agreed to unite, but Singapore withdrew in 1965.

From 1981, under the leadership of Dr Mahathir bin Mohamad, Malaysia achieved rapid economic progress. However, together with other countries in eastern Asia, it experienced an economic recession in 1997. In response to the crisis, the government ordered the repatriation of many foreign workers and initiated measures aimed at restoring confidence and avoiding the chronic debt problems affecting some other Asian countries. Mahathir bin Mohamad retired in 2003. Abdullah Ahmad Badawi, who became prime minister, won a landslide election victory in 2004.

The World Bank classifies Malaysia as an "upper-middle-income" developing country. Palm oil, rubber, and tin are major products. Manufactures include cars, chemicals, a wide range of electronic goods, plastics, textiles, rubber, and wood products.

AREA 127,320 sq mi [329,758 sq km] **POPULATION** 23,953,000 **CAPITAL (POPULATION)** Kuala Lumpur (1,145,000); Putrajaya (administrative capital awaiting completion) **GOVERNMENT** Federal constitutional monarchy **ETHNIC GROUPS** Malay and other indigenous groups 58%, Chinese 24%, Indian 8%, others **LANGUAGES** Malay (official), Chinese, English **RELIGIONS** Islam, Buddhism, Daoism, Hinduism, Christianity, Sikhism **CURRENCY** Ringgit = 100 cents

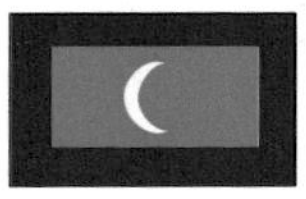

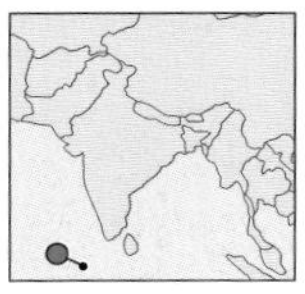

MALDIVES

The Republic of the Maldives consists of about 1,200 low-lying coral islands, south of India. The highest point is 79 ft [24 m], but most of the land is only 6 ft [1.8 m] above sea level. The islands became a British territory in 1887 and independence was achieved in 1965. Tourism and fishing are the main industries.

AREA 115 sq mi [298 sq km] **POPULATION** 349,000 **CAPITAL** Malé

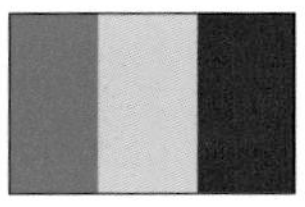

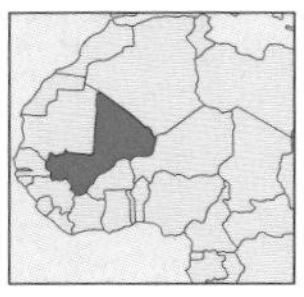

MALI

GEOGRAPHY The Republic of Mali is a landlocked country in northern Africa. The land is generally flat, with the highest land in the north. Northern Mali is hot and practically rainless. The south has enough rain for farming.

POLITICS & ECONOMY Between the 4th and 16th centuries, Mali was part of three African empires – ancient Ghana, ancient Mali, and Songhay. However, after 1591, when Songhay was defeated by Morocco, the area was divided into small kingdoms. France ruled the area, then known as French Sudan, from 1893 until the country became independent as Mali in 1960.

The first socialist government was overthrown in 1968 by an army group led by Moussa Traoré, but he was ousted in 1991. Multiparty democracy was restored in 1992 and Alpha Oumar Konaré was elected president. Konaré stood down in 2002 and Ahmadou Toure, who had restored democracy in 1992, was elected president.

Mali is one of the world's poorest countries and 70% of the land is desert or semidesert. Only about 2% of the land is used for growing crops, while 25% is used for grazing animals. Despite this, agriculture employs nearly 80% of the people, many of whom subsist by nomadic livestock rearing.

AREA 478,838 sq mi [1,240,192 sq km] **POPULATION** 12,292,000 **CAPITAL (POPULATION)** Bamako (1,016,000) **GOVERNMENT** Multiparty republic **ETHNIC GROUPS** Mande 50% (Bambara, Malinke, Soninke), Peul 17%, Voltaic 12%, Songhai 6%, Tuareg and Moor 10%, others **LANGUAGES** French (official), many African languages **RELIGIONS** Islam 90%, traditional beliefs 9%, Christianity 1% **CURRENCY** CFA franc = 100 centimes

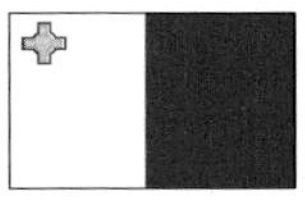

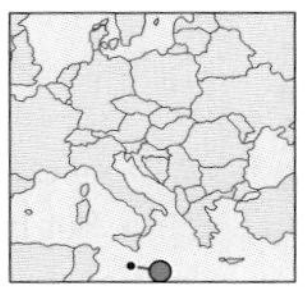

MALTA

GEOGRAPHY The Republic of Malta consists of two main islands, Malta and Gozo, a third, much smaller island called Comino lying between the two large islands and two islets. The climate is typically Mediterranean, with hot, dry summers and mild, moist winters.

POLITICS & ECONOMY Malta has fascinating Stone and Bronze age remains. The islands later came under Phoenician, Greek, Carthaginian, Roman, and Arab rule. In about 1090, Malta came under the Norman kings of Sicily and, from 1530, the Knights Hospitallers (also called the Knights of St John of Jerusalem). France took the islands in 1798, but the British drove them out in 1800. British rule was officially recognized in 1815.

During World War I (1914–18), Malta was an important naval base. In World War II (1939–45), Italian and German aircraft bombed the islands. In recognition of the islanders' bravery, the British King George VI awarded the George Cross to Malta in 1942. In 1953, Malta became a base for NATO (North Atlantic Treaty Organization). Malta became independent in 1964 and a republic in 1974. In 1979, Malta ceased to be a British military base and all British forces withdrew. Malta was declared a neutral country in the 1980s. It became a member of the European Union on May 1, 2004.

The World Bank classifies Malta as an "upper-middle-income" developing country. It lacks natural resources, and most people work in the former naval dockyards, which are now used for commercial shipbuilding and repair, in manufacturing industries, and in the tourist industry.

Manufactures include chemicals, processed food, and chemicals. Farming is difficult, because of the rocky soils. Crops include barley, fruits, potatoes, and wheat. Malta also has a small fishing industry.

AREA 122 sq mi [316 sq km] **POPULATION** 399,000 **CAPITAL (POPULATION)** Valletta (9,000) **GOVERNMENT** Multiparty republic **ETHNIC GROUPS** Maltese 96%, British 2% **LANGUAGES** Maltese and English (both official) **RELIGIONS** Roman Catholic 98% **CURRENCY** Maltese lira = 100 cents

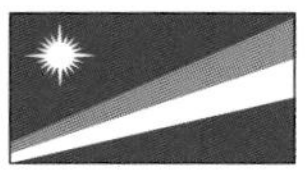

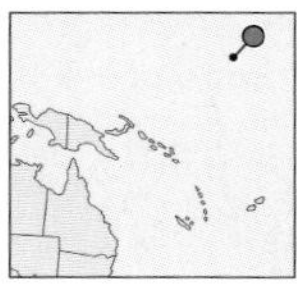

MARSHALL ISLANDS

The Republic of the Marshall Islands, a former US territory, became fully independent in 1991. This island nation, lying north of Kiribati in a region known as Micronesia, is heavily dependent on US aid. The main activities are agriculture and tourism.

AREA 70 sq mi [181 sq km] **POPULATION** 59,000 **CAPITAL** Majuro

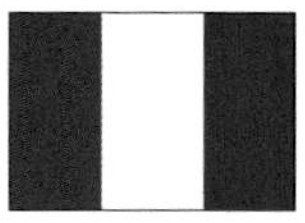

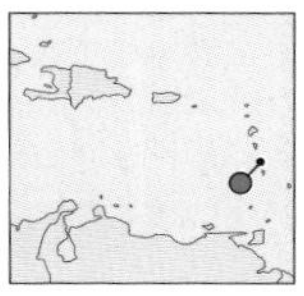

MARTINIQUE

Martinique, a volcanic island nation in the Caribbean, was colonized by France in 1635. It became a French overseas department in 1946. Tourism and agriculture are major activities. About 70% of Martinique's gross domestic product is provided by the French government, allowing for a good standard of living.

AREA 425 sq mi [1,102 sq km] **POPULATION** 433,000 **CAPITAL** Fort-de-France

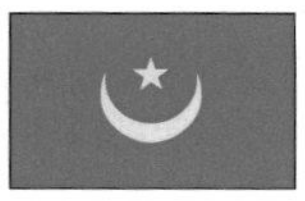

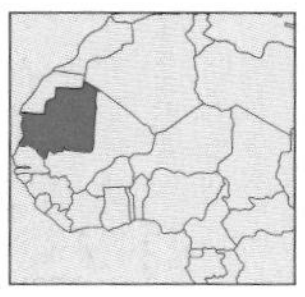

MAURITANIA

GEOGRAPHY The Islamic Republic of Mauritania in northwestern Africa is nearly twice the size of France. But France has more than 28 times as many people. Part of the world's largest desert, the Sahara, covers northern Mauritania and most Mauritanians live in the southwest. The amount of rainfall and the length of the rainy season increase from north to south. Much of the land is desert, but southwesterly winds bring summer rain to the south.

POLITICS & ECONOMY Originally part of the great African empires of Ghana and Mali, France set up a protectorate in Mauritania in 1903, attempting to exploit the trade in gum arabic. The country became a territory of French West Africa and a French colony in 1920. French West Africa was a huge territory, which included present-day Benin, Burkina Faso, Guinea, Ivory Coast, Mali, Niger, and Senegal, as well as Mauritania. In 1958, Mauritania became a self-governing territory in the French Union and it became fully independent in 1960.

In 1976, Spain withdrew from Spanish (now Western) Sahara, a territory bordering Mauritania to the north. Morocco occupied the northern two-thirds of this territory, while Mauritania took the rest. But Saharan guerrillas belonging to POLISARIO (the Popular Front for the Liberation of Saharan Territories) began an armed struggle for independence. In 1979, Mauritania withdrew from the southern part of Western Sahara, which was then occupied by Morocco. Democracy was restored after a new constitution was adopted in 1991. However, in 2005, a military group overthrew the elected government headed by President Maaouiya Ould Sid'Ahmed Taya.

Mauritania is a "low-income" developing country. Nearly half of the people are engaged in agriculture. In 2006, Mauritania became Africa's newest oil producer, when an offshore platform came online for the first time.

AREA 395,953 sq mi [1,025,520 sq km] **POPULATION** 3,087,000 **CAPITAL (POPULATION)** Nouakchott (735,000) **GOVERNMENT** Multiparty Islamic republic **ETHNIC GROUPS** Mixed Moor/Black 40%, Moor 30%, Black 30% **LANGUAGES** Arabic and Wolof (both official), French **RELIGIONS** Islam **CURRENCY** Ouguiya = 5 khoums

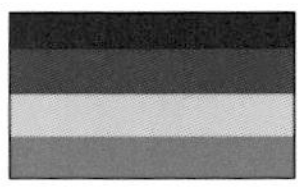

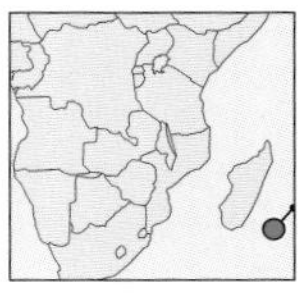

MAURITIUS

The Republic of Mauritius, an Indian Ocean nation lying east of Madagascar, was previously ruled by France and Britain until it achieved independence in 1968. It became a republic in 1992. Sugar production is in decline but tourism is vital to the economy.

AREA 788 sq mi [2,040 sq km] **POPULATION** 1,231,000 **CAPITAL** Port Louis

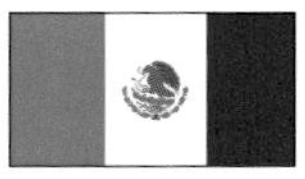

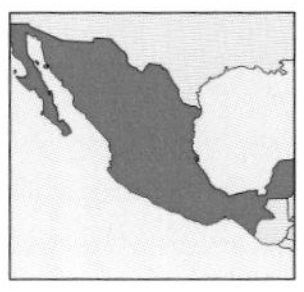

MEXICO

GEOGRAPHY The United Mexican States, as Mexico is officially named, is the world's most populous Spanish-speaking country. Much of the land is mountainous, although most people live on the central plateau. Mexico contains two large peninsulas, Lower (or Baja) California in the northwest and the flat Yucatán peninsula in the southeast.

The climate varies according to the altitude. The resort of Acapulco on the southwest coast has a dry and sunny climate. Mexico City, at about 7,546 ft [2,300 m] above sea level, is much cooler. Most rain occurs between June and September. The rainfall decreases north of Mexico City and northern Mexico is mainly arid.

POLITICS & ECONOMY In the mid-19th century, Mexico lost land to the United States, and between 1910 and 1921 violent revolutions created chaos.

Reforms were introduced in the 1920s and, in 1929, the Institutional Revolutionary Party (PRI) was formed. The PRI ruled Mexico effectively as a one-party state until it was finally defeated in 2001. The new president, Vicente Fox, faced many problems, including unemployment and rapid urbanization especially around Mexico City, demands for indigenous rights by Amerindian groups, and illegal emigration to the United States.

The World Bank classifies Mexico as an "upper-middle-income" developing country. Agriculture is important. Food crops include beans, maize, rice, and wheat, while cash crops include coffee, cotton, fruits, and vegetables. Beef cattle, dairy cattle, and other livestock are raised and fishing is also important.

But oil and oil products are the chief exports, while manufacturing is the most valuable activity. Mexico is the world's leading silver producer, and it also mines copper, gold, lead, zinc, and other minerals. Many factories near the northern border assemble goods, such as car parts and electrical products, for US companies. These factories are called *maquiladoras*. Hope for the future lies in increasing economic cooperation with the USA and Canada

through NAFTA (North American Free Trade Agreement), which came into being on January 1, 1994.

AREA 756,061 sq mi [1,958,201 sq km] **POPULATION** 106,203,000
CAPITAL (POPULATION) Mexico City (8,236,000)
GOVERNMENT Federal republic
ETHNIC GROUPS Mestizo 60%, Amerindian 30%, White 9%
LANGUAGES Spanish (official)
RELIGIONS Roman Catholic 90%, Protestant 6%
CURRENCY Mexican peso = 100 centavos

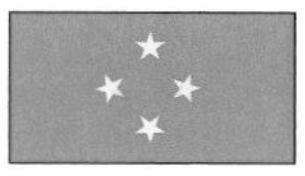
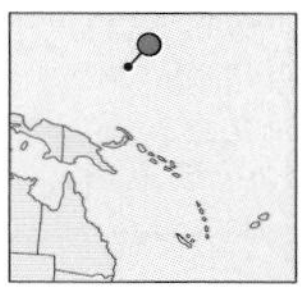

MICRONESIA

The Federated States of Micronesia, a former US territory covering a vast area in the western Pacific Ocean, became fully independent in 1991. The main export is copra. Fishing and tourism are also important.

AREA 271 sq mi [702 sq km]
POPULATION 108,000 **CAPITAL** Palikir

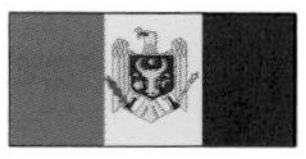
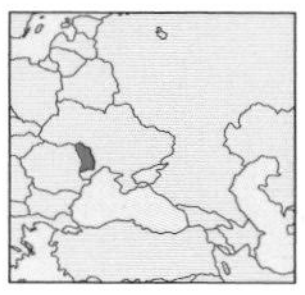

MOLDOVA

GEOGRAPHY The Republic of Moldova is a small country sandwiched between Ukraine and Romania. It was formerly one of the 15 republics that made up the Soviet Union. Much of the land is hilly and the highest areas are near the center of the country.

Moldova has a moderately continental climate, with warm summers and fairly cold winters when temperatures dip below freezing point. Most of the rain comes in the warmer months.

POLITICS & ECONOMY In the 14th century, the Moldavians formed a state called Moldavia. It included part of Romania and Bessarabia (now the modern country of Moldova). The Ottoman Turks took the area in the 16th century, but in 1812 Russia took over Bessarabia. In 1861, Moldavia and Walachia united to form Romania. Russia retook southern Bessarabia in 1878.

After World War I (1914–18), all of Bessarabia was returned to Romania, but the Soviet Union did not recognize this act. From 1944, the Moldovan Soviet Socialist Republic was part of the Soviet Union.

In 1989, the Moldovans asserted their independence and ethnicity by making Romanian the official language and, at the end of 1991, Moldova became an independent country. In 1992, fighting occurred between Moldovans and Russians in Trans-Dniester, a mainly Russian-speaking area east of the River Dniester. The first multiparty elections were held in 1994, but economic problems made the government unpopular. In 2001, Moldova became the first former Soviet republic to return the Communist Party to power in a general election. The Communist Party was re-elected in 2005, though it then advocated closer ties with the West, a matter of some concern to Russia.

In terms of its GNP per capita, Moldova is Europe's poorest country. Agriculture is the leading activity and products include fruits, maize, tobacco, and wine. Moldova has few natural resources and it imports materials and fuels for its industries. Light industries, such as food processing and factories making household appliances, are increasing.

AREA 13,070 sq mi [33,851 sq km] **POPULATION** 4,455,000
CAPITAL (POPULATION) Chişinău (658,000)
GOVERNMENT Multiparty republic
ETHNIC GROUPS Moldovan/Romanian 65%, Ukrainian 14%, Russian 13%, others
LANGUAGES Moldovan/Romanian and Russian (official)
RELIGIONS Eastern Orthodox 98%
CURRENCY Moldovan leu = 100 bani

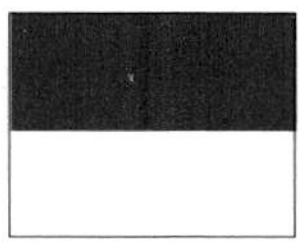
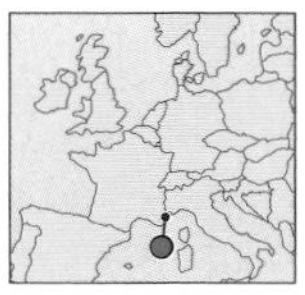

MONACO

The tiny Principality of Monaco consists of a narrow strip of coastline and a rocky peninsula on the French Riviera. Its considerable wealth is derived largely from banking, finance, gambling, and tourism. Monaco's citizens do not pay any state tax. The reigning prince is Albert II, son of Prince Rainier III, who died in 2005, and his wife, the American actress Grace Kelly.

AREA 0.4 sq mi [1 sq km] **POPULATION** 32,000 **CAPITAL** Monaco

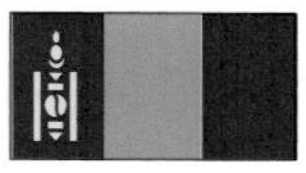
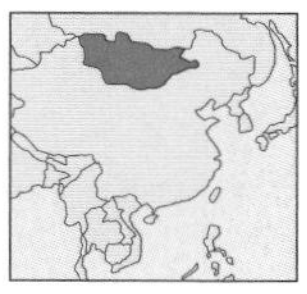

MONGOLIA

GEOGRAPHY The State of Mongolia is the world's largest landlocked country. It consists mainly of high plateaux, with the Gobi Desert in the southeast.

Ulan Bator lies on the northern edge of a desert plateau. It has bitterly cold winters. Summer temperatures are moderated by the altitude.

POLITICS & ECONOMY In the 13th century, Genghis Khan united the Mongolian peoples and built up a great empire. Under his grandson, Kublai Khan, the Mongol empire extended from Korea and China to eastern Europe and present-day Iraq.

The Mongol empire broke up in the late 14th century. In the early 17th century, Inner Mongolia came under Chinese control, and by the late 17th century Outer Mongolia had become a Chinese province. In 1911, the Mongolians drove the Chinese out of Outer Mongolia and made the area a Buddhist kingdom. But in 1924, under Russian influence, the Communist Mongolian People's Republic was set up. From the 1950s, Mongolia supported the Soviet Union in its disputes with China. In 1990, the people demonstrated for more freedom, and free elections in June 1990 were won by the Communist Mongolian People's Revolutionary Party (MPRP). The Democratic Union coalition won power in 1996, but the MPRP regained power in 2000. In 2004, after disputed elections, a coalition government was set up. In 2005, the MPRP candidate, Nambaryn Enkhbayar, became president.

The World Bank classifies Mongolia as a "lower-middle-income" developing country. Most people were once nomads, who moved around with their herds of sheep, cattle, goats, and horses. Under Communist rule, most people were moved into permanent homes on government-owned farms. But livestock and animal products remain leading exports. The Communists also developed industry, especially the mining of coal, copper, gold, molybdenum, tin, and tungsten, and manufacturing. Minerals and fuels now account for around half of Mongolia's exports.

AREA 604,826 sq mi [1,566,500 sq km] **POPULATION** 2,791,000
CAPITAL (POPULATION) Ulan Bator (760,000)
GOVERNMENT Multiparty republic **ETHNIC GROUPS** Khalkha Mongol 85%, Kazakh 6% **LANGUAGES** Khalkha Mongolian (official), Turkic, Russian **RELIGIONS** Tibetan Buddhist Lamaism 96%
CURRENCY Tugrik = 100 möngös

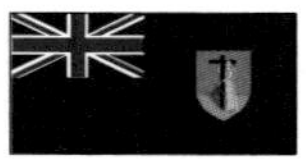
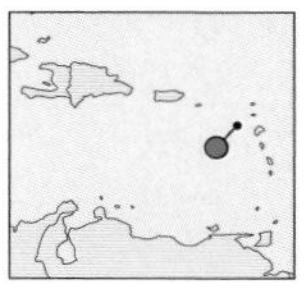

MONTSERRAT

Monserrat is a British overseas territory in the Caribbean Sea. The climate is tropical and hurricanes often cause much damage. Intermittent eruptions of the Soufrière Hills volcano between 1995 and 1998, and again in 2003, led to the emigration of many people and the virtual destruction of Plymouth, the capital. A new airport was opened in 2005.

AREA 39 sq mi [102 sq km] **CAPITAL** Plymouth

MONTENEGRO – SEE SERBIA AND MONTENEGRO

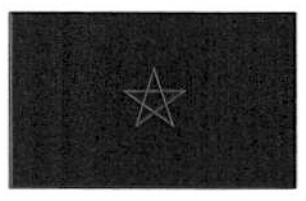
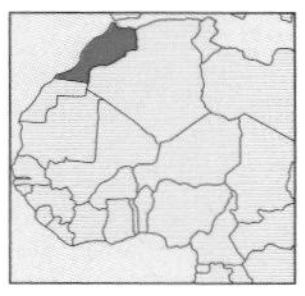

MOROCCO

GEOGRAPHY The Kingdom of Morocco lies in northwestern Africa. Its name comes from the Arabic Maghreb-el-Aksa, meaning "the farthest west." Behind the western coastal plain the land rises to a broad plateau and ranges of the Atlas Mountains. The High (Haut) Atlas contains the highest peak, Djebel Toubkal, at 13,665 ft [4,165 m]. East of the mountains, the land descends to the Sahara. The Canaries Current cools the Atlantic coast. Inland, summers are hot and dry. Winters are mild, with moderate rainfall. Snow often falls on the High Atlas Mountains.

POLITICS & ECONOMY The original people of Morocco were the Berbers. But in the 680s, Arab invaders introduced Islam and the Arabic language. By the early 20th century, France and Spain controlled Morocco, which became an independent kingdom in 1956. Although Morocco is a constitutional monarchy, King Hassan II ruled the country in a generally authoritarian way from the time of his accession to the throne in 1961 to his death in 1999. His successor, Mohamed VI, faced several problems, including that of Western Sahara, which he claimed for Morocco, and the activities of Islamic extremists. In 2004, Morocco's opposition to extremism led the USA to designate it a major non-NATO ally.

Morocco is classified as a "lower-middle-income" developing country. It is the world's third largest producer of phosphate rock, which is used to make fertilizer. One of the reasons why Morocco wants to keep Western Sahara is that it, too, has large phosphate reserves. Farming employs 17% of Moroccans. Chief crops include barley, beans, citrus fruits, maize, olives, sugar beet, and wheat. Processed phosphates are exported, but most of Morocco's manufactures are for home consumption. Fishing and tourism are also important.

AREA 172,413 sq mi [446,550 sq km] **POPULATION** 32,726,000
CAPITAL (POPULATION) Rabat (1,220,000)
GOVERNMENT Constitutional monarchy
ETHNIC GROUPS Arab-Berber 99%
LANGUAGES Arabic (official), Berber dialects, French
RELIGIONS Islam 99% **CURRENCY** Moroccan dirham = 100 centimes

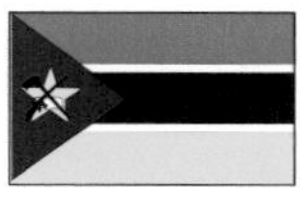
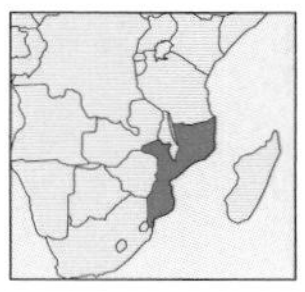

MOZAMBIQUE

GEOGRAPHY The Republic of Mozambique borders the Indian Ocean in southeastern Africa. The coastal plains are narrow in the north but broaden in the south. Inland lie plateaux and hills, which make up another two-fifths of Mozambique.

Mozambique has a mostly tropical climate. The capital Maputo, which lies outside the tropics, has hot and humid summers, though the winters are mild and fairly dry.

POLITICS & ECONOMY In 1885, when the European powers divided Africa, Mozambique was recognized as a Portuguese colony. But black African opposition to European rule gradually increased. In 1961, the Front for the Liberation of Mozambique (FRELIMO) was founded to oppose Portuguese rule. In 1964, FRELIMO launched a guerrilla war, which continued for ten years. Mozambique became independent in 1975.

After independence, Mozambique became a one-party state. Its government aided African nationalists in Rhodesia (now Zimbabwe) and South Africa. But the white governments of these countries helped an opposition group, the Mozambique National Resistance Movement (RENAMO) to lead an armed struggle against Mozambique's government. Civil war, combined with droughts, caused much suffering in the 1980s. In 1989, FRELIMO declared that it had dropped its Communist policies and ended one-party rule. The war ended in 1992 and multiparty elections in 1994 heralded more stable conditions. In 1995 Mozambique became the 53rd member of the Commonwealth.

In the early 1990s, the UN rated Mozambique as one of the world's poorest countries. The second half of the 1990s saw the start of renewed economic growth, but floods in 2000–1 and prolonged droughts in the mid-2000s proved to be major setbacks. About 80% of the people are poor farmers. Crops include cassava, cotton, maize, rice, and tea.

AREA 309,494 sq mi [801,590 sq km] **POPULATION** 19,407,000
CAPITAL (POPULATION) Maputo (1,015,000)
GOVERNMENT Multiparty republic **ETHNIC GROUPS** Indigenous tribal groups (Shangaan, Chokwe, Manyika, Sena, Makua, others) 99%
LANGUAGES Portuguese (official), many others
RELIGIONS Traditional beliefs 50%, Christianity 30%, Islam 20%
CURRENCY Metical = 100 centavos

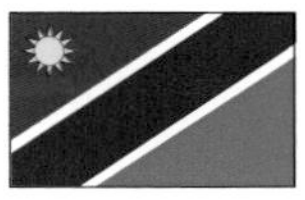
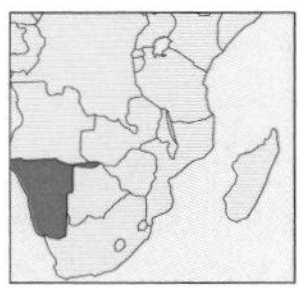

NAMIBIA

GEOGRAPHY The Republic of Namibia was formerly ruled by South Africa, which called it South West Africa. The country became independent in 1990. The coastal region contains the arid Namib Desert, which is virtually uninhabited. Inland is a central plateau, bordered by a rugged spine of mountains stretching north–south. Eastern Namibia contains part of the Kalahari Desert, a semidesert area which extends into Botswana. Namibia is a warm and arid country. Lying at 5,500 ft [1,700 m] above sea level, Windhoek has an average annual rainfall of about 15 inches [370 mm], often occurring during thunderstorms in the hot summer months.

POLITICS & ECONOMY During World War I, South African troops defeated the Germans who ruled what is now Namibia. After World War II, many people challenged South Africa's right to govern the territory and a civil war began in the 1960s between African guerrillas and South African troops. A ceasefire was agreed in 1989 and Namibia became independent in 1990. In the 1990s, the government pursued a policy of "national reconciliation." An enclave on the coast, called Walvis Bay (Walvisbaai), remained part of South Africa until 1994, when it was transferred to Namibia. In 2004, the nationalist leader,

Sam Nujoma, president since 1990, retired and was succeeded by Hifikepunye Pohama. In 2005, as part of a policy of land reform, the government began to expropriate white-owned farms.

Namibia has reserves of diamonds, uranium, zinc, and copper. Minerals make up 80% of the exports, though agriculture employs about 20% of the people. Sea fishing is important, but overfishing has reduced the yields of the fishing fleet. The country has few industries, but tourism is expanding.

AREA 318,259 sq mi [824,292 sq km] **POPULATION** 2,031,000
CAPITAL (POPULATION) Windhoek (147,000)
GOVERNMENT Multiparty republic **ETHNIC GROUPS** Ovambo 50%, Kavango 9%, Herero 7%, Damara 7%, White 6%, Nama 5%
LANGUAGES English (official), Afrikaans, German, indigenous dialects **RELIGIONS** Christianity 90% (Lutheran 51%)
CURRENCY Namibian dollar = 100 cents

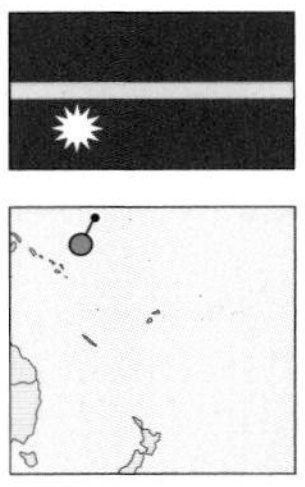

NAURU

Nauru is the world's smallest republic, located in the western Pacific Ocean, close to the equator. Independent since 1968, Nauru's prosperity is based on phosphate mining, but the reserves are running out.

AREA 8 sq mi [21 sq km]
POPULATION 13,000 **CAPITAL** Yaren

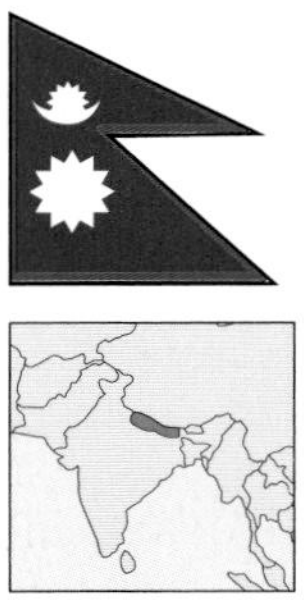

NEPAL

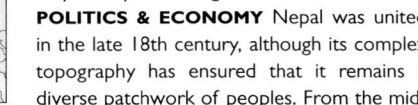

GEOGRAPHY Over three-quarters of Nepal lies in the Himalayan region, culminating in the world's highest peak (Mount Everest, or Chomolongma in Nepali) at 29,035 ft [8,850 m]. As a result, climatic conditions vary widely according to the altitude.

POLITICS & ECONOMY Nepal was united in the late 18th century, although its complex topography has ensured that it remains a diverse patchwork of peoples. From the mid-19th century to 1951, power was held by the royal Rana family. Attempts to introduce a democratic system in the 1950s failed. The first democratic elections in 32 years were held in 1991, but, by the early 21st century, Nepal faced many problems, including an uprising of Maoist guerrillas. In 2005, King Gyanendra seized power and sacked the government. But he failed to stop the fighting and, in 2006, he was forced to hand power back to the parliament, which declared that it would curtail the king's powers.

Agriculture remains the chief activity in this overwhelmingly rural country and the government is heavily dependent on aid. Tourism, centered around the high Himalaya, grows in importance each year, although Nepal was closed to foreigners until 1951. There are also ambitious plans to exploit the hydroelectric potential offered by the ferocious Himalayan rivers.

AREA 56,827 sq mi [147,181 sq km] **POPULATION** 27,677,000
CAPITAL (POPULATION) Katmandu (695,000)
GOVERNMENT Constitutional monarchy **ETHNIC GROUPS** Brahman, Chetri, Newar, Gurung, Magar, Tamang, Sherpa, and others
LANGUAGES Nepali (official), local languages
RELIGIONS Hinduism 86%, Buddhism 8%, Islam 4%
CURRENCY Nepalese rupee = 100 paisa

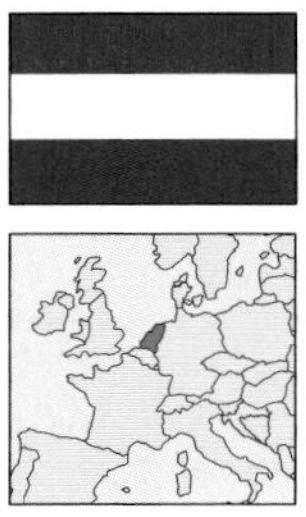

NETHERLANDS

GEOGRAPHY The Netherlands lies at the western end of the North European Plain, which extends to the Ural Mountains in Russia. Except for the far southeastern corner, the Netherlands is flat and about 40% lies below sea level at high tide. To prevent flooding, the Dutch have built dykes (sea walls) to hold back the waves. Large areas which were once under the sea, but which have been reclaimed, are called polders. Because of its position on the North Sea, the Netherlands has a temperate climate, with mild, rainy winters.

POLITICS & ECONOMY Before the 16th century, the area that is now the Netherlands was under a succession of foreign rulers, including the Romans, the Germanic Franks, the French, and the Spanish. The Dutch declared their independence from Spain in 1581 and their status was finally recognized by Spain in 1648. In the 17th century, the Dutch built up a great overseas empire, especially in Southeast Asia. But in the early 18th century, the Dutch lost control of the seas to England.

France controlled the Netherlands from 1795 to 1813. In 1815, the Netherlands, then containing Belgium and Luxembourg, became an independent kingdom. Belgium broke away in 1830 and Luxembourg followed in 1890.

The Netherlands was neutral in World War I (1914–18), but was occupied by Germany in World War II (1939–45). After the war, the Netherlands Indies became independent as Indonesia. The Netherlands became active in West European affairs. With Belgium and Luxembourg, it formed a customs union called Benelux in 1948. In 1949, it joined NATO (the North Atlantic Treaty Organization), and the European Coal and Steel Community (ECSC) in 1953. In 1957, it became a founder member of the European Economic Community (now the European Union) and, in 2002, it adopted the euro as its sole unit of currency. In 2002, an anti-immigration group made sweeping gains in national elections. It joined a coalition government, which collapsed later that year. Following elections in 2003, a center-right coalition took office.

The Netherlands is a highly industrialized country and industry and commerce are the most valuable activities. Its resources include natural gas, some oil, salt, and china clay. But the Netherlands imports many of the materials needed by its industries and it is, therefore, a major trading country. Industrial products are wide-ranging, including aircraft, chemicals, electronic equipment, machinery, textiles, and vehicles. Agriculture employs only 5% of the people, but scientific methods are used and yields are high. Dairy farming is the leading farming activity. Major products include barley, flowers and bulbs, potatoes, sugar beet, and wheat.

AREA 16,033 sq mi [41,526 sq km] **POPULATION** 16,407,000
CAPITAL (POPULATION) Amsterdam (729,000); The Hague (seat of government, 440,000)
GOVERNMENT Constitutional monarchy
ETHNIC GROUPS Dutch 83%, Indonesian, Turkish, Moroccan, and others **LANGUAGES** Dutch (official), Frisian
RELIGIONS Roman Catholic 31%, Protestant 21%, Islam 4%, others
CURRENCY Euro = 100 cents

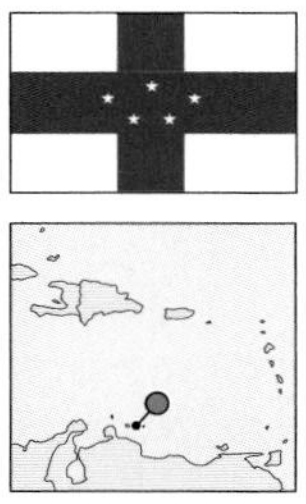

NETHERLANDS ANTILLES

The Netherlands Antilles consists of two different island groups; one off the coast of Venezuela, and the other at the northern end of the Leeward Islands, some 500 mi [800 km] away. They remain a self-governing Dutch territory. The island of Aruba was once part of the territory, but it broke away in 1986. Oil refining and tourism are important activities.

AREA 309 sq mi [800 sq km] **POPULATION** 220,000 **CAPITAL** Willemstad

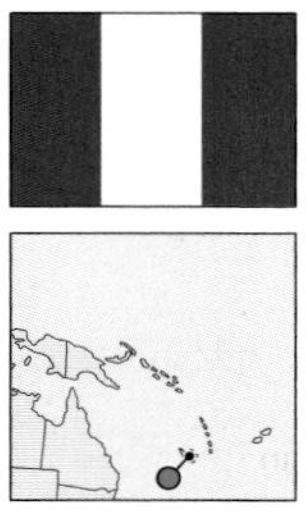

NEW CALEDONIA

New Caledonia is the most southerly of the Melanesian countries in the Pacific. A French possession since 1853 and an Overseas Territory since 1958. In 1998, France announced an agreement with local Melanesians that a vote on independence would be postponed until 2014. The country is rich in mineral resources, especially nickel.

AREA 7,172 sq mi [18,575 sq km] **POPULATION** 216,000 **CAPITAL** Nouméa

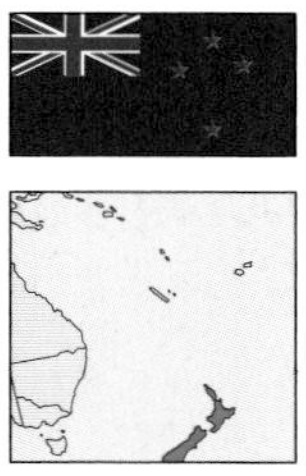

NEW ZEALAND

GEOGRAPHY New Zealand lies about 994 mi [1,600 km] southeast of Australia. It consists of two main islands and several other small ones. Much of North Island is volcanic. Active volcanoes include Ngauruhoe and Ruapehu. Hot springs and geysers are common, and steam from the ground is used to produce electricity. The Southern Alps, which contain the country's highest peak, Aoraki Mount Cook, at 12,313 ft [3,753 m], form the backbone of South Island. The island also has some large, fertile plains.

Auckland in the north has a warm, humid climate throughout the year. Wellington has cooler summers, while in Dunedin, in the southeast, temperatures sometimes dip below freezing in winter. The rainfall is heaviest on the western highlands.

POLITICS & ECONOMY Evidence suggests that early Maori settlers arrived in New Zealand more than 1,000 years ago. The Dutch navigator Abel Tasman reached New Zealand in 1642, but his discovery was not followed up. In 1769, the British Captain James Cook rediscovered the islands. In the early 19th century, British settlers arrived and, in 1840, under the Treaty of Waitangi, Britain took possession of the islands. From the 1870s, the Maoris were gradually integrated into colonial society.

In 1907, New Zealand became a self-governing dominion in the British Commonwealth. The country's economy developed quickly and the people became increasingly prosperous. However, after Britain joined the European Economic Community in 1973, New Zealand's exports to Britain shrank and the country had to reassess its economic and defense strategies and seek new markets. The world recession led the government to cut back on welfare spending in the 1990s. The preservation of Maori culture and Maori rights are also major issues. Ties with Britain have been gradually reduced. In 2005, the country's prime minister, Helen Clark, stated her view that New Zealand would eventually abolish the monarchy. In 2005, her Labor Party won a narrow victory in national elections and formed a coalition with two minor parties.

The economy once depended on agriculture, but manufacturing now employs twice as many people as farming. Meat and dairy products are leading commodities. Sheep rearing has declined as the area under cattle, deer, and vines has expanded. Crops include barley, fruits, potatoes and other vegetables, and wheat.

AREA 104,453 sq mi [270,534 sq km] **POPULATION** 4,035,000
CAPITAL (POPULATION) Wellington (167,000)
GOVERNMENT Constitutional monarchy
ETHNIC GROUPS New Zealand European 74%, New Zealand Maori 10%, Polynesian 4% **LANGUAGES** English and Maori (both official) **RELIGIONS** Anglican 24%, Presbyterian 18%, Roman Catholic 15%, others
CURRENCY New Zealand dollar = 100 cents

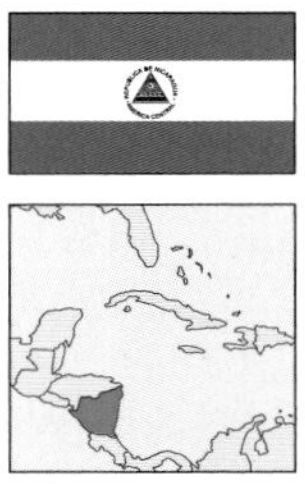

NICARAGUA

GEOGRAPHY The Republic of Nicaragua is a large country in Central America. In the east is a broad plain bordering the Caribbean Sea. The plain is drained by rivers that flow from the Central Highlands. The fertile western Pacific region contains about 40 volcanoes, many of which are active, and earthquakes are common.

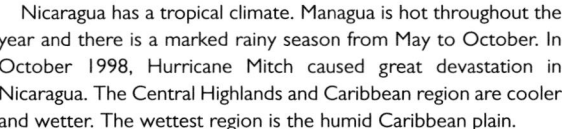

Nicaragua has a tropical climate. Managua is hot throughout the year and there is a marked rainy season from May to October. In October 1998, Hurricane Mitch caused great devastation in Nicaragua. The Central Highlands and Caribbean region are cooler and wetter. The wettest region is the humid Caribbean plain.

POLITICS & ECONOMY In 1502, Christopher Columbus claimed the area for Spain, which ruled Nicaragua until 1821. By the early 20th century, the United States had considerable influence in the country and, in 1912, US forces entered Nicaragua to protect US interests. From 1927 to 1933, rebels under General Augusto César Sandino, tried to drive US forces out of the country. In 1933, US marines set up a Nicaraguan army, the National Guard, to help to defeat the rebels. Its leader, Anastasio Somoza Garcia, had Sandino murdered in 1934 and, from 1937, Somoza ruled as a dictator.

In the mid-1970s, many people began to protest against Somoza's rule. Many joined a guerrilla force, called the Sandinista National Liberation Front, named after General Sandino. The rebels defeated the Somoza regime in 1979. In the 1980s, the US-supported forces, called the "Contras," launched a campaign against the Sandinista government. The US government opposed the Sandinista regime, under Daniel José Ortega Saavedra, claiming that it was a Communist dictatorship. A coalition, the National Opposition Union, defeated the Sandinistas in 1990. In 2001, the Sandinista candidate, Daniel Ortega, was defeated in presidential elections by the Liberal Constitutionalist Party candidate, Enrique Solaños.

In the early 1990s, Nicaragua faced many problems in rebuilding its shattered economy. Agriculture is the main activity, employing more than a third of the population. Coffee, cotton, sugar, and bananas are grown for export, while rice is the main food crop.

AREA 50,193 sq mi [130,000 sq km] **POPULATION** 5,465,000
CAPITAL (POPULATION) Managua (1,009,000)
GOVERNMENT Multiparty republic
ETHNIC GROUPS Mestizo 69%, White 17%, Black 9%, Amerindian 5%
LANGUAGES Spanish (official)
RELIGIONS Roman Catholic 85%, Protestant
CURRENCY Córdoba oro (gold córdoba) = 100 centavos

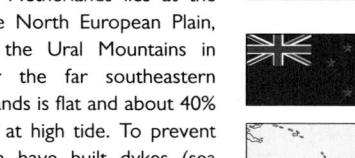

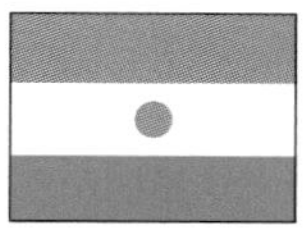
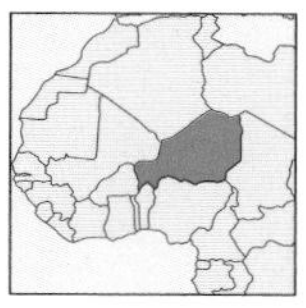

NIGER

GEOGRAPHY The Republic of Niger is a landlocked nation in north-central Africa. The northern plateaux lie in the Sahara Desert, while Central Niger contains the rugged Aïr Mountains. The most fertile, densely populated region is the Niger valley in the southwest.

Niger has a tropical climate and the south has a rainy season between June and September. The north is practically rainless.

POLITICS & ECONOMY Since independence in 1960, Niger, a French territory from 1900, has suffered severe droughts. Food shortages and the collapse of the traditional nomadic way of life of some of Niger's people have caused political instability. After a period of military rule, a multiparty constitution was adopted in 1992, but the military again seized power in 1996. Later that year, the coup leader, Colonel Ibrahim Barre Mainassara, was elected president. He was assassinated in 1999, but parliamentary rule was rapidly restored and Tandja Mamadou was elected president. He was re-elected in December 2004.

Niger's chief resource is uranium and the country is the fourth largest producer. In 2003, accusations that Niger supplied uranium to Iraq for its nuclear program proved to be baseless. Some tin and tungsten are also mined, though other mineral reserves are largely untouched. Despite its resources, Niger is one of the world's poorest countries. Farming employs 76% of the people, but only 3% of the land can be used for crops and 8% for grazing.

AREA 489,189 sq mi [1,267,000 sq km] **POPULATION** 11,665,000
CAPITAL (POPULATION) Niamey (732,000)
GOVERNMENT Multiparty republic **ETHNIC GROUPS** Hausa 56%, Djerma 22%, Tuareg 8%, Fula 8%, others **LANGUAGES** French (official), Hausa, Djerma **RELIGIONS** Islam 80%, indigenous beliefs, Christianity **CURRENCY** CFA franc = 100 centimes

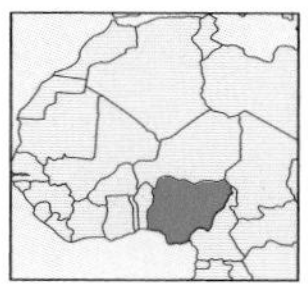

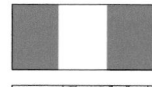

NIGERIA

GEOGRAPHY The Federal Republic of Nigeria is the most populous nation in Africa. The country's main rivers are the Niger and Benue, which meet in central Nigeria. North of the two river valleys are high plains and plateaux. The Lake Chad basin is in the northeast, with the Sokoto plains in the northwest. The south contains hilly uplands and plains. The south has a hot, rainy climate. The north is drier and often hotter than the south.

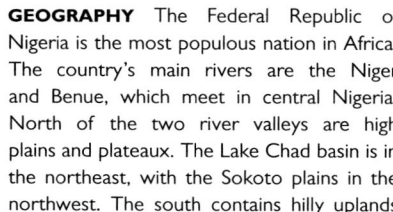

POLITICS & ECONOMY Nigeria has a long artistic tradition. Major cultures include the Nok (500 BC to AD 200), the Ife, a major Yoruba culture which developed about 1,000 years ago, and the Benin (15th to 17th centuries). Britain gradually extended its influence over the area in the second half of the 19th century.

Nigeria became independent in 1960 and a federal republic in 1963. A federal constitution dividing the country into regions was necessary because Nigeria contains more than 250 ethnic and linguistic groups, as well as several religious ones. Local rivalries have long been a threat to national unity, and six new states were created in 1996 in an attempt to overcome this. Civil war occurred between 1967 and 1970, when the people of the southeast attempted unsuccessfully to secede during the Biafran War. Between 1960 and 1998, Nigeria had only nine years of civilian government.

In 1998–9, civilian rule was restored and Olusegun Obasanjo became president. Re-elected in 2003, he faced many problems, including religious clashes in the north, where some states adopted *sharia* (Islamic law). In 2005–6, separatists in the Niger delta region demanded a greater share of the area's oil wealth. They committed acts of violence, sabotaged oil wells and kidnapped foreign workers.

Nigeria is a developing country with great potential. Its chief natural resource is oil, which accounts for most of its exports. Agriculture employs 43% of the people and the country is a major producer of cocoa, palm oil and palm kernels, groundnuts (peanuts), and rubber. Industry is increasing and manufactures include cement, chemicals, fertilizers, textiles, and timber.

AREA 356,667 sq mi [923,768 sq km] **POPULATION** 128,772,000
CAPITAL (POPULATION) Abuja (339,000)
GOVERNMENT Federal multiparty republic
ETHNIC GROUPS Hausa and Fulani 29%, Yoruba 21%, Ibo (or Igbo) 18%, Ijaw 10%, Kanuri 4%, many others
LANGUAGES English (official), Hausa, Yoruba, Ibo
RELIGIONS Islam 50%, Christianity 40%, traditional beliefs 10%
CURRENCY Naira = 100 kobo

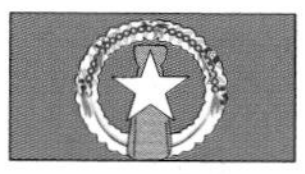
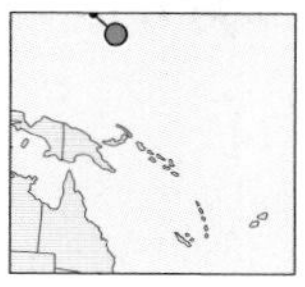

NORTHERN MARIANA ISLANDS

The Commonwealth of the Northern Mariana Islands contains 16 mountainous islands north of Guam in the western Pacific Ocean. In a 1975 plebiscite, the islanders voted for Commonwealth status in union with the United States and, in 1986, they were granted US citizenship.

AREA 179 sq mi [464 sq km] **POPULATION** 80,000 **CAPITAL** Saipan

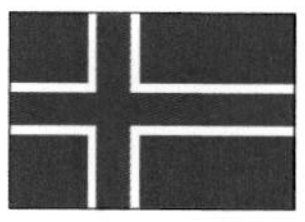
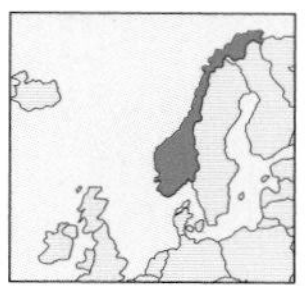

NORWAY

GEOGRAPHY The Kingdom of Norway forms the western part of the rugged Scandinavian peninsula. The deep inlets along the highly indented coastline were worn out by glaciers during the Ice Age. The warm North Atlantic Drift off the coast of Norway moderates the climate, with mild winters and cool summers. Nearly all the ports are ice-free throughout the year. Inland, winters are colder and snow cover lasts for at least three months a year.

POLITICS & ECONOMY Between about AD 800 and 1100, Norwegian Vikings ravaged western Europe. In 1380, Norway was united with Denmark. But in 1814, Denmark handed Norway over to Sweden, though it kept Norway's colonies – Greenland, Iceland, and the Færoe Islands. Norway briefly became independent, but Swedish forces defeated the Norwegians and Norway had to accept Sweden's king as its ruler. The union with Sweden ended in 1903. Germany occupied Norway during World War II (1939–45). Norway recovered quickly after the war and it now has one of the world's highest standards of living. In 1960, Norway and six other countries formed the European Free Trade Association (EFTA). But, in 1994, Norway voted against joining the European Union. In the 1990s and 2000s, Norwegian diplomats sought to broker peace deals in Palestine and Sri Lanka.

Norway's chief resources and exports are oil and natural gas which come from wells under the North Sea. Farmland covers only 3% of the land. Dairy farming and meat production are important, but Norway has to import food. Norway has many industries powered by cheap hydroelectricity.

AREA 125,049 sq mi [323,877 sq km] **POPULATION** 4,593,000
CAPITAL (POPULATION) Oslo (513,000)
GOVERNMENT Constitutional monarchy
ETHNIC GROUPS Norwegian 97%
LANGUAGES Norwegian (official)
RELIGIONS Evangelical Lutheran 86%
CURRENCY Norwegian krone = 100 ore

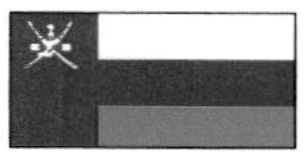
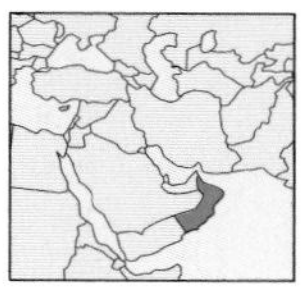

OMAN

GEOGRAPHY The Sultanate of Oman occupies the southeastern corner of the Arabian peninsula. It also includes the tip of the Musandam peninsula, overlooking the strategic Strait of Hormuz.

Oman has a hot tropical climate. In Muscat, temperatures may reach 117°F [47°C] in the summer months.

POLITICS & ECONOMY British influence in Oman dates back to the end of the 18th century, but the country became fully independent in 1971. Since then, using revenue from oil, which was discovered in 1964, the absolute ruler, Qaboos ibn Said, and his government have sought to modernize Oman. In 2000, Oman held elections to its consultative parliament. In 2004, the Sultan appointed Oman's first woman minister without portfolio. In 2005, 31 Islamists were convicted of trying to overthrow the government, but they were later pardoned.

Oman has an "upper-middle-income" economy. Oil accounts for the bulk of the exports and huge natural gas deposits were discovered in 1991. But agriculture remains important. Crops include alfalfa, bananas, coconuts, dates, limes, tobacco, vegetables, and wheat. Fishing is also important, but Oman imports food.

AREA 119,498 sq mi [309,500 sq km] **POPULATION** 3,002,000
CAPITAL (POPULATION) Muscat (41,000)
GOVERNMENT Monarchy with consultative council
ETHNIC GROUPS Arab, Baluchi, Indian, Pakistani
LANGUAGES Arabic (official), Baluchi, English
RELIGIONS Islam (mainly Ibadhi), Hinduism
CURRENCY Omani rial = 100 baizas

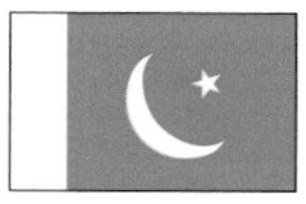
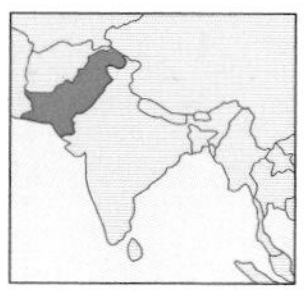

PAKISTAN

GEOGRAPHY The Islamic Republic of Pakistan contains high mountains, fertile plains and rocky deserts. The Karakoram range, which contains K2, the world's second highest peak, lies in the northern part of Jammu and Kashmir, which is occupied by Pakistan but claimed by India. Other mountains rise in the west. Plains, drained by the River Indus and its tributaries, occupy much of eastern Pakistan. Arid areas include the Thar Desert and the Baluchistan plateau. Most of Pakistan has hot summers and mild winters, though the mountains have cold winters. The rainfall is generally sparse.

POLITICS & ECONOMY Pakistan was the site of the Indus Valley civilization which developed about 4,500 years ago. But Pakistan's modern history dates from 1947, when British India was divided into India and Pakistan. Muslim Pakistan was divided into two parts: East and West Pakistan, but East Pakistan broke away in 1971 to become Bangladesh. In 1948–9, 1965, and 1971, Pakistan and India clashed over Kashmir. In 1998, Pakistan responded in kind to India's nuclear weapons tests, but, in 2003–5, Pakistan and India launched a series of initiatives aimed at achieving peace.

Pakistan has been subject to several periods of military rule, but elections in 1988 led to Benazir Bhutto becoming prime minister. She was removed from office in 1990, but she returned as prime minister between 1993 and 1996. In 1997, Narwaz Sharif was elected prime minister, but a military coup in 1999 brought General Pervez Musharraf to power. Musharraf's powers were increased by constitutional changes in 2002. In 2004, Musharraf announced that he would remain the army chief, despite international criticism. In 2005, an earthquake in the north caused great destruction. More than 73,000 Pakistanis and 1,400 Indians in Indian-ruled Kashmir died in the disaster.

According to the World Bank, Pakistan is a "low-income" developing country. The economy is based on farming or rearing goats and sheep. Agriculture employs nearly half the people. Major crops include cotton, fruits, rice, sugarcane, and wheat.

AREA 307,372 sq mi [796,095 sq km] **POPULATION** 162,420,000
CAPITAL (POPULATION) Islamabad (529,000)
GOVERNMENT Military regime **ETHNIC GROUPS** Punjabi, Sindhi, Pashtun (Pathan), Baluchi, Muhajir
LANGUAGES Urdu (official), many others
RELIGIONS Islam 97%, Christianity, Hinduism
CURRENCY Pakistani rupee = 100 paisa

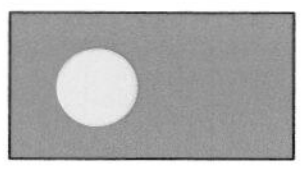
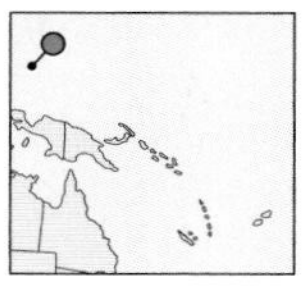

PALAU

The Republic of Palau became fully independent in 1994, after the USA refused to accede to a 1979 referendum that declared this island nation a nuclear-free zone. In December 1994 Palau joined the United Nations. The economy relies heavily on US aid, tourism, fishing, and subsistence agriculture. The main crops include cassava, coconuts, and copra.

AREA 177 sq mi [459 sq km] **POPULATION** 20,000 **CAPITAL** Koror

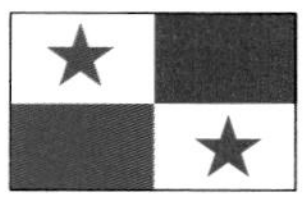
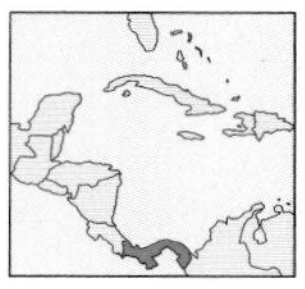

PANAMA

GEOGRAPHY The Republic of Panama forms an isthmus linking Central America to South America. The Panama Canal, which is 50.7 mi [81.6 km] long, cuts across the isthmus. It has made the country a major transport center.

Panama has a tropical climate. Temperatures are high, though the mountains are much cooler than the coastal plains. The main rainy season is between May and December.

POLITICS & ECONOMY Christopher Columbus landed in Panama in 1502 and Spain soon took the area. In 1821, Panama became independent from Spain and a province of Colombia.

In 1903, Colombia refused a request by the United States to build a canal. Panama then revolted against Colombia, and became independent. The United States then began to build the canal, which was opened in 1914. The United States administered the Panama Canal Zone, a strip of land along the canal. But many Panamanians resented US influence and, in 1979, the Canal Zone was returned to Panama. Control of the canal itself was handed over by the USA to Panama on December 31, 1999.

Panama's government has changed many times since independence, and there have been periods of military dictatorships. In 1983, General Manuel Antonio Noriega became Panama's leader. In 1988, two US grand juries in Florida indicted

Noriega on charges of drug trafficking. In 1989, Noriega was apparently defeated in a presidential election, but the government declared the election invalid. After the killing of a US marine, US troops entered Panama and arrested Noriega, who was convicted by a Miami court of drug offences in 1992. However, Panama held national elections in 1994. In 1999, Mireya Moscoso became Panama's first woman president. She was succeeded in 2004 by Martin Torrijos, son of a former military dictator.

The World Bank classifies Panama as a "lower-middle-income" developing country. The Panama Canal is an important source of revenue. In 2006, a plan was announced to widen the canal to take giant container ships. Away from the canal, the main activity is agriculture, which employs 15% of the people.

AREA 29,157 sq mi [75,517 sq km] **POPULATION** 3,039,000 **CAPITAL (POPULATION)** Panamá (484,000) **GOVERNMENT** Multiparty republic **ETHNIC GROUPS** Mestizo 70%, Black and Mulatto 14%, White 10%, Amerindian 6% **LANGUAGES** Spanish (official), English **RELIGIONS** Roman Catholic 85%, Protestant 15% **CURRENCY** US dollar; Balboa = 100 centésimos

PAPUA NEW GUINEA

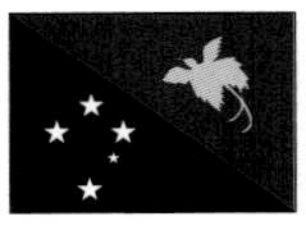

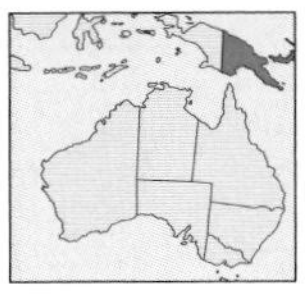

GEOGRAPHY Papua New Guinea is an independent country in the Pacific Ocean, north of Australia. It is part of a Pacific island region called Melanesia. Papua New Guinea includes the eastern part of New Guinea, the Bismarck Archipelago, the northern Solomon Islands, the D'Entrecasteaux Islands, and the Louisiade Archipelago. The land is largely mountainous.

Papua New Guinea has a tropical climate, with high temperatures throughout the year. Most of the rain occurs during the monsoon season (from December to April), when the northwesterly winds blow. Winds blow from the south-east during the dry season.

POLITICS & ECONOMY The Dutch took western New Guinea (now part of Indonesia) in 1828, but it was not until 1884 that Germany took northeastern New Guinea and Britain took the southeast. In 1906, Britain handed the southeast over to Australia. It then became known as the Territory of Papua. When World War I broke out in 1914, Australia took German New Guinea and, in 1921, the League of Nations gave Australia a mandate to rule the area, which was named the Territory of New Guinea.

Japan invaded New Guinea in 1942, but the Allies reconquered the area in 1944. In 1949, Papua and New Guinea were combined into the Territory of Papua and New Guinea. Papua New Guinea became fully independent in 1975.

Since independence, the government has worked to develop its mineral reserves. One of the most valuable mines was on Bougainville, in the northern Solomon Islands. But the people of Bougainville demanded a larger share in the profits of the mine. Conflict broke out and a secessionist group declared the island independent. Under a peace treaty in 2001, Bougainville became autonomous and held elections in 2005. In 2004, Australia sent police to Papua New Guinea to help fight crime, but they were withdrawn in 2005 following a Supreme Court ruling that their presence was unconstitutional.

Papua New Guinea has a "lower-middle-income" economy. Agriculture employs three out of every four people, but most of them live at subsistence level. Petroleum and minerals, notably copper, are the leading exports.

AREA 178,703 sq mi [462,840 sq km] **POPULATION** 5,545,000 **CAPITAL (POPULATION)** Port Moresby (193,000) **GOVERNMENT** Constitutional monarchy **ETHNIC GROUPS** Papuan, Melanesian, Micronesian **LANGUAGES** English (official), Melanesian Pidgin; more than 700 indigenous languages **RELIGIONS** Traditional beliefs 34%, Roman Catholic 22%, Lutheran 16% **CURRENCY** Kina = 100 toea

PARAGUAY

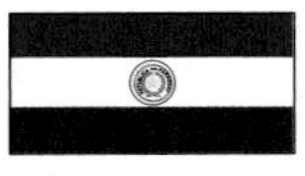

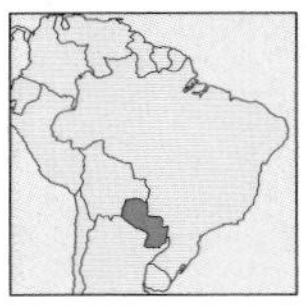

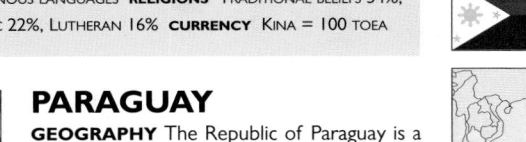

GEOGRAPHY The Republic of Paraguay is a landlocked country and rivers, notably the Paraná, Pilcomayo (Brazo Sur) and Paraguay, form most of its borders. A flat region called the Gran Chaco lies in the northwest, while the southeast contains plains, hills, and plateaux. Northern Paraguay lies in the tropics, while the south is subtropical. Most of the country has a warm, humid climate.

POLITICS & ECONOMY In 1776, Paraguay became part of a large colony called the Vice-royalty of La Plata, with Buenos Aires as the capital. Paraguayans opposed this move and the country declared its independence in 1811.

For many years, Paraguay was torn by internal strife and conflict with its neighbors. A war against Brazil, Argentina, and Uruguay (1865–70) led to the deaths of more than half of Paraguay's population, and a great loss of territory.

General Alfredo Stroessner took power in 1954 and ruled as a dictator. His government imprisoned many opponents. Stroessner was overthrown in 1989. However, the return of democracy in the 1990s and 2000s often seemed precarious because of rivalries between politicians and army leaders, together with economic problems arising partly from the severe problems experienced in neighboring Argentina and Brazil.

The World Bank classifies Paraguay as a "lower-middle-income" developing country. Farming and forestry are important. Paraguay produces hydroelectricity and exports power to its neighbors.

AREA 157,047 sq mi [406,752 sq km] **POPULATION** 6,348,000 **CAPITAL (POPULATION)** Asunción (547,000) **GOVERNMENT** Multiparty republic **ETHNIC GROUPS** Mestizo 95% **LANGUAGES** Spanish and Guaraní (both official) **RELIGIONS** Roman Catholic 90%, Protestant **CURRENCY** Guaraní = 100 céntimos

PERU

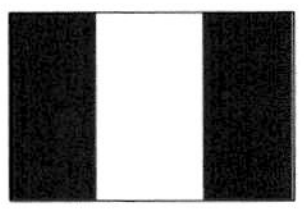

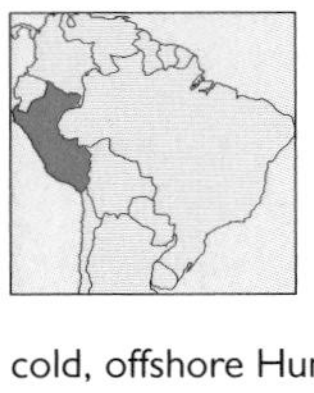

GEOGRAPHY The Republic of Peru lies in the tropics in western South America. A narrow coastal plain borders the Pacific Ocean in the west. Inland are ranges of the Andes Mountains, which rise to 22,205 ft [6,768 m] at Mount Huascarán, an extinct volcano. East of the Andes lies the Amazon basin.

Lima, on the coastal plain, has an arid climate. The coastal region is chilled by the cold, offshore Humboldt Current. The rainfall increases inland and many mountains in the high Andes are snow-capped.

POLITICS & ECONOMY Spanish conquistadors conquered Peru in the 1530s. In 1820, an Argentinian, José de San Martín, led an army into Peru and declared it independent. But Spain still held large areas. In 1823, the Venezuelan Simon Bolívar led another army into Peru and, in 1824, one of his generals defeated the Spaniards at Ayacucho. The Spaniards surrendered in 1826. Peru suffered much instability throughout the 19th century.

Instability continued in the 20th century. In 1980, when civilian rule was restored, a left-wing group called the Sendero Luminoso, or the "Shining Path," began guerrilla warfare against the government. In 1990, Alberto Fujimori, son of Japanese immigrants, became president. In 1992, he suspended the constitution and dismissed the legislature. The guerrilla leader, Abimael Guzmán, was arrested in 1992, but instability continued. Following his victory in disputed presidential elections in 2000, Fujimori resigned and left the country. Between 2001 and 2006, Alejandro Toledo was the first Peruvian of Amerindian descent to serve as president. In 2006, a state of emergency was declared in six central provinces after suspected "Shining Path" guerrilla activity.

The World Bank classifies Peru as a "lower-middle-income" developing country. Major food crops include beans, maize, potatoes and rice. Fish products are exported, but the most valuable export is copper. Peru also produces lead, silver, zinc, and iron ore.

AREA 496,222 sq mi [1,285,216 sq km] **POPULATION** 27,926,000 **CAPITAL (POPULATION)** Lima (5,681,000) **GOVERNMENT** Transitional republic **ETHNIC GROUPS** Amerindian 45%, Mestizo 37%, White 15% **LANGUAGES** Spanish and Quechua (both official), Aymara, other Amazonian languages **RELIGIONS** Roman Catholic 90% **CURRENCY** New sol = 100 centavos

PHILIPPINES

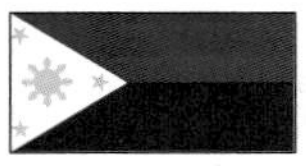

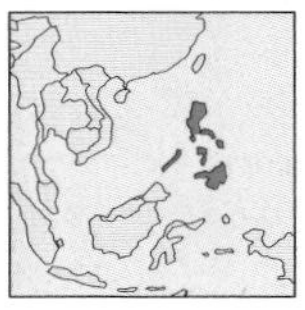

GEOGRAPHY The Republic of the Philippines is an island country in southeastern Asia. It includes about 7,100 islands, of which 2,770 are named and about 1,000 are inhabited. Luzon and Mindanao, the two largest islands, make up more than two-thirds of the country. The land is mainly mountainous.

The country has a hot tropical climate. The dry season runs from December to April. The rest of the year is wet. Much of the rainfall comes from the typhoons which periodically strike the east coast.

POLITICS & ECONOMY The first European to reach the Philippines was the Portuguese navigator Ferdinand Magellan in 1521. Spanish explorers claimed the region in 1565 when they established a settlement on Cebu. The Spaniards ruled the country until 1898, when the United States took over at the end of the Spanish–American War. Japan invaded the Philippines in 1941, but US forces returned in 1944. The country became fully independent as the Republic of the Philippines in 1946.

Since independence, the country's problems have included armed uprisings by left-wing guerrillas demanding land reform, and Muslim separatist groups, crime, corruption, and unemployment. The dominant figure in recent times was Ferdinand Marcos, who ruled in a dictatorial manner from 1965 to 1986. His successors were Corazon Aquino (1986–92), Fidel Ramos (1992–8), and Joseph Estrada, who resigned following accusations of corruption. He was succeeded by Vice-President Gloria Arroyo, who was re-elected president in 2004. Conflict continued in the south and, in 2006, the government declared a state of emergency after the army said that it had prevented a planned coup.

The Philippines is a developing country. Agriculture employs around 30% of the people. The main foods are rice and maize, while bananas, cocoa, coffee, sugarcane, and tobacco are grown commercially. Manufacturing plays an increasingly important role in the economy.

AREA 115,830 sq mi [300,000 sq km] **POPULATION** 87,857,000 **CAPITAL (POPULATION)** Manila (1,581,000) **GOVERNMENT** Multiparty republic **ETHNIC GROUPS** Christian Malay 92%, Muslim Malay 4%, Chinese and others **LANGUAGES** Filipino (Tagalog) and English (both official), Spanish, many others **RELIGIONS** Roman Catholic 83%, Protestant 9%, Islam 5% **CURRENCY** Philippine peso = 100 centavos

PITCAIRN

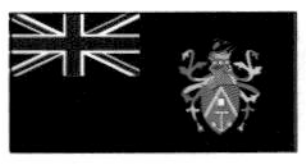

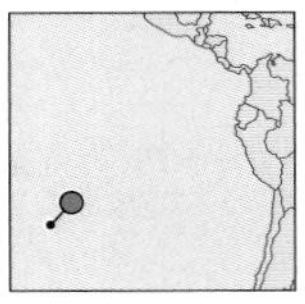

Pitcairn Island is a British overseas territory in the Pacific Ocean. Its inhabitants are descendants of the original settlers – nine mutineers from HMS *Bounty* and 18 Tahitians who arrived in 1790.

AREA 21 sq mi [55 sq km] **POPULATION** 46 **CAPITAL** Adamstown

POLAND

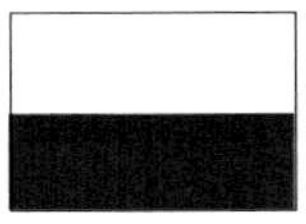

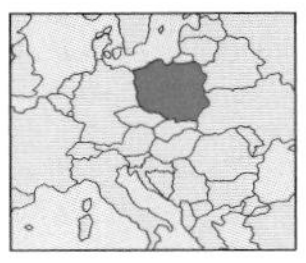

GEOGRAPHY The Republic of Poland faces the Baltic Sea and, behind its lagoon-fringed coast, lies a broad plain. A plateau lies in the southeast, while the Sudeten Highlands straddle part of the border with the Czech Republic. Part of the Carpathian Range (the Tatra) lies in the southeast.

Poland's climate is influenced by its position in Europe. Warm, moist air masses come from the west, while cold air masses come from the north and east. Summers are warm, but winters are cold and snowy.

POLITICS & ECONOMY Poland's boundaries have changed several times in the last 200 years, partly as a result of its geographical location between the powers of Germany and Russia. It disappeared from the map in the late 18th century, when a Polish state called the Grand Duchy of Warsaw was set up. But in 1815, the country was partitioned, between Austria, Prussia, and Russia. Poland became independent in 1918, but in 1939 it was divided between Germany and the Soviet Union. The country again became independent in 1945, when it lost land to Russia but gained some from Germany. Communists took power in 1948, but opposition mounted and eventually became focused through an organization called Solidarity.

Solidarity was led by a trade unionist, Lech Walesa. A coalition government was formed between Solidarity and the Communists in 1989. In 1990, the Communist Party was dissolved and Walesa became president. But Walesa faced many problems in turning Poland toward a market economy. In presidential elections in 1995, Walesa was defeated by ex-Communist Aleksander Kwasniewski, but he followed westward-looking policies. Poland joined NATO in 1999 and the European Union on May 1, 2004. In 2005, conservative and liberal parties defeated the left in national elections. A nationalist, Lech Kaczynski, was elected president.

Poland has large reserves of coal and deposits of various minerals which are used in its factories. Manufactures include chemicals, processed food, machinery, ships, steel, and textiles.

AREA 124,807 sq mi [323,250 sq km] **POPULATION** 38,635,000 **CAPITAL (POPULATION)** Warsaw (1,615,000) **GOVERNMENT** Multiparty republic **ETHNIC GROUPS** Polish 97%, Belarusian, Ukrainian, German **LANGUAGES** Polish (official) **RELIGIONS** Roman Catholic 95%, Eastern Orthodox **CURRENCY** Zloty = 100 groszy

PORTUGAL

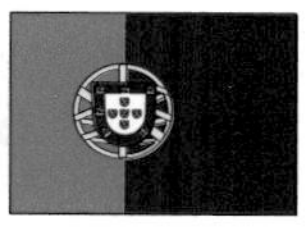

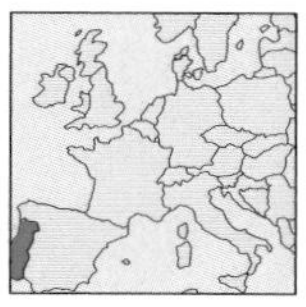

GEOGRAPHY The Republic of Portugal is the most westerly of Europe's mainland countries. The land rises from the coastal plains on the Atlantic Ocean to the western edge of the huge plateau, or Meseta, which occupies most of the Iberian peninsula. The climate is moderated by winds blowing from the Atlantic Ocean. Summers are cooler and winters are milder than in other Mediterranean lands. Portugal also contains two autonomous regions, the Azores and Madeira island groups.

POLITICS & ECONOMY Portugal became a separate country, independent of Spain, in 1143. In the 15th century, Portugal led the "Age of European Exploration." This led to the growth of a large Portuguese empire, with colonies in Africa, Asia and, most valuable of all, Brazil in South America. Portuguese power began to decline in the 16th century and, between 1580 and 1640, Portugal was ruled by Spain. Portugal lost Brazil in 1822 and, in 1910, Portugal became a republic. Instability hampered progress and army officers seized power in 1926. In 1928, they chose Antonio de Salazar to be minister of finance.

Salazar became prime minister in 1932 and ruled as a dictator from 1933 until 1968. In 1974, army officers mounted a coup. The new regime made most of Portugal's colonies independent and held free elections in 1978. Portugal joined the European Community (now the European Union) in 1986 and, in 2002, the euro became the sole unit of currency. In 2005, the Socialists, led by a moderate, José Socrates, won a decisive victory in parliamentary elections.

Agriculture and fishing were the mainstays of the economy until the mid-20th century, when manufacturing became the most valuable activity. The timber industry received a major setback in 2003 and again in 2005 when forest fires caused great damage.

AREA 34,285 sq mi [88,797 sq km] **POPULATION** 10,566,000
CAPITAL (POPULATION) Lisbon (663,000)
GOVERNMENT Multiparty republic **ETHNIC GROUPS** Portuguese 99%
LANGUAGES Portuguese (official) **RELIGIONS** Roman Catholic 94%, Protestant **CURRENCY** Euro = 100 cents

PUERTO RICO

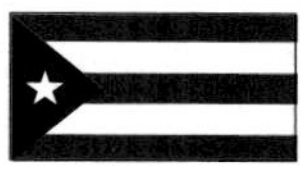

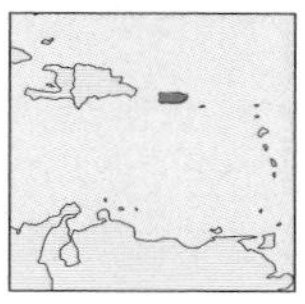

The Commonwealth of Puerto Rico, a mainly mountainous island, is the easternmost of the Greater Antilles chain. The climate is hot and wet. Puerto Rico is a dependent territory of the USA and the people are US citizens. In 1998, 50.2% of the population voted in a referendum on possible statehood to maintain the status quo.

Puerto Rico is the most industrialized country in the Caribbean. Tax exemptions attract US companies to the island and manufacturing is expanding. The chief exports are chemicals and chemical products, machinery, and food.

AREA 3,427 sq mi [8,875 sq km] **POPULATION** 3,917,000
CAPITAL (POPULATION) San Juan (422,000)

QATAR

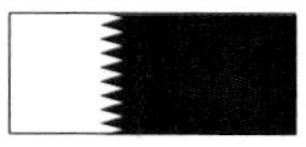

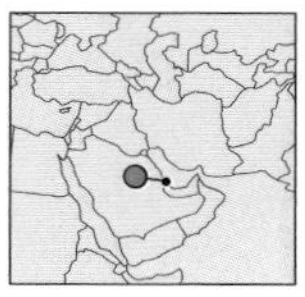

The State of Qatar occupies a low, barren peninsula that extends northward from the Arabian peninsula into the Persian Gulf. The climate is hot and dry. Qatar became a British protectorate in 1916, but it became fully independent in 1971. Oil, first discovered in 1939, is the mainstay of the economy of this prosperous nation.

AREA 4,247 sq mi [11,000 sq km] **POPULATION** 863,000 **CAPITAL** Doha

RÉUNION

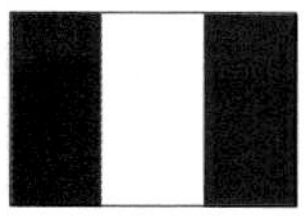

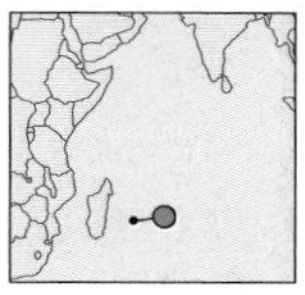

Réunion is a French overseas department in the Indian Ocean. The land is mainly mountainous, though the lowlands are intensely cultivated. Sugar and sugar products are the main exports, but French aid, given to the island in return for its use as a military base, is important to the economy.

AREA 969 sq mi [2,510 sq km]
POPULATION 777,000 **CAPITAL** St-Denis

ROMANIA

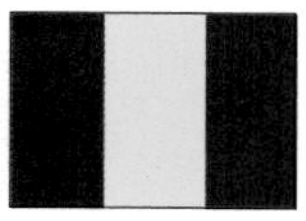

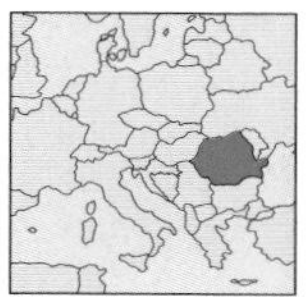

GEOGRAPHY Romania is a country on the Black Sea in eastern Europe. Eastern and southern Romania form part of the Danube river basin. The delta region, near the mouths of the Danube, where the river flows into the Black Sea, is one of Europe's finest wetlands. The southern part of the coast contains several resorts. The heart of the country is called Transylvania. It is ringed in the east, south and west by scenic mountains which are part of the Carpathian mountain system. Romania has hot summers and cold winters. The rainfall is heaviest in spring and early summer.

POLITICS & ECONOMY From the late 18th century, the Turkish empire began to break up. The modern history of Romania began in 1861 when Walachia and Moldavia united. After World War I (1914–18), Romania, which had fought on the side of the victorious Allies, obtained large areas, including Transylvania, where most people were Romanians. This almost doubled the country's size and population. In 1939, Romania lost territory to Bulgaria, Hungary and the Soviet Union. Romania fought alongside Germany in World War II, and Soviet troops occupied the country in 1944. Hungary returned northern Transylvania to Romania in 1945, but Bulgaria and the Soviet Union kept former Romanian territory. In 1947, Romania officially became a Communist country.

In 1990, Romania held its first free elections since the end of World War II. The National Salvation Front, led by Ion Iliescu and containing many former Communist leaders, won a large majority. A new constitution, approved in 1991, made the country a democratic republic. Elections held under this constitution in 1992 again resulted in victory for Ion Iliescu, whose party was renamed the Party of Social Democracy (PDSR) in 1993. But the government faced many problems. Iliescu was defeated in 1996, but he served again as president between 2000 and 2004, when he stood down. Romania became a member of the North Atlantic Treaty Organization in 2004. Its efforts to establish good relations with the West led observers to forecast that Romania would be admitted to the European Union in 2007, provided it met certain conditions.

According to the World Bank, Romania is a "lower-middle-income" economy. Under Communist rule, industry, including mining and manufacturing, became more important than agriculture.

AREA 92,043 sq mi [238,391 sq km] **POPULATION** 22,330,000
CAPITAL (POPULATION) Bucharest (2,001,000)
GOVERNMENT Multiparty republic
ETHNIC GROUPS Romanian 89%, Hungarian 7%, Roma 2%, Ukrainian **LANGUAGES** Romanian (official), Hungarian, German **RELIGIONS** Eastern Orthodox 87%, Protestant 7%, Roman Catholic 5% **CURRENCY** Leu = 100 bani

RUSSIA

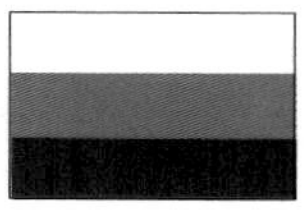

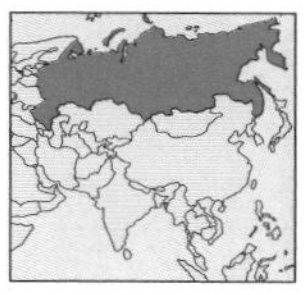

GEOGRAPHY Russia is the world's largest country. About 25% lies west of the Ural Mountains in European Russia, where 80% of the population lives. It is mostly flat or undulating, but the land rises to the Caucasus Mountains in the south, where Russia's highest peak, Elbrus, at 18,481 ft [5,633 m], is found. Asian Russia, or Siberia, contains vast plains and plateaux, with mountains in the east and south. The Kamchatka peninsula in the far east has many active volcanoes. Russia contains many of the world's longest rivers, including the Yenisey-Angara and the Ob-Irtysh. It also includes part of the world's largest inland body of water, the Caspian Sea, and Lake Baikal, the world's deepest lake.

Moscow has a continental climate with cold and snowy winters and warm summers. Siberia has a harsher, drier climate.

POLITICS & ECONOMY In the 9th century AD, a state called Kievan Rus was formed by a group of people called the East Slavs. Kiev, now capital of Ukraine, became a major trading center, but, in 1237, Mongol armies conquered Russia and destroyed Kiev. Russia was part of the Mongol empire until the late 15th century. Under Mongol rule, Moscow became the leading Russian city.

In the 16th century, Moscow's grand prince was retitled "tsar." The first tsar, Ivan the Terrible, expanded Russian territory. In 1613, after a period of civil war, Michael Romanov became tsar, founding a dynasty which ruled until 1917. In the early 18th century, Tsar Peter the Great began to westernize Russia and, by 1812, when Napoleon failed to conquer the country, Russia was a major European power. But during the 19th century, many Russians demanded reforms and discontent was widespread.

In World War I (1914–18), the Russian people suffered great hardships and, in 1917, Tsar Nicholas II was forced to abdicate. In November 1917, the Bolsheviks seized power under Vladimir Lenin. In 1922, the Bolsheviks set up a new nation, the Union of Soviet Socialist Republics (also called the USSR or the Soviet Union).

From 1924, Joseph Stalin introduced a socialist economic program, suppressing all opposition. In 1939, the Soviet Union and Germany signed a non-aggression pact, but Germany invaded the Soviet Union in 1941. Soviet forces pushed the Germans back, occupying eastern Europe. They reached Berlin in May 1945. From the late 1940s, tension between the Soviet Union and its allies and Western nations developed into a "Cold War." This continued until 1991, when the Soviet Union was dissolved.

The Soviet Union collapsed because of the failure of its economic policies. From 1991, President Boris Yeltsin introduced democratic and economic reforms. Yeltsin retired in 1999 and, in 2000, was succeeded by Vladimir Putin. Putin, who was re-elected in 2004, has sought to develop contacts with the West. He supported the US-declared "war on terrorism," though he opposed the invasion of Iraq in 2003. The secessionist conflict in Chechenia, including the occupation of a school by Muslim extremists in 2004, causing more than 330 deaths, provoked outrage. In 2005, violent incidents in the republics of Dagestan, Ingushetia and Kabardino-Balkaria further confirmed that Russia's size and diversity make national unity hard to achieve.

Russia's economy was thrown into disarray after the collapse of the Soviet Union, and in the early 1990s the World Bank described Russia as a "lower-middle-income" economy. Russia was admitted to the Council of Europe in 1997, essentially to discourage instability in the Caucasus. More significantly still, Boris Yeltsin was invited to attend the G7 summit in Denver in 1997. The summit became known as "the Summit of the Eight" and it appeared that Russia will now be included in future meetings of the world's most powerful economies. Industry is the most valuable activity, though, under Communist rule, manufacturing was less efficient than in the West, and the emphasis was on heavy industry. Today, light industries producing consumer goods are becoming important. Russia's abundant resources include oil and natural gas, coal, timber, metal ores, and hydroelectric power.

Russia is a major producer of farm products, though it imports grains. Major crops include barley, flax, fruits, oats, rye, potatoes, sugar beet, sunflower seeds, vegetables, and wheat.

AREA 6,592,812 sq mi [17,075,400 sq km] **POPULATION** 143,420,000
CAPITAL (POPULATION) Moscow (8,297,000) **GOVERNMENT** Federal multiparty republic **ETHNIC GROUPS** Russian 82%, Tatar 4%, Ukrainian 3%, Chuvash 1%, more than 100 others
LANGUAGES Russian (official), many others
RELIGIONS Mainly Russian Orthodox, Islam, Judaism
CURRENCY Russian ruble = 100 kopeks

RWANDA

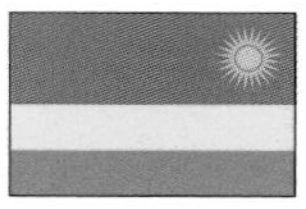

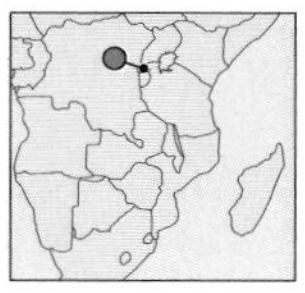

GEOGRAPHY The Republic of Rwanda is a small, landlocked country in east-central Africa. Lake Kivu and the River Ruzizi in the Great African Rift Valley form the country's western border.

Kigali stands on the central plateau of Rwanda. Here, temperatures are moderated by the altitude. The rainfall is abundant, but much heavier rain falls on the western mountains.

POLITICS & ECONOMY Germany conquered the area, called Ruanda-Urundi, in the 1890s. However, Belgium occupied the region during World War I (1914–18) and ruled it until 1961, when the people of Ruanda voted for their country to become a republic, called Rwanda. This decision followed a rebellion by the majority Hutu people against the Tutsi monarchy. About 150,000 deaths resulted from this conflict. Many Tutsis fled to Uganda, where they formed a rebel army. Relations between Hutus and Tutsis deteriorated and, in 1994, between 500,000 and 800,000 people were massacred in Rwanda. After the Tutsis had restored order, Hutu rebels fled into the Democratic Republic of the Congo (then Zaïre). Rwanda intervened in the Congo in 1996–2002. In the 2000s, Paul Kagame, Rwanda's leader since 1994, worked to create unity and restore stability.

According to the World Bank, Rwanda is a "low-income" developing country. Most people are poor farmers. Food crops include bananas, beans, cassava, and sorghum. Some cattle are raised.

AREA 10,169 sq mi [26,338 sq km] **POPULATION** 8,441,000
CAPITAL (POPULATION) Kigali (234,000)
GOVERNMENT Republic **ETHNIC GROUPS** Hutu 84%, Tutsi 15%, Twa 1% **LANGUAGES** French, English and Kinyarwanda (all official) **RELIGIONS** Roman Catholic 57%, Protestant 26%, Adventist 11%, Islam 5% **CURRENCY** Rwandan franc = 100 centimes

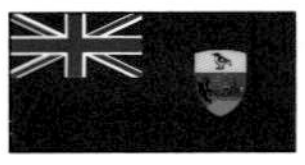
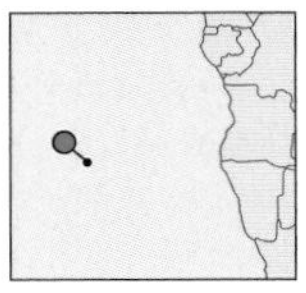

ST HELENA

St Helena, which became a British colony in 1834, is an isolated volcanic island in the south Atlantic Ocean. Now a British overseas territory, it is also the administrative center of Ascension and Tristan da Cunha.

AREA 47 SQ MI [122 SQ KM]
POPULATION 7,000 **CAPITAL** JAMESTOWN

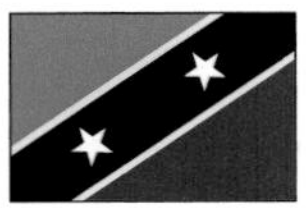
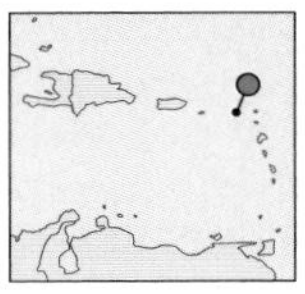

ST KITTS AND NEVIS

The Federation of St Kitts and Nevis comprises two well-watered volcanic islands, with mountains rising to around 3,300 ft [1,000 m]. The islands were the first in the Caribbean to be colonized by Britain (in 1623 and 1628), and they became an independent country in 1983. In 1998, a vote for the secession of Nevis fell short of the two-thirds majority required. Tourism has replaced sugar as the principal earner.

AREA 101 SQ MI [261 SQ KM] **POPULATION** 39,000
CAPITAL (POPULATION) BASSETERRE (12,000)

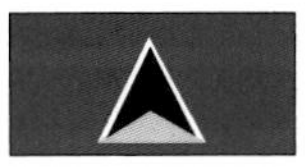
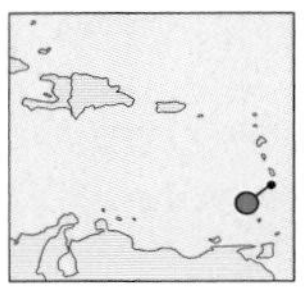

ST LUCIA

St Lucia, which became independent from Britain in 1979, is a mountainous, forested island of extinct volcanoes. It exports bananas and coconuts, and now attracts many tourists.

AREA 208 SQ MI [539 SQ KM]
POPULATION 166,000 **CAPITAL** CASTRIES

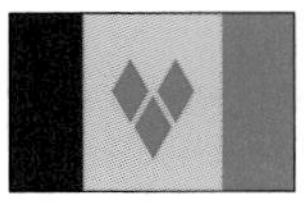
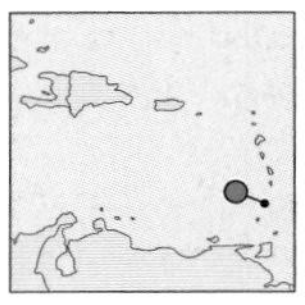

ST VINCENT AND THE GRENADINES

St Vincent and the Grenadines achieved its independence from Britain in 1979. Tourism is growing, but the territory is less prosperous than its neighbors.

AREA 150 SQ MI [388 SQ KM]
POPULATION 118,000 **CAPITAL** KINGSTOWN

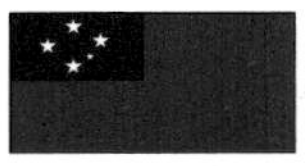
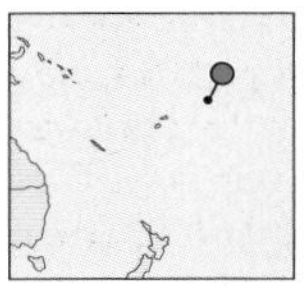

SAMOA

The Independent State of Samoa (formerly Western Samoa) comprises two islands in the South Pacific Ocean. Governed by New Zealand from 1920, the territory became independent in 1962. Exports include coconut cream and beer.

AREA 1,093 SQ MI [2,831 SQ KM]
POPULATION 177,000 **CAPITAL** APIA

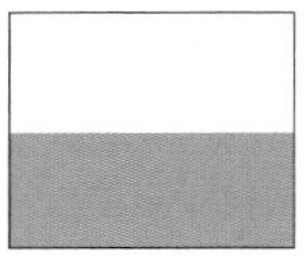
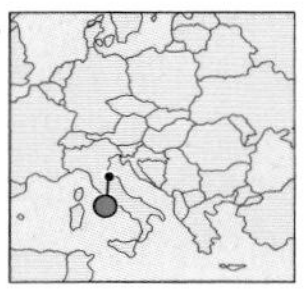

SAN MARINO

San Marino in northern Italy has been independent since 885 and a republic since the 14th century. It is the world's oldest republic. It has a friendship and cooperation treaty with Italy dating back to 1862. The state is governed by an elected council and has its own legal system. It has no armed forces and the police are "hired" from the Italian constabulary. The chief occupations are tourism, limestone quarrying, textiles, and wine-making.

AREA 24 SQ MI [61 SQ KM] **POPULATION** 29,000 **CAPITAL** SAN MARINO

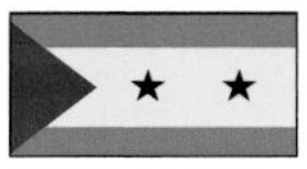
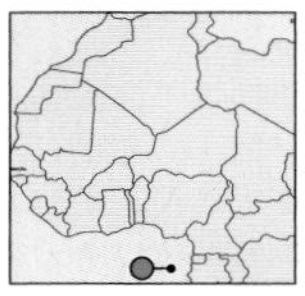

SÃO TOMÉ AND PRÍNCIPE

The Democratic Republic of São Tomé and Príncipe, a mountainous island territory west of Gabon, became a Portuguese colony in 1522. Following independence in 1975, the islands became a one-party Marxist state, but multiparty elections were held in 1991.

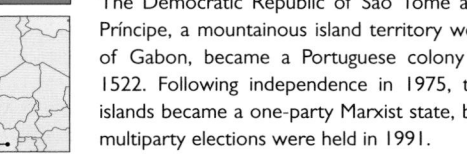

AREA 372 SQ MI [964 SQ KM] **POPULATION** 187,000 **CAPITAL** SÃO TOMÉ

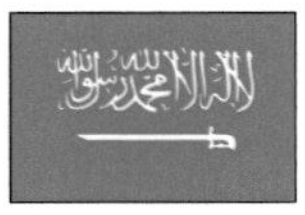
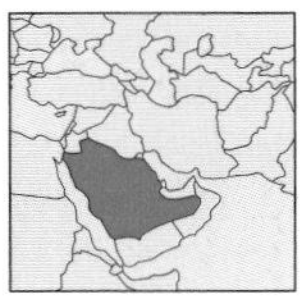

SAUDI ARABIA

GEOGRAPHY The Kingdom of Saudi Arabia occupies about three-quarters of the Arabian peninsula in southwest Asia. Deserts cover most of the land. Mountains border the Red Sea plains in the west. In the north is the sandy Nafud Desert (An Nafud). In the south is the Rub' al Khali (the "Empty Quarter"), one of the world's bleakest deserts.

Saudi Arabia has a hot, dry climate. In the summer months, the temperatures in Riyadh often exceed 104°F [40°C], though the nights are cool.

POLITICS & ECONOMY Saudi Arabia contains the two holiest places in Islam – Mecca (or Makka), the birthplace of the Prophet Muhammad in AD 570, and Medina (Al Madinah) where Muhammad went in 622. These places are visited by many pilgrims.

Saudi Arabia was poor until the oil industry began to operate on the eastern plains in 1933. Oil revenues have been used to develop the country and Saudi Arabia has given aid to poorer Arab nations. The monarch has supreme authority and Saudi Arabia has no formal constitution. Saudi Arabia supported Iraq against Iran in 1980–8. But when Iraq invaded Kuwait in 1990, it joined the alliance against Iraq. Many of the alleged terrorists involved in the terrorist attacks on the US on September 11, 2001, were Saudi nationals, but Saudi Arabia condemned the violence. In 2003–5, Saudi Arabia was itself hit by Islamic attacks. In 2005, King Fahd, the country's monarch since 1982, died. He was succeeded by Prince Abdullah, who had been *de facto* ruler for the previous decade.

Saudi Arabia has about 25% of the world's known oil reserves and oil products make up about 90% of its exports. Agriculture remains important. Irrigation and desalination schemes have increased crop production.

AREA 829,995 SQ MI [2,149,690 SQ KM] **POPULATION** 26,418,000
CAPITAL (POPULATION) RIYADH (3,000,000)
GOVERNMENT ABSOLUTE MONARCHY WITH CONSULTATIVE ASSEMBLY
ETHNIC GROUPS ARAB 90%, AFRO-ASIAN 10%
LANGUAGES ARABIC (OFFICIAL)
RELIGIONS ISLAM 100%
CURRENCY SAUDI RIYAL = 100 HALALAS

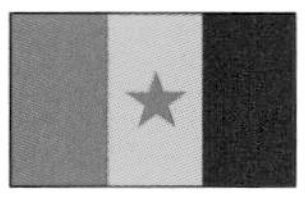
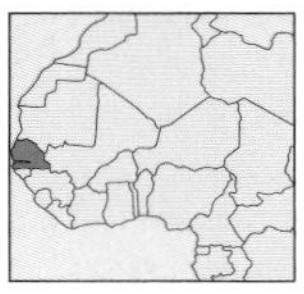

SENEGAL

GEOGRAPHY The Republic of Senegal is on the northwest coast of Africa. The volcanic Cape Verde (Cap Vert), on which Dakar stands, is the most westerly point in Africa. Plains cover most of Senegal, though the land rises gently in the southeast.

Dakar has a tropical climate, with a short rainy season between July and October.

POLITICS & ECONOMY In 1882, Senegal became a French colony, and from 1895 it was ruled as part of French West Africa, the capital of which, Dakar, developed as a major port and city.

In 1959, Senegal joined French Sudan (now Mali) to form the Federation of Mali. But Senegal withdrew in 1960 and became the separate Republic of Senegal. Its first president, Léopold Sédar Senghor, served until 1981, when he was succeeded by Abdou Diouf. However, in 2000, Diouf was defeated in elections by Abdoulaye Wade.

In the past, Senegal has usually enjoyed close relations with The Gambia, despite their differing traditions. In 1981, Senegalese troops put down an attempted coup in The Gambia and, in 1982, the countries set up a defense alliance, called the Confederation of Senegambia. But this alliance was dissolved in 1989. In 2005, a dispute with The Gambia over ferry tariffs on the border damaged the economies of both countries.

According to the World Bank, Senegal is a "lower-middle-income" developing country. It was badly hit in the 1960s and 1970s by droughts, which caused starvation. Agriculture still employs 65% of the population, though many farmers produce little more than they need to feed their families. Food crops include groundnuts, millet, and rice. Phosphates are the country's chief resource, but Senegal also refines oil which it imports from Gabon and Nigeria. Dakar is a busy port and has many industries.

AREA 75,954 SQ MI [196,722 SQ KM] **POPULATION** 11,127,000
CAPITAL (POPULATION) DAKAR (880,000)
GOVERNMENT MULTIPARTY REPUBLIC
ETHNIC GROUPS WOLOF 44%, PULAR 24%, SERER 15%
LANGUAGES FRENCH (OFFICIAL), TRIBAL LANGUAGES
RELIGIONS ISLAM 94%, CHRISTIANITY (MAINLY ROMAN CATHOLIC) 5%, TRADITIONAL BELIEFS 1%
CURRENCY CFA FRANC = 100 CENTIMES

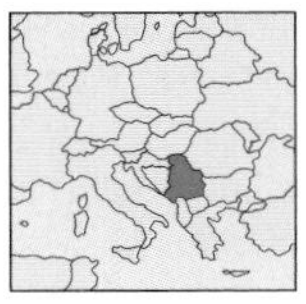

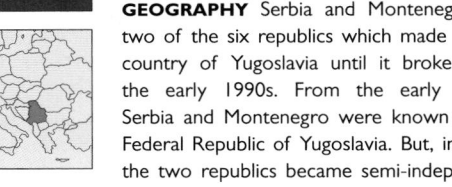

SERBIA AND MONTENEGRO

GEOGRAPHY Serbia and Montenegro are two of the six republics which made up the country of Yugoslavia until it broke up in the early 1990s. From the early 1990s, Serbia and Montenegro were known as the Federal Republic of Yugoslavia. But, in 2003, the two republics became semi-independent and adopted the name of the Union of Serbia and Montenegro.

Behind the coastline on the Adriatic Sea lies an upland region, including the Dinaric Alps and part of the Balkan Mountains. The Pannonian plains, which are drained by the River Danube, are in the north. The coast has a Mediterranean climate. The interior highlands have bitterly cold winters and cool summers. The wettest season is the summer, but there is also plenty of sunshine.

POLITICS & ECONOMY People who became known as the South Slavs began to move into the region around 1,500 years ago. Each group, including the Serbs and Croats, founded its own state. But, by the 15th century, foreign countries controlled the region. Serbia and Montenegro were under the Turkish Ottoman empire.

In the 19th century, many Slavs worked for independence and Slavic unity. In 1914, Austria-Hungary declared war on Serbia, blaming it for the assassination of Archduke Francis Ferdinand of Austria-Hungary. This led to World War I and the defeat of Austria-Hungary. In 1918, the South Slavs united in the Kingdom of the Serbs, Croats, and Slovenes, which consisted of Bosnia-Herzegovina, Croatia, Dalmatia, Montenegro, Serbia, and Slovenia. The country was renamed Yugoslavia in 1929. Germany occupied Yugoslavia during World War II, but partisans, including a Communist force led by Josip Broz Tito, fought the invaders.

From 1945, the Communists controlled the country, which was called the Federal People's Republic of Yugoslavia. But after Tito's death in 1980, the country faced many problems. In 1990, non-Communist parties were permitted and non-Communists won majorities in elections in all but Serbia and Montenegro, where Socialists (former Communists) won control. Yugoslavia split apart in 1991–2 with Bosnia-Herzegovina, Croatia, Macedonia and Slovenia proclaiming their independence. The two remaining republics of Serbia and Montenegro became the new Yugoslavia.

Fighting broke out in Croatia and Bosnia-Herzegovina as rival groups struggled for power. In 1992, the United Nations withdrew recognition of Yugoslavia because of its failure to halt atrocities committed by Serbs living in Croatia and Bosnia. In 1995, Yugoslavia was involved in the talks that led to the Dayton Peace Accord, which brought peace to Bosnia-Herzegovina. But the issue of Yugoslav repression of minorities flared up again in 1998 in Kosovo, a province where the majority are ethnic Albanians. In response to Serb ethnic cleansing, NATO forces began an offensive against Yugoslavia. However, Kosovar demands for independence persisted. Many Montenegrins also expressed a wish to secede from Yugoslavia. In 2003, Serbia and Montenegro set up a loose union and the name Yugoslavia passed into history. In a referendum in 2006, the people of Montenegro voted by a narrow majority to make Montenegro an independent nation.

Under Communist rule, manufacturing became increasingly important in Yugoslavia. But in the early 1990s, the World Bank described what is now Serbia and Montenegro as a "lower-middle-income" economy. Resources include bauxite, coal, copper and other metals, oil, and natural gas. Manufactures, which form the main exports, include aluminum, machinery, plastics, steel, textiles, and vehicles. Farming remains important. Crops include fruits, maize, potatoes, tobacco, and wheat. Cattle, pigs, and sheep are raised.

AREA 39,449 SQ MI [102,173 SQ KM] **POPULATION** 10,829,000
CAPITAL (POPULATION) BELGRADE (1,594,000)
GOVERNMENT FEDERAL REPUBLIC
ETHNIC GROUPS SERB 62%, ALBANIAN 17%, MONTENEGRIN 5%, HUNGARIAN 3%, OTHERS
LANGUAGES SERBIAN (OFFICIAL), ALBANIAN
RELIGIONS ORTHODOX 65%, ISLAM 19%, ROMAN CATHOLIC 4%, OTHERS
CURRENCY NEW DINAR = 100 PARAS

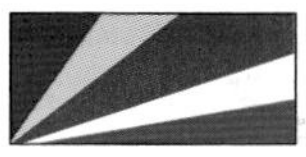
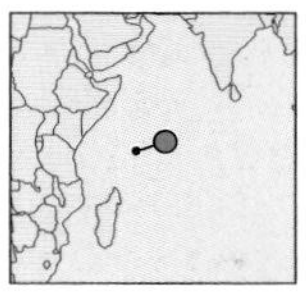

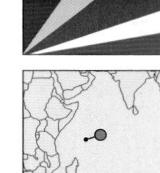

SEYCHELLES

The Republic of Seychelles in the western Indian Ocean achieved independence from Britain in 1976. Coconuts are the main cash crop, and fishing and tourism are important to the country's economy.

AREA 176 SQ MI [455 SQ KM]
POPULATION 81,000 **CAPITAL** VICTORIA

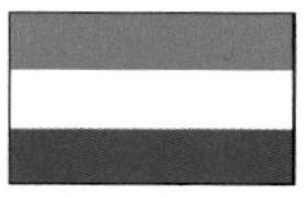

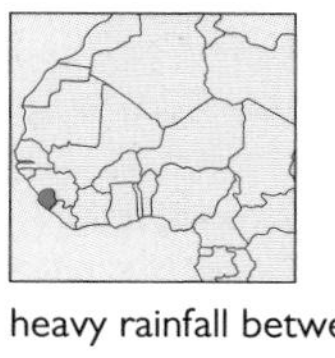

SIERRA LEONE

GEOGRAPHY The Republic of Sierra Leone in West Africa is about the same size as the Republic of Ireland. The coast contains several deep estuaries in the north, with lagoons in the south. The most prominent feature is the mountainous Freetown (or Sierra Leone) peninsula.

Sierra Leone has a tropical climate, with heavy rainfall between April and November.

POLITICS & ECONOMY A former British territory, Sierra Leone became independent in 1961 and a republic in 1971. It became a one-party state in 1978, but, in 1991, the people voted for the restoration of democracy. The military seized power in 1992 and a civil war caused much destruction in 1994–5. Elections in 1996 were followed by another military coup. In 1998, the West African Peace Force restored the deposed President Ahmed Tejan Kabbah. In 1999, a peace agreement followed further conflict. As part of this agreement, Foday Sankoh, one of the rebel leaders, became vice-president. However, he was arrested in 2000 and charged with war crimes. Conflict resumed, but another ceasefire was agreed. In 2004, President Kabbah declared a successful end to the disarmament process. In December 2005, the last of the UN forces, who had been helping to restore peace, left the country.

Sierra Leone has a "low-income" economy. More than 60% of the people live by farming, mainly at subsistence level. The leading exports are minerals, including diamonds, bauxite, and rutile (titanium ore). The country has few manufacturing industries.

AREA 27,699 SQ MI [71,740 SQ KM] **POPULATION** 6,018,000
CAPITAL (POPULATION) FREETOWN (470,000)
GOVERNMENT SINGLE-PARTY REPUBLIC **ETHNIC GROUPS** NATIVE AFRICAN TRIBES 90% **LANGUAGES** ENGLISH (OFFICIAL), MENDE, TEMNE, KRIO
RELIGIONS ISLAM 60%, TRADITIONAL BELIEFS 30%, CHRISTIANITY 10%
CURRENCY LEONE = 100 CENTS

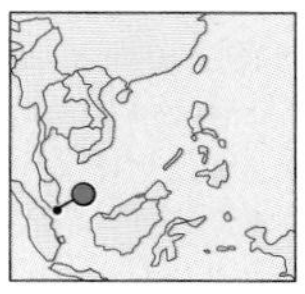

SINGAPORE

GEOGRAPHY The Republic of Singapore is an island country at the southern tip of the Malay peninsula. It consists of the large Singapore Island and 58 small islands, 20 of which are inhabited. The climate is hot and humid. Temperatures are high and rainfall is heavy throughout the year.

POLITICS & ECONOMY In 1819, Sir Thomas Stamford Raffles (1781–1826), agent of the British East India Company, made a treaty with the Sultan of Johor allowing the British to build a settlement on Singapore Island. Singapore soon became the leading British trading center in Southeast Asia and it later became a naval base. Japanese forces seized the island in 1942, but British rule was restored in 1945.

In 1963, Singapore became part of the Federation of Malaysia, which also included Malaya and the territories of Sabah and Sarawak on Borneo. In 1965, Singapore broke away and became independent.

The People's Action Party (PAP) has ruled Singapore since 1959. Its leader, Lee Kuan Yew, served as prime minister from 1959 until 1990, when he resigned and was succeeded by Goh Chok Tong. In 2004, Lee Hsien Loong, eldest son of Lee Kuan Yew, succeeded Goh Chok Tong as prime minister. His ruling People's Action Party won 82 out of 84 seats in parliament in 2006.

The World Bank classifies Singapore as a "high-income" economy. A skilled work force has created a fast-growing economy, but the recession in 1997–8 was a setback. Trade and finance are leading activities. Manufactures include electronic products, machinery, scientific instruments, textiles, and ships. Singapore has a large oil refinery. Petroleum products and manufactures are the main exports.

AREA 264 SQ MI [683 SQ KM] **POPULATION** 4,426,000
CAPITAL (POPULATION) SINGAPORE CITY (3,894,000)
GOVERNMENT MULTIPARTY REPUBLIC
ETHNIC GROUPS CHINESE 77%, MALAY 14%, INDIAN 8%
LANGUAGES CHINESE, MALAY, TAMIL, AND ENGLISH (ALL OFFICIAL)
RELIGIONS BUDDHISM, ISLAM, CHRISTIANITY, HINDUISM
CURRENCY SINGAPORE DOLLAR = 100 CENTS

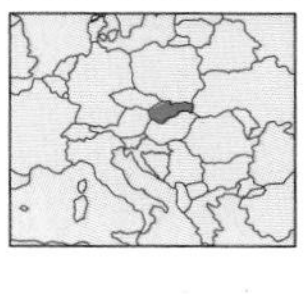

SLOVAK REPUBLIC

GEOGRAPHY The Slovak Republic is a predominantly mountainous country, consisting of part of the Carpathian range. The highest peak is Gerlachovsky in the Tatra Mountains, which reaches 8,711 ft [2,655 m]. The south is a fertile lowland. The Slovak Republic has cold winters and warm summers. Kosice, in the east, has average temperatures ranging from 27°F [–3°C] in January to 68°F [20°C] in July. The highland areas are much colder. Snow or rain falls throughout the year. Kosice has an average annual rainfall of 24 inches [600 mm], the wettest months being July and August.

POLITICS & ECONOMY Slavic peoples settled in the region in the 5th century AD. They were subsequently conquered by Hungary, beginning a millennium of Hungarian rule and suppression of Slovak culture.

In 1867, Hungary and Austria united to form Austria–Hungary, of which the present-day Slovak Republic was a part. Austria–Hungary collapsed at the end of World War I (1914–18). The Czech and Slovak people then united to form a new nation, Czechoslovakia. But Czech domination led to resentment by many Slovaks. In 1939, the Slovak Republic declared itself independent, but Germany occupied the country. At the end of World War II, the Slovak Republic again became part of Czechoslovakia.

The Communist Party took control in 1948. In the 1960s, many people sought reform, but they were crushed by the Russians. In the late 1980s, demands for democracy mounted and a non-Communist government took office in 1990. Elections in 1992 led to victory for the Movement for a Democratic Slovakia headed by a former Communist and nationalist, Vladimir Meciar, and the independent Slovak Republic came into existence on January 1, 1993.

Independence raised national aspirations among Slovakia's Magyar-speaking community, but relations with Hungary deteriorated when the Magyars felt that administrative changes under-represented them politically. The government also made Slovak the only official language. The government's autocratic rule and human rights record provoked international criticism. In 1998, Meciar's party was defeated and Mikulas Dzurinda replaced Meciar as prime minister. The government strengthened its ties with the West, and in 2004 it joined both NATO and the European Union. In 2005, it joined the European Exchange Rate.

Before 1948, the Slovak Republic's economy was based on farming, but Communist governments developed manufacturing industries, producing such things as chemicals, machinery, steel, and weapons. Since the late 1980s, many state-run businesses have been handed over to private owners.

AREA 18,924 SQ MI [49,012 SQ KM] **POPULATION** 5,431,000
CAPITAL (POPULATION) BRATISLAVA (449,000)
GOVERNMENT MULTIPARTY REPUBLIC
ETHNIC GROUPS SLOVAK 86%, HUNGARIAN 11%
LANGUAGES SLOVAK (OFFICIAL), HUNGARIAN
RELIGIONS ROMAN CATHOLIC 60%, PROTESTANT 8%, ORTHODOX 4%, OTHERS **CURRENCY** SLOVAK KORUNA = 100 HALIEROV

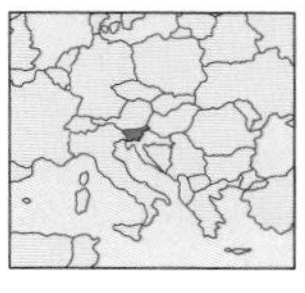

SLOVENIA

GEOGRAPHY The Republic of Slovenia was one of the six republics which made up the former Yugoslavia. Much of the land is mountainous, rising to 9,393 ft [2,863 m] at Mount Triglav in the Julian Alps (Julijske Alpe) in the northwest. Central Slovenia contains the limestone Karst region. The Postojna caves near Ljubljana are among the largest in Europe.

The coast has a mild Mediterranean climate, but inland the climate is more continental. The mountains are snow-capped in winter.

POLITICS & ECONOMY In the last 2,000 years, the Slovene people have been independent as a nation for less than 50 years. The Austrian Habsburgs ruled over the region from the 13th century until World War I. Slovenia became part of the Kingdom of the Serbs, Croats, and Slovenes (later called Yugoslavia) in 1918. During World War II, Slovenia was invaded and partitioned between Italy, Germany and Hungary, but, after the war, Slovenia again became part of Yugoslavia.

From the late 1960s, some Slovenes demanded independence, but the central government opposed the breakup of the country. In 1990, when Communist governments had collapsed throughout Eastern Europe, elections were held and a non-Communist coalition government was set up. Slovenia then declared itself independent. This led to fighting between Slovenes and the federal army, but Slovenia did not become a battlefield. Slovenia's independence was recognized in 1992 and a coalition led by the Liberal Democrats was elected in 1992, 1996 and 2000. In 2004, Slovenia became a member of the North Atlantic Treaty Organization and the European Union. In 2004, following elections, a center-right coalition was formed, but it stated that it would continue Slovenia's westward-leaning stance.

The reform of the formerly state-run economy caused problems for Slovenia. However, it has enjoyed considerable economic progress, with one of Europe's fastest growing economies. In 1992, the World Bank classified Slovenia's economy as "upper-middle-income."

Manufacturing is the leading activity and manufactures are the main exports. Manufactures include chemicals, machinery and transport equipment, metal goods, and textiles. Slovenia mines some iron ore, lead, lignite, and mercury. Agriculture and forestry employ 9% of the people. Fruits, maize, potatoes, and wheat are major crops, and many farmers raise animals.

AREA 7,821 SQ MI [20,256 SQ KM] **POPULATION** 2,011,000
CAPITAL (POPULATION) LJUBLJANA (264,000)
GOVERNMENT MULTIPARTY REPUBLIC
ETHNIC GROUPS SLOVENE 92%, CROAT 1%, SERB, HUNGARIAN, BOSNIAK
LANGUAGES SLOVENIAN (OFFICIAL), SERBO-CROATIAN
RELIGIONS MAINLY ROMAN CATHOLIC
CURRENCY TOLAR = 100 STOTIN

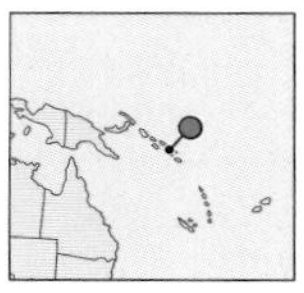

SOLOMON ISLANDS

The Solomon Islands, a chain of mainly volcanic islands in the Pacific Ocean, were a British territory between 1893 and 1978. The chain extends for some 1,400 mi [2,250 km]. They were the scene of fierce fighting during World War II. Most people are Melanesians, and the islands have a young population profile, with half the people aged under 20. Fish, coconuts and cocoa are leading products, though development is hampered by mountainous, forested terrain.

AREA 11,157 SQ MI [28,896 SQ KM] **POPULATION** 538,000
CAPITAL (POPULATION) HONIARA (49,000)

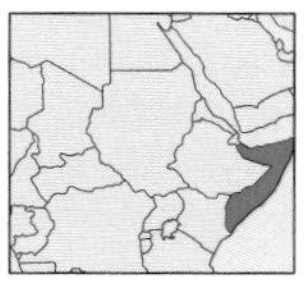

SOMALIA

GEOGRAPHY The Somali Democratic Republic, or Somalia, is in a region known as the "Horn of Africa." It is more than twice the size of Italy, the country which once ruled the southern part of Somalia. The most mountainous part of the country is in the north, behind the narrow coastal plains that border the Gulf of Aden.

Rainfall is light throughout Somalia. The wettest regions are the south and the northern mountains, but droughts often occur. Temperatures are high on the low plateaux and plains.

POLITICS & ECONOMY European powers became interested in the Horn of Africa in the 19th century. In 1884, Britain made the northern part of what is now Somalia a protectorate, while Italy took the south in 1905. The new boundaries divided the Somalis into five areas: the two Somalilands, Djibouti (which was taken by France in the 1880s), Ethiopia, and Kenya. Since then, many Somalis have wanted to create a Greater Somalia. Italy invaded British Somaliland in 1940, but was defeated in 1941. Britain ruled both Somalilands until 1950, when the United Nations asked Italy to take over the former Italian Somaliland for ten years. In 1960, the two Somalilands united to become Somalia.

Somalia has faced many problems. Economic difficulties led a military group to seize power in 1969. In the 1970s, Somalia supported an uprising of Somali-speaking people in the Ogaden region of Ethiopia. But, in 1988, Somalia and Ethiopia signed a peace treaty. In the 1990s, Somalia gradually broke apart. In 1991, the people in what was once British Somaliland set up the "Somaliland Republic," but it failed to get international recognition. The northeast, called Puntland, also seceded, while the south was riven by clan warfare. US troops sent into the south by the UN in 1993 were forced to withdraw in 1994 and clan fighting continued. A transitional government set up in 2000 failed to bring peace. A parliament, with a president and cabinet, was set up in Kenya in 2004–5. In 2006, because it could not meet in the capital, Mogadishu, which was regarded as unsafe, it convened instead in the southern town of Baidoa.

Somalia is a developing country, whose economy has been shattered by drought, floods, and war. Many Somalis are nomads. Live animals, meat, and hides and skins are exported. Crops include bananas, citrus fruits, cotton, maize, and sugarcane. Mining and manufacturing are relatively unimportant.

AREA 246,199 SQ MI [637,657 SQ KM] **POPULATION** 8,592,000
CAPITAL (POPULATION) MOGADISHU (900,000) **GOVERNMENT** SINGLE-PARTY REPUBLIC, MILITARY DOMINATED **ETHNIC GROUPS** SOMALI 85%, BANTU, ARAB **LANGUAGES** SOMALI (OFFICIAL), ARABIC **RELIGIONS** ISLAM (SUNNI MUSLIM) **CURRENCY** SOMALI SHILLING = 100 CENTS

SOUTH AFRICA

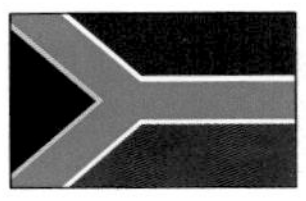

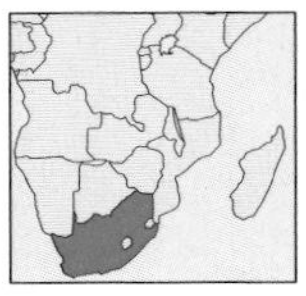

GEOGRAPHY The Republic of South Africa is made up largely of the southern part of the huge plateau which makes up most of southern Africa. The highest peaks are in the Drakensberg range, which is formed by the uplifted rim of the plateau. The coastal plains include part of the Namib Desert in the northwest. Most of South Africa has a mild, sunny climate. Much of the coastal strip, including Cape Town, has warm, dry summers and mild, rainy winters. Inland, large areas are arid.

POLITICS & ECONOMY Early inhabitants in South Africa were the Khoisan. In the last 2,000 years, Bantu-speaking people moved into the area. Their descendants include the Zulu, Xhosa, Sotho and Tswana. The Dutch founded a settlement at the Cape in 1652, but Britain took over in the early 19th century, making the area a colony. The Dutch, called Boers or Afrikaners, resented British rule and moved inland. Rivalry between the groups led to Anglo-Boer Wars in 1880–1 and 1899–1902.

In 1910, the country was united as the Union of South Africa. In 1948, the National Party won power and introduced a policy known as apartheid, under which non-whites had no votes and their human rights were strictly limited. In 1990, Nelson Mandela, leader of the African National Congress (ANC), was released from prison. Multiracial elections were held in 1994 and Mandela became president. After Mandela's retirement in 1999, his successor, Thabo Mbeki, led the ANC to victory in national elections. In 2004, the ANC won again by a landslide. Taking almost 70% of the vote, it was far ahead of its nearest rival, the Democratic Alliance, which polled only 13%. However, the government faced massive problems of poverty and underdevelopment, and maintaining national unity. South Africa also faces a major health crisis. With about 11% of its people infected with the HIV virus, it has a greater number of infected people than any other country. Until 2004, anti-retroviral drugs to slow down the effects of the virus were unavailable.

South Africa is Africa's most developed country. However, most of the black people are poor, with low standards of living. Natural resources include diamonds, gold, and many other metals. Mining and manufacturing are the most valuable activities.

AREA 471,442 sq mi [1,221,037 sq km] **POPULATION** 44,344,000
CAPITAL (POPULATION) Cape Town (legislative, 855,000); Pretoria/Tshwane (administrative, 692,000); Bloemfontein (judiciary, 350,000) **GOVERNMENT** Multiparty republic **ETHNIC GROUPS** Black 76%, White 13%, Colored 9%, Asian 2% **LANGUAGES** Afrikaans, English, Ndebele, Pedi, Sotho, Swazi, Tsonga, Tswana, Venda, Xhosa, and Zulu (all official) **RELIGIONS** Christianity 68%, Islam 2%, Hinduism 1% **CURRENCY** Rand = 100 cents

SPAIN

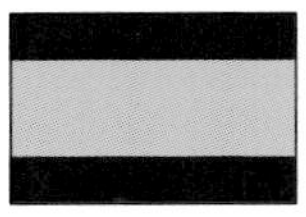

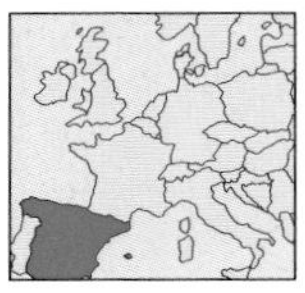

GEOGRAPHY The Kingdom of Spain is the second largest country in Western Europe after France. It shares the Iberian peninsula with Portugal. A large plateau, called the Meseta, covers most of Spain. Much of the Meseta is flat, but it is crossed by several mountain ranges, called sierras.

The northern highlands include the Cantabrian Mountains (Cordillera Cantabrica) and the high Pyrenees, which form Spain's border with France. But Mulhacén, the highest peak on the Spanish mainland, is in the Sierra Nevada in the southeast. Spain also contains fertile coastal plains. Other major lowlands are the Ebro river basin in the northeast and the Guadalquivir river basin in the southwest. Spain also includes the Balearic Islands in the Mediterranean Sea and the Canary Islands off the northwest coast of Africa.

The Meseta has a continental climate, with hot summers and cold winters, when temperatures often fall below freezing point. Snow frequently covers the mountain ranges on the Meseta. The Mediterranean coasts have hot, dry summers and mild winters.

POLITICS & ECONOMY In the 16th century, Spain became a world power. At its peak, it controlled much of Central and South America, parts of Africa and the Philippines in Asia. Spain began to decline in the late 16th century. Its sea power was destroyed by a British fleet in the Battle of Trafalgar (1805). By the 20th century, it was a poor country.

Spain became a republic in 1931, but the republicans were defeated in the Spanish Civil War (1936–9). General Francisco Franco (1892–1975) became the country's dictator, though, technically, it was a monarchy. When Franco died, the monarchy was restored. Prince Juan Carlos became king.

Spain has several groups with their own languages and cultures. Some of these people want to run their own regional affairs. In the northern Basque region, some nationalists have waged a terrorist campaign. A truce in 1998 was ended in 1999 when talks failed to produce results. In 2003, Spain's Supreme Court voted to ban Batasuna, the Basque separatist party.

Since the 1970s, regional parliaments with a considerable degree of autonomy have been set up in the Basque Country (called Euskadi in the indigenous language and Pais Vasco in Spanish), in Catalonia in the northeast, and in Galicia in the northwest. From the 1960s, Eta, a Basque terrorist group, waged a violent campaign for the secesssion of the Basque Country and, in 2003, Batasuna, the Basque separatist party, was banned. In March 2004, bombings attributed to al Qaida terrorists killed about 200 people in Madrid. The opposition socialists won the parliamentary elections that followed. In 2005, the government rejected proposals to make the Basque Country a "free state" associated with Spain, but, in 2006, Eta declared a permanent ceasefire.

Since the 1950s, Spain, then one of Europe's poorest countries, has become a prosperous nation and major vacation destination. By 2003, agriculture employed 5% of the people, as compared with 16% in mining and manufacturing. Arable and grazing land make up two-thirds of Spain, while forests cover most of the rest of the land. Crops include barley, citrus fruits, grapes for wine-making, olives, potatoes, and wheat. Apart from some high-grade iron ore in the north, Spain lacks natural resources. Its many manufacturing industries make such products as cars, chemicals, clothing electronic goods, processed food, metal goods, steel, and textiles.

AREA 192,103 sq mi [497,548 sq km] **POPULATION** 40,341,000
CAPITAL (POPULATION) Madrid (2,939,000)
GOVERNMENT Constitutional monarchy
ETHNIC GROUPS Composite of Mediterranean and Nordic types
LANGUAGES Castilian Spanish (official) 74%, Catalan 17%, Galician 7%, Basque 2%
RELIGIONS Roman Catholic 94%, others
CURRENCY Euro = 100 cents

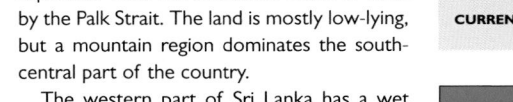

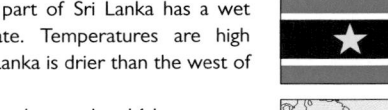

SRI LANKA

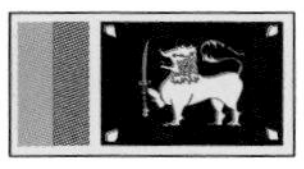

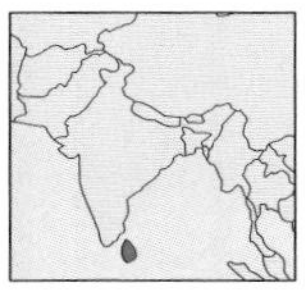

GEOGRAPHY The Democratic Socialist Republic of Sri Lanka is an island nation, separated from the southeast coast of India by the Palk Strait. The land is mostly low-lying, but a mountain region dominates the south-central part of the country.

The western part of Sri Lanka has a wet equatorial climate. Temperatures are high and the rainfall is heavy. Eastern Sri Lanka is drier than the west of the country.

POLITICS & ECONOMY From the early 16th century, Ceylon (as Sri Lanka was then known) was ruled successively by the Portuguese, Dutch and British. Independence was achieved in 1948 and the country was renamed Sri Lanka in 1972.

After independence, rivalries between the two main ethnic groups, the Sinhalese and Tamils, marred progress. In the 1950s, the government made Sinhala the official language. Following protests, the prime minister made provisions for Tamil to be used in some areas. In 1959, the prime minister was assassinated by a Sinhalese extremist and he was succeeded by Sirimavo Bandanaraike, the world's first woman prime minister.

Conflict between Tamils and Sinhalese continued in the 1970s and 1980s. In 1987, India helped to engineer a ceasefire. Indian troops arrived to enforce the agreement, but withdrew in 1990 after failing to subdue the main guerrilla group, the Tamil Tigers, who wanted to set up an independent Tamil homeland in northern Sri Lanka. In 1993, the country's president was assassinated by a suspected Tamil separatist. Offensives against the Tamil Tigers continued until hopes of peace were raised in 2002, with the signing of a ceasefire. In late 2004, a tsunami, caused by a sudden movement of the plates underlying the eastern Indian Ocean, struck parts of the coast of Sri Lanka, killing more than 30,000 people. Some hoped that the tragedy might lead to a reconciliation, but the conflict continued despite attempts to set up peace talks in 2005 and 2006.

Sri Lanka is classed as a "low-income" economy. Agriculture employs about 33% of the people. Coconuts, rubber, and tea are exported, but rice is the main food crop. Factories process farm products and manufacture textiles.

AREA 25,332 sq mi [65,610 sq km] **POPULATION** 20,065,000
CAPITAL (POPULATION) Colombo (642,000)
GOVERNMENT Multiparty republic
ETHNIC GROUPS Sinhalese 74%, Tamil 18%, Moor 7%
LANGUAGES Sinhala and Tamil (both official)
RELIGIONS Buddhism 70%, Hinduism 15%, Christianity 8%, Islam 7%
CURRENCY Sri Lankan rupee = 100 cents

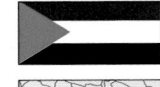

SUDAN

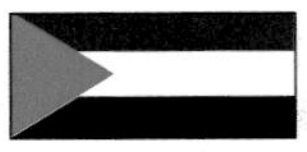

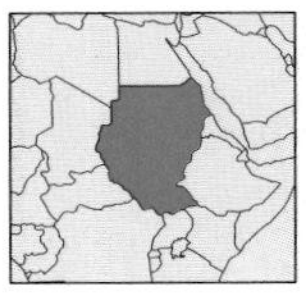

GEOGRAPHY The Republic of Sudan is the largest country in Africa. From north to south, it spans a vast area extending from the arid Sahara in the north to the wet equatorial region in the south. The land is mostly flat, with the highest mountains in the far south. The main physical feature is the River Nile. The north is virtually rainless, while the south has a wet equatorial climate.

POLITICS & ECONOMY In the 19th century, Egypt gradually took over Sudan. In 1881, a Muslim religious teacher, the Mahdi ("divinely appointed guide"), led an uprising. Britain and Egypt put the rebellion down in 1898. In 1899, they agreed to rule Sudan jointly as a condominium. After independence in 1952, the black Africans in the south, who were either Christians or followers of traditional religions, feared domination by the Muslim north. They objected to Arabic becoming the sole official language and, in 1964, civil war broke out. The war ended in 1972, when the south was granted regional self-government.

In 1983, the announcement that Islamic law would apply throughout Sudan sparked off further resistance from the rebel Sudan People's Liberation Army (SPLA) in the south. In 1998, Sudan's government announced that it accepted the idea of a referendum in the south. In 2005, a peace agreement was signed, bringing peace to the south. Since 2003, another conflict has raged in the western province of Darfur, where government-backed militias have attacked the population in an operation described as genocide and ethnic cleansing. Thousands of refugees fled into Chad and fighting spilled over the border in 2005–6.

Agriculture employs 60% of the people and cotton is the chief crop. Cotton, gum arabic and sesame seeds are exported, but the most valuable exports are oil and oil products. Manufacturing industries produce items mainly for home consumption.

AREA 967,494 sq mi [2,505,813 sq km] **POPULATION** 40,187,000
CAPITAL (POPULATION) Khartoum (947,000)
GOVERNMENT Military regime **ETHNIC GROUPS** Black 52%, Arab 39%, Beja 6%, others **LANGUAGES** Arabic (official), Nubian, Ta Bedawie **RELIGIONS** Islam 70%, traditional beliefs 25%
CURRENCY Sudanese dinar = 10 Sudanese pounds

SURINAME

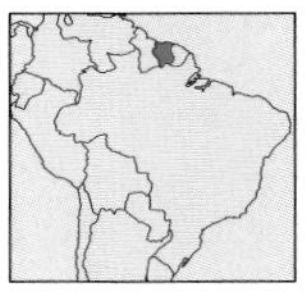

GEOGRAPHY The Republic of Suriname is sandwiched between French Guiana and Guyana in northeastern South America. The narrow coastal plain was once swampy, but it has been drained and now consists mainly of farmland. Inland lie hills and low mountains, which rise to 4,199 ft [1,280 m].

Suriname has a hot, wet and humid climate. Temperatures are high throughout the year.

POLITICS & ECONOMY In 1667, the British handed Suriname to the Dutch in return for New Amsterdam, an area that is now the state of New York. Slave revolts and Dutch neglect hampered development. In the early 19th century, Britain and the Netherlands disputed the ownership of the area. The British gave up their claims in 1813. Slavery was abolished in 1863 and, soon afterward, Indian and Indonesian laborers were introduced to work on the plantations. Suriname became fully independent in 1975, but the economy was weakened when thousands of skilled people emigrated from Suriname to the Netherlands. Following a coup in 1980, Suriname was ruled by a military dictator, Dési Bouterse. The adoption of a new constitution led to the restoration of democracy in 1988, though another military coup occurred in 1990. Ronald Venetiaan was elected president in 2000 and his government replaced the guilder with the Surinamese dollar in 2004. Venetiaan was re-elected in 2005, when his New Front coalition won a narrow majority in elections. Severe flooding in lowland areas in 2006 left more than 20,000 people homeless.

The World Bank classifies Suriname as an "upper-middle-income" developing country. Its economy is based on mining and metal processing. Suriname is a leading producer of bauxite, from which the metal aluminum is made.

AREA 63,037 sq mi [163,265 sq km] **POPULATION** 438,000
CAPITAL (POPULATION) Paramaribo (216,000)
GOVERNMENT Multiparty republic
ETHNIC GROUPS Hindustani/East Indian 37%, Creole (mixed White and Black) 31%, Javanese 15%, Black 10%, Amerindian 2%, Chinese 2%, others **LANGUAGES** Dutch (official), Sranang Tonga
RELIGIONS Hinduism 27%, Protestant 25%, Roman Catholic 23%, Islam 20% **CURRENCY** Surinamese dollar= 100 cents

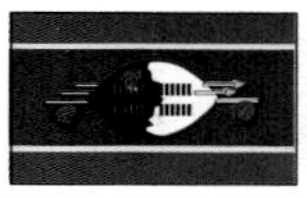

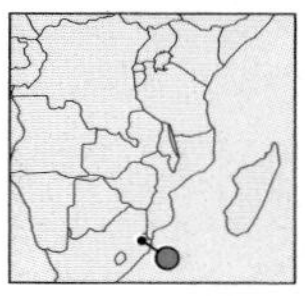

SWAZILAND

GEOGRAPHY The Kingdom of Swaziland is a small, landlocked country in southern Africa. The country has four regions which run north–south. In the west, the Highveld, with an average height of 3,950 ft [1,200 m], makes up 30% of Swaziland. The Middleveld, between 1,150 ft and 3,280 ft [350 m to 1,000 m], covers 28% of the country. The Lowveld, with an average height of 886 ft [270 m], covers another 33%. Finally, the Lebombo Mountains reach 2,600 ft [800 m] along the eastern border. The Lowveld is almost tropical, with average temperatures of 72°F [22°C] and low rainfall. The altitude moderates the climate in the west.

POLITICS & ECONOMY In 1894, Britain and the Boers of South Africa agreed to put Swaziland under the control of the South African Republic (the Transvaal). But at the end of the Anglo–Boer War (1899–1902), Britain took control of the country. In 1968, when Swaziland became fully independent as a constitutional monarchy, the head of state was King Sobhuza II. Sobhuza died in 1982 and was succeeded by his son, who, in 1986, became King Mswati III. Political parties were banned in elections in 1993 and 1998. Mswati ruled by decree. In 2005, Mswati signed a new constitution, combining traditional and modern values, though political parties remain banned.

The World Bank classifies Swaziland as a "lower-middle-income" developing country. Agriculture employs 50% of the people, and farm products and processed foods, including soft drink concentrates, sugar, wood pulp, citrus fruits, and canned fruit, are the leading exports. Many farmers live at subsistence level. Swaziland is heavily dependent on South Africa and the two countries are linked through a customs union. Swaziland shares two major problems with South Africa – the widespread poverty and the high incidence of HIV/AIDS. Experts have reported that Swaziland has the world's highest HIV infection rate of 42.6%.

AREA 6,704 sq mi [17,364 sq km] **POPULATION** 1,174,000
CAPITAL (POPULATION) Mbabane (38,000)
GOVERNMENT Monarchy **ETHNIC GROUPS** African 97%, European 3% **LANGUAGES** Siswati and English (both official)
RELIGIONS Zionist (a mix of Christianity and traditional beliefs) 40%, Roman Catholic 20%, Islam 10% **CURRENCY** Lilangeni = 100 cents

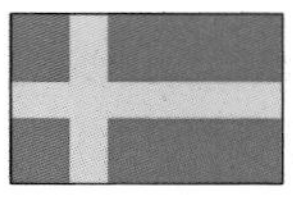

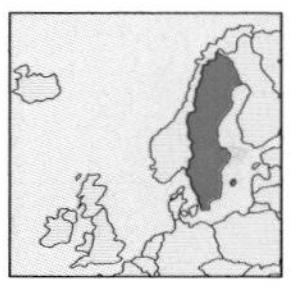

SWEDEN

GEOGRAPHY The Kingdom of Sweden is the largest of the countries of Scandinavia in both area and population. It shares the Scandinavian peninsula with Norway. The western part of the country, along the border with Norway, is mountainous. The highest point is Kebnekaise, which reaches 6,946 ft [2,117 m] in the northwest.

The climate of Sweden becomes more severe from south to north. Stockholm has cold winters and cool summers. The far south is much milder.

POLITICS & ECONOMY Swedish Vikings plundered areas to the south and east between the 9th and 11th centuries. Sweden, Denmark and Norway were united in 1397, but Sweden regained its independence in 1523. In 1809, Sweden lost Finland to Russia, but, in 1814, it gained Norway from Denmark. The union between Sweden and Norway was dissolved in 1905. Sweden was neutral in World Wars I and II. Since 1945, Sweden has become a prosperous country. In 1995, it joined the European Union. However, many people were sceptical about the advantages of EU membership and Sweden did not adopt the euro, the single EU currency, in 1999.

Sweden has wide-ranging welfare services. But many people are concerned about the high cost of these services and the high taxes they must pay. In 1991, the Social Democrats, who had built up the welfare state, were defeated. They were re-elected in 1994. In 2003, the government held a referendum on replacing the country's currency with the EU's unit of currency, the euro, but the electorate rejected the proposal.

Sweden is a highly developed industrial country. Major products include steel and steel goods. Steel is used in the engineering industry to manufacture aircraft, cars, machinery, and ships. Sweden has some of the world's richest iron ore deposits. They are located near Kiruna in the far north. But most of this ore is exported, and Sweden imports most of the materials needed by its industries. Sweden also has a major forestry industry. Development of hydroelectricity has made up for the lack of oil and coal. In 1996, a decision was taken to decommission all of Sweden's nuclear power stations. The first reactor closed in 1999, followed by a second in 2005. Another ten reactors remain to be decommissioned.

AREA 173,731 sq mi [449,964 sq km] **POPULATION** 9,002,000
CAPITAL (POPULATION) Stockholm (744,000)
GOVERNMENT Constitutional monarchy **ETHNIC GROUPS** Swedish 91%, Finnish, Sami **LANGUAGES** Swedish (official), Finnish, Sami
RELIGIONS Lutheran 87%, Roman Catholic, Orthodox
CURRENCY Swedish krona = 100 öre

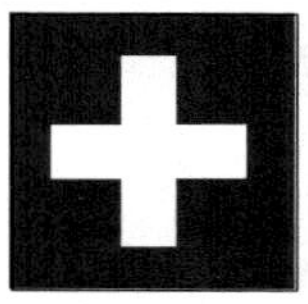

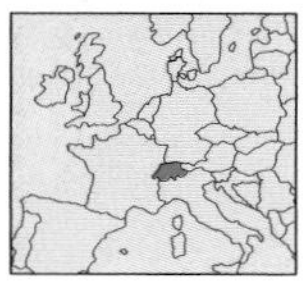

SWITZERLAND

GEOGRAPHY The Swiss Confederation is a landlocked country in Western Europe. Much of the land is mountainous. The Jura Mountains lie along Switzerland's western border with France, while the Swiss Alps make up about 60% of the country in the south and east. Four-fifths of the people of Switzerland live on the fertile Swiss plateau, which contains most of Switzerland's large cities.

The climate of Switzerland varies greatly according to the height of the land. The plateau region has a central European climate with warm summers, but cold and snowy winters. Rain occurs all through the year. The rainiest months are in summer.

POLITICS & ECONOMY In 1291, three small cantons (states) united to defend their freedom against the Habsburg rulers of the Holy Roman Empire. They were Schwyz, Uri and Unterwalden, and they called the confederation they formed "Switzerland." Switzerland expanded and, in the 14th century, defeated Austria in three wars of independence. After a defeat by the French in 1515, the Swiss adopted a policy of neutrality, which they still follow. In 1815, the Congress of Vienna expanded Switzerland to 22 cantons and guaranteed its neutrality. Switzerland's 23rd canton, Jura, was created in 1979 from part of Bern. Neutrality combined with the vigor and independence of its people have made Switzerland prosperous. The Swiss have voted against joining the European Union, although, in 2002, the country joined the United Nations. In 2005, it also joined the Schengen group, a European passport-free zone.

Although lacking in natural resources, Switzerland is a wealthy, industrialized country. Many workers are highly skilled. Major products include chemicals, electrical equipment, machinery and machine tools, precision instruments, processed food, watches, and textiles. Farmers produce about three-fifths of the country's food – the rest is imported. Livestock raising, especially dairy farming, is the chief agricultural activity. Crops include fruits, potatoes, and wheat. Tourism and banking are also important. Swiss banks attract investors from all over the world.

AREA 15,940 sq mi [41,284 sq km] **POPULATION** 7,489,000
CAPITAL (POPULATION) Bern (124,000) **GOVERNMENT** Federal republic **ETHNIC GROUPS** German 65%, French 18%, Italian 10%, Romansch 1%, others **LANGUAGES** French, German, Italian, and Romansch (all official) **RELIGIONS** Roman Catholic 46%, Protestant 40% **CURRENCY** Swiss franc = 100 centimes

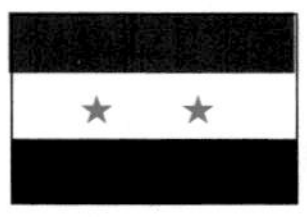

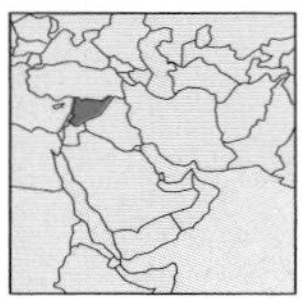

SYRIA

GEOGRAPHY The Syrian Arab Republic is a country in southwestern Asia. The narrow coastal plain is overlooked by a low mountain range which runs north–south. Another range, the Jabal ash Sharqi, runs along the border with Lebanon. South of this range is the Golan Heights, which Israel has occupied since 1967.

The coast has a Mediterranean climate, with dry, warm summers and wet, mild winters. The low mountains cut off Damascus from the sea. It has less rainfall than the coastal areas. To the east, the land becomes drier.

POLITICS & ECONOMY After the collapse of the Turkish Ottoman empire in World War I, Syria was ruled by France. Since independence in 1946, Syria has been involved in the Arab–Israeli wars and, in 1967, it lost a strategic border area, the Golan Heights, to Israel. In 1970, Lieutenant-General Hafez al-Assad took power, establishing a stable but repressive regime. Syria sent troops into Lebanon in 1976 in an effort to halt the civil war there. In 2005, following demonstrations against its continuing military presence in Lebanon, Syria executed a phased withdrawal of its troops. Hafez al-Assad died in 2000. He was succeeded by his son, Bashar Assad.

The World Bank classifies Syria as a "lower-middle-income" developing country. But it has great potential for development. Its main resources are oil, hydroelectricity from the dam at Lake Assad, and fertile land. Oil is the main export; farm products, textiles, and phosphates are also important. Agriculture employs about 27% of the work force.

AREA 71,498 sq mi [185,180 sq km] **POPULATION** 18,449,000
CAPITAL (POPULATION) Damascus (1,394,000)
GOVERNMENT Multiparty republic **ETHNIC GROUPS** Arab 90%, Kurdish, Armenian, others **LANGUAGES** Arabic (official), Kurdish, Armenian **RELIGIONS** Sunni Muslim 74%, other Islam 16%
CURRENCY Syrian pound = 100 piastres

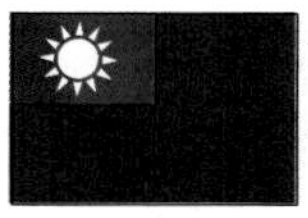

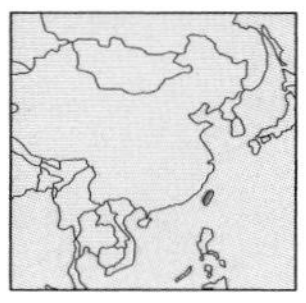

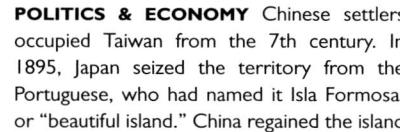

TAIWAN

GEOGRAPHY High mountain ranges run down the length of the island, with dense forest in many areas. The climate is warm, moist and suitable for agriculture.

POLITICS & ECONOMY Chinese settlers occupied Taiwan from the 7th century. In 1895, Japan seized the territory from the Portuguese, who had named it Isla Formosa, or "beautiful island." China regained the island after World War II. In 1949, it became the refuge of the Nationalists who had been driven out of China by the Communists. They set up the Republic of China, which, with US help, began to expand its economy. Today, it produces a wide range of manufactured goods.

In the early 21st century, the Taiwanese declared full nationhood for Taiwan. But the government of mainland China threatened to attack the territory if it did not accept the fact that it was a self-governing province of China. But reunification seemed a remote prospect.

AREA 13,900 sq mi [36,000 sq km] **POPULATION** 22,894,000
CAPITAL (POPULATION) Taipei (2,550,000)
GOVERNMENT Unitary multiparty republic
ETHNIC GROUPS Taiwanese 84%, mainland Chinese 14%
LANGUAGES Mandarin Chinese (official), Min, Hakka
RELIGIONS Buddhism, Taoism, Confucianism
CURRENCY New Taiwan dollar = 100 cents

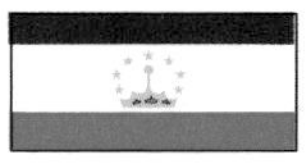

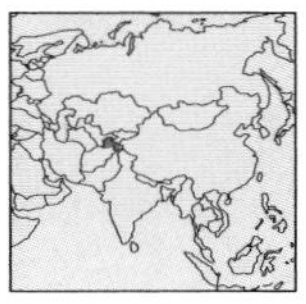

TAJIKISTAN

GEOGRAPHY The Republic of Tajikistan is one of the five central Asian republics that formed part of the former Soviet Union. Only 7% of the land is below 3,280 ft [1,000 m], while almost all of eastern Tajikistan is above 9,840 ft [3,000 m]. The highest point is Pik Imeni Ismail Samani (formerly known as Communism Peak or Pik Kommunizma), which reaches 24,590 ft [7,495 m]. The main ranges are the westward extension of the Tian Shan Range in the north and the snow-capped Pamirs in the southeast. Earthquakes are common throughout the country. The climate is continental, with hot, dry summers in the lower valleys and bitterly cold winters, especially in the mountains.

POLITICS & ECONOMY Russia conquered parts of Tajikistan in the late 19th century and, by 1920, Russia took complete control. In 1924, Tajikistan became part of the Uzbek Soviet Socialist Republic, but, in 1929, it was expanded, taking in some areas populated by Uzbeks, becoming the Tajik Soviet Socialist Republic.

While the Soviet Union began to introduce reforms during the 1980s, many Tajiks demanded freedom. In 1989, the Tajik government made Tajik the official language instead of Russian and, in 1990, it stated that its local laws overruled Soviet laws. Tajikistan became fully independent in 1991, following the breakup of the Soviet Union. In 1992, civil war broke out between the government, which was run by former Communists, and an alliance of democrats and Islamic forces. A ceasefire was agreed in 1996 and, in 1997, opposition leaders were brought into the government. In 2003, changes to the constitution enabled President Emomali Rakhmanov, president since 1994, to serve two more seven-year terms in office after elections in 2006. In 2005. Rakhmanov's party won the parliamentary elections.

The World Bank classifies Tajikistan as a "low-income" developing country. Agriculture, mainly on irrigated land, is the main activity and cotton is the chief product. Other crops include fruits, grains, and vegetables. The country has large hydroelectric power resources and it produces aluminum.

AREA 55,521 sq mi [143,100 sq km] **POPULATION** 7,164,000
CAPITAL (POPULATION) Dushanbe (529,000)
GOVERNMENT Transitional democracy
ETHNIC GROUPS Tajik 65%, Uzbek 25%, Russian
LANGUAGES Tajik (official), Russian
RELIGIONS Islam (Sunni Muslim 85%)
CURRENCY Somoni = 100 dirams

TANZANIA

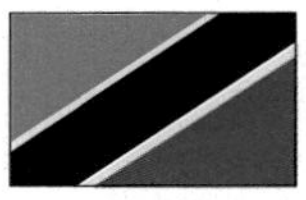

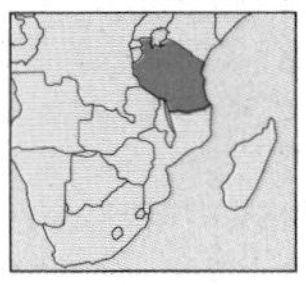

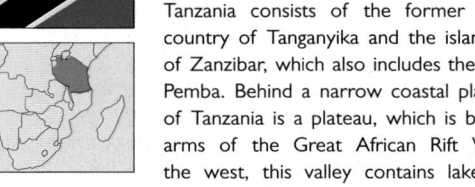

GEOGRAPHY The United Republic of Tanzania consists of the former mainland country of Tanganyika and the island nation of Zanzibar, which also includes the island of Pemba. Behind a narrow coastal plain, most of Tanzania is a plateau, which is broken by arms of the Great African Rift Valley. In the west, this valley contains lakes Nyasa and Tanganyika. The highest peak is Kilimanjaro, Africa's tallest mountain.

The coast has a hot and humid climate, with the greatest rainfall in April and May. The inland plateaux and mountains are cooler and less humid.

POLITICS & ECONOMY Mainland Tanganyika became a German territory in the 1880s, while Zanzibar and Pemba became a British protectorate in 1890. Following Germany's defeat in World War I, Britain took over Tanganyika, which remained a British territory until its independence in 1961. In 1964, Tanganyika and Zanzibar united to form the United Republic of Tanzania. The country's president, Julius Nyerere, pursued socialist policies of self-help (*ujamaa*) and egalitarianism. Many of its social reforms were successful, though the country failed to make economic progress. Nyerere resigned as president in 1985. His successors, Ali Hassan Mwinyi and Benjamin Mkapa (1995–2006), followed more liberal economic policies. In 2006, Jakaya Kikwete, leader of the ruling party, Chama Cha Mapinduzi, was elected president.

Tanzania is a poor country. Crops are grown on only 4.2% of the land, yet agriculture employs nearly 80% of the people. Food crops include bananas, cassava, maize, millet, and rice. Minerals, including gold, as well as cashews, tobacco, coffee, and tea are exported.

AREA 364,899 sq mi [945,090 sq km] **POPULATION** 36,766,000
CAPITAL (POPULATION) Dodoma (204,000)
GOVERNMENT Multiparty republic
ETHNIC GROUPS Native African 99% (of whch 95% are Bantu consisting of more than 130 tribes)
LANGUAGES Swahili (Kiswahili) and English (both official)
RELIGIONS Islam 35% (99% in Zanzibar), traditional beliefs 35%, Christianity 30%
CURRENCY Tanzanian shilling = 100 cents

THAILAND

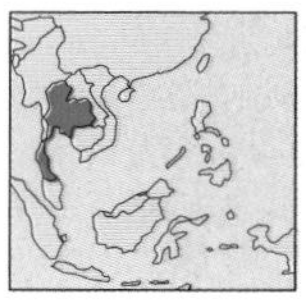

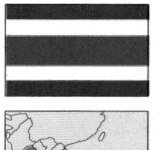

GEOGRAPHY The Kingdom of Thailand is one of the ten countries in Southeast Asia. The highest land is in the north, where Doi Inthanon, the highest peak, reaches 8,514 ft [2,595 m]. The Khorat plateau, in the north-east, makes up about 30% of the country and is the most heavily populated part of Thailand. In the south, Thailand shares the finger-like Malay peninsula with Burma and Malaysia.

Thailand has a tropical climate. Monsoon winds from the south-west bring heavy rains in May to October. Mountains shelter the central plains from the rain-bearing winds.

POLITICS & ECONOMY The first Thai state was set up in the 13th century. By 1350, it included most of what is now Thailand. European contact began in the early 16th century. But, in the late 17th century, the Thais, fearing interference in their affairs, forced all Europeans to leave. This policy continued for 150 years. In 1782, a Thai General, Chao Phraya Chakkri, became king, founding a dynasty which continues today. The country became known as Siam, and Bangkok became its capital. From the mid-19th century, contacts with the West were restored. In World War I, Siam supported the Allies against Germany and Austria-Hungary. But in 1941, the country was conquered by Japan and became its ally. After 1945, it became an ally of the United States.

After 1967, when Thailand became a member of ASEAN (Association of Southeast Asian Nations), its economy expanded rapidly, especially in manufacturing and service industries. However, in 1997, it suffered a recession along with other eastern Asian economies. From 1997, Thailand suffered economic recession. In 2001, a businessman, Thaksin Shinawatra, became prime minister. In 2006, Thaksin's party won a comfortable majority, the result of a boycott by opposition parties. Thaksin stood down in the interests of national stability. New elections were then ordered. Southern Thailand, where the largely Muslim population claims that the government discriminates against them, has been hit by violence.

Agriculture employs 45% of the people and rice is the chief crop. Cassava, cotton, maize, rubber, sugarcane, and tobacco are also grown. Tin is mined, but the chief exports are manufactures and food products. Tourism is important, but the devastating tsunami in December 2004 cast a shadow over its future growth.

AREA 198,114 sq mi [513,115 sq km] **POPULATION** 65,444,000
CAPITAL (POPULATION) Bangkok (6,320,000)
GOVERNMENT Constitutional monarchy
ETHNIC GROUPS Thai 75%, Chinese 14%, others 11%
LANGUAGES Thai (official), English, ethnic and regional dialects
RELIGIONS Buddhism 95%, Islam, Christianity
CURRENCY Baht = 100 satang

TOGO

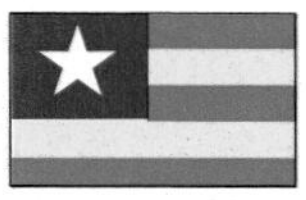

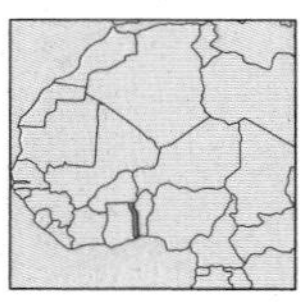

GEOGRAPHY The Republic of Togo is a long, narrow country in West Africa. From north to south, it extends about 311 mi [500 km]. Its coastline on the Gulf of Guinea is only 40 mi [64 km] long and it is only 90 mi [145 km] at its widest point.

Togo has high temperatures all through the year. The main wet season is from March to July, with a minor wet season in October and November.

POLITICS & ECONOMY Togo became a German protectorate in 1884 but, in 1919, Britain took over the western third of the territory, while France took over the eastern two-thirds. In 1956, the people of British Togoland voted to join Ghana, while French Togoland became an independent republic in 1960.

A military regime took power in 1963. In 1967, General Gnassingbé Eyadéma became head of state and suspended the constitution. Under a new constitution adopted in 1992, multiparty elections were held in 1994. However, in 1998, the count in the presidential elections was stopped when it became clear that Eyadéma had been defeated. The opposition boycotted subsequent elections. Eyadéma died in 2005. His son, Faure, took over as president, but international pressure forced him to step down. However, Faure was elected president in April 2005.

Togo is a poor, developing country dependent on agriculture. Major food crops include cassava, maize, millet, and yams. Phosphate rock is the leading export.

AREA 21,925 sq mi [56,785 sq km] **POPULATION** 5,682,000
CAPITAL (POPULATION) Lomé (658,000)
GOVERNMENT Multiparty republic **ETHNIC GROUPS** Native African 99% (largest tribes are Ewe, Mina, and Kabre) **LANGUAGES** French (official), African languages **RELIGIONS** Traditional beliefs 51%, Christianity 29%, Islam 20% **CURRENCY** CFA franc = 100 centimes

TONGA

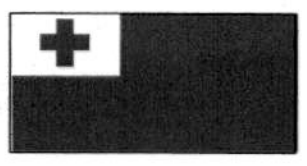

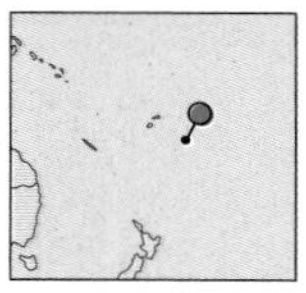

The Kingdom of Tonga, a former British protectorate, became independent in 1970. Situated in the South Pacific Ocean, it contains more than 170 islands, 36 of which are inhabited. Agriculture is the main activity; coconuts, copra, fruits, and fish are leading products.

AREA 251 sq mi [650 sq km] **POPULATION** 112,000 **CAPITAL** Nuku'alofa

TRINIDAD AND TOBAGO

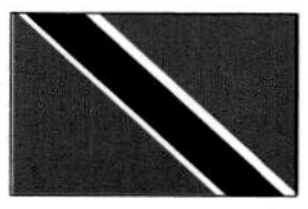

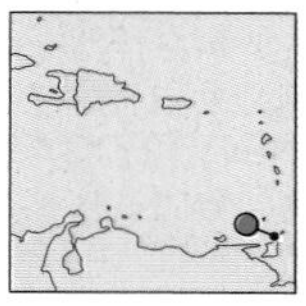

The Republic of Trinidad and Tobago became independent from Britain in 1962. These tropical islands, populated by people of African, Asian (mainly Indian), and European origin, are hilly and forested, though there are some fertile plains. Oil production is the mainstay of the economy.

AREA 1,981 sq mi [5,130 sq km]
POPULATION 1,089,000 **CAPITAL** Port of Spain

TUNISIA

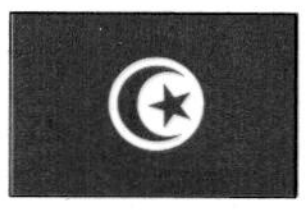

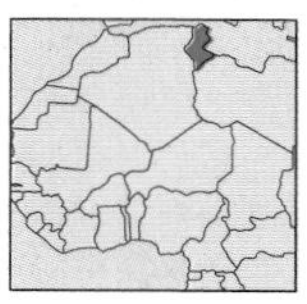

GEOGRAPHY The Republic of Tunisia is the smallest country in North Africa. The mountains in the north are an eastward and comparatively low extension of the Atlas Mountains. To the north and east of the mountains lie fertile plains, especially between Sfax, Tunis and Bizerte. In the south, low-lying regions contain a vast salt pan, called the Chott Djerid, and part of the Sahara Desert.

Northern Tunisia has a Mediterranean climate, with dry, sunny summers, and mild winters with a moderate rainfall. The average yearly rainfall decreases toward the south.

POLITICS & ECONOMY In 1881, France established a protectorate over Tunisia and ruled the country until 1956. The new parliament abolished the monarchy and declared Tunisia to be a republic in 1957, with the nationalist leader, Habib Bourguiba, as president. His government introduced many reforms, including votes for women, but various problems arose, including unemployment among the middle class and fears that Western values introduced by tourists might undermine Muslim values. In 1987, the prime minister Zine el Abidine Ben Ali removed Bourguiba and succeeded him as president. In 2002, the bombing of a synagogue on Djerba, believed to be the work of al Qaida, led to a major crackdown on dissidents.

The World Bank classifies Tunisia as a "middle-income" developing country. The main resources and chief exports are phosphates and oil. Most industries are concerned with food processing. Agriculture employs 21% of the people; major crops being barley, dates, grapes, olives, and wheat. Fishing is important, as is tourism.

AREA 63,170 sq mi [163,610 sq km] **POPULATION** 10,075,000
CAPITAL (POPULATION) Tunis (702,000) **GOVERNMENT** Multiparty republic **ETHNIC GROUPS** Arab 98%, European 1% **LANGUAGES** Arabic (official), French **RELIGIONS** Islam 98%, Christianity 1%, others **CURRENCY** Tunisian dinar = 1,000 millimes

TURKEY

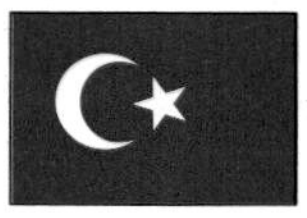

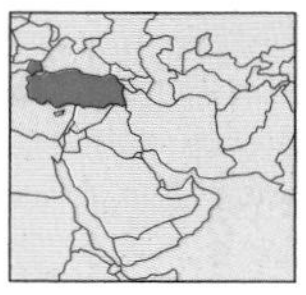

GEOGRAPHY The Republic of Turkey lies in two continents. European Turkey, also called Thrace, lies west of a waterway linking the Mediterranean and Black seas. Most of Asian Turkey consists of plateaux and mountains, which rise to 16,945 ft [5,165 m] at Mount Ararat (Agri Dagi) near the border with Armenia. Earthquakes are common. Central Turkey has a dry climate, with hot, sunny summers and cold winters. The west has a Mediterranean climate, but the Black Sea coast has cooler summers.

POLITICS & ECONOMY In AD 330, the Roman empire moved its capital to Byzantium, which it renamed Constantinople. Constantinople became capital of the East Roman (or Byzantine) empire in 395. Muslim Seljuk Turks from central Asia invaded Anatolia in the 11th century. In the 14th century, another group of Turks, the Ottomans, conquered the area. In 1453, the Ottoman Turks took Constantinople, which they called Istanbul. The Ottomans built up a vast empire which finally collapsed during World War I (1914–18). Turkey became a republic in 1923. Its leader, Mustafa Kemal, or Atatürk ("father of the Turks") began to modernize and secularize the country.

Since the 1940s, Turkey has sought to strengthen its ties with Western powers. It joined NATO (North Atlantic Treaty Organization) in 1951 and it applied to join the European Economic Community in 1987. But Turkey's conflict with Greece, together with its invasion of northern Cyprus in 1974, have led many Europeans to treat Turkey's aspirations with caution. Political instability, military coups, conflict with Kurdish nationalists in eastern Turkey, and concern about the country's record on human rights are other problems. Turkey has enjoyed democracy since 1983, though, in 1998, the government banned the Islamist Welfare Party, which it accused of violating secular principles. In 1999, the Muslim Virtue Party (successor to Islamist Welfare Party) lost ground. The largest numbers of parliamentary seats were won by the ruling Democratic Left Party and the far-right National Action Party. However, in the elections in 2002, the moderate Islamic Justice and Development Party (AKP) won 362 of the 500 seats in parliament, while none of the parties in the former ruling coalition won 10% of the vote. In 2003, Turkey opened its airspace to American aircraft during the Iraq war. Turkey hopes to join the European Union. Negotiations began in 2005, but they were expected to continue for around ten years.

The World Bank classifies Turkey as a "lower-middle-income" developing country. Agriculture employs 40% of the people, and barley, cotton, fruits, maize, tobacco, and wheat are major crops. Livestock farming is important and wool is a leading product. Turkey produces chromium, but manufacturing is the chief activity. Manufactures include processed farm products and textiles, cars, fertilizers, iron and steel, machinery, metal products, and paper products.

AREA 299,156 sq mi [774,815 sq km] **POPULATION** 69,661,000
CAPITAL (POPULATION) Ankara (2,984,000)
GOVERNMENT Multiparty republic **ETHNIC GROUPS** Turkish 80%, Kurdish 20% **LANGUAGES** Turkish (official), Kurdish, Arabic
RELIGIONS Islam (mainly Sunni Muslim) 99%
CURRENCY New Turkish lira = 100 kurus

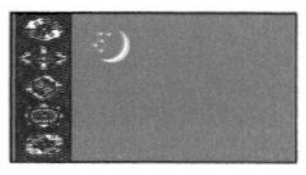
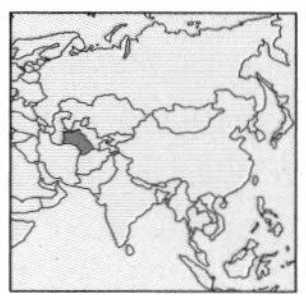

TURKMENISTAN

GEOGRAPHY The Republic of Turkmenistan is one of the five central Asian republics which once formed part of the former Soviet Union. Most of the land is low-lying, with mountains lying on the southern and southwestern borders. In the west lies the salty Caspian Sea. Most of Turkmenistan is arid and the Garagum, Asia's largest sand desert, covers about 80% of the country. Turkmenistan has a continental climate, with average annual rainfall varying from 3 inches [80 mm] in the desert to 12 inches [300 mm] in the mountains. Summer months are hot, but winter temperatures drop well below freezing point.

POLITICS & ECONOMY Just over 1,000 years ago, Turkic people settled in the lands east of the Caspian Sea and the name "Turkmen" comes from this time. Mongol armies conquered the area in the 13th century and Islam was introduced in the 14th century. Russia took over the area in the 1870s and 1880s. After the Russian Revolution of 1917, the area came under Communist rule and, in 1924, it became the Turkmen Soviet Socialist Republic. The Communists strictly controlled all aspects of life and discouraged religion. But they improved such services as education, health, housing, and transport.

In the 1980s, when the Soviet Union began to introduce reforms, the Turkmen began to demand more freedom. In 1990, the Turkmen government stated that its laws overruled Soviet laws. In 1991, Turkmenistan became fully independent after the breakup of the Soviet Union. But the country kept ties with Russia through the Commonwealth of Independent States (CIS).

In 1992, Turkmenistan adopted a new constitution, allowing for the setting up of political parties, providing that they were not ethnic or religious in character. But, effectively, Turkmenistan remained a one-party state and, in 1992, Saparmurad Niyazov, the former Communist and now Democratic Party leader, was the only candidate. In 1994, a referendum prolonged Niyazov's term of office to 2002, while, in 1999, the parliament declared him president for life. Parliamentary elections in 2004 were described as a "sham," because all the candidates supported the president.

Faced with many economic problems, Turkmenistan began to look south rather than to the CIS for support. As part of this policy, it joined the Economic Cooperation Organization, which had been set up in 1985 by Iran, Pakistan, and Turkey. In 1996, the completion of a rail link from Turkmenistan to the Iranian coast was an important step in the development of Central Asia. Oil and natural gas are Turkmenistan's chief resources, but agriculture is the main activity. Cotton, grown on irrigated land, is the main crop. Manufactures include cement, glass, petrochemicals, and textiles.

AREA 188,455 SQ MI [488,100 SQ KM] **POPULATION** 4,952,000 **CAPITAL (POPULATION)** ASHKHABAD (521,000) **GOVERNMENT** SINGLE-PARTY REPUBLIC **ETHNIC GROUPS** TURKMEN 85%, UZBEK 5%, RUSSIAN 4% **LANGUAGES** TURKMEN (OFFICIAL), RUSSIAN, UZBEK **RELIGIONS** ISLAM 89%, EASTERN ORTHODOX 9% **CURRENCY** TURKMEN MANAT = 100 TENESI

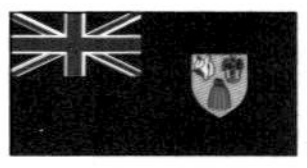
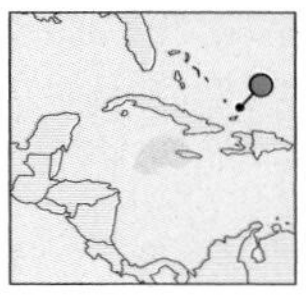

TURKS AND CAICOS ISLANDS

The Turks and Caicos Islands, a British territory in the Caribbean since 1776, are a group of about 30 islands. Fishing and tourism are major activities.

AREA 166 SQ MI [430 SQ KM]
POPULATION 21,000 **CAPITAL** COCKBURN TOWN

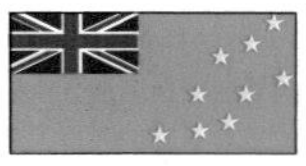
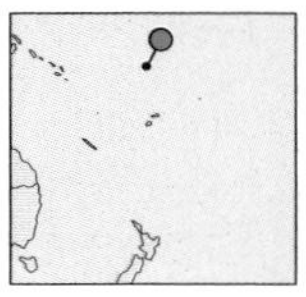

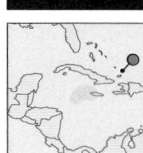

TUVALU

Tuvalu, formerly called the Ellice Islands, was a British territory from the 1890s until it became independent in 1978. It consists of nine low-lying coral atolls in the southern Pacific Ocean. Copra is the chief export.

AREA 10 SQ MI [26 SQ KM]
POPULATION 12,000 **CAPITAL** FONGAFALE

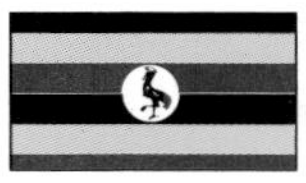
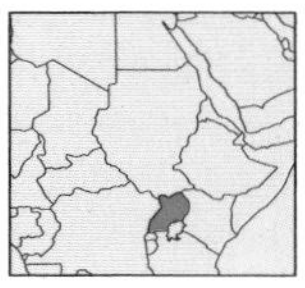

UGANDA

GEOGRAPHY The Republic of Uganda is a landlocked country on the East African plateau. It contains part of Lake Victoria, Africa's largest lake and a source of the River Nile, which occupies a shallow depression in the plateau.

The equator runs through Uganda and the country is warm throughout the year, though the high altitude moderates the temperature. The wettest regions are the lands to the north of Lake Victoria, where Kampala is situated, and the western mountains, especially the high Ruwenzori range.

POLITICS & ECONOMY Little is known of the early history of Uganda. When Europeans first reached the area in the 19th century, many of the people were organized in kingdoms, the most powerful of which was Buganda, the home of the Baganda people. Britain took over the country between 1894 and 1914, and ruled it until independence in 1962.

In 1967, Uganda became a republic and Buganda's Kabaka (king), Sir Edward Mutesa II, was made president. But tensions between the Kabaka and the prime minister, Apollo Milton Obote, led to the dismissal of the Kabaka in 1966. Obote also abolished the traditional kingdoms, including Buganda. Obote was overthrown in 1971 by an army group led by General Idi Amin Dada. Amin ruled as a dictator. He forced most of the Asians who lived in Uganda to leave the country and had many of his opponents killed.

In 1978, a border dispute between Uganda and Tanzania led Tanzanian troops to enter Uganda. With help from Ugandan opponents of Amin, they overthrew Amin's government. In 1980, Obote led his party to victory in national elections. But after charges of fraud, Obote's opponents began guerrilla warfare. A military group overthrew Obote in 1985, though strife continued until 1986, when Yoweri Museveni's National Resistance Movement seized power. In 1993, Museveni restored the traditional kingdoms. Elections were held in 1994, but political parties were forbidden. Museveni was elected in 1996, 2001 and again in 2006, when political parties were permitted. In recent years, Uganda has suffered from a conflict with a rebel force in the north, known as the Lord's Resistance Army. The objectives of this anarchic organization remain unclear.

Internal strife since the 1960s has greatly damaged the economy, but conditions improved during the relative stability of the 1990s and 2000s. Agriculture dominates the economy, employing 80% of the people. The chief export is coffee.

AREA 93,065 SQ MI [241,038 SQ KM] **POPULATION** 27,269,000
CAPITAL (POPULATION) KAMPALA (774,000)
GOVERNMENT REPUBLIC IN TRANSITION
ETHNIC GROUPS BAGANDA 17%, ANKOLE 8%, BASOGO 8%, ITESO 8%, BAKIGA 7%, LANGI 6%, RWANDA 6%, BAGISU 5%, ACHOLI 4%, LUGBARA 4%, AND OTHERS
LANGUAGES ENGLISH AND SWAHILI (BOTH OFFICIAL), GANDA
RELIGIONS ROMAN CATHOLIC 33%, PROTESTANT 33%, TRADITIONAL BELIEFS 18%, ISLAM 16%
CURRENCY UGANDAN SHILLING = 100 CENTS

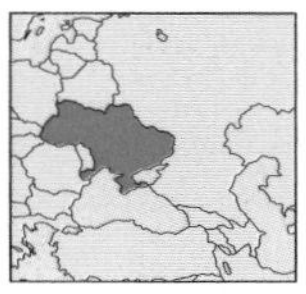

UKRAINE

GEOGRAPHY Ukraine is the second largest country in Europe after Russia. It was formerly part of the Soviet Union, which split apart in 1991. This mostly flat country faces the Black Sea in the south. The Crimean peninsula includes a highland region overlooking Yalta. Ukraine has warm summers, but the winters are cold, becoming more severe from west to east. In the summer, the east of the country is often warmer than the west. The heaviest rainfall occurs in the summer.

POLITICS & ECONOMY Kiev was the original capital of the early Slavic civilization known as Kievan Rus. In the 17th and 18th centuries, parts of Ukraine came under Polish and Russian rule. But Russia gained most of Ukraine in the late 18th century. In 1918, Ukraine became independent, but in 1922 it became part of the Soviet Union. Millions of people died in the 1930s as a result of Soviet policies, while millions more died during the Nazi occupation (1941–4).

In the 1980s, Ukrainian people demanded more say over their affairs. The country became independent in 1991. Leonid Kuchma, who became president in 1994, came under fire in the early 2000s for maladministration and for his alleged involvement in the murder of a journalist. In 2005, the pro-Western leader Victor Yuschenko was elected president. Economic problems and political infighting led to a Russian-leaning party, led by Viktor Yanukovich, winning the highest number of seats in parliament in 2006. Yuschenko then had the difficult task of forming a coalition.

The World Bank classifies Ukraine as a "lower-middle-income" economy. Agriculture is important. Wheat and sugar are exported. Barley, maize, potatoes, sunflowers, and tobacco are also grown. Livestock rearing and fishing are also important.

Manufacturing is the chief economic activity. Major manufactures include iron and steel, machinery, and vehicles. Ukraine has large coalfields. The country imports oil and natural gas, but it has hydroelectric and nuclear power stations. In 1986, an accident at the Chernobyl (Chornobyl) nuclear power plant caused widespread nuclear radiation. The plant was finally closed in 2001.

AREA 233,089 SQ MI [603,700 SQ KM] **POPULATION** 47,425,000
CAPITAL (POPULATION) KIEV (2,590,000)
GOVERNMENT MULTIPARTY REPUBLIC
ETHNIC GROUPS UKRAINIAN 78%, RUSSIAN 17%, BELARUSIAN, MOLDOVAN, BULGARIAN, HUNGARIAN, POLISH
LANGUAGES UKRAINIAN (OFFICIAL), RUSSIAN
RELIGIONS MOSTLY UKRAINIAN ORTHODOX
CURRENCY HRYVNIA = 100 KOPIYKAS

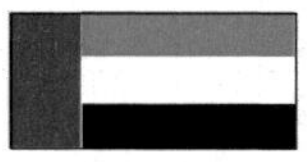
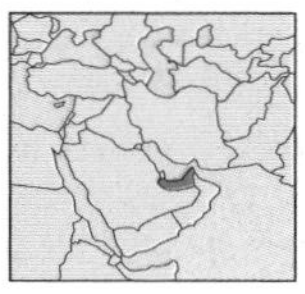

UNITED ARAB EMIRATES

The United Arab Emirates were formed in 1971 when the seven Trucial States of the Persian Gulf (Abu Dhabi, Dubai, Sharjah, Ajman, Umm al Qawayn, Ra's al Khaymah, and Al Fujayrah) opted to join together and form an independent country. The economy of this hot and dry country depends on oil production, and oil revenues give the United Arab Emirates one of the highest per capita GNPs in Asia.

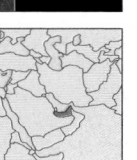

AREA 32,278 SQ MI [83,600 SQ KM] **POPULATION** 2,563,000
CAPITAL (POPULATION) ABU DHABI (363,000)

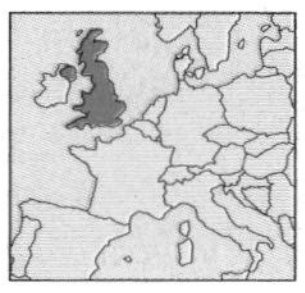

UNITED KINGDOM

GEOGRAPHY The United Kingdom (or UK) is a union of four countries. Three of them – England, Scotland, and Wales – make up Great Britain. The fourth country is Northern Ireland. The Isle of Man and the Channel Islands, including Jersey and Guernsey, are not part of the UK. They are self-governing British dependencies.

The land is highly varied. Much of Scotland and Wales is mountainous, and the highest peak is Scotland's Ben Nevis at 4,404 ft [1,342 m]. England has some highland areas, including the Cumbrian Mountains (or Lake District) and the Pennine range in the north. But England also has large areas of fertile lowland. Northern Ireland is also a mixture of lowlands and uplands. It contains the UK's largest lake, Lough Neagh.

The UK has a mild climate, influenced by the warm Gulf Stream which flows across the Atlantic from the Gulf of Mexico, then past the British Isles. Moist winds from the southwest bring rain, but the rainfall decreases from west to east. Winds from the east and north bring cold weather in winter.

POLITICS & ECONOMY In ancient times, Britain was invaded by many peoples, including Iberians, Celts, Romans, Angles, Saxons, Jutes, Norsemen, Danes, and Normans, who arrived in 1066. The evolution of the United Kingdom spanned hundreds of years. The Normans finally overcame Welsh resistance in 1282, when King Edward I annexed Wales and united it with England. Union with Scotland was achieved by the Act of Union of 1707. This created a country known as the United Kingdom of Great Britain.

Ireland came under Norman rule in the 11th century, and much of its later history was concerned with a struggle against English domination. In 1801, Ireland became part of the United Kingdom of Great Britain and Ireland. But in 1921, southern Ireland broke away to become the Irish Free State. Most of the people in the Irish Free State were Roman Catholics. In Northern Ireland, where the majority of the people were Protestants, most people wanted to remain citizens of the United Kingdom. As a result, the country's official name changed to the United Kingdom of Great Britain and Northern Ireland.

The modern history of the UK began in the 18th century when the British empire began to develop, despite the loss in 1783 of its 13 North American colonies which became the core of the modern United States. The other major event occurred in the late 18th century, when the UK became the first country to industrialize its economy.

The British empire broke up after World War II (1939–45), though the UK still administers many small, mainly island, territories around the world. The empire was transformed into the Commonwealth of Nations, a free association of independent countries which numbered 53 in 2006.

The UK has retained an important world role. For example, in 2001, it played a prominent role in creating a broad alliance to counter international terrorism following the attacks on the United

States. It was also a prominent member of the coalition force which invaded Iraq in 2003. However, the UK has recognized that its economic future lies within Europe. It became a member of the European Economic Community (now the European Union) in 1973. Membership of the EU has been important to the British economy, but some people fear a loss of British identity should the EU ever evolve into a political union. Another matter of public concern is large-scale immigration, both from the EU and outside.

The UK is a major industrial and trading nation. It lacks natural resources apart from coal, iron ore, oil, and natural gas, and has to import most of the materials it needs for its industries. The UK also has to import food, because it produces only about two-thirds of the food it needs. In the first half of the 20th century, Britain was a major exporter of cars, ships, steel, and textiles. But many industries have suffered from competition from other countries, with lower labor costs. Today, industries have to use high-technology in order to compete on the world market.

The UK is one of the world's most urbanized countries, and agriculture employs only 1% of the people. Production is high because of the use of scientific methods and modern machinery. However, in the early 21st century, especially following the outbreak of foot-and-mouth disease in 2001, questions were raised about the future of rural industries. Major crops include barley, potatoes, sugar beet, and wheat. Sheep are the leading livestock, but beef and dairy cattle, pigs, and poultry are also important. Fishing is another major activity and the UK is one of the largest fishing countries in the EU. Important catches include cod, haddock, plaice, and mackerel.

Service industries play a major part in the UK's economy. Financial and insurance services bring in much-needed foreign exchange, while tourism has become a major earner.

AREA 93,381 sq mi [241,857 sq km] **POPULATION** 60,441,000
CAPITAL (POPULATION) London (8,089,000)
GOVERNMENT Constitutional monarchy
ETHNIC GROUPS English 82%, Scottish 10%, Irish 2%, Welsh 2%, Ulster 2%, West Indian, Indian, Pakistani, and others **LANGUAGES** English (official), Welsh, Gaelic
RELIGIONS Christianity (Anglican, Roman Catholic, Presbyterian, Methodist), Islam, Sikhism, Hinduism, Judaism
CURRENCY Pound sterling = 100 pence

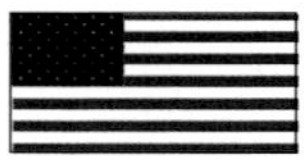

UNITED STATES OF AMERICA

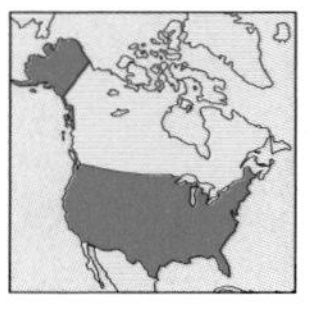

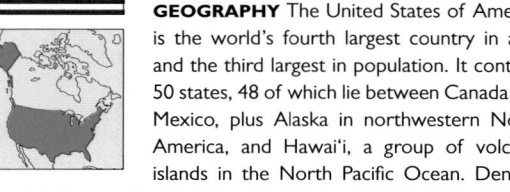

GEOGRAPHY The United States of America is the world's fourth largest country in area and the third largest in population. It contains 50 states, 48 of which lie between Canada and Mexico, plus Alaska in northwestern North America, and Hawai'i, a group of volcanic islands in the North Pacific Ocean. Densely populated coastal plains lie to the east and south of the Appalachian Mountains. The central lowlands drained by the Mississippi–Missouri rivers stretch from the Appalachians to the Rocky Mountains in the west. The Pacific region contains fertile valleys, separated by mountain ranges.

The climate varies greatly, ranging from the Arctic cold of Alaska to the intense heat of Death Valley, a bleak desert in California. Of the 48 states between Canada and Mexico, winters are cold and snowy in the north, but mild in the south, a region which is often called the "Sun Belt."

POLITICS & ECONOMY The first people in North America, the ancestors of the Native Americans (or American Indians) arrived perhaps 40,000 years ago from Asia. Although Vikings probably reached North America 1,000 years ago, European exploration proper did not begin until the late 15th century.

The first Europeans to settle in large numbers were the British, who founded settlements on the eastern coast in the early 17th century. British rule ended in the War of Independence (1775–83). The country expanded in 1803 when a vast territory in the south and west was acquired through the Louisiana Purchase, while the border with Mexico was fixed in the mid-19th century. The Civil War (1861–5) ended slavery and the serious threat that the nation might split into two parts. In the late 19th century, the West was opened up, while immigrants flooded in from Europe and elsewhere.

During the late 19th and early 20th centuries, industrialization led to the United States becoming the world's leading economic superpower and a pioneer in science and technology. It took on the mantle of the champion of Western democracy and, following the breakup of the former Soviet Union, it became the world's only superpower. But the attacks on the country on September 11, 2001, revealed its vulnerability to terrorists and rogue states. The response was vigorous. In 2001, it attacked the Taliban government in Afghanistan, which was protecting al Qaida terrorists. Then, in 2003, it led a coalition force to invade Iraq and overthrow Saddam Hussein. President George W. Bush was re-elected in 2004. The formation of an Iraqi government in 2006, following democratic elections, was hailed as a sign of the success of his policies. However, other observers were concerned that the ongoing conflict in Iraq might develop into civil war.

The United States has the world's largest economy in terms of the total value of its production. Although agriculture employs only about 2% of the people, farming is highly mechanized and scientific, and the United States leads the world in farm production. Major products include beef and dairy cattle, together with such crops as cotton, fruits, groundnuts, maize, potatoes, soybeans, tobacco, and wheat.

Natural resources include oil, natural gas, coal, a wide range of metal ores, and timber, especially from the Pacific northwest. Manufacturing is the single most valuable activity, employing 11.5% of the people. Major products include vehicles, food products, chemicals, machinery, printed goods, metal products, and scientific instruments. California, with its high-tech electronics industries, is the top manufacturing state. Many southern states, petroleum-rich and climatically favored, have also become highly prosperous in recent years.

AREA 3,717,792 sq mi [9,629,091 sq km] **POPULATION** 295,734,000
CAPITAL (POPULATION) Washington, DC (572,000)
GOVERNMENT Federal republic
ETHNIC GROUPS White 77%, African American 13%, Asian 4%, Amerindian 2%, others **LANGUAGES** English (official), Spanish, more than 30 others **RELIGIONS** Protestant 56%, Roman Catholic 28%, Islam 2%, Judaism 2%
CURRENCY US dollar = 100 cents

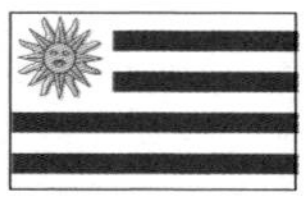

URUGUAY

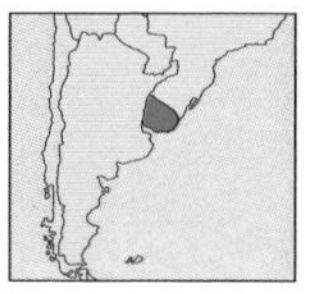

GEOGRAPHY Uruguay is South America's second smallest independent country after Suriname. The land consists mainly of flat plains and hills. The River Uruguay, which forms the country's western border, flows into the Río de la Plata, a large estuary which leads into the South Atlantic Ocean.

Uruguay has a mild climate, with rain in every month, though droughts sometimes occur. Summers are pleasantly warm, especially near the coast. The weather remains relatively mild throughout the winter.

POLITICS & ECONOMY In 1726, Spanish settlers founded Montevideo in order to halt the Portuguese gaining influence in the area. By the late 18th century, Spaniards had settled in most of the country. Uruguay became part of a colony called the Vice-royalty of La Plata, which also included Argentina, Paraguay, and parts of Bolivia, Brazil and Chile. In 1820 Brazil annexed Uruguay, ending Spanish rule. In 1825, Uruguayans, supported by Argentina, began a struggle for independence. Finally, in 1828, Brazil and Argentina recognized Uruguay as an independent republic. Social and economic developments were slow, but, from 1903, Uruguay became stable and democratic.

From the 1950s, economic problems caused unrest. Terrorist groups, notably the Tupumaros, carried out murders and kidnappings. The army crushed the Tupumaros in 1972, but the army took over the government in 1973. Military rule continued until 1984 when elections were held. In the early 21st century, Uruguay faced many economic problems, many of which were the result of the economic crisis in its neighbor, Argentina, and its imposition of banking controls in 2004. In 2005, Uruguay's first leftist president, Tabare Vasquez, was sworn in. He restored ties with Cuba and introduced measures to combat poverty.

The World Bank classifies Uruguay as an "upper-middle-income" developing country. Agriculture employs only 3.8% of the people, but farm products, notably hides and leather goods, beef, and wool, are the main exports, while many manufacturing industries process farm products. Crops include maize, potatoes, wheat, and sugar beet. Uruguay depends largely on hydroelectric power for energy; it exports electricity to Argentina.

AREA 67,574 sq mi [175,016 sq km] **POPULATION** 3,416,000
CAPITAL (POPULATION) Montevideo (1,303,000)
GOVERNMENT Multiparty republic
ETHNIC GROUPS White 88%, Mestizo 8%, Mulatto or Black 4%
LANGUAGES Spanish (official)
RELIGIONS Roman Catholic 66%, Protestant 2%, Judaism 1%
CURRENCY Uruguayan peso = 100 centésimos

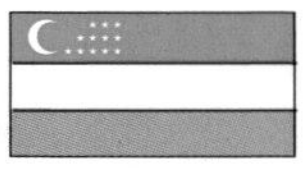

UZBEKISTAN

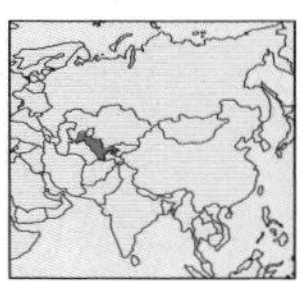

GEOGRAPHY The Republic of Uzbekistan is one of the five republics in Central Asia which were once part of the Soviet Union. Plains cover most of western Uzbekistan, with highlands in the east. The main rivers, the Amu (or Amu Darya) and Syr (or Syr Darya), drain into the Aral Sea. So much water has been taken from these rivers to irrigate the land that the Aral Sea has now shrunk to about a quarter of its size in 1960. The dried-up lake area has become desert, like much of the rest of the country. Uzbekistan has a continental climate with cold winters and hot summers. The west is extremely arid, with an average annual rainfall of about 8 inches [200 mm].

POLITICS & ECONOMY Russia took the area in the 19th century. After the Russian Revolution of 1917, the Communists took over and, in 1924, they set up the Uzbek Soviet Socialist Republic. Under Communism, all aspects of Uzbek life were controlled and religious worship was discouraged. But education, health, housing, and transport were improved. In the late 1980s, the people demanded more freedom and, in 1990, the government stated that its laws overruled those of the Soviet Union. Uzbekistan became independent in 1991 when the Soviet Union broke up, but it retained links with Russia through the Commonwealth of Independent States. Islam Karimov, leader of the People's Democratic Party (formerly the Communist Party), was elected president in December 1991. In 1992–3, many opposition leaders were arrested because the government said that they threatened national stability. In 1994–5, the PDP was victorious in national elections and, in 1995, a referendum extended Karimov's term in office until 2000, when he was again re-elected. In 2001, Uzbekistan allowed the United States to use bases in Uzbekistan for its military campaign in Afghanistan, but it demanded that US forces leave in 2005. International groups continued to criticize Uzbekistan's poor record on human rights.

The World Bank classifies Uzbekistan as a "lower-middle-income" developing country and the government still controls most economic activity. The country produces coal, copper, gold, oil, and natural gas.

AREA 172,741 sq mi [447,400 sq km] **POPULATION** 26,851,000
CAPITAL (POPULATION) Tashkent (2,143,000)
GOVERNMENT Socialist republic **ETHNIC GROUPS** Uzbek 80%, Russian 5%, Tajik 5%, Kazakh 3%, Tatar 2%, Kara-Kalpak 2%
LANGUAGES Uzbek (official), Russian **RELIGIONS** Islam 88%, Eastern Orthodox 9% **CURRENCY** Uzbekistani sum = 100 tyiyn

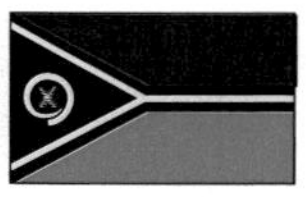

VANUATU

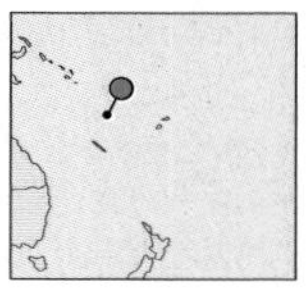

The Republic of Vanuatu, formerly the Anglo-French Condominium of the New Hebrides, became independent in 1980. It consists of a chain of 80 islands in the South Pacific Ocean. Its economy is based on agriculture and it exports copra, beef and veal, timber, and cocoa.

AREA 4,706 sq mi [12,189 sq km]
POPULATION 206,000 **CAPITAL** Port-Vila

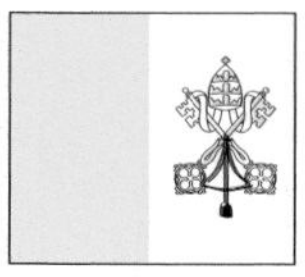

VATICAN CITY

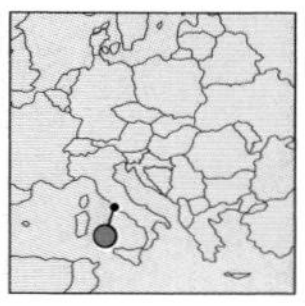

Vatican City State, the world's smallest independent nation, is an enclave on the west bank of the River Tiber in Rome. It forms an independent base for the Holy See, the governing body of the Roman Catholic Church.

AREA 0.17 sq mi [0.44 sq km]
POPULATION 1,000

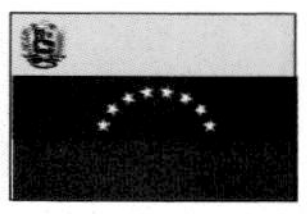

VENEZUELA

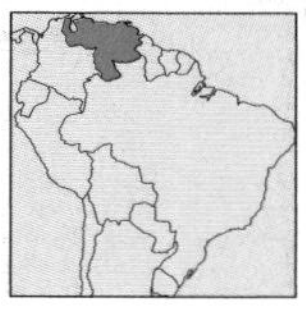

GEOGRAPHY The Bolivarian Republic of Venezuela, in northern South America, contains the Maracaibo lowlands around the oil-rich Lake Maracaibo in the west. Andean ranges enclose the lowlands and extend across most of northern Venezuela. The Orinoco river basin, containing tropical grasslands called *llanos*, lies between the northern highlands and the Guiana Highlands in the southeast. The Orinoco is Venezuela's longest river.

Venezuela has a tropical climate. Temperatures are high

throughout the year on the lowlands, though the mountains are much cooler. The rainfall is heaviest in the mountains. But much of the country has a marked dry season between December and April.

POLITICS & ECONOMY In the early 19th century, Venezuelans, such as Simón Bolívar and Francisco de Miranda, began a struggle against Spanish rule. Venezuela declared its independence in 1811. But it only became truly independent in 1821, when the Spanish were defeated in a battle near Valencia.

The development of Venezuela in the 19th and the first half of the 20th centuries was marred by instability, violence and periods of harsh dictatorial rule. But Venezuela has had elected governments since 1958. The country has greatly benefited from its oil resources which were first exploited in 1917. In 1960, Venezuela helped to form OPEC (the Organization of Petroleum Exporting Countries) and, in 1976, the government of Venezuela took control of the entire oil industry. In 1999, Hugo Chavez, who had staged an unsuccessful coup in 1992, was elected president. Chavez survived an attempted coup in 2002 and, in 2004, he won a majority in a referendum that had been intended by the opposition to remove him from office. In 2005–6, his left-wing policies and support for other left-wing regimes in Latin America continued to arouse US hostility.

With oil accounting for 80% of its exports, Venezuela has an "upper-middle-income" economy. Other exports include bauxite and aluminum, iron ore, and farm products. Beef cattle, dairy cattle, and poultry are raised. Crops include bananas, cassava, citrus fruits, coffee, and rice. The main industry is petroleum refining. Cement, steel, and textiles are also produced.

AREA 352,143 SQ MI [912,050 SQ KM] **POPULATION** 25,375,000 **CAPITAL (POPULATION)** CARACAS (1,823,000) **GOVERNMENT** FEDERAL REPUBLIC **ETHNIC GROUPS** SPANISH, ITALIAN, PORTUGUESE, ARAB, GERMAN, AFRICAN, INDIGENOUS PEOPLE **LANGUAGES** SPANISH (OFFICIAL), INDIGENOUS DIALECTS **RELIGIONS** ROMAN CATHOLIC 96% **CURRENCY** BOLÍVAR = 100 CÉNTIMOS

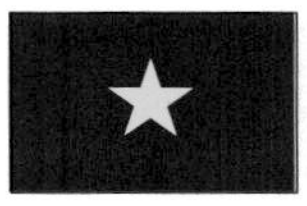
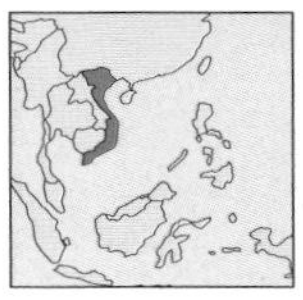

VIETNAM

GEOGRAPHY The Socialist Republic of Vietnam occupies an S-shaped strip of land facing the South China Sea in Southeast Asia. The coastal plains include two densely populated, fertile delta regions: the Red (Hong) delta facing the Gulf of Tonkin in the north, and the Mekong delta in the south.

Vietnam has a tropical climate, though the driest months of January to March are a little cooler than the wet, hot summer months, when monsoon winds blow from the southwest. Typhoons (cyclones or hurricanes) sometimes hit the coast, causing extensive flooding and much damage.

POLITICS & ECONOMY China dominated Vietnam for a thousand years before AD 939, when a Vietnamese state was founded. The French took over the area between the 1850s and 1880s. They ruled Vietnam as part of French Indochina, which also included Cambodia and Laos.

Japan conquered Vietnam during World War II (1939–45). In 1946, war broke out between a nationalist group, called the Vietminh, and the French colonial government. France withdrew in 1954 and Vietnam was divided into a Communist North Vietnam, led by the Vietminh leader, Ho Chi Minh, and a non-Communist South.

A force called the Viet Cong rebeled against South Vietnam's government in 1957 and a war began, which gradually increased in intensity. The United States aided the South, but after it withdrew in 1975, South Vietnam surrendered. In 1976, the united Vietnam became a Socialist Republic.

Vietnamese troops intervened in Cambodia in 1978 to defeat the Communist Khmer Rouge government, but it withdrew its troops in 1989. In the 1990s, Vietnam began to introduce reforms. In 1995, the United States opened an embassy in Hanoi and, in 2002, trade relations with the US were normalized. In 2004, the first US commercial flight since 1975 touched down in Ho Chi Minh City.

Agriculture is the main activity. Rice is the main food crop. Vietnam also produces chromium, oil (located off the south coast), tin, and phosphates.

AREA 128,065 SQ MI [331,689 SQ KM] **POPULATION** 83,536,000 **CAPITAL (POPULATION)** HANOI (1,074,000) **GOVERNMENT** SOCIALIST REPUBLIC **ETHNIC GROUPS** VIETNAMESE 87%, CHINESE, HMONG, THAI, KHMER, CHAM, MOUNTAIN GROUPS **LANGUAGES** VIETNAMESE (OFFICIAL), ENGLISH, CHINESE **RELIGIONS** BUDDHISM, CHRISTIANITY, INDIGENOUS BELIEFS **CURRENCY** DONG = 10 HAO = 100 XU

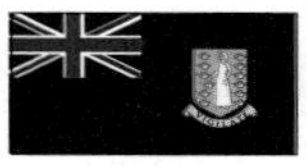
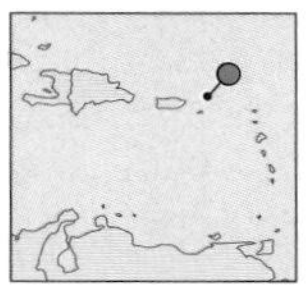

VIRGIN ISLANDS, BRITISH

The British Virgin Islands, the most northerly of the Lesser Antilles, are a British overseas territory, with a substantial measure of self-government.

AREA 58 SQ MI [151 SQ KM] **POPULATION** 23,000 **CAPITAL** ROAD TOWN

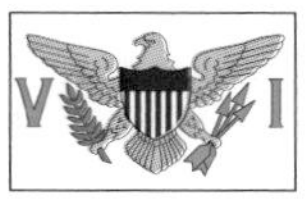
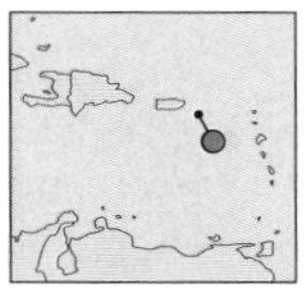

VIRGIN ISLANDS, US

The Virgin Islands of the United States, a group of three islands and 65 small islets, are a self-governing US territory. Purchased from Denmark in 1917, its residents are US citizens and they elect a non-voting delegate to the US House of Representatives.

AREA 134 SQ MI [347 SQ KM] **POPULATION** 109,000 **CAPITAL** CHARLOTTE AMALIE

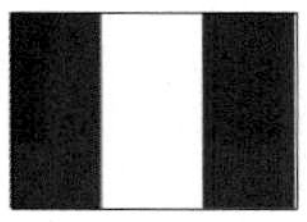
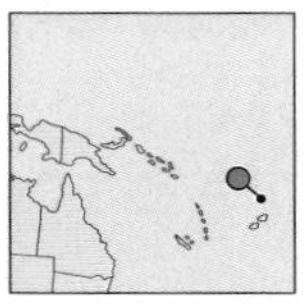

WALLIS AND FUTUNA

Wallis and Futuna, in the South Pacific Ocean, is the smallest and the poorest of France's overseas territories. French aid remains vital to an economy based on subsistence agriculture.

AREA 77 SQ MI [200 SQ KM] **POPULATION** 16,000 **CAPITAL** MATA-UTU

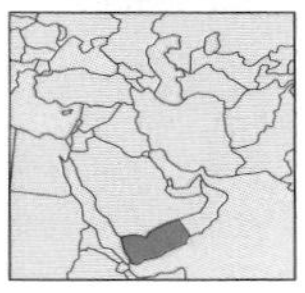

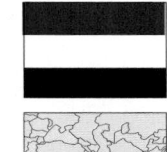

YEMEN

GEOGRAPHY The Republic of Yemen faces the Red Sea and the Gulf of Aden in the southwestern corner of the Arabian peninsula. Behind the narrow coastal plain along the Red Sea, the land rises to a mountain region called High Yemen. The climate ranges from hot and often humid conditions on the coast to the cooler highlands. Most of the country is arid. The south coasts are particularly hot and humid.

POLITICS & ECONOMY After World War I, northern Yemen, which had been ruled by Turkey, began to evolve into a separate state from the south, where Britain was in control. Britain withdrew in 1967 and a left-wing government took power in the south. In North Yemen, the monarchy was abolished in 1962 and the country became a republic.

Clashes occurred between the traditionalist Yemen Arab Republic in the north and the formerly British Marxist People's Democratic Republic of Yemen but, in 1990, the two Yemens merged to form a single country. Further conflict occurred in 1994, when southern secessionist forces were defeated. In 1998 and 1999, militants in the Aden-Abyan Islamic army sought to destabilize the country. In 2000, suicide bombers, thought to be part of the al Qaida network, steered a craft into a US destroyer in Aden harbor, killing 17 sailors. Hundreds of Yemenis were killed in 2004–5 during an uprising by Shia Muslims in the north. (Most Yemenis are Sunni Muslims.)

Yemen is a developing country and agriculture employs nearly half of the people. Sheep are reared and such crops as barley, fruits, wheat, and vegetables are grown in highland valleys and around oases. Cash crops include coffee and cotton.

Imported oil is refined at Aden and petroleum extraction began in the northwest in the 1980s. Handicrafts, leather goods, and textiles are manufactured. Remittances from Yemenis abroad are a major source of revenue.

AREA 203,848 SQ MI [527,968 SQ KM] **POPULATION** 20,727,000 **CAPITAL (POPULATION)** SANA' (954,000) **GOVERNMENT** MULTIPARTY REPUBLIC **ETHNIC GROUPS** PREDOMINANTLY ARAB **LANGUAGES** ARABIC (OFFICIAL) **RELIGIONS** ISLAM **CURRENCY** YEMENI RIAL = 100 FILS

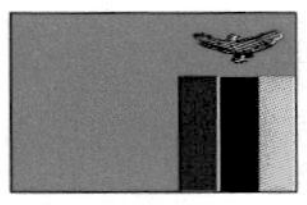
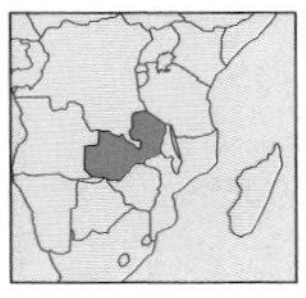

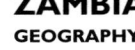

ZAMBIA

GEOGRAPHY The Republic of Zambia is a landlocked country in southern Africa. Zambia lies on the plateau that makes up most of southern Africa. Much of the land is between 2,950 ft and 4,920 ft [900 m to 1,500 m] above sea level. The Muchinga Mountains in the northeast rise above this flat land. Lakes include Bangweulu, which is entirely within Zambia, together with parts of lakes Mweru and Tanganyika in the north. Zambia lies in the tropics, but temperatures are moderated by the altitude.

POLITICS & ECONOMY European contact with Zambia began in the 19th century, when the explorer David Livingstone crossed the River Zambezi. In the 1890s, the British South Africa Company, set up by Cecil Rhodes (1853–1902), the British financier and statesman, made treaties with local chiefs and gradually took over the area. In 1911, the Company named the area Northern Rhodesia. In 1924, Britain took over the government of the country.

In 1953, Britain formed a federation of Northern Rhodesia, Southern Rhodesia (now Zimbabwe), and Nyasaland (now Malawi). Because of African opposition, the federation was dissolved in 1963 and Northern Rhodesia became independent as Zambia in 1964. Kenneth Kaunda became president and one-party rule was introduced in 1972. Under a new constitution, Frederick Chiluba was elected president in 1996. He stood down in 2001 and Levy Mwanawasa became president. In 2005, the Supreme Court rejected a challenge to Mwanawasa's election, but stated that the 2001 ballot had been flawed.

Copper, the main resource, accounted for 55% of the exports in 2001. Zambia also produces cobalt, lead, zinc, and gemstones. Agriculture employs 69% of the people, as compared with 4% in industry and mining. Food crops include cassava, fruits and vegetables, maize, millet, and sorghum, while cash crops include coffee, sugarcane, and tobacco.

AREA 290,586 SQ MI [752,618 SQ KM] **POPULATION** 11,262,000 **CAPITAL (POPULATION)** LUSAKA (1,270,000) **GOVERNMENT** MULTIPARTY REPUBLIC **ETHNIC GROUPS** NATIVE AFRICAN (BEMBA, TONGA, MARAVI/NYANJA) **LANGUAGES** ENGLISH (OFFICIAL), BEMBA, KAONDA, NYANJA, AND ABOUT 70 OTHERS **RELIGIONS** CHRISTIANITY 70%, ISLAM, HINDUISM **CURRENCY** ZAMBIAN KWACHA = 100 NGWEE

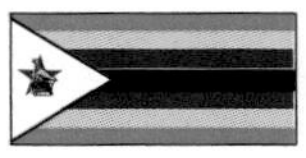
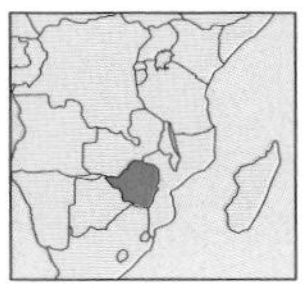

ZIMBABWE

GEOGRAPHY The Republic of Zimbabwe is a landlocked country in southern Africa. Most of the country lies on a high plateau between the Zambezi and Limpopo rivers between 2,950 ft and 4,920 ft [900 m to 1,500 m] above sea level. From October to March, the weather is hot and wet, but in the winter, daily temperatures can vary greatly.

POLITICS & ECONOMY The Shona people became dominant in the region about 1,000 years ago. The British South Africa Company, under the statesman Cecil Rhodes (1853–1902), occupied the area in the 1890s, after obtaining mineral rights from local chiefs. The area was named Rhodesia and later Southern Rhodesia. It became a self-governing British colony in 1923. Between 1953 and 1963, Southern and Northern Rhodesia (now Zambia) were joined to Nyasaland (Malawi) in the Central African Federation.

In 1965, the European government of Southern Rhodesia (then called Rhodesia) declared their country independent but Britain refused to accept this. Finally, after a civil war, the country became legally independent in 1980, though rivalries between the Shona and Ndebele people threatened stability. Order was restored when the Shona prime minister, Robert Mugabe, brought his Ndebele rivals into his government. In 1987, Mugabe became the country's executive president and, in 1991, the government renounced its Marxist ideology. Mugabe was re-elected president in 1990 and 1996. During the late 1990s, Mugabe threatened to seize white-owned farms without paying compensation to the owners. Despite international pressure, landless "war veterans" began to occupy white farms. In 2002, Mugabe was re-elected amid accusations of electoral irregularities. The Commonwealth suspended Zimbabwe's membership and, in 2004, the European Union renewed sanctions against the country. In 2005, the USA named Zimbabwe as one of the world's six "outposts of tyranny." Zimbabwe rejected this accusation and Mugabe's party won the 2005 parliamentary elections.

The World Bank classifies Zimbabwe as a "low-income" developing country. The country has valuable mineral resources and mining accounts for a fifth of the country's exports. Agriculture employs about half of the working people. Maize is the chief food crop, while cash crops include cotton, sugar, and tobacco. Cattle ranching is another important activity.

AREA 150,871 SQ MI [390,757 SQ KM] **POPULATION** 12,747,000 **CAPITAL (POPULATION)** HARARE (1,189,000) **GOVERNMENT** MULTIPARTY REPUBLIC **ETHNIC GROUPS** SHONA 82%, NDEBELE 14%, OTHER AFRICAN GROUPS 2%, MIXED AND ASIAN 1% **LANGUAGES** ENGLISH (OFFICIAL), SHONA, NDEBELE **RELIGIONS** CHRISTIANITY, TRADITIONAL BELIEFS **CURRENCY** ZIMBABWEAN DOLLAR = 100 CENTS

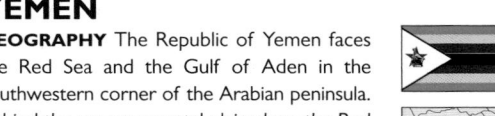

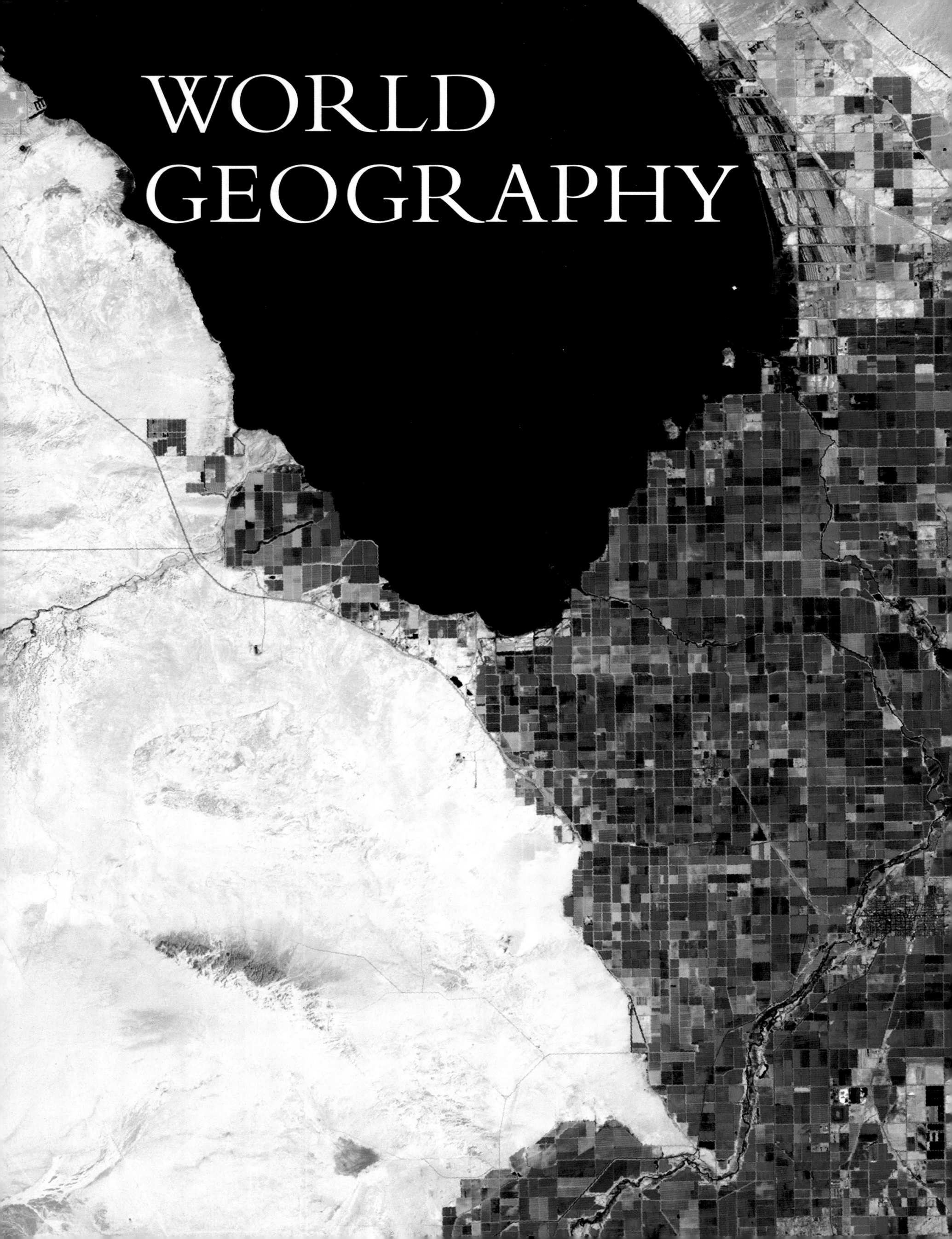

WORLD GEOGRAPHY

– IMPERIAL VALLEY, USA/MEXICO –
The dark area at top left of this false-color image is the Salton Sea. It is the largest lake in California but was created inadvertently in 1905 during an attempt to divert the flow of the Colorado River for irrigation. The resultant floodwaters filled part of the Imperial Valley. It lies 236 ft [72 m] below sea level and is very saline. To the south is a large area of productive land, which uses irrigated water from the river. The vegetation appears bright red on this image. [Map page 307]

For more information:
66 Orbits of the planets
Planetary data

About 13.7 billion years ago, time and space began with the most colossal explosion in cosmic history: the so-called Big Bang that is believed to have initiated the Universe. According to current theory, in the first millionth of a second of its existence it expanded from a dimensionless point of infinite mass and density into a fireball about 19 billion miles across – and it has been expanding ever since.

It took about 300,000 years for the primal fireball to cool enough for atoms to form. They were mostly hydrogen, which is still the most abundant material in the Universe. But the new matter was not evenly distributed around the young Universe, and by another billion years or so, atoms in relatively dense regions had begun to cling together under the influence of gravity, forming distinct masses of gas separated by vast expanses of empty space. To begin with, these first protogalaxies were dark places: the Universe had cooled. But gravitational attraction continued, condensing matter into coherent lumps inside the galactic gas clouds. By about 3 billion years later, some of these masses had contracted so much that their internal pressure created the high temperatures necessary to bring about nuclear fusion: the first stars were born.

There were several generations of stars, each feeding on the wreckage of its extinct predecessors as well as the original galactic gas swirls. With each new generation, progressively larger atoms were forged in stellar furnaces, and the galaxy's range of elements, once restricted to hydrogen and helium, grew larger. About 9 billion years after the Big Bang, a star formed on the outskirts of our galaxy with enough matter left over to create a retinue of planets. Nearly 5 billion years after that, human beings evolved.

The Sun is one of more than 100 billion stars in the home galaxy alone. Our galaxy, in turn, forms part of a local group consisting of approximately 30 similar structures, mostly small "dwarf" galaxies but a few large ones, and one – the Andromeda Galaxy – larger than our own. There are at least 100 billion galaxies in the Universe, many of which are members of huge galaxy clusters.

LIFE OF A STAR

For most of its existence, a star produces energy by the nuclear fusion of hydrogen into helium at its core. The duration of this hydrogen-burning period – known as the *main sequence* – depends on the star's mass; the greater the mass, the higher the core temperatures and the sooner the star's supply of hydrogen is exhausted. Dim, dwarf stars consume their hydrogen slowly, eking it out over billions of years. The Sun, like other stars of its mass, should spend about 10 billion years on the main sequence; since it was formed less than 5 billion years ago, it still has half its life left.

Once all of a star's core hydrogen has been fused into helium, nuclear activity moves outward into layers of unconsumed hydrogen. For a time, energy production sharply increases: the star grows hotter and expands enormously, turning into a so-called red giant. Its energy output will increase a thousandfold, and it will swell to a hundred times its former diameter.

After a few hundred million years, helium in the core will become sufficiently compressed to initiate a new cycle of nuclear fusion: from helium to carbon. The star will contract somewhat, before beginning its last expansion, in the Sun's case engulfing the Earth and perhaps Mars. In this bloated condition, the Sun's outer layers will break off into space, leaving a tiny inner core, mainly of carbon, that shrinks progressively under its own gravity. The white dwarf star thus formed can attain a density more than 10,000 times that of normal matter, with crushing surface gravity to match. Gradually, the nuclear fires will die down, and the Sun will reach its terminal stage: a black dwarf, emitting insignificant amounts of energy.

Black holes

However, stars more massive than the Sun may undergo a different transformation. The additional mass allows gravitational collapse to continue indefinitely: eventually, all the star's remaining matter shrinks to a point, and its density approaches infinity – a state that will not permit even subatomic structures to survive.

The star has become a *black hole*: an anomalous "singularity" in the fabric of space and time. Although vast coruscations of radiation will be emitted by any matter falling into its grasp, the singularity itself has an escape velocity that exceeds the speed of light, and nothing can ever be released from it. Within the boundaries of the black hole, the laws of physics are suspended.

GALACTIC STRUCTURES

Many of the Universe's 100 billion galaxies show clear structural patterns, originally classified by the American astronomer Edwin Hubble in 1925. Spiral galaxies like our own have a central, almost spherical bulge and a surrounding disk composed of spiral arms. Barred spirals have a central bar of stars across the nucleus, with spiral arms trailing from the ends of the bar. Elliptical galaxies have a more uniform appearance, ranging from a flattened disk to a near sphere.

▲ M51, the Whirlpool Nebula, comprises the large spiral galaxy NGC 5194 and its smaller, barred companion NGC 5195. M51 was the first astronomical object in which a spiral structure was identified, in 1845. Although smaller and less massive than our own Galaxy, M51 is much brighter, due to recent star formation.

Most galaxies, however, have no obvious structure at all. Galaxies also vary enormously in size, from dwarf galaxies only 2,000 light-years across to great assemblies of stars 80 or more times larger.

THE HOME GALAXY

The Sun and its planets are located in one of the spiral arms of the Galaxy, about 26,000 light-years from the galactic center and orbiting around it in a period of about 220 million years. The center is invisible from the Earth, masked by vast, light-absorbing clouds of interstellar dust.

The Galaxy is probably around 12 billion years old and, like other spiral galaxies, has three distinct regions. The central bulge is about 30,000 light-years in diameter. The disk in which the Sun is located is not much more than 1,000 light-years thick, but approximately 100,000 light-years from end to end. Around the Galaxy is the halo, a spherical zone 300,000 light-years across, studded with globular star clusters and sprinkled with individual suns.

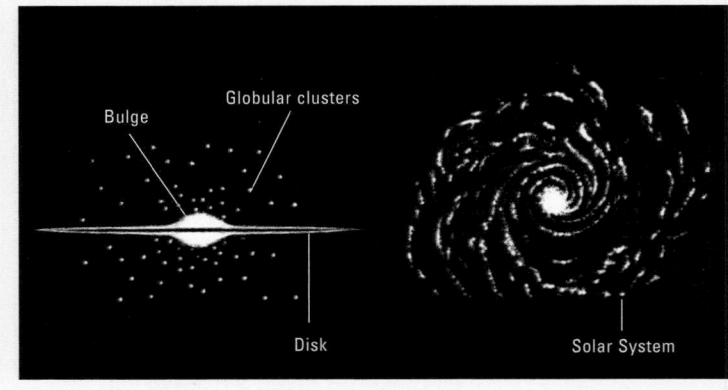

THE END OF THE UNIVERSE

The likely fate of the Universe is disputed. According to one theory (*top of diagram, below*), the expansion begun at the time of the Big Bang will continue "indefinitely," with aging galaxies moving further and further apart in an immense, dark graveyard.

Alternatively, gravity may overcome the expansion (*bottom of diagram*). Galaxies will fall back together until everything is again concentrated at a single point, followed by a new Big Bang and a new expansion, in an endlessly repeated cycle.

The first theory is supported by the amount of visible matter in the Universe; the second theory assumes that there is enough dark material in the Universe to bring about the gravitational collapse.

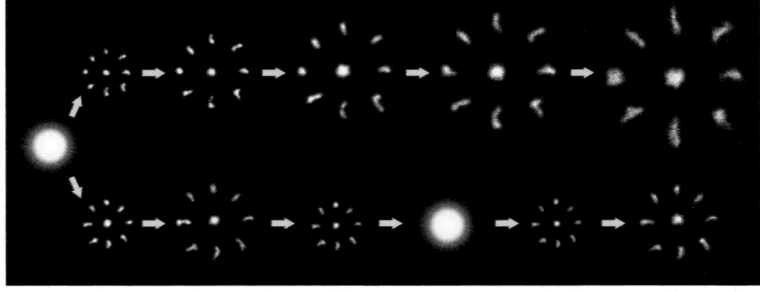

THE NEAREST STARS

The 22 nearest stars, excluding the Sun, with their distance from Earth in light-years*

Proxima Centauri	4.2	UV Ceti A	8.7	61 Cygni A	11.4
Alpha Centauri A	4.4	UV Ceti B	8.7	Procyon A	11.4
Alpha Centauri B	4.4	Ross 154	9.7	Procyon B	11.4
Barnard's Star	5.9	Ross 248	10.3	61 Cygni B	11.4
Wolf 359	7.8	Epsilon Eridani	10.5	HD 173740	11.5
Lalande 21185	8.3	HD 217987	10.7	HD 173739	11.7
Sirius A	8.6	Ross 128	10.9	* A light-year is about 5,900	
Sirius B	8.6	L789-6	11.2	billion miles [9,500 billion km]	

Many of the nearest stars, like Alpha Centauri A and B, are double stars, orbiting about their common center of gravity and to all intents and purposes equidistant from Earth. Many of them are dim objects, with no name other than the designation given to them by the astronomers who first investigated them.

However, they include Sirius, the brightest star in the sky, and Procyon, the seventh brightest. Both are larger than the Sun; of the nearest stars, only Epsilon Eridani is similar in size and luminosity. Most of the other bright stars in the sky are within 500 light-years of the Sun – a small fraction of the diameter of our Galaxy.

STAR CHARTS

NORTHERN HEMISPHERE SKY

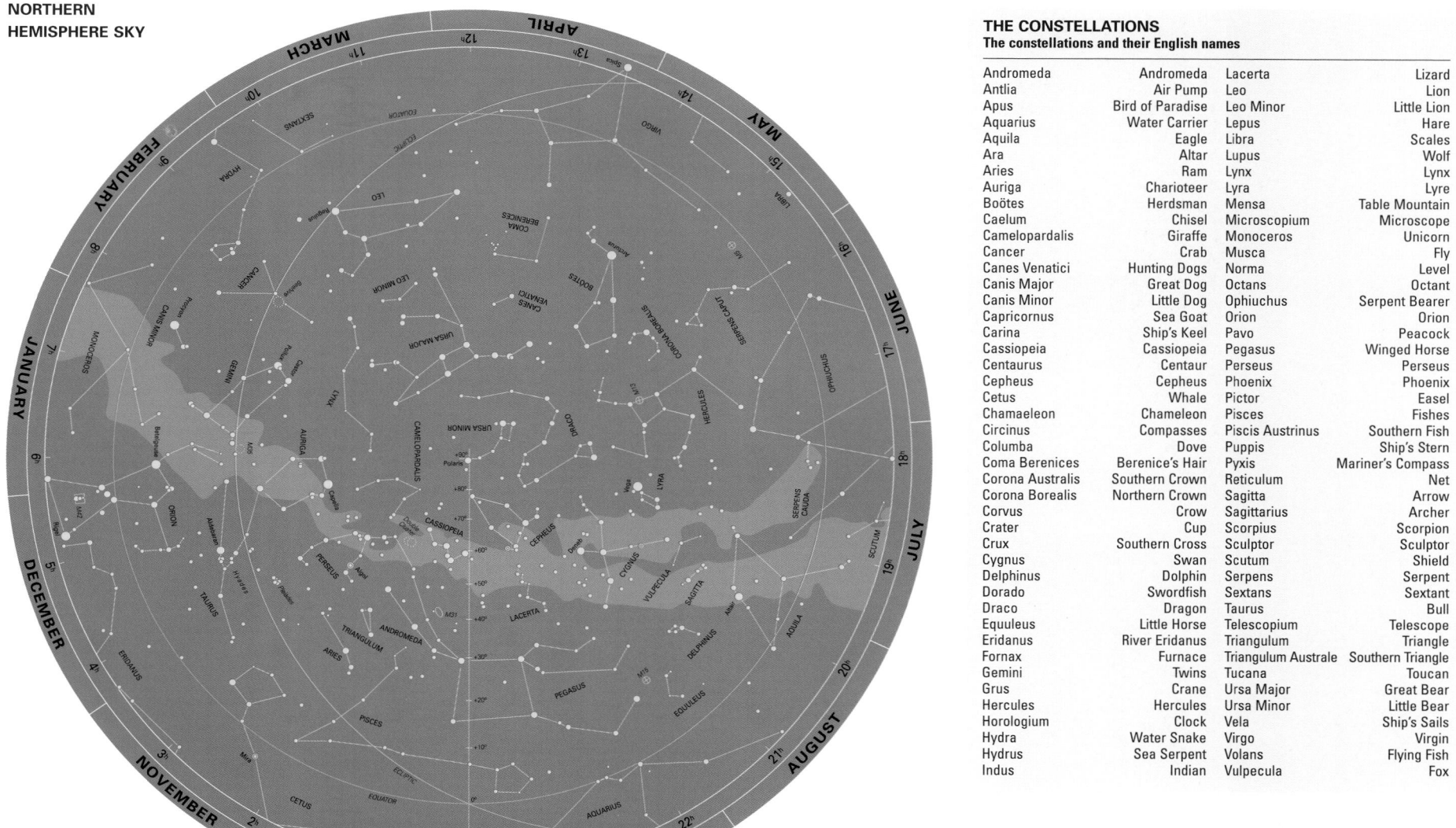

THE CONSTELLATIONS
The constellations and their English names

Andromeda	Andromeda	Lacerta	Lizard
Antlia	Air Pump	Leo	Lion
Apus	Bird of Paradise	Leo Minor	Little Lion
Aquarius	Water Carrier	Lepus	Hare
Aquila	Eagle	Libra	Scales
Ara	Altar	Lupus	Wolf
Aries	Ram	Lynx	Lynx
Auriga	Charioteer	Lyra	Lyre
Boötes	Herdsman	Mensa	Table Mountain
Caelum	Chisel	Microscopium	Microscope
Camelopardalis	Giraffe	Monoceros	Unicorn
Cancer	Crab	Musca	Fly
Canes Venatici	Hunting Dogs	Norma	Level
Canis Major	Great Dog	Octans	Octant
Canis Minor	Little Dog	Ophiuchus	Serpent Bearer
Capricornus	Sea Goat	Orion	Orion
Carina	Ship's Keel	Pavo	Peacock
Cassiopeia	Cassiopeia	Pegasus	Winged Horse
Centaurus	Centaur	Perseus	Perseus
Cepheus	Cepheus	Phoenix	Phoenix
Cetus	Whale	Pictor	Easel
Chamaeleon	Chameleon	Pisces	Fishes
Circinus	Compasses	Piscis Austrinus	Southern Fish
Columba	Dove	Puppis	Ship's Stern
Coma Berenices	Berenice's Hair	Pyxis	Mariner's Compass
Corona Australis	Southern Crown	Reticulum	Net
Corona Borealis	Northern Crown	Sagitta	Arrow
Corvus	Crow	Sagittarius	Archer
Crater	Cup	Scorpius	Scorpion
Crux	Southern Cross	Sculptor	Sculptor
Cygnus	Swan	Scutum	Shield
Delphinus	Dolphin	Serpens	Serpent
Dorado	Swordfish	Sextans	Sextant
Draco	Dragon	Taurus	Bull
Equuleus	Little Horse	Telescopium	Telescope
Eridanus	River Eridanus	Triangulum	Triangle
Fornax	Furnace	Triangulum Australe	Southern Triangle
Gemini	Twins	Tucana	Toucan
Grus	Crane	Ursa Major	Great Bear
Hercules	Hercules	Ursa Minor	Little Bear
Horologium	Clock	Vela	Ship's Sails
Hydra	Water Snake	Virgo	Virgin
Hydrus	Sea Serpent	Volans	Flying Fish
Indus	Indian	Vulpecula	Fox

SOUTHERN HEMISPHERE SKY

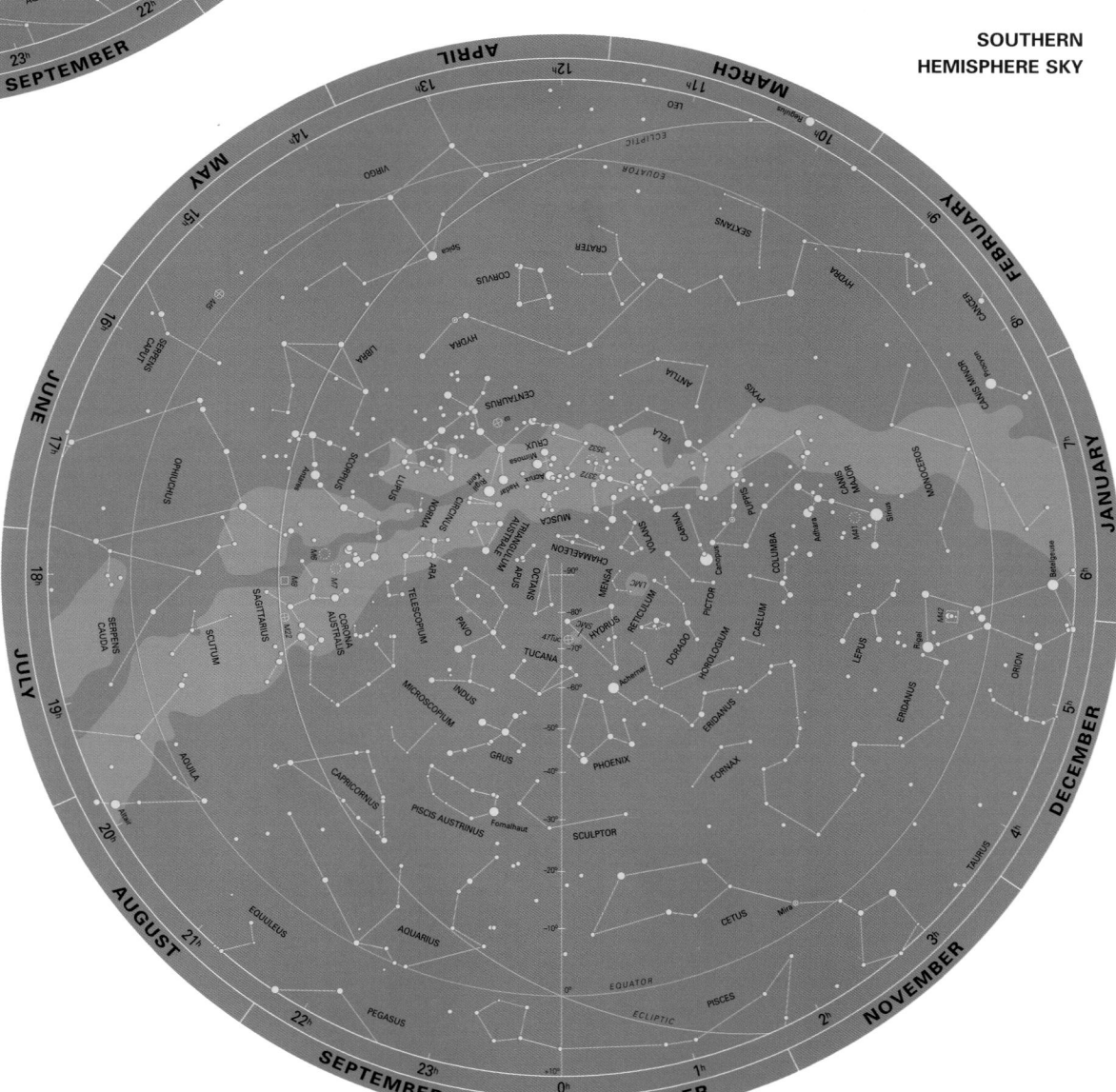

The charts on this page show the entire heavens divided into northern and southern hemispheres, with 10° of overlap between them around the perimeter of each one. However, the view from any particular location on Earth will be different, and will change both hourly as the Earth turns, and throughout the year as the Earth goes around the Sun.

The Sun's annual path through the heavens is known as the "ecliptic," and is shown here by an orange line. When the Sun is in the sky its light drowns out our view of the stars, so only that part of the heavens opposite the Sun is visible at a particular time. The sky's equivalent of longitude is known as "right ascension." As the stars appear to rotate around the Earth once every 24 hours, right ascension is measured eastward in hours and minutes and is marked around the edge of the maps. The equivalent of latitude is "declination," measured in degrees north or south of the celestial equator, and shown by the vertical line on each chart.

Using the charts

At any place and time you can see half of the whole sky, assuming a flat horizon. If you were at one of the poles your view would be shown as a circle centered on the middle of the map for the appropriate hemisphere, with the horizon marked by the celestial equator. From all other locations the center of your view (your overhead point) will be at some other point on the map whose location changes with time. The closer you are to Earth's equator, the closer the center will be to the edge of the map and more stars in the opposite hemisphere will be visible.

So first choose the appropriate chart for your hemisphere and hold it with the month at the bottom. At 11 p.m., not allowing for daylight saving time (Summer Time), your overhead point will be at the same declination as your geographical latitude and stars lower on the map will be due south (or north in the southern hemisphere). From latitude 50° in mid August, for example, your overhead point will be close to the star Deneb in the constellation of Cygnus. Stars on the opposite side of the map will be below your northern horizon, while stars below Deneb will be due south.

STAR MAGNITUDES
Apparent visual magnitudes

The magnitude scale of star brightnesses is developed from the system used by the Ancient Greeks in which the brightest stars were first magnitude and the faintest visible to the naked eye were sixth. Today the scale has a mathematical basis and extends, at the brightest end, through to negative magnitudes.

The Milky Way is shown in light blue on these charts.

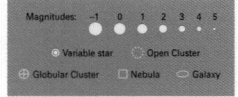

For more information:
64 The Home Galaxy
68 The seasons
   Day and night
69 The Moon

Lying about halfway from the center of one of billions of galaxies that populate the observable Universe, our Solar System contains nine planets and their moons, innumerable asteroids and comets, and a miscellany of dust and gas, all tethered by the immense gravitational field of the Sun, the middling-sized star whose thermonuclear furnaces provide them all with heat and light.

The Solar System was formed about 5 billion years ago, when a spinning cloud of gas, mostly hydrogen but seeded with other heavier elements, condensed enough to ignite a nuclear reaction and create a star. The Sun still accounts for almost 99.9% of the system's total mass.

By composition as well as distance, the planetary array divides quite neatly in two: an inner system of four small, solid planets, including the Earth, and an outer system, from Jupiter to Neptune, of four much larger planets composed of lighter materials, such as gas, liquid, and ice. Lying mostly between the two groups is a scattering of rocky asteroids, numbering perhaps a million or more. They may be debris left over from the formation of the inner Solar System. The outermost planet, Pluto, may simply be the largest member of the Kuiper Belt of rock–ice bodies orbiting beyond Neptune, left over from the formation of the outer Solar System.

Much of the early history of science is the story of people trying to make sense of the wandering points of light that were all they knew of the planets. Now, men have themselves stood on the Earth's Moon, space probes have landed on Mars and Venus, and distant landscapes have been mapped with astonishing accuracy, transforming our knowledge of our celestial environment.

In the 1980s, the Voyager space probes skimmed all four major planets of the outer Solar System, bringing new revelations with each close approach. The Magellan (Venus), Galileo (Jupiter), and Cassini–Huygens (Saturn) missions have transformed our knowledge of those planets and the giants' moons, and a host of orbiters and landers have shown us Mars in a new light. There are even plans to visit distant Pluto.

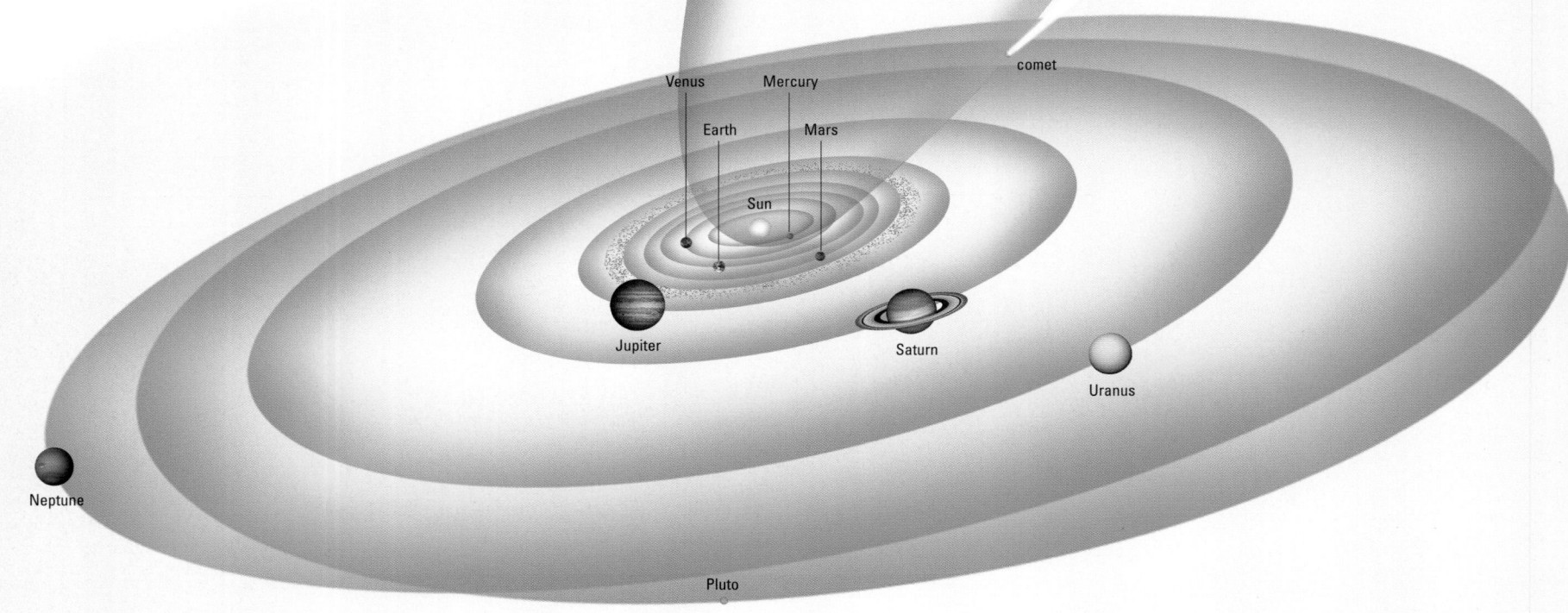

Diagram not drawn to scale

ORBITS OF THE PLANETS

The diagram above shows the Solar System as it might appear to an observer a few light-hours away in the direction of the constellation Hercules. Seen from such a position, above the plane of the ecliptic, all the planets revolve about the Sun in a counterclockwise direction. The perspective view exaggerates the elliptical form of all the planetary orbits: only Pluto and Mercury follow paths that deviate noticeably from circularity.

Near perihelion – its closest approach to the Sun – Pluto actually passes inside the orbit of Neptune, an event that last occurred in 1979. Pluto did not regain its station as the Sun's outermost planet until February 1999. The diagram also shows the main swarm of asteroids between Mars and Jupiter, and the orbit of a comet. Comets reside in a vast spherical halo beyond the Solar System, and are occasionally diverted toward the Sun on highly elliptical orbits.

PLANETARY DATA

	Mean distance from Sun (million miles)	Mass (Earth = 1)	Period of orbit (Earth days/years)	Period of rotation (Earth days)	Equatorial diameter (miles)	Average density (water = 1)	Surface gravity (Earth = 1)	Number of known satellites*
Sun	–	332,946	–	25.38	865,000	1.41	27.9	–
Mercury	36.0	0.06	87.97d	58.65	3,032	5.43	0.38	0
Venus	67.2	0.82	224.7d	243.02	7,521	5.24	0.91	0
Earth	93.0	1.00	365.3d	1.00	7,926	5.52	1.00	1
Mars	141.6	0.11	687.0d	1.029	4,220	3.94	0.38	2
Jupiter	483.7	317.8	11.86y	0.411	88,848	1.33	2.36	63
Saturn	886.6	95.2	29.45y	0.428	74,900	0.69	0.91	47
Uranus	1,784.0	14.5	84.02y	0.720	31,764	1.27	0.89	27
Neptune	2,795.2	17.2	164.8y	0.673	30,776	1.64	1.13	13
Pluto	3,670.2	0.002	247.9y	6.39	1,485	1.8	0.07	3

Planetary days are given in sidereal time – that is, with respect to the stars rather than the Sun. Most of the information in the table was confirmed by spacecraft and often obtained from photographs and other data transmitted back to the Earth. In the case of Pluto, however, only Earthbound observations have been made, and no spacecraft will encounter it until well into the 21st century. Given the planet's small size and great distance, figures for its diameter and rotation period have only recently been confirmed. Pluto is not massive enough to account for the perturbations in the orbits of Uranus and Neptune that led to its discovery in 1930, but it is now widely believed that these perturbations can be explained away as observational errors made by the earlier observers.

* Number of known satellites at mid-2006

THE PLANETS

Mercury is the closest planet to the Sun and hence the fastest-moving. It is very hot, with a cratered, wrinkled surface very similar to that of Earth's Moon. It is small and has low gravity, so there is no significant atmosphere.

Venus has much the same physical dimensions as Earth. Its dense atmosphere is composed of 97% carbon dioxide resulting in a runaway greenhouse effect that makes the surface, at 890°F, the hottest of all the planets in the Solar System. Radar mapping revealed a terrain consisting of highland regions and vast, rolling plains crossed by volcanic flows and dotted with craters. Discharges from volcanic regions could explain the sulfuric-acid rain detected by spacecraft. Soft-landers last less than an hour in Venus's fierce climate.

Earth seen from space is easily the most beautiful of the inner planets; it is also, and more objectively, the largest, as well as the only known home of life. Living things are the main reason why the Earth is able to retain a substantial proportion of reactive oxygen in its atmosphere; the oxygen in turn supports the life that constantly regenerates it. The Earth's natural satellite, the Moon, is believed to have been created when an asteroid struck our planet in its infancy.

Mars, smaller and cooler than the Earth, is nevertheless the most likely planet other than Earth where life may have formed. The planet was until recently (in astronomical terms) a geologically active world with water on its surface: rivers, lakes, and even an ocean. Liquid water may well exist today, but trapped beneath its dusty, boulder-strewn surface. The Martian landscape features huge extinct volcanoes, a giant canyon system, craters, and sand dunes. Its thin atmosphere is mostly carbon dioxide, and its polar caps are of frozen carbon dioxide and water ice. It has two tiny moons, probably captured asteroids.

Jupiter has about three times the mass of all the other planets combined. The planet is mostly gas, under intense pressure in the lower atmosphere above a core of fiercely compressed hydrogen and helium. The upper layers form strikingly colored rotating belts, the outward sign of the intense storms created by Jupiter's rapid rotation. The Great Red Spot is a storm feature that has persisted for at least 170 years. Jupiter has at least 63 moons. Most are very small, but the four largest – Io, Europa, Ganymede, and Callisto – are fascinating worlds in their own right. Io is the most volcanically active world known, and Europa possesses an ocean deep below its icy surface. The planet also has a system of rings, though nowhere near as prominent as Saturn's.

Saturn is structurally similar to Jupiter, rotating fast enough to produce an obvious bulge at its equator. It is composed of 89% hydrogen and 11% helium, and has wind velocities in the outer atmosphere of 1,600ft/sec. Ever since the invention of the telescope, Saturn's rings have been the feature that has most attracted observers. The rings consist of thousands of individual ringlets, composed of icy particles ranging in size from 30 feet down to microscopic. Titan, the largest of Saturn's 46 known moons, has a dense atmosphere.

Uranus was unknown to the ancients. Although it is faintly visible to the naked eye, it was not established as a planet until 1781. In its interior is probably a rocky core surrounded by frozen methane, water, and ammonia; the atmosphere is of hydrogen, helium, and some methane, which gives the planet its greenish-blue color. There is a system of thin, dark rings and a retinue of 27 moons, all but five of which are small.

Neptune is always more than 2.5 billion miles from Earth, and despite its diameter of nearly 31,000 miles, it can only be seen by telescope. Its discovery in 1846 was the result of mathematical predictions by astronomers seeking to explain irregularities in the orbit of Uranus. Like Uranus, it has a ring system; recent observations have revealed a total of 13 moons.

Pluto is the most mysterious of the solar planets, if only because even the most powerful telescopes can scarcely resolve it from a point of light to a disk. It was discovered as recently as 1930, as the result of a search based on analysing irregularities in the orbits of Uranus and Neptune. One of its moons, Charon, is the largest in the Solar System with respect to its parent planet. Pluto is the only planet yet to be visited by spacecraft.

Mean distance from the Sun in millions of miles

Mercury	36.0 Mercury
Venus	67.2 Venus
Earth	93.0 Earth
Mars	141.6 Mars
Jupiter	483.7 Jupiter
Saturn	886.6 Saturn
Uranus	1,784.0 Uranus
Neptune	2,795.2 Neptune
Pluto	3,670.2 Pluto

Diagrams not drawn to scale

Uranus   Neptune   Pluto

For more information:

66 Orbits of the planets

75 Ocean currents

76 Circulation of the air

78 Climate

The basic units of time measurement are the day and the year. The day is one rotation of the Earth on its axis. Our present calendar is based on the solar year of 365.24 days, the time taken by the Earth to orbit the Sun. Calendars based on the movements of the Sun and Moon have been used since ancient times. The length of the year, reckoned by the Julian Calendar introduced by Julius Caesar, was about 11 minutes too long. The cumulative error was rectified in 1582 by the Gregorian Calendar, when Pope Gregory XIII decreed that the day following October 4 was October 15, and that century years did not count as leap years unless they were divisible by 400. England finally adopted the reformed calendar in 1752, when it was 11 days behind the European mainland.

The rotation of the Earth on its axis causes day and night. The Earth rotates through 360° every 24 hours, and the world is divided into 24 time zones centered on lines of longitude at 15° intervals.

The tilt of the Earth's axis, which is also called the "obliquity of the ecliptic," accounts for the seasons which are so familiar in the middle latitudes. However, geological evidence shows that, over long periods of time, climates change, and the advances and retreats of the ice during the Pleistocene Ice Age may have been caused by regular variations in the Earth's tilt, its orbit around the Sun, and changes in the season when it is closest to the Sun (perihelion).

THE SEASONS

Seasons occur because the Earth's axis is tilted at an angle of approximately 23½°. When the northern hemisphere is tilted to a maximum extent toward the Sun, on June 21, the Sun is overhead at the Tropic of Cancer (latitude 23½° North). This is midsummer, or the summer solstice, in the northern hemisphere.

On September 22 or 23, the Sun is overhead at the equator, and day and night are of equal length throughout the world. This is the autumnal equinox in the northern hemisphere.

On December 21 or 22, the Sun is overhead at the Tropic of Capricorn (23½° South), the winter solstice in the northern hemisphere. The overhead Sun then tracks north until, on March 21, it is overhead at the equator. This is the spring (vernal) equinox in the northern hemisphere.

In the southern hemisphere, the seasons are the reverse of those in the north.

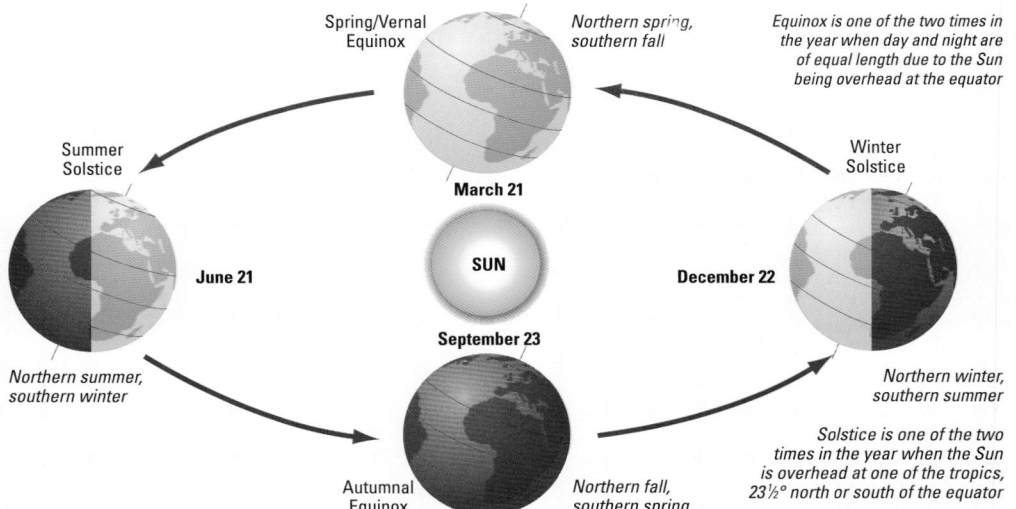

DAY AND NIGHT

The Sun appears to rise in the east, reach its highest point at noon, and then set in the west, to be followed by night. In reality, it is not the Sun that is moving but the Earth rotating from west to east. The moment when the Sun's upper limb first appears above the horizon is termed sunrise; the moment when the Sun's upper limb disappears below the horizon is sunset.

At the summer solstice in the northern hemisphere (June 21), the Arctic has total daylight and the Antarctic total darkness. The opposite occurs at the winter solstice (December 21 or 22). At the equator, the length of day and night are almost equal all year.

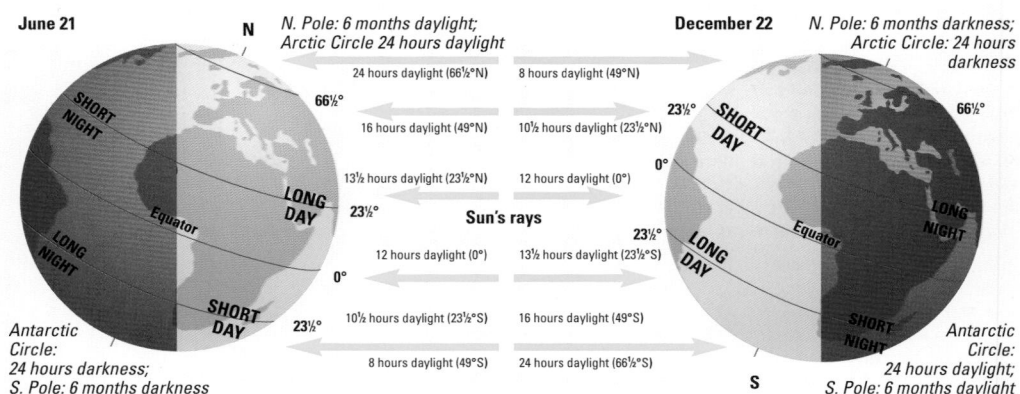

EARTH DATA

Aphelion (maximum distance from Sun):	94,508,166 miles	**Length of year:**	365 days, 5 hours, 48 minutes, 46 seconds of mean solar time	**Polar circumference:**	24,860 miles
Perihelion (minimum distance from Sun):	91,403,477 miles			**Equatorial diameter:**	7,926 miles
		Superficial area:	197,000,000 sq miles	**Polar diameter:**	7,900 miles
Angle of tilt (obliquity of the ecliptic):	23° 27' 08"	**Land surface:**	57,500,000 sq miles (29.2%)	**Equatorial radius:**	3,963 miles
				Polar radius:	3,950 miles
Length of year – solar tropical (equinox to equinox):	365.24 days	**Water surface:**	139,500,000 sq miles (70.8%)	**Volume of the Earth:**	$259,880 \times 10^{6}$ cu miles
		Equatorial circumference:	24,901 miles	**Mass of the Earth:**	5.97×10^{24} kg

SUNRISE AND SUNSET

The term "equinox" comes from the Latin for "equal night." At the spring and autumnal equinoxes, the Sun is vertically overhead at midday at the equator and all places on Earth have 12 hours of darkness and 12 hours of daylight. The graphs of sunrise and sunset show that these occasions occur on March 21 and on September 22 or 23. The graphs also show that, because the Sun remains high in the sky at the equator throughout the year, the length of day and night there remains roughly the same throughout the year, with sunrise around 6 a.m. and sunset around 6 p.m.

The further north or south one travels, the greater the difference between the number of hours of daylight and darkness. For example, the graph (right) shows that at latitude 60°N sunrise varies from just after 9 a.m. in midwinter (on December 22 or 23) to about 2.30 a.m. in midsummer (around the summer solstice on June 21). By contrast, the second graph (far right) shows that sunset at latitude 60°N occurs at about 2.45 p.m. in midwinter and 9.20 p.m. in midsummer.

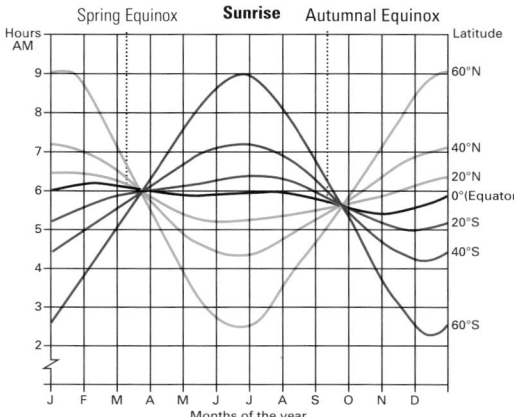

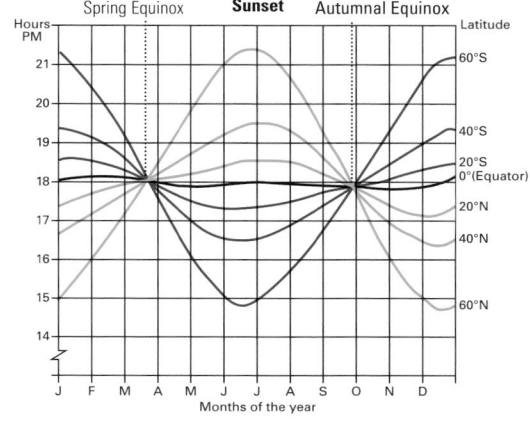

THE MOON

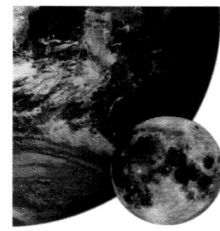

The Moon rotates more slowly than the Earth, taking just over 27 days to make one complete rotation on its axis. Since this corresponds to the Moon's orbital period around the Earth, the Moon always presents the same hemisphere toward us, and we never see the far side. The interval between one New Moon and the next is 29½ days – this is called a lunation, or lunar month. The Moon shines only by reflected sunlight, and emits no light of its own. During each lunation the Moon displays a complete cycle of phases, caused by the changing angle of illumination from the Sun.

PHASES OF THE MOON

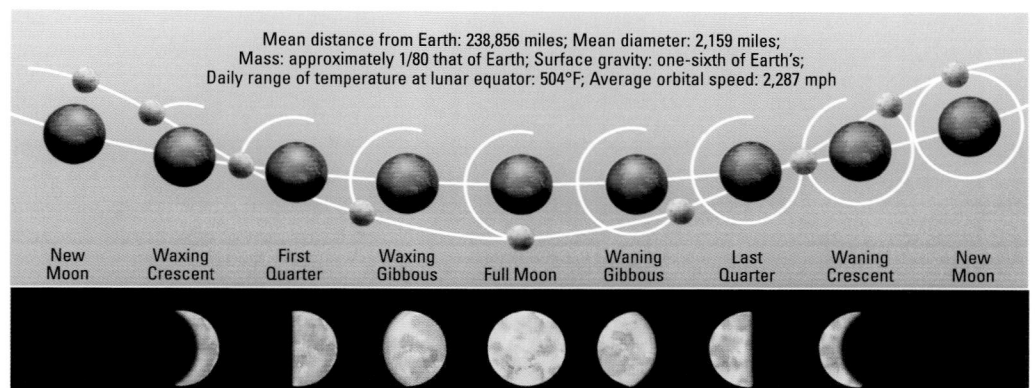

Mean distance from Earth: 238,856 miles; Mean diameter: 2,159 miles; Mass: approximately 1/80 that of Earth; Surface gravity: one-sixth of Earth's; Daily range of temperature at lunar equator: 504°F; Average orbital speed: 2,287 mph

New Moon | Waxing Crescent | First Quarter | Waxing Gibbous | Full Moon | Waning Gibbous | Last Quarter | Waning Crescent | New Moon

ECLIPSES

When the Moon passes between the Sun and the Earth, the Sun becomes partially eclipsed (1). A partial eclipse can become a total eclipse if the Moon covers the Sun completely (2) and the dark central part of the lunar shadow touches the Earth. The broad geographical zone covered by the Moon's outer shadow (P) has only a very small central area (often less than 62 miles wide) that experiences totality. Totality can never last for more than 7½ minutes, and it is usually briefer than this. Lunar eclipses take place when the Moon moves through the shadow of the Earth, and can also be partial or total. Any single location on Earth can experience a maximum of four solar and three lunar eclipses in any single year, while a total solar eclipse occurs an average of once every 360 years for any given location.

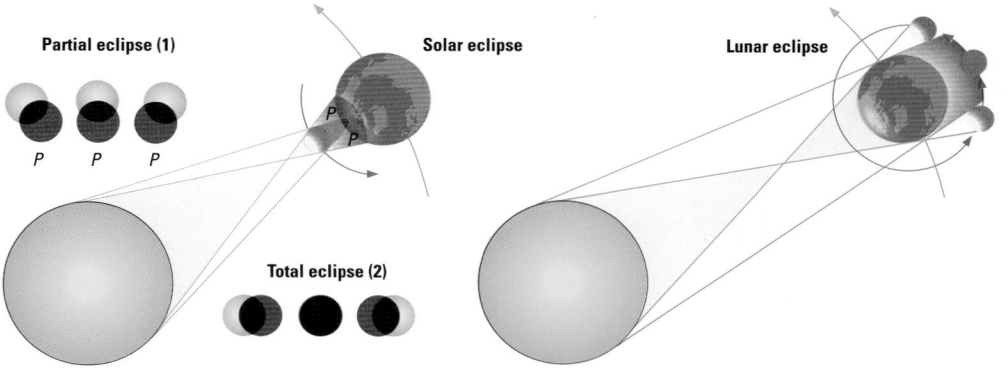

Partial eclipse (1) P P P

Solar eclipse P P

Total eclipse (2)

Lunar eclipse

TIDES

The daily rise and fall of the ocean's tides are the result of the gravitational pull of the Moon and that of the Sun, though the effect of the latter is not as strong as that of the Moon. This effect is greatest on the hemisphere facing the Moon and causes a tidal "bulge." When the Sun, Earth, and Moon are in line, spring tides occur: high tide reaches the highest values, and low tide falls to low levels. When lunar and solar forces are least coincidental with the Sun and Moon at an angle (near the Moon's first and third quarters), neap tides occur, which have a small tidal range.

Spring tide

Last Quarter

Neap tide

Spring tide

New Moon

Full Moon

Gravitational pull by the Sun

Neap tide

First Quarter

MOON DATA

Distance from Earth
The Moon orbits at a mean distance of 238,856 miles, at an average speed of 2,287 mph in relation to the Earth.

Size and mass
The average diameter of the Moon is 2,159 miles. It is 400 times smaller than the Sun but is about 400 times closer to the Earth, so we see them as the same size. The Moon has a mass of 7.35×10^{22} kg, with a density 3.344 times that of water.

Visibility
Only 59% of the Moon's surface is visible from the Earth over time. Sunlight reflected from the Moon takes 1.3 seconds to reach the Earth (the Sun itself is around 8½ light-minutes away).

Temperature
With the Sun overhead, the temperature on the lunar equator can reach 243°F [117°C]. At night it can sink to −261°F [−163°C].

TIME ZONES

The Earth rotates through 360° in 24 hours, and so moves 15° every hour. The world is divided into 24 standard time zones, each centered on lines of longitude at 15° intervals. At the center of the first zone is the prime meridian, or Greenwich meridian. All places to the west of Greenwich are one hour behind for every 15° of longitude; places to the east are ahead by one hour for every 15°.

International Date Line
When it is 12 noon on the Greenwich meridian, 180° east it is midnight of the same day – while 180° west the day is just beginning. To overcome this, the International Date Line was established, approximately following the 180° meridian. Thus, if you were to travel eastward from Japan (140°E) to Samoa (170°W), you would pass from Sunday night into Sunday morning.

10   Hours behind or ahead of UT or Coordinated Universal Time

Zones using UT (GMT)

Zones behind UT (GMT)

International boundaries

Zones ahead of UT (GMT)

Half-hour zones

Time-zone boundaries

International Date Line

Actual solar time when time at Greenwich is 12:00 (noon)

Note: Some of the above time zones are affected by the incidence of daylight saving time in countries where it is adopted.

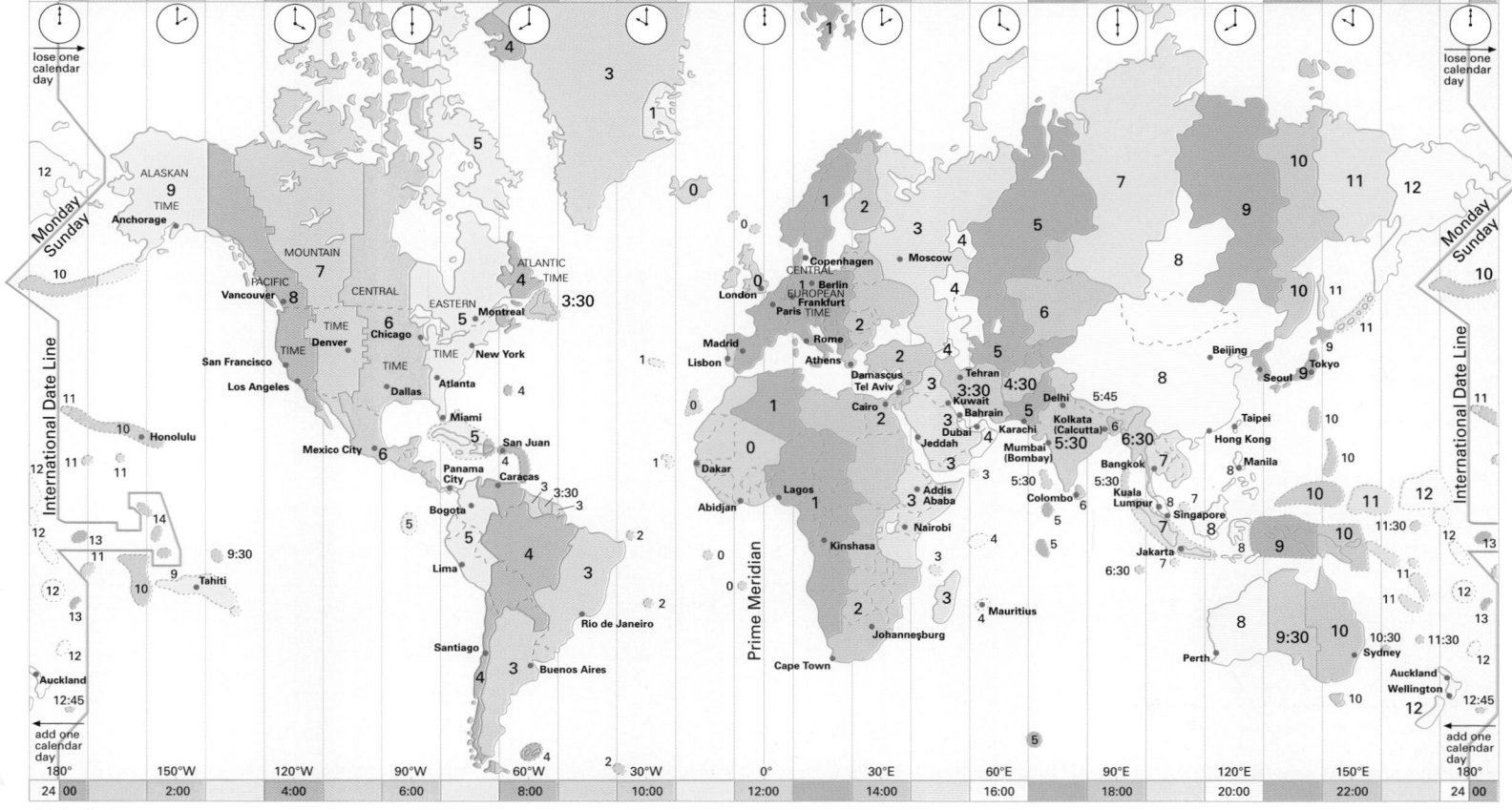

Projection: Mercator

For more information:
72 Types of rock
   Mountain building
73 Surface processes
83 The carbon cycle
98 Minerals

Every year, earthquakes and volcanic eruptions cause much destruction throughout the world. Such phenomena were once thought to be unconnected, but since the late 1960s, scientists have understood that these events are surface manifestations of the tremendous forces operating in the Earth's interior that are slowly but constantly changing the face of our planet.

The Earth is divided into three zones. The crust, a brittle, low-density zone, overlies the dense mantle. Separating the crust from the mantle is a distinct boundary called the Mohorovičić (or Moho) discontinuity. Enclosed by the mantle is the Earth's core, which consists mainly of iron and nickel.

Temperatures inside the Earth range from about 1,600°F in the upper mantle to perhaps 9,000°F in the core. Heat creates convection currents in a semimolten part of the mantle called the asthenosphere. Above the asthenosphere is the lithosphere, a solid layer about 40 miles thick, consisting of the crust and part of the mantle. The lithosphere is divided into rigid plates, moved around by the currents in the asthenosphere, a process named plate tectonics.

The Earth was formed around 4.6 billion years ago. Lighter elements floated toward the surface, where they formed crustal rocks. The oldest rocks so far discovered are about 4 billion years old, while the oldest fossils occur in rocks formed around 3.5 billion years ago. An explosion of life occurred at the start of the Cambrian period, 570 million years ago. The fossil record since the start of the Cambrian has enabled scientists to piece together the story of life on Earth.

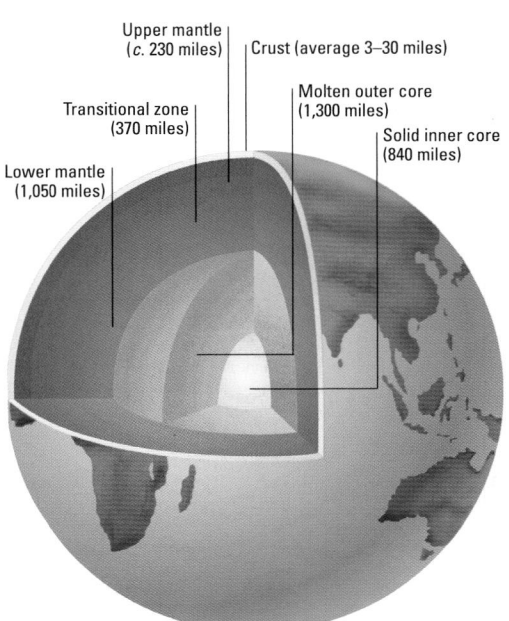

Upper mantle (c. 230 miles)
Crust (average 3–30 miles)
Transitional zone (370 miles)
Molten outer core (1,300 miles)
Solid inner core (840 miles)
Lower mantle (1,050 miles)

CONTINENTAL DRIFT

——— Trench
——— Rift
▨ New ocean floor
——— Zones of slippage

In 1915, Alfred Wegener produced a series of world maps proposing that, around 200 million years ago, the continents had been joined together in a supercontinent that he called Pangaea. This land mass started to break up about 180 million years ago and the parts drifted to their present positions. In the 1950s and 1960s, evidence from studies of the ocean floor suggested that the low-density continents rest on huge slow-moving plates. The arrows on the present-day world map (*below*) show that the continents are still on the move.

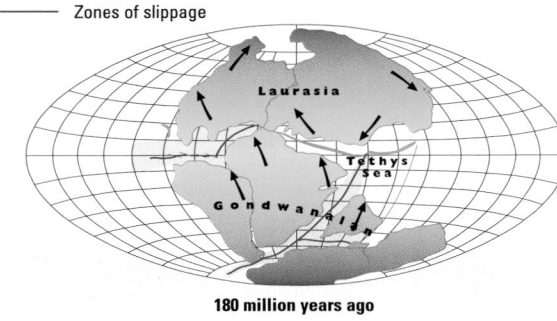

180 million years ago

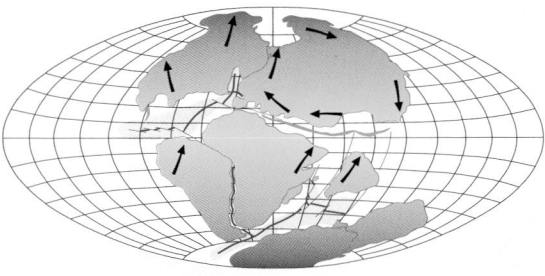

135 million years ago

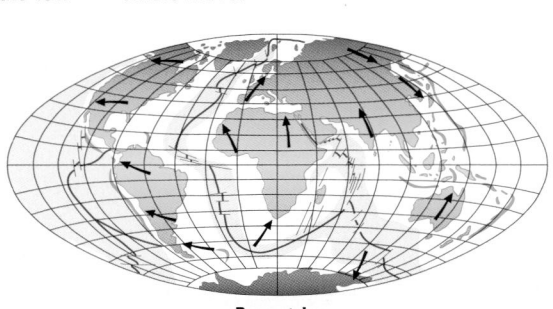

Present day

DISTRIBUTION OF VOLCANOES

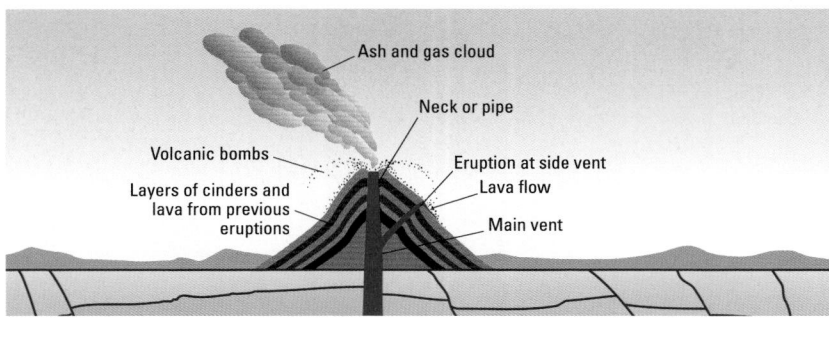

Ash and gas cloud
Neck or pipe
Volcanic bombs
Eruption at side vent
Lava flow
Layers of cinders and lava from previous eruptions
Main vent

Volcanoes occur when hot liquefied rock beneath the Earth's crust is pushed up by pressure to the surface as molten lava. There are some 550 known active volcanoes, around 20 of which are erupting at any one time.

○ Submarine volcanoes

▲ Land volcanoes active since 1700

— Boundaries of tectonic plates

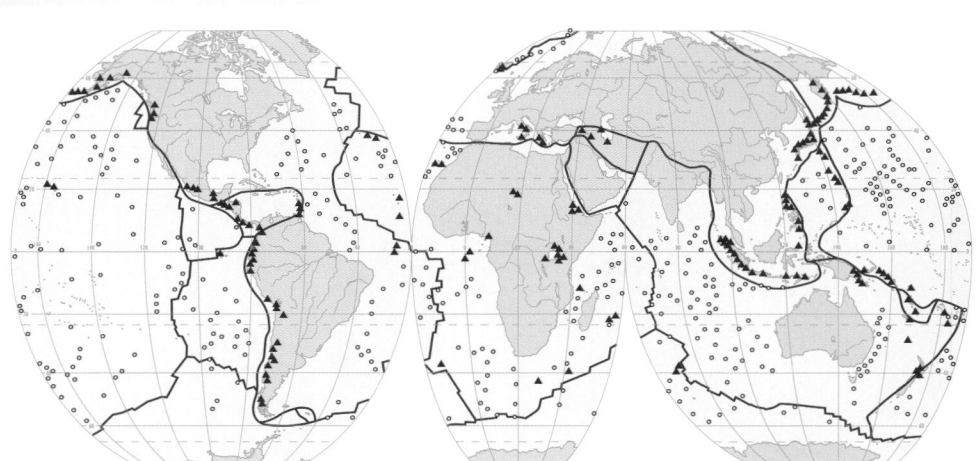

PLATE TECTONICS

The huge ridges that run through the oceans represent boundaries between plates. Here plates are diverging and molten magma from the mantle rises along a central rift valley to form new crustal rock. These ocean ridges, which are active zones where earthquakes and volcanic eruptions are common, are called constructive plate margins. Destructive plate margins, which occur when two plates converge, are marked by deep-ocean trenches as one plate is forced under the other. The descending plate is melted to produce the magma that fuels volcanoes alongside the trenches. Movements of descending plates are often sudden, triggering earthquakes in overlying continental areas.

Sea-floor spreading in the Atlantic Ocean and plate collision

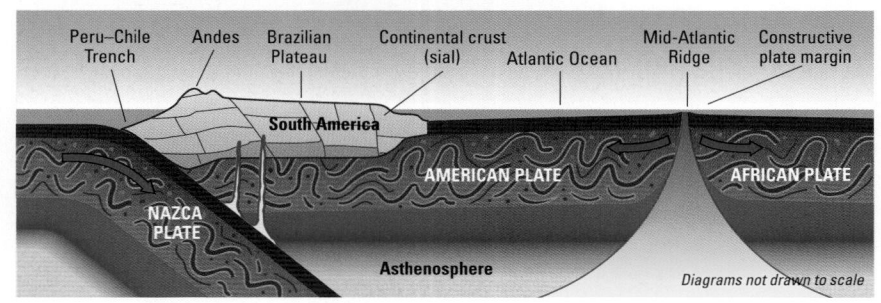

Peru–Chile Trench
Andes
Brazilian Plateau
Continental crust (sial)
Atlantic Ocean
Mid-Atlantic Ridge
Constructive plate margin
South America
AMERICAN PLATE
AFRICAN PLATE
NAZCA PLATE
Asthenosphere
Diagrams not drawn to scale

Sea-floor spreading in the Indian Ocean and continental plate collision

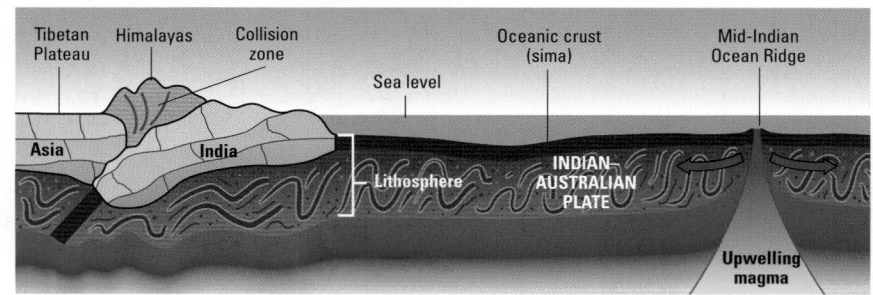

Tibetan Plateau
Himalayas
Collision zone
Sea level
Oceanic crust (sima)
Mid-Indian Ocean Ridge
Asia
India
Lithosphere
INDIAN–AUSTRALIAN PLATE
Upwelling magma

GEOLOGICAL TIME

Time, in millions of years before the present, is shown on a sliding scale, greatly compressed in the distant past.

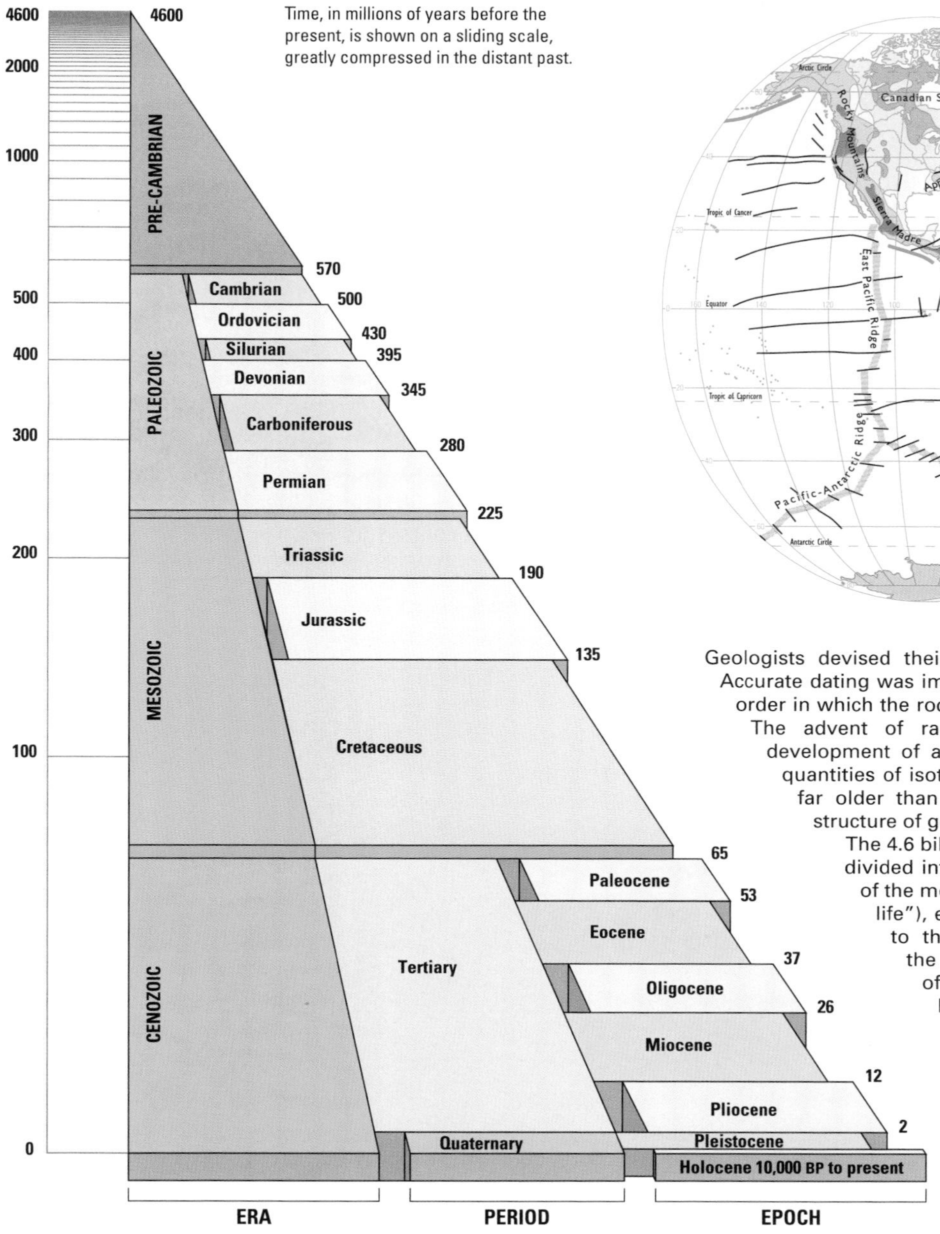

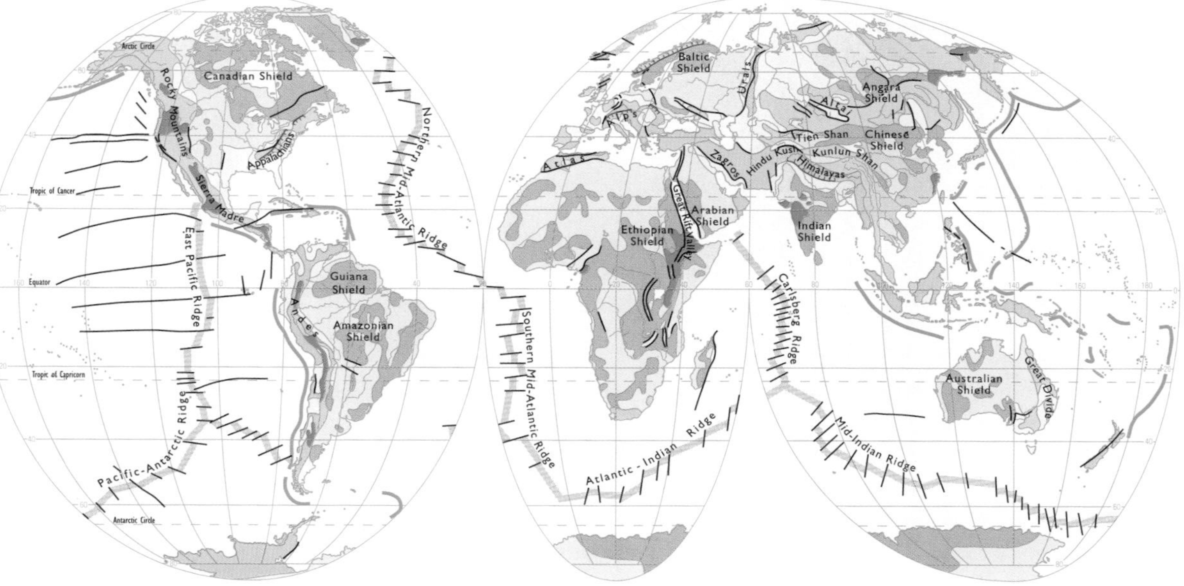

Geological time chart:

ERA	PERIOD	EPOCH
PRE-CAMBRIAN (4600)		
PALEOZOIC	Cambrian (570→500)	
	Ordovician (500→430)	
	Silurian (430→395)	
	Devonian (395→345)	
	Carboniferous (345→280)	
	Permian (280→225)	
MESOZOIC	Triassic (225→190)	
	Jurassic (190→135)	
	Cretaceous (135→65)	
CENOZOIC	Tertiary	Paleocene (65→53)
		Eocene (53→37)
		Oligocene (37→26)
		Miocene (26→12)
		Pliocene (12→2)
	Quaternary	Pleistocene (2)
		Holocene 10,000 BP to present

Geologists devised their timescale on the basis of relative, not calendar, ages. Accurate dating was impossible and estimates were often bitterly disputed, but the order in which the rocks were formed could be deduced from careful observation. The advent of radioactive dating – culminating in the 1950s with the development of a mass spectrometer capable of accurately measuring tiny quantities of isotopes – appears to have settled the arguments. The Earth is far older than geologists first imagined, but their painstakingly-created structure of geological time has withstood the advent of high technology.

The 4.6 billion (4,600 million) years since the formation of the Earth are divided into four great eras, further split into periods and, in the case of the most recent era, epochs. The present era is the Cenozoic ("new life"), extending backward through "middle life" and "ancient life" to the Pre-Cambrian, named after the Latin word for Wales, the location of some of the earliest known fossils. Most of the Earth's geological history is encompassed by the Pre-Cambrian: though traces of ancient life have since been found, it was largely the proliferation of fossils from the beginning of the Paleozoic era onward, some 570 million years ago, which first allowed precise subdivisions to be made.

Like the Cambrian, most are named after regions exemplifying a period's geology. Others – such as the Carboniferous ("coal-bearing") or the Cretaceous ("chalk-bearing") – are more directly descriptive.

Map legend:
- Pre-Cambrian shields
- Sedimentary cover on Pre-Cambrian shields
- Paleozoic (Caledonian and Hercynian) folding
- Sedimentary cover on Paleozoic folding
- Mesozoic folding
- Sedimentary cover on Mesozoic folding
- Cenozoic (Alpine) folding
- Sedimentary cover on Cenozoic folding
- Intensive Mesozoic and Cenozoic vulcanism
- Principal faults
- Oceanic marginal troughs
- Midoceanic ridges
- Overthrust faults

EARTHQUAKES

Earthquake magnitude is usually rated according to either the Richter or the Modified Mercalli scale, both devised by seismologists in the 1930s. The Richter scale measures absolute earthquake power with mathematical precision: each step upward represents a tenfold increase in the amplitude of the shockwave. Theoretically, there is no upper limit, but most of the largest earthquakes measured have been rated at between 8.8 and 8.9. The 12-point Mercalli scale, based on observed effects, is often more meaningful, ranging from I (earthquakes noticed only by seismographs) to XII (total destruction); intermediate points include V (people awakened at night; unstable objects overturned), VII (collapse of ordinary buildings; chimneys and monuments fall), and IX (conspicuous cracks in ground; serious damage to reservoirs).

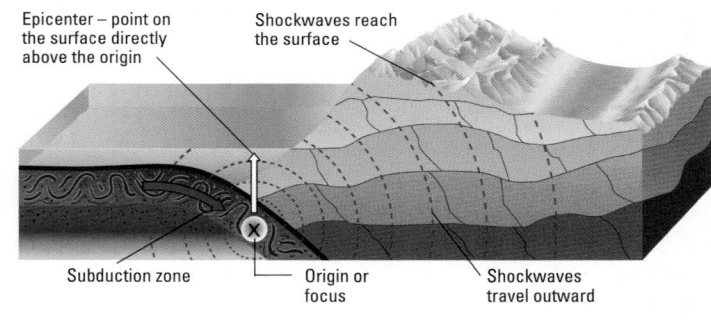

Epicenter – point on the surface directly above the origin
Shockwaves reach the surface
Subduction zone
Origin or focus
Shockwaves travel outward

Map legend:
- Mobile land areas
- Submarine zones of mobile land areas
- Stable land platforms
- Submarine extensions of land platforms
- Midoceanic volcanic ridges
- Oceanic platforms
- Principal earthquakes and dates (since 1900)

Earthquakes are a series of rapid vibrations originating from the slipping or faulting of parts of the Earth's crust when stresses within build up to breaking point. They usually happen at depths varying from 5 to 20 miles. Severe earthquakes cause extensive damage when they take place in populated areas, destroying structures and severing communications. Most initial loss of life occurs due to secondary causes such as falling masonry, fires, and flooding.

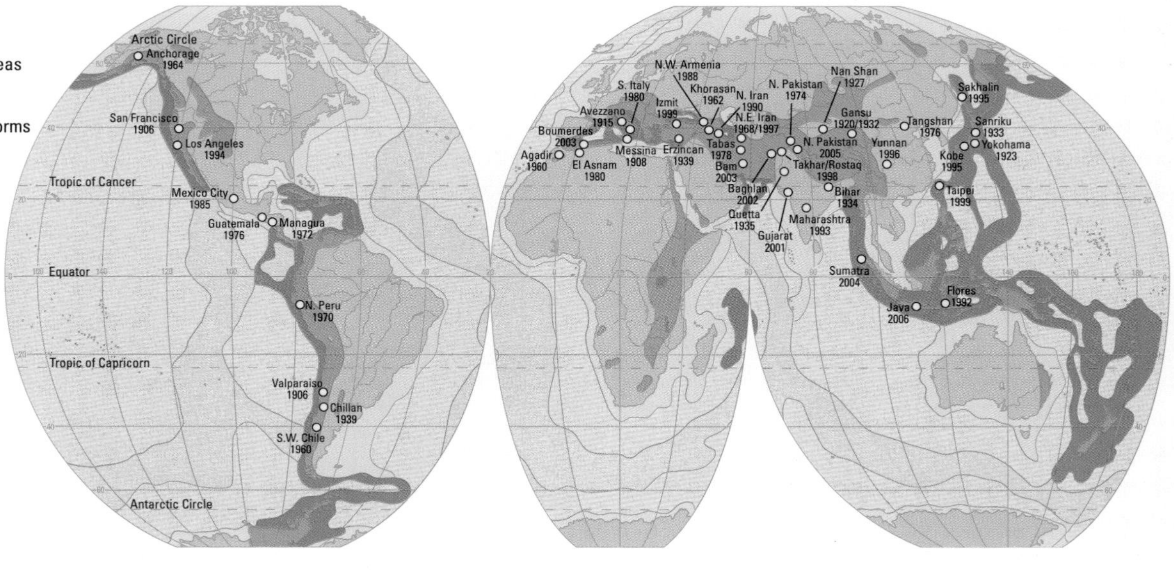

Notable Earthquakes Since 1900

Year	Location	Mag.	Deaths
1906	San Francisco, USA	8.3	3,000
1906	Valparaiso, Chile	8.6	22,000
1908	Messina, Italy	7.5	83,000
1915	Avezzano, Italy	7.5	30,000
1920	Gansu (Kansu), China	8.6	180,000
1923	Yokohama, Japan	8.3	143,000
1927	Nan Shan, China	8.3	200,000
1932	Gansu (Kansu), China	7.6	70,000
1933	Sanriku, Japan	8.9	2,990
1934	Bihar, India/Nepal	8.4	10,700
1935	Quetta, India*	7.5	60,000
1939	Chillan, Chile	8.3	28,000
1939	Erzincan, Turkey	7.9	30,000
1960	S. W. Chile	9.5	2,200
1960	Agadir, Morocco	5.8	12,000
1962	Khorasan, Iran	7.1	12,230
1964	Anchorage, USA	9.2	125
1968	N. E. Iran	7.4	12,000
1970	N. Peru	7.8	70,000
1972	Managua, Nicaragua	6.2	5,000
1974	N. Pakistan	6.3	5,200
1976	Guatemala	7.5	22,500
1976	Tangshan, China	8.2	255,000
1978	Tabas, Iran	7.7	25,000
1980	El Asnam, Algeria	7.3	20,000
1980	S. Italy	7.2	4,800
1985	Mexico City, Mexico	8.1	4,200
1988	N.W. Armenia	6.8	55,000
1990	N. Iran	7.7	36,000
1992	Flores, Indonesia	6.8	1,895
1993	Maharashtra, India	6.4	30,000
1994	Los Angeles, USA	6.6	51
1995	Kobe, Japan	7.2	5,000
1995	Sakhalin Is., Russia	7.5	2,000
1996	Yunnan, China	7.0	240
1997	N. E. Iran	7.1	2,400
1998	Takhar, Afghanistan	6.1	4,200
1998	Rostaq, Afghanistan	7.0	5,000
1999	Izmit, Turkey	7.4	15,000
1999	Taipei, Taiwan	7.6	1,700
2001	Gujarat, India	7.7	14,000
2002	Baghlan, Afghanistan	6.1	1,000
2003	Boumerdes, Algeria	6.8	2,200
2003	Bam, Iran	6.6	30,000
2004	Sumatra, Indonesia	9.0	250,000
2005	N. Pakistan	7.6	74,000
2006	Java, Indonesia	6.4	6,200

An earthquake off the coast of Sumatra on December 26, 2004, triggered a deadly tsunami that swept across the Indian Ocean, causing devastation in many countries, in particular Sri Lanka, India, Thailand, and Indonesia, where the loss of life was greatest.

* now Pakistan

For more information:
70 The Earth's structure
   Plate tectonics
   Volcanoes
71 Geological time
74 Oceans
80 Hydrological cycle
99 Structural regions

The theory of plate tectonics has offered new insights into how the Earth works, elucidating mysteries concerning continental drift, volcanic eruptions, and earthquakes. It has also contributed to our understanding of how collisions between plates can squeeze up layers of sediments on seabeds, forming fold mountain ranges, such as the Himalayas.

Yet even as mountains rise, natural forces are wearing them away. In hot, dry climates, mechanical weathering (a result of rapid temperature changes) causes the outer layers of rocks to peel away, while, in cold mountain regions, boulders are prised apart when water freezes in cracks in rocks. Chemical weathering is responsible for hollowing out limestone caves and decomposing granites.

Climatic conditions have a great bearing on the principal agent of erosion in any particular area. Running water is most important in moist temperate regions. In cold regions, ice is the major agent of erosion, and in many mountain ranges, U-shaped valleys are evidence of the erosive power of valley glaciers.

Ice sheets molded much of the Earth's surface during the Ice Ages, the most recent of which, in the northern hemisphere, ended only 10,000 years ago. Polar climates also shape the scenery of the periglacial areas that border bodies of ice. Such areas are subject to constant freeze-thaw action, which creates such features as pingos (domed mounds).

Climatic change has also affected many of the landforms in hot deserts, which were shaped by running water at a time when the deserts enjoyed much wetter climates. However, the major agent of erosion in deserts today is wind-blown sand, which erodes rock strata to form mushroom-shaped rocks and caves.

The surface of the Earth is under constant assault from tectonic processes and the agents of erosion. The products of erosion, fragments of rock such as sand, are deposited to form sedimentary rocks. Metamorphic rocks are created when igneous or sedimentary rocks are buried and metamorphosed by heat and pressure. Eventually the rocks are recycled to form magma, which rises upward to start the rock cycle all over again.

THE ROCK CYCLE

James Hutton first proposed the rock cycle in the late 1700s after he observed the slow but steady effects of erosion.

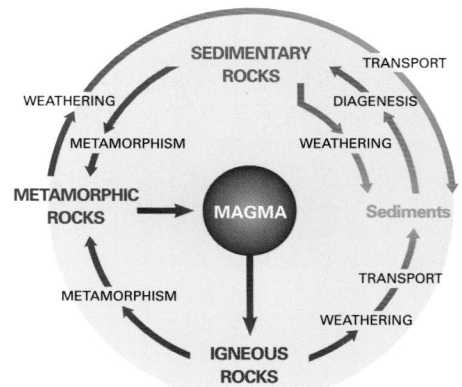

Rocks are divided into three types, according to the way in which they are formed:

Igneous rocks, including granite and basalt, are formed when magma cools inside the Earth's crust or on the surface.

Metamorphic rocks, such as slate, marble, and quartzite, are formed below the Earth's surface by the compression or baking of existing rocks.

Sedimentary rocks, like sandstone and limestone, are formed on the surface of the Earth from the remains of living organisms and eroded fragments of older rocks.

MOUNTAIN BUILDING

Mountains are formed when pressures on the Earth's crust caused by continental drift become so intense that the surface buckles or cracks. This happens where oceanic crust is subducted by continental crust or, more dramatically, where two tectonic plates collide: the Rockies, Andes, Alps, Urals, and Himalayas resulted from such impacts. These are known as fold mountains because they were formed by the compression of the rocks. The Himalayas were formed from the folded former sediments of the Tethys Sea, which was trapped in the collision zone between the Indian–Australian and Eurasian plates.

The other main mountain-building processes occur when the crust fractures to create faults, allowing rock to be forced upward in large blocks, or when the pressure of magma within the crust forces the surface to bulge into a dome, or erupts to form a volcano.

Large mountain ranges may reveal a combination of these features. The Alps, for example, have been compressed so violently that the folds are fragmented by numerous faults and intrusions of molten igneous rock.

Over millions of years, even the greatest mountain ranges can be reduced by the agents of erosion (especially rivers) to a low, rugged landscape known as a peneplain.

Types of faults: Faults occur where the crust is being stretched or compressed so violently that the rock strata break in a horizontal or vertical movement. They are classified by the direction in which the blocks of rock have moved. A normal fault results when a vertical movement causes the surface to break apart; compression causes a reverse fault. Horizontal movement causes shearing, known as a strike-slip fault. When the rock breaks in two places, the central block may be pushed up in a horst fault, or sink (creating a rift valley) in a graben fault.

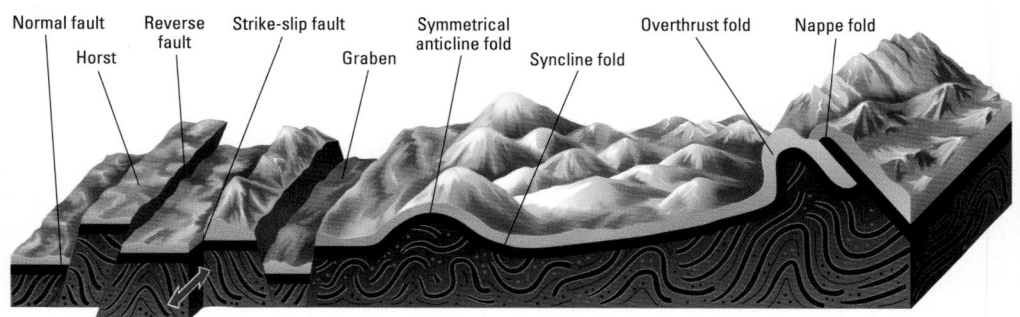

Types of fold: Folds occur when rock strata are squeezed and compressed. They are common, therefore, at destructive plate margins and where plates have collided, forcing the rocks to buckle into mountain ranges. Geographers give different names to the degrees of fold that result from continuing pressure on the rock. A simple fold may be symmetric, with even slopes on either side, but as the pressure builds up, one slope becomes steeper and the fold becomes asymmetric. Later, the ridge or "anticline" at the top of the fold may slide over the lower ground or "syncline" to form a recumbent fold. Eventually, the rock strata may break under the pressure to form an overthrust and finally a nappe fold.

CONTINENTAL GLACIATION

Many landforms in the northern hemisphere were shaped by ice sheets and meltwater during the Pleistocene Ice Age, which began about 2 million years ago. During the Ice Age, the ice sheets periodically advanced and retreated. The first map (*below left*) shows the ice cover at its greatest extent about 200,000 years BP (before the present), when it covered about 30% of the land surface, as compared with 10% today. About 18,000 years BP, the ice covered most of Canada and extended as far south as the Bristol Channel in England. Around the ice sheets, land areas experienced periglacial conditions.

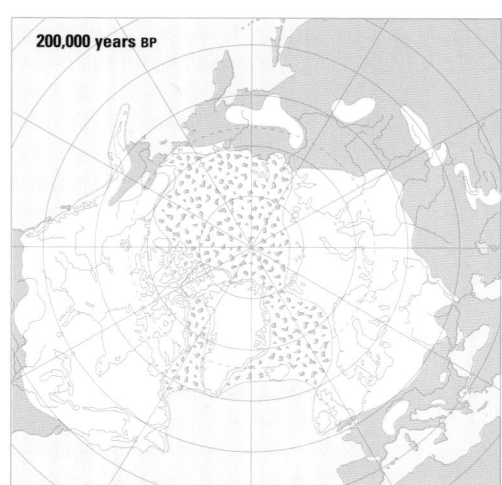

200,000 years BP

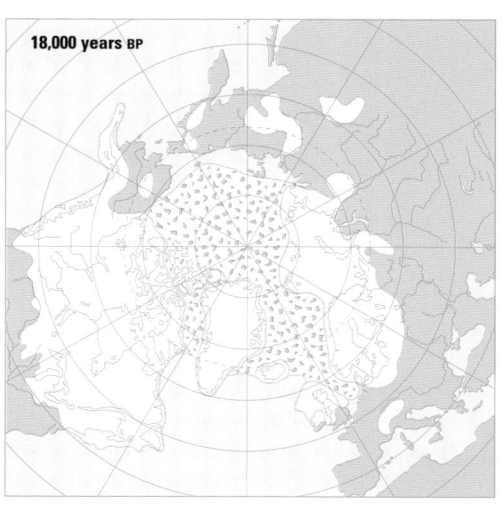

18,000 years BP

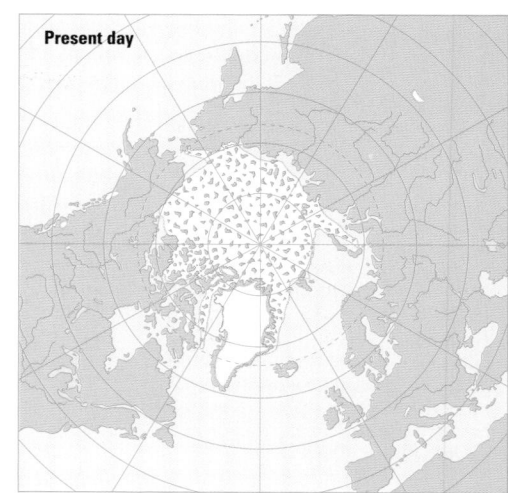

Present day

NATURAL LANDFORMS

Natural landforms reflect the influence of plate tectonics, through mountain-building and the generation of new rocks from the Earth's interior, together with the agents of erosion – running water, ice, winds, and coastal waves. Over millions of years, mountains are gradually eroded, with the eroded material redistributed, usually at lower levels. The resultant landforms reflect the major forces that have been at work, as well as the underlying geology, the climatic conditions, which often vary over time, and the vegetation cover. The study of these processes and the landforms they create is called geomorphology. The stylized diagram (*below*) shows some major natural landforms found in the mid-latitudes.

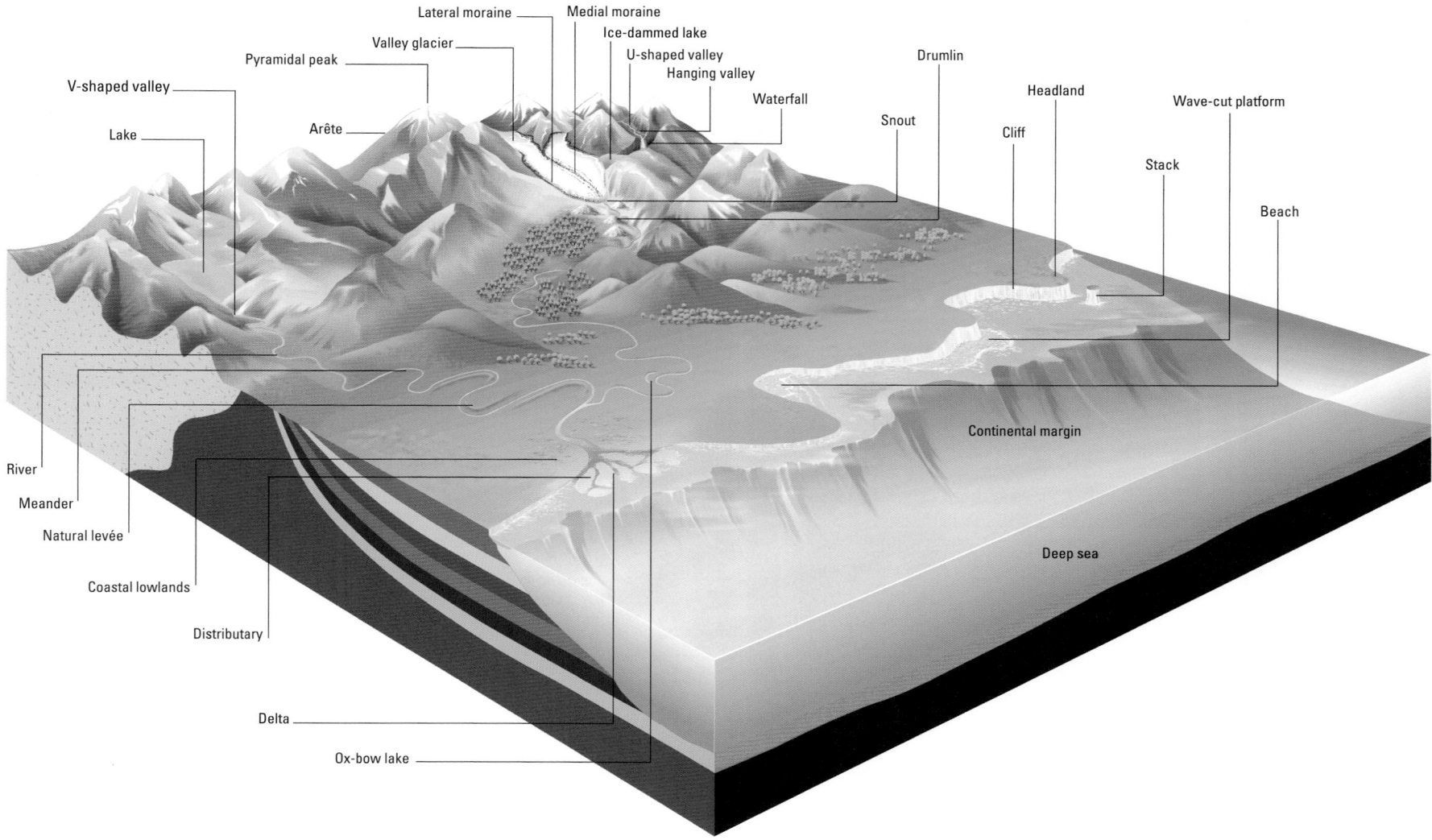

SURFACE PROCESSES

Catastrophic changes to landforms are caused periodically by such phenomena as avalanches, landslides, and volcanic eruptions, but most of the processes that shape the Earth's surface operate extremely slowly in human terms.

Chemical weathering is at its greatest in warm, humid regions, while mechanical weathering (the physical breakup of rocks) predominates in cold mountain or hot desert regions. The most familiar type of chemical weathering is caused by the reaction of rainwater containing dissolved carbon dioxide on limestone; this leads to the creation of labyrinthine cave networks dissolved by groundwater. Mechanical weathering includes frost action, while in hot deserts, rapid temperature changes cause the outer layers of rocks to expand and contract until they crack and peel away, a process called exfoliation.

Running water is probably the world's leading agent of erosion and transportation. The energy of a river depends on several factors, including its velocity and volume, and its erosive power is at its peak when it is in full flood, sweeping soil, pebbles and even boulders along its course, cutting downward into the bedrock or widening its valley.

Sea waves also exert tremendous erosive power during storms, when they hurl pebbles and large rocks against the shore, undercutting cliffs and hollowing out caves. Headlands are often attacked on both sides, forming caves, then a natural arch and eventually an isolated stack.

Glacier ice forms in mountain hollows, called cirques, and spills out to form valley glaciers, which transport rocks shattered by frost action. As a glacier moves, rocks embedded in the base and sides scrape away bedrock, eroding steep-sided, flat-bottomed, U-shaped valleys. Evidence of past glaciation in mountain regions includes cirques, knife-edged ridges, or arêtes, and pyramidal peaks, or horns.

DESERT LANDFORMS

Deserts are defined as places with an average annual precipitation of 10 inches [250 mm] per year, though places with a higher rainfall and a high evaporation rate may also qualify as deserts.

The three types of desert landforms are known by their Arabic names, a reflection of the fact that the Sahara in North Africa is the world's largest desert. Sand desert, called *erg*, covers about one-fifth of the world's deserts. The rest is divided between *hammada* (areas of bare rock) and *reg* (broad plains covered by loose gravel or pebbles).

The shapes of dunes in sand deserts reflect the character of local winds. Where winds are constant in direction, the sand often piles up in crescent-shaped dunes, called *barchans*. Barchans are constantly on the move and their forward march, unless halted by vegetation, may overwhelm settlements at oases. *Seif* dunes, named after the Arabic word for "sword," are long ridges of sand that lie parallel to the direction of the wind, but where winds are variable, the sand sheets are often featureless.

Wind-blown sand is an effective agent of erosion, but because of the weight of sand grains, this type of erosion is confined to within approximately 7 feet [2 meters] of the land surface, creating caves and mushroom-shaped rocks.

In assessing desert landforms, it is important to remember that other processes were at work in the past when the climate was very different from today. For example, cave paintings suggest that the Sahara had a much wetter climate after the end of the Ice Age and only began to dry up after about 5000 BC. However, human action, including overgrazing and the cutting down of trees for firewood, can turn a grassland region into desert – a process known as desertification.

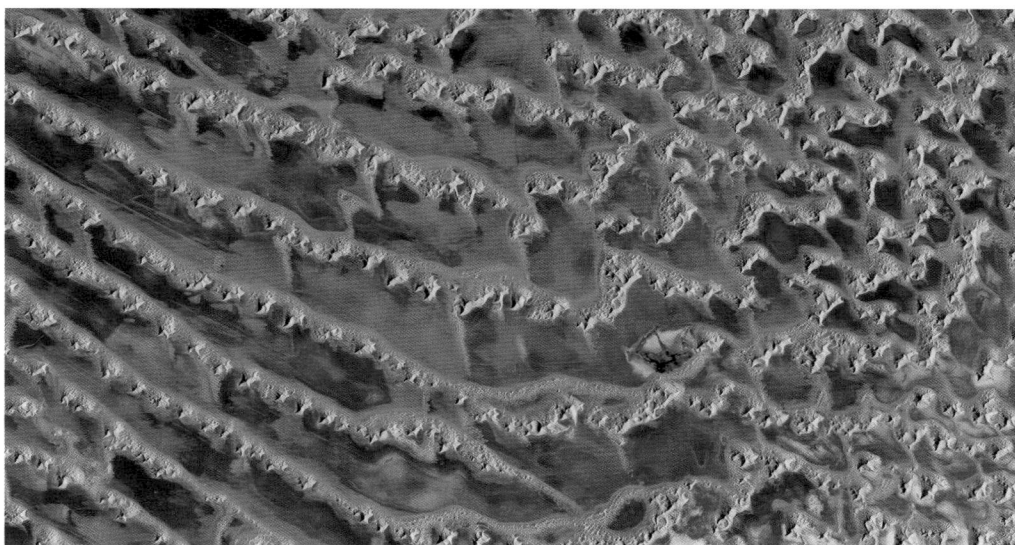

◄ This false-color satellite image of part of the Rub' al Khali, or "Empty Quarter," in Saudi Arabia shows part of the world's largest sand sea (*erg*), which covers almost 232,000 sq miles [600,000 sq km]. Showing many different types of sand dune, the image enhances the difference in color between the dune sand and the interdune areas, which have a higher clay composition. The blue "eye" is a partially flooded clay basin (*playa*).

For more information:
69 Tides
70 Plate tectonics
76 Atmosphere
80 Hydrological cycle
   Water distribution
81 Watersheds
85 Water pollution
103 World shipping

The last 40 years have been described as the "Space Age," but another exciting and perhaps even more important area of discovery, proceeding at the same time, has been the exploration of the oceans which cover more than 70% of our planet. Studies of the ocean floor and oceanic islands have revealed features that help to explain how continents move, and how the movements are related to earthquakes and volcanic activity.

Manned submersibles have established that life exists even in the deepest trenches, where the pressure reaches 1,000 atmospheres, the equivalent of the force of six and a half tons bearing down on every square inch. Further exploration in the pitch-black environment of the ocean ridges has revealed strange forms of marine life around scalding hot vents. The creatures include giant tubeworms, blind shrimps, and bacteria, some of which are genetically very different from any other known life forms. In 1996, an analysis of one micro-organism revealed that at least half of its 1,700 or so genes were hitherto unknown. This environment, which is based on chemicals, not sunlight, may resemble the places where life on Earth first began.

Another vital area of contemporary research concerns the interactions between the oceans and the atmosphere, as exemplified in the El Niño–Southern Oscillation (ENSO) cycle, and the bearing that these have on climatic change (*see below*).

Most geographers divide the world's ocean waters into five areas: the Pacific, Atlantic, Indian, Southern, and Arctic oceans. The most active zone in the oceans is the sunlit upper layer, where the water is moved around by wind-blown currents. It is the home of most sea life and acts as a membrane through which the ocean breathes, absorbing great quantities of carbon dioxide and partly exchanging it for oxygen.

As the depth increases, so light fades and temperatures fall until just before 3,000 feet where there is a marked temperature change at the thermocline, the boundary between the warm surface zone and the cold deep zone. Below the thermocline, slow currents are caused by density differences between bodies of water with varying temperatures and salinity.

LIFE IN THE OCEANS

An imaginary profile of the typical coastal and oceanic zones is shown, with a selection of the life forms that might occur in the waters off the Pacific Coast of Central America. The animals illustrated are not drawn to scale as the range of sizes is too great. Most marine life is confined to the first 650 feet, the upper sunlit (photic) zone, where sunlight can still penetrate. Plant and animal plankton, the basis of life in the oceans, occur in great quantities in all zones.

In the pelagic environment (open sea), vertical gradients, including those of light, temperature, and salinity, determine the distribution of organisms. From the tidal zone at the coastline, the continental shelf, geologically still part of the continental land mass, drops gently to about 650 feet – the sunlit zone. At the end of the shelf, the seabed falls away in the steeper angle of the continental slope. The subsequent descent to the deep-ocean floor, known as the continental rise, is more gentle, with gradients between 1 in 100 and 1 in 700 until the abyssal plains and hills between 8,000 and 19,500 feet below the surface.

The deep-sea floor contains seamounts, some of which are capped by coral reefs, ocean ridges – the longest mountain chains on Earth – and deep-ocean trenches, especially in the Pacific Ocean where six trenches reach depths of more than 33,000 feet, including the Mariana Trench at 36,161 feet deep .

Each of these zones contains a distinctive community of species adapted to the different conditions of salinity, temperature, and light intensity. Indeed, a few organisms have been found even in the abyssal darkness of the great ocean trenches.

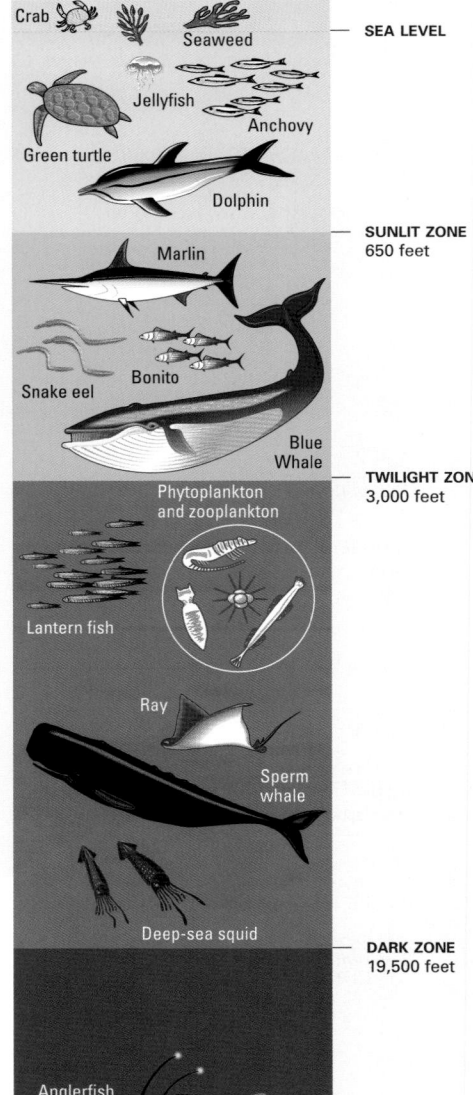

ATOLL BUILDING

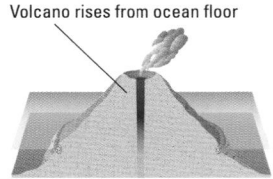

Volcano rises from ocean floor

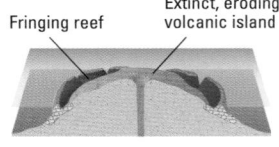

Fringing reef — Extinct, eroding volcanic island

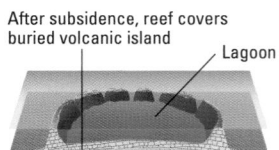

After subsidence, reef covers buried volcanic island — Lagoon

A coral atoll usually begins existence as a bare volcanic peak, thrusting above the surface of the ocean. A colony of coral – organisms with calcium carbonate skeletons – forms itself in the shallow water around the peak. The volcano is eroded and slowly sinks, leaving the coral forming a ring of hard limestone around its remnant. In time, the barrier reef of an atoll is all that remains.

EL NIÑO PHENOMENON

Normal year – Walker Circulation Cell   **El Niño event**

The importance of the ocean–atmosphere interaction is nowhere more dramatically demonstrated than in the El Niño phenomenon of the southern Pacific Ocean. Under normal conditions, called La Niña, cold, nutrient-rich water rises to the surface and spreads westward. In the western Pacific, sea surface temperatures reach 82°F or more and warm air rises, creating a low-pressure air system and causing heavy rains. The rising air spreads out and some of it descends over South America and the eastern Pacific, creating a high-pressure air system from which winds blow westward. This rotating system is called a Walker Circulation Cell.

An El Niño event is characterized by a reversal of currents. The upwelling of cold water off South America is greatly reduced and surface water temperatures rise, causing a drastic reduction in fish life. The heaviest rainfall is over the eastern Pacific, while Southeast Asia is drier than usual.

During an intense El Niño, the effects of the current and wind reversals affect the weather around the world. In 1982–3, the monsoon rainfall was reduced in Australia and Southeast Asia, while in 1983–4 a severe drought occurred in the Sahel, south of the Sahara, and also in southern Africa. The southeast coast of the United States suffered storms and heavy rainfall, and even Europe experienced changes in weather patterns, possibly as a result of consequent changes in the course of the jet stream.

Scientists have found evidence that the frequency of the El Niño event, which normally occurs every three to seven years, and lasts between 12–18 months, may have increased in recent years. Another intense El Niño occurred in 1997–8, with resultant freak weather conditions across the entire Pacific region.

We do not fully understand the causes of the El Niño event, though some researchers are investigating possible connections between major volcanic eruptions in the tropical Pacific region, the ENSO cycle, and atmospheric circulation.

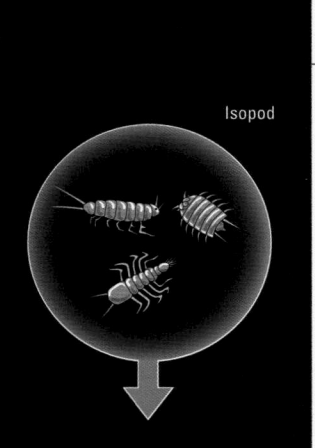

OCEAN CURRENTS

JANUARY CURRENTS AND TEMPERATURES
(Northern Hemisphere: winter)

ACTUAL SURFACE
TEMPERATURE

°F

| 86 |
| 68 |
| 50 |
| 32 |
| 14 |
| -4 |
| -22 |
| -40 |

OCEAN CURRENTS

Cold	Warm	Speed (knots)
←– –	←–	Less than 0.5
←	←	0.5 – 1.0
←	←	Over 1.0

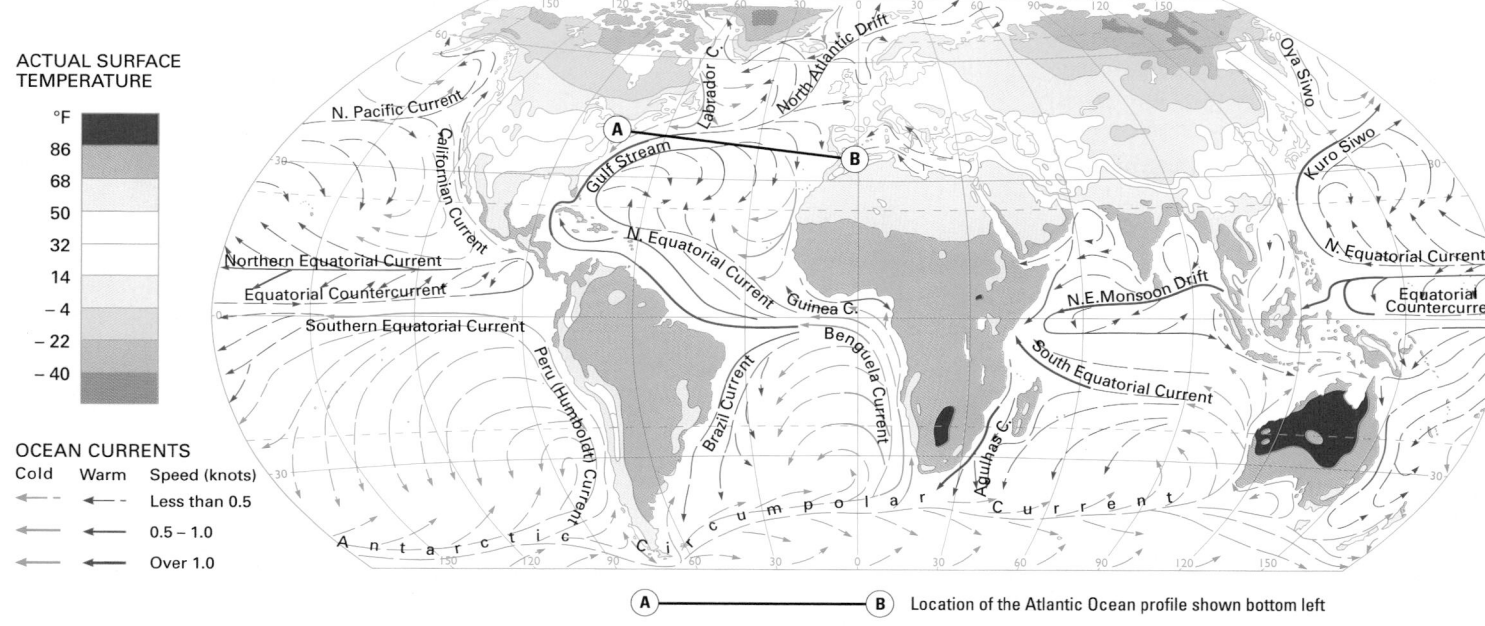

Ⓐ———————Ⓑ Location of the Atlantic Ocean profile shown bottom left

JULY CURRENTS AND TEMPERATURES
(Northern Hemisphere: summer)

ACTUAL SURFACE
TEMPERATURE

°F

| 86 |
| 68 |
| 50 |
| 32 |
| 14 |

OCEAN CURRENTS

Cold	Warm	Speed (knots)
←– –	←–	Less than 0.5
←	←	0.5 – 1.0
←	←	Over 1.0

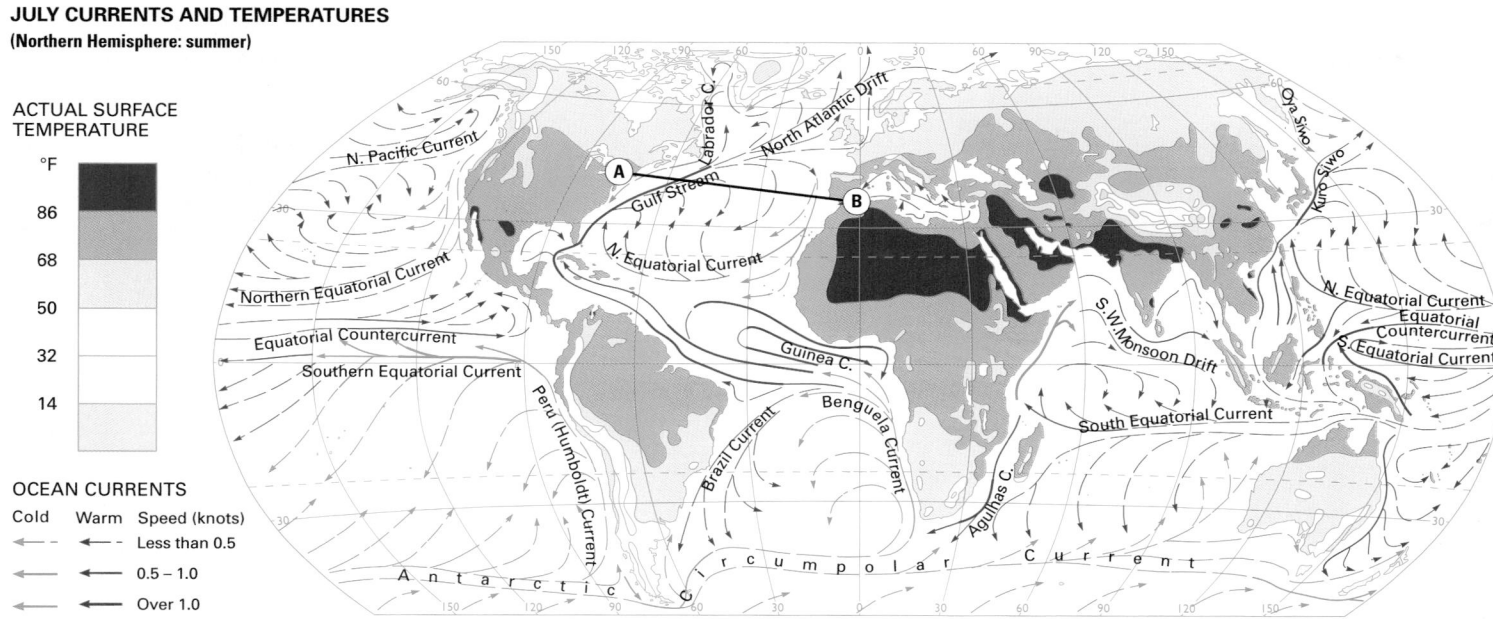

Moving immense quantities of energy as well as billions of tons of water every hour, the ocean currents are a vital part of the great heat engine that drives the Earth's climate. They themselves are produced by a twofold mechanism. At the surface, winds push huge masses of water before them; in the deep ocean, below an abrupt temperature gradient that separates the churning surface waters from the still depths, density variations cause slow vertical movements.

Coriolis effect
The pattern of circulation of the great surface currents is determined by the displacement known as the *Coriolis effect.* As the Earth turns, the vast mass of ocean water is deflected to one side. The deflection is most obvious near the equator, where the Earth's surface is spinning eastward at 1,000 mph; currents moving poleward are curved clockwise in the northern hemisphere and counterclockwise in the southern hemisphere.

Ocean currents
The result is a system of spinning circles known as "gyres." Warm currents move constantly from the equator toward the poles, while cold water moves in the reverse direction. In this way, ocean currents act like a thermostat, helping to regulate temperatures around the world.
    Depending on the annual movements of the prevailing wind belts, some currents on or near the equator may reverse their direction in the course of the year, a variation on which Asia's monsoon rains depend and whose occasional failure has brought disaster to millions of people.

TOPOGRAPHY OF THE OCEAN FLOOR

Profile of the Atlantic Ocean

The deep-ocean floor was once believed to be flat, but sonar readings have shown that it is no more uniform than the surface of the continents. The profile (*below*) shows some of the features on the Atlantic Ocean floor between Massachusetts in North America and Gibraltar (*for location of profile, see maps above*).

Around the continents are shallow continental shelves composed of rocks that are less dense than the underlying oceanic crust. The continents end at

the top of the steep continental slope, which descends to the abyss via the continental rise, made up of sediments washed down from the continental shelves.

The abyss contains large plains overlain by oozes but broken by volcanic seamounts and guyots (flat-topped seamounts), a few of which reach the surface as islands. The Mid-Atlantic Ridge contains a rift valley where new crustal rock is being formed as the plates on either side move apart.

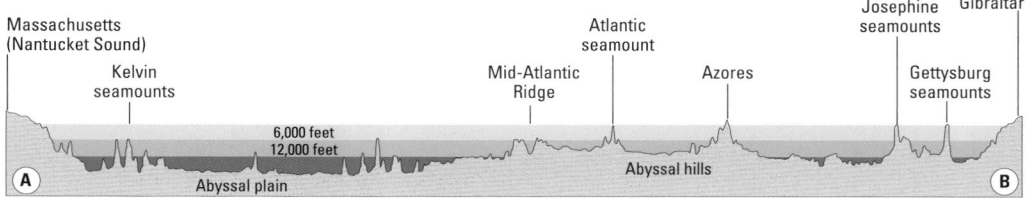

Topography of the ocean floor around Australia

In the image on the right, land areas are shown in gray, with shaded relief. The colors represent sea depths, with red representing the shallowest areas, through yellow and green to dark blue (the deepest).

The data for the sea topography are from the Seasat radar satellite. The deep blue area in the upper left is the Java Trench, which forms the boundary

between the Indian–Australian plate and the Eurasian plate. In the top right, the New Guinea trench, which has a maximum depth of 29,865 feet, forms the border of the Indian–Australian and Pacific plates. Alongside the trenches are volcanic islands formed from magma, created as the edge of the Indian–Australian plate is subducted and melted.

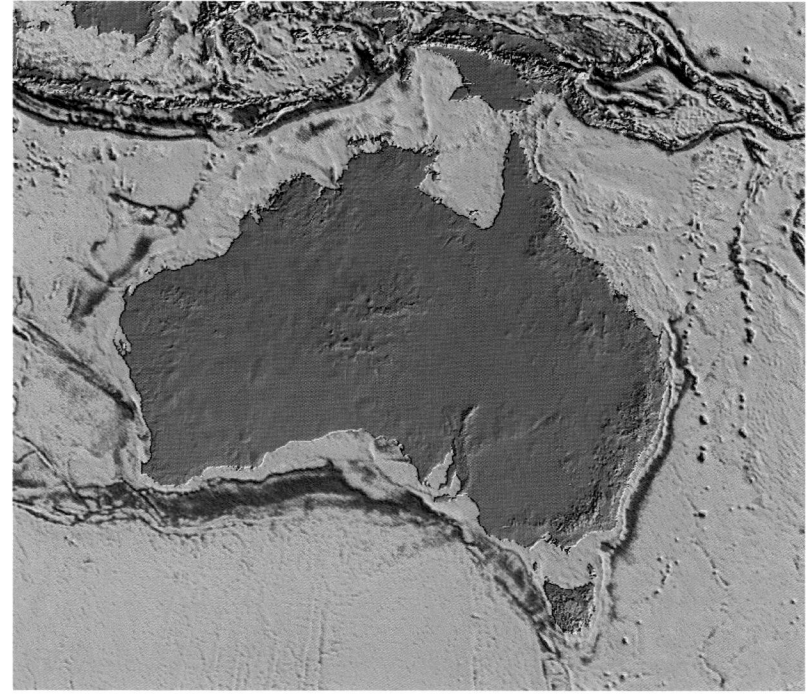

For more information:
75 Ocean currents
79 Beaufort wind scale
   Climate change
   Monsoon
83 Solar energy
   Greenhouse effect
84 Greenhouse power
85 Acid rain

The atmosphere is a meteor shield, a radiation deflector, a thermal blanket, and a source of chemical energy for the Earth's diverse life forms. Five-sixths of its mass is in the lowest layer, the troposphere, which ranges in thickness from 11–6 miles between the equator and the poles. Powered by the Sun, the air is always on the move, flowing generally from high- to low-pressure areas. The troposphere is the layer where virtually all weather phenomena, including clouds, precipitation and winds, occur. Above the troposphere is the stratosphere, which contains the important ozone layer and extends to about 30 miles above the Earth's surface. Beyond 60 miles, atmospheric density is lower than most laboratory vacuums.

STRUCTURE OF THE ATMOSPHERE

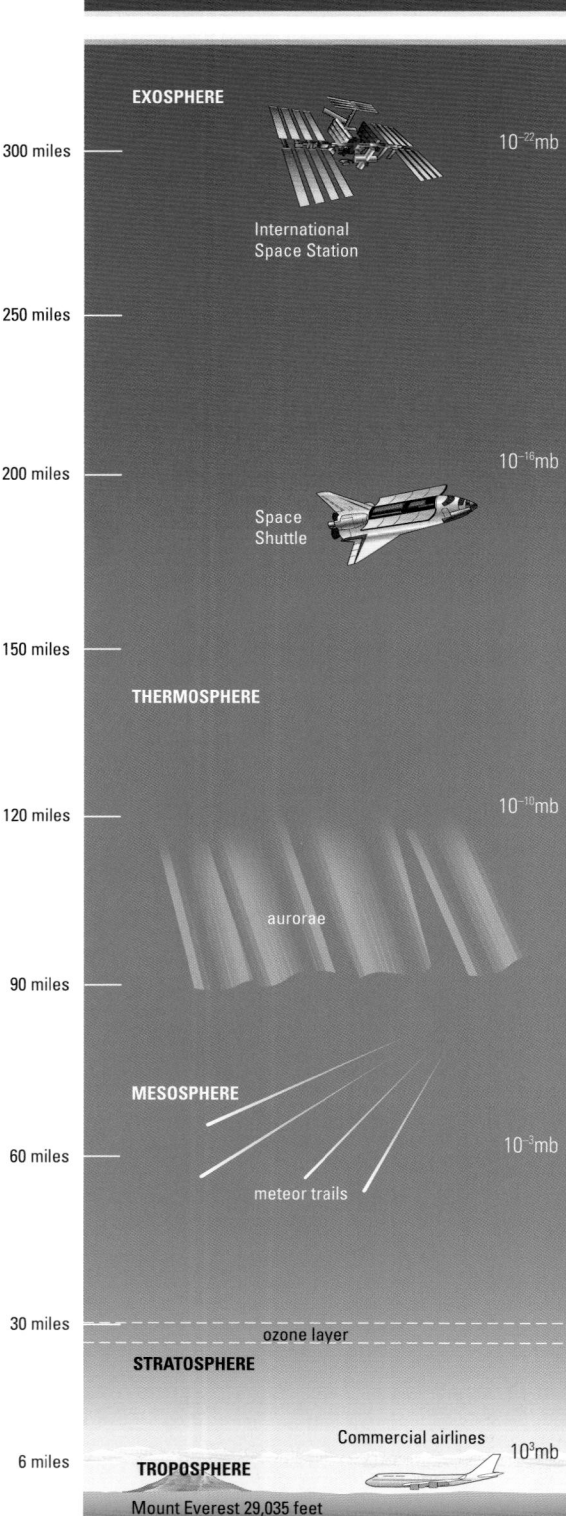

CIRCULATION OF THE AIR

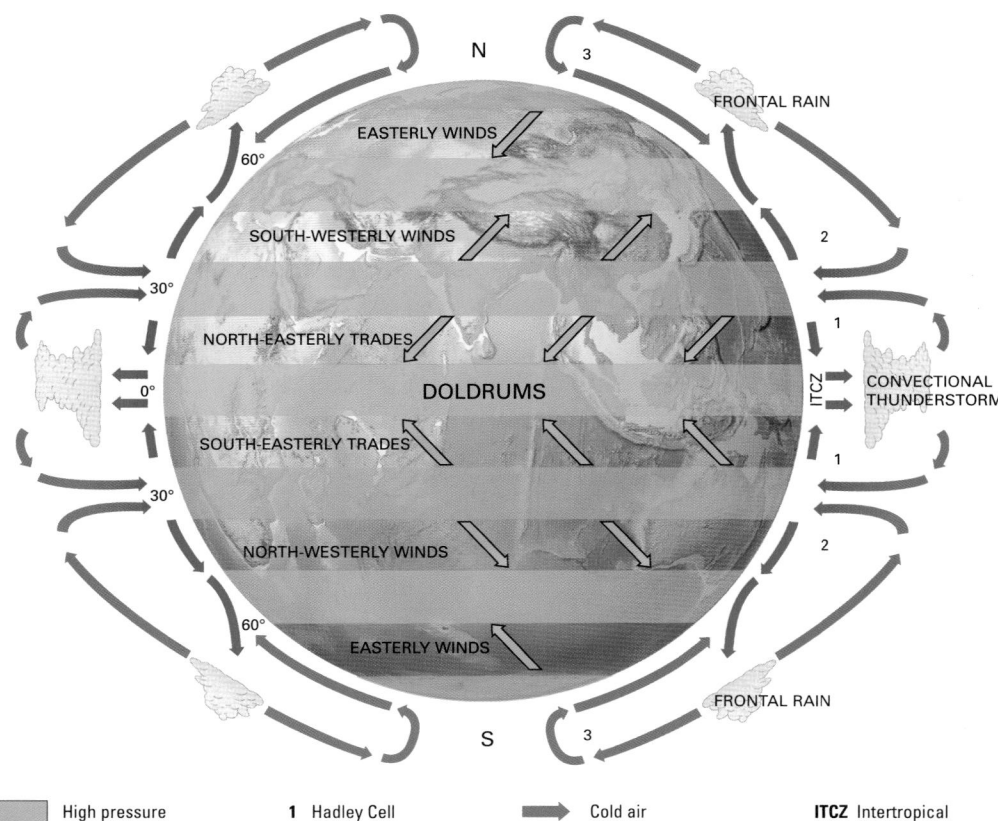

▨ High pressure	**1** Hadley Cell
▨ Low pressure	**2** Ferrel Cell
➡ Warm air	**3** Polar Cell

➡ Cold air	**ITCZ** Intertropical convergence zone
➡ Surface winds	
☁ Clouds	

FRONTAL SYSTEMS

Depressions, or cyclones, form along the polar front where dense polar easterlies meet warm subtropical westerlies. Depressions occur when warm air flows into waves in the polar front, while cold air flows in behind it, creating rotating air systems that bring changeable weather.

Along the warm front (the boundary on the ground between the warm and cold air), the warm air flows upward over the cold air, producing a sequence of clouds that help forecasters to predict a depression's advance. Along the cold front, the advancing cold air forces warm air to rise steeply. Towering cumulonimbus clouds form in the rising air.

When the cold front overtakes the warm front, the warm air is pushed above ground level to form an occluded front. Cloud and rain persist along occlusions until temperatures equalize, the air mixes, and the depression dies out.

Depressions with these distinctive features are known as "frontal." The diagram below shows a cross-section through a depression and the associated cloud types and weather conditions that may be experienced.

CHEMICAL COMPOSITION

Gaseous composition of the principal atmospheric layers

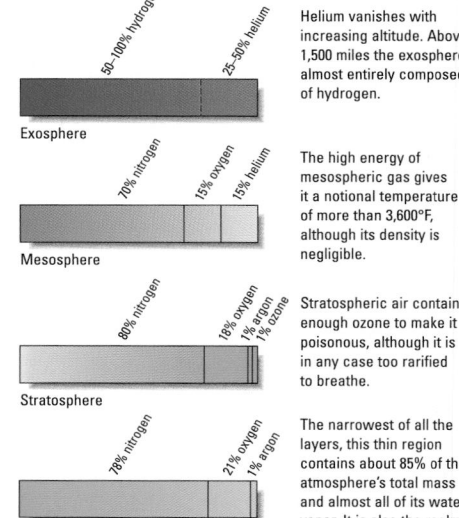

Helium vanishes with increasing altitude. Above 1,500 miles the exosphere is almost entirely composed of hydrogen.

The high energy of mesospheric gas gives it a notional temperature of more than 3,600°F, although its density is negligible.

Stratospheric air contains enough ozone to make it poisonous, although it is in any case too rarified to breathe.

The narrowest of all the layers, this thin region contains about 85% of the atmosphere's total mass and almost all of its water vapor. It is also the realm of the Earth's weather.

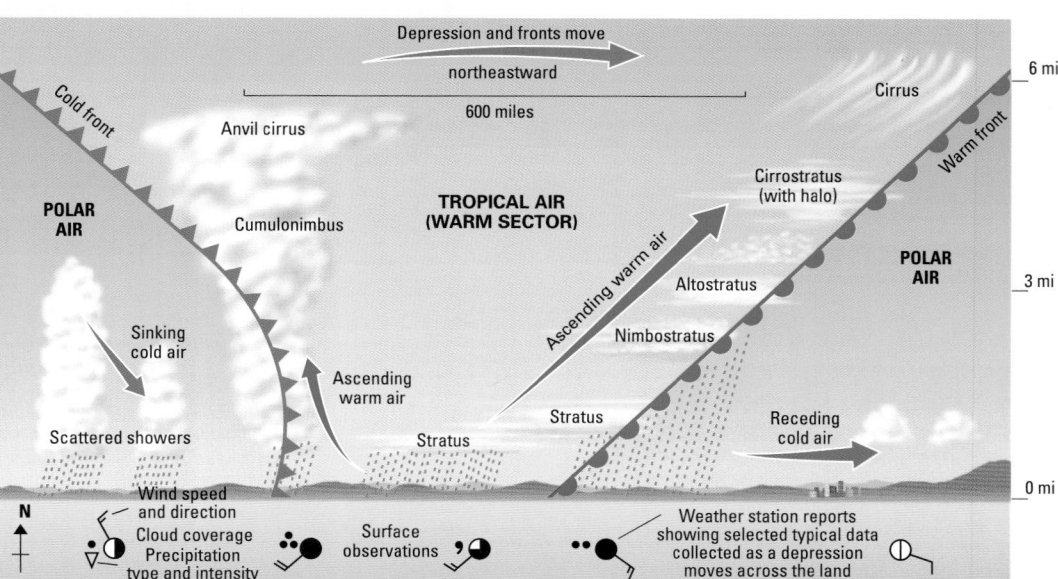

COPYRIGHT PHILIP'S

AIR MASSES

Air masses are bodies of air whose characteristics are broadly the same over a large area. Around the equator, where the Sun's heat creates relatively high surface temperatures, warm air rises to create a zone of low pressure called the doldrums. The air cools and finally spreads out toward the poles. Around latitudes 30° north and south, the air sinks back to the surface, becoming warmer as it descends and creating zones of high pressure called the horse latitudes.

The high- and low-pressure zones are both areas of comparative calm, but between them lie the prevailing trade wind belts. Air also flows north and south from the high-pressure horse latitudes and these airflows meet up with cold, dense air flowing from the poles along the polar front.

This basic circulatory system is complicated by the Coriolis effect, brought about by the spinning Earth. Because of the Coriolis effect, the prevailing winds do not flow directly north–south but are deflected to the right in the northern hemisphere and to the left in the southern. Along the polar front, depressions form where the polar easterlies meet the westerlies.

The first classification of clouds was developed by a London chemist, Luke Howard, in 1803, and it was later modified by the World Meteorological Organization. The main types are divided into three groups according to their altitude, and into sub-groups according to their shape, which vary from hairlike filaments (cirrus), heaps or piles (cumulus), and layers (stratus). Each cloud carries some kind of message, though not always a clear one, to weather forecasters.

CLASSIFICATION OF CLOUDS

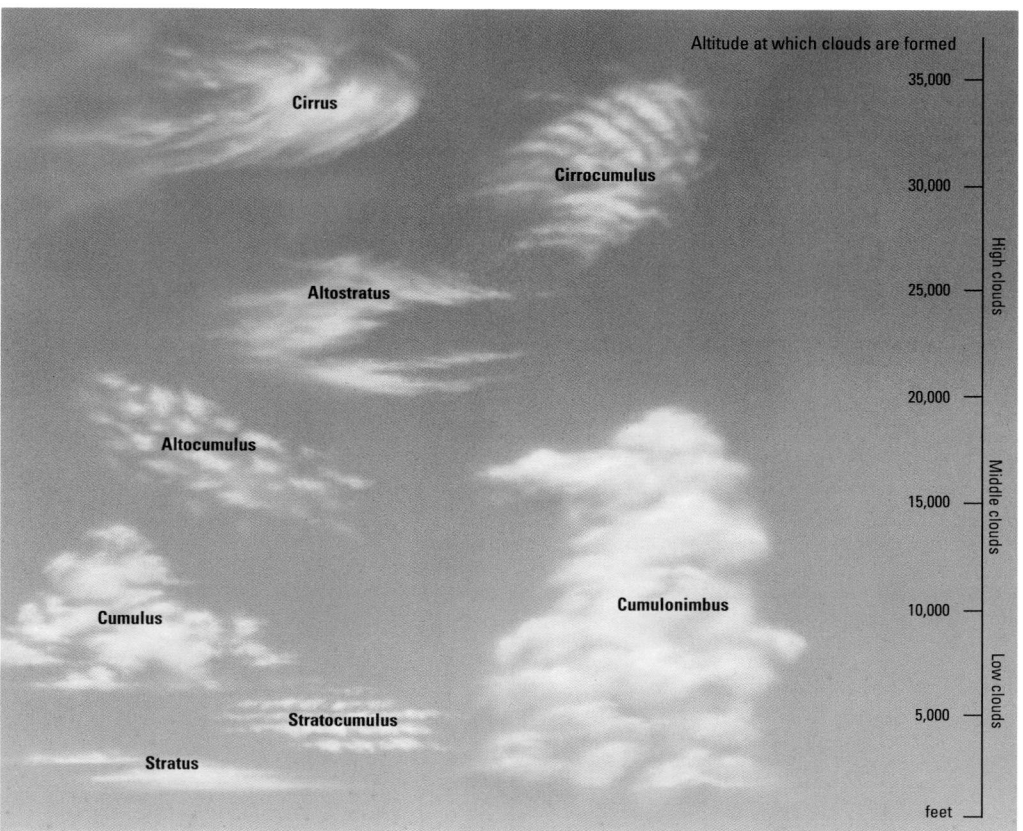

Clouds form when damp, usually rising, air is cooled. Thus they form when a wind rises to cross hills or mountains; when a mass of air rises over, or is pushed up by, another mass of denser air; or when local heating of the ground causes convection currents.

The types of clouds are classified according to altitude as high, middle, or low. The high ones, composed of ice crystals, are cirrus, cirrostratus, and cirrocumulus.

The middle clouds are altostratus – a gray or bluish striated, fibrous or uniform sheet producing light drizzle – and altocumulus, a thicker and fluffier version of cirrocumulus.

Low clouds include nimbostratus, a dark gray layer that brings rain or snow; cumulus, a detached heap, dark at the base; stratus, which forms dull, overcast skies at low levels; and stratocumulus, which consists of fluffy grayish-white layers.

Cumulonimbus, associated with storms and rains, heavy and dense with a flat base and a high, fluffy outline, can be tall enough to occupy middle as well as low altitudes.

PRESSURE AND SURFACE WINDS

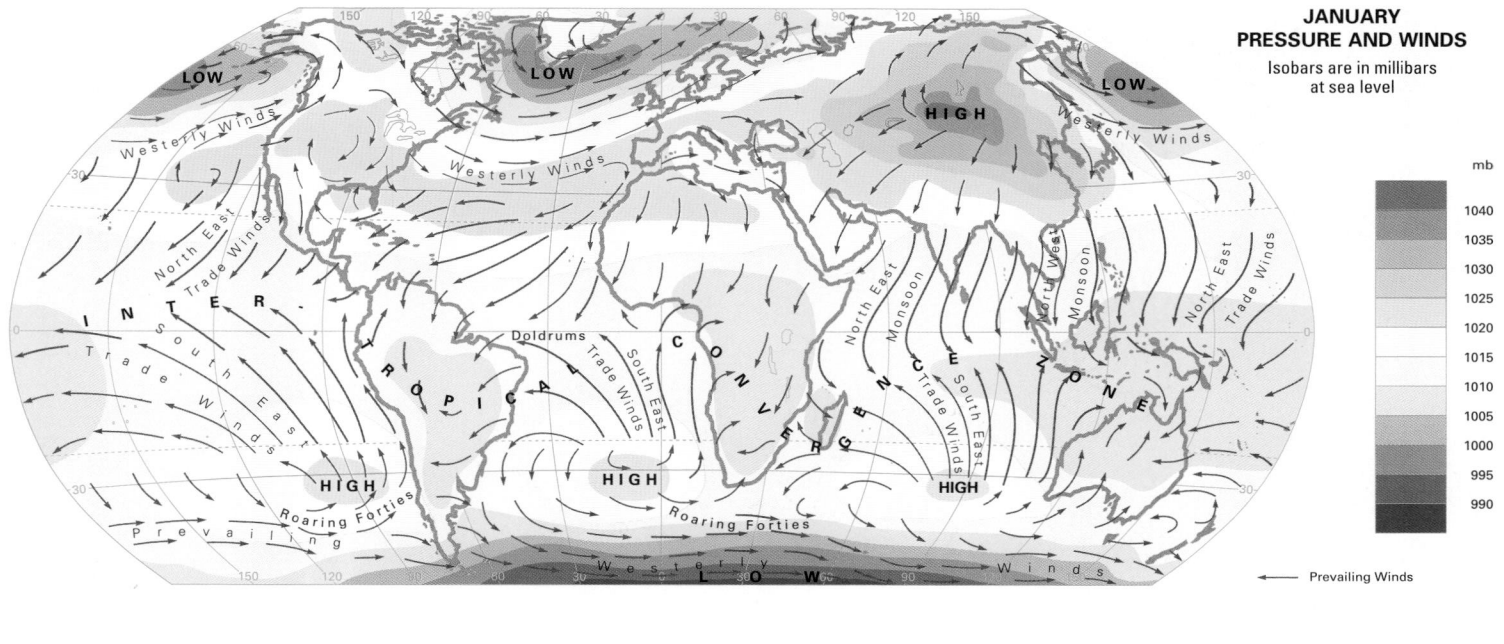

JANUARY PRESSURE AND WINDS
Isobars are in millibars at sea level

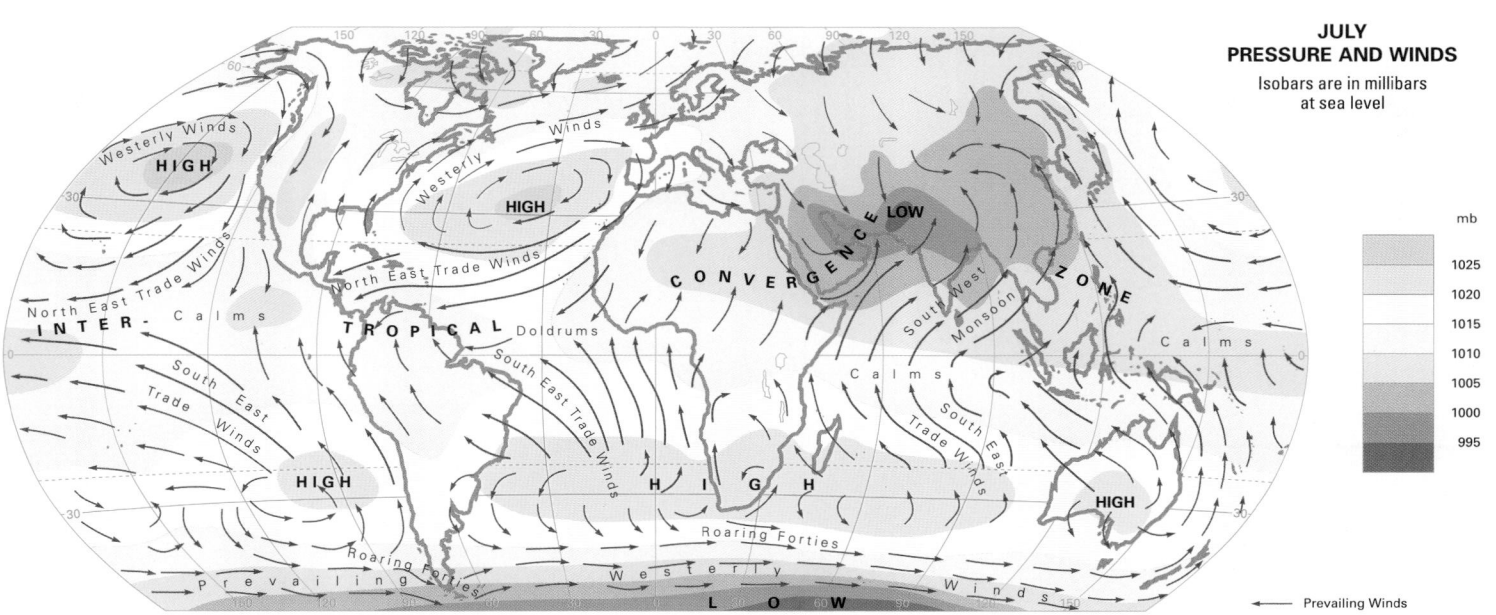

JULY PRESSURE AND WINDS
Isobars are in millibars at sea level

WEATHER RECORDS

Pressure and winds

Highest barometric pressure:
Agata, Siberia, 1,083.8 mb at altitude 862 ft [262 m], December 31, 1968.

Lowest barometric pressure:
Typhoon Tip, 300 mi [480 km] west of Guam, Pacific Ocean, 870 mb, October 12, 1979.

Highest recorded wind speed:
Mt Washington, New Hampshire, USA, 231 mph [371 km/h], April 12, 1934. This is three times as strong as hurricane force on the Beaufort Scale.

Windiest place:
Commonwealth Bay, George V Coast, Antarctica, where gales frequently reach over 200 mph [320 km/h].

Worst recorded storm:
Bangladesh (then East Pakistan) cyclone*, November 13, 1970 – over 300,000 dead or missing. The 1991 cyclone, Bangladesh's and the world's second worst in terms of loss of life, killed an estimated 138,000 people.

Worst recorded tornado:
Missouri/Illinois/Indiana, USA, March 18, 1925 – 792 deaths. The tornado was only 300 yds [275 m] wide.

* Tropical cyclones are known as hurricanes in Central and North America, as typhoons in the Far East, and as willy-willies in northern Australia.

For more information:
75 Ocean currents
76 Circulation of the air
77 Classification of clouds
   Pressure and winds
80 Hydrological cycle
81 Natural vegetation
83 Greenhouse effect
84 Global warming

Weather is the day-to-day or hour-to-hour condition of the air, while climate is weather in the long term – the seasonal pattern of hot and cold, wet and dry, averaged over a long period.

Most classifications of climate are based on a system developed in the early 19th century by Vladimir Köppen, a Russian meteorologist. Using a code based on letters and a classification centered on two main features, temperature and precipitation, he identified five main climatic types: tropical (A), dry (B), warm temperate (C), cold temperate (D), and polar (E). A highland mountain climate (H) was added later to account for the variety of altitudinal climatic zones on high mountains. Each of these main regions was then further subdivided.

Latitude is a major factor in determining climate, but other factors add to the complexity. These include the differential heating of land and sea, the distance from the sea, the effect of mountains on winds, and the influence of ocean currents. For example, New York City, Naples, and the Gobi Desert share almost the same latitude, but their climates are very different.

During the last Ice Age, the Earth underwent alternating cold periods, called glacials, separated by warm interglacials. The Milankovich theory suggests such cycles may be caused by variations in the Earth's path around the Sun, changing from almost circular to elliptical every 95,000 years, and variations in the Earth's tilt from 21.5° to 24.5° every 42,000 years. Another factor is that the Earth is now closest to the Sun in the middle of winter in the northern hemisphere and furthest away in summer. But 12,000 years ago, at the height of the last glacial period, the northern winter fell with the Sun at its most distant.

Studies of these cycles suggest that we are now in an interglacial with a new glacial period on the way. However, scientists believe that global warming, largely a result of burning fossil fuels and deforestation, may be occurring much faster than the great, slow cycles of the Solar System.

Tropical rainy climates
All mean monthly temperatures above 64°F.

Af	Rain forest climate
Am	Monsoon climate
Aw	Savanna climate

Dry climates
Low rainfall combined with a wide range of temperatures

BS	Steppe climate
BW	Desert climate

Warm temperate rainy climates
The mean temperature is below 64°F but above 26°F and that of the warmest month is over 50°F.

Cw	Dry winter climate
Cs	Dry summer climate
Cf	Climate with no dry season

Cold temperate rainy climates
The mean temperature of the coldest month is below 26°F but that of the warmest month is still over 50°F.

Dw	Dry winter climate
Df	Climate with no dry season

Polar climates
The mean temperature of the warmest month is below 50°F, giving permanently frozen subsoil.

ET	Tundra climate

The mean temperature of the warmest month is below 32°F, giving permanent ice and snow.

EF	Polar climate

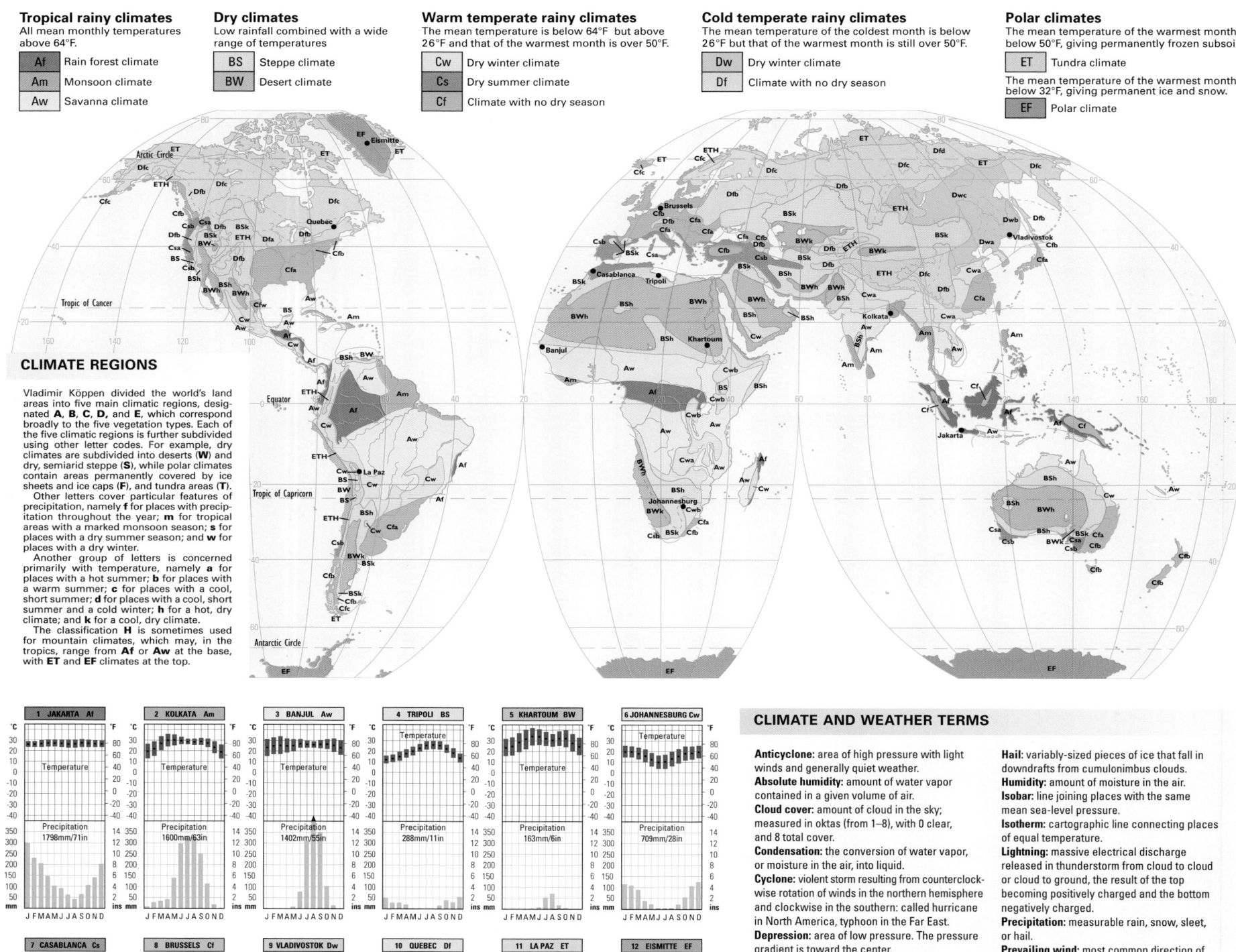

CLIMATE REGIONS

Vladimir Köppen divided the world's land areas into five main climatic regions, designated **A, B, C, D,** and **E,** which correspond broadly to the five vegetation types. Each of the five climatic regions is further subdivided using other letter codes. For example, dry climates are subdivided into deserts (**W**) and dry, semiarid steppe (**S**), while polar climates contain areas permanently covered by ice sheets and ice caps (**F**), and tundra areas (**T**).

Other letters cover particular features of precipitation, namely **f** for places with precipitation throughout the year; **m** for tropical areas with a marked monsoon season; **s** for places with a dry summer season; and **w** for places with a dry winter.

Another group of letters is concerned primarily with temperature, namely **a** for places with a hot summer; **b** for places with a warm summer; **c** for places with a cool, short summer; **d** for places with a cool, short summer and a cold winter; **h** for a hot, dry climate; and **k** for a cool, dry climate.

The classification **H** is sometimes used for mountain climates, which may, in the tropics, range from **Af** or **Aw** at the base, with **ET** and **EF** climates at the top.

CLIMATE AND WEATHER TERMS

Anticyclone: area of high pressure with light winds and generally quiet weather.
Absolute humidity: amount of water vapor contained in a given volume of air.
Cloud cover: amount of cloud in the sky; measured in oktas (from 1–8), with 0 clear, and 8 total cover.
Condensation: the conversion of water vapor, or moisture in the air, into liquid.
Cyclone: violent storm resulting from counterclockwise rotation of winds in the northern hemisphere and clockwise in the southern: called hurricane in North America, typhoon in the Far East.
Depression: area of low pressure. The pressure gradient is toward the center.
Dew: water droplets condensed out of the air after the ground has cooled at night.
Dew point: temperature at which air becomes saturated (reaches a relative humidity of 100%) at a constant pressure.
Drizzle: precipitation where drops are less than 0.02 inches [0.5 mm] in diameter.
Evaporation: conversion of water from liquid into vapor or moisture in the air.
Front: the dividing line between two air masses.
Frost: the surface deposition of water vapor as minute ice crystals, when temperature reaches the frost point.

Hail: variably-sized pieces of ice that fall in downdrafts from cumulonimbus clouds.
Humidity: amount of moisture in the air.
Isobar: line joining places with the same mean sea-level pressure.
Isotherm: cartographic line connecting places of equal temperature.
Lightning: massive electrical discharge released in thunderstorm from cloud to cloud or cloud to ground, the result of the top becoming positively charged and the bottom negatively charged.
Precipitation: measurable rain, snow, sleet, or hail.
Prevailing wind: most common direction of wind at a given location.
Rain: precipitation of liquid particles with diameter larger than 0.02 inches [0.5 mm].
Relative humidity: observed quantity of water vapor in a mass of air over the saturation value at a given temperature (as a percentage).
Snow: flake-like coagulations of ice crystals that fall from clouds in subzero temperatures.
Thunder: sound produced by the rapid expansion of air heated by lightning.
Tornado: rapidly-rotating funnel-shaped cloud or debris column that must reach the surface and be attached to a parent cumulonimbus cloud.

CLIMATE CHANGE

Human factors, such as the emission of greenhouse gases through the burning of fossil fuels and deforestation, have contributed to global warming. The histogram (below) shows in blue the average global temperatures from 1860 to 1996. The red line is a 10-year running average. Overall, there is an upward trend, particularly so since the 1970s, when global warming became a matter of concern in scientific circles. The large year-to-year changes indicate the Earth's natural climatic variability and the influence of such factors as major volcanic eruptions.

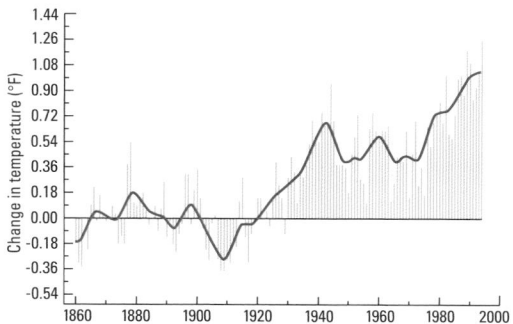

Data from the Hadley Centre for Climate Research and Prediction

BEAUFORT WIND SCALE

Named after Admiral Sir Francis Beaufort, the 19th-century British naval officer who devised it, the Beaufort Scale assesses wind speed according to its effects. It was originally designed as an aid for sailors, but has since been adapted for use on the land. It is used internationally.

Scale	Wind speed mph	km/h	Effect
0	0–1	0–1	**Calm** Smoke rises vertically
1	1–3	1–5	**Light air** Wind direction shown only by smoke drift
2	4–7	6–11	**Light breeze** Wind felt on face; leaves rustle; vanes moved by wind
3	8–12	12–19	**Gentle breeze** Leaves and small twigs in constant motion; wind extends small flag
4	13–18	20–28	**Moderate** Raises dust and loose paper; small branches move
5	19–24	29–38	**Fresh** Small trees in leaf sway; crested wavelets on inland waters
6	25–31	39–49	**Strong** Large branches move; difficult to use umbrellas; overhead wires whistle
7	32–38	50–61	**Near gale** Whole trees in motion; difficult to walk against wind
8	39–46	62–74	**Gale** Twigs break from trees; walking very difficult
9	47–54	75–88	**Strong gale** Slight structural damage
10	55–63	89–102	**Storm** Trees uprooted; serious structural damage
11	64–72	103–117	**Violent storm** Widespread damage
12	73+	118+	**Hurricane**

THE MONSOON

Monsoon is the term given to the seasonal reversal of wind direction, most noticeably in Southeast Asia. It results from a combination of factors: the extreme heating and cooling of large land masses in relation to the less marked changes in temperature of the adjacent seas; the northward movement of the Intertropical Convergence Zone (ITCZ); and the effect of the Himalayas on the circulation of the air.

In March, winds blow outward from the mainland. But as the Sun and the ITCZ move northward, the land is intensely heated, and a low-pressure system develops. The southeast trade winds change direction and are sucked into the interior to become southwesterlies, bringing heavy rain. By November, the Sun and the ITCZ have again moved south and the wind directions are again reversed. Cool winds blow from the Asian interior to the sea, losing any moisture on the Himalayas before descending to the coast.

TEMPERATURE

Average temperature in January

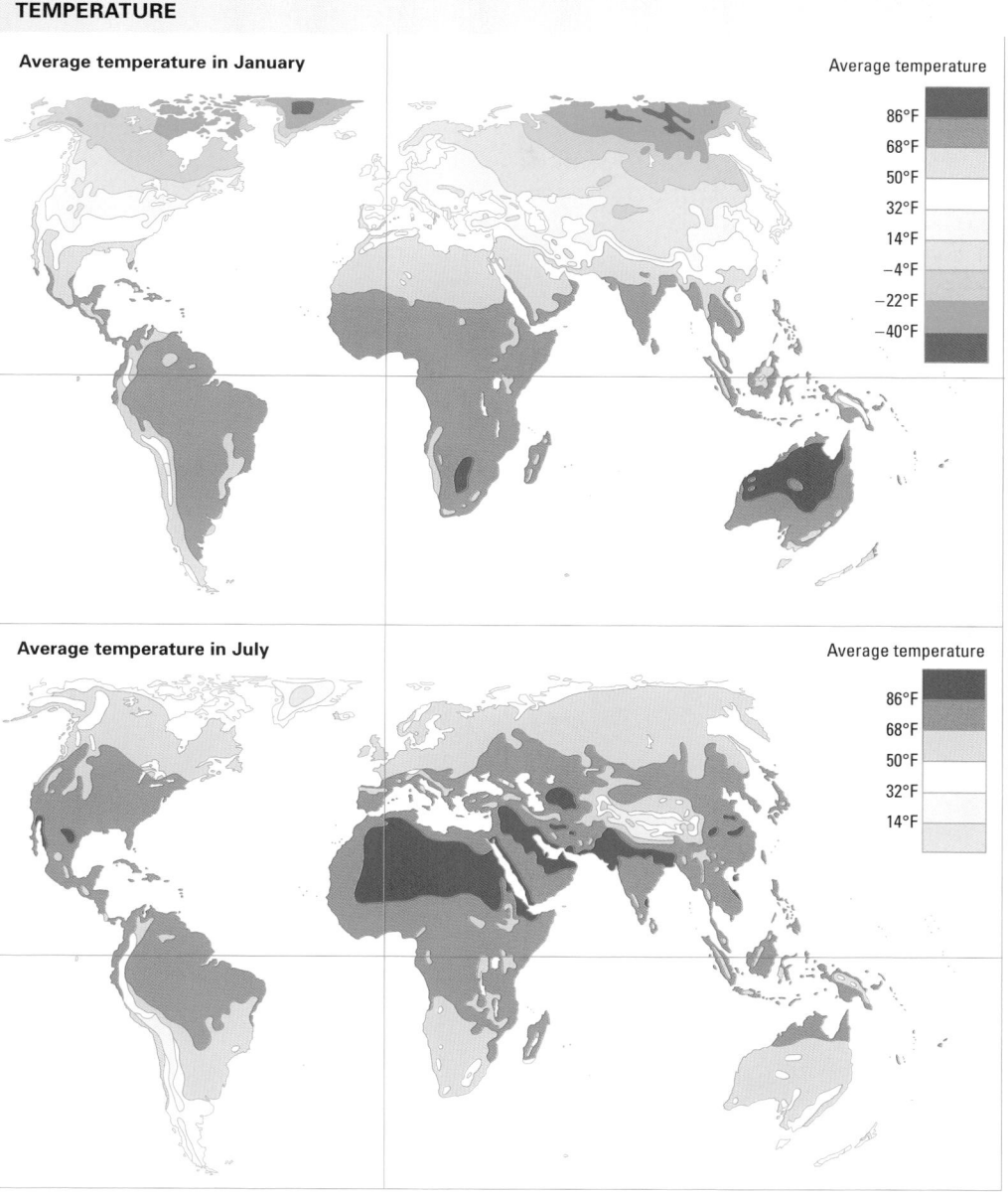

Average temperature

	86°F
	68°F
	50°F
	32°F
	14°F
	−4°F
	−22°F
	−40°F

Average temperature in July

Average temperature

	86°F
	68°F
	50°F
	32°F
	14°F

PRECIPITATION (RAINFALL AND SNOW)

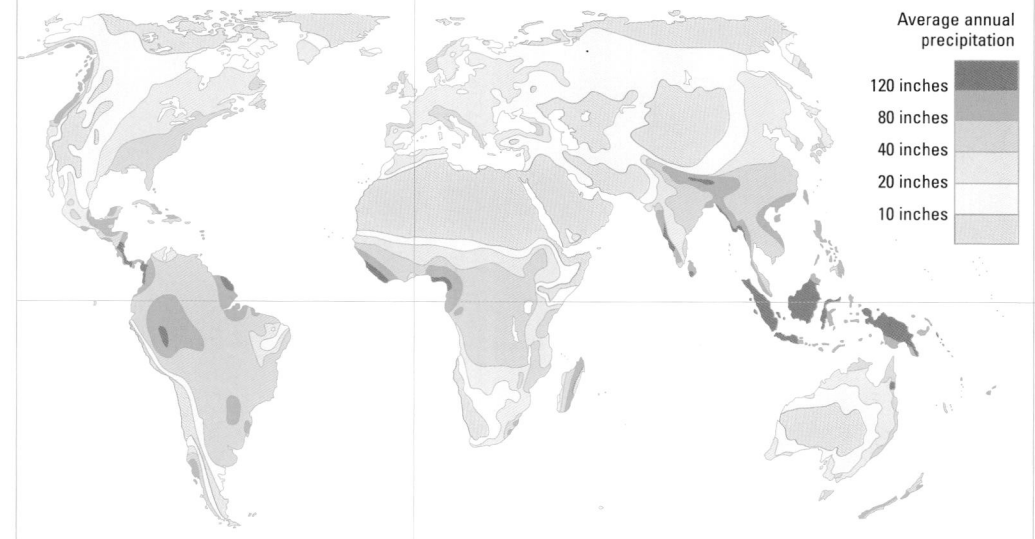

Average annual precipitation

	120 inches
	80 inches
	40 inches
	20 inches
	10 inches

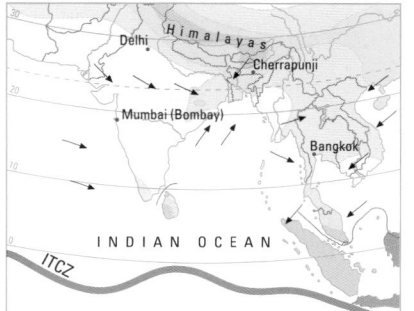

March – Start of the hot, dry season. The ITCZ is over the southern Indian Ocean.

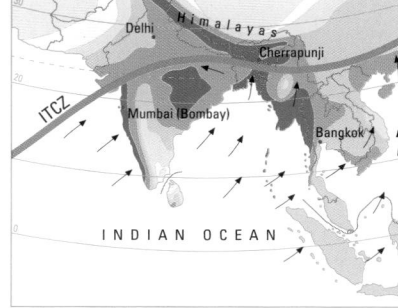

July – The rainy season. The ITCZ has migrated northward; winds blow onshore.

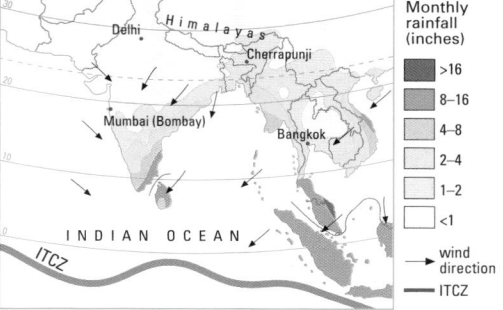

November – The ITCZ has returned south. The offshore winds are cool and dry.

Monthly rainfall (inches)

	>16
	8–16
	4–8
	2–4
	1–2
	<1

→ wind direction
━ ITCZ

CLIMATE RECORDS

TEMPERATURE

Highest recorded temperature:
Al Aziziyah, Libya, 136.4°F [58°C], September 13, 1922.

Highest mean annual temperature:
Dallol, Ethiopia, 94°F [34.4°C], 1960–6.

Longest heatwave:
Marble Bar, W. Australia, 162 days over 100°F [38°C], October 23, 1923 to April 7, 1924.

Lowest recorded temperature (outside poles):
Verkhoyansk, Siberia, −90°F [−68°C], February 6, 1933. Verkhoyansk also registered the greatest annual range of temperature: −90°F to 98°F [−68°C to 37°C].

Lowest mean annual temperature:
Polus Nedostupnosti, Pole of Cold, Antarctica, −72°F [−57.8°C].

PRECIPITATION

Driest place:
Calama, N. Chile: no recorded rainfall in 400 years to 1971.

Wettest place (average):
Tututendo, Colombia: mean annual rainfall 463.4 inches [11,770 mm].

Wettest place (12 months):
Cherrapunji, Meghalaya, N.E. India, 1,040 inches [26,470 mm], August 1860 to August 1861. Cherrapunji also holds the record for rainfall in one month: 115 inches [2,930 mm], July 1861. (*See maps below.*)

Wettest place (24 hours):
Cilaos, Réunion, Indian Ocean, 73.6 inches [1,870 mm], March 15–16, 1952.

Heaviest hailstones:
Gopalganj, Bangladesh, up to 2.25 lb [1.02 kg], April 14, 1986 (killed 92 people).

Heaviest snowfall (continuous):
Bessans, Savoie, France, 68 inches [1,730 mm] in 19 hours, April 5–6, 1969.

Heaviest snowfall (season/year):
Paradise Ranger Station, Mt Rainier, Washington, USA, 1,224.5 inches [31,102 mm], February 19, 1971, to February 18, 1972.

For more information:

78 Climate regions

79 Precipitation

82 Biodiversity

85 Water pollution

Deforestation

Without the hydrological cycle, by which water is constantly recycled between the oceans, the atmosphere and the land, the continents would be barren. Precipitation enables plants to grow and soils to form, creating the world's natural vegetation regions and the ecosystems that support animal life.

Running water also plays a major role in shaping landforms. Yet in many parts of the world, people do not have safe water to drink and suffer from diseases caused by water-borne organisms and pollution. In 2005, an estimated 1.1 billion people lacked access to safe water and 2.6 billion people lacked basic sanitation.

Experts argue that world demand for water is increasing at about twice the rate of population growth. It is predicted that, by 2025, half the world's population will face water shortages. This could lead to conflict and even boundary wars – 300 major rivers cross national frontiers and access to their water is likely to be disputed.

THE HYDROLOGICAL CYCLE

The world's water balance is regulated by the constant recycling of water between the oceans, the atmosphere and the land. The movement of water between these three reservoirs is known as the *hydrological cycle*. The oceans play a vital role in the hydrological cycle: 74% of the total precipitation falls over the oceans and 84% of the total evaporation comes from the oceans. Water vapor in the atmosphere circulates around the planet, transporting energy as well as the water itself. When the vapor cools, it falls as rain or snow. The whole cycle is driven by the Sun.

WATER DISTRIBUTION

The distribution of planetary water, by percentage. Oceans and ice caps together account for more than 99% of the total; the breakdown of the remainder is estimated.

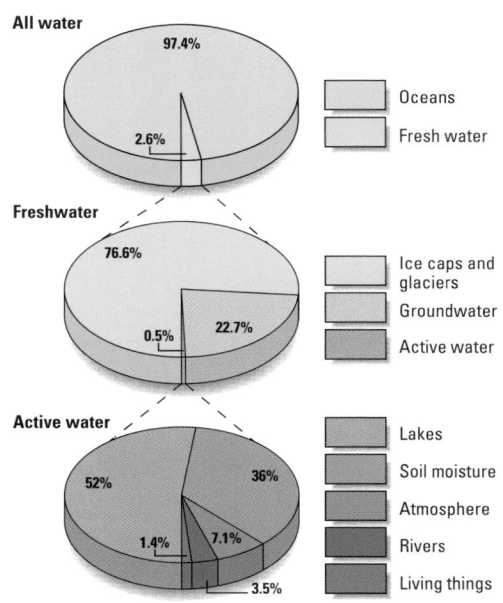

Almost all the world's water is 3,000 million years old, and all of it cycles endlessly through the hydrosphere, though at different rates. Water vapor circulates over days, even hours; deep-ocean water circulates over millennia; and ice-cap water remains solid for millions of years.

ANNUAL SEDIMENT YIELD

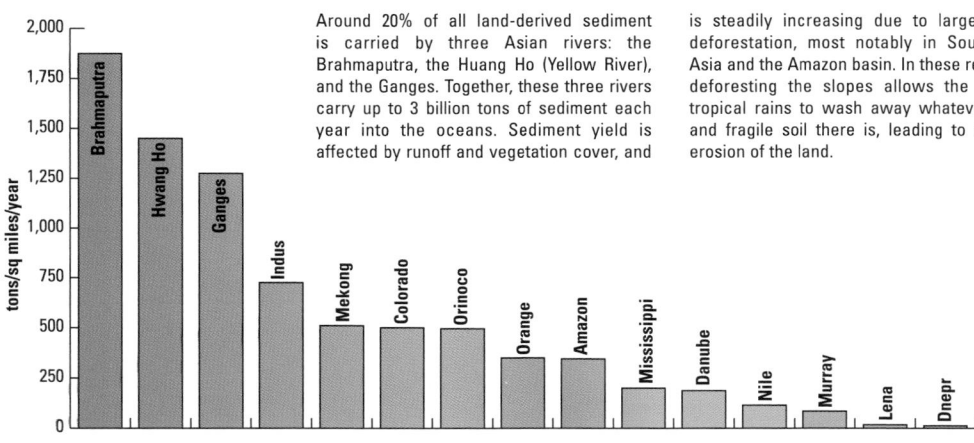

Around 20% of all land-derived sediment is carried by three Asian rivers: the Brahmaputra, the Huang Ho (Yellow River), and the Ganges. Together, these three rivers carry up to 3 billion tons of sediment each year into the oceans. Sediment yield is affected by runoff and vegetation cover, and is steadily increasing due to large-scale deforestation, most notably in Southeast Asia and the Amazon basin. In these regions, deforesting the slopes allows the heavy tropical rains to wash away whatever thin and fragile soil there is, leading to severe erosion of the land.

WATER RUNOFF

Annual freshwater runoff by continent in cubic miles

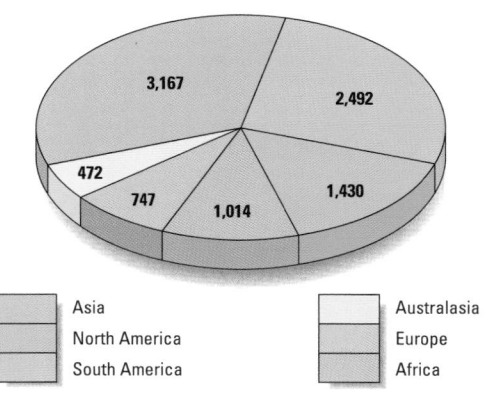

▶ The River Amazon is the world's second-longest river (after the River Nile), draining the vast rain forest basin of northern South America. The Amazon carries by far the greatest volume of water of any river in the world: the average rate of discharge is approximately 3,355,000 cu ft [95,000 cu m] per second, nearly three times as much as its nearest rival, the Congo. The flow is so great that its silt discolors the water up to 125 miles [200 km] into the Atlantic. At approximately 2.7 million sq miles [7 million sq km], the Amazon basin comprises nearly 40% of the whole of South America.

WATERSHEDS

The map below shows the world's major rivers, with the ranking of the 20 longest rivers shown in square brackets after their name, led by the Nile [1] and the Amazon [2].

The map shows the direction of freshwater flow on a continental scale, whereas the water runoff chart on the facing page indicates the quantities involved annually.

The rate of runoff varies seasonally and is affected by the surface vegetation and climate. Most of the world's major rivers discharge into the Atlantic Ocean.

Where the rivers run

- Pacific Ocean
- Indian Ocean
- Arctic Ocean
- Atlantic Ocean
- Caribbean Sea–Gulf of Mexico
- Mediterranean Sea
- Inland basins, ice caps, and deserts

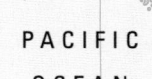

NATURAL VEGETATION

The map below illustrates the natural "climax vegetation" of a region, as dictated by its climate and topography. In most cases, human agricultural activity has drastically altered the pattern of the vegetation. Western Europe, for example, lost most of its broadleaf forests many centuries ago, while elsewhere irrigation has turned some natural semideserts into productive land. The various vegetation regions support different kinds of animals and wildlife, and, in an undisturbed state, they are highly developed biological communities, or "biomes."

The blue line on the map represents the northern limit of tree growth, and the red lines indicate the northern and southern limits of palm growth.

- Tropical rain forest
- Subtropical and temperate rain forest
- Monsoon woodland and open jungle
- Subtropical and temperate woodland, scrub, and bush
- Tropical savanna, with low trees and bush
- Tropical savanna and grasslands
- Dry semidesert, with shrub and grass
- Desert shrub
- Desert
- Dry steppe and shrub
- Temperate grasslands, prairie, and steppe
- Mediterranean hardwood forest and scrub
- Temperate deciduous forest and meadow
- Temperate deciduous and coniferous forest
- Northern coniferous forest (taïga)
- Mountainous forest, mainly coniferous
- High plateau steppe and tundra
- Arctic tundra
- Polar and mountainous ice desert

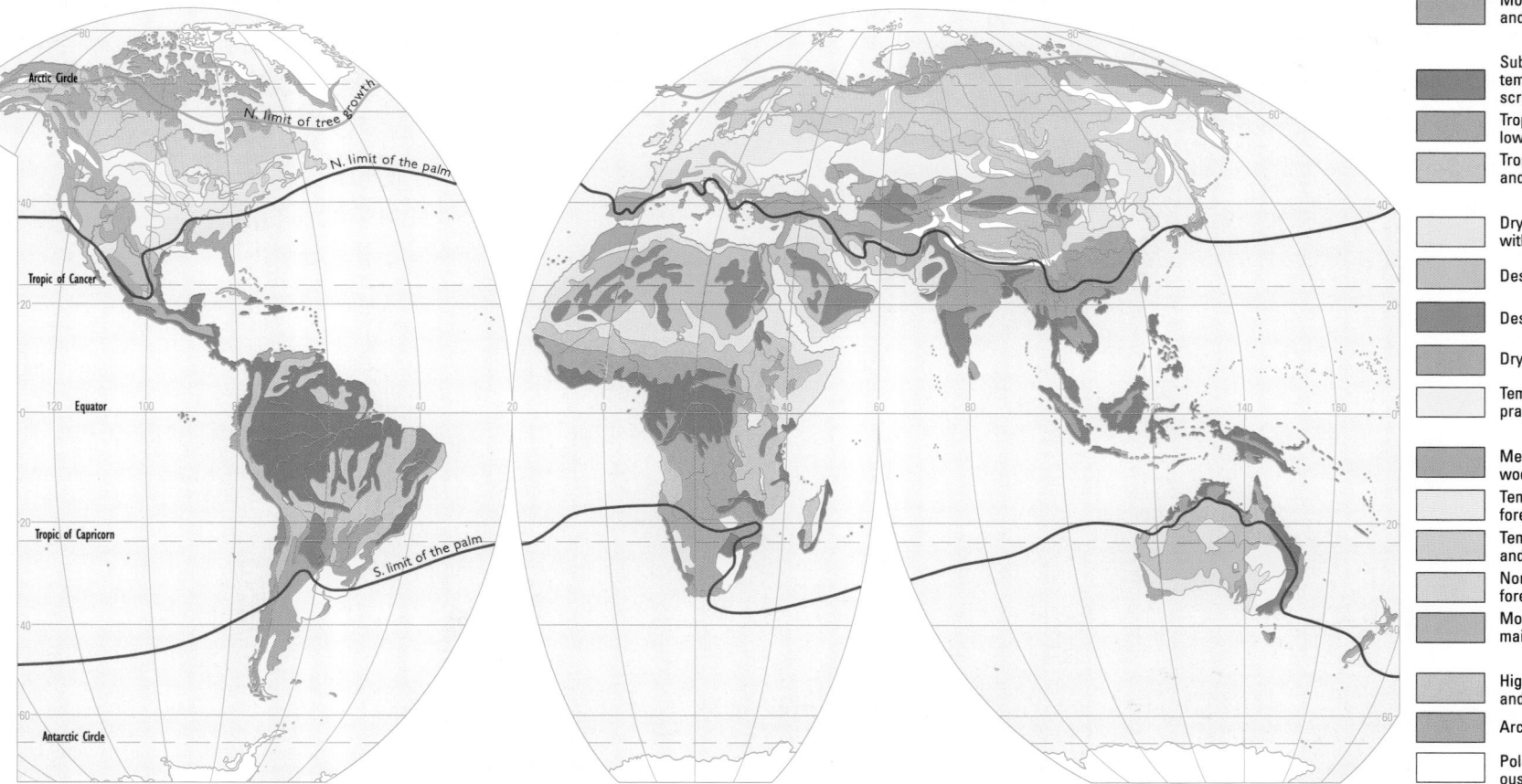

For more information:
74 Oceans
76 Atmosphere
81 Natural vegetation
84 Carbon dioxide
   Greenhouse power
   Global warming
85 Acid rain
   Desertification
   Deforestation
   Water pollution

Recent discoveries of life forms in some of the world's most hostile environments, such as around the black smokers along the ocean ridges, prepared the way for the announcement by NASA scientists in 1996 that they had found microfossils in a Martian meteorite. But other scientists were sceptical, believing them to be natural mineral structures and not evidence of extraterrestrial life.

Until further evidence is available, the Earth remains the only planet where we know for sure that life exists. According to the fossil record, life on Earth appeared at least 3,500 million years ago. Since then, it has evolved from its primitive beginnings to its modern biodiversity, including millions of plants, animals and micro-organisms. Living organisms have not only adapted to the environment, but they have also changed their environment to suit themselves. For example, the Earth's early atmosphere contained little oxygen, but the emergence of multicelled, oxygen-producing algae, around 2,000 million years ago, led to the creation of an oxygen-rich atmosphere. This enabled land animals to populate the ancient continents.

The amount of the greenhouse-gas carbon dioxide in the atmosphere would steadily increase from its present 0.03% were it not for plants. Without them, the Earth's atmosphere would, in a few million years, be similar to that of Venus, where surface temperatures reach 890°F. The Earth has evolved into a complex control system, sensing and reacting to changes and tending always to maintain the balance it has achieved.

Much discussion has centered on how that balance changes. Only recently, scientists were suggesting that we may be living in an interglacial stage of the Pleistocene Ice Age. Since the 1980s, however, predictions of future climate patterns have concentrated more on global warming, caused by pollution that has led to an increase in greenhouse gases in the atmosphere. Interference in the natural cycles that control the environment may have consequences that are hard to predict.

Furthermore, we are currently experiencing a period of mass extinction of species, causing a rapid reduction in our planet's biodiversity. In 2004, a report by the International Union for the Conservation of Nature listed 15,589 organisms facing extinction. This was 1,000 more than in 2003.

THREATENED MAMMALS

The map shows the number of mammal species threatened with extinction in 2004. Many experts believe we are currently experiencing a period of mass extinction of species, rivaling five other periods in the past half a billion years. Among the most threatened mammals today are elephants, primates, and rhinoceroses.

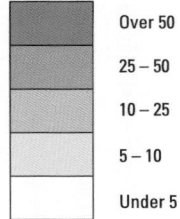

Over 50

25 – 50

10 – 25

5 – 10

Under 5

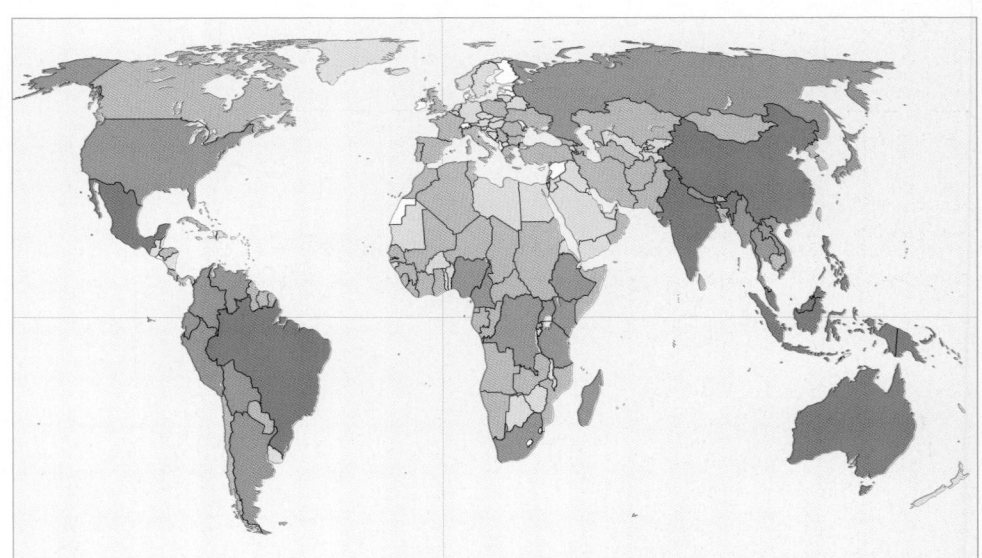

BIODIVERSITY IN CALIFORNIA, USA

This false-color satellite image of central California shows San Francisco lying just below the entrance to San Francisco Bay, with Oakland on the far side and San Jose to the southeast. California, nick-named the Golden State, is the third largest state in the United States and the most populous.

Due to its varied terrain and climate, California has a wide range of diverse habitats within a relatively small area. East of the forested Coast Ranges (the gray and red areas just inland from the bay) lies the fertile Central Valley, which appears as a red-and-blue checkerboard. In the northwest and southwest of the state (*not shown here*) lie parts of the Basin and Range region, much of which is desert. It includes Death Valley, which contains the country's lowest point on land, at 282 feet below sea level.

Natural vegetation

Forests cover about 40% of California and they include bristlecone pines, thought to be the oldest living things on Earth, together with coastal red-woods, the world's tallest trees. Wildlife is still abundant, though some species, such as the rare California condor, are on the endangered list.

The state has achieved much to protect its biodiversity. It contains eight of the 56 national parks in the United States. Two of them, Death Valley and Joshua Tree, were designated national parks as recently as 1994, as part of a conservation measure, including the protection of large areas of wilderness in the deserts.

California has vast resources and, were it a separate nation, it would rank among the world's ten most productive in terms of the total value of its goods and services. This means that, like the United States as a whole, it has resources, which many developing countries lack, to finance conservation measures. For example, the World Conservation Union reported in the late 1990s that 8% of mammals were threatened in the US, as compared with 32% in the Philippines and 44% in Madagascar, two countries where habitat destruction has been proceeding on a large scale.

THE EARTH'S ENERGY BALANCE

Apart from a modest quantity of internal heat from its molten core, the Earth receives all of its energy from the Sun. If the planet is to remain at a constant temperature, it must reradiate exactly as much energy as it receives. Even a minute surplus would lead to a warmer Earth, a deficit to a cooler one. The temperature at which thermal equilibrium is reached depends on many factors, including the relative brightness of the Earth (its index of reflectivity, called the "albedo") and the heat-trapping capacity of the atmosphere (the "greenhouse effect").

Most of the Sun's energy arrives in the form of short-wave radiation. Some of the energy is reflected straight back into space, while some is absorbed by the atmosphere or by the Earth itself. Absorbed energy heats the Earth and its atmosphere alike, but since its temperature is much lower than that of the Sun, the outgoing energy is emitted at longer infrared wavelengths.

The diagram (*right*) shows short-wave radiation in yellow, with long-wave radiation in orange.

THE GREENHOUSE EFFECT

Constituting less than 1% of the atmosphere, the natural greenhouse gases (water vapor, carbon dioxide, methane, nitrous oxide, and ozone) have a disproportionate effect on the Earth's climate, and even its habitability. Like the glass panes in a greenhouse, the gases are transparent to most incoming short-wave radiation, which passes freely to heat the planet beneath. But when the warmed Earth retransmits that energy, in the form of longer-wave infrared radiation, the gases function as an opaque shield, preventing some of it from escaping, so that the planetary surface (like the interior of a greenhouse) stays relatively hot.

Over the last 150 years, there has been a gradual increase in the levels of greenhouse gases (with the exception of water vapor, which remains a constant in the system). Current predictions suggest that there could be a further rise of 2.5–8°F by the year 2100. A serious reduction in the greenhouse gases would be just as damaging, though. A total absence of carbon dioxide, for example, would leave the planet with a temperature roughly 60°F colder than it is at present.

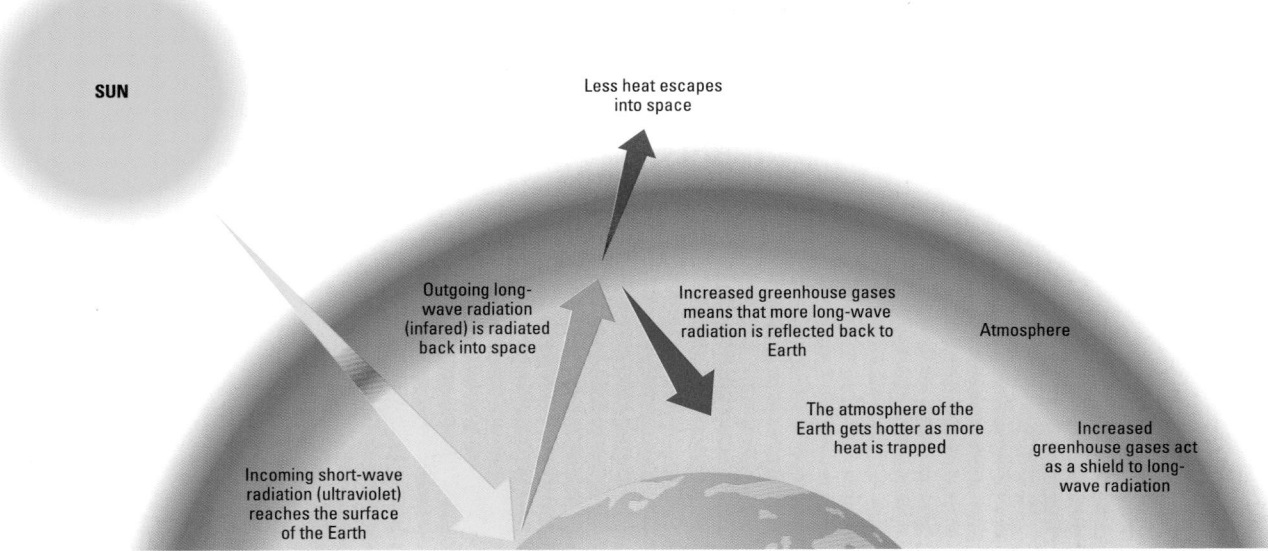

THE CARBON CYCLE

The Earth has a huge supply of carbon, only a small quantity of which is in the form of carbon dioxide. Of that, around 98% is dissolved in the sea; the fraction circulating in the air amounts to only 340 parts per million of the atmosphere, where its capacity as a greenhouse gas is the key regulator of the planetary temperature.

Living things, however, circulate carbon. Plants absorb carbon dioxide from the atmosphere and the carbon is then returned to circulation when the plants die, or is passed up the food chain to the herbivores, and then to the carnivores that feed on them. As organisms at each of these trophic levels die, they decay, releasing the carbon, which then combines once more with the oxygen released during life. However, a small proportion of carbon is removed almost permanently, buried beneath mud on land or at sea, sinking as dead matter to the ocean floor. In time, it is slowly compressed into sedimentary rocks, such as limestone and chalk.

The carbon cycle has continued for a very long time. However, human beings have found a way to release fixed carbon at a faster rate than existing global systems can recirculate it. It has taken only a few human generations to deplete the fossil fuels that represent many millions of years of carbon accumulation.

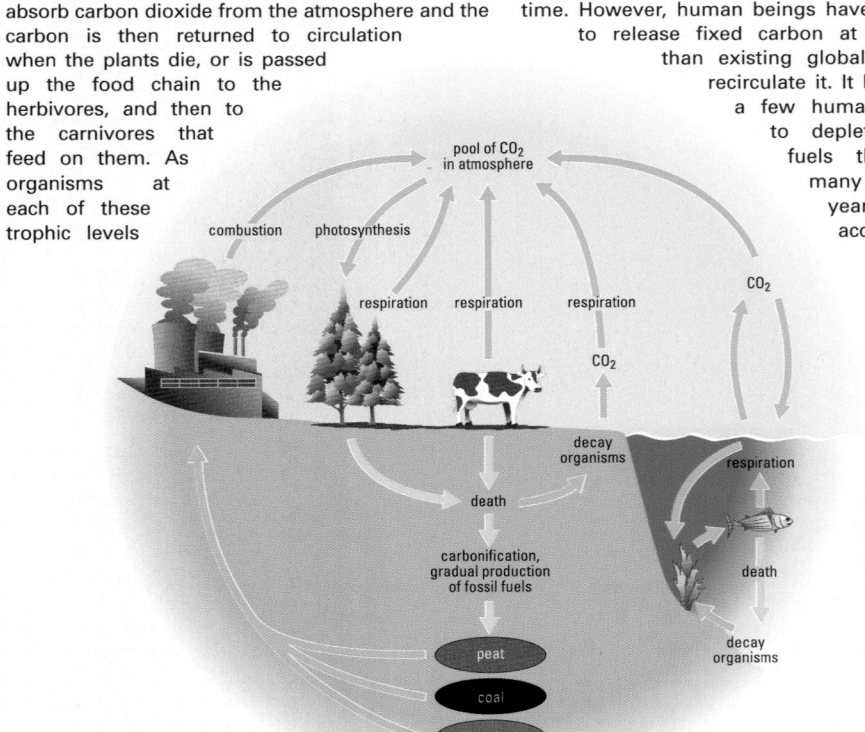

CARBON MONOXIDE CONCENTRATION

A colorless, odorless and poisonous gas, carbon monoxide (CO) is formed during the incomplete combustion of fossil fuels, occurring, for example, in coal gas and the exhaust fumes of cars. It is a major air pollutant and is now regulated by many world nations. The images below show the seasonal amounts and geographical sources of atmospheric carbon monoxide in the spring and summer months. Progressively higher levels of carbon monoxide are shown in green, yellow, orange, and red, while the blue areas have little or no atmospheric carbon monoxide.

Carbon monoxide can remain in the atmosphere for up to several months and can affect air quality in regions that are a long way from the original source of the pollution emissions.

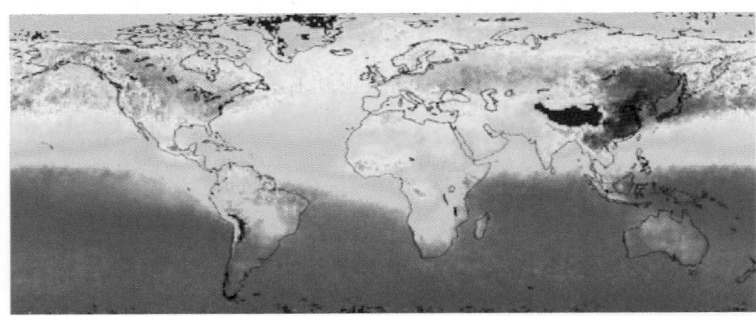

April, May, June

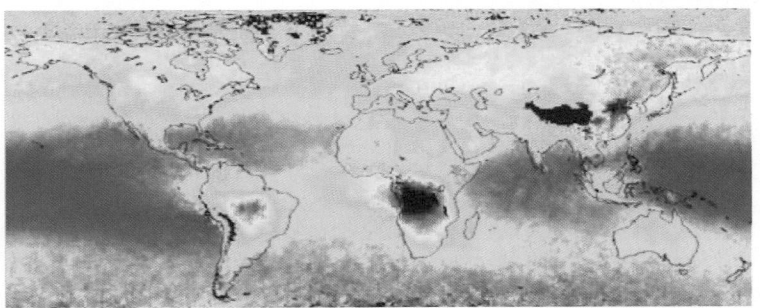

July, August, September

Carbon monoxide concentration (parts per billion by volume)

| 0 | 50 | 100 | 150 | 200 | >250 | no data |

For more information:

74 Oceans

76 Atmosphere

78 Climate

83 Greenhouse effect

88 Urban pollution

In 1996, the Intergovernmental Panel on Climate Change issued a report stating that "The balance of evidence suggests a discernible human influence on global climate through emissions of carbon dioxide and other greenhouse gases." The report acknowledged that average global temperatures had risen by about 0.9°F since the mid-19th century, though there were still reasons for caution on attributing this entirely to actions taken by humans.

Human interference with nature is nothing new, at least since people turned from hunting and gathering to agriculture more than 10,000 years ago. At first, human actions seemed to have no ill effects because the systems that regulate the global environment were able to absorb damage. But from the late 18th century, the Industrial Revolution and the population explosion have caused massive pollution that threatens to overwhelm the Earth's ability to cope.

The 20th century experienced many disasters, including the dumping of industrial wastes in rivers and seas, accidents at nuclear power stations, and the creation of acid rain through the release of sulfur dioxides and nitrous oxides by the burning of fossil fuels. The release of greenhouse gases are held to be the main reason for global warming, while CFCs (chlorofluorocarbons) have damaged the ozone layer in the stratosphere, the planet's screen against ultraviolet radiation.

In December 1998, an international conference in Kyoto, Japan, reached an agreement to reduce the emission of greenhouse gases by 5.2% by 2012. But, in the early 21st century, the United States, which produces about a third of all emissions, opposed the Kyoto protocol.

Global warming will lead to melting ice sheets and the flooding of fertile coastal plains. Computer models suggest that it might affect ocean currents so that northwestern Europe, which owes its mild climate to the Gulf Stream, could expect bitterly cold winters. Some models have also suggested that cloud cover could increase, reflecting more solar energy back into space and thus start a new Ice Age.

In many tropical areas, deforestation is making productive land barren, while in the dry grasslands bordering deserts, the removal of plant cover is causing desertification. But human ingenuity can respond to this crisis in planet management.

GLOBAL WARMING

High atmospheric concentrations of heat-absorbing gases appear to be causing a rise in average temperatures worldwide – up to 3°F [1.5°C] by the year 2020, according to some estimates. Global warming is likely to bring about a rise in sea levels that may flood some of the world's densely populated coastal areas.

Evidence of global warming is attributed mainly to the "greenhouse effect," caused by the emission of certain gases, notably carbon dioxide, into the atmosphere (*see page 83*). Despite international action to control emissions of some greenhouse gases, carbon dioxide levels are still rising.

Carbon dioxide emissions in metric tons per capita (2003)

	Over 15
	10 – 15
	5 – 10
	1 – 5
	Under 1

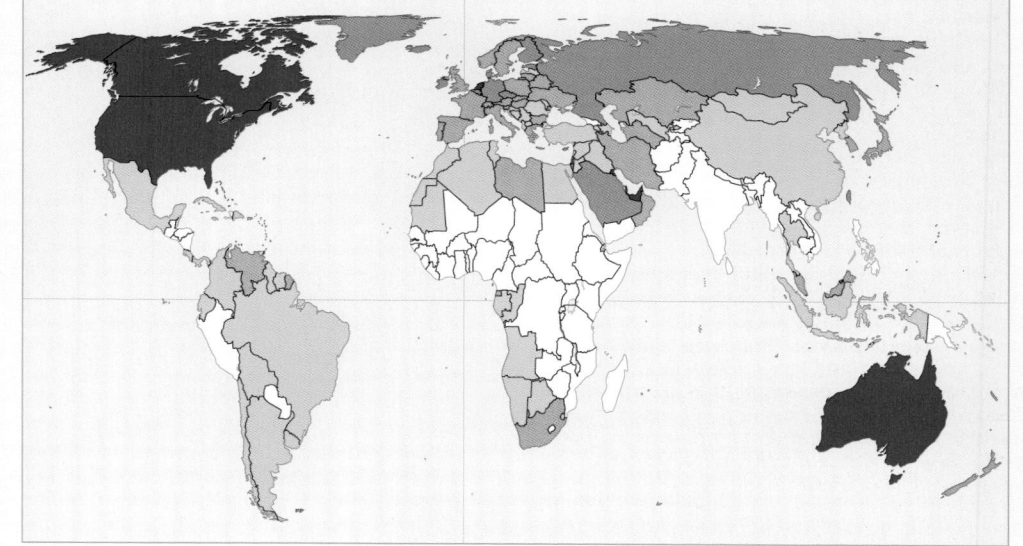

GREENHOUSE POWER

Relative contributions to the "greenhouse effect" by the major heat-absorbing gases in the atmosphere The chart combines greenhouse potency and volume. Carbon dioxide has a greenhouse potential of only 1, but its concentration of 350 parts per million makes it predominate. CFC 12, with 25,000 times the absorption capacity of CO_2, is present only as 0.00044 ppm.

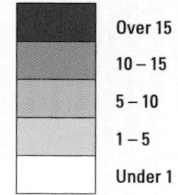

Carbon dioxide (CO_2)

Ozone

Methane

Nitrous oxide

CFC 12

CFC 11

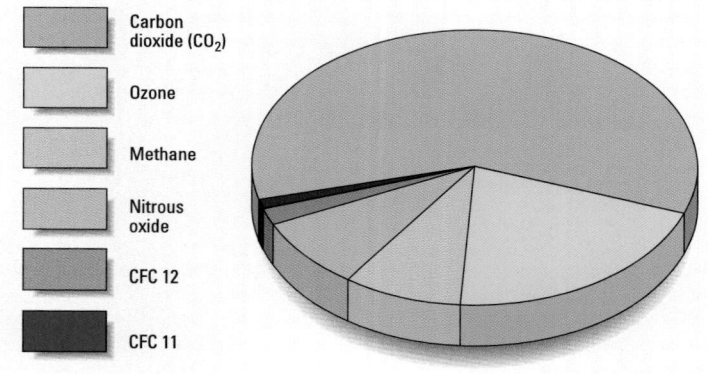

CARBON DIOXIDE
Estimated percentage share of total world CO_2 emissions (2003)

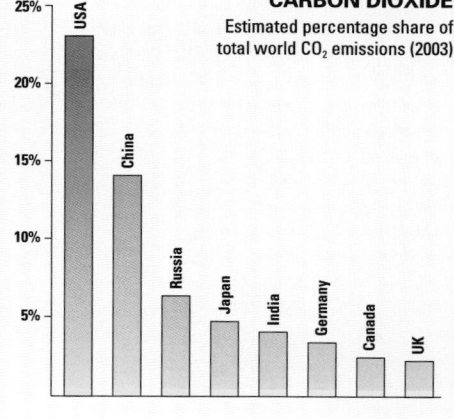

USA · China · Russia · Japan · India · Germany · Canada · UK

TEMPERATURE RISE
The rise in average temperatures caused by carbon dioxide and other greenhouse gases, assuming present trends continue (1960–2020)

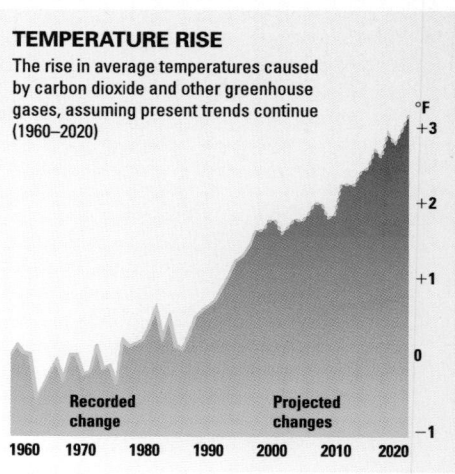

Recorded change · Projected changes

1960 1970 1980 1990 2000 2010 2020

THE THINNING OZONE LAYER

Total atmospheric ozone concentration in the southern and northern hemispheres (Dobson Units)
In 1985, scientists working in Antarctica discovered a thinning of the ozone layer, commonly known as an "ozone hole." This caused immediate alarm because the ozone layer absorbs most of the Sun's dangerous ultraviolet radiation, which is believed to cause an increase in skin cancer, cataracts, and damage to the immune system.

Since 1985, ozone depletion has increased and, by 2002, the ozone hole over the South Pole was estimated to be three times as large as the USA. The false-color images (*right*) show the total atmospheric ozone concentration in the southern hemisphere (in September 2000) and the northern hemisphere (in March 2000) with the ozone hole clearly identifiable at the center. The data is from the Tiros weather satellite. The colors represent the ozone concentration in Dobson Units (DU).

Scientists agree that ozone depletion is caused by CFCs, a group of manufactured chemicals used in air-conditioning systems and refrigerators. In a 1987 treaty most industrial nations agreed to phase out CFCs and a complete ban on most CFCs was agreed after the end of 1995. However, scientists believe that the chemicals will remain in the atmosphere for 50 to 100 years. As a result, ozone depletion will continue for many years.

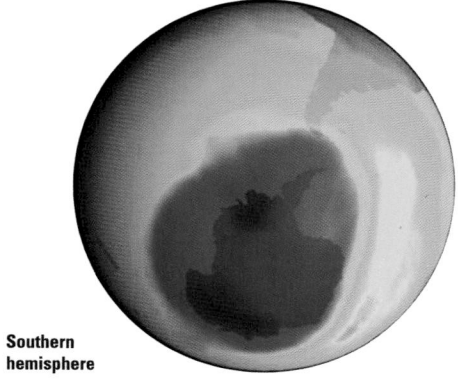

Southern hemisphere

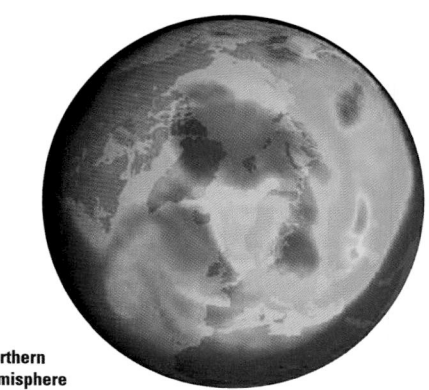

Northern hemisphere

WORLD POLLUTION

Acid rain and sources of acidic emissions (latest available year)
Acid rain is caused by high levels of sulfur and nitrogen in the atmosphere. They combine with water vapor and oxygen to form acids (H_2SO_4 and HNO_3) which fall as precipitation.

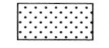 Regions where sulfur and nitrogen oxides are released in high concentrations, mainly from fossil fuel combustion

• Major cities with high levels of air pollution (including nitrogen and sulfur emissions)

Areas of heavy acid deposition
pH numbers indicate acidity, decreasing from a neutral 7. Normal rain, slightly acid from dissolved carbon dioxide, never exceeds a pH of 5.6.

 pH less than 4.0 (most acidic)

 pH 4.0 to 4.5

 pH 4.5 to 5.0

 Areas where acid rain is a potential problem

WATER POLLUTION

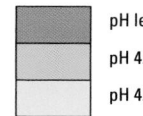

Severely polluted sea areas and lakes

Polluted sea areas and lakes

Areas of frequent oil pollution by shipping

▶ Major oil tanker spills

▲ Major oil rig blowouts

▼ Offshore dumpsites for industrial and municipal waste

— Severely polluted rivers and estuaries

In December 2002, oil slicks from the 77,000-ton *Prestige* tanker, which broke up off Spain, caused environmental damage to the north coast of Spain and, in 2003, to the southwest coast of France. This was a small incident by comparison with some earlier events, such as the collision between the *Atlantic Empress* and the *Aegean Captain* in July 1979. This was the worst tanker incident ever, polluting the Caribbean with 1,890,000 barrels of crude oil.

Oil spills, however, declined in the 1980s, from a peak of 750,000 tons in 1979 to less than 50,000 tons in 1990. The most notorious spill of that period – when the *Exxon Valdez* ran aground in Prince William Sound, Alaska, in March 1989 – released only 267,000 barrels, a relatively small amount when compared with the 2,500,000 barrels spilled during the Gulf War of 1991. Oil spillage, poisoned rivers, and domestic sewage have in recent years badly contaminated parts of the oceans.

DESERTIFICATION

 Existing deserts

Areas with a high risk of desertification

Areas with a moderate risk of desertification

 Former areas of rain forest

 Existing rain forest

DEFORESTATION

Bolivia has over 100,000 sq miles [250,000 sq km] of dry tropical forest, home to animals such as jaguars and ocelots. It is, however, being cleared at a rate of over 2% per annum. This false-color image shows an area that has been almost completely cleared. The darkest areas are remnants of the original forest, some retained as wind breaks between newly created arable fields, growing such crops as soybeans.

Where deforestation occurs, there is an immediate danger that the vital topsoil will be eroded by wind or by rain. Proposals to clear large regions of the Amazonian rain forests, which play a key role in maintaining the Earth's oxygen balance, could cause an environmental catastrophe.

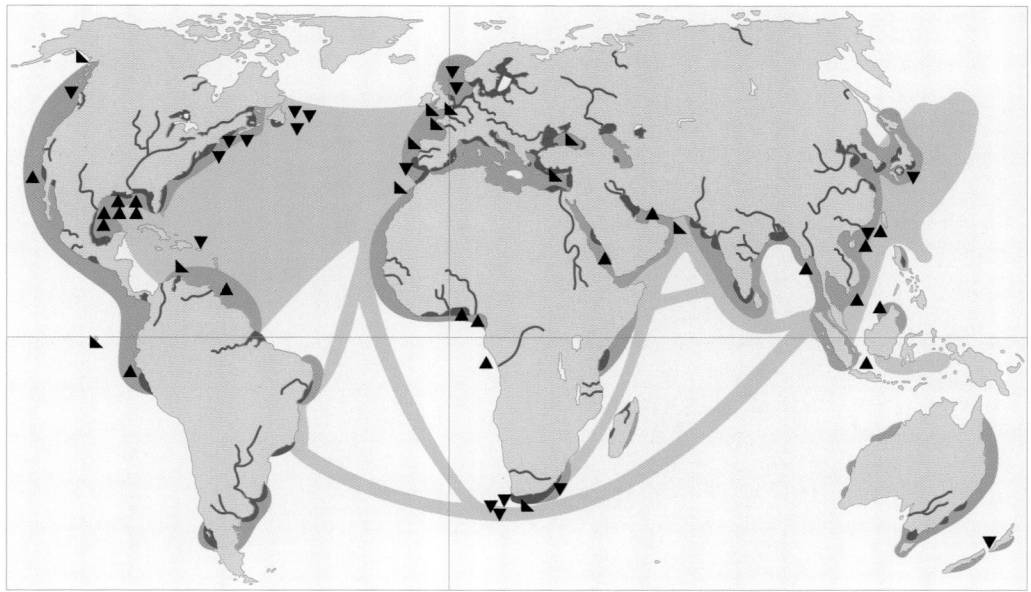

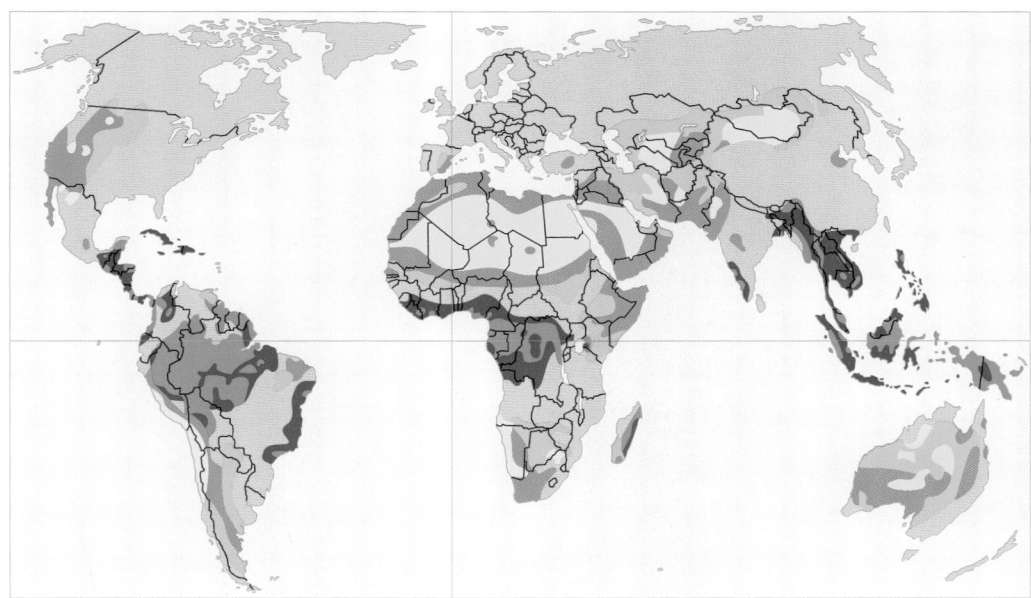

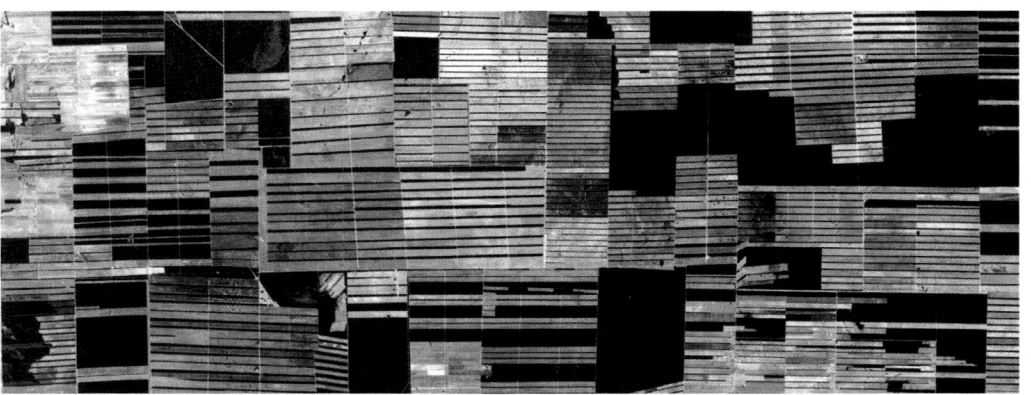

ANTARCTICA

The vast Antarctic ice sheet, containing some 70% of the Earth's fresh water, plays a crucial role in the circulation of the atmosphere and oceans, and hence the Earth's climate. The frozen southern continent is also the last remaining wilderness – the largest area to remain free from human colonization.

Various countries have pressed territorial claims over sections of Antarctica, spurred in recent years by its known and suspected mineral wealth: enough iron ore to supply the world at present levels for 200 years, large oil reserves and, probably, the biggest coal deposits on Earth.

The 1961 Antarctic Treaty set aside the area for peaceful uses only, guaranteeing freedom of scientific investigation, banning waste disposal and nuclear testing, and suspending the issue of territorial rights. By 1990, the original 12 signatories had grown to 25; a further 15 nations were granted observer status in subsequent deliberations.

In July 1991, a new accord banned all mineral exploration for a further 50 years. The ban can only be rescinded if all the present signatories, plus a majority of any future adherents, agree.

While the treaty has always lacked a formal mechanism for enforcement, it is firmly underwritten by public concern generated by the efforts of environmental pressure groups such as Greenpeace, which have campaigned vigorously to have Antarctica declared a "World Park."

However, from the mid-1990s, the continent appeared to be under threat from global warming, which some scientists believe was the cause of the breakup of ice shelves along the Antarctic peninsula. Rising temperatures have also disturbed the breeding patterns of Adelie penguins.

For more information:

88	Urbanization of the Earth
	Urban population
89	Largest cities
95	Food and population
106	Wealth and population

In 8000 BC, following the development of agriculture, the world had an estimated population of 8 million and by AD 1000 it was about 300 million. The onset of the Industrial Revolution in the late 18th century led to a population explosion. The 1,000 million mark was passed by 1850, it doubled by the 1920s, and doubled again to 4,000 million by 1975.

In the 1990s, demographers estimated that the world's population, which passed the 6 billion mark in 1999, would reach 9.3 billion by 2050 and only level out in 2200, at a peak of around 11 billion. However, in the early 21st century, after the rate of population growth had shown signs of decline, the Institute for Applied Systems Analysis suggested that the world's population might peak at about 9 billion in 2070. Whatever the global projections, everyone agreed that the greatest population growth would be in the developing countries.

The developing world includes what the World Bank (2004) describes as low-income economies (average per capita GNI of US $507), lower-middle-income economies (average per capita GNI of US $1,686) and upper-middle-income economies (average per capita GNI of US $4,769). Most developing countries are in Africa, Asia, and Latin America. The developed world, made up of high-income, industrialized economies (average per capita GNI of US $32,112), contains Australasia, most of Europe and North America, and Japan.

In developing countries, a high proportion of the population is young and so these countries face high expenditure on health and education. In developed countries, the population pyramids are becoming top-heavy, with increasingly aging populations.

LARGEST NATIONS

The world's most populous nations, in millions (2005 est.)

1.	China	1,306
2.	India	1,080
3.	USA	296
4.	Indonesia	242
5.	Brazil	186
6.	Pakistan	162
7.	Bangladesh	144
8.	Russia	143
9.	Nigeria	129
10.	Japan	127
11.	Mexico	106
12.	Philippines	88
13.	Vietnam	84
14.	Germany	82
15.	Egypt	78
16.	Ethiopia	73
17.	Turkey	70
18.	Iran	68
19.	Thailand	65
20.	France	61
21.	UK	60
22.	Congo (Dem. Rep.)	60
23.	Italy	58
24.	South Korea	48
25.	Ukraine	47

MOST CROWDED NATIONS

Population per square mile (2005 est.)

1.	Monaco	80,000
2.	Singapore	16,540
3.	Vatican City	5,000
4.	Malta	3,267
5.	Maldives	3,013
6.	Bahrain	2,680
7.	Bangladesh	2,595
8.	Barbados	1,678
9.	Taiwan	1,648
10.	Nauru	1,609

LEAST CROWDED NATIONS

Population per square mile (2005 est.)

1.	Western Sahara	2.7
2.	Mongolia	4.6
3.	Namibia	6.4
4.	Australia	6.8
5.	Suriname	7.0
6.	Botswana	7.1
7.	Iceland	7.5
8.	Mauritania	7.8
9.	Libya	8.5
10.	Canada	8.5

POPULATION DENSITY

The places marked on the map reflect the size of the urban agglomerations and conurbations, rather than the actual city limits. San Francisco itself, for example, has an official population of less than a million people.

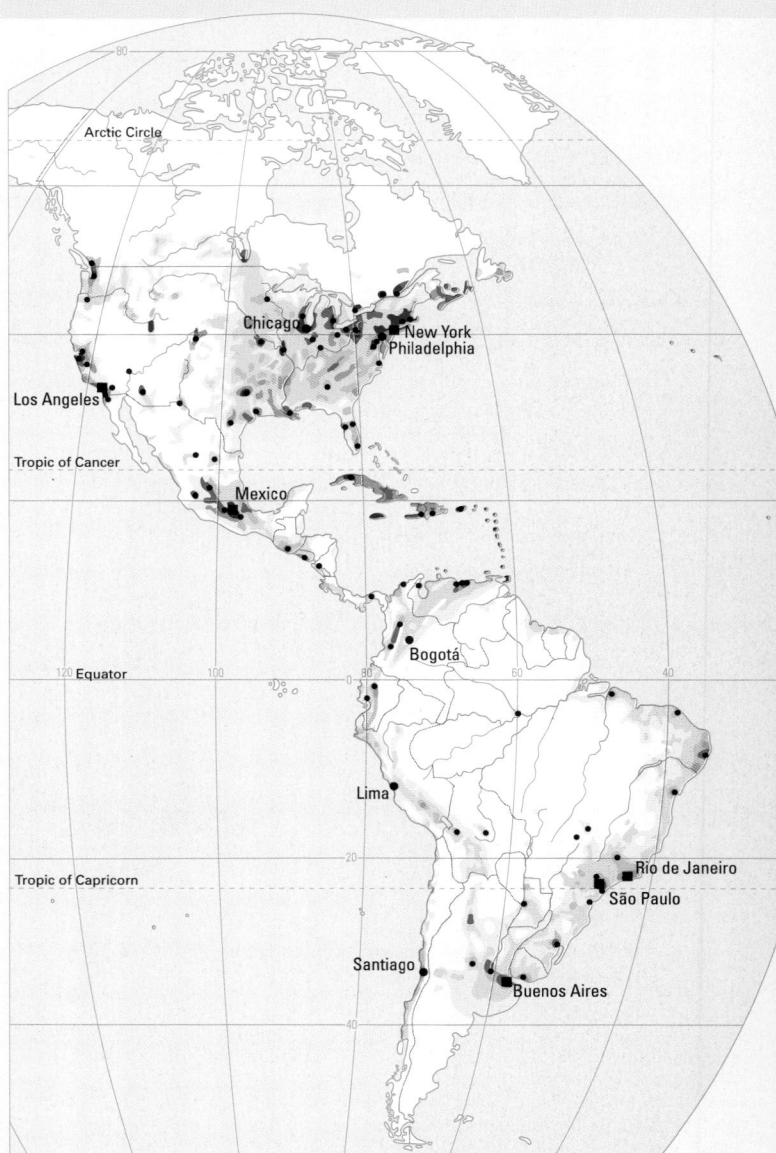

Inhabitants per square mile

▉	Over 500
	250 – 500
	125 – 250
	65 – 125
	15 – 65
	8 – 15
	3 – 8
	Under 3

Urban population

■	Over 10,000,000
●	5,000,000 – 10,000,000
•	1,000,000 – 5,000,000

POPULATION CHANGE

The projected population change for the years 2004–2050

	Over 125% population gain
	100 – 125% population gain
	50 – 100% population gain
	25 – 50% population gain
	0 – 25% population gain
	No change or population loss
	No data available

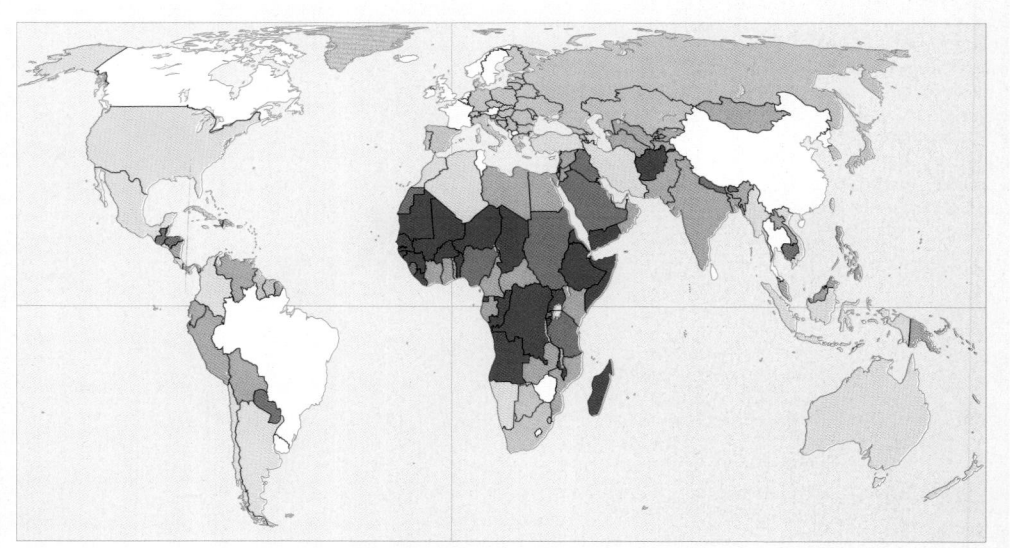

Based on estimates for the year 2050, below are listed the ten most populous nations in the world, in millions:

1.	India	1,628	6.	Pakistan	295
2.	China	1,437	7.	Bangladesh	280
3.	USA	420	8.	Brazil	221
4.	Indonesia	308	9.	Congo (Dem. Rep.)	181
5.	Nigeria	307	10.	Ethiopia	173

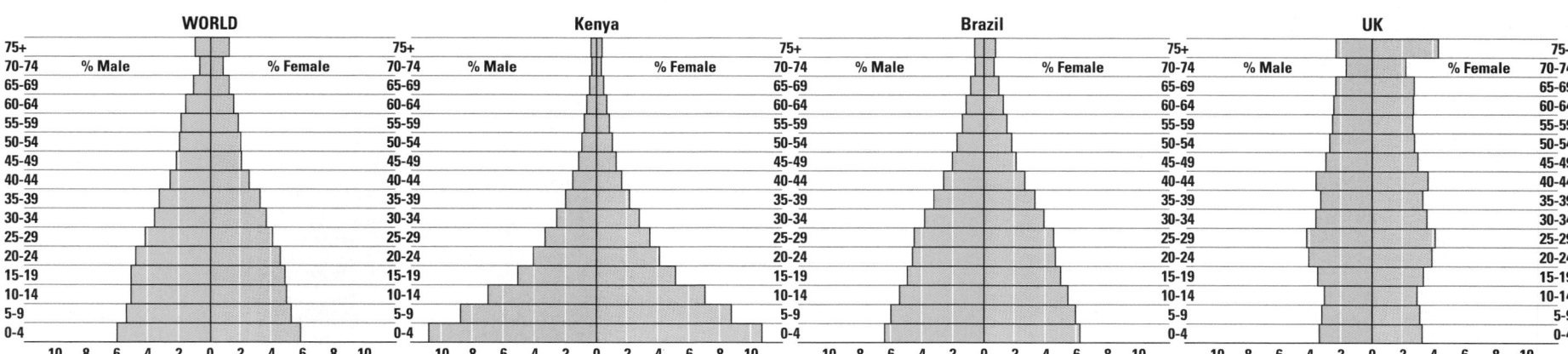

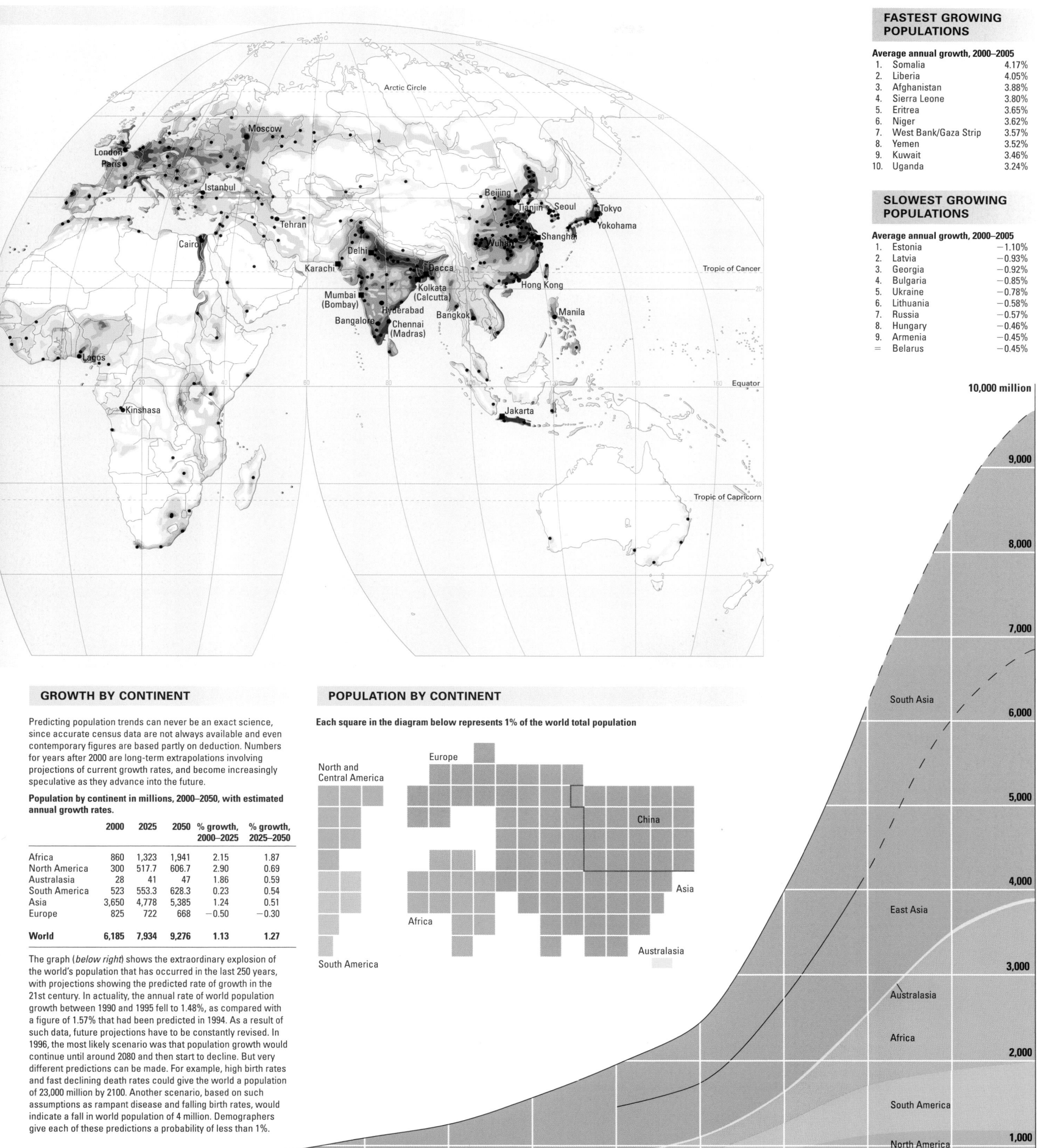

FASTEST GROWING POPULATIONS

Average annual growth, 2000–2005

1.	Somalia	4.17%
2.	Liberia	4.05%
3.	Afghanistan	3.88%
4.	Sierra Leone	3.80%
5.	Eritrea	3.65%
6.	Niger	3.62%
7.	West Bank/Gaza Strip	3.57%
8.	Yemen	3.52%
9.	Kuwait	3.46%
10.	Uganda	3.24%

SLOWEST GROWING POPULATIONS

Average annual growth, 2000–2005

1.	Estonia	−1.10%
2.	Latvia	−0.93%
3.	Georgia	−0.92%
4.	Bulgaria	−0.85%
5.	Ukraine	−0.78%
6.	Lithuania	−0.58%
7.	Russia	−0.57%
8.	Hungary	−0.46%
9.	Armenia	−0.45%
=	Belarus	−0.45%

GROWTH BY CONTINENT

Predicting population trends can never be an exact science, since accurate census data are not always available and even contemporary figures are based partly on deduction. Numbers for years after 2000 are long-term extrapolations involving projections of current growth rates, and become increasingly speculative as they advance into the future.

Population by continent in millions, 2000–2050, with estimated annual growth rates.

	2000	2025	2050	% growth, 2000–2025	% growth, 2025–2050
Africa	860	1,323	1,941	2.15	1.87
North America	300	517.7	606.7	2.90	0.69
Australasia	28	41	47	1.86	0.59
South America	523	553.3	628.3	0.23	0.54
Asia	3,650	4,778	5,385	1.24	0.51
Europe	825	722	668	−0.50	−0.30
World	**6,185**	**7,934**	**9,276**	**1.13**	**1.27**

The graph (*below right*) shows the extraordinary explosion of the world's population that has occurred in the last 250 years, with projections showing the predicted rate of growth in the 21st century. In actuality, the annual rate of world population growth between 1990 and 1995 fell to 1.48%, as compared with a figure of 1.57% that had been predicted in 1994. As a result of such data, future projections have to be constantly revised. In 1996, the most likely scenario was that population growth would continue until around 2080 and then start to decline. But very different predictions can be made. For example, high birth rates and fast declining death rates could give the world a population of 23,000 million by 2100. Another scenario, based on such assumptions as rampant disease and falling birth rates, would indicate a fall in world population of 4 million. Demographers give each of these predictions a probability of less than 1%.

POPULATION BY CONTINENT

Each square in the diagram below represents 1% of the world total population

For more information:
80 Water distribution
83 Population density
103 The world's ports

Following the development of agriculture more than 10,000 years ago, people began to live in farming villages. Around 5,500 years ago, the world's first cities appeared in the lower Tigris and Euphrates valleys in Mesopotamia. Cities were founded in Ancient Egypt around 5,000 years ago and in China around 3,600 years ago. By contrast with the villages, most people in the early cities were not engaged in farming. Instead, they worked in craft industries, in government services, in religion, and in trade. The cities became centers of early civilizations and, through trade, their influence spread far and wide. However, they were dependent on the surrounding farming communities for their food and other materials.

In 1750, prior to the start of the Industrial Revolution, barely 3% of the world's population lived in urban areas. By 1850, London and Paris had more than a million people, and, by 1900, 14% of the world's population lived in cities. By 1950, the world had 83 cities with more than a million people, and by 1996 there were 280; by 2015, experts predict there will be more than 500. New York City was the only city with a population in excess of 10 million in 1950; by 2015, experts predict there will be 27 such cities worldwide, the majority located in the developing world.

However, predictions have to be constantly revised in light of new data. For example, in the late 1990s, demographers calculated that urban areas then accounted for 50% of the world's population. But after much lower census figures emerged for many cities in the early 21st century, the estimated date by which half of the world's population would be living in cities was pushed back to 2007.

Urbanization is greatest in industrialized countries. For example, in 2003, 80% of the people in the United States lived in urban areas. However, in low-income countries, which contained nearly 40% of the world's population in the early 21st century, only 31% lived in urban areas.

The rapid rate of urbanization has created many social problems, especially in cities that have been unable to provide enough jobs and services for the new arrivals. Many of the new city dwellers come from rural areas and take time to adjust to urban life and employment possibilities.

A typical city in a developing country contains millions of people living, often illegally, in shanty towns (or "informal settlements"), while thousands live on the streets. Yet many of these shanty towns are healthier than the industrial cities of 19th-century Europe and North America. Indeed, surveys have shown that migrants to cities in developing countries are less likely to face poverty than they are in rural areas, while benefiting from greater access to healthcare services and education.

Modern cities face many problems today, including pollution, crime, and unemployment. Yet, given competent central and local government, they are capable of generating the wealth they need to solve them, as well as making a major contribution to the nation's economy.

URBAN POPULATION

Percentage of total population living in towns and cities (2003)

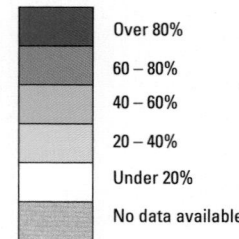

- Over 80%
- 60 – 80%
- 40 – 60%
- 20 – 40%
- Under 20%
- No data available

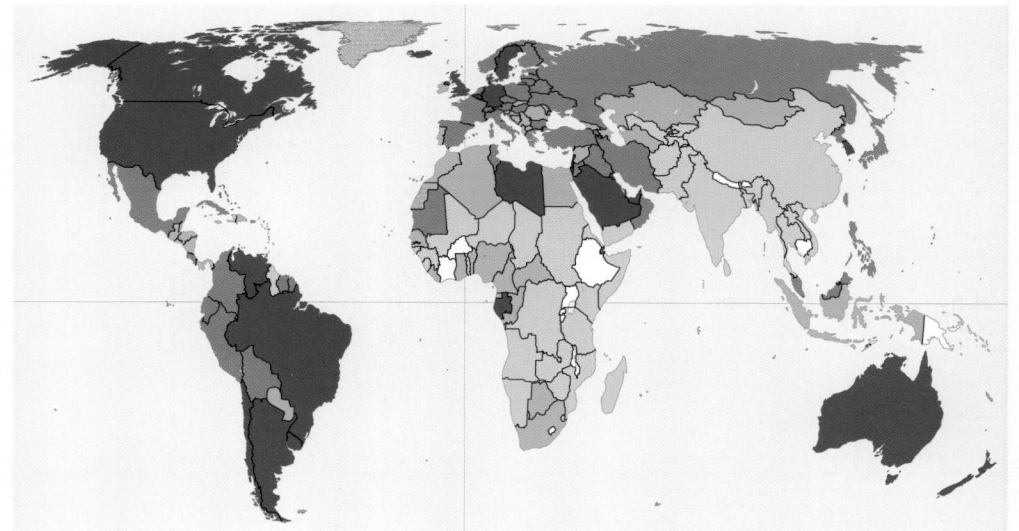

Most urbanized		Least urbanized	
Singapore	100%	East Timor	8%
Belgium	97%	Bhutan	8%
Kuwait	96%	Burundi	10%
Iceland	93%	Uganda	12%
Uruguay	92%	Papua New Guinea	13%

THE URBANIZATION OF THE EARTH

City-building, 1850–2000; each white spot represents a city of at least 1 million inhabitants

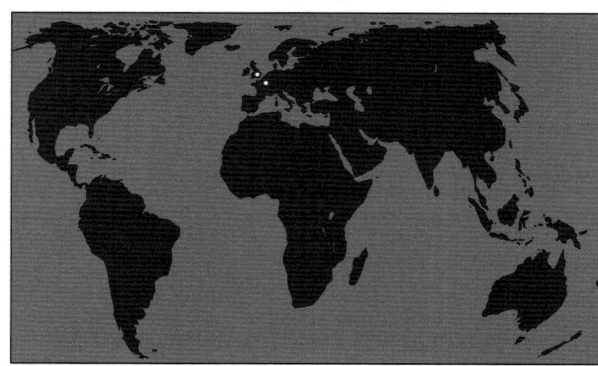

1850

1900

1925

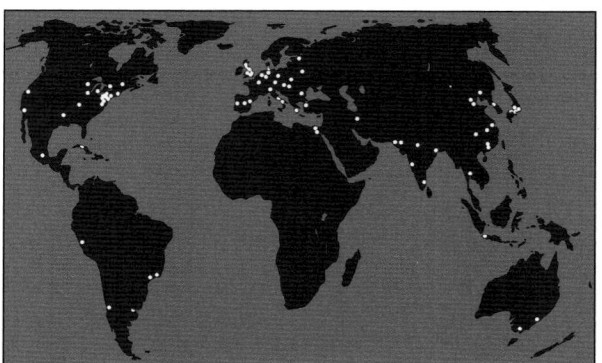

1950

1975

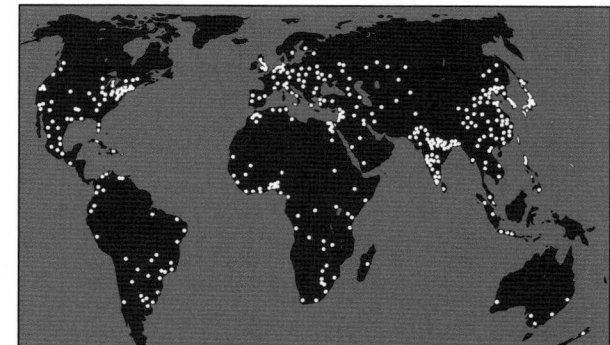

2005

EXPANDING CITIES

These graphs show the projected growth of some of the world's megacities between 1950 and 2015. New York City, the world's largest city in 1950, reached a peak in 1970, but it has since experienced periods of negative growth. London's population also declined between 1970 and 1985, before resuming a modest rate of increase.

In both cases, the divergence from world trends is explained in part by counting methods. Each lies at the center of a great agglomeration, and definitions of the "city limits" may vary over time. Also, in developing countries, many areas around the megacities, which are counted as urban, are in fact rural in character.

The rates of city population growth in developing countries have also often been overestimated. For example, it was once predicted that Kolkata (Calcutta) would have a population of 40 million by the late 1990s. The reason why many estimates have proven incorrect is partly explained by a new trend, namely that rapid urban growth is now greatest, in some regions, in the smaller cities. For example, the main expansion in West Bengal is no longer in Kolkata, but in a rash of small cities across the state.

The growth of some of the world's largest cities in millions, 1950–2015
Comparisons of city populations over time are problematic due to changes in the definition of the city limits. These figures attempt to take such changes into consideration. The figure for London is the metropolitan region.

1950   2015

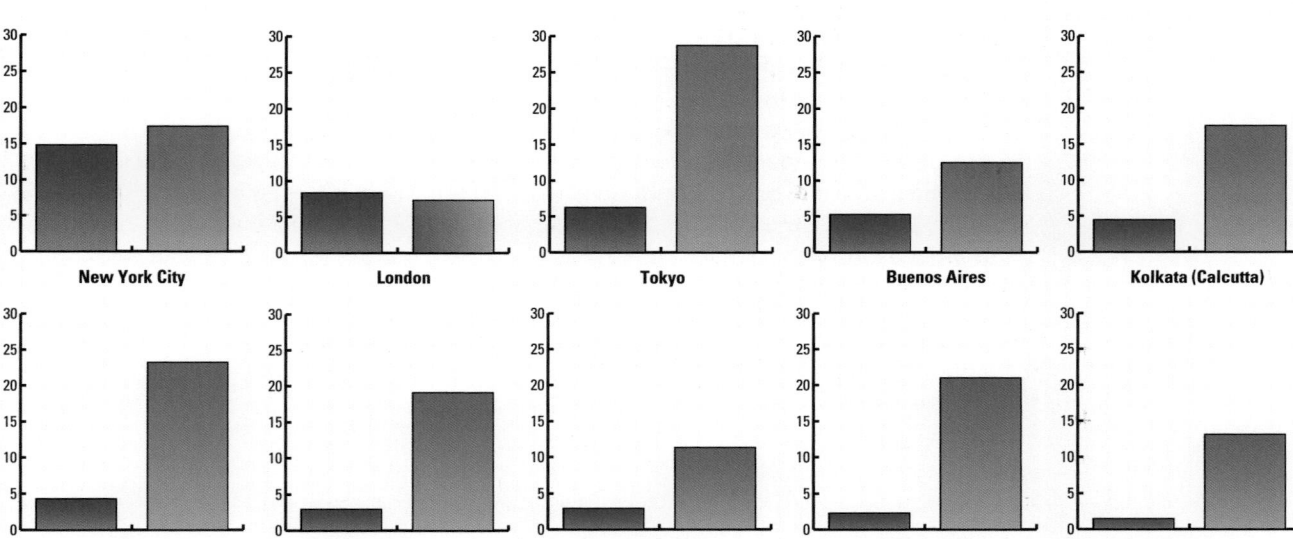

New York City   London   Tokyo   Buenos Aires   Kolkata (Calcutta)

Shanghai   Mexico City   Rio de Janeiro   São Paulo   Seoul

CITIES IN DANGER

In mid-2002, a "brown haze." stretching 2 miles [3 km] high, covered much of southern Asia. Caused mainly by the burning of coal and biomass, it caused respiratory diseases and many deaths. Alarm concerning urban air pollution had been expressed much earlier, but controls since the 1980s had proved difficult to enforce and expensive to introduce.

Those cities taking part in the United Nation's Global Environment Monitoring System frequently show dangerous levels of pollutants, ranging from soot to sulfur dioxide and photochemical smog. Air in the majority of cities without such sampling equipment is likely to be at least as bad. Traffic, a major source of air pollution worldwide, loses Thailand's work force 44 working days each year.

URBAN HOUSING NEEDS

Urbanization in most developing countries has been proceeding so rapidly that local governments have been unable to provide the necessary services and housing to meet demand.

In some cities, many people make their homes in squatter settlements, which are frequently without power, water, and sanitation. Yet these communities are often a dynamic part of the city's economy, while their inhabitants sometimes take the initiative in setting up their own local government and self-help associations.

Some of the world's richest cities also have a homeless underclass, although calculating the numbers of people involved is problematic. Yet it is the case that homelessness and unemployment are currently affecting an increasing number of people in the developed world.

LARGEST CITIES

◄ The business district of Hong Kong City is located on the northern shore of Hong Kong Island. The cluster of modern high-rise buildings reflects the financial success of this tiny region, which has one of the strongest economies in Asia.

Early in the 21st century for the first time in history, the majority of the world's population will live in cities. Below is a list of all the cities with more than 10 million inhabitants, based on estimates for the year 2015.

1. Tokyo–Yokohama	28.7
2. Mumbai (Bombay)	27.4
3. Lagos	24.1
4. Shanghai	23.2
5. Jakarta	21.5
6. São Paulo	21.0
7. Karachi	20.6
8. Beijing	19.6
9. Dhaka	19.2
10. Mexico City	19.1
11. Kolkata (Calcutta)	17.6
12. Delhi	17.5
13. New York City	17.4
14. Tianjin	17.1
15. Manila	14.9
16. Cairo	14.7
17. Los Angeles	14.5
18. Seoul	13.1
19. Buenos Aires	12.5
20. Istanbul	12.1
21. Rio de Janeiro	11.3
22. Lahore	10.9
23. Hyderabad	10.6
24. Bangkok	10.4
25. Osaka	10.2
26. Lima	10.1
27. Tehran	10.0

The city populations above are based on urban agglomerations rather than legal city limits. In some cases, where two adjacent cities have merged into one concentration, such as Tokyo–Yokohama, they have been regarded as a single unit.

URBAN ADVANTAGES

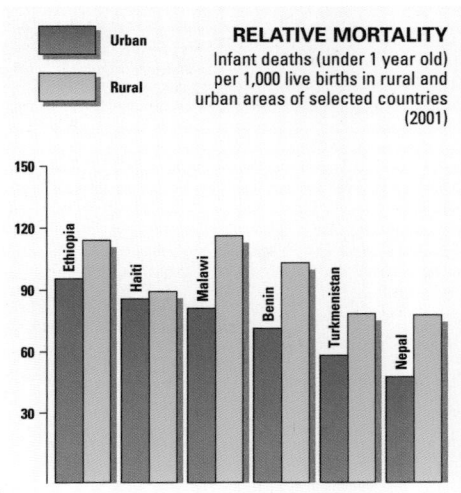

Urban   Rural

RELATIVE MORTALITY
Infant deaths (under 1 year old) per 1,000 live births in rural and urban areas of selected countries (2001)

Ethiopia, Haiti, Malawi, Benin, Turkmenistan, Nepal

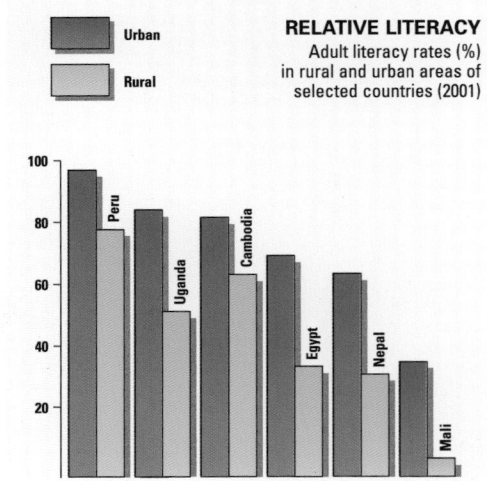

Urban   Rural

RELATIVE LITERACY
Adult literacy rates (%) in rural and urban areas of selected countries (2001)

Peru, Uganda, Cambodia, Egypt, Nepal, Mali

Despite overcrowding and poor housing, living standards in the developing world's cities are almost invariably better than in the surrounding countryside. Resources – financial, material, and administrative – are concentrated in the towns, which are usually also the centers of political activity and pressure. Governments – frequently unstable, and rarely established on a solid democratic base – are usually more responsive to urban discontent than to rural misery.

In many developing countries, especially in Africa, food prices are kept artificially low, thus appeasing the underemployed urban masses at the expense of agricultural development.

This imbalance encourages further cityward migration, helping to account for the astonishing rate of post-1950 urbanization and putting great strain on the ability of many nations to provide even modest improvements for their people.

For more information:
86 Population density
92 The world's refugees
   War since 1945
93 United Nations
   International
   organizations

Racial, language, and religious differences have led to appalling acts of inhumanity throughout history. Yet, strictly speaking, all human beings belong to one species, *Homo sapiens*, which has no sub-species. The differences between the three racial types which most people identify – Caucasoid, Mongoloid, and Negroid – reflect not so much evolutionary differences as long periods of separation.

Migration has recently mingled the various groups to an unprecedented extent, and most nations now have some degree of racial mixing. For example, the USA has often been called a melting pot, because of the large numbers of people from various geographical locations which make up the population. The country has no official language but, until recently, English was spoken by the vast majority of the people. But in recent years, some of the immigrants from Mexico, Cuba, and other parts of Latin America have not learned English and speak only Spanish. This development disturbs those Americans who believe that the use of English binds the nation together, and several states have passed laws stating that English is their only official language.

Language is fundamental to human culture. Because definitions of languages vary, estimates of the total number range from 3,000 to 6,000, although most are spoken by only a few people. Chinese is spoken by more people as a first language than any other, while English ranks second, but English is the leading international language, because so many people speak it as their second tongue.

Like language, religion encourages cohesion in single human groups and it satisfies a deep human need by assigning people a place in a divinely ordered world. Religion is a way in which a culture can express its individuality. For example, the rise of Islamic fundamentalism in the late 20th century was partly an expression of resentment that secular Western values were being imposed on Muslims.

WORLD MIGRATION

The greatest voluntary migration was the colonization of North America by 30–35 million European settlers during the 19th century. The greatest forced migration involved 9–11 million Africans taken as slaves to America between 1550 and 1860. The migrations shown on the map below are mostly international, as population movements within borders are not usually recorded. Many of the statistics are necessarily estimates as so many refugees and migrant workers enter countries illegally and unrecorded. Emigrants may have a variety of motives for leaving, thus making it difficult to distinguish between voluntary and involuntary migrations.

Foreign born, as a % of total population (2005)
- More than 20%
- 10 – 20%
- 5 – 10%
- 2 – 5%
- Less than 2%
- No available data

Migration
- Over 2,000,000 people
- 1 – 2,000,000 people
- 500,000 – 1,000,000 people
- Under 500,000 people

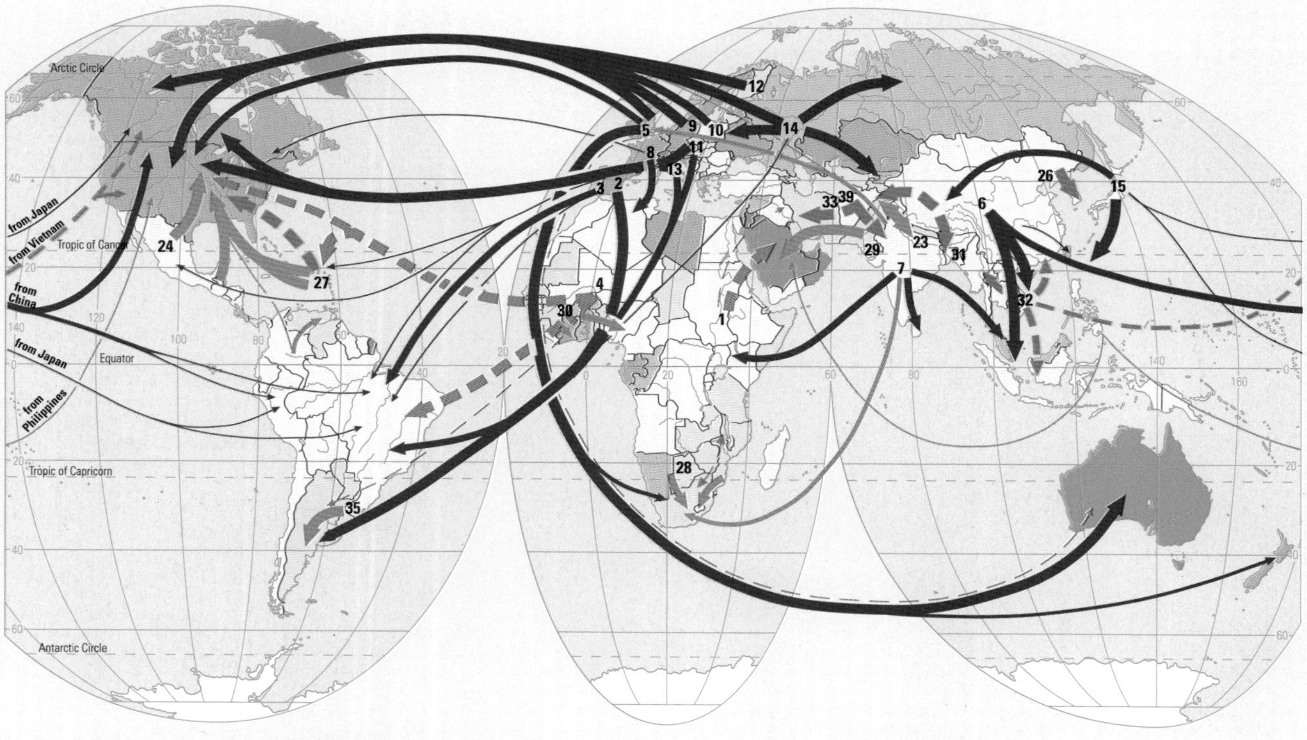

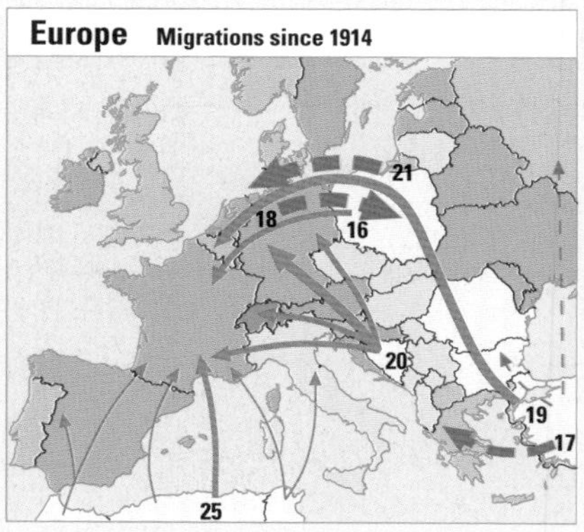

	1500 – 1914		Since 1914	
	Voluntary	Involuntary	Voluntary	Involuntary

Europe Migrations since 1914

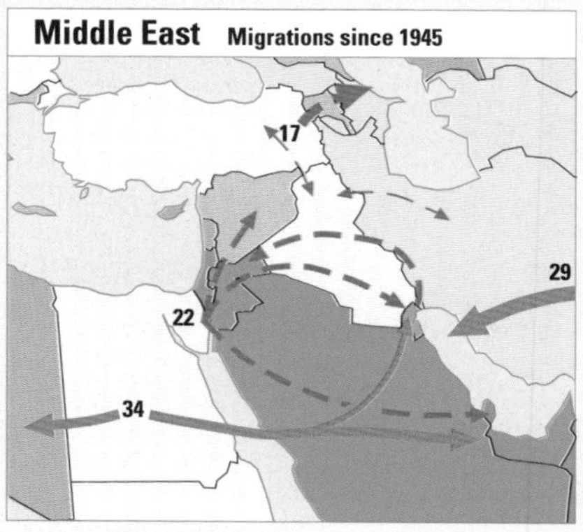

Middle East Migrations since 1945

Major world migrations since 1500 (over 1 million people)

1. North and East African slaves to Arabia (4.3m) 1500–1900
2. Spanish to South and Central America (2.3m) 1530–1914
3. Portuguese to Brazil (1.4m)..1530–1914
4. West African slaves to South America (4.6m) 1550–1860
   to Caribbean (4m) 1580–1860
   to North/Central America (1m) 1650–1820
5. British and Irish to North America (13.5m) 1620–1914
   to Australasia and South Africa (3m) 1790–1914
6. Chinese to Southeast Asia (22m) 1820–1914
   to North America (1m) 1880–1914
7. Indian migrant workers (3m) 1850–1914
8. French to North Africa (1.5m) 1850–1914
9. Germans to North America (5m) 1850–1914
10. Poles to North America (3.6m) 1850–1914
11. Austro-Hungarians to North America (3.2m) 1850–1914
    to Western Europe (3.4m) 1850–1914
    to South America (1.8m) 1850–1914
12. Scandinavians to North America (2.7m) 1850–1914
13. Italians to North America (5m) 1860–1914
    to South America (3.7m) 1860–1914
14. Russians to North America (2.2m) 1880–1914
    to Western Europe (2.2m) 1880–1914
    to Siberia (6m) 1880–1914
    to Central Asia (4m) 1880–1914
15. Japanese to Eastern Asia, Southeast Asia and America (8m) 1900–1914
16. Poles to Western Europe (1m) 1920–1940
17. Greeks and Armenians from Turkey (1.6m) 1922–1923
18. European Jews to extermination camps (5m) 1940–1944
19. Turks to Western Europe (1.9m) 1940–
20. Yugoslavs to Western Europe (2m) 1940–
21. Germans to Western Europe (9.8m) 1945–1947
22. Palestinian refugees (2m) 1947–
23. Indian and Pakistani refugees (15m) 1947
24. Mexicans to North America (9m) 1950–
25. North Africans to Western Europe (1.1m) 1950–
26. Korean refugees (5m) 1950–1954
27. Latin Americans and West Indians to North America (4.7m) 1960–
28. Migrant workers to South Africa (1.5m) 1960–
29. Indians and Pakistanis to the Persian Gulf (2.4m) 1970–
30. Migrant workers to Nigeria and Ivory Coast (3m) 1970–
31. Bangladeshi and Pakistani refugees (2m) 1972
32. Vietnamese and Cambodian refugees (1.5m) 1975–
33. Afghan refugees (6.1m) 1979–
34. Egyptians to the Persian Gulf and Libya (2.9m) 1980–
35. Migrant workers to Argentina (2m)...1980–
36. Mozambique refugees (1.7m) 1985–
37. Yugoslav/Balkan refugees (1.7m) 1992–
38. Rwanda/Burundi refugees (2.6m) 1994–
39. Afghan refugees (2.1m) 2001–

BUILDING THE USA

US Immigration, 1920 and 2004

For decades the USA was the magnet that attracted millions of immigrants, notably from Central and Eastern Europe, the flow peaking in the early years of the 20th century. By the mid-1990s the proportion of immigrants had increased again to pre-World War II rates, reaching over 11% by 2004. However, the balance of origin had swung from Europe to Latin America and Asia, as the graphs indicate.

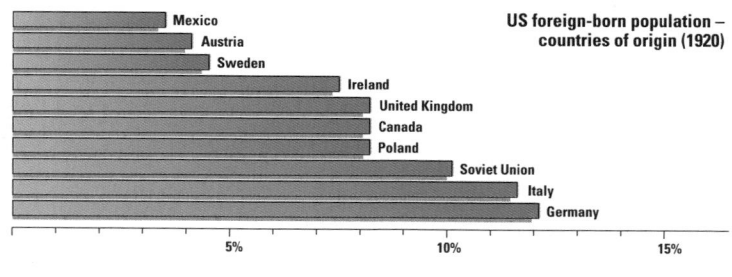

US foreign-born population – countries of origin (1920)

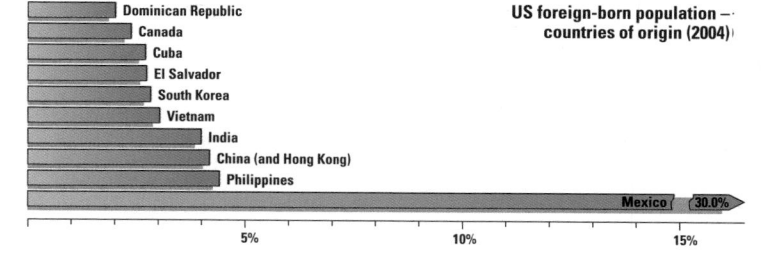

US foreign-born population – countries of origin (2004)

PREDOMINANT LANGUAGES

INDO-EUROPEAN FAMILY

1	Balto-Slavic group (incl. Russian, Ukrainian)
2	Germanic group (incl. English, German)
3	Celtic group
4	Greek
5	Albanian
6	Iranian group
7	Armenian
8	Romance group (incl. Spanish, Portuguese, French, Italian)
9	Indo-Aryan group (incl. Hindi, Bengali, Urdu, Punjabi, Marathi)

10	CAUCASIAN FAMILY

AFRO-ASIATIC FAMILY

11	Semitic group (incl. Arabic)
12	Kushitic group
13	Berber group

14	KHOISAN FAMILY
15	NIGER-CONGO FAMILY
16	NILO-SAHARAN FAMILY
17	URALIC FAMILY

ALTAIC FAMILY

18	Turkic group (incl. Turkish)
19	Mongolian group
20	Tungus-Manchu group
21	Japanese and Korean

SINO-TIBETAN FAMILY

22	Sinitic (Chinese) languages (incl. Mandarin, Wu, Yue)
23	Tibetic-Burmic languages

24	TAI FAMILY

AUSTRO-ASIATIC FAMILY

25	Mon-Khmer group
26	Munda group
27	Vietnamese

28	DRAVIDIAN FAMILY (incl. Telugu, Tamil)

29	AUSTRONESIAN FAMILY (incl. Malay-Indonesian, Javanese)

30	OTHER LANGUAGES

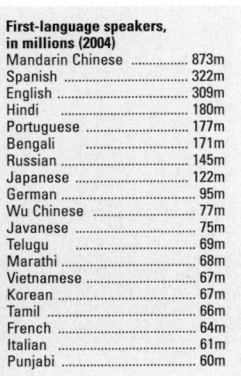

First-language speakers, in millions (2004)

Mandarin Chinese	873m
Spanish	322m
English	309m
Hindi	180m
Portuguese	177m
Bengali	171m
Russian	145m
Japanese	122m
German	95m
Wu Chinese	77m
Javanese	75m
Telugu	69m
Marathi	68m
Vietnamese	67m
Korean	67m
Tamil	66m
French	64m
Italian	61m
Punjabi	60m

Languages form a kind of tree of development, splitting from a few ancient proto-tongues into branches that have grown apart and further divided with the passage of time. English and Hindi, for example, both belong to the great Indo-European family, although the relationship is only apparent after much analysis and comparison with non-Indo-European languages such as Chinese or Arabic. Hindi is part of the Indo-Aryan subgroup, whereas English is a member of Indo-European's Germanic branch. French, another Indo-European tongue, traces its descent through the Latin, or Romance, branch. A few languages – Basque is one example – have no apparent links with any other, living or dead. Most modern languages, of course, have acquired enormous quantities of vocabulary from each other.

DISTRIBUTION OF LIVING LANGUAGES

The figures refer to the number of languages currently in use in the regions shown

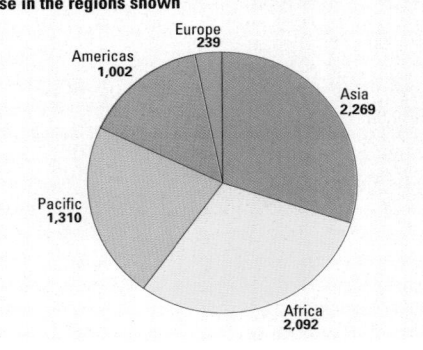

- Europe **239**
- Americas **1,002**
- Asia **2,269**
- Pacific **1,310**
- Africa **2,092**

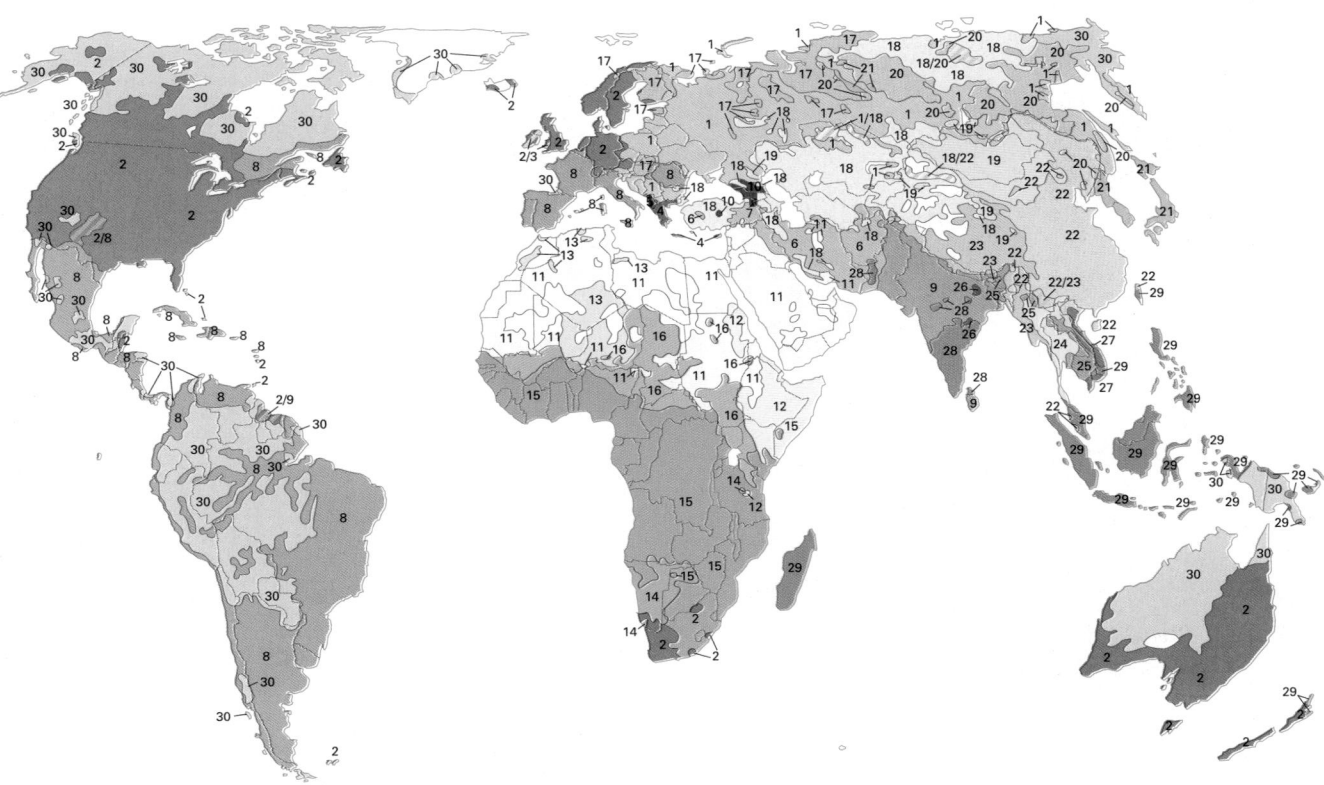

PREDOMINANT RELIGIONS

- Roman Catholicism
- Orthodox and other Eastern Churches
- Protestantism
- Sunni Islam
- Shia Islam
- Buddhism
- Hinduism
- Confucianism
- Judaism
- Shintoism
- Tribal Religions

Religions are not as easily mapped as the physical contours of the land. Divisions are often blurred and frequently overlapping: most nations include people of many different faiths – or no faith at all. Some religions, like Islam and Christianity, have proselytes worldwide; others, like Hinduism and Confucianism, are restricted to a particular area, though modern migrations have taken some Indians and Chinese very far from their cultural origins. It is also difficult to show the degree to which religion controls daily life: Christian Western Europe, for example, is now far less dominated by its religion than are the Islamic nations of the Middle East. Similarly, figures for the major faiths' adherents make no distinction between nominal believers enrolled at birth and those for whom religion is a vital part of their existence.

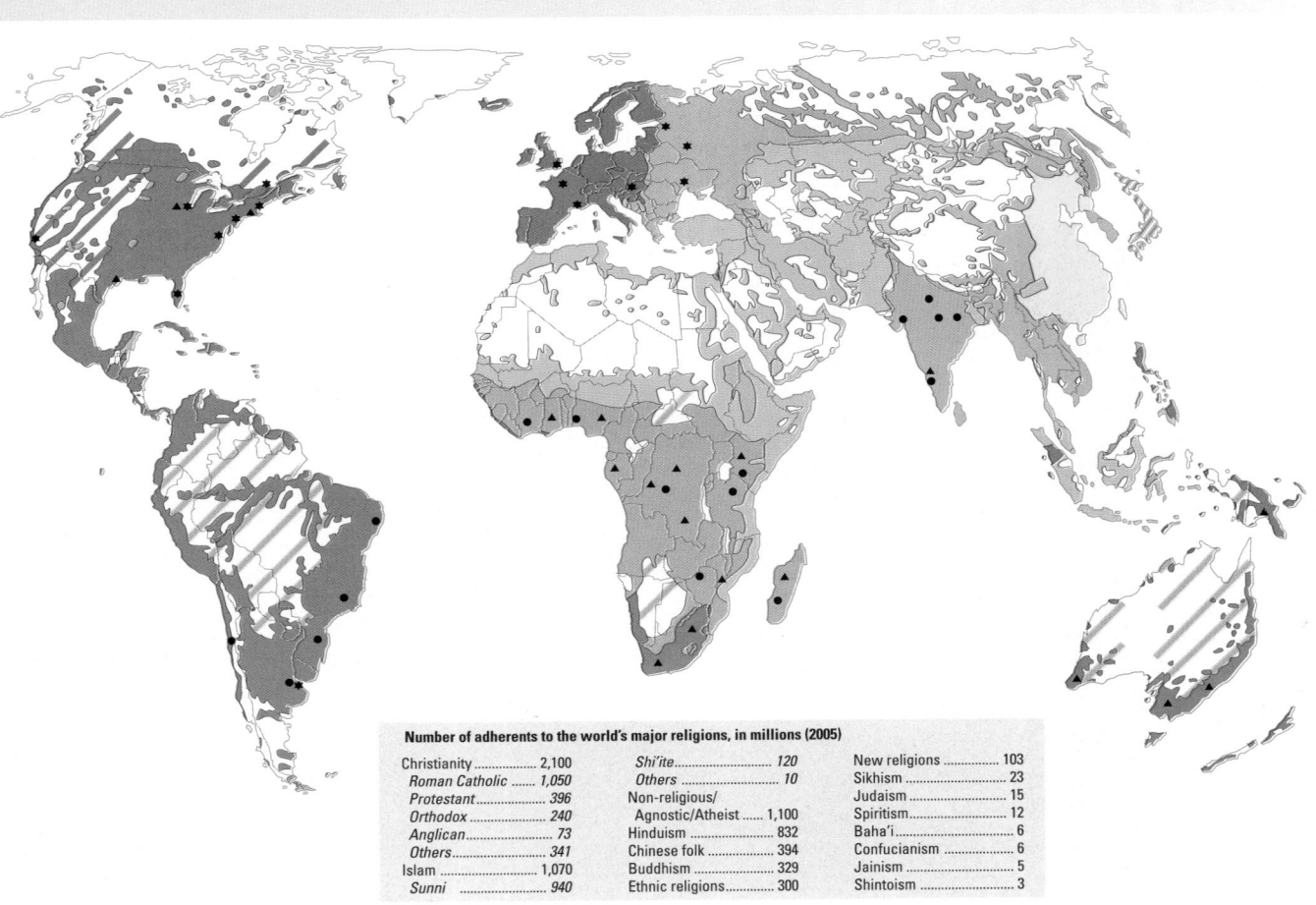

Number of adherents to the world's major religions, in millions (2005)

Christianity	2,100	Shi'ite	120	New religions	103
Roman Catholic	1,050	Others	10	Sikhism	23
Protestant	396	Non-religious/		Judaism	15
Orthodox	240	Agnostic/Atheist	1,100	Spiritism	12
Anglican	73	Hinduism	832	Baha'i	6
Others	341	Chinese folk	394	Confucianism	6
Islam	1,070	Buddhism	329	Jainism	5
Sunni	940	Ethnic religions	300	Shintoism	3

For more information:
90 Migration
91 Religion

The 20th century witnessed two world wars, followed by a Cold War which several times threatened to erupt into a third world war, fought with nuclear weapons. The Cold War was marked by a great number of conflicts. Some were colonial wars, as the empires of the first half of the century fell apart, some were border wars, and some were civil wars. All the wars have caused great suffering among civilians, many of whom were forced to join the ranks of the world's refugees.

In the late 1980s, many people hoped that the end of the Cold War, following the collapse of Communist regimes in the former Soviet Union and Eastern Europe, would herald a new era of international stability. Instead, old ethnic and religious antagonisms surfaced in many areas, leading to civil war in such places as Chechenia, in Russia, and the former Yugoslavia. Nationalist rivalries, suppressed under Communist rule, replaced ideological factors as the major cause of conflict.

War is a very human activity, with no real equivalent in any other species. Yet humans also function well when they cooperate. Evolution has made this so. Hunter-gatherers in cooperative bands were far more effective than animals that prowled. Agriculture, urbanization, and industrialization all depend on the ability of humans to cooperate.

The creation of the United Nations in 1945 held out hope that the world's nations, tired of war, would have the means to control humanity's aggressive instincts. Although the UN lacks the power to halt conflicts, it has often helped to achieve negotiation. Economic pressures have led to another kind of cooperation, resulting in the creation of common markets and economic unions, such as ASEAN in Southeast Asia, the European Union, and NAFTA in North America.

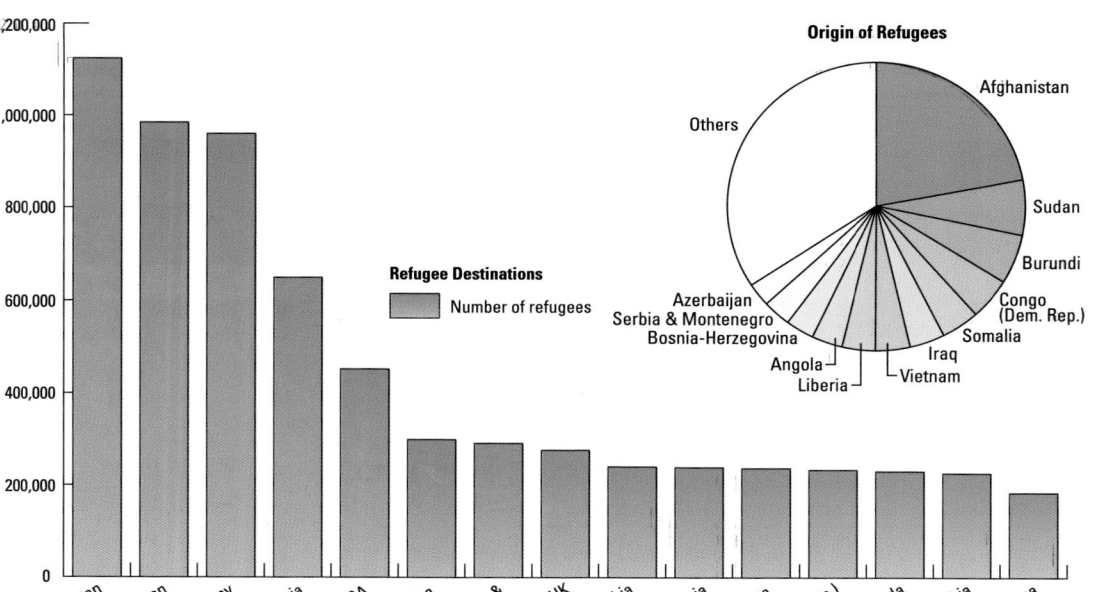

THE WORLD'S REFUGEES

Refugees by host nation (bar chart, left) and by nation of origin (pie chart, left) (2003). The source is the United Nations High Commission for Refugees (UNHCR). The 3.2 million Palestinian refugees living in Jordan, Syria, Lebanon, Gaza, and the West Bank fall under the mandate of United Nations Relief and Works Agency (UNRWA) and are not included on the graphs.

The pie chart shows the origins of the world's refugees, while the bar chart below shows their destinations. According to the United Nations High Commission for Refugees (UNHCR) in 2003 there were 9.7 million refugees. However, the UNHCR definition of a refugee, "a person who has left or remains outside their own country because they have a well-founded fear of persecution, or because their safety is threatened by events seriously disturbing public order," does not include people who are in a refugee-like situation but who have not been formally recognized. In 2003, there were a further 5.6 million people who were internally displaced, and a total "population of concern" of 17 million people, worldwide.

All but a few who cross international boundaries seek asylum in neighboring countries, which are often the least equipped to deal with them. Lacking any rights or power, they frequently become an unwelcome burden to their hosts. Usually, the best any refugee can hope for is rudimentary food and shelter in temporary camps. Many Palestinians have been forced to live in camps since 1948.

WAR SINCE 1945

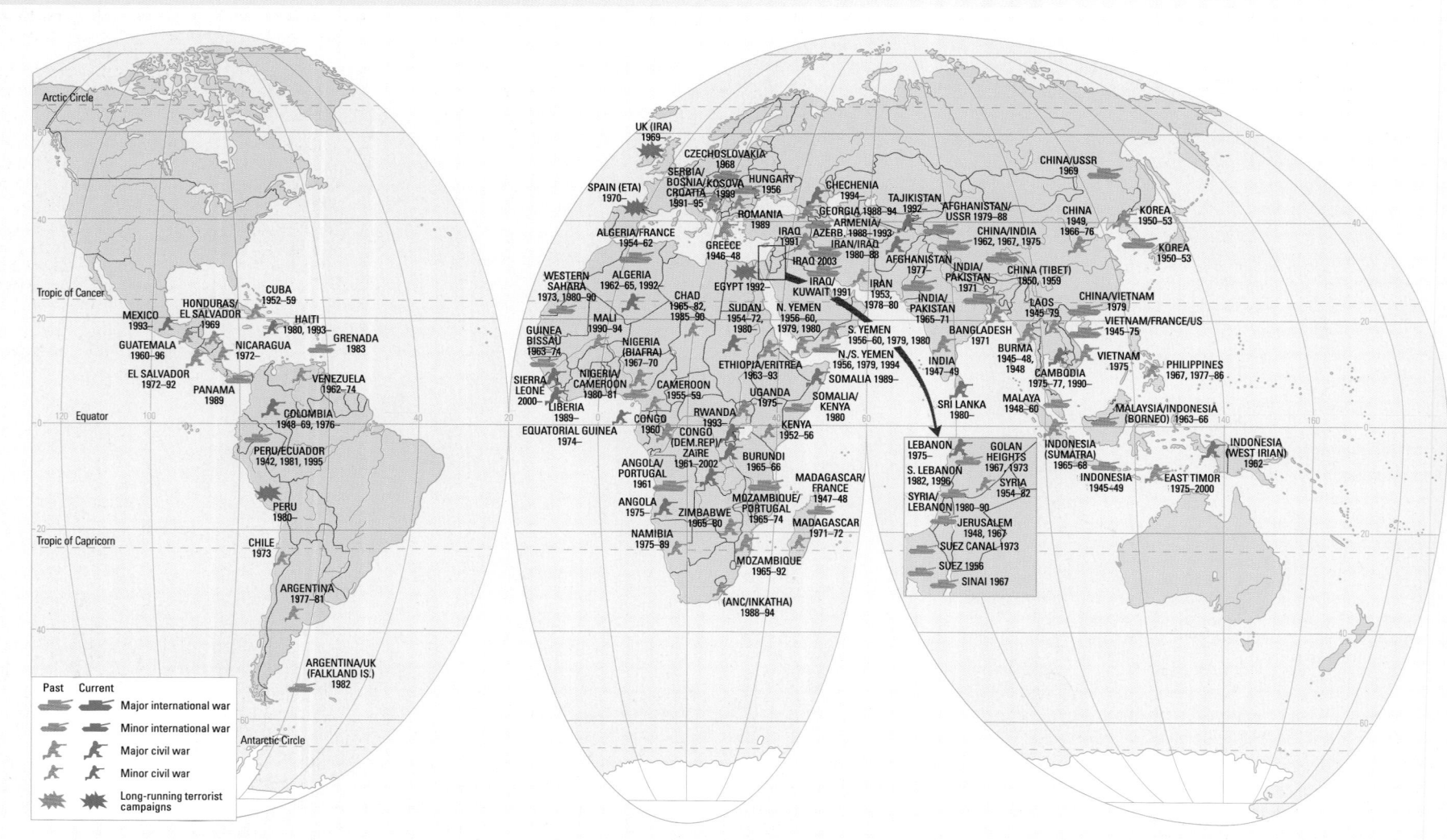

INTERNATIONAL ORGANIZATIONS

OAS Organization of American States (formed in 1948). It aims to promote social and economic cooperation between countries in the developed North America and developing Latin America.
EU European Union (evolved from the European Community in 1993). Cyprus, the Czech Republic, Estonia, Hungary, Latvia, Lithuania, Malta, Poland, the Slovak Republic, and Slovenia joined the EU in May 2004. The other 15 members of the EU are Austria, Belgium, Denmark, Finland, France, Germany, Greece, Ireland, Italy, Luxembourg, Netherlands, Portugal, Spain, Sweden, and the UK – together they aim to integrate economies, coordinate social developments, and bring about political union. Bulgaria and Romania are expected to join in 2007.
AU The African Union was set up in 2002, taking over from the Organization of African Unity (1963). It has 53 members. Working languages are Arabic, English, French, and Portuguese.
COLOMBO PLAN (formed in 1951) Its 25 members aim to promote economic and social development in Asia and the Pacific.

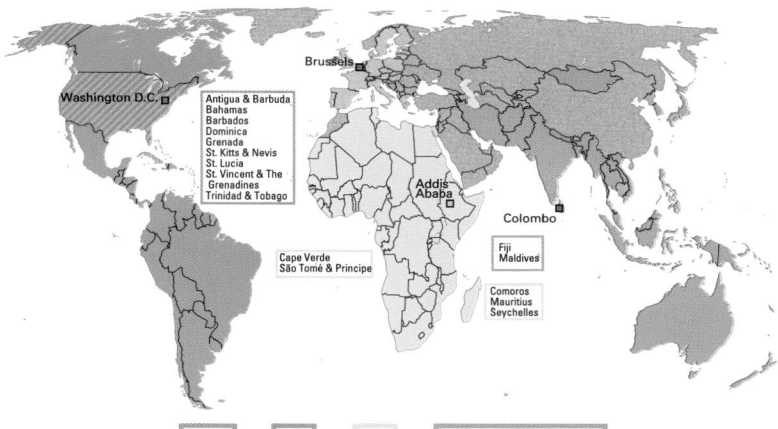

| OAS | EU | AU | COLOMBO PLAN |

G8 Group of eight leading industrialized nations, comprising Canada, France, Germany, Italy, Japan, Russia, the UK, and the USA. Periodic meetings are held to discuss major world issues, such as world recessions.
APEC Asia-Pacific Economic Cooperation (formed in 1989). It aims to enhance economic growth and prosperity for the region and to strengthen the Asia-Pacific community. APEC is the only intergovernmental grouping in the world operating on the basis of non-binding commitments, open dialogue, and equal respect for the views of all participants. There are 21 member economies.
OECD Organization for Economic Cooperation and Development (formed in 1961). It comprises 30 major free-market economies. The "G8" is its "inner group" of leading industrial nations, comprising Canada, France, Germany, Italy, Japan, Russia, the UK, and the USA.
ACP African-Caribbean-Pacific (formed in 1963). Members enjoy economic ties with the EU.
OPEC Organization of Petroleum Exporting Countries (formed in 1960). It controls about three-quarters of the world's oil supply. Gabon formally withdrew from OPEC in August 1996.

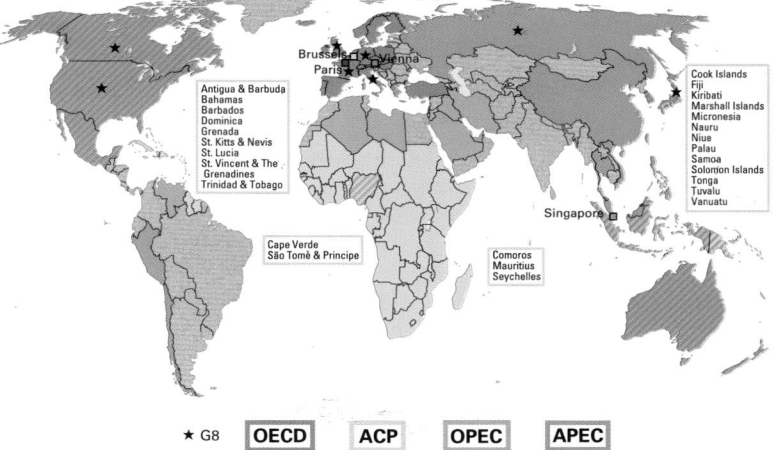

| ★ G8 | OECD | ACP | OPEC | APEC |

NATO North Atlantic Treaty Organization (formed in 1949). It continues despite the winding up of the Warsaw Pact in 1991. Bulgaria, Estonia, Latvia, Lithuania, Romania, the Slovak Republic, and Slovenia became members in 2004.
LAIA The Latin American Integration Association (formed in 1980) superceded the Latin American Free Trade Association formed in 1961. Its aim is to promote freer regional trade.
ARAB LEAGUE (1945) Aims to promote economic, social, political, and military cooperation. There are 22 member nations.
COMMONWEALTH The Commonwealth of Nations evolved from the British Empire. Pakistan was suspended in 1999, but reinstated in 2004. Zimbabwe was suspended in 2002 and, in response to its continued suspension, Zimbabwe left the Commonwealth in December 2003. It now comprises 16 Queen's realms, 31 republics, and 6 indigenous monarchies, giving a total of 53 member states.
ASEAN Association of Southeast Asian Nations (formed in 1967). Cambodia joined in 1999.

| NATO | LAIA | ARAB LEAGUE | COMMONWEALTH | ASEAN |

UNITED NATIONS

The United Nations Organization was born as World War II drew to its conclusion. Six years of strife had strengthened the world's desire for peace, but an effective international organization was needed to help achieve it. That body would replace the League of Nations which, since its inception in 1920, had failed to curb the aggression of at least some of its member nations. At the United Nations Conference on International Organization held in San Francisco, the United Nations Charter was drawn up. Ratified by the Security Council and signed by the 51 original members, it came into effect on October 24, 1945.

The Charter set out the aims of the organization: to maintain peace and security, and develop friendly relations between nations; to achieve international cooperation in solving economic, social, cultural, and humanitarian problems; to promote respect for human rights and fundamental freedoms; and to harmonize the activities of nations in order to achieve these common goals.

The United Nations has five principal organs:

The General Assembly The forum at which member nations discuss moral and political issues affecting world development, peace and security meets annually in September, under a newly-elected President whose tenure lasts one year. Any member can bring business to the agenda, and each member nation has one vote.

The Security Council A legislative and executive body, the Security Council is the primary instrument for establishing and maintaining international peace by attempting to settle disputes between nations. It has the power to dispatch UN forces, and member nations undertake to provide armed forces, assistance and facilities. The Security Council has ten temporary members elected by the General Assembly for two-year terms, and five permanent members – China, France, Russia, the UK, and the USA.

The Economic and Social Council By far the largest United Nations executive, the Council operates as a conduit between the General Assembly and the many United Nations agencies it instructs to implement Assembly decisions, and whose work it coordinates. The Council also commissions studies on economic conditions, collects data and makes recommendations to the Assembly.

The Secretariat This is the staff of the United Nations, and its task is to administer the policies and programs of the UN and its organs, and assist and advise the Head of the Secretariat, the Secretary-General – a full-time, non-political appointment made by the General Assembly.

The Trusteeship Council This no longer administers any of the original 11 trust territories as they are all now independent.

The International Court of Justice (the World Court) The World Court is the judicial organ of the United Nations. It deals only with United Nations disputes and all members are subject to its jurisdiction. There are 15 judges, elected for nine-year terms by the General Assembly and the Security Council.

The social and humanitarian operations of the UN include:

United Nations Development Program (UNDP) Plans and funds projects to help developing countries make better use of their resources.
United Nations International Childrens' Fund (UNICEF) Created at the General Assembly's first session in 1945 to help children in the aftermath of World War II, it now provides basic health care and aid worldwide.
Food and Agriculture Organization (FAO) Aims to raise living standards and nutrition levels in rural areas by improving food production and distribution.
United Nations Educational, Scientific and Cultural Organization (UNESCO) Promotes international cooperation through broader and better education.
World Health Organization (WHO) Promotes and provides for better health care, public and environmental health, and medical research.

United Nations agencies are involved in many aspects of international trade, safety, and security:

International Maritime Organization (IMO) Promotes unity amongst merchant shipping, especially in regard to safety, marine pollution, and standardization.
International Labor Organization (ILO) Seeks to improve labor conditions and promote productive employment to raise living standards.
World Meteorological Organization (WMO) Promotes cooperation in weather observation, reporting, and forecasting.
World Trade Organization (WTO) On January 1, 1995, the WTO replaced GATT. It advocates a common code of conduct and its aim is the liberalization of world trade.
Disarmament Commission Considers and makes recommendations to the General Assembly on disarmament issues.
International Atomic Energy Agency (IAEA) Fosters development of peaceful uses for nuclear energy and establishes safety standards.

The World Bank comprises three United Nations agencies:

International Monetary Fund (IMF) Cultivates international monetary cooperation and the expansion of trade.
International Bank for Reconstruction and Development (IBRD) Provides funds and technical assistance to developing countries.
International Finance Corporation (IFC) Encourages the growth of productive private enterprise in less developed countries.

Membership There are two independent states which are not members of the UN – Taiwan and Vatican City. Official languages are Chinese, English, French, Russian, Spanish, and Arabic.

Funding The UN regular budget for 2005 was US$1.8 billion. Contributions are assessed by the members' ability to pay, with the maximum 24% of the total (USA's share), the minimum 0.01%. The EU pays over 37% of the budget.

Peacekeeping The UN has been involved in 54 peacekeeping operations worldwide since 1948.

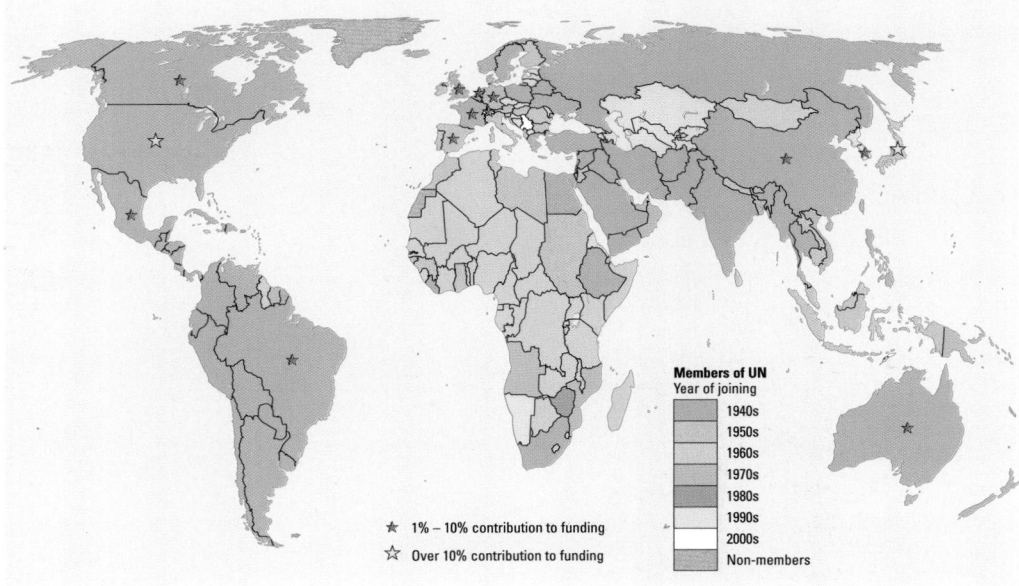

★ 1% – 10% contribution to funding
☆ Over 10% contribution to funding

Members of UN
Year of joining
1940s
1950s
1960s
1970s
1980s
1990s
2000s
Non-members

For more information:

78 Climate regions

79 Temperature and precipitation

80 Water distribution

81 Natural vegetation

100 Division of employment

When harvests are bad and world grain reserves fall, an old debate is revived, namely whether the population explosion will cause major food crises in the 21st century. Experts estimate that 3 billion tons of cereals will be needed to feed the world's population in 25 years' time, as compared with 1.9 billion tons at present. To expand food production to this extent, some argue, will place great strain on the environment.

Other experts, however, argue that there should be no food crises. World grain production tripled between 1950 and 1990, largely as a result of the Green Revolution, during which genetically improved, high-yield varieties of maize, rice, and wheat, the world's three leading staple crops, were developed.

These new varieties have helped many developing countries achieve food surpluses and prevent widespread starvation. Some people, however, oppose the use of genet-ically modified crops. In 2002, with severe droughts causing widespread starvation, Zambia and Zimbabwe both refused large maize donations from the USA because they might be genetically modified.

The only region of the world which seems likely to suffer food shortages in the 21st century is sub-Saharan Africa, where in the late 1990s the average daily calorie intake was 6% less than what was needed and where the population is expected to double in 20 years. Improved land management and a huge increase in global trade, especially in food distribution, is necessary if sub-Saharan Africans are not to go hungry.

The development of agriculture more than 10,000 years ago transformed human existence more than any other major advance. By supporting larger populations, it led to the growth of early civilizations and later it sustained people in the industrial cities that sprang up in the 19th century.

Today, agricultural production varies a great deal between the developed world, where it is highly mechanized and employs few people, such as 2% of the work force in the United States, and the developing world, such as sub-Saharan Africa, where it employs 66% of the work force. Many Africans are engaged in subsistence farming, providing the basic needs of their families but not con-tributing to the national economy. Much of Africa also suffers from economic misman-agement, as well as civil war and corruption.

Political problems have also affected food production in other parts of the world. The former USSR had much excellent farmland, but the failure of the collectives and state farms to maintain sufficiently high levels of production helped to bring about the collapse of Communism.

Farmers are under pressure not only to maintain high levels of production but also to increase them. However, the cultivation of marginal areas is one of the prime causes of soil erosion and desertification.

► The wheat harvest – photographed in Oregon, USA. Wheat, corn, rye, oats, and barley are grown in temperate regions, whereas rice, millet, sorghum, and maize require more tropical climates. Cereal cultivation was the basis of early civilizations, and, with the development of high-yielding strains, remains the world's most important food source today.

LAND USE

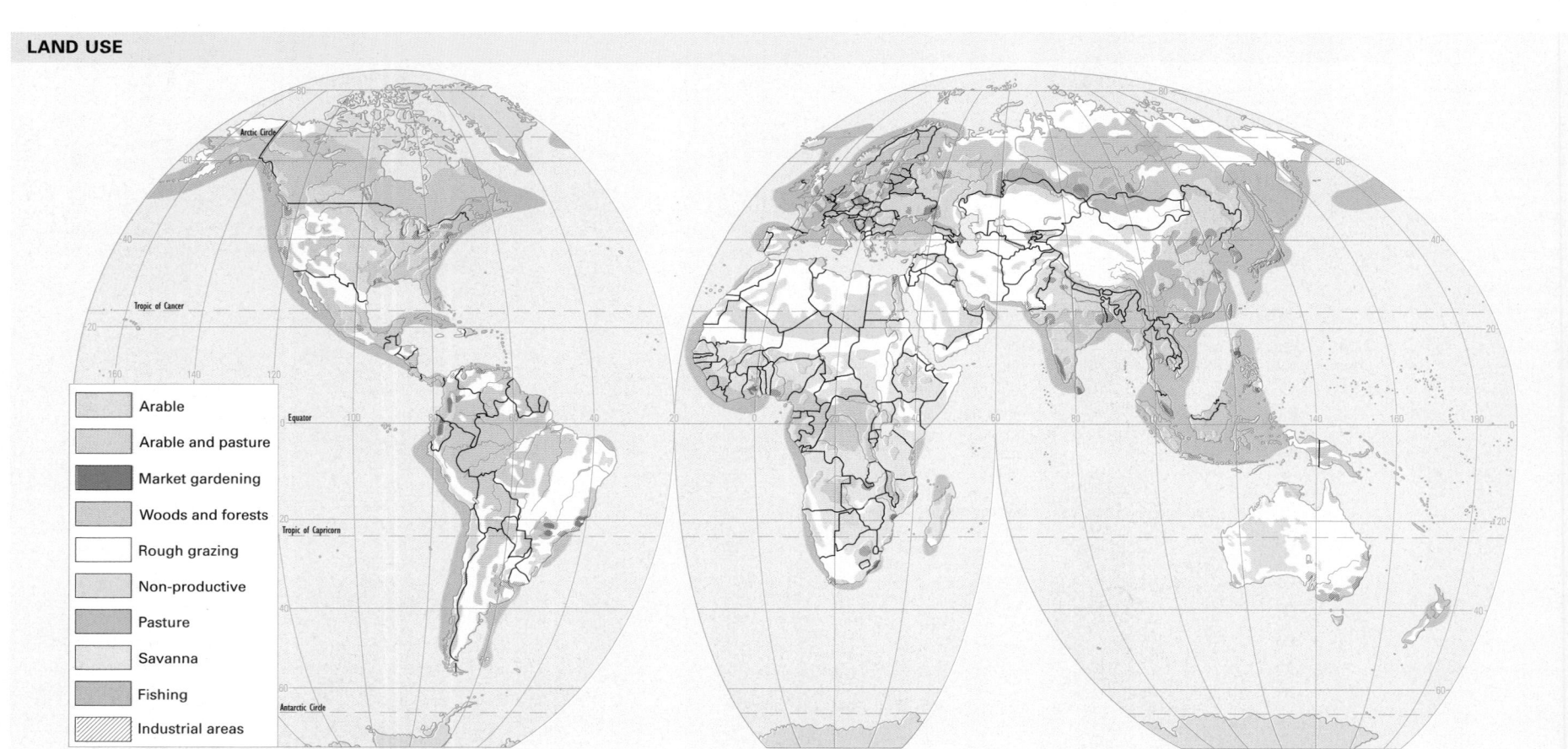

Arable

Arable and pasture

Market gardening

Woods and forests

Rough grazing

Non-productive

Pasture

Savanna

Fishing

Industrial areas

STAPLE CROPS

Wheat: Grown in a range of climates, with most varieties – including the highest-quality bread wheats – requiring temperate conditions. Mainly used in baking, it is also used for pasta and breakfast cereals.

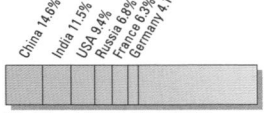

World total (2004): 624,093,000 tons

Maize: Originating in the New World and still an important human food in Africa and Latin America, in the developed world it is processed into breakfast cereals, oil, starches and adhesives. It is also used for animal feed.

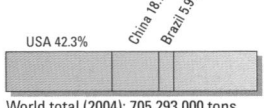

World total (2004): 705,293,000 tons

Oats: Most widely used to feed livestock, but eaten by humans as oatmeal or porridge. Oats have a beneficial effect on the cardiovascular system, and human consumption is likely to increase.

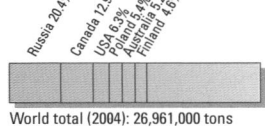

World total (2004): 26,961,000 tons

Millet: The name covers a number of small-grained cereals, members of the grass family with a short growing season. Used to produce flour, meal and animal feed, and fermented to make beer, especially in Africa.

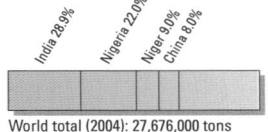

World total (2004): 27,676,000 tons

Rice: Thrives on the high humidity and temperatures of the Far East, where it is the traditional staple food of half the human race. Usually grown standing in water, rice responds well to continuous cultivation, with three or four crops annually.

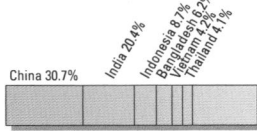

World total (2004): 608,496,000 tons

Potatoes: The most important of the edible tubers, potatoes grow in well-watered, temperate areas. Though weight for weight less nutritious than grain, they are a human staple as well as an important animal feed.

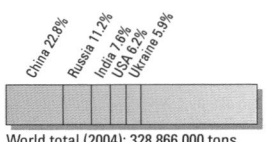

World total (2004): 328,866,000 tons

Soya: Beans from soya bushes (soybeans) are very high (30–40%) in protein. Most are processed into oil and proprietary protein foods. Consumption since 1950 has tripled, mainly due to the health-conscious developed world.

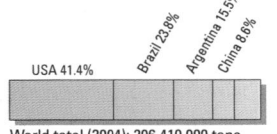

World total (2004): 206,410,000 tons

Cassava: A tropical shrub that needs high rainfall (over 1,000 mm annually) and a 10–30 month growing season to produce its large, edible tubers. Used as flour by humans, as cattle feed and in industrial starches.

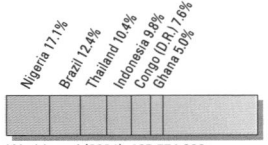

World total (2004): 195,574,000 tons

SUGARS

Sugarcane: Confined to tropical regions, cane sugar accounts for the bulk of international trade in sugar. Most is produced as a foodstuff, but some countries, notably Brazil and South Africa, distil sugarcane to make motor fuels.

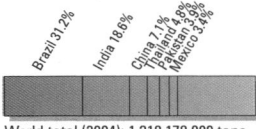

World total (2004): 1,318,178,000 tons

Sugar beet: Closely related to the beetroot, sugar beet's yield after processing is indistinguishable from cane sugar. It is replacing sugarcane imports in Europe, to the detriment of the developing countries that rely on it as a major cash crop.

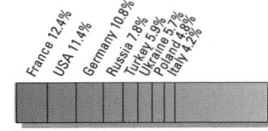

World total (2004): 237,858,000 tons

CEREALS & TUBERS

Cereals: These are grasses with starchy, edible seeds; every important civilization has depended on them as a source of food. The major cereal grains contain about 10% protein and 75% carbohydrate. Grain contributes more than any other group of foods to the energy and protein content of the human diet.

Starchy tuber crops or root crops: Second in importance after cereals as staple foods; easily cultivated, they provide high yields for little effort.

FOOD & POPULATION

Comparison of food production and population by continent
The left column indicates the % of world food production and the right shows population in proportion.

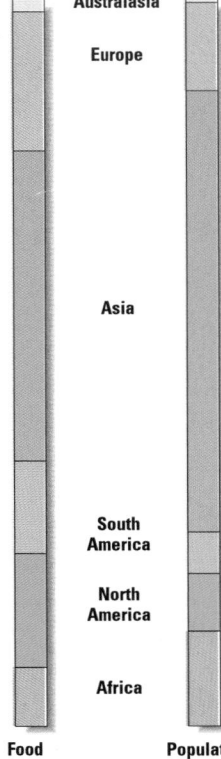

Food   Population

AGRICULTURAL WORK FORCE

Percentage of the total work force dependent on agriculture for their livelihood (2003)

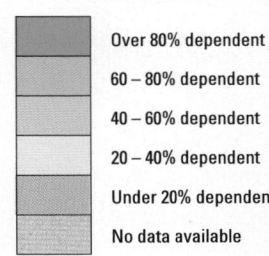

Over 80% dependent

60 – 80% dependent

40 – 60% dependent

20 – 40% dependent

Under 20% dependent

No data available

Top 5 countries		Bottom 5 countries	
Burundi	94%	USA	0.7%
Bhutan	93%	Singapore	1.0%
Burkina Faso	90%	Luxembourg	1.0%
Malawi	90%	Kuwait	1.0%
Niger	90%	Bahrain	1.0%

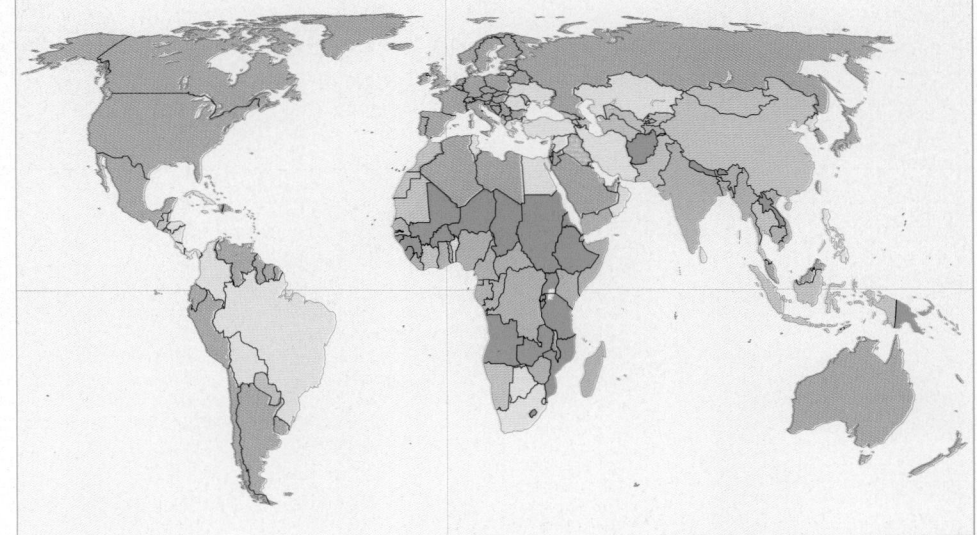

ANIMAL PRODUCTS

Traditionally, food animals subsisted on land unsuitable for cultivation, supporting agricultural production with their fertilizing dung. But free-ranging animals grow slowly and yield less meat than those more intensively reared; the demands of urban markets in the developed world have encouraged the growth of factory-like production methods.

A large proportion of staple crops, especially cereals, are fed to animals – an inefficient way to produce protein, but one likely to continue as long as people value meat and dairy products in their diet.

Cheese: Least perishable of all dairy products, cheese is milk fermented with selected bacterial strains to produce a foodstuff with a potentially immense range of flavors and textures. The vast majority of cheeses are made from cow's milk, although sheep and goat cheeses are highly prized.

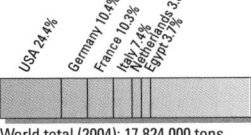

World total (2004): 17,824,000 tons

Beef and Veal: Most beef and veal is reared for home markets, and the top five producers are also the biggest consumers. The United States produces nearly a quarter of the world's beef and eats even more.

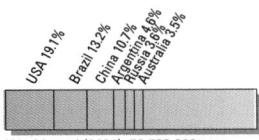

World total (2004): 58,702,000 tons

Milk: Many human groups, including most Asians, find raw milk indigestible after infancy, and it is often only the starting point for other dairy products such as butter, cheese, and yoghurt. Most world production comes from cows, but sheep's milk and goats' milk are also important.

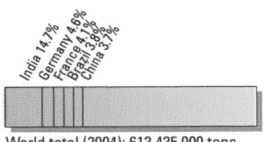

World total (2004): 613,435,000 tons

Butter: A traditional source of vitamin A as well as calories, butter has lost much popularity in the developed world for health reasons, although it remains a valuable food. Most butter from India, the world's largest producer, is clarified into ghee, which has religious as well as nutritional importance.

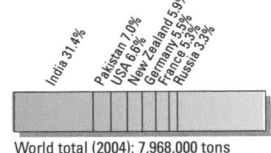

World total (2004): 7,968,000 tons

Pork: Although pork is forbidden to many millions, notably Muslims, on religious grounds, more is produced than any other meat in the world, mainly because it is the cheapest. It accounts for about 90% of China's meat output, although the per capita meat consumption is relatively low.

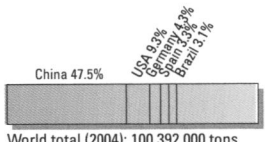

World total (2004): 100,392,000 tons

CRISIS IN AFRICA

Each year 40 million people, almost half of whom are children, die from starvation and related diseases. In 2000, 600 million people worldwide were estimated to be suffering from malnutrition. Africa suffers from more natural disasters than any other continent; pests such as locusts destroy crops, and tropical storms and floods ruin harvests. Famines periodically affect parts of Africa causing widespread hardship, even though enough food is produced worldwide to feed everyone.

A major phenomenon that affects the weather over tropical and subtropical regions areas around the world is called El Niño *(see page 74).* It occurs when there is unusual warming in the tropical eastern Pacific Ocean, causing changes in the wind and pressure systems. Normal years are called La Niña. El Niño years included 1973–4, 1982–3, 1986–7, 1992, 1997–8, and 2002.

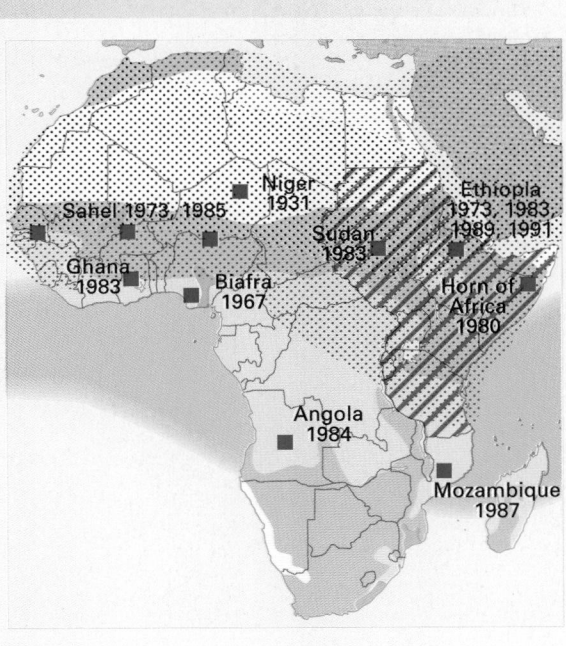

Ocean areas affected by El Niño and La Niña temperature fluctuations

Countries affected by 4 years of continuous drought, 1996–2000

Areas liable to flood

Crop Failure

Areas liable to periodic crop failure

Areas where crop failures are rare

Desert

Desert Locusts

Areas liable to invasions by desert locusts

Areas affected by 1993 swarm of desert locusts

Major famines since 1900 (with dates)

For more information:
83 The carbon cycle
84 Global warming
   Carbon dioxide
   Greenhouse power
85 Water pollution
98 Minerals
103 World shipping

Every year, the world's energy consumption is about the equivalent of what would come from burning 9,000 million tons of oil (9,000 MtOe) – a 20-fold increase since 1850. Two-fifths of this total actually comes from burning oil and most of the rest comes from coal and natural gas.

The oil crises in the 1970s precipitated concern over dependence on finite fossil fuels as the primary source of energy, and growing environmental awareness has added impetus to the search for alternative energy resources. Fossil fuel combustion damages the environment through the release of gases and particulate matter, but two other major sources of energy, hydroelectricity and nuclear power, are also controversial. Hydroelectricity production involves flooding large areas to create reservoirs, while nuclear power stations generate dangerous radioactive wastes and can cause major disasters. Significantly, by 2002, Belgium, Germany, the Netherlands, Spain, and Sweden had plans to phase out the use of nuclear energy. However, Finland decided to construct a new one.

Alternative energy resources may soon provide a much larger proportion of the world's energy consumption. Solar and wind energy may become important in such countries as China and India, while tidal, wave, and geothermal energy all have potential in appropriate areas. Experts calculate that solar power could, in theory, supply between five and ten times the present electricity supply of developing countries.

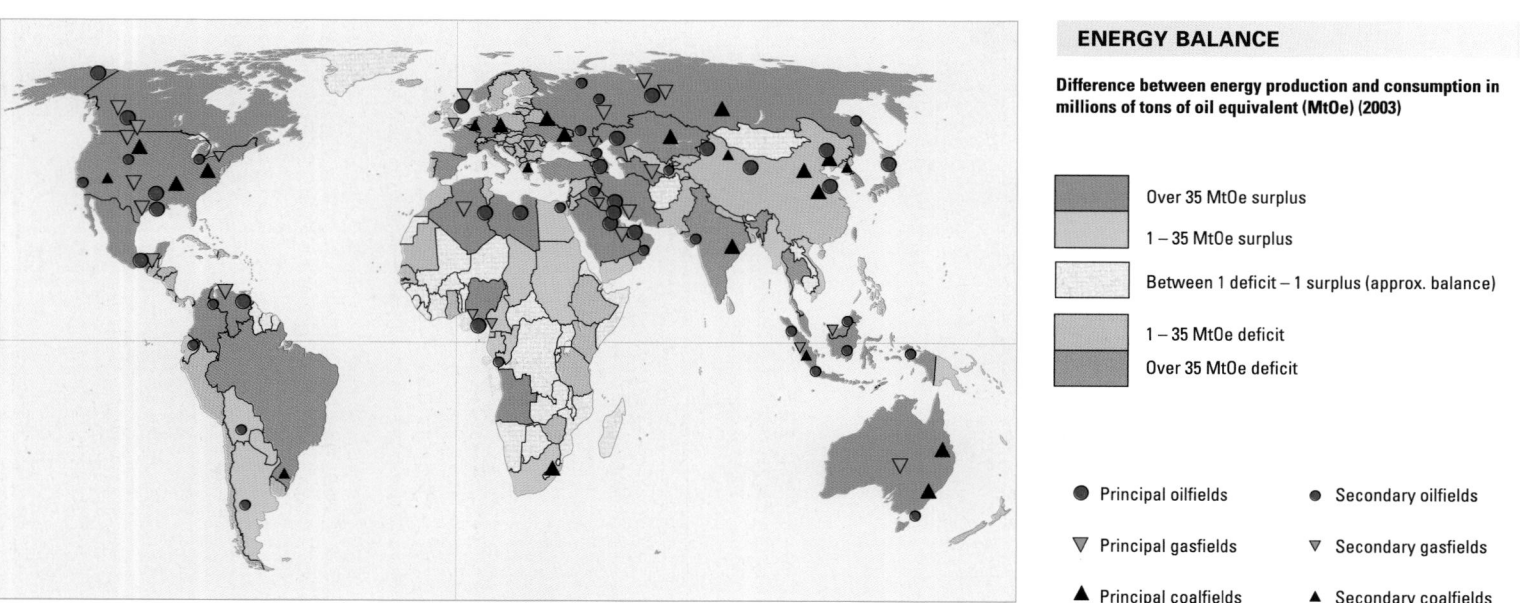

ENERGY BALANCE

Difference between energy production and consumption in millions of tons of oil equivalent (MtOe) (2003)

- Over 35 MtOe surplus
- 1 – 35 MtOe surplus
- Between 1 deficit – 1 surplus (approx. balance)
- 1 – 35 MtOe deficit
- Over 35 MtOe deficit

- ● Principal oilfields
- ● Secondary oilfields
- ▽ Principal gasfields
- ▽ Secondary gasfields
- ▲ Principal coalfields
- ▲ Secondary coalfields

ENERGY CONSUMPTION

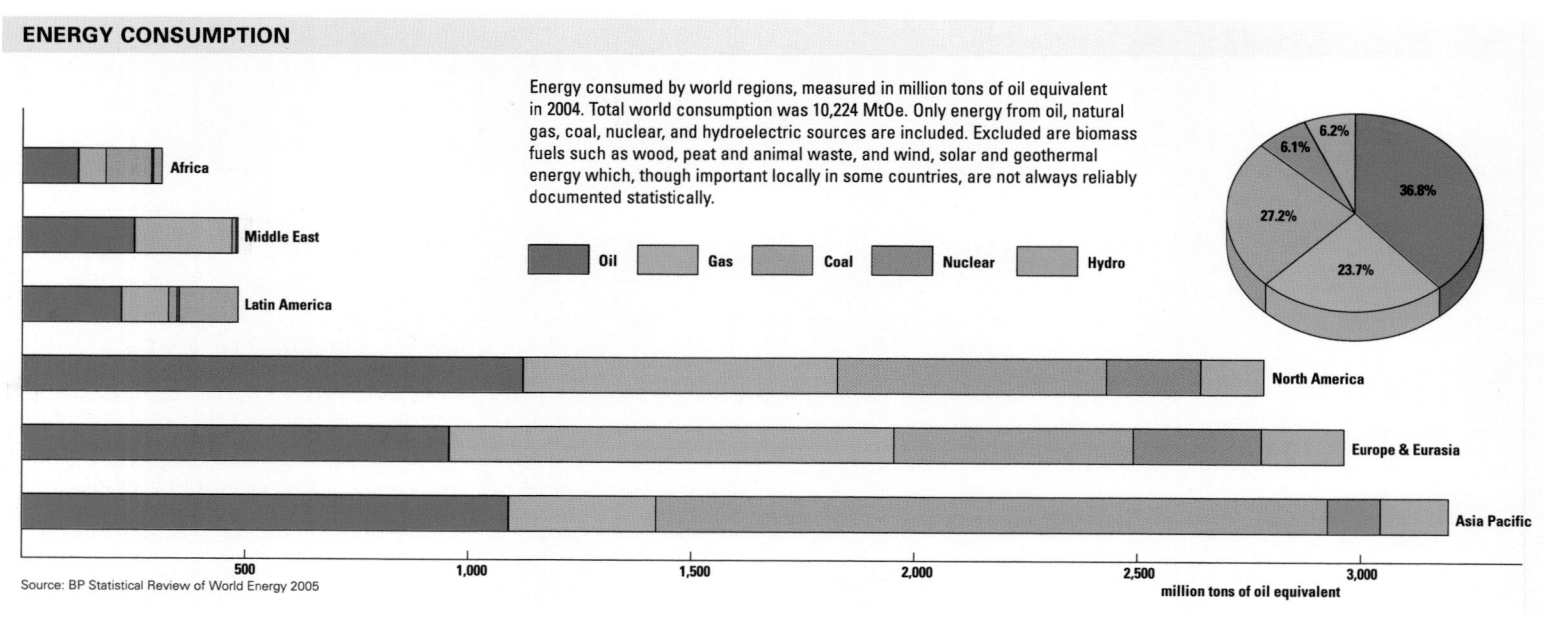

Energy consumed by world regions, measured in million tons of oil equivalent in 2004. Total world consumption was 10,224 MtOe. Only energy from oil, natural gas, coal, nuclear, and hydroelectric sources are included. Excluded are biomass fuels such as wood, peat and animal waste, and wind, solar and geothermal energy which, though important locally in some countries, are not always reliably documented statistically.

Oil | Gas | Coal | Nuclear | Hydro

Africa
Middle East
Latin America
North America
Europe & Eurasia
Asia Pacific

6.2%
6.1%
27.2%
36.8%
23.7%

Source: BP Statistical Review of World Energy 2005

million tons of oil equivalent

ENERGY PRODUCTION

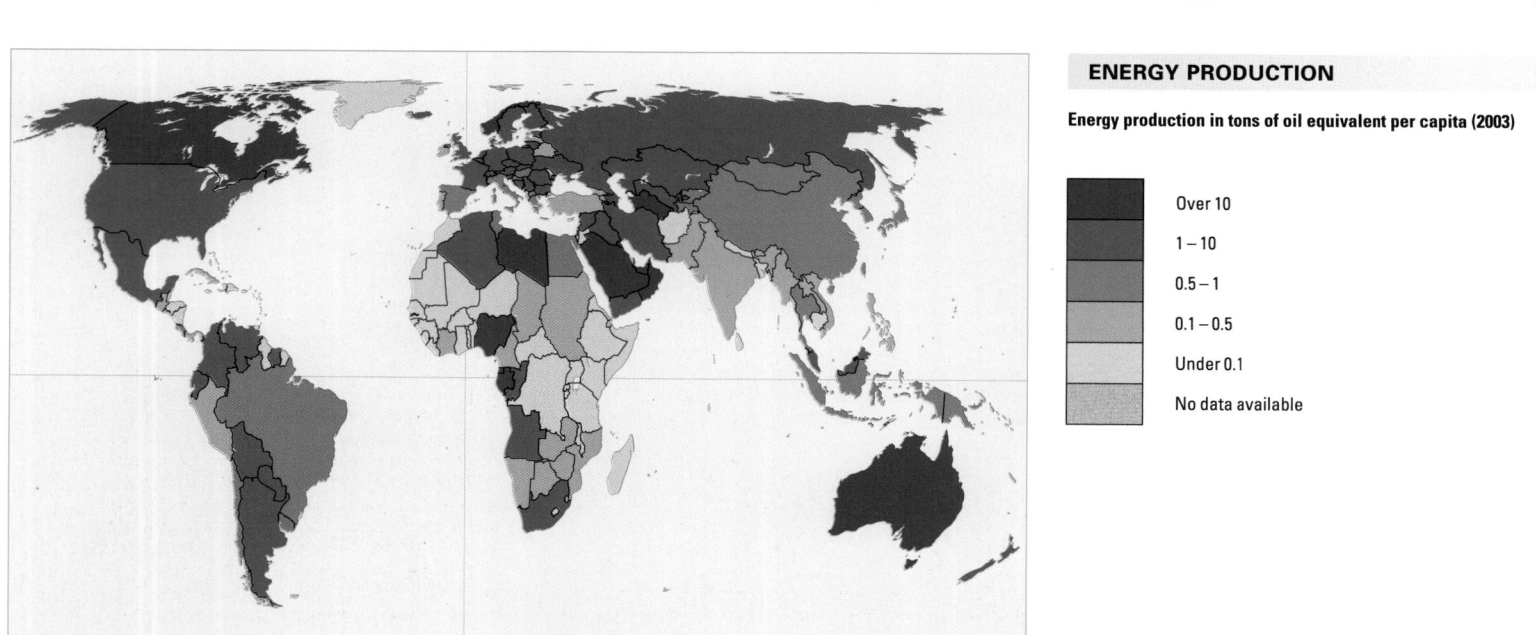

Energy production in tons of oil equivalent per capita (2003)

- Over 10
- 1 – 10
- 0.5 – 1
- 0.1 – 0.5
- Under 0.1
- No data available

OIL MOVEMENTS

Major world movements of oil in millions of tons (2004)

1.	Middle East to Asia (not China or Japan)	357.4
2.	Former Soviet Union to Europe	269.9
3.	Middle East to Japan	208.5
4.	Middle East to Europe	159.6
5.	South and Central America to USA	130.6
6.	Middle East to USA	124.9
7.	Canada to USA	104.8
8.	North Africa to Europe	95.5
9.	Mexico to USA	81.9
10.	West Africa to USA	81.6
11.	Middle East to China	62.8
12.	Europe to USA	48.1
13.	West Africa to Asia (not China or Japan)	42.5
14.	Asia (not China) to China	40.0
15.	Middle East to Africa	35.9
16.	East and Southern Africa to China	27.5
Total world imports		**2,380,700,000 tons**

◄ With many of the world's onshore oilfields reaching their maturity, exploration and production in ever-deeper ocean waters is taking place to try to satisfy demand. The current deepest production well is in 6,004 ft [1,829 m] of water, offshore of Brazil. However, exploration wells off the coasts of Angola and Nigeria are already being drilled in water 8,000 ft [2,438 m] deep, and it is believed that wells in 10,000 ft [3,048 m] of water will soon be developed.

ENERGY RESERVES

WORLD OIL RESERVES
World oil reserves by region and country, thousand million tons (2004)

World total: 156.7 thousand million tons

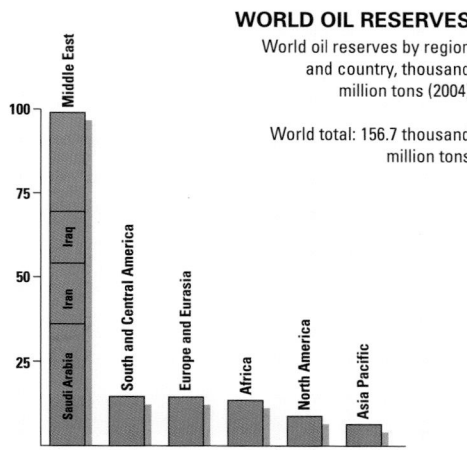

WORLD GAS RESERVES
World natural gas reserves by region and country, thousand million tons of oil equivalent (2004)

World total: 164.8 thousand million tons of oil equivalent

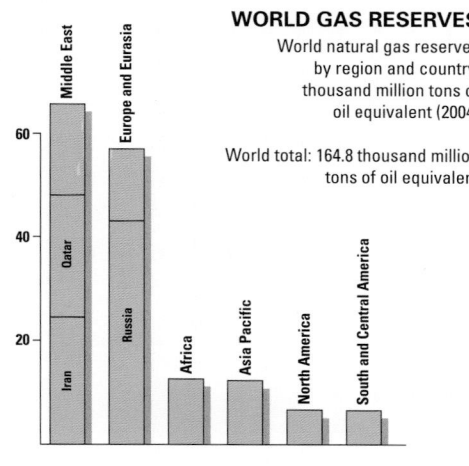

WORLD COAL RESERVES
World coal reserves (including lignite) by region and country, thousand million tons (2004)

World total: 984.45 thousand million tons

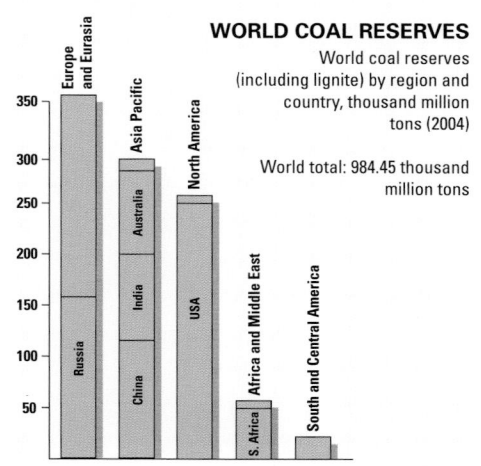

NUCLEAR POWER

Major producers by percentage of world total and by percentage of domestic electricity generation (2003)

Country	% of world total production	Country	% of nuclear as proportion of domestic electricity
1. USA	30.4%	1. Lithuania	79.9%
2. France	16.7%	2. France	77.7%
3. Japan	8.7%	3. Slovak Rep.	57.4%
4. Germany	6.2%	4. Belgium	55.5%
5. Russia	5.7%	5. Sweden	50.0%
6. South Korea	4.9%	6. Ukraine	45.9%
7. UK	3.4%	7. Slovenia	40.4%
8. Ukraine	3.1%	8. South Korea	40.0%
9. Canada	2.8%	9. Switzerland	39.7%
10. Sweden	2.6%	10. Bulgaria	37.7%

Although the 1980s were a bad time for the nuclear power industry (major projects ran over budget and fears of long-term environmental damage were heavily reinforced by the 1986 disaster at Chernobyl), the industry picked up in the early 1990s. However, while the number of reactors is still increasing, orders for new plants have shrunk. Sixteen countries currently rely on nuclear power to supply over 25% of their total electricity requirements.

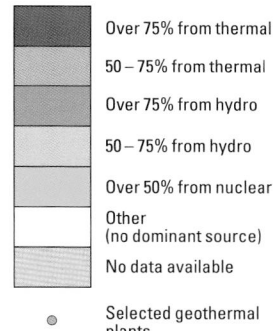

ELECTRICITY PRODUCTION

Percentage of electricity generated by source (2004)

- Over 75% from thermal
- 50 – 75% from thermal
- Over 75% from hydro
- 50 – 75% from hydro
- Over 50% from nuclear
- Other (no dominant source)
- No data available
- Selected geothermal plants
- Selected hydroelectric plants

HYDROELECTRICITY

Major producers by percentage of world total and by percentage of domestic electricity generation (2003)

Country	% of world total production	Country	% of hydroelectric as proportion of domestic electricity
1. Canada	11.5%	1. Bhutan	99.9%
2. USA	10.2%	2. Paraguay	99.8%
3. Brazil	11.6%	= Zambia	99.8%
4. China	10.8%	4. Norway	99.1%
5. Russia	6.0%	5. Ethiopia	98.1%
6. Norway	4.0%	6. Congo (Rep. Dem.)	97.9%
7. Japan	3.8%	7. Tajikistan	97.8%
8. India	2.6%	8. Cameroon	97.3%
9. France	2.5%	9. Albania	97.2%
10. Venezuela	2.3%	= Laos	97.2%

Countries heavily reliant on hydroelectricity are usually small and non-industrial: a high proportion of hydroelectric power more often reflects a modest energy budget than vast hydroelectric resources. The USA, for instance, produces only 8.5% of its power requirements from hydroelectricity; yet that 8.5% amounts to more than three times the hydropower generated by most of Africa.

ALTERNATIVE ENERGY RESOURCES

Solar: Each year the Sun bestows upon the Earth almost a million times as much energy as is locked up in all the planet's oil reserves, but only an insignificant fraction is trapped and used commercially. In a few installations around the world, mirrors focus the Sun's rays on to boilers, whose steam generates electricity by spinning turbines.

Wind: Caused by uneven heating of the Earth, winds are themselves a form of solar energy. Windmills have been long used for wind power; recent models, often arranged in banks on wind-swept high ground or off coastlines, usually generate electricity. Wind-power figures are given in the table (*right*) – it is the world's fastest growing energy source. In 2004, Germany, the USA, Spain, and Denmark produced nearly 39,000 MW.

Tidal: The energy from tides is potentially enormous, although only a few installations have so far been built to exploit it. In theory at least, waves and currents could also provide almost unimaginable power, and the thermal differences in the ocean depths are another huge well of potential energy. But work on extracting it is still at the experimental stage.

Geothermal: The Earth's temperature rises by 1°F for every 50 feet descent, with much steeper temperature gradients in geologically active areas. El Salvador, for example, produces 39% of its electricity from geothermal power stations, whilst the USA is the world's leading producer. Some of the oldest and most successful applications are in Iceland, where 86% of all households are heated by geothermal energy.

Biomass: The oldest of human fuels ranges from animal dung, still burned in cooking fires in much of North Africa and elsewhere, to sugarcane plantations feeding high-technology distilleries to produce ethanol for motor-vehicle engines. In Brazil and South Africa, plant ethanol provides up to 25% of motor fuel. Throughout the developing world, most biomass energy comes from firewood: although accurate figures are impossible to obtain, it may yield as much as 10% of the world's total energy consumption.

WIND POWER

World wind energy generating capacity, in megawatts

1980	10
1982	90
1984	600
1986	1,270
1988	1,580
1990	1,930
1992	2,510
1994	3,710
1995	4,820
1996	6,115
1997	7,630
1998	9,600
1999	11,700
2000	17,800
2001	23,300
2002	31,000
2003	39,300
2004	47,671
2005	58,982

For more information:
70 Geology
101 Patterns of production
103 World shipping

The use of metals played a vital part in the evolving technologies of early peoples. Copper first came into use around 10,000 years ago, bronze about 5,000 years ago, and iron 3,300 years ago. In the early stages of the Industrial Revolution, the location of coal, iron ore, and water power usually determined the location of new industries. But due to continuing improvements in transport, including oil pipelines, industries can now be located almost anywhere.

Minerals are distributed unevenly and some industrial countries, lacking their own mineral resources, import most of the raw materials they need. Some imports come from mineral-rich countries, such as Australia, but others come from developing countries, especially in Africa and South America. Most developing countries export unprocessed ores, losing out on the higher revenues gained from exporting metals.

Most minerals come from land deposits, because undersea deposits, with the exception of oil reserves under the continental shelves, have been inaccessible. But shortages of terrestrial minerals may one day encourage exploitation of the ocean floor.

► An aerial view of gold mine excavations in Zimbabwe, for extraction both above and below ground. Once a major producer of gold, Zimbabwe's gold mining industry has greatly declined in recent years as a result of political and social unrest.

URANIUM

Uranium was first discovered by the German chemist Martin Klaproth in 1789. In its pure state, uranium is an immensely heavy, white metal. But although spent uranium is employed as a projectile in anti-missile cannons, where its mass ensures a lethal punch, its main use is as a fuel in nuclear reactors, and in nuclear weaponry.

Uranium is very scarce: the main source is the rare ore pitchblende, which itself contains only 0.2% uranium oxide. This blackish, lustrous ore occurs in quartz veins. Only a minute fraction of that is the radioactive U^{235} isotope, though so-called breeder reactors can transmute the more common U^{238} into highly radioactive plutonium.

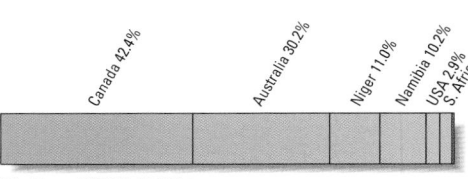

World total (2004): 29,700 tons

DIAMOND

Most of the world's diamond is found in kimberlite, or "blue ground," a basic peridotite rock; erosion may wash the diamond from its kimberlite matrix and deposit it with sand or gravel on river beds. Only a small proportion of the world's diamond, the most flawless, is cut into gemstones – "diamonds"; most are used in industry, where the material's remarkable hardness and abrasion resistance finds a use in cutting tools, drills, and dies. The world's major producers are Australia (24%), Botswana (17.5%), Democratic Republic of the Congo (14.6%), Russia (15.5%), and South Africa (9.25%). Natural diamonds now account for less than 10% of all industrial diamond output. Synthetic diamond production in centers such as Ireland, Japan, Russia, and the USA far exceeds it.

METALS

Figures refer to ore production unless otherwise specified after the world total figure.

The world's leading producers of aluminum ore (bauxite) in 2004 were as follows:

1. Australia 35.6%
2. Brazil 11.6%
3. Guinea 10.1%
4. China 9.4%
5. Jamaica 8.4%
6. India 7.1%
7. Russia 3.8%
8. Venezuela 3.5%
9. Kazakhstan 3.0%
10. Suriname 2.5%

The figures shown above are in stark contrast to the figures showing aluminum production (*see above right*). Australia, for example, produces 35.6% of the world's bauxite but only 6.4% of aluminum. Guinea and Jamaica account for almost 20% of the bauxite mined but have no smelters and export virtually all of it to countries like the USA and Canada.

Aluminum: Produced mainly from its oxide, bauxite, which yields 25% of its weight in aluminum. The cost of refining and production is often too high for producer-countries to bear, so bauxite is largely exported. Lightweight and corrosion resistant, aluminum alloys are widely used in aircraft, vehicles, cans, and packaging.

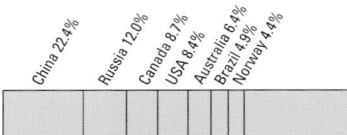

World total (2004): 29,800,000 tons

Lead: A soft metal, obtained mainly from galena (lead sulfide), which occurs in veins associated with iron, zinc and silver sulfides. Its use in vehicle batteries accounts for the USA's prime consumer status; lead is also made into sheeting and piping. Its use as an additive to paints and petrol is decreasing.

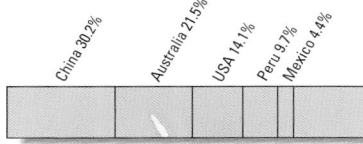

World total (2004): 3,150,000 tons

Tin: Soft, pliable and non-toxic, used to coat "tin" (tin-plated steel) cans, in the manufacture of foils and in alloys. The principal tin-bearing mineral is cassiterite (SnO_2), found in ore formed from molten rock. Producers and refiners were hit by a price collapse in 1991.

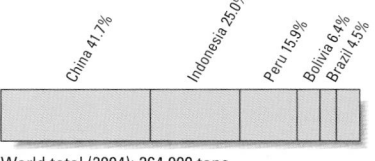

World total (2004): 264,000 tons

Gold: Regarded for centuries as the most valuable metal in the world and used to make coins, gold is still recognized as the monetary standard. A soft metal, it is alloyed to make jewelry; the electronics industry values its corrosion resistance and conductivity.

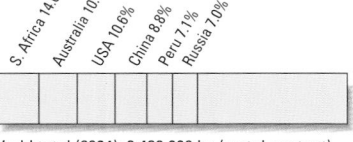

World total (2004): 2,430,000 kg (metal content)

Copper: Derived from low-yielding sulfide ores, copper is an important export for several developing countries. An excellent conductor of heat and electricity, it forms part of most electrical items, and is used in the manufacture of brass and bronze. Major importers include Japan and Germany.

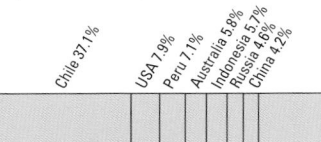

World total (2004): 14,600,000 tons

Mercury: The only metal that is liquid at normal temperatures, most is derived from its sulfide, cinnabar, found only in small quantities in volcanic areas. Apart from its value in thermometers and other instruments, most mercury production is used in antifungal and antifouling preparations, and to make detonators.

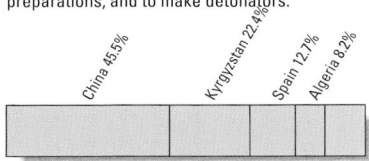

World total (2004): 1,340,000 kg

Zinc: Often found in association with lead ores, zinc is highly resistant to corrosion, and about 40% of the refined metal is used to plate sheet steel, particularly vehicle bodies – a process known as galvanizing. Zinc is also used in dry batteries, paints, and dyes.

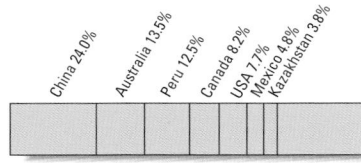

World total (2004): 9,600,000 tons

Silver: Most silver comes from ores mined and processed for other metals (including lead and copper). Pure or alloyed with harder metals, it is used for jewelry and ornaments. Industrial use includes dentistry, electronics, photography, and as a chemical catalyst.

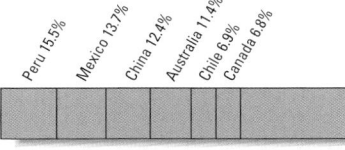

World total (2004): 19,700,000 kg (metal content)

DISTRIBUTION OF MINERALS

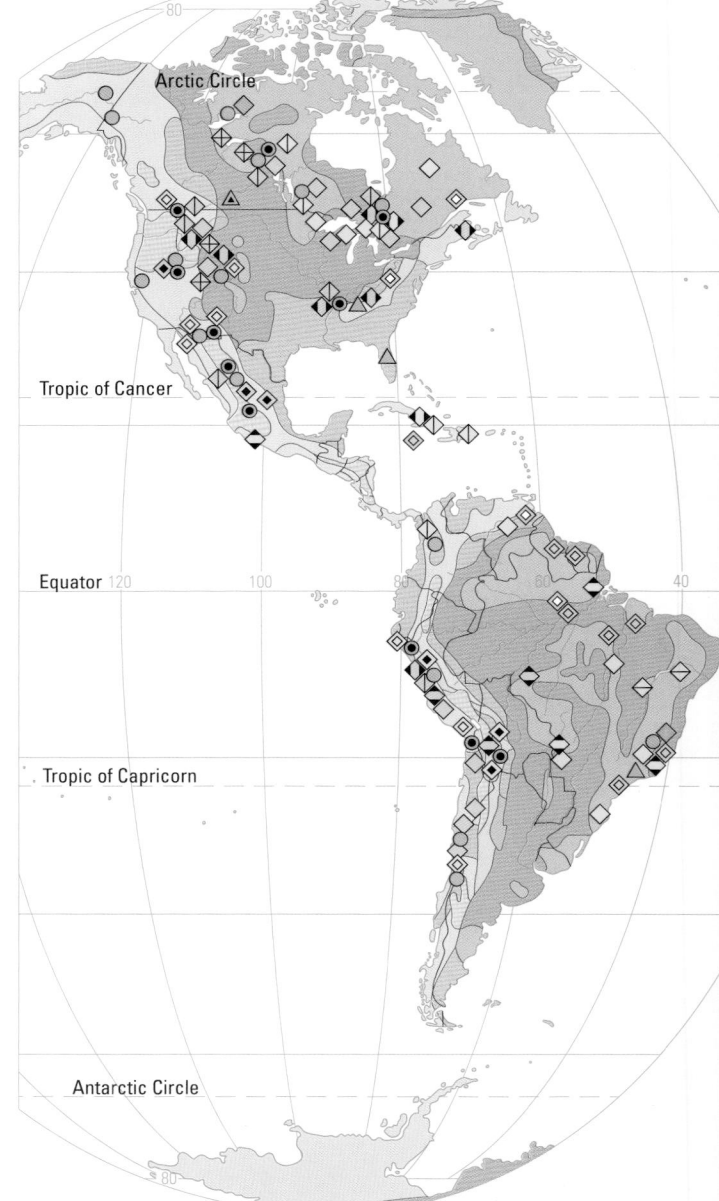

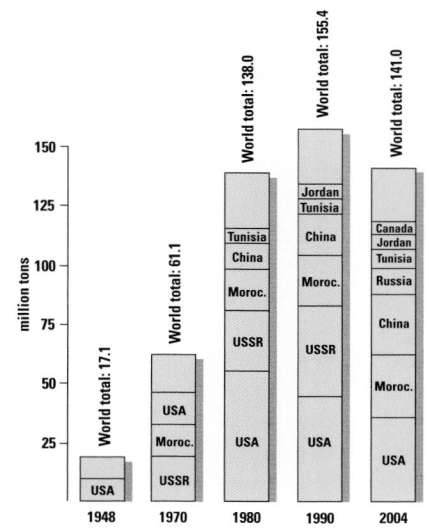

World production of phosphates in millions of tons (2004): Phosphate production is vital to the economies of several small countries. Nauru, for example, was heavily dependent on phosphate exports – the island had one of the world's richest deposits. In 1999, 500,000 tons were mined, employing 1,000 people, but by 2003 production had fallen to 22,000 tons owing to depletion of the deposits.

Percentage of total world phosphate production (2004)

1. USA	25.4%	7. Canada	3.8%
2. Morocco	16.2%	8. Israel	2.1%
3. China	19.5%	9. Syria	1.7%
4. Russia	7.8%	10. South Africa	1.9%
5. Tunisia	5.7%	11. Egypt	1.6%
6. Jordan	4.4%	12. Australia	1.4%

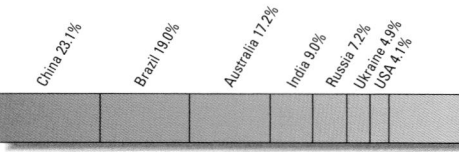

World total production of iron ore (2004): 1,340,000,000 tons

IRON ORE

Ever since the art of high-temperature smelting was discovered, some time in the second millennium BC, iron has been by far the most important metal known to man. The earliest iron plows transformed primitive agriculture and led to the first human population explosion, while iron weapons – or the lack of them – ensured the rise or fall of entire cultures.

Widely distributed around the world, iron ores usually contain 25–60% iron; blast furnaces process the raw product into pig-iron, which is then alloyed with carbon and other minerals to produce steels of various qualities. From the time of the first Industrial Revolution, steel has been almost literally the backbone of modern civilization, the prime structural material on which all else is built.

Iron smelting usually developed close to the sources of ore and, later, to the coalfields that fueled the furnaces. Today, most ore comes from a few richly-endowed locations where large-scale mining is possible.

Iron and steel plants are generally built at coastal sites so that giant ore carriers, which account for a sizable proportion of the world's merchant fleet, can easily discharge their cargoes.

Manganese: In its pure state, manganese is a hard, brittle metal. Alloyed with chromium, iron, and nickel, it produces abrasion-resistant steels; manganese-aluminum alloys are light but tough. Found in batteries and inks, manganese is also used in glass production. Manganese ores are frequently found in the same location as sedimentary iron ores. Pyrolusite (MnO_2) and psilomelane are the main economically-exploitable sources.

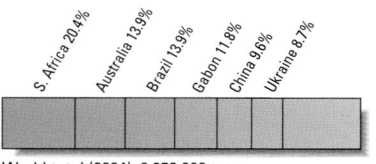

World total (2004): 9,350,000 tons

World production of pig-iron (2004)

Total world production: 712 million tons

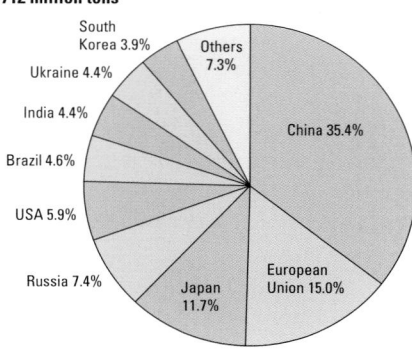

Chromium: Most of the world's chromium production is alloyed with iron and other metals to produce steels with various different properties. Combined with iron, nickel, cobalt, and tungsten, chromium produces an exceptionally hard steel, resistant to heat; chrome steels are used for many household items where utility must be matched with appearance – cutlery, for example. Chromium is also used in the production of refractory bricks, and its salts for tanning and dyeing leather and cloth.

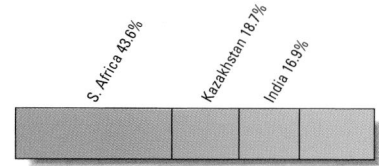

World total (2004): 17,500,000 tons

Nickel: Combined with chromium and iron, nickel produces stainless and high-strength steels; similar alloys go to make magnets and electrical heating elements. Nickel combined with copper is widely used to make coins; cupro-nickel alloy is very resistant to corrosion. Its ores yield only modest quantities of nickel – 0.5% to 3% – but also contain copper, iron, and small amounts of precious metals. Japan, USA, UK, Germany, and France are the principal importers.

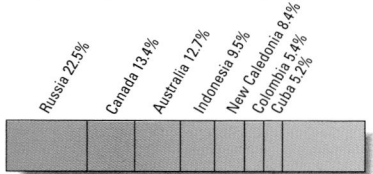

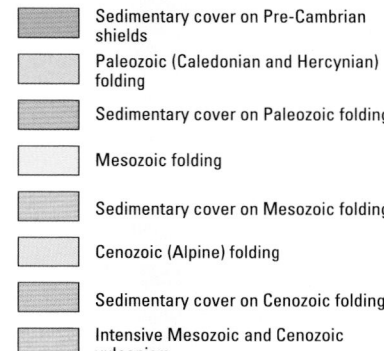

World total (2004): 1,400,000 tons (metal content)

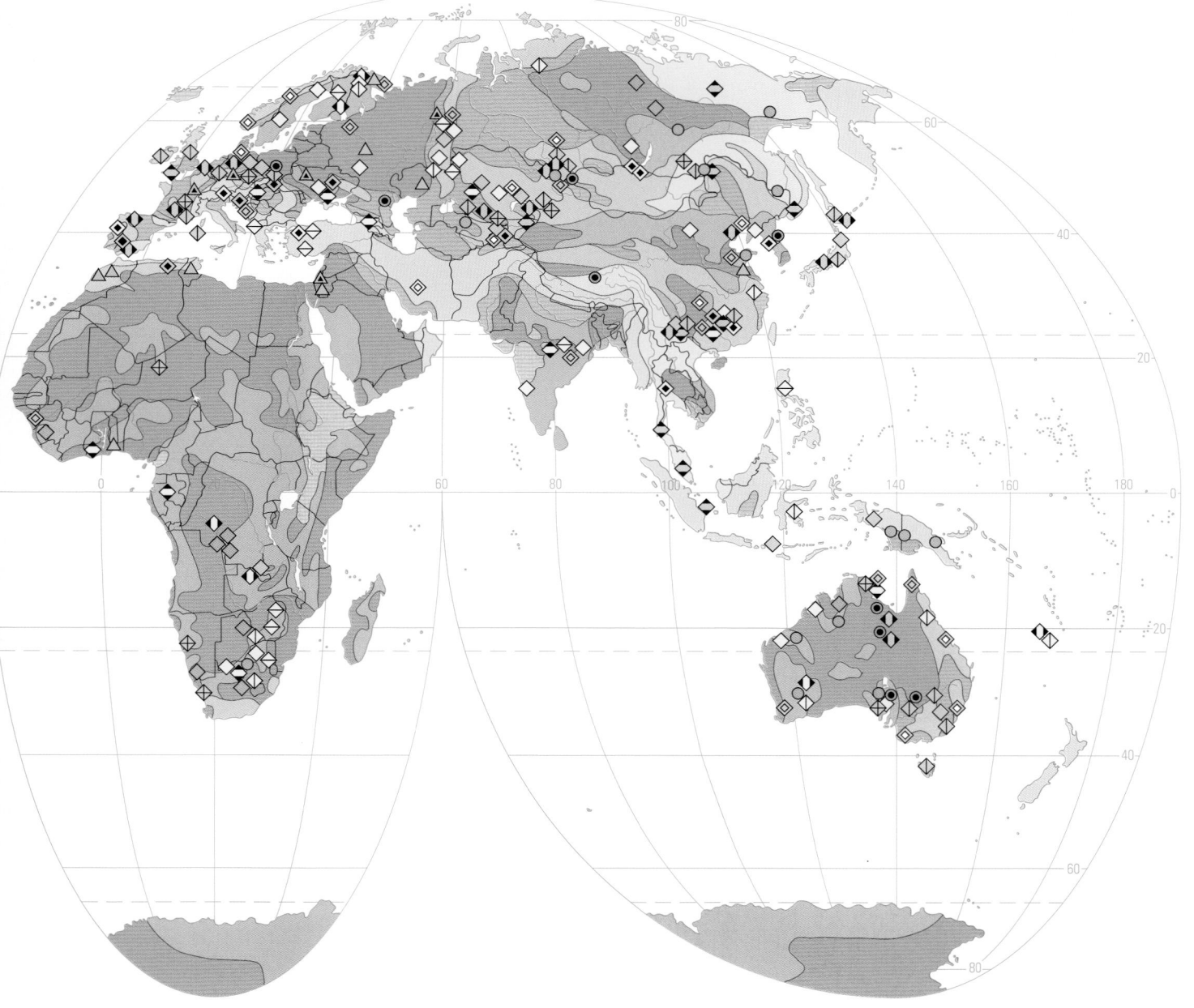

STRUCTURAL REGIONS

- Pre-Cambrian shields
- Sedimentary cover on Pre-Cambrian shields
- Paleozoic (Caledonian and Hercynian) folding
- Sedimentary cover on Paleozoic folding
- Mesozoic folding
- Sedimentary cover on Mesozoic folding
- Cenozoic (Alpine) folding
- Sedimentary cover on Cenozoic folding
- Intensive Mesozoic and Cenozoic vulcanism

DISTRIBUTION

Iron and ferroalloys

- Chromium
- Cobalt
- Iron ore
- Manganese
- Molybdenum
- Nickel ore
- Tungsten

Non-ferrous metals

- Bauxite (Aluminum)
- Copper
- Lead
- Mercury
- Tin
- Zinc
- Uranium

Precious metals and stones

- Diamonds
- Gold
- Silver

Fertilizers

- Phosphates
- Potash

For more information:

80 Water distribution
94 Land use
98 Minerals
99 Iron and ferroalloys
102 Major exports
Traded products

The Industrial Revolution, which began in Britain in the late 18th century, represented a major technological advance in the evolution of human society. It enabled a group of countries to become prosperous by replacing expensive human labor with increasingly sophisticated machinery. In economic terms, manufacturing is the transformation of raw materials, energy, labor, and machines into finished goods, which have a higher value than the various elements used in production.

The economies of countries can be compared by reference to their per capita Gross Domestic Products (GDPs), namely, the total value of goods and services produced within a country in a year, divided by the population. The industrialized, or developed, countries accounted for 16% of the world's population in 2004 with an average per capita GDP of more than US $30,000. On the other hand, low-income developing countries, with small industrial sectors, accounted for 37% of the world's population. Their per capita GDPs are less than $2,000, with some as low as $500.

Kenya, with its low-income economy, had a per capita GDP in 2004 of US $1,200. Agriculture employs 75% of the people, while industry together with services employs 25%. The main industries are the processing of agricultural imports and import substitution (making such necessities as cement, footwear, and textiles). Heavy industry plays only a small part. By contrast, Germany had a per capita GDP in 2004 of $29,800. Agriculture employs only 3% of the population, with 33% in industry and 64% in services. Germany's industrial sector differs greatly from Kenya's, with its emphasis on vehicles, machinery, chemicals, and electronics.

Since the 1970s, some former developing countries in eastern Asia achieved rapid economic growth through industrialization. Despite setbacks in the late 1990s, they demonstrated that a developing industrial sector can transform an economy, which starts off with certain advantages, such as low labor costs. But economic success also depends on such factors as education to provide skills, and regulations that attract foreign investors. China, whose economy grew by more than 9% per year between 2001 and 2005, satisfies many of these criteria, though its record on human rights leaves much to be desired.

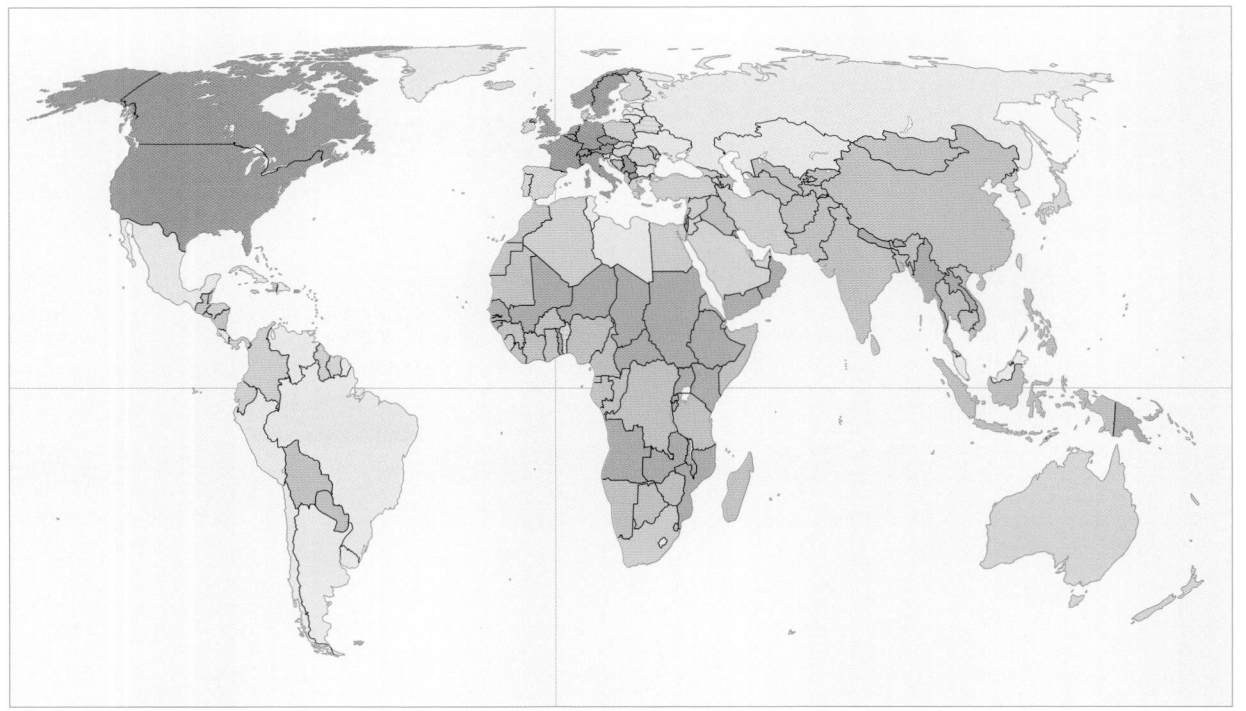

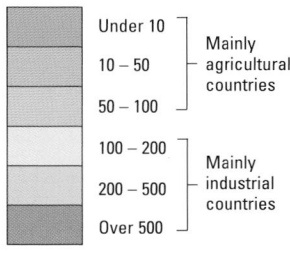

EMPLOYMENT

The number of workers employed in manufacturing for every 100 workers engaged in agriculture (2003)

Under 10	
10 – 50	Mainly agricultural countries
50 – 100	
100 – 200	
200 – 500	Mainly industrial countries
Over 500	

Countries with the highest number of workers employed in manufacturing per 100 workers in agriculture (2003)

Bahrain	3,900
Liechtenstein	3,646
USA	3,242
UK	2,500
Andorra	2,100
Belgium	1,884
Sweden	1,200
Germany	1,193
Israel	777
Austria	725

DIVISION OF EMPLOYMENT

Distribution of workers between agriculture, industry and services, selected countries (2004)

The six countries selected illustrate the usual stages of economic development, from dependence on agriculture through industrial growth to the expansion of the service sector.

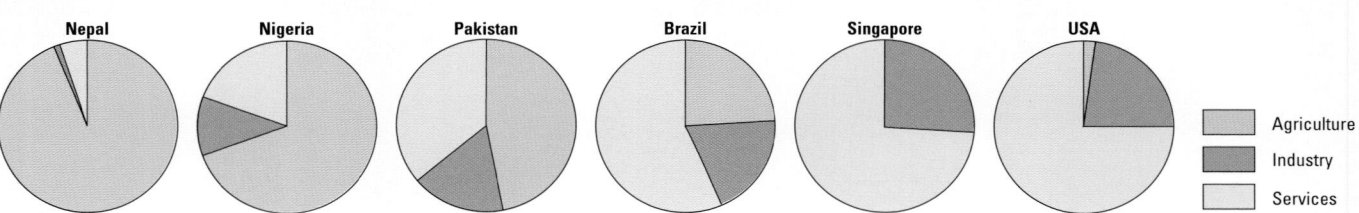

Nepal   Nigeria   Pakistan   Brazil   Singapore   USA

Agriculture
Industry
Services

THE WORK FORCE

Percentages of men and women between 15 and 64 in employment (selected countries)

The figures include employees and the self-employed, who in developing countries are often subsistence farmers. People in full-time education are excluded. Because of the population age structure in developing countries, the employed population has to support a far larger number of non-workers than its industrial equivalent. For example, more than 52% of Kenya's people are under 15, an age group that makes up less than a tenth of the UK population.

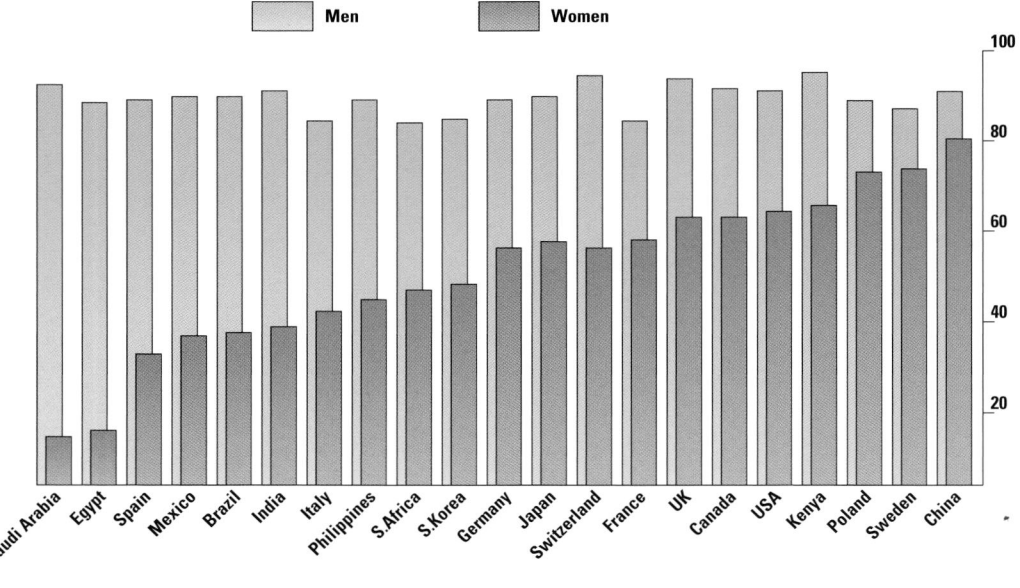

Men   Women

Saudi Arabia, Egypt, Spain, Mexico, Brazil, India, Italy, Philippines, S.Africa, S.Korea, Germany, Japan, Switzerland, France, UK, Canada, USA, Kenya, Poland, Sweden, China

WEALTH CREATION

The Gross National Income (GNI) of the world's largest economies, US $ million (2004)

1.	USA	12,168,500	21.	Austria	263,900
2.	Japan	4,734,300	22.	Indonesia	248,000
3.	Germany	2,532,300	23.	Saudi Arabia	242,900
4.	UK	2,013,400	24.	Norway	237,800
5.	China	1,938,000	25.	Poland	232,900
6.	France	1,888,400	26.	Denmark	220,200
7.	Italy	1,513,100	27.	Greece	185,000
8.	Spain	919,100	28.	Hong Kong	183,500
9.	Canada	905,000	29.	Finland	171,900
10.	Mexico	704,900	30.	South Africa	165,300
11.	India	673,200	31.	Thailand	158,400
12.	South Korea	673,100	32.	Iran	155,300
13.	Brazil	551,700	33.	Portugal	149,300
14.	Australia	544,300	34.	Ireland	139,600
15.	Netherlands	523,100	35.	Argentina	137,300
16.	Russia	488,500	36.	Israel	118,000
17.	Switzerland	366,500	37.	Malaysia	112,600
18.	Belgium	326,000	38.	Venezuela	105,300
19.	Sweden	322,300	39.	Singapore	105,000
20.	Turkey	269,000	40.	UAE	102,700

INDUSTRIAL OUTPUT

Largest industrial output (mining, manufacturing, construction, energy, and water production), US $ billion (2003)

1.	USA	2,256	22.	Belgium	75
2.	Japan	1,120	23.	Switzerland	73
3.	China	746	24.	Austria	61
4.	Germany	693	25.	Thailand	59
5.	UK	475	26.	Poland	56
6.	France	432	27.	Denmark	53
7.	Italy	427	28.	Malaysia	50
8.	Canada	256	29.	Finland	49
9.	Spain	240	30.	Iran	48
10.	South Korea	209	31.	South Africa	45
11.	Brazil	196	32.	Ireland	44
12.	Mexico	150	=	Portugal	44
13.	India	142	=	Turkey	44
14.	Australia	138	35.	Argentina	42
15.	Russia	132	36.	Venezuela	40
16.	Netherlands	127	37.	Greece	39
17.	Saudi Arabia	120	38.	Czech Republic	35
18.	Indonesia	91	39.	Algeria	34
19.	Taiwan	87	40.	Singapore	30
20.	Sweden	85	41.	Egypt	26
21.	Norway	79	=	Philippines	26

INDUSTRY AND TRADE

Manufactured goods (including machinery and transport) as a percentage of total exports (2003)

- Over 75%
- 50 – 75%
- 25 – 50%
- 10 – 25%
- Under 10%
- No data available

Countries most dependent on the export of manufactured goods

Malta	96%
Israel	93%
Japan	93%
South Korea	93%
Switzerland	93%
China	91%

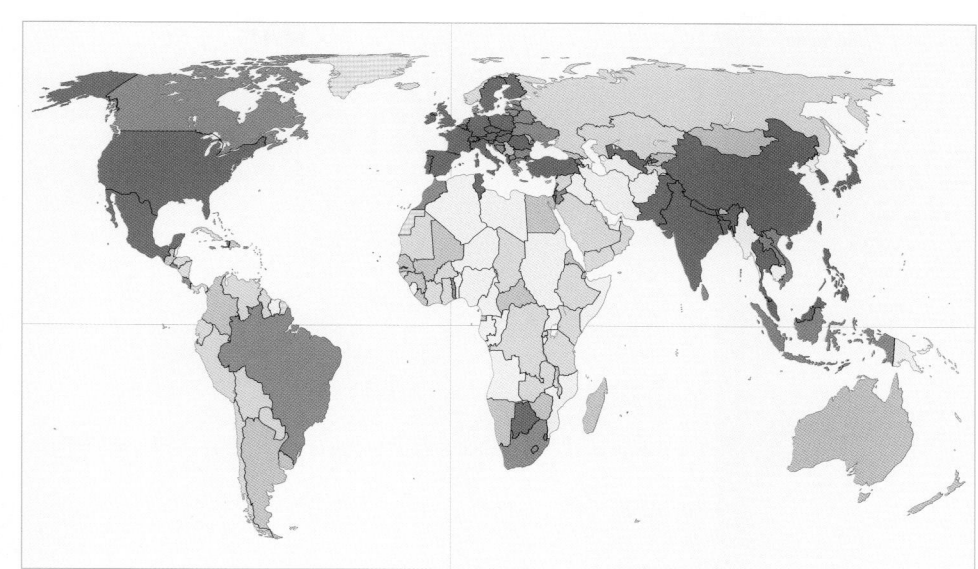

UNEMPLOYMENT

Highest rates of unemployment, percentage of the labor force (2003)

1.	Macedonia	36.7%
2.	Namibia	33.8%
3.	South Africa	29.7%
4.	Algeria	27.3%
5.	Guadeloupe	25.7%
6.	West Bank and Gaza	25.6%
7.	Martinique	22.3%
8.	Botswana	19.6%
=	Poland	19.6%
10.	Bulgaria	17.6%
11.	Slovakia	17.5%
12.	Uruguay	16.9%
13.	Venezuela	15.8%
14.	Argentina	15.6%
=	Dominican Republic	15.6%
16.	Albania	15.2%
=	Serbia & Montenegro	15.2%
18.	Jamaica	15.0%
19.	Croatia	14.3%
=	Tunisia	14.3%

◄ This photograph shows a cement-manufacturing plant in Riverside, California, USA. Cement production figures are often an indicator of the relative prosperity of a country, since they show the construction of roads, dams, and other infrastructure projects (*see the graph below*).

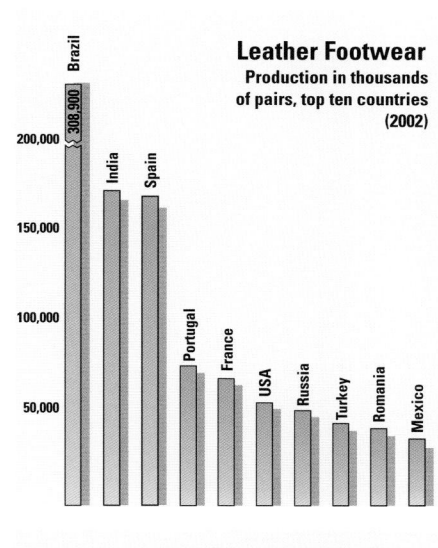

Leather Footwear
Production in thousands of pairs, top ten countries (2002)

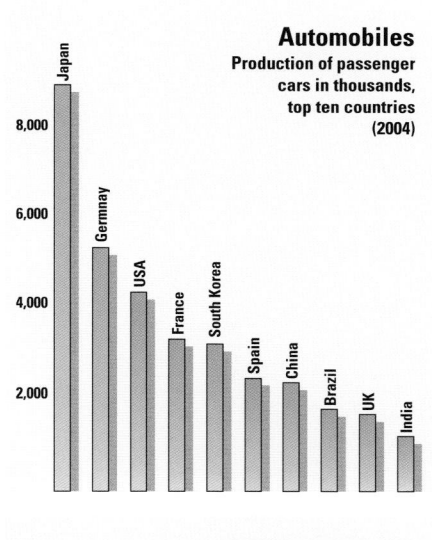

Automobiles
Production of passenger cars in thousands, top ten countries (2004)

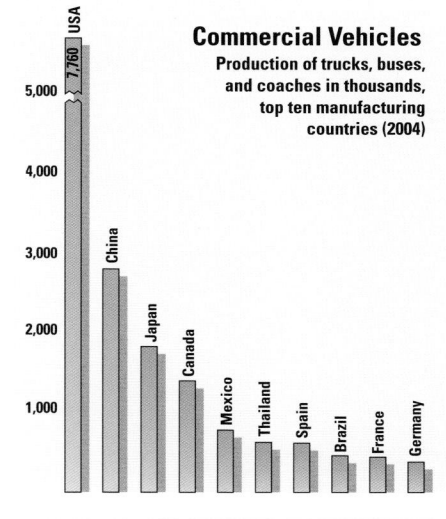

Commercial Vehicles
Production of trucks, buses, and coaches in thousands, top ten manufacturing countries (2004)

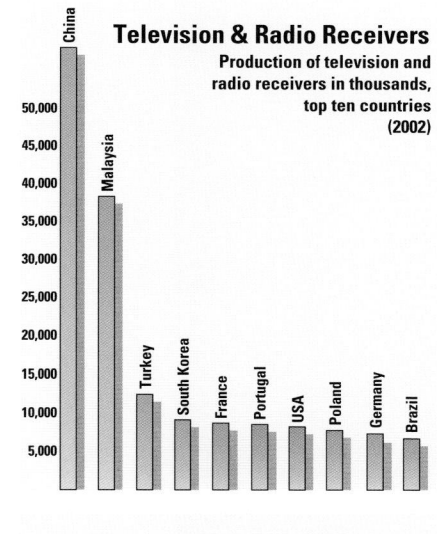

Television & Radio Receivers
Production of television and radio receivers in thousands, top ten countries (2002)

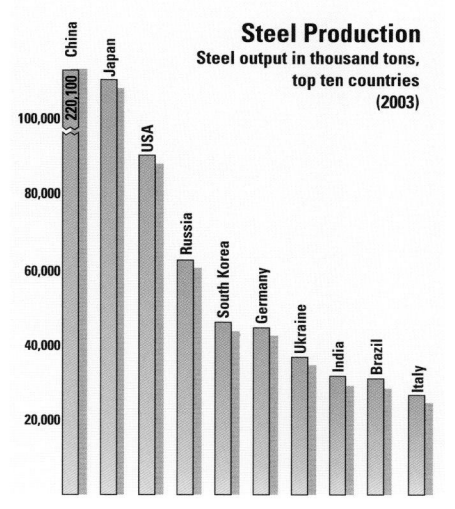

Steel Production
Steel output in thousand tons, top ten countries (2003)

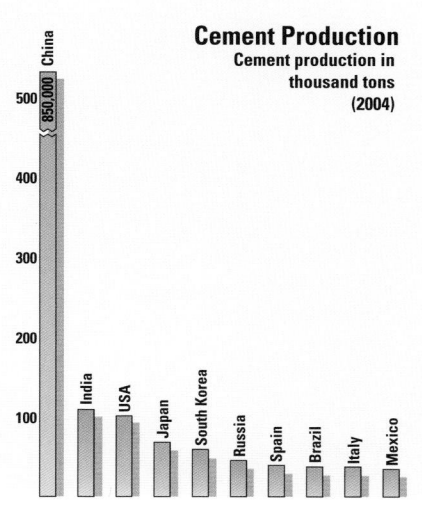

Cement Production
Cement production in thousand tons (2004)

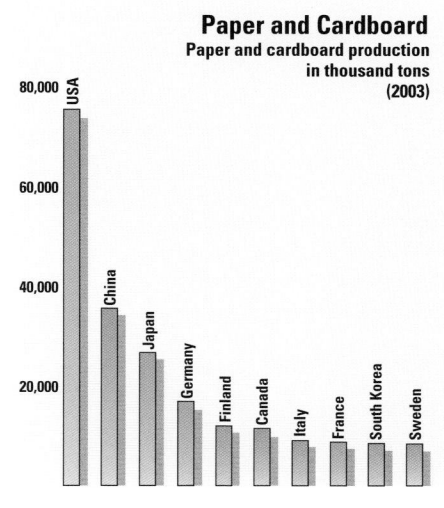

Paper and Cardboard
Paper and cardboard production in thousand tons (2003)

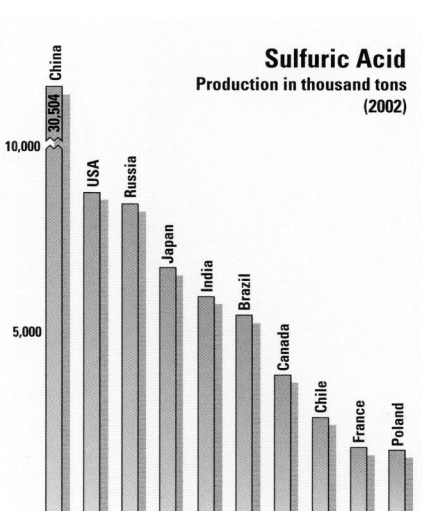

Sulfuric Acid
Production in thousand tons (2002)

For more information:

93 International organizations
97 Movements of oil
98 Minerals
100 Wealth creation
101 Industry and trade
107 Air travel and tourism
   Inflation

Trade played a vital role in the growth of early civilizations and it was later a spur to European exploration and colonization. The colonial powers grew rich by exporting cheap manufactures, such as clothing and footwear, while obtaining primary products from their colonies.

From the late 19th century to the early 1950s, as transport technology improved, primary products, especially oil in the later stages of this period, dominated world trade. However, since that time, manufactures have become the chief commodities in world trade, which is dominated by the industrialized countries. Nearly half of all world trade flows between the developed market economies of the European Union, the United States, and Japan, although a number of Asian economies, notably China, Malaysia, Singapore, South Korea, Taiwan, and Thailand, increased their share in the 1990s.

China's remarkable economic growth meant that, by 2004, it had become the second highest exporter to the United States after Canada. China's low production costs, especially its cheap labor, were estimated to be one-twentieth of those of Japan, making its high-quality exports highly competitive in price. Growth in world trade is regarded as a sign of economic health, as is a favorable balance of trade (or trade surplus) in any country.

WORLD TRADE

Percentage share of total world exports by value (2005)

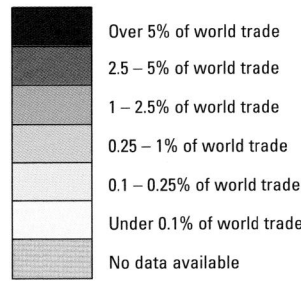

- Over 5% of world trade
- 2.5 – 5% of world trade
- 1 – 2.5% of world trade
- 0.25 – 1% of world trade
- 0.1 – 0.25% of world trade
- Under 0.1% of world trade
- No data available

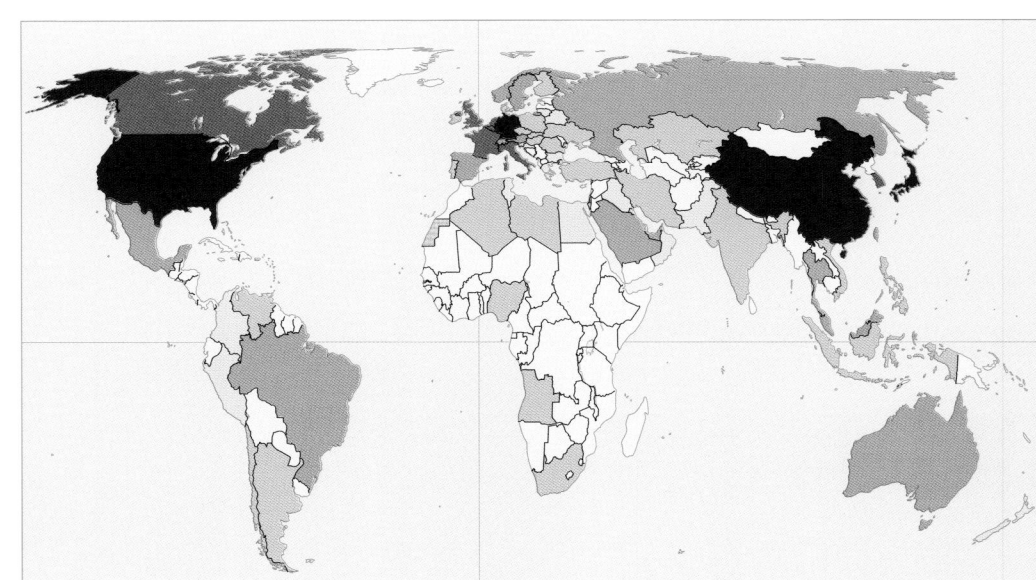

International trade is dominated by a handful of powerful maritime nations. The members of "G8" (Canada, France, Germany, Italy, Japan, Russia, the United Kingdom, and the United States) account for more than half the total. The majority of nations contribute less than a quarter of 1% to the worldwide total of exports. The countries of the European Union account for 35%, whereas the Pacific Rim nations account for over 50%.

DEPENDENCE ON TRADE

Exports as a percentage of GDP (2005)

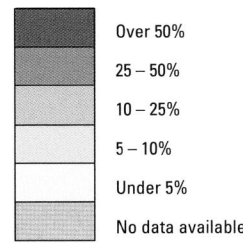

- Over 50%
- 25 – 50%
- 10 – 25%
- 5 – 10%
- Under 5%
- No data available

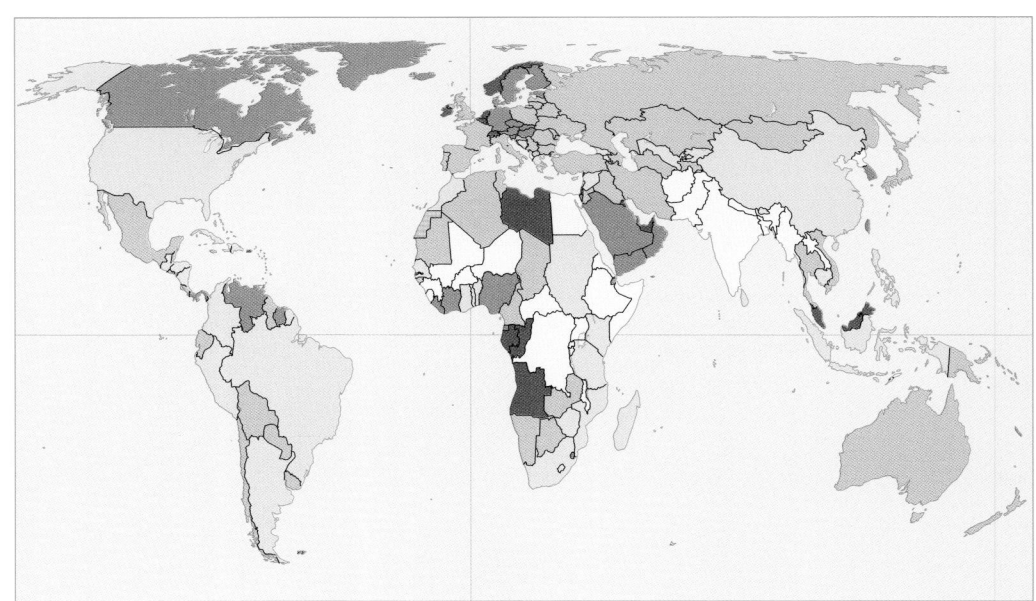

The character of world trade has changed a great deal in the last 50 years or so. While many developing countries still remain heavily dependent on exporting mineral ores, fossil fuels or farm products, such as coffee or cocoa, world trade is now dominated by manufactured goods. Since the 1980s, high-tech products, such as computer equipment, telecommunications gear, and transistors, have become increasingly important.

TRADED PRODUCTS

World merchandise exports by product, percentage of total value (2004)

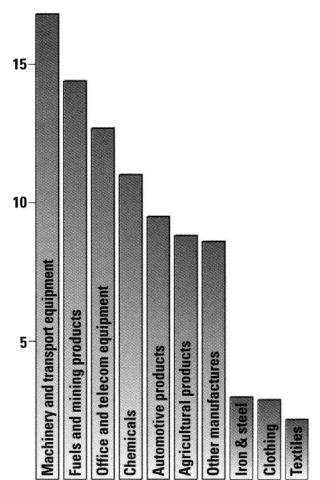

MAJOR EXPORTS

Leading manufactured items and their exporters (2004)

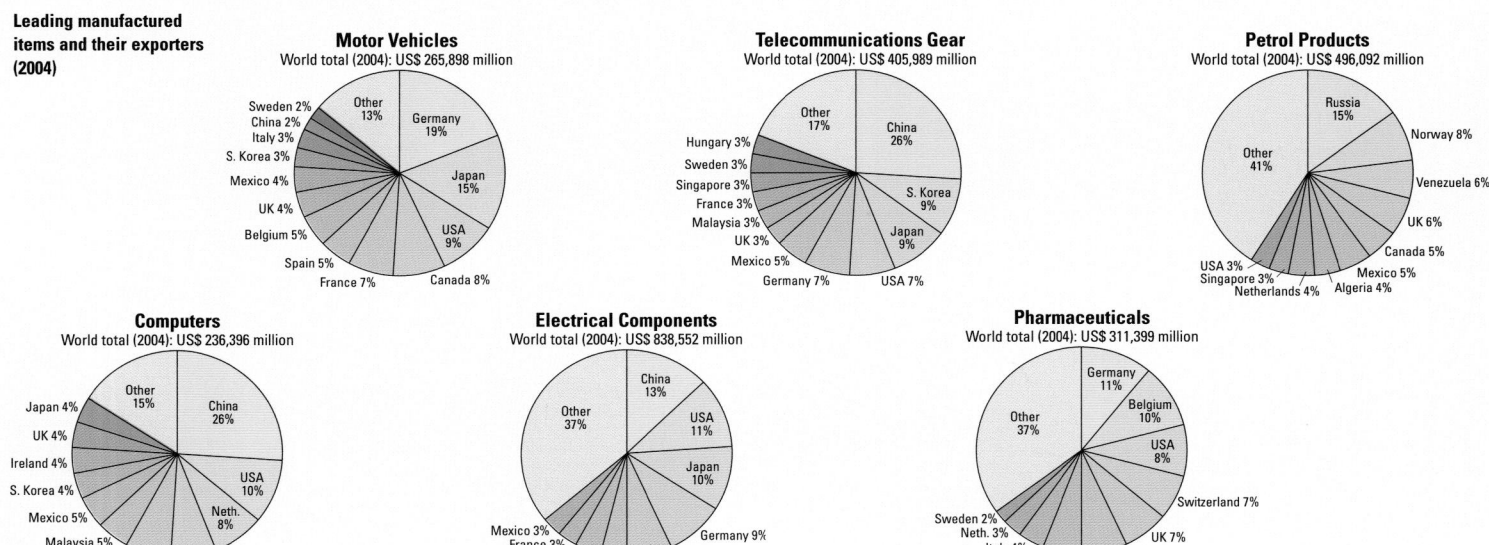

Motor Vehicles
World total (2004): US$ 265,898 million

Germany 19%, Japan 15%, USA 9%, Canada 8%, France 7%, Spain 5%, Belgium 5%, UK 4%, Mexico 4%, S. Korea 3%, Italy 3%, China 2%, Sweden 2%, Other 13%

Telecommunications Gear
World total (2004): US$ 405,989 million

China 26%, S. Korea 9%, Japan 9%, USA 7%, Germany 7%, Mexico 5%, UK 3%, Malaysia 3%, France 3%, Singapore 3%, Sweden 3%, Hungary 3%, Other 17%

Petrol Products
World total (2004): US$ 496,092 million

Russia 15%, Norway 8%, Venezuela 6%, UK 6%, Canada 5%, Mexico 5%, Algeria 4%, Netherlands 4%, Singapore 3%, USA 3%, Other 41%

Computers
World total (2004): US$ 236,396 million

China 26%, USA 10%, Neth. 8%, Germany 7%, Singapore 7%, Malaysia 5%, Mexico 5%, S. Korea 4%, Ireland 4%, UK 4%, Japan 4%, Other 15%

Electrical Components
World total (2004): US$ 838,552 million

China 13%, USA 11%, Japan 10%, Germany 9%, Singapore 7%, S. Korea 4%, Malaysia 4%, France 3%, Mexico 3%, Other 37%

Pharmaceuticals
World total (2004): US$ 311,399 million

Germany 11%, Belgium 10%, USA 8%, Switzerland 7%, UK 7%, France 7%, Ireland 6%, Italy 4%, Neth. 3%, Sweden 2%, Other 37%

WORLD SHIPPING

While ocean passenger traffic is relatively modest nowadays, sea transport still carries most of the world's trade. Oil and bulk carriers make up the majority of the world fleet, although the general cargo category is the fastest growing. Two innovations have revolutionized sea transport. The first is the development of the roll-on/roll-off (Ro-Ro) method where trucks or even trains loaded with freight are driven straight on to the ship, thus saving time. The second is containerization in which goods are packed into containers (the dimensions of which are fixed) at the factory, driven to the port, and loaded on board by specialist machinery.

Almost 30% of world shipping today sails under a "flag of convenience," whereby owners take advantage of low taxes by registering their vessels in a foreign country the ships will never see, notably Panama and Liberia.

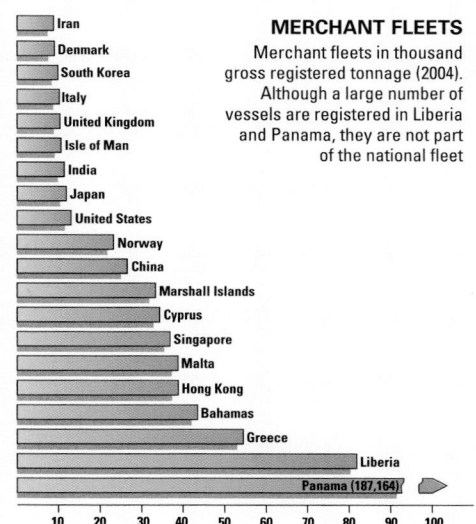

MERCHANT FLEETS

Merchant fleets in thousand gross registered tonnage (2004). Although a large number of vessels are registered in Liberia and Panama, they are not part of the national fleet

Iran
Denmark
South Korea
Italy
United Kingdom
Isle of Man
India
Japan
United States
Norway
China
Marshall Islands
Cyprus
Singapore
Malta
Hong Kong
Bahamas
Greece
Liberia
Panama (187,164)

10 20 30 40 50 60 70 80 90 100

TOP TEN PORTS

Total container traffic, in million TEU (2003)

("TEU" stands for Twenty-foot Equivalent Unit, the equivalent of a standard container)

Hong Kong
Singapore
Shanghai
Shenzhen
Busan
Kaohsiung
Los Angeles
Rotterdam
Hamburg
Antwerp

TYPES OF VESSELS

World merchant fleet by type of vessel and deadweight tonnage (2003)

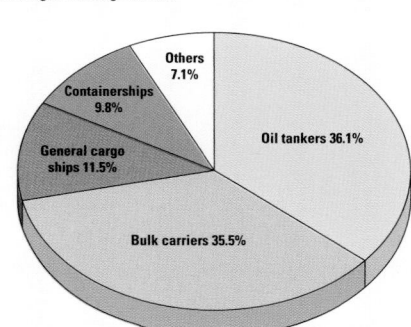

Others 7.1%
Containerships 9.8%
General cargo ships 11.5%
Oil tankers 36.1%
Bulk carriers 35.5%

▲ Shanghai is the largest port in China, lying on the Yangtze River, which is navigable for over 600 miles [1,000 km]. In this image more modern shipping can be seen alongside smaller traditional craft, which are used to trans-ship cargoes to smaller ports.

TRADE IN PRIMARY EXPORTS

Primary exports as a percentage of total export value (2003)

Over 75%
50 – 75%
25 – 50%
10 – 25%
Under 10%
No data available

Primary exports are raw materials or partly processed products that form the basis for manufacturing. They are the necessary requirements of industries and include agricultural products, minerals, fuels and timber, as well as many semimanufactured goods such as cotton, which has been spun but not woven, wood pulp or flour. Many developed countries have few natural resources and rely on imports for the majority of their primary products. The countries of Southeast Asia export hardwoods to the rest of the world, while many South American countries are heavily dependent on coffee exports.

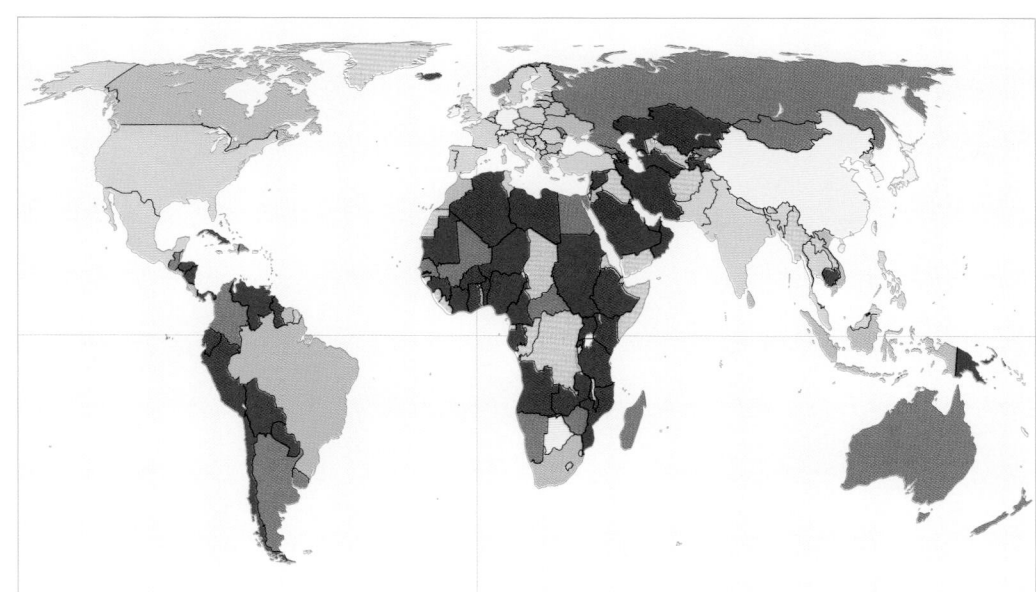

BALANCE OF TRADE

Value of exports in proportion to the value of imports (2005)

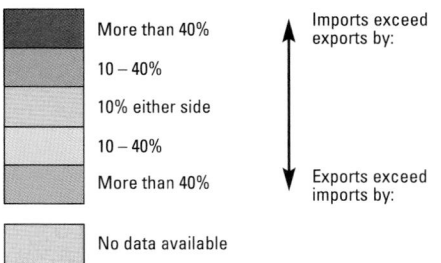

More than 40%   Imports exceed exports by:
10 – 40%
10% either side
10 – 40%
More than 40%   Exports exceed imports by:

No data available

The total world trade balance should amount to zero, since exports must equal imports on a global scale. In practice, though, at least US $100 billion in exports go unrecorded, leaving the world with an apparent deficit and many countries in a better position than public accounting reveals. However, a favorable trade balance is not necessarily a sign of prosperity: many poorer countries must maintain a high surplus in order to service debts, and do so by restricting imports below the levels needed to sustain successful economies.

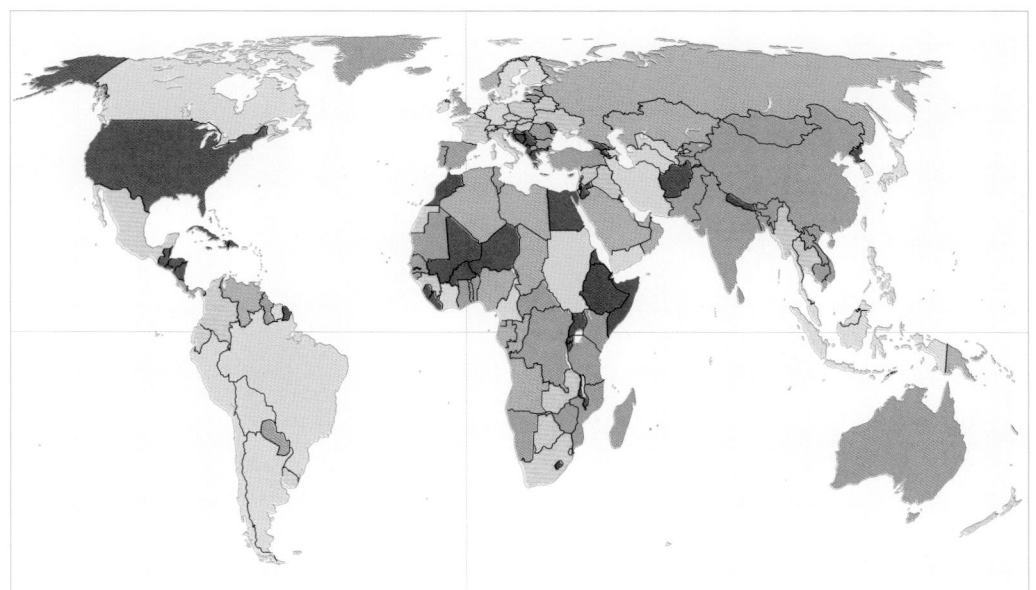

For more information:

80 Water distribution
89 Urban pollution
   Urban advantages
95 Crisis in Africa
   Food and
   population
109 Distribution of
   spending

Until the late 1990s, when the full extent of the AIDS crisis emerged, average life expectancies at birth were rising almost everywhere. By 2003, they ranged from 78 years in high-income economies to 48 in sub-Saharan Africa. These figures represented an enormous advance on the situation in 1880, when citizens of Berlin had an estimated life expectancy of 30 years.

The ravages of AIDS have been greatest in southern Africa. One of the worst affected countries is Botswana, where nearly 40% of the adult population were thought to be infected by 2003. In Botswana, life expectancies were expected to fall to 27 years in 2010 instead of an original estimate of 74 years. However, in much of the world, average life expectancies are still increasing. The rises are attributed to improvements in agriculture and, hence, nutrition, as well as health education, improved sanitation and the quality of drinking water, together with advances in medicine.

Besides AIDS, the people of the developing world are subject to another affliction – malnutrition. The map below shows that in most of Africa, Asia, and Latin America, the average daily calorie supply per person is so low as to cause malnutrition. Malnutrition is a serious condition – among pregnant women it causes high rates of child mortality.

Deficiency diseases occur when people do not have a balanced diet. Protein deficiency causes stunting and kwashiorkor, which can be fatal, especially among young children, while vitamin deficiencies cause such illnesses as beri beri, pellagra, scurvy, and rickets. Iron deficiency causes anemia, while a lack of iodine causes mental retardation.

Infectious diseases, in association with deficient diets, continue to affect people in developing countries. Around the turn of the century, a WHO report stated that infectious diseases cause over 16 million deaths a year. Most of the victims are young and otherwise fit people in developing countries. The major killers are AIDS, cholera, dysentery, malaria, measles, pneumonia, respiratory infections, tuberculosis, and typhoid.

Infectious diseases are much less important as causes of death in developed countries, where cancer and circulatory diseases, such as atherosclerosis and hypertension, which cause strokes and heart attacks, are the most common causes of fatality. Because these diseases tend to kill older people, they are relatively less important in the developing countries where people have shorter lifespans.

Harmful habits are also generally practiced more by the rich than the poor. For example, smoking is an important cause of death in developed countries, while poor diet and high alcohol consumption can badly affect health.

▲ Almost 17% of the world's population does not have access to safe water (the diagram at the bottom left-hand corner of this page shows how this breaks down by continent). This places a huge strain on the millions of mainly women and children who have to walk, collect and carry drinkable water in order to survive. UNICEF is dedicated to help improve this situation and to react swiftly in the case of emergencies such as civil war, as with the case of this man in Liberia.

FOOD CONSUMPTION

Average daily food intake in calories per person (2003)

- Over 3,500 calories
- 3,000 – 3,500 calories
- 2,500 – 3,000 calories
- 2,000 – 2,500 calories
- Under 2,000 calories
- No data available

The daily food intake rated adequate by the World Health Organization is between 2,300 and 2,500 calories per day. Approximately 6 million children under the age of 5 years die of starvation each year, the vast majority in Africa. In 2005, the FAO estimated that 780 million people were undernourished, contrasting sharply with the overconsumption of food in some Western cultures.

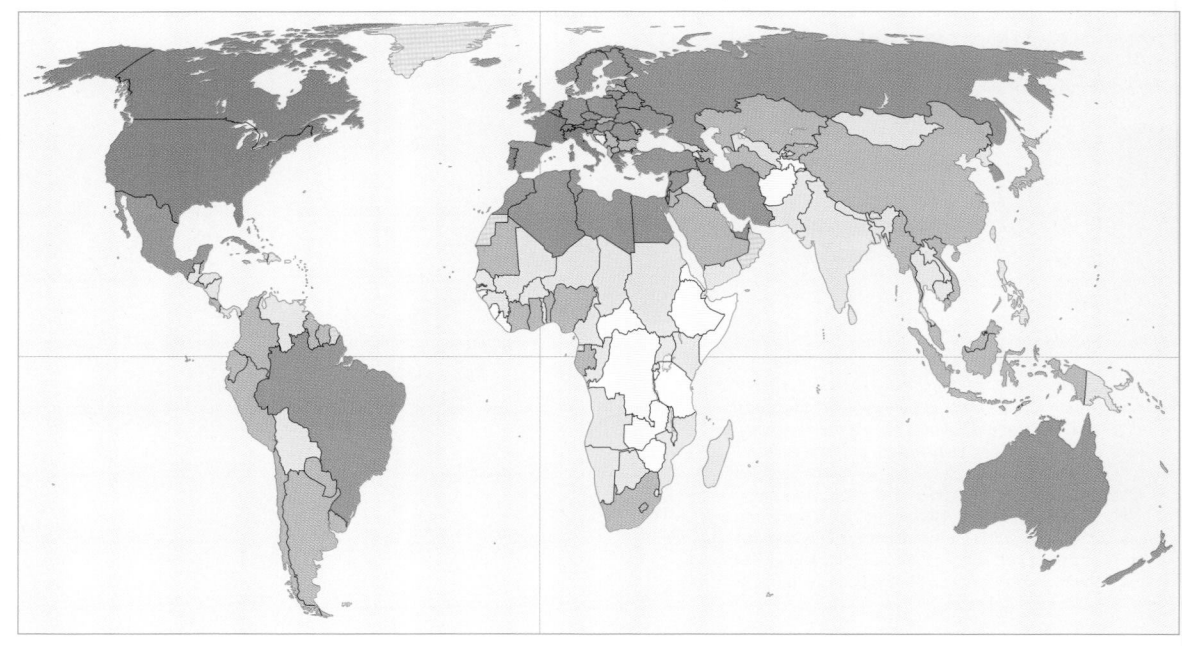

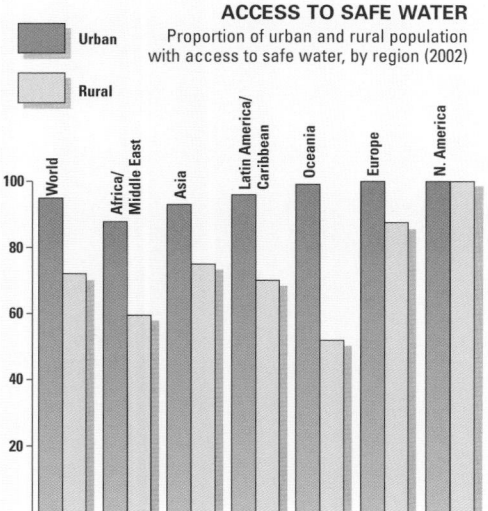

ACCESS TO SAFE WATER

- Urban
- Rural

Proportion of urban and rural population with access to safe water, by region (2002)

Regions: World, Africa/Middle East, Asia, Latin America/Caribbean, Oceania, Europe, N. America

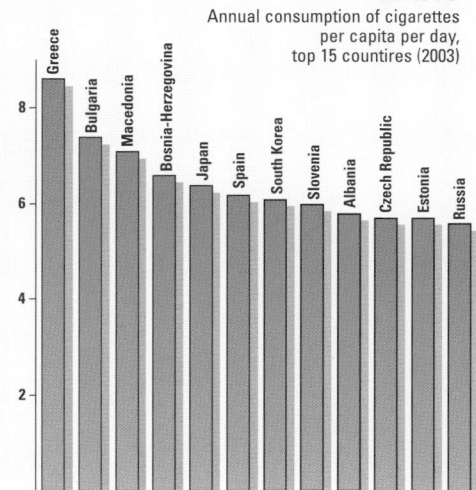

TOBACCO

Annual consumption of cigarettes per capita per day, top 15 countries (2003)

Countries: Greece, Bulgaria, Macedonia, Bosnia-Herzegovina, Japan, Spain, South Korea, Slovenia, Albania, Czech Republic, Estonia, Russia

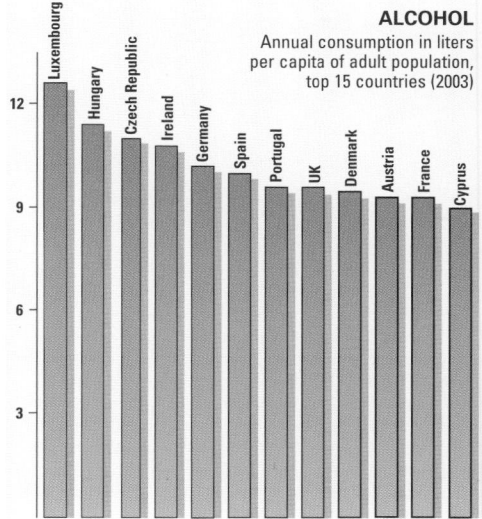

ALCOHOL

Annual consumption in liters per capita of adult population, top 15 countries (2003)

Countries: Luxembourg, Hungary, Czech Republic, Ireland, Germany, Spain, Portugal, UK, Denmark, Austria, France, Cyprus

INFANT MORTALITY

Number of babies who died under the age of one, per 1,000 live births (2004)

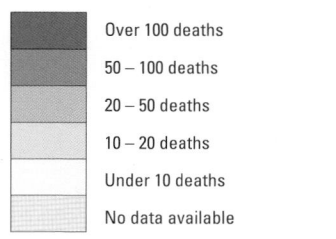

Over 100 deaths
50 – 100 deaths
20 – 50 deaths
10 – 20 deaths
Under 10 deaths
No data available

Highest infant mortality
Angola .... 193 deaths
Afghanistan .... 166 deaths
Sierra Leone .... 145 deaths

Lowest infant mortality
Singapore .... 2 deaths
Sweden .... 3 deaths
Japan .... 3 deaths

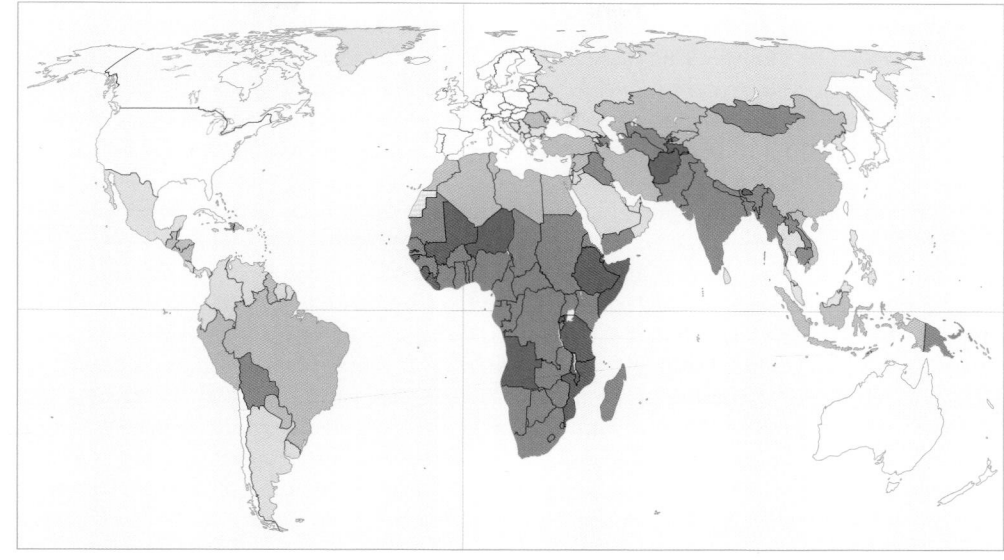

THE AIDS CRISIS

The Acquired Immune Deficiency Syndrome (AIDS) was first identified in 1981 when American doctors found otherwise healthy young men succumbing to rare infections. By 1984 the cause had been traced to the Human Immunodeficiency Virus (HIV), which can remain dormant for many years and perhaps indefinitely: only half of those known to carry the virus in 1981 had developed AIDS ten years later.

In Western countries in the 1990s, most AIDS deaths were among male homosexuals or needle-sharing drug-users. However, the disease is spreading fastest among heterosexual men and women, which is its usual vector in the developing world where most of its victims live.

In 2005, over 20 million people had already died of AIDS and another 40 million were infected with the HIV virus. Around 26 million of them live in sub-Saharan Africa. In some southern African countries, more than a third of the population carries the virus. In South Africa, which has the largest number of HIV infections, about 6 million people were expected to die of the disease between 2002 and 2012.

AIDS also has other serious consequences. A report by UNAIDS and UNICEF stated that, by 2005, 15 million children under the age of 18 had been orphaned by HIV/AIDS.

MEDICAL PROVISION

Doctors per 100,000 population, selected countries (2003)

Although the ratio of people to doctors gives a good approximation of a country's health provision, it is not an absolute indicator. Raw numbers may mask inefficiency and other weaknesses: the high proportion of physicians in Hungary, for example, has not prevented infant mortality rates more than twice as high as in the United Kingdom.

The definition of a doctor also varies from nation to nation. As well as registered medical practitioners, it may include trained medical assistants – an especially important category in developing countries, where they provide many of the same services as fully qualified physicians, including simple operations.

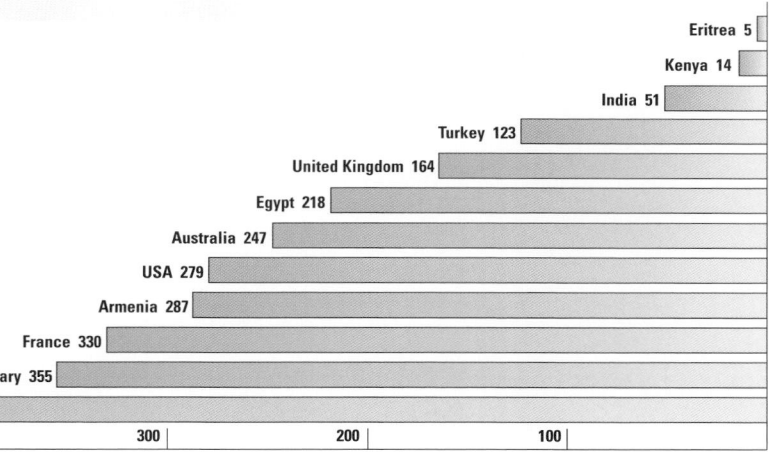

Eritrea 5
Kenya 14
India 51
Turkey 123
United Kingdom 164
Egypt 218
Australia 247
USA 279
Armenia 287
France 330
Hungary 355
Italy 607

600   500   400   300   200   100

AIDS
Cases reported in 2003

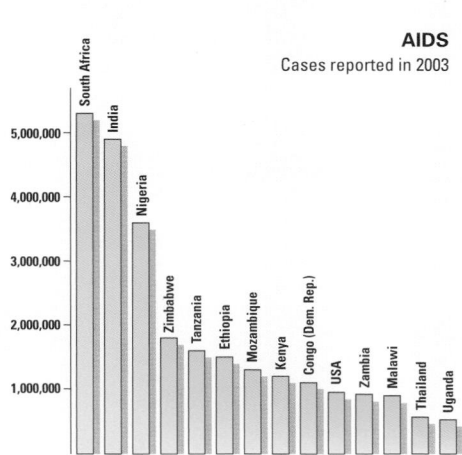

South Africa
India
Nigeria
Zimbabwe
Tanzania
Ethiopia
Mozambique
Kenya
Congo (Dem. Rep.)
USA
Zambia
Malawi
Thailand
Uganda

CAUSES OF DEATH

■ Accidents, poisoning, and violence   ■ Metabolic disorders

■ Respiratory and digestive diseases   ■ Cancers

■ Nervous and circulatory diseases   ■ Infectious and parasitic diseases

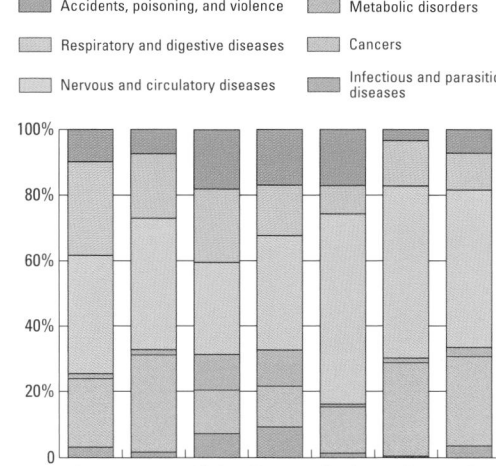

China   Japan   Mexico   Morocco   Russia   UK   USA

EXPENDITURE ON HEALTH

Public health expenditure per capita, in US$ (2001)

Countries with the highest spending		Countries with the lowest spending	
USA	$4,887	Congo (Dem. Rep.)	$12
Switzerland	$3,322	Ethiopia	$14
Norway	$2,920	Chad	$17
Luxembourg	$2,905	Burundi	$19
Germany	$2,820	Madagascar	$20
Canada	$2,792	São Tomé & Príncipe	$22
Iceland	$2,643	Niger	$22
Netherlands	$2,612	Congo	$22
France	$2,567	Tanzania	$26
Australia	$2,532	Sierra Leone	$26

The allocation of limited funds for health care in developing countries is rarely evenly spread – the quality of treatment can vary enormously from place to place within the same country. Urban dwellers tend to have much better access to health provisions than those living in rural areas.

SANITATION
Percentage of population with access to sanitation services, selected countries (2002)

■ Urban
■ Rural

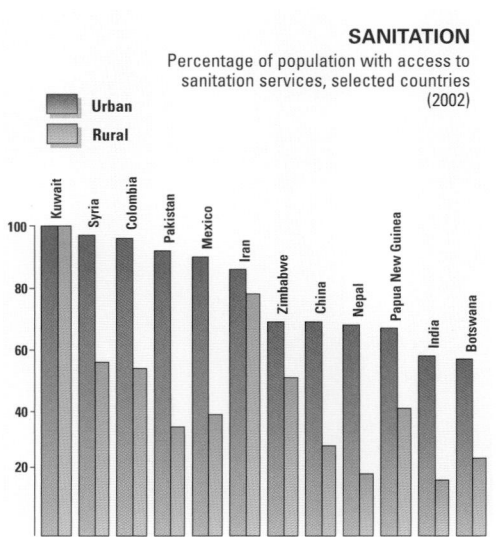

Kuwait
Syria
Colombia
Pakistan
Mexico
Iran
Zimbabwe
China
Nepal
Papua New Guinea
India
Botswana

MALARIA
Reported cases of malaria in millions, selected countries (2003)

Uganda
Tanzania
Mozambique
Congo (Dem. Rep.)
Ghana
Sudan
Nigeria
Madagascar
India
Rwanda
Mali

CIRCULATORY DISEASE IN EUROPE

Diseases of the circulatory system per 100,000 people (latest available year)

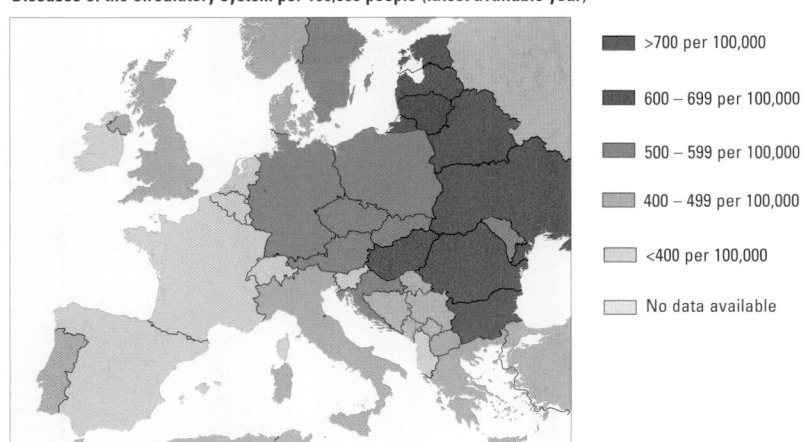

>700 per 100,000
600 – 699 per 100,000
500 – 599 per 100,000
400 – 499 per 100,000
<400 per 100,000
No data available

For more information:
100 Wealth creation
101 Industrial output
102 World trade
    Major exports
103 Balance of trade
109 Distribution of spending

Perhaps the most glaring differences in the world today are those between the rich and the poor. The World Bank divides countries into three main groups based on average economic production expressed in terms of per capita GNI (Gross National Income). They are the low-income economies, including most African countries and much of Asia; the middle-income economies, including most of Latin America and most of the former USSR; and the high-income economies of Canada, the United States, Western Europe, Japan, and Australia.

Per capita GNIs are a measure of the total goods and services produced by a country divided by the population, and then converted into US dollars at official exchange rates. They are useful indicators of a country's prosperity, though, like all statistics, they must be treated with care. For example, the prices for goods and services in China are far cheaper than they are in the United States. China's per capita GNI in 2004 was $1,500 (as compared with $41,440 in the US), but the PPP (Purchasing Power Parity – which adjusts the figure for cost-of-living differences) estimate of China's per capita GNI was considerably higher at $5,890. Another problem with per capita GNIs is that they are averages, which often conceal wide internal variations.

The pattern of poverty varies from region to region. In Latin America, much progress has been made through industrialization, though startling inequalities still exist between rich and poor. China and other countries in eastern Asia, including South Korea and Taiwan, have followed Japan's example in pursuing export-led industrial policies. The success of China's Special Economic Zones, where foreign investment is encouraged, has led to a huge rise in China's per capita GNI.

Solutions to poverty in Africa are much harder to find because of its high population growth, civil wars, natural disasters, and high inflation rates. Although Africa receives more aid than any other continent, aid is only a partial solution. Much aid has been wasted on overambitious projects, in the servicing of huge national debts, or lost by inexperienced or corrupt governments. One initiative in some African countries has been to improve the infrastructure and develop tourism, creating employment and providing much-needed foreign currency.

The International Monetary Fund and the World Bank argue that real economic progress in Africa will be achieved only when African countries create market-friendly economies that encourage trade through export-led manufacturing, while at the same time strictly controlling public spending.

CONTINENTAL SHARES

Shares of population and of wealth (GNI) by continent

These generalized continental figures show the startling difference between rich and poor, but mask the successes or failures of individual countries. Japan, for example, with less than 4% of Asia's population, produces almost 70% of the continent's output. Within countries, the difference between rich and poor can also be startling. In Brazil, for example, the richest 20% of the population own 60% of the wealth.

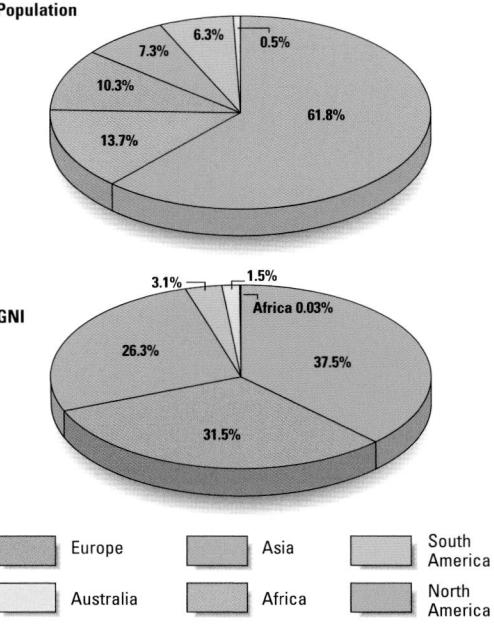

LEVELS OF INCOME

Gross National Income per capita: the value of total production divided by the population (2003)

- Over 400% of world average
- 200 – 400%
- 100 – 200%
- 50 – 100%
- 25 – 50%
- 10 – 25%
- Under 10%
- No data available

Top 5 countries
Luxembourg	$43,940
Norway	$43,350
Switzerland	$39,880
USA	$37,610
Japan	$34,510

Bottom 5 countries
Ethiopia	$90
Congo (Dem. Rep.)	$100
Burundi	$100
Liberia	$130
Guinea-Bissau	$140

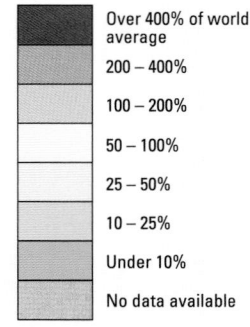
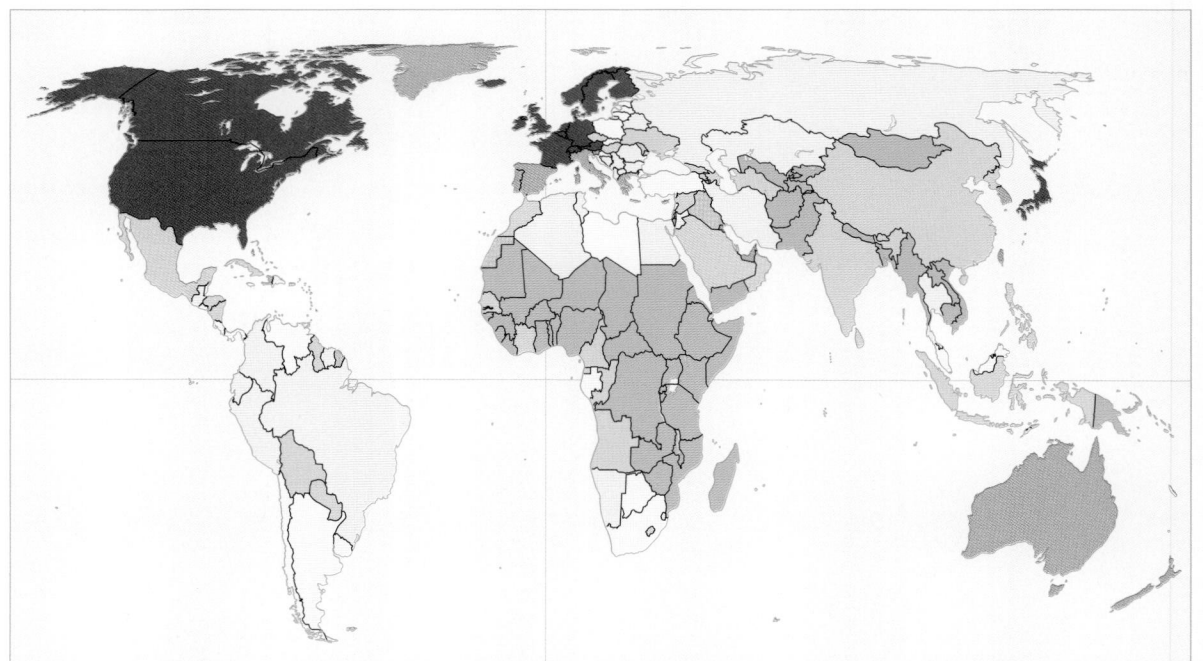

INDICATORS

The gap between the world's rich and poor is now so great that it is difficult to illustrate on a single graph. Within each income group (as defined by the World Bank), however, comparisons have some meaning. The wealth gap in many developing countries, though, is wide, with a small, rich class and a large, impoverished majority, while many high-income countries contain an underclass of unemployed and homeless people.

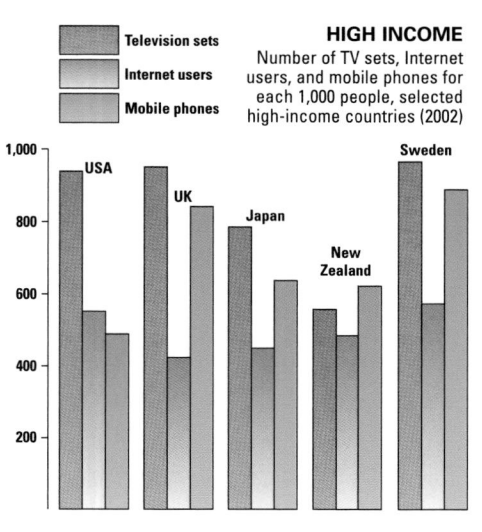
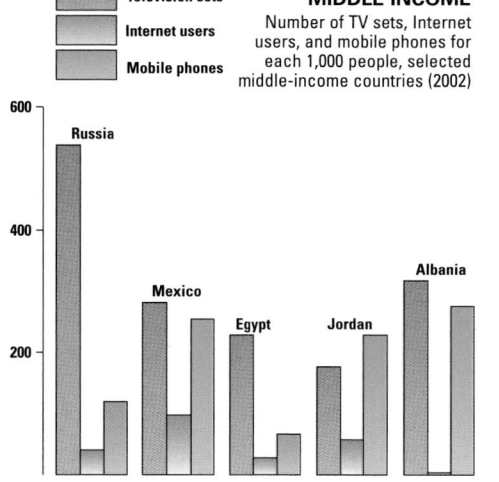
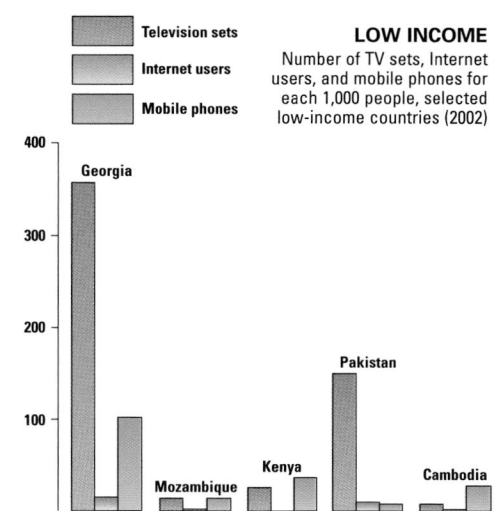

STATE FINANCE

Inflation rates (*shown on the map, right*) are an indication of a country's financial stability and, usually, of its prosperity. Annual inflation rates above 20% are usually marked by slow or even negative growth of the GNI. Above 50%, it becomes hyperinflation and an economy is left reeling.

In the late 1980s and early 1990s, many high-income countries had to contend with annual inflation rates of 10% or more, while Japan, the growth leader, had an average inflation rate of just 1.3% between 1985 and 1994.

Market-friendly policies, including low taxes and state spending, liberal trade policies and a warm welcome for foreign investors, are major factors in countries that have enjoyed rapid economic growth in the decades since 1980. For example, the setting up of Special Economic Zones in eastern China has led to a spectacular rise in that country's per capita GNI.

Other successful countries include South Korea and Singapore, although an Asian market crash in 1997 temporarily halted the dramatic economic expansion of these countries.

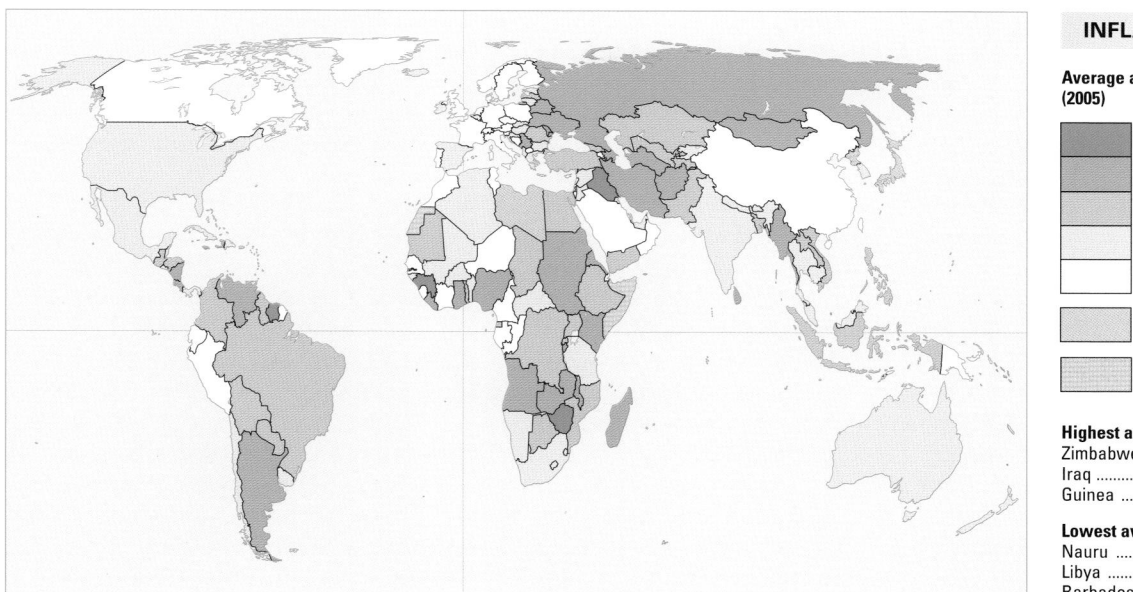

INFLATION

Average annual rate of inflation (2005)

- Over 20%
- 10 – 20%
- 5 – 10%
- 2.5 – 5%
- Under 2.5%
- Negative inflation
- No data available

Highest average inflation

Zimbabwe	246%
Iraq	40%
Guinea	25%

Lowest average inflation

Nauru	–3.6%
Libya	–1.0%
Barbados	–0.5%

GROWTH IN GNI

GNI per capita annual growth rate (1999–2003)

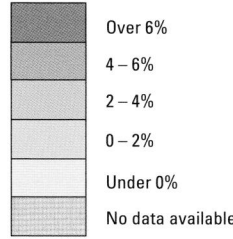

- Over 6%
- 4 – 6%
- 2 – 4%
- 0 – 2%
- Under 0%
- No data available

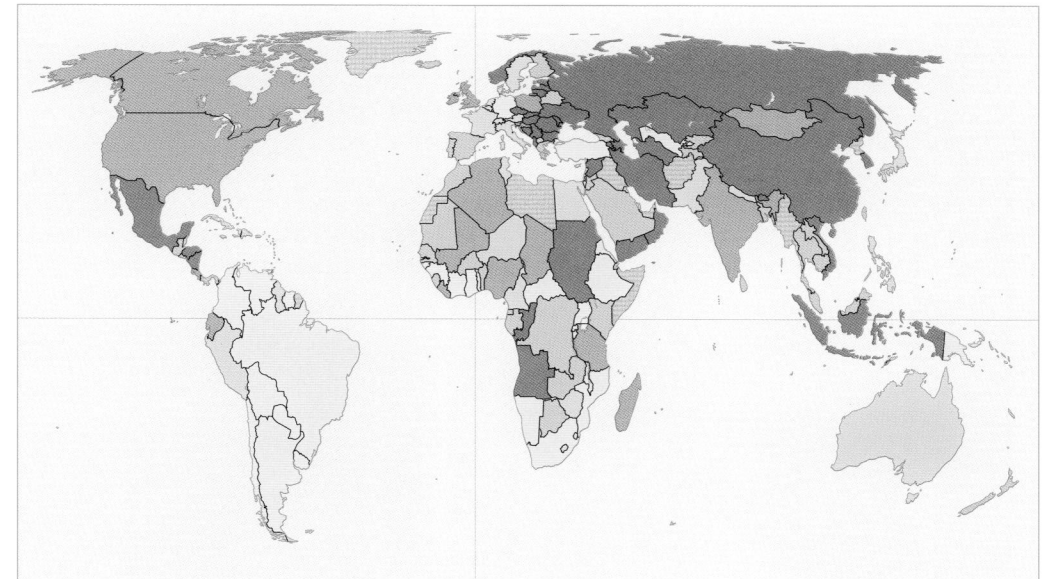

Countries with highest growth rates

Turkmenistan	20.9%
Nicaragua	20.6%
Albania	19.9%
Angola	18.0%
Latvia	14.6%

WORLD AIR TRAVEL

Traffic in passenger miles
Passengers carried (international and local) multiplied by distance flown from airport of origin

- 30,000 million and over
- 6,000 – 30,000 million
- 600 – 6,000 million
- Under 600 million

Major airports
Number of passengers (international and domestic) per year

- ○ Over 50 million
- ○ 25 – 50 million
- ○ 15 – 25 million
- ○ 10 – 15 million

Major air routes
Number of international flights per year

- Over 50 million
- 10 – 50 million
- 5 – 10 million

Projection: Peirce

Leisure and tourism is the world's second largest industry in terms of revenue generated. Small economies in attractive areas are often completely dominated by tourism: in some Caribbean islands, tourist spending provides over 90% of the total income and is the biggest foreign exchange earner. In cash terms, the USA is the world leader: its 2004 earnings exceeded US $74 billion, though that sum amounted to approximately 0.6% of its total GNI. Of the 46 million visitors to the USA, 29% came from Canada and 20% from Mexico. Germany spends the most on overseas tourism; this amounts to US $71,000 million. The next biggest spenders are the USA, the UK, and Japan.

The world's busiest airport in terms of total number of passengers is Atlanta (83.6 million passengers in 2004); London's Heathrow handles the most international passengers.

WORLD'S BUSIEST AIRPORTS
Total passengers in millions (2004)

1.	Atlanta Hartsfield Intl. (ATL)	83.6
2.	Chicago O'Hare Intl. (ORD)	75.4
3.	London Heathrow (LHR)	67.3
4.	Tokyo Haneda (HND)	62.3
5.	Los Angeles Intl. (LAX)	60.7
6.	Dallas/Fort Worth Intl. (DFW)	59.4
7.	Frankfurt Intl. (FRA)	51.1
8.	Paris Charles de Gaulle (CDG)	50.9
9.	Amsterdam Schiphol (AMS)	42.5
10.	Denver Intl. (DEN)	42.4

For more information:

80   Water supply
86   Population density
88   Urban population
89   Urban advantages
92   World's refugees
     War since 1945
100 Employment
     The work force
105 Infant mortality
106 Wealth

Wealth is a basic factor in determining standards of living. Everywhere, the rich have more of everything, including higher average life expectancies, while the poor have to spend most of their income on basic human needs, such as food and clothing. Yet poverty and wealth are relative terms: slum dwellers living on social security in an industrial society feel their poverty acutely, but have far more resources than an average African living in a rural area.

In 1990 the United Nations Development Program published its first Human Development Index (HDI), an attempt to construct a comparative scale by which a simplified form of well-being might be measured. The HDI, expressed as a value between 0 and 0.999, combines figures for life expectancy and literacy with a wealth scale, based on Purchasing Power Parity.

The world's countries are divided into three groups, those with a high HDI (0.800 and above); those with a medium HDI (0.500 to 0.799); and those with a low HDI (below 0.500). In 2003, Norway was top in the world rankings and Niger was bottom. In fact, of the 32 countries with a low HDI, 30 were from Africa, one from Asia, plus Haiti from the Caribbean. Besides having low per capita GNIs, the average life expectancy in these countries was 46 years, while the adult literacy rate was 57%. By comparison, the average life expectancy at birth in countries in the high HDI group was 78 years, while the literacy rate was 98%.

Comparisons between countries with similar per capita GNIs reveal the effects of government actions. For example, the World Bank classifies both India and China as low-income economies, but India's HDI at 0.602 is much lower than that of China, at 0.755. This reflects not only China's economic progress in the 1980s and 1990s, but also differences in average life expectancies (64 years in India and 72 years in China), and adult literacy rates (61% in India and 90% in China).

Disparities in standards of living exist not only between countries but also between individuals, groups and regions within countries. For example, income distribution figures for 2003 show that, in the United States, the poorest 20% of households received less than 4% of the income.

Other contrasts exist in developing countries between rural communities, where incomes are low and basic services are often in short supply, and urban areas, where even those living in slums are generally better off than their rural neighbors. Other striking differences exist between men and women. For example, while adult literacy rates for men and women living in developed countries are more or less the same, large differences exist in many developing countries. In 2003, in countries in the lowest HDI category, only 64% of women were literate, as compared with 73% of men.

Female education is a factor in population control, especially as women's fertility rates appear to fall in direct proportion to the amount of secondary education they receive. This point was acknowledged in 2004 by the UN Population Fund, which defined four main objectives relating to women and population control: the reduction of maternal, infant, and child mortality; better education, especially for girls; universal access to reproductive health services; and gender equality.

Statistical analysis presents many problems of interpretation, especially when trying to define such intangible factors as a sense of well-being. For example, education helps create wealth; but are rich countries wealthy because their people are well educated, or are they well educated because they are rich?

HUMAN DEVELOPMENT INDEX

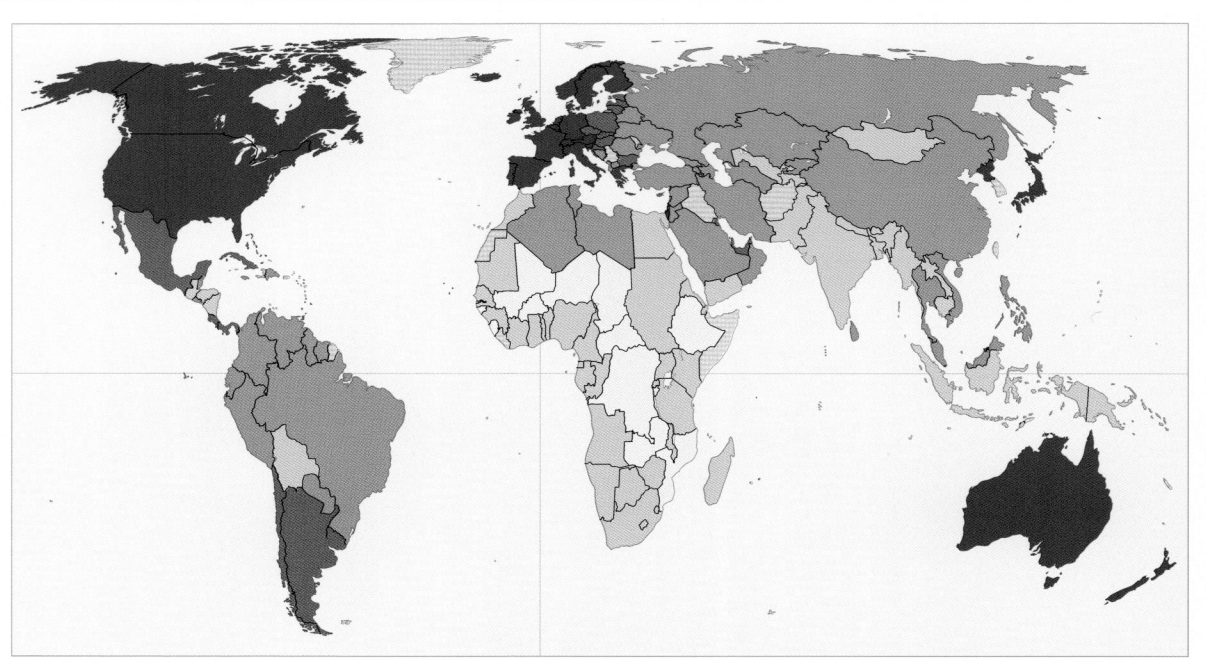

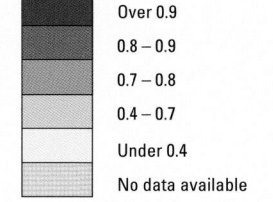

The Human Development Index (HDI), calculated by the UN Development Program (UNDP), gives a value to countries using indicators of life expectancy, education and standards of living in 2003. Higher values show more developed countries.

■	Over 0.9
■	0.8 – 0.9
■	0.7 – 0.8
▨	0.4 – 0.7
□	Under 0.4
▨	No data available

Highest values
Norway 0.963
Iceland 0.956
Australia 0.955
Canada 0.949
Luxembourg 0.949

Lowest values
Niger 0.281
Sierra Leone 0.298
Burkina Faso 0.317
Mali 0.333
Chad 0.341

EDUCATION

The developing countries made great efforts in the 1970s and 1980s to bring at least a basic education to their people. In all but the poorest nations, primary school enrolments rose above 60%. However, figures often include teenagers or young adults, and there are still 300 million children worldwide who receive no schooling at all. A lack of resources has restricted the development of secondary and higher education. Most primary school education is free in the poorer countries, but fees are often paid for secondary and higher education, thus heightening the differences between rich and poor.

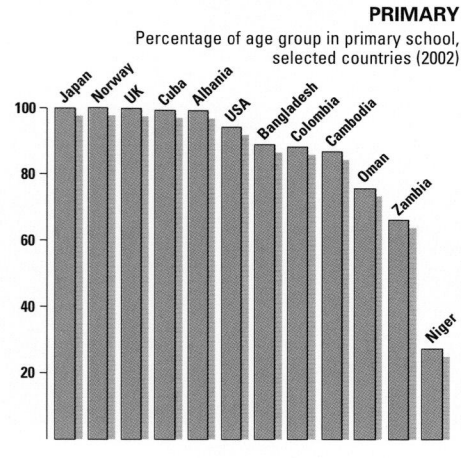

PRIMARY
Percentage of age group in primary school, selected countries (2002)

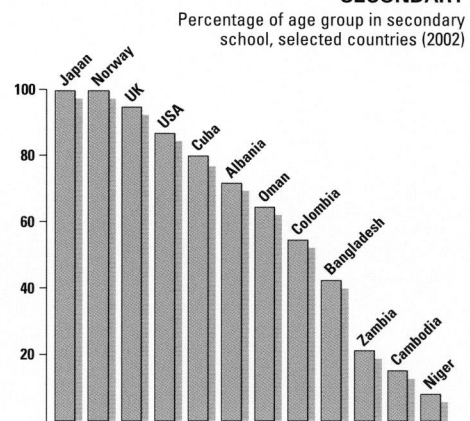

SECONDARY
Percentage of age group in secondary school, selected countries (2002)

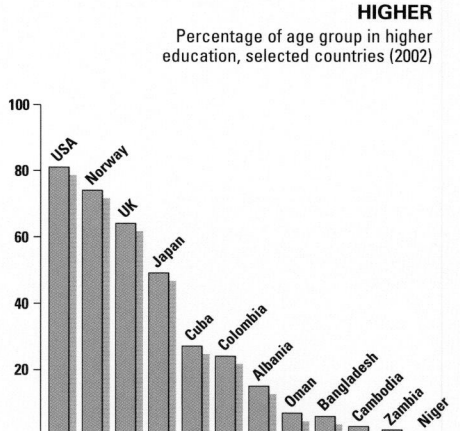

HIGHER
Percentage of age group in higher education, selected countries (2002)

DISTRIBUTION OF SPENDING

Percentage share of household spending

A high proportion of the average income of households in developing nations is spent on basic needs such as food and clothing. In most Western countries food and clothing account for less than 25% of expenditure.

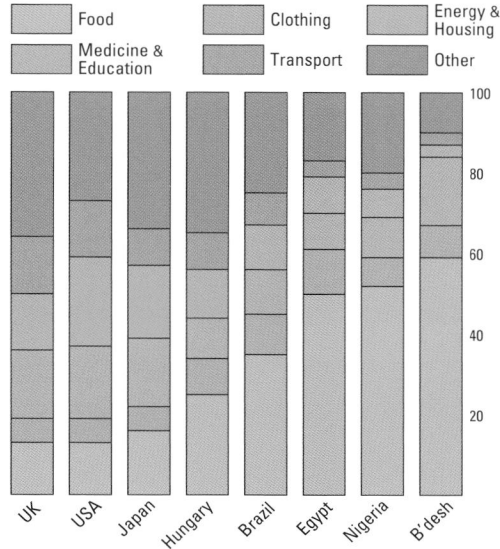

- Food
- Medicine & Education
- Clothing
- Transport
- Energy & Housing
- Other

STANDARDS OF LIVING IN THE USA BY RACE, AGE, AND REGION

A comparison of measures of income and education, by selected characteristics (2003)

Median income per household (US $), by age and region

15–24 years	27,053
25–34 years	44,779
35–44 years	55,044
45–54 years	60,252
55–64 years	49,215
65 years and over	23,787
Northeast	46,742
Midwest	44,732
South	39,823
West	46,820

Per capita income (US $), by race and Hispanic origin of householder

ALL RACES	23,276
White	24,442
Black	15,583
Asian and Pacific Is.	23,654
Hispanic (any race)	13,492

The poorest 20% of households received just 3.6% of the income, whereas the richest 20% received 48.2%.

Percentage of persons aged 25 and over who have completed High School, by race or origin

ALL RACES	1975	62.5
	2004	85.2
White	1975	64.5
	2004	85.8
Black	1975	42.5
	2004	80.6
Hispanic	1975	37.9
	2004	58.4

FERTILITY AND EDUCATION

Fertility rates compared with female education, selected countries (2000–2005)

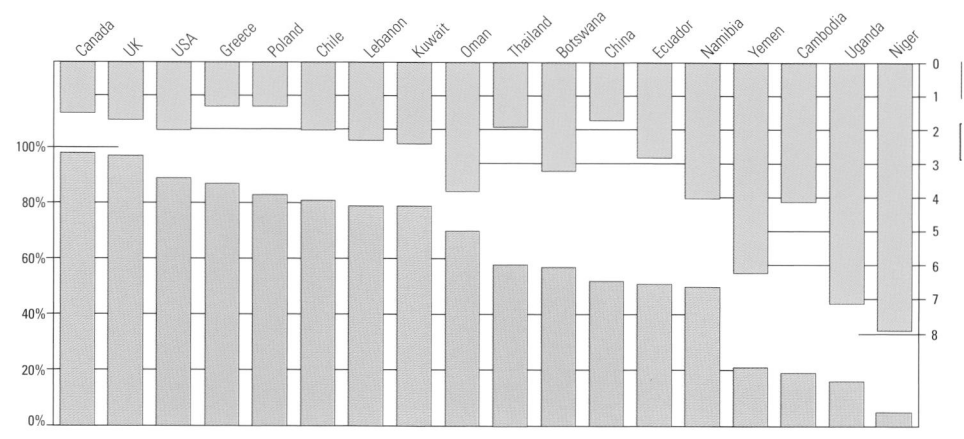

Access to secondary education is closely linked to low fertility rates in developed countries. By contrast, in many developing countries, women's lives are dominated by agriculture, or they lack access to secondary and higher education for cultural reasons, as in Muslim countries. Such disparities are reflected in women's parliamentary representation which is only one-seventh that of men, despite the emergence of such figures as Mrs Indira Gandhi, India's former prime minister. Female wages are also, on average, only two-thirds of those of men.

- Fertility rate: average number of children borne per woman
- Percentage of females aged 12–17 in secondary education

GENDER DEVELOPMENT INDEX

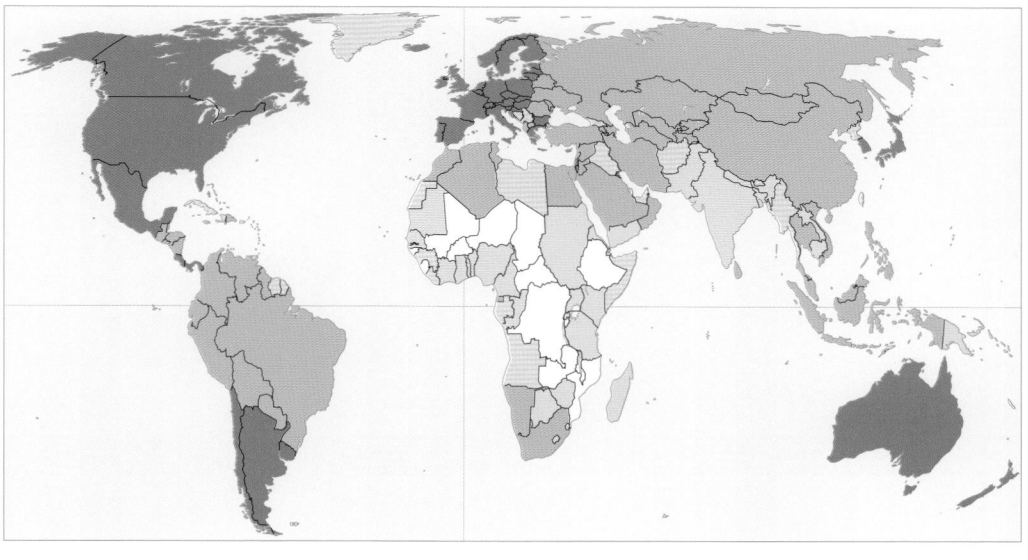
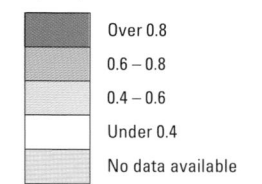

The Gender Development Index (GDI) shows economic and social differences between men and women by using various UNDP indicators (2003). Countries with higher values of GDI have more equality between men and women.

- Over 0.8
- 0.6 – 0.8
- 0.4 – 0.6
- Under 0.4
- No data available

Highest values

Norway	0.960
Australia	0.954
Iceland	0.953
Sweden	0.947

Lowest values

Niger	0.271
Sierra Leone	0.279
Burkina Faso	0.311
Chad	0.322

REGIONAL INEQUALITY IN ITALY

The southern part of Italy, known as the *Mezzogiorno*, has been described as one of the poorest parts of the European Union. It is identifiable on the map (*right*) as all the regions with a GDP per capita of less than US $25,000 (including the two islands of Sicily and Sardinia), plus Abruzzi whose capital is L'Aquila.

The *Mezzogiorno* region suffers from a lack of energy resources, minerals, industry, commerce, services, and skilled labor. As a result, standards of living in the region are well below the rest of Italy. Employment is predominantly agricultural and small-scale.

The north of Italy accounts for 60% of the population but 80% of the GDP, whereas the *Mezzogiorno* accounts for 40% of the population and only 20% of the GDP. Manpower surpluses in the south led to emigration to other parts of Europe and the Americas.

It has also led, especially in the last 50 years, to inter-regional migration from the islands and the southern mainland to the north. The main regions attracting migrants are the northwest (the prosperous Liguria–Piedmont–Lombardy triangle, with its great industrial cities of Genoa, Milan, and Turin) and the Venetia region in the northeast.

As a result, the north has experienced much higher population growth rates than the rest of Italy.

Gross Domestic Product (GDP) per capita in Italy, by region (2002)

- Over US $35,000
- $30,000 – $35,000
- $25,000 – $30,000
- $20,000 – $25,000
- Under $20,000

The average GNI (Gross National Income) per capita for Italy was US $21,560. By comparison, the GNI for the UK was $28,350; for the USA $37,610; and for the EU $22,850.

The number of inhabitants per doctor, another social indicator, varies from less than 500 in the northwest of Italy to over 800 in the far south (the *Mezzogiorno*), with a national average of 607.

◄ These two images illustrate the reality of suburban life for people at either end of the economic scale. On the far left is part of a huge area of "tract housing" in California, where large houses of a similar design are laid out by a developer, complete with gardens, drives, and swimming pools. On the right is a much more haphazard arrangement of home-built, rudimentary shelters, many without sanitation and most with no electricity, in Crossroads Township, outside Cape Town in South Africa.

– CHICAGO, ILLINOIS, USA –
At the southern end of Lake Michigan, Chicago is the third largest metropolitan area in the US, with a total population of over 8 million people. The central area of the agglomeration is covered in this image. The town developed as a major transport hub for the Midwest, with a complex road and rail network, and a large port trading on a global scale. The runway pattern of the second busiest airport in the world, O'Hare International, can be seen at the top of the image. [Map page 119]

WORLD
CITIES

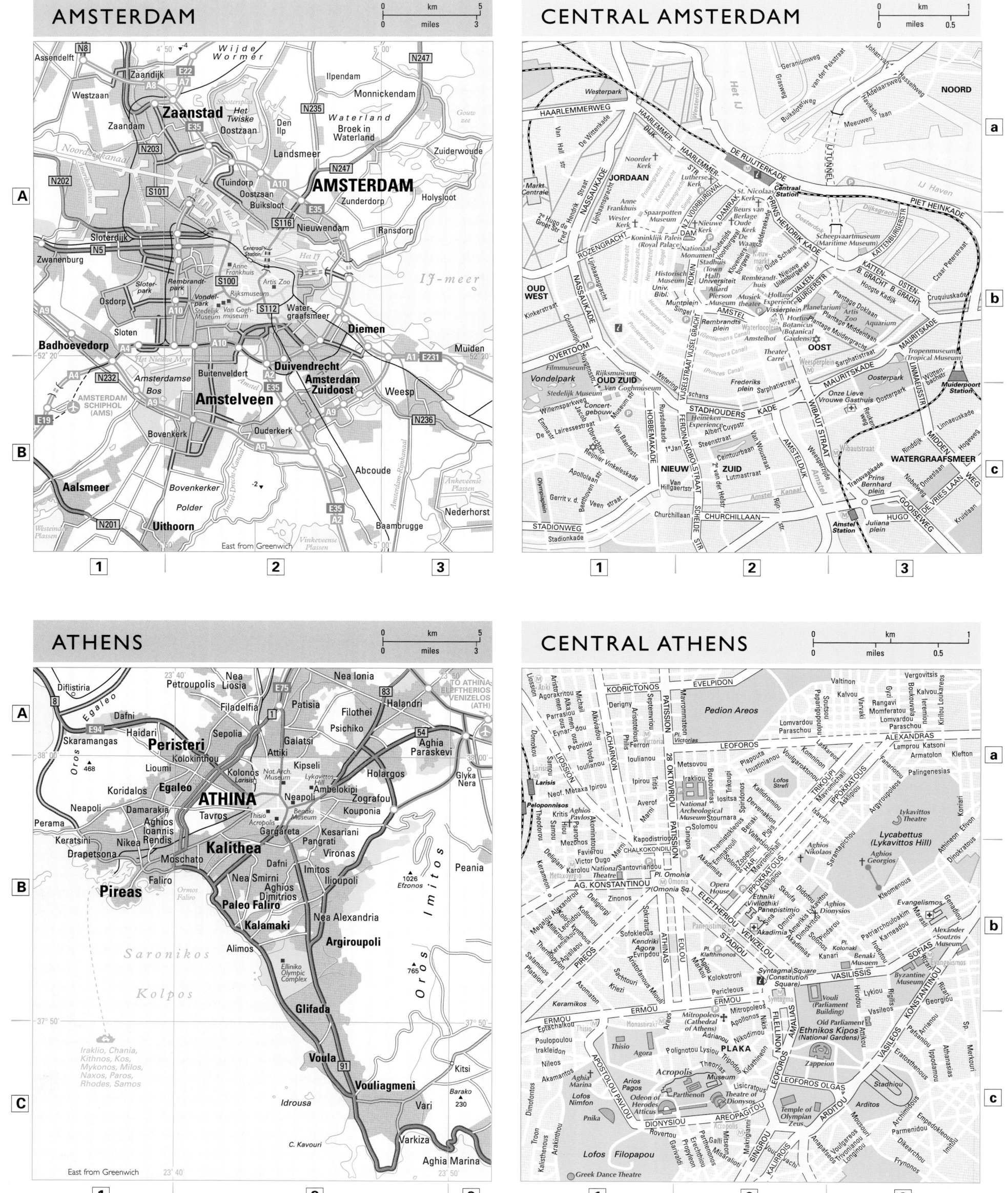

AMSTERDAM

CENTRAL AMSTERDAM

ATHENS

CENTRAL ATHENS

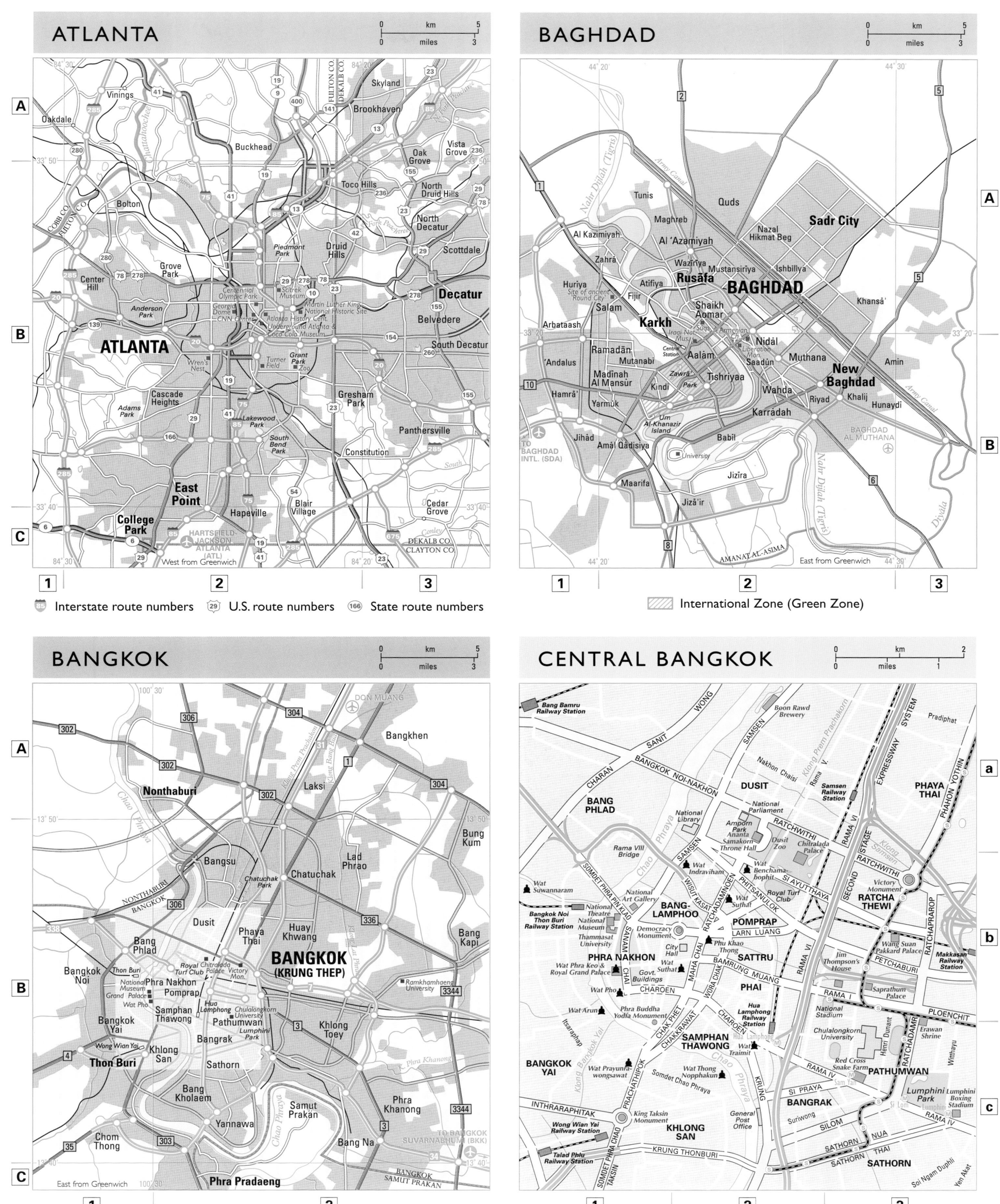

BARCELONA

CENTRAL BARCELONA

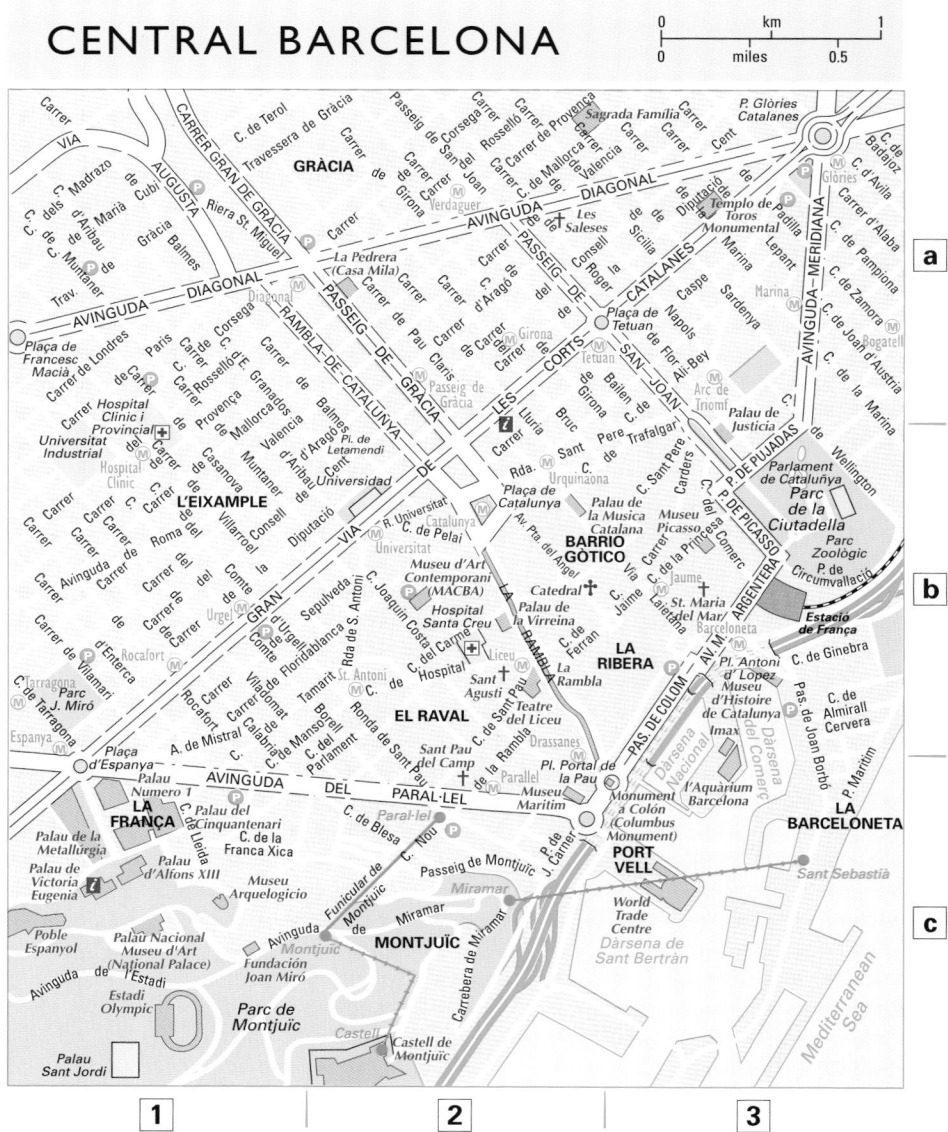

BEIJING

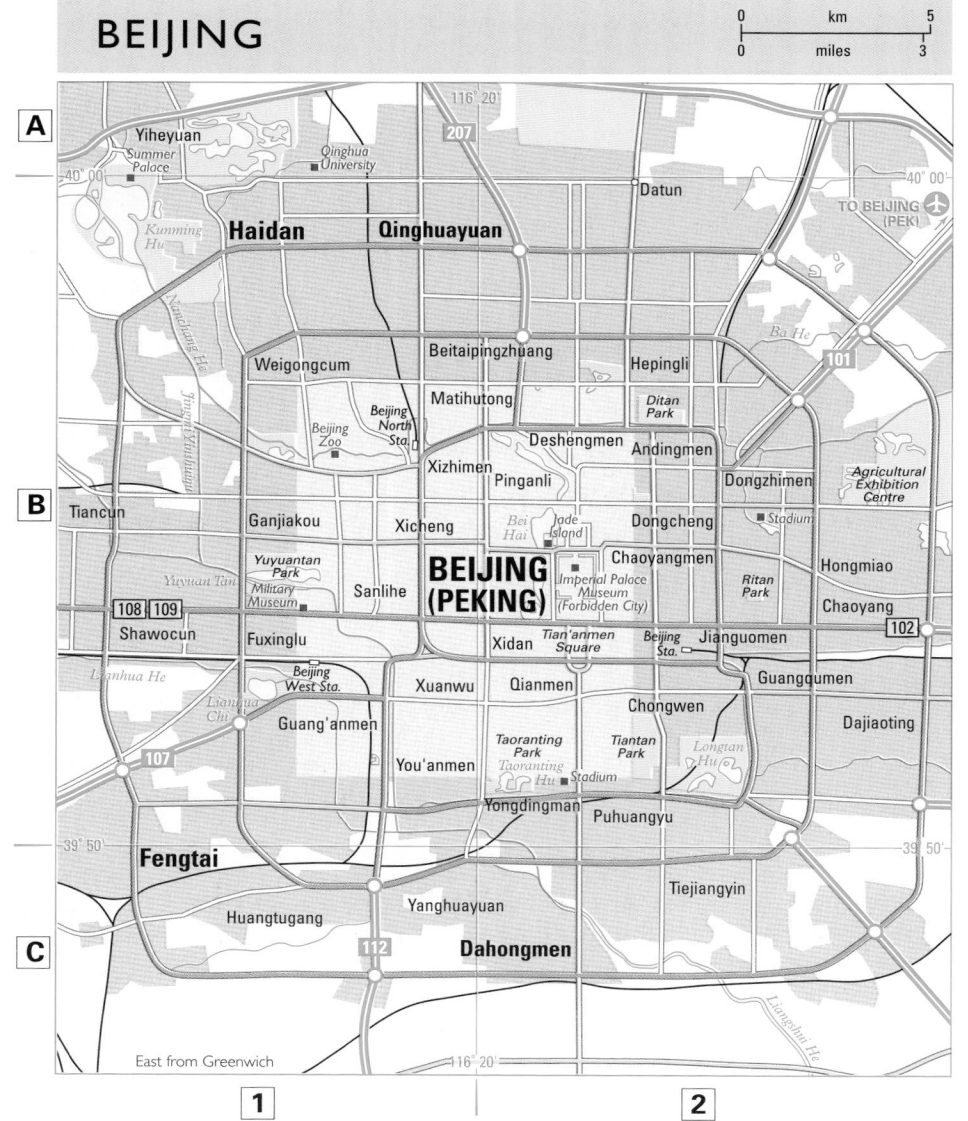

CENTRAL BEIJING

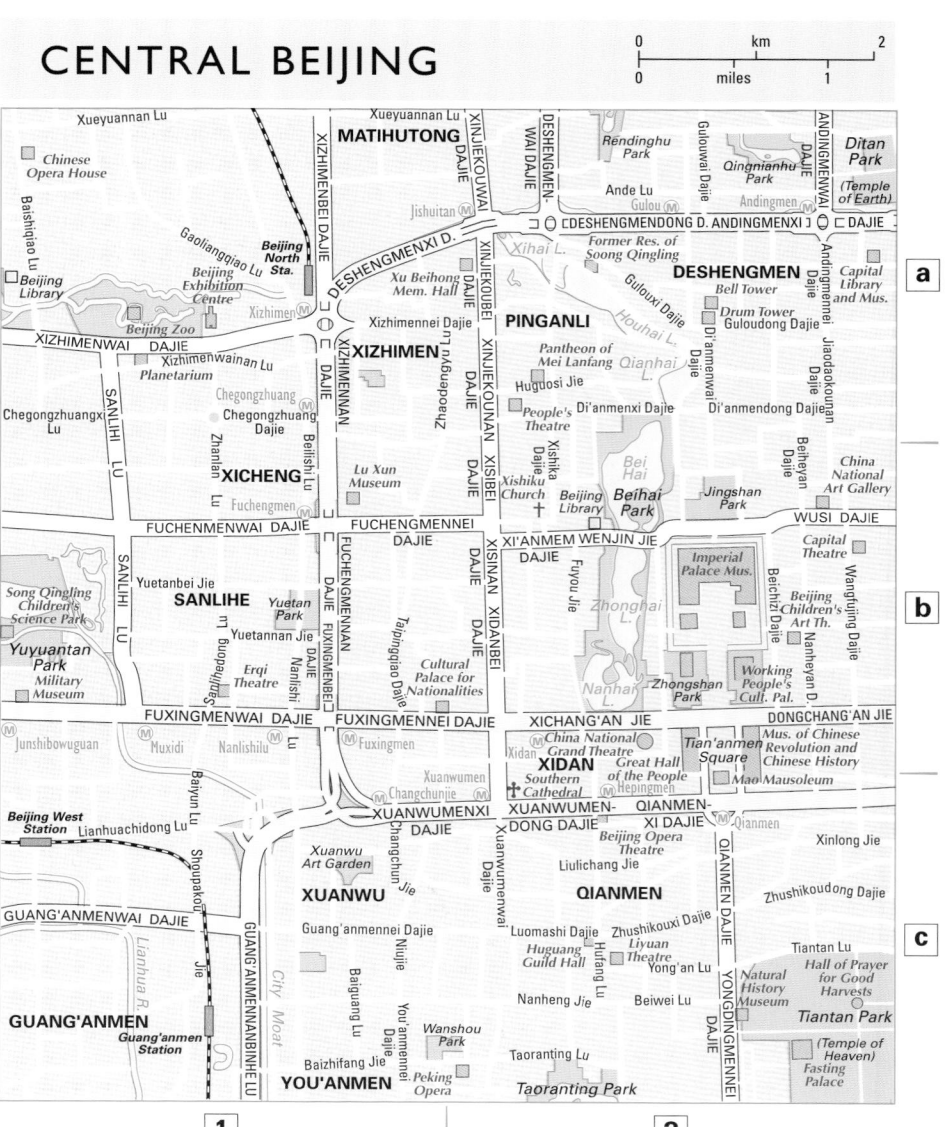

BERLIN

km 5
miles 3

Schönwalde · Hennigsdorf · Hermsdorf · Lübars · Blankenfelde · Karow · Schwaneck · Birkholzaue · Löhme · Werneuchen
Nieder Neuendorf · Schulzendorf · Heiligensee · Waidmannslust · Bucholz · Neu Buch · Lindenberg · Birkholz · Seefeld · Rudolfshöhe
Alter Finkenkrug · Siedlung Schönwalde · Tegelort · Scharfenberg · Tegel · Wittenau · Niederschönhausen · Rosenthal · Blankenburg · Neu Lindenberg · Wegendorf · Krummensee · Neuhönow
Waldheim · Falkensee · Johannesstift · Haselhorst · BERLIN-TEGEL (TXL) · Pankow · Heinersdorf · Malchow · Wartenberg · Ahrensfelde · Trappenfelde · Altlandsberg Nord
Falkenhagen · Reinickendorf · Weissensee · Hohenschönhausen · Marzahn · Mehrow · Eiche · Eiche Süd · Seeberg · Friedrichslust · Altlandsberg
Döberitz · Spandau · Zitadelle · Volkspark Jungfernheide · Siemensstadt · Wedding · Prenzlauerberg · Hellersdorf · Hönow · Friedersdorf Nord
Dallgow · Staaken · Charlottenburg · Schlossgarten Charlottenburg · Tiergarten · Mitte · Volkspark Friedrichshain · Lichtenburg · Neuenhagen · Birkenstein · Bollensdorf
Seeburg · Olympia Stadion · Deutsche Oper · Berlin Dom · Friedrichshain · Wuhlgarten · Dahlwitz-Hoppegarten
Universität · Zoo · Tiergarten · Brandenburger Tor · BERLIN · Kreuzberg · Friedrichsfelde · Kaulsdorf · Mahlsdorf · Vogelsdorf
Teufelsberg · Wilmersdorf · Schöneberg · Treptow · Karlshorst · Biesdorf · Münchehofe
Gatow · Grunewald · Schmargendorf · Neukölln · BERLIN TEMPELHOF (THF) · Heidemühle · Kleinschönebeck
Krampnitz · Gross Glienicke · Dahlem · Friedenau · Tempelhof · Niederschöneweide · Oberschöneweide · Waldesruh · Schöneiche · Gratzwalde
Neu Fahrland · Steglitz · Britz · Johannisthal · Fichtenau · Schönblick
Nedlitz · Sacrow · Pfaueninsel · Schwanenwerder · Zehlendorf · Mariendorf · Aldershof · Köpenick · Friedrichshagen · Woltersdorf
Nikolassee · Lichterfelde · Lankwitz · Buckow · Grünau · Grosse Müggelsee · Rahnsdorf · Wilhelmshagen · Springeberg
Schloss Babelsberg · Wannsee · Buckow · Rudow · Altglienicke · Wendenschloss · Müggelberge · Müggelheim · Erkner · Neu Buchhorst
Potsdam · Klein Gleinicke · Kleinmachnow · Seehof · Osdorf · Marienfelde · Grossziethen · Bohnsdorf · Karolinenhof · Gosen
Potsdam Museum · Teltow · BERLIN-SCHÖNEFELD (SXF)

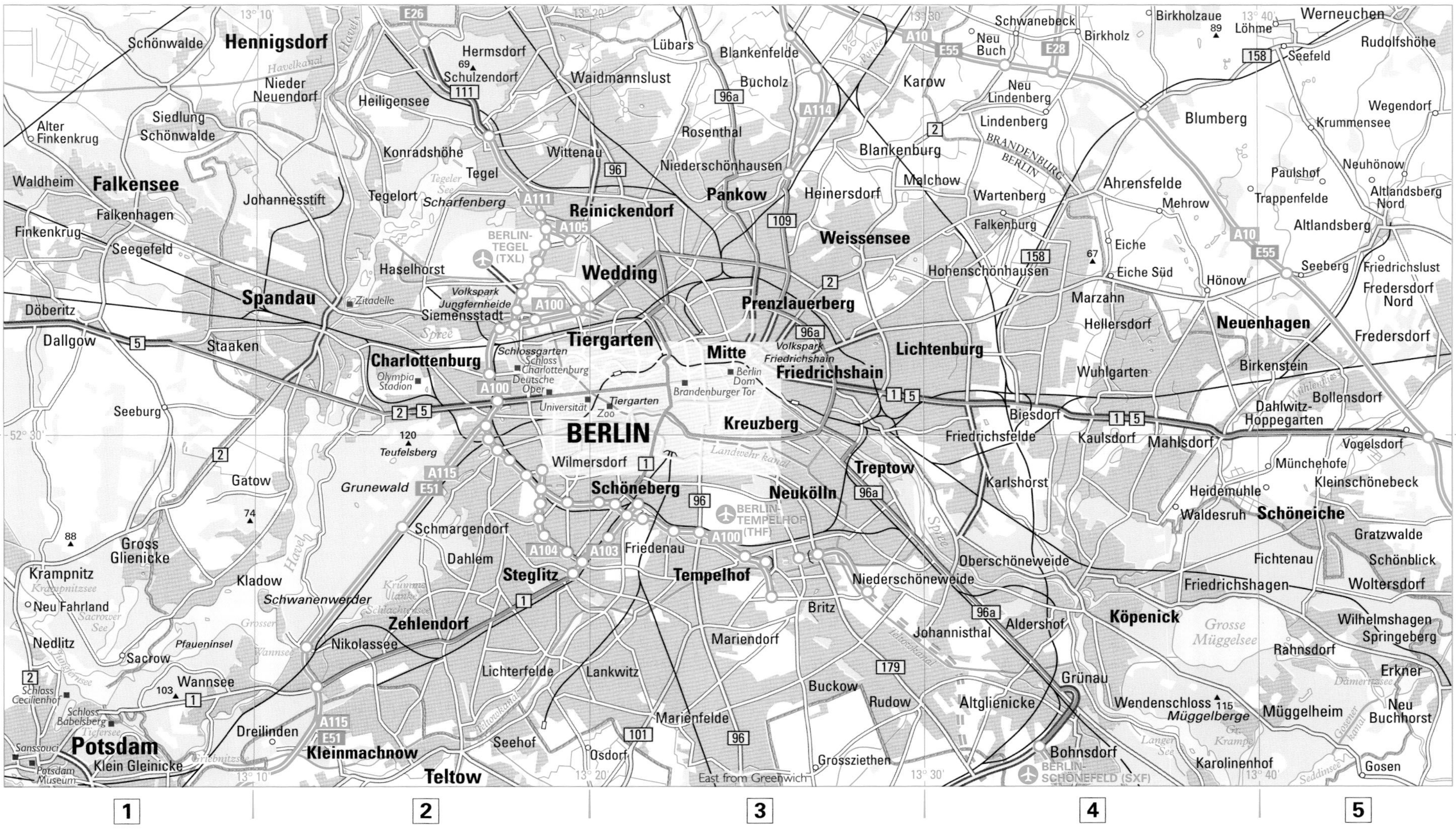

East from Greenwich

CENTRAL BERLIN

km 1
miles 0.5

CHARLOTTENBURG · TIERGARTEN · SCHEUNENVIERTEL · Hauptbahnhof Lehrter Bahnhof · Oranienburger Str. · Hackescher Mkt. · Alexanderplatz
Deutsche Oper · Technische Universität · Bellevue · Schloss Bellevue · Bundeskanzleramt · Paul-Löbe-Haus · Haus der Kulturen der Welt · Reichstag · Friedrichstr. · Pergamonmuseum · Fernsehturm (T.V. Tower) · Rathaus
Zoologischer Garten · Siegessäule · Tiergarten · Brandenburger Tor (Brandenburg Gate) · Pariser Platz · Unter den Linden · Staatsoper · Berliner Dom (Cathedral) · Museuminsel · Poliklinik
Kaiser Wilhelm Gedächtniskirche · Europa-Kurfürsten-center · Philharmonie · Gemäldegalerie · Neue Nationalgalerie · Sony Centre · Holocaust Memorial · MITTE · Deutscher Dom
Savignypl. · KURFÜRSTENDAMM · Zoologischer Garten · Potsdamer Platz · Checkpoint Charlie · KREUZBERG
WILMERSDORF · Urania · Anhalter Bf. · Martin-Gropius-Bau · Topography of Terror · Jüdisches Museum (Jewish Museum)
Deutsches Technikmuseum Berlin · Tempodrom · Anhalter Bf. · Halleschen Tor
Yorckstrasse · Kreuzberg · Viktoriapark · HASEN-HEIDE

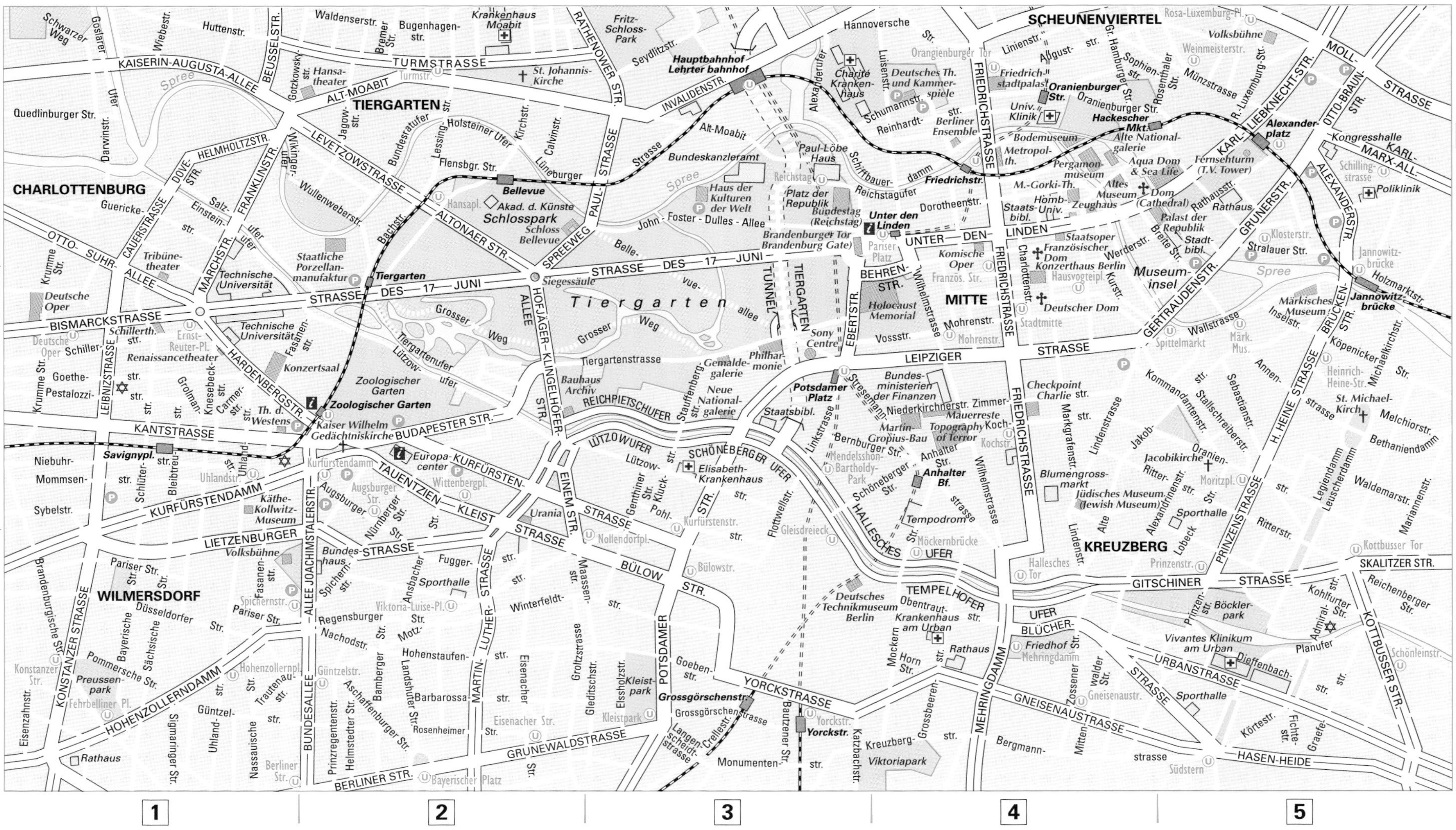

COPYRIGHT PHILIP'S

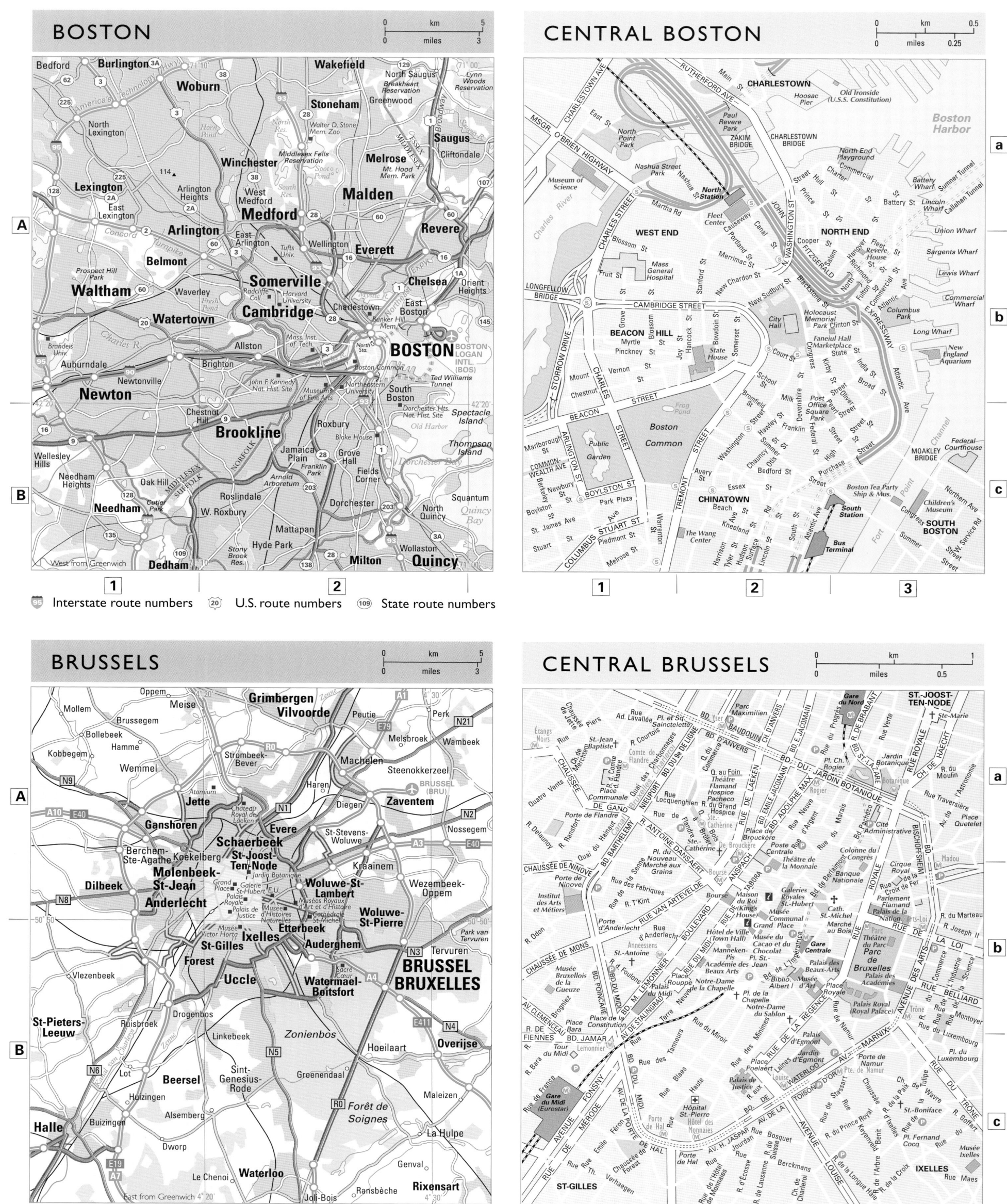

BUDAPEST

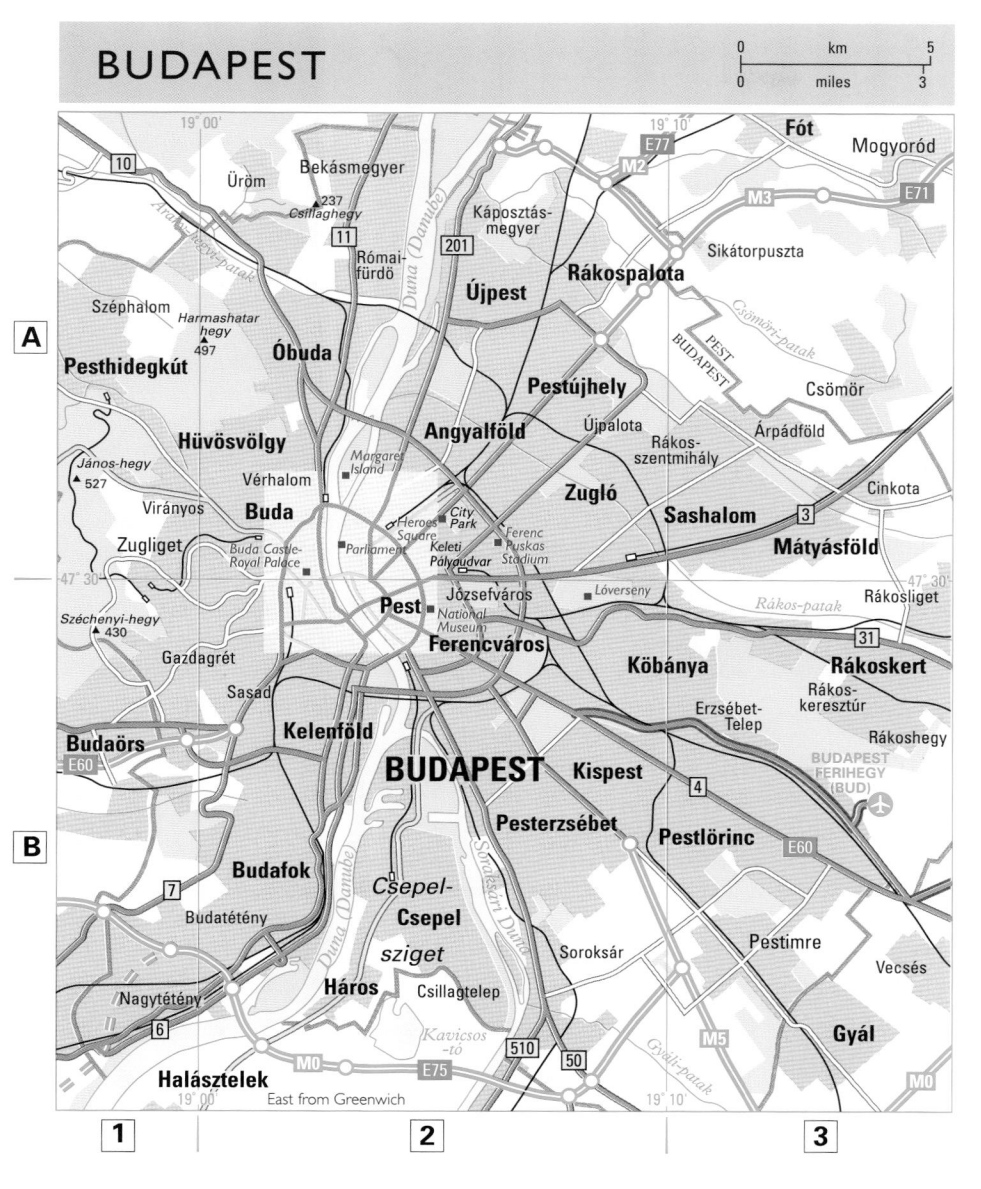

CENTRAL BUDAPEST

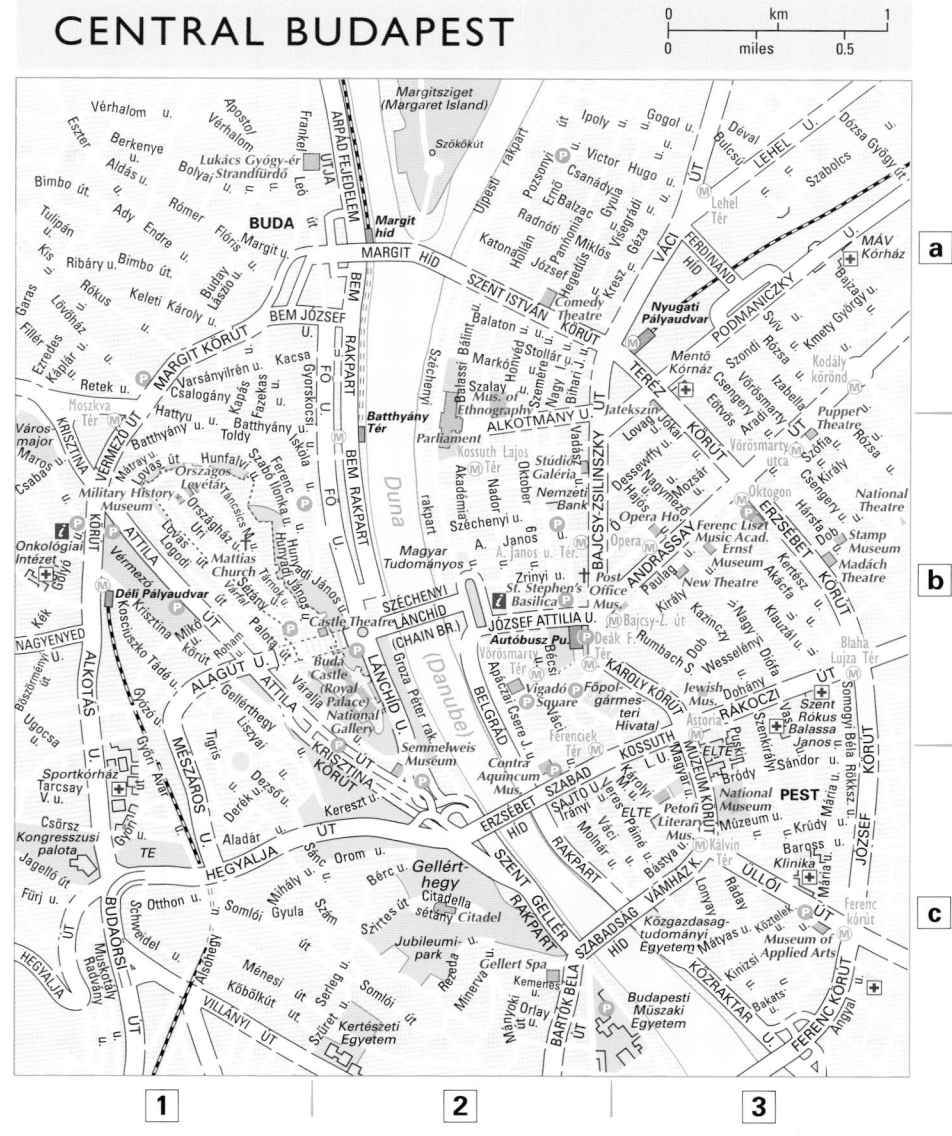

BUENOS AIRES

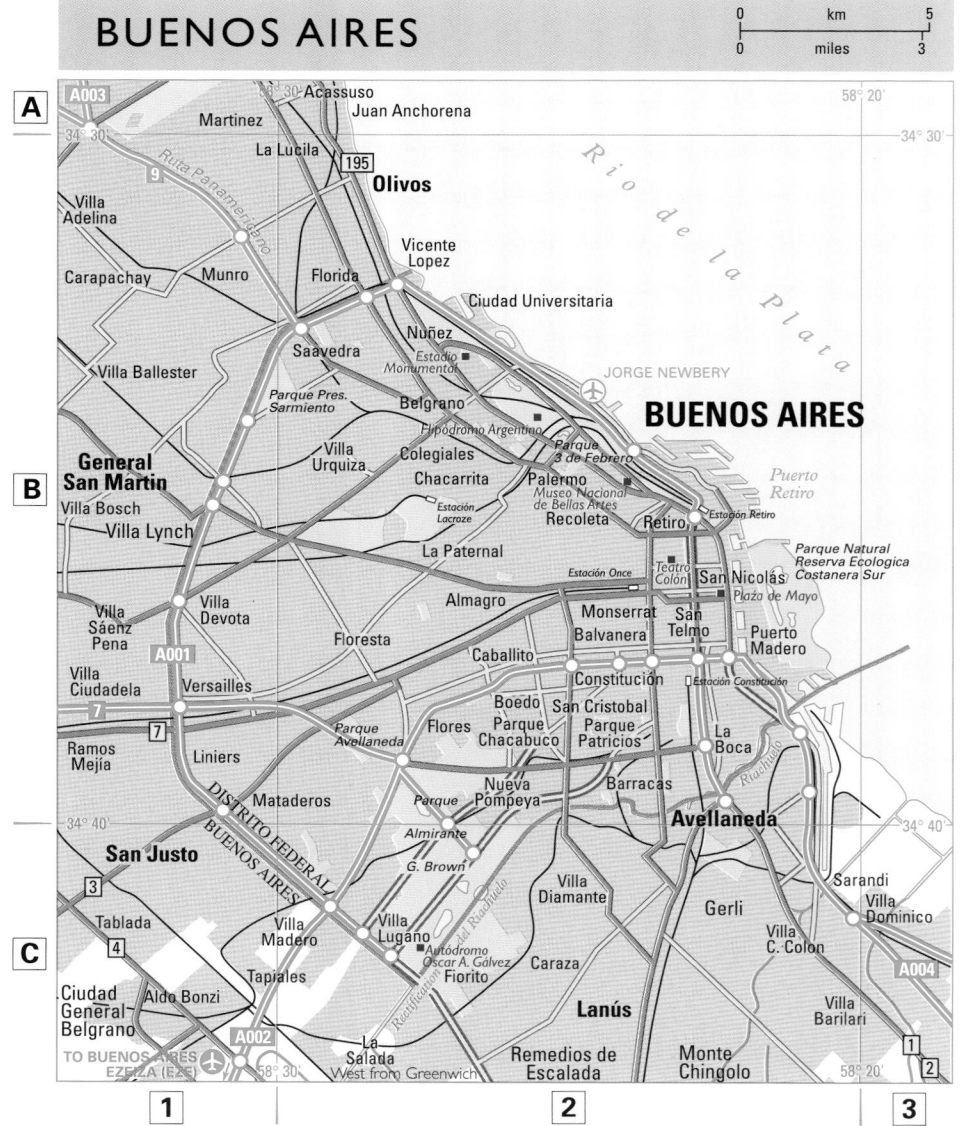

CAIRO

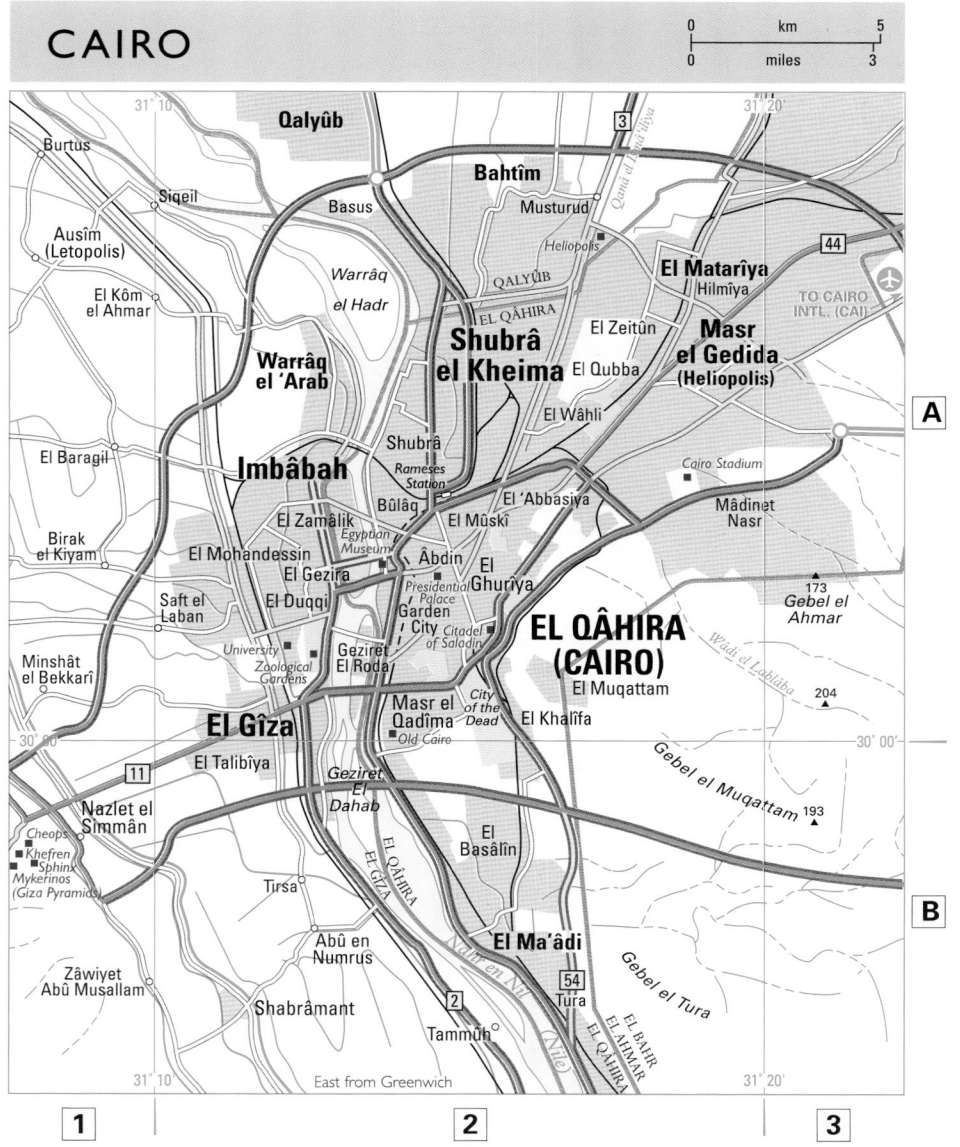

CAPE TOWN

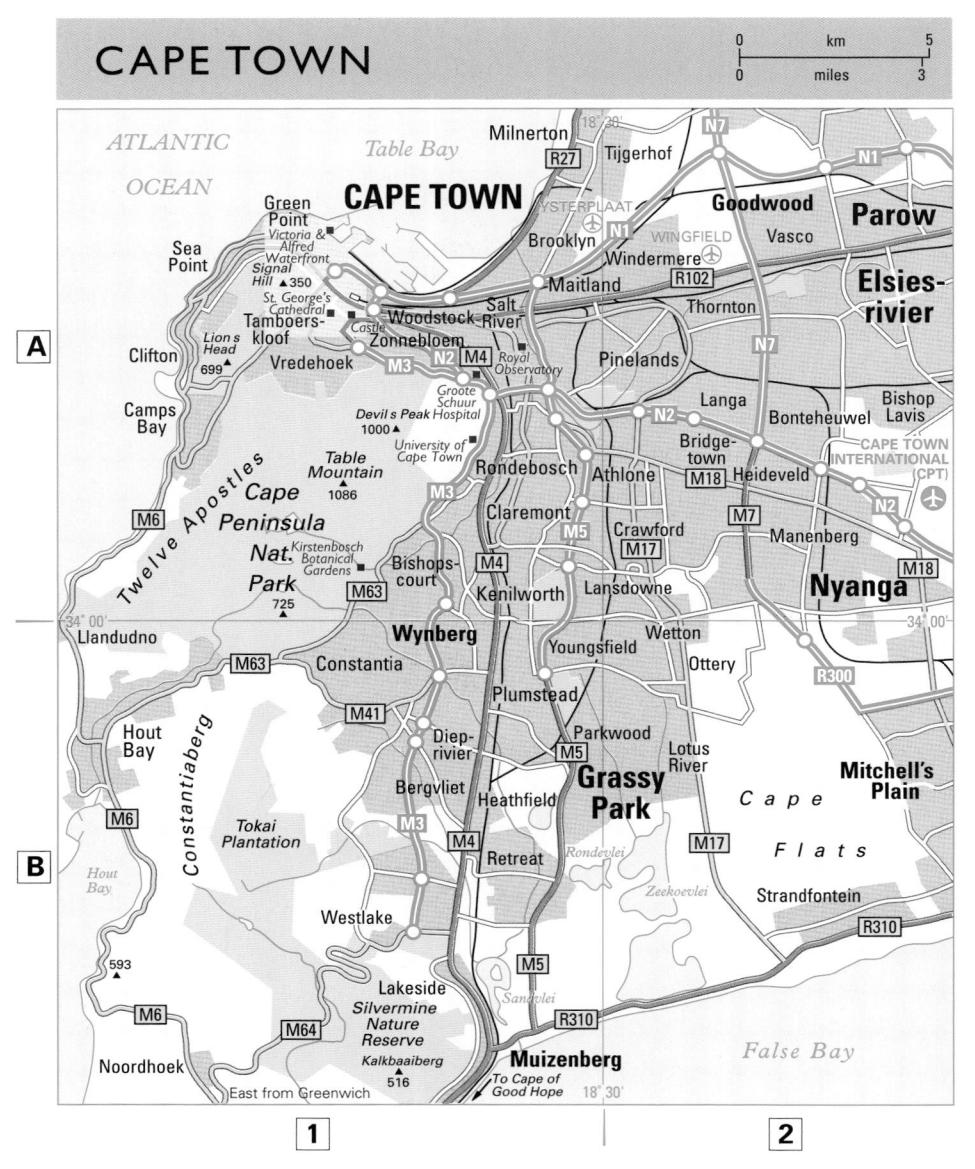

ATLANTIC OCEAN
Table Bay
Milnerton
Tijgerhof
R27
N7
N1
CAPE TOWN
Goodwood
Parow
Green Point Victoria & Alfred Waterfront
Sea Point
Signal Hill ▲350
Brooklyn
Windermere
Vasco
Elsies-rivier
Clifton
Lion's Head 699
Tamboers-kloof
Woodstock
Salt River
Zonnebloem
Maitland
Thornton
Bishop Lavis
A
Vredehoek
M3
Castle
N2
M4
Pinelands
N7
Camps Bay
Devil's Peak 1000
Groote Schuur Hospital
Royal Observatory
Langa
Bonteheuwel
CAPE TOWN INTERNATIONAL (CPT)
Table Mountain 1086
University of Cape Town
Rondebosch
Bridge-town
Heideveld
Cape Peninsula Nat. Park
Kirstenbosch Botanical Gardens
Claremont
Athlone
Crawford
Manenberg
M18
Bishops-court
725
Kenilworth
Lansdowne
Nyanga
M6
M63
Wynberg
Wetton
34° 00'
Llandudno
M63
Constantia
Youngsfield
Ottery
R300
Plumstead
B
Hout Bay
Constantiaberg
M41
Diep-rivier
Parkwood
Lotus River
Mitchell's Plain
M6
Tokai Plantation
Bergvliet
Heathfield
Grassy Park
Cape Flats
Retreat
M4
M3
Westlake
Strandfontein
R310
593
M6
M64
Lakeside Silvermine Nature Reserve
M5
Sandvlei
False Bay
Noordhoek
Kalkbaaiberg 516
Muizenberg
East from Greenwich
To Cape of Good Hope
18° 30'

CENTRAL CAPE TOWN

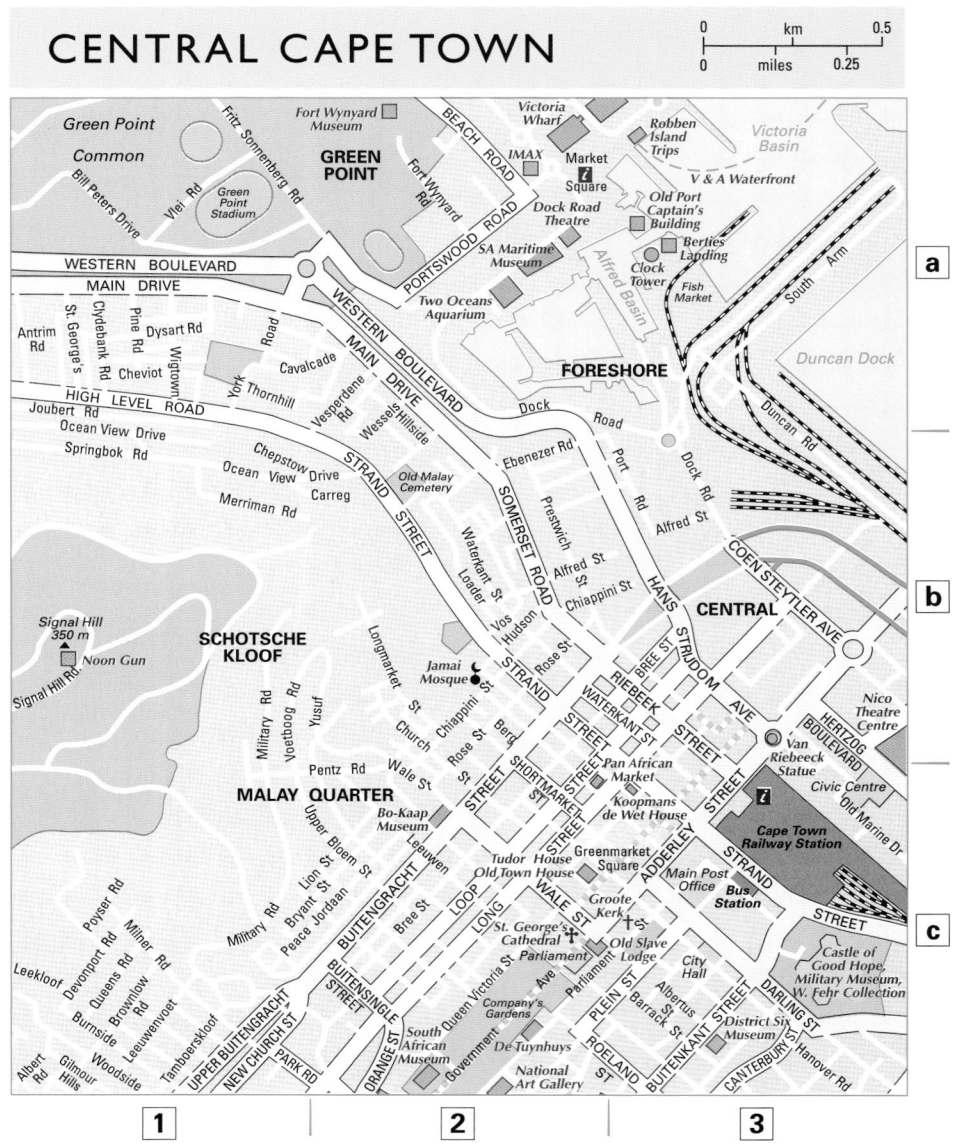

Green Point Common
Fort Wynyard Museum
Victoria Wharf
Robben Island Trips
V & A Waterfront
Victoria Basin
GREEN POINT
IMAX
Market Square
Old Port Captain's Building
WESTERN BOULEVARD
MAIN DRIVE
Two Oceans Aquarium
Clock Tower
Berties Landing
Fish Market
a
FORESHORE
Duncan Dock
HIGH LEVEL ROAD
Ocean View Drive
Springbok Rd
Old Malay Cemetery
CENTRAL
b
Signal Hill 350 m
Noon Gun
SCHOTSCHE KLOOF
Jamai Mosque
Nico Theatre Centre
Van Riebeeck Statue
Civic Centre
MALAY QUARTER
Bo-Kaap Museum
Pan African Market
Koopmans de Wet House
Cape Town Railway Station
Tudor House
Greenmarket Square
Old Town House
Main Post Office
Bus Station
St. George's Cathedral
Parliament
Old Slave Lodge
Castle of Good Hope, Military Museum, W. Fehr Collection
c
Company's Gardens
De Tuynhuys
City Hall
District Six Museum
South African Museum
Governmentt
National Art Gallery

COPENHAGEN

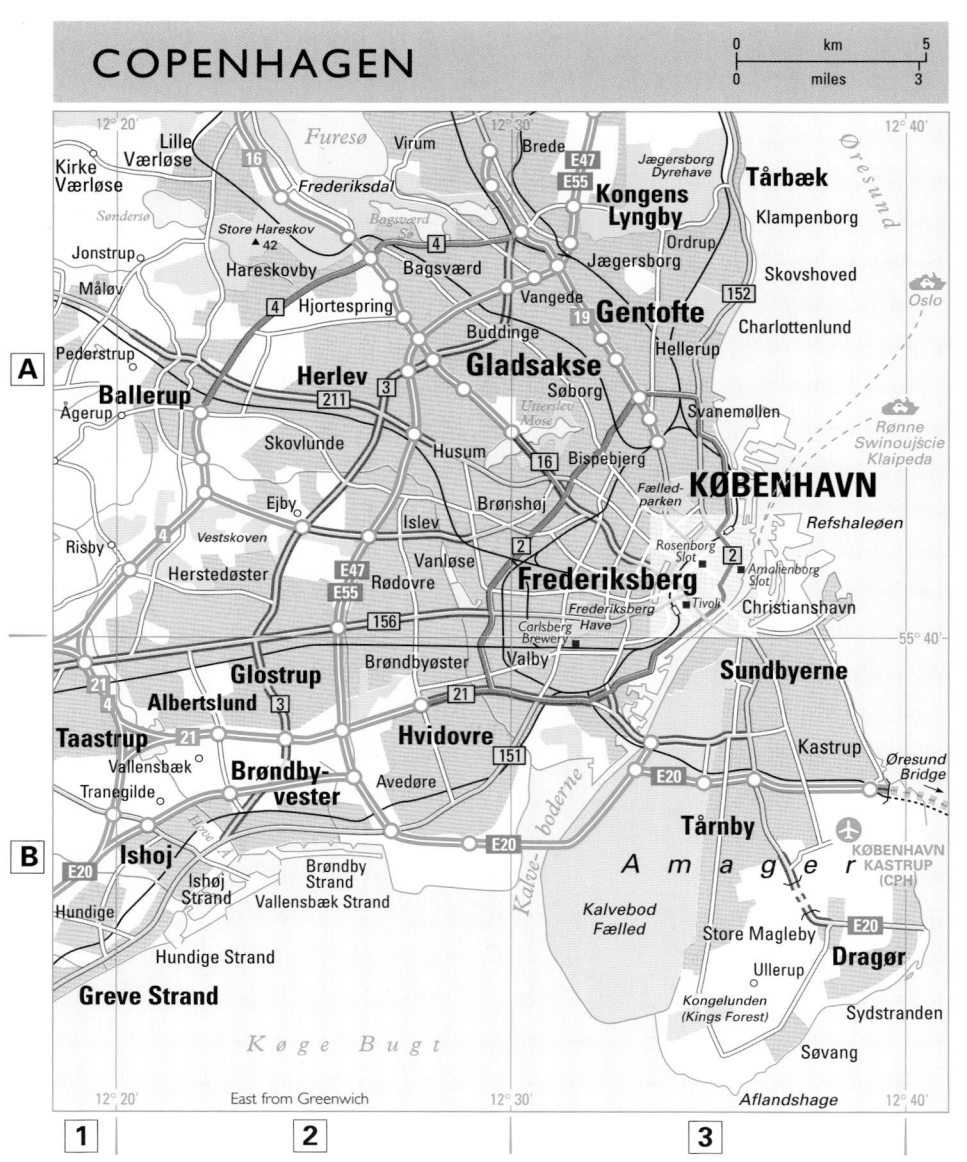

Furesø
Øresund
Lille Værløse
16
E47
E55
Brede
Kongens Lyngby
Tårbæk
Kirke Værløse
Frederiksdal
Klampenborg
Store Hareskov ▲42
Bagsværd
Ordrup
Jonstrup
Hareskovby
Bagsværd
Jægersborg
Skovshoved
Målov
Hjortespring
Vangede
Gentofte
152
Oslo
Ballerup
Buddinge
Hellerup
Herlev
Gladsakse
211
Søborg
Svanemøllen
Rønne Swinoujscie Klaipeda
Skovlunde
Husum
16
Bispebjerg
Fælled-parken
Refshaleøen
Ejby
Islev
Brønshøj
KØBENHAVN
Risby
Vanløse
2
Rosenborg Slot
2
Herstedøster
E47
E55
Rødovre
Frederiksberg
Amalienborg Slot
Christianshavn
156
Frederiksberg Have
Tivoli
Glostrup
Carlsberg Brewery
Valby
Sundbyerne
Albertslund
3
Brøndbyøster
21
Taastrup
21
Hvidovre
151
Kastrup
Vallensbæk
Avedøre
E20
Øresund Bridge
Brøndby-vester
Tårnby
Ishøj
E20
KØBENHAVN KASTRUP (CPH)
Ishøj Strand
Brøndby Strand
Amager
Greve Strand
Vallensbæk Strand
Kalvebod Fælled
Store Magleby
E20
Dragør
Kongelunden (Kings Forest)
Sydstranden
Køge Bugt
Ullerup
Søvang
Aflandshage

CENTRAL COPENHAGEN

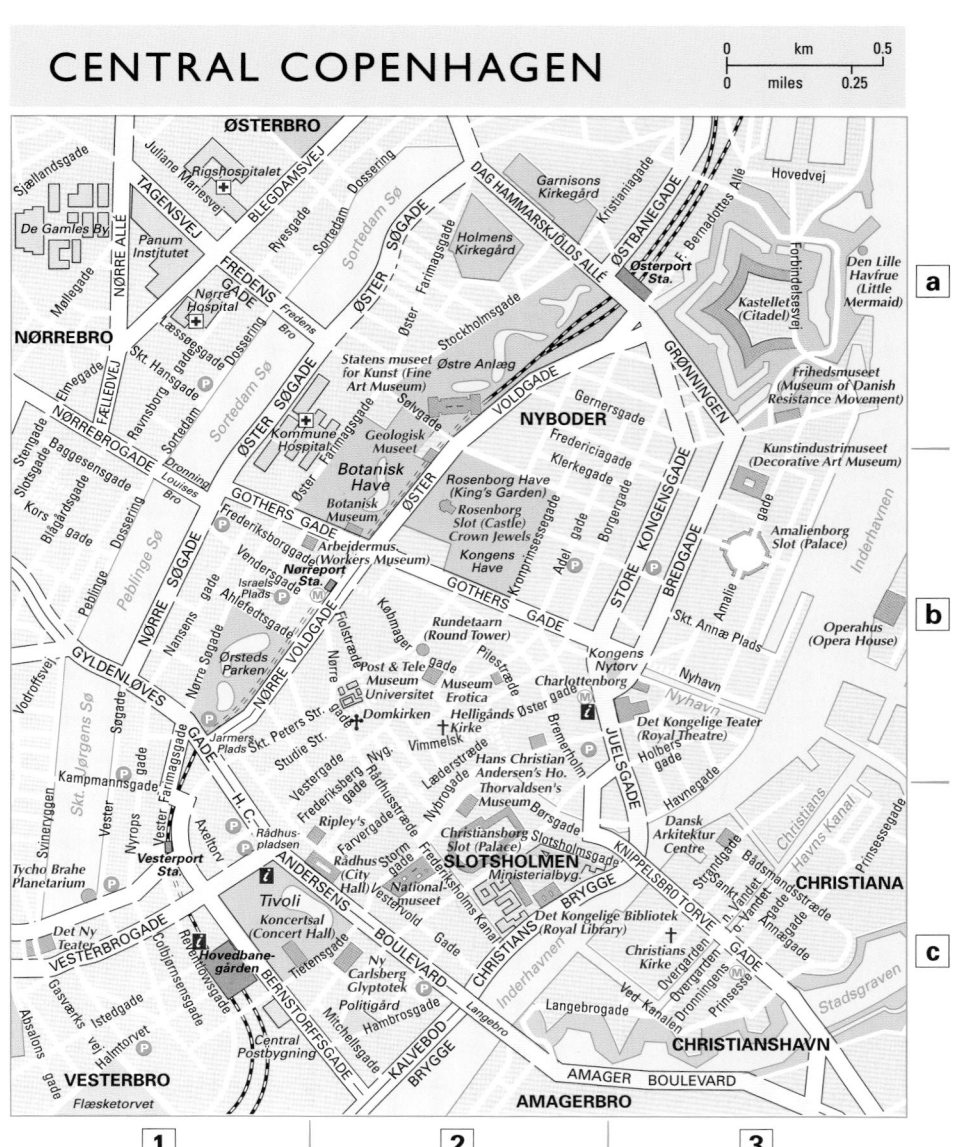

ØSTERBRO
Rigshospitalet
Hovedvej
De Gamles By
Garnisons Kirkegård
Den Lille Havfrue (Little Mermaid)
NØRREBRO
Panum Institutet
Holmens Kirkegård
Kastellet (Citadel)
a
Statens museum for Kunst (Fine Art Museum)
Frihedsmuseet (Museum of Danish Resistance Movement)
NYBODER
Kunstindustrimuseet (Decorative Art Museum)
Botanisk Have
Botanisk Museum
Rosenborg Have (King's Garden)
Rosenborg Slot (Castle) Crown Jewels
Amalienborg Slot (Palace)
Geologisk Museet
Nørreport
Arbejdermus (Workers Museum)
Kongens Have
b
Rundetaarn (Round Tower)
Kongens Nytorv
Operahus (Opera House)
Ørsteds Parken
Museum Universitet
Museum Erotica
Charlottenborg
Det Kongelige Teater (Royal Theatre)
Domkirken
Helligånds
Hans Christian Andersen's Ho.
Thorvaldsen's Museum
Ripley's
Christiansborg Slotsholmen
Dansk Arkitektur Centre
CHRISTIANA
Vesterport Sta.
Rådhus (City Hall)
National
SLOTSHOLMEN
Ministerialbyg
c
Tivoli
Det Kongelige Bibliotek (Royal Library)
Christians Kirke
Tycho Brahe Planetarium
Ny Carlsberg Glyptotek
Hovedbane-gården
CHRISTIANSHAVN
VESTERBRO
Central Postbygning
AMAGER BOULEVARD
Flæsketorvet
AMAGERBRO

CHICAGO

km 0 5
miles 0 3

LAKE MICHIGAN

CHICAGO

Evanston
Wilmette
Skokie
Morton Grove
Niles
Glenview
Glenview Countryside
Park Ridge
Des Plaines
Rosemont
Schiller Park
Franklin Park
Northlake
Stone Park
Melrose Park
Bellwood
Maywood
Broadview
Westchester
La Grange Park
La Grange
Brookfield
Riverside
North Riverside
Lyons
Forest View
Stickney
Summit
Bedford Park
Bridgeview
Justice
Hickory Hills
Palos Hills
Hodgkins
Countryside
Willow Springs
Palos Park
Palos Heights
Worth
Chicago Ridge
Burbank
Oak Lawn
Evergreen Park
Mount Greenwood
Merrionette Park
Beverly
Morgan Park
Alsip
Robbins
Blue Island
Calumet Park
Roseland
South Deering
South Shore
Hyde Park
Chatham
Englewood
Gage Park
Chicago Lawn
Ashburn
Hometown
Marquette Park
Brighton Park
McKinley Park
Bridgeport
Chinatown
Lawndale
Douglas Park
Garfield Park
Humboldt Park
West Town
Near North
Gold Coast
Old Town
Lincoln Park
Lakeview
Uptown
Rogers Park
Lincolnwood
Edison Park
Norwood Park
Harwood Heights
Norridge
Dunning
Belmont Cragin
Austin
Oak Park
River Forest
Elmwood Park
River Grove
Forest Park
Berwyn
Cicero
Portage Park
Irving Park
Jefferson Park
Avondale
Logan Square

Loyola University
Northwestern University
Wrigley Field
Lincoln Park Zoo
Navy Pier
John Hancock Center
Lincoln Park
Grant Park
Art Institute
Field Museum
Soldier Field
Adler Planetarium
Shedd Aquarium
Burnham Park
Univ. of Chicago
Washington Park
U.S. Cellular Field
Dan Ryan Woods
Pullman Historic District
Beverly Arts Center
Argonne Forest
Palos Forest

Baha'i Temple
Grosse Point Lighthouse & Lakefront
Mitchell Museum of the American Indian
Charles Gates Dawes House
Skokie Heritage Museum
Lincolnwood Town Center
Frank Lloyd Wright Home
Brookfield Chicago Zoological Park
Hawthorne Racecourse
Ford City Shopping Center
Little Red School House Nature Center

CHICAGO O'HARE INTERNATIONAL (ORD)
CHICAGO MIDWAY (MDW)

Dan Ryan Expwy
Kennedy Expwy
Eisenhower Expwy
Dwight D. Eisenhower Expwy
Stevenson Expwy
Bishop Ford Mem. Expwy
Chicago Skyway
Tri-State Tollway

North Shore Channel
Des Plaines River
Chicago River
Calumet Sag Channel
Sanitary & Ship Canal

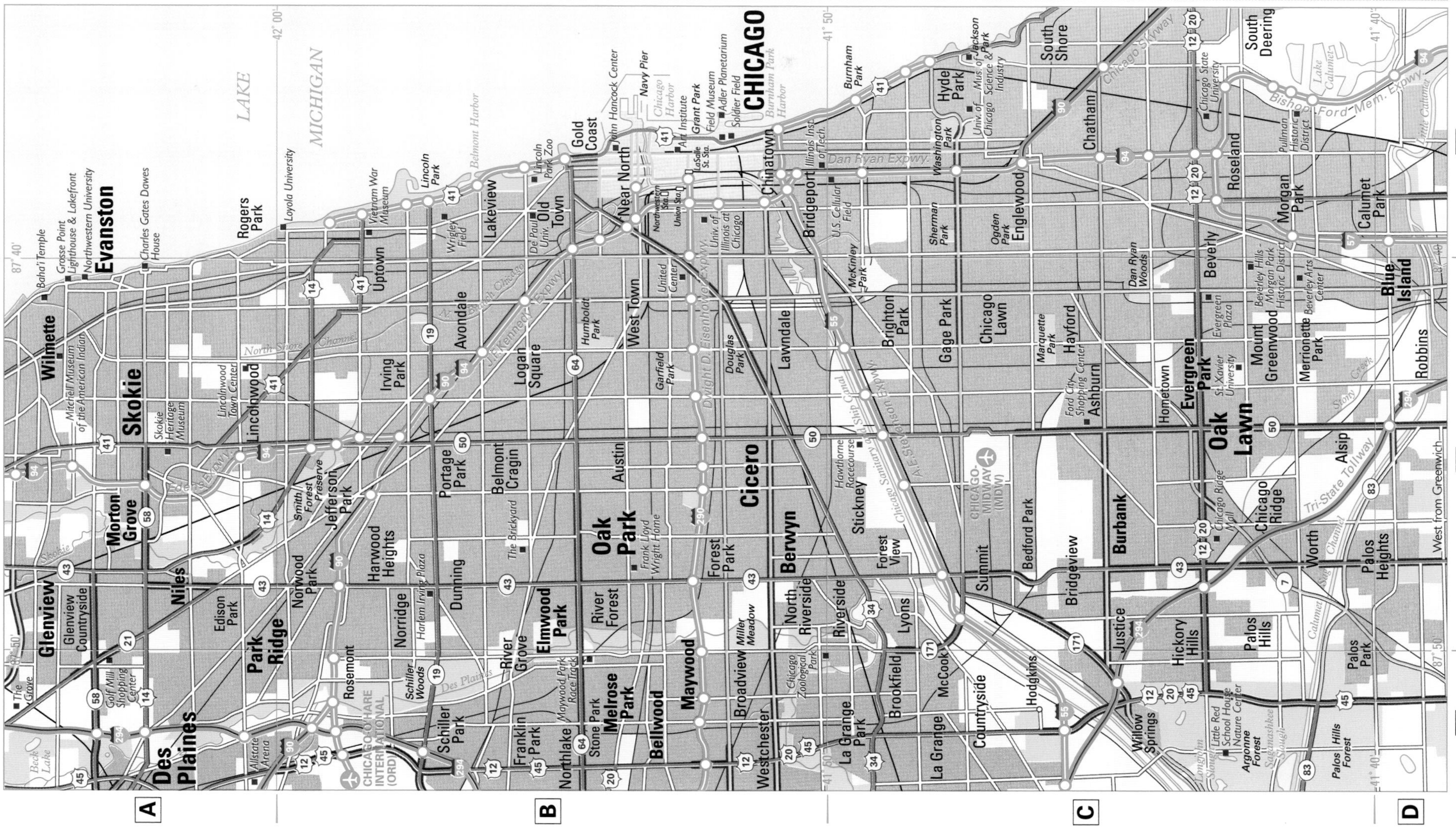

Interstate route numbers
U.S. route numbers
State route numbers

CENTRAL CHICAGO

km 0 1
miles 0 0.5

LAKE MICHIGAN

Outer Harbor
Navy Pier
Streeter Dr
Olive Park
Lake Point Tower
Ohio St Beach
Chicago Yacht Club
Chicago Harbor
Adler Planetarium
Meigs Field (Closed)
Merrill C. Meigs Field
Shedd Aquarium
Field Museum of Nat. History
Soldier Field
Burnham Park
Burnham Harbor
McCormick Place East
McCormick Place North
McCormick Place South
Lakeside Center

John Hancock Center
Water Tower Place
Chestnut St
Delaware Pl
Memorial Hospital
Northwestern Memorial Hosp.
Tribune Tower
Wrigley Bldg.
Marshall Field's
Prudential Building
Art Institute of Chicago
Buckingham Fountain
Grant Park
Sears Tower
City Hall & County Bldg.
Daley Center
Randolph St. Sta.
Van Buren St. Sta.
Roosevelt Road Sta.
LaSalle St. Sta.
Northwestern Sta.
Union Sta.
Main Post Office
Opera Ho.
Merchandise Mart

GOLD COAST
NEAR NORTH
RIVER NORTH
THE LOOP
PRINTER'S ROW
SOUTH LOOP
CHINATOWN

GEORGE HALAS DRIVE
N LAKE SHORE DRIVE
S LAKE SHORE DRIVE
SOUTH LAKE SHORE DRIVE
Old Lake Shore Drive
E SOLIDARITY DR
E RANDOLPH DRIVE
MONROE DRIVE
COLUMBUS DRIVE
JACKSON DR
CONGRESS PKWY
ROOSEVELT ROAD
CERMAK ROAD
WENTWORTH AVE
WENTWORTH ARCH VIADUCT

N MICHIGAN AVENUE
E CHICAGO AVE
E OAK ST
E DIVISION ST
E DELAWARE PL
E CHESTNUT ST
E SUPERIOR ST
E HURON ST
E ERIE ST
E ONTARIO ST
E OHIO ST
E GRAND AVE
E ILLINOIS ST
E NORTH WATER ST
E SOUTH WATER ST
E WACKER DR
E LAKE ST
E RANDOLPH ST
E WASHINGTON ST
E MADISON ST
E MONROE ST
E ADAMS ST
E JACKSON BLVD
E VAN BUREN ST
E CONGRESS PKWY
E HARRISON ST
E BALBO AVE
E 8TH ST
E 9TH ST
E 11TH ST
E 13TH ST
E 14TH ST
E 16TH ST
E 18TH ST
E 21ST ST
E 23RD ST

N State St
N Dearborn St
N Clark St
N LaSalle St
N Wells St
N Franklin St
N Wacker Dr
N Orleans St
N Kingsbury St
N Canal St
N Clinton St
N Jefferson St
N Desplaines St
N Milwaukee Ave
N Hudson Ave
N Larrabee St
N Kinzie St

S State Street
S Wabash Ave
S Michigan Avenue
S Indiana Ave
S Prairie Ave
S Calumet Ave
S Dearborn St
S Clark St
S LaSalle St
S Wells Street
S Franklin St
S Wacker Dr
S Canal Street
S Clinton St
S Jefferson St
S Grove St
S Princeton Ave
S Wentworth Ave

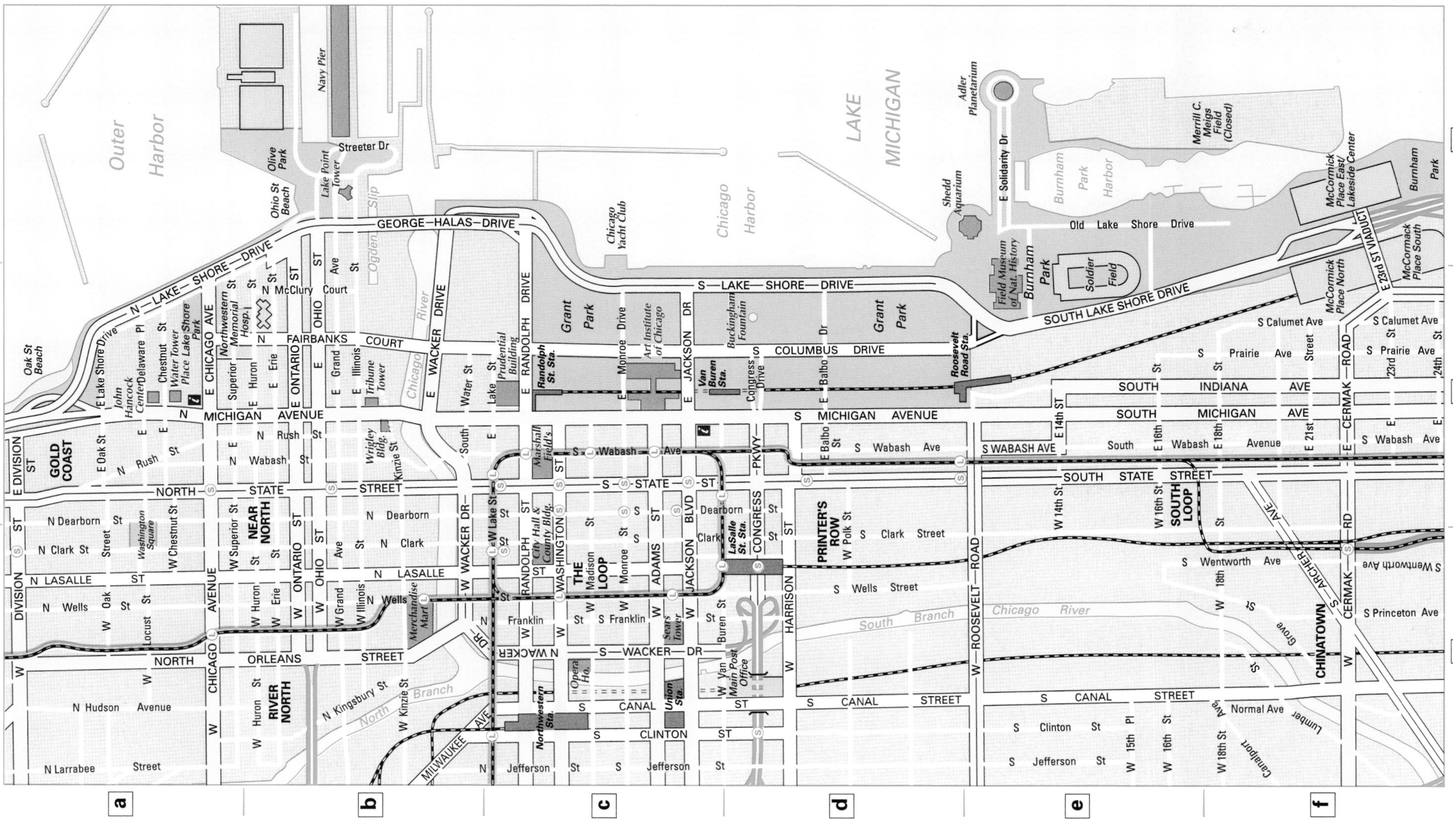

Elevated rail lines

COPYRIGHT PHILIP'S

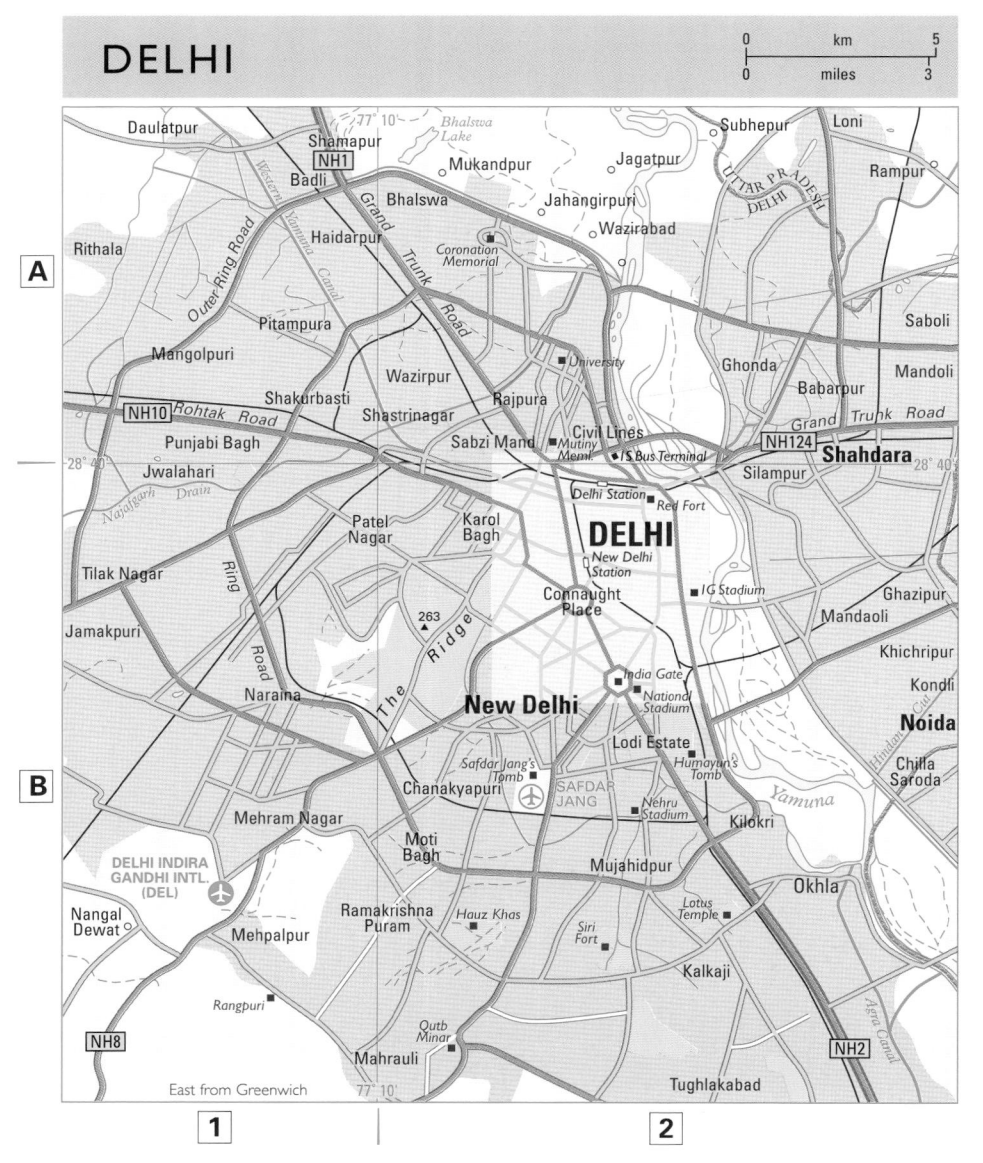

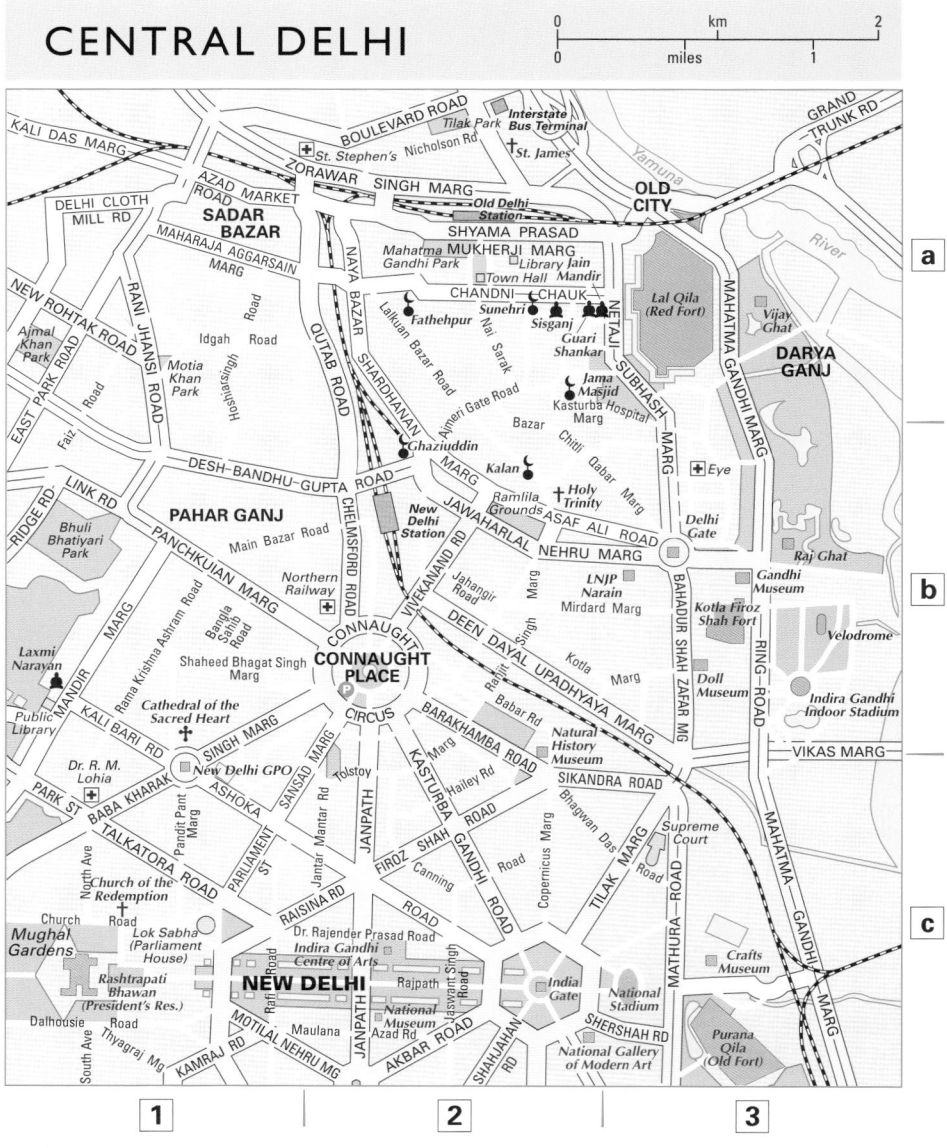

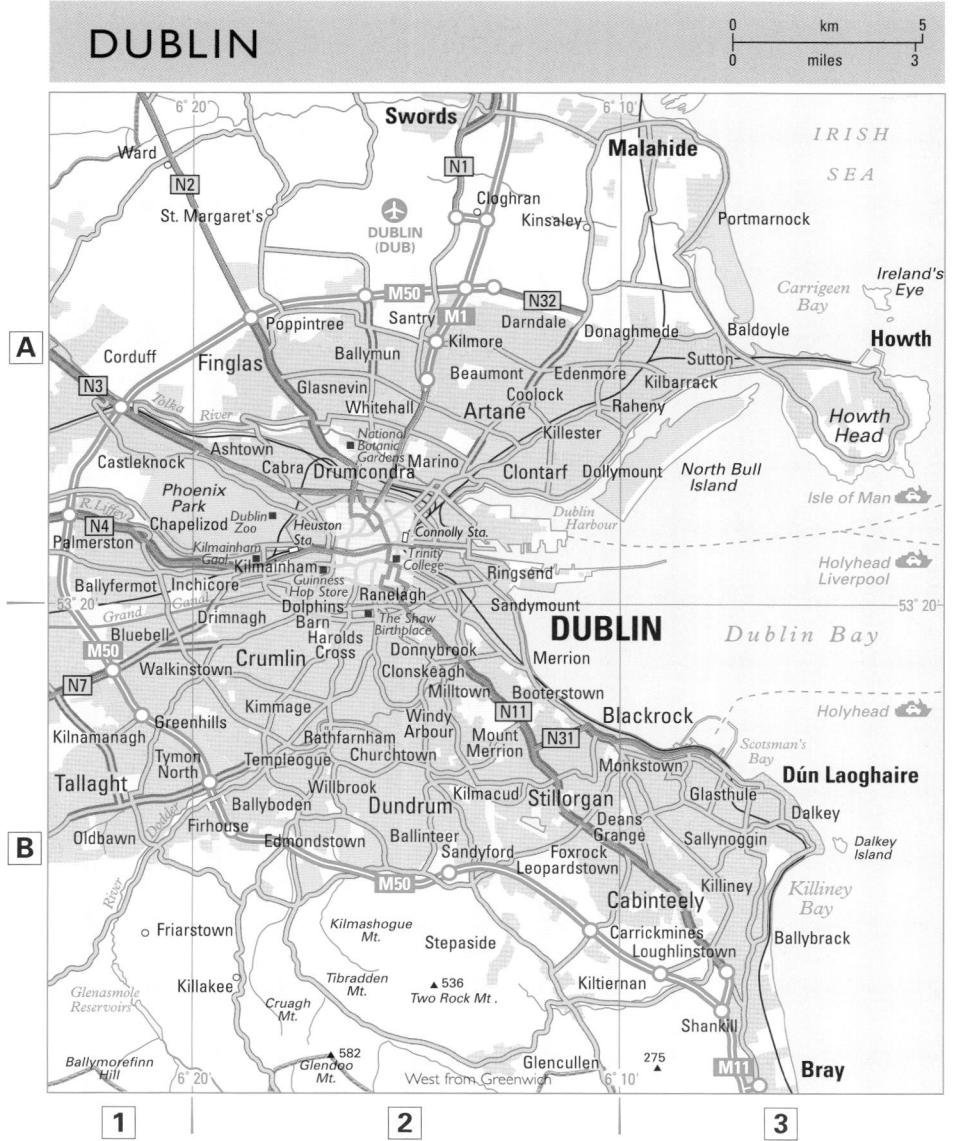

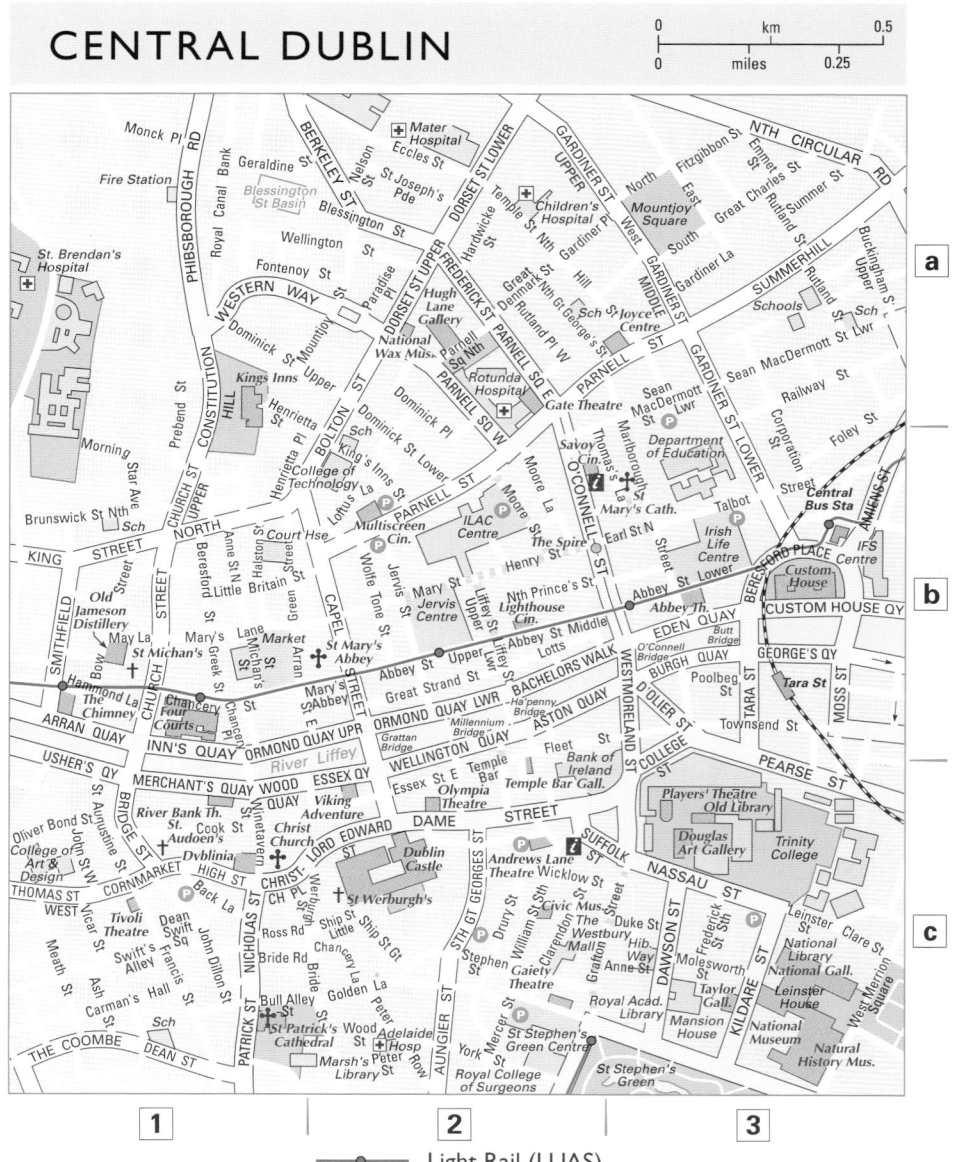

Light Rail (LUAS)

EDINBURGH

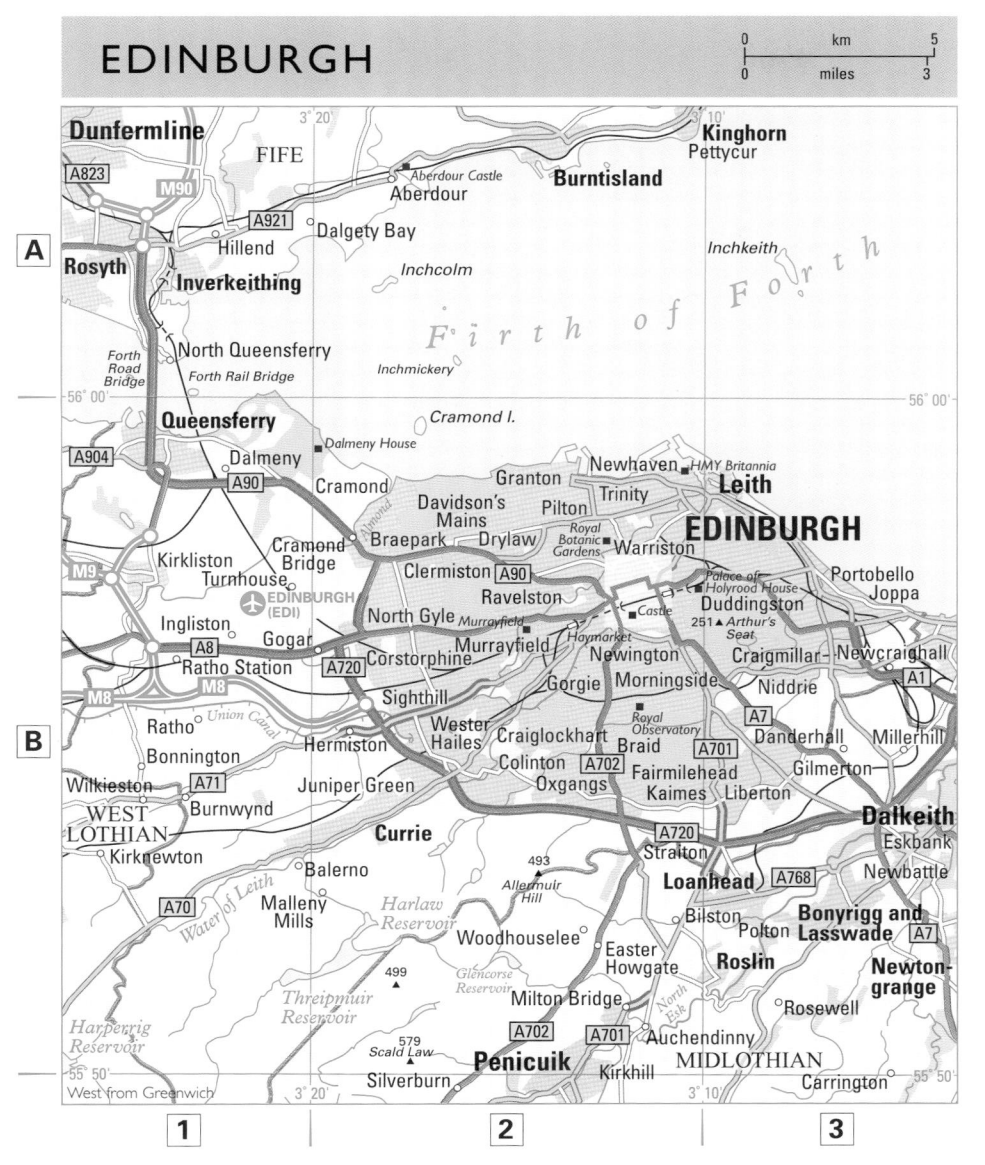

CENTRAL EDINBURGH

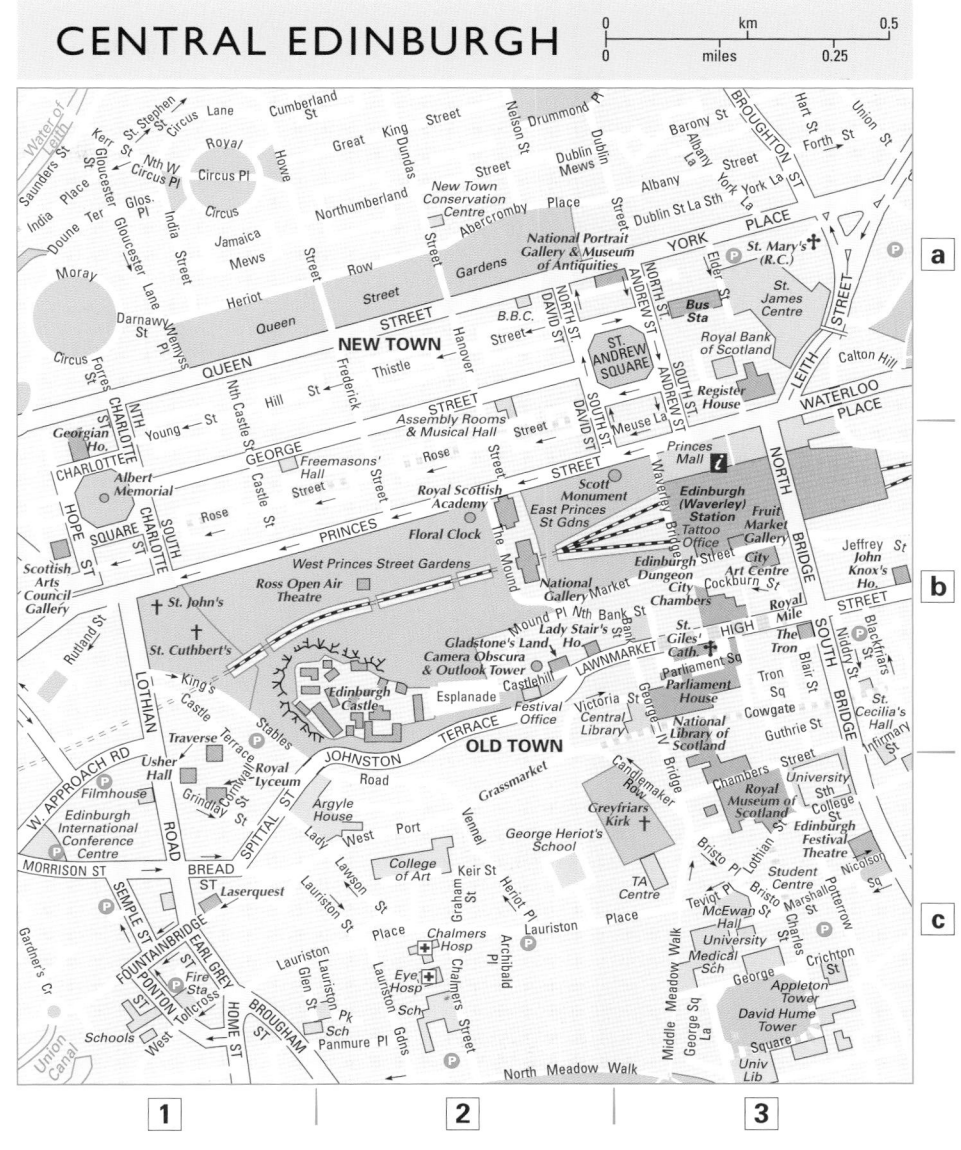

GUANGZHOU

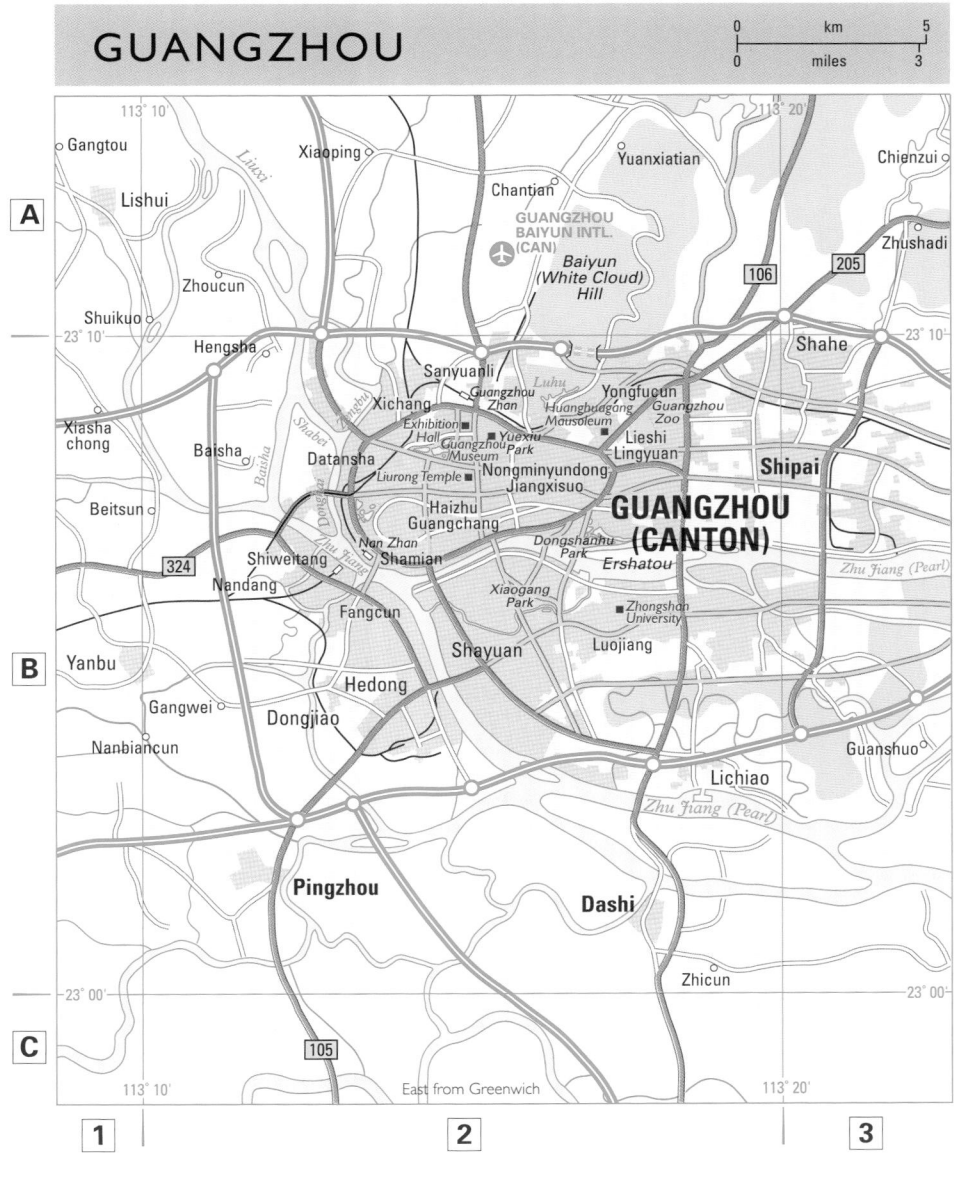

HELSINKI

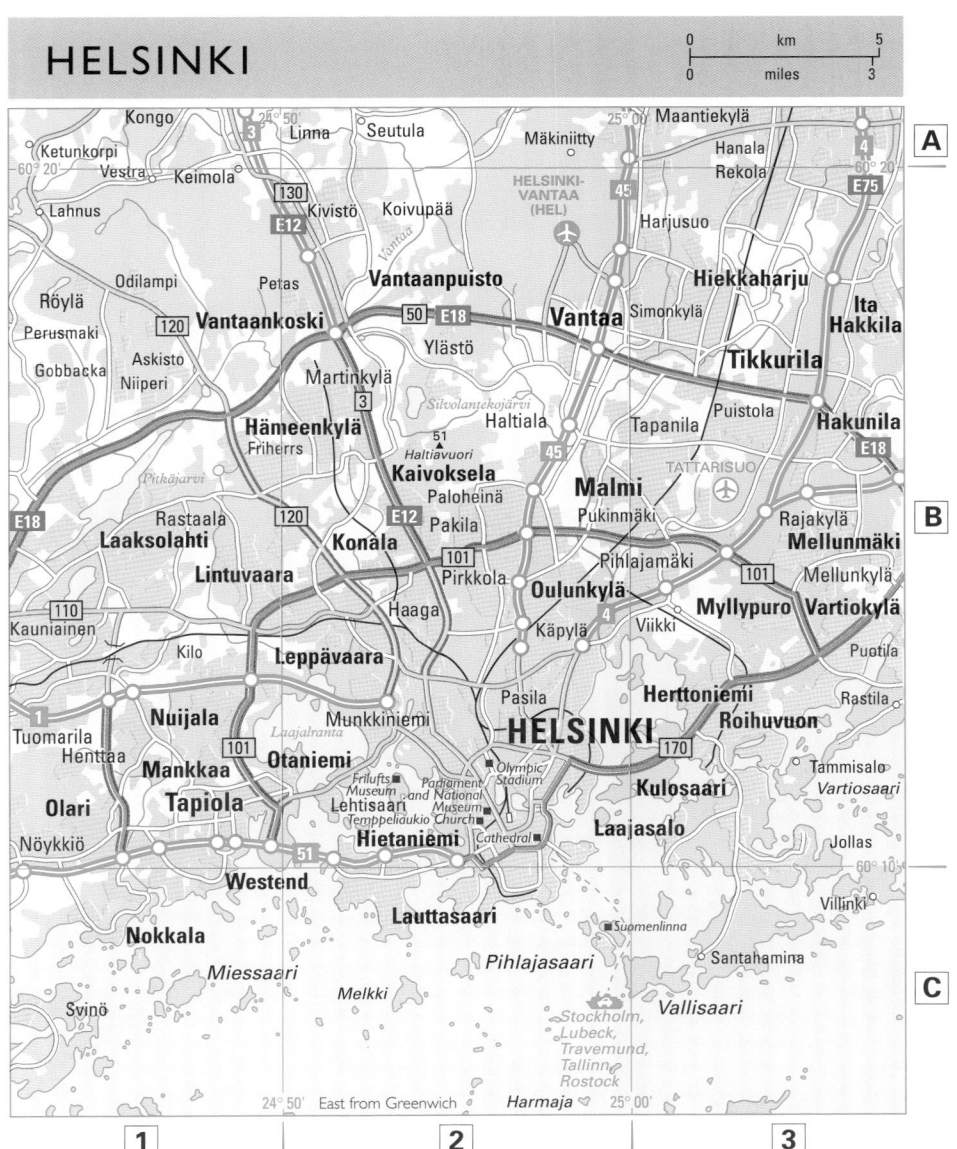

HONG KONG

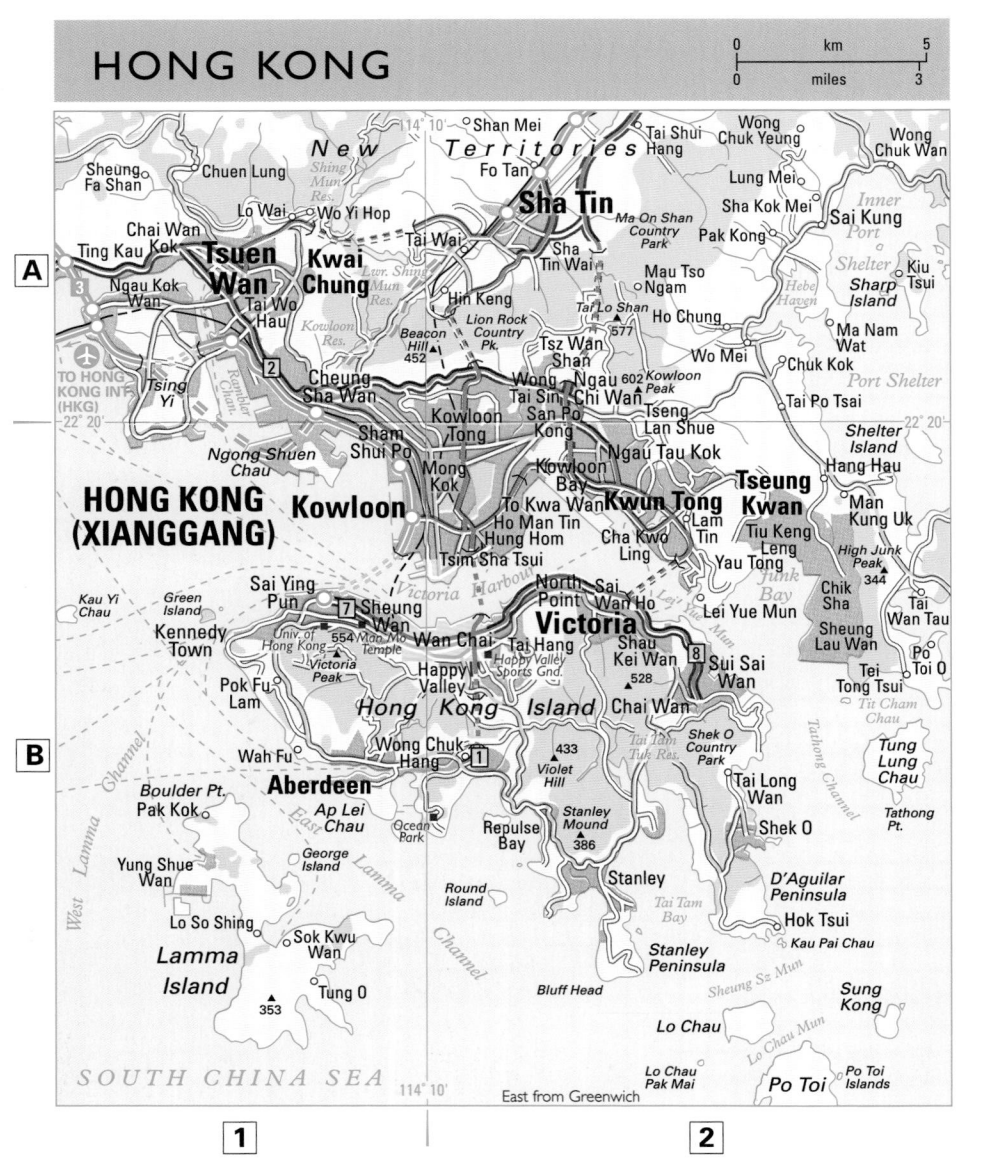

CENTRAL HONG KONG

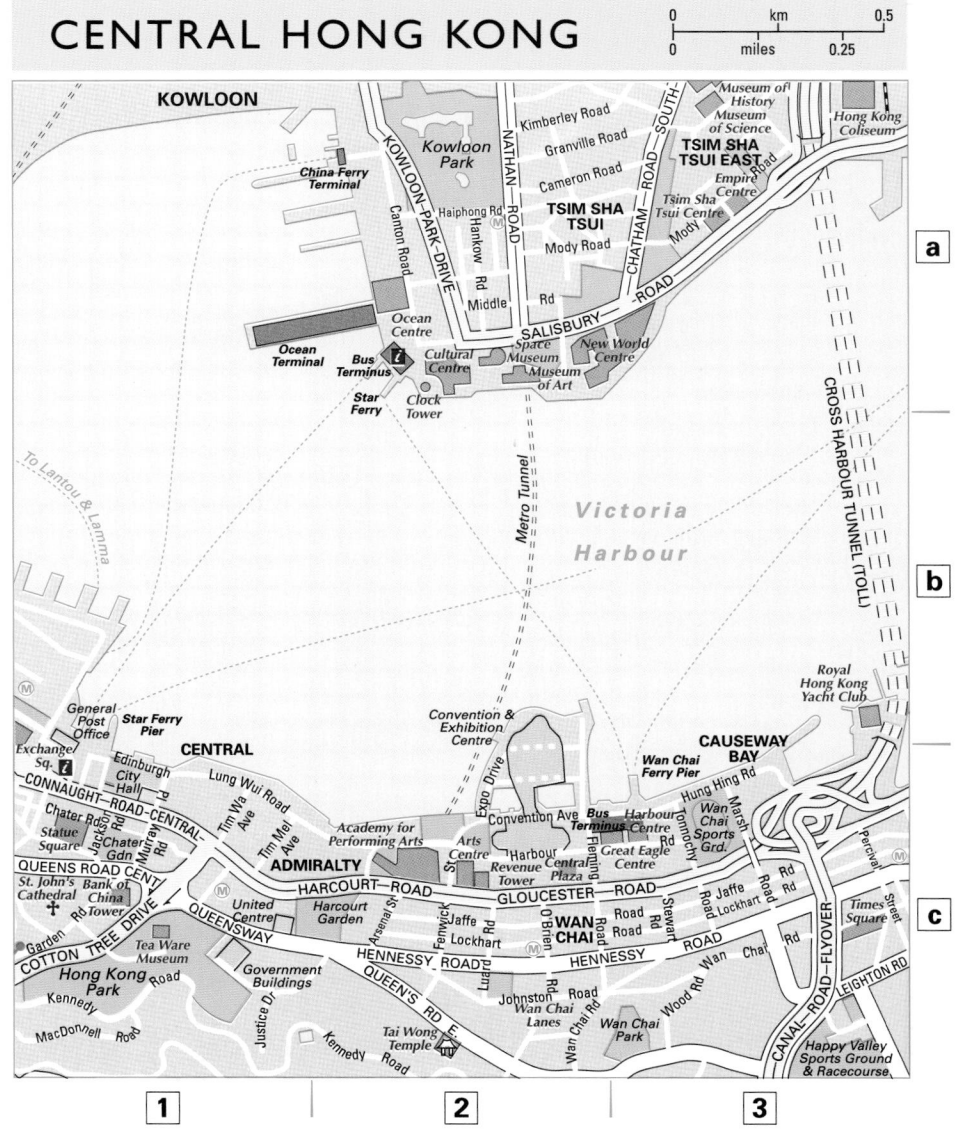

ISTANBUL

JAKARTA

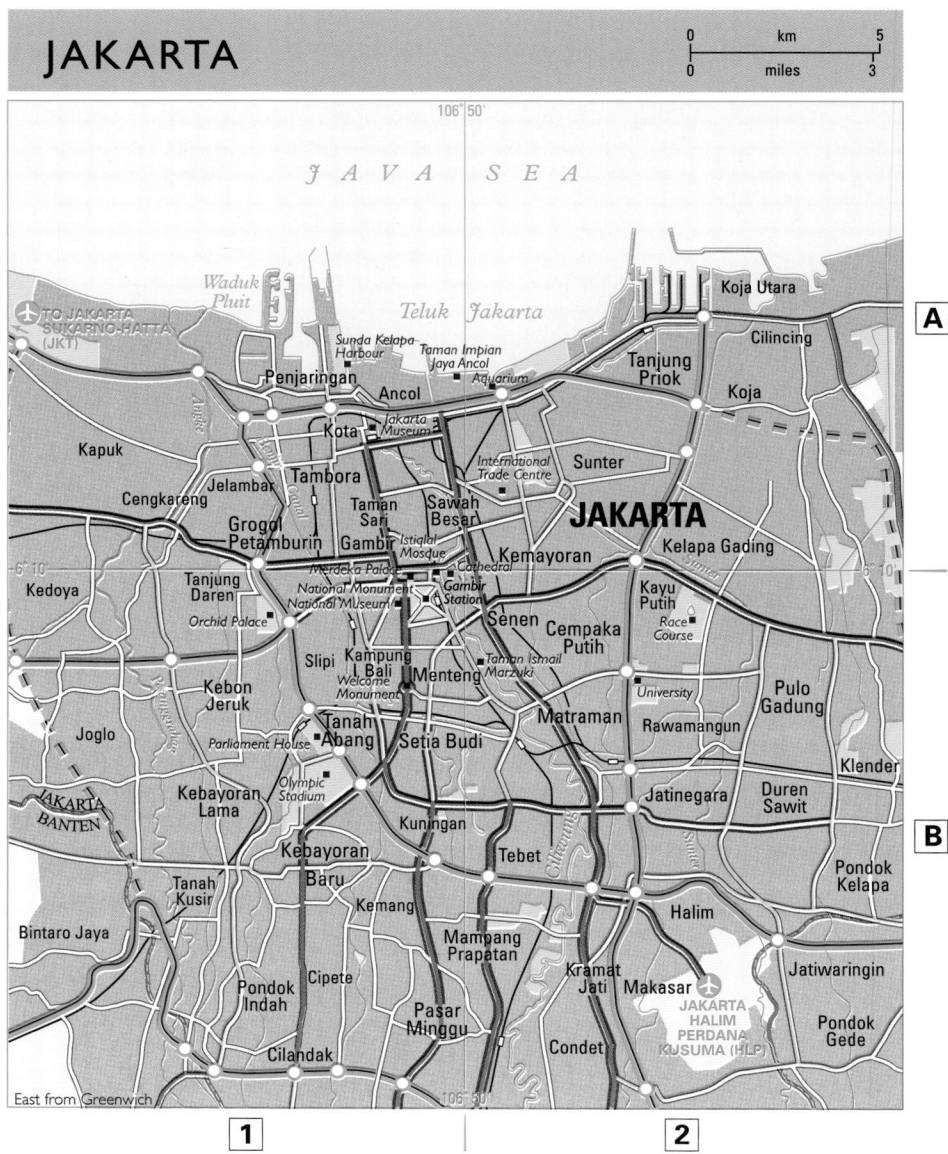

JERUSALEM

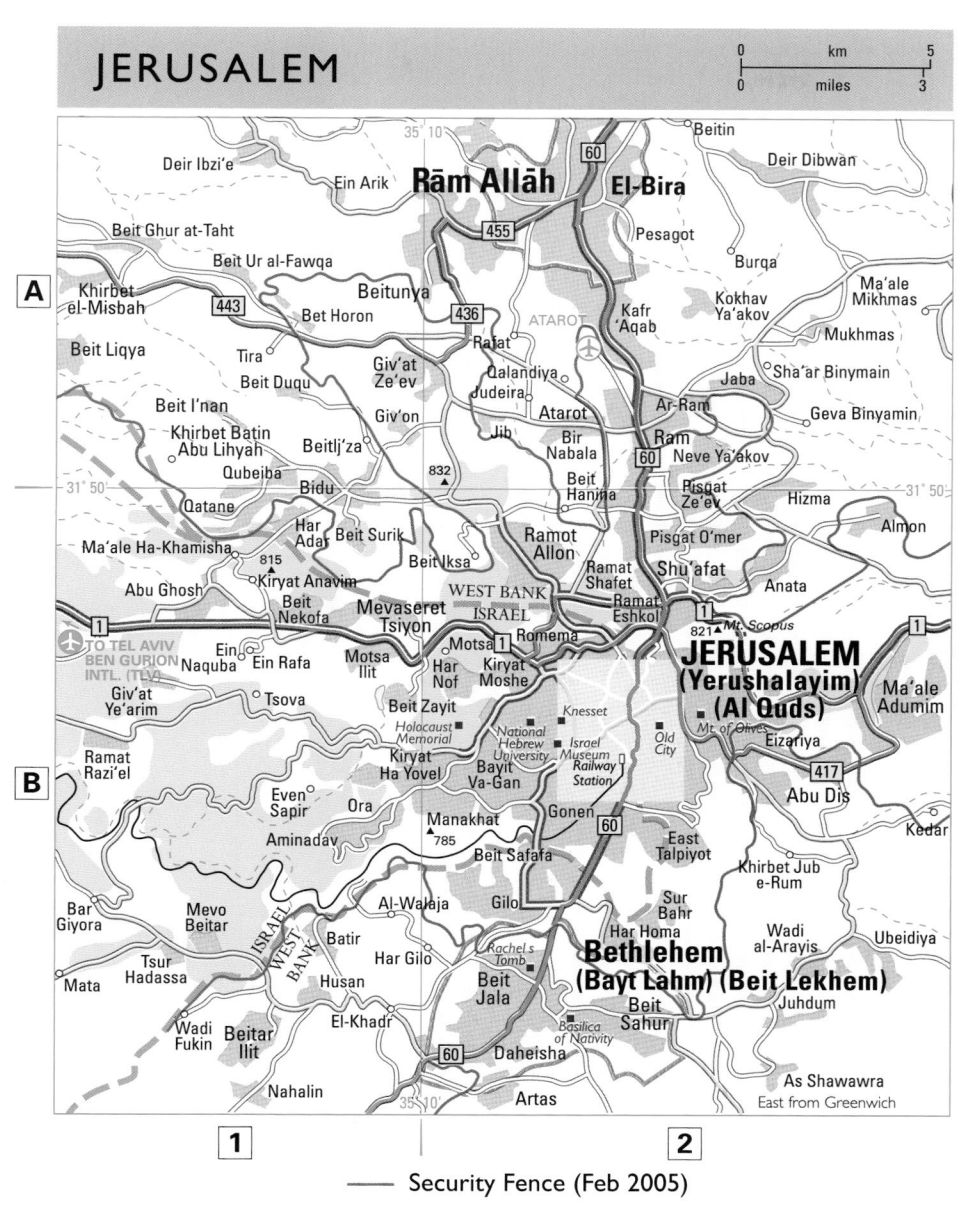

km 5 / miles 3

Security Fence (Feb 2005)

CENTRAL JERUSALEM

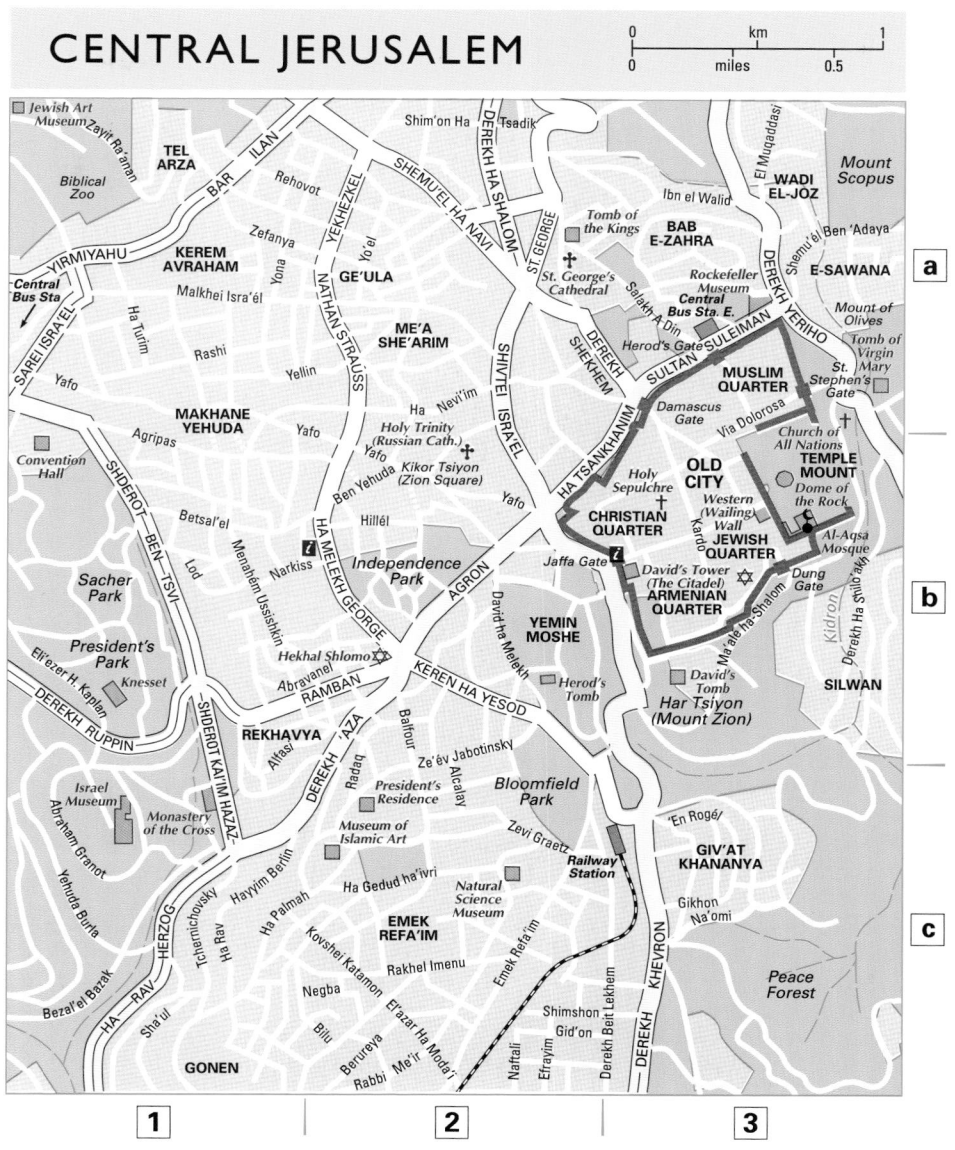

km 1 / miles 0.5

JOHANNESBURG

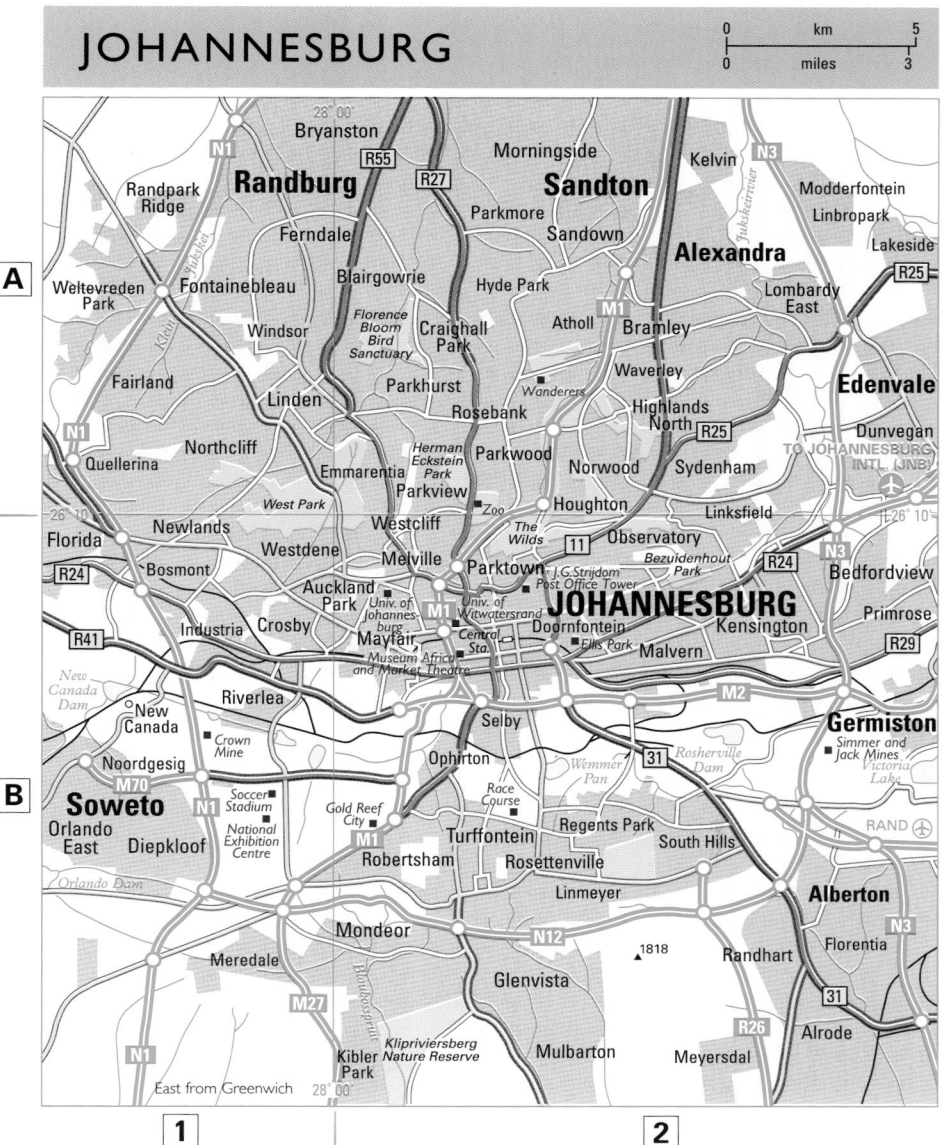

km 5 / miles 3

KARACHI

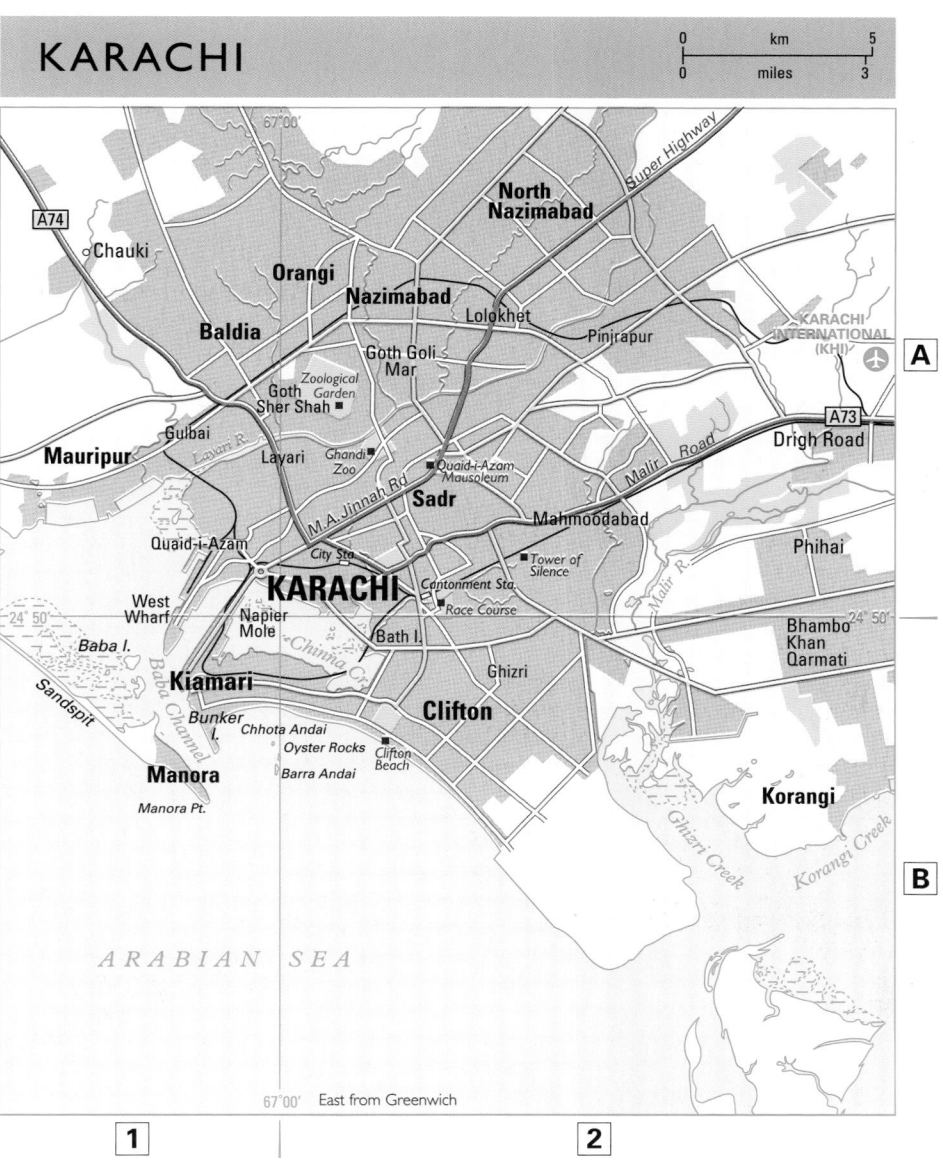

km 5 / miles 3

COPYRIGHT PHILIP'S

KOLKATA

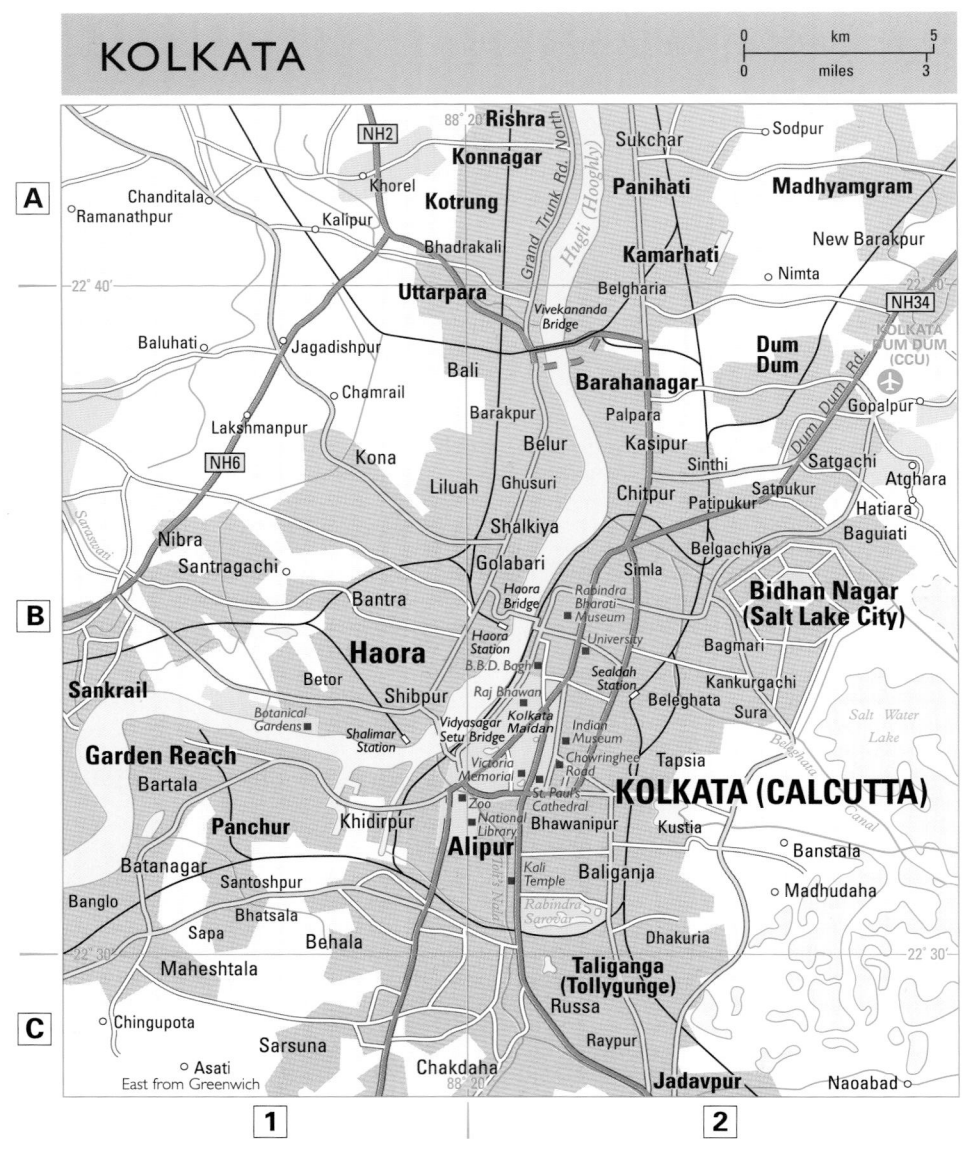

LAGOS

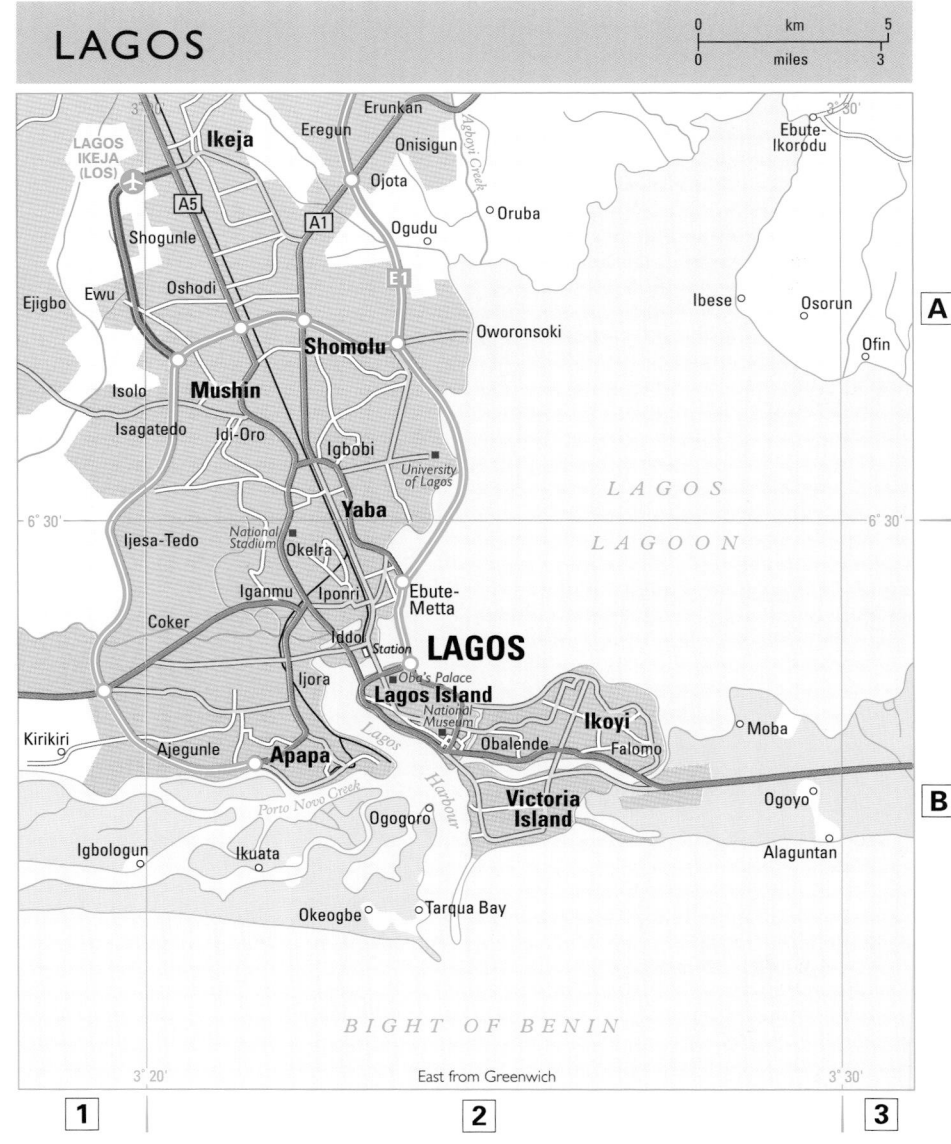

LAS VEGAS

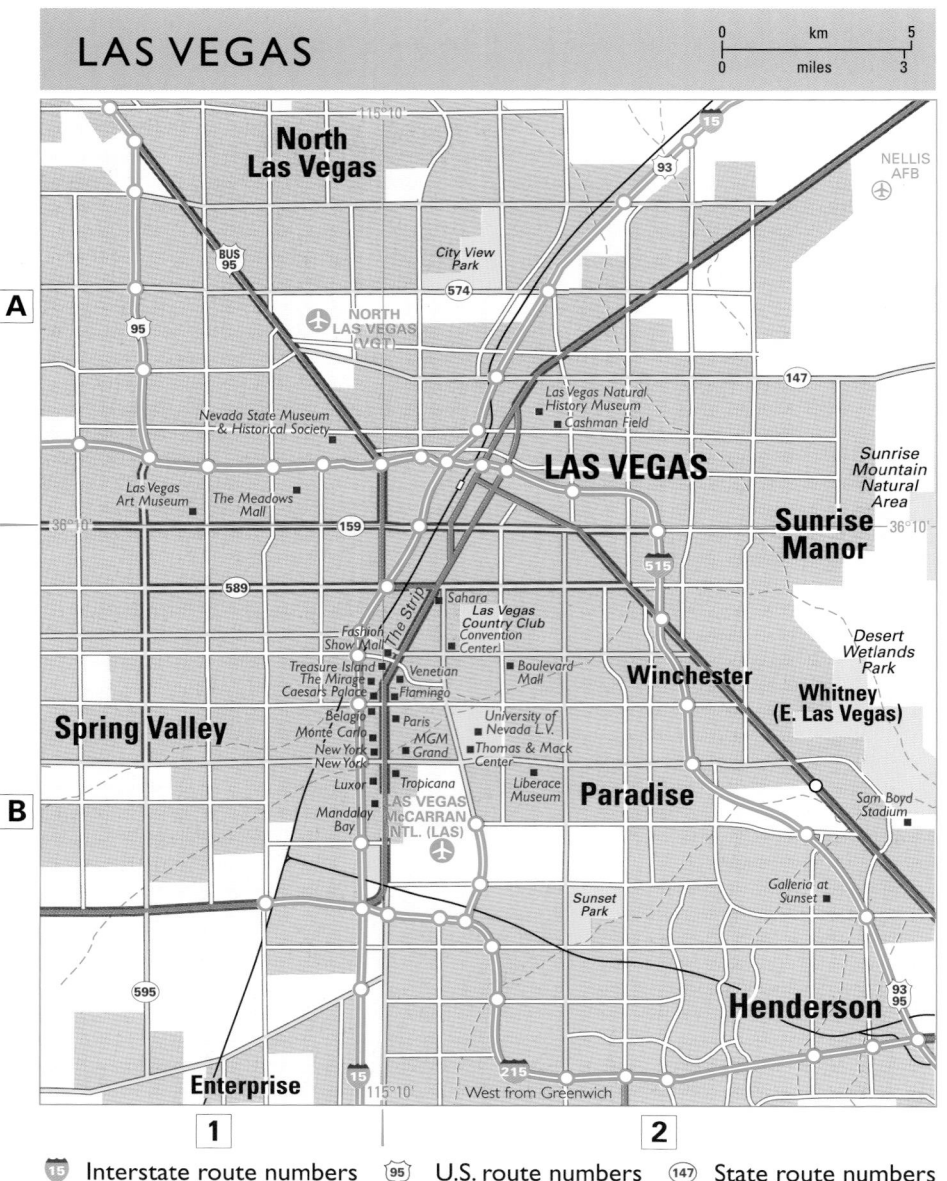

LIMA

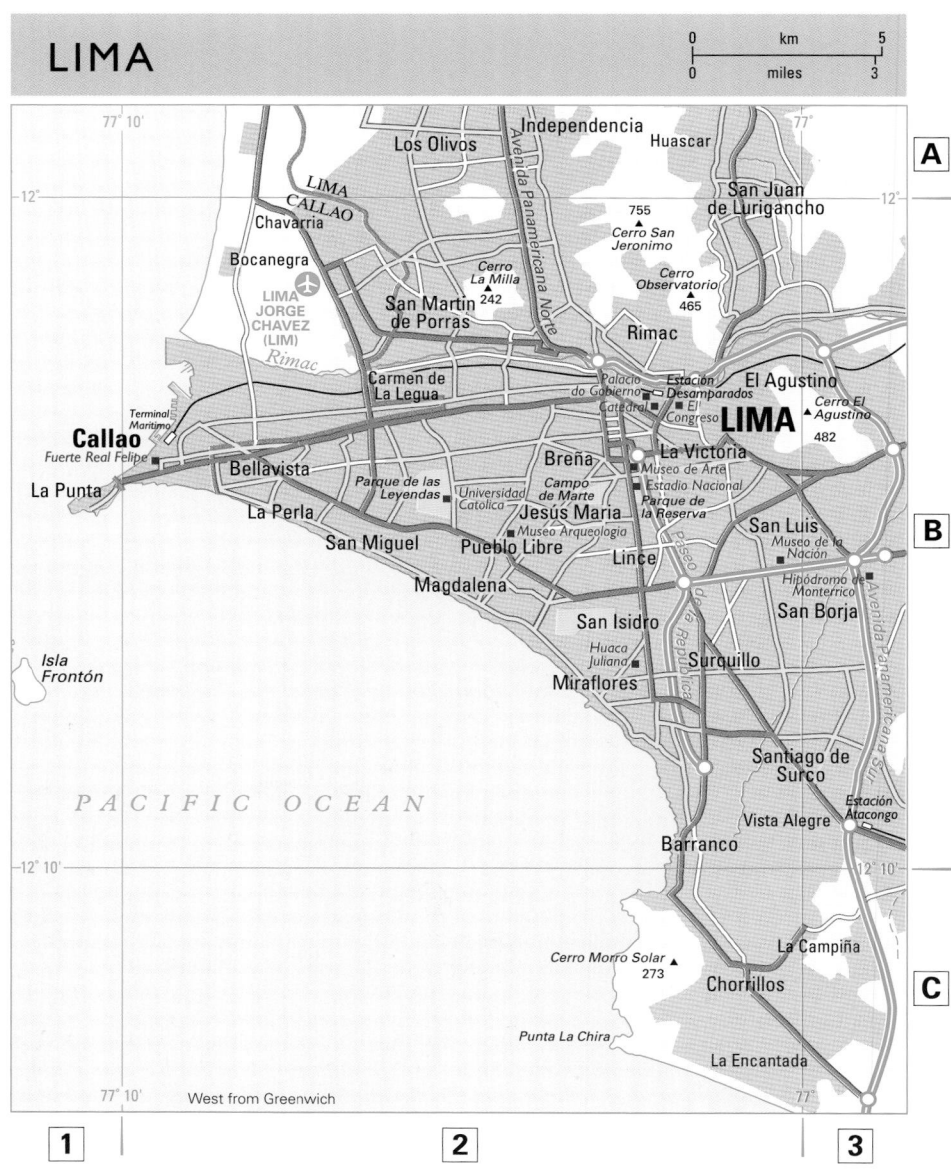

15 Interstate route numbers   95 U.S. route numbers   147 State route numbers

LONDON

km 5
miles 3

A

B

1 2 3 4 5

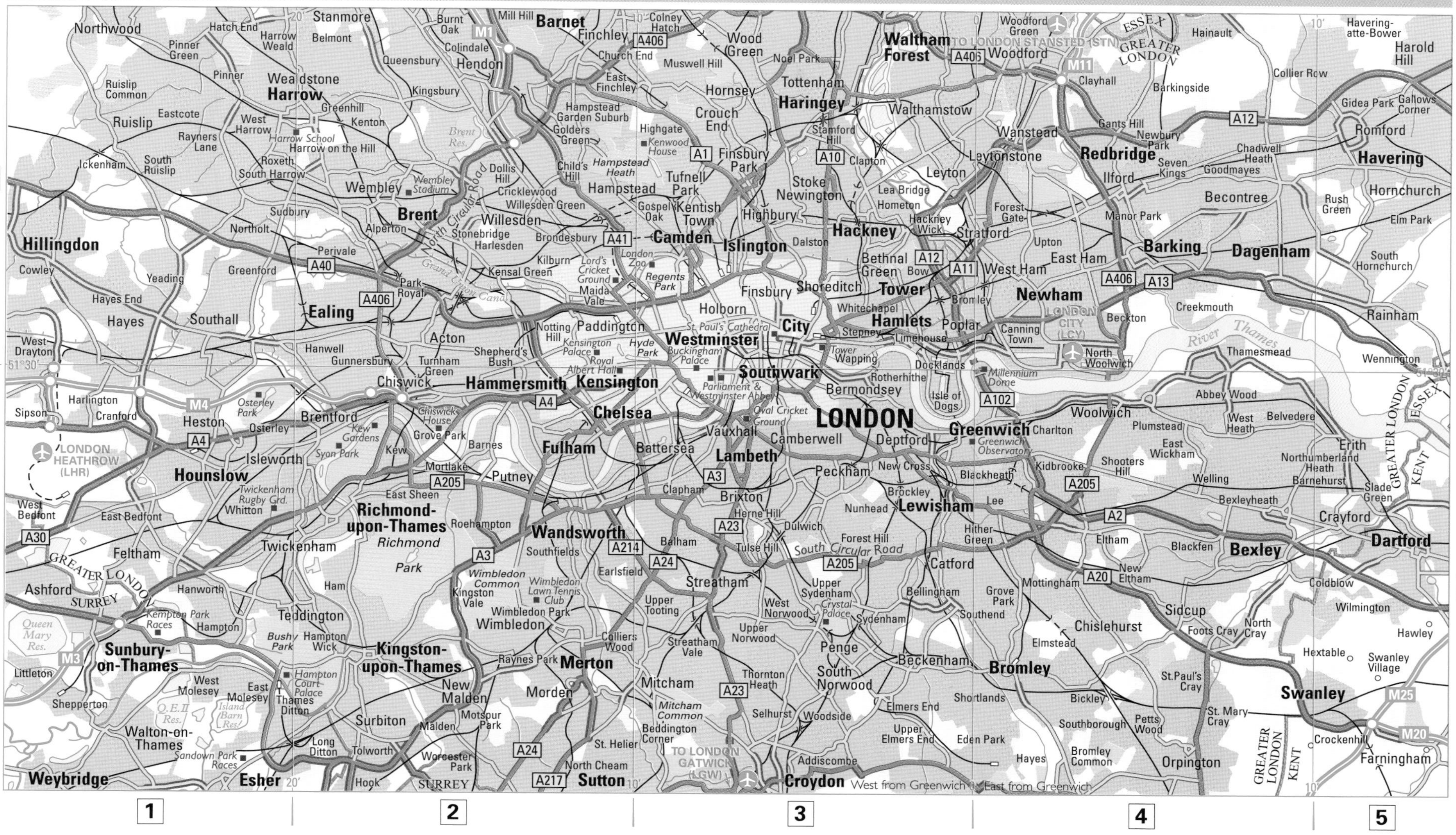

CENTRAL LONDON

km 2
miles 1

a

b

c

1 2 3 4 5

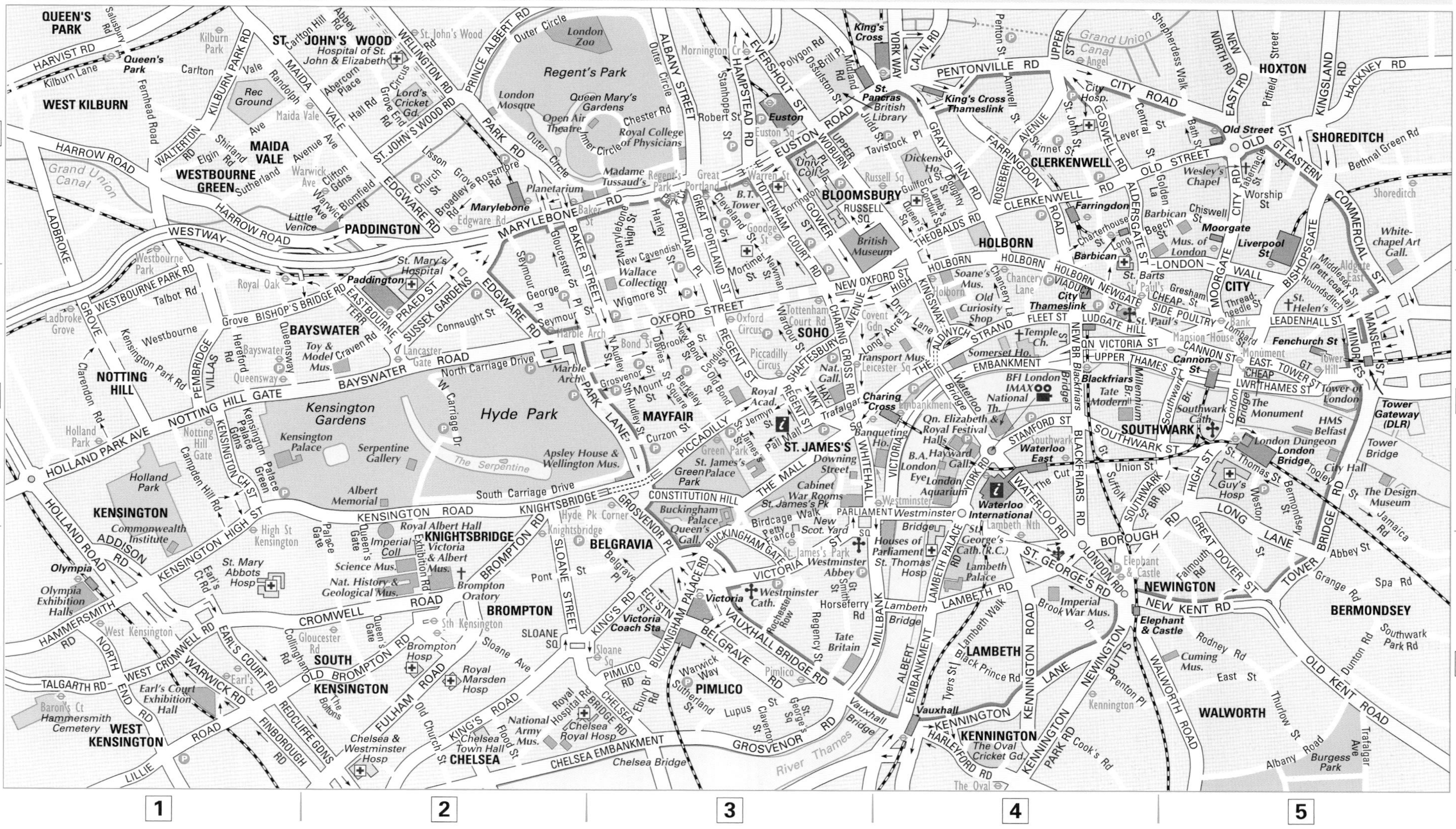

— Congestion Charging Zone

COPYRIGHT PHILIP'S

LISBON

km 5
miles 3

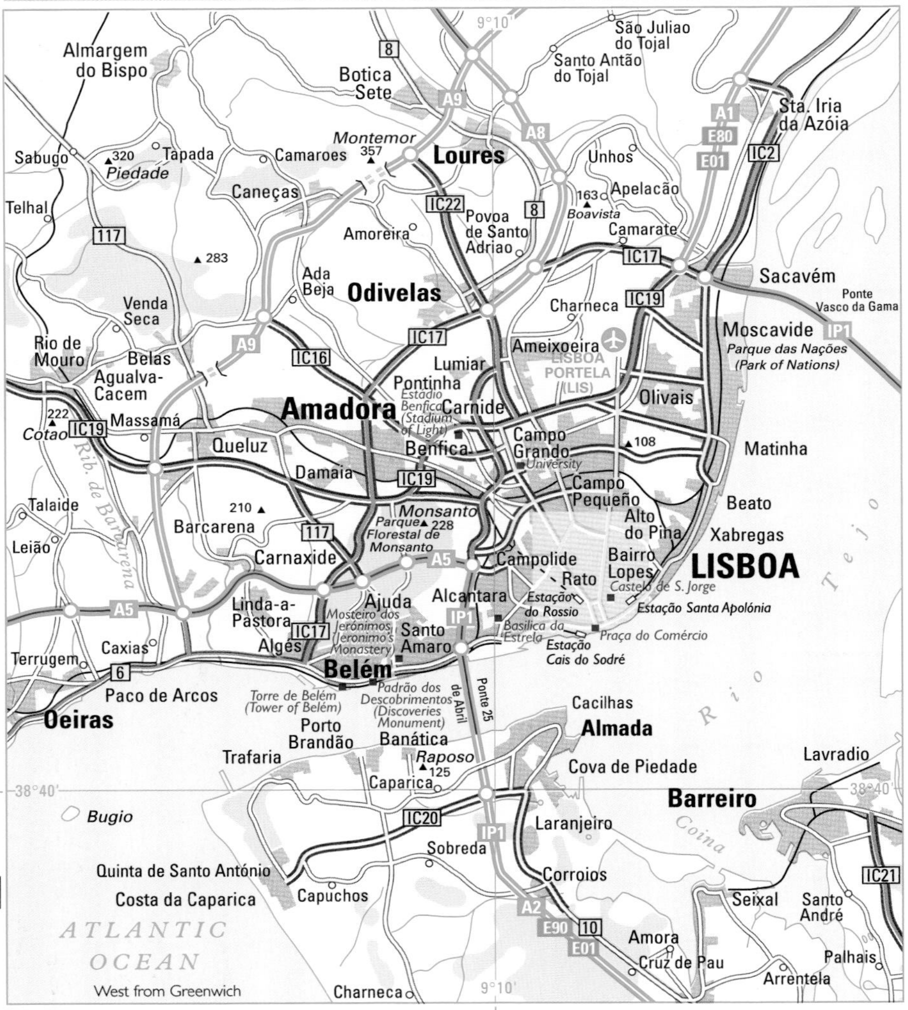

Almargem do Bispo
Botica Sete
Sabugo
Piedade ▲320
Tapada
Telhal
Camaroes ▲357
Montemor
Caneças
Loures
São Julião do Tojal
Santo Antão do Tojal
Unhos
Apelação
Sta. Iria da Azóia
Odivelas
Povoa de Santo Adrião
Amoreira
Camarate
Sacavém
Ponte Vasco da Gama
Venda Seca
Belas
Aguava-Cacem
Massamá
Ada Beja
Lumiar
Carnide
Pontinha
Charneca
Moscavide
Parque das Nações (Park of Nations)
Rio de Mouro
Amadora
Queluz
Benfica
Campo Grande
Olivais
Matinha
Damaia
▲210
Monsanto
Campo Pequeno
Alto do Pina
Beato
Xabregas
Carnaxide
Parque Florestal de Monsanto
▲228
Campolide
Rato
Bairro Lopes
LISBOA
Linda-a-Pastora
Algés
Ajuda
Alcántara
Santo Amaro
Belém
Estação do Rossio
Estação Santa Apolónia
Praça do Comércio
Caxias
Paco de Arcos
Torre de Belém (Tower of Belém)
Porto Brandão
Banática
Raposo ▲125
Almada
Lavradio
Oeiras
Terrugem
Trafaria
Caparica
Cova de Piedade
38°40'
Bugio
Quinta de Santo António
Costa da Caparica
Capuchos
Sobreda
Laranjeiro
Corroios
Barreiro
Coina
ATLANTIC OCEAN
West from Greenwich
Amora
Cruz de Pau
Seixal
Santo André
Palhais
Arrentela
Charneca

CENTRAL LISBON

km 1
miles 0.5

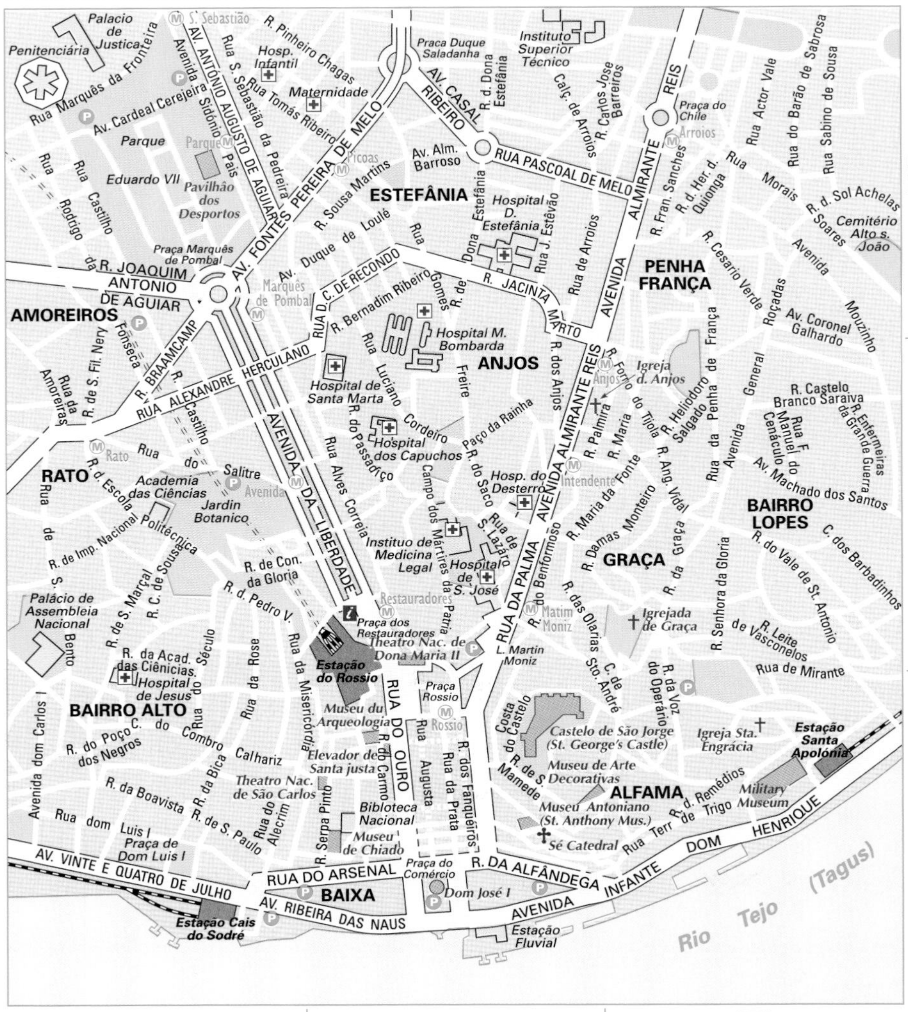

Palacio de Justiça
Penitenciária
Praça Duque Saldanha
Instituto Superior Técnico
Maternidade
ESTEFÂNIA
Parque Eduardo VII
Pavilhão dos Desportos
PENHA FRANÇA
Praça Marquês de Pombal
AMOREIROS
Hospital M. Bombarda
ANJOS
Hospital de Santa Marta
RATO
Jardim Botânico
Academia das Ciências
Instituto de Medicina Legal
GRAÇA
Palácio de Assembleia Nacional
BAIRRO ALTO
Museu do Arqueológico
Praça dos Restauradores
Teatro Nac. de Dona Maria II
Estação do Rossio
Castelo de São Jorge (St. George's Castle)
Museu de Arte Decorativas
ALFAMA
Museu Antoniano (St. Anthony Mus.)
Military Museum
Estação Santa Apolónia
Elevador de Sta. Justa
Theatro Nac. de São Carlos
Biblioteca Nacional
Sé Catedral
BAIXA
RUA DO ARSENAL
Praça do Comércio
Estação Cais do Sodré
Estação Fluvial
Rio Tejo (Tagus)

LOS ANGELES

km 5
miles 3

Tarzana
Sepulveda Dam Rec. Area
San Fernando Valley
Van Nuys
North Hollywood
Burbank
Verdugo Mts.
San Gabriel Mts.
Altadena
Eaton Canyon Park
Encino
▲216
Sherman Oaks
Studio City
N.B.C. Studios
Disney Studios
Flint Peak 575
Rose Bowl
Pasadena
Sierra Madre
Colorado Fwy.
Monrovia
Encino Reservoir
C.B.S. Fox Studios
Universal Studios
Warner Brothers Studios
Zoo
Glendale
Glendale Galleria
California Institute of Technology
Santa Anita Park
Topanga State Park
Cahuenga Peak 555
Griffith Park
Eagle Rock
South Pasadena
Arcadia
Santa Monica Mts.
Beverly Glen
Hollywood
Griffith Observatory
Highland Park
Garvanza
San Marino
Temple City
▲459
Bel Air
Hollywood Bowl
Mann's Chinese Theatre
Sunset Blvd.
Southwest Museum
El Sereno
Arroyo Seco Park
The Getty Center
University of California Los Angeles
Beverly Hills
West Hollywood
Santa Monica Blvd.
Paramount Studios
Alhambra
San Gabriel
Rosemead
Will Rogers State Historical Park
Westwood Village
Los Angeles County Art Museum
Wilshire Blvd.
MacArthur Park
Elysian Park
Dodger Stadium
Lincoln Heights
California State University
San Bernardino Fwy.
Pacific Palisades
Santa Monica
Museum of Art
Hollywood Fwy.
LOS ANGELES
Civic Center
Union Sta.
Monterey Park
South San Gabriel
El Monte
South El Monte
Brentwood Park
Whittier Narrows
Flood Control Basin
Bicentennial Park
Santa Monica Fwy.
Convention Center
Boyle Heights
Montebello Town Center
Culver City
Sony Picture Studio
University of Southern California
California Space & Science Center
Memorial Coliseum
Exposition Park
East Los Angeles
Montebello
Puente Hills
View Park
Vernon
Commerce
Pio Pico State Historic Park
Pico Rivera
Santa Monica Pier
California Heritage Museum
Baldwin Hills Reservoir
Windsor Hills
Maywood
Bell Gardens
Whittier
Venice
Venice Boardwalk
Ladera Heights
Huntington Park
Florence
Bell
Cudahy
Los Nietos
PACIFIC OCEAN
Marina del Rey
Westchester
University of West Los Angeles
Great Western Forum
Inglewood
Walnut Park
Santa Fe Springs
LOS ANGELES INTERNATIONAL (LAX)
Lennox
South Gate
Downey

Interstate route numbers   State route numbers

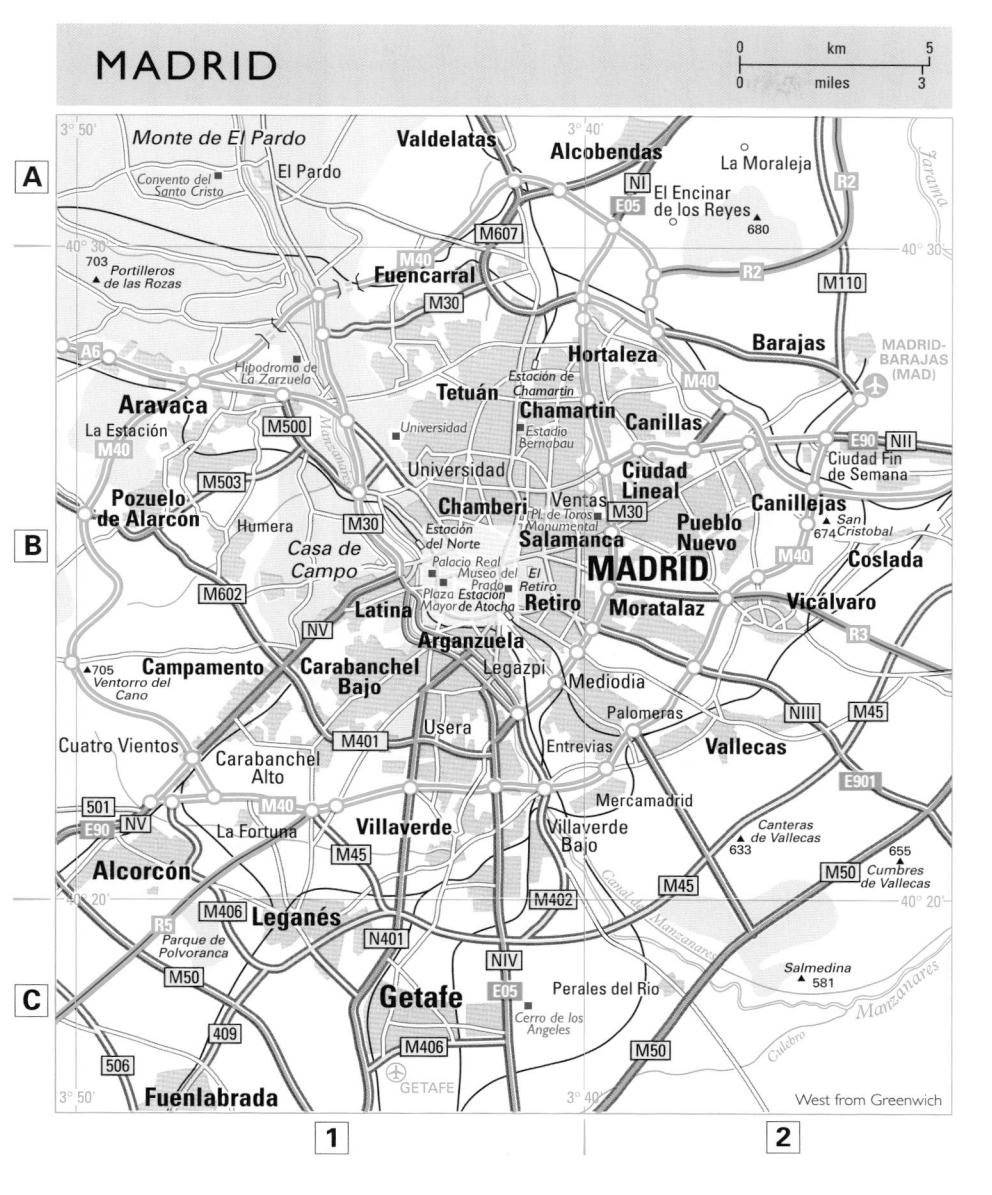

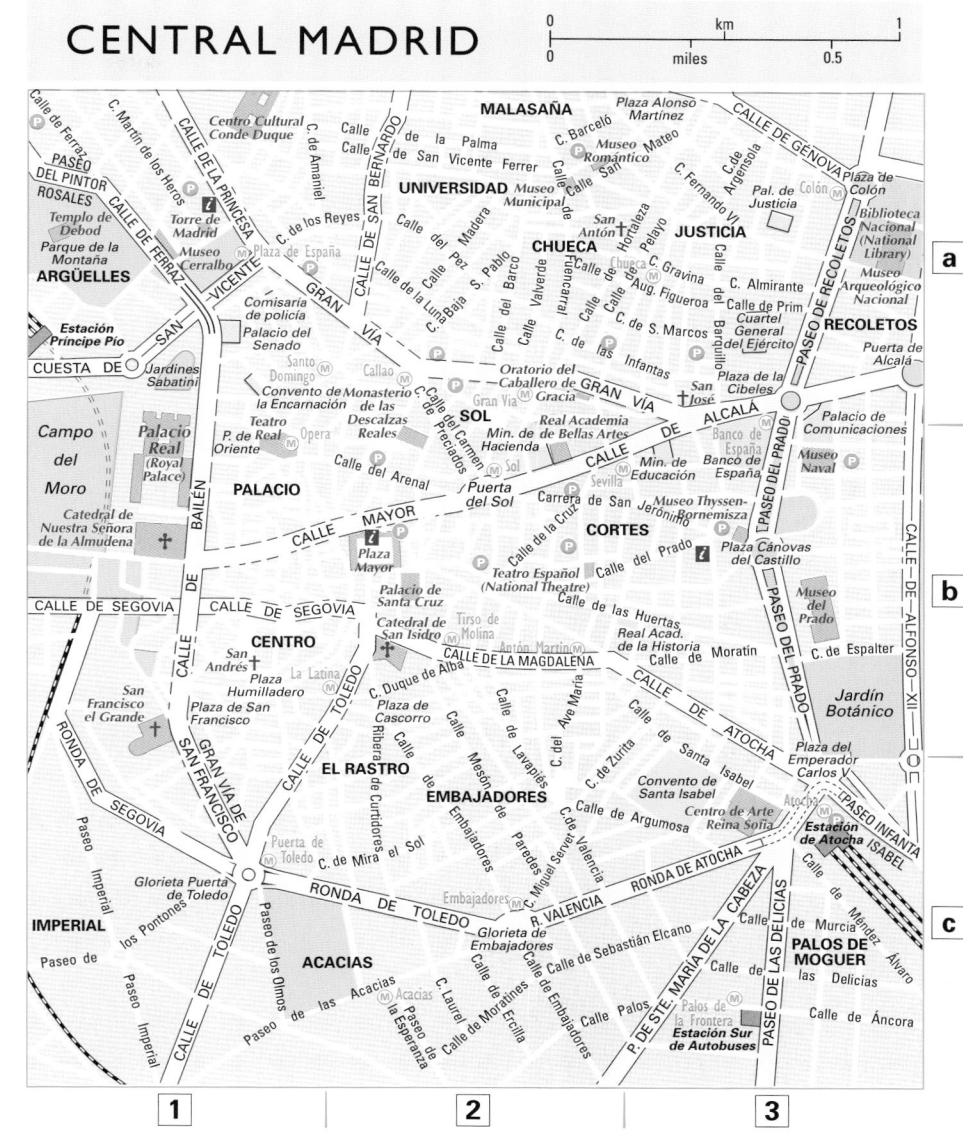

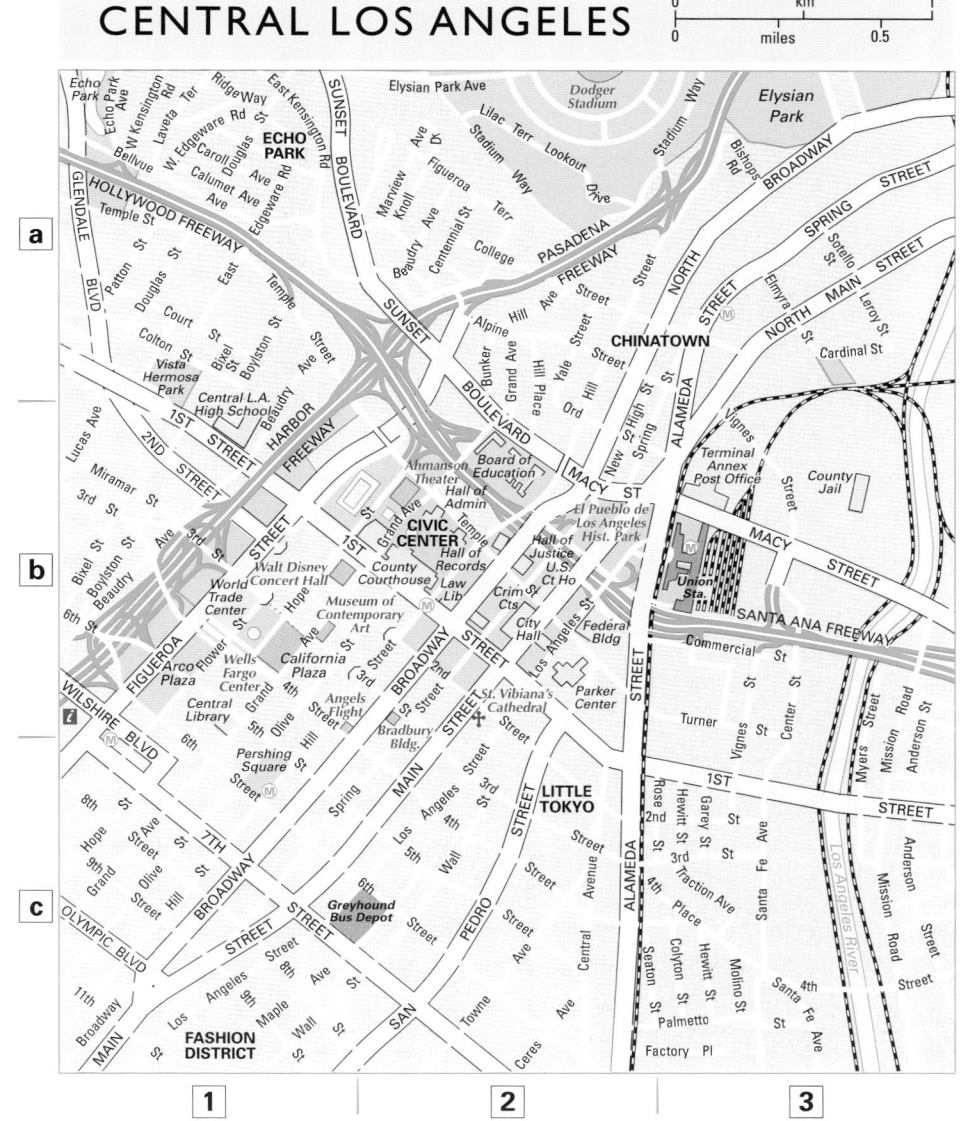

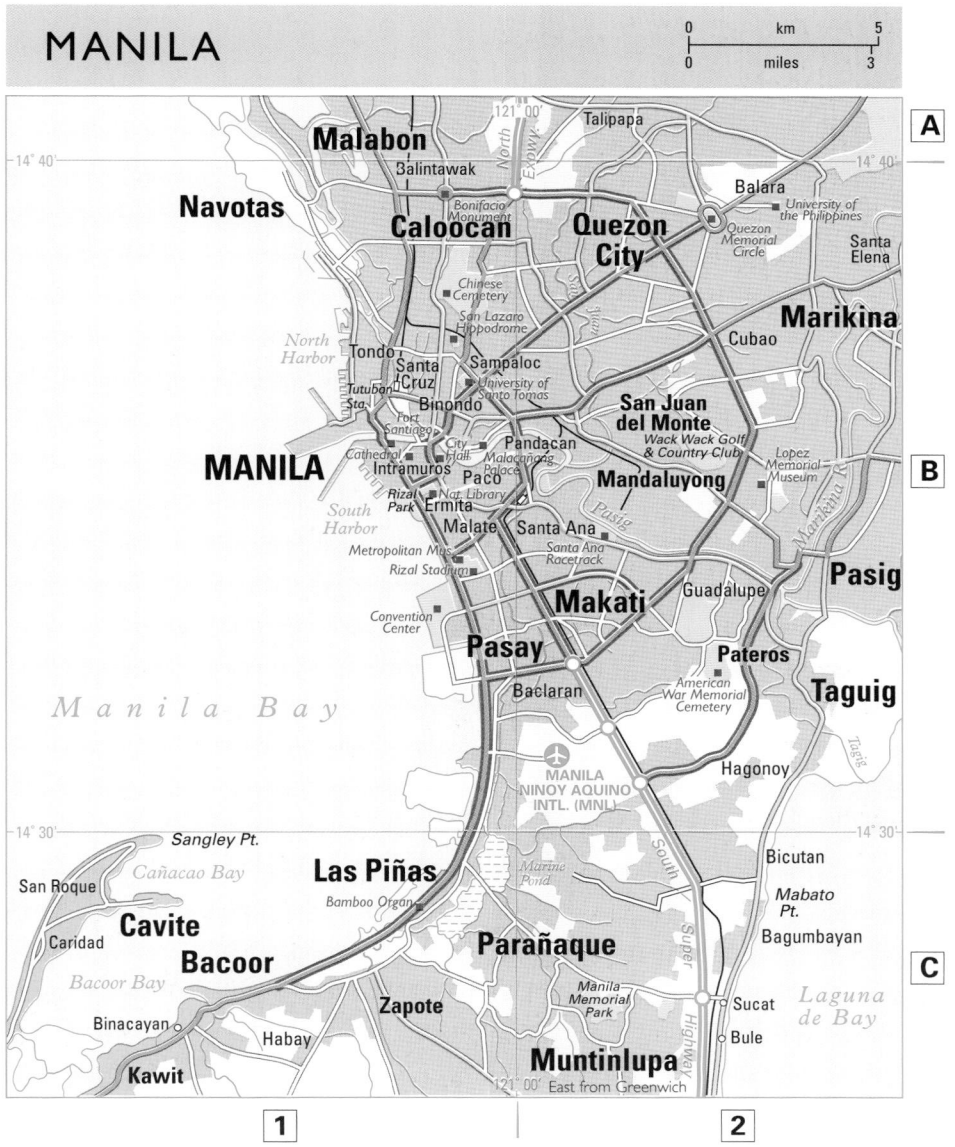

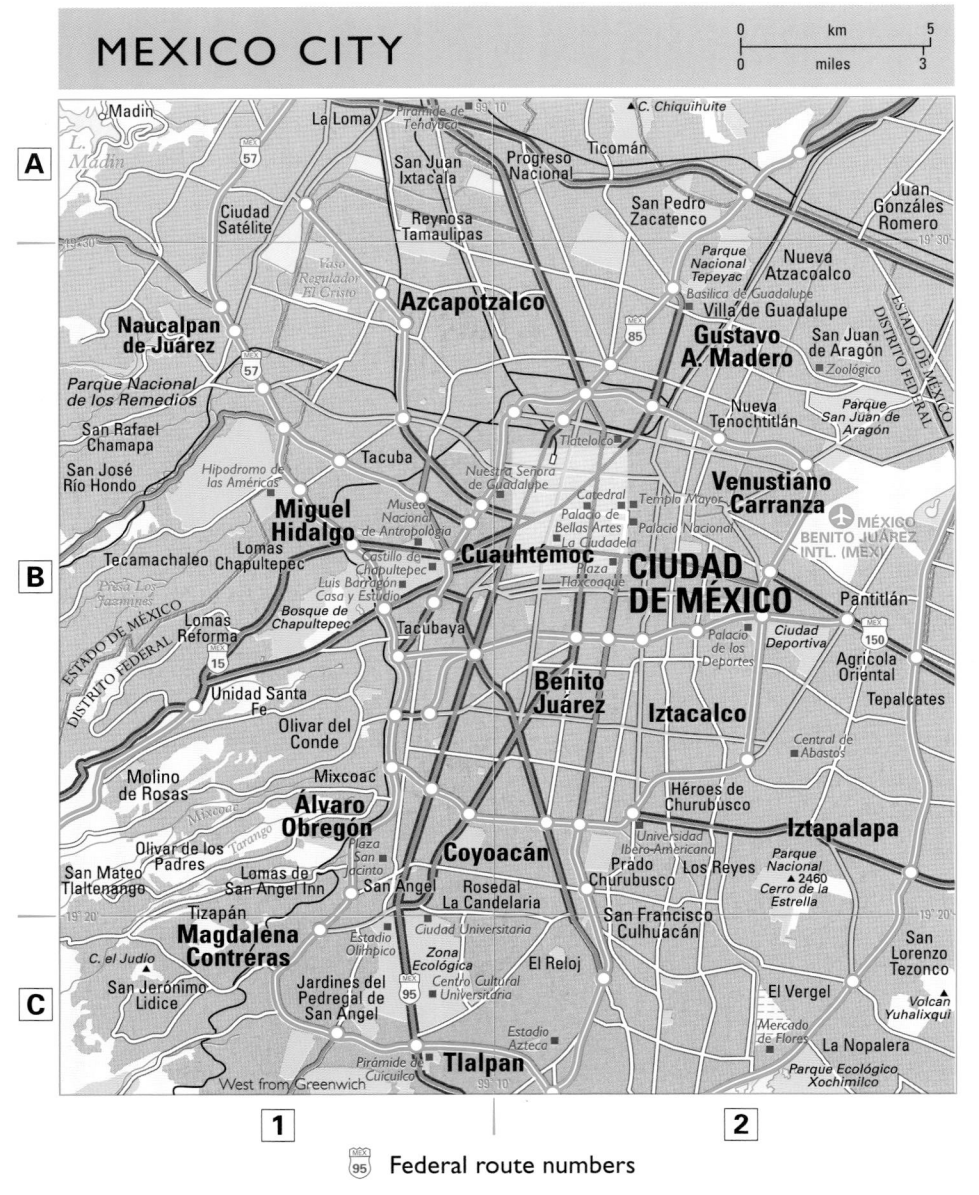

MEXICO CITY

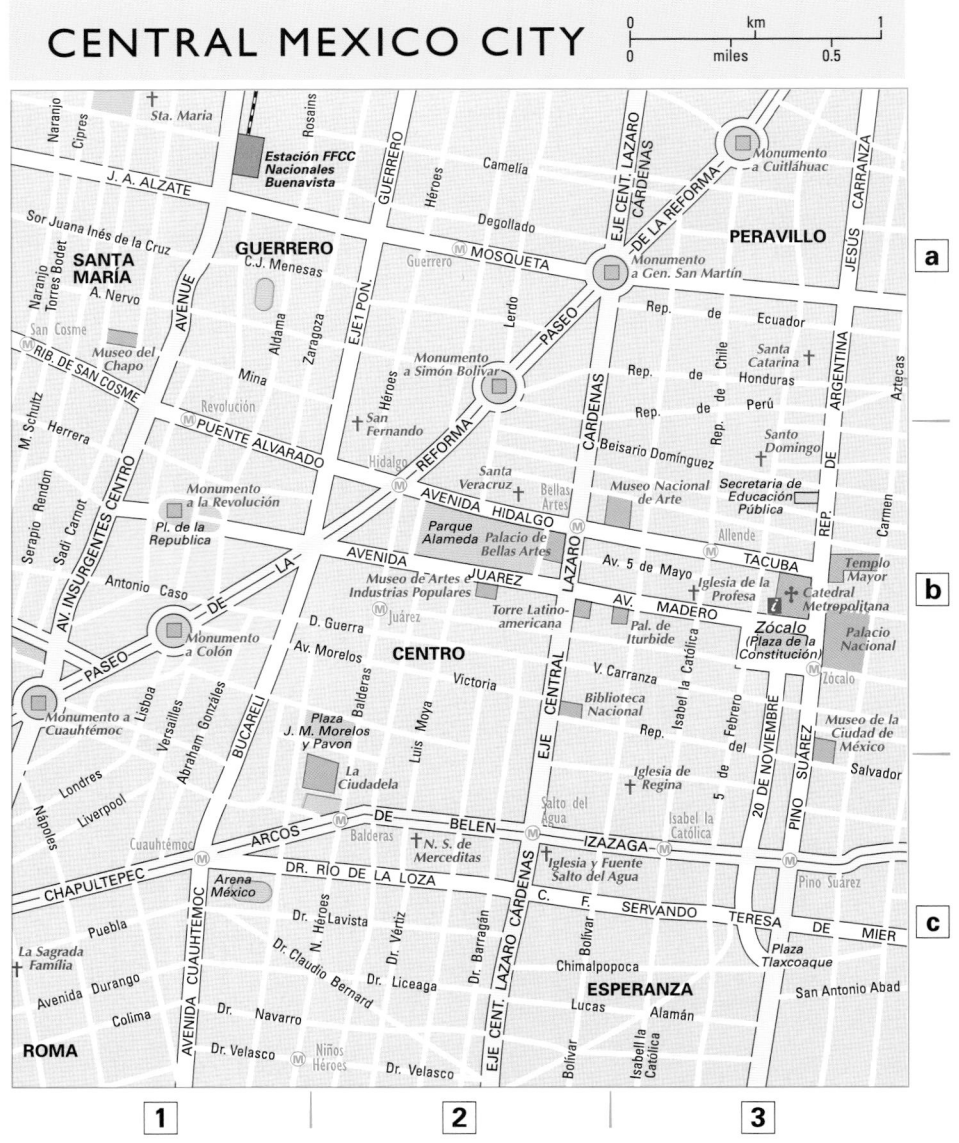

CENTRAL MEXICO CITY

95 Federal route numbers

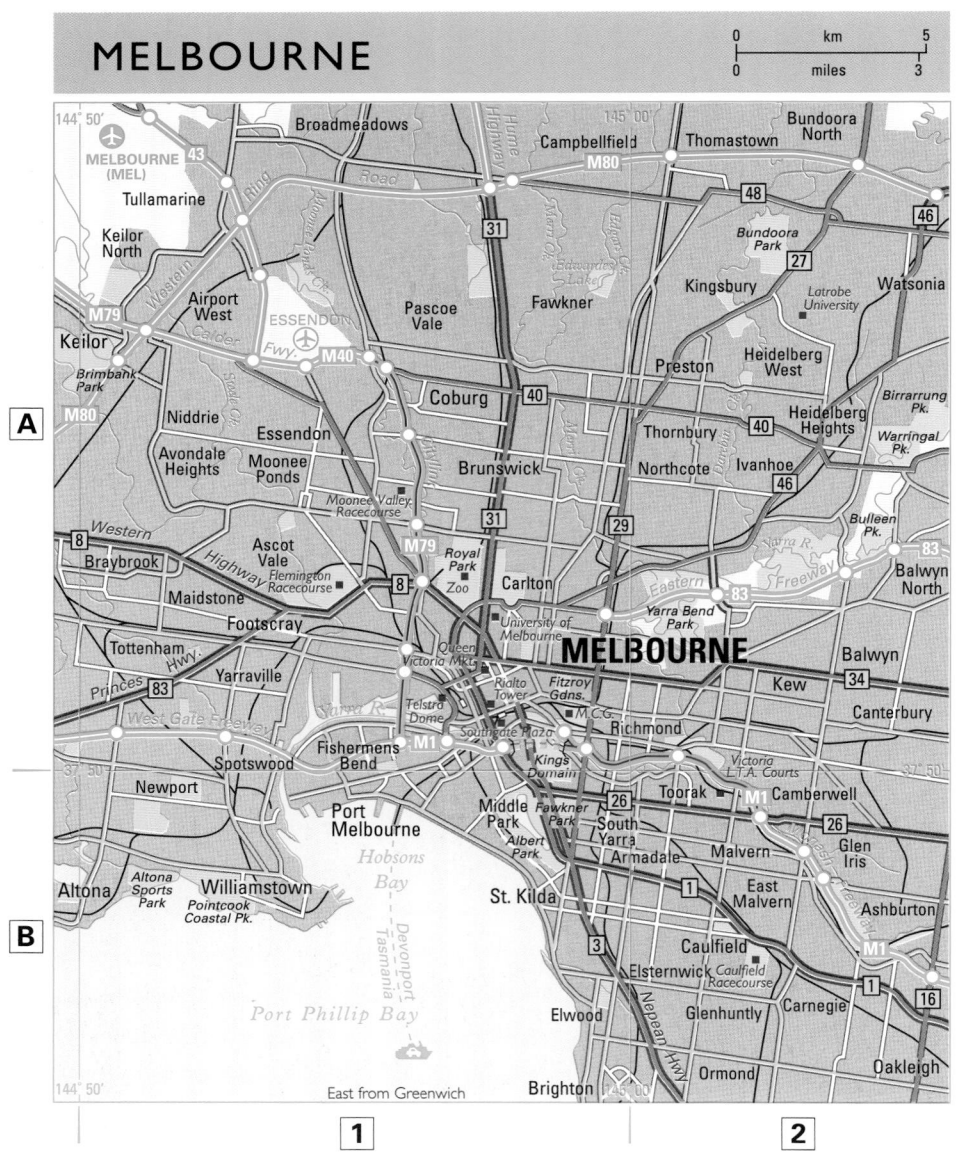

MELBOURNE

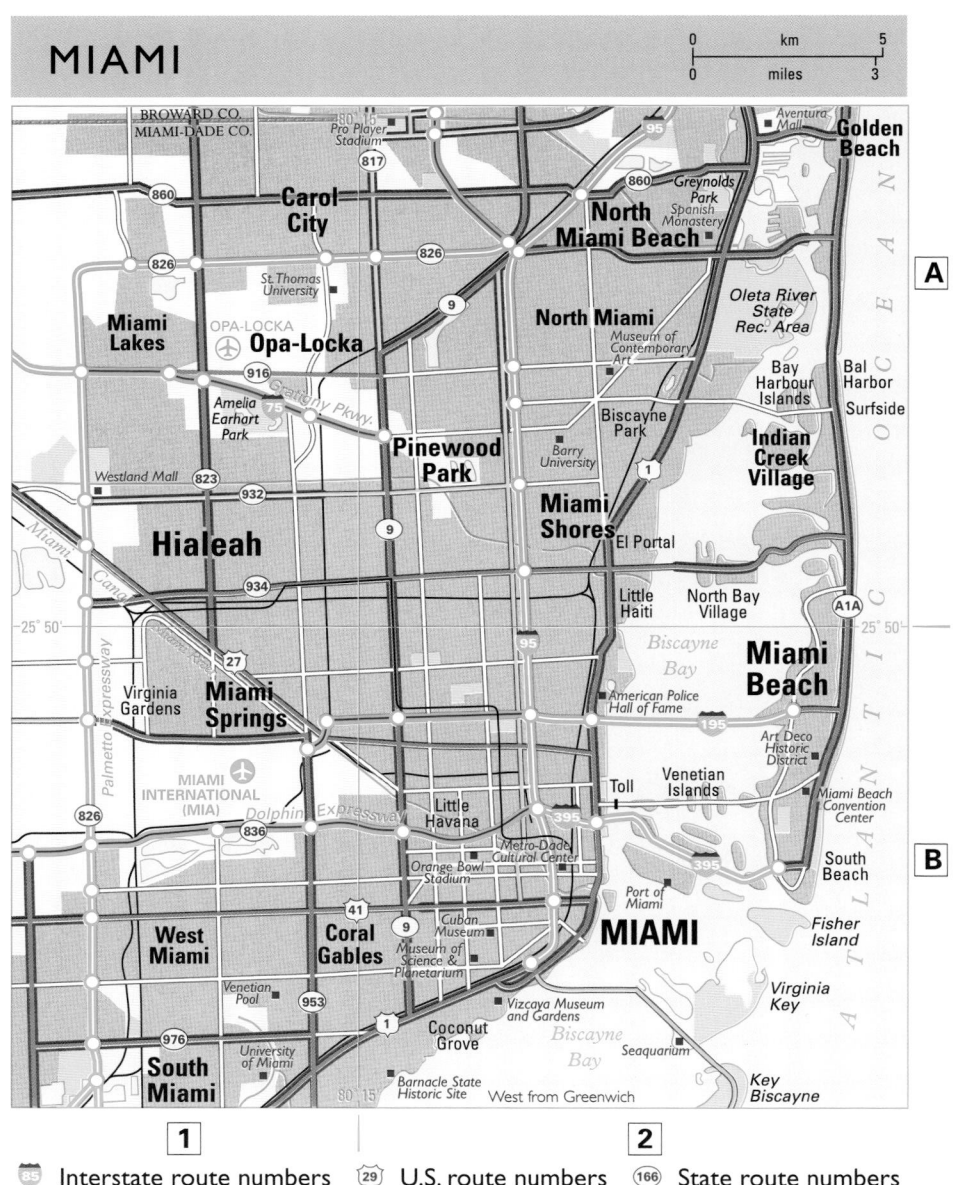

MIAMI

Interstate route numbers   29 U.S. route numbers   166 State route numbers

MILAN

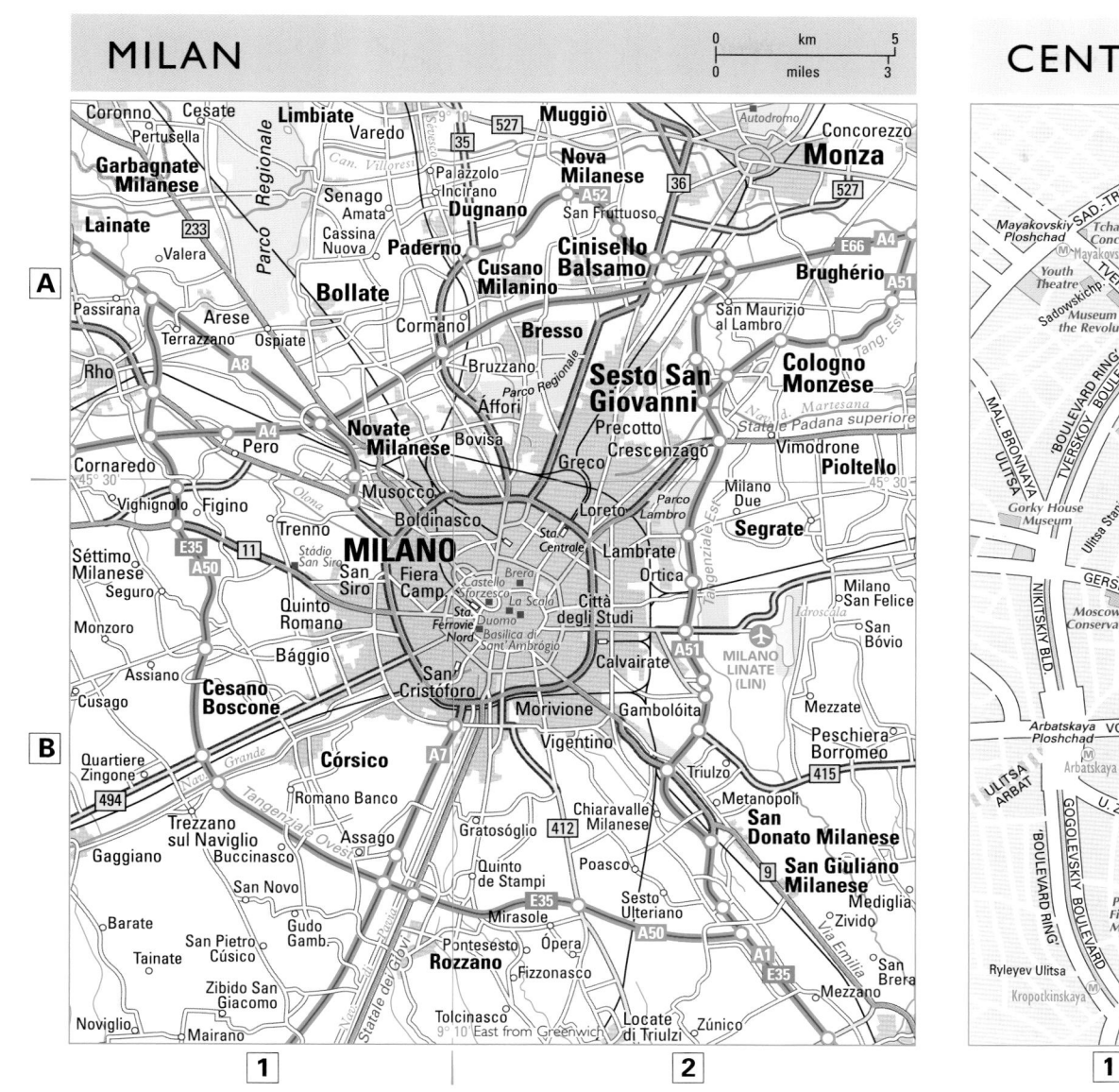

CENTRAL MOSCOW

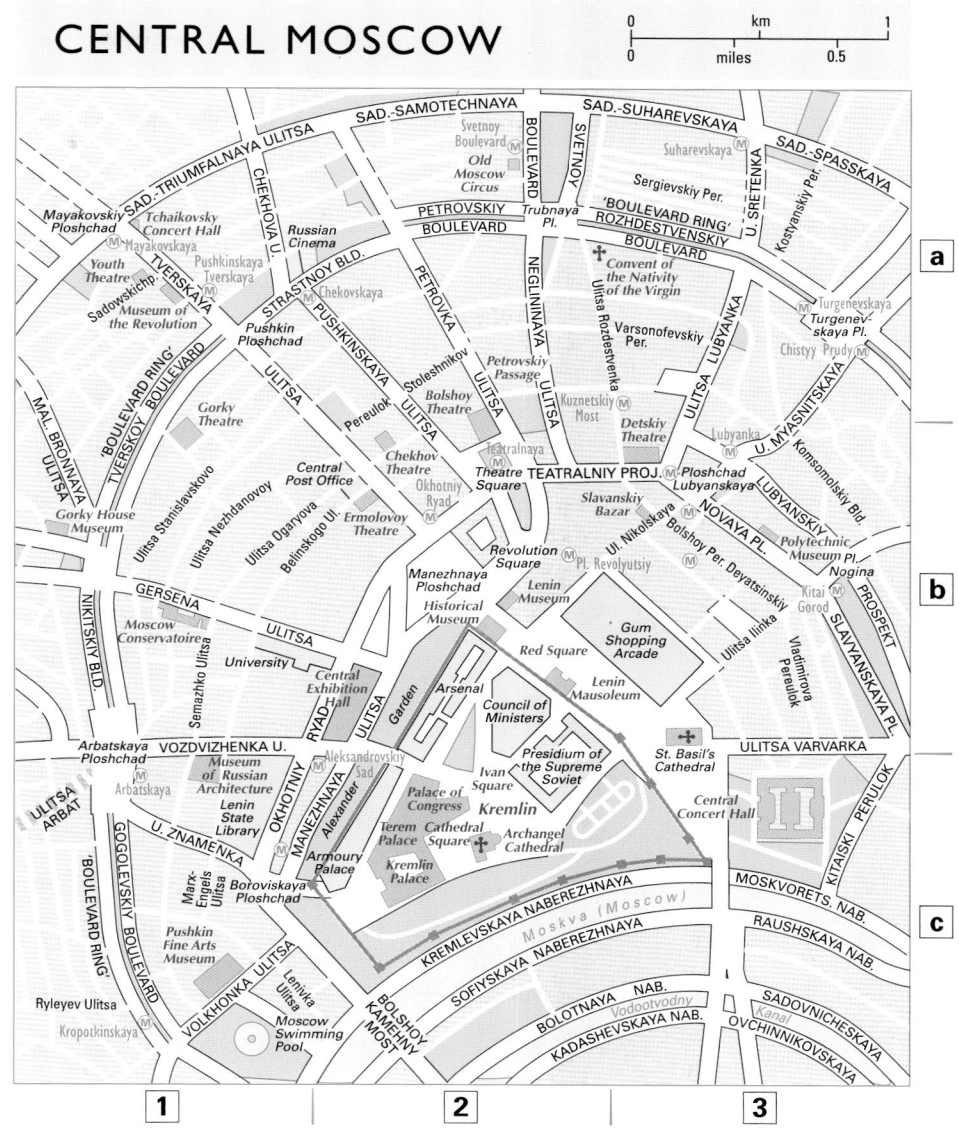

MOSCOW

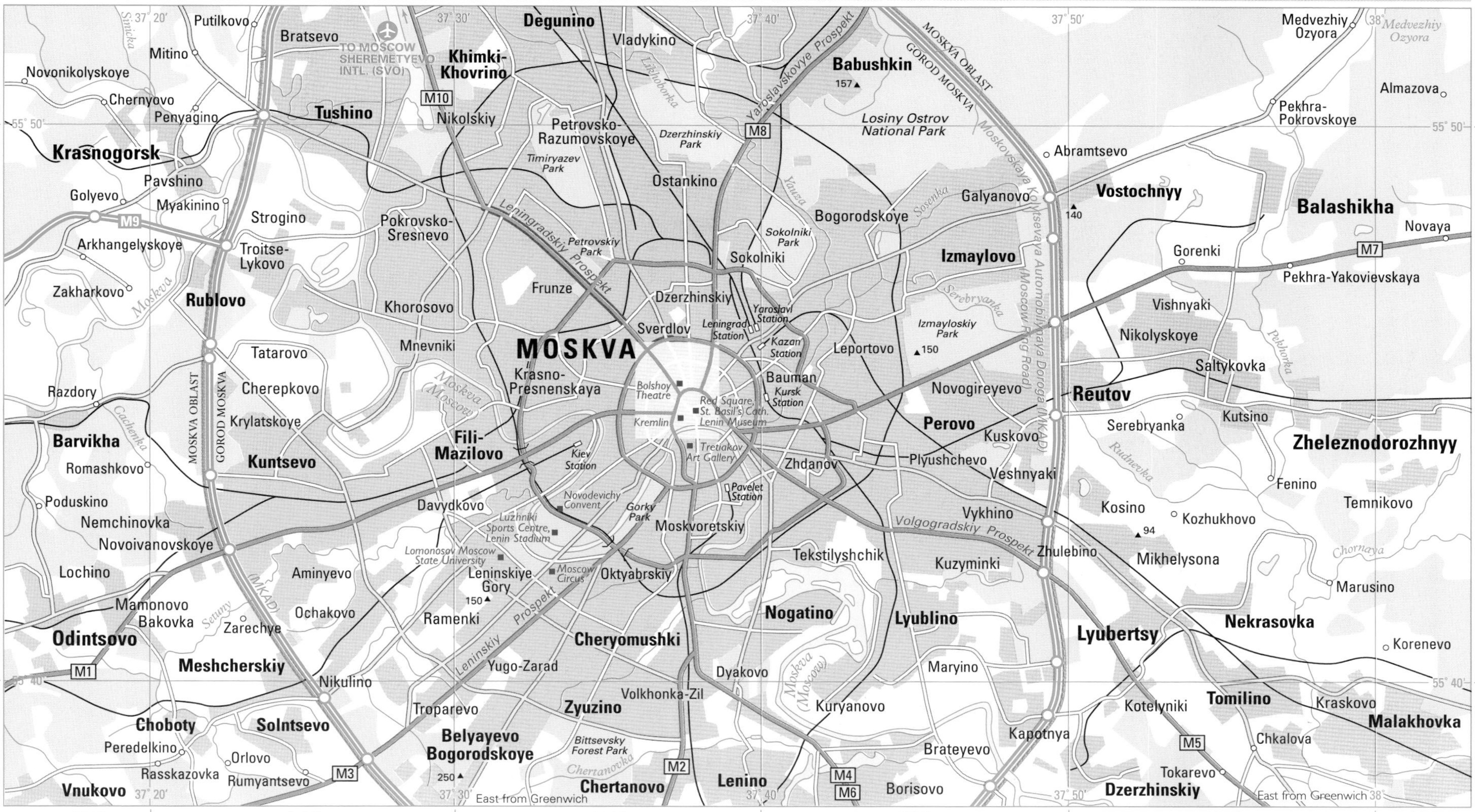

COPYRIGHT PHILIP'S

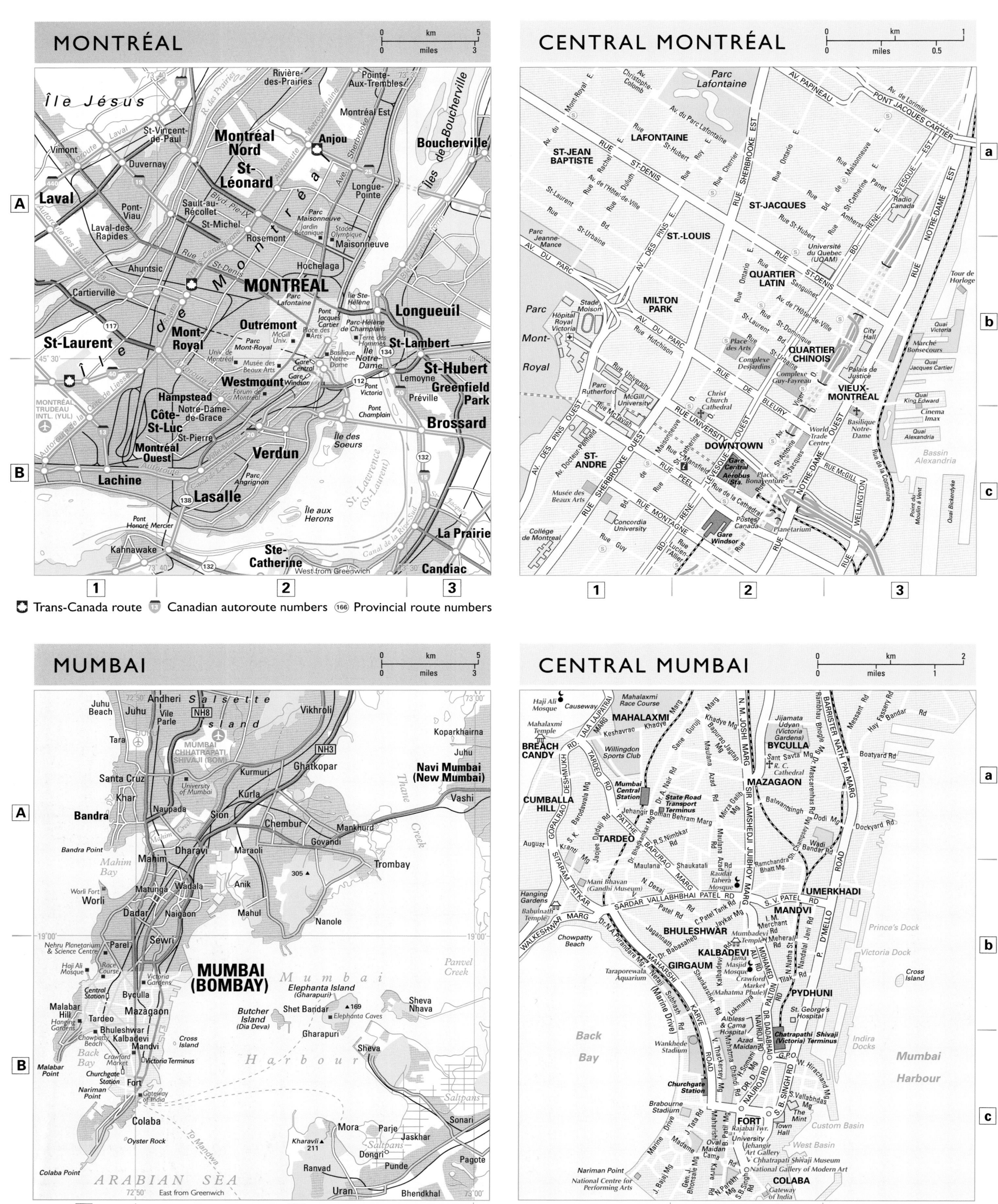

MONTRÉAL

km 5 / miles 3

Île Jésus · Laval · Rivière-des-Prairies · Pointe-Aux-Trembles · Boucherville · Montréal Est · Montréal Nord · St-Léonard · Anjou · Longue-Pointe · Boucherville · Îles de Boucherville · Vimont · St-Vincent-de-Paul · Duvernay · Laval · Laval-des-Rapides · Pont-Viau · Sault-au-Récollet · St-Michel · Rosemont · Hochelaga · Maisonneuve · Longueuil · Laval · Ahuntsic · MONTRÉAL · St-Lambert · Cartierville · Outremont · St-Hubert · St-Laurent · Mont-Royal · Lemoyne · Greenfield Park · Préville · Hampstead · Westmount · Brossard · Côte-St-Luc · Notre-Dame-de-Grâce · St-Pierre · Montréal Ouest · Verdun · Lachine · Lasalle · Île des Soeurs · Île aux Herons · Kahnawake · Ste-Catherine · La Prairie · Candiac · West from Greenwich

Trans-Canada route · Canadian autoroute numbers · Provincial route numbers

CENTRAL MONTRÉAL

km 1 / miles 0.5

Parc Lafontaine · LAFONTAINE · ST-JEAN BAPTISTE · ST-JACQUES · ST-LOUIS · Université du Québec (UQAM) · MILTON PARK · QUARTIER LATIN · Parc Jeanne-Mance · QUARTIER CHINOIS · City Hall · VIEUX-MONTRÉAL · Marché Bonsecours · Parc du Mont-Royal · Place des Arts · Christ Church Cathedral · Complexe Desjardins · Palais de Justice · Hôpital Royal Victoria · McGill University · Parc Rutherford · DOWNTOWN · Basilique Notre-Dame · World Trade Centre · ST-ANDRÉ · Musée des Beaux Arts · Gare Central · Gare Aérobus Sta. · Cinéma Imax · Bassin Alexandria · Collège de Montréal · Concordia University · Postes Canada · Gare Windsor · Planétarium · Quai Victoria · Quai Jacques Cartier · Quai King Edward · Quai Alexandria

MUMBAI

km 5 / miles 3

Salsette Island · Juhu Beach · Andheri · Vile Parle · Vikhroli · NH8 · Juhu · Tara · MUMBAI CHHATRAPATI SHIVAJI (BOM) · Koparkhairna · Santa Cruz · Kurmuri · Ghatkopar · NH3 · Navi Mumbai (New Mumbai) · University of Mumbai · Kurla · Juhu · Khar · Naupada · Sion · Vashi · Bandra · Dharavi · Chembur · Govandi · Mankhurd · Thane Creek · Bandra Point · Mahim · Maraoli · 305 · Trombay · Mahim Bay · Matunga · Wadala · Anik · Worli Fort · Worli · Dadar · Naigaon · Mahul · Nanole · Nehru Planetarium & Science Centre · Parel · Sewri · Panvel Creek · Haji Ali Mosque · Race Course · MUMBAI (BOMBAY) · Mumbai Harbour · Central Station · Victoria Gardens · Elephanta Island (Gharapuri) · Byculla · Malabar Hill · Hanging Gardens · Mazagaon · Elephanta Caves · Cross Island · Sheva Nhava · Chowpatty Beach · Bhuleshwar · Kalbadevi · Mandvi · Butcher Island (Dia Deva) · Gharapuri · Crawford Market · Victoria Terminus · Sheva · Malabar Point · Back Bay · Churchgate Station · Fort · Harbour · Nariman Point · Gateway of India · Saltpans · Colaba · Mora · Parje · Sonari · Oyster Rock · Jaskhar · Kharavli 211 · Dongri · Punde · Pagote · Colaba Point · ARABIAN SEA · Ranvad · Uran · Bhendkhal · East from Greenwich

CENTRAL MUMBAI

km 2 / miles 1

Haji Ali Mosque · Mahalaxmi Race Course · Causeway · MAHALAXMI · Jijamata Udyan (Victoria Gardens) · Mahalaxmi Temple · BYCULLA · BREACH CANDY · Willingdon Sports Club · R. C. Cathedral · MAZAGAON · CUMBALLA HILL · Mumbai Central Station · State Road Transport Terminus · UMERKHADI · TARDEO · Mani Bhavan (Gandhi Museum) · Raudat Tahera Mosque · MANDVI · Hanging Gardens · SARDAR VALLABHBHAI · BHULESHWAR · Babulnath Temple · Chowpatty Beach · Mumbadevi Temple · KALBADEVI · GIRGAUM · Taraporewala Aquarium · Crawford Market · Mahatma Phule · PYDHUNI · Cross Island · St. George's Hospital · Albless & Cama Hospital · Azad Maidan · Chatrapathi Shivaji (Victoria) Terminus · Indira Docks · Wankhede Stadium · G.P.O. · Mumbai Harbour · Back Bay · Churchgate Station · Brabourne Stadium · FORT · The Mint · Town Hall · West Basin · Custom Basin · Jehangir Art Gallery · Chhatrapati Shivaji Museum · National Gallery of Modern Art · Nariman Point · National Centre for Performing Arts · COLABA · Gateway of India

MUNICH

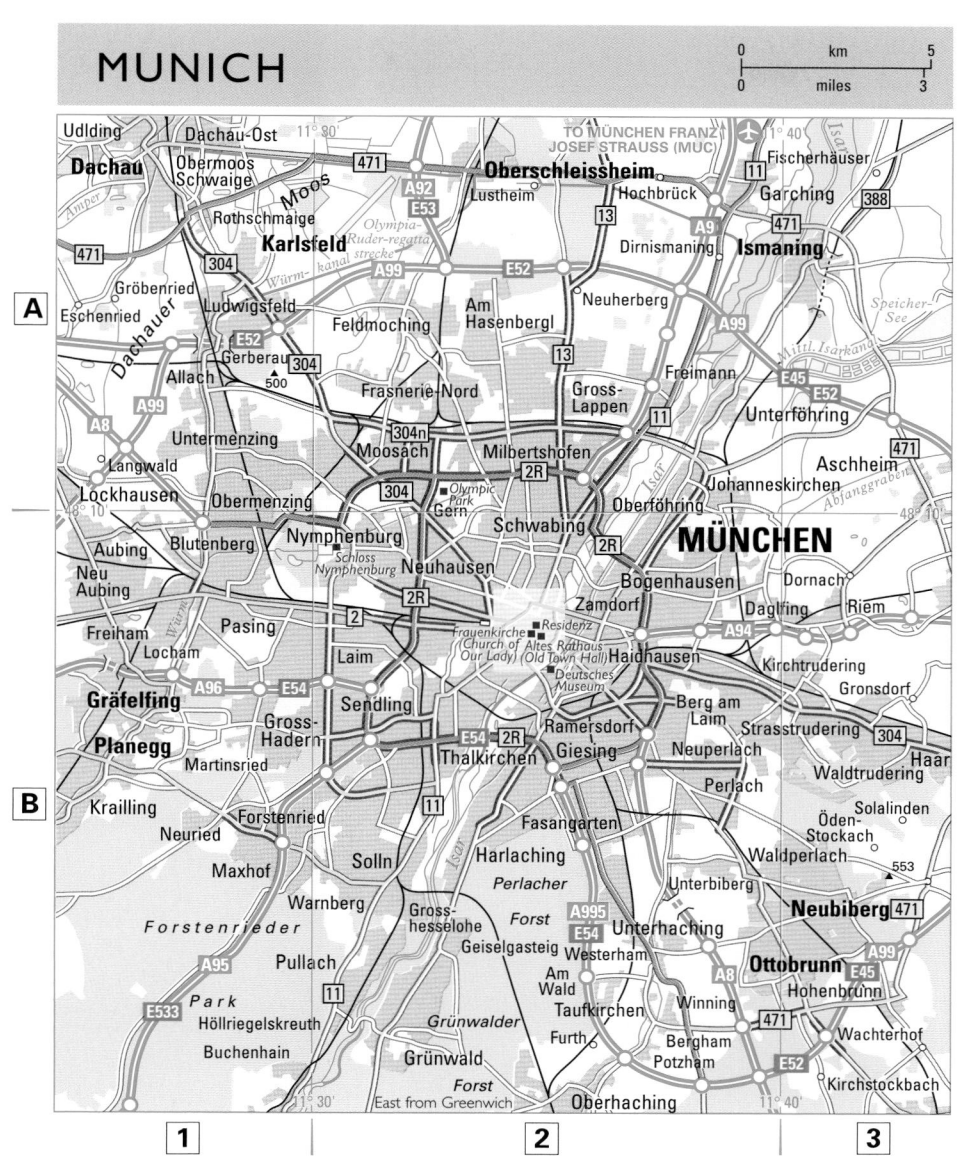

CENTRAL MUNICH

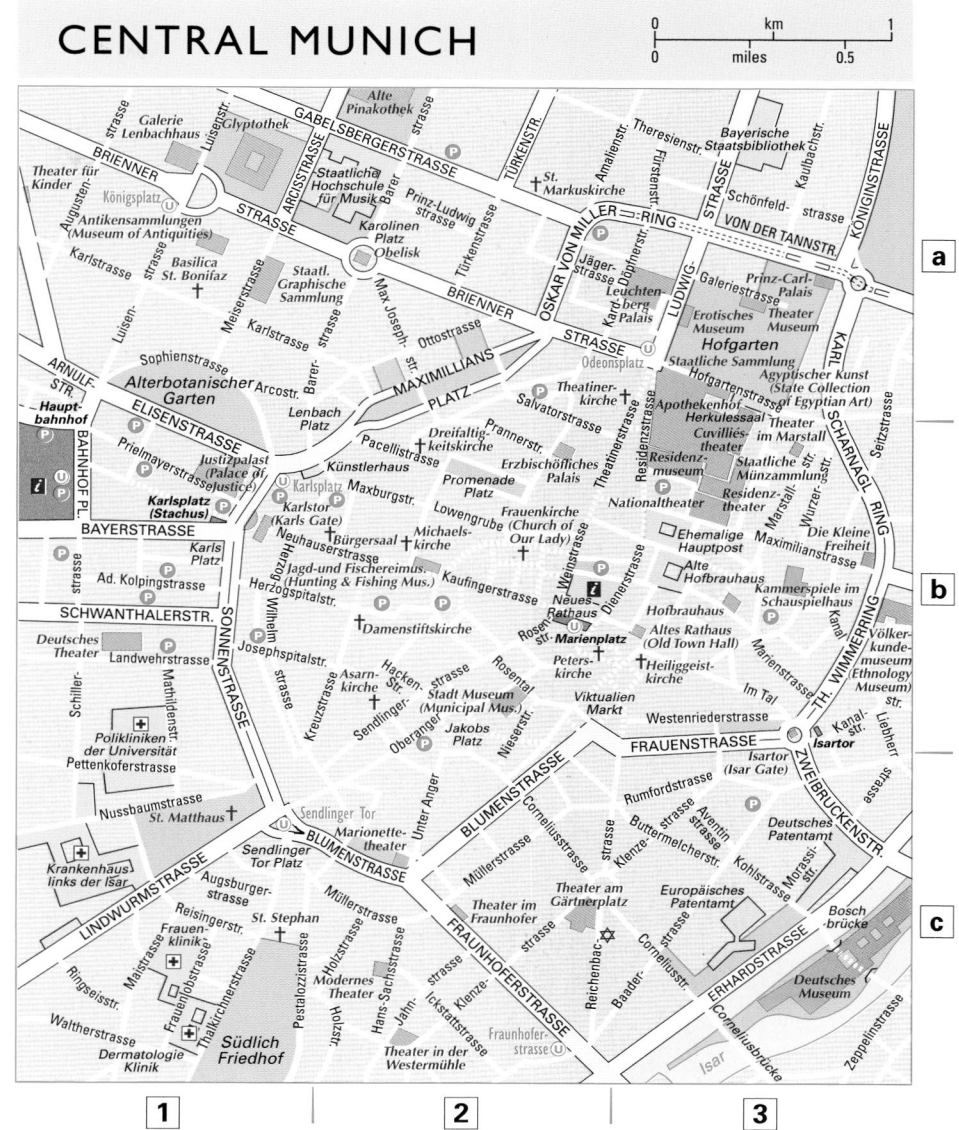

NEW ORLEANS

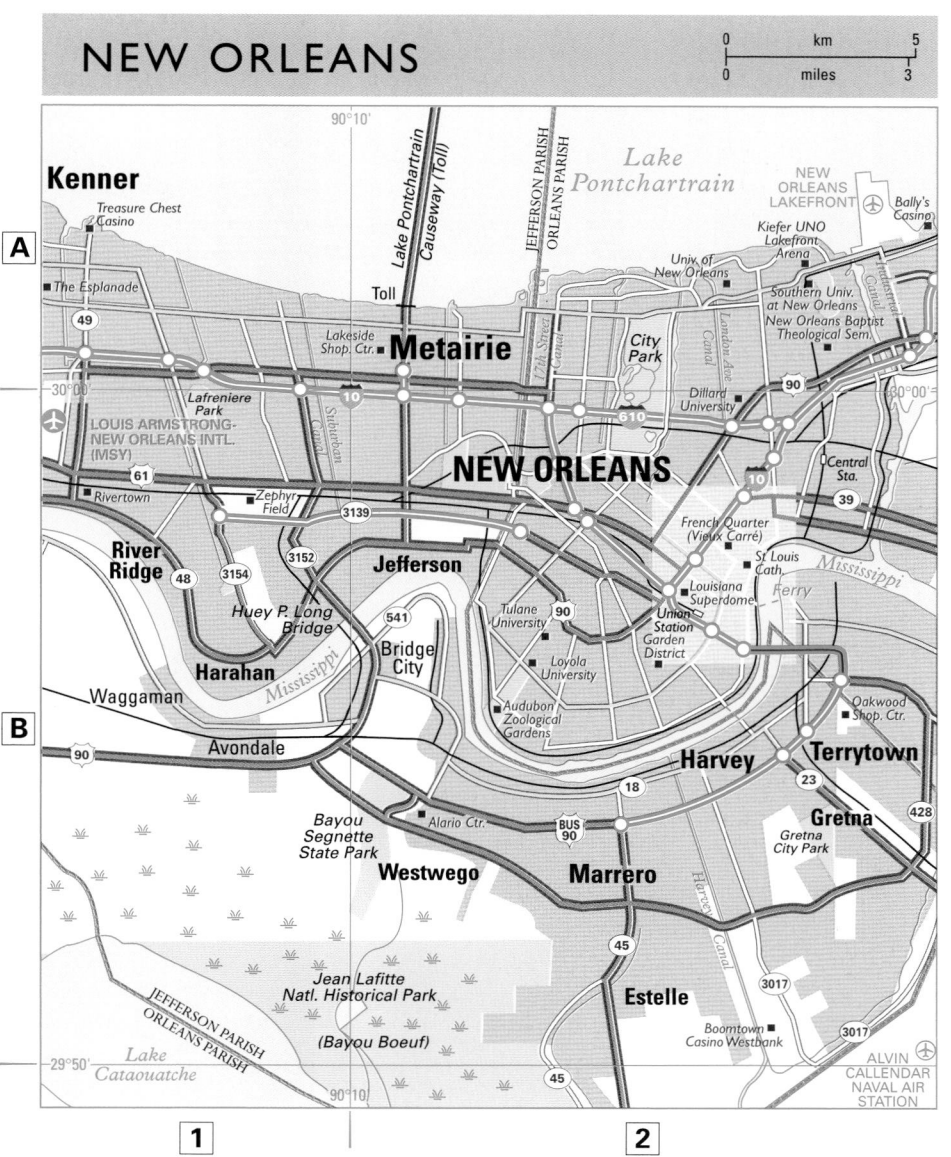

CENTRAL NEW ORLEANS

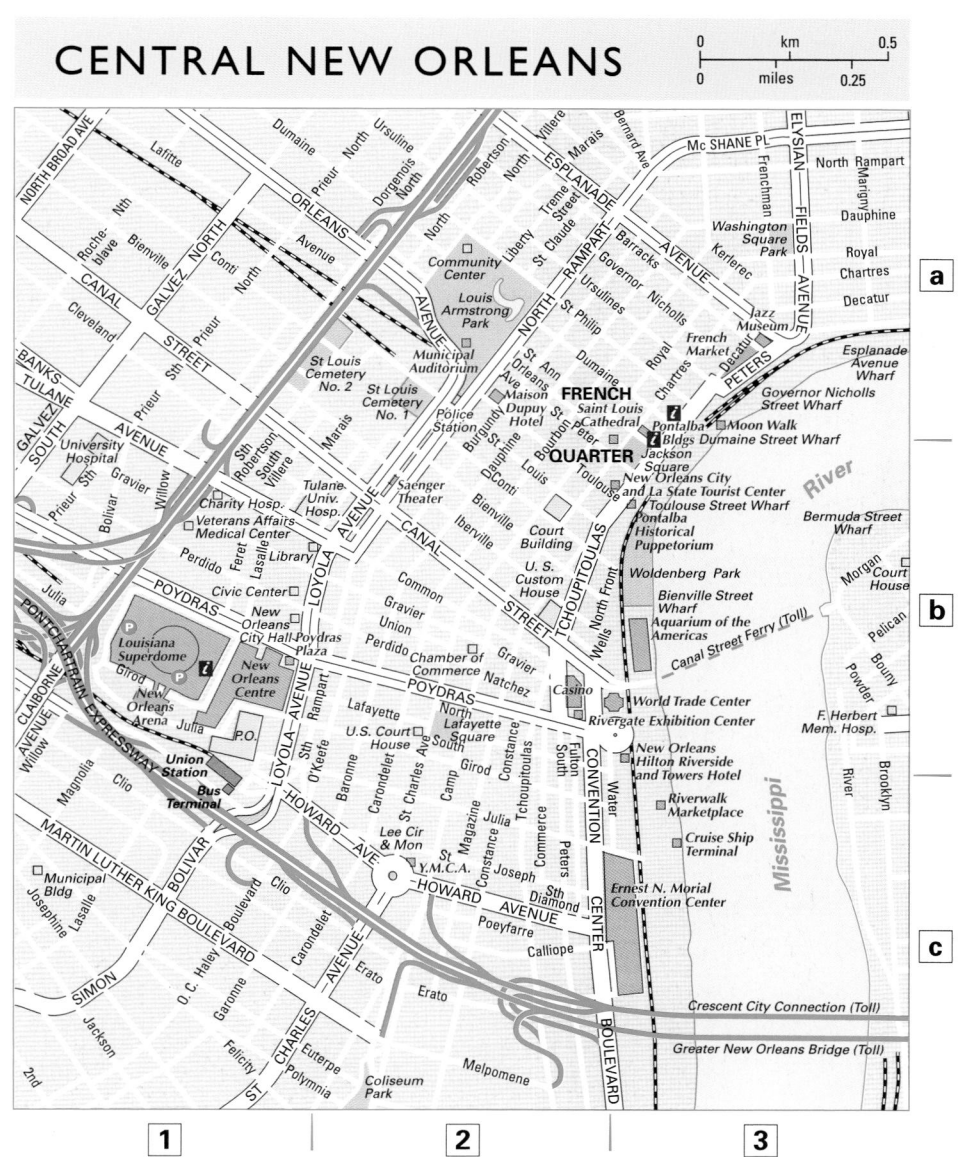

4 Interstate route numbers   17 U.S. route numbers   417 State route numbers

COPYRIGHT PHILIP'S

NEW YORK

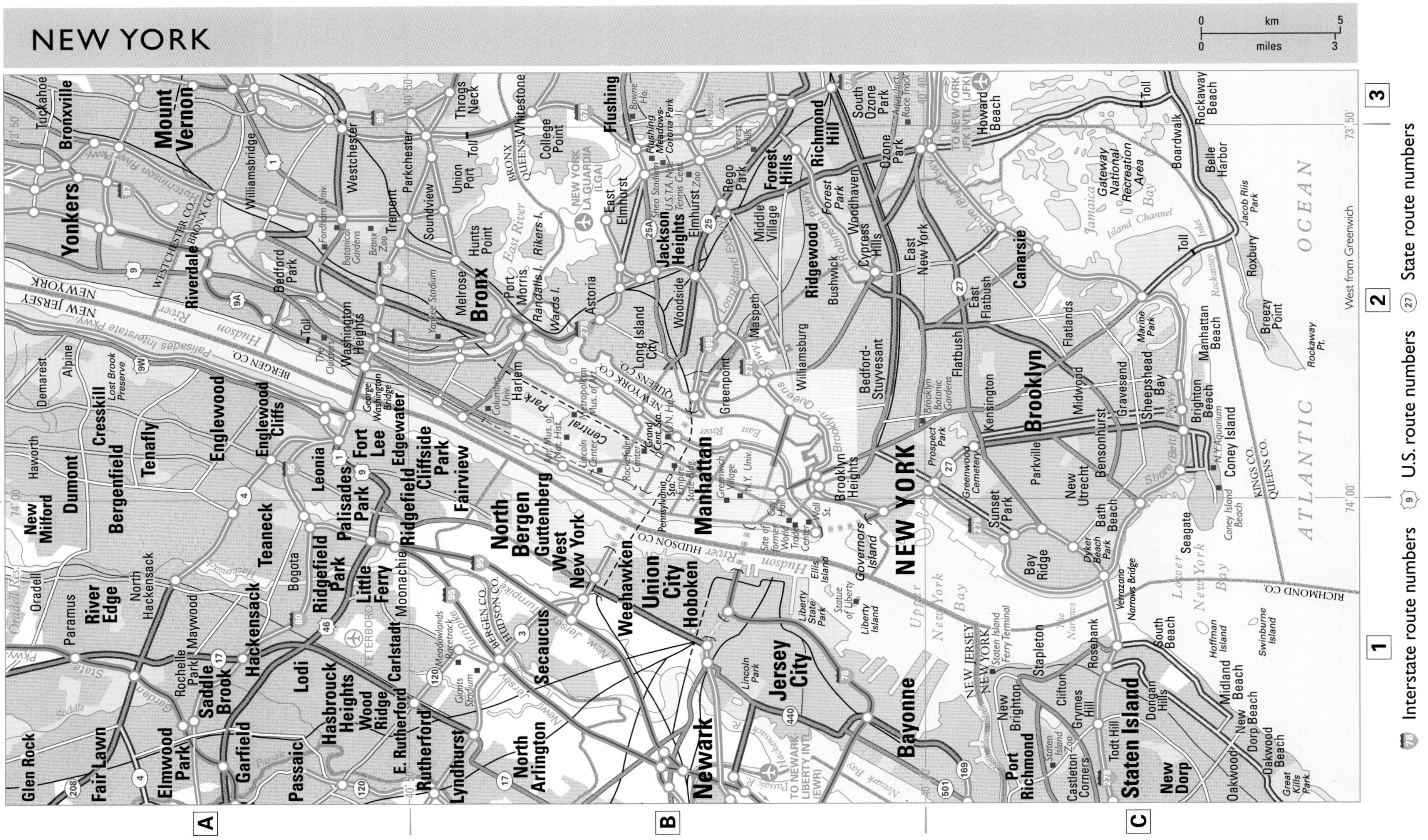

km 5
miles 3

Tuckahoe · Bronxville · Mount Vernon · Yonkers · Riverdale · Williamsbridge · Westchester · Parkchester · Southview · Trogg's Neck · Flushing · Whitestone · College Point · QUEENS · South Ozone Park · Richmond Hill · Forest Hills · Rego Park · Howard Beach · Rockaway Beach

Demarest · Alpine · Haworth · Cresskill · Dumont · New Milford · Bergenfield · Tenafly · Englewood · Englewood Cliffs · Leonia · Fort Lee · Palisades Park · Edgewater · Cliffside Park · Fairview · Melrose · Bronx · Hunts Point · Astoria · Long Island City · Woodside · Jackson Heights · Elmhurst · Middle Village · Ridgewood · Bushwick · Cypress Hills · East New York · Canarsie

New Milford · River Edge · Teaneck · Hackensack · Bogota · Ridgefield Park · Little Ferry · Moonachie · Ridgefield · North Bergen · Guttenberg · West New York · Washington Heights · Harlem · Central Park · Manhattan · Greenpoint · Williamsburg · Bedford-Stuyvesant · Brooklyn · Prospect Park · Kensington · Flatbush · Flatlands

Paramus · Rochelle Park · Maywood · Saddle Brook · Lodi · Garfield · Passaic · Hasbrouck Heights · Wood Ridge · E. Rutherford · Rutherford · North Arlington · Lyndhurst · Secaucus · North Bergen · Weehawken · Union City · Hoboken · Jersey City · NEW YORK · Sunset Park · New Utrecht · Bath Beach · Bensonhurst · Gravesend · Sheepshead Bay · Brighton Beach · Coney Island · Manhattan Beach

Glen Rock · Fair Lawn · Elmwood Park · Garfield · Passaic · North Arlington · Lyndhurst · Newark · Bayonne · Port Richmond · Staten Island · New Dorp · New Brighton · Stapleton · Rosebank · South Beach · Midland Beach · Oakwood Beach · Great Kills Park

ATLANTIC OCEAN

Legend: Interstate route numbers · U.S. route numbers (9) · State route numbers (27)

A · B · C

CENTRAL NEW YORK

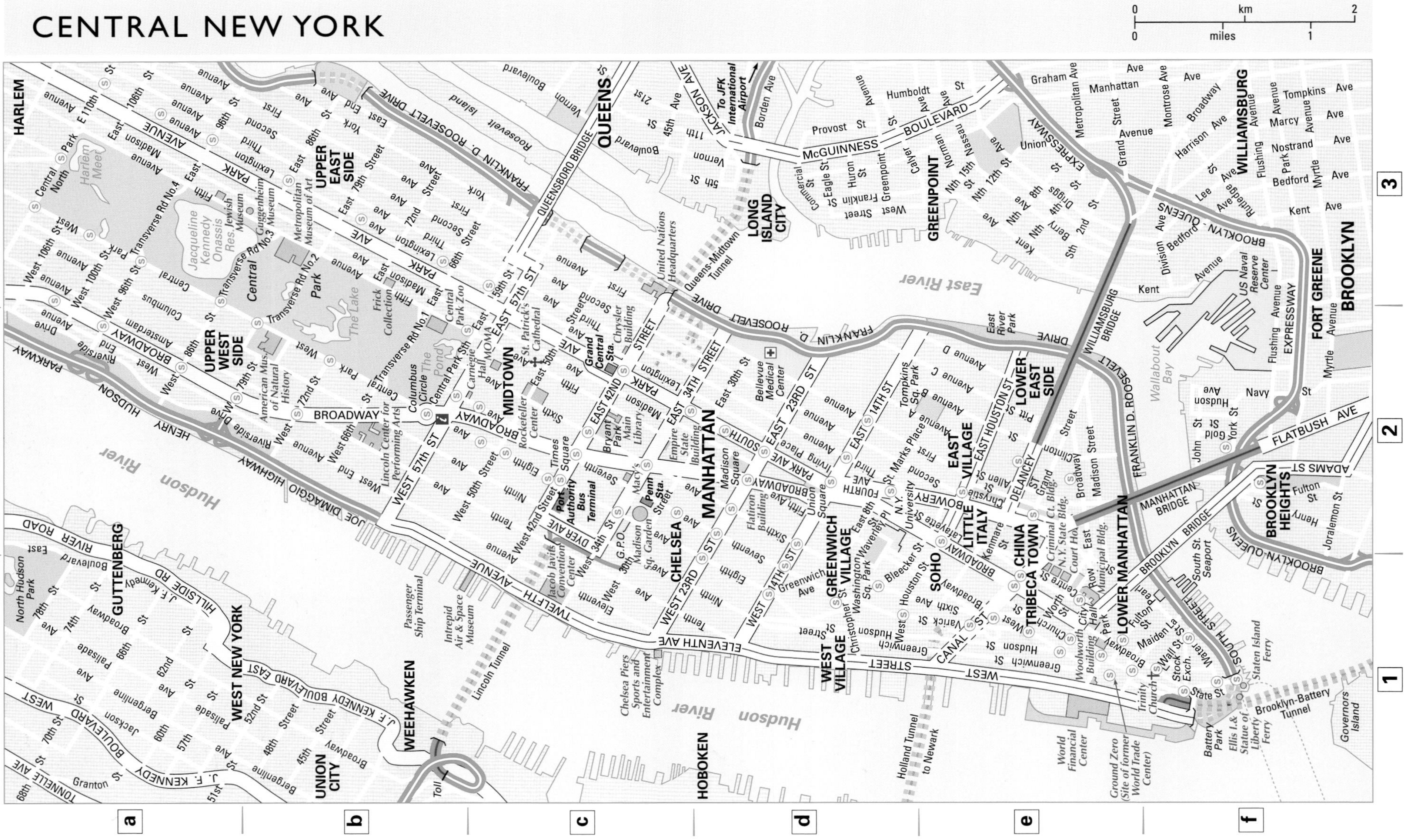

km 2
miles 1

HARLEM · Harlem Meer · Central Park · UPPER WEST SIDE · UPPER EAST SIDE · Metropolitan Museum of Art · The Lake · The Reservoir · American Museum of Natural History · Lincoln Center for the Performing Arts · Columbus Circle · MIDTOWN · St. Patrick's Cathedral · Rockefeller Center · Grand Central Sta. · Chrysler Building · United Nations Headquarters · Times Square · Bryant Park · New York Public Library · Empire State Building · Penn Sta. · Madison Square Garden · Port Authority Bus Terminal · CHELSEA · MANHATTAN · Bellevue Medical Center · Gramercy Park · Stuyvesant Sq. · Tompkins Sq. Park · EAST VILLAGE · GREENWICH VILLAGE · Washington Square · WEST VILLAGE · LITTLE ITALY · SOHO · NOHO · LOWER EAST SIDE · Delancey St. · TRIBECA · CHINA TOWN · Criminal Ct. Bldg. · Municipal Bldg. · Woolworth Bldg. · World Financial Center · Ground Zero Site of former World Trade Center · LOWER MANHATTAN · City Hall · Trinity Church · N.Y. Stock Exch. · Battery Park · Ellis I. & Statue of Liberty · Staten Island Ferry · South Street Seaport

QUEENS · LONG ISLAND CITY · Roosevelt Island · Queensboro Bridge · Queens-Midtown Tunnel · East River · Franklin D. Roosevelt Drive · To JFK International Airport · McGuinness Boulevard · GREENPOINT · WILLIAMSBURG · BROOKLYN · FORT GREENE · Williamsburg Bridge · Brooklyn-Queens Expressway · Manhattan Bridge · Brooklyn Bridge · BROOKLYN HEIGHTS · Wallabout Bay · US Naval Reserve Center · Flatbush Ave. · Adams St. · Brooklyn-Battery Tunnel · Governors Island

HUDSON · GUTTENBERG · WEST NEW YORK · North Hudson Park · Joe DiMaggio Highway · Henry Hudson Parkway · Riverside Drive · Hudson River · WEEHAWKEN · UNION CITY · HOBOKEN · Lincoln Tunnel · Holland Tunnel · To Newark · Chelsea Piers Sports and Entertainment Complex · Jacob Javits Convention Center · Intrepid Air & Space Museum · Passenger Ship Terminal

a · b · c · d · e · f

ORLANDO

Interstate route numbers • U.S. route numbers • State route numbers

OSAKA

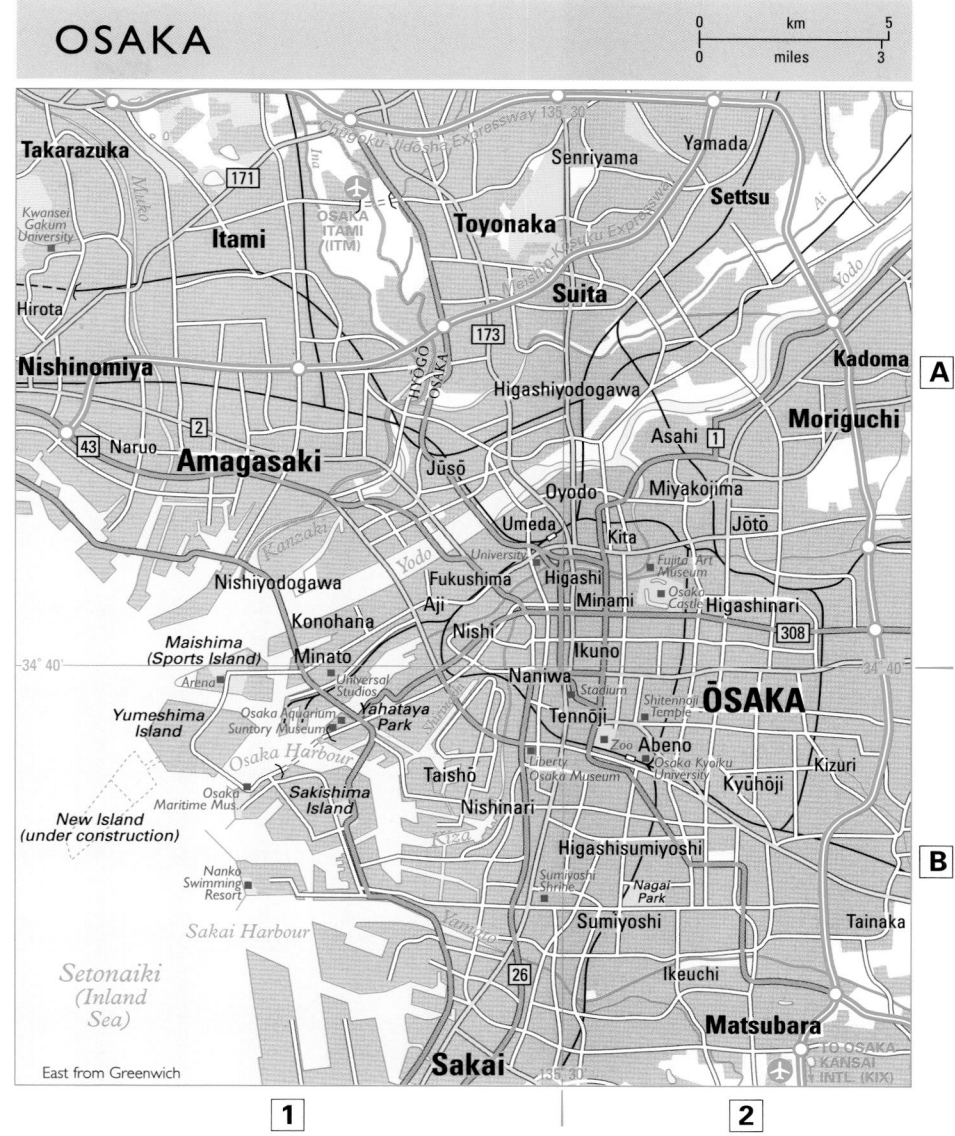

OSLO

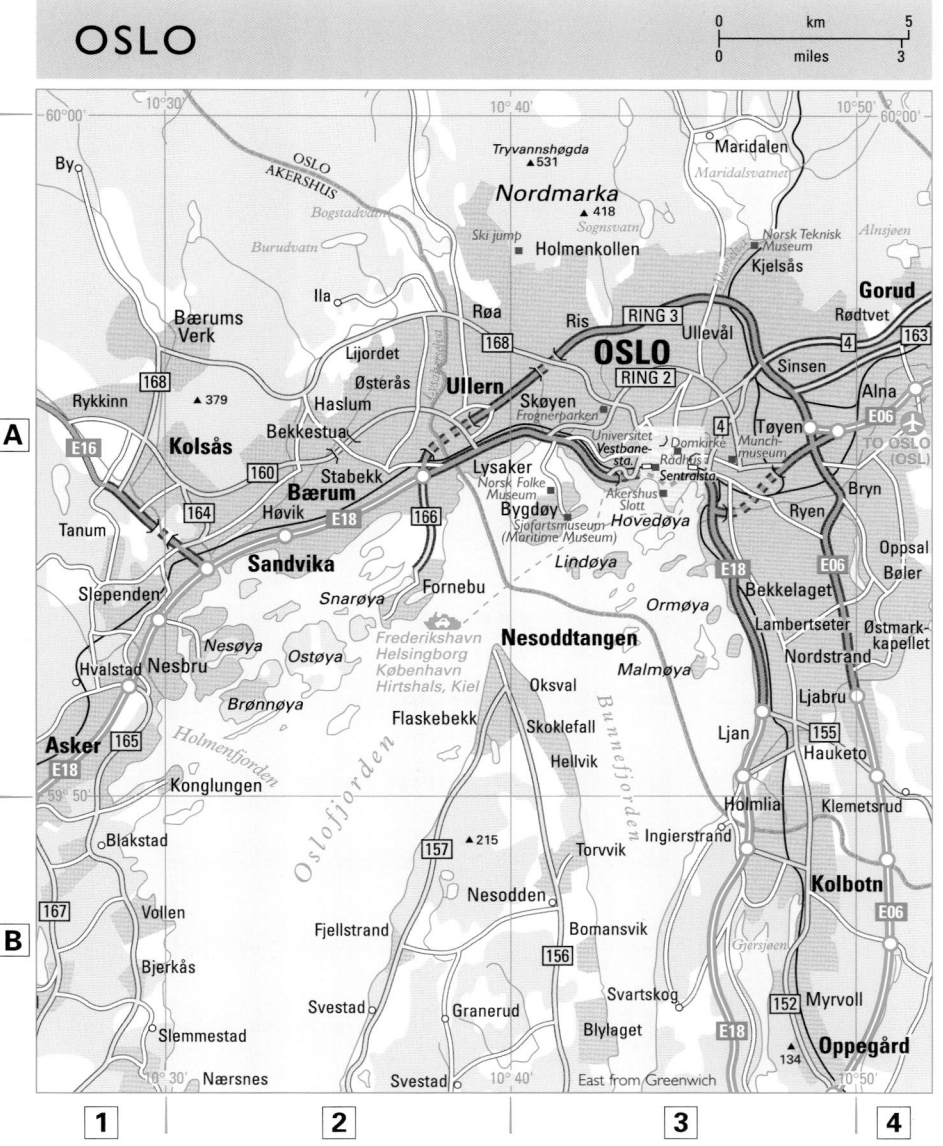

CENTRAL OSLO

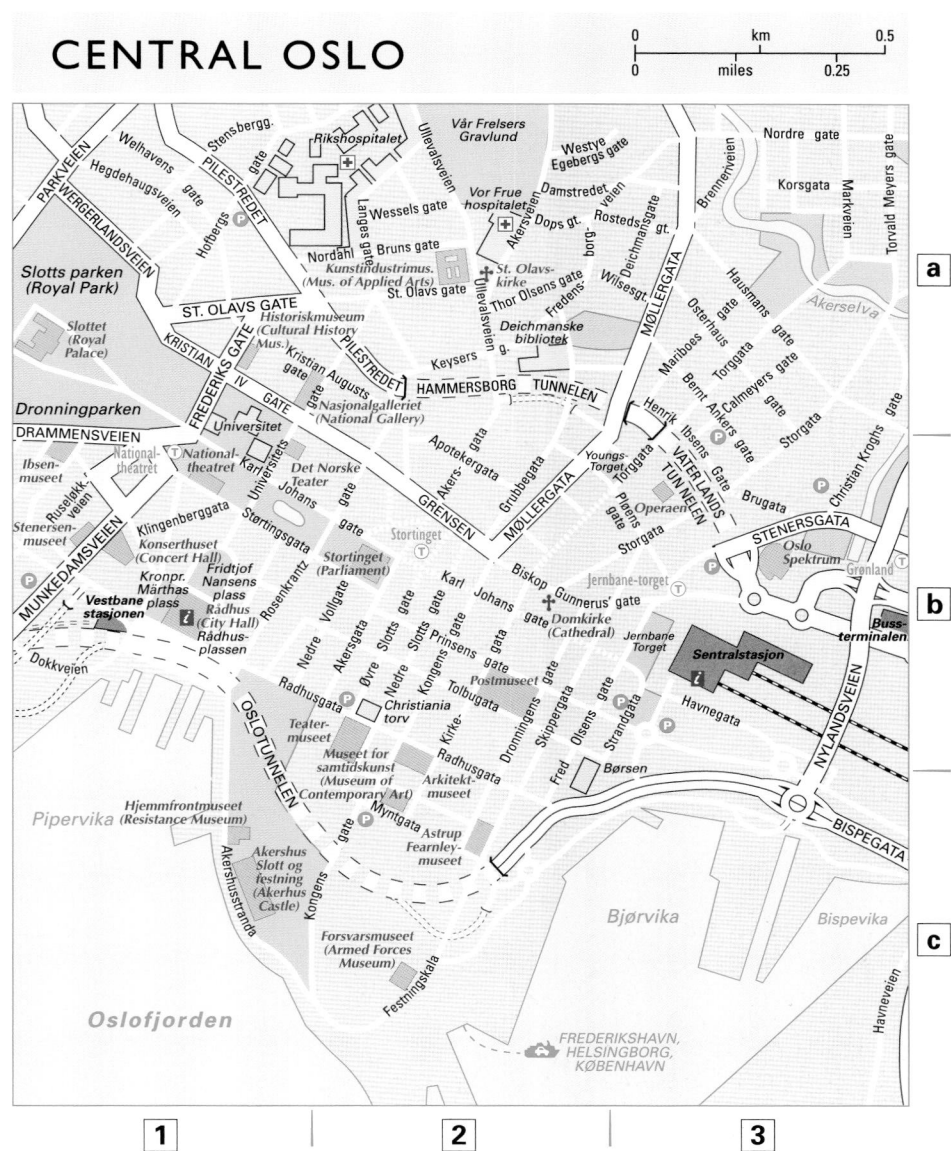

PARIS

0 km 5
0 miles 3

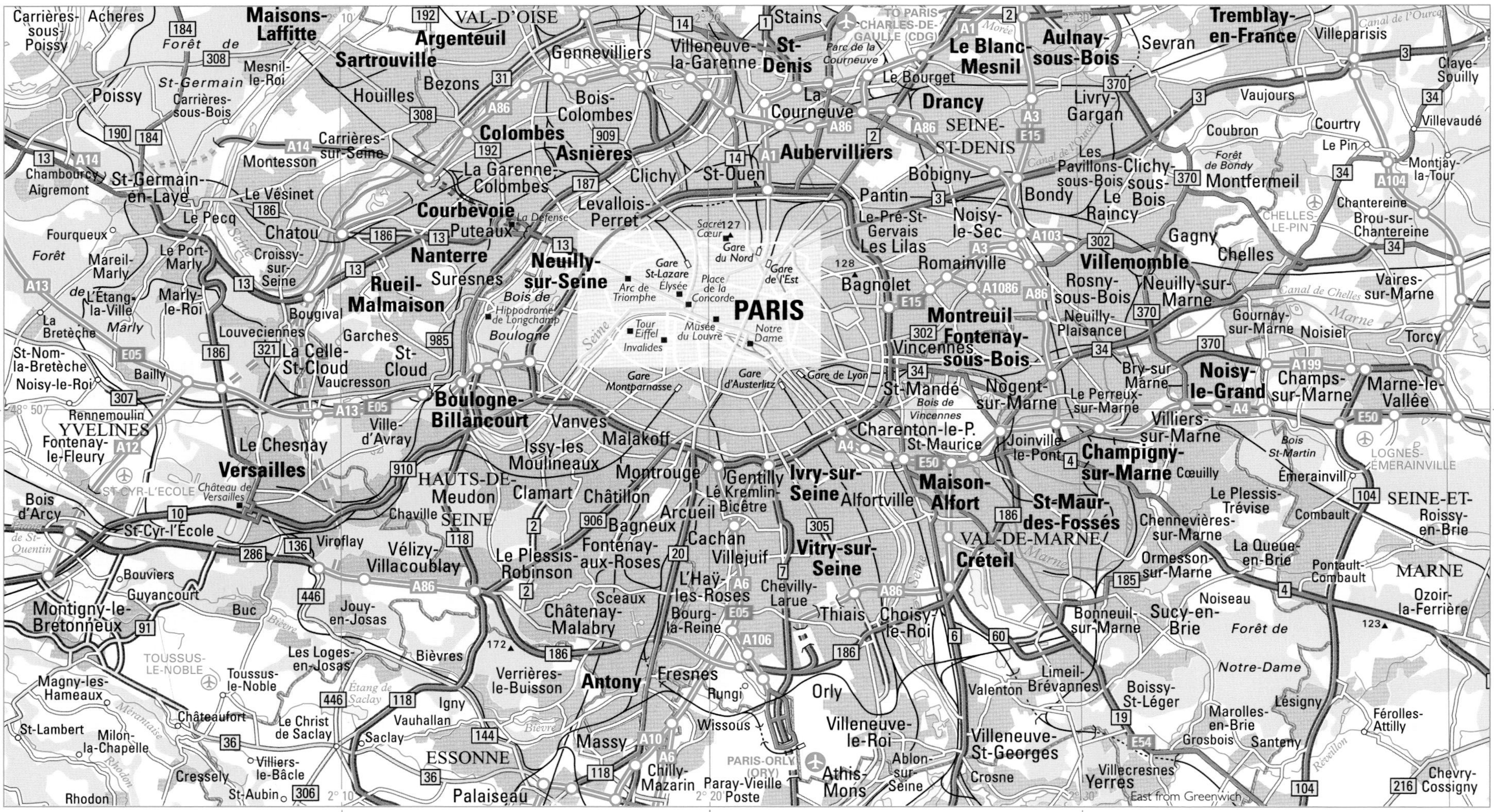

Carrières-sous-Poissy · Achères · Maisons-Laffitte · 184 · Forêt · 192 · VAL-D'OISE · 14 · Villeneuve-la-Garenne · 1 · Stains · TO PARIS CHARLES-DE-GAULLE (CDG) · A1 · Tremblay-en-France · Villeparisis · 3 · Claye-Souilly

Poissy · Mesnil-le-Roi · Argenteuil · Sartrouville · Bezons · Gennevilliers · St-Denis · Parc de la Courneuve · Le Bourget · Le Blanc Mesnil · Aulnay-sous-Bois · Sevran · Vaujours · 34 · Villevaudé

190 · 184 · St-Germain-en-Laye · Houilles · 308 · Bois-Colombes · La Courneuve · Drancy · 370 · Livry-Gargan · Montfermeil · Coubron · Courtry · Le Pin · Montjay-la-Tour · A104

13 · A14 · Chambourcy · Aigremont · Fourqueux · Le Vésinet · Chatou · Colombes · 909 · Asnières · Clichy · St-Ouen · Aubervilliers · SEINE-ST-DENIS · Bobigny · Le Pré-St-Gervais · Les Lilas · Pavillons-sous-Bois · Bondy · Le Bois Raincy · Gagny · Chelles · Chanterine · Brou-sur-Chanterine · 34

A Poissy · Montesson · Carrières-sur-Seine · Courbevoie · Puteaux · La Garenne-Colombes · Levallois-Perret · Clichy · Pantin · Romainville · Noisy-le-Sec · Rosny-sous-Bois · Neuilly-sur-Marne · Gournay-sur-Marne · Noisiel · Torcy **A**

Le Pecq · Nanterre · Suresnes · Neuilly-sur-Seine · Arc de Triomphe · Gare St-Lazare · PARIS · Notre Dame · Bagnolet · Montreuil · Fontenay-sous-Bois · Bry-sur-Marne · Noisy-le-Grand · Champs-sur-Marne · Marne-la-Vallée

Rueil-Malmaison · Bois de Boulogne · Tour Eiffel · Invalides · Musée du Louvre · Vincennes · Neuilly-Plaisance · Le Perreux-sur-Marne · A4

Versailles · Boulogne-Billancourt · Vanves · Issy-les-Moulineaux · Malakoff · Gare Montparnasse · Gare d'Austerlitz · Gare de Lyon · St-Mandé · Charenton-le-P. · St-Maurice · Joinville-le-Pont · Champigny-sur-Marne · Cœuilly · Emerainvill · LOGNES EMERAINVILLE

B Le Chesnay · Ville-d'Avray · Montrouge · Gentilly · Ivry-sur-Seine · Maison-Alfort · Nogent-sur-Marne · Villiers-sur-Marne · Le Plessis-Trévise · SEINE-ET-ROISSY-EN-BRIE **B**

Bois d'Arcy · St-Cyr-l'Ecole · HAUTS-DE-SEINE · Clamart · Châtillon · Arcueil · Le Kremlin-Bicêtre · Alfortville · Charenton · St-Maur-des-Fossés · Chennevières-sur-Marne · Ormesson-sur-Marne · La Queue-en-Brie · Combault · MARNE

Viroflay · Vélizy-Villacoublay · Le Plessis-Robinson · Bagneux · Fontenay-aux-Roses · Cachan · Villejuif · Vitry-sur-Seine · Créteil · VAL-DE-MARNE · Bonneuil-sur-Marne · Sucy-en-Brie · Noiseau · Ozoir-la-Ferrière

Montigny-le-Bretonneux · Guyancourt · Jouy-en-Josas · Sceaux · L'Haÿ-les-Roses · Bourg-la-Reine · Chevilly-Larue · Thiais · Choisy-le-Roi · Forêt de Notre-Dame · Boissy-St-Léger · Lésigny · Férolles-Attilly

Magny-les-Hameaux · Toussus-le-Noble · Les Loges-en-Josas · Bièvres · Châtenay-Malabry · Antony · Fresnes · Orly · Valenton · Brévannes · Limeil-Brévannes · Marolles-en-Brie · Santeny

St-Lambert · Châteaufort · Le Christ de Saclay · Igny · Vauhallan · Verrières-le-Buisson · Rungi · Villeneuve-le-Roi · Villeneuve-St-Georges · Crosne · Villecresnes · Yerres · Chevry-Cossigny

Cressely · Villiers-le-Bâcle · Saclay · ESSONNE · Massy · PARIS-ORLY (ORY) · Athis-Mons · Ablon-sur-Seine · 104 · 216

Rhodon · St-Aubin · 306 · Palaiseau · Chilly-Mazarin · Wissous · Paray-Vieille Poste · East from Greenwich

1 · 2 · 3 · 4

CENTRAL PARIS

0 km 1
0 miles 0.5

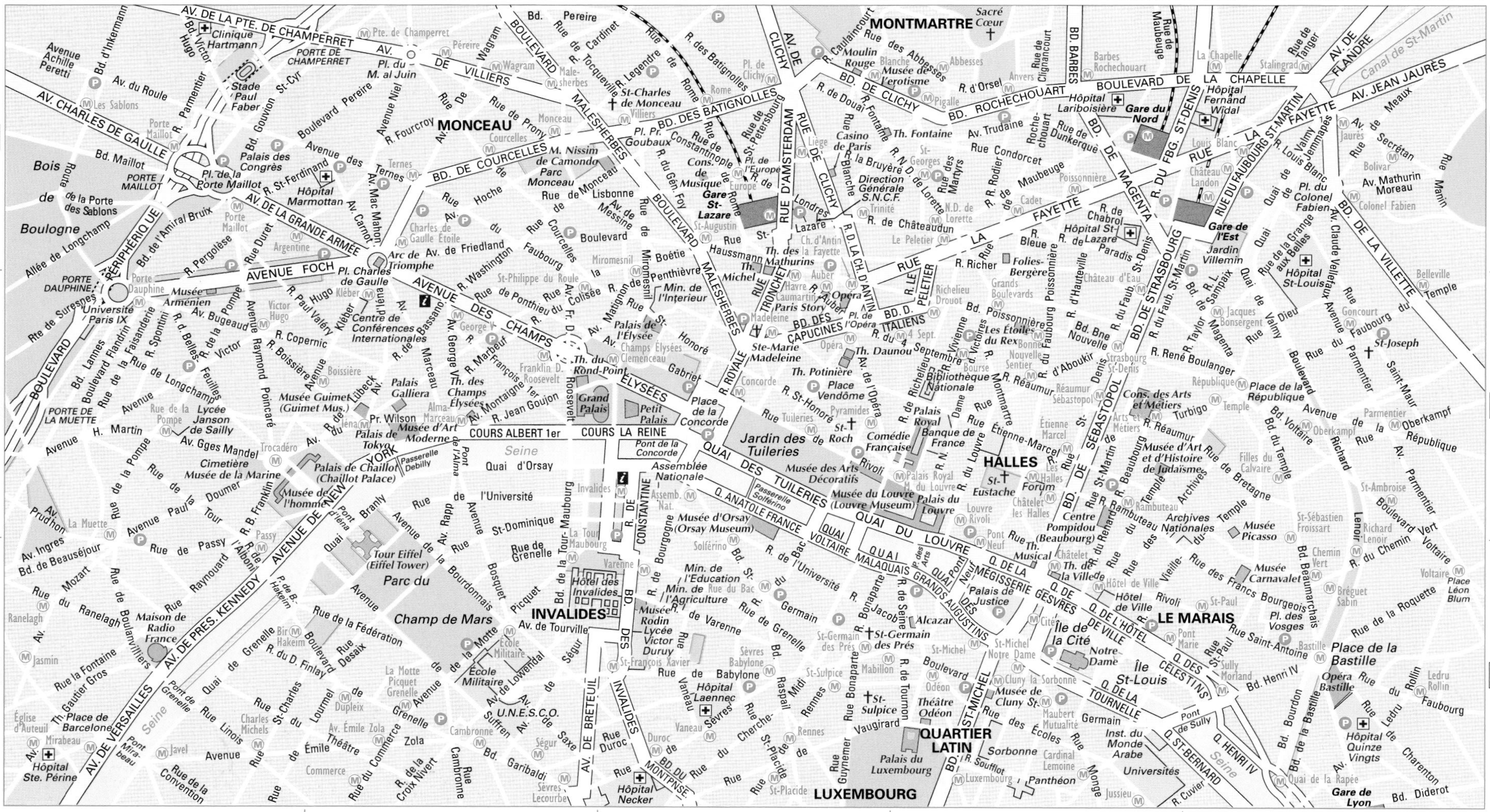

a MONTMARTRE · Sacré Cœur · MONCEAU · Parc Monceau · Gare St-Lazare · Gare du Nord · Gare de l'Est · Canal St-Martin **a**

b Arc de Triomphe · AVENUE FOCH · AVENUE DES CHAMPS ELYSÉES · ELYSÉES · Place de la Concorde · Jardin des Tuileries · HALLES · Place de la République **b**

c Tour Eiffel (Eiffel Tower) · Parc du Champ de Mars · INVALIDES · Musée d'Orsay (Orsay Museum) · Ile de la Cité · Notre Dame · LE MARAIS · Place de la Bastille · QUARTIER LATIN · LUXEMBOURG · Palais du Luxembourg · Gare de Lyon **c**

1 · 2 · 3 · 4 · 5

PRAGUE

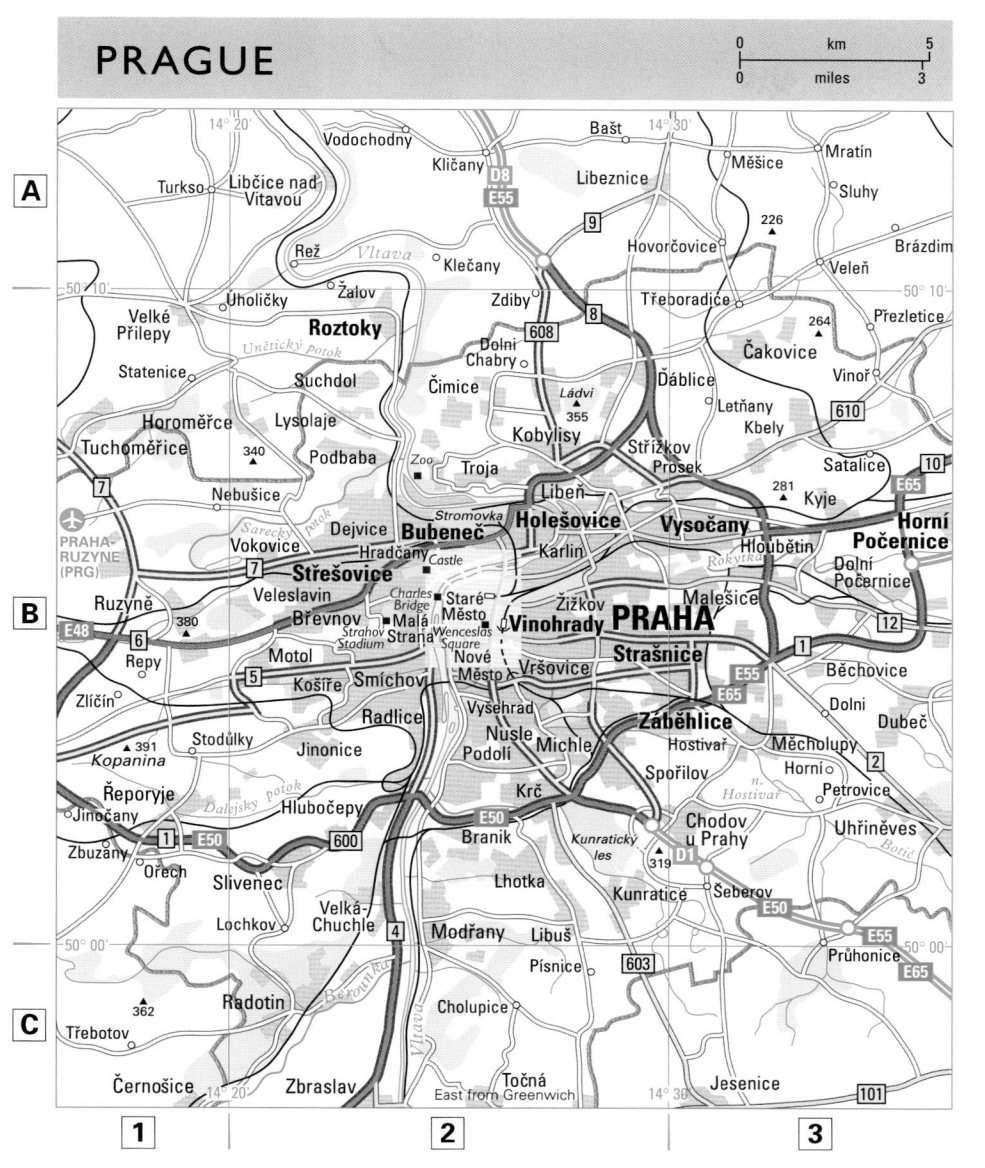

CENTRAL PRAGUE

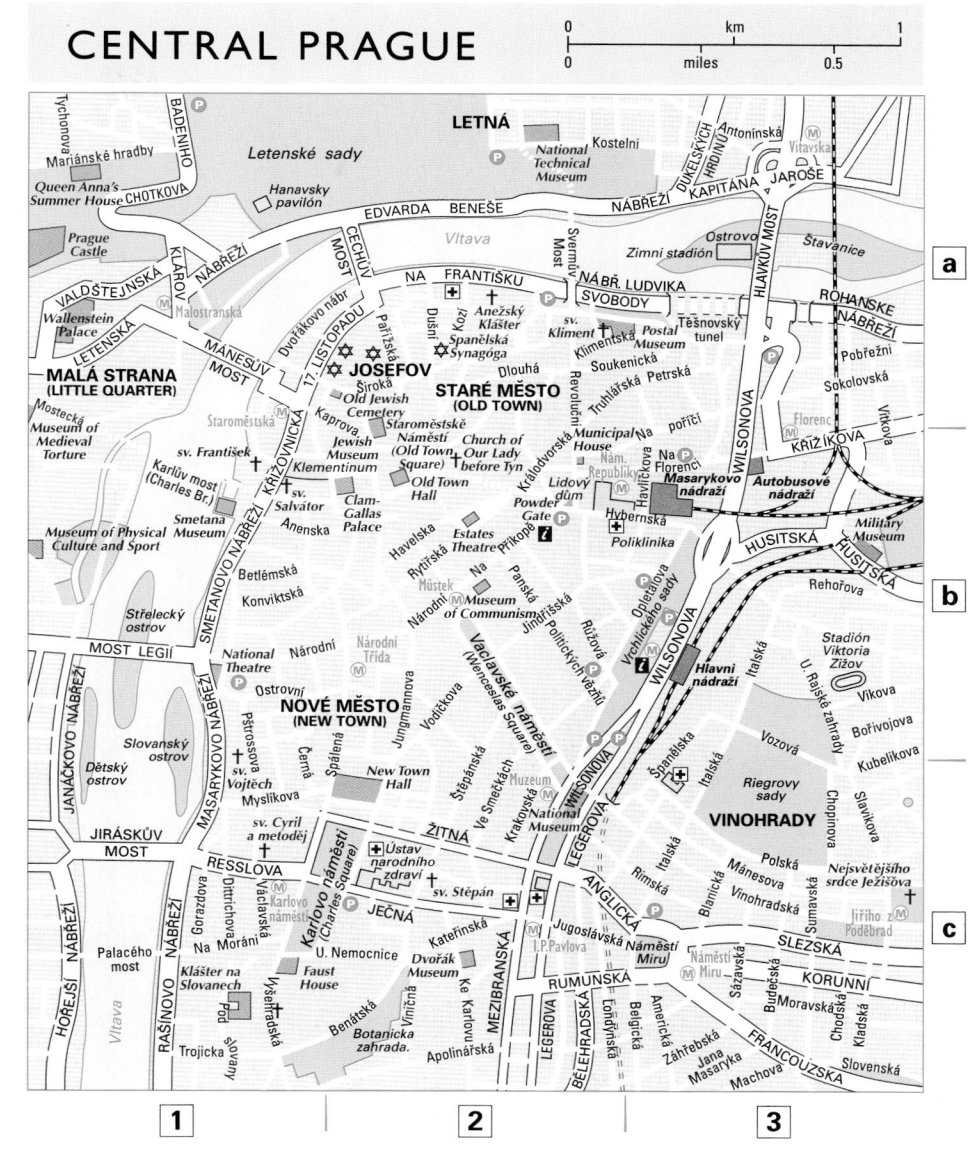

RIO DE JANEIRO

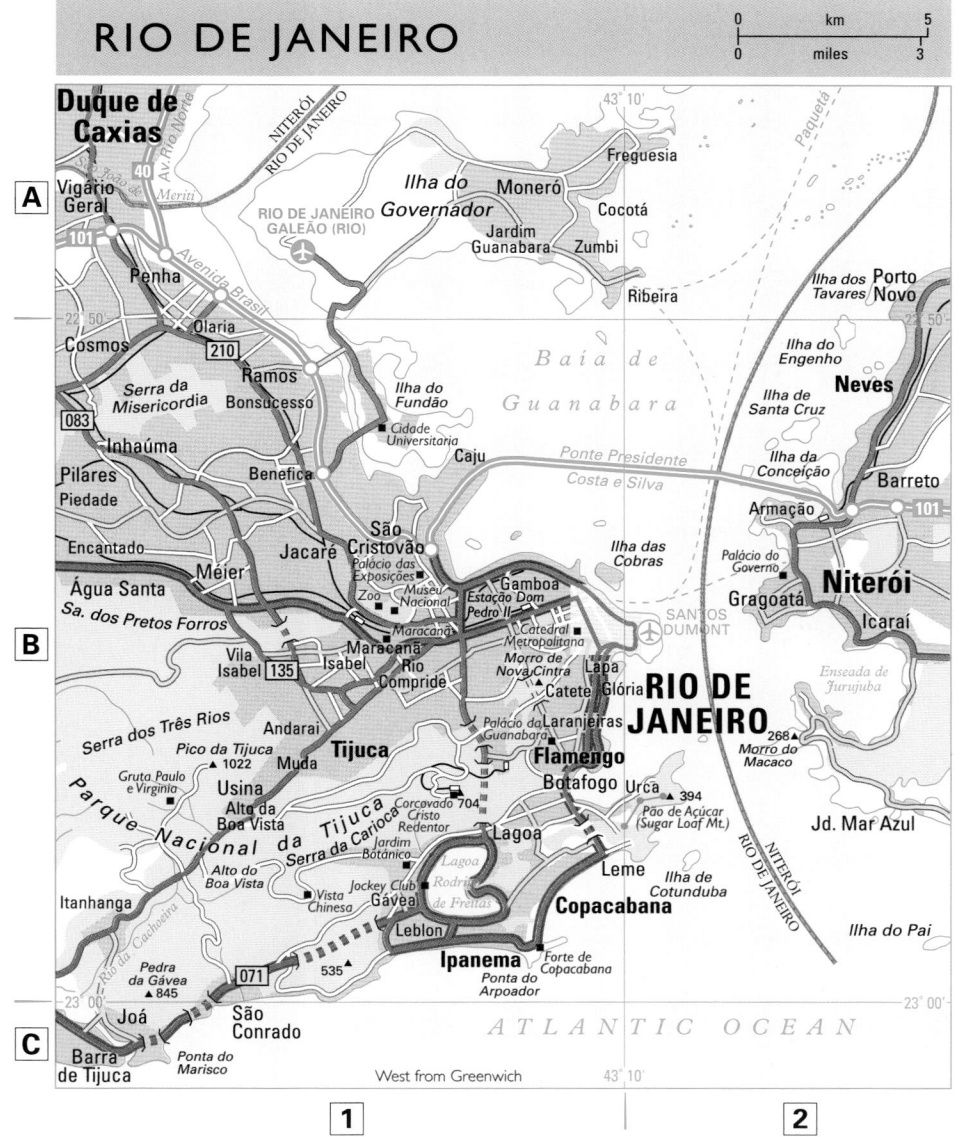

CENTRAL RIO DE JANEIRO

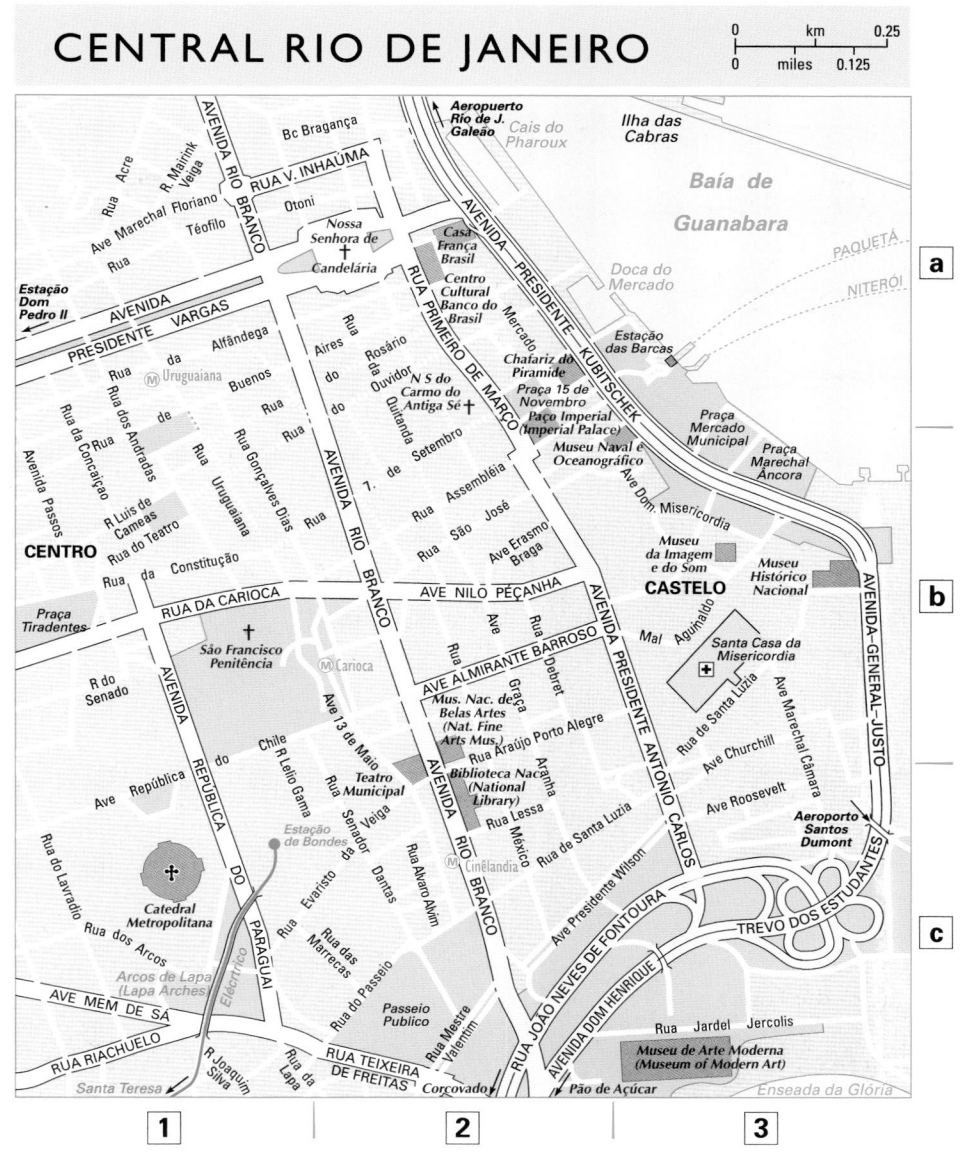

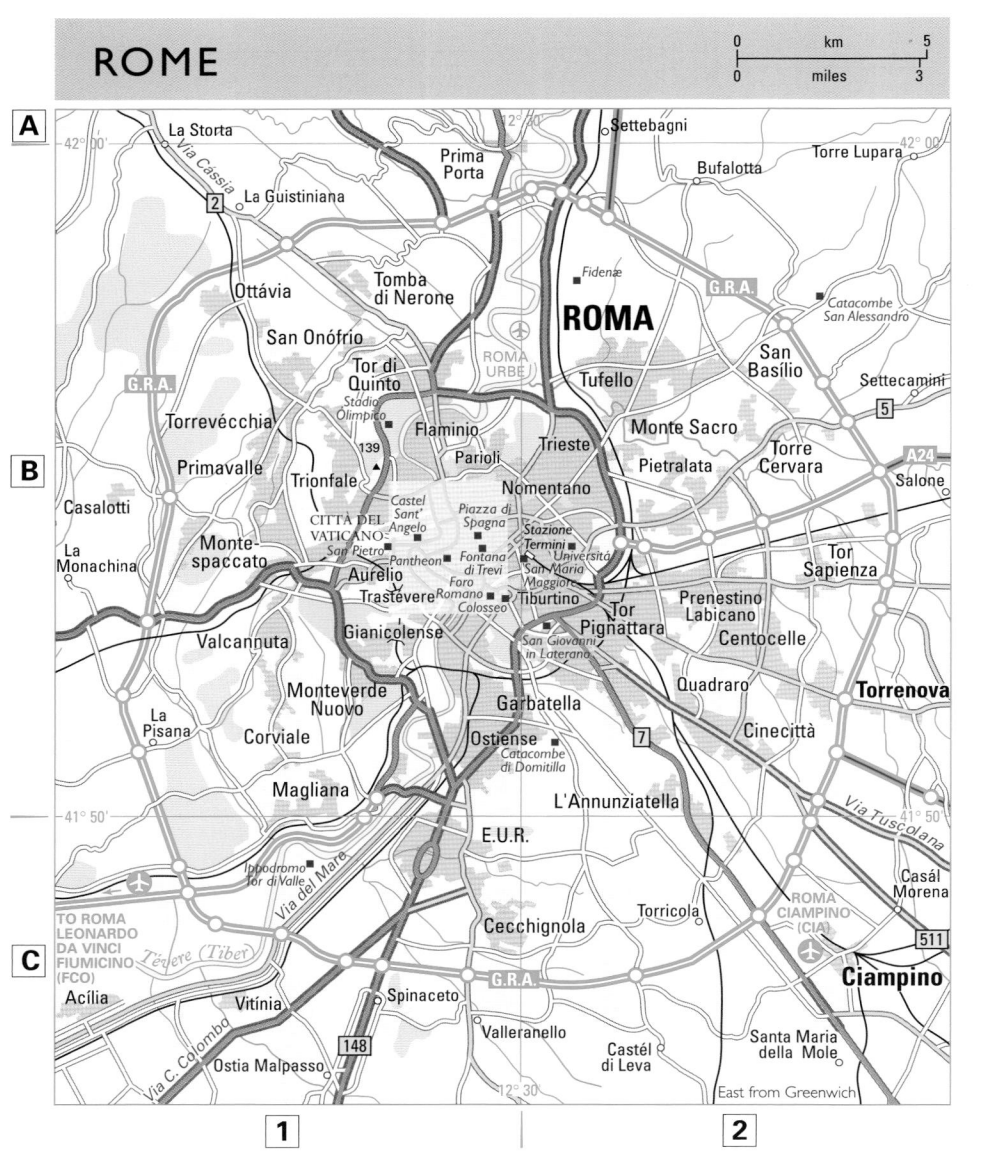

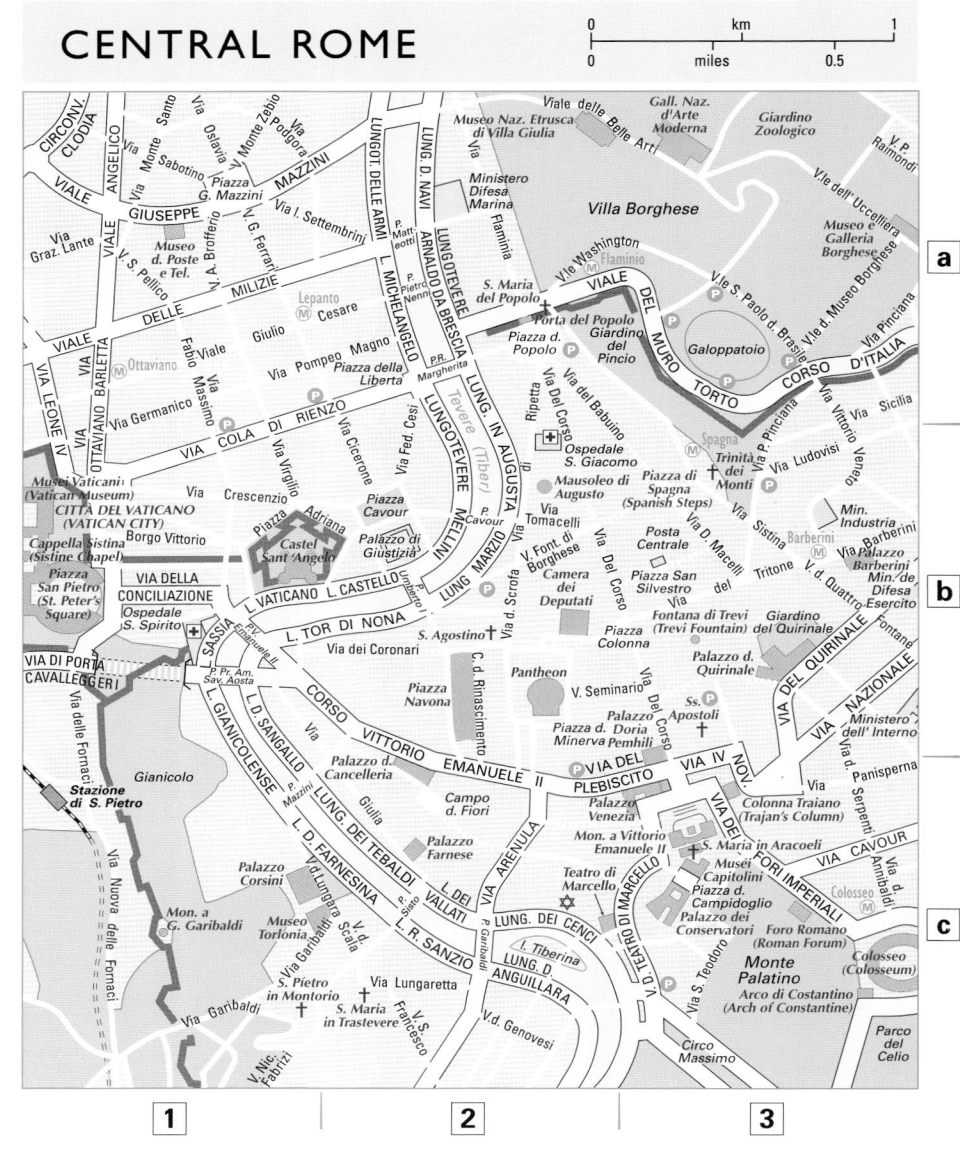

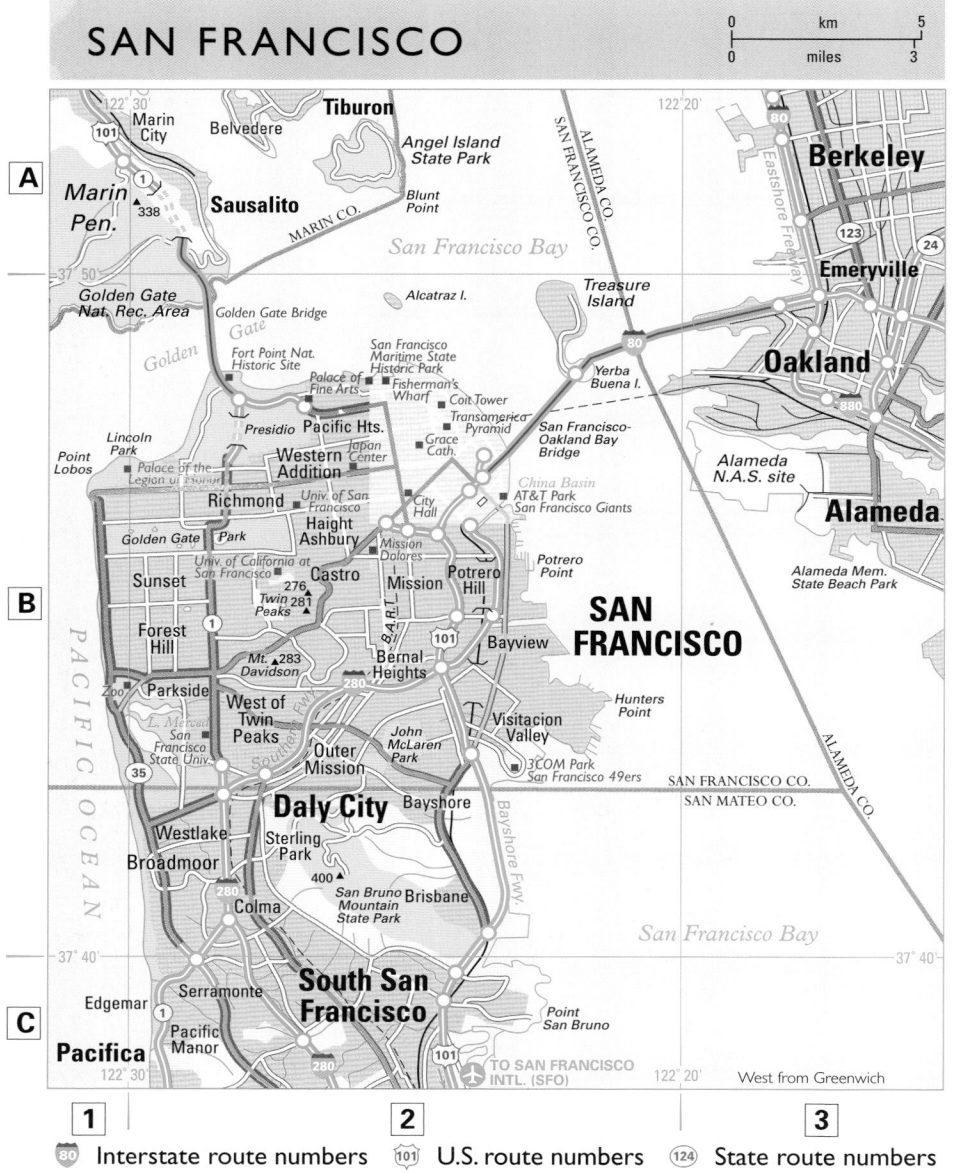

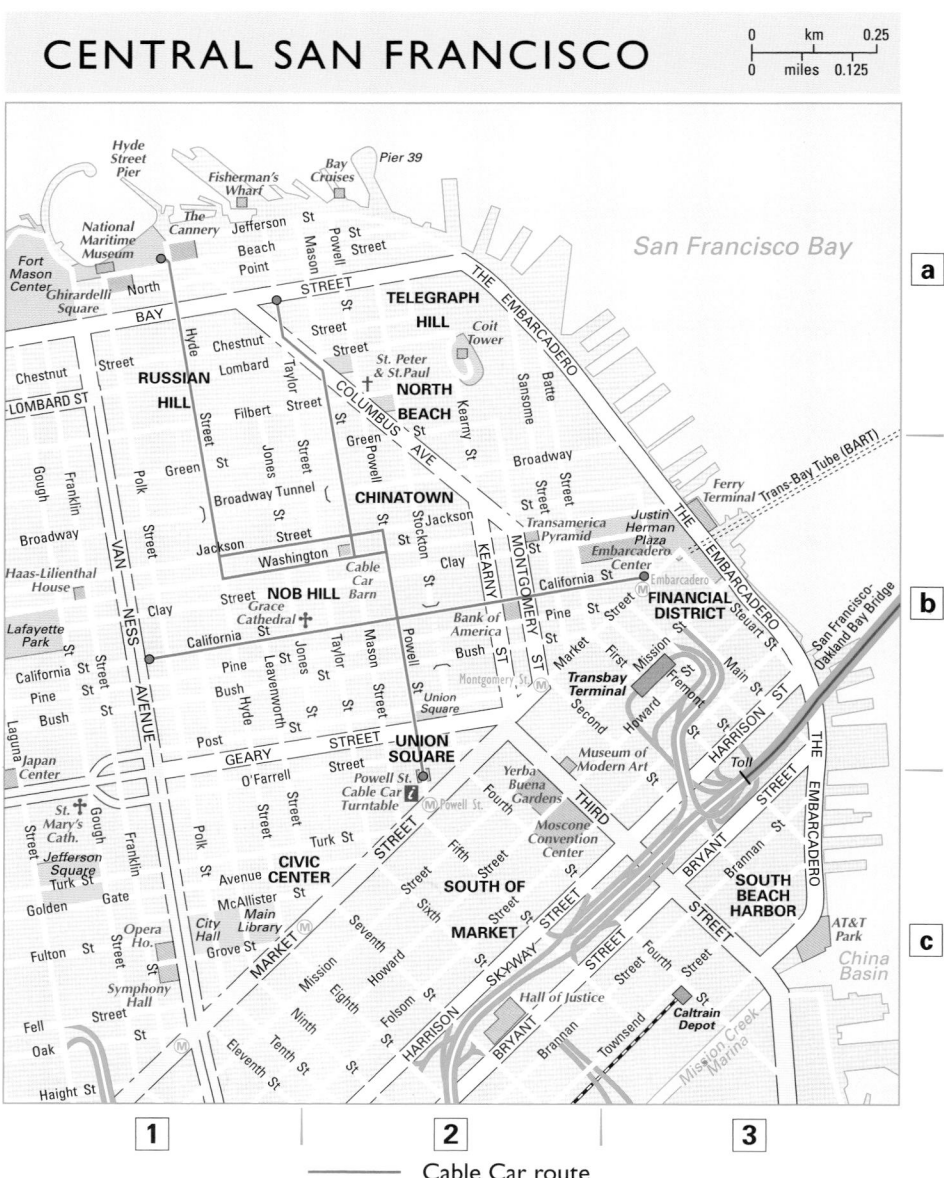

Interstate route numbers U.S. route numbers State route numbers

Cable Car route

COPYRIGHT PHILIP'S

ST PETERSBURG

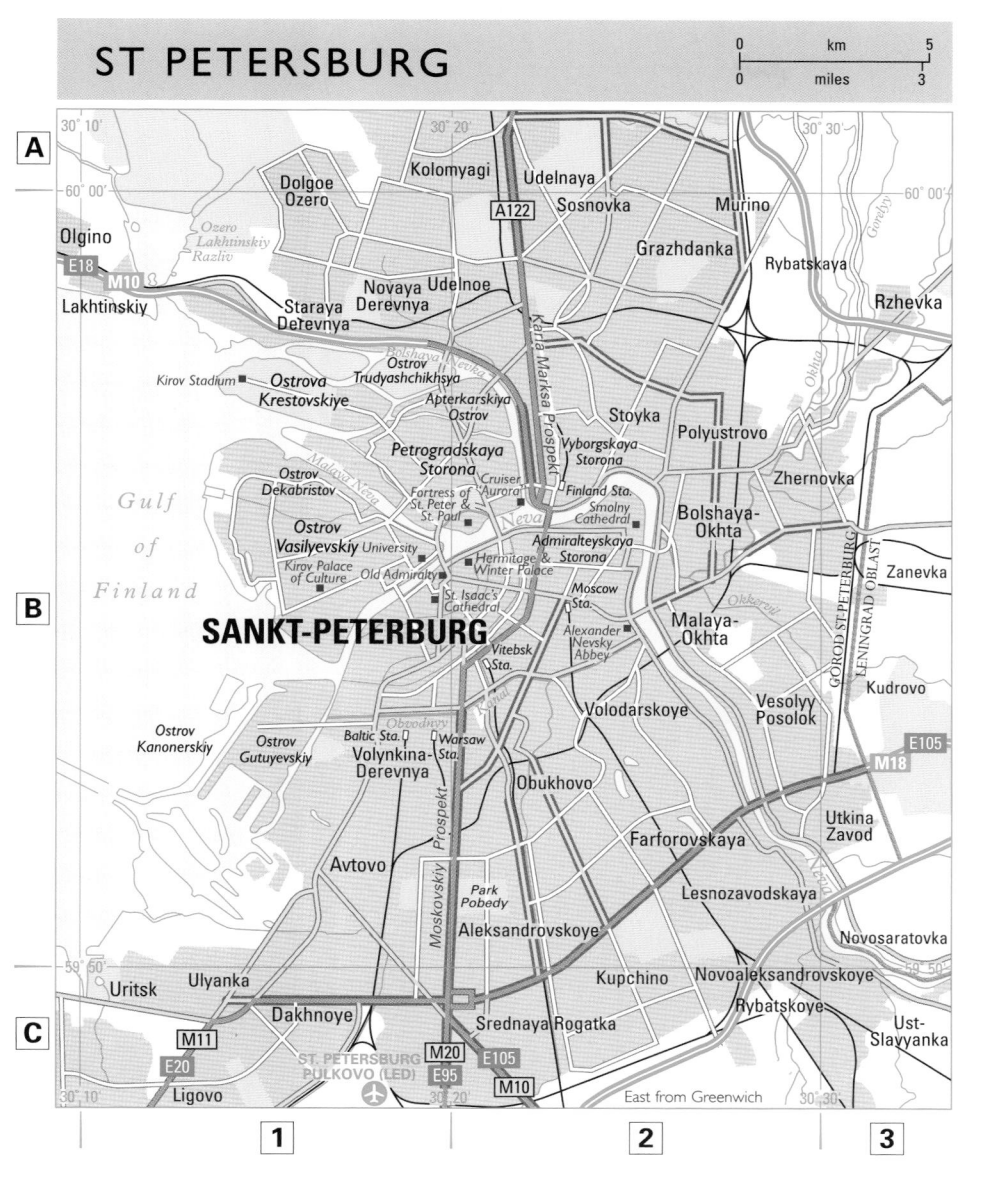

SANTIAGO

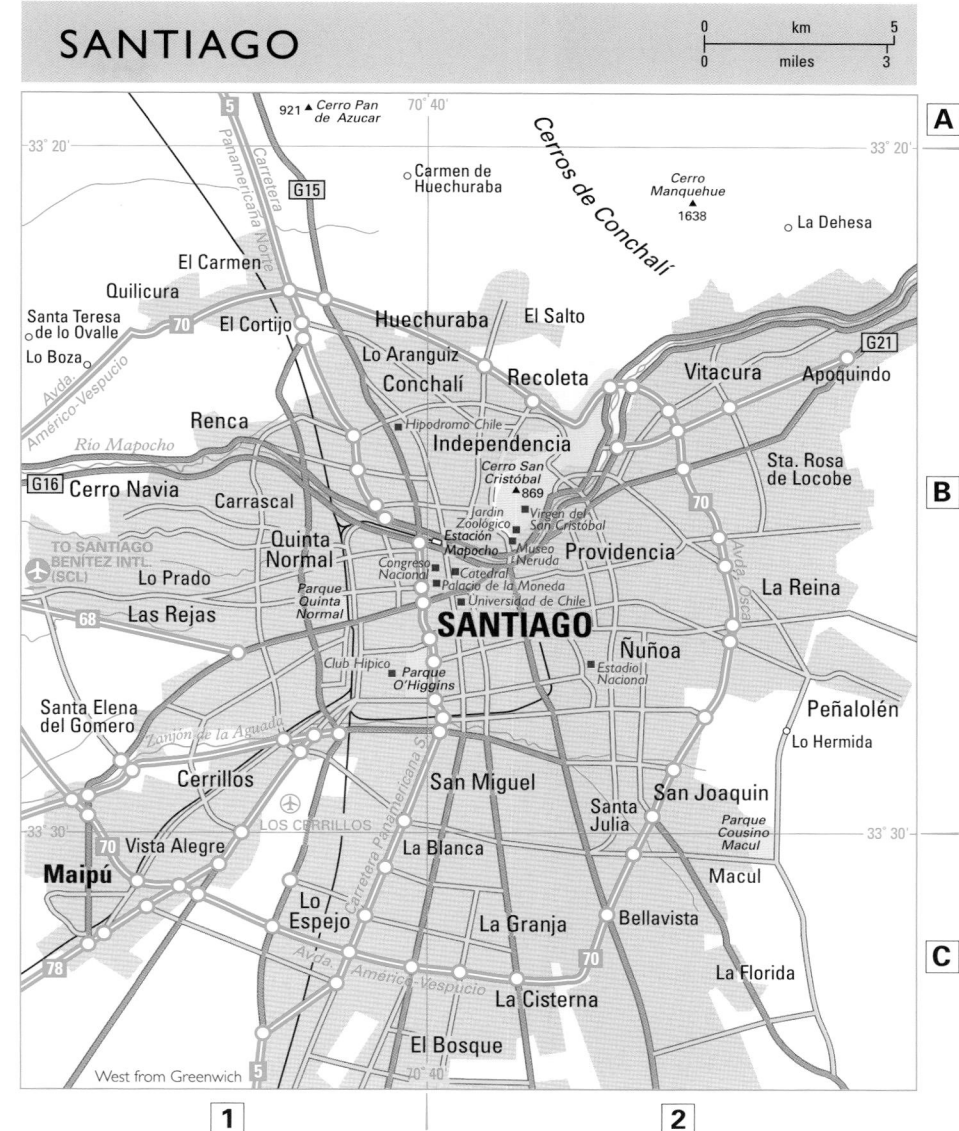

SÃO PAULO

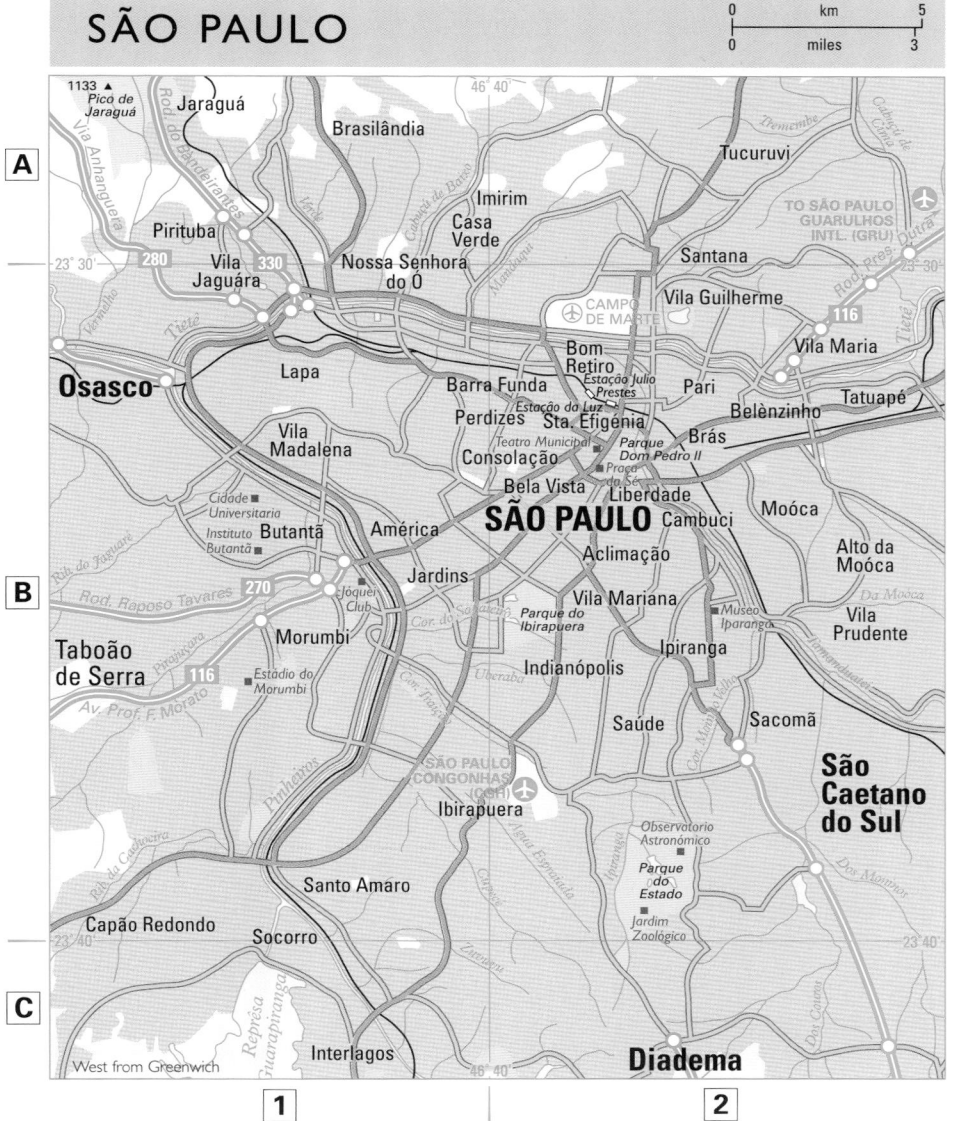

SEOUL

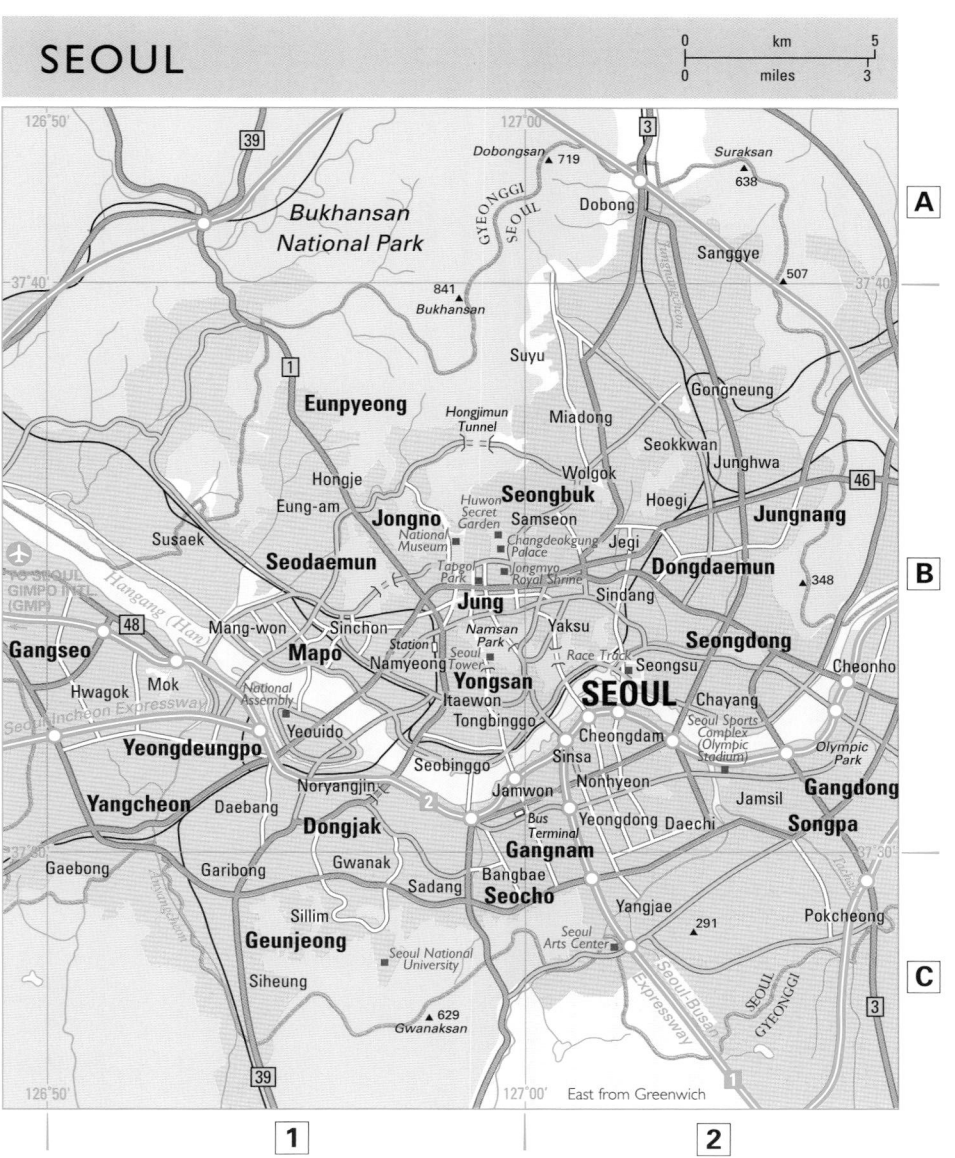

SHANGHAI

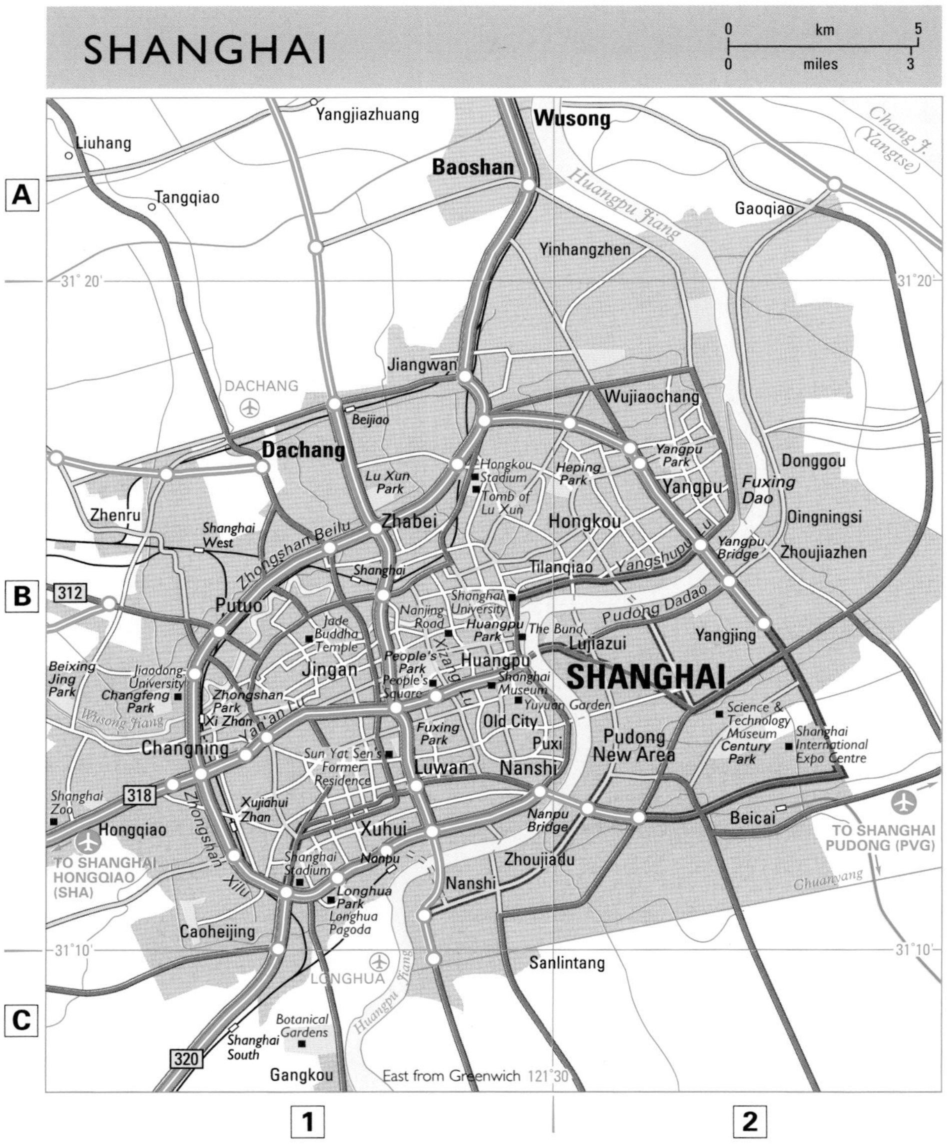

km 0 — 5
miles 0 — 3

Liuhang
Tangqiao
Yangjiazhuang
Wusong
Baoshan
Gaoqiao
Yinhangzhen
Chang J. (Yangtze)
Huangpu Jiang

31°20'

Jiangwan
DACHANG
Wujiaochang
Donggou
Qingningsi
Dachang
Beijiao
Lu Xun Park
Yangpu Park
Yangpu
Fuxing Dao
Lu Xun Tomb of
Hongkou Stadium
Heping Park
Zhongshan Beilu
Zhenru
Zhabei
Hongkou
Yangpu Bridge
Zhoujiazhen
Shanghai West
Shanghai University
Tilangiao
Yangshupu
Yangjing
312
Putuo
Jade Buddha Temple
Nanjing Road
Shanghai
Huangpu Park
The Bund
Lujiazui
Beixing Jing Park
Jingan
People's Park
People's Square
Huangpu
Shanghai Museum
Jiaodong University
Changfeng Park
Zhongshan Park
Xi Zhan
Zhongshan Park
Yuyuan Garden
Yangjing
Changning
Old City
Puxi
SHANGHAI
Science & Technology Museum
Shanghai International Expo Centre
318
Xujiahui Zhan
Fuxing Park
Luwan
Nanshi
Pudong New Area
Century Park
Sun Yat-Sen's Former Residence
Whangpu River
Hongqiao
Shanghai Zoo
TO SHANGHAI HONGQIAO (SHA)
Xinhua
Shanghai Stadium
Nanpu
Xuhui
Nanpu Bridge
Beicai
Chuanyang
Caoheijing
Longhua Temple Longhua Pagoda
Nanshi
Zhoujiadu
TO SHANGHAI PUDONG (PVG)

31°10'

LONGHUA
Sanlintang
320
Botanical Gardens
Shanghai South
Gangkou
East from Greenwich 121°30'

1 | 2

— Magnetic Levitation (Maglev) Railway

CENTRAL SINGAPORE

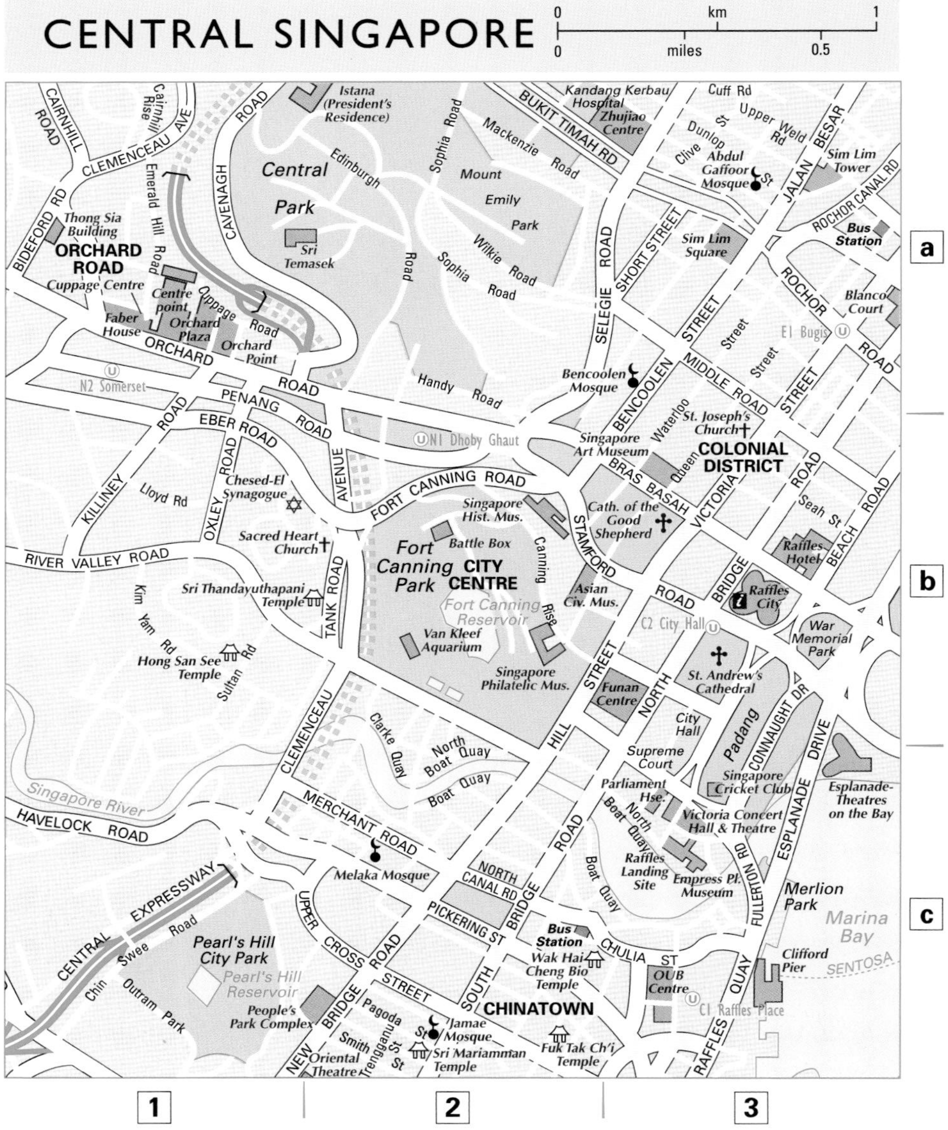

km 0 — 1
miles 0 — 0.5

CAIRNHILL ROAD
CLEMENCEAU
Istana (President's Residence)
Cairnhill Rise
BUKIT TIMAH RD
Kandang Kerbau Hospital
Cuff Rd
Upper Weld Rd
Sim Lim Tower
BIDEFORD RD
Thong Sia Building
CAVENAGH
Central Park
Edinburgh
Sophia Road
Mackenzie Road
Clive
Dunlop
Abdul Gaffoor Mosque
JALAN BESAR
ROCHOR CANAL RD
ORCHARD ROAD
Sri Temasek
Emerald Hill
Mount Emily
Wilkie Road
Sophia Road
Handy Road
SELEGIE ROAD
SHORT STREET
Sim Lim Square
Bus Station
a
Cuppage Centre
Centre point
Orchard
Cuppage Road
Blanco Court
Faber House
Orchard Plaza
ORCHARD ROAD
N2 Somerset
PENANG ROAD
EBER ROAD
KILLINEY ROAD
Lloyd Rd
OXLEY ROAD
Chesed-El Synagogue
FORT CANNING ROAD
Singapore Hist. Mus.
Bencoolen Mosque
BENCOOLEN STREET
Waterloo
Singapore Art Museum
St. Joseph's Church
BRAS BASAH
Cath. of the Good Shepherd
COLONIAL DISTRICT
VICTORIA STREET
MIDDLE ROAD
El Bugu
Raffles Hotel
BEACH ROAD
b
RIVER VALLEY ROAD
Sacred Heart Church
Sri Thandayuthapani Temple
TANK ROAD
Fort Canning Park CITY CENTRE
Battle Box
Fort Canning Reservoir
Van Kleef Aquarium
CANNING
Asian Civ. Mus.
STAMFORD ROAD
HILL STREET
City Hall
St. Andrew's Cathedral
CONNAUGHT DR
Raffles City
War Memorial Park
Kim
Yam Rd
Hong San See Temple
Sultan Rd
Singapore Philatelic Mus.
Funan Centre
NORTH BRIDGE ROAD
Supreme Court
Padang
Singapore Cricket Club
Esplanade Theatres on the Bay
CLEMENCEAU AVENUE
Clarke Quay
North Boat Quay
Parliament Hse.
Victoria Concert Hall & Theatre
Empress Pl. Museum
FULLERTON RD
Merlion Park
c
HAVELOCK ROAD
Singapore River
MERCHANT ROAD
South Boat Quay
Boat Quay
Raffles Landing Site
Marina Bay
CENTRAL EXPRESSWAY
Swee Road
Chin
Melaka Mosque
UPPER CROSS ROAD
NORTH CANAL RD
Boat Quay
SOUTH BRIDGE ROAD
CHULIA STREET
Clifford Pier
SENTOSA
Pearl's Hill City Park
Pearl's Hill Reservoir
PICKERING STREET
Bus Station
Wak Hai Cheng Bio Temple
OUB Centre
RAFFLES QUAY
Pagoda
Chin Outram Park
People's Park Complex
Smith
Trengganu
Jamae Mosque
Sri Mariamman Temple
CHINATOWN
Fuk Tak Ch'i Temple
OUB Centre
C1 Raffles Place
Oriental Theatre
NEW BRIDGE ROAD
Pagoda St
St
Mosque St
Oriental

1 | 2 | 3

SINGAPORE

km 0 — 5
miles 0 — 3

103°40'E
103°50'E
104°00'E

Malayu
Johor Bahru
Senoko Ind. Est.
Sembawang
Selat Johor
Sungei Buloh Nature Park
Kranji Ind. Est.
Woodlands
Chong Pang
Yishun
Pulau Seletar
MALAYSIA SINGAPORE
A
Lim Chu Kang
Singapore Turf Club
Sungei Kadut Ind. Est.
Zoological Gardens
Nee Soon
Sungai Seletar Reservoir
Dam
SELETAR
Seletar Golf Course
Jalan Kayu
Punggol Point
Pulau Serangoon
Pulau Ketam
Pulau Ubin
Pulau Tekong Kechil
Pulau Tekong
Sarimbun Res.
Sarimbun 85
Ama Keng
Choa Chu Kang
Punggol
Sengkang
Serangoon Harbour
Tg. Ladang
Murai Res.
Choa Chu Kang
Bukit Timah Expy.
Choa Chu Kang
Central Catchment Nature Reserve
Yio Chu Kang
Pasir Ris Park
Pasir Ris
Loyang Ind. Est.
Changi
SINGAPORE CHANGI (SIN)
Poyan Res.
Bukit Panjang
132
Bt. Panjang
Upper Peirce Reservoir
Ang Mo Kio
Hougang
Chia Keng
Yan Kit
Chongji Prison Museum
Tengeh Res.
Choa Chu Kang 88
Nanyang University
Bukit Batok Nature Parks 106
162
MacRitchie Reservoir
Serangoon
Bishan
Paya Lebar
Tai Seng
Simei
Tampines
Reclaimed Land
Raffles Golf Course & Country Club
Boon Lay
Singapore Discovery Centre
Chinese & Japanese Gardens
Jurong West
Air View Park
Raffles Park
Toa Payoh
Kg Landang
Tanah Merah Golf Course
Jurong
Jurong Industrial Estate
Jurong Bird Park
Tang Dynasty Museum
Jurong East
Ayer Rajah Expy.
Dunearn
Victoria Park
University of Singapore
Botanic Gardens
Geylang Serai
Chai Chee
Bedok
Frankel
Singapore Expo
1°20'N
Tuas
Pandan Res.
Clementi
Maryland
Holland Village
Queenstown
Katong
East Coast Park
Kg Tanjong Penjuru
Pasir Panjang
National University of Singapore
Telok Blangah
National Stadium
Kallang Park
East Coast Pkwy.
Buona Vista Park
Mt. 105 Faber
St Andrew's Cathedral
City Hall
National Museum
Thian Hock Keng Temple
SINGAPORE
Pulau Jurong
Seraya
Pasir Panjang Terminal
Buona Vista Park
Cable Car
Underwater World
World Trade Centre
P. Brani
Harbour
B
Reclaimed Land
Sakra
Sentosa Gardens
Sentosa
Tanjong Golf Course
Straits of Singapore
Pulau Busing
Pulau Bukum

1 | 2 | 3 | 4

East from Greenwich

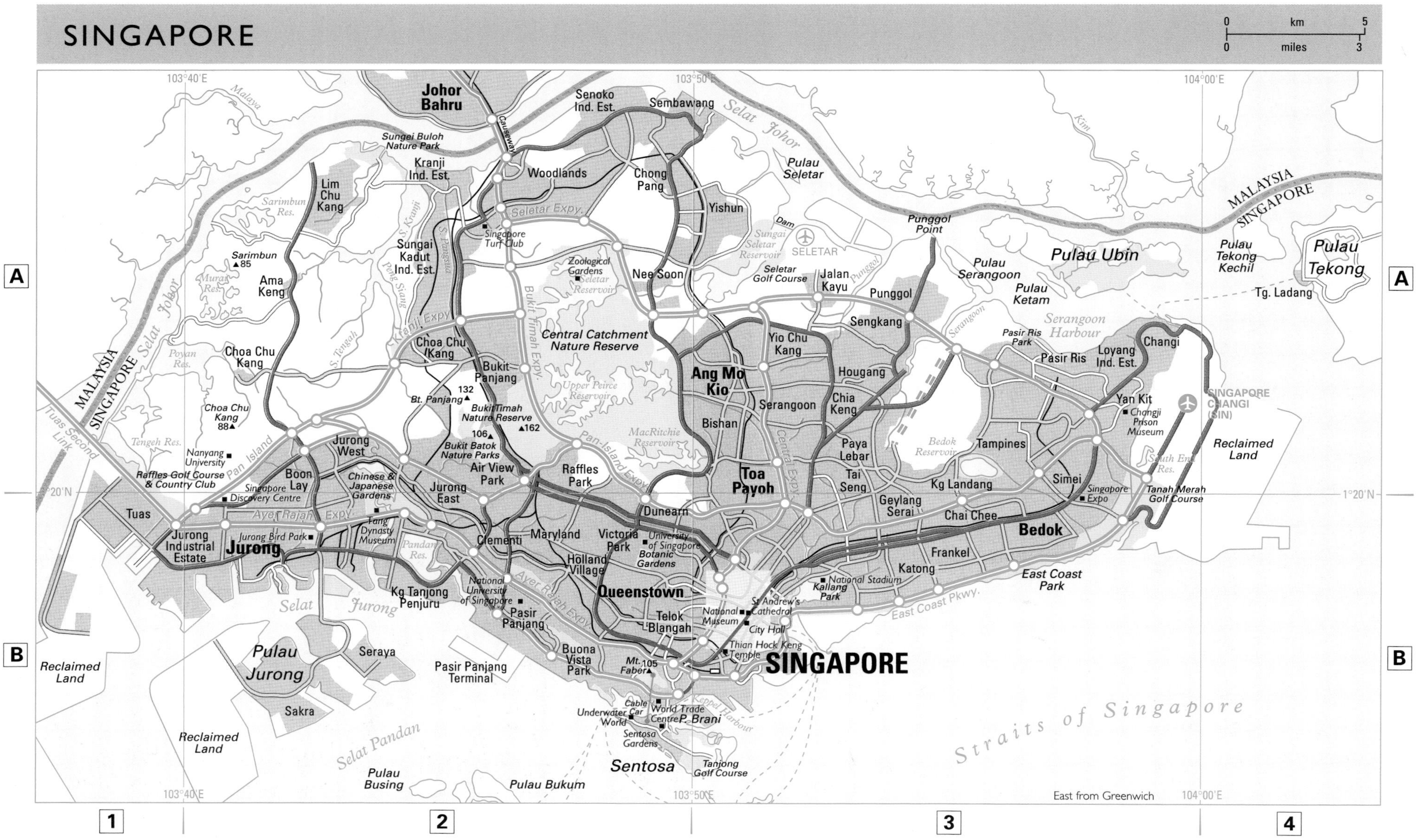

COPYRIGHT PHILIP'S

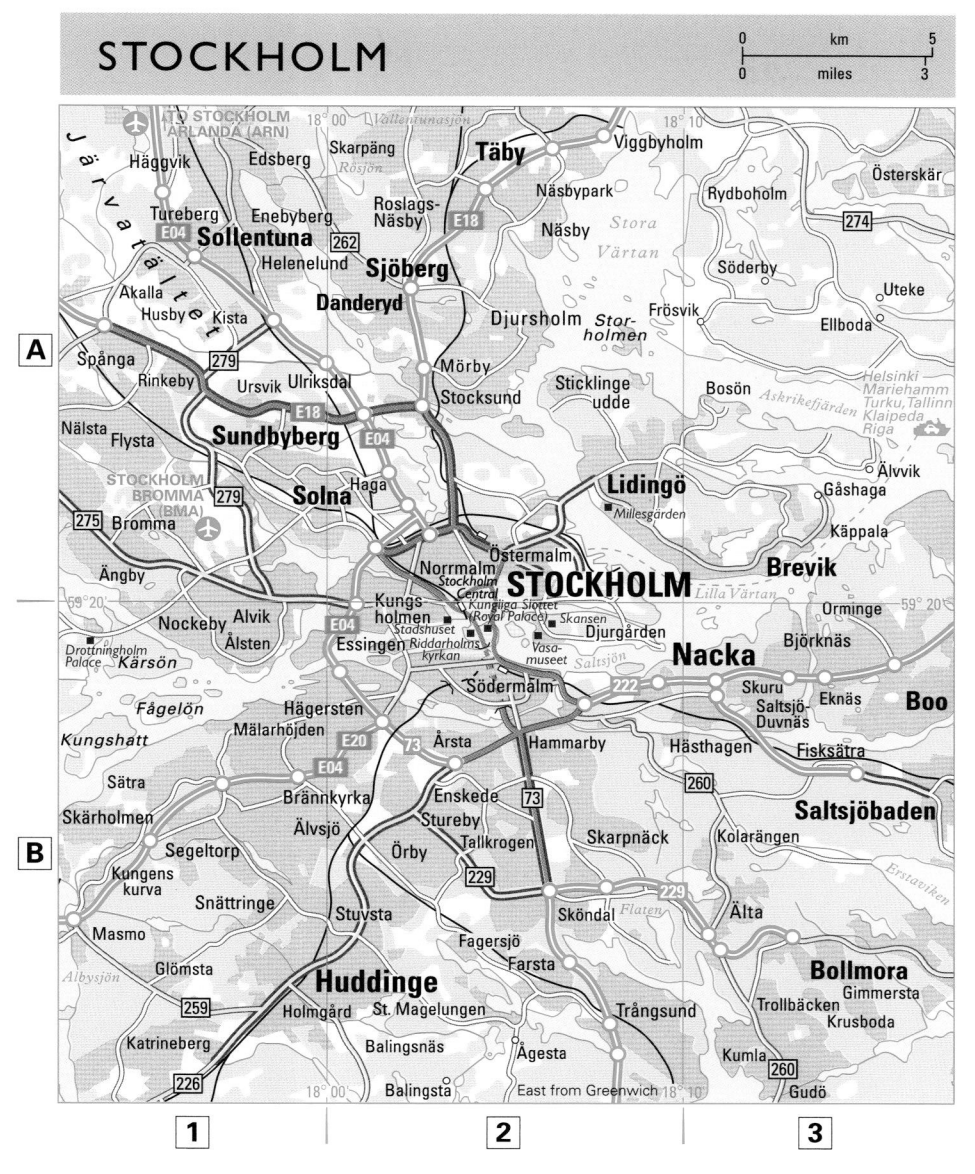

STOCKHOLM

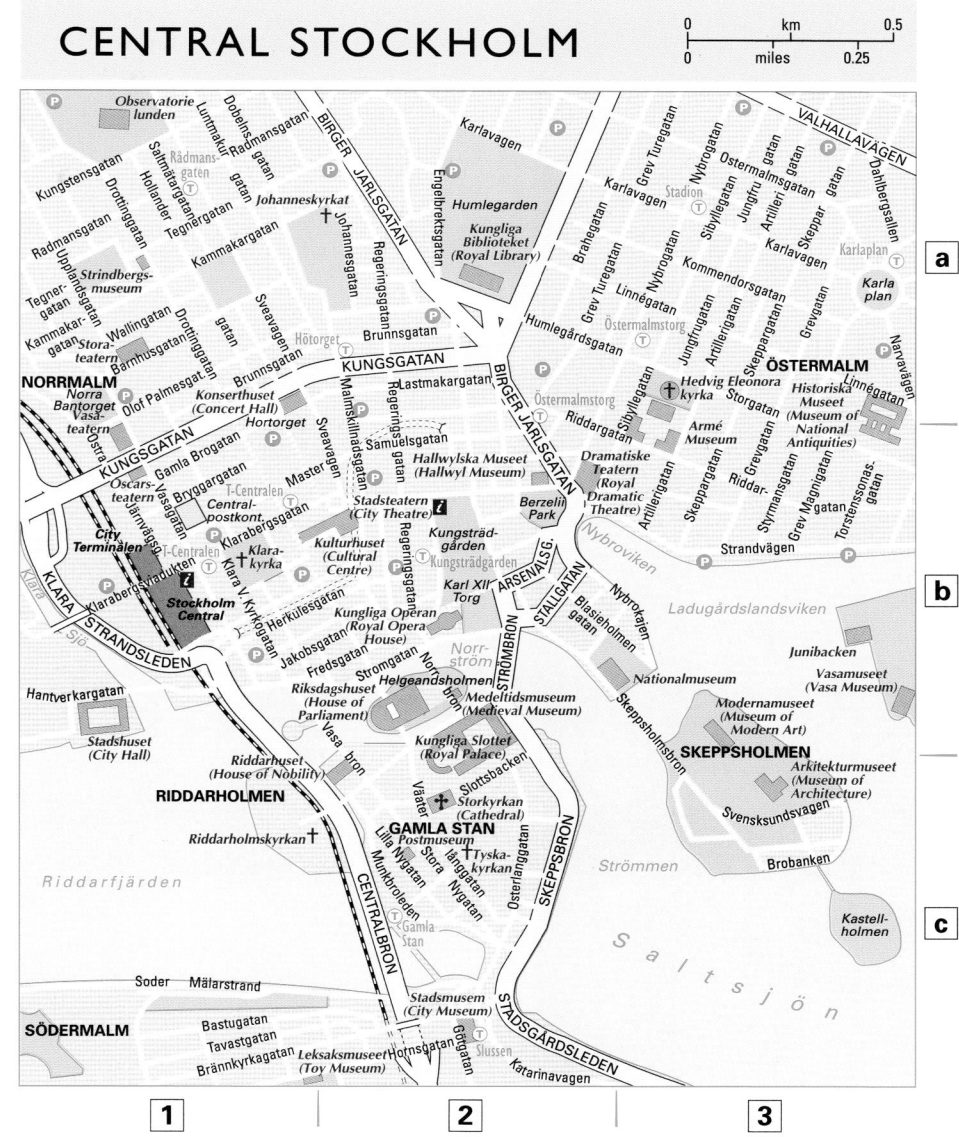

CENTRAL STOCKHOLM

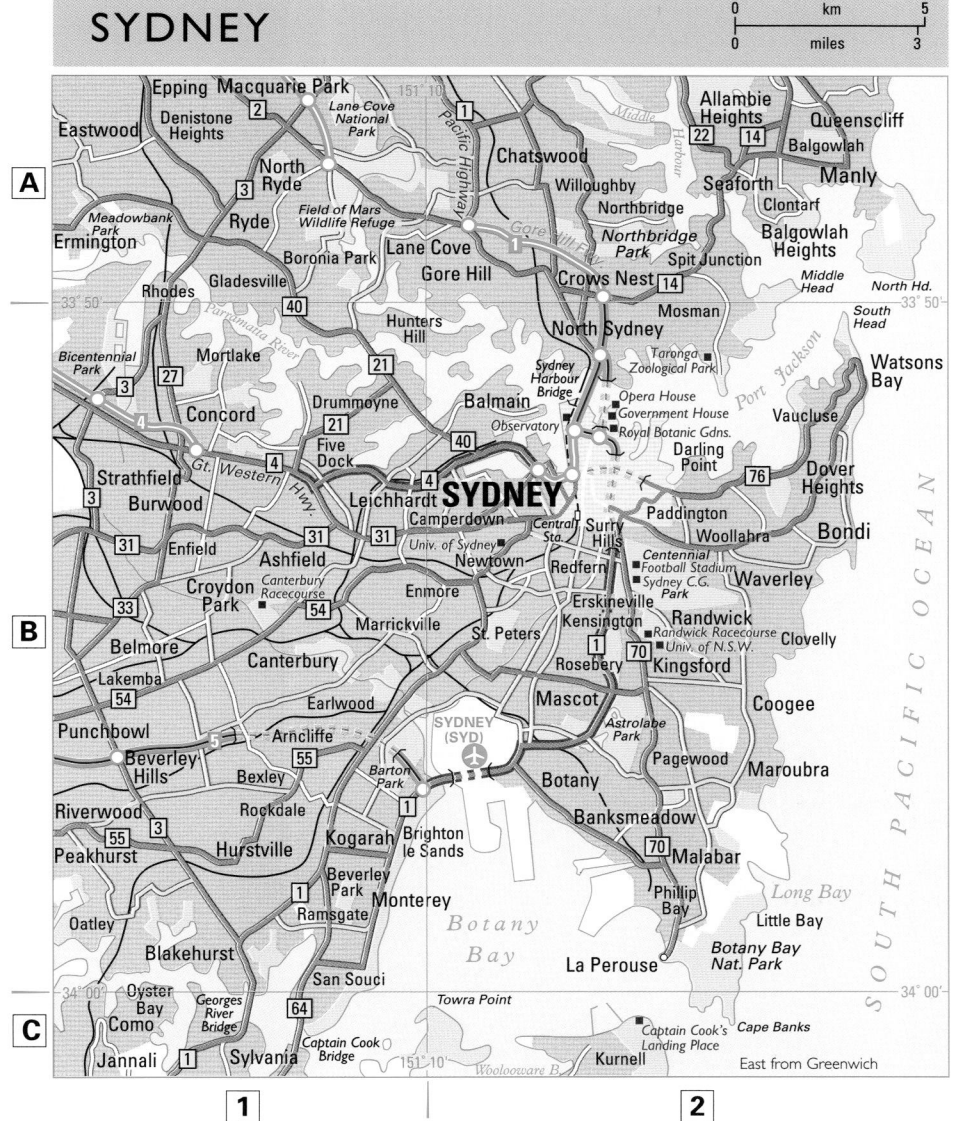

SYDNEY

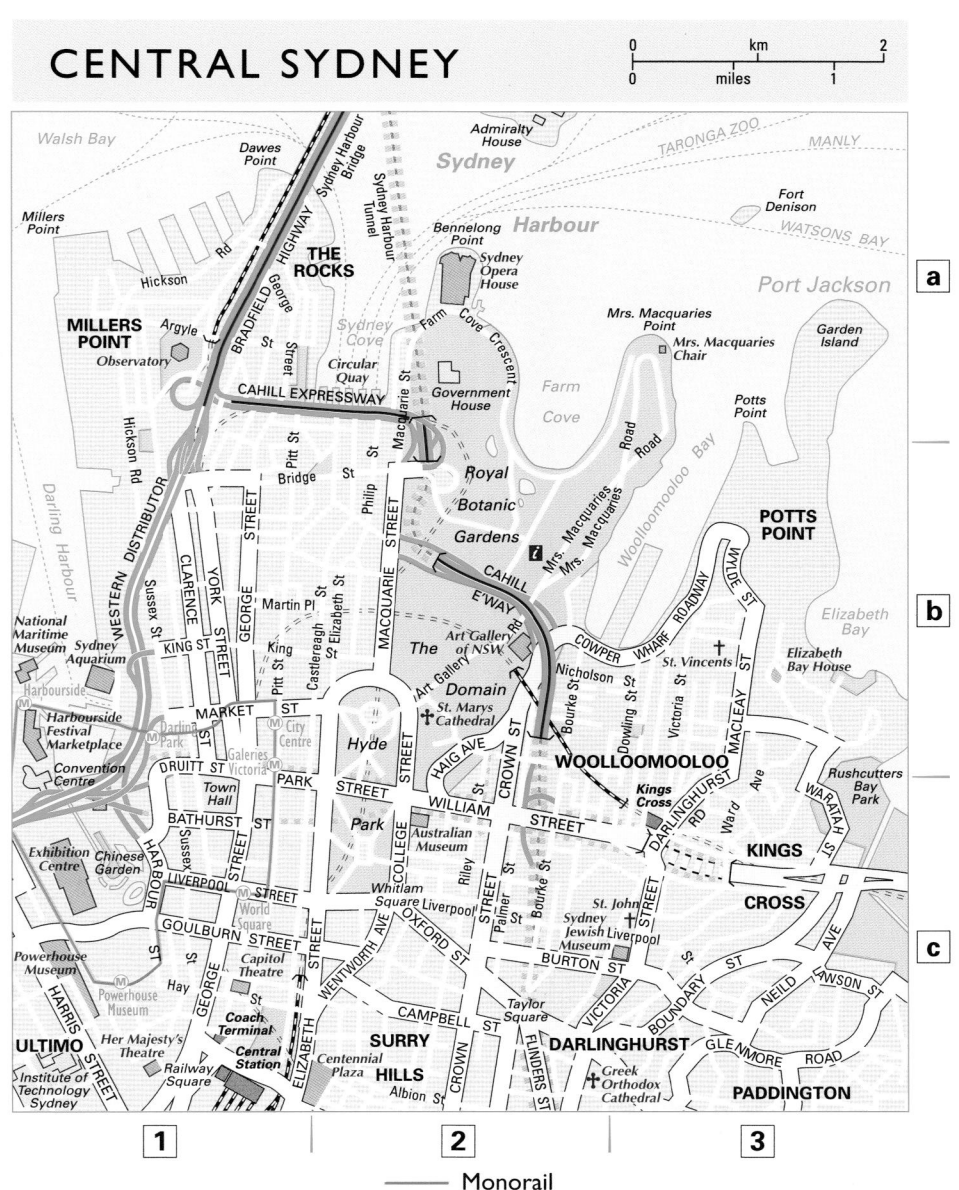

CENTRAL SYDNEY

— Monorail

CENTRAL TOKYO

km 0 5
miles 0 3

A

Higashimurayama Kurume Shimosato Kasuga Itabashi Jūjō Takinogawa Kasuge Kameari Yakire
Kodaira Kurihara Yahara Ōyama Kita Tabata Senju Takasago Soya
Higashimurayama Hōya Shimo-shakuji Nerima Ikebukuro Sugamo Arakawa Horikiri Katsushika Takasago
Ogawa Nonakashinden Suzuki-shinden Tanashi Toshimaen Ōtsuka Nippori Honden Shinkoiwa Ichikawa
Kodaira Kokobunji Koganei Ogikubo Nakano Toshima Mejiro Komagome Asakusa Sumida Kameido Mizue Edogawa
Kunitachi Yaho Fuchū Mitaka Asagaya Suginami Shinnakano Shinjuku Chiyoda Nihonbashi Ryogoku Funabori Tōkagi
Koremasa Takaido Honancho Honcho Meiji Shrine Akasaka Imperial Palace Chūō Kōto Urayasu
Shimogawara Kamikitazawa Shibuya Aoyama Roppongi Ginza Fukagawa Kasai
Tama Inagi Suge Komae Tamaden Minato Ebisu Shiba Harumi TŌKYŌ
Chōfu Setagaya Sangenjaya Shirogane Rainbow Bridge Tokyo Disneyland
Hosoyama Ikuta Komazawa Meguro Gotanda Port of Tokyo Tokyo Disney Sea
Takaishi Mampukuji Takatsu-Ku Futago-tamagawaen Ōokayama Ōsaki Shinagawa
Mizonokuchi Kodanaka Jiyūgaoka Ebara Ōimachi Tokyo Bay
Machida Sugō Maginu Arima Chitose Nakahara-Ku Maruko Ōta Ōmori
Nagatsuta Eda Ōdana Yamada Hiyoshi Kosugi Ikegami Kamata Haneda
Kanamori Takeshita Ichgao Minami-tsunashima Saiwai TOKYO-HANEDA INTL. (HND) Hamano
Kamitsuruma Tōkaichiba Ikebe Nippa Kikuna Kawasaki Kisarazu East from Greenwich

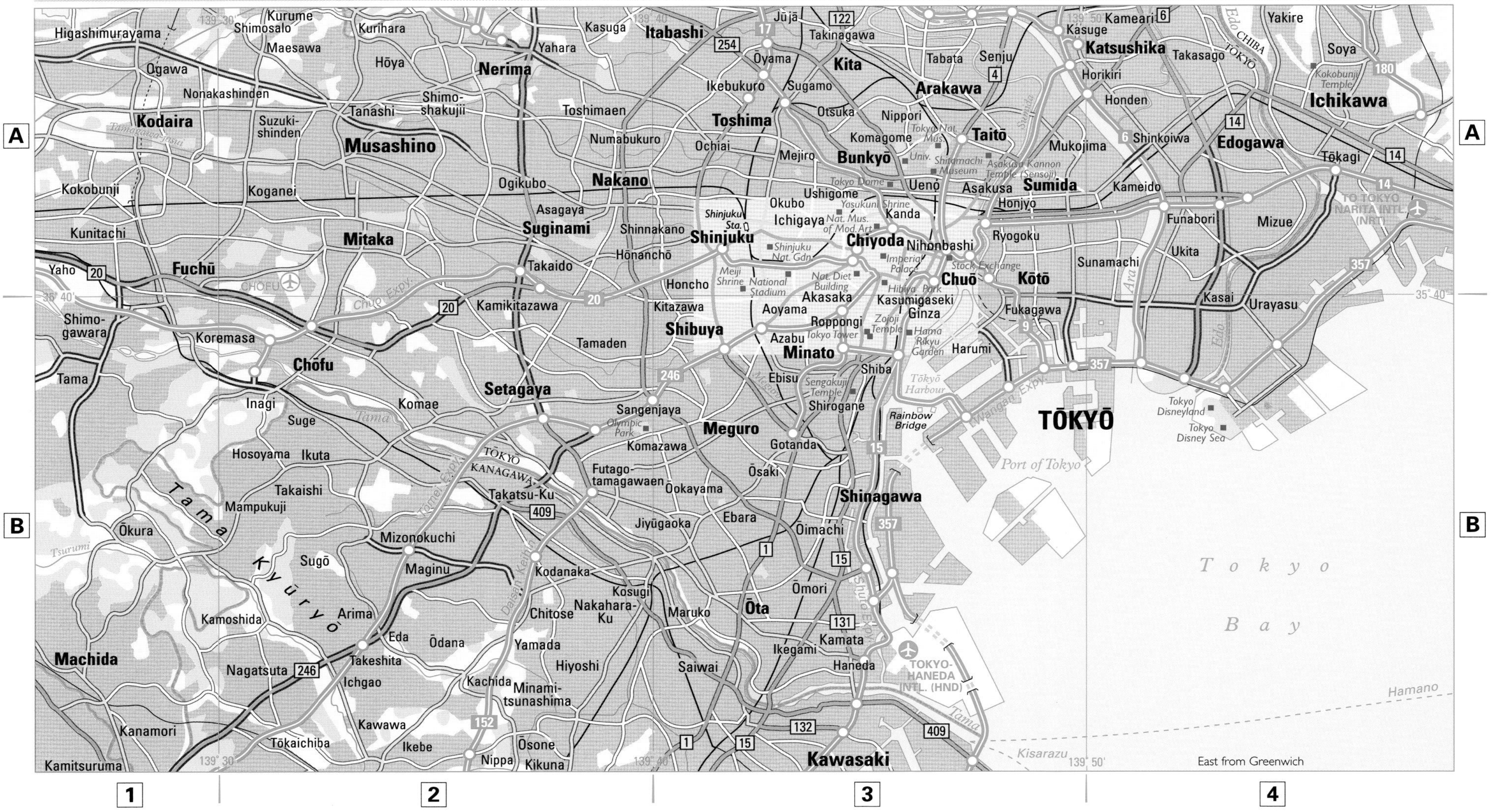

1 2 3 4

CENTRAL TOKYO

km 0 0.5
miles 0 0.25

SHINJUKU ŌKUBO AKIHABARA ASAKUSABASHI
ICHIGAYA KUDANKITA JIMBŌCHŌ KANDA KODENMACHO
YOTSUYA SANBANCHO CHIYODA MARUNOUCHI NIHONBASHI
AOYAMA AKASAKA CHŪŌ
SHIBUYA KASUMIGASEKI GINZA
TORANOMON SHIMBASHI TSUKIJI
ROPPONGI MINATO SHIBA HARUMI
AZABU

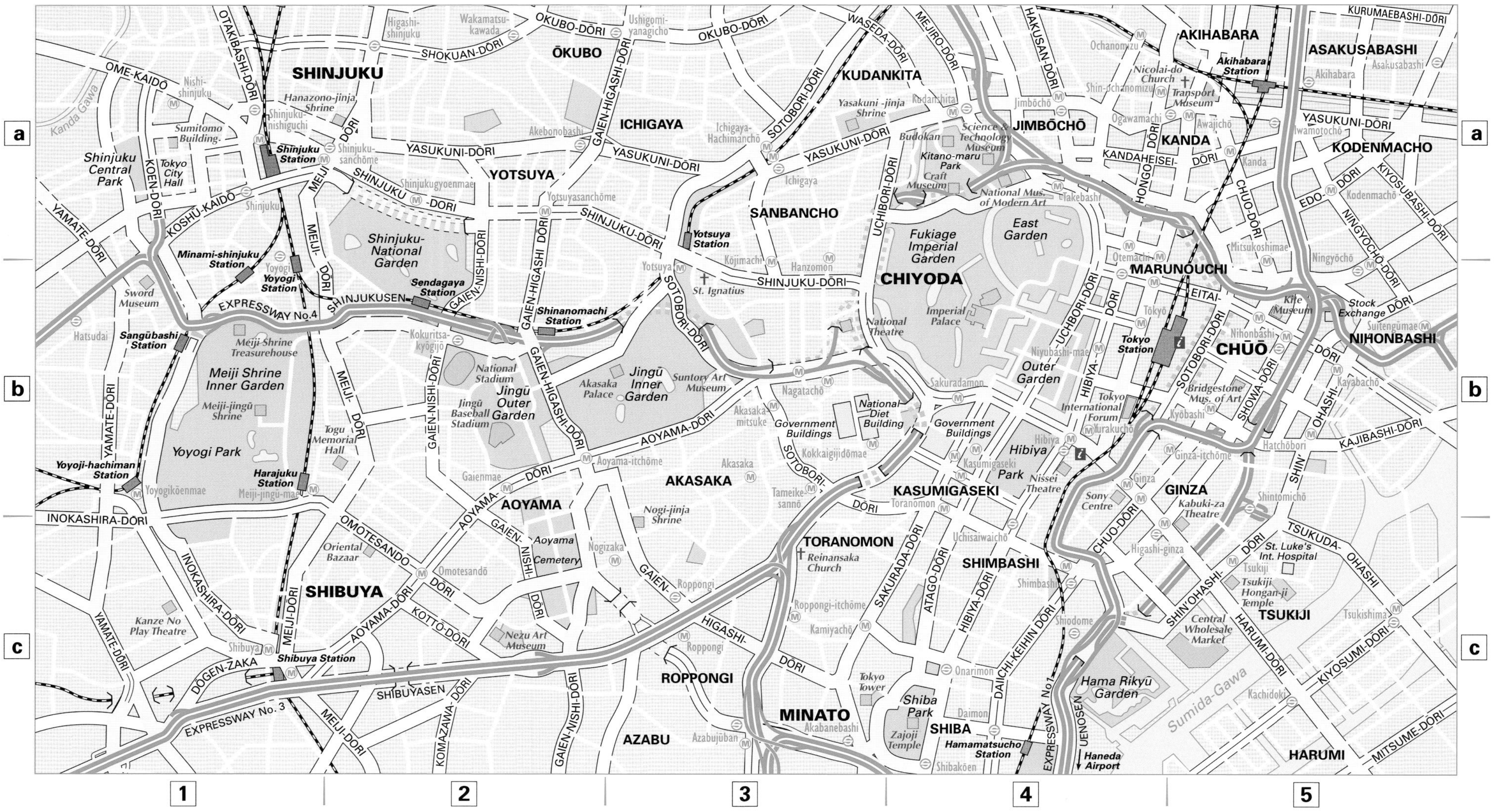

Toei Subway Ⓜ Tokyo Metro

TEHRAN

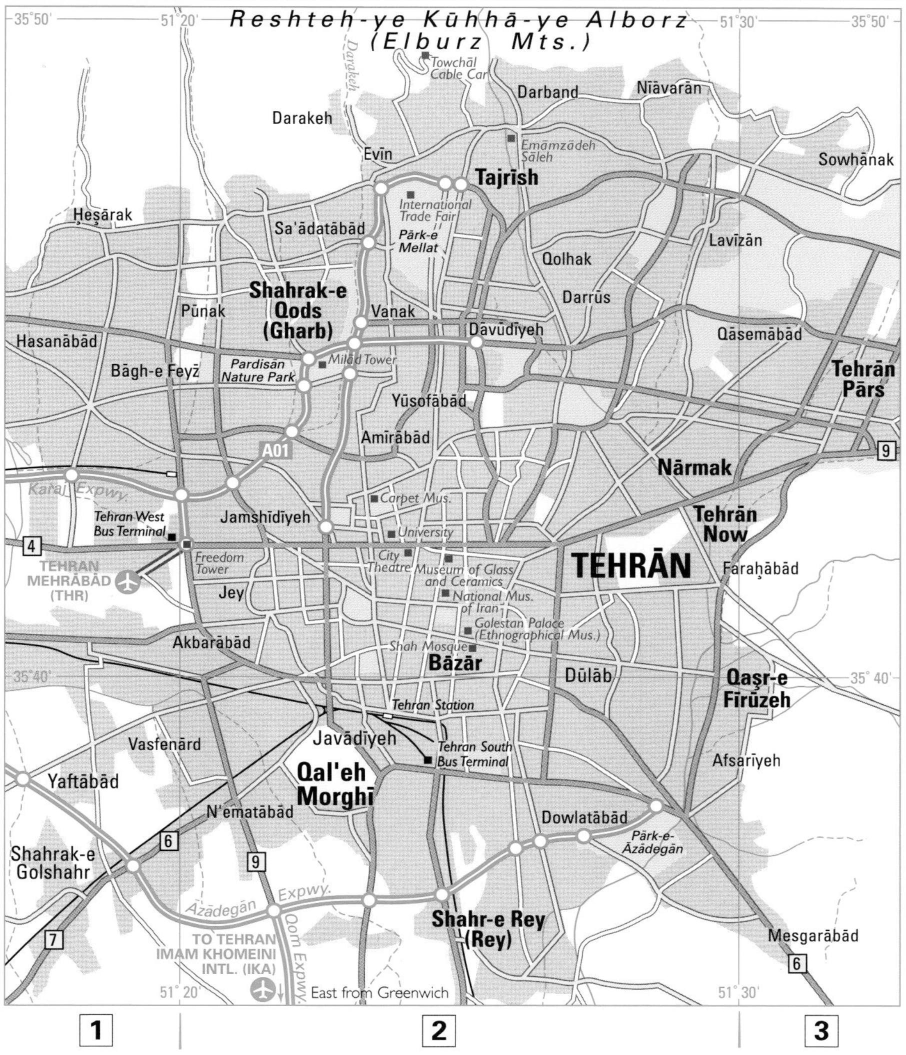

km 0 — 5
miles 0 — 3

Reshteh-ye Kūhhā-ye Alborz
(Elburz Mts.)

Towchāl Cable Car
Darakeh
Darband
Niāvarān
Emāmzādeh Sāleh
Sowhānak
Evin
Tajrish
Sa'ādatābād
Qolhak
Lavīzān
Darrūs
Qāsemābād
Tehrān Pārs
Hesārak
Bāgh-e Feyż
Shahrak-e Qods (Gharb)
Pūnak
Vanak
Davūdīyeh
Hasanābād
Pardisān Nature Park
Milad Tower
Yūsofābād
Amirābād
Nārmak
Tehrān West Bus Terminal
Jamshīdīyeh
Carpet Mus.
University
Tehrān Now
TEHRAN MEHRĀBĀD (THR)
Freedom Tower
Akbarābād
City Theatre
Museum of Glass and Ceramics
National Mus. of Iran
Shah Mosque
Golestan Palace (Ethnographical Mus.)
Farahābād
Jey
Bāzār
Dūlāb
Qasr-e Firūzeh
Vasfenārd
Tehran Station
Javādīyeh
Tehran South Bus Terminal
Afsarīyeh
Yaftābād
Qal'eh Morghī
N'ematābād
Dowlatābād
Pārk-e Āzādegān
Shahrak-e Golshahr
Shahr-e Rey (Rey)
Mesgarābād
TO TEHRAN IMAM KHOMEINI INTL. (IKA)
East from Greenwich

TEHRĀN

CENTRAL TORONTO

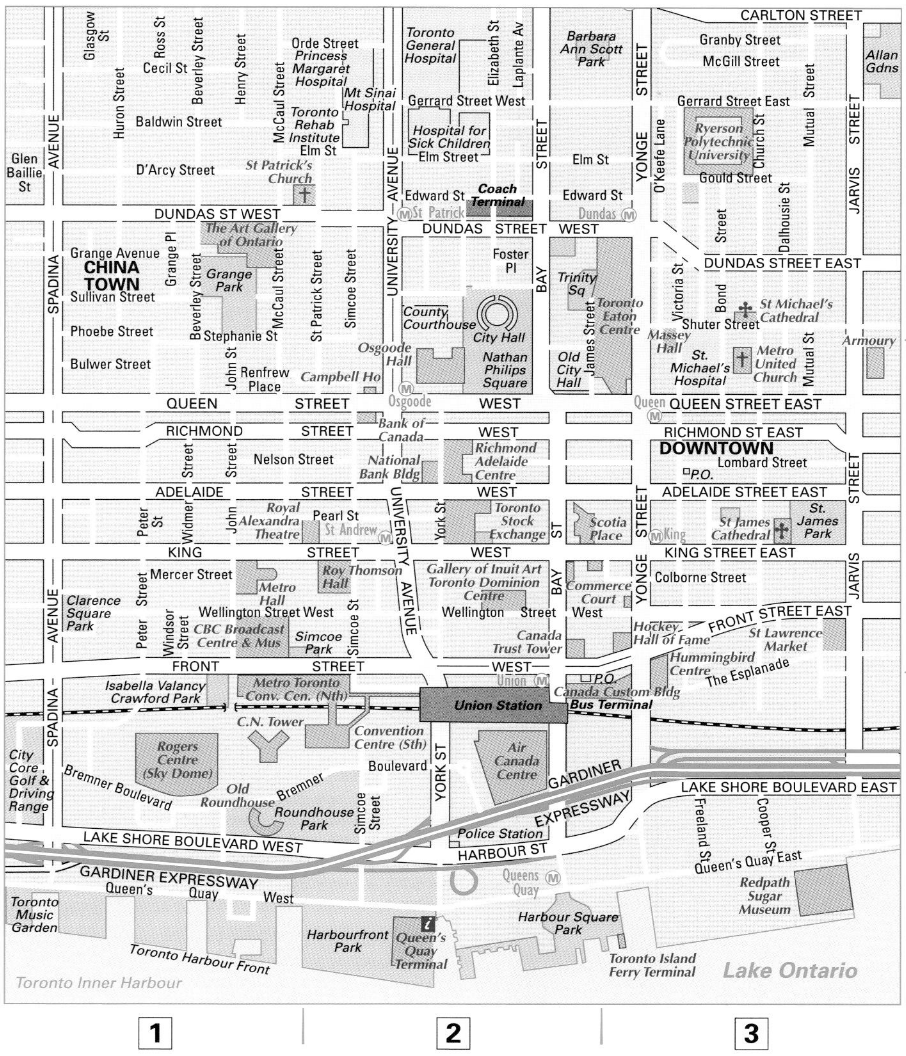

km 0 — 0.5
miles 0 — 0.25

Glasgow St
Ross St
Cecil St
Orde Street
CARLTON STREET
Toronto General Hospital
Granby Street
Allan Gdns
Huron Street
Baldwin Street
Henry Street
Princess Margaret Hospital
Elizabeth St
Laplante Av
Barbara Ann Scott Park
McGill Street
Glen Baillie St
D'Arcy Street
Beverley Street
McCaul Street
Gerrard Street West
Mt Sinai Hospital
Gerrard Street East
Toronto Rehab Institute
Hospital for Sick Children
Elm Street
Mutual Street
SPADINA
AVENUE
St Patrick's Church
Edward Street
Coach Terminal
Elm St
Edward St
Gould Street
Jarvis St
DUNDAS ST WEST
DUNDAS STREET WEST
DUNDAS STREET EAST
Grange Avenue
The Art Gallery of Ontario
Grange Pl
Foster Pl
Trinity Sq
Dalhousie St
CHINA TOWN
Sullivan Street
Grange Park
BAY
Toronto Eaton Centre
St Michael's Cathedral
Beverley Street
McCaul Street
St Patrick Street
Simcoe Street
County Courthouse
City Hall
Victoria St
Bond
Phoebe Street
Stephanie St
Osgoode Hall
Nathan Phillips Square
Old City Hall
Massey Hall
St. Michael's Hospital
Metro United Church
Bulwer Street
John St
Renfrew Place
Campbell Ho
Church St
Armoury
QUEEN
STREET
WEST
QUEEN STREET EAST
RICHMOND
STREET
WEST
Bank of Canada
RICHMOND ST EAST
DOWNTOWN
Lombard Street
Peter St
Nelson Street
York St
National Bank Bldg
Richmond Adelaide Centre
ADELAIDE
STREET
WEST
ADELAIDE STREET EAST
Widmer St
John
Pearl St
Scotia Place
St James Cathedral
St. James Park
KING
STREET
WEST
Royal Alexandra Theatre
Toronto Stock Exchange
KING STREET EAST
Clarence Square Park
Mercer Street
Metro Hall
Roy Thomson Hall
Gallery of Inuit Art
Colborne Street
Windsor Street
CBC Broadcast Centre & Mus
Wellington Street West
Simcoe Park
Toronto Dominion Centre
Commerce Court West
Hockey Hall of Fame
FRONT STREET EAST
St Lawrence Market
Canada Trust Tower
Hummingbird Centre
The Esplanade
Isabella Valancy Crawford Park
Metro Toronto Conv. Cen. (Nth)
P.O.
Canada Custom Bldg
C.N. Tower
Union Station
Bus Terminal
City Core Golf & Driving Range
Bremner Boulevard
Rogers Centre (Sky Dome)
Convention Centre (Sth)
Air Canada Centre
LAKE SHORE BOULEVARD EAST
Old Roundhouse
Roundhouse Park
Simcoe Park
Boulevard
GARDINER EXPRESSWAY
Police Station
HARBOUR ST
Redpath Sugar Museum
LAKE SHORE BOULEVARD WEST
GARDINER EXPRESSWAY
Toronto Music Garden
Queen's Quay West
Harbourfront Park
Queen's Quay Terminal
Harbour Square Park
Queen's Quay East
Toronto Harbour Front
Toronto Island Ferry Terminal
Toronto Inner Harbour
Lake Ontario

TORONTO

km 0 — 5
miles 0 — 3

Boyd Conservation Area
Thornhill
Markham
Metro Toronto Zoo
Fairport
Vaughan
The Promenade
Concord
Brown
Glen Rouge Park
West Rouge
Pine Grove
Edgeley
Newtonbrook
Agincourt
Malvern
Rouge Hill
Woodbridge
Fisherville
Willowdale
Port Union
Humber Summit
G. Ross Lord Park
East Don Parkland
Fairview Mall
Scarborough Town Centre
Morningside Park
Highland Creek
Beaumonte Heights
Black Creek Pioneer Village
York University
Northwood Park
North York
Lansing
Woburn
Bendale
West Hill
Thistletown
Downsview
Armour Heights
York Mills
Wexford
Scarborough
Eastpoint Park
Claireville Reservoir
DOWNSVIEW C.A.F.B.
Don Mills
Cliffside
Humberwood Park
Woodbine Centre
Kipling Heights
Rexdale
Humberlea
Lawrence Heights
York Univ Sunnybrook Health Science Centre
Wilket Creek Park
Ontario Science Centre
Thorncliffe
Danforth
Bluffers Park
Malton
Woodbine Race Track
Weston
Forest Hill
Leaside
Dentonia Park
Scarborough Bluffs
TORONTO LESTER B. PEARSON INTL. (YYZ)
Cedarvale Park
York
East York
Birch Cliff
Humber Valley Village
Mount Dennis
Casa Loma
Royal Ontario Museum
Riverdale Park
Kew Gardens
Hanlon
Lambton Mills
Swansea
University of Toronto
Old City Hall
Ashbridge's Bay Park
Etobicoke
High Park
Parliament Buildings
Islington
Kingsway
C.N. Tower & Rogers Centre
Union Sta
TORONTO
Markland Wood
Humber Bay
Old Fort York
Parkdale
TORONTO CITY CENTRE (ISLAND)
Tommy Thompson Park
Burnhamthorpe
Summerville
Exhibition Place
Ontario Place
Island Park
Toronto Harbour
LAKE ONTARIO
Mimico
New Toronto
Humber Bay Park
Toronto Islands
Gibraltar Point
Square One
Dixon Mall
Humber College
Samuel Smith Park
Cooksville
Mississauga
Long Branch
West from Greenwich

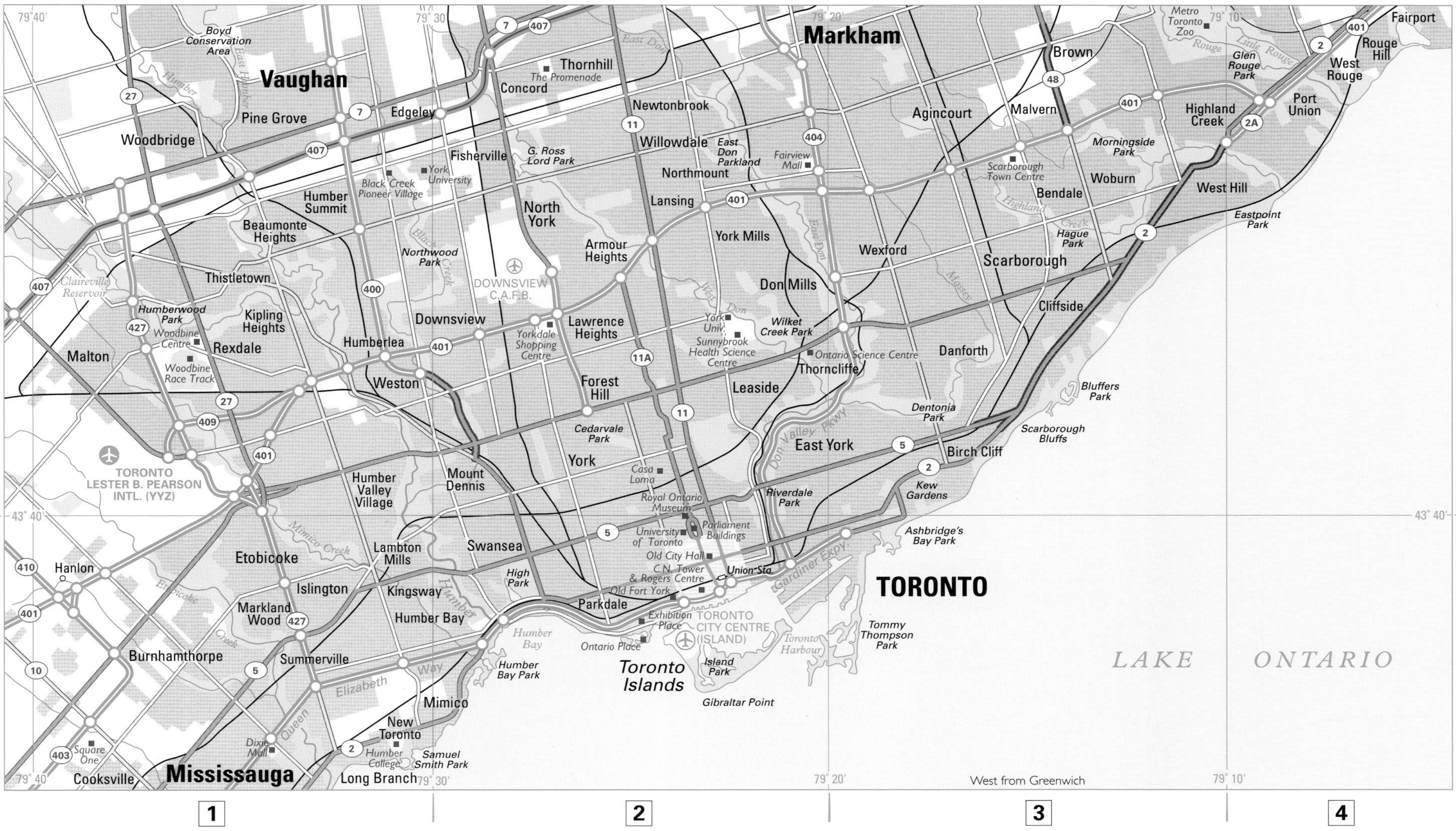

427 Provincial route numbers

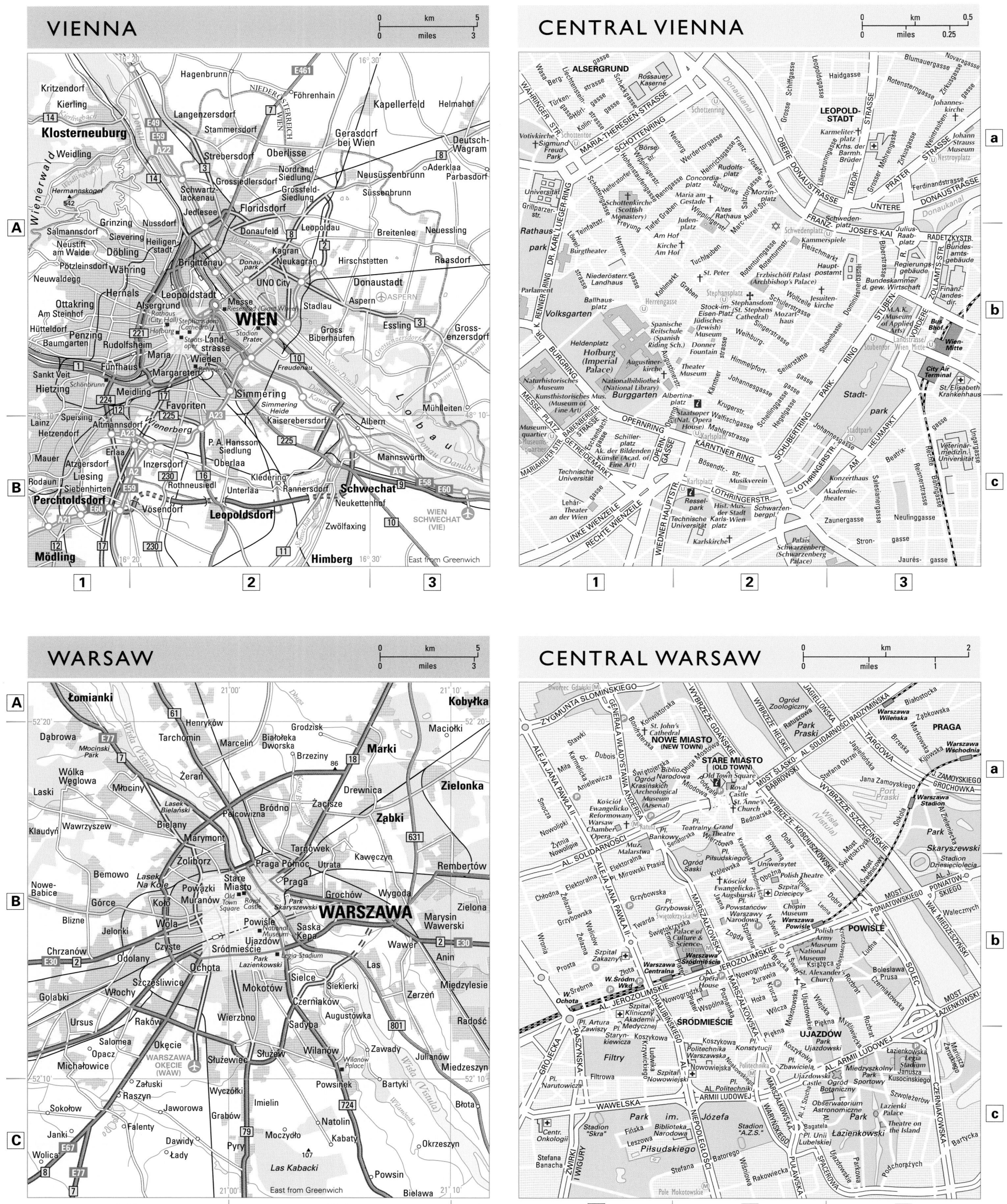

WASHINGTON

km 5
miles 3

A
Dranesville · Great Falls · Potomac · Cabin John Regional Park · Oak View · Greenbelt · 39°00'
Woodmont · Silver Spring · Adelphi
Bethesda · Chevy Chase · Langley Park · College Park · Lanham-Seabrook
Reston · MARYLAND · VIRGINIA · Cabin John · Glen Echo · Glen Mar Park · Somerset · Rock Creek Park · Takoma Park · Univ. of Maryland · Berwyn Heights · East Pines · New Carrollton
Belle View · Langley · Westgate · Brookmont · Brightwood · Chillum · Hyattsville · Riverdale · Edmonston · Landover Hills · Glenarden
B
Tysons Corner · McLean · Franklin Park · WASHINGTON · Mount Rainier · Bladensburg · Kent Village
Pimmit Hills · Georgetown · The White House · Trinidad · Fairmount Heights · Cheverly · Palmer Park
Hunters Valley · Vienna · Dunn Loring · Vietnam Veterans Mem. · Union Station · U.S. Capitol · Seat Pleasant · FedEx Field
Oakton · Falls Church · Arlington · Rosslyn · Lincoln Memorial · Library of Congress · Kettering
Seven Corners · Arlington Blvd. · Broyhill Park · Hillwood · Arlington Nat. Cemetery · Pentagon · Jefferson Memorial · Fort Dupont Park · Capitol Heights · Millwood · Ritchie
Fairfax · Holmes Run Acres · Annalee Heights · Culmore · Baileys Crossroads · East Arlington · Anacostia · Coral Hills · District Heights · Forestville
Parklawn · Suitland
Annandale · Kings Park · Alexandria · Hillcrest Heights · Silver Hill · Morningside · 38°50'
North Springfield · Glassmanor · Camp Springs
West Springfield · Springfield · Franconia · Huntington · Rose Hill · Groveton · Temple Hills · Oxon Hill · ANDREWS AIR FORCE BASE
Butts Corner · Fairfax Station · Kings Park West · Woodrow Wilson Memorial Bridge · Fort Foote Village · South Lawn · Oaklawn · West from Greenwich
C

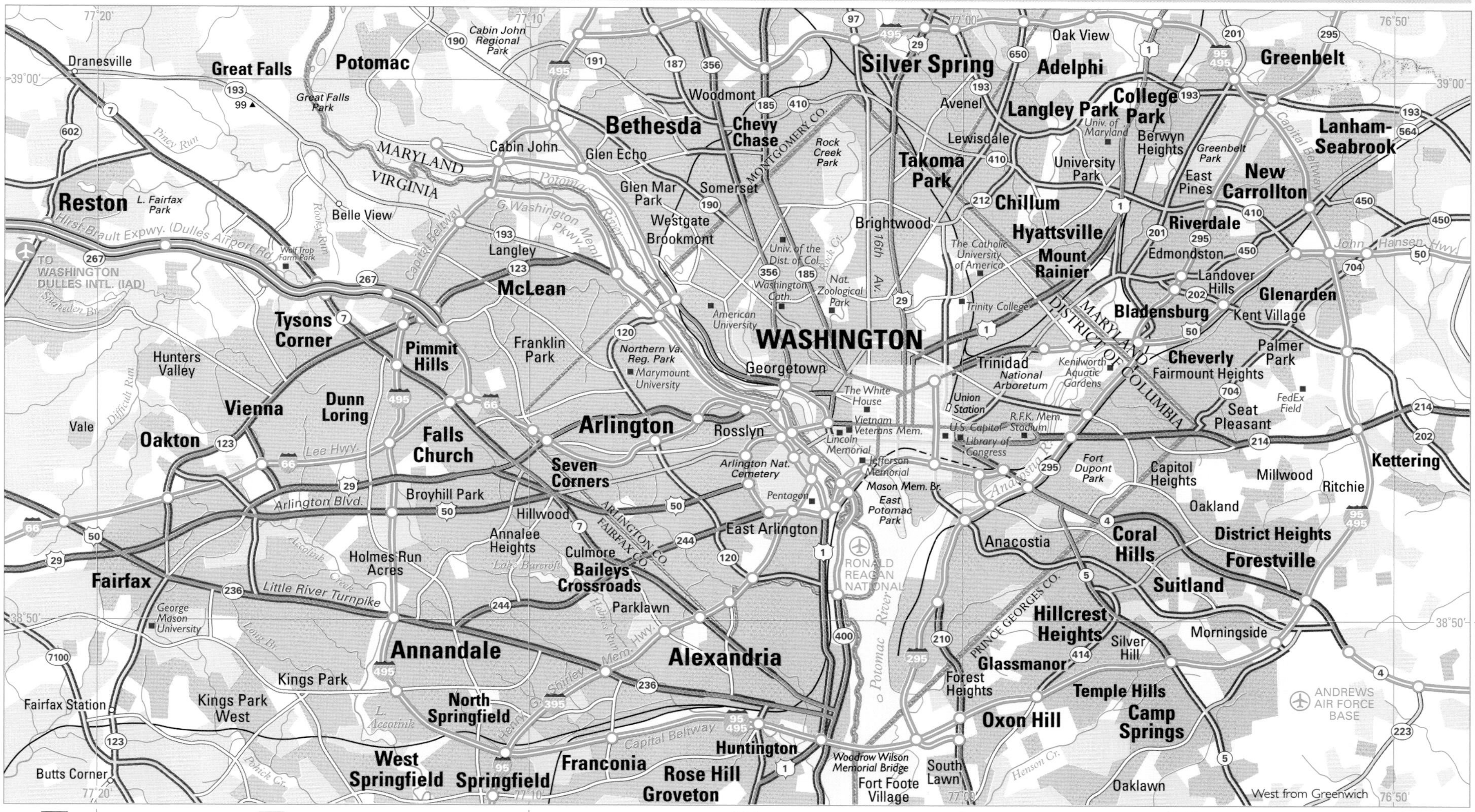

🛡 Interstate route numbers   29 U.S. route numbers   166 State route numbers

CENTRAL WASHINGTON

km
miles 0.5

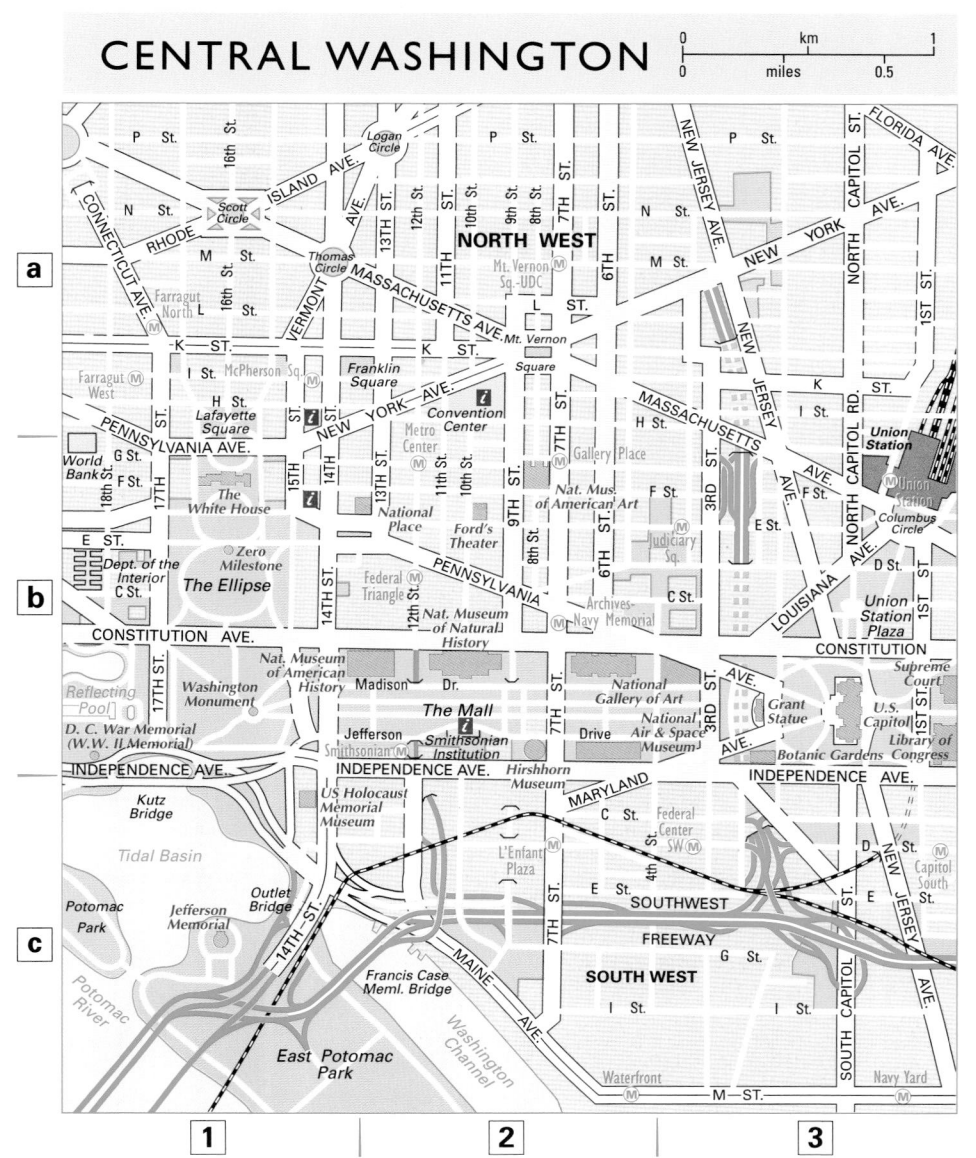

WELLINGTON

km 5
miles 3

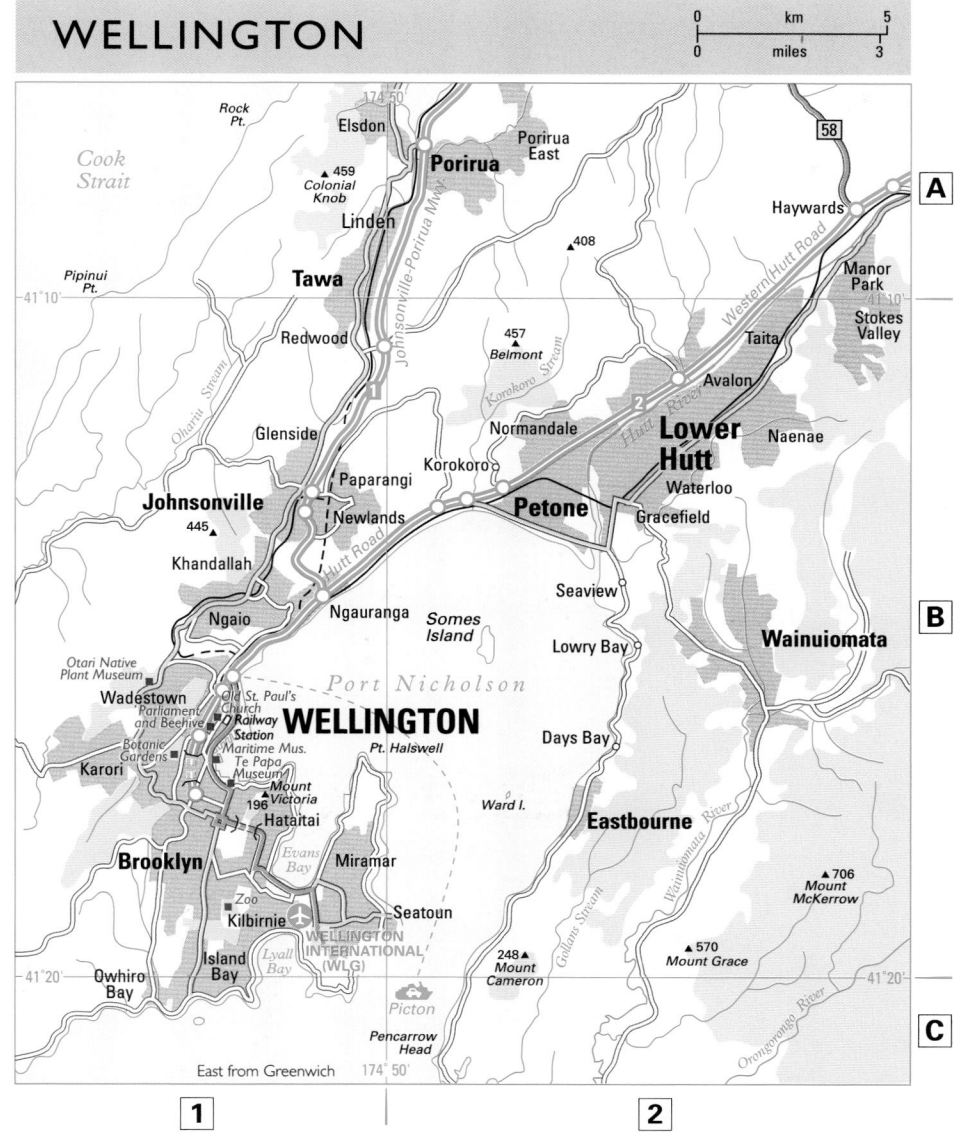

Cook Strait · Rock Pt. · Elsdon · Porirua · Porirua East · Haywards · A
Pipinui Pt. · Colonial Knob · Linden · Tawa · Manor Park · Stokes Valley
Redwood · Belmont · Taita · Avalon · Naenae
Glenside · Normandale · Lower Hutt · Waterloo
Johnsonville · Korokoro · Petone · Gracefield · B
Khandallah · Paparangi · Newlands · Ngauranga · Somes Island · Seaview
Ngaio · Otari Native Plant Park · Wadestown · Port Nicholson · Lowry Bay · Wainuiomata
Karori · Old St. Paul's Church · WELLINGTON · Days Bay
Botanic Gardens · Parliament · Maritime Mus. · Te Papa Museum · Mount Victoria · Ward I. · Eastbourne
Brooklyn · Hataitai · Miramar · Evans Bay · Pt. Halswell · C
Zoo · Kilbirnie · Seatoun · Mount McKerrow
Owhiro Bay · Island Bay · Lyall Bay · WELLINGTON INTERNATIONAL (WLG) · Mount Cameron · Mount Grace
Pencarrow Head · Picton · East from Greenwich

COPYRIGHT PHILIP'S

WORLD
MAPS

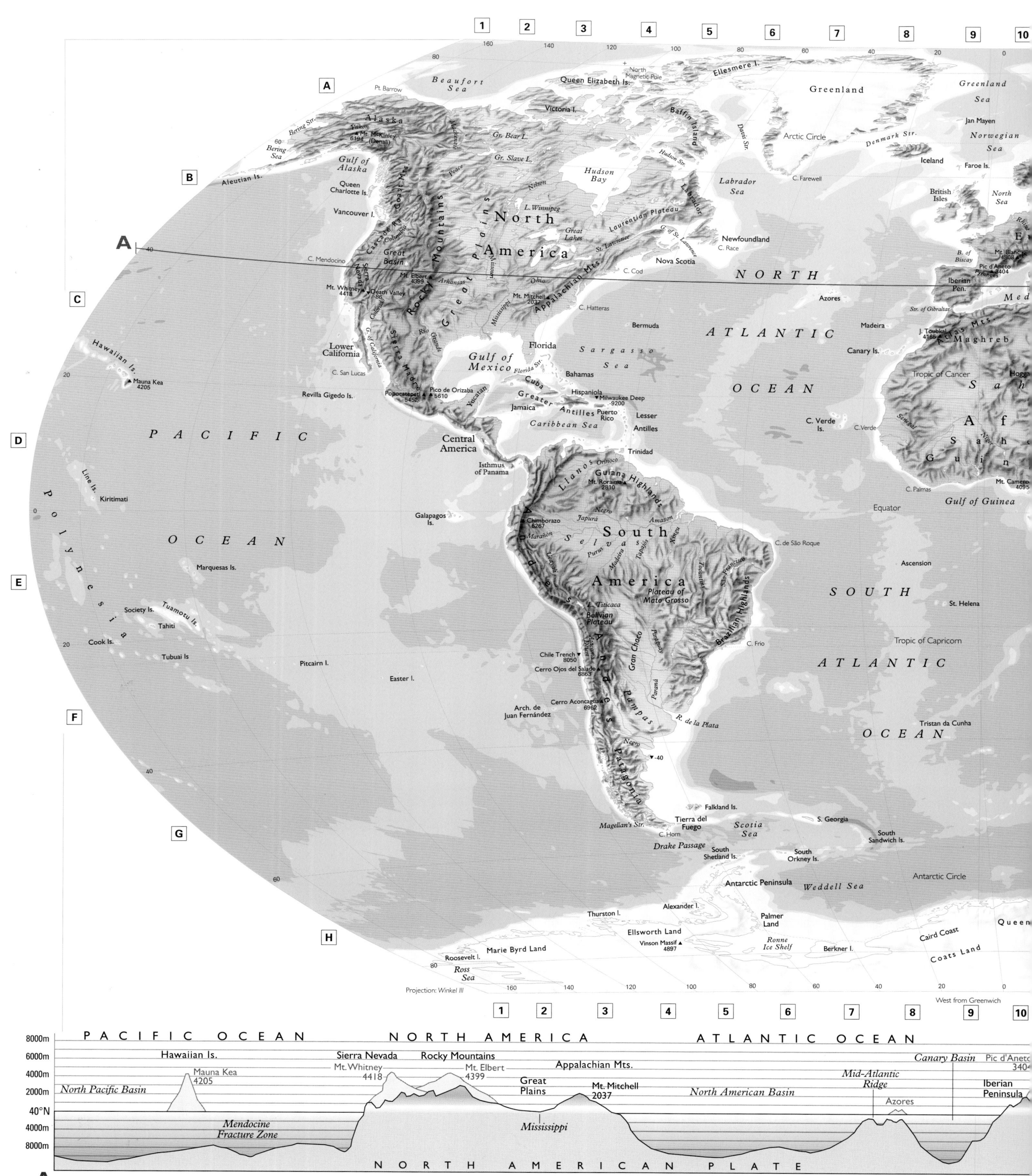

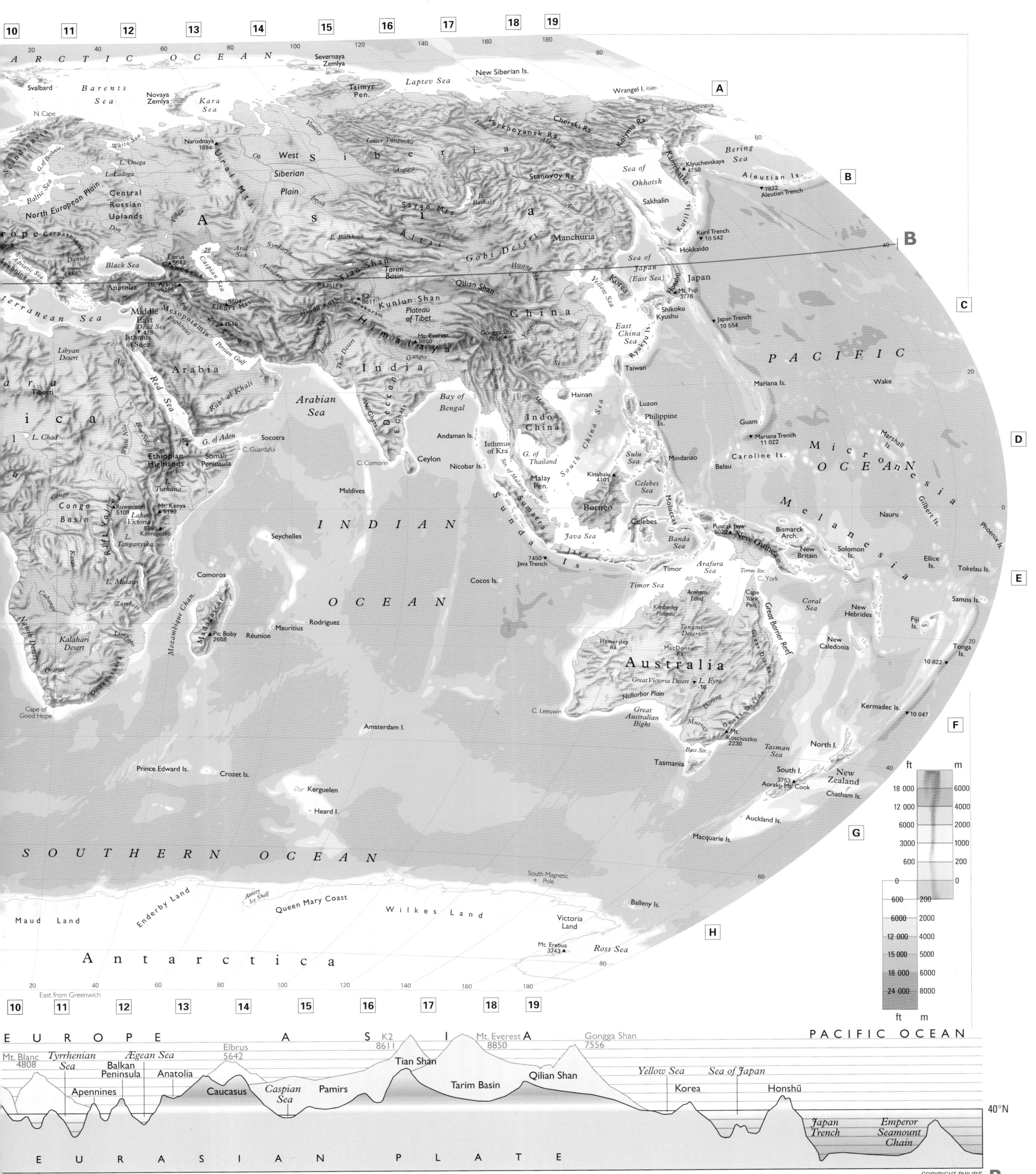

A R C T I C   O C E A N

Svalbard
N. Cape
Barents
Sea
Novaya
Zemlya
Kara
Sea
Severnaya
Zemlya
Laptev Sea
New Siberian Is.
Wrangel I.
Dezhneva

A

Scandinavia
G. of Bothnia
White Sea
L. Onega
L. Ladoga
Narodnaya
1894
Ob
West
Siberian
Plain
Irtysh
Yenisey
Lower Tunguska
Angara
Taimyr
Pen.
Verkhoyansk Ra.
Cherski Ra.
Stanovoy Ra.
Kolyma Ra.
Kamchatka
Klyuchevskaya
4750
Bering
Sea
Aleutian Is.
7822
Aleutian Trench

B

North European Plain
Central Russian Uplands
Don
Volga
S i b e r i a
Sayan Mts.
Baikal
Amur
Sea of Okhotsk
Sakhalin
Kuril Is.
Kuril Trench
10 542
Hokkaido

B

Europe
Carpathians
Black Sea
Danube
Caucasus
Elbrus
5642
Aral Sea
Caspian Sea
Syrdarya
Amudarya
L. Balkhash
A s i a
Altai
Tian Shan
Tarim Basin
Gobi Desert
Hwang Ho
Manchuria
Korea
Yellow Sea
Sea of Japan (East Sea)
Japan
Mt. Fuji
3776
Japan Trench
10 554

C

Mediterranean Sea
Anatolia
Mt. Ararat
5165
Middle East
Dead Sea
-418
Isthmus of Suez
Mesopotamia
Euphrates
Byrjian Gulf
Elbruz Mts.
5604
Hindu Kush
Karakoram
8611
K2
4548
Pamirs
Kunlun Shan
Plateau of Tibet
Qilian Shan
H i m a l a y a
Mt. Everest
8850
Gongga Shan
7556
China
Si
Yangtze
East China Sea
Shikoku
Kyushu
Ryukyu Is.
PACIFIC

Libyan Desert
Tibesti
Arabia
Red Sea
Blue Nile
White Nile
Nile
Rub' al Khali
G. of Aden
Socotra
C. Guardafui
Ethiopian Highlands
Somali Peninsula
Turkana
Indus
Thar Desert
Deccan
W. Ghats
E. Ghats
India
Ganges
Brahmaputra
Arabian Sea
Bay of Bengal
Andaman Is.
C. Comorin
Ceylon
Nicobar Is.
Isthmus of Kra
G. of Thailand
Indo-China
Malay Pen.
South China Sea
Hainan
Luzon
Philippine Is.
Taiwan
Mariana Is.
Guam
Mariana Trench
11 022
Belau
Caroline Is.
Wake
Marshall Is.
Gilbert Is.
M i c r o n e s i a

D

L. Chad
Congo Basin
Rift Valley
Ruwenzori
5109
Lake Victoria
Kilimanjaro
5895
Mt. Kenya
5199
L. Tanganyika
L. Malawi
Seychelles
Comoros
Maldives
I N D I A N
O C E A N
Cocos Is.
Java Trench
7450
Sumatra
Sunda Is.
Java Sea
Java
Borneo
Celebes
Celebes Sea
Sulu Sea
Mindanao
Moluccas
Banda Sea
Timor
Arafura Sea
New Guinea
Puncak Jaya
5029
Bismarck Arch.
New Britain
Solomon Is.
Nauru
Ellice Is.
Tokelau Is.
M e l a n e s i a
Phoenix Is.

E

Angola
Kalahari Desert
Zambezi
Okavango
Limpopo
Orange
Mozambique Chan.
Madagascar
Pic Boby
2658
Réunion
Mauritius
Rodriguez
Rodrigues
Amsterdam I.
Timor Sea
Arnhem Land
Kimberley Plateau
Hamersley Ra.
Tanami Desert
MacDonnell Ra.
Cape York Pen.
C. York
Torres Str.
Great Barrier Reef
Coral Sea
New Hebrides
Fiji Is.
New Caledonia
Samoa Is.
Tonga Is.
10 822

Cape of Good Hope
Prince Edward Is.
Crozet Is.
Kerguelen
Heard I.
C. Leeuwin
Great Victoria Desert
Nullarbor Plain
Great Australian Bight
A u s t r a l i a
L. Eyre
-16
Darling
Murray
Murray
Great Dividing Ra.
Mt. Kosciuszko
2230
Bass Str.
Tasmania
Tasman Sea
North I.
South I.
New Zealand
Aoraki/ Mt. Cook
3753
Chatham Is.
Kermadec Is.
10 047

F

G

S O U T H E R N   O C E A N
Macquarie Is.
Auckland Is.

Maud Land
Enderby Land
Amery Ice Shelf
Queen Mary Coast
W i l k e s   L a n d
South Magnetic Pole
Balleny Is.
Victoria Land
Ross Sea
Mt. Erebus
3743

H

A n t a r c t i c a

Cross-section

E U R O P E   A S I A   PACIFIC OCEAN

K2
8611
Mt. Everest
8850
Gongga Shan
7556

Mt. Blanc
4808
Tyrrhenian Sea
Balkan Peninsula
Apennines
Ægean Sea
Anatolia
Elbrus
5642
Caucasus
Caspian Sea
Pamirs
Tian Shan
Tarim Basin
Qilian Shan
Yellow Sea
Korea
Sea of Japan
Honshū

40°N

Japan Trench
Emperor Seamount Chain

E U R A S I A N   P L A T E

B

ft   m
18 000   6000
12 000   4000
6000   2000
3000   1000
600   200
0   0
600   200
6000   2000
12 000   4000
15 000   5000
18 000   6000
24 000   8000
ft   m

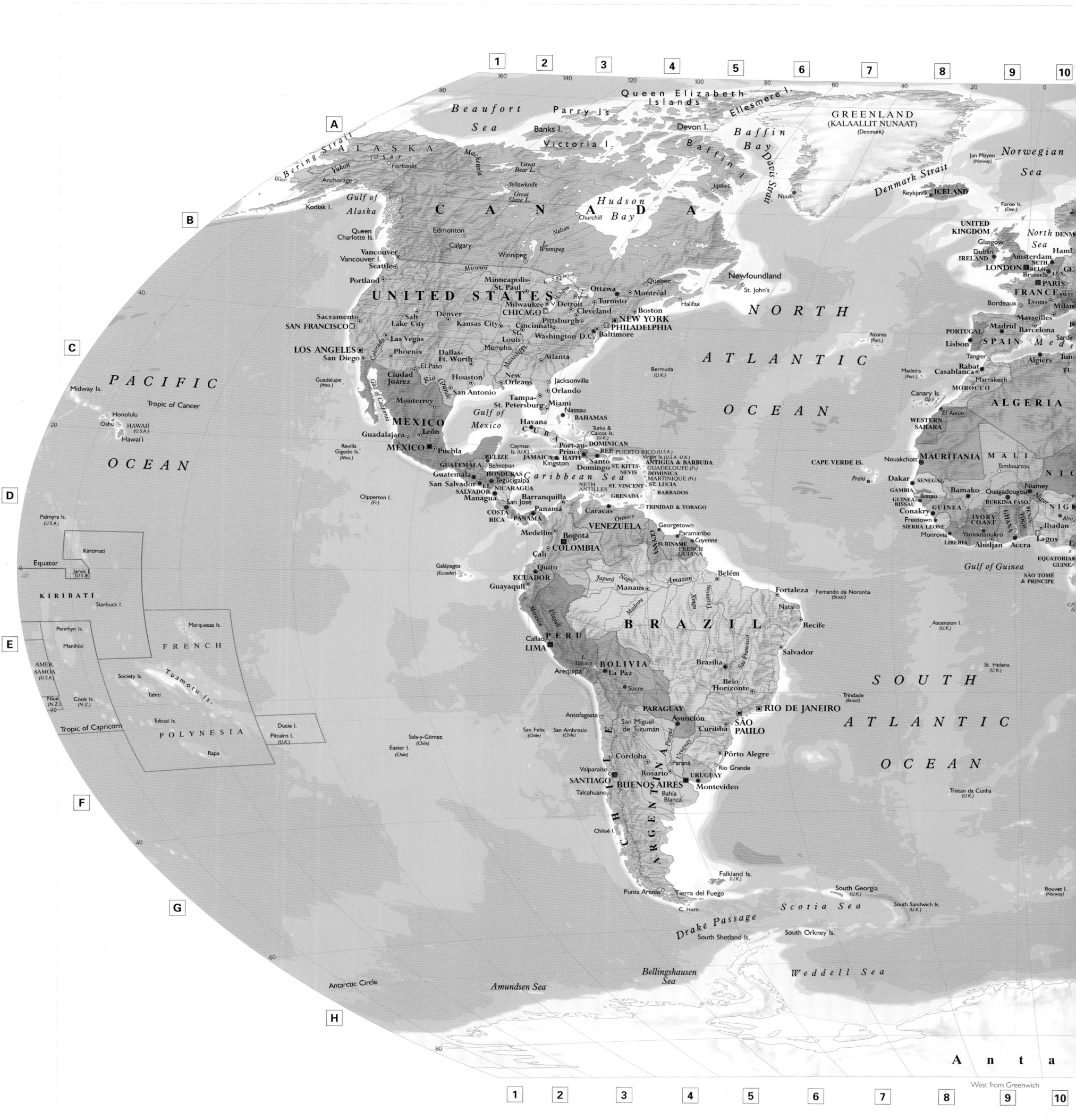

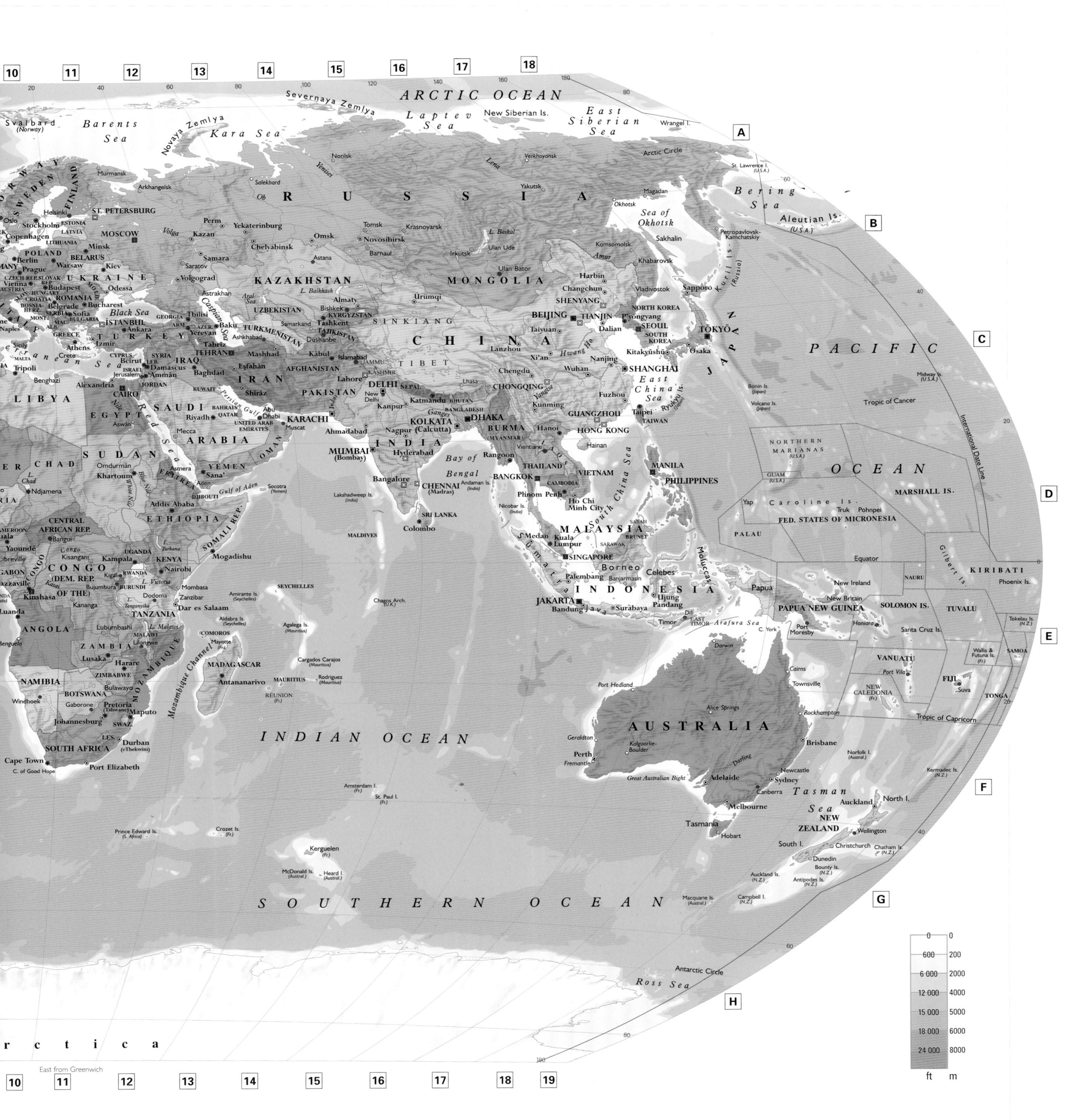

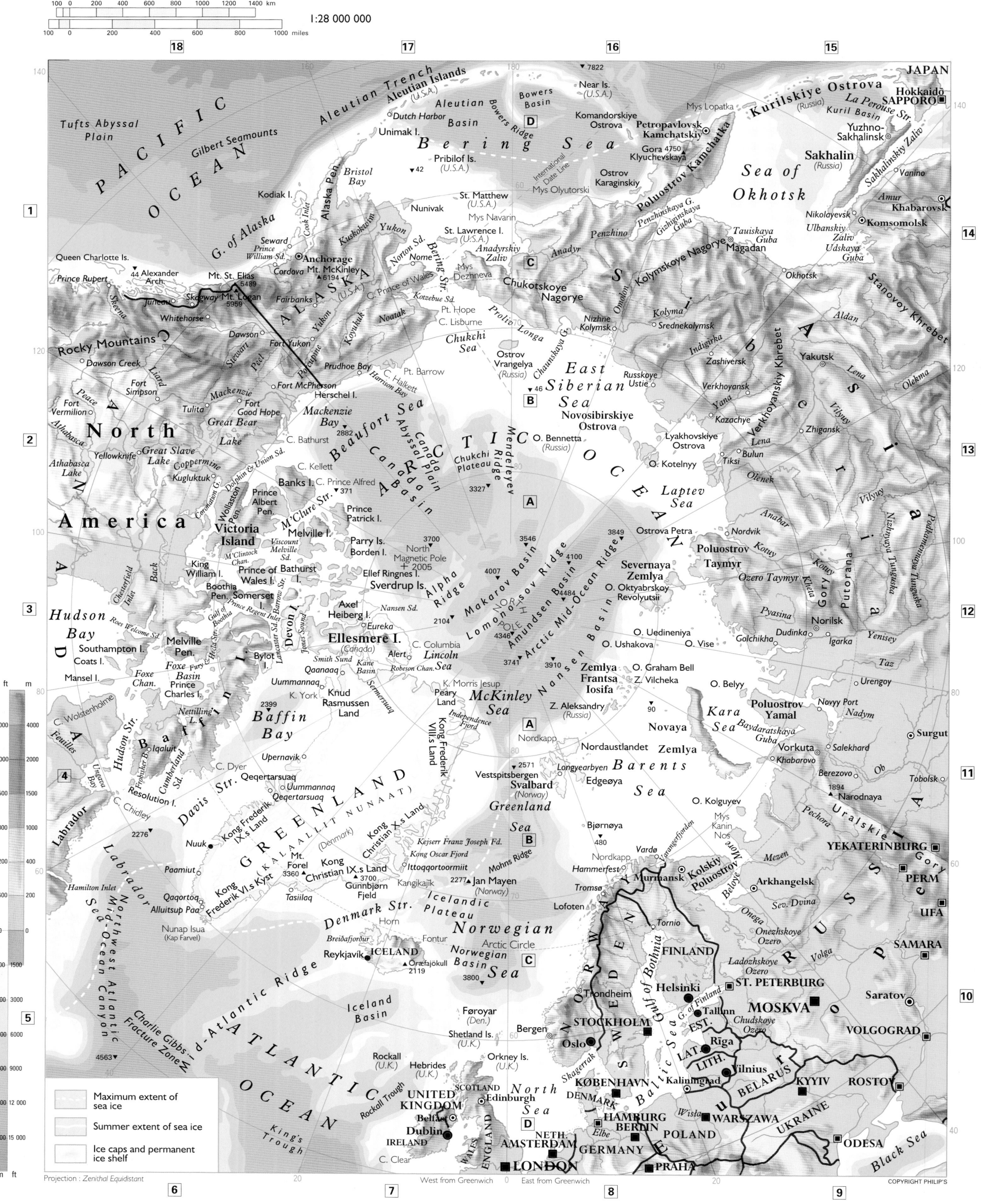

100 0   200 400 600 800 1000 1200 1400 km

1:28 000 000

100 0   200   400   600   800   1000 miles

PACIFIC OCEAN

Tufts Abyssal Plain

Gilbert Seamounts

Aleutian Trench

Aleutian Islands (U.S.A.)

Dutch Harbor

Unimak I.

Aleutian Basin

Bowers Basin

Bowers Ridge

7822

Bering Sea

Komandorskiye Ostrova

Petropavlovsk Kamchatskiy

Mys Lopatka

Kurilskiye Ostrova (Russia)

Kuril Basin

La Perouse Str.

SAPPORO

Hokkaidō

JAPAN

Bristol Bay

Pribilof Is. (U.S.A.)

42

St. Matthew (U.S.A.)

Gora 4750 Klyuchevskaya

Poluostrov Kamchatka

Ostrov Karaginskiy

Mys Olyutorski

Penzhinskaya G.

Gizhiginskaya Guba

Tauiskaya Guba

Magadan

Sakhalin (Russia)

Sakhalinskiy Zaliv

Vanino

Amur

Khabarovsk

Kodiak I.

Queen Charlotte Is.

44 Alexander Arch.

Prince Rupert

Nunivak

Norton Sd.

St. Lawrence I. (U.S.A.)

Bering Str.

Mys Navarin

Anadyrskiy Zaliv

Penzhino

Kolymskoye Nagorye

Nikolayevsk

Ulbanskiy Zaliv

Udskaya Guba

Okhotsk

Sea of Okhotsk

Yuzhno-Sakhalinsk

Komsomolsk

Seward

Prince William Sd.

Cook Inlet

Anchorage

Cordova

Mt. McKinley 6194

Nome

Prince of Wales

Kotzebue Sd.

Mys Dezhneva

Chukotskoye Nagorye

Anadyr

Omolon

Magadan

Stanovoy Khrebet

G. of Alaska

Mt. St. Elias 5489

Skagway Mt. Logan 5959

Juneau

Fairbanks

ALASKA (U.S.A.)

Yukon

Kuskokwim

Pt. Hope

C. Lisburne

Prolив Longa

Nizhne Kolymsk

Srednekolymsk

Kolyma

Russkoye Ustie

Verkhoyansk

Yakutsk

Whitehorse

Dawson

Rocky Mountains

Fort Yukon

Fort McPherson

Koyukuk

Noatak

Yukon

Chukchi Sea

Ostrov Vrangelya (Russia)

46

Chaunskaya G.

Indigirka

Zashiversk

Verkhoyanskiy Khrebet

Yana

Kazachye

Lena

Zhigansk

Olekma

Aldan

120

Dawson Creek

Liard

Peace

Fort Simpson

Fort Good Hope

Mackenzie

Prudhoe Bay

C. Halkett

Harrison Bay

Pt. Barrow

East Siberian Sea

Novosibirskiye Ostrova

Lyakhovskiye Ostrova

Bulun

Tiksi

Vilyuy

Fort Vermilion

Athabasca

North

Yellowknife

Great Slave Lake

Coppermine

Kugluktuk

Tulita

Fort Good Hope

Great Bear Lake

Mackenzie Bay

2882

C. Bathurst

Beaufort Sea

Canada Abyssal Plain

Canada Basin

Chukchi Plateau

3327

Mendeleyev Ridge

O. Bennetta (Russia)

Laptev Sea

Kotelnyy

Olenek

Anabar

Zhigansk

Verkhoyanskiy

America

Athabasca Lake

C. Kellett

Banks I.

C. Prince Alfred

371

A R C T I C

Prince Patrick I.

3700

North Magnetic Pole 2005

4007

3546

Norвеgian Ridge

4100

Lomonosov Ridge

3849

Amundsen Ridge

Ostrova Petra

Nordvik

Poluostrov Taymyr

Severnaya Zemlya

O. Oktyabrskoy Revolyutsii

Ozero Taymyr

Khatanga

Kotuy

Gory Byrranga

Putorana

Nizhnyaya Tunguska

A

C a n a d a

Victoria Island

M'Clure Str.

Melville I.

Viscount Melville Sd.

Prince Albert Pen.

King William I.

Prince of Wales I.

Prince of Bathurst I.

Parry Is.

Borden I.

Ellef Ringnes I.

Sverdrup Is.

Alpha Ridge

O C E A N

4484

Makarov Basin

4346

North Pole

2104

Nansen Basin

3741

3910

Zemlya Frantsa Iosifa

O. Graham Bell

Z. Vilcheka

Ozero Taymyr

Pyasina

Dudinka

Norilsk

Golchikha

Igarka

Yenisey

Taz

100

S i b e r i a

North Magnetic Pole 2005

Boothia Pen.

Somerset I.

Axel Heiberg I.

Nansen Sd.

Hudson Bay

Chesterfield Inlet

Back

Roes Welcome Sd.

Gulf of Boothia

Gulf of Prince Regent Inlet

Barrow Str.

Lancaster Sound

Devon I.

Eureka

Alert

C. Columbia

Lincoln Sea

4346

O. Uedineniya

O. Ushakova

O. Vise

Dudinka

Igarka

Ellesmere I. (Canada)

Jones Sound

Z. Aleksandry (Russia)

90

O. Belyy

Novaya Zemlya

Kara Sea

Poluostrov Yamal

Novyy Port

Nadym

Urengoy

Surgut

Southampton I.

Coats I.

Melville Pen.

Mansel I.

Foxe Basin

Foxe Chan.

Prince Charles I.

Bylot I.

K. York

Smith Sund

Kane Basin

Robeson Chan.

Sermersuaq

K. Morris Jesup

Peary Land

McKinley Sea

A

Independence Fjord

Kong Frederik VIII.s Land

3910

Nordkapp

Z. Vilcheka

Baydaratskaya Guba

O. Belyy

Vorkuta

Khabarovo

80

Baffin I.

C. Wolstenholme

Nettilling L.

Iqaluit

Frobisher Bay

Resolution I.

Baffin Bay

2399

Knud Rasmussen Land

Qaanaaq

Uummannaq

K. York

Kong Frederik IX.s Land

Kong Christian X.s Land

Kong Oscar Fjord

Kejser Franz Joseph Fd.

Greenland Sea

B

Nordkapp

Nordaustlandet

Vestspitsbergen

Svalbard (Norway)

2571

Edgeøya

Longyearbyen

Barents Sea

O. Kolguyev

Mys Kanin Nos

Pechora

Narodnaya 1894

Berezovo

Tobolsk

YEKATERINBURG

R U S S I A

Ungava Bay

C. Dyer

Cumberland Sd.

C. Chidley

Labrador

Davis Str.

Upernavik

Qeqertarsuaq

Uummannaq

Qeqertarsuaq

Nuuk

GREENLAND (KALAALLIT NUNAAT)

Kong Frederik IX.s Land

Mt. Forel 3360

Kong Christian IX.s Land

Ittoqqortoormiit

480

Bjørnøya

O. Kanin

Vardø

Varangerfjorden

Mezen

Mys Kanin Nos

Onega

Sev. Dvina

Arkhangelsk

PERM

UFA

60

2276

Labrador Sea

Hamilton Inlet

Paamiut

Qaqortoq

Alluitsup Paa

Nunap Isua (Kap Farvel)

Kong Frederik VI.s Kyst

Tasiilaq

Denmark Str.

Breiðafjörður

Horn

Fontur

3700

Kangikajik

Gunnbjørn Fjeld

2277

Jan Mayen (Norway)

Mohns Ridge

Hammerfest

Tromsø

Lofoten

Murmansk

Kolskiy Poluostrov

Beloye More

Onega

Onezhskoye Ozero

SAMARA

Northwest Atlantic Mid-Ocean Canyon

Mid-Atlantic Ridge

2119

Óræfajökull

ICELAND

Reykjavik

Icelandic Plateau

Norwegian Sea

3800

Arctic Circle

Trondheim

Bergen

FINLAND

Helsinki

Ladozhskoye Ozero

ST. PETERBURG

MOSKVA

Ladozhskoye Ozero

Volga

Saratov

VOLGOGRAD

Charlie Gibbs Fracture Zone

4563

ATLANTIC

Iceland Basin

Føroyar (Den.)

Shetland Is. (U.K.)

Norwegian Basin

N o r w a y

S w e d e n

Oslo

STOCKHOLM

Gulf of Bothnia

Tornio

Gulf of Finland

Tallinn

EST.

Chudskoye Ozero

Riga

LAT.

ROSTOV

OCEAN

King's Trough

Rockall (U.K.)

Hebrides (U.K.)

Orkney Is. (U.K.)

North Sea

SCOTLAND

Edinburgh

Rockall Trough

Skagerrak

DENMARK

KØBENHAVN

Baltic Sea

Kaliningrad

LITH.

Vilnius

BELARUS

KYYIV

UKRAINE

ODESA

Black Sea

Belfast

Dublin

IRELAND

UNITED KINGDOM

ENGLAND

WALES

C. Clear

LONDON

NETH.

AMSTERDAM

HAMBURG

BERLIN

GERMANY

Elbe

POLAND

WARSZAWA

Wisła

PRAHA

Projection : Zenithal Equidistant

West from Greenwich 0 East from Greenwich

COPYRIGHT PHILIP'S

Maximum extent of sea ice

Summer extent of sea ice

Ice caps and permanent ice shelf

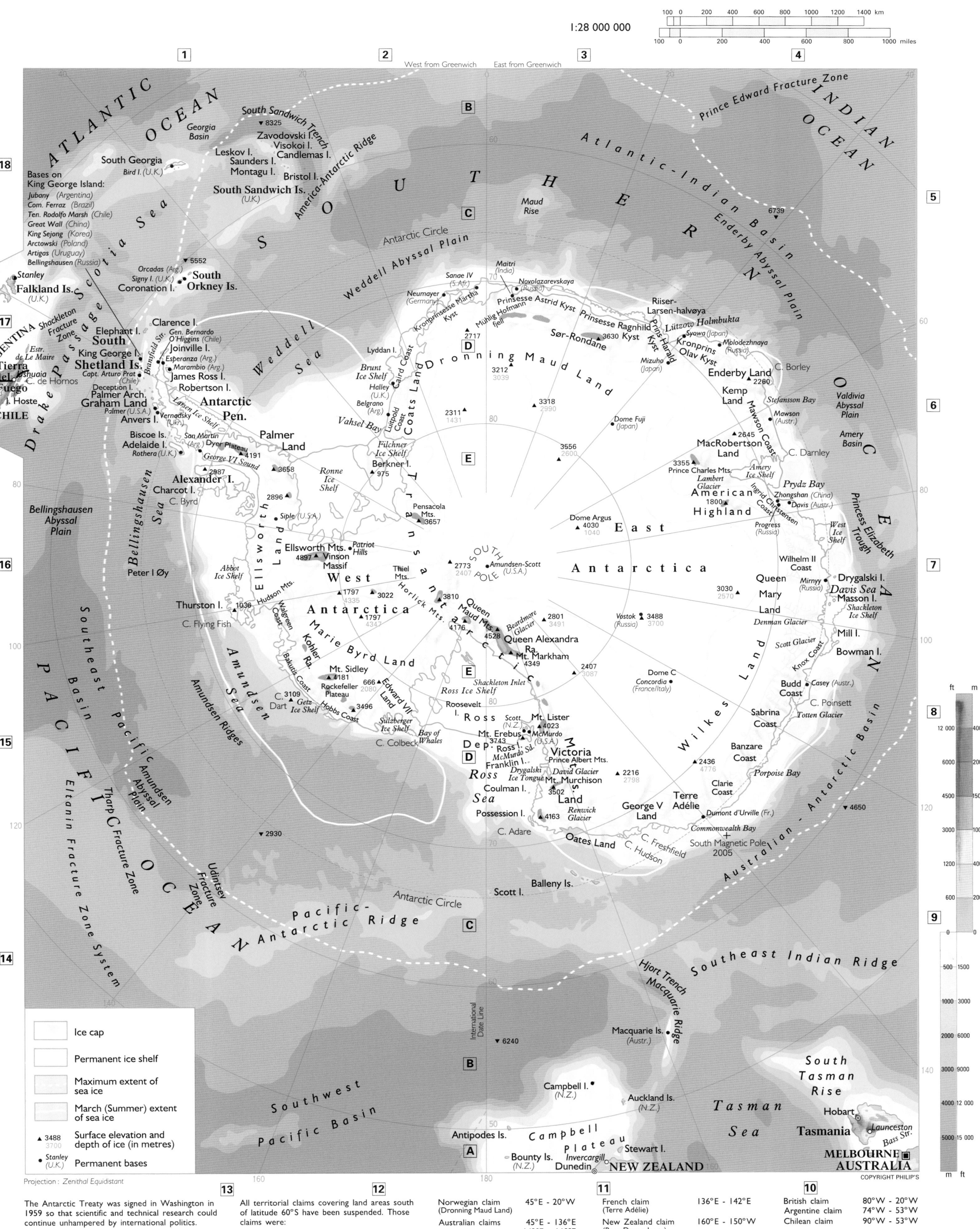

1:28 000 000

Projection: Zenithal Equidistant

The Antarctic Treaty was signed in Washington in 1959 so that scientific and technical research could continue unhampered by international politics.

All territorial claims covering land areas south of latitude 60°S have been suspended. Those claims were:

Norwegian claim (Dronning Maud Land)	45°E - 20°W
Australian claims	45°E - 136°E 142°E - 160°E
French claim (Terre Adélie)	136°E - 142°E
New Zealand claim (Ross Dependency)	160°E - 150°W
British claim	80°W - 20°W
Argentine claim	74°W - 53°W
Chilean claim	90°W - 53°W

COPYRIGHT PHILIP'S

Legend:

Ice cap

Permanent ice shelf

Maximum extent of sea ice

March (Summer) extent of sea ice

▲ 3488 / 3700 Surface elevation and depth of ice (in metres)

• Stanley (U.K.) Permanent bases

Bases on King George Island:
Jubany (Argentina)
Com. Ferraz (Brazil)
Ten. Rodolfo Marsh (Chile)
Great Wall (China)
King Sejong (Korea)
Arctowski (Poland)
Artigas (Uruguay)
Bellingshausen (Russia)

Equatorial Scale 1:41 000 000

NORTH ATLANTIC OCEAN

SOUTH ATLANTIC OCEAN

PACIFIC OCEAN

CANADA

Hudson Bay

Churchill
Regina
Winnipeg
Minneapolis
Chicago
Omaha
Detroit
Toronto
Montréal
Ottawa
Québec
Boston
New York
Philadelphia
Baltimore
Washington D.C.
Pittsburgh
St. Louis
Atlanta
Charleston
Jacksonville
Houston
Galveston
New Orleans
Miami
Nassau
La Habana
Tampico
Veracruz

UNITED STATES

MEXICO

GUATEMALA
HONDURAS
EL SALVADOR
NICARAGUA
COSTA RICA
PANAMA
BELIZE

Gulf of Mexico
Sigsbee • 3504
Deep
Canal de Yucatán
G. de Campeche
CUBA
BAHAMAS
JAMAICA
Santiago de Cuba
Kingston
HAITI
DOM. REP.
Milwaukee Deep • 9200
Puerto Rico Trench
PUERTO RICO (U.S.A.)
ANTIGUA
ST. KITTS
GUADELOUPE (Fr.)
DOMINICA
MARTINIQUE (Fr.)
ST. LUCIA
BARBADOS
ST. VINCENT
GRENADA
Leeward Is.
Windward Is.
West Indies
Cayman Trough

Caribbean Sea
Colombia Basin
Venezuela Basin
Barranquilla
Caracas
TRINIDAD & TOBAGO
Curaçao

VENEZUELA
COLOMBIA
Bogotá
Cali
Quito
ECUADOR
Guayaquil
PERU
Lima
Callao
Trujillo
Iquitos

GUYANA
Georgetown
SURINAME
Paramaribo
GUYANA (Fr.)
Cayenne
C. Orange
Mt. Roraima

BRAZIL
Manaus
Santarém
Belém
São Luís
Fortaleza
Natal
Recife
Maceió
Salvador
Brasília
Goiânia
Belo Horizonte
São Paulo
Rio de Janeiro
Santos
Curitiba
Pôrto Alegre

Amazonas
Orinoco
Negro
Japurá
Purus
Madeira
Tapajós
Xingu
Tocantins
São Francisco

BOLIVIA
La Paz
L. Titicaca
Nevado Ancohuma 6550

PARAGUAY
Asunción

ARGENTINA
CHILE
URUGUAY
Córdoba
Rosario
Santa Fe
San Miguel de Tucumán
Mendoza
Buenos Aires
Montevideo
Bahía Blanca
Santiago
Valparaíso
Concepción
Aconcagua 6962
Antofagasta
Iquique
Arica

Pampas
Gran Chaco
Paraná
Uruguay
Río de la Plata
Colorado

Puerto Montt
I. de Chiloé
Arch. de los Chonos
Pen. de Taitao
Golfo San Jorge
Pen. Valdés
G. San Matías
L. dos Patos

Punta Arenas
Tierra del Fuego
Est. de Magallanes
C. de Hornos

GREENLAND (Denmark)
Nuuk
Nunap Isua (K. Farvell)
Tasiilaq
Davis Strait
Denmark Strait
Hudson Str.
C. Chidley
Labrador Sea
Hamilton Inlet
Str. of Belle Isle
Newfoundland
C. Race
Cape Breton I.
Halifax
Grand Banks of Newfoundland
Flemish Cap
St. John's

ICELAND
Reykjavík
Öræfajökull 2119
Norwegian Sea
Norwegian Basin
Tórshavn
Føroyar (Den.)
Trondheim

NORWAY
Bergen
Oslo
Stockholm
Göteborg
DENMARK
København
Malmö
POLAND
Warszawa
Gdańsk

UNITED KINGDOM
Glasgow
Dublin
IRELAND
Liverpool
London
North Sea
Celtic Sea
Rockall (U.K.)
Rockall Trough

GERMANY
Hamburg
Berlin
Amsterdam
NETH.
BELG.
Brussel
Le Havre
Paris
FRANCE
Bordeaux
Marseille
Bay of Biscay
Biscay Abyssal Plain
A Coruña
C. Fisterra
Vigo
Porto
PORTUGAL
Lisboa
C. de São Vicente
SPAIN
Madrid
Barcelona
Is. Baleares
Corse
Sardegna
Roma
Nápoli
ITALY
Milano
Wien
AUSTRIA
CZECH REP.
SLOVAK REP.
HUNGARY
Zagreb
Mt. Blanc 4808
Adriatic Sea
Mediterranean Sea

MALTA
Sicilia
Alger
Tunis
TUNISIA
Tarābulus
ALGERIA
Sahara
MOROCCO
Rabat
Casablanca
Marrakech
Tanger
Str. of Gibraltar
Chott Djerid
Chott ech Chergui
Funchal
Madeira (Port.)
Is. Canarias (Sp.) 3718
Las Palmas
Saharan Seamounts
WESTERN SAHARA
El Aaiún
Ras Nouâdhibou
MAURITANIA
Nouâdhibou
Nouakchott
Tombouctou
MALI
NIGER
Kano
NIGERIA
Kayes
Bamako
Ouagadougou
BURKINA FASO
SENEGAL
Dakar
C. Vert
St-Louis
GAMBIA
Banjul
GUINEA-BISSAU
GUINEA
Conakry
SIERRA LEONE
Freetown
LIBERIA
Monrovia
IVORY COAST
Abidjan
GHANA
Accra
Sekondi-Takoradi
TOGO
BENIN
Lagos
Port Harcourt
CAMEROON
Douala
Bioko
EQUATORIAL GUINEA
Libreville
GABON
C. Lopez
Annobón
São Tomé & Príncipe
Pointe Noire
ANGOLA
Luanda
Lobito
Benguela
Namibe
NAMIBIA
Walvis Bay
Lüderitz
Port Nolloth
SOUTH AFRICA
Cape Town
C. of Good Hope
C. Fria

Cape Verde Abyssal Plain
Cape Verde Plateau
CAPE VERDE IS.
Praia
Gulf of Guinea
Guinea Basin
Sierra Leone Rise
Sierra Leone Basin
Ceara Rise
Ceara Abyssal Plain
Demerara Abyssal Plain
Pernambuco Abyssal Plain
Fernando de Noronha
C. de São Roque
São Pedro & São Paulo (Brazil)
Brazil Basin
Ascension I. (U.K.)
St. Helena (U.K.)
Hotspur Seamount
Banco Abrolhos
Martin Vaz
Trindade (Brazil)
Vitória Seamount
Rio Grande Rise
Argentine Basin
Argentine Abyssal Plain
Falkland Plateau
Falkland Ridge
Falkland Is. (U.K.)
Stanley
Burdwood Bank
Shag Rocks
Georgia Basin
South Georgia
South Sandwich Trench
Tristan da Cunha (U.K.)
Gough I. (U.K.)
Discovery Seamount
Bouvetøya (Norw.)
Angola Basin
Angola Abyssal Plain
Cape Basin
Nambia Abyssal Plain
Walvis Ridge
Agulhas Ridge

Mid-Atlantic Ridge
Charlie Gibbs Fracture Zone
Reykjanes Ridge
Northwest Atlantic Mid-Ocean Canyon
Porcupine Abyssal Plain
King's Trough
Azores-Biscay Rise 5225
Açores (Port.) 2351
Ponta Delgada
Corner Seamounts
New England Seamounts
Sohm Abyssal Plain
Bermuda (U.K.) 6028
Bermuda Rise
Sargasso Sea
Hatteras Abyssal Plain
Nares Abyssal Plain
Tropic of Cancer
Tropic of Capricorn
Equator

Lac Superior
L. Michigan
L. Huron
L. Erie
L. Ontario
L. Winnipeg
Nelson
Missouri
Mississippi
Ohio
Tennessee
Arkansas
Red
Alabama
Appalachian Mts.
Andes
Nazca Ridge
Peru-Chile Trench
Chile Rise

Projection: Mollweide
West from Greenwich
COPYRIGHT PHILIP'S

ft m
12000 4000
9000 3000
6000 2000
3000 1000
1500 500
600 200
0 0
-200 600
1000 3000
2000 6000
4000 12000
6000 18000
8000 24000
m ft

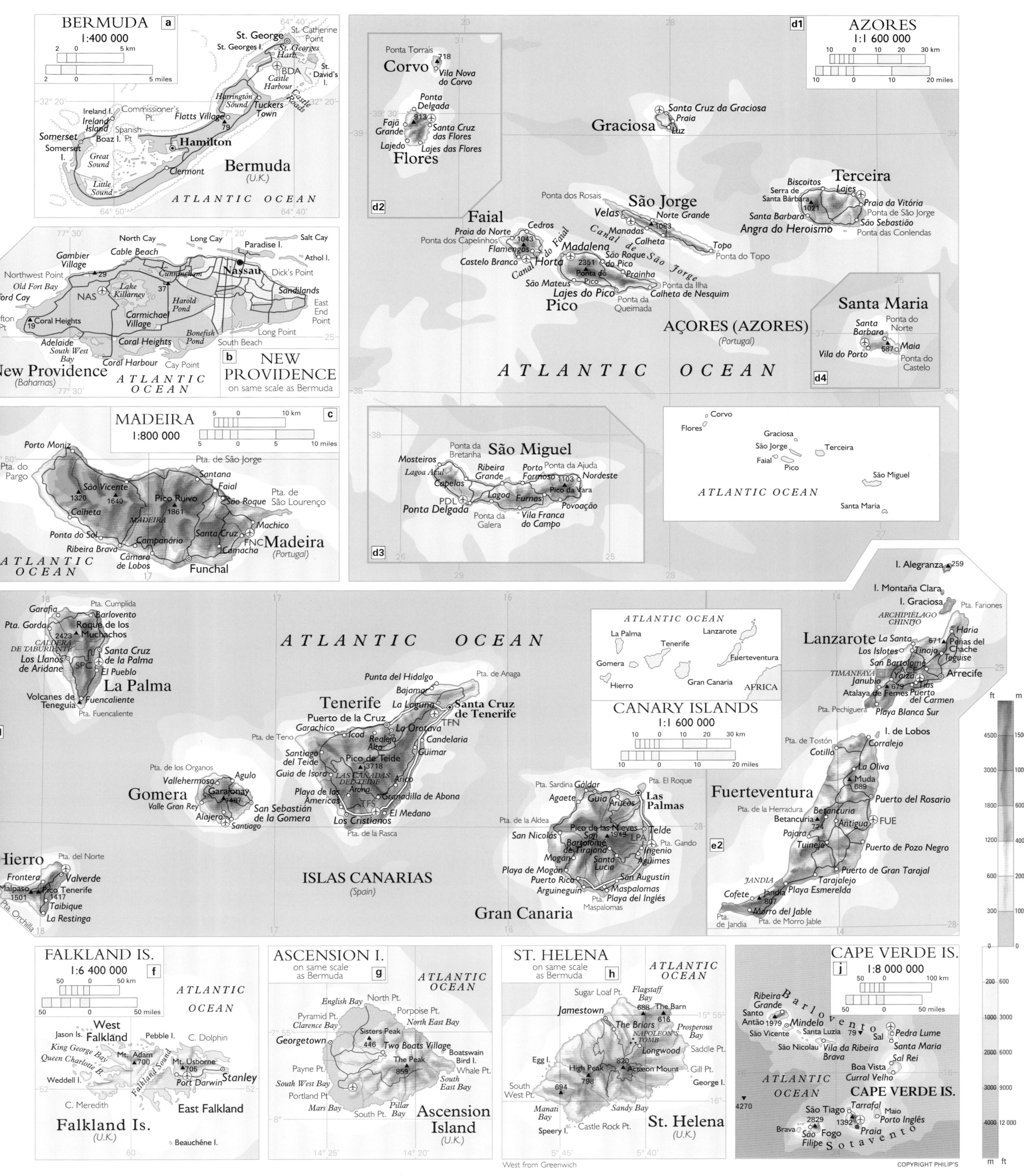

BERMUDA
1:400 000

St. Catherine Point
St. George
St. Georges I.
St. Georges Harb.
St. Georges
BDA
St. David's
Castle Roads
Castle Harbour
Harrington Sound
Flatts Village
Tuckers Town
Commissioner's Pt.
Ireland I.
Ireland Island
Spanish
Somerset
Boaz I. Pt.
Somerset I.
Hamilton
Great Sound
Little Sound
Clermont
BERMUDA
(U.K.)
ATLANTIC OCEAN

NEW PROVIDENCE
North Cay
Long Cay
Paradise I.
Salt Cay
Gambier Village
Cable Beach
Nassau
Athol I.
Northwest Point
Cunningham
Dick's Point
Old Fort Bay
NAS
Lake Killarney
Sandilands
Gambier
Harold Pond
East End Point
Coral Heights
Carmichael Village
Long Point
Adelaide
Coral Heights
Bonefish Pond
South West Bay
Coral Harbour
South Beach
Cay Point
NEW PROVIDENCE
(Bahamas)
ATLANTIC OCEAN
NEW PROVIDENCE
on same scale as Bermuda

MADEIRA
1:800 000

Porto Moniz
Pta. de São Jorge
Pta. do Pargo
Santana
São Vicente
Faial
1320
1640
Pico Ruivo 1861
São Roque
Pta. de São Lourenço
Calheta
MADEIRA
Machico
Ponta do Sol
Campanário
Santa Cruz
Ribeira Brava
Câmara de Lobos
Camacha
Madeira
(Portugal)
Funchal
FNC
ATLANTIC OCEAN

AZORES
1:1 600 000

Ponta Torrais
Corvo
718
Vila Nova do Corvo
Ponta Delgada
813
Fajã Grande
Santa Cruz das Flores
Lajedo
Lajes das Flores
Flores

Santa Cruz da Graciosa
Praia
Graciosa
Luz

Ponta dos Rosais
Velas
São Jorge
Norte Grande
1083
Manadas
Calheta
Topo
Ponta do Topo

Faial
Cedros
Praia do Norte
Ponta dos Capelinhos
1043
Flamengos
Horta
Castelo Branco
São Mateus
Madalena
São Roque do Pico
2351
Ponta do Pico
Prainha
Ponta da Ilha
Calheta de Nesquim
Lajes do Pico
Pico
Ponta da Queimada

Terceira
Biscoitos
Serra de Santa Bárbara
Lajes
1021
Praia da Vitória
Santa Bárbara
Ponta de São Jorge
São Sebastião
Angra do Heroismo
Ponta das Conlendas

AÇORES (AZORES)
(Portugal)

Santa Maria
Santa Barbara
Ponta do Norte
Maia
Vila do Porto
587
Ponta do Castelo

ATLANTIC OCEAN

São Miguel
Mosteiros
Ponta da Bretanha
Lagoa Azul
Ribeira Grande
Porto
Ponta da Ajuda
Capelas
Formoso
Nordeste
PDL
Lagoa
Furnas
Pico da Vara 1103
Ponta Delgada
Povoação
Ponta da Galera
Vila Franca do Campo

Corvo
Flores
Graciosa
São Jorge
Terceira
Faial
Pico
São Miguel
Santa Maria
ATLANTIC OCEAN

CANARY ISLANDS
ATLANTIC OCEAN
La Palma
Lanzarote
Tenerife
Gomera
Fuerteventura
Hierro
Gran Canaria
AFRICA
CANARY ISLANDS
1:1 600 000

Garafia
Pta. Cumplida
Pta. Gorda
Barlovento
Roque de los Muchachos
CALDERA DE TABURIENTE
2423
Santa Cruz de la Palma
Los Llanos de Aridane
SPC
El Pueblo
La Palma
Volcanes de Teneguia
Fuencaliente
Pta. Fuencaliente

Punta del Hidalgo
Pta. de Anaga
Bajamar
La Laguna
Tenerife
Santa Cruz de Tenerife
Puerto de la Cruz
TFN
Garachico
La Orotava
Icod
Realejo Alta
Candelaria
Santiago del Teide
Pico de Teide 3718
Güimar
Guia de Isora
LAS CAÑADAS DEL TEIDE
Arico
Pta. de Teno
Pta. de los Organos
Vallehermoso
Agulo
Playa de las Americas
Garajonay 1487
Aroña
Granadilla de Abona
Gomera
Valle Gran Rey
San Sebastián de la Gomera
AGS
Alajero
Los Cristianos
Santiago
Pta. de la Rasca

Hierro
Pta. del Norte
Frontera
Valverde
Malpaso 1501
Pico Tenerife 1417
Taibique
La Restinga
Pta. Orchilla

ISLAS CANARIAS
(Spain)

Pta. Sardina
Gáldar
Pta. El Roque
Agaete
Guia
Arucas
Las Palmas
San Nicolás
Pico de las Nieves
San Bartolomé de Tirajana 1949
Telde
LPL
Mogán
Ingenio
Playa de Mogán
Santa Lucia
Aguimes
Puerto Rico
San Augustín
Arguineguin
Maspalomas
Pta. de la Aldea
Playa del Inglés
Pta. Playa de Maspalomas
Gran Canaria

I. Alegranza 259
I. Montaña Clara
I. Graciosa
Pta. Fariones
ARCHIPIÉLAGO CHINIJO
Haria
Lanzarote
La Santa
671
Peñas del Chache
Los Islotes
Tinajo
Teguise
San Bartolomé
Yaiza
Arrecife
TIMANFAYA
Janubio
Tias
Atalaya de Femes
Puerto del Carmen
Pta. Pechiguera
Playa Blanca Sur

Pta. de Tostón
I. de Lobos
Corralejo
Cotillo
La Oliva
Muda 689
Puerto del Rosario
Fuerteventura
Betancuria
Antigua
FUE
Pta. de la Herradura
Betancuria 724
Pajara
Tuineje
Puerto de Pozo Negro
JANDIA
Tarajalejo
Playa Esmerelda
Cofete
Jandia 807
Morro del Jable
Pta. de Jandia
Pta. de Morro Jable

FALKLAND IS.
1:6 400 000
ATLANTIC OCEAN
Jason Is.
West Falkland
King George Bay
Pebble I.
C. Dolphin
Queen Charlotte B.
Mt. Adam 700
Falkland Sound
Mt. Usborne 705
Weddell I.
Stanley
Port Darwin
C. Meredith
East Falkland
Falkland Is.
(U.K.)
Beauchêne I.

ASCENSION I.
on same scale as Bermuda
English Bay
North Pt.
Pyramid Pt.
Porpoise Pt.
Clarence Bay
North East Bay
Georgetown
Sisters Peak 446
Boatswain Bird I.
Payne
Two Boats Village
The Peak 859
Whale Pt.
South West Bay
South East Bay
Portland Pt
Pillar Bay
Mars Bay
South Pt.
Ascension Island
(U.K.)
ATLANTIC OCEAN

ST. HELENA
on same scale as Bermuda
ATLANTIC OCEAN
Sugar Loaf Pt.
Flagstaff Bay
Jamestown
688
The Barn
616
The Briars
Prosperous Bay
NAPOLEON'S TOMB
Longwood
Saddle Pt.
Egg I.
High Peak 820
Acteaon Mount
Gill Pt.
694
High Peak 798
George I.
South West Pt.
Manati Bay
Sandy Bay
Speery I.
Castle Rock Pt.
St. Helena
(U.K.)

CAPE VERDE IS.
1:8 000 000
Ribeira Grande
Barlovento
Santo Antão 1979
Mindelo
Pedra Lume
São Vicente
Santa Luzia
Sal
Santa Maria
São Nicolau
Vila da Ribeira Brava
Sal Rei
Boa Vista
CAPE VERDE IS.
ATLANTIC OCEAN
Curral Velho
São Tiago
Tarrafal
Maio
Porto Inglês
Brava 2829
Praia
São Filipe
Fogo 1392
Sotavento
4270

West from Greenwich

100   0   100   200   300   400   500 km
100   0   50   100   150   200   250   300   350 miles

1:10 000 000

A

150

A

ARCTIC OCEAN

3548

1626

Meighen I.

Axel Heiberg I.
Eureka
2616
QUTTINIRPAAQ NAT. PARK

Cape Columbia

Lincoln Sea

Kap Morris Jesup

Nansen Land   Peary Land
1920   Frederick E. Hyde Fjord

CANADA

Ellesmere Island

Alert

Robeson Chan.
Nyeboe Land
Hall Land
Wulff Land
Warming Land

J.P. Koch Fjord
Jørgen Brønlund Fjord

Independence Fjord

Station Nord
Nordostrundingen

Nansen Basin

McKinley Sea

Nordkapp
Nordaust-landet
Kong Karls Land
Kvitøya
Olgastredet
Barentsøya
Edgeøya

Vestspitsbergen
1717 Newtontoppen
Longyearbyen
Storfjorden

Prins Karls Forland
Barentsburg

Svalbard
(Spitsbergen)
(Norway)
Sørkapp

B

Nares Str.
Kane Basin
Kennedy Chan.
Hans I.
Washington Land

Heilprin Land

Mylius Erichsen Land
Kronprins Christian Land

Denmark Fjord

Kronprins Frederik Land

Ingolf Fjord
Mallemukfjeld

2571

GREENLAND SEA

Grise Fjord
Smith Sound
Siorapaluk
Qeqertarsuaq (Thule)

Inglefield Land
Knud Rasmussen Land
Sermersuaq

Lambert Land

Hovgaard Ø
Nioghalvfjerdsfjorden
Norske Øer

Jones Sd. Coburg I.
Devon Island
Kap Atholl
Pituffik (Thule Air Base)
Kap York

2170
Lauge Koch Kyst

Kong Frederik VIII.s Land

Franske Øer
Île de France
Germania Land
Danmarkshavn

C

Uummannaq (Dundas)

Melville Bugt

Steenstrup Gletscher

Dove Bugt   Store Koldewey
Hochstetter Forland

Baffin Bay

Nuussuaq (Kraulshavn)

2469

Dronning Margrethe II Land
Shannon

Zackenberg
Wollaston Forland
Clavering Ø

Clyde River

Upernavik
Kangersuatsiaq
Upernavik Kujalleq

NATIONALPARKEN I NORD-OG ØSTGRØNLAND

2935

Ole Rømer Land

Andrée Land

Kejser Franz Joseph Fd.

Baffin I.

Nunavik
Illorsuit

Maarmorilik

KITAA (VESTGRØNLAND)
TUNU (ØSTGRØNLAND)

3238

2940
Petermann Bjerg

Traill Ø
Mestersvig
Kong Oscar Fjord

Haakon VII Topp
2277

Jan Mayen
(Norway)

D

295

Qeqertarsuaq (Disko)
Ikerasak
2092
Uummannaq
Saqqaq
Kangerluk
Ilulissat (Jakobshavn)
Qeqertarsuaq (Godhavn)
Aasiaat (Egedesminde)
Disko Bugt
Qasigiannguit
Kangaatsiaq
Ikamiut
Qeqertarsuatsiaat (Christianshåb)

GREENLAND (KALAALLIT NUNAAT)

Stauning Alper

Renland
Milne Land

Jameson Land
Ittaajimmiut
Scoresby Sund

Ittoqqortoormiit (Scoresbysund)

Uunarteq
Kangikajik (Kap Brewster)

Iceland Plateau

Baffin I.

Nordre Strømfjord
Kong Frederik IX.s Land
Sisimiut (Holsteinsborg)
Kangerlussuaq (Søndre Strømfjord)
Itilleq
Kangaamiut
Søndre Strømfjord

(Denmark)

Gunnbjørn Field
3700
Blosseville Kyst

Kap Dalton

Kong Christian IX.s Land

Arctic Circle

E

Davis Strait

Maniitsoq (Sukkertoppen)

Dronning Ingrid Land

Nuuk (Godthåb)
Kapisillit
Kangerluarsoruseq (Færingehavn)
Qeqertarsuatsiaat (Fiskenæsset)

2850

Kangerdlugssuaq

Mt. Forel
3560
Kap Gustav Holm

Ikkatteq
Isortoq
Kuummiut
Kulusuk
Tasiilaq (Ammassalik)

ICELAND

Horn
Hornafjörður
Húsavík
Akureyri
Neskaupstaður

Ísafjörður
Blönduós
Breiðafjörður
Vatnajökull
2119
Höfn
Öræfajökull

Faxaflói
Reykjavík

Denmark Strait

F

Paamiut (Frederikshåb)
Narsalik

Gyldenløve Fjord
Kap Møsting
Kap Moltke
Kap Skjold

Frederik VI.s Kyst

Timmiarmiut
Mogens Heinesen Fjord

Vestmannaeyjar
Surtsey
Heimaey

ATLANTIC OCEAN

Labrador Sea

Kangilinnguit (Grønnedal)
Arsuk
Ivittuut
Narsaq
Narsarsuaq
Qaqortoq (Julianehåb)
Alluitsup Paa (Sydprøven)
Nanortalik

Lindenow Fjord

Prins Christian Sund

Reykjanes Ridge

Nunap Isua (Kap Farvel)

ft   m
3000   1000
1200   400
600   200
0   0
200   600
500   1500
1000   3000
2000   6000
4000   12000
m   ft

Projection: Conic with two standard parallels

West from Greenwich

COPYRIGHT PHILIP'S

Underlined towns give their name to the administrative area in which they stand.

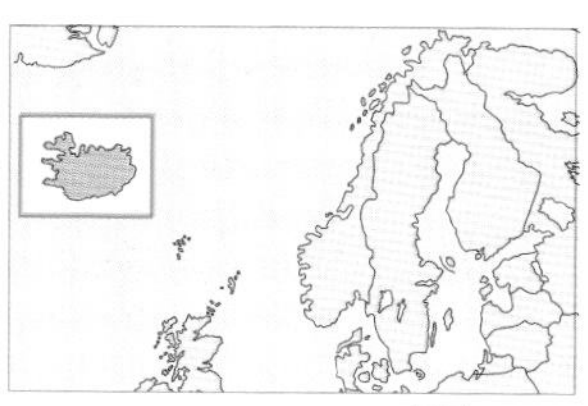

1:2 000 000

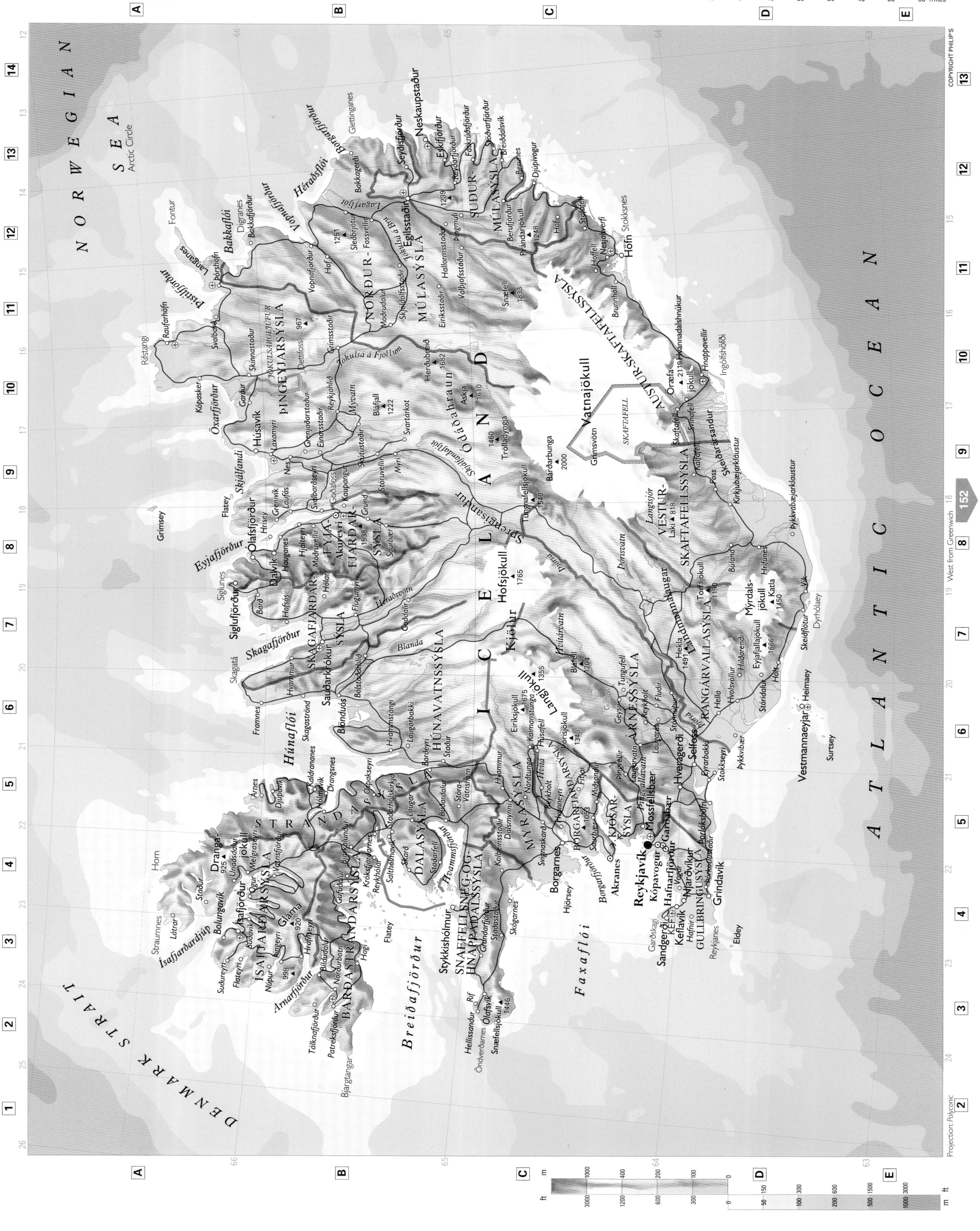

10 0 10 20 30 40 50 60 70 80 100 km
10 0 10 20 30 40 50 60 miles

NORWEGIAN SEA

Arctic Circle

ATLANTIC OCEAN

DENMARK STRAIT

I C E L A N D

Vatnajökull

Faxaflói

Breiðafjörður

Húnaflói

Skagafjörður

Eyjafjörður

Héraðsflói

Bakkaflói

Þistilfjörður

Öxarfjörður

Reykjavík
Kópavogur
Hafnarfjörður
Garðabær
Mosfellsbær
Njarðvík
Keflavík
Sandgerði
Grindavík
Akranes
Borgarnes

Ísafjörður
Bolungarvík
Suðureyri
Flateyri
Patreksfjörður
Tálknafjörður
Bíldudalur

Stykkishólmur
Ólafsvík
Hellissandur
Rif

Sauðárkrókur
Blönduós
Skagaströnd

Siglufjörður
Dalvík
Ólafsfjörður
Akureyri
Húsavík
Raufarhöfn
Þórshöfn
Vopnafjörður

Egilsstaðir
Seyðisfjörður
Neskaupstaður
Eskifjörður
Reyðarfjörður
Fáskrúðsfjörður
Breiðdalsvík
Djúpivogur
Höfn

Selfoss
Hveragerði
Þorlákshöfn
Eyrarbakki
Stokkseyri
Hella
Hvolsvöllur
Vík

Vestmannaeyjar
Heimaey
Surtsey

Grímsey

Hofsjökull 1765
Langjökull
Mýrdalsjökull
Eyjafjallajökull 1666
Hekla 1491
Katla 1450
Bárðarbunga 2000
Öræfajökull 2119 Hvannadalshnúkur
Snæfell 1833
Herðubreið 1682
Askja 1510

Drangajökull
Snæfellsjökull 1446
Eiríksjökull 1675

ÍSAFJARÐARSÝSLA
STRANDASÝSLA
BARÐASTRANDARSÝSLA
DALASÝSLA
SNÆFELLSNES-OG-HNAPPAÐALSSÝSLA
MÝRASÝSLA
BORGARFJARÐARSÝSLA
KJÓSAR-SÝSLA
GULLBRINGUSÝSLA
ÁRNESSÝSLA
RANGARVALLASÝSLA
VESTUR-SKAFTAFELLSSÝSLA
AUSTUR-SKAFTAFELLSSÝSLA
SUÐUR-MÚLASÝSLA
NORÐUR-MÚLASÝSLA
ÞINGEYJARSÝSLA
EYJAFJARÐAR-SÝSLA
SKAGAFJARÐAR-SÝSLA
HÚNAVATNSSÝSLA

Jökulsá á Fjöllum
Þjórsá
Blanda
Héraðsvötn

Sprengisandur
Kjölur
Ódáðahraun

Projection: Polyconic

West from Greenwich

152

m / ft
3000
1200 / 400
600 / 200
300 / 100
150 / 50
0
-50 / -150
100 / 300
200 / 600
500 / 1500
1000 / 3000
ft / m

1:16 000 000

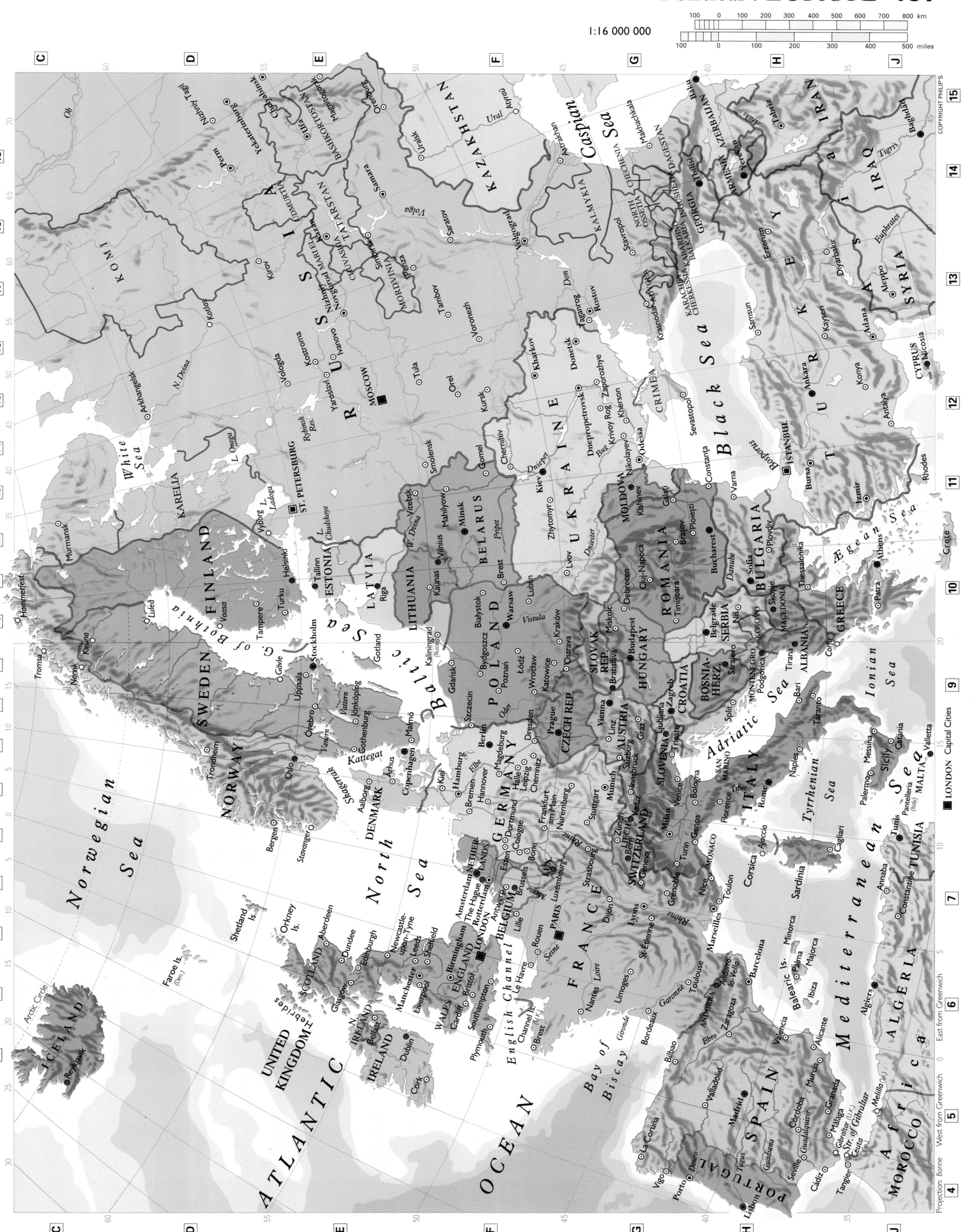

1:16 000 000

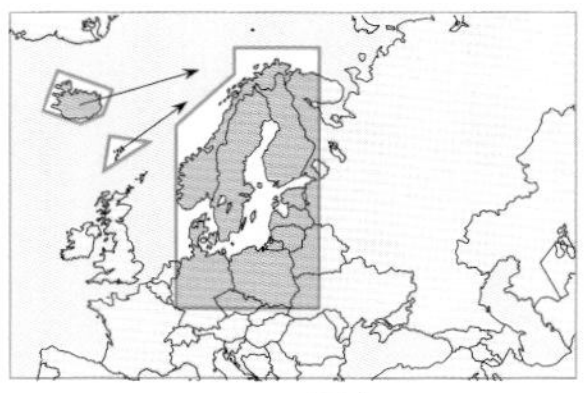

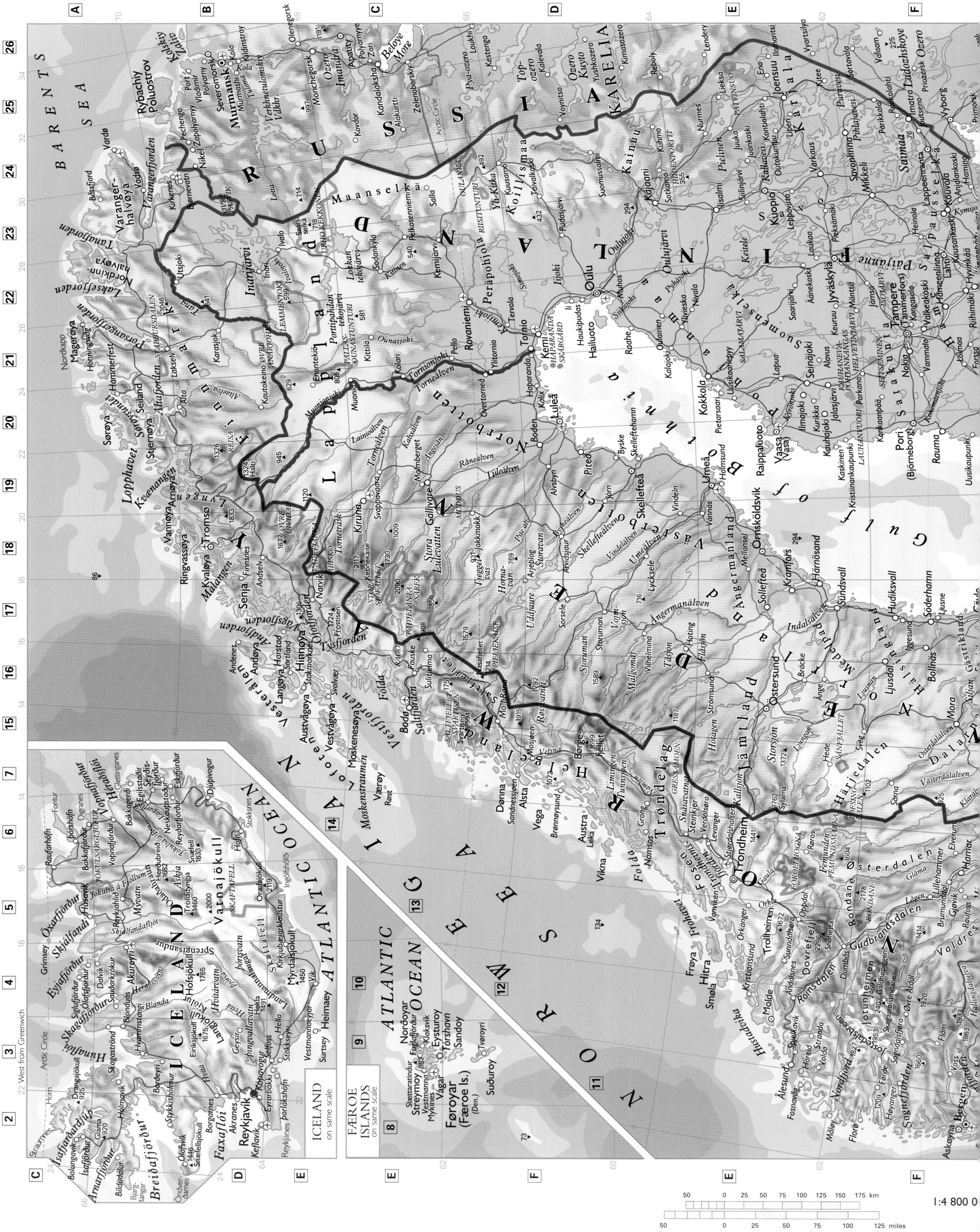
BARENTS SEA
NORWEGIAN SEA
ATLANTIC OCEAN
Gulf of Bothnia
RUSSIA
FINLAND
SWEDEN
NORWAY
KARELIA
Lapland
Finnmark
Norrbotten
Västerbotten
Ångermanland
Jämtland
Härjedalen
Trøndelag
Lofoten
Vesterålen
Maanselkä
Suomenselkä
Murmansk
Kola
Monchegorsk
Kandalaksha
Kirkenes
Hammerfest
Tromsø
Narvik
Bodø
Kiruna
Gällivare
Luleå
Umeå
Oulu
Kemi
Tornio
Rovaniemi
Kajaani
Kuopio
Joensuu
Jyväskylä
Tampere
Vaasa
Kokkola
Pori
Östersund
Sundsvall
Trondheim
Molde
Ålesund
Bergen
Vardø
Nordkapp
Alta
ICELAND
Reykjavík
Akureyri
Vatnajökull
FÆROE ISLANDS on same scale
ICELAND on same scale
Føroyar (Færoe Is.) (Den.)
Tórshavn
Arctic Circle
1:4 800 000
50 0 25 50 75 100 125 150 175 km
50 0 25 50 75 100 125 miles

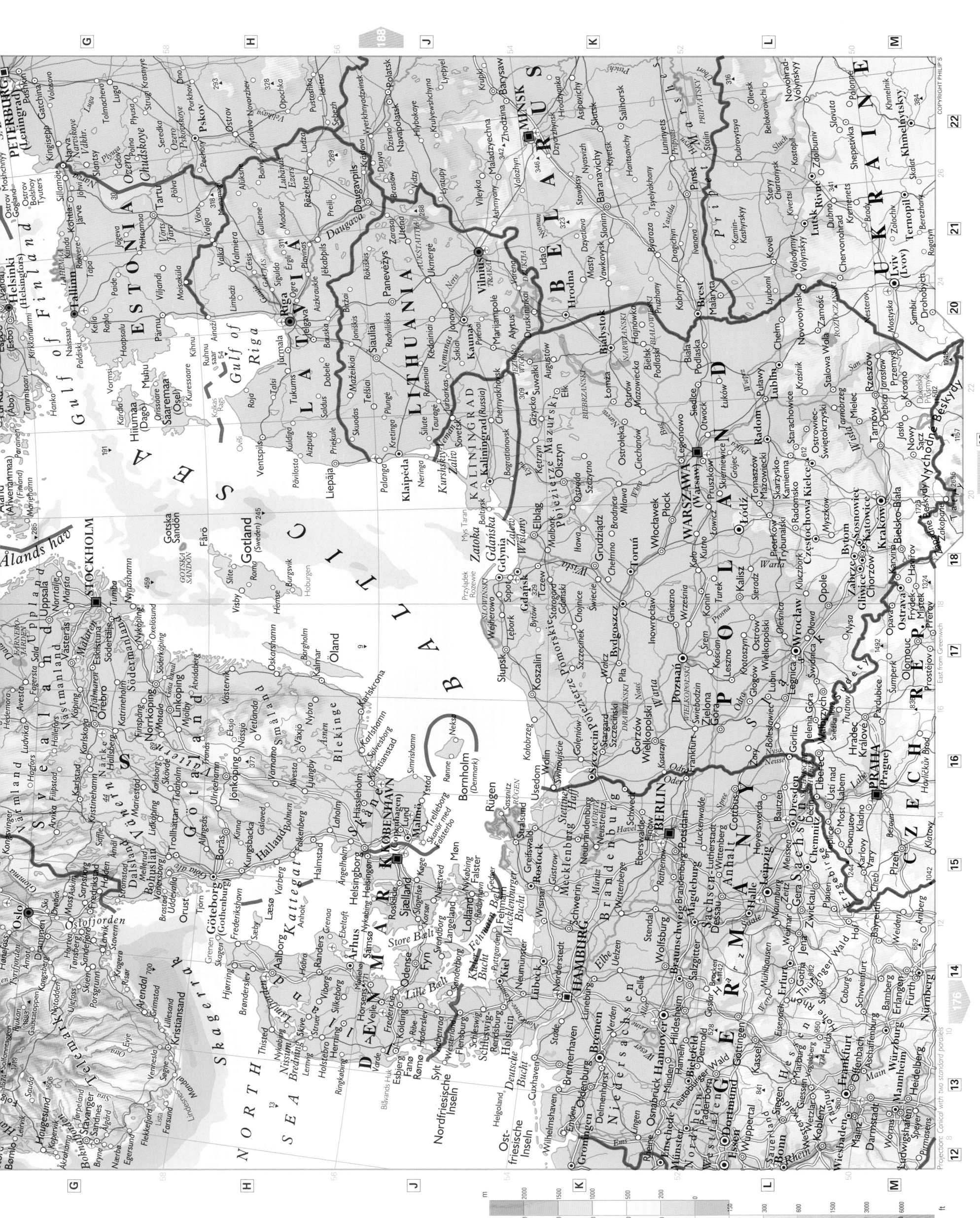

Projection: Conical with two standard parallels

East from Greenwich

1:2 000 000

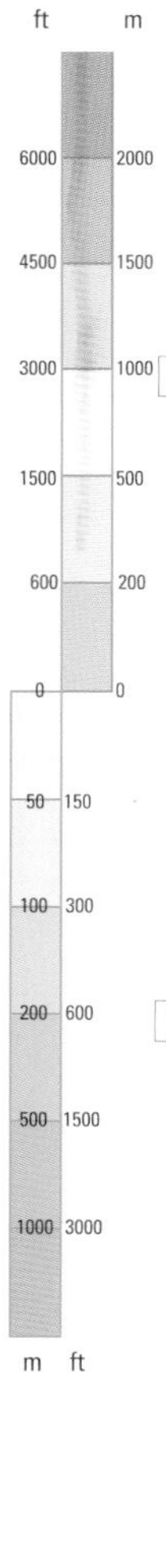

10 0 10 20 30 40 50 60 70 80 90 km

10 0 10 20 30 40 50 60 miles

NORWEGIAN SEA

Projection: Lambert's Conformal Conic

East from Greenwich

COPYRIGHT PHILIP'S

National Parks

1:4 000 000

50 0 25 50 75 100 125 150 175 km
50 0 25 50 75 100 125 miles

ATLANTIC OCEAN

NORWAY
Askøyna
Bergen
Osøyro
Stord
Bømlo Leirvik
Haugesund
Kopervik Åkrahamn
Stavanger
Sandnes
Bryne
Nærbø
Boknafjorden

Shetland Is.
Yell Unst
Fetlar
Mainland
Foula Lerwick
Fair Isle

1224
316

Orkney Is.
Westray Sanday
Stronsay
Mainland Kirkwall
Hoy South
Ronaldsay

Pentland Firth
C. Wrath Thurso
Lewis Wick
Stornoway Helmsdale
789 Lairg
Harris Ullapool Golspie
St. Kilda North West Highlands Tain Invergordon
North Moray Firth
Uist Portree Dingwall Nairn Elgin Buckie Banff Fraserburgh
Benbecula Skye Inverness Peterhead
South Uist 1182 Glen More CAIRNGORMS Huntly
Barra Aviemore Spey Don Inverurie
L. Ness 1311 Dee Aberdeen
Malaig SCOTLAND Ballater Stonehaven
Rhum Eigg Ben Nevis Grampian Mts.
Coll Fort William 1342 Forfar Montrose
Tobermory 1214 Arbroath
Mull Oban L. Lomond Perth St. Andrews
Colonsay L. Awe L. TROSSACHS Dundee
Jura 973 Stirling Glenrothes
Islay Dumbarton Dunfermline Kirkcaldy
L. Fyne Greenock Glasgow Edinburgh Dunbar
Campbeltown Paisley Motherwell Berwick-upon-Tweed
Arran East Kilbride Hamilton Galashiels
Kilmarnock Southern Uplands
Ayr 840 Jedburgh Cheviot Hills 816
Malin Hd. Girvan Hawick Alnwick
North Channel Dumfries NORTHUMBERLAND
Buncrana Stranraer Carlisle Hexham Newcastle-upon-Tyne
Aran I. Coleraine Kirkcudbright Gateshead South Shields Sunderland
Letterkenny Ballymena Mull of Galloway Workington Durham Hartlepool
GLENVEAGH NORTHERN IRELAND Larne Whitehaven 893 Darlington Redcar
Donegal Omagh Antrim Bangor Cumbrian Stockton-on-Tees Middlesbrough
Lough Belfast Mts. 978 Lancaster N. YORK MOORS Scarborough
Bundoran Enniskillen Lough Neagh Lisburn Lurgan Lake District YORKSHIRE
Ballina Sligo Clones Armagh Newry Barrow-in-Furness DALES Bridlington
L. Conn Castleblaney Douglas I. of Man Harrogate York Beverley Kingston upon Hull
Castlebar Leitrim Cavan Dundalk UNITED Blackpool Barnley Leeds Humber Grimsby
Westport Roscommon Drogheda KINGDOM Preston Keighley Bradford Doncaster Scunthorpe Louth
Lough Mask Longford Boyne IRISH Blackburn Halifax Huddersfield Barnsley Rotherham
Connemara Lough Athlone Mullingar SEA Bolton Oldham 636 Sheffield Lincoln Skegness
Galway B. Corrib Lough Ree Anglesey MANCHESTER Stockport Boston Cromer
Galway Ballinasloe Holyhead Liverpool Warrington Chesterfield Mansfield THE
Aran Is. BURREN Birr Tullamore Bangor Colwyn Bay Chester Crewe Derby The Wash BROADS
Ennis Lough Derg Port Laoise Liffey Snowdon Wrexham PEAK Stoke- Nottingham King's Lynn Great Yarmouth
Kilrush Nenagh Carlow 1085 926 DISTRICT on-Trent Trent Grantham Norwich Lowestoft
Shannon Limerick Thurles Kilkenny Wicklow Mts. SNOWDONIA Stafford Telford ENGLAND Ely Bury St. Edmunds THE
Listowel Tipperary Arklow Pwllheli Cambrian Mts. Shrewsbury Leicester Peterborough Thetford Ipswich
953 Tralee Cashel Carrick-on-Suir Cardigan Welshpool Wolverhampton Nuneaton Corby Cambridge Harwich
Dingle Mallow Clonmel Bay Aberystwyth BIRMINGHAM Coventry Rugby Bedford Colchester
Killarney Blackwater Waterford Wexford 886 Redditch Royal Northampton Milton Keynes Felixstowe
Carrantoohill Dungarvan Rosslare WALES Brecon Worcester Leamington Spa Stevenage Southend-on-Sea
1041 Killorglin Youghal BRECON Hereford Cheltenham Luton Harlow 36
Macgillycuddy's Reeks St. George's Channel Carmarthen BEACONS Gloucester Oxford Hempstead Chelmsford
Kenmare Cork Haverfordwest Merthyr Tydfil Neath Cotswold Hills High Wycombe Watford Basildon Margate
Bantry Bandon Kinsale Milford Haven Llanelli Rhondda Cwmbran Newport Swindon Reading LONDON Chatham Canterbury Dover
C. Clear Cóbh Pembroke Swansea Port Talbot Cardiff Bristol Bath Newbury Slough Reigate Maidstone Folkestone
99 PEMBROKESHIRE Barry Weston-super- Basingstoke Guildford Crawley Ashford Str. of Dover
COAST Bristol Channel Mare Salisbury Winchester Fareham Hastings Worthing Eastbourne
EXMOOR Exmoor Taunton Yeovil Southampton Havant Brighton Dunkerque
Barnstaple Bournemouth Isle of Portsmouth Boulogne Calais
Bude 618 Poole Wight Newport sur-Mer Gris St-Omer
DARTMOOR Exeter Weymouth 33 English Channel Nez Le Touquet- Béthune
CELTIC Newquay Dartmoor Torquay Paris-Plage Bruay-la- Lens
Truro Exmouth Abbeville Buissière Valenciennes
SEA St. Austell Plymouth Dieppe Amiens Cambrai
Falmouth Penzance Fécamp St-Quentin
Land's End Rouen FRANCE Laon
Isles of Scilly C. de la Pte. de Le Havre Picardie
Hague Barfleur Pays de Seine 171
Alderney St. Peter Cherbourg Caux East from Greenwich
Guernsey Port Valognes Trouville-sur-Mer COPYRIGHT PHILIP'S
Sark Cotentin Bolbec
Channel Is. St. Helier Bayeux Elbeuf
(U.K.) Jersey Lisieux Caen
West from Greenwich

NORTH SEA

16 238

NETHERLANDS
Texel
Den Helder
Alkmaar
Haarlem
's-Gravenhage
(Den Haag)
Hoek van Holland
ROTTERDAM
Dordrecht

BELGIUM
Zeebrugge
Oostende
Vlissingen
Antwerpen
Brugge Mechelen
Gent **Brussel**
(Bruxelles)
Flandre Tourcoing
St-Amand Lille
Tournai
176

161

161

1:1 600 000

Projection: Lambert's Conformal Conic

West from Greenwich

COPYRIGHT PHILIP'S

National Parks

ATLANTIC OCEAN

CELTIC SEA

IRISH SEA

North Channel

St. George's Channel

IRELAND

NORTHERN IRELAND

Ulster

Leinster

Munster

Connacht

DONEGAL
LONDONDERRY
ANTRIM
TYRONE
FERMANAGH
MONAGHAN
ARMAGH
DOWN
CAVAN
LEITRIM
SLIGO
MAYO
ROSCOMMON
LONGFORD
WESTMEATH
MEATH
LOUTH
GALWAY
OFFALY
KILDARE
DUBLIN
WICKLOW
CLARE
LIMERICK
TIPPERARY
LAOIS
CARLOW
KILKENNY
WEXFORD
KERRY
CORK
WATERFORD

Dublin
Belfast
Londonderry
Cork
Limerick
Galway
Waterford
Dun Laoghaire
Dundalk
Drogheda
Sligo
Killarney

Kintyre
Arran
Brodick
Campbeltown
Firth of Clyde

Malin Hd.
Bloody Foreland
Tory I.
Erris Hd.
Achill I.
Clew Bay
Connemara
Aran Is.
Galway Bay
Dingle Bay
Bantry Bay
Mizen Hd.
Fastnet Rock
Carrauntoohill 1041
Macgillycuddy's Reeks
Mweelrea 819
Errigal 752
Slieve Donard 852
Lugnaquilla 926
Mt. Leinster 794
Galtymore 920

Lough Neagh
Lough Erne
Lower L. Erne
Upper L. Erne
Lough Corrib
Lough Mask
Lough Derg
Lough Ree
Lough Allen
Lough Melvin
Donegal Bay
Sligo Bay
Clew Bay
Dundalk Bay
Carlingford L.
Strangford L.
Wexford Harbour
Waterford Harbour
Cork Harbour
Dundalk

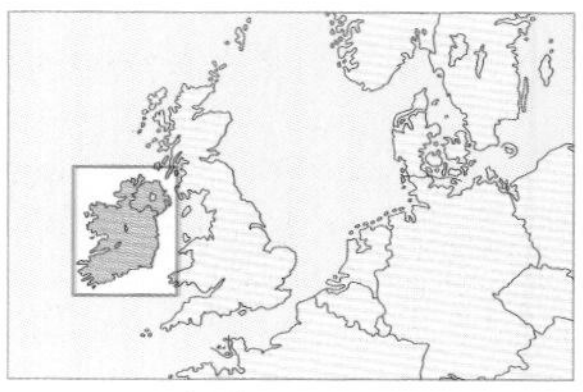

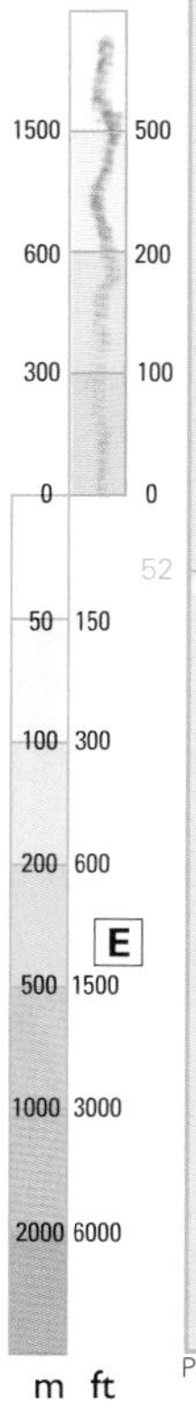

Mull of Oa
Giants Causeway
Rathlin I.
Mull of Kintyre
Ailsa Craig
Cairnryan
Stranraer
Portpatrick
L. Ryan

1:1 600 000

166
168

National Parks and Forest Parks in Scotland

Key to Scottish unitary authorities on map

1 CITY OF ABERDEEN
2 DUNDEE CITY
3 WEST DUNBARTONSHIRE
4 EAST DUNBARTONSHIRE
5 CITY OF GLASGOW
6 INVERCLYDE
7 RENFREWSHIRE
8 EAST RENFREWSHIRE
9 NORTH LANARKSHIRE
10 FALKIRK
11 CLACKMANNANSHIRE
12 WEST LOTHIAN
13 CITY OF EDINBURGH
14 MIDLOTHIAN

ORKNEY IS.
on same scale

SHETLAND IS.
on same scale

Projection : Lambert's Conformal Conic

West from Greenwich

COPYRIGHT PHILIP'S

10 0 10 20 30 40 50 60 70 80 km
10 0 10 20 30 40 50 miles

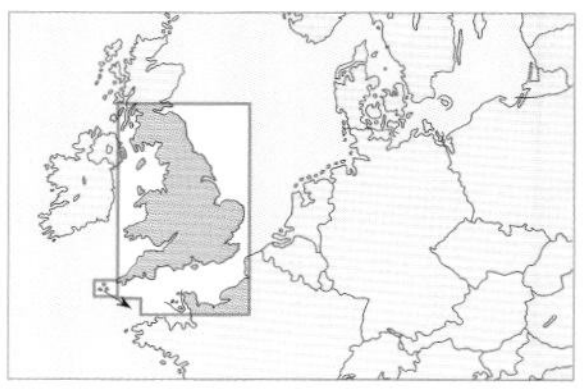

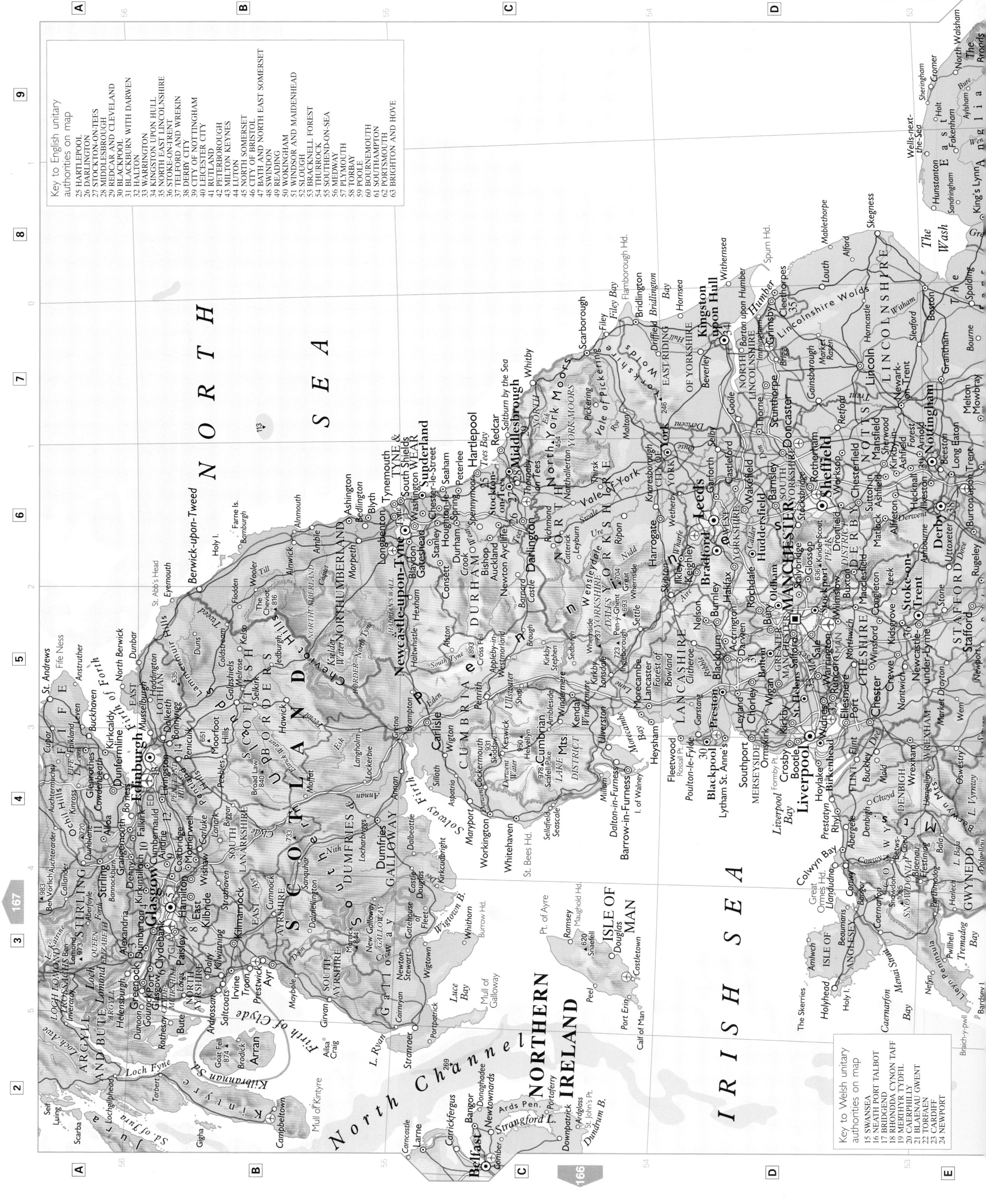

1:1 600 000

Key to English unitary
authorities on map

25 HARTLEPOOL
26 DARLINGTON
27 STOCKTON-ON-TEES
28 MIDDLESBROUGH
29 REDCAR AND CLEVELAND
30 BLACKPOOL
31 BLACKBURN WITH DARWEN
32 HALTON
33 WARRINGTON
34 KINGSTON UPON HULL
35 NORTH EAST LINCOLNSHIRE
36 STOKE-ON-TRENT
37 TELFORD AND WREKIN
38 DERBY CITY
39 CITY OF NOTTINGHAM
40 LEICESTER CITY
41 RUTLAND
42 PETERBOROUGH
43 MILTON KEYNES
44 LUTON
45 NORTH SOMERSET
46 CITY OF BRISTOL
47 BATH AND NORTH EAST SOMERSET
48 SWINDON
49 READING
50 WOKINGHAM
51 WINDSOR AND MAIDENHEAD
52 SLOUGH
53 BRACKNELL FOREST
54 THURROCK
55 SOUTHEND-ON-SEA
56 MEDWAY
57 PLYMOUTH
58 TORBAY
59 POOLE
60 BOURNEMOUTH
61 SOUTHAMPTON
62 PORTSMOUTH
63 BRIGHTON AND HOVE

Key to Welsh unitary
authorities on map

15 SWANSEA
16 NEATH PORT TALBOT
17 BRIDGEND
18 RHONDDA CYNON TAFF
19 MERTHYR TYDFIL
20 CAERPHILLY
21 TORFAEN
22 BLAENAU GWENT
23 CARDIFF
24 NEWPORT

NORTH SEA

IRISH SEA

North Channel

NORTHERN IRELAND

SCOTLAND

ISLE OF MAN

ENGLAND

WALES

CUMBRIA

NORTHUMBERLAND

DURHAM

NORTH YORKSHIRE

LANCASHIRE

LINCOLNSHIRE

GWYNEDD

Newcastle-upon-Tyne
Sunderland
Middlesbrough
Hartlepool
Darlington
York
Leeds
Bradford
Sheffield
Manchester
Liverpool
Blackpool
Preston
Lancaster
Carlisle
Chester
Stoke-on-Trent
Derby
Nottingham
Kingston upon Hull
Lincoln
Edinburgh
Glasgow
Stirling
Dumfries
Belfast
Holyhead
Cardiff

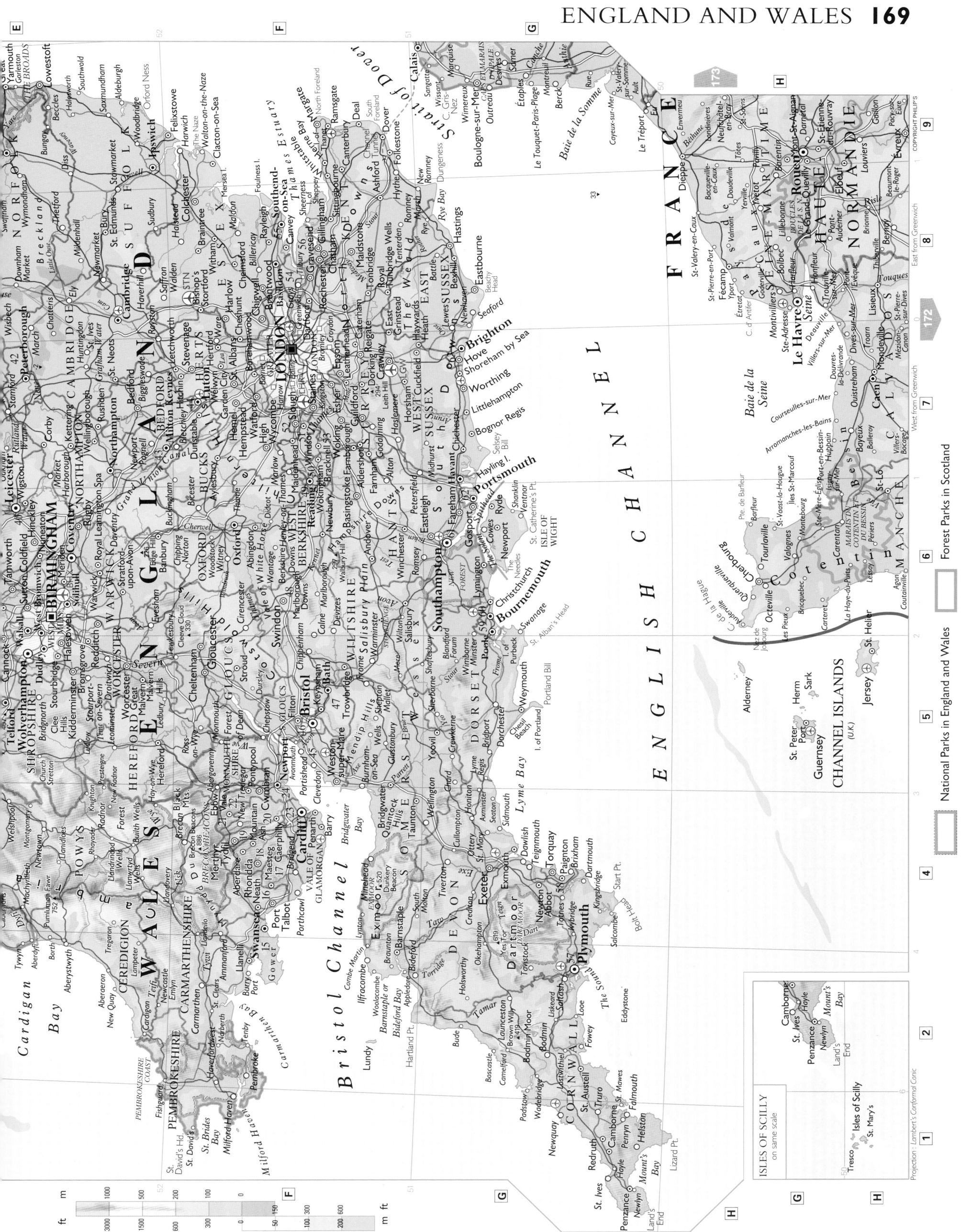

1:2 000 000

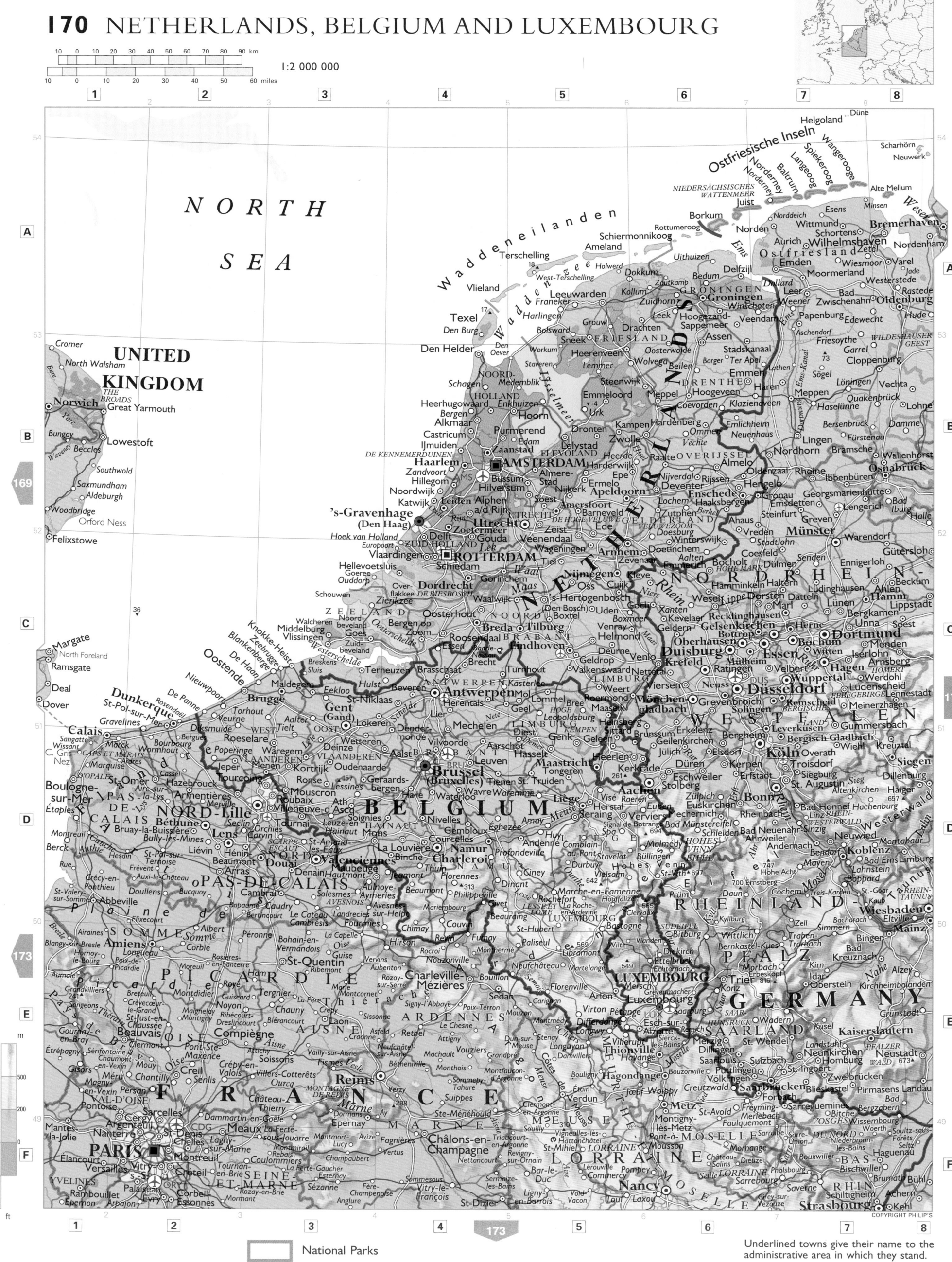

National Parks

Underlined towns give their name to the
administrative area in which they stand.

COPYRIGHT PHILIP'S

1:4 000 000

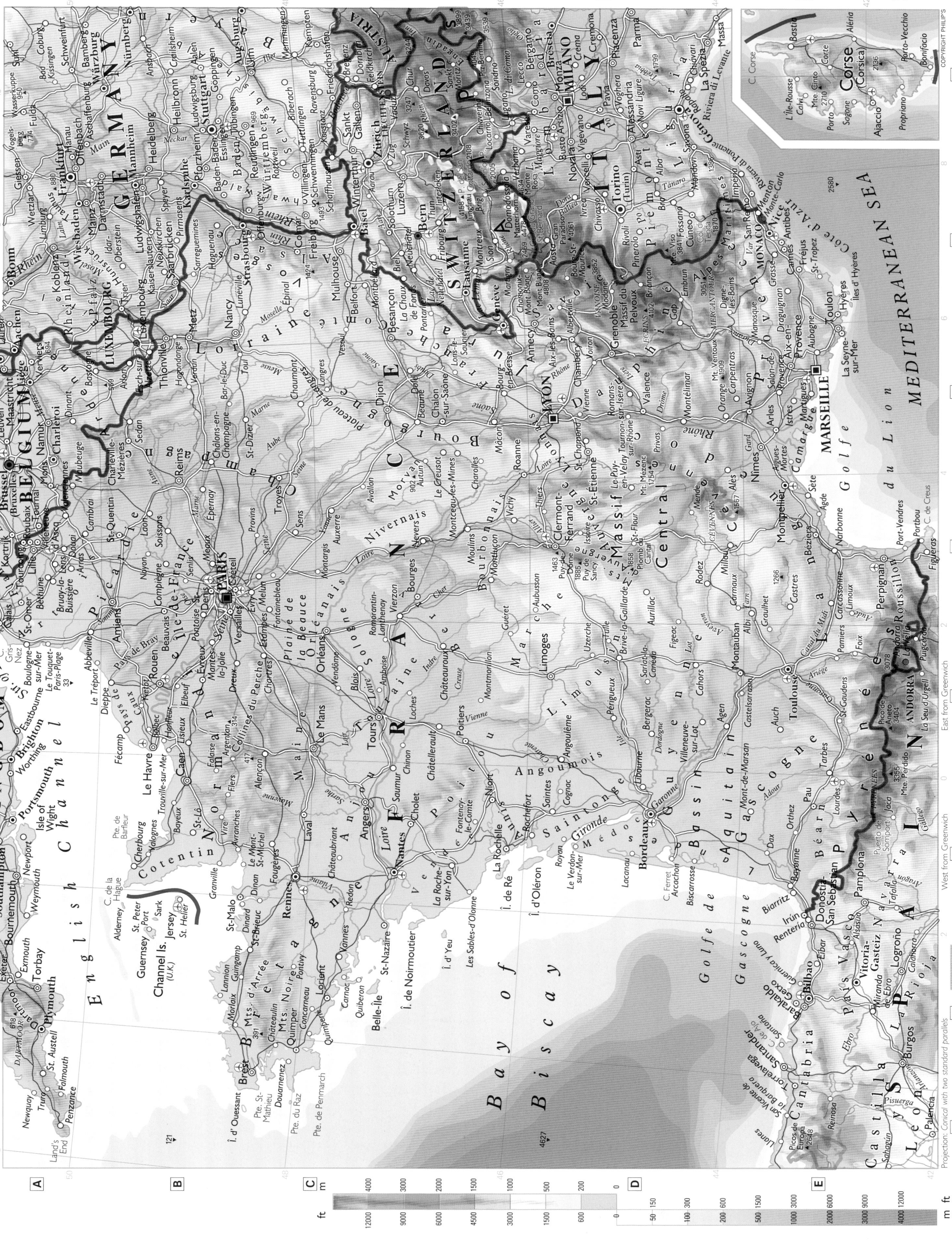

Projection: Conical with two standard parallels

COPYRIGHT PHILIP'S

Countries and regions

UNITED KINGDOM

GERMANY

BELGIUM

LUXEMBOURG

SWITZERLAND

AUSTRIA

ITALY

FRANCE

ANDORRA

SPAIN

Corse (Corsica)

Seas and water bodies

English Channel

Bay of Biscay

MEDITERRANEAN SEA

Golfe du Lion

Golfe de Gascogne

Physical regions

Normandie

Bretagne

Île-de-France

Picardie

Champagne

Lorraine

Alsace

Bourgogne

Nivernais

Bourbonnais

Massif Central

Provence

Côte d'Azur

Languedoc

Roussillon

Pyrénées

Gascogne

Aquitaine

Bassin

Aquitain

Béarn

País Vasco

Navarra

Cantabria

Castilla y León

La Rioja

Touraine

Anjou

Maine

Poitou

Angoumois

Limousin

Marche

Berry

Orléanais

Plaine de la Beauce

Collines du Perche

Cotentin

Cities and towns

PARIS

Brussel (Bruxelles)

Frankfurt

Stuttgart

München

MILANO

Torino (Turin)

Genova

LYON

MARSEILLE

Bordeaux

Toulouse

Nantes

Rennes

Brest

Le Havre

Rouen

Caen

Amiens

Reims

Strasbourg

Metz

Nancy

Dijon

Besançon

Grenoble

Nice

MONACO

Montpellier

Nîmes

Avignon

Clermont-Ferrand

Limoges

Poitiers

Orléans

Tours

Angers

Le Mans

Pamplona

Bilbao

ANDORRA

La Seu d'Urgell

Geneva

Bern

Zürich

Basel

Lausanne

East from Greenwich

West from Greenwich

ft 12000 9000 6000 4500 3000 1500 600 200 0

m 4000 3000 2000 1500 1000 500 200 0

km 50 0 25 50 75 100 125 150 175 km

miles 50 0 25 50 75 100 125 miles

10 0 10 20 30 40 50 60 70 80 90 km

1:2 000 000

10 0 10 20 30 40 50 60 miles

1 **2** **3** **4** 169 **5** **6** **7**

UNITED KINGDOM

Taunton · Salisbury · Winchester · Crawley · Royal Tunbridge Wells · Ashford

Bideford · Wellington · Yeovil · Sherborne · Southampton · Eastleigh · Horsham · East Grinstead · Dover · Folkestone

Bude · Holsworthy · Crewkerne · Blandford Forum · Fareham · Gosport · Chichester · Worthing · Brighton · Hastings · Eastbourne · Boulogne-sur-M

CORNWALL · **DEVON** · **DORSET** · Poole · Bournemouth · **ISLE OF WIGHT** · Newport · Ryde

E n g l i s h   C h a n n e l

Guernsey · **CHANNEL ISLANDS (U.K.)** · Jersey

Cherbourg · **Baie de la Seine** · Le Havre · Dieppe

BASSE-NORMANDIE · Caen · **HAUTE-NORMANDIE** · Rouen

St-Malo · Dinard · Avranches · St-Lô · Bayeux · Lisieux · Évreux

CÔTES-D'ARMOR · St-Brieuc · Dinan · **BRETAGNE** · Rennes · **MAYENNE** · Laval · Le Mans · **SARTHE**

Brest · Morlaix · **FINISTÈRE** · **ILLE-ET-VILAINE** · **PAYS DE LA LOIRE**

Quimper · **MORBIHAN** · Vannes · **LOIRE-ATLANTIQUE** · **MAINE-ET-LOIRE** · Angers · Tours · **INDRE-ET-LOIRE**

Lorient · Redon · St-Nazaire · Nantes · **LOIRE** · Saumur

Belle-Île · **Baie de Bourgneuf** · Cholet · **VIENNE** · Poitiers

A T L A N T I C

VENDÉE · La Roche-sur-Yon · **DEUX-SÈVRES** · Niort · **POITOU-**

Les Sables-d'Olonne · Île d'Yeu

O C E A N

Île de Ré · La Rochelle · **CHARENTE** · Angoulême

Île d'Oléron · Rochefort · Saintes · Cognac · **LIMOUSIN** · Limoges

1 **2** **3** **4** 174 **5** **6** **7** **8**

Projection : Lambert's Conformal Conic · West from Greenwich

DÉPARTEMENTS IN THE PARIS AREA
1 Ville de Paris   3 Val-de-Marne
2 Seine-St-Denis   4 Hauts-de-Seine

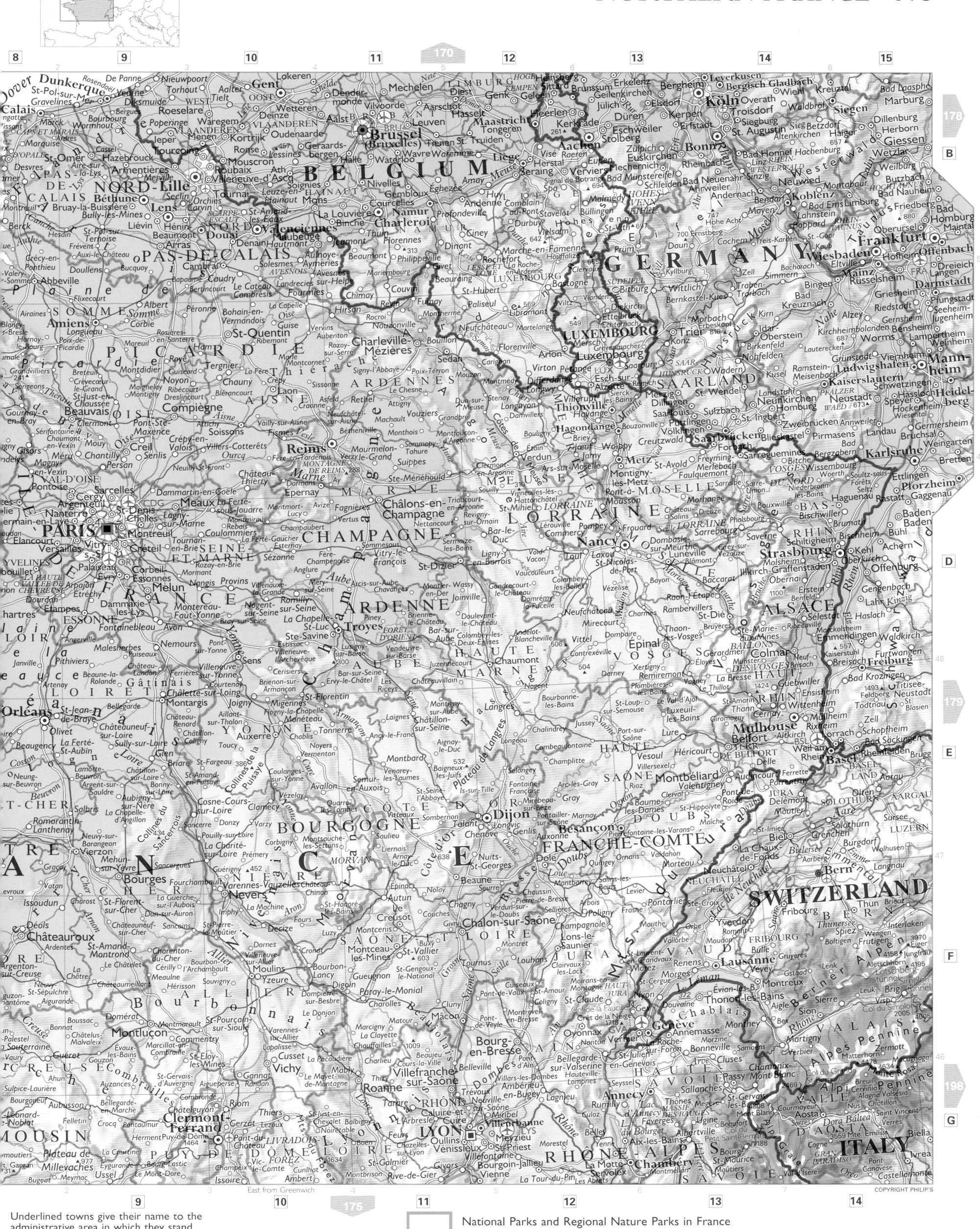

National Parks and Regional Nature Parks in France

COPYRIGHT PHILIP'S

1:2 000 000

Projection : Lambert's Conformal Conic

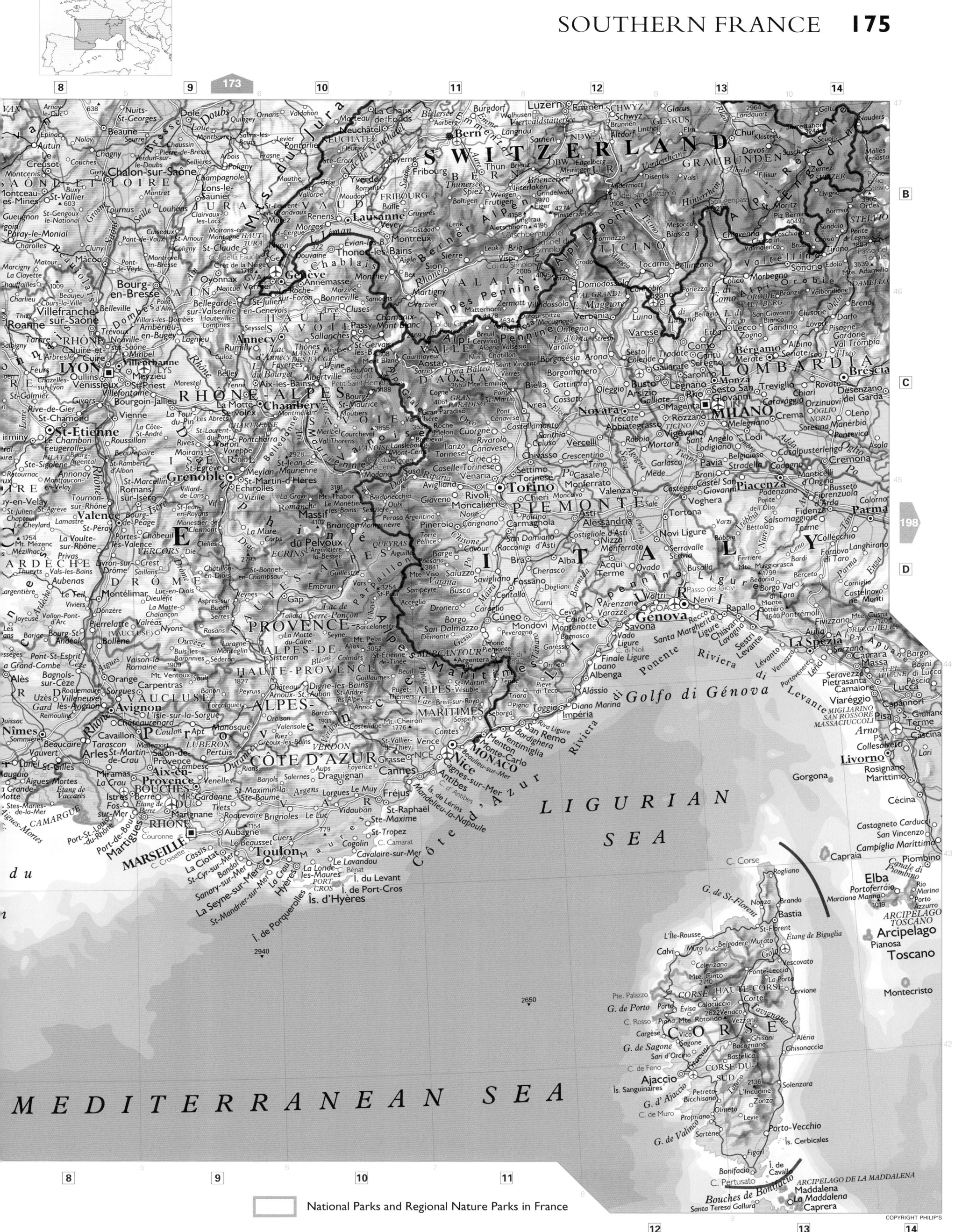

National Parks and Regional Nature Parks in France

50 0 25 50 75 100 125 150 175 km
50 0 25 50 75 100 125 miles

1:4 000 000

1 **2** **3** **4** **5** **6** **7** **8** 161

N O R T H   S E A

B

DENMARK

Sylt
Westerland
Föhr
Nordfriesische
Inseln
Helgoland
Ost-
friesische
Inseln
Norderney
Borkum
Terschelling
Ameland
Schiermonnikoog

Aabenraa
Flensburg
Schleswig
Rendsburg
Holstein
Neumünster
Itzehoe
Elmshorn
Norderstedt
HAMBURG

Sønderborg
Kiel
Lübeck
Travemünde
Wismar
Schwerin

Svendborg
Nakskov
Lolland
Nykøbing
Fehmarn
Mecklenburger
Bucht
Rostock
Güstrow
Neubrandenburg
Neustrelitz

Møn
Falster
Gedser
Stralsund
Greifswald
Usedom

BALTIC SEA
Rügen
Sassnitz
RÜGEN

Kołobrzeg
Koszal
Wolin
Świnoujście
WOLIŃSKI
Szczecin
Police
Stettiner
Haff
Goleniów
Stargard
Szczeciński
Białogard

UNITED
KINGDOM
Cromer
THE
BROADS
Great Yarmouth
Lowestoft
Norwich
Ipswich
Felixstowe
Harwich
Margate
Dover

NETHERLANDS
AMSTERDAM
's-Gravenhage
(Den Haag)
Hoek van Holland
ROTTERDAM
Dordrecht
Leiden
Gouda
Utrecht
Hilversum
Arnhem
Nijmegen
Den Helder
Alkmaar
Hoorn
Haarlem
Kampen
Zwolle
Almelo
Deventer
Apeldoorn
Enschede
Groningen
Assen
Emmen
Leeuwarden
Sneek
Meppel
Leer
Oldenburg
Delmenhorst
Bremen
Bremerhaven
Wilhelmshaven
Emden
Aurich
Cuxhaven
Stade
Buxtehude
Lüneburg
Lüneburger
Heide
Uelzen
Celle
Hannover
Wolfsburg
Braunschweig
Magdeburg

Mecklenburg
Brandenburg
Wittenberge
Neuruppin
Oranienburg
Rathenow
Stendal
Salzwedel
Eberswalde-
Finow
BERLIN
Potsdam
Fürstenwalde
Frankfurt

Gorzów
Wielkopolski
Kostrzyn
Nowy Tomyśl
Międzychód
Zielona
Góra
Świebodzin

GERMANY

Osnabrück
Münster
Rheine
Lingen
Nordhorn
Gütersloh
Bielefeld
Herford
Minden
Hameln
Hildesheim
Salzgitter
Goslar
Halberstadt
Bernburg
Dessau
Wittenberg
Lutherstadt
Cottbus

Dortmund
Essen
Bochum
Duisburg
Oberhausen
Gelsenkirchen
Hagen
Wuppertal
Düsseldorf
Krefeld
Mönchengladbach
Köln
(Cologne)
Bonn
Aachen
Düren
Siegen
Paderborn
Kassel
Göttingen
Nordhausen
Mühlhausen
Halle
Leipzig
Merseburg
Naumburg
Riesa
Meissen
Dresden
Görlitz
Zgorzelec
Bautzen
Hoyerswerda
Lauchhammer

BELGIUM
BRUSSEL
(Bruxelles)
Gent
Brugge
Antwerpen
Mechelen
Leuven
Liège
Namur
Charleroi
Mons
Tournai
Kortrijk
Roeselare
Hasselt
Maastricht
Verviers
Eupen

Oostende
Calais
Dunkerque
Zeebrugge
Vlissingen
Breda
Tilburg
's-Hertogenbosch
Eindhoven
Venlo
Roermond
Heerlen

Erfurt
Weimar
Jena
Gera
Zwickau
Chemnitz
Gotha
Eisenach
Suhl
Plauen
Hof
Bamberg
Bayreuth
Coburg
Würzburg
Schweinfurt
Fulda
Marburg
Giessen
Wetzlar
Koblenz
Frankfurt
Hanau
Offenbach
Darmstadt
Mainz
Wiesbaden
Worms
Mannheim
Ludwigshafen
Heidelberg
Speyer
Karlsruhe
Pforzheim
Heilbronn

LUXEMBOURG
Luxembourg
Trier
Saarbrücken
Kaiserslautern
Pirmasens
Esch-sur-Alzette
Thionville
Metz
Nancy
Saarlouis
Saarguemines
Haguenau
Strasbourg
Offenburg
Freiburg
Colmar
Mulhouse
Basel

CZECH
PRAHA
(Prague)
Plzeň
Karlovy Vary
Cheb
Klatovy
Most
Teplice
Ústí nad Labem
Děčín
Liberec
Jablonec nad Nisou
Hradec
Králové
Pardubice
Jihlava
Kolín
Kladno
Beroun
Příbram
Tábor
Písek
České
Budějovice

FRANCE
PARIS
Créteil
St-Denis
Reims
Épernay
Meaux
Melun
Provins
Troyes
Sens
Auxerre
Chaumont
Dijon
Beaune
Chalon-sur-Saône
Mâcon
Besançon
Montbéliard
Belfort
Vesoul
Nancy
Épinal
Verdun
Bar-le-Duc
Châlons-en-Champagne
Fontainebleau
Nevers
Moulins
Roanne
Vichy
Clermont

SWITZERLAND
Bern
Zürich
Basel
Genève
Lausanne
Neuchâtel
Fribourg
Thun
Interlaken
Luzern
Winterthur
Sankt Gallen
Chur
Davos
St. Moritz
Montreux
Sion
Brig
Bellinzona
Lugano
Locarno

AUSTRIA
Innsbruck
Salzburg
Linz
Wels
Steyr
Amstetten
Wiener
Neustadt
Graz
Klagenfurt
Villach
Leoben
Bruck an der Mur
Judenburg
Bregenz
Feldkirch
Landeck
Badgastein
Lienz
Wolfsberg

LIECHTENSTEIN
Vaduz

München
(Munich)
Augsburg
Ingolstadt
Regensburg
Nürnberg
Fürth
Erlangen
Ansbach
Amberg
Weiden
Straubing
Passau
Landshut
Deggendorf
Freising
Dachau
Rosenheim
Traunstein
Garmisch-Partenkirchen
Kempten
Memmingen
Kaufbeuren
Ulm
Stuttgart
Esslingen
Göppingen
Tübingen
Reutlingen
Aalen
Schwäbisch
Crailsheim
Baden-Baden
Rastatt
Villingen-Schwenningen
Konstanz
Friedrichshafen
Ravensburg
Biberach

ITALY
MILANO
Torino
(Turin)
Genova
Novara
Vercelli
Bergamo
Brescia
Como
Lecco
Varese
Busto Arsizio
Alessandria
Asti
Cuneo
Savona
Imperia
San Remo
Pavia
Lodi
Cremona
Mantova
Piacenza
Parma
Reggio nell'Emilia
Modena
Bologna
Ferrara
Ravenna
Forlì
Rimini
Carrara
Massa
La Spézia
Verona
Vicenza
Padova
Venézia
(Venice)
Treviso
Belluno
Trento
Rovereto
Bolzano
Merano
Brunico
Udine
Pordenone
Gorizia
Trieste

SLOVENIA
Ljubljana
Maribor
Celje
Kranj
Koper
Nova Gorica

MARSEILLE
Toulon
Nice
Monaco
Monte-Carlo
Menton
Cannes
Antibes
Fréjus
Aix-en-Provence
Avignon
Arles
Nîmes
Orange
Carpentras
Gap
Briançon
Grenoble
Valence
Lyon
St-Étienne
Chambéry
Annecy
Aix-les-Bains
Bourg-en-Bresse
Albertville

ADRIATIC
SEA

CRO...
Zagreb
Rijeka
Pula
Rovinj
Krk
Cres
Lošinj

Golfo di
Génova

Projection: Conical with two standard parallels

1 **2** **3** **4** **5** **6** **7** 192 **8**

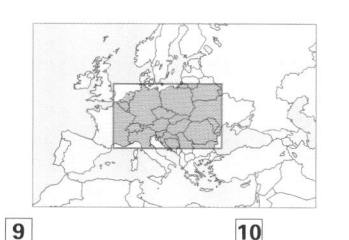

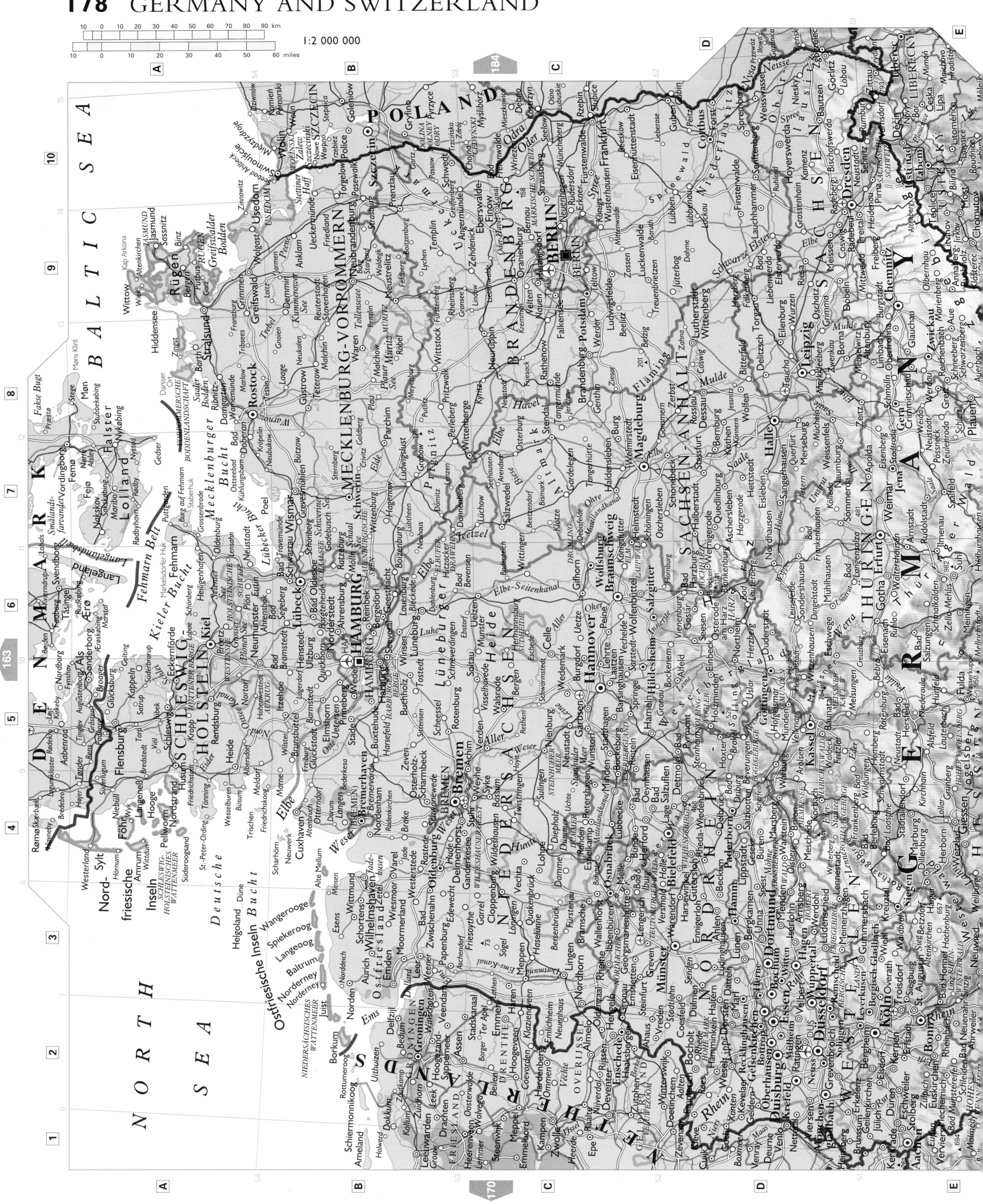

Underlined towns give their name to the
administrative area in which they stand.

National Parks and Nature Parks in Germany

Projection: Lambert's Conformal Conic

East from Greenwich

National Parks

Underlined towns give their name to the
administrative area in which they stand.

1:2 000 000

Administrative divisions in Croatia:
1 Brodsko-Posavska   5 Osječko-Baranjska   9 Vukovarsko-Srijemska
2 Koprivničko-Križevačka 6 Požeško-Slavonska
4 Medimurska   8 Virovitičko-Podravska

– – – – – Inter-entity boundaries as agreed
at the 1995 Dayton Peace Agreement

National Parks

Underlined towns give their name to the administrative area in which they stand.

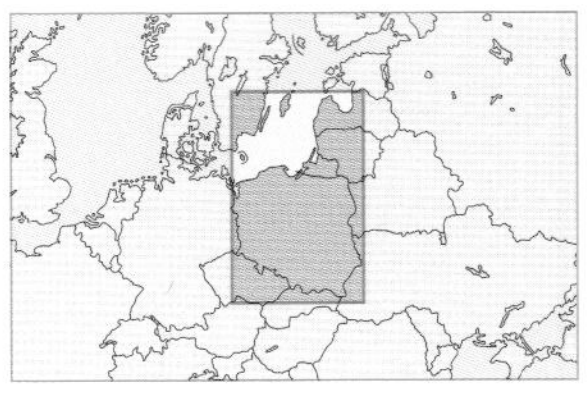

10 0 10 20 30 40 50 60 70 80 90 km

1:2 000 000

10 0 10 20 30 40 50 60 miles

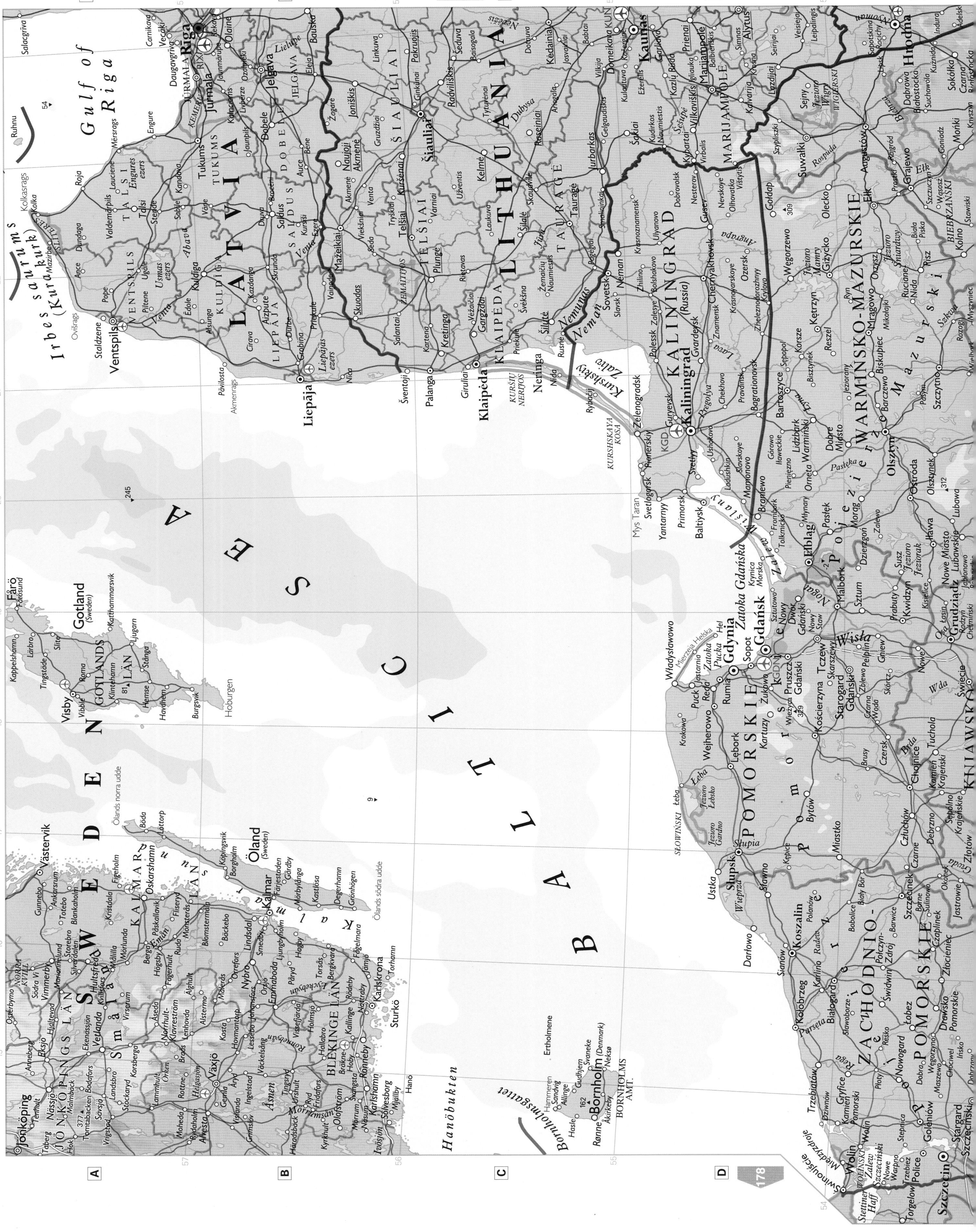

Gulf of Riga

LATVIA

LITHUANIA

KALININGRAD (Russia)

SWEDEN

Gotland (Sweden)

Öland (Sweden)

BALTIC SEA

WARMIŃSKO-MAZURSKIE

POMORSKIE

ZACHODNIO-POMORSKIE

Riga
Jūrmala
Jelgava
Ventspils
Liepāja
Klaipėda
Šiauliai
Kaunas
Marijampolė
Kaliningrad
Gdańsk
Gdynia
Sopot
Elbląg
Malbork
Słupsk
Koszalin
Szczecin
Hrodna
Kalmar
Visby
Bornholm (Denmark)

Underlined towns give their name to the administrative area in which they stand.

National Parks

East from Greenwich

Projection: Lambert's Conformal Conic

COPYRIGHT PHILIP'S

GERMANY

CZECH REP.

SLOVAK REP.

AUSTRIA

UKRAINE

BELARUS

P O L A N D

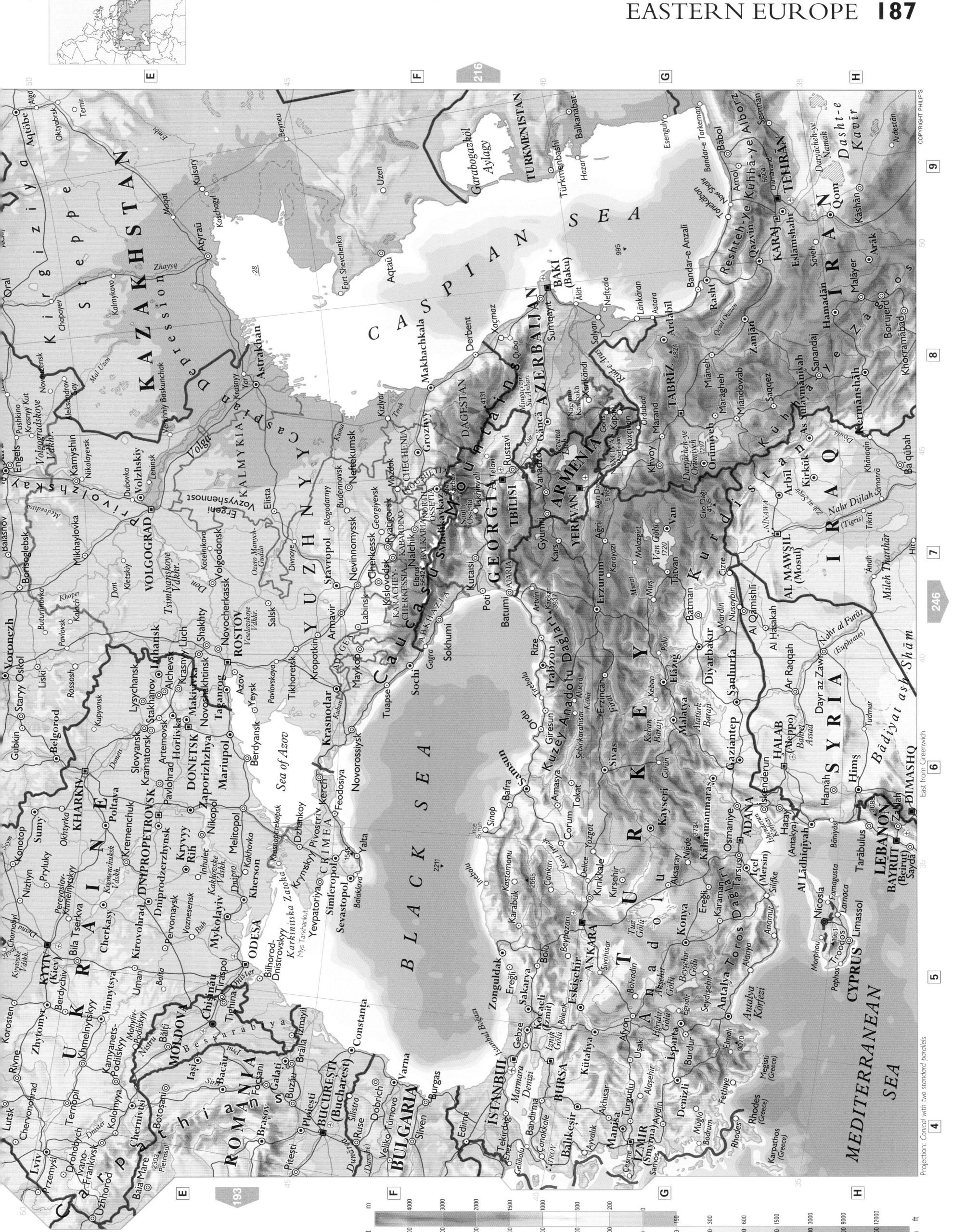

Projection: Conical with two standard parallels

East from Greenwich

ft
m
4000
3000
2000
1500
1000
500
200
0
ft

m
12 000
9000
6000
4500
3000
1500
600
300
150
50
0
50
150
300
600
1500
3000
6000
9000
12000
ft

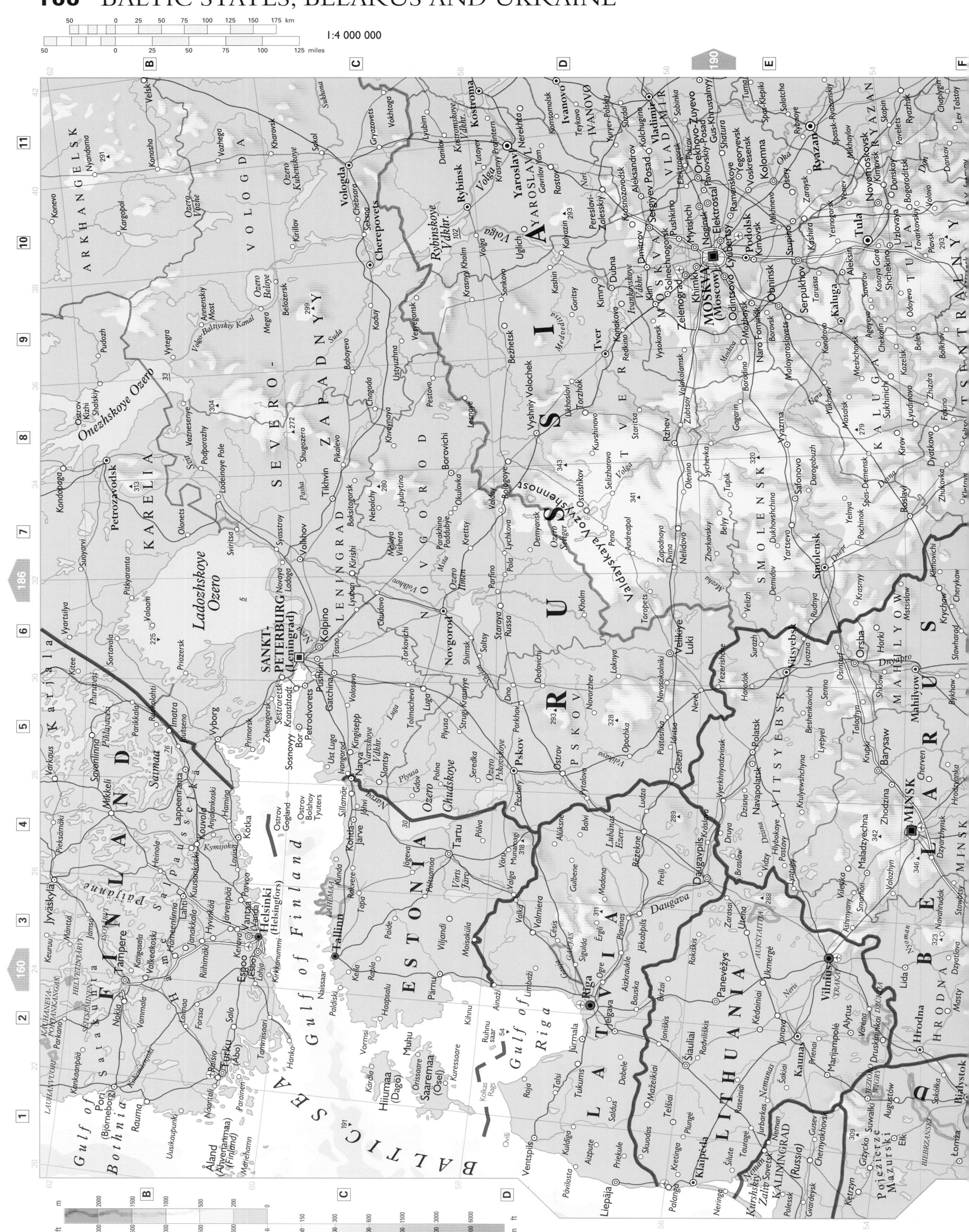

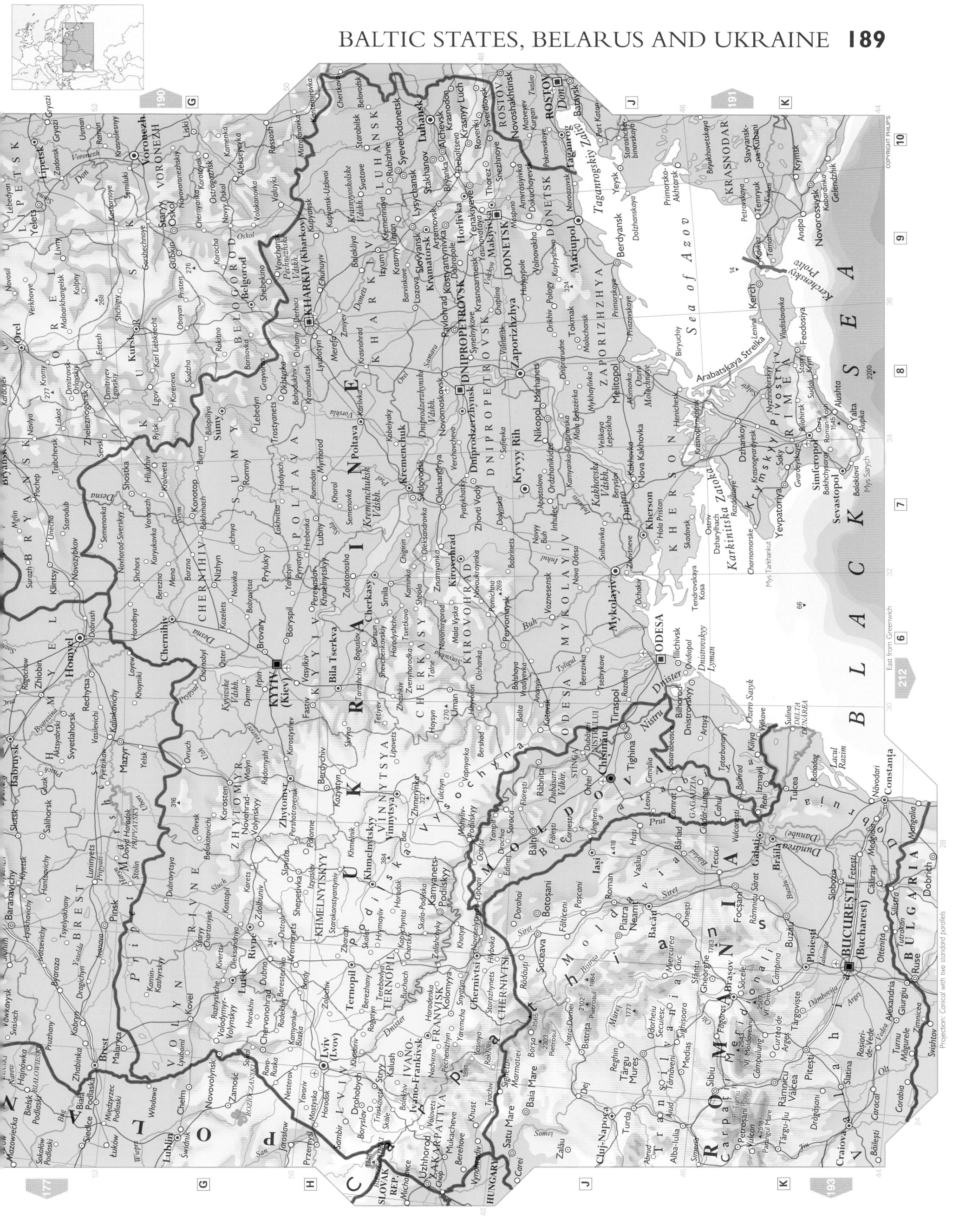

Projection: Conical with two standard parallels

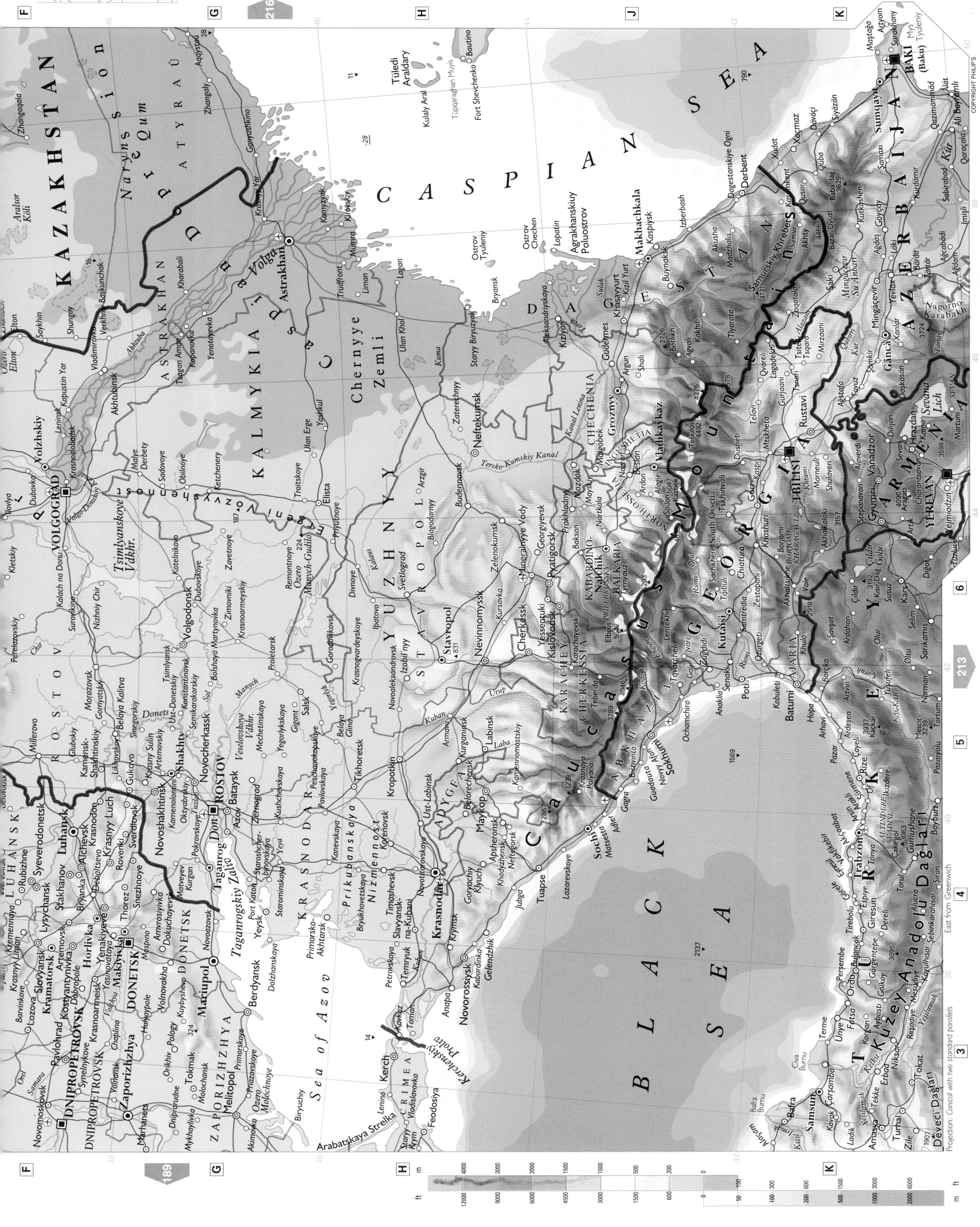

F G H J K

C A S P I A N   S E A

K A Z A K H S T A N

Narynskiye Peski

P r i k a s p i y s k a y a   N i z m e n n o s t

ASTRAKHAN

Astrakhan

Volga

KALMYKIA

Chernyye Zemli

Yergeni Vozvyshennost

VOLGOGRAD

Volzhskiy

Tsimlyanskoye Vdkhr.

ROSTOV

Tsimlyanskoye Vdkhr.

Don

Taganrogskiy Zaliv

Taganrog

DONETSK

Novoshakhtinsk

Shakhty

Novocherkassk

Bataysk

Rostov

Azov

LUHANSK

Luhansk

D A G E S T A N

Makhachkala

Derbent

Kizlyar

CHECHENIA

Grozny

INGUSHETIA

NORTH OSSETIA

Vladikavkaz

KABARDINO-BALKARIA

Nalchik

Elbrus 5642

KARACHEY-CHERKESSIA

STAVROPOL

Stavropol

Nevinnomyssk

Cherkessk

Kislovodsk

Pyatigorsk

Mineralnyye Vody

Georgiyevsk

KRASNODAR

Krasnodar

ADYGEA

Maykop

A B K H A Z I A

C a u c a s u s   M o u n t a i n s

G E O R G I A

TBILISI

Rustavi

Kutaisi

Batumi

AJARIA

Poti

SOUTH OSSETIA

Tskhinvali

A Z E R B A I J A N

Sumqayit

BAKI (Baku)

Gäncä

Mingäçevir

Nagorno-Karabakh

A R M E N I A

YEREVAN

Sevana Lich

Gyumri

Vanadzor

T U R K E Y

Trabzon

Kuzey Anadolu Dağları

Devecı Dağı

B L A C K   S E A

Novorossiysk

Sochi

Tuapse

Sea of Azov

Kerch

CRIMEA

Feodosiya

DNIPROPETROVSK

Zaporizhzhya

Melitopol

Mariupol

Berdyansk

ZAPORIZHZHYA

COPYRIGHT PHILIP'S

213

189

East from Greenwich

Projection: Conical with two standard parallels

9 8 7 6 5 4 3

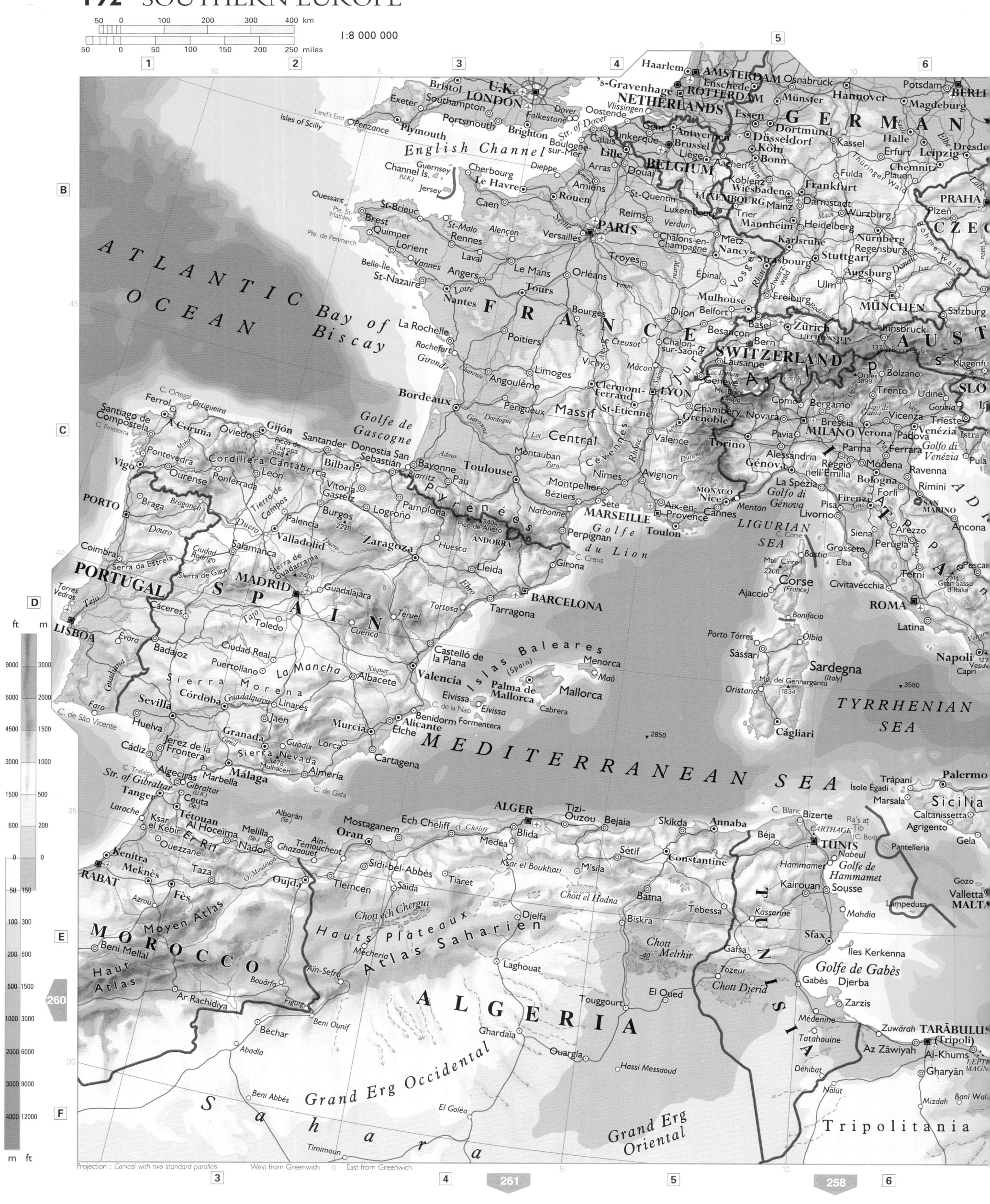

50 0 100 200 300 400 km
1:8 000 000
50 0 50 100 150 200 250 miles

|1| **|2|** **|3|** **|4|** **|5|** **|6|**

ATLANTIC
OCEAN

Bay of
Biscay

English Channel

A T L A N T I C
O C E A N

Land's End
Isles of Scilly
Penzance
Plymouth
Exeter
Bristol
Southampton
LONDON
U.K.
Portsmouth
Brighton
Folkestone
Dover
Str. of Dover
Calais
Boulogne-sur-Mer
Dunkerque
Dieppe
Arras
Douai
Lille
Gent
Ostende
Vlissingen
's-Gravenhage
ROTTERDAM
NETHERLANDS
Enschede
Haarlem
AMSTERDAM
Osnabrück
Münster
Essen
Dortmund
Hannover
Magdeburg
Potsdam
BERLI
G E R M A N Y

Cherbourg
Le Havre
Rouen
Caen
St-Brieuc
Brest
Quimper
Lorient
Belle-Île
St-Nazaire
Vannes
Angers
Nantes

Channel Is.
(U.K.)
Guernsey
Jersey
Pte. St-Mathieu
Pte. de Penmarch
Ouessant

Amiens
St-Quentin
Reims
PARIS
Versailles
Rennes
St-Malo
Alençon
Laval
Le Mans
Tours
Orléans
Troyes
Bourges

Antwerpen
Brussel
BELGIUM
Liège
LUXEMBOURG
Luxembourg
Aachen
Köln
Bonn
Koblenz
Wiesbaden
Mainz
Frankfurt
Darmstadt
Heidelberg
Mannheim
Würzburg
PRAHA
Plzeň
CZE
Kassel
Halle
Erfurt
Leipzig
Dresden
Plauen
Chemnitz
Thüringer Wald
Fulda
Trier
Verdun
Metz
Nancy
Châlons-en-Champagne
Épinal
Strasbourg
Karlsruhe
Stuttgart
Nürnberg
Regensburg
Augsburg
Ulm
Schwarzwald
Freiburg

F R A N C E
Nantes
Poitiers
Angoulême
Limoges
La Rochelle
Rochefort
Bordeaux
Périgueux
Clermont-Ferrand
St-Étienne
LYON
Vichy
Mâcon
Chalon-sur-Saône
Dijon
Belfort
Besançon
Mulhouse
Basel
Bern
Zürich
SWITZERLAND
Lausanne
Genève
Mont Blanc
MÜNCHEN
Salzburg
Innsbruck
AUS
Klagenfu
SLO
Bolzano
Trento
Brennerp.
Ortles
3899
3371

Massif
Central
Yonne
Loire
Cher
Seine
Marne
Rhin
Donau
Isar
Inn

Golfe de
Gascogne

C. Ortegal
Ortigueira
C. Finisterra
Santiago de Compostela
A Coruña
Ferrol
Pontevedra
Vigo
Ourense
Braga
Bragança
PORTO
Ponferrada
León
Oviedo
Gijón
Santander
Donostia San Sebastián
Bilbao
Vitoria Gasteiz
Logroño
Pamplona
Huesca
Bayonne
Biarritz
Pau
Pyrénées
Pico de Aneto 3404
Lleida
Zaragoza
Tudela
Toulouse
Montauban
Tarn
Lot
C E V E N N E S
Nîmes
Montpellier
Béziers
Narbonne
Perpignan
ANDORRA
Girona
C. de Creus
Montpellier
Valence
Avignon
Aix-en-Provence
MARSEILLE
Toulon
Cannes
Menton
MONACO
Nice
Golfe du Lion
LIGURIAN SEA
C. Corse
Bastia
Mte. Cinto 2706
Corse
(France)
Ajaccio
Bonifacio
Porto Tórres
Sássari
Oristano
Sardegna
(Italy)
Mti. del Gennargentu 1834
Cágliari
TYRRHENIAN SEA
Génova
Torino
Novara
Pavia
Alessándria
Bergamo
Brescia
MILANO
Como
Verona
Vicenza
Pádova
Venézia
Trieste
Gorízia
Údine
Treviso
Parma
Réggio nell'Emília
Módena
Bologna
Ferrara
Ravenna
Rímini
SAN MARINO
Forlì
Pisa
Livorno
Firenze
Siena
Arezzo
Perúgia
Grosseto
Elba
Civitavécchia
ROMA
Latina
Ancona
I T A L Y

Picos de Europa 2648
Cordillera Cantábrica
Tierra de Campos
Palencia
Burgos
Valladolid
Salamanca
Ciudad Rodrigo
Sierra de Guadarrama 2430
MADRID
Guadalajara
Cuenca
Teruel
Tortosa
Tarragona
BARCELONA
Ebro
Duero
Sierra de Gredos 2228
Douro

C. de São Vicente
Faro
Huelva
Sevilla
Cádiz
C. Trafalgar
Str. of Gibraltar
Tánger
Tétouan
Gibraltar
(U.K.)
Ceuta
(Sp.)
Algeciras
Marbella
Málaga
Granada
Sierra Nevada
Mulhacén 3478
Guadix
C. de Gata
Almería
Lorca
Cartagena
Murcia
Alicante
Elche
Benidorm
C. de la Nao
Valencia
Xúquer
Albacete
La Mancha
Alcázar
Islas Baleares
(Spain)
Eivissa
Formentera
Cabrera
Palma de Mallorca
Mallorca
Menorca
Maó

SPAIN
PORTUGAL
Torres Vedras
LISBOA
Setúbal
Évora
Serra da Estrela
Coimbra
Guadiana
Badajoz
Cáceres
Toledo
Ciudad Real
Puertollano
Sierra Morena
Córdoba
Jaén
Linares
Guadalquivir
Jerez de la Frontera
Tejo
Tajo

MEDITERRANEAN SEA

M O R O C C O
Kénitra
RABAT
Meknès
Fès
Azrou
Taza
Oujda
Ksar el Kebir
Larache
Al Hoceima
El Rif
Melilla
(Sp.)
Nador
Alborán
(Sp.)
Ouezzane
Beni Mellal
Moyen Atlas
Haut Atlas
Ar Rachidia
Béchar
Abadla
Beni Ounif
Bouárfa
Figuig
Aïn-Sefra
Atlas Saharien
Méchéria
Hauts Plateaux
Chott ech Chergui
Saïda
Tlemcen
Sidi-bel-Abbès
Aïn-Témouchent
Ghazaouet
Oran
Mostaganem
Ech Chéliff
O. Chéliff
Médéa
ALGER
Blida
Tizi-Ouzou
Bejaïa
Skikda
Sétif
Constantine
M'sila
Ksar el Boukhari
Djelfa
Laghouat
Chott el Hodna
Batna
Biskra
Chott Melrhir
El Oued
Touggourt
Ouargla
Hassi Messaoud
Ghardaïa
El Goléa
Timimoun
A L G E R I A
Grand Erg Occidental
Beni Abbès
S a h a r a
Tamimoun

Annaba
Béja
Bizerte
CARTHAGE
C. Blanc
Ra's aṭ Ṭib
C. Bon
TUNIS
Nabeul
Golfe de Hammamet
Hammamet
Sousse
Mahdia
Kairouan
Kasserine
T U N I S I A
Gafsa
Tozeur
Chott Djerid
Gabès
Djerba
Golfe de Gabès
Sfax
Îles Kerkenna
Médenine
Zarzis
Tatahouine
Dehibat
Nalūt
Bani Walīd
Mizdah
Tripolitania
Grand Erg Oriental
Trápani
Ísole Égadi
Marsala
Palermo
Sicilia
Caltanissetta
Agrigento
Gela
Pantelleria
Lampedusa
Gozo
Valletta
MALTA
Zuwārah
TARĀBULUS
(Tripoli)
Az Zāwiyah
Al-Khums
Gharyān
LEPTIS MAGNA
Napoli
Capri
Vésuv

West from Greenwich   East from Greenwich
Projection : Conical with two standard parallels

|3| 261 **|4|** 258 **|5|** **|6|**

ft   m
9000   3000
6000   2000
4500   1500
3000   1000
1500   500
600   200
0   0
0   0
50   150
100   300
200   600
500   1500
1000   3000
2000   6000
3000   9000
4000   12000
m   ft

260

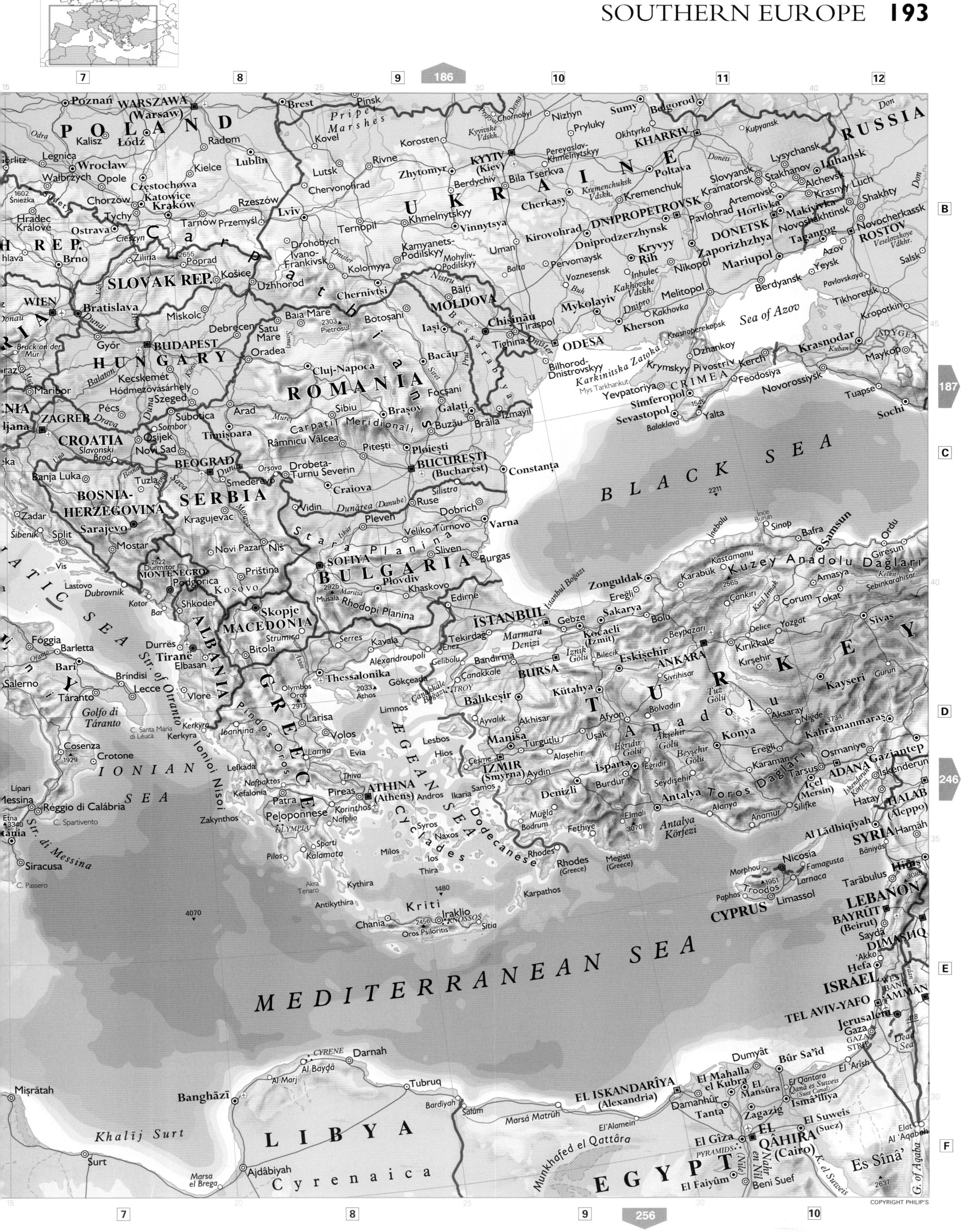

SOUTHERN EUROPE

POLAND
Poznań
WARSZAWA (Warsaw)
Brest
Pinsk
Pripet Marshes
Nizhyn
Chornobyl
Sumy
Begorod
Don
RUSSIA
Kalisz
Łódź
Radom
Kovel
Korosten
Kyyivske Vdskh.
Pryluky
Okhtyrka
Kupyansk
Legnica
Wrocław
Kielce
Lublin
Rivne
Zhytomyr
KYYIV (Kiev)
Bila Tserkva
Pereyaslav-Khmelnytskyy
Poltava
KHARKIV
Lysychansk
Lohansk
Walbrzych
Opole
Częstochowa
Katowice
Kraków
Tarnów
Przemyśl
Lviv
Chervonohrad
Lutsk
Khmelnytskyy
Vinnytsya
Cherkasy
Kremenchuksk Vdskh.
Kremenchuk
Kramatorsk
Slovyansk
Stakhanov
Krasnyy Luch
Alchevsk
Hradec Králové
Ostrava
Tychy
Cieszyn
Żylina
Poprad
Košice
Uzhhorod
Drohobych
Ivano-Frankivsk
Ternopil
Kamyanets-Podilskyy
Kolomyya
Uman
Kirovohrad
Dniprodzerzhynsk
DNIPROPETROVSK
Pavlohrad
Horlivka
Artemovsk
DONETSK
Makiyvka
Novoshakhtinsk
Shakhty
Brno
Žilina
SLOVAK REP.
Miskolc
Baia Mare
Botoşani
MOLDOVA
Balta
Pervomaysk
Voznesensk
Kryvyy Rih
Nikopol
Zaporizhzhya
Mariupol
Taganrog
ROSTOV
Novocherkassk
Yeysk
Salsk
WIEN
Bratislava
Győr
BUDAPEST
Satu Mare
Oradea
Cluj-Napoca
Bacău
Iaşi
Chişinău
Tiraspol
Mykolayiv
Kakhovka
Kherson
Krasnoperekopsk
Dzhankoy
Berdyansk
Azov
Pavlovskaya
Tikhoretsk
Kropotkin
Bruck an der Mur
HUNGARY
Kecskemét
Hódmezővásárhely
Szeged
Debrecen
Subotica
Arad
Sibiu
Braşov
Galaţi
Bîrlad
Tighina
ODESA
Bilhorod-Dnistrovskyy
Kakhovske Vdskh.
Dnipro
Sea of Azov
Kerch
Krasnodar
ADYGEA
Maykop
Maribor
Pécs
ZAGREB
Balaton
ROMANIA
Timişoara
Sombor
Novi Sad
Focşani
Bessarabiya
Izmayil
Kakhovka
Karkinitska Zatoka
Mys Tarkhankut
Yevpatoriya
Simferopol
CRIMEA
Feodosiya
Novorossiysk
Tuapse
CROATIA
Slavonski Brod
Osijek
BEOGRAD
Duna
Smederevo
Drobeta-Turnu Severin
Craiova
Piteşti
Ploieşti
BUCUREŞTI (Bucharest)
Constanţa
Sevastopol
Balaklava
Yalta
Sochi
Banja Luka
SERBIA
Orşova
Dunărea (Danube)
Silistra
Ruse
Dobrich
BLACK SEA
Zadar
BOSNIA-HERZEGOVINA
Sarajevo
Kragujevac
Niš
Vidin
Pleven
Veliko Tŭrnovo
Varna
Ince Burun
Sinop
Bafra
Samsun
Ordu
Giresun
Šibenik
Split
MONTENEGRO
Durmitor
Podgorica
Priština
Kosovo
SOFIYA
Stara Planina
BULGARIA
Plovdiv
Sliven
Burgas
Zonguldak
Karabük
Kastamonu
Kuzey Anadolu Dağları
Amasya
Sivas
Vis
Lastovo
Dubrovnik
Kotor
Bar
Shkodër
Novi Pazar
Musala
Marisa
Rhodopi Planina
Khaskovo
Edirne
Ereğli
Sakarya
Bolu
Çankırı
Çorum
Tokat
Fóggia
Barletta
ALBANIA
Skopje
MACEDONIA
Bitola
Strumica
Serres
Kavala
İSTANBUL
İstanbul Boğazı
Gebze
Kocaeli (İzmit)
Beypazarı
Delice
Yozgat
Kırıkkale
ANKARA
Kırşehir
Bari
Bríndisi
Durrës
Tiranë
Elbasan
GREECE
Olymbos Oros
Thessaloníki
Gökçeada
Tekirdağ
Marmara Denizi
Bandırma
İznik Gölü
Bilecik
Eskişehir
Sivrihisar
Kayseri
Lecce
Táranto
Str. of Otranto
Vlorë
Pindos Oros
Olympos Oros
Athos
Limnos
Gelibolu
Çanakkale
BURSA
Balıkesir
Kütahya
Afyon
Bolvadin
Aksaray
Niğde
Kahramanmaraş
ADANA
Gaziantep
Golfo di Táranto
Kerkyra
Ioánnina
Lárisa
Évia
Lesbos
Ayvalık
Akhisar
Uşak
TURKEY
Anadolu
Konya
Ereğli
Karaman
Tarsus
İçel (Mersin)
İskenderun
Cosenza
Crotone
Lefkáda
Nafpaktos
Thíva
Vólos
Lamía
Ikaría
Híos
Çeşme
Manisa
Turgutlu
Alaşehir
Egridir Gölü
Beyşehir Gölü
Isparta
Seydişehir
Antalya
Toros Dağları
Hatay
HALAB (Aleppo)
Lípari
Messina
Réggio di Calábria
IONIAN SEA
Pátra
Korinthos
Peloponnese
OLYMPIA
Pireás
ATHINA (Athens)
Ándros
Sámos
İZMIR (Smyrna)
Aydın
Denizli
Muğla
Burdur
Elmalı
Antalya Körfezi
Alanya
Anamur
Silifke
Al Lādhiqiyah
SYRIA
Hamāh
Etna
Stretto di Messina
Sparti
Nafplio
Kalámata
Kythira
Náxos
Íos
Bodrum
Fethiye
Rhodes (Greece)
Megísti (Greece)
Morphou
Famagusta
Nicosia
Larnaca
Tarābulus
Hims
Siracusa
C. Passero
Pílos
Milos
AEGEAN SEA
CYCLADES
Thíra
Dodecanese
Rhodes
CYPRUS
Troodos
Limassol
Paphos
LEBANON
BAYRŪT (Beirut)
DIMASHQ
Antikythira
Kríti
Chaniá
Iráklio
KNOSSOS
Sitía
Karpathos
Oros Psilóritis
MEDITERRANEAN SEA
Hefa
'Akko
ISRAEL
WEST BANK
AMMAN
TEL AVIV-YAFO
Jerusalem
Gaza
GAZA STRIP
Dead Sea
CYRENE
Darnah
Dumyât
Bûr Sa'id
El 'Arîsh
Al Baydā
Al Marj
Tubruq
El ISKANDARÎYA (Alexandria)
Damanhûr
El Mahalla el Kubra
El Mansûra
El Qantara
Qanâ es Suweis
Ismâ'îliya
Misrâtah
Banghāzī
Bardiyah
Salûm
Marsá Matrûh
El'Alamein
Tanta
Zagazig
El Suweis (Suez)
Es Sînâ'
LIBYA
Ajdābiyah
Cyrenaica
Munkhafed el Qattâra
EGYPT
El Gîza
EL QÂHIRA (Cairo)
El 'Aqabah
Surt
Khalij Surt
Marsa el Brega
Bardiyah
El Faiyûm
Beni Suef
G. of Aqaba

1:2 000 000

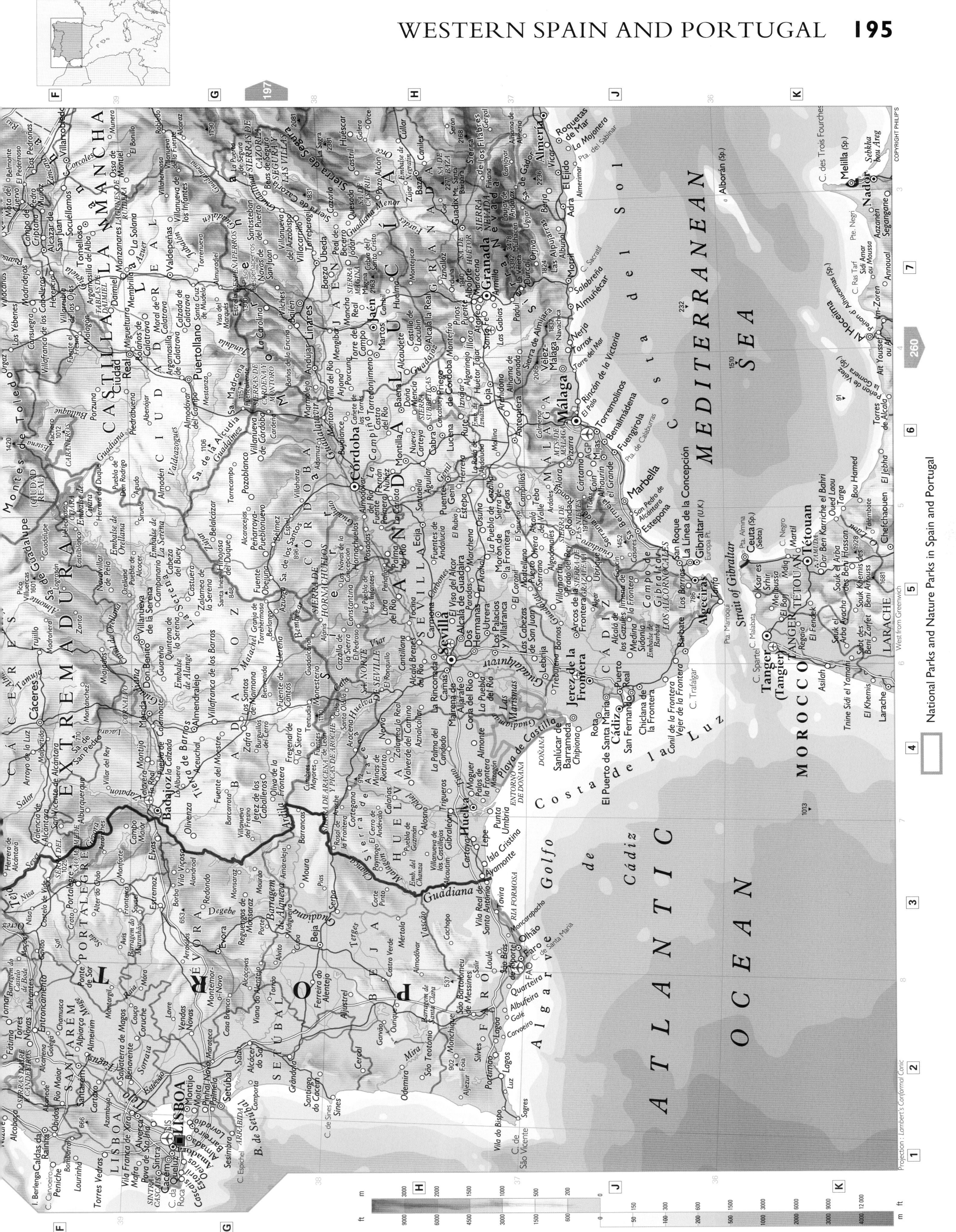

National Parks and Nature Parks in Spain and Portugal

Projection : Lambert's Conformal Conic

1:2 000 000

National Parks and Nature Parks in Spain

1:2 000 000

Projection : Lambert's Conformal Conic

East from Greenwich

Underlined towns give their name to the
administrative area in which they stand.

Administrative divisions in Croatia:

Brodsko-Posavska
Koprivničko-Križevačka
Krapinsko-Zagorska

4 Medimurska
6 Požeško-Slavonska
7 Varaždinska

8 Virovitičko-Podravska
10 Zagreba čka

National Parks and Nature Parks in Italy

Inter-entity boundaries as agreed
at the 1995 Dayton Peace Agreement

COPYRIGHT PHILIP'S

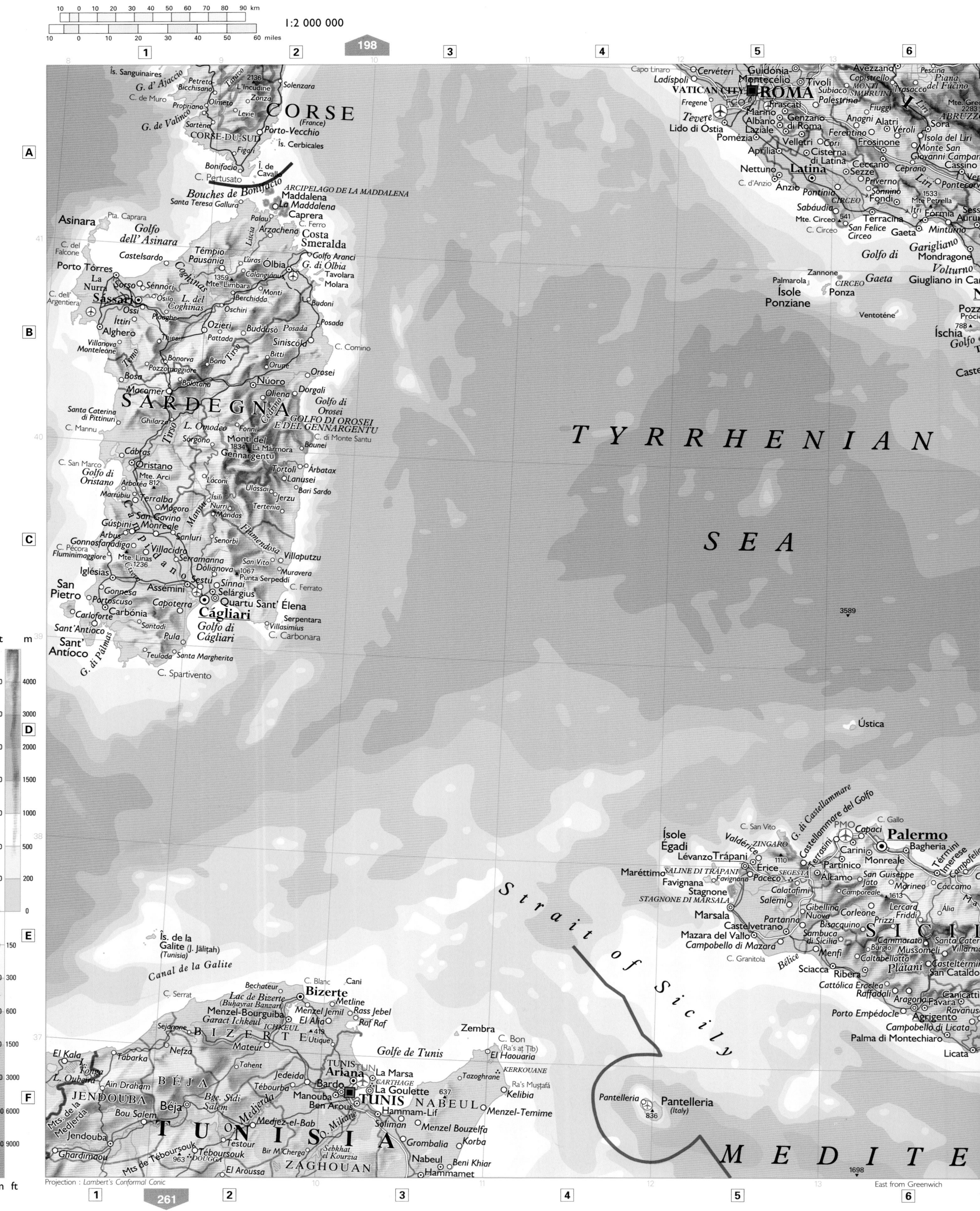

1:2 000 000

Projection : Lambert's Conformal Conic

East from Greenwich

National Parks and Nature Parks in Italy

Underlined towns give their name to the
administrative area in which they stand.

1 : 2 000 000

Projection : Lambert's Conformal Conic

East from Greenwich

- - - - Inter-entity boundaries as agreed
at the 1995 Dayton Peace Agreement

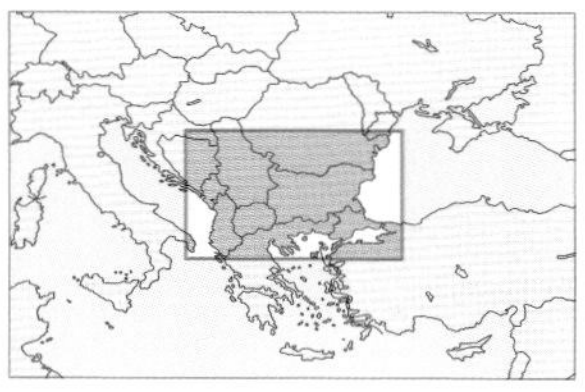

BLACK SEA

TURKEY

BULGARIA

MANIA

Valla hia

DELTA DUNĂREA

BUCUREŞTI
(Bucharest)

Ploieşti
Piteşti
Buzău
Brăila
Galaţi
Constanţa
Mangalia
Dobrich
Varna
Burgas
Shumen
Veliko Tŭrnovo
Gabrovo
Sliven
Stara Zagora
Plovdiv
Pazardzhik
Asenovgrad
Dimitrovgrad
Khaskovo
Edirne
Kırklareli
Lüleburgaz
Çorlu
Tekirdağ
İSTANBUL
Üsküdar
Kartal
Gebze
Kocaeli (İzmit)
BURSA
İnegöl
Çanakkale
Gökçeada
Limnos
Samothraki
Thasos

Marmara Denizi
(Sea of Marmara)

Çanakkale Boğazı (Dardanelles)

İstanbul Boğazı
(Bosporus)

Kamchiya
Aytoska Planina
Kotlenska Planina
Balkan
Udvoy Balkan
Sredna Gora

ANATOLIKI MAKEDONIA
RODOPI
EVROS
THRAKI
KAVALA

Sea of Thrace

Dunay (Dunărea) (Danube)

National Parks

Underlined towns give their name to the
administrative area in which they stand.

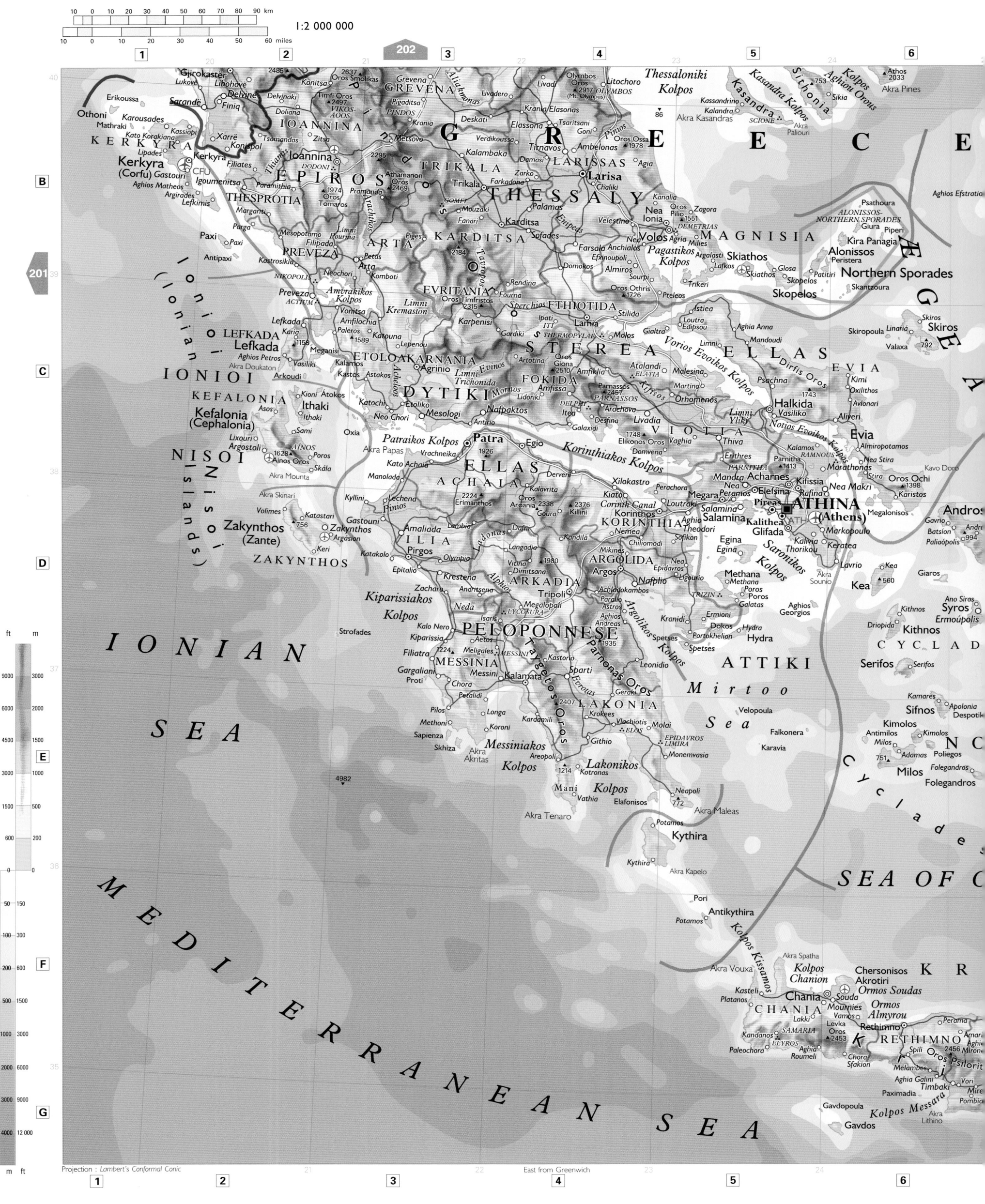

1:2 000 000

Projection : Lambert's Conformal Conic

East from Greenwich

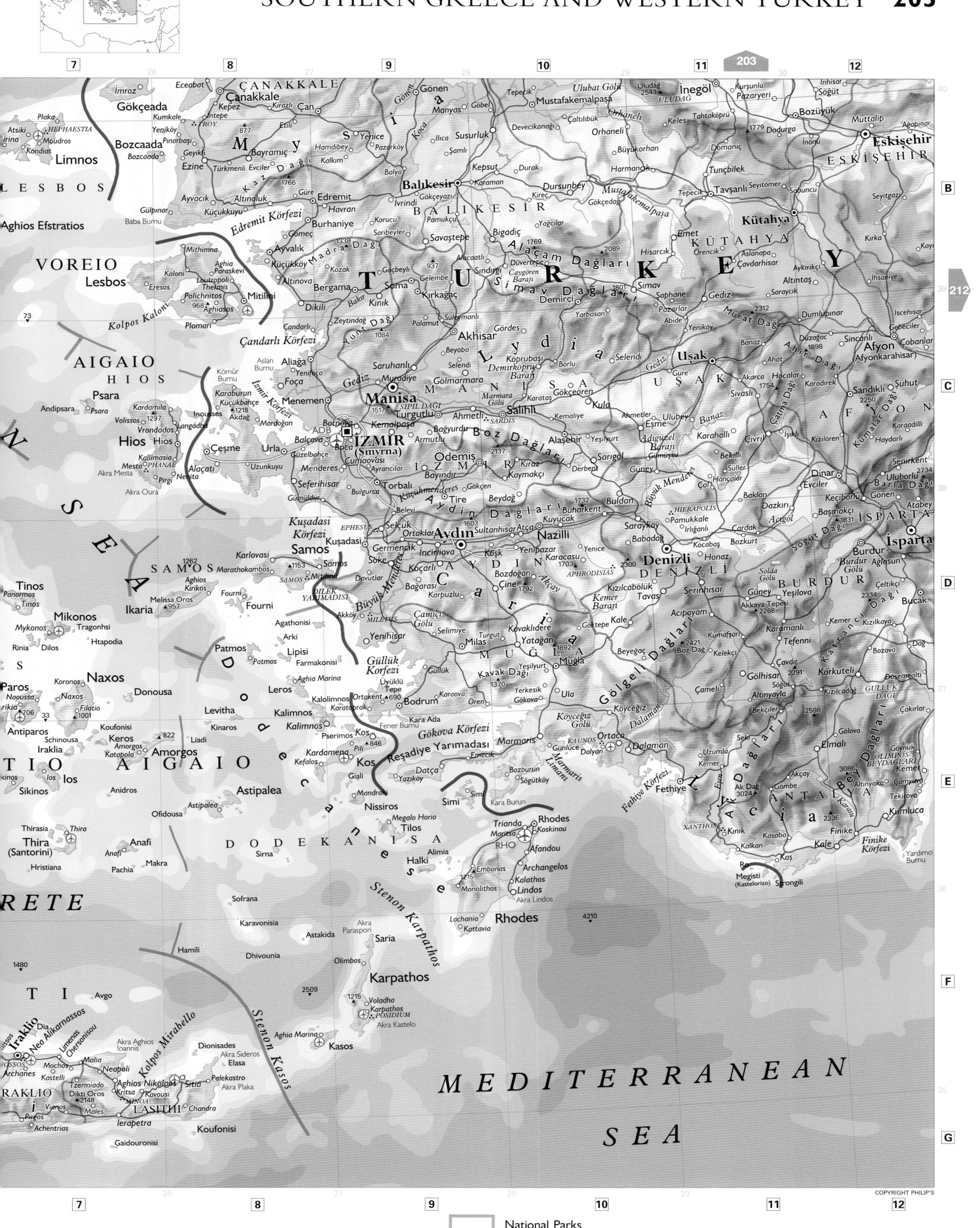

National Parks

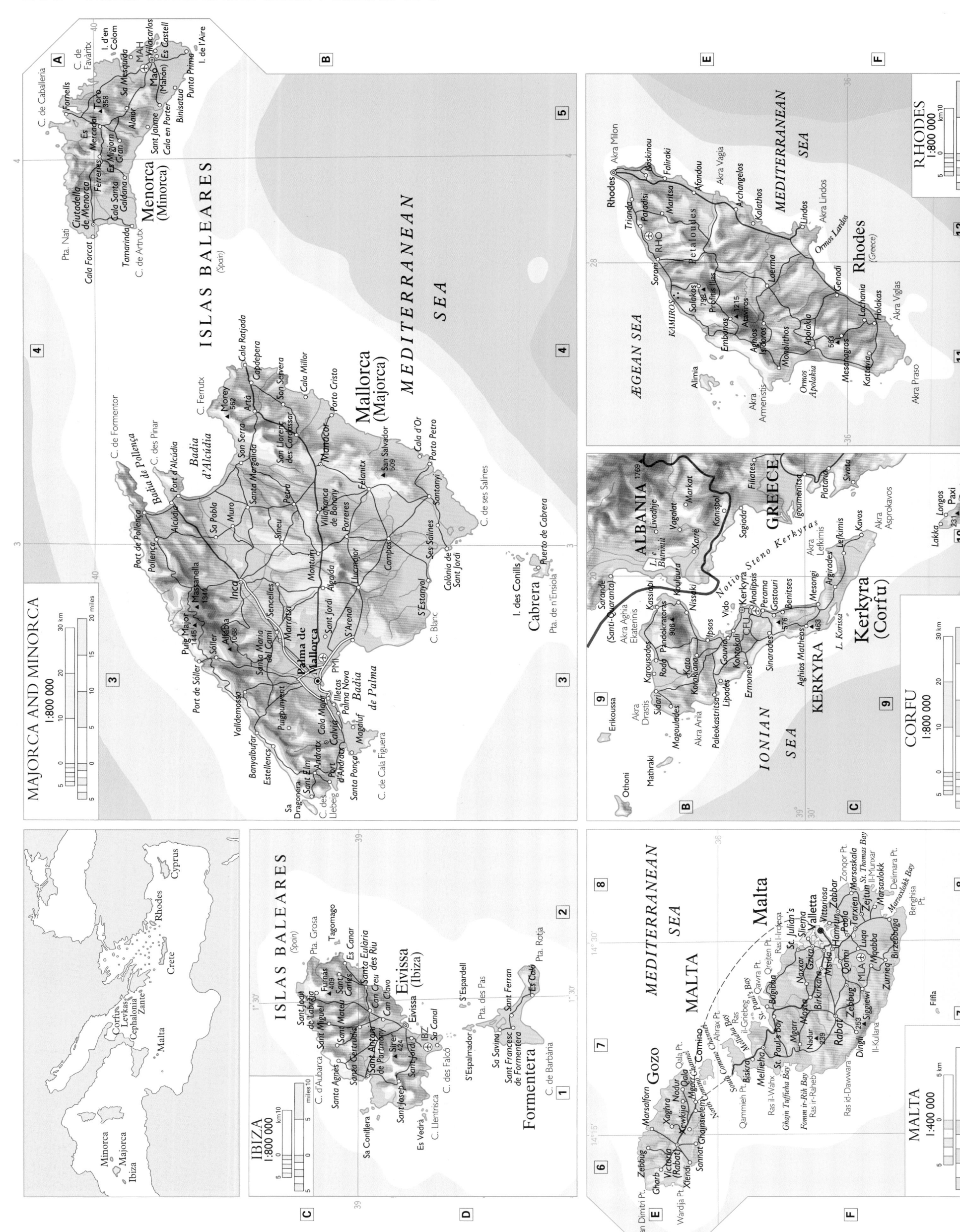

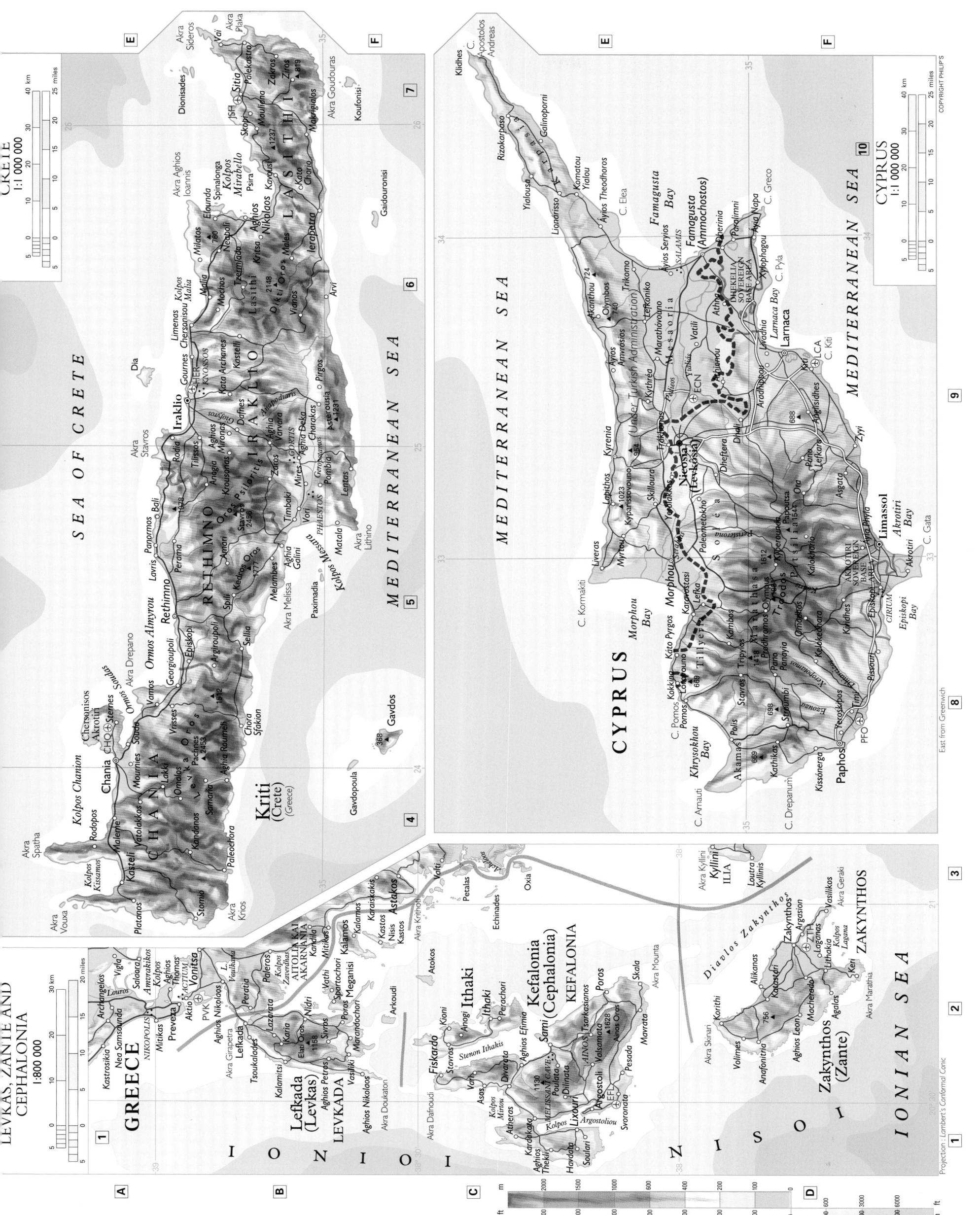

CRETE
1:1 000 000

Akra Sideros
Akra Plaka
Vai
Dionisades
Sitia
Palekastro
Skopi
Zakros
Kolpos Kavousi
Spinalonga
Elounda
Mirabello
Chrissi
Neapoli
Kritsa
Ziros
819
Milatos
Agios Nikolaos
1237
Skopi
Moutiana
L A S I T H I
Akra Agios
Ioannis
780
Tzermiado
Males
Akra Goudouras
Koufonisi
Limenas Chersonisou
Kolpos Dikti Oros
Malia
Mochos
2148
Ierapetra
Gournes
Kato Chorio
Arvi
Knossos
Kata Arhanes
Vianos
Iraklio
Kastelli
Radia
Anogia
I R A K L I O
Akra Stavros
1678
Aghios Mironas
Agia Varvara
Arkalochori
Dafnes
Zaros
1231
Charakas
Oros Psiloritis
Asterousia
Zaros
Timbaki
Agia Deka
Pombia
Tilissos
2456
Vori
GORTIS
Melambes
Spili
Kedros Oros
777
PHAESTOS
Lentas
Matala
Melissa
Akra Lithino
Agia Galini
Kolpos Mesaras
Paximadia

SEA OF CRETE

Dia

CHANIA
Akra Spatha
Akra Vouxa
Kolpos Kissamos
Rodopos
Kasteli
Malame
Platanos
Stomio
Akra Krios
Kandanos
Samaria
Omalos
Lakki
Mournies
Chania
Souda
Akrotiri
Mouries
Chersonisos
Vamos
Georgioupoli
Rethimno
Episkopi
Argiroupoli
Sellia
Chora Sfakion
Agia Roumeli
Pachnes
2453
L e v k a O r o s
R E T H I M N O
Perama
Spili
Amari
Lavris
Panormos
Bali
Vrisses
Vatolakos
Ormos Almyrou
Akra Drepano

Kriti
(Crete)
(Greece)

Gavdopoula
Gavdos
368

MEDITERRANEAN SEA

CYPRUS
1:1 000 000

C. Apostolos
Andreas
Klidhes
Rizokarpaso
Galinoporni
Komi Kebir
Yialousa
Komatou
Yialou
Liandrisso
Ayios
Theodoros
Famagusta
Bay
C. Elea
Ayios Seryios
SALAMIS
Famagusta
(Ammochostos)
Akanthou
724
Trikomo
Dherinia
Olympos
746
Marathóvouno
Vatili
Paralimni
Tekhrea
Ayia Napa
C. Greco
Kythrea
Yialias
Xylophagou
Nicosia
(Lefkosia)
ECN
DHEKELIA
SOVEREIGN
BASE AREA
Pyla
Dhiorios
Lapithos
Kyrenia
1023
Skilloura
Mora
C. Kormakiti
Morphou
Bay
Kyparissovouno
981
Paleometokho
Dhali
Pyroi
Larnaca
Kiti
LCA
C. Kiti
Morphou
Morphou
Karavostasi
Lefka
Dheftera
Athienou
Larnaca Bay
Liveras
Myrtou
Kato Pyrgos
Karavostasi
Peristerona
Kakopetria
Pano Panayia
Pedhoulas
1612
Kalo Chorio
Troodos
Khirokitia
Pera Oria
Paphos
C. Pomos
Pomos
Loukrounou
Staurós
669
M a s s i f
Olympos
1951
Tillyria
Kampos
T r o o d o s
Pano
Platres
Asgata
Zyyi
C. Drepanum
Kissónerga
698
Kathikas
669
Akamas
Pólis
Khrysokhou
Bay
C. Arnauti
C. Pomos
Kelokedhara
Omodhos
Kouklia
Episkopi
Kolossi
Limassol
Akrotiri
Bay
AKROTIRI
SOVEREIGN
BASE
CIRIUM
Episkopi
Bay
C. Gata

C Y P R U S

MEDITERRANEAN SEA

CYPRUS
1:1 000 000

COPYRIGHT PHILIP'S

East from Greenwich

LEVKAS, ZANTE AND
CEPHALONIA
1:800 000

GREECE

Kastrosikia
Archangelos
Vigla
Nea Samsounda
Louros
NIKOPOLIS
Preveza
Aktio
PVK
Vonitsa
ACTIUM
Salaora
Kolpos
Thomas
Amfilochia
Vouliagme
AITOLIA KAI
AKARNANIA
Paleros
Loutraki
Zaverdhas
Peratia
Aghios Nikolaos
Mitikas
Astakos
Lefkada
(Levkas)
Lefkada
Karia
Nidri
Sivros
1158
Elati Oros
Spartochori
Poros Meganisi
Marandochori
Vasiliki
Kalamos
Nisis
Kastos
Kastos
Aghios Petros
Kardákis
Vathi
Arkoudi
Akra Krithoni
Oxia
Petalas
Echinades
Akra Mounta

Fiskardo
Stavros
Anogi
Ithaki
Kioni
Perachori
Sami
(Cephalonia)
Kefalonia
(Cephalonia)
KEFALONIA
Divarata
AINOS
1628
Aghios Efimia
Tsarkasianos
1130
Valsamata
Poros
Skala
Argostoli
Lixouri
Dilinata
Pesada
Mavrata
Argostoliou
Kolpos Mironu
Athiras
Kolpos
Karakandia
Aghios
Theklia
Havdata
Soulari
LEVKADA

Akra Kyllini
ILIA
Loutra
Kyllinis
Diavlos Zakynthos
Akra Skinari
Korithi
ZTI
Zakynthos
Alikanas
Lithakia
Kolpos
Laganas
Lagana
ZAKYNTHOS
Zakynthos
(Zante)
Volimes
Anafonitria
756
Macherado
Vasilikos
Akra Geraki
Aghios Leon
Argasion
Keri
Agalas
Akra Marathia

IONIAN
SEA

I O N I O I   N I S O I

Projection: Lambert's Conformal Conic

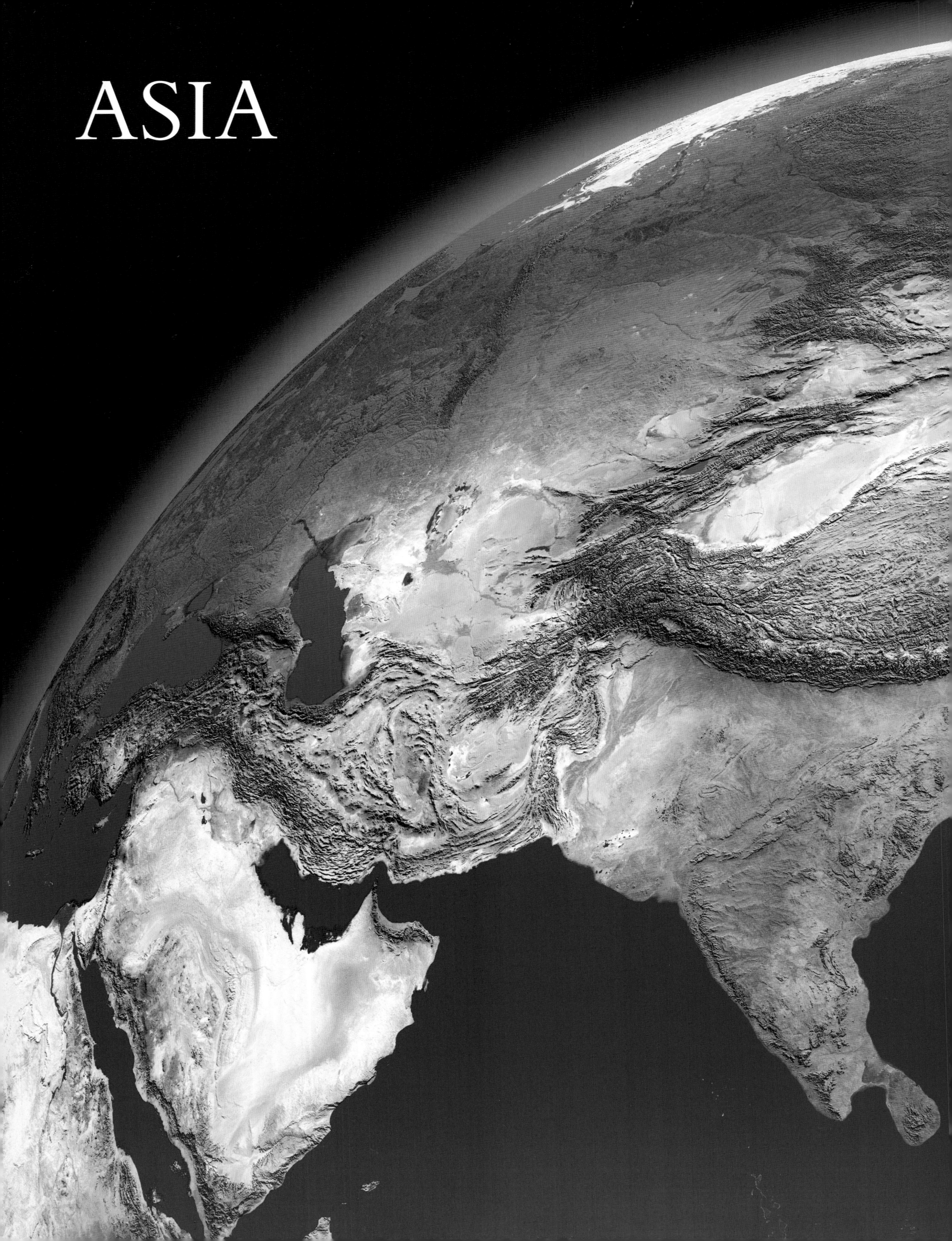

ASIA

100 0 200 400 600 800 1000 1200 1400 km

100 0 200 400 600 800 1000 miles

1:40 000 000

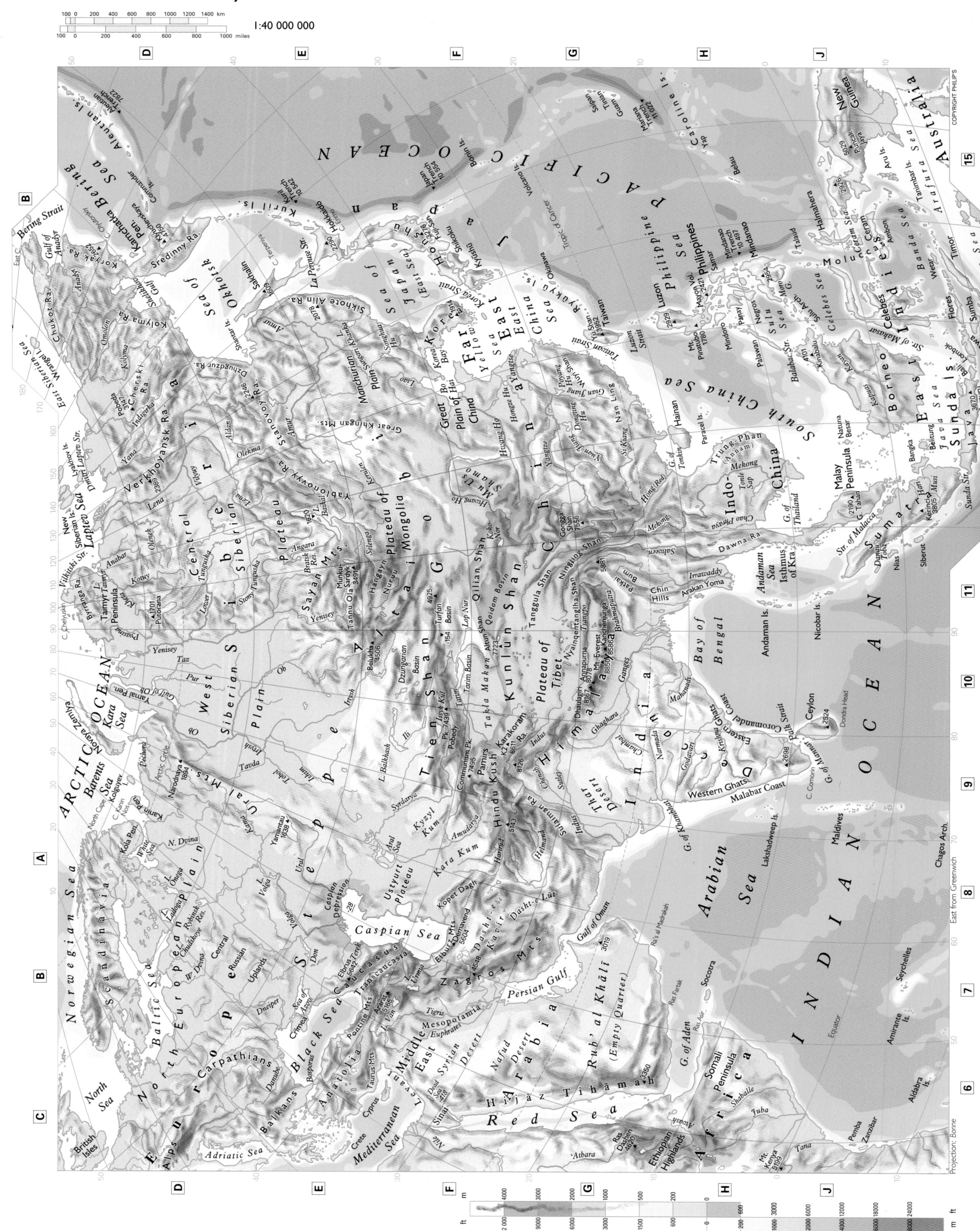

Projection: Bonne

East from Greenwich

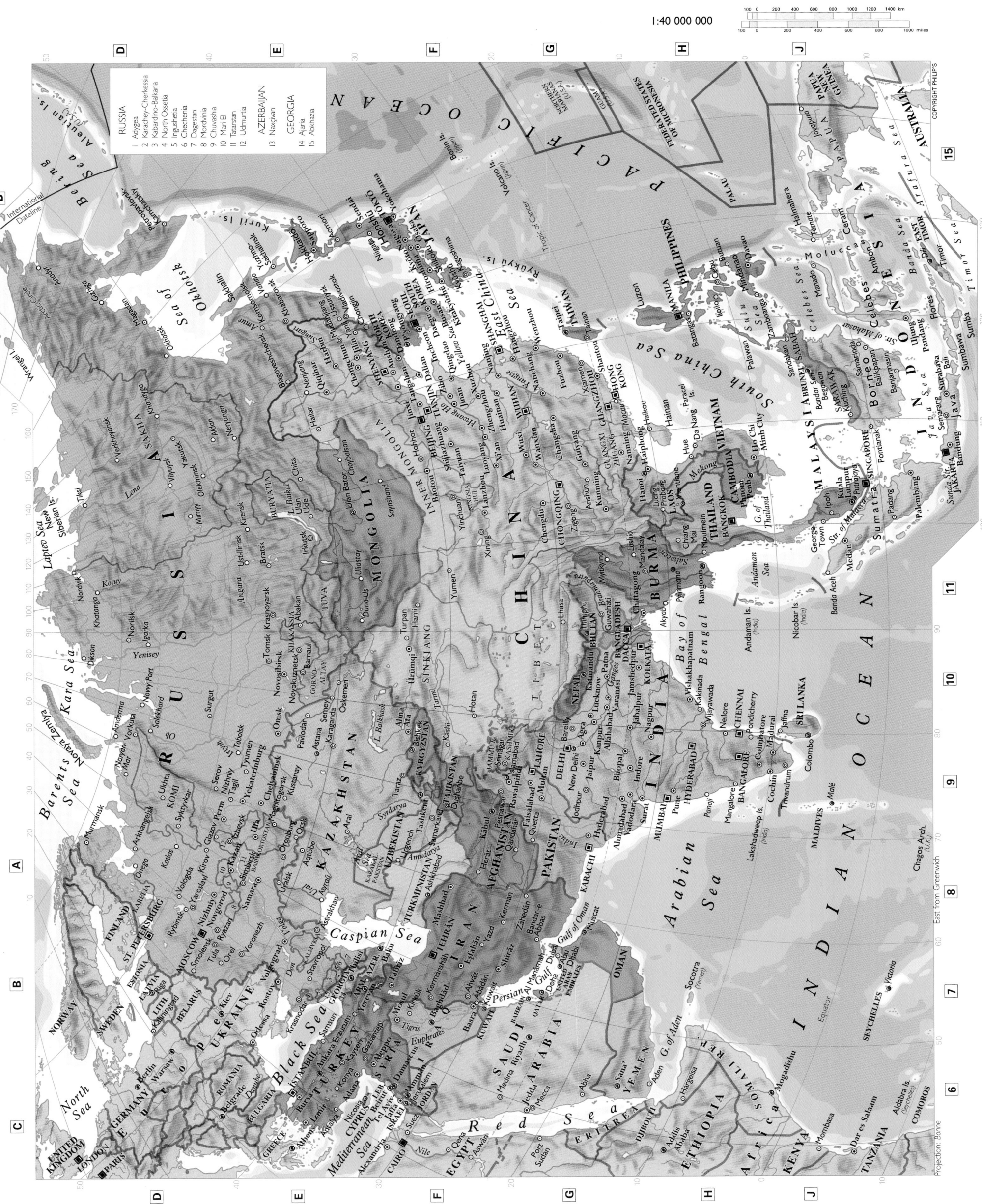

1: 4 000 000

50   0   25   50   75   100   125   150   175 km

50   0   25   50   75   100   125 miles

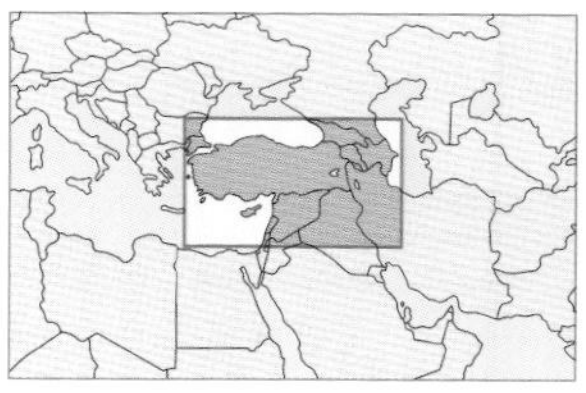

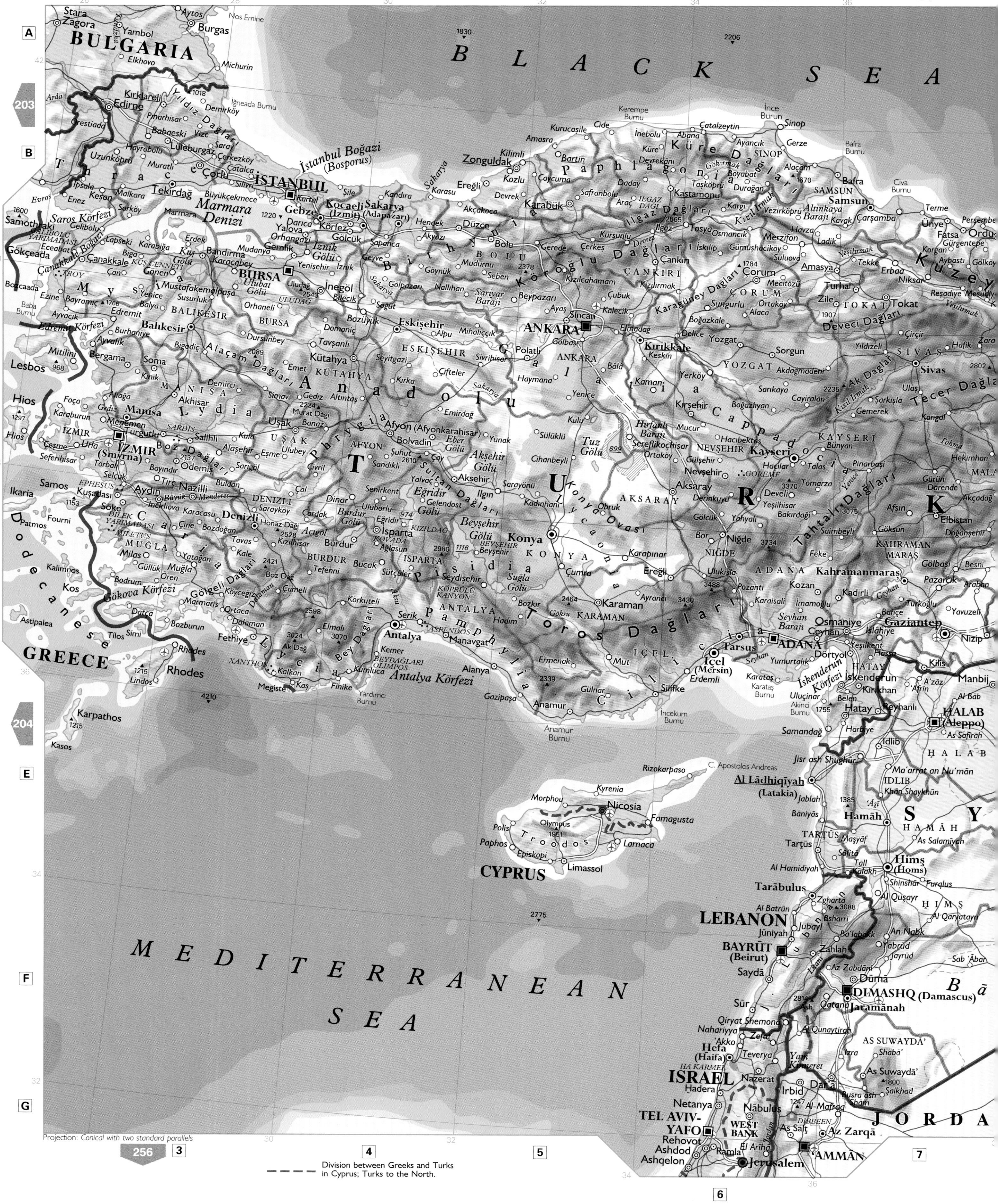

189

BULGARIA

B L A C K   S E A

Stara Zagora
Yambol
Aytos
Burgas
Nos Emine
Michurin
Elkhovo
Arda
Kırklareli
Edirne
Demirköy
İğneada Burnu
Orestiada
Pınarhisar
Babaeski
Vize
Saray
Çerkezköy
Uzunköprü
Murath
Çatalca
İstanbul Boğazı (Bosporus)
Hayrabolu
Lüleburgaz
Çorlu
İSTANBUL
Keremçe Burnu
Kurucaşile
Cide
İnebolu
Abana
Çatalzeytin
Sinop
İnce Burun
Amasra
Küre
Ayancık
Gerze
Kilimli
Devrekâni
Bartın
Kastamonu
Bafra Burnu
SAMSUN
Samsun
Terme
Ünye
Fatsa
Ordu

Tekirdağ
Büyükçekmece
Kartal
Gebze
Darıca
Kocaeli (İzmit)
Sakarya (Adapazarı)
Sile
Kandıra
Karasu
Zonguldak
Ereğli
Akçakoca
Kozlu
Çaycuma
Düzce
Devrek
Karabük
Safranbolu
Araç
İLGAZ DAĞI
Tosya
Osmancık
Vezirköprü
Merzifon
Kargı
Altınkaya Barajı
Kavak
Çarşamba
Persembe
Gürgentepe
Korgan
Aybastı
Gölköy

Malkara
Şarköy
Marmara
Erdek
Bandırma
Mudanya
Yalova
Körfez
Orhangazi
Gemlik
İznik Gölü
Geyve
Akyazı
Hendek
Bolu
Gerede
Çerkeş
Çankırı
Kızılcahamam
Çubuk
Sungurlu
Alaca
ÇORUM
Mecitözü
Amasya
Turhal
Zile
Erbaa
Niksar
Tekke
Reşadiye
Mesudiye

Keşan
Enez
Saros Körfezi
Gelibolu
Lapseki
Karabiga
Gönen
Manyas Gölü
KUŞ CENNETİ
Karacabey
Yenişehir
İnegöl
Bozüyük
Bilecik
Söğüt
Nallıhan
Beypazarı
Ayaş
Sincan
ANKARA
Kırıkkale
Keskin
Yozgat
Sorgun
Yıldızeli
SİVAS
Sivas
Hafik

Gökçeada
Çanakkale
Çan
Mustafakemalpaşa
Ulubat Gölü
BURSA
Uludağ
ULUDAĞ
Domaniç
Tavşanlı
Eskişehir
Alpu
Mihalıççık
Sivrihisar
Polatlı
Gölbaşı
Elmadağ
Bâlâ
Kaman
Yerköy
Kırşehir
Boğazlıyan
Çayıralan
Gemerek
Şarkışla
Kangal
TECER DAĞLARI

Bozcaada
Ezine
Bayramiç
Edremit
Balya
Susurluk
BALIKESİR
Dursunbey
Emet
Kütahya
KÜTAHYA
Seyitgazi
Çifteler
ESKİŞEHİR
Kırka
Sakarya
Yunak
Cihanbeyli
Tuz Gölü
Şereflikoçhisar
Hacıbektaş
NEVŞEHİR
Nevşehir
GÖREME
Gülşehir
Talas
KAYSERİ
Kayseri
Pınarbaşı
Hekimhan
Gürün
Darende
MALA

Edremit Körfezi
Ayvacık
Burhaniye
Bergama
Soma
Kınık
ALAÇAM DAĞLARI
Demirci
Simav
Gediz
Banaz
Murat Dağı
Uşak
UŞAK
Banaz
Afyon (Afyonkarahisar)
Bolvadin
Emirdağ
AFYON
Sandıklı
Şuhut
Akşehir Gölü
Akşehir
Ilgın
Sarayönü
Kadınhanı
AKSARAY
Aksaray
Derinkuyu
Yeşilhisar
Develi
Tomarza
Afşin
Elbistan
Doğanşehir
KAHRAMAN-MARAŞ

Mitilini
Lesbos
Hios
Foça
Karaburun
Manisa
Menemen
MANISA
Akhisar
Salihli
Alaşehir
Eşme
Uşak
Sivrihisar
Kütahya
Kula
Ulubey
Çivril
Dinar
Senirkent
Yalvaç
Gelendost
Eğirdir
Beyşehir Gölü
Cihanbeyli
Obruk
Kulu
KONYA
Konya
Karapınar
Ereğli
Bor
Niğde
NİĞDE
Ulukışla
Pozantı
ADANA
Kozan
Kadirli
İmamoğlu
Feke
Saimbeyli
Göksun
KAHRAMANMARAŞ
Pazarcık
Besni
Araban
Yavuzeli

İZMİR (Smyrna)
Çeşme
Urla
Seferihisar
Torbalı
Ödemiş
Tire
Bayındır
Nazilli
Aydın
AYDIN
Denizli
DENİZLİ
Sarayköy
Çal
Çardak
Acıpayam
Burdur
BURDUR
Tefenni
Bucak
Sütçüler
Isparta
ISPARTA
Eğirdir Gölü
Beyşehir
Seydişehir
Bozkır
Hadim
Karaman
KARAMAN
Mut
Ermenek
Gülnar
Silifke
Erdemli
İçel (Mersin)
İÇEL
Tarsus
Seyhan Barajı
Yumurtalık
Dörtyol
İskenderun
İskenderun Körfezi
HATAY
Hatay
Reyhanlı
Kırıkhan
Belen
Kilis
Gaziantep
Nizip

Samos
Kuşadası
DİLEK YARIMADASI
EPHESUS
Söke
MILETUS
İncirliova
Karacasu
Bozdoğan
Çine
MUĞLA
Milas
Yatağan
Muğla
Ören
Bodrum
Güllük
GÖKOVA KÖRFEZİ
Köyceğiz
Ortaca
Dalaman
Fethiye
Kalkan
Kaş
Finike
Kumluca
Kemer
Antalya
ANTALYA
Manavgat
Serik
Side
ASPENDOS
Alanya
Gazipaşa
Anamur
Anamur Burnu
İncekum Burnu

GREECE

Rhodes
Lindos

DODECANESE

M E D I T E R R A N E A N   S E A

CYPRUS
Morphou
Kyrenia
Nicosia
Famagusta
Polis
Paphos
Troodos
Olympus 1951
Episkopi
Limassol
Larnaca
Rizokarpaso
C. Apostolos Andreas

LEBANON
BAYRÛT (Beirut)
Ṣaydā
Ṣūr
Jûniyah
Jubayl
Zahlah
Baʿlabak

SYRIA
Al Lādhiqīyah (Latakia)
Jablah
Bāniyās
Hamāh
HAMĀH
Ṭarṭūs
TARTŪS
Ḥimṣ (Homs)
ḤIMṢ
HALAB (Aleppo)
IDLIB
Idlib
Maʿarrat an Nuʿmān

DIMASHQ (Damascus)
Dūmā
AS SUWAYDĀʾ
As Suwaydāʾ

ISRAEL
Hefa (Haifa)
Nazerat
HA KARMEL
Hadera
Netanya
TEL AVIV-YAFO
Rehovot
Ashdod
Ashqelon
WEST BANK
Jerusalem
AMMAN
JORDAN

Projection: Conical with two standard parallels

256

Division between Greeks and Turks
in Cyprus; Turks to the North.

203
204

191

247

246

CASPIAN SEA

Underlined towns give their name
to the administrative area in which they stand

COPYRIGHT PHILIP'S

East from Greenwich

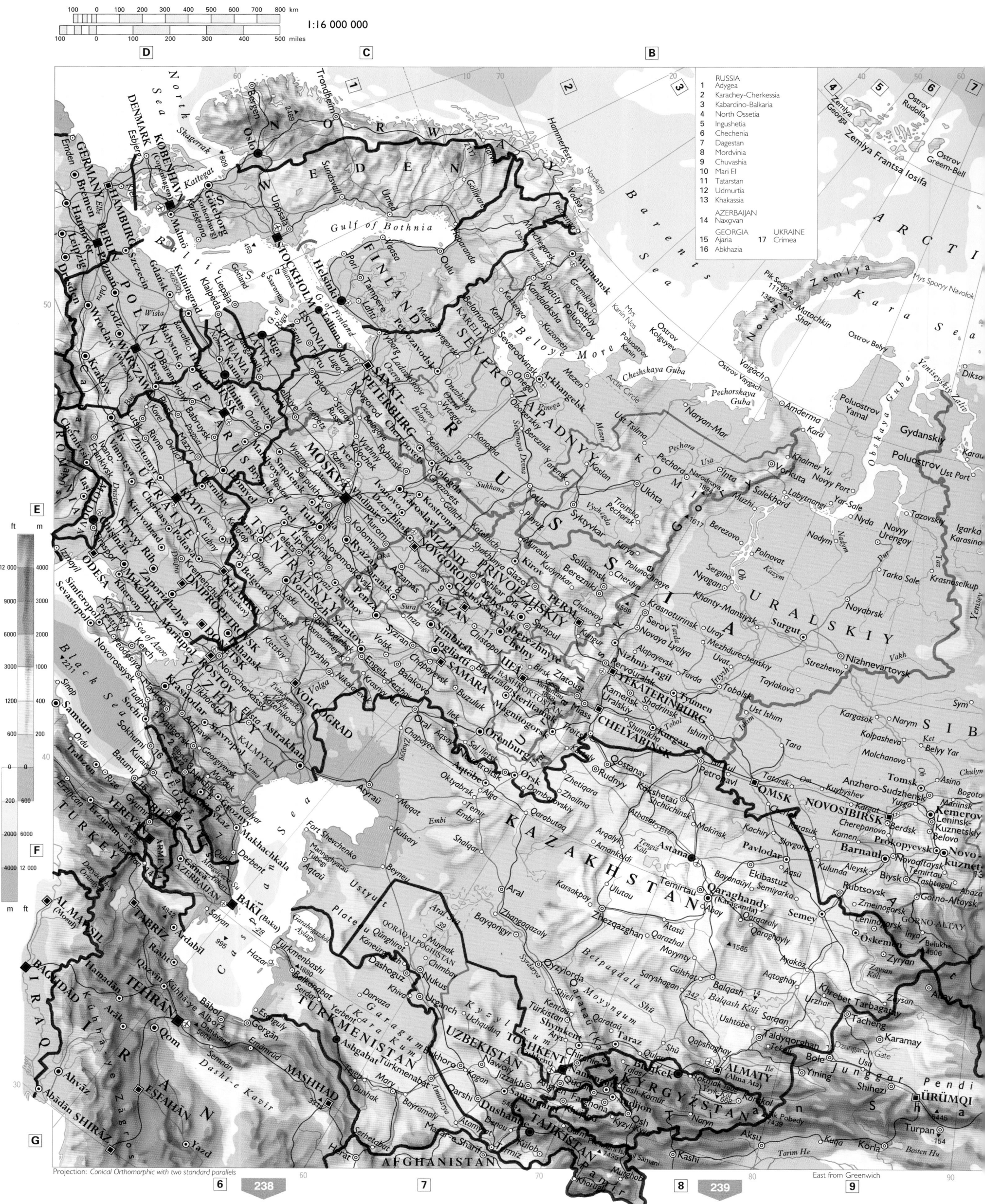

RUSSIA
1 Adygea
2 Karachey-Cherkessia
3 Kabardino-Balkaria
4 North Ossetia
5 Ingushetia
6 Chechenia
7 Dagestan
8 Mordvinia
9 Chuvashia
10 Mari El
11 Tatarstan
12 Udmurtia
13 Khakassia

AZERBAIJAN
14 Naxçivan

GEORGIA   UKRAINE
15 Ajaria   17 Crimea
16 Abkhazia

Projection: Conical Orthomorphic with two standard parallels

East from Greenwich

A   150   B   C

8 9 10 11 12 13 14 15 16 17 18 19

ARCTIC OCEAN

Laptev Sea

East Siberian Sea

Bering Sea

Severnaya Zemlya

Ostrov Shmidta
Ostrov Komsomolets
Ostrov Pioner
Ostrov Oktyabrskoy Revolyutsii
Ostrov Bolshevik

Mys Arkticheskiy
Proliv Vilkitskogo
Mys Chelyuskin

Poluostrov Taymyr
Gory Byrranga
Oz. Taymyr
Nordvik

Novosibirskiye Ostrova
Ostrov Belkovskiy
Ostrov Kotelnyy
Ostrov Stolbovoy
Lyakhovskiye Ostrova
Ostrov Malyy Lyakhovskiy
Ostrov Bolshoy Lyakhovskiy

Ostrov Bennetta
Ostrova Delonga
Ostrov Zhokhova

Ostrov Genriyetty
Ostrov Znamenty

Ostrov Vrangelya

Ostrova Medvezhi
Ostrov Ayon

Mys Dezhneva (East C.)
St. Lawrence I. (U.S.A.)

Chukchi Sea

Koryakskoye Nagorye
Chukotskoye Nagorye
Anadyrskiy Zaliv
Anadyr
Pevek

Sredinnyy Khrebet
Poluostrov Kamchatka
Petropavlovsk-Kamchatskiy

Kolymskoye Nagorye

Sea of Okhotsk

Khrebet Cherskogo
Verkhoyanskiy Khrebet

Norilsk
Dudinka
Turukhansk

R U S S I A

Yakutsk
Vilyuysk
Olekminsk
Lensk
Mirnyy
Vitim

Lena
Vilyuy
Aldan

Magadan
Ust-Omchug

Sakhalin
Yuzhno-Sakhalinsk
Aleksandrovsk-Sakhalinskiy

Khabarovsk
Komsomolsk
Birobidzhan
Sikhote Alin
Blagoveshchensk
Skovorodino

Krasnoyarsk
Achinsk
Kansk
Yeniseysk
Bratsk
Ust-Ilimsk
Tayshet
Nizhneudinsk
Tulun
Zima

Irkutsk
Angarsk
Ulan Ude
Chita

Zapadnyy Sayan
Vostochnyy Sayan
Abakan
Minusinsk

TUVA
Kyzyl

Sea of Japan (East Sea)

Hokkaidō
SAPPORO
Hakodate
Honshū

Kurilskiye Ostrova

M O N G O L I A
Ulaanbaatar
Hentiyn Nuruu
Hangayn Nuruu
Choybalsan
Ondörhaan
Uliastay
Altay
Tsetserleg

Gobi

C H I N A

BEIJING
BAOTOU Hohhot Zhangjiakou
Chengde
SHENYANG
JINXI ANSHAN
CHIFENG
CHANGCHUN
JILIN
HARBIN
QIQIHAR
DAQING
Yichun
Jiamusi
Jixi
Mudanjiang
Dong bei (Manchuria)
Da Hinggai Ling
Hailar
Manzhouli
Hulun Nur

NORTH KOREA
PYŏNGYANG
Nampo
Hamhŭng
Wŏnsan
Ch'ŏngjin
Kimch'aek

SOUTH KOREA
SEOUL
INCHEON
DAEJEON
DAEGU
BUSAN
GWANGJU

DALIAN
Dandong
Dalian

JAPAN
KYOTO
OSAKA
KOBE
Kanazawa
Toyama
Niigata
Akita
Aomori
Hachinohe

Vladivostok
Nakhodka
Ussuriysk
Artem

10   218   11   219   12   13   14

COPYRIGHT PHILIP'S

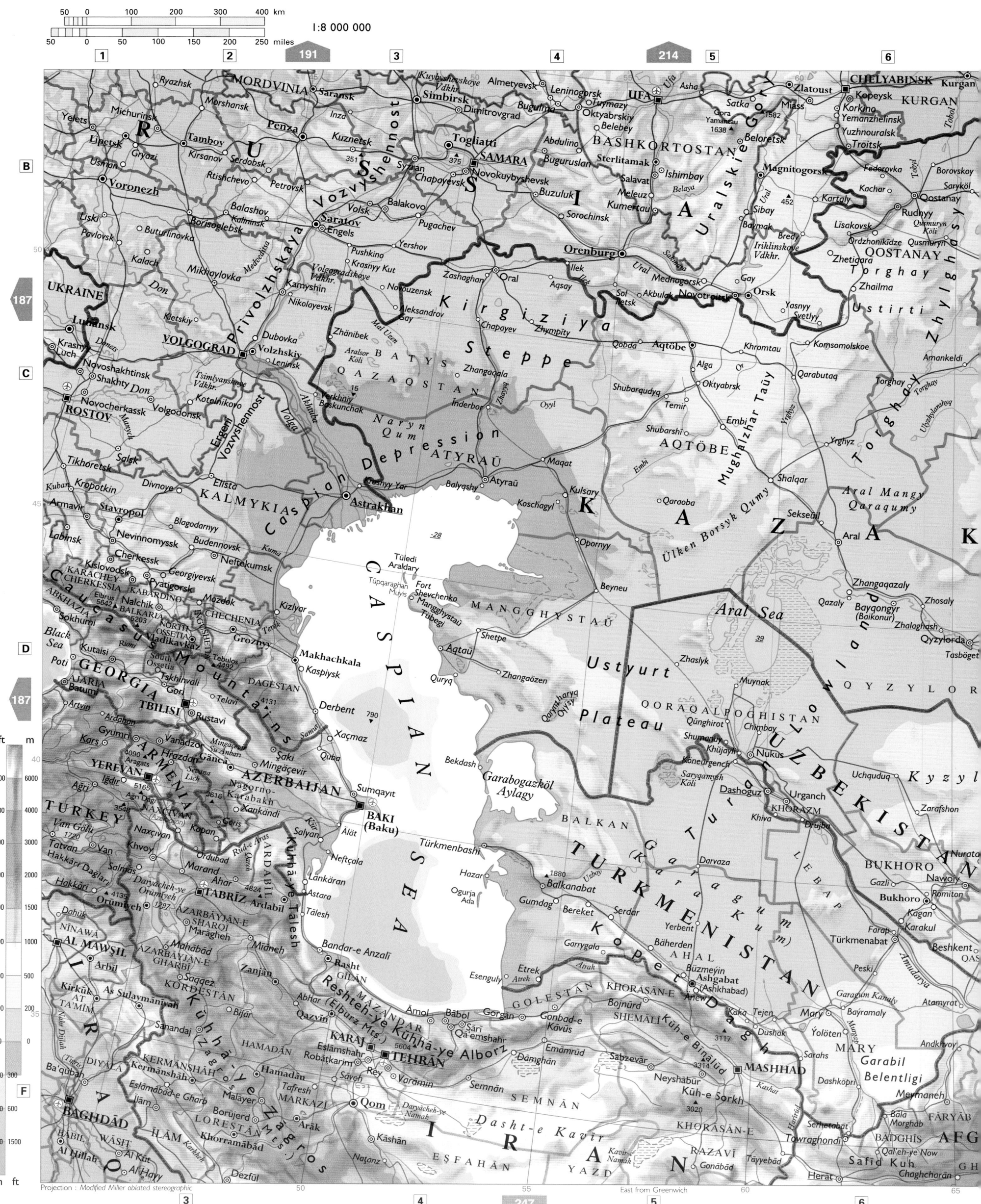

Projection : Modified Miller oblated stereographic

East from Greenwich

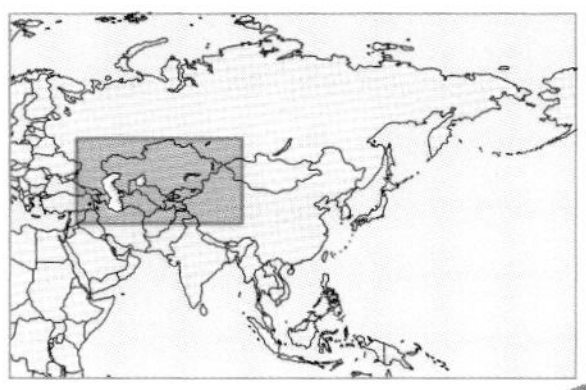

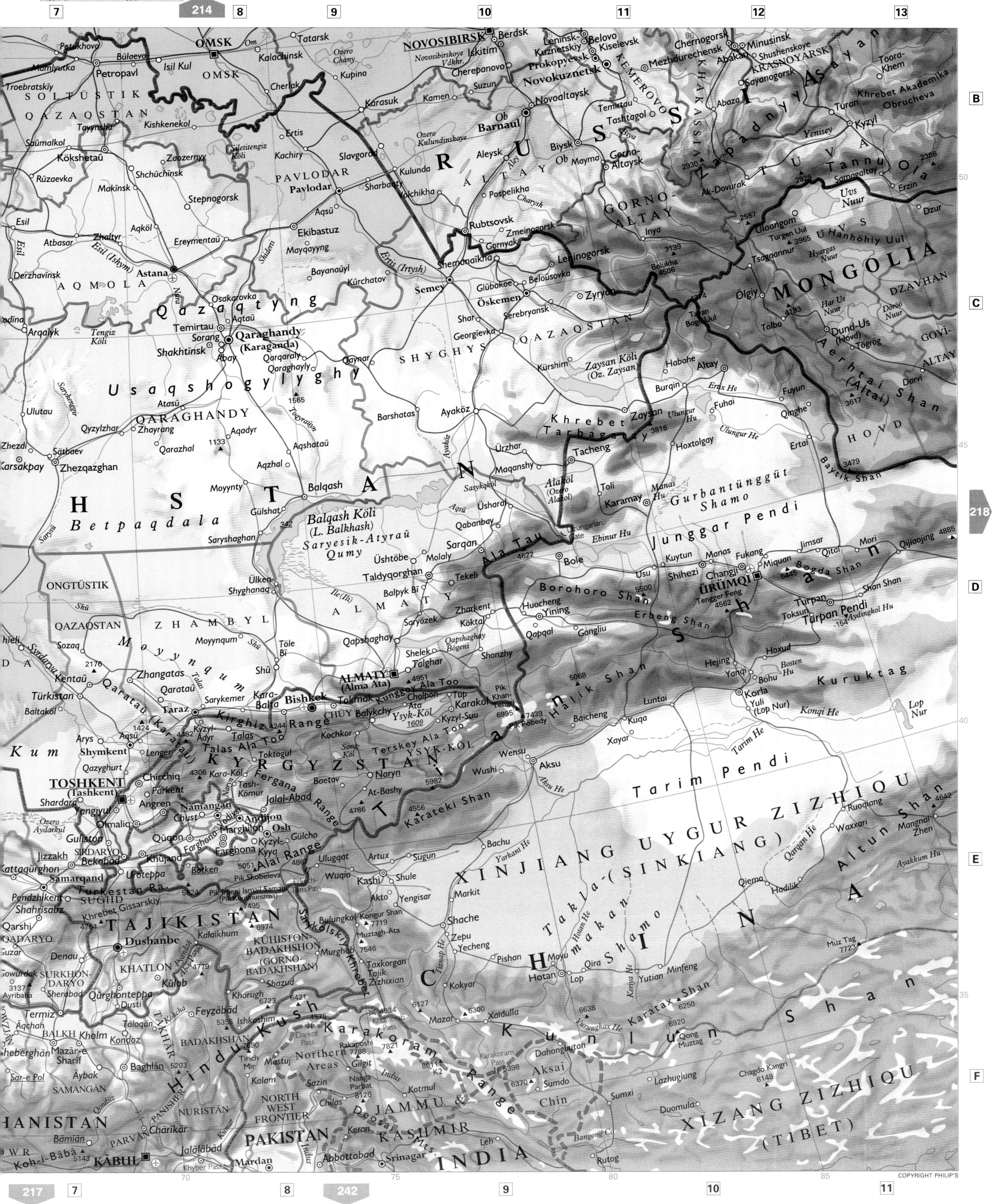

214 · 7 · 8 · 9 · 10 · 11 · 12 · 13

Countries, regions and major labels:

RUSSIA · MONGOLIA · KAZAKHSTAN · KYRGYZSTAN · TAJIKISTAN · PAKISTAN · INDIA · AFGHANISTAN

SOLTÜSTIK QAZAQSTAN · PAVLODAR · AQMOLA · QARAGHANDY · ONGTÜSTIK QAZAQSTAN · ZHAMBYL · ALMATY · SHYGHYS QAZAQSTAN · GORNO-ALTAY · TUVA · DZAVHAN · GOVI-ALTAY · HOVD

XINJIANG UYGUR ZIZHIQU (SINKIANG) · XIZANG ZIZHIQU (TIBET) · CHINA

SIRDARYO · SUGHD · KHATLON · SURKHON-DARYO · QADARYO · SAMANGĀN · TAKHĀR · BADAKHSHAN · KŪHISTON-BADAKHSHON (GORNO-BADAKHSHON) · NURISTĀN · NORTH WEST FRONTIER · NORTHERN AREAS · JAMMU & KASHMIR · PARVAN

Cities and towns:

OMSK · NOVOSIBIRSK · KEMEROVO · KRASNOYARSK · Astana · Qaraghandy (Karaganda) · Semey · Öskemen · Pavlodar · Barnaul · Novokuznetsk · Prokopyevsk · Abakan · Petropavl · Kökshetaū · Temirtaū · Almaty (Alma Ata) · Bishkek · TOSHKENT (Tashkent) · Dushanbe · Samarqand · Shymkent · Taraz · Türkistan · ÜRÜMQI · KĀBUL · Mardan · Srinagar

Physical features:

Ob · Ertis (Irtysh) · Ertis (Irtysh) · Yenisey · Tengiz Köli · Balqash Köli (L. Balkhash) · Zaysan Köli (Oz. Zaysan) · Ysyk-Köl · Uvs Nuur · Lop Nur (Lop Nur) · Betpaqdala · Saryesik-Atyraū Qumy · Moyynqum · Gurbantünggüt Shamo · Junggar Pendi · Tarim Pendi · Turpan Pendi · Takla-Makan (Taklamakan) Shamo · Kuruktag · Tien Shan · Altai Shan · Altyn Shan · Kunlun Shan · Karakoram Range · Hindu Kush · Alai Range · Fergana · Tarbagatay · Khrebet Zaysan · Borohoro Shan · Bogda Shan · Halik Shan

Underlined towns give their name to the administrative area in which they stand.

COPYRIGHT PHILIP'S

1:12 000 000

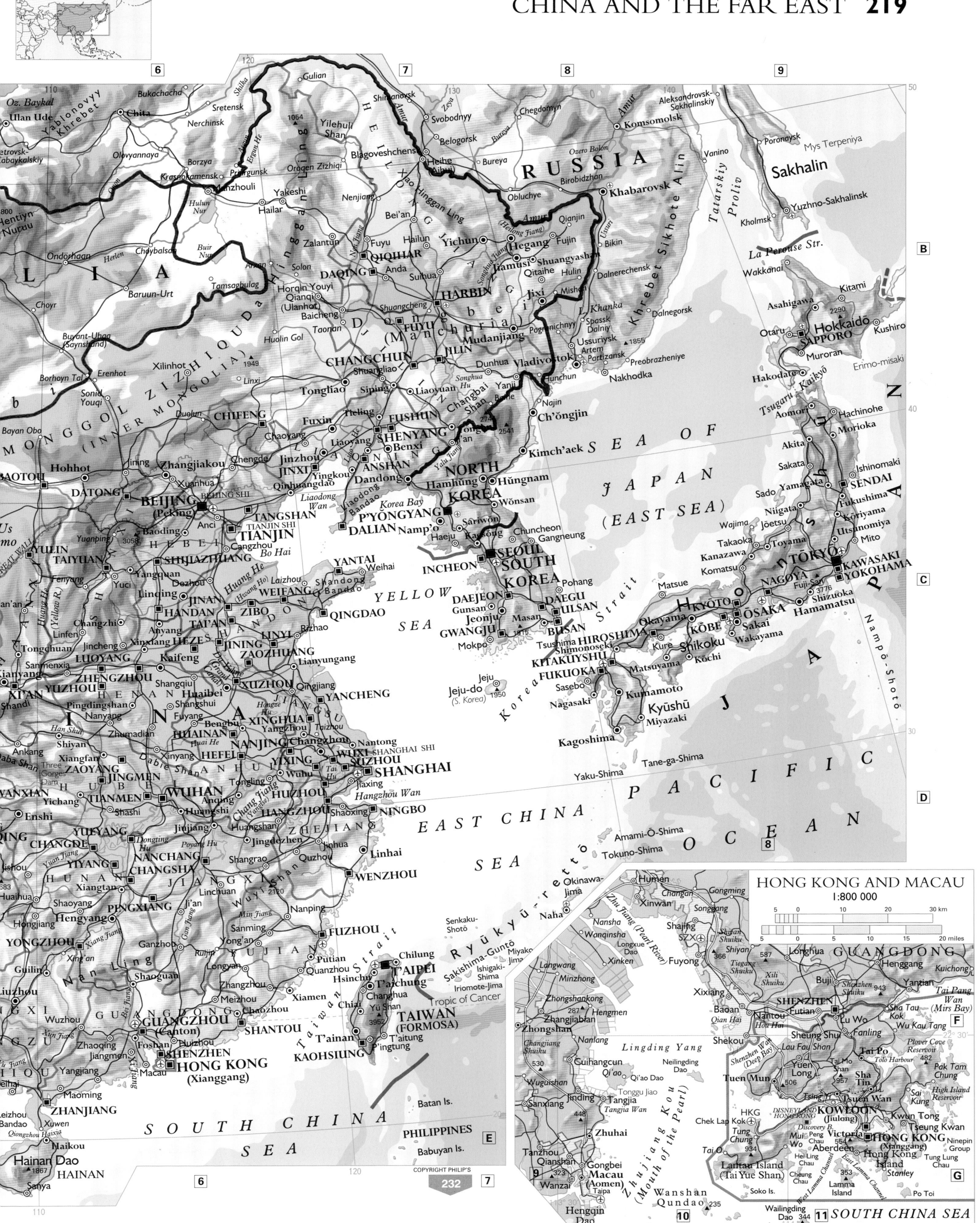

50 0 25 50 75 100 125 150 175 km
50 0 25 50 75 100 125 miles

1:4 000 000

B C D E F

12
11
10
9
8 219
7
6
5

SEA OF OKHOTSK

Sakhalin
(Russia)

La Perouse Strait
(Sōya-Kaikyō)

Ostrov Moneron
(Russia)

Ostrov Kunashir

Wakkanai
RISHIRI-
REBUN-
SAROBETSU

Shiretoko-Misaki

Abashiri
Abashiri-Wan

Nemuro
Nosappu-Misaki

Kushiro

HOKKAIDŌ

SAPPORO
Otaru
Ebetsu
Tomakomai
SHIKOTSU-
TOYA

Ishikari-Wan
(Otaru-Wan)

Kitami-Sammyaku

Hakodate
Muroran
Uchiura-
Wan

Ō-Shima
Okushiri-Tō

RUSSIA

CHINA

HEILONG-
JIANG

Songhua Jiang

Jiamusi
Shuangyashan
Jixi

Lake
Khanka

JILIN

Vladivostok
Ussuriysk
Nakhodka

Zaliv
Petra Velikogo

NORTH
KOREA

Ch'ŏngjin

Najin

SEA
OF
JAPAN
(EAST SEA)

Yamato
Rise

TŌHOKU
HONSHŪ
CHŪBU

Aomori
Hachinohe
Morioka
Akita
SENDAI
Niigata
Sado

RIKUCHŪ-
KAIGAN

A B C 227 D E

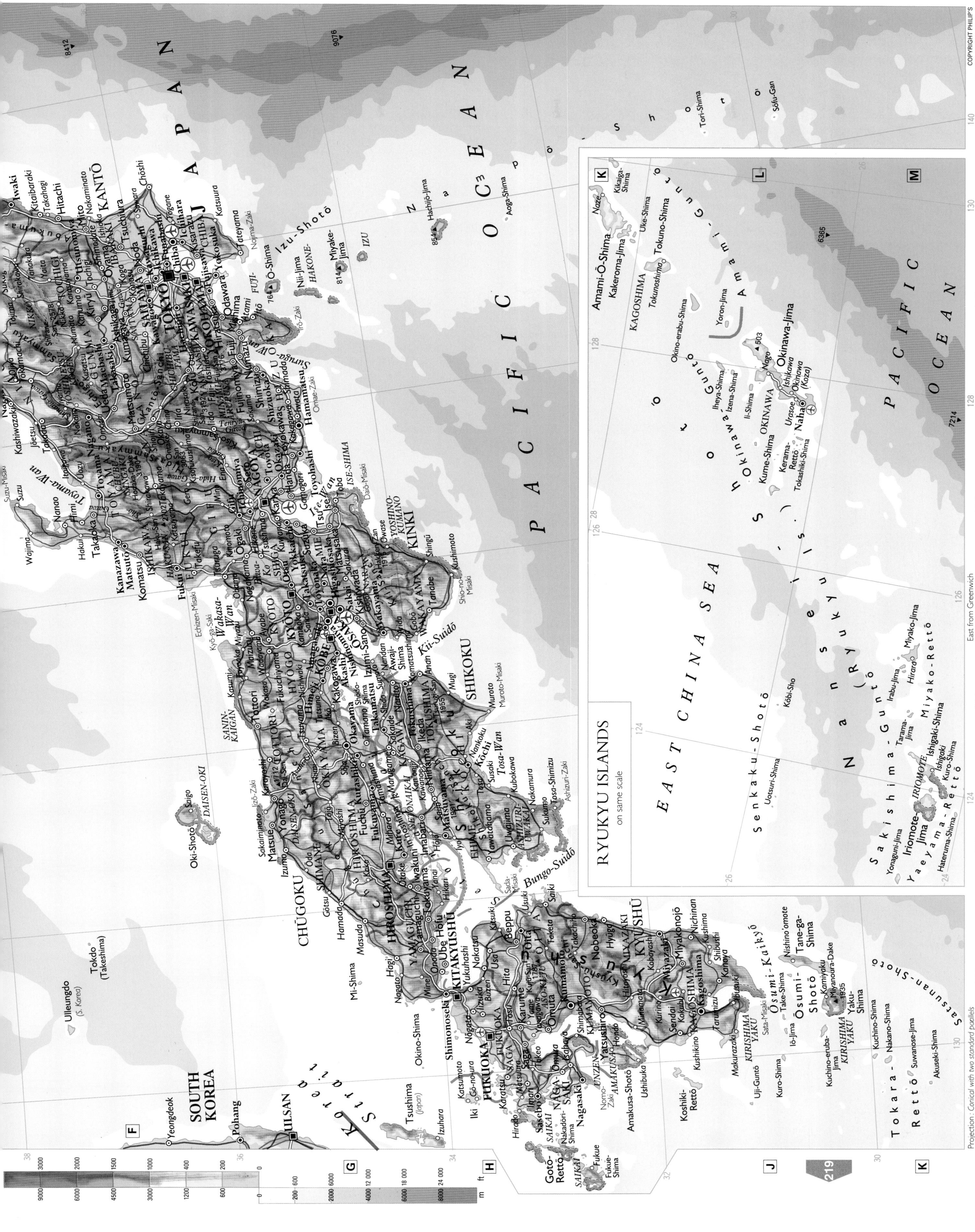

G H J K

8412▼
9076▼

J A P A N

KANTŌ
TOKYO
PACIFIC OCEAN

Iwaki
Kitaibaraki
Takahagi
Hitachi
Mito
Nakaminato
Chōshi
Katsuura
Kashima
Chiba
Yokohama
Yokosuka
Odawara
Tateyama
Nojima-Zaki

Izu-Shotō
Ō-Shima
Nii-Jima
Miyake-Jima
HAKONE
IZU
FUJI
Hachijō-Jima
Aoga-Shima

KINKI
NAGOYA
KYOTO
OSAKA
KOBE
ISE-SHIMA
Ise-Wan
Daiō-Misaki
YOSHINO-KUMANO
Kii-Suidō
Shio-no-Misaki

SHIKOKU
TOKUSHIMA
KŌCHI
Muroto-Misaki
Ashizuri-Zaki
Tosa-Wan
Bungo-Suidō

CHŪGOKU
HIROSHIMA
OKAYAMA
TOTTORI
SHIMANE
Matsue
Yonago
DAISEN-OKI
Oki-Shotō
DAISEN-OKI

SOUTH KOREA
Yeongdeok
Pohang
ULSAN
 Tokdo
(Takeshima)
Ulleungdo
(S. Korea)

Tsushima
(Japan)
Izuhara

KITAKYUSHU
FUKUOKA
SAGA
NAGASAKI
SAIKAI
UNZEN-AMAKUSA
KUMAMOTO
ŌITA
Beppu
MIYAZAKI
KAGOSHIMA
KYŪSHŪ
KIRISHIMA-YAKU

Goto-Rettō
SAIKAI
Fukue-Shima

Ōsumi-Kaikyō
Ōsumi-Shotō
Tane-ga-Shima
Yaku-Shima
KIRISHIMA YAKU

Tokara-Rettō
Nakano-Shima
Suwanose-Jima
Akuseki-Shima
Satsunan-Shotō

P A C I F I C   O C E A N

Sōfu-Gan
Tori-Shima

RYUKYU ISLANDS
on same scale

E A S T   C H I N A   S E A

Amami-Ō-Shima
Naze
Kikaiga-Shima
Uke-Shima
Tokuno-Shima
KAGOSHIMA
Kakeroma
Okino-erabu-Shima
Yoron-Jima
OKINAWA
Okinawa-Jima
Naha

N a n s u k y u   (R y u k y u)   I s .
O k i n a w a - G u n t ō

Senkaku-Shotō
Uotsuri-Shima
Kōbi-Sho

Sakishima-Guntō
Miyako-Rettō
Miyako-Jima
IRIOMOTE
Iriomote-Jima
Ishigaki-Shima
Ishigaki
Yaeyama-Rettō
Yonaguni-Jima

P A C I F I C   O C E A N

10 0 10 20 30 40 50 60 70 80 90 km
1:2 000 000
10 0 10 20 30 40 50 60 miles

SEA OF JAPAN
(EAST SEA)

Yeongdeok

Heunghae

Pohang

SOUTH KOREA

Oki-Shotō
Daimanji-San
Dōgo 608
Saigō
DAISEN-OKI
Dōzen

H O N S H U

CHŪGOKU-DISTRICT

DAISEN-OKI
Shimane-Hantō
Jizō-Zaki
Iwami
SANIN-KAIGAN
Kasumi

Hi-no-Misaki
Hirata
Matsue
Shinji-Ko
Sakaiminato
Yonago
TOTTORI
Toyooka
Hidaka
Tottori

Taisha
Shinji
Yasugi
Dai-Sen
1729
Kurayoshi
Suga-no-Sen
1510
Wadayama

Izumo
Daito
Kisuki

Kara-Saki
Kamitsushima

Kamiagata

Tsushima

Mitsushima
Izuhara

Kō-Saki

Higasi-Suidō

Iki

Katsumoto

Korea Strait

Gō-no-ura
Iki-Kaikyō

Ō-Shima
Ikitsuki-Shima
Hirado
Matsuura
Imari
SAIKAI
Saza
Sasebo
Takeo
Arita

Higasi-Suidō

Genkai-Nada

FUKUOKA
FUK.
Dazaifu
Kasuga
Chikushino
Sefuri-San
1055
Tosu
Kurume

Hibiki-Nada

Nagato
Yamaguchi
Mine
San'yō
Onoda
Ube
Hōfu
Shin-Nan'yō
Tokuyama
Yanai

KITAKYŪSHŪ

Shimonoseki
Nakama
Munakata
Fukuma
Nōgata
Miyata
Yukuhashi
Iizuka
Tagawa
Yamada
Buzen
Nakatsu
Usa
Bungotakada
Kitsuki

Suō-Nada

Naga-Shima
Iwai-Jima

Hime-Jima

Kyūshū
KYŪSHŪ-DISTRICT

Shikoku
SHIKOKU-DISTRICT

Kagoshima

Shinkansen line   National Parks

Projection:
Lambert's Conformal Conic

1:3 100 000

SEA OF JAPAN
(EAST SEA)

Korea
Bay

NORTH
KOREA

P'YŎNGYANG

SOUTH
KOREA

YELLOW SEA
(HUANG HAI)

SEOUL
INCHEON
SUWŎN
DAEJEON
DAEGU
ULSAN
GWANGJU
BUSAN

Korea Strait

JAPAN

JEJU-DO on same scale

Jeju
Jeju-do
(S. Korea)
Hallasan
HALLASAN
Seogwipo Namjeju

Projection : Conical with two standard parallels

East from Greenwich

COPYRIGHT PHILIP'S

1:1 400 000

5 0 10 20 30 40 50 60 70 km
5 0 10 20 30 40 50 miles

CHINA FUJIAN
Jimei
Shijing
Xinglin
Jinjing
XMN
Kuahao
Chinmen (Quemoy)
Xiamen
Hsiao-chinmen Tao
Chinmen Tao (Taiwan)
Zhenhai
Taiwan Strait
CHINMEN
on same scale

CHINA FUJIAN
Huangqi
Liang Tao
Tungyin Tao
Lianjiang
Peikant'ang Tao
Tongsha Tao
Langqi *Min Jiang*
Matsu Tao (Taiwan)
Changle
Paichuan
Liehtao
Taiwan Strait
MATSU
on same scale

229

T A I W A N   S T R A I T

Fukuei Chiao
Shihmen
Sanchih
Chinshan
T'AIPEI
Tanshui
YANGMINGSHAN
Pali
Chilung (Keelung)
Tanshui Kang
Peitou
Wanli
Pitou Chiao
Kuanyin
Sanchung
Nankang
Maoao
Santiao Chiao
TAOYUAN
Panch'iao
T'AIPEI
Chungho
Kungliao
Chungli
T'aoyüan
Sanhsia
Hsintien
Pinglin
Talichien
Yingmei
Tach'i
Wulai
Waiao
Hsinfeng
Huk'ou
Fuhsing
Chiaohsi
Kueishan Tao
Nanliao
Kuanhsi
Ilan
T'ouch'eng
Hsinchu
Chupei
Shihmen
Yuanshan
Chuangwei
Hsiangshan
Chutung
T'aman Shan 2731
Sanhsing
Wuchieh
Chunan
Toufen
Neiwan
Paleng
Chingshui
Lotung
HSINCHU
Suao
Houlung
MIAOLI
Shihtan
Chittan
T'uch'ang
Nanao
Kungssuliao
Tsaochiao
Shihliu 2573
Tungshan
Chungtungwan
Miaoli
Kungkuan
3886 **HSUEH**
Tungao
T'unghsiao
Yüanli
Sani
Tahu
Hsueh Shan
ILAN
Kuanyin
Taan
Jihnan
Tachia
Houli
Cholan
Hsueh Kang
3740 Nanhunan Shan
Fachoshui
Ch'ingshui
Fengyüan
Tantzu
Tungshih
Kukuan
Ushan
2646 Chingshui
Wuch'i Hsi
Shalu
Peitun
Hsinche
Hoping
Tayüling
TAROKO
Shenkang
Taichung
Taping
3605 T'ailuko
Hsinch'eng
Homei
Wujih
Kuohsing
Peipu
Changhua
Wufeng
Wantouliu
Jenai
HUALIEN
Lukang
Hsiushui
Shihkongkeng
Hualien
Fuhsing
Fenyüan
Jenho
Wangkung
CHANGHUA
Puyen
Chihu
Pitou
Peitou
NANTOU
Puli
Fangyüan
Yüanlin
Shetou
Mingchien
Yüchih
Shoufeng
Erhlin
Tengchung
Nant'ou
3349 Choshota Shan
Fenglin
T'ai'ou'un
Ch'ich'u
Echshui
Shuili
Chichi
Wulicheng
Chichi
Maliao
Lunpei
Hsilo
Tzutun
Chushan
Tingkan
Fenglin
Taihsi
YUNLIN
Huwei
Linnei
Luku
Hsini
Wanjung
Kuangfu
Santiaolun
Touliu
Kukeng
2480 Fengpin
Ssuhu
Yüanch'ang
Tounan
Meishan
3833 Tafu
K'ouhu
Kanghsi
Talin
Minhsiung
Fenchih
Luyeh
Takangkou
Peikang
Chiai
Chüchi
Leyeh
3952 Jade Mt.
Chingpu
Putai
CHIAI
Hsingying
Kuchia
Yunshui
KAO-
Choch'i
Changyuan
Peimen
Yenshui
Liuying
Paiho
Meishan
Yüli
Ch'angpin
Ichu
Shuishang
Houpi
Topu
HSIUNG
1331
Hsüehchia
Chiangchun
Hsiaying
Kuan Shan
Antung
Chiali
Tan Shanhu
Tsengwen Shui
Fuli
Shajuwan
Chiku
T'AINAN
Yüching
Wulu
Sanhsien
Matou
Shanshang
Taoyüan
Ch'ihshang
1682
Sanhsien
Chengnan
Anting
Hsinshih
Shanlin
Hsinfa
Ch'engkung
Hsinhua
Nanhua
Peinanchu Shan
Kuanshan
Hoping
T'ainan
Jente
Yungk'ang
Liukuei
T'AITUNG
Chiehting
Kuanmiao
Meinung
Tungho
Lunei
Ch'ishan
Luyeh
Tulan
Luchu
Yungan
Alien
Kaoshu
Chianapu
Lichia
Chialulantsun
Kangshan
Yenchu
P'ING-
Santi
Peinan
Tzukuan
Jenvu
Chuju
Yenpu
Ch'ihpen
Nantzu
Changchih
Peinan
Tsoying
Tashu
Pingtung
Peiawu Shan
KAOHSIUNG
Fengshan
Taliao
Neipu
3090
T'aimali
Chienchen
Wantan
TUNG
Hsiaokang
Wanluan
Ch'aochou
Hsinchuang
Hsinyuan
Ch'inlun
Linyuan
Hsinpi
Hsiatahsi
Tungkang
Limpien
Shuitiliao
Taniao
Chiatung
Tawu
Liuch'iu Yü
Fangliao
Tajen
Liuch'iu
Fangshan
Shouchia
Fengkang
Tanlu
Hsühaitsun
Ch'ulin
Mutanshe
Fengkang
Kangtzu
Hengch'un
Manchou
KENTING
Naowan
Oluanpi
Maopi T'ou
Oluan Pi

Bashi Channel

Lü Tao (Green I.)
Lütao

Lan Yü (Orchid I.)
Lanyu
Hsiaohungt'ou Hsü

P A C I F I C   O C E A N

Tropic of Cancer

T A I W A N   S T R A I T

P'enghu
Chipei Tao
Paisha
Yüweng Tao
Hsiyu
Huhsi
Makung
P'enghu Tao
P'ENGHU
Ch'üntou (Pescadores)
Hua Yü
Wangan
Pachao Yü
Ch'imei Yü
Tungchi Yü
Ch'imei
Waisanting

T A I W A N

ft m
9000 3000
6000 2000
4500 1500
3000 1000
1200 400
600 200
0 0
200 600
2000 6000
4000 12 000
m ft

Projection: Lambert Conformal Conic

East from Greenwich

COPYRIGHT PHILIP'S

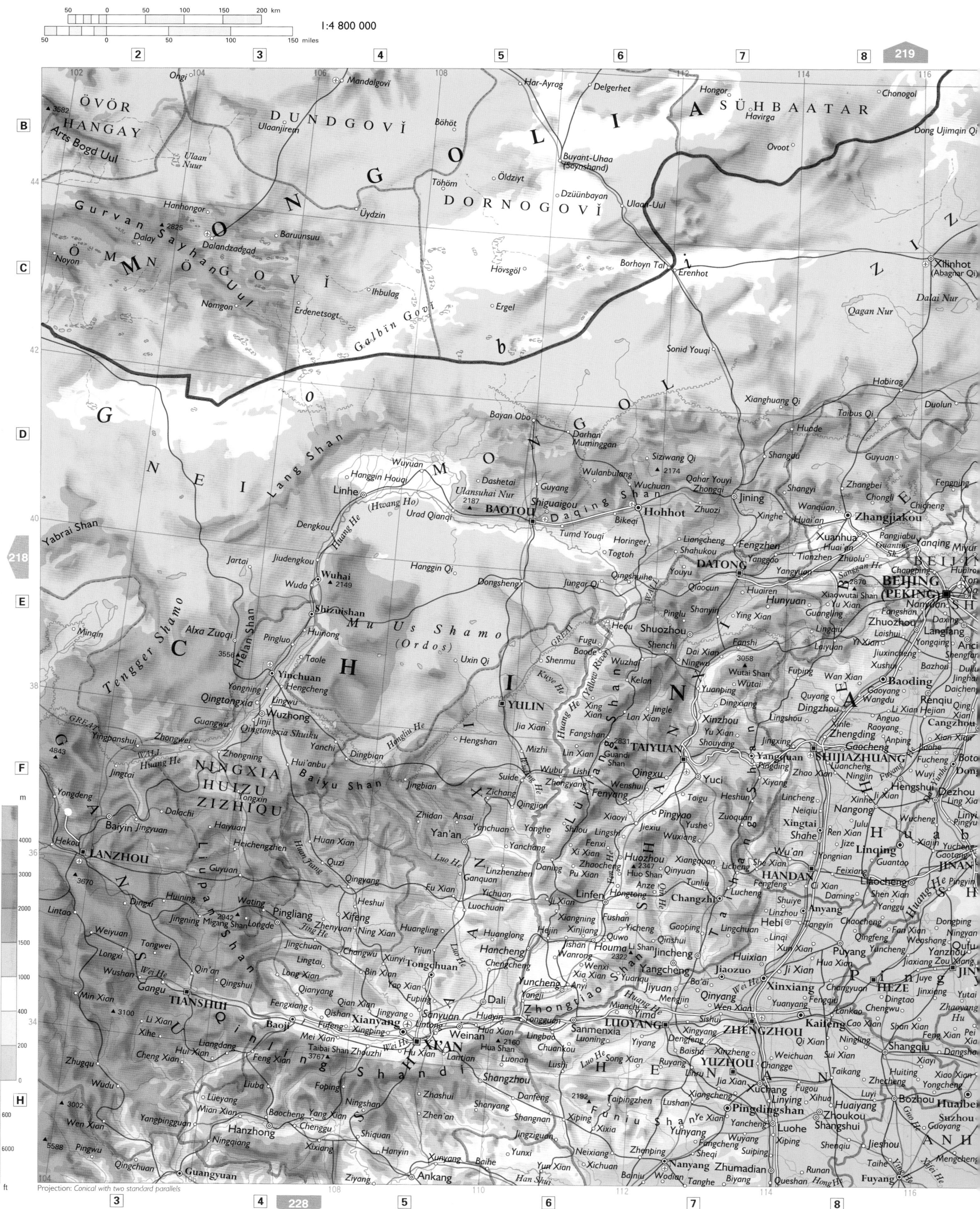

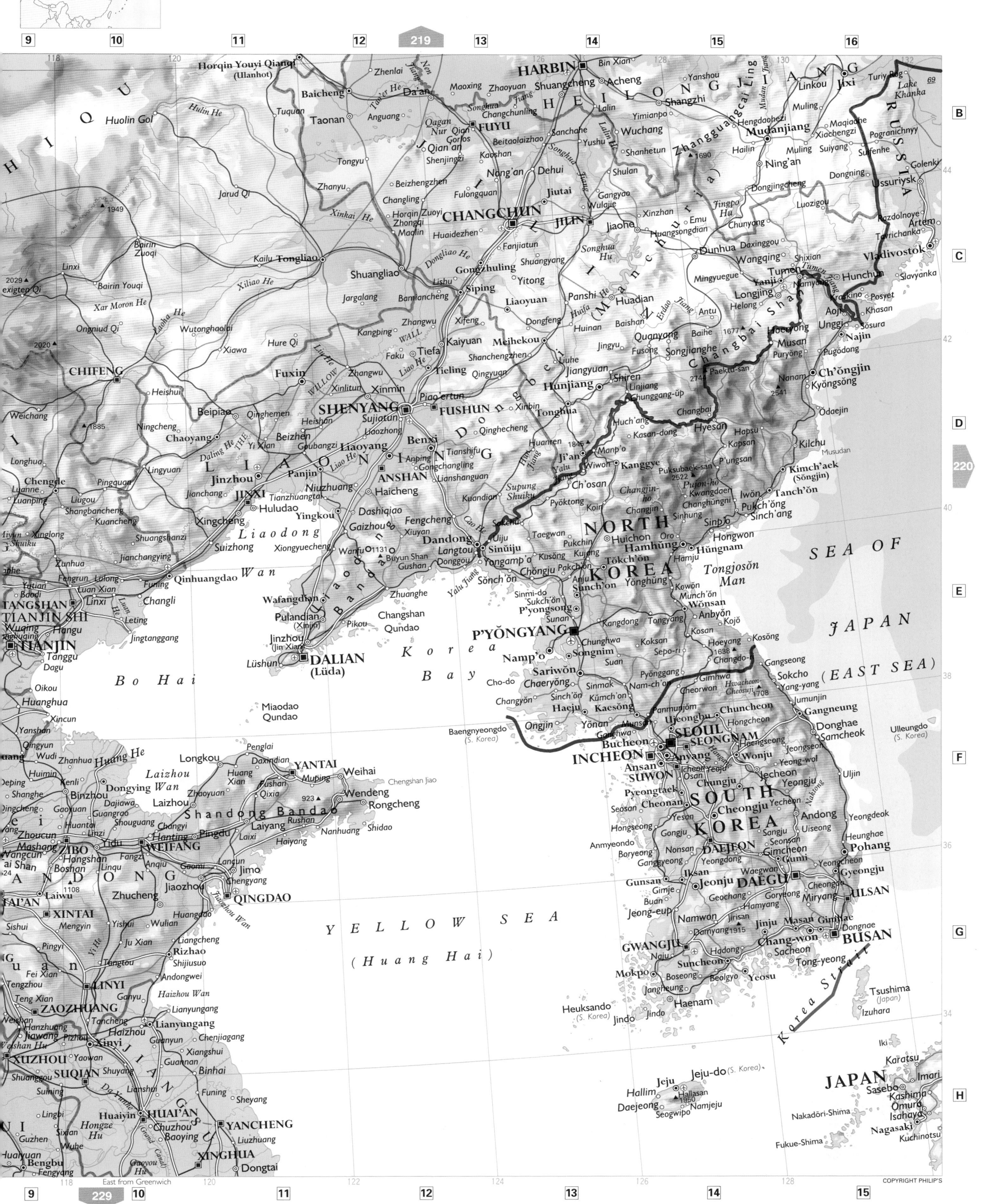

50 0 50 100 150 200 km

1:4 800 000

50 0 50 100 150 miles

Projection: Conical with two standard parallels

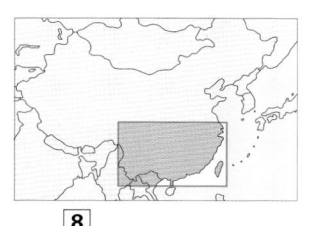

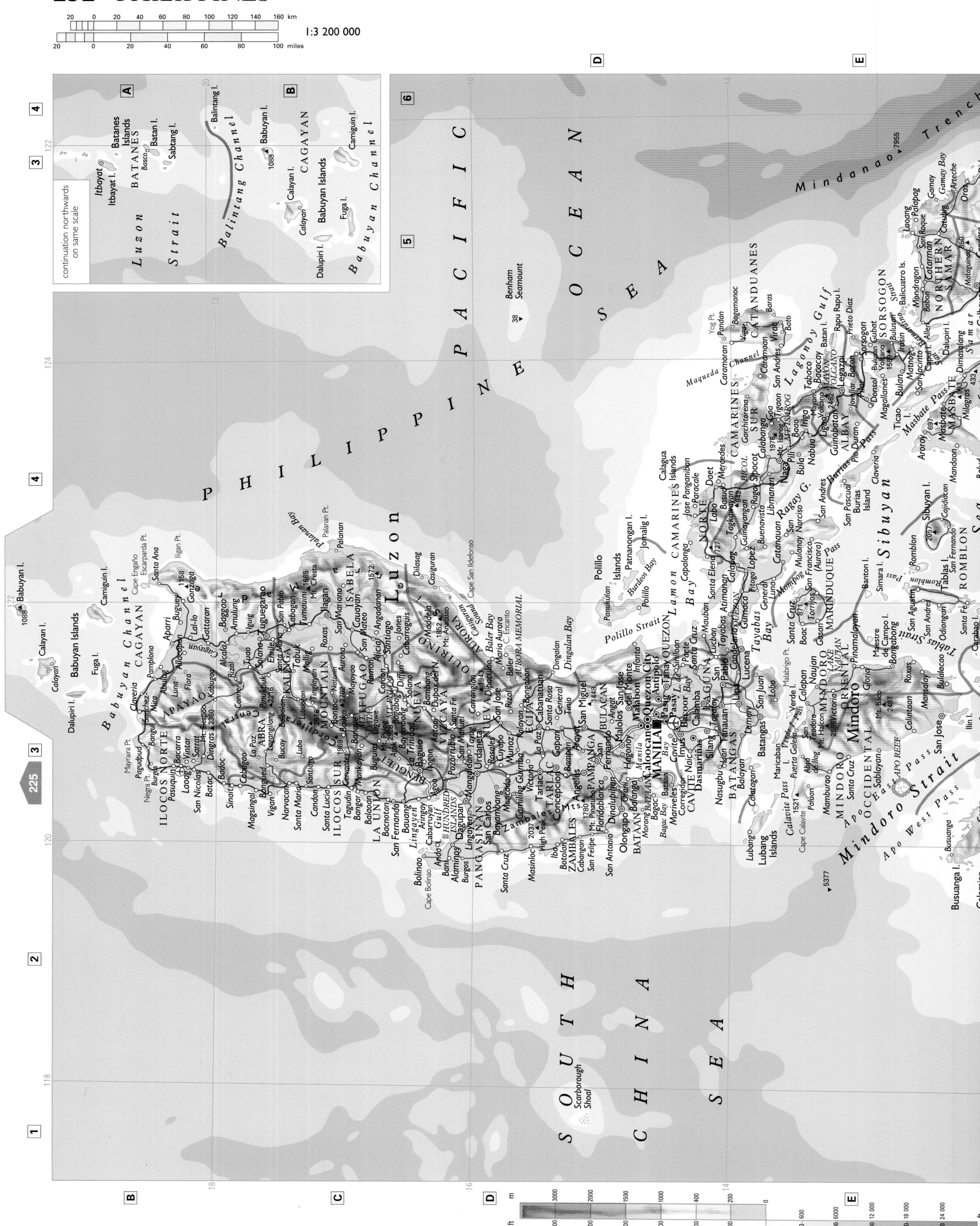

1:3 200 000

continuation northwards
on same scale

Batanes
Islands
Itbayat I.
Itbayat
Batan I.
Basco
Sabtang I.
Luzon
Strait
BATANES
Balintang I.
Balintang Channel
Babuyan I.
1088▲
Calayan I.
CAGAYAN
Camiguin I.
Babuyan Islands
Babuyan Channel
Dalupiri I.
Fuga I.

PHILIPPINE PACIFIC OCEAN SEA

SOUTH
CHINA
SEA

Benham
Seamount
38▶

Mindanao Trench
7955▲

Scarborough
Shoal

Luzon

Mindoro

MINDORO
OCCIDENTAL

MINDORO
ORIENTAL

Mindoro Strait

SORSOGON

CATANDUANES

MASBATE

SIBUYAN
SEA

ROMBLON

SAMAR

NORTHERN
SAMAR

CAMARINES
SUR

CAMARINES
NORTE

ALBAY

QUEZON

BULACAN

BATANGAS

LAGUNA

MANILA■

CAGAYAN

ISABELA

KALINGA

APAYAO

ABRA

ILOCOS
NORTE

ILOCOS
SUR

MOUNTAIN
PROVINCE

IFUGAO

NUEVA
VIZCAYA

QUIRINO

AURORA

NUEVA
ECIJA

TARLAC

PAMPANGA

ZAMBALES

BATAAN

PANGASINAN

LA UNION

BENGUET

m ft
3000 9000
2000 6000
1500 4500
1000 3000
400 1200
200 600
0
200 600
2000 6000
4000 12 000
6000 18 000
8000 24 000 m

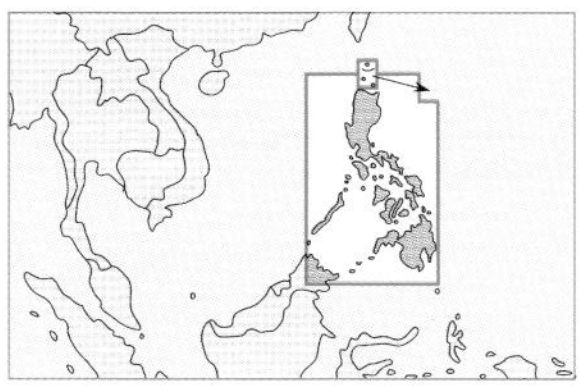

CELEBES SEA

SULU SEA

Mindanao

MALAYSIA

Borneo

SABAH

Palawan Passage

Sulu Archipelago

TAWI-TAWI

SULU

BASILAN

Zamboanga

DAVAO ORIENTAL

DAVAO DEL SUR

DAVAO DEL NORTE

DAVAO

BUKIDNON

COTABATO

SOUTH COTABATO

SULTAN KUDARAT

MAGUINDANAO

LANAO DEL SUR

LANAO DEL NORTE

MISAMIS ORIENTAL

MISAMIS OCCIDENTAL

ZAMBOANGA DEL NORTE

ZAMBOANGA DEL SUR

AGUSAN DEL SUR

AGUSAN DEL NORTE

SURIGAO DEL SUR

SURIGAO DEL NORTE

CAMIGUIN

BOHOL

CEBU

NEGROS ORIENTAL

NEGROS OCCIDENTAL

SIQUIJOR

LEYTE

SOUTHERN LEYTE

BILIRAN

EASTERN SAMAR

SAMAR

AKLAN

CAPIZ

ILOILO

ANTIQUE

GUIMARAS

Panay

Negros

Bohol Sea

Visayan Sea

Mindanao Sea

Moro Gulf

Davao Gulf

Leyte Gulf

Illana Bay

Panay Gulf

Tañon Strait

Cuyo East Pass

Cuyo West Pass

Linapacan Strait

Balabac Strait

Sibutu Passage

Basilan Strait

Sarangani Islands

Cagayan Sulu I.

Mt. Apo 2954

Copyright Philip's

Projection: Lambert Conformal Conic

East from Greenwich

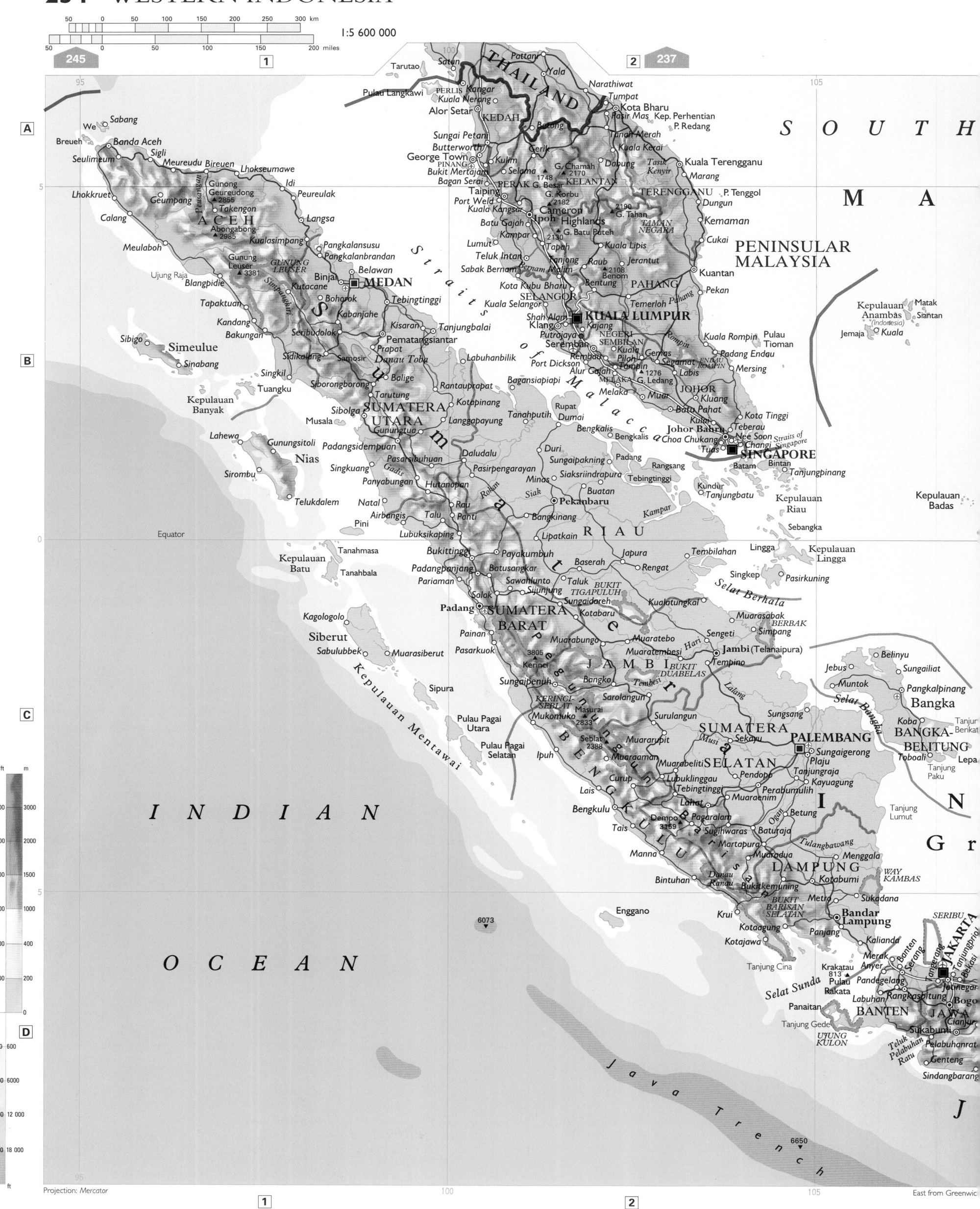

Projection: Mercator

East from Greenwic

CHINA SEA

SULU SEA

MALAYSIA

LAYSIA

Laut

Telukbutun

Kepulauan Natuna Besar
Ranai
Natuna Besar
Binjai
(Indonesia)

Midai

Subi

Kepulauan Natuna Selatan
(Indonesia)

Serasan

Kepulauan Tambelan
(Indonesia)

Singkawang

Sambas

Tanjung Datu

Tanjung Sipang

Tanjong Po

Paloh

Lundu

Sekatan

KUBAH

Batu

Bungo

Niut

Tebakang

Sanggau

Bengkayang

Ngabang

Mempawah

Jungkat

Pontianak

Sungaidurian

Tayan

KALIMANTAN BARAT

Kapuas

Padangtikar

Maya

Telukbatang

Sukadana

Sandai

GUNUNG PALUNG

Nangatayap

Kepulauan Karimata
Padang

Ketapang

Kualapesaguan

Marau

Riam

Panopah

Rantaupulut

Sukaraja

Kendawangan

Kotawaringin

Sukamara

Marau

Kualajelai

Kumai

Pangkalanbuun

Semuda

Kualapembuang

TANJUNG PUTING
Tanjung Puting

Teluk Sampit

Tanjung Selatan

Kepulauan Laut Kecil

Kepulauan Laut Kecil

Kepulauan Tambelan

Tanjungpandan
Manggar

Gantung

Belitung

Membalong
Dendang

Selat Karimata

BRUNEI
Bandar Seri Begawan
Kuala Belait
Lutong
Miri
Seria
LAMBIR HILLS
Niah
SIMILAJAU
Tanjong Kidurong
Bintulu
Tatau
Mukah
Oya
Dalat
Sibu
Bintangau
Kanowit
Kapit
Sarikei
RANJANG MANGROVES
Saratok
Debak
Betong
Sri Aman
Simunjan
Serian
Kuching

SARAWAK

Belaga

Bukit Batu Boga

Long Akah

Marudi

GUNUNG MULU
G. Mulu

KAYAN MENTARANG

Longjelai

Datadian

Longagung

Longnawan

Kongkemul

KALIMANTAN TIMUR

Tanjungselor

Nameh

Longbia

Berau

Telukbayur
Tanjungredeb

Tanjungbatu

Maratua

Tarakan

Bunyu

Longberang

Sesayap

Atap

Teluk Sebuku

Sipadan

SABAH

Kota Kinabalu
Penampang
Papar
Beaufort
Sipitang
Lawas
CROCKER RANGE
KINABALU
Mt. Palin
Kota Belud
Tuaran
Ranau
Tambunan
Keningau
Tenom
Melalap
Sapulut
Pensiangan
Lumbis
Kalabakan
Tawau
Alang
Semporna
Sipitang

PHILIPPINES

P. Balambangan
Tg. Sempang
Mengayou
Langkon
Kudat
P. Banggi
P. Malawali
Senaja
P. Jambongan
Datong
Klogan
Telok Labuk
Sandakan
Tanjong Pisau
Turtle Islands
Lamag
Batu Puteh
Beluran
Lahad Datu
Kunak
Tungku
Tanjong Labian
Sibutu
Tumindao
Sibutu Passage

SULAWESI (Celebes)

SULAWESI BARAT

Mamuju

Malunda

Onang

Majene

Donggala

Palu

Lariang

Karosa

Mamasa

Makale

Polewali

Pinrang

Enrekang

Rapang

Parepare

Pangkajene

Watansoppeng

Sumpangbinangae

Maros

UJUNG PANDANG
(Makasar)

Sungguminasa

Patalasang

Bontosunggu

Bantaeng

KALIMANTAN

Pegunungan Iran

Putussibau

Nangamentebah

Danau Luar

Kuda

KARIMUN

Liangpran

Nahabuan

Longboh

Kubumesaai

Muarawahau

Sangkulirang

Tanjung Mangkalihat

Batuputih

Sepasu

Bontang

Equator

Santan

Muarakaman

Tenggarong

Samarinda

Sangasangadalam

Sungaitiram

Samboja

Balikpapan

Menyapa

Tabang

Muarabenangin

Muaratewe

Teweh

Sebakung

Tanahgrogot

Tanjung

Amuntai

Barabai

Kandangan

Marabahan

Banjarmasin

Banjarbaru

Martapura

Rantau

KALIMANTAN SELATAN

Pegunungan Meratus

Kotabaru

Sebuku

Pagatan

Karambu

Pelaihari

Satui

Pulau Laut

Kintap

Batakan

Jorong

Tanjung Selatan

KALIMANTAN TENGAH

Palangkaraya

Kualakurun

Kahayan

Buntok

Ampah

Pujon

Bawan

Pulangpisau

Kualakapuas

Pangkoh

Seipinang

Purukcahu

Tumbangsamba

Kasongan

Sampit

Kotabesi

Mendawai

Tumbangsamba

Kepulauan Balabalangan

SELAT MAKASAR
Selat Makasar

KUTAI

Danau Jempang

Longiram

Klampo

Muarajuloi

Murung

Mahakam

Barito

BUKIT BAKA
BUKIT RAYA

Pegunungan Schwaner

Pegunungan Muller

Gunung Saran

Kotabaru

Nangapinoh

Melawi

Menate

Nangamau

Sekadau

Sintang

Semitau

Danau Sentarum

Balaikarangan

Balaisabut

Nangamentebah

Selimbau

BENTUANG

GREATER SUNDA

Greater Sunda Islands

JAVA SEA

Kepulauan Masalembo

Kepulauan Karimunjawa

Bawean
Sangkapura

BALI SEA

FLORES SEA

Kepulauan Sabalana

Kepulauan Masalima

Kepulauan Kangean

Pabean

Sepanjang

Kepulauan Tengah

Kepulauan Balabalangan

Karawang
Pamanukan
Subang
Indramayu
Jatibarang
Cirebon
Kuningan
Majalengka
Sumedang
BANDUNG
Garut
Ciamis
Banjar
Tasikmalaya
Cijulang
Pameungpeuk
Nusa Kambangan
Cilacap
Kroya
Banyumas
Purwokerto
Purwodadi
Wonosobo
Slamet
Kebumen
Karanganyar
Wates
YOGYAKARTA
Sleman
Magelang
Merapi
Surakarta
Klaten
Pacitan
Wonogiri
Ponorogo
Trenggalek
Tulungagung
Blitar
Wlingi
Kediri
JAWA TIMUR
Malang
Lumajang
Semeru
MERU BETIRI
Pasirian
Nusa Barung
Jember
Rambipuji
Bondowoso
Kraksaan
Probolinggo
Pasuruan
Bangil
BALURAN
Panarukan
Banyuwangi
Pekalongan
Batang
Pemalang
Tegal
Brebes
Demak
SEMARANG
JAWA TENGAH
Kudus
Muria
Pati
Blora
Cepu
Bojonegoro
Ngawi
Sragen
Madiun
Jombang
Mojokerto
Gresik
SURABAYA
Sidoarjo
Selat Madura
Pasuruan
Jepara
Rembang
Kragan
Tuban
Lamongan
Bangkalan
Sampang
Pamekasan
Sumenep
MADURA
Puteran
Sapudi
Tanjung Pangkah
Tanjung Bugel

Lesser Sunda Islands

BALI
Singaraja
Agung
Karangasem
RINJANI
Tabanan
Denpasar
Negara
Gilimanuk
BALI BARAT
Klungkung
Tanjung
Mataram
Lombok
Lembar
Praya
Selong
Alas
Taliwang
Sumbawa Besar
Moyo
Tambora
KOMODO
Komodo
Rinca
Flores
Sape
Plampang
Dompu
Raba
Sangeang
Labuhanbajo
Tente
Bima

NUSA TENGGARA BARAT

(Java)

JAVA SEA

J A V A   S E A

INDONESIA

eater Sunda Islands

COPYRIGHT PHILIP'S

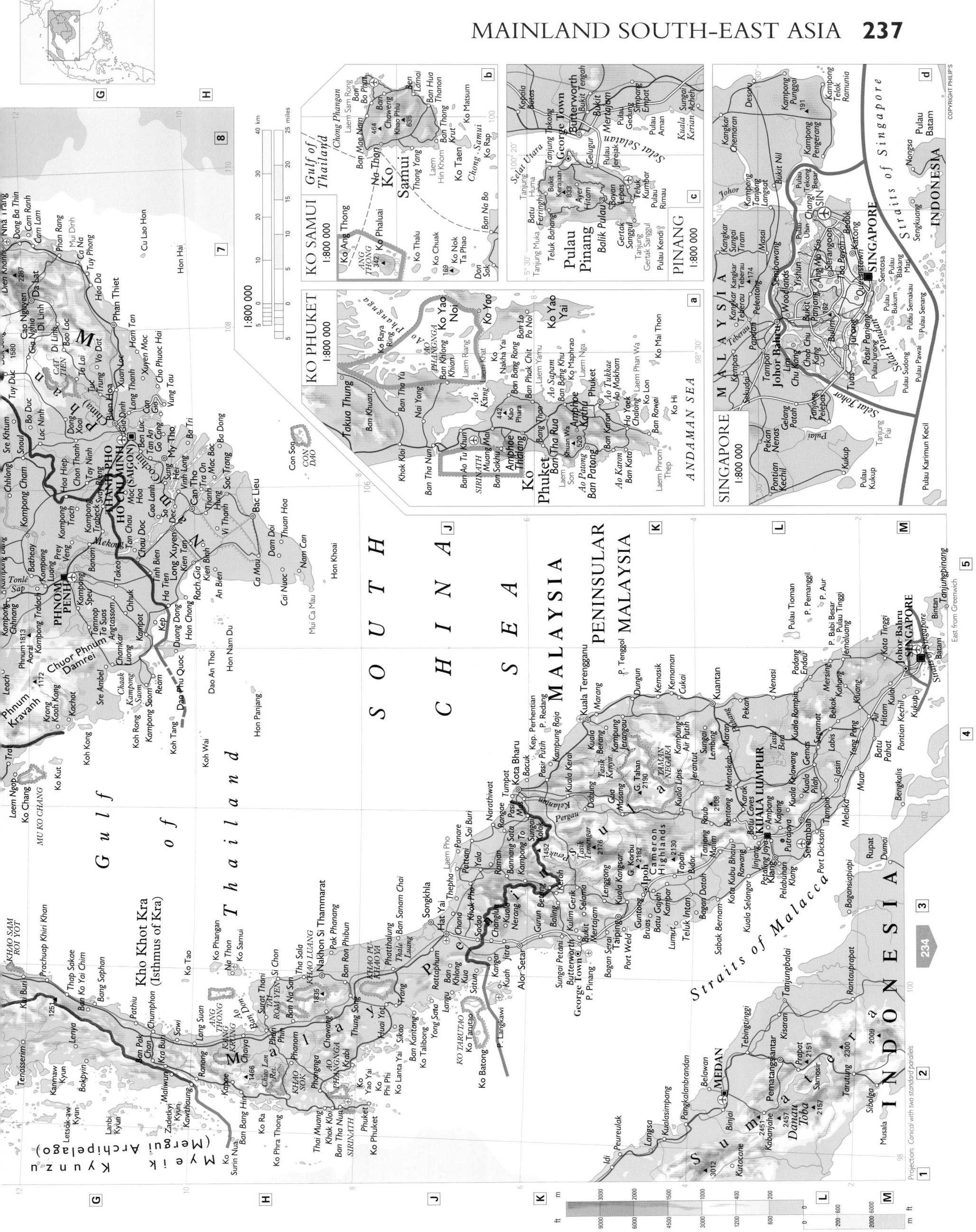

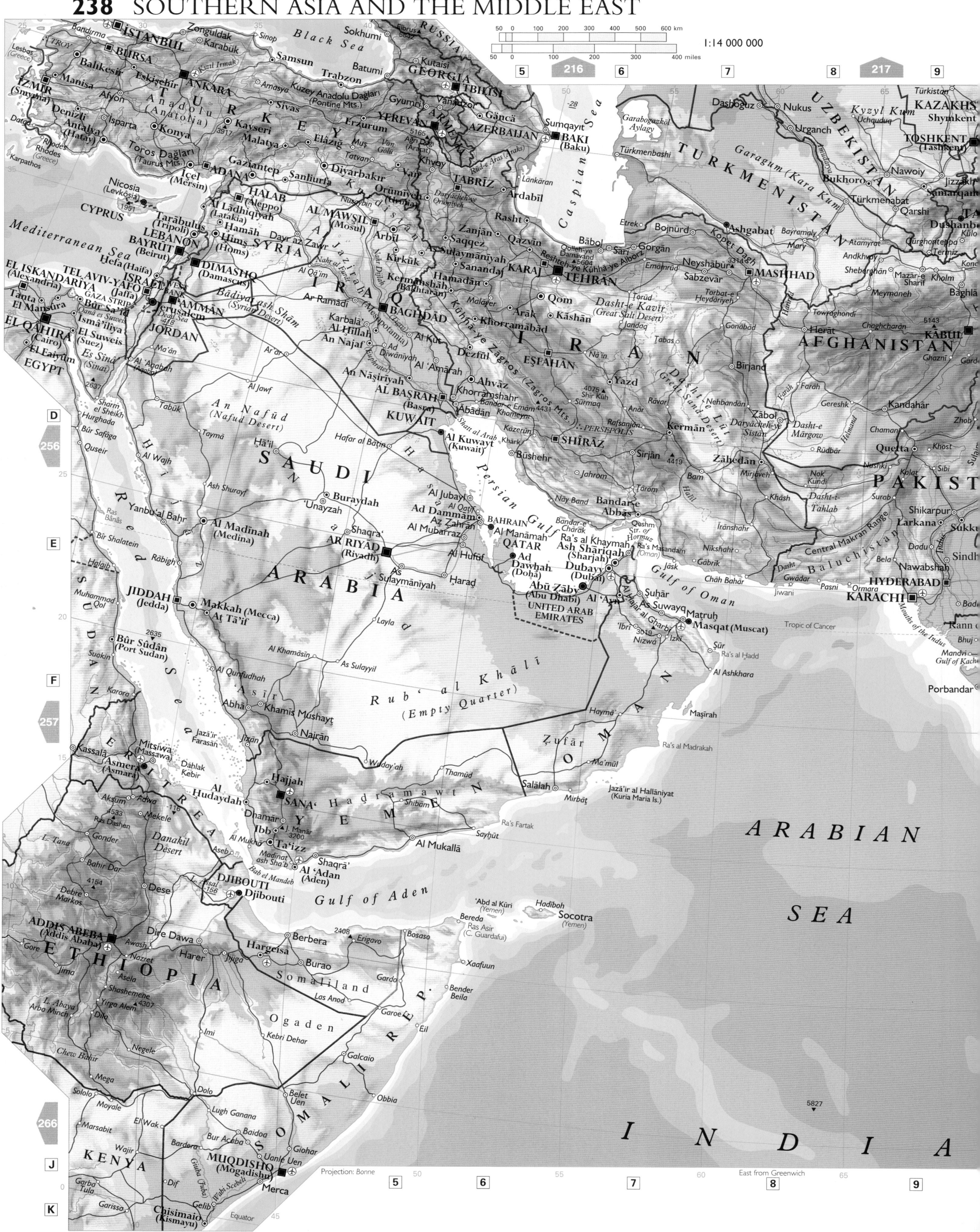

1:14 000 000

218
219
230
272
230
COPYRIGHT PHILIP'S

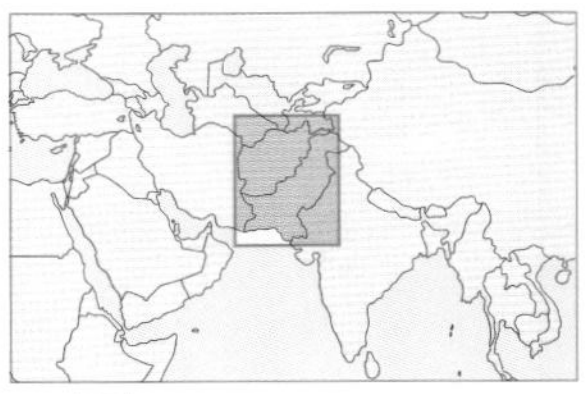

50 0 50 100 150 200 250 300 km

50 0 50 100 150 200 miles

1:5 600 000

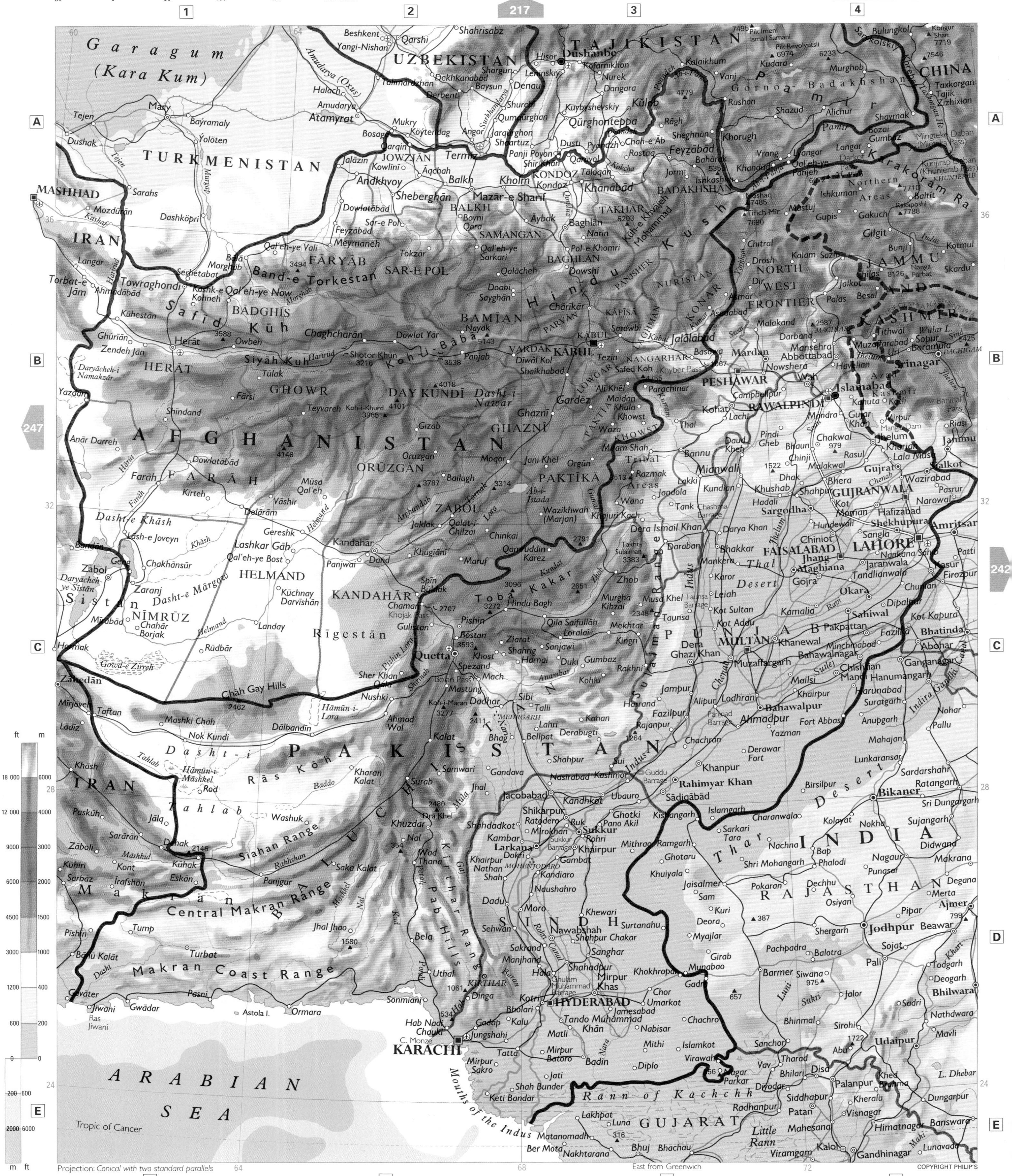

217
247
242
A
B
C
D
E
1
2
3
4
TURKMENISTAN
UZBEKISTAN
TAJIKISTAN
CHINA
IRAN
AFGHANISTAN
PAKISTAN
INDIA
ARABIAN SEA
Garagum (Kara Kum)
Hindu Kush
Pamir
Karakoram Ra.
Safid Kūh
Band-e Torkestan
Siyāh Kuh
Koh-i-Bābā
Dasht-e Mārgow
Rīgestān
Sīstān
Chāh Gay Hills
Dasht-i Tahlab
Rās Koh
Siahan Range
Central Makran Range
Makran Coast Range
Kirthar Range
Pab Hills
Thal Desert
Thar Desert
Rann of Kachchh
Mouths of the Indus
Tropic of Cancer
HERĀT
GHOWR
FARĀH
NĪMRŪZ
HELMAND
KANDAHĀR
ORŪZGĀN
ZĀBOL
GHAZNĪ
PAKTĪKĀ
BAMĪĀN
BADAKHSHĀN
BALKH
JOWZJĀN
FĀRYĀB
BĀDGHĪS
SAR-E POL
SAMANGĀN
BAGHLĀN
TAKHĀR
KONDOZ
NORTH WEST FRONTIER
JAMMU AND KASHMIR
BALUCHISTAN
PUNJAB
SINDH
RAJASTHAN
GUJARAT
Dushanbe
Mary
MASHHAD
Herāt
Kandahār
KĀBUL
Mazār-e Sharif
Jalālābād
Ghaznī
PESHAWAR
Islamabad
RAWALPINDI
Quetta
LAHORE
FAISALABAD
MULTĀN
Gujranwala
Srinagar
Amritsar
Hyderabad
KARACHI
Bikaner
Jodhpur
Bahawalpur
Sukkur
Zāhedān
Gwādar
Astola I.
Ras Jiwani
C. Monze
ft m
18 000 6000
12 000 4000
9000 3000
6000 2000
4500 1500
3000 1000
1200 400
600 200
0 0
200 600
2000 6000
m ft

Projection: Conical with two standard parallels

East from Greenwich

COPYRIGHT PHILIP'S

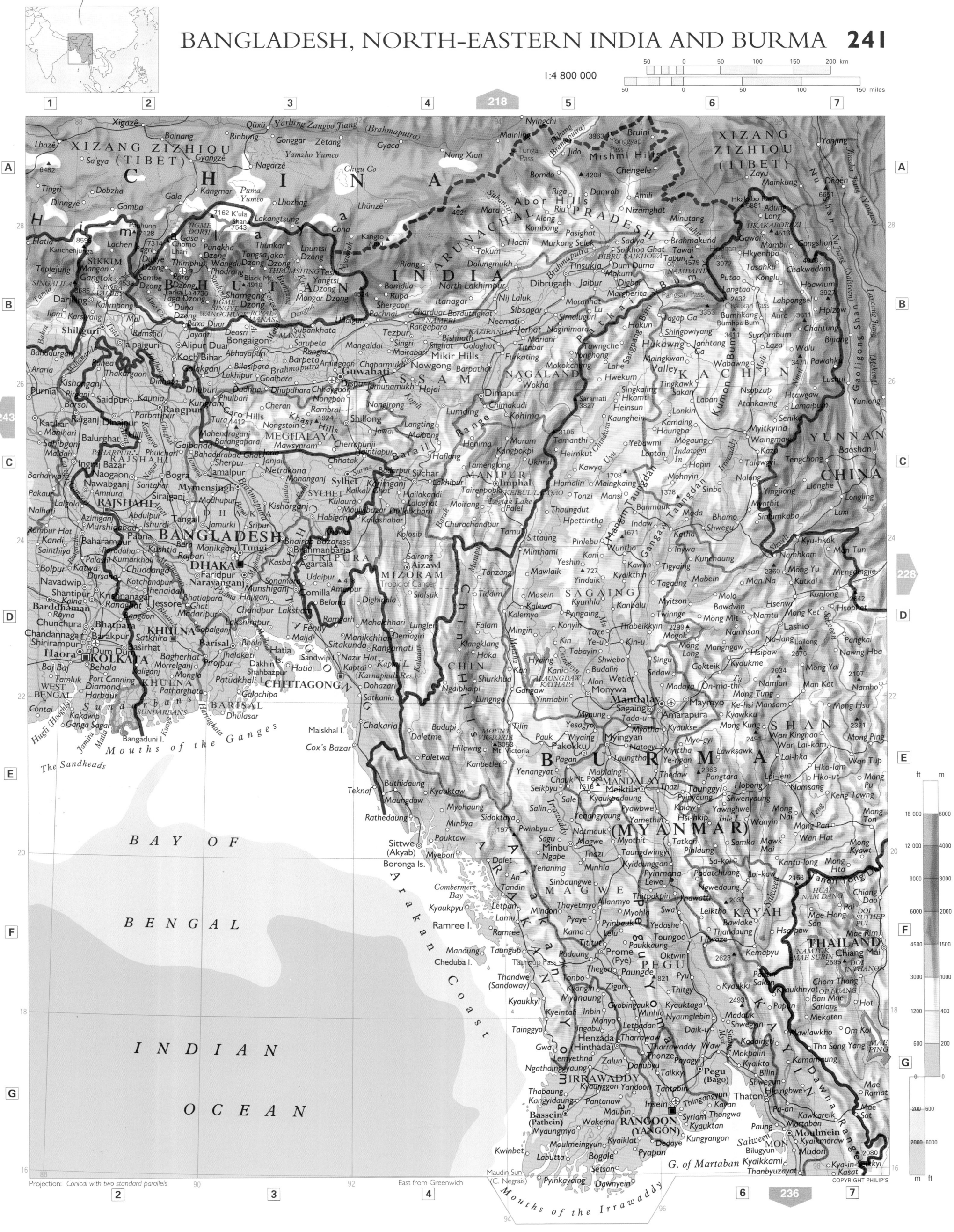

1:4 800 000

50 0 50 100 150 200 km
50 0 50 100 150 miles

CHINA

XIZANG ZIZHIQU (TIBET)

Lhazê 6482 Sa'gya Xigazê Bainang Qüxü Yarlung Zangbo Jiang (Brahmaputra) Nyingchi Mainling Bruini XIZANG ZIZHIQU (TIBET)

Tingri Dinggyê Dobzha Gala Rinbung Gonggar Zêtang Gyaca Nang Xian 3963 Yonggyap Pass Yanjing

Dobzha Kangmar Puma Yumco Lhozhag Chigu Co Tunga Pass Mishmi Hills Zayu Mainkung

Hatia 8598 Kanchenjunga Lachen Gamba Cona Kangto Bomdo 4208 Chengele Gawai Dêqên 6651

Tigme Dorji Gasa Chomo Lhari Thunkar Lhuntsi Dzong Abor Hills Riga Damroh Amili Nizamghat Hkakabo Razi 5881 Adung Long Gongshan

ARUNACHAL PRADESH

Darjiling Gangtok Thimphu BHUTAN Tashigang Takum Dolungmukh Pasighat Brahmakund Sadiya Saikhoa Ghat Tawai Putao Konglu Chakwadam

SIKKIM Mangan Paro Black Mt Mongar Dzong Tawang Bomdila Rupa Along Murkong Selek Tinsukia Dibru-Saikhowa Tapun Tasahku

INDIA

Shiliguri Jalpaiguri Buxa Duar MANAS Bongaigaon Shergaon North Lakhimpur Brahmaputra Dibrugarh Jaipur Margherita Namdapha Hkyenhpa Hpizow

Araria Kishanganj Koch Bihar Abhayapuri Barpeta Rangia Tezpur Singri Bishnath Jorhat Titabar Hukawng Valley KACHIN

Purnia Katihar Thakurganj Dhuburi Goalpara Dispur GUWAHATI Nowgong Golaghat Mariani Sibsagar Tagap Ga Shingbwiyang Sumprabum

Rangpur Kurigram Mangaldai Barpathar NAGALAND Wokha Kohima Saramati 3827 Singkaling Hkamti Myitkyina YUNNAN

ASSAM Mikir Hills Dimapur Chimakudi Hkamti Mogaung Indawgyi In Talawgyi Tengchong CHINA

MEGHALAYA Nongpoh Shillong Manipur Imphal Homalin Mohnyin Hopin Lienghe

Rajshahi Bogra Tura 4412 Cheran Mawphlang Jowai Marbong Langting Maram Tamanthi Indaw Katha Shwegu Longling

Naogaon Mymensingh Khasi Hills Cherrapunji Jaintia Hills Haflong Silchar Tamenglong Kangpokpi Ukhrul Kawya Uyu Sinbo Luxi

BANGLADESH Sylhet Kailashahar Hailakandi Churachandpur Tonzi Mansi Banmauk Myothit Sinlumkaba

DHAKA Narayanganj Comilla TRIPURA Agartala Aizawl MIZORAM Tropic of Cancer Tamu Kalewa Shwebo Bhamo Man Tun Namhkam

KHULNA BARISAL Chandpur Lakshmipur Feni CHITTAGONG CHIN HILLS Falam Kalemyo Monywa MANDALAY Lashio Pangkai

KOLKATA Haora Sundarbans Patuakhali Cox's Bazar MOUNT VICTORIA 3053 Pagan Sagaing Amarapura Kyaukse SHAN Hsipaw

BAY OF BENGAL

Teknaf Maungdaw Buthidaung Rathedaung Kanpetlet Yenangyat Meiktila Taunggyi Inle Lake Keng Tawng

Sittwe (Akyab) Myebon ARAKAN BURMA (MYANMAR) Magwe Pyinmana KAYAH Loi-kaw

Ramree I. Kyaukpyu Manaung Cheduba I. MAGWE Prome (Pye) PEGU THAILAND Chiang Mai

Thandwe (Sandoway) Taungup IRRAWADDY Henzada (Hinthada) Pegu (Bago) MON

INDIAN OCEAN

Bassein (Pathein) Myaungmya RANGOON (YANGON) Syriam Moulmein Mudon

Mouths of the Ganges The Sandheads Mouths of the Irrawaddy G. of Martaban

ft m
18 000 6000
12 000 4000
9000 3000
6000 2000
4500 1500
3000 1000
1200 600
600 200
0 0
200 600
2000 6000
m ft

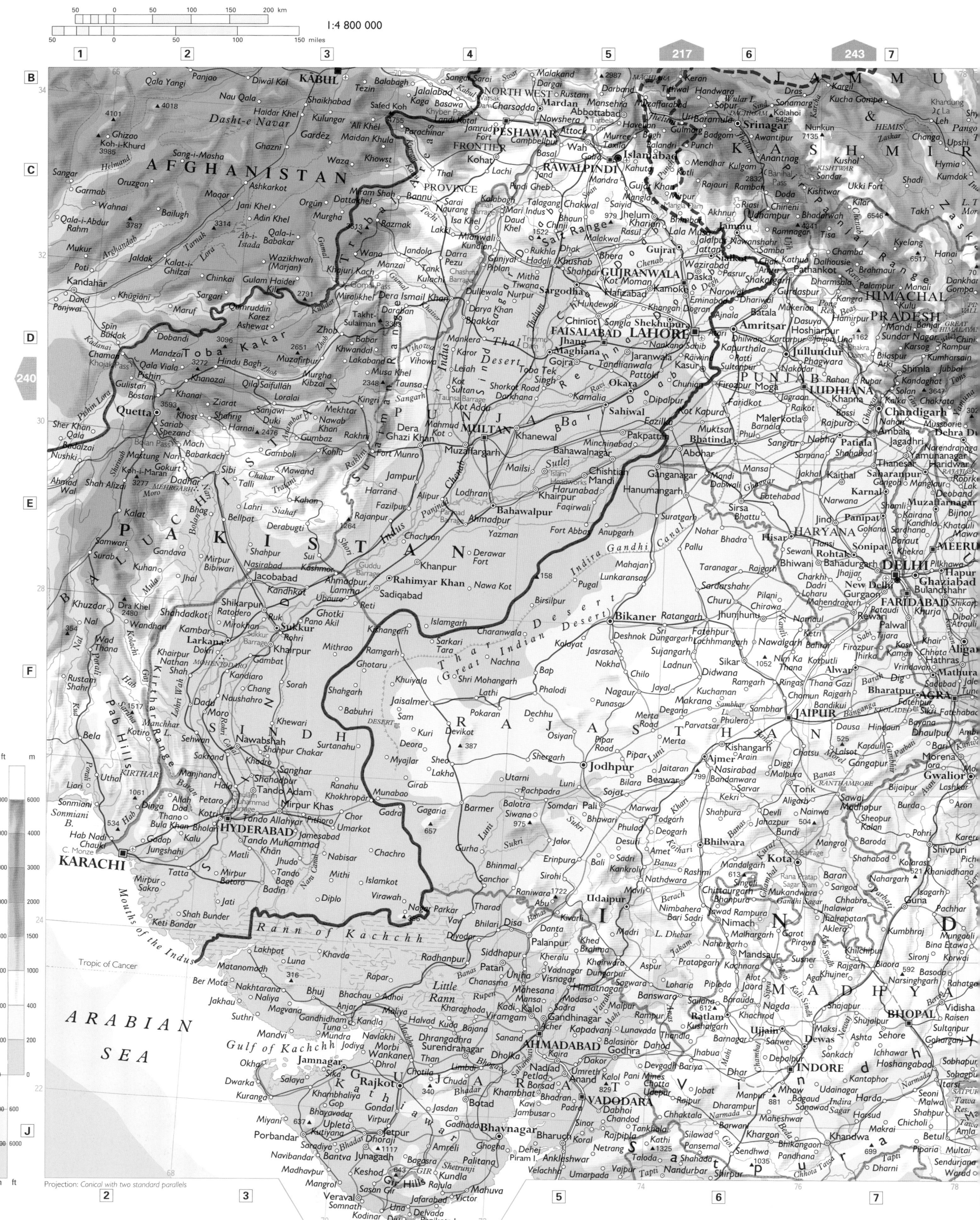

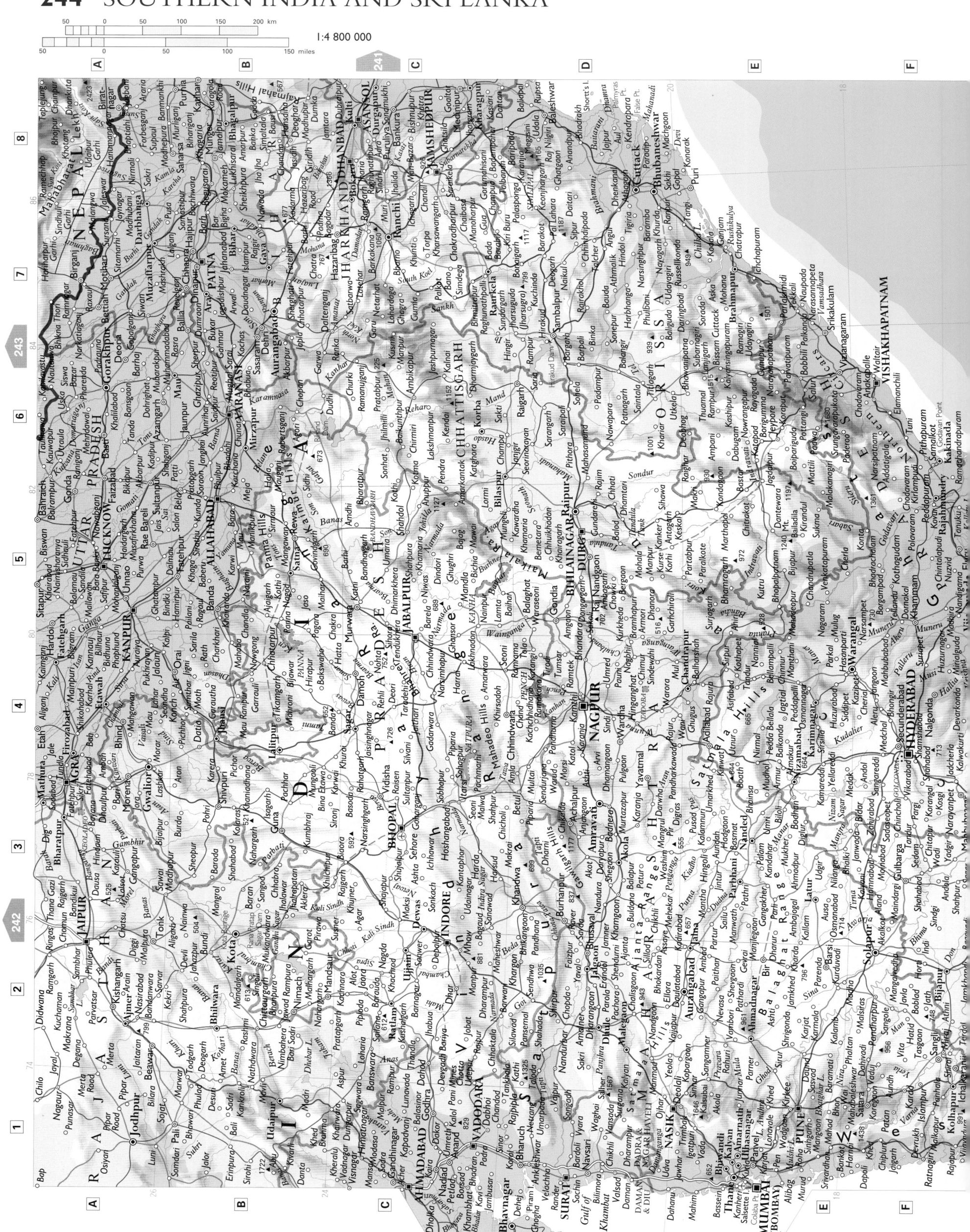

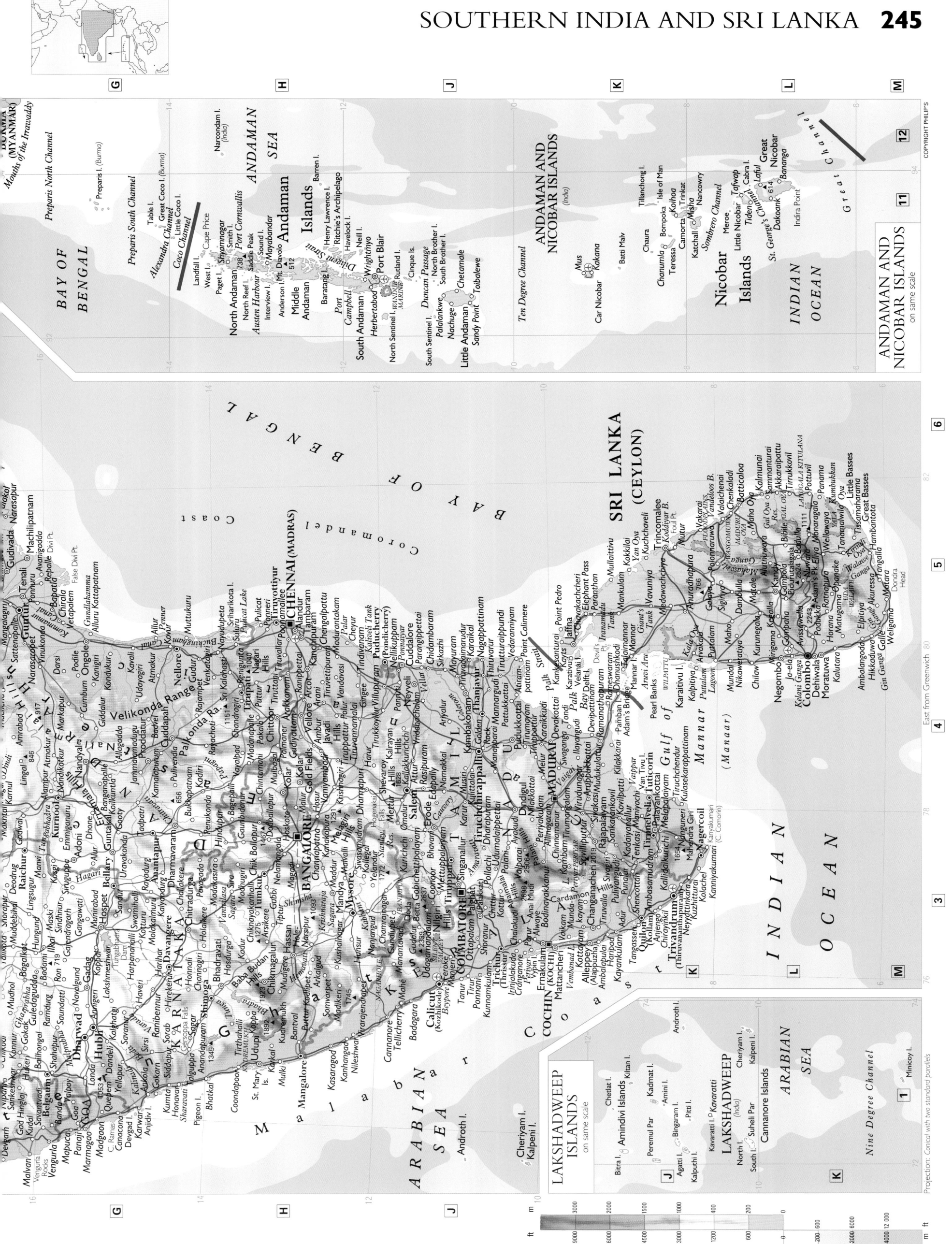

ANDAMAN AND
NICOBAR ISLANDS
on same scale

LAKSHADWEEP
ISLANDS
on same scale

Projection: Conical with two standard parallels

East from Greenwich

1:5 600 000

Projection: Conical with two standard parallels

Underlined towns in Iraq give their name
to the administrative area in which they stand

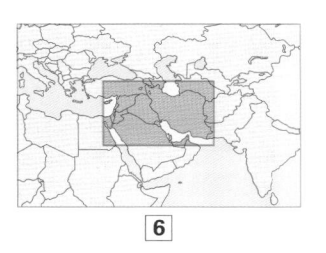

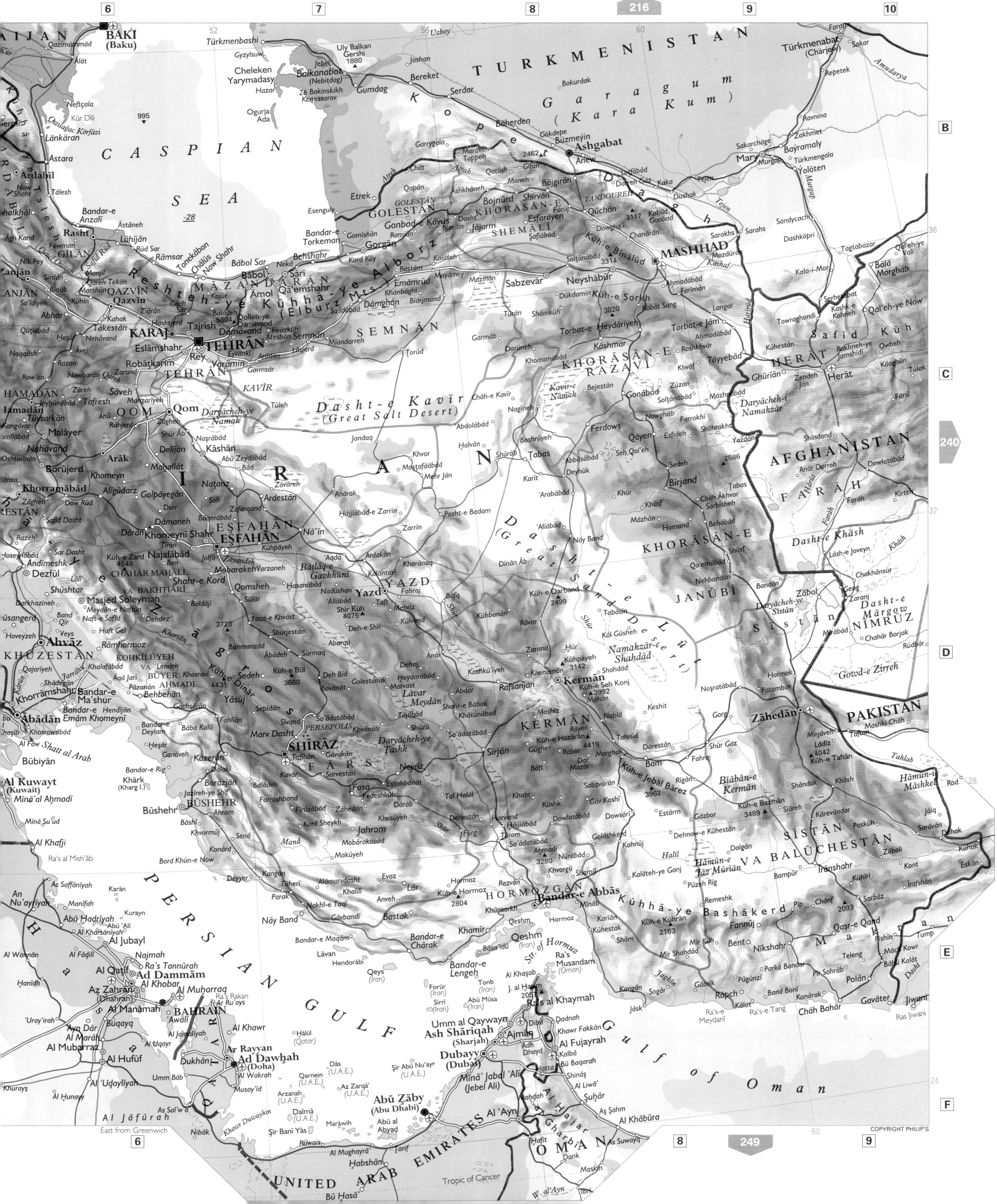

Projection: Conical with two standard parallels

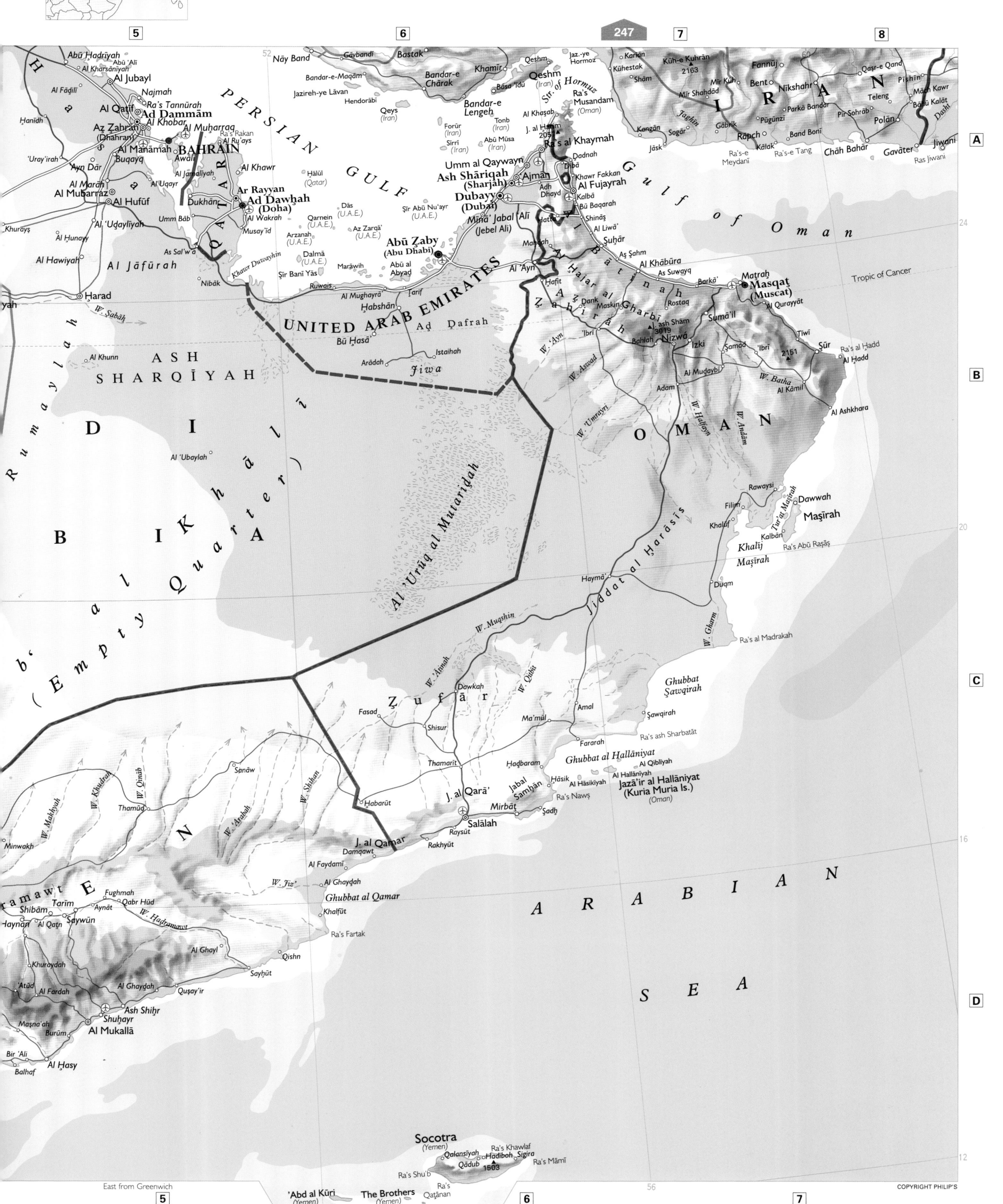

IRAN

Abū Hadrīyah
Al Kharsānīyah
Al Jubayl
Najmah
Abū 'Alī
Al Fāḍilī
Ḥanīdh
Ra's Tannūrah
Ad Dammām
Al Qaṭīf
Al Khobar
Az Zahrān
(Dhahran)
Al Muḥarraq
Ra's Rakan
Al Manāmah
BAHRAIN
Awalī
Ra's al Ruʿays
'Uray'irah
Buqayq
Ayn Dār
Al Jamalīyah
Al Khawr
Al Maraħ
Ar Rayyan
Al Mubarraz
Dukhān
Ad Dawḥah
(Doha)
Al Hufūf
Al Wakrah
Musay'īd
Al 'Uqayr
Al 'Uḍaylīyah
Umm Bāb
As Sal'w a

PERSIAN GULF

Nāy Band
Gāybandī
Bastak
Qeshm
Bandar-e-Maqām
Jazireh-ye Lāvan
Bandar-e Chārak
Khamīr
Hendorābī
Bandar-e
Lengeh
Qeys
(Iran)
Forūr
(Iran)
Sirrī
(Iran)
Tonb
(Iran)
Abū Mūsā
(Iran)
Qeshm
(Iran)
Bāsa Īdu
Jaz.-ye
Hormoz
Str. of Hormuz
Ra's
Musandam
(Oman)
Al Khaşab
J. al Ḥarīm
2051

Kārān
Kūhestak
Mīr Kūh
Sogar
Kūh-e Kuhrān
2163
Fannūj
Nīkshahr
Qaşr-e Qand
Bent
Teleng
Māēn Kawr
Bāhū Kalāt
Rāpch
Gābrīk
Pīr Sohrāb
Polān
Dashtī
Jāsk
Kālak
Gāvāter
Ras Jiwani
Jiwani

A

Umm al Qaywayn
Ash Shāriqah
(Sharjah)
Ajman
Khawr Fakkan
Al Fujayrah
Dubayy
(Dubai)
Adh Dhayd
Kalbā
Mīnā' Jabal 'Alī
(Jebel Ali)
Bū Baqarah
Shināş
Ra's al Khaymah
Dadnah
Dibā

Abū Ẓaby
(Abu Dhabi)
Dās
(U.A.E.)
Şīr Abū Nu'ayr
(U.A.E.)
Az Zarqā'
(U.A.E.)
Arzanah
(U.A.E.)
Dalmā
(U.A.E.)
Marāwih
Abū
al Abyaḍ
Şīr Banī Yās
Ruwais
Al Mughayrā
Ţarīf
Qarnein

Gulf of Oman

As Şahm
Al Khābūra
As Suwayq
Barkā'
Maţrah
Masqaţ
(Muscat)
Al Qurayyāt

Tropic of Cancer

24

Khuwr Duwayhin
Nibāk
Khurayş
Al Hawiyah
Ḥarad
W. Sabāh

UNITED ARAB EMIRATES

Al Liwā'
Ḥabshān
Bū Ḥaşā'
Arādah
Istaihah
Aḍ Ḍafrah

Ḥafīt
Al 'Ayn
Ḥattā
Suḥār
Maḥdah
Dank
Maskin
Rostaq
Sumā'il
Nizwā
Ibrī
Adam
Bahlah
Izkī
Samad
'Ibrī
2151
Şūr
Ra's al Ḥadd
Al Ḥadd

Bāţinah
Ḥajar al Gharbī
Aẕ Ẕāhirah
J. ash Shām
3019

B

Al Khunn
ASH
SHARQĪYAH
Al 'Ubaylah
Jiwa
W. 'Ayn
W. Asnad
Al Muḍaybī
W. Ḥalfayn
OMAN
Adam
Al Kāmil
Al Ashkhara

Rumaylah
D
I
B
a
l
K
h
a
l
ī
(Empty Quarter)
Empty
Al 'Urūq al Mutariḍah

SA U D I

ARABIA

W. Umtayri
W. Andām
Rawaysi
Filim
Khalūf
Kalbān
Khalīj
Maşīrah
Ra's Abū Raşāş
Dawwah
Maşīrah
Tui'al Maşīrah
20

Haymā'
Jiddat al Ḥarāsīs
Ḍuqm
Ra's al Madrakah

C

W. Muqshin
W. 'Aynah
W. Qabīt
Ghubbat
Şawqirah

Zufār
Dawkah
Shisur
Ma'mūl
Amal
Şawqirah
Ra's ash Sharbatāt

Fasad
Ḥabarūt
Thamarīt
Ḥaqbaram
Ghubbat al Hallāniyat
Al Qibliyah
Al Hallāniyah
Jazā'ir al Hallāniyat
(Kuria Muria Is.)
(Oman)

Sanāw
J. al Qarā'
Jabal
Samhan
Ḥāsik
Ra's Nawş
Ra's al Ḥadd

Minwakh
W. Mahiyah
W. Khudrah
W. Qināb
W. Shiḥan
W. 'Arabah
Thamūd
Damqawt
J. al Qamar
Ḥabarūt
Mirbāţ
Şadḥ

YEMEN

Salālah
Raysūt
Rakhyūt
16

Al Faydamī
W. Jīz'
Al Ghaydah
Ghubbat al Qamar
Khalfūt

Fughmah
Qabr Hūd
Tarīm
Shibām
Aynāt
Saywūn
W. Ḥadramawt
Al Qaţn
Ḥaynān
ramawt
Al Ghayl
Qishn
Sayḥūt
Ra's Fartak

ARABIAN

SEA

D

Khuraydah
Al Ghaydah
Quşay'ir
Aţūd
Al Fardah
Maşna'ah
Burūm
Ash Shiḥr
Shuḥayr
Al Mukallā
Bir 'Ali
Balḥaf
Al Ḥaşy

Socotra
(Yemen)
Qalansīyah
Qādub
Ra's Khawlaf
Hadiboh
Sigira
1503
Ra's Māmī
12

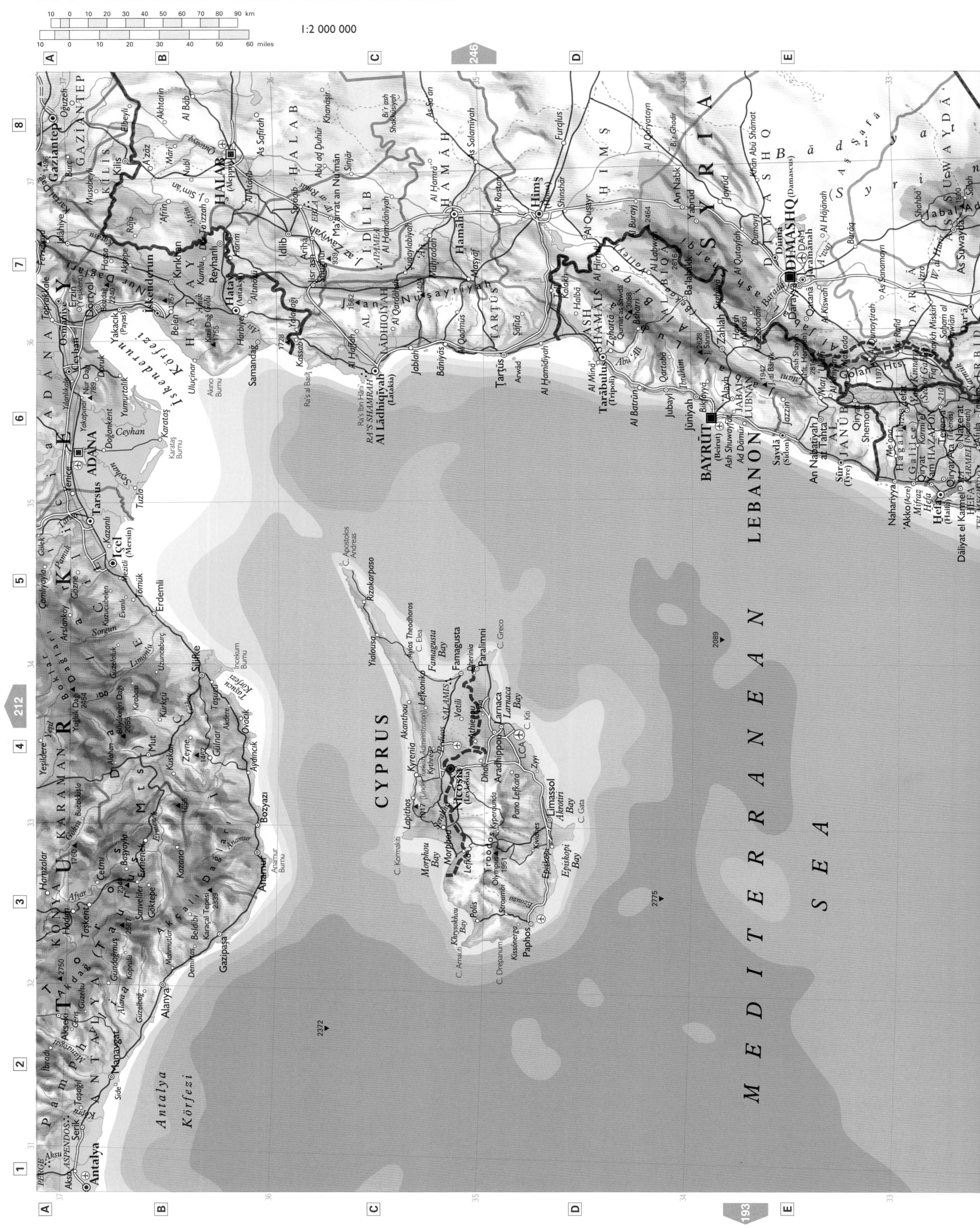

1:2 000 000

MEDITERRANEAN SEA

CYPRUS

SYRIA

LEBANON

TURKEY

1974 Cease Fire Lines

Projection : Polyconic

East from Greenwich

AFRICA

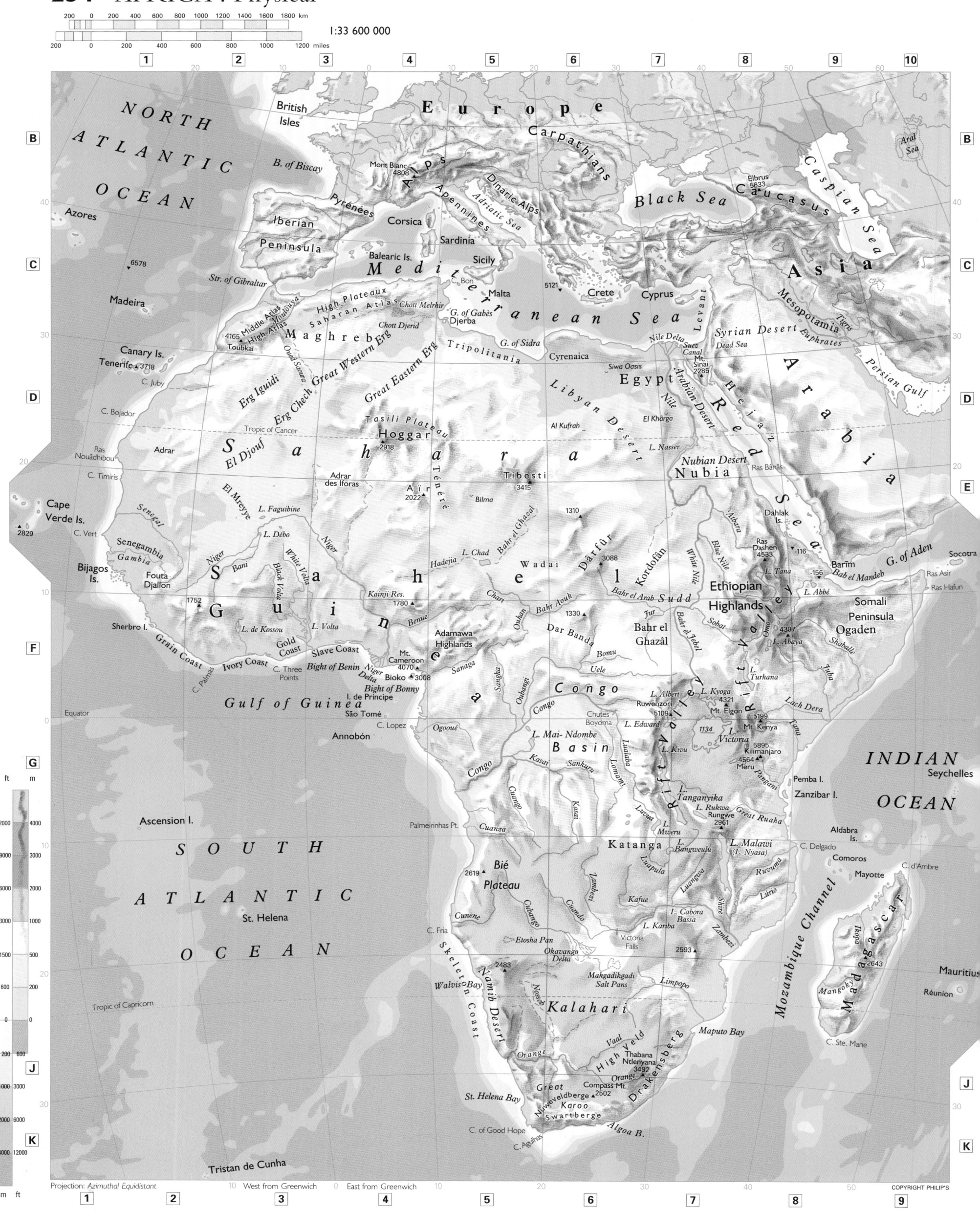

1:33 600 000

Projection: *Azimuthal Equidistant*

West from Greenwich   East from Greenwich

COPYRIGHT PHILIP'S

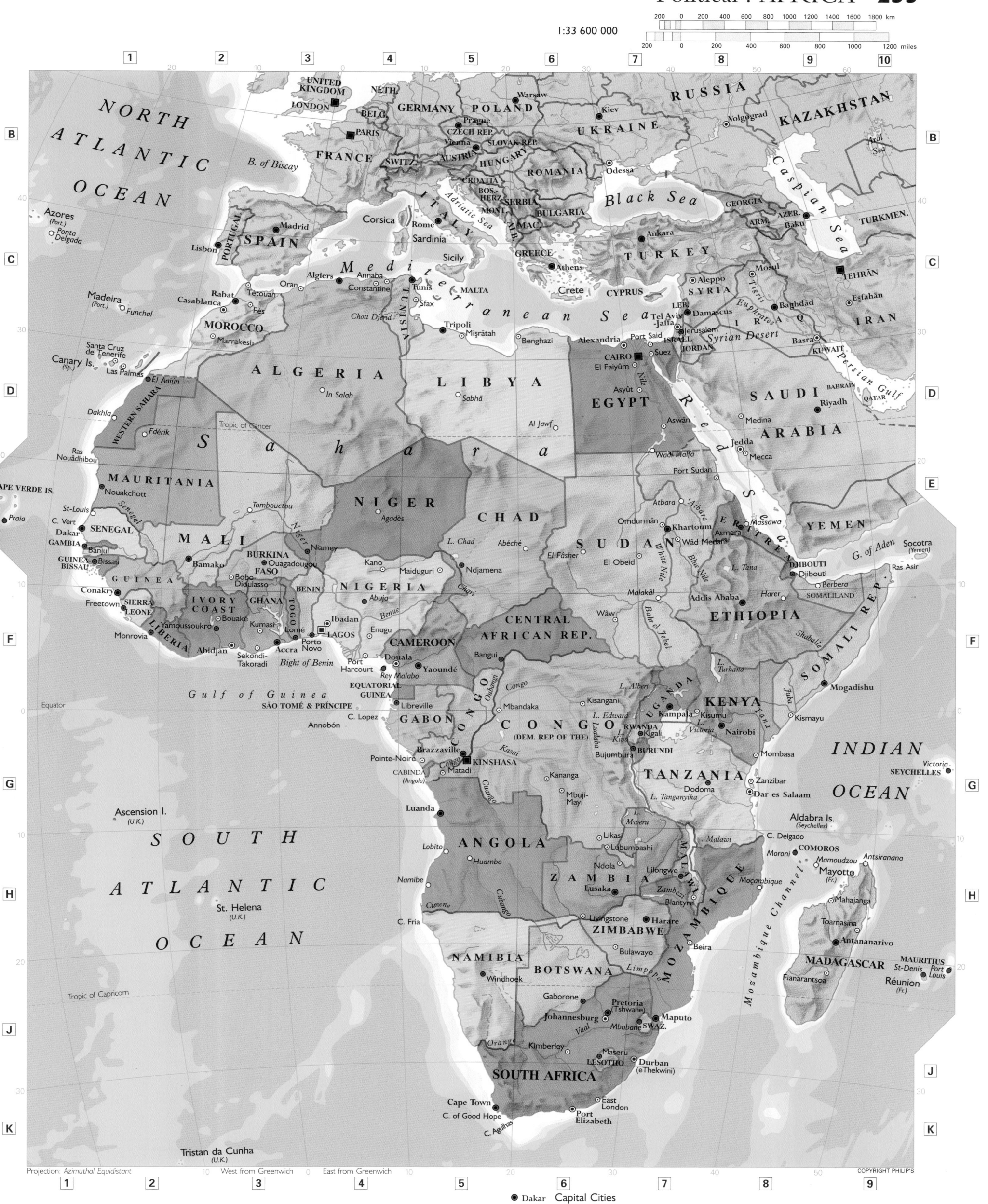

1:33 600 000

200 0 200 400 600 800 1000 1200 1400 1600 1800 km
200 0 200 400 600 800 1000 1200 miles

NORTH ATLANTIC OCEAN

UNITED KINGDOM
LONDON
NETH.
BELG.
FRANCE
B. of Biscay
PORTUGAL
Lisbon
SPAIN
Madrid
GERMANY
Prague
CZECH REP.
Vienna
SWITZ.
AUSTRIA
SLOVAK REP.
HUNGARY
CROATIA
BOS.-HERZ.
MONT.
SERBIA
M.B.
MAC.
Warsaw
POLAND
Kiev
UKRAINE
ROMANIA
BULGARIA
Odessa
RUSSIA
Volgograd
KAZAKHSTAN
Aral Sea
Black Sea
GEORGIA
ARM.
AZER.
Baku
Caspian Sea
TURKMEN.
Corsica
Rome
Sardinia
Italy
Adriatic Sea
Sicily
GREECE
Athens
Crete
Mediterranean Sea
CYPRUS
TURKEY
Ankara
SYRIA
Aleppo
Mosul
Tehrān
LEB.
Tel Aviv-Jaffa
Damascus
Baghdād
Eşfahān
IRAN
Tigris
Euphrates

Azores (Port.)
Ponta Delgada
Madeira (Port.)
Funchal
Santa Cruz de Tenerife
Canary Is. (Sp.)
Las Palmas
Casablanca
Rabat
Tétouan
Fès
MOROCCO
Marrakesh
Algiers
Oran
Annaba
Constantine
Tunis
Sfax
TUNISIA
Tripoli
Mişrātah
Benghazi
Chott Djerid
MALTA
ALGERIA
LIBYA
EGYPT
Alexandria
CAIRO
El Faiyûm
Port Said
Suez
ISRAEL
JORDAN
Jerusalem
Syrian Desert
Basra
KUWAIT
BAHRAIN
QATAR
Persian Gulf
Riyadh
SAUDI ARABIA
Medina
Mecca
Jedda

Dakhla
Ras Nouâdhibou
CAPE VERDE IS.
Praia
St-Louis
C. Vert
Dakar
SENEGAL
GAMBIA
Banjul
GUINEA-BISSAU
Bissau
Conakry
SIERRA LEONE
Freetown
Monrovia
LIBERIA
Fdérik
WESTERN SAHARA
El Aaiún
Tropic of Cancer
Sahara
MAURITANIA
Nouakchott
Tombouctou
MALI
Bamako
GUINEA
Yamoussoukro
IVORY COAST
Bouaké
Kumasi
GHANA
Abidjan
Sekondi-Takoradi
Accra
BURKINA FASO
Ouagadougou
Bobo-Dioulasso
BENIN
TOGO
Lomé
Porto Novo
LAGOS
Ibadan
Enugu
NIGERIA
Abuja
Kano
Maiduguri
Niger
Namey
NIGER
Agadès
L. Chad
Ndjamena
Abéché
CHAD
El Fâsher
SUDAN
El Obeid
Wâw
Malakâl
White Nile
Khartoum
Omdurmán
Atbara
'Atbara
ERITREA
Massawa
Asmera
L. Tana
Blue Nile
DJIBOUTI
Djibouti
Berbera
SOMALILAND
Harer
Addis Ababa
ETHIOPIA
YEMEN
Socotra (Yemen)
Ras Asir
G. of Aden
Red Sea
Wâdi Halfa
Port Sudan
Aswân
Asyût
Al Jawf
In Salah
Sabhā
Nile

CENTRAL AFRICAN REP.
Bangui
CAMEROON
Douala
Yaoundé
Rey Malabo
EQUATORIAL GUINEA
SÃO TOMÉ & PRÍNCIPE
Libreville
GABON
C. Lopez
Annobón
Port Harcourt
Bight of Benin
Gulf of Guinea
Benue
Chari
Oubangui
Congo
Mbandaka
Kisangani
CONGO (DEM. REP. OF THE)
L. Albert
L. Edward
L. Kivu
UGANDA
Kampala
RWANDA
Kigali
BURUNDI
Bujumbura
L. Victoria
Kisumu
Nairobi
KENYA
Mombasa
SOMALI REP.
Mogadishu
Kismayu
Juba
Shabeelle
L. Turkana
Bahr el Jebel
Equator

Ascension I. (U.K.)
SOUTH ATLANTIC OCEAN
St. Helena (U.K.)
Pointe-Noire
Brazzaville
CONGO
KINSHASA
Matadi
CABINDA (Angola)
Luanda
Lobito
Namibe
C. Fria
Huambo
ANGOLA
Kasai
Kananga
Mbuji-Mayi
Likasi
Lubumbashi
Ndola
ZAMBIA
Lusaka
Kwango
Cubango
Cunene
Cuanza
Congo
TANZANIA
Dodoma
Dar es Salaam
Zanzibar
L. Tanganyika
L. Mweru
Malawi
MALAWI
Lilongwe
Blantyre
Zambezi
Moçambique
C. Delgado
Moroni
COMOROS
Mamoudzou
Mayotte (Fr.)
Antsiranana
MOZAMBIQUE
INDIAN OCEAN
SEYCHELLES
Victoria
Aldabra Is. (Seychelles)

NAMIBIA
Windhoek
BOTSWANA
Gaborone
Tropic of Capricorn
Livingstone
Bulawayo
ZIMBABWE
Harare
Beira
Mozambique Channel
Limpopo
Mahajanga
Toamasina
Antananarivo
MADAGASCAR
Fianarantsoa
MAURITIUS
St-Denis
Réunion (Fr.)
Port Louis
Johannesburg
Pretoria (Tshwane)
Maputo
Mbabane
SWAZ.
Maseru
LESOTHO
Durban (eThekwini)
SOUTH AFRICA
Kimberley
Orange
Vaal
East London
Cape Town
C. of Good Hope
Port Elizabeth
C. Agulhas

Tristan da Cunha (U.K.)

Projection: *Azimuthal Equidistant*   West from Greenwich   East from Greenwich   COPYRIGHT PHILIP'S

● Dakar   Capital Cities

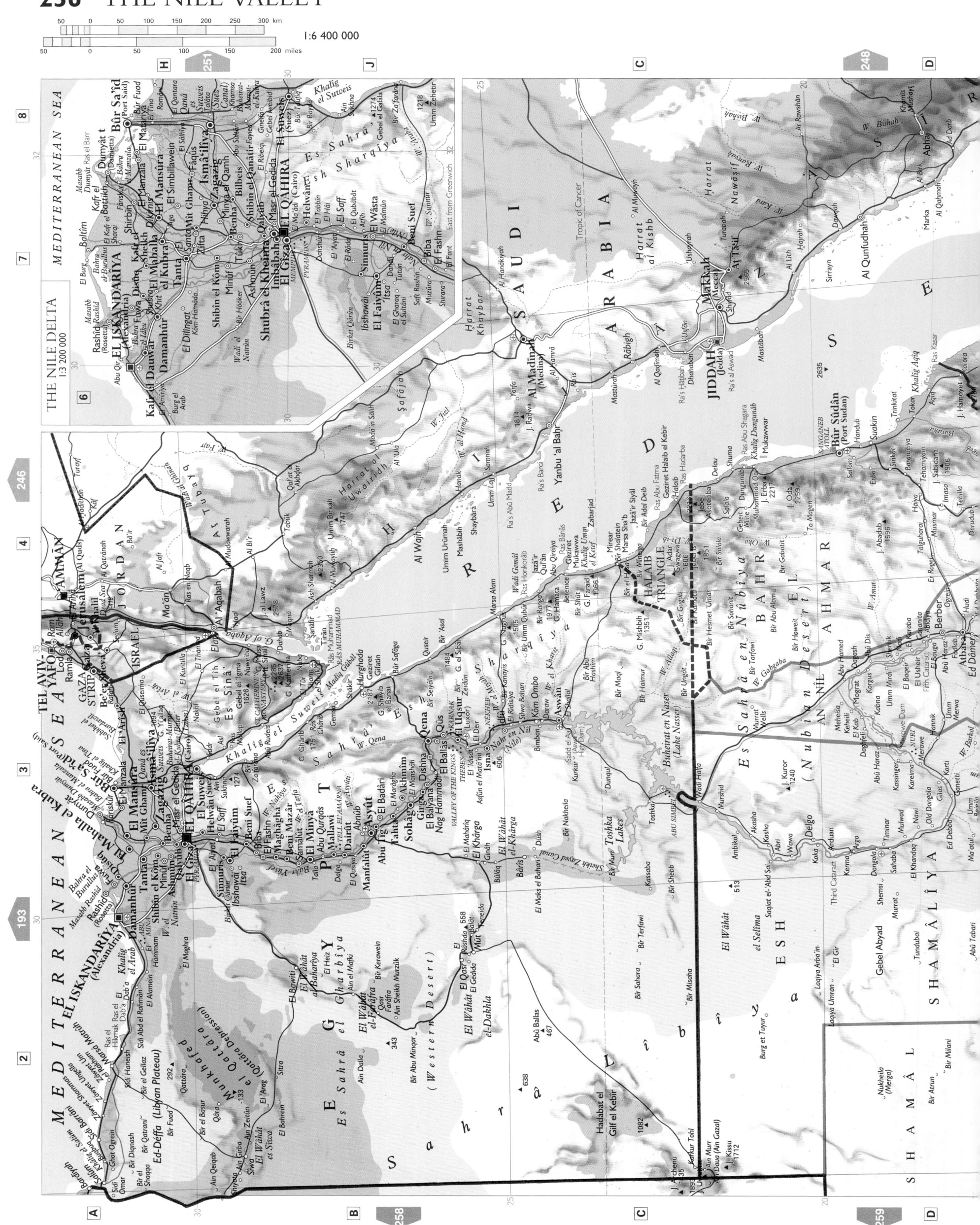

1:6 400 000

50   0   50   100   150   200   250   300 km

50   0   50   100   150   200 miles

THE NILE DELTA
1:3 200 000

MEDITERRANEAN SEA

Bûr Sa'îd (Port Said)

ELISKANDARIYA
(Alexandria)

EL QAHIRA (Cairo)

SAUDI ARABIA

Makkah (Mecca)

JIDDAH (Jedda)

Bûr Sûdân (Port Sudan)

Buheirat en Naser (Lake Nasser)

HALAIB TRIANGLE

Es Sahrâ en Nûbîya
(Nubian Desert)

BAHR EL AHMAR

Es Sahrâ el Gharbîya
(Western Desert)

EL WÂHÂT

Sahra el Kubra

Libyan Plateau

Qattara Depression
(Munkhafad el Qattâra)

S a h r a   L i b i y a

SHAMÂLÎYA

SHAMÂL

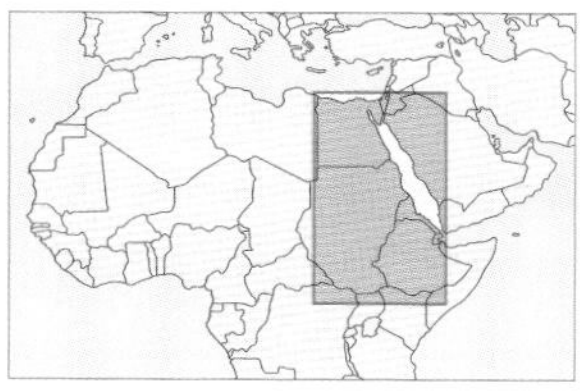

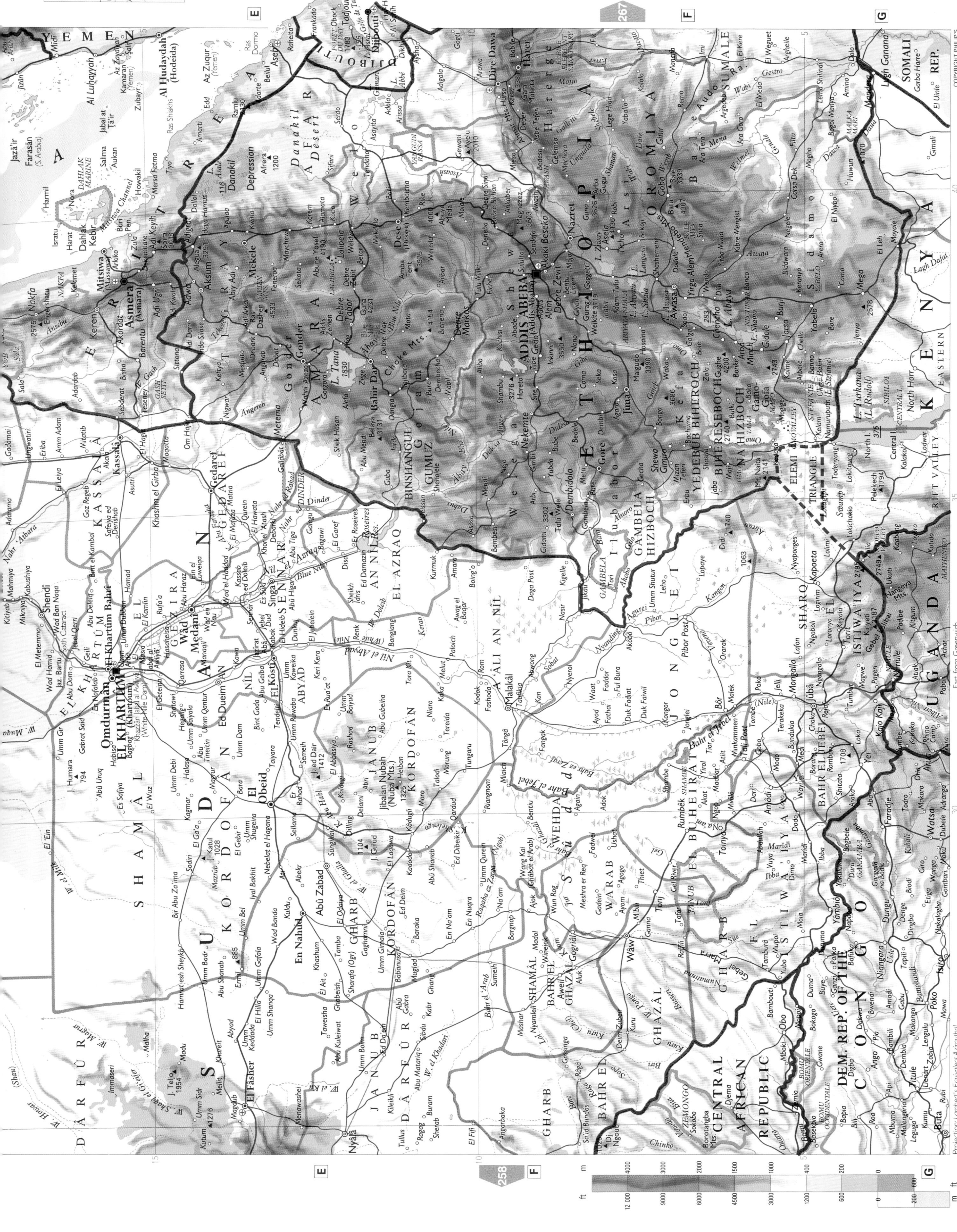

∴ UNESCO World Heritage Sites

National Parks

Nature Reserves and Game Reserves

COPYRIGHT PHILIP'S

Projection: Lambert's Equivalent Azimuthal

East from Greenwich

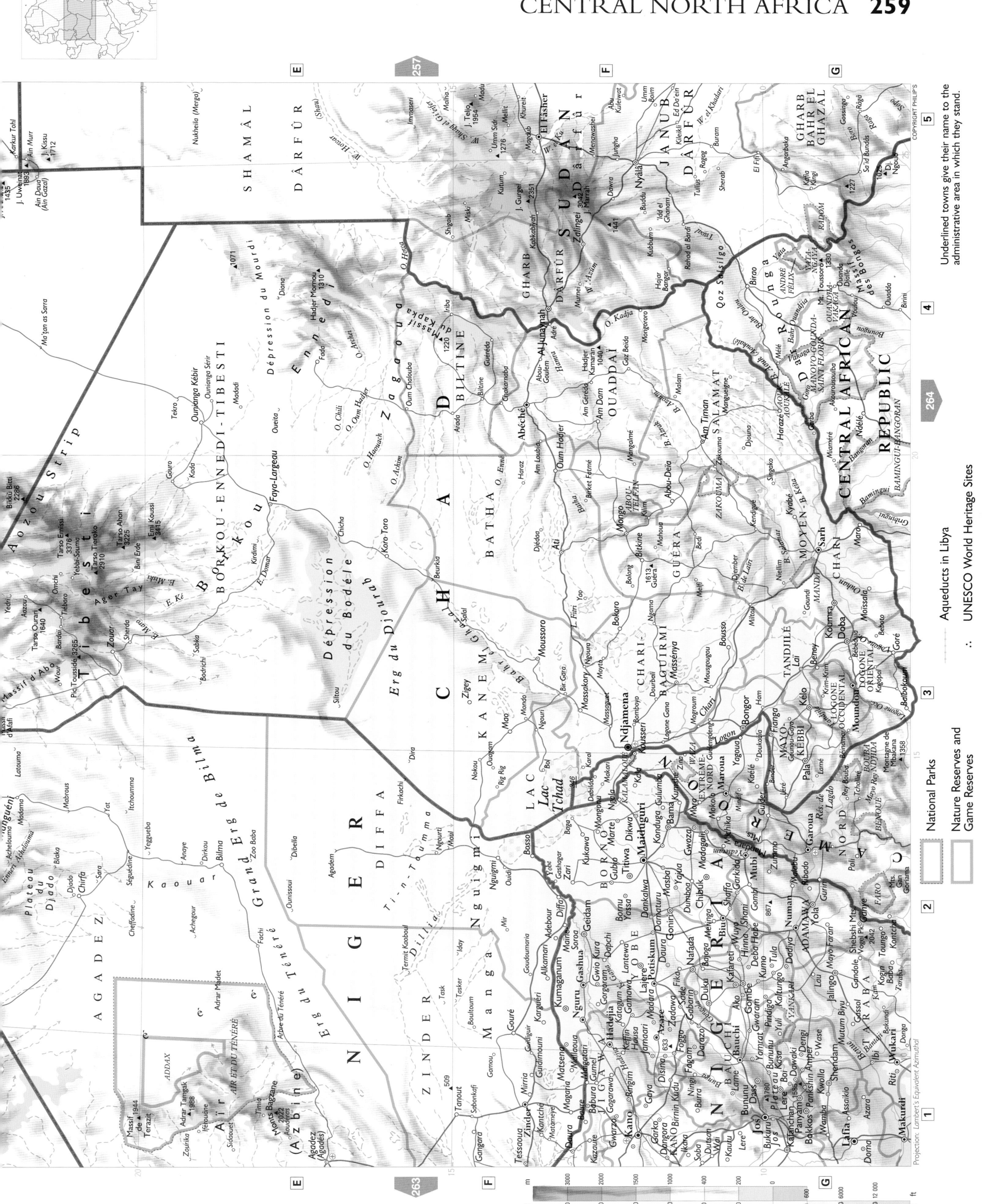

Underlined towns give their name to the administrative area in which they stand.

Aqueducts in Libya

:: UNESCO World Heritage Sites

National Parks

Nature Reserves and Game Reserves

50 0 50 100 150 200 250 300 km

1:6 400 000

50 0 50 100 150 200 miles

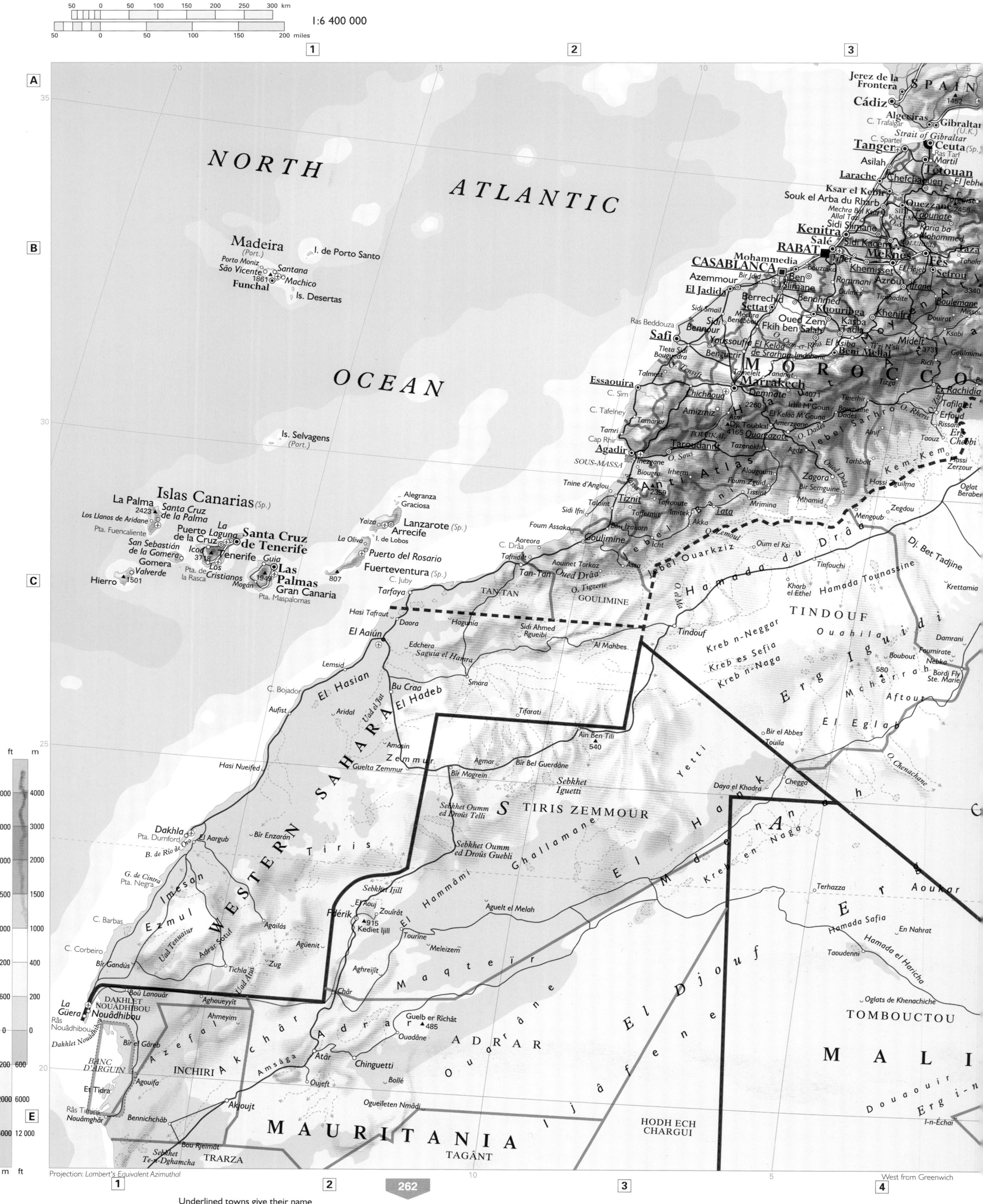

NORTH

ATLANTIC

OCEAN

SPAIN
Jerez de la Frontera
Cádiz
C. Trafalgar
Algeciras · **Gibraltar** (U.K.)
Strait of Gibraltar
C. Spartel · **Ceuta** (Sp.)
Tanger · Ras Tarf · Martil
Asilah · **Tétouan**
Larache · Chefchaouen · El Jebha
Ksar el Kebir · **Ouezzane** · Taounate
Souk el Arba du Rharb · **Taza**
Mechra Bel Ksiri · Sidi Slimane
Kenitra · **Salé** · Sidi Kacem · **Meknès** · **Fès**
RABAT · Rommani · **Khemisset** · Azrou · **Sefrou**
Mohammedia · Boulemane
CASABLANCA · Ben Slimane · Khouribga · **Khénifra**
Azemmour · Berrechid · Benahmed · Kasba Tadla · Midelt
El Jadida · **Settat** · Oued Zem · Fkih ben Salah · El Ksiba
Sidi Smaïl · Beni Mellal · Er Rachidia
Ras Beddouza · **Safi** · Youssoufia · El Kelaâ des Srarhna · Tafilalet · Erfoud
Tleta Sidi Bouguedra · **Marrakech** · Demnate · Rissani
Essaouira · C. Sim · Chichaoua · Amizmiz · El Kelaâ M'Goune · **MOROCCO**
C. Tafelney · Tamanar · Dj. Toubkal 4165 · Ouarzazate · Zagora
Agadir · Taroudant · Tazenakht
SOUS-MASSA · Inezgane · Irherm · Foum Zguid · Tissint · Mhamid
Tamri · O. Sous · Tnine d'Anglou
Tiznit · Tafraoute · Tata
Sidi Ifni · Foum Assaka · Akka · Oglat Beraber
Goulimine · Assa · Zegdou
Tan-Tan · Oued Drâa · Tindouf · Mengoub
Tarfaya · GOULIMINE · Kreb n-Neggar · **Erg Iguidi**
Hasi Tafraut · Daora · Hagunia · Sidi Ahmed Rgueibi · Al Mahbes · Kreb es Sefia · Bordj Fly Ste. Marie
El Aaiún · Edchera · Tindouf · Kreb n-Naga · **TINDOUF**
Lemsid · Saguia el Hamra · Smara · Tifariti · **Aftout**
C. Bojador · **El Hasian** · Bu Craa · El Hadeb · **El Eglab**
Aufist · Aridal · Ain Ben Tili 540 · Bir el Abbes · Touila
WESTERN SAHARA · Amosin · Agmar · Bîr Bel Guerdâne
Hasi Nueifed · Guelta Zemmur · Zemmur · Bîr Mogrein · Daya el Khadra · Chegga
S TIRIS ZEMMOUR · Terhazza
Dakhla · Pta. Durnford · El Aargub · Bîr Enzarân · Sebkhet Iguetti · Chenachane
B. de Rio de Oro · Tiris · Sebkhet Oumm ed Droûs Telli · **Ghallamane** · **El Hank** · **Adrar**
G. de Cintra · Pta. Negra · Sebkhet Oumm ed Droûs Guebli · Hamada Safia · En Nahrat
Imeson · Sebkhet Ijill · Hammâmi · Hamada el Haricha
C. Barbas · El Aouj · Zouîrât · El Aouguelt el Melah · Meleizem · Taoudenni
Ezmul · Agaïlás · Kediet Ijill 915 · Tourine
C. Corbeiro · Bîr Gandús · Adrar Atâr · Tichla · Aguenit · Zug · **El Djouf** · **TOMBOUCTOU**
Bou Lanouâr · Aghoueyyit · Maqtëir · Oglats de Khenachiche
La Güera · Nouâdhibou · Ahmeyim · Char · Ouadâne · **MALI**
Râs Nouâdhibou · DAKHLET NOUÂDHIBOU · Aghreijît
Dakhlet Nouâdhibou · Bîr el Gâreb · Tichla · Atár · Chinguetti · Guelb er Richât 485
BANC D'ARGUIN · INCHIRI · Amsâga · Bollé
Et Tidra · Agouifa · Oujeft · Ogueïleten Nmâdi · I-n-Échai
Râs Tidra · Akjoujt · **ADRAR** · **Douaouir**
Nouâmghâr · Bennichâb · **MAURITANIA**
Sebkha Te-n-Dghamcha · HODH ECH CHARGUI
Bou Rjeimât · **TRARZA** · **TAGÂNT**

West from Greenwich

Projection: Lambert's Equivalent Azimuthal

Underlined towns give their name
to the administrative area in which they stand

ft m

12 000 — 4000
9000 — 3000
6000 — 2000
4500 — 1500
3000 — 1000
1200 — 400
600 — 200
0 — 0
200 — 600
2000 — 6000
4000 — 12 000

m ft

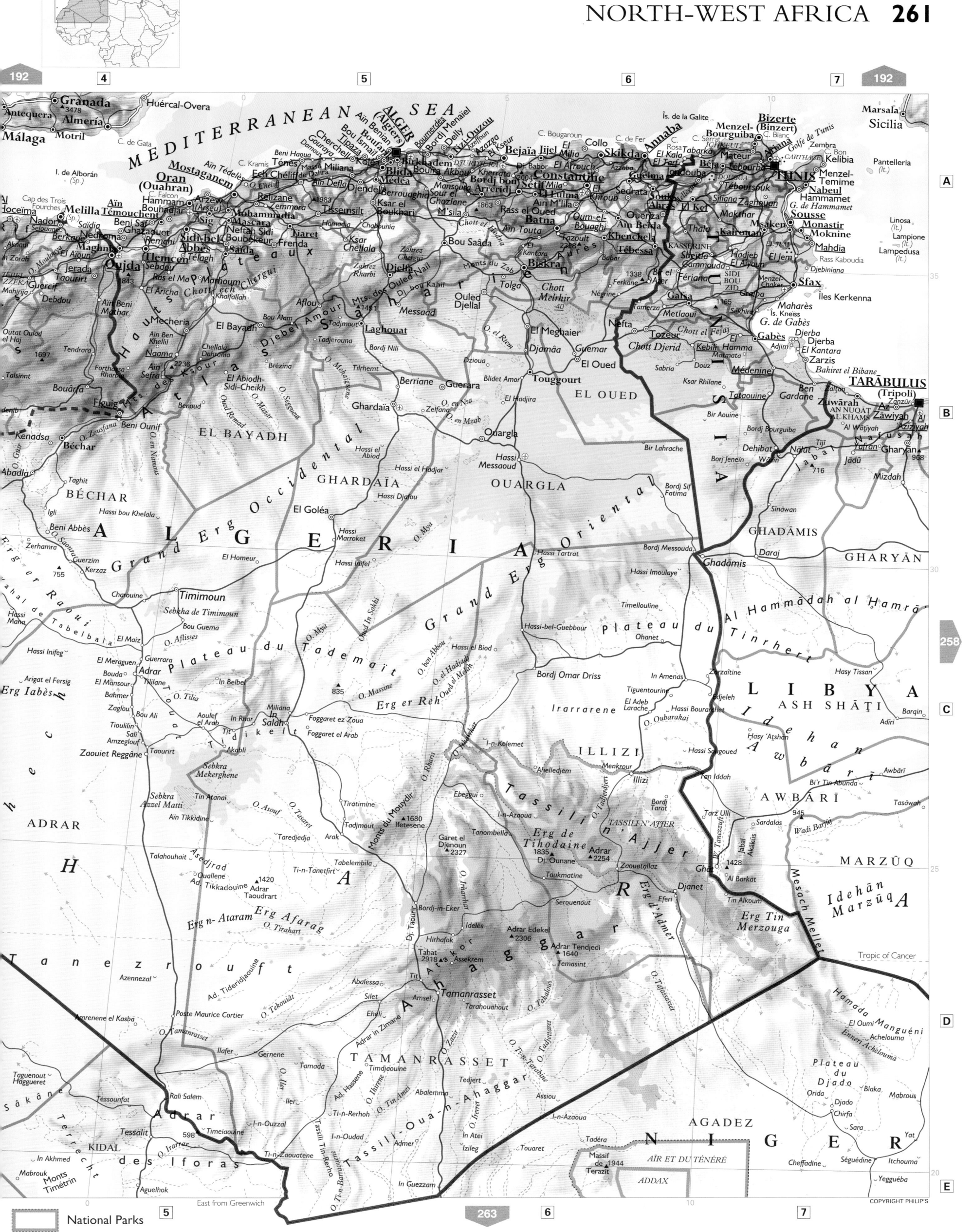

National Parks

Nature Reserves and
Game Reserves

◇∴ UNESCO World Heritage Sites

COPYRIGHT PHILIP'S

1:6 400 000

260

Projection : Lambert's Equivalent Azimuthal

Underlined towns give their name to the
administrative area in which they stand.

West from Greenw

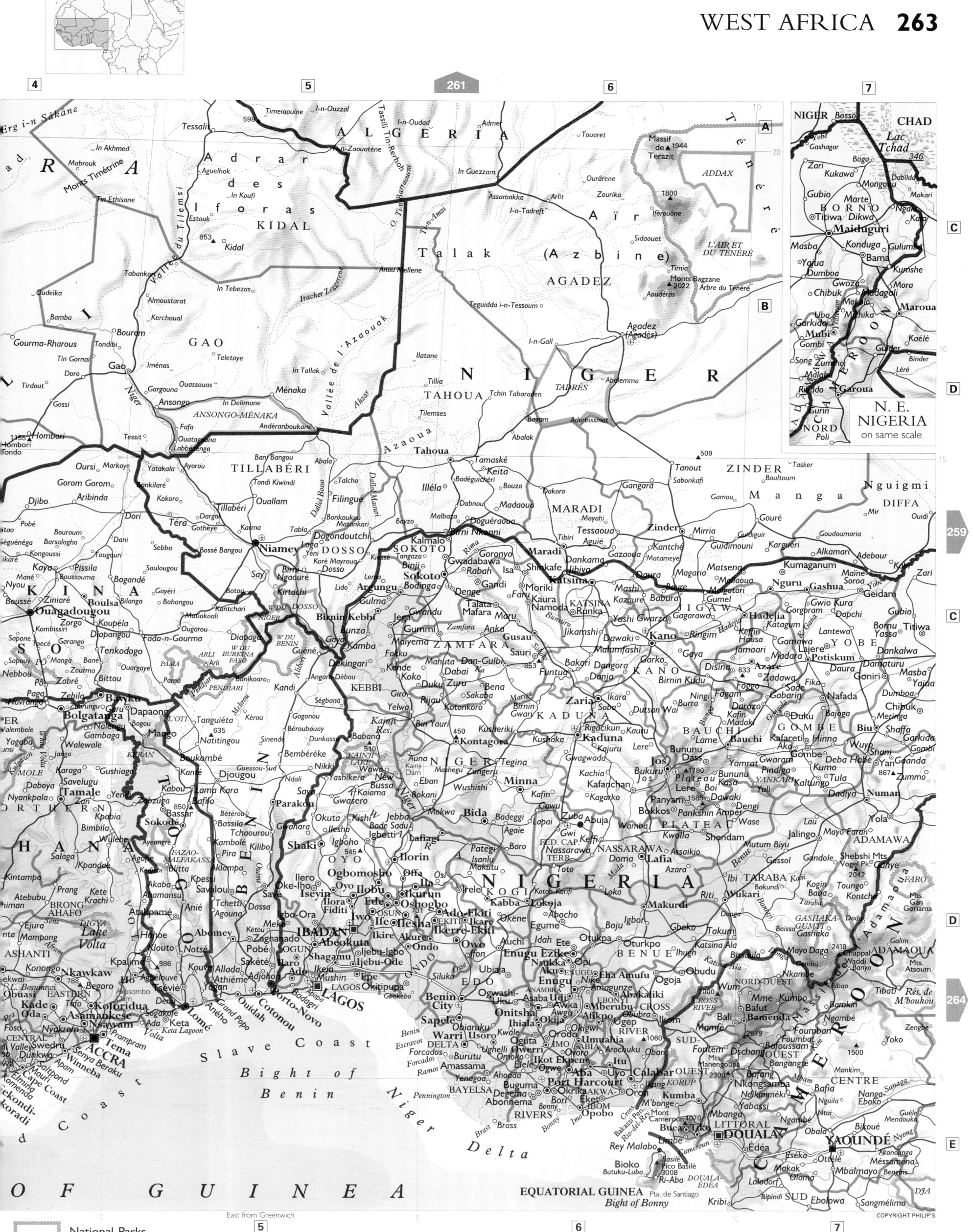

National Parks

Nature Reserves and
Game Reserves

∴ UNESCO World Heritage Sites

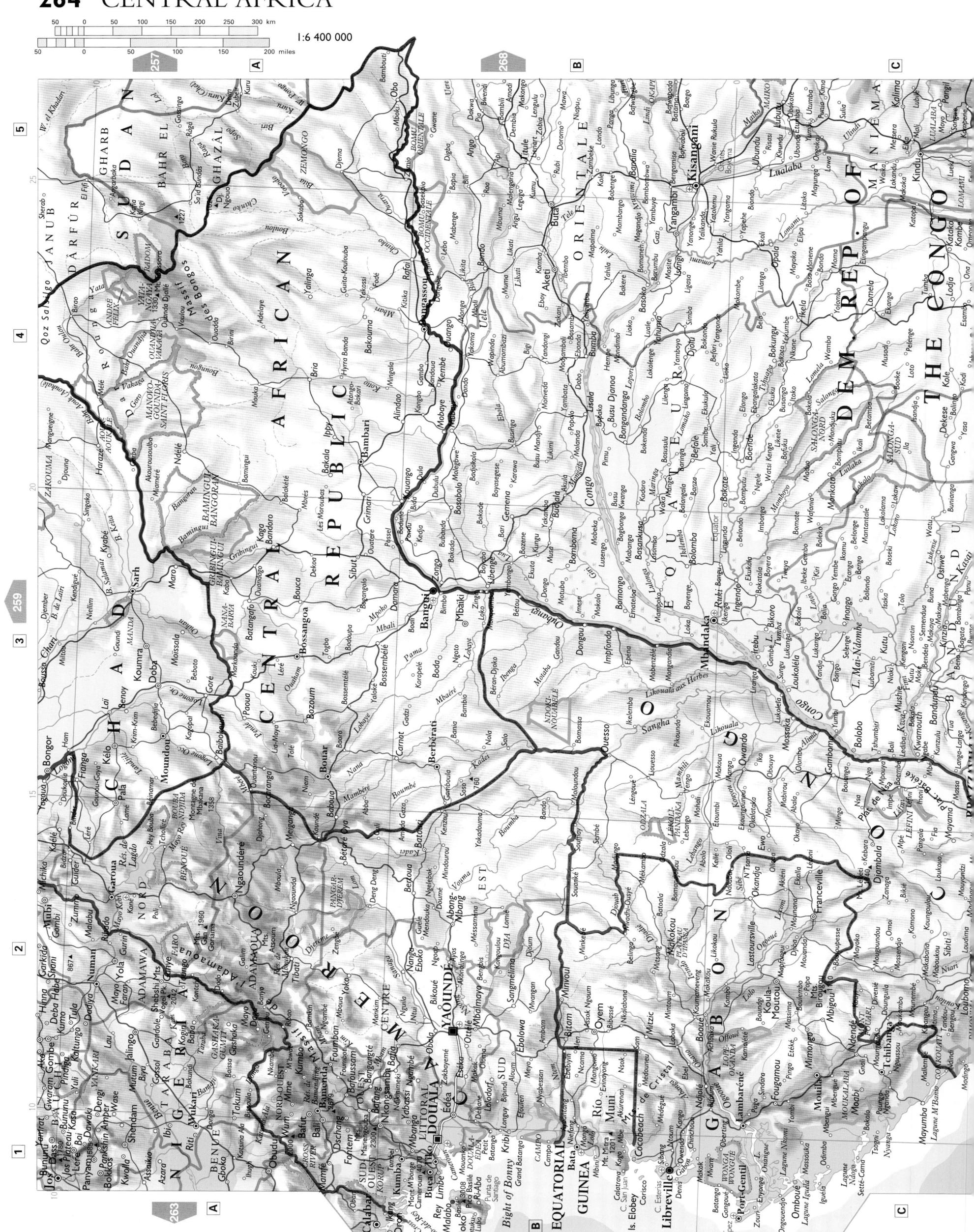

National Parks

Nature Reserves and
Game Reserves

∴ UNESCO World Heritage Sites

SÃO TOMÉ
AND PRÍNCIPE
on same scale

Projection: Lambert's Equivalent Azimuthal

COPYRIGHT PHILIP'S

1:6 400 000

National Parks

Nature Reserves and
Game Reserves

∴ UNESCO World Heritage Sites

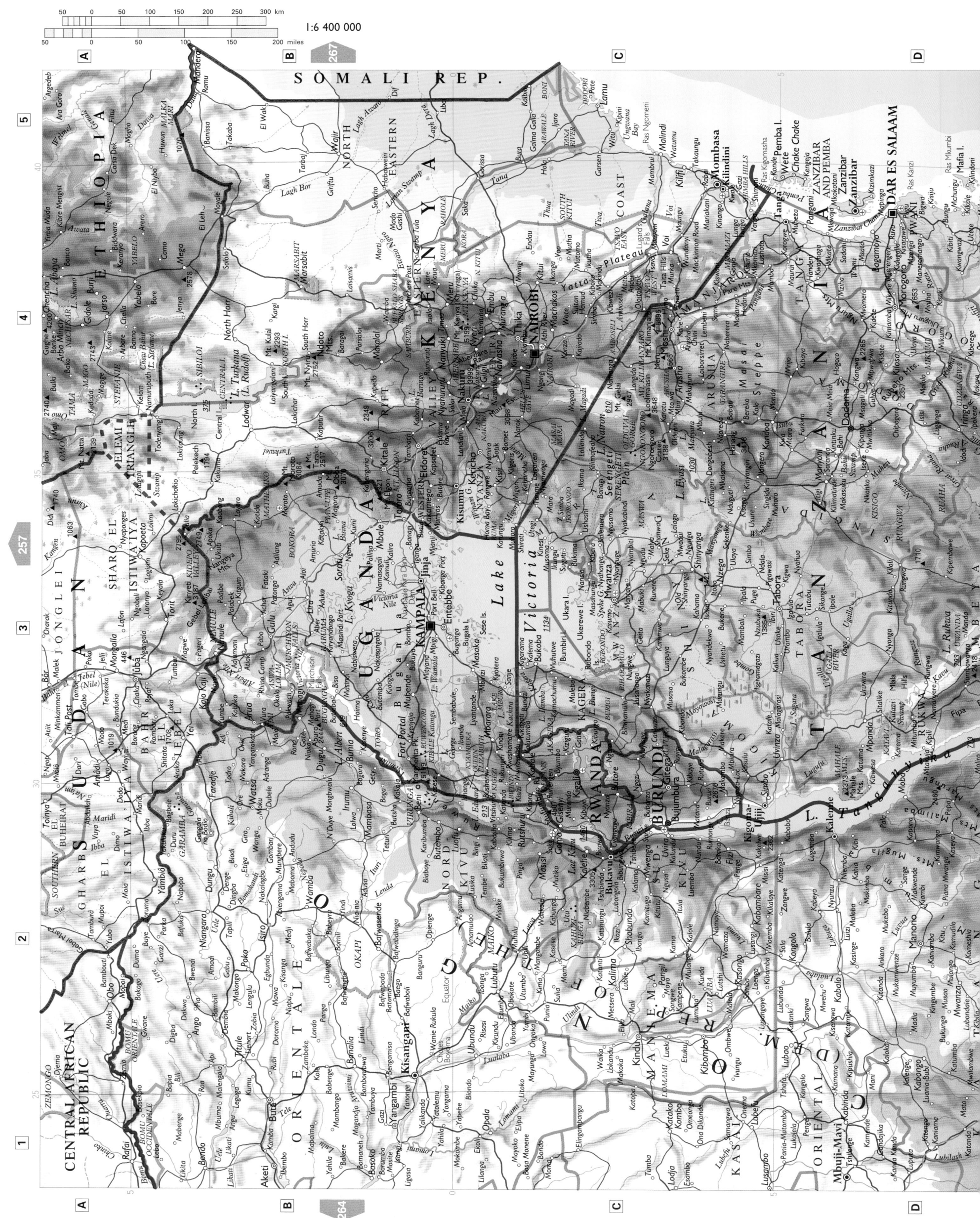

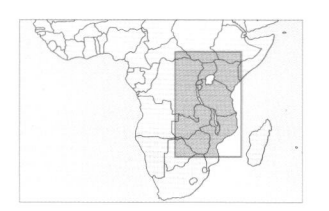

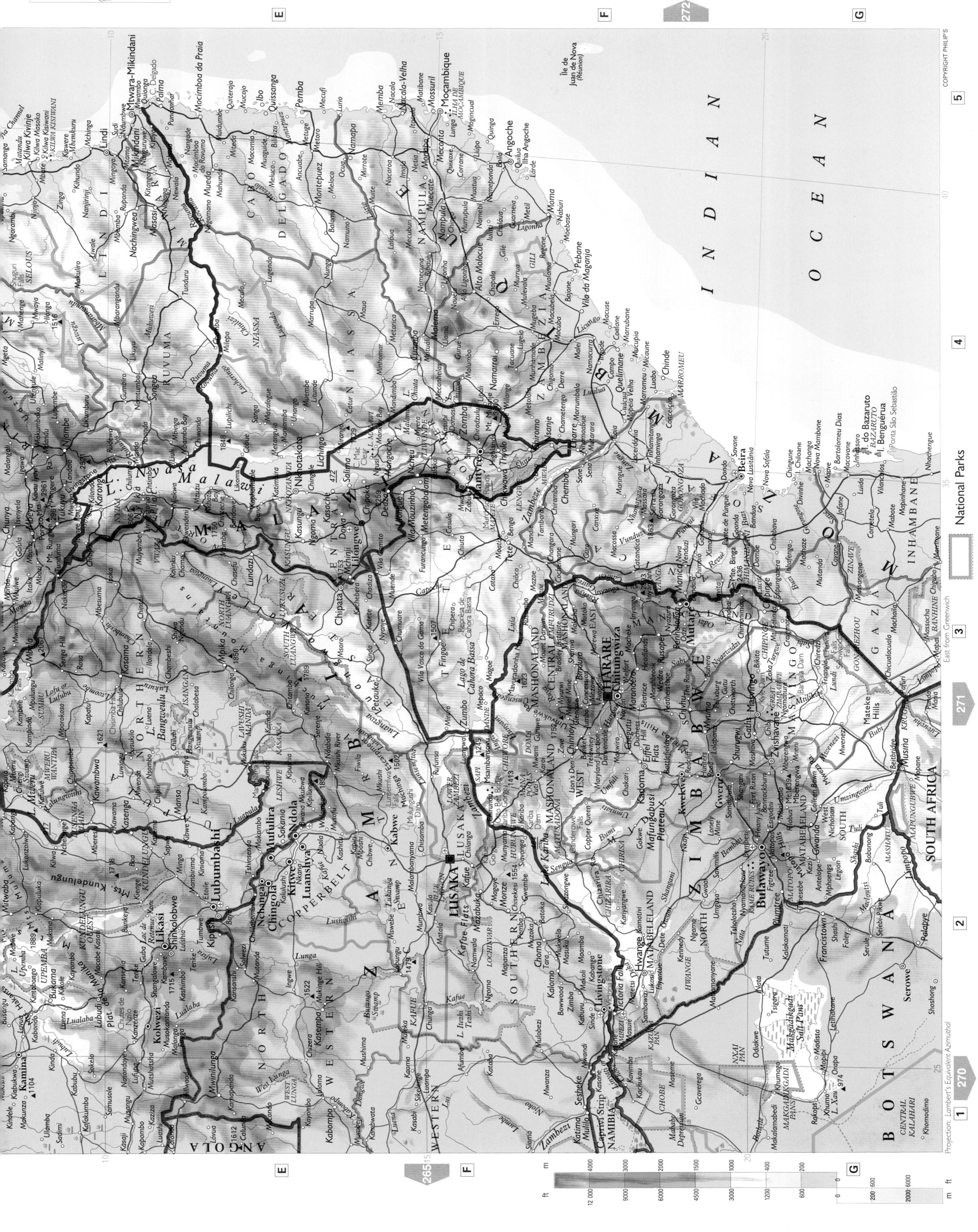

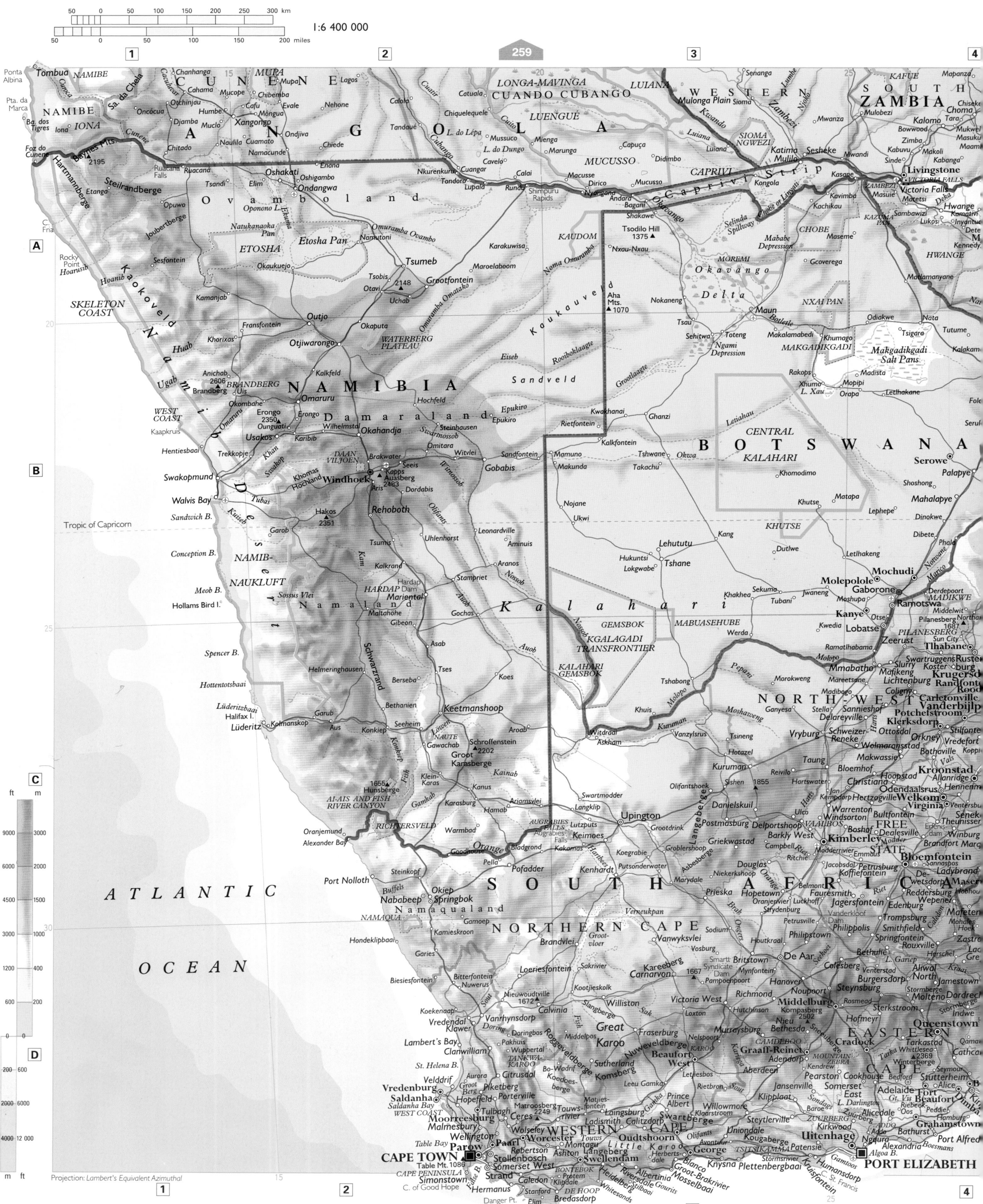

1:6 400 000

Projection: Lambert's Equivalent Azimuthal

MALAWI

ZAMBEZIA

MOZAMBIQUE

CHANNEL

Bassas da India
(Fr.)

Île de Júan de Nova
(Fr.)

Île Europa
(Fr.)

Tropic of Capricorn

ZIMBABWE

HARARE
Chitungwiza

Bulawayo

Beira

LIMPOPO

PRETORIA
(Tshwane)

JOHANNESBURG

MAPUTO

SWAZILAND

LESOTHO

KWAZULU NATAL

PIETERMARITZBURG

DURBAN (eThekwini)
Umlazi

East London

INDIAN

OCEAN

National Parks

Nature Reserves and
Game Reserves   ∴ UNESCO World Heritage Sites

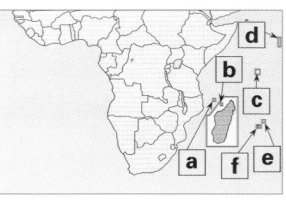

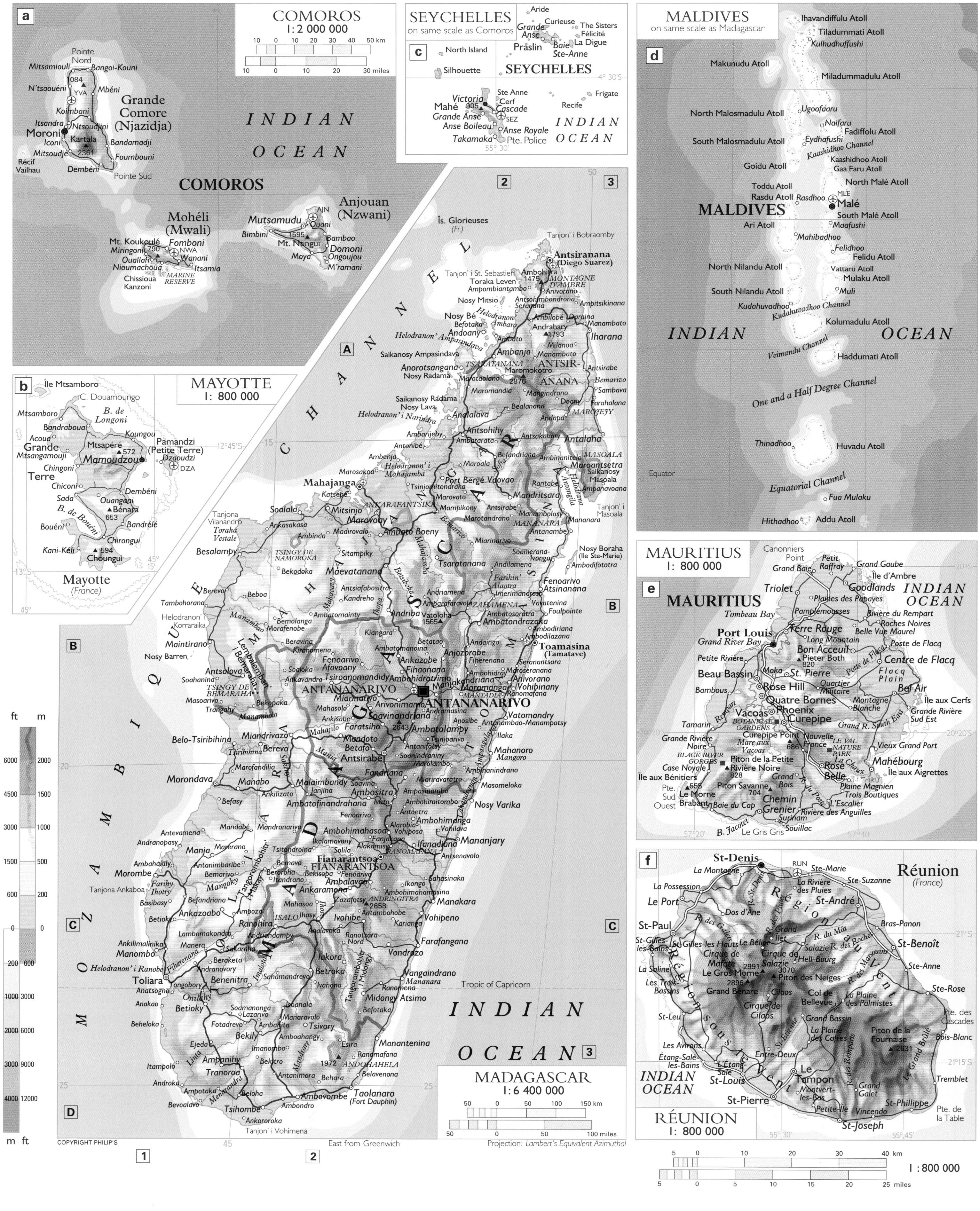

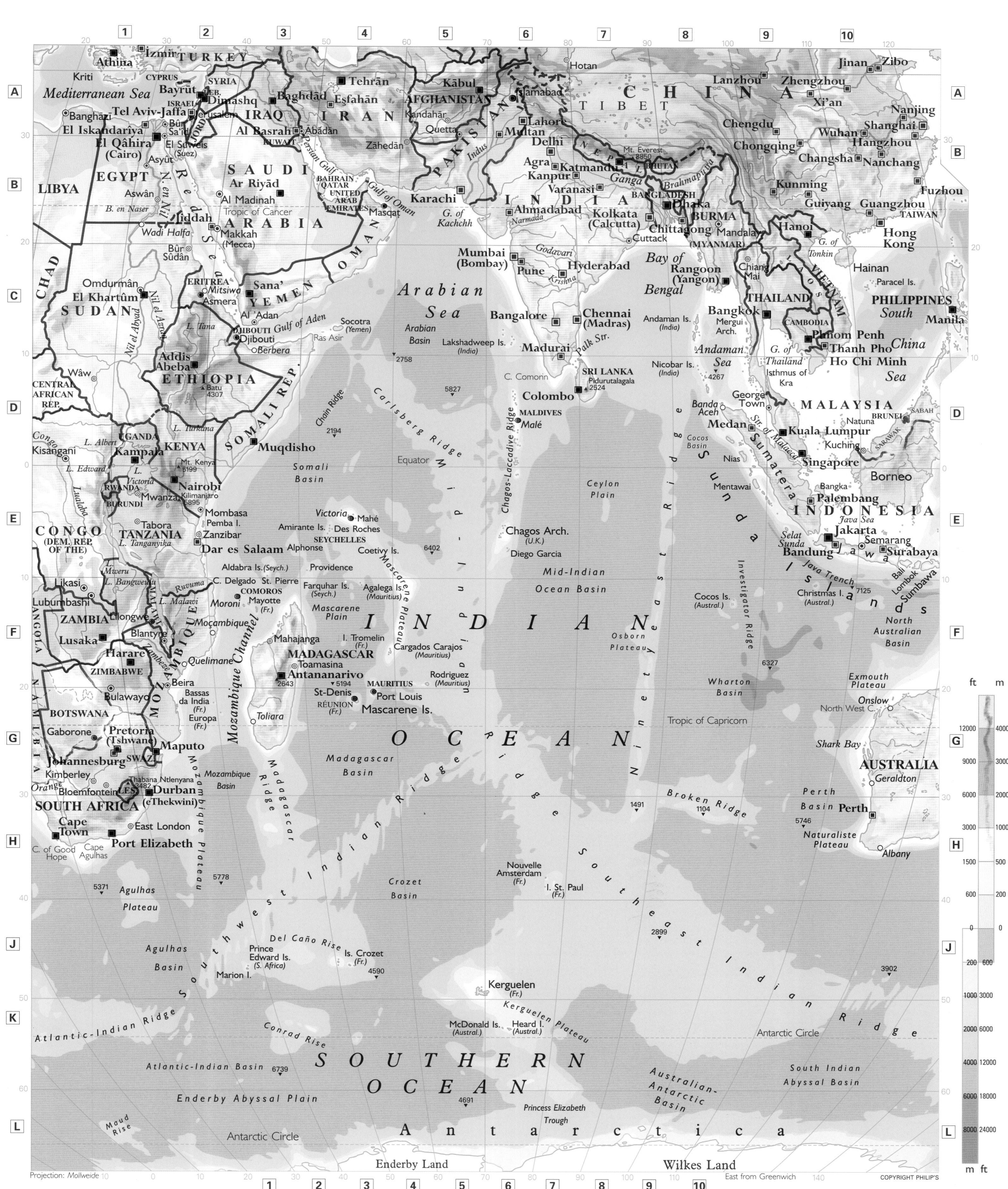

Athína
Kríti
Mediterranean Sea
Banghāzī
El Iskandarîya
(Cairo)
El Qâhira
(Cairo)
Asyût
EGYPT
Aswân
B. en Naser
Wadi Halfa
Bûr Sûdân
CHAD
Omdurmân
El Khartûm
SUDAN
Wâw
CENTRAL AFRICAN REP.
Kisangani
CONGO (DEM. REP. OF THE)
Likasi
Lubumbashi
ANGOLA
ZAMBIA
Lusaka
NAMIBIA
Gaborone
BOTSWANA
Johannesburg
Kimberley
Bloemfontein
SOUTH AFRICA
Cape Town
C. of Good Hope
Cape Agulhas

İzmir
TURKEY
CYPRUS
Bayrût
Tel Aviv-Jaffa
ISRAEL
Jerusalem
LEB.
Dimashq
SYRIA
Baghdād
IRAQ
Al Basrah
KUWAIT
Jiddah
SAUDI ARABIA
Ar Riyāḍ
Al Madinah
Makkah (Mecca)
Bûr Sa'îd
El Suweis (Suez)
Tropic of Cancer
Nîl el Azraq
Nîl el Abyad
L. Tana
ERITREA
Mitsiwa
Asmera
YEMEN
Sana'
Al 'Adan
Gulf of Aden
Socotra (Yemen)
Ras Asir
Berbera
DJIBOUTI
Djibouti
Addis Abeba
ETHIOPIA
Batu 4307
L. Turkana
SOMALI REP.
UGANDA
Kampala
L. Albert
L. Edward
RWANDA
BURUNDI
L. Victoria
Mwanza
Mt. Kenya 5199
Nairobi
KENYA
Kilimanjaro 5895
Mombasa
TANZANIA
Tabora
L. Tanganyika
Dar es Salaam
Zanzibar
Pemba I.
L. Mweru
L. Bangweulu
L. Malawi
Lilongwe
MALAWI
Blantyre
Ruvuma
Moçambique
MOZAMBIQUE
Mahajanga
Mozambique Channel
Quelimane
Beira
ZIMBABWE
Harare
Bulawayo
Thabana Ntlenyana 3482
LESOTHO
Durban (eThekwini)
Maputo
SWAZ.
Pretoria (Tshwane)
Orange
East London
Port Elizabeth
Agulhas Plateau
5371
5778

TEHRĀN
Eşfahān
IRAN
Zāhedān
Abādān
Persian Gulf
BAHRAIN
QATAR
UNITED ARAB EMIRATES
Masqat
Gulf of Oman
OMAN
Red Sea

Hotan
TIBET
CHINA
AFGHANISTAN
Kābul
ISLAMABAD
Kandahar
Quetta
PAKISTAN
Multan
Lahore
Delhi
Karachi
Ahmadabad
Indus
G. of Kachchh
Narmada
Mumbai (Bombay)
Pune
Hyderabad
Godavari
Krishna
INDIA
Bangalore
Chennai (Madras)
Madurai
Palk Str.
SRI LANKA
Pidurutalagala 2524
Colombo
Agra
Kanpur
Varanasi
Ganga
Katmandu
NEPAL
Mt. Everest 8850
BHUTAN
Brahmaputra
BANGLADESH
Dhaka
Kolkata (Calcutta)
Cuttack
Chittagong
BURMA (MYANMAR)
Mandalay
Bay of Bengal
Rangoon (Yangon)
Andaman Is. (India)
Nicobar Is. (India)
Lakshadweep Is. (India)
Maldives
Malé
Chagos-Laccadive Ridge
Chagos Arch. (U.K.)
Diego Garcia
Ceylon Plain
Mid-Indian Ocean Basin

Jinan
Zibo
Lanzhou
Zhengzhou
Chengdu
Chongqing
Changsha
Kunming
Guiyang
Guangzhou
Xi'an
Nanjing
Wuhan
Hangzhou
Nanchang
Fuzhou
TAIWAN
Hong Kong
Hainan
Paracel Is.
South China Sea
Hanoi
G. of Tonkin
Chiang Mai
THAILAND
Bangkok
Mergui Arch.
VIETNAM
LAOS
CAMBODIA
Phnom Penh
Thanh Pho Ho Chi Minh
G. of Thailand
Isthmus of Kra
Andaman Sea
George Town
Banda Aceh
Medan
MALAYSIA
Kuala Lumpur
Kuching
Singapore
BRUNEI
SABAH
SARAWAK
Borneo
Natuna
Bangka
Palembang
INDONESIA
Nias
Mentawai
Selat Sunda
Bandung
Jakarta
Semarang
Surabaya
Bali
Lombok
Sumbawa
Java Sea
Java Trench
Christmas I. (Austral.)
PHILIPPINES
Manila

Lanzhou
Zhengzhou

Arabian Sea
Arabian Basin
2758
5827
6402
Carlsberg Ridge
Chain Ridge
2194
Equator
Somali Basin
Victoria
Mahé
Amirante Is.
Des Roches
SEYCHELLES
Alphonse
Coetivy Is.
Aldabra Is. (Seych.)
Providence
C. Delgado
St. Pierre
Farquhar Is. (Seych.)
Agalega Is. (Mauritius)
I. Tromelin (Fr.)
Cargados Carajos (Mauritius)
Mascarene Plateau
Mascarene Plain
COMOROS
Moroni
Mayotte (Fr.)
MADAGASCAR
Toamasina
Antananarivo 2643
MAURITIUS
St-Denis
RÉUNION (Fr.)
Port Louis
Mascarene Is.
5194
Rodriguez (Mauritius)
Bassas da India (Fr.)
Europa (Fr.)
Toliara
Madagascar Ridge
Mozambique Basin
Madagascar Basin
I N D I A N
O C E A N

Sumatera
Sunda Strait
Cocos Basin
Ninety East Ridge
Investigator Ridge
6327
Cocos Is. (Austral.)
Osborn Plateau
Wharton Basin
7125
Exmouth Plateau
North West C.
Onslow
AUSTRALIA
Shark Bay
Geraldton
Perth
Perth Basin
5746
Naturaliste Plateau
Albany
Tropic of Capricorn

Mid-Indian Ridge

Southwest Indian Ridge
Agulhas Basin
Prince Edward Is. (S. Africa)
Marion I.
Is. Crozet (Fr.)
Del Caño Rise
Crozet Basin
4590
Kerguelen (Fr.)
Kerguelen Plateau
McDonald Is. (Austral.)
Heard I. (Austral.)
Nouvelle Amsterdam (Fr.)
I. St. Paul (Fr.)
2899
Southeast Indian Ridge
1491
1104
Broken Ridge
Australian-Antarctic Basin
South Indian Abyssal Basin
Southeast Indian Ridge
3902

Atlantic-Indian Ridge
Conrad Rise
Atlantic-Indian Basin
6739
Enderby Abyssal Plain
4691
Maud Rise
Antarctic Circle
SOUTHERN OCEAN
Princess Elizabeth Trough
Antarctic Circle
A n t a r c t i c a
Enderby Land
Wilkes Land
East from Greenwich

Projection: Mollweide   COPYRIGHT PHILIP'S

ft   m
12000   4000
9000   3000
6000   2000
3000   1000
1500   500
600   200
0
200   600
1000   3000
2000   6000
4000   12000
6000   18000
8000   24000
m   ft

AUSTRALIA AND OCEANIA

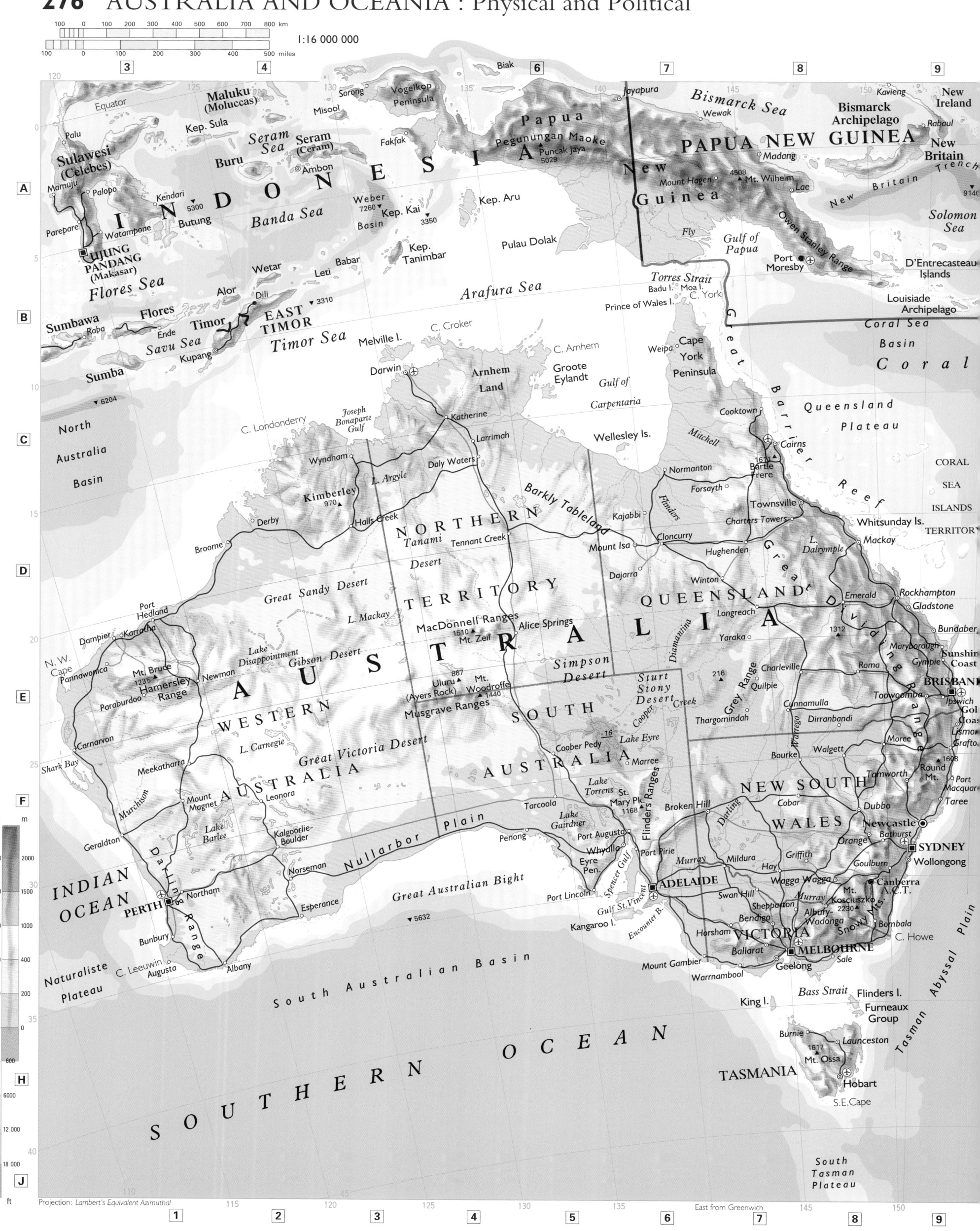

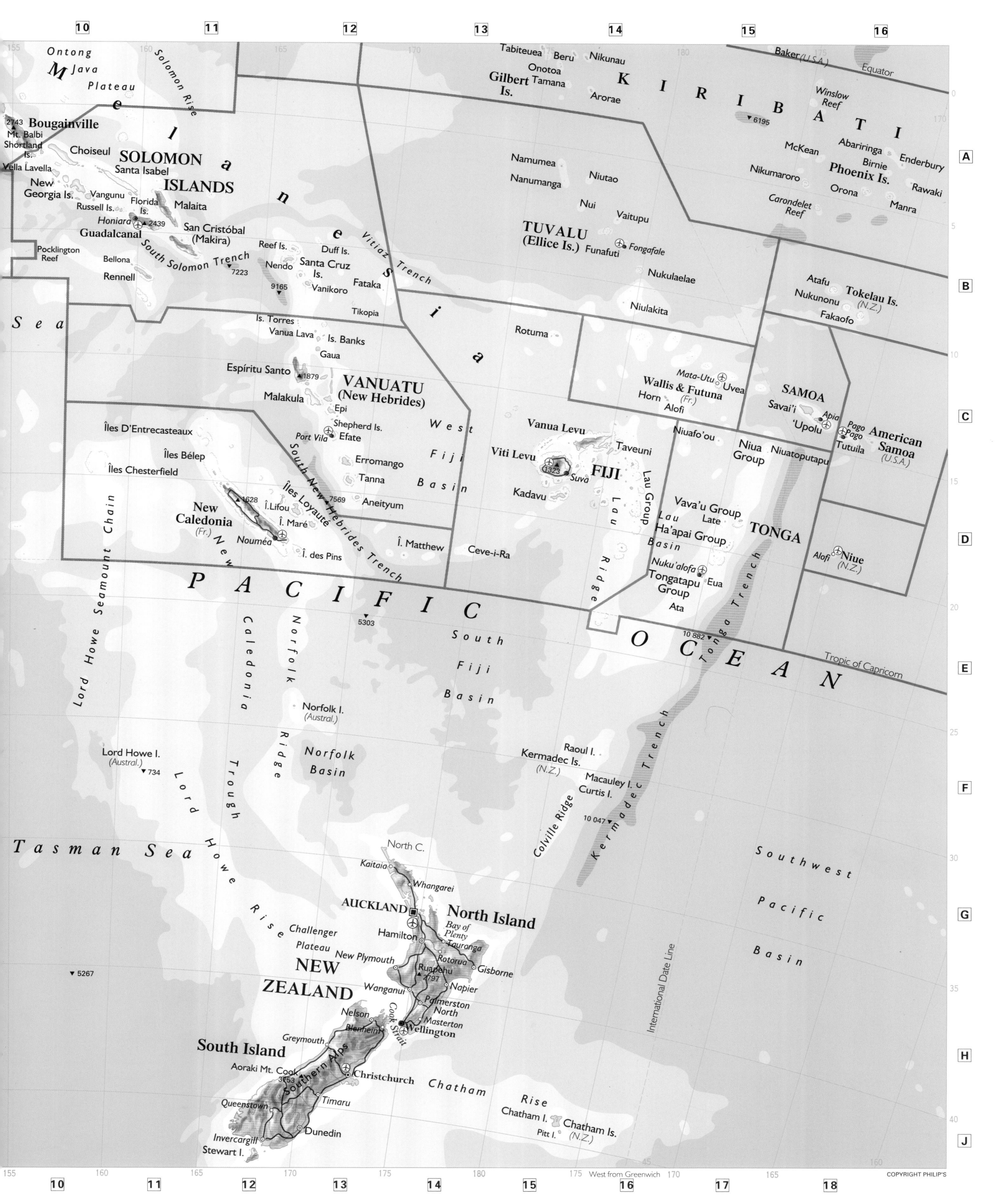

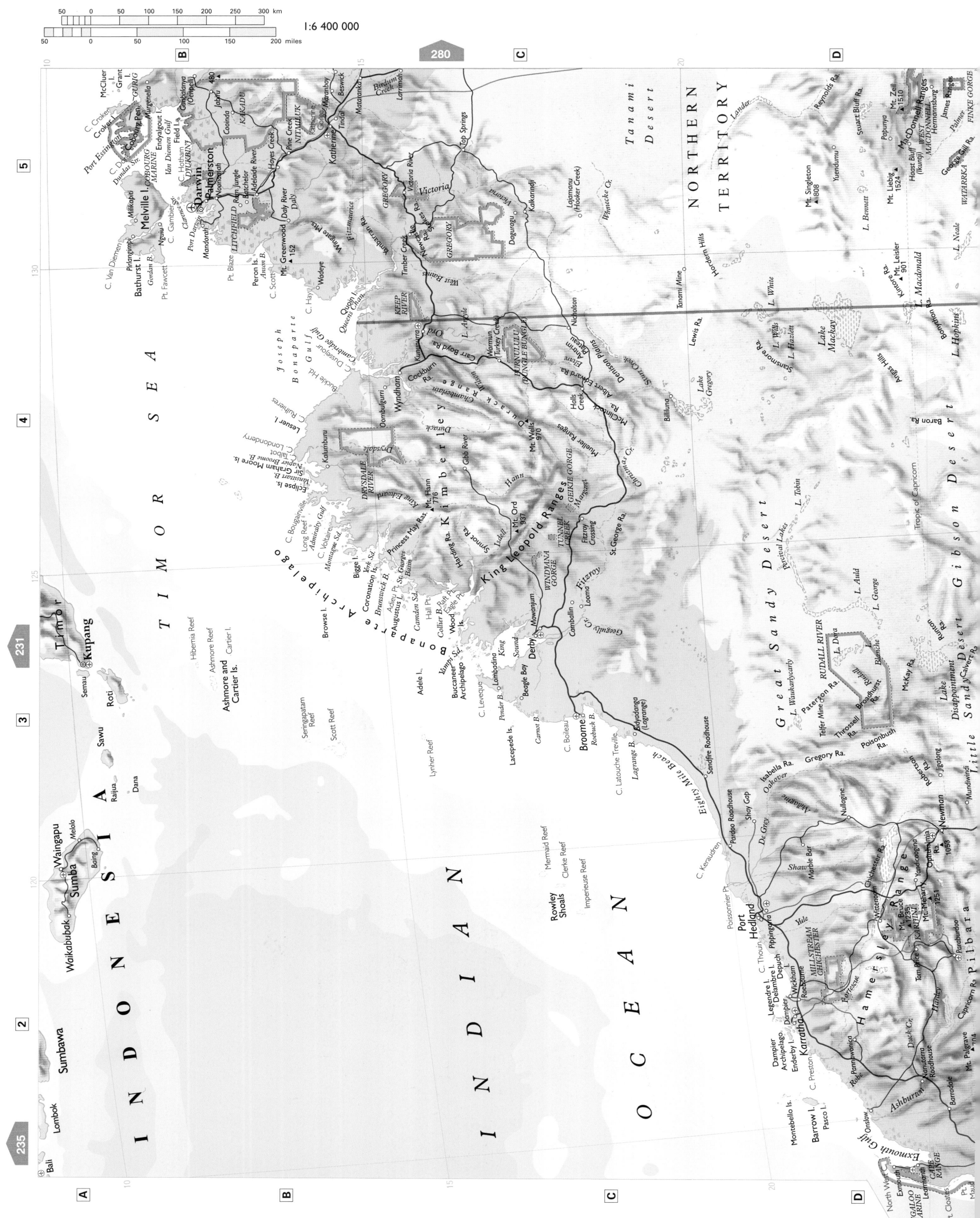

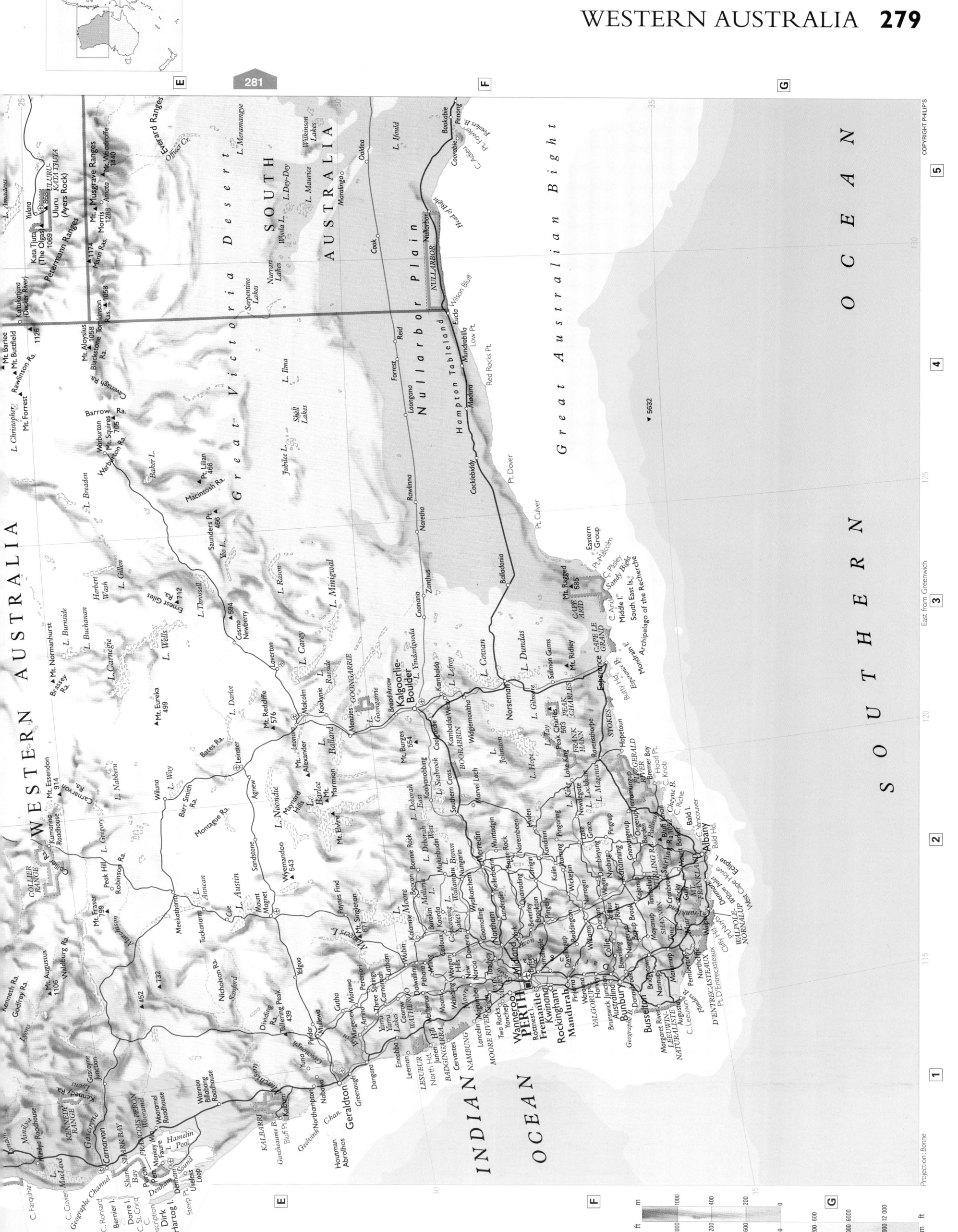

INDIAN OCEAN

SOUTHERN OCEAN

WESTERN AUSTRALIA

SOUTH AUSTRALIA

Great Victoria Desert

Nullarbor Plain

Great Australian Bight

Hampton Tableland

PERTH

Kalgoorlie-Boulder

Geraldton

Albany

Esperance

Projection: Bonne

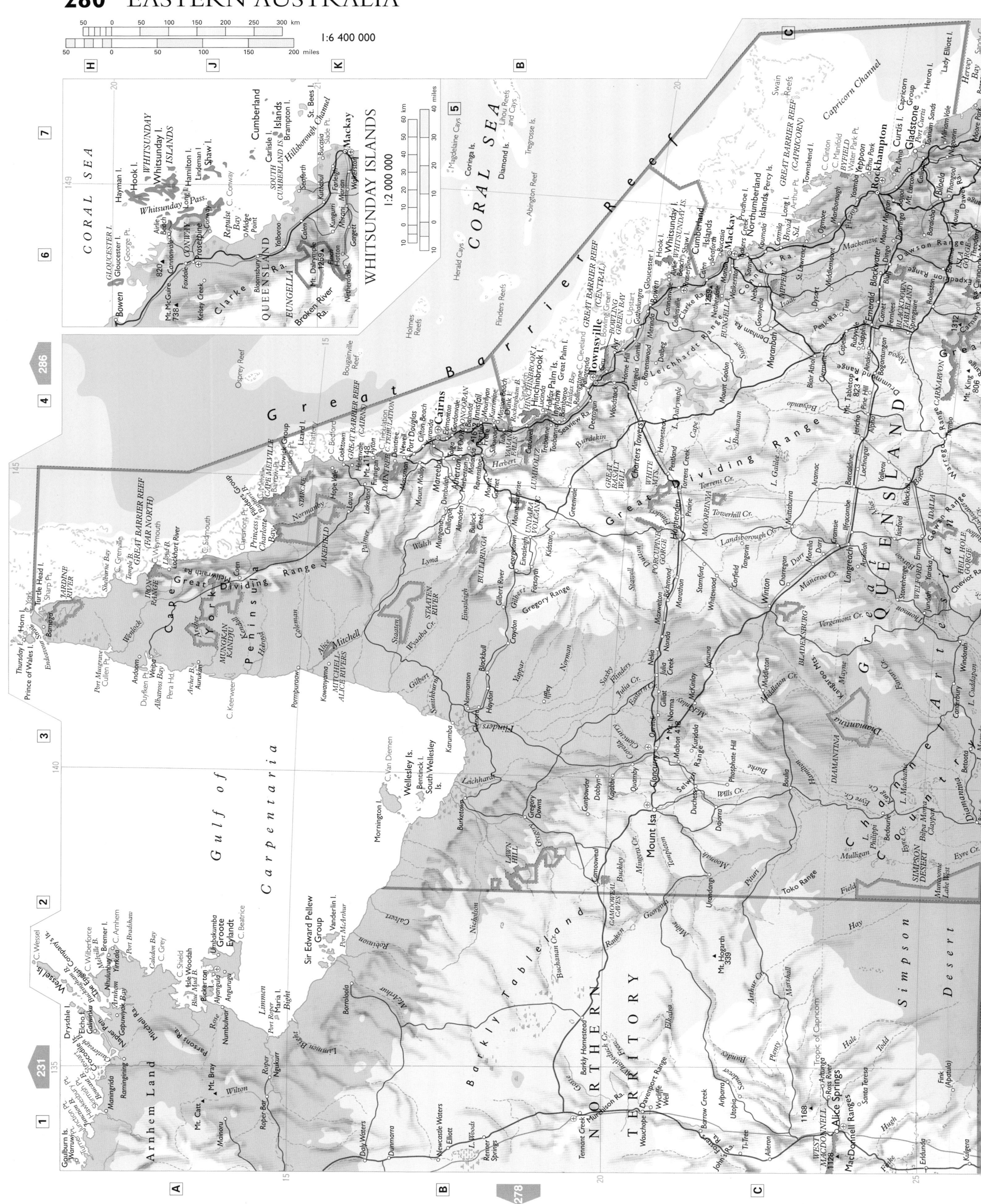

1:6 400 000

50 0 50 100 150 200 250 300 km
50 0 50 100 150 200 miles

H   **J**   **K**   **B**

WHITSUNDAY ISLANDS

1:2 000 000

10 0 10 20 30 40 50 60 km
0 10 20 30 40 miles

CORAL SEA

CORAL SEA

WHITSUNDAY ISLANDS

Gulf of Carpentaria

Arnhem Land

NORTHERN TERRITORY

QUEENSLAND

Great Dividing Range

Cape York Peninsula

Great Barrier Reef

Simpson Desert

Barkly Tableland

Alice Springs

MacDonnell Ranges

Cairns

Townsville

Mackay

Rockhampton

Gladstone

Mount Isa

Tropic of Capricorn

COPYRIGHT, GEORGE PHILIP LTD.

TASMAN SEA

QUEENSLAND

NEW SOUTH WALES

SOUTH AUSTRALIA

VICTORIA

TASMANIA

Brisbane
Gold Coast
Sunshine Coast
Toowoomba
Maryborough
Bundaberg
Hervey Bay
Gympie
Caloundra
Maroochydore
Redcliffe
Ipswich
Southport
Coolangatta
Ballina
Coffs Harbour
Grafton
Lismore
Tweed Heads
Byron Bay
Port Macquarie
Taree
Forster
Tamworth
Armidale
Inverell
Moree
Narrabri
Gunnedah
Newcastle
Gosford
Maitland
Cessnock
SYDNEY
Blacktown
Penrith
Campbelltown
Wollongong
Shellharbour
Nowra
Goulburn
Bathurst
Orange
Dubbo
Lithgow
Katoomba
Canberra
Queanbeyan
Wagga Wagga
Albury
Wodonga
Shepparton
Bendigo
Echuca
Ballarat
MELBOURNE
Geelong
Warrnambool
Mount Gambier
Horsham
Mildura
Broken Hill
Bourke
Cobar
Dubbo
ADELAIDE
Gawler
Elizabeth
Salisbury
Port Pirie
Port Augusta
Whyalla
Port Lincoln
Murray Bridge
Kangaroo I.
Eyre Peninsula
Yorke Peninsula
Spencer Gulf
Gulf St. Vincent
Lake Eyre (North)
Lake Eyre (South)
Lake Torrens
Lake Gairdner
Lake Frome
Lake Blanche
Flinders Ranges
Gammon Ranges
Strzelecki Desert
Sturt Stony Desert
Simpson Desert
Cooper Cr.
Darling
Murray R.
Murrumbidgee R.
Lachlan R.
Macquarie R.
Great Dividing Range
Fraser I.
Moreton Bay
Fraser Sandy
Great Sandy

Launceston
Devonport
Burnie
Hobart
Flinders Island
Furneaux Group
King Island
Cape Barren I.
Bass Strait
Wilsons Promontory

Projection: Borne

East from Greenwich

279

ft m
4500 1500
3000 1000
1200 400
600 200
0
200 600
2000 6000
4000 12 000
m ft

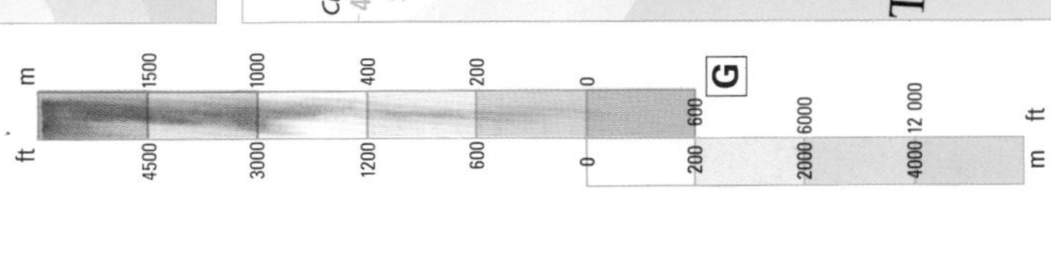

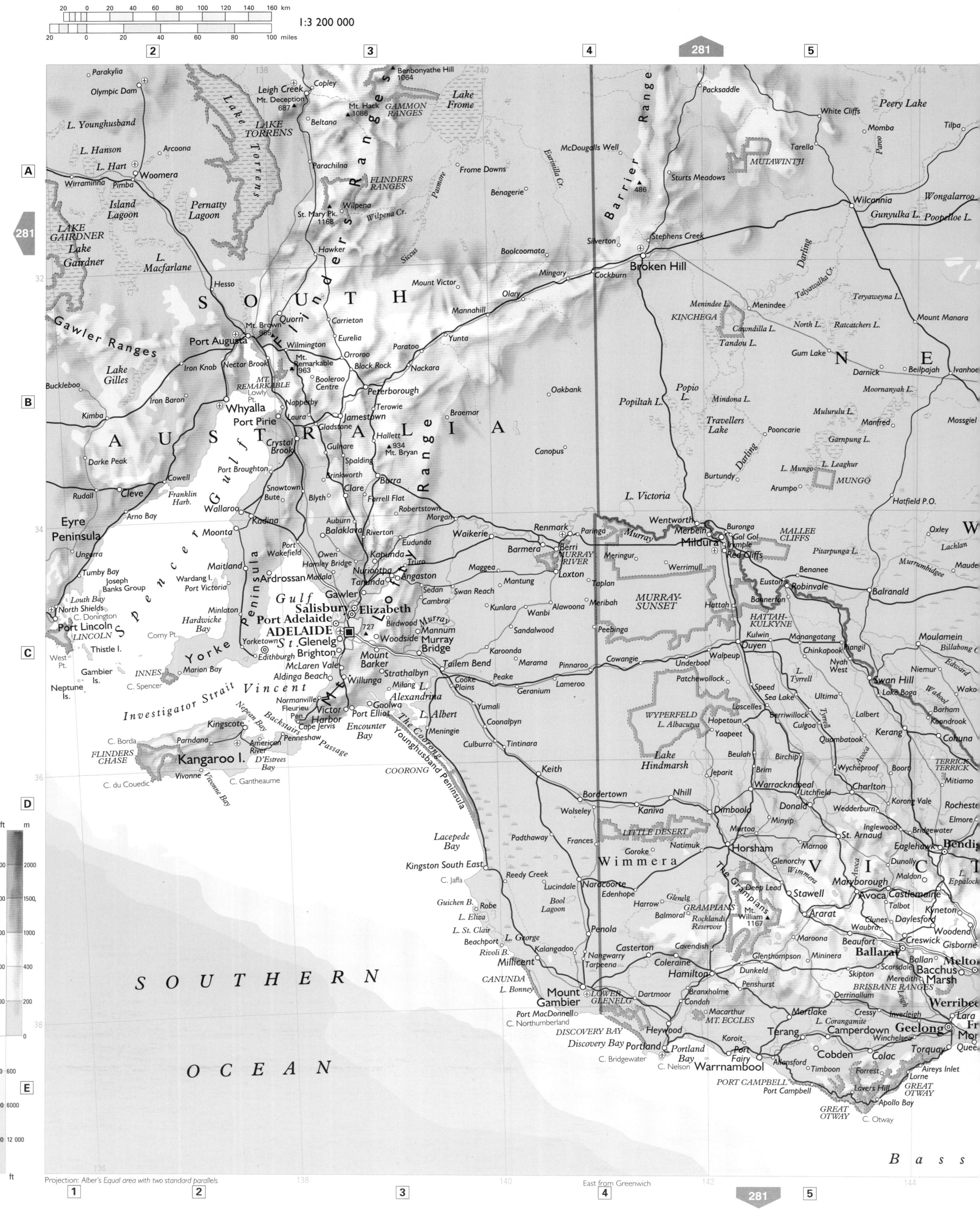

20 0 20 40 60 80 100 120 140 160 km
1:3 200 000
20 0 20 40 60 80 100 miles

2 3 4 281 5

281

| A |
281

| B |

32

| C |

34

| D |

| E |

36

38

Projection: Alber's Equal area with two standard parallels

East from Greenwich

1 2 138 3 140 4 142 5 144

281

National Parks

East from Greenwich

COPYRIGHT PHILIP'S

1:2 800 000

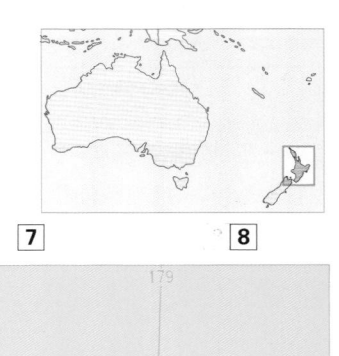

A
C. Reinga
North C.
C. Maria van Diemen
Parengarenga Harbour
Houhora Heads
Ninety Mile Beach
Ranganui B.
C. Karikari
Doubless B.
Whangaroa Harb.
Awanui
Mongonui
Cavalli Is.
Ahipara B.
Kaitaia
Kaeo
Waitongi
B. of Islands
C. Brett

B
Herekino
Kohukohu
Kerikeri
Russell
Kawakawa
Whangaruru Harb.
Rawene
Kaikohe
Moerewa
Poor Knights Is.
Hokianga Harbour
Omapere
▲ 781
Wairoa
Hikurangi
Waipoua Forest
Donnelly's Crossing
Whangarei
Aranga
Kamo
Onerahi
Dargaville
Kirikopuni
Whangarei Harb.
Bream B.
Hen & Chickens Is.

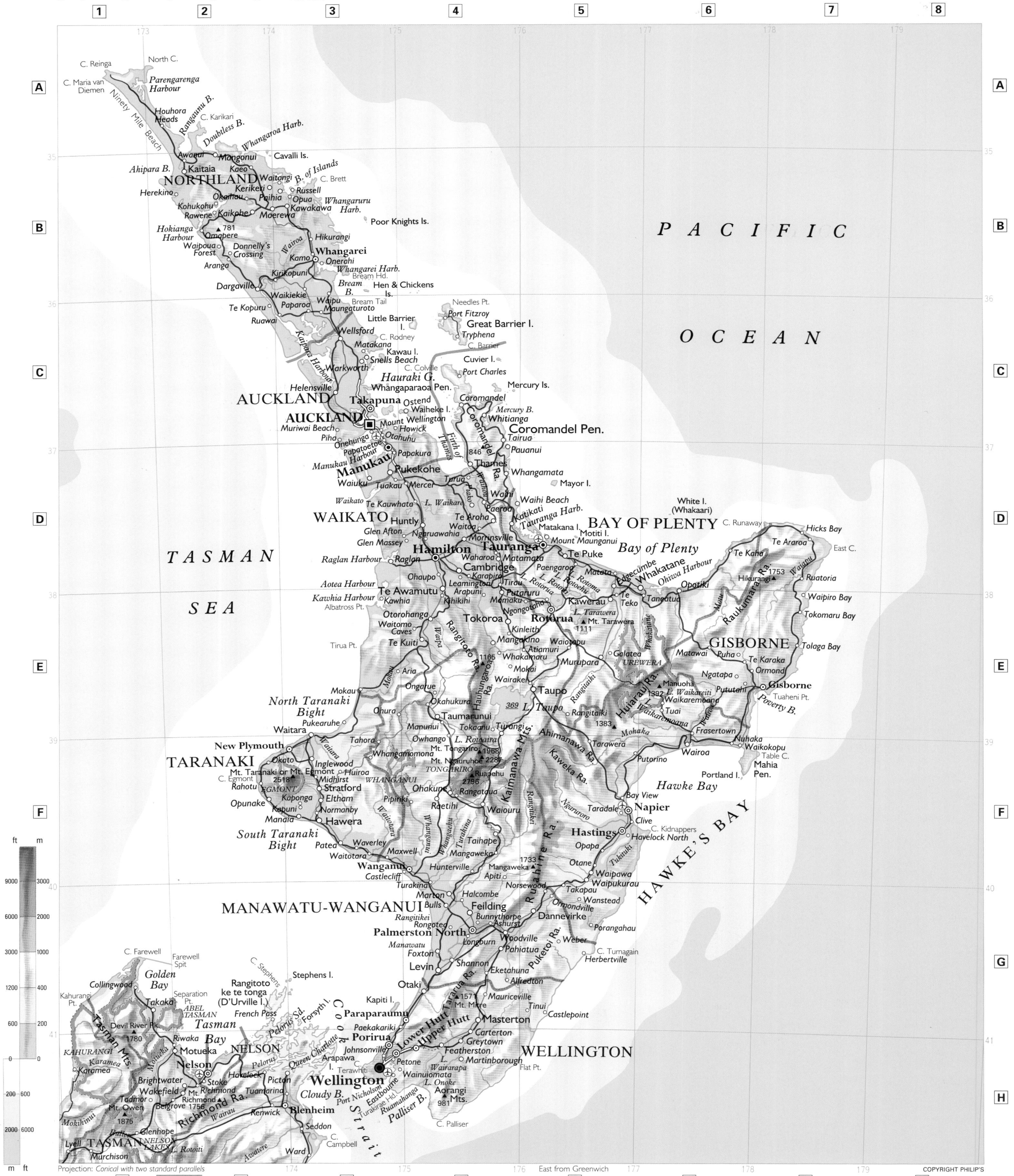

C
TASMAN
SEA

NORTHLAND

AUCKLAND

D
WAIKATO
Hamilton

TARANAKI

E

F

G

H

PACIFIC

OCEAN

BAY OF PLENTY

GISBORNE

HAWKE'S BAY

WELLINGTON

National Parks

1:2 800 000

10 0 20 40 60 80 100 120 140 km
10 0 20 40 60 80 100 miles

284

TASMAN SEA

PACIFIC OCEAN

C. Farewell
Farewell Spit
Golden Bay
Collingwood
Takaka
Kahurangi Pt.
Separation Pt.
ABEL TASMAN
C. Stephens
Rangitoto ke te tonga (D'Urville I.)
Stephens I.
French Pass
Pelorus Sd.
Forsyth I.
C. Jackson
Queen Charlotte Sd.
Arapawa I.
Picton
Tuamarina
Blenheim
Seddon
C. Campbell
Ward
Wharanui
Kekerengu

Kahurangi Pt.
Devil River Pk. 1780
KAHURANGI
Tasman Mts.
Riwaka
Motueka
Nelson
Stoke
Richmond
Mt Richmond 1756
Wakefield
Brightwater
Waimea
Geddonville
Tadmor
Glenhope
Richmond Ra.
Havelock
Renwick
Wairau
NELSON
MARLBOROUGH

Karamea Bight
Karamea
Granity
Millerton
Westport
C. Foulwind
Waimarie
Waimangaroa
Mokihinui
Lyell
Buller
Gorge
Murchison
L. Rotoroa
Inangahua
TASMAN
Mt Owen 1875
Belgrove
Glenhope
Molesworth
Inland Kaikoura Ra.
2885 Tapuaeo
Benmuku

PAPAROA
Punakaiki
Paparoa Ra.
Reefton
Grey
Ahaura
Maruia Springs
Mt. Franklin 2340
Mt Travers 2337
Spenser Mts.
St. Arnaud Ra.
NELSON LAKES
Hanmer Springs
Clarence
Seaward Kaikoura Ra.
Manakau 2608
Kaikoura

Blackball
Ikamatua
Lewis Pass
Waiau
Kaikoura Pen.

Greymouth
Runanga
Taramakau
L. Kaimata
Mt Ajax 1834
Culverden
Waiau
Parnassus

Hokitika
Kumara
Jacksons
Otira
ARTHUR'S PASS
L. Brunner
L. Sumner
Hurunui
Domett
Seargill

Ross
L. Kaniere
Otira Gorge
Arthur's Pass 926
Mt Crossley 1980
Hawarden
Waikari
Waipara
Amberley
Mt Somers
Scargill

WESTLAND BIGHT

Wanganui
Abut Hd.
Harihari
Whataroa
Okarito
L. Mapourika
Gillespies Pt.
Whitcombe Pass
Mt Murchison 2408
Whitcombe
Lake Coleridge
L. Coleridge
Springfield
Sheffield
Whitecliffs
Darfield
Oxford
Rangiora
Kaiapoi
Belfast
Riccarton
Christchurch
New Brighton
Sumner
Lyttelton
Banks Pen.
Akaroa
Little River

PEGASUS BAY

WESTLAND
Bruce B.
Tititira Hd.
Fox Glacier
Franz Josef 2781
Mt Tasman 3497
Aorata Mount Cook 3753
Tasman Gl.
Mount Cook
MT COOK
Mt. Taylor 2333
Methven
Highbank
Rakaia
Rolleston
Hornby
Lincoln
Leeston
Southbridge
L. Ellesmere
Akaroa Harbour
919

THE SOUTHERN ALPS
Haast
Okuru
Jackson Hd. B.
Jackson
Cascade Pt.
Glenmary
2590
Haast Pass
L. Tekapo
L. Pukaki
Mckenzie
Two Thumbs Ra.
Mount Somers
Geraldine
Hinds
Ashburton
Tinwald
Winchester
Temuka
Pleasant Point
Timaru

MOUNT ASPIRING
Olivine Ra.
Barrier Ra.
Mt Aspiring 3033
Awarua Pt.
Awarua B.
Yates Pt.
Milford Sd.
Mt. McKerrow 2723
Mt. Tutoko 2723
L. Wanaka
Wanaka
L. Hawea
Hawea
Hawea Flat
Mt St. Bathan's 2087
Lindis Pass
L. Ohau
Lake Pukaki
Benmore Pk. 1894
The Hunter Hills
Waitaki Plains
Kirkliston Ra.
St. Andrews
Studholme
Waimate

Mitre Peak 1683
Bligh Sound
George Sound
Caswell Sound
Charles Sound
Thompson Sd.
Secretary I.
Doubtful Sd.
Dagg Sd.
Breaksea Sd.
Resolution I.
Dusky Sd.
Milford Sound
Sutherland Falls
Darran Mts.
Franklin Mts.
Stuart Mts.
Murchison Mts.
Kepler Mts.
Livingstone Mts.
Mt Earnslaw 2819
Richardson Mts.
Harris Mts.
Glenorchy
Queenstown
Arrowtown
Cromwell
Clyde
Alexandra
Roxburgh
Pisa Ra.
Dunstan Mts.
St. Bathans
Hawkdun Ra.
Kakanui Mts.
Naseby
Ranfurly
Windsor
Mahena
Pukeuri
Oamaru
Kurow
Duntroon
Ngapara
Tokarahi
Hampden

FIORDLAND
C. Providence
Chalky Inlet
Preservation Coal
Puysegur Pt.
Te Waewae B.
Pahia Pt.
Heath Mts.
Hunter Mts.
Kaherekoau Mts.
Takitimu Mts.
Caroline Pk. 1704
Mt Lyall 1892
Te Anau
L. Te Anau
L. Manapouri
Manapouri
Mavora
2022 Jane Pk.
Eyre Mts.
The Remarkables 2315
Double Cone
Garvie Mts.
Umbrella Mts.
Rough Ridge 1449
Middlemarch
Sutton
Waikouaiti
Waikouaiti Downs
Warrington
Port Chalmers
Otago Harbour
Otago Pen.
C. Saunders
St. Kilda

SOUTHLAND
OTAGO
Mossburn
Lumsden
Athol
Kingston
Dipton
Birchwood
Ohai
Nightcaps
Monowai
Clifden
Tuatapere
Orawia
Otautau
Winton
Makarewa
Gore
Mataura
Waikaka
Edievale
Beaumont
Miller's Flat
Roxburgh
Tapanui
Waipahi
Clinton
Balclutha
Owaka
Nugget Pt.
Lawrence
Kelso
L. Mahinerangi
Riversdale

L. Hauroko
Te Waewae B.
Riverton
Thornbury
Wairio
Wrey's Bush
Hedgehope
Edendale
Wyndham
Stirling
Kaitangata
L. Waihola
Waihola
Mosgiel
Allanton
Taieri
Dunedin

Invercargill
South Invercargill
Wallacetown
Glenham
Waimatua
Fortrose
Tokanui
Tahakopa
Catlins
Chaslands Mistake
Long Pt.
Waipapa Pt.

Solander I.
Codfish I.
Mt Anglem 980
Foveaux Str.
Bluff
Bluff Harbour
Ruapuke I.
Mason B.
Halfmoon Bay
Paterson Inlet
Doughboy B.
RAKIURA
Port Pegasus
South West C.
Stewart I. (Rakiura)

PACIFIC OCEAN

Projection: Conical with two standard parallels
East from Greenwich
National Parks

COPYRIGHT PHILIP'S

CHATHAM ISLANDS
on same scale

PACIFIC OCEAN

The Sisters
C. Young
Munning Pt.
Western Reef
Te One
Waitangi
Owenga
C. Fournier
Chatham I. (Rekohua)
The Forty Fours
The Horns
Pitt Strait
Mangere I.
Pitt I.
Rangatira I.
The Pyramid
Star Keys

Chatham Islands (Wharekauri)

West from Greenwich

ft m
9000 3000
6000 2000
3000 1000
1200 400
600 200
0 0
200 600
2000 6000
4000 12 000
m ft

1:5 200 000

50 0 50 100 150 200 km
50 0 50 100 150 miles

287

m / ft
4000 / 12 000
2000 / 6000
1000 / 3000
400 / 1200
200 / 600
0 / 0

200 / 600
600 / 2000
2000 / 6000
4000 / 12 000
6000 / 18 000
m / ft

PACIFIC OCEAN

NORTH SOLOMONS

Nuguria Is.
Sable I.
Kilinailau Is.
C. Haripan
Buka I.
Sohano
Hutjena
Kunua
Torokina
Bougainville I.
Matupena Pt.
Kieta
Arawa
Panguna
Mt. Takuan 2275
Buin
Boku
225 I.
C. L'Averdy
Tinputz
Wakunai
Mt. Balbi
Toki

Shortland I. (Solomon Is.)
Treasury Is. (Solomon Is.)

Solomon Islands

Bougainville Trench 9140

Green Is.
Lemankoa

Feni Is.
Babase I.
Ambitle I.
Tanga Is.
Boang I.
Malendok I.
Lihir Group
Lihir I.
Tabar Is.
Tabar I.
Tabar I.
Simberi I.

Lyra Reef

NEW IRELAND

Hans Meyer Ra.
Verron Ra.
Lossu
Konos
Namatanai
New Ireland
Lokuramau
Tatau I.
Metai
St. George's Channel
C. St. George
Kavieng
North C.
Taskul I.
Ungat
Konogogo
Api
Lambu

St. Matthias Group
Mussau I.
Tabalo
Eloaua I.
Emirau I.
Tench I.
Tong I.
Lou I.
Baluan I.
Rambutyo I.
Muschu I.

New Hanover
Tingwon Group
Noipuos 895
Ysabel Channel

BISMARCK ARCHIPELAGO

Bismarck Sea

NEW BRITAIN
EAST NEW BRITAIN
WEST NEW BRITAIN

Rabaul
Kokopo
Gazelle Peninsula
Mt. Sinewit 2438
Watom I.
Kerevat
Pondo
Lolobau I.
Ulamona
Talasea
Kimbe
Kimbe Bay
Hoskins
Williamez Pen. 2027
Whiteman Ra.
Nukuhu
Ewasse
Ubai
Pomio
Matong
Tacquinot Bay
Wide Bay
Sampun
Gasmata
C. Anukur
C. Kablungu
Woku
Sog Sog
Kandrian
Aumo
Arawe Is.
Awawe
Dampier Strait
C. Gloucester

Nakanai Ra.

WEST SOLOMON SEA

New Britain 8320

MANUS
Admiralty Islands
Sori
Lorengau
Momote
Manus I.
South West Pt.
Kabul I.
Los Negros I.

Hermit Is.
Ninigo Group
Aua I.
Wuvulu I.

Schouten Is.
Vokeo I.
Kairiru I.
Walis I.
Tarawai I.
Muschu I.
Wewak
Dagua
Boram

MADANG
Manam I.
Karkar I.
Bagabag I.
Madang
Bogia
Matuka
Bibi
Saidor
Crown I.
Long I.
Umboi I.
Tolokiwa I.
Sakar I.
Siassi I.
Vitiaz Strait
Finschhafen
Sialum
Kabwum
Wasu
Finisterre Ra.
Dumpu

New Guinea

WEST SEPIK
Sissano
Aitape
Wutung
Vanimo
Torricelli Mts.
Nuku
Lumi
Maprik
Angoram
Keram
Yuat
Sepik

EAST SEPIK

Central Range

Mt. Capella 3993
Mt. Ayang 3505
Victor Emanuel Ra.
Telefomin
Oksapmin
Tabubil
Mt. Bosavi 2507

PAPUA NEW GUINEA

WESTERN HIGHLANDS
SOUTHERN HIGHLANDS
Mount Hagen
Mendi
Tari
Kundiawa
Mt. Giluwe 4368
Mt. Ialibu
CHIMBU
Mt. Wilhelm 4508
Mt. Kubor 4359
EASTERN HIGHLANDS
Goroka
Kainantu
Kerowagi
Kagua
Nipa
Koroba
ENGA
Wabag
Wapenamanda
Laiagam

Bismarck Range

Adelbert Range

MOROSE / MOROBE
Lae
Wau
Bulolo
Menyamya
Aseki
Mumeng
Wonenara
Markham
Huon Peninsula
Huon Gulf
Morobe
Lasanga I.
Salamaua
Markham R.
Bowatu Mts.

NORTHERN
Popondetta
Buna
Gona
Kokoda
Mt. Albert Edward 3990
Mt. Victoria 4035
Mt. St. Mary
Mt. Suckling 3676
Owen Stanley Ra.
Mt. Simpson 2883
Tufi
Gobe
C. Nelson
Dyke Ackland Bay
Afore
Sibium Mts.
Wanigela
Rabaraba
Dogura
Kwikila
C. Ward Hunt

Gulf of Papua
GULF
Kerema
Kikori
Ihu
Kukipi
Malalaua
Baimuru
Kikori R.
Turama R.
Vailala

CENTRAL
Port Moresby
Hood Pt.
Hula
Abau
Kupiano
Kapa Kapagere
Rigo
Berehia

SOUTHERN HIGHLANDS
Darai Hills

WESTERN
Kikori
Daru
Kiwai I.
Bristow I.
Parama I.
Purutu I.
Wabuda I.
Deception Bay
Umuda I.
Morehead
Nomad
Lake Murray
L. Murray
Balimo
Suki
Aramia
Wasua
Fly
Fly R.
Strickland R.
Bamu R.
Aworra

Coral Sea
CENTRAL

CORAL SEA

Louisiade Archipelago
MILNE BAY
Woodlark I.
Laughlan Is.
Rossel I.
Tagula I.
Tagula
Misima I.
Tawa Tawa Mal Reef
Sudest I.
The Calvados Chain
Deboyne Is.
Conflict Group
Samarai
Alotau
Normanby I.
Fergusson I.
Goodenough I.
D'Entrecasteaux Islands
Dobu
Esa'ala
Sehulea
Suau
East C.
Basilaki I.
Engineer Group
Dumoulin Is.

Trobriand Is.
Kiriwina I.
Kitava I.
Vakuta I.
Kaileuna I.
Losuia
Lusancay Is. and Reefs
Marshall Bennett Is.
Alcester I.
Madau I.
Egum Atoll
Guasopa
Kulumadau

Pocklington Reef

SOLOMON SEA

AUSTRALIA
QUEENSLAND
Cape York Peninsula
Torres Strait
Prince of Wales I.
Thursday I.
Wednesday I.
Horn I.
C. York
Turtle Head I.
Moa I.
Badu I.
Saibai I. (Australia)
Boigu I. (Australia)
Endeavour Strait
Sharp Pt.
Cullen Pt.
Shelburne Bay
Temple Bay
C. Grenville

Great Barrier Reef

INDONESIA
PAPUA

231
280

Projection: Lambert Conformal Conic
East from Greenwich

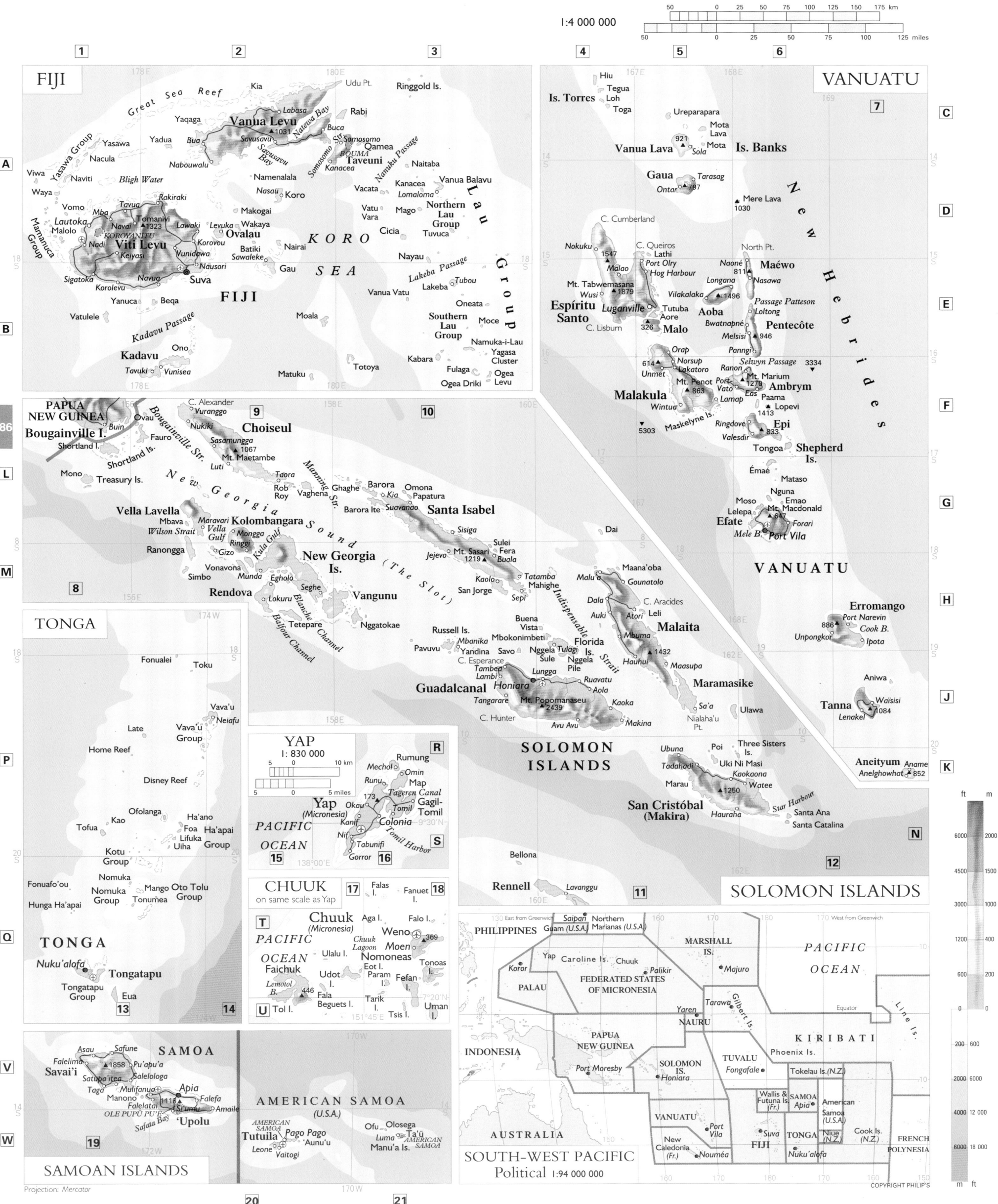

Equatorial Scale 1:43 200 000

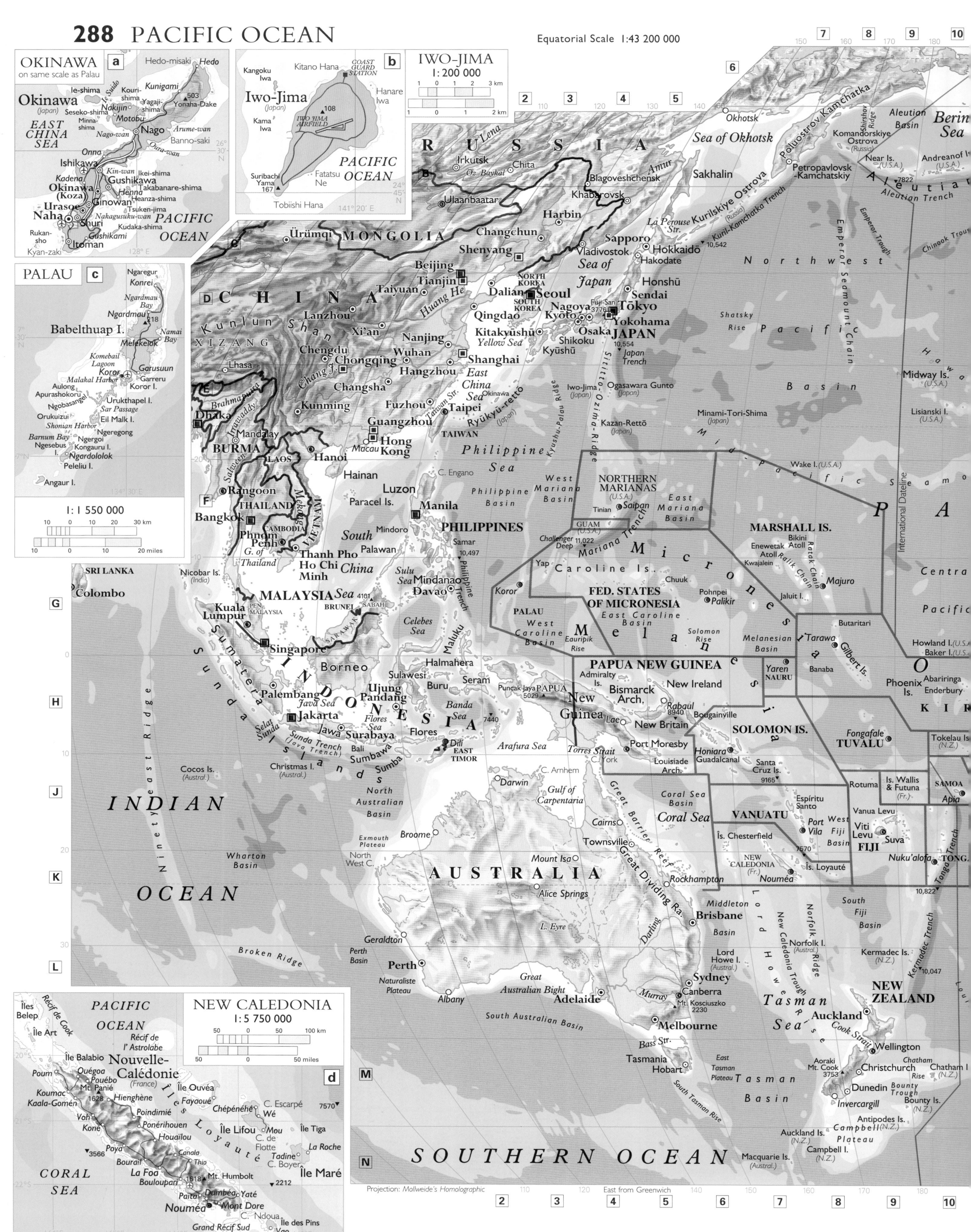

OKINAWA on same scale as Palau [a]

Okinawa *(Japan)*

Hedo-misaki Hedo
Kangoku Iwa
le-shima
Kouri-shima
Kunigami
Yagaji-shima
Yonaha-Dake 503
Nakijin
Motobu
Nago
Arume-wan
Banno-saki
Onna
Ishikawa
Kin-wan
Ikei-shima
Kadena
Minna-shima
Nago-wan
Ouna-zaki
Gushikawa
Okinawa *(Koza)*
Ginowan
Tsuken-shima
Urasoe
Shuri
Naha
Nakagusuku-wan
Gushikami
Rukan-sho
Kyan-zaki
Itoman
Kudaka-shima

EAST CHINA SEA

PACIFIC OCEAN

IWO-JIMA [b] 1:200 000

Iwo-Jima *(Japan)*
Kitano Hana
COAST GUARD STATION
Kangoku Iwa
Kama Iwa
IWO JIMA AIRFIELD 108
Suribachi Yama 167
Fatatsu Ne
Tobiishi Hana
Hanare Iwa

PACIFIC OCEAN

PALAU [c]

Ngaregur
Konrei
Ngardmau Bay
Ngardmau 218
Babelthuap I.
Namai Bay
Komebail Lagoon
Melekeok
Aulong
Apurashokoru
Koror I.
Ngobasangel
Uruhthapel I.
Garusuun
Garreru
Koror I.
Sar Passage
Eil Malk I.
Barnum Bay
Shonian Harbor
Orukuizui
Ngeregong
Ngesebus I.
Kongauru I.
Ngardololok
Ngergoi I.
Peleliu I.
Angaur I.

1:1 550 000

NEW CALEDONIA [d] 1:5 750 000

PACIFIC OCEAN
Îles Belep
Île Art
Récif de l'Astrolabe
Nouvelle-Calédonie *(France)*
Île Balabio
Poum
Quégoa
Pouébo
Koumac
Mt. Panié 1628
Hienghène
Kaala-Gomén
Voh
Poindimié
3566
Kone
Ponérihouen
Houailou
Bourail
La Foa
Boulouparis
Poya
Canala
Thio
Mt. Humbolt 1618
Dumbéa
Yaté
Paita
Mont Dore
Nouméa
Ndoua
Grand Récif Sud
Île Ouvéa
Fayaoué
Chépénéhé
Wé
Mou
C. de Flotte
Tadine
Île Lifou
Île Tiga
La Roche
C. Boyer
Île Maré
C. Escarpé 7570

CORAL SEA

RUSSIA
Sea of Okhotsk
Poluostrov Kamchatka
Okhotsk
Irkutsk
Oz. Baykal
Chita
Blagoveshchensk
Khabarovsk
Amur
Sakhalin
Petropavlovsk-Kamchatskiy
Komandorskiye Ostrova *(Russia)*
Near Is. *(U.S.A.)*
Aleutian Basin
Bering Sea
Andreanof Is. *(U.S.A.)*
Ulaanbaatar
MONGOLIA
Ürümqi
Changchun
Harbin
La Perouse Str.
Kurilskiye Ostrova *(Russia)*
Kuril-Kamchatka Trench
Shirshov Ridge
7822
Aleutian Trench
Emperor Seamount Chain
Northwest
Shenyang
Beijing
Tianjin
Taiyuan
NORTH KOREA
Vladivostok
Sea of Japan
Sapporo
Hokkaido
Hakodate
10,542
CHINA
Lanzhou
Kunlun Shan
XIZANG
Dalian
SOUTH KOREA
Seoul
Sendai
Honshū
Qingdao
Nagoya
Kyoto
Tokyo
Fuji-San 3776
Yokohama
Osaka JAPAN
Shikoku
Shatsky Rise
Pacific
Basin
Midway Is. *(U.S.A.)*
Xi'an
Nanjing
Kitakyūshū
Yellow Sea
Kyūshū
10,554
Japan Trench
Howl
Chengdu
Chongqing
Wuhan
Shanghai
East China Sea
Okinawa
Iwo-Jima *(Japan)*
Ogasawara Gunto *(Japan)*
Lisianski I. *(U.S.A.)*
Lhasa
Changsha
Hangzhou
Kazan-Rettō *(Japan)*
Minami-Tori-Shima *(Japan)*
Brahmaputra
Chang J.
Fuzhou
Taipei
Ryukyu-retto *(Japan)*
Kyushu-Palau Ridge
Sitito-Ozima-Ridge
Wake I. *(U.S.A.)*
Mid-Pacific
Dhaka
Kunming
Guangzhou
TAIWAN
Philippine Sea
West Mariana Basin
NORTHERN MARIANAS *(U.S.A.)*
East Mariana Basin
Mandalay
Irrawaddy
Macau
Hong Kong
Philippine Basin
Tinian
Saipan
BURMA
LAOS
Hanoi
Luzon
Paracel Is.
GUAM
Challenger Deep 11,022
Rangoon
THAILAND
Salween
Mekong
VIETNAM
Manila
PHILIPPINES
Mariana Trench
Micronesia
Yap
Caroline Is.
MARSHALL IS.
Bikini Atoll
Bangkok
CAMBODIA
Mindoro
Samar
10,497
Enewetak Atoll
Kwajalein
Ralik Chain
Ratak Chain
Majuro
Phnom Penh
G. of Thailand
Palawan
South China Sea
Mindanao 4101
Davao
Philippine Trench
Koror
FED. STATES OF MICRONESIA
Chuuk
Pohnpei
Palikir
East Caroline Basin
Jaluit I.
Thanh Pho Ho Chi Minh
SRI LANKA
Nicobar Is. *(India)*
Sulu Sea
PALAU
West Caroline Basin
Eauripik Rise
Solomon Rise
Butaritari
Pacific
Colombo
MALAYSIA
PEN. MALAYSIA
BRUNEI
SABAH
Celebes Sea
Melanesian Basin
Tarawa
Gilbert Is.
Howland I. *(U.S.A.)*
Central
Kuala Lumpur
SARAWAK
Sulawesi
Halmahera
PAPUA NEW GUINEA
Melanesia
Banaba
Baker I. *(U.S.A.)*
Singapore
Borneo
Buru
Seram
Admiralty Is.
New Ireland
Yaren NAURU
KIRIBATI
Sumatera
INDONESIA
Java Sea
Ujung Pandang
Maluku
Banda Sea
7440
Puncak Jaya PAPUA 5029
Bismarck Arch.
New Guinea
Rabaul 8940
Bougainville
SOLOMON IS.
Phoenix Is.
Abariringa Enderbury
Palembang
Jakarta
Jawa
Surabaya
Flores Sea
Flores
New Britain
Lae
SOLOMON IS.
Fongafale
TUVALU
Ninetyeast Ridge
Selat Sunda
Sunda Strait
Bali
Sumbawa
Sumba
Dili
EAST TIMOR
Arafura Sea
Port Moresby
Torres Strait
Honiara
Guadalcanal
Santa Cruz Is. 9165
Funafuti
Tokelau Is. *(N.Z.)*
INDIAN
OCEAN
Cocos Is. *(Austral.)*
Christmas I. *(Austral.)*
North Australian Basin
Darwin
C. York
C. Arnhem
Louisiade Arch.
Coral Sea Basin
Rotuma
Is. Wallis & Futuna *(Fr.)*
SAMOA
Apia
Wharton Basin
Gulf of Carpentaria
Broome
VANUATU
Espíritu Santo
Port Vila
West Fiji Basin
Vanua Levu
Viti Levu
Suva
FIJI
Broken Ridge
Exmouth Plateau
North West C.
Cairns
Mount Isa
AUSTRALIA
Townsville
Great Barrier Reef
Coral Sea
Îs. Chesterfield
7670
NEW CALEDONIA *(Fr.)*
Nouméa
Is. Loyauté
Nuku'alofa
TONGA
10,822
OCEAN
Geraldton
Perth Basin
L. Eyre
Alice Springs
Great Dividing Ra.
Rockhampton
Middleton Basin
South Fiji Basin
Kermadec Is. *(N.Z.)*
10,047
Kermadec Trench
Naturaliste Plateau
Perth
Great Australian Bight
Darling
Brisbane
Lord Howe I. *(Austral.)*
New Caledonia Trough
Norfolk Ridge
Norfolk I. *(Austral.)*
South Fiji Basin
NEW ZEALAND
Albany
South Australian Basin
Murray
Sydney
Canberra
Mt. Kosciuszko 2230
Tasman Sea
Auckland
Melbourne
Bass Str.
Adelaide
Tasmania
Hobart
Mt. Cook
Aoraki 3753
Christchurch
Chatham Is. *(N.Z.)*
Chatham I.
East Tasman Plateau
South Tasman Rise
Tasman Basin
Wellington
Dunedin
Bounty Trough
Invercargill
Bounty Is. *(N.Z.)*
Auckland Is. *(N.Z.)*
Campbell *(N.Z.)*
Macquarie Is. *(Austral.)*
Campbell I. *(N.Z.)*
Antipodes Is. *(N.Z.)*

SOUTHERN OCEAN

Projection: Mollweide's Homolographic
East from Greenwich

ALASKA (U.S.A.)
Arctic Circle
Anchorage
Bristol Bay
Juneau
Gulf of Alaska
CANADA
Prince of Wales I.
Prince Rupert
Queen Charlotte Is. (Canada)
Vancouver
Vancouver I.
Victoria
Seattle
Portland
Edmonton
Calgary
Boise
Tufts
Abyssal
Plain
Snake
Salt Lake City
Denver
Sacramento
San Francisco
6741
Murray Fracture Zone
Mendocino Fracture Zone
C. Mendocino
4418
Colorado
UNITED STATES
Los Angeles
San Diego
Phoenix
Oklahoma City
Memphis
Atlanta
Dallas
Houston
Jacksonville
Ciudad Juárez
San Antonio
New Orleans
Gulf of Mexico
Miami
BAHAMAS
Monterrey
3504
Guadalupe (Mex.)
Molokai Fracture Zone
Baja California
Golfo de California
Tropic of Cancer
C. San Lucas
Sigsbee Deep
La Habana
CUBA
Canal de Yucatán
HAITI
Kingston
JAMAICA
Honolulu
O'ahu
4205
HAWAI'I (U.S.A.)
Hawai'i
Clarion Fracture Zone
Is. de Revillagigedo (Mex.)
Guadalajara
Mexico
5610
Puebla
Mérida
7680
Acapulco
BELIZE
Middle America Trench
GUATEMALA
Guatemala
HONDURAS
San Salvador
EL SALVADOR
Managua
NICARAGUA
Caribbean Sea
Guatemala Basin
Barranquilla
San José
COSTA RICA
Colón
Panamá
PANAMA
Panama Basin
Medellín
Cali
COLOMBIA
I. del Coco (Costa Rica)
I. de Malpelo (Colombia)
Cocos Ridge
Clipperton Fracture Zone
Î. Clipperton (Fr.)
Galápagos Fracture Zone
Galápagos (Ecuador)
Carnegie Ridge
Quito
ECUADOR
Guayaquil
C. Pariñas

Johnston I. (U.S.A.)
Palmyra Is. (U.S.A.)
Teraina
Tabuaeran
Kiritimati
KIRIBATI
Jarvis I. (U.S.A.)
Phoenix Is.
Malden I.
Starbuck I.
Caroline I. (Millennium I.)
Vostok I.
Flint I.
Nuku Hiva
Îs. Marquises
Hiva Oa
Marquesas Fracture Zone
Cooper Ridge
Equator
North West Christmas I. Ridge
Line Islands
Pacific Ocean
Manihiki
Pukapuka
Manihiki
Suwarrow Is.
Îs. de la Société
Bora Bora
Huahine
Raiatea
Papeete
Tahiti
Îs. Tuamotu
Aitutaki
Cook Is. (N.Z.)
Atiu
Rarotonga
Mangaia
Mururoa
Îs. Gambier
FRENCH POLYNESIA
Austral Seamount Chain
Îs. Tubuaï
Oeno I.
Henderson I.
Ducie I.
Pitcairn I. (U.K.)
Rapa
Yupanqui Basin
Mendaña Fracture Zone
Peru Basin
Galápagos Fracture Zone
Peru Rise
Tropic of Capricorn
Sala y Gómez Ridge
Sala-y-Gómez (Chile)
I. de Pascua (Chile)
Easter Fracture Zone
San Félix (Chile)
San Ambrosio (Chile)
Nazca Ridge
Trujillo
6369
PERU
Lima
Cuzco
L. Titicaca
Arequipa
6866
Peru-Chile Trench
Arica
Nevado Ancohuma 6550
La Paz
BOLIVIA
Iquique
Chile Basin
Antofagasta
8064
PARAGUAY
Asunción
San Miguel de Tucumán
Córdoba
Aconcagua 6960
Valparaíso
Rosario
Santiago
URUGUAY
Buenos Aires
Montevideo
Río de la Plata
Concepción
ARGENTINA
Arch. de Juan Fernández (Chile)
Roggeveen Basin
Easter Fracture Zone
Challenger Fracture Zone
Chile Rise
Menard Fracture Zone
Pacific Antarctic Ridge
East Pacific Rise
Southwest Pacific Basin
Southeast Pacific Basin
114
Pacific Basin
Patagonia
Cordillera
SOUTH ATLANTIC OCEAN
Argentine Basin
6212
Falkland Plateau
Punta Arenas
Est. de Magallanes
Tierra del Fuego
4402
C. de Hornos
Drake Passage
Falkland Is. (U.K.)
Georgia Basin
South Georgia (U.K.)
South Georgia Ridge

Niue (N.Z.)
American Samoa (U.S.A.)
Swains I.

TAHITI [e]
Pte. Aroa
B. de Matavai
Pte. Vénus
Mahina
Papenoo
Papeari
Pte. Aroa
Mt. Tohiea 1207
Papao
Aruė
Papeete
Pirae
Tiarei
Afareaitu
Faaa
Tahiti (France)
Hitiaa
Moorea
Haapiti
Nuupere
Paea
Mt. Aorai 2060
Mt. Orohena 2241
Punaauia
Mt. Tetufera 1799
Faaone
Lac Vaihiria
Taravao
Isthme de Taravao
Maraa
Paea
Papara
Atimaono
Mataiea
Vairao
Pueu
Afaahiti
Tatutu
Tautira
Teahupoo
Mt. Rooniu 1332
Presqu'île de Taiarapu
PACIFIC OCEAN

FRENCH POLYNESIA [f]
1:26 000 000
200 0 200 400 km
200 0 200 400 miles
Hatutu
Eiao
Îles Marquises
Nuku Hiva
Ua Huka
Ua Pu
Hiva Oa
Tahuata
Motané
4884
6513
Flint I. (U.K.)
Îles du Roi-Georges
Manihi
Takaroa
Îles du Désappointement
Puka Puka
Tikahau
Ahé
Takapoto
Rangiroa
Apataki
Kaukura
Raroia
Makemo
Fangatau
Tatakoto
Îles Sous-le-Vent
Matahiva
Îles du Vent
Maupiti
Huahine
Fakarava
Ile Raeuki
Tekokota
Tahiti
Moorea
Anaa
Haraiki
Marokau
Amanu
Puka Ruha
Maupihaa
Méhétia
Ravahere
Hao
Paraoa
Vahitahi
Réao
Nengonengo
Héréhérétué
Ahunui
Vairaatea
Îles de la Société
Îles Maria
Rimatara
Rurutu
Tubuaï
Raivavae
Vanavana
Turéia
Groupe Actéon
Mururoa
Fangataufa
Morane
Tematagi
Îles Gambier
Tropic of Capricorn
Récif Président-Thiers
Îles Tubuaï (Îles Australes)
Rapa
Récif Neilson
Îlots de Bass
Morané
Récif Portland
PACIFIC OCEAN

1:1 150 000
10 0 10 km
10 0 10 miles

NIUE [g]
1:830 000
5 0 10 km
3 0 5 miles
Hikutavake
Mutalau
Namukulu
Toi
Tuapa
Makefu
Lakepa
Alofi Bay
Alofi
Liku
Niue (N.Z.)
Halangingie Pt.
Fonuakula
Tamakautoga
Avatele
Tepa Pt.
Vaiea
Hakupu
PACIFIC OCEAN

RAROTONGA [h]
1:415 000
5 km 0
5 miles 0
Rarotonga (N.Z.)
Avarua Harbour
Nikaō
Avatiu
Avarua
Pue
Aroa
Matavera
Arorangi
509
Maungaroa
588
Te Manga 653
Ngatangiia
222
Te Kou
Acuana
Motu Tapu
Oneroa
Maungatongariti
329
Muri
Koromiri
Taakoka
Taroume
Titikaveka
PACIFIC OCEAN

West from Greenwich

ft m
12 000 4000
9000 3000
6000 2000
3000 1000
0 0
200 600
1000 3000
2000 6000
4000 12 000
6000 18 000
8000 24 000
m ft

NORTH AMERICA

100 0 200 400 600 800 1000 1200 1400 km
100 0 200 400 600 800 1000 miles

1:28 000 000

ft m
9000 3000
6000 2000
3000 1000
1500 500
600 200
0 0
200 600
1000 3000
2000 6000
4000 12000
6000 18000
8000 24000
m ft

Projection: Bonne

West from Greenwich

COPYRIGHT PHILIP'S

1:28 000 000

100 0   200   400   600   800   1000 1200 1400 km

100 0   200   400   600   800   1000 miles

ARCTIC OCEAN

RUSSIA

Asia

St. Lawrence I.

Bering Strait

Bering Sea

GREENLAND
(Denmark)

ICELAND
Reykjavik

Denmark Strait

Queen Elizabeth Is.

Ellesmere I.

Baffin Bay

Beaufort Sea

Victoria I.

Baffin Island

Nuuk

International Date Line

ALASKA
(USA)

Yukon

Porcupine

Fairbanks

Anchorage

Kodiak I.

Gulf of Alaska

Juneau

Whitehorse

Arctic Circle

YUKON TERRITORY

NORTHWEST

Mackenzie

Great Bear L.

Back

Liard

Great Slave L.

Yellowknife

TERRITORIES

Dubawnt

NUNAVUT

Hudson Strait

Iqaluit

Davis Strait

Baffin Island

Hudson Bay

CANADA

BRITISH COLUMBIA

Skeena

Fraser

Peace

Athabasca

L. Athabasca

Churchill

Nelson

Eastmain

St. Lawrence

NEWFOUNDLAND & LABRADOR

ALBERTA

Edmonton

Calgary

Saskatchewan

SASKATCHEWAN

MANITOBA

L. Winnipeg

ONTARIO

QUÉBEC

St. John's

Victoria

Vancouver

Regina

Winnipeg

Québec

Fredericton

PRINCE EDWARD

Charlottetown

St-Pierre et Miquelon (Fr.)

NEW BRUNSWICK

NOVA SCOTIA

Halifax

WASHINGTON

Seattle

Olympia

Portland

Salem

Columbia

OREGON

IDAHO

Boise

Snake

MONTANA

Helena

Missouri

WYOMING

NORTH DAKOTA

Bismarck

SOUTH DAKOTA

MINNESOTA

L. Superior

Minneapolis-St. Paul

WISCONSIN

Madison

MICHIGAN

L. Michigan

Lansing

L. Huron

Toronto

L. Ontario

Ottawa

Montréal

VER.

N.H.

Concord

MAINE

Augusta

Boston

Providence

MASS.

CONN.

R.I.

Detroit

Buffalo

NEW YORK

Hartford

NEW YORK

N.J.

PHILADELPHIA

PA.

Pittsburgh

Cleveland

Erie

Toledo

Milwaukee

CHICAGO

IOWA

OHIO

Columbus

Baltimore

Washington D.C.

DE.

MD.

W.V.

Richmond

UNITED STATES

Sacramento

San Francisco

San Jose

CALIFORNIA

LOS ANGELES

San Diego

Tijuana

Carson City

NEVADA

Las Vegas

Salt Lake City

UTAH

Denver

COLORADO

Santa Fe

Albuquerque

ARIZONA

Phoenix

Tucson

NEW MEXICO

El Paso

Ciudad Juárez

Colorado

Mexicali

Hermosillo

NEBRASKA

Lincoln

KANSAS

Kansas City

Topeka

OKLAHOMA

Oklahoma City

TEXAS

Dallas-Ft. Worth

Austin

San Antonio

Houston

Baton Rouge

LOUISIANA

New Orleans

ILLINOIS

Springfield

INDIANA

Indianapolis

St. Louis

MISSOURI

KENTUCKY

Cincinnati

Nashville

TENNESSEE

ARKANSAS

Little Rock

Memphis

Mississippi

Birmingham

MISSISSIPPI

Jackson

ALABAMA

Montgomery

GEORGIA

Atlanta

Columbia

SOUTH CAROLINA

NORTH CAROLINA

Raleigh

Charlotte

VIRGINIA

Charleston

Tallahassee

Jacksonville

FLORIDA

Tampa-St. Petersburg

Orlando

Miami

NORTH ATLANTIC OCEAN

Bermuda (U.K.)

PACIFIC OCEAN

Guadalupe (Mex.)

Revilla Gigedo Is. (Mex.)

Tropic of Cancer

Culiacan

MEXICO

Torreón

Monterrey

Rio Grande

San Luis Potosí

León

Guadalajara

MÉXICO

Toluca

Puebla

Acapulco

Mérida

Gulf of Mexico

Florida Str.

Havana

CUBA

BAHAMAS

Nassau

Turks & Caicos Is. (U.K.)

Cayman Is. (U.K.)

JAMAICA

Kingston

HAITI

Port-au-Prince

DOMINICAN REP.

Santo Domingo

PUERTO RICO (U.S.A.)

San Juan

Caribbean Sea

BELIZE

Belmopan

GUATEMALA

Guatemala

San Salvador

EL SALVADOR

HONDURAS

Tegucigalpa

NICARAGUA

Managua

L. Nicaragua

COSTA RICA

San José

PANAMA

Panamá

Barranquilla

Maracaibo

VENEZUELA

COLOMBIA

Medellín

South America

Projection: Bonne

West from Greenwich

COPYRIGHT PHILIP'S

7   ■ MÉXICO Capital Cities   8   9   10   11   12

Scale 1:12 000 000

Projection : Bonne

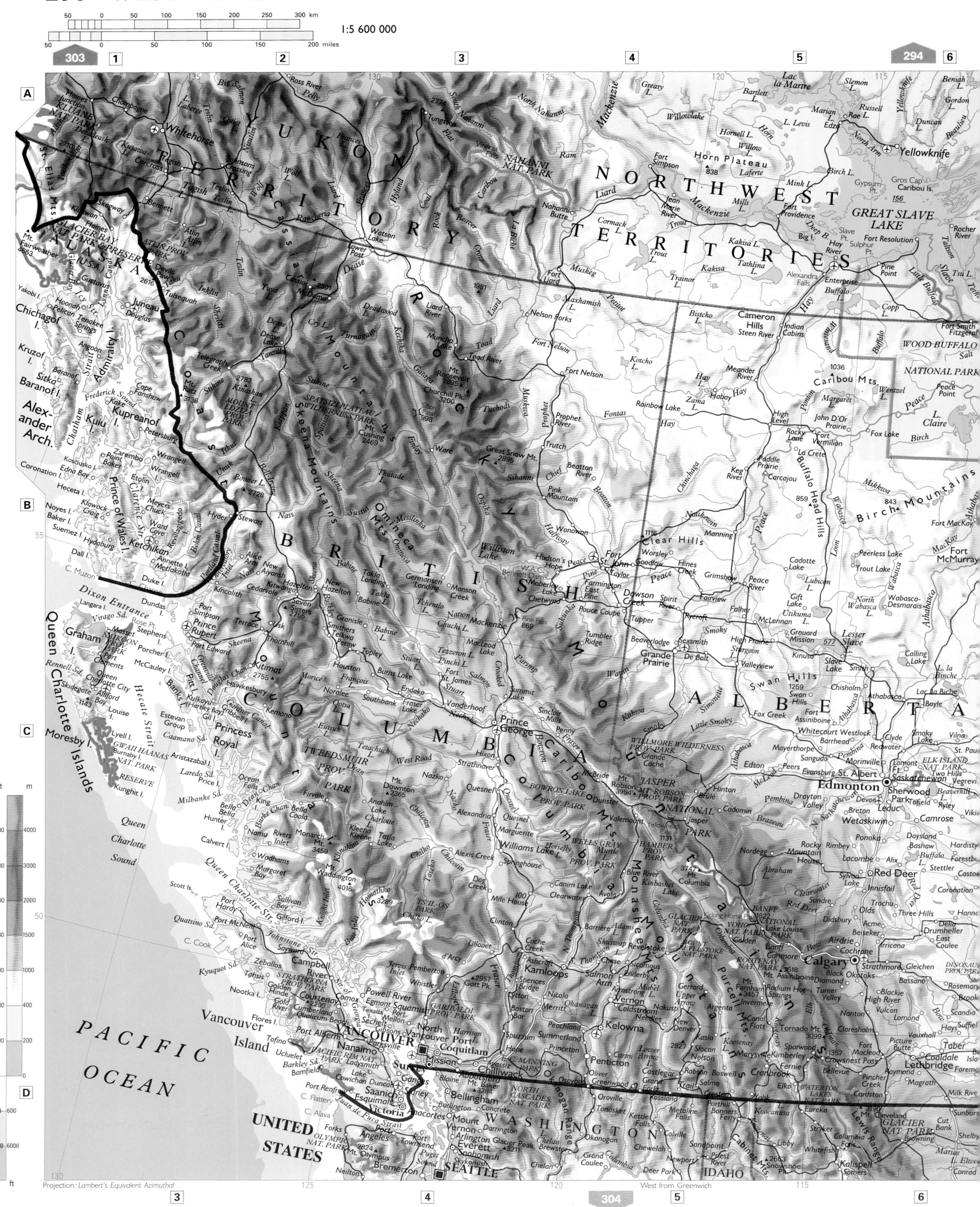

Projection: Lambert's Equivalent Azimuthal   West from Greenwich

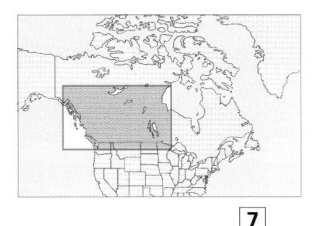

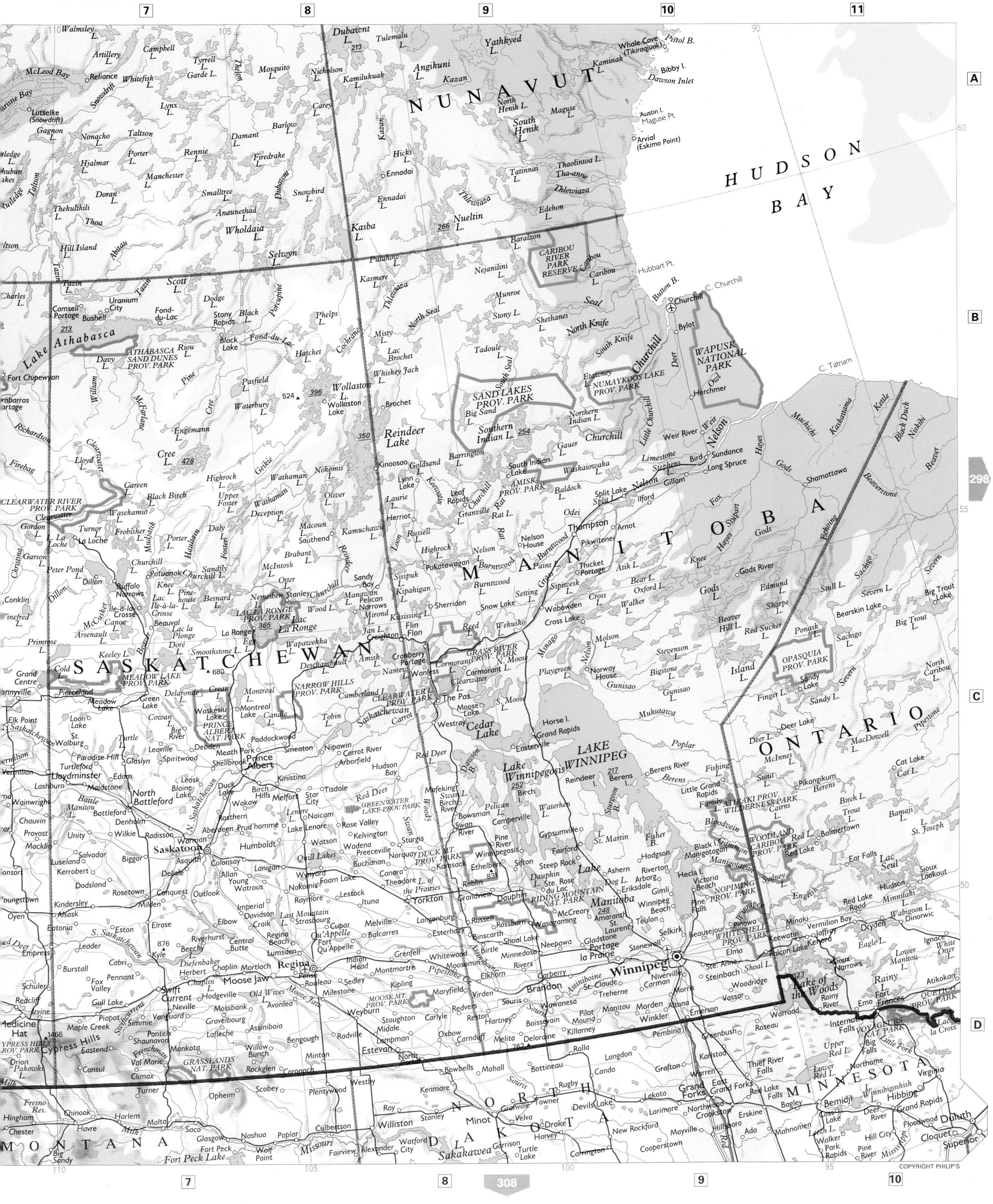

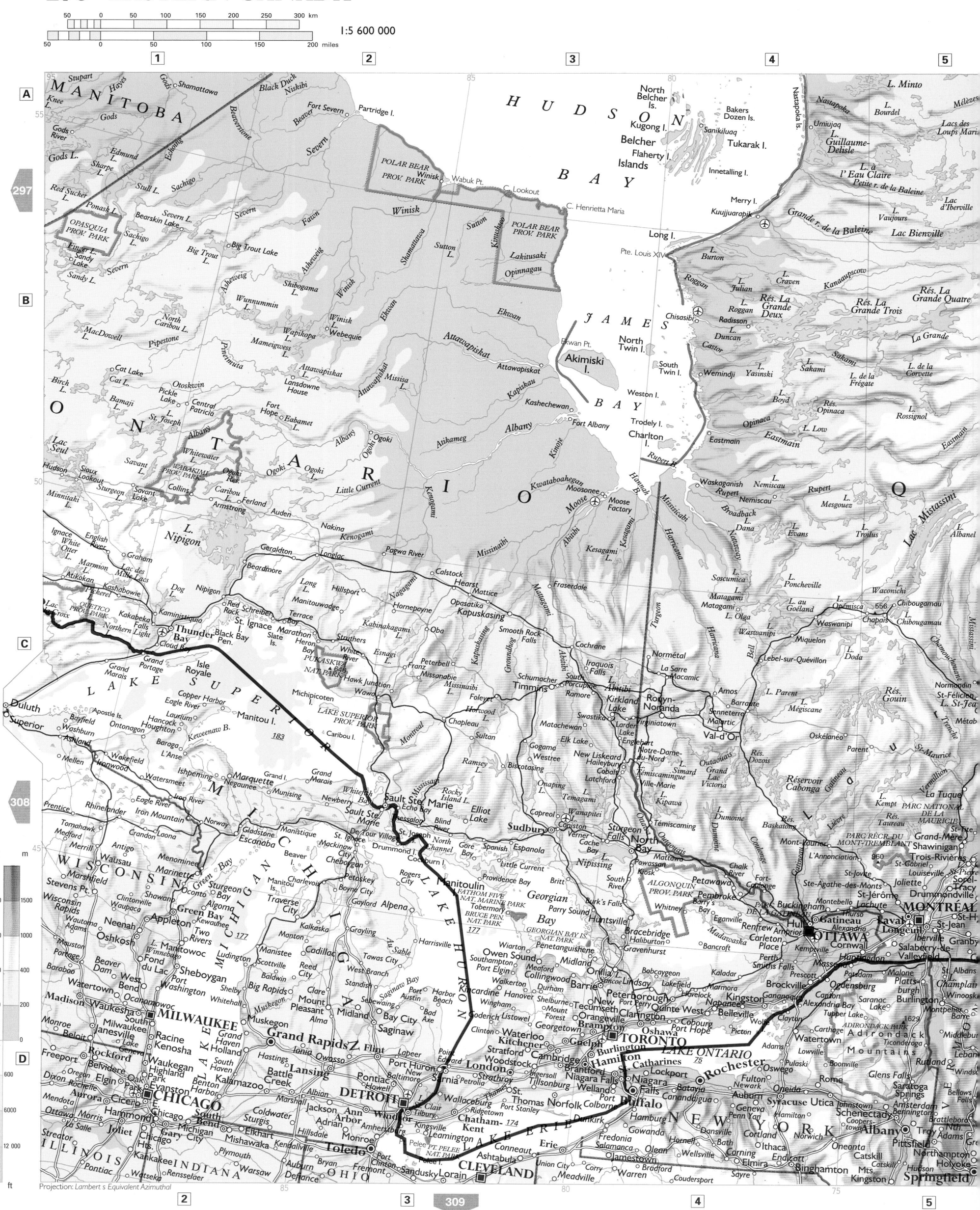

1:5 600 000

Projection: Lambert's Equivalent Azimuthal

6 295 7 8 9

A

LABRADOR SEA

LABRADOR

NEWFOUNDLAND &

Labrador

QUÉBEC

B

Smallwood Reservoir

Schefferville
Kawawachikamach

Petitsikapau L.

Menihek

L. Caniapiscau

Twin Falls
Churchill Falls
Churchill
North West River
Goose
Happy Valley-Goose Bay

L. Melville 1128
Mealy Mts.

Nain
Paul I.
Voisey B.
Davis Inlet
Hopedale
Postville
Makkovik
Adlavik Is.
C. Harrison
Holton
Indian Harbour
Groswater B.
North River
Cartwright
Sandwich B.
Table B.
Black Tickle
Island of Ponds
Paradise River
Charlottetown
Alexis
Williams Harbour
Port Hope Simpson
Battle Harbour
Lodge Bay
St. Lewis Mary's Harbour
Red Bay
L'Anse au Loup
Forteau
Lourdes-de-Blanc-Sablon
St. Barbe
Belle Isle
Str. of Belle Isle
L'Anse aux Meadows
St. Anthony
Hare B.
Groais I.
Roddickton
Bell I.

Labrador City
Wabush
Fermont

L. Ashuanipi
Atikonak L.
Burnt L.
Natashquan
Little Mécatina
Minipi
L.

Labrador Plateau

LABRADOR

NEWFOUNDLAND

C

Î. d'Anticosti

GULF OF ST. LAWRENCE

Long Range Mts.

Corner Brook
Stephenville
Grand Falls
Windsor
Gander
Buchans
Red Indian L.
L. Meelpaeg
St. George's
Channel-Port aux Basques
Burgeo
François
Cabot Strait

Sept-Îles
Port-Cartier
Baie-Comeau
Matane
Gaspé
Percé
Chic-Chocs
Pén. de la Gaspésie
Rimouski
Mont-Joli

Îs. de la Madeleine (Québec)
Cap-aux-Meules
Havre-Aubert

St-Pierre et Miquelon (France)

D

NEW BRUNSWICK
Fredericton
Moncton
Saint John
Edmundston
Campbellton
Bathurst
Miramichi

PRINCE EDWARD ISLAND
Charlottetown
Summerside

NOVA SCOTIA
Halifax
Dartmouth
Truro
New Glasgow
Sydney
Glace Bay
Cape Breton Island
Louisbourg
Yarmouth

MAINE
Bangor
Augusta
Portland

NEW HAMPSHIRE

UNITED STATES

BOSTON
Worcester
Quincy
Brockton

ATLANTIC OCEAN

Sable I. (Nova Scotia)

St. John's
Avalon Peninsula
Placentia
Conception B.
Trinity B.
Bonavista

West from Greenwich

COPYRIGHT PHILIP'S

Projection: Albers' Equal Area with two standard parallels

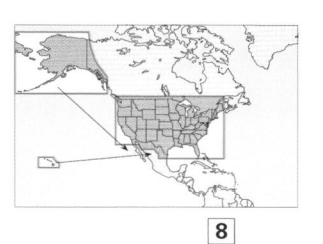

Tallahassee ⭐ U.S. state capitals

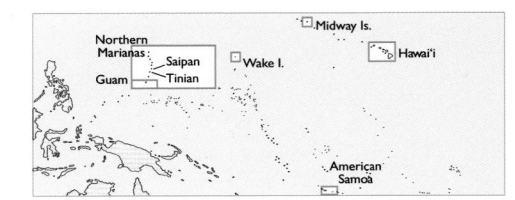

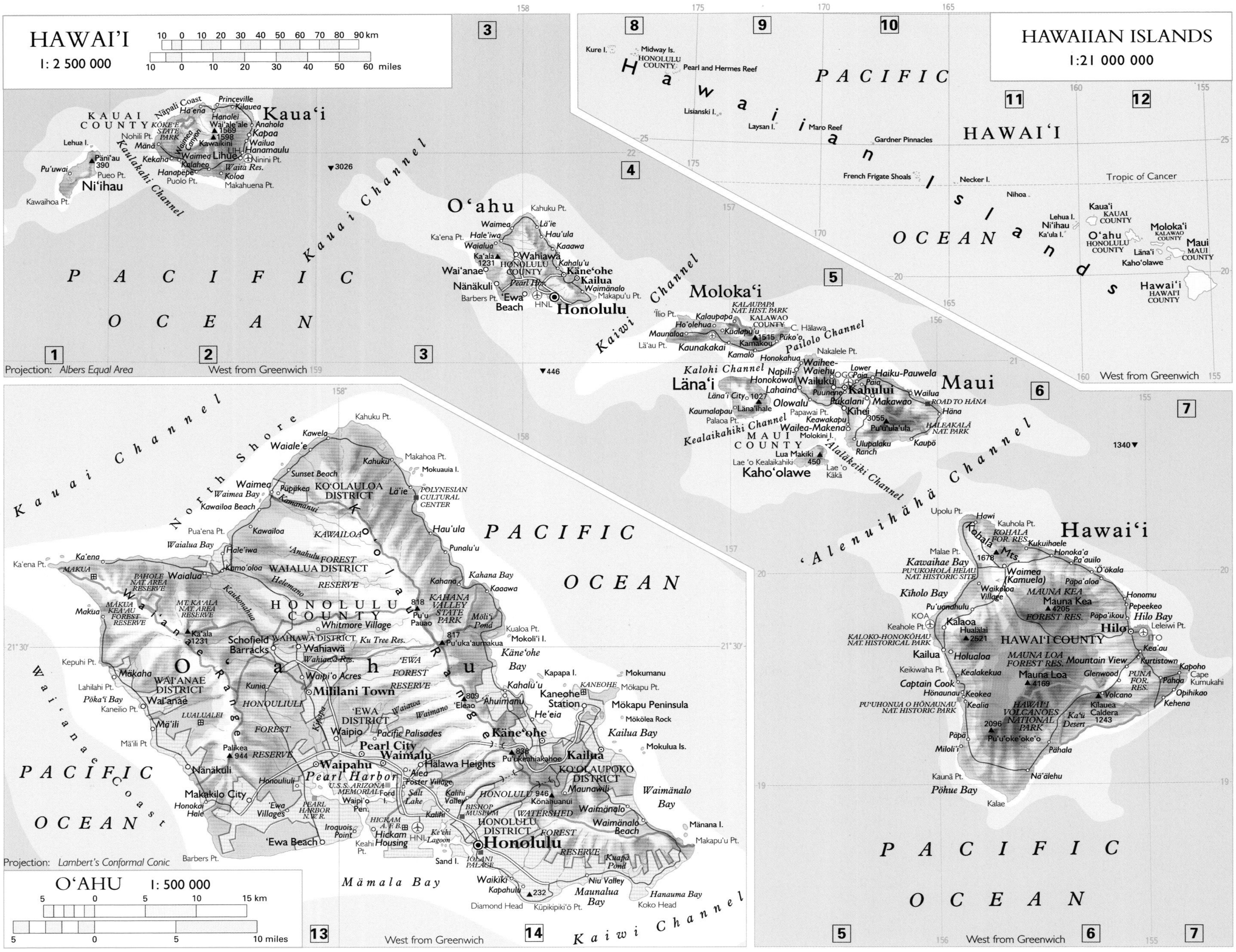

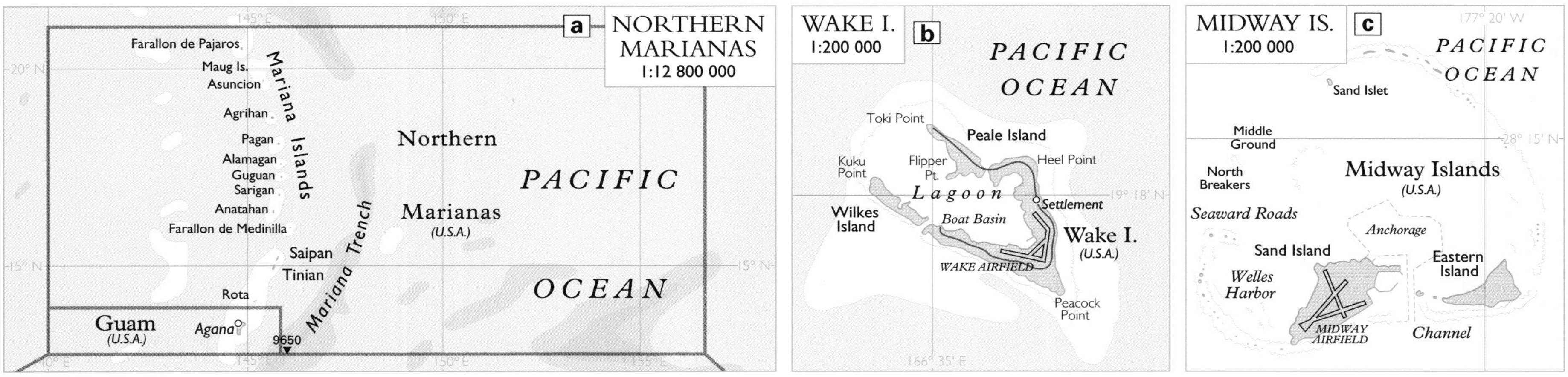

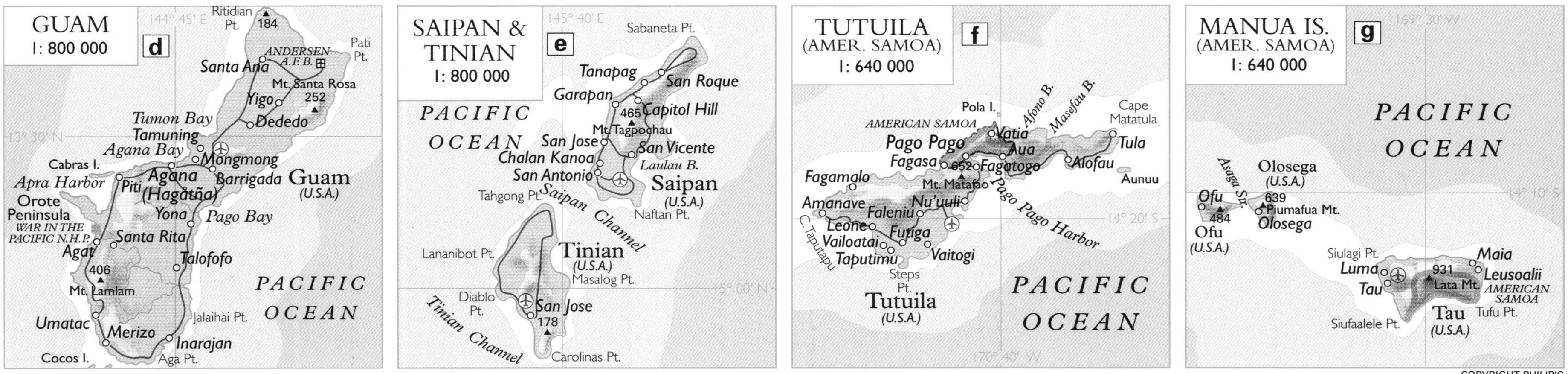

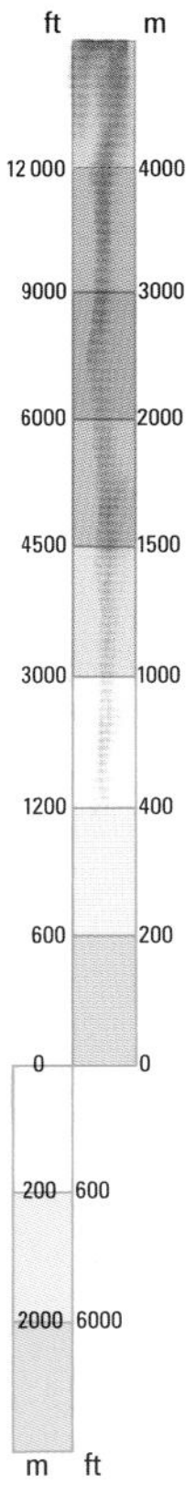

HAWAI'I
1: 2 500 000

10 0 10 20 30 40 50 60 70 80 90 km
10 0 10 20 30 40 50 60 miles

Projection: Albers Equal Area   West from Greenwich 159

KAUAI COUNTY
Kaua'i
Princeville · Kilauea
Nāpali Coast · Ha'ena · Hanalei · Anahola
KŌKE'E STATE PARK · Wai'ale'ale 1569 · Kapaa
Kalalau · Waimea Canyon · Kawaikini 1598 · Wailua · Hanamaulu
Nohili Pt. · Mānā · Kekaha · Waimea · Kalaheo · Lihue · Wailua
Pani'au 390 · Hanapepe · Koloa
Pu'uwai · Makahuena Pt.
Lehua I. · Pueo Pt. · Puolo Pt.
Ni'ihau
Kawaihoa Pt.

Kauai Channel · Kealakahiki Channel

▼3026

O'ahu
Kahuku Pt.
Wai'anae · Waimea · Lā'ie · Hau'ula
Ka'ena Pt. · Hale'iwa · Kaaawa
Waialua · Wahiawā · Kāne'ohe
Nānākuli · HONOLULU COUNTY · Kailua
Barbers Pt. · 'Ewa Beach · Waimānalo
Pearl Hbr. · Makapu'u Pt.
Honolulu · HNL

Kaiwi Channel

Moloka'i
'Ilio Pt. · Kalaupapa · KALAUPAPA NAT. HIST. PARK · KALAWAO COUNTY
Ho'olehua · Kualapu'u · Hālawa · Kamalo
Kaunakakai · Pohakuloa · Nakelele Pt.
Lā'au Pt. · Kolohi Channel · Pailolo Channel

Lāna'i
Lāna'i City 1027 · Waikapu · Waihe'e · Haiku-Pauwela
Kaumalapau · Lāna'ihale · Lahaina · Puunene · Kahului · Wailua
Kaumalapau Pt. · Papawai Pt. · Kihei · Makawao · Hāna
Kaho'olawe · Wailea-Makena · Puunene · HALEAKALĀ NAT. PARK
Lae 'o Kealaikahiki · Molokini I. · 3055 · Kaupō
MAUI COUNTY
Lae 'o Kala · Lua Makiki 450
Kealaikahiki Channel · Alalākeiki Channel · 'Alenuihāhā Channel

1340▼

Maui

HAWAIIAN ISLANDS
1:21 000 000

Kure I. · Midway Is. · HONOLULU COUNTY · Pearl and Hermes Reef
Lisianski I. · Maro Reef · Gardner Pinnacles
Laysan I.
French Frigate Shoals · Necker I. · Nihoa · Tropic of Cancer
Niihoa
HAWAI'I
Lehua I. · Kaua'i · KAUAI COUNTY
Ni'ihau · O'ahu · HONOLULU COUNTY · Moloka'i · KALAWAO COUNTY
Ka'ula I. · Lāna'i · Maui · MAUI COUNTY
Kaho'olawe · **Hawai'i** · HAWAI'I COUNTY

PACIFIC OCEAN
West from Greenwich 155

O'AHU
1: 500 000

Kahuku Pt.
North Shore · Kawela · Kahuku
Waialua · Waimea · Makahoa Pt.
Sunset Beach · Pupukea · KO'OLAULOA DISTRICT · Mokuauia I.
Waialua Bay · Hale'iwa · Lā'ie · POLYNESIAN CULTURAL CENTER
Kawailoa Beach · KAWAILOA · Hau'ula
Ka'ena · Pua'ena Pt. · Kawailoa · Punalu'u
Ka'ena Pt. · MAKUA · WAIALUA DISTRICT · Kahana Bay
PAHOLE NAT. AREA RESERVE · 'ĀLIŌLANI FOREST · KAHANA VALLEY STATE PARK
Makua · Waialua · Mt. Ka'ala · HONOLULU COUNTY · Kaaawa
WAI'ANAE · Ka'ala 1231 · NAT. AREA RESERVE · Whitmore Village · Kualoa Pt.
Mākaha · Schofield Barracks · WAIAWA DISTRICT · Wahiawā · Moku'oloe I.
Kepuhi Pt. · Mililani Town · Ku Tree Res.
O'ahu · Waipi'o Acres · 'EWA FOREST RESERVE · Kapapa I. · Mokumanu
Lahilahi Pt. · WAI'ANAE DISTRICT · Kunia · Wahiawa · Kahalu'u · Mōkapu Pt.
Pōka'i Bay · Kaneohe · Mōkapu Peninsula
Wai'anae · HONOULIULI · Mākua · Pearl City · Mokolii I. · He'eia
Mā'ili · FOREST · Waipio · Kāne'ohe · KĀNEOHE · Kailua Bay
Mā'ili Pt. · 944 · RESERVE · Waipahu · Waimalu · Mokulua Is.
Nanakuli · Pearl Harbor · Halawa Heights · KO'OLAUPOKO DISTRICT
WAIANAE COAST · Honouliuli · Foster Village · Puukeahiakahoe 946
Makakilo City · 'Ewa Villages · U.S.S. ARIZONA MEMORIAL · Bishop Museum
Honokai Hale · PEARL HARBOR N.W.R. · WAR MEMORIAL · Waimānalo
Iroquois Pt. · HICKAM A.F.B. · Salt Lake · HONOLULU DISTRICT · Waimānalo Beach
'Ewa Beach · Kaehi Lagoon · HNL · Ka'ohi Housing · FOREST RESERVE · Mānana I.
Barbers Pt. · Keahi Pt. · **Honolulu** · 'IOLANI PALACE
Māmala Bay · Waikīkī · 232 · Kapahulu · Hawaii Kai
Diamond Head · Kūpikipiki'o Pt. · Maunalua Bay · Koko Head
Niu Valley · Hanauma Bay
Kaiwi Channel

Projection: Lambert's Conformal Conic

5 0 5 10 15 km
5 0 5 10 miles

Hawai'i (island)
Hāwī · KOHALA · 1678 Mts · Kukuihaele
Kawaihae Bay · KOHALA FOR. RES. · Honoka'a · Pa'auilo
PU'UKOHOLĀ HEIAU NAT. HISTORIC SITE · Honomu · Pepeekeo
Kawaihae · Waimea (Kamuela) · Pāpa'aloa
Kīholo Bay · MAUNA KEA FOREST RES. · Pāpa'ikou · Hilo
Pu'uanahulu · 4205 Mauna Kea · Hilo Bay
Kalaoa · Hualalai · Wailuku · Leleiwi Pt.
KOA · 2521 · Kurtistown · Kea'au
KALOKO-HONOKŌHAU NAT. HISTORICAL PARK · Keahole Pt. · Mountain View
Kailua · HAWAII COUNTY · Kapoho Cape
Holualoa · 2096 · Glenwood · Kumukahi
Keikewaha Pt. · Kealakekua · Mauna Loa 4169 · PUNA FOR. RES.
Captain Cook · HAWAI'I VOLCANOES · Pāhoa · Opihikao
Kealia · NATIONAL PARK · Kehena
Hōnaunau · Kilauea Caldera 1243
PU'UHONUA O HŌNAUNAU NAT. HISTORICAL PARK · Volcano
Pāpā · Ka'ū Desert · Pu'u 'ōke'oke'o
Keokea · Mili'oli'i · Pāhala
Kaunā Pt. · Pōhue Bay · Nā'ālehu
Kalae

PACIFIC OCEAN
West from Greenwich

NORTHERN MARIANAS
1:12 800 000

Farallon de Pajaros
Maug Is.
Asuncion
Agrihan
Pagan
Alamagan · Mariana Islands
Guguan
Sarigan
Anatahan
Farallon de Medinilla

Northern Marianas (U.S.A.)

Saipan
Tinian
Rota
Guam (U.S.A.) · Agana

Mariana Trench
▼9650

PACIFIC OCEAN

WAKE I.
1:200 000

PACIFIC OCEAN
Toki Point
Peale Island
Kuku Point · Flipper Pt. · Heel Point
Lagoon · Settlement
Wilkes Island · Boat Basin · Wake I. (U.S.A.)
WAKE AIRFIELD
Peacock Point

MIDWAY IS.
1:200 000

PACIFIC OCEAN
Sand Islet
Middle Ground
North Breakers · Midway Islands (U.S.A.)
Seaward Roads · Anchorage
Sand Island · Eastern Island
Welles Harbor · Channel
MIDWAY AIRFIELD

GUAM
1: 800 000

Ritidian Pt. · 184
Santa Ana · ANDERSEN A.F.B. · Pati Pt.
Yigo · Mt. Santa Rosa 252 · Dededo
Tumon Bay · Tamuning
Agana Bay · Mongmong
Cabras I. · Barrigada Pt. · Guam (U.S.A.)
Apra Harbor · Agana (Hagåtña)
Orote Peninsula · Piti · Yona · Pago Bay
WAR IN THE PACIFIC N.H.P. · Agat · Santa Rita
406 · Talofofo
Umatac · Mt. Lamlam
Merizo · Inarajan
Cocos I. · Aga Pt.
PACIFIC OCEAN

SAIPAN & TINIAN
1: 800 000

Sabaneta Pt.
Tanapag · San Roque
Garapan · 465 Capitol Hill
San Jose · Mt. Tagpochau
Chalan Kanoa · San Vicente
San Antonio · Laulau B.
Tahgong Pt. · Saipan · Saipan Channel · (U.S.A.) · Naftan Pt.

Lananibot Pt.
Tinian (U.S.A.)
Masalog Pt.
Diablo Pt. · San Jose · 178
Tinian Channel · Carolinas Pt.

PACIFIC OCEAN

TUTUILA
(AMER. SAMOA)
1: 640 000

Pola I. · Cape Matatula
AMERICAN SAMOA · Vatia · Masefau B. · Tula
Pago Pago · Afono B. · Aoa
Fagamalo · Fagasa · 652 Fagatogo · Alofau
Amanave · Nu'uuli · Aua · Aunuu
Leone · Faleniu · Pago Pago Harbor
C. Taputapu · Vailoatai · Futiga
Taputimu · Vaitogi
Steps

PACIFIC OCEAN
Tutuila (U.S.A.)

MANUA IS.
(AMER. SAMOA)
1: 640 000

PACIFIC OCEAN
Asaga Str. · Olosega
Ofu · 639 Piumafua Mt. · Olosega
484 · Ofu (U.S.A.)
Siulagi Pt. · Maia
Luma · Leusoalii
Tau · 931 Lata Mt. · AMERICAN SAMOA
Siufaalele Pt. · Tau (U.S.A.) · Tufu Pt.

COPYRIGHT PHILIP'S

---

ft / m
12 000 / 4000
9000 / 3000
6000 / 2000
4500 / 1500
3000 / 1000
1200 / 400
600 / 200
0 / 0
200 / 600
2000 / 6000
m / ft

100 0 100 200 300 km
100 0 100 200 miles
1: 12 800 000

5 0 5 10 15 20 km
5 0 5 10 15 miles
1: 800 000

1 0 1 2 3 km
0 1 2 miles
1: 200 000

5 0 5 10 km
5 0 5 10 miles
1: 640 000

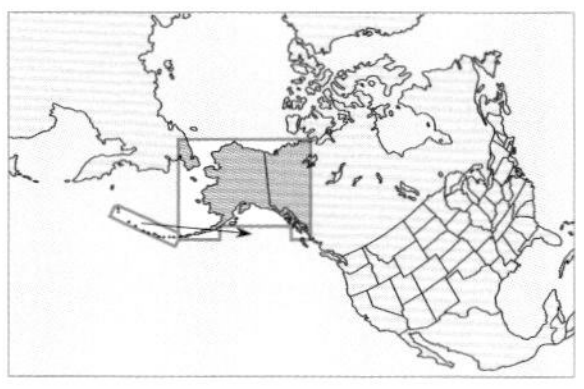

1:8 000 000

50 0 100 200 300 400 km
50 0 50 100 150 200 250 miles

National Parks

continuation westwards
on same scale

Projection: Bipolar oblique conic conformal

ARCTIC OCEAN

BEAUFORT SEA

CHUKCHI SEA

BERING SEA

RUSSIA

NORTH-WEST TERRITORIES

CANADA

YUKON TERRITORY

BRITISH COLUMBIA

ALASKA (U.S.A.)

Gulf of Alaska

PACIFIC OCEAN

Aleutian Islands

Alexander Archipelago

Brooks Range

Mackenzie Mountains

Selwyn Mountains

Alaska Range

Kuskokwim Mountains

Denali Nat. Park and Preserve

Mt. McKinley

Fairbanks

Anchorage

Juneau

Kodiak I.

Nunivak I.

St. Lawrence I.

Pribilof Is.

Seward Peninsula

Nome

Barrow

Prudhoe Bay

Bristol Bay

West from Greenwich

East from Greenwich

1:5 360 000

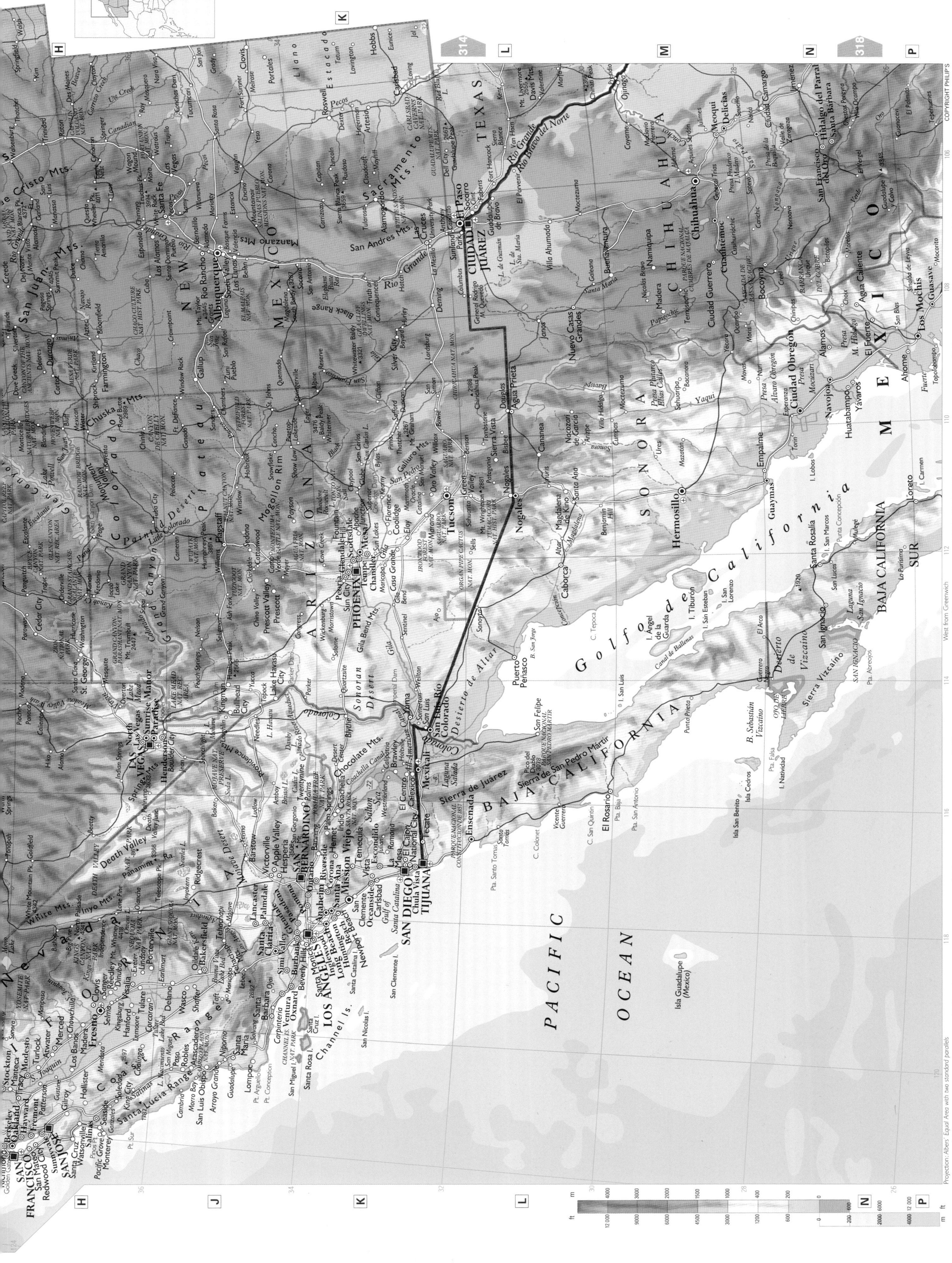

K L M N P

TEXAS

NEW MEXICO

ARIZONA

CALIFORNIA

Nevada

CHIHUAHUA

SONORA

BAJA CALIFORNIA

BAJA CALIFORNIA SUR

MEXICO

Golfo de California

PACIFIC OCEAN

Colorado Plateau

Sonoran Desert

Mojave Desert

DEATH VALLEY

Sacramento Mts.

San Juan Mts.

SAN FRANCISCO
SAN JOSE
LAS VEGAS
LOS ANGELES
SAN DIEGO
TIJUANA
PHOENIX
Tucson
Albuquerque
Santa Fe
El Paso
CIUDAD JUÁREZ
Las Cruces
Mexicali
Ensenada
Hermosillo
Chihuahua
Ciudad Obregón
Los Mochis
Nogales
Agua Prieta

Rio Grande / Rio Bravo del Norte

West from Greenwich

Projection: Albers' Equal Area with two standard parallels

COPYRIGHT PHILIP'S

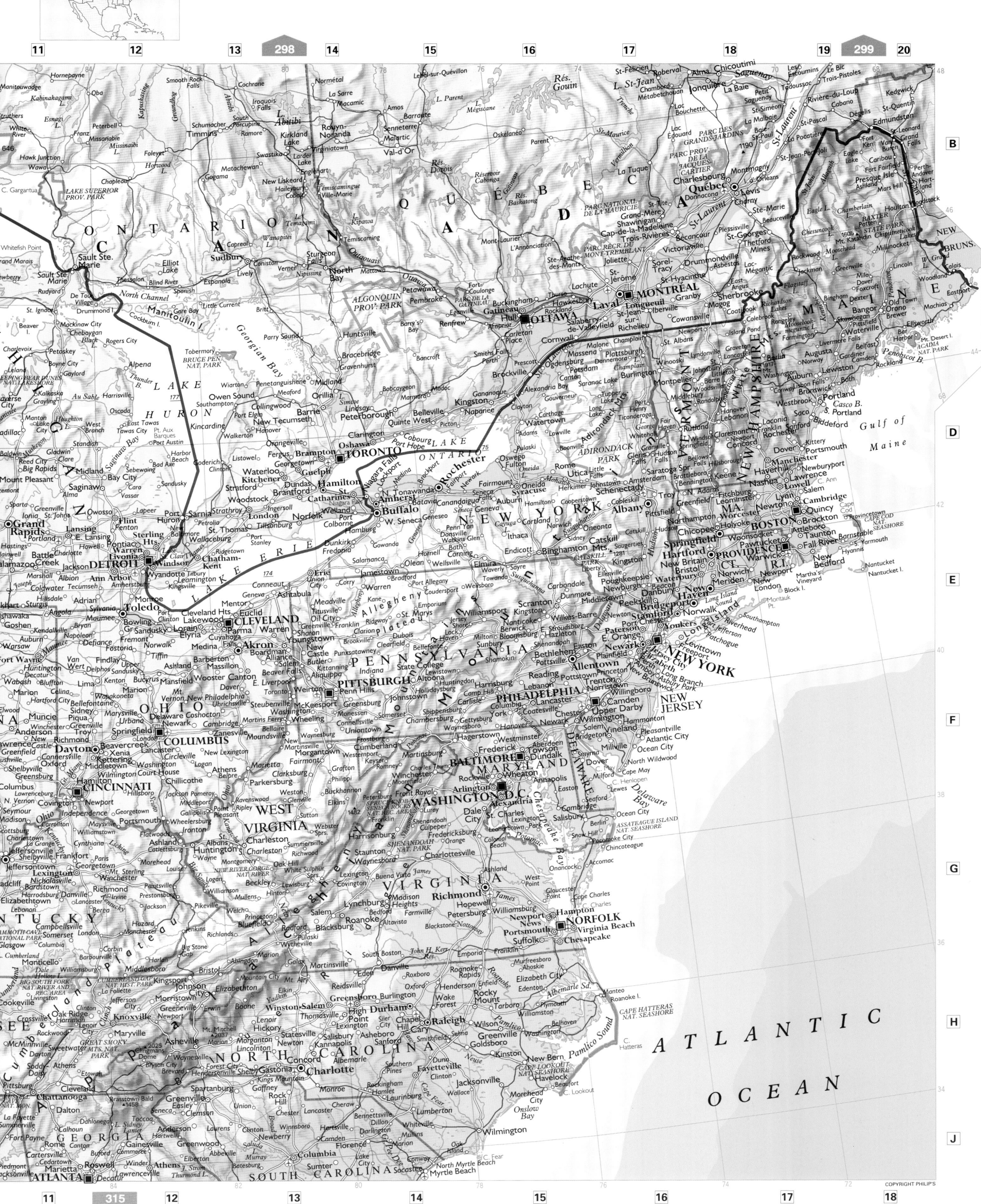

National Parks

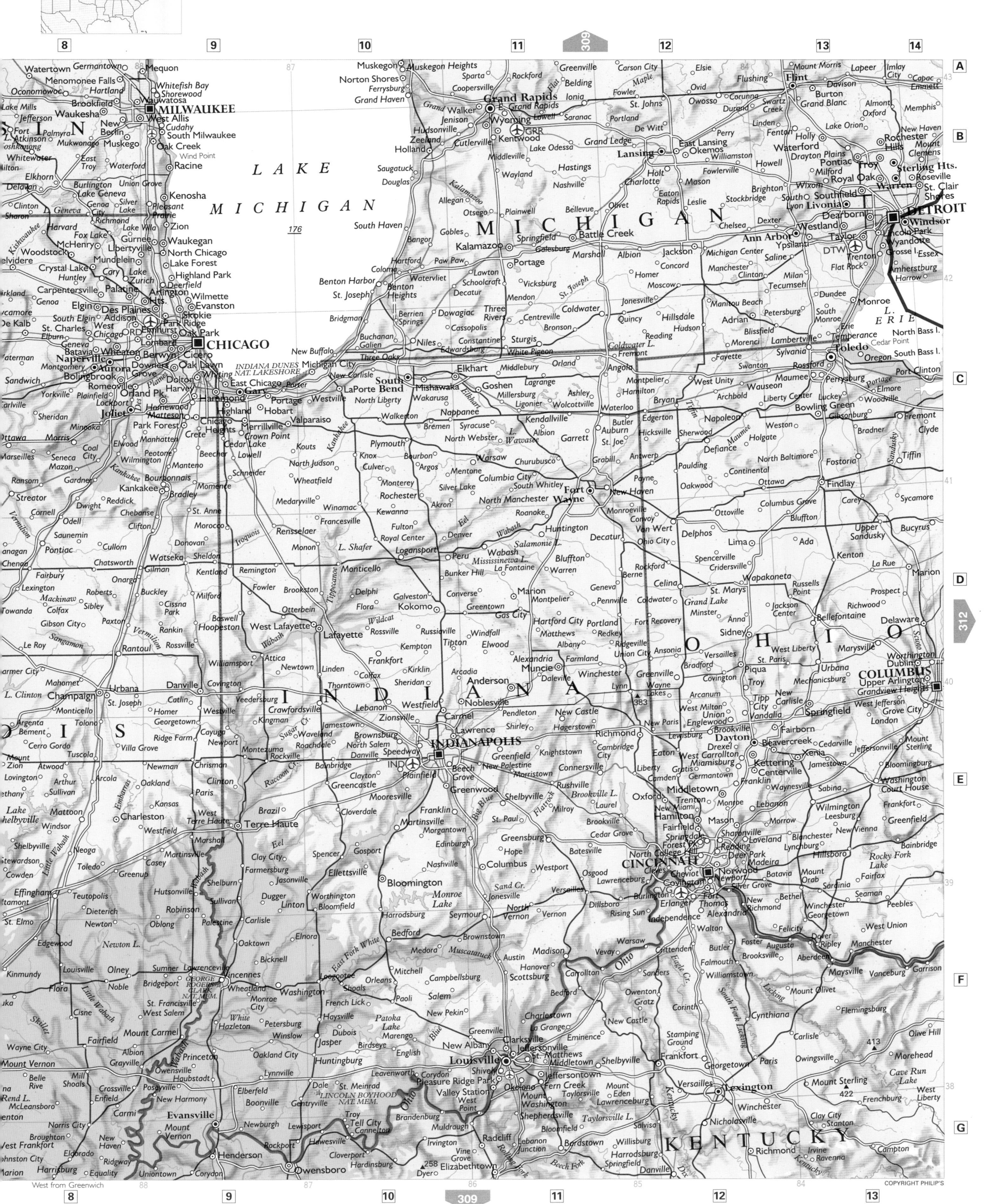

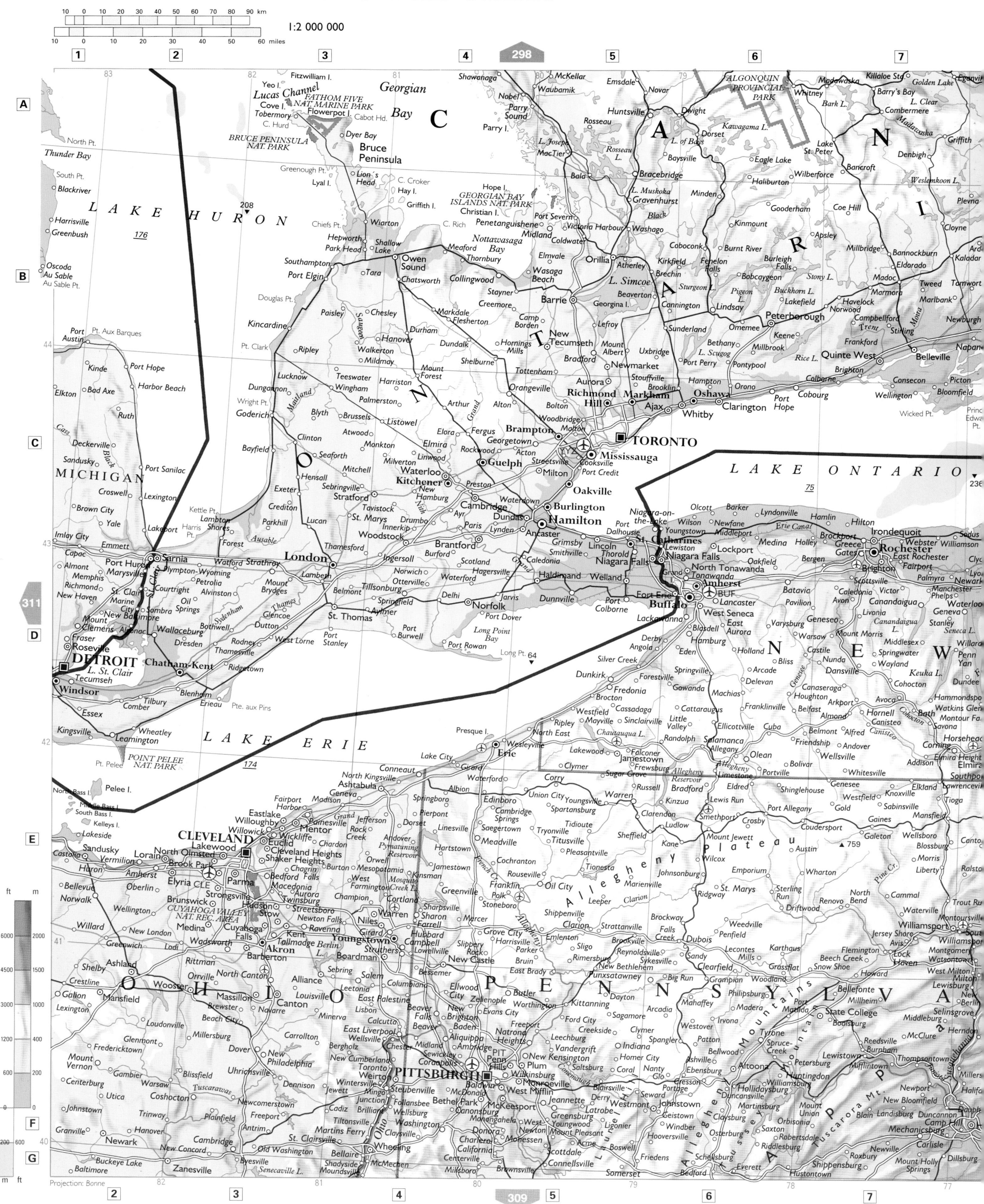

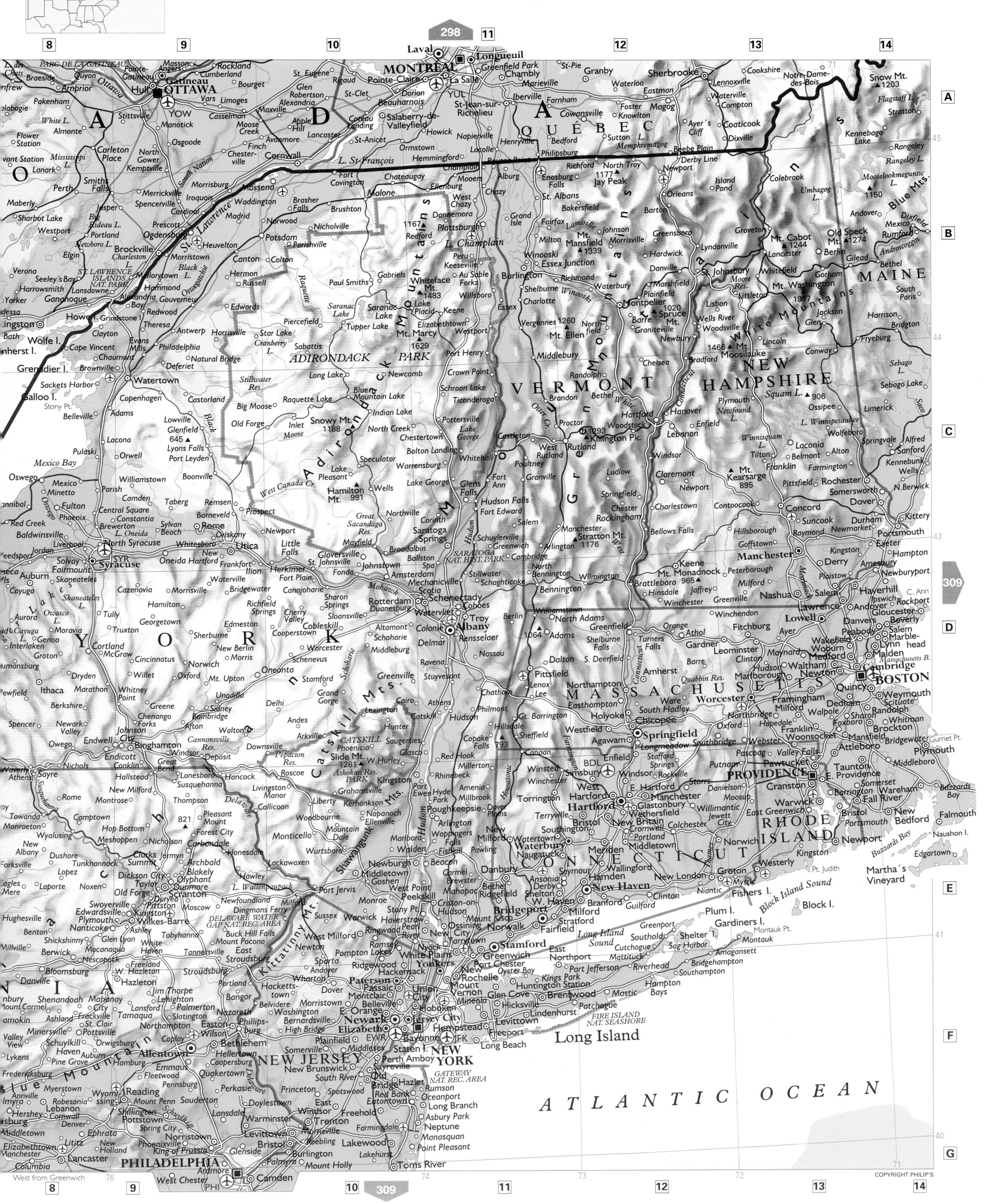

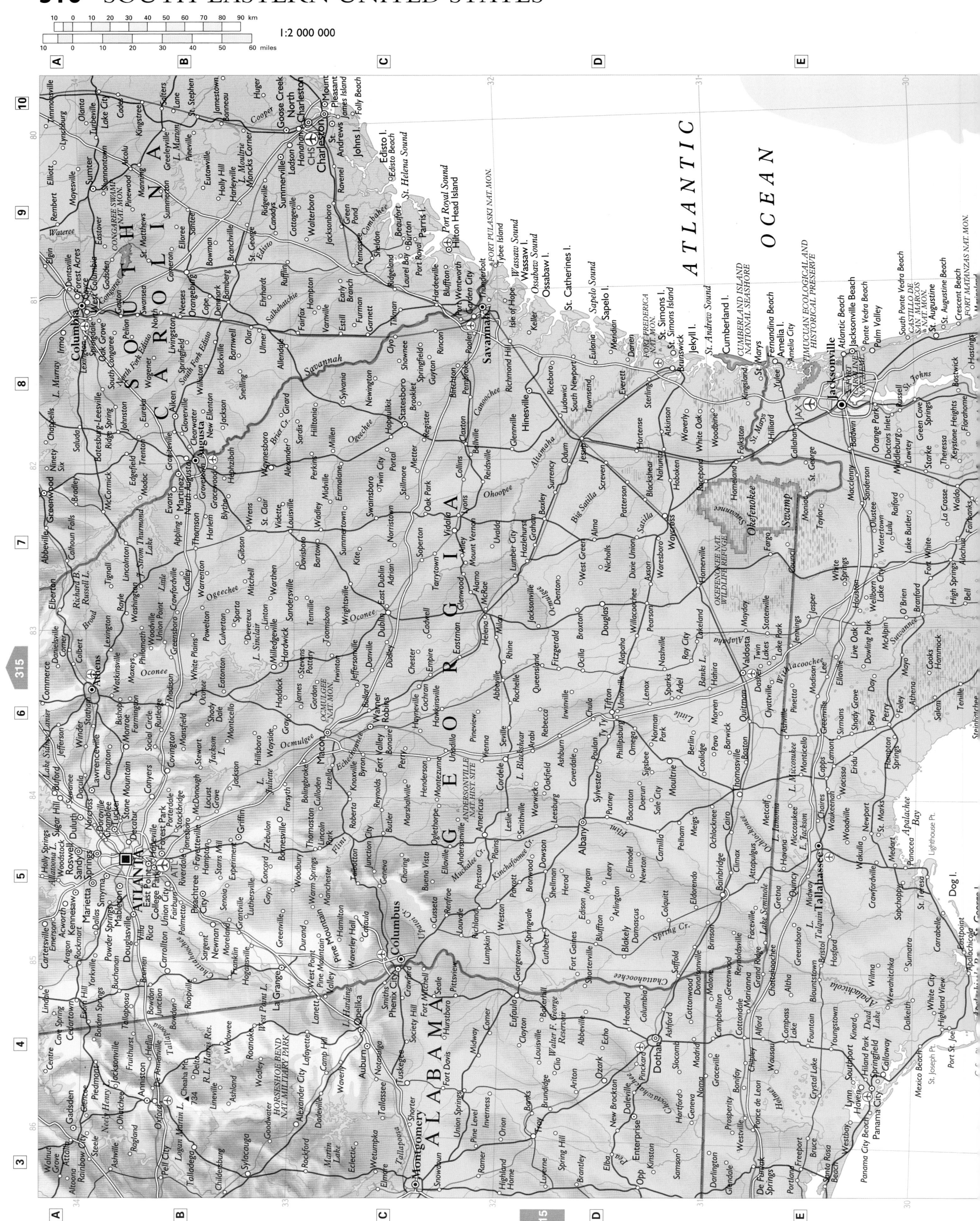

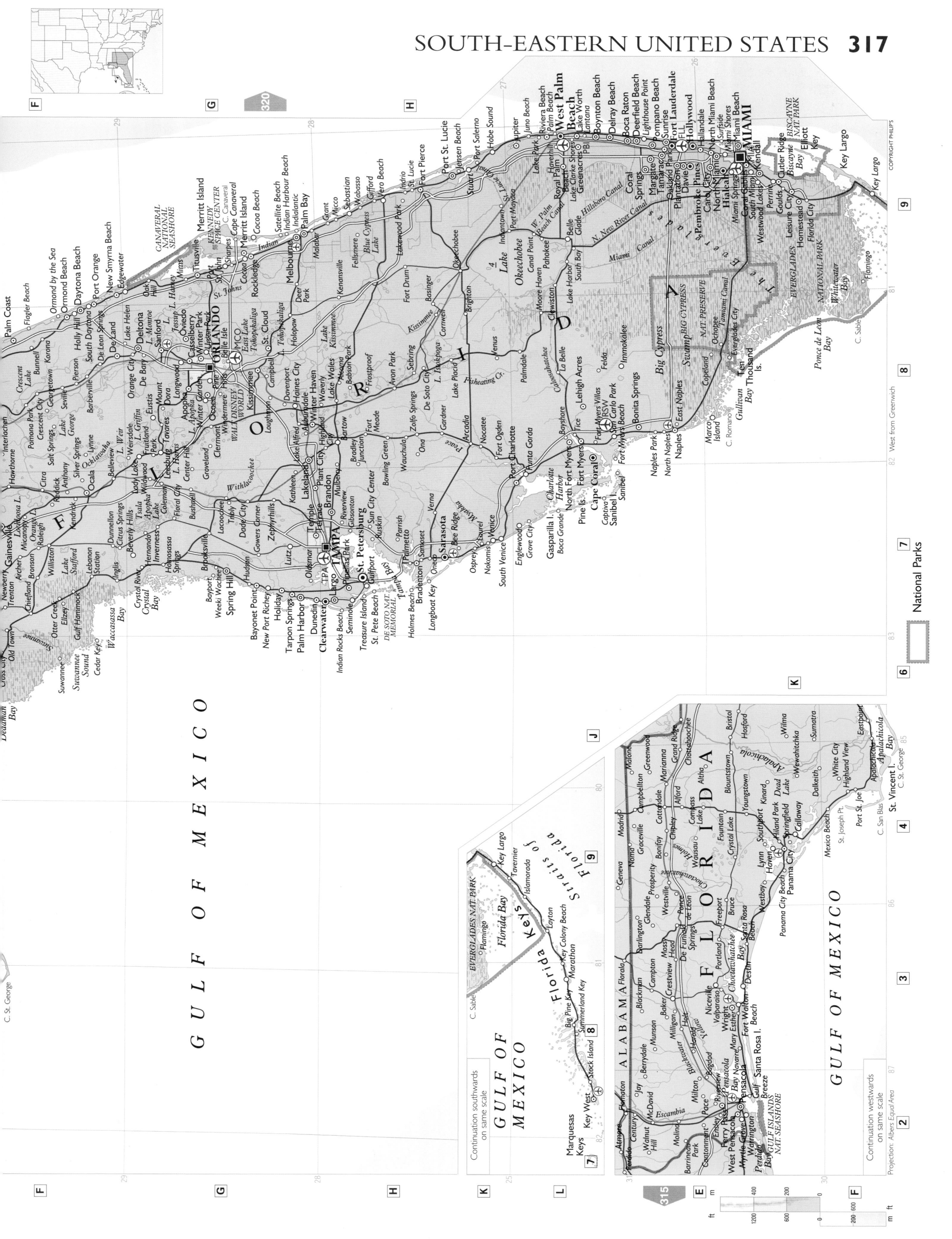

GULF OF MEXICO

GULF OF MEXICO

National Parks

Continuation southwards
on same scale

Continuation westwards
on same scale

Projection: Albers Equal Area

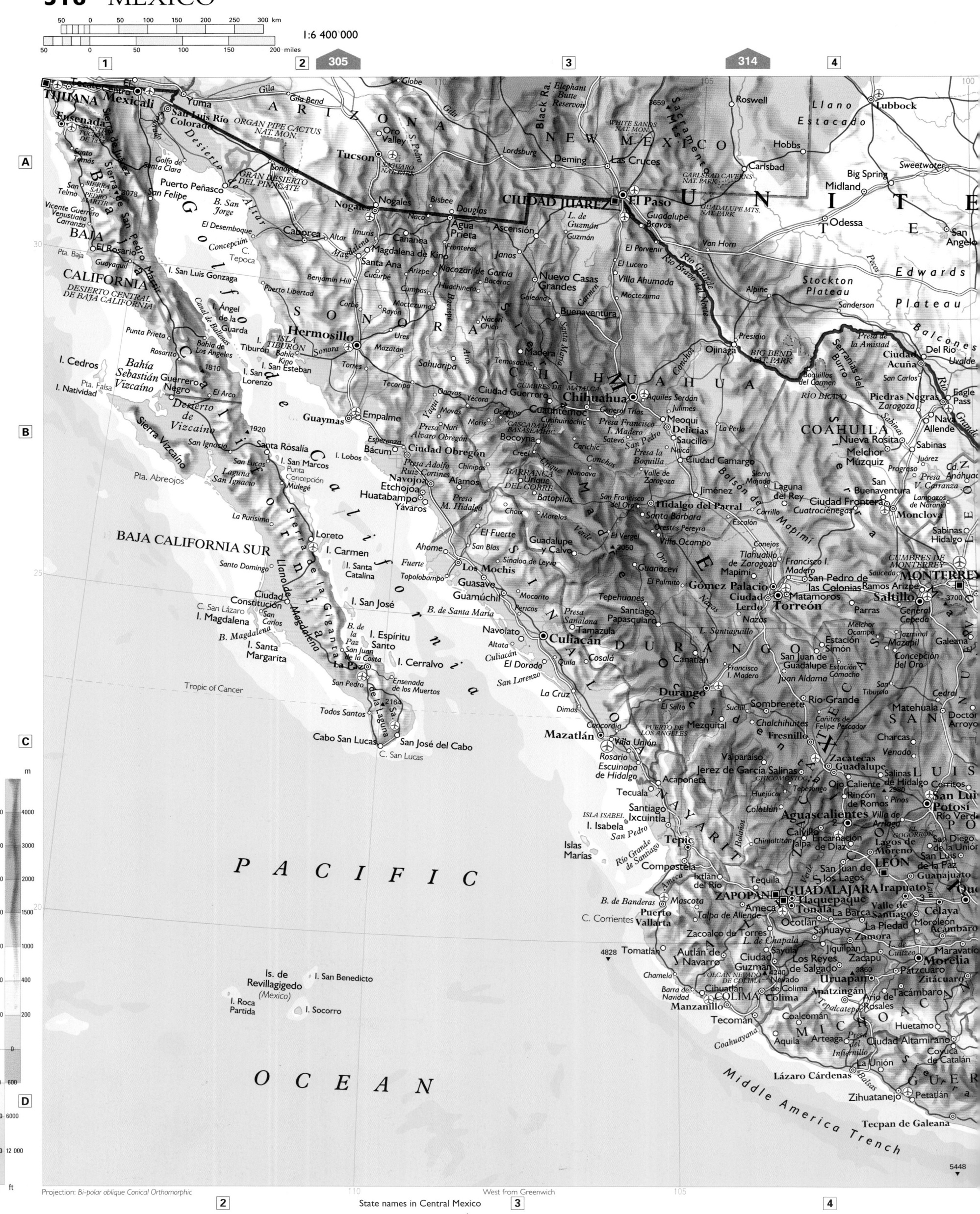

50 0 50 100 150 200 250 300 km

1:6 400 000

50 0 50 100 150 200 miles

1 | **2** | 305 | **3** | 314 | **4**

States / Regions

ARIZONA

NEW MEXICO

UNITED STATES

TIJUANA **Mexicali**
Ensenada
Yuma
San Luis Río Colorado

BAJA CALIFORNIA

SONORA

CHIHUAHUA

COAHUILA

Hermosillo

Chihuahua

CIUDAD JUAREZ El Paso

Roswell Lubbock

Hobbs

Carlsbad

Big Spring Sweetwater

Midland

Odessa San Angelo

Edwards Plateau

Del Rio

Piedras Negras

MONTERREY Saltillo

DURANGO

SINALOA

NAYARIT

Durango

Mazatlán

Culiacán

Los Mochis

Guadalajara

ZAPOPAN

León

San Luis Potosí

Aguascalientes

Zacatecas

BAJA CALIFORNIA SUR

La Paz

Cabo San Lucas San José del Cabo

Tropic of Cancer

PACIFIC

OCEAN

Is. de Revillagigedo
(Mexico)
I. San Benedicto
I. Roca Partida
I. Socorro

MICHOACAN

Morelia

Colima

Manzanillo

Lázaro Cárdenas

Middle America Trench

ft   m
12 000 4000
9000   3000
6000   2000
4500   1500
3000   1000
1200   400
600   200
0   0
200   600
2000   6000
4000   12 000
m   ft

Projection: Bi-polar oblique Conical Orthomorphic

West from Greenwich

2 | **3** | **4**

State names in Central Mexico
1 DISTRITO FEDERAL   5 MÉXICO
2 AGUASCALIENTES   6 MORELOS
3 GUANAJUATO   7 QUERÉTARO
4 HIDALGO   8 TLAXCALA

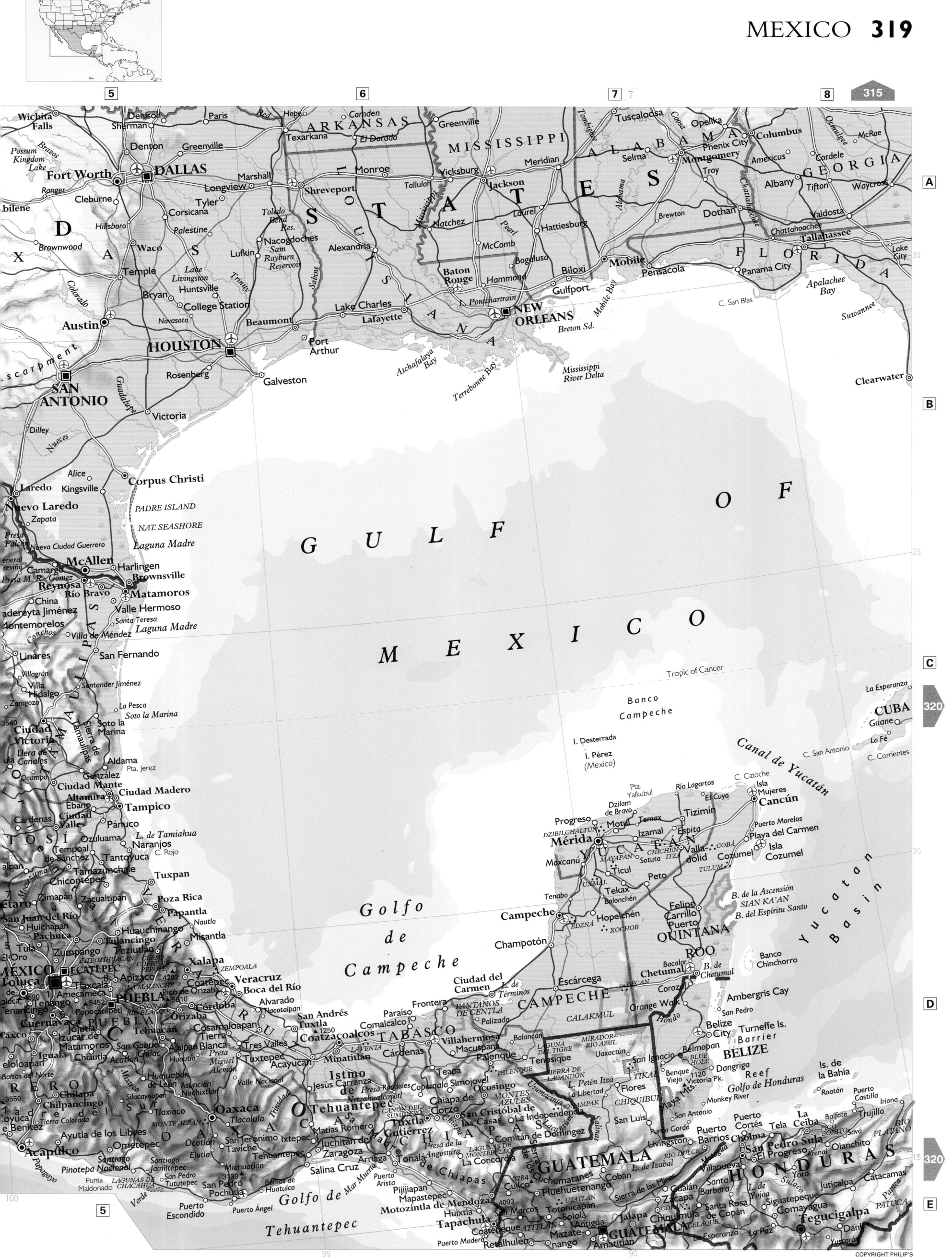

COPYRIGHT PHILIP'S

JAMAICA

1 : 1 600 000

Projection: Conical Equidistant

West from Greenwich

Projection: Bi-polar oblique Conical Orthomorphic

1 : 6 400 000

328

PUERTO RICO AND THE VIRGIN IS.
b 1:1 600 000

10   0   10   20   30   40   60   70 km
10   0   10   20   30   40   50 miles

ATLANTIC OCEAN

VIRGIN ISLANDS (U.K.)

Ruffling Pt. · Anegada · The Settlement · East Pt.
Jost Van Dyke I. · Guana I. · Great Camanoe · Virgin Gorda
Hans Lollik I. · Tortola · Road Town · Spanish Town · Beef I.
Charlotte Amalie · Cruz Bay · VIRGIN IS. NAT. PARK · Peter I.
St. Thomas I. · St. John I.
VIRGIN ISLANDS (U.S.A.)

Pta. Agujereada · Quebradillas · Camuy · Arecibo
Isabela · Moca · Barceloneta · Vega Baja · Levittown · **SAN JUAN**
Aguadilla · Pta. Higuero · PARQUE DE LAS CAVERNAS DEL RIO CAMUY · OBSERVATORIO DE ARECIBO · Manatí · Vega Alta · Cataño · SJU · Carolina · Río Grande
Aguada · San Sebastián · Florida · Ciales · Guaynabo · **Bayamón** · Trujillo Alto · Luquillo · Fajardo
Rincon · Lares · **PUERTO RICO** (U.S.A.) · Comerio · Gurabo · Sierra de Luquillo · EL YUNQUE · Ceiba · Dewey
Mayagüez · Maricao · Utuado · Adjuntas · Cordillera Central · Barranquitas · Juncos · Las Piedras · Naguabo · Culebra
Añasco · Hormigueros · 1338 Cerro de Punta · Villalba · Cayey · Cidra · Humacao
Cabo Rojo · San German · Sabana Grande · Yauco · Juana Dias · Coamo · Pta. Puerca
Parguera · Guayanilla · Guánica · **Ponce** · Salinas · Guayama · Yabucoa · Pta. Arenas
Pta. Aguila · Santa Isabel · I. Caja de Muertos · Patillas · Maunabo · Isabel Segunda · Esperanza · Vieques

CARIBBEAN SEA

▲353 Mt. Eagle · Christiansted · East Pt.
Frederiksted · St. Croix I. (U.S.A.)
Southwest Pt.

West from Greenwich

Main map

ATLANTIC OCEAN

Puerto Rico Trench · Milwaukee Deep 9200

Turks & Caicos (U.K.) · Caicos Is. · Cockburn Town · Turks Is.
Little Inagua I. · Great Inagua I. · Lake Rose · Matthew Town · INAGUA
Mouchoir Bank · Silver Bank · Navidad Bank

Guantánamo · GUANTANAMO BAY (U.S.A.) · Baracoa · Maisí
Pta. de Maisi · Î. de la Tortue · Monte Cristi · LA ISABELA · Puerto Plata · Santiago de los Caballeros · San Francisco de Macorís · Samaná
Cap-Haïtien · Port-de-Paix · Fort Liberté · La Vega · Nagua · Sánchez · Sabana de la Mar · C. Engaño
Jean Rabel · Cap-à-Foux · G. de la Gonâve · Gonaïves · Hinche · Cord. Central · Pico Duarte 3175 · HAITISES · Hato Mayor · Higuey
St-Marc · ARMANDO BERMÚDEZ · San Juan · **DOMINICAN REP.** · San Pedro de Macorís · La Romana
HAITI · L. Enriquillo · Azua · Bani · San Cristóbal · **SANTO DOMINGO** · B. de Yuma · I. Saona
Jérémie · Î. de la Gonâve · **PORT-AU-PRINCE** · Petit Goâve · Jacmel · Barahona · Compostela · Isla Mona (U.S.A.)
Dame Marie · C. Carcasse · Les Cayes · Aquin · Pedernales · SIERRA DE BAHORUCO
Avassal I. (U.S.A.) · Pointe-à-Gravois · Î. à Vache

Bayamón · SAN JUAN · Virgin Gorda · Anegada Is. (U.K.) · Sombrero (U.K.)
Aguadilla · Arecibo · Carolina · St. Thomas · Tortola · Road Town · Anguilla (U.K.)
Ponce · Fajardo · Charlotte Amalie · St.-Martin (Fr.)
Mayagüez · Caguas · Virgin Is. (U.S.A.) · St. Maarten (Neth.) · St.-Barthélemy (Fr.)
PUERTO RICO (U.S.A.) · Guayama · Christiansted · Saba (Neth.) · St. Eustatius (Neth.) · Barbuda
St. Croix (U.S.A.) · Basseterre · **ST. KITTS & NEVIS** · **ANTIGUA & BARBUDA**
Frederiksted · Nevis · Redonda · St. John's · Antigua
Montserrat (U.K.)

Hispaniola · *Antilles* · *Greater* · *Antilles*

Beata Ridge · I. Beata · C. Beata

Venezuelan Sea Basin

Leeward Islands · *Lesser Antilles*
I. de Aves (Venezuela)
Gde. Guadeloupe Passage · Ste.-Rose · Le Moule · La Désirade
GUADELOUPE (Fr.) · 1467 · Pointe-à-Pitre · Marie-Galante (Fr.)
Basse-Terre · I. des Saintes (Fr.) · Grand-Bourg
Dominica Passage · Portsmouth · 1447 · **DOMINICA**
Roseau · MORNE TROIS PITONS
Martinique Passage · Mt. Pelée 1397 · Ste.-Marie · Le François
Fort-de-France · Rivière-Pilote · **MARTINIQUE**
St. Lucia Channel · Castries · 950 · **ST. LUCIA**
Soufrière · St. Vincent Passage
Soufrière 1234 · **St. Vincent** · Speightstown · Bridgetown · **BARBADOS**
Kingstown · Grenadines · **ST. VINCENT & THE GRENADINES**
Hillsborough

Windward Islands · *Aves Ridge*

Colombian Basin · *CARIBBEAN Sea* · *Bean Basin*

ABC Islands · *Lesser Antilles*
Aruba (Neth.) · Curaçao · Bonaire
Oranjestad · NETH. · ANTILLES · Willemstad

St. George's · **GRENADA**
I. Blanquilla (Ven.) · I. Los Hermanos (Ven.)
I. Orchila (Ven.) · I. Los Testigos (Ven.) · Tobago
NUEVA ESPARTA · Scarborough
ARC. LOS ROQUES (Ven.) · I. Los Roques (Ven.) · I. La Tortuga (Ven.) · I. de Margarita · La Asunción · Port of Spain · Galera Point
Pta. Gallinas · MACUIRA · Porlamar · Pen. de Paria · **TRINIDAD**
Ríohacha · Uribia · Pta. Espada · Pen. de Paraguaná · Punto Fijo · Cumaná · Carúpano · Güiria · Arima · Río Claro
COLOMBIA · Pen. de la Guajira · Punta Cardón · MÉDANOS DE CORO · Puerto Cumarebo · Río Caribe · San Fernando · **TRINIDAD & TOBAGO**
Santa Marta · TAYRONA · Golfo de Venezuela · La Vela de Coro · Barcelona · Guanta · Maturín · Serpent's Mouth
Barranquilla · NEVADA DE STA. MARTA · San Rafael · **FALCÓN** · Tucacas · Puerto La Cruz · Caripito · **SUCRE** · **DELTA AMACURO**
Soledad · Sabanalarga · Sierra Nevada de Santa Marta 5800 · Altagracia · Mene de Mauroa · **LARA** · **CARABOBO** · Los Teques · Río Chico · **MIRANDA** · Anaco · **MONAGAS** · Tucupita
ATLÁNTICO · Ciénaga · La Concepción · Villa del Rosario · Cabimas · Coro · Barquisimeto · Valencia · San Juan de los Morros · El Tigre · Los Barrancos
MAGDALENA · Fundación · MARACAIBO · Ciudad Ojeda · Carora · San Felipe · **VALENCIA** · Aragua de Barcelona · **ANZOÁTEGUI** · Sierra Imataca
Calamar · Agustín Codazzi · Machiques · Lago de Maracaibo · El Tocuyo · Villa de Cura · Calabozo · Valle de la Pascua · Ciudad Guayana · Soledad
Plato · Zambrano · **CÉSAR** · **ZULIA** · Trujillo · **PORTUGUESA** · **COJEDES** · Santa María de Ipire · El Pao · Upata
Mompós · El Banco · PERIJÁ · Valera · El Baúl · **GUÁRICO** · Ciudad Bolívar · Tumeremo
Magangué · Valledupar · CIÉNAGAS DEL CATATUMBO · Betijoque · **TRUJILLO** · Acarigua · El Sombrero · Guasipati
San Carlos · **NORTE DE SANTANDER** · CATATUMBO-BARI · MÉRIDA · **BARINAS** · Guanare · San Carlos · Los Pijiguaos · El Callao
Ocaña · Cúcuta · San Cristóbal · **TÁCHIRA** · **MÉRIDA** · Barinas · Libertad · Calabozo · Caicara · Embalse de Guri
BOLÍVAR · Simití · **SANTANDER** · Santa Bárbara · Puerto de Nutrias · San Fernando de Apure · Mapire · Orinoco · Guasipati
VENEZUELA · Achaguas · **APURE** · Calcara

West from Greenwich

Elevation scale
4000 3000 2000 1500 1000 400 200 600 6000 12 000 18 000 24 000 ft
12 000 9000 6000 4500 3000 1500 600 200 2000 4000 6000 8000 m

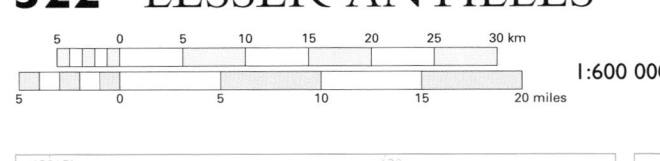

5 0 5 10 15 20 25 30 km
1:600 000
5 0 5 10 15
20 miles

a
Prickly Pear
Cays
Seal I.
Grafton's Pt.
Snake Pt.
Scrub I.
Island Harbour
59
Anguilla
Crocus Bay
The
Quarter
(U.K.)
Sandy I.
The Valley
Sandy Hill Bay
Sandy Ground Village
South Hill Village
West End Village
Blowing Point Village
Anguillita
I.
Blowing Rock
Île
Tintamarre
Grand Case
Cul de Sac
Pte. du
Canonnier
Marigot
Quartier
Saint Martin
Sandy Ground
D'Orléans
(France)
Simpson Bay
Colombier
Mulletbaai
Cul de Sac
Simsonbaai
Sentry Hill
St. Maarten
Philipsburg
(Netherlands)
Pte. Blanche

Anegada Passage

Saint Barthélemy Channel
Île Fourchue

b
ATLANTIC
OCEAN
Dickinson Bay
Boon Pt.
Beggars Pt.
Long I.
Runaway Bay
St. Johnston
Village
Crabs
Pen.
Guiana I.
Antigua
ANU
Indian
Town Pt.
St.
John's
Potters
Village
Willikies
DEVIL'S
BRIDGE
Five I. Harbour
Nonsuch Bay
York I.
Boggy Peak
English
Harbour
Town
Green I.
Freetown
Soldier Pt.
402
Johnsons
Pt.
368
Willoughby
Bay
Old Road
Bluff
NELSON'S
DOCKYARD
Nanton Pt.
West from Greenwich

ANTIGUA AND BARBUDA

c
Goat Pt.
Billy Pt.
Goat
I.
Kid I.
Hog Pt.
Cedar
Tree Pt.
39
The Highlands
Low
Bay
Codrington
Dulcina
Palmetto Pt.
Barbuda
Cocoa Point
Spanish
Pt.
West from Greenwich

d
ST. KITTS AND NEVIS
Helden's
Pt.
Dieppe Bay Town
Sadlers
Tabernacle
Sandy Point
Town
Mt. Liamuiga
1156
Cayon
ATLANTIC
OCEAN
BRIMSTONE
HILL FORT
847
Old Road Town
Middle
Island
St. Kitts
Palmetto Pt.
Basseterre
Frigate Bay
Sand Bank Bay
Friar's Bay
CARIBBEAN
SEA
Gt. Salt Pond
319
The Narrows
Nags Head
Round Hill
305
Cotton Ground
Newcas
Nevis
Peak
98
Nevis
873
Charlestown
Fig Tree
381
Sher
Bath
Saddle Hill
West from Greenwich

St. Kitts & Nevis
Antigua

e
Guadeloupe Passage
Pte. de la Grande Vigie
Anse-
Bertrand
Haut de la
Montagne
Campêche
Pte. du Piton
Pte. d'Antigues
Port-Louis
Beauport
Gros Cap
Les Mangles
Petit-Canal
Ste-Marguerite
Pte. Macou
Îlet à
Kahouanne
Pointe
Allègre
Îlet à Fajou
Bazin
Morne-
à-l'Eau
L'Autre Bord
La
Désirade
Grande
Anse
Duzer
611
Ste-Rose
Château
Gaillard
Le Moule
Le Souffleur
MAISON
COLONIALE
MUSÉE
DU RHUM
Vieux
Bourg
Deshaies
Sofaia
Grand Cul-de-Sac Marin
Grande-
Terre
Zévallos
Ste-Marthe
715
Pointe-
Noire
Goyaves
Castel
Les Abymes
PTP
Les Grands Fonds
Douville
Plaine de la
Simonière
Pte. des
Colibris
Beauséjour
Baille-
Argent
744 Ravine
Chaude
Mahaut
Baie
Mahault
Pointe-
à-Pitre
Ste-Anne
Kahouanne
Pointe des
Châteaux
St-François
Morne
Jeanneton
631
Petit
Bourg
Bas du Fort
Petit Cul-de-Sac Marin
Le Gosier
Îles de la
Petite Terre
Mahaut
Montebello
Terre de Bas
Pigeon
Pitons (ou Sauts)
de Bouillante
Morne Moustique
ou Joffre
1088
Goyave
Pte. de la
Rivière à Goyave
Bouillante
1354
PARC
Ste-Marie
Marigot
1263
Montagne
Guadeloupe
Vieux-
Habitants
NATIONAL
DE LA Capesterre
1467 CHUTES DU
Pte. de la Capesterre
(France)
Matouba
DE LA
GUADELOUPE
CARBET
Capesterre-
Belle-Eau
Baillif
St-Claude
Soufrière
Bananier
Basse-Terre
Courbeyre
Grande Pte.
Grosse Pointe
Vieux Fort
Pte. du
Monts
Caraïbes
Vieux-Fort
Trois-Rivières
St-Louis
Marie-
Galante
LE TROU
À DIABLE
204
Pte.
Pisiou
Pte. du Vieux
Fort
Pte. de
Folle Anse
Canal des Saintes
Canal de
Marie-Galante
Grand
Bourg
CHÂTEAU
MURAT
Capesterre-
de-Marie-Galante
Pte. des Basses
Îles des Saintes
Terre-de-Bas
309
FORT NAPOLÉON
Terre-de-Haute
Petites-Anses
Le Chameau
Grand Îlet
West from Greenwich
Dominica Passage

Basse-Terre

Guadeloupe

Guadeloupe
Martinique

GUADELOUPE
MARTINIQUE

Northern
Leewards

CARIBBEAN
SEA

Mt. Scenery
871
Saba
(Netherlands)
The
Bottom
Hells Gate
Fort Bay
Windward Side

Zeelandia
St. Eustatius (Statia)
(Netherlands)
Oranjestad
304
The Quill

NORTHERN
LEEWARDS
West from Greenwich

f
Kudarebe
CARIBBEAN
SEA
Malmok
Palm Beach
Noord
Bushiribana
Eagle Beach
BUBALI BIRDS
SANCTUARY
Noordkaap
Oranjestad
Paradera
AUA
165
ARIKOK
Santa Cruz
188
Jamanota
Spaans Lagoen
Pos Chiquito
Savaneta
Aruba
(Netherlands)
Sint Nicolaas
Seroe Colorado
Punta Basora

ARUBA

g
Noordpunt
Westpunt
BOKA TABLA
CHRISTOFFEL
Savonet
Lagún
375
St. Christoffelberg
B. Santa Cruz
Bartolbaai
Santa Cruz
St. Nicolaas
Soto
Barber
St. Marthabaai
San
Juan
Siberië
Pt. Halve Dag
St. Willibrordus
Hato
CUR
K. St. Marie
HATO
CAVES
Stenen Koraal
Julandorp
Brievengat
St. Michiel
Gasparito
Buena Vista
Emmastad
Santa Rosa
St. Jorisbaai
Otrobanda
Punda
Santa
Barbara
Willemstad
Bottelier
Schottegat
Bullenbaai
St. Annabaai
SEAQUARIUM
Tafelberg
193
Spaanse Water
Lagún
Blanku
Nieuwpoort
Oostpunt
West from Greenwich

CARIBBEAN
SEA

Curaçao (Netherlands)

Projection: Conical with two standard parallels

h
Noordpunt
CARIBBEAN
SEA
Boca
Slagbaai
740
Washington
Brandaris
WASHINGTON
SLAGBAAI
Onima
Bonaire
(Netherlands)
Goto
Meer
Rincon
Wekeowa Pt.
115
Noord Saliña
Hato
Punto Blanco
Klein
Bonaire
Antriol
Nikiboko
Tera Kora
Kralendijk
Wanapa
Bachelor's Beach
Vierkant Pt.
Fuoop
Key Bay
Pink
Beach
Witte
Pan
(Salt Flats)
Lacre Punt
West from Greenwich

NETHERLANDS
ANTILLES

Aruba
Curaçao
Bonaire

j
Martinique Passage
Grand'
Rivière
Macouba
Cap St-Martin
GORGES DE
LA FALAISE
Basse-Pointe
Le Lorrain
Le Marigot
Le Prêcheur
1397
Montagne
Pelée
Ajoupa-
Bouillon
Ste-Marie
CHÂTEAU
DUBUC
Pte. du Diable
Presqu'île de
la Caravelle
Pte. Caracoli
St-Pierre
Le Morne
Rouge
884
Morne des Esses
Tartane
Rade de St-Pierre
Fonds-St-Denis
La Trinité
Le Carbet
1109
Le Morne-
Vert
Gros-Morne
ARBORÉTUM
Le Robert
Îlet Chancel
ou Ramville
Bellefontaine
Pitons
du Carbet
Case-Pilote
Fond Rousseau
St-Joseph
334
B. du François
Schoelcher
Le Lamentin
Le François
Îlet Long
Fort-de-
France
FDF
Ducos
Montagne
du Vauclin
504
Pte. de Vauclin
L'Anse Mitan
Baie de Fort-de-France
Pte. du Bout
B. de
Génipa
Les Trois-Îlets
Le St-Esprit
Le Vauclin
L'Anse à l'Âne
LA PAGERIE
Rivière-Salée
Cap Salomon
460
Grande Anse
359
Rivière-Pilote
Le Marin
Les Anses-d'Arlet
Le Diamant
Barrière-la-Croix
Cap Ferré
Petite Anse
Trois Rivières
Ste-Luce
Rocher du
Diamant
Pte. du Diamant
Pte. Borgnesse
Ste-Anne
Îlet Chevalier
Étang des
Salines
Pte. Baham
Cul-de-Sac du Marin
Pte. d'Enfer
Des
Salines
Îlet Cabrits
St. Lucia Channel

Martinique
(France)

CARIBBEAN
SEA

ATLANTIC
OCEAN

West from Greenwich

ft m
3000 1000
1200 400
600
0
200 600
500 1500
1000 300
2000 6000
m ft

■ Place of interest

▨ Mangrove

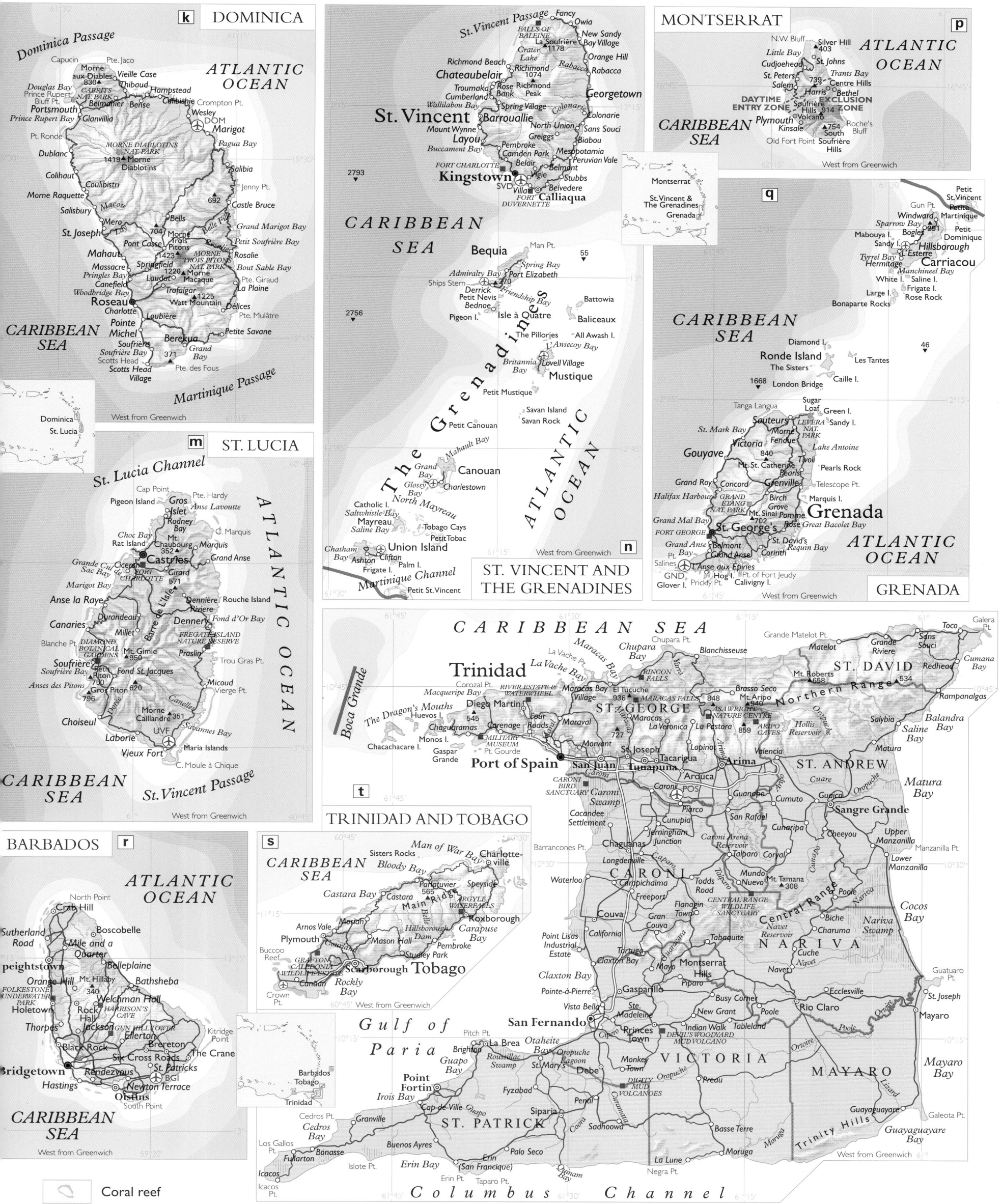

Coral reef

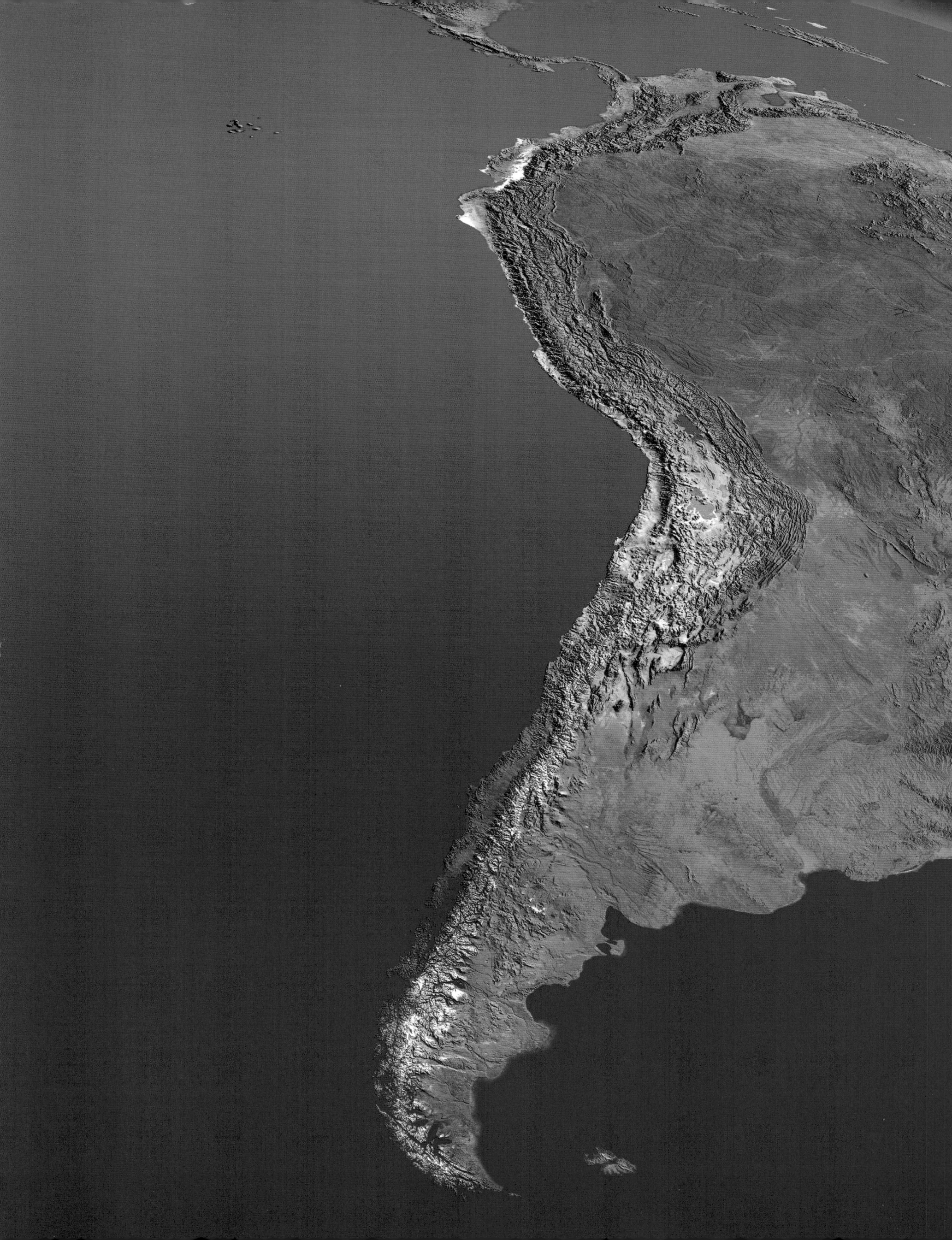

SOUTH AMERICA

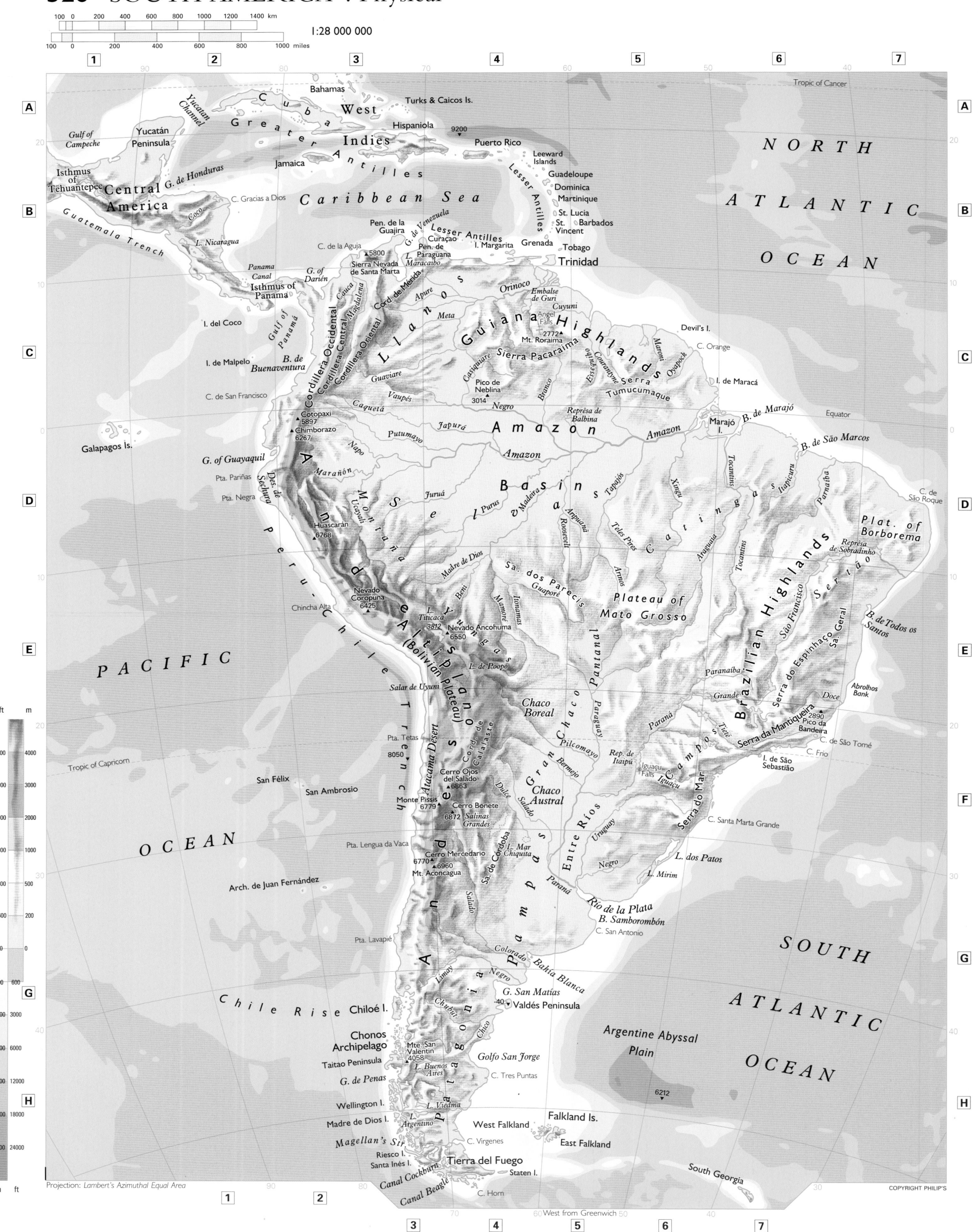

100 0   200   400   600   800 1000 1200 1400 km
100 0   200   400   600   800   1000 miles

1:28 000 000

Projection: Lambert's Azimuthal Equal Area

COPYRIGHT PHILIP'S

ft   m
12000   4000
9000   3000
6000   2000
3000   1000
1500   500
600   200
0   0
200   600
1000   3000
2000   6000
4000   12000
6000   18000
8000   24000
m   ft

Tropic of Cancer

NORTH ATLANTIC OCEAN

Bahamas
Cuba
West Indies
Greater Antilles
Turks & Caicos Is.
Hispaniola
Puerto Rico
Jamaica
9200
Leeward Islands
Guadeloupe
Dominica
Martinique
St. Lucia
St. Vincent
Barbados
Grenada
Tobago
Trinidad
Lesser Antilles

Yucatán Channel
Gulf of Campeche
Yucatán Peninsula
Isthmus of Tehuantepec
Central America
G. de Honduras
C. Gracias a Dios
Coco
L. Nicaragua
Guatemala Trench
Panama Canal
Isthmus of Panama
Gulf of Panamá
I. del Coco
I. de Malpelo
B. de Buenaventura

Caribbean Sea

Pen. de la Guajira
G. de Venezuela
Curaçao
Pen. de Paraguaná
I. Margarita
C. de la Aguja
5800
Sierra Nevada de Santa Marta
L. Maracaibo
Cord. de Mérida
Cordillera Occidental
Cordillera Central
Cordillera Oriental
G. of Darién
Cauca
Magdalena
Apure
Meta
Llanos
Orinoco
Embalse de Guri
Cuyuni
Angel Falls
Mt. Roraima 2772
Guiana Highlands
Sierra Pacaraima
Casiquiare
Branco
Negro
Pico de Neblina 3014
Devil's I.
C. Orange
I. de Maracá
Maroni
Oyapock
Essequibo
Courantyne
Serra Tumucumaque

Guaviare
Vaupés
Caquetá
Putumayo
Japurá
Napo
Marañón
Ucayali
Juruá
Purus
Amazon
Represa de Balbina
Amazon
Marajó
B. de Marajó
Equator
B. de São Marcos

Cotopaxi 5897
Chimborazo 6267
G. of Guayaquil
Pta. Pariñas
Pta. Negra
Des. de Sechura
Montaña
Madeira
Madre de Dios
Beni
Mamoré
Roosevelt
Tapajós
Xingu
Tocantins
Araguaia
Tocantins
Parnaíba
Itapicuru
C. de São Roque

Galapagos Is.
C. de San Francisco

Amazon Basins
Sa. dos Parecis
Guaporé
Iquitos
Teles Pires
Arinos
Caatinga
Represa de Sobradinho
Plat. of Borborema

PACIFIC

Huascarán 6768
Nevado Coropuna 6425
Chincha Alta
L. Titicaca 3812
Nevado Ancohuma 6550
L. de Poopó
Salar de Uyuni
Yungas
Altiplano (Bolivian Plateau)
Plateau of Mato Grosso
Paraná
Brazilian Highlands
São Francisco
Serra do Espinhaço
Sertão
Serra Geral
Abrolhos Bank
B. de Todos os Santos

Peru-Chile Trench
Andes
Chaco Boreal
Gran Chaco
Paraguay
Pilcomayo
Bermejo
Chaco Austral
Cord. de Calalaste
Cord. de Atacama
Grande
Serra da Mantiqueira
Pico da Bandeira 2890
C. de São Tomé
C. Frio
I. de São Sebastião

Tropic of Capricorn
San Félix
San Ambrosio
Pta. Tetas 8050
Atacama Desert
Cerro Ojos del Salado 6863
Monte Pissis 6779
Cerro Bonete 6872
Salinas Grandes
Dulce
Salado
Rep. de Itaipú
Iguaçu Falls
Iguaçu
Campos
Serra do Mar
C. Santa Marta Grande

OCEAN

Arch. de Juan Fernández
Pta. Lengua da Vaca
Cerro Mercedario 6770
Mt. Aconcagua 6960
Sa. de Córdoba
L. Mar Chiquita
Córdoba
Salado
Paraná
Entre Ríos
Uruguay
Negro
L. Mirim
L. dos Patos
Pampas
Rio de la Plata
B. Samborombón
C. San Antonio

SOUTH ATLANTIC OCEAN

Colorado
Bahía Blanca
Limay
Negro
G. San Matías
Valdés Peninsula 40
Argentine Abyssal Plain

Chile Rise
Chiloé I.
Chonos Archipelago
Taitao Peninsula
Mte. San Valentín 4058
L. Buenos Aires
Chubut
Chico
Golfo San Jorge
C. Tres Puntas
Patagonia
6212

G. de Penas
Wellington I.
Madre de Dios I.
L. Viedma
L. Argentino
West Falkland
East Falkland
Falkland Is.

Magellan's Str.
Riesco I.
Santa Inés I.
Tierra del Fuego
Canal Cockburn
Canal Beagle
C. Virgenes
C. Horn
Staten I.
South Georgia

West from Greenwich

1:28 000 000

| 100 | 0 | 200 | 400 | 600 | 800 | 1000 | 1200 | 1400 km |
| 100 | 0 | 200 | 400 | 600 | 800 | 1000 miles |

1 **2** **3** **4** **5** **6** **7**

Tropic of Cancer

A

Havana
BAHAMAS
Turks & Caicos Is.
(U.K.)

N O R T H

CUBA

20

Cayman Is.
(U.K.)

HAITI   DOMINICAN
REP.
San Juan
Virgin Is. (U.S.A.-U.K.)
Anguilla (U.K.)
St. Martin (Fr.-Neth.)
ANTIGUA &
BARBUDA

A T L A N T I C

B

MEXICO
BELIZE
Kingston
JAMAICA
Port-au-
Prince
Santo
Domingo
PUERTO
RICO
(U.S.A.)
ST. KITTS
& NEVIS
Basse-Terre
GUADELOUPE
(Fr.)
DOMINICA
MARTINIQUE
(Fr.)
Fort-de-France
Castries ST. LUCIA

O C E A N

GUATEMALA
HONDURAS
Guatemala
Tegucigalpa
San Salvador
EL SALVADOR
NICARAGUA
Managua
C a r i b b e a n   S e a
ST. VINCENT
Kingstown
GRENADA
St. George's
BARBADOS
Bridgetown

COSTA
RICA
San José
Panamá
Barranquilla
C. de
la Aguja
Aruba
(Neth.)
NETH.
ANTILLES
Oranjestad
Willemstad
Port of
Spain
TRINIDAD &
TOBAGO

C

I. del Coco
(Costa Rica)
PANAMA
G. of
Darién
Cartagena
Maracaibo
Caracas
Valencia

Gulf of Panama
Medellín
Cúcuta
San Cristóbal
Barquisimeto
Orinoco
Ciudad Guayana

I. de Malpelo
(Colombia)
Bucaramanga
VENEZUELA
Georgetown
Paramaribo

Cali
BOGOTÁ
GUYANA
Cayenne
C. Orange

SURINAME
FRENCH
GUIANA

C

COLOMBIA
RORAIMA

Branco
AMAPÁ

Galapagos Is.
(Ecuador)
Quito
Equator

ECUADOR
Putumayo
Japurá
Amazon
Marajó
I.
Belém

Guayaquil
Napo
Manaus
Santarém
São Luís

G. of Guayaquil
Iquitos
AMAZONAS
Amazon
PARÁ
Fortaleza
C. de
São Roque

D

Marañón
Chiclayo
Juruá
Purus
Madeira
Tapajós
Xingu
Tocantins
MARANHÃO
Teresina
CEARÁ
RIO G.
DO NORTE
Natal

Trujillo
Ucayali
ACRE
Pôrto Velho
PIAUÍ
PARAÍBA
Campina Grande
Chimbote
RONDÔNIA
Parnaíba
PERNAMBUCO
Recife

E

PERU
Callao LIMA
Cuzco
Madre de Dios
Mamoré
B R A Z I L
TOCANTINS
São Francisco
BAHIA
ALAGOAS
SERGIPE
Maceió
Aracaju
Salvador

L.
Titicaca
MATO GROSSO
GOIÁS
DIS. FED.
Brasília

Arequipa
BOLIVIA
La Paz
Cochabamba
Santa Cruz
Cuiabá
Goiânia
MINAS GERAIS
Iquique
Sucre
Paraguay
MATO GROSSO
DO SUL
Belo
Horizonte
ESPÍRITO
SANTO
Vitória

F

Antofagasta
PARAGUAY
Paraná
Ribeirão
Prêto
Juiz
de Fora
Campos
San Félix
(Chile)
San Ambrosio
(Chile)
Salta
Pilcomayo
Asunción
SÃO PAULO
Campinas
SÃO
PAULO
Niterói
RIO DE
JANEIRO
Santos
San Miguel
de Tucumán
Resistencia
Corrientes
PARANÁ
Curitiba
SANTA CATARINA

P A C I F I C
O C E A N
Arch. de Juan Fernández
(Chile)

Córdoba
San Juan
Santa Fe
Paraná
Salado
URUGUAY
RIO GRANDE
DO SUL
Pôrto Alegre
Viña del Mar
Valparaíso
SANTIAGO
Mendoza
Rosario
Pelotas

G

Talca
Concepción
BUENOS AIRES
La Plata
Montevideo
Rio de la Plata

ARGENTINA
Bahía
Blanca
Mar del Plata

S O U T H

Valdivia
Colorado
A T L A N T I C

Puerto Montt
Negro
Viedma
Chubut

H

Gulf of Penas
Comodoro Rivadavia
Gulf of San Jorge
O C E A N

Magellan's Str.
West Falkland
FALKLAND IS.
(U.K.)
Stanley
East Falkland

Punta Arenas
Tierra del Fuego
South Georgia
(U.K.)

C. Horn
West from Greenwich

Tropic of Capricorn

1 **2** **3** **4** **5** **6** **7**

■ LIMA Capital Cities

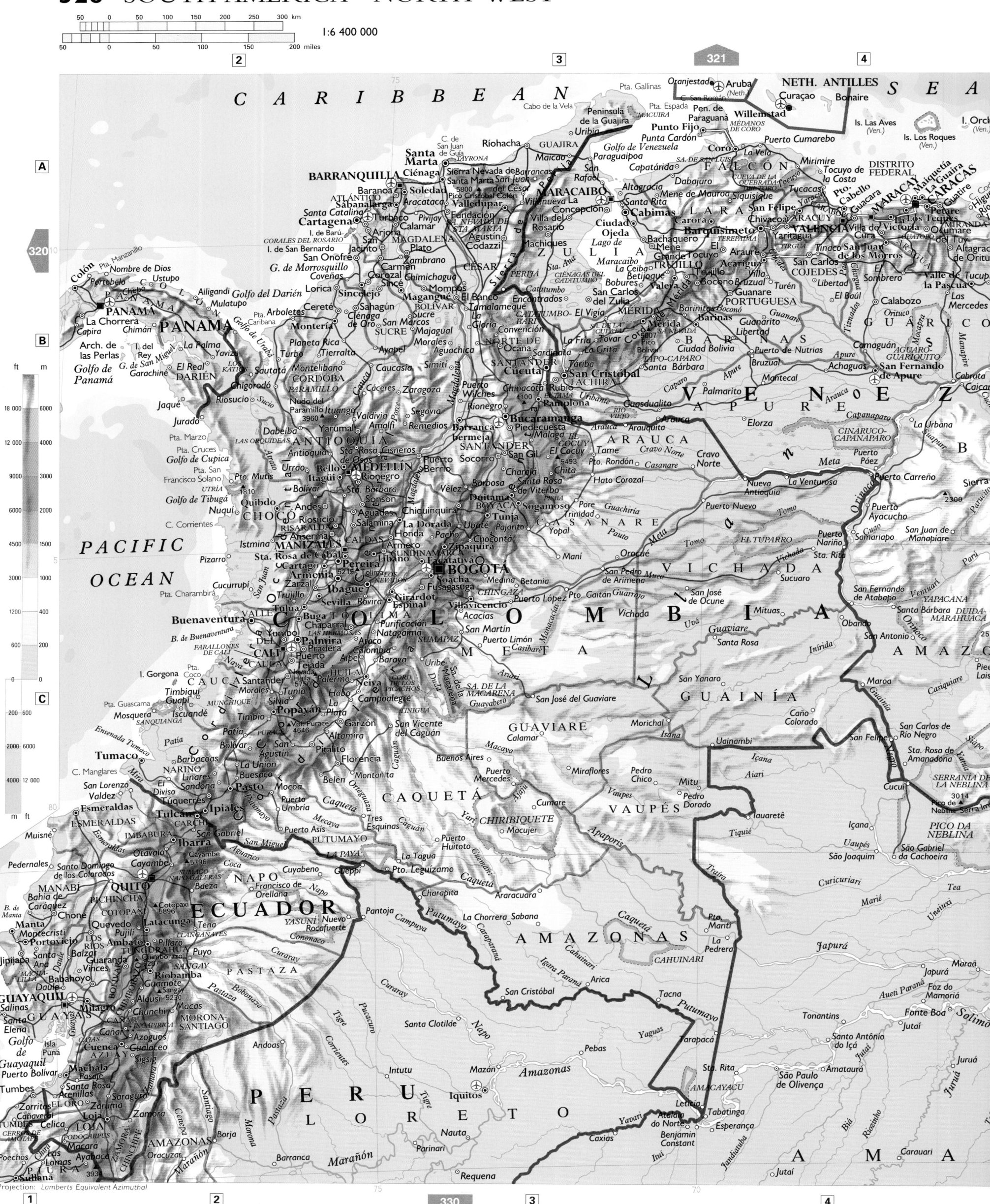

Projection: Lamberts Equivalent Azimuthal

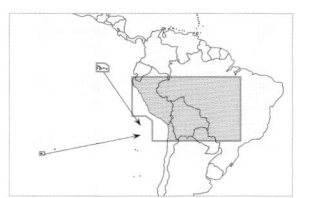

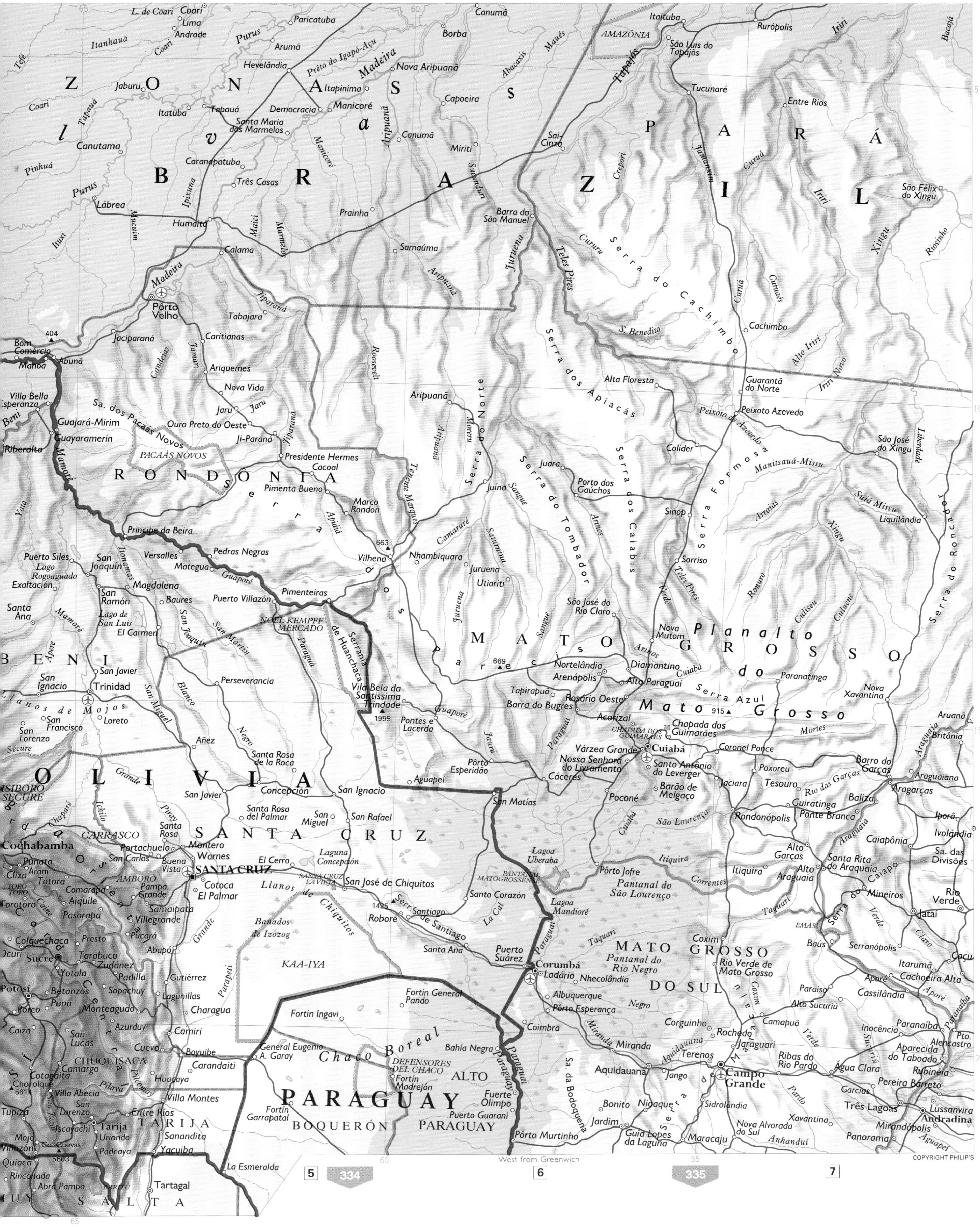

West from Greenwich

COPYRIGHT PHILIP'S

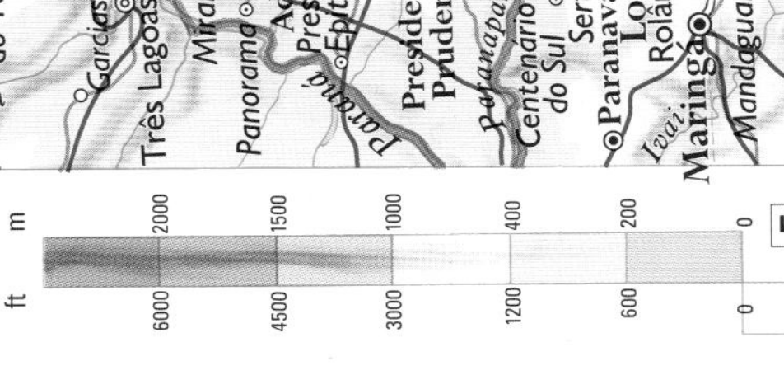

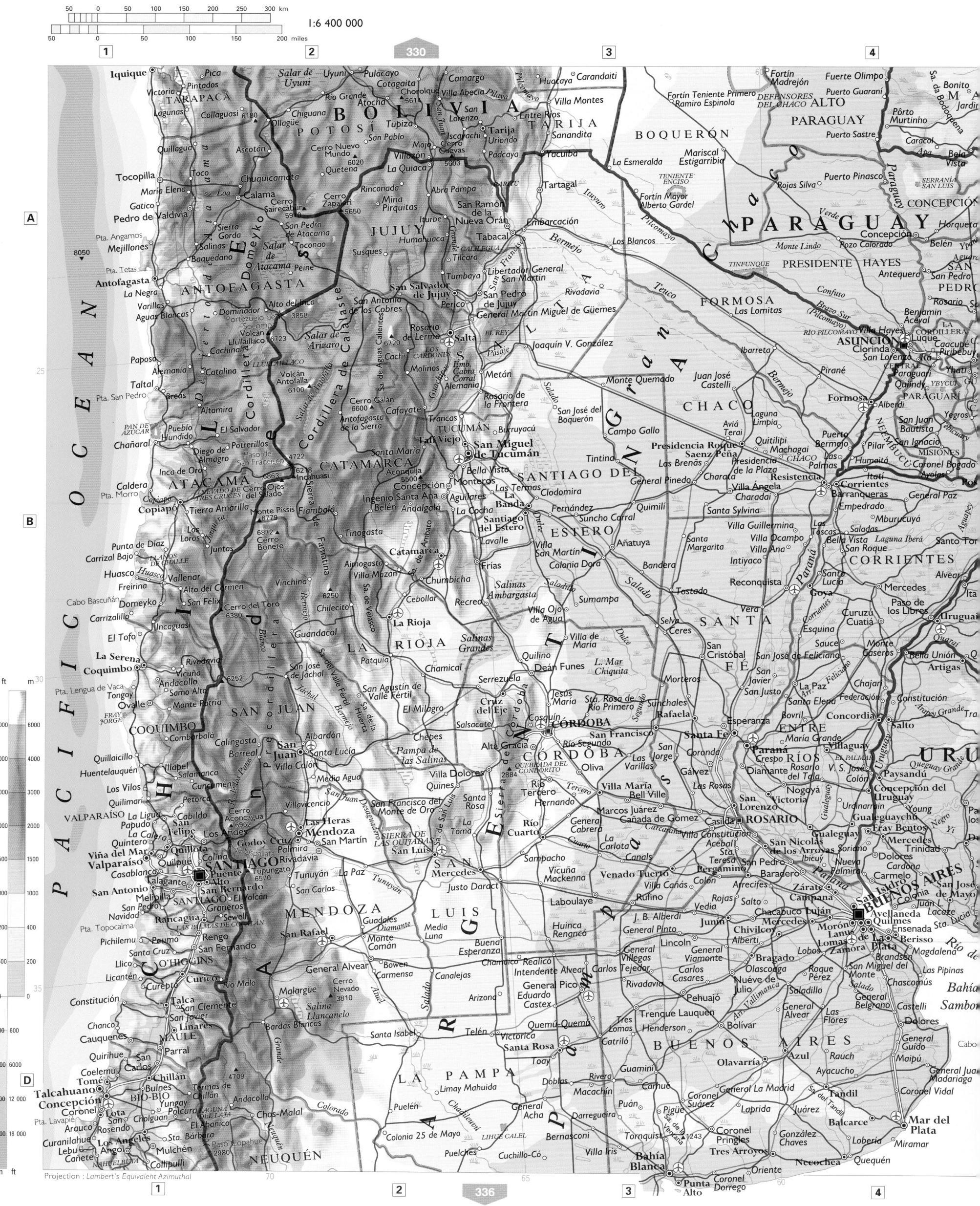

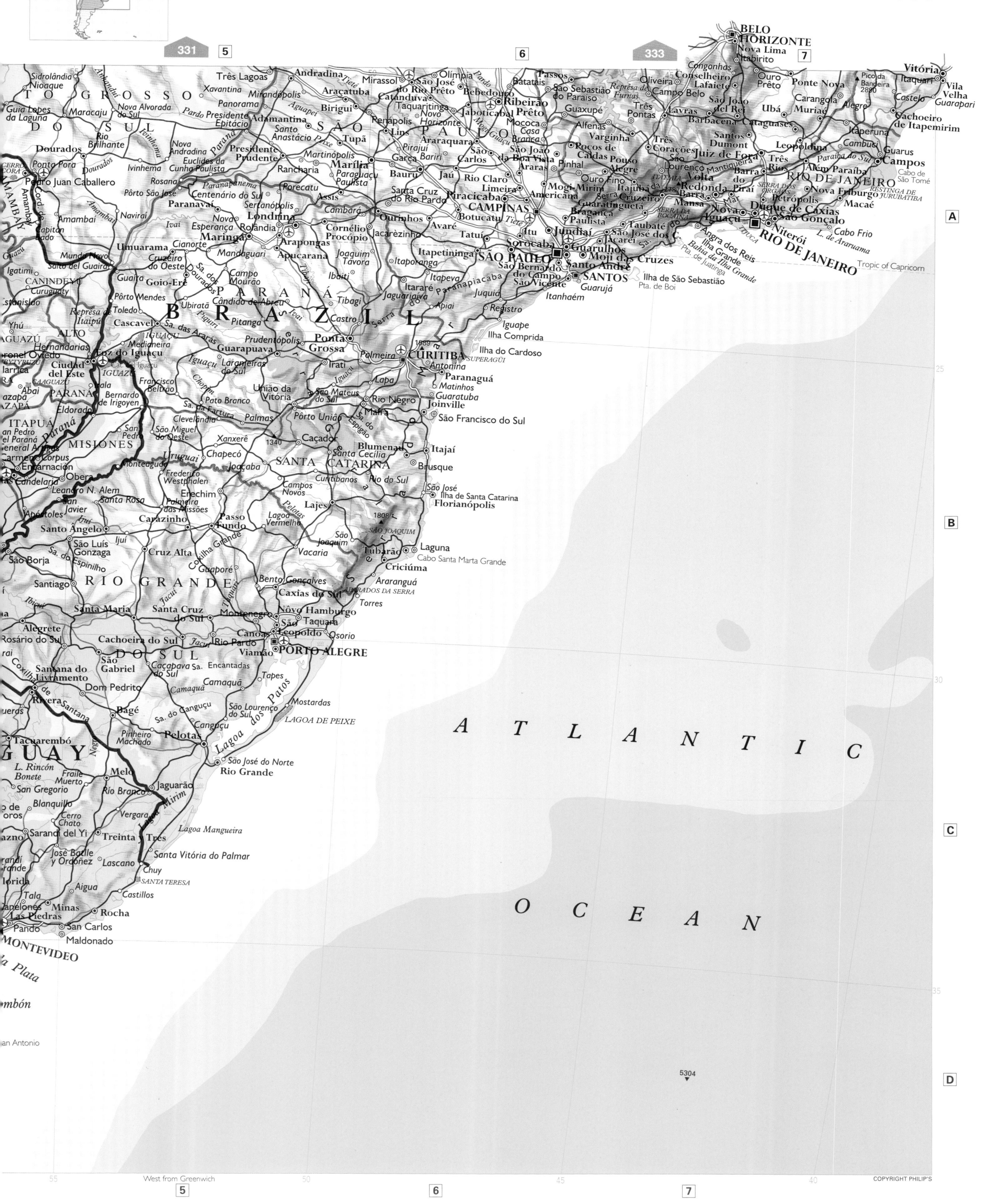

A T L A N T I C

O C E A N

BELO HORIZONTE
Nova Lima
Itabirito
Vitória
Vila Velha
Guarapari
Sachoeiro de Itapemirim

MATO GROSSO DO SUL

Sidrolândia
Nioaque
Guia Lopes da Laguna
Maracaju
Dourados
Nova Alvorada do Sul
Três Lagoas
Andradina
Mirandópolis
Aracatuba
Araçatuba
Andradina
Olímpia
São José do Rio Prêto
Bebedouro
Ribeirão Prêto
Passos
São Sebastião do Paraíso
Campo Belo
Conselheiro Lafaiete
Congonhas
Oliveira
Ouro Prêto
Ponte Nova
Itaquari

Xavantina
Panorama
Presidente Epitácio
Adamantina
Tupã
Lins
Araraquara
Taquaritinga
Jaboticabal
Mococa
Casa Branca
Guaxupé
Três Pontas
Lavras
Barbacena
Cataguases
Cambuí

Pôrto Pora
Dourados
Ivinhema
Euclides da Cunha Paulista
Rancharia
Marília
Paraguaçu Paulista
Bauru
Jaú
Rio Claro
Araras
Limeira
Americana
Mogi-Mirim
Alfenas
Varginha
Poços de Caldas
Pouso Alegre
Santos
Leopoldina
Ubá
Além Paraíba
Muriaé
Campos

Pedro Juan Caballero
Rosana
Nova Andradina
Presidente Prudente
Martinópolis
Garça
Bariri
São Carlos
São João da Boa Vista
Santa Cruz do Rio Pardo
Ouro Fino
Itajubá
Cruzeiro
Guaratinguetá
Redonda
Barra do Piraí
Nova Friburgo
Macaé

Paranavaí
Goio-Erê
Cornélio Procópio
Jacarèzinho
Piracicaba
CAMPINAS
Botucatu
Avaré
Tatuí
São Paulo
Sorocaba
GUARULHOS
Itu
Jundiaí
Moji das Cruzes
Angra dos Reis
Duque de Caxias
RIO DE JANEIRO

BRAZIL

PARANÁ

Foz do Iguaçu
Cascavel
Guarapuava
Ponta Grossa
CÚRITIBA
Paranaguá
Ilha de São Sebastião

Ciudad del Este
Medianeira
Francisco Beltrão
Pato Branco
União da Vitória
São Mateus do Sul
Irati
Palmeira
Antonina
Matinhos
Guaratuba
Joinville
São Francisco do Sul

MISIONES
Xanxerê
Chapecó
Concordia
Joaçaba
SANTA CATARINA
Blumenau
Brusque
Itajaí

RIO GRANDE DO SUL

Passo Fundo
Carazinho
Cruz Alta
Vacaria
Lajes
Florianópolis
Ilha de Santa Catarina

URUGUAY

MONTEVIDEO

Porto Alegre
Pelotas
Rio Grande
Laguna

Tropic of Capricorn

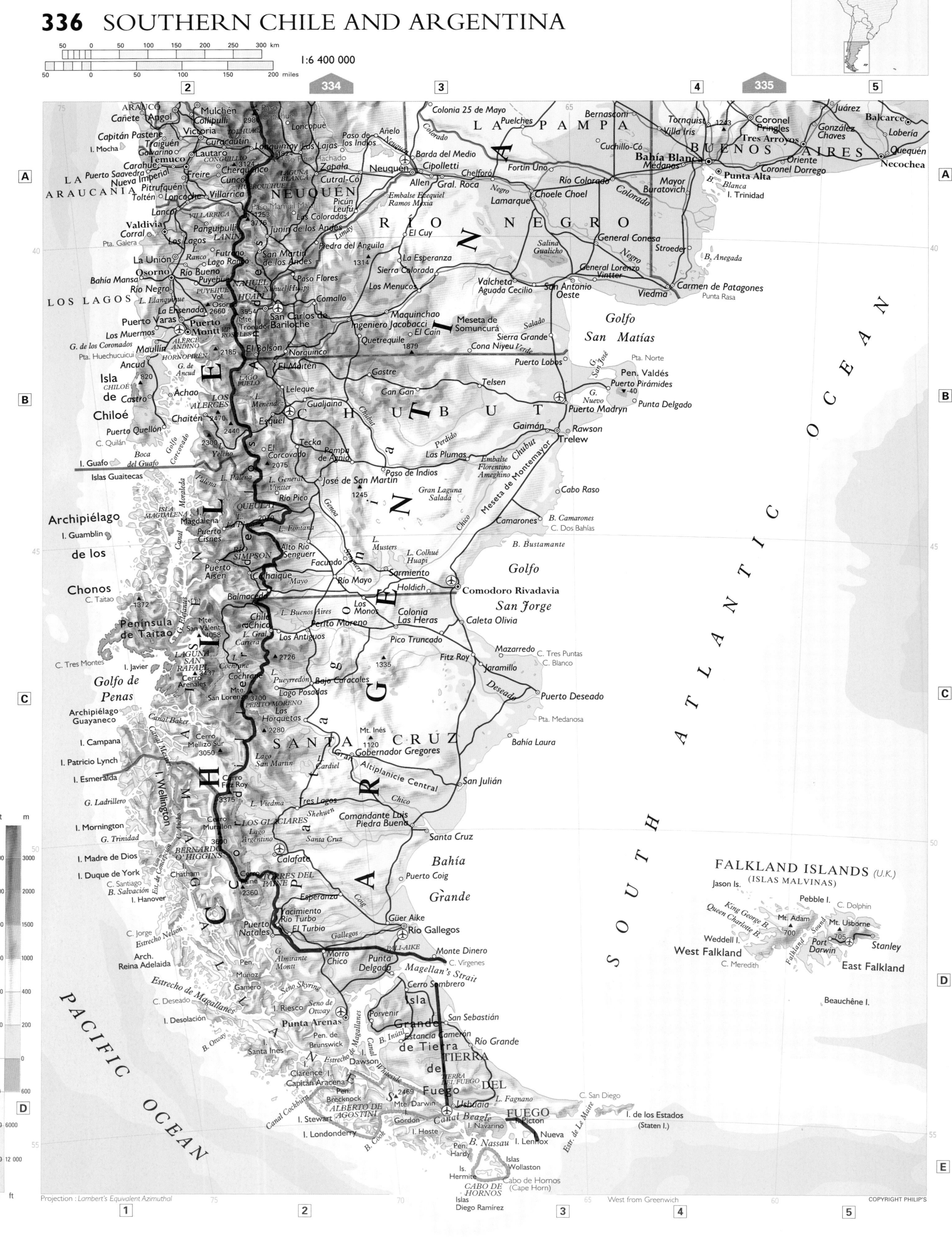

1:6 400 000

50   0   50   100   150   200   250   300 km
50   0   50   100   150   200 miles

ft   m
9000 3000
6000 2000
4500 1500
3000 1000
1200   400
600   200
0   0
-200   -600
2000   6000
4000 12 000
m   ft

PACIFIC OCEAN

SOUTH ATLANTIC OCEAN

FALKLAND ISLANDS (U.K.)
(ISLAS MALVINAS)

Jason Is.
Pebble I.
King George B.   C. Dolphin
Queen Charlotte B.   Mt. Adam
                     700
Weddell I.   Mt. Usborne
                     ▲705
West Falkland   Port   Stanley
                     Darwin
C. Meredith   East Falkland

Beauchêne I.

LA   PAMPA

RIO   NEGRO

ARGENTINA

Golfo
San Matías

Pen. Valdés

Golfo
San Jorge

CHUBUT

SANTA   CRUZ

Golfo de
Penas

MAGALLANES

TIERRA   DEL   FUEGO

Magellan's Strait

CABO DE
HORNOS

Projection : Lambert's Equivalent Azimuthal

West from Greenwich

COPYRIGHT PHILIP'S

GEOGRAPHICAL GLOSSARY

This is a list of the geographical terms from various foreign languages that are found in the place names on the maps and in the index. Each is followed by the language and its English meaning.

Afr. Afrikaans
Alb. Albanian
Amh. Amharic
Ar. Arabic
Belo. Belorussian
Berb. Berber
Bulg. Bulgarian
Burm. Burmese
Cam. Cambodian
Cat. Catalan
Chin. Chinese
Czec. Czech
Dan. Danish
Dut. Dutch
Est. Estonian
Fin. Finnish
Fr. French
Gae. Gaelic
Ger. German
Gr. Greek
Heb. Hebrew
Hin. Hindi
Hung. Hungarian
I.-C. Indo-Chinese
Ice. Icelandic
It. Italian
Indo. Indonesian
Jap. Japanese
Kaz. Kazakh
Kor. Korean
Kyrg. Kyrgyz
Lapp. Lapp (Sami)
Lat. Latvian
Lith. Lithuanian
Malag. Malagasy
Mong. Mongolian
Nor. Norway
Pash. Pashto
Per. Persian
Pol. Polish
Port. Portuguese
Rom. Romanian
Russ. Russian
Sin. Sinhalese
Ser.-Cr. Serbo-Croat
Slov. Slovene
Som. Somali
Span. Spanish
Swe. Swedish
Tib. Tibetan
Turk. Turkish
Ukr. Ukrainian
Viet. Vietnamese

-á *Ice.* river
-å *Dan., Nor., Swe.* stream
-abad *Farsi, Russ.* town
Abyad *Ar.* white mountain
Ada, Adasi *Turk.* island
Addis *Amh.* new
Adrar *Ar., Berb.* mountains
Aiguille *Fr.* peak
Aïn, Aîn (A.) *Ar.* spring
Ákra *Gr.* cape, point
Akrotíri *Gr.* cape, point
Alb *Ger.* mountains
Albufera *Span.* lagoon
-ålen *Nor.* islands
Alpen *Ger.* mountain ranges
Alpes *Fr.* mountains
Alpi *It.* mountains
Alt *Ger.* old
Alta, Alto *Port.* high, upper
Altos *Span.* mountains
-älv, -älven *Swe.* stream, river
Amtskommune (Amt.) *Dan.* first-order administrative division
-ån *Swe.* river
Anse *Fr.* bay
Ao *Thai* bay
Appennino *It.* mountain range
Archipel *Fr.* archipelago
Archipiélago (Arch.) *Span.* archipelago
Arcipélago *It.* archipelago
Arquipélago (Arq.) *Port.* archipelago
Arrecife *Span.* reef
Arroyo (Arr.) *Span.* stream
-ås, -åsen *Nor., Swe.* hill
Ayios *Gr.* island
Ayn *Ar.* well, waterhole

Baai, -baai *Afr., Dut.* bay
Bāb *Ar.* gate, strait
Bäck, -bäcken *Swe.* stream
Back, -backen, *Swe.* hill
Bad, -baden *Ger.* spa
Badia *Cat.* bay
Bādiyah, Bādiyat *Ar.* desert
Bæk *Dan.* stream
Bælt *Dan.* strait
Baharu *Malay* new
Bahía (B.) *Span.* bay
Bahiret *Ar.* lagoon
Bahr *Ar.* sea, lake, river
Bahra Bahrat *Ar.* lake
Baía (B.) *Port.* bay
Baie (B.) *Fr.* bay
Baixa, Baixo *Port.* lower
Baja, Bajo *Span.* lower
Bakke *Nor.* hill
Bala *Farsi* upper
Ballon *Fr.* dome
Baltă *Rom.* marsh, lake
Ban *Lao, Thai* village
-Bana *Jap.* cape
Banc *Fr.* bank
Banco *Span.* bank
Bandao *Chin.* peninsula
Bandar *Ar., Malay* port, harbour
Bandar *Farsi* bay
Banja *Ser.-Cr.* spa, resort
Banjaran *Malay* mountain range
Baraji *Turk.* dam
Barat *Indo., Malay* western
Barrage (Barr.) *Fr.* dam
Barragem (Barr.) *Port.* dam, reservoir
Bas, basse *Fr.* lower
Bassin *Fr.* basin
-batang *Indo.* river
Baţlaq *Farsi* marsh
Batu *Malay* mountain
Bayt *Heb.* house, village
Bazar *Hin.* market, bazaar
-beek *Afr., Dut.* river
Be'er *Heb.* well
Bei *Chin.* north, northern
Beinn, Ben *Gae.* mountain
Beit *Heb.* village
Belaya, Belo, Beloye, Belyy *Russ.* white
Belogorye *Russ.* hills, mountain range
Bender *Som.* harbour
Berg(e), -berg(e) *Afr., Ger.* mountain(s)
-berg, -en, -et *Nor., Swe.* hill, mountain, rock
Besar *Indo., Malay* big
Bet *Heb.* house, village
Bir, Bîr, Bi'r *Ar.* well
Birkat, Birket *Ar.* lake, marsh, well
Bishti *Alb.* cape
-bjerg *Dan.* hill, point
Blaenau *Welsh* upland
-bo *Chin.* lake
Boca *Port., Span.* river mouth, inlet
Bodden *Ger.* bay, inlet
Bogaz, Boğazı *Turk.* channel, strait
Bogd *Mong.* mountain range
Bois *Fr.* woods
Boka *Ser.-Cr.* gulf, inlet
Bolshoi, Bolshaya, Bolshoye (Bol.) *Russ.* great, large
Bordj (Bj.) *Ar.* fort
-borg *Dan., Nor., Swe.* castle, fort
Bory *Pol.* woods
Bosque *Span.* woods
-botn *Nor.* valley floor
Bouche(s) *Fr.* mouth(s)
Braţul *Rom.* distributary stream, branch
-bre, -breen *Nor.* glacier
Bredning *Dan.* bay
Brücke *Ger.* bridge
-brug *Dut.* bridge
-brunn *Swe.* well, spring
Bucht *Ger.* bay
Bugt *Dan.* bay
-bugten *Dan.* bay
Buheirat *Ar.* lake, reservoir
Bukit *Malay* hill
-bukt, -a *Nor.* bay
-bukten *Swe.* bay
-bulag *Mong.* spring
Bulag *Chin.* lake
Bulu *Malay* mountain
Bum *Burm.* mountain
Bûr *Ar.* port
Burg. *Ar.* fort
Burg, -burg *Ger.* castle
Burnu, Burun *Turk.* cape
Butt *Gae.* promontory
Büyük *Turk.* big
-by *Dan., Nor., Swe.* town
-byen *Nor., Swe.* town

Cabeza *Span.* peak, hill
Cabo (C.) *Port., Span.* headland, cape
Cachoeira *Port.* waterfall
Cala Cat. *It.* bay
Camp Port. *Span.* land, field
Câmpia *Rom.* plain
Campo *It., Port., Span.* plain
Campos *Span.* upland
Canal (Can.) *Fr., Port., Span.* canal, channel
Canale (Can.) *It.* channel
Canalul (Can.) *Ser.-Cr.* canal
Cao Nguyen *Thai* plateau, tableland
Cap (C.) *Cat., Fr.* cape
Capo (C) *It.* cape
Carn *Gae.* hill
Carse *Gae.* valley
Catarata *Port., Span.* cataract
Cauce *Span.* intermittent stream
Causse *Fr.* limestone plateau
Cay, Cayi, -cay, -cayi *Turk.* river
Cayo(s) *Span.* rock(s), islet(s)
Cefn *Welsh* hill
Cerro *Span.* hill, peak
Česká, Český, České *Czec.* Czech
Chaco *Span.* jungle
Chaîne(s) *Fr.* mountain range(s)
Chang *Chin.* mountain
Chapa *Span.* hills, upland
Chapada *Port.* hills, upland
Chaung *Burm.* stream, river
Chi *Chin.* small lake
-ch'ŏn *Kor.* river
-chŏsuji *Kor.* reservoir
Chott *Ar.* salt lake, depression
Chu *Tib.* river
Chute *Fr.* waterfall
Città *It.* city
Ciudad *Span.* city
Co *Tib.* lake
Cochilla (Coch.) *Port.* hills
Col *Fr., It.* pass
Colina(s) *Span.* hill(s)
Colle *It.* pass
Colline(s) *Fr.* hill(s)
Conca *It.* plain, basin
Cordillera (Cord.) *Span.* mountain range
Costa *It., Port., Span.* coast
Côte *Fr.* coast, slope, hill
Coteaux *Fr.* hills
Cuchilla *Span.* hills
Cuenca *Span.* river basin
Cu-Lao *Viet.* island

Da *Chin.* big
Da *Viet.* river
Daban *Mong.* pass
Dağ(i) *Turk.* mountain(s)
Dāgh *Farsi* mountain
Dağları *Turk.* mountain range
-dai, -daichi *Jap.* plateau
-Dake *Jap.* mountain
-dal, -e *Dan., Swe.* valley
-dal, -en *Swe., Nor.* valley, stream
Dalay Mong. large lake
-ðalir, -ðalur *Ice.* valley
-damm, -en *Swe.* lake
Danau *Malay* lake
Dao *Chin., Viet.* island
Dar *Ar.* region
Darya *Russ.* river
Daryācheh *Farsi* marshy lake, lake
Dasht *Farsi* desert, steppe
Daung *Burm.* mountain, hill
Dayr *Ar.* monastery
Debre *Amh.* hill
Deli *Ser.-Cr.* mountain
Deniz, -i *Turk.* sea
Département (Dépt.) *Fr.* first-order administrative division
Dere *Turk.* stream
Desierto (Des.) *Span.* desert
Détroit *Fr.* strait
Dhar *Ar.* region, mountain range
Diep *Dut.* channel
Dijk *Dut.* dyke
Ding *Chin.* mountain
Dingzi *Chin.* hill, mountain
Djebel (Dj.) *Ar.* mountain
-djúp *Ice.* fjord
-djupet *Swe.* channel, sound
-Do *Jap., Kor.* island
Dolina *Russ.* valley
Dolna, Dolni *Bulg.* lower
Dolna, Dolne, Dolny *Russ.* lower
Dolní *Czec.* lower
Dolok (D.) *Malay* mountain
-dong *Kor.* village, town
Dong *Chin.* east, eastern
Donja, Donji *Ser.-Cr.* lower
-dorf *Ger.* village
-dorp *Afr.* village
-drif *Afr.* ford
-dybet *Dan.* marine channel
Dzong *Tib.* town, settlement
Dzüün *Mong.* east, eastern

-egga *Nor.* peak
-eiland, -en (eil.) *Afr., Dut.* island(s)
Eilean *Gae.* island
-elv, -a *Nor.* river
Embalse *Span.* reservoir
'Emeq *Heb.* plain, valley
Ensenada *Span.* bay
Erg *Ar.* sand desert
Estero *Span.* estuary
Estrada *Span.* bay
Estrecho *Span.* strait
Estuaire *Fr.* estuary
Estuario *Span.* estuary
Étang *Fr.* lagoon, lake
-ey, -jar *Ice.* island(s)
-ežeras *Lith.* lake
-ezers *Lat.* lake

Falaise *Fr.* cliff
-fallet *Swe.* waterfall
Farihy *Malag.* lake
Faro *Span.* lighthouse
-feld *Ger.* field
-fell *Ice.* mountain, hill
Feng *Chin.* mountain range
Fiume (F.) *It.* river
-fjäll, -en, -et *Swe.* hill(s), mountain(s), ridge
-fjärden *Swe.* fjord
Fjeld *Dan.* mountain
-fjell, -et *Nor.* mountain range
-fjord, -en *Dan., Nor., Swe.* fjord
-fjorður *Ice.* fjord, bay, inlet
Fleuve (Fl.) *Fr.* river
-flói *Ice.* bay, marshy country
Fluss (F.) *Ger.* river
Foce, Foci *It.* mouth(s)
Folyó (F.) *Hung.* river
-fonn *Nor.* glacier
-fontein *Afr.* fountain, spring
Forêt *Fr.* forest
-fors, -en *Swe.* waterfall, rapids
-foss, -en *Ice., Nor.* waterfall
Forst *Ger.* forest
Foum *Ar.* pass
Fuente *Span.* source
-furt *Ger.* ford
Fylke *Nor.* first-order administrative division

-gang *Chin.* bay, harbour
-gang *Kor.* river
Ganga *Hin., Sin.* river
Gangri *Tib.* mountain
Gaoyuan *Chin.* plateau
-gat *Dan.* sound
-Gata *Jap.* lake
-gau *Ger.* district
-Gawa *Jap.* river
Gebel (G.) *Ar.* mountain
Gebirge (Geb.) *Ger.* hills, mountains
Gezirat, Geziret *Ar.* island
Ghat *Hin.* range of hills
Ghiol *Rom.* lake
Ghubbat *Ar.* bay, inlet
Gjiri *Alb.* bay
Gjol *Alb.* lagoon, lake
Glava (Gl.) *Ser.-Cr.* mountain, peak
Glen *Gae.* valley
Gletscher (Gl.) *Ger.* glacier
Gobi *Mong.* desert
Gol *Mong.* river
Göl *Azeri, Turk.* lake
Golfe (G.) *Fr.* gulf
Golfo (G.) *It., Span.* gulf
Gölü *Turk.* lake
Gomba *Tib.* settlement
Gora, Góra *Bulg., Russ., Ser.-Cr., Pol.* mountain
Gorje *Ser.-Cr.* hills, mountains
Gorno *Russ.* mountainous
-gorod *Russ.* small town
Gory, Góry *Pol., Russ.* mountain
-grad *Bulg. Russ., Ser.-Cr.* town, city
-grada *Russ.* ridge
Gran *It., Span.* big, great
Grand, -e *Fr.* big, great
Groot (Gt.) *Afr., Dut.* big, great
Gross, -e, -en, -er *Ger.* big, great(er)
Grupo *Span.* group
Gruppo *It.* group
Guan *Chin.* pass
Guba (G.) *Russ.* bay
-Guntō *Jap.* island group
Gunong, Gunung (G.) *Indo., Malay* mountain
Gură *Rom.* passage

Hadabat *Ar.* plateau
Hadjer *Ar.* mountain
-hafen *Ger.* harbour, port
Haff *Ger.* bay, lagoon
Hai *Chin.* lake, sea
Haixia *Chin.* channel, strait
Halbinsel *Ger.* peninsula
Halvø *Dan.* peninsula
Halvøya *Nor.* peninsula
Hāmad, Hamada, Hammādah, Hammādat *Ar.* stony desert, plateau
-hamn *Swe., Nor.* harbour, anchorage
Hāmūn *Farsi* marsh, lake
-Hantō *Jap.* peninsula
Har(e) *Heb.* hill(s), mountain(s)
Hassi (Hi.) *Ar.* well
-haug *Nor.* hill
Hav, Havet *Nor., Swe.* sea
-havn *Dan., Nor.* bay, harbour
Havre *Fr.* harbour
Hawd *Ar.* oasis
Hawr *Ar.* lake, marsh
He *Chin.* river
-hegység *Hung.* hills, forest
Heide *Ger.* heath, moor
Helodranon' *Malag.* bay
Higashi *Jap.* east, eastern
-ho *Kor.* lake
-hø *Nor.* peak
Hoch *Ger.* high
Hochland *Afr.* highland
Hoek, -hoek *Afr., Dut.* cape, point
-höfn *Ice.* harbour, port
-hög, -en, -högar, -högarna *Swe.* hill(s), peak, mountain
Höhe *Ger.* height
Hohen *Ger.* high, upper
-hoi *Chin.* bay
-høj, -e *Dan.* hills
-holm, -holme, -holmen *Dan., Nor., Swe.* island
Hon *Viet.* island
Hoog *Dut.* high
Hora *Czec., Ukr.* mountain
-horn *Ger.* peak
Hory *Czec.* mountains, hills
-hot *Mong.* town
-hoved *Dan.* point, headland, peninsula
-hrad *Czec.* town
Hráun *Ice.* lava
-hsi *Chin.* river
-hsia *Chin.* gorge, strait
-hsien *Chin.* district
Hu *Chin.* lake, reservoir
Huk *Dan., Ger.* cape
-huk *Swe.* cape
Huken *Nor.* cape

Idd *Ar.* well
Idehan *Ar., Berb.* sandy plain, dunes
-ike *Jap.* lake
Île(s) (I(s).) *Fr.* island(s)
Ilha(s) (I(s).) *Port.* island(s)
imeni *Russ.* 'in the name of'
Inish *Gae.* island
Insel(n) (I.) *Ger.* island(s)
Irmak *Turk.* river
'Irq *Ar.* dunes
Isla(s) (I(s).) *Span.* island(s)
Iso *Fin.* big, great
Isol, -a, -e (I.) *It.* island(s)
Isthme *Fr.* isthmus
Istmo *Span.* isthmus
-iwa *Jap.* island

Jabal *Ar.* mountain range
Järv *Est.* lake
järvi *Fin.* lake, bay, pond
-jaur, -javre *Lapp.* lake
Jazā'ir *Ar.* islands
Jazīra, jazīrat *Ar.* island
Jazireh *Farsi* island
Jebel *Ar.* mountain
Jezero *Ser.-Cr.* lake
Jezioro *Pol.* lake
Jiang *Chin.* river
Jiao *Chin.* cape
-Jima *Jap.* island
Jøkulen *Nor.* glacier, ice cap
-joki *Fin.* river
-jökull *Ice.* glacier, ice cap
Jūras Līcis *Lat.* bay, gulf

Kaap (K.) *Afr.* cape
-kai *Jap.* bay, channel, sea
-kaikyō *Jap.* strait
-kaise *Lapp.* mountain
kalnas *Lith.* hill
Kamennyy *Russ.* stony
Kampong *Cam.* village
Kampung *Malay* village
-kanaal *Dut.* canal
Kanal *Dan.* channel, gulf
Kanal *Ger., Swe.* canal
-kanal *Ser.-Cr.* channel, canal
Kanava *Fin.* canal
Kang *Kor.* river, bay
Kap (K.) *Dan., Ger.* cape, point
-kapp *Nor.* cape, point
-kaupstaður *Ice.* market town
-kaupunki *Fin.* town
Kavīr *Farsi* salt desert
Kébir *Ar.* great
Kecil *Malay* lesser, little
Kefar *Heb.* village, hamlet
-Ken *Jap.* first-order administrative division
Kep, -i (K.) *Alb.* cape
Kepulauan (Kep.) *Indo., Malay* archipelago
Keski- *Fin.* middle, central
Khalīg, Khalīj *Ar.* gulf
-khamba *Tib.* source, spring
Khawr *Ar.* bay, channel, wadi
Khlong *Thai* river
Kho Khot *Thai* isthmus
Khōr *Farsi* bay, estuary
Khrebet *Russ.* mountain range
Kita- *Jap.* north
Klein,-e, -er *Ger.* small
-klint *Dan.* cliff
Klintar *Swe.* hills
-kloof *Afr.* gorge, pass
Knude *Dan.* point
-Ko *Jap.* lake
Ko *Thai* island
-kōchi *Jap.* mountainous region
-kōgen *Jap.* plateau
Kohi *Pash.* mountains
Kol *Kaz., Kyrg.* lake
Kólpos *Gr., Turk.* gulf, bay
Kolymskoye *Russ.* mountain range
Kompong *Malay* landing place
-kop *Afr.* hill
-kopf *Ger.* hill
-köping *Swe.* market town
Körfäzi *Azeri* gulf
Körfezi *Turk.* gulf
Kosa *Russ., Ukr.* spit
-koski *Fin.* rapids
-kraal *Afr.* native village
-kraj *Czec., Pol., Ser.-Cr.* region
Krasnyy *Russ.* red
Kryazh *Russ.* ridge, hills
Kuala *Malay* bay
-kuan *Chin.* pass
Kūh(ha) *Farsi* mountain(s)
Kul *Russ.* lake
-kulle *Swe.* hill
Kum *Russ.* sandy desert
Kumpu *Fin.* hill
Kwe *Burm.* bay, gulf
-kylä *Fin.* village
Kyst, -en *Dan., Nor.* coast
Kyun(zu) *Burm.* island(s)

La *Tib.* pass
-laagte *Afr.* watercourse

Lääni *Fin.* first-order administrative division
Lac (L.) *Fr.* lake
Lacul (L.) *Rom.* lake, lagoon
Lago (L.) *It., Port., Span.* lake, lagoon
Lagoa (L.) *Port.* lagoon
Lagos *Port., Span.* lakes
Laguna (L.) *It., Span.* lagoon, lake
Lagune (L.) *Fr.* lake
-laht *Est.* bay
Lahti *Fin.* bay, gulf, cove
Lakhti *Russ.* bay, gulf
Lam *Thai* river
Lampi *Fin.* lake
Län *Swe.* first-order administrative division
Land *Ger.* first-order administrative division
-land *Dan.* region
-land *Afr., Nor.* land, province
Lande *Fr.* heath
Laut *Indo.* sea
Law *Gae.* hill, mountain
Līcis *Lat.* gulf
Lido *It.* beach, shore
Liedao *Chin.* islands
Lilla *Swe.* small
Lille *Dan., Nor.* small
Liman *Russ.* bay, gulf
Límni (L.) *Gr.* lake
Ling *Chin.* mountain range
-linna *Fin.* fort
Llano *Span.* prairie, plain
Llyn *Welsh* lake
Loch (L.) *Gae.* lake, inlet
Lough (L.) *Gae.* lake, inlet
Lum *Alb.* river
Lund *Dan.* forest
-lund, -en *Swe.* wood(s)
-luoto *Fin.* island

-maa *Est.* island
Madīnat *Ar.* town, city
Madiq *Ar.* strait
Maja *Alb.* mountains
-mäki *Fin.* hill, hillside
Mal *Alb.* mountain
Maloye, Malyy, Malyya *Russ.* little, small
Mala, Mali, Malo *Ser.-Cr.* little, small
Malaya *Belo.* small
Malé *Czec., Slovak* small
Mali *Alb.* mountain
-man *Kor.* bay
Mar *Span.* lagoon, sea
Marais *Fr.* marsh
Mare *It.* sea
Mare *Rom.* great
Marisma *Span.* marsh
-mark *Dan., Nor.* land
Marsâ *Ar.* anchorage, bay, inlet
Masabb *Ar.* river mouth, estuary
Massif *Fr.* upland, mountains
Mato *Port.* forest
Mazar *Farsi* shrine, tomb
Meer, -meer *Afr., Dut., Ger.* lake, sea
-men *Chin.* bay, gorge, channel
Mesto *Ser.-Cr., Czec.* town
Mezzo *It.* middle
Midbar *Heb.* wilderness
Mierzeja *Pol.* spit
Mifraz *Heb.* bay
Mina *Ar.* port
Minami *Jap.* south, southern
-misaki *Jap.* cape, point
Mittel *Ger.* central, middle
-mo *Nor., Swe.* heath, island
-mon *Swe.* heath
Mong *Burm.* town
Mont(s) (Mt(s).) *Fr.* hill(s), mountain(s)
Montagna (Mt.) *It.* mountain
Montagne(s) (Mt(s).) *Fr.* hill(s), mountain(s)
Montaña(s) (Mt(s).) *Span.* mountain(s)
Montanyes *Cat.* mountains
Monte(s) (Mte(s).) *It., Port., Span.* mountain(s)
Monti (Mti.) *It.* mountains
More *Russ.* sea
Mörön *Mong.* river
Moyen *Fr.* central, middle
Muang *Malay* town
Mui *Viet.* cape
Mull *Gae.* promontory
Mund, -mund *Afr.* mouth
Munkhafed *Ar.* depression
Munte (Mte.) *Rom.* mount
Munţi(i) (Mti.) *Rom.* mountain(s)
Muong *Malay* village
Myit *Burm.* river
Myitwanya *Burm.* mouths of river
Mynydd *Welsh* mountain
-myr *Nor., Swe.* swamp
-mýri *Ice.* swamp
Mys (M.) *Russ.* cape

-Nada *Jap.* bay, gulf
-næs *Dan.* point, cape
Nafūd *Ar.* sandy desert
Nagorye *Russ.* hills, mountains
Nagy *Hung.* big
Nahal (N.) *Heb.* river
Nahr (N.) *Ar.* river, stream
Najd *Ar.* plateau, pass
Nakhon *Thai* town
Nam *Kor., Viet.* river
-nam *Kor.* south
Namakzār *Per.* salt flat
Nan *Chin.* south, southern
-nao *Chin.* lake
-näs *Swe.* cape
Neder *Dut.* lower
Nedre *Nor.* lower
Nei *Chin.* inner
Nek *Afr.* pass
-nes *Ice., Nor.* cape
Ness, -ness *Gae.* promontory, cape
Nevada, Nevado *Span.* snow-capped mountain
Nez *Fr.* cape
Nieder *Ger.* lower
-niemi *Fin.* cape, point, peninsula, island
Nieuw, -e *Dut.* new
Nishi *Jap.* west, western
Nisos, Nisoi *Gr.* island(s)
Nizhneye, Nizhniy *Russ.* lower
Nizina *Belo., Pol.* lowland
Nizmennost *Russ.* plain, lowland
Nízní *Czec.* lower
Noord *Dut.* north, northern
Nord *Fr.* north, northern
Norra *Swe.* north, northern
Nørre *Dan.* north, northern
Norte *Port., Span.* north, northern
Nos *Bulg., Russ.* cape, point
Nosy *Malag.* island
Nouveau, Nouvelle *Fr.* new
Nova, Novi *Bulg., Port., Serb.-Cr.* new
Novaya, Novo, Novoye, Novyy *Russ.* new
Nové, Novy *Czec., Slovak* new
Novo *Port.* new
Nowa, Nowe, Nowy *Pol.* new
Nudo *Span.* mountain
Nueva, Nuevo *Span.* new
Nur *Chin.* lake
Nur *Tib.* peak
Nuruu *Mong.* mountain range
Nusa *Indo.* island
Nuur *Mong.* lake
Ny *Dan., Nor., Swe.* new

-ø *Dan., Nor.* island
-ö *Swe.* island,
-öar, -na *Swe.* islands
Ober *Ger., Ukr.* upper
Oblast *Russ.* administrative division
Öbor *Mong.* inner
Occidental *Fr., Span.* western
-odde *Dan., Nor.* point, peninsula, cape
Oeste *Span.* west, western
Oglat *Ar.* well
Oji *Alb.* bay
Ojo *Span.* spring
-Oki *Jap.* bay
-ön *Swe.* island
Ondör *Mong.* upper
Oost(er) *Dut.* east(ern)
Oraşu *Rom.* city
Ord *Gae.* point
Óri *Gr.* mountains
Oriental, -e *Fr., Span.* east, eastern
Órmos *Gr.* bay
Óros *Gr.* mountain(s)
Ort *Ger.* point, cape
Ost *Ger.* east
Øst(er) *Den., Nor.* east(ern)
Öst(ra) *Swe.* east(ern)
Ostriv *Ukr.* island
Ostrov(a) *Russ.* island(s)
Otok(i) *Ser.-Cr.* island(s)
Ouabi, Ouadi (O.) *Ar.* dry watercourse, wadi
Oud, -e *Dut.* old
Oued, -i (O.) *Ar.* watercourse
Ouest *Fr.* west, western
Ouzan *Farsi* river
Ova, -si *Turk.* plains, lowlands
Over- *Dan., Dut.* upper
Över-, Övre *Nor., Swe.* upper
-øy, -a *Nor.* island(s)
Oya *Hin.* point
Oya *Sin.* river
Ozero, Ozera (Oz.) *Russ., Ukr.* lake(s)

-pää *Fin.* hill(s), mountain
Pahta *Lapp.* hill
Pampa(s) *Span.* plain(s)
Pantanal *Port.* marsh
Pantano *Span.* reservoir
Pantao *Chin.* peninsula
Parbat *Urdu* mountain
Pas *Fr.* strait
Paso (P.) *Span.* pass
Passage *Fr.* channel
Passe *Fr.* channel
Passo (P.) *It.* pass
Pasul (P.) *Rom.* pass
Patam *Hin.* small village
Patna, -patnam *Hin.* small village
Pegunungan *Indo., Malay* mountain range
Pei, -pei *Chin.* north
Pélagos *Gr.* sea
Pen *Welsh* hill
Peña *Span.* rock, peak
Pendi *Chin.* basin, depression
Péninsule *Fr.* peninsula
Penisola (Pen.) *It.* peninsula
Pereval (Per.) *Russ.* pass
Pervo-, Pervyy- *Russ.* first
Pertuis *Fr.* channel, strait
Peski *Russ.* sand desert
Petit, -e *Fr.* small
Phanom *Thai* mountain
Phnum *Cam.* mountain
Phou *Lao.* mountain
Phu *Thai, Viet.* mountain
Piano *It.* plain
Pic *Cat., Fr.* peak
Pico(s) *Span.* peak(s)
-piggen *Dan.* peak
Pik *Russ.* peak
Pingyuan *Chin.* plain
Pique *Fr.* peak
Piton *Fr.* peak
Pivostriv *Ukr.* peninsula
Piz, Pizzo *It.* peak
Plage *Fr.* beach
Plaine *Fr.* plain
Planalto *Port.* plateau
Planina (Pl.) *Bulg., Ser.-Cr.* mountain range
Plato *Russ., Bulg.* plateau
Playa *Span.* beach
-po *Chin.* lake, wetland
Pointe (Pte.) *Fr.* point, cape
Pojezierze *Pol.* lakes
Polder *Dut.* reclaimed farmland
-pólis *Gr.* city, town
Poluostrov (Pov.) *Russ.* peninsula
Połwysep *Pol.* peninsula
Pont *Fr.* bridge
Ponta (Pta.) *Port.* point, cape
Ponte *Port.* bridge
Poort *Afr.* passage, gate
-poort *Dut.* port
Porta *Port.* pass
Porţile *Rom.* gate
Portillo *Span.* pass
Porto *It., Port., Span.* port
Potámi, Potamós *Gr.* river
Pradesh *Hin.* state
Praia *Port.* beach, shore
Presa *Span.* reservoir
Presqu'île *Fr.* peninsula
Prokhod *Bulg.* pass
Proliv *Russ.* strait
Promontorio *Span.* promontory
Průsmyk (Pr.) *Czec.* pass
Pueblo *Span.* village
Puerto (Pto.) *Span.* port
Puig *Cat.* peak
Pulau (P.) *Indo., Malay* island
Puna *Span.* desert plateau
Puncak *Indo.* peak
Punta (Pta.) *It., Span.* point, peak
Puy *Fr.* peak

Qal'at *Ar.* fort
Qanat *Ar.* canal
Qasr *Ar.* fort
Qiryat *Heb.* town
Qiuling *Chin.* plateau
Qolleh *Farsi* mountain
-qundao *Chin.* islands

Rach *Viet.* river
Rags *Lat.* cape
Rambla *Cat.* river
Ramlat *Ar.* sandy desert
Rão (R.) *Port.* river
Rann *Hin.* swampy region
Rao *I.-C.* river
Ras *Amh., Ar., Farsi* cape, point
Récif(s) *Fr.* reef(s)
Recife(s) *Port.* reef(s)
Reka *Bulg.* river
Repede *Rom.* rapids
Reprêsa *Port.* reservoir
Reshteh *Farsi* mountain range
-rettō *Jap.* group of islands, chain
Ria *Port., Span.* estuary, bay
Ribeirão (R.) *Port.* river
Ribera (R.) *Span.* river bank
Rijeka *Ser.-Cr.* river
Rio (R.) *Port., Span.* river
Rivier (R.) *Afr., Dut.* river
Riviera *It.* coastal plain, coast
Rivière (R.) *Fr.* river
Roca *Span.* rock
Rocca *It.* rock, peak
Roche *Fr.* rock
Rt *Ser.-Cr.* cape, point
Rubh', Rubha *Gae.* cape, point
-rück *Ger.* ridge
Rūd *Farsi* stream, river
Rudohorie *Slovak* mountains
Rzeka (R.) *Pol.* river

-saar *Est.* island
-saari *Fin.* island
Sabkhat, Sabkhet *Ar.* salt flats
Sadd *Ar.* dam
Sagar,-a *Hin., Urdu* lake
Sahrâ *Ar.* desert
-Saki *Jap.* cape, point
Salar *Span.* salt flat
Salina(s) *Span.* salt marsh(es)
-salmi *Fin.* strait, sound, lake, channel
Saltsjöbad *Swe.* resort
-Sammyaku *Jap.* mountain range
Samut *Thai* gulf
San (S.) *It., Port., Span.* saint
-San *Jap., Kor.* hill, mountain
-Sanchi *Jap.* mountain range
Sankt (St.) *Ger., Russ.* saint
-sanmaek *Kor.* mountain range
-sanmyaku *Jap.* mountain range
Santa (Sta.) *It., Port., Span.* saint
Santo (Sto.) *It. Port., Span.* saint
São (S.) *Port.* saint
Sarīr *Ar.* desert
Sasso *It.* mountain
Satu *Rom.* village
Saurums *Lat.* strait
Sebkha, Sebkhet *Ar.* salt flat
See, -see *Ger.* lake
-şehir *Turk.* town
Selat *Indo., Malay* strait
Selatan *Indo.* southern
-selkä *Fin.* bay, lake, ridge, hills
Selo *Ser.-Cr., Russ.* village
Selva *Port., Span.* forest, wood
Seno *Span.* bay, sound
Serir *Ar.* stony desert
Serra (Sa.) *Cat., Port.* range of hills
Serranía *Span.* mountain ridge
Severo, Severnaya, Severnoye, Severnyy (Sev.) *Russ.* north, northern
Sfântu *Rom.* saint
Shahr, -shahr *Farsi* city, town
Shamo *Chin.* desert
Shan *Chin.* hills, mountains
Shankou *Chin.* pass
Shanmo *Chin.* mountain range
Sharm *Ar.* bay
Shatt *Ar.* river mouth, estuary
-Shima *Jap.* island
Shimāli *Ar.* northern
-Shotō *Jap.* group of islands
-shui *Chin.* river
-shuiku *Chin.* reservoir
Sierra (Sa.) *Span.* mountain range
-sjö, -sjön, -sjø *Swe., Nor.* lake
-sjøen *Dan.* sea
-sjór *Ice.* lake
-sker *Ice.* island
-skär *Swe.* island, rock, cape
-skog, -skogen *Nor., Swe.* wood(s)
-skov *Dan.* forest
Slieve *Gae.* hill, mountain
Sø *Dan., Nor.* lake
Söder, Södra *Swe.* south, southern
Sør *Nor.* south, southern
Solonchak *Russ.* salt lake, marsh
Sønder, Søndra *Dan.* south, southern
Song *Viet.* river
Souk *Ar.* market
-spitze *Ger.* peak, mountain
-spruit *Afr.* stream
Sredna, Sredno *Bulg.* middle, central
Sredne, Sredneye *Russ.* middle, central
Srednja *Ser.-Cr.* middle, central
-stad *Afr., Nor., Swe.* town
-stadt *Ger.* town
-staður *Ice.* town
Stara, Stari *Ser.-Cr.* old
Stará, Staré, Stary *Czec.* old
Staraya, Staroye, Staryy *Russ.* old
Stare, Staro, Stary *Ukr.* old
Stausee *Ger.* reservoir
Stenón *Gr.* strait, pass
Step *Russ.* steppe
Stor, -a *Swe.* big
Store *Dan.* big
-strand *Dan., Ger., Nor., Swe.* beach
-strede *Nor.* straits
Strelka *Russ.* spit
-strete *Nor.* straits
Stretto (Str.) *It.* strait
Strædet (Str.) *Dan.* strait
-ström, -strömmen *Swe.* stream(s)
-stroom *Afr.* large river
Sud *Fr.* south, southern
Süd, -er *Ger.* south, southern
Suid *Afr.* south, southern
-Suidō *Jap.* strait, channel
Sul *Port.* south, southern
Sûn *Burm.* cape
-sund, -et *Swe., Nor.* sound, estuary, inlet
Sungai *Indo., Malay* river
Sur *Span.* south, southern
Sveti *Bulg.* saint
Syd *Dan., Swe.* south, southern
Sýsla *Ice.* first-order administrative division

-tag *Uighur* mountain
Tai -tai *Chin.* tower
-Take *Jap.* mountain
Tal *Mong.* plain, steppe
-tal *Ger.* valley
Tall *Ar.* hills
Tanjona *Malag.* cape, point
Tanjung, Tanjong (Tg.) *Indo., Malay.* cape, point
Tao *Chin.* island
Tasik *Malay* lake
Tassili *Ar.* rocky plateau
Tau *Russ.* mountain range
Taung *Burm.* mountain
Taungdan. *Burm.* mountain range
Taunggya *Burm.* pass
-tekojärvi *Fin.* reservoir
Teluk *Indo., Malay* bay, gulf
Ténéré *Berb.* desert
Tengah *Indo.* middle, central
-thal *Ger.* valley
Thok *Tib.* town
Tien *Chin.* lake, marsh
Tierra *Span.* land, country
Timur *Indo.* eastern
-tind *Nor.* peak
-ting *Chin.* mountain
Tjärn, -en, -et *Swe.* lake
-Tō *Jap.* island
Tong *Kor.* village, town
Tong *Burm., Thai, Kor.* mountain range
Tonlé *Cam.* lake
Top *Dut.* peak
-topp, -en *Nor.* peak
-träsk *Swe.* lake, swamp
Tsangpo *Tib.* large river
Tso *Tib.* lake
Tsu *Jap.* entrance, bay
Tsui *Chin.* cape, point
Tulur *Ar.* hill
-tunturi *Fin.* hill(s), mountain(s), ridge

Uad *Ar.* dry watercourse, wadi
Über *Ger.* upper
-udde, -udden *Swe.* point, cape
Uebi *Som.* river
Ujung *Indo., Malay* cape
Unter- *Ger.* lower
Us *Mong.* water
Ust, Ustye *Russ.* river mouth
Utara *Indo.* north, northern
Uttar *Hin.* north, northern
Uul *Mong., Russ.* mountain range

-vaara *Fin.* hill, mountain ridge, peak
Vaart *Dut.* canal
-våg *Nor.* bay
Val *Fr., Port., Span.* valley
Valea *Rom.* valley
-vall, -en *Swe.* mountain
Valle *It., Span.* valley
Vallée *Fr.* valley
Valli *It.* lake, lagoon
-város *Hung.* town
-varre *Nor.* mountain
Väst, Västra *Swe.* west, western
-vatn *Ice., Nor.* lake
-vatnet *Nor.* lake
-vatten, vattnet *Swe.* lake
-vecchio *It.* old
Vechi *Rom.* old
-ved, -veden *Swe.* hills
Veld, -veld *Afr.* field
Velha, Velho *Port.* old
Velika, Velike, Veliki, Veliko *Ser.-Cr., Slov.* big, large
Velikaya, Velikiy *Russ.* big, large
Velká, Velké, Velký *Czec.* big, large
Verkhne, Verkhniy *Russ.* upper
-vesi *Fin.* water, lake, bay, sound, strait
Vest, Vester, Vestre *Dan., Nor.* west, western
-vidda *Nor.* plateau
Vieille, Vieux *Fr.* old
Vieja, Vejo *Span.* old
Vig *Dan.* bay, inlet, cove, lagoon, lake
-vík *Ice.* bay
-vik, -a, -en *Nor., Swe.* bay, gulf, inlet, lake
Vila *Port.* small town
Villa *Span.* town
Ville *Fr.* town
Vinh *Viet.* bay
Vîrful (Vf.) *Rom.* peak, mountain
-viz *Hung.* river
-víztároló *Hung.* reservoir
-vlei *Afr.* lake, salt pan
-vliet *Dut.* canal
-vloer *Afr.* salt pan
Vodokhranilishche (Vdkhr.) *Russ.* reservoir
Vodoskovyshche (Vdskh.) *Ukr.* reservoir
Volcán (Vol.) *Span.* volcano, mountain
Vorota *Russ.* pass, channel, strait
Vostochno, Vostochnyy *Russ.* east, eastern
-vötn *Ice.* lakes
Vozvyshennost *Russ.* heights, uplands
Vozyera *Belo.* lake
Vrata *Bulg.* gate, pass
Vrchovina *Czec.* mountainous country
Vrch(y) *Czec.* mountain (range)
Vung *Viet.* bay, gulf
-vuori *Fin.* mountain, hill
Vychodné *Slovak* east, eastern
Vysochyna *Ukr.* upland

-waard *Dut.* polder
Wadi (W.) *Ar.* dry watercourse
Wâhât *Ar.* oasis
Wald *Ger.* forest, mountains
-Wan *Chin., Jap.* bay, harbour
Wāw *Ar.* well
Webi *Amh.* river
Wes *Afr.* west, western
Wielka, Wielki, Wielko *Pol.* big, large
Woestyn *Afr.* desert
Wysoka, Wysoki *Pol.* upper
Wyżyna *Pol.* plateau

Xi *Chin.* river
Xia *Chin.* gorge, strait
Xiao *Chin.* small

Yam *Heb.* sea
-Yama *Jap.* mountain
-yan *Chin.* gorge, island
Yang *Chin.* bay, sea, sound
Yangi *Russ.* new
Yazovir *Bulg.* reservoir
Yeni *Turk.* new
Yli *Fin.* upper
Ynys *Welsh* island
Yoma *Burm.* mountain range
Ytre-, Ytter- *Nor., Swe.* outer
-yuan *Chin.* stream
Yugo- *Ser.-Cr.* south, southern
Yunhe *Chin.* canal
Yuzhni, Yuzhno *Russ.* south, southern

-Zaki *Jap.* point
Zalew *Pol.* lagoon, swamp
Zaliv *Russ.* bay, gulf
-Zan *Jap.* mountain
Zangbo *Tib.* stream, river
Zapadnaya, Zapadno, Zapadnyi (Zap.) *Russ.* west, western
Zatoka *Pol., Ukr.* bay, gulf
-zee *Dut.* lake, sea
Zemlya *Russ.* land, island(s)
Zhang *Chin.* mountain
-zhou *Chin.* island
Zhong *Chin.* middle, central
Zhou *Chin.* island
Zizhiqu *Chin.* autonomous region
Zuid, Zuider *Dut.* south, southern

INDEX TO WORLD MAPS

HOW TO USE THE INDEX

The index contains the names of all the principal places and features shown on the World and City Maps. Each name is followed by an additional entry in italics giving the country or region within which it is located. The alphabetical order of names composed of two or more words is governed primarily by the first word, then by the second, and then by the country or region name that follows. This is an example of the rule:

Mir *Niger*	14°5N 11°59E	**259** F2
Mīr Kūh *Iran*	26°22N 58°55E	**247** E8
Mīr Shahdād *Iran*	26°15N 58°29E	**247** E8
Mira *Italy*	45°26N 12°8E	**199** C9

Physical features composed of a proper name (Erie) and a description (Lake) are positioned alphabetically by the proper name. The description is positioned after the proper name and is usually abbreviated:

Erie, L. *N. Amer.*	42°15N 81°0W	**312** D4

Where a description forms part of a settlement or administrative name, however, it is always written in full and put in its true alphabetical position:

Mount Olive *U.S.A.*	39°4N 89°44W	**310** E7

Names beginning with M' and Mc are indexed as if they were spelled Mac. Names beginning St. are alphabetized under Saint, but Sankt, Sint, Sant', Santa and San are all spelt in full and are alphabetized accordingly. If the same place name occurs two or more times in the index and all are in the same country, each is followed by the name of the administrative subdivision in which it is located.

The geographical co-ordinates which follow each name in the index give the latitude and longitude of each place. The first co-ordinate indicates latitude – the distance north or south of the Equator. The second co-ordinate indicates longitude – the distance east or west of the Greenwich Meridian. Both latitude and longitude are measured in degrees and minutes (there are 60 minutes in a degree). Latitude and longitude references are not used on the Central Area City Maps.

The latitude is followed by N(orth) or S(outh) and the longitude by E(ast) or W(est).

The number in bold type which follows the geographical co-ordinates refers to the number of the map page where that feature or place will be found. This is usually the largest scale at which the place or feature appears.

The letter and figure that are immediately after the page number give the grid square on the map page, within which the feature is situated. The letter represents the latitude and the figure the longitude. A lower-case letter immediately after the page number refers to an inset map on that page.

In some cases the feature itself may fall within the specified square, while the name is outside. This is usually the case only with features that are larger than a grid square.

Rivers are indexed to their mouths or confluences, and carry the symbol ➔ after their names. The following symbols are also used in the index: ■ country, ⧄ overseas territory or dependency, ▢ first-order administrative area, △ national park, ⌓ other park (provincial park, nature reserve or game reserve), ✈ (LHR) principal airport (and location identifier).

HOW TO PRONOUNCE PLACE NAMES

English-speaking people usually have no difficulty in reading and pronouncing correctly English place names. However, foreign place name pronunciations may present many problems. Such problems can be minimized by following some simple rules. However, these rules cannot be applied to all situations, and there will be many exceptions.

1. In general, stress each syllable equally, unless your experience suggests otherwise.
2. Pronounce the letter 'a' as a broad 'a' as in 'arm'.
3. Pronounce the letter 'e' as a short 'e' as in 'elm'.
4. Pronounce the letter 'i' as a cross between a short 'i' and long 'e', as the two 'i's in 'California'.
5. Pronounce the letter 'o' as an intermediate 'o' as in 'soft'.
6. Pronounce the letter 'u' as an intermediate 'u' as in 'sure'.
7. Pronounce consonants hard, except in the Romance-language areas where 'g's are likely to be pronounced softly like 'j' in 'jam'; 'j' itself may be pronounced as 'y'; and 'x's may be pronounced as 'h'.
8. For names in mainland China, pronounce 'q' like the 'ch' in 'chin', 'x' like the 'sh' in 'she', 'zh' like the 'j' in 'jam', and 'z' as if it were spelled 'dz'. In general, pronounce 'a' as in 'father', 'e' as in 'but', 'i' as in 'keep', 'o' as in 'or', and 'u' as in 'rule'.

Moreover, English has no diacritical marks (accent and pronunciation signs), although some languages do. The following is a brief and general guide to the pronunciation of those most frequently used in the principal Western European languages.

		Pronunciation as in
French	é	day and shows that the 'e' is to be pronounced; e.g. Orléans.
	è	mare
	î	used over any vowel and does not affect pronunciation; shows contraction of the name, usually omission of 's' following a vowel.
	ç	's' before 'a', 'o' and 'u'.
	ë, ï, ü	over 'e', 'i' and 'u' when they are used with another vowel and shows that each is to be pronounced.
German	ä	fate
	ö	fur
	ü	no English equivalent; like French 'tu'.
Italian	à, é	over vowels and indicates stress.
Portuguese	ã, õ	vowels pronounced nasally.
	ç	boss
	á	shows stress.
	ô	shows that a vowel has an 'i' or 'u' sound combined with it.
Spanish	ñ	canyon
	ü	pronounced as 'w' and separately from adjoining vowels.
	á	usually indicates that this is a stressed vowel.

ABBREVIATIONS

A.C.T. – Australian Capital Territory	*El Salv.* – El Salvador	*Man.* – Manitoba	*Okla.* – Oklahoma	*Sask.* – Saskatchewan
A.R. – Autonomous Region	*Eq. Guin.* – Equatorial Guinea	*Mass.* – Massachusetts	*Ont.* – Ontario	*Scot.* – Scotland
Afghan. – Afghanistan	*Est.* – Estrecho	*Md.* – Maryland	*Or.* – Orientale	*Sd.* – Sound
Afr. – Africa	*Falk. Is.* – Falkland Is.	*Me.* – Maine	*Oreg.* – Oregon	*Sev.* – Severnaya
Ala. – Alabama	*Fd.* – Fjord	*Medit. S.* – Mediterranean Sea	*Os.* – Ostrov	*Sib.* – Siberia
Alta. – Alberta	*Fla.* – Florida	*Mich.* – Michigan	*Oz.* – Ozero	*Sprs.* – Springs
Amer. – America(n)	*Fr.* – French	*Minn.* – Minnesota	*P.* – Pass, Passo, Pasul, Pulau	*St.* – Saint
Ant. – Antilles	*G.* – Golfe, Golfo, Gulf, Guba, Gebel	*Miss.* – Mississippi	*P.E.I.* – Prince Edward Island	*Sta.* – Santa
Arch. – Archipelago		*Mo.* – Missouri	*Pa.* – Pennsylvania	*Ste.* – Sainte
Ariz. – Arizona	*Ga.* – Georgia	*Mont.* – Montana	*Pac. Oc.* – Pacific Ocean	*Sto.* – Santo
Ark. – Arkansas	*Gt.* – Great, Greater	*Mozam.* – Mozambique	*Papua N.G.* – Papua New Guinea	*Str.* – Strait, Stretto
Atl. Oc. – Atlantic Ocean	*Guinea-Biss.* – Guinea-Bissau	*Mt.(s)* – Mont, Montaña, Mountain	*Pass.* – Passage	*Switz.* – Switzerland
B. – Baie, Bahía, Bay, Bucht, Bugt	*H.K.* – Hong Kong	*Mte.* – Monte	*Peg.* – Pegunungan	*Tas.* – Tasmania
B.C. – British Columbia	*H.P.* – Himachal Pradesh	*Mti.* – Monti	*Pen.* – Peninsula, Péninsule	*Tenn.* – Tennessee
Bangla. – Bangladesh	*Hants.* – Hampshire	*N.* – Nord, Norte, North, Northern, Nouveau, Nahal, Nahr	*Phil.* – Philippines	*Terr.* – Territory, Territoire
Barr. – Barrage	*Harb.* – Harbor, Harbour		*Pk.* – Peak	*Tex.* – Texas
Bos.-H. – Bosnia-Herzegovina	*Hd.* – Head	*N.B.* – New Brunswick	*Plat.* – Plateau	*Tg.* – Tanjung
C. – Cabo, Cap, Cape, Coast	*Hts.* – Heights	*N.C.* – North Carolina	*Prov.* – Province, Provincial	*Trin. & Tob.* – Trinidad & Tobago
C.A.R. – Central African Republic	*I.(s).* – Île, Ilha, Insel, Isla, Island, Isle	*N. Cal.* – New Caledonia	*Pt.* – Point	*U.A.E.* – United Arab Emirates
C. Prov. – Cape Province		*N. Dak.* – North Dakota	*Pta.* – Ponta, Punta	*U.K.* – United Kingdom
Calif. – California	*Ill.* – Illinois	*N.H.* – New Hampshire	*Pte.* – Pointe	*U.S.A.* – United States of America
Cat. – Catarata	*Ind.* – Indiana	*N.I.* – North Island	*Qué.* – Québec	*Ut. P.* – Uttar Pradesh
Cent. – Central	*Ind. Oc.* – Indian Ocean	*N.J.* – New Jersey	*Queens.* – Queensland	*Va.* – Virginia
Chan. – Channel	*Ivory C.* – Ivory Coast	*N. Mex.* – New Mexico	*R.* – Rio, River	*Vdkhr.* – Vodokhranilishche
Colo. – Colorado	*J.* – Jabal, Jebel	*N.S.* – Nova Scotia	*R.I.* – Rhode Island	*Vdskh.* – Vodoskhovyshche
Conn. – Connecticut	*Jaz.* – Jazīrah	*N.S.W.* – New South Wales	*Ra.* – Range	*Vf.* – Vírful
Cord. – Cordillera	*Junc.* – Junction	*N.W.T.* – North West Territory	*Raj.* – Rajasthan	*Vic.* – Victoria
Cr. – Creek	*K.* – Kap, Kapp	*N.Y.* – New York	*Recr.* – Recreational, Récréatif	*Vol.* – Volcano
Czech. – Czech Republic	*Kans.* – Kansas	*N.Z.* – New Zealand	*Reg.* – Region	*Vt.* – Vermont
D.C. – District of Columbia	*Kep.* – Kepulauan	*Nac.* – Nacional	*Rep.* – Republic	*W.* – Wadi, West
Del. – Delaware	*Ky.* – Kentucky	*Nat.* – National	*Res.* – Reserve, Reservoir	*W. Va.* – West Virginia
Dem. – Democratic	*L.* – Lac, Lacul, Lago, Lagoa, Lake, Limni, Loch, Lough	*Nebr.* – Nebraska	*Rhld-Pfz.* – Rheinland-Pfalz	*Wall. & F. Is.* – Wallis and Futuna Is.
Dep. – Dependency		*Neths.* – Netherlands	*S.* – South, Southern, Sur	*Wash.* – Washington
Des. – Desert	*La.* – Louisiana	*Nev.* – Nevada	*Si. Arabia* – Saudi Arabia	*Wis.* – Wisconsin
Dét. – Détroit	*Ld.* – Land	*Nfld & L.* – Newfoundland and Labrador	*S.C.* – South Carolina	*Wlkp.* – Wielkopolski
Dist. – District	*Liech.* – Liechtenstein		*S. Dak.* – South Dakota	*Wyo.* – Wyoming
Dj. – Djebel	*Lux.* – Luxembourg	*Nic.* – Nicaragua	*S.I.* – South Island	*Yorks.* – Yorkshire
Dom. Rep. – Dominican Republic	*Mad. P.* – Madhya Pradesh	*O.* – Oued, Ouadi	*S. Leone* – Sierra Leone	
E. – East	*Madag.* – Madagascar	*Occ.* – Occidentale	*Sa.* – Serra, Sierra	

A

A 'Âli an Nîl □ *Sudan* 9°30N 33°0E **257** F3
A Baña *Spain* 42°58N 8°46W **194** C2
A Cañiza *Spain* 42°13N 8°16W **194** C2
A Estrada *Spain* 42°43N 8°27W **194** C2
A Fonsagrada *Spain* 43°8N 7°4W **194** B3
A Guarda *Spain* 41°56N 8°52W **194** D2
A Gudiña *Spain* 42°4N 7°8W **194** C3
A Rúa *Spain* 42°24N 7°6W **194** C3
Aabenraa *Denmark* 55°3N 9°25E **163** J3
Aabybro *Denmark* 57°10N 9°44E **163** G3
Aachen *Germany* 50°45N 6°6E **178** E2
Aalâm *Iraq* 33°19N 44°23E **113** B2
Aalborg *Denmark* 57°2N 9°54E **163** G3
Aalborg Bugt *Denmark* 56°48N 10°35E **163** H3
Aalen *Germany* 48°51N 10°6E **179** G6
Aalestrup *Denmark* 56°42N 9°29E **163** H3
Aalsmeer *Neths.* **112** B
Aalst *Belgium* 50°56N 4°2E **170** C4
Aalten *Neths.* 51°56N 6°35E **170** C4
Aalter *Belgium* 51°5N 3°28E **170** C3
Äänekoski *Finland* 62°36N 25°44E **160** E21
Aarau *Switz.* 47°23N 8°4E **179** H4
Aarberg *Switz.* 47°2N 7°16E **179** H3
Aare → *Switz.* 47°33N 8°14E **179** H4
Aargau □ *Switz.* 47°26N 8°10E **179** H4
Aarhus = Århus *Denmark* 56°8N 10°11E **163** H4
Aarlen = Arlon *Belgium* 49°42N 5°49E **170** E5
Aars *Denmark* 56°48N 9°30E **163** H3
Aarschot *Belgium* 50°59N 4°49E **170** D4
Aasiaat *Greenland* 68°43N 52°56W **154** C5
Ab-i-Istada □ *Afghan.* 32°29N 67°55E **240** B3
Ab-i-Panja = Pyandzh →
    Asia 37°6N 68°20E **240** A2
Aba *Sichuan, China* 32°59N 101°42E **228** A3
Aba *Dem. Rep. of the Congo* 5°10N 30°17E **268** B3
Aba *Nigeria* 5°10N 7°19E **263** D6
Âbâ, Jazîrat *Sudan* 13°30N 32°31E **257** E3
Abacaxis → *Brazil* 3°54S 58°47W **329** D6
Abaco I. *Bahamas* 26°25N 77°10W **320** A4
Abadab, J. *Sudan* 18°54N 35°56E **256** D4
Âbâdân *Iran* 30°22N 48°20E **247** D6
Abade *Ethiopia* 9°22N 38°3E **257** F4
Âbâdeh *Iran* 31°8N 52°40E **247** C7
Abadin *Spain* 43°21N 7°29W **194** B3
Abadla *Algeria* 31°2N 2°45W **261** B4
Abaeté *Brazil* 19°9S 45°27W **333** E2
Abaeté → *Brazil* 18°2S 45°12W **333** E2
Abaetetuba *Brazil* 1°40S 48°50W **332** B2
Abagnar Qi = Xilinhot
    China 43°52N 116°2E **226** C9
Abah, Tanjung
    Indonesia 8°46S 115°38E **231** K18
Abai *Paraguay* 25°58S 55°54W **335** B4
Abak *Nigeria* 4°58N 7°50E **263** D6
Abakaliki *Nigeria* 6°22N 8°2E **263** D6
Abakan *Russia* 53°40N 91°10E **217** D11
Abala *Congo* 1°17S 15°35E **264** C3
Abala *Niger* 14°56N 3°22E **263** C5
Abalak *Niger* 15°22N 6°21E **263** B6
Abalemma *Algeria* 20°51N 5°59E **261** D6
Abalemma *Niger* 16°12N 7°50E **263** B6
Abalessa *Algeria* 22°58N 4°47E **261** D5
Abana *Turkey* 41°59N 34°1E **212** B6
Abancay *Peru* 13°35S 72°55W **330** C3
Abanga → *Gabon* 0°20S 10°30E **264** C2
Abano Terme *Italy* 45°22N 11°46E **199** C8
Abapó *Bolivia* 18°48S 63°25W **331** D5
Abarán *Spain* 38°12N 1°23W **197** G3
Abariringa *Kiribati* 2°50S 171°40W **277** A16
Abarqú *Iran* 31°10N 53°20E **247** D7
Abashiri *Japan* 44°0N 144°15E **220** B12
Abashiri-Wan *Japan* 44°0N 144°30E **220** C12
Abau *Papua N. G.* 10°11S 148°46E **286** F5
Abaújszántó *Hungary* 48°16N 21°12E **182** B6
Abava → *Latvia* 57°6N 21°54E **184** A8
Âbay = Nîl el Azraq →
    Sudan 15°38N 32°31E **257** D3
Abay *Kazakhstan* 49°38N 72°53E **217** C8
Abaya, L. *Ethiopia* 6°30N 37°50E **257** F4
Abaza *Russia* 52°39N 90°6E **217** B12
Abba *C.A.R.* 5°20N 15°11E **264** A3
Abbadia di Fiastra △
    Italy 43°12N 13°24E **199** E10
Abbadia San Salvatore
    Italy 42°53N 11°41E **199** F8
'Abbâsâbâd *Iran* 33°34N 58°23E **247** C8
Abbay = Nîl el Azraq →
    Sudan 15°38N 32°31E **257** D3
Abbaye, Pt. *U.S.A.* 46°58N 88°8W **308** B9
Abbazia = Opatija
    Croatia 45°21N 14°17E **199** C11
Abbé, L. *Ethiopia* 11°8N 41°47E **257** E5
Abbeville *Somme, France* 50°6N 1°49E **173** B8
Abbeville *Ala., U.S.A.* 31°34N 85°15W **316** D4
Abbeville *Ga., U.S.A.* 31°59N 83°18W **316** D6
Abbeville *La., U.S.A.* 29°58N 92°8W **314** G8
Abbeville *S.C., U.S.A.* 34°11N 82°23W **316** A7
Abbey Wood *U.K.* 51°29N 0°7E **125** B4
Abbeyfeale *Ireland* 52°23N 9°18W **166** D2
Abbiategrasso *Italy* 45°24N 8°54E **198** C5
Abbot Ice Shelf *Antarctica* 73°0S 92°0W **151** D16
Abbotsford *Canada* 49°5N 122°20W **296** D4
Abbottabad *Pakistan* 34°10N 73°15E **242** B5
Abbou, O. Ben *Algeria* 28°32N 5°14E **261** C5
ABC Islands = Netherlands
    Antilles □ *W. Indies* 12°15N 69°0W **328** A4
Abcoude *Neths.* 52°17N 4°59E **112** B2
Abd al Kûrî *Yemen* 12°5N 52°20E **249** D6
Âbdar *Iran* 30°16N 55°19E **247** D7
'Âbdîn *Iran* 30°2N 31°14E **117** A2
'Abdolâbâd *Iran* 34°12N 56°30E **247** C8
Abdulpur *Russia* 53°42N 53°40E **216** B4
Abdulpur *Bangla.* 24°15N 88°59E **244** C2
Abéché *Chad* 13°50N 20°35E **259** F4
Abejar *Spain* 41°48N 2°47W **196** D2
Abekr *Sudan* 12°45N 28°50E **257** E2
Abel Tasman △ *N.Z.* 40°59S 173°3E **285** A8
Abengourou *Ivory C.* 6°42N 3°27W **262** D4
Abeno *Japan* 34°38N 135°31E **133** B2
Abenójar *Spain* 38°53N 4°21W **195** G6
Äbenrå = Aabenraa
    Denmark 55°3N 9°25E **163** J3
Abensberg *Germany* 48°48N 11°51E **179** G7
Abeokuta *Nigeria* 7°3N 3°19E **263** D5
Aber *Uganda* 2°12N 32°25E **268** B3
Aberaeron *U.K.* 52°15N 4°15W **169** E3
Aberayron = Aberaeron
    U.K. 52°15N 4°15W **169** E3
Aberchirder *U.K.* 57°34N 2°37W **167** D6
Abercorn = Mbala *Zambia* 8°46S 31°24E **269** D3
Abercrombie River △
    Australia 34°5S 149°40E **283** B4
Aberdare *U.K.* 51°43N 3°27W **169** F4
Aberdare △ *Kenya* 0°35S 36°44E **268** C4
Aberdare Ra. *Kenya* 0°15S 36°50E **268** C4
Aberdeen *N.S.W.,*
    Australia 32°9S 150°56E **283** B9

Aberdeen *Sask., Canada* 52°20N 106°8W **297** C7
Aberdeen *Hong Kong,*
    China 22°14N 114°8E **122** B1
Aberdeen *Eastern Cape,*
    S. Africa 32°28S 24°2E **270** C3
Aberdeen *C. of Aberd., U.K.* 57°9N 2°5W **167** D6
Aberdeen *Idaho, U.S.A.* 42°57N 112°50W **304** E7
Aberdeen *Md., U.S.A.* 39°31N 76°10W **309** F15
Aberdeen *Miss., U.S.A.* 33°49N 88°33W **315** E10
Aberdeen *Ohio, U.S.A.* 38°39N 83°46W **311** F13
Aberdeen *S. Dak., U.S.A.* 45°28N 98°29W **306** C5
Aberdeen *Wash., U.S.A.* 46°59N 123°50W **306** D3
Aberdeen, City of □ *U.K.* 57°10N 2°10W **167** D6
Aberdeenshire □ *U.K.* 57°17N 2°36W **167** D6
Aberdour *U.K.* 56°3N 3°18W **121** A2
Aberdour Castle *U.K.* 56°3N 3°18W **121** A2
Aberdovey = Aberdyfi
    U.K. 52°33N 4°3W **169** E3
Aberdyfi *U.K.* 52°33N 4°3W **169** E3
Aberfeldy *U.K.* 56°37N 3°51W **167** E5
Aberfoyle *U.K.* 56°11N 4°23W **167** E4
Abergavenny *U.K.* 51°49N 3°1W **169** F4
Abergele *U.K.* 53°17N 3°35W **168** D4
Abernathy *U.S.A.* 33°50N 101°51W **314** E4
Aberystwyth *U.K.* 52°25N 4°5W **169** E3
Abfanggraben →
    Germany 48°10N 11°41E **131** A2
Abhā *Si. Arabia* 18°0N 42°34E **248** C3
Abhar *Iran* 36°9N 49°13E **213** D13
Abhayapuri *India* 26°24N 90°38E **241** B3
Abia □ *Nigeria* 5°30N 7°35E **263** D6
Abidiya *Sudan* 18°18N 34°3E **256** D3
Abidjan *Ivory C.* 5°26N 3°58W **262** D4
Abilene *Kans., U.S.A.* 38°55N 97°13W **308** F5
Abilene *Tex., U.S.A.* 32°28N 99°43W **314** E5
Abingdon *Oxon., U.K.* 51°40N 1°17W **169** F6
Abingdon *Ill., U.S.A.* 40°48N 90°24W **310** D8
Abingdon *Va., U.S.A.* 36°43N 81°59W **309** G13
Abingdon, I. = Pinta, I.
    Ecuador 0°35N 90°44W **330** a
Abington Reef *Australia* 18°0S 149°35E **280** B4
Abitau → *Canada* 59°53N 109°3W **297** B7
Abitibi → *Canada* 51°3N 80°55W **298** B3
Abitibi, L. *Canada* 48°40N 79°40W **304** E3
Abiy Adi *Ethiopia* 13°39N 39°3E **257** E4
Abiyata, L. *Ethiopia* 7°37N 38°36E **257** F4
Abiyata-Shala △ *Ethiopia* 7°40N 38°37E **257** F4
Abkhaz Republic = Abkhazia □
    Georgia 43°12N 41°5E **191** J5
Abkhazia □ *Georgia* 43°12N 41°5E **191** J5
Ablon-sur-Seine *France* 48°43N 2°25E **134** B3
Abminga *Australia* 26°8S 134°51E **281** D1
Abnûb *Egypt* 27°18N 31°4E **256** B3
Âbo = Turku *Finland* 60°30N 22°19E **188** B2
Abo, Massif d' *Chad* 21°41N 16°8E **259** D3
Abocho *Nigeria* 7°35N 6°56E **263** D6
Abohar *India* 30°10N 74°10E **242** D6
Aboisso *Ivory C.* 5°30N 3°5W **262** D4
Abolo *Congo* 0°8N 14°16E **264** B2
Abomey *Benin* 7°10N 2°5E **263** D5
Abong-Mbang *Cameroon* 4°0N 13°8E **264** B2
Abongabong *Indonesia* 4°15N 96°48E **234** B1
Abonnema *Nigeria* 4°41N 6°49E **263** E6
Abony *Hungary* 47°12N 20°3E **182** C5
Abor Hills *India* 28°25N 94°46E **241** A5
Aborlan *Phil.* 9°26N 118°33E **233** G2
Aboso *Ghana* 5°23N 1°57W **262** D4
Abou-Deïa *Chad* 11°20N 19°20E **259** F3
Abou-Goulem *Chad* 13°37N 21°38E **259** F4
Abou-Telfan △ *Chad* 12°2N 18°58E **259** F3
Aboyne *U.K.* 57°4N 2°47W **167** D6
Abra → *Phil.* 17°35N 120°45E **232** C3
Abra de Ilog *Phil.* 13°27N 120°4E **232** E3
Abra Pampa *Argentina* 22°43S 65°42W **334** A2
Abraham L. *Canada* 52°15N 116°35W **296** C5
Abramtsevo *Russia* 56°14N 37°58E **137** A5
Abreojos, Pta. *Mexico* 26°50N 113°40W **318** B2
Abri *North Kordofân, Sudan* 20°50N 30°27E **256** C3
Abri *Junub Kordofân, Sudan* 11°40N 30°21E **257** E3
Abrolhos, Banco *Brazil* 18°0S 38°30W **333** D4
Abrud *Romania* 46°19N 23°5E **182** D8
Abruzzo □ *Italy* 42°15N 14°0E **199** F10
Absaroka Range *U.S.A.* 44°45N 109°50W **304** D9
Abtenau *Austria* 47°33N 13°21E **180** D6
Abu *India* 24°41N 72°50E **242** G5
Abû al Abyad *U.A.E.* 24°11N 53°50E **247** E7
Abû al Khaşîb *Iraq* 30°25N 48°0E **247** D6
Abû 'Alî *Si. Arabia* 27°20N 49°27E **247** D6
Abû 'Alî → *Lebanon* 34°25N 35°50E **250** C2
Abû 'Arîsh *Si. Arabia* 16°53N 42°48E **248** C3
Abû 'Aweigîla *Egypt* 30°50N 34°7E **251** H5
Abu Ballas *Egypt* 24°26N 27°36E **256** C2
Abu Deleiq *Sudan* 15°57N 33°48E **257** D3
Abu Dhabi = Abû Z̧aby
    U.A.E. 24°28N 54°22E **247** E7
Abu Dis *Sudan* 19°12N 33°38E **256** D3
Abu Dis *West Bank* 31°46N 35°16E **123** B2
Abu Dom *Sudan* 16°18N 32°25E **257** D3
Abû Du'ân *Syria* 36°25N 38°15E **213** D8
Abû el Gaïn, W. → *Egypt* 29°35N 33°30E **251** J4
Abu Fatma, Ras *Sudan* 22°25N 36°56E **256** C4
Abû Gabra *Sudan* 11°2N 26°50E **257** E2
Abu Ga'da, W. → *Egypt* 29°15N 32°53E **251** J3
Abu Gelba *Sudan* 13°11N 31°52E **257** E3
Abu Ghosh *Israel* 31°48N 35°6E **123** B1
Abu Gubeiha *Sudan* 11°30N 31°15E **257** E3
Abu Habl, Khawr →
    Sudan 12°37N 31°0E **257** E3
Abû Ḩadrîyah *Si. Arabia* 27°20N 48°58E **247** E6
Abu Hamed *Sudan* 19°32N 33°13E **256** D3
Abu Haraz *An Nîl al Azraq,*
    Sudan 18°1N 33°58E **256** D3
Abu Haraz *El Gezira,*
    Sudan 14°35N 33°30E **257** E3
Abu Haraz Esh Shamâliya,
    Sudan 19°8N 32°18E **256** D3
Abû Ḩigar *Sudan* 12°50N 33°59E **257** E3
Abu Kebir *Egypt* 30°43N 31°40E **251** H2
Abu Kuleiwat *Sudan* 10°47N 29°32E **268** B2
Abû Madd, Ra's *Si. Arabia* 24°50N 37°7E **246** E3
Abu Matariq *Sudan* 10°59N 26°9E **257** E2
Abû Mendi *Ethiopia* 11°48N 35°42E **257** E4
Abû Mûsá *U.A.E.* 25°52N 55°3E **247** E8
Abû Nûjaym *Libya* 30°35N 15°24E **258** B3
Abû Qaşr *Si. Arabia* 31°18N 30°0E **246** D2
Abu Qireiya *Sudan* 24°5N 35°28E **256** C4
Abû Qurqâş *Egypt* 28°1N 30°44E **256** B3
Abû Raşaş, Ra's *Oman* 20°10N 58°38E **249** B7
Abu Rudeis *Egypt* 28°54N 33°11E **251** K4
Abu Shagara, Ras *Sudan* 21°4N 37°19E **256** C4
Abû Shanab *Junub Kordofân,*
    Sudan 10°47N 29°32E **268** B2
Abû Shanab *Shamâl Kordofân,*
    Sudan 13°18N 27°49E **256** E2
Abu Simbel *Egypt* 22°31N 31°40E **256** C3

Abû Şukhayr *Iraq* 31°54N 44°30E **213** G11
Abu Sultân *Egypt* 30°24N 32°21E **256** H8
Abu Tabari *Sudan* 17°32N 28°30E **256** D2
Abu Tig *Egypt* 27°4N 31°15E **256** B3
Abu Tineitin *Sudan* 14°24N 31°1E **257** E3
Abû Uruq *Sudan* 15°52N 30°25E **257** D3
Abû Zabad *Sudan* 12°25N 29°10E **257** E2
Abû Zeydâbâd *Iran* 33°54N 51°45E **247** C6
Abufari *Brazil* 5°22S 62°59W **331** B5
Abuja *Nigeria* 9°5N 7°32E **263** D6
Abukuma-Gawa →
    Japan 38°6N 140°52E **220** E10
Abukuma-Sammyaku
    Japan 37°30N 140°45E **220** F10
Abulug *Phil.* 18°27N 121°27E **232** B3
Abumombazi
    Dem. Rep. of the Congo 3°42N 22°10E **264** B4
Abunã *Brazil* 9°40S 65°20W **331** B4
Abunã → *Brazil* 9°41S 65°20W **331** B4
Abune Yosef *Ethiopia* 12°5N 39°12E **257** E4
Aburatsu *Japan* 31°34N 131°24E **222** D3
Abut Hd. *N.Z.* 43°7S 170°15E **285** D5
Abuye Meda *Ethiopia* 10°30N 39°49E **257** E4
Abuyog *Phil.* 10°45N 125°0E **233** F5
Abybro *Sweden* 9°2N 32°14E **257** F3
Aby, Lagune *Ivory C.* 5°15N 3°14W **262** D4
Abyad *Sudan* 13°47N 26°24E **257** E2
Acacías *Colombia* 3°59N 73°46W **328** C3
Acacias *Madrid, Spain* 40°24N 3°42W **127** C2
Acadia □ *U.S.A.* 44°20N 68°13W **309** C19
Açailândia *Brazil* 5°0S 47°30W **332** C2
Acámbaro *Mexico* 20°2N 100°44W **318** D4
Acanthus *Greece* 40°27N 23°47E **202** F7
Acaponeta *Mexico* 22°30N 105°22W **318** C3
Acapulco *Mexico* 16°51N 99°55W **319** D5
Acapulco Trench *Pac. Oc.* 15°0N 98°0W **320** D2
Acará *Brazil* 1°57S 48°11W **332** B2
Acarai, Serra *Brazil* 1°50N 57°50W **329** C6
Acaraú *Brazil* 2°53S 40°7W **332** B3
Acaraú → *Brazil* 6°31S 36°30W **332** C4
Acari *Peru* 15°25S 74°36W **330** D3
Acariguá *Venezuela* 9°33N 69°12W **328** B4
Acassuso *Argentina* 34°29S 58°30W **117** A2
Acatlán *Mexico* 18°12N 98°3W **319** D5
Acayucán *Mexico* 17°57N 94°55W **319** D6
Accéglio *Italy* 44°28N 7°0E **198** D4
Accomac *U.S.A.* 37°43N 75°40W **309** G16
Accotink, L. *U.S.A.* 38°47N 77°13W **143** C2
Accotink Cr. → *U.S.A.* 38°51N 77°15W **143** B2
Accous *France* 43°0N 0°36W **174** E3
Accra *Ghana* 5°35N 0°6W **263** D4
Accrington *U.K.* 53°45N 2°22W **168** D5
Acebal *Argentina* 33°20S 60°50W **334** C3
Aceh □ *Indonesia* 4°15N 97°30E **234** B1
Acerra *Italy* 40°57N 14°22E **201** B7
Aceuchal *Spain* 38°39N 6°30W **195** G4
Achacachi *Bolivia* 16°3S 68°43W **330** D4
Achaguas *Venezuela* 7°46N 68°14W **328** B4
Achaia □ *Greece* 38°5N 21°45E **204** C3
Achao *Chile* 42°28S 73°30W **336** B2
Acharnes *Greece* 38°5N 23°44E **204** C5
Achegour *Niger* 19°10N 11°54E **259** E2
Acheloos → *Greece* 38°19N 21°7E **204** C3
Achelouma *Niger* 22°12N 12°50E **259** D2
Achelouma, E. → *Niger* 21°55N 13°35E **259** D2
Acheng *China* 45°30N 126°58E **227** B14
Achenkirch *Austria* 47°32N 11°45E **180** D4
Achensee *Austria* 47°26N 11°45E **180** D4
Achentrias *Greece* 34°59N 25°13E **205** D7
Acher *India* 23°10N 72°32E **242** H5
Achères *France* 48°57N 2°3E **134** A3
Achern *Germany* 48°37N 8°4E **179** G4
Acheron → *N.Z.* 42°16S 173°4E **285** C8
Achill Hd. *Ireland* 53°58N 10°15W **166** C1
Achill I. *Ireland* 53°58N 10°1W **166** C1
Achim *Germany* 53°1N 9°3E **178** B5
Achinsk *Russia* 56°20N 90°20E **215** D10
Achladokambos *Greece* 37°31N 22°35E **204** D4
Achouka *Gabon* 0°52S 9°45E **264** C2
Acıgöl *Turkey* 37°50N 29°50E **205** D11
Acıpayam *Turkey* 37°26N 29°22E **205** D11
Acireale *Italy* 37°37N 15°10E **201** F8
Ackerman *U.S.A.* 33°19N 89°11W **315** E10
Ackley *U.S.A.* 42°33N 93°3W **310** B3
Acklins I. *Bahamas* 22°30N 74°0W **321** B5
Acme *Alta., Canada* 51°33N 113°30W **296** C6
Acme *Pa., U.S.A.* 40°8N 79°26W **312** F5
Acobamba *Peru* 12°52S 74°3W **330** C3
Acomayo *Peru* 13°55S 71°39W **330** C3
Aconcagua, Cerro
    Argentina 32°39S 70°0W **334** C2
Aconquija, Mt. *Argentina* 27°0S 66°0W **334** B2
Açores, Is. dos *Atl. Oc.* 38°0N 27°0W **153** d1
Acorizal *Brazil* 15°12S 56°22W **331** D6
Acornhoek *S. Africa* 24°37S 31°2E **271** B5
Acoua *Mayotte* 12°43S 45°4E **272** b
Acquapendente *Italy* 42°44N 11°50E **199** F8
Acquasanta Terme *Italy* 42°46N 13°24E **199** F10
Acquasparta *Italy* 42°41N 12°33E **199** F9
Acquaviva delle Fonti
    Italy 40°54N 16°50E **201** B9
Acqui Terme *Italy* 44°41N 8°28E **198** D5
Acraman, L. *Australia* 32°2S 135°23E **281** E2
Acre = 'Akko *Israel* 32°55N 35°4E **250** F6
Acre □ *Brazil* 9°1S 71°0W **330** B3
Acre → *Brazil* 8°45S 67°22W **330** B4
Acri *Italy* 39°29N 16°23E **201** C9
Acropolis *Athens, Greece* **112** c2
Acs *Hungary* 47°42N 18°0E **182** C3
Actéon, Groupe
    French Polynesia 21°5S 136°30W **289** f
Actium *Greece* 38°57N 20°45E **207** B2
Acton *Ont., Canada* 43°38N 80°3W **312** C4
Acton *London, U.K.* 51°30N 0°16W **125** A2
Açu *Brazil* 5°34S 36°54W **332** C4
Açu, Pão de *Brazil* 22°26S 43°9W **135** B2
Acuã → *Brazil* 5°0S 43°30W **332** C3
Acuña *Argentina* 29°55S 57°58W **335** B1
Acworth *U.S.A.* 34°4N 84°41W **316** A1
Ad Dafinah *Si. Arabia* 23°18N 41°58E **248** B3
Ad Dafrah *U.A.E.* 23°21N 52°55E **247** E7
Ad Dahnā *Si. Arabia* 24°30N 48°10E **249** A5
Ad Dammām *Si. Arabia* 26°20N 50°5E **247** E6
Ad Dāmūr *Lebanon* 33°30N 35°27E **250** F6
Ad Darb *Si. Arabia* 18°2N 43°7E **248** C3
Ad Dawādimī *Si. Arabia* 24°35N 44°15E **248** B4
Ad Dawḩah *Qatar* 25°15N 51°35E **247** E6
Ad Dawr *Iraq* 34°27N 43°47E **213** E10
Ad Diffah = Libya 30°30N 24°30E **258** B4
Ad Dir'īyah *Si. Arabia* 24°44N 46°35E **248** B5
Ad Dīwānīyah *Iraq* 32°0N 45°0E **213** F11
Ad Dujayl *Iraq* 33°51N 44°14E **213** F11

Ad Duwayd *Si. Arabia* 30°15N 42°17E **246** D4
Adra □ *Algeria* 27°51N 0°11E **261** C4
Adrar □ *Algeria* 25°45N 1°0E **261** C5
Adrar *Mauritania* 20°30N 7°30W **260** D2
Adrar des Iforas *Africa* 19°40N 1°40E **261** D5
Adrar Madet *Niger* 18°54N 10°35E **259** E2
Adré *Chad* 13°40N 22°20E **259** F4
Âdria *Italy* 45°3N 12°3E **199** C9
Adrian *Ga., U.S.A.* 32°33N 82°35W **316** C7
Adrian *Mich., U.S.A.* 41°54N 84°2W **311** G12
Adrian *Mo., U.S.A.* 38°24N 94°21W **310** F2
Adrian *Tex., U.S.A.* 35°16N 102°40W **314** D3
Adrianople = Edirne
    Turkey 41°40N 26°34E **203** D10
Adriatic Sea *Medit. S.* 43°0N 16°0E **193** C7
Adua *Indonesia* 1°45S 129°50E **231** E7
Adung Long *Burma* 28°7N 97°42E **241** A6
Adur *India* 9°8N 76°40E **245** K3
Adwa *Ethiopia* 14°15N 38°52E **257** E4
Adygea □ *Russia* 45°0N 40°0E **191** H5
Adzhar Republic = Ajaria □
    Georgia 41°30N 42°0E **191** K6
Adzhikabul = Qazımämmäd
    Azerbaijan 40°3N 49°0E **191** K9
Adzopé *Ivory C.* 6°7N 3°49W **262** D4
Ægean Sea *Medit. S.* 38°30N 25°0E **205** C2
Aerhtai Shan *Mongolia* 46°40N 92°45E **217** C12
Ærø *Denmark* 54°52N 10°25E **163** K4
Ærøskøbing *Denmark* 54°53N 10°24E **163** K4
Aetos *Greece* 37°15N 21°50E **204** D3
Afaahiti *Tahiti* 17°45S 149°17W **289** e
Afabet *Eritrea* 16°51N 38°58E **257** D4
'Afak *Iraq* 32°4N 45°15E **213** F11
Afandou *Greece* 36°18N 28°12E **206** E12
Afar *Ethiopia* 12°0N 41°0E **257** E5
Afarag, Erg *Algeria* 23°50N 2°47E **261** D5
Afareaitu *Moorea* 17°33S 149°47W **289** e
Âfarnes *Norway* 62°40N 7°32E **164** B4
Afdega *Ethiopia* 6°4N 43°30E **267** C5
Affori *Italy* 45°31N 9°10E **129** A2
Affton *U.S.A.* 38°33N 90°20W **310** f6
Afghanistan ■ *Asia* 33°0N 65°0E **240** B2
Afgoi *Somali Rep.* 2°7N 44°59E **267** C5
'Afif *Si. Arabia* 23°53N 42°56E **248** B3
Afikpo *Nigeria* 5°53N 7°54E **263** D6
Aflandshage *Denmark* 55°33N 12°35E **118** B3
Aflisses, O. → *Algeria* 28°40N 0°50E **261** C5
Aflou *Algeria* 34°7N 2°3E **261** B5
Afmadu *Somali Rep.* 0°31N 42°4E **267** D5
Afogados da Ingàzeira
    Brazil 7°45S 37°39W **332** C4
Afognak I. *U.S.A.* 58°15N 152°30W **303** D9
Afono B. *Amer. Samoa* 14°15S 170°38W **302** f
Afore *Papua N. G.* 9°9S 148°23E **286** C5
Afragola *Italy* 40°55N 14°18E **201** B7
Afram → *Ghana* 7°0N 0°52W **263** D4
Afrera *Ethiopia* 13°16N 41°5E **257** E5
Africa 10°0N 20°0E **254** E6
'Afrīn *Syria* 36°32N 36°50E **250** B7
'Afrīn → *Syria* 36°20N 36°55E **250** B7
Afsarīyeh *Iran* 35°39N 51°30E **141** B2
Afşin *Turkey* 38°14N 36°55E **212** C7
Afton *Italy* 40°13N 16°44E **201** B9
Afton *Iowa, U.S.A.* 41°2N 94°12W **310** C2
Afton *N.Y., U.S.A.* 42°14N 75°32W **313** D9
Afton *Wyo., U.S.A.* 42°44N 110°56W **304** E8
Aftout *Algeria* 26°50N 3°45W **260** C4
Afuá *Brazil* 0°15S 50°20W **329** D7
'Afula *Israel* 32°37N 35°17E **250** F6
Afyon *Turkey* 38°45N 30°33E **205** C12
Afyon □ *Turkey* 38°45N 30°30E **205** C12
Afyonkarahisar = Afyon
    Turkey 38°45N 30°33E **205** C12
Aga *Egypt* 30°55N 31°10E **256** H7
Aga I. *Micronesia* 7°29N 151°43E **287** T18
Agadem *Niger* 16°50N 13°51E **259** E3
Agadès = Agadez *Niger* 16°58N 7°59E **259** E1
Agadez *Niger* 16°58N 7°59E **259** E1
Agadir *Morocco* 30°28N 9°55W **260** B3
Agadir *Morocco* 30°42N 9°0W **260** B3
Agaie *Nigeria* 9°1N 6°18E **263** D6
Agailâs *Mauritania* 22°37N 14°22E **260** D2
Agaïn *Sudan* 8°28N 29°5E **257** F3
Agalas *Greece* 37°44N 20°47E **207** B2
Agalega Is. *Mauritius* 11°0S 57°0E **273** F4
Agam *Guam* 13°28N 144°45E **302** a
Agana B. *Guam* 13°29N 144°45E **302** a
Aganjur *Turkey* 39°48N 30°47E **205** C12
Agar *India* 23°40N 76°2E **242** H7
Agar → *India* 21°0N 82°57E **244** D6
Agaro *Ethiopia* 7°50N 36°38E **257** F4
Agartala *India* 23°50N 91°23E **241** D2
Agăş *Romania* 46°28N 26°15E **183** D11
Agassiz *Canada* 49°14N 121°46W **296** D4
Agats *Indonesia* 5°33S 138°0E **231** F9
Agatti I. *India* 10°50N 72°12E **245** J1
Agawam *U.S.A.* 42°5N 72°37W **313** D12
Agawâm → *Italy* 45°9N 12°0E **199** C9
Agboville *Ivory C.* 5°55N 4°15W **262** D4
Agboyi Cr. → *Nigeria* 6°33N 3°24E **124** A2
Ağcabädi *Azerbaijan* 40°5N 47°27E **191** K8
Ağdam *Azerbaijan* 40°0N 46°58E **191** L8
Ağdaş *Azerbaijan* 40°44N 47°22E **191** K8
Agde *France* 43°19N 3°28E **174** E7
Agde, C. d' *France* 43°16N 3°28E **174** E7
Agdz *Morocco* 30°47N 6°30W **260** B3
Agdzhabedi = Ağcabädi
    Azerbaijan 40°5N 47°27E **191** K8
Agen *France* 44°12N 0°38E **174** D4
Ageo *Japan* 35°58N 139°36E **223** B11
Ager Tay *Chad* 20°0N 17°41E **259** E3
Agerbæk *Denmark* 55°36N 8°48E **163** J2
Agersø *Denmark* 55°13N 11°12E **163** J5
Agerup *Denmark* 55°43N 12°19E **118** A1
Ages *Sweden* 59°12N 18°6E **139** B2
Aggeneys *S. Africa* 29°12N 18°49E **270** D2
Ággtelek △ *Hungary* 48°31N 20°30E **182** B5
Âgh Kand *Iran* 37°15N 48°4E **213** D13
Aghagallon *U.K.* 54°35N 6°16W **166** B5
Aghaghallon *U.K.* 54°35N 6°16W **166** B5
Aghia Anna *Greece* 38°52N 23°24E **204** C5
Aghia Deka *Greece* 35°3N 24°58E **205** E7
Aghia Ekaterinis, Akra
    Greece 39°50N 19°50E **207** A3
Aghia Galini *Greece* 35°6N 24°41E **205** E7
Aghia Marina *Athina,*
    Greece 37°48N 23°51E **112** C1
Aghia Marina *Kasos,*
    Greece 35°27N 26°53E **205** E9
Aghia Marina *Leros,*
    Greece 37°11N 26°43E **206** E10
Aghia Paraskevi *Athina,*
    Greece 38°1N 23°49E **112** A2
Aghia Paraskevi *Voreio Aigaio,*
    Greece 39°14N 26°16E **206** C8
Aghia Roumeli *Greece* 35°15N 23°58E **205** E6
Aghia Varvara *Greece* 35°8N 25°1E **205** E7
Aghiasos *Greece* 39°5N 26°21E **206** C8
Aghio Theodori *Greece* 37°55N 23°9E **204** D5
Aghion Oros □ *Greece* 40°25N 24°6E **203** F8
Aghios Andreas *Greece* 37°21N 22°45E **204** D4

Aghios Dimitrios *Greece* 37°53N 23°44E **112** B2
Aghios Efimia *Greece* 38°18N 20°36E **207** C2
Aghios Efstratios *Greece* 39°34N 24°58E **206** D8
Aghios Georgios *Greece* 38°28N 23°57E **204** C5
Aghios Ioannis, Akra
    Greece 35°20N 25°40E **207** E6
Aghios Ioannis Rendis
    Greece 37°57N 23°39E **112** B1
Aghios Isidoros *Greece* 36°9N 27°51E **206** E11
Aghios Kirikos *Greece* 37°34N 26°17E **205** D8
Aghios Leon *Greece* 37°47N 20°43E **207** B2
Aghios Matheos *Greece* 39°30N 19°47E **206** C4
Aghios Mironas *Greece* 35°15N 25°1E **207** E6
Aghios Nikolaos *Etoloakarnania,*
    Greece 38°52N 20°48E **207** B2
Aghios Nikolaos *Kriti,*
    Greece 35°11N 25°41E **207** E6
Aghios Nikolaos *Lefkada,*
    Greece 38°36N 20°34E **207** B2
Aghios Oros = Athos
    Greece 40°9N 24°22E **203** F8
Aghios Petros *Greece* 38°39N 20°33E **207** B2
Aghios Thekli *Greece* 38°15N 20°23E **207** C1
Aghios Thomas *Greece* 38°58N 24°7E **207** B2
Aghiou Orous, Kolpos
    Greece 40°6N 24°0E **202** F7
Aghireşu *Romania* 46°53N 23°15E **183** D8
Aghoueyyit *Mauritania* 21°10N 15°56W **260** D1
Aghreïjît *Mauritania* 21°58N 12°11W **260** D2
Agia *Greece* 39°43N 22°45E **204** B4
Agincourt *Canada* 43°47N 79°16W **141** A3
Aginskoye *Russia* 51°6N 114°32E **215** D12
Ağlasun *Turkey* 37°39N 30°31E **205** D12
Agly → *France* 42°46N 3°3E **174** F7
Agmar *Mauritania* 25°18N 10°50W **260** C2
Agnew *Australia* 28°1S 120°31E **279** E3
Agnibilékrou *Ivory C.* 7°10N 3°11W **262** D4
Agnita *Romania* 45°59N 24°40E **183** E9
Agnone *Italy* 41°48N 14°22E **199** G11
Ago *Japan* 34°20N 136°51E **223** C8
Agofie *Ghana* 8°27N 0°15E **263** D5
Agogna → *Italy* 45°4N 8°54E **198** C5
Agogo *Sudan* 7°50N 28°45E **257** F2
Agön *Sweden* 61°34N 17°23E **162** C11
Agon Coutainville *France* 49°2N 1°34W **172** C5
Agoo *Phil.* 16°20N 120°22E **232** C3
Agora *Athens, Greece* **112** c1
Âgordo *Italy* 46°18N 12°2E **199** B9
Agori *India* 24°33N 82°57E **243** G10
Agouffa *Mauritania* 19°57N 16°10W **260** D1
Agouna *Benin* 7°39N 1°47E **263** D5
Agour → *France* 43°47N 1°41E **174** E5
Agra *India* 27°17N 77°58E **242** F7
Agra Canal *India* 27°9N 77°47E **129** A2
Agrakhanskiuy Poluostrov
    Russia 43°42N 47°38E **199** C12
Agram = Zagreb *Croatia* 45°50N 15°58E **199** C12
Agramunt *Spain* 41°48N 1°6E **196** D6
Agreda *Spain* 41°51N 1°55W **196** D3
Ağri *Turkey* 39°44N 43°3E **213** C10
Ağri → *Italy* 40°13N 16°44E **201** B9
Ağri Daği *Turkey* 39°50N 44°15E **213** C11
Ağri Karakose = Ağri
    Turkey 39°44N 43°3E **213** C10
Agria *Greece* 39°20N 23°1E **204** B5
Agricola Oriental *Mexico* 19°23N 99°4E **128** B2
Agrigento *Italy* 37°19N 13°34E **201** F6
Agrihan N. Marianas 18°46N 145°40E **302** a
Agrinio *Greece* 38°37N 21°27E **204** C3
Agrópoli *Italy* 40°21N 14°59E **201** B7
Agstafa *Azerbaijan* 41°7N 45°27E **191** K7
Água Branca *Brazil* 7°32S 37°37W **332** C4
Agua Caliente *Mexico* 32°29N 116°59W **307** N10
Agua Caliente Springs
    U.S.A. 32°56N 116°19W **307** N10
Água Clara *Brazil* 20°25S 52°45W **331** E7
Água Espraiada →
    Brazil 23°36S 46°41W **137** B2
Agua Fria □ *U.S.A.* 34°14N 112°0W **305** J8
Agua Hechicera
    Mexico 32°28N 116°15W **307** N10
Água Preta → *Brazil* 1°41S 63°48W **329** D5
Agua Prieta *Mexico* 31°18N 109°34W **318** A3
Aguachica *Colombia* 8°19N 73°38E **328** B4
Aguada *Puerto Rico* 18°23N 67°11W **321** b
Aguada Cecilio *Argentina* 40°51S 65°51W **336** B3
Aguadas *Colombia* 5°40N 75°38W **328** B2
Aguadilla *Puerto Rico* 18°26N 67°10W **321** C6
Aguadulce *Panama* 8°15N 80°32W **321** E4
Agualva-Cacem *Portugal* 38°46N 9°15W **126** A1
Aguanga *U.S.A.* 33°27N 116°51W **307** M10
Aguanish *Canada* 50°14N 62°2W **299** B7
Aguanus → *Canada* 50°13N 62°5W **299** B7
Aguapeí *Brazil* 16°12S 59°43E **331** D6
Aguapeí → *Brazil* 21°0S 51°0W **331** F7
Aguapey → *Argentina* 29°7S 56°36W **334** C4
Aguaray Guazú →
    Paraguay 24°47S 57°19W **334** B4
Aguarico → *Ecuador* 0°59S 75°11W **328** D2
Aguaro-Guariquito △
    Venezuela 8°20N 66°35W **328** B4
Aguas → *Spain* 41°20N 0°30W **196** D4
Aguas Blancas *Chile* 24°15S 69°55W **334** A2
Aguas Calientes, Sierra de
    Argentina 25°26S 66°40W **334** B2
Águas Formosas *Brazil* 17°5S 40°57W **333** E3
Aguascalientes *Mexico* 21°53N 102°12W **318** C4
Aguascalientes □
    Mexico 22°0N 102°20W **318** C4
Agudo *Spain* 38°59N 4°52W **195** G6
Águeda *Portugal* 40°34N 8°27W **194** E2
Agueda → *Spain* 41°2N 6°56W **194** D4
Aguelhok *Mali* 19°29N 0°52E **261** D5
Aguenit *W. Sahara* 22°11N 13°8W **260** D2
Aguié *Niger* 13°31N 7°46E **263** C6
Aguila, Punta *Puerto Rico* 17°57N 67°13W **321** b
Aguilafuente *Spain* 41°13N 4°7W **194** D6
Aguilar de Campóo *Spain* 42°47N 4°15W **194** C6
Aguilares *Argentina* 27°26S 65°35W **334** B2
Águilas *Spain* 37°23N 1°25W **197** H3
Agüímes *Canary Is.* 27°58N 15°27W **153** e1
Aguja, C. de la *Colombia* 11°18N 74°12W **328** A3
Agula'a *Ethiopia* 13°40N 39°40E **257** E4
Agulhas, C. *S. Africa* 34°52S 20°0E **270** E3
Agulhas Ridge *Atl. Oc.* 42°0N 15°0E **152** L13
Agulo *Canary Is.* 28°11N 17°12W **153** e1
Agung, Gunung
    Indonesia 8°20S 115°28E **231** J18
Agur *Uganda* 2°28N 32°55E **268** B3
Agusan → *Phil.* 9°0N 125°1E **233** G6
Agusan del Norte □ *Phil.* 9°20N 125°10E **233** G6
Agusan del Sur □ *Phil.* 8°30N 126°0E **233** H6
Agustín Codazzi *Colombia* 10°2N 73°14W **328** A4
Agutaya I. *Phil.* 11°9N 120°58E **233** F3
Agva *Turkey* 41°8N 29°52E **213** B8
Aha Mts. *Botswana* 19°45S 21°0E **270** A4

INDEX
Albert Town 341

Ahad Rifaydah Si. Arabia 17°50N 42°50E 248 C3
Ahaggar Algeria 23°0N 6°30E 261 D6
Ahal □ Turkmenistan 37°0N 57°0E 216 E5
Ahamansu Ghana 7°38N 0°35E 263 D5
Ahar Iran 38°35N 47°0E 213 C12
Ahat Turkey 38°39N 29°47E 205 C11
Ahaura → N.Z. 42°21S 171°34E 285 C6
Ahaus Germany 52°4N 7°0E 178 C2
Ahé French Polynesia 14°30S 146°18W 289 f
Åheim Norway 62°2N 5°13E 164 B2
Ahelledjem Algeria 26°37N 6°58E 261 C6
Ahimanawa Ra. N.Z. 39°3S 176°30E 284 F5
Ahioma Papua N. G. 10°20S 150°33E 286 F6
Ahipara B. N.Z. 35°5S 173°5E 284 B2
Ahir Dağı Turkey 38°45N 30°10E 205 C12
Ahiri India 19°30N 80°0E 244 E5
Ahlat Turkey 38°45N 42°29E 213 C10
Ahlen Germany 51°45N 7°53E 178 D3
Ahmad Wal Pakistan 29°18N 65°58E 242 E1
Ahmadabad India 23°0N 72°40E 242 H5
Aḩmadābād Khorāsān, Iran 35°3N 60°50E 247 C9
Aḩmadābād Khorāsān, Iran 35°49N 59°42E 247 C8
Aḩmadī Iran 27°56N 56°42E 247 E8
Ahmadnagar India 19°7N 74°46E 244 E2
Ahmadpur India 18°40N 76°57E 244 E3
Ahmadpur Pakistan 29°12N 71°10E 242 E4
Ahmadpur Lamma Pakistan 28°19N 70°3E 242 E4
Ahmanson Theater Los Angeles, U.S.A. 127 b2
Ahmar, Mts. Ethiopia 9°20N 41°15E 257 F5
Ahmedabad = Ahmadabad India 23°0N 72°40E 242 H5
Ahmednagar = Ahmadnagar India 19°7N 74°46E 244 E2
Ahmetbey Turkey 41°26N 27°34E 203 E11
Ahmetler Turkey 38°28N 29°5E 205 C11
Ahmetli Turkey 38°32N 27°57E 205 C9
Ahmeyim Mauritania 20°51N 14°25W 260 D2
Ahoada Nigeria 5°8N 6°36E 263 D6
Ahome Mexico 25°55N 109°11W 318 B3
Ahon, Tarso Chad 20°23N 18°18E 259 D3
Ahoskie U.S.A. 36°17N 76°59W 315 C16
Ahr → Germany 50°32N 7°16E 178 E3
Ahram Iran 28°52N 51°16E 247 D6
Ahrax Pt. Malta 36°0N 14°22E 206 F7
Ahrensbök Germany 54°2N 10°35E 178 A6
Ahrensburg Germany 53°40N 10°13E 178 B6
Ahrensfelde Germany 52°34N 13°34E 115 A4
Āhū Iran 34°33N 50°2E 247 C6
Ahu Akivi Chile 27°7S 109°24W 330 b
Ahu Tepeu Chile 27°6S 109°25W 330 b
Ahu Tongariki Chile 27°8S 109°17W 330 b
Ahu Vinapu Chile 27°10S 109°25W 330 b
Ahuachapán El Salv. 13°54N 89°52W 320 D2
'Āhuimanu U.S.A. 21°26N 157°50W 302 K14
Ahun France 46°4N 2°5E 173 F9
Ahuntsic Canada 45°32N 73°41W 130 A1
Ahunui French Polynesia 19°39S 140°25W 289 f
Ahuriri → N.Z. 44°31S 170°12E 285 E5
Åhus Sweden 55°56N 14°18E 163 J8
Ahvāz Iran 31°20N 48°40E 247 D6
Ahvenanmaa = Åland Finland 60°15N 20°0E 161 F19
Aḩwar Yemen 13°30N 46°40E 248 D4
Ahzar → Mali 15°30N 3°20E 263 B5
Ai → India 26°26N 90°44E 241 B3
Ai → Ōsaka, Japan 34°46N 135°35E 133 A2
Ai-Ais Namibia 27°54S 17°59E 270 C2
Ai-Ais and Fish River Canyon △ Namibia 24°45S 17°15E 270 B2
Aiari → Brazil 1°22N 68°36W 328 C4
Aichach Germany 48°27N 11°8E 179 G7
Aichi □ Japan 35°0N 137°15E 223 C9
'Aiea U.S.A. 21°23N 157°56W 302 K14
Aigle Switz. 46°18N 6°58E 179 J2
Aignay-le-Duc France 47°40N 4°43E 173 E11
Aigoual, Mt. France 44°8N 3°35E 174 D7
Aigre France 45°54N 0°1E 174 C4
Aigremont France 48°54N 2°1E 134 A1
Aigrettes, Île aux Mauritius 20°25S 57°43E 272 e
Aigua Uruguay 34°13S 54°46W 335 C5
Aigueperse France 46°3N 3°13E 173 F10
Aigues → France 44°7N 4°43E 175 D8
Aigues-Mortes France 43°35N 4°12E 175 E8
Aigues-Mortes, G. d' France 43°31N 4°3E 175 E8
Aigües Tortes y Lago San Mauricio △ Spain 42°38N 0°31W 196 C4
Aiguilles France 44°47N 6°51E 175 D10
Aiguillon France 44°18N 0°21E 174 D4
Aigurande France 46°27N 1°49E 173 F8
Aihui = Heihe China 50°10N 127°30E 219 A7
Aija Peru 9°50S 77°45W 330 B2
Aikawa Japan 38°2N 138°15E 220 E9
Aiken U.S.A. 33°34N 81°43W 316 B8
Ailao Shan China 24°0N 101°20E 228 F3
Aileron Australia 22°39S 133°20E 280 C1
Ailey U.S.A. 32°11N 82°34W 316 C7
Ailigandi Panama 9°14N 78°1W 328 B2
Aillant-sur-Tholon France 47°52N 3°20E 173 E10
Aillik Canada 55°11N 59°18W 299 A8
Ailsa Craig U.K. 55°15N 5°6W 167 F3
Ailulual Papua N. G. 9°38S 150°35E 286 E6
Aim Russia 59°0N 133°55E 215 D14
Aimere Indonesia 8°45S 121°3E 231 F6
Aimogasta Argentina 28°33S 66°50W 334 B2
Aimorés Brazil 19°30S 41°4W 333 E3
Ain □ France 46°5N 5°20E 173 F12
Ain → France 45°45N 5°11E 175 C9
Aïn Beïda Algeria 35°50N 7°29E 261 A6
Aïn Ben Khellil Algeria 33°15N 0°49W 261 B4
Aïn Ben Tili Mauritania 25°59N 9°27W 260 C3
Aïn Beni Mathar Morocco 34°1N 2°0W 261 B4
Aïn Benian Algeria 36°48N 2°55E 261 A5
Ain Dalla Egypt 27°20N 27°23E 256 B2
Ain Defla Algeria 36°16N 1°58E 261 A5
Ain Defla □ Algeria 36°10N 2°10E 261 A5
'Ain el Akhḑar Egypt 28°50N 33°55E 251 K4
Ain el Mafki Egypt 27°30N 28°15E 256 B2
Ain Girba Egypt 29°20N 25°14E 256 B2
Aïn M'lila Algeria 36°2N 6°35E 261 A6
Ain Murr Sudan 21°50N 25°9E 256 C2
Ain Qeiqab Egypt 29°42N 24°55E 256 B1
Aïn Salah = In Salah Algeria 27°10N 2°32E 261 C5
Aïn Sefra Algeria 32°47N 0°37W 261 B4
Ain Sheikh Murzûk Egypt 26°47N 27°45E 256 B2
Ain Sudr Egypt 29°50N 33°6E 251 J4
Ain Sukhna Egypt 29°32N 32°20E 256 J8
Aïn Tédelès Algeria 36°0N 0°21E 261 A5
Aïn Témouchent Algeria 35°16N 1°8W 261 A4
Aïn Témouchent □ Algeria 35°20N 1°5W 261 A4
Aïn Tikkidine Algeria 25°33N 1°24E 261 C5
Aïn Touta Algeria 35°26N 5°54E 261 A6
Ain Zeitûn Egypt 29°10N 25°48E 256 B2
Aïn Zorah Morocco 34°37N 3°32W 261 B4
Ainabo Somali Rep. 9°0N 46°25E 267 C6
Ainaži Latvia 57°50N 24°24E 188 D3
Ainos Oros Greece 38°9N 20°40E 207 C2
Ainsworth U.S.A. 42°33N 99°52W 308 D4
Aintab = Gaziantep Turkey 37°6N 37°23E 250 A8
Aioi Japan 34°48N 134°28E 222 C6
Aiome Papua N. G. 5°8S 144°44E 286 C3
Aipe Colombia 3°13N 75°15W 328 C2
Aiquile Bolivia 18°10S 65°10W 331 D4
Aïr Niger 18°30N 8°0E 259 E1
Air Canada Centre Toronto, Canada 141 c2
Aïr et du Ténéré ⌂ Niger 18°12N 9°56E 259 E1
Air Force I. Canada 67°58N 74°5W 295 C12
Air Hitam Malaysia 1°55N 103°11E 237 M4
Air View Park Singapore 1°20N 103°46E 138 A2
Aira Japan 31°43N 130°43E 222 F2
Airaines France 49°58N 1°55E 173 C8
Airão Brazil 1°56S 61°22W 329 D5
Airdrie Alta., Canada 51°18N 114°2W 296 C6
Airdrie N. Lanarks., U.K. 55°52N 3°57W 167 F5
Aire → Meuse, France 49°18N 4°49E 173 C11
Aire → N. Yorks., U.K. 53°43N 0°55W 168 D7
Aire, I. de l' Spain 39°48N 4°16E 206 B5
Aire-sur-la-Lys France 50°37N 2°22E 173 B9
Aire-sur-l'Adour France 43°42N 0°15W 174 E3
Aireys Inlet Australia 38°29S 144°5E 282 E6
Airlie Beach Australia 20°16S 148°43E 280 J6
Airport West Australia 37°42S 144°52E 128 A1
Airvault France 46°50N 0°8W 172 F6
Aisch → Germany 49°49N 10°58E 179 F6
Aisen □ Chile 46°30S 73°0W 336 C2
Aisne □ France 49°42N 3°40E 173 C10
Aisne → France 49°26N 2°50E 173 C9
Ait India 25°54N 79°14E 243 G8
Aitana, Sierra de Spain 38°35N 0°24W 197 G4
Aitape Papua N. G. 3°11S 142°22E 286 B2
Aitkin U.S.A. 46°32N 93°42W 308 B7
Aitutaki Cook Is. 18°52S 159°45W 289 J12
Aiuaba Brazil 6°38S 40°7W 332 C3
Aiud Romania 46°19N 23°44E 183 D8
Aix-en-Provence France 43°32N 5°27E 175 E9
Aix-la-Chapelle = Aachen Germany 50°45N 6°6E 178 E2
Aix-les-Bains France 45°41N 5°53E 175 C9
Aixe-sur-Vienne France 45°47N 1°9E 174 C5
Aiyang, Mt. Papua N. G. 5°10S 141°20E 286 C1
Aíyina = Egina Greece 37°45N 23°26E 204 D5
Aizawl India 23°40N 92°44E 241 D4
Aizenay France 46°44N 1°38W 172 F5
Aizkraukle Latvia 56°36N 25°11E 188 D3
Aizpute Latvia 56°43N 21°40E 184 B8
Aizuwakamatsu Japan 37°30N 139°56E 220 F9
Ajaccio France 41°55N 8°40E 175 G12
Ajaccio, G. d' France 41°52N 8°40E 175 G12
Ajai ⌂ Uganda 2°52N 31°16E 268 B3
Ajaigarh India 24°52N 80°16E 243 G9
Ajaju → Colombia 0°59N 72°20W 328 C3
Ajalpan Mexico 18°22N 97°15W 319 D5
Ajanta India 20°30N 75°48E 244 D2
Ajanta Ra. India 20°28N 75°50E 244 D2
Ajari Rep. = Ajaria □ Georgia 41°30N 42°0E 191 K6
Ajaria □ Georgia 41°30N 42°0E 191 K6
Ajax Canada 43°50N 79°1W 312 C5
Ajax, Mt. N.Z. 42°35S 172°5E 285 C7
Ajdābiyā Libya 30°54N 20°4E 258 B4
Ajdovščina Slovenia 45°54N 13°54E 199 C10
Ajegunle Nigeria 6°26N 3°20E 124 B2
Aji Japan 34°40N 135°27E 133 A1
Ajibar Ethiopia 10°35N 38°36E 257 E4
Ajka Hungary 47°4N 17°31E 182 C2
'Ajlūn Jordan 32°18N 35°47E 251 F6
'Ajmān U.A.E. 25°25N 55°30E 247 E7
Ajmer India 26°28N 74°37E 242 F6
Ajnala India 31°50N 74°48E 242 D6
Ajo U.S.A. 32°22N 112°52W 305 K7
Ajo, C. de Spain 43°31N 3°35W 194 B7
Ajok Sudan 9°15N 28°28E 257 F2
Ajoupa-Bouillon Martinique 14°49N 61°7W 322 j
Ajuda Portugal 38°42N 9°12W 126 A1
Ajuda, Pta. da Azores 37°52N 25°19W 153 d3
Ajuy Phil. 11°10N 123°1E 233 F4
Ak Dağ Turkey 36°30N 29°32E 205 E11
Ak Dağları Muğla, Turkey 36°30N 29°30E 205 E11
Ak Dağları Sivas, Turkey 39°32N 36°12E 212 C7
Ak-Dovurak Russia 51°11N 90°36E 217 B12
Ak-Mechet = Qyzylorda Kazakhstan 44°48N 65°28E 217 D7
Ak-Mednet = Chornomorske Ukraine 45°31N 32°40E 189 K7
Ak-Sheikh = Razdolnoye Ukraine 45°46N 33°29E 189 K7
Akaba Togo 8°10N 1°2E 263 D5
Akabira Japan 43°33N 142°5E 220 C11
Akabli Algeria 26°49N 1°31E 261 C5
Akademika Obrucheva, Khrebet Russia 51°50N 96°0E 217 B13
Akagera △ Rwanda 1°31S 30°33E 268 C3
Akaishi-Dake Japan 35°27N 138°9E 223 B10
Akaishi-Sammyaku Japan 35°25N 138°10E 223 B10
Akaki Beseka Ethiopia 8°55N 38°45E 257 F4
Akākūs, Jabal Libya 25°20N 10°30E 261 C7
Akala Sudan 15°39N 36°13E 257 D4
Akalkot India 17°32N 76°13E 244 F3
Akalla Sweden 59°24N 17°55E 139 A1
Akamas Cyprus 35°3N 32°18E 207 E8
Akan △ Japan 43°20N 144°20E 220 C12
Akanthou Cyprus 35°22N 33°45E 207 E9
Akarca Turkey 38°35N 29°35E 205 C11
Akaroa N.Z. 43°49S 172°59E 285 D7
Akaroa Harbour N.Z. 43°50S 172°55E 285 D7
Akasaka Tokyo, Japan 140 b3
Akasha Sudan 21°10N 30°32E 256 C3
Akashi Japan 34°45N 134°58E 222 C6
Akbarābād Iran 35°40N 51°20E 141 A2
Akbarpur Bihar, India 24°39N 83°58E 243 G10
Akbarpur Ut. P., India 26°25N 82°32E 243 F10
Akbou Algeria 36°31N 4°31E 261 A5
Akbulak Russia 51°1N 55°37E 216 B5
Akçaabat Turkey 41°1N 39°34E 213 B8
Akçadağ Turkey 38°27N 37°43E 212 C7
Akçakale Turkey 36°41N 38°56E 213 D8
Akçakoca Turkey 41°5N 31°8E 212 B4
Akçalı Dağları Turkey 36°18N 33°21E 250 B4
Akçaova Turkey 41°3N 29°57E 203 E13
Akçay Turkey 36°36N 29°45E 205 E11
Akçay → Turkey 37°50N 28°15E 205 D10
Akchâr Mauritania 20°20N 14°28W 260 D2
Akchi-Karasu = Toktogul Kyrgyzstan 41°50N 72°50E 217 D8
Akdağ Antalya, Turkey 37°0N 32°0E 250 B3
Akdağ İzmir, Turkey 38°33N 26°30E 205 C8
Akdağmadeni Turkey 39°39N 35°53E 212 C6
Akdere Turkey 36°14N 33°46E 250 B4
Akechi Japan 35°18N 137°23E 223 B9
Akelamo Indonesia 1°35N 129°40E 231 D7
Åkernes = Åknes Norway 58°45N 7°30E 164 F4
Åkers styckebruk Sweden 59°15N 17°5E 162 E11
Åkersberga Sweden 59°29N 18°18E 162 E12
Akershus □ Norway 60°0N 11°10E 164 D8
Akershus Slott Oslo, Norway 133 c1
Akeru → India 17°25N 80°5E 244 F5
Aketi Dem. Rep. of the Congo 2°38N 23°47E 264 B4
Akhalkalaki Georgia 41°27N 43°25E 191 K6
Akhaltsikhe Georgia 41°40N 43°0E 191 K6
Akhḑar, W. al → Si. Arabia 28°36N 36°36E 251 K7
Akhiok U.S.A. 56°57N 154°10W 303 H9
Akhisar Turkey 38°56N 27°48E 205 C9
Akhmîm Egypt 26°31N 31°47E 256 B3
Akhnur India 32°52N 74°45E 243 C6
Akhtarīn Syria 36°31N 37°20E 250 B8
Akhtopol Bulgaria 42°6N 27°56E 203 D11
Akhtuba → Russia 47°41N 46°55E 191 G8
Akhtubinsk Russia 48°13N 46°7E 191 F8
Akhty Russia 41°30N 47°45E 191 K8
Akhtyrka = Okhtyrka Ukraine 50°25N 35°0E 189 G8
Aki Japan 33°30N 133°54E 222 D5
Aki-Nada Japan 34°5N 132°40E 222 C4
Akiachak U.S.A. 60°55N 161°26W 303 F7
Akiak U.S.A. 60°55N 161°13W 303 F7
Akiéni Gabon 1°11S 13°53E 264 C2
Akihabara Tokyo, Japan 140 a5
Akimiski I. Canada 52°50N 81°30W 298 B3
Akimovka Ukraine 46°44N 35°0E 189 J8
Akıncı Burnu Turkey 36°19N 35°46E 250 B6
Åkirkeby Denmark 55°4N 14°55E 163 J8
Akita Japan 39°45N 140°7E 220 E10
Akita □ Japan 39°40N 140°30E 220 E10
Akjoujt Mauritania 19°45N 14°15W 262 B2
Akka Mali 15°24N 4°11W 262 B4
Akka Morocco 29°22N 8°9W 260 C3
Akkaraipattu Sri Lanka 7°13N 81°51E 245 L5
Akkaya Tepesi Turkey 37°25N 29°38E 205 D11
Akkerman = Bilhorod-Dnistrovskyy Ukraine 46°11N 30°23E 189 J6
Akkeshi Japan 43°2N 144°51E 220 C12
'Akko Israel 32°55N 35°4E 250 F6
Akköy Turkey 37°29N 27°15E 205 D9
Aklampa Benin 8°15N 2°10E 263 D5
Aklan □ Phil. 11°50N 122°30E 233 F4
Aklavik Canada 68°12N 135°0W 294 C6
Aklera India 24°26N 76°32E 242 G7
Akmenė Lithuania 56°15N 22°45E 184 B9
Akmenrags Latvia 56°50N 21°4E 184 B8
Akmolinsk = Astana Kazakhstan 51°10N 71°30E 217 B8
Akmonte = Almonte Spain 37°13N 6°38W 195 H4
Åknes Norway 58°45N 7°30E 164 F4
Aknoul Morocco 34°40N 3°55W 261 B4
Akō Japan 34°45N 134°24E 222 C6
Ako Nigeria 10°19N 10°48E 263 C7
Akôbô Sudan 7°47N 33°1E 257 F3
Akobo → Ethiopia 7°48N 33°3E 257 F3
Akola Maharashtra, India 20°42N 77°2E 244 D3
Akola Maharashtra, India 19°32N 74°3E 244 E2
Akolmiut U.S.A. 60°55N 162°20W 303 F7
Akonolinga Cameroon 3°50N 12°18E 263 E7
Akor Mali 14°59N 6°58W 262 C3
Akordat Eritrea 15°30N 37°40E 257 D4
Akosombo Dam Ghana 6°20N 0°5E 263 D5
Akot India 21°10N 77°10E 244 D3
Akot Sudan 6°31N 30°9E 257 F3
Akoupé Ivory C. 6°23N 3°54W 262 D4
Akourousoulba C.A.R. 8°58N 20°46E 264 A4
Akpatok I. Canada 60°25N 68°8W 295 C13
Åkrahamn Norway 59°15N 5°10E 164 E2
'Akramah Libya 32°2N 23°41E 258 B4
Akranes Iceland 64°19N 22°5W 155 C4
Akreïjit Mauritania 18°19N 9°11W 262 B3
Akritas, Akra Greece 36°43N 21°54E 204 E3
Akron Colo., U.S.A. 40°10N 103°13W 304 F12
Akron Ind., U.S.A. 41°2N 86°1W 311 C10
Akron Ohio, U.S.A. 41°5N 81°31W 312 E3
Akrotiri Cyprus 34°36N 32°57E 207 F8
Akrotiri, Akra Greece 40°26N 25°27E 203 F9
Akrotiri Bay Cyprus 34°35N 33°10E 207 F9
Aksai Chin China 35°15N 79°55E 243 B8
Aksaray Turkey 38°25N 34°2E 212 C6
Aksaray □ Turkey 38°20N 33°45E 212 C5
Aksay = Aqsay Kazakhstan 51°11N 53°0E 187 D9
Akşehir Turkey 38°18N 31°30E 212 C4
Akşehir Gölü Turkey 38°30N 31°25E 212 C4
Akseki Turkey 37°2N 31°47E 250 A2
Akstafa = Ağstafa Azerbaijan 41°7N 45°27E 191 K7
Aksu Xinjiang Uygur, China 41°5N 80°10E 217 D10
Aksu Turkey 36°57N 30°50E 250 B1
Aksu → Turkey 36°52N 30°57E 250 B1
Aksu He → China 40°26N 80°59E 217 D10
Aksum Ethiopia 14°5N 38°40E 257 E4
Aktash Russia 55°2N 52°3E 190 C11
Aktepe Turkey 36°42N 36°27E 250 B7
Aktio Greece 38°57N 20°46E 207 B2
Akto China 39°5N 75°59E 217 E9
Aktsyabrski Belarus 52°38N 28°53E 177 B15
Aktyubinsk = Aqtöbe Kazakhstan 50°17N 57°10E 187 D10
Aku Nigeria 6°40N 7°18E 263 D6
Akula Dem. Rep. of the Congo 2°22N 20°12E 264 B4
Akun I. U.S.A. 54°11N 165°32W 303 J6
Akune Japan 32°1N 130°12E 222 E2
Akure Nigeria 7°15N 5°5E 263 D6
Akurenan Eq. Guin. 1°2N 10°40E 264 B2
Akuressa Sri Lanka 6°5N 80°29E 245 L5
Akureyri Iceland 65°40N 18°6W 155 B8
Akuseki-Shima Japan 29°27N 129°37E 221 K4
Akusha Russia 42°18N 47°30E 191 J8
Akutan U.S.A. 54°8N 165°46W 303 J6
Akutan I. U.S.A. 54°7N 165°55W 303 J6
Akwa-Ibom □ Nigeria 4°30N 7°30E 263 E6
Akyab = Sittwe Burma 20°18N 92°45E 241 E4
Akyazı Turkey 40°40N 30°38E 212 B4
Ål Norway 60°38N 8°33E 164 D5
Al Abyaḑ Libya 26°49N 14°1E 258 C2
Al Abyār Libya 32°9N 20°29E 258 B4
Al 'Adam Libya 31°51N 23°55E 258 B4
Al 'Adan Yemen 12°45N 45°0E 248 D4
Al Aḩsā = Hasa Si. Arabia 25°50N 49°0E 247 E6
Al Ajfar Si. Arabia 27°26N 43°0E 246 E4
Al Amādīyah Iraq 37°5N 43°30E 213 D10
Al 'Amārah Iraq 31°55N 47°15E 213 G12
Al Anbār □ Iraq 33°25N 42°0E 246 C4
Al 'Aqabah Jordan 29°31N 35°0E 251 J6
Al 'Aqabah □ Jordan 29°30N 35°0E 251 J6
Al 'Aqīq Si. Arabia 20°39N 41°25E 248 B3
Al Arak Syria 34°38N 38°35E 213 E8
Al 'Aramah Si. Arabia 25°30N 46°0E 246 E5
Al 'Ariḑah Si. Arabia 17°3N 43°5E 248 C3
Al 'Arţāwīyah Si. Arabia 26°31N 45°20E 246 E5
Al Ashkhara Oman 21°50N 59°30E 249 B7
Al 'Āşimah = 'Ammān □ Jordan 31°40N 36°30E 251 G7
Al 'Assāfīyah Si. Arabia 28°17N 38°59E 246 D3
Al Atārib Syria 36°9N 36°49E 250 B7
Al 'Ayn Si. Arabia 25°4N 38°6E 246 E3
Al 'Ayn U.A.E. 24°15N 55°45E 247 E7
Al 'Azamīyah Iraq 33°22N 44°22E 113 A2
Al 'Azīzīyah Iraq 32°54N 45°4E 213 F11
Al 'Azīzīyah Libya 32°30N 13°1E 258 B2
Al 'Azīzīyah □ Libya 32°31N 13°1E 261 B7
Al Bāb Syria 36°23N 37°29E 250 B8
Al Bad' Si. Arabia 28°28N 35°1E 246 D2
Al Bādī Iraq 35°56N 41°32E 246 C4
Al Badī' Si. Arabia 22°0N 46°35E 248 B4
Al Bāḩah □ Si. Arabia 20°30N 41°30E 248 B3
Al Baḩrah Kuwait 29°40N 47°52E 246 D5
Al Baḩral Mayyit = Dead Sea Asia 31°30N 35°30E 251 G6
Al Balqā' □ Jordan 32°5N 35°45E 251 F6
Al Barkāt Libya 24°56N 10°14E 258 D2
Al Bārūk, J. Lebanon 33°39N 35°40E 250 E6
Al Başrah Iraq 30°30N 47°50E 246 D5
Al Baţḩā Iraq 31°6N 45°53E 246 D5
Al Batinah Oman 24°10N 56°50E 249 A7
Al Batrūn Lebanon 34°15N 35°40E 250 D6
Al Bayāḑ Si. Arabia 22°0N 47°0E 248 B4
Al Bayḑā Libya 32°50N 21°44E 258 B4
Al Bayḑā' Yemen 14°5N 45°42E 248 D4
Al Bi'ār Si. Arabia 22°39N 39°40E 248 B2
Al Biqā Lebanon 34°10N 36°10E 250 D7
Al Biqā □ Lebanon 34°0N 36°5E 250 E7
Al Bi'r Si. Arabia 28°51N 36°16E 251 K7
Al Birk Si. Arabia 18°13N 41°33E 248 C3
Al Bu'ayrāt al Ḩasūn Libya 31°24N 15°44E 258 B3
Al Bukayrīyah Si. Arabia 26°9N 43°40E 246 E4
Al Bumbah Libya 32°24N 23°8E 258 B4
Al Burayj Syria 34°15N 36°46E 250 D7
Al Faḑilī Si. Arabia 26°58N 49°10E 247 E6
Al Fallūjah Iraq 33°20N 43°55E 213 F10
Al Fātiḩ □ Libya 32°0N 21°0E 258 B4
Al Fāw Iraq 30°0N 48°30E 247 D6
Al Faydamī Yemen 16°25N 52°26E 249 C6
Al Fujayrah U.A.E. 25°7N 56°18E 247 E8
Al Fuqahā' Libya 27°50N 16°23E 258 C3
Al Ghadaf, W. → Jordan 31°26N 36°43E 251 G7
Al Ghammās Iraq 31°45N 44°37E 246 D5
Al Gharīb Libya 32°35N 21°11E 258 B4
Al Ghayḑah Ḩaḑramaut, Yemen 14°55N 50°0E 249 D5
Al Ghayḑah Qamar, Yemen 16°13N 52°11E 249 C6
Al Ghayl Yemen 15°30N 50°54E 249 D5
Al Ghazālah Si. Arabia 26°48N 41°19E 246 E4
Al Ḩadd Oman 22°32N 59°48E 249 B7
Al Ḩaddār Si. Arabia 21°58N 45°57E 248 B4
Al Ḩadīthah Iraq 34°0N 41°13E 213 E10
Al Ḩadīthah Si. Arabia 31°28N 37°8E 246 D3
Al Ḩaḑr Iraq 35°35N 42°44E 213 E10
Al Ḩaffah Syria 35°36N 36°1E 250 C7
Al Ḩājānah Syria 33°20N 36°33E 250 E7
Al Ḩajar al Gharbī Oman 24°10N 56°15E 247 E8
Al Hallānīyah Oman 17°30N 56°1E 249 C7
Al Hāmad Si. Arabia 31°30N 39°30E 246 D3
Al Ḩamar Si. Arabia 22°26N 46°12E 248 B4
Al Ḩamdānīyah Syria 35°25N 36°50E 250 C7
Al Ḩamīdīyah Syria 34°42N 35°57E 250 D6
Al Hammādat al Ḩamrā' Libya 29°30N 12°0E 258 C2
Al Ḩammār Iraq 30°57N 46°51E 246 D5
Al Ḩamrā' Si. Arabia 24°2N 38°55E 246 E3
Al Ḩamrā' Syria 35°19N 37°5E 250 C8
Al Ḩamzah Iraq 31°43N 44°58E 246 D5
Al Ḩanākīyah Si. Arabia 24°51N 40°31E 246 E4
Al Ḩarīq Si. Arabia 23°29N 46°27E 248 B4
Al Harūj al Aswad Libya 27°0N 17°10E 258 C3
Al Ḩasakah Syria 36°35N 40°45E 213 D9
Al Ḩasakah □ Syria 36°40N 40°50E 213 D9
Al Hāsikīyah Oman 17°28N 55°36E 249 C6
Al Ḩasy Yemen 14°3N 48°40E 249 D5
Al Hawīyah Ash Sharqīyah, Si. Arabia 24°45N 49°6E 249 A5
Al Hawīyah Makkah, Si. Arabia 21°26N 40°30E 248 B3
Al Ḩawrah Yemen 13°50N 47°35E 248 D4
Al Hawtah = Laḩij Yemen 13°4N 44°53E 248 D4
Al Ḩawţah Si. Arabia 23°30N 47°0E 248 B4
Al Ḩayy Iraq 32°5N 46°5E 213 F12
Al Ḩijarah Asia 30°0N 44°0E 246 D4
Al Ḩillah Iraq 32°30N 44°25E 213 F11
Al Ḩillah Si. Arabia 23°35N 46°50E 248 B4
Al Hindīyah Iraq 32°30N 44°10E 213 F11
Al Hirmil Lebanon 34°26N 36°24E 250 D7
Al Hoceïma Morocco 35°8N 3°58W 261 A4
Al Ḩudaydah Yemen 14°50N 43°0E 248 D3
Al Ḩudūd ash Shamālīyah □ Si. Arabia 29°10N 42°30E 246 D4
Al Ḩufrah Libya 25°32N 14°1E 258 C2
Al Hufūf Si. Arabia 25°25N 49°45E 247 E6
Al Ḩulwah Si. Arabia 23°24N 46°48E 248 B4
Al Ḩumayḑah Si. Arabia 29°14N 34°56E 251 J5
Al Ḩunayy Si. Arabia 25°58N 48°45E 247 E6
Al Husayyāt Libya 30°24N 20°37E 258 B4
Al 'Irqah Yemen 13°39N 47°22E 248 D4
Al Īsāwīyah Si. Arabia 30°43N 37°59E 246 D3
Al Ittihad = Madīnat ash Sha'b Yemen 12°50N 45°0E 248 D4
Al Jabal al Akhḑar Libya 32°30N 21°30E 258 B4
Al Jabal al Akhḑar □ Libya 32°30N 21°41E 258 B4
Al Jafr Jordan 30°18N 36°14E 251 H7
Al Jāfūrah Si. Arabia 25°0N 50°15E 247 E7
Al Jaghbūb Libya 29°42N 24°38E 258 C4
Al Jahrah Kuwait 29°25N 47°40E 246 D5
Al Jalāmīd Si. Arabia 31°20N 40°6E 246 D3
Al Jamalīyah Qatar 25°37N 51°5E 247 E6
Al Janūb □ Lebanon 33°20N 35°20E 250 E6
Al Jawf Libya 24°10N 23°24E 258 D4
Al Jawf Si. Arabia 29°55N 39°40E 246 D3
Al Jawf □ Si. Arabia 29°30N 39°30E 246 D3
Al Jazair = Algeria ■ Africa 28°30N 2°0E 261 C5
Al Jazirah Iraq 33°30N 44°0E 213 E10
Al Jithāmīyah Si. Arabia 27°41N 41°43E 246 E4
Al Jubayl Si. Arabia 27°0N 49°50E 247 E6
Al Jubaylah Si. Arabia 24°55N 46°25E 246 E5
Al Jubb Si. Arabia 27°11N 42°17E 246 E4
Al Jufrah Libya 29°10N 16°0E 258 C3
Al Jufrah □ Libya 27°30N 17°30E 258 C3
Al Jumūm Si. Arabia 21°37N 39°42E 248 B2
Al Junaynah Sudan 13°27N 22°45E 259 F4
Al Kabā'ish Iraq 30°58N 47°0E 246 D5
Al Kāmil Oman 22°13N 59°12E 249 B7
Al Karak Jordan 31°11N 35°42E 251 G6
Al Karak □ Jordan 31°0N 36°0E 251 H7
Al Kāẓimīyah Iraq 33°22N 44°18E 213 F11
Al Khābūra Oman 23°57N 57°5E 247 F8
Al Khafji Si. Arabia 28°24N 48°29E 247 E6
Al Khalīl West Bank 31°32N 35°6E 251 G6
Al Khāliş Iraq 33°49N 44°32E 213 F11
Al Khamāsīn Si. Arabia 20°29N 44°46E 248 B4
Al Kharj Si. Arabia 24°0N 47°0E 248 B4
Al Kharsānīyah Si. Arabia 27°13N 49°18E 247 E6
Al Khaşab Oman 26°14N 56°15E 247 E8
Al Khāşirah Si. Arabia 23°30N 43°47E 248 B3
Al Khawr Qatar 25°41N 51°30E 247 E6
Al Khiḑr Iraq 31°12N 45°33E 246 D5
Al Khiyām Lebanon 33°20N 35°36E 250 E6
Al Khobar Si. Arabia 26°17N 50°12E 247 E6
Al Khums Libya 32°40N 14°17E 258 B2
Al Khums □ Libya 31°20N 14°10E 258 B2
Al Kiswah Syria 33°23N 36°14E 250 E7
Al Kūfah Iraq 32°2N 44°24E 213 F11
Al Kufrah Libya 24°17N 23°15E 258 D4
Al Kuhayfiyah Si. Arabia 27°12N 43°3E 246 E4
Al Kūt Iraq 32°30N 46°0E 213 F11
Al Kuwayt Kuwait 29°30N 48°0E 246 D5
Al Labwah Lebanon 34°11N 36°20E 250 D7
Al Lādhiqīyah Syria 35°30N 35°45E 250 C6
Al Lādhiqīyah □ Syria 35°45N 36°0E 250 C7
Al Līth Si. Arabia 20°9N 40°15E 248 B3
Al Liwā' Oman 24°31N 56°36E 247 E8
Al Luḩayyah Yemen 15°45N 42°40E 248 D3
Al Madīnah Iraq 30°57N 47°16E 246 D5
Al Madīnah Si. Arabia 24°35N 39°52E 246 E3
Al Madīnah □ Si. Arabia 23°50N 40°30E 248 B3
Al Mafraq Jordan 32°17N 36°14E 251 F7
Al Mafraq □ Jordan 32°17N 36°15E 251 F7
Al Maghārīm Yemen 15°1N 47°49E 248 D4
Al Maghreb = Morocco ■ N. Afr. 32°0N 5°50W 260 B3
Al Mahbes W. Sahara 27°10N 9°50W 260 C3
Al Maḩmūdīyah Iraq 33°3N 44°21E 213 F11
Al Majma'ah Si. Arabia 25°57N 45°22E 246 E5
Al Makhruq, W. → Jordan 31°28N 37°0E 251 G8
Al Makḩūl Si. Arabia 26°37N 42°39E 246 E4
Al Manāmah Bahrain 26°10N 50°30E 247 E6
Al Maqwa' Kuwait 29°10N 47°59E 246 D5
Al Marāḩ Si. Arabia 25°35N 49°35E 247 E6
Al Marj Libya 32°25N 20°30E 258 B4
Al Maţlā Kuwait 29°24N 47°40E 246 D5
Al Mawşil Iraq 36°15N 43°5E 213 D10
Al Mayādin Syria 35°1N 40°27E 213 E9
Al Mazār Jordan 31°4N 35°41E 251 G6
Al Midhnab Si. Arabia 25°50N 44°18E 246 E5
Al Minā' Lebanon 34°24N 35°49E 250 D6
Al Miqdādīyah Iraq 34°0N 45°0E 213 E11
Al Mubarraz Si. Arabia 25°30N 49°40E 247 E6
Al Mudawwarah Jordan 29°19N 36°0E 251 J7
Al Muḑaybī Oman 22°34N 58°7E 249 B7
Al Mughayrā' U.A.E. 24°5N 53°32E 247 E7
Al Muḩarraq Bahrain 26°15N 50°40E 247 E6
Al Mukallā Yemen 14°33N 49°2E 249 D5
Al Mukhā Yemen 13°18N 43°15E 248 D3
Al Mukhaylī Libya 32°10N 22°17E 258 B4
Al Musayjīd Si. Arabia 24°5N 39°5E 246 E3
Al Musayyib Iraq 32°49N 44°20E 213 F11
Al Muthanná □ Iraq 30°30N 45°15E 246 D5
Al Muwayh Si. Arabia 22°41N 41°37E 256 C5
Al Muwayliḩ Si. Arabia 27°40N 35°30E 246 E2
Al Muzāḩimīyah Si. Arabia 24°29N 46°18E 248 A4
Al Owuho = Otukpa Nigeria 7°9N 7°41E 263 D6
Al Qaddāḩīyah Libya 31°15N 15°9E 258 B3
Al Qaḑīmah Si. Arabia 22°20N 39°13E 248 B2
Al Qādisīyah □ Iraq 32°0N 45°0E 246 D5
Al Qadmūs Syria 35°5N 36°10E 250 C7
Al Qaḩmah Si. Arabia 18°0N 41°41E 248 C3
Al Qā'im Iraq 34°21N 41°7E 213 E9
Al Qā'iyah Si. Arabia 24°33N 43°15E 248 A3
Al Qalībah Si. Arabia 28°24N 37°42E 246 D3
Al Qāmishlī Syria 37°2N 41°14E 213 D9
Al Qardāḩah Syria 35°27N 36°3E 250 C7
Al Qaryah ash Sharqīyah Libya 30°28N 13°40E 258 B2
Al Qaryatayn Syria 34°12N 37°13E 250 D8
Al Qaşabát Libya 32°39N 14°1E 258 B2
Al Qaşīm □ Si. Arabia 26°0N 43°0E 246 E4
Al Qaţ'ā Syria 34°40N 40°48E 213 E9
Al Qaţīf Si. Arabia 26°35N 50°0E 247 E6
Al Qaţn Yemen 15°51N 48°26E 249 D5
Al Qatrānah Jordan 31°12N 36°6E 251 G7
Al Qaţrūn Libya 24°56N 15°3E 258 D3
Al Qawz Si. Arabia 18°58N 41°26E 248 C3
Al Qayşūmah Si. Arabia 28°20N 46°7E 246 D5
Al Qiblīyah Oman 17°30N 56°20E 249 C7
Al Quds = Jerusalem Israel/West Bank 31°47N 35°10E 123 B2
Al Qunayţirah Syria 32°55N 35°45E 250 F6
Al Qunfudhah Si. Arabia 19°3N 41°4E 248 C3
Al Qurayyāt Oman 23°17N 58°53E 249 B7
Al Qurḩ Yemen 16°44N 51°29E 249 C5
Al Qurnah Iraq 31°1N 47°25E 246 D5
Al Quşayr Iraq 30°39N 45°50E 246 D5
Al Quşayr Syria 34°31N 36°34E 250 D7
Al Qutayfah Syria 33°44N 36°36E 250 E7
Al Quway'īyah Si. Arabia 24°3N 45°15E 248 A4
Al 'Ubaylah Si. Arabia 21°59N 50°57E 249 B5
Al 'Uḑaylīyah Si. Arabia 25°8N 49°18E 247 E6
Al 'Ulā Si. Arabia 26°35N 38°0E 246 E3
Al 'Ulayyah Si. Arabia 19°39N 41°54E 248 C3
Al Uqaylah ash Sharqīgah Libya 30°12N 19°10E 258 B3
Al 'Uqayr Si. Arabia 25°40N 50°15E 247 E6
Al 'Urūq al Mutariḑah Si. Arabia 21°0N 53°30E 249 B6
Al 'Uwaynat Libya 25°47N 10°33E 258 C2
Al 'Uwaynid Si. Arabia 24°50N 46°0E 246 E5
Al 'Uwayqīlah Si. Arabia 30°30N 42°10E 246 D4
Al 'Uyūn Ḩijāz, Si. Arabia 24°33N 39°35E 246 E3
Al 'Uyūn Najd, Si. Arabia 26°30N 43°50E 246 E4
Al 'Uzayr Iraq 31°19N 47°25E 246 D5
Al Wajh Si. Arabia 26°10N 36°30E 246 E3
Al Wakrah Qatar 25°10N 51°40E 247 E6
Al-Walaja West Bank 31°44N 35°9E 123 B1
Al Waqbah Si. Arabia 28°48N 45°33E 246 D5
Al Wari'āh Si. Arabia 27°51N 47°25E 246 E5
Al Wāţīyah Libya 32°28N 11°57E 258 B2
Al Yaman = Yemen ■ Asia 15°0N 44°0E 248 D4
Ala Italy 45°45N 11°0E 198 C8
Ala Dağ Turkey 37°44N 35°9E 246 B2
Ala Dağları Turkey 39°15N 43°33E 213 C10
Ala Tau Asia 45°30N 80°40E 217 C10
Ala Tau Shankou = Dzungarian Gate Asia 45°10N 82°0E 217 C10
Alabama □ U.S.A. 33°0N 87°0W 315 E11
Alabama → U.S.A. 31°8N 87°57W 315 F11
Alabaster U.S.A. 33°15N 86°49W 315 E11
Alabat I. Phil. 14°7N 122°3E 232 D4
Alabel Phil. 6°4N 125°16E 233 H5
Alabule → Papua N. G. 8°31S 146°56E 286 E4
Alaca Turkey 40°10N 34°51E 212 B6
Alacaatlı Turkey 39°15N 28°3E 205 B10
Alaçam Turkey 41°36N 35°36E 212 B6
Alaçam Dağları Turkey 39°18N 28°49E 205 B10
Alacant = Alicante Spain 38°23N 0°30W 197 G4
Alaçatı Turkey 38°15N 26°22E 205 C8
Alachua U.S.A. 29°47N 82°30W 316 F7
Alaejos Spain 41°18N 5°13W 194 D5
Alagir Russia 43°3N 44°14E 191 J7
Alagna Valsésia Italy 45°51N 7°56E 198 C4
Alagoa de Baixo = Sertânia Brazil 8°5S 37°20W 332 C4
Alagoa Grande Brazil 7°3S 35°35W 332 C4
Alagoas = Marechal Deodoro Brazil 9°43S 35°54W 332 C4
Alagoas □ Brazil 9°0S 36°0W 332 C4
Alagoinhas Brazil 12°7S 38°20W 333 D4
Alagón Spain 41°46N 1°12W 196 D3
Alagón → Spain 39°44N 6°53W 194 F4
Alaguntan Nigeria 6°25N 3°29E 124 B2
Alagyoz = Aragats Armenia 40°30N 44°15E 191 K7
Alahan Turkey 36°46N 33°19E 250 B4
Alai Range Asia 39°45N 72°0E 217 E8
Alaior Spain 39°57N 4°8E 206 B5
Alajero Canary Is. 28°3N 17°13W 153 e1
Alajuela Costa Rica 10°2N 84°8W 320 D3
Alakamisy Madag. 21°19S 47°14E 272 C2
Alakanuk U.S.A. 62°41N 164°37W 303 E6
Alaknanda → India 30°8N 78°36E 243 D8
Alaköl Kazakhstan 46°0N 81°5E 217 C10
Alakurtti Russia 66°58N 30°25E 160 C24
'Alaläkeiki Channel U.S.A. 20°30N 156°30W 302 C5
Alalapura Suriname 2°20N 56°25W 329 C6
Alalaú → Brazil 0°30S 61°9W 329 D5
Alamagan N. Marianas 17°36N 145°50E 302 a
Alamarvdasht Iran 27°37N 52°59E 247 E7
Alamata Ethiopia 12°25N 39°33E 257 E4
Alameda Calif., U.S.A. 37°46N 122°15W 136 B3
Alameda N. Mex., U.S.A. 35°11N 106°37W 305 J10
Alameda, Parque Mexico City, Mexico 128 b2
Alameda Memorial State Beach Park U.S.A. 37°45N 122°16W 136 B3
Alaminos Phil. 16°10N 119°59E 232 C2
Alamo Ga., U.S.A. 32°9N 82°47W 316 C7
Alamo Nev., U.S.A. 37°22N 115°10W 307 H11
Alamogordo U.S.A. 32°54N 105°57W 305 K11
Alamos Mexico 27°1N 108°56W 318 B3
Alamosa U.S.A. 37°28N 105°52W 305 H11
Alampur India 15°55N 78°6E 245 G4
Åland Finland 60°15N 20°0E 161 F19
Aland India 17°36N 76°35E 244 F3
Alandroal Portugal 38°41N 7°24W 195 G3
Ålands hav Europe 60°0N 19°30E 161 G18
Alandur India 13°0N 80°15E 245 H5
Alange, Embalse d' Spain 38°45N 6°18W 195 G4
Alania = North Ossetia □ Russia 43°30N 44°30E 191 J7
Alanís Spain 38°3N 5°43W 195 G5
Alanya Turkey 36°38N 32°0E 250 B3
Alaotra, Farihin' Madag. 17°30S 48°30E 272 B2
Alapaha U.S.A. 31°23N 83°13W 316 D6
Alapayevsk Russia 57°52N 61°42E 214 D7
Alappuzha = Alleppey India 9°30N 76°28E 245 K3
'Alāqán Si. Arabia 29°10N 35°21E 251 J6
Alar del Rey Spain 42°38N 4°20W 194 C6
Alara → Turkey 36°38N 31°39E 250 B2
Alaraz Spain 40°45N 5°17W 194 E5
Alarcón, Embalse de Spain 39°36N 2°10W 196 F2
Alarobia-Vohiposa Madag. 20°59S 47°9E 272 C2
Alaşehir Turkey 38°23N 28°30E 205 C10
Alaska □ U.S.A. 64°0N 154°0W 303 D9
Alaska, G. of Pac. Oc. 58°0N 145°0W 303 G11
Alaska Maritime Nat. Wildlife Refuge ⌂ U.S.A. 52°0N 174°0W 303 L4
Alaska Peninsula U.S.A. 56°0N 159°0W 303 H8
Alaska Peninsula Nat. Wildlife Refuge ⌂ U.S.A. 56°0N 159°0W 303 J8
Alaska Range U.S.A. 62°50N 151°0W 303 E10
Alássio Italy 44°0N 8°10E 198 E5
Älät Azerbaijan 39°58N 49°25E 191 L9
Alatau Shan = Ala Tau Asia 45°30N 80°40E 217 C10
Alatri Italy 41°43N 13°21E 199 G10
Alatyr Russia 54°55N 46°35E 190 C8
Alatyr → Russia 54°52N 46°36E 190 C8
Alaungdaw Kathapa △ Burma 22°30N 94°30E 241 D5
Alausi Ecuador 2°0S 78°50W 328 D2
Álava □ Spain 42°48N 2°28W 196 C2
Alava, C. U.S.A. 48°10N 124°44W 304 B1
Alaverdi Armenia 41°15N 44°37E 191 K7
Alavo = Alavus Finland 62°35N 23°36E 160 E20
Alavus Finland 62°35N 23°36E 160 E20
Alawoona Australia 34°45S 140°30E 282 C4
'Alayh Lebanon 33°46N 35°33E 250 E6
Alazani → Azerbaijan 41°5N 46°40E 191 K8
Alba Italy 44°42N 8°2E 198 D5
Alba □ Romania 46°10N 23°30E 183 D8
Alba Adriática Italy 42°50N 13°56E 199 F10
Alba de Tormes Spain 40°50N 5°30W 194 E5
Alba-Iulia Romania 46°8N 23°39E 183 D8
Albac Romania 46°28N 22°58E 182 D7
Albacete Spain 39°0N 1°50W 197 F3
Albacete □ Spain 38°50N 2°0W 197 G3
Albacutya, L. Australia 35°45S 141°58E 282 C4
Ålbæk Denmark 57°36N 10°25E 163 G4
Ålbæk Bugt Denmark 57°35N 10°40E 163 G4
Albaida Spain 38°51N 0°31W 197 G4
Albalate de las Nogueras Spain 40°22N 2°18W 196 E2
Albalate del Arzobispo Spain 41°6N 0°31W 196 D4
Alban France 43°53N 2°28E 174 E6
Albanel, L. Canada 50°55N 73°12W 298 B5
Albania ■ Europe 41°0N 20°0E 202 E4
Albano Laziale Italy 41°44N 12°39E 199 G9
Albany W. Austral., Australia 35°1S 117°58E 279 G2
Albany Ga., U.S.A. 31°35N 84°10W 316 D5
Albany Ind., U.S.A. 40°18N 85°14W 311 D11
Albany Mo., U.S.A. 40°15N 94°20W 310 D2
Albany N.Y., U.S.A. 42°39N 73°45W 313 D11
Albany Oreg., U.S.A. 44°38N 123°6W 304 D2
Albany Tex., U.S.A. 32°44N 99°18W 314 E5
Albany Wis., U.S.A. 42°42N 89°26W 310 B7
Albany → Canada 52°17N 81°31W 298 B3
Albardón Argentina 31°20S 68°30W 334 C2
Albarracín Spain 40°25N 1°26W 196 E3
Albarracín, Sierra de Spain 40°30N 1°30W 196 E3
Albatera Spain 38°11N 0°52W 197 G4
Albatross B. Australia 12°45S 141°30E 280 A3
Albatross Pt. N.Z. 38°7S 174°44E 284 E3
Albay □ Phil. 13°13N 123°33E 232 E4
Albegna → Italy 42°30N 11°11E 199 F8
Albemarle U.S.A. 35°21N 80°12W 315 D14
Albemarle, I. = Isabela, I. Ecuador 0°30S 91°4W 330 a
Albemarle, Pta. Ecuador 0°11N 91°21W 330 a
Albemarle Sd. U.S.A. 36°5N 76°0W 315 C16
Albenga Italy 44°3N 8°13E 198 D5
Alberche → Spain 39°58N 4°46W 194 F6
Alberdi Paraguay 26°14S 58°20W 334 B4
Albères, Mts. France 42°28N 2°56E 174 F6
Ålberga Sweden 58°44N 16°35E 163 F10
Alberga → Australia 27°6S 135°33E 281 D2
Albern Austria 48°9N 16°29E 142 B2
Albersdorf Germany 54°8N 9°17E 178 A5
Albert France 50°0N 2°38E 173 C9
Albert, L. Africa 1°30N 31°0E 268 B3
Albert, L. S. Austral., Australia 35°30S 139°10E 282 C3
Albert Edward, Mt. Papua N. G. 8°20S 147°24E 286 E4
Albert Edward Ra. Australia 18°17S 127°57E 278 C4
Albert Lea U.S.A. 43°39N 93°22W 308 D7
Albert National Park = Virunga △ Dem. Rep. of the Congo 0°5N 29°38E 268 B2
Albert Nile → Uganda 3°36N 32°2E 268 B3
Albert Park Australia 37°51S 144°58E 128 B1
Albert Town Bahamas 22°37N 74°33W 321 B5

342 Albert Town INDEX

Albert Town *Jamaica* 18°17N 77°33W **320** a
Alberta □ *Canada* 54°40N 115°0W **296** C6
Alberti *Argentina* 35°1S 60°16W **334** D3
Albertinia *S. Africa* 34°11S 21°34E **270** D3
Albertirsa *Hungary* 47°14N 19°37E **182** C4
Alberto de Agostini △ *Chile* 54°38S 71°37W **336** D2
Alberton *P.E.I., Canada* 46°50N 64°0W **299** C7
Alberton *Gauteng, S. Africa* 26°15S 28°7E **123** B2
Albertslund *Denmark* 55°39N 12°21E **118** B2
Albertville = Kalemie *Dem. Rep. of the Congo* 5°55S 29°9E **268** D2
Albertville *Savoie, France* 45°40N 6°22E **175** C10
Albertville *Ala., U.S.A.* 34°16N 86°13W **315** D11
Albi *France* 43°56N 2°9E **174** E6
Albia *U.S.A.* 41°2N 92°48W **310** C4
Albina *Suriname* 5°37N 54°15W **329** B7
Albina, Ponta *Angola* 15°52S 11°44E **265** F2
Albino *Italy* 45°46N 9°47E **198** C6
Albion *Ill., U.S.A.* 38°23N 88°4W **311** F8
Albion *Ind., U.S.A.* 41°24N 85°25W **311** C11
Albion *Mich., U.S.A.* 42°15N 84°45W **311** B12
Albion *Nebr., U.S.A.* 41°42N 98°0W **308** E4
Albion *Pa., U.S.A.* 41°53N 80°22W **312** E4
Albocácer *Spain* 40°21N 0°1E **196** E5
Albolote *Spain* 37°14N 3°39W **195** H7
Alborán *Medit. S.* 35°57N 3°0W **195** K7
Alborea *Spain* 39°17N 1°24W **197** F3
Ålborg = Aalborg *Denmark* 57°2N 9°54E **163** G3
Ålborg Bugt = Aalborg Bugt *Denmark* 56°50N 10°35E **163** H4
Alborz, Reshteh-ye Kūhhā-ye *Iran* 36°0N 52°0E **247** C7
Albox *Spain* 37°23N 2°8W **197** H2
Albuera *Phil.* 10°55N 124°42E **233** F5
Albufeira *Portugal* 37°5N 8°15W **195** H2
Albula → *Switz.* 46°38N 9°28E **179** J5
Albuñol *Spain* 36°48N 3°11W **195** J7
Albuquerque *Brazil* 19°23S 57°26W **331** D6
Albuquerque *N. Mex., U.S.A.* 35°5N 106°39W **305** J10
Albuquerque, Cayos de *Caribbean* 12°10N 81°50W **320** D3
Alburg *U.S.A.* 44°59N 73°18W **313** B11
Alburno, Mte. *Italy* 40°33N 15°17E **201** B8
Alburquerque *Spain* 39°15N 6°59W **195** F4
Albury *Australia* 36°3S 146°56E **283** D7
Albysjön *Sweden* 59°14N 17°52E **139** B1
Alcácer do Sal *Portugal* 38°22N 8°33W **195** G2
Alcáçovas *Portugal* 38°23N 8°9W **195** G2
Alcala *Phil.* 17°54N 121°39E **232** C3
Alcalá de Chivert *Spain* 40°19N 0°13E **196** E5
Alcalá de Guadaira *Spain* 37°20N 5°50W **195** H5
Alcalá de Henares *Spain* 40°28N 3°22W **194** E7
Alcalá de los Gazules *Spain* 36°29N 5°43W **195** J5
Alcalá del Júcar *Spain* 39°12N 1°26W **197** F3
Alcalá del Río *Spain* 37°31N 5°59W **195** H5
Alcalá del Valle *Spain* 36°54N 5°10W **195** J5
Alcalá la Real *Spain* 37°27N 3°57W **195** H7
Álcamo *Italy* 37°59N 12°55E **200** E5
Alcanadre *Spain* 42°24N 2°7W **196** C2
Alcanadre → *Spain* 41°43N 0°12W **196** D4
Alcanar *Spain* 40°33N 0°28E **196** E5
Alcanede *Portugal* 39°25N 8°49W **195** F2
Alcanena *Portugal* 39°27N 8°40W **195** F2
Alcañices *Spain* 41°41N 6°21W **194** D4
Alcaníz *Spain* 41°2N 0°8W **196** D4
Alcântara *Brazil* 2°20S 44°30W **332** B3
Alcantara *Lisboa, Portugal* 38°43N 9°10W **126** A1
Alcántara *Spain* 39°41N 6°57W **194** F4
Alcántara, Embalse de *Spain* 39°44N 6°50W **194** F4
Alcantarilla *Spain* 37°59N 1°12W **197** H3
Alcaracejos *Spain* 38°24N 4°58W **195** G6
Alcaraz *Spain* 38°40N 2°29W **197** G2
Alcaraz, Sierra de *Spain* 38°40N 2°20W **197** G2
Alcatraz I. *U.S.A.* 37°49N 122°25W **136** B2
Alcaudete *Spain* 37°35N 4°5W **195** H6
Alcázar de San Juan *Spain* 39°24N 3°12W **195** F7
Alcazarquivir = Ksar el Kebir *Morocco* 35°0N 6°0W **260** B3
Alcedo, Volcán *Ecuador* 0°24S 91°6W **330** a
Alchevsk *Ukraine* 48°30N 38°45E **189** H10
Alcira = Alzira *Spain* 39°9N 0°30W **197** F4
Alcobaça = Tucuruí *Brazil* 3°42S 49°44W **332** B2
Alcobaça *Portugal* 39°32N 8°58W **195** F2
Alcobendas *Spain* 40°32N 3°38W **127** A2
Alcolea del Pinar *Spain* 41°2N 2°28W **196** D2
Alcoma *U.S.A.* 27°54N 81°29W **317** H8
Alcora *Spain* 40°5N 0°14W **196** E4
Alcorcón *Spain* 40°20N 3°48W **127** B1
Alcoutim *Portugal* 37°25N 7°28W **195** H3
Alcova *U.S.A.* 42°34N 106°43W **304** E10
Alcoy *Spain* 38°43N 0°30W **197** G4
Alcubierre, Sierra de *Spain* 41°45N 0°22W **196** D4
Alcublas *Spain* 39°48N 0°43W **196** F4
Alcúdia *Spain* 39°51N 3°7E **206** B4
Alcúdia, B. d' *Spain* 39°47N 3°15E **206** B4
Alcudia, Sierra de la *Spain* 38°34N 4°30W **195** G6
Aldabra Is. *Seychelles* 9°22S 46°28E **255** G8
Aldama *Mexico* 22°55N 98°4W **319** C5
Aldan *Russia* 58°40N 125°30E **215** D13
Aldan → *Russia* 63°28N 129°35E **215** C13
Aldea, Pta. de la *Canary Is.* 28°0N 15°50W **153** e1
Aldeburgh *U.K.* 52°10N 1°37E **169** E9
Alden *Norway* 61°19N 4°45E **164** C1
Alder Pk. *U.S.A.* 35°53N 121°22W **306** K5
Alderney *U.K.* 49°42N 2°11W **169** H5
Aldershof *Germany* 52°26N 13°33E **115** B4
Aldershot *U.K.* 51°15N 0°44W **169** F7
Aldinga Beach *Australia* 35°17S 138°27E **282** C3
Aldo Bonzi *Argentina* 34°42S 58°31W **117** C1
Åled *Sweden* 56°44N 12°57E **163** H6
Aledo *U.S.A.* 41°12N 90°45W **310** C6
Alefa *Ethiopia* 11°55N 36°55E **257** E4
Aleg *Mauritania* 17°3N 13°55W **262** B2
Alegranza *Canary Is.* 29°23N 13°32W **260** C2
Alegranza, I. *Canary Is.* 29°23N 13°32W **153** e2
Alegre *Brazil* 20°50S 41°30W **333** F3
Alegrete *Brazil* 29°40S 56°0W **335** B4
Aleknagik *U.S.A.* 59°17N 158°36W **303** G8
Aleksandriya = Oleksandriya *Kirovohrad, Ukraine* 48°42N 33°3E **189** H7
Aleksandriya = Oleksandriya *Rivne, Ukraine* 50°37N 26°19E **177** C14
Aleksandriyskaya *Russia* 43°58N 47°14E **191** J8
Aleksandropol = Gyumri *Armenia* 40°47N 43°50E **191** K6
Aleksandrov *Russia* 56°23N 38°44E **188** D10
Aleksandrov Gay *Russia* 50°9N 48°34E **190** E9
Aleksandrovac *Serbia* 43°28N 21°3E **202** C5
Aleksandrovac *Serbia* 44°28N 21°13E **202** B5
Aleksandrovka = Oleksandrovka *Ukraine* 48°55N 32°20E **189** H7
Aleksandrovka = Ordzhonikidze *Ukraine* 47°39N 34°3E **189** J8
Aleksandrovo *Bulgaria* 43°14N 24°51E **203** C8
Aleksandrovsk = Belogorsk *Russia* 51°0N 128°20E **215** D13
Aleksandrovsk = Polyarny *Russia* 69°8N 33°20E **160** B25
Aleksandrovsk = Zaporizhzhya *Ukraine* 47°50N 35°10E **189** J8
Aleksandrovsk-Grushevsky = Shakhty *Russia* 47°40N 40°16E **191** G5
Aleksandrovsk-Sakhalinskiy *Russia* 50°50N 142°20E **215** D15
Aleksandrovskoye *Russia* 59°51N 30°20E **137** B2
Aleksandrów Kujawski *Poland* 52°53N 18°43E **185** F5
Aleksandrów Łódźki *Poland* 51°49N 19°17E **185** G6
Aleksandry, Zemlya *Russia* 80°25N 48°0E **150** A10
Alekseyevka *Samara, Russia* 52°35N 51°17E **190** D10
Alekseyevka *Voronezh, Russia* 50°43N 38°40E **189** G10
Alekseyevsk = Svobodnyy *Russia* 51°20N 128°0E **215** D13
Alekseyevskoye = Qazyghurt *Kazakhstan* 41°45N 69°23E **217** D7
Aleksin *Russia* 54°31N 37°9E **188** E9
Aleksinac *Serbia* 43°31N 21°42E **202** C5
Além Paraíba *Brazil* 21°52S 42°41W **333** F3
Alemania *Argentina* 25°40S 65°30W **334** B2
Alemania *Chile* 25°10S 69°55W **334** B2
Alen *Eq. Guin.* 1°58N 11°19E **264** B2
Alençon *France* 48°27N 0°4E **172** D7
'Alenuihähä Channel *U.S.A.* 20°30N 156°0W **302** C5
Alépé *Ivory C.* 5°29N 3°40W **262** D4
Aleppo = Ḥalab *Syria* 36°10N 37°15E **250** B8
Alerce Andino △ *Chile* 41°33S 72°29W **336** B2
Aléria *France* 42°5N 9°26E **175** F13
Alert *Canada* 83°2N 60°0W **295** A13
Aleru *India* 17°39N 79°3E **244** F4
Alès *France* 44°9N 4°5E **175** D8
Aleşd *Romania* 47°3N 22°22E **182** C7
Alessándria *Italy* 44°54N 8°37E **198** D5
Ålesund *Norway* 62°28N 6°12E **164** B3
Alet-les-Bains *France* 42°59N 2°14E **174** F6
Aletschhorn *Switz.* 46°28N 8°0E **179** J4
Aleutian Basin *Pac. Oc.* 57°0N 177°0E **288** B9
Aleutian Is. *Pac. Oc.* 52°0N 175°0W **303** K3
Aleutian Range *U.S.A.* 60°0N 154°0W **303** G9
Aleutian Trench *Pac. Oc.* 48°0N 180°0E **150** D17
Alexander *Ga., U.S.A.* 33°1N 81°53W **316** B8
Alexander *N. Dak., U.S.A.* 47°51N 103°39W **308** B2
Alexander, C. *Solomon Is.* 6°34S 156°32E **287** L9
Alexander, Mt. *Australia* 28°58S 120°16E **279** E3
Alexander Arch. *U.S.A.* 56°0N 136°0W **303** J14
Alexander Bay *S. Africa* 28°40S 16°30E **270** C2
Alexander City *U.S.A.* 32°56N 85°58W **316** C4
Alexander I. *Antarctica* 69°0S 70°0W **151** C17
Alexander Nevsky Abbey *Russia* 59°54N 30°23E **137** B2
Alexander Soutzos Moussio *Athens, Greece* **112** b3
Alexandra *Vic., Australia* 37°8S 145°40E **283** D6
Alexandra *N.Z.* 45°14S 169°25E **285** F4
Alexandra *Singapore, Singapore* 1°17N 103°49E **138** B2
Alexandra *Gauteng, S. Africa* 26°6S 28°5E **123** A2
Alexandra Channel *Burma* 14°7N 93°13E **245** G11
Alexandra Falls *Canada* 60°29N 116°18W **296** A5
Alexandretta = İskenderun *Turkey* 36°32N 36°10E **250** B7
Alexandria = El Iskandarîya *Egypt* 31°13N 29°58E **256** H7
Alexandria *B.C., Canada* 52°35N 122°27W **296** C4
Alexandria *Ont., Canada* 45°19N 74°38W **313** A10
Alexandria *Romania* 43°57N 25°24E **183** G10
Alexandria *Eastern Cape, S. Africa* 33°38S 26°28E **270** D4
Alexandria *W. Dunb., U.K.* 55°59N 4°35W **167** F4
Alexandria *Ind., U.S.A.* 40°16N 85°41W **311** D11
Alexandria *Ky., U.S.A.* 38°58N 84°23W **311** F12
Alexandria *La., U.S.A.* 31°18N 92°27W **314** F8
Alexandria *Minn., U.S.A.* 45°53N 95°22W **308** C6
Alexandria *Mo., U.S.A.* 40°27N 91°28W **310** D5
Alexandria *S. Dak., U.S.A.* 43°39N 97°47W **308** D5
Alexandria *Va., U.S.A.* 38°49N 77°5W **143** C3
Alexandria Bay *U.S.A.* 44°20N 75°55W **313** B9
Alexandrina, L. *Australia* 35°25S 139°10E **282** C3
Alexandroupoli *Greece* 40°50N 25°54E **203** F9
Alexis *U.S.A.* 41°4N 90°33W **310** C6
Alexis → *Canada* 52°33N 56°8W **299** B8
Alexis Creek *Canada* 52°10N 123°20W **296** C4
Aley → *Russia* 52°51N 83°36E **217** B10
Aleysk *Russia* 52°40N 83°0E **217** B10
Alfabia *Spain* 39°44N 2°44E **206** B3
Alfama *Lisbon, Portugal* **126** c3
Alfambra *Spain* 40°33N 1°5W **196** E3
Alfândega da Fé *Portugal* 41°20N 6°59W **194** D4
Alfaro *Spain* 42°10N 1°50W **196** C3
Alfatar *Bulgaria* 43°59N 27°13E **203** C11
Alfaz del Pi *Spain* 38°35N 0°5W **197** G4
Alfeld *Germany* 51°59N 9°50E **178** D5
Alfenas *Brazil* 21°20S 46°10W **335** A6
Alföld *Hungary* 46°30N 20°0E **182** D5
Alfonsine *Italy* 44°30N 12°3E **199** D9
Alford *Aberds., U.K.* 57°14N 2°41W **167** D6
Alford *Lincs., U.K.* 53°15N 0°10E **168** D8
Alford *Fla., U.S.A.* 30°42N 85°24W **316** E4
Alfortville *France* 48°48N 2°24E **134** B3
Ålfotbreen *Norway* 61°45N 5°39E **164** C2
Ålfoten *Norway* 61°51N 5°41E **164** C2
Alfred *Maine, U.S.A.* 43°29N 70°43W **313** C14
Alfred *N.Y., U.S.A.* 42°16N 77°48W **312** D7
Alfredton *N.Z.* 40°41S 175°54E **284** G4
Alfreton *U.K.* 53°6N 1°24W **168** D6
Alfta *Sweden* 61°21N 16°4E **162** C10
Alga *Kazakhstan* 49°53N 57°20E **187** E10
Algaida *Spain* 39°33N 2°53E **206** B3
Algar *Spain* 36°40N 5°39W **195** J5
Ålgård *Norway* 58°46N 5°53E **164** F2
Algarinejo *Spain* 37°19N 4°9W **195** H6
Algarve *Portugal* 36°58N 8°20W **195** J2
Algeciras *Spain* 36°9N 5°28W **195** J5
Algemesí *Spain* 39°11N 0°27W **197** F4
Alger *Algeria* 36°42N 3°8E **261** A5
Alger □ *Algeria* 36°45N 3°10E **197** J8
Alger ✈ (ALG) *Algeria* 36°39N 3°13E **197** J8
Algeria ■ *Africa* 28°30N 2°0E **261** C5
Algés *Portugal* 38°42N 9°13W **126** A1
Alghero *Italy* 40°33N 8°19E **200** B1
Älghult *Sweden* 57°0N 15°35E **163** G9
Algiers = Alger *Algeria* 36°42N 3°8E **261** A5
Algoa B. *S. Africa* 33°50S 25°45E **270** D4
Algodonales *Spain* 36°54N 5°24W **195** J5
Algodor → *Spain* 39°55N 3°53W **194** F7
Algoma *U.S.A.* 44°36N 87°26W **308** C10
Algona *U.S.A.* 43°4N 94°14W **310** A2
Algonac *U.S.A.* 42°37N 82°32W **312** D2
Algonquin ⌂ *Canada* 45°50N 78°30W **298** C4
Alhama de Almería *Spain* 36°57N 2°34W **195** J8
Alhama de Aragón *Spain* 41°18N 1°54W **196** D3
Alhama de Granada *Spain* 37°0N 3°59W **195** H7
Alhama de Murcia *Spain* 37°51N 1°25W **197** H3
Alhambra *U.S.A.* 34°5N 118°7W **126** B4
Alhaurín el Grande *Spain* 36°39N 4°41W **195** J6
Alhucemas = Al Hoceïma *Morocco* 35°8N 3°58W **261** A4
'Alī al Gharbī *Iraq* 32°30N 46°45E **213** F12
'Alī ash Sharqī *Iraq* 32°7N 46°44E **213** F12
Äli Bayramlı *Azerbaijan* 39°59N 48°52E **191** L9
'Alī Khēl *Afghan.* 33°57N 69°43E **242** C3
Ali Sahîh *Djibouti* 11°10N 42°44E **257** E5
Alī Shāh *Iran* 38°9N 45°50E **246** B5
Ália *Italy* 37°47N 13°43E **200** E6
'Alīābād *Khorāsān, Iran* 32°30N 57°30E **247** C8
'Alīābād *Kordestān, Iran* 35°4N 46°58E **246** C5
'Alīābād *Yazd, Iran* 31°41N 53°49E **247** D7
Aliaga *Spain* 40°40N 0°42W **196** E4
Aliağa *Turkey* 38°47N 26°59E **205** C8
Aliakmonas → *Greece* 40°30N 22°36E **202** F6
Alibag *India* 18°38N 72°56E **244** E1
Alibey → *Turkey* 41°3N 28°56E **122** B1
Alibey Barajı *Turkey* 41°8N 28°53E **122** B1
Alibeyköy *Turkey* 41°4N 28°56E **122** B1
Alibo *Ethiopia* 9°52N 37°5E **257** F4
Alibori → *Benin* 11°56N 3°17E **263** C5
Alibunar *Serbia* 45°5N 20°57E **182** E5
Alicante *Spain* 38°23N 0°30W **197** G4
Alicante □ *Spain* 38°30N 0°37W **197** G4
Alicante ✈ (ALC) *Spain* 38°14N 0°36W **197** G4
Alice *Eastern Cape, S. Africa* 32°48S 26°55E **270** D4
Alice *Tex., U.S.A.* 27°45N 98°5W **314** H5
Alice → *Queens., Australia* 24°2S 144°50E **280** C3
Alice → *Queens., Australia* 15°35S 142°20E **280** B3
Alice → *Papua N. G.* 6°10S 141°8E **286** D1
Alice, Punta *Italy* 39°24N 17°9E **201** C10
Alice Arm *Canada* 55°29N 129°31W **296** B3
Alice Springs *Australia* 23°40S 133°50E **280** C1
Alicedale *S. Africa* 33°15S 26°4E **270** D4
Aliceville *U.S.A.* 33°8N 88°9W **315** E10
Alicia *Bohol, Phil.* 9°54N 124°26E **233** G5
Alicia *Isabela, Phil.* 16°46N 121°42E **232** C3
Alicudi *Italy* 38°33N 14°20E **201** D7
Alien *Taiwan* 22°52N 120°19E **225** D2
Aliganj *India* 27°30N 79°10E **243** F8
Aligarh *Raj., India* 25°55N 76°15E **242** G7
Aligarh *Ut. P., India* 27°55N 78°10E **242** F8
Alīgūdarz *Iran* 33°25N 49°45E **247** C6
Alijó *Portugal* 41°16N 7°27W **194** D3
Alikanas *Greece* 37°51N 20°47E **207** D2
Alima → *Congo* 1°35S 16°37E **264** C3
Alimia *Greece* 36°16N 27°43E **206** E11
Alimodian *Phil.* 10°49N 122°26E **233** F4
Alimos *Greece* 37°52N 23°43E **112** B2
Alindao *C.A.R.* 5°2N 21°13E **264** A4
Alingsås *Sweden* 57°56N 12°31E **163** G6
Alipur *W. Bengal, India* 22°43N 88°12E **124** B1
Alipur *Pakistan* 29°25N 70°55E **242** E4
Alipur Duar *India* 26°30N 89°35E **241** B2
Aliquippa *U.S.A.* 40°37N 80°15W **312** F4
Alishan *Taiwan* 23°31N 120°48E **225** C2
Aliste → *Spain* 41°34N 5°58W **194** D5
Alitus = Alytus *Lithuania* 54°24N 24°3E **188** E3
Aliveri *Greece* 38°24N 24°2E **204** C6
Aliwal North *S. Africa* 30°45S 26°45E **270** D4
Alix *Canada* 52°24N 113°11W **296** C6
Aljezur *Portugal* 37°18N 8°49W **195** H2
Aljustrel *Portugal* 37°55N 8°10W **195** H2
Alkamari *Niger* 13°27N 11°10E **259** F2
Alkmaar *Neths.* 52°37N 4°45E **170** B4
All American Canal *U.S.A.* 32°45N 115°15W **305** K6
Allacapan *Phil.* 18°15N 121°35E **232** B3
Allach *Germany* 48°11N 11°27E **131** A1
Allada *Benin* 6°41N 2°9E **263** D5
Allagadda *India* 15°8N 78°30E **245** G4
Allagash → *U.S.A.* 47°5N 69°3W **309** B19
Allah Dad *Pakistan* 25°38N 67°34E **242** G2
Allahabad *India* 25°25N 81°58E **243** G9
Allakaket *U.S.A.* 66°34N 152°39W **303** C9
Allal Tazi *Morocco* 34°30N 6°20W **260** B3
Allambie Heights *Australia* 33°46S 151°15E **139** A2
Allan *Canada* 51°53N 106°4W **297** C7
Allanche *France* 45°14N 2°57E **174** C6
Allanmyo *Burma* 19°30N 95°17E **241** F5
Allanridge *S. Africa* 27°45S 26°40E **270** C4
Allansford *Australia* 38°26S 142°39E **282** E5
Allanton *N.Z.* 45°55S 170°15E **285** F5
Allaqi, Wadi → *Egypt* 23°7N 32°47E **256** C3
Allard Pierson Museum *Amsterdam, Neths.* **112** b2
Allariz *Spain* 42°11N 7°50W **194** C3
Allassac *France* 45°15N 1°29E **174** C5
Allatoona L. *U.S.A.* 34°10N 84°44W **316** A5
Ålleberg *Sweden* 58°8N 13°36E **163** F7
Allegan *U.S.A.* 42°32N 85°51W **311** B11
Allegany *U.S.A.* 42°6N 78°30W **312** D6
Allegheny → *U.S.A.* 40°27N 80°1W **312** F5
Allegheny Mts. *U.S.A.* 38°15N 80°10W **309** F13
Allegheny Plateau *U.S.A.* 41°30N 78°30W **309** E14
Allegheny Res. *U.S.A.* 41°50N 79°0W **312** E6
Allègre *France* 45°12N 3°41E **174** C7
Allègre, Pte. *Guadeloupe* 16°22N 61°46W **322** e
Allen *Argentina* 38°58S 67°50W **336** A3
Allen *Phil.* 12°30N 124°17E **232** E5
Allen, Bog of *Ireland* 53°15N 7°0W **166** C5
Allen, L. *Ireland* 54°8N 8°4W **166** B3
Allendale *U.S.A.* 33°1N 81°18W **316** B8
Allende *Mexico* 28°20N 100°51W **318** B4
Allenstein = Olsztyn *Poland* 53°48N 20°29E **184** E7
Allentown *U.S.A.* 40°37N 75°29W **313** F9
Allentsteig *Austria* 48°41N 15°20E **180** C8
Alleppey *India* 9°30N 76°28E **245** K3
Allepuz *Spain* 40°29N 0°44W **196** E4
Aller → *Germany* 52°56N 9°12E **178** C5
Allermuir Hill *U.K.* 55°53N 3°14W **121** B2
Alley, The *Jamaica* 17°48N 77°17W **320** a
Alliance *Suriname* 5°50N 54°50W **329** B7
Alliance *Nebr., U.S.A.* 42°6N 102°52W **308** D2
Alliance *Ohio, U.S.A.* 40°55N 81°6W **312** F3
Allier □ *France* 46°25N 2°40E **173** F9
Allier → *France* 46°57N 3°4E **173** F10
Alliford Bay *Canada* 53°12N 131°58W **296** C2
Alligator Pond *Jamaica* 17°52N 77°34W **320** a
Allinagaram *India* 10°2N 77°30E **245** J3
Allinge *Denmark* 55°17N 14°50E **163** J8
Allison *U.S.A.* 42°45N 92°48W **310** B4
Alliston = New Tecumseth *Canada* 44°9N 79°52W **312** B5
Alloa *U.K.* 56°7N 3°47W **167** E5
Allones *France* 48°20N 1°40E **172** D8
Allora *Australia* 28°2S 152°0E **281** D5
Allos *France* 44°15N 6°38E **175** D10
Allstate Arena *U.S.A.* 42°2N 87°54W **119** A1
Allston *U.S.A.* 42°21N 71°7W **116** A2
Alluitsup Paa *Greenland* 60°30N 45°35W **154** E6
Allur *India* 14°40N 80°4E **245** G5
Alluru Kottapatnam *India* 15°24N 80°7E **245** G5
Alma *Qué., Canada* 48°35N 71°40W **299** C5
Alma *Ga., U.S.A.* 31°33N 82°28W **316** D7
Alma *Kans., U.S.A.* 39°1N 96°17W **308** F5
Alma *Mich., U.S.A.* 43°23N 84°39W **309** D11
Alma *Nebr., U.S.A.* 40°6N 99°22W **308** E4
Alma *Wis., U.S.A.* 44°20N 91°55W **308** C8
Alma Ata = Almaty *Kazakhstan* 43°15N 76°57E **217** D9
Almacelles *Spain* 41°43N 0°27E **196** D5
Almada *Portugal* 38°41N 9°8W **126** A2
Almaden *Queens., Australia* 17°22S 144°40E **280** B3
Almadén *Spain* 38°49N 4°52W **195** G6
Almagro *Argentina* 34°38S 58°24W **117** B2
Almalyk = Olmaliq *Uzbekistan* 40°50N 69°35E **217** D7
Almanor, L. *U.S.A.* 40°14N 121°9W **304** F3
Almansa *Spain* 38°51N 1°5W **197** G3
Almanza *Spain* 42°39N 5°3W **194** C5
Almanzor, Pico *Spain* 40°15N 5°18W **194** E5
Almanzora → *Spain* 37°14N 1°46W **197** H3
Almargem do Bispo *Portugal* 38°49N 9°17W **126** A1
Almas *Brazil* 11°33S 47°9W **333** D2
Almaş, Munţii *Romania* 44°49N 22°12E **182** F7
Almassora *Spain* 39°57N 0°3W **196** F4
Almaty *Kazakhstan* 43°15N 76°57E **217** D9
Almaty □ *Kazakhstan* 44°30N 78°0E **217** D9
Almazán *Spain* 41°30N 2°30W **196** D2
Almazovo *Russia* 55°50N 38°3E **129** A6
Almeirim *Brazil* 1°30S 52°34W **329** D7
Almeirim *Portugal* 39°12N 8°37W **195** F2
Almelo *Neths.* 52°22N 6°42E **170** B6
Almenar de Soria *Spain* 41°43N 2°12W **196** D2
Almenara *Brazil* 16°11S 40°42W **333** E3
Almenara *Spain* 39°46N 0°14W **196** F4
Almenara, Sierra de la *Spain* 37°34N 1°32W **197** H3
Almendra, Embalse de *Spain* 41°10N 6°5W **194** D4
Almendralejo *Spain* 38°41N 6°26W **195** G4
Almere-Stad *Neths.* 52°20N 5°15E **170** B5
Almería *Spain* 36°52N 2°27W **195** J8
Almería □ *Spain* 37°20N 2°20W **197** H2
Almería, G. de *Spain* 36°41N 2°28W **197** J2
Almetyevsk *Russia* 54°53N 52°20E **190** C11
Älmhult *Sweden* 56°33N 14°8E **163** H8
Almirante *Panama* 9°10N 82°30W **320** E3
Almirante G. Brown, Parque *Argentina* 34°40S 58°28W **117** C2
Almirante Montt, G. *Chile* 51°52S 72°50W **336** D2
Almiropotamos *Greece* 38°16N 24°11E **204** C6
Almiros *Greece* 39°11N 22°45E **204** B4
Almodôvar *Portugal* 37°31N 8°2W **195** H2
Almodóvar del Campo *Spain* 38°43N 4°10W **195** G6
Almodóvar del Río *Spain* 37°48N 5°1W **195** H5
Almon *West Bank* 31°49N 35°17E **123** B2
Almond *U.S.A.* 42°19N 77°44W **312** D7
Almond → *U.K.* 55°58N 3°18W **121** B2
Almont *U.S.A.* 42°55N 83°3W **312** D1
Almonte *Ont., Canada* 45°14N 76°12W **313** A8
Almonte *Spain* 37°13N 6°38W **195** H4
Almora *India* 29°38N 79°40E **243** E8
Almoradí *Spain* 38°7N 0°46W **197** G4
Almorox *Spain* 40°14N 4°24W **194** E6
Almoustarat *Mali* 17°35N 0°8E **263** B5
Älmsta *Sweden* 59°58N 18°50E **162** E12
Almudévar *Spain* 42°3N 0°35W **196** C4
Almuñécar *Spain* 36°43N 3°41W **195** J7
Almunge *Sweden* 59°53N 18°3E **162** E12
Almuradiel *Spain* 38°32N 3°28W **195** G7
Almyrou, Ormos *Greece* 35°23N 24°20E **207** E5
Alna *Norway* 59°55N 10°50E **133** A4
Alness *U.K.* 57°41N 4°16W **167** D4
Alnif *Morocco* 31°10N 5°8W **260** B3
Alnmouth *U.K.* 55°24N 1°37W **168** B6
Alnsjøen *Norway* 59°57N 10°51E **133** A4
Alnwick *U.K.* 55°24N 1°42W **168** B6
Alofau *Amer. Samoa* 14°16S 170°36W **302** f
Alofi *Niue* 19°1S 169°55W **289** g
Alofi, I. *Wall. & F. Is.* 14°27S 178°5W **277** C15
Alofi B. *Niue* 19°1S 169°56W **289** g
Aloi *Uganda* 2°16N 33°10E **268** B3
Alon *Burma* 22°12N 95°5E **241** D5
Along *India* 28°10N 94°46E **241** A5
Alonissos *Greece* 39°12N 23°50E **204** B5
Alonissos-Northern Sporades △ *Greece* 39°15N 24°5E **204** B6
Alor *Indonesia* 8°15S 124°30E **231** F6
Alor Setar *Malaysia* 6°7N 100°22E **237** J3
Álora *Spain* 36°49N 4°46W **195** J6
Alosno *Spain* 37°33N 7°7W **195** H3
Alost = Aalst *Belgium* 50°56N 4°2E **170** D4
Alot *India* 23°56N 75°40E **242** H6
Alotau *Papua N. G.* 10°16S 150°30E **286** F6
Alougoum *Morocco* 30°17N 6°56W **260** B3
Aloum *Cameroon* 2°16N 10°34E **264** B2
Aloysius, Mt. *Australia* 26°0S 128°38E **279** E4
Alpaugh *U.S.A.* 35°53N 119°29W **306** K7
Alpe Apuane ⌂ *Italy* 44°4N 10°15E **198** D7
Alpedrinha *Portugal* 40°6N 7°27W **194** E3
Alpena *U.S.A.* 45°4N 83°27W **309** C12
Alpercatas → *Brazil* 6°2S 44°19W **332** C3
Alperton *U.K.* 51°32N 0°17W **125** A2
Alpes-de-Haute-Provence □ *France* 44°8N 6°10E **175** D10
Alpes-Maritimes □ *France* 43°55N 7°10E **175** E11
Alpha *Queens., Australia* 23°39S 146°37E **280** C4
Alpha *Ill., U.S.A.* 41°12N 90°23W **310** C6
Alpha Ridge *Arctic* 84°0N 118°0W **150** A2
Alphen aan den Rijn *Neths.* 52°7N 4°40E **170** B4
Alphios → *Greece* 37°40N 21°33E **204** D3
Alphonse *Seychelles* 7°0S 52°45E **273** E4
Alpiarça *Portugal* 39°15N 8°35W **195** F2
Alpine *Ariz., U.S.A.* 33°51N 109°9W **305** K9
Alpine *Calif., U.S.A.* 32°50N 116°46W **307** N10
Alpine *N.J., U.S.A.* 40°57N 73°57W **132** A2
Alpine *Tex., U.S.A.* 30°22N 103°40W **314** F3
Alpine △ *Australia* 36°56S 148°10E **283** D7
Alps *Europe* 46°30N 9°30E **171** C8
Alpu *Turkey* 39°46N 30°58E **212** C4
Alqueta, Barragem do *Portugal* 38°20N 7°25W **195** G3
Alrø *Denmark* 55°52N 10°5E **163** J4
Alrode *S. Africa* 26°17S 28°7E **123** B2
Als *Denmark* 54°59N 9°55E **163** K3
Alsace □ *France* 48°15N 7°25E **173** D14
Alsask *Canada* 51°21N 109°59W **297** C7
Alsasua *Spain* 42°54N 2°10W **196** C2
Alsek → *U.S.A.* 59°10N 138°12W **296** B1
Alsemberg *Belgium* 50°44N 4°20E **116** B2
Alsergrund *Austria* 48°13N 16°21E **142** A2
Alsfeld *Germany* 50°44N 9°16E **178** E5
Alsip *U.S.A.* 41°40N 87°44W **119** C2
Alsta *Norway* 65°58N 12°40E **160** D15
Ålsten *Sweden* 59°19N 17°57E **139** B1
Alstermo *Sweden* 56°58N 15°38E **163** H9
Alston *U.K.* 54°49N 2°25W **168** C5
Alta *Finnmark, Norway* 69°57N 23°10E **160** B20
Älta *Sweden* 59°15N 18°11E **139** B3
Alta, Sierra *Spain* 40°31N 1°30W **196** E3
Alta Floresta *Brazil* 9°57S 55°58W **331** B6
Alta Gracia *Argentina* 31°40S 64°30W **334** C3
Alta Sierra *U.S.A.* 35°42N 118°33W **307** K8
Altadena *U.S.A.* 34°11N 118°8W **126** A4
Altaelva → *Norway* 69°54N 23°17E **160** B20
Altafjorden *Norway* 70°5N 23°5E **160** A20
Altagracia *Venezuela* 10°45N 71°30W **328** A3
Altagracia de Orituco *Venezuela* 9°52N 66°23W **328** B4
Altai = Aerhtai Shan *Mongolia* 46°40N 92°45E **217** C12
Altai = Gorno-Altay □ *Russia* 51°0N 86°0E **217** B11
Altamachi → *Bolivia* 16°8S 66°50W **330** D4
Altamaha → *U.S.A.* 31°20N 81°20W **316** D8
Altamira *Brazil* 3°12S 52°10W **329** D7
Altamira *Chile* 25°47S 69°51W **334** B2
Altamira *Colombia* 2°3N 75°47W **328** C2
Altamira *Tamaulipas, Mexico* 22°24N 97°55W **319** C5
Altamira, Cuevas de *Spain* 43°20N 4°5W **194** B6
Altamont *Ill., U.S.A.* 39°4N 88°45W **311** E8
Altamont *N.Y., U.S.A.* 42°42N 74°2W **313** D10
Altamura *Italy* 40°49N 16°33E **201** B9
Altanbulag *Mongolia* 50°16N 106°30E **218** A5
Altar *Mexico* 30°43N 111°44W **318** A2
Altar, Gran Desierto de *Mexico* 31°50N 114°10W **318** B2
Altata *Mexico* 24°40N 107°55W **318** C3
Altavas *Phil.* 11°32N 122°29E **233** F4
Altavista *U.S.A.* 37°6N 79°17W **309** G14
Altay *China* 47°48N 88°10E **217** C11
Altdorf *Switz.* 46°52N 8°36E **179** J4
Alte-Donau → *Austria* 48°14N 16°25E **142** A2
Alte Mellum *Germany* 53°43N 8°10E **178** B4
Altea *Spain* 38°38N 0°2W **197** G4
Altenberg *Germany* 50°45N 13°45E **178** E9
Altenbruch *Germany* 53°49N 8°46E **178** B4
Altenburg *Germany* 50°59N 12°25E **178** E8
Altenkirchen *Mecklenburg-Vorpommern, Germany* 54°38N 13°22E **178** A9
Altenkirchen *Rhld-Pfz., Germany* 50°41N 7°39E **178** E3
Altenmarkt *Austria* 47°43N 14°39E **180** D7
Alter do Chão *Brazil* 2°31S 54°57W **329** D6
Alter do Chão *Portugal* 39°12N 7°40W **195** F3
Alter Finkenkrug *Germany* 52°35N 13°3E **115** A1
Altes Rathaus *Munich, Germany* **131** b3
Altglienicke *Germany* 52°25N 13°32E **115** B4
Altha *U.S.A.* 30°34N 85°8W **316** E4
Altınkaya Barajı *Turkey* 41°18N 35°30E **212** B6
Altınoluk *Turkey* 39°34N 26°45E **205** B8
Altınova *Turkey* 39°12N 26°47E **205** B8
Altınözü *Turkey* 36°7N 36°14E **250** B7
Altıntaş *Turkey* 39°4N 30°7E **205** B12
Altınyaka *Turkey* 36°33N 30°20E **205** E12
Altınyayla *Turkey* 37°0N 29°33E **205** D11
Altiplano *Bolivia* 17°0S 68°0W **330** D4
Altkirch *France* 47°37N 7°15E **173** E14
Altlandsberg *Germany* 52°33N 13°43E **115** A5
Altlandsberg Nord *Germany* 52°34N 13°43E **115** A5
Altmannsdorf *Austria* 48°9N 16°18E **142** B1
Altmark *Germany* 52°45N 11°30E **178** C7
Altmühl → *Germany* 48°54N 11°52E **179** G7
Altmühltal ⌂ *Germany* 48°55N 11°15E **179** G7
Altmunster *Austria* 47°54N 13°45E **180** D6
Alto Adige = Trentino-Alto Adige □ *Italy* 46°30N 11°20E **199** B8
Alto Alegre *Brazil* 2°50N 61°20W **329** C5
Alto Araguaia *Brazil* 17°15S 53°20W **331** D7
Alto Chicapa *Angola* 10°52S 19°17E **265** E3
Alto Cuchumatanes = Cuchumatanes, Sierra de los *Guatemala* 15°35N 91°25W **320** C1
Alto Cuito = Tempué *Angola* 13°27S 18°49E **265** E3
Alto da Boa Vista *Brazil* 22°57S 43°16W **135** B1
Alto da Moóca *Brazil* 23°34S 46°33W **137** B2
Alto del Carmen *Chile* 28°46S 70°30W **334** B1
Alto del Inca *Chile* 24°10S 68°10W **334** A2
Alto do Pina *Portugal* 38°44N 9°7W **126** A2
Alto Garças *Brazil* 16°56S 53°32W **331** D7
Alto Garda Bresciano ⌂ *Italy* 45°42N 10°38E **198** C7
Alto Iriri → *Brazil* 8°50S 53°25W **331** B7
Alto Ligonha *Mozam.* 15°30S 38°11E **269** F4
Alto Molocue *Mozam.* 15°50S 37°35E **269** F4
Alto Paraguai *Brazil* 14°30S 56°31W **331** C6
Alto Paraguay □ *Paraguay* 21°0S 58°30W **334** A4
Alto Paraiso de Goiás *Brazil* 14°7S 47°31W **333** D2
Alto Paraná □ *Paraguay* 25°30S 54°50W **335** B5
Alto Parnaíba *Brazil* 9°6S 45°57W **332** C2
Alto Purús → *Peru* 9°12S 70°28W **330** B3
Alto Río Senguerr *Argentina* 45°2S 70°50W **336** C2
Alto Santo *Brazil* 5°31S 38°15W **332** C4
Alto Sucuriú *Brazil* 19°19S 52°47W **331** D7
Alto Turi *Brazil* 2°54S 45°38W **332** B2
Alton *Ont., Canada* 43°54N 80°5W **312** C4
Alton *Hants., U.K.* 51°9N 0°59W **169** F7
Alton *Ill., U.S.A.* 38°53N 90°11W **310** F6
Alton *N.H., U.S.A.* 43°27N 71°13W **313** C13
Altona *Vic., Australia* 37°51S 144°49E **128** B1
Altona *Man., Canada* 49°6N 97°33W **297** D9
Altoona *Ala., U.S.A.* 34°2N 86°20W **316** A3
Altoona *Iowa, U.S.A.* 41°39N 93°28W **310** C3
Altoona *Pa., U.S.A.* 40°31N 78°24W **312** F6
Altos *Brazil* 5°3S 42°28W **332** C3
Altötting *Germany* 48°12N 12°39E **179** G8
Altstätten *Switz.* 47°22N 9°33E **179** H5
Altun Kupri *Iraq* 35°45N 44°9E **213** E11
Altun Shan *China* 38°30N 88°0E **217** E11
Alturas *U.S.A.* 41°29N 120°32W **304** F3
Altus *U.S.A.* 34°38N 99°20W **314** D5
Alubijid *Phil.* 8°35N 124°29E **233** G5
Alucra *Turkey* 40°22N 38°47E **213** B8
Aluk *Sudan* 8°25N 27°30E **257** F2
Alūksne *Latvia* 57°24N 27°3E **188** D4
Alùla *Somali Rep.* 11°50N 50°45E **267** B7
Alunda *Sweden* 60°4N 18°5E **162** D12
Alunite *U.S.A.* 35°59N 114°55W **307** K12
Aluoro → *Ethiopia* 8°26N 33°24E **257** F3
Alupka *Ukraine* 44°23N 34°2E **189** K8
Alur *India* 15°24N 77°15E **245** E3
Alur Gajah *Malaysia* 2°23N 102°13E **234** B2
Alushta *Ukraine* 44°40N 34°25E **189** K8
Alusi *Indonesia* 7°35S 131°40E **231** F8
Alustante *Spain* 40°36N 1°40W **196** E3
Alutgama *Sri Lanka* 6°26N 79°59E **245** L4
Alutnuwara *Sri Lanka* 7°19N 80°59E **245** L5
Alva *U.S.A.* 36°48N 98°40W **314** C5
Alvaiázere *Portugal* 39°49N 8°23W **194** F2
Älvängen *Sweden* 57°58N 12°8E **163** G6
Alvão ⌂ *Portugal* 41°22N 7°48W **194** D3
Alvarado *Veracruz, Mexico* 18°46N 95°46W **319** D5
Alvarado *Tex., U.S.A.* 32°24N 97°13W **314** E6
Alvarães *Brazil* 3°12S 64°50W **329** D5
Alvaro Obregón, Presa *Mexico* 27°52N 109°52W **318** B3
Alvdal *Norway* 62°6N 10°37E **164** B7
Älvdalen *Sweden* 61°13N 14°4E **162** C8
Alvear *Argentina* 29°5S 56°30W **334** B4
Alverca *Portugal* 38°56N 9°1W **195** G1
Alvesta *Sweden* 56°54N 14°35E **163** H8
Alvik *Sweden* 59°19N 17°58E **139** B1
Alvin *U.S.A.* 29°26N 95°15W **314** G7
Alvin Callendar Naval Air Station *U.S.A.* 29°50N 90°1W **131** B2
Alvinston *Canada* 42°49N 81°52W **312** D3
Alvito *Portugal* 38°15N 7°58W **195** G3
Älvkarleby *Sweden* 60°34N 17°26E **162** D11
Alvorado *Brazil* 12°28S 49°6W **333** D2
Alvord Desert *U.S.A.* 42°30N 118°25W **304** E4
Älvros *Sweden* 62°3N 14°38E **162** B8
Älvsbyn *Sweden* 65°40N 21°0E **160** D19
Älvsjo *Sweden* 59°16N 18°0E **139** B2
Ålvundeid *Norway* 62°45N 8°33E **164** B5
Älvvik *Sweden* 59°21N 18°15E **139** A3
Alwar *India* 27°38N 76°34E **242** F7
Alwaye *India* 10°8N 76°24E **245** J3
Alxa Zuoqi *China* 38°50N 105°40E **226** E3
Alyangula *Australia* 13°55S 136°30E **280** A2
Alyata = Älät *Azerbaijan* 39°58N 49°25E **191** L9
Alyth *U.K.* 56°38N 3°13W **167** E5
Alytus *Lithuania* 54°24N 24°3E **188** E3
Alzada *U.S.A.* 45°2N 104°25W **304** D11
Alzey *Germany* 49°45N 8°7E **179** F4
Alzira *Spain* 39°9N 0°30W **197** F4
Am Dam *Chad* 12°40N 20°35E **259** F4
Am Géréda *Chad* 12°53N 21°14E **259** F4
Am Hasenbergl *Germany* 48°12N 11°33E **131** A2
Am Loubia *Chad* 13°39N 20°8E **259** F4
Am Steinhof *Austria* 48°12N 16°17E **142** A1
Am Timan *Chad* 11°0N 20°10E **259** F4
Am Wald *Germany* 48°3N 11°36E **131** B2
Ama Keng *Singapore* 1°23N 103°41E **138** A2
Amacayacu △ *Colombia* 3°21S 70°8W **328** D3
Amada Gaza *C.A.R.* 4°46N 15°9E **264** B3
Amadeus, L. *Australia* 24°54S 131°0E **279** D5
Amadi *Dem. Rep. of the Congo* 3°40N 26°40E **268** B2
Amâdi *Sudan* 5°29N 30°25E **257** F3
Amadjuak L. *Canada* 65°0N 71°8W **295** C12
Amadora *Portugal* 38°45N 9°13W **126** A1
Amagansett *U.S.A.* 40°59N 72°9W **313** F12
Amagasaki *Japan* 34°42N 135°23E **133** A1
Amager *Denmark* 55°36N 12°35E **118** B3
Amagi *Japan* 33°25N 130°39E **222** D2
Amagunze *Nigeria* 6°20N 7°40E **263** D6
Amahai *Indonesia* 3°20S 128°55E **231** E7
Amaile *Samoa* 13°59S 171°22W **287** V20
Amaimon *Papua N. G.* 5°12S 145°30E **286** C3
Amakusa-Nada *Japan* 32°35N 130°5E **222** E2
Amakusa-Shotō *Japan* 32°15N 130°10E **222** E2
Amal *Oman* 18°21N 55°39E **249** C6
Åmål *Sweden* 59°3N 12°42E **162** E6
Amāl Qādisiya *Iraq* 33°16N 44°20E **113** B2
Amalapuram *India* 16°35N 81°55E **245** F5
Amalfi *Colombia* 6°55N 75°4W **328** B2
Amalfi *Italy* 40°38N 14°36E **201** B7
Amaliada *Greece* 37°47N 21°22E **204** D3
Amalienborg Slot *Copenhagen, Denmark* **118** b3
Amalner *India* 21°5N 75°5E **244** D2
Amamapare *Indonesia* 4°53S 136°38E **231** E9
Amambaí *Brazil* 23°5S 55°13W **335** A4
Amambaí → *Brazil* 23°22S 53°56W **335** A5
Amambay □ *Paraguay* 23°0S 56°0W **335** A4
Amambay, Cordillera de *S. Amer.* 23°0S 55°45W **335** A4
Amami-Guntō *Japan* 27°16N 129°21E **221** L4
Amami-Ō-Shima *Japan* 28°16N 129°21E **221** K4
Aman, Pulau *Malaysia* 5°16N 100°24E **237** c
Amana → *Venezuela* 9°45N 62°39W **329** B5
Amaná, L. *Brazil* 2°35S 64°40W **329** D5
Amanab *Papua N. G.* 3°40S 141°14E **286** B1
Amanat → *India* 24°7N 84°4E **243** G11
Amanave *Amer. Samoa* 14°20S 170°50W **302** f
Amanda Park *U.S.A.* 47°28N 123°55W **306** C3
Amankeldi *Kazakhstan* 50°10N 65°10E **217** B7
Amantea *Italy* 39°8N 16°4E **201** C9
Amanu *French Polynesia* 17°48S 140°46W **289** f
Amapá *Brazil* 2°5N 50°50W **329** C7
Amapá □ *Brazil* 1°40N 52°0W **329** C7
Amapari = Ferreira Gomes *Brazil* 0°48N 51°8W **332** A1
Amapari *Brazil* 0°37N 51°39W **329** C7
Amara *Sudan* 10°25N 34°10E **257** E3
Amara □ *Ethiopia* 12°30N 37°30E **257** E4
Amaração = Luís Correia *Brazil* 3°0S 41°35W **332** B3
Amarante *Brazil* 6°14S 42°50W **332** C3
Amarante *Portugal* 41°16N 8°5W **194** D2
Amarante do Maranhão *Brazil* 5°36S 46°45W **332** C2
Amaranth *Canada* 50°36N 98°43W **297** C9
Amarapura *Burma* 21°54N 96°3E **241** E6
Amaravati → *India* 11°0N 78°15E **245** J4
Amareleja *Portugal* 38°12N 7°13W **195** G3
Amargosa *Brazil* 13°2S 39°36W **333** D4
Amargosa → *U.S.A.* 36°14N 116°51W **307** J10
Amargosa Desert *U.S.A.* 36°40N 116°30W **307** J10
Amargosa Range *U.S.A.* 36°20N 116°45W **307** J10
Amari *Greece* 35°13N 24°40E **207** E5
Amarillo *U.S.A.* 35°13N 101°50W **314** D4
Amarkantak *India* 22°40N 81°45E **243** H9
Amârna, Tell el' *Sudan* 27°38N 30°52E **256** B3
Amarnath *India* 19°12N 73°22E **244** E1
Amaro, Mte. *Italy* 42°5N 14°5E **199** F11
Amaro Leite *Brazil* 13°58S 49°9W **333** D2
Amarpur *Bihar, India* 25°5N 87°0E **243** G12
Amarpur *Tripura, India* 23°31N 91°39E **241** D3
Amarti *Eritrea* 14°17N 41°6E **257** E5
Amarwara *India* 22°18N 79°10E **243** H8
Amasin *W. Sahara* 25°45N 13°20W **260** C2
Amasra *Turkey* 41°45N 32°23E **212** B5
Amassama *Nigeria* 5°1N 6°2E **263** D6
Amasya *Turkey* 40°40N 35°50E **212** B6
Amasya □ *Turkey* 40°40N 35°50E **212** B6
Amata *S. Austral., Australia* 26°9S 131°9E **279** E5
Amata *Piemonte, Italy* 45°34N 9°8E **129** A1
Amataurá *Brazil* 3°29S 68°6W **328** D4
Amatignak I. *U.S.A.* 51°16N 179°6W **303** L3
Amatikulu *S. Africa* 29°3S 31°33E **271** C5
Amatitlán *Guatemala* 14°29N 90°38W **320** D1
Amatrice *Italy* 42°38N 13°17E **199** F10
Amau *Papua N. G.* 10°2S 148°34E **286** F5
Amay *Belgium* 50°33N 5°19E **170** D5
Amazon = Amazonas → *S. Amer.* 0°5S 50°0W **329** D8
Amazonas □ *Brazil* 5°0S 65°0W **331** B5
Amazonas □ *Peru* 5°0S 78°0W **330** B2
Amazonas □ *Venezuela* 3°30N 66°0W **328** C4
Amazonas → *S. Amer.* 0°5S 50°0W **329** D8
Amba Ferit *Ethiopia* 10°55N 38°50E **257** E4
Ambad *India* 19°38N 75°50E **244** E2
Ambagarh Chowki *India* 20°47N 80°43E **244** D5

Ambah India 26°43N 78°13E 242 F8
Ambahakily Madag. 21°36S 43°41E 272 C1
Ambahita Madag. 24°1S 45°16E 272 C2
Ambajogal India 18°44N 76°23E 244 F3
Ambala India 30°23N 76°56E 242 D7
Ambalangoda Sri Lanka 6°15N 80°5E 245 L5
Ambalapulai India 9°25N 76°25E 245 K3
Ambalavao Madag. 21°50S 46°56E 272 C2
Ambam Cameroon 2°20N 11°15E 264 B2
Ambanja Madag. 13°40S 48°27E 272 A2
Ambararata Madag. 15°3S 48°33E 272 B2
Ambarchik Russia 69°40N 162°20E 215 C17
Ambarijeby Madag. 14°56S 47°41E 272 A2
Ambaro, Helodranon'
 Madag. 13°23S 48°38E 272 A2
Ambasamudram India 8°43N 77°25E 245 K3
Ambato Ecuador 1°5S 78°42W 328 D2
Ambato Madag. 13°24S 48°29E 272 A2
Ambato, Sierra de
 Argentina 28°25S 66°10W 334 B2
Ambato Boeny Madag. 16°28S 46°43E 272 B2
Ambatofinandrahana
 Madag. 20°33S 46°48E 272 C2
Ambatolampy Madag. 19°20S 47°35E 272 B2
Ambatomainty Madag. 17°55S 45°40E 272 B2
Ambatomanoina Madag. 18°18S 47°37E 272 B2
Ambatondrazaka Madag. 17°55S 48°28E 272 B2
Ambatosoratra Madag. 17°37S 48°31E 272 B2
Ambelokipi Greece 23°37N 23°47E 112 B2
Ambelonas Greece 39°45N 22°22E 204 B4
Ambenja Madag. 15°17S 46°58E 272 B2
Amberg Germany 49°26N 11°52E 179 F7
Ambergris Cay Belize 18°0N 87°55W 319 D7
Ambérieu-en-Bugey
 France 45°57N 5°20E 175 C9
Amberley N.Z. 43°9S 172°44E 285 D7
Ambert France 45°33N 3°44E 174 C7
Ambidédi Mali 14°35N 11°47W 262 C2
Ambikapur India 23°15N 83°15E 243 H10
Ambikol Sudan 21°20N 30°50E 256 C3
Ambilobé Madag. 13°10S 49°3E 272 A2
Ambinanindrano Madag. 18°25S 48°23E 272 C2
Ambinda Madag. 16°25S 45°52E 272 B2
Ambitle I. Papua N. G. 4°5S 153°37E 286 C7
Amble U.K. 55°20N 1°36W 168 B6
Ambler U.S.A. 67°5N 157°52W 303 C8
Ambleside U.K. 54°26N 2°58W 168 C5
Ambo Peru 10°5S 76°10W 330 C2
Amboahangy Madag. 24°15S 46°22E 272 C2
Ambodifototra Madag. 16°59S 49°52E 272 B2
Ambodilazana Madag. 18°6S 49°10E 272 B2
Ambodiriana Madag. 17°55S 49°18E 272 B2
Ambohidray Madag. 18°36S 48°18E 272 B2
Ambohimahamasina
 Madag. 21°56S 47°11E 272 C2
Ambohimahasoa Madag. 21°7S 47°13E 272 C2
Ambohimanga Madag. 20°52S 47°36E 272 C2
Ambohimitombo Madag. 20°43S 47°26E 272 C2
Ambohitra Madag. 12°30S 49°10E 272 A2
Amboise France 47°24N 1°2E 172 E8
Amboiva Angola 11°33S 14°43E 266 E2
Ambon Indonesia 3°43S 128°12E 231 E7
Ambondro Madag. 25°13S 45°44E 272 D2
Amboró △ Bolivia 17°39S 64°3W 331 D5
Amboseli, I. Kenya 2°40S 37°10E 268 C4
Amboseli △ Kenya 2°37S 37°13E 268 C4
Ambositra Madag. 20°31S 47°25E 272 C2
Ambovombe Madag. 25°11S 46°5E 272 D2
Amboy Calif., U.S.A. 34°33N 115°45W 307 L11
Amboy Ill., U.S.A. 41°44N 89°20W 310 C7
Amboyna Cay
 S. China Sea 7°50N 112°50E 230 C4
Ambre, Île d' Mauritius 20°2S 57°41E 272 e
Ambridge U.S.A. 40°36N 80°14W 312 F4
Ambriz Angola 7°48S 13°8E 265 D2
Ambriz △ Angola 7°56S 10°27E 265 D2
Ambrym Vanuatu 16°15S 168°10E 287 F6
Ambunti Papua N. G. 4°13S 142°52E 286 A6
Ambur India 12°48N 78°43E 245 H4
Amchitka I. Russia 51°32N 179°0E 303 L2
Amderma Russia 69°45N 61°30E 214 C7
Amdhi India 23°51N 81°27E 243 H9
Ameca Mexico 20°33N 104°2W 318 C4
Ameca → Mexico 20°41N 105°18W 318 C3
Amecameca de Juárez
 Mexico 19°8N 98°46W 319 D5
Ameixoeira Portugal 38°46N 9°8W 126 A2
Ameland Neths. 53°27N 5°45E 170 A5
Amélia Italy 42°33N 12°25E 199 F9
Amelia City U.S.A. 30°35N 81°26W 316 E8
Amelia I. U.S.A. 30°40N 81°25W 316 E8
Amendolara Italy 39°57N 16°35E 201 C9
Amenia U.S.A. 41°51N 73°33W 313 E11
América Brazil 23°35S 46°41W 137 B1
America-Antarctica Ridge
 S. Ocean 59°0S 16°0W 151 B2
American Falls U.S.A. 42°47N 112°51W 304 E7
American Falls Res.
 U.S.A. 42°47N 112°52W 304 E7
American Fork U.S.A. 40°23N 111°48W 304 F8
American Highland
 Antarctica 73°0S 75°0E 151 D6
American Museum of Natural
 History New York, U.S.A. 132 b2
American Police Hall of Fame
 U.S.A. 25°49N 80°11W 128 B2
American River
 Australia 35°47S 137°46E 282 C2
American Samoa ☑
 Pac. Oc. 14°20S 170°0W 302 f
American Samoa △
 Amer. Samoa 14°15S 170°28W 302 g
American University
 U.S.A. 38°56N 77°5W 143 B3
Americana Brazil 22°45S 47°20W 335 A6
Americus U.S.A. 32°4N 84°14W 316 C5
Amerigo Vespucci, Firenze ✈ (FLR)
 Italy 43°49N 11°13E 199 E8
Amerika = Nakhodka
 Russia 42°53N 132°54E 220 C6
Amersfoort Mpumalanga,
 S. Africa 26°59S 29°53E 271 C4
Amery Basin S. Ocean 68°0S 74°30E 151 C6
Amery Ice Shelf Antarctica 69°30S 72°0E 151 D6
Amerzgane Morocco 31°4N 7°14W 260 B3
Ames Spain 42°54N 8°38W 194 C2
Ames Iowa, U.S.A. 42°2N 93°37W 310 C3
Amesbury U.S.A. 42°51N 70°56W 313 D14
Amet India 25°18N 73°56E 242 G5
Amfíklia Greece 38°38N 22°36E 204 C4
Amfilochia Greece 38°52N 21°9E 204 C3
Amfípoli Greece 40°48N 23°52E 202 F7
Amfissa Greece 38°32N 22°22E 204 C4
Amga Russia 60°50N 132°0E 215 C14
Amga → Russia 62°38N 134°32E 215 C14
Amgaoon India 21°22N 80°22E 243 J12
Amgu Russia 45°45N 137°15E 220 B8
Amgun → Russia 52°56N 139°38E 215 D14
Amherst = Kyaikkami
 Burma 16°4N 97°34E 241 G6

Amherst N.S., Canada 45°48N 64°8W 299 C7
Amherst Mass., U.S.A. 42°23N 72°31W 313 D12
Amherst N.Y., U.S.A. 42°59N 78°48W 312 D6
Amherst Ohio, U.S.A. 41°24N 82°14W 312 E2
Amherst I. Canada 44°8N 76°43W 313 B8
Amherstburg Canada 42°6N 83°6W 311 B13
Amidon U.S.A. 46°29N 103°19W 308 B2
Amiens France 49°54N 2°16E 173 C9
Amik Gölü Turkey 36°22N 36°17E 250 B7
Amili India 28°25N 95°52E 241 A5
Amin Iraq 33°19N 44°29E 113 B2
Amindeo Greece 40°42N 21°42E 202 F5
Amindivi Is. India 11°23N 72°23E 245 J1
Amingaon India 26°11N 91°40E 241 B3
Amini I. India 11°6N 72°45E 245 J1
Âminne Sweden 57°7N 14°0E 163 G7
Amino Ethiopia 4°25N 41°52E 257 G5
Aminuis Namibia 23°43S 19°21E 270 B2
Aminyevo Russia 55°41N 37°25E 129 B2
Âmir, Ras Libya 32°57N 21°43E 258 B4
Amīrābād Īlām, Iran 33°20N 46°16E 246 C5
Amīrābād Tehrān, Iran 35°43N 51°24E 141 A2
Amirante Is. Seychelles 6°0S 53°0E 210 J7
Amisk Canada 52°34N 111°3W 306 C6
Amisk L. Canada 54°35N 102°15W 297 C8
Amistad, Presa de la
 Mexico 29°26N 101°3W 318 B4
Amistad U.S.A. 29°32N 101°12W 314 G4
Amite U.S.A. 30°44N 90°30W 315 F9
Amizmiz Morocco 31°12N 8°15W 260 B3
Amla India 21°56N 78°7E 242 J8
Amlapura = Karangasem
 Indonesia 8°27S 115°37E 231 J18
Amli Norway 58°45N 8°32E 164 F5
Amlia I. U.S.A. 52°4N 173°30W 303 K4
Amlwch U.K. 53°24N 4°20W 168 D3
Amm Adam Sudan 16°20N 36°1E 257 D4
'Ammān Jordan 31°57N 35°52E 251 G6
'Ammān △ Jordan 31°40N 36°30E 251 G7
Ammanford U.K. 51°48N 3°59W 169 F4
Ammassalik = Tasiilaq
 Greenland 65°40N 37°20W 154 D7
Ammerån → Sweden 63°9N 16°13E 162 A10
Ammersee Germany 48°0N 11°7E 179 F7
Ammochostos = Famagusta
 Cyprus 35°8N 33°55E 207 E9
Ammon U.S.A. 43°28N 111°58W 304 E8
Amnat Charoen
 Thailand 15°51N 104°38E 236 E5
Amnura Bangla. 24°37N 88°25E 243 G13
Amo Jiang → China 23°0N 101°50E 228 F3
Āmol Iran 36°23N 52°20E 247 B7
Amora Portugal 38°37N 9°6W 126 B2
Amoreira Portugal 38°48N 9°11W 126 A1
Amoret U.S.A. 38°15N 94°35W 310 F2
Amorgós Greece 36°50N 25°57E 205 E7
Amory U.S.A. 33°59N 88°29W 315 E10
Amos Canada 48°35N 78°5W 298 C4
Åmot Buskerud, Norway 59°57N 9°54E 164 E6
Åmot Oppland, Norway 61°0N 10°2E 164 D7
Åmot Telemark, Norway 59°34N 8°0E 164 E5
Åmotfors Sweden 59°47N 12°22E 162 E6
Åmotsdal Norway 59°37N 8°26E 164 E5
Amour, Djebel Algeria 33°42N 1°37E 261 B5
Amoy = Xiamen China 24°25N 118°4E 229 E12
Ampanavoana Madag. 15°41S 50°22E 272 B3
Ampang Malaysia 3°8N 101°45E 237 L3
Ampangalana, Lakandranon'
 Madag. 22°48S 47°50E 272 C2
Ampanihy Madag. 24°40S 44°45E 272 C1
Amparafaravola Madag. 17°35S 48°13E 272 B2
Amparihy Madag. 20°31S 48°0E 272 C2
Ampasinambo Madag. 20°31S 48°0E 272 C2
Ampasindava, Helodranon'
 Madag. 13°40S 48°15E 272 A2
Ampasindava, Saikanosy
 Madag. 13°42S 47°55E 272 A2
Ampenan Indonesia 8°34S 116°4E 231 K18
Ampère Nigeria 9°25N 9°40E 263 D6
Amper → Germany 48°29N 11°55E 179 G7
Amper → Oberbayern,
 Germany 48°14N 11°25E 131 A1
Ampezzo Italy 46°25N 12°48E 199 B9
Amphoe Kathu Thailand 7°55N 98°21E 237 a
Amphoe Thalang Thailand 8°1N 98°20E 237 a
Ampitsikinana Madag. 12°57S 49°49E 272 A2
Ampombiantambo
 Madag. 12°42S 47°55E 272 A2
Ampani India 19°35N 82°38E 244 E6
Ampanihy Madag. 24°40S 44°45E 272 C1
Ampoza Madag. 22°20S 44°44E 272 C1
Amqui Canada 48°28N 67°27W 299 C6
Amrabad India 16°23N 78°50E 245 F4
'Amrān Yemen 15°41N 43°55E 248 D3
Amraoti = Amravati
 India 20°55N 77°45E 244 D3
Amravati India 20°55N 77°45E 244 D3
Amreli India 21°35N 71°17E 242 J4
Amrenene el Kasba
 Algeria 22°10N 0°30E 261 D5
Amritsar India 31°35N 74°57E 242 D6
Amroha India 28°53N 78°30E 243 E8
Amrum Germany 54°38N 8°21E 178 A4
Amsâga Mauritania 20°7N 14°10W 260 D2
Amsel Algeria 22°47N 5°29E 261 D6
Amstel Amsterdam, Neths. 112 b2
Amstel → Amsterdam, Neths. 112 c2
Amstel-Drecht-Kanaal
 Neths. 52°18N 4°54E 112 B2
Amstel Station Amsterdam, Neths. 112 b3
Amstelhof Amsterdam, Neths. 112 b2
Amstelveen Neths. 52°18N 4°51E 112 B2
Amsterdam N.Y.,
 U.S.A. 42°56N 74°11W 313 D10
Amsterdam, I. = Nouvelle
 Amsterdam, Î. Ind. Oc. 38°30S 77°30E 273 H6
Amsterdam-Rijnkanaal
 Neths. 52°18N 4°58E 112 B2
Amsterdam Zoo Amsterdam, Neths. 112 b3
Amsterdam Zuidoost
 Neths. 52°18N 4°58E 112 B2
Amsterdamse Bos Neths. 52°18N 4°50E 112 B2
Amstetten Austria 48°7N 14°51E 180 C7
Amudarya → Uzbekistan 43°58N 59°34E 226 E6
Amukta I. U.S.A. 52°30N 171°16W 303 K5
Amuku Guyana 3°43N 59°28W 135 b
Amulung Phil. 17°50N 121°43E 232 C3
Amund Ringnes I.
 Canada 78°20N 96°25W 295 B10
Amundsen Abyssal Plain
 S. Ocean 65°0S 125°0W 151 C14
Amundsen Basin Arctic 87°30N 80°0E 150 A14
Amundsen Gulf Canada 71°0N 124°0W 294 B7
Amundsen Ridges
 S. Ocean 69°15S 123°0W 151 C14
Amundsen-Scott Antarctica 90°0S 166°0E 151 E

Amundsen Sea
 Antarctica 72°0S 115°0W 151 D15
Amungen Sweden 61°10N 15°40E 162 C9
Amuntai Indonesia 2°28S 115°25E 235 C5
Amur Somali Rep. 5°16N 46°30E 267 C6
Amur → Russia 52°56N 141°10E 215 D15
Amur, W. → Sudan 18°56N 33°34E 256 D3
Amurang Indonesia 1°5N 124°40E 231 D6
Amurrio Spain 43°3N 3°0W 196 B1
Amursk Russia 50°14N 136°54E 215 D14
Amusco Spain 42°10N 4°28W 194 C6
Amvrakikos Kolpos
 Greece 39°0N 20°55E 204 C2
Amvrosiyivka Ukraine 47°43N 38°30E 189 J10
Amyderya = Amudarya →
 Uzbekistan 43°58N 59°34E 216 D5
Amzeglouf Algeria 26°50N 0°1E 261 C5
An Burma 19°48N 94°0E 241 F5
An Bien Vietnam 9°45N 105°0E 237 H5
An Hoa Vietnam 15°40N 108°5E 236 E7
An Nabatīyah at Tahta
 Lebanon 33°23N 35°27E 250 B6
An Nabk Si. Arabia 31°20N 37°20E 246 D3
An Nabk Syria 34°2N 36°44E 250 D7
An Nafūd Si. Arabia 28°15N 41°0E 246 D4
An Najaf Iraq 32°3N 44°15E 213 G11
An Namās Si. Arabia 19°7N 42°8E 248 C3
An Nāşirīyah Iraq 31°0N 46°15E 246 D5
An Nawfaliyah Libya 30°54N 17°58E 258 B3
An Nhon Vietnam 13°55N 109°7E 236 F7
An Nīl □ Sudan 19°30N 33°0E 256 D3
An Nīl al Abyaḍ □ Sudan 14°0N 32°15E 257 E3
An Nīl al Azraq □ Sudan 11°30N 34°30E 257 E3
An Nu'ayrīyah Si. Arabia 27°30N 48°30E 247 E6
An Nu'mānīyah Iraq 32°32N 45°25E 213 F11
An Nuqat Alkhams □
 Libya 32°42N 11°57E 261 B7
An Thoi, Dao Vietnam 9°58N 104°0E 237 H5
An Uaimh Ireland 53°39N 6°41W 166 C5
Anaa French Polynesia 17°25S 145°30W 289 f
Anabar Russia 73°8N 113°36E 215 B12
Anaco Venezuela 9°27N 64°28W 334 B3
Anaconda U.S.A. 46°8N 112°57W 304 C7
Anacortes U.S.A. 48°30N 122°37W 306 B3
Anacosta → U.S.A. 38°52N 77°1W 143 B4
Anacostia U.S.A. 38°51N 76°59W 143 B4
Anacuao, Mt. Phil. 16°16N 121°53E 232 C3
Anadarko U.S.A. 35°4N 98°15W 314 D5
Anadia Brazil 9°42S 36°18W 332 C4
Anadia Portugal 40°26N 8°27W 194 E2
Anadolu Turkey 39°0N 30°0E 212 C5
Anadolukavağı Turkey 41°4N 29°3E 122 A2
Anadyr Russia 64°35N 177°20E 215 C18
Anadyr → Russia 64°55N 176°5E 215 C18
Anadyrskiy Zaliv Russia 64°0N 180°0E 215 C19
Anafi Greece 36°22N 25°48E 205 E7
Anafiotitra Greece 37°51N 20°39E 207 D8
Anaga, Pta. de Canary Is. 28°34N 16°9W 153 e1
Anagni Italy 41°44N 13°9E 199 G10
Anaheim U.S.A. 33°50N 117°55W 307 M9
Anahim Lake Canada 52°28N 125°18W 296 C3
Anaholu → U.S.A. 22°9N 159°19W 302 A2
'Anahulu → U.S.A. 21°37N 158°6W 302 J13
Anai Mudi India 10°12N 77°4E 245 J3
Anaichak △ U.S.A. 56°50N 158°15W 303 H8
Anaimalai Hills India 10°20N 76°40E 245 J3
Anajás Brazil 0°59S 49°57W 332 B2
Anajatuba Brazil 3°16S 44°37W 332 B3
Anakao Chile 27°5S 109°20W 330 b
Anakapalle India 17°42N 83°6E 244 F6
Anakie Australia 23°32S 147°45E 280 C4
Anaklia Georgia 42°22N 41°35E 191 J5
Anaktuvuk Pass
 U.S.A. 68°8N 151°45W 303 B10
Analalava Madag. 14°35S 48°0E 272 C2
Analavoka Madag. 23°25S 46°30E 272 C2
Analipsis Greece 39°36N 19°55E 206 B9
Anamã Brazil 3°35S 61°22W 329 D5
Anambar → Pakistan 30°15N 68°50E 242 D3
Anambas, Kepulauan
 Indonesia 3°20N 106°30E 234 B3
Anambas Is. = Anambas,
 Kepulauan Indonesia 3°20N 106°30E 234 B3
Anambra □ Nigeria 6°20N 7°0E 263 D6
Anamé Vanuatu 20°8S 169°47E 287 K7
Anamosa U.S.A. 42°7N 91°17W 310 D8
Anamur Turkey 36°8N 32°58E 250 D5
Anamur Burnu Turkey 36°3N 32°47E 250 D5
Anan Japan 33°54N 134°40E 222 D6
Anand India 22°32N 72°59E 242 H5
Anandapuram India 14°5N 75°12E 242 H5
Anandpur India 14°5N 75°12E 244 D8
Ananes Greece 36°33N 24°9E 204 E6
Anantapur India 14°39N 77°42E 245 G3
Anantnag India 33°45N 75°10E 243 C6
Ananyiv Ukraine 47°44N 29°58E 183 C14
Anapa Russia 44°55N 37°25E 189 K9
Anapodiaris → Greece 34°59N 25°20E 207 F6
Anápolis = Simão Dias
 Brazil 10°44S 37°49W 332 D4
Anápolis Brazil 16°15S 48°50W 333 E2
Anapu → Brazil 1°53S 50°53W 329 D7
Anār Iran 30°55N 55°13E 247 D7
Anār Darreh Afghan. 32°55N 61°50E 247 C9
Anārak Iran 33°25N 53°40E 247 C7
Anarisfjällen Sweden 63°6N 13°10E 162 A7
Anas → India 23°26N 74°0E 242 H6
Añasco Puerto Rico 18°17N 67°8W 321 b
Anatah West Bank 31°49N 35°16E 123 B2
Anatahan N. Marianas 16°21N 145°40E 302 a
Anatolia = Anadolu Turkey 39°0N 30°0E 212 C5
Anatsogno Madag. 23°33S 43°46E 272 C1
Añatuya Argentina 28°20S 62°50W 334 B3
Anauá → Brazil 0°58N 61°21W 329 C5
Anaunethad L. Canada 60°55N 104°25W 297 A8
Anavilhanas, Arquipélago das
 Brazil 2°42S 60°45W 329 D5
Anaye Niger 19°15N 12°50E 259 E2
Anbyŏn N. Korea 39°1N 127°35E 224 C2
Ancares, Sierra de Spain 42°50N 6°40W 194 B3
Ancares □ Spain 42°50N 6°40W 194 C4
Ancaster Canada 43°13N 79°59W 312 D5
Ancenis France 47°21N 1°10W 172 E5
Anchieta = Piatã Brazil 13°9S 41°48W 333 D3
Anch'ing = Anqing
 China 30°30N 117°3E 229 B11
Ancho, Canal Chile 50°0S 75°0W 335 D2
Anchor Bay U.S.A. 38°48N 123°34W 306 G3
Anchorage U.S.A. 61°13N 149°54W 303 F10
Anchorage ✈ (ANC)
 U.S.A. 61°10N 150°0W 303 F10
Anci China 39°20N 116°40E 228 F8
Ancohuma, Nevado
 Bolivia 16°0S 68°50W 330 D4
Ancón Peru 11°50S 77°10W 330 C2
Ancona Italy 43°38N 13°30E 199 E10

Ancud Chile 42°0S 73°50W 336 B2
Ancud, G. de Chile 42°0S 73°0W 336 B2
Ancy-le-Franc France 47°46N 4°10E 173 E11
Anda Heilongjiang, China 46°24N 125°19E 219 B7
Anda Phil. 16°17N 119°57E 232 C2
Andacollo Argentina 37°10S 70°42W 334 D1
Andacollo Chile 30°14S 71°6W 334 C1
Andahuaylas Peru 13°40S 73°25W 330 C3
Andaingo Madag. 18°12S 48°17E 272 B2
Andalgalá Argentina 27°40S 66°30W 334 B2
Åndalsnes Norway 62°35N 7°43E 164 B4
Andalucía □ Spain 37°35N 5°0W 195 H6
Andalucía U.S.A. 31°18N 86°29W 315 F11
Andalusia = Andalucía □
 Spain 37°35N 5°0W 195 H6
Andalusia U.S.A. 31°18N 86°29W 315 F11
Andaman & Nicobar Is. □
 India 10°0N 93°0E 245 K11
Andaman Is. Ind. Oc. 12°30N 92°45E 245 H11
Andaman Sea Ind. Oc. 13°0N 96°0E 230 B1
Andamooka Australia 30°27S 137°9E 281 E2
Andapa Madag. 14°39S 49°39E 272 A2
Andara Namibia 18°2S 21°9E 270 A3
Andaraí Bahia, Brazil 12°48S 41°20W 333 D3
Andaraí Rio de J., Brazil 22°56S 43°14W 135 B1
Andelot-Blancheville
 France 48°15N 5°18E 173 D12
Andenes Norway 69°19N 16°18E 160 B17
Andenne Belgium 50°28N 5°5E 170 D5
Andéranboukane Mali 15°26N 3°2E 263 B5
Anderlecht Belgium 50°50N 4°19E 116 A1
Andermatt Switz. 46°38N 8°35E 179 J4
Andernach Germany 50°26N 7°24E 178 E3
Anderø-les-Bains France 44°44N 1°6W 174 D2
Andersen Air Force Base
 Guam 13°35N 144°55E 302 d
Anderslöv Sweden 55°26N 13°19E 163 J7
Anderson Alaska,
 U.S.A. 64°25N 149°15W 303 D10
Anderson Calif., U.S.A. 40°27N 122°18W 304 F2
Anderson Ind., U.S.A. 40°10N 85°41W 311 D11
Anderson Mo., U.S.A. 36°39N 94°27W 308 G6
Anderson S.C., U.S.A. 34°31N 82°39W 315 D13
Anderson → Canada 69°42N 129°0W 294 C7
Anderson I. India 12°46N 92°43E 245 H11
Anderson Park U.S.A. 33°45N 84°21W 116 C3
Andersonville U.S.A. 32°12N 84°9W 316 C5
Anderstorp Sweden 57°19N 13°39E 163 G7
Andes Colombia 5°39N 75°54W 328 B2
Andes, Cord. de los
 S. Amer. 20°0S 68°0W 330 E4
Andfjorden Norway 69°10N 16°20E 160 B17
Andhra, L. India 18°54N 73°32E 244 F1
Andhra Pradesh □ India 18°0N 79°0E 244 F4
Andijon Uzbekistan 41°10N 72°15E 217 D8
Andijon = Uzbekistan 40°45N 72°20E 217 D8
Andikíthira = Antikythira
 Greece 35°52N 23°15E 204 F5
Andímilos Greece 36°47N 24°12E 204 E6
Andímilos = Antimilos
 Greece 36°47N 24°12E 204 E6
Andine China 39°55N 116°23E 114 B2
Andine = Antiparos
 Greece 37°0N 25°3E 205 D7
Andipaxoi = Antipaxi
 Greece 39°9N 20°13E 204 C2
Andizhan = Andijon
 Uzbekistan 41°10N 72°15E 217 D8
Andkhvoy Afghan. 36°52N 65°8E 240 A2
Andoain Spain 43°13N 2°1W 196 B2
Andoany Madag. 13°25S 48°16E 272 A2
Andoas Peru 2°55S 76°25W 328 D2
Andóhahela △ Madag. 24°45S 46°44E 272 C2
Andol India 17°51N 78°4E 244 F4
Andong S. Korea 36°40N 128°43E 224 D4
Andong S. Korea 35°6N 119°20E 227 G10
Andoom Australia 12°25S 141°53E 280 A3
Andorra Spain 40°59N 0°28W 196 E4
Andorra ■ Europe 42°30N 1°30E 174 E5
Andorra La Vella Andorra 42°31N 1°32E 174 F5
Andover Hants., U.K. 51°12N 1°29W 169 F6
Andover Maine, U.S.A. 44°38N 70°45W 313 B14
Andover Mass., U.S.A. 42°40N 71°8W 313 D13
Andover N.J., U.S.A. 40°59N 74°45W 313 F10
Andover N.Y., U.S.A. 42°10N 77°48W 312 D7
Andover Ohio, U.S.A. 41°36N 80°34W 312 E4
Andøya Norway 69°10N 15°50E 160 B16
Andrade Brazil 1°0S 50°0W 137 B1
Andradina Brazil 20°54S 51°23W 333 H8
Andrahary Madag. 13°37S 49°17E 272 A2
Andramasina Madag. 19°11S 47°35E 272 B2
Andranopasy Madag. 21°17S 43°44E 272 C1
Andranovory Madag. 23°8S 44°10E 272 C1
Andratx Spain 39°39N 2°25E 206 B9
Andreanof Is. U.S.A. 51°30N 176°0W 303 L4
Andreápoli Russia 56°40N 32°17E 188 C7
Andrée Land Greenland 73°40N 26°0W 154 C8
Andrews Tex., U.S.A. 32°19N 102°33W 314 E3
Andreyev = Jędrzejów
 Poland 50°35N 20°15E 185 H7
Andreyevka Russia 52°19N 51°55E 190 D10
Ándria Italy 41°13N 16°17E 201 A9
Andriamena Madag. 22°45S 45°41E 272 C2
Andriba Madag. 17°30S 46°58E 272 B2
Andrijevica Montenegro 42°45N 19°48E 202 D3
Andringitra △ Madag. 22°13S 46°58E 272 C2
Andritsena Greece 37°29N 21°52E 204 D3
Andropov = Rybinsk
 Russia 58°5N 38°50E 188 C10
Ándros Greece 37°50N 24°57E 204 D6
Andros I. Bahamas 24°30N 78°0W 320 B4
Andros Town Bahamas 24°43N 77°47W 320 B4
Androscoggin →
 U.S.A. 43°58N 69°52W 313 C14
Androth I. India 10°50N 73°41E 245 J1
Andselv Norway 69°4N 18°34E 160 B18
Andújar Spain 38°3N 4°5W 195 G6
Andulo Angola 11°25S 16°45E 265 E3
Aneby Akershus, Norway 60°10N 11°16E 164 D7
Aneby Sweden 57°48N 14°49E 163 G8
Anegada Br. Virgin Is. 18°45N 64°20W 321 C7
Anegada, B. Argentina 40°35S 62°0W 336 B4
Anegada Passage
 W. Indies 18°15N 63°45W 321 C7
Aneho Togo 6°12N 1°34E 263 D5
Aneityum Vanuatu 20°12S 169°45E 287 K7
Aneigbovohat Vanuatu 21°57S 169°36E 287 F5
Anemni-Noi Moldova 46°5N 28°45E 183 B13
Aneiti Togo 7°42N 1°9E 263 D5
Anembo Australia 35°53S 149°23E 283 C4
Aneto, Pico de Spain 42°37N 0°40E 196 C5
Aney Turkmenistan 21°52S 58°31E 176 E5
Ankara Turkey 39°57N 32°54E 212 C5

Ankilimalinika Madag. 22°58S 43°45E 272 C1
Ankilizato Madag. 20°25S 45°1E 272 C2
Anking = Anqing China 30°30N 117°3E 229 B11
Ankisabe Madag. 19°17S 46°29E 272 B2
Anklam Germany 53°51N 13°41E 178 B9
Ankleshwar India 21°38N 73°3E 244 D1
Ankober Ethiopia 9°35N 39°40E 257 F4
Ankola India 14°40N 74°18E 245 G2
Ankoro
 Dem. Rep. of the Congo 6°45S 26°55E 268 D2
Ankororoka Madag. 25°30S 45°11E 272 D2
Anlong China 25°2N 105°27E 228 E5
Anlu China 31°15N 113°45E 229 B9
Anmyeondo S. Korea 36°25N 126°25E 224 F2
Ånn Sweden 63°19N 12°33E 162 A6
Ann, C. U.S.A. 42°38N 70°35W 313 D14
Ann Arbor U.S.A. 42°17N 83°45W 311 D13
Anna Russia 51°28N 40°23E 190 D6
Anna Ill., U.S.A. 37°28N 89°15W 308 G9
Anna Ohio, U.S.A. 40°24N 84°11W 311 D12
Anna Regina Guyana 7°10N 58°30W 329 B6
Annaba Algeria 36°50N 7°46E 261 A6
Annaba □ Algeria 36°12N 7°45E 261 A6
Annaberg-Buchholz
 Germany 50°34N 13°0E 178 E9
Annai Guyana 3°57N 59°8W 329 C6
Annaka Japan 36°19N 138°54E 223 A10
Annalee → Ireland 54°2N 7°24W 166 B4
Annalee Heights U.S.A. 38°51N 77°14W 143 B2
Annam Vietnam 16°0N 108°0E 236 E7
Annamitique, Chaîne
 Asia 17°0N 106°0E 236 D6
Annan U.K. 54°59N 3°16W 167 G5
Annan → U.K. 54°58N 3°16W 167 G5
Annanberg Papua N. G. 4°52S 144°42E 286 C3
Annandale U.S.A. 38°50N 77°11W 143 C2
Annapolis U.S.A. 38°59N 76°30W 309 F15
Annapolis Royal Canada 44°44N 65°32W 299 D6
Annapurna Nepal 28°34N 83°50E 243 E10
Anne Frankhuis Amsterdam, Neths. 112 a1
Annean, L. Australia 26°54S 118°14E 279 E2
Anneberg Sweden 57°44N 14°49E 163 G8
Annecy France 45°55N 6°8E 175 C10
Annecy, Lac d' France 45°52N 6°10E 175 C10
Annemasse France 46°12N 6°16E 173 F13
Annenfeld = Şämkir
 Azerbaijan 40°50N 46°0E 191 K8
Annenskiy Most Russia 60°45N 37°10E 188 B9
Annette France 55°9N 131°28W 296 B2
Annette Island Indian Reservation
 U.S.A. 55°9N 131°28W 303 J15
Annigeri India 15°26N 75°26E 245 G2
Anniston U.S.A. 33°39N 85°50W 316 B4
Annobón Atl. Oc. 1°25S 5°36E 255 G4
Annonay France 45°15N 4°40E 175 C8
Annot France 43°58N 6°38E 175 E10
Annotto Bay Jamaica 18°16N 76°47W 320 a
Ånnsjön Sweden 63°19N 12°34E 162 A6
Annville U.S.A. 40°20N 76°31W 313 F8
Annweiler Germany 49°12N 7°57E 179 F3
Ano Poroia Greece 41°17N 23°2E 202 E7
Ano Siros Greece 37°29N 24°56E 204 D6
Anogi Greece 38°25N 20°40E 207 C2
Anorotsangana Madag. 13°56S 47°55E 272 A2
Anosibe Madag. 19°26S 48°13E 272 B2
Anou Mellene Mali 17°29N 0°33E 263 B5
Anoumaba Ivory C. 6°23N 4°38E 262 D4
Anping Hebei, China 38°15N 115°30E 228 E8
Anping Liaoning, China 41°5N 123°30E 227 D13
Anpu Gang China 21°25N 109°56E 228 G7
Anqiu China 30°30N 117°3E 229 B11
Anren China 26°43N 113°18E 229 D9
Ansager Denmark 55°43N 8°45E 163 J2
Ansai China 36°50N 109°20E 226 G6
Ansan S. Korea 37°21N 126°52E 224 D3
Ansbach Germany 49°28N 10°34E 179 F6
Anse-Bertrand Guadeloupe 16°28N 61°32W 322 a
Anse Boileau Seychelles 4°43S 55°29E 272 c
Anse Royale Seychelles 4°44S 55°31E 272 c
Anseba → Eritrea 16°0N 38°30E 257 D4
Anseong S. Korea 37°0N 127°16E 224 D3
Anserma Colombia 5°13N 75°48W 328 B2
Ansfelden Austria 48°12N 14°17E 180 C7
Anshan China 41°5N 122°58E 227 D13
Anshun China 26°18N 105°57E 228 D5
Ansião Portugal 39°56N 8°27W 194 F2
Ansley U.S.A. 41°18N 99°23W 308 E5
Ansó Spain 42°51N 0°48W 196 C4
Ansoain Spain 42°50N 1°38W 196 C3
Anson B. Australia 13°20S 130°6E 278 B5
Ansongo Mali 15°25N 0°35E 263 B5
Ansonia Conn., U.S.A. 41°21N 73°5W 313 E11
Ansonia Ohio, U.S.A. 40°13N 84°38W 311 D12
Anstruther U.K. 56°14N 2°41W 167 E6
Ansudu Indonesia 2°11S 139°22E 231 E9
Antabamba Peru 14°40S 73°0W 330 C3
Antagarh India 20°6N 81°4E 244 D5
Antakya = Hatay Turkey 36°14N 36°10E 250 B7
Antalaha Madag. 14°57S 50°20E 272 A3
Antalló Libya 31°8N 20°42E 258 B4
Antalya Turkey 36°52N 30°45E 250 D1
Antalya □ Turkey 36°52N 30°45E 250 D1
Antalya Körfezi Turkey 36°15N 31°30E 250 D2
Antambohobe Madag. 22°20S 46°47E 272 C2
Antanambao-Manampotsy
 Madag. 19°29S 48°34E 272 B2
Antanambe Madag. 16°26S 49°52E 272 B2
Antananarivo Madag. 18°55S 47°31E 272 B2
Antananarivo □ Madag. 19°0S 47°0E 272 B2
Antanifotsy Madag. 19°39S 47°19E 272 B2
Antanimbaribe Madag. 21°30S 44°48E 272 C1
Antanimora Madag. 24°49S 45°40E 272 C2
Antarctic Pen. Antarctica 67°0S 60°0W 151 C18
Antarctica 90°0S 0°0 151 E3
Antécume Pata Fr. Guiana 3°1N 54°4W 329 C7
Antelope Zimbabwe 21°2S 28°31E 271 A4
Antenor Navarro Brazil 6°44S 38°27W 332 C4
Antequera Paraguay 24°8S 57°7W 334 A4
Antequera Spain 37°5N 4°33W 195 H6
Antero, Mt. U.S.A. 38°41N 106°15W 304 G10
Anti Atlas Morocco 30°0N 8°30W 260 C3
Anti-Lebanon = Sharqi, Al Jabal
 ash Lebanon 33°40N 36°10E 250 E7
Antibes France 43°34N 7°6E 175 E11
Antibes, C. d' France 43°31N 7°7E 175 E11
Anticosti, Î. d' Canada 49°30N 63°0W 299 C7
Antifer, C. d' France 49°41N 0°10E 172 C7
Antigo U.S.A. 45°9N 89°9W 310 C9
Antigonish Canada 45°38N 61°58W 299 C7
Antigua Canary Is. 28°24N 14°1W 153 f
Antigua Guatemala 14°34N 90°41W 320 D1
Antigua ☑ W. Indies 17°0N 61°50W 322 a
Antigua & Barbuda ■
 W. Indies 17°20N 61°48W 322 b

Antigua Int. ✈ (ANU) *Antigua & B.* 17°8N 61°47W **322** b
Antigues, Pte. d' *Guadeloupe* 16°26N 61°32W **322** e
Antikythira *Greece* 35°52N 23°15E **204** F5
Antilla *Cuba* 20°40N 75°50W **320** B4
Antilles = West Indies *Cent. Amer.* 15°0N 65°0W **321** D7
Antimilos *Greece* 36°47N 24°12E **204** E6
Anting *Taiwan* 23°7N 120°14E **225** C2
Antioch = Hatay *Turkey* 36°14N 36°10E **250** B7
Antioch *U.S.A.* 38°1N 121°48W **306** G5
Antioche, Pertuis d' *France* 46°6N 1°20W **174** B2
Antioquia *Colombia* 6°40N 75°55W **328** B2
Antioquia □ *Colombia* 7°0N 75°30W **328** B2
Antiparos *Greece* 37°0N 25°3E **205** D7
Antipaxi *Greece* 39°9N 20°13E **204** B2
Antipodes Is. *Pac. Oc.* 49°45S 178°40E **288** M9
Antipolo *Phil.* 14°35N 121°10E **232** D3
Antique □ *Phil.* 11°10N 122°5E **233** F4
Antirio *Greece* 38°20N 21°46E **204** C3
Antlers *U.S.A.* 34°14N 95°37W **314** D7
Antoetra *Madag.* 20°46S 47°20E **272** C2
Antofagasta *Chile* 23°50S 70°30W **334** A1
Antofagasta □ *Chile* 24°0S 69°0W **334** A2
Antofagasta de la Sierra *Argentina* 26°5S 67°20W **334** B2
Antofalla *Argentina* 25°30S 68°5W **334** B2
Antofalla, Salar de *Argentina* 25°40S 67°45W **334** B2
Antoine, L. *Grenada* 12°11N 61°36W **323** q
Anton *U.S.A.* 33°49N 102°10W **314** E3
Antongila, Helodrano *Madag.* 15°30S 49°50E **272** B2
Antonibé *Madag.* 15°7S 47°24E **272** B2
Antonina *Brazil* 25°26S 48°42W **335** B6
Antonio B. Won Pat Int. ✈ (GUM) *Guam* 13°29N 144°48E **302** d
António Enes = Angoche *Mozam.* 16°8S 39°55E **269** F4
Antony *France* 48°44N 2°17E **134** B2
Antrain *France* 48°28N 1°30W **172** D5
Antrim *U.K.* 54°43N 6°14W **166** B5
Antrim *Ohio, U.S.A.* 40°7N 81°21W **312** F3
Antrim □ *U.K.* 54°56N 6°25W **166** B5
Antrim, Mts. of *U.K.* 55°3N 6°14W **166** A5
Antrim Plateau *Australia* 18°8S 128°20E **278** C4
Antriol *Neth. Ant.* 12°12N 68°16W **322** h
Antrodoco *Italy* 42°25N 13°5E **199** F10
Antropovo *Russia* 58°24N 43°6E **190** A6
Antsakabary *Madag.* 15°3S 48°56E **272** B2
Antsalova *Madag.* 18°40S 44°37E **272** B1
Antsenavolo *Madag.* 21°24S 48°3E **272** C2
Antsiafabositra *Madag.* 17°18S 46°57E **272** B2
Antsirabe *Antananarivo, Madag.* 19°55S 47°2E **272** B2
Antsirabe *Antsiranana, Madag.* 14°0S 49°59E **272** A2
Antsirabe *Mahajanga, Madag.* 15°57S 48°58E **272** B2
Antsiranana *Madag.* 12°25S 49°20E **272** A2
Antsiranana □ *Madag.* 12°16S 49°17E **272** A2
Antsohihy *Madag.* 14°50S 47°59E **272** A2
Antsohimbondrona Seranana *Madag.* 13°7S 48°48E **272** A2
Antu *China* 42°30N 128°20E **227** C15
Antufash *Yemen* 15°42N 42°25E **248** D3
Antung *Taiwan* 23°18N 121°20E **225** C3
Antwerp = Antwerpen *Belgium* 51°13N 4°25E **170** C4
Antwerp *N.Y., U.S.A.* 44°12N 75°37W **313** B9
Antwerp *Ohio, U.S.A.* 41°11N 84°45W **311** C12
Antwerpen *Belgium* 51°13N 4°25E **170** C4
Antwerpen □ *Belgium* 51°15N 4°40E **170** C4
Anukur, C. *Papua N. G.* 6°18S 149°37E **286** D5
Anupgarh *India* 29°10N 73°10E **242** E5
Anuppur *India* 23°6N 81°41E **243** H9
Anuradhapura *Sri Lanka* 8°22N 80°28E **245** K5
Anveh *Iran* 27°23N 54°11E **247** E7
Anvers = Antwerpen *Belgium* 51°13N 4°25E **170** C4
Anvers I. *Antarctica* 64°30S 63°40W **151** C17
Anvik *U.S.A.* 62°39N 160°13W **303** E7
Anwen *China* 29°4N 120°26E **229** C13
Anxi *Fujian, China* 25°2N 118°12E **229** E12
Anxi *Gansu, China* 40°30N 95°43E **218** B4
Anxian *China* 31°40N 104°25E **228** B5
Anxiang *China* 29°27N 112°11E **229** C9
Anxious B. *Australia* 33°24S 134°45E **281** E1
Anyama *Ivory C.* 5°30N 4°3W **262** D4
Anyang *Henan, China* 36°5N 114°21E **226** F8
Anyang *S. Korea* 37°23N 126°55E **224** D3
Anyer *Indonesia* 6°4S 105°53E **234** D3
Anyi *Jiangxi, China* 28°49N 115°25E **229** C10
Anyi *Shanxi, China* 35°2N 111°2E **226** G6
Anyuan *China* 25°9N 115°21E **229** E10
Anyue *China* 30°9N 105°50E **228** B5
Anza *U.S.A.* 33°35N 116°39W **307** M10
Anze *China* 36°10N 112°12E **226** F7
Anzhero-Sudzhensk *Russia* 56°10N 86°0E **214** D9
Ánzio *Italy* 41°27N 12°37E **200** A5
Anzoátegui □ *Venezuela* 9°0N 64°30W **329** B5
Ao Makham *Thailand* 7°50N 98°24E **237** a
Ao Phangnga △ *Thailand* 8°10N 98°32E **237** a
Aoba *Vanuatu* 15°25S 167°50E **287** E5
Aoga-Shima *Japan* 32°28N 139°46E **223** E11
Aoiz *Spain* 42°46N 1°22W **196** C3
Aoji *N. Korea* 42°31N 130°23E **224** A5
Aola *Solomon Is.* 9°30S 160°30E **287** M11
Aomen = Macau *China* 22°12N 113°33E **219** G10
Aomori *Japan* 40°45N 140°45E **220** D10
Aomori □ *Japan* 40°45N 140°40E **220** D10
Aonla *India* 28°16N 79°11E **243** E8
Aono-Yama *Japan* 34°28N 131°48E **222** C3
Aorai, Mt. *Tahiti* 17°34S 149°30W **289** e
Aoraki Mount Cook *N.Z.* 43°36S 170°9E **285** D5
Aoral, Phnum *Cambodia* 12°0N 104°15E **237** G5
Aorangi Ra. *N.Z.* 41°28S 175°22E **284** H4
Aore *Vanuatu* 15°35S 167°10E **287** E5
Aoreora *Morocco* 28°51N 10°53W **260** C2
Aosta *Italy* 45°45N 7°20E **198** C4
Aotea Harbour *N.Z.* 38°0S 174°50E **284** E3
Aotearoa = New Zealand ■ *Oceania* 40°0S 176°0E **284** G5
Aoudéras *Niger* 17°45N 8°20E **259** E1
Aouinet Torkoz *Morocco* 28°31N 9°46W **260** C2
Aouk, Bahr → *Africa* 8°51N 18°53E **259** G3
Aouk-Aoukalé △ *C.A.R.* 9°52N 21°25E **264** A4
Aoukar *Mali* 23°50N 2°45W **260** D4
Aoukâr *Mauritania* 17°40N 10°0W **262** B3
Aoulef el Arab *Algeria* 26°55N 1°2E **261** C5
Aoyama *Tokyo, Japan* **140** b
Aozou *Chad* 21°45N 17°28E **259** D3
Aozou Strip *Chad* 22°0N 19°0E **259** D3
Ap Lei Chau *China* 22°14N 114°9E **122** B1
Apa → *S. Amer.* 22°6S 58°2W **334** A4
Apache *U.S.A.* 34°54N 98°22W **314** D5
Apache Junction *U.S.A.* 33°25N 111°33W **305** K8
Apalachee B. *U.S.A.* 30°0N 84°0W **316** E5
Apalachicola *U.S.A.* 29°43N 84°59W **316** F5
Apalachicola → *U.S.A.* 29°43N 84°58W **316** F5
Apalachicola B. *U.S.A.* 29°40N 85°0W **316** F3
Apam *Ghana* 5°19N 0°42W **263** D4
Apamea *Syria* 35°31N 36°28E **250** C7
Apapa *Nigeria* 6°26N 3°21E **124** B2
Apaporis → *Colombia* 1°23S 69°25W **328** D4
Aparados da Serra △ *Brazil* 29°10S 50°8W **335** B5
Aparecida = Bertolínia *Brazil* 7°38S 43°57W **332** C3
Aparecida do Taboado *Brazil* 20°5S 51°5W **333** F1
Aparri *Phil.* 18°22N 121°38E **232** B3
Aparurén *Venezuela* 5°6N 62°8W **329** B5
Apataki *French Polynesia* 15°26S 146°20W **289** f
Apateu *Romania* 46°36N 21°47E **182** D6
Apatin *Serbia* 45°40N 19°0E **182** E4
Apatity *Russia* 67°34N 33°22E **160** C25
Apatou *Fr. Guiana* 5°9N 54°20W **329** B7
Apatula = Finke *Australia* 25°34S 134°35E **280** D1
Apatzingán *Mexico* 19°5N 102°21W **318** D4
Apayao □ *Phil.* 18°10N 121°10E **232** B3
Apelacão *Portugal* 38°48N 9°7W **126** A2
Apeldoorn *Neths.* 52°13N 5°57E **170** B5
Apen *Germany* 53°13N 7°48E **178** B3
Apennines = Appennini *Italy* 44°30N 10°0E **198** D7
Apenrade = Aabenraa *Denmark* 55°3N 9°25E **163** J3
Apere → *Bolivia* 13°44S 65°18W **331** C4
Aphrodisias *Turkey* 37°42N 28°46E **205** D10
Api *Nepal* 30°0N 80°57E **218** C3
Apia *Samoa* 13°50S 171°50W **287** V20
Apiacás, Serra dos *Brazil* 9°50S 57°0W **331** B6
Apiaí *Brazil* 24°31S 48°50W **333** F2
Apiaú → *Brazil* 2°39N 61°12W **329** C5
Apiaú, Serra do *Brazil* 2°30N 62°0W **329** C5
Apidiá → *Brazil* 11°39S 61°11W **331** C5
Apies → *S. Africa* 25°15S 28°8E **271** C4
Apinajé *Brazil* 11°31S 48°18W **333** D2
Apiti *N.Z.* 39°58S 175°54E **284** F4
Apizaco *Mexico* 19°25N 98°8W **319** D5
Aplao *Peru* 16°0S 72°40W **330** D3
Apo, Mt. *Phil.* 6°53N 125°14E **233** H5
Apo East Pass *Phil.* 12°40N 120°40E **232** E3
Apo Reef ⌂ *Phil.* 12°50N 120°50E **232** E3
Apo West Pass *Phil.* 12°31N 120°22E **232** E3
Apodi *Brazil* 5°39S 37°48W **332** C4
Apoera *Suriname* 5°12N 57°10W **329** B6
Apolakia *Greece* 36°5N 27°48E **206** E11
Apolakia, Ormos *Greece* 36°5N 27°45E **206** E11
Apolda *Germany* 51°2N 11°32E **178** D7
Apollo Bay *Australia* 38°45S 143°40E **282** E5
Apollonia = Marsá Susah *Libya* 32°52N 21°59E **258** B4
Apolo *Bolivia* 14°30S 68°30W **330** C4
Apolonia *Greece* 36°58N 24°43E **204** E6
Apónguao → *Venezuela* 4°48N 61°36W **329** C5
Apopka *U.S.A.* 28°40N 81°31W **317** G8
Apopka, L. *U.S.A.* 28°37N 81°37W **133** A1
Apoquindo *Chile* 33°24S 70°32W **137** B2
Aporé *Brazil* 18°58S 52°1W **331** D7
Aporé → *Brazil* 19°27S 50°57W **333** E1
Aporema *Brazil* 1°14N 50°49W **332** A1
Apostle Is. *U.S.A.* 47°0N 90°40W **308** B8
Apostle Islands ⌂ *U.S.A.* 46°55N 91°0W **308** B8
Apóstoles *Argentina* 28°0S 56°0W **335** B4
Apostolos Andreas, C. *Cyprus* 35°42N 34°35E **207** E10
Apostolovo *Ukraine* 47°39N 33°39E **189** J7
Apoteri *Guyana* 4°2N 58°32W **329** C6
Appalachian Mts. *U.S.A.* 38°0N 80°0W **309** G14
Äppelbo *Sweden* 60°29N 14°1E **162** D8
Appennini *Italy* 44°30N 10°0E **198** D7
Appennino Ligure *Italy* 44°30N 9°0E **198** D6
Appenzell-Ausser Rhoden □ *Switz.* 47°23N 9°23E **179** H5
Appenzell-Inner Rhoden □ *Switz.* 47°20N 9°25E **179** H5
Appiano *Italy* 46°28N 11°15E **199** B8
Apple Hill *Canada* 45°13N 74°46W **313** A10
Apple Valley *U.S.A.* 34°32N 117°14W **307** L9
Appleby-in-Westmorland *U.K.* 54°35N 2°29W **168** C5
Appledore *U.K.* 51°3N 4°13W **169** F3
Appleton *U.S.A.* 44°16N 88°25W **308** C9
Appleton City *U.S.A.* 38°11N 94°2W **310** F2
Appleton Rum Distillery *Jamaica* 18°10N 77°44W **320** a
Appling *U.S.A.* 33°33N 82°19W **316** B7
Approuague *Fr. Guiana* 4°20N 52°0W **329** C7
Apra Harbor *Guam* 13°26N 144°40E **302** d
Apricena *Italy* 41°47N 15°27E **199** G12
April → *Papua N. G.* 4°18S 142°26E **286** C2
Aprilia *Italy* 41°36N 12°39E **200** A5
Apsheronsk *Russia* 44°28N 39°42E **191** H4
Apsley *Canada* 44°45N 78°6W **312** B6
Apt *France* 43°53N 5°24E **175** E9
Apterkarskiy Ostrov *Russia* 59°57N 30°20E **137** B2
Apuane, Alpi *Italy* 44°7N 10°14E **198** D7
Apuaú *Brazil* 2°25S 60°53W **329** D5
Apucarana *Brazil* 23°55S 51°33W **335** A5
Apulia = Púglia □ *Italy* 41°15N 16°15E **201** A9
Apurashokoru *Palau* 7°16N 134°17E **288** c
Apurauan *Phil.* 9°35N 118°20E **233** G2
Apure □ *Venezuela* 7°10N 68°50W **328** B4
Apure → *Venezuela* 7°37N 66°25W **328** B4
Apurímac □ *Peru* 14°0S 73°0W **330** C3
Apurímac → *Peru* 12°17S 73°56W **330** C3
Apuseni, Munţii *Romania* 46°30N 22°45E **182** D7
Āqā Jarī *Iran* 30°42N 49°50E **247** D6
Aqaba = Al 'Aqabah *Jordan* 29°31N 35°0E **251** J6
Aqaba, G. of *Red Sea* 29°0N 34°40E **251** K5
'Aqabah, Khalīj al = Aqaba, G. of *Red Sea* 29°0N 34°40E **251** K5
Aqadyr *Kazakhstan* 48°17N 74°50E **217** C8
Āqchah *Afghan.* 36°56N 66°11E **240** A2
'Aqdā *Iran* 32°26N 53°37E **247** C7
Aqiq *Sudan* 18°14N 38°12E **256** D4
Aqiq, Khalîg *Sudan* 18°20N 38°10E **256** D4
'Aqīq, W. al → *Si. Arabia* 20°16N 41°40E **248** B3
Aqköl *Kazakhstan* 51°59N 70°56E **217** B8
Aqmola = Astana *Kazakhstan* 51°10N 71°30E **217** B8
Aqmola □ *Kazakhstan* 51°30N 70°0E **217** B8
'Aqrah *Iraq* 36°46N 43°45E **213** D10
Aqsay *Kazakhstan* 51°11N 53°0E **187** D9
Aqshatau *Kazakhstan* 47°59N 74°3E **217** C8
Aqsū *Ongtüstik Qazaqstan, Kazakhstan* 42°25N 69°50E **217** D7
Aqsū *Pavlodar, Kazakhstan* 52°2N 76°55E **217** B9
Aqsūat *Kazakhstan* 48°16N 80°9E **217** C10
Aqsüyek *Kazakhstan* 44°37N 74°30E **217** D8
Aqtaū *Mangghystaū, Kazakhstan* 43°39N 51°12E **187** F9
Aqtaū *Qaraghandy, Kazakhstan* 50°14N 73°3E **217** B8
Aqtöbe *Kazakhstan* 50°17N 57°10E **187** D10
Aqtoghay *Kazakhstan* 46°57N 79°40E **217** C9
Aquarium of the Americas *New Orleans, U.S.A.* **131** b3
Aquidauana *Brazil* 20°30S 55°50W **331** E6
Aquidauana → *Brazil* 19°44S 56°50W **331** D6
Aquila *Mexico* 18°36N 103°30W **318** D4
Aquiles Serdán *Mexico* 28°36N 105°53W **318** B3
Aquin *Haiti* 18°16N 73°24W **321** C5
Aquitain, Bassin *France* 44°0N 0°30W **174** D3
Aquitaine □ *France* 44°25N 0°30W **174** D3
Ar Kazimiyah *Iraq* 33°22N 44°20E **113** B1
Ar Rachidiya = Er Rachidia *Morocco* 31°58N 4°20W **260** B4
Ar Rafid *Syria* 32°57N 35°52E **250** F6
Ar Rahhālīyah *Iraq* 32°44N 43°23E **213** F10
Ar Ram *West Bank* 31°51N 35°15E **123** A2
Ar Ramādī *Iraq* 33°25N 43°20E **213** F10
Ar Raml *Libya* 26°45N 19°40E **258** C3
Ar Ramthā *Jordan* 32°34N 36°0E **251** F7
Ar Raqqah *Syria* 35°59N 39°8E **213** E8
Ar Raqqah □ *Syria* 36°20N 39°10E **213** D8
Ar Rass *Si. Arabia* 25°50N 43°40E **246** E4
Ar Rastan *Syria* 34°55N 36°43E **250** D7
Ar Rawdah *Si. Arabia* 21°16N 42°50E **248** B3
Ar Rawdah *Yemen* 14°28N 47°17E **248** D4
Ar Rawshān *Si. Arabia* 20°2N 42°36E **256** C5
Ar Rayyān *Qatar* 25°17N 51°25E **247** E6
Ar Rifā'ī *Iraq* 31°50N 46°10E **246** D5
Ar Rijā' *Yemen* 13°1N 44°35E **248** D4
Ar Riyāḍ *Si. Arabia* 24°41N 46°42E **246** E5
Ar Riyāḍ □ *Si. Arabia* 23°0N 45°50E **248** B4
Ar Rmās, W. → *Syria* 35°47N 36°50E **250** C7
Ar Ru'ays *Qatar* 26°8N 51°12E **247** E6
Ar Rukhaymīyah *Iraq* 29°22N 45°38E **246** D5
Ar Ruṣāfah *Syria* 35°45N 38°49E **213** E8
Ar Ruṭbah *Iraq* 33°0N 40°15E **213** F9
Ar Ruwaydah *Si. Arabia* 23°40N 44°40E **248** B4
Ara *India* 25°35N 84°32E **243** G11
Ara → *Japan* 35°41N 139°50E **140** A4
Ara Goro *Ethiopia* 5°48N 41°18E **257** F5
Ara Tera *Ethiopia* 6°38N 40°57E **257** F5
Arab *U.S.A.* 34°19N 86°30W **315** D11
'Arab, Bahr el → *Sudan* 9°0N 29°30E **257** F2
Arab, Khalîg el *Egypt* 30°55N 29°0E **256** A2
Arab, Shatt al → *Asia* 29°57N 48°34E **247** D6
'Araba, W. → *Egypt* 28°19N 33°21E **256** J8
'Arabābād *Iran* 33°2N 57°41E **247** C8
'Arabah, W. → *Yemen* 18°5N 51°26E **249** C5
Araban *Turkey* 37°28N 37°44E **212** D7
Arabatskaya Strelka *Ukraine* 45°40N 35°0E **189** K8
Arabba *Italy* 46°30N 11°52E **199** B8
Arabelo *Venezuela* 4°55N 64°13W **329** C5
Arabi *U.S.A.* 31°50N 83°44W **316** D6
Arabia *Asia* 25°0N 45°0E **210** F6
Arabian Basin *Ind. Oc.* 11°30N 65°0E **273** C5
Arabian Desert = Es Sahrâ' Esh Sharqîya *Egypt* 27°30N 32°30E **256** B3
Arabian Gulf = Persian Gulf *Asia* 27°0N 50°0E **247** E6
Arabian Sea *Ind. Oc.* 16°0N 65°0E **238** F9
Arabistan = Khūzestān □ *Iran* 31°0N 49°0E **247** D6
Araç *Turkey* 41°15N 33°21E **212** B5
Aracaju *Brazil* 10°55S 37°4W **332** D4
Aracataca *Colombia* 10°38N 74°9W **328** A3
Aracati *Brazil* 4°30S 37°44W **332** B4
Araçatuba *Brazil* 21°10S 50°30W **335** A5
Araceli *Phil.* 10°33N 119°59E **233** F2
Aracena *Spain* 37°53N 6°38W **195** H4
Aracena, Sierra de *Spain* 37°50N 6°50W **195** H4
Arachova *Greece* 38°28N 22°35E **204** C4
Arachthos → *Greece* 39°20N 21°4E **204** B3
Aracides, C. *Solomon Is.* 8°21S 161°0E **287** M11
Aračinovo *Macedonia* 42°1N 21°34E **202** D5
Araçuaí *Brazil* 16°52S 42°4W **333** E3
Araçuaí → *Brazil* 16°46S 42°2W **333** E3
'Arad *Israel* 31°15N 35°12E **251** G6
Arad *Romania* 46°10N 21°20E **182** D6
Arad □ *Romania* 46°20N 22°0E **182** D6
Arada *Chad* 15°0N 20°20E **259** E4
Arādān *Iran* 35°21N 52°30E **247** C7
Aradhippou *Cyprus* 34°57N 33°36E **207** F9
Arafura Sea *E. Indies* 9°0S 135°0E **288** H5
Aragarças *Brazil* 15°55S 52°15W **331** D7
Aragats *Armenia* 40°30N 44°15E **191** K7
Aragon *U.S.A.* 34°2N 85°3W **316** A4
Aragón □ *Spain* 41°25N 0°40W **196** D4
Aragón → *Spain* 42°13N 1°44W **196** C3
Aragona *Italy* 37°24N 13°27E **200** E6
Aragua □ *Venezuela* 10°0N 67°10W **328** B4
Aragua de Barcelona *Venezuela* 9°28N 64°49W **329** B5
Araguacema *Brazil* 8°50S 49°20W **332** C2
Araguaçu = Paraguaçu Paulista *Brazil* 22°22S 50°35W **335** A5
Araguaçu *Brazil* 12°49S 49°51W **333** D2
Araguaia → *Brazil* 5°21S 48°41W **332** C2
Araguaia △ *Brazil* 10°30S 50°0W **333** D2
Araguaiana *Brazil* 15°43S 51°51W **331** D7
Araguaína *Brazil* 7°12S 48°12W **332** C2
Araguari *Brazil* 18°38S 48°11W **333** E2
Araguari → *Brazil* 1°15N 49°55W **329** C8
Araguatins *Brazil* 5°38S 48°7W **332** C2
Arain *India* 26°27N 75°2E **242** F6
Araioses *Brazil* 2°53S 41°55W **332** B3
Arak *Algeria* 25°20N 3°45E **261** C5
Arāk *Iran* 34°0N 49°40E **247** C6
Araka *Sudan* 4°20N 30°23E **257** G3
Arakan □ *Burma* 19°0N 94°15E **241** F5
Arakan Coast *Burma* 19°0N 94°0E **241** F5
Arakan Yoma *Burma* 20°0N 94°40E **241** F5
Arakawa *Japan* 35°44N 139°48E **140** A3
Arakkonam *India* 13°7N 79°43E **245** H4
Araklı *Turkey* 41°6N 40°2E **213** B9
Araks = Aras, Rūd-e → *Asia* 40°5N 48°29E **191** K9
Araks → *Iran* 39°10N 47°10E **216** E3
Aral *Kazakhstan* 46°41N 61°45E **216** C6
Aral Mangy Qaraqumy *Kazakhstan* 46°50N 63°10E **216** C6
Aral Sea *Asia* 44°30N 60°0E **216** E5
Aral Tengizi = Aral Sea *Asia* 44°30N 60°0E **216** C5
Aralsk = Aral *Kazakhstan* 46°41N 61°45E **216** C6
Aralskoye More = Aral Sea *Asia* 44°30N 60°0E **216** C5
Aralsor, Ozero = Aralsor Köli *Kazakhstan* 49°5N 48°12E **191** F9
Aralsor Köli *Kazakhstan* 49°5N 48°12E **191** F9
Aramac *Australia* 22°58S 145°14E **280** C4
Aramia → *Papua N. G.* 7°55S 143°22E **286** D2
Aran → *India* 19°55N 78°12E **244** E4
Aran Areh *Ethiopia* 6°3N 42°54E **267** C5
Aran I. *Ireland* 55°0N 8°30W **166** A3
Aran Is. *Ireland* 53°6N 9°38W **166** C2
Aranda de Duero *Spain* 41°39N 3°42W **194** D7
Arandān *Iran* 35°23N 46°55E **246** C5
Aranđelovac *Serbia* 44°18N 20°34E **202** B4
Aranga *N.Z.* 35°44S 173°40E **284** B2
Arani *Bolivia* 17°34S 65°46W **331** D4
Arani *India* 12°43N 79°19E **245** H4
Aranjuez *Spain* 40°1N 3°40W **194** E7
Aranos *Namibia* 24°9S 19°7E **270** B2
Aransas Pass *U.S.A.* 27°55N 97°9W **314** H6
Arany-hegyi-patak → *Hungary* 47°34N 19°4E **117** A2
Aranyaprathet *Thailand* 13°41N 102°30E **236** F4
Arao *Japan* 32°59N 130°25E **222** E2
Araouane *Mali* 18°55N 3°30W **262** B4
Arapahoe *U.S.A.* 40°18N 99°54W **308** E4
Arapari *Brazil* 5°34S 49°15W **332** C2
Arapawa I. *N.Z.* 41°11S 174°17E **285** B9
Arapey Grande → *Uruguay* 30°55S 57°49W **334** C4
Arapgir *Turkey* 39°5N 38°30E **213** C8
Arapiraca *Brazil* 9°45S 36°39W **332** C4
Arapis, Akra *Greece* 40°27N 24°0E **203** F8
Arapongas *Brazil* 23°29S 51°28W **335** A5
Arapuni *N.Z.* 38°4S 175°39E **284** E4
Ar'ar *Si. Arabia* 30°59N 41°2E **246** D4
Araracuara *Colombia* 0°24S 72°17W **328** D3
Araranguá *Brazil* 29°0S 49°30W **335** B6
Araraquara *Brazil* 21°50S 48°0W **333** F2
Ararás, Serra das *Brazil* 25°0S 53°10W **335** B5
Ararat *Armenia* 39°48N 44°50E **213** C11
Ararat *Vic., Australia* 37°16S 142°58E **282** D5
Ararat, Mt. = Ağrı Dağı *Turkey* 39°50N 44°15E **213** C11
Arari *Brazil* 3°28S 44°47W **332** B3
Araria *India* 26°9N 87°33E **243** F12
Araripe, Chapada do *Brazil* 7°20S 40°0W **332** C4
Araripina *Brazil* 7°33S 40°34W **332** C3
Araruama, L. de *Brazil* 22°53S 42°12W **333** F3
Araruna *Brazil* 6°52S 35°44W **332** C4
Aras, Rūd-e → *Asia* 40°5N 48°29E **191** K9
Arataca *Brazil* ...
Aratāne *Mauritania* 18°24N 8°32W **262** B3
Araticu = Oeiras do Para *Brazil* 1°58S 49°51W **329** D8
Arauca *Colombia* 7°0N 70°40W **328** B3
Arauca □ *Colombia* 6°40N 71°0W **328** B3
Arauca → *Venezuela* 7°24N 66°35W **328** B4
Arauco *Chile* 37°16S 73°25W **334** D1
Araújos *Brazil* 19°56S 45°14W **333** E2
Arauquita *Colombia* 7°2N 71°25W **328** B3
Araure *Venezuela* 9°34N 69°13W **328** B4
Arauzo *Spain* 40°27N 3°47W **127** B1
Arawa *Ethiopia* 9°57N 41°58E **257** F5
Arawale ⌂ *Kenya* 1°24S 40°9E **268** C5
Arawe Is. *Papua N. G.* 6°6S 149°0E **286** D5
Arawhata → *N.Z.* 44°0S 168°40E **285** E3
Araxá *Brazil* 19°35S 46°55W **333** E2
Araya, Pen. de *Venezuela* 10°40N 64°0W **329** A5
Arayat *Phil.* 15°10N 120°46E **232** D3
Arba Gugu *Ethiopia* 8°40N 40°15E **257** F5
Arba Minch *Ethiopia* 6°0N 37°30E **257** F4
Arbat *Iraq* 35°25N 45°35E **213** E11
Arbataash *Iraq* 33°20N 44°19E **113** A1
Árbatax *Italy* 39°56N 9°42E **200** C2
Arbi *Ethiopia* 9°4N 35°7E **257** F4
Arbīl *Iraq* 36°15N 44°5E **213** D11
Arbīl □ *Iraq* 36°20N 44°20E **213** D11
Arboga *Sweden* 59°24N 15°52E **162** E9
Arbois *France* 46°55N 5°46E **173** F12
Arboletes *Colombia* 8°51N 76°26W **328** B2
Arbore *Ethiopia* 5°3N 36°50E **257** F4
Arboréa *Italy* 39°46N 8°35E **200** C1
Arborfield *Canada* 53°6N 103°39W **297** C8
Arborg *Canada* 50°54N 97°13W **297** C9
Arbre du Ténéré *Niger* 17°50N 10°4E **259** E2
Arbroath *U.K.* 56°34N 2°35W **167** E6
Arbuckle *U.S.A.* 39°1N 122°3W **306** F4
Arbus *Italy* 39°30N 8°33E **200** C1
Arc → *France* 45°34N 6°12E **175** C10
Arc de Triomphe *Paris, France* **134** a2
Arc-lès-Gray *France* 47°28N 5°34E **173** E12
Arcachon *France* 44°40N 1°10W **174** D2
Arcachon, Bassin d' *France* 44°42N 1°10W **174** D2
Arcade *U.S.A.* 42°32N 78°25W **312** D6
Arcadia *Calif., U.S.A.* 34°7N 118°1W **126** B4
Arcadia *Fla., U.S.A.* 27°13N 81°52W **317** H8
Arcadia *Ind., U.S.A.* 40°11N 86°1W **311** D10
Arcadia *Iowa, U.S.A.* 42°5N 95°3W **310** B1
Arcadia *La., U.S.A.* 32°33N 92°55W **314** E8
Arcadia *Pa., U.S.A.* 40°47N 78°51W **312** F6
Arcadia *Wis., U.S.A.* 44°15N 91°30W **308** C8
Arcanum *U.S.A.* 39°59N 84°33W **311** E12
Arcata *U.S.A.* 40°52N 124°5W **304** F1
Arcévia *Italy* 43°30N 12°56E **199** E9
Archanes *Greece* 35°16N 25°11E **205** F7
Archangel = Arkhangelsk *Russia* 64°38N 40°36E **186** B7
Archangelos *Preveza, Greece* 39°6N 20°42E **207** A2
Archangelos *Rhodes, Greece* 36°13N 28°7E **206** E12
Archar *Bulgaria* 43°50N 22°54E **202** C6
Archbald *U.S.A.* 41°30N 75°32W **313** E9
Archbold *U.S.A.* 41°31N 84°18W **311** C12
Archena *Spain* 38°9N 1°16W **197** G3
Archenu, J. *Chad* 21°55N 24°45E **259** D4
Archer *U.S.A.* 29°32N 82°32W **317** F7
Archer → *Australia* 13°28S 141°41E **280** A3
Archer B. *Australia* 13°20S 141°30E **280** A3
Archer Bend = Mungkan Kandju △ *Australia* 13°35S 142°52E **280** A3
Archers Post *Kenya* 0°35N 37°35E **268** B4
Arches △ *U.S.A.* 38°45N 109°25W **304** G9
Archidona *Spain* 37°6N 4°22W **195** H6
Archipel-de-Mingan △ *Canada* 50°13N 63°10W **299** B7
Archipiélago Chinijo △ *Canary Is.* 29°20N 13°30W **153** e2
Archipiélago Los Roques △ *Venezuela* 11°50N 66°44W **328** A4
Archives Navy Memorial *Washington, D.C., U.S.A.* **143** b2
Arci, Mte. *Italy* 39°47N 8°45E **200** C1
Arcidosso *Italy* 42°52N 11°33E **199** F8
Arcila = Asilah *Morocco* 35°29N 6°0W **260** A3
Arcipelago de la Maddalena △ *Italy* 41°14N 9°24E **200** A2
Arcipelago Toscano △ *Italy* 42°45N 10°15E **198** F7
Arcis-sur-Aube *France* 48°32N 4°10E **173** D11
Arckaringa Cr. → *Australia* 28°10S 135°22E **281** D2
Arco *Italy* 45°55N 10°53E **198** C7
Arco *Idaho, U.S.A.* 43°38N 113°18W **304** E7
Arco Plaza *Los Angeles, U.S.A.* **127** b1
Arcola *U.S.A.* 39°41N 88°19W **311** E8
Arcoona *Australia* 31°2S 137°1E **282** A2
Arcos de Jalón *Spain* 41°12N 2°16W **196** D2
Arcos de la Frontera *Spain* 36°45N 5°49W **195** J5
Arcos de Valdevez *Portugal* 41°55N 8°22W **194** D2
Arcot *India* 12°53N 79°20E **245** H4
Arcoverde *Brazil* 8°25S 37°4W **332** C4
Arcozelo *Portugal* 40°32N 7°47W **194** E3
Arctic Bay *Canada* 73°1N 85°7W **295** B11
Arctic Mid-Ocean Ridge *Arctic* 87°0N 90°0E **150** A3
Arctic Ocean *Arctic* 78°0N 160°0W **150** B18
Arctic Red River = Tsiigehtchic *Canada* 67°15N 134°0W **294** C6
Arctic Village *U.S.A.* 68°8N 145°32W **303** B11
Arctowski *Antarctica* 62°30S 58°0W **151** C18
Arcueil *France* 48°48N 2°19E **134** B2
Arda → *Bulgaria* 41°40N 26°30E **203** E10
Arda → *Italy* 45°2N 10°2E **198** C7
Ardabīl *Iran* 38°15N 48°18E **213** C13
Ardabīl □ *Iran* 38°15N 48°20E **247** B6
Ardahan *Turkey* 41°7N 42°41E **213** B10
Ardahan □ *Turkey* 41°10N 42°50E **213** B10
Ardakān = Sepīdān *Iran* 30°20N 52°5E **247** D7
Ardakān *Iran* 32°19N 53°59E **247** C7
Ardala *Sweden* 58°22N 13°19E **163** F7
Ardales *Spain* 36°53N 4°51W **195** J6
Ardalstangen *Norway* 61°14N 7°43E **164** C4
Ardara *Ireland* 54°46N 8°25W **166** B3
Ardas → *Greece* 41°40N 26°30E **203** E10
Ardèche □ *France* 44°42N 4°16E **175** D8
Ardèche → *France* 44°16N 4°39E **175** D8
Ardee *Ireland* 53°52N 6°33W **166** C5
Arden *Ont., Canada* 44°43N 76°56W **312** B8
Arden *Denmark* 56°46N 9°52E **163** H3
Arden *Calif., U.S.A.* 38°36N 121°33W **306** G5
Arden *Nev., U.S.A.* 36°1N 115°14W **307** J11
Ardenne *Belgium* 49°50N 5°5E **170** E5
Ardennes = Ardenne *Belgium* 49°50N 5°5E **170** E5
Ardennes □ *France* 49°35N 4°40E **173** C11
Ardentes *France* 46°45N 1°50E **173** F8
Arderin *Ireland* 53°2N 7°39W **166** C4
Ardeşen *Turkey* 41°12N 41°2E **213** B9
Ardestān *Iran* 33°20N 52°25E **247** C7
Ardfert *Ireland* 52°20N 9°47W **166** D2
Ardglass *U.K.* 54°17N 5°36W **166** B6
Ardhéa = Aridea *Greece* 40°58N 22°3E **202** F6
Ardila → *Portugal* 38°12N 7°28W **195** G3
Ardino *Bulgaria* 41°34N 25°9E **203** E9
Ardivachar Pt. *U.K.* 57°23N 7°26W **167** D1
Ardlethan *Australia* 34°22S 146°53E **283** C7
Ardmore *Okla., U.S.A.* 34°10N 97°8W **314** D6
Ardmore *Pa., U.S.A.* 40°2N 75°17W **313** F9
Ardnamurchan, Pt. of *U.K.* 56°43N 6°14W **167** E2
Ardnave Pt. *U.K.* 55°53N 6°20W **167** F2
Ardon *Russia* 43°10N 44°18E **191** J7
Ardore *Italy* 38°11N 16°10E **201** D9
Ardres *France* 50°50N 1°59E **173** B8
Ardrossan *S. Austral., Australia* 34°26S 137°53E **282** C2
Ardrossan *N. Ayrs., U.K.* 55°39N 4°49W **167** F4
Ards Pen. *U.K.* 54°33N 5°34W **166** B6
Arduan *Sudan* 19°54N 30°20E **256** D3
Ardud *Romania* 47°37N 22°52E **182** C7
Åre *Sweden* 63°22N 13°15E **162** A7
Arecibo *Puerto Rico* 18°29N 66°43W **321** C6
Areia Branca *Brazil* 5°0S 37°0W **332** C4
Arena, Pt. *U.S.A.* 38°57N 123°44W **306** G3
Arenal *Honduras* 15°21N 86°50W **320** C2
Arenales, Cerro *Chile* 47°5S 73°40W **336** C2
Arenápolis *Brazil* 14°26S 56°49W **331** C6
Arenas = Las Arenas *Spain* 43°17N 4°50W **194** B6
Arenas, Pta. *Venezuela* 10°31N 64°14W **329** A5
Arenas de San Pedro *Spain* 40°12N 5°5W **194** E5
Arendal *Norway* 58°28N 8°46E **164** F5
Arendsee *Germany* 52°52N 11°27E **178** C7
Arenillas *Ecuador* 3°33S 80°10W **328** D1
Arensburg = Kuressaare *Estonia* 58°15N 22°30E **188** C2
Arenys de Mar *Spain* 41°35N 2°33E **196** D7
Arenzano *Italy* 44°24N 8°41E **198** D5
Arenzville *U.S.A.* 39°53N 90°22W **310** E6
Areopoli *Greece* 36°40N 22°22E **204** E4
Arequipa *Peru* 16°20S 71°30W **330** D3
Arequipa □ *Peru* 16°0S 72°50W **330** D3
Arere *Brazil* 0°16S 53°52W **329** D7
Arero *Ethiopia* 4°41N 38°50E **257** G4
Arès *France* 44°47N 1°8W **174** D2
Ares *Spain* 43°25N 8°14W 194 B2
Arévalo *Spain* 41°3N 4°43W **194** D6
Arezzo *Italy* 43°25N 11°53E **199** E8
Arga *Turkey* 38°21N 37°59E **246** B3
Arga → *Spain* 42°18N 1°47W **196** C3
Argalasti *Greece* 39°13N 23°13E **204** B5
Argamakmur *Indonesia* 3°35S 102°0E **234** C2
Argamasilla de Alba *Spain* 39°8N 3°5W **195** F7
Argamasilla de Calatrava *Spain* 38°44N 4°4W **195** G6
Arganda *Spain* 40°19N 3°26W **194** E7
Arganil *Portugal* 40°13N 8°3W **194** E2
Arganzuela *Spain* 40°23N 3°42W **127** B1
Argao *Phil.* 9°52N 123°36E **233** G4
Argasion *Greece* 37°45N 20°56E **207** D2
Argedeb *Ethiopia* 6°11N 41°13E **257** F5
Argelès-Gazost *France* 43°0N 0°6W **174** E3
Argelès-sur-Mer *France* 42°34N 3°1E **174** F7
Argens → *France* 43°24N 6°44E **175** E10
Argent-sur-Sauldre *France* 47°33N 2°25E **173** E9
Argenta = North Little Rock *U.S.A.* 34°45N 92°16W **314** D8
Argenta *B.C., Canada* 50°11N 116°56W **296** C5
Argenta *Italy* 44°37N 11°50E **199** D8
Argenta *Ill., U.S.A.* 39°59N 88°49W **311** E8
Argentan *France* 48°45N 0°1W **172** D6
Argentário, Mte. *Italy* 42°24N 11°9E **199** F8
Argentat *France* 45°6N 1°56E **174** C5
Argentera *Italy* 44°24N 7°5E **198** D4
Argenteuil *France* 48°56N 2°15E **134** A2
Argentia *Canada* 47°18N 53°58W **299** C9
Argentiera, C. dell' *Italy* 40°44N 8°8E **200** B1
Argentina ■ *S. Amer.* 35°0S 66°0W **336** A3
Argentine Abyssal Plain *Atl. Oc.* 46°0S 52°0W **152** L6
Argentine Basin *Atl. Oc.* 45°0S 45°0W **152** L7
Argentino, L. *Argentina* 50°10S 73°0W **336** D2
Argenton-Château *France* 46°59N 0°27W **172** F6
Argenton-sur-Creuse *France* 46°36N 1°30E **173** F8
Argeş □ *Romania* 45°0N 24°45E **183** F9
Argeş → *Romania* 44°5N 26°38E **183** F11
Arghandab → *Afghan.* 31°30N 64°15E **242** D1
Argheile *Ethiopia* 5°19N 42°4E **257** F5
Argirades *Greece* 39°27N 19°58E **206** C9
Argiroupoli *Athina, Greece* 37°52N 23°44E **112** B2
Argiroupoli *Kriti, Greece* 35°17N 24°20E **207** E5
Argo *Sudan* 19°28N 30°30E **256** D3
Argolida □ *Greece* 37°38N 22°50E **204** D4
Argolikos Kolpos *Greece* 37°20N 22°52E **204** D4
Argonne *France* 49°10N 5°0E **173** C12
Argonne Forest *U.S.A.* 41°42N 87°53W **119** C1
Argos *Greece* 37°40N 22°43E **204** D4
Argos *Ind., U.S.A.* 41°14N 86°15W **311** C10
Argos Orestiko *Greece* 40°27N 21°18E **202** F5
Argostoli *Greece* 38°11N 20°29E **207** C2
Argostoliou, Kolpos *Greece* 38°10N 20°27E **207** C1
Arguedas *Spain* 42°11N 1°36W **196** C3
Argüelles *Madrid, Spain* **127** a1
Arguineguín *Canary Is.* 27°46N 15°41W **153** e1
Argun *Russia* 43°18N 45°55E **191** J7
Argun → *Russia* 53°20N 121°28E **215** D13
Argungu *Nigeria* 12°40N 4°31E **263** C5
Argus Pk. *U.S.A.* 35°52N 117°26W **307** K9
Argyle, L. *Australia* 16°20S 128°40E **278** C4
Argyle Waterfalls *Trin. & Tob.* 11°15N 60°35W **323** s
Argyll ⌂ *U.K.* 56°6N 5°0W **167** E4
Argyll & Bute □ *U.K.* 56°13N 5°28W **167** E3
Arhavi *Turkey* 41°21N 41°18E **213** B9
Århus *Denmark* 56°8N 10°11E **163** H4
Ari Atoll *Maldives* 3°53N 72°50E **272** d
Aria *N.Z.* 38°33S 175°0E **284** E4
Ariadnoye *Russia* 45°8N 134°25E **220** B7
Ariamsvlei *Namibia* 28°9S 19°51E **270** C2
Ariana *Tunisia* 36°52N 10°12E **258** A2
Ariana □ *Tunisia* 36°50N 9°52E **261** A6
Ariano Irpino *Italy* 41°9N 15°5E **201** A8
Ariari → *Colombia* 2°35N 72°47W **328** C3
Aribinda *Burkina Faso* 14°17N 0°52W **263** C4
Arica *Chile* 18°32S 70°20W **330** D3
Arica *Colombia* 2°0S 71°50W **328** D3
Arico *Canary Is.* 28°9N 16°29W **153** e1
Arid, C. *Australia* 34°1S 123°10E **279** F3
Arida *Japan* 34°5N 135°8E **223** C7
Aridal *W. Sahara* 25°59N 13°54W **260** C2
Aride *Seychelles* 4°13S 55°40E **272** c
Aridea *Greece* 40°58N 22°3E **202** F6
Ariège □ *France* 42°56N 1°30E **174** F5
Ariège → *France* 43°30N 1°25E **174** E5
Aries → *Romania* 46°24N 23°20E **183** D8
Arigat el Fersig *Algeria* 27°35N 2°7W **261** C4
Arīhā *Israel* 31°51N 35°27E **256** A4
Arīḥā *Syria* 35°49N 36°35E **250** C7
Arikok △ *Aruba* 12°31N 69°56W **322** f
Arila, Akra *Greece* 39°43N 19°39E **206** B9
Arilje *Serbia* 43°44N 20°7E **202** C4
Arima *Kanagawa, Japan* 35°33N 139°33E **140** B2
Arima *Trin. & Tob.* 10°38N 61°17W **323** t
Arima → *Trin. & Tob.* 10°35N 61°16W **323** t
Aringay *Phil.* 16°26N 120°21E **232** C3
Arinos → *Brazil* 10°25S 58°20W **331** C6
Ario de Rosales *Mexico* 19°12N 101°43W **318** D4
Ariogala *Lithuania* 55°16N 23°28E **184** C10
Arios Pagos *Athens, Greece* **112** c1
Aripo → *Trin. & Tob.* 10°35N 61°14W **323** t
Aripo, Mt. *Trin. & Tob.* 10°45N 61°15W **323** t
Aripo Caves *Trin. & Tob.* 10°43N 61°14W **323** t
Aripuanã *Brazil* 9°25S 60°30W **331** B5
Aripuanã → *Brazil* 5°7S 60°25W **331** B5
Ariquemes *Brazil* 9°55S 63°6W **331** B5
Arisaig *U.K.* 56°55N 5°51W **167** E3
Arîsh, W. el → *Egypt* 31°9N 33°49E **256** A3
Arissa *Ethiopia* 11°10N 41°35E **257** E5
Aristazabal I. *Canada* 52°40N 129°10W **296** C3
Arita *Japan* 33°11N 129°54E **222** D1
Aritao *Phil.* 16°18N 121°2E **232** C3
Ariton *U.S.A.* 31°36N 85°43W **316** D4
Arivonimamo *Madag.* 19°1S 47°11E **272** B2
Ariyalur *India* 11°8N 79°8E **245** J4
Ariza *Spain* 41°19N 2°3W **196** D2
Arizaro, Salar de *Argentina* 24°40S 67°50W **334** A2
Arizona *Argentina* 35°45S 65°25W **334** D2
Arizona □ *U.S.A.* 34°0N 112°0W **305** J8
Arizpe *Mexico* 30°20N 110°10W **318** A2
Årjäng *Sweden* 59°24N 12°8E **162** E6
Arjeplog *Sweden* 66°3N 17°54E **160** C17
Arjepluovve = Arjeplog *Sweden* 66°3N 17°54E **160** C17
Arjona *Colombia* 10°14N 75°22W **328** A2
Arjona *Spain* 37°56N 4°4W **195** H6
Arjuna *Indonesia* 7°49S 112°34E **235** D4
Arka *Russia* 60°15N 142°0E **215** C15
Arkadak *Russia* 51°58N 43°30E **190** E6
Arkadelphia *U.S.A.* 34°7N 93°4W **314** D8
Arkadia □ *Greece* 37°30N 22°20E **204** D4
Arkaig, L. *U.K.* 56°59N 5°10W **167** E3
Arkalgud *India* 12°46N 76°3E **245** H3
Arkalyk = Arqalyk *Kazakhstan* 50°13N 66°50E **217** B7
Arkansas □ *U.S.A.* 35°0N 92°30W **314** D8
Arkansas → *U.S.A.* 33°47N 91°4W **314** E9
Arkansas City *U.S.A.* 37°4N 97°2W **308** G5
Arkaroola *Australia* 30°20S 139°22E **281** E2
Arkhangelsk *Russia* 64°38N 40°36E **186** B7
Arkhangelskoye *Russia* 51°32N 40°58E **190** E5
Arkhangelyskoye *Russia* 55°47N 37°17E **129** B1
Arki *Greece* 37°24N 26°44E **205** D8
Arki *India* 31°9N 76°58E **242** D7
Arkiko *Eritrea* 15°33N 39°30E **257** D4
Arklow *Ireland* 52°48N 6°10W **166** D5
Arkona, Kap *Germany* 54°41N 13°26E **178** A9
Arkösund *Sweden* 58°29N 16°56E **163** F10
Arkoudi *Greece* 38°33N 20°43E **207** B2
Arkport *U.S.A.* 42°24N 77°42W **312** D7
Arkticheskiy, Mys *Russia* 81°10N 95°0E **215** A10
Arkul *Russia* 57°17N 50°3E **190** B10
Arkville *U.S.A.* 42°9N 74°37W **313** D10
Årla *Sweden* 59°17N 16°40E **162** E10
Arlanda, Stockholm ✈ (ARN) *Sweden* 59°41N 17°56E **139** A1
Arlanza → *Spain* 42°6N 4°9W **194** C6
Arlanzón → *Spain* 42°3N 4°17W **194** C6
Arlbergpass *Austria* 47°9N 10°12E **180** D3
Arles *France* 43°41N 4°40E **175** E8
Arli *Burkina Faso* 11°35N 1°28E **263** C5
Arli △ *Burkina Faso* 11°35N 1°28E **263** C5
Arlington *Free State, S. Africa* 28°1S 27°53E **271** C4
Arlington *Ga., U.S.A.* 31°26N 84°44W **316** D5
Arlington *Mass., U.S.A.* 42°24N 71°10W **116** A1
Arlington *N.Y., U.S.A.* 41°42N 73°54W **313** E11
Arlington *Oreg., U.S.A.* 45°43N 120°12W **304** D3
Arlington *S. Dak., U.S.A.* 44°22N 97°8W **308** C5
Arlington *Tex., U.S.A.* 32°44N 97°6W **314** E6
Arlington *Va., U.S.A.* 38°53N 77°7W **143** B3
Arlington *Vt., U.S.A.* 43°5N 73°9W **313** C11
Arlington *Wash., U.S.A.* 48°12N 122°8W **306** B4
Arlington Heights *Ill., U.S.A.* 42°5N 87°59W **311** B9
Arlington Heights *Mass., U.S.A.* 42°25N 71°10W **116** A1
Arlington Nat. Cemetery *U.S.A.* 38°52N 77°4W **143** B3
Arlon *Belgium* 49°42N 5°49E **170** E5
Arlparra *Australia* 22°11S 134°30E **280** C1
Arltunga *Australia* 23°26S 134°41E **280** C1
Armação *Brazil* 22°52S 43°6W **135** B2
Armadale *Australia* 32°9S 116°0E **279** F2
Armadale *U.K.* 55°54N 3°41W **167** F5
Armagh *U.K.* 54°21N 6°39W **166** B5
Armagh □ *U.K.* 54°18N 6°37W **166** B5
Armagnac *France* 43°50N 0°10E **174** E4
Armançon → *France* 47°59N 3°30E **173** E10
Armando Bermudez △ *Dom. Rep.* 19°3N 71°0W **321** C5
Armatree *Australia* 31°26S 148°28E **283** A8
Armavir *Russia* 45°2N 41°7E **191** H5
Armenia *Colombia* 4°35N 75°45W **328** C2
Armenia ■ *Asia* 40°20N 45°0E **191** K7
Armenian Quarter *Jerusalem* **123** b3
Armeniş *Romania* 45°13N 22°17E **182** E7
Armenistis, Akra *Greece* 36°8N 27°42E **206** E11
Armentières *France* 50°40N 2°50E **173** B9
Armero *Colombia* 4°58N 74°54W **328** C3
Armidale *Australia* 30°30S 151°40E **283** A9
Armilla *Spain* 37°9N 3°37W **195** H7
Armori *India* 20°28N 79°59E **244** D4
Armorique ⌂ *France* 48°22N 3°50W **172** D3
Armour *U.S.A.* 43°19N 98°21W **308** D4

Armour Heights Canada 43°45N 79°25W 141 A2
Armstrong B.C., Canada 50°25N 119°10W 296 C5
Armstrong Ont., Canada 50°18N 89°4W 298 B2
Armur India 18°48N 78°16E 244 E4
Armutlu Bursa, Turkey 40°31N 28°50E 203 F12
Armutlu İzmir, Turkey 38°24N 27°34E 205 C9
Arnarfjörður Iceland 65°48N 23°40W 155 B3
Arnaud ➔ Canada 59°59N 69°46W 295 D13
Arnauti, C. Cyprus 35°6N 32°17E 207 E8
Arnay-le-Duc France 47°10N 4°27E 173 E11
Arncliffe Australia 33°56S 151°8E 139 B1
Arnea Greece 40°30N 23°38E 202 F7
Arnedillo Spain 42°13N 2°14W 196 C2
Arnedo Spain 42°12N 2°5W 196 C2
Arnes Iceland 66°1N 21°31W 155 A5
Årnes Akershus, Norway 60°7N 11°28E 164 D8
Árnessýsla □ Iceland 64°15N 20°30W 155 C6
Arnett U.S.A. 36°8N 99°46W 314 C5
Arnhem Neths. 51°58N 5°55E 170 C5
Arnhem, C. Australia 12°20S 137°30E 280 A2
Arnhem B. Australia 12°20S 136°10E 280 A2
Arnhem Land Australia 13°10S 134°30E 280 A1
Arnissa Greece 40°47N 21°49E 202 F5
Arno ➔ Italy 43°41N 10°17E 198 E7
Arno Bay Australia 33°54S 136°34E 282 B2
Arnold Notts., U.K. 53°1N 1°7W 168 D6
Arnold Calif., U.S.A. 38°15N 120°21W 306 G6
Arnold Mo., U.S.A. 38°26N 90°23W 310 F6
Arnold Arboretum U.S.A. 42°18N 71°8W 116 B2
Arnoldstein Austria 46°33N 13°43E 180 E6
Arnon ➔ France 47°13N 2°1E 173 E9
Arnos Vale Trin. & Tob. 11°13N 60°45W 323 s
Arnot Canada 55°56N 96°41W 297 B9
Arnøya Norway 70°9N 20°40E 160 A19
Arnprior Canada 45°26N 76°21W 313 A8
Arnsberg Germany 51°24N 8°5E 178 D4
Arnsberger Wald ⌓ Germany 51°25N 8°20E 178 D4
Arnstadt Germany 50°50N 10°56E 178 E6
Arnswalde = Choszczno Poland 53°7N 15°25E 185 E2
Aro ➔ Venezuela 8°1N 64°11W 329 B5
Aroa, Pte. Moorea 17°28S 149°46W 289 e
Aroab Namibia 26°41S 19°39E 270 C2
Aroania Oros Greece 37°56N 22°12E 204 D4
Aroche Spain 37°56N 6°57W 195 H4
Arochuku Nigeria 5°21N 7°54E 263 D6
Aroeiras Brazil 7°31S 35°41W 332 C4
Arolsen Germany 51°23N 9°2E 178 D5
Aron India 25°57N 77°56E 242 G6
Aron ➔ France 46°50N 3°28E 173 F10
Arona Canary Is. 28°6N 16°40W 153 e1
Arona Italy 45°46N 8°34E 198 C5
Arorae Kiribati 2°38S 176°49E 277 A14
Arorangi Cook Is. 21°13S 159°49W 289 h
Aroroy Phil. 12°31N 123°24E 232 E4
Aros ➔ Mexico 29°9N 107°57W 318 B3
Arosa, Ría de Spain 42°28N 8°57W 194 C2
Arouca Trin. & Tob. 10°38N 61°20W 323 t
Årøysund Norway 59°10N 10°27E 164 F7
Árpádföld Hungary 47°32N 19°8E 117 A3
Arpajon France 48°36N 2°15E 173 D9
Arpajon-sur-Cère France 44°53N 2°28E 174 D6
Arpaşu de Jos Romania 45°47N 24°37E 183 E9
Arqalyk Kazakhstan 50°13N 66°50E 217 B7
Arque Bolivia 17°48S 66°23W 330 D4
Arrah = Ara India 25°35N 84°32E 243 G11
Arrah Ivory C. 6°40N 3°58W 262 D4
Arraias Brazil 12°56S 46°57W 333 D2
Arraias ➔ Mato Grosso, Brazil 11°10S 53°35W 331 C7
Arraias ➔ Pará, Brazil 7°30S 49°20W 332 C2
Arraiolos Portugal 38°44N 7°59W 195 G3
Arran U.K. 55°34N 5°12W 167 F3
Arras France 50°17N 2°46E 173 B9
Arrasate Spain 43°4N 2°30W 196 B2
Arrats ➔ France 44°6N 0°52E 174 D4
Arreau France 42°54N 0°22E 174 F4
Arrecife Canary Is. 28°57N 13°37W 153 e2
Arrecifes Argentina 34°6S 60°9W 334 C3
Arrée, Mts. d' France 48°26N 3°55W 172 D3
Arrentela Portugal 38°37N 9°6W 126 B2
Arresø Denmark 55°58N 12°6E 163 J6
Arriaga Mexico 16°14N 93°54W 319 D6
Arribes del Duero ⌓ Spain 41°11N 6°39W 194 D4
Arrilalah Australia 23°43S 143°54E 280 C3
Arrino Australia 29°30S 115°40E 279 E2
Arriondas Spain 43°23N 5°11W 194 B5
Arrojado ➔ Brazil 13°24S 44°20W 333 D3
Arromanches-les-Bains France 49°20N 0°38W 172 C6
Arronches Portugal 39°8N 7°16W 195 F3
Arros ➔ France 43°40N 0°2W 174 E3
Arrow, L. Ireland 54°3N 8°19W 166 B3
Arrowsmith, Mt. N.Z. 43°20S 170°55E 285 D5
Arrowtown N.Z. 44°57S 168°50E 285 E3
Arroyo de la Luz Spain 39°30N 6°38W 195 F4
Arroyo del Puerco = Arroyo de la Luz Spain 39°30N 6°38W 195 F4
Arroyo Grande U.S.A. 35°7N 120°35W 307 K6
Arroyo Seco Park U.S.A. 34°6N 118°11W 126 B3
Ars Iran 37°9N 47°46E 246 B5
Ars-sur-Moselle France 49°5N 6°4E 173 C13
Arsenault L. Canada 55°6N 108°32W 297 B7
Arsenev Russia 44°10N 133°15E 220 B6
Arsi Ethiopia 7°45N 39°0E 257 F4
Arsiero Italy 45°48N 11°21E 199 C8
Arsikere India 13°15N 76°15E 245 H3
Arsin Turkey 41°8N 39°55E 213 B8
Arsk Russia 56°10N 49°50E 190 B9
Arslanköy Turkey 37°0N 34°17E 250 B5
Årsta Sweden 59°17N 18°3E 139 B2
Årsunda Sweden 60°31N 16°45E 162 D10
Art, Î. N. Cal. 19°43S 163°38E 288 d
Art Institute Chicago, U.S.A. 119 c2
Arta Greece 39°8N 21°2E 204 B3
Artà Spain 39°41N 3°21E 206 B4
Arta □ Greece 39°15N 21°5E 204 B3
Artane Ireland 53°22N 6°12W 120 A2
Artas West Bank 31°41N 35°11E 123 B2
Arteaga Mexico 18°28N 102°25W 318 D4
Arteche Phil. 12°17N 125°22E 232 E5
Arteijo = Arteixo Spain 43°19N 8°29W 194 B2
Arteixo Spain 43°19N 8°29W 194 B2
Artem = Artyom Azerbaijan 40°28N 50°20E 191 K10
Artem Russia 43°22N 132°13E 220 C6
Artemovsk Sib., Russia 54°45N 93°35E 215 D10
Artemovsk Ukraine 48°35N 38°0E 189 H9
Artemovskiy Russia 47°45N 40°16E 191 G5
Artenay France 48°5N 1°50E 173 D8
Artern Germany 51°22N 11°18E 178 D7
Artesa de Segre Spain 41°54N 1°3E 196 D6
Artesia = Mosomane Botswana 24°2S 26°19E 270 B4
Artesia U.S.A. 32°51N 104°24W 305 K11
Arthington Liberia 6°35N 10°45W 262 D2
Arthur Ont., Canada 43°50N 80°32W 312 C4
Arthur Ill., U.S.A. 39°43N 88°28W 311 E8
Arthur ➔ Australia 41°2S 144°40E 281 G3
Arthur Cr. ➔ Australia 22°30S 136°25E 280 C2
Arthur Pt. Australia 22°7S 150°3E 280 C5
Arthur River Australia 33°20S 117°2E 279 F2
Arthur's Pass N.Z. 42°54S 171°35E 285 C6
Arthur's Pass △ N.Z. 42°53S 171°42E 285 C6
Arthur's Seat U.K. 55°56N 3°9W 121 B3
Arthur's Town Bahamas 24°38N 75°42W 321 B4
Artigas = Río Branco Uruguay 32°40S 53°40W 335 C5
Artigas Antarctica 62°30S 58°0W 151 C18
Artigas Uruguay 30°20S 56°30W 334 C4
Artik Armenia 40°38N 43°58E 191 K6
Artillery L. Canada 63°9N 107°52W 297 A7
Artois France 50°20N 2°30E 173 B9
Artotina Greece 38°42N 22°2E 204 C4
Artrutx, C. de Spain 39°55N 3°49E 206 B4
Arts, Place des Montréal, Canada 130 b2
Artsyz Ukraine 46°4N 29°26E 183 D14
Artux China 39°40N 76°10E 217 E9
Artvin Turkey 41°14N 41°44E 213 B9
Artvin □ Turkey 41°10N 41°50E 213 B9
Artyom Azerbaijan 40°28N 50°20E 191 K10
Aru, Kepulauan Indonesia 6°0S 134°30E 231 F8
Aru Is. = Aru, Kepulauan Indonesia 6°0S 134°30E 231 F8
Arua Uganda 3°1N 30°58E 268 B3
Aruanã Brazil 14°54S 51°10W 333 D1
Aruba ☒ W. Indies 12°30N 70°0W 322 f
Arudy France 43°7N 0°28W 174 E3
Arué Tahiti 17°31S 149°30W 289 e
Arumã Brazil 4°44S 62°8W 329 D5
Arume-wan Japan 26°35N 128°8E 288 a
Arumpo Australia 33°48S 142°55E 282 B5
Arun ➔ Nepal 26°55N 87°10E 243 F12
Arun ➔ W. Susx., U.K. 50°49N 0°33W 169 G7
Arunachal Pradesh □ India 28°0N 95°0E 241 B5
Aruppukkottai India 9°31N 78°8E 245 K4
Arusha Tanzania 3°20S 36°40E 268 C4
Arusha □ Tanzania 4°0S 36°30E 268 C4
Arusha △ Tanzania 3°16S 36°47E 268 C4
Arusha Chini Tanzania 3°32S 37°20E 268 C4
Arut ➔ Indonesia 2°42S 111°34E 235 C4
Aruvi ➔ Sri Lanka 8°48N 79°53E 245 K4
Aruwimi ➔ Dem. Rep. of the Congo 1°13N 23°36E 264 B4
Arvada Colo., U.S.A. 39°48N 105°5W 304 G11
Arvada Wyo., U.S.A. 44°39N 106°8W 304 D10
Arvakalu Sri Lanka 8°20N 79°58E 245 K4
Arvayheer Mongolia 46°15N 102°48E 218 B5
Arve ➔ France 46°11N 6°8E 173 F13
Arvi Kriti, Greece 34°59N 25°28E 207 F6
Arvi India 20°59N 78°16E 244 D4
Arviat Canada 61°6N 93°59W 297 A10
Arvidsjaur Sweden 65°35N 19°10E 160 D18
Arvika Sweden 59°40N 12°36E 162 E6
Arvin U.S.A. 35°12N 118°50W 307 K8
Arwad Syria 34°51N 35°51E 250 D6
Arwal India 25°15N 84°41E 243 G11
Arxan China 47°11N 119°57E 219 B6
Åryd Sweden 56°49N 14°59E 163 H8
Arys Kazakhstan 42°26N 68°48E 217 D7
Arzachena Italy 41°5N 9°23E 200 A2
Arzamas Russia 55°27N 43°55E 190 C6
Arzanah U.A.E. 24°47N 52°34E 247 E7
Arzew Algeria 35°50N 0°23W 261 A4
Arzgir Russia 45°18N 44°23E 191 H7
Arzignano Italy 45°31N 11°20E 199 C8
Arzúa Spain 42°56N 8°9W 194 C2
Aš Czech Rep. 50°13N 12°12E 180 A5
Ås Akershus, Norway 59°40N 10°48E 164 E7
Ås Sweden 63°15N 14°34E 162 A8
As Pontes de García Rodríguez Spain 43°27N 7°50W 194 B3
As Sa'an Syria 35°16N 37°22E 250 C8
Aş Şafā Syria 33°10N 37°0E 250 E8
As Saffānīyah Si. Arabia 27°55N 48°50E 247 E6
As Safirah Syria 36°5N 37°21E 250 B8
Aş Şahm Oman 24°10N 56°53E 247 E8
As Sājir Si. Arabia 25°11N 44°36E 246 E5
As Salamīyah Syria 35°1N 37°2E 250 C8
As Salmān Iraq 30°30N 44°32E 246 D5
As Salţ Jordan 32°2N 35°43E 251 E5
As Sal'w'a Qatar 24°23N 50°50E 247 E6
As Samāwah Iraq 31°15N 45°15E 246 D5
As Sanamayn Syria 33°3N 36°10E 250 E7
As Sawādah Si. Arabia 22°24N 44°28E 248 B4
As Sayl al Kabīr Si. Arabia 21°38N 40°25E 248 B3
As Shawawra West Bank 31°41N 35°15E 123 B2
As Sohar = Şuḩār Oman 24°20N 56°40E 247 E8
As Sukhnah Syria 34°52N 38°52E 213 E8
As Sulaymānīyah Iraq 35°35N 45°29E 213 E11
As Sulaymānīyah Si. Arabia 24°9N 47°18E 248 A4
As Sulaymānīyah □ Iraq 35°50N 45°30E 213 E11
As Sulaymī Si. Arabia 26°17N 41°21E 246 E4
As Sulayyil Si. Arabia 20°27N 45°34E 248 B4
As Sulţān Libya 31°4N 17°8E 258 B3
As Summān Si. Arabia 25°0N 47°0E 246 E5
Aş Şurrah Yemen 13°57N 46°14E 248 D4
As Suwaydā' Syria 32°40N 36°30E 250 F7
As Suwaydā' □ Syria 32°45N 36°45E 250 F7
As Suwayq Oman 23°51N 57°26E 247 F8
Aş Şuwayrah Iraq 32°55N 45°0E 213 F11
Åsa Sweden 57°21N 12°8E 163 G6
Asa Wright Nature Centre Trin. & Tob. 10°43N 61°17W 323 t
Asab Namibia 25°30S 18°0E 270 C2
Asaba Nigeria 6°12N 6°38E 263 D6
Asad, Buḩayrat al Syria 36°0N 38°15E 213 D8
Asadābād Iran 34°47N 48°7E 213 E13
Asafo Ghana 6°20N 2°40W 262 D4
Asaga Str. Amer. Samoa 14°10S 169°37W 302 g
Asagaya Japan 35°41N 139°38E 140 A2
Asahi Chiba, Japan 35°43N 140°39E 223 B12
Asahi Ōsaka, Japan 34°43N 135°31E 133 A2
Asahi-Gawa ➔ Japan 34°36N 133°58E 222 C5
Asahigawa Japan 43°46N 142°22E 220 C11
Asakusa Japan 35°42N 139°47E 140 A3
Asakusabashi Tokyo, Japan 140 a5
Asale, L. Ethiopia 14°0N 40°20E 257 E5
Asama-Yama Japan 36°24N 138°31E 223 A10
Asamankese Ghana 5°50N 0°40W 263 D4
Asan S. Korea 36°48N 127°1E 224 D3
Asan ➔ India 26°37N 78°24E 243 F8
Asansol India 23°40N 87°1E 243 H12
Åsarna Sweden 62°39N 14°22E 162 B8
Asati India 22°28N 88°15E 124 C1
Asau Samoa 13°27S 172°33W 287 V19
Asayita Ethiopia 11°35N 41°23E 257 E5
Asba Littoria = Asbe Teferi Ethiopia 9°4N 40°49E 257 F5
Asbe Teferi Ethiopia 9°4N 40°49E 257 F5
Asbesberge S. Africa 29°0S 23°0E 270 C3
Asbestos Canada 45°47N 71°58W 299 C5
Asbury Park U.S.A. 40°13N 74°1W 313 F10
Ascea Italy 40°8N 15°11E 201 B8
Ascensión Mexico 31°6N 107°59W 318 A3
Ascensión, B. de la Mexico 19°40N 87°30W 319 D7
Ascension I. Atl. Oc. 7°57S 14°23W 153 g
Aschach an der Donau Austria 48°22N 14°2E 180 C7
Aschaffenburg Germany 49°58N 9°6E 179 F5
Aschendorf Germany 53°3N 7°19E 178 B3
Aschersleben Germany 51°45N 11°29E 178 D7
Aschheim Germany 48°10N 11°42E 131 A3
Asciano Italy 43°14N 11°33E 199 E8
Áscoli Piceno Italy 42°51N 13°34E 199 F10
Áscoli Satriano Italy 41°11N 15°32E 201 A8
Ascope Peru 7°46S 79°8W 330 B2
Ascot Vale Australia 37°46S 144°53E 128 A1
Ascotán Chile 21°45S 68°17W 334 A2
Ascuncion Phil. 7°35N 125°45E 233 H5
Aseb Eritrea 13°0N 42°40E 257 E5
Åseda Sweden 57°10N 15°20E 163 G9
Asedjrad Algeria 24°51N 1°29E 261 D5
Aseki Papua N. G. 7°21S 146°12E 286 D4
Asela Ethiopia 8°0N 39°0E 257 F4
Åsen Sweden 61°17N 13°50E 162 C7
Asenovgrad Bulgaria 42°1N 24°51E 203 D8
Asfeld France 49°27N 4°5E 173 C11
Asfûn el Matâ'na Egypt 25°26N 32°30E 256 B3
Asgabat = Ashgabat Turkmenistan 38°0N 57°50E 247 B8
Åsgårdstrand Norway 59°22N 10°27E 164 E7
Asgata Cyprus 34°46N 33°15E 207 F9
Ash Fork U.S.A. 35°13N 112°29W 305 J7
Ash Grove U.S.A. 37°19N 93°35W 308 G7
Ash Shabakah Iraq 30°49N 43°39E 246 D4
Ash Shafa Si. Arabia 21°27N 39°49E 248 B2
Ash Shamāl □ Lebanon 34°25N 36°0E 250 D7
Ash Shāmīyah Iraq 31°55N 44°35E 213 G11
Ash Sha'rā' Si. Arabia 24°16N 44°11E 248 A4
Ash Shāriqah U.A.E. 25°23N 55°26E 247 E7
Ash Sharmah Si. Arabia 28°1N 35°16E 251 K6
Ash Sharqāt Iraq 35°27N 43°16E 213 E10
Ash Sharqīyah □ Si. Arabia 23°0N 50°30E 249 B6
Ash Shāţi Libya 27°30N 12°30E 258 C2
Ash Shaţi □ Libya 27°27N 13°37E 261 C7
Ash Shaţrah Iraq 31°30N 46°10E 246 D5
Ash Shawbak Jordan 30°32N 35°34E 246 D2
Ash Shaykh Ḩumayd Si. Arabia 28°6N 34°33E 251 K5
Ash Shifā' Si. Arabia 28°30N 35°30E 251 K6
Ash Shiḩr Yemen 14°45N 49°36E 249 D5
Ash Shināfiyah Iraq 31°35N 44°39E 246 D5
Ash Shu'bah Si. Arabia 28°54N 44°44E 246 D5
Ash Shumlūl Si. Arabia 26°31N 47°20E 246 E5
Ash Shuqayq Si. Arabia 17°44N 42°1E 248 C3
Ash Shūr'a Iraq 35°58N 43°13E 246 C4
Ash Shurayf Si. Arabia 25°43N 39°14E 246 E3
Ash Shuwayfāt Lebanon 33°45N 35°30E 250 E6
Ash Shuwayrif Libya 29°59N 14°16E 258 C2
Asha Russia 55°0N 57°16E 186 D10
Ashanti □ Ghana 7°30N 1°30W 263 D4
Ashau Vietnam 16°6N 107°22E 236 D6
Ashbourne U.K. 53°2N 1°43W 168 D6
Ashbridge's Bay Park Canada 43°40N 79°18W 141 B3
Ashburn Ga., U.S.A. 31°43N 83°39W 316 D6
Ashburn Ill., U.S.A. 41°45N 87°43W 119 C2
Ashburton Vic., Australia 37°51S 145°4E 128 B2
Ashburton N.Z. 43°53S 171°48E 285 D6
Ashburton ➔ Australia 21°40S 114°56E 278 D1
Ashburton, North Branch ➔ N.Z. 43°54S 171°44E 285 D6
Ashburton, South Branch ➔ N.Z. 43°54S 171°44E 285 D6
Ashcroft Canada 50°40N 121°20W 296 C4
Ashdod Israel 31°49N 34°35E 251 G5
Ashdown U.S.A. 33°40N 94°8W 314 E7
Asheboro U.S.A. 35°43N 79°49W 315 D15
Åsheim Norway 61°42N 11°11E 164 C8
Ashern Canada 51°11N 98°21W 297 C9
Asherton U.S.A. 28°27N 99°46W 314 G5
Asheville U.S.A. 35°36N 82°33W 315 D13
Ashewat Pakistan 31°22N 68°32E 242 D3
Asheweig ➔ Canada 54°17N 87°12W 298 B2
Ashfield Australia 33°53S 151°7E 139 B1
Ashford N.S.W., Australia 29°15S 151°3E 281 D5
Ashford Kent, U.K. 51°8N 0°53E 169 F8
Ashford Surrey, U.K. 51°25N 0°26W 125 B1
Ashford Ala., U.S.A. 31°11N 85°14W 316 D4
Ashgabat Turkmenistan 38°0N 57°50E 247 B8
Ashhurst N.Z. 40°16S 175°45E 284 G4
Ashibetsu Japan 43°31N 142°11E 220 C11
Ashikaga Japan 36°28N 139°29E 223 A11
Ashington U.K. 55°11N 1°33W 168 B6
Ashio Japan 36°38N 139°27E 223 A11
Ashizuri-Uwakai △ Japan 32°56N 132°32E 222 E4
Ashizuri-Zaki Japan 32°44N 133°0E 222 E5
Ashkarkot Afghan. 33°3N 67°58E 242 C2
Ashkhabad = Ashgabat Turkmenistan 38°0N 57°50E 247 B8
Āshkhāneh Iran 37°26N 56°55E 247 B8
Ashland Ala., U.S.A. 33°16N 85°50W 316 B4
Ashland Ill., U.S.A. 39°53N 90°1W 310 E7
Ashland Kans., U.S.A. 37°11N 99°46W 308 G4
Ashland Ky., U.S.A. 38°28N 82°38W 309 F12
Ashland Maine, U.S.A. 46°38N 68°24W 309 B19
Ashland Mont., U.S.A. 45°36N 106°16W 304 D10
Ashland Ohio, U.S.A. 40°52N 82°19W 312 F2
Ashland Oreg., U.S.A. 42°12N 122°43W 304 E2
Ashland Pa., U.S.A. 40°45N 76°22W 313 F8
Ashland Va., U.S.A. 37°46N 77°29W 309 G15
Ashland Wis., U.S.A. 46°35N 90°53W 308 B8
Ashley Ill., U.S.A. 38°20N 89°11W 310 F7
Ashley Ind., U.S.A. 41°32N 85°4W 311 C11
Ashley N. Dak., U.S.A. 46°2N 99°22W 308 B4
Ashley Pa., U.S.A. 41°12N 75°55W 313 E9
Ashley ➔ N.Z. 43°17S 172°44E 285 D7
Ashmore and Cartier Is. Ind. Oc. 12°15S 123°0E 278 B3
Ashmore Reef Australia 12°14S 123°5E 278 B3
Ashmûn Egypt 30°18N 30°58E 251 H1
Ashmyany Belarus 54°26N 25°52E 177 A13
Ashokan Res. U.S.A. 41°56N 74°13W 313 E10
Ashqelon Israel 31°42N 34°35E 251 G5
Ashraf = Behshahr Iran 36°45N 53°35E 247 B7
Ashta India 23°1N 76°43E 242 H7
Ashtabula U.S.A. 41°52N 80°47W 312 E4
Ashti Maharashtra, India 21°12N 78°11E 244 D4
Ashti Maharashtra, India 18°50N 75°15E 244 E2
Ashton Western Cape, S. Africa 33°50S 20°5E 270 D3
Ashton Idaho, U.S.A. 44°4N 111°27W 304 D8
Ashtown Ireland 53°22N 6°19W 120 A2
Ashuanipi, L. Canada 52°45N 66°15W 299 B6
Ashuapmushuan ➔ Canada 48°37N 72°20W 298 C5
Ashville Ala., U.S.A. 33°50N 86°15W 316 B3
Ashville Fla., U.S.A. 30°37N 83°39W 316 D6
Ashville Pa., U.S.A. 40°34N 78°33W 312 F6
'Āşī ➔ Asia 36°1N 35°59E 250 B6
Asia 45°0N 75°0E 210 E9
Asia, Kepulauan Indonesia 1°0N 131°13E 231 D8
Āsīā Bak Iran 35°19N 50°30E 247 C6
Asidonhoppo Suriname 3°50N 55°30W 329 C6
Asifabad India 19°20N 79°24E 244 E4
Asilah Morocco 35°29N 6°0W 260 A3
Asinara Italy 41°4N 8°16E 200 A1
Asinara, G. dell' Italy 41°0N 8°30E 200 A1
Asino Russia 57°0N 86°0E 214 D9
Asipovichy Belarus 53°19N 28°33E 177 B15
'Asīr Si. Arabia 18°40N 42°30E 248 C3
Asir, Ras Somali Rep. 11°55N 51°10E 267 B7
Aska India 19°2N 84°42E 244 E7
Aşkale Turkey 39°55N 40°41E 213 C9
Asker Norway 59°50N 10°29E 164 E7
Askersund Sweden 58°53N 14°55E 163 F8
Askham S. Africa 26°59S 20°47E 270 C3
Askim Norway 59°35N 11°10E 164 E8
Askio, Oros Greece 40°25N 21°35E 202 F5
Askisto Finland 60°16N 24°47E 121 B1
Askja Iceland 65°3N 16°48W 155 B10
Askøyna Norway 60°29N 5°10E 164 D2
Askrikefjärden Sweden 59°22N 18°13E 139 A3
Askvoll Norway 61°21N 5°4E 164 C2
Asl Egypt 29°33N 32°44E 256 B3
Aslan Burnu Turkey 38°44N 26°45E 205 C8
Aslanapa Turkey 39°13N 29°52E 205 B11
Asmār Afghan. 35°10N 71°27E 240 B3
Asmara = Asmera Eritrea 15°19N 38°55E 257 D4
Asmera Eritrea 15°19N 38°55E 257 D4
Asnæs Denmark 55°40N 11°0E 163 J4
Åsnen Sweden 56°37N 14°45E 163 H8
Asni Morocco 31°17N 7°58W 260 B3
Asnières France 48°54N 2°16E 134 A2
Aso Japan 32°55N 131°5E 222 E3
Aso Kuju △ Japan 32°53N 131°6E 222 E3
Aso-Zan Japan 32°53N 131°6E 222 E3
Asola Italy 45°13N 10°24E 198 C7
Asos Greece 38°22N 20°33E 207 C2
Asosa Ethiopia 10°3N 34°32E 257 E3
Asoteriba, Jebel Sudan 21°51N 36°30E 256 C4
Asouf, O. ➔ Algeria 25°40N 2°8E 261 C5
Aspatria U.K. 54°47N 3°19W 168 C4
Aspe Spain 38°20N 0°40W 197 G4
Aspen U.S.A. 39°11N 106°49W 304 G10
Aspendos Turkey 36°54N 31°7E 250 B2
Aspermont U.S.A. 33°8N 100°14W 314 E4
Aspern Austria 48°13N 16°29E 142 A2
Aspern ✕ Austria 48°13N 16°30E 142 A3
Aspet France 43°1N 0°48E 174 E4
Aspiring, Mt. N.Z. 44°23S 168°46E 285 E3
Aspres-sur-Buëch France 44°32N 5°44E 175 D9
Asprokavos, Akra Greece 39°21N 20°6E 206 C10
Aspromonte △ Italy 38°9N 15°58E 201 D8
Aspur India 23°58N 74°7E 242 H6
Asquith Canada 52°8N 107°13W 297 C7
Assa Morocco 28°35N 9°6W 260 C3
Assab = Aseb Eritrea 13°0N 42°40E 257 E5
Assâba □ Mauritania 16°40N 11°40W 262 B2
Assâba, Massif de l' Mauritania 16°10N 11°45W 262 B2
Assagny △ Ivory C. 5°10N 4°48W 262 D4
Assago Italy 45°24N 9°7E 129 B1
Assaikio Nigeria 8°34N 8°55E 263 D6
Assal, L. Djibouti 11°40N 42°26E 257 E5
Assam □ India 26°0N 93°0E 241 C3
Assamakka Niger 19°21N 5°38E 263 B6
Assateague Island ⌓ U.S.A. 38°15N 75°10W 309 F16
Assaye India 20°15N 75°53E 244 D2
Asse Belgium 50°24N 4°10E 170 D4
Assekrem Algeria 23°16N 5°49E 261 D6
Assemblée Nationale Paris, France 134 b3
Assémini Italy 39°17N 9°0E 200 C1
Assen Neths. 53°0N 6°35E 170 A6
Assendelft Neths. 52°28N 4°45E 112 A1
Assens Denmark 55°16N 9°55E 163 J3
Assiano Italy 45°27N 9°12E 129 B1
Assini Ivory C. 5°9N 3°17W 262 D4
Assiniboia Canada 49°40N 105°59W 297 D7
Assiniboine ➔ Canada 49°53N 97°8W 297 D9
Assiniboine, Mt. Canada 50°52N 115°39W 296 C5
Assiou Algeria 21°7N 7°36E 261 D6
Assis Brazil 22°40S 50°20W 335 A5
Assis Brasil Brazil 10°55S 69°32W 330 C4
Assisi Italy 43°4N 12°37E 199 E9
Åsskard Norway 63°1N 8°30E 164 A5
Assok Ngoum Gabon 1°45N 11°39E 264 B2
Assumption U.S.A. 39°31N 89°3W 310 E7
Assynt, L. U.K. 58°10N 5°3W 167 C3
Astaffort France 44°4N 0°40E 174 D4
Astakida Greece 35°53N 26°50E 205 F8
Astakos Greece 38°32N 21°5E 204 C3
Astana Kazakhstan 51°10N 71°30E 217 B8
Āstāneh Iran 37°17N 49°59E 247 B6
Astapovo = Lev Tolstoy Russia 53°13N 39°29E 188 F10
Astara Azerbaijan 38°30N 48°50E 213 C13
Āstārā Iran 38°20N 48°52E 213 C13
Astarabad = Gorgān Iran 36°55N 54°30E 247 B7
Asterousia Greece 34°59N 25°3E 207 F6
Asti Italy 44°54N 8°12E 198 D5
Astipalea Greece 36°32N 26°22E 205 E8
Astola I. Pakistan 25°7N 63°51E 240 D1
Astorga Davao del S., Phil. 6°54N 125°27E 233 H5
Astorga Spain 42°29N 6°8W 194 C4
Astoria Ill., U.S.A. 40°14N 90°21W 310 D6
Astoria N.Y., U.S.A. 40°46N 73°55W 132 B2
Astoria Oreg., U.S.A. 46°11N 123°50W 306 D3
Åstorp Sweden 56°6N 12°55E 163 H6
Astrakhan Russia 46°25N 48°5E 191 G9
Astrakhan □ Russia 47°45N 46°30E 191 G8
Astrolabe, Récifs de l' N. Cal. 19°48S 165°37E 288 d
Astrolabe Park Australia 33°57S 151°12E 139 B2
Astudillo Spain 42°12N 4°22W 194 C6
Asturias □ Spain 43°15N 6°0W 194 B5
Asturias ✕ (OVD) Spain 43°33N 6°3W 194 B4
Asumman S. Korea 37°4N 126°40E 224 D3
Asunción Bolivia 11°46S 67°50W 330 C4
Asuncion N. Marianas 19°40N 145°24E 302 a
Asunción Paraguay 25°10S 57°30W 334 B4
Asunción Nochixtlán Mexico 17°28N 97°14W 319 D5
Åsunden Sweden 58°0N 15°51E 163 F9
Asurit Sudan 15°25N 35°45E 257 D4
Aswa ➔ Uganda 3°43N 31°55E 268 B3
Aswa-Lolim △ Uganda 2°43N 31°35E 268 B3
Aswad, Ra's al Si. Arabia 21°20N 39°0E 248 B2
Aswân Egypt 24°4N 32°57E 256 C3
Aswan Dam = Sadd el Aali Egypt 23°54N 32°54E 256 C3
Asyût Egypt 27°11N 31°4E 256 B3
Asyûti, Wadi ➔ Egypt 27°11N 31°16E 256 B3
Aszód Hungary 47°39N 19°28E 182 C4
At-Bashy Kyrgyzstan 41°10N 75°48E 217 D9
Aţ Ţafilah Jordan 30°45N 35°30E 251 E4
Aţ Ţafilah □ Jordan 30°45N 35°30E 251 E4
Aţ Ţā'if Si. Arabia 21°5N 40°27E 248 B3
At Tāj Libya 24°13N 23°18E 258 D4
At Ta'mīm □ Iraq 35°30N 44°20E 246 C5
At Tamīmī Libya 32°20N 23°4E 258 B4
Aţ Ţirāq Si. Arabia 27°19N 44°33E 246 E5
Aţ Ţubayq Si. Arabia 29°30N 37°0E 251 J8
Aţ Ţunayb Jordan 31°48N 35°57E 251 D4
At Turbah Lahij, Yemen 12°40N 43°30E 248 D3
At Turbah Ta'izz, Yemen 13°13N 44°7E 248 D4
Atabey Turkey 37°57N 30°39E 205 D12
Atacama □ Chile 27°30S 70°0W 334 B2
Atacama, Desierto de Chile 24°0S 69°20W 334 A2
Atacama, Salar de Chile 23°30S 68°20W 334 A2
Ataco Colombia 3°35N 75°23W 328 C2
Atafu Pac. Oc. 8°32S 172°31W 277 B16
Atakor Algeria 23°27N 5°31E 261 D6
Atakpamé Togo 7°31N 1°13E 263 D5
Atalaia do Norte Brazil 4°20S 70°12W 328 D3
Atalandi Greece 38°39N 22°58E 204 C4
Atalaya Peru 10°45S 73°50W 330 C3
Atalaya de Femes Canary Is. 28°56N 13°47W 153 e2
Ataléia Brazil 18°3S 41°6W 333 E3
Atami Japan 35°5N 139°4E 223 B11
Atamyrat Turkmenistan 37°50N 65°12E 217 E7
Atankawng Burma 25°50N 97°47E 241 C6
Atapupu Indonesia 9°0S 124°51E 231 F6
Atâr Mauritania 20°30N 13°5W 260 D2
Ataram, Erg n- Algeria 23°57N 2°0E 261 D5
Atarfe Spain 37°13N 3°40W 195 H7
Atari Pakistan 30°56N 74°2E 242 D6
Atarot West Bank 31°52N 35°13E 123 A2
Atarot ✕ West Bank 31°52N 35°14E 123 A2
Atascadero U.S.A. 35°29N 120°40W 306 K6
Atasū Kazakhstan 48°30N 71°0E 217 C8
Atatürk, İstanbul ✕ (IST) Turkey 40°59N 28°49E 203 F12
Atatürk Barajı Turkey 37°28N 38°30E 213 D8
Atauro E. Timor 8°10S 125°30E 231 F7
Ataviros Greece 36°12N 27°50E 206 E11
Atbara Sudan 17°42N 33°59E 256 D3
'Atbara, Nahr ➔ Sudan 17°40N 33°56E 256 D3
Atbasar Kazakhstan 51°48N 68°20E 217 B7
Atbashi = At-Bashy Kyrgyzstan 41°10N 75°48E 217 D9
Atça Turkey 37°53N 28°13E 205 D10
Atchafalaya B. U.S.A. 29°25N 91°25W 314 G9
Atchison U.S.A. 39°34N 95°7W 308 F6
Atebubu Ghana 7°47N 1°0W 263 D4
Ateca Spain 41°20N 1°49W 196 D3
Aterno ➔ Italy 42°11N 13°51E 199 F10
Āteshān Iran 35°35N 52°37E 247 C7
Atesine, Alpi Italy 46°55N 11°30E 199 B8
Atessa Italy 42°4N 14°27E 199 F11
Atfîh Egypt 29°25N 31°15E 256 J7
Atghara India 22°37N 88°26E 124 B2
Ath Belgium 50°38N 3°47E 170 D3
Athabasca Canada 54°45N 113°20W 296 C6
Athabasca ➔ Canada 58°40N 110°50W 297 B6
Athabasca, L. Canada 59°15N 109°15W 297 B7
Athabasca Sand Dunes ⌓ Canada 59°4N 108°43W 297 B7
Athagarh India 20°32N 85°37E 244 D7
Athamanon Oros Greece 39°30N 21°26E 204 B3
Athboy Ireland 53°37N 6°56W 166 C5
Athena U.S.A. 29°59N 83°30W 316 F6
Athenry Ireland 53°18N 8°44W 166 C3
Athens = Athina Greece 37°58N 23°43E 112 B2
Athens Ala., U.S.A. 34°48N 86°58W 315 D11
Athens Ga., U.S.A. 33°57N 83°23W 316 B6
Athens N.Y., U.S.A. 42°16N 73°49W 313 D11
Athens Ohio, U.S.A. 39°20N 82°6W 309 F12
Athens Pa., U.S.A. 41°57N 76°31W 313 E8
Athens Tenn., U.S.A. 35°27N 84°36W 315 D12
Athens Tex., U.S.A. 32°12N 95°51W 314 E7
Atheras Greece 38°19N 20°25E 207 C1
Atherley Canada 44°37N 79°20W 312 B5
Atherton Australia 17°17S 145°30E 280 B4
Athi River Kenya 1°28S 36°58E 268 C4
Athiéme Benin 6°37N 1°40E 263 D5
Athienou Cyprus 35°3N 33°32E 207 E9
Athina Greece 37°58N 23°43E 112 B2
Athina ✕ (ATH) Greece 37°56N 23°56E 112 A3
Athínai = Athina Greece 37°58N 23°43E 112 B2
Athis-Mons France 48°42N 2°23E 134 B3
Athlone Westmeath, Ireland 53°25N 7°56W 166 C4
Athlone Western Cape, S. Africa 33°57S 18°30E 118 A2
Athmalik India 20°43N 84°32E 244 D7
Athna Cyprus 35°3N 33°47E 207 E9
Athni India 16°44N 75°6E 244 F2
Athol N.Z. 45°30S 168°35E 285 F3
Athol Mass., U.S.A. 42°36N 72°14W 313 D12
Athol I. Bahamas 25°5N 77°16W 153 b
Atholl S. Africa 26°7S 28°3E 123 A2
Atholl, Forest of U.K. 56°51N 3°50W 167 E5
Atholl, Kap Greenland 76°25N 69°30W 154 B4
Atholville Canada 47°59N 66°43W 299 C6
Athos Greece 40°9N 24°22E 203 F8
Athy Ireland 53°0N 7°0W 166 C5
Ati Chad 13°13N 18°20E 259 F3
Ati Sudan 13°5N 29°2E 257 E2
Atiak Uganda 3°12N 32°2E 268 B3
Atiamuri N.Z. 38°24S 176°5E 284 E5
Atico Peru 16°14S 73°40W 330 D3
Atienza Spain 41°12N 2°52W 196 D2
Atifiya Iraq 33°21N 44°21E 113 A2
Atiit Sudan 6°10N 30°35E 257 F3
Atik L. Canada 55°15N 96°0W 297 B9
Atikaki ⌓ Canada 51°30N 95°31W 297 C9
Atikameg ➔ Canada 52°30N 82°46W 298 B3
Atikokan Canada 48°45N 91°37W 298 C1
Atikonak L. Canada 52°40N 64°32W 299 B7
Atimaono Tahiti 17°46S 149°28W 289 e
Atimonan Phil. 14°0N 121°55E 232 D3
'Ātinah, W. ➔ Oman 18°23N 53°28E 249 C6
Atirampattinam India 10°28N 79°20E 245 J4
Atişalen Turkey 41°3N 28°52E 122 B1
Atitlán △ Cent. Amer. 14°38N 91°10W 319 E6
Atiu Cook Is. 20°0S 158°10W 289 J12
Atka Russia 60°50N 151°48E 215 C16
Atka Alaska, U.S.A. 52°12N 174°12W 303 K4
Atka I. U.S.A. 52°7N 174°30W 303 K4
Atkarsk Russia 51°55N 45°2E 190 E7
Atkinson Ga., U.S.A. 31°13N 81°47W 316 D8
Atkinson Ill., U.S.A. 41°25N 90°1W 310 C6
Atkinson Nebr., U.S.A. 42°32N 98°59W 308 D4
Atlanta Ga., U.S.A. 33°45N 84°23W 113 B2
Atlanta Ill., U.S.A. 40°16N 89°14W 310 D7
Atlanta Mo., U.S.A. 39°54N 92°29W 310 E4
Atlanta Tex., U.S.A. 33°7N 94°10W 314 E7
Atlanta Hartsfield Int. ✕ (ATL) U.S.A. 33°38N 84°26W 113 C2
Atlanta Zoo U.S.A. 33°44N 84°22W 113 B2
Atlantic U.S.A. 41°24N 95°1W 310 C2
Atlantic Beach U.S.A. 30°20N 81°24W 316 E8
Atlantic City U.S.A. 39°21N 74°27W 309 F16
Atlantic-Indian Basin Antarctica 60°0S 30°0E 151 B4
Atlantic Ocean 0°0 20°0W 152 F8
Atlántico □ Colombia 10°45N 75°0W 328 A3
Atlas Mts. = Haut Atlas Morocco 32°30N 5°0W 260 B4
Atlin Canada 59°31N 133°41W 296 B2
Atlin, L. Canada 59°26N 133°45W 296 B2
Atlin ⌓ Canada 59°10N 134°30W 296 B2
Atløyna Norway 61°21N 4°58E 164 C1
Atmakur Andhra Pradesh, India 18°45N 78°39E 244 E4
Atmakur Andhra Pradesh, India 14°37N 79°40E 245 G4
Atmakur Andhra Pradesh, India 15°53N 78°35E 245 G4
Atmore U.S.A. 31°2N 87°29W 315 F11
Atna Norway 61°44N 10°49E 164 C7
Atna ➔ Norway 61°44N 10°49E 164 C7
Atō Japan 34°25N 131°40E 222 C3
Atocha Bolivia 20°56S 66°14W 330 E4
Atok Phil. 16°35N 120°41E 232 C3
Atoka U.S.A. 34°23N 96°8W 314 D6
Atokos Greece 38°28N 20°49E 207 C2
Atolia U.S.A. 35°19N 117°37W 307 K9
Atomium Belgium 50°54N 4°20E 116 A2
Atongo-Bakari C.A.R. 5°49N 21°35E 264 A4
Atori Solomon Is. 8°42S 160°59E 287 M11
Atqasuk U.S.A. 70°28N 157°24W 303 A8
Atqasuk ➔ U.S.A. 70°52N 155°59W 303 A9
Atrå Norway 59°59N 8°45E 164 E5
Atrai ➔ Bangla. 24°7N 89°22E 241 C2
Atrak = Atrek ➔ Turkmenistan 37°35N 53°58E 247 B8
Ätran Sweden 57°7N 12°57E 163 G6
Ätran ➔ Sweden 56°53N 12°30E 163 H6
Atrato ➔ Colombia 8°17N 76°58W 328 B2
Atrauli India 28°2N 78°20E 242 E8
Atrek ➔ Turkmenistan 37°35N 53°58E 247 B8
Atri Italy 42°35N 13°58E 199 F10
Atsiki Greece 39°56N 25°13E 205 B7
Atsoum, Mts. Cameroon 6°41N 12°57E 263 D7
Atsugi Japan 35°25N 139°21E 223 B11
Atsumi Japan 34°35N 137°4E 223 C9
Atsumi-Wan Japan 34°44N 137°13E 223 C9
Atsuta Japan 43°24N 141°26E 220 C10
Attalla U.S.A. 34°1N 86°6W 316 A3
Attapu Laos 14°48N 106°50E 236 E6
Attapulgus U.S.A. 30°45N 84°29W 316 E5
Attawapiskat Canada 52°56N 82°24W 298 B3
Attawapiskat ➔ Canada 52°57N 82°18W 298 B3
Attawapiskat L. Canada 52°18N 87°54W 298 B2
Attersee Austria 47°55N 13°32E 180 D6
Attica Ind., U.S.A. 40°18N 87°15W 311 D9
Attica Ohio, U.S.A. 41°4N 82°53W 312 E2
Attichy France 49°25N 3°3E 173 C10
Attigny France 49°28N 4°35E 173 C11
Attika = Attiki □ Greece 37°10N 23°40E 204 D5
Attikamagen L. Canada 55°0N 66°30W 299 B6
Attiki Greece 38°0N 23°43E 112 A2
Attiki □ Greece 37°10N 23°40E 204 D5
Attleboro U.S.A. 41°57N 71°17W 313 E13
Attock Pakistan 33°52N 72°20E 242 C5
Attopeu = Attapu Laos 14°48N 106°50E 236 E6
Attu U.S.A. 52°56N 173°15E 303 K1
Attu I. U.S.A. 52°55N 172°55E 303 K1
Attunga Australia 30°55S 150°50E 283 A9
Attur India 11°35N 78°30E 245 J4
'Atūd Yemen 14°53N 48°10E 249 D5
Atuel ➔ Argentina 36°17S 66°50W 334 D2
Åtvidaberg Sweden 58°12N 16°0E 163 F10
Atwater U.S.A. 37°21N 120°37W 306 H6
Atwood Ont., Canada 43°40N 81°1W 312 C3
Atwood Ill., U.S.A. 39°48N 88°28W 311 E8
Atwood Kans., U.S.A. 39°48N 101°3W 308 F3
Atyraū Kazakhstan 47°5N 52°0E 187 E9
Atzgersdorf Austria 48°8N 16°18E 142 B1
Au Sable U.S.A. 44°25N 83°20W 312 B1
Au Sable ➔ U.S.A. 44°25N 83°20W 309 C12
Au Sable Forks U.S.A. 44°27N 73°41W 313 B11
Au Sable Pt. U.S.A. 44°20N 83°20W 312 B1
Au Vent, Région Réunion 21°0S 55°35E 272 f
Aua Amer. Samoa 14°17S 170°40W 302 f
Auasberg Namibia 22°37S 17°13E 270 B2
Aubagne France 43°17N 5°37E 175 E9
Aubarca, C. d' Spain 39°4N 1°22E 206 C1
Aube □ France 48°15N 4°10E 173 D11
Aube ➔ France 48°34N 3°43E 173 D10
Aubenas France 44°37N 4°24E 175 D8
Aubenton France 49°50N 4°12E 173 C11
Auberry U.S.A. 37°7N 119°29W 306 H7
Aubervilliers France 48°54N 2°22E 134 A3
Aubigny-sur-Nère France 47°30N 2°24E 173 E9
Aubin France 44°33N 2°15E 174 D6
Aubing Germany 48°9N 11°25E 131 B1
Aubrac, Mts. d' France 44°40N 3°2E 174 D7
Auburn S. Austral., Australia 34°1S 138°42E 282 C3
Auburn Ala., U.S.A. 32°36N 85°29W 316 C4
Auburn Calif., U.S.A. 38°54N 121°4W 306 G5
Auburn Ill., U.S.A. 39°36N 89°45W 310 E7
Auburn Ind., U.S.A. 41°22N 85°4W 311 C11
Auburn Maine, U.S.A. 44°6N 70°14W 309 C18
Auburn N.Y., U.S.A. 42°56N 76°34W 313 D8
Auburn Nebr., U.S.A. 40°23N 95°51W 308 E6
Auburn Pa., U.S.A. 40°36N 76°6W 313 F8
Auburn Wash., U.S.A. 47°18N 122°14W 306 C4
Auburn Ra. Australia 25°15S 150°30E 281 D5
Auburndale Fla., U.S.A. 28°4N 81°48W 317 G8
Auburndale Mass., U.S.A. 42°20N 71°14W 116 A1
Aubusson France 45°57N 2°11E 174 C6
Auce Latvia 56°28N 22°53E 184 B9
Auch France 43°39N 0°36E 174 E4
Auchendinny U.K. 55°51N 3°11W 121 B2
Auchi Nigeria 7°6N 6°13E 263 D6
Auchterarder U.K. 56°18N 3°41W 167 E5
Auchtermuchty U.K. 56°18N 3°13W 167 E5
Auckland N.Z. 36°52S 174°46E 284 C3
Auckland □ N.Z. 36°50S 175°0E 284 C3
Auckland Is. Pac. Oc. 50°40S 166°5E 288 N8
Auckland Park S. Africa 26°11S 28°0E 123 B2
Aude □ France 43°8N 2°28E 174 E6
Aude ➔ France 43°13N 3°14E 174 E7
Audegle Somali Rep. 1°59N 44°50E 267 D5
Auden Canada 50°14N 87°53W 298 B2
Auderghem Belgium 50°49N 4°26E 116 B2
Auderville France 49°43N 1°57W 172 C5
Audierne France 48°1N 4°34W 172 D2
Audincourt France 47°30N 6°50E 173 E13
Audo Ra. Ethiopia 6°20N 41°50E 257 F5
Audubon U.S.A. 41°43N 94°56W 310 C2
Aue Germany 50°35N 12°41E 178 E8
Auerbach Germany 50°30N 12°24E 178 E8
Aueti Paraná ➔ Brazil 1°51S 65°37W 328 D4
Aufist W. Sahara 25°44N 14°39W 260 C2
Augathella Australia 25°48S 146°35E 281 D4
Aughnacloy U.K. 54°25N 6°59W 166 B5
Aughrim Ireland 53°18N 8°19W 166 C3
Augrabies Falls S. Africa 28°35S 20°20E 270 C3
Augrabies Falls △ S. Africa 28°40S 20°22E 270 C3
Augsburg Germany 48°25N 10°52E 179 G6
Augsburg-Westliche Wälder ⌓ Germany 48°22N 10°40E 179 G6
August Town Jamaica 17°59N 76°44W 320 a
Augusta W. Austral., Australia 34°19S 115°9E 279 F2
Augusta Italy 37°13N 15°13E 201 E8
Augusta Ark., U.S.A. 35°17N 91°22W 314 D9
Augusta Ga., U.S.A. 33°28N 81°58W 316 B8
Augusta Ill., U.S.A. 40°14N 90°57W 310 D6
Augusta Kans., U.S.A. 37°41N 96°59W 308 G5
Augusta Ky., U.S.A. 38°47N 84°0W 311 F12
Augusta Maine, U.S.A. 44°19N 69°47W 309 C19
Augusta Mont., U.S.A. 47°30N 112°24W 304 C7
Augusta, Mausoleo di Rome, Italy 136 b2
Augustenborg Denmark 54°57N 9°53E 163 K3
Augustine I. U.S.A. 59°22N 153°26W 303 G9
Augusto Cardosa = Metangula Mozam. 12°40S 34°50E 269 E3

Augustów *Poland* 53°51N 23°0E **184** E9
Augustówka *Poland* 52°11N 21°5E **142** B2
Augustus, Mt. *Australia* 24°20S 116°50E **279** D2
Augustus I. *Australia* 15°20S 124°30E **278** C3
Aujuittuq = Grise Fiord
Canada 76°25N 82°57W **295** B11
Aukan *Eritrea* 15°29N 40°50E **257** D5
Auki *Solomon Is.* 8°45S 160°42E **287** M11
Aukra *Norway* 62°47N 6°55E **164** B3
Aukrug △ *Germany* 54°5N 9°45E **178** A5
Aukštaitija △ *Lithuania* 55°15N 26°0E **161** J22
Aukum *U.S.A.* 38°34N 120°43W **306** G6
Aul *India* 20°41N 86°39E **244** D8
Auld, L. *Australia* 22°25S 123°50E **278** D3
Aulifeltet *Norway* 60°30N 11°21E **162** D5
Auliye-Ata = Taraz
Kazakhstan 42°54N 71°22E **217** D8
Aulla *Italy* 44°12N 9°58E **198** D6
Aulnay *France* 46°2N 0°22W **174** B3
Aulnay-sous-Bois *France* 48°56N 2°29E **134** A3
Aulne → *France* 48°17N 4°16W **172** D2
Aulnoye-Aymeries
France 50°12N 3°50E **173** B10
Aulong *Palau* 7°16N 134°17E **288** c
Ault *Somme, France* 50°8N 1°26E **172** B8
Ault *Colo., U.S.A.* 40°35N 104°44W **304** F11
Aulus-les-Bains *France* 42°49N 1°19E **174** F5
Aumale = Sour el Ghozlane
Algeria 36°10N 3°45E **261** A5
Aumale *France* 49°46N 1°46E **173** C8
Aumo *Papua N. G.* 5°44S 148°30E **286** C5
Aumont-Aubrac *France* 44°43N 3°17E **174** D7
Auna *Nigeria* 10°9N 4°42E **263** C5
Aundah *India* 19°32N 77°3E **244** E3
Aundh *India* 17°33N 74°23E **244** F2
Auning *Denmark* 56°26N 10°22E **163** H4
Aunis *France* 46°5N 0°50W **174** B3
Aunu'u *Amer. Samoa* 14°20S 170°31W **302** f
Auponhia *Indonesia* 1°58S 125°27E **231** E7
Aups *France* 43°37N 6°15E **175** E10
Aur, Pulau *Malaysia* 2°35N 104°10E **237** L5
Aura *Burma* 26°59N 97°57E **241** B6
Auraiya *India* 26°28N 79°33E **243** F8
Aurangabad *Bihar, India* 24°45N 84°18E **243** G11
Aurangabad *Maharashtra,*
India 19°50N 75°23E **244** E2
Auray *France* 47°40N 2°59W **172** E4
Aurdal *Norway* 60°55N 9°26E **164** D6
Aure *Norway* 63°16N 8°33E **164** A5
Aurelio *Italy* 41°54N 12°26E **136** B1
Aurès *Algeria* 35°8N 6°30E **261** A6
Aurich *Germany* 53°28N 7°28E **178** B3
Aurilândia *Brazil* 16°44S 50°28W **333** E1
Aurillac *France* 44°55N 2°26E **174** D6
Aurlandsfjorden *Norway* 61°3N 7°1E **164** C4
Aurlandsvangen *Norway* 60°55N 7°12E **164** D4
Auronzo di Cadore *Italy* 46°33N 12°26E **199** B9
Aurora = Maéwo
Vanuatu 15°10S 168°10E **287** E6
Aurora = San Francisco
Phil. 13°21N 122°31E **232** E4
Aurora *Ont., Canada* 44°0N 79°28W **312** C5
Aurora *Isabela, Phil.* 16°59N 121°38E **232** C3
Aurora *Zamboanga del S.,*
Phil. 7°57N 123°36E **233** H4
Aurora *Western Cape,*
S. Africa 32°40S 18°29E **270** D2
Aurora *Colo., U.S.A.* 39°43N 104°49W **304** G11
Aurora *Ill., U.S.A.* 41°45N 88°19W **311** C8
Aurora *Mo., U.S.A.* 36°58N 93°43W **308** G7
Aurora *N.Y., U.S.A.* 42°45N 76°42W **313** D8
Aurora *Nebr., U.S.A.* 40°52N 98°0W **308** E5
Aurora *Ohio, U.S.A.* 41°21N 81°20W **312** E3
Aurora □ *Phil.* 15°30N 121°30E **232** D3
Aurora △ *Phil.* 15°40N 121°20E **232** D3
Aursmoen *Norway* 59°55N 11°26E **164** E8
Aursunden *Norway* 62°40N 11°40E **164** B8
Aurukun *Australia* 13°20S 141°45E **280** A3
Aus *Namibia* 26°35S 16°12E **270** C2
Ausa *India* 18°15N 76°30E **244** E3
Ausable → *Canada* 43°19N 81°46W **312** C3
Auschwitz = Oświęcim
Poland 50°2N 19°11E **185** H6
Ausîm *Egypt* 30°7N 31°8E **117** A1
Auspitz = Hustopeče
Czech Rep. 48°57N 16°43E **181** C9
Aussig = Ústí nad Labem
Czech Rep. 50°41N 14°3E **180** A7
Aust-Agder □ *Norway* 58°45N 8°0E **164** F4
Austad *Norway* 58°58N 7°37E **164** F4
Austen Harbour *India* 12°55N 92°45E **245** H11
Austerlitz = Slavkov u Brna
Czech Rep. 49°10N 16°52E **181** B9
Austerlitz, Gare d' *France* 48°50N 2°22E **134** A3
Austevoll *Norway* 60°5N 5°13E **164** D2
Austin *Ill., U.S.A.* 41°53N 87°45W **119** B2
Austin *Ind., U.S.A.* 38°45N 85°49W **311** F11
Austin *Minn., U.S.A.* 43°40N 92°58W **308** D7
Austin *Nev., U.S.A.* 39°30N 117°4W **304** G5
Austin *Pa., U.S.A.* 41°38N 78°6W **312** E6
Austin *Tex., U.S.A.* 30°17N 97°45W **314** F6
Austin, L. *Australia* 27°40S 118°0E **279** E2
Austin I. *Canada* 61°10N 94°0W **297** A10
Austmarka *Norway* 60°6N 12°21E **164** D9
Austnes *Norway* 62°38N 6°16E **164** B3
Austra *Norway* 65°8N 11°55E **160** D14
Austral Is. = Tubuaï, Îs.
French Polynesia 25°0S 150°0W **289** f
Austral Seamount Chain
Pac. Oc. 24°0S 150°0W **289** K13
Australia ■ *Oceania* 23°0S 135°0E **276** E3
Australian-Antarctic Basin
S. Ocean 60°0S 120°0E **151** C9
Australian Capital Territory □
Australia 35°30S 149°0E **283** C8
Australind *Australia* 33°17S 115°42E **279** F2
Austria ■ *Europe* 47°0N 14°0E **180** E7
Austur-Skaftafellssýsla □
Iceland 64°15N 16°0W **155** C10
Austvågøya *Norway* 68°20N 14°40E **160** B16
Autazes *Brazil* 3°35S 59°8W **329** D6
Auterive *France* 43°21N 1°29E **174** E5
Authie → *France* 50°22N 1°38E **173** B8
Authon-du-Perche *France* 48°12N 0°54E **172** D7
Autlán de Navarro
Mexico 19°46N 104°22W **318** D4
Autun *France* 46°58N 4°17E **173** F11
Auvergne □ *France* 45°20N 3°15E **174** C7
Auvergne, Mts. d' *France* 45°20N 2°55E **174** C6
Auvézère → *France* 45°12N 0°50E **174** C4
Auxerre *France* 47°48N 3°32E **173** E10
Auxi-le-Château *France* 50°15N 2°8E **173** B9
Auxonne *France* 47°10N 5°20E **173** E12
Auxvasse *U.S.A.* 39°1N 91°54W **310** E5
Auzances *France* 46°2N 2°30E **173** F9
Ava *Ill., U.S.A.* 37°53N 89°30W **310** G7
Ava *Mo., U.S.A.* 36°57N 92°40W **308** G7
Avaldsnes *Norway* 59°21N 5°20E **164** E2
Avallon *France* 47°30N 3°53E **173** E10
Avalon *N.Z.* 41°12S 174°56E **143** B2
Avalon *Calif., U.S.A.* 33°21N 118°20W **307** M8
Avalon Pen. *Canada* 47°30N 53°20W **299** C9
Avana → *Cook Is.* 21°14S 159°43W **289** h
Avanavero *Suriname* 4°51N 57°22W **329** C6
Avanigadda *India* 16°0N 80°56E **245** G5
Avannaarsua □ *Greenland* 80°0N 55°0W **154** B5
Avanos *Turkey* 38°43N 34°51E **246** B2
Avantas *Greece* 40°57N 25°56E **203** F9
Avaré *Brazil* 23°4S 48°58W **335** A6
Avarua *Cook Is.* 21°12S 159°46W **289** h
Avarua Harb. *Cook Is.* 21°12S 159°46W **289** h
Avatele *Cook Is.* 19°6S 169°55W **289** g
Avatiu *Cook Is.* 21°12S 159°47W **289** h
Avawatz Mts. *U.S.A.* 35°40N 116°30W **307** K10
Avdan Dağı *Turkey* 40°23N 29°46E **203** F13
Avedøre *Denmark* 55°37N 12°27E **118** B2
Aveiro *Brazil* 3°10S 55°5W **329** D6
Aveiro *Portugal* 40°37N 8°38W **194** E2
Aveiro □ *Portugal* 40°40N 8°35W **194** E2
Āvej *Iran* 35°40N 49°15E **247** C6
Avellaneda *Argentina* 34°40S 58°22W **117** C2
Avellino *Italy* 40°54N 14°47E **201** B7
Avenal *U.S.A.* 36°0N 120°8W **306** K6
Avenel *U.S.A.* 38°59N 76°59W **143** B4
Averøya *Norway* 63°0N 7°35E **164** A4
Aversa *Italy* 40°58N 14°12E **201** B7
Avery *U.S.A.* 47°15N 115°49W **304** C6
Aves, I. de *W. Indies* 15°45N 63°55W **321** C7
Aves, Is. las *Venezuela* 12°0N 67°30W **321** D6
Aves Ridge *W. Indies* 14°0N 63°30W **321** D7
Avesnes-sur-Helpe *France* 50°8N 3°55E **173** B10
Avesnois △ *France* 50°10N 3°45E **173** B10
Avesta *Sweden* 60°9N 16°10E **162** D10
Aveyron □ *France* 44°22N 2°45E **174** D6
Aveyron → *France* 44°5N 1°16E **174** D5
Avezzano *Italy* 42°2N 13°25E **199** F10
Avgo *Greece* 35°33N 25°37E **205** F7
Aviá Terai *Argentina* 26°45S 60°50W **334** B3
Aviano *Italy* 46°4N 12°36E **199** B9
Aviatu → *Cook Is.* 21°12S 159°49W **289** h
Aviemore *U.K.* 57°12N 3°50W **167** D5
Aviemore, L. *N.Z.* 44°37S 170°18E **285** E5
Avigliana *Italy* 45°5N 7°23E **198** C4
Avigliano *Italy* 40°44N 15°43E **201** B8
Avignon *France* 43°57N 4°50E **175** E8
Ávila *Spain* 40°39N 4°43W **194** E6
Ávila □ *Spain* 40°30N 5°0W **194** E6
Ávila, Sierra de *Spain* 40°40N 5°15W **194** E5
Avila Beach *U.S.A.* 35°11N 120°44W **307** K6
Avilés *Spain* 43°35N 5°57W **194** B5
Avintes *Portugal* 41°7N 8°33W **194** D2
Avis *Portugal* 39°4N 7°53W **195** F3
Avis *Pa., U.S.A.* 41°11N 77°19W **312** E7
Avísio → *Italy* 46°7N 11°5E **198** B8
Avissawella *Sri Lanka* 6°56N 80°11E **245** L5
Aviston *U.S.A.* 38°36N 89°36W **310** F7
Aviz = Avis *Portugal* 39°4N 7°53W **195** F3
Avize *France* 48°59N 4°1E **173** D11
Avlona = Vlorë *Albania* 40°32N 19°28E **202** F3
Avlonari *Greece* 38°31N 24°8E **204** C6
Avlum *Denmark* 56°16N 8°47E **163** H2
Avoca *Vic., Australia* 37°5S 143°26E **282** D5
Avoca *N.Y., U.S.A.* 42°25N 77°25W **312** D7
Avoca → *Vic., Australia* 35°40S 143°43E **282** C5
Avoca → *Wicklow, Ireland* 52°48N 6°10W **166** D5
Avola *B.C., Canada* 51°45N 119°19W **296** C5
Avola *Italy* 36°56N 15°7E **201** F8
Avon *Ill., U.S.A.* 40°40N 90°26W **310** D6
Avon *N.Y., U.S.A.* 42°55N 77°45W **312** D7
Avon → *W. Austral.,*
Australia 31°40S 116°7E **279** F2
Avon → *Bristol, U.K.* 51°29N 2°41W **169** F5
Avon → *Dorset, U.K.* 50°44N 1°46W **169** G6
Avon → *Warks., U.K.* 52°0N 2°8W **169** E5
Avon Park *U.S.A.* 27°36N 81°31W **317** H8
Avondale *Ill., U.S.A.* 41°56N 87°41W **119** B2
Avondale *La., U.S.A.* 29°54N 90°12W **131** B1
Avondale *Zimbabwe* 17°43S 30°58E **269** F3
Avondale Heights
Australia 37°45S 144°52E **128** A1
Avonlea *Canada* 50°0N 105°0W **297** D8
Avonmore *Canada* 45°10N 74°58W **313** A10
Avonmouth *U.K.* 51°30N 2°42W **169** F5
Avramov *Bulgaria* 42°45N 26°38E **203** D10
Avranches *France* 48°40N 1°20W **172** D5
Avre → *France* 48°47N 1°22E **172** D8
Avrig *Romania* 45°43N 24°21E **183** E9
Avrillé *France* 47°30N 0°35W **172** E6
Avtovac *Bos.-H.* 43°9N 18°35E **202** C2
Avtovo *Russia* 59°51N 30°15E **137** B1
Avu Avu *Solomon Is.* 9°50S 160°22E **287** M11
Awa-Shima *Japan* 38°27N 139°14E **220** E9
Awag el Baqar *Sudan* 10°10N 33°10E **257** E3
A'waj → *Syria* 33°23N 36°20E **250** E7
Awaji *Japan* 34°32N 135°1E **223** C7
Awaji-Shima *Japan* 34°30N 134°50E **222** C6
'Awālī *Bahrain* 26°0N 50°30E **247** E6
Awantipur *India* 33°55N 75°3E **243** C6
Awanui *N.Z.* 35°4S 173°17E **284** B2
Aware *Ethiopia* 8°16N 44°9E **257** F6
Awarja → *India* 17°5N 76°15E **244** F3
Awarua B. *N.Z.* 44°28S 168°4E **285** E3
Awarua Pt. *N.Z.* 44°15S 168°5E **285** E3
Awasa *Ethiopia* 7°2N 38°28E **257** F4
Awasa, L. *Ethiopia* 7°0N 38°30E **257** F4
Awash *Ethiopia* 9°1N 40°10E **257** F5
Awash → *Ethiopia* 11°45N 41°5E **257** E5
Awash △ *Ethiopia* 9°8N 40°0E **257** F5
Awaso *Ghana* 6°15N 2°22W **262** D4
Awat *China* 40°35N 80°24E **216** E5
Awatere → *N.Z.* 41°37S 174°10E **285** B9
Awbārī *Libya* 26°46N 12°57E **258** C2
Awbārī □ *Libya* 26°35N 12°46E **258** C2
Awbārī, Idehan *Libya* 27°10N 11°30E **258** C2
Awe, L. *U.K.* 56°17N 5°16W **167** E3
Aweil *Sudan* 8°42N 27°20E **257** F2
Awgu *Nigeria* 6°4N 7°24E **263** D6
Awjilah *Libya* 29°8N 21°7E **258** C4
Awka *Nigeria* 6°12N 7°5E **263** D6
Aworro *Papua N. G.* 7°43S 143°11E **286** D2
Ax-les-Thermes *France* 42°44N 1°50E **174** F5
Axat *France* 42°48N 2°13E **174** F6
Axe → *U.K.* 50°42N 3°4W **169** G5
Axel Heiberg I. *Canada* 80°0N 90°0W **295** B11
Axim *Ghana* 4°51N 2°15W **262** E4
Axinim *Brazil* 4°2S 59°22W **329** D6
Axintele *Romania* 44°37N 26°47E **183** F11
Axioma *Brazil* 6°45S 64°31W **331** B5
Axios → *Greece* 40°57N 22°35E **202** F6
Axminster *U.K.* 50°46N 3°0W **169** G4
Axson *U.S.A.* 31°17N 82°44W **316** D7
Axvall *Sweden* 58°23N 13°34E **163** F7
Ay *France* 49°3N 4°1E **173** C11
Ayaantang *Eq. Guin.* 1°58N 10°24E **264** B2
Ayabaca *Peru* 4°40S 79°53W **330** A2
Ayabe *Japan* 35°20N 135°20E **223** B7
Ayacucho *Argentina* 37°5S 58°20W **334** D4
Ayacucho *Peru* 13°0S 74°0W **330** C3
Ayacucho □ *Peru* 14°0S 74°0W **330** C3
Ayaguz = Ayakōz
Kazakhstan 48°10N 80°10E **217** C10
Ayakkum Hu *China* 37°30N 89°20E **217** E11
Ayakōz *Kazakhstan* 48°10N 80°10E **217** C10
Ayakōz → *Kazakhstan* 46°40N 79°14E **217** C9
Ayakudi *India* 10°28N 77°56E **245** J3
Ayala *Phil.* 6°57N 121°57E **233** H3
Ayamé *Ivory C.* 5°35N 3°9W **262** D4
Ayamonte *Spain* 37°12N 7°24W **195** H3
Ayan *Russia* 56°30N 138°16E **215** D14
Ayancık *Turkey* 41°57N 34°35E **212** B6
Ayapel *Colombia* 8°19N 75°9W **328** B2
Ayas *Turkey* 40°2N 32°21E **212** B5
Ayaviri *Peru* 14°50S 70°35W **330** C3
Ayazağa *Turkey* 41°6N 28°59E **122** B1
Āybak *Afghan.* 36°15N 68°5E **240** A3
Aybastı *Turkey* 40°41N 37°23E **212** B7
Aydarkul, Ozero
Uzbekistan 40°50N 67°10E **217** D7
Aydın *Turkey* 37°51N 27°51E **212** D2
Aydın □ *Turkey* 37°50N 28°0E **205** D9
Aydın Dağları *Turkey* 38°0N 28°0E **205** D10
Aydıncık *Turkey* 36°9N 33°21E **250** B4
Aydingkol Hu *China* 42°40N 89°15E **217** D11
Ayelu *Ethiopia* 10°5N 40°42E **257** E5
Ayenngré *Togo* 8°40N 1°1E **263** D5
Ayer *U.S.A.* 42°34N 71°35W **313** D13
Ayer Chawan, Pulau
Singapore 1°16N 103°41E **138** B2
Ayer Hitam *Malaysia* 5°24N 100°16E **237** c
Ayer Merbau, Pulau
Singapore 1°16N 103°42E **138** B2
Ayerbe *Spain* 42°17N 0°41W **196** C4
Ayer's Cliff *Canada* 45°10N 72°3W **313** A12
Ayers Rock = Uluru
Australia 25°23S 131°5E **279** E5
Ayeyarwady = Irrawaddy →
Burma 15°50N 95°6E **241** G5
Áyia Napa *Cyprus* 34°59N 34°0E **207** F10
Áyia Phyla *Cyprus* 34°43N 33°1E **207** F9
Áyios Amvrósios *Cyprus* 35°20N 33°35E **207** E9
Áyios Seryios *Cyprus* 35°12N 33°53E **207** E9
Áyios Theodhoros *Cyprus* 35°22N 34°1E **207** E10
Áyios Yeóryios = Aghios Georgios
Greece 37°28N 23°57E **204** D5
Aykino *Russia* 62°15N 49°56E **186** B8
Aylesbury *Turkey* 39°8N 30°9E **205** B12
Aylesbury *U.K.* 51°49N 0°49W **169** F7
Aylmer *Canada* 42°46N 80°59W **312** D4
Aylmer, L. *Canada* 64°5N 108°30W **294** C9
'Ayn, Wādī al *Oman* 22°15N 55°28E **247** F7
'Ayn al Ghazālah *Libya* 32°10N 23°20E **258** B4
Ayn Dār *Si. Arabia* 25°55N 49°10E **247** E7
Ayn Zālah *Iraq* 36°45N 42°35E **213** D10
Ayna *Spain* 38°34N 2°3W **197** G2
Aynāt *Yemen* 16°4N 49°9E **249** C5
'Aynūnah *Si. Arabia* 28°5N 35°8E **251** K6
Ayod *Sudan* 8°7N 31°26E **257** F3
Ayolas *Paraguay* 27°10S 56°59W **334** B4
Ayom *Sudan* 7°49N 28°23E **257** F2
Ayon, Ostrov *Russia* 69°50N 169°0E **215** C17
Ayora *Spain* 39°3N 1°3W **197** F3
Ayorou *Niger* 14°53N 1°0E **263** C5
Ayos *Cameroon* 3°53N 12°31E **264** B2
'Ayoûn el 'Atroûs
Mauritania 16°38N 9°37W **262** B3
Ayr *Queens., Australia* 19°35S 147°25E **280** B4
Ayr *Ont., Canada* 43°17N 80°27W **312** C4
Ayr *S. Ayrs., U.K.* 55°28N 4°38W **167** F4
Ayr → *U.K.* 55°28N 4°38W **167** F4
Ayrancı *Turkey* 37°21N 33°41E **212** D5
Ayrancılar *Turkey* 38°15N 27°18E **205** C9
Ayre, Pt. of *I. of Man* 54°25N 4°21W **168** C3
Ayribaba *Turkmenistan* 37°50N 66°34E **217** E7
Aysha *Ethiopia* 10°50N 42°23E **257** E5
Ayton *Australia* 15°56S 145°22E **280** B4
Aytos *Bulgaria* 42°42N 27°16E **203** D11
Aytoska Planina
Bulgaria 42°45N 27°30E **203** D11
Ayu, Kepulauan *Indonesia* 0°35N 131°5E **231** D8
Ayutla *Guatemala* 14°40N 92°10W **320** D1
Ayutla de los Libres
Mexico 16°54N 99°13W **319** D5
Ayvacık *Turkey* 39°36N 26°24E **212** C2
Ayvalık *Turkey* 39°20N 26°46E **205** B8
Az Zabadānī *Syria* 33°43N 36°5E **250** E7
Az Zahirīah *Asia* 23°40N 56°10E **249** B7
Az Zāhirīyah *West Bank* 31°25N 34°58E **251** G3
Az Zahrān *Si. Arabia* 26°10N 50°7E **247** E6
Az Zarqā *Jordan* 32°5N 36°4E **251** F7
Az Zarqā' *U.A.E.* 24°53N 53°4E **247** E7
Az Zāwiyah *Libya* 32°52N 12°56E **258** B2
Az Zāwiyah □ *Libya* 32°44N 12°43E **261** B7
Az Zaydīyah *Yemen* 15°20N 43°1E **248** D3
Az Zībār *Iraq* 36°52N 44°4E **213** D11
Az Zilfī *Si. Arabia* 26°12N 44°52E **246** E5
Az Zubayr *Iraq* 30°26N 47°40E **246** D5
Az Zuqur *Yemen* 14°0N 42°45E **248** D3
Az Zuwaytīnah *Libya* 30°58N 20°7E **258** B4
Azabu *Tokyo, Japan* **140** c3
Azad Kashmir □
Pakistan 33°50N 73°50E **243** C5
Azambuja *Portugal* 39°4N 8°51W **195** F2
Azamgarh *India* 26°5N 83°13E **243** F10
Azangaro *Peru* 14°55S 70°13W **330** C3
Azaouad *Mali* 19°0N 3°0W **262** B4
Azaouak, Vallée de l' *Mali* 15°50N 3°20E **263** B5
Āzār Shahr *Iran* 37°45N 45°59E **213** D11
Azara *Nigeria* 8°22N 9°12E **263** D6
Azarān *Iran* 37°25N 47°16E **213** D12
Azärbayjan = Azerbaijan ■
Asia 40°20N 48°0E **191** K9
Āzarbāyjān-e Gharbī □
Iran 37°0N 44°30E **246** B5
Āzarbāyjān-e Sharqī □
Iran 37°20N 47°0E **246** B5
Azare *Nigeria* 11°55N 10°10E **263** C7
Azay-le-Rideau *France* 47°16N 0°30E **172** E7
A'zāz *Syria* 36°36N 37°4E **250** B8
Azazga *Algeria* 36°48N 4°22E **261** A5
Azbine = Aïr *Niger* 18°30N 8°0E **259** E1
Azcapotzalco *Mexico* 19°28N 99°10W **128** B1
Azefal *Mauritania* 21°0N 14°45W **260** D2
Azeffoun *Algeria* 36°51N 4°26E **261** A5
Azemmour *Morocco* 33°20N 9°20W **260** B3
Azennezal *Algeria* 22°58N 0°43E **261** D5
Azerbaijan ■ *Asia* 40°20N 48°0E **191** K9
Azezo *Ethiopia* 12°28N 37°15E **257** E4
Azimganj *India* 24°14N 88°16E **243** G13
Aznalcóllar *Spain* 37°32N 6°17W **195** H4
Azogues *Ecuador* 2°35S 78°0W **328** D2
Azores = Açores, Is. dos
Atl. Oc. 38°0N 27°0W **153** d1
Azores-Biscay Rise *Atl. Oc.* 42°0N 20°0W **152** B9
Azoum, B. → *Chad* 10°53N 20°15E **259** F4
Azov *Russia* 47°3N 39°25E **191** J4
Azov, Sea of *Europe* 46°0N 36°30E **188** J9
Azovskoye More = Azov, Sea of
Europe 46°0N 36°30E **189** J9
Azpeitia *Spain* 43°12N 2°19W **196** B2
Azrak, B. → *Chad* 10°52N 20°35E **259** F4
Azraq ash Shīshān
Jordan 31°50N 36°49E **251** G7
Azrou *Morocco* 33°28N 5°19W **260** B4
Aztec *U.S.A.* 36°49N 107°59W **305** H10
Azteca, Estadio *Mexico* 19°19N 99°9W **128** C2
Azúa de Compostela
Dom. Rep. 18°25N 70°44W **321** C5
Azuaga *Spain* 38°16N 5°39W **195** G5
Azuara *Spain* 41°15N 0°53W **196** D4
Azuay □ *Ecuador* 2°55S 79°0W **328** D2
Azucar, Cerro Pan de
Chile 33°19S 70°41W **137** A1
Azuer → *Spain* 39°8N 3°36W **195** F7
Azuero, Pen. de *Panama* 7°30N 80°30W **320** E3
Azuga *Romania* 45°27N 25°33E **183** E10
Azul *Argentina* 36°42S 59°43W **334** D4
Azul, Laguna *Azores* 37°52N 25°47W **153** d3
Azul, Serra *Brazil* 14°50S 54°50W **331** C7
Azurduy *Bolivia* 19°59S 64°29W **331** D5
Azusa *U.S.A.* 34°8N 117°52W **307** L9
Azzaba *Algeria* 36°48N 7°6E **261** A6
Azzano Décimo *Italy* 45°52N 12°56E **199** C9
Azzel Matti, Sebkra
Algeria 26°10N 0°43E **261** C5

B

Ba Be △ *Vietnam* 22°25N 105°37E **236** A5
Ba Don *Vietnam* 17°45N 106°26E **236** D6
Ba Dong *Vietnam* 9°40N 106°33E **237** H6
Ba Ngoi = Cam Lam
Vietnam 11°54N 109°10E **237** G7
Ba Tri *Vietnam* 10°2N 106°36E **237** G6
Ba Vi △ *Vietnam* 21°1N 105°22E **236** B5
Ba Xian = Bazhou *China* 39°8N 116°22E **226** E9
Baa *Indonesia* 10°50S 123°0E **231** F6
Baambrugge *Neths.* 52°15N 4°59E **112** B2
Baamonde *Spain* 43°7N 7°44W **194** B3
Baao *Phil.* 13°27N 123°22E **232** E4
Baardeere = Bardera
Somali Rep. 2°20N 42°27E **267** D5
Baarle-Nassau *Belgium* 51°27N 4°56E **170** C4
Bab el Mandeb *Red Sea* 12°35N 43°25E **248** D3
Baba *Bulgaria* 42°44N 23°59E **202** D7
Baba, B. do *Angola* 14°50S 12°14E **265** E2
Bābā, Koh-i- *Afghan.* 34°30N 67°0E **240** B2
Baba Budan Hills *India* 13°30N 75°44E **245** H2
Baba Burnu *Turkey* 39°29N 26°2E **205** B8
Baba Channel *Pakistan* 24°48N 66°58E **123** B1
Baba dag *Azerbaijan* 41°0N 48°19E **191** K9
Baba I. *Pakistan* 24°49N 66°57E **123** B1
Bābā Kalū *Iran* 30°7N 50°49E **247** D6
Babaçulândia *Brazil* 7°13S 47°46W **332** C2
Babadag *Romania* 44°53N 28°44E **183** F13
Babadağ *Turkey* 37°49N 28°52E **205** D10
Babaeski *Turkey* 41°26N 27°6E **203** E11
Babahoyo *Ecuador* 1°40S 79°30W **328** D2
Babai = Sarju → *India* 27°21N 81°23E **243** F9
Babak *Phil.* 7°8N 125°41E **233** H5
Babana *Nigeria* 10°31N 3°46E **263** C5
Babanusa *Sudan* 11°20N 27°48E **257** E2
Babar *Algeria* 35°10N 7°6E **261** A6
Babar *Indonesia* 8°0S 129°30E **231** F7
Babar *Pakistan* 31°7N 69°32E **242** D3
Babarkach *Pakistan* 29°45N 68°0E **242** E3
Babarpur *India* 28°41N 77°16E **120** A2
Babase I. *Papua N. G.* 4°0S 153°42E **286** B7
Babayevo *Russia* 59°24N 35°55E **188** C8
Babb *U.S.A.* 48°51N 113°27W **304** B7
Babelthuap *Palau* 7°30N 134°36E **288** c
Babenhausen *Germany* 49°57N 8°57E **179** F4
Băbeni *Romania* 44°59N 24°11E **183** F9
Baberu *India* 25°33N 80°43E **243** G9
Babi Besar, Pulau
Malaysia 2°25N 103°59E **237** L4
Babia Gora *Europe* 49°38N 19°38E **185** J6
Babian Jiang → *China* 22°55N 101°47E **228** F3
Bābil □ *Iraq* 32°30N 44°30E **246** C5
Babile *Ethiopia* 9°16N 42°11E **257** F5
Babile △ *Ethiopia* 8°45N 42°20E **267** C5
Babimost *Poland* 52°10N 15°49E **185** F2
Babinda *Australia* 17°20S 145°56E **280** B4
Babine *Canada* 55°22N 126°37W **296** B3
Babine → *Canada* 55°45N 127°44W **296** B3
Babine L. *Canada* 54°48N 126°0W **296** C3
Babiogórski △ *Poland* 49°38N 19°39E **185** J6
Babo *Indonesia* 2°30S 133°30E **231** E8
Babócsa *Hungary* 46°2N 17°21E **182** D2
Bābol *Iran* 36°40N 52°50E **247** B7
Bābol Sar *Iran* 36°45N 52°45E **247** B7
Babor, Dj. *Algeria* 36°31N 5°25E **261** A6
Baborów *Poland* 50°7N 18°1E **185** H5
Baboua *C.A.R.* 5°49N 14°58E **264** A2
Babruysk *Belarus* 53°10N 29°15E **177** B15
Babson Park *U.S.A.* 27°49N 81°32W **317** H8
Babuhri *India* 26°49N 69°43E **242** F3
Babuna *Macedonia* 41°30N 21°40E **202** E5
Babura *Nigeria* 12°51N 8°59E **263** C6
Babusar Pass *Pakistan* 35°12N 73°59E **243** B5
Babushkin *Russia* 55°51N 37°42E **129** A4
Babušnica *Serbia* 43°7N 22°27E **202** C6
Babuyan *Phil.* 10°0N 118°54E **233** F2
Babuyan Chan. *Phil.* 18°40N 121°30E **232** B3
Babuyan I. *Phil.* 19°32N 121°57E **232** B3
Babuyan Is. *Phil.* 19°10N 121°40E **232** B3
Babylon *Iraq* 32°34N 44°22E **213** F11
Bač *Serbia* 45°29N 19°17E **182** E4
Bâc → *Moldova* 46°55N 29°26E **183** D14
Bac Can *Vietnam* 22°8N 105°49E **236** A5
Bac Giang *Vietnam* 21°16N 106°11E **228** G6
Bac Lieu *Vietnam* 9°17N 105°43E **237** H5
Bac Ninh *Vietnam* 21°13N 106°4E **228** G6
Bac Phan *Vietnam* 22°0N 105°0E **236** B5
Bac Quang *Vietnam* 22°30N 104°48E **228** F5
Bacabal *Brazil* 4°15S 44°45W **332** B3
Bacacay *Phil.* 13°18N 123°47E **232** E4
Bacajá → *Brazil* 3°25S 51°50W **329** D7
Bacalar *Mexico* 18°43N 88°27W **319** D7
Bacan, Kepulauan
Indonesia 0°35S 127°30E **231** E7
Bacarra *Phil.* 18°15N 120°37E **232** B3
Bacău *Romania* 46°35N 26°55E **183** D11
Bacău □ *Romania* 46°30N 26°45E **183** D11
Baccarat *France* 48°28N 6°42E **173** D13
Bacchus Marsh
Australia 37°43S 144°27E **282** D6
Bacerac *Mexico* 30°18N 108°50W **318** A3
Băcești *Romania* 46°50N 27°11E **183** D12
Bach Long Vi, Dao
Vietnam 20°10N 107°40E **236** B6
Bach Ma △ *Vietnam* 16°11N 107°49E **236** D6
Bachaquero *Venezuela* 9°56N 71°8W **328** B3
Bacharach *Germany* 50°3N 7°46E **179** E3
Bachelor's Beach
Neth. Ant. 12°11N 68°18W **322** h
Bachhwara *India* 25°35N 85°54E **243** G11
Bachu *China* 39°46N 78°34E **217** E9
Bachuma *Ethiopia* 6°48N 35°53E **257** F4
Bačina *Serbia* 43°42N 21°23E **202** C5
Back → *Canada* 65°10N 104°0W **294** C9
Back B. *India* 18°56N 72°48E **130** B1
Bačka Palanka *Serbia* 45°17N 19°27E **182** E4
Bačka Topola *Serbia* 45°49N 19°39E **182** E4
Bäckebo *Sweden* 56°53N 16°4E **163** H10
Bäckefors *Sweden* 58°48N 12°9E **163** F6
Bäckhammar *Sweden* 59°10N 14°11E **162** E8
Bački Petrovac *Serbia* 45°29N 19°32E **182** E4
Backnang *Germany* 48°56N 9°26E **179** G5
Backstairs Passage
Australia 35°40S 138°5E **282** C3
Baclaran *Phil.* 14°31N 121°0E **127** B2
Baco, Mt. *Phil.* 12°49N 121°10E **232** E3
Bacolod *Phil.* 10°40N 122°57E **233** F4
Bacon *Phil.* 13°3N 124°3E **232** E5
Baconton *U.S.A.* 31°23N 84°10W **316** D5
Bacoor *Phil.* 14°27N 120°56E **127** C1
Bacoor B. *Phil.* 14°27N 120°54E **127** C1
Bacqueville-en-Caux
France 49°47N 1°0E **172** C8
Bács-Kiskun □ *Hungary* 46°43N 19°30E **182** D4
Bácsalmás *Hungary* 46°8N 19°17E **182** D4
Bacuag = Placer *Phil.* 9°36N 125°38E **233** G5
Bacuit = El Nido *Phil.* 11°10N 119°25E **233** F2
Bacuk *Malaysia* 6°4N 102°25E **237** J4
Bacum *Mexico* 27°33N 110°5W **318** B2
Bād *Iran* 33°41N 52°1E **247** C7
Bad → *U.S.A.* 44°21N 100°22W **308** C3
Bad Aussee *Austria* 47°43N 13°45E **180** D6
Bad Axe *U.S.A.* 43°48N 83°0W **312** C2
Bad Bergzabern *Germany* 49°6N 7°59E **179** F3
Bad Berleburg *Germany* 51°2N 8°26E **178** D4
Bad Bevensen *Germany* 53°5N 10°35E **178** B6
Bad Bramstedt *Germany* 53°55N 9°53E **178** B5
Bad Brückenau *Germany* 50°18N 9°47E **179** E5
Bad Doberan *Germany* 54°6N 11°53E **178** A7
Bad Driburg *Germany* 51°43N 9°1E **178** D5
Bad Ems *Germany* 50°20N 7°43E **179** E3
Bad Frankenhausen
Germany 51°21N 11°5E **178** D7
Bad Freienwalde
Germany 52°46N 14°1E **178** C10
Bad Goisern *Austria* 47°38N 13°38E **180** D6
Bad Harzburg *Germany* 51°52N 10°34E **178** D6
Bad Hersfeld *Germany* 50°52N 9°42E **178** E5
Bad Hofgastein *Austria* 47°17N 13°6E **180** D6
Bad Homburg *Germany* 50°13N 8°38E **179** E4
Bad Honnef *Germany* 50°38N 7°13E **178** E3
Bad Iburg *Germany* 52°10N 8°3E **178** C4
Bad Ischl *Austria* 47°44N 13°38E **180** D6
Bad Kissingen *Germany* 50°11N 10°4E **179** E6
Bad Königshofen
Germany 50°17N 10°28E **179** E6
Bad Kreuznach *Germany* 49°50N 7°51E **179** F3
Bad Krozingen *Germany* 47°54N 7°42E **179** H3
Bad Kudowa = Kudowa-Zdrój
Poland 50°27N 16°15E **185** H3
Bad Laasphe *Germany* 50°56N 8°25E **178** E4
Bad Landeck = Lądek-Zdrój
Poland 50°21N 16°53E **185** H3
Bad Langensalza *Germany* 51°5N 10°38E **178** D6
Bad Lauterberg *Germany* 51°38N 10°28E **178** D6
Bad Leonfelden *Austria* 48°31N 14°18E **180** C7
Bad Liebenwerda
Germany 51°31N 13°24E **178** D9
Bad Mergentheim
Germany 49°28N 9°46E **179** F5
Bad Münstereifel *Germany* 50°33N 6°46E **178** E2
Bad Nauheim *Germany* 50°21N 8°43E **179** E4
Bad Neuenahr-Ahrweiler
Germany 50°32N 7°5E **178** E3
Bad Neustadt *Germany* 50°18N 10°13E **179** E6
Bad Oeynhausen *Germany* 52°12N 8°46E **178** C4
Bad Oldesloe *Germany* 53°48N 10°22E **178** B6
Bad Orb *Germany* 50°12N 9°22E **179** E5
Bad Polzin = Polanica-Zdrój
Poland 50°24N 16°32E **185** H3
Bad Pyrmont *Germany* 51°59N 9°16E **178** D5
Bad Reichenhall
Germany 47°43N 12°54E **179** H8
Bad Reinerz = Duszniki-Zdrój
Poland 50°24N 16°24E **185** H3
Bad Säckingen *Germany* 47°33N 7°56E **179** H3
Bad St. Leonhard *Austria* 46°58N 14°47E **180** E7
Bad Salzuflen *Germany* 52°5N 8°44E **178** C4
Bad Salzungen *Germany* 50°48N 10°14E **178** E6
Bad Schönfliess = Trzcińsko Zdrój
Poland 52°58N 14°35E **185** F1
Bad Schwartau *Germany* 53°55N 10°41E **178** B6
Bad Segeberg *Germany* 53°56N 10°17E **178** B6
Bad Tölz *Germany* 47°45N 11°34E **179** H7
Bad Urach *Germany* 48°29N 9°23E **179** G5
Bad Vöslau *Austria* 47°58N 16°12E **181** D9
Bad Waldsee *Germany* 47°55N 9°45E **179** H5
Bad Wildungen *Germany* 51°6N 9°7E **178** D5
Bad Wimpfen *Germany* 49°13N 9°11E **179** F5
Bad Windsheim *Germany* 49°36N 10°25E **179** F6
Bad Zwischenahn *Germany* 53°12N 8°1E **178** B4
Bada Barabil *India* 22°7N 85°24E **243** H11
Badagara *India* 11°35N 75°40E **245** J2
Badagri *Nigeria* 6°25N 2°55E **263** D5
Badain Jaran Shamo
China 40°23N 102°0E **218** B5
Badajós, L. *Brazil* 3°15S 62°50W **329** D5
Badajoz *Spain* 38°50N 6°59W **195** G4
Badajoz □ *Spain* 38°40N 6°30W **195** G4
Badakhshān □ *Afghan.* 36°30N 71°0E **240** A3
Badalona *Spain* 41°26N 2°15E **114** A2
Badalzai *Afghan.* 29°50N 65°35E **242** E1
Badami *India* 15°55N 75°41E **245** G2
Badampahar *India* 22°10N 86°10E **244** C8
Badanah *Si. Arabia* 30°58N 41°30E **246** D4
Badarinath *India* 30°45N 79°30E **243** D8
Badarpur *India* 24°54N 92°36E **241** C4
Badas, Kepulauan
Indonesia 0°45N 107°5E **234** B3
Baddo → *Pakistan* 28°0N 64°20E **240** D2
Bade *Indonesia* 7°10S 139°35E **231** F9
Badeggi *Nigeria* 9°1N 6°8E **263** D6
Badéguichéri *Niger* 14°30N 5°22E **263** C6
Baden *Austria* 48°1N 16°13E **181** C9
Baden *Switz.* 47°28N 8°18E **179** H4
Baden *Pa., U.S.A.* 40°38N 80°14W **312** F4
Baden-Baden *Germany* 48°44N 8°13E **179** G4
Baden-Württemberg □
Germany 48°20N 8°40E **179** G4
Badgastein *Austria* 47°7N 13°9E **180** D6
Badger *Nfld. & L., Canada* 49°0N 56°4W **299** C8
Badger *Calif., U.S.A.* 36°38N 119°1W **306** J7
Bādghīs □ *Afghan.* 35°0N 63°0E **240** B1
Badgingarra △ *Australia* 30°23S 115°22E **279** F2
Badgom *India* 34°1N 74°45E **243** B6
Badhoevedorp *Neths.* 52°20N 4°47E **112** A1
Badia Polésine *Italy* 45°5N 11°29E **199** C8
Badian *Phil.* 9°55N 123°24E **233** G4
Badiar △ *Guinea* 13°37N 13°11W **262** C2
Badin *Pakistan* 24°38N 68°54E **242** G3
Badinka △ *Mali* 13°31N 9°28W **262** C3
Badjokola
Dem. Rep. of the Congo 3°54N 20°17E **264** B4
Badlands *U.S.A.* 43°55N 102°30W **308** D2
Badlands △ *U.S.A.* 43°38N 102°56W **308** D2
Badli *India* 28°44N 77°8E **120** A1
Badnera *India* 20°48N 77°44E **244** D3
Badoc *Phil.* 17°56N 120°28E **232** C3
Badogo *Mali* 11°2N 8°13W **262** C3
Badoumbé *Mali* 13°42N 10°15W **262** C2
Badr Ḥunayn *Si. Arabia* 23°44N 38°46E **248** B2
Badrah *Iraq* 33°6N 45°58E **213** F11
Badrinath *India* 30°44N 79°29E **243** D8
Badu I. *Papua N. G.* 10°5S 142°10E **286** F2
Baduen *Somali Rep.* 7°15N 47°40E **267** C6
Badulla *Sri Lanka* 7°1N 81°7E **245** L5
Badung, Selat *Indonesia* 8°40S 115°22E **231** K18
Badupi *Burma* 21°36N 93°27E **241** E4
Badvel *India* 14°45N 79°3E **245** G4
Baena *Spain* 37°37N 4°20W **195** H6
Baengnyeongdo
S. Korea 37°57N 124°40E **224** D2
Baerami *Australia* 32°27S 150°27E **283** B9
Bærum *Norway* 59°54N 10°36E **133** A2
Baetov *Kyrgyzstan* 41°13N 74°54E **217** D8
Baeza *Ecuador* 0°25S 77°53W **328** D2
Baeza *Spain* 37°57N 3°25W **195** H7
Bafang *Cameroon* 5°9N 10°11E **263** D7
Bafatá *Guinea-Biss.* 12°8N 14°40W **262** C2
Baffin B. *N. Amer.* 72°0N 64°0W **295** B13
Baffin I. *Canada* 68°0N 75°0W **295** C12
Bafia *Cameroon* 4°40N 11°10E **263** E7
Bafilo *Togo* 9°22N 1°22E **263** D5
Bafing → *Mali* 13°49N 10°50W **262** C2
Bafing △ *Mali* 12°38N 10°28W **262** C2
Bafliyūn *Syria* 36°37N 36°59E **246** B3
Bafoulabé *Mali* 13°50N 10°55W **262** C2
Bafoussam *Cameroon* 5°28N 10°25E **263** D7
Bāfq *Iran* 31°40N 55°25E **247** D7
Bafra *Turkey* 41°34N 35°54E **212** B6
Bafra Burnu *Turkey* 41°45N 36°2E **212** B7
Bāft *Iran* 29°15N 56°38E **247** D8
Bafut *Cameroon* 6°6N 10°2E **263** D7
Bafwasende
Dem. Rep. of the Congo 1°3N 27°5E **268** B2
Bagabag *Phil.* 16°30N 121°15E **232** C3
Bagabag I. *Papua N. G.* 4°48S 146°14E **286** C4
Bagac *Phil.* 14°36N 120°23E **232** D3
Bagac Bay *Phil.* 14°36N 120°20E **232** D3
Bagalkot *India* 16°10N 75°40E **245** F2
Bagam *Niger* 15°43N 6°35E **263** B6
Bagamanoc *Phil.* 13°57N 124°17E **232** E5
Bagamoyo *Tanzania* 6°28S 38°55E **268** D4
Bagan Datoh *Malaysia* 3°59N 100°47E **237** L3
Bagan Serai *Malaysia* 5°1N 100°32E **237** K3
Baganga *Phil.* 7°34N 126°33E **233** H6
Bagani *Namibia* 18°7S 21°41E **270** A3
Bagansiapiapi *Indonesia* 2°12N 100°50E **234** B2
Bagasra *India* 21°30N 71°0E **242** J4
Bagata
Dem. Rep. of the Congo 3°44S 17°57E **264** C3
Bagaud *India* 22°19N 75°53E **242** H6
Bagawi *Sudan* 12°20N 34°18E **257** E3
Bagbag *Sudan* 15°23N 31°30E **257** D3
Bağcılar *Turkey* 41°2N 28°49E **122** B1
Bagdad *Calif., U.S.A.* 34°35N 115°53W **307** L11
Bagdad *Fla., U.S.A.* 30°36N 87°2W **317** E2
Bagdarin *Russia* 54°26N 113°36E **215** D12
Bagé *Brazil* 31°20S 54°15W **335** C5
Bagenalstown = Muine Bheag
Ireland 52°42N 6°58W **166** D5
Bagepalli *India* 13°47N 77°47E **245** H3
Bagevadi *India* 16°35N 75°58E **244** F2
Baggao *Phil.* 17°56N 121°46E **232** C3
Bággio *Italy* 45°27N 9°6E **121** B1
Baggs *U.S.A.* 41°2N 107°39W **304** F10
Bagh *Pakistan* 33°59N 73°45E **243** C5
Bāgh-e-Feyz *Iran* 35°44N 51°19E **141** A1
Baghain → *India* 25°32N 81°1E **243** G9
Baghdād *Iraq* 33°20N 44°23E **113** A2
Baghdad al Muthana ✈
Iraq 33°17N 44°30E **113** B2
Baghdad Int. ✈ (SDA)
Iraq 33°15N 44°14E **113** B1
Bagherhat *Bangla.* 22°40N 89°47E **241** D2
Bagheria *Italy* 38°5N 13°30E **200** D6
Baghlān *Afghan.* 32°12N 68°46E **240** A3
Baghlān □ *Afghan.* 36°0N 68°30E **240** B3
Bagley *U.S.A.* 47°32N 95°24W **308** B6
Bagmari *India* 22°34N 88°23E **124** B2
Bagn *Norway* 60°49N 9°34E **164** D6
Bagnara Cálabra *Italy* 38°17N 15°48E **201** D8
Bagnasco *Italy* 44°18N 8°2E **198** D5
Bagnell Dam *U.S.A.* 38°14N 92°36W **310** F4
Bagnères-de-Bigorre *France* 43°5N 0°9E **174** E4
Bagnères-de-Luchon
France 42°47N 0°38E **174** F4
Bagneux *France* 48°47N 2°18E **134** B2
Bagni di Lucca *Italy* 44°1N 10°35E **198** D7
Bagno di Romagna *Italy* 43°50N 11°57E **199** E8
Bagnoles-de-l'Orne
France 48°32N 0°25W **172** D6
Bagnolet *France* 48°52N 2°25E **134** A3
Bagnols-sur-Cèze *France* 44°10N 4°36E **175** D8
Bagnorea = Bagnorégio
Italy 42°37N 12°5E **199** F9
Bagnorégio *Italy* 42°37N 12°5E **199** F9
Bago = Pegu *Burma* 17°20N 96°29E **241** G6
Bago *Phil.* 10°32N 122°50E **233** F4
Bagodar *India* 24°5N 85°52E **243** G11
Bagrationovsk *Russia* 54°23N 20°39E **184** D7
Bagrdan *Serbia* 44°5N 21°11E **202** B5
Bagsværd *Denmark* 55°45N 12°27E **118** A2
Bagsværd Sø *Denmark* 55°46N 12°28E **118** A2
Bagua *Peru* 5°35S 78°22W **330** B2
Baguiati *India* 22°36N 88°25E **124** B2
Baguio *Phil.* 16°26N 120°34E **232** C3
Bagumbayan *Phil.* 14°28N 121°3E **127** C2
Bağyurdu *Turkey* 38°25N 27°41E **205** C9
Bagzane, Monts *Niger* 17°43N 8°45E **259** E1
Bah *India* 26°53N 78°36E **243** F8
Bahabón de Esgueva
Spain 41°52N 3°43W **194** D7
Bahadurabad Ghat
Bangla. 25°11N 89°44E **241** C2
Bahadurganj *India* 26°16N 87°49E **243** F12
Bahadurgarh *India* 28°40N 76°57E **242** E7
Baha'i Temple *U.S.A.* 42°4N 87°41W **119** A2
Bahaja *Somali Rep.* 11°16N 49°50E **267** B6
Baham, Pte. *Martinique* 14°24N 60°50W **322** j
Bahama, Canal Viejo de
W. Indies 22°10N 77°30W **320** B4
Bahamas ■ *N. Amer.* 24°0N 75°0W **321** B5
Bahār *Iran* 34°54N 48°26E **213** E13
Bahārak *Afghan.* 37°0N 70°53E **240** A4
Baharampur *India* 24°2N 88°27E **243** G13
Baharîya, El Wâhât al
Egypt 28°0N 28°50E **256** B2
Baharu Pandan = Pandan
Malaysia 1°32N 103°46E **237** d
Bahawalnagar *Pakistan* 30°0N 73°15E **242** E5
Bahawalpur *Pakistan* 29°24N 71°40E **242** E4
Bahçe *Turkey* 37°13N 36°34E **212** D7
Bahçecik *Turkey* 40°41N 29°44E **203** F13
Bahçeköy *Turkey* 41°10N 28°59E **122** A1
Bahçelievler *Turkey* 41°0N 28°50E **122** B1
Baheli *Phil.* 10°0N 118°47E **233** F2
Bäherden *Turkmenistan* 38°25N 57°26E **247** B8
Baheri *India* 28°45N 79°34E **243** E8
Bahgul → *India* 27°45N 79°36E **243** F8
Bahi *Tanzania* 5°58S 35°21E **268** D4
Bahi Swamp *Tanzania* 6°10S 35°0E **268** D4
Bahía = Salvador *Brazil* 13°0S 38°30W **333** D4
Bahía □ *Brazil* 12°0S 42°0W **333** D3
Bahía, Is. de la *Honduras* 16°45N 86°15W **320** C2
Bahía Blanca *Argentina* 38°35S 62°13W **334** D3
Bahía de Caráquez
Ecuador 0°40S 80°27W **328** D1
Bahía Kino *Mexico* 28°47N 111°58W **318** B2
Bahía Laura *Argentina* 48°10S 66°30W **336** C3

Bahía Mansa Chile 40°33S 73°46W 336 B2
Bahía Negra Paraguay 20°5S 58°5W 331 E6
Bahir Dar Ethiopia 11°37N 37°10E 257 E4
Bahlah Oman 22°58N 57°18E 249 B7
Bahmanzād Iran 31°15N 51°47E 247 D6
Bahmer Algeria 27°32N 0°10W 261 C4
Bahr el Ahmar □ Egypt 28°40N 31°30E 251 K2
Bahr el Ahmar □ Sudan 20°0N 35°0E 256 D4
Bahr el Jabal □ Sudan 4°0N 31°0E 257 G3
Bahraich India 27°38N 81°37E 243 F9
Bahrain ■ Asia 26°0N 50°35E 247 E6
Bahror India 27°51N 76°20E 242 F7
Bahtîm Egypt 30°8N 31°16E 117 A2
Bāhū Kalāt Iran 25°43N 61°25E 247 E9
Bai Mali 13°35N 3°28W 262 C4
Bai Bung, Mui = Ca Mau, Mui
Vietnam 8°38N 104°44E 237 H5
Bai Duc Vietnam 18°3N 105°49E 236 C5
Bai Thuong Vietnam 19°54N 105°23E 236 C5
Baia de Aramă Romania 45°0N 22°50E 182 E7
Baía dos Tigres Angola 16°40S 11°47E 265 F2
Baia Farta Angola 12°40S 13°11E 265 E2
Baia Mare Romania 47°40N 23°35E 183 C8
Baia-Sprie Romania 47°41N 23°43E 183 C8
Baião Brazil 2°40S 49°40W 332 B2
Baïbokoum Chad 7°46N 15°43E 259 G3
Baicheng Jilin, China 45°38N 122°42E 227 B12
Baicheng Xinjiang Uygur,
China 41°46N 81°52E 217 D10
Băicoi Romania 45°3N 25°52E 183 E10
Baidoa Somali Rep. 3°8N 43°30E 267 D5
Baie-Comeau Canada 49°12N 68°10W 299 C6
Baie du Cap Mauritius 20°29S 57°22E 272 e
Baie-Mahault Guadeloupe 16°16N 61°35W 322 e
Baie-St-Paul Canada 47°28N 70°32W 299 C5
Baie Ste-Anne Seychelles 4°18S 55°45E 272 c
Baie-Trinité Canada 49°25N 67°20W 299 C6
Baie Verte Canada 49°55N 56°12W 299 C8
Baignes-Ste-Radegonde
France 45°23N 0°25W 174 C3
Baigneux-les-Juifs France 47°31N 4°39E 173 E11
Baihar India 22°6N 80°33E 243 H9
Baihe China 32°50N 110°5E 226 H6
Ba'ījī Iraq 35°0N 43°30E 213 E10
Baijnath India 29°55N 79°37E 243 E8
Baikal, L. = Baykal, Oz.
Russia 53°0N 108°0E 215 D11
Baikonur = Bayqongyr
Kazakhstan 45°40N 63°20E 216 C6
Baikunthpur India 23°15N 82°33E 243 H10
Bailadila, Mt. India 18°43N 81°15E 244 E5
Baile Atha Cliath = Dublin
Ireland 53°21N 6°15W 120 A2
Băile Govora Romania 45°5N 24°11E 183 E9
Băile Herculane Romania 44°53N 22°26E 182 F7
Băile Olănești Romania 45°12N 24°14E 183 E9
Băile Tușnad Romania 46°9N 25°51E 183 D10
Bailén Spain 38°8N 3°48W 195 G7
Băilești Romania 44°1N 23°20E 183 F8
Baileys Crossroads U.S.A. 38°50N 77°6W 143 B3
Bailhongal India 15°55N 74°53E 245 G2
Bailique, Ilha Brazil 1°2N 49°58W 332 A2
Baille-Argent Guadeloupe 16°15N 61°48W 322 e
Baillif Guadeloupe 16°1N 61°44W 322 e
Bailly France 48°50N 2°4E 134 A1
Bailugh Afghan. 32°40N 66°47E 240 B2
Bailundo = Luau Angola 10°40S 22°10E 265 E4
Bailundo Angola 12°10S 15°50E 265 E3
Baima China 33°0N 100°26E 228 A3
Baimuru Papua N. G. 7°35S 144°51E 286 D3
Bain-de-Bretagne France 47°50N 1°40W 172 E5
Bainbridge Ga., U.S.A. 30°55N 84°35W 316 E5
Bainbridge Ind., U.S.A. 39°46N 86°49W 311 E10
Bainbridge N.Y., U.S.A. 42°18N 75°29W 313 D9
Bainbridge Ohio, U.S.A. 39°14N 83°16W 311 E13
Bainbridge Island
U.S.A. 47°38N 122°32W 306 C4
Baing Indonesia 10°14S 120°34E 231 F6
Bainiu China 32°50N 112°15E 226 H7
Baiyik Papua N. G. 3°40S 143°4E 286 B2
Baiona Spain 42°6N 8°52W 194 C2
Bā'ir Jordan 30°45N 36°55E 251 H7
Bā'ir, W. → Jordan 30°59N 37°24E 251 H8
Baird Mts. U.S.A. 67°0N 160°0W 303 C7
Bairiki = Tarawa Kiribati 1°30N 173°0E 288 G9
Bairin Youqi China 43°30N 118°35E 227 C10
Bairin Zuoqi China 43°58N 119°15E 227 C10
Bairnsdale Australia 37°48S 147°36E 283 D7
Bairro Alto Lisbon, Portugal 126 c1
Bairro Lopes Lisbon, Portugal 126 b3
Bais Phil. 9°35N 123°7E 233 G4
Baisha Guangdong, China 23°8N 113°11E 121 B2
Baisha Henan, China 34°20N 112°32E 226 G7
Baissa Nigeria 7°14N 10°38E 263 D7
Baitadi Nepal 29°35N 80°25E 243 E9
Baitarani → India 20°45N 86°48E 244 D8
Baixa Lisbon, Portugal 126 c2
Baixa Grande Brazil 11°57S 40°11W 333 D3
Baixa Limia-Sierra do Xurés △
Spain 41°59N 8°2W 194 D2
Baixo-Longa Angola 15°41S 18°45E 265 F3
Baiyer River Papua N. G. 5°32S 144°9E 286 C3
Baiyin China 36°45N 104°14E 226 F3
Baiyü China 31°16N 98°50E 228 B2
Baiyu Shan China 37°15N 107°30E 226 F4
Baiyuda Sudan 17°35N 32°7E 256 D3
Baiyun Hill China 23°8N 113°15E 121 B2
Baiyun Int. ✕ (CAN)
China 23°10N 113°15E 121 A2
Baj Baj India 22°30N 88°5E 243 H13
Baja Hungary 46°12N 18°59E 182 D3
Baja, Pta. Easter I., Chile 27°10S 109°22W 330 b
Baja, Pta. Baja Calif.,
Mexico 29°58N 115°49W 318 B1
Baja California Mexico 31°10N 115°12W 318 A1
Baja California □ Mexico 30°0N 115°0W 318 B2
Baja California Sur □
Mexico 25°50N 111°50W 318 B2
Bajag India 22°40N 81°21E 243 H9
Bajamar Canary Is. 28°33N 16°20W 153 e1
Bajana India 23°7N 71°49E 242 H4
Bajatrejo Indonesia 8°29S 114°19E 231 J17
Bajera Indonesia 8°31S 115°2E 231 J18
Bājgīrān Iran 37°36N 58°24E 247 B8
Bājil Yemen 15°4N 43°17E 248 D3
Bajimba, Mt. Australia 29°17S 152°6E 281 D5
Bajina Bašta Serbia 43°58N 19°35E 202 C3
Bajmok Serbia 45°57N 19°24E 182 E4
Bajo Caracoles Argentina 47°27S 70°56W 336 C2
Bajo Nuevo Caribbean 15°40N 78°50W 320 C4
Bajoga Nigeria 10°57N 11°20E 263 C7
Bajool Australia 23°40S 150°35E 280 C5
Bak Hungary 46°43N 16°51E 182 D1
Bakala C.A.R. 6°15N 20°20E 264 A4
Bakar Croatia 45°18N 14°32E 199 C11
Bakassi Pen. Cameroon 4°42N 8°20E 263 E6
Bakel Senegal 14°56N 12°20W 262 C2
Baker Calif., U.S.A. 35°16N 116°4W 307 K10
Baker Fla., U.S.A. 30°48N 86°41W 317 E3
Baker Mont., U.S.A. 46°22N 104°17W 304 C11
Baker, Canal Chile 47°45S 74°45W 336 C2
Baker, L. Canada 64°0N 96°0W 294 C10
Baker, Mt. U.S.A. 48°50N 121°49W 304 B3
Baker City U.S.A. 44°47N 117°50W 304 D5
Baker I. Pac. Oc. 0°10N 176°35W 277 A15
Baker I. Alaska, U.S.A. 55°20N 133°40W 296 B2
Baker L. Australia 26°54S 126°5E 279 E4
Baker Lake Canada 64°20N 96°3W 294 C10
Bakere
Dem. Rep. of the Congo 1°36N 23°50E 264 B4
Bakerhill U.S.A. 31°47N 85°18W 316 D4
Bakers Creek Australia 21°13S 149°7E 280 C4
Bakers Dozen Is. Canada 56°45N 78°45W 298 A4
Bakersfield Calif., U.S.A. 35°23N 119°1W 307 K8
Bakersfield Vt., U.S.A. 44°45N 72°48W 313 B12
Bakharden = Bäherden
Turkmenistan 38°25N 57°26E 247 B8
Bakhchysaray Ukraine 44°40N 33°45E 189 K7
Bakhmach Ukraine 51°10N 32°45E 189 G7
Bakhmut = Artemovsk
Ukraine 48°35N 38°0E 189 H9
Bākhtarān = Kermānshāh
Iran 34°23N 47°0E 213 E12
Bākhtarān = Kermānshāh □
Iran 34°0N 46°30E 246 C5
Baki = Krasnyye Baki
Russia 57°8N 45°10E 190 B7
Bakı Azerbaijan 40°29N 49°56E 191 K9
Bakır → Turkey 38°55N 27°0E 205 C9
Bakırdağı Turkey 38°13N 35°46E 212 C6
Bakırköy Turkey 40°58N 28°52E 122 C1
Bakkafjörður Iceland 66°2N 14°48W 155 A12
Bakkaflói Iceland 66°10N 14°45W 155 A12
Bakkagerði Iceland 65°31N 13°49W 155 B13
Baklan Turkey 38°0N 29°36E 205 C11
Bako Ethiopia 5°51N 36°23E 257 F4
Bako Ivory C. 9°8N 7°40W 262 D3
Bako △ Malaysia 1°43N 110°28E 235 B4
Bakony Hungary 47°10N 17°30E 182 C2
Bakony Forest = Bakony
Hungary 47°10N 17°30E 182 C2
Bakori Nigeria 11°34N 7°25E 263 C6
Bakouma C.A.R. 5°40N 22°56E 264 A4
Bakovka Russia 55°40N 37°19E 129 B2
Baksan Russia 43°42N 43°32E 191 J6
Bakswaho India 24°15N 79°18E 243 G8
Baku = Bakı Azerbaijan 40°29N 49°56E 191 K9
Bakundi Nigeria 8°2N 10°45E 263 D7
Bakutis Coast Antarctica 74°0S 120°0W 151 D15
Bakwa-Kenge
Dem. Rep. of the Congo 4°51S 22°4E 265 C4
Bakwanga = Mbuji-Mayi
Dem. Rep. of the Congo 6°9S 23°40E 265 D4
Baky = Bakı Azerbaijan 40°29N 49°56E 191 K9
Bal Harbour U.S.A. 25°53N 80°7W 128 A2
Bala Ont., Canada 45°1N 79°37W 312 A5
Bala Senegal 14°1N 13°8W 262 C2
Bâlâ Turkey 39°32N 33°6E 212 C5
Bala Gwynedd, U.K. 52°54N 3°36W 168 E4
Bala, L. U.K. 52°53N 3°37W 168 E4
Bālā Morghāb Afghan. 35°35N 63°20E 240 B1
Balabac Phil. 7°59N 117°4E 233 H1
Balabac I. Phil. 8°0N 117°0E 233 G1
Balabac Str. E. Indies 7°53N 117°5E 230 C5
Balabagh Afghan. 34°25N 70°12E 242 B4
Ba'labakk Lebanon 34°0N 36°10E 250 E7
Balabalangan, Kepulauan
Indonesia 2°20S 117°30E 235 C5
Balabio, Î. N. Cal. 20°7S 164°11E 288 d
Bălăcița Romania 44°23N 23°8E 183 F8
Balad Iraq 34°0N 44°9E 213 F11
Balad Rūz Iraq 33°42N 45°5E 213 F11
Bālādeh Fārs, Iran 29°17N 51°56E 247 D6
Bālādeh Māzandaran, Iran 36°12N 51°48E 247 B6
Balaghat India 21°49N 80°12E 244 D5
Balaghat Ra. India 18°50N 76°30E 244 E3
Balaguer Spain 41°50N 0°50E 196 D5
Balaka
Dem. Rep. of the Congo 4°52S 19°57E 265 C3
Balakété C.A.R. 6°56N 19°54E 264 A3
Balakhna Russia 56°25N 43°32E 190 B6
Balaklava S. Austral.,
Australia 34°7S 138°22E 282 C3
Balaklava Ukraine 44°30N 33°30E 189 K7
Balakliya Ukraine 49°28N 36°55E 189 H9
Balakovo Russia 52°4N 47°55E 190 D8
Balamau India 27°10N 80°21E 243 F9
Balamban Phil. 10°30N 123°43E 233 F4
Balambangan Malaysia 7°17N 116°55E 235 A5
Balan Romania 46°39N 25°49E 183 D10
Balancán Mexico 17°48N 91°32W 319 D6
Balanda = Kalininsk
Russia 51°30N 44°40E 190 E7
Balandra B. Trin. & Tob. 10°42N 61°0W 323 t
Balanga Phil. 14°41N 120°32E 232 D3
Balangala
Dem. Rep. of the Congo 0°30N 19°56E 264 B3
Balangiga Phil. 11°7N 125°23E 233 F5
Balangir India 20°43N 83°35E 244 D6
Balanivka Ukraine 48°24N 29°24E 183 B14
Balaoan Phil. 16°49N 120°24E 232 C3
Balapur India 20°40N 76°45E 244 D3
Balara Phil. 14°39N 121°3E 127 B2
Balashikha Russia 55°48N 37°58E 129 B5
Balashov Russia 51°30N 43°10E 190 E6
Balasinor India 22°57N 73°23E 242 H5
Balasore = Baleshwar
India 21°35N 87°3E 244 D8
Balassagyarmat Hungary 48°4N 19°15E 182 B4
Balât Egypt 25°36N 29°19E 256 B2
Balaton Hungary 46°50N 17°40E 182 D2
Balaton-Felvidéki △
Hungary 46°52N 17°30E 182 D2
Balatonboglár Hungary 46°46N 17°40E 182 D2
Balatonfüred Hungary 46°58N 17°54E 182 D2
Balatonszentgyörgy
Hungary 46°41N 17°19E 182 D2
Balayan Phil. 13°57N 120°44E 232 E3
Balazote Spain 38°54N 2°9W 197 G2
Balbal Phil. 17°27N 121°12E 232 C3
Balbi, Mt. Papua N. G. 5°55S 154°58E 286 C8
Balbieriškis Lithuania 54°32N 23°52E 184 D10
Balbigny France 45°49N 4°11E 175 C8
Balbina Brazil 1°58S 59°29W 329 D6
Balbina, Represa de Brazil 2°0S 59°30W 329 D6
Balboa Panama 8°57N 79°34W 320 E4
Balbriggan Ireland 53°37N 6°11W 166 C5
Balcarce Argentina 38°0S 58°10W 334 D4
Balcarres Canada 50°50N 103°35W 297 C8
Bălcești Romania 44°37N 23°57E 183 F8
Balchik Bulgaria 43°28N 28°11E 203 C12
Balclutha N.Z. 46°15S 169°45E 285 G4
Balcones Escarpment
U.S.A. 29°30N 99°15W 314 G5
Balçova Turkey 38°22N 27°4E 205 C9
Bald Hd. Australia 35°6S 118°1E 279 G2
Bald I. Australia 34°57S 118°27E 279 F2
Bald Knob U.S.A. 35°19N 91°34W 314 D9
Baldenburg = Biały Bór
Poland 53°53N 16°51E 184 E3
Baldia Pakistan 24°54N 66°58E 123 A1
Baldock L. Canada 56°33N 97°57W 297 B9
Baldoyle Ireland 53°24N 6°8W 120 A3
Baldwin Fla., U.S.A. 30°18N 81°59W 316 E8
Baldwin Mich., U.S.A. 43°54N 85°51W 309 D11
Baldwin Pa., U.S.A. 40°21N 79°58W 312 F5
Baldwin, L. U.S.A. 28°34N 81°19W 133 A3
Baldwin Hills U.S.A. 34°0N 118°21W 126 B2
Baldwin Hills Res.
U.S.A. 34°0N 118°21W 126 B2
Baldwinsville U.S.A. 43°10N 76°20W 313 C8
Baldy Peak U.S.A. 33°54N 109°34W 305 K9
Bale Croatia 45°4N 13°46E 199 C10
Bale Oromiya, Ethiopia 6°57N 40°8E 257 F5
Bale Oromiya, Ethiopia 6°20N 41°30E 257 F5
Bale Mts. △ Ethiopia 6°59N 39°52E 257 F4
Baleares □ Spain 39°30N 3°0E 206 B4
Balearic Is. = Baleares, Is.
Spain 39°30N 3°0E 206 B4
Baleia, Pta. da Brazil 17°40S 39°7W 333 E4
Baleine = Whale →
Canada 58°15N 67°40W 299 A6
Baleine, Petite R. de la →
Canada 56°0N 76°45W 298 A4
Băleni Romania 45°48N 27°51E 183 E12
Baler Phil. 15°46N 121°34E 232 D3
Baler Bay Phil. 15°50N 121°35E 232 D3
Balerne Suisse U.K. 57°31N 7°22W 167 D1
Baleshwar India 21°35N 87°3E 244 D8
Balestrand Norway 61°11N 6°31E 164 C3
Balezino Russia 58°2N 53°6E 190 B11
Balfate Honduras 15°48N 86°25W 320 C2
Balfour Channel
Solomon Is. 8°43S 157°27E 287 M9
Balgowlah Australia 33°47S 151°16E 139 A2
Balgowlah Heights
Australia 33°48S 151°16E 139 A2
Balham U.K. 51°26N 0°8W 125 B3
Balharshah India 19°50N 79°23E 244 E4
Bali Cameroon 5°54N 10°0E 263 D7
Bali Dem. Rep. of the Congo 2°50S 16°12E 264 C3
Bali Kriti, Greece 35°25N 24°47E 207 E5
Bali Raj., India 25°11N 73°17E 242 G5
Bali W. Bengal, India 22°39N 88°20E 124 B1
Bali Indonesia 8°20S 115°0E 231 J18
Bali □ Indonesia 8°20S 115°0E 231 J18
Bali, Selat Indonesia 8°18S 114°25E 231 J17
Bali Barat △ Indonesia 8°12S 114°35E 235 D4
Bali Sea Indonesia 8°0S 115°0E 231 J17
Balia S. Leone 9°22N 11°1W 262 D2
Baliapal India 21°40N 87°17E 243 J12
Baliceaux St. Vincent 12°57N 61°8W 323 n
Balicuatro Is. Phil. 12°39N 124°24E 232 E5
Baliganja India 22°31N 88°22E 124 B2
Baligród Poland 49°20N 22°17E 185 J9
Baliguda India 20°12N 83°55E 244 D6
Balik Pulau Malaysia 5°21N 100°14E 237 c
Balıkeşir Turkey 39°39N 27°53E 205 B9
Balıkesir □ Turkey 39°45N 28°0E 205 B9
Balıkliçeşme Turkey 40°18N 27°5E 203 F11
Balikpapan Indonesia 1°10S 116°55E 235 C5
Balimbing Phil. 5°5N 119°58E 233 J2
Balimo Papua N. G. 8°6S 142°57E 286 E2
Baling Malaysia 5°41N 100°55E 237 K3
Balingasag Phil. 8°45N 124°47E 233 G5
Balingen Germany 48°16N 8°51E 179 G4
Balingsnäs Sweden 59°13N 18°0E 139 B2
Balingsta Sweden 59°12N 18°3E 139 B2
Balinț Romania 45°48N 21°54E 182 E6
Balintang Channel Phil. 19°49N 121°40E 232 B3
Balintang I. Phil. 19°58N 122°9E 232 B4
Balintawak Phil. 14°39N 120°59E 127 B1
Baliza Brazil 16°0S 52°20W 331 D7
Baljurashī Si. Arabia 19°51N 41°33E 248 C3
Balkan □ Turkmenistan 40°0N 54°30E 216 D5
Balkan Mts. = Stara Planina
Bulgaria 43°15N 23°0E 202 C7
Balkanabat Turkmenistan 39°30N 54°22E 247 B7
Balkh Afghan. 36°44N 66°47E 217 E7
Balkh □ Afghan. 36°50N 67°0E 240 A2
Balkhash = Balqash
Kazakhstan 46°50N 74°50E 214 E8
Balkhash, Ozero = Balqash Köli
Kazakhstan 46°0N 74°50E 217 C8
Balkonda India 18°52N 78°21E 244 E4
Balla Bangla. 24°10N 91°35E 241 G4
Ballachulish U.K. 56°41N 5°8W 167 E3
Balladonia Australia 32°27S 123°51E 279 F3
Ballaghaderreen Ireland 53°55N 8°34W 166 C3
Ballan Australia 37°35S 144°13E 282 D6
Ballarat Australia 37°33S 143°50E 282 D5
Ballard, L. Australia 29°20S 120°40E 279 E3
Ballater U.K. 57°3N 3°3W 167 D5
Ballé Mali 15°18N 8°33W 262 B3
Ballenas, Canal de
Mexico 29°10N 113°29W 318 B2
Balleny Is. Antarctica 66°30S 163°0E 151 C11
Balleroy France 49°11N 0°50W 172 C6
Ballerup Denmark 55°43N 12°21E 118 A2
Ballı Turkey 40°50N 27°3E 203 F11
Ballia India 25°46N 84°12E 243 G11
Ballina N.S.W., Australia 28°50S 153°31E 281 D5
Ballina Mayo, Ireland 54°7N 9°9W 166 B2
Ballinasloe Ireland 53°20N 8°13W 166 C3
Ballinger U.S.A. 31°45N 99°57W 314 F5
Ballinrobe Ireland 53°38N 9°13W 166 C2
Ballinskelligs B. Ireland 51°48N 10°13W 166 E1
Ballinteer Ireland 53°17N 6°15W 120 B2
Ballon France 48°10N 0°14E 172 D7
Ballons des Vosges △
France 48°0N 7°0E 173 E14
Ballsh Albania 40°36N 19°44E 202 F3
Ballston Spa U.S.A. 43°0N 73°51W 313 D11
Ballyboden Ireland 53°17N 6°18W 120 B2
Ballyboghil Ireland 53°32N 6°16W 166 C5
Ballybrack Ireland 53°15N 6°7W 120 B3
Ballybunion Ireland 52°31N 9°40W 166 D2
Ballycanew Ireland 52°37N 6°19W 166 D5
Ballycastle U.K. 55°12N 6°15W 166 A5
Ballyclare U.K. 54°46N 6°0W 166 B5
Ballydehob Ireland 51°34N 9°28W 166 E2
Ballyfermot Ireland 53°20N 6°21W 120 A1
Ballygawley U.K. 54°27N 7°2W 166 B4
Ballyhaunis Ireland 53°46N 8°46W 166 C3
Ballyheige Ireland 52°23N 9°49W 166 D2
Ballymena U.K. 54°52N 6°17W 166 B5
Ballymoney U.K. 55°5N 6°31W 166 A5
Ballymorefinn Hill Ireland 53°14N 6°22W 120 B1
Ballymote Ireland 54°5N 8°31W 166 B3
Ballymun Ireland 53°23N 6°16W 120 A2
Ballynahinch U.K. 54°24N 5°54W 166 B6
Ballyquintin Pt. U.K. 54°20N 5°30W 166 B6
Ballyshannon Ireland 54°30N 8°11W 166 B3
Balmaceda Chile 46°0S 71°50W 336 C2
Balmain Australia 33°51S 151°11E 139 B2
Balmaseda Spain 43°11N 3°12W 196 B1
Balmazújváros Hungary 47°37N 21°21E 182 C6
Balmertown Canada 51°4N 93°41W 297 C10
Balmoral Australia 37°15S 141°48E 282 D4
Balmorhea U.S.A. 30°59N 103°45W 314 F3
Balochistan = Baluchistan □
Pakistan 27°30N 65°0E 240 D2
Balod India 20°44N 81°13E 244 D5
Balombo Angola 12°21S 14°46E 265 E2
Balombo → Angola 11°57S 13°46E 265 E2
Balonne → Australia 28°47S 147°56E 281 D4
Balotra India 25°50N 72°14E 242 G5
Balpyq Bī Kazakhstan 44°52N 78°12E 217 D9
Balqash Kazakhstan 46°50N 74°50E 214 E8
Balqash Köli Kazakhstan 46°0N 74°50E 217 C8
Balrampur India 27°30N 82°20E 243 F10
Balranald Australia 34°38S 143°33E 282 C5
Balș Romania 44°22N 24°5E 183 F9
Balsapuerto Peru 5°48S 76°33W 330 B2
Balsas → Maranhão,
Brazil 7°15S 44°35W 332 C3
Balsas → Tocantins, Brazil 9°58S 47°52W 332 C2
Balsas → Michoacan,
Mexico 17°55N 102°10W 318 D4
Balsas del Norte Mexico 18°0N 99°46W 319 D5
Bålsta Sweden 59°35N 17°30E 162 E11
Balta Romania 44°54N 22°38E 182 F7
Balta Ukraine 48°2N 29°45E 183 B14
Baltakôl Kazakhstan 43°7N 67°46E 217 D7
Baltanás Spain 41°56N 4°15W 194 D6
Bălți Moldova 47°48N 27°58E 183 C12
Baltic Sea Europe 57°0N 19°0E 161 H18
Baltîm Egypt 31°35N 31°10E 256 H7
Baltimore Cork, Ireland 51°29N 9°22W 166 E2
Baltimore Md., U.S.A. 39°17N 76°36W 309 F15
Baltimore Ohio, U.S.A. 39°51N 82°36W 312 G2
Baltinglass Ireland 52°56N 6°43W 166 D5
Baltit Pakistan 36°15N 74°40E 243 A6
Baltiysk Russia 54°41N 19°58E 184 D6
Baltiyskiy = Paldiski
Estonia 59°23N 24°9E 188 C3
Baltra, I. Ecuador 0°26S 90°16W 330 a
Baltrum Germany 53°43N 7°24E 178 B3
Baluan I. Papua N. G. 2°33S 147°17E 286 B4
Baluchistan □ Pakistan 27°30N 65°0E 240 D2
Balud Phil. 12°2N 123°12E 232 E4
Baluhati India 22°39N 88°15E 124 B1
Baluran △ Indonesia 7°50S 114°23E 235 D4
Balurghat India 25°15N 88°44E 241 C2
Balvanera Argentina 34°37S 58°23W 117 B2
Balvi Latvia 57°8N 27°15E 188 D4
Balwyn Australia 37°48S 145°4E 128 A2
Balwyn North Australia 37°47S 145°4E 128 A2
Balya Turkey 39°44N 27°35E 205 B9
Balykchy Kyrgyzstan 42°26N 76°12E 217 D9
Balyqshy Kazakhstan 47°4N 51°52E 216 C4
Balzar Ecuador 2°2S 79°54W 328 D2
Bam Iran 29°7N 58°14E 247 D8
Bama Guangxi Zhuangzu,
China 24°8N 107°12E 228 E6
Bama Nigeria 11°33N 13°41E 263 C7
Bamaga Australia 10°50S 142°25E 280 A3
Bamaji L. Canada 51°9N 91°25W 298 B1
Bamako Mali 12°34N 7°55W 262 C3
Bamba
Dem. Rep. of the Congo 5°45S 18°23E 265 D3
Bamba Mali 17°5N 1°24W 262 B4
Bambamarca Peru 6°36S 78°32W 330 B2
Bambang Phil. 16°23N 121°6E 232 C3
Bambannan I. Phil. 5°37N 120°17E 233 J3
Bambao Comoros Is. 12°11S 44°31E 272 a
Bambara Maoundé Mali 13°26N 4°3W 262 B4
Bambari C.A.R. 5°40N 20°35E 264 A4
Bambaroo Australia 18°50S 146°10E 280 B4
Bambaya Guinea 10°55N 13°38W 262 D2
Bamberg Bayern, Germany 49°54N 10°54E 179 F6
Bamberg S.C., U.S.A. 33°18N 81°2W 316 B8
Bambesi Ethiopia 9°45N 34°40E 257 F3
Bambey Senegal 14°42N 16°28W 262 C1
Bambili
Dem. Rep. of the Congo 3°40N 26°0E 268 B2
Bambinga
Dem. Rep. of the Congo 3°43S 18°53E 264 C3
Bambio C.A.R. 3°55N 16°57E 264 B3
Bamboi Ghana 8°13N 2°1W 262 D4
Bamboo Avenue Jamaica 18°6N 77°47W 320 a
Bambous Mauritius 20°15S 57°24E 272 e
Bambouti C.A.R. 5°24N 27°12E 264 A5
Bambuí Brazil 20°1S 45°58W 333 F2
Bamburgh U.K. 55°37N 1°43W 168 B6
Bamenda Cameroon 5°57N 10°11E 263 D7
Bamfield Canada 48°45N 125°10W 296 D3
Bāmīān Afghan. 34°49N 67°49E 217 F7
Bāmīān □ Afghan. 35°0N 67°0E 240 B2
Bamiancheng China 43°15N 124°2E 227 C13
Bamingui C.A.R. 7°34N 20°11E 264 A4
Bamingui → C.A.R. 8°33N 19°5E 264 A3
Bamingui-Bangoran △
C.A.R. 8°30N 19°46E 264 A3
Bamkin Cameroon 6°3N 11°27E 263 D7
Bampan Phil. 15°40N 120°20E 232 D3
Bampūr Iran 27°15N 60°21E 247 E9
Bamu → Papua N. G. 8°1S 143°33E 286 E2
Ban Burkina Faso 14°5N 2°27W 262 C4
Ban Ao Tu Khun Thailand 8°9N 98°20E 237 a
Ban Ban Laos 19°31N 103°30E 236 C4
Ban Bang Hin Thailand 9°32N 98°35E 237 H2
Ban Bang Khu Thailand 7°57N 98°23E 237 a
Ban Bang Rong Thailand 8°3N 98°25E 237 a
Ban Bo Phut Thailand 9°33N 100°2E 237 b
Ban Chaweng Thailand 9°32N 100°3E 237 b
Ban Chiang Klang
Thailand 19°25N 100°55E 236 C3
Ban Chik Laos 17°15N 102°22E 236 D4
Ban Choho Thailand 15°2N 102°9E 236 E4
Ban Dan Lan Hoi Thailand 17°0N 99°35E 236 D2
Ban Don = Surat Thani
Thailand 9°6N 99°20E 237 H2
Ban Don Vietnam 12°53N 107°48E 236 F6
Ban Don, Ao → Thailand 9°20N 99°25E 237 H2
Ban Dong Thailand 19°30N 100°59E 236 C3
Ban Hong Thailand 18°18N 98°50E 236 C2
Ban Hua Thanon Thailand 9°26N 100°1E 237 b
Ban Kaeng Thailand 17°29N 100°7E 236 D3
Ban Kantang Thailand 7°25N 99°31E 237 J2
Ban Karon Thailand 7°51N 98°18E 237 a
Ban Kata Thailand 7°50N 98°18E 237 a
Ban Keun Laos 18°22N 102°35E 236 C4
Ban Khai Thailand 12°46N 101°18E 236 F3
Ban Kheun Laos 20°13N 101°7E 236 B3
Ban Khlong Khian Thailand 8°10N 98°26E 237 a
Ban Khlong Kua Thailand 6°57N 100°8E 237 J3
Ban Khuan Thailand 8°20N 98°25E 237 a
Ban Khuan Mao Thailand 7°50N 99°37E 237 J2
Ban Ko Yai Chim
Thailand 11°17N 99°26E 237 G2
Ban Kok Thailand 16°40N 103°40E 236 D4
Ban Laem Thailand 13°13N 99°59E 236 F2
Ban Lamai Thailand 9°28N 100°3E 237 b
Ban Lao Ngam Laos 15°28N 106°10E 236 E6
Ban Le Kathe Thailand 15°49N 98°53E 236 E2
Ban Lo Po Noi Thailand 8°1N 98°34E 237 a
Ban Mae Chedi Thailand 19°11N 99°31E 236 C2
Ban Mae Laeng Thailand 20°1N 99°17E 236 B2
Ban Mae Nam Thailand 9°34N 100°0E 237 b
Ban Mae Sariang
Thailand 18°10N 97°56E 236 C1
Ban Mê Thuôt = Buon Ma Thuot
Vietnam 12°40N 108°3E 236 F7
Ban Mi Thailand 15°3N 100°32E 236 E3
Ban Muong Mo Laos 19°4N 103°58E 236 C4
Ban Na Bo Thailand 9°19N 99°41E 237 b
Ban Na Mo Laos 17°7N 105°40E 236 D5
Ban Na San Thailand 8°53N 99°52E 237 H2
Ban Na Tong Laos 20°56N 101°47E 236 B3
Ban Nam Bac Laos 20°38N 102°20E 236 B4
Ban Nam Ma Laos 22°2N 101°37E 236 A3
Ban Ngang Laos 15°59N 106°11E 236 E6
Ban Nong Bok Laos 17°5N 104°48E 236 D5
Ban Nong Boua Laos 15°40N 106°33E 236 E6
Ban Nong Pling Thailand 15°40N 100°10E 236 E3
Ban Pak Chan Thailand 10°32N 98°51E 237 G2
Ban Patong Thailand 7°54N 98°18E 237 a
Ban Phai Thailand 16°4N 102°44E 236 D4
Ban Phak Chit Thailand 8°0N 98°24E 237 a
Ban Pong Thailand 13°50N 99°55E 236 F2
Ban Rawai Thailand 7°47N 98°20E 237 a
Ban Ron Phibun Thailand 8°9N 99°51E 237 H2
Ban Sakhu Thailand 8°4N 98°18E 237 a
Ban Sanam Chai Thailand 7°33N 100°25E 237 J3
Ban Sangkha Thailand 14°37N 103°52E 236 E4
Ban Tak Thailand 17°2N 99°4E 236 D2
Ban Tako Thailand 14°5N 102°40E 236 E4
Ban Tha Dua Thailand 17°59N 98°39E 236 D2
Ban Tha Li Thailand 17°37N 101°25E 236 D3
Ban Tha Nun Thailand 8°12N 98°18E 237 a
Ban Tha Rua Thailand 7°59N 98°22E 237 a
Ban Tha Yu Thailand 8°17N 98°22E 237 a
Ban Thahine Laos 14°12N 105°33E 236 E5
Ban Thong Krut Thailand 9°25N 99°57E 237 b
Ban Xien Kok Laos 20°54N 100°39E 236 B3
Ban Yen Nhan Vietnam 20°57N 106°2E 236 B6
Banā, W. → Yemen 13°3N 45°24E 248 D4
Banaba Kiribati 0°45S 169°50E 288 H8
Banalia
Dem. Rep. of the Congo 1°32N 25°5E 268 B2
Banam Cambodia 11°20N 105°17E 237 G5
Banamba Mali 13°29N 7°22W 262 C3
Banana Is. S. Leone 8°7N 13°15W 262 D2
Bananal, I. do Brazil 11°30S 50°30W 333 D1
Bananga India 6°57N 93°54E 245 L11
Bananier Guadeloupe 16°0N 61°36W 322 e
Banaras = Varanasi
India 25°22N 83°0E 243 G10
Banas → Gujarat, India 23°45N 71°25E 242 H4
Banas → Mad. P., India 24°15N 81°30E 243 G9
Bânâs, Ras Egypt 23°57N 35°59E 256 C4
Banatica Portugal 38°40N 9°11W 126 A1
Banaue Phil. 16°55N 121°4E 232 C3
Banaz Turkey 38°46N 29°46E 205 C11
Banaz → Turkey 38°12N 29°14E 205 C11
Banbridge U.K. 54°22N 6°16W 166 B5
Banbury U.K. 52°4N 1°20W 169 E6
Banc d'Arguin △
Mauritania 20°10N 16°20W 260 D1
Banchory U.K. 57°3N 2°29W 167 D6
Banco Ethiopia 6°12N 38°13E 257 F4
Banco do Brasil, Centro Cultural
Rio de J., Brazil 135 a2
Bancoran Phil. 7°45N 118°30E 233 H2
Bancroft = Chililabombwe
Zambia 12°18S 27°43E 269 E2
Bancroft Canada 45°3N 77°51W 312 A7
Band Romania 46°30N 24°25E 183 D9
Band Bonī Iran 25°30N 59°33E 247 E8
Band-e Torkestan Afghan. 35°30N 64°0E 240 B2
Band Qīr Iran 31°39N 48°53E 247 D6
Banda Cameroon 3°58N 14°32E 264 B2
Banda Mad. P., India 24°3N 78°57E 243 G8
Banda Maharashtra, India 15°49N 73°52E 245 G1
Banda Ut. P., India 25°30N 80°26E 243 G9
Banda, Kepulauan
Indonesia 4°37S 129°50E 231 E7
Banda Aceh Indonesia 5°35N 95°20E 234 A1
Banda Banda, Mt.
Australia 31°10S 152°28E 283 A10
Banda Elat Indonesia 5°40S 133°5E 231 F8
Banda Is. = Banda, Kepulauan
Indonesia 4°37S 129°50E 231 E7
Banda Kani
Dem. Rep. of the Congo 4°48S 13°52E 265 C2
Banda Sea Indonesia 6°0S 130°0E 231 F8
Bandai-Asahi △ Japan 37°38N 140°5E 220 F10
Bandai-San Japan 37°36N 140°4E 220 F10
Bandak Norway 59°23N 8°29E 164 E5
Bandama → Ivory C. 6°32N 4°30W 262 D3
Bandama Blanc →
Ivory C. 6°55N 5°30W 262 D4
Bandama Rouge →
Ivory C. 6°55N 5°30W 262 D4
Bandamadji Comoros Is. 11°47S 43°26E 272 a
Bandān Iran 31°23N 60°44E 247 D9
Bandanaira Indonesia 4°32S 129°54E 231 E7
Bandanwara India 26°9N 74°38E 242 F6
Bandar = Machilipatnam
India 16°12N 81°8E 245 F5
Bandar-e Abbās Iran 27°15N 56°15E 247 E8
Bandar-e Anzalī Iran 37°30N 49°30E 213 D13
Bandar-e Bushehr = Būshehr
Iran 28°55N 50°55E 247 D6
Bandar-e Chārak Iran 26°45N 54°20E 247 E7
Bandar-e Deylam Iran 30°5N 50°10E 247 D6
Bandar-e Emām Khomeynı
Iran 30°30N 49°5E 247 D6
Bandar-e Lengeh Iran 26°35N 54°58E 247 E7
Bandar-e Maqām Iran 26°56N 53°29E 247 E7
Bandar-e Ma'shur Iran 30°35N 49°10E 247 D6
Bandar-e Rīg Iran 29°29N 50°38E 247 D6
Bandar-e Torkeman Iran 37°0N 54°10E 247 B7
Bandar Lampung =
Tanjungkarang Telukbetung
Indonesia 5°20S 105°10E 234 D3
Bandar Maharani = Muar
Malaysia 2°3N 102°34E 237 L4
Bandar Penggaram = Batu Pahat
Malaysia 1°50N 102°56E 237 M4
Bandar Seri Begawan
Brunei 4°52N 115°0E 235 B4
Bandar Sri Aman = Sri Aman
Malaysia 1°15N 111°32E 235 B4
Bandawe Malawi 11°58S 34°5E 269 E3
Bande Spain 42°3N 7°58W 194 C3
Bandeira, Pico da Brazil 20°26S 41°47W 333 F3
Bandeirante Brazil 13°41S 50°48W 333 D1
Bandera Argentina 28°55S 62°20W 334 B3
Banderas, B. de Mexico 20°40N 105°25W 318 C3
Bandhavgarh India 23°40N 81°2E 243 H9
Bandhavgarh △ India 23°45N 81°10E 244 C5
Bandi → India 26°12N 75°47E 242 F6
Bandia → India 19°2N 80°28E 244 E5
Bandiagara Mali 14°12N 3°29W 262 C4
Bandikui India 27°3N 76°34E 242 F7
Bandipur △ India 11°45N 76°30E 245 J3
Bandırma Turkey 40°20N 28°0E 203 F11
Bandjarmasin = Banjarmasin
Indonesia 3°20S 114°35E 235 C4
Bandol France 43°8N 5°46E 175 E9
Bandon Ireland 51°44N 8°44W 166 E3
Bandon → Ireland 51°43N 8°37W 166 E3
Bandoua C.A.R. 4°39N 21°42E 264 B4
Bandra India 19°3N 72°49E 130 A1
Bandra Pt. India 19°2N 72°49E 130 A1
Bandraboua Mayotte 12°42S 45°8E 272 b
Bandrélé Mayotte 12°54S 45°11E 272 b
Bandula Mozam. 19°0S 33°7E 269 F3
Bandundu
Dem. Rep. of the Congo 3°15S 17°22E 264 C3
Bandundu □
Dem. Rep. of the Congo 3°30S 17°30E 264 C3
Bandung Indonesia 6°54S 107°36E 235 D3
Bané Burkina Faso 11°42N 0°15W 263 C4
Băneasa Romania 45°56N 27°55E 183 E12
Bāneh Iran 35°59N 45°53E 213 E11
Bañeres Spain 38°44N 0°38W 197 G4
Banes Cuba 21°0N 75°42W 320 B4
Banff Alta., Canada 51°10N 115°34W 296 C5
Banff Aberds., U.K. 57°40N 2°33W 167 D6
Banff △ Canada 51°30N 116°15W 296 C5
Banfora Burkina Faso 10°40N 4°40W 262 C4
Bang Fai → Laos 16°57N 104°45E 236 D5
Bang Hieng → Laos 16°10N 105°10E 236 D5
Bang Kapi Thailand 13°45N 100°38E 113 B2
Bang Krathum Thailand 16°34N 100°18E 236 D3
Bang Lamung Thailand 13°3N 100°56E 236 F3
Bang Mun Nak Thailand 16°2N 100°23E 236 D3
Bang Na Thailand 13°40N 100°36E 113 B2
Bang Pa In Thailand 14°14N 100°35E 236 E3
Bang Phlad Bangkok, Thailand 113 a1
Bang Rakam Thailand 16°45N 100°7E 236 D3
Bang Saphan Thailand 11°14N 99°28E 237 G2
Bang Thao Thailand 7°59N 98°18E 237 a
Banga Angola 8°43S 15°13E 265 D3
Banga
Dem. Rep. of the Congo 5°25S 20°28E 265 D4
Banga Aklan, Phil. 11°38N 122°20E 233 F4
Banga S. Cotabato, Phil. 6°21N 124°47E 233 H5
Bangaduni I. India 21°34N 88°52E 241 E2
Bangala Dam Zimbabwe 21°7S 31°25E 269 G3
Bangalore India 12°59N 77°40E 245 H3
Banganapalle India 15°19N 78°14E 245 G4
Banganga → India 27°6N 77°25E 242 F6
Bangangté Cameroon 5°8N 10°32E 263 D7
Bangaon India 23°0N 88°47E 243 H13
Bangar Phil. 16°54N 120°25E 232 C3
Bangassou C.A.R. 4°55N 23°7E 264 B4
Bangbae S. Korea 37°29N 126°59E 137 C1
Bangeta, Mt. Papua N. G. 6°21S 147°3E 286 D4
Banggai Indonesia 1°34S 123°30E 231 E6
Banggai, Kepulauan
Indonesia 1°40S 123°30E 231 E6
Banggai Arch. = Banggai,
Kepulauan Indonesia 1°40S 123°30E 231 E6
Banggi, Pulau Malaysia 7°17N 117°12E 235 A5
Banghāzī Libya 32°11N 20°3E 258 B4
Banghāzī □ Libya 32°7N 20°4E 258 B4
Bangil Indonesia 7°36S 112°50E 235 D4
Bangjang Sudan 11°23N 32°41E 257 E3
Bangka Sulawesi, Indonesia 1°50N 125°5E 231 D7
Bangka Sumatera, Indonesia 2°0S 105°50E 234 C3
Bangka, Selat Indonesia 2°30S 105°30E 234 C3
Bangka-Belitung □
Indonesia 2°30S 107°0E 234 C3
Bangkalan Indonesia 7°2S 112°46E 235 D4
Bangkhen Thailand 13°52N 100°36E 113 A2
Bangkinang Indonesia 0°18N 101°5E 234 B2
Bangko Indonesia 2°5S 102°9E 234 C2
Bangkok Thailand 13°45N 100°35E 113 B2
Bangkok Don Muang Int. ✕ (BKK)
Thailand 13°53N 100°36E 113 A2
Bangkok Noi Thailand 13°45N 100°29E 113 B1
Bangkok Yai Thailand 13°43N 100°29E 113 B1
Bangladesh ■ Asia 24°0N 90°0E 241 D3
Banglamphoo Bangkok, Thailand 113 b2
Bangli Indonesia 8°27S 115°21E 231 J18
Bangloo India 22°31N 88°14E 124 B1
Bangoi-Kouni Comoros Is. 11°22S 43°23E 272 a
Bangolo Ivory C. 7°1N 7°29W 262 D3
Bangong Co China 33°45N 78°43E 243 B8
Bangor Down, U.K. 54°40N 5°40W 166 B6
Bangor Gwynedd, U.K. 53°14N 4°8W 168 D3
Bangor Maine, U.S.A. 44°48N 68°46W 309 C19
Bangor Mich., U.S.A. 42°18N 86°7W 311 B10
Bangor Pa., U.S.A. 40°52N 75°13W 313 F9
Bangoran → C.A.R. 8°42N 19°6E 264 A3
Bangrak Thailand 13°43N 100°31E 113 B2
Bangsu Thailand 13°49N 100°31E 113 B2
Bangu Dem. Rep. of the Congo 0°3S 19°12E 264 C3
Bangued Phil. 17°40N 120°37E 232 C3
Bangui C.A.R. 4°23N 18°35E 264 B3
Bangui Phil. 18°32N 120°46E 232 B3
Banguru
Dem. Rep. of the Congo 0°30N 27°10E 268 B2
Bangweulu, L. Zambia 11°0S 30°0E 269 E3
Bangweulu Swamp
Zambia 11°20S 30°15E 269 E3
Banhine △ Mozam. 22°49S 32°55E 271 B5
Baní Dom. Rep. 18°16N 70°22W 321 C5
Bani Phil. 16°11N 119°52E 232 C2
Bani → Mali 14°30N 4°12W 262 C4
Bani, Jebel Morocco 29°16N 8°0W 260 C3
Bani Bangou Niger 15°3N 2°42E 263 B5
Banī Sa'd Iraq 33°34N 44°32E 213 F11
Bania C.A.R. 4°1N 16°7E 264 B3
Bania Ivory C. 9°4N 3°6W 262 D4
Baniara Papua N. G. 9°44S 149°54E 286 E5
Banihal Pass India 33°30N 75°12E 243 C6
Banikoara Benin 11°18N 2°26E 263 C5
Banīnah Libya 32°0N 20°12E 258 B4
Banissa Kenya 3°55N 40°19E 268 B4
Bāniyās Syria 35°10N 36°0E 250 C7
Banja Luka Bos.-H. 44°49N 17°11E 182 F2
Banjar India 31°38N 77°21E 242 D7
Banjar Indonesia 7°24S 108°30E 235 D3
Banjar → India 22°36N 80°22E 243 H9
Banjarmasin Indonesia 3°20S 114°35E 235 C4
Banjarnegara Indonesia 7°24S 109°42E 235 D3
Banjul Gambia 13°28N 16°40W 262 C1
Bank London, U.K. 125 b5
Bank of America San Francisco, U.S.A. 136 b2
Bank of China Tower Hong Kong, China 122 c1
Banka India 24°53N 86°55E 243 G12
Bankas Mali 14°4N 3°31W 262 C4
Bankeryd Sweden 57°53N 14°6E 163 G8
Banket Zimbabwe 17°27S 30°19E 269 F3
Bankilaré Niger 14°35N 0°44E 263 C5
Bankot India 17°58N 73°2E 244 F1
Banks U.S.A. 31°49N 85°51W 316 D4
Banks, C. Australia 34°0S 151°16E 139 C2
Banks I. = Moa, I.
Papua N. G. 10°10S 142°15E 286 F2
Banks I. B.C., Canada 53°20N 130°0W 296 C3
Banks I. N.W.T., Canada 73°15N 121°30W 294 B7
Banks Is. Vanuatu 13°50S 167°30E 287 C5
Banks L. U.S.A. 31°2N 83°6W 316 D6
Banks Pen. N.Z. 43°45S 173°15E 285 D8
Banks Str. Australia 40°40S 148°10E 281 G4
Banksmeadow Australia 33°57S 151°13E 139 B2
Bankumuna
Dem. Rep. of the Congo 4°28S 19°57E 265 C3
Bankura India 23°11N 87°18E 243 H12
Bankya Bulgaria 42°43N 23°8E 202 D7
Banmankhi India 25°53N 87°11E 243 G12
Banmauk Burma 24°24N 95°51E 241 C5
Bann → Armagh, U.K. 54°30N 6°31W 166 B5
Bann → L'derry., U.K. 55°8N 6°41W 166 A5
Bannaanka Saraar
Somali Rep. 9°25N 46°17E 267 C6
Bannalec France 47°57N 3°42W 172 E3
Bannang Sata Thailand 6°16N 101°16E 237 J3
Bannerton Australia 34°42S 142°47E 282 C5
Banning U.S.A. 33°56N 116°53W 307 M10
Banningville = Bandundu
Dem. Rep. of the Congo 3°15S 17°22E 264 C3
Banno Ethiopia 4°51N 37°24E 257 G4

Banno-saki Japan 26°33N 128°8E 288 a
Bannockburn Ont., Canada 44°39N 77°33W 312 B7
Bannockburn Stirling, U.K. 56°5N 3°55W 167 E5
Bannockburn Zimbabwe 20°17S 29°48E 269 G2
Bannu Pakistan 33°0N 70°18E 240 B3
Bano India 22°40N 84°55E 243 H11
Bañolas = Banyoles Spain 42°16N 2°44E 196 C7
Banon France 44°2N 5°38E 175 D9
Baños de la Encina Spain 38°10N 3°46W 195 G7
Baños de Molgas Spain 42°15N 7°40W 194 C3
Bánovce nad Bebravou Slovak Rep. 48°44N 18°16E 181 C11
Banovići Bos.-H. 44°25N 18°32E 182 F3
Bansalan Phil. 6°55N 125°13E 233 H5
Bansgaon India 26°33N 83°21E 243 F10
Banská Bystrica Slovak Rep. 48°46N 19°14E 181 C12
Banská Štiavnica Slovak Rep. 48°25N 18°55E 181 C11
Bansko Bulgaria 41°52N 23°28E 202 E7
Banskobystrický □ Slovak Rep. 48°20N 19°0E 181 C12
Banstala India 22°31N 88°24E 124 B2
Banswara India 23°32N 74°24E 242 H6
Bantaeng Indonesia 5°32S 119°56E 231 F5
Bantaji Nigeria 8°6N 10°5E 263 D7
Bantayan Phil. 11°10N 123°43E 233 F4
Bantayan I. Phil. 11°13N 123°44E 233 F4
Banten Indonesia 6°5S 106°8E 234 D3
Banten □ Indonesia 6°30S 106°0E 231 G11
Banton I. Phil. 12°56N 122°4E 232 E4
Bantra India 22°35N 88°18E 124 B1
Bantry Ireland 51°41N 9°27W 166 E2
Bantry B. Ireland 51°37N 9°44W 166 E2
Bantul Indonesia 7°55S 110°19E 235 D4
Bantva India 21°29N 70°12E 242 J4
Bantval India 12°55N 75°0E 245 H2
Banya Bulgaria 42°33N 24°50E 203 D8
Banyak, Kepulauan Indonesia 2°10N 97°10E 234 B1
Banyalbufar Spain 39°42N 2°31E 206 B3
Banyo Cameroon 6°52N 11°45E 263 D7
Banyoles Spain 42°16N 2°44E 196 C7
Banyuls-sur-Mer France 42°28N 3°8E 174 F7
Banyumas Indonesia 7°32S 109°18E 235 D3
Banyuwangi Indonesia 8°13S 114°21E 231 J17
Banz Papua N. G. 5°47S 144°37E 286 C4
Banza Dem. Rep. of the Congo 0°28N 20°10E 264 B4
Banzare Coast Antarctica 68°0S 125°0E 151 C9
Banzyville = Mobayi Dem. Rep. of the Congo 4°15N 21°8E 264 B4
Bao Ha Vietnam 22°11N 104°21E 228 F5
Bao Lac Vietnam 22°57N 105°40E 236 A5
Bao Loc Vietnam 11°32N 107°48E 237 G6
Bao'an = Shenzhen China 22°32N 114°5E 219 F10
Baocheng China 33°12N 106°56E 226 H4
Baode China 39°1N 111°5E 226 E6
Baodi China 39°38N 117°20E 227 E9
Baoding China 38°50N 115°28E 226 E8
Baoji China 34°20N 107°5E 226 G4
Baojing China 28°45N 109°41E 228 C7
Baokang China 31°54N 111°12E 229 B8
Baoro C.A.R. 5°40N 15°58E 264 A3
Baoshan Shanghai, China 31°24N 121°28E 138 A1
Baoshan Yunnan, China 25°10N 99°5E 228 E2
Baotou China 40°32N 110°2E 226 D6
Baotow = Baotou China 40°32N 110°2E 226 D6
Baoxing China 30°24N 102°50E 228 B4
Baoying China 33°17N 119°20E 227 H10
Baoyou = Ledong China 18°41N 109°5E 236 C7
Bap India 27°23N 72°18E 242 F5
Bapatla India 15°55N 80°30E 245 G5
Bapaume France 50°7N 2°50E 173 B9
Baqar, Bahr el → Egypt 31°7N 32°6E 251 G3
Bāqerābād Iran 33°2N 51°58E 247 C6
Ba'qūbah Iraq 33°45N 44°50E 213 F11
Baquedano Chile 23°20S 69°52W 334 A2
Bar Montenegro 42°8N 19°6E 202 D3
Bar Ukraine 49°4N 27°40E 177 D14
Bar Bigha India 25°21N 85°47E 243 G11
Bar Giyora Israel 31°45N 35°5E 123 B1
Bar Harbor U.S.A. 44°23N 68°13W 309 C19
Bar-le-Duc France 48°47N 5°10E 173 D12
Bar-sur-Aube France 48°14N 4°40E 173 D11
Bar-sur-Seine France 48°7N 4°20E 173 D11
Bara India 25°16N 81°43E 243 G9
Bara Romania 47°2N 27°3E 183 C12
Bara Sudan 13°42N 30°22E 266 B3
Bara Banki India 26°55N 81°12E 243 F9
Barabai Indonesia 2°32S 115°34E 235 C5
Baraboo U.S.A. 43°28N 89°45W 308 D9
Baracoa Cuba 20°20N 74°30W 321 B5
Baradā → Syria 33°33N 36°34E 250 E7
Baradero Argentina 33°52S 59°29W 334 C4
Baradine Australia 30°56S 149°4E 283 A8
Baraga U.S.A. 46°47N 88°30W 308 B9
Bărăganul Romania 44°49N 27°31E 183 F12
Baragoi Kenya 1°47N 36°47E 268 B4
Barah → India 27°42N 77°5E 242 F6
Barahanagar India 22°39N 88°22E 124 B2
Barahona Dom. Rep. 18°13N 71°7W 321 C5
Barahona Spain 41°17N 2°39W 196 D2
Barail Range India 25°15N 93°20E 241 C4
Barajas Spain 40°28N 3°34W 127 B2
Barajas, Madrid ✈ (MAD) Spain 40°26N 3°34W 127 B2
Barak → India 24°52N 92°30E 241 C4
Baraka Sudan 10°59N 27°59E 257 E2
Baraka → Sudan 18°13N 37°35E 256 D4
Barakaldo Spain 43°18N 2°59W 196 B2
Barakar → India 24°7N 86°14E 243 G12
Barakee △ Australia 31°37S 151°53E 283 A9
Barakot India 21°33N 84°59E 243 J11
Barakpur India 22°47N 88°21E 124 A2
Baralaba Australia 24°13S 149°50E 280 C4
Baralla Spain 42°53N 7°15W 194 C3
Baralzon L. Canada 60°0N 98°3W 297 B9
Baram → Malaysia 4°35N 113°58E 235 B4
Baramati India 18°11N 74°33E 244 E2
Baramba India 20°25N 85°23E 244 D7
Barameiya Sudan 18°32N 36°38E 256 D4
Baramula India 34°15N 74°20E 242 B3
Baran India 25°9N 76°40E 242 G7
Baran → Pakistan 25°13N 68°17E 242 G3
Barañain Spain 42°48N 1°40W 196 C3
Baranavichy Belarus 53°10N 26°0E 177 B14
Barani Burkina Faso 13°9N 3°51W 262 C4
Baranoa Colombia 10°48N 74°55W 328 A3
Baranof U.S.A. 57°5N 134°50W 296 B2
Baranof I. U.S.A. 57°0N 135°0W 303 H14
Baranów Sandomierski Poland 50°29N 21°30E 185 H8
Baranowicze = Baranavichy Belarus 53°10N 26°0E 177 B14
Baranya □ Hungary 46°0N 18°15E 182 E3
Barão de Cocais Brazil 19°56S 43°28W 333 E2
Barão de Grajaú Brazil 6°45S 43°1W 332 C3
Barão de Melgaço Mato Grosso, Brazil 16°14S 55°52W 331 D6
Barão de Melgaço Rondônia, Brazil 11°50S 60°45W 331 C5
Baraolt Romania 46°5N 25°34E 183 D10
Barapasi Indonesia 2°15S 137°5E 231 E9
Barapina = Panguna Papua N. G. 6°21S 155°25E 286 D8
Baras Phil. 13°40N 124°22E 232 E5
Barasat India 22°46N 88°31E 243 H13
Barat Daya, Kepulauan Indonesia 7°30S 128°0E 231 F7
Baratang I. India 12°13N 92°45E 245 H11
Barataria B. U.S.A. 29°20N 89°55W 315 G10
Barauda India 23°33N 75°15E 242 H6
Baraut India 29°13N 77°7E 242 E7
Baraya Colombia 3°10N 75°4W 328 C2
Barbacan = Roxas Phil. 10°20N 119°21E 233 F2
Barbacena Brazil 21°15S 43°56W 333 F3
Barbacoas Colombia 1°45N 78°0W 328 C2
Barbados ■ W. Indies 13°10N 59°30W 323 r
Barbalha Brazil 7°19S 39°17W 332 C4
Barban Croatia 45°5N 14°2E 199 C11
Barbària, C. de Spain 38°39N 1°24E 206 D1
Barbaros Turkey 40°54N 27°27E 203 F11
Barbas, C. W. Sahara 22°20N 16°42W 260 D1
Barbastro Spain 42°2N 0°5E 196 C5
Barbate Spain 36°13N 5°56W 195 J5
Barbaza Phil. 11°12N 122°2E 233 F4
Barber Neth. Ant. 12°17N 69°4W 322 g
Barber, L. U.S.A. 28°30N 81°19W 133 A3
Barberini, Palazzo Rome, Italy 136 b3
Barberino di Mugello Italy 44°0N 11°15E 199 E8
Barbers Pt. U.S.A. 21°18N 158°7W 302 K13
Barberton Mpumalanga, S. Africa 25°42S 31°2E 271 C5
Barberton Ohio, U.S.A. 41°1N 81°39W 312 E3
Barberville U.S.A. 29°11N 81°26W 317 F8
Barbezieux-St-Hilaire France 45°28N 0°9W 174 C3
Barbican London, U.K. 125 a4
Barbosa Colombia 5°57N 73°37W 328 B3
Barbourville U.S.A. 36°52N 83°53W 309 G12
Barbuda W. Indies 17°30N 61°40W 322 c
Bârca Romania 43°59N 23°36E 183 G8
Barcaldine Australia 23°43S 145°6E 280 C4
Barcarena Brazil 1°30S 48°40W 332 B2
Barcarena Lisboa, Portugal 38°43N 9°16W 126 A1
Barcarena, Rib. de → Portugal 38°41N 9°16W 126 A1
Barcarrota Spain 38°31N 6°51W 195 G4
Barce = Al Marj Libya 32°25N 20°30E 258 B4
Barcellona Pozzo di Gotto Italy 38°9N 15°13E 201 D8
Barcelona Spain 41°22N 2°10E 114 A2
Barcelona Venezuela 10°10N 64°40W 329 A5
Barcelona □ Spain 41°30N 2°0E 196 D7
Barcelona-Prat ✈ (BCN) Spain 41°18N 2°5E 114 B1
Barceloneta Puerto Rico 18°27N 66°32W 321 b
Barceloneta Barcelona, Spain 41°22N 2°11E 114 A2
Barcelonette France 44°23N 6°40E 175 D10
Barcelos Brazil 1°0S 63°0W 329 D5
Barcin Poland 52°52N 17°55E 185 F4
Barclayville Liberia 4°48N 8°10W 262 E3
Barcoo → Australia 25°30S 142°50E 280 D3
Barcroft, L. U.S.A. 38°52N 77°9W 143 B3
Barcs Hungary 45°58N 17°28E 182 E2
Barczewo Poland 53°50N 20°42E 184 E7
Bärdä Azerbaijan 40°25N 47°10E 191 K8
Barda del Medio Argentina 38°45S 68°11W 336 A3
Bardaï Chad 21°25N 17°0E 259 D3
Bardas Blancas Argentina 35°49S 69°45W 334 D2
Bardawîl, Sabkhet el Egypt 31°10N 33°15E 251 G4
Barddhaman India 23°14N 87°39E 243 H12
Bardejov Slovak Rep. 49°18N 21°15E 181 B14
Bardera Somali Rep. 2°20N 42°27E 267 D5
Barð Iceland 66°3N 19°8W 155 A7
Barðarbunga Iceland 64°38N 17°32W 155 C9
Barðastrandarsýsla □ Iceland 65°40N 23°0W 155 B3
Bardi Italy 44°38N 9°44E 198 D6
Bardīyah Libya 31°45N 25°5E 258 B5
Bardoli India 21°12N 73°5E 244 D1
Bardolino Italy 45°33N 10°43E 198 C7
Bardonécchia Italy 45°5N 6°42E 198 C3
Bardsey I. U.K. 52°45N 4°47W 168 E3
Bardstown U.S.A. 37°49N 85°28W 311 G11
Bareilly India 28°22N 79°27E 243 E8
Barela India 23°6N 80°3E 243 H9
Barellan Australia 34°16S 146°24E 283 C7
Barengapara India 25°14N 90°14E 243 G14
Barentin France 49°33N 0°58E 172 C7
Barenton France 48°38N 0°50W 172 D6
Barents Sea Arctic 73°0N 39°0E 150 B9
Barentsøya Svalbard 78°25N 21°20E 154 B13
Barentu Eritrea 15°2N 37°35E 257 D4
Barfleur France 49°40N 1°17W 172 C5
Barfleur, Pte. de France 49°42N 1°16W 172 C5
Barfurush = Bābol Iran 36°40N 52°50E 247 B7
Barga Italy 44°4N 10°29E 198 D7
Bargal Somali Rep. 11°25N 51°0E 267 B7
Bargara Australia 24°50S 152°25E 280 C5
Bargarh India 21°20N 83°37E 244 D6
Bargas Spain 39°56N 4°3W 194 F6
Bărgăului Bistriţa Romania 47°13N 24°46E 183 C9
Barge Italy 44°43N 7°20E 198 D4
Bargnop Sudan 9°32N 28°25E 257 F2
Bargo Australia 34°18S 150°35E 283 C9
Bargteheide Germany 53°44N 10°14E 178 B6
Barguzin Russia 53°37N 109°37E 215 D11
Barh India 25°29N 85°46E 243 G11
Barhaj India 26°18N 83°44E 243 F10
Barham Australia 35°36S 144°8E 282 C6
Barharwa India 24°52N 87°47E 243 G12
Barhi India 24°15N 85°25E 243 G11
Bari Dem. Rep. of the Congo 3°20N 19°25E 264 B3
Bari India 26°39N 77°39E 242 F7
Bari Italy 41°8N 16°51E 201 A9
Bari Doab Pakistan 30°20N 73°0E 242 D5
Bari Sadri India 24°28N 74°30E 242 G6
Bari Sardo Italy 39°50N 9°38E 200 C2
Barīdī, Ra's Si. Arabia 24°17N 37°31E 246 E3
Barīm Yemen 12°39N 43°25E 248 D3
Barima → Guyana 8°33N 60°25W 329 B5
Barinas Venezuela 8°36N 70°15W 328 B3
Barinas □ Venezuela 8°10N 69°50W 328 B4
Baring U.S.A. 40°15N 92°12W 310 D4
Baring, C. Canada 70°0N 117°30W 294 C8
Baringa Dem. Rep. of the Congo 0°45N 20°52E 264 B4
Baringo Kenya 0°38N 36°16E 266 D4
Baringo, L. Kenya 0°47N 36°16E 268 B4
Barinitas Venezuela 8°45N 70°25W 328 B3
Baripada India 21°57N 86°45E 244 D8
Bariri Brazil 22°4S 48°44W 333 F2
Bâris Egypt 24°42N 30°31E 256 C3
Barisal Bangla. 22°45N 90°20E 241 D3
Barisal □ Bangla. 22°45N 90°20E 241 D3
Barisan, Pegunungan Indonesia 3°30S 102°15E 230 E2
Barito → Indonesia 4°0S 114°50E 235 C4
Baritú △ Argentina 23°43S 64°40W 334 A3
Barjac France 44°20N 4°22E 175 D8
Barjols France 43°34N 6°2E 175 E10
Barjūj, Wadi → Libya 25°26N 12°12E 258 C2
Bark L. Canada 45°27N 77°51W 312 A7
Barka = Baraka → Sudan 18°13N 37°35E 256 D4
Barkā' Oman 23°40N 58°0E 249 B7
Barkakana India 23°37N 85°29E 243 H11
Barkald Norway 61°59N 10°53E 164 C7
Barkam China 31°51N 102°28E 228 B4
Barker U.S.A. 43°20N 78°33W 312 C6
Barking U.K. 51°32N 0°5E 125 A4
Barkingside U.K. 51°35N 0°4E 125 A4
Barkley, L. U.S.A. 37°1N 88°14W 315 C10
Barkley Sound Canada 48°50N 125°10W 296 D3
Barkly East S. Africa 30°58S 27°33E 270 D4
Barkly Homestead Australia 19°52S 135°50E 280 B2
Barkly Tableland Australia 17°50S 136°40E 280 B2
Barkly West S. Africa 28°5S 24°31E 270 C3
Barkol, Wadi → Sudan 17°40N 32°0E 256 D3
Barkol Kazak Zizhixian China 43°37N 93°2E 218 B4
Barla Dağı Turkey 38°5N 30°40E 205 C12
Bârlad Romania 46°15N 27°38E 183 D12
Bârlad → Romania 45°38N 27°32E 183 E12
Barlee, L. Australia 29°15S 119°30E 279 E2
Barlee, Mt. Australia 24°38S 128°13E 279 D4
Barletta Italy 41°19N 16°17E 201 A9
Barlinek Poland 53°0N 15°15E 185 F2
Barlovento Canary Is. 28°48N 17°48W 153 e1
Barlovento C. Verde Is. 17°0N 25°0W 153 j
Barlow L. Canada 62°0N 103°0W 297 A8
Barmedman Australia 34°9S 147°21E 283 C7
Barmer India 25°45N 71°20E 242 G4
Barmera Australia 34°15S 140°28E 282 C4
Barmouth U.K. 52°44N 4°4W 168 E3
Barmstedt Germany 53°47N 9°46E 178 B5
Barn, The St. Helena 15°55S 5°40W 153 h
Barna → India 25°21N 83°3E 243 G10
Barnagar India 23°7N 75°19E 242 H6
Barnala India 30°23N 75°33E 242 D6
Barnard → Australia 31°34S 151°25E 283 A9
Barnard Castle U.K. 54°33N 1°55W 168 C6
Barnato Australia 31°38S 145°0E 283 A6
Barnaul Russia 53°20N 83°40E 217 B10
Barnes N.S.W., Australia 36°2S 144°49E 282 D6
Barnes London, U.K. 51°28N 0°14W 125 B2
Barnesville Ga., U.S.A. 33°3N 84°9W 316 B5
Barnesville Minn., U.S.A. 46°43N 96°28W 308 B5
Barnet U.K. 51°39N 0°11W 125 A2
Barnet □ U.K. 51°38N 0°9W 169 F7
Barneveld Neths. 52°7N 5°36E 170 B5
Barneveld N.Y., U.S.A. 43°16N 75°14W 313 C9
Barneville-Cartevert France 49°23N 1°46W 172 C5
Barnhart U.S.A. 31°8N 101°10W 314 F4
Barnsley U.K. 53°34N 1°27W 168 D6
Barnstable U.S.A. 41°42N 70°18W 309 E18
Barnstaple U.K. 51°5N 4°4W 169 F3
Barnstaple Bay = Bideford Bay U.K. 51°5N 4°20W 169 F3
Barnum B. Palau 7°6N 134°15E 288 c
Barnwell U.S.A. 33°15N 81°23W 316 B8
Baro Nigeria 8°35N 6°18E 263 D6
Baro → Ethiopia 8°26N 33°13E 257 F3
Barobo Phil. 8°33N 126°7E 233 G6
Baroda = Vadodara India 22°20N 73°10E 242 H5
Baroda India 25°29N 76°35E 242 G7
Baroe S. Africa 33°13S 24°33E 270 D3
Baron Ra. Australia 23°30S 127°45E 278 D4
Barong China 31°3N 99°20E 228 B2
Barora Solomon Is. 7°30S 158°20E 287 L10
Barora Ite Solomon Is. 7°36S 158°24E 287 L10
Barotse = Western □ Zambia 15°0S 24°4E 265 F4
Barotseland Zambia 15°0S 24°0E 265 F4
Barouéli Mali 13°4N 6°50W 262 C3
Barpali India 21°11N 83°35E 244 D6
Barpathar India 26°17N 93°53E 241 B4
Barpeta India 26°20N 91°10E 241 B3
Barqin Libya 27°33N 13°34E 258 C2
Barques, Pt. Aux U.S.A. 44°4N 82°58W 312 B2
Barquísimeto Venezuela 10°4N 69°19W 328 A4
Barr, Ras el Egypt 31°32N 31°50E 256 H7
Barr Smith Range Australia 27°4S 120°20E 279 E3
Barra Brazil 11°5S 43°10W 332 D3
Barra U.K. 57°0N 7°29W 167 E1
Barra, Sd. of U.K. 57°4N 7°25W 167 D1
Barra Andai Pakistan 24°47N 66°59E 123 B2
Barra Bonita = Ibaiti Brazil 23°50S 50°10W 333 F1
Barra da Estiva Brazil 13°38S 41°19W 333 D3
Barra de Navidad Mexico 19°12N 104°41W 318 D4
Barra do Bugres Brazil 15°0S 57°11W 331 D6
Barra do Corda Brazil 5°30S 45°10W 332 C2
Barra do Dande Angola 8°28S 13°22E 265 D2
Barra do Mendes Brazil 11°43S 42°4W 333 D3
Barra do Piraí Brazil 22°30S 43°50W 333 F3
Barra Falsa, Pta. da Mozam. 22°58S 35°37E 271 B6
Barra Funda Brazil 23°31S 46°39W 137 B2
Barra Hd. U.K. 56°47N 7°40W 167 E1
Barra Mansa Brazil 22°35S 44°12W 333 F3
Barraba Australia 30°21S 150°35E 283 A9
Barracão do Barreto Brazil 8°48S 58°24W 331 B6
Barracas Argentina 34°39S 58°24W 117 B2
Barracas al Sur = Avellaneda Argentina 34°40S 58°22W 117 C2
Barrackpur = Barakpur India 22°47N 88°21E 124 A2
Barradale Australia 22°42S 114°58E 278 D1
Barrafranca Italy 37°22N 14°12E 201 E7
Barraigh = Barra U.K. 57°0N 7°29W 167 E1
Barranca Lima, Peru 10°45S 77°50W 330 C2
Barranca Loreto, Peru 4°50S 76°50W 328 D2
Barranca del Cobre ⌂ Mexico 27°18N 107°40W 318 B3
Barrancabermeja Colombia 7°0N 73°50W 328 B3
Barrancas Colombia 10°57N 72°50W 328 A3
Barrancas Venezuela 8°55N 62°5W 329 B5
Barranco Peru 12°9S 77°2W 120 B2
Barrancones Pt. Trin. & Tob. 10°31N 61°28W 323 t
Barrancos Portugal 38°10N 6°58W 195 G4
Barranqueras Argentina 27°30S 59°0W 334 B4
Barranquilla Colombia 11°0N 74°50W 328 A3
Barranquitas Puerto Rico 18°11N 66°19W 321 b
Barras Brazil 4°15S 42°18W 332 B3
Barras Colombia 1°45S 73°13W 328 D3
Barraute Canada 48°26N 77°38W 298 C4
Barre Mass., U.S.A. 42°25N 72°6W 313 D12
Barre Vt., U.S.A. 44°12N 72°30W 313 B12
Barre de l'Isle Ridge St. Lucia 13°55N 60°58W 323 m
Barreal Argentina 31°33S 69°28W 334 C2
Barrei Ethiopia 6°10N 42°49E 267 C5
Barreiras Brazil 12°8S 45°0W 333 D3
Barreirinha Brazil 2°47S 57°3W 329 D6
Barreirinhas Brazil 2°30S 42°50W 332 B3
Barreiro Portugal 38°39N 9°5W 126 B2
Barreiros Brazil 8°49S 35°12W 332 C4
Barrême France 43°57N 6°23E 175 E10
Barren I. India 12°16N 93°51E 245 H11
Barren Is. U.S.A. 58°55N 152°15W 303 G9
Barreto Brazil 22°50S 43°5W 135 B2
Barretos Brazil 20°30S 48°35W 333 F2
Barrhead Canada 54°10N 114°24W 296 C6
Barrie Canada 44°24N 79°40W 312 B5
Barrier, C. N.Z. 36°25S 175°32E 284 C4
Barrier Ra. N.S.W., Australia 31°0S 141°30E 282 A4
Barrier Ra. Otago, N.Z. 44°15S 169°32E 285 E4
Barrier Ra. W. Coast, N.Z. 44°30S 168°30E 285 E3
Barrier Reef Belize 17°9N 88°3W 319 D7
Barrière Canada 51°12N 120°7W 296 C4
Barrière-la-Croix Martinique 14°27N 60°51W 322 j
Barrigada Guam 13°28N 144°48E 302 d
Barrineau Park U.S.A. 30°42N 87°26W 317 E2
Barrington U.S.A. 41°44N 71°18W 313 E13
Barrington, I. = Santa Fé, I. Ecuador 0°49S 90°5W 330 a
Barrington L. Canada 56°55N 100°15W 297 B8
Barrington Tops Australia 32°6S 151°28E 283 B9
Barrington Tops △ Australia 32°4S 151°25E 283 B9
Barringun Australia 29°1S 145°41E 281 D4
Barrit-Luluno = Luba Phil. 17°19N 120°42E 232 C3
Barro do Garças Brazil 15°54S 52°16W 331 D7
Barron U.S.A. 45°24N 91°51W 308 C8
Barrouallie St. Vincent 13°14N 61°17W 323 n
Barrow U.S.A. 71°18N 156°47W 303 A8
Barrow → Ireland 52°25N 6°58W 166 D5
Barrow, Pt. U.S.A. 71°23N 156°29W 303 A8
Barrow Creek Australia 21°30S 133°55E 280 C1
Barrow I. Australia 20°45S 115°20E 278 D2
Barrow-in-Furness U.K. 54°7N 3°14W 168 C4
Barrow Pt. Australia 14°20S 144°40E 280 A3
Barrow Ra. Australia 26°0S 127°40E 279 E4
Barrow Str. Canada 74°20N 95°0W 150 B3
Barruecopardo Spain 41°4N 6°40W 194 D4
Barruelo de Santullán Spain 42°54N 4°17W 194 C6
Barry V. of Glam., U.K. 51°24N 3°16W 169 F4
Barry Ill., U.S.A. 39°42N 91°2W 310 E5
Barry's Bay Canada 45°29N 77°41W 312 A7
Barsalogho Burkina Faso 13°25N 1°3W 263 C4
Barsat Pakistan 36°10N 72°45E 243 A5
Barsham Syria 35°21N 40°33E 213 E9
Barshatas Kazakhstan 48°10N 78°39E 217 C9
Barsi India 18°10N 75°50E 244 E2
Barsinghausen Germany 52°18N 9°28E 178 C5
Barsoi India 25°48N 87°57E 241 C1
Barstow U.S.A. 34°54N 117°1W 307 L9
Bartala India 22°32N 88°15E 124 B1
Bartenstein = Bartoszyce Poland 54°15N 20°55E 184 D7
Bartfeld = Bardejov Slovak Rep. 49°18N 21°15E 181 B14
Barth Germany 54°22N 12°42E 178 A8
Barthélemy, Col Vietnam 19°26N 104°6E 236 C5
Bartica Guyana 6°25N 58°40W 329 B6
Bartin Turkey 41°38N 32°21E 212 B5
Bartle Frere Australia 17°27S 145°50E 280 B4
Bartlesville U.S.A. 36°45N 95°59W 314 C7
Bartlett Calif., U.S.A. 36°29N 118°2W 306 J8
Bartlett Tenn., U.S.A. 35°12N 89°52W 315 D10
Bartlett, L. Canada 63°5N 118°20W 296 A5
Bartolbaai Neth. Ant. 12°20N 69°2W 322 g
Bartolo = Betanzos Bolivia 19°34S 65°27W 331 D4
Bartolomeu Dias Mozam. 21°10S 35°8E 269 G4
Barton Phil. 10°24N 119°8E 233 F2
Barton Vt., U.S.A. 44°45N 72°11W 313 B12
Barton, L. U.S.A. 28°33N 81°18W 133 A3
Barton Park Australia 33°56S 151°9E 139 B1
Barton upon Humber U.K. 53°41N 0°25W 168 D7
Bartonville U.S.A. 40°39N 89°39W 310 D7
Bartoszyce Poland 54°15N 20°55E 184 D7
Bartow Fla., U.S.A. 27°54N 81°50W 317 H8
Bartow Ga., U.S.A. 32°53N 82°29W 316 C7
Bartyki Poland 52°10N 21°6E 122 C2
Barú, I. de Colombia 10°15N 75°35W 328 A2
Barú, Volcan Panama 8°55N 82°35W 320 E3
Barumba Dem. Rep. of the Congo 1°3N 23°37E 268 B1
Barumbu Dem. Rep. of the Congo 1°14N 23°31E 264 B4
Baruth Germany 52°4N 13°30E 178 C9
Baruunsuu Mongolia 43°43N 105°35E 226 C3
Barvikha Russia 55°44N 37°16E 129 B1
Barvinkove Ukraine 48°57N 37°0E 189 H9
Bärwalde = Barwice Poland 53°44N 16°21E 184 E3
Barwani India 22°2N 74°57E 242 H6
Barwice Poland 53°44N 16°21E 184 E3
Barwick U.S.A. 30°54N 83°44W 316 E6
Barycz → Poland 51°42N 16°15E 185 G3
Barysaw Belarus 54°17N 28°28E 177 A15
Barysh Russia 53°39N 47°8E 190 D8
Barzān Iraq 36°55N 44°3E 246 B5
Bârzava Romania 46°7N 21°59E 182 D6
Bas-Congo □ Dem. Rep. of the Congo 5°0S 15°0E 265 D2
Bas du Fort Guadeloupe 16°13N 61°30W 322 e
Bas-Kouilou Congo 4°28S 11°42E 265 C2
Bas-Rhin □ France 48°40N 7°30E 173 D14
Bašaid Serbia 45°38N 20°25E 182 E5
Bāsa'idū Iran 26°35N 55°20E 247 E7
Basal Pakistan 33°33N 72°13E 242 C5
Basankusa Dem. Rep. of the Congo 1°5N 19°50E 264 B3
Basarabeasca Moldova 46°21N 28°58E 183 D13
Basarabi Romania 44°10N 28°26E 183 F13
Basarabia = Bessarabiya Moldova 47°0N 28°10E 177 E15
Basauri Spain 43°13N 2°53W 196 B2
Basawa Afghan. 34°15N 70°50E 242 B4
Basco Phil. 20°27N 121°58E 232 A3
Bascuñán, C. Chile 28°52S 71°35W 334 B1
Basekpio Dem. Rep. of the Congo 4°43N 24°36E 264 B4
Basel Switz. 47°35N 7°35E 179 H3
Basel, Euroairport ✈ (BSL) Europe 47°36N 7°33E 173 E14
Basel-Landschaft □ Switz. 47°26N 7°45E 179 H3
Basento → Italy 40°20N 16°49E 201 B9
Basey Phil. 11°17N 125°4E 233 F5
Bashākerd, Kūhhā-ye Iran 26°42N 58°35E 247 E8
Bashanta = Gorodovikovsk Russia 46°8N 41°58E 191 G5
Bashaw Canada 52°35N 112°58W 296 C6
Bāshī Iran 28°41N 51°4E 247 D6
Bashi Channel Taiwan 21°25N 121°30E 225 E3
Bashkir Republic = Bashkortostan □ Russia 54°0N 57°0E 186 D10
Bashkortostan □ Russia 54°0N 57°0E 186 D10
Bashtanivka Ukraine 45°46N 29°29E 183 E14
Basibasy Madag. 22°10S 43°40E 272 C7
Basilaki I. Papua N. G. 10°35S 151°0E 286 F6
Basilan Phil. 6°35N 122°0E 233 H4
Basilan □ Phil. 6°33N 122°4E 233 H4
Basilan Str. Phil. 6°50N 122°0E 233 H4
Basildon U.K. 51°34N 0°28E 169 F8
Basile Eq. Guin. 3°42N 8°48E 263 E6
Basilé, Pico Eq. Guin. 3°36N 8°49E 263 E6
Basilicata □ Italy 40°30N 16°0E 201 B9
Basim = Washim India 20°3N 77°0E 244 D3
Basin U.S.A. 44°23N 108°2W 304 D9
Basinger U.S.A. 27°23N 81°2W 317 H8
Basingstoke U.K. 51°15N 1°5W 169 F6
Basirhat Bangla. 22°40N 88°54E 241 D2
Basīt, Ra's al Syria 35°51N 35°48E 250 C6
Baška Croatia 44°58N 14°45E 199 D11
Başkale Turkey 38°2N 43°59E 213 C10
Baskatong, Rés. Canada 46°46N 75°50W 298 C4
Basle = Basel Switz. 47°35N 7°35E 179 H3
Başmakçı Turkey 37°54N 30°1E 205 D12
Basmat India 19°15N 77°12E 244 E3
Basoda India 23°52N 77°54E 242 H7
Basoko Dem. Rep. of the Congo 1°16N 23°40E 264 B4
Basongo Dem. Rep. of the Congo 4°15S 20°20E 265 C4
Basora, Pta. Aruba 12°25N 69°51W 322 f
Basque, Pays France 43°15N 1°20W 174 E2
Basque Provinces = País Vasco □ Spain 42°50N 2°45W 196 C2
Basra = Al Başrah Iraq 30°30N 47°50E 246 D5
Bass, Îs. de French Polynesia 27°55S 143°26W 289 f
Bass Str. Australia 39°15S 146°30E 281 F4
Bassano Canada 50°48N 112°20W 296 C6
Bassano del Grappa Italy 45°46N 11°44E 199 C8
Bassar Togo 9°19N 0°57E 263 D5
Bassas da India Ind. Oc. 22°0S 39°0E 271 B6
Basse-Normandie □ France 48°45N 0°30W 172 D6
Basse-Pointe Martinique 14°52N 61°8W 322 j
Basse Santa-Su Gambia 13°13N 14°15W 262 C2
Basse-Terre Guadeloupe 16°0N 61°44W 322 e
Basse Terre Trin. & Tob. 10°7N 61°19W 323 t
Bassein Burma 16°45N 94°30E 241 G5
Bassein India 19°26N 72°48E 244 E1
Basses, Pte. des Guadeloupe 15°52N 61°17W 322 e
Basses-Alpes = Alpes-de-Haute-Provence □ France 44°8N 6°10E 175 D10
Basses-Pyrénées = Pyrénées-Atlantiques □ France 43°10N 0°50W 174 E3
Basseterre St. Kitts & Nevis 17°17N 62°43W 322 d
Bassett U.S.A. 42°35N 99°32W 308 D4
Bassi India 30°44N 76°21E 242 D7
Bassigny France 48°0N 5°30E 173 E12
Bassikounou Mauritania 15°55N 6°1W 262 B3
Bassila Benin 9°1N 1°46E 263 D5
Bassum Germany 52°50N 8°40E 178 C4
Båstad Sweden 56°25N 12°51E 163 H6
Bastak Iran 27°15N 54°25E 247 E7
Baştām Iran 36°29N 55°4E 247 B7
Bastar India 19°15N 81°40E 244 E5
Bastelica France 42°1N 9°3E 175 F13
Basti India 26°52N 82°55E 243 F10
Bastia France 42°40N 9°30E 175 F13
Bastille, Place de la Paris, France 134 c5
Bastogne Belgium 50°1N 5°43E 170 D5
Bastrop La., U.S.A. 32°47N 91°55W 314 E9
Bastrop Tex., U.S.A. 30°7N 97°19W 314 F6
Basud Phil. 14°4N 122°58E 232 D4
Basuo = Dongfang China 18°50N 108°33E 236 C7
Basus Egypt 30°7N 31°12E 117 A2
Basutoland = Lesotho ■ Africa 29°40S 28°0E 271 C4
Başyayla Turkey 36°45N 32°40E 250 B3
Bat Yam Israel 32°2N 34°44E 251 F5
Bata Eq. Guin. 1°57N 9°50E 264 B1
Bata Romania 46°1N 22°4E 182 D7
Bataan □ Phil. 14°40N 120°25E 232 D3
Bataan △ Phil. 14°45N 120°27E 232 D3
Batabanó Cuba 22°41N 82°18W 320 B3
Batabanó, G. de Cuba 22°30N 82°30W 320 B3
Batac Phil. 18°3N 120°34E 232 B3
Batagai Russia 67°38N 134°38E 215 C14
Batajnica Serbia 44°54N 20°17E 202 B4
Batak Bulgaria 41°57N 24°12E 203 E8
Batala India 31°48N 75°12E 242 D6
Batalha Portugal 39°40N 8°50W 194 F2
Batalpashinsk = Cherkessk Russia 44°15N 42°5E 191 H6
Batam Indonesia 1°5N 104°3E 234 B2
Batama Dem. Rep. of the Congo 0°58N 26°33E 268 B2
Batamay Russia 63°30N 129°15E 215 C13
Batan I. Albay, Phil. 13°15N 124°0E 232 E5
Batan I. Batanes, Phil. 20°26N 121°58E 232 A3
Batanagar India 22°31N 88°15E 124 B1
Batanes □ Phil. 20°40N 121°55E 232 A3
Batanes Is. Phil. 20°30N 122°0E 232 A3
Batang Sichuan, China 30°1N 99°0E 228 B2
Batang Indonesia 6°55S 109°45E 235 D3
Batanga Gabon 0°21S 9°18E 264 C1
Batangafo C.A.R. 7°25N 18°20E 264 A3
Batangas Phil. 13°35N 121°10E 232 E3
Batangas □ Phil. 13°40N 121°20E 232 E3
Batanghari Indonesia 1°36S 103°37E 234 C2
Batanta Indonesia 0°55S 130°40E 231 E8
Bataraza Phil. 8°40N 117°37E 233 G1
Batas I. Phil. 11°10N 119°36E 233 F2
Batatais Brazil 20°54S 47°37W 335 A6
Batavia = Jakarta Indonesia 6°9S 106°52E 122 A2
Batavia Ill., U.S.A. 41°51N 88°19W 311 C8
Batavia N.Y., U.S.A. 43°0N 78°11W 312 D6
Batavia Ohio, U.S.A. 39°5N 84°11W 311 E12
Bataysk Russia 47°3N 39°45E 189 J10
Batbakara = Amankeldi Kazakhstan 50°10N 65°10E 217 B7
Batchelor Australia 13°4S 131°1E 278 B5
Batdambang Cambodia 13°7N 103°12E 236 F4
Batéké, Plateau Congo 3°30S 15°45E 264 C3
Batemans B. Australia 35°40S 150°12E 283 C9
Batemans Bay Australia 35°44S 150°11E 283 C9
Bates Ra. Australia 27°27S 121°5E 279 E3
Batesburg-Leesville U.S.A. 33°54N 81°33W 316 B8
Batesville Ark., U.S.A. 35°46N 91°39W 314 D9
Batesville Ind., U.S.A. 39°18N 85°13W 311 E11
Batesville Miss., U.S.A. 34°19N 89°57W 315 D10
Batesville Tex., U.S.A. 28°58N 99°37W 314 G5
Bath Ont., Canada 44°11N 76°47W 313 B8
Bath St. Kitts & Nevis 17°8N 62°37W 322 d
Bath Bath & N.E. Somerset, U.K. 51°23N 2°22W 169 F5
Bath Maine, U.S.A. 43°55N 69°49W 309 D19
Bath N.Y., U.S.A. 42°20N 77°19W 312 D7
Bath & North East Somerset □ U.K. 51°21N 2°27W 169 F5
Bath Beach U.S.A. 40°36N 74°0W 132 C1
Bath I. Pakistan 24°49N 67°1E 123 B2
Batha □ Chad 14°0N 19°0E 259 F3
Batha → Chad 12°47N 17°34E 259 F3
Batheay Cambodia 11°59N 104°57E 237 G5
Bathsheba Barbados 13°13N 59°32W 323 r
Bathurst = Banjul Gambia 13°28N 16°40W 262 C1
Bathurst N.S.W., Australia 33°25S 149°31E 283 B8
Bathurst N.B., Canada 47°37N 65°43W 299 C6
Bathurst Eastern Cape, S. Africa 33°30S 26°50E 270 D4
Bathurst, C. Canada 70°34N 128°0W 294 B7
Bathurst B. Australia 14°16S 144°25E 280 A3
Bathurst Harb. Australia 43°15S 146°10E 281 G4
Bathurst I. N. Terr., Australia 11°30S 130°10E 278 B5
Bathurst I. Nunavut, Canada 76°0N 100°30W 295 B11
Bathurst Inlet Canada 66°50N 108°1W 294 C9
Bati Ethiopia 11°10N 40°0E 257 E5
Batie Burkina Faso 9°53N 2°53W 262 D4
Batiki Fiji 17°48S 179°10E 287 a2
Batir West Bank 31°43N 35°8E 123 B1
Batken Kyrgyzstan 40°3N 70°50E 217 D8
Batken □ Kyrgyzstan 39°50N 71°0E 217 E8
Batlow Australia 35°31S 148°9E 283 C8
Batman Turkey 37°55N 41°5E 213 D9
Baţn al Ghūl Jordan 29°36N 35°56E 251 J6
Batna Algeria 35°34N 6°15E 261 A6
Batna □ Algeria 35°30N 5°55E 261 A6
Batnfjordsøra Norway 62°53N 7°42E 164 B4
Bato Catanduanes, Phil. 13°36N 124°18E 232 E5
Bato Leyte, Phil. 10°13N 124°48E 233 F5
Bato Bato Phil. 5°6N 119°49E 233 J2
Batoala Gabon 0°48N 13°27E 264 B2
Batobato = San Isidro Phil. 6°50N 126°5E 233 H6
Batočina Serbia 44°7N 21°5E 202 B5
Batok, Bukit Singapore 1°21N 103°46E 138 A2
Batoka Zambia 16°45S 27°15E 269 F2
Baton Rouge U.S.A. 30°27N 91°11W 314 F9
Batong, Ko Thailand 6°32N 99°12E 237 J2
Bátonyterenye Hungary 47°59N 19°50E 182 C4
Batopilas Mexico 27°1N 107°44W 318 B3
Batouri Cameroon 4°30N 14°25E 264 B2
Batovany = Partizánske Slovak Rep. 48°38N 18°23E 181 C11
Båtsfjord Norway 70°38N 29°39E 160 A23
Battambang = Batdambang Cambodia 13°7N 103°12E 236 F4
Battersea U.K. 51°28N 0°9W 125 B3
Battery Park New York, U.S.A. 132 f1
Batti Malv India 8°50N 92°51E 245 K11
Batticaloa Sri Lanka 7°43N 81°45E 245 L5
Battipáglia Italy 40°37N 14°58E 201 B7
Battle U.K. 50°55N 0°30E 169 G8
Battle → Canada 52°43N 108°15W 297 C7
Battle Creek U.S.A. 42°19N 85°11W 311 B11
Battle Ground U.S.A. 45°47N 122°32W 306 E4
Battle Harbour Canada 52°16N 55°35W 299 B8
Battle Lake U.S.A. 46°17N 95°43W 308 B6
Battle Mountain U.S.A. 40°38N 116°56W 304 F5
Battlefields Zimbabwe 18°37S 29°47E 269 F2
Battleford Canada 52°45N 108°15W 297 C7
Battonya Hungary 46°16N 21°3E 182 D6
Batu Ethiopia 6°55N 39°45E 257 F4
Batu, Bukit Malaysia 2°16N 113°43E 235 B4
Batu, Kepulauan Indonesia 0°30S 98°25E 234 C1
Batu Bora, Bukit Malaysia 2°43N 114°43E 235 B4
Batu Caves Malaysia 3°15N 101°40E 237 L3
Batu Ferringhi Malaysia 5°28N 100°15E 237 c
Batu Gajah Malaysia 4°28N 101°3E 237 K3
Batu Is. = Batu, Kepulauan Indonesia 0°30S 98°25E 234 C1
Batu Pahat Malaysia 1°50N 102°56E 237 M4
Batu Puteh, Gunung Malaysia 4°15N 101°31E 234 B2
Batuata Indonesia 6°12S 122°42E 231 F6
Batugondang, Tanjung Indonesia 8°6S 114°29E 231 J17
Batukau, Gunung Indonesia 8°20S 115°5E 231 J18
Batulaki Phil. 5°34N 125°19E 233 J5
Batuli = San Isidro Phil. 6°50N 126°5E 233 H6
Batumi Georgia 41°39N 41°44E 191 K5
Batur Indonesia 8°15S 115°20E 231 J18
Batur, Danau Indonesia 8°15S 115°24E 231 J18
Batur, Gunung Indonesia 8°14S 115°23E 231 J18
Baturaja Indonesia 4°11S 104°15E 234 C2
Baturité Brazil 4°28S 38°45W 332 B4
Baturiti Indonesia 8°19S 115°11E 231 J18
Batusangkar Indonesia 0°27S 100°35E 234 C2
Batys Qazaqstan □ Kazakhstan 50°0N 50°0E 216 C3
Bau Malaysia 1°25N 110°9E 235 B4
Bauang Phil. 16°31N 120°20E 232 C3
Baubau Indonesia 5°25S 122°38E 231 F6
Baucau E. Timor 8°27S 126°27E 231 F7
Bauchi Nigeria 10°22N 9°48E 263 C6
Bauchi □ Nigeria 10°30N 10°0E 263 C7
Baud France 47°52N 3°1W 172 E3
Bauda India 20°50N 84°25E 244 D7
Baudette U.S.A. 48°43N 94°36W 308 A6
Bauer, C. Australia 32°44S 134°4E 281 E1
Bauerwitz = Baborów Poland 50°7N 18°1E 185 H5
Bauguen = Salcedo Phil. 11°9N 125°40E 233 F5
Bauhinia Australia 24°35S 149°18E 280 C4
Baukau = Baucau E. Timor 8°27S 126°27E 231 F7
Bauko Phil. 17°0N 120°52E 232 C3
Baulai → Bangla. 24°22N 91°1E 241 C3
Bauld, C. Canada 51°38N 55°26W 295 D14
Bauman Russia 55°45N 37°40E 129 B4
Baume-les-Dames France 47°22N 6°22E 173 E13
Baumgarten Austria 48°12N 16°17E 142 A1
Baunatal Germany 51°14N 9°24E 178 D5
Baunei Italy 40°2N 9°40E 200 B2
Baure Nigeria 12°52N 8°50E 263 C6
Baures Bolivia 13°35S 63°35W 331 C5
Bauru Brazil 22°10S 49°0W 335 A6
Baús Brazil 18°22S 52°47W 331 D7
Bausi India 24°48N 87°1E 243 G12
Bauska Latvia 56°24N 24°15E 184 B11
Bautino Kazakhstan 44°35N 50°14E 191 H10
Bautzen Germany 51°10N 14°26E 178 D10
Bauya S. Leone 8°12N 12°38W 262 D2
Bavānāt Iran 30°28N 53°27E 247 D7
Bavaništé Serbia 44°49N 20°55E 182 F5
Bavaria = Bayern □ Germany 48°50N 12°0E 179 G7
Båven Sweden 59°0N 16°56E 162 E10
Bavispe → Mexico 29°15N 109°11W 318 B3
Baw Baw △ Australia 37°50S 146°17E 283 D7
Bawdwin Burma 23°5N 97°20E 241 D6
Bawean Indonesia 5°46S 112°35E 235 D4
Bawku Ghana 11°3N 0°19W 263 C4
Bawlake Burma 19°11N 97°21E 241 F6
Bawolung China 28°50N 101°16E 228 C3
Baxley U.S.A. 31°47N 82°21W 316 D7
Baxoi China 30°1N 96°50E 228 B1

Baxter *Iowa, U.S.A.* 41°49N 93°9W **310** C3
Baxter *Minn., U.S.A.* 46°21N 94°17W **308** B6
Baxter Springs *U.S.A.* 37°2N 94°44W **308** G6
Baxter State □ *U.S.A.* 46°5N 68°57W **309** B19
Bay, L. *U.S.A.* 28°25N 81°34W **133** A2
Bay, L. de *Phil.* 14°20N 121°11E **232** D3
Bay City *Mich., U.S.A.* 43°36N 83°54W **309** D12
Bay City *Tex., U.S.A.* 28°59N 95°58W **314** G7
Bay Harbour Islands *U.S.A.* 25°53N 80°7W **128** A2
Bay Hill *U.S.A.* 28°28N 81°30W **133** B1
Bay Minette *U.S.A.* 30°53N 87°46W **315** F11
Bay of Plenty □ *N.Z.* 38°0S 177°0E **284** D5
Bay Ridge *U.S.A.* 40°37N 74°1W **132** C1
Bay Roberts *Canada* 47°36N 53°16W **299** C9
Bay St. Louis *U.S.A.* 30°19N 89°20W **315** F10
Bay Springs *U.S.A.* 31°59N 89°17W **315** F10
Bay View *N.Z.* 39°25S 176°50E **284** F5
Baya *Dem. Rep. of the Congo* 11°53S 27°25E **269** E2
Bayambang *Phil.* 15°49N 120°27E **232** D3
Bayamo *Cuba* 20°20N 76°40W **320** B4
Bayamón *Puerto Rico* 18°24N 66°9W **321** C6
Bayan Har Shan *China* 34°0N 98°0E **218** C4
Bayan Hot = Alxa Zuoqi *China* 38°50N 105°40E **226** E3
Bayan Lepas *Malaysia* 5°17N 100°16E **237** c
Bayan Obo *China* 41°52N 109°59E **226** D5
Bayan-Ovoo = Erdenetsogt *Mongolia* 42°55N 106°5E **226** C4
Bayan-Tumen = Choybalsan *Mongolia* 48°4N 114°30E **219** B6
Bayana *India* 26°55N 77°18E **242** F7
Bayanaūyl *Kazakhstan* 50°45N 75°45E **217** B9
Bayandalay *Mongolia* 43°30N 103°29E **226** C2
Bayanhongor *Mongolia* 46°8N 102°43E **218** B5
Bayard *N. Mex., U.S.A.* 32°46N 108°8W **305** K9
Bayard *Nebr., U.S.A.* 41°45N 103°20W **308** E2
Bayawan *Phil.* 9°46N 122°45E **233** G4
Baybay *Phil.* 10°40N 124°55E **233** F5
Bayburt *Turkey* 40°15N 40°20E **213** B9
Bayburt □ *Turkey* 40°35N 39°25E **213** B8
Baydhabo = Baidoa *Somali Rep.* 3°8N 43°30E **267** D5
Bayelsa □ *Nigeria* 4°30N 6°0E **263** E6
Bayerische Alpen *Germany* 47°35N 11°30E **179** H7
Bayerische Rhön ⌓ *Germany* 50°15N 10°5E **179** E6
Bayerischer Spessart ⌓ *Germany* 49°58N 10°15E **179** F6
Bayerischer Wald *Germany* 48°56N 12°50E **179** G8
Bayern □ *Germany* 48°50N 12°0E **179** G7
Bayeux *France* 49°17N 0°42W **172** C6
Bayfield *Ont., Canada* 43°34N 81°42W **312** C3
Bayfield *Wis., U.S.A.* 46°49N 90°49W **308** B8
Bayḥān al Qiṣāb *Yemen* 15°48N 45°44E **248** D4
Bayındır *Turkey* 38°13N 27°39E **205** C9
Bayit Va-Gan *Israel* 31°46N 35°11E **123** B2
Baykal, Oz. *Russia* 53°0N 108°0E **215** D11
Baykan *Turkey* 38°7N 41°44E **246** B4
Baymak *Russia* 52°36N 58°19E **186** D10
Baynes Mts. *Namibia* 17°15S 13°0E **270** A1
Bayombong *Phil.* 16°30N 121°10E **232** C3
Bayon *France* 48°30N 6°20E **173** D13
Bayona = Baiona *Spain* 42°6N 8°52W **194** C2
Bayonet Point *U.S.A.* 28°20N 82°41W **317** G7
Bayonne *Pyrénées-Atlantiques, France* 43°30N 1°28W **174** E2
Bayonne *N.J., U.S.A.* 40°40N 74°6W **132** B1
Bayou Boeuf *U.S.A.* 29°50N 90°10W **131** B1
Bayou Segnette State Park ⌓ *U.S.A.* 29°53N 90°10W **131** B2
Bayovar *Peru* 5°50S 81°0W **330** B1
Bayport *U.S.A.* 28°32N 82°39W **317** G7
Bayqongyr *Kazakhstan* 45°40N 63°20E **216** C6
Bayram-Ali = Baýramaly *Turkmenistan* 37°37N 62°10E **247** B9
Baýramaly *Turkmenistan* 37°37N 62°10E **247** B9
Bayramiç *Turkey* 39°48N 26°36E **205** B8
Bayrampaşa *Turkey* 41°1N 28°56E **122** B1
Bayreuth *Germany* 49°56N 11°35E **179** F7
Bayrischzell *Germany* 47°41N 12°0E **179** H8
Bayrūt *Lebanon* 33°53N 35°31E **250** E6
Bays, L. of *Canada* 45°15N 79°4W **312** A5
Bayshore *Calif., U.S.A.* 37°42N 122°24W **136** B2
Bayshore *Fla., U.S.A.* 26°43N 81°50W **317** J8
Baysville *Canada* 45°9N 79°7W **312** A5
Bayswater *London, U.K.* **125** b2
Bayt al Faqīh *Yemen* 14°31N 43°19E **248** D3
Bayt Lahm *West Bank* 31°43N 35°12E **123** B2
Baytik Shan *China* 45°15N 90°50E **217** C12
Baytown *U.S.A.* 29°43N 94°59W **314** G7
Bayugan *Phil.* 8°43N 125°42E **233** G5
Bayun *Indonesia* 8°11S 115°16E **231** J18
Bayview *U.S.A.* 37°44N 122°23W **136** B2
Bayville = Kirkwood *S. Africa* 33°22S 25°15E **270** D4
Bayy al Kabir, W. *Libya* 31°10N 15°53E **258** B3
Bayy al Khā'ib, Wādī → *Libya* 30°55N 15°29E **258** B3
Bazar *Niger* 13°52N 4°35E **263** C5
Baza *Spain* 37°30N 2°47W **195** H8
Bāzār *Iran* 35°40N 51°25E **141** A2
Bazar Dyuzi *Russia* 41°12N 47°50E **191** K8
Bazardüzü = Bazar Dyuzi *Russia* 41°12N 47°50E **191** K8
Bazargic = Dobrich *Bulgaria* 43°37N 27°49E **203** C11
Bazarny Karabulak *Russia* 52°20N 46°29E **190** D8
Bazarnyy Syzgan *Russia* 53°45N 46°40E **190** D8
Bazaruto, I. do *Mozam.* 21°40S 35°28E **271** B6
Bazaruto △ *Mozam.* 21°42S 35°26E **271** B6
Bazas *France* 44°27N 0°13W **174** D3
Bazhong *China* 31°52N 106°46E **228** B6
Bazhou *China* 39°8N 116°22E **226** E9
Bazin *Guadeloupe* 16°22N 61°26W **322** e
Bazmān, Kūh-e *Iran* 28°4N 60°1E **247** D9
Beach *U.S.A.* 46°58N 104°0W **308** B2
Beach City *U.S.A.* 40°39N 81°35W **312** F3
Beachport *Australia* 37°29S 140°0E **282** D3
Beachy Hd. *U.K.* 50°44N 0°15E **169** G8
Beacon *W. Austral., Australia* 30°26S 117°52E **279** F2
Beacon *N.Y., U.S.A.* 41°30N 73°58W **313** E11
Beacon Hill *Hong Kong, China* 22°21N 114°10E **122** A2
Beacon Hill *Boston, U.S.A.* **116** b1
Beaconsfield *Australia* 41°11S 146°48E **281** G4
Beagle, Canal *S. Amer.* 55°0S 68°30W **336** E3
Beagle Bay *Australia* 16°58S 122°40E **278** C3
Bealanana *Madag.* 14°33S 48°44E **272** A2
Beals Cr. → *U.S.A.* 32°10N 100°51W **314** E4
Beamsville = Lincoln *Canada* 43°12N 79°28W **312** C5
Bear → *Calif., U.S.A.* 38°56N 121°36W **306** G5
Bear → *Utah, U.S.A.* 41°30N 112°8W **300** B4
Béar, C. *France* 42°31N 3°8E **174** F7
Bear I. *Ireland* 51°38N 9°50W **166** E2
Bear L. *Man., Canada* 55°8N 96°0W **297** B9
Bear L. *Utah, U.S.A.* 41°59N 111°21W **304** F8
Beardmore *Canada* 49°36N 87°57W **298** C2
Beardmore Glacier *Antarctica* 84°30S 170°0E **151** E11
Beardstown *U.S.A.* 40°1N 90°26W **310** E6
Bearma → *India* 24°20N 79°51E **243** G8
Béarn *France* 43°20N 0°30W **174** E3
Bearpaw Mts. *U.S.A.* 48°12N 109°30W **304** B9
Bearskin Lake *Canada* 53°58N 91°2W **298** B1
Beas → *India* 31°10N 74°59E **242** D6
Beas de Segura *Spain* 38°15N 2°53W **195** G8
Beasain *Spain* 43°3N 2°11W **196** B2
Beata, C. *Dom. Rep.* 17°40N 71°30W **321** C5
Beata, I. *Dom. Rep.* 17°34N 71°31W **321** C5
Beata Ridge *W. Indies* 16°0N 72°30W **321** C5
Beato *Portugal* 38°44N 9°5W **126** A2
Beatrice *Nebr., U.S.A.* 40°16N 96°45W **308** E5
Beatrice *Zimbabwe* 18°15S 30°55E **269** F3
Beatrice, C. *Australia* 14°20S 136°55E **280** A2
Beatton → *Canada* 56°15N 120°45W **296** B4
Beatton River *Canada* 57°26N 121°20W **296** B4
Beatty *U.S.A.* 36°54N 116°46W **306** J10
Beau Bassin *Mauritius* 20°13S 57°27E **272** e
Beauaraba = Pittsworth *Australia* 27°41S 151°37E **281** D5
Beaucaire *France* 43°48N 4°39E **175** E8
Beauce, Plaine de la *France* 48°10N 1°45E **173** D8
Beauceville *Canada* 46°13N 70°46W **299** C5
Beauchêne, I. *Falk. Is.* 52°55S 59°15W **153** f
Beaudesert *Australia* 27°59S 153°0E **281** D5
Beaufort *Vic., Australia* 37°25S 143°25E **282** D5
Beaufort *Savoie, France* 45°44N 6°34E **175** C10
Beaufort *Malaysia* 5°30N 115°40E **235** A5
Beaufort *N.C., U.S.A.* 34°43N 76°40W **315** D16
Beaufort *S.C., U.S.A.* 32°26N 80°40W **316** C9
Beaufort Sea *Arctic* 72°0N 140°0W **292** B5
Beaufort West *S. Africa* 32°18S 22°36E **270** D3
Beaugency *France* 47°47N 1°38E **173** E8
Beauharnois *Canada* 45°20N 73°52W **313** A11
Beaujeu *France* 46°10N 4°35E **173** F11
Beaujolais *France* 46°0N 4°22E **173** F11
Beaulieu → *Canada* 62°3N 113°11W **296** A6
Beaulieu-sur-Dordogne *France* 44°58N 1°50E **174** D5
Beaulieu-sur-Mer *France* 43°42N 7°20E **175** E11
Beauly *U.K.* 57°30N 4°28W **167** D4
Beauly → *U.K.* 57°29N 4°27W **167** D4
Beaumaris *U.K.* 53°16N 4°6W **168** D3
Beaumont *Belgium* 50°15N 4°14E **170** D4
Beaumont *Dordogne, France* 44°45N 0°46E **174** D4
Beaumont *Dublin, Ireland* 53°23N 6°13W **120** A2
Beaumont *N.Z.* 45°50S 169°33E **285** F4
Beaumont *Tex., U.S.A.* 30°5N 94°6W **314** F7
Beaumont-de-Lomagne *France* 43°53N 1°0E **174** E5
Beaumont-le-Roger *France* 49°4N 0°47E **172** C7
Beaumont-sur-Sarthe *France* 48°13N 0°8E **172** D7
Beaumonte Heights *Canada* 43°45N 79°34W **141** A1
Beaune *France* 47°2N 4°50E **173** E11
Beaune-la-Rolande *France* 48°4N 2°25E **173** D9
Beauport *Guadeloupe* 16°25N 61°30W **322** e
Beaupré *Canada* 47°3N 70°54W **299** C5
Beaupréau *France* 47°12N 1°0W **172** E6
Beauraing *Belgium* 50°7N 4°57E **170** D4
Beaurepaire *France* 45°22N 5°1E **175** C9
Beausejour *Man., Canada* 50°5N 96°35W **297** C9
Beauséjour *Guadeloupe* 16°18N 61°48W **322** e
Beauséjour *Martinique* 14°44N 60°57W **322** j
Beauvais *France* 49°25N 2°8E **173** C9
Beauval *Canada* 55°9N 107°37W **297** B7
Beauvoir-sur-Mer *France* 46°55N 2°2W **172** F4
Beauvoir-sur-Niort *France* 46°12N 0°30W **174** B3
Beaux Arts, Musée des *Montréal, Canada* **130** c1
Beaver *Alaska, U.S.A.* 66°22N 147°24W **303** C11
Beaver *Okla., U.S.A.* 36°49N 100°31W **314** C4
Beaver *Pa., U.S.A.* 40°42N 80°19W **312** F4
Beaver *Utah, U.S.A.* 38°17N 112°38W **304** G7
Beaver → *B.C., Canada* 59°52N 124°20W **296** B4
Beaver → *Ont., Canada* 55°55N 87°48W **298** A2
Beaver → *Sask., Canada* 55°26N 107°45W **297** B7
Beaver → *Okla., U.S.A.* 36°35N 99°30W **314** C5
Beaver City *U.S.A.* 40°8N 99°50W **308** E4
Beaver Creek *Canada* 63°0N 141°0W **294** C5
Beaver Dam *U.S.A.* 43°28N 88°50W **308** D9
Beaver Falls *U.S.A.* 40°46N 80°20W **312** F4
Beaver Hill L. *Canada* 54°5N 94°50W **297** C10
Beaver I. *U.S.A.* 45°40N 85°33W **309** C11
Beavercreek *U.S.A.* 39°43N 84°11W **311** E12
Beaverhill L. *Canada* 53°27N 112°32W **296** C6
Beaverlodge *Canada* 55°11N 119°29W **296** B5
Beaverstone → *Canada* 54°59N 89°25W **298** B2
Beaverton *Ont., Canada* 44°26N 79°9W **312** B5
Beaverton *Oreg., U.S.A.* 45°29N 122°48W **306** E4
Beawar *India* 26°3N 74°18E **242** F6
Bebedouro *Brazil* 21°0S 48°25W **335** A6
Bebek *Turkey* 41°4N 29°2E **122** B2
Bebera, Tanjung *Indonesia* 8°44S 115°51E **231** K18
Beboa *Madag.* 17°22S 44°33E **272** B1
Beboto *Chad* 8°16N 16°55E **259** G3
Bebra *Germany* 50°58N 9°48E **178** E5
Becán *Mexico* 18°34N 89°31W **319** D7
Bécancour *Canada* 46°20N 72°26W **309** B17
Beccles *U.K.* 52°27N 1°35E **169** E9
Bečej *Serbia* 45°36N 20°3E **182** E5
Beceni *Romania* 45°23N 26°48E **183** E11
Becerreá *Spain* 42°51N 7°10W **194** C3
Béchar *Algeria* 31°38N 2°18W **261** B4
Béchar □ *Algeria* 30°15N 3°5E **261** B5
Becharof L. *U.S.A.* 57°56N 156°23W **303** H8
Becharof Nat. Wildlife Refuge ⌓ *U.S.A.* 58°0N 156°15W **303** H8
Běchovice *Czech Rep.* 50°4N 14°36E **135** B3
Bechuanaland = Botswana ■ *Africa* 22°0S 24°0E **270** B3
Bechyně *Czech Rep.* 49°17N 14°29E **180** B7
Beck L. *U.S.A.* 42°4N 87°52W **119** A1
Beckenham *U.K.* 51°24N 0°1W **125** B3
Bečkerek = Zrenjanin *Serbia* 45°22N 20°23E **182** E5
Beckley *U.S.A.* 37°47N 81°11W **309** G13
Beckton *U.K.* 51°30N 0°4E **125** A4
Beckum *Germany* 51°45N 8°3E **178** D4
Beclean *Romania* 47°11N 24°11E **183** C9
Becontree *U.K.* 51°33N 0°7E **125** A4
Bečov nad Teplou *Czech Rep.* 50°5N 12°49E **180** A5
Bečva → *Czech Rep.* 49°31N 17°20E **181** B10
Bédar *Spain* 37°11N 1°59W **197** H3
Bédarieux *France* 43°37N 3°10E **174** E7
Beddington Corner *U.K.* 51°23N 0°9W **125** B3
Beddouza, Ras *Morocco* 32°33N 9°9W **260** B3
Bedeau = Ras el Ma *Algeria* 34°26N 0°50W **261** B4
Bedele *Ethiopia* 8°31N 36°23E **257** F4
Bederkesa *Germany* 53°37N 8°50E **178** B4
Bederwanak *Somali Rep.* 9°34N 44°23E **267** C5
Bedesso *Ethiopia* 9°58N 40°52E **257** F5
Bedford *Qué., Canada* 45°7N 72°59W **313** A12
Bedford *Eastern Cape, S. Africa* 32°40S 26°10E **270** D4
Bedford *Beds., U.K.* 52°8N 0°28W **169** E7
Bedford *Ind., U.S.A.* 38°52N 86°29W **311** F10
Bedford *Iowa, U.S.A.* 40°40N 94°44W **310** D2
Bedford *Ky., U.S.A.* 38°36N 85°19W **311** F11
Bedford *Mass., U.S.A.* 42°27N 71°15W **116** A1
Bedford *Ohio, U.S.A.* 41°23N 81°32W **312** E3
Bedford *Pa., U.S.A.* 40°1N 78°30W **312** F6
Bedford *Va., U.S.A.* 37°20N 79°31W **309** G14
Bedford, C. *Australia* 15°14S 145°21E **280** B4
Bedford Park *Ill., U.S.A.* 41°46N 87°46W **119** C2
Bedford Park *N.Y., U.S.A.* 40°52N 73°52W **132** A2
Bedford Stuyvesant *U.S.A.* 40°41N 73°56W **132** B2
Bedford View *S. Africa* 26°10S 28°7E **123** B2
Bedfordshire □ *U.K.* 52°4N 0°28W **169** E7
Bedi *Chad* 11°6N 18°33E **259** F3
Będków *Poland* 51°36N 19°44E **185** G6
Bednja → *Croatia* 46°20N 16°52E **199** B13
Bednodemyanovsk *Russia* 53°55N 43°15E **190** D6
Bedok *Singapore* 1°19N 103°56E **138** B3
Bedok, Res. *Singapore* 1°20N 103°56E **138** A3
Bedónia *Italy* 44°30N 9°38E **198** D6
Bedourie *Australia* 24°30S 139°30E **280** C2
Bedum *Neths.* 53°18N 6°36E **170** A6
Będzin *Poland* 50°19N 19°7E **185** H6
Bee Ridge *U.S.A.* 27°17N 82°29W **317** H7
Beebe Plain *Canada* 45°1N 72°9W **313** A12
Beech Creek *U.S.A.* 41°5N 77°36W **312** E7
Beech Fork → *U.S.A.* 37°46N 85°41W **311** G11
Beech Grove *U.S.A.* 39°43N 86°5W **311** E10
Beecher *U.S.A.* 41°21N 87°38W **311** C9
Beechey Point *U.S.A.* 70°29N 149°9W **303** A10
Beechworth *Australia* 36°22S 146°43E **283** D7
Beechy *Canada* 50°53N 107°24W **297** C7
Beef I. *Br. Virgin Is.* 18°26N 64°30W **321** b
Beelitz *Germany* 52°14N 12°58E **178** C8
Beenleigh *Australia* 27°43S 153°10E **281** D5
Be'er Menuḥa *Israel* 30°19N 35°8E **246** D2
Be'er Sheva *Israel* 31°15N 34°48E **251** G5
Beersel *Belgium* 50°46N 4°18E **116** B1
Beersheba = Be'er Sheva *Israel* 31°15N 34°48E **251** G5
Beeskow *Germany* 52°10N 14°15E **178** C10
Beestekraal *S. Africa* 25°23S 27°38E **271** C4
Beeston *U.K.* 52°56N 1°14W **168** E6
Beetaloo *Australia* 17°15S 133°50E **280** B1
Beetzendorf *Germany* 52°42N 11°6E **178** C7
Beeville *U.S.A.* 28°24N 97°45W **314** G6
Befale *Dem. Rep. of the Congo* 0°25N 20°45E **264** B4
Befandriana *Mahajanga, Madag.* 15°16S 48°32E **272** B2
Befandriana *Toliara, Madag.* 21°55S 44°0E **272** C1
Befasy *Madag.* 20°33S 44°23E **272** C1
Befori *Dem. Rep. of the Congo* 0°8N 22°22E **264** B4
Befotaka *Antsiranana, Madag.* 13°15S 48°16E **272** A2
Befotaka *Fianarantsoa, Madag.* 23°49S 47°0E **272** C2
Bega *Australia* 36°41S 149°51E **283** D8
Bega, Canalul *Romania* 45°37N 20°46E **182** E5
Bégard *France* 48°38N 3°18W **172** D3
Beğendik *Turkey* 40°55N 26°34E **203** F10
Beggars Pt. *Antigua & B.* 17°10N 61°48W **322** b
Begndal *Norway* 60°49N 9°46E **164** D6
Begoro *Ghana* 6°23N 0°23W **263** D4
Begusarai *India* 25°24N 86°9E **243** G12
Behābād *Iran* 32°24N 59°47E **247** C8
Behala *India* 22°30N 88°18E **124** B1
Behara *Madag.* 24°55S 46°20E **272** C2
Behbehān *Iran* 30°30N 50°15E **247** D6
Beheloka *Madag.* 23°54S 43°40E **272** C1
Behm Canal *U.S.A.* 55°10N 131°0W **296** B2
Behshahr *Iran* 36°45N 53°35E **247** B7
Bei Hai *China* 39°54N 116°21E **114** B2
Bei Jiang → *China* 23°2N 112°58E **229** F9
Bei Shan *China* 41°30N 96°0E **218** B4
Bei'an *China* 48°10N 126°20E **219** B7
Beibei *China* 29°47N 106°22E **228** C6
Beicai *China* 31°11N 121°32E **138** B2
Beichuan *China* 31°55N 104°39E **228** B5
Beihai *China* 21°28N 109°6E **228** G7
Beihai Park *Beijing, China* **114** b2
Beijing *China* 39°53N 116°21E **114** B1
Beijing □ *China* 39°55N 116°20E **226** E9
Beijing Zoo *Beijing, China* **114** a1
Beilau = Piława *Poland* 51°57N 21°32E **185** G8
Beilen *Neths.* 52°52N 6°27E **170** B6
Beiliu *China* 22°41N 110°21E **229** F8
Beilngries *Germany* 49°2N 11°28E **179** F7
Beilpajah *Australia* 32°54S 143°52E **282** B5
Beilul *Eritrea* 13°2N 42°20E **257** E5
Béinamar *Chad* 8°40N 15°23E **259** G3
Beinn na Faoghla = Benbecula *U.K.* 57°26N 7°21W **167** D1
Beipan Jiang *China* 25°7N 106°1E **228** E5
Beipiao *China* 41°52N 120°32E **227** D11
Beira *Mozam.* 19°50S 34°52E **269** F3
Beira *Somali Rep.* 6°57N 47°19E **267** C6
Beirut = Bayrūt *Lebanon* 33°53N 35°31E **250** E6
Beiseker *Canada* 51°23N 113°32W **296** C6
Beit Duqu *West Bank* 31°51N 35°6E **123** A1
Beit Ghur at-Taht *West Bank* 31°54N 35°5E **123** A1
Beit Ghur el-Fawqa *West Bank* 31°53N 35°5E **123** A1
Beit Hanina *West Bank* 31°50N 35°12E **123** B2
Beit Ij'za *West Bank* 31°51N 35°9E **123** A1
Beit Iksa *West Bank* 31°49N 35°11E **123** B2
Beit I'nan *West Bank* 31°51N 35°7E **123** A1
Beit Jala *West Bank* 31°43N 35°11E **123** B2
Beit Lekhem = Bayt Lahm *West Bank* 31°43N 35°12E **123** B2
Beit Liqya *West Bank* 31°52N 35°4E **123** A1
Beit Nekofa *Israel* 31°49N 35°7E **123** B1
Beit Sahur *West Bank* 31°42N 35°13E **123** B2
Beit Sofafa *West Bank* 31°45N 35°12E **123** B2
Beit Surik *West Bank* 31°50N 35°9E **123** B1
Beit Ur al-Fawqa *West Bank* 31°53N 35°7E **123** A1
Beit Zayit *Israel* 31°47N 35°9E **123** B1
Beitaipingzhuan *China* 39°57N 116°20E **114** B1
Beitaolaizhao *China* 44°58N 125°58E **227** B13
Beitar Illit *West Bank* 31°42N 35°7E **123** B1
Beitbridge *Zimbabwe* 22°12S 30°0E **269** G3
Beitin *West Bank* 31°56N 35°14E **123** A2
Beitsun *China* 23°7N 113°12E **121** B2
Beitunya *West Bank* 31°53N 35°10E **123** A2
Beiuş *Romania* 46°40N 22°21E **182** D7
Beixing Jing Park *China* 31°14N 121°21E **138** B1
Beizhen = Binzhou *China* 37°20N 118°2E **227** F10
Beizhen *China* 41°38N 121°54E **227** D11
Beizhengzhen *China* 44°31N 123°30E **227** B12
Beja *Portugal* 38°2N 7°53W **195** G3
Béja *Tunisia* 36°43N 9°12E **261** A6
Beja □ *Portugal* 37°55N 7°55W **195** H3
Béja □ *Tunisia* 36°40N 9°29E **261** A6
Bejaïa *Algeria* 36°42N 5°2E **261** A5
Bejaïa □ *Algeria* 36°40N 4°55E **261** A5
Béjar *Spain* 40°23N 5°46W **194** E5
Bejestān *Iran* 34°30N 58°5E **247** C8
Bek-Budi = Qarshi *Uzbekistan* 38°53N 65°48E **217** E7
Bekaa Valley = Al Biqā *Lebanon* 34°10N 36°10E **250** D7
Bekasi *Indonesia* 6°14S 106°59E **234** D3
Békásmegyer *Hungary* 47°35N 19°3E **117** A2
Bekçiler *Turkey* 36°56N 29°44E **205** E11
Bekdash *Turkmenistan* 41°34N 52°32E **216** D4
Békés *Hungary* 46°47N 21°9E **182** D6
Békés □ *Hungary* 46°45N 21°0E **182** D6
Békéscsaba *Hungary* 46°40N 21°5E **182** D6
Bekilli *Turkey* 38°17N 29°27E **205** C11
Bekily *Madag.* 24°13S 45°19E **272** C2
Bekisopa *Madag.* 21°40S 45°54E **272** C2
Bekitro *Madag.* 24°33S 45°18E **272** C2
Bekkelaget *Norway* 59°53N 10°47E **133** A3
Bekkestua *Norway* 59°55N 10°35E **133** A2
Bekodoka *Madag.* 16°58S 45°7E **272** B2
Bekoji *Ethiopia* 7°40N 39°17E **257** F4
Bekok *Malaysia* 2°20N 103°7E **237** L4
Bekopaka *Madag.* 19°9S 44°48E **272** B1
Bekuli *Indonesia* 8°22S 114°13E **231** J17
Bekwai *Ghana* 6°30N 1°34W **263** D4
Bel Air *Mauritius* 20°15S 57°44E **272** e
Bel Air *Calif., U.S.A.* 34°4N 118°27W **126** B2
Bela *India* 25°50N 82°0E **243** G10
Bela *Pakistan* 26°12N 66°20E **242** F2
Bela Aliança = Rio do Sul *Brazil* 27°13S 49°37W **335** B6
Bela Bela *S. Africa* 24°51S 28°19E **271** B4
Bela Crkva *Serbia* 44°55N 21°27E **182** F6
Bela Palanka *Serbia* 43°13N 22°17E **202** C6
Bela Vista *Mato Grosso do Sul, Brazil* 22°12S 56°20W **334** A4
Bela Vista *São Paulo, Brazil* 23°33S 46°38W **137** B2
Bela Vista *Mozam.* 26°10S 32°44E **271** C5
Bélâbre *France* 46°34N 1°8E **174** B5
Belaga *Malaysia* 2°42N 113°47E **235** B4
Belalcázar *Spain* 38°35N 5°10W **195** G5
Belan → *India* 24°2N 81°45E **243** G9
Bélanger *Canada* 45°35N 73°42W **130** A1
Belanovica *Serbia* 44°15N 20°23E **202** B4
Belarus ■ *Europe* 53°30N 27°0E **177** B14
Belas *Angola* 8°55S 13°9E **265** D2
Belas *Lisboa, Portugal* 38°46N 9°17W **126** A1
Belas Artes, Museu Nacional de *Rio de J., Brazil* **135** b2
Belau = Palau ■ *Palau* 7°30N 134°30E **288** c
Belavenona *Madag.* 24°50S 47°4E **272** C2
Belawan *Indonesia* 3°33N 98°32E **234** B1
Belaya *Ethiopia* 11°25N 36°8E **257** E4
Belaya → *Russia* 54°40N 56°0E **186** C9
Belaya Glina *Russia* 46°5N 40°48E **191** G5
Belaya Kalitva *Russia* 48°13N 40°50E **191** F5
Belaya Tserkov = Bila Tserkva *Ukraine* 49°45N 30°10E **177** D16
Belayan → *Indonesia* 0°14S 116°36E **235** C5
Belceşti *Romania* 47°19N 27°7E **183** C12
Bełchatów *Poland* 51°21N 19°22E **185** G6
Belcher Chan. *Canada* 77°15N 95°0W **295** B10
Belcher Is. *Canada* 56°15N 78°45W **298** A3
Belchite *Spain* 41°18N 0°43W **196** D4
Belden *U.S.A.* 40°2N 121°17W **306** E5
Beldibi *Turkey* 36°25N 30°26E **250** B3
Belding *U.S.A.* 43°6N 85°14W **311** A11
Belebey *Russia* 54°7N 54°7E **186** D9
Beled Weyne = Belet Uen *Somali Rep.* 4°30N 45°5E **267** D6
Beleghata *India* 22°33N 88°22E **124** B2
Belém = Palmeirais *Brazil* 6°0S 43°0W **332** C3
Belém *Brazil* 1°20S 48°30W **332** B2
Belém *Lisboa, Portugal* 38°41N 9°12W **126** A1
Belém, Torre de *Portugal* 38°41N 9°12W **126** A1
Belém de São Francisco *Brazil* 8°46S 38°58W **332** C4
Belén *Argentina* 27°40S 67°5W **334** B2
Belén *Colombia* 1°26N 75°56W **328** C2
Belén *Paraguay* 23°30S 57°6W **334** A4
Belen *Turkey* 36°31N 36°10E **250** B7
Belen *N. Mex., U.S.A.* 34°40N 106°46W **305** J10
Belene *Bulgaria* 43°39N 25°10E **203** C9
Belênzinho *Brazil* 23°32S 46°34W **137** B2
Belep, Îs. *N. Cal.* 19°45S 163°40E **288** d
Bélesta *France* 42°55N 1°56E **174** F5
Belet Uen *Somali Rep.* 4°30N 45°5E **267** D6
Belev *Russia* 53°50N 36°5E **188** F9
Belevi *Turkey* 38°0N 27°28E **205** C9
Belfair *U.S.A.* 47°27N 122°50W **306** C4
Belfast *N.Z.* 43°27S 172°39E **285** D7
Belfast *Mpumalanga, S. Africa* 25°42S 30°2E **271** C5
Belfast *Antrim, U.K.* 54°37N 5°56W **166** B6
Belfast *Maine, U.S.A.* 44°26N 69°1W **309** C19
Belfast *N.Y., U.S.A.* 42°21N 78°7W **312** D6
Belfast L. *U.K.* 54°40N 5°50W **166** B6
Belfield *U.S.A.* 46°53N 103°12W **308** B2
Belfort *France* 47°38N 6°50E **173** E13
Belfort, Territoire de □ *France* 47°40N 6°55E **173** E13
Belfry *U.S.A.* 45°9N 109°1W **304** D9
Belgachiya *India* 22°36N 88°23E **124** B2
Belgard = Białogard *Poland* 54°2N 15°58E **184** D2
Belgaum *India* 15°55N 74°35E **245** G2
Belgharia *India* 22°39N 88°22E **124** B2
Belgian Congo = Congo, Dem. Rep. of the ■ *Africa* 3°0S 23°0E **265** C4
Belgioioso *Italy* 45°10N 9°19E **198** C6
Belgium ■ *Europe* 50°30N 5°0E **170** D4
Belgodère *France* 42°35N 9°1E **175** F13
Belgorod *Russia* 50°35N 36°35E **189** G9
Belgorod □ *Russia* 50°45N 36°45E **189** G9
Belgorod-Dnestrovskiy = Bilhorod-Dnistrovskyy *Ukraine* 46°11N 30°23E **189** J6
Belgrade = Beograd *Serbia* 44°50N 20°37E **202** B4
Belgrade *U.S.A.* 45°47N 111°11W **304** D8
Belgrano *Antarctica* 77°52S 34°37W **151** D1
Belgrano *B. Aires, Argentina* 34°33S 58°27W **117** B2
Belgravia *London, U.K.* **125** c3
Belgrove *N.Z.* 41°27S 172°59E **285** B7
Belhaven *U.S.A.* 35°33N 76°37W **315** D16
Beli Drim → *Europe* 42°6N 20°25E **202** D4
Beli Manastir *Croatia* 45°45N 18°36E **182** E3
Beli Timok → *Serbia* 43°53N 22°14E **202** C6
Bélice → *Italy* 37°35N 12°55E **200** E5
Belimbing *Indonesia* 8°24S 115°2E **231** J18
Belinga *Gabon* 1°10N 13°2E **264** B2
Belinskiy *Russia* 53°0N 43°25E **190** D6
Belinyu *Indonesia* 1°35S 105°50E **234** C3
Beliton Is. = Belitung *Indonesia* 3°10S 107°50E **235** C3
Belitung *Indonesia* 3°10S 107°50E **235** C3
Beliu *Romania* 46°30N 22°0E **182** D6
Belize *Angola* 4°39S 12°46E **265** C2
Belize ■ *Cent. Amer.* 17°0N 88°30W **319** D7
Belize City *Belize* 17°25N 88°10W **319** D7
Beljakovci *Macedonia* 42°6N 21°59E **202** D5
Beljanica *Serbia* 44°8N 21°43E **202** B5
Belkovskiy, Ostrov *Russia* 75°32N 135°44E **215** B14
Bell *Calif., U.S.A.* 33°58N 118°11W **126** C3
Bell *Fla., U.S.A.* 29°45N 82°52W **316** F7
Bell → *Canada* 49°48N 77°38W **298** C4
Bell Gardens *U.S.A.* 33°58N 118°9W **126** C4
Bell I. *Canada* 50°46N 55°35W **299** B8
Bell-Irving → *Canada* 56°12N 129°5W **296** B3
Bell Peninsula *Canada* 63°50N 82°0W **295** C11
Bell Tower *Beijing, China* **114** a2
Bell Ville *Argentina* 32°40S 62°40W **334** C3
Bella *Italy* 40°45N 15°32E **201** B8
Bella Bella *Canada* 52°10N 128°10W **296** C3
Bella Coola *Canada* 52°25N 126°40W **296** C3
Bella Flor *Bolivia* 11°9S 67°49W **330** C4
Bella Unión *Uruguay* 30°15S 57°40W **334** C4
Bella Vista *Corrientes, Argentina* 28°33S 59°0W **334** B4
Bella Vista *Tucuman, Argentina* 27°10S 65°25W **334** B2
Bellac *France* 46°7N 1°3E **174** B5
Bellágio *Italy* 45°59N 9°15E **198** C6
Bellaire *U.S.A.* 40°1N 80°45W **312** F4
Bellária *Italy* 44°9N 12°28E **199** D9
Bellary *India* 15°10N 76°56E **245** G3
Bellas Artes, Palacio de *Mexico City, Mexico* **128** b2
Bellata *Australia* 29°53S 149°46E **281** D4
Bellavista *Santiago, Chile* 33°31S 70°35W **137** C2
Bellavista *Galápagos Is., Ecuador* 0°41S 90°18W **330** a
Bellavista *Lima, Peru* 12°4S 77°8W **124** B2
Belle *U.S.A.* 38°17N 91°43W **310** F5
Belle → *Trin. & Tob.* 11°14N 60°37W **323** s
Belle Fille → *Dominica* 15°25N 61°16W **323** k
Belle Fourche *U.S.A.* 44°40N 103°51W **308** C2
Belle Fourche → *U.S.A.* 44°26N 102°18W **300** B6
Belle Glade *U.S.A.* 26°41N 80°40W **317** J9
Belle Harbor *U.S.A.* 40°34N 73°51W **132** C2
Belle-Île *France* 47°20N 3°10W **172** E3
Belle Isle *Nfld. & L., Canada* 51°57N 55°25W **299** B8
Belle Isle *Fla., U.S.A.* 28°27N 81°12W **317** G8
Belle Isle, Str. of *Canada* 51°30N 56°30W **299** B8
Belle Plaine *U.S.A.* 41°54N 92°17W **310** C4
Belle Rive *U.S.A.* 38°14N 88°45W **311** F8
Belle View *U.S.A.* 38°57N 77°14W **143** B2
Belle Vue Mauret *Mauritius* 20°7S 57°39E **272** e
Belle Yella *Liberia* 7°24N 10°0W **262** D3
Belledonne *France* 45°20N 6°10E **175** C10
Bellefontaine *Martinique* 14°39N 61°10W **322** j
Bellefontaine *Ohio, U.S.A.* 40°22N 83°46W **311** D13
Bellefonte *U.S.A.* 40°55N 77°47W **312** F7
Bellegarde *France* 47°59N 2°26E **173** E9
Bellegarde-en-Marche *France* 45°59N 2°18E **174** C6
Bellegarde-sur-Valserine *France* 46°4N 5°50E **173** F12
Bellême *France* 48°22N 0°34E **172** D7
Belleoram *Canada* 47°31N 55°25W **299** C8
Belleplaine *Barbados* 13°15N 59°34W **323** r
Belleview *U.S.A.* 29°4N 82°3W **317** F7
Belleville *Ont., Canada* 44°10N 77°23W **312** B7
Belleville *Rhône, France* 46°7N 4°45E **173** F11
Belleville *Ill., U.S.A.* 38°31N 89°59W **310** F7
Belleville *Kans., U.S.A.* 39°50N 97°38W **308** F5
Belleville *N.J., U.S.A.* 40°47N 74°9W **313** F10
Belleville *N.Y., U.S.A.* 43°46N 76°10W **313** C8
Belleville-sur-Vie *France* 46°46N 1°25W **172** F5
Bellevue *Alta., Canada* 49°35N 114°22W **296** D6
Bellevue *Idaho, U.S.A.* 43°28N 114°16W **304** E6
Bellevue *Iowa, U.S.A.* 42°16N 90°26W **310** B6
Bellevue *Mich., U.S.A.* 42°27N 85°1W **311** B11
Bellevue *Nebr., U.S.A.* 41°9N 95°54W **308** E6
Bellevue *Ohio, U.S.A.* 41°17N 82°51W **312** E2
Bellevue *Wash., U.S.A.* 47°37N 122°12W **306** C4
Bellevue, Col de *Réunion* 21°9S 55°36E **272** f
Bellevue, Schloss *Berlin, Germany* **115** a2
Belley *France* 45°46N 5°41E **175** C9
Bellin = Kangirsuk *Canada* 60°0N 70°0W **295** D13
Bellinge *Denmark* 55°20N 10°20E **163** J4
Bellingen *Australia* 30°25S 152°50E **283** A10
Bellingham *London, U.K.* 51°25N 0°1W **125** B3
Bellingham *Wash., U.S.A.* 48°46N 122°29W **306** B4
Bellingshausen Abyssal Plain *S. Ocean* 64°0S 90°0W **151** C16
Bellingshausen Sea *Antarctica* 66°0S 80°0W **151** C17
Bellinzona *Switz.* 46°11N 9°1E **179** J5
Bello *Colombia* 6°20N 75°33W **328** B2
Bellona *Solomon Is.* 11°17S 159°47E **287** N10
Bellows Falls *U.S.A.* 43°8N 72°27W **313** C12
Bellpat *Pakistan* 29°0N 68°5E **242** E3
Bellpuig d'Urgell *Spain* 41°37N 1°1E **196** D6
Bells *Dominica* 15°25N 61°21W **323** k
Belluno *Italy* 46°9N 12°13E **199** B9
Bellville *U.S.A.* 32°9N 81°59W **316** C8
Bellwood *Ill., U.S.A.* 41°52N 87°53W **119** B1
Bellwood *Pa., U.S.A.* 40°36N 78°20W **312** F6
Belmanier *Dominica* 15°21N 61°24W **323** k
Bélmez *Spain* 38°17N 5°17W **195** G5
Belmond *U.S.A.* 42°51N 93°37W **310** B3
Belmont *N.S.W., Australia* 33°4S 151°42E **283** B9
Belmont *Ont., Canada* 42°53N 81°5W **312** D3
Belmont *Grenada* 12°2N 61°45W **323** q
Belmont *Northern Cape, S. Africa* 29°28S 24°22E **270** C3
Belmont *London, U.K.* 51°36N 0°18W **125** A2
Belmont *Mass., U.S.A.* 42°23N 71°10W **116** A1
Belmont *N.Y., U.S.A.* 42°14N 78°2W **312** D6
Belmont, Mt. *N.Z.* 41°11S 174°53E **143** B2
Belmont Cragin *U.S.A.* 41°55N 87°45W **119** B2
Belmont Harbor *U.S.A.* 41°56N 87°38W **119** B3
Belmonte *Brazil* 16°0S 39°0W **333** E4
Belmonte *Portugal* 40°21N 7°20W **194** E3
Belmonte *Spain* 39°34N 2°43W **197** F2
Belmopan *Belize* 17°18N 88°30W **319** D7
Belmore *Australia* 33°55S 151°5E **139** B1
Belmullet *Ireland* 54°14N 9°58W **166** B2
Belo *Dem. Rep. of the Congo* 0°32S 23°13E **264** C4
Belo Horizonte *Brazil* 19°55S 43°56W **333** E3
Belo Jardim *Brazil* 8°20S 36°26W **332** C4
Belo Monte *Brazil* 3°5S 51°46W **329** D7
Belo-Tsiribihina *Madag.* 19°40S 44°30E **272** B1
Belogorsk = Bilohirsk *Ukraine* 45°3N 34°35E **189** K8
Belogorsk *Russia* 51°0N 128°20E **215** D13
Belogradchik *Bulgaria* 43°53N 22°42E **202** C6
Belogradets *Bulgaria* 43°22N 27°18E **203** C11
Beloha *Madag.* 25°10S 45°3E **272** D2
Beloit *Kans., U.S.A.* 39°28N 98°6W **308** F4
Beloit *Wis., U.S.A.* 42°31N 89°2W **310** B7
Belokalitvenskaya = Belaya Kalitva *Russia* 48°13N 40°50E **191** F5
Belokorovichi *Ukraine* 51°7N 28°2E **177** C15
Belomorsk *Russia* 64°35N 34°54E **186** B5
Belondo *Dem. Rep. of the Congo* 0°19S 19°31E **264** C3
Belonge *Dem. Rep. of the Congo* 2°7S 19°33E **264** C3
Belonia *India* 23°15N 91°30E **241** D3
Belopolye = Bilopillya *Ukraine* 51°14N 34°20E **189** G8
Belorechensk *Russia* 44°46N 39°52E **191** H4
Beloretsk *Russia* 53°58N 58°24E **186** D10
Belorussia = Belarus ■ *Europe* 53°30N 27°0E **177** B14
Beloshchelye = Naryan-Mar *Russia* 67°42N 53°12E **186** A9
Beloslav *Bulgaria* 43°11N 27°42E **203** C11
Belotsarsk = Kyzyl *Russia* 51°50N 94°30E **217** B12
Beloūsovka *Kazakhstan* 50°8N 82°31E **217** B10
Belovo *Bulgaria* 42°13N 24°1E **203** D8
Belovo *Russia* 54°30N 86°0E **217** B11
Belovodsk *Ukraine* 49°13N 39°36E **189** H10
Beloye, Ozero *Russia* 60°10N 37°35E **188** B9
Beloye More *Russia* 66°30N 38°0E **160** C25
Belozem *Bulgaria* 42°12N 25°2E **203** D9
Belozersk *Russia* 60°1N 37°45E **188** B9
Belpasso *Italy* 37°35N 14°58E **201** E7
Belpre *U.S.A.* 39°17N 81°34W **309** F13
Belrain *India* 28°23N 80°55E **243** E9
Belt *U.S.A.* 47°23N 110°55W **304** C8
Beltana *Australia* 30°48S 138°25E **282** A3
Belterra *Brazil* 2°45S 55°0W **329** D7
Beltinci *Slovenia* 46°37N 16°20E **199** B13
Belton *Mo., U.S.A.* 38°49N 94°32W **310** F2
Belton *Tex., U.S.A.* 31°3N 97°28W **314** F6
Belton L. *U.S.A.* 31°6N 97°28W **314** F6
Beltsy = Bălţi *Moldova* 47°48N 27°58E **183** C12
Belturbet *Ireland* 54°6N 7°26W **166** B4
Belukha *Russia* 49°50N 86°50E **217** C11
Belur *India* 22°37N 88°21E **124** B2
Beluran *Malaysia* 5°48N 117°35E **235** A5
Beluša *Slovak Rep.* 49°5N 18°17E **181** B11
Belušić *Serbia* 43°50N 21°10E **202** C5
Belvedere *St. Vincent* 13°8N 61°11W **323** n
Belvedere *London, U.K.* 51°29N 0°9E **125** B4
Belvedere *Calif., U.S.A.* 37°52N 122°27W **136** A2
Belvedere *Georgia, U.S.A.* 33°45N 84°16W **113** B3
Belvedere Marittimo *Italy* 39°37N 15°52E **201** C8
Belvès *France* 44°46N 1°0E **174** D5
Belvidere *Ill., U.S.A.* 42°15N 88°50W **311** B8
Belvidere *N.J., U.S.A.* 40°50N 75°5W **313** F9
Belvis de la Jara *Spain* 39°45N 4°57W **194** F6
Bely Bychek = Chagoda *Russia* 59°10N 35°15E **188** C8
Belyando → *Australia* 21°38S 146°50E **280** C4
Belyayevo Bogorodskoye *Russia* 55°39N 37°31E **129** C3
Belyy *Russia* 55°49N 33°3E **188** E7
Belyy, Ostrov *Russia* 73°30N 71°0E **214** B8
Belyy Yar *Russia* 58°26N 84°39E **214** D9
Belyye Vody = Aqsū *Kazakhstan* 42°25N 69°50E **217** D7
Belz *Ukraine* 50°23N 24°1E **185** H11
Bełżec *Poland* 50°23N 23°26E **185** H10
Belzig *Germany* 52°8N 12°35E **178** C8
Belzoni *U.S.A.* 33°11N 90°29W **315** E9
Bełżyce *Poland* 51°11N 22°17E **185** G9
Bemaraha, Lembalemban' i *Madag.* 18°40S 44°45E **272** B1
Bemarivo *Madag.* 21°45S 44°45E **272** C1
Bemarivo → *Antsiranana, Madag.* 14°9S 50°9E **272** A3
Bemarivo → *Mahajanga, Madag.* 15°27S 47°40E **272** B2
Bemavo *Madag.* 21°33S 45°25E **272** C2
Bembe *Angola* 7°3S 14°25E **265** D2
Bembèrèke *Benin* 10°11N 2°43E **263** C5
Bembesi *Zimbabwe* 20°0S 28°58E **269** G2
Bembesi → *Zimbabwe* 18°57S 27°47E **269** F2
Bembézar → *Spain* 37°45N 5°13W **195** H5
Bembibre *Spain* 42°37N 6°25W **194** C4
Bemboka △ *Australia* 36°35S 149°41E **283** D8
Bement *U.S.A.* 39°55N 88°34W **311** E8
Bemetara *India* 21°42N 81°32E **243** J9
Bemidji *U.S.A.* 47°28N 94°53W **308** B6
Bemolanga *Madag.* 17°44S 45°6E **272** B2
Bemowo *Poland* 52°15N 20°53E **142** B1
Ben *Iran* 32°32N 50°45E **247** C6
Ben Boyd △ *Australia* 37°0S 149°55E **283** D8
Ben Cruachan *U.K.* 56°26N 5°8W **167** E3
Ben Dearg *U.K.* 57°47N 4°56W **167** D4
Ben En △ *Vietnam* 19°37N 105°30E **236** C5
Ben Gardane *Tunisia* 33°11N 11°11E **258** B2
Ben Halls Gap △ *Australia* 31°37S 151°1E **283** A9
Ben Hope *U.K.* 58°25N 4°36W **167** C4
Ben Lawers *U.K.* 56°32N 4°14W **167** E4
Ben Lomond *N.S.W., Australia* 30°1S 151°43E **281** E5
Ben Lomond *Tas., Australia* 41°38S 147°42E **281** G4
Ben Lomond *Stirling, U.K.* 56°11N 4°38W **167** E4
Ben Lomond △ *Australia* 41°33S 147°39E **281** G4
Ben Luc *Vietnam* 10°39N 106°29E **237** G6
Ben Macdhui *U.K.* 57°4N 3°40W **167** D5
Ben Mhor *U.K.* 57°15N 7°18W **167** D1
Ben More *Argyll & Bute, U.K.* 56°26N 6°1W **167** E2
Ben More *Stirling, U.K.* 56°23N 4°32W **167** E4
Ben More Assynt *U.K.* 58°8N 4°52W **167** C4
Ben Nevis *U.K.* 56°48N 5°1W **167** E3
Ben Ohau Ra. *N.Z.* 44°1S 170°4E **285** E5
Ben Quang *Vietnam* 17°3N 106°55E **236** D6
Ben Slimane *Morocco* 33°38N 7°7W **260** B3
Ben Slimane □ *Morocco* 33°30N 7°10W **260** B3
Ben Vorlich *U.K.* 56°21N 4°14W **167** E4
Ben Wyvis *U.K.* 57°40N 4°35W **167** D4
Bena *Nigeria* 11°20N 5°50E **263** C6
Bena-Dibele *Dem. Rep. of the Congo* 4°4S 22°50E **265** C4
Bena-Leka *Dem. Rep. of the Congo* 5°8S 22°10E **265** D4
Bena-Tshadi *Dem. Rep. of the Congo* 4°40S 22°49E **265** C4
Benadir *Somali Rep.* 1°30N 44°30E **267** D5
Benagerie *Australia* 31°25S 140°22E **282** A4
Benahmed *Morocco* 33°4N 7°9W **260** B3
Benaki Museum *Athens, Greece* **112** b3
Benalla *Australia* 36°30S 146°0E **283** D7
Benalmádena *Spain* 36°36N 4°34W **195** J6
Benambra, Mt. *Australia* 36°31S 147°34E **283** D7
Benanee *Australia* 34°31S 142°52E **282** C5
Benares = Varanasi *India* 25°22N 83°0E **243** G10
Bénat, C. *France* 43°5N 6°22E **175** E10
Benavente *Portugal* 38°59N 8°49W **195** G2
Benavente *Spain* 42°2N 5°43W **194** C5
Benavides *U.S.A.* 27°36N 98°25W **314** H5
Benavides de Órbigo *Spain* 42°30N 5°54W **194** C5
Benbecula *U.K.* 57°26N 7°21W **167** D1
Benbonyathe Hill *Australia* 30°25S 139°11E **282** A3
Bend *U.S.A.* 44°4N 121°19W **304** D3

Bendale Canada 43°45N 79°13W 141 A3
Bendela
Dem. Rep. of the Congo 3°18S 17°36E 264 C3
Bendemeer Australia 30°53S 151°8E 283 A9
Bender Beila Somali Rep. 9°30N 50°48E 267 C7
Bender Merchagno
Somali Rep. 11°41N 50°34E 267 B7
Bendery = Tighina
Moldova 46°50N 29°30E 183 D14
Bendigo Australia 36°40S 144°15E 282 D6
Bendin = Będzin Poland 50°19N 19°7E 185 H6
Bendorf Germany 50°25N 7°35E 178 E3
Bendsburg = Będzin
Poland 50°19N 19°7E 185 H6
Benë Beraq Israel 32°6N 34°51E 251 F5
Beneditinos Brazil 5°27S 42°22W 332 C3
Benedito Leite Brazil 7°13S 44°34W 332 C3
Benefica Brazil 22°52S 43°14W 135 B1
Bénéna Mali 13°9N 4°17W 262 C4
Benenitra Madag. 23°27S 45°5E 272 C2
Beneŝov Czech Rep. 49°46N 14°41E 180 B7
Benevento Italy 41°8N 14°45E 201 A7
Benfeld France 48°22N 7°34E 173 D14
Benfica Portugal 38°45N 9°11W 126 A1
Benga Mozam. 16°11S 33°40E 269 F3
Bengal = West Bengal □
India 23°0N 88°0E 243 H13
Bengal, Bay of Ind. Oc. 15°0N 90°0E 239 F14
Bengalūru = Bangalore
India 12°59N 77°40E 245 H3
Bengbis Cameroon 3°27N 12°36E 263 E7
Bengbu China 32°58N 117°20E 227 H9
Benghazi = Banghāzī
Libya 32°11N 20°3E 258 B4
Benghisa Point Malta 35°49N 14°33E 206 F8
Bengkalis Indonesia 1°30N 102°10E 234 B2
Bengkulu Indonesia 3°50S 102°12E 234 C2
Bengkulu □ Indonesia 3°48S 102°16E 234 C2
Bengo Dem. Rep. of the Congo 2°11S 19°5E 264 C3
Bengo □ Angola 9°0S 13°10E 265 D2
Bengough Canada 49°25N 105°10W 297 D7
Bengtsfors Sweden 59°2N 12°14E 162 E6
Benguela Angola 12°37S 13°25E 265 E2
Benguela □ Angola 13°0S 13°30E 265 E2
Benguerir Morocco 32°16N 7°56W 260 B3
Benguérua, I. Mozam. 21°58S 35°28E 271 B6
Benguet □ Phil. 16°30N 120°40E 232 C3
Benha Egypt 30°26N 31°8E 256 H7
Benham Seamount
Pac. Oc. 15°40N 124°30E 232 D5
Beni Dem. Rep. of the Congo 0°30N 29°27E 268 B2
Beni □ Bolivia 14°0S 65°0W 331 C5
Beni → Bolivia 10°23S 65°24W 331 C4
Beni Abbès Algeria 30°5N 2°5W 261 B4
Beni Haoua Algeria 36°30N 1°30E 261 A5
Beni Mazâr Egypt 28°32N 30°44E 256 B3
Beni Mellal Morocco 32°21N 6°21W 260 B3
Beni Mellal □ Morocco 32°0N 6°30W 260 B3
Beni Ounif Algeria 32°0N 1°10W 261 B4
Beni Saf Algeria 35°17N 1°15W 261 A4
Beni Suef Egypt 29°5N 31°6E 256 J7
Beniah L. Canada 63°23N 112°17W 296 A6
Benicarló Spain 40°23N 0°23E 196 E5
Benicássim Spain 40°3N 0°4E 196 E5
Benidorm Spain 38°33N 0°9W 197 G4
Benin ■ Africa 10°0N 2°0E 263 D5
Benin → Nigeria 5°45N 5°4E 263 D6
Benin, Bight of W. Afr. 5°0N 3°0E 263 E5
Benin City Nigeria 6°20N 5°31E 263 D6
Benisa Spain 38°43N 0°3E 197 G5
Benitez Int. ✈ (SCL)
Chile 33°33S 70°42W 137 B1
Bénitiers, Île aux Mauritius 20°24S 57°20E 272 e
Benito Juárez, Int. ✈ (MEX)
Mexico 19°25N 99°5W 128 B2
Benitses Greece 39°32N 19°55E 206 B9
Benjamin Aceval
Paraguay 24°58S 57°34W 334 A4
Benjamin Constant Brazil 4°40S 70°15W 328 D3
Benjamín Hill Mexico 30°9N 111°7W 318 A2
Benkelman U.S.A. 40°3N 101°32W 308 E3
Benkovac Croatia 44°2N 15°37E 199 D12
Benmore Pk. N.Z. 44°25S 170°8E 285 E5
Bennett Canada 59°51N 135°0W 296 B2
Bennett, L. Australia 22°50S 131°2E 278 D5
Bennetta, Ostrov
Russia 76°21N 148°56E 215 B15
Bennettsville U.S.A. 34°37N 79°41W 315 D15
Bennichchâb Mauritania 19°32N 15°12W 262 B1
Bennington N.H., U.S.A. 43°0N 71°55W 313 D11
Bennington Vt., U.S.A. 42°53N 73°12W 313 D11
Beno Dem. Rep. of the Congo 3°41S 17°49E 264 C3
Bénodet France 47°53N 4°7W 172 E2
Benoni S. Africa 26°11S 28°18E 271 C4
Benoud Algeria 32°20N 0°16E 261 B5
Benoué △ Cameroon 8°30N 13°55E 264 A2
Benoy Chad 8°59N 16°19E 259 G3
Benque Viejo Belize 17°5N 89°8W 319 D7
Bense Dominica 15°35N 61°22W 323 k
Bensheim Germany 49°40N 8°38E 179 F4
Benson Ariz., U.S.A. 31°58N 110°18W 305 L8
Benson Minn., U.S.A. 45°19N 95°36W 308 C6
Bensonhurst U.S.A. 40°35N 73°59W 132 C2
Bent Iran 26°20N 59°31E 247 E8
Benteng Indonesia 6°10S 120°30E 231 F6
Bentiaba Angola 14°15S 12°21E 265 E2
Bentinck I. Australia 17°3S 139°35E 280 B2
Bentiu Sudan 9°10N 29°55E 257 F2
Bento Gonçalves Brazil 29°10S 51°31W 335 B5
Benton Ark., U.S.A. 34°34N 92°35W 314 D8
Benton Calif., U.S.A. 37°48N 118°32W 306 H8
Benton Ill., U.S.A. 38°0N 88°55W 310 G8
Benton Pa., U.S.A. 41°12N 76°23W 313 E8
Benton Harbor U.S.A. 42°6N 86°27W 311 B10
Benton Heights U.S.A. 42°7N 86°24W 311 B10
Bentong Malaysia 3°31N 101°55E 237 L3
Bentonville U.S.A. 36°22N 94°13W 314 C7
Bentu Liben Ethiopia 8°32N 38°21E 257 F4
Bentuang Karimun △
Indonesia 1°11N 113°38E 235 B4
Benue □ Nigeria 7°20N 8°45E 263 D6
Benue → Nigeria 7°48N 6°46E 263 D6
Benxi China 41°20N 123°48E 224 B1
Benza
Dem. Rep. of the Congo 4°49S 13°17E 265 D2
Benzdorp Suriname 3°44N 54°5W 329 C7
Beo Indonesia 4°25N 126°50E 231 D7
Beograd Serbia 44°50N 20°37E 202 B4
Beograd ✈ (BEG) Serbia 43°49N 20°17E 202 C4
Beolgyo S. Korea 34°51N 127°21E 224 E3
Beoumi Ivory C. 7°45N 5°23W 262 D3
Bepan Jiang → China 24°55N 106°5E 228 E6
Beppu Japan 33°15N 131°30E 222 D3
Beppu-Wan Japan 33°18N 131°34E 222 D3
Beqa Fiji 18°23S 178°8E 287 B2
Beqaa Valley = Al Biqā
Lebanon 34°10N 36°10E 250 D7
Bequia St. Vincent 13°0N 61°15W 323 n
Ber Mota India 23°27N 68°34E 242 H3
Bera Bangla. 24°5N 89°37E 241 C2
Berach → India 25°15N 75°2E 242 G6
Beraketa Madag. 23°7S 44°25E 272 C1
Béran-Djoko Congo 3°15N 17°0E 264 B3
Berane Montenegro 42°51N 19°52E 202 D3
Berat Albania 40°43N 19°59E 202 F3
Berau → Indonesia 2°10N 117°42E 235 B5
Berau, Teluk Indonesia 2°30S 132°30E 231 E8
Beravina Madag. 18°10S 45°14E 272 B2
Berback △ Indonesia 1°27S 104°19E 234 C2
Berber Sudan 18°0N 34°0E 256 D3
Berbera Somali Rep. 10°30N 45°2E 267 B6
Berbérati C.A.R. 4°15N 15°40E 264 B3
Berbice → Guyana 6°20N 57°32W 329 B6
Berceto Italy 44°31N 9°51E 198 D6
Berchem-Ste-Agathe
Belgium 50°52N 4°17E 116 A1
Berchidda Italy 40°47N 9°10E 200 B2
Berchtesgaden Germany 47°38N 13°0E 179 H8
Berchtesgaden △
Germany 47°34N 12°55E 179 H8
Berck France 50°25N 1°36E 173 B8
Berdale Somali Rep. 7°4N 47°51E 267 C6
Berdichev = Berdychiv
Ukraine 49°57N 28°30E 177 D15
Berdsk Russia 54°47N 83°2E 217 B10
Berdyansk Ukraine 46°45N 36°50E 189 J9
Berdychiv Ukraine 49°57N 28°30E 177 D15
Berea U.S.A. 37°34N 84°17W 309 G11
Berebere Indonesia 2°25N 128°45E 231 D7
Bereda Somali Rep. 11°45N 51°0E 267 B7
Berehomet Ukraine 48°10N 25°19E 183 B10
Berehove Ukraine 48°15N 22°35E 182 B7
Bereina Papua N. G. 8°39S 146°30E 286 E4
Bereket Turkmenistan 39°16N 55°32E 247 B7
Berekua Dominica 15°14N 61°20W 323 k
Berekum Ghana 7°29N 2°34W 262 D4
Berenice Egypt 24°2N 35°25E 256 C4
Berens → Canada 52°25N 97°2W 297 C9
Berens I. Canada 52°18N 97°18W 297 C9
Berens River Canada 52°25N 97°0W 297 C9
Beresford U.S.A. 43°5N 96°47W 308 D5
Berestechko Ukraine 50°22N 25°5E 177 C13
Bereşti Romania 46°6N 27°50E 183 D12
Beretău → Romania 47°10N 21°50E 182 C6
Berettyó → Hungary 46°59N 21°7E 182 D6
Berettyóújfalu Hungary 47°13N 21°33E 182 C6
Berevo Mahajanga, Madag. 17°14S 44°17E 272 B1
Berevo Toliara, Madag. 19°44S 44°58E 272 B1
Bereza = Byaroza Belarus 52°31N 24°51E 189 F3
Berezhany Ukraine 49°26N 24°58E 177 D13
Berezina = Byarezina →
Belarus 52°33N 30°14E 177 B16
Berezivka Ukraine 47°14N 30°55E 189 J6
Berezna Ukraine 51°35N 31°46E 189 G6
Bereznik Russia 62°51N 42°40E 186 B7
Berezniki Russia 59°24N 56°46E 186 C10
Berezovo Russia 64°0N 65°0E 214 C7
Berezyne Ukraine 46°14N 29°12E 183 D14
Berg am Laim Germany 48°7N 11°38E 131 B2
Berga Spain 42°6N 1°48E 196 C6
Berga Kalmar, Sweden 57°14N 16°3E 163 G10
Bergama Turkey 39°8N 27°11E 205 B9
Bérgamo Italy 45°41N 9°43E 198 C6
Bergaon India 20°41N 80°27E 244 D5
Bergara Spain 43°9N 2°28W 196 B2
Bergby Sweden 60°57N 17°2E 162 D11
Berge Norway 59°34N 8°10E 162 E2
Bergedorf Germany 53°28N 10°6E 178 B6
Bergeforsen Sweden 62°32N 17°23E 162 B11
Bergen Mecklenburg-Vorpommern,
Germany 54°25N 13°25E 178 A9
Bergen Niedersachsen,
Germany 52°49N 9°57E 178 C5
Bergen Neths. 52°40N 4°43E 170 B4
Bergen Hordaland, Norway 60°20N 5°20E 164 D2
Bergen N.Y., U.S.A. 43°5N 77°57W 312 C7
Bergen ✈ (BGO) Norway 60°17N 5°19E 164 D2
Bergen op Zoom Neths. 51°28N 4°18E 170 C4
Bergenfield U.S.A. 40°55N 73°59W 132 A2
Bergerac France 44°51N 0°30E 174 D4
Bergham Germany 48°2N 11°37E 131 B2
Bergheim Germany 50°57N 6°38E 178 E2
Bergholz U.S.A. 40°31N 80°53W 312 F4
Bergisch Gladbach
Germany 50°59N 7°8E 170 D7
Bergisches Land ⌂
Germany 51°0N 7°30E 178 E3
Bergkamen Germany 51°37N 7°38E 178 D3
Bergkvara Sweden 56°23N 16°5E 163 H10
Bergshamra Sweden 59°38N 18°37E 162 E12
Bergsjö Sweden 61°59N 17°3E 162 C11
Bergstadt = Leśnica
Poland 50°26N 18°11E 185 H5
Bergstrasse-Odenwald ⌂
Germany 49°45N 5°55E 179 F1
Bergues France 50°58N 2°24E 173 B9
Bergviken Sweden 61°15N 16°40E 162 C10
Bergville S. Africa 28°52S 29°18E 271 C4
Bergvliet S. Africa 34°2S 18°25E 118 B1
Berhala, Selat Indonesia 1°0S 104°15E 234 C2
Berhampore = Baharampur
India 24°2N 88°27E 243 G13
Berhampur = Brahmapur
India 19°15N 84°54E 244 E7
Berheci → Romania 45°58N 27°28E 183 E12
Beri Spain 41°20N 2°1E 114 A1
Bering Glacier U.S.A. 60°20N 143°30W 303 F12
Bering Land Bridge ⌂
U.S.A. 66°20N 165°0W 303 C6
Bering Sea Pac. Oc. 58°0N 171°0W 300 a
Bering Strait Pac. Oc. 65°30N 169°0W 303 D5
Beringovskiy Russia 63°3N 179°19E 215 C18
Berisso Argentina 34°56S 57°50W 334 C4
Berja Spain 36°50N 2°56W 195 J8
Berkåk Norway 62°50N 10°0E 164 B6
Berkane Morocco 34°52N 2°20W 261 B4
Berkeley U.S.A. 37°51N 122°16W 136 A3
Berkeley, C. Ecuador 0°1N 91°35W 330 a
Berkner I. Antarctica 79°30S 50°0W 151 D18
Berkovitsa Bulgaria 43°16N 23°8E 202 C7
Berkshire U.S.A. 42°19N 76°11W 313 D8
Berkshire Downs U.K. 51°33N 1°29W 169 F6
Berlanga Spain 38°17N 5°50W 195 G5
Berlenga, I. Portugal 39°25N 9°30W 195 F1
Berlengas = Valença do Piaui
Brazil 6°20S 41°45W 332 C3
Berlin = Kitchener
Canada 43°27N 80°29W 312 C4
Berlin Berlin, Germany 52°31N 13°23E 115 A3
Berlin Ga., U.S.A. 31°4N 83°37W 316 D6
Berlin Md., U.S.A. 38°20N 75°13W 309 F16
Berlin N.H., U.S.A. 44°28N 71°11W 313 B13
Berlin N.Y., U.S.A. 42°42N 73°23W 313 D11
Berlin Wis., U.S.A. 43°58N 88°57W 308 D9
Berlin □ Germany 52°30N 13°20E 178 C9
Berlin Dom Germany 52°31N 13°24E 115 A3
Berlin L. U.S.A. 41°3N 81°0W 312 E4
Berlin Tegel ✈ (TXL)
Germany 52°35N 13°14E 115 A2
Berlin Tempelhof ✈ (THF)
Germany 52°28N 13°27E 115 B3
Berlinchen = Barlinek
Poland 53°0N 15°15E 185 F2
Bermagui Australia 36°25S 150°4E 283 D9
Bermeja, Sierra Spain 36°30N 5°11W 195 J5
Bermejo → Formosa,
Argentina 26°51S 58°23W 334 B4
Bermejo → San Juan,
Argentina 32°30S 67°30W 334 C2
Bermejo, Paso = Uspallata, P. de
Argentina 32°37S 69°22W 334 C2
Bermen, L. Canada 53°35N 68°55W 299 B6
Bermeo Spain 43°25N 2°47W 196 B2
Bermillo de Sayago Spain 41°22N 6°8W 194 D4
Bermondsey U.K. 51°29N 0°3W 125 B3
Bermuda ☑ Atl. Oc. 32°45N 65°0W 153 a
Bermuda Int. ✈ (BDA)
Bermuda 32°22N 64°41W 153 a
Bermuda Rise Atl. Oc. 32°30N 65°0W 152 C5
Bern Switz. 46°57N 7°28E 179 J3
Bern □ Switz. 46°45N 7°40E 179 J3
Bernabeu, Estadio Spain 40°27N 3°41W 127 B1
Bernal Heights U.S.A. 37°44N 122°24W 136 B2
Bernalda Italy 40°24N 16°41E 201 B9
Bernalillo U.S.A. 35°18N 106°33W 305 J10
Bernam → Malaysia 3°45N 101°5E 234 B2
Bernardo de Irigoyen
Argentina 26°15S 53°40W 335 B5
Bernardo O'Higgins □
Chile 34°15S 70°45W 334 C1
Bernardo O'Higgins △
Chile 48°50S 75°36W 336 C1
Bernardsville U.S.A. 40°43N 74°34W 313 F10
Bernasconi Argentina 37°55S 63°44W 334 D3
Bernau Bayern, Germany 47°47N 12°22E 179 H8
Bernau Brandenburg,
Germany 52°40N 13°35E 178 C9
Bernay France 49°5N 0°35E 172 C7
Bernburg Germany 51°47N 11°44E 178 D7
Berndorf Austria 47°59N 16°1E 180 D9
Berne = Bern Switz. 46°57N 7°28E 179 J3
Berne = Bern □ Switz. 46°45N 7°40E 179 J3
Berne U.S.A. 40°39N 84°57W 311 D12
Berner Alpen Switz. 46°27N 7°35E 179 J3
Berneray U.K. 57°43N 7°11W 167 D1
Bernier I. Australia 24°50S 113°12E 279 D1
Bernina, Piz Switz. 46°20N 9°54E 179 J5
Bernkastel-Kues Germany 49°55N 7°3E 179 F3
Bernstadt = Bierutów
Poland 51°7N 17°32E 185 G4
Bernstein = Pełczyce
Poland 53°3N 15°16E 185 E2
Bero → Angola 15°10S 12°9E 265 F2
Beroroha Madag. 21°40S 45°10E 272 C2
Béroubouay Benin 10°34N 2°46E 263 C5
Beroun Czech Rep. 49°57N 14°5E 180 B7
Berounka → Czech Rep. 50°0N 14°22E 180 B7
Berovo Macedonia 41°38N 22°51E 202 E6
Berre, Étang de France 43°27N 5°5E 175 E9
Berre-l'Étang France 43°27N 5°10E 175 E9
Berrechid Morocco 33°18N 7°36W 260 B3
Berri Australia 34°14S 140°35E 282 C4
Berriane Algeria 32°50N 3°46E 261 B5
Berridale Australia 36°22S 148°48E 283 D8
Berrien Springs U.S.A. 41°57N 86°20W 311 C10
Berrigan Australia 35°38S 145°49E 283 C6
Berriwillock Australia 35°36S 142°59E 282 C5
Berrouaghia Algeria 36°10N 2°53E 261 A5
Berry N.S.W., Australia 34°46S 150°43E 283 C9
Berry France 46°50N 2°0E 173 F8
Berry Is. Bahamas 25°40N 77°50W 320 A4
Berrydale U.S.A. 30°53N 87°3W 317 E2
Berryessa, L. U.S.A. 38°31N 122°6W 306 G4
Berryville U.S.A. 36°22N 93°34W 314 C8
Berseba Namibia 26°0S 17°46E 270 C2
Bersenbrück Germany 52°34N 7°56E 178 C3
Bershad Ukraine 48°22N 29°31E 183 B14
Berthold U.S.A. 48°19N 101°44W 308 A3
Berthoud U.S.A. 40°19N 105°5W 304 F11
Bertincourt France 50°5N 2°58E 173 B9
Bertolínia Brazil 7°38S 43°57W 332 C3
Bertoua Cameroon 4°30N 13°45E 264 B2
Bertraghboy B. Ireland 53°22N 9°54W 166 C2
Bertys = Balqash
Kazakhstan 46°50N 74°50E 214 E8
Beru Kiribati 1°20S 176°0E 277 A14
Berufjörður Iceland 64°48N 14°29W 155 C12
Berunes Iceland 64°42N 14°16W 155 C12
Beruri Brazil 3°54S 61°22W 329 D5
Berwick U.S.A. 41°3N 76°14W 313 E8
Berwick-upon-Tweed
U.K. 55°46N 2°0W 168 B6
Berwyn U.S.A. 41°50N 87°47W 119 B2
Berwyn Heights U.S.A. 38°59N 76°55W 143 B4
Berwyn Mts. U.K. 52°54N 3°26W 168 E4
Beryslav Ukraine 46°50N 33°30E 189 J7
Berzasca Romania 44°39N 21°58E 182 F6
Berzence Hungary 46°12N 17°11E 182 D2
Besal Pakistan 35°4N 73°56E 243 B5
Besalampy Madag. 16°43S 44°29E 272 B1
Besançon France 47°15N 6°2E 173 E13
Besar Indonesia 2°40S 116°0E 235 C5
Besar, Gunong Malaysia 5°10N 101°18E 234 A2
Beshenkovichi Belarus 55°2N 29°29E 188 E5
Besiktas Turkey 41°2N 29°0E 122 B2
Beška Serbia 45°8N 20°6E 182 E5
Beslan Russia 43°15N 44°28E 191 J7
Besna Kobila Serbia 42°31N 22°10E 202 D6
Besnard L. Canada 55°25N 106°0W 297 B7
Besni Turkey 37°41N 37°52E 212 D7
Besor, N. → Egypt 31°28N 34°22E 251 G5
Besós → Spain 41°24N 2°13E 114 A2
Bessa Monteiro Angola 7°7S 13°44E 265 D2
Bessarabiya Moldova 47°0N 28°10E 177 E15
Bessarabka = Basarabeasca
Moldova 46°21N 28°58E 183 D13
Bessèges France 44°18N 4°8E 175 D8
Bessemer Ala., U.S.A. 33°24N 86°58W 315 E11
Bessemer Mich., U.S.A. 46°29N 90°3W 308 B8
Bessemer Pa., U.S.A. 40°59N 80°30W 312 F4
Bessie, L. U.S.A. 28°29N 81°31W 133 B1
Bessin France 49°18N 1°0W 172 C6
Bessines-sur-Gartempe
France 46°6N 1°22E 174 B5
Beswick Australia 14°34S 132°53E 278 B5
Bet Horon West Bank 31°52N 35°7E 123 B1
Bet She'an Israel 32°30N 35°30E 251 F6
Bet Shemesh Israel 31°44N 35°0E 251 G6
Bet Tadjine, Djebel Algeria 29°0N 3°30W 260 C4
Betafo Madag. 19°50S 46°51E 272 B2
Betamba
Dem. Rep. of the Congo 2°17S 21°24E 264 C4
Betancuria Canary Is. 28°25N 14°3W 153 e2
Betancuria, Mt. Canary Is. 28°25N 14°6W 153 e2
Betania Colombia 4°22N 72°54W 328 C3
Betanzos Bolivia 19°34S 65°27W 331 D4
Betanzos Spain 43°15N 8°12W 194 B2
Bétaré Oya Cameroon 5°40N 14°5E 264 A2
Betatao Madag. 18°11S 47°52E 272 B2
Betera Spain 39°35N 0°28W 197 F4
Bétérou Benin 9°12N 2°16E 263 D5
Bethal S. Africa 26°27S 29°28E 271 C4
Bethalto U.S.A. 38°55N 90°2W 310 F6
Bethanien Namibia 26°31S 17°8E 270 C2
Bethany Ont., Canada 44°11N 78°34W 312 B6
Bethany Ill., U.S.A. 39°39N 88°45W 311 E8
Bethany Mo., U.S.A. 40°16N 94°2W 310 D2
Bethany Okla., U.S.A. 35°31N 97°38W 314 D6
Bethel Montserrat 16°44N 62°9W 323 p
Bethel Alaska, U.S.A. 60°48N 161°45W 303 F7
Bethel Conn., U.S.A. 41°22N 73°25W 313 E11
Bethel Maine, U.S.A. 44°25N 70°47W 313 B14
Bethel Ohio, U.S.A. 38°58N 84°5W 311 F12
Bethel Vt., U.S.A. 43°50N 72°38W 313 C12
Bethel Park U.S.A. 40°19N 80°2W 312 F4
Béthenville France 49°18N 4°23E 173 C11
Bethesda U.S.A. 38°59N 77°6W 143 B3
Bethlehem = Bayt Lahm
West Bank 31°43N 35°12E 123 B2
Bethlehem Free State,
S. Africa 28°14S 28°18E 271 C4
Bethlehem Pa., U.S.A. 40°37N 75°23W 313 F9
Bethnal Green U.K. 51°31N 0°2W 125 A3
Bethulie S. Africa 30°30S 25°59E 270 D4
Béthune France 50°30N 2°38E 173 B9
Béthune → France 49°53N 1°4E 172 C8
Bethungra Australia 34°45S 147°51E 283 C7
Betijoque Venezuela 9°23N 70°44W 328 B3
Betioky Toliara, Madag. 23°48S 44°20E 272 C1
Betioky Toliara, Madag. 22°27S 43°43E 272 C1
Betong Malaysia 1°24N 111°31E 235 B4
Betong Thailand 5°45N 101°5E 237 K3
Betoota Australia 25°45S 140°42E 280 D3
Betor Ethiopia 11°37N 39°2E 257 E4
Betor W. Bengal, India 22°34N 88°17E 124 B1
Bétou Congo 3°2N 18°32E 264 B3
Betpaqdala Kazakhstan 45°45N 70°30E 217 C8
Betroka Madag. 23°16S 46°0E 272 C2
Betsiamites Canada 48°56N 68°40W 299 C6
Betsiamites → Canada 48°56N 68°38W 299 C6
Betsiboka → Madag. 16°3S 46°36E 272 B2
Bettendorf U.S.A. 41°32N 90°30W 310 C6
Bettiah India 26°48N 84°33E 243 F11
Bettna Sweden 58°55N 16°38E 163 F10
Béttola Italy 44°47N 9°36E 198 D6
Betul India 21°58N 77°59E 244 D3
Betws-y-Coed U.K. 53°5N 3°48W 168 D4
Betxi Spain 39°56N 0°12W 196 F4
Betzdorf Germany 50°46N 7°52E 178 E3
Béu Angola 6°15S 15°32E 265 D3
Beuil France 44°6N 6°59E 175 D10
Beulah Vic., Australia 35°58S 142°29E 282 C5
Beulah Fla., U.S.A. 28°32N 81°34W 133 A1
Beulah Mich., U.S.A. 44°38N 86°6W 308 C10
Beulah N. Dak., U.S.A. 47°16N 101°47W 308 B3
Beulah, L. U.S.A. 28°32N 81°33W 133 A1
Beurkia Chad 15°20N 17°56E 259 E3
Beurs Amsterdam, Neths. 112 b2
Beuthen = Bytom Poland 50°25N 18°54E 185 H5
Beuthen an der Oder = Bytom
Odrzański Poland 51°44N 15°48E 185 G2
Beuvron → France 47°29N 1°15E 172 E8
Beveren Belgium 51°12N 4°16E 170 C4
Beverley W. Austral.,
Australia 32°9S 116°56E 279 F2
Beverley E. Riding, U.K. 53°51N 0°26W 168 D7
Beverley Hills Australia 33°56S 151°5E 139 B1
Beverley Park Australia 33°58S 151°8E 139 B1
Beverly Ill., U.S.A. 41°42N 87°39W 119 C3
Beverly Mass., U.S.A. 42°33N 70°53W 313 D14
Beverly Arts Center
U.S.A. 41°41N 87°40W 119 C2
Beverly Glen U.S.A. 34°6N 118°26W 126 B2
Beverly Hills Calif.,
U.S.A. 34°5N 118°24W 126 B2
Beverly Hills Fla., U.S.A. 28°55N 82°28W 317 G7
Beverly Hills -Morgan Park Historic
District U.S.A. 41°41N 87°40W 119 C2
Beverungen Germany 51°39N 9°22E 178 D5
Bevoalavo Madag. 25°13S 45°26E 272 D2
Bewas → India 23°59N 79°21E 243 H8
Bex Switz. 46°15N 7°1E 179 J3
Bexhill U.K. 50°51N 0°29E 169 G8
Bexley Australia 33°56S 151°7E 139 B1
Bexley □ U.K. 51°27N 0°9E 125 B4
Bexleyheath U.K. 51°27N 0°8E 125 B4
Bey Dağları Turkey 36°38N 30°29E 205 E12
Beyānlū Iran 36°0N 47°51E 246 C5
Beyazköy Turkey 41°21N 27°42E 203 E11
Beyçayırı Turkey 40°15N 26°55E 203 F10
Beydağ Turkey 38°5N 28°13E 205 C10
Beyeğaç Turkey 37°14N 28°53E 205 D10
Beyin Ghana 5°1N 2°41W 262 D4
Beykoz Turkey 41°7N 29°7E 122 B2
Beyla Guinea 8°30N 8°38W 262 D3
Beylerbeyi Turkey 41°2N 29°2E 122 B2
Beynat France 45°8N 1°44E 174 C5
Beyneu Kazakhstan 45°18N 55°9E 187 E10
Beyoba Turkey 38°48N 27°47E 205 C9
Beyoğlu Turkey 41°1N 28°58E 122 B1
Beypazarı Turkey 40°10N 31°56E 212 B4
Beypore → India 11°10N 75°47E 245 J2
Beyşehir Turkey 37°41N 31°43E 212 D4
Beyşehir Gölü Turkey 37°41N 31°33E 212 D4
Beytüşşebap Turkey 37°35N 43°10E 213 D10
Bezdan Serbia 45°50N 18°57E 182 E3
Bezhetsk Russia 57°47N 36°39E 188 D9
Béziers France 43°20N 3°12E 174 E7
Bezons France 48°56N 2°13E 134 A2
Bezuidenhout Park
S. Africa 26°10S 28°5E 123 B2
Bezwada = Vijayawada
India 16°31N 80°39E 244 F5
Bhabua India 25°3N 83°37E 243 G10
Bhadar → Gujarat, India 22°17N 72°20E 242 H5
Bhadar → Gujarat, India 21°27N 69°47E 242 J3
Bhadarwah India 32°58N 75°46E 243 C6
Bhadgaon = Bhaktapur
Nepal 27°38N 85°24E 243 F11
Bhadohi India 25°25N 82°34E 243 G10
Bhadra India 29°8N 75°14E 242 E6
Bhadra → India 14°0N 75°20E 245 H2
Bhadrachalam India 17°40N 80°53E 244 F5
Bhadrakali India 22°40N 88°20E 124 A2
Bhadrakh India 21°10N 86°30E 244 D8
Bhadran India 22°19N 72°6E 242 H5
Bhadravati India 13°49N 75°40E 245 H2
Bhag Pakistan 29°2N 67°49E 242 E2
Bhagalpur India 25°10N 87°0E 243 G12
Bhagirathi → Uttaranchal,
India 30°8N 78°35E 243 D8
Bhagirathi → W. Bengal,
India 23°25N 88°23E 243 H13
Bhainsa India 19°10N 77°58E 244 E3
Bhairab → Bangla. 22°51N 89°34E 241 D2
Bhairab Bazar Bangla. 24°4N 90°58E 241 C3
Bhakkar Pakistan 31°40N 71°5E 242 D4
Bhakra Dam India 31°30N 76°45E 242 D7
Bhaktapur Nepal 27°38N 85°24E 243 F11
Bhalki India 18°2N 77°13E 244 E3
Bhalswa India 28°44N 77°10E 120 A2
Bhambo Khan Qarmati
Pakistan 24°49N 67°7E 123 B2
Bhamo Burma 24°15N 97°15E 241 C6
Bhamragarh India 19°30N 80°40E 244 E5
Bhandara India 21°5N 79°42E 244 D4
Bhanpura India 24°31N 75°44E 242 G6
Bhanrer Ra. India 23°40N 79°45E 243 H8
Bhaptiahi India 26°19N 86°44E 243 F12
Bharat = India ■ Asia 20°0N 78°0E 239 F11
Bharatpur Chhattisgarh,
India 23°44N 81°46E 243 H9
Bharatpur Raj., India 27°15N 77°30E 242 F7
Bharno India 23°14N 84°53E 243 H11
Bharuch India 21°47N 73°0E 244 D1
Bhatghar L. India 18°10N 73°48E 244 E1
Bhatiapara Ghat Bangla. 23°13N 89°42E 241 D2
Bhatinda India 30°15N 74°57E 242 D6
Bhatkal India 13°58N 74°35E 245 H2
Bhatpara India 22°50N 88°25E 243 H13
Bhatsala India 22°30N 88°16E 124 B1
Bhattu India 29°36N 75°19E 242 E6
Bhaun Pakistan 32°55N 72°40E 242 C5
Bhaunagar = Bhavnagar
India 21°45N 72°10E 244 D1
Bhavani India 11°27N 77°43E 245 J3
Bhavnagar India 21°45N 72°10E 244 D1
Bhawanipatna India 19°55N 83°10E 244 E6
Bhawanipur India 22°32N 88°21E 124 B2
Bhawari India 25°42N 73°4E 242 G5
Bhayavadar India 21°51N 70°15E 242 J4
Bhendkhal India 18°52N 72°59E 130 B2
Bhera Pakistan 32°29N 72°57E 242 C5
Bhikangaon India 21°52N 75°57E 242 J6
Bhilai = Bhilainagar-Durg
India 21°13N 81°26E 244 D5
Bhilainagar-Durg India 21°13N 81°26E 244 D5
Bhilsa = Vidisha India 23°28N 77°53E 242 H7
Bhilwara India 25°25N 74°38E 242 G6
Bhima → India 16°25N 77°17E 244 F3
Bhimavaram India 16°30N 81°30E 245 F5
Bhimbar Pakistan 32°59N 74°3E 243 C6
Bhind India 26°30N 78°46E 243 F8
Bhinga India 27°43N 81°56E 243 F9
Bhinmal India 25°0N 72°15E 242 G5
Bhisho S. Africa 32°50S 27°23E 270 D4
Bhiwandi India 19°20N 73°0E 244 E1
Bhiwani India 28°50N 76°9E 242 E7
Bhogava → India 22°26N 72°20E 242 H5
Bhokardan India 20°16N 75°46E 244 D2
Bhola Bangla. 22°45N 90°35E 241 D3
Bholari Pakistan 25°19N 68°13E 242 G3
Bhongir India 17°30N 78°56E 244 F4
Bhopal India 23°20N 77°30E 242 H7
Bhopalpatnam India 18°52N 80°23E 244 E5
Bhor India 18°12N 73°53E 244 E1
Bhubaneshwar India 20°15N 85°50E 244 D7
Bhuj India 23°15N 69°49E 242 H3
Bhuleshwar Mumbai, India 130 b2
Bhumiphol Res. Thailand 17°20N 98°40E 236 D2
Bhusawal India 21°3N 75°46E 244 D2
Bhutan ■ Asia 27°25N 90°30E 241 B3
Biá → Brazil 3°28S 67°23W 328 D4
Biafra, B. of = Bonny, Bight of
Africa 3°30N 9°20E 263 E6
Biak Indonesia 1°10S 136°6E 231 E9
Biała Poland 50°24N 17°40E 185 H4
Biała → Poland 50°3N 20°55E 185 H7
Biała Piska Poland 53°37N 22°5E 184 E9
Biała Podlaska Poland 52°4N 23°6E 185 F10
Biała Rawska Poland 51°48N 20°29E 185 G7
Białobrzegi Poland 51°39N 20°57E 185 G7
Białogard Poland 54°2N 15°58E 184 D2
Białołeka Dworska Poland 52°19N 21°1E 142 B2
Białowieski △ Poland 52°43N 23°50E 185 F10
Białowieża Poland 52°41N 23°49E 185 F10
Biały Bór Poland 53°53N 16°51E 184 E3
Białystok Poland 53°10N 23°10E 185 E10
Biancavilla Italy 37°38N 14°52E 201 E7
Bianco Italy 38°5N 16°9E 201 D9
Biankouma Ivory C. 7°50N 7°40W 262 D3
Biaora India 23°56N 76°56E 242 H7
Biārjmand Iran 36°6N 55°53E 247 B7
Biaro Indonesia 2°5N 125°26E 231 D7
Biarritz France 43°29N 1°33W 174 E2
Bias Indonesia 8°24S 115°36E 231 J18
Biasca Switz. 46°22N 8°58E 179 J4
Biavela Angola 14°43S 19°47E 265 E3
Biba Egypt 28°55N 31°0E 256 J7
Bibai Japan 43°19N 141°52E 220 C10
Bibala Angola 14°44S 13°24E 265 E2
Bibane, Bahiret el Tunisia 33°16N 11°13E 258 B2
Bibassé Gabon 1°27N 11°37E 264 B2
Bibbiena Italy 43°42N 11°49E 199 E8
Bibby I. Canada 61°55N 93°0W 297 A10
Bibel → Spain 42°24N 7°13W 194 C3
Biberach Germany 48°5N 9°47E 179 G5
Bibi Papua N. G. 5°30S 146°2E 286 D4
Bibiani Ghana 6°30N 2°8W 262 D4
Bibile Sri Lanka 7°10N 81°25E 245 L5
Biblioteca Nacional Rio de J., Brazil 135 c2
Bibungwa
Dem. Rep. of the Congo 2°40S 28°15E 268 C2
Bicaj Albania 41°58N 20°25E 202 E4
Bicaz Romania 46°53N 26°5E 183 D11
Bicazu Ardelean
Romania 46°51N 25°56E 183 D10
Biccari Italy 41°23N 15°12E 201 A8
Bicentennial Park N.S.W.,
Australia 33°51S 151°5E 139 B1
Bicentennial Park Calif.,
U.S.A. 34°1N 118°1W 126 B4
Bicester U.K. 51°54N 1°9W 169 F6
Biche Trin. & Tob. 10°26N 61°8W 323 t
Bichena Ethiopia 10°28N 38°10E 257 E4
Bicheno Australia 41°52S 148°18E 281 G4
Bichia India 22°27N 80°42E 243 H9
Bichvinta Georgia 43°9N 40°21E 191 J5
Bickerton I. Australia 13°45S 136°10E 280 A2
Bickley U.K. 51°23N 0°3E 125 B4
Bicknell U.S.A. 38°47N 87°19W 311 F9
Bicske Hungary 47°29N 18°38E 182 C3
Bicuar △ Angola 15°14S 14°45E 265 F2
Bicutan Phil. 14°30N 121°3E 127 C2
Bida Dem. Rep. of the Congo 4°55N 19°56E 264 B3
Bida Nigeria 9°3N 5°58E 263 D6
Bidar India 17°55N 77°35E 244 F3
Biddeford U.S.A. 43°30N 70°28W 309 D18
Biddwara Ethiopia 5°11N 38°34E 257 F4
Bideford U.K. 51°1N 4°13W 169 F3
Bideford Bay U.K. 51°5N 4°20W 169 F3
Bidhan Nagar India 22°35N 88°25E 124 B2
Bidhuna India 26°49N 79°31E 243 F8
Bidi Burkina Faso 0°58N 42°37E 267 D5
Bidon 5 = Poste Maurice Cortier
Algeria 22°14N 1°2E 261 D5
Bidor Malaysia 4°6N 101°15E 237 K3
Bidu West Bank 31°50N 35°9E 123 B1
Bidyadanga Australia 18°45S 121°43E 278 C3
Bidzar Cameroon 9°54N 14°7E 264 A2
Bie Sweden 59°5N 16°12E 162 E10
Bié □ Angola 12°30S 17°0E 265 E3
Bié, Planalto de Angola 12°0S 16°0E 265 E3
Bieber U.S.A. 41°7N 121°8W 304 F3
Biebrza → Poland 53°13N 22°25E 185 E9
Biebrzański △ Poland 53°36N 22°45E 184 E9
Biecz Poland 49°44N 21°15E 185 J8
Biel Switz. 47°8N 7°14E 179 H3
Bielany Poland 52°17N 20°57E 142 B1
Bielawa Dolnośląskie,
Poland 50°43N 16°37E 185 H3
Bielawa Warszawa, Poland 52°8N 21°9E 142 C2
Bielefeld Germany 52°1N 8°33E 178 C4
Bielersee Switz. 47°6N 7°5E 179 H3
Bielitz = Bielsko-Biała
Poland 49°50N 19°2E 185 J6
Biella Italy 45°34N 8°3E 198 C5
Bielsk Podlaski Poland 52°47N 23°12E 185 F10
Bielsko-Biała Poland 49°50N 19°2E 185 J6
Bien Hoa Vietnam 10°57N 106°49E 237 G6
Bienne = Biel Switz. 47°8N 7°14E 179 H3
Bienvenida Spain 38°18N 6°12W 195 G4
Bienvenue Fr. Guiana 3°0N 52°30W 329 C7
Bienville, L. Canada 55°5N 72°40W 298 A5
Bierné France 47°48N 0°33W 172 E6
Bierun Poland 50°6N 19°6E 185 H6
Bierutów Poland 51°7N 17°32E 185 G4
Biescas Spain 42°37N 0°20W 196 C4
Biesdorf Germany 52°30N 13°33E 115 A4
Biese → Germany 52°53N 11°46E 178 C7
Biesiesfontein S. Africa 30°57S 17°58E 270 D2
Bieszczadzki △ Poland 49°5N 22°43E 185 J9
Bietigheim-Bissingen
Germany 48°58N 9°8E 179 G5
Bièvre → France 48°44N 2°9E 134 B1
Bièvres France 48°45N 2°13E 134 B2
Bieżuń Poland 52°58N 19°55E 185 F6
Biferno → Italy 41°59N 15°2E 199 G12
Bifoum Gabon 0°20S 10°23E 264 C2
Big → Nfld. & L., Canada 54°50N 58°55W 299 B8
Big → Mo., U.S.A. 38°28N 90°37W 310 F6
Big B. = Awarua B. N.Z. 44°28S 168°4E 285 E3
Big B. Canada 55°43N 60°35W 299 A7
Big Bear City U.S.A. 34°16N 116°51W 307 L10
Big Bear Lake U.S.A. 34°15N 116°56W 307 L10
Big Belt Mts. U.S.A. 46°30N 111°25W 304 C8
Big Bend Swaziland 26°50S 31°58E 271 C5
Big Bend △ U.S.A. 29°20N 103°5W 314 G3
Big Blue → Ind., U.S.A. 39°12N 85°56W 311 E11
Big Blue → Kans., U.S.A. 39°35N 96°34W 308 F5
Big Creek U.S.A. 37°11N 119°14W 306 H7
Big Cypress ⌂ U.S.A. 26°0N 81°10W 317 J8
Big Cypress Swamp
U.S.A. 26°15N 81°30W 317 J8
Big Delta U.S.A. 64°10N 145°51W 303 D11
Big Desert Australia 35°45S 141°10E 281 F3
Big Falls U.S.A. 48°12N 93°48W 308 A7
Big Fork → U.S.A. 48°31N 93°43W 308 A7
Big Horn Mts. = Bighorn Mts.
U.S.A. 44°25N 107°0W 304 D10
Big I. Canada 61°7N 116°45W 296 A5
Big Lake Alaska, U.S.A. 61°20N 150°20W 303 F10
Big Lake Tex., U.S.A. 31°12N 101°28W 314 F4
Big Moose U.S.A. 43°49N 74°58W 313 C10
Big Muddy → U.S.A. 37°33N 89°32W 310 G8
Big Muddy Cr. →
U.S.A. 48°8N 104°36W 304 B11
Big Pine U.S.A. 37°10N 118°17W 306 H8
Big Pine Key U.S.A. 24°40N 81°21W 317 L8
Big Piney U.S.A. 42°32N 110°7W 304 E8
Big Rapids U.S.A. 43°42N 85°29W 309 D11
Big Rideau L. Canada 44°40N 76°15W 313 B8
Big River Canada 53°50N 107°0W 297 C7
Big Run U.S.A. 40°57N 78°55W 312 F6
Big Sable Pt. U.S.A. 44°3N 86°1W 308 C10
Big Salmon → Canada 61°52N 134°55W 296 A2
Big Sand L. Canada 57°45N 99°45W 297 B9
Big Sand Lake U.S.A. 28°25N 81°29W 133 B2
Big Sandy U.S.A. 48°11N 110°7W 304 B8
Big Sandy → U.S.A. 38°25N 82°36W 309 F12
Big Sandy Cr. = Sandy Cr. →
U.S.A. 41°51N 109°47W 304 F9
Big Sandy Cr. →
U.S.A. 38°7N 102°29W 304 G12
Big Satilla Cr. → U.S.A. 31°27N 82°3W 316 D7
Big Sioux → U.S.A. 42°29N 96°27W 308 D5
Big South Fork ⌂
U.S.A. 36°27N 84°47W 315 C12
Big Spring U.S.A. 32°15N 101°28W 314 E4
Big Stone City U.S.A. 45°18N 96°28W 308 C5
Big Stone Gap U.S.A. 36°52N 82°47W 309 G12
Big Stone L. U.S.A. 45°18N 96°27W 308 C5
Big Sur U.S.A. 36°15N 121°48W 306 J5
Big Timber U.S.A. 45°50N 109°57W 304 D9
Big Trout L. Canada 53°40N 90°0W 298 B2
Big Trout Lake Canada 53°45N 90°0W 298 B2
Biğa Turkey 40°13N 27°14E 203 F11
Biga → Turkey 40°20N 27°14E 203 F11
Bigadiç Turkey 39°22N 28°7E 205 B10
Biganos France 44°39N 0°59W 174 D3
Bigeumdo S. Korea 34°45N 126°56E 224 E3
Biggar Sask., Canada 52°4N 108°0W 297 C7
Biggar S. Lanarks., U.K. 55°38N 3°32W 167 F5
Bigge I. Australia 14°35S 125°10E 278 B4
Biggenden Australia 25°31S 152°4E 281 D5
Biggleswade U.K. 52°5N 0°14W 169 E7
Biggs U.S.A. 39°25N 121°43W 306 F5
Bighorn U.S.A. 46°10N 107°27W 304 C10
Bighorn → U.S.A. 46°10N 107°28W 304 C10
Bighorn Canyon ⌂
U.S.A. 45°10N 108°0W 304 D10
Bighorn L. U.S.A. 44°55N 108°15W 304 D9
Bighorn Mts. U.S.A. 44°25N 107°0W 304 D10
Bigi Dem. Rep. of the Congo 3°2N 22°25E 264 B4
Bignona Senegal 12°52N 16°14W 262 C1
Bigorre France 43°10N 0°5E 174 E4
Bigstone L. Canada 53°42N 95°44W 297 C9
Biguglia, Étang de France 42°36N 9°29E 175 F13
Bigwa Tanzania 7°10S 39°10E 268 D4
Bihać Bos.-H. 44°49N 15°57E 199 D12
Bihar India 25°5N 85°40E 243 G11
Bihar □ India 25°0N 86°0E 243 G12
Biharamulo Tanzania 2°25S 31°25E 268 C3
Biharamulo ⌂ Tanzania 2°24S 31°26E 268 C3
Bihariganj India 25°44N 86°59E 243 G12
Biharkeresztes Hungary 47°8N 21°44E 182 C6
Bihor □ Romania 47°0N 22°10E 182 D7
Bihor, Munţii Romania 46°29N 22°47E 182 D7
Bijagós, Arquipélago dos
Guinea-Biss. 11°15N 16°10W 262 C1
Bijaipur India 26°2N 77°20E 242 F7
Bijapur Chhattisgarh, India 18°50N 80°50E 244 E5
Bijapur Karnataka, India 16°50N 75°55E 244 F2
Bījār Iran 35°52N 47°35E 213 E12
Bijawar India 24°38N 79°30E 243 G8
Bijela Montenegro 42°28N 18°39E 202 D2
Bijeljina Bos.-H. 44°46N 19°14E 182 F4
Bijelo Polje Montenegro 43°1N 19°45E 202 C3
Bijie China 27°20N 105°16E 228 D5
Bijnor India 29°27N 78°11E 242 E8
Bikaner India 28°2N 73°18E 242 E5
Bikapur India 26°30N 82°7E 243 F10
Bikeqi China 40°43N 111°20E 226 D6
Bikfayyā Lebanon 33°55N 35°41E 250 E6
Bikié Congo 3°7S 13°52E 264 C2
Bikin Russia 46°50N 134°20E 220 A7
Bikin → Russia 46°51N 134°2E 220 A7
Bikini Atoll Marshall Is. 12°0N 167°30E 288 F8
Bikita Zimbabwe 20°6S 31°41E 271 B5
Bīkkū Bīttī Libya 22°0N 19°12E 259 D3
Bikoro
Dem. Rep. of the Congo 0°48S 18°15E 264 C3
Bikoué Cameroon 3°55N 11°50E 263 E7
Bila Tserkva Ukraine 49°45N 30°10E 177 D16
Bilanga Burkina Faso 12°40N 0°1W 263 C4
Bilara India 26°14N 73°53E 242 F5
Bilaspara India 26°13N 90°14E 241 B3
Bilaspur Chhattisgarh,
India 22°2N 82°15E 243 H10

Bilaspur *Punjab, India* 31°19N 76°50E **242** D7
Biläsuvar *Azerbaijan* 39°27N 48°33E **213** C13
Bilauk Taungdan *Thailand* 13°0N 99°0E **236** F2
Bilbao *Spain* 43°16N 2°56W **196** B2
Bilbao ✈ (BIO) *Spain* 43°18N 2°57W **196** B2
Bilbeis *Egypt* 30°25N 31°34E **256** H7
Bilbor *Romania* 43°16N 0°56W **196** B2
Bilce-Zolote *Ukraine* 48°47N 25°53E **183** B10
Bilciurești *Romania* 44°44N 25°48E **183** F10
Bildudalur *Iceland* 65°41N 23°36W **155** B3
Bilé Karpaty *Europe* 49°5N 18°0E **181** D11
Bileća *Bos.-H.* 42°53N 18°27E **202** D7
Bilecik *Turkey* 40°5N 30°5E **212** B4
Bilecik □ *Turkey* 40°0N 30°0E **212** B3
Bilećko Jezero *Bos.-H.* 42°48N 18°20E **202** D7
Bilgoraj *Poland* 50°33N 22°42E **185** H9
Bilgram *India* 27°11N 80°2E **243** F9
Bilhaur *India* 26°51N 80°5E **243** F9
Bilhorod-Dnistrovskyy
  Ukraine 46°11N 30°23E **189** J6
Bili → *Dem. Rep. of the Congo* 4°9N 22°29E **264** D4
Bilibino *Russia* 68°3N 166°20E **215** C17
Bilibiza *Mozam.* 12°30S 40°20E **269** E5
Bilimora *India* 20°45N 72°57E **244** D1
Bilin *Burma* 17°14N 97°15E **241** G6
Biliran □ *Phil.* 11°35N 124°28E **233** C10
Bilisht *Albania* 40°37N 21°2E **202** F5
Billabong Cr. → *Australia* 35°5S 144°2E **282** C6
Billdal *Sweden* 57°35N 11°57E **163** G5
Billiluna *Australia* 19°37S 127°41E **278** C4
Billings *U.S.A.* 45°47N 108°30W **304** D9
Billiton Is. = Belitung
  Indonesia 3°10S 107°50E **235** C3
Billsta *Sweden* 63°20N 18°28E **162** A12
Billund *Denmark* 55°44N 9°6E **163** J3
Billy Pt. *Antigua & B.* 17°44N 61°52W **322** c
Bilma *Niger* 18°50N 13°30E **259** E2
Bilo Gora *Croatia* 45°53N 17°15E **184** E2
Biloela *Australia* 24°24S 150°31E **280** C5
Bilohirsk *Ukraine* 45°3N 34°35E **189** K8
Biloku *Guyana* 1°50N 58°25W **329** C6
Biloli *India* 18°46N 77°44E **244** E3
Bilopillya *Ukraine* 51°14N 34°20E **189** G8
Biloxi *U.S.A.* 30°24N 88°53W **315** F10
Bilpa Morea Claypan
  Australia 25°0S 140°0E **280** D3
Bilqās Qism Auwal *Egypt* 31°12N 31°21E **251** G2
Bilston *U.K.* 55°52N 3°10W **121** B2
Biltine *Chad* 14°40N 20°50E **259** F4
Biltine □ *Chad* 15°0N 21°0E **259** F4
Bilugyun *Burma* 16°24N 97°32E **241** G6
Bilyarsk *Russia* 54°58N 50°22E **190** C10
Bima *Indonesia* 8°22S 118°49E **235** D5
Bimban *Egypt* 24°24N 32°54E **256** C3
Bimbe *Angola* 11°50S 15°50E **266** E3
Bimberi Pk. *Australia* 35°44S 148°51E **283** C8
Bimbila *Ghana* 8°54N 0°5E **263** D5
Bimini Comoros Is. *Comoros Is.* 12°11S 44°14E **272** a
Bimbo *C.A.R.* 4°15N 18°33E **264** D3
Bimini Is. *Bahamas* 25°42N 79°25W **320** A4

Bin Xian *Heilongjiang,*
  China 45°42N 127°32E **227** B14
Bin Xian *Shaanxi, China* 35°2N 108°4E **226** G5
Bin Yauri *Nigeria* 10°46N 4°45E **263** C5
Bina-Etawah *India* 24°13N 78°14E **242** G8
Bināb *Iran* 36°35N 48°41E **213** D12
Binacayan *Phil.* 14°27N 120°55E **127** C1
Binalbagan *Phil.* 10°12N 122°50E **233** F4
Binalong *Australia* 34°40S 148°39E **283** C8
Bīnālūd, Kūh-e *Iran* 36°30N 58°30E **247** B8
Binangonan de Lampon =
  Infanta
  Phil. 14°45N 121°39E **232** D3
Binatang = Bintangau
  Malaysia 2°10N 111°40E **235** B4
Binche *Belgium* 50°26N 4°10E **170** D4
Binchuan *China* 25°42N 100°38E **228** E3
Binda
  Dem. Rep. of the Congo 5°52S 13°14E **265** D2
Binder *Chad* 9°56N 14°27E **259** G2
Bindki *India* 26°2N 80°36E **243** F9
Bindloe, I. = Marchena, I.
  Ecuador 0°19N 90°29W **330** a
Bindoy *Phil.* 9°48N 123°5E **233** G4
Bindslev *Denmark* 57°33N 10°11E **163** G4
Bindura *Zimbabwe* 17°18S 31°18E **269** F3
Binefar *Spain* 41°51N 0°18E **196** D5
Bingara *Australia* 29°52S 150°36E **281** D5
Bingaram I. *India* 10°56N 72°17E **245** J1
Bingen *Germany* 49°57N 7°55E **179** F3
Bingerau = Węgrów
  Poland 52°24N 22°0E **185** F9
Bingerville *Ivory C.* 5°18N 3°49W **262** D4
Bingham *U.S.A.* 45°3N 69°53W **309** C19
Binghamton *U.S.A.* 42°6N 75°55W **313** D9
Bingo-Ochiai *Japan* 34°59N 133°8E **222** C4
Bingöl *Turkey* 38°53N 40°29E **213** C9
Bingöl □ *Turkey* 38°55N 40°40E **213** C9
Bingöl Dağları *Turkey* 39°16N 41°9E **213** C9
Bingsjö *Sweden* 61°1N 15°39E **162** C9
Binh Dinh = An Nhon
  Vietnam 13°55N 109°7E **236** F7
Binh Khe *Vietnam* 13°57N 108°51E **236** F7
Binh Son *Vietnam* 15°20N 108°40E **236** E7
Binhai *China* 34°2N 119°49E **227** G10
Bini Erde *Chad* 20°6N 18°1E **259** D3
Binic *France* 48°46N 2°50W **172** D4
Binisatua *Spain* 39°50N 4°11E **206** B5
Binjai *Indonesia* 3°20N 98°30E **234** B1
Binji *Nigeria* 13°10N 4°55E **263** C5
Binka *India* 21°2N 83°58E **244** D6
Binnah, Ras *Somali Rep.* 11°9N 51°10E **267** F5
Binnaway *Australia* 31°28S 149°24E **283** A8
Binondo *Phil.* 14°36N 120°58E **127** B1
Binongko *Indonesia* 5°57S 124°2E **231** F6
Binscarth *Canada* 50°37N 101°17W **297** C8
Binshangul Gumuz □
  Ethiopia 11°0N 35°30E **257** E4
Bint Goda *Sudan* 13°17N 31°33E **257** E3
Bintan *Indonesia* 1°0N 104°0E **234** B2
Bintangau *Malaysia* 2°10N 111°40E **235** B4
Bintaro Jaya *Indonesia* 6°16S 106°44E **122** B1
Bintulu *Malaysia* 3°10N 113°0E **235** B4
Bintuni *Indonesia* 2°7S 133°32E **231** E8
Binyang *China* 23°12N 108°47E **228** F7
Binz *Germany* 54°24N 13°37E **181** A9
Binza *Dem. Rep. of the Congo* 4°21S 15°14E **265** C3
Binzert = Bizerte *Tunisia* 37°15N 9°50E **261** A1
Binzhou *China* 37°20N 118°2E **227** F10
Bio Bío □ *Chile* 37°35N 72°0W **334** D1
Biograd na Moru
  Croatia 43°56N 15°29E **199** E12
Biogradska Gora △
  Montenegro 42°55N 19°40E **202** D3
Bioko *Eq. Guin.* 3°30N 8°40E **263** E6
Biokovo *Croatia* 30°15N 9°14W **260** B3
Bipindi *Cameroon* 3°6N 10°30E **263** E7
Bir *India* 19°4N 75°46E **244** E2
Bir, Ras *Djibouti* 12°0N 43°20E **257** E5
Bīr Abu Hashim *Egypt* 23°42N 34°6E **256** D3
Bîr Abu Minqar *Egypt* 26°33N 27°33E **256** B2
Bîr Abu Muhammad
  Egypt 29°44N 34°14E **251** J5

Bîr Abu Sandûq *Egypt* 29°24N 32°30E **251** J3
Bir Adal Deib *Sudan* 22°35N 36°10E **256** D3
Bi'r al Butayyihāt *Jordan* 29°47N 35°20E **251** J4
Bi'r al Ḩamdah *Si. Arabia* 28°30N 34°55E **251** K5
Bi'r al Māri *Jordan* 30°4N 35°33E **251** H6
Bi'r al Musallam
  Si. Arabia 28°56N 35°38E **251** K6
Bi'r al Qaṭṭār *Jordan* 29°47N 35°32E **251** J4
Bi'r 'Ali *Yemen* 14°1N 48°20E **249** D5
Bir Aouine *Tunisia* 32°25N 9°18E **258** B1
Bi'r 'Asal *Egypt* 25°55N 34°20E **256** B3
Bir Atrun *Sudan* 18°15N 26°40E **256** D2
Bîr Beiḑa *Egypt* 30°25N 34°29E **251** H5
Birnin Gwari *Nigeria* 11°0N 6°45E **263** C6
Birnin Kebbi *Nigeria* 12°32N 4°12E **263** C5
Birnin Kudu *Nigeria* 11°30N 9°29E **263** C6
Birougou, Mts. *Gabon* 1°51S 12°20E **264** C2
Birr *Ireland* 53°6N 7°54W **166** C4
Birrarrung Park *Australia* 37°45S 145°4E **128** A2
Birrie → *Australia* 29°43S 146°37E **281** D4
Birsilpur *India* 28°11N 72°15E **242** E5
Birsk *Russia* 55°25N 55°30E **186** D6
Birṣtonas *Lithuania* 54°37N 24°2E **184** D11
Birtle *Canada* 50°30N 101°5W **297** C8
Biryuchiy *Ukraine* 46°10N 35°0E **189** J8
Biržai *Lithuania* 56°11N 24°45E **183** D11
Birzebbuga *Malta* 35°50N 14°32E **206** F8
Birzhi = Madona *Latvia* 56°53N 26°5E **188** D4
Birzula = Kotovsk
  Ukraine 47°45N 29°35E **177** E15
Bisa *Indonesia* 1°15S 127°28E **231** E7
Bisáccia *Italy* 41°1N 15°22E **201** A8
Bisacquino *Italy* 37°42N 13°15E **200** E6
Bisai *Japan* 35°16N 136°44E **222** B4
Bisalpur *India* 28°14N 79°48E **243** E8
Bisbee *U.S.A.* 31°27N 109°55W **305** L9
Biscarrosse *France* 44°22N 1°20W **174** D2
Biscarrosse et de Parentis, Étang de
  France 44°21N 1°10W **174** D2
Biscay, B. of *Atl. Oc.* 45°0N 2°0W **171** D1
Biscay Abyssal Plain
  Atl. Oc. 45°0N 8°0W **152** B11
Biscayne B. → *U.S.A.* 25°25N 80°12W **317** K9
Biscayne B. *U.S.A.* 25°40N 80°12W **317** K9
Biscayne Park *U.S.A.* 25°52N 80°10W **128** A2
Biscéglie *Italy* 41°14N 16°30E **201** A9
Bischheim *France* 48°37N 7°46E **179** D14
Bischofsburg = Biskupiec
  Poland 53°53N 20°58E **184** E7
Bischofshofen *Austria* 47°26N 13°14E **180** D6
Bischofstal = Ujazd
  Poland 50°23N 18°21E **185** H5
Bischofswerda *Germany* 51°7N 14°10E **178** D10
Bischofswerda *Germany* 54°8N 20°53E **184** D7
Bischwiller *France* 48°46N 7°50E **179** D14
Biscoe Is. *Antarctica* 66°0S 67°0W **5** C17
Biscoitos *Azores* 38°47N 27°15W **153** d1
Biscostasing *Canada* 47°18N 82°9W **298** C3
Biševo *Croatia* 42°57N 16°3E **199** F13
Bisha *Eritrea* 15°30N 37°31E **257** D4
Bishah, W. → *Si. Arabia* 21°24N 43°26E **248** B3
Bishan *China* 29°33N 106°12E **228** C6
Bishanga
  Dem. Rep. of the Congo 4°31S 21°2E **265** C4
Bishkek *Kyrgyzstan* 42°54N 74°46E **214** E8
Bishnath *India* 26°40N 93°10E **241** B4
Bishnupur *India* 23°8N 87°20E **243** H12
Bisho = Bhisho *S. Africa* 32°50S 27°23E **270** E4
Bishop *Calif., U.S.A.* 37°22N 118°24W **306** H8
Bishop *Ga., U.S.A.* 33°49N 83°26W **316** B6
Bishop *Tex., U.S.A.* 27°35N 97°48W **314** H6
Bishop Auckland *U.K.* 54°39N 1°40W **168** C6
Bishop Lavis *S. Africa* 33°56S 18°35E **118** A2
Bishop Museum
  U.S.A. 21°20N 157°52W **302** K14
Bishop's Falls *Canada* 49°2N 55°30W **298** C8
Bishop's Stortford *U.K.* 51°52N 0°10E **169** F8
Bishopscourt *S. Africa* 33°59S 18°27E **118** A1
Bisignano *Italy* 39°36N 16°17E **201** C9
Bisina, L. *Uganda* 1°38N 33°56E **268** B3
Biskra *Algeria* 34°50N 5°44E **261** B6
Biskra □ *Algeria* 34°40N 5°25E **261** B6
Biskupiec *Poland* 53°53N 20°58E **184** E7
Bismarck *Mo., U.S.A.* 37°46N 90°38W **310** G6
Bismarck *N. Dak.,*
  U.S.A. 46°48N 100°47W **308** B3
Biräk *Libya* 27°31N 14°20E **258** C2
Birak el Kiyam *Egypt* 30°2N 31°9E **117** A1
Biramféro *Guinea* 11°40N 9°10W **262** C3
Birao *C.A.R.* 10°20N 22°47E **264** A4
Biratnagar *Nepal* 26°27N 87°17E **243** F12
Birawa
  Dem. Rep. of the Congo 2°20S 28°48E **268** C2
Bircao *Somali Rep.* 1°13S 41°51E **267** E5
Birch → *Canada* 58°28N 112°17W **296** B6
Birch Cliff *Canada* 43°41N 79°16W **141** A3
Birch Grove *Grenada* 12°6N 61°40W **323** q
Birch Hills *Canada* 52°59N 105°25W **297** C7
Birch I. *Canada* 52°26N 99°54W **297** C9
Birch L. *N.W.T., Canada* 62°4N 116°33W **296** A5
Birch L. *Ont., Canada* 51°23N 92°18W **298** B1
Birch Mts. *Canada* 57°30N 113°10W **296** B6
Birch River *Canada* 52°24N 101°6W **297** C8
Birchip *Australia* 35°56S 142°55E **282** C5
Birchis *Romania* 45°58N 22°9E **182** E7
Birchwood *N.Z.* 46°4S 168°8E **285** F2
Birchwood *Alaska,*
  U.S.A. 61°24N 149°28W **303** F10
Bird *Canada* 56°30N 94°13W **297** B10
Bird I. = Aves, I. de
  W. Indies 15°45N 63°55W **321** C7
Bird I. *Antarctica* 54°0S 38°0W **151** B1
Birdseye *U.S.A.* 38°19N 86°42W **311** F10
Birdsville *Australia* 25°51S 139°20E **280** D2
Birdum Cr. → *Australia* 15°14S 133°0E **278** C5
Birdwood *Australia* 34°51S 138°58E **282** C3
Birecik *Turkey* 37°2N 38°0E **213** D8
Biren *Israel* 30°50N 34°28E **251** H5
Bireuen *Indonesia* 5°14N 96°39E **234** A1
Biri → *Vittoriosa Malta* 35°54N 14°31E **206** F8
Biri *Norway* 60°58N 10°35E **164** D7
Birifo *Gambia* 13°30N 14°0W **262** C2
Birigui *Brazil* 21°18S 50°16W **335** A5
Birjand *Iran* 32°53N 59°13E **247** C8
Birkan *C.A.R.* 7°51N 22°22E **264** A4
Birkdale *U.K.* 53°38N 3°2W **168** D5
Birkenfeld *Germany* 49°38N 7°9E **179** F3
Birkenhead *U.K.* 53°23N 3°2W **168** D4
Birkenstein *Germany* 52°31N 13°40E **115** A6
Birkerød *Denmark* 55°50N 12°25E **163** J6
Birket Fatmé *Chad* 12°57N 17°0E **259** F3
Birket Qârûn *Egypt* 29°30N 30°40E **256** J7
Birkfeld *Austria* 47°21N 15°45E **180** D8
Birkhadem *Algeria* 36°43N 3°3E **261** A5
Birkholz *Germany* 52°37N 13°34E **115** A5

Birkholzaue *Germany* 52°38N 13°36E **115** A4
Birkirkara *Malta* 35°54N 14°28E **206** F7
Bîrlad = Bârlad *Romania* 46°15N 27°38E **183** D12
Birmingham *W. Mids.,*
  U.K. 52°29N 1°52W **169** E6
Birmingham *Ala.,*
  U.S.A. 33°31N 86°48W **315** E11
Birmingham *Iowa,*
  U.S.A. 40°53N 91°57W **310** D5
Birmingham Int. ✈ (BHX)
  U.K. 52°26N 1°45W **169** E6
Birmitrapur *India* 22°24N 84°46E **244** C7
Birni Ngaouré *Niger* 13°5N 2°51E **263** C5
Birni Nkonni *Niger* 13°55N 5°15E **263** C6
Birnie *Kiribati* 3°35S 171°31W **277** A16

Bitterfeld *Germany* 51°37N 12°20E **178** D8
Bitterfontein *S. Africa* 31°1S 18°32E **270** D2
Bitterroot → *U.S.A.* 46°52N 114°7W **304** C6
Bitterroot Range *U.S.A.* 46°0N 114°20W **304** C6
Bitterwater *U.S.A.* 36°23N 121°0W **306** J6
Bitti *Italy* 40°29N 9°23E **200** B2
Bittou *Burkina Faso* 11°17N 0°18W **263** C4
Biu *Nigeria* 10°40N 12°3E **263** C7
Bivolari *Romania* 47°31N 27°27E **183** C12
Bivolu, Vf. *Romania* 47°16N 25°58E **183** C10
Biwa-Ko *Japan* 35°15N 136°10E **223** B8
Biwabik *U.S.A.* 47°32N 92°21W **308** B7
Bixad *Romania* 47°56N 23°28E **183** B8
Bixby *U.S.A.* 35°57N 95°53W **314** D7
Biya → *Russia* 52°25N 85°0E **217** B11
Biyang *China* 32°38N 113°21E **226** H7
Biysk *Russia* 52°40N 85°0E **217** B11
Bizana *S. Africa* 30°50S 29°52E **271** D4
Bizen *Japan* 34°43N 134°8E **222** C6
Bizerte *Tunisia* 37°15N 9°50E **261** A6
Bizerte □ *Tunisia* 37°5N 9°35E **261** A6
Bjäen fjellstove *Norway* 59°37N 7°26E **164** E4
Bjargtangar *Iceland* 65°30N 24°30W **155** B2
Bjarkalundur *Iceland* 65°33N 22°9W **155** B4
Bjärnum *Sweden* 56°17N 13°43E **163** H7
Bjästa *Sweden* 63°12N 18°29E **162** A12
Bjelasica *Montenegro* 42°50N 19°40E **202** D3
Bjelašnica *Bos.-H.* 43°43N 18°9E **182** G3
Bjelland *Norway* 58°23N 7°32E **164** F4
Bjelovar *Croatia* 45°56N 16°49E **199** C13
Bjervamoen *Norway* 59°17N 9°5E **164** E6
Bjøberg *Norway* 60°56N 8°13E **164** D5
Bjørkelangen *Norway* 59°53N 11°34E **164** E8
Bjørklinge *Sweden* 60°2N 17°33E **162** D11
Bjørknäs *Sweden* 59°19N 18°12E **139** B3
Bjørnafjorden *Norway* 60°7N 5°28E **164** D2
Bjørneborg = Pori
  Finland 61°29N 21°48E **188** E1
Bjørneborg *Sweden* 59°14N 14°16E **162** E8
Bjørnevatn *Norway* 69°40N 30°0E **160** B24
Bjørnøya *Arctic* 74°30N 19°0E **150** B8
Bjursås *Sweden* 60°44N 15°25E **162** D9
Bjuv *Sweden* 56°5N 12°55E **163** H6
Bla *Mali* 12°56N 5°47W **262** C3
Blace *Serbia* 43°18N 21°17E **202** C5
Blachownia *Poland* 50°49N 18°56E **185** H5
Black = Da → *Vietnam* 21°15N 105°20E **228** G5
Black → *Ont., Canada* 44°42N 79°19W **312** B5
Black → *Man.,*
  U.S.A. 66°42N 144°42W **303** C11
Black → *Ariz., U.S.A.* 33°44N 110°13W **305** K8
Black → *Ark., U.S.A.* 35°38N 91°20W **314** D9
Black → *La., U.S.A.* 31°16N 91°50W **314** F9
Black → *Mich., U.S.A.* 42°59N 82°27W **312** D2
Black → *N.Y., U.S.A.* 43°59N 76°4W **313** C8
Black → *Wis., U.S.A.* 43°57N 91°22W **308** D8
Black Bay Pen. *Canada* 48°38N 88°21W **298** C2
Black Birch L. *Canada* 56°53N 107°45W **297** B7
Black Canyon of the Gunnison
  U.S.A. 38°40N 107°35W **304** G10
Black Cr. → *U.S.A.* 44°30N 79°30W **141** A2
Black Diamond = Pittsburg
  U.S.A. 38°2N 121°53W **306** G5
Black Diamond *Canada* 50°45N 114°14W **296** D6
Black Duck → *Canada* 56°51N 89°2W **298** A2
Black Forest = Schwarzwald
  Germany 48°30N 8°20E **179** G4
Black Forest *U.S.A.* 39°0N 104°43W **304** G11
Black Hd. *Ireland* 53°9N 9°16W **166** C2
Black Hills *U.S.A.* 44°0N 103°45W **308** C2
Black I. *Canada* 51°12N 96°30W **297** C9
Black L. *Sask., Canada* 59°12N 105°15W **297** B7
Black L. *Mich., U.S.A.* 45°28N 84°16W **309** C11
Black L. *N.Y., U.S.A.* 44°31N 75°36W **313** B9
Black Lake *Canada* 59°11N 105°20W **297** B7
Black Mesa *U.S.A.* 36°58N 102°58W **314** C3
Black Mountain
  Australia 30°18S 151°39E **283** A9
Black Mt. = Mynydd Du
  U.K. 51°52N 3°50W **169** F4
Black Mt. *Bhutan* 27°20N 90°25E **241** B3
Black Mts. *U.K.* 51°55N 3°7W **169** F4
Black Range *U.S.A.* 33°15N 107°50W **305** K10
Black River *Jamaica* 18°0N 77°50W **320** a
Black River Falls *U.S.A.* 44°18N 90°51W **308** D8
Black River Gorges
  Mauritius 20°24S 57°25E **272** a
Black Rock *S. Austral.,*
  Australia 32°50S 138°44E **282** B2
Black Rock *Barbados* 13°7N 59°37W **323** g
Black Sea *Eurasia* 43°30N 35°0E **187** f6
Black Tickle *Canada* 53°28N 55°45W **299** B8
Black Volta → *Africa* 8°41N 1°33W **262** D4
Black Warrior →
  U.S.A. 32°32N 87°51W **315** E11
Blackall *Australia* 24°25S 145°45E **280** C4
Blackball *N.Z.* 42°22S 171°26E **285** C6
Blackbull *Australia* 17°55S 141°45E **280** B3
Blackburn *U.K.* 53°45N 2°29W **168** D5
Blackbutt *Australia* 26°51S 152°6E **281** D5
Blackdown Tableland △
  Australia 23°35S 149°45E **280** C4
Blackfen *U.K.* 51°26N 0°6E **125** B4
Blackfoot *U.S.A.* 43°11N 112°21W **304** E7
Blackfoot → *U.S.A.* 46°52N 113°53W **304** C7
Blackfoot Res. *U.S.A.* 42°55N 111°39W **304** E8
Blackheath *U.K.* 51°28N 0°0 **125** B3
Blackman *U.S.A.* 30°56N 86°38W **317** A3
Blackpool *U.K.* 53°49N 3°3W **168** D4
Blackpool □ *U.K.* 53°49N 3°3W **168** D4
Blackriver *U.S.A.* 44°46N 83°17W **312** B1
Blackrock *Ireland* 53°18N 6°11W **120** B2
Blackrock *U.K.* 54°6N 10°0W **166** C1
Blacks Harbour *Canada* 45°3N 66°49W **299** D6
Blacksburg *U.S.A.* 37°14N 80°25W **309** G14
Blackshear *U.S.A.* 31°18N 82°14W **316** D7
Blacksod B. *Ireland* 54°6N 10°0W **166** B1
Blackstairs Mt. *Ireland* 52°33N 6°48W **166** D5
Blackstone Ra. *Australia* 26°0S 128°30E **279** E4
Blacktown *Australia* 33°48S 150°55E **281** E5
Blackville *Canada* 46°44N 65°50W **299** C6
Blackwater = West Road →
  Canada 53°18N 122°53W **296** C4
Blackwater *Meath,*
  Ireland 53°39N 6°41W **166** C5
Blackwater *Waterford,*
  Ireland 52°4N 7°52W **166** D4
Blackwater → *Armagh,*
  U.K. 54°31N 6°35W **166** B5
Blackwater → *Fla.,*
  U.S.A. 30°36N 87°2W **317** A2
Blackwater → *Mo.,*
  U.S.A. 38°58N 92°59W **310** F5

Blackwells Corner
  U.S.A. 35°37N 119°47W **307** K7
Blackwood, C.
  Papua N. G. 7°49S 144°31E **286** B7
Bladensburg *U.S.A.* 38°55N 76°55W **143** B4
Bladensburg △ *Australia* 22°30S 142°59E **280** C3
Bladenbury *U.K.* 53°0N 3°56W **168** E4
Blaenau Ffestiniog *U.K.* 53°0N 3°56W **168** E4
Blaenau Gwent □ *U.K.* 51°48N 3°12W **169** F4
Blåfell *Iceland* 64°30N 19°51W **155** C7
Bláfjall *Iceland* 65°26N 16°50W **155** B10
Blagaj *Bos.-H.* 43°16N 17°55E **202** D6
Blagnac *France* 43°37N 1°23E **174** E5
Blagnac, Toulouse ✈ (TLS)
  France 43°37N 1°22E **174** E5
Blagodarnoye = Blagodarnyy
  Russia 45°7N 43°37E **191** H6
Blagodarnyy *Russia* 45°7N 43°37E **191** H6
Blagoevgrad *Bulgaria* 42°2N 23°5E **202** D7
Blagoveshchensk
  Russia 50°20N 127°30E **215** D13
Blahkiuh *Indonesia* 8°31S 115°12E **231** J18
Blain *Loire-Atlantique,*
  France 47°29N 1°45W **172** E5
Blain *Pa., U.S.A.* 40°20N 77°31W **312** F7
Blaine *Minn., U.S.A.* 45°10N 93°13W **308** C7
Blaine *Wash., U.S.A.* 48°59N 122°45W **306** B4
Blaine Lake *Canada* 52°51N 106°52W **297** C7
Blair *Australia* 22°42S 147°31E **280** C4
Blair *U.S.A.* 41°33N 96°8W **308** E5
Blair Athol *Australia* 22°42S 147°31E **280** C4
Blair Atholl *U.K.* 56°46N 3°50W **167** E5
Blair Village *U.S.A.* 33°40N 84°23W **113** C2
Blairgowrie *Gauteng,*
  S. Africa 26°6S 28°0E **123** A2
Blairgowrie *Perth & Kinr.,*
  U.K. 56°35N 3°21W **167** E5
Blairsden *U.S.A.* 39°47N 120°37W **306** F6
Blairsville *U.S.A.* 40°26N 79°16W **312** F5
Blaj *Romania* 46°10N 23°57E **182** E7
Blaka *Niger* 21°21N 12°47E **259** D2
Blakang Mati, Pulau
  Singapore 1°15N 103°50E **237** d
Blake House *U.S.A.* 42°19N 71°3W **116** B2
Blake Pt. *U.S.A.* 48°11N 88°25W **308** A9
Blakehurst *Australia* 33°59S 151°6E **139** E1
Blakely *Ga., U.S.A.* 31°23N 84°56W **316** D5
Blakely *Pa., U.S.A.* 41°28N 75°37W **313** E9
Blakesburg *U.S.A.* 40°58N 92°38W **310** D4
Blakstad *Akershus,*
  Norway 59°49N 10°28E **133** B1
Blåmont *France* 48°35N 6°50E **173** D13
Blanc, C. *Spain* 39°21N 2°51E **206** B3
Blanc, Mont *Europe* 45°48N 6°50E **175** C10
Blanca, B. *Argentina* 39°10S 61°30W **336** D4
Blanca Peak *U.S.A.* 37°35N 105°29W **305** H11
Blanchardville *U.S.A.* 42°48N 89°52W **308** D8
Blanche, C. *Australia* 33°1S 134°9E **281** E1
Blanche, L. *S. Austral.,*
  Australia 29°15S 139°40E **281** D2
Blanche, L. *W. Austral.,*
  Australia 22°25S 123°17E **278** D3
Blanche, L. *Fla., U.S.A.* 28°28N 81°30W **133** B5
Blanche Channel
  Solomon Is. 8°30S 157°30E **287** M9
Blanchester *U.S.A.* 39°17N 83°59W **311** E13
Blanchisseuse *Trin. & Tob.* 10°48N 61°18W **323** t
Blanco *Western Cape,*
  S. Africa 33°55S 22°23E **270** D3
Blanco → *Argentina* 30°20S 68°42W **334** C2
Blanco → *Bolivia* 12°30S 64°18W **331** C5
Blanco, C. *Costa Rica* 9°34N 85°8W **322** D2
Blanco, C. *U.S.A.* 42°51N 124°34W **304** E1
Blanco, Pta. *Neth. Ant.* 12°13N 68°14W **322** h
Blanda → *Iceland* 65°37N 20°9W **155** B8
Blandford Forum *U.K.* 50°51N 2°9W **169** G5
Blanding *U.S.A.* 37°37N 109°29W **305** H9
Blandinsville *U.S.A.* 40°33N 90°52W **310** D6
Blanes *Spain* 41°40N 2°48E **196** D7
Blangy-sur-Bresle *France* 49°56N 1°38E **172** D4
Blanice → *Czech Rep.* 49°10N 14°5E **180** C8
Blankaholm *Sweden* 57°36N 16°31E **163** G11
Blankenberge *Belgium* 51°20N 3°9E **170** C3
Blankenburg *Berlin,*
  Germany 52°35N 13°27E **115** A3
Blankenburg *Sachsen-Anhalt,*
  Germany 51°47N 10°57E **178** D6
Blankenfelde *Germany* 52°19N 13°24E **115** B3
Blanku, L. *Neth. Ant.* 12°20N 68°47W **322** j
Blanquefort *France* 44°55N 0°39W **174** D3
Blanquilla *Venezuela* 11°51N 64°37W **329** A5
Blanquillo *Uruguay* 32°53S 55°37W **337** B4
Blansko *Czech Rep.* 49°22N 16°40E **181** B9
Blantyre *Malawi* 15°45S 35°0E **269** F4
Blarney *Ireland* 51°56N 8°33W **166** E3
Blasdell *U.S.A.* 42°48N 78°50W **312** D6
Blåsjø *Norway* 59°36N 6°50E **164** E3
Blaszki *Poland* 51°38N 18°30E **185** G5
Blatná *Czech Rep.* 49°25N 13°52E **180** B7
Blato *Croatia* 42°56N 16°48E **199** F13
Blaubeuren *Germany* 48°24N 9°46E **179** G5
Blaustein *Germany* 48°25N 9°47E **179** G5
Blåvands Huk *Denmark* 55°33N 8°4E **163** J2
Blaydon *U.K.* 54°58N 1°42W **168** C6
Blaye *France* 45°8N 0°40W **174** C3
Blaye-les-Mines *France* 44°1N 2°8E **174** D6
Blayney *Australia* 33°32S 149°14E **283** B8
Blaze, Pt. *Australia* 12°56S 130°11E **278** B5
Blazowa *Poland* 49°53N 22°7E **185** d9
Blechhammer = Blachownia
  Poland 50°49N 18°56E **185** H5
Bleckede *Germany* 53°17N 10°43E **178** B6
Bled *Slovenia* 46°27N 14°7E **199** B11
Bleiburg *Austria* 46°35N 14°49E **180** E7
Blejești *Romania* 44°19N 25°27E **183** F10
Blekinge *Sweden* 56°20N 15°20E **163** H7
Blekinge län □ *Sweden* 56°20N 15°20E **163** H7
Blenheim *Ont., Canada* 42°20N 82°0W **312** D3
Blenheim *N.Z.* 41°38S 173°57E **285** B8
Bléone → *France* 44°5N 6°0E **175** D10
Blérancourt *France* 49°31N 3°9E **173** C10
Bletchley *U.K.* 51°59N 0°44W **169** F7
Blida *Algeria* 36°30N 2°49E **261** A5
Blida □ *Algeria* 36°35N 3°0E **261** A5
Blidö *Sweden* 59°37N 18°53E **162** D12
Blidsberg *Sweden* 57°56N 13°30E **163** G7
Blieskastel *Germany* 49°14N 7°12E **179** F3
Bligh Sound *N.Z.* 44°47S 167°32E **285** E2
Bligh Water *Fiji* 17°0S 178°0E **287** a2
Blind River *Canada* 46°10N 82°58W **298** C3
Blinisht *Albania* 41°52N 19°58E **202** E3
Bliss *Idaho, U.S.A.* 42°56N 114°57W **304** E6
Bliss *N.Y., U.S.A.* 42°34N 78°15W **312** D6
Blissfield *Ohio, U.S.A.* 40°24N 81°58W **312** F3
Blitar *Indonesia* 8°5S 112°11E **235** D4
Blitchton *U.S.A.* 32°12N 81°26W **316** D8

Blitta *Togo* 8°23N 1°6E **263** D5
Blizne *Poland* 52°14N 20°52E **142** B1
Block I. *U.S.A.* 41°11N 71°35W **313** E13
Block Island Sd. *U.S.A.* 41°15N 71°40W **313** E13
Bloemfontein *S. Africa* 29°6S 26°7E **270** C4
Bloemhof *S. Africa* 27°38S 25°32E **270** C4
Blois *France* 47°35N 1°20E **172** E8
Blokhus *Denmark* 57°15N 9°34E **163** G3
Blomskog *Sweden* 59°16N 12°2E **162** E6
Blomstermåla *Sweden* 56°59N 16°21E **163** H10
Blomvåg *Norway* 60°32N 4°56E **164** D1
Blönduós *Iceland* 65°40N 20°12W **155** B6
Blongas *Indonesia* 8°53S 116°2E **231** K19
Blonie *Poland* 52°12N 20°37E **185** F7
Bloodvein → *Canada* 51°47N 96°43W **297** C9
Bloody B. *Trin. & Tob.* 11°18N 60°38W **323** s
Bloody Foreland *Ireland* 55°10N 8°17W **166** A3
Bloom = Chicago Heights
  U.S.A. 41°30N 87°38W **311** C9
Bloomburg *U.S.A.* 45°6N 91°29W **308** C8
Bloomfield *Ont., Canada* 43°59N 77°14W **312** C7
Bloomfield *Australia* 39°1N 86°57W **311** E10
Bloomfield *Iowa, U.S.A.* 40°45N 92°25W **310** D4
Bloomfield *Ky., U.S.A.* 37°55N 85°19W **311** G11
Bloomfield *N. Mex.,*
  U.S.A. 36°43N 107°59W **305** H10
Bloomfield *Nebr., U.S.A.* 42°36N 97°39W **308** D5
Bloomingburg *U.S.A.* 39°36N 83°24W **311** E13
Bloomington *Ill., U.S.A.* 40°28N 89°0W **310** D8
Bloomington *Ind.,*
  U.S.A. 39°10N 86°32W **311** E10
Bloomington *Minn.,*
  U.S.A. 44°50N 93°17W **308** C7
Bloomington *Wis.,*
  U.S.A. 42°53N 90°55W **310** B6
Bloomsburg *U.S.A.* 41°0N 76°27W **313** E8
Bloomsbury *Australia* 20°48S 148°38E **280** C4
Bloomsbury *London, U.K.* **125** a3
Blora *Indonesia* 6°57S 111°25E **235** D4
Blossburg *U.S.A.* 41°41N 77°4W **312** E7
Blosseville Kyst
  Greenland 68°50N 26°30W **154** D8
Blota *Poland* 52°9N 21°11E **142** C3
Blouberg *S. Africa* 23°8S 28°59E **271** B4
Blountstown *U.S.A.* 30°27N 85°3W **316** D4
Blowing Point Village
  Anguilla 18°11N 63°6W **322** a
Blowing Rock *Anguilla* 18°9N 63°10W **322** a
Bludenz *Austria* 47°10N 9°50E **180** D2
Blue → *U.S.A.* 38°11N 86°19W **311** F10
Blue Cypress L. *U.S.A.* 27°44N 80°45W **317** H9
Blue Earth *U.S.A.* 43°38N 94°6W **308** D6
Blue Hole △ *Belize* 18°10N 76°24W **320** a
Blue Hole △ *Belize* 17°24N 88°30W **320** C2
Blue Island *U.S.A.* 41°40N 87°40W **119** D2
Blue Lagoon △ *Zambia* 15°28S 27°26E **269** F2
Blue Mesa Res. *U.S.A.* 38°28N 107°20W **304** G10
Blue Mosque = Sultanahme Camil
  Turkey 41°0N 28°58E **122** B1
Blue Mound *U.S.A.* 39°42N 89°7W **310** E7
Blue Mountain Lake
  U.S.A. 43°51N 74°27W **313** C10
Blue Mountain Pk. *Jamaica* 18°3N 76°36W **320** a
Blue Mountains and John Crow
  Mountains Nat. Park △
  Jamaica 18°5N 76°34W **320** a
Blue Mt. *U.S.A.* 40°30N 76°30W **313** F8
Blue Mts. *N.S.W.,*
  Australia 33°40S 150°15E **283** B9
Blue Mts. *Jamaica* 18°3N 76°34W **320** a
Blue Mts. *Oreg., U.S.A.* 45°0N 118°20W **304** D4
Blue Mts. △ *Australia* 34°2S 150°15E **283** C9
Blue Mud B. *Australia* 13°0S 136°0E **280** A2
Blue Nile = Nil el Azraq →
  Sudan 15°38N 32°31E **257** D3
Blue Nile Falls *Ethiopia* 11°25N 37°45E **257** E4
Blue Rapids *U.S.A.* 39°41N 96°39W **308** E6
Blue Ridge *U.S.A.* 36°40N 80°50W **309** G13
Blue Ridge *Canada* 52°9N 119°18W **296** C5
Blue Springs *U.S.A.* 39°1N 94°17W **310** E2
Bluebell *Ireland* 53°19N 6°21W **120** B1
Bluefield *U.S.A.* 37°15N 81°17W **309** G13
Bluefields *Nic.* 12°20N 83°50W **320** D3
Bluff *Queens., Australia* 23°35S 149°4E **280** C4
Bluff *N.Z.* 46°37S 168°20E **285** G3
Bluff *Utah, U.S.A.* 37°17N 109°33W **305** H9
Bluff Harbour *N.Z.* 46°36S 168°21E **285** G3
Bluff Hole *Jamaica* 18°9N 76°56W **320** a
Bluff Hd. *China* 22°11N 114°12E **124** F2
Bluff Knoll *Australia* 34°24S 118°15E **279** F2
Bluff Pt. *Australia* 27°50S 114°5E **279** E1
Bluffers Park *Canada* 43°43N 79°14W **141** A3
Bluffs *U.S.A.* 39°45N 90°33W **310** E6
Bluffton *Ga., U.S.A.* 31°31N 84°52W **316** D5
Bluffton *Ind., U.S.A.* 40°44N 85°11W **311** D11
Bluffton *Ohio, U.S.A.* 40°54N 83°54W **311** D13
Bluffton *S.C., U.S.A.* 32°14N 80°52W **316** D9
Blumberg *Germany* 47°49N 8°32E **179** H4
Blumenau = Stettler
  Canada 52°19N 112°40W **296** C6
Blumenau *Brazil* 27°0S 49°0W **335** B6
Blunt *U.S.A.* 44°31N 99°59W **308** C4
Blunt Pt. *U.S.A.* 37°51N 122°25W **136** A2
Blutenberg *Germany* 48°9N 11°27E **131** B1
Bly *U.S.A.* 42°24N 121°3W **304** E3
Blyde River Canyon △
  S. Africa 24°37S 31°2E **271** B5
Blylaget *Norway* 59°46N 10°41E **133** B3
Blyth *S. Austral.,*
  Australia 33°49S 138°28E **282** B3
Blyth *Ont., Canada* 43°44N 81°26W **312** C3
Blyth *Northumberland, U.K.* 55°8N 1°31W **168** B6
Blyth → *U.K.* 52°25N 1°45E **169** E9
Blythe *Calif., U.S.A.* 33°37N 114°36W **307** M12
Blythe *Ga., U.S.A.* 33°17N 82°12W **316** B7
Blytheville *U.S.A.* 35°56N 89°55W **315** D10
Bø *Norway* 59°25N 9°3E **164** E6
Bo *S. Leone* 7°55N 11°50W **262** D2
Bo Duc *Vietnam* 11°58N 106°50E **237** G6
Bo-eun *S. Korea* 36°29N 127°44E **227** G14
Bo Hai *China* 39°0N 119°0E **227** E10
Bo-Kaap Museum *Cape Town, S. Africa* **118** c2
Bo-no-Misaki *Japan* 31°15N 130°13E **222** F2
Bo Xian = Bozhou *China* 33°55N 115°41E **226** H8
Boa Esperança *Brazil* 21°3N 61°23W **329** C5
Boa Esperança, Reprêsa
  Brazil 6°5S 43°50W **332** C3
Boa Nova *Brazil* 14°22S 40°10W **335** D6
Boa Viagem *Brazil* 5°7S 39°44W **332** C4
Boa Vista = Tocantinópolis
  Brazil 6°50S 47°25W **332** C2
Boa Vista *Brazil* 2°48N 60°30W **332** B2
Boa Vista, C. *Verde Is.* 16°0N 22°49W **153** j
Boa Vista, Alto do *Brazil* 22°58S 43°16W **135** B1
Boa Vista do Erechim = Erechim
  Brazil 27°35S 52°15W **335** B5
Boac *Phil.* 13°27N 121°50E **232** D3
Boaco *Nic.* 12°29N 85°35W **320** D2
Bo'ai *China* 35°10N 113°3E **226** G7
Boal *Spain* 43°25N 6°49W **196** B3
Boali *C.A.R.* 4°48N 18°7E **264** D3
Boane *Mozam.* 26°6S 32°19E **271** D5
Boang I. *Papua N. G.* 3°23S 153°18E **286** E4
Boardman *U.S.A.* 41°2N 80°40W **312** E4

Boardwalk U.S.A. 40°34N 73°49W **132** C3
Boath India 19°20N 78°20E **244** E4
Boatswain Bird I.
  Ascension I. 7°56S 14°18W **153** g
Boavista Portugal 38°48N 9°8W **126** A2
Boaz I. Bermuda 32°18N 64°51W **153** a
Bob Marley Mausoleum
  Jamaica 18°18N 77°18W **320** a
Bobadah Australia 32°19S 146°41E **283** B7
Bobai China 22°17N 109°59E **228** F7
Bobbili India 18°35N 83°30E **244** E6
Bóbbio Italy 44°46N 9°23E **198** D6
Bobcaygeon Canada 44°33N 78°33W **312** B6
Bobigny France 48°54N 2°26E **134** A3
Boblad India 17°13N 75°26E **244** F2
Böblingen Germany 48°40N 9°1E **179** G5
Bobo-Dioulasso
  Burkina Faso 11°8N 4°13W **262** C4
Bobolice Poland 53°58N 16°37E **184** E3
Bobon Phil. 12°32N 124°34E **232** E5
Bobonaza → Ecuador 2°36S 76°38W **328** D3
Boboshevo Bulgaria 42°9N 23°0E **202** D7
Bobov Dol Bulgaria 42°20N 23°0E **202** D7
Bóbr → Poland 52°4N 15°4E **185** F2
Bobraomby, Tanjon' i
  Madag. 12°40S 49°10E **272** A2
Bobrinets Ukraine 48°4N 32°5E **189** H7
Bobrov Russia 51°5N 40°2E **190** E5
Bobrovitsa Ukraine 50°44N 31°23E **189** G6
Bobruysk = Babruysk
  Belarus 53°10N 29°15E **177** B15
Bobures Venezuela 9°15N 71°11W **328** B3
Boca de Drago Venezuela 11°0N 61°50W **323** t
Boca del Río Mexico 19°5N 96°4W **319** D5
Bôca do Acre Brazil 8°50S 67°27W **328** E5
Bôca do Jari Brazil 1°7S 51°58W **329** D7
Bôca do Moaco Brazil 7°41S 68°17W **328** E5
Boca Grande Trin. & Tob. 10°40N 61°50W **323** t
Boca Grande Fla., U.S.A. 26°45N 82°16W **317** J7
Boca Grande Venezuela 8°40N 60°40W **329** B5
Boca Raton U.S.A. 26°21N 80°5W **317** J7
Bocaiúva Brazil 17°7S 43°49W **333** E3
Bocanda Ivory C. 7°5N 4°31W **262** D4
Bocanegra Peru 12°1S 77°7W **124** B2
Bocaranga C.A.R. 7°0N 15°35E **264** A3
Bocas del Toro Panama 9°15N 82°20W **320** E3
Boceguillas Spain 41°20N 3°39W **194** D7
Bochkarevo = Belogorsk
  Russia 51°0N 128°20E **215** D13
Bochmanivka Ukraine 47°40N 29°34E **183** C14
Bochnia Poland 49°58N 20°27E **185** J7
Bocholt Germany 51°50N 6°36E **178** D2
Bochum = Senwabarana
  S. Africa 23°17S 29°7E **271** B4
Bochum Germany 51°28N 7°13E **178** D3
Bockenem Germany 52°1N 10°8E **178** C6
Bočki Poland 52°39N 23°3E **185** F10
Bocognano France 42°5N 9°4E **175** F13
Bocoio Angola 12°28S 14°10E **268** B1
Bocoio Brazil 9°15N 70°16W **328** B3
Bocono → Venezuela 9°43N 69°34W **328** B4
Bocoyna Mexico 27°52N 107°35W **318** B3
Boçsa C.A.R. 45°21N 21°47E **182** E6
Boda C.A.R. 4°19N 17°26E **264** B3
Boda Dalarna, Sweden 61°1N 15°13E **162** C9
Böda Kalmar, Sweden 57°15N 17°3E **163** G11
Boda Västernorrland,
  Sweden 62°52N 16°39E **162** B10
Bodafors Sweden 57°48N 14°23E **163** G8
Bodaybo Russia 57°50N 114°0E **215** D12
Boddam U.K. 59°56N 1°17W **167** B7
Boddington Australia 32°50S 116°30E **279** F2
Bode Sadu Nigeria 9°0N 4°47E **263** D5
Bodega Bay U.S.A. 38°20N 123°3W **306** G3
Boden Sweden 65°50N 21°42E **160** D19
Bodensee Europe 47°35N 9°25E **179** H5
Bodenteich Germany 52°50N 10°42E **178** C6
Bodhan India 18°40N 77°44E **244** E3
Bodinayakkanur India 10°2N 77°10E **245** J3
Bodinga Nigeria 12°58N 5°10E **263** C6
Bodmin U.K. 50°28N 4°43W **169** G3
Bodmin Moor U.K. 50°33N 4°36W **169** G4
Bodo Australia 67°17N 14°24E **160** C16
Bodø Norway
Bodoquena, Serra da
  Brazil 21°0S 56°50W **331** E6
Bodoupa C.A.R. 5°43N 17°36E **264** A3
Bodrichi Chad 19°11N 15°54E **259** E3
Bodrog → Hungary 48°11N 21°22E **182** B6
Bodrum Turkey 37°3N 27°30E **205** D9
Boduna
  Dem. Rep. of the Congo 5°5N 19°44E **264** A3
Bódva → Hungary 48°19N 20°45E **182** B5
Boedo Argentina 34°38S 58°26W **117** B2
Boembé Congo 2°54S 15°39E **264** C3
Boën France 45°44N 4°1E **175** C8
Boende
  Dem. Rep. of the Congo 0°24S 21°12E **264** C4
Boerne U.S.A. 29°47N 98°44W **314** G5
Boesmans → S. Africa 33°42S 26°39E **270** C4
Boffa Guinea 10°16N 14°3W **262** C2
Bofuku
  Dem. Rep. of the Congo 0°57S 20°53E **264** C4
Bog Walk Jamaica 18°6N 77°1W **320** a
Bogal, Lagh → Kenya 0°41N 40°57E **267** D5
Bogale Burma 16°17N 95°24E **241** G5
Bogalusa U.S.A. 30°47N 89°52W **315** F10
Bogan → Australia 30°20S 146°55E **283** A7
Bogan Gate Australia 33°7S 147°49E **283** B7
Bogandé Burkina Faso 13°2N 0°8W **263** C4
Bogantungan Australia 23°41S 147°17E **280** C4
Bogata U.S.A. 33°28N 95°13W **314** E7
Bogatić Serbia 44°51N 19°30E **202** B3
Boğazkale Turkey 40°2N 34°37E **212** C6
Boğazlıyan Turkey 39°11N 35°14E **212** C6
Bogbonga
  Dem. Rep. of the Congo 1°36N 19°24E **264** B3
Bogda Shan China 43°35N 89°40E **217** D11
Bogen Sweden 60°4N 12°33E **162** D6
Bogenhausen Germany 48°8N 11°36E **182** D2
Bogense Denmark 55°34N 10°5E **163** J4
Bogetići Montenegro 42°41N 18°58E **202** D2
Boggabilla Australia 28°36S 150°24E **281** D5
Boggabri Australia 30°45S 150°5E **283** B8
Boggeragh Mts. Ireland 52°2N 8°55W **166** D3
Boggy Creek Swamp
  U.S.A. 28°52N 81°19W **133** B2
Boggy Peak Antigua & B. 17°2N 61°52W **322** b
Boghari = Ksar el Boukhari
  Algeria 35°51N 2°52E **261** A5
Bogia Papua N. G. 4°9S 145°0E **286** C3
Bogildo S. Korea 34°9N 126°32E **234** H4
Boglan = Solhan Turkey 38°57N 41°3E **213** C9
Bogles Grenada 12°30N 61°26W **323** q
Bognor Regis U.K. 50°47N 0°40W **169** G7
Bogo Phil. 11°3N 124°0E **233** F4
Bogodukhov = Bohodukhiv
  Ukraine 50°9N 35°33E **189** G8
Bogól Manya Ethiopia 4°34N 41°29E **257** G5
Bogong, Mt. Australia 36°47S 147°17E **283** D7
Bogor Indonesia 6°36S 106°48E **234** D3
Bogorodsk Russia 53°27N 38°38E **188** D14
Bogorodsk = Noginsk
  Russia 55°50N 38°25E **188** E10

Bogorodsk Russia 56°4N 43°30E **190** B6
Bogorodskoye = Kamskoye Ustye
  Russia 55°10N 49°20E **190** C9
Bogorodskoye = Leninskoye
  Russia 58°23N 47°3E **190** A8
Bogoslovsky = Karpinsk
  Russia 59°45N 60°1E **186** C11
Bogoso Ghana 5°38N 2°3W **262** D4
Bogotá Colombia 4°34N 74°0W **328** C3
Bogota N.J., U.S.A. 40°52N 74°2W **132** A1
Bogotol Russia 56°15N 89°50E **214** D9
Bogou Togo 10°40N 0°12E **263** C5
Bogra Bangla. 24°51N 89°22E **241** C2
Bogstadvatnet Norway 59°58N 10°37E **163** D3
Boguchany Russia 58°40N 97°30E **215** D10
Boguchar Russia 49°55N 40°32E **190** F5
Boguslav = Bohuslav
  Ukraine 49°47N 30°57E **189** H6
Boguszów-Gorce Poland 50°45N 16°12E **185** H3
Bohain-en-Vermandois
  France 49°59N 3°28E **173** C10
Bohan Ukraine 48°2N 24°22E **183** B9
Bohemian Forest = Böhmerwald
  Germany 49°8N 13°14E **179** F9
Bohena Cr. → Australia 30°17S 149°42E **283** A8
Bohinjska Bistrica
  Slovenia 46°17N 14°1E **199** B11
Böhmerwald Germany 49°8N 13°14E **179** F9
Böhmisch-Brod = Český Brod
  Czech Rep. 50°4N 14°57E **180** A7
Böhmisch-Leipa = Česká Lípa
  Czech Rep. 50°45N 14°30E **180** A7
Böhmisch-Trübau = Česká Třebová
  Czech Rep. 49°54N 16°27E **181** B9
Bohmte Germany 52°22N 8°19E **178** C4
Bohnsdorf Germany 52°23N 13°34E **115** B4
Bohodukhiv Ukraine 50°9N 35°33E **189** G8
Bohol → Phil. 9°50N 124°10E **233** G5
Bohol Sea Phil. 9°0N 124°0E **233** G5
Bohol Str. Phil. 9°45N 123°40E **233** G4
Bohongou Burkina Faso 12°30N 0°40E **263** C5
Böhönye Hungary 46°25N 17°28E **182** D2
Bohorodchany Ukraine 48°48N 24°32E **183** B9
Bohotleh Somali Rep. 8°20N 46°25E **267** C4
Bohu China 41°58N 86°37E **217** D11
Bohuslän Sweden 58°25N 12°0E **163** F5
Boi Nigeria 9°35N 9°27E **263** D6
Boi, Pta. de Brazil 23°55S 45°15W **335** A6
Boiaçu Brazil 0°27S 61°46W **329** D5
Boigu I. Australia 9°15S 142°14E **286** E2
Boileau, C. Australia 17°40S 122°7E **278** C3
Boim Brazil 2°49S 55°10W **329** D6
Boing'o Sudan 9°58N 33°44E **257** F3
Boipariguda India 18°46N 82°26E **244** E6
Boipeba, I. de Brazil 13°39S 38°55W **333** D4
Boiro Spain 42°39N 8°54W **194** C2
Bois → Brazil 18°35S 50°2W **333** E1
Bois-Blanc Réunion 21°11S 55°49E **272** t
Bois-Colombes France 48°55N 2°16E **134** A2
Bois-d'Arcy France 48°48N 2°1E **134** B1
Boise U.S.A. 43°37N 116°13W **304** E5
Boise City U.S.A. 36°44N 102°31W **314** C3
Boissevain Canada 49°15N 100°5W **297** D8
Boissy-St-Léger France 48°44N 2°31E **134** B4
Böite → Italy 46°5N 12°5E **199** B9
Boitzenburg Germany 53°16N 13°35E **178** B9
Boizenburg Germany 53°23N 10°43E **178** B6
Bojador, C. W. Sahara 26°0N 14°30W **260** C2
Bojana → Albania 41°52N 19°22E **202** E3
Bojanowo Poland 51°43N 16°42E **185** G3
Bojden Denmark 55°6N 10°7E **163** J4
Bojnürd Iran 37°30N 57°20E **247** B8
Bojonegoro Indonesia 7°11S 111°54E **235** D4
Boju Nigeria 7°22N 7°55E **263** D6
Boka Serbia 45°22N 20°52E **182** E5
Boka Kotorska
  Montenegro 42°23N 18°32E **202** D2
Boka Tabla Neth. Ant. 12°22N 69°8W **322** g
Bokada
  Dem. Rep. of the Congo 4°8N 19°23E **264** B3
Bokala Dem. Rep. of the Congo 3°8S 17°4E **264** C3
Bokani Ivory C. 8°31N 4°33W **262** D4
Bokani Nigeria 9°28N 5°10E **263** D6
Bokaro India 23°46N 85°55E **243** H11
Bokatola
  Dem. Rep. of the Congo 0°38S 18°46E **264** C3
Boké Guinea 10°56N 14°17W **262** C2
Bokela
  Dem. Rep. of the Congo 1°10S 21°59E **264** C4
Bokenda
  Dem. Rep. of the Congo 1°16N 21°22E **264** B4
Bokkos Nigeria 9°17N 9°1E **263** D6
Bokhara → Australia 29°55S 146°42E **281** D4
Bokhara → Australia 29°55S 146°42E **281** D4
Bokkos Nigeria 9°17N 9°1E **263** D6
Boknafjorden Norway 59°14N 5°40E **164** E2
Bokode
  Dem. Rep. of the Congo 3°55N 19°30E **264** B3
Bokolo Gabon 2°40S 10°10E **264** C2
Bokondo
  Dem. Rep. of the Congo 0°15N 22°32E **264** B4
Bokora → Uganda 2°12N 31°32E **268** B3
Bokoro Chad 12°25N 17°14E **259** F3
Bokota
  Dem. Rep. of the Congo 0°56S 22°24E **264** C4
Bokote
  Dem. Rep. of the Congo 0°12S 21°8E **264** C4
Bokpyin Burma 11°18N 98°42E **237** G2
Boksitogorsk Russia 59°22N 33°50E **188** C7
Boku Papua N. G. 6°34S 155°21E **286** D8
Bokungu
  Dem. Rep. of the Congo 0°35S 22°50E **264** C4
Bol Chad 13°30N 14°40E **259** F2
Bol Croatia 43°18N 16°38E **199** E13
Bolama Guinea-Biss. 11°30N 15°30W **262** C1
Bolan → Pakistan 28°38N 67°42E **242** E2
Bolan Pass Pakistan 29°50N 67°20E **240** C2
Bolaños → Mexico 21°12N 104°5W **318** C4
Bolaños de Calatrava
  Spain 38°54N 3°40W **195** C7
Bolayır Turkey 40°31N 26°45E **203** F10
Bolbec France 49°30N 0°30E **172** C7
Boldāji Iran 31°56N 51°3E **247** D6
Boldești-Scăeni Romania 45°3N 26°2E **183** E11
Boldeslato Italy 45°39N 9°8E **129** B1
Bole Xinjiang Uygur, China
  45°11N 81°37E **217** C10
Bole Ethiopia 6°36N 37°20E **257** F4
Bole Ghana 9°2N 2°7W **262** D4
Bolekhiv Ukraine 49°0N 23°57E **177** D12
Boleko
  Dem. Rep. of the Congo 1°35S 19°50E **264** C3
Boler Norway 59°53N 10°50E **163** J4
Boleslawiec Poland 51°17N 15°37E **185** G2
Bolgatanga Ghana 10°44N 0°53W **263** C4
Bolgrad = Bolhrad
  Ukraine 45°40N 28°32E **183** E13
Bolia Dem. Rep. of the Congo 1°35S 18°22E **264** C3
Boliden Phil. 16°23N 119°54E **232** C2
Bolinao, C. Phil. 16°23N 119°55E **232** C2

Bolingbroke U.S.A. 32°57N 83°48W **316** C6
Bolingbrook U.S.A. 41°42N 88°4W **311** C8
Bolingo
  Dem. Rep. of the Congo 5°0N 25°50E **264** B2
Bolintin-Vale Romania 44°27N 25°46E **183** F10
Bolívar Argentina 36°15S 60°53W **334** D3
Bolívar Antioquia, Colombia 5°50N 76°1W **328** B2
Bolívar Cauca, Colombia 2°0N 77°0W **328** C2
Bolívar Peru 7°18S 77°48W **330** B2
Bolivar Mo., U.S.A. 37°37N 93°25W **308** G7
Bolivar N.Y., U.S.A. 42°4N 78°10W **312** D6
Bolivar Tenn., U.S.A. 35°12N 89°0W **315** D10
Bolívar □ Colombia 9°0N 74°40W **328** B3
Bolívar □ Ecuador 1°15S 79°0W **328** D2
Bolívar □ Venezuela 6°20N 63°30W **329** B5
Bolivian Plateau = Altiplano
  Bolivia 17°0S 68°0W **330** D4
Bolipúblico Brazil 10°0S 40°10W **333** D3
Boljevac Serbia 43°51N 21°58E **202** C5
Bolkhov Russia 53°25N 36°0E **188** F9
Bolków Poland 50°55N 16°6E **185** H3
Bollate Italy 45°32N 9°7E **129** A1
Bollé Mauritania 20°8N 11°40W **260** D2
Bollebeek Belgium 50°55N 4°14E **116** A1
Bolleboygd Sweden 57°40N 12°35E **163** F6
Bollmora Sweden 59°14N 18°14E **115** B3
Bollnäs Sweden 61°21N 16°24E **162** C10
Bollon Australia 28°2S 147°29E **281** D4
Bollstabruk Sweden 62°59N 17°40E **162** B11
Bolmen Sweden 56°55N 13°40E **163** H7
Bologna Italy 44°29N 11°20E **199** D8
Bologna ✈ (BLQ) Italy 44°34N 11°16E **198** D8
Bologoye Russia 57°55N 34°5E **188** D8
Bolomba
  Dem. Rep. of the Congo 0°35N 19°0E **264** B3
Bolombo →
  Dem. Rep. of the Congo 1°32N 21°14E **264** B4
Bolonchén Mexico 20°1N 89°45W **319** D7
Bolondo
  Dem. Rep. of the Congo 2°12S 18°42E **264** C3
Boloven, Cao Nguyen
  Laos 15°10N 106°30E **236** E6
Bolpur India 23°40N 87°45E **243** H12
Bolsena Italy 42°39N 11°59E **199** F8
Bolsena, L. di Italy 42°36N 11°56E **199** F8
Bolshakovo Russia 54°53N 21°40E **184** D8
Bolshaya Chernigovka
  Russia 52°6N 50°52E **190** D10
Bolshaya Garmanda = Evensk
  Russia 62°12N 159°30E **215** C16
Bolshaya Glushitsa
  Russia 52°28N 50°30E **190** D10
Bolshaya Martynovka
  Russia 47°19N 41°37E **191** G5
Bolshaya Okhta Russia 59°56N 30°26E **137** B2
Bolshaya Tsaryovshchina =
  Volzhskiy Russia 48°56N 44°46E **191** F7
Bolshaya Vradiyevka
  Ukraine 47°50N 30°40E **189** J6
Bolshevik, Ostrov
  Russia 78°30N 102°0E **215** B11
Bolshoy Anyuy →
  Russia 68°30N 160°49E **215** C17
Bolshoy Begichev, Ostrov
  Russia 74°20N 112°30E **215** B12
Bolshoy Kavkas = Caucasus
  Mountains Eurasia 42°50N 44°0E **191** J7
Bolshoy Lyakhovskiy, Ostrov
  Russia 73°35N 142°0E **215** B15
Bolshoy Theatre Moscow, Russia **129** b2
Bolshoy Tokmak = Tokmak
  Kyrgyzstan 42°49N 75°15E **217** D9
Bolshoy Tyuters, Ostrov
  Russia 59°51N 27°13E **188** C4
Bólstaðarhlíð Iceland 65°31N 19°49W **155** B7
Bolsward Neths. 53°3N 5°32E **170** A5
Bolt Head U.K. 50°12N 3°48W **169** G4
Boltaña Spain 42°28N 0°4E **196** C5
Boltigen Switz. 46°38N 7°24E **179** J3
Boltonville France 46°4N 6°24E **173** F13
Bolton Canada 43°54N 79°45W **312** C5
Bolton Gt. Man., U.K. 53°35N 2°26W **168** D5
Bolton Landing U.S.A. 43°32N 73°35W **313** C11
Bolton Georgia, U.S.A. 33°48N 84°28W **113** B2
Bolu Turkey 40°45N 31°35E **212** B4
Bolu □ Turkey 40°45N 31°30E **212** B4
Bolubulu Papua N. G. 9°21S 150°20E **286** E6
Bolungavík Iceland 66°9N 23°15W **155** A2
Boluo China 23°3N 114°21E **229** F10
Bolvadin Turkey 38°45N 31°4E **212** C4
Bolzano Italy 46°31N 11°22E **199** B8
Bom Comércio Brazil 9°45S 65°54W **331** B4
Bom Conselho Brazil 9°10S 36°41W **333** D4
Bom Despacho Brazil 19°43S 45°15W **333** E2
Bom Jesus Brazil 9°10S 44°0E **333** D3
Bom Jesus Brazil 9°4S 44°22W **332** C3
Bom Jesus da Gurguéia, Serra
  Brazil 9°0S 43°0W **332** C3
Bom Jesus da Lapa
  Brazil 13°15S 43°25W **333** D3
Bom Retiro Brazil 13°58S 38°15W **137** B2
Dem. Rep. of the Congo 5°50S 13°4E **266** D2
Bomaderry Australia 34°52S 150°37E **283** C9
Bomandjokou Congo 3°39N 26°8E **268** B2
Bomaneh
  Dem. Rep. of the Congo 1°18N 23°47E **264** B4
Bomassa Congo 2°12N 16°12E **264** B3
Bomate
  Dem. Rep. of the Congo 2°14N 25°15E **264** C2
Bombala Australia 36°56S 149°15E **283** C8
Bombarral Portugal 39°15N 9°9W **195** C1
Bombay = Mumbai India 18°55N 72°50E **244** F1
Bombedor, Pta. Venezuela 9°53N 61°37W **329** C6
Bombo Kasani
  Dem. Rep. of the Congo 5°51S 21°54E **266** D4
Bomboma
  Dem. Rep. of the Congo 2°25S 18°55E **264** B3
Bombowa
  Dem. Rep. of the Congo 2°14N 25°15E **264** C2
Bomboyo Chad 12°1N 15°28E **259** F3
Bomdila India 28°44N 94°12E **241** A8
Bomet Kenya 0°47N 35°21E **266** C4
Bomi Hills Liberia 7°1N 10°38W **262** D2
Bomili Dem. Rep. of the Congo 1°45N 27°5E **268** B2
Bomlo Norway 59°37N 5°13E **164** E2
Bomokandi →
  Dem. Rep. of the Congo 3°39N 26°8E **268** B2
Bomongo
  Dem. Rep. of the Congo 1°27N 18°21E **264** B3
Bomu →
  Dem. Rep. of the Congo 4°40N 22°30E **264** B4
Bon, C. Tunisia 37°1N 11°2E **258** A2

Bomu Orientale □
  Dem. Rep. of the Congo 5°0N 25°50E **264** B2
Bon Acceuil Mauritius 20°10S 57°39E **272** d
Bon Sar Pa Vietnam 12°24N 107°35E **236** F6
Bonāb Iran 37°20N 46°4E **213** D12
Bonaigarh India 21°50N 84°57E **243** J11
Bonaire Neth. Ant. 12°10N 68°15W **322** h
Bonampak Mexico 16°45N 91°1W **319** D6
Bonang Australia 37°11S 148°41E **283** D8
Bonanza Nic. 13°54N 84°35W **320** D3
Bonaparte →
  Australia 14°0S 124°30E **278** B3
Bonaparte Arch.
  Australia 14°0S 124°30E **278** B3
Bonaparte Rocks Grenada 12°24N 61°30W **323** q
Bonar Bridge U.K. 57°54N 4°20W **167** D4
Bonasse Trin. & Tob. 10°5N 61°54W **323** t
Bonaventure Canada 48°5N 65°32W **299** C6
Bonaventure, Place Montréal, Canada **130** C2
Bonavista Canada 48°40N 53°5W **299** C9
Bonavista, C. Canada 48°42N 53°5W **299** C9
Bonavista B. Canada 48°45N 53°25W **299** C9
Bondeno Italy 44°53N 11°25E **199** D8
Bondi Australia 33°53S 151°16E **139** A3
Bondo
  Dem. Rep. of the Congo 1°22S 23°54E **264** C4
Bondo Équateur,
  Dem. Rep. of the Congo 3°55N 23°53E **264** B4
Bondoukou Ivory C. 8°2N 2°47W **262** D4
Bondowoso Indonesia 7°55S 113°49E **235** D4
Bondy France 48°54N 2°28E **134** A4
Bondy, Forêt de France 48°54N 2°33E **134** A4
Bône = Annaba Algeria 36°50N 7°46E **261** A6
Bonefish Pond Bahamas 25°59N 77°23W **153** b
Bonerate Indonesia 7°25S 121°5E **231** F6
Bonerate, Kepulauan
  Indonesia 6°30S 121°10E **231** F6
Bo'ness U.K. 56°1N 3°37W **167** E5
Bonete, Cerro Argentina 27°55S 68°40W **334** B2
Bonfim Brazil 3°33N 59°25W **329** C6
Bonfim = Senhor-do-Bonfim
  Brazil 10°30S 40°10W **333** D3
Bong Son = Hoai Nhon
  Vietnam 14°28N 109°1E **236** E7
Bonga Ethiopia 7°15N 36°1E **257** F4
Bongabon Phil. 15°38N 121°8E **232** D3
Bongaigaon India 26°28N 90°34E **241** A3
Bongandanga
  Dem. Rep. of the Congo 1°24N 21°3E **264** B4
Bongao Phil. 5°2N 119°46E **233** J2
Bongo, Sa. de Angola 10°35S 15°15E **266** D3
Bongor Chad 10°35N 15°20E **259** F3
Bongouanou Ivory C. 6°42N 4°15E **262** D4
Bonham U.S.A. 33°35N 96°11W **314** E6
Boni Mali 15°3N 2°10W **262** B4
Boni → Kenya 1°35S 41°18E **268** C5
Bonifacio France 41°24N 9°10E **175** G13
Bonifacio, Bouches de
  Medit. S. 41°12N 9°15E **175** G13
Bonifacio Monument
  Phil. 14°38N 120°58E **127** B1
Bonifay U.S.A. 30°47N 85°41W **316** E4
Bonin Is. = Ogasawara Gunto
  Pac. Oc. 27°0N 142°0E **288** E6
Bonita Springs U.S.A. 26°21N 81°47W **317** J8
Bonito Brazil 21°8S 56°28W **331** E6
Bonke Ethiopia 6°5N 37°16E **257** F4
Bonkoukou Niger 14°0N 3°15E **263** C5
Bonn Germany 50°46N 7°6E **178** E3
Bonnat France 46°20N 1°54E **173** B4
Bonne Terre U.S.A. 37°55N 90°33W **310** G9
Bonne B. Canada 49°42N 116°13W **297** D5
Bonners Ferry U.S.A. 48°42N 116°19W **304** B5
Bonnétable France 48°11N 0°25E **172** D7
Bonneuil-sur-Marne
  France 48°46N 2°30E **134** B4
Bonneval France 48°11N 1°24E **172** D8
Bonneval-sur-Arc France 45°22N 7°3E **175** C11
Bonneville France 46°4N 6°24E **173** F13
Bonney, L. Australia 37°50S 140°20E **282** D4
Bonnie Doon Australia 37°2S 145°53E **283** D6
Bonnie Rock Australia 30°29S 118°22E **279** F2
Bonnington U.S.A. 55°54N 3°25W **121** B1
Bonny Nigeria 4°25N 7°13E **263** E6
Bonny → Nigeria 4°20N 7°10E **263** E6
Bonny, Bight of Africa 3°30N 9°20E **263** E6
Bonny Hills Australia 31°36S 152°51E **283** A10
Bonny-sur-Loire France 47°33N 2°50E **173** E9
Bonnyrigg U.K. 55°53N 3°6W **167** F5
Bonnyrigg and Lasswade
  U.K. 55°53N 3°6W **121** B3
Bonnyville Canada 54°20N 110°45W **297** C6
Bono Italy 40°25N 9°2E **200** B2
Bonoi Indonesia 1°45S 137°41E **231** E9
Bonorva Italy 40°25N 8°46E **200** B1
Bonsall U.S.A. 33°16N 117°14W **307** M9
Bontang Indonesia 0°10N 117°30E **235** B5
Bontebok △ S. Africa 34°5S 20°28E **270** D3
Bonthe S. Leone 7°30N 12°33W **262** D2
Bontoc U.S.A. 17°7N 120°58E **232** C3
Bonyeri Ghana 5°1N 2°46E **262** D4
Bonyhád Hungary 46°18N 18°32E **182** D3
Bonython Ra. Australia 23°40S 128°45E **278** D4
Boo Sweden 59°20N 18°16E **139** A3
Booderee △ Australia 35°12S 150°42E **283** D9
Bookabie Australia 31°50S 132°41E **279** F5
Booke Dem. Rep. of the Congo 2°34S 22°32E **264** C4
Booker U.S.A. 36°27N 100°32W **314** C4
Bool Lagoon Australia 37°7S 140°40E **282** D4
Boola Guinea 8°26N 8°41E **262** D3
Boolcoomata Australia 31°57S 140°33E **282** B4
Booligal Australia 33°58S 144°53E **283** B6
Boon Pt. Antigua & B. 17°10N 61°50W **322** b
Boone Iowa, U.S.A. 42°4N 93°53W **310** D3
Boone N.C., U.S.A. 36°13N 81°41W **315** C14
Booneville Ark., U.S.A. 35°8N 93°55W **314** D8
Booneville Miss., U.S.A. 34°39N 88°34W **315** D10
Boonville Calif., U.S.A. 39°1N 123°22W **306** F3
Boonville Ind., U.S.A. 38°3N 87°16W **311** F10
Boonville Mo., U.S.A. 38°58N 92°44W **310** F7
Boonville N.Y., U.S.A. 43°29N 75°20W **313** C9
Boorabbin △ Australia 31°22N 120°18E **279** F3
Boorindal Australia 30°22S 146°11E **281** E4
Boorowa Australia 34°28S 148°44E **283** B8
Boort Australia 36°7S 143°42E **282** D5
Boosaaso = Bosaso
  Somali Rep. 11°12N 49°18E **267** E4
Boostoun Ireland
Boothia, Gulf of Canada 71°0N 90°0W **295** B11

Boothia Pen. Canada 71°0N 94°0W **294** B10
Bootle U.K. 53°28N 3°1W **168** D4
Booué Gabon 0°5S 11°55E **264** C2
Bopako
  Dem. Rep. of the Congo 1°53N 21°13E **264** B4
Boppard Germany 50°13N 7°35E **179** E3
Boquerón □ Paraguay 23°0S 60°0W **331** H5
Boquete Panama 8°46N 82°27W **320** E3
Boquilla, Presa de la
  Mexico 27°31N 105°30W **318** B3
Boquillas del Carmen
  Mexico 29°11N 102°58W **318** B4
Bor Czech Rep. 49°41N 12°45E **180** B5
Bor Serbia 44°5N 22°7E **202** B6
Bôr Sudan 6°10N 31°40E **257** F3
Bor Sweden 57°9N 14°10E **163** H8
Bor Turkey 37°54N 34°32E **212** D6
Bor, Lagh → Kenya 1°18N 40°40E **267** D5
Bor Mashash Israel 31°7N 34°50E **251** G5
Bor u Ceske Lipy = Nový Bor
  Czech Rep. 50°46N 14°35E **180** A7
Bora Bora
  French Polynesia 16°30S 151°45W **289** f
Borah Peak U.S.A. 44°8N 113°47W **304** D7
Borama Somali Rep. 9°55N 43°7E **267** C5
Borang Sudan 4°50N 30°59E **257** G3
Borangapara India 25°14N 90°14E **241** C3
Borås Sweden 57°43N 12°56E **163** H6
Borāzjān Iran 29°22N 51°10E **247** D6
Borba Brazil 4°12S 59°34W **329** D6
Borba Portugal 38°50N 7°26E **195** G3
Borbon Phil. 10°50N 124°2E **233** F5
Borborema, Planalto da
  Brazil 7°0S 37°0W **332** C4
Borcea Romania 44°20N 27°45E **183** F12
Borzna Ukraine 51°18N 32°26E **189** G7
Borzya Russia 50°24N 116°31E **215** D12
Bosa Italy 40°18N 8°30E **200** B1
Bosa Monene
  Dem. Rep. of the Congo 1°16S 23°40E **264** C4
Bosaga Turkmenistan 37°33N 65°41E **240** A2
Bosambi
  Dem. Rep. of the Congo 2°24N 22°39E **264** B4
Bosanska Dubica
  Bos.-H. 45°10N 16°50E **199** C13
Bosanska Gradiška
  Bos.-H. 45°10N 17°15E **182** E2
Bosanska Kostajnica
  Bos.-H. 45°11N 16°33E **199** C13
Bosanska Krupa
  Bos.-H. 44°25N 16°10E **198** C12
Bosanski Brod Bos.-H. 45°10N 18°0E **182** E2
Bosanski Novi Bos.-H. 45°2N 16°22E **199** C13
Bosanski Petrovac
  Bos.-H. 44°35N 16°21E **199** C13
Bosanski Šamac Bos.-H. 45°3N 18°29E **182** E3
Bosanско Grahovo
  Bos.-H. 44°12N 16°26E **198** B6
Bosaso Somali Rep. 11°12N 49°18E **267** B6
Bosavi, Mt. Papua N. G. 6°30S 142°49E **286** D2
Boscastle U.K. 50°41N 4°42W **169** G3
Boscobel U.S.A. 43°8N 90°42W **310** A6
Boscobelle Barbados 13°17N 59°35W **323** t
Bose China 23°53N 106°35E **228** F6
Boseki
  Dem. Rep. of the Congo 2°34S 19°38E **264** C3
Bosobong S. Korea 34°46N 127°5E **234** H3
Boshan China 36°28N 117°49E **227** F9
Boshof S. Africa 28°31S 25°13E **270** C4
Boshrūyeh Iran 33°50N 57°30E **247** C8
Bosilegrad Serbia 42°30N 22°27E **202** D6
Boskovice Czech Rep. 49°29N 16°40E **181** B9
Bosmont S. Africa 26°10S 27°57E **123** B1
Bosna → Bos.-H. 45°4N 18°29E **182** E3
Bosna i Hercegovina = Bosnia-
  Herzegovina ■ Europe 44°0N 18°0E **182** G2
Bosnia-Herzegovina ■
  Europe 44°0N 18°0E **182** G2
Bosnik Indonesia 1°5S 136°10E **231** E9
Bōsō-Hantō Japan 35°20N 140°20E **223** B12
Bosobolo
  Dem. Rep. of the Congo 4°15N 19°50E **264** B3
Bosön Sweden 59°22N 18°11E **139** A3
Bosporus = İstanbul Boğazı
  Turkey 41°5N 29°3E **122** B2
Bosque Farms U.S.A. 35°51N 106°42W **305** J10
Bossangoa C.A.R. 6°35N 17°30E **264** A3
Bossé Bangou Niger 13°20N 1°16E **263** C5
Bossembélé C.A.R. 5°25N 17°40E **264** A3
Bossemtélé C.A.R. 5°2N 17°6E **264** A3
Bossier City U.S.A. 32°31N 93°44W **314** E8
Bosso Niger 13°43N 13°19E **259** F2
Bosso, Dallol → Niger 12°25N 2°50E **263** C5
Bostan Pakistan 30°26N 67°2E **242** D2
Bostānābād Iran 37°50N 46°50E **213** D12
Bostancı Turkey 40°57N 29°5E **122** C2
Bosten Hu China 41°55N 87°40E **217** D11
Boston U.K. 52°59N 0°2W **168** E7
Boston Lincs., U.S.A. 52°59N 0°2W **168** E7
Boston Ga., U.S.A. 30°47N 83°47W **316** F6
Boston Mass., U.S.A. 42°22N 71°3W **313** D13
Boston Bar Canada 49°52N 121°30W **296** D4
Boston Bay Jamaica 18°9N 76°22W **320** a
Boston Logan Int. ✈ (BOS)
  U.S.A. 42°22N 71°1W **116** b2
Boston Mts. U.S.A. 35°42N 93°15W **314** D8
Boston, U.S.A. **116** c3
Boston Tea Party Ship & Museum
  U.S.A. **116** c3
Bostwick U.S.A. 29°46N 81°38W **316** F8
Bosumtwi, L. Ghana 6°30N 1°25W **263** D4
Bosusulu
  Dem. Rep. of the Congo 0°50N 20°45E **264** B4
Bosut → Croatia 45°20N 18°45E **182** E3
Boswell B.C., Canada 49°28N 116°45W **296** D5
Boswell Ind., U.S.A. 40°31N 87°23W **311** D9
Boswell Pa., U.S.A. 40°10N 79°2W **312** E5
Bosworth U.S.A. 39°28N 93°20W **310** F7
Botad India 22°15N 71°40E **242** H4
Botafogo Brazil 22°56S 43°10W **135** B1
Botan → Turkey 37°57N 42°2E **213** D10
Botanic Gardens
  Washington, D.C., U.S.A. **143** b3
Botanic Have Copenhagen, Denmark **118** b2
Botany B. Australia 33°58S 151°11E **139** B3
Botany B. Australia 33°58S 151°11E **139** B2
Botany Bay Nat. Park △
  Australia 34°0S 151°10E **139** B3
Botene Laos 17°35N 101°12E **236** D3
Botev Bulgaria 42°44N 24°45E **203** D8
Botevgrad Bulgaria 42°55N 23°47E **203** D8
Bothaville S. Africa 27°23S 26°34E **270** C4
Bothnia, G. of Europe 62°0N 20°0E **160** F19
Bothwell Tas., Australia 42°20S 147°1E **285** G4
Bothwell Ont., Canada 42°38N 81°52W **312** D3
Botić → Czech Rep. **128** B2
Botica Sete Portugal 38°49N 9°10W **126** A1
Boticas Portugal 41°41N 7°40W **194** D3
Botletle → Botswana 20°10S 23°15E **270** C3
Botlikh Russia 42°40N 46°11E **213** A12
Botna → Moldova 46°45N 29°34E **183** D14
Botola
  Dem. Rep. of the Congo 1°17S 18°13E **264** C3

Botolan *Phil.* 15°17N 120°1E **232** D3
Botoroaga *Romania* 44°8N 25°32E **183** F10
Botoşani *Romania* 47°42N 26°41E **183** C11
Botoşani □ *Romania* 47°50N 26°50E **183** C11
Botou *Burkina Faso* 12°42N 1°59E **263** C5
Botricello *Italy* 38°56N 16°51E **201** D9
Botro *Ivory C.* 7°51N 5°19W **262** D3
Botswana ■ *Africa* 22°0S 24°0E **270** B3
Bottellier *Neth. Ant.* 12°6N 68°54W **322** g
Bottineau *U.S.A.* 48°50N 100°27W **308** A3
Bottnaryd *Sweden* 57°47N 13°50E **163** G7
Bottom, The *Neth. Ant.* 17°38N 63°15W **322** a
Bottopassi *Suriname* 4°14N 55°27W **329** C6
Bottrop *Germany* 51°31N 6°58E **170** C6
Botucatu *Brazil* 22°55S 48°30W **335** A6
Botwood *Canada* 49°6N 55°23W **299** C8
Bou Alam *Algeria* 33°50N 1°26E **261** B5
Bou Ali *Algeria* 27°11N 0°4W **261** C4
Bou Djébéha *Mali* 18°25N 2°45W **262** B4
Bou Guema *Algeria* 28°49N 0°19E **261** C5
Bou Ismaïl *Algeria* 36°38N 2°42E **261** A5
Bou Izakarn *Morocco* 29°12N 9°46W **260** C3
Boû Lanouâr *Mauritania* 21°12N 16°34W **260** D1
Boû Rjeïmât *Mauritania* 19°4N 15°3W **262** B1
Bou Saâda *Algeria* 35°11N 4°9E **261** A5
Bou Salem *Tunisia* 36°45N 9°2E **258** A1
Bouaflé *Ivory C.* 7°1N 5°47W **262** D3
Bouaké *Ivory C.* 7°40N 5°2W **262** D3
Bouanga *Congo* 2°7S 16°8E **264** C3
Bouar *C.A.R.* 6°0N 15°40E **264** A3
Bouârfa *Morocco* 32°32N 1°58W **261** B4
Bouba Ndjida △ *Cameroon* 8°50N 14°45E **264** A2
Boubout *Algeria* 27°26N 4°30W **260** C4
Bouca *C.A.R.* 6°45N 18°25E **264** A3
Boucaut B. *Australia* 12°0S 134°25E **280** A1
Boucherville *Canada* 45°36N 73°28W **130** A3
Boucherville, Îs. de *Canada* 45°36N 73°28W **130** A3
Bouches-du-Rhône □ *France* 43°37N 5°2E **175** E9
Boucle de Baoule △ *Mali* 13°53N 9°0W **262** C3
Boucles de la Seine Normande ⌓ *France* 49°32N 0°35E **172** C7
Bouctouche *Canada* 46°30N 64°45W **299** C7
Bouda *Algeria* 27°50N 0°27W **261** C4
Boudenib *Morocco* 31°59N 3°31W **260** B4
Bouéni *Mayotte* 12°54S 45°4E **272** b
Bouéni, B. de *Mayotte* 12°55S 45°7E **272** b
Boufarik *Algeria* 36°34N 2°58E **261** A5
Bougainville, C. *Australia* 13°57S 126°4E **278** B4
Bougainville I. *Papua N. G.* 6°0S 155°0E **287** L8
Bougainville Reef *Australia* 15°30S 147°5E **280** B4
Bougainville Str. *Solomon Is.* 6°40S 156°10E **287** L9
Bougaroun, C. *Algeria* 37°6N 6°30E **261** A6
Bougie = Bejaïa *Algeria* 36°42N 5°2E **261** A6
Bougival *France* 48°51N 2°8E **134** A1
Bougouni *Mali* 11°30N 7°20W **262** C3
Bouillante *Guadeloupe* 16°8N 61°46W **322** e
Bouillante, Pitons de *Guadeloupe* 16°8N 61°43W **322** e
Bouillon *Belgium* 49°44N 5°3E **170** E5
Bouïra *Algeria* 36°20N 3°59E **261** A5
Bouïra □ *Algeria* 36°15N 3°55E **261** A5
Boukombé *Benin* 10°13N 1°9E **263** C5
Boulal *Mali* 15°8N 8°21W **262** B3
Boulazac *France* 45°10N 0°47E **174** C4
Boulder *Colo., U.S.A.* 40°1N 105°17W **304** F11
Boulder *Mont., U.S.A.* 46°14N 112°7W **304** C7
Boulder City *U.S.A.* 35°58N 114°49W **307** K12
Boulder Creek *U.S.A.* 37°7N 122°7W **306** H4
Boulder Dam = Hoover Dam *U.S.A.* 36°1N 114°44W **307** K12
Boulder Pt. *China* 22°14N 114°6E **122** B1
Boulemane □ *Morocco* 33°10N 4°0W **260** B4
Boulembo *Gabon* 1°26S 12°0E **264** C2
Bouli *Mauritania* 15°17N 12°18W **262** B2
Boulia *Australia* 22°52S 139°51E **280** C2
Bouligny *France* 49°17N 5°45E **173** C12
Boulogne → *France* 47°12N 1°47W **172** E5
Boulogne, Bois de *France* 48°51N 2°14E **134** A2
Boulogne-Billancourt *France* 48°50N 2°14E **134** A2
Boulogne-sur-Gesse *France* 43°18N 0°38E **174** E4
Boulogne-sur-Mer *France* 50°42N 1°36E **173** B8
Bouloire *France* 47°59N 0°45E **172** E7
Boulou → *C.A.R.* 6°45N 24°16E **264** A4
Boulouli *Mali* 15°30N 9°25W **262** B3
Bouloupari *N. Cal.* 21°52S 166°4E **288** d
Bouloupesse *Congo* 1°58S 12°40E **264** C2
Boulsa *Burkina Faso* 12°39N 0°34W **263** C4
Boultoum *Niger* 14°45N 10°25E **259** F2
Bouma △ *Fiji* 16°50S 179°52E **287** A2
Boumalne Dadès *Morocco* 31°25N 6°0W **260** B3
Boumba → *Cameroon* 2°2N 15°12E **264** B2
Boumbé → *C.A.R.* 4°4N 15°23E **264** B3
Boûmdeïd *Mauritania* 17°25N 9°50W **262** B2
Boumerdès *Algeria* 36°46N 3°28E **261** A5
Boumerdès □ *Algeria* 36°45N 3°40E **261** A5
Boun Neua *Laos* 21°38N 101°54E **236** B3
Boun Tai *Laos* 21°23N 101°58E **236** B3
Bouna *Ivory C.* 9°10N 3°0W **262** D4
Boundary *U.S.A.* 64°5N 141°1W **303** D12
Boundary Peak *U.S.A.* 37°51N 118°21W **306** H8
Boundgi *Gabon* 1°0S 11°51E **264** C2
Boundiali *Ivory C.* 9°30N 6°20W **262** D3
Boungou → *C.A.R.* 8°21N 23°48E **264** A4
Bountiful *U.S.A.* 40°53N 111°52W **304** F8
Bounty Is. *Pac. Oc.* 48°0S 178°30E **288** M9
Bounty Trough *Pac. Oc.* 46°0S 178°0E **288** M9
Boura *Mali* 12°25N 4°33W **262** C4
Bourail *N. Cal.* 21°34S 165°30E **288** d
Bourbeuse → *U.S.A.* 38°24N 90°53W **310** F6
Bourbon *U.S.A.* 41°18N 86°7W **311** C10
Bourbon-Lancy *France* 46°37N 3°45E **173** F10
Bourbon-l'Archambault *France* 46°36N 3°4E **173** F10
Bourbon Street *New Orleans, U.S.A.* **131** b2
Bourbonnais *Allier, France* 46°28N 3°0E **173** F10
Bourbonnais *Ill., U.S.A.* 41°9N 87°52W **311** C9
Bourbonne-les-Bains *France* 47°54N 5°45E **173** E12
Bourbourg *France* 50°56N 2°12E **173** B9
Bourdel L. *Canada* 56°43N 74°10W **298** A5
Bourem *Mali* 17°0N 0°24W **263** B4
Bourg *France* 45°3N 0°34W **174** C3
Bourg-Argental *France* 45°18N 4°32E **175** C8
Bourg-de-Péage *France* 45°2N 5°3E **175** C9
Bourg-en-Bresse *France* 46°13N 5°12E **173** F12
Bourg-la-Reine *France* 48°46N 2°19E **134** B2
Bourg-Lastic *France* 45°39N 2°35E **174** C6
Bourg-Madame *France* 42°26N 1°55E **174** F5
Bourg-St-Andéol *France* 44°23N 4°39E **175** D8
Bourg-St-Maurice *France* 45°35N 6°46E **175** C10
Bourganeuf *France* 45°57N 1°45E **174** C5
Bourgas = Burgas *Bulgaria* 42°33N 27°29E **203** D11
Bourges *France* 47°9N 2°25E **173** E9
Bourget *Canada* 45°26N 75°9W **313** A9
Bourget, Lac du *France* 45°44N 5°52E **175** C9
Bourgneuf, B. de *France* 47°3N 2°10W **172** E4
Bourgneuf-en-Retz *France* 47°2N 1°58W **172** E5
Bourgogne □ *France* 47°0N 4°50E **173** F11
Bourgoin-Jallieu *France* 45°36N 5°17E **175** C9
Bourgueil *France* 47°17N 0°10E **172** E7
Bourke *Australia* 30°8S 145°55E **281** E4
Bourne *U.K.* 52°47N 0°22W **168** E7
Bournemouth *U.K.* 50°43N 1°52W **169** G6
Bournemouth □ *U.K.* 50°43N 1°52W **169** G6
Bouroum *Burkina Faso* 13°37N 0°39W **263** C4
Bouse *U.S.A.* 33°56N 114°0W **307** M13
Boussac *France* 46°22N 2°13E **173** F9
Boussé *Burkina Faso* 12°39N 1°53W **263** C4
Bousso *Chad* 10°34N 16°52E **259** F3
Boussouma *Burkina Faso* 12°52N 1°13W **263** C4
Bout, Pte. du *Martinique* 14°33N 61°3W **322** j
Bout Stable Bay *Dominica* 15°21N 61°15W **323** k
Boutilimit *Mauritania* 17°45N 14°40W **262** B2
Boutonne → *France* 45°54N 0°50W **174** C3
Bouvet I. = Bouvetøya *Antarctica* 54°26S 3°24E **152** M12
Bouvetøya *Antarctica* 54°26S 3°24E **152** M12
Bouviers *France* 48°46N 2°4E **134** B1
Bouxwiller *France* 48°49N 7°27E **173** D14
Bouza *Niger* 14°29N 6°2E **263** C6
Bouznika *Morocco* 33°46N 7°6W **260** B3
Bouzonville *France* 49°17N 6°32E **173** C13
Bova Marina *Italy* 37°56N 15°55E **201** E8
Bovalino Marina *Italy* 38°10N 16°10E **201** D9
Bovec *Slovenia* 46°20N 13°33E **199** B10
Boven Kapuas, Pegunungan *Malaysia* 1°25N 113°15E **235** B4
Bovenkerk *Neths.* 52°18N 4°51E **112** B2
Bovenkerker Polder *Neths.* 52°16N 4°52E **112** B2
Bøverdal *Norway* 61°44N 8°20E **164** C5
Bøverfjorden *Norway* 63°1N 8°32E **164** A5
Bovill *U.S.A.* 46°51N 116°24W **304** C5
Bovino *Italy* 41°15N 15°20E **201** A8
Bovisa *Italy* 45°30N 9°10E **129** A2
Bovril *Argentina* 31°21S 59°26W **334** C4
Bow *U.K.* 51°31N 0°1W **125** A3
Bow → *Canada* 49°57N 111°41W **296** C6
Bow Island *Canada* 49°50N 111°23W **304** B8
Bowbells *U.S.A.* 48°48N 102°15W **308** A2
Bowdle *U.S.A.* 45°27N 99°39W **308** C4
Bowdon *U.S.A.* 33°32N 85°15W **316** B4
Bowdon Junction *U.S.A.* 33°40N 85°9W **316** B4
Bowelling *Australia* 33°25S 116°30E **279** F2
Bowen *Argentina* 35°0S 67°31W **334** D2
Bowen *Queens., Australia* 20°0S 148°16E **280** J6
Bowen Mts. *Australia* 37°0S 147°50E **283** D7
Bowers Basin *Pac. Oc.* 53°45N 176°0E **150** D16
Bowers Ridge *Pac. Oc.* 54°0N 180°0E **150** D17
Bowery *New York, U.S.A.* **132** e2
Bowie *Ariz., U.S.A.* 32°19N 109°29W **305** K9
Bowie *Tex., U.S.A.* 33°34N 97°51W **314** E6
Bowland, Forest of *U.K.* 54°0N 2°30W **168** D5
Bowling Green *Fla., U.S.A.* 27°38N 81°50W **317** H8
Bowling Green *Ky., U.S.A.* 36°59N 86°27W **308** G10
Bowling Green *Mo., U.S.A.* 39°21N 91°12W **310** E5
Bowling Green *Ohio, U.S.A.* 41°23N 83°39W **311** C13
Bowling Green, C. *Australia* 19°19S 147°25E **280** B4
Bowling Green Bay △ *Australia* 19°26S 146°57E **280** B4
Bowman *N. Dak., U.S.A.* 46°11N 103°24W **308** B2
Bowman *S.C., U.S.A.* 33°21N 80°41W **316** B9
Bowman I. *Antarctica* 65°0S 104°0E **151** C8
Bowmanville = Clarington *Canada* 43°55N 78°41W **312** C6
Bowmore *U.K.* 55°45N 6°17W **167** F2
Bowral *Australia* 34°26S 150°27E **283** C9
Bowraville *Australia* 30°37S 152°52E **281** E5
Bowron → *Canada* 54°3N 121°50W **296** C4
Bowron Lake ⌓ *Canada* 53°10N 121°5W **296** C4
Bowser L. *Canada* 56°30N 129°30W **296** B3
Bowsman *Canada* 52°14N 101°12W **297** C8
Bowutu Mts. *Papua N. G.* 7°45S 147°10E **286** D4
Bowwood *Zambia* 17°5S 26°20E **269** F2
Box Cr. → *Australia* 34°10S 143°50E **281** E3
Boxholm *Sweden* 58°12N 15°3E **163** F9
Boxmeer *Neths.* 51°38N 5°56E **170** C5
Boxtel *Neths.* 51°36N 5°20E **170** C5
Boyabat *Turkey* 41°28N 34°47E **212** B6
Boyabo *Dem. Rep. of the Congo* 3°43N 18°46E **264** B3
Boyaca □ *Colombia* 5°30N 73°20W **328** B3
Boyacıköy *Turkey* 41°5N 29°2E **122** B2
Boyalıca *Turkey* 40°29N 29°33E **203** F13
Boyang *China* 29°0N 116°38E **229** C11
Boyany *Ukraine* 48°17N 26°8E **183** B11
Boyasegese *Dem. Rep. of the Congo* 3°29N 20°33E **264** B4
Boyce *U.S.A.* 31°23N 92°40W **314** F8
Boyd *U.S.A.* 30°11N 83°37W **316** E6
Boyd Conservation Area *Canada* 43°49N 79°35W **141** A1
Boyd L. *Canada* 52°46N 76°42W **298** B4
Boyenge *Dem. Rep. of the Congo* 0°14N 18°55E **264** B3
Boyer, C. *N. Cal.* 21°37S 168°6E **288** d
Boyera *Dem. Rep. of the Congo* 0°40S 19°23E **264** C3
Boyle *Alta., Canada* 54°35N 112°49W **296** C6
Boyle *Roscommon, Ireland* 53°59N 8°18W **166** C3
Boyle Heights *U.S.A.* 34°1N 118°12W **126** B3
Boyne → *Ireland* 53°43N 6°15W **166** C5
Boyne City *U.S.A.* 45°13N 85°1W **309** C11
Boyni Qara *Afghan.* 36°20N 67°0E **240** A2
Boynitsa *Bulgaria* 43°58N 22°32E **202** C6
Boynton Beach *U.S.A.* 26°32N 80°4W **317** J9
Boyolali *Indonesia* 7°32S 110°35E **235** D4
Boyoma, Chutes *Dem. Rep. of the Congo* 0°35N 25°23E **264** B5
Boysen Res. *U.S.A.* 43°25N 108°11W **304** E9
Boyup Brook *Australia* 33°50S 116°23E **279** F2
Boz Burun *Turkey* 40°32N 28°46E **203** F12
Boz Dağ *Turkey* 37°18N 29°11E **205** D11
Boz Dağları *Turkey* 38°20N 28°0E **205** C10
Bozai Gumbaz *Afghan.* 37°8N 74°0E **240** A4
Bozburun *Turkey* 36°43N 28°4E **205** E10
Bozcaada *Turkey* 39°49N 26°3E **212** C2
Bozdağ *Turkey* 36°50N 36°22E **250** B7
Bozdoğan *Turkey* 37°40N 28°17E **205** D10
Boze *Papua N. G.* 9°3S 143°3E **286** E2
Bozeman *U.S.A.* 45°41N 111°2W **304** D8
Bozen = Bolzano *Italy* 46°31N 11°22E **199** B8
Bozene *Dem. Rep. of the Congo* 2°56N 19°12E **264** B3
Boževac *Serbia* 44°32N 21°24E **202** B5
Bozhou *China* 33°55N 115°41E **226** H8
Bozkır *Turkey* 37°11N 32°14E **212** D5
Bozkurt *Turkey* 37°50N 29°37E **205** D11
Bozouls *France* 44°28N 2°43E **174** D6
Bozoum *C.A.R.* 6°25N 16°35E **264** A3
Bozova *Antalya, Turkey* 37°13N 30°18E **205** D12
Bozova *Sanliurfa, Turkey* 37°21N 38°32E **213** D8
Bozovici *Romania* 44°56N 22°0E **182** F7
Bozüyük *Turkey* 39°54N 30°3E **205** B12
Bozyazı *Turkey* 36°6N 33°0E **250** B4
Bra *Italy* 44°42N 7°51E **198** D4
Braås *Sweden* 57°4N 15°3E **163** G9
Brabant □ *Belgium* 50°46N 4°30E **170** D4
Brabant L. *Canada* 55°58N 103°43W **297** B8
Brabrand *Denmark* 56°9N 10°7E **163** H4
Brač *Croatia* 43°20N 16°40E **199** E13
Bracadale, L. *U.K.* 57°20N 6°30W **167** D2
Bracciano *Italy* 42°6N 12°10E **199** F9
Bracciano, L. di *Italy* 42°7N 12°14E **199** F9
Bracebridge *Canada* 45°2N 79°19W **312** A5
Bracieux *France* 47°30N 1°30E **172** E8
Bräcke *Sweden* 62°45N 15°26E **162** B9
Brackettville *U.S.A.* 29°19N 100°25W **314** G4
Bracki Kanal *Croatia* 43°24N 16°40E **199** E13
Bracknell *U.K.* 51°25N 0°43W **169** F7
Bracknell Forest □ *U.K.* 51°25N 0°44W **169** F7
Brad *Romania* 46°10N 22°50E **182** D7
Brádano → *Italy* 40°23N 16°51E **201** B9
Bradbury Building *Los Angeles, U.S.A.* **127** b2
Bradenton *U.S.A.* 27°30N 82°34W **317** H7
Bradford *Ont., Canada* 44°7N 79°34W **312** B5
Bradford *W. Yorks., U.K.* 53°47N 1°45W **168** D6
Bradford *Ill., U.S.A.* 41°11N 89°39W **310** C7
Bradford *Ohio, U.S.A.* 40°8N 84°27W **311** D12
Bradford *Pa., U.S.A.* 41°58N 78°38W **312** E6
Bradford *Vt., U.S.A.* 43°59N 72°9W **313** C12
Bradley *Ark., U.S.A.* 33°6N 93°39W **314** E8
Bradley *Calif., U.S.A.* 35°52N 120°48W **306** K6
Bradley *Ill., U.S.A.* 41°9N 87°52W **311** C9
Bradley Institute *Zimbabwe* 17°7S 31°25E **269** F3
Bradley Junction *U.S.A.* 27°48N 81°59W **317** H8
Bradner *U.S.A.* 41°20N 83°26W **311** C13
Brady *U.S.A.* 31°9N 99°20W **314** F5
Brædstrup *Denmark* 55°58N 9°37E **163** J3
Braemar *Australia* 33°12S 139°35E **282** B3
Braepark *U.K.* 55°58N 3°18W **121** B2
Braeside *Canada* 45°28N 76°24W **313** A8
Braeton *Jamaica* 17°57N 76°53W **320** a
Braga *Portugal* 41°35N 8°25W **194** D2
Braga □ *Portugal* 41°30N 8°30W **194** D2
Bragadiru *Romania* 43°46N 25°31E **183** G10
Bragado *Argentina* 35°2S 60°27W **334** D3
Bragança *Brazil* 1°0S 47°2W **332** B2
Bragança *Portugal* 41°48N 6°50W **194** D4
Bragança □ *Portugal* 41°30N 6°45W **194** D4
Bragança Paulista *Brazil* 22°55S 46°32W **335** A6
Bragg's Spur = West Memphis *U.S.A.* 35°8N 90°10W **315** D9
Brahestad = Raahe *Finland* 64°40N 24°28E **160** D21
Brahmakund *India* 27°52N 96°22E **241** B6
Brahmanbaria *Bangla.* 23°58N 91°15E **241** D3
Brahmani → *India* 20°39N 86°46E **244** D8
Brahmapur *India* 19°15N 84°54E **244** E7
Brahmaputra → *Asia* 23°40N 90°35E **241** D3
Braich-y-pwll *U.K.* 52°47N 4°46W **168** E3
Braid *U.K.* 55°55N 3°11W **121** B2
Braidwood *Australia* 35°27S 149°49E **283** C8
Brăila *Romania* 45°19N 27°59E **183** E12
Brăila □ *Romania* 45°5N 27°30E **183** E12
Brainerd *U.S.A.* 46°22N 94°12W **308** B6
Braintree *Essex, U.K.* 51°53N 0°34E **169** F8
Braintree *Mass., U.S.A.* 42°13N 71°0W **313** D14
Brak → *S. Africa* 29°35S 22°55E **270** C3
Brake *Germany* 53°20N 8°28E **178** B4
Brakel *Germany* 51°42N 9°11E **178** D5
Brakna □ *Mauritania* 17°0N 13°20W **262** B2
Bräkne-Hoby *Sweden* 56°14N 15°6E **163** H9
Brakwater *Namibia* 22°28S 17°3E **270** B2
Brålanda *Sweden* 58°34N 12°21E **163** F6
Bramberg *Germany* 50°6N 10°40E **179** E6
Bramdrupdam *Denmark* 55°31N 9°28E **163** J3
Bramhapuri *India* 20°36N 79°52E **244** D4
Bramley *S. Africa* 26°7S 28°4E **123** A2
Bramming *Denmark* 55°28N 8°42E **163** J2
Brämön *Sweden* 62°14N 17°40E **162** B11
Brampton *Ont., Canada* 43°45N 79°45W **312** C5
Brampton *Cumb., U.K.* 54°57N 2°44W **168** C5
Bramsche *Germany* 52°24N 7°59E **178** C3
Bramton I. *Australia* 20°50S 149°17E **280** J7
Branchville *U.S.A.* 33°15N 80°49W **316** B9
Branco → *Brazil* 1°20S 61°50W **329** D5
Branco, C. *Brazil* 7°9S 34°47W **332** C5
Brandaris *Neth. Ant.* 12°16N 68°23W **322** h
Brandberg *Namibia* 21°10S 14°33E **270** B1
Brandberg ⌓ *Namibia* 21°10S 14°30E **270** B1
Brandbu *Norway* 60°26N 10°28E **164** D7
Brande *Denmark* 55°57N 9°8E **163** J3
Brandeis University *U.S.A.* 42°21N 71°17W **116** A1
Brandenburg = Neubrandenburg *Germany* 53°33N 13°15E **178** B9
Brandenburg *Brandenburg, Germany* 52°25N 12°33E **178** C8
Brandenburg *Ky., U.S.A.* 38°0N 86°10W **311** G10
Brandenburg □ *Germany* 52°50N 13°0E **178** C9
Brandenburger Tor *Germany* 52°30N 13°21E **115** A3
Brandfort *S. Africa* 28°40S 26°30E **270** C4
Brando *France* 42°47N 9°27E **175** F13
Brandon *Man., Canada* 49°50N 99°57W **297** D9
Brandon *Fla., U.S.A.* 27°56N 82°17W **317** H7
Brandon *Vt., U.S.A.* 43°48N 73°6W **313** C11
Brandon B. *Ireland* 52°17N 10°8W **166** D1
Brandon Mt. *Ireland* 52°15N 10°15W **166** D1
Brandsen *Argentina* 35°10S 58°15W **334** D4
Brandvlei *S. Africa* 30°25S 20°30E **270** D3
Brandýs nad Labem *Czech Rep.* 50°10N 14°40E **180** A7
Brăneşti *Romania* 44°27N 26°20E **183** F11
Branford *Conn., U.S.A.* 41°17N 72°49W **313** E12
Branford *Fla., U.S.A.* 29°58N 82°56W **316** F7
Brani, Pulau *Singapore* 1°15N 103°50E **138** B3
Braniewo *Poland* 54°25N 19°50E **184** D6
Branik *Czech Rep.* 50°1N 14°25E **135** B2
Brännkyrka *Sweden* 59°17N 18°0E **139** B2
Bransfield Str. *Antarctica* 63°0S 59°0W **151** C18
Brańsk *Poland* 52°45N 22°50E **185** F9
Branson *U.S.A.* 36°39N 93°13W **308** G7
Brantford *Canada* 43°10N 80°15W **312** C4
Brantley *U.S.A.* 31°35N 86°16W **316** D3
Brantôme *France* 45°22N 0°39E **174** C4
Branxholme *Australia* 37°52S 141°49E **282** D4
Branxton *Australia* 32°38S 151°21E **283** B9
Branzi *Italy* 46°1N 9°46E **198** B6
Brás *Amazonas, Brazil* 2°5S 58°10W **329** D6
Brás *São Paulo, Brazil* 23°32S 46°36W **137** B2
Bras d'Or L. *Canada* 45°50N 60°50W **299** C7
Bras-Panon *Réunion* 20°59S 55°41E **272** f
Brasher Falls *U.S.A.* 44°49N 74°47W **313** B10
Brasil = Brazil ■ *S. Amer.* 12°0S 50°0W **333** D2
Brasil, Planalto *Brazil* 18°0S 46°30W **326** E6
Brasil Novo *Brazil* 3°19S 52°38W **329** D7
Brasilândia *Brazil* 23°28S 46°42W **137** A1
Brasiléia *Brazil* 11°0S 68°45W **330** C4
Brasília *Distrito Federal, Brazil* 15°47S 47°55W **333** E2
Brasília *Minas Gerais, Brazil* 16°12S 44°26W **333** E3
Brasília △ *Brazil* 15°41S 48°8W **333** E2
Brasília Legal *Brazil* 3°49S 55°36W **329** D6
Braskereidfoss *Norway* 60°44N 11°46E **164** D8
Braslaw *Belarus* 55°38N 27°0E **188** E4
Braslovče *Slovenia* 46°21N 15°3E **199** B12
Braşov *Romania* 45°38N 25°35E **183** E10
Braşov □ *Romania* 45°45N 25°15E **183** E10
Brass *Nigeria* 4°35N 6°14E **263** E6
Brass → *Nigeria* 4°15N 6°13E **263** E6
Brassac-les-Mines *France* 45°24N 3°20E **174** C7
Brasschaat *Belgium* 51°19N 4°27E **170** C4
Brassey, Banjaran *Malaysia* 5°0N 117°15E **235** B5
Brassey Ra. *Australia* 25°8S 122°15E **279** E3
Brasso Seco *Trin. & Tob.* 10°45N 61°16W **323** t
Brasstown Bald *U.S.A.* 34°53N 83°49W **315** D13
Brastad *Sweden* 58°23N 11°30E **163** F5
Brastavăţu *Romania* 43°55N 24°24E **183** G9
Bratan = Morozov *Bulgaria* 42°30N 25°10E **203** D9
Brateş *Romania* 45°50N 26°4E **183** E11
Brateyevo *Russia* 55°39N 37°45E **129** C4
Bratislava *Slovak Rep.* 48°10N 17°7E **181** C10
Bratislava M.R. Stefanik ✈ **(BTS)** *Slovak Rep.* 48°11N 17°9E **181** C10
Bratislavský □ *Slovak Rep.* 48°15N 17°20E **181** C10
Bratsberg = Telemark □ *Norway* 59°25N 8°30E **164** E5
Bratsevo *Russia* 55°51N 37°24E **129** A2
Bratsigovo *Bulgaria* 42°1N 24°22E **203** D8
Bratsk *Russia* 56°10N 101°30E **215** D11
Brattleboro *U.S.A.* 42°51N 72°34W **313** D12
Brattvåg *Norway* 62°37N 6°25E **164** B3
Bratunac *Bos.-H.* 44°13N 19°21E **182** F4
Braunau *Austria* 48°15N 13°3E **180** C6
Braunsberg = Braniewo *Poland* 54°25N 19°50E **184** D6
Braunschweig *Germany* 52°15N 10°31E **178** C6
Braunton *U.K.* 51°7N 4°10W **169** F3
Brava *C. Verde Is.* 15°0N 24°40W **153** j
Brava *Somali Rep.* 1°20N 44°8E **267** D5
Bravicea *Moldova* 47°22N 28°27E **183** C13
Bråviken *Sweden* 58°38N 16°32E **163** F10
Bravo del Norte, Rio = Grande, Rio → *N. Amer.* 25°58N 97°9W **314** J6
Brawley *U.S.A.* 32°59N 115°31W **307** N11
Bray *Ireland* 53°13N 6°7W **166** C5
Bray, Mt. *Australia* 14°0S 134°30E **280** A1
Bray, Pays de *France* 49°46N 1°26E **171** B4
Bray-sur-Seine *France* 48°25N 3°14E **173** D10
Braybrook *Australia* 37°46S 144°51E **128** A1
Braymer *U.S.A.* 39°35N 93°48W **310** E3
Brázdim *Czech Rep.* 50°10N 14°35E **135** A3
Brazeau → *Canada* 52°55N 115°14W **296** C5
Brazil *U.S.A.* 39°32N 87°8W **311** E9
Brazil ■ *S. Amer.* 12°0S 50°0W **333** D2
Brazil Basin *Atl. Oc.* 15°0S 25°0W **152** H9
Brazilian Highlands = Brasil, Planalto *Brazil* 18°0S 46°30W **326** E6
Brazo Sur → *S. Amer.* 25°21S 57°42W **334** B4
Brazos → *U.S.A.* 28°53N 95°23W **314** G7
Brazzaville *Congo* 4°9S 15°12E **265** C3
Brčko *Bos.-H.* 44°54N 18°46E **182** F3
Brda → *Poland* 53°8N 18°8E **185** E5
Brdy *Czech Rep.* 49°43N 13°55E **180** B6
Brea *Peru* 4°40S 81°7W **330** A1
Breach Candy *Mumbai, India* **130** a1
Breaden, L. *Australia* 25°51S 125°28E **279** E4
Breakheart Reservation *U.S.A.* 42°28N 71°1W **116** A2
Breaksea Sd. *N.Z.* 45°35S 166°35E **285** F1
Bream B. *N.Z.* 35°56S 174°28E **284** B3
Bream Hd. *N.Z.* 35°51S 174°36E **284** B3
Bream Tail *N.Z.* 36°3S 174°36E **284** C3
Breas *Chile* 25°29S 70°24W **334** B1
Breaza *Romania* 45°11N 25°40E **183** E10
Brebes *Indonesia* 6°52S 109°3E **235** D3
Brechin *Ont., Canada* 44°32N 79°10W **312** B5
Brechin *Angus, U.K.* 56°44N 2°39W **167** E6
Brecht *Belgium* 51°21N 4°38E **170** C4
Breckenridge *Colo., U.S.A.* 39°29N 106°3W **304** G10
Breckenridge *Minn., U.S.A.* 46°16N 96°35W **308** B5
Breckenridge *Tex., U.S.A.* 32°45N 98°54W **314** E5
Breckland *U.K.* 52°30N 0°40E **169** E8
Brecknock, Pen. *Chile* 54°35S 71°30W **336** D2
Břeclav *Czech Rep.* 48°46N 16°53E **181** C9
Brecon *U.K.* 51°57N 3°23W **169** F4
Brecon Beacons *U.K.* 51°53N 3°26W **169** F4
Brecon Beacons △ *U.K.* 51°50N 3°30W **169** F4
Breda *Neths.* 51°35N 4°45E **170** C4
Bredaryd *Sweden* 57°10N 13°45E **163** G7
Bredasdorp *S. Africa* 34°33S 20°2E **270** D3
Bredbo *Australia* 35°58S 149°10E **283** C8
Brede *Denmark* 55°47N 12°30E **118** A3
Bredebro *Denmark* 55°4N 8°50E **163** J2
Bredstedt *Germany* 54°37N 8°55E **178** A4
Bredy *Russia* 52°26N 60°21E **216** B6
Bree *Belgium* 51°8N 5°35E **170** C5
Breezy Point *U.S.A.* 40°33N 73°56W **132** C2
Bregalnica → *Macedonia* 41°43N 22°9E **202** E6
Bregenz *Austria* 47°30N 9°45E **180** D2
Bregovo *Bulgaria* 44°9N 22°39E **202** B6
Bréhal *France* 48°53N 1°30W **172** D5
Bréhat, Î. de *France* 48°51N 3°0W **172** D4
Breiðafjörður *Iceland* 65°15N 23°15W **155** B3
Breiðdalsvík *Iceland* 64°44N 14°0W **155** C13
Breil-sur-Roya *France* 43°56N 7°31E **175** E11
Breim *Norway* 61°44N 6°25E **164** C3
Breisach *Germany* 48°1N 7°36E **179** G3
Breitenlee *Austria* 48°15N 16°30E **142** A3
Brejinho de Nazaré *Brazil* 11°1S 48°34W **332** D2
Brejo *Brazil* 3°41S 42°47W **332** B3
Brekke *Norway* 61°1N 5°26E **164** C2
Brekken *Norway* 62°40N 11°51E **164** B8
Brekkestø *Norway* 58°11N 8°22E **164** F5
Bremanger *Norway* 61°51N 4°58E **164** C1
Bremangerlandet *Norway* 61°51N 5°0E **164** C1
Bremen *Bremen, Germany* 53°4N 8°47E **178** B4
Bremen *Ga., U.S.A.* 33°43N 85°9W **316** B4
Bremen *Ind., U.S.A.* 41°27N 86°9W **311** C10
Bremen □ *Germany* 53°4N 8°50E **178** B4
Bremer Bay *Australia* 34°21S 119°20E **279** F2
Bremer I. *Australia* 12°5S 136°45E **280** A2
Bremerhaven *Germany* 53°33N 8°36E **178** B4
Bremersdorp = Manzini *Swaziland* 26°30S 31°25E **271** C5
Bremerton *U.S.A.* 47°34N 122°37W **306** C4
Bremervörde *Germany* 53°29N 9°8E **178** B5
Bremnes *Norway* 59°47N 5°8E **164** E2
Bremsnes *Norway* 63°6N 7°40E **164** A4
Breña *Peru* 12°3S 77°3W **124** B2
Brenes *Spain* 37°32N 5°54W **195** H5
Brenham *U.S.A.* 30°10N 96°24W **314** F6
Brenne *France* 46°44N 1°14E **174** B5
Brenne ⌓ *France* 46°40N 1°15E **174** B5
Brennerpass *Austria* 47°2N 11°30E **180** D4
Brennhaug *Norway* 61°54N 9°21E **164** C6
Breno *Italy* 45°57N 10°18E **198** C7
Brent *U.S.A.* 32°56N 87°10W **315** E11
Brent □ *U.K.* 51°33N 0°16W **125** A2
Brent Res. *U.K.* 51°34N 0°14W **125** A2
Brenta → *Italy* 45°11N 12°18E **199** C9
Brentford *U.K.* 51°28N 0°18W **125** B2
Brentwood *Essex, U.K.* 51°37N 0°19E **169** F8
Brentwood *Calif., U.S.A.* 37°56N 121°42W **306** H5
Brentwood *N.Y., U.S.A.* 40°47N 73°15W **313** F11
Brentwood Park *U.S.A.* 34°3N 118°29W **126** B2
Brera *Italy* 45°28N 9°11E **129** B2
Brereton *Barbados* 13°7N 59°30W **323** r
Bréscia *Italy* 45°33N 10°15E **198** C7
Breskens *Neths.* 51°23N 3°33E **170** C3
Breslau = Wrocław *Poland* 51°5N 17°5E **185** G4
Bresle → *France* 50°4N 1°22E **172** B8
Bressanone *Italy* 46°43N 11°39E **199** B8
Bressay *U.K.* 60°9N 1°6W **167** A7
Bresse *France* 46°50N 5°10E **173** F12
Bresso *Italy* 45°32N 9°11E **129** A2
Bressuire *France* 46°51N 0°30W **172** F6
Brest *Belarus* 52°10N 23°40E **177** B12
Brest *Finistère, France* 48°24N 4°31W **172** D2
Brest □ *Belarus* 52°30N 26°10E **189** F4
Brest-Litovsk = Brest *Belarus* 52°10N 23°40E **177** B12
Bretagne □ *France* 48°10N 3°0W **172** D3
Bretanha, Pta. da *Azores* 37°54N 25°47W **153** d3
Bretçu *Romania* 46°7N 26°18E **183** D11
Bretenoux *France* 44°54N 1°51E **174** D5
Breteuil *Eure, France* 48°50N 0°57E **172** D7
Breteuil *Oise, France* 49°38N 2°18E **173** C9
Breton *Canada* 53°7N 114°28W **296** C6
Breton, Pertuis *France* 46°17N 1°25W **174** B2
Breton Sd. *U.S.A.* 29°35N 89°15W **315** G10
Brett, C. *N.Z.* 35°10S 174°20E **284** B3
Bretten *Germany* 49°2N 8°42E **179** F4
Breuil-Cervínia *Italy* 45°56N 7°38E **198** C4
Brevard *U.S.A.* 35°14N 82°44W **315** D13
Breves *Brazil* 1°40S 50°29W **332** B1
Brevig Mission *U.S.A.* 65°20N 166°29W **303** D6
Brevik *Telemark, Norway* 59°4N 9°42E **164** E6
Brevik *Stockholm, Sweden* 59°20N 18°12E **139** A3
Břevnov *Czech Rep.* 50°4N 14°22E **135** B2
Brewarrina *Australia* 30°0S 146°51E **281** E4
Brewer *U.S.A.* 44°48N 68°46W **309** C19
Brewer, Mt. *U.S.A.* 36°44N 118°28W **306** J8
Brewerville *Liberia* 6°26N 10°47W **262** D2
Brewster *N.Y., U.S.A.* 41°24N 73°36W **313** E11
Brewster *Ohio, U.S.A.* 40°43N 81°36W **312** F3
Brewster *Wash., U.S.A.* 48°6N 119°47W **304** B4
Brewster, Kap = Kangikajik *Greenland* 70°7N 22°0W **154** C8
Brewton *U.S.A.* 31°7N 87°4W **315** F11
Breyten *S. Africa* 26°16S 30°0E **271** C5
Breza *Bos.-H.* 44°2N 18°16E **182** F3
Brežice *Slovenia* 45°54N 15°35E **199** C12
Brézina *Algeria* 33°4N 1°14E **261** B5
Březnice *Czech Rep.* 49°32N 13°57E **180** B6
Breznik *Bulgaria* 42°44N 22°55E **202** D6
Brezno *Slovak Rep.* 48°50N 19°40E **181** C12
Brezoi *Romania* 45°21N 24°15E **183** E9
Brezovica *Serbia* 42°15N 21°3E **202** D5
Brezovo *Bulgaria* 42°21N 25°5E **203** D9
Bria *C.A.R.* 6°30N 21°58E **264** A4
Briançon *France* 44°54N 6°39E **175** D10
Briare *France* 47°38N 2°45E **173** E9
Briars, The *St. Helena* 15°56S 5°43W **153** h
Briático *Italy* 38°43N 16°2E **201** D9
Bribie I. *Australia* 27°0S 153°10E **281** D5
Bribri *Costa Rica* 9°38N 82°50W **320** E3
Briceni *Moldova* 48°22N 27°6E **183** B12
Brickyard, The *U.S.A.* 41°55N 87°47W **119** B2
Bricquebec *France* 49°28N 1°38W **172** C5
Bridge City *U.S.A.* 29°55N 90°9W **131** B2
Bridgehampton *U.S.A.* 40°56N 72°19W **313** F12
Bridgend *U.K.* 51°30N 3°34W **169** F4
Bridgend □ *U.K.* 51°36N 3°36W **169** F4
Bridgeport *Calif., U.S.A.* 38°15N 119°14W **306** G7
Bridgeport *Conn., U.S.A.* 41°11N 73°12W **313** E11
Bridgeport *Ill., U.S.A.* 41°50N 87°38W **119** B3
Bridgeport *Ill., U.S.A.* 38°43N 87°46W **311** F9
Bridgeport *Nebr., U.S.A.* 41°40N 103°6W **308** E2
Bridgeport *Tex., U.S.A.* 33°13N 97°45W **314** E6
Bridger *U.S.A.* 45°18N 108°55W **304** D9
Bridgeton *U.S.A.* 39°26N 75°14W **309** F16
Bridgetown *W. Austral., Australia* 33°58S 116°7E **279** F2
Bridgetown *Barbados* 13°6N 59°37W **323** r
Bridgetown *N.S., Canada* 44°55N 65°18W **299** D6
Bridgetown *Western Cape, S. Africa* 33°58S 18°33E **118** A2
Bridgeview *U.S.A.* 41°45N 87°48W **119** C2
Bridgewater *Tas., Australia* 42°44S 147°14E **281** G4
Bridgewater *Vic., Australia* 36°36S 143°59E **282** D5
Bridgewater *N.S., Canada* 44°25N 64°31W **299** D7
Bridgewater *Mass., U.S.A.* 41°59N 70°58W **313** E14
Bridgewater *N.Y., U.S.A.* 42°53N 75°15W **313** D9
Bridgewater, C. *Australia* 38°23S 141°23E **282** E4
Bridgman *U.S.A.* 41°57N 86°33W **311** C10
Bridgnorth *U.K.* 52°32N 2°25W **169** E5
Bridgton *U.S.A.* 44°3N 70°42W **313** B14
Bridgwater *U.K.* 51°8N 2°59W **169** F5
Bridgwater B. *U.K.* 51°15N 3°15W **169** F4
Bridlington *U.K.* 54°5N 0°12W **168** C7
Bridlington B. *U.K.* 54°4N 0°10W **168** C7
Bridport *Tas., Australia* 40°59S 147°23E **281** G4
Bridport *Dorset, U.K.* 50°44N 2°45W **169** G5
Briec *France* 48°6N 4°0W **172** D2
Brieg = Brzeg *Poland* 50°52N 17°30E **185** H4
Brienne-le-Château *France* 48°24N 4°30E **173** D11
Brienon-sur-Armançon *France* 47°59N 3°38E **173** E10
Brienz *Switz.* 46°46N 8°2E **179** J4
Brienzersee *Switz.* 46°44N 7°53E **179** J3
Brier Cr. → *U.S.A.* 32°44N 81°26W **316** C8
Brière ⌓ *France* 47°22N 2°13W **172** E4
Brievengat *Neth. Ant.* 12°9N 68°54W **322** g
Brig *Switz.* 46°18N 7°59E **179** J3
Brigg *U.K.* 53°34N 0°28W **168** D7
Brigham City *U.S.A.* 41°31N 112°1W **304** F7
Bright *Australia* 36°42S 146°56E **283** D7
Brighton *S. Austral., Australia* 35°5S 138°30E **282** C3
Brighton *Vic., Australia* 37°55S 144°59E **128** B1
Brighton *Ont., Canada* 44°2N 77°44W **312** B7
Brighton *Trin. & Tob.* 10°13N 61°39W **323** t
Brighton *Brighton & Hove, U.K.* 50°49N 0°7W **169** G7
Brighton *Fla., U.S.A.* 27°14N 81°6W **317** H8
Brighton *Ill., U.S.A.* 39°2N 90°8W **310** E6
Brighton *Iowa, U.S.A.* 41°10N 91°49W **310** C5
Brighton *Mass., U.S.A.* 42°21N 71°9W **116** A2
Brighton *Mich., U.S.A.* 42°32N 83°47W **311** B13
Brighton *N.Y., U.S.A.* 43°8N 77°34W **312** C7
Brighton Beach *U.S.A.* 40°34N 73°57W **132** C2
Brighton le Sands *Australia* 33°57S 151°9E **139** B1
Brighton Park *U.S.A.* 41°48N 87°41W **119** C2
Brightwater *N.Z.* 41°22S 173°9E **285** B8
Brightwood *U.S.A.* 38°57N 77°1W **143** B3
Brigittenau *Austria* 48°14N 16°22E **142** A2
Brignogan-Plage *France* 48°40N 4°20W **172** D2
Brignoles *France* 43°25N 6°5E **175** E10
Brihuega *Spain* 40°45N 2°52W **196** E2
Brikama *Gambia* 13°15N 16°45W **262** C1
Brilliant *U.S.A.* 40°15N 80°39W **312** F4
Brilon *Germany* 51°23N 8°35E **178** D4
Brim *Australia* 36°3S 142°27E **282** D5
Brimbank Park *Australia* 37°43S 144°50E **128** A1
Brimfield *U.S.A.* 40°50N 89°53W **310** D7
Brimstone Hill Fort *St. Kitts & Nevis* 17°20N 62°50W **322** d
Brindabella △ *Australia* 35°14S 148°5E **283** C8
Bríndisi *Italy* 40°39N 17°55E **201** B10
Brinje *Croatia* 44°59N 15°9E **199** D12
Brinkley *U.S.A.* 34°53N 91°12W **314** D9
Brinkworth *Australia* 33°42S 138°26E **282** B3
Brinnon *U.S.A.* 47°41N 122°54W **306** C4
Brinson *U.S.A.* 30°59N 84°44W **316** E5
Brion, Î. *Canada* 47°46N 61°26W **299** C7
Brionne *France* 49°11N 0°43E **172** C7
Brionski *Croatia* 44°55N 13°45E **199** D10
Brioude *France* 45°18N 3°24E **174** C7
Briouze *France* 48°42N 0°23W **172** D6
Brisbane *Queens., Australia* 27°25S 153°2E **281** D5
Brisbane *Calif., U.S.A.* 37°40N 122°23W **136** B2
Brisbane → *Australia* 27°24S 153°9E **281** D5
Brisbane Ranges △ *Australia* 37°47S 144°16E **282** D6
Brisbane Water △ *Australia* 33°26S 151°13E **283** B9
Brisighella *Italy* 44°13N 11°46E **199** D8
Bristol *Bristol, U.K.* 51°26N 2°35W **169** F5
Bristol *Conn., U.S.A.* 41°40N 72°57W **313** E12
Bristol *Fla., U.S.A.* 30°26N 84°59W **316** E5
Bristol *Pa., U.S.A.* 40°6N 74°51W **313** F10
Bristol *R.I., U.S.A.* 41°40N 71°16W **313** E13
Bristol *Tenn., U.S.A.* 36°36N 82°11W **315** C13
Bristol, City of □ *U.K.* 51°27N 2°36W **169** F5
Bristol B. *U.S.A.* 58°0N 160°0W **303** H8
Bristol Channel *U.K.* 51°18N 4°30W **169** F3
Bristol I. *Antarctica* 58°45S 28°0W **151** B1
Bristol L. *U.S.A.* 34°28N 115°41W **305** J6
Bristow *U.S.A.* 35°50N 96°23W **314** D6
Bristow I. *Papua N. G.* 9°8S 143°14E **286** E2
Britain = Great Britain *Europe* 54°0N 2°15W **158** E5
Britânia *Brazil* 15°14S 51°9W **331** D7
British Central Africa = Malawi ■ *Africa* 11°55S 34°0E **269** E3
British Columbia □ *Canada* 55°0N 125°15W **296** C3
British East Africa = Kenya ■ *Africa* 1°0N 38°0E **268** B4
British Guiana = Guyana ■ *S. Amer.* 5°0N 59°0W **329** C6
British Honduras = Belize ■ *Cent. Amer.* 17°0N 88°30W **319** D7
British Indian Ocean Terr. = Chagos Arch. ⧄ *Ind. Oc.* 6°0S 72°0E **210** J9
British Isles *Europe* 54°0N 4°0W **165** D5
British Museum *London, U.K.* **125** a3
British Virgin Is. ⧄ *W. Indies* 18°30N 64°30W **321** C7
Brits *S. Africa* 25°37S 27°48E **271** C4
Britstown *S. Africa* 30°37S 23°30E **270** D3
Britt *Ont., Canada* 45°46N 80°34W **298** C3
Britt *Iowa, U.S.A.* 43°6N 93°48W **310** A3
Brittany = Bretagne □ *France* 48°10N 3°0W **172** D3
Britton *U.S.A.* 45°48N 97°45W **308** C5
Britz *Germany* 52°26N 13°27E **115** B3
Brive-la-Gaillarde *France* 45°10N 1°32E **174** C5
Briviesca *Spain* 42°32N 3°19W **194** C7
Brixen = Bressanone *Italy* 46°43N 11°39E **199** B8
Brixham *U.K.* 50°23N 3°31W **169** G4
Brixton *U.K.* 51°27N 0°8W **125** B3
Brnaze *Croatia* 43°41N 16°40E **199** E13
Brnenský □ *Czech Rep.* 49°10N 16°40E **181** B9
Brno *Czech Rep.* 49°10N 16°35E **181** B9
Broach = Bharuch *India* 21°47N 73°0E **244** D1
Broad → *Ga., U.S.A.* 33°59N 82°39W **316** B7
Broad → *S.C., U.S.A.* 34°1N 81°4W **315** D14
Broad Arrow *Australia* 30°23S 121°15E **279** F3
Broad B. *U.K.* 58°14N 6°18W **167** C2
Broad Haven *Ireland* 54°20N 9°55W **166** B2
Broad Law *U.K.* 55°30N 3°21W **167** F5
Broad Sd. *Australia* 22°0S 149°45E **280** C4
Broadalbin *U.S.A.* 43°4N 74°12W **313** C10
Broadback → *Canada* 51°21N 78°52W **298** B4
Broadford *Australia* 37°14S 145°4E **283** D6
Broadhurst Ra. *Australia* 22°30S 122°30E **278** D3
Broadmeadows *Australia* 37°40S 144°55E **128** A1
Broadmoor *U.S.A.* 37°41N 122°29W **136** B2
Broads, The *U.K.* 52°45N 1°30E **168** E9
Broadus *U.S.A.* 45°27N 105°25W **304** D11
Broadview *U.S.A.* 41°51N 87°52W **119** B1
Broadway *New York, U.S.A.* **132** d2
Broager *Denmark* 54°53N 9°40E **163** K3
Broby *Sweden* 56°15N 14°4E **163** H8
Brocēni *Latvia* 56°42N 22°32E **184** B9
Brochet *Canada* 57°53N 101°40W **297** B8
Brochet, L. *Canada* 58°36N 101°35W **297** B8
Brock I. *Canada* 77°52N 114°19W **295** B8
Brocken *Germany* 51°47N 10°37E **178** D6
Brocklehurst *Australia* 32°9S 148°38E **283** B8
Brocklesby *Australia* 35°48S 146°40E **283** C7
Brockley *U.K.* 51°27N 0°2W **125** B3
Brockport *U.S.A.* 43°13N 77°56W **312** C7
Brockton *U.S.A.* 42°5N 71°1W **313** D13
Brockville *Canada* 44°35N 75°41W **313** B9
Brockway *Mont., U.S.A.* 47°18N 105°45W **304** C11
Brockway *Pa., U.S.A.* 41°15N 78°47W **312** E6
Brocton *U.S.A.* 42°23N 79°26W **312** D5
Brod *Macedonia* 41°32N 21°17E **202** E5
Brodarevo *Serbia* 43°14N 19°44E **202** C3
Brodeur Pen. *Canada* 72°30N 88°10W **295** B11
Brodhead *U.S.A.* 42°37N 89°22W **310** B7
Brodick *U.K.* 55°35N 5°9W **167** F3
Brodnica *Poland* 53°15N 19°25E **185** E6
Bródno *Poland* 52°17N 21°1E **142** B2
Bródnowski, Kanal *Poland* 52°17N 21°3E **142** B2
Brody *Ukraine* 50°5N 25°10E **177** C13
Broek *Neths.* 52°26N 5°0E **112** A2
Brogan *U.S.A.* 44°15N 117°31W **304** D5
Broglie *France* 49°2N 0°30E **172** C7
Brok *Poland* 52°43N 21°52E **185** F8
Broken Arrow *U.S.A.* 36°3N 95°48W **314** C7
Broken Bow *Nebr., U.S.A.* 41°24N 99°38W **308** E4
Broken Bow *Okla., U.S.A.* 34°2N 94°44W **314** D7
Broken Bow Lake *U.S.A.* 34°9N 94°40W **314** D7
Broken Hill = Kabwe *Zambia* 14°30S 28°29E **269** E2
Broken Hill *Australia* 31°58S 141°29E **282** A4
Broken River Ra. *Australia* 21°0S 148°22E **280** K6
Brokind *Sweden* 58°13N 15°42E **163** F9
Brokopondo *Suriname* 5°3N 54°59W **329** B7

354 Bromberg
INDEX

Bromberg = Bydgoszcz Poland 53°10N 18°0E 185 E5
Bromley □ U.K. 51°24N 0°2E 125 B4
Bromley Common U.K. 51°22N 0°2E 125 B4
Bromma Sweden 59°21N 17°55E 139 A1
Bromma ✕ Sweden 59°21N 17°56E 139 A1
Bromo Indonesia 7°55S 112°55E 231 G15
Bromölla Sweden 56°5N 14°28E 163 H8
Brompton London, U.K. 125 c2
Bromsgrove U.K. 52°21N 2°2W 169 E5
Bronaugh U.S.A. 37°41N 94°28W 310 G2
Brøndby Strand Denmark 55°36N 12°25E 118 B2
Brøndbyøster Denmark 55°39N 12°26E 118 B2
Brøndbyvester Denmark 55°37N 12°23E 118 B2
Brønderslev Denmark 57°16N 9°57E 163 G3
Brondesbury U.K. 51°32N 0°12W 125 A2
Brong-Ahafo □ Ghana 7°50N 2°0W 262 D4
Broni Italy 45°4N 9°16E 198 C6
Bronkhorstspruit S. Africa 25°46S 28°45E 271 C4
Brønnøya Norway 59°51N 10°32E 133 A2
Brønnøysund Norway 65°28N 12°14E 160 D15
Brønshøj Denmark 55°41N 12°29E 118 A2
Bronson Fla., U.S.A. 29°27N 82°39W 317 F7
Bronson Mich., U.S.A. 41°52N 85°12W 311 C11
Bronte Italy 37°47N 14°50E 201 E7
Bronwood U.S.A. 31°50N 84°22W 316 D5
Bronxville U.S.A. 40°56N 73°49W 132 A3
Brook Park U.S.A. 41°23N 81°48W 312 E4
Brooke's Point Phil. 8°47N 117°50E 233 G1
Brookfield Ill., U.S.A. 41°48N 87°50W 119 C1
Brookfield Mo., U.S.A. 39°47N 93°4W 310 E3
Brookfield Wis., U.S.A. 43°4N 88°9W 311 A8
Brookhaven Georgia, U.S.A. 33°52N 84°19W 113 A2
Brookhaven Miss., U.S.A. 31°35N 90°26W 315 F9
Brookings Oreg., U.S.A. 42°3N 124°17W 304 E1
Brookings S. Dak., U.S.A. 44°19N 96°48W 308 C5
Brookland = West Columbia U.S.A. 33°59N 81°4W 316 B8
Brooklet U.S.A. 32°23N 81°40W 316 C8
Brooklin Canada 43°55N 78°55W 312 C6
Brookline U.S.A. 42°19N 71°8W 116 B2
Brooklyn N.Z. 41°18S 174°46E 143 B1
Brooklyn Western Cape, S. Africa 33°54S 18°29E 118 A1
Brooklyn Iowa, U.S.A. 41°44N 92°27W 310 C4
Brooklyn New York, U.S.A. 132 f3
Brooklyn-Battery Tunnel New York, U.S.A. 132 f1
Brooklyn Bridge New York, U.S.A. 132 f2
Brooklyn Heights New York, U.S.A. 132 f2
Brooklyn Park U.S.A. 45°6N 93°23W 308 C7
Brookmont U.S.A. 38°57N 77°7W 143 B3
Brooks Canada 50°35N 111°55W 296 C6
Brooks Range U.S.A. 68°0N 152°0W 303 C9
Brookston U.S.A. 40°36N 86°52W 311 D10
Brooksville Fla., U.S.A. 28°33N 82°23W 317 G7
Brooksville Ky., U.S.A. 38°41N 84°4W 311 F12
Brookton Australia 32°22S 117°0E 279 F2
Brookville Ind., U.S.A. 39°25N 85°1W 311 E12
Brookville Ohio, U.S.A. 39°50N 84°24W 311 E12
Brookville Pa., U.S.A. 41°10N 79°5W 312 E5
Brookville L. U.S.A. 39°28N 85°0W 311 E11
Broom, L. U.K. 57°55N 5°15W 167 D3
Broome Australia 18°0S 122°15E 278 C3
Broons France 48°20N 2°16W 172 D4
Brora U.K. 58°0N 3°52W 167 C5
Brora → U.K. 58°0N 3°51W 167 C5
Brørup Denmark 55°29N 9°1E 163 J2
Brösarp Sweden 55°43N 14°6E 163 J8
Brosna → Ireland 53°14N 7°58W 166 C4
Brossard Canada 45°27N 73°28W 130 B3
Broşteni Mehedinţi, Romania 44°45N 22°59E 182 F7
Broşteni Suceava, Romania 47°14N 25°43E 183 C10
Brøsterud Norway 60°18N 8°34E 164 D5
Brotas de Macaúbas Brazil 12°0S 42°38W 333 D3
Brothers U.S.A. 43°49N 120°36W 304 E3
Brothers, The Yemen 12°8N 53°10E 249 D6
Brøttum Norway 61°2N 10°34E 164 C7
Brou France 48°13N 1°11E 172 D8
Brou-sur-Chantereine France 48°53N 2°37E 134 A4
Brouage France 45°52N 1°4W 174 C2
Brough U.K. 54°32N 2°18W 168 C5
Brough Hd. U.K. 59°8N 3°20W 167 B5
Broughton U.S.A. 37°56N 88°27W 311 G8
Broughton Island = Qikiqtarjuaq Canada 67°33N 63°0W 295 C13
Broumov Czech Rep. 50°35N 16°20E 181 A9
Brovary Ukraine 50°34N 30°48E 189 G6
Brovst Denmark 57°6N 9°31E 163 G3
Brown Canada 43°48N 79°14W 141 A3
Brown, L. Australia 31°5S 118°15E 279 F2
Brown, Mt. Australia 32°30S 138°0E 282 B3
Brown, Pt. Australia 32°32S 133°50E 281 E1
Brown City U.S.A. 43°13N 82°59W 312 C2
Brown Willy U.K. 50°35N 4°37W 169 G3
Brownfield U.S.A. 33°11N 102°17W 314 E3
Browning Ill., U.S.A. 40°8N 90°22W 310 D6
Browning Mo., U.S.A. 40°3N 93°12W 310 D3
Browning Mont., U.S.A. 48°34N 113°1W 304 B7
Browns Town Jamaica 18°24N 77°22W 320 a
Brownsburg U.S.A. 39°51N 86°24W 311 E10
Brownstown U.S.A. 38°53N 86°3W 311 F10
Brownsville Oreg., U.S.A. 44°24N 122°59W 304 D2
Brownsville Pa., U.S.A. 40°1N 79°53W 312 F5
Brownsville Tenn., U.S.A. 35°36N 89°16W 315 D10
Brownsville Tex., U.S.A. 25°54N 97°30W 314 J6
Brownsweg Suriname 5°5N 55°15W 329 B6
Brownville U.S.A. 44°0N 75°59W 313 C9
Brownwood U.S.A. 31°43N 98°59W 314 F5
Browse I. Australia 14°7S 123°33E 278 B3
Broxton U.S.A. 31°38N 82°53W 316 D7
Broyhill Park U.S.A. 38°52N 77°12W 143 B2
Bru Norway 61°32N 5°11E 164 C2
Bruas Malaysia 4°30N 100°47E 237 K3
Bruay-la-Buissière France 50°29N 2°33E 173 B9
Bruce U.S.A. 30°28N 85°58W 316 E4
Bruce, Mt. Australia 22°37S 118°8E 278 D2
Bruce B. N.Z. 43°35S 169°42E 285 D4
Bruce Pen. Canada 45°0N 81°30W 312 B3
Bruce Peninsula △ Canada 45°14N 81°36W 312 A3
Bruce Rock Australia 31°52S 118°8E 279 F2
Bruche → France 48°34N 7°43E 173 D14
Bruchsal Germany 49°7N 8°35E 179 F4
Bruck an der Leitha Austria 48°1N 16°47E 181 C9
Bruck an der Mur Austria 47°24N 15°16E 180 D8
Brue → U.K. 51°13N 2°59W 169 F5
Bruflat Norway 60°53N 9°37E 164 D6
Bruges = Brugge Belgium 51°13N 3°13E 170 C3
Brugg Switz. 47°29N 8°11E 179 H4
Brugge Belgium 51°13N 3°13E 170 C3
Brughério Italy 45°33N 9°17E 129 A2
Bruin U.S.A. 41°3N 79°43W 312 E5
Bruini India 29°10N 96°11E 241 A6
Brûk, W. el → Egypt 30°15N 33°50E 251 H4
Brûlé Canada 53°15N 117°58W 296 C5
Brûlon France 47°58N 0°15W 172 E6
Brumado Brazil 14°14S 41°40W 333 D3
Brumado → Brazil 14°13S 41°40W 333 D3
Brumath France 48°43N 7°40E 173 D14
Brumunddal Norway 60°53N 10°56E 164 D7
Brundidge U.S.A. 31°43N 85°49W 316 D4
Bruneau U.S.A. 42°53N 115°48W 304 E6
Bruneau → U.S.A. 42°56N 115°57W 304 E6
Bruneck = Brunico Italy 46°48N 11°56E 199 B8
Brunei = Bandar Seri Begawan Brunei 4°52N 115°0E 235 B4
Brunei ■ Asia 4°50N 115°0E 235 B4
Brunflo Sweden 63°5N 14°50E 162 A8
Brunico Italy 46°48N 11°56E 199 B8
Brünn = Brno Czech Rep. 49°10N 16°35E 181 B9
Brunna Sweden 59°52N 17°25E 162 E11
Brunnen Switz. 46°59N 8°37E 179 J4
Brunner, L. N.Z. 42°37S 171°27E 285 C6
Brunnhóll Iceland 64°17N 15°26W 155 C11
Brunsbüttel Germany 53°53N 9°6E 178 B5
Brunssum Neths. 50°57N 5°59E 170 D5
Brunswick = Braunschweig Germany 52°15N 10°31E 178 C6
Brunswick Vic., Australia 37°45S 144°57E 128 A1
Brunswick Ga., U.S.A. 31°10N 81°30W 316 D8
Brunswick Maine, U.S.A. 43°55N 69°58W 309 D19
Brunswick Md., U.S.A. 39°19N 77°38W 309 F15
Brunswick Mo., U.S.A. 39°26N 93°8W 310 E3
Brunswick Ohio, U.S.A. 41°14N 81°51W 312 E3
Brunswick, Pen. de Chile 53°30S 71°30W 336 D2
Brunswick B. Australia 15°15S 124°50E 278 C3
Brunswick Junction Australia 33°15S 115°50E 279 F2
Brunt Ice Shelf Antarctica 75°30S 25°0W 151 D2
Bruntál Czech Rep. 49°59N 17°27E 181 B10
Brus Laguna Honduras 15°47N 84°35W 320 C3
Brusa = Bursa Turkey 40°15N 29°5E 203 F13
Brusartsi Bulgaria 43°40N 23°5E 202 C7
Brush U.S.A. 40°15N 103°37W 304 F12
Brushton U.S.A. 44°50N 74°31W 313 B10
Brusio Switz. 46°14N 10°8E 179 J6
Brusque Brazil 27°5S 49°0W 335 B6
Brussegem Belgium 50°56N 4°16E 116 A1
Brussel Belgium 50°51N 4°21E 116 A2
Brussel ✕ (BRU) Belgium 50°54N 4°29E 116 A2
Brussels = Brussel Belgium 50°51N 4°21E 116 A2
Brussels Canada 43°44N 81°15W 312 C3
Brusy Poland 53°53N 17°43E 184 E4
Bruthen Australia 37°42S 147°50E 283 D7
Bruvoll Norway 60°27N 11°29E 164 D8
Bruxelles = Brussel Belgium 50°51N 4°21E 116 A2
Bruyères France 48°10N 6°40E 173 D13
Bruz France 48°1N 1°46W 172 D5
Bruzzano Italy 45°31N 9°10E 129 A2
Brwinów Poland 52°9N 20°40E 185 F7
Bry-sur-Marne France 48°50N 2°32E 134 A4
Bryagovo Bulgaria 41°58N 25°8E 203 E9
Bryan Ohio, U.S.A. 41°28N 84°33W 311 C12
Bryan Tex., U.S.A. 30°40N 96°22W 314 F6
Bryan, L. U.S.A. 28°22N 81°29W 133 B2
Bryan, Mt. Australia 33°30S 139°5E 282 B3
Bryanka Ukraine 48°32N 38°45E 189 H10
Bryansk Bryansk, Russia 53°13N 34°25E 189 F8
Bryansk Dagestan, Russia 44°20N 47°10E 191 H8
Bryansk □ Russia 53°10N 33°10E 189 F7
Bryanskoye = Bryansk Russia 44°20N 47°10E 191 H8
Bryanston S. Africa 26°4S 28°0E 123 A1
Bryant Park New York, U.S.A. 132 c2
Bryce Canyon △ U.S.A. 37°30N 112°10W 305 H7
Bryn Norway 59°55N 10°27E 133 A1
Bryne Norway 58°44N 5°38E 164 F2
Bryson City U.S.A. 35°26N 83°27W 315 D13
Bryukhovetskaya Russia 45°48N 39°0E 189 K10
Brza Palanka Serbia 44°28N 22°27E 202 B6
Brzeg Poland 50°52N 17°30E 185 H4
Brzeg Dolny Poland 51°16N 16°41E 185 G3
Brześć Kujawski Poland 52°36N 18°55E 185 F5
Brzešč nad Bugiem = Brest Belarus 52°10N 23°40E 177 B12
Brzesko Poland 49°59N 20°34E 185 J7
Brzeziny Łódzkie, Poland 51°49N 19°42E 185 G6
Brzeziny Warszawa, Poland 52°19N 21°2E 142 B2
Brzozów Poland 49°41N 22°3E 185 J9
Bsharri Lebanon 34°15N 36°0E 250 D7
Bū al Ḩīdān, W. → Libya 27°25N 19°22E 258 C3
Bū Athlah Libya 30°9N 15°39E 258 B3
Bū Baqarah U.A.E. 25°35N 56°25E 247 E8
Bu Craa W. Sahara 26°45N 12°50W 260 C2
Bū Ḩasā U.A.E. 23°30N 53°20E 247 F7
Bū Tummayyim, W. → Libya 26°56N 19°13E 258 C3
Bua Fiji 16°48S 178°37E 287 A2
Bua Sweden 57°14N 12°7E 163 G6
Bua Yai Thailand 15°33N 102°26E 236 E4
Buad I. Phil. 11°40N 124°51E 233 F5
Buala Solomon Is. 8°10S 159°35E 287 M10
Buan S. Korea 35°44N 126°44E 224 E3
Buapinang Indonesia 4°40S 121°30E 231 E6
Buayan = General Santos Phil. 6°5N 125°14E 233 H5
Buba Guinea-Biss. 11°40N 14°59W 262 C2
Bubali Bird Sanctuary Aruba 12°33N 70°2W 322 f
Bubanda Dem. Rep. of the Congo 4°14N 19°38E 264 B3
Bubanza Burundi 3°6S 29°23E 268 C2
Bubaque Guinea-Biss. 11°16N 15°51W 262 C1
Bube Ethiopia 8°46N 35°48E 257 F4
Bubeneč Czech Rep. 50°6N 14°24E 135 B2
Bubi → Zimbabwe 22°20S 31°7E 271 B5
Būbiyān Kuwait 29°45N 48°15E 247 D6
Buc France 48°46N 2°7E 134 B1
Buca Fiji 16°38S 179°52E 287 A2
Buca Turkey 38°22N 27°11E 205 C9
Bucaco Angola 11°26S 20°10E 265 E4
Bucak Turkey 37°28N 30°36E 205 D12
Bucakkışla Turkey 36°57N 33°1E 250 B4
Bucaramanga Colombia 7°0N 73°0W 328 B3
Bucas Grande I. Phil. 9°40N 125°57E 233 G5
Bucasia Australia 21°2S 149°10E 280 K7
Bucay Phil. 17°32N 120°43E 232 C3
Buccaneer Arch. Australia 16°7S 123°20E 278 C3
Buccino Italy 40°38N 15°22E 201 B8
Buccoo Reef Trin. & Tob. 11°10N 60°51W 323 s
Bucecea Romania 47°47N 26°28E 183 C11
Bucegi △ Romania 45°25N 25°25E 183 E10
Buchach Ukraine 49°5N 25°25E 177 D13
Buchan Vic., Australia 37°30S 148°12E 283 D8
Buchan Aberds., U.K. 57°32N 2°21W 167 D6
Buchan Ness U.K. 57°29N 1°46W 167 D7
Buchanan Sask., Canada 51°40N 102°45W 297 C8
Buchanan Liberia 5°57N 10°2W 262 D2
Buchanan Ga., U.S.A. 33°48N 85°11W 316 B4
Buchanan Mich., U.S.A. 41°50N 86°22W 311 C10
Buchanan, L. Queens., Australia 21°35S 145°52E 280 C4
Buchanan, L. W. Austral., Australia 25°33S 123°2E 279 E3
Buchanan, L. Tex., U.S.A. 30°45N 98°25W 314 F5
Buchanan Cr. → Australia 19°13S 136°33E 280 B2
Buchans Canada 48°50N 56°52W 299 C8
Bucharest = Bucureşti Romania 44°27N 26°10E 183 F11
Buchen Germany 49°32N 9°20E 179 F5
Buchenhain Germany 48°1N 11°29E 131 B1
Bucheon S. Korea 37°28N 126°45E 224 D3
Buchholz Berlin, Germany 52°36N 13°25E 115 A3
Buchholz Niedersachsen, Germany 53°19N 9°52E 178 B5
Buchloe Germany 48°1N 10°44E 179 G6
Buchon, Pt. U.S.A. 35°15N 120°54W 306 K6
Buciumi Romania 47°3N 23°1E 182 C8
Buck Hill Falls U.S.A. 41°11N 75°16W 313 E9
Bückeburg Germany 52°16N 9°7E 178 C5
Buckeye Lake U.S.A. 39°55N 82°29W 312 G2
Buckhannon U.S.A. 39°0N 80°8W 309 F13
Buckhaven U.K. 56°11N 3°3W 167 E5
Buckhead U.S.A. 33°51N 84°24W 113 A2
Buckhorn L. Canada 44°29N 78°23W 312 B6
Buckie U.K. 57°41N 2°58W 167 D6
Buckingham Qué., Canada 45°37N 75°24W 298 C4
Buckingham Bucks., U.K. 51°59N 0°57W 169 F7
Buckingham B. Australia 12°10S 135°40E 280 A2
Buckingham Canal India 14°0N 80°5E 245 H5
Buckingham Fountain Chicago, U.S.A. 119 d2
Buckingham Palace London, U.K. 125 b3
Buckinghamshire □ U.K. 51°53N 0°55W 169 F7
Buckland U.S.A. 65°59N 161°8W 303 D7
Buckle Hd. Australia 14°26S 127°52E 278 B4
Buckleboo Australia 32°54S 136°12E 282 B2
Buckley Flints., U.K. 53°10N 3°5W 168 D4
Buckley Ill., U.S.A. 40°36N 88°2W 311 D8
Buckley → Australia 20°10S 138°49E 280 C2
Bucklin Kans., U.S.A. 37°33N 99°38W 308 G4
Bucklin Mo., U.S.A. 39°47N 92°53W 310 E4
Buckow Germany 52°25N 13°26E 115 B3
Bucks L. U.S.A. 39°54N 121°12W 306 F5
Buco Zau Angola 4°46S 12°33E 265 C2
Bucquoy France 50°9N 2°43E 173 B9
Bucureşti Romania 44°27N 26°10E 183 F11
Bucureşti Otopeni ✕ (OTP) Romania 44°30N 26°11E 183 F11
Bucyrus U.S.A. 40°48N 82°59W 311 D14
Bud Norway 62°55N 6°55E 164 B3
Bud Bud Somali Rep. 4°11N 46°28E 267 D6
Buda Hungary 47°30N 19°2E 117 A2
Buda Castle = Budavári palota Budapest, Hungary 117 b2
Budacu, Vf. Romania 47°7N 25°41E 183 C10
Budafok Hungary 47°25N 19°2E 117 B2
Budalin Burma 22°20N 95°10E 241 D5
Budaörs Hungary 47°27N 18°57E 117 B1
Budapest Hungary 47°29N 19°3E 117 B2
Budapest □ Hungary 47°29N 19°5E 182 C4
Budapest ✕ (BUD) Hungary 47°26N 19°14E 117 B3
Budatétény Hungary 47°25N 19°1E 117 B2
Budaun India 28°5N 79°10E 243 E8
Budavári palota Budapest, Hungary 117 b2
Budawang △ Australia 35°10S 150°12E 283 C9
Budd Coast Antarctica 68°0S 112°0E 151 C8
Buddenbrock = Brodnica Poland 53°15N 19°25E 185 E6
Budderoo △ Australia 35°40S 150°41E 283 C9
Buddinge Denmark 55°44N 12°30E 118 A3
Buddusò Italy 40°35N 9°15E 200 B2
Bude U.K. 50°49N 4°34W 169 G3
Budennovsk Russia 44°50N 44°10E 191 H7
Budeşti Romania 44°13N 26°30E 183 F11
Budeyi Ukraine 48°3N 29°16E 183 B14
Budge Budge = Baj Baj India 22°30N 88°5E 243 H13
Budgewoi Australia 33°13S 151°34E 283 B9
Búðardalur Iceland 65°7N 21°46W 155 B5
Budia Spain 40°38N 2°46W 196 E2
Büdingen Germany 50°16N 9°7E 179 E5
Budjala Dem. Rep. of the Congo 2°50N 19°40E 264 B3
Budokan Tokyo, Japan 140 a4
Budoni Italy 40°40N 9°45E 200 B2
Búdrio Italy 44°32N 11°32E 199 D8
Bűdszentmihály = Tiszavasvári Hungary 47°58N 21°18E 182 C6
Budva Montenegro 42°17N 18°50E 202 D2
Budweis = České Budějovice Czech Rep. 48°55N 14°25E 180 C7
Budyonnovka = Novoazovsk Ukraine 47°15N 38°4E 189 J10
Budzyń Poland 52°54N 16°59E 185 F3
Bue Norway 58°40N 5°58E 164 F2
Buea Cameroon 4°10N 9°9E 263 E6
Buela Angola 5°54S 14°40E 265 D2
Buellton U.S.A. 34°37N 120°12W 307 L6
Buena Esperanza Argentina 34°45S 65°15W 334 C2
Buena Park U.S.A. 33°52N 117°59W 307 M9
Buena Ventura Lakes U.S.A. 28°21N 81°21W 133 B2
Buena Vista Bolivia 17°27S 63°40W 331 D5
Buena Vista Neth. Ant. 12°8N 68°57W 322 g
Buena Vista Solomon Is. 8°52S 160°3E 287 M11
Buena Vista Calif., U.S.A. 37°45N 122°26W 136 B2
Buena Vista Colo., U.S.A. 38°51N 106°8W 304 G10
Buena Vista Ga., U.S.A. 32°19N 84°31W 316 C5
Buena Vista Va., U.S.A. 37°44N 79°21W 309 G14
Buena Vista Lake Bed U.S.A. 35°12N 119°18W 307 K7
Buenaventura Colombia 3°53N 77°4W 328 C2
Buenaventura Chihuahua, Mexico 29°51N 107°29W 318 B3
Buenaventura, B. de Colombia 3°48N 77°17W 328 C2
Buenavista Agusan del N., Phil. 8°59N 125°24E 233 G5
Buenavista Quezon, Phil. 13°35N 122°34E 232 E4
Buendía, Embalse de Spain 40°25N 2°43W 196 E2
Buenópolis Brazil 17°54S 44°11W 333 E3
Buenos Aires Argentina 34°36S 58°22W 117 B2
Buenos Aires Colombia 1°36N 73°18W 328 C3
Buenos Aires Costa Rica 9°10N 83°20W 320 E3
Buenos Aires □ Argentina 36°30S 60°0W 334 D4
Buenos Aires, L. Argentina 46°35S 72°30W 336 C2
Buenos Aires Ezeiza ✕ (EZE) Argentina 34°49S 58°32W 117 B2
Buenos Ayres Trin. & Tob. 10°6N 61°41W 323 t
Buesaco Colombia 1°23N 77°9W 328 C2
Bufalotta Italy 41°59N 12°33E 136 B2
Buff Bay Jamaica 18°14N 76°40W 320 a
Buffalo Mo., U.S.A. 37°39N 93°6W 310 G3
Buffalo N.Y., U.S.A. 42°53N 78°53W 312 D6
Buffalo Okla., U.S.A. 36°50N 99°38W 314 C5
Buffalo S. Dak., U.S.A. 45°35N 103°33W 308 C2
Buffalo Wyo., U.S.A. 44°21N 106°42W 304 D10
Buffalo → Alta., Canada 60°5N 115°5W 296 A5
Buffalo → S. Africa 28°43S 30°37E 271 C5
Buffalo ⌓ U.S.A. 36°14N 92°36W 314 C8
Buffalo Head Hills Canada 57°25N 115°55W 296 B5
Buffalo L. Alta., Canada 52°27N 112°54W 296 C6
Buffalo L. N.W.T., Canada 60°12N 115°25W 296 A5
Buffalo Narrows Canada 55°51N 108°29W 297 B7
Buffalo Springs ⌓ Kenya 0°32N 37°35E 268 B4
Buffels → S. Africa 29°36S 17°3E 270 C2
Buford U.S.A. 34°10N 84°0W 315 D12
Bug = Buh → Ukraine 46°59N 31°58E 189 J6
Bug → Poland 52°31N 21°5E 185 F8
Buga Colombia 4°0N 76°15W 328 C2
Bugala I. Uganda 0°40S 32°20E 268 C3
Buganda Uganda 0°0 31°30E 268 C3
Buganga Uganda 0°3S 32°0E 268 C3
Bugasong Phil. 11°3N 122°4E 233 F4
Bugda Acable Somali Rep. 4°4N 45°15E 267 D6
Bugeat France 45°36N 1°55E 174 C5
Bugel, Tanjung Indonesia 6°26S 111°3E 235 D4
Bugibba Malta 35°57N 14°25E 206 F7
Bugio Portugal 38°39N 9°18W 126 B1
Bugojno Bos.-H. 44°2N 17°25E 182 F2
Bugsuk I. Phil. 8°12N 117°18E 233 G1
Buguey Phil. 18°17N 121°50E 232 B3
Buguias Phil. 16°43N 120°50E 232 C3
Bugulma Russia 54°33N 52°48E 186 D9
Buguma Nigeria 4°42N 6°55E 263 E6
Bugungu ⌓ Uganda 2°17N 31°50E 268 B3
Buguruslan Russia 53°39N 52°26E 186 D9
Buh → Ukraine 46°59N 31°58E 189 J6
Buharkent Turkey 37°58N 28°44E 205 D10
Buheirat-Murrat-el-Kubra Egypt 30°18N 32°26E 256 H8
Buhera Zimbabwe 19°18S 31°29E 271 A5
Bühl Baden-W., Germany 48°40N 8°8E 179 G4
Buhl Idaho, U.S.A. 42°36N 114°46W 304 E6
Buhuşi Romania 46°41N 26°45E 183 D11
Bui △ Ghana 8°21N 2°21W 262 D4
Buiksloot Neths. 52°24N 4°55E 112 A2
Builth Wells U.K. 52°9N 3°25W 169 E4
Buin Papua N. G. 6°48S 155°42E 287 L8
Buinsk Russia 55°0N 48°18E 190 C9
Buíque Brazil 8°37S 37°9W 332 C4
Buir Nur Mongolia 47°50N 117°42E 219 B6
Buis-les-Baronnies France 44°17N 5°16E 175 D9
Buitenveldert Neths. 52°20N 4°53E 112 B2
Buitenzorg = Bogor Indonesia 6°36S 106°48E 234 D3
Buitrago del Lozoya Spain 40°58N 3°38W 194 E7
Buizingen Belgium 50°44N 4°15E 116 B1
Bujalance Spain 37°54N 4°23W 195 H6
Bujanovac Serbia 42°28N 21°44E 202 D5
Bujaraloz Spain 41°29N 0°10W 196 D4
Buje Croatia 45°24N 13°39E 199 C10
Buji China 22°37N 114°5E 219 F11
Bujumbura Burundi 3°16S 29°18E 268 C2
Bük Hungary 47°22N 16°45E 182 C1
Buk Poland 52°21N 16°30E 185 F3
Buka I. Papua N. G. 5°10S 154°35E 286 C8
Bukachacha Russia 52°55N 116°50E 215 D12
Bukama Dem. Rep. of the Congo 9°10S 25°50E 269 D2
Būkān Iran 36°31N 46°12E 213 D12
Bukavu Dem. Rep. of the Congo 2°20S 28°52E 268 C2
Bukene Tanzania 4°15S 32°48E 268 C3
Bukhansan S. Korea 37°38N 126°58E 137 B1
Bukhara = Bukhoro Uzbekistan 39°48N 64°25E 216 E6
Bukhoro Uzbekistan 39°48N 64°25E 216 E6
Bukidnon □ Phil. 8°0N 125°0E 233 H5
Bukima Tanzania 1°50S 33°25E 268 C3
Bukit Badung Indonesia 8°49S 115°10E 231 K18
Bukit Baka Bukit Raya △ Indonesia 0°43S 112°40E 235 C4
Bukit Barisan Selatan △ Indonesia 5°8S 104°4E 234 D2
Bukit Duabelas △ Indonesia 2°3S 102°48E 234 C2
Bukit Kerajaan Malaysia 5°25N 100°15E 237 c
Bukit Mertajam Malaysia 5°22N 100°28E 237 c
Bukit Ni Malaysia 1°22N 104°12E 237 d
Bukit Panjang Singapore 1°23N 103°46E 237 d
Bukit Panjang Nature Reserve Singapore 1°22N 103°45E 138 A2
Bukit Tengah Malaysia 5°22N 100°25E 237 c
Bukit Tiban △ Malaysia 3°31N 113°53E 235 B4
Bukit Tigapuluh △ Indonesia 1°15S 102°25E 234 C2
Bukit Timah Nature Reserve Singapore 1°20N 103°47E 138 A2
Bukittinggi Indonesia 0°20S 100°20E 234 C2
Bükk Hungary 48°0N 20°30E 182 B5
Bukkapatnam India 14°14N 77°46E 245 G3
Bükki △ Hungary 48°3N 20°30E 182 B5
Bukoba Tanzania 1°20S 31°49E 268 C3
Bukum, Pulau Singapore 1°14N 103°46E 138 B2
Bukuru Nigeria 9°42N 8°48E 263 D6
Bukuya Uganda 0°40N 31°52E 268 B3
Būl, Kuh-e Iran 30°48N 52°45E 247 D7
Bula Guinea-Biss. 12°7N 15°43W 262 C1
Bula Indonesia 3°6S 130°30E 231 E8
Bula Camarines S., Phil. 13°28N 123°16E 232 E4
Bula-Atumba Angola 8°41S 14°52E 265 D2
Bulacan □ Phil. 15°0N 121°5E 232 D3
Bülach Switz. 47°31N 8°32E 179 H4
Būlaevo Kazakhstan 54°54N 70°26E 217 B8
Bulahdelah Australia 32°23S 152°13E 283 B10
Bulalacao Phil. 12°31N 121°26E 232 E3
Bulan Phil. 12°40N 123°52E 232 E4
Bulancak Turkey 40°56N 38°14E 213 B8
Búland Iceland 63°46N 18°30W 155 D8
Bulandshahr India 28°28N 77°51E 242 E7
Bulanık Turkey 39°4N 42°14E 213 C10
Bûlâq El Khârga, Egypt 25°10N 30°38E 256 B3
Bûlâq El Qâhira, Egypt 30°3N 31°14E 117 A2
Bulawayo Zimbabwe 20°7S 28°32E 269 G2
Buldan Turkey 38°2N 28°50E 205 C10
Buldana India 20°30N 76°18E 244 D3
Buldir I. U.S.A. 52°21N 175°56E 303 K1
Buldon Phil. 7°33N 124°25E 233 H5
Bule Phil. 14°26N 121°2E 127 C2
Bulgan Mongolia 48°45N 103°34E 218 B5
Bulgar Russia 54°57N 49°4E 190 C9
Bulgaria ■ Europe 42°35N 25°30E 203 D9
Bulgheria, Monte Italy 40°4N 15°26E 201 B8
Bulgurca Turkey 38°9N 27°9E 205 C9
Bulhale Somali Rep. 5°20N 46°29E 267 C6
Bulhar Somali Rep. 10°25N 44°30E 267 B5
Buli, Teluk Indonesia 0°48N 128°25E 231 D7
Buliluyan, C. Phil. 8°20N 117°15E 233 G1
Bulim Singapore 1°22N 103°43E 138 A2
Bulki Ethiopia 6°11N 36°31E 257 F4
Bulkley → Canada 55°15N 127°40W 296 B3
Bull Head Jamaica 18°10N 77°16W 320 a
Bull Savanna Jamaica 17°53N 77°35W 320 a
Bull Shoals L. U.S.A. 36°22N 92°35W 314 C8
Bullaque → Spain 38°59N 4°17W 195 G6
Bullard U.S.A. 32°38N 83°30W 316 C6
Bullas Spain 38°2N 1°40W 197 G3
Bulle Switz. 46°37N 7°3E 179 J3
Bullen Park Australia 37°46S 145°4E 128 A2
Bullenbaai Neth. Ant. 12°11N 69°2W 322 g
Buller → N.Z. 41°44S 171°36E 285 B6
Buller, Mt. Australia 37°10S 146°28E 283 D7
Buller Gorge N.Z. 41°40S 172°10E 285 B7
Bulleringa △ Australia 17°39S 143°56E 280 B3
Bullhead City U.S.A. 35°8N 114°32W 307 K12
Bulli Australia 34°15S 150°57E 283 C9
Büllingen Belgium 50°25N 6°16E 170 D6
Bullock Creek Australia 17°43S 144°31E 280 B3
Bulloo → Australia 28°43S 142°30E 281 D3
Bulloo L. Australia 28°43S 142°25E 281 D3
Bulls N.Z. 40°10S 175°24E 284 G4
Bully-les-Mines France 50°27N 2°44E 173 B9
Bulnes Chile 36°42S 72°19W 334 D1
Bulo Burti Somali Rep. 3°50N 45°33E 267 D6
Bulo Ghedudo Somali Rep. 2°52N 43°1E 267 D5
Bulolo Papua N. G. 7°10S 146°40E 286 D4
Bulongo Dem. Rep. of the Congo 4°45S 21°30E 265 C4
Bulqizë Albania 41°30N 20°21E 202 E4
Bulsar = Valsad India 20°40N 72°58E 244 D1
Bultfontein S. Africa 28°18S 26°10E 270 C4
Buluan Phil. 6°44N 124°47E 233 H5
Buluan, L. Phil. 6°40N 124°49E 233 H5
Bulukumba Indonesia 5°33S 120°11E 231 F6
Bulun Russia 70°37N 127°30E 215 B13
Bulungkol China 38°36N 74°58E 217 E8
Bulungu Dem. Rep. of the Congo 6°4S 21°54E 265 D4
Bulusan Phil. 12°45N 124°8E 232 E5
Bulusan Vol. Phil. 12°46N 124°3E 232 E5
Bumba Bandundu, Dem. Rep. of the Congo 6°58S 19°19E 265 D3
Bumba Équateur, Dem. Rep. of the Congo 2°13N 22°30E 264 B4
Bumbeşti-Jiu Romania 45°10N 23°24E 183 E8
Bumbiri I. Tanzania 1°40S 31°55E 268 C3
Bumbuna S. Leone 9°2N 11°49W 262 D2
Bumhkang Burma 26°51N 97°40E 241 B6
Bumhpa Bum Burma 26°51N 97°14E 241 B6
Bumi → Zimbabwe 17°0S 28°20E 269 F2
Bumtang → Bhutan 26°56N 90°53E 241 B3
Bumthang = Jakar Dzong Bhutan 27°33N 90°43E 241 B3
Buna Dem. Rep. of the Congo 3°14S 18°59E 264 C3
Buna North Eastern, Kenya 2°58N 39°30E 268 B4
Buna Papua N. G. 8°42S 148°27E 286 E5
Bunaken Indonesia 1°37N 124°46E 231 D6
Bunama Papua N. G. 10°9S 151°9E 286 F6
Bunawan Phil. 8°12N 125°57E 233 G5
Bunazi Tanzania 1°3S 31°23E 268 C3
Bunbah, Khalīj Libya 32°20N 23°15E 258 B4
Bunbury Australia 33°20S 115°35E 279 F2
Bunclody Ireland 52°39N 6°40W 166 D5
Buncrana Ireland 55°8N 7°27W 166 A4
Bund, The China 31°14N 121°30E 138 B1
Bunda Dem. Rep. of the Congo 4°58S 14°29E 265 C3
Bundaberg Australia 24°54S 152°22E 281 C5
Bundanoon Australia 34°40S 150°16E 283 C9
Bünde Germany 52°11N 8°35E 178 C4
Bundestag = Reichstag Berlin, Germany 115 a3
Bundey → Australia 21°46S 135°37E 280 C2
Bundi India 25°30N 75°35E 242 G6
Bundjalung △ Australia 29°16S 153°21E 281 D5
Bundoora North Australia 37°41S 145°2E 128 A2
Bundoora Park Australia 37°42S 145°2E 128 A2
Bundoran Ireland 54°28N 8°16W 166 B3
Bundukia Sudan 5°14N 30°55E 257 F3
Bundure Australia 35°10S 146°1E 283 C7
Bung Kan Thailand 18°23N 103°37E 236 C4
Bunga → Nigeria 11°23N 9°56E 263 C6
Bungay U.K. 52°27N 1°28E 169 E9
Bungendore Australia 35°14S 149°30E 283 C8
Bungil Cr. → Australia 27°5S 149°5E 281 D4
Bungle Bungle = Purnululu △ Australia 17°20S 128°20E 278 C4
Bungo Angola 7°26S 15°33E 265 D3
Bungo, Gunung Malaysia 1°16N 110°9E 235 B4
Bungo-Suidō Japan 33°0N 132°15E 222 E4
Bungoma Kenya 0°34N 34°34E 268 B3
Bungotakada Japan 33°35N 131°25E 222 D3
Bungu Tanzania 7°35S 39°0E 268 D4
Bunia Dem. Rep. of the Congo 1°35N 30°20E 268 B3
Bunianga Dem. Rep. of the Congo 3°28S 20°11E 264 C4
Bunji Pakistan 35°45N 74°40E 243 B6
Bunker Hill Ill., U.S.A. 39°3N 89°57W 310 E7
Bunker Hill Ind., U.S.A. 40°40N 86°6W 311 D10
Bunker Hill Memorial U.S.A. 42°22N 71°4W 116 A2
Bunker I. Pakistan 24°48N 66°57E 123 B1
Bunkie U.S.A. 30°57N 92°11W 314 F8
Bunkyō Japan 35°42N 139°45E 140 A3
Bunnefjorden Norway 59°50N 10°44E 133 A3
Bunnell U.S.A. 29°28N 81°16W 317 F8
Bunnythorpe N.Z. 40°16S 175°39E 284 G4
Buñol Spain 39°25N 0°47W 197 F4
Bunsuru Nigeria 13°21N 6°23E 263 C5
Buntok Indonesia 1°40S 114°58E 235 C4
Bununu Dass Nigeria 10°5N 9°31E 263 C6
Bununu Kasa Nigeria 9°51N 9°32E 263 D6
Bunya Mts. △ Australia 26°51S 151°34E 281 D5
Bünyan Turkey 38°51N 35°51E 212 C6
Bunyu Indonesia 3°35N 117°50E 235 B5
Bunza Nigeria 12°8N 4°0E 263 C5
Bunzlau = Bolesławiec Poland 51°17N 15°37E 185 G2
Buol Indonesia 1°15N 121°32E 231 D6
Buon Brieng Vietnam 13°9N 108°12E 236 F7
Buon Ma Thuot Vietnam 12°40N 108°3E 236 F7
Buona Vista Park Singapore 1°16N 103°47E 138 B2
Buong Long Cambodia 13°44N 106°59E 236 F6
Buorkhaya, Mys Russia 71°50N 132°40E 215 B14
Buqayq Si. Arabia 26°0N 49°45E 247 E6
Buqbuq Egypt 31°29N 25°29E 256 A2
Bur Acaba Somali Rep. 3°12N 44°20E 267 D5
Bûr Fuad Egypt 31°15N 32°20E 256 H8
Bur Ghibi Somali Rep. 3°56N 45°7E 267 D6
Bûr Safâga Egypt 26°43N 33°57E 246 E2
Bûr Sa'îd Egypt 31°16N 32°18E 256 H8
Bûr Sûdân Sudan 19°32N 37°9E 256 D4
Bûr Taufiq Egypt 29°54N 32°32E 256 J8
Bura Kenya 1°4S 39°58E 268 C4
Burakin Australia 30°31S 117°10E 279 F2
Buram Sudan 10°51N 25°9E 257 E2
Buran Somali Rep. 10°14N 48°44E 267 B6
Burao Somali Rep. 9°32N 45°32E 267 C6
Burāq Syria 33°11N 36°29E 250 E7
Burauen Phil. 10°58N 124°53E 233 F5
Buraydah Si. Arabia 26°20N 43°59E 246 E4
Burbank Calif., U.S.A. 34°12N 118°18W 126 A3
Burbank Ill., U.S.A. 41°44N 87°46W 119 C2
Burç Turkey 36°59N 37°8E 250 B8
Burcher Australia 33°30S 147°16E 283 B7
Burda India 25°50N 77°35E 242 G6
Burdekin → Australia 19°38S 147°25E 280 B4
Burden, L. U.S.A. 28°27N 81°33W 133 B1
Burdeos Bay Phil. 14°44N 122°6E 232 D4
Burdur Turkey 37°45N 30°17E 205 D12
Burdur □ Turkey 37°45N 30°0E 205 D12
Burdur Gölü Turkey 37°44N 30°10E 205 D12
Burdwan = Barddhaman India 23°14N 87°39E 243 H12
Burdwood Bank Atl. Oc. 54°0S 59°0W 152 M6
Bure Gojam, Ethiopia 10°40N 37°4E 257 E4
Bure Ilubabor, Ethiopia 8°19N 35°8E 257 F4
Bure → U.K. 52°38N 1°43E 168 E9
Büren Germany 51°33N 8°35E 178 D4
Bureya → Russia 49°27N 129°30E 215 E13
Burford Canada 43°7N 80°27W 312 C4
Burg Germany 52°16N 11°51E 178 C7
Burg auf Fehmarn Germany 54°28N 11°9E 178 A7
Burg el Arab Egypt 30°54N 29°32E 256 H6
Burg et Tuyur Sudan 20°55N 27°56E 256 C2
Burg Stargard Germany 53°29N 13°18E 178 B9
Burgas Bulgaria 42°33N 27°29E 203 D11
Burgas □ Bulgaria 42°30N 26°50E 203 D10
Burgaski Zaliv Bulgaria 42°30N 27°39E 203 D11
Burgdorf Niedersachsen, Germany 52°27N 10°1E 178 C6
Burgdorf Switz. 47°3N 7°37E 179 H3
Burgenland □ Austria 47°20N 16°20E 181 D9
Burgeo Canada 47°37N 57°38W 299 C8
Burgersdorp S. Africa 31°0S 26°20E 270 D4
Burges, Mt. Australia 30°50S 121°5E 279 F3
Burghausen Germany 48°9N 12°49E 179 G8
Burghead U.K. 57°43N 3°30W 167 D5
Búrgio Italy 37°36N 13°17E 200 E6
Burglengenfeld Germany 49°12N 12°2E 179 F8
Burgohondo Spain 40°26N 4°47W 194 E6
Burgos Ilocos N., Phil. 18°31N 120°39E 232 B3
Burgos Pangasinan, Phil. 16°4N 119°52E 232 C2
Burgos Spain 42°21N 3°41W 194 C7
Burgos □ Spain 42°21N 3°42W 194 C7
Burgstädt Germany 50°54N 12°49E 178 E8
Burgsvik Sweden 57°3N 18°19E 163 G12
Burguillos del Cerro Spain 38°23N 6°35W 195 G4
Burgundy = Bourgogne □ France 47°0N 4°50E 173 F11
Burhaniye Turkey 39°30N 26°58E 205 B8
Burhanpur India 21°18N 76°14E 244 D3
Burhi Gandak → India 25°20N 86°37E 243 G12
Burhner → India 22°43N 80°31E 243 H9
Buri Pen. Eritrea 15°25N 39°55E 257 D4
Burias I. Phil. 12°55N 123°5E 232 E4
Burias Pass Phil. 13°0N 123°15E 232 E4
Burica, Pta. Costa Rica 8°3N 82°51W 320 E3
Burien U.S.A. 47°28N 122°20W 306 C4
Burigi, L. Tanzania 2°2S 31°22E 268 C3
Burigi ⌓ Tanzania 2°20S 31°6E 268 C3
Burin Canada 47°1N 55°14W 299 C8
Buriram Thailand 15°0N 103°0E 236 E4
Buriti Alegre Brazil 18°9S 49°3W 333 E2
Buriti Bravo Brazil 5°50S 43°50W 332 C3
Buriti dos Lopes Brazil 3°10S 41°52W 332 B3
Burji Ethiopia 5°29N 37°51E 257 F4
Burkburnett U.S.A. 34°6N 98°34W 314 D5
Burke → Australia 23°12S 139°33E 280 C2
Burke Chan. Canada 52°10N 127°30W 296 C3
Burketown Australia 17°45S 139°33E 280 B2
Burkina Faso ■ Africa 12°0N 1°0W 262 C4
Burk's Falls Canada 45°37N 79°24W 298 C4
Burlada Spain 42°49N 1°36W 196 C3
Burleigh Falls Canada 44°33N 78°12W 312 B6
Burley U.S.A. 42°32N 113°48W 304 E7
Burlingame U.S.A. 37°35N 122°21W 306 H4
Burlington Ont., Canada 43°18N 79°45W 312 C5
Burlington Colo., U.S.A. 39°18N 102°16W 304 G12
Burlington Iowa, U.S.A. 40°49N 91°14W 310 D5
Burlington Kans., U.S.A. 38°12N 95°45W 308 F6
Burlington Ky., U.S.A. 39°2N 84°43W 311 E12
Burlington Mass., U.S.A. 42°30N 71°13W 116 A1
Burlington N.C., U.S.A. 36°6N 79°26W 315 C15
Burlington N.J., U.S.A. 40°4N 74°51W 313 F10
Burlington Vt., U.S.A. 44°29N 73°12W 313 B11
Burlington Wash., U.S.A. 48°28N 122°20W 306 B4
Burlington Wis., U.S.A. 42°41N 88°17W 311 B8
Burma ■ Asia 21°0N 96°30E 241 E6
Burnaby I. Canada 52°25N 131°19W 296 C2
Burnet U.S.A. 30°45N 98°14W 314 F5
Burney U.S.A. 40°53N 121°40W 304 F3
Burnham U.S.A. 40°38N 77°34W 312 F7
Burnham-on-Sea U.K. 51°14N 3°0W 169 F5
Burnham Park U.S.A. 41°49N 87°35W 119 C3
Burnham Park Harbor Chicago, U.S.A. 119 e3
Burnhamthorpe Canada 43°37N 79°35W 141 B1
Burnie Australia 41°4S 145°56E 281 G4
Burnley U.K. 53°47N 2°14W 168 D5
Burns U.S.A. 43°35N 119°3W 304 E4
Burns Junction U.S.A. 42°47N 117°51W 304 E5
Burns Lake Canada 54°14N 125°45W 296 C3
Burnside → Canada 66°51N 108°4W 294 C9
Burnside, L. Australia 25°22S 123°0E 279 E3
Burnsville U.S.A. 44°47N 93°17W 308 C7
Burnt, L. Canada 53°35N 64°4W 299 B7
Burnt Oak U.K. 51°36N 0°15W 125 A2
Burnt Paw U.S.A. 66°54N 143°44W 303 C12
Burnt River Canada 44°41N 78°42W 312 B6
Burntisland U.K. 56°4N 3°13W 121 A2
Burntwood → Canada 56°8N 96°34W 297 B9
Burntwood L. Canada 55°22N 100°26W 297 B8
Burnwynd U.K. 55°54N 3°23W 121 B1
Buronga Australia 34°18S 142°20E 282 C5
Burqa West Bank 31°54N 35°15E 123 A2
Burqān Kuwait 29°0N 47°57E 246 D5
Burqin China 47°43N 87°0E 217 C11
Burra S. Austral., Australia 33°40S 138°55E 282 B3
Burra Nigeria 11°0N 8°56E 263 C6
Burragorang, L. Australia 33°52S 150°37E 283 B9
Burray U.K. 58°51N 2°54W 167 C6
Burrel Albania 41°36N 20°1E 202 E4
Burren Ireland 53°9N 9°5W 166 C2
Burren △ Ireland 53°1N 8°58W 166 C3
Burren Junction Australia 30°7S 148°58E 281 E4
Burrendong, L. Australia 32°45S 149°10E 283 B8
Burriana Spain 39°50N 0°4W 196 F4
Burrinjuck Res. Australia 35°0S 148°36E 283 C8
Burro, Serranías del Mexico 28°56N 102°5W 318 B4
Burrow Hd. U.K. 54°41N 4°24W 167 G4
Burrowa-Pine Mountain △ Australia 36°6S 147°45E 283 D7
Burrum Coast △ Australia 25°13S 152°36E 281 D5
Burruyacú Argentina 26°30S 64°40W 334 B3
Burry Port U.K. 51°41N 4°15W 169 F3
Bursa Turkey 40°15N 29°5E 203 F13

Bursa □ *Turkey* 40°10N 29°5E **212** B3
Burseryd *Sweden* 57°12N 13°17E **163** G7
Burstall *Canada* 50°39N 109°54W **297** C7
Burton *Mich., U.S.A.* 43°0N 83°40W **311** B13
Burton *Ohio, U.S.A.* 41°28N 81°8W **312** E3
Burton *S.C., U.S.A.* 32°26N 80°43W **315** E14
Burton, L. *Canada* 54°45N 78°20W **298** B4
Burton upon Trent *U.K.* 52°48N 1°38W **168** E6
Burtundy *Australia* 33°45S 142°15E **282** B5
Burtus *Egypt* 30°8N 31°8E **117** A1
Buru *Indonesia* 3°30S 126°30E **231** E7
Buruanga *Phil.* 11°51N 121°53E **233** F3
Burudvatn *Norway* 59°58N 10°35E **133** A2
Burullus, Bahra el *Egypt* 31°25N 31°0E **256** H7
Burûm *Yemen* 14°22N 48°59E **249** D5
Burûn, Râs *Egypt* 31°14N 33°7E **251** G4
Burundi ■ *Africa* 3°15S 30°0E **268** C3
Burunny = Tsagan Aman
Russia 47°34N 46°43E **191** G8
Bururi *Burundi* 3°57S 29°37E **268** C2
Burutu *Nigeria* 5°20N 5°29E **263** D6
Burwell *U.S.A.* 41°47N 99°8W **308** E4
Burwick *U.K.* 58°45N 2°58W **167** C5
Burwood *Australia* 33°52S 151°5E **139** B1
Bury *U.K.* 53°35N 2°17W **168** D5
Bury St. Edmunds *U.K.* 52°15N 0°43E **169** E8
Buryatia □ *Russia* 53°0N 110°0E **215** D12
Buryn *Ukraine* 51°13N 33°50E **189** G7
Burzenin *Poland* 51°28N 18°47E **185** G5
Busa, Mt. *Phil.* 6°8N 124°39E **233** H5
Busalla *Italy* 44°34N 8°57E **198** D5
Busan *S. Korea* 35°5N 129°0E **224** E4
Busanga
Dem. Rep. of the Congo 0°53S 22°7E **264** C4
Busango Swamp *Zambia* 14°15S 25°45E **269** E2
Buşayrah *Syria* 35°9N 40°26E **213** E9
Busca *Italy* 44°31N 7°29E **198** D4
Bûsh *Egypt* 29°9N 31°8E **251** J2
Bushat *Albania* 41°58N 19°34E **202** E3
Būshehr *Iran* 28°55N 50°55E **247** D6
Būshehr □ *Iran* 28°20N 51°45E **247** D6
Bushell *Canada* 59°31N 108°45W **297** B7
Bushenyi *Uganda* 0°35S 30°10E **268** C3
Bushimaie →
Dem. Rep. of the Congo 6°2S 23°45E **265** D4
Bushire = Būshehr *Iran* 28°55N 50°55E **247** D6
Bushiribana *Aruba* 12°33N 69°58W **322** f
Bushnell *Fla., U.S.A.* 28°40N 82°7W **317** G7
Bushnell *Ill., U.S.A.* 40°33N 90°31W **310** D6
Bushtyna *Ukraine* 48°3N 23°28E **183** B8
Bushwick *U.S.A.* 40°41N 73°54W **132** B2
Bushy Park *U.K.* 51°24N 0°20W **125** B1
Busie *Ghana* 10°29N 2°22W **262** C4
Businga
Dem. Rep. of the Congo 3°16N 20°59E **264** B4
Buskerud □ *Norway* 60°20N 9°0E **164** D5
Busko-Zdrój *Poland* 50°28N 20°42E **185** H7
Buslei *Ethiopia* 5°28N 44°25E **267** C5
Busovača *Bos.-H.* 44°6N 17°53E **182** F2
Buşra ash Shām *Syria* 32°30N 36°25E **251** F7
Busselton *Australia* 33°42S 115°15E **279** F2
Busseri → *Sudan* 7°41N 28°3E **257** F2
Busseto *Italy* 44°59N 10°2E **198** D7
Bussière-Badil *France* 45°39N 0°36E **174** C4
Bussolengo *Italy* 45°28N 10°51E **198** C7
Bussum *Neths.* 52°16N 5°10E **170** B5
Bustamante, B. *Argentina* 45°5S 66°18W **336** C3
Buşteni *Romania* 45°24N 25°32E **183** E10
Busto, C. *Spain* 43°34N 6°28W **194** B4
Busto Arsizio *Italy* 45°37N 8°51E **198** C5
Busu Djanoa
Dem. Rep. of the Congo 1°43N 21°23E **264** B4
Busu Kwanga
Dem. Rep. of the Congo 1°48N 20°21E **264** B4
Busu Mandji
Dem. Rep. of the Congo 2°52N 21°14E **264** B4
Busuanga *Phil.* 12°14N 119°52E **232** E2
Busuanga I. *Phil.* 12°10N 120°0E **232** E2
Büsum *Germany* 54°7N 8°51E **178** A4
Busungbiu *Indonesia* 8°16S 114°58E **231** J17
Busy Corner *Trin. & Tob.* 10°18N 61°17W **323** t
Buta *Dem. Rep. of the Congo* 2°50N 24°53E **264** B4
Butantã *Brazil* 23°34S 46°42W **137** B1
Butare *Rwanda* 2°31S 29°52E **268** C2
Butaritari *Kiribati* 3°30N 174°0E **288** G9
Butcher I. *India* 18°57N 72°53E **130** B2
Bute *S. Austral., Australia* 33°51S 138°2E **282** B3
Bute *Scotland, U.K.* 55°48N 5°2W **167** F3
Bute Inlet *Canada* 50°40N 124°53W **296** C4
Butemba *Uganda* 1°9N 31°37E **268** B3
Butembo
Dem. Rep. of the Congo 0°9N 29°18E **268** B2
Buteni *Romania* 46°19N 22°7E **182** D7
Butera *Italy* 37°11N 14°11E **201** E7
Butere *Kenya* 0°13N 34°30E **268** B3
Butha Qi *China* 48°0N 122°32E **219** B7
Buthidaung *Burma* 20°52N 92°32E **241** E4
Butiaba *Uganda* 1°50N 31°20E **268** B3
Butler *Ga., U.S.A.* 32°33N 84°14W **316** C5
Butler *Ind., U.S.A.* 41°26N 84°52W **311** C12
Butler *Ky., U.S.A.* 38°47N 84°22W **311** F12
Butler *Mo., U.S.A.* 38°16N 94°20W **310** F2
Butler *Pa., U.S.A.* 40°52N 79°54W **312** F5
Butler, L. *U.S.A.* 28°29N 81°33W **133** B1
Buton *Indonesia* 5°0S 122°45E **231** F6
Bütow = Bytów *Poland* 54°10N 17°30E **184** D4
Butrintit, L. e *Albania* 39°43N 20°5E **206** B10
Butte *Mont., U.S.A.* 46°0N 112°32W **304** C7
Butte *Nebr., U.S.A.* 42°58N 98°51W **308** D4
Butte Creek → *U.S.A.* 39°12N 121°56W **306** F5
Butterworth = Gcuwa
S. Africa 32°20S 28°11E **271** D4
Butterworth *Malaysia* 5°24N 100°23E **237** c
Buttevant *Ireland* 52°14N 8°40W **166** D3
Buttfield, Mt. *Australia* 24°45S 128°9E **279** D4
Button B. *Canada* 58°45N 94°23W **297** B10
Buttonwillow *U.S.A.* 35°24N 119°28W **307** K7
Butts Corner *U.S.A.* 38°46N 77°19W **143** C2
Butty Hd. *Australia* 33°54S 121°39E **279** F3
Butuan *Phil.* 8°57N 125°33E **233** G5
Butuku-Luba *Eq. Guin.* 3°29N 8°33E **263** E6
Butung = Buton *Indonesia* 5°0S 122°45E **231** F6
Buturlinovka *Russia* 50°50N 40°35E **190** E5
Butzbach *Germany* 50°25N 8°40E **179** E4
Bützow *Germany* 53°50N 11°58E **178** B7
Buulobarde = Bulo Burti
Somali Rep. 3°50N 45°33E **267** D6
Buur Hakaba = Bur Acaba
Somali Rep. 3°12N 44°20E **267** D5
Buvika *Norway* 63°18N 10°11E **164** A7
Buxa Duar *India* 27°45N 89°35E **243** F13
Buxar *India* 25°34N 83°58E **243** G10
Buxoro = Bukhoro
Uzbekistan 39°48N 64°25E **216** E6
Buxtehude *Germany* 53°28N 9°39E **178** B5
Buxton *Guyana* 6°48N 58°2W **329** B6
Buxton *Derby, U.K.* 53°16N 1°54W **168** D6
Buxy *France* 46°44N 4°40E **173** F11
Buy *Russia* 58°28N 41°28E **190** A5
Buyant-Uhaa *Mongolia* 44°55N 110°11E **219** B6
Buynaksk *Russia* 42°48N 47°7E **191** J8
Buyo *Ivory C.* 6°21N 7°5W **262** D3
Buyo, L. de *Ivory C.* 6°16N 7°10W **262** D3
Büyük Menderes →
Turkey 37°28N 27°11E **205** D9
Büyükçekmece *Turkey* 41°2N 28°35E **203** E12
Büyükdere *Turkey* 41°9N 29°2E **122** B2
Büyükeğri Dağı *Turkey* 36°45N 33°33E **250** B4
Büyükkariştiran *Turkey* 41°18N 27°33E **203** E11
Büyükkemikli Burnu
Turkey 40°18N 26°14E **203** F10
Büyükorhan *Turkey* 39°46N 28°56E **205** B10
Büyükyoncalı *Turkey* 41°20N 27°55E **203** E11
Buzançais *France* 46°54N 1°25E **172** F8
Buzău *Romania* 45°10N 26°50E **183** E11
Buzău □ *Romania* 45°20N 26°30E **183** E11
Buzău → *Romania* 45°26N 27°44E **183** E12
Buzău, Pasul *Romania* 45°35N 26°12E **183** E11
Buzen *Japan* 33°35N 131°5E **222** D3
Buzet *Croatia* 45°24N 13°58E **199** C10
Buzi → *Mozam.* 19°50S 34°43E **269** F3
Buziaş *Romania* 45°38N 21°36E **182** E6
Bŭzmeyin *Turkmenistan* 38°3N 58°12E **247** B8
Buzuluk *Russia* 52°48N 52°12E **186** D9
Buzuluk → *Russia* 50°15N 42°7E **190** E6
Buzzards Bay *U.S.A.* 41°45N 70°37W **313** E14
Bwagaoia *Papua N. G.* 10°40S 152°52E **286** F7
Bwana Mkubwe
Dem. Rep. of the Congo 13°8S 28°38E **269** E2
Bwasa
Dem. Rep. of the Congo 3°55S 18°24E **264** C3
Bwatnapné *Vanuatu* 15°41S 168°9E **287** E6
Bwindi △ *Uganda* 1°2S 29°42E **268** C2
Byakar Dzong = Jakar Dzong
Bhutan 27°33N 90°43E **241** B3
Byala *Ruse, Bulgaria* 43°28N 25°44E **203** C9
Byala *Varna, Bulgaria* 42°53N 27°55E **203** D11
Byala Slatina *Bulgaria* 43°26N 23°58E **202** C7
Byarezina → *Belarus* 52°33N 30°14E **177** B16
Byaroza *Belarus* 52°31N 24°51E **189** F3
Bychawa *Poland* 51°1N 22°36E **185** G9
Byculla *India* 18°58N 72°50E **130** B2
Byczyna *Poland* 51°7N 18°12E **185** G5
Bydgoszcz *Poland* 53°10N 18°0E **185** E5
Byelorussia = Belarus ■
Europe 53°30N 27°0E **177** B14
Byeonsan Peninsula △
S. Korea 35°40N 126°30E **224** E3
Byers *U.S.A.* 39°43N 104°14W **304** G11
Byesville *U.S.A.* 39°58N 81°32W **312** G3
Byfield △ *Australia* 22°52S 150°45E **280** C5
Byford *Australia* 32°15S 116°0E **279** F2
Bygdin *Norway* 61°21N 8°32E **164** C5
Bygdøy *Norway* 59°54N 10°40E **133** A3
Bygland *Norway* 58°50N 7°48E **164** F4
Byglandsfjorden *Norway* 58°44N 7°50E **164** F4
Bygstad *Norway* 61°23N 5°40E **164** C2
Bykhaw *Belarus* 53°31N 30°14E **177** B16
Bykhov = Bykhaw
Belarus 53°31N 30°14E **177** B16
Bykle *Norway* 59°20N 7°22E **164** E4
Bykovo *Russia* 49°50N 45°25E **190** F7
Bylas *U.S.A.* 33°8N 110°7W **305** K8
Bylot *Canada* 58°25N 94°8W **297** B10
Bylot I. *Canada* 73°13N 78°34W **295** B12
Byrd, C. *Antarctica* 69°38S 76°7W **151** C17
Byrock *Australia* 30°40S 146°27E **283** A7
Byron *Ga., U.S.A.* 32°39N 83°46W **316** C6
Byron *Ill., U.S.A.* 42°8N 89°15W **310** B7
Byron, C. *Australia* 28°43S 153°38E **281** D5
Byron Bay *Australia* 28°43S 153°37E **281** D5
Byrranga, Gory *Russia* 75°0N 100°0E **215** B11
Byrranga Mts. = Byrranga, Gory
Russia 75°0N 100°0E **215** B11
Byrum *Denmark* 57°16N 11°0E **163** G5
Byske *Sweden* 64°57N 21°11E **160** D19
Byskeälven → *Sweden* 64°57N 21°13E **160** D19
Bystrytsya *Ukraine* 48°27N 24°14E **183** B9
Bystrzyca → *Dolnośląskie,*
Poland 51°12N 16°55E **185** G3
Bystrzyca → *Lubelskie,*
Poland 51°21N 22°46E **185** G9
Bystrzyca Kłodzka
Poland 50°19N 16°39E **185** H3
Bytča *Slovak Rep.* 49°13N 18°34E **181** B11
Bytkiv *Ukraine* 48°38N 24°28E **183** B9
Bytom *Poland* 50°25N 18°54E **185** H5
Bytom Odrzański *Poland* 51°44N 15°48E **185** G2
Bytów *Poland* 54°10N 17°30E **184** D4
Byumba *Rwanda* 1°35S 30°4E **268** C3
Bzenec *Czech Rep.* 48°58N 17°18E **181** C10
Bzura → *Poland* 52°25N 20°15E **185** F7

C

C.B.S. Fox Studios
U.S.A. 34°9N 118°24W **126** B2
C.N.N. Center *U.S.A.* 33°45N 84°23W **113** B2
C.N. Tower *Toronto, Canada* **141** c1
C.W. McConaughy, L.
U.S.A. 41°14N 101°40W **308** E3
Ca → *Vietnam* 18°45N 105°45E **236** C5
Ca Mau *Vietnam* 9°7N 105°8E **237** H5
Ca Mau, Mui *Vietnam* 8°38N 104°44E **237** H5
Ca Na *Vietnam* 11°20N 108°54E **237** G7
Caacupé *Paraguay* 25°23S 57°5W **334** B4
Caaguazú △ *Paraguay* 26°5S 55°31W **335** B4
Caála *Angola* 12°46S 15°30E **265** E3
Caamaño Sd. *Canada* 52°55N 129°25W **296** C3
Caapiranga *Brazil* 3°18S 61°13W **329** D5
Caazapá *Paraguay* 26°8S 56°19W **334** B4
Caazapá □ *Paraguay* 26°10S 56°0W **335** B4
Cabadbaran *Phil.* 9°10N 125°38E **233** G5
Cabagan *Phil.* 17°26N 121°46E **232** C3
Cabalian = San Juan
Phil. 10°16N 125°10E **233** F5
Caballeria, C. de *Spain* 40°5N 4°5E **206** A5
Caballito *Argentina* 34°37S 58°25W **117** B2
Cabana *Peru* 8°25S 78°5W **330** B2
Cabana *Spain* 43°13N 8°54W **194** B2
Cabanaconde *Peru* 15°38S 71°58W **330** D3
Cabanaquinta *Spain* 43°10N 5°38W **194** B5
Cabanatuan *Phil.* 15°30N 120°58E **232** D3
Cabañeros △ *Spain* 39°18N 4°35W **195** F6
Cabanes *Spain* 40°9N 0°2E **196** E5
Cabangon *Phil.* 15°10N 120°3E **232** D3
Cabanillas *Peru* 15°36S 70°28W **330** D3
Cabano *Canada* 47°40N 68°56W **299** C6
Čabar *Croatia* 45°36N 14°39E **199** C11
Cabarroguis *Phil.* 16°50N 121°30E **232** C3
Cabarruyan I. *Phil.* 16°18N 119°59E **232** C2
Cabazon *U.S.A.* 33°55N 116°47W **307** M10
Cabedelo *Brazil* 7°0S 34°50W **332** C5
Cabeza del Buey *Spain* 38°44N 5°13W **195** G5
Cabezón de la Sal *Spain* 43°18N 4°14W **194** B6
Cabildo *Chile* 32°30S 71°5W **334** C1
Cabimas *Venezuela* 10°23N 71°25W **328** A3
Cabin John *U.S.A.* 38°58N 77°10W **143** B2
Cabin John Regional Park ⌂
U.S.A. 39°0N 77°10W **143** A2
Cabinda *Angola* 5°33S 12°11E **265** D2
Cabinda □ *Angola* 5°0S 12°30E **265** D2
Cabinet Mts. *U.S.A.* 48°10N 115°50W **304** B6
Cabinteely *Ireland* 53°16N 6°9W **120** B3
Cabiri *Angola* 8°52S 13°39E **265** D2
Cable Beach *Bahamas* 25°4N 77°24W **153** b
Cabo Blanco *Argentina* 47°15S 65°47W **336** C3
Cabo de Gata-Níjar ⌂
Spain 36°51N 2°6W **197** J2
Cabo de Hornos △ *Chile* 55°42S 67°20W **336** E3
Cabo Frio *Brazil* 22°51S 42°3W **333** F3
Cabo Pantoja *Peru* 1°0S 75°10W **328** D2
Cabo Raso *Argentina* 44°20S 65°15W **336** B3
Cabo Rojo *Puerto Rico* 18°5N 67°9W **321** b
Cabo San Lucas *Mexico* 22°53N 109°54W **318** C3
Cabo Verde = Cape Verde Is. ■
Atl. Oc. 16°0N 24°0W **153** j
Cabo Yubi = Tarfaya
Morocco 27°55N 12°55W **260** C2
Cabonga, Réservoir
Canada 47°20N 76°40W **298** C4
Cabool *U.S.A.* 37°7N 92°6W **308** G7
Caboolture *Australia* 27°5S 152°58E **281** D5
Cabora Bassa Dam = Cahora Bassa,
Represa de *Mozam.* 15°20S 32°50E **269** F3
Caborca *Mexico* 30°37N 112°6W **318** A2
Cabot, Mt. *U.S.A.* 44°30N 71°25W **313** B13
Cabot Hd. *Canada* 45°14N 81°17W **312** A3
Cabot Str. *Canada* 47°15N 59°40W **299** C8
Cabra *Dublin, Ireland* 53°21N 6°18W **120** A2
Cabra *Spain* 37°30N 4°28W **195** H6
Cabra del Santo Cristo
Spain 37°42N 3°16W **195** H7
Cabra I. *India* 7°18N 93°50E **245** L11
Cábras *Italy* 39°56N 8°32E **200** C1
Cabras I. *Guam* 13°27N 144°44E **302** d
Cabrera *Spain* 39°8N 2°57E **206** B3
Cabrera, Sierra *Spain* 42°12N 6°40W **194** C4
Cabrera △ *Spain* 39°13N 2°53E **197** F7
Cabri *Canada* 50°35N 108°25W **297** C7
Cabriel → *Spain* 39°14N 1°3W **197** F3
Cabrits, Î. *Martinique* 14°23N 60°52W **322** j
Cabrits △ *Dominica* 15°35N 61°26W **323** k
Cabruta *Venezuela* 7°50N 66°10W **328** B4
Cabucgayan *Phil.* 11°29N 124°34E **233** F5
Cabuçú de Baixo →
Brazil 23°30S 46°40W **137** A1
Cabuçú de Cima →
Brazil 23°30S 46°33W **137** A2
Cabugao *Phil.* 17°48N 120°27E **232** C3
Cabulauan Is. *Phil.* 11°25N 120°8E **233** F3
Cabulo *Angola* 10°18S 16°22E **265** E3
Caburan = Jose Abad Santos
Phil. 5°55N 125°39E **233** J5
Cabuta *Angola* 9°48S 14°58E **265** D2
Cabuyaro *Colombia* 4°18N 72°49W **328** C3
Cacabelos *Spain* 42°36N 6°44W **194** C4
Caçador *Brazil* 26°47S 51°0W **335** B5
Čačak *Serbia* 43°54N 20°20E **202** C4
Cacandee Settlement
Trin. & Tob. 10°33N 61°26W **323** t
Cacao *Fr. Guiana* 4°33N 52°26W **329** C7
Caçapava do Sul *Brazil* 30°30S 53°30W **335** C5
Cáccamo *Italy* 37°56N 13°40E **200** E6
Cacém *Portugal* 38°46N 9°18W **195** G1
Cáceres *Brazil* 16°5S 57°40W **331** D6
Cáceres *Colombia* 7°35N 75°20W **328** B2
Cáceres *Spain* 39°26N 6°23W **195** F4
Cáceres □ *Spain* 39°45N 6°0W **194** F5
Cachan *France* 48°47N 2°19E **134** B2
Cache Bay *Canada* 46°22N 80°0W **298** C4
Cache Cr. → *U.S.A.* 38°42N 121°42W **306** G5
Cache Creek *Canada* 50°48N 121°19W **296** C4
Cachenka → *Russia* 55°46N 37°17E **129** B1
Cacheu *Guinea-Biss.* 12°14N 16°8W **262** C1
Cachi *Argentina* 25°5S 66°10W **334** B2
Cachimbo *Brazil* 8°57S 54°54W **331** B7
Cachimbo, Serra do *Brazil* 9°30S 55°30W **331** B6
Cachimo *Angola* 8°21S 21°24E **265** D4
Cachinal de la Sierra
Chile 24°58S 69°32W **334** A2
Cachingues *Angola* 13°5S 16°43E **265** E3
Cachoeira = Solonópole
Brazil 5°44S 39°1W **332** C4
Cachoeira *Brazil* 12°30S 39°0W **333** D4
Cachoeira, Rib. da →
Brazil 23°38S 46°43W **137** B1
Cachoeira Alta *Brazil* 18°48S 50°58W **333** E1
Cachoeira do Sul *Brazil* 30°3S 52°53W **335** C5
Cachoeiro de Itapemirim
Brazil 20°51S 41°7W **333** F3
Cachoeiro do Arari *Brazil* 1°1S 48°58W **332** B2
Cachopo *Portugal* 37°20N 7°49W **195** H3
Cachuela Esperanza
Bolivia 10°32S 65°38W **331** C4
Cacilhas *Portugal* 38°41N 9°8W **126** A2
Cacine *Guinea-Biss.* 11°8N 14°57W **262** C1
Cacoal *Brazil* 11°32S 61°18W **331** C5
Cacólo *Angola* 10°9S 19°21E **265** E3
Caconda *Angola* 13°48S 15°8E **265** E3
Cacongo *Angola* 5°11S 12°5E **265** D2
Caçu *Brazil* 18°37S 51°4W **333** E1
Cacuaco *Angola* 8°47S 13°21E **265** D2
Cacuchi → *Angola* 14°26S 16°46E **265** E3
Cacula *Angola* 14°29S 14°10E **265** E2
Caculé *Brazil* 14°30S 42°13W **333** D3
Caculuvar → *Angola* 16°47S 14°56E **265** F2
Cacuso *Angola* 9°25S 15°45E **265** D3
Čadca *Slovak Rep.* 49°26N 18°45E **181** B11
Caddo *U.S.A.* 34°7N 96°16W **314** D6
Cader Idris *U.K.* 52°42N 3°53W **169** E4
Cadereyta de Jiménez
Mexico 25°36N 100°0W **318** B5
Cades *U.S.A.* 33°47N 79°47W **316** B10
Cadí, Sierra del *Spain* 42°17N 1°42E **196** C6
Cadí-Moixeró ⌂ *Spain* 42°17N 1°44E **196** C6
Cadibarrawirracanna, L.
Australia 28°52S 135°27E **281** D2
Cadillac *Gironde, France* 44°38N 0°20W **174** D3
Cadillac *Mich., U.S.A.* 44°15N 85°24W **309** C11
Cadiz *Phil.* 10°57N 123°15E **233** F4
Cádiz *Spain* 36°30N 6°20W **195** J4
Cadiz *Calif., U.S.A.* 34°30N 115°28W **307** L11
Cadiz *Ohio, U.S.A.* 40°22N 81°0W **312** F4
Cádiz □ *Spain* 36°36N 5°45W **195** J5
Cádiz, G. de *Spain* 36°40N 7°0W **195** J3
Cadiz L. *U.S.A.* 34°18N 115°24W **305** J6
Cadley *U.S.A.* 33°32N 82°40W **316** B7
Cadney Park *Australia* 27°55S 134°3E **281** D1
Cadomin *Canada* 53°2N 117°20W **296** C5
Cadotte Lake *Canada* 56°26N 116°23W **296** B5
Cadours *France* 43°44N 1°2E **174** E5
Cadoux *Australia* 30°46S 117°7E **279** F2
Cadwell *U.S.A.* 32°20N 83°3W **316** C6
Caen *France* 49°10N 0°22W **172** C6
Caernarfon *U.K.* 53°8N 4°16W **168** D3
Caernarfon B. *U.K.* 53°4N 4°40W **168** D3
Caernarvon = Caernarfon
U.K. 53°8N 4°16W **168** D3
Caerphilly *U.K.* 51°35N 3°13W **169** F4
Caerphilly □ *U.K.* 51°37N 3°12W **169** F4
Caesarea *Israel* 32°30N 34°53E **251** F5
Caeté *Brazil* 19°55S 43°40W **333** E3
Caetité *Brazil* 13°50S 42°32W **333** D3
Cafayate *Argentina* 26°2S 66°0W **334** B2
Cafu *Angola* 16°30S 15°8E **265** F3
Cagayan □ *Phil.* 18°0N 121°50E **232** C3
Cagayan → *Phil.* 18°25N 121°42E **232** B3
Cagayan de Oro *Phil.* 8°30N 124°40E **233** G5
Cagayan Is. *Phil.* 9°40N 121°16E **233** G4
Cagayan Sulu I. *Phil.* 7°1N 118°30E **233** H2
Cagli *Italy* 43°33N 12°39E **199** E9
Cágliari *Italy* 39°13N 9°7E **200** C2
Cágliari, G. di *Italy* 39°8N 9°11E **200** C2
Cagnano Varano *Italy* 41°49N 15°47E **199** G12
Cagnes-sur-Mer *France* 43°40N 7°9E **175** E11
Caguán → *Colombia* 0°8S 74°18W **328** D3
Caguas *Puerto Rico* 18°14N 66°2W **321** C6
Caha Mts. *Ireland* 51°45N 9°40W **166** E2
Cahama *Angola* 16°17S 14°19E **265** F2
Caher *Ireland* 52°22N 7°56W **166** D4
Cahersiveen *Ireland* 51°56N 10°14W **166** E1
Cahora Bassa, L. de
Mozam. 15°35S 32°0E **269** F3
Cahora Bassa, Represa de
Mozam. 15°20S 32°50E **269** F3
Cahore Pt. *Ireland* 52°33N 6°12W **166** D5
Cahors *France* 44°27N 1°27E **174** D5
Cahuapanas *Peru* 5°15S 77°0W **330** B2
Cahuenga Park *U.S.A.* 34°8N 118°19W **126** B3
Cahuinari → *Colombia* 1°21S 70°44W **328** D3
Cahuinari △ *Colombia* 1°20S 71°10W **328** D3
Cahul *Moldova* 45°50N 28°15E **183** E13
Cai Bau, Dao *Vietnam* 21°10N 107°27E **228** G6
Cai Nuoc *Vietnam* 8°56N 105°1E **237** H5
Caia *Mozam.* 17°51S 35°24E **269** F4
Caiabis, Serra dos *Brazil* 11°30S 56°30W **331** C6
Caianda *Angola* 11°2S 23°31E **265** E4
Caiapó, Serra do *Brazil* 17°0S 52°0W **331** D7
Caiapônia *Brazil* 16°57S 51°49W **331** D7
Caibarién *Cuba* 22°30N 79°30W **320** B4
Caibiran *Phil.* 11°34N 124°35E **233** F5
Caiçara = Alvarães *Brazil* 3°12S 64°50W **329** D5
Caicara *Bolívar, Venezuela* 7°38N 66°10W **328** B4
Caicara *Monagas,*
Venezuela 9°52N 63°38W **329** B5
Caicó *Brazil* 6°20S 37°0W **332** C5
Caicos Is. *Turks & Caicos* 21°40N 71°40W **321** B5
Caicos Passage *W. Indies* 22°45N 72°45W **321** B5
Caidian *China* 30°35N 114°2E **229** B10
Caillandre, Morne
St. Lucia 13°46N 60°57W **323** m
Cailloma *Peru* 15°9S 71°45W **330** D3
Cain, L. *U.S.A.* 28°28N 81°28W **133** B2
Căinari *Moldova* 46°41N 29°13E **183** D14
Cainde *Angola* 15°29S 13°24E **265** F2
Caine → *Bolivia* 18°23S 65°21W **331** D4
Caird Coast *Antarctica* 75°0S 25°0W **151** D1
Cairn Gorm *U.K.* 57°7N 3°39W **167** D5
Cairngorm Mts. *U.K.* 57°6N 3°42W **167** D5
Cairngorms △ *U.K.* 57°10N 3°50W **167** D5
Cairnryan *U.K.* 54°59N 5°1W **167** G3
Cairns *Australia* 16°57S 145°45E **280** B4
Cairns L. *Canada* 51°42N 94°30W **297** C10
Cairo = El Qâhira *Egypt* 30°1N 31°13E **117** A2
Cairo *Ga., U.S.A.* 30°52N 84°13W **316** E5
Cairo *Ill., U.S.A.* 37°0N 89°11W **308** G9
Cairo *N.Y., U.S.A.* 42°18N 74°0W **313** D10
Cairo Int. ✈ (CAI) *Egypt* 30°7N 31°24E **117** A3
Cairo Montenotte *Italy* 44°23N 8°16E **198** D5
Cairofa *Angola* 14°3S 12°54E **265** E2
Caithness *U.K.* 58°25N 3°35W **167** C5
Caithness, Ord of *U.K.* 58°8N 3°36W **167** C5
Caitou *Angola* 14°28S 13°7E **265** E2
Caiuás = Rio Brilhante
Brazil 21°48S 54°33W **335** A5
Caiundo *Angola* 15°50S 17°28E **265** F3
Caiza *Bolivia* 20°2S 65°40W **331** E4
Caja de Muertos, I.
Puerto Rico 17°54N 66°32W **321** b
Cajabamba *Peru* 7°38S 78°4W **330** B2
Cajamarca *Peru* 7°5S 78°28W **330** B2
Cajamarca □ *Peru* 6°15S 78°50W **330** B2
Cajamarquilla = Bolívar
Peru 7°18S 77°48W **330** B2
Cajapió *Brazil* 2°58S 44°48W **332** B3
Cajarc *France* 44°29N 1°50E **174** D5
Cajas △ *Ecuador* 2°48S 79°15W **328** D2
Cajatambo *Peru* 10°30S 77°2W **330** C2
Cajàzeiras *Brazil* 6°52S 38°30W **332** C4
Čajetina *Serbia* 43°47N 19°42E **202** C3
Cajidiocan *Phil.* 12°22N 122°41E **232** E4
Caju *Brazil* 22°52S 43°12W **135** B1
Çakırgöl *Turkey* 40°33N 39°40E **213** B8
Çakırlar *Turkey* 36°52N 30°33E **205** E12
Čakovec *Croatia* 46°23N 16°26E **199** B13
Čakovice *Czech Rep.* 50°9N 14°31E **135** B3
Çal *Turkey* 38°4N 29°23E **205** C11
Cala *Spain* 37°59N 6°21W **195** H4
Cala → *Spain* 37°38N 6°5W **195** H4
Cala Cadolar, Punta de = Rotja,
Pta. *Spain* 38°38N 1°35E **206** D2
Cala d'Or *Spain* 39°23N 3°14E **206** B4
Cala en Porter *Spain* 39°52N 4°8E **206** B5
Cala Figuera, C. de *Spain* 39°27N 2°31E **206** B3
Cala Forcat *Spain* 40°0N 3°47E **206** B4
Cala Major *Spain* 39°33N 2°37E **206** B3
Cala Mezquida = Sa Mesquida
Spain 39°55N 4°16E **206** B5
Cala Millor *Spain* 39°35N 3°22E **206** B4
Cala Ratjada *Spain* 39°43N 3°27E **206** B4
Cala Santa Galdana *Spain* 39°56N 3°58E **206** B4
Calabanga *Phil.* 13°42N 123°17E **232** E4
Calabar *Nigeria* 4°57N 8°20E **263** E6
Calabogie *Canada* 45°18N 76°43W **313** A8
Calabozo *Venezuela* 9°0N 67°28W **328** B4
Calábria □ *Italy* 39°0N 16°30E **201** C9
Calábria △ *Italy* 39°6N 16°35E **201** C9
Calaburras, Pta. de *Spain* 36°30N 4°38W **195** J6
Calaceite *Spain* 41°1N 0°11E **196** D5
Calacoto *Bolivia* 17°16S 68°38W **330** D4
Calacuccia *France* 42°21N 9°1E **175** F13
Calafat *Romania* 43°58N 22°59E **182** G7
Calafate *Argentina* 50°19S 72°15W **336** D2
Calafell *Spain* 41°11N 1°34E **196** D6
Calagua Is. *Phil.* 14°30N 122°55E **232** D4
Calahorra *Spain* 42°18N 1°59W **196** C3
Calai *Angola* 17°47S 19°41E **265** F3
Calais *Pas-de-Calais, France* 50°57N 1°56E **173** B8
Calais *Maine, U.S.A.* 45°11N 67°17W **309** C20
Calakmul ⌂ *Mexico* 18°14N 89°48W **319** D7
Calalaste, Cord. de
Argentina 25°0S 67°0W **334** B2
Calama *Brazil* 8°0S 62°50W **331** B5
Calama *Chile* 22°30S 68°55W **334** A2
Calamar *Bolívar,*
Colombia 10°15N 74°55W **328** A3
Calamar *Vaupés, Colombia* 1°58N 72°32W **328** C3
Calamarca *Bolivia* 16°55S 68°9W **330** D4
Calamba *Cavite, Phil.* 14°13N 121°10E **232** D3
Calamba *Mis. Occ., Phil.* 8°35N 123°39E **233** G4
Calamian Group *Phil.* 11°50N 119°55E **233** F2
Calamocha *Spain* 40°50N 1°17W **196** E3
Calamonte *Spain* 38°53N 6°23W **195** G4
Călan *Romania* 45°44N 22°59E **182** E7
Calañas *Spain* 37°40N 6°53W **195** H4
Calanda *Spain* 40°56N 0°15W **196** E4
Calandagan I. *Phil.* 10°39N 120°15E **233** F3
Calandula *Angola* 9°6S 15°57E **265** D3
Calang *Indonesia* 4°37N 95°37E **234** B1
Calangiánus *Italy* 40°56N 9°11E **200** B2
Calanscio, Sarīr *Libya* 27°30N 21°30E **258** C4
Calapan *Phil.* 13°25N 121°7E **232** E3
Călăraşi *Moldova* 47°16N 28°19E **183** C13
Călăraşi *Romania* 44°12N 27°20E **183** F12
Călăraşi □ *Romania* 44°10N 27°0E **183** F12
Calasparra *Spain* 38°14N 1°41W **197** G3
Calatafimi *Italy* 37°55N 12°52E **200** E5
Calatagan *Phil.* 13°50N 120°38E **232** E3
Calatayud *Spain* 41°20N 1°40W **196** D3
Călăţele *Romania* 46°46N 23°1E **182** D8
Calato = Kalathos *Greece* 36°9N 28°8E **206** E12
Calatrava *Eq. Guin.* 1°6N 9°25E **264** B1
Calauag *Phil.* 13°55N 122°15E **232** E4
Calavà, C. *Italy* 38°11N 14°55E **201** D7
Calavite, C. *Phil.* 13°26N 120°20E **232** E3
Calavite Pass *Phil.* 13°36N 120°25E **232** E3
Calayan *Phil.* 19°16N 121°28E **232** B3
Calayan I. *Phil.* 19°20N 121°27E **232** B3
Calbayog *Phil.* 12°4N 124°38E **232** E5
Calbiga *Phil.* 11°38N 125°0E **233** F5
Calca *Peru* 13°22S 72°0W **330** C3
Calcasieu L. *U.S.A.* 29°55N 93°18W **314** G8
Calcutta = Kolkata *India* 22°34N 88°21E **124** B2
Calcutta *U.S.A.* 40°40N 80°34W **312** F4
Caldaro *Italy* 46°25N 11°14E **199** B8
Caldas □ *Colombia* 5°15N 75°30W **328** B2
Caldas da Rainha *Portugal* 39°24N 9°8W **195** F1
Caldas de Reis *Spain* 42°36N 8°39W **194** C2
Caldas Novas *Brazil* 17°45S 48°38W **333** E2
Calder → *U.K.* 53°44N 1°22W **168** D6
Caldera *Chile* 27°5S 70°55W **334** B1
Caldera de Taburiente △
Canary Is. 28°43N 17°52W **153** e1
Caldwell *Idaho, U.S.A.* 43°40N 116°41W **304** E5
Caldwell *Kans., U.S.A.* 37°2N 97°37W **308** G5
Caldwell *Tex., U.S.A.* 30°32N 96°42W **314** F6
Caledon *S. Africa* 34°14S 19°26E **270** D2
Caledon → *S. Africa* 30°31S 26°5E **270** D4
Caledon B. *Australia* 12°45S 137°0E **280** A2
Caledonia *Ont., Canada* 43°7N 79°58W **312** C5
Caledonia *Mo., U.S.A.* 37°45N 90°48W **310** G6
Caledonia *N.Y., U.S.A.* 42°58N 77°51W **312** D7
Calella *Spain* 41°37N 2°40E **196** D7
Calemba *Angola* 16°0S 15°44E **270** A2
Calen *Australia* 20°56S 148°48E **280** J6
Calenzana *France* 42°31N 8°51E **175** F12
Caleta Olivia *Argentina* 46°25S 67°25W **336** C3
Caletones *Chile* 34°6S 70°27W **334** C1
Calexico *U.S.A.* 32°40N 115°30W **307** N11
Calf of Man *I. of Man* 54°3N 4°48W **168** C3
Calgary *Canada* 51°0N 114°10W **296** C6
Calheta *Azores* 38°36N 28°1W **153** d1
Calheta *Madeira* 32°44N 17°11W **153** c
Calheta de Nesquim
Azores 38°24N 28°5W **153** d1
Calhoun *U.S.A.* 34°30N 84°57W **315** D12
Calhoun Falls *U.S.A.* 34°6N 82°36W **316** A7
Cali *Colombia* 3°25N 76°35W **328** C2
Calibishie *Dominica* 15°35N 61°21W **323** k
Calicut *India* 11°15N 75°43E **245** J2
Caliente *U.S.A.* 37°37N 114°31W **305** H6
California *Trin. & Tob.* 10°24N 61°28W **323** t
California *Mo., U.S.A.* 38°38N 92°34W **310** F4
California *Pa., U.S.A.* 40°4N 79°54W **312** F5
California □ *U.S.A.* 37°30N 119°30W **306** H7
California, Baja, T.N. = Baja
California □ *Mexico* 30°0N 115°0W **318** B2
California, Baja, T.S. = Baja
California Sur □
Mexico 25°50N 111°50W **318** B2
California, G. de *Mexico* 27°0N 111°0W **318** B2
California City *U.S.A.* 35°10N 117°55W **307** K9
California Hot Springs
U.S.A. 35°51N 118°41W **307** K8
California Inst. of Tech.
U.S.A. 34°8N 118°8W **126** B4
California Los Angeles, University
of *U.S.A.* 34°4N 118°27W **126** B2
California Plaza *Los Angeles, U.S.A.* **127** b1
California State University
U.S.A. 34°4N 118°10W **126** B3
Calilegua △ *Argentina* 25°36S 64°50W **334** B3
Călimăneşti *Romania* 45°14N 24°20E **183** E9
Călimani, Munţii
Romania 47°12N 25°0E **183** C10
Calingasta *Argentina* 31°15S 69°30W **334** C2
Calinog *Phil.* 11°7N 122°32E **233** F4
Calintaan *Phil.* 12°35N 120°57E **232** E3
Calipatria *U.S.A.* 33°8N 115°31W **307** M11
Calistoga *U.S.A.* 38°35N 122°35W **306** G4
Calitri *Italy* 40°54N 15°26E **201** B8
Calitzdorp *S. Africa* 33°33S 21°42E **270** D3
Calivigny I. *Grenada* 12°0N 61°43W **323** q
Callabonna, L. *Australia* 29°40S 140°5E **281** D3
Callac *France* 48°25N 3°27W **172** D3
Callahan *U.S.A.* 30°34N 81°50W **316** E8
Callahan Tunnel *Boston, U.S.A.* **116** a3
Callan *Ireland* 52°32N 7°24W **166** D4
Callander *U.K.* 56°15N 4°13W **167** E4
Callang = San Manuel
Phil. 16°4N 120°40E **232** C3
Callao *Peru* 12°3S 77°8W **124** B2
Callaway *U.S.A.* 30°8N 85°36W **316** E4
Calliaqua *St. Vincent* 13°8N 61°12W **323** n
Callicoon *U.S.A.* 41°46N 75°3W **313** E9
Calling Lake *Canada* 55°15N 113°12W **296** B6
Calliope *Australia* 24°0S 151°16E **280** C5
Callosa de Ensarriá *Spain* 38°40N 0°8W **197** G4
Callosa de Segura *Spain* 38°7N 0°53W **197** G4
Calmar *U.S.A.* 43°11N 91°52W **310** A5
Calne *U.K.* 51°26N 2°0W **169** F6
Calola *Angola* 16°25S 17°48E **265** F3
Calolbon = San Andres
Phil. 13°36N 124°6E **232** E5
Calonge *Spain* 41°52N 3°5E **196** D8
Caloocan *Phil.* 14°39N 120°58E **127** B1
Caloosahatchee →
U.S.A. 26°31N 82°1W **317** J7
Calore → *Italy* 41°11N 14°28E **201** A7
Caloundra *Australia* 26°45S 153°10E **281** D5
Calpe *Spain* 38°39N 0°3E **197** G5
Calpella *U.S.A.* 39°14N 123°12W **306** F3
Calpine *U.S.A.* 39°40N 120°27W **306** F6
Calstock *Canada* 49°47N 84°9W **298** C3
Caltabellotta *Italy* 37°34N 13°13E **200** E6
Caltagirone *Italy* 37°14N 14°31E **201** E7
Caltanissetta *Italy* 37°29N 14°4E **201** E7
Çaltılıbük *Turkey* 39°57N 28°36E **203** G12
Caluango *Angola* 8°20S 19°39E **265** D3
Calubian *Phil.* 11°27N 124°26E **233** F5
Calucinga *Angola* 11°18S 16°12E **265** E3
Caluire-et-Cuire *France* 45°48N 4°52E **173** G11
Calulo *Angola* 10°1S 14°56E **265** E2
Calumet L. *U.S.A.* 41°41N 87°35W **119** C3
Calumet Park *U.S.A.* 41°40N 87°39W **119** C3
Calumet Sag Channel →
U.S.A. 41°40N 87°47W **119** C2
Calunda *Angola* 12°7S 23°36E **265** E4
Caluquembe *Angola* 13°47S 14°44E **265** E2
Caluso *Italy* 45°18N 7°53E **198** C4
Caluya I. *Phil.* 11°55N 121°34E **233** F3
Calvados □ *France* 49°5N 0°15W **172** C6
Calvados Chain, The
Papua N. G. 11°10S 152°45E **286** F7
Calvairate *Italy* 45°27N 9°13E **129** B2
Calvert → *Australia* 16°17S 137°44E **280** B2
Calvert I. *Canada* 51°30N 128°0W **296** C3
Calvert Ra. *Australia* 24°0S 122°30E **278** D3
Calvi *France* 42°34N 8°45E **175** F12
Calviá *Spain* 39°33N 2°31E **206** B3
Calvillo *Mexico* 21°51N 102°43W **318** C4
Calvinia *S. Africa* 31°28S 19°45E **270** D2
Calvo, Mte. *Italy* 41°44N 15°46E **199** G12
Calwa *U.S.A.* 36°42N 119°46W **306** J7
Calzada Almuradiel = Almuradiel
Spain 38°32N 3°28W **195** G7
Calzada de Calatrava
Spain 38°42N 3°46W **195** G7
Cam → *U.K.* 52°21N 0°16E **169** E8
Cam Lam *Vietnam* 11°54N 109°10E **237** G7
Cam Pha *Vietnam* 21°7N 107°18E **228** G6
Cam Ranh *Vietnam* 11°54N 109°12E **237** G7
Cam Xuyen *Vietnam* 18°15N 106°0E **236** C6
Camabatela *Angola* 8°20S 15°26E **265** D3
Camacã *Brazil* 15°24S 39°30W **333** E4
Camaçari *Brazil* 12°41S 38°18W **333** D4
Camacha *Madeira* 32°41N 16°49W **153** c
Camacupa *Angola* 11°58S 17°22E **265** E3
Camaguán *Venezuela* 8°6N 67°36W **328** B4
Camagüey *Cuba* 21°20N 77°55W **320** B4
Camagüey, Arch. de
Cuba 22°18N 78°0W **320** B4
Camaiore *Italy* 43°56N 10°18E **198** E7
Camamu *Brazil* 13°57S 39°7W **333** D4
Camaná *Peru* 16°30S 72°50W **330** D3
Camanche *U.S.A.* 41°47N 90°15W **310** C6
Camanche Res. *U.S.A.* 38°14N 121°1W **306** G6
Camapuã *Brazil* 19°30S 54°5W **331** D7
Camaquã *Brazil* 30°51S 51°49W **335** C5
Camaquã → *Brazil* 31°17S 51°47W **335** C5
Câmara de Lobos *Madeira* 32°39N 16°59W **153** c
Camararé → *Brazil* 12°15S 58°55W **331** C6
Camarat, C. *France* 43°12N 6°41E **175** E10
Camarate *Portugal* 38°48N 9°7W **126** A2
Camarès *France* 43°49N 2°53E **174** E6
Camaret-sur-Mer *France* 48°16N 4°37W **172** D2
Camargo *Bolivia* 20°38S 65°15W **331** E4
Camargo *Tamaulipas,*
Mexico 26°19N 98°50W **319** B5
Camargue *France* 43°34N 4°34E **175** E8
Camargue ⌂ *France* 43°30N 4°40E **175** E8
Camarillo *U.S.A.* 34°13N 119°2W **307** L7
Camariñas *Spain* 43°8N 9°12W **194** B1
Camarines Norte □
Phil. 14°10N 122°45E **232** D4
Camarines Sur □ *Phil.* 13°40N 123°20E **232** E4
Camarões *Portugal* 38°49N 9°14W **126** A1
Camarón, C. *Honduras* 16°0N 85°5W **320** C2
Camarones *Argentina* 44°50S 65°40W **336** B3
Camarones, B. *Argentina* 44°45S 65°35W **336** B3
Camas *Spain* 37°24N 6°2W **195** H4
Camas *Wash., U.S.A.* 45°35N 122°24W **306** E4
Camas Valley *U.S.A.* 43°2N 123°40W **304** E2
Camatambo *Angola* 6°31S 15°21E **265** D3
Camataquí = Villa Abecia
Bolivia 21°0S 68°18W **334** A2
Camaxilo *Angola* 8°21S 18°56E **265** D3
Camba Cassai *Angola* 9°47S 19°9E **265** D3
Camballin *Australia* 17°59S 124°12E **278** C3
Cambamba *Angola* 8°53S 14°44E **265** D2
Cambará *Brazil* 23°2S 50°5W **335** A5
Cambay = Khambhat
India 22°23N 72°33E **242** H5
Cambay, G. of = Khambhat, G. of
India 20°45N 72°30E **239** E10
Camberwell *Vic.,*
Australia 37°50S 145°5E **128** B2
Camberwell *London, U.K.* 51°28N 0°5W **125** B3
Cambil *Spain* 37°40N 3°33W **195** H7
Cambo *Angola* 10°55S 20°6E **265** D3
Cambo-les-Bains *France* 43°22N 1°23W **174** E2
Cambodia ■ *Asia* 12°15N 105°0E **236** F5
Camborne *U.K.* 50°12N 5°19W **169** G2
Cambrai *S. Austral.,*
Australia 34°40S 139°16E **282** C3
Cambrai *Nord, France* 50°11N 3°14E **173** B10
Cambre *Spain* 43°17N 8°20W **194** B2
Cambria *U.S.A.* 35°34N 121°5W **306** K5
Cambrian Mts. *U.K.* 52°3N 3°57W **169** E4
Cambridge *Ont., Canada* 43°23N 80°15W **312** C4
Cambridge *N.Z.* 37°54S 175°29E **284** D4
Cambridge *Cambs., U.K.* 52°12N 0°8E **169** E8
Cambridge *Ill., U.S.A.* 41°18N 90°12W **310** C6
Cambridge *Iowa, U.S.A.* 41°54N 93°32W **310** C3
Cambridge *Mass., U.S.A.* 42°23N 71°7W **116** A2
Cambridge *Minn., U.S.A.* 45°34N 93°13W **308** C7
Cambridge *N.Y., U.S.A.* 43°2N 73°22W **313** C11
Cambridge *Nebr., U.S.A.* 40°17N 100°10W **308** E3
Cambridge *Ohio, U.S.A.* 40°2N 81°35W **312** F3
Cambridge Bay = Ikaluktutiak
Canada 69°10N 105°0W **294** C9
Cambridge City *U.S.A.* 39°49N 85°10W **311** E11
Cambridge G. *Australia* 14°55S 128°15E **278** B4
Cambridge Springs *U.S.A.* 41°48N 80°4W **312** E4
Cambridgeshire □ *U.K.* 52°25N 0°7W **169** E7
Cambrils *Spain* 41°8N 1°3E **196** D6
Cambuci *Rio de J., Brazil* 21°35S 41°55W **333** F3
Cambuci *São Paulo, Brazil* 23°33S 46°47W **137** B2
Cambundi-Catembo
Angola 10°10S 17°35E **265** E3
Camdeboo △ *S. Africa* 32°28S 24°25E **270** D3
Camden *N.S.W., Australia* 34°1S 150°43E **283** C9
Camden *Ala., U.S.A.* 31°59N 87°17W **315** F11
Camden *Ark., U.S.A.* 33°35N 92°50W **314** E8
Camden *Maine, U.S.A.* 44°13N 69°4W **309** C19
Camden *N.J., U.S.A.* 39°55N 75°7W **313** G9
Camden *N.Y., U.S.A.* 43°20N 75°45W **313** C9
Camden *Ohio, U.S.A.* 39°38N 84°39W **311** E12
Camden *S.C., U.S.A.* 34°16N 80°36W **315** D14
Camden □ *U.K.* 51°32N 0°8W **125** A3
Camden Bay *U.S.A.* 70°10N 145°15W **303** A11
Camden Sd. *Australia* 15°27S 124°25E **278** C3
Camdenton *U.S.A.* 38°1N 92°45W **310** F4
Cameia △ *Angola* 12°5S 21°40E **265** E4
Camelford *U.K.* 50°37N 4°42W **169** G3
Çameli *Turkey* 37°5N 29°24E **205** D11
Camenca *Moldova* 48°3N 28°42E **183** B13
Camerino *Italy* 43°8N 13°4E **199** E10
Cameron *Ariz., U.S.A.* 35°53N 111°25W **305** J8
Cameron *La., U.S.A.* 29°48N 93°20W **314** G8
Cameron *Mo., U.S.A.* 39°44N 94°14W **310** E2
Cameron *S.C., U.S.A.* 33°34N 80°43W **316** B9
Cameron *Tex., U.S.A.* 30°51N 96°59W **314** F6
Cameron, Mt. *N.Z.* 41°20S 174°52E **143** B2
Cameron Highlands
Malaysia 4°27N 101°22E **237** K3
Cameron Hills *Canada* 59°48N 118°0W **296** B5
Cameron Mts. *N.Z.* 46°1S 167°0E **285** G2
Cameroon ■ *Africa* 6°0N 12°30E **264** A2
Camerota *Italy* 40°2N 15°22E **201** B8
Cameroun → *Cameroon* 4°0N 9°35E **263** E6
Cameroun, Mt. *Cameroon* 4°13N 9°10E **263** E6
Cametá *Brazil* 2°12S 49°30W **332** B2
Çamiçi Gölü *Turkey* 37°29N 27°28E **205** D9

Camiguin □ Phil. 9°11N 124°42E 233 G5
Camiguin I. Phil. 18°56N 121°55E 232 B3
Camiling Phil. 15°42N 120°24E 232 D3
Camilla U.S.A. 31°14N 84°12W 316 D5
Caminha Portugal 41°50N 8°50W 194 D2
Camino U.S.A. 38°44N 120°41W 306 G6
Camira Creek Australia 29°15S 152°58E 281 D5
Camiranga Brazil 1°48S 46°17W 332 B2
Camiri Bolivia 20°3S 63°31W 331 E5
Camissombo Angola 8°7S 20°38E 265 D4
Çamlıca Turkey 41°1N 29°3E 122 B2
Çamlıyayla Turkey 37°10N 34°36E 250 A5
Cammal U.S.A. 41°24N 77°28W 312 E7
Cammarata Italy 37°38N 13°38E 200 E6
Cammin = Kamień Pomorski Poland 53°57N 14°43E 184 E1
Camo Ethiopia 4°29N 38°24E 266 D4
Camocim Brazil 2°55S 40°50W 332 B3
Camooweal Australia 19°56S 138°7E 280 B2
Camooweal Caves △ Australia 20°1S 138°11E 280 C2
Camopi Fr. Guiana 3°12N 52°17W 329 C7
Camopi ➝ Fr. Guiana 3°10N 52°20W 329 C7
Camorta India 8°8N 93°30E 245 K11
Camotes Is. Phil. 10°40N 124°24E 233 F5
Camotes Sea Phil. 10°30N 124°15E 233 F5
Camp Borden Canada 44°18N 79°56W 312 B5
Camp Coulter = Powell U.S.A. 44°45N 108°46W 304 D9
Camp Hill Ala., U.S.A. 32°48N 85°39W 316 C4
Camp Hill Pa., U.S.A. 40°14N 76°55W 312 F8
Camp Nelson U.S.A. 36°8N 118°39W 307 J8
Camp Pendleton U.S.A. 33°13N 117°24W 307 M9
Camp Point U.S.A. 40°3N 91°4W 310 D5
Camp Springs U.S.A. 38°48N 76°55W 143 C4
Camp Verde U.S.A. 34°34N 111°51W 305 J8
Camp Wood U.S.A. 29°40N 100°1W 314 G4
Campagna Italy 40°40N 15°6E 201 B8
Campamento Spain 40°23N 3°46W 127 B1
Campana Argentina 34°10S 58°55W 334 C4
Campana, I. Chile 48°20S 75°20W 336 C1
Campanário Madeira 32°39N 17°2W 153 c
Campanario Spain 38°52N 5°36W 195 G5
Campánia □ Italy 41°0N 14°30E 201 B7
Campbell Northern Cape, S. Africa 28°48S 23°44E 270 C3
Campbell Calif., U.S.A. 37°17N 121°57W 306 H5
Campbell Fla., U.S.A. 28°16N 81°27W 317 G8
Campbell Ohio, U.S.A. 41°5N 80°37W 312 E4
Campbell, C. N.Z. 41°47S 174°18E 285 B9
Campbell I. Pac. Oc. 52°30S 169°0E 288 N8
Campbell L. Canada 63°14N 106°55W 297 A7
Campbell Plateau S. Ocean 50°0S 170°0E 151 A11
Campbell River Canada 50°5N 125°20W 296 C3
Campbell Town Australia 41°52S 147°30E 281 G4
Campbellfield Australia 37°41S 144°57E 128 A1
Campbellford Canada 44°18N 77°48W 312 B7
Campbellpur Pakistan 33°46N 72°26E 242 C5
Campbellsburg U.S.A. 38°39N 86°16W 311 F10
Campbellsville U.S.A. 37°21N 85°20W 309 G11
Campbellton N.B., Canada 47°57N 66°43W 299 C6
Campbellton Fla., U.S.A. 30°57N 85°24W 316 E4
Campbelltown = Bluff N.Z. 46°37S 168°20E 285 G3
Campbelltown Australia 34°4S 150°49E 283 C9
Campbeltown U.K. 55°26N 5°36W 167 F3
Campêche Guadeloupe 16°26N 61°26W 322 e
Campeche Campeche, Mexico 19°51N 90°32W 319 D6
Campeche □ Mexico 19°0N 90°30W 319 D6
Campeche, Banco Mexico 22°30N 88°0W 320 B2
Campeche, Golfo de Mexico 19°30N 93°0W 319 D6
Campello Spain 38°26N 0°24W 197 G4
Câmpeni Romania 46°22N 23°3E 182 D8
Camperdown N.S.W., Australia 33°53S 151°11E 139 B2
Camperdown Vic., Australia 38°14S 143°9E 282 E5
Camperville Canada 51°59N 100°9W 297 C8
Campi Salentina Italy 40°24N 18°1E 201 B11
Câmpia Turzii Romania 46°34N 23°53E 183 D8
Campidano Italy 39°30N 8°47E 200 C1
Campidoglio, Piazza de Rome, Italy 136 c3
Campíglia Marittima Italy 43°4N 10°37E 198 E7
Campillo de Altobuey Spain 39°36N 1°49W 197 F3
Campillos Spain 37°4N 4°51W 195 H6
Câmpina Romania 45°10N 25°45E 183 E10
Campina Grande Brazil 7°20S 35°47W 332 C4
Campina Verde Brazil 19°31S 49°28W 333 E2
Campinas Brazil 22°50S 47°0W 335 A6
Campli Italy 42°43N 13°41E 199 F10
Campo = Ntem ➝ Cameroon 2°21N 9°49E 264 B2
Campo Cameroon 2°22N 9°50E 264 B1
Campo Spain 42°25N 0°24E 196 C5
Campo, Casa de Spain 40°25N 3°45W 127 B1
Campo △ Cameroon 2°23N 10°5E 264 B2
Campo Belo Brazil 20°52S 45°16W 333 F2
Campo de Criptana Spain 39°24N 3°7W 195 F7
Campo de Diauarum Brazil 11°12S 53°14W 331 C7
Campo de Gibraltar Spain 36°15N 5°25W 195 J5
Campo F.C. Barcelona Spain 41°22N 2°7E 114 A1
Campo Flórido Brazil 19°47S 48°35W 333 E2
Campo Formoso = Campo Flórido Brazil 19°47S 48°35W 333 E2
Campo Formoso Brazil 10°30S 40°20W 332 D3
Campo Grande Brazil 20°25S 54°40W 331 E7
Campo Grande Portugal 38°45N 9°9W 126 A2
Campo Maior Brazil 4°50S 42°12W 332 B3
Campo Maior Portugal 39°2N 7°7W 195 F3
Campo Mourão Brazil 24°3S 52°22W 335 A5
Campo Pequeño Portugal 38°44N 9°8W 126 A2
Campo Túres Italy 46°53N 11°55E 199 B8
Campoalegre Colombia 2°41N 75°20W 328 C2
Campobasso Italy 41°34N 14°39E 201 A7
Campobello di Licata Italy 37°15N 13°55E 200 E6
Campobello di Mazara Italy 37°38N 12°45E 200 E5
Campofelice di Roccella Italy 37°59N 13°53E 200 E6
Campolide Portugal 38°43N 9°9W 126 A2
Campomarino Italy 41°57N 15°2E 199 G12
Camporeale Italy 37°54N 13°6E 200 E6
Camporrobles Spain 39°39N 1°24W 196 F3
Campos Brazil 21°50S 41°20W 333 F3
Campos Spain 39°26N 3°1E 206 B4
Campos Altos Brazil 19°47S 46°10W 333 E2
Campos Belos Brazil 13°10S 47°3W 333 D2
Campos Novos Brazil 27°21S 51°50W 335 B5
Campos Sales Brazil 7°4S 40°23W 332 C3
Camprodón Spain 42°19N 2°23E 196 C7
Camps Bay S. Africa 33°57S 18°23E 118 A1
Campton Fla., U.S.A. 30°53N 86°31W 317 E3
Campton Ga., U.S.A. 33°52N 83°43W 316 B6
Campton Ky., U.S.A. 37°44N 83°33W 311 G13
Camptonville U.S.A. 39°27N 121°3W 306 F5
Camptown U.S.A. 41°44N 76°14W 313 E8
Câmpulung Argeş, Romania 45°17N 25°3E 183 E10
Câmpulung Suceava, Romania 47°32N 25°30E 183 C10
Câmpuri Romania 46°0N 26°50E 183 D11
Campuya ➝ Peru 1°40S 73°30W 328 D3
Campville U.S.A. 29°40N 82°7W 316 F7
Camrose Canada 53°0N 112°50W 296 C6
Camsell Portage Canada 59°37N 109°15W 297 B7
Camucuio Angola 14°7S 13°15E 265 E2
Camuy Puerto Rico 18°29N 66°51W 321 b
Çamyuva Turkey 36°30N 30°30E 205 E12
Çan Turkey 40°2N 27°3E 203 F11
Can Clavo Spain 38°57N 1°27E 206 D1
Can Creu Spain 38°58N 1°28E 206 D1
Can Gio Vietnam 10°25N 106°58E 237 G6
C'an San Joan Spain 41°28N 2°11E 114 A2
Can Tho Vietnam 10°2N 105°46E 237 G5
Canaan Trin. & Tob. 11°9N 60°49W 323 s
Canaan Conn., U.S.A. 42°2N 73°20W 313 D11
Canaan Hill Jamaica 18°23N 77°14W 320 a
Cañacao B. Phil. 14°29N 120°54E 127 C1
Canacona India 15°1N 74°4E 245 G2
Canada ■ N. Amer. 60°0N 100°0W 294 D10
Canada Abyssal Plain Arctic 80°0N 140°0W 150 B18
Canada Basin Arctic 80°0N 145°0W 150 B18
Cañada de Gómez Argentina 32°40S 61°30W 334 C3
Canadian U.S.A. 35°55N 100°23W 314 D4
Canadian ➝ U.S.A. 35°28N 95°3W 314 D7
Canadian Shield Canada 53°0N 75°0W 292 D12
Canadys U.S.A. 33°3N 80°37W 316 B9
Canajoharie U.S.A. 42°54N 74°35W 313 D10
Çanakkale Turkey 40°8N 26°24E 203 F10
Çanakkale □ Turkey 40°10N 26°25E 203 F10
Çanakkale Boğazı Turkey 40°17N 26°32E 203 F10
Canal Flats Canada 50°10N 115°48W 296 C5
Canal Point U.S.A. 26°52N 80°38W 317 J9
Canal Street New Orleans, U.S.A. 131 b2
Canala N. Cal. 21°32S 165°57E 288 d
Canalejas Argentina 35°15S 66°34W 334 D2
Canals Argentina 33°35S 62°53W 334 C3
Canals Spain 38°58N 0°35W 197 G4
Canandaigua U.S.A. 42°54N 77°17W 312 D7
Canandaigua L. U.S.A. 42°47N 77°19W 312 D7
Cananea Mexico 31°0N 110°18W 318 A2
Cañar Ecuador 2°33S 78°56W 328 D2
Cañar □ Ecuador 2°30S 79°0W 328 D2
Canarias, Is. Atl. Oc. 28°30N 16°0W 153 e1
Canaries St. Lucia 13°55N 61°4W 323 m
Canarreos, Arch. de los Cuba 21°35N 81°40W 320 B3
Canarsie U.S.A. 40°38N 73°53W 132 C2
Canary Is. = Canarias, Is. Atl. Oc. 28°30N 16°0W 153 e1
Canaseraga U.S.A. 42°27N 77°45W 312 D7
Canastra, Serra da Brazil 20°0S 46°20W 333 F2
Canatlán Mexico 24°31N 104°47W 318 C4
Cañaveral Peru 3°56S 80°39W 328 D1
Canaveral, C. U.S.A. 28°27N 80°32W 317 G9
Canaveral △ U.S.A. 28°28N 80°34W 317 G9
Cañaveruelas Spain 40°24N 2°38W 196 E2
Canavieiras Brazil 15°39S 39°0W 333 E4
Canbelego Australia 31°32S 146°18E 283 A7
Canberra Australia 35°15S 149°8E 283 C8
Canby Calif., U.S.A. 41°27N 120°52W 304 F3
Canby Minn., U.S.A. 44°43N 96°16W 308 C5
Canby Oreg., U.S.A. 45°16N 122°42W 306 E4
Cancale France 48°40N 1°50W 172 D5
Cancellería, Palazzo dei Rome, Italy 136 c2
Canche ➝ France 50°31N 1°39E 173 B8
Canchungo = Teixeira Pinto Guinea-Biss. 12°3N 16°0W 262 C1
Canchyuaya, Cordillera de Peru 7°30S 74°0W 330 B3
Cancún Mexico 21°8N 86°44W 319 C7
Candala Somali Rep. 11°30N 49°58E 267 B6
Candanchu Spain 42°47N 0°32W 196 C4
Candarave Peru 17°15S 70°13W 330 D3
Çandarlı Turkey 38°56N 26°56E 205 C8
Çandarlı Körfezi Turkey 38°52N 26°55E 205 C8
Candas Spain 43°35N 5°45W 194 B5
Candé France 47°34N 1°2W 172 E5
Candeias ➝ Brazil 8°39S 63°31W 331 B5
Candela Italy 41°8N 15°31E 201 A8
Candelaria Argentina 27°29S 55°44W 335 B4
Candelaria Canary Is. 28°22N 16°22W 153 e1
Candelaria Phil. 13°56N 121°25E 232 E3
Candelario △ Spain 40°20N 5°46W 194 E5
Candeleda Spain 40°10N 5°14W 194 E5
Candelo Australia 36°47S 149°43E 283 D8
Candi Dasa Indonesia 8°30S 115°34E 231 J18
Candia = Iraklio Greece 35°20N 25°12E 207 E6
Candia, Sea of = Crete, Sea of Greece 36°0N 25°0E 205 E7
Candiac Canada 45°23N 73°29W 130 B3
Cândido de Abreu Brazil 24°35S 51°20W 333 F1
Cândido Mendes Brazil 1°27S 45°43W 332 B2
Candle U.S.A. 65°55N 161°56W 303 D7
Candle L. Canada 53°50N 105°18W 297 C7
Candlemas I. Antarctica 57°3S 26°40W 151 B1
Cando U.S.A. 48°32N 99°12W 308 A4
Candon Phil. 17°12N 120°27E 232 C3
Canea = Chania Greece 35°30N 24°4E 207 E5
Caneças Portugal 38°48N 9°13W 126 A1
Canefield Dominica 15°20N 61°24W 323 k
Canela Brazil 10°15S 48°25W 332 D2
Canelles ➝ St. Lucia 13°47N 60°55W 323 m
Canelli Italy 44°43N 8°17E 198 D5
Canelones Uruguay 34°32S 56°17W 335 C4
Canet-Plage France 42°41N 3°2E 174 F7
Cañete Chile 37°50S 73°30W 334 D1
Cañete Peru 13°8S 76°30W 330 C2
Cañete Spain 40°3N 1°54W 196 E3
Cañete de las Torres Spain 37°53N 4°19W 195 H6
Cangamba Angola 13°40S 19°54E 265 E3
Cangandala Angola 9°45S 16°33E 265 D3
Cangandala △ Angola 9°53S 16°42E 265 D3
Cangas Spain 42°16N 8°47W 194 C2
Cangas de Narcea Spain 43°10N 6°32W 194 B4
Cangas de Onís Spain 43°21N 5°8W 194 B5
Cangas de Tineo = Cangas de Narcea Spain 43°10N 6°32W 194 B4
Cangnan China 27°30N 120°23E 229 D13
Cangoa Angola 13°8S 18°30E 265 E3
Cangola Angola 7°58S 15°53E 265 D3
Cangolo Angola 15°0S 13°52E 265 E2
Cangombe Angola 14°24S 19°59E 265 E3
Cangongo Angola 9°24S 17°30E 265 D3
Canguaretama Brazil 6°20S 35°5W 332 C4
Canguçu Brazil 31°22S 52°43W 335 C5
Canguçu, Serra do Brazil 31°20S 52°40W 335 C5
Cangumbe Angola 11°58S 19°12E 265 E3
Cangwu China 23°25N 111°17E 229 F8
Cangxi China 31°47N 105°59E 228 B5
Cangyuan China 23°12N 99°14E 228 F2
Cangzhou China 38°19N 116°52E 226 E9
Canhoca Angola 9°15S 14°41E 265 D2
Cani, I. Tunisia 36°21N 10°5E 258 A2
Caniapiscau ➝ Canada 56°40N 69°30W 299 A6
Caniapiscau, L. Canada 54°10N 69°55W 299 B6
Canicattì Italy 37°21N 13°51E 200 E6
Canicattini Bagni Italy 37°2N 15°4E 201 E8
Canigao Channel Phil. 10°15N 124°42E 233 F5
Caniles Spain 37°26N 2°43W 195 H8
Canillas Spain 40°27N 3°38W 127 B2
Canillejas Spain 40°26N 3°36W 127 B2
Canim Lake Canada 51°47N 120°54W 296 C4
Canindé Brazil 4°22S 39°19W 332 B4
Canindé ➝ Brazil 6°15S 42°52W 332 C3
Canindeyu □ Paraguay 24°10S 55°0W 335 A5
Canino Italy 42°28N 11°45E 199 F8
Canisteo U.S.A. 42°16N 77°36W 312 D7
Canisteo ➝ U.S.A. 42°7N 77°8W 312 D7
Cañitas de Felipe Pescador Mexico 23°36N 102°43W 318 C4
Cañizal Spain 41°12N 5°22W 194 D5
Canjáyar Spain 37°1N 2°44W 195 H8
Canjinge Angola 10°12S 21°17E 265 E4
Çankırı Turkey 40°40N 33°37E 212 B5
Çankırı □ Turkey 40°40N 33°30E 212 B5
Cankuzo Burundi 3°10S 30°31E 268 C3
Canlaon Phil. 10°22N 123°12E 233 F4
Canlaon Volcano Phil. 10°25N 123°8E 233 F4
Canmore Canada 51°7N 115°18W 296 C5
Cann River Australia 37°35S 149°7E 283 D8
Canna U.K. 57°3N 6°33W 167 D2
Cannanore India 11°53N 75°27E 245 J2
Cannanore Is. India 10°30N 72°30E 245 J1
Cannelton U.S.A. 37°55N 86°45W 311 G10
Cannery, The San Francisco, U.S.A. 136 a1
Cannes France 43°32N 7°1E 175 E11
Canning Town = Port Canning India 22°23N 88°40E 243 H13
Canning Town U.K. 51°30N 0°1E 125 A4
Cannington Canada 44°20N 79°2W 312 B5
Cannóbio Italy 46°4N 8°42E 198 B5
Cannock U.K. 52°41N 2°1W 169 E5
Cannonball ➝ U.S.A. 46°26N 100°35W 308 B3
Cannondale Mt. Australia 25°13S 148°57E 280 D4
Cannonsville Res. U.S.A. 42°4N 75°22W 313 D9
Cannonvale Australia 20°17S 148°43E 280 J6
Caño Colorado Colombia 2°18N 68°22W 328 C4
Canoas Brazil 29°56S 51°11W 335 B5
Canoe L. Canada 55°10N 108°15W 297 B7
Cañon City U.S.A. 38°27N 105°14W 304 G11
Cañón de Río Blanco △ Mexico 18°43N 97°15W 319 D5
Cañón del Río Lobos △ Spain 41°46N 3°28W 194 D7
Cañón del Sumidero △ Mexico 19°22N 96°24W 319 D5
Canonnier, Pte. du St.-Martin 18°4N 63°7W 322 a
Canonniers Pt. Mauritius 20°2S 57°32E 272 e
Canoochee ➝ U.S.A. 31°59N 81°19W 316 D8
Canopus Australia 33°29S 140°42E 282 B4
Canora Canada 51°40N 102°30W 297 C8
Canosa di Púglia Italy 41°13N 16°4E 201 A9
Canouan St. Vincent 12°43N 61°20W 323 n
Canowindra Australia 33°35S 148°38E 283 B8
Canso Canada 45°20N 61°0W 299 C7
Canta Peru 11°29S 76°37W 330 C2
Cantabria □ Spain 43°10N 4°0W 194 B7
Cantabria, Sierra de Spain 42°40N 2°30W 196 C2
Cantabrian Mts. = Cantábrica, Cordillera Spain 43°0N 5°10W 194 C5
Cantábrica, Cordillera Spain 43°0N 5°10W 194 C5
Cantal □ France 45°5N 2°45E 174 C6
Cantal, Plomb du France 45°3N 2°45E 174 C6
Cantanhede Portugal 40°20N 8°36W 194 E2
Cantaura Venezuela 9°19N 64°21W 329 B5
Cantavieja Spain 40°31N 0°25W 196 E4
Čantavir Serbia 45°55N 19°46E 182 E4
Cantemir Moldova 46°17N 28°14E 183 D13
Canteras de Vallecas Spain 40°20N 3°37W 127 B2
Canterbury = Invermere Canada 50°30N 116°2W 296 C5
Canterbury N.S.W., Australia 33°55S 151°7E 139 B1
Canterbury Queens., Australia 25°23S 141°53E 280 D3
Canterbury Vic., Australia 37°49S 145°4E 128 A2
Canterbury Kent, U.K. 51°16N 1°6E 169 F9
Canterbury □ N.Z. 43°45S 171°19E 285 D6
Canterbury Bight N.Z. 44°16S 171°55E 285 E6
Canterbury Plains N.Z. 43°55S 171°22E 285 D6
Cantil U.S.A. 35°18N 117°58W 307 K9
Cantilan Phil. 9°20N 125°58E 233 G5
Cantillana Spain 37°36N 5°50W 195 H5
Canto do Buriti Brazil 8°7S 42°58W 332 C3
Canton = Guangzhou China 23°6N 113°13E 121 B2
Canton Ga., U.S.A. 34°14N 84°29W 315 D12
Canton Ill., U.S.A. 40°33N 90°2W 310 D6
Canton Miss., U.S.A. 32°37N 90°2W 315 E9
Canton Mo., U.S.A. 40°8N 91°32W 310 D5
Canton N.Y., U.S.A. 44°36N 75°10W 313 B9
Canton Ohio, U.S.A. 40°48N 81°23W 312 F3
Canton Pa., U.S.A. 41°39N 76°51W 312 E8
Canton S. Dak., U.S.A. 43°18N 96°35W 308 D5
Canton L. U.S.A. 36°6N 98°35W 314 C5
Cantonment U.S.A. 30°37N 87°20W 317 E2
Cantù Italy 45°44N 9°8E 198 C6
Cantwell U.S.A. 63°24N 148°57W 303 E10
Canudos Brazil 7°13S 58°5W 331 B6
Canumã Amazonas, Brazil 4°2S 59°4W 329 D6
Canumã Amazonas, Brazil 6°8S 60°10W 331 B5
Canumã ➝ Brazil 3°55S 59°10W 331 A6
Canunda △ Australia 37°42S 140°15E 282 D3
Canutama Brazil 6°30S 64°20W 331 B5
Canutillo U.S.A. 31°55N 106°36W 314 F1
Canvey U.K. 51°31N 0°37E 169 F8
Canyon U.S.A. 34°59N 101°55W 314 D4
Canyon De Chelly △ U.S.A. 36°10N 109°20W 305 H9
Canyonlands △ U.S.A. 38°15N 110°0W 305 G9
Canyons of the Ancients △ U.S.A. 37°30N 108°55W 305 H9
Canyonville U.S.A. 42°56N 123°17W 304 E2
Canzar Angola 7°35S 21°34E 265 D4
Cao Bang Vietnam 22°40N 106°15E 236 A6
Cao He ➝ China 40°10N 124°32E 227 D13
Cao Lanh Vietnam 10°27N 105°38E 237 G5
Cao Xian China 34°50N 115°35E 226 G8
Caoheijing China 31°10N 121°25E 138 B1
Caombo Angola 8°42S 16°33E 265 D3
Cáorle Italy 45°36N 12°53E 199 C9
Cap-aux-Meules Canada 47°23N 61°52W 299 C7
Cap-Chat Canada 49°6N 66°40W 299 C6
Cap-de-la-Madeleine Canada 46°22N 72°31W 298 C5
Cap de Ville Trin. & Tob. 10°9N 61°42W 323 t
Cap-Haïtien Haiti 19°40N 72°20W 321 C5
Cap I. Phil. 5°57N 120°6E 233 J3
Cap Pt. St. Lucia 14°7N 60°57W 323 m
Capac U.S.A. 43°1N 82°56W 312 C2
Capáccio Italy 40°25N 15°5E 201 B8
Capaci Italy 38°10N 13°14E 200 D6
Capaia Angola 8°27S 20°13E 265 D4
Capalonga Phil. 14°20N 122°30E 232 D4
Capanaparo ➝ Venezuela 7°1N 67°7W 328 B4
Capanema Brazil 1°12S 47°11W 332 B2
Capangombe Angola 15°6S 13°6E 265 F2
Capánnori Italy 43°50N 10°34E 198 E7
Capão Redondo Brazil 23°39S 46°45W 137 B1
Caparaó △ Brazil 20°25S 41°46W 333 F3
Caparica Portugal 38°40N 9°9W 126 A2
Caparica, Costa da Portugal 38°38N 9°15W 126 B1
Caparo ➝ Trin. & Tob. 10°31N 61°28W 323 t
Caparo ➝ Barinas, Venezuela 7°46N 70°23W 328 B3
Caparo ➝ Bolívar, Venezuela 7°30N 64°0W 329 B5
Capatárida Venezuela 11°11N 70°37W 328 A3
Capayas Phil. 10°28N 119°39E 233 F2
Capbreton France 43°39N 1°26W 174 E2
Capdenac France 44°34N 2°5E 174 D6
Capdepera Spain 39°42N 3°26E 206 B4
Cape ➝ Australia 20°59S 146°51E 280 C4
Cape Arid △ Australia 33°58S 123°13E 279 F3
Cape Barren I. Australia 40°25S 148°15E 281 G4
Cape Basin Atl. Oc. 34°0S 7°0W 152 K12
Cape Breton Highlands △ Canada 46°50N 60°40W 299 C7
Cape Breton I. Canada 46°0N 60°30W 299 C7
Cape Canaveral U.S.A. 28°24N 80°36W 317 G9
Cape Charles U.S.A. 37°16N 76°1W 309 G15
Cape Coast Ghana 5°5N 1°15W 263 D4
Cape Cod △ U.S.A. 41°56N 70°6W 309 E18
Cape Coral U.S.A. 26°33N 81°57W 317 J8
Cape Dorset Canada 64°14N 76°32W 295 C12
Cape Fear ➝ U.S.A. 33°53N 78°1W 315 E15
Cape Flats S. Africa 34°3S 18°33E 118 B2
Cape Girardeau U.S.A. 37°19N 89°32W 308 G9
Cape Hatteras △ U.S.A. 35°30N 75°28W 315 D17
Cape Jervis Australia 35°40S 138°5E 282 C3
Cape Krusenstern △ U.S.A. 67°30N 163°30W 303 C7
Cape Le Grand △ Australia 33°54S 122°26E 279 F3
Cape Lisburne = Wevok U.S.A. 68°53N 166°13W 303 B6
Cape Lookout △ U.S.A. 35°45N 76°25W 315 D16
Cape May U.S.A. 38°56N 74°56W 309 F16
Cape May Point U.S.A. 38°56N 74°58W 309 F16
Cape Melville △ Australia 14°26S 144°28E 280 A3
Cape Mount △ Liberia 6°44N 11°24W 262 D2
Cape Peninsula △ S. Africa 34°20S 18°28E 118 A1
Cape Pole U.S.A. 55°58N 133°48W 303 J14
Cape Range △ Australia 22°3S 114°0E 278 D1
Cape Tormentine Canada 46°8N 63°47W 299 C7
Cape Town S. Africa 33°55S 18°22E 118 A1
Cape Town Int. ✕ (CPT) S. Africa 33°58S 18°35E 118 A2
Cape Tribulation △ Australia 16°5S 145°25E 280 B4
Cape Verde Abyssal Plain Atl. Oc. 23°0N 26°0W 152 D9
Cape Verde Is. ■ Atl. Oc. 16°0N 24°0W 153 j
Cape Verde Plateau Atl. Oc. 18°0N 20°0W 152 E10
Cape Vincent U.S.A. 44°8N 76°20W 313 B8
Cape Yakataga U.S.A. 60°4N 142°26W 303 F12
Cape York Peninsula Australia 12°0S 142°30E 286 F2
Capela Brazil 10°30S 37°0W 332 D4
Capela de Campo Brazil 4°40S 41°55W 332 B3
Capelas Azores 37°50N 25°41W 153 d3
Capele Angola 13°39S 14°53E 265 E2
Capelengue Angola 8°53S 19°42E 265 D3
Capelinha Brazil 17°42S 42°31W 333 E3
Capelinhos, Pta. dos Azores 38°36N 28°50W 153 d1
Capella Australia 23°2S 148°1E 280 C4
Capella, Mt. Papua N. G. 5°4S 141°8E 286 C1
Capelongo Angola 14°54S 15°8E 265 E3
Capenda Camulemba Angola 9°24S 18°27E 265 D3
Capendu France 43°11N 2°31E 174 E6
Capertree Australia 33°6S 149°58E 283 B8
Capestang France 43°20N 3°2E 174 E7
Capesterre, Grande Rivière de la ➝ Guadeloupe 16°3N 61°33W 322 e
Capesterre, Pte. de la Guadeloupe 16°3N 61°33W 322 e
Capesterre-Belle-Eau Guadeloupe 16°4N 61°36W 322 e
Capesterre-de-Marie-Galante Guadeloupe 15°53N 61°14W 322 e
Capim Brazil 1°41S 47°47W 332 B2
Capim ➝ Brazil 1°40S 47°47W 332 B2
Capinópolis Brazil 18°41S 49°35W 333 E2
Capinota Bolivia 17°43S 66°14W 330 D4
Capira Panama 8°45N 79°53W 328 B2
Capistrello Italy 41°57N 13°23E 199 G10
Capitan U.S.A. 33°35N 105°35W 305 K11
Capitán Aracena, I. Chile 54°10S 71°20W 336 D2
Capitán Arturo Prat Antarctica 63°0S 61°0W 151 C17
Capitán Pastene Chile 38°13S 73°1W 336 A2
Capitol Heights U.S.A. 38°52N 76°55W 143 B4
Capitol Hill N. Marianas 15°13N 145°45E 302 e
Capitol Reef △ U.S.A. 38°15N 111°10W 305 G8
Capitola U.S.A. 36°59N 121°57W 306 J5
Capitolini, Musei Rome, Italy 136 c3
Capivara, Serra da Brazil 14°35S 45°0W 333 D3
Capiz □ Phil. 11°35N 122°30E 233 F4
Capizzi Italy 37°51N 14°29E 201 E7
Capoche ➝ Mozam. 15°35S 33°0E 269 F3
Capodichino, Nápoli ✕ (NAP) Italy 40°53N 14°16E 201 B7
Capoeira Brazil 5°37S 59°33W 331 B6
Capolo Angola 10°22S 14°7E 265 E2
Caporetto = Kobarid Slovenia 46°15N 13°30E 199 B10
Caporolo ➝ Angola 12°56S 12°58E 265 E2
Capot ➝ Martinique 14°50N 61°5W 322 j
Capoterra Italy 39°11N 8°58E 200 C1
Cappadocia Turkey 39°0N 35°0E 212 C6
Capps U.S.A. 30°24N 83°54W 316 E6
Capraia Italy 43°2N 9°50E 198 E6
Capraia, Pta. Italy 41°7N 8°19E 200 A1
Caprarola Italy 42°19N 12°14E 199 F9
Capreol Canada 46°43N 80°56W 298 C3
Caprera Italy 41°12N 9°28E 200 A2
Capri Italy 40°33N 14°14E 201 B7
Capricorn Group Australia 23°30S 151°55E 280 C5
Capricorn Ra. Australia 23°20S 116°50E 278 D2
Caprino Veronese Italy 45°36N 10°47E 198 C7
Caprivi Game △ Namibia 17°55S 22°37E 270 A3
Caprivi Strip Namibia 18°0S 23°0E 270 A3
Caps et Marais d'Opale △ France 50°40N 2°0E 173 B9
Captain Cook U.S.A. 19°30N 155°55W 302 D6
Captain Cook Bridge Australia 34°0S 151°7E 139 C1
Captain Cook Landing Place Park Australia 34°1S 151°14E 139 C2
Captain's Flat Australia 35°35S 149°27E 283 C8
Captieux France 44°18N 0°16W 174 D3
Captiva U.S.A. 26°31N 82°11W 317 J7
Capuça Angola 17°22S 21°18E 265 F4
Capuchos Portugal 38°38N 9°16W 126 B1
Capucin Dominica 15°38N 61°28W 323 k
Capul I. Phil. 12°26N 124°10E 232 E5
Capulin Volcano △ U.S.A. 36°47N 103°58W 314 C3
Capunda Angola 10°41S 17°23E 265 E3
Caquetá □ Colombia 1°0N 74°0W 328 C3
Caquetá ➝ Colombia 1°15S 69°15W 328 D4
Car Nicobar India 9°10N 92°47E 245 K11
Carabanchel Alto Spain 40°22N 3°44W 127 B1
Carabanchel Bajo Spain 40°23N 3°44W 127 B1
Carabao I. Phil. 12°4N 121°56E 232 E3
Carabobo □ Venezuela 10°10N 68°5W 328 A4
Caracal Romania 44°8N 24°22E 183 F9
Caracaraí Brazil 1°50N 61°8W 329 C5
Caracas Venezuela 10°30N 66°55W 328 A4
Caracol Mato Grosso do Sul, Brazil 22°18S 57°1W 334 A4
Caracol Piauí, Brazil 9°15S 43°22W 332 C3
Caracoli, Pte. Martinique 14°45N 60°52W 322 j
Caracollo Bolivia 17°39S 67°10W 330 D4
Caraga Phil. 7°20N 126°34E 233 H6
Caragabal Australia 33°49S 147°45E 283 B7
Caráglio Italy 44°25N 7°26E 198 D4
Carahue Chile 38°43S 73°12W 336 A2
Caraí Brazil 17°12S 41°42W 333 E3
Caraïbes, Mts. Guadeloupe 15°58N 61°41W 322 e
Carajás Brazil 2°57S 51°22W 332 C1
Carajás, Serra dos Brazil 6°0S 51°30W 332 C1
Caramoan Phil. 13°46N 123°52E 232 E4
Caramoran Phil. 14°0N 124°8E 232 D5
Carandaiti Bolivia 20°45S 63°4W 331 E5
Carangola Brazil 20°44S 42°5W 333 F3
Caransebeş Romania 45°28N 22°18E 182 E7
Carantec France 48°40N 3°55W 172 D3
Carapachay Argentina 34°31S 58°32W 117 B1
Caraparaná ➝ Colombia 1°45S 73°13W 328 D3
Carapichaima Trin. & Tob. 10°28N 61°27W 323 t
Carapuse B. Trin. & Tob. 11°11N 60°35W 323 s
Caraquet Canada 47°48N 64°57W 299 C6
Caras Peru 9°3S 77°47W 330 B2
Caraş Severin □ Romania 45°10N 22°10E 182 E7
Caraşova Romania 45°11N 21°51E 182 E6
Caratasca, L. Honduras 15°20N 83°40W 320 C3
Caratinga Brazil 19°50S 42°10W 333 E3
Carauari Brazil 4°52S 66°54W 328 D4
Caraúbas Brazil 5°43S 37°33W 332 C4
Caravaca de la Cruz Spain 38°8N 1°52W 197 G3
Caravággio Italy 45°30N 9°38E 198 C6
Caravela Guinea-Biss. 11°30N 16°30W 262 C1
Caravelas Brazil 17°45S 39°15W 333 E4
Caraveli Peru 15°45S 73°25W 330 D3
Caravelle, Presqu'île de la Martinique 14°46N 60°48W 322 j
Caraza Argentina 34°41S 58°25W 117 C2
Carazinho Brazil 28°16S 52°46W 335 B5
Carballino = O Carballiño Spain 42°26N 8°5W 194 C2
Carballo Spain 43°13N 8°41W 194 B2
Carberry Canada 49°50N 99°25W 297 D9
Carbet, Chutes du Guadeloupe 16°2N 61°38W 322 e
Carbet, Pitons du Martinique 14°42N 61°7W 322 j
Carbó Mexico 29°42N 110°58W 318 B2
Carbonara, C. Italy 39°6N 9°31E 200 C2
Carbondale Colo., U.S.A. 39°24N 107°13W 304 G10
Carbondale Ill., U.S.A. 37°44N 89°13W 310 G7
Carbondale Pa., U.S.A. 41°35N 75°30W 313 E9
Carbonear Canada 47°42N 53°13W 299 C9
Carboneras Spain 36°59N 1°53W 197 J3
Carboneras de Guadazaón Spain 39°54N 1°50W 196 F3
Carbónia Italy 39°10N 8°30E 200 C1
Carcabuey Spain 37°27N 4°17W 195 H6
Carcagente = Carcaixent Spain 39°8N 0°28W 197 F4
Carcaixent Spain 39°8N 0°28W 197 F4
Carcajou Canada 57°47N 117°6W 296 B5
Carcar Phil. 10°6N 123°38E 233 F4
Carcarana ➝ Argentina 32°27S 60°48W 334 C3
Carcasse, C. Haiti 18°30N 74°28W 321 C5
Carcassonne France 43°13N 2°20E 174 E6
Carchi □ Ecuador 0°45N 78°0W 328 C2
Carcoar Australia 33°36S 149°8E 283 B8
Carcross Canada 60°13N 134°45W 296 A2
Çardak Çanakkale, Turkey 40°22N 26°43E 203 F10
Çardak Denizli, Turkey 37°49N 29°39E 205 D11
Cardamon Hills India 9°30N 77°15E 245 K3
Cardeña Spain 38°16N 4°20W 195 G6
Cárdenas Cuba 23°0N 81°30W 320 B3
Cárdenas San Luis Potosí, Mexico 22°0N 99°38W 319 C5
Cárdenas Tabasco, Mexico 17°59N 93°22W 319 D6
Cardenete Spain 39°46N 1°41W 196 F3
Cardiel, L. Argentina 48°55S 71°10W 336 C2
Cardiff U.K. 51°29N 3°10W 169 F4
Cardiff □ U.K. 51°31N 3°12W 169 F4
Cardiff-by-the-Sea U.S.A. 33°1N 117°17W 307 M9
Cardigan U.K. 52°5N 4°40W 169 E3
Cardigan B. U.K. 52°30N 4°30W 169 E3
Cardinal Canada 44°47N 75°23W 313 B9
Cardón, Punta Venezuela 11°37N 70°14W 328 A3
Cardona Spain 41°56N 1°40E 196 D6
Cardona Uruguay 33°53S 57°18W 334 C4
Cardoner ➝ Spain 41°41N 1°51E 196 D6
Cardoso, Ilha do Brazil 25°8S 47°58W 335 B5
Cardston Canada 49°15N 113°20W 296 D6
Cardwell Australia 18°14S 146°2E 280 B4
Careen L. Canada 57°0N 108°11W 297 B7
Carei Romania 47°40N 22°29E 182 C7
Careiro Brazil 3°12S 59°45W 329 D6
Careme = Ciremay Indonesia 6°55S 108°27E 235 D3
Carenage Trin. & Tob. 10°41N 61°36W 323 t
Carentan France 49°19N 1°15W 172 C5
Carey Idaho, U.S.A. 43°19N 113°57W 304 E7
Carey Ohio, U.S.A. 40°57N 83°23W 311 D13
Carey, L. Australia 29°0S 122°15E 279 E3
Carey L. Canada 62°12N 102°55W 297 A8
Careysburg Liberia 6°34N 10°30W 262 D2
Cargados Garajos Ind. Oc. 17°0S 59°0E 273 F4
Cargèse France 42°7N 8°35E 175 F12
Carhaix-Plouguer France 48°18N 3°36W 172 D3
Carhuamayo Peru 10°51S 76°4W 330 C2
Carhuas Peru 9°15S 77°39W 330 B2
Carhué Argentina 37°10S 62°50W 334 D3
Caria Turkey 37°20N 28°10E 205 D10
Cariacica Brazil 20°16S 40°25W 333 F3
Cariaco Venezuela 10°29N 63°33W 329 A5
Cariango Angola 10°37S 15°20E 265 E3
Cariati Italy 39°30N 16°57E 201 C9
Caribbean Sea W. Indies 15°0N 75°0W 320 C4
Cariboo Mts. Canada 53°0N 121°0W 296 C4
Caribou U.S.A. 46°52N 68°1W 309 B19
Caribou ➝ Man., Canada 59°20N 94°44W 297 B10
Caribou ➝ N.W.T., Canada 61°27N 125°45W 296 A3
Caribou I. Canada 47°22N 85°49W 298 C2
Caribou Is. Canada 61°55N 113°15W 296 A6
Caribou L. Man., Canada 59°21N 96°10W 297 B9
Caribou L. Ont., Canada 50°25N 89°5W 298 B2
Caribou Mts. Canada 59°12N 115°40W 296 B5
Caribou River △ Canada 59°35N 96°35W 297 B9
Caribrod = Dimitrovgrad Serbia 43°2N 22°48E 202 C6
Carichic Mexico 27°56N 107°3W 318 B3
Caridad Phil. 14°28N 120°53E 127 C1
Carigara Phil. 11°18N 124°41E 233 F5
Carignan France 49°38N 5°10E 173 C12
Carignano Italy 44°55N 7°40E 198 D4
Carin Somali Rep. 10°59N 49°13E 267 B6
Carinda Australia 30°28S 147°41E 283 A7
Cariñena Spain 41°20N 1°13W 196 D3
Carinhanha Brazil 14°15S 44°46W 333 D3
Carinhanha ➝ Brazil 14°20S 43°47W 333 D3
Carini Italy 38°8N 13°11E 200 D6
Cariño Spain 43°45N 7°52W 194 B3
Carínola Italy 41°11N 13°58E 200 A6
Carinthia = Kärnten □ Austria 46°52N 13°30E 180 E6
Carioca, Sa. da Brazil 22°57S 43°13W 135 B1
Caripito Venezuela 10°8N 63°6W 329 A5
Cariré Brazil 3°57S 40°27W 332 B3
Caritianas Brazil 9°20S 63°6W 331 B5
Carles Phil. 11°34N 123°8E 233 F4
Carlet Spain 39°14N 0°31W 197 F4
Carleton, Mt. Canada 47°23N 66°53W 299 C6
Carleton Place Canada 45°8N 76°9W 313 A8
Carletonville S. Africa 26°23S 27°22E 270 C4
Cârlibaba Romania 47°35N 25°8E 183 C10
Carlin U.S.A. 40°43N 116°7W 304 F5
Carlingford L. U.K. 54°3N 6°9W 166 B5
Carlinville U.S.A. 39°17N 89°53W 310 E7
Carlisle Cumb., U.K. 54°54N 2°56W 168 C5
Carlisle Ind., U.S.A. 38°58N 87°24W 311 F9
Carlisle Ky., U.S.A. 38°19N 84°1W 311 F12
Carlisle Pa., U.S.A. 40°12N 77°12W 312 F7
Carlisle I. Australia 20°49S 149°18E 280 J7
Carlit, Pic France 42°35N 1°55E 174 F5
Carloforte Italy 39°8N 8°18E 200 C1
Carlos Casares Argentina 35°32S 61°20W 334 D3
Carlos Chagas Brazil 17°43S 40°45W 333 E3
Carlos Tejedor Argentina 35°25S 62°25W 334 D3
Carlow Ireland 52°50N 6°56W 166 D5
Carlow □ Ireland 52°43N 6°50W 166 D5
Carlsbad = Karlovy Vary Czech Rep. 50°13N 12°51E 180 A5
Carlsbad Calif., U.S.A. 33°10N 117°21W 307 M9
Carlsbad N. Mex., U.S.A. 32°25N 104°14W 305 K11
Carlsbad Caverns △ U.S.A. 32°10N 104°35W 305 K11
Carlsberg Ridge Ind. Oc. 1°0N 66°0E 273 D5
Carlstadt U.S.A. 40°50N 74°6W 132 A1
Carlton Australia 37°47S 144°57E 128 A1
Carluke U.K. 55°45N 3°50W 167 F5
Carlyle Sask., Canada 49°40N 102°20W 297 D8
Carlyle Ill., U.S.A. 38°37N 89°22W 310 F7
Carlyle L. U.S.A. 38°37N 89°21W 310 F7
Carmacks Canada 62°5N 136°16W 294 C6
Carmagnola Italy 44°51N 7°43E 198 D4
Carman Canada 49°30N 98°0W 297 D9
Carmarthen U.K. 51°52N 4°19W 169 F3
Carmarthen B. U.K. 51°40N 4°30W 169 F3
Carmarthenshire □ U.K. 51°55N 4°13W 169 F3
Carmaux France 44°3N 2°10E 174 D6
Carmel Ind., U.S.A. 39°58N 86°7W 311 E10
Carmel N.Y., U.S.A. 41°26N 73°41W 313 E11
Carmel-by-the-Sea U.S.A. 36°33N 121°55W 306 J5
Carmel Valley U.S.A. 36°29N 121°43W 306 J5
Carmelo Uruguay 34°0S 58°20W 334 C4
Carmen Bolivia 11°40S 67°51W 330 C4
Carmen Colombia 9°43N 75°8W 328 B2
Carmen Paraguay 27°13S 56°12W 335 B4
Carmen Bohol, Phil. 9°50N 124°12E 233 G5
Carmen Cebu, Phil. 10°35N 124°1E 233 F5
Carmen Cotabato, Phil. 7°13N 124°45E 233 H5
Carmen Venezuela 1°16N 66°52W 328 C4
Carmen ➝ Mexico 30°42N 106°29W 318 A3
Carmen, I. Mexico 25°57N 111°12W 318 B2
Carmen de Huechuraba Chile 33°20S 70°40W 137 B1
Carmen de la Legua Peru 12°3S 77°7W 124 B2
Carmen de Patagones Argentina 40°50S 63°0W 336 B4
Cármenes Spain 42°58N 5°34W 194 C5
Carmensa Argentina 35°15S 67°40W 334 D2
Carmi B.C., Canada 49°36N 119°8W 296 D5
Carmi Ill., U.S.A. 38°5N 88°10W 311 F8
Carmichael U.S.A. 38°38N 121°19W 306 G5
Carmichael Village Bahamas 25°0N 77°26W 153 b
Carmila Australia 21°55S 149°24E 280 C4
Carmona Costa Rica 10°0N 85°15W 320 E2
Carmona Spain 37°28N 5°42W 195 H5
Carn Ban U.K. 57°7N 4°15W 167 D4
Carn Eige U.K. 57°17N 5°8W 167 D3
Carnac France 47°35N 3°6W 172 E3
Carnamah Australia 29°41S 115°53E 279 E2
Carnarvon W. Austral., Australia 24°51S 113°42E 279 D1
Carnarvon Northern Cape, S. Africa 30°56S 22°8E 270 D3
Carnarvon △ Australia 24°54S 148°2E 280 C4
Carnarvon Ra. Queens., Australia 25°15S 148°30E 280 D4
Carnarvon Ra. W. Austral., Australia 25°20S 120°45E 279 E3
Carnatic India 9°40N 77°50E 245 K3
Carnation U.S.A. 47°39N 121°55W 306 C5
Carnaxide Portugal 38°43N 9°14W 126 A1
Carncastle U.K. 54°54N 5°53W 166 B6
Carndonagh Ireland 55°16N 7°15W 166 A4
Carnduff Canada 49°10N 101°50W 297 D8
Carnegie Vic., Australia 37°53S 145°3E 128 B2
Carnegie Pa., U.S.A. 40°24N 80°5W 312 F4
Carnegie, L. Australia 26°5S 122°30E 279 E3
Carnegie Hall New York, U.S.A. 132 c2
Carnegie Ridge Pac. Oc. 1°0S 87°0W 289 H19
Carnic Alps = Karnische Alpen Europe 46°36N 13°0E 180 E6
Carniche Alpi = Karnische Alpen Europe 46°36N 13°0E 180 E6
Carnide Portugal 38°45N 9°10W 126 A1
Carnot C.A.R. 4°59N 15°56E 264 B3
Carnot, C. Australia 34°57S 135°38E 281 E2
Carnot B. Australia 17°20S 122°15E 278 C3
Carnoustie U.K. 56°30N 2°42W 167 E6
Carnsore Pt. Ireland 52°10N 6°22W 166 D5
Caro U.S.A. 43°29N 83°24W 309 D12
Caroço São Tomé & Príncipe 1°32N 7°27E 265 a
Carol City U.S.A. 25°56N 80°14W 128 A1

Carolina Brazil 7°10S 47°30W 332 C2
Carolina Puerto Rico 18°23N 65°58W 321 C6
Carolina Mpumalanga, S. Africa 26°5S 30°6E 271 C5
Carolinas Pt. N. Marianas 14°55N 145°38E 302 e
Caroline I. Kiribati 9°58S 150°13W 289 H12
Caroline Is. Micronesia 8°0N 150°0E 288 G6
Caroline Pk. N.Z. 45°57S 167°15E 285 F2
Carondelet Reef Kiribati 5°33S 173°50E 277 B16
Caroni Trin. & Tob. 10°34N 61°23W 323 t
Caroni □ Trin. & Tob. 10°30N 61°22W 323 t
Caroni → Trin. & Tob. 10°37N 61°30W 323 t
Caroni → Venezuela 8°21N 62°43W 329 B5
Caroni Arena Res. Trin. & Tob. 10°33N 61°15W 323 t
Caroni Bird Sanctuary Trin. & Tob. 10°36N 61°28W 323 t
Caroni Swamp Trin. & Tob. 10°36N 61°27W 323 t
Caronie = Nébrodi, Monti Italy 37°54N 14°35E 201 E7
Caroona Australia 31°24S 150°26E 283 A9
Carora Venezuela 10°11N 70°5W 328 A3
Carpathians Europe 49°30N 21°0E 177 D11
Carpaţii Meridionali Romania 45°30N 25°0E 183 E9
Carpentaria, G. of Australia 14°0S 139°0E 280 A2
Carpentersville U.S.A. 42°6N 88°17W 311 B8
Carpentras France 44°3N 5°2E 175 D9
Carpi Italy 44°47N 10°53E 198 D7
Carpina Brazil 7°51S 35°15W 332 C4
Cărpineni Moldova 46°46N 28°22E 183 D13
Carpinteria U.S.A. 34°24N 119°31W 307 L7
Carpio Spain 41°13N 5°7W 194 D5
Carr Boyd Ra. Australia 16°15S 128°35E 278 C4
Carra, L. Ireland 53°41N 9°14W 166 C2
Carrabelle U.S.A. 29°51N 84°40W 316 F5
Carral Spain 43°14N 8°21W 194 B2
Carranglan Phil. 15°58N 121°4E 232 D3
Carranza, Presa V. Mexico 27°20N 100°50W 318 B4
Carrara Italy 44°5N 10°6E 198 D7
Carrascal Santiago, Chile 33°25S 70°42W 137 B1
Carrascal Phil. 9°22N 125°56E 233 G5
Carrasco △ Bolivia 17°23S 64°59W 331 D5
Carrascosa del Campo Spain 40°2N 2°45W 196 E2
Carrauntoohill Ireland 52°0N 9°45W 166 D2
Carretas, Punta Peru 14°12S 76°17W 330 C2
Carriacou Grenada 12°29N 61°26W 323 q
Carrick-on-Shannon Ireland 53°57N 8°5W 166 C3
Carrick-on-Suir Ireland 52°21N 7°24W 166 D4
Carrickfergus U.K. 54°43N 5°49W 166 B6
Carrickmacross Ireland 53°59N 6°43W 166 C5
Carrickmines Ireland 53°15N 6°10W 120 B3
Carrières-sous-Bois France 48°55N 2°6E 134 A1
Carrières-sous-Poissy France 48°56N 2°2E 134 A1
Carrières-sur-Seine France 48°55N 2°11E 134 A2
Carrieton Australia 32°25S 138°31E 282 B3
Carrigeen B. Ireland 53°24N 6°5W 120 A3
Carrillo Mexico 26°54N 103°55W 318 B4
Carrington U.S.A. 47°27N 99°8W 308 B4
Carrión → Spain 41°53N 4°32W 194 D6
Carrión de los Condes Spain 42°20N 4°37W 194 C6
Carrizal Bajo Chile 28°5S 71°20W 334 B1
Carrizalillo Chile 29°5S 71°30W 334 B1
Carrizo Cr. → U.S.A. 36°55N 103°55W 305 H12
Carrizo Plain △ U.S.A. 35°11N 119°47W 306 K7
Carrizo Springs U.S.A. 28°31N 99°52W 314 G5
Carrizozo U.S.A. 33°38N 105°53W 305 K11
Carroll U.S.A. 42°4N 94°52W 310 B2
Carrollton Ga., U.S.A. 33°35N 85°5W 316 B4
Carrollton Ill., U.S.A. 39°18N 90°24W 310 E8
Carrollton Ky., U.S.A. 38°41N 85°11W 311 F11
Carrollton Mo., U.S.A. 39°22N 93°30W 310 E3
Carrollton Ohio, U.S.A. 40°34N 81°5W 312 F3
Carron → U.K. 57°53N 4°22W 167 D4
Carron, L. U.K. 57°22N 5°35W 167 D3
Carrot → Canada 53°50N 101°17W 297 C8
Carrot River Canada 53°17N 103°35W 297 C8
Carrouges France 48°34N 0°10W 172 D6
Carrù Italy 44°29N 7°52E 198 D4
Carruthers Canada 52°52N 109°16W 297 C7
Carsa Dek Ethiopia 5°13N 39°50E 257 F4
Çarşamba Turkey 41°11N 36°44E 212 B7
Carsóli Italy 42°6N 13°5E 199 F10
Carson Calif., U.S.A. 33°49N 118°16W 307 M8
Carson N. Dak., U.S.A. 46°25N 101°34W 308 B3
Carson → U.S.A. 39°45N 118°40W 306 F8
Carson City Mich., U.S.A. 43°11N 84°51W 311 A12
Carson City Nev., U.S.A. 39°10N 119°46W 306 F7
Carson Sink U.S.A. 39°50N 118°25W 304 G4
Carstensz Pyramid = Jaya, Puncak Indonesia 3°57S 137°17E 231 E9
Cartagena Colombia 10°25N 75°33W 328 A2
Cartagena Spain 37°38N 0°59W 197 H4
Cartago Colombia 4°45N 75°55W 328 C2
Cartago Costa Rica 9°50N 83°55W 320 E3
Cártama Spain 36°43N 4°39W 195 J6
Cartaxo Portugal 39°10N 8°47W 195 F2
Cartaya Spain 37°16N 7°9W 195 H3
Cartersville U.S.A. 34°10N 84°48W 316 A5
Carterton N.Z. 41°2S 175°31E 284 H4
Carterville U.S.A. 37°46N 89°5W 310 G7
Carthage Tunisia 36°52N 10°20E 200 F3
Carthage Ill., U.S.A. 40°25N 91°8W 310 D5
Carthage Mo., U.S.A. 37°11N 94°19W 308 G6
Carthage N.Y., U.S.A. 43°59N 75°37W 309 D16
Carthage Tex., U.S.A. 32°9N 94°20W 314 E7
Cartier I. Australia 12°31S 123°29E 278 B3
Cartierville Canada 45°31N 73°42W 130 A1
Cartwright Canada 53°41N 56°58W 299 B8
Caruaru Brazil 8°15S 35°55W 332 C4
Carúpano Venezuela 10°39N 63°15W 329 A5
Caruray Phil. 10°20N 119°0E 233 F2
Carutapera Brazil 1°13S 46°1W 332 B2
Caruthersville U.S.A. 36°11N 89°39W 308 G9
Carvalho Brazil 2°16S 51°29W 329 D7
Carvin France 50°30N 2°57E 173 B9
Carvoeiro Brazil 1°30S 61°59W 329 D5
Carvoeiro, C. Portugal 39°21N 9°24W 195 F1
Cary Ill., U.S.A. 42°13N 88°14W 311 B8
Cary N.C., U.S.A. 35°47N 78°46W 315 D15
Casa, Pas de la = Envalira, Port d' Europe 42°33N 1°43E 196 C6
Casa Branca Brazil 21°46S 47°4W 333 F2
Casa Branca Portugal 38°29N 8°12W 195 G2
Casa Grande U.S.A. 32°53N 111°45W 305 K8
Casa Loma Canada 43°41N 79°24W 141 A2
Casa Verde Brazil 23°29S 46°40W 137 A1
Casablanca Chile 33°20S 71°25W 334 C1
Casablanca Morocco 33°36N 7°36W 260 B3
Casablanca □ Morocco 33°38N 7°35W 260 B3
Casacalenda Italy 41°44N 14°51E 199 G11
Casal Morena Italy 41°49N 12°37E 136 C2
Casalbordino Italy 42°9N 14°35E 199 F11
Casale Monferrato Italy 45°8N 8°27E 198 C5
Casalmaggiore Italy 44°59N 10°26E 198 D7
Casalotti Italy 41°54N 12°22E 136 B1
Casalpusterlengo Italy 45°11N 9°39E 198 C6
Casamance → Senegal 12°33N 16°46W 262 C1
Casanare □ Colombia 5°30N 72°0W 328 B3
Casanare → Colombia 6°2N 69°51W 328 B4
Casarano Italy 40°0N 18°10E 201 B11
Casares Spain 36°27N 5°16W 195 J5
Casas Ibáñez Spain 39°17N 1°30W 197 F3
Casasimarro Spain 39°22N 2°3W 197 F2
Casatejada Spain 39°54N 5°40W 194 F5
Casavieja Spain 40°17N 4°46W 194 E6
Cascada de Basaseachic △ Mexico 28°9N 108°15W 318 B3
Cascade Seychelles 4°39S 55°29E 272 c
Cascade Idaho, U.S.A. 44°31N 116°2W 304 D5
Cascade Iowa, U.S.A. 42°18N 91°0W 310 B6
Cascade Mont., U.S.A. 47°16N 111°42W 304 C8
Cascade Locks U.S.A. 45°40N 121°54W 306 E5
Cascade Heights U.S.A. 33°43N 84°26W 113 B2
Cascade Pt. N.Z. 44°1S 168°20E 285 E3
Cascade Ra. U.S.A. 47°0N 121°30W 306 D5
Cascade Res. U.S.A. 44°32N 116°3W 304 D5
Cascades, Pte. des Réunion 21°9S 55°51E 272 f
Cascais Portugal 38°41N 9°25W 195 G1
Cascavel Ceará, Brazil 4°7S 38°14W 332 B4
Cascavel Paraná, Brazil 24°57S 53°28W 335 A5
Cáscina Italy 43°41N 10°33E 198 E7
Casco B. U.S.A. 43°45N 70°0W 309 D19
Case Noyale Mauritius 20°23S 57°22E 272 e
Case-Pilote Martinique 14°38N 61°9W 322 j
Caselle Torinese Italy 45°10N 7°39E 198 C4
Caserta Italy 41°4N 14°20E 201 A7
Casey Antarctica 66°0S 76°0E 151 C8
Casey Ill., U.S.A. 39°18N 87°59W 311 E9
Caseyr, Raas = Asir, Ras Somali Rep. 11°55N 51°10E 267 B7
Cashel Ireland 52°30N 7°53W 166 D4
Casibare → Colombia 3°48N 72°18W 328 C3
Casiguran Phil. 16°22N 122°7E 232 C4
Casiguran Sound Phil. 16°16N 121°58E 232 C3
Casilda Argentina 33°10S 61°10W 334 C3
Casim = General Toshevo Bulgaria 43°42N 28°6E 203 C12
Casimcea Romania 44°45N 28°23E 183 F13
Casino N.S.W., Australia 28°52S 153°3E 281 D5
Casino New Orleans, U.S.A. 131 b2
Casiquiare → Venezuela 2°1N 67°7W 328 C4
Casitas Peru 3°54S 80°39W 330 A1
Čáslav Czech Rep. 49°54N 15°22E 180 B8
Casma Peru 9°30S 78°20W 330 B2
Casmalia U.S.A. 34°50N 120°32W 307 L6
Cásola Valsénio Italy 44°12N 11°40E 199 D8
Cásoli Italy 42°7N 14°18E 199 F11
Caspe Spain 41°14N 0°1W 196 D4
Casper U.S.A. 42°51N 106°19W 304 E10
Caspian Depression Eurasia 47°0N 48°0E 191 G9
Caspian Sea Eurasia 43°0N 50°0E 187 F9
Cass Lake U.S.A. 47°23N 94°37W 308 B6
Cassà de la Selva Spain 41°53N 2°52E 196 D7
Cassadaga U.S.A. 42°20N 79°19W 312 D5
Cassai Angola 10°33S 21°59E 265 E4
Cassai → Angola 3°2S 16°57E 265 E4
Cassamba Angola 13°6S 20°18E 265 E4
Cassano allo Iónio Italy 39°47N 16°20E 201 C9
Cassel France 50°48N 2°30E 173 B9
Casselberry U.S.A. 28°41N 81°20W 317 G8
Casselman Canada 45°19N 75°5W 313 A9
Casselton U.S.A. 46°54N 97°13W 308 B5
Cassiar Canada 59°16N 129°40W 296 B3
Cassiar Mts. Canada 59°30N 130°30W 296 B2
Cassilândia Brazil 19°9S 51°45W 331 D7
Cassilis Australia 32°3S 149°58E 283 B8
Cassinga Angola 15°5S 16°4E 265 F3
Cassino Italy 41°30N 13°49E 200 A6
Cassis France 43°14N 5°32E 175 E9
Cassoalala Angola 9°30S 14°22E 265 D2
Cassoango Angola 13°42S 20°56E 265 E4
Cassongue Angola 11°53S 15°2E 265 E3
Cassopolis U.S.A. 41°55N 86°1W 311 C10
Cassunda Angola 10°57S 21°3E 265 E4
Cassville Mo., U.S.A. 36°41N 93°52W 308 G7
Cassville Wis., U.S.A. 42°43N 90°59W 310 B6
Castagneto Carducci Italy 43°9N 10°36E 198 E7
Castaic U.S.A. 34°30N 118°38W 307 L8
Castalia U.S.A. 41°24N 82°49W 312 E2
Castanhal Brazil 1°18S 47°55W 332 B2
Castara Trin. & Tob. 11°17N 60°42W 323 s
Castara B. Trin. & Tob. 11°17N 60°42W 323 s
Castéggio Italy 45°0N 9°7E 198 C6
Castejón de Monegros Spain 41°37N 0°15W 196 D4
Castel Guadeloupe 16°15N 61°35W 322 e
Castèl di Leva Italy 41°46N 12°33E 136 C2
Castèl di Sangro Italy 41°47N 14°6E 199 G11
Castèl San Giovanni Italy 45°4N 9°26E 198 C6
Castèl San Pietro Terme Italy 44°24N 11°35E 199 D8
Castèl Sant'Angelo Rome, Italy 136 b1
Castelbuono Italy 37°56N 14°5E 201 E7
Castelfidardo Italy 43°28N 13°33E 199 E10
Castelfiorentino Italy 43°36N 10°58E 198 E7
Castelfranco Emília Italy 44°37N 11°3E 198 D8
Castelfranco Véneto Italy 45°40N 11°55E 199 C8
Casteljaloux France 44°19N 0°6E 174 D4
Castellabate Italy 40°17N 14°57E 201 B7
Castellammare, G. di Italy 38°8N 12°54E 200 D5
Castellammare del Golfo Italy 38°1N 12°53E 200 D5
Castellammare di Stábia Italy 40°42N 14°29E 201 B7
Castellamonte Italy 45°23N 7°42E 198 C4
Castellane France 43°50N 6°31E 175 E10
Castellaneta Italy 40°38N 16°56E 201 B9
Castelli Argentina 36°7S 57°47W 334 D4
Castelló de la Plana Spain 39°58N 0°3W 196 F4
Castellón de la Plana □ Spain 40°15N 0°5W 196 E4
Castellote Spain 40°48N 0°15W 196 E4
Castelmáuro Italy 41°50N 14°43E 199 G11
Castelnau-de-Médoc France 45°2N 0°48W 174 C3
Castelnau-Magnoac France 43°17N 0°31E 174 E4
Castelnaudary France 43°20N 1°58E 174 E5
Castelnovo ne' Monti Italy 44°26N 10°24E 198 D7
Castelnuovo di Val di Cécina Italy 43°12N 10°59E 198 E7
Castelo = Manuel Urbano Brazil 8°53S 69°18W 330 B4
Castelo Brazil 20°33S 41°14W 333 F3
Castelo, Pta. do Azores 36°56N 25°1W 153 d4
Castelo Branco Azores 38°31N 28°44W 153 d1
Castelo Branco Portugal 39°50N 7°31W 194 F3
Castelo Branco □ Portugal 39°52N 7°45W 194 F3
Castelo de Paiva Portugal 41°2N 8°16W 194 D2
Castelo de Vide Portugal 39°25N 7°27W 195 F3
Castelo do Piauí Brazil 5°20S 41°33W 332 C3
Castelrosso = Megisti Greece 36°8N 29°34E 205 E11
Castelsardo Italy 40°55N 8°43E 200 B1
Castelsarrasin France 44°2N 1°7E 174 D5
Casteltérmini Italy 37°32N 13°39E 200 E6
Castelvetrano Italy 37°41N 12°47E 200 E5
Castendo Angola 8°39S 14°10E 265 D2
Casterton Australia 37°30S 141°30E 282 D4
Castets France 43°52N 1°6W 174 E2
Castiglion Fiorentino Italy 43°20N 11°55E 199 E8
Castiglione = Bou Ismaïl Algeria 36°38N 2°42E 261 A5
Castiglione del Lago Italy 43°7N 12°3E 199 E9
Castiglione della Pescáia Italy 42°46N 10°53E 198 F7
Castiglione delle Stiviere Italy 45°23N 10°29E 198 C7
Castilblanco Spain 39°17N 5°5W 195 F5
Castile U.S.A. 42°38N 78°3W 312 D6
Castilla Peru 5°12S 80°38W 330 B1
Castilla, Playa de Spain 37°0N 6°33W 195 J4
Castilla-La Mancha □ Spain 39°30N 3°30W 195 F7
Castilla y Leon □ Spain 42°0N 5°0W 194 D6
Castillo de Locubín Spain 37°32N 3°56W 195 H7
Castillo de San Marcos △ U.S.A. 29°54N 81°19W 316 F8
Castillon-en-Couserans France 42°56N 1°1E 174 F5
Castillonès France 44°39N 0°37E 174 D4
Castillos Uruguay 34°12S 53°52W 335 C5
Castle Bruce Dominica 15°26N 61°16W 323 k
Castle Dale U.S.A. 39°13N 111°1W 304 G8
Castle Douglas U.K. 54°56N 3°56W 167 G5
Castle Harbour Bermuda 32°21N 64°40W 153 a
Castle Mt. Jamaica 18°8N 76°22W 320 a
Castle of Good Hope Cape Town, S. Africa 118 c3
Castle Roads Bermuda 32°20N 64°40W 153 a
Castle Rock Colo., U.S.A. 39°22N 104°51W 304 G11
Castle Rock Wash., U.S.A. 46°17N 122°54W 306 D4
Castle Rock Pt. St. Helena 16°1S 5°45W 153 h
Castlebar Ireland 53°52N 9°18W 166 C2
Castlebay U.K. 56°57N 7°31W 167 E1
Castleblaney Ireland 54°7N 6°44W 166 B5
Castlecliff N.Z. 39°57S 175°5E 284 F4
Castlederg U.K. 54°42N 7°35W 166 B4
Castleford U.K. 53°43N 1°21W 168 D6
Castlegar Canada 49°20N 117°40W 296 D5
Castleknock Ireland 53°22N 6°21W 120 A1
Castlemaine Vic., Australia 37°2S 144°12E 282 D6
Castlemaine Kerry, Ireland 52°10N 9°42W 166 D2
Castlepoint N.Z. 40°54S 176°15E 284 G5
Castlepollard Ireland 53°41N 7°19W 166 C4
Castlerea Ireland 53°46N 8°29W 166 C3
Castlereagh → Australia 30°12S 147°32E 283 A7
Castlereagh B. Australia 12°10S 135°10E 280 A2
Castleton U.S.A. 43°37N 73°11W 313 C11
Castleton Corners U.S.A. 40°36N 74°8W 132 C1
Castletown I. of Man 54°5N 4°38W 168 C3
Castletown Bearhaven Ireland 51°39N 9°55W 166 E2
Castor Canada 52°15N 111°50W 296 C6
Castor → Canada 53°24N 78°58W 298 B4
Castorland U.S.A. 43°53N 75°31W 313 C9
Castres France 43°37N 2°13E 174 E6
Castricum Neths. 52°33N 4°40E 170 B4
Castries St. Lucia 14°2N 60°58W 323 m
Castril Spain 37°48N 2°46W 195 H8
Castro Brazil 24°45S 50°0W 335 A6
Castro Chile 42°30S 73°50W 336 B2
Castro Alves Brazil 12°46S 39°33W 333 D4
Castro del Río Spain 37°41N 4°29W 195 H6
Castro-Urdiales Spain 43°23N 3°11W 194 B7
Castro Valley U.S.A. 37°41N 122°5W 306 H4
Castro Verde Portugal 37°41N 8°4W 195 H2
Castrogiovanni = Enna Italy 37°34N 14°16E 201 E7
Castrojeriz Spain 42°17N 4°9W 194 C6
Castropol Spain 43°32N 7°0W 194 B4
Castroreale Italy 38°6N 15°12E 201 D8
Castrovíllari Italy 39°49N 16°12E 201 C9
Castroville U.S.A. 36°46N 121°45W 306 J5
Castrovirreyna Peru 13°20S 75°18W 330 C2
Castuera Spain 38°43N 5°37W 195 G5
Caswell Sound N.Z. 44°59S 167°8E 285 E2
Çat Turkey 39°40N 41°3E 213 C9
Cat Ba, Dao Vietnam 20°50N 107°0E 236 B6
Cat Ba △ Vietnam 20°47N 107°3E 236 B6
Cat I. Bahamas 24°30N 75°30W 321 B4
Cat L. Canada 51°40N 91°50W 298 B1
Cat Lake Canada 51°40N 91°50W 298 B1
Cat Tien △ Vietnam 11°25N 107°17E 237 G6
Čata Slovak Rep. 47°58N 18°38E 181 D11
Catabola Angola 12°9S 17°16E 265 E3
Catacamas Honduras 14°54N 85°56W 320 D2
Catacáos Peru 5°20S 80°45W 330 B1
Cataguases Brazil 21°23S 42°39W 333 F3
Catagupan Phil. 8°1N 116°58E 233 G1
Cataingan Phil. 12°0N 124°0E 232 E4
Çatak Turkey 38°1N 43°8E 213 C10
Catalão Brazil 18°10S 47°57W 333 E2
Çatalca Turkey 41°8N 28°27E 203 E12
Catalina Nfld. & L., Canada 48°31N 53°4W 299 C9
Catalina Chile 25°13S 69°43W 334 B2
Catalina Ariz., U.S.A. 32°30N 110°50W 305 K8
Catalonia = Cataluña □ Spain 41°40N 1°15E 196 D6
Cataluña □ Spain 41°40N 1°15E 196 D6
Çatalzeytin Turkey 41°57N 34°12E 212 B6
Catamarca Argentina 28°30S 65°50W 334 B2
Catamarca □ Argentina 27°0S 65°50W 334 B2
Catanauan Phil. 13°36N 122°19E 232 E4
Catanduanes □ Phil. 13°50N 124°20E 232 E5
Catanduva Brazil 21°5S 48°58W 335 A6
Catânia Italy 37°30N 15°6E 201 E8
Catânia, G. di Italy 37°24N 15°9E 201 E8
Cataño Puerto Rico 18°27N 66°7W 321 b
Catanzaro Italy 38°54N 16°35E 201 D9
Cataouatche, L. U.S.A. 29°50N 90°14W 131 B1
Catarman Camiguin, Phil. 9°8N 124°40E 233 G5
Catarman N. Samar, Phil. 12°28N 124°35E 232 E5
Catatumbo → Venezuela 9°21N 71°45W 328 B3
Catauala U.S.A. 32°39N 84°52W 316 C5
Catbalogan Phil. 11°46N 124°53E 233 F5
Cateco Cangola Angola 8°28S 15°51E 265 D3
Catedral Metropolitana Rio de J., Brazil 135 c1
Catedral Metropolitana Mexico City, Mexico 128 b3
Cateel Phil. 7°47N 126°24E 233 H6
Cateel Bay Phil. 7°54N 126°25E 233 H6
Catembe Mozam. 26°0S 32°33E 271 C5
Catende Angola 11°14S 21°30E 265 E4
Catende Brazil 8°40S 35°43W 332 C4
Caterham U.K. 51°15N 0°4W 169 F7
Catete Angola 9°6S 13°43E 265 D2
Catete Rio de J., Brazil 22°54S 43°10W 135 B1
Catford U.K. 51°26N 0°1W 125 B3
Cathcart N.S.W., Australia 36°52S 149°24E 283 D8
Cathcart Eastern Cape, S. Africa 32°18S 27°10E 270 D4
Cathedral City U.S.A. 33°47N 116°28W 307 M10
Cathedral Rock △ Australia 30°24S 152°15E 283 A10
Catherine, L. U.S.A. 28°30N 81°24W 133 B2
Cathlamet U.S.A. 46°12N 123°23W 306 D3
Catio Guinea-Biss. 11°17N 15°15W 262 C1
Catisimiña Venezuela 4°5N 63°40W 329 C5
Catita Brazil 9°31S 43°1W 332 C3
Catlettsburg U.S.A. 38°25N 82°36W 309 F12
Catlin U.S.A. 40°4N 87°42W 311 D9
Catlins N.Z. 46°22S 169°17E 285 G4
Çatma Dağı Turkey 38°25N 29°50E 205 C11
Catmon Phil. 10°43N 124°1E 233 F5
Catoche, C. Mexico 21°35N 87°5W 319 C7
Catolé do Rocha Brazil 6°21S 37°45W 332 C4
Catota Angola 13°57S 17°30E 265 E3
Cátria, Mte. Italy 43°28N 12°42E 199 E9
Catriló Argentina 36°26S 63°24W 334 D3
Catrimani Brazil 0°27N 61°41W 329 C5
Catrimani → Brazil 0°28N 61°44W 329 C5
Catskill U.S.A. 42°14N 73°52W 313 D11
Catskill △ U.S.A. 42°8N 74°39W 313 D10
Catskill Mts. U.S.A. 42°10N 74°25W 313 D10
Catt, Mt. Australia 13°49S 134°23E 280 A1
Cattaraugus U.S.A. 42°20N 78°52W 312 D6
Cattaro = Kotor Montenegro 42°25N 18°47E 202 D2
Catterick U.K. 54°23N 1°37W 168 C6
Cattólica Italy 43°58N 12°44E 199 E9
Cattólica Eraclea Italy 37°26N 13°24E 200 E6
Catu Brazil 12°21S 38°23W 333 D4
Catuala Angola 16°25S 19°2E 265 F3
Catuane Mozam. 26°48S 32°18E 271 C5
Catubig Phil. 12°24N 125°3E 232 E5
Catumbela Angola 12°25S 13°34E 265 E2
Catumbela → Angola 12°29S 13°28E 265 E2
Catur Mozam. 13°45S 35°30E 269 E4
Catwick Is. = Hon Hai Vietnam 10°0N 109°0E 237 H7
Cauayan Isabela, Phil. 16°56N 121°46E 232 C3
Cauayan Neg. Occ., Phil. 9°58N 122°37E 233 G4
Cauca □ Colombia 2°30N 76°50W 328 C2
Cauca → Colombia 8°54N 74°28W 328 B3
Caucaia Brazil 3°40S 38°35W 332 B4
Caucasia Colombia 8°0N 75°12W 328 B2
Caucasus Mountains Eurasia 42°50N 44°0E 191 J7
Caudete Spain 38°42N 1°2W 197 G3
Caudry France 50°7N 3°22E 173 B10
Caulfield Australia 37°52S 145°1E 128 B2
Caulnes France 48°18N 2°10W 172 D4
Caulónia Italy 38°23N 16°24E 201 D9
Caungula Angola 8°26S 18°38E 265 D3
Cauquenes Chile 36°0S 72°22W 334 D1
Caura → Venezuela 7°38N 64°53W 329 B5
Caurés → Brazil 1°21S 62°20W 329 D5
Cauresi → Mozam. 17°8S 33°0E 269 F3
Căuşani Moldova 46°38N 29°25E 183 D14
Causapscal Canada 48°19N 67°12W 299 C6
Causeway Bay Hong Kong, China 122 c3
Caussade France 44°10N 1°33E 174 D5
Causse-Méjean France 44°18N 3°42E 174 D7
Causses du Quercy △ France 44°35N 1°35E 174 D5
Cauterets France 42°52N 0°8W 174 F3
Cauvery → India 11°9N 78°52E 245 J4
Caux, Pays de France 49°38N 0°35E 172 C7
Cava de' Tirreni Italy 40°42N 14°42E 201 B7
Cávado → Portugal 41°32N 8°48W 194 D2
Cavagrande del Cassibile △ Italy 36°58N 15°6E 201 F8
Cavaillon France 43°50N 5°2E 175 E9
Cavalaire-sur-Mer France 43°10N 6°33E 175 E10
Cavalcante Brazil 13°48S 47°30W 333 D2
Cavalese Italy 46°17N 11°27E 199 B8
Cavalier U.S.A. 48°48N 97°37W 308 A5
Cavalla = Cavally → Africa 4°22N 7°32W 262 E3
Cavalli Is. N.Z. 35°0S 173°58E 284 B2
Cavallo, Î. de France 41°22N 9°16E 175 G13
Cavally → Africa 4°22N 7°32W 262 E3
Cavan Ireland 54°0N 7°22W 166 B4
Cavan □ Ireland 54°1N 7°16W 166 C4
Cavárzere Italy 45°8N 12°5E 199 C9
Cavazzucherina = Iésolo Italy 45°32N 12°38E 199 C9
Çavdarhisar Turkey 39°12N 29°37E 205 B11
Çavdır Turkey 37°10N 29°42E 205 D11
Cave Creek U.S.A. 33°50N 111°57W 305 K8
Cave Run L. U.S.A. 38°5N 83°25W 311 F13
Cave Spring U.S.A. 34°6N 85°20W 316 A4
Cavenagh Ra. Australia 26°12S 127°55E 279 E4
Cavendish Australia 37°31S 142°2E 282 D5
Caviana, I. Brazil 0°10N 50°10W 329 C7
Cavite Phil. 14°29N 120°54E 127 C1
Cavite □ Phil. 14°15N 120°50E 232 D3
Caviúna = Rolândia Brazil 23°18S 51°23W 335 A5
Cavnic Romania 47°40N 23°52E 183 C8
Cavour Italy 44°47N 7°22E 198 D4
Cavtat Croatia 42°35N 18°13E 202 D2
Cawayan Phil. 11°56N 123°46E 233 F4
Cawayanon = Vintar Phil. 18°14N 120°39E 232 B3
Cawndilla L. Australia 32°30S 142°15E 282 B5
Cawnpore = Kanpur India 26°28N 80°20E 243 F9
Caxias Brazil 4°55S 43°20W 332 B3
Caxias Lisboa, Portugal 38°42N 9°16W 126 A1
Caxias do Sul Brazil 29°10S 51°10W 335 B5
Caxito Angola 8°30S 13°30E 265 D2
Caxopa Angola 11°52S 20°52E 265 E4
Çay Turkey 38°35N 31°1E 212 C4
Cay Pt. Bahamas 25°59N 77°25W 153 b
Cay Sal Bank Bahamas 23°45N 80°0W 320 B4
Cayambe Napo, Ecuador 0°2N 77°59W 328 C2
Cayambe Quito, Ecuador 0°3N 78°8W 328 C2
Cayce U.S.A. 33°58N 81°4W 316 B8
Çaycuma Turkey 41°25N 32°4E 212 B5
Çayeli Turkey 41°5N 40°45E 213 B9
Cayenne Fr. Guiana 5°5N 52°18W 329 B7
Cayenne □ Fr. Guiana 5°0N 53°0W 329 C7
Cayey Puerto Rico 18°7N 66°10W 321 b
Caygören Barajı Turkey 39°15N 28°12E 205 B10
Cayiralan Turkey 39°17N 35°38E 212 C6
Caylus France 44°15N 1°47E 174 D5
Cayman Brac Cayman Is. 19°43N 79°49W 320 C4
Cayman Is. ☑ W. Indies 19°40N 80°30W 320 C3
Cayman Trench Caribbean 17°0N 83°0W 320 C3
Cayman Trough Caribbean 19°0N 81°0W 292 H11
Cayon St. Kitts & Nevis 17°21N 62°52W 322 d
Cayres France 44°55N 3°48E 174 D7
Cayuga Ind., U.S.A. 39°57N 87°28W 311 E9
Cayuga N.Y., U.S.A. 42°54N 76°44W 313 D8
Cayuga L. U.S.A. 42°41N 76°41W 313 D8
Cazage Angola 11°2S 20°45E 265 E4
Cazalla de la Sierra Spain 37°56N 5°45W 195 H5
Căzăneşti Romania 44°36N 27°3E 183 F12
Cazaubon France 43°56N 0°3W 174 E3
Cazaux et de Sanguinet, Étang de France 44°29N 1°10W 174 D2
Cazenovia U.S.A. 42°56N 75°51W 313 D9
Cazères France 43°13N 1°5E 174 E5
Cazin Bos.-H. 44°57N 15°57E 199 D12
Čazma Croatia 45°45N 16°39E 199 C13
Cazombo Angola 11°54S 22°56E 265 E4
Cazorla Spain 37°55N 3°2W 195 H7
Cazorla, Sierra de Spain 38°5N 2°55W 195 G8
Cea → Spain 42°0N 5°36W 194 C5
Ceamurlia de Jos Romania 44°43N 28°47E 183 F13
Ceanannus Mor Ireland 53°44N 6°53W 166 C5
Ceará = Fortaleza Brazil 3°45S 38°35W 332 B4
Ceará □ Brazil 5°0S 40°0W 332 C4
Ceara Abyssal Plain Atl. Oc. 0°0 36°30W 152 F7
Ceará Mirim Brazil 5°38S 35°25W 332 C4
Ceara Rise Atl. Oc. 4°30N 43°30W 152 F7
Ceauru, L. Romania 44°58N 23°11E 183 F8
Cebaco, I. de Panama 7°33N 81°9W 320 E3
Cebeci Turkey 41°7N 28°52E 122 B1
Cebollar Argentina 29°10S 66°35W 334 B2
Cebollera, Sierra de Spain 42°0N 2°30W 196 D2
Cebreros Spain 40°27N 4°28W 194 E6
Cebu Phil. 10°18N 123°54E 233 F4
Cebu □ Phil. 10°20N 123°40E 233 F4
Čečava Bos.-H. 44°42N 17°44E 182 F2
Ceccano Italy 41°34N 13°20E 200 A6
Cecchignola Italy 41°48N 12°29E 136 C2
Cece Hungary 46°46N 18°39E 182 D3
Cechi Ivory C. 6°15N 4°25W 262 D4
Cecil Plains Australia 27°30S 151°11E 281 D5
Cecilienhof, Schloss Germany 52°35N 13°5E 115 B1
Cécina Italy 43°19N 10°31E 198 E7
Cécina → Italy 43°18N 10°29E 198 E7
Ceclavín Spain 39°50N 6°45W 194 F4
Cedar → U.S.A. 41°17N 91°21W 310 C5
Cedar City U.S.A. 37°41N 113°4W 305 H7
Cedar Creek Res. U.S.A. 32°11N 96°4W 314 E6
Cedar Falls Iowa, U.S.A. 42°32N 92°27W 310 B4
Cedar Falls Wash., U.S.A. 47°25N 121°45W 306 C5
Cedar Grove Georgia, U.S.A. 33°40N 84°16W 113 C3
Cedar Grove Ind., U.S.A. 39°22N 84°56W 311 E12
Cedar Key U.S.A. 29°8N 83°2W 317 G6
Cedar L. Canada 53°10N 100°0W 297 C9
Cedar Lake U.S.A. 41°22N 87°26W 311 C9
Cedar Park U.S.A. 30°30N 97°49W 314 F6
Cedar Point U.S.A. 41°44N 83°21W 311 C13
Cedar Rapids U.S.A. 41°59N 91°40W 310 C5
Cedar Tree Pt. Antigua & B. 17°42N 61°53W 322 c
Cedartown U.S.A. 34°1N 85°15W 316 A4
Cedarvale Canada 55°1N 128°22W 296 B3
Cedarvale Park Canada 43°42N 79°36W 141 A2
Cedarville KwaZulu Natal, S. Africa 30°23S 29°3E 271 D4
Cedarville Ill., U.S.A. 42°23N 89°38W 310 B7
Cedarville Ohio, U.S.A. 39°44N 83°49W 311 E13
Cedeira Spain 43°39N 8°2W 194 B2
Cedral Mexico 23°50N 100°45W 318 C4
Cedrino → Italy 40°11N 9°24E 200 B2
Cedro Brazil 6°34S 39°3W 332 C4
Cedros Azores 38°38N 28°42W 153 d1
Cedros, I. Mexico 28°12N 115°15W 318 B1
Cedros B. Trin. & Tob. 10°16N 61°54W 323 t
Cedros Pt. Trin. & Tob. 10°7N 61°49W 323 t
Ceduna Australia 32°7S 133°46E 281 E1
Cedynia Poland 52°53N 14°12E 185 F1
Cée Spain 42°57N 9°10W 194 C1
Ceel Dheere = El Dere Somali Rep. 5°22N 46°11E 267 C6
Ceerigaabo = Erigavo Somali Rep. 10°35N 47°20E 267 B6
Cefalù Italy 38°2N 14°1E 201 D7
Cega → Spain 41°33N 4°46W 194 D6
Cegléd Hungary 47°11N 19°47E 182 C4
Céglie Messápico Italy 40°39N 17°31E 201 B10
Cehegín Spain 38°6N 1°48W 197 G3
Ceheng China 24°58N 105°48E 228 E5
Cehu-Silvaniei Romania 47°24N 23°9E 183 C8
Ceiba Puerto Rico 18°16N 65°39W 321 b
Ceica Romania 46°53N 22°10E 182 D7
Ceira → Portugal 40°13N 8°16W 194 E2
Cekik Indonesia 8°12S 114°27E 231 J17
Cela Angola 11°25S 15°7E 265 E3
Čelákovice Czech Rep. 50°10N 14°46E 180 A7
Celano Italy 42°5N 13°33E 199 F10
Celanova Spain 42°9N 7°58W 194 C3
Celaque △ Honduras 14°30N 88°43W 320 D2
Celaya Mexico 20°31N 100°37W 318 C4
Celebes = Sulawesi Indonesia 2°0S 120°0E 231 E6
Celebes Sea Indonesia 3°0N 123°0E 231 D6
Celendín Peru 6°52S 78°10W 330 B2
Čelić Bos.-H. 44°43N 18°49E 182 F3
Celica Ecuador 4°7S 79°59W 328 D2
Celina U.S.A. 40°33N 84°35W 311 D12
Celinac Bos.-H. 44°44N 17°22E 182 F2
Celje Slovenia 46°16N 15°18E 199 B12
Celldömölk Hungary 47°16N 17°10E 182 C2
Celle Germany 52°37N 10°4E 178 C6
Celorico da Beira Portugal 40°38N 7°24W 194 E3
Celtic Sea Atl. Oc. 50°9N 9°34W 165 F2
Çeltikçi Turkey 37°32N 30°29E 205 D12
Çemişgezek Turkey 39°3N 38°56E 213 C8
Cempaka Putih Indonesia 6°10S 106°51E 122 B2
Cenderwasih, Teluk Indonesia 3°0S 135°20E 231 E9
Cenepa → Peru 4°40S 78°10W 328 D2
Çengelköy Turkey 41°2N 29°3E 122 B2
Cengkareng Indonesia 6°9S 106°45E 122 A1
Cengong China 27°13N 108°44E 228 D7
Ceno → Italy 44°43N 10°5E 198 D7
Centallo Italy 44°30N 7°35E 198 D4
Centelles Spain 41°50N 2°14E 196 D7
Centenário do Sul Brazil 22°48S 51°36W 333 F1
Centennial Olympic Park U.S.A. 33°46N 84°23W 113 B2
Centennial Park Australia 33°53S 151°14E 139 B2
Center N. Dak., U.S.A. 47°7N 101°18W 308 B3
Center Tex., U.S.A. 31°48N 94°11W 314 F7
Center Hill Fla., U.S.A. 28°38N 82°3W 317 G7
Center Hill Georgia, U.S.A. 33°46N 84°29W 113 B2
Center Point U.S.A. 42°12N 91°46W 310 B5
Centerburg U.S.A. 40°18N 82°42W 312 F2
Centerville Calif., U.S.A. 36°44N 119°30W 306 J7
Centerville Iowa, U.S.A. 40°44N 92°52W 310 D4
Centerville Ohio, U.S.A. 39°38N 84°8W 311 E12
Centerville Pa., U.S.A. 40°3N 79°59W 312 F5
Centerville Tenn., U.S.A. 35°47N 87°28W 315 D11
Centerville Tex., U.S.A. 31°16N 95°59W 314 F7
Cento Italy 44°43N 11°17E 199 D8
Centocelle Italy 41°52N 12°34E 136 B2
Centraal Station Amsterdam, Neths. 112 a2
Central = Tsentralnyy □ Russia 52°0N 40°0E 190 D4
Central Brazil 11°8S 42°8W 332 D3
Central Alaska, U.S.A. 65°35N 144°48W 303 D11
Central □ Ghana 5°30N 1°0W 263 D4
Central □ Kenya 0°30S 37°30E 268 C4
Central □ Malawi 13°30S 33°30E 269 E3
Central □ Papua N. G. 10°0S 148°0E 286 F5
Central □ Zambia 14°25S 28°50E 269 E2
Central, Cordillera Bolivia 18°30S 64°55W 331 D5
Central, Cordillera Colombia 5°0N 75°0W 328 C3
Central, Cordillera Costa Rica 10°10N 84°5W 320 D3
Central, Cordillera Dom. Rep. 19°15N 71°0W 321 C5
Central, Cordillera Peru 7°0S 77°30W 330 B2
Central, Cordillera Phil. 17°20N 120°57E 232 C3
Central, Cordillera Puerto Rico 18°8N 66°35W 321 b
Central, Gare Montréal, Canada 130 c2
Central African Empire = Central African Rep. ■ Africa 7°0N 20°0E 264 A4
Central African Rep. ■ Africa 7°0N 20°0E 264 A4
Central America America 12°0N 85°0W 292 H11
Central Butte Canada 50°48N 106°31W 297 C7
Central City Colo., U.S.A. 39°48N 105°31W 304 G11
Central City Iowa, U.S.A. 42°12N 91°32W 310 B5
Central City Ky., U.S.A. 37°18N 87°7W 308 G10
Central City Nebr., U.S.A. 41°7N 98°0W 308 E4
Central I. Kenya 3°30N 36°0E 268 B4
Central Island △ Kenya 2°33N 36°1E 268 B4
Central Japan Int. ✈ (CJI) Japan 34°53N 136°45E 223 C8
Central Kalahari △ Botswana 22°36S 23°58E 270 B3
Central Makran Range Pakistan 26°30N 64°15E 240 D2
Central Pacific Basin Pac. Oc. 8°0N 175°0W 288 G10
Central Park New York, U.S.A. 132 a3
Central Park Zoo New York, U.S.A. 132 b2
Central Patricia Canada 51°30N 90°9W 298 B1
Central Point U.S.A. 42°23N 122°55W 304 E2
Central Provinces = Madhya Pradesh □ India 22°50N 78°0E 242 J8
Central Ra. Papua N. G. 5°0S 143°0E 286 C2
Central Range Trin. & Tob. 10°25N 61°15W 323 t
Central Range Wildlife Sanctuary Trin. & Tob. 10°27N 61°14W 323 t
Central Russian Uplands Europe 54°0N 36°0E 158 E13
Central Siberian Plateau Russia 65°0N 105°0E 210 B12
Central Square U.S.A. 43°17N 76°9W 313 C8
Central Village Jamaica 17°59N 76°55W 320 a
Centralia Ill., U.S.A. 38°32N 89°8W 310 F7
Centralia Mo., U.S.A. 39°13N 92°8W 310 E4
Centralia Wash., U.S.A. 46°43N 122°58W 306 D4
Centre U.S.A. 34°9N 85°41W 316 A4
Centre □ Cameroon 4°45N 12°0E 263 E7
Centre de Flacq Mauritius 20°12S 57°43E 272 e
Centreville U.S.A. 41°55N 85°32W 311 C11
Century U.S.A. 30°58N 87°16W 317 E2
Cenxi China 22°57N 110°57E 229 F8
Ceotina → Bos.-H. 43°36N 18°50E 202 C2
Cephalonia = Kefalonia Greece 38°15N 20°30E 207 C2
Čepin Croatia 45°32N 18°34E 182 E3
Ceprano Italy 41°33N 13°31E 200 A6
Ceptia Angola 12°56S 17°35E 265 E3
Ceptura Romania 45°1N 26°21E 183 E11
Cepu Indonesia 7°9S 111°35E 235 D4
Ceram = Seram Indonesia 3°10S 129°0E 231 E7
Ceram Sea = Seram Sea Indonesia 2°30S 128°30E 231 E7
Cerbère France 42°26N 3°10E 174 F7
Cerbicales, Îs. France 41°33N 9°22E 175 G13
Cercal Portugal 37°48N 8°40W 195 H2
Cerdaña Spain 42°22N 1°35E 196 C6
Cerdanyola del Vallès Spain 41°27N 2°8W 114 A1
Cère → France 44°55N 1°49E 174 D5
Cerea Italy 45°12N 11°13E 199 C8
Ceredigion □ U.K. 52°16N 4°15W 169 E3
Ceres Argentina 29°55S 61°55W 334 B3
Ceres Brazil 15°17S 49°35W 333 E2
Ceres Western Cape, S. Africa 33°21S 19°18E 270 D2
Ceres Calif., U.S.A. 37°35N 120°57W 306 H6
Céret France 42°30N 2°42E 174 F6
Cereté Colombia 8°53N 75°48W 328 B2
Cerf Seychelles 4°38S 55°40E 272 c
Cerfs, Îs. aux Mauritius 20°16S 57°47E 272 e
Cergy France 49°2N 2°4E 173 C9
Cerignola Italy 41°17N 15°53E 201 A8
Cerigo = Kythira Greece 36°8N 23°0E 204 E5
Cerillos Chile 33°29S 70°42W 137 B1
Cérilly France 46°37N 2°50E 173 F9
Cerisiers France 48°8N 3°30E 173 D10
Cerizay France 46°50N 0°40W 172 F6
Çerkeş Turkey 40°49N 32°52E 212 B5
Çerkezköy Turkey 41°17N 28°0E 203 E12
Cerknica Slovenia 45°48N 14°21E 199 C11
Cerkovica Bulgaria 43°41N 24°50E 203 C8
Cermerno Serbia 43°35N 20°25E 202 C4
Çermik Turkey 38°8N 39°26E 213 C8
Cerna Romania 45°4N 28°17E 183 E13
Cerna → Romania 44°38N 23°48E 183 F8
Cernauti = Chernivtsi Ukraine 48°15N 25°52E 183 B10
Cernavodă Romania 44°22N 28°3E 183 F13
Cernay France 47°44N 7°10E 173 E14
Cernik Croatia 45°17N 17°22E 182 E2
Cerralvo, I. Mexico 24°15N 109°55W 318 C3
Cërrik Albania 41°2N 19°58E 202 E3
Cerritos Mexico 22°25N 100°16W 318 C4
Cerro Chato Uruguay 33°6S 55°8W 335 C4
Cerro Cofre de Perote △ Mexico 19°29N 97°8W 319 D5
Cerro Corá △ Paraguay 22°35S 56°2W 335 A4
Cerro de la Estrella, Parque Nacional △ Mexico 19°23N 99°5W 128 B2
Cerro de los Angeles Spain 40°18N 3°41W 127 C1
Cerro Gordo U.S.A. 39°53N 88°44W 311 E8
Cerro Hoyo △ Panama 7°17N 80°45W 320 E3
Cerro Navia Chile 33°25S 70°42W 137 B1
Cerro Sombrero Chile 52°45S 69°15W 336 D3
Certaldo Italy 43°33N 11°2E 198 E8
Cervantes Phil. 17°0N 120°44E 232 C3
Cervaro → Italy 41°30N 15°52E 201 A8
Cervati, Monte Italy 40°17N 15°29E 201 B8
Cerventes Australia 30°31S 115°3E 279 F2
Cervera Spain 41°40N 1°16E 196 D6
Cervera de Pisuerga Spain 42°51N 4°30W 194 C6
Cervera del Río Alhama Spain 42°2N 1°58W 196 C3
Cervéteri Italy 42°0N 12°6E 199 F9
Cérvia Italy 44°15N 12°22E 199 D9
Cervignano del Friuli Italy 45°49N 13°20E 199 C10
Cervinara Italy 41°1N 14°37E 201 A7
Cervione France 42°20N 9°29E 175 F13
Cervo Spain 43°40N 7°24W 194 B3
Cesano Boscone Italy 45°26N 9°5E 129 B1
César □ Colombia 9°0N 73°30W 328 B3
Cesarò Italy 37°50N 14°38E 201 E7
Cesate Italy 45°35N 9°4E 129 A1

Cesena Italy 44°8N 12°15E 199 D9
Cesenático Italy 44°12N 12°24E 199 D9
Cēsis Latvia 57°18N 25°15E 188 D3
Česká Lipa Czech Rep. 50°45N 14°30E 180 A7
Ceská Rep. = Czech Rep. ■ Europe 50°0N 15°0E 180 B8
Česká Třebová Czech Rep. 49°54N 16°27E 181 B9
České Budějovice Czech Rep. 48°55N 14°25E 180 C7
České Velenice Czech Rep. 48°45N 14°57E 180 C7
Českobudějovický □ Czech Rep. 49°10N 14°30E 180 B7
Českomoravská Vrchovina Czech Rep. 49°30N 15°40E 180 B8
Český Brod Czech Rep. 50°4N 14°52E 180 A7
Český Krumlov Czech Rep. 48°43N 14°21E 180 C7
Český Těšín Czech Rep. 49°45N 18°39E 181 B11
Česma → Croatia 45°35N 16°29E 199 C13
Çeşme Turkey 38°20N 26°23E 205 C8
Cessnock Australia 32°50S 151°21E 283 B9
Cesson-Sévigné France 48°7N 1°36W 172 D5
Cestas France 44°44N 0°41W 174 D3
Cestos → Liberia 5°40N 9°10W 262 D3
Cestos Sehnkwehn △ Liberia 5°40N 9°10W 262 D3
Cetate Romania 44°7N 23°2E 182 F8
Cetatea-Albă = Bilhorod-Dnistrovskyy Ukraine 46°11N 30°23E 189 J6
Cetin Grad Croatia 45°9N 15°45E 199 C12
Cetina → Croatia 43°26N 16°42E 199 E13
Cetinje Montenegro 42°23N 18°59E 202 D2
Çetmi Turkey 36°52N 32°38E 250 B3
Cetraro Italy 39°31N 15°55E 201 C8
Ceuta N. Afr. 35°52N 5°18W 260 A3
Ceva Italy 44°23N 8°2E 198 D5
Ceve-i-Ra Fiji 21°46S 174°31E 277 E13
Cévennes France 44°10N 3°50E 174 D7
Cévennes △ France 44°15N 3°45E 174 D7
Ceyhan Turkey 37°4N 35°47E 250 A6
Ceyhan → Turkey 36°38N 35°40E 250 B6
Ceylânpınar Turkey 36°50N 40°2E 213 D9
Ceylon = Sri Lanka ■ Asia 7°30N 80°50E 245 L5
Ceylon Plain Ind. Oc. 4°0S 82°0E 273 E7
Cèze → France 44°6N 4°43E 175 D8
Cha-am Thailand 12°48N 99°58E 236 F2
Cha Kwo Ling China 22°18N 114°13E 122 B2
Cha Pa Vietnam 22°20N 103°47E 236 A4
Chá Pungana Angola 13°44S 18°39E 265 E3
Chabanais France 45°52N 0°48E 174 C4
Chabeuil France 44°54N 5°3E 175 D9
Chablais France 46°20N 6°36E 173 F13
Chablis France 47°47N 3°48E 173 E10
Chabounia Algeria 35°30N 2°38E 261 A5
Chacabuco Argentina 34°40S 60°27W 334 C3
Chacachacare I. Trin. & Tob. 10°41N 61°45W 323 t
Chacarrita Argentina 34°35S 58°27W 117 B2
Chachapoyas Peru 6°15S 77°50W 330 B2
Chachasp Peru 15°30S 72°15W 330 D3
Chachoengsao Thailand 13°42N 101°5E 236 F3
Chachran Pakistan 28°55N 70°30E 242 E4
Chachro Pakistan 25°5N 70°15E 242 G4
Chaco □ Argentina 26°30S 61°0W 334 B3
Chaco □ Paraguay 26°0S 60°0W 334 B4
Chaco → U.S.A. 36°46N 108°39W 305 H9
Chaco △ Argentina 27°0S 59°30W 334 B4
Chaco Culture ⌂ U.S.A. 36°3N 107°58W 305 H10
Chacon, C. U.S.A. 54°42N 132°0W 296 C2
Chad ■ Africa 15°0N 17°15E 259 F3
Chad, L. = Tchad, L. Chad 13°30N 14°30E 259 F2
Chadan Russia 51°17N 91°35E 215 D10
Chadileuvú → Argentina 37°46S 66°0W 334 D2
Chadiza Zambia 14°45S 32°27E 269 E3
Chadron U.S.A. 42°50N 103°0W 308 D2
Chadwell Heath U.K. 51°34N 0°8E 125 A4
Chadyr-Lunga = Ciadâr-Lunga Moldova 46°3N 28°51E 183 D13
Chae Hom Thailand 18°43N 99°35E 236 C2
Chae Son △ Thailand 18°42N 99°20E 236 C2
Chaem → Thailand 18°11N 98°38E 236 C2
Chaeryŏng N. Korea 38°24N 125°36E 224 C2
Chagai Hills = Chāh Gay Hills Afghan. 29°30N 64°0E 240 C2
Chagang-do □ N. Korea 40°50N 126°30E 224 B3
Chagda Russia 58°45N 130°38E 215 D14
Chagdo Kangri China 34°15N 84°10E 217 F10
Chaghcharān Afghan. 34°31N 65°15E 240 B2
Chagny France 46°57N 4°45E 173 F11
Chagoda Russia 59°10N 35°15E 188 C8
Chagos Arch. ☒ Ind. Oc. 6°0S 72°0E 210 J9
Chagos-Laccadive Ridge Ind. Oc. 3°0N 73°0E 273 D6
Chagrin Falls U.S.A. 41°26N 81°24W 312 E3
Chaguanas Trin. & Tob. 10°30N 61°26W 323 t
Chaguaramas Trin. & Tob. 10°41N 61°38W 323 t
Chāh Ākhvor Iran 32°41N 59°40E 247 C8
Chāh Bahar Iran 25°20N 60°40E 247 E9
Chāh-e Āb Afghan. 37°23N 69°48E 240 A3
Chāh-e Kavīr Iran 34°29N 56°52E 247 C8
Chāh Gay Hills Afghan. 29°30N 64°0E 240 C2
Chahār Borjak Afghan. 30°17N 62°3E 240 C1
Chahār Mahāll va Bakhtīarī □ Iran 32°0N 49°0E 247 C6
Chahtung Burma 26°41N 98°10E 241 B7
Chai Chee Singapore 1°19N 103°46E 138 B3
Chai Wan China 22°16N 114°14E 122 B2
Chai Wan Kok China 22°22N 114°6E 122 A1
Chaibasa India 22°42N 85°49E 243 H11
Chaillé-les-Marais France 46°25N 1°2W 174 B2
Chaillot, Palais de Paris, France 134 b2
Chain Ridge Ind. Oc. 6°0N 54°0E 273 D4
Chainat Thailand 15°11N 100°8E 236 E3
Chaires U.S.A. 30°26N 84°7W 316 E5
Chaitén Chile 42°55S 72°43W 336 B2
Chaiya Thailand 9°23N 99°14E 237 H2
Chaiyaphum Thailand 15°48N 102°2E 236 E4
Chaj Doab Pakistan 32°15N 73°0E 242 C5
Chajari Argentina 30°42S 58°0W 334 C4
Chak Amru Pakistan 32°22N 75°11E 242 C6
Chaka Sudan 4°49N 31°14E 257 G3
Chakar → Pakistan 29°29N 68°2E 242 E3
Chakari Zimbabwe 18°5S 29°51E 271 A4
Chakaria Bangla. 21°45N 92°5E 241 E4
Chakarnaba Chad 14°13N 20°51E 259 F4
Chakdaha India 22°28N 88°19E 124 C1
Chake Chake Tanzania 5°15S 39°45E 268 D4
Chakhānsūr Afghan. 31°10N 62°0E 240 C1
Chakonipau, L. Canada 56°18N 68°30W 299 A6
Chakradharpur India 22°45N 85°40E 243 H11
Chakrata India 30°42N 77°51E 242 D7
Chakwadam Burma 27°29N 98°31E 241 B7
Chakwal Pakistan 32°56N 72°53E 242 C5
Chala Peru 15°48S 74°20W 330 D3
Chalais France 45°16N 0°3E 174 C4
Chalakudi India 10°18N 76°20E 245 J3
Chalan Kanoa N. Marianas 15°9N 145°42E 302 e
Chalchihuites Mexico 23°29N 103°53W 318 C4
Chalcis = Halkida Greece 38°27N 23°42E 204 C5
Châlette-sur-Loing France 48°1N 2°44E 173 D9
Chaleur B. Canada 47°55N 65°30W 299 C6
Chalfant U.S.A. 37°32N 118°21W 306 H8
Chalhuanca Peru 14°15S 73°15W 330 C3
Chaliki Greece 39°36N 22°30E 204 B4
Chalindrey France 47°43N 5°26E 173 E12
Chaling China 26°58N 113°30E 229 D9
Chalisgaon India 20°30N 75°10E 244 D2
Chalk River Canada 46°1N 77°27W 298 C4
Chalky Inlet N.Z. 46°3S 166°31E 285 G1
Chalkyitsik U.S.A. 66°39N 143°43W 303 C12
Challakere India 14°19N 76°39E 245 G3
Challans France 46°50N 1°52W 172 F5
Challapata Bolivia 18°53S 66°50W 330 D4
Challenger Deep Pac. Oc. 11°30N 142°0E 288 F6
Challenger Fracture Zone Pac. Oc. 35°0S 105°0W 289 L17
Challis U.S.A. 44°30N 114°14W 304 D6
Chalmette U.S.A. 29°56N 89°57W 315 G10
Chalon-sur-Saône France 46°48N 4°50E 173 F11
Chalonnes-sur-Loire France 47°20N 0°45W 172 E6
Châlons-en-Champagne France 48°58N 4°20E 173 D11
Chálten, Cerro = Fitz Roy, Cerro Argentina 49°17S 73°5W 336 C2
Châlus Haute-Vienne, France 45°39N 0°58E 174 C4
Chālūs Iran 36°38N 51°26E 247 B6
Cham Germany 49°13N 12°39E 179 F8
Cham, Cu Lao Vietnam 15°57N 108°30E 236 E7
Chama U.S.A. 36°54N 106°35W 305 H10
Chamah, Gunong Malaysia 5°13N 101°35E 237 K3
Chamaicó Argentina 35°3S 64°58W 334 D3
Chaman Pakistan 30°58N 66°25E 240 C2
Chamartin Spain 40°27N 3°40W 127 B1
Chamba India 32°35N 76°10E 242 C7
Chamba Tanzania 11°37S 37°0E 269 E4
Chambal → India 26°29N 79°15E 243 F8
Chamberí Spain 40°26N 3°42W 127 B1
Chamberlain U.S.A. 43°49N 99°20W 308 D4
Chamberlain → Australia 15°30S 127°54E 278 C4
Chamberlain L. U.S.A. 46°14N 69°19W 309 B19
Chambers U.S.A. 35°11N 109°26W 305 J9
Chambersburg U.S.A. 39°56N 77°40W 309 F15
Chambéry France 45°34N 5°55E 175 C9
Chamblee U.S.A. 33°53N 84°18W 316 B5
Chambly Canada 45°27N 73°17W 313 A11
Chambord Canada 48°25N 72°6W 299 C5
Chamboulive France 45°26N 1°42E 174 C5
Chambourcy France 48°54N 2°2E 134 A1
Chambri L. Papua N. G. 4°15S 143°10E 286 C2
Chamchamal Iraq 35°32N 44°50E 213 E11
Chamela Mexico 19°32N 105°5W 318 D3
Chamical Argentina 30°22S 66°27W 334 C2
Chamkar Luong Cambodia 11°0N 103°45E 237 G4
Chamois U.S.A. 38°41N 91°46W 310 F5
Chamoli India 30°24N 79°21E 243 D8
Chamonix-Mont Blanc France 45°55N 6°51E 175 C10
Champ de Mars, Parc du Paris, France 134 c2
Champa India 22°2N 82°43E 243 H10
Champagne Canada 60°49N 136°30W 296 A1
Champagne France 48°40N 4°20E 173 D11
Champagnole France 46°45N 5°55E 173 F12
Champaign U.S.A. 40°7N 88°15W 311 D8
Champassak Laos 14°53N 105°52E 236 E5
Champaubert France 48°50N 3°45E 173 D10
Champawat India 29°20N 80°6E 243 E9
Champdeniers-St-Denis France 46°29N 0°25W 174 B3
Champdoré, L. Canada 55°55N 65°49W 299 A6
Champeix France 45°37N 3°8E 174 C7
Champigny-sur-Marne France 48°49N 2°30E 134 B4
Champion U.S.A. 41°19N 80°51W 312 E4
Champlain U.S.A. 44°59N 73°27W 313 B11
Champlain, L. U.S.A. 44°40N 73°20W 313 B11
Champlain, Pont Canada 45°28N 73°31W 130 B2
Champlitte France 47°32N 5°31E 173 E12
Champotón Mexico 19°21N 90°43W 319 D6
Champs Elysées, Avenue des Paris, France 134 b2
Champs-sur-Marne France 48°50N 2°34E 134 A4
Champua India 22°5N 85°40E 243 H11
Chamrail India 22°38N 88°17E 124 B1
Chamrajnagar India 11°52N 76°52E 245 J3
Chamusca Portugal 39°21N 8°29W 195 F2
Chan Chan Peru 8°7S 79°0W 330 B2
Chana Thailand 6°55N 100°44E 237 J3
Chanakyapuri India 28°35N 77°11E 120 B2
Chañaral Chile 26°23S 70°40W 334 B1
Chanārān Iran 36°39N 59°6E 247 B8
Chanasma India 23°44N 72°5E 242 H5
Chancay Peru 11°32S 77°25W 330 C2
Chancel, Î. Martinique 14°41N 60°53W 322 j
Chanchiang = Zhanjiang China 21°15N 110°20E 229 G8
Chanco Chile 35°44S 72°32W 334 D1
Chand India 21°57N 79°7E 243 J8
Chandalar → U.S.A. 66°37N 146°0W 303 C11
Chandan India 24°38N 86°40E 243 G12
Chandan Chauki India 28°33N 80°47E 243 E9
Chandannagar India 22°52N 88°24E 243 H13
Chandausi India 28°27N 78°49E 243 E8
Chandeleur Is. U.S.A. 29°55N 88°57W 315 G10
Chandeleur Sd. U.S.A. 29°55N 89°0W 315 G10
Chandigarh India 30°43N 76°47E 242 D7
Chandil India 22°58N 86°3E 243 H12
Chanditala India 22°41N 88°15E 124 A1
Chandler S. Austral., Australia 27°0S 133°19E 281 D1
Chandler Qué., Canada 48°18N 64°46W 299 C7
Chandler Ariz., U.S.A. 33°18N 111°50W 305 K8
Chandler Okla., U.S.A. 35°42N 96°53W 314 D6
Chandless → Brazil 9°8S 69°51W 330 B4
Chandod India 21°59N 73°28E 242 J5
Chandpur Bangla. 23°8N 90°45E 241 D3
Chandra Greece 35°3N 26°8E 205 F8
Chandragiri India 13°35N 79°19E 245 H4
Chandrapur India 19°57N 79°25E 244 E4
Chandrupatla India 18°33N 80°24E 244 E5
Chānf Iran 26°38N 60°29E 247 E9
Chang Pakistan 26°59N 68°30E 242 F3
Chang, Ko Thailand 12°0N 102°23E 237 G4
Ch'ang Chiang = Chang Jiang → China 31°48N 121°10E 229 B13
Chang Jiang → China 31°48N 121°10E 229 B13
Chang-won S. Korea 35°16N 128°37E 224 E4
Changa India 33°53N 77°35E 243 C7
Changan China 22°48N 113°48E 219 F10
Changanacheri India 9°25N 76°31E 245 K3
Changane → Mozam. 24°30S 33°30E 271 B5
Changbai China 41°25N 128°5E 224 B4
Changbai Shan China 42°20N 129°0E 224 A4
Changchiak'ou = Zhangjiakou China 40°48N 114°55E 226 D8
Changchih = Changzhi China 36°10N 113°6E 226 F7
Changchih Taiwan 22°41N 120°32E 225 D2
Ch'angchou = Changzhou China 31°47N 119°58E 229 B12
Changchow = Changzhou China 31°47N 119°58E 229 B12
Changchun China 43°57N 125°17E 227 C13
Changchunling China 45°18N 125°27E 227 B13
Changde China 29°4N 111°35E 229 C8
Changdo-ri N. Korea 38°30N 127°40E 224 C3
Changfeng China 32°28N 117°10E 229 A11
Changfeng Park China 31°14N 121°24E 138 B1
Changhai = Shanghai China 31°15N 121°26E 138 B2
Changhua Zhejiang, China 30°12N 119°12E 229 B12
Changhua Taiwan 24°2N 120°30E 225 B2
Changhua □ Taiwan 24°15N 120°55E 225 B2
Changhŭngni N. Korea 40°24N 128°19E 224 B4
Changi Singapore 1°23N 103°59E 138 A3
Changi, Singapore ✈ (SIN) Singapore 1°23N 103°59E 138 A3
Changji China 44°1N 87°19E 217 D11
Changjiang China 19°20N 108°55E 236 C7
Changjiang Shuiku China 22°29N 113°27E 219 G10
Changjin N. Korea 40°23N 127°15E 224 B3
Changjin-ho N. Korea 40°30N 127°15E 224 B3
Changle China 25°59N 119°27E 229 E12
Changli China 39°40N 119°13E 227 E10
Changling China 44°20N 123°58E 227 B12
Changlun Malaysia 6°25N 100°26E 237 J3
Changning Hunan, China 26°28N 112°22E 229 D9
Changning Shanghai, China 31°13N 121°24E 138 B1
Changning Sichuan, China 28°40N 104°56E 228 C5
Changning Yunnan, China 24°45N 99°30E 228 E2
Ch'angpin Taiwan 23°19N 121°27E 225 C3
Changping China 40°14N 116°12E 226 D9
Changsha China 28°12N 113°0E 229 C9
Changshan China 28°55N 118°27E 229 C12
Changshan Qundao China 39°11N 122°32E 227 E12
Changshu China 31°38N 120°43E 229 B13
Changshun China 26°3N 106°25E 228 D6
Changtai China 24°35N 117°42E 229 E11
Changt'e = Chongde China 30°32N 120°26E 229 B13
Changting China 25°50N 116°22E 229 E11
Changwu China 35°10N 107°45E 226 G4
Changxing China 31°0N 119°55E 229 B12
Changyang China 30°30N 111°10E 229 B8
Changyi China 36°40N 119°30E 227 F10
Changyŏn N. Korea 38°15N 125°6E 224 C2
Changyuan Henan, China 35°15N 114°42E 226 G8
Changyuan Taiwan 23°25N 121°29E 225 C3
Changzhi China 36°10N 113°6E 226 F7
Changzhou China 31°47N 119°58E 229 B12
Chanhanga Angola 16°0S 14°8E 265 F2
Chania Greece 35°30N 24°4E 207 E5
Chania □ Greece 35°30N 24°0E 207 E5
Chania ✈ (CHQ) Greece 35°30N 24°6E 207 E5
Chanion, Kolpos Greece 35°33N 23°55E 207 E4
Chanlar = Xanlar Azerbaijan 40°37N 46°12E 191 K8
Channagiri India 14°2N 75°56E 245 G2
Channapatna India 12°40N 77°15E 245 H3
Channel Is. U.K. 49°19N 2°24W 169 H5
Channel Is. Calif., U.S.A. 33°40N 119°15W 307 M7
Channel Islands △ U.S.A. 34°0N 119°24W 307 L7
Channel-Port aux Basques Canada 47°30N 59°9W 299 C8
Channel Tunnel Europe 51°0N 1°30E 169 F9
Channing U.S.A. 35°41N 102°20W 314 D3
Chantada Spain 42°36N 7°46W 194 C3
Chantereine France 48°53N 2°37E 134 A4
Chanthaburi Thailand 12°38N 102°12E 236 F4
Chantian China 23°12N 113°16E 121 A2
Chantilly France 49°12N 2°29E 173 C9
Chantonnay France 46°40N 1°3W 172 F5
Chantrey Inlet Canada 67°48N 96°20W 294 C10
Chanumla India 8°19N 93°5E 245 K11
Chanute U.S.A. 37°41N 95°27W 308 G6
Chany, Ozero Russia 54°49N 77°29E 217 B9
Chanza → Spain 37°32N 7°30W 195 H3
Chao Hu China 31°30N 117°30E 229 B11
Chao Phraya → Thailand 13°40N 100°31E 236 F3
Chao Phraya Lowlands Thailand 15°30N 100°0E 236 E3
Chaocheng China 36°4N 115°37E 226 F8
Ch'aochou Taiwan 22°33N 120°32E 225 D2
Chaohu China 31°38N 117°50E 229 B11
Chaoyang Beijing, China 39°53N 116°26E 114 B2
Chaoyang Guangdong, China 23°17N 116°30E 229 F11
Chaoyang Liaoning, China 41°35N 120°22E 227 D11
Chaoyangmen China 39°54N 116°23E 114 B2
Chaozhou China 23°42N 116°32E 229 F11
Chapada Diamantina △ Brazil 12°52S 41°30W 333 D3
Chapada dos Guimarães Brazil 15°26S 55°45W 331 D6
Chapada dos Guimarães △ Brazil 15°18S 55°54W 331 D6
Chapada dos Veadeiros △ Brazil 14°0S 47°30W 333 D2
Chapais Canada 49°47N 74°51W 298 C5
Chapala Mozam. 15°50S 37°35E 269 F4
Chapala, L. de Mexico 20°15N 103°0W 318 C4
Chaparé → Bolivia 15°58S 64°42W 331 D5
Chaparmukh India 26°12N 92°31E 241 B4
Chaparral Colombia 3°43N 75°28W 328 C2
Chapayev Kazakhstan 50°25N 51°10E 190 E10
Chapayevsk Russia 53°0N 49°40E 190 D9
Chapecó Brazil 27°14S 52°41W 335 B5
Chapel Hill U.S.A. 35°55N 79°4W 315 D15
Chapelizod Ireland 53°21N 6°21W 120 A1
Chapelton Jamaica 18°5N 77°16W 320 a
Chapin = Edinburg U.S.A. 26°18N 98°10W 314 H5
Chapin U.S.A. 39°46N 90°24W 310 E6
Chapleau Canada 47°50N 83°24W 298 C3
Chaplin Canada 50°28N 106°40W 297 C7
Chaplin L. Canada 50°22N 106°36W 297 C7
Chaplino Ukraine 48°8N 36°15E 189 H9
Chaplygin Russia 53°15N 40°0E 188 F11
Chappell U.S.A. 41°6N 102°28W 308 E2
Chappells U.S.A. 34°11N 81°52W 316 A8
Chapra = Chhapra India 25°48N 84°44E 243 G11
Chapultepec, Bosque de Mexico 19°25N 99°11W 128 B1
Chapultepec, Castillo de Mexico 19°25N 99°10W 128 B1
Châr Mauritania 21°32N 12°45W 260 D2
Chara Russia 56°54N 118°20E 215 D12
Charadai Argentina 27°35S 59°55W 334 B4
Charagua Bolivia 19°45S 63°10W 331 D5
Charakas Greece 35°1N 25°7E 207 E6
Charalá Colombia 6°17N 73°10W 328 B3
Charambirá, Punta Colombia 4°16N 77°32W 328 C2
Charaña Bolivia 17°30S 69°25W 330 D4
Charantsavan Armenia 40°35N 44°41E 191 K7
Charanwala India 27°51N 72°10E 242 F5
Charapita Colombia 0°37S 74°21W 328 D3
Charata Argentina 27°13S 61°14W 334 B3
Charcas Mexico 23°8N 101°7W 318 C4
Charcot I. Antarctica 70°0S 70°0W 151 C17
Chard U.K. 50°52N 2°58W 169 G5
Chardon U.S.A. 41°35N 81°12W 312 E3
Charduar India 26°51N 92°46E 241 B4
Chardzhou = Türkmenabat Turkmenistan 39°6N 63°34E 247 B9
Charente □ France 45°50N 0°16E 174 C4
Charente → France 45°57N 1°5W 174 C2
Charente-Inférieure = Charente-Maritime □ France 45°45N 0°45W 174 C3
Charente-Maritime □ France 45°45N 0°45W 174 C3
Charenton-du-Cher France 46°44N 2°39E 173 F9
Charenton-le-Pont France 48°49N 2°25E 134 B3
Chari → Chad 12°58N 14°31E 259 F2
Chari-Baguirmi □ Chad 11°0N 17°0E 259 F3
Chārīkār Afghan. 35°0N 69°10E 240 B3
Charing U.S.A. 32°28N 84°22W 316 C5
Charing Cross London, U.K. 125 b4
Chariton U.S.A. 41°1N 93°19W 310 C3
Chariton → U.S.A. 39°19N 92°58W 310 E4
Charity Guyana 7°24N 58°36W 329 B6
Chärjew = Türkmenabat Turkmenistan 39°6N 63°34E 247 B9
Charkhari India 25°24N 79°45E 243 G8
Charkhi Dadri India 28°37N 76°17E 242 E7
Charleroi Belgium 50°24N 4°27E 170 D4
Charleroi Pa., U.S.A. 40°9N 79°57W 312 F5
Charleroi, Kanal de → Belgium 50°51N 4°19E 116 B1
Charles, C. U.S.A. 37°7N 75°58W 309 G16
Charles, I. = Santa María, I. Ecuador 1°17S 90°26W 330 a
Charles, Peak Australia 32°52S 121°11E 279 F3
Charles Bridge = Karlův most Prague, Czech Rep. 135 b1
Charles City U.S.A. 43°4N 92°41W 310 A4
Charles de Gaulle, Paris ✈ (CDG) France 49°0N 2°32E 173 D9
Charles Gates Dawes House U.S.A. 42°2N 87°40W 119 A2
Charles L. Canada 59°50N 110°33W 297 B6
Charles Sound N.Z. 45°2S 167°4E 285 F2
Charles Square = Karlovo náměstí Prague, Czech Rep. 135 c1
Charles Town U.S.A. 39°17N 77°52W 309 F15
Charlesbourg Canada 46°51N 71°16W 309 B18
Charleston Ill., U.S.A. 39°30N 88°10W 311 E8
Charleston Miss., U.S.A. 34°1N 90°4W 315 D9
Charleston Mo., U.S.A. 36°55N 89°21W 308 G9
Charleston S.C., U.S.A. 32°46N 79°56W 316 C10
Charleston W. Va., U.S.A. 38°21N 81°38W 309 F13
Charleston L. Canada 44°32N 76°0W 313 B9
Charleston Peak U.S.A. 36°16N 115°42W 307 J11
Charlestown Mayo, Ireland 53°58N 8°48W 166 C3
Charlestown St. Kitts & Nevis 17°8N 62°37W 322 d
Charlestown KwaZulu Natal, S. Africa 27°26S 29°53E 271 C4
Charlestown Ind., U.S.A. 38°27N 85°40W 311 F11
Charlestown Mass., U.S.A. 42°22N 71°4W 116 A2
Charlestown N.H., U.S.A. 43°14N 72°25W 313 C12
Charlestown Bridge Boston, U.S.A. 116 a2
Charlestown of Aberlour U.K. 57°28N 3°14W 167 D5
Charleville = Rath Luirc Ireland 52°21N 8°40W 166 D3
Charleville Australia 26°24S 146°15E 281 D4
Charleville-Mézières France 49°44N 4°40E 173 C11
Charlevoix U.S.A. 45°19N 85°16W 309 C11
Charlie Gibbs Fracture Zone Atl. Oc. 52°45N 35°30W 152 A8
Charlieu France 46°10N 4°10E 173 F11
Charlotte Dominica 15°17N 61°24W 323 k
Charlotte Mich., U.S.A. 42°34N 84°50W 311 B12
Charlotte N.C., U.S.A. 35°13N 80°50W 315 D14
Charlotte Vt., U.S.A. 44°19N 73°16W 313 B11
Charlotte Amalie U.S. Virgin Is. 18°21N 64°56W 321 C7
Charlotte Harbor U.S.A. 26°57N 82°4W 317 J7
Charlotte L. Canada 52°12N 125°19W 296 C3
Charlottenberg Sweden 59°54N 12°17E 162 E6
Charlottenburg Germany 52°31N 13°14E 115 A2
Charlottenburg, Schloss Germany 52°31N 13°18E 115 A2
Charlottenlund Denmark 55°44N 12°35E 118 A3
Charlottesville U.S.A. 38°2N 78°30W 309 F14
Charlottetown Nfld. & L., Canada 52°46N 56°7W 299 B8
Charlottetown P.E.I., Canada 46°14N 63°8W 299 C7
Charlotteville Trin. & Tob. 11°20N 60°33W 323 s
Charlton Vic., Australia 36°16S 143°24E 282 D5
Charlton London, U.K. 51°29N 0°1E 125 B4
Charlton I. Canada 52°0N 79°20W 298 B4
Charmes France 48°22N 6°17E 173 D13
Charneca Lisboa, Portugal 38°47N 9°8W 126 A2
Charneca Setúbal, Portugal 38°37N 9°12W 126 B1
Charny Canada 46°43N 71°15W 299 C5
Charnyany Belarus 51°59N 24°12E 185 G11
Charolles France 46°27N 4°16E 173 F11
Chârost France 47°0N 2°7E 173 F9
Charouine Algeria 29°0N 0°15W 261 C4
Charre Mozam. 17°13S 35°10E 269 F4
Charroux France 46°9N 0°25E 174 B4
Charsadda Pakistan 34°7N 71°45E 242 B4
Charshanga = Köýtendag Turkmenistan 37°30N 66°1E 240 A2
Charters Towers Australia 20°5S 146°13E 280 C4
Chartres France 48°29N 1°30E 172 D8
Chartreuse △ France 45°22N 5°42E 175 C9
Charuma Trin. & Tob. 10°24N 61°9W 323 t
Charysh → Russia 52°22N 83°45E 217 B10
Chascomús Argentina 35°30S 58°0W 334 D4
Chase Canada 50°50N 119°41W 296 C5
Chase, L. U.S.A. 28°28N 81°31W 133 B1
Chasefu Zambia 11°55S 33°8E 269 E3
Chashma Barrage Pakistan 32°27N 71°20E 242 C4
Chaslands Mistake N.Z. 46°38S 169°22E 285 G4
Chasong N. Korea 41°27N 126°38E 224 B3
Chasseneuil-sur-Bonnieure France 45°52N 0°29E 174 C4
Chāt Iran 37°59N 55°16E 247 B7
Chatal Balkan = Udvoy Balkan Bulgaria 42°50N 26°50E 203 D10
Chatanika U.S.A. 65°7N 147°28W 303 D11
Château-Arnoux-St-Auban France 44°6N 6°0E 175 D10
Château-Chinon France 47°4N 3°56E 173 E10
Château-d'Olonne France 46°30N 1°44W 174 B2
Château-du-Loir France 47°40N 0°25E 172 E7
Château Dubug Martinique 14°46N 60°55W 322 j
Château Gaillard Guadeloupe 16°18N 61°23W 322 e
Château-Gontier France 47°50N 0°48W 172 E6
Château-la-Vallière France 47°30N 0°20E 172 E7
Château-Landon France 48°8N 2°40E 173 D9
Château Murat Guadeloupe 15°52N 61°17W 322 e
Château-Renard France 47°56N 2°55E 173 E9
Château-Renault France 47°36N 0°56E 172 E7
Château-Salins France 48°50N 6°30E 173 D13
Château-Thierry France 49°3N 3°20E 173 C10
Chateaubelair St. Vincent 13°17N 61°15W 323 n
Châteaubourg France 48°7N 1°25W 172 D5
Châteaubriant France 47°43N 1°23W 172 E5
Châteaudun France 48°3N 1°20E 172 D8
Chateaufort France 48°44N 2°5E 134 B1
Chateaugay U.S.A. 44°56N 74°5W 313 B10
Châteaugiron France 48°3N 1°30W 172 D5
Châteauguay, L. Canada 56°26N 70°3W 299 A5
Châteaulin France 48°11N 4°8W 172 D2
Châteaumeillant France 46°35N 2°12E 173 F9
Châteauneuf-du-Faou France 48°11N 3°50W 172 D3
Châteauneuf-sur-Charente France 45°36N 0°3W 174 C3
Châteauneuf-sur-Cher France 46°52N 2°18E 173 F9
Châteauneuf-sur-Loire France 47°52N 2°13E 173 E9
Châteaurenard France 43°53N 4°51E 175 E8
Châteauroux France 46°50N 1°40E 173 F8
Châteauvillain France 48°2N 4°55E 173 D11
Châteaux, Pte. des Guadeloupe 16°15N 61°10W 322 e
Châtelaillon-Plage France 46°5N 1°5W 174 B2
Châtelguyon France 45°55N 3°4E 174 C7
Châtellerault France 46°50N 0°30E 172 F7
Châtelus-Malvaleix France 46°18N 2°1E 173 F9
Châtenay-Malabry France 48°46N 2°16E 134 B2
Chatham = Chatham-Kent Canada 42°24N 82°11W 312 D2
Chatham = Miramichi Canada 47°2N 65°28W 299 C6
Chatham Medway, U.K. 51°22N 0°32E 169 F8
Chatham Ill., U.S.A. 41°45N 87°36W 119 C3
Chatham Ill., U.S.A. 39°40N 89°42W 310 E7
Chatham N.Y., U.S.A. 42°21N 73°36W 313 D11
Chatham, I. = San Cristóbal, I. Ecuador 0°50S 89°26W 330 a
Chatham, I. Chile 50°40S 74°25W 336 D2
Chatham I. N.Z. 43°50S 176°20W 285 a
Chatham Is. Pac. Oc. 44°0S 176°40W 285 a
Chatham-Kent Canada 42°24N 82°11W 312 D2
Chatham Rise Pac. Oc. 43°30S 180°0E 288 M10
Châtillon Hauts-de-Seine, France 48°48N 2°17E 134 B2
Châtillon Italy 45°45N 7°37E 198 C4
Châtillon-Coligny France 47°50N 2°51E 173 E9
Châtillon-en-Diois France 44°41N 5°29E 175 D9
Châtillon-sur-Indre France 46°59N 1°10E 172 F8
Châtillon-sur-Loire France 47°35N 2°44E 173 E9
Châtillon-sur-Seine France 47°50N 4°33E 173 E11
Chatmohar Bangla. 24°15N 89°15E 243 G13
Chatou France 48°53N 2°9E 134 A1
Chatpur India 22°36N 88°22E 124 B2
Chatra India 24°12N 84°56E 243 G11
Chatrapur India 19°22N 85°2E 244 E7
Chats, L. des Canada 45°30N 76°20W 313 A8
Chatsu India 26°36N 75°57E 242 F6
Chatswood Australia 33°47S 151°11E 139 A2
Chatsworth Ont., Canada 44°27N 80°54W 312 B4
Chatsworth Ill., U.S.A. 40°45N 88°18W 311 D8
Chatsworth Zimbabwe 19°38S 31°13E 269 F3
Chatta-Hantō Japan 34°45N 136°55E 223 C8
Chāttagām = Chittagong Bangla. 22°19N 91°48E 241 D3
Chattahoochee U.S.A. 30°42N 84°51W 316 E5
Chattahoochee → U.S.A. 30°54N 84°57W 316 E5
Chattanooga U.S.A. 35°3N 85°19W 315 D12
Chatteris U.K. 52°28N 0°2E 169 E8
Chatuchak Thailand 13°48N 100°33E 113 B2
Chatuchak Park Thailand 13°48N 100°32E 113 B2
Chaturat Thailand 15°40N 101°51E 236 E3
Chau Doc Vietnam 10°42N 105°7E 237 G5
Chaubourg, Mt. St. Lucia 14°2N 60°57W 323 m
Chaudes-Aigues France 44°51N 3°1E 174 D7
Chauffailles France 46°13N 4°20E 173 F11
Chauk Burma 20°53N 94°49E 241 E5
Chaukan Pass Burma 27°8N 97°10E 241 B6
Chauki Pakistan 24°55N 66°56E 123 A1
Chaumont Haute-Marne, France 48°7N 5°8E 173 D12
Chaumont N.Y., U.S.A. 44°4N 76°8W 313 B8
Chaumont-en-Vexin France 49°16N 1°53E 173 C8
Chaumont-sur-Loire France 47°29N 1°11E 172 E8
Chaunay France 46°13N 0°9E 174 B4
Chaunskaya G. Russia 69°0N 169°0E 150 C16
Chauny France 49°37N 3°12E 173 C10
Chaura India 8°27N 93°2E 245 K11
Chausey, Îs. France 48°52N 1°49W 172 D5
Chaussin France 46°59N 5°22E 173 F12
Chautauqua L. U.S.A. 42°10N 79°24W 312 D5
Chauvigny France 46°34N 0°39E 172 F7
Chauvin Canada 52°45N 110°10W 297 C6
Chavakachcheri Sri Lanka 9°39N 80°9E 245 K5
Chavanges France 48°30N 4°35E 173 D11
Chavantina Brazil 14°40S 52°21W 331 C7
Chavarria Peru 12°0S 77°7W 124 B2
Chaves Brazil 0°15S 49°55W 332 B2
Chaves Portugal 41°45N 7°32W 194 D3
Chaville France 48°48N 2°11E 134 B2
Chavuma Zambia 13°4S 22°40E 265 E4
Chawang Thailand 8°25N 99°30E 237 H2
Chayang S. Korea 37°32N 127°3E 137 B2
Chaykovskiy Russia 56°47N 54°9E 186 C9
Chazelles-sur-Lyon France 45°39N 4°22E 175 C8
Chazuta Peru 6°30S 76°0W 330 B2
Chazy U.S.A. 44°53N 73°26W 313 B11
Cheaha Mt. U.S.A. 33°29N 85°49W 316 B4
Cheb Czech Rep. 50°9N 12°28E 180 A5
Chebanse U.S.A. 41°0N 87°54W 311 D9
Chebbi, Erg Africa 31°12N 3°58W 260 B3
Cheboksarskoye Vdkhr. Russia 56°13N 46°58E 190 B8
Cheboksary Russia 56°8N 47°12E 190 B8
Cheboygan U.S.A. 45°39N 84°29W 309 C11
Chebsara Russia 59°10N 38°59E 188 C10
Chech, Erg Africa 25°0N 2°15W 260 D4
Chechelnyk Ukraine 48°13N 29°22E 183 B14
Chechen, Ostrov Russia 43°59N 47°40E 191 H8
Ch'ech'eng Taiwan 22°52N 120°42E 225 D2
Chechenia □ Russia 43°30N 45°29E 191 J7
Checheno-Ingush Republic = Chechenia □ Russia 43°30N 45°29E 191 J7
Chechnya = Chechenia □ Russia 43°30N 45°29E 191 J7
Chęciny Poland 50°46N 20°28E 185 H7
Checotah U.S.A. 35°28N 95°31W 314 D7
Chedabucto B. Canada 45°25N 61°8W 299 C7
Cheduba I. Burma 18°45N 93°40E 241 F4
Cheepie Australia 26°33S 145°1E 281 D4
Cheeyou Trin. & Tob. 10°33N 61°8W 323 t
Chef-Boutonne France 46°7N 0°4W 174 B3
Chefchaouen Morocco 35°9N 5°15W 260 A3
Chefchaouen □ Morocco 35°10N 5°15W 260 A3
Cheffadine Niger 19°57N 12°11E 259 D2
Chefoo = Yantai China 37°34N 121°22E 227 F11
Chefornak U.S.A. 60°13N 164°12W 303 F6
Chegdomyn Russia 51°7N 133°1E 215 D14
Chegga Mauritania 25°27N 5°40W 260 C3
Chegutu Zimbabwe 18°10S 30°14E 269 F3
Chehalis U.S.A. 46°40N 122°58W 306 D4
Chehalis → U.S.A. 46°57N 123°50W 306 D3
Cheile Nerei-Beusnita △ Romania 44°56N 21°52E 182 F6
Cheiron, Mt. France 43°49N 6°58E 175 E10
Cheju = Jeju S. Korea 33°31N 126°32E 224 a
Cheju-do = Jeju-do S. Korea 33°29N 126°34E 224 a
Chekalin Russia 54°10N 36°10E 188 E9
Chekhovo Russia 54°33N 20°43E 184 D7
Chekiang = Zhejiang □ China 29°0N 120°0E 229 C13
Chel = Kuru, Bahr el → Sudan 8°10N 26°50E 257 F2
Chela, Sa. da Angola 16°20S 13°20E 265 F2
Chelan U.S.A. 47°51N 120°1W 304 C3
Chelan, L. U.S.A. 48°11N 120°30W 304 B3
Cheleken = Hazar Turkmenistan 39°34N 53°16E 187 G9
Cheleken Yarymadasy Turkmenistan 39°30N 53°15E 247 B7
Chelforó Argentina 39°0S 66°33W 336 A3
Chéliff, O. → Algeria 36°0N 0°8E 261 A5
Chelkar = Shalqar Kazakhstan 47°48N 59°39E 216 C5
Chella Ethiopia 5°0N 37°26E 257 F4
Chellala Dahrania Algeria 33°2N 0°1E 261 B5
Chelles France 48°53N 2°35E 134 A4
Chelles, Canal de France 48°51N 2°35E 134 A4
Chelles-le-Pin ✈ France 48°53N 2°36E 134 A4
Chelm Poland 51°8N 23°30E 185 G10
Chelmno Poland 53°20N 18°30E 185 E5
Chelmsford U.K. 51°44N 0°29E 169 F8
Chelmża Poland 53°10N 18°39E 185 E5
Chelny = Naberezhnyye Chelny Russia 55°42N 52°19E 190 C11
Chelsea Vic., Australia 38°5S 145°8E 283 E6
Chelsea London, U.K. 51°29N 0°10W 125 B2
Chelsea Mass., U.S.A. 42°23N 71°1W 116 A2
Chelsea Mich., U.S.A. 42°19N 84°1W 311 B12
Chelsea New York, U.S.A. 132 c1
Chelsea Vt., U.S.A. 43°59N 72°27W 313 C12
Cheltenham U.K. 51°54N 2°4W 169 F5
Chelva Spain 39°45N 1°0W 196 F4
Chelyabinsk Russia 55°10N 61°24E 216 A6
Chelyakobi = Kopeysk Russia 55°7N 61°37E 216 A6
Chelyuskin, C. = Chelyuskin, Mys Russia 77°30N 103°0E 215 B11
Chelyuskin, Mys Russia 77°30N 103°0E 215 B11
Chemainus Canada 48°55N 123°42W 306 B3
Chembar = Belinskiy Russia 53°0N 43°25E 190 D6
Chembur India 19°3N 72°53E 130 A2
Chemillé France 47°14N 0°45W 172 E6
Chemin Grenier Mauritius 20°29S 57°28E 272 e
Chemnitz Germany 50°51N 12°54E 178 E8
Chemulpho = Incheon S. Korea 37°27N 126°40E 224 D3
Chemult U.S.A. 43°14N 121°47W 304 E3
Chen, Gora Russia 65°16N 141°50E 215 C15
Chenab → Pakistan 30°23N 71°2E 242 D4
Chenachane, O. → Algeria 25°20N 3°20W 260 C4
Chenango Forks U.S.A. 42°15N 75°51W 313 D9
Chencha Ethiopia 6°15N 37°32E 257 F4
Chenchiang = Zhenjiang China 32°11N 119°26E 229 A12
Cheney U.S.A. 47°30N 117°35W 304 C5
Cheng Xian China 33°43N 105°42E 226 H3
Chengalpattu India 12°42N 79°58E 245 H4
Chengbu China 26°18N 110°16E 229 D8
Chengcheng China 35°8N 109°56E 226 G5
Chengchou = Zhengzhou China 34°45N 113°34E 226 G7
Chengde China 40°59N 117°58E 227 D9
Chengdong Hu China 32°15N 116°20E 229 A11
Chengdu China 30°38N 104°2E 228 B5
Chengele India 28°47N 96°16E 241 A6
Chenggong China 24°52N 102°56E 228 E4
Chenggu China 33°10N 107°21E 226 H4
Chenghai China 23°30N 116°42E 229 F11
Chengjiang China 24°39N 103°0E 228 E4
Chengkou China 31°54N 108°31E 228 B7
Ch'engkung Taiwan 23°6N 121°22E 225 C3
Chengmai China 19°50N 109°58E 236 C7
Chengnan Taiwan 23°3N 120°7E 225 C2
Chengteh = Chengde China 40°59N 117°58E 227 D9
Ch'engtu = Chengdu China 30°38N 104°2E 228 B5
Chengwu China 34°58N 115°50E 226 G8
Chengxi Hu China 32°15N 116°10E 229 A11
Chengyang China 36°18N 120°21E 227 F11
Chenjiagang China 34°23N 119°47E 227 G10
Chenkaladi Sri Lanka 7°47N 81°35E 245 L5
Chennai India 13°8N 80°19E 245 H5
Chennevières-sur-Marne France 48°47N 2°31E 134 B4
Chenoa U.S.A. 40°45N 88°43W 311 D8
Chenôve France 47°16N 5°1E 173 E12
Chenxi China 28°2N 110°12E 229 C8
Chenzhou China 25°47N 113°1E 229 E9
Cheom Ksan Cambodia 14°13N 104°56E 236 E5
Cheonan S. Korea 36°48N 127°9E 224 D3
Cheongdam S. Korea 37°31N 127°3E 137 B2
Cheongdo S. Korea 35°38N 128°42E 224 E4
Cheongju S. Korea 36°39N 127°27E 224 D3
Cheongsando S. Korea 34°11N 126°53E 224 E3
Cheongsong S. Korea 36°25N 129°3E 224 D4
Cheonho S. Korea 37°32N 127°6E 137 B2
Cheonsumman S. Korea 36°33N 126°27E 224 D3
Cheops Egypt 29°58N 31°8E 117 B1
Cheorwon S. Korea 38°15N 127°10E 224 C3
Chepelare Bulgaria 41°44N 24°40E 203 E8
Chepén Peru 7°15S 79°23W 330 B2
Chépénéhé N. Cal. 20°47S 167°9E 288 d
Chepes Argentina 31°20S 66°35W 334 C2
Chepo Panama 9°10N 79°6W 320 E4

Chepstow *U.K.* 51°38N 2°41W **169** F5
Chequamegon B. *U.S.A.* 46°39N 90°51W **308** B8
Cher □ *France* 47°10N 2°30E **173** E9
Cher ➔ *France* 47°21N 0°29E **172** E7
Chéradi *Italy* 40°27N 17°10E **201** B10
Cheran *India* 25°45N 90°44E **241** C3
Cherasco *Italy* 44°39N 7°51E **198** D4
Cheraw *U.S.A.* 34°42N 79°53W **315** D15
Cherbourg *France* 49°39N 1°40W **172** C5
Cherchell *Algeria* 36°35N 2°12E **261** A5
Cherdakly *Russia* 54°25N 48°50E **190** C9
Cherdyn *Russia* 60°24N 56°29E **186** B10
Cheremkhovo *Russia* 53°8N 103°1E **215** D11
Cherepanovo *Russia* 54°15N 83°30E **217** B10
Cherepkovo *Russia* 55°45N 37°21E **129** B2
Cherepovets *Russia* 59°5N 37°55E **188** C9
Chergui, Chott ech *Algeria* 34°21N 0°25E **261** B5
Chergui, Zahrez *Algeria* 35°11N 3°31E **261** B5
Cherial *India* 17°55N 78°59E **244** F4
Cheribon = Cirebon
Indonesia 6°45S 108°32E **235** D3
Cherikov = Cherykaw
Belarus 53°32N 31°20E **177** B16
Cheriyam I. *India* 10°9N 73°40E **245** J1
Cherkasy *Ukraine* 49°27N 32°4E **189** H7
Cherkasy □ *Ukraine* 48°55N 30°50E **189** H6
Cherkessk *Russia* 44°15N 42°5E **191** H6
Cherla *India* 18°5N 80°49E **244** E5
Cherlak *Russia* 54°15N 74°55E **217** B8
Chernaya *Russia* 70°30N 89°10E **215** B9
Chernelytsya *Ukraine* 48°49N 25°26E **183** B10
Cherni *Bulgaria* 42°35N 23°18E **202** D7
Chernigov = Chernihiv
Ukraine 51°28N 31°20E **189** G6
Chernihiv *Ukraine* 51°28N 31°20E **189** G6
Chernihiv □ *Ukraine* 51°10N 32°55E **189** G7
Chernivtsi *Chernivtsi, Ukraine* 48°15N 25°52E **183** B10
Chernivtsi *Vinnyts'ka, Ukraine* 48°32N 28°9E **183** B13
Chernivtsi □ *Ukraine* 48°5N 25°30E **183** B10
Chernobyl = Chornobyl
Ukraine 51°20N 30°15E **177** C16
Chernogorsk *Russia* 53°49N 91°18E **217** B12
Chernomorskoye = Chornomorske
Ukraine 45°31N 32°40E **189** K7
Chernorechye = Dzerzhinsk
Russia 56°14N 43°30E **190** B6
Chernovtsy = Chernivtsi
Ukraine 48°15N 25°52E **183** B10
Chernyakhovsk *Russia* 54°36N 21°48E **184** D8
Chernyanka *Russia* 50°56N 37°49E **189** G9
Chernyovo *Russia* 55°50N 37°17E **129** A1
Chernysheyskiy *Russia* 63°0N 112°30E **215** C12
Chernyye Zemli *Russia* 46°10N 46°0E **191** H8
Cherokee *Iowa, U.S.A.* 42°45N 95°33W **308** D6
Cherokee *Okla., U.S.A.* 36°45N 98°21W **314** C5
Cherokee Village *U.S.A.* 36°18N 91°31W **314** C9
Cherokees, Grand Lake O' The
U.S.A. 36°28N 94°55W **314** C7
Cherquenco *Chile* 38°35S 72°0W **336** A2
Cherrapunji *India* 25°17N 91°47E **241** C3
Cherry Valley *U.S.A.* 42°48N 74°45W **313** D10
Cherryvile *U.S.A.* 37°51N 91°16W **310** G5
Cherskiy *Russia* 68°45N 161°18E **215** C17
Cherskogo Khrebet
Russia 65°0N 143°0E **215** C15
Chersonisos Akrotiri
Greece 35°30N 24°10E **207** E5
Chertanovka ➔ *Russia* 55°38N 37°48E **129** C3
Chertanovo *Russia* 55°38N 37°36E **129** C3
Chertkov = Chortkiv
Ukraine 49°2N 25°46E **177** D13
Chertkovo *Russia* 49°25N 40°19E **189** H11
Cherven *Belarus* 53°45N 28°28E **177** B15
Cherven-Bryag *Bulgaria* 43°17N 24°7E **203** C8
Chervonoarmeyskoye = Volnansk
Ukraine 48°2N 35°29E **189** H8
Chervonoarmiyske
Ukraine 45°47N 28°44E **183** E13
Chervonohrad *Ukraine* 50°25N 24°10E **177** C13
Cherwell ➔ *U.K.* 51°44N 1°14W **169** F6
Cherykaw *Belarus* 53°32N 31°20E **177** B16
Cheryomushki *Russia* 55°40N 37°35E **129** B3
Chesapeake *U.S.A.* 36°49N 76°16W **309** G15
Chesapeake B. *U.S.A.* 38°0N 76°10W **309** F14
Cheshire □ *U.K.* 53°14N 2°30W **168** D5
Cheshskaya Guba *Russia* 67°20N 47°0E **186** A8
Cheshunt *U.K.* 51°43N 0°1W **169** F7
Chesil Beach *U.K.* 50°37N 2°33W **169** G5
Chesley *Canada* 44°17N 81°5W **312** B3
Chesnokovka = Novoaltaysk
Russia 53°30N 84°0E **217** B10
Cheste *Spain* 39°30N 0°41W **197** F4
Chester *Ches., U.K.* 53°12N 2°53W **168** D5
Chester *Calif., U.S.A.* 40°19N 121°14W **304** F3
Chester *Ga., U.S.A.* 32°24N 83°9W **316** C6
Chester *Ill., U.S.A.* 37°55N 89°49W **310** G7
Chester *Mont., U.S.A.* 48°31N 110°58W **304** B8
Chester *Pa., U.S.A.* 39°51N 75°22W **309** F16
Chester *S.C., U.S.A.* 34°43N 81°12W **315** D14
Chester *Vt., U.S.A.* 43°16N 72°36W **313** C12
Chester *W. Va., U.S.A.* 40°37N 80°34W **312** F4
Chester-le-Street *U.K.* 54°51N 1°34W **168** C6
Chesterfield *Derby, U.K.* 53°15N 1°25W **168** D6
Chesterfield *Mo., U.S.A.* 38°40N 90°35W **310** F6
Chesterfield, Îs. *N. Cal.* 19°52S 158°15E **277** D10
Chesterfield Inlet
Canada 63°30N 90°45W **294** C10
Chesterton Ra. *Australia* 25°30S 147°27E **281** D4
Chesterton Range △
Australia 26°16S 147°22E **281** D4
Chestertown *U.S.A.* 43°40N 73°48W **313** C11
Chesterville *Canada* 45°6N 75°14W **313** A9
Chestnut Hill *U.S.A.* 42°19N 71°10W **116** B1
Chesuncook L. *U.S.A.* 46°0N 69°21W **309** C19
Chetamale *India* 10°43N 92°33E **245** J11
Chéticamp *Canada* 46°37N 60°59W **299** C7
Chetlat I. *India* 11°42N 72°42E **245** J1
Chetrosu *Moldova* 48°5N 27°54E **183** B12
Chetumal *Mexico* 18°30N 88°20W **319** D7
Chetumal, B. de
Cent. Amer. 18°40N 88°10W **319** D7
Chetwynd *Canada* 55°45N 121°36W **296** B4
Cheung Sha Wan *China* 22°20N 114°8E **122** A1
Chevak *U.S.A.* 61°32N 165°35W **303** F6
Chevalier, Î. de *Martinique* 14°25N 60°50W **322** j
Chevanceaux *France* 45°18N 0°14W **174** C3
Cheverly *U.S.A.* 38°55N 76°54W **143** B4
Chevilly-Larue *France* 48°46N 2°21E **134** E2
Cheviot *U.S.A.* 39°9N 84°36W **311** E12
Cheviot, The *U.K.* 55°29N 2°9W **168** B5
Cheviot Hills *U.K.* 55°20N 2°30W **168** B5
Cheviot Ra. *Australia* 25°20S 143°45E **280** D3
Chevry-Cossigny *France* 48°43N 2°39E **134** B4
Chevy Chase *U.S.A.* 38°59N 77°4W **143** B3
Chew Bahir *Ethiopia* 4°40N 36°50E **257** G4
Chewelah *U.S.A.* 48°17N 117°43W **304** B5
Chewore △ *Zimbabwe* 16°0S 29°52E **269** F2
Cheyenne *Okla., U.S.A.* 35°37N 99°40W **314** D5
Cheyenne *Wyo., U.S.A.* 41°8N 104°49W **304** F11
Cheyenne ➔ *U.S.A.* 44°41N 101°18W **308** C3
Cheyenne Wells
U.S.A. 38°49N 102°21W **304** G12
Cheyne B. *Australia* 34°35S 118°50E **279** F2
Cheyur *India* 12°21N 80°0E **245** H5
Chhabra *India* 24°40N 76°54E **242** G7
Chhaktala *India* 22°6N 74°11E **242** H6
Chhapra *India* 25°48N 84°44E **243** G11
Chhata *India* 27°42N 77°30E **242** F7
Chhatak *Bangla.* 25°5N 91°37E **241** C3
Chhatarpur *Jharkhand, India* 24°23N 84°11E **243** G11
Chhatarpur *Mad. P., India* 24°55N 79°35E **243** G8
Chhati *India* 20°47N 81°40E **244** D5
Chhatrapati Shivaji, Mumbai ✈
(BOM) *India* 19°5N 72°51E **130** A2
Chhattisgarh □ *India* 22°0N 82°0E **243** J10
Chhaygaon *India* 26°3N 91°24E **241** B3
Chhep *Cambodia* 13°45N 105°24E **236** F5
Chhindwara *Mad. P., India* 23°3N 79°29E **243** H8
Chhindwara *Mad. P., India* 22°2N 78°59E **243** H8
Chhinhdipada *India* 21°6N 84°52E **244** D7
Chhlong *Cambodia* 12°15N 105°58E **237** F5
Chhota Tawa ➔ *India* 22°14N 76°36E **242** H7
Chhoti Kali Sindh ➔
India 24°2N 75°31E **242** G6
Chhuikhadan *India* 21°32N 80°59E **243** J9
Chhuk *Cambodia* 10°46N 104°28E **237** G5
Chi ➔ *Thailand* 15°11N 104°43E **236** E5
Chia Keng *Singapore* 1°21N 103°52E **138** A3
Chiahsien *Taiwan* 23°5N 120°35E **225** C2
Chiai *Taiwan* 23°29N 120°25E **225** C2
Chiai □ *Taiwan* 23°30N 120°30E **225** C2
Chiaksan △ *S. Korea* 37°15N 128°0E **224** D4
Chiali *Taiwan* 23°9N 120°10E **225** C2
Chialulantsun *Taiwan* 22°49N 121°11E **225** D3
Chiamboni *Somali Rep.* 1°39S 41°35E **267** E5
Chiamussu = Jiamusi
China 46°40N 130°26E **219** B8
Chian *Taiwan* 23°59N 121°33E **225** C3
Chianapu *Taiwan* 22°47N 120°36E **225** D2
Chianciano Terme *Italy* 43°2N 11°49E **199** E8
Chiang Dao *Thailand* 19°22N 98°58E **236** C2
Chiang Kham *Thailand* 19°32N 100°18E **236** C3
Chiang Khan *Thailand* 17°52N 101°36E **236** D3
Chiang Khong *Thailand* 20°17N 100°24E **228** G3
Chiang Mai *Thailand* 18°47N 98°59E **236** C2
Chiang Rai *Thailand* 19°52N 99°50E **228** H2
Chiang Saen *Thailand* 20°16N 100°5E **228** G3
Chiangchun *Taiwan* 23°12N 120°9E **225** C2
Chiange *Angola* 15°35S 13°40E **265** F2
Chianti *Italy* 43°32N 11°25E **199** E8
Chiaohsi *Taiwan* 24°49N 121°46E **225** B3
Chiaotou *Taiwan* 22°45N 120°18E **225** D2
Chiapa ➔ *Mexico* 16°42N 93°0W **319** D6
Chiapa de Corzo *Mexico* 16°42N 93°0W **319** D6
Chiapas □ *Mexico* 16°30N 92°30W **319** D6
Chiapas, Sa. Madre de
Mexico 15°40N 93°0W **319** D6
Chiaramonte Gulfi *Italy* 37°2N 14°42E **201** E7
Chiaravalle *Italy* 43°36N 13°19E **199** E10
Chiaravalle Centrale
Italy 38°41N 16°25E **201** D9
Chiaravalle Milanese *Italy* 45°24N 9°16E **129** B2
Chiari *Italy* 45°32N 9°56E **198** C6
Chiatung *Taiwan* 22°25N 120°32E **225** D2
Chiatura *Georgia* 42°15N 43°17E **191** J6
Chiautla de Tapia
Mexico 18°18N 98°36W **319** D5
Chiávari *Italy* 44°19N 9°19E **198** D6
Chiavenna *Italy* 46°19N 9°24E **198** B6
Chiba *Japan* 35°30N 140°7E **223** B12
Chiba □ *Japan* 35°30N 140°20E **223** B12
Chibabava *Mozam.* 20°17S 33°35E **271** B5
Chibango *Angola* 13°38S 21°56E **265** E4
Chibemba *Cunene, Angola* 15°48S 14°8E **265** F2
Chibemba *Huila, Angola* 16°20S 15°20E **265** F3
Chibi *Zimbabwe* 20°18S 30°25E **271** B5
Chibia *Angola* 15°10S 13°42E **265** F2
Chibizovka = Zherdevka
Russia 51°56N 41°29E **190** E5
Chibougamau *Canada* 49°56N 74°24W **298** C5
Chibougamau, L. *Canada* 49°50N 74°20W **298** C5
Chibuk *Nigeria* 10°52N 12°50E **263** C7
Chibuto *Mozam.* 24°40S 33°33E **271** B5
Chibyu = Ukhta *Russia* 63°34N 53°41E **186** B9
Chic-Chocs, Mts. *Canada* 48°55N 66°0W **299** C6
Chicacole = Srikakulam
India 18°14N 83°58E **244** E6
Chicago *U.S.A.* 41°52N 87°38W **119** B3
Chicago, University of
U.S.A. 41°47N 87°35W **119** C3
Chicago Harbor *Chicago, U.S.A.* **119** d3
Chicago Heights *U.S.A.* 41°30N 87°38W **311** C9
Chicago Lawn *U.S.A.* 41°47N 87°40W **119** C2
Chicago-Midway ✈ **(MDW)**
U.S.A. 41°47N 87°45W **119** C2
Chicago O'Hare Int. ✈ **(ORD)**
U.S.A. 41°59N 87°54W **119** B1
Chicago Ridge *U.S.A.* 41°41N 87°46W **119** C2
Chicago River ➔ *Chicago, U.S.A.* **119** b2
Chicago River, North Branch ➔
U.S.A. 41°53N 87°42W **119** B2
Chicago Sanitary and Ship Canal
U.S.A. 41°49N 87°45W **119** C2
Chicago State University
U.S.A. 41°43N 87°36W **119** C3
Chicago Zoo *U.S.A.* 41°50N 87°50W **119** B1
Chicapa ➔
Dem. Rep. of the Congo 6°25S 20°48E **265** D4
Chicha *Chad* 16°57N 18°34E **259** E3
Chichagof I. *U.S.A.* 57°30N 135°30W **303** H14
Chichaoua *Morocco* 31°32N 8°44W **260** B3
Chichaoua □ *Morocco* 31°32N 8°45W **260** B3
Chichén-Itzá *Mexico* 20°37N 88°35W **319** C7
Chicheng *China* 40°55N 115°55E **226** D8
Chichester *U.K.* 50°50N 0°47W **169** G7
Chichester Ra. *Australia* 22°12S 119°15E **278** D2
Chichi *Hualien, Taiwan* 23°44N 121°33E **225** C3
Chichi *Nant'ou, Taiwan* 23°49N 120°47E **225** C2
Chichibu *Japan* 35°59N 139°10E **223** A11
Chichibu-Tama △
Japan 35°52N 138°42E **223** B10
Ch'ich'ihaerh = Qiqihar
China 47°26N 124°0E **219** B7
Chicholi *India* 22°1N 77°40E **242** H8
Chich'ou *Taiwan* 23°45N 120°33E **225** C2
Chickasaw △ *U.S.A.* 34°26N 97°0W **314** D6
Chickasha *U.S.A.* 35°3N 97°58W **314** D6
Chicken *U.S.A.* 64°5N 141°56W **303** D12
Chiclana de la Frontera
Spain 36°26N 6°9W **195** J4
Chiclayo *Peru* 6°42S 79°50W **330** B2
Chico *U.S.A.* 39°44N 121°50W **306** F5
Chico ➔ *Chubut, Argentina* 44°0S 67°0W **336** B3
Chico ➔ *Santa Cruz, Argentina* 50°0S 68°30W **336** D3
Chicomba *Angola* 14°10S 14°52E **265** E2
Chicomo *Mozam.* 24°31S 34°6E **271** B5
Chicomostoc *Mexico* 22°28N 102°46W **318** C4
Chiconi *Mayotte* 12°50S 45°7E **272** b
Chicontepec *Mexico* 20°58N 98°10W **319** C5
Chicopee *U.S.A.* 42°9N 72°37W **313** D12
Chicoutimi *Canada* 48°28N 71°5W **299** C5
Chicualacuala *Mozam.* 22°6S 31°42E **271** B5
Chicuma *Angola* 13°26S 14°50E **265** E2
Chidambaram *India* 11°20N 79°45E **245** J4
Chidenguele *Mozam.* 24°55S 34°11E **271** B5
Chidley, C. *Canada* 60°23N 64°26W **295** C13
Chiducuane *Mozam.* 24°35S 34°25E **271** B5
Chiede *Angola* 17°15S 16°22E **265** F3
Chiefland *U.S.A.* 29°29N 82°52W **317** F7
Chiefs Pt. *Canada* 44°41N 81°18W **312** B3
Chiehting *Taiwan* 22°54N 120°11E **225** D2
Chiem Hoa *Vietnam* 22°12N 105°17E **236** A5
Chiemsee *Germany* 47°53N 12°28E **179** H8
Chienchen *Taiwan* 22°35N 120°18E **225** D2
Chiengi *Zambia* 8°45S 29°10E **269** D2
Chiengmai = Chiang Mai
Thailand 18°47N 98°59E **236** C2
Chiengo *Angola* 13°20S 21°55E **265** E4
Chienti ➔ *Italy* 43°18N 13°45E **199** E10
Chienzui *China* 23°12N 113°22E **121** A3
Chieri *Italy* 45°1N 7°49E **198** C4
Chiers ➔ *France* 49°39N 4°59E **173** C11
Chiesa in Valmalenco
Italy 46°16N 9°51E **198** B6
Chiese ➔ *Italy* 45°8N 10°25E **198** C7
Chieti *Italy* 42°21N 14°10E **199** F11
Chifeng *China* 42°18N 118°58E **227** C10
Chigasaki *Japan* 35°19N 139°24E **223** B11
Chigirin *Ukraine* 49°4N 32°38E **189** H7
Chignecto B. *Canada* 45°30N 64°40W **299** C7
Chignik *U.S.A.* 56°18N 158°24W **303** H8
Chigorodó *Colombia* 7°41N 76°42W **328** B2
Chiguana *Bolivia* 21°0S 67°58W **334** A2
Chigwell *U.K.* 51°37N 0°6E **169** F8
Chihli, G. of = Bo Hai
China 39°0N 119°0E **227** E10
Ch'ihpen *Taiwan* 22°42N 121°2E **225** D3
Ch'ihshang *Taiwan* 23°7N 121°12E **225** C3
Chihsi = Jixi *China* 45°20N 130°50E **227** B16
Chihtan *Taiwan* 23°54N 120°24E **225** C2
Chihuahua *Mexico* 28°38N 106°5W **318** B3
Chihuahua □ *Mexico* 28°30N 106°0W **318** B3
Chiili = Shieli *Kazakhstan* 44°20N 66°15E **217** D7
Chik Bollapur *India* 13°25N 77°45E **245** H3
Chik Sha *China* 22°17N 114°16E **122** B2
Chikalda *India* 21°24N 77°19E **244** D3
Chikhli *Ahmadabad, India* 20°45N 73°4E **244** D1
Chikhli *Maharashtra, India* 20°20N 76°18E **244** D3
Chikmagalur *India* 13°15N 75°45E **245** H2
Chiknayakanhalli *India* 13°26N 76°37E **245** H3
Chikodi *India* 16°26N 74°38E **245** F2
Chiku *Taiwan* 23°8N 120°7E **225** C2
Chikugo *Japan* 33°14N 130°28E **222** D2
Chikuma-Gawa ➔
Japan 36°59N 138°35E **223** A10
Chikushino *Japan* 33°30N 130°30E **222** D2
Chikwawa *Malawi* 16°2S 34°50E **269** F3
Chila *Angola* 12°3S 14°29E **265** E2
Ch'ilaichu Shan *Taiwan* 24°5N 121°20E **225** B3
Chilam Chavki *Pakistan* 35°5N 75°5E **243** B6
Chilanga *Zambia* 15°33S 28°16E **269** F2
Chilapa *Mexico* 17°36N 99°10W **319** D5
Chilas *Pakistan* 35°25N 74°5E **243** B6
Chilaw *Sri Lanka* 7°30N 79°50E **245** L4
Chilcotin ➔ *Canada* 51°44N 122°23W **296** C4
Childers *Australia* 25°15S 152°17E **281** D5
Childersburg *U.S.A.* 33°16N 86°21W **316** B3
Children's Museum *Boston, U.S.A.* **116** c3
Childress *U.S.A.* 34°25N 100°13W **314** D4
Child's Hill *U.K.* 51°33N 0°12W **125** A2
Chile ■ *S. Amer.* 35°0S 72°0W **336** A2
Chile, Universidad de
Chile 33°26S 70°39W **137** B2
Chile Basin *Pac. Oc.* 33°0S 80°0W **289** L20
Chile Chico *Chile* 46°33S 71°44W **336** C2
Chile Rise *Pac. Oc.* 38°0S 92°0W **289** L18
Chilecito *Argentina* 29°10S 67°30W **334** B2
Chilengue, Serra do
Angola 13°18S 15°22E **265** E2
Chilesso *Angola* 11°35S 16°34E **265** E3
Chilete *Peru* 7°10S 78°50W **330** B2
Chilhowee *U.S.A.* 38°36N 93°51W **310** F3
Chilia, Braţul ➔
Romania 45°14N 29°42E **183** E14
Chilik = Shelek
Kazakhstan 43°33N 78°17E **217** D9
Chililabombwe *Zambia* 12°18S 27°43E **269** E2
Chilin = Jilin *China* 43°44N 126°30E **227** C14
Chiliomodi *Greece* 37°48N 22°51E **204** D4
Chilka L. *India* 19°40N 85°25E **244** E7
Chilko ➔ *Canada* 52°0N 123°40W **296** C4
Chilko L. *Canada* 51°20N 124°10W **296** C4
Chilla Saroda *India* 28°35N 77°18E **120** B2
Chillagoe *Australia* 17°7S 144°33E **280** B3
Chillán *Chile* 36°40S 72°10W **334** D1
Chillicothe *Ill., U.S.A.* 40°55N 89°29W **310** D7
Chillicothe *Mo., U.S.A.* 39°48N 93°33W **310** E3
Chillicothe *Ohio, U.S.A.* 39°20N 82°59W **309** F12
Chilliwack *Canada* 49°10N 121°54W **296** D4
Chillum *U.S.A.* 38°56N 76°58W **143** B4
Chilly-Mazarin *France* 48°42N 2°17E **134** B2
Chilo *India* 27°25N 73°32E **242** F5
Chiloane, I. *Mozam.* 20°40S 34°55E **271** B5
Chiloé, I. de *Chile* 42°30S 73°50W **336** B2
Chiloé △ *Chile* 42°11S 73°59W **336** B2
Chilonda *Angola* 11°19S 16°12E **265** E3
Chilongo *Angola* 13°55S 16°35E **265** E3
Chilpancingo *Mexico* 17°33N 99°30W **319** D5
Chiltern *Australia* 36°10S 146°36E **283** D7
Chiltern Hills *U.K.* 51°40N 0°53W **169** F7
Chilton *U.S.A.* 44°2N 88°10W **308** C9
Chiluage *Angola* 9°30S 21°50E **265** D4
Chilubi *Zambia* 11°5S 29°58E **269** E2
Chilubula *Zambia* 10°14S 30°51E **269** E3
Chilumba *Malawi* 10°28S 34°12E **269** E3
Chilung *Taiwan* 25°3N 121°45E **225** A3
Chilwa, L. *Malawi* 15°15S 35°40E **269** F4
Chimaltitán *Mexico* 21°35N 103°50W **318** C4
Chimán *Panama* 8°45N 78°40W **320** E4
Chimanimani *Zimbabwe* 19°48S 32°52E **271** A5
Chimanimani △ *Zimbabwe* 19°48S 33°0E **271** A5
Chimay *Belgium* 50°3N 4°20E **170** D4
Chimayo *U.S.A.* 36°0N 105°56W **305** J11
Chimbay *Uzbekistan* 42°57N 59°47E **216** D5
Chimborazo *Ecuador* 1°29S 78°55W **328** D2
Chimborazo □ *Ecuador* 1°0S 78°40W **328** D2
Chimbote *Peru* 9°0S 78°35W **330** B2
Chimbu □ *Papua N. G.* 6°15S 144°50E **286** D3
Ch'imei *Taiwan* 23°12N 119°25E **225** C1
Ch'imei Yü *Taiwan* 23°13N 119°26E **225** C1
Chimichagua *Colombia* 9°15N 73°49W **328** B3
Chimkent = Shymkent
Kazakhstan 42°18N 69°36E **217** D7
Chimoio *Mozam.* 19°4S 33°30E **269** F3
Chimpembe *Zambia* 9°31S 29°33E **269** D2
Chimur *India* 20°30N 79°23E **244** D4
Chin □ *Burma* 22°0N 93°0E **241** E4
Chin Hills *Burma* 22°30N 93°30E **241** D4
Chin Ling Shan = Qinling Shandi
China 33°50N 108°10E **226** H5
China *Mexico* 25°42N 99°14W **319** B5
China ■ *Asia* 30°0N 110°0E **219** C6
China, Great Plain of
Asia 35°0N 115°0E **210** E13
China Basin *San Francisco, U.S.A.* **136** c3
China Lake *U.S.A.* 35°44N 117°37W **307** K9
China Town *Toronto, Canada* **141** a1
Chinacota *Colombia* 7°37N 72°36W **328** B3
Chinan = Jinan *China* 36°38N 117°1E **226** F9
Chinandega *Nic.* 12°35N 87°12W **320** D2
Chinati Peak *U.S.A.* 29°57N 104°29W **314** G2
Chinatown *Singapore* **138** c2
Chinatown *Boston, U.S.A.* **116** c2
Chinatown *Chicago, U.S.A.* **119** f1
Chinatown *Los Angeles, U.S.A.* **127** a3
Chinatown *New York, U.S.A.* **132** e2
Chinatown *San Francisco, U.S.A.* **136** b2
Chincha Alta *Peru* 13°25S 76°7W **330** C2
Chinchaga ➔ *Canada* 58°53N 118°20W **296** B5
Chincheros *Peru* 13°30S 73°44W **330** C3
Chinchilla *Australia* 26°45S 150°38E **281** D5
Chinchilla de Monte Aragón
Spain 38°53N 1°40W **197** G3
Chincholi *India* 17°28N 77°26E **244** E3
Chinchorro, Banco
Mexico 18°35N 87°22W **319** D7
Chinchou = Jinzhou
China 41°5N 121°3E **227** D11
Chinchoua *Gabon* 0°1N 9°48E **264** B1
Chincoteague *U.S.A.* 37°56N 75°23W **309** G16
Chinde *Mozam.* 18°35S 36°30E **269** F4
Chindwin ➔ *Burma* 21°26N 95°15E **241** E5
Chineni *India* 33°2N 75°15E **243** C6
Chinga *Mozam.* 15°13S 38°35E **269** F4
Chingaza △ *Colombia* 4°30N 73°40W **328** C3
Chingola *Zambia* 12°31S 27°53E **269** E2
Chingole *Malawi* 13°4S 34°17E **269** E3
Chingoni *Mayotte* 12°48S 45°8E **272** b
Chingoroi *Angola* 13°37S 14°1E **265** E2
Chingpu *Taiwan* 23°28N 121°29E **225** C3
Ch'ingshui *Changhua, Taiwan* 24°16N 120°34E **225** B2
Chingshui *Hualien, Taiwan* 24°13N 121°41E **225** B3
Chingshui *Ilan, Taiwan* 24°39N 121°35E **225** B3
Ch'ingtao = Qingdao
China 36°5N 120°20E **227** F11
Chinguar *Angola* 12°25S 16°45E **265** E3
Chinguetti *Mauritania* 20°25N 12°24W **260** D2
Chingune *Mozam.* 20°33S 34°58E **271** B5
Chingupota *India* 22°29N 88°14E **124** C1
Chinhanguanine *Mozam.* 25°21S 32°30E **271** C5
Chinhoyi *Zimbabwe* 17°20S 30°8E **269** F3
Chinhsien = Jinxian
China 28°26N 116°17E **229** C11
Chini *India* 31°32N 78°15E **242** D8
Chiniot *Pakistan* 31°45N 73°0E **242** D5
Chinipas *Mexico* 27°23N 108°32W **318** B3
Chinji *Pakistan* 32°42N 72°22E **242** C5
Chinju = Jinju *S. Korea* 35°12N 128°2E **224** E4
Chinkai *Afghan.* 31°57N 67°26E **240** C2
Chinkapook *Australia* 35°11S 142°57E **282** C5
Chinkiang = Zhenjiang
China 32°11N 119°26E **229** A12
Chinko ➔ *C.A.R.* 4°50N 23°53E **264** B4
Chinle *U.S.A.* 36°9N 109°33W **305** H9
Ch'inlun *Taiwan* 22°32N 120°57E **225** D2
Chinmen *Taiwan* 24°26N 118°19E **225** a
Chinmen Tao *Taiwan* 24°26N 118°22E **225** a
Chinna Cr. ➔ *Pakistan* 24°50N 67°0E **123** B2
Chinnamanur *India* 9°50N 77°24E **245** K3
Chinnampo = Namp'o
N. Korea 38°52N 125°10E **224** C2
Chinnur *India* 18°57N 79°49E **244** E4
Chino *Japan* 35°59N 138°9E **223** B10
Chino *Calif., U.S.A.* 34°1N 117°41W **307** L9
Chino Valley *U.S.A.* 34°45N 112°27W **305** J7
Chinois, Quartier *Montréal, Canada* **130** b2
Chinon *France* 47°10N 0°15E **172** E7
Chinook *U.S.A.* 48°35N 109°14W **304** B9
Chinook Trough *Pac. Oc.* 44°0N 175°0W **288** C10
Chinoya *Zambia* 13°55S 23°16E **265** E4
Chinsali *Zambia* 10°30S 32°2E **269** E3
Chinshan *Taiwan* 25°13N 121°38E **225** A3
Chintalapudi *India* 17°4N 80°59E **244** F5
Chintamani *India* 13°26N 78°3E **245** H4
Chinwangtao = Qinhuangdao
China 39°56N 119°30E **227** E10
Chióggia *Italy* 45°13N 12°17E **199** C9
Chios = Hios *Greece* 38°27N 26°9E **205** C8
Chipata *Zambia* 13°38S 32°28E **269** E3
Chipei Tao *Taiwan* 23°45N 119°37E **225** C1
Chiperceni *Moldova* 47°31N 28°50E **183** C13
Chipindo *Angola* 13°49S 15°48E **265** E3
Chipinge *Zimbabwe* 20°13S 32°28E **269** G3
Chipinge △ *Zimbabwe* 20°14S 33°0E **269** G3
Chipiona *Spain* 36°44N 6°26W **195** J4
Chipley *U.S.A.* 30°47N 85°32W **316** E4
Chiplun *India* 17°31N 73°34E **244** F1
Chipman *Canada* 46°6N 65°53W **299** C6
Chipoka *Malawi* 13°57S 34°28E **269** E3
Chippenham *U.K.* 51°27N 2°6W **169** F5
Chippewa ➔ *U.S.A.* 44°25N 92°5W **308** C7
Chippewa Falls *U.S.A.* 44°56N 91°24W **308** C8
Chipping Norton *U.K.* 51°56N 1°32W **169** F6
Chiprovtsi *Bulgaria* 43°24N 22°52E **202** C6
Chiputneticook Lakes
N. Amer. 45°35N 67°35W **309** C20
Chiputo = Vila Vasco da Gama
Mozam. 14°54S 32°14E **269** E3
Chiquelequele *Angola* 16°44S 19°5E **265** F3
Chiquián *Peru* 10°10S 77°0W **330** C2
Chiquibul △ *Belize* 16°49N 88°52W **320** C2
Chiquihuite, Cerro
Mexico 19°32N 99°8W **128** A2
Chiquimula *Guatemala* 14°51N 89°37W **320** D2
Chiquinquira *Colombia* 5°37N 73°50W **328** B3
Chiquitos, Llanos de
Bolivia 18°0S 61°30W **331** D5
Chir ➔ *Russia* 48°30N 43°0E **191** F6
Chira ➔ *Peru* 4°54S 81°8W **328** D1
Chirala *India* 15°50N 80°26E **245** G5
Chiramba *Mozam.* 16°55S 34°39E **269** F3
Chirawa *India* 28°14N 75°42E **242** E6
Chirayinkil *India* 8°41N 76°49E **245** K3
Chirchiq *Uzbekistan* 41°29N 69°35E **217** D7
Chiredzi *Zimbabwe* 21°0S 31°38E **271** B5
Chirfa *Niger* 20°55N 12°22E **259** D2
Chirgua ➔ *Venezuela* 8°54N 67°58W **328** B4
Chiribiquete △ *Colombia* 0°31N 72°50W **328** C3
Chiricahua △ *U.S.A.* 32°0N 109°20W **305** K9
Chiricahua Peak *U.S.A.* 31°51N 109°18W **305** L9
Chiriquí, G. de *Panama* 8°0N 82°10W **320** E3
Chiriquí, L. de *Panama* 9°10N 82°0W **320** E3
Chirisa △ *Zimbabwe* 17°53S 28°15E **269** F2
Chirivira Falls *Zimbabwe* 21°10S 32°12E **269** G3
Chirmiri *India* 23°15N 82°20E **243** H10
Chirnogi *Romania* 44°7N 26°32E **183** F11
Chirongui *Mayotte* 12°55S 45°9E **272** b
Chirpan *Bulgaria* 42°10N 25°19E **203** D9
Chirripó Grande, Cerro
Costa Rica 9°29N 83°29W **320** E3
Chirundu *Zimbabwe* 16°3S 28°50E **271** A4
Chisamba *Zambia* 14°55S 28°20E **269** E2
Chisapani *Nepal* 28°37N 81°16E **243** E9
Chisasibi *Canada* 53°50N 79°0W **298** B4
Ch'ishan *Taiwan* 22°44N 120°31E **225** D2
Ch'ishan Hsi ➔ *Taiwan* 22°51N 120°28E **225** C2
Chisholm *Alta., Canada* 54°55N 114°10W **296** C6
Chisholm *Minn., U.S.A.* 47°29N 92°53W **308** B7
Chishtian Mandi *Pakistan* 29°50N 72°55E **242** E5
Chishui *China* 28°30N 105°42E **228** C5
Chishui He ➔ *China* 28°49N 105°50E **228** C5
Chisimaio *Somali Rep.* 0°22S 42°32E **267** E5
Chisimba Falls *Zambia* 10°12S 30°56E **269** E3
Chişinău *Moldova* 47°2N 28°50E **183** C13
Chişinău ✈ **(KIV)**
Moldova 47°3N 28°46E **183** C13
Chişineu Criş *Romania* 46°32N 21°37E **182** D6
Chislehurst *U.K.* 51°24N 0°6E **125** B4
Chisone ➔ *Italy* 44°49N 7°25E **198** D4
Chisos Mts. *U.S.A.* 29°5N 103°15W **314** G3
Chissengue *Angola* 9°13S 20°34E **265** D4
Chissilo *Angola* 13°48S 16°31E **265** E3
Chistochina *U.S.A.* 62°34N 144°40W **303** E11
Chistopol *Russia* 55°25N 50°38E **190** C10
Chiswick *U.K.* 51°29N 0°16W **125** B2
Chiswick House *U.K.* 51°28N 0°15W **125** B2
Chita *Colombia* 6°11N 72°28W **328** B3
Chita *Russia* 52°0N 113°35E **215** D12
Chitado *Angola* 17°10S 14°8E **265** F2
Chitaldrug = Chitradurga
India 14°14N 76°24E **245** G3
Chitan *Taiwan* 24°35N 121°29E **225** B3
Chitanda ➔ *Angola* 16°1S 15°12E **265** F3
Chitapur *India* 17°10N 77°5E **244** F3
Chitembo *Angola* 13°30S 16°50E **265** E3
Chitina *U.S.A.* 61°31N 144°26W **303** F11
Chitipa *Malawi* 9°41S 33°19E **269** D3
Chitose *Hokkaidō, Japan* 42°49N 141°39E **220** C10
Chitose *Kanagawa, Japan* 35°33N 139°37E **140** B2
Chitradurga *India* 14°14N 76°24E **245** G3
Chitrakot *India* 19°10N 81°40E **244** E5
Chitral *Pakistan* 35°50N 71°56E **240** B3
Chitralada Palace
Thailand 13°45N 100°31E **113** B2
Chitravati ➔ *India* 14°45N 78°15E **245** G4
Chitré *Panama* 7°59N 80°27W **320** E3
Chittagong *Bangla.* 22°19N 91°48E **241** D3
Chittagong □ *Bangla.* 24°5N 91°0E **241** C3
Chittaurgarh *India* 24°52N 74°38E **242** G6
Chittoor *India* 13°15N 79°5E **245** H4
Chittur *India* 10°40N 76°45E **245** J3
Chitungwiza *Zimbabwe* 18°0S 31°6E **269** F3
Chiuju *Taiwan* 22°44N 120°29E **225** D2
Chiumbe ➔
Dem. Rep. of the Congo 6°59S 21°12E **265** D4
Chiumbo *Angola* 12°29S 16°8E **265** E3
Chiume *Angola* 15°3S 21°14E **265** F4
Chiusi *Italy* 43°1N 11°57E **199** E8
Chiva *Spain* 39°27N 0°41W **197** F4
Chivacoa *Venezuela* 10°10N 68°54W **328** A4
Chivasso *Italy* 45°11N 7°53E **198** C4
Chivay *Peru* 15°40S 71°35W **330** D3
Chivé *Bolivia* 12°23S 68°35W **330** C4
Chivhu *Zimbabwe* 19°2S 30°52E **269** F3
Chivilcoy *Argentina* 34°55S 60°0W **334** C4
Chiwanda *Tanzania* 11°23S 34°55E **269** E3
Chixi *China* 22°0N 112°58E **229** G9
Chiyoda *Tokyo, Japan* **140** b4
Chizarira *Zimbabwe* 17°36S 27°45E **269** F2
Chizarira △ *Zimbabwe* 17°44S 27°52E **269** F2
Chizela *Zambia* 13°8S 25°0E **265** E4
Chizu *Japan* 35°16N 134°14E **222** B6
Chkalov = Orenburg
Russia 51°45N 55°6E **186** D10
Chkalova *Russia* 55°39N 37°56E **129** C5
Chkolovsk *Russia* 56°50N 43°10E **190** B6
Chloride *U.S.A.* 35°25N 114°12W **307** K12
Chlumec nad Cidlinou
Czech Rep. 50°9N 15°29E **180** A8
Chmielnik *Poland* 50°37N 20°43E **185** H7
Cho Bo *Vietnam* 20°46N 105°10E **228** G5
Cho-do *N. Korea* 38°30N 124°40E **224** C2
Cho Phuoc Hai *Vietnam* 10°26N 107°18E **237** G6
Choa Chu Kang
Singapore 1°22N 103°41E **138** A2
Choba *Kenya* 2°30N 38°5E **268** B4
Chobe △ *Botswana* 18°37S 24°23E **270** A4
Choboty *Russia* 55°39N 37°21E **129** C2
Choc B. *St. Lucia* 14°3N 60°59W **323** m
Choch'i *Taiwan* 23°20N 121°16E **225** C3
Chociańów *Poland* 51°27N 15°55E **182** G2
Chociwel *Poland* 53°29N 15°21E **184** E2
Chocó □ *Colombia* 6°0N 77°0W **328** B2
Chocolate Mts. *U.S.A.* 33°15N 115°15W **307** M11
Chocontá *Colombia* 5°9N 73°41W **328** B3
Choctawhatchee ➔
U.S.A. 30°25N 86°8W **316** E3
Choctawhatchee B.
U.S.A. 30°20N 86°20W **317** E3
Chodavaram *Andhra Pradesh, India* 17°50N 82°57E **244** F6
Chodavaram *Andhra Pradesh, India* 17°27N 81°46E **244** F5
Chodecz *Poland* 52°24N 19°2E **185** F6
Chodov *Czech Rep.* 50°15N 12°45E **180** A5
Chodov u Prahy
Czech Rep. 50°1N 14°30E **135** B3
Chodziez *Poland* 52°58N 16°58E **185** F3
Choele Choel *Argentina* 39°11S 65°40W **336** A3
Chōfu *Japan* 35°38N 139°32E **140** B2
Choiseul *St. Lucia* 13°47N 61°3W **323** m
Choiseul *Solomon Is.* 7°0S 156°40E **287** L9
Choisy-le-Roi *France* 48°46N 2°24E **134** B3
Choix *Mexico* 26°43N 108°17W **318** B3
Chojna *Poland* 52°58N 14°25E **185** F1
Chojnice *Poland* 53°42N 17°32E **184** E4
Chojnów *Poland* 51°18N 15°58E **185** G2
Chōkai-San *Japan* 39°6N 140°3E **220** E10
Choke Canyon Res.
U.S.A. 28°30N 98°20W **314** G5
Choke Mts. *Ethiopia* 11°18N 37°15E **257** E4
Chokurdakh *Russia* 70°38N 147°55E **215** B16
Cholame *U.S.A.* 35°44N 120°18W **306** K6
Cholan *Taiwan* 24°18N 120°49E **225** B2
Cholet *France* 47°4N 0°52W **172** E6
Cholguan *Chile* 37°10S 72°3W **334** D1
Cholpon-Ata *Kyrgyzstan* 42°40N 77°6E **217** D9
Cholupice *Czech Rep.* 49°59N 14°27E **135** C2
Choluteca *Honduras* 13°20N 87°14W **320** D2
Choluteca ➔ *Honduras* 13°0N 87°20W **320** D2
Chom Bung *Thailand* 13°37N 99°36E **236** F2
Chom Thong *Bangkok, Thailand* 13°41N 100°29E **113** B1
Chom Thong *Chiang Mai, Thailand* 18°25N 98°41E **236** C2
Choma *Zambia* 16°48S 26°59E **269** F2
Chomolungma = Everest, Mt.
Nepal 28°5N 86°58E **243** E12
Chomun *India* 27°15N 75°40E **242** F6
Chomutov *Czech Rep.* 50°28N 13°23E **180** A6
Chon Buri *Thailand* 13°21N 101°1E **236** F3
Chon Thanh *Vietnam* 11°24N 106°36E **237** G6
Chone *Ecuador* 0°40S 80°0W **328** D2
Chong Kai *Cambodia* 13°57N 103°35E **236** F4
Chong Mek *Thailand* 15°10N 105°27E **236** E5
Chong Pang *Singapore* 1°26N 103°49E **138** A2
Chong Phangan *Thailand* 9°39N 100°0E **237** b
Chong Samui *Thailand* 9°21N 99°50E **237** b
Chongde *China* 30°32N 120°26E **229** B13
Ch'ŏngjin *N. Korea* 41°47N 129°50E **224** B4
Chŏngju *N. Korea* 39°40N 125°5E **224** C2
Chongli *China* 40°58N 115°15E **226** D8
Chongming *China* 31°38N 121°23E **229** B13
Chongming Dao *China* 31°40N 121°30E **229** B13
Chongoyape *Peru* 6°35S 79°25W **330** B2
Chongp'yŏng *N. Korea* 39°47N 127°23E **224** C3
Chongqing *Chongqing, China* 29°35N 106°25E **228** C6
Chongqing *Sichuan, China* 30°38N 103°40E **228** B4
Chongqing Shi □ *China* 30°0N 108°0E **228** C6
Chongren *China* 27°46N 116°3E **229** D11
Chonguene *Mozam.* 25°3S 33°49E **271** C5
Chongwen *China* 39°52N 116°23E **114** B2
Chongyi *China* 25°45N 114°29E **229** E10
Chongzuo *China* 22°23N 107°20E **228** F6
Chonos, Arch. de los *Chile* 45°0S 75°0W **336** C2
Chop *Ukraine* 48°26N 22°12E **182** B7
Chopda *India* 21°20N 75°15E **244** D2
Chopim ➔ *Brazil* 25°35S 53°5W **335** B5
Chopin Museum *Warsaw, Poland* **142** b2
Chor *Pakistan* 25°31N 69°46E **242** G3
Chora *Greece* 37°3N 21°42E **204** D3
Chora Sfakion *Greece* 35°15N 24°9E **207** E5
Chorbat La *India* 34°42N 76°37E **243** B7
Chorley *U.K.* 53°39N 2°38W **168** D5
Chorna *Ukraine* 47°36N 29°20E **183** C14
Chornaya ➔ *Russia* 55°41N 38°0E **129** B6
Chornobyl *Ukraine* 51°20N 30°15E **177** C16
Chornomorske *Ukraine* 45°31N 32°40E **189** K7
Chorolque, Cerro *Bolivia* 20°59S 66°5W **334** A2
Choroszcz *Poland* 53°10N 22°59E **185** E9
Chorregon *Australia* 22°40S 143°32E **280** C3
Chorrillos *Peru* 12°10S 77°1W **124** C2
Chortkiv *Ukraine* 49°2N 25°46E **177** D13
Chorzele *Poland* 53°15N 20°55E **185** E7
Chorzów *Poland* 50°18N 18°57E **185** H5
Chos-Malal *Argentina* 37°20S 70°15W **334** D1
Ch'osan *N. Korea* 40°50N 125°47E **224** B2
Chosheta Shan *Taiwan* 23°50N 121°6E **225** C3
Chōshi *Japan* 35°45N 140°51E **223** B12
Choshui Hsi ➔ *Taiwan* 23°50N 120°15E **225** C2
Choszczno *Poland* 53°7N 15°25E **185** E2
Chota *Peru* 6°33S 78°39W **330** B2
Choteau *U.S.A.* 47°49N 112°11W **304** C7
Chotěboř *Czech Rep.* 49°43N 15°40E **180** B8
Chotila *India* 22°23N 71°15E **242** H4
Chotta Udepur *India* 22°19N 74°1E **242** H6
Choungui *Mayotte* 12°57S 45°8E **272** b
Chowchilla *U.S.A.* 37°7N 120°16W **306** H6
Chowpatty Beach *Mumbai, India* **130** b1
Choybalsan *Mongolia* 48°4N 114°30E **219** B6
Chrisman *U.S.A.* 39°48N 87°41W **311** E9
Christ Church Cathedral
Montréal, Canada **130** c2
Christburg = Dzierzgoń
Poland 53°58N 19°20E **184** E6
Christchurch *N.Z.* 43°33S 172°47E **285** D7
Christchurch *Dorset, U.K.* 50°44N 1°47W **169** G6
Christian I. *Canada* 44°50N 80°12W **312** B4
Christian Quarter *Jerusalem* **123** b3
Christian Sd. *U.S.A.* 55°56N 134°40W **303** J14
Christiana *Jamaica* 18°10N 77°29W **320** a
Christiana *North West, S. Africa* 27°52S 25°8E **270** C4
Christiansborg Slot
Copenhagen, Denmark **118** c2
Christiansfeld *Denmark* 55°21N 9°29E **163** J3
Christianshåb = Qasigiannguit
Greenland 68°50N 51°18W **154** D5
Christianshavn *Denmark* 55°40N 12°35E **118** A3
Christiansted
U.S. Virgin Is. 17°45N 64°42W **321** C7
Christie B. *Canada* 62°32N 111°10W **297** A6
Christina ➔ *Canada* 56°40N 111°3W **297** B6
Christmas Cr. ➔
Australia 18°29S 125°23E **278** C4
Christmas I. = Kiritimati
Kiribati 1°58N 157°27W **289** G12
Christmas I. *Ind. Oc.* 10°30S 105°40E **273** F9
Christoffel Nat. Park △
Neth. Ant. 12°21N 69°8W **322** g
Christopher *U.S.A.* 37°59N 89°3W **310** G7
Christopher, L. *Australia* 24°49S 127°42E **279** D4
Christyakovo = Thorez
Ukraine 48°4N 38°34E **189** H10
Chrudim *Czech Rep.* 49°58N 15°43E **180** B8
Chrysler Building *New York, U.S.A.* **132** c2
Chrzanów *Małopolskie, Poland* 50°10N 19°21E **185** H6
Chrzanów *Warszawa, Poland* 52°13N 20°53E **142** B1
Chtimba *Malawi* 10°35S 34°13E **269** E3
Chū = Shū *Kazakhstan* 43°36N 73°42E **217** D8
Chū = Shū ➔ *Kazakhstan* 45°0N 67°44E **217** D7
Chu ➔ *Vietnam* 19°53N 105°45E **236** C5
Chu Lai *Vietnam* 15°28N 108°45E **236** E7
Chuadanga *Bangla.* 23°38N 88°51E **241** D2
Chuak, Ko *Thailand* 9°28N 99°41E **237** b
Ch'uanchou = Quanzhou
China 24°55N 118°34E **229** E12
Chüanchow = Quanzhou
China 24°55N 118°34E **229** E12
Chuangwei *Taiwan* 24°45N 121°47E **225** B3
Chuankou *China* 34°20N 110°59E **226** G6
Chuathbaluk *U.S.A.* 61°40N 159°15W **303** F8
Chubarovka = Pology
Ukraine 47°29N 36°15E **189** J9
Chubbuck *U.S.A.* 42°55N 112°28W **304** E7
Chūbu □ *Japan* 36°45N 137°30E **223** A9
Chubu-Sangaku △
Japan 36°30N 137°40E **223** A9
Chubut □ *Argentina* 43°30S 69°0W **336** B3
Chubut ➔ *Argentina* 43°20S 65°5W **336** B3
Chuchi'i *Taiwan* 23°31N 120°33E **225** C2
Chuchi L. *Canada* 55°12N 124°30W **296** B4
Chuchow = Zhuzhou
China 27°49N 113°12E **229** D9
Chuda *India* 22°29N 71°41E **242** H4
Chudovo *Russia* 59°10N 31°41E **188** C6
Chudskoye, Ozero *Russia* 58°13N 27°30E **188** C4
Chuen Lung *China* 22°23N 114°6E **122** A1
Chugach Mts. *U.S.A.* 60°45N 147°0W **303** F11
Chuginadak I. *U.S.A.* 52°50N 169°45W **303** K5
Chūgoku □ *Japan* 35°0N 133°0E **222** B5
Chūgoku-Sanchi *Japan* 35°0N 133°0E **222** B5
Chuguyev = Chuhuyiv
Ukraine 49°55N 36°45E **189** H9
Chugwater *U.S.A.* 41°46N 104°50W **304** F11
Chuhuyiv *Ukraine* 49°55N 36°45E **189** H9
Chuk Kok *China* 22°20N 114°15E **122** A2
Chuka *Kenya* 0°20S 37°39E **268** C4
Chukchi Plateau *Arctic* 78°0N 165°0W **150** B17
Chukchi Sea *Russia* 68°0N 175°0W **215** C19
Chukotskoye Nagorye
Russia 68°0N 175°0E **215** C18
Chula *U.S.A.* 31°33N 83°32W **316** D6
Chula Vista *U.S.A.* 32°38N 117°5W **307** N9
Chulalongkorn University
Thailand 13°44N 100°31E **113** B2
Chulband ➔ *India* 20°40N 79°54E **244** D4

College Park *Md., U.S.A.* 38°59N 76°55W **143** B4
College Point *U.S.A.* 40°47N 73°50W **132** B2
College Station *U.S.A.* 30°37N 96°21W **314** F6
Collégien *France* 48°50N 2°41E **134** A4
Collesalvetti *Italy* 43°34N 10°27E **198** E7
Colli Euganei ⌓ *Italy* 45°18N 11°43E **199** C8
Collie *N.S.W., Australia* 31°41S 148°18E **283** A8
Collie *W. Austral., Australia* 33°22S 116°8E **279** F2
Collier B. *Australia* 16°10S 124°15E **278** C3
Collier Ra. *Australia* 24°45S 119°10E **279** D2
Collier Range △ *Australia* 24°39S 119°7E **279** D2
Collier Row *U.K.* 51°35N 0°9E **125** A4
Colliers Wood *U.K.* 51°24N 0°10W **125** B2
Collierville *U.S.A.* 35°3N 89°40W **315** D10
Collina, Passo di *Italy* 44°2N 10°56E **198** D7
Collingwood *Ont., Canada* 44°29N 80°13W **312** B4
Collingwood *N.Z.* 40°41S 172°40E **285** A7
Collins *Ont., Canada* 50°17N 89°27W **298** B2
Collins *Ga., U.S.A.* 32°11N 82°7W **316** C7
Collins *Mo., U.S.A.* 37°54N 93°37W **310** G3
Collinsville *Queens., Australia* 20°30S 147°56E **280** C4
Collinsville *Ill., U.S.A.* 38°40N 89°59W **310** F7
Collipulli *Chile* 37°55S 72°30W **334** D1
Collo *Algeria* 36°58N 6°37E **261** A6
Collooney *Ireland* 54°11N 8°29W **166** B3
Colma *U.S.A.* 37°40N 122°27W **136** B2
Colmar *France* 48°5N 7°20E **173** D14
Colmars *France* 44°11N 6°39E **175** D10
Colmenar *Spain* 36°54N 4°20W **195** J6
Colmenar de Oreja *Spain* 40°6N 3°25W **194** E7
Colmenar Viejo *Spain* 40°39N 3°47W **194** E7
Colney Hatch *U.K.* 51°36N 0°9W **125** A3
Colo → *Australia* 33°25S 150°52E **283** B9
Cologne = Köln *Germany* 50°56N 6°57E **178** E2
Cologno Monzese *Italy* 45°31N 9°16E **129** A2
Colom, I. d'en *Spain* 39°58N 4°16E **206** B5
Coloma *Calif., U.S.A.* 38°48N 120°53W **306** G6
Coloma *Mich., U.S.A.* 42°11N 86°19W **311** B10
Colomb-Béchar = Béchar *Algeria* 31°38N 2°18W **261** B4
Colombes *France* 48°55N 2°15E **134** A2
Colombey-les-Belles *France* 48°32N 5°54E **173** D12
Colombey-les-Deux-Églises *France* 48°13N 4°50E **173** D11
Colômbia *Brazil* 20°10S 48°40W **333** F2
Colombia ■ *S. Amer.* 3°45N 73°0W **328** C3
Colombian Basin *S. Amer.* 14°0N 76°0W **321** D5
Colombier *St.-Martin* 18°5N 63°4W **322** a
Colombo *Sri Lanka* 6°56N 79°58E **245** L4
Colomiers *France* 43°36N 1°21E **174** E5
Colón *B. Aires, Argentina* 33°53S 61°7W **334** C3
Colón *Entre Ríos, Argentina* 32°12S 58°10W **334** C4
Colón *Cuba* 22°42N 80°54W **320** B3
Colón *Panama* 9°20N 79°54W **320** E4
Colón *Peru* 5°0S 81°0W **330** B1
Colón, Arch. de *Ecuador* 0°0 91°0W **330** a
Colón, Monumente a *Barcelona, Spain* **114** c3
Colon, Plaza de *Madrid, Spain* **127** a3
Colón Ridge *Pac. Oc.* 2°0N 96°0W **289** G18
Colonarie *St. Vincent* 13°14N 61°8W **323** n
Colonia *Micronesia* 9°30N 138°10E **287** R16
Colonia 25 de Mayo *Argentina* 37°48S 67°41W **336** A3
Colònia de Sant Jordi *Spain* 39°19N 2°59E **206** B3
Colonia del Sacramento *Uruguay* 34°25S 57°50W **334** C4
Colonia Dora *Argentina* 28°34S 62°59W **334** B3
Colonia Güell *Spain* 41°21N 2°2E **114** A1
Colonia Las Heras *Argentina* 46°33S 68°57W **336** C3
Colonial Beach *U.S.A.* 38°15N 76°58W **309** F15
Colonial Knob *N.Z.* 41°9S 174°48E **143** A1
Colonie *U.S.A.* 42°43N 73°50W **313** D11
Colonna, C. *Italy* 39°2N 17°12E **201** C10
Colonsay *Sask., Canada* 51°59N 105°52W **297** C7
Colonsay *Argyll & Bute, U.K.* 56°5N 6°12W **167** E2
Colorado □ *U.S.A.* 39°30N 105°30W **304** G11
Colorado → *Argentina* 39°50S 62°8W **336** A4
Colorado → *N. Amer.* 31°45N 114°40W **305** L6
Colorado → *Tex., U.S.A.* 28°36N 95°59W **314** G7
Colorado City *U.S.A.* 32°24N 100°52W **314** E4
Colorado Plateau *U.S.A.* 37°0N 111°0W **305** H8
Colorado River Aqueduct *U.S.A.* 33°50N 117°23W **307** L12
Colorado Springs *U.S.A.* 38°50N 104°49W **304** G11
Colorno *Italy* 44°56N 10°23E **198** D7
Colosseo *Rome, Italy* **136** c3
Colosseum = Colosseo *Rome, Italy* **136** c3
Colotlán *Mexico* 22°6N 103°16W **318** C4
Colquechaca *Bolivia* 18°40S 66°1W **331** D4
Colquitt *U.S.A.* 31°10N 84°44W **316** D5
Colstrip *U.S.A.* 45°53N 106°38W **304** D10
Colton *U.S.A.* 44°33N 74°56W **313** B10
Columbia *Ala., U.S.A.* 31°18N 85°7W **316** D4
Columbia *Ill., U.S.A.* 38°27N 90°12W **310** F6
Columbia *Ky., U.S.A.* 37°6N 85°18W **309** G11
Columbia *La., U.S.A.* 32°6N 92°5W **314** E8
Columbia *Miss., U.S.A.* 31°15N 89°50W **315** F10
Columbia *Mo., U.S.A.* 38°57N 92°20W **310** F4
Columbia *Pa., U.S.A.* 40°2N 76°30W **313** F8
Columbia *S.C., U.S.A.* 34°0N 81°2W **316** A8
Columbia *Tenn., U.S.A.* 35°37N 87°2W **315** D11
Columbia → *N. Amer.* 46°15N 124°5W **306** D2
Columbia, C. *Canada* 83°6N 69°57W **295** A11
Columbia, District of □ *U.S.A.* 38°55N 77°0W **309** F15
Columbia, Mt. *Canada* 52°8N 117°20W **296** C5
Columbia Basin *U.S.A.* 46°45N 119°5W **304** C4
Columbia City *U.S.A.* 41°10N 85°29W **311** C11
Columbia Falls *U.S.A.* 48°23N 114°11W **304** B6
Columbia Mts. *Canada* 52°0N 119°0W **296** C5
Columbia Plateau *U.S.A.* 44°0N 117°30W **304** E5
Columbiana *U.S.A.* 40°53N 80°42W **312** F4
Columbretes, Is. *Spain* 39°50N 0°50E **196** F5
Columbus *Ga., U.S.A.* 32°28N 84°59W **316** C5
Columbus *Ind., U.S.A.* 39°13N 85°55W **311** E11
Columbus *Kans., U.S.A.* 37°10N 94°50W **308** G6
Columbus *Miss., U.S.A.* 33°30N 88°25W **315** E10
Columbus *Mont., U.S.A.* 45°38N 109°15W **304** D9
Columbus *N. Mex., U.S.A.* 31°50N 107°38W **305** L10
Columbus *Nebr., U.S.A.* 41°26N 97°22W **308** E5
Columbus *Ohio, U.S.A.* 39°58N 83°0W **311** E13
Columbus *Tex., U.S.A.* 29°42N 96°33W **314** G6
Columbus Circle *Washington, D.C., U.S.A.* **143** b3
Columbus Circle *New York, U.S.A.* **132** b2
Columbus Grove *U.S.A.* 40°55N 84°4W **311** D12
Columbus Junction *U.S.A.* 41°17N 91°22W **310** C5
Columbus Monument = Colón, Monumente a *Barcelona, Spain* **114** c3
Columbus Park *Jamaica* 18°28N 77°25W **320** a
Columbus Park *Boston, U.S.A.* **116** b3
Colunga *Spain* 43°29N 5°16W **194** B5
Colusa *U.S.A.* 39°13N 122°1W **306** F4
Colville *U.S.A.* 48°33N 117°54W **304** B5
Colville → *U.S.A.* 70°25N 150°30W **303** A10
Colville, C. *N.Z.* 36°29S 175°21E **284** C4
Colville Ridge *Pac. Oc.* 30°0S 180°0E **277** G15
Colwood *Canada* 48°26N 123°29W **306** B3
Colwyn Bay *U.K.* 53°18N 3°44W **168** D4
Coma *Ethiopia* 8°29N 36°53E **257** F4
Comácchio *Italy* 44°42N 12°11E **199** D9
Comalcalco *Mexico* 18°16N 93°13W **319** D6
Comallo *Argentina* 41°0S 70°5W **336** B2
Comana *Romania* 44°10N 26°10E **183** F11
Comanche *U.S.A.* 31°54N 98°36W **314** F5
Comandante Arbues = Mirandópolis *Brazil* 21°9S 51°6W **335** A5
Comandante Ferraz *Antarctica* 62°30S 58°0W **151** C18
Comandante Luis Piedrabuena *Argentina* 49°59S 68°54W **336** C3
Comănești *Romania* 46°25N 26°26E **183** D11
Comarapa *Bolivia* 17°54S 64°29W **331** D5
Comarnic *Romania* 45°15N 25°38E **183** E10
Comayagua *Honduras* 14°25N 87°37W **320** D2
Combahee → *U.S.A.* 32°31N 80°31W **315** E14
Combara *Australia* 31°10S 148°22E **283** A8
Combarbalá *Chile* 31°11S 71°2W **334** C1
Combault *France* 48°48N 2°37E **134** B4
Combe Martin *U.K.* 51°12N 4°3W **169** F3
Combeaufontaine *France* 47°38N 5°54E **173** E12
Comber *Ont., Canada* 42°14N 82°33W **312** D2
Comber *Down, U.K.* 54°33N 5°45W **166** B6
Combermere *Canada* 45°22N 77°37W **312** A7
Combermere Bay *Burma* 19°37N 93°34E **241** F4
Comblain-au-Pont *Belgium* 50°29N 5°35E **170** D5
Combourg *France* 48°25N 1°46W **172** D5
Comboyne *Australia* 31°34S 152°27E **283** A10
Combrailles *France* 46°8N 2°8E **173** F9
Combronde *France* 45°58N 3°5E **174** C7
Comer *Ala., U.S.A.* 32°2N 85°23W **316** C4
Comer *Ga., U.S.A.* 34°4N 83°8W **316** A6
Comeragh Mts. *Ireland* 52°18N 7°34W **166** D4
Comércio, Praça do *Portugal* 38°41N 9°9W **126** A2
Comerío *Puerto Rico* 18°12N 66°12W **321** b
Comet *Australia* 23°36S 148°38E **280** C4
Comilla *Bangla.* 23°28N 91°10E **241** D3
Comino *Malta* 36°1N 14°20E **206** E7
Comino, C. *Italy* 40°32N 9°49E **200** B2
Cómiso *Italy* 36°56N 14°36E **201** F7
Comitán de Domínguez *Mexico* 16°15N 92°8W **319** D6
Commentry *France* 46°20N 2°46E **173** F9
Commerce *Calif., U.S.A.* 34°0N 118°9W **126** B4
Commerce *Ga., U.S.A.* 34°12N 83°28W **315** D13
Commerce *Tex., U.S.A.* 33°15N 95°54W **314** E7
Commercy *France* 48°43N 5°34E **173** D12
Commissioner's Pt. *Bermuda* 32°19N 64°49W **153** a
Committee B. *Canada* 68°30N 86°30W **295** C11
Commonwealth B. *Antarctica* 67°0S 144°0E **151** C10
Commoron Cr. → *Australia* 28°22S 150°8E **281** D5
Communism Pk. = imeni Ismail Samani, Pik *Tajikistan* 39°0N 72°2E **217** E8
Como *N.S.W., Australia* 34°0S 151°4E **139** C1
Como *Italy* 45°47N 9°5E **198** C6
Como, Lago di *Italy* 46°0N 9°11E **198** B6
Comodoro Rivadavia *Argentina* 45°50S 67°40W **336** C3
Comoé △ *Ivory C.* 9°0N 3°35W **262** D4
Comorâște *Romania* 45°10N 21°35E **182** E6
Comorin, C. = Kanyakumari *India* 8°3N 77°40E **245** K3
Comoros ■ *Ind. Oc.* 12°10S 44°15E **272** a
Comox *Canada* 49°42N 124°55W **296** D4
Company's Gardens *Cape Town, S. Africa* **118** c2
Compass Lake *U.S.A.* 30°36N 85°24W **316** E4
Compiègne *France* 49°24N 2°50E **173** C9
Comporta *Portugal* 38°22N 8°46W **195** G2
Compostela *Nayarit, Mexico* 21°14N 104°55W **318** C4
Compostela *Phil.* 7°40N 126°2E **233** H6
Comprida, I. *Brazil* 24°50S 47°42W **335** A6
Compton *Qué., Canada* 45°14N 71°49W **313** A13
Compton *Calif., U.S.A.* 33°53N 118°13W **307** M8
Comrat *Moldova* 46°18N 28°40E **183** D13
Con Cuong *Vietnam* 19°2N 104°54E **236** C5
Con Dao △ *Vietnam* 8°42N 106°35E **237** H6
Con Son *Vietnam* 8°41N 106°37E **237** H6
Cona Niyeu *Argentina* 41°58S 67°0W **336** B3
Conakry *Guinea* 9°29N 13°49W **262** D2
Conara *Australia* 41°50S 147°26E **281** G4
Conargo *Australia* 35°16S 145°10E **283** C6
Concarneau *France* 47°52N 3°56W **172** E3
Conceição *Paraíba, Brazil* 7°33S 38°31W **332** C4
Conceição *Mozam.* 18°47S 36°7E **269** F4
Conceição, I. da *Brazil* 22°52S 43°6W **135** B2
Conceição da Barra *Brazil* 18°35S 39°45W **333** E4
Conceição do Araguaia *Brazil* 8°0S 49°2W **332** C2
Conceição do Canindé *Brazil* 7°54S 41°34W **332** C3
Conceição do Maú *Brazil* 3°35N 59°53W **329** C6
Conceição do Paraíba = Capela *Brazil* 10°30S 37°0W **332** D4
Concepción *Argentina* 27°20S 65°35W **334** B2
Concepción *Bolivia* 16°15S 62°8W **331** D5
Concepción *Chile* 36°50S 73°0W **334** D1
Concepción *Mexico* 18°15N 90°5W **319** D6
Concepción *Paraguay* 23°22S 57°26W **334** A4
Concepción *Peru* 11°54S 75°19W **330** C2
Concepcion *Tarlac, Phil.* 15°27N 120°47E **232** D3
Concepción □ *Chile* 37°0S 72°30W **334** D1
Concepción → *Mexico* 30°32N 113°2W **318** A2
Concepción, Est. de *Chile* 50°30S 74°55W **336** D2
Concepción, L. *Bolivia* 17°20S 61°20W **331** D5
Concepción, Pta. *Mexico* 26°53N 111°50W **318** B2
Concepción del Oro *Mexico* 24°38N 101°25W **318** C4
Concepción del Uruguay *Argentina* 32°35S 58°20W **334** C4
Conception, Pt. *U.S.A.* 34°27N 120°28W **307** L6
Conception B. *Nfld. & L., Canada* 47°45N 53°0W **299** C9
Conception B. *Namibia* 23°55S 14°22E **270** B1
Conception I. *Bahamas* 23°52N 75°9W **321** B4
Concertgebouw *Amsterdam, Neths.* **112** c1
Concession *Zimbabwe* 17°27S 30°56E **269** F3
Conchalí *Chile* 33°22S 70°39W **137** B2
Conchas Dam *U.S.A.* 35°22N 104°11W **305** J11
Conches-en-Ouche *France* 48°58N 0°56E **172** D7
Concho *U.S.A.* 34°28N 109°36W **305** J9
Concho → *U.S.A.* 31°34N 99°43W **314** F5
Conchos → *Chihuahua, Mexico* 29°35N 104°25W **318** B4
Conchos → *Chihuahua, Mexico* 27°29N 106°45W **318** B3
Conchos → *Tamaulipas, Mexico* 24°55N 97°38W **319** B5
Concord *N.S.W., Australia* 33°52S 151°6E **139** B1
Concord *Ont., Canada* 43°48N 79°29W **141** A2
Concord *Grenada* 12°17N 61°44W **323** q
Concord *Calif., U.S.A.* 37°59N 122°2W **306** H4
Concord *Ga., U.S.A.* 33°5N 84°27W **316** B5
Concord *Mich., U.S.A.* 42°11N 84°38W **311** B12
Concord *Mo., U.S.A.* 38°32N 90°23W **310** F6
Concord *N.C., U.S.A.* 35°25N 80°35W **315** D14
Concord *N.H., U.S.A.* 43°12N 71°32W **313** C13
Concorde, Place de la *Paris, France* **134** b3
Concordia *Antarctica* 75°6S 123°23E **151** D17
Concordia *Argentina* 31°20S 58°2W **334** C4
Concórdia *Brazil* 4°36S 66°36W **328** D4
Concordia *Sinaloa, Mexico* 23°17N 106°4W **318** C3
Concordia *Kans., U.S.A.* 39°34N 97°40W **308** F5
Concordia *Mo., U.S.A.* 38°59N 93°34W **310** F3
Concordia University *Montréal, Canada* **130** c1
Concorezzo *Italy* 45°35N 9°19E **129** A2
Concrete *U.S.A.* 48°32N 121°45W **304** B3
Conda *Angola* 11°9S 14°20E **265** E2
Condah *Australia* 37°57S 141°44E **282** D4
Condamine *Australia* 26°56S 150°9E **281** D5
Condat *France* 45°21N 2°46E **174** C6
Condé *Angola* 10°50S 14°37E **265** E2
Conde *Brazil* 11°49S 37°37W **333** D4
Conde *S. Dak., U.S.A.* 45°9N 98°6W **308** C4
Condé-sur-Noireau *France* 48°51N 0°33W **172** D6
Condet *Indonesia* 6°17S 106°51E **122** A2
Condeúba *Brazil* 14°52S 42°0W **333** D3
Condobolin *Australia* 33°4S 147°6E **283** B7
Condom *France* 43°57N 0°22E **174** E4
Condon *U.S.A.* 45°14N 120°11W **304** D3
Conegliano *Italy* 45°53N 12°18E **199** C9
Conejera, I. = Conills, I. des *Spain* 39°11N 2°58E **206** B3
Conejos *Mexico* 26°14N 103°53W **318** B4
Conemaugh → *U.S.A.* 40°28N 79°19W **312** F5
Conero ⌓ *Italy* 43°32N 13°35E **199** E10
Coney Island *U.S.A.* 40°34N 74°0W **132** C2
Conflict Group *Papua N. G.* 10°47S 151°45E **286** F6
Confolens *France* 46°2N 0°40E **174** B4
Confuso → *Paraguay* 25°9S 57°34W **334** B4
Congaree → *U.S.A.* 33°44N 80°38W **316** B9
Congaree Swamp ⌓ *U.S.A.* 33°47N 80°47W **316** B9
Congaz *Moldova* 46°7N 28°36E **183** D13
Congerville *U.S.A.* 40°38N 89°11W **310** D7
Conghua *China* 23°36N 113°31E **229** F9
Congjiang *China* 25°43N 108°52E **228** E7
Congleton *U.K.* 53°10N 2°13W **168** D5
Congo *Brazil* 7°48S 36°40W **332** C4
Congo (Brazzaville) = Congo ■ *Africa* 1°0S 16°0E **264** C3
Congo (Kinshasa) = Congo, Dem. Rep. of the ■ *Africa* 3°0S 23°0E **265** C4
Congo ■ *Africa* 1°0S 16°0E **264** C3
Congo → *Africa* 6°4S 12°24E **265** D2
Congo, Dem. Rep. of the ■ *Africa* 3°0S 23°0E **265** C4
Congo Basin *Africa* 0°10S 24°30E **254** G6
Congo Free State = Congo, Dem. Rep. of the ■ *Africa* 3°0S 23°0E **265** C4
Congonhas *Brazil* 20°30S 43°52W **333** F3
Congonhas São Paulo ✈ **(CGH)** *Brazil* 23°38S 46°39W **137** B2
Congress *U.S.A.* 34°9N 112°51W **305** J7
Conguillio △ *Chile* 38°40S 71°42W **336** A2
Conil de la Frontera *Spain* 36°17N 6°10W **195** J4
Conills, I. des *Spain* 39°11N 2°58E **206** B3
Conimbla △ *Australia* 33°45S 148°28E **283** B8
Coniston *Canada* 46°29N 80°51W **298** C3
Conjeeveram = Kanchipuram *India* 12°52N 79°45E **245** H4
Conklin *Alta., Canada* 55°38N 111°5W **297** B6
Conklin *N.Y., U.S.A.* 42°2N 75°49W **313** D9
Conkouati ⌓ *Congo* 3°50S 11°28E **264** C2
Conlendas, Pta. das *Azores* 38°38N 27°14W **153** d1
Conley → *U.S.A.* 33°40N 84°17W **113** C3
Conn, L. *Ireland* 54°3N 9°15W **166** B2
Connacht □ *Ireland* 53°43N 9°12W **166** C2
Connaught Place *Delhi, India* **120** b2
Conneaut *U.S.A.* 41°57N 80°34W **312** E4
Connecticut □ *U.S.A.* 41°30N 72°45W **313** E12
Connecticut → *U.S.A.* 41°16N 72°20W **313** E12
Connell *U.S.A.* 46°40N 118°52W **304** C4
Connellsville *U.S.A.* 40°1N 79°35W **312** F5
Connemara *Ireland* 53°29N 9°45W **166** C2
Connemara △ *Ireland* 53°32N 9°52W **166** C2
Conner *Phil.* 17°48N 121°19E **232** C3
Connerré *France* 48°3N 0°30E **172** D7
Connersville *U.S.A.* 39°39N 85°8W **311** E11
Connors Ra. *Australia* 21°40S 149°10E **280** C4
Conoble *Australia* 32°55S 144°33E **283** B6
Cononaco → *Ecuador* 1°32S 75°35W **328** D2
Conques *France* 44°36N 2°23E **174** D6
Conquest *Canada* 51°32N 107°14W **297** C7
Conquista = Vitória da Conquista *Brazil* 14°51S 40°51W **333** D3
Conrad *Iowa, U.S.A.* 42°14N 92°52W **310** B4
Conrad *Mont., U.S.A.* 48°10N 111°57W **304** B8
Conrad Rise *S. Ocean* 53°0S 41°0E **273** K3
Conran, C. *Australia* 37°49S 148°44E **283** D8
Conroe *U.S.A.* 30°19N 95°27W **314** F7
Consecon *Canada* 44°0N 77°31W **312** C7
Conselheiro Lafaiete *Brazil* 20°40S 43°48W **333** F3
Conselheiro Pena *Brazil* 19°10S 41°30W **333** E3
Conselve *Italy* 45°14N 11°52E **199** C8
Conservatori, Palazzo dei *Rome, Italy* **136** c3
Consett *U.K.* 54°51N 1°50W **168** C6
Consolação *Brazil* 23°32S 46°38W **137** B2
Consort *Canada* 52°1N 110°46W **297** C6
Constance = Konstanz *Germany* 47°40N 9°10E **179** H5
Constance, L. = Bodensee *Europe* 47°35N 9°25E **179** H5
Constanța *Romania* 44°14N 28°38E **183** F13
Constanța □ *Romania* 44°15N 28°15E **183** F13
Constantia *Western Cape, S. Africa* 34°2S 18°26E **118** B1
Constantia *N.Y., U.S.A.* 43°15N 76°1W **313** C8
Constantina *Spain* 37°51N 5°40W **195** H5
Constantine *Algeria* 36°25N 6°42E **261** A6
Constantine *Mich., U.S.A.* 41°50N 85°40W **311** C11
Constantine □ *Algeria* 36°30N 6°40E **261** A6
Constantine, Arch of = Costantino, Arco di *Rome, Italy* **136** c3
Constantine, C. *U.S.A.* 58°24N 158°54W **303** G8
Constantinople = İstanbul *Turkey* 41°0N 28°58E **122** C1
Constitución *B. Aires, Argentina* 34°38S 58°23W **117** B2
Constitución *Chile* 35°20S 72°30W **334** D1
Constitución *Uruguay* 31°0S 57°50W **334** C4
Constitución de 1857 △ *Mexico* 32°4N 115°55W **318** A1
Constitution *U.S.A.* 33°42N 84°20W **113** B2
Constitution Avenue *Washington, D.C., U.S.A.* **143** b2
Constitution Square = Syntagma Square *Athens, Greece* **112** b3
Consuegra *Spain* 39°28N 3°36W **195** F7
Consul *Canada* 49°20N 109°30W **297** D7
Contact *U.S.A.* 41°46N 114°45W **304** F6
Contai *India* 21°54N 87°46E **243** J12
Contamana *Peru* 7°19S 74°55W **330** B3
Contarina *Italy* 45°1N 12°13E **199** C9
Contas → *Brazil* 14°17S 39°1W **333** D4
Contes *France* 43°49N 7°19E **175** E11
Continental *U.S.A.* 41°6N 84°16W **311** C12
Contoocook *U.S.A.* 43°13N 71°45W **313** C13
Contra Costa *Mozam.* 25°9S 33°30E **271** C5
Contres *France* 47°24N 1°26E **172** E8
Contrexéville *France* 48°10N 5°53E **173** D12
Controller B. *U.S.A.* 60°7N 144°15W **303** F11
Contumaza *Peru* 7°23S 78°57W **330** B2
Contwoyto L. *Canada* 65°42N 110°50W **294** C8
Convención *Colombia* 8°28N 73°21W **328** B3
Convention and Exhibition Centre *Hong Kong, China* **122** b2
Convention Center *Calif., U.S.A.* 34°3N 118°16W **126** B3
Convention Center *Washington, D.C., U.S.A.* **143** a2
Conversano *Italy* 40°58N 17°7E **201** B10
Converse *U.S.A.* 40°35N 85°52W **311** D11
Convoy *U.S.A.* 40°55N 84°43W **311** D12
Conway = Conwy *U.K.* 53°17N 3°50W **168** D4
Conway = Conwy → *U.K.* 53°17N 3°50W **168** D4
Conway *Australia* 20°24S 148°41E **280** J6
Conway *Ark., U.S.A.* 35°5N 92°26W **314** D8
Conway *Fla., U.S.A.* 28°30N 81°19W **133** B2
Conway *N.H., U.S.A.* 43°59N 71°7W **313** C13
Conway *S.C., U.S.A.* 33°51N 79°3W **315** E15
Conway, C. *Australia* 20°34S 148°46E **280** J6
Conway, L. *S. Austral., Australia* 28°17S 135°35E **281** D2
Conway, L. *Fla., U.S.A.* 28°28N 81°21W **133** B2
Conwy *U.K.* 53°17N 3°50W **168** D4
Conwy □ *U.K.* 53°10N 3°44W **168** D4
Conwy → *U.K.* 53°17N 3°50W **168** D4
Conyers *U.S.A.* 33°40N 84°1W **316** B5
Coober Pedy *Australia* 29°1S 134°43E **281** D1
Cooch Behar = Koch Bihar *India* 26°22N 89°29E **241** B2
Coogee *Australia* 33°55S 151°16E **139** B2
Cooinda *Australia* 13°15S 130°5E **278** B5
Cook *S. Austral., Australia* 30°37S 130°25E **279** F5
Cook *Minn., U.S.A.* 47°51N 92°41W **308** B7
Cook, B. *Chile* 55°10S 70°0W **336** E3
Cook, C. *Canada* 50°8N 127°55W **296** C3
Cook, Mt. = Aoraki Mount Cook *N.Z.* 43°36S 170°9E **285** D5
Cook, Récif de *N. Cal.* 19°25S 163°50E **288** d
Cook B. *Vanuatu* 18°46S 169°15E **287** H7
Cook Inlet *U.S.A.* 60°0N 152°0W **303** G10
Cook Is. *Pac. Oc.* 17°0S 160°0W **289** J12
Cook Strait *N.Z.* 41°15S 174°29E **284** H3
Cooke Plains *Australia* 35°23S 139°34E **282** C3
Cookeville *U.S.A.* 36°10N 85°30W **315** C12
Cookhouse *S. Africa* 32°44S 25°47E **270** D4
Cooks Hammock *U.S.A.* 29°56N 83°17W **316** F6
Cookshire *Canada* 45°25N 71°38W **313** A13
Cookstown *U.K.* 54°39N 6°45W **166** B5
Cooksville *Canada* 43°35N 79°38W **141** B1
Cooktown *Australia* 15°30S 145°16E **280** B4
Coolabah *Australia* 31°1S 146°43E **283** A7
Cooladdi *Australia* 26°37S 145°23E **281** D4
Coolah *Australia* 31°48S 149°41E **283** A8
Coolah Tops △ *Australia* 31°52S 150°0E **283** A9
Coolamon *Australia* 34°46S 147°8E **283** C7
Coolgardie *Australia* 30°55S 121°8E **279** F3
Coolidge *Ariz., U.S.A.* 32°59N 111°31W **305** K8
Coolidge *Ga., U.S.A.* 31°1N 83°52W **316** D6
Coolidge Dam *U.S.A.* 33°10N 110°32W **305** K8
Coolock *Ireland* 53°22N 6°12W **120** A2
Cooma *Australia* 36°12S 149°8E **283** D8
Coon Rapids *Iowa, U.S.A.* 41°53N 94°41W **310** C2
Coon Rapids *Minn., U.S.A.* 45°9N 93°19W **308** C7
Coonabarabran *Australia* 31°14S 149°18E **283** A8
Coonalpyn *Australia* 35°43S 139°52E **282** C3
Coonamble *Australia* 30°56S 148°27E **283** A8
Coonana *Australia* 31°0S 123°0E **279** F3
Coondapoor *India* 13°42N 74°40E **245** H2
Cooninnie, L. *Australia* 26°4S 139°59E **281** D2
Coonoor *India* 11°21N 76°45E **245** J3
Cooper *U.S.A.* 33°23N 95°42W **314** E7
Cooper → *U.S.A.* 32°50N 79°56W **316** C10
Cooper Cr. → *Australia* 28°29S 137°46E **281** D2
Cooper Ridge *Pac. Oc.* 10°0N 150°30W **289** G12
Cooper's Hill *Jamaica* 18°4N 76°51W **320** a
Cooperstown *N. Dak., U.S.A.* 47°27N 98°8W **308** B4
Cooperstown *N.Y., U.S.A.* 42°42N 74°56W **313** D10
Coopersville *U.S.A.* 43°4N 85°57W **311** A11
Coopracambra △ *Australia* 37°20S 149°20E **283** D8
Coora → *Trin. & Tob.* 10°10N 61°28W **323** t
Coorabie *Australia* 31°54S 132°18E **279** F5
Coorong, The *Australia* 35°50S 139°20E **282** C3
Coorong △ *Australia* 36°0S 139°29E **282** D3
Coorow *Australia* 29°53S 116°2E **279** E2
Cooroy *Australia* 26°22S 152°54E **281** D5
Coos Bay *U.S.A.* 43°22N 124°13W **304** E1
Coosa → *U.S.A.* 32°30N 86°16W **315** E11
Cootamundra *Australia* 34°36S 148°1E **283** C8
Cootehill *Ireland* 54°4N 7°5W **166** B4
Copacabana *Brazil* 22°58S 43°11W **135** B1
Copahue Paso *Argentina* 37°49S 71°8W **334** D1
Copainalá *Mexico* 17°4N 93°18W **319** D6
Copake *U.S.A.* 42°7N 73°31W **313** D11
Copalnic Mănăștur *Romania* 47°30N 23°41E **183** C8
Copán *Honduras* 14°50N 89°9W **320** D2
Copatana *Brazil* 2°48S 67°4W **328** D4
Cope *Colo., U.S.A.* 39°40N 102°51W **304** G12
Cope *S.C., U.S.A.* 33°23N 81°0W **316** B8
Cope, C. *Spain* 37°26N 1°28W **197** H3
Copeland *U.S.A.* 25°57N 81°22W **317** K8
Copenhagen = København *Denmark* 55°40N 12°26E **118** A2
Copenhagen *U.S.A.* 43°54N 75°41W **313** C9
Copertino *Italy* 40°16N 18°3E **201** B11
Copiapó *Chile* 27°30S 70°20W **334** B1
Copiapó → *Chile* 27°19S 70°56W **334** B1
Coplay *U.S.A.* 40°44N 75°29W **313** F9
Copley *Australia* 30°36S 138°26E **282** A3
Copp L. *Canada* 60°14N 114°40W **296** A6
Copparo *Italy* 44°54N 11°49E **199** D8
Coppename → *Suriname* 5°48N 55°55W **329** B6
Copper → *U.S.A.* 60°18N 145°3W **303** F11
Copper Canyon = Barranca del Cobre ⌓ *Mexico* 27°18N 107°40W **318** B3
Copper Center *U.S.A.* 61°58N 145°18W **303** F11
Copper City = Invermere *Canada* 50°30N 116°2W **296** C5
Copper Harbor *U.S.A.* 47°28N 87°53W **308** B10
Copper Queen *Zimbabwe* 17°29S 29°18E **269** F2
Copperas Cove *U.S.A.* 31°8N 97°54W **314** F6
Copperbelt □ *Zambia* 13°15S 27°30E **269** E2
Coppermine = Kugluktuk *Canada* 67°50N 115°5W **294** C8
Coppermine → *Canada* 67°49N 116°4W **294** C8
Copperopolis *U.S.A.* 37°58N 120°38W **306** H6
Copșa Mică *Romania* 46°7N 24°15E **183** D9
Coquet → *U.K.* 55°20N 1°32W **168** B6
Coquilhatville = Mbandaka *Dem. Rep. of the Congo* 0°1N 18°18E **264** B3
Coquille *U.S.A.* 43°11N 124°11W **304** E1
Coquimbo *Chile* 30°0S 71°20W **334** C1
Coquimbo □ *Chile* 31°0S 71°0W **334** C1
Corabia *Romania* 43°48N 24°30E **183** G9
Coração de Jesus *Brazil* 16°43S 44°22W **333** E3
Coracora *Peru* 15°5S 73°45W **330** D3
Coraki *Australia* 28°59S 153°17E **281** D5
Coral *U.S.A.* 40°29N 79°10W **312** F5
Coral Bay *Phil.* 8°25N 117°20E **233** G1
Coral Gables *U.S.A.* 25°43N 80°16W **128** B2
Coral Harbour *Bahamas* 24°58N 77°28W **153** b
Coral Harbour *Nunavut, Canada* 64°8N 83°10W **295** C11
Coral Heights *Bahamas* 25°0N 77°27W **153** b
Coral Hills *U.S.A.* 38°51N 76°55W **143** B4
Coral Sea *Pac. Oc.* 15°0S 150°0E **286** F4
Coral Sea Basin *Pac. Oc.* 14°0S 152°0E **288** J7
Coral Sea Islands Terr. □ *Australia* 20°0S 155°0E **276** D9
Coral Springs *U.S.A.* 26°16N 80°16W **317** J9
Corales del Rosario △ *Colombia* 10°8N 75°46W **328** A2
Coralville *U.S.A.* 41°40N 91°35W **310** C5
Coralville L. *U.S.A.* 41°42N 91°33W **310** C5
Corangamite, L. *Australia* 38°5S 143°30E **282** E5
Corantijn → *Suriname* 5°50N 57°8W **329** B6
Coraopolis *U.S.A.* 40°31N 80°10W **312** F4
Corato *Italy* 41°9N 16°25E **201** A9
Corbeil-Essonnes *France* 48°36N 2°26E **173** D9
Corbeiro, C. *W. Sahara* 21°50N 17°0W **260** D1
Corbett △ *India* 29°20N 79°0E **243** E8
Corbie *France* 49°54N 2°30E **173** C9
Corbières *France* 42°55N 2°35E **174** F6
Corbigny *France* 47°16N 3°40E **173** E10
Corbin *U.S.A.* 36°57N 84°6W **309** G11
Corbones → *Spain* 37°36N 5°39W **195** H5
Corbu *Romania* 44°25N 28°39E **183** F13
Corby *U.K.* 52°30N 0°41W **169** E7
Corcaigh = Cork *Ireland* 51°54N 8°29W **166** E3
Corcoran *U.S.A.* 36°6N 119°33W **306** J7
Corcovado, Cristo Redentar *Brazil* 22°57S 43°12W **135** B1
Corcovado △ *Costa Rica* 8°33N 83°35W **320** E3
Cordele *U.S.A.* 31°58N 83°47W **316** D6
Cordell *U.S.A.* 35°17N 98°59W **314** D5
Cordenòns *Italy* 45°59N 12°42E **199** C9
Cordes-sur-Ciel *France* 44°5N 1°57E **174** D5
Cordillera de los Picachos △ *Colombia* 2°39N 74°30W **328** C3
Cordisburgo *Brazil* 19°7S 44°21W **333** E3
Córdoba *Argentina* 31°20S 64°10W **334** C3
Córdoba *Veracruz, Mexico* 18°53N 96°56W **319** D5
Córdoba *Spain* 37°50N 4°50W **195** H6
Córdoba □ *Argentina* 31°22S 64°15W **334** C3
Córdoba □ *Colombia* 8°20N 75°40W **328** B2
Córdoba □ *Spain* 38°5N 5°0W **195** G6
Córdoba, Sierra de *Argentina* 31°10S 64°25W **334** C3
Cordon *Phil.* 16°42N 121°32E **232** C3
Cordova *U.S.A.* 60°33N 145°45W **303** F11
Corduff *Ireland* 53°23N 6°21W **120** A1
Corella *Spain* 42°7N 1°48W **196** C3
Corella → *Australia* 19°34S 140°47E **280** B3
Coremas *Brazil* 7°1S 37°58W **332** C4
Corentyne → *Guyana* 5°50N 57°8W **329** B6
Corfield *Australia* 21°40S 143°21E **280** C3
Corfu = Kerkyra *Greece* 39°38N 19°50E **206** B9
Corfu ✈ **(CFU)** *Greece* 39°35N 19°54E **204** B1
Corfu, Str. of = Kerkyras, Notio Steno *Greece* 39°34N 20°0E **206** B10
Corgo = O Corgo *Spain* 42°56N 7°25W **194** C3
Corguinho *Brazil* 19°53S 54°52W **331** D7
Cori *Italy* 41°39N 12°55E **200** A5
Coria *Spain* 39°58N 6°33W **194** F4
Coria del Río *Spain* 37°16N 6°3W **195** H4
Coricudgy *Australia* 32°51S 150°24E **283** B9
Corigliano Cálabro *Italy* 39°36N 16°31E **201** C9
Corimba, Barra de *Angola* 8°52S 13°9E **265** D2
Coringa Is. *Australia* 16°58S 149°58E **280** B4
Corinth = Korinthos *Greece* 37°56N 22°55E **204** D4
Corinth *Grenada* 12°2N 61°40W **323** q
Corinth *Ky., U.S.A.* 38°30N 84°34W **311** F12
Corinth *Miss., U.S.A.* 34°56N 88°31W **315** D10
Corinth *N.Y., U.S.A.* 43°15N 73°49W **313** C11
Corinth, G. of = Korinthiakos Kolpos *Greece* 38°16N 22°30E **204** C4
Corinth Canal *Greece* 37°58N 23°0E **204** D4
Corinto *Brazil* 18°20S 44°30W **333** E3
Corinto *Nic.* 12°30N 87°10W **320** D2
Corisco *Eq. Guin.* 0°55N 9°18E **264** B1
Cork *Ireland* 51°54N 8°29W **166** E3
Cork □ *Ireland* 51°57N 8°40W **166** E3
Cork Harbour *Ireland* 51°47N 8°16W **166** E3
Corlay *France* 48°20N 3°5W **172** D3
Corleone *Italy* 37°49N 13°18E **200** E6
Corleto Perticara *Italy* 40°23N 16°2E **201** B9
Çorlu *Turkey* 41°11N 27°49E **203** E11
Cormack L. *Canada* 60°56N 121°37W **296** A4
Cormano *Italy* 45°32N 9°10E **129** A2
Cormòns *Italy* 45°58N 13°28E **199** C10
Cormorant *Canada* 54°14N 100°35W **297** C8
Cormorant L. *Canada* 54°15N 100°50W **297** C8
Corn Is. = Maiz, Is. del *Nic.* 12°15N 83°4W **320** D3
Cornalvo ⌓ *Spain* 39°1N 6°13W **195** F4
Cornaredo *Italy* 45°30N 9°1E **129** A1
Cornélio Procópio *Brazil* 23°7S 50°40W **335** A5
Cornell *U.S.A.* 41°0N 88°44W **311** D8
Corner Brook *Canada* 48°57N 57°58W **299** C8
Corner Inlet *Australia* 38°45S 146°20E **283** E7
Corner Seamounts *Atl. Oc.* 35°0N 52°0W **152** C6
Cornești *Moldova* 47°21N 28°1E **183** C13
Corneto = Tarquínia *Italy* 42°15N 11°45E **199** F8
Corníglio *Italy* 44°29N 10°5E **198** D7
Corning *Ark., U.S.A.* 36°25N 90°35W **315** C9
Corning *Calif., U.S.A.* 39°56N 122°11W **304** G2
Corning *Iowa, U.S.A.* 40°59N 94°44W **310** D2
Corning *N.Y., U.S.A.* 42°9N 77°3W **312** D7
Corno Grande *Italy* 42°28N 13°34E **199** F10
Cornwall *Ont., Canada* 45°2N 74°44W **313** A10
Cornwall *Pa., U.S.A.* 40°17N 76°25W **313** F8
Cornwall □ *Jamaica* 18°15N 77°54W **320** a
Cornwall □ *U.K.* 50°26N 4°40W **169** G3
Cornwall I. *Canada* 77°37N 94°38W **295** B10
Cornwallis I. *Canada* 75°8N 95°0W **295** B10
Cornwell *U.S.A.* 27°23N 81°6W **317** H8
Corny Pt. *Australia* 34°55S 137°0E **282** C2
Coro *Venezuela* 11°25N 69°41W **328** A4
Coroaci *Brazil* 18°35S 42°17W **333** E3
Coroatá *Brazil* 4°8S 44°0W **332** B3
Coroban *Somali Rep.* 3°58N 42°44E **267** D5
Corocoro *Bolivia* 17°15S 68°28W **330** D4
Corocoro, I. *Venezuela* 8°30N 60°10W **329** B5
Coroico *Bolivia* 16°0S 67°50W **330** D4
Coromandel *Brazil* 18°28S 47°13W **333** E2
Coromandel *N.Z.* 36°45S 175°31E **284** C4
Coromandel Coast *India* 12°30N 81°0E **245** H5
Coromandel Pen. *N.Z.* 37°0S 175°45E **284** D4
Coromandel Ra. *N.Z.* 37°0S 175°40E **284** D4
Coron *Phil.* 12°1N 120°12E **232** E3
Coron Bay *Phil.* 11°54N 120°8E **233** F3
Coron I. *Phil.* 11°55N 120°14E **233** F3
Corona *Calif., U.S.A.* 33°53N 117°34W **307** M9
Corona *N. Mex., U.S.A.* 34°15N 105°36W **305** J11
Coronach *Canada* 49°7N 105°31W **297** D7
Coronado *U.S.A.* 32°41N 117°10W **307** N9
Coronado, B. de *Costa Rica* 9°0N 83°40W **320** E3
Coronados, G. de los *Chile* 41°40S 74°0W **336** B2
Coronados, Is. Los *Mexico* 32°26N 117°19W **307** N9
Coronation *Canada* 52°5N 111°27W **296** C6
Coronation Gulf *Canada* 68°25N 110°0W **294** C9
Coronation I. *Antarctica* 60°45S 46°0W **151** C18
Coronation Is. *Australia* 14°57S 124°55E **278** B3
Coronda *Argentina* 31°58S 60°56W **334** C3
Coronel *Chile* 37°0S 73°10W **334** D1
Coronel Bogado *Paraguay* 27°11S 56°18W **334** B4
Coronel Dorrego *Argentina* 38°40S 61°10W **334** D3
Coronel Fabriciano *Brazil* 19°31S 42°38W **333** E3
Coronel Murta *Brazil* 16°37S 42°11W **333** E3
Coronel Oviedo *Paraguay* 25°24S 56°30W **334** B4
Coronel Ponce *Brazil* 15°34S 55°1W **331** D6
Coronel Pringles *Argentina* 38°0S 61°30W **334** D3
Coronel Suárez *Argentina* 37°30S 61°52W **334** D3
Coronel Vidal *Argentina* 37°28S 57°45W **334** D4
Corongo *Peru* 8°30S 77°53W **330** B2
Coropuna, Nevado *Peru* 15°30S 72°41W **330** D3
Corossol *St.-Martin* 17°54N 62°51W **322** a
Çorovodë *Albania* 40°31N 20°14E **202** F4
Corowa *Australia* 35°58S 146°21E **283** C7
Corozal *Colombia* 9°19N 75°18W **328** B2
Corozal *Puerto Rico* 18°21N 66°19W **321** b
Corozal □ *Belize* 18°23N 88°23W **319** D7
Corozal Pt. *Trin. & Tob.* 10°45N 61°37W **323** t
Corps *France* 44°50N 5°56E **175** D9
Corpus *Argentina* 27°10S 55°30W **335** B4
Corpus Christi *U.S.A.* 27°47N 97°24W **314** H6
Corpus Christi, L. *U.S.A.* 28°2N 97°52W **314** G6
Corque *Bolivia* 18°20S 67°41W **330** D4
Corral *Chile* 39°52S 73°26W **336** A2
Corral de Almaguer *Spain* 39°45N 3°10W **194** F7
Corralejo *Canary Is.* 28°43N 13°53W **153** e2
Corraun Pen. *Ireland* 53°54N 9°54W **166** C2
Corréggio *Italy* 44°46N 10°47E **198** D7
Corregidor *Phil.* 14°23N 120°35E **232** D3
Corrente *Brazil* 10°27S 45°10W **332** D2
Corrente → *Brazil* 13°8S 43°28W **333** D3
Correntes → *Brazil* 17°38S 55°8W **331** D6
Correntes, C. das *Mozam.* 24°6S 35°34E **271** B6
Correntina *Brazil* 13°20S 44°39W **333** D3
Corrèze □ *France* 45°20N 1°45E **174** C5
Corrèze → *France* 45°10N 1°28E **174** C5
Corrib, L. *Ireland* 53°27N 9°16W **166** C2
Corridónia *Italy* 43°15N 13°30E **199** E10
Corrientes *Argentina* 27°30S 58°45W **334** B4
Corrientes □ *Argentina* 28°0S 57°0W **334** B4
Corrientes → *Argentina* 30°42S 59°38W **334** C4
Corrientes → *Peru* 3°43S 74°35W **328** D3
Corrientes, C. *Colombia* 5°30N 77°34W **328** B2
Corrientes, C. *Cuba* 21°43N 84°30W **320** B3
Corrientes, C. *Jalisco, Mexico* 20°25N 105°42W **318** C3
Corrigan *U.S.A.* 31°0N 94°52W **314** F7
Corrigin *Australia* 32°20S 117°53E **279** F2
Corriverton *Guyana* 5°55N 57°20W **329** B6
Corry *U.S.A.* 41°55N 79°39W **312** E5
Corryong *Australia* 36°12S 147°53E **283** D7
Corse □ *France* 42°0N 9°0E **175** G13
Corse, C. *France* 43°1N 9°25E **175** E13
Corse ⌓ *France* 42°14N 9°10E **175** F13
Corse-du-Sud □ *France* 41°45N 9°0E **175** G13
Corsica = Corse □ *France* 42°0N 9°0E **175** G13
Corsicana *U.S.A.* 32°6N 96°28W **314** E6
Córsico *Italy* 45°25N 9°6E **129** B1
Corsini, Palazzo *Rome, Italy* **136** c1
Corstorphine *U.K.* 55°56N 3°17W **121** B2
Corte *France* 42°19N 9°11E **175** F13
Corte Pinto *Portugal* 37°42N 7°29W **195** H3
Cortegana *Spain* 37°52N 6°49W **195** H4
Cortes *Phil.* 9°17N 126°11E **233** G6
Cortés, Mar de = California, G. de *Mexico* 27°0N 111°0W **318** B2
Cortez *U.S.A.* 37°21N 108°35W **305** H9
Cortina d'Ampezzo *Italy* 46°32N 12°8E **199** B9
Cortland *N.Y., U.S.A.* 42°36N 76°11W **313** D8
Cortland *Ohio, U.S.A.* 41°20N 80°44W **312** E4
Cortona *Italy* 43°16N 11°59E **199** E8
Corubal → *Guinea-Biss.* 11°57N 15°5W **262** C2
Coruche *Portugal* 38°57N 8°30W **195** G2
Çoruh → *Turkey* 41°38N 41°38E **191** K5
Çorum *Turkey* 40°30N 34°57E **212** B6
Çorum □ *Turkey* 40°40N 35°0E **212** B6
Corumbá *Brazil* 19°0S 57°30W **331** D6
Corumbá → *Brazil* 18°19S 48°55W **333** E2
Corumbá de Goiás *Brazil* 16°0S 48°50W **333** E2
Corumbaíba *Brazil* 18°9S 48°34W **333** E2
Corund *Romania* 46°30N 25°13E **183** D10
Corunna = A Coruña *Spain* 43°20N 8°25W **194** B2
Corunna *U.S.A.* 42°59N 84°7W **311** B12
Corvallis *U.S.A.* 44°34N 123°16W **304** D2
Corvette, L. de la *Canada* 53°25N 74°3W **298** B5
Corviale *Italy* 41°51N 12°25E **136** B1
Corvo *Azores* 39°42N 31°6W **153** d2
Coryal *Trin. & Tob.* 10°30N 61°11W **323** t
Corydon *Ind., U.S.A.* 38°13N 86°7W **311** F10
Corydon *Iowa, U.S.A.* 40°46N 93°19W **310** D3
Corydon *Ky., U.S.A.* 37°44N 87°43W **311** G9
Cosalá *Mexico* 24°23N 106°41W **318** C3
Cosamaloapan de Carpio *Mexico* 18°22N 95°48W **319** D5
Cosenza *Italy* 39°18N 16°15E **201** C9
Coșereni *Romania* 44°38N 26°35E **183** F11
Coshocton *U.S.A.* 40°16N 81°51W **312** F3
Coslada *Spain* 40°25N 3°35W **127** B2
Cosmo Newberry *Australia* 28°0S 122°54E **279** E3
Cosne-Cours-sur-Loire *France* 47°24N 2°54E **173** E9
Coso Junction *U.S.A.* 36°3N 117°57W **307** J9
Coso Pk. *U.S.A.* 36°13N 117°44W **307** J9
Cospeito *Spain* 43°12N 7°34W **194** B3
Cosquín *Argentina* 31°15S 64°30W **334** C3
Cossato *Italy* 45°34N 8°10E **198** C5
Cossé-le-Vivien *France* 47°57N 0°54W **172** E6
Cossigny *France* 48°43N 2°40E **134** B4
Cosson → *France* 47°30N 1°15E **172** E8
Costa Blanca *Spain* 38°25N 0°10W **197** G4
Costa Brava *Spain* 41°30N 3°0E **196** D8
Costa del Sol *Spain* 36°30N 4°30W **195** J6
Costa Dorada *Spain* 41°12N 1°15E **196** D6

Costa Mesa *U.S.A.* 33°38N 117°55W **307** M9
Costa Rica ■ *Cent. Amer.* 10°0N 84°0W **320** E3
Costa Smeralda *Italy* 41°5N 9°35E **200** A2
Costantino, Arco di *Rome, Italy* **136** c3
Costermansville = Bukavu *Dem. Rep. of the Congo* 2°20S 28°52E **268** C2
Costeşti *Romania* 44°40N 24°53E **183** F9
Costigliole d'Asti *Italy* 44°47N 8°11E **198** D5
Cosumnes → *U.S.A.* 38°16N 121°26W **306** G5
Coswig *Sachsen, Germany* 51°7N 13°34E **178** D9
Coswig *Sachsen-Anhalt, Germany* 51°53N 12°27E **178** D8
Cotabato *Phil.* 7°14N 124°15E **233** H5
Cotabato □ *Phil.* 7°10N 125°0E **233** H5
Cotacajes → *Bolivia* 16°0S 67°1W **330** D4
Cotagaita *Bolivia* 20°45S 65°40W **334** A2
Cotahuasi *Peru* 15°12S 72°50W **330** D3
Cotao *Portugal* 38°45N 9°17W **126** A1
Côte d'Azur *France* 43°25N 7°10E **175** E11
Côte-d'Ivoire = Ivory Coast ■ *Africa* 7°30N 5°0W **262** D4
Côte d'Or *France* 47°10N 4°50E **173** E11
Côte-d'Or □ *France* 47°30N 4°50E **173** E11
Côte-St-Luc *Canada* 45°28N 73°39W **130** B2
Coteau des Prairies *U.S.A.* 45°20N 97°50W **308** C5
Coteau du Missouri *U.S.A.* 47°0N 100°0W **308** B4
Cotegipe *Brazil* 12°2S 44°15W **333** D3
Cotentin *France* 49°15N 1°30W **172** C5
Côtes-d'Armor □ *France* 48°25N 2°40W **172** D4
Côtes de Meuse *France* 49°15N 5°22E **173** C12
Côtes-du-Nord = Côtes-d'Armor □ *France* 48°25N 2°40W **172** D4
Cotiella *Spain* 42°31N 0°19E **196** C5
Cotillo *Canary Is.* 28°41N 14°1W **153** e2
Cotiujeni *Moldova* 47°51N 28°33E **183** C13
Cotoca *Bolivia* 17°49S 63°3W **331** D5
Cotonou *Benin* 6°20N 2°25E **263** D5
Cotopaxi *Ecuador* 0°40S 78°30W **328** D2
Cotopaxi □ *Ecuador* 0°5S 78°55W **328** D2
Cotopaxi △ *Ecuador* 0°39S 78°24W **328** D2
Cotronei *Italy* 39°9N 16°47E **201** C9
Cotswold Hills *U.K.* 51°42N 2°10W **169** F5
Cottage Grove *U.S.A.* 43°48N 123°3W **304** E2
Cottageville *U.S.A.* 32°56N 80°29W **316** C9
Cottbus *Germany* 51°45N 14°20E **178** D10
Cotton Ground *St. Kitts & Nevis* 17°11N 62°36W **322** d
Cottondale *U.S.A.* 30°48N 85°23W **316** E4
Cottonwood *Ala., U.S.A.* 31°3N 85°18W **316** D4
Cottonwood *Ariz., U.S.A.* 34°45N 112°1W **305** J7
Cotulla *U.S.A.* 28°26N 99°14W **314** G5
Cotunduba, I. de *Brazil* 22°57S 43°8W **135** B2
Coubre, Pte. de la *France* 45°42N 1°15W **174** C2
Coubron *France* 48°54N 2°34E **134** A4
Couches *France* 46°53N 4°30E **173** F11
Couço *Portugal* 38°59N 8°17W **195** G2
Coudersport *U.S.A.* 41°46N 78°1W **312** E6
Couedic, C. du *Australia* 36°5S 136°40E **282** D2
Couëron *France* 47°13N 1°44W **172** E5
Couesnon → *France* 48°38N 1°32W **172** D5
Couhé *France* 46°17N 0°11E **174** B4
Coulanges-sur-Yonne *France* 47°31N 3°33E **173** E10
Coulee City *U.S.A.* 47°37N 119°17W **304** C4
Coulee Dam Nat. Recr. Area = Lake Roosevelt ⌓ *U.S.A.* 48°5N 118°14W **304** B4
Coulibistri *Dominica* 15°27N 61°28W **323** k
Coulman I. *Antarctica* 73°35S 170°0E **151** D11
Coulommiers *France* 48°50N 3°3E **173** D10
Coulon → *France* 43°51N 5°6E **175** E9
Coulonge → *Canada* 45°52N 76°46W **298** C4
Coulonges-sur-l'Autize *France* 46°29N 0°36W **174** B3
Coulounieix-Chamiers *France* 45°11N 0°42E **174** C4
Coulterville *Calif., U.S.A.* 37°43N 120°12W **306** H6
Coulterville *Ill., U.S.A.* 38°11N 89°36W **310** F7
Council *Alaska, U.S.A.* 64°53N 163°41W **303** D7
Council *Ga., U.S.A.* 30°37N 82°31W **316** E7
Council *Idaho, U.S.A.* 44°44N 116°26W **304** D5
Council Bluffs *U.S.A.* 41°16N 95°52W **308** E6
Council Grove *U.S.A.* 38°40N 96°29W **308** F5
Countryside *U.S.A.* 41°47N 87°52W **119** C1
County Art Museum *U.S.A.* 34°4N 118°21W **126** B2
Coupeville *U.S.A.* 48°13N 122°41W **306** B4
Courantyne → *S. Amer.* 5°55N 57°5W **329** B6
Courbevoie *France* 48°53N 2°14E **134** A2
Courcelles *Belgium* 50°28N 4°22E **170** D4
Courchevel *France* 45°25N 6°36E **175** C10
Courçon *France* 46°15N 0°50W **174** B3
Courland → *Trin. & Tob.* 11°13N 60°47W **323** s
Courmayeur *Italy* 45°47N 6°58E **198** C3
Couronne, C. *France* 43°19N 5°3E **175** E9
Cours-la-Ville *France* 46°7N 4°19E **173** F11
Coursan *France* 43°14N 3°4E **174** E7
Courseulles-sur-Mer *France* 49°20N 0°29W **172** C6
Courtenay *B.C., Canada* 49°45N 125°0W **296** D4
Courtenay *Loiret, France* 48°2N 3°3E **173** D10
Courtland *U.S.A.* 38°20N 121°34W **306** G5
Courtrai = Kortrijk *Belgium* 50°50N 3°17E **170** D3
Courtright *Canada* 42°49N 82°28W **312** D2
Courtry *France* 48°55N 2°35E **134** A4
Coushatta *U.S.A.* 32°1N 93°21W **314** E8
Coutances *France* 49°3N 1°28W **172** C5
Coutras *France* 45°3N 0°8W **174** C3
Coutts Crossing *Australia* 29°49S 152°55E **281** D5
Couva *Trin. & Tob.* 10°25N 61°27W **323** t
Couvin *Belgium* 50°3N 4°29E **170** D4
Covarrubias *Spain* 42°4N 3°31W **194** C7
Covasna *Romania* 45°50N 26°10E **183** E11
Covasna □ *Romania* 45°50N 26°0E **183** E10
Cove I. *Canada* 45°17N 81°44W **312** A3
Coveñas *Colombia* 9°24N 75°44W **328** B2
Covent Garden *London, U.K.* **125** b4
Coventry *U.K.* 52°25N 1°28W **169** E6
Coverdale *U.S.A.* 31°38N 83°58W **316** D6
Covilhã *Portugal* 40°17N 7°31W **194** E3
Covington *Ga., U.S.A.* 33°36N 83°51W **316** B6
Covington *Ind., U.S.A.* 40°9N 87°24W **311** D9
Covington *Ky., U.S.A.* 39°5N 84°30W **311** E12
Covington *Ohio, U.S.A.* 40°7N 84°21W **311** D12
Covington *Tenn., U.S.A.* 35°34N 89°39W **315** D10
Covington *Va., U.S.A.* 37°47N 79°59W **309** G14
Cowal, L. *Australia* 33°40S 147°25E **283** B7
Cowan, Cerro *Ecuador* 0°12S 90°48W **330** a
Cowan, L. *Australia* 31°45S 121°45E **279** F3
Cowan L. *Canada* 54°0N 107°15W **297** C7
Cowangie *Australia* 35°12S 141°26E **282** C4
Cowansville *Canada* 45°14N 72°46W **313** A12
Coward Springs *Australia* 29°24S 136°49E **281** D2
Cowcowing Lakes *Australia* 30°55S 117°20E **279** F2
Cowden *U.S.A.* 39°15N 88°52W **311** E8
Cowdenbeath *U.K.* 56°7N 3°21W **167** E5
Cowell *Australia* 33°39S 136°56E **282** B2
Cowes *Vic., Australia* 38°28S 145°14E **283** E6
Cowes *I. of W., U.K.* 50°45N 1°18W **169** G6
Cowgate *Edinburgh, U.K.* **121** b3
Cowichan L. *Canada* 48°53N 124°17W **306** B2
Cowley *U.K.* 51°31N 0°28W **125** A1
Cowlitz → *U.S.A.* 46°6N 122°55W **306** D4
Cowra *Australia* 33°49S 148°42E **283** B8
Cox *Spain* 38°8N 0°53W **197** G4
Coxilha Grande *Brazil* 28°18S 51°30W **335** B5
Coxim *Brazil* 18°30S 54°55W **331** D7
Coxim → *Brazil* 18°34S 54°46W **331** D7
Cox's Bazar *Bangla.* 21°26N 91°59E **241** E3
Coyoacán *Mexico* 19°21N 99°9W **128** B2
Coyote Wells *U.S.A.* 32°44N 115°58W **307** N11
Coyuca de Benitez *Mexico* 17°2N 100°4W **319** D4
Coyuca de Catalán *Mexico* 18°20N 100°39W **318** D4
Cozad *U.S.A.* 40°52N 99°59W **308** E4
Cozes *France* 45°34N 0°49W **174** C3
Cozumel *Mexico* 20°31N 86°55W **319** C7
Cozumel, Isla *Mexico* 20°30N 86°40W **319** C7
Crab Hill *Barbados* 13°19N 59°38W **323** r
Crabs Pen. *Antigua & B.* 17°7N 61°45W **322** b
Cracow = Kraków *Poland* 50°4N 19°57E **185** H6
Cracow *Australia* 25°17S 150°17E **281** D5
Cradle Mt.-Lake St. Clair △ *Australia* 41°49S 147°56E **281** G4
Cradock *S. Austral., Australia* 32°6S 138°31E **281** E2
Cradock *Eastern Cape, S. Africa* 32°8S 25°36E **270** D4
Craig *Alaska, U.S.A.* 55°29N 133°9W **303** J14
Craig *Colo., U.S.A.* 40°31N 107°33W **304** F10
Craigavon *U.K.* 54°27N 6°23W **166** B5
Craighall Park *S. Africa* 26°7S 28°1E **123** A2
Craigieburn *Australia* 37°36S 144°56E **283** D6
Craiglockhart *U.K.* 55°55N 3°14W **121** B2
Craigmillar *U.K.* 55°56N 3°9W **121** B3
Craigmore *Zimbabwe* 20°28S 32°50E **269** G3
Craik *Canada* 51°3N 105°49W **297** C7
Crailsheim *Germany* 49°8N 10°5E **179** F6
Craiova *Romania* 44°21N 23°48E **183** F8
Cramond *U.K.* 55°58N 3°18W **121** B2
Cramond Bridge *U.K.* 55°57N 3°19W **121** B1
Cramond I. *U.K.* 55°59N 3°17W **121** B2
Cramsie *Australia* 23°20S 144°15E **280** C3
Cranberry L. *U.S.A.* 44°11N 74°50W **313** B10
Cranberry Portage *Canada* 54°35N 101°23W **297** C8
Cranbrook *W. Austral., Australia* 34°18S 117°33E **279** F2
Cranbrook *B.C., Canada* 49°30N 115°46W **296** D5
Crandon *U.S.A.* 45°34N 88°54W **308** C9
Crane *Oreg., U.S.A.* 43°25N 118°35W **304** E4
Crane *Tex., U.S.A.* 31°24N 102°21W **314** F3
Crane, The *Barbados* 13°6N 59°27W **323** r
Cranford *U.K.* 51°29N 0°25W **125** B1
Cranganore *India* 10°13N 76°13E **245** J3
Cranston *U.S.A.* 41°47N 71°26W **313** E13
Craon *France* 47°50N 0°58W **172** E6
Craonne *France* 49°27N 3°46E **173** C10
Craponne-sur-Arzon *France* 45°19N 3°51E **174** C7
Crasna *Romania* 46°32N 27°51E **183** D12
Crasna → *Romania* 47°44N 22°35E **182** C7
Crasnei, Munţii *Romania* 47°0N 23°20E **183** C8
Crater L. *St. Vincent* 13°17N 61°13W **323** n
Crater L. *Oreg., U.S.A.* 42°56N 122°6W **304** E2
Crater Lake △ *U.S.A.* 42°55N 122°10W **304** E2
Crater Mt. *Papua N. G.* 6°37S 145°7E **286** D3
Crater Pt. *Papua N. G.* 5°25S 152°9E **286** C7
Craters of the Moon ⌓ *U.S.A.* 43°25N 113°30W **304** E7
Crateús *Brazil* 5°10S 40°39W **332** C3
Crati → *Italy* 39°43N 16°31E **201** C9
Crato *Brazil* 7°10S 39°25W **332** C4
Crato *Portugal* 39°16N 7°39W **195** F3
Craven, L. *Canada* 54°20N 76°56W **298** B4
Cravo Norte *Colombia* 6°18N 70°12W **328** B3
Cravo Norte → *Colombia* 6°18N 70°12W **328** B3
Crawford *Western Cape, S. Africa* 33°59S 18°30E **118** A2
Crawford *Ala., U.S.A.* 32°27N 85°11W **316** C4
Crawford *Nebr., U.S.A.* 42°41N 103°25W **308** D2
Crawfordsville *Ind., U.S.A.* 40°2N 86°54W **311** D10
Crawfordsville *Iowa, U.S.A.* 41°12N 91°32W **310** C5
Crawfordville *Fla., U.S.A.* 30°11N 84°23W **316** E5
Crawfordville *Ga., U.S.A.* 33°33N 82°54W **316** B7
Crawley *U.K.* 51°7N 0°11W **169** F7
Crayford *U.K.* 51°27N 0°11E **125** B5
Crazy Mts. *U.S.A.* 46°12N 110°20W **304** C8
Crean L. *Canada* 54°5N 106°9W **297** C7
Crécy-en-Ponthieu *France* 50°15N 1°53E **173** B8
Crediton *Ont., Canada* 43°17N 81°33W **312** C3
Crediton *Devon, U.K.* 50°47N 3°40W **169** G4
Cree → *Sask., Canada* 58°57N 105°47W **297** B7
Cree → *Dumf. & Gall., U.K.* 54°55N 4°25W **167** G4
Cree L. *Canada* 57°30N 106°30W **297** B7
Creede *U.S.A.* 37°51N 106°56W **305** H10
Creekmouth *U.K.* 51°30N 0°6E **125** A4
Creekside *U.S.A.* 40°40N 79°11W **312** F5
Creel *Mexico* 27°45N 107°38W **318** B3
Creemore *Canada* 44°19N 80°6W **312** B4
Creighton *Sask., Canada* 54°45N 101°54W **297** C8
Creighton *Nebr., U.S.A.* 42°28N 97°54W **308** D5
Creil *France* 49°15N 2°29E **173** C9
Crema *Italy* 45°22N 9°41E **198** C6
Cremona *Italy* 45°7N 10°2E **198** C7
Crepaja *Serbia* 45°1N 20°38E **182** E5
Crepori → *Brazil* 5°42S 57°8W **331** B6
Crépy *France* 49°35N 3°32E **173** C10
Crépy-en-Valois *France* 49°14N 2°54E **173** C9
Cres *Croatia* 44°58N 14°25E **199** D11
Crescent, L. *U.S.A.* 28°30N 81°33W **133** A1
Crescent Beach *U.S.A.* 29°46N 81°15W **316** F8
Crescent City *Calif., U.S.A.* 41°45N 124°12W **304** F1
Crescent City *Fla., U.S.A.* 29°26N 81°31W **317** F8
Crescent Hd. *Australia* 31°11S 152°59E **283** A10
Crescent L. *U.S.A.* 29°28N 81°30W **317** F8
Crescentino *Italy* 45°11N 8°6E **198** C5
Crescenzago *Italy* 45°30N 9°14E **129** A2
Crespo *Argentina* 32°2S 60°19W **334** C3
Cressely *France* 48°44N 2°6E **134** B1
Cresskill *U.S.A.* 40°56N 73°57W **132** A2
Cresson *U.S.A.* 40°28N 78°36W **312** F6
Cressy *Australia* 38°2S 143°40E **282** E5
Crest *France* 44°44N 5°2E **175** D9
Cresta, Mt. *Phil.* 17°17N 122°6E **232** C4
Crestline *Calif., U.S.A.* 34°14N 117°18W **307** L9
Crestline *Ohio, U.S.A.* 40°47N 82°44W **312** F2
Creston *B.C., Canada* 49°10N 116°31W **296** D5
Creston *Calif., U.S.A.* 35°32N 120°33W **306** K6
Creston *Iowa, U.S.A.* 41°4N 94°22W **310** C2
Crestview *Calif., U.S.A.* 37°46N 118°58W **306** H8
Crestview *Fla., U.S.A.* 30°46N 86°34W **317** E3
Creswick *Australia* 37°25S 143°58E **282** D5
Crêt de la Neige *France* 46°16N 5°58E **173** F12
Crete = Kriti *Greece* 35°15N 25°0E **207** E6
Crete *Ill., U.S.A.* 41°27N 87°38W **311** C9
Crete *Nebr., U.S.A.* 40°38N 96°58W **308** E5
Crete, Sea of *Greece* 36°0N 25°0E **205** E7
Créteil *France* 48°47N 2°27E **134** B3
Cretin, C. *Papua N. G.* 6°40S 147°53E **286** D4
Creus, C. de *Spain* 42°20N 3°19E **196** C8
Creuse □ *France* 46°10N 2°0E **173** F9
Creuse → *France* 47°0N 0°34E **174** B4
Creutzwald *France* 49°12N 6°42E **173** C13
Creuzburg *Germany* 51°3N 10°14E **178** D6
Crèvecœur-le-Grand *France* 49°37N 2°5E **173** C9
Crevillente *Spain* 38°12N 0°48W **197** G4
Crewe *U.K.* 53°6N 2°26W **168** D5
Crewkerne *U.K.* 50°53N 2°48W **169** G5
Crianlarich *U.K.* 56°24N 4°37W **167** E4
Criciúma *Brazil* 28°40S 49°23W **335** B6
Cricklewood *U.K.* 51°33N 0°13W **125** A2
Cricova *Moldova* 47°8N 28°52E **183** C13
Cridersville *U.S.A.* 40°39N 84°9W **311** D12
Crieff *U.K.* 56°22N 3°50W **167** E5
Crikvenica *Croatia* 45°11N 14°40E **199** C11
Crimea □ *Ukraine* 45°30N 33°10E **189** K8
Crimean Pen. = Krymskyy Pivostriv *Ukraine* 45°0N 34°0E **189** K8
Crimmitschau *Germany* 50°48N 12°24E **178** E8
Cristal, Mts. de *Gabon* 0°30N 10°30E **264** B2
Cristalândia *Brazil* 10°36S 49°11W **332** D2
Cristino Castro *Brazil* 8°49S 44°13W **332** C3
Cristo Redentor, Corcovado *Brazil* 22°56S 43°12W **135** B1
Cristóbal, Pta. *Ecuador* 0°54S 91°31W **330** a
Cristuru Secuiesc *Romania* 46°17N 25°2E **183** D10
Crişul Alb → *Romania* 46°42N 21°17E **182** D6
Crişul Negru → *Romania* 46°42N 21°16E **182** D6
Crişul Repede → *Romania* 46°55N 20°59E **182** D5
Crittenden *U.S.A.* 38°47N 84°36W **311** F12
Criuleni *Moldova* 47°13N 29°10E **183** C14
Crivitz *Germany* 53°34N 11°39E **178** B7
Crixás *Brazil* 14°27S 49°58W **333** D2
Crna → *Macedonia* 41°33N 21°59E **202** E5
Crna Gora = Montenegro ■ *Europe* 42°40N 19°20E **202** D3
Crna Gora *Macedonia* 42°10N 21°30E **202** D5
Crna Reka = Crna → *Macedonia* 41°33N 21°59E **202** E5
Crna Trava *Serbia* 42°49N 22°19E **202** D6
Crni Drim → *Macedonia* 41°17N 20°40E **202** E4
Crni Timok → *Serbia* 43°53N 22°15E **202** C6
Crnoljeva Planina *Serbia* 42°20N 21°0E **202** D5
Črnomelj *Slovenia* 45°33N 15°10E **199** C12
Croagh Patrick *Ireland* 53°46N 9°40W **166** C2
Croajingolong △ *Australia* 37°45S 149°26E **283** D8
Croatia ■ *Europe* 45°20N 16°0E **199** C13
Crockenhill *U.K.* 51°22N 0°9E **125** B4
Crocker *U.S.A.* 37°57N 92°16W **310** G4
Crocker, Banjaran *Malaysia* 5°40N 116°30E **235** A5
Crocker, Cerro *Ecuador* 0°36S 90°21W **330** a
Crocker Range △ *Malaysia* 5°33N 116°8E **235** A5
Crockett *U.S.A.* 31°19N 95°27W **314** F7
Crocodile = Umgwenya → *Mozam.* 25°14S 32°18E **271** C5
Crocodile Is. *Australia* 12°3S 134°58E **280** A1
Crocq *France* 45°52N 2°21E **174** C6
Crocus B. *Anguilla* 18°13N 63°5W **322** a
Crodo *Italy* 46°13N 8°19E **198** B5
Crohy Hd. *Ireland* 54°55N 8°26W **166** B3
Croisette, C. *France* 43°14N 5°22E **175** E9
Croisic, Pte. du *France* 47°19N 2°31W **172** E4
Croissy-Beaubourg *France* 48°49N 2°39E **134** B4
Croissy-sur-Seine *France* 48°52N 2°8E **134** A1
Croix, L. la *Canada* 48°20N 92°15W **298** C1
Croker, C. *N. Terr., Australia* 10°58S 132°35E **278** B5
Croker, C. *Ont., Canada* 44°58N 80°59W **312** B4
Croker I. *Australia* 11°12S 132°32E **278** B5
Cromarty *U.K.* 57°40N 4°2W **167** D4
Cromer *U.K.* 52°56N 1°17E **168** E9
Crompton Pt. *Dominica* 15°35N 61°19W **323** k
Cromwell *N.Z.* 45°3S 169°14E **285** F4
Cromwell *Conn., U.S.A.* 41°36N 72°39W **313** E12
Cronat *France* 46°43N 3°40E **173** F10
Crook *U.K.* 54°43N 1°45W **168** C6
Crooked → *B.C., Canada* 54°50N 122°54W **296** C4
Crooked → *Oreg., U.S.A.* 44°32N 121°16W **304** D3
Crooked Creek *U.S.A.* 61°52N 158°7W **303** F8
Crooked I. *Bahamas* 22°50N 74°10W **321** B5
Crooked Island Passage *Bahamas* 22°55N 74°35W **321** B5
Crookston *Minn., U.S.A.* 47°47N 96°37W **308** B5
Crookston *Nebr., U.S.A.* 42°56N 100°45W **308** D3
Crookwell *Australia* 34°28S 149°24E **283** C8
Cropane-Micone ⌓ *Italy* 38°31N 16°18E **201** D9
Crosby *Gauteng, S. Africa* 26°11S 27°59E **123** B1
Crosby *Mersey., U.K.* 53°30N 3°3W **168** D4
Crosby *N. Dak., U.S.A.* 48°55N 103°18W **308** A2
Crosby *Pa., U.S.A.* 41°45N 78°23W **312** E6
Crosbyton *U.S.A.* 33°40N 101°14W **314** E4
Crosía *Italy* 39°35N 16°45E **201** C9
Crosne *France* 48°43N 2°27E **134** B3
Cross → *Nigeria* 4°42N 8°21E **263** E6
Cross City *U.S.A.* 29°38N 83°7W **317** F6
Cross Fell *U.K.* 54°43N 2°28W **168** C5
Cross I. *India* 18°56N 72°51E **130** B2
Cross L. *Canada* 54°45N 97°30W **297** C9
Cross Lake *Canada* 54°37N 97°47W **297** C9
Cross River □ *Nigeria* 6°0N 8°0E **263** D6
Cross River △ *Nigeria* 5°50N 9°50E **263** D6
Cross Sound *U.S.A.* 58°0N 135°0W **303** G14
Cross Timbers *U.S.A.* 38°1N 93°14W **310** F3
Crossen = Krosno Odrzańskie *Poland* 52°3N 15°7E **185** F2
Crossett *U.S.A.* 33°8N 91°58W **314** E9
Crosshaven *Ireland* 51°47N 8°17W **166** E3
Crossley, Mt. *N.Z.* 42°50S 172°5E **285** C7
Crossmaglen *U.K.* 54°5N 6°36W **166** B5
Crossmolina *Ireland* 54°6N 9°20W **166** B2
Crossville *Ill., U.S.A.* 38°10N 88°4W **311** F8
Crossville *Tenn., U.S.A.* 35°57N 85°2W **315** D12
Croswell *U.S.A.* 43°16N 82°37W **312** C2
Croton-on-Hudson *U.S.A.* 41°12N 73°55W **313** E11
Crotone *Italy* 39°5N 17°8E **201** C10
Crouch End *U.K.* 51°34N 0°7W **125** A3
Crow → *Canada* 59°41N 124°20W **296** B4
Crow Agency *U.S.A.* 45°36N 107°28W **304** D10
Crow Hd. *Ireland* 51°35N 10°9W **166** E1
Crowdy Bay △ *Australia* 31°45S 152°45E **283** A10
Crowell *U.S.A.* 33°59N 99°43W **314** E5
Crowl Cr. → *Australia* 32°0S 145°30E **283** B6
Crowley *U.S.A.* 30°13N 92°22W **314** F8
Crowley, L. *U.S.A.* 37°35N 118°42W **306** H8
Crown I. *Papua N. G.* 5°7S 146°58E **286** C4
Crown Mine *S. Africa* 26°12S 27°57E **123** B1
Crown Point *Ind., U.S.A.* 41°25N 87°22W **311** C9
Crown Point *N.Y., U.S.A.* 43°57N 73°26W **313** C11
Crown Point ✕ (TAB) *Trin. & Tob.* 11°9N 60°50W **323** s
Crown Pt. *Trin. & Tob.* 11°18N 60°51W **323** s
Crownpoint *U.S.A.* 35°41N 108°9W **305** J9
Crows Landing *U.S.A.* 37°23N 121°6W **306** H5
Crows Nest *N.S.W., Australia* 33°49S 151°12E **139** A2
Crows Nest *Queens., Australia* 27°16S 152°4E **281** D5
Crowsnest Pass *Canada* 49°40N 114°40W **296** D6
Croydon *Queens., Australia* 18°13S 142°14E **280** B3
Croydon *London, U.K.* 51°22N 0°5W **125** B3
Croydon □ *U.K.* 51°22N 0°5W **169** F7
Croydon Park *Australia* 33°55S 151°7E **139** B1
Crozet, Is. *Ind. Oc.* 46°27S 52°0E **273** J4
Crozet Basin *Ind. Oc.* 39°0S 60°0E **273** H5
Crozon *France* 48°15N 4°30W **172** D2
Cruagh Mt. *Ireland* 53°14N 6°17W **120** B2
Cruces, Punta *Colombia* 6°39N 77°32W **328** B2
Crumlin *Ireland* 53°19N 6°19W **120** B2
Crusheen *Ireland* 52°57N 8°53W **166** D3
Cruz, C. *Cuba* 19°50N 77°50W **320** C4
Cruz Alta *Brazil* 28°45S 53°40W **335** B5
Cruz Bay *U.S. Virgin Is.* 18°20N 64°48W **321** b
Cruz das Almas *Brazil* 12°0S 39°6W **333** D4
Cruz de Incio *Spain* 42°39N 7°21W **194** C3
Cruz de Malta *Brazil* 8°15S 40°20W **332** C3
Cruz de Pau *Portugal* 38°37N 9°7W **126** B2
Cruz del Eje *Argentina* 30°45S 64°50W **334** C3
Cruzeiro *Brazil* 22°33S 45°0W **333** F3
Cruzeiro do Oeste *Brazil* 23°46S 53°4W **335** A5
Cruzeiro do Sul = Joaçaba *Brazil* 27°5S 51°31W **335** B5
Cruzeiro do Sul *Brazil* 7°35S 72°35W **330** B3
Cry L. *Canada* 58°45N 129°0W **296** B3
Crystal B. *U.S.A.* 28°50N 82°45W **317** G7
Crystal Bay *U.S.A.* 39°15N 120°0W **306** F7
Crystal Brook *Australia* 33°21S 138°12E **282** B3
Crystal City *Mo., U.S.A.* 38°13N 90°23W **310** F6
Crystal City *Tex., U.S.A.* 28°41N 99°50W **314** G5
Crystal Falls *U.S.A.* 46°5N 88°20W **308** B9
Crystal Lake *Fla., U.S.A.* 30°26N 85°42W **316** E4
Crystal Lake *Ill., U.S.A.* 42°14N 88°19W **311** B8
Crystal Palace *U.K.* 51°25N 0°4W **125** B3
Crystal River *U.S.A.* 28°54N 82°35W **317** G7
Crystal Springs *U.S.A.* 31°59N 90°21W **315** F9
Csenger *Hungary* 47°50N 22°41E **182** C7
Csepel *Hungary* 47°25N 19°4E **117** B2
Csepelsziget *Hungary* 47°25N 19°4E **117** B2
Csillaghegy *Hungary* 47°35N 19°2E **117** A2
Csillagtelep *Hungary* 47°24N 19°5E **117** B2
Csömör *Hungary* 47°33N 19°14E **117** A3
Csömöri-patak → *Hungary* 47°35N 19°5E **117** A3
Csongrád *Hungary* 46°43N 20°12E **182** D5
Csongrád □ *Hungary* 46°32N 20°15E **182** D5
Csorna *Hungary* 47°38N 17°18E **182** C2
Csurgo *Hungary* 46°16N 17°9E **182** D2
Cu Lao Hon *Vietnam* 10°54N 108°18E **237** G7
Cua Rao *Vietnam* 19°16N 104°27E **236** C5
Cuácua → *Mozam.* 17°54S 37°0E **269** F4
Cuále *Angola* 8°22S 16°10E **265** D3
Cuále → *Angola* 8°29S 15°1E **265** D3
Cuamato *Angola* 17°2S 15°7E **265** F3
Cuamba *Mozam.* 14°45S 36°22E **269** E4
Cuando *Angola* 14°34S 19°1E **265** E3
Cuando → *Angola* 17°30S 23°15E **265** F4
Cuando Cubango □ *Angola* 16°25S 20°0E **265** F4
Cuangar *Angola* 17°36S 18°39E **265** F3
Cuango = Kwango → *Dem. Rep. of the Congo* 3°14S 17°22E **264** C3
Cuango *Lunda Norte, Angola* 9°8S 18°3E **265** D3
Cuango *Moxico, Angola* 14°30S 19°0E **265** E3
Cuango *Uíge, Angola* 6°15S 16°42E **265** D3
Cuanza → *Angola* 9°21S 13°9E **265** D2
Cuanza Norte □ *Angola* 8°50S 14°30E **265** D2
Cuanza Sul □ *Angola* 10°50S 14°50E **265** E2
Cuao → *Venezuela* 4°55N 67°40W **328** C4
Cuare → *Trin. & Tob.* 10°36N 61°6W **323** t
Cuarto → *Argentina* 33°25S 63°2W **334** C3
Cuatir → *Angola* 17°1S 18°9E **265** F3
Cuatro Vientos *Spain* 40°22N 3°47W **127** B1
Cuatrociénegas *Mexico* 26°59N 102°5W **318** B4
Cuauhtémoc *Chihuahua, Mexico* 28°25N 106°52W **318** B3
Cuauhtémoc *México, Mexico* 19°25N 99°9W **128** B2
Cuba *Portugal* 38°10N 7°54W **195** G3
Cuba *Mo., U.S.A.* 38°4N 91°24W **310** F5
Cuba *N. Mex., U.S.A.* 36°1N 107°4W **305** H10
Cuba *N.Y., U.S.A.* 42°13N 78°17W **312** D6
Cuba ■ *W. Indies* 22°0N 79°0W **320** B4
Cuba City *U.S.A.* 42°36N 90°26W **310** B6
Cubal *Angola* 12°26S 14°3E **265** E2
Cubal → *Angola* 12°13S 13°39E **265** E2
Cuban Museum *U.S.A.* 25°45N 80°13W **128** B2
Cubango → *Africa* 18°50S 22°25E **265** F4
Cubanja *Angola* 14°49S 21°20E **265** E4
Cubao *Phil.* 14°37N 121°3E **127** B2
Cubia *Angola* 15°58S 21°42E **265** F4
Çubuk *Turkey* 40°14N 33°3E **212** B5
Çubuklu *Turkey* 41°5N 29°4E **122** B2
Cuc Phuong △ *Vietnam* 20°17N 105°38E **236** B5
Cuche *Trin. & Tob.* 10°22N 61°10W **323** t
Cuchi *Angola* 14°37S 16°58E **265** E3
Cuchi → *Angola* 15°13S 17°20E **265** F3
Cuchillo-Có *Argentina* 38°20S 64°37W **336** A4
Cuchivero → *Venezuela* 7°40N 65°57W **328** B4
Cuchumatanes, Sierra de los *Guatemala* 15°35N 91°25W **320** C1
Cuckfield *U.K.* 51°1N 0°8W **169** F7
Cucuí *Brazil* 1°12N 66°50W **328** C4
Cucumbi *Angola* 10°17S 19°5E **265** E3
Cucurpé *Mexico* 30°20N 110°43W **318** A2
Cucurrupí *Colombia* 4°23N 76°56W **328** C2
Cúcuta *Colombia* 7°54N 72°31W **328** B3
Cudahy *Calif., U.S.A.* 33°57N 118°11W **126** C3
Cudahy *Wis., U.S.A.* 42°57N 87°51W **311** B9
Cudalbi *Romania* 45°46N 27°41E **183** E12
Cudarebe = Kudarebe *Aruba* 12°37N 70°4W **322** f
Cuddalore *India* 11°46N 79°45E **245** J4
Cuddapah *India* 14°30N 78°47E **245** G4
Cuddapan, L. *Australia* 25°45S 141°26E **280** D3
Cudgewa *Australia* 36°10S 147°42E **283** D7
Cudillero *Spain* 43°33N 6°9W **194** B4
Cudjoehead *Montserrat* 16°47N 62°12W **323** p
Cue *Australia* 27°25S 117°54E **279** E2
Cuebe → *Angola* 15°46S 17°32E **265** F3
Cuéllar *Spain* 41°23N 4°21W **194** D6
Cuemba *Angola* 11°50S 17°42E **265** E3
Cuenca *Ecuador* 2°50S 79°9W **328** D2
Cuenca *Spain* 40°5N 2°10W **196** E2
Cuenca □ *Spain* 40°0N 2°0W **196** F3
Cuenca, Serranía de *Spain* 39°55N 1°50W **196** F3
Cuenca Alta del Manzanares ⌓ *Spain* 40°40N 3°55W **194** E7
Cuerdo del Pozo, Embalse de la *Spain* 41°51N 2°44W **196** D2
Cuernavaca *Mexico* 18°55N 99°15W **319** D5
Cuero *U.S.A.* 29°6N 97°17W **314** G6
Cuers *France* 43°14N 6°5E **175** E10
Cueva de la Quebrada del Toro △ *Venezuela* 10°46N 69°3W **328** A4
Cueva de los Guácharos △ *Colombia* 1°35N 76°1W **328** C2
Cuevas, Cerro *Bolivia* 22°0S 65°12W **331** E4
Cuevas de Vera = Cuevas del Almanzora *Spain* 37°18N 1°58W **197** H3
Cuevas del Almanzora *Spain* 37°18N 1°58W **197** H3
Cuevo *Bolivia* 20°15S 63°30W **331** E5
Cugir *Romania* 45°48N 23°25E **183** E8
Cugnaux *France* 43°32N 1°20E **174** E5
Cuhai-Bakony → *Hungary* 47°35N 17°54E **182** C2
Cuiabá *Brazil* 15°30S 56°0W **331** D6
Cuiabá → *Brazil* 17°5S 56°36W **331** D6
Cuicuilco, Pirámide de *Mexico* 19°18N 99°11W **128** C1
Cuihangcun *China* 22°27N 113°32E **219** G10
Cuijk *Neths.* 51°44N 5°50E **170** C5
Cuilco *Guatemala* 15°24N 91°58W **320** C1
Cuillin Hills *U.K.* 57°13N 6°15W **167** D2
Cuillin Sd. *U.K.* 57°4N 6°20W **167** D2
Cuilo = Kwilu → *Dem. Rep. of the Congo* 3°22S 17°22E **265** C3
Cuilo *Angola* 8°12S 19°28E **265** D3
Cuilo-Futa *Angola* 6°28S 15°51E **265** D3
Cuima *Angola* 13°25S 15°45E **265** E3
Cuimba *Angola* 6°10S 14°41E **265** D2
Cuiseaux *France* 46°30N 5°22E **173** F12
Cuité *Brazil* 6°29S 36°9W **332** C4
Cuito → *Angola* 18°1S 20°48E **265** F4
Cuito Cuanavale *Angola* 15°10S 19°10E **265** F3
Cuitzeo, L. de *Mexico* 19°55N 101°5W **318** D4
Cuiuni → *Brazil* 0°45S 63°7W **329** D5
Cuivre → *U.S.A.* 38°56N 90°41W **310** F6
Cujmir *Romania* 44°13N 22°57E **182** F7
Cukai *Malaysia* 4°13N 103°25E **237** K4
Cul-de-Sac *St.-Maarten* 18°2N 63°4W **322** a
Cul de Sac *St.-Martin* 18°6N 63°2W **322** a
Culasi *Phil.* 11°26N 122°3E **233** F4
Culbertson *U.S.A.* 48°9N 104°31W **304** B11
Culburra *N.S.W., Australia* 34°56S 150°46E **283** C9
Culburra *S. Austral., Australia* 35°50S 139°58E **282** C3
Culcairn *Australia* 35°41S 147°3E **283** C7
Culebra *Puerto Rico* 18°19N 65°18W **321** b
Culebra, Sierra de la *Spain* 41°55N 6°20W **194** D4
Culfa *Azerbaijan* 38°57N 45°38E **213** C11
Culgoa *Australia* 35°44S 143°6E **282** C5
Culgoa → *Australia* 29°56S 146°20E **281** D4
Culgoa Flood Plain △ *Australia* 28°58S 147°5E **281** D4
Culiacán *Mexico* 24°50N 107°23W **318** C3
Culiacán → *Mexico* 24°30N 107°42W **318** C3
Culik *Indonesia* 8°21S 115°37E **231** J18
Culion *Phil.* 11°54N 119°58E **233** F3
Culion I. *Phil.* 11°50N 120°0E **233** F2
Culiseu → *Brazil* 12°14S 53°17W **331** C7
Cúllar *Spain* 37°35N 2°34W **195** H8
Cullarin Ra. *Australia* 34°30S 149°30E **283** C8
Cullen *U.K.* 57°42N 2°49W **167** D6
Cullen Bullen *Australia* 33°18S 150°2E **283** B9
Cullen Pt. *Australia* 11°57S 141°54E **286** F1
Cullera *Spain* 39°9N 0°17W **197** F4
Cullman *U.S.A.* 34°11N 86°51W **315** D11
Culloden *U.S.A.* 32°52N 84°6W **316** C5
Cullom *U.S.A.* 40°53N 88°16W **311** D8
Cullompton *U.K.* 50°51N 3°24W **169** G4
Culmore *U.S.A.* 38°51N 77°8W **143** B3
Culo → *Angola* 6°13S 15°34E **265** D3
Culoz *France* 45°47N 5°46E **175** C9
Culpeper *U.S.A.* 38°30N 78°0W **309** F14
Culture and Science, Palace of *Warsaw, Poland* **142** b2
Culuene → *Brazil* 12°56S 52°51W **331** C7
Culver *U.S.A.* 41°13N 86°25W **311** C10
Culver, Pt. *Australia* 32°54S 124°43E **279** F3
Culver City *U.S.A.* 34°1N 118°24W **126** B2
Culverden *N.Z.* 42°47S 172°49E **285** C7
Culverton *U.S.A.* 33°19N 82°54W **316** B7
Cuma *Angola* 12°52S 15°5E **265** E3
Cumaná *Venezuela* 10°30N 64°5W **329** A5
Cumana B. *Trin. & Tob.* 10°48N 60°56W **323** t
Cumaovası *Turkey* 38°15N 27°9E **205** C9
Cumare *Colombia* 0°49N 72°32W **328** C3
Cumari *Brazil* 18°16S 48°11W **333** E2
Cumballa Hill *Mumbai, India* **130** a1
Cumbe = Euclides da Cunha *Brazil* 10°31S 39°1W **332** D4
Cumberland *B.C., Canada* 49°40N 125°0W **296** D4
Cumberland *Ont., Canada* 45°29N 75°24W **313** A9
Cumberland *St. Vincent* 13°16N 61°16W **323** n
Cumberland *Iowa, U.S.A.* 41°16N 94°52W **310** C2
Cumberland *Md., U.S.A.* 39°39N 78°46W **309** F14
Cumberland → *U.S.A.* 37°9N 88°25W **308** G9
Cumberland, C. *Vanuatu* 14°39S 166°37E **287** D4
Cumberland, L. *U.S.A.* 36°52N 85°9W **309** G11
Cumberland Gap ⌓ *U.S.A.* 36°36N 83°40W **309** G12
Cumberland I. *U.S.A.* 30°50N 81°25W **316** E8
Cumberland Is. *Australia* 20°35S 149°10E **280** J7
Cumberland Island ⌓ *U.S.A.* 30°12N 81°24W **316** E8
Cumberland L. *Canada* 54°3N 102°18W **297** C8
Cumberland Pen. *Canada* 67°0N 64°0W **295** C13
Cumberland Plateau *U.S.A.* 36°0N 85°0W **315** D12
Cumberland Sd. *Canada* 65°30N 66°0W **295** C13
Cumbernauld *U.K.* 55°57N 3°58W **167** F5
Cumbira *Angola* 12°11S 15°8E **265** E3
Cumborah *Australia* 29°40S 147°45E **281** D4
Cumbres de Majalca △ *Mexico* 28°48N 106°30W **318** B3
Cumbres de Monterrey △ *Mexico* 25°26N 100°25W **318** B4
Cumbres de Vallecas *Spain* 40°20N 3°33W **127** B2
Cumbres Mayores *Spain* 38°4N 6°39W **195** G4
Cumbria □ *U.K.* 54°42N 2°52W **168** C5
Cumbrian Mts. *U.K.* 54°30N 3°0W **168** C5
Cumbum *India* 15°40N 79°10E **245** G4
Cuminá *Brazil* 1°57S 56°2W **329** D6
Cuminá → *Brazil* 1°30S 56°0W **329** D6
Cuminapanema → *Brazil* 1°9S 54°54W **329** D7
Cumming, C. *Chile* 27°6S 109°14W **330** b
Cummings Mt. *U.S.A.* 35°2N 118°34W **307** K8
Cummins *Australia* 34°16S 135°43E **281** E2
Cumnock *N.S.W., Australia* 32°59S 148°46E **283** B8
Cumnock *E. Ayrs., U.K.* 55°28N 4°17W **167** F4
Cumpas *Mexico* 30°2N 109°48W **318** B3
Cumplida, Pta. *Canary Is.* 28°50N 17°48W **153** e1
Çumra *Turkey* 37°34N 32°45E **212** D5
Cumuto *Trin. & Tob.* 10°35N 61°12W **323** t
Cunapo → *Trin. & Tob.* 10°35N 61°8W **323** t
Cunaripa *Trin. & Tob.* 10°33N 61°10W **323** t
Cuncumén *Chile* 31°53S 70°38W **334** C1
Cunderdin *Australia* 31°37S 117°12E **279** F2
Cundinamarca □ *Colombia* 5°0N 74°0W **328** C3
Cunene □ *Angola* 16°30S 15°0E **265** F3
Cunene → *Angola* 17°20S 11°50E **265** F2
Cúneo *Italy* 44°23N 7°32E **198** D4
Çüngüş *Turkey* 38°13N 39°17E **246** B3
Cunhinga *Angola* 12°11S 16°47E **265** E3
Cunillera, I. = Sa Conillera *Spain* 38°59N 1°13E **206** D1
Cunjamba *Angola* 15°27S 20°10E **265** F4
Cunlhat *France* 45°38N 3°32E **174** C7
Cunnamulla *Australia* 28°2S 145°38E **281** D4
Cunningham *Bahamas* 25°5N 77°26W **153** b
Cunupia *Trin. & Tob.* 10°32N 61°22W **323** t
Cuorgnè *Italy* 45°23N 7°39E **198** C4
Cupar *Sask., Canada* 50°57N 104°10W **297** C8
Cupar *Fife, U.K.* 56°19N 3°1W **167** E5
Cupcini *Moldova* 48°6N 27°23E **183** B12
Cupecé → *Brazil* 23°39S 46°40W **137** B1
Cupertino *U.S.A.* 37°19N 122°2W **306** H4
Cupica, G. de *Colombia* 6°25N 77°30W **328** B2
Čuprija *Serbia* 43°57N 21°26E **202** C5
Curaçá *Brazil* 8°59S 39°54W **332** C4
Curaçao *Neth. Ant.* 12°10N 69°0W **322** g
Curaçao Int. ✕ (CUR) *Neth. Ant.* 12°11N 68°57W **322** g
Curacautín *Chile* 38°26S 71°53W **336** A2
Curador = Presidente Dutra *Brazil* 5°15S 44°30W **332** C3
Curahuara de Carangas *Bolivia* 17°52S 68°26W **330** D4
Curalhinho = Coelho Neto *Brazil* 4°15S 43°0W **332** B3
Curamata → *Trin. & Tob.* 10°11N 61°28W **323** t
Curanilahue *Chile* 37°29S 73°28W **334** D1
Curaray → *Peru* 2°20S 74°5W **328** D3
Curatabaca *Venezuela* 6°19N 62°51W **329** B5
Cure → *France* 47°40N 3°41E **173** E10
Curepipe *Mauritius* 20°19S 57°31E **272** e
Curepipe Point *Mauritius* 20°21S 57°31E **272** e
Curepto *Chile* 35°8S 72°1W **334** D1
Curiapo *Venezuela* 8°33N 61°5W **329** B5
Curicó *Chile* 34°55S 71°20W **334** C1
Curicuriari → *Brazil* 0°14S 66°48W **328** D4
Curieuse *Seychelles* 4°15S 55°44E **272** c
Curimatá *Brazil* 10°2S 44°17W **332** D3
Curinga *Italy* 38°49N 16°19E **201** D9
Curiplaya *Colombia* 0°16N 74°52W **328** C3
Curitiba *Brazil* 25°20S 49°10W **335** B6
Curitibanos *Brazil* 27°18S 50°36W **335** B5
Curlewis *Australia* 31°7S 150°16E **283** A9
Curoca → *Angola* 15°43S 11°55E **265** F2
Currabubula *Australia* 31°16S 150°44E **283** A9
Currais Novos *Brazil* 6°13S 36°30W **332** C4
Curral Velho *C. Verde Is.* 16°8N 22°48W **153** j
Curralinho *Brazil* 1°45S 49°46W **332** B2
Currane, L. *Ireland* 51°49N 10°4W **166** E1
Currant *U.S.A.* 38°44N 115°28W **304** G6
Curraweena *Australia* 30°47S 145°54E **283** A6
Currawinya △ *Australia* 28°55S 144°27E **281** D3
Current → *U.S.A.* 36°15N 90°55W **314** C9
Currie *Tas., Australia* 39°56S 143°53E **281** F3
Currie *Edinburgh, U.K.* 55°54N 3°17W **121** B2
Currie *Nev., U.S.A.* 40°16N 114°45W **304** F6
Cursole *Somali Rep.* 2°14N 45°25E **267** D6
Curt-Bunar = Tervel *Bulgaria* 43°45N 27°28E **203** C11
Curtea de Argeş *Romania* 45°12N 24°42E **183** E9
Curtici *Romania* 46°21N 21°18E **182** D6
Curtis *U.S.A.* 40°38N 100°31W **308** E3
Curtis Group *Australia* 39°30S 146°37E **281** F4
Curtis I. *Queens., Australia* 23°35S 151°10E **280** C5
Curtis I. *Pac. Oc.* 30°30S 178°34W **277** G15
Curuá → *Pará, Brazil* 2°24S 54°5W **329** D7
Curuá → *Pará, Brazil* 5°23S 54°22W **331** B7
Curuá, I. *Brazil* 0°48N 50°10W **332** A1
Curuaés → *Brazil* 7°30S 54°45W **331** B7
Curuaí *Brazil* 2°17S 55°29W **329** D6
Curuápanema → *Brazil* 2°25S 55°2W **329** D6
Curuçá *Brazil* 0°43S 47°50W **332** B2
Curuçá → *Brazil* 4°27S 71°23W **330** B3
Curuguaty *Paraguay* 24°31S 55°42W **335** A4
Curup *Indonesia* 4°26S 102°13E **234** C2
Curupira, Serra *S. Amer.* 1°25N 64°30W **329** C5
Cururu → *Brazil* 7°12S 58°3W **331** B6
Cururupu *Brazil* 1°50S 44°50W **332** B3
Curuzú Cuatiá *Argentina* 29°50S 58°5W **334** B4
Curvelo *Brazil* 18°45S 44°27W **333** E3
Cusago *Italy* 45°26N 9°1E **129** B1
Cusano Milanino *Italy* 45°33N 9°11E **129** A2
Cusco = Cuzco *Peru* 13°32S 72°0W **330** C3
Cushendall *U.K.* 55°5N 6°4W **166** A5
Cushing *U.S.A.* 35°59N 96°46W **314** D6
Cushing, Mt. *Canada* 57°35N 126°57W **296** B3
Cusihuiriáchic *Mexico* 28°14N 106°50W **318** B3
Cusna, Mte. *Italy* 44°17N 10°23E **198** D7
Cussabat = Al Qaşabát *Libya* 32°39N 14°1E **258** B2
Cusset *France* 46°8N 3°28E **173** F10
Cusseta *U.S.A.* 32°18N 84°47W **316** C5
Cusso, Sa. do *Angola* 6°30S 14°58E **265** D2
Custer *U.S.A.* 43°46N 103°36W **308** D2
Custom House *Dublin, Ireland* **120** b3
Cut Bank *U.S.A.* 48°38N 112°20W **304** B7
Cutchogue *U.S.A.* 41°1N 72°30W **313** E12
Cutervo *Peru* 6°25S 78°55W **330** B2
Cuthbert *U.S.A.* 31°46N 84°48W **316** D5
Cutler *U.S.A.* 36°31N 119°17W **306** J7
Cutler Park *U.S.A.* 42°17N 71°12W **116** B1
Cutler Ridge *U.S.A.* 25°35N 80°20W **317** K9
Cutlerville *U.S.A.* 42°50N 85°40W **311** B11
Cutral-Có *Argentina* 38°58S 69°15W **336** A3
Cutro *Italy* 39°2N 16°59E **201** C9
Cuttaburra → *Australia* 29°43S 144°22E **281** D3
Cuttack *India* 20°25N 85°57E **244** D7
Cuva → *Angola* 11°42S 14°52E **265** E2
Cuvelai *Angola* 15°44S 15°50E **265** F3
Cuvier, C. *Australia* 23°14S 113°22E **279** D1
Cuvier I. *N.Z.* 36°27S 175°50E **284** C4
Çuvuşabaşi → *Turkey* 40°58N 28°51E **122** B1
Cuxhaven *Germany* 53°51N 8°41E **178** B4
Cuyabeno *Ecuador* 0°16S 75°53W **328** D2
Cuyahoga Falls *U.S.A.* 41°8N 81°29W **312** E3
Cuyahoga Valley △ *U.S.A.* 41°14N 81°33W **312** E3
Cuyapo *Phil.* 15°46N 120°40E **232** D3
Cuyo *Phil.* 10°51N 121°2E **233** F3
Cuyo East Pass *Phil.* 11°0N 121°28E **233** F3
Cuyo Islands *Phil.* 11°4N 120°57E **233** F3
Cuyo West Pass *Phil.* 11°0N 120°30E **233** F3
Cuyuni → *Guyana* 6°23N 58°41W **329** B6
Cuzco *Bolivia* 20°0S 66°50W **330** E4
Cuzco *Peru* 13°32S 72°0W **330** C3
Cuzco □ *Peru* 13°31S 71°59W **330** C3
Čvrsnica *Bos.-H.* 43°36N 17°35E **182** G2
Cwmbran *U.K.* 51°39N 3°2W **169** F4
Cyangugu *Rwanda* 2°29S 28°54E **268** C2
Cybinka *Poland* 52°12N 14°46E **185** F1
Cyclades *Greece* 37°0N 24°30E **204** E6
Cyclades □ *Greece* 37°0N 25°0E **204** D6
Cygnet *Australia* 43°8S 147°1E **281** G4
Cynthiana *U.S.A.* 38°23N 84°18W **311** F12

Cypress Hills *Canada* 49°40N 109°30W **297** D7
Cypress Hills *N.Y., U.S.A.* 40°41N 73°53W **132** B2
Cypress Hills △ *Canada* 49°40N 109°30W **297** D7
Cyprus ■ *Asia* 35°0N 33°0E **207** F9
Cyrenaica *Libya* 27°0N 23°0E **258** B4
Cyrene *Libya* 32°53N 21°52E **258** B4
Czaplinek *Poland* 53°34N 16°14E **184** E3
Czar *Canada* 52°27N 110°50W **297** C6
Czarna → *Łódzkie, Poland* 51°18N 19°55E **185** G6
Czarna → *Świętokrzyskie, Poland* 50°28N 21°21E **185** H8
Czarna Białostocka *Poland* 53°18N 23°17E **185** E10
Czarna Woda *Poland* 53°51N 18°6E **184** E5
Czarne *Poland* 53°42N 16°58E **184** E3
Czarnków *Poland* 52°55N 16°38E **185** F3
Czaslau = Čáslav *Czech Rep.* 49°54N 15°22E **180** B8
Czech Rep. ■ *Europe* 50°0N 15°0E **180** B8
Czechowice-Dziedzice *Poland* 49°54N 18°59E **185** J5
Czempiń *Poland* 52°9N 16°43E **185** F3
Czeremcha *Poland* 52°31N 23°21E **185** F10
Czerniejewo *Poland* 52°26N 17°30E **185** F4
Czernowitz = Chernivtsi *Ukraine* 48°15N 25°52E **183** B10
Czerniaków *Poland* 52°11N 21°3E **142** B2
Czersk *Poland* 53°46N 17°58E **184** E4
Czerwieńsk *Poland* 52°1N 15°23E **185** F2
Czerwionka-Leszczyny *Poland* 50°7N 18°37E **185** H5
Częstochowa *Poland* 50°49N 19°7E **185** H6
Człopa *Poland* 53°6N 16°6E **185** E3
Człuchów *Poland* 53°41N 17°22E **184** E4
Czortów = Chortkiv *Ukraine* 49°2N 25°46E **177** D13
Czyste *Poland* 52°13N 20°57E **142** B1
Czyżew-Osada *Poland* 52°48N 22°19E **185** F9

D

D.C. War Memorial *Washington, D.C., U.S.A.* **143** b1
Da → *Vietnam* 21°15N 105°20E **228** G5
Da Hinggan Ling *China* 48°0N 121°0E **219** B7
Da Lat *Vietnam* 11°56N 108°25E **237** G7
Da Mócca → *Brazil* 23°35S 46°35W **137** B2
Da Nang *Vietnam* 16°4N 108°13E **236** D7
Da Qaidam *China* 37°50N 95°15E **218** C4
Da Yunhe → *Hopei, China* 39°10N 117°10E **227** E9
Da Yunhe → *Jiangsu, China* 34°25N 120°5E **227** G11
Da'an *China* 45°30N 124°7E **227** B13
Daan Viljoen △ *Namibia* 22°2S 16°45E **270** B2
Daanbantayan *Phil.* 11°17N 124°2E **233** F5
Dab'a, Ras el *Egypt* 31°3N 28°31E **256** H6
Daba Shan *China* 32°0N 109°0E **228** B7
Dabai *Nigeria* 11°25N 5°15E **263** C6
Dabajuro *Venezuela* 11°2N 70°40W **328** A3
Dabakala *Ivory C.* 8°15N 4°20W **262** D4
Dabaro *Somali Rep.* 6°21N 48°43E **267** C6
Dabas *Hungary* 47°11N 19°19E **182** C4
Dabat *Ethiopia* 12°58N 37°41E **257** E4
Dabbagh, Jabal *Si. Arabia* 27°52N 35°45E **246** E2
Dabeiba *Colombia* 7°1N 76°16W **328** B2
Daber = Dobra *Poland* 53°34N 15°20E **184** E2
Dabhoi *India* 22°10N 73°20E **242** H5
Dąbie *Poland* 52°5N 18°50E **185** F5
Dabie Shan *China* 31°20N 115°20E **229** B10
Dabilda *Cameroon* 12°45N 14°35E **259** F2
Dabl, W. → *Si. Arabia* 29°5N 36°16E **251** J7
Ďablice *Czech Rep.* 50°8N 14°29E **135** B2
Dabnou *Niger* 14°10N 5°22E **263** C6
Dabo = Pasirkuning *Indonesia* 0°30S 104°33E **234** C2
Dabola *Guinea* 10°50N 11°5W **262** C2
Dabou *Ivory C.* 5°20N 4°23W **262** D4
Daboya *Ghana* 9°30N 1°20W **263** D4
Dabravolya *Belarus* 52°55N 23°59E **185** F10
Dąbrowa *Poland* 52°19N 20°52E **142** B1
Dąbrowa Białostocka *Poland* 53°40N 23°21E **184** E10
Dąbrowa Górnicza *Poland* 50°15N 19°10E **185** H6
Dąbrowa Tarnowska *Poland* 50°10N 20°59E **185** H7
Dabu *China* 24°22N 116°41E **229** E11
Dabugam *India* 19°27N 82°26E **244** E6
Dabung *Malaysia* 5°23N 102°1E **237** K4
Dabus → *Ethiopia* 10°48N 35°10E **257** E4
Dacato → *Ethiopia* 7°25N 42°40E **257** F5
Dacca = Dhaka *Bangla.* 23°43N 90°26E **241** D3
Dacca = Dhaka □ *Bangla.* 24°25N 90°25E **241** C3
Dachang *China* 31°17N 121°24E **138** B1
Dachang ✕ *China* 31°18N 121°25E **138** B1
Dachau *Germany* 48°15N 11°26E **131** A1
Dachau-Ost *Germany* 48°15N 11°27E **131** A1
Dachauer Moos *Germany* 48°13N 11°27E **131** A1
Dachigam △ *India* 34°10N 75°0E **242** B6
Dachstein, Hoher *Austria* 47°28N 13°35E **180** D6
Dačice *Czech Rep.* 49°5N 15°26E **180** B8
Dacula *U.S.A.* 33°59N 83°54W **316** B6
Dadanawa *Guyana* 2°50N 59°30W **329** C6
Dadar *India* 19°0N 72°49E **130** A1
Daday *Turkey* 41°28N 33°27E **212** B5
Dade City *U.S.A.* 28°22N 82°11W **317** G7
Dadès, Oued → *Morocco* 30°58N 6°44W **260** B3
Dadeville *U.S.A.* 32°50N 85°46W **316** C4
Dadhar *Pakistan* 29°28N 67°39E **242** E2
Dadiya *Nigeria* 9°35N 11°24E **263** D7
Ḍadnah *U.A.E.* 25°32N 56°22E **247** E8
Dadohae Maritime National Park △ *S. Korea* 34°0N 126°0E **224** E3
Dadra = Achalpur *India* 21°22N 77°32E **244** D3
Dadra & Nagar Haveli □ *India* 20°5N 73°0E **244** D1
Dadri = Charkhi Dadri *India* 28°37N 76°17E **242** E7
Dadu *Pakistan* 26°45N 67°45E **242** F2
Dadu He → *China* 29°31N 103°46E **228** C4
Daebang *S. Korea* 37°30N 126°55E **137** B1
Daebudo *S. Korea* 37°14N 126°35E **224** D3
Daecheongdo *S. Korea* 37°49N 124°42E **224** D2
Daechi *S. Korea* 37°30N 127°2E **137** B2
Daegu *S. Korea* 35°50N 128°37E **224** E4
Daejeon *S. Korea* 36°20N 127°28E **224** D3
Daejeon □ *S. Korea* 36°20N 127°25E **224** D3
Daejeong *S. Korea* 33°8N 126°17E **224** a
Daemodo *S. Korea* 34°11N 126°45E **224** E3
Daet *Phil.* 14°2N 122°55E **232** D4
Dafang *China* 27°9N 105°39E **228** D5
Dafdaf, J. *Si. Arabia* 28°16N 35°35E **251** K6
Dafnes *Greece* 35°13N 25°3E **207** E6
Dafni *Athina, Greece* 37°55N 23°44E **112** B2
Dafni *Peloponnese, Greece* 37°48N 22°1E **204** D4
Dafnoudi, Akra *Greece* 38°28N 20°32E **202** C2
Dağ *Turkey* 37°12N 30°31E **205** D12
Daga Post *Sudan* 9°13N 33°58E **266** C3
Dagali *Norway* 60°25N 8°28E **164** D5
Dagana *Senegal* 16°30N 15°35W **262** B1
Dagash *Sudan* 19°19N 33°25E **256** D3
Dagenham *U.K.* 51°32N 0°8E **125** A4
Dagestan □ *Russia* 42°30N 47°0E **191** J8
Dagestanskiye Ogni *Russia* 42°6N 48°12E **191** J9
Dagg Sd. *N.Z.* 45°23S 166°45E **285** F1
Daggett *U.S.A.* 34°52N 116°52W **307** L10
Daghestan Republic = Dagestan □ *Russia* 42°30N 47°0E **191** J8
Daghfeli *Sudan* 19°18N 32°40E **256** D3
Daglfing *Germany* 48°8N 11°39E **131** B2
Dağlıq Qarabağ = Nagorno-Karabakh □ *Azerbaijan* 39°55N 46°45E **213** C12
Dagö = Hiiumaa *Estonia* 58°50N 22°45E **188** C2
Dagu *China* 38°59N 117°40E **227** E9
Dagua *Papua N. G.* 3°27S 143°20E **286** B2
Daguan *China* 27°43N 103°56E **228** D4
Dagupan *Phil.* 16°3N 120°20E **232** C3
Daguragu *Australia* 17°33S 130°30E **278** C5
Dahab *Egypt* 28°31N 34°31E **251** K5
Dahab, Gezîret el *Egypt* 29°59N 31°13E **117** B2
Dahanu *India* 19°58N 72°44E **244** E1
Daheisha *West Bank* 31°42N 35°11E **123** B2
Dahivadi *India* 17°43N 74°33E **244** F2
Dahlak △ *Eritrea* 15°35N 40°1E **257** D5
Dahlak Kebir *Eritrea* 15°50N 40°10E **257** D5
Dahlem *Germany* 52°27N 13°16E **115** B2
Dahlenburg *Germany* 53°11N 10°44E **178** B6
Dahlonega *U.S.A.* 34°32N 83°59W **315** D13
Dahlwitz-Hoppegarten *Germany* 52°30N 13°41E **115** A5
Dahme *Germany* 51°52N 13°25E **178** D9
Dahod *India* 22°50N 74°15E **242** H6
Dahomey = Benin ■ *Africa* 10°0N 2°0E **263** D5
Dahong Shan *China* 31°25N 113°0E **229** B9
Dahongliutan *China* 35°45N 79°20E **243** B8
Dahongmen *China* 39°48N 116°21E **114** C2
Dahra *Libya* 29°30N 17°50E **258** C3
Dahra *Senegal* 15°22N 15°30W **262** B1
Dahra, Massif de *Algeria* 36°7N 1°21E **261** A5
Dahshûr *Egypt* 29°45N 31°14E **256** J7
Dahūk *Iraq* 36°50N 43°1E **213** D10
Dahūk □ *Iraq* 36°50N 42°50E **213** D10
Dahuofan Shuiku *China* 41°52N 124°12E **224** B2
Daḥy, Nafūd ad *Si. Arabia* 22°20N 45°25E **248** B4
Dai *Solomon Is.* 7°54S 160°40E **287** L11
Dai Hao *Vietnam* 18°1N 106°25E **236** C6
Dai-Sen *Japan* 35°22N 133°32E **222** B5
Dai Shan *China* 30°25N 122°10E **229** B14
Dai Xian *China* 39°4N 112°58E **226** E7
Daicheng *China* 38°42N 116°38E **226** E9
Daigo *Japan* 36°46N 140°21E **223** A12
Daik-u *Burma* 17°47N 96°40E **241** G6
Daikondi = Day Kundī □ *Afghan.* 34°0N 66°0E **240** B2
Daimanji-San *Japan* 36°14N 133°20E **222** A5
Daimiel *Spain* 39°5N 3°35W **195** F7
Daingean *Ireland* 53°18N 7°17W **166** C4
Dainkog *China* 32°30N 97°58E **228** A1
Daintree *Australia* 16°20S 145°20E **280** B4
Daintree △ *Australia* 16°8S 145°2E **280** B4
Daiō-Misaki *Japan* 34°15N 136°45E **223** C8
Dair, J. ed *Sudan* 12°27N 30°42E **257** E3
Dairen = Dalian *China* 38°50N 121°40E **227** E11
Dairût *Egypt* 27°34N 30°43E **256** B3
Daisen-Oki △ *Japan* 35°23N 133°34E **222** B5
Daisetsu-Zan *Japan* 43°30N 142°57E **220** C11
Daisetsu-Zan △ *Japan* 43°30N 142°55E **220** C11
Daitari *India* 21°10N 85°46E **244** D7
Daito *Japan* 35°19N 132°58E **222** B4
Dajarra *Australia* 21°42S 139°30E **280** C2
Dajiaoting *China* 39°51N 116°27E **114** B2
Dajiawa *China* 37°9N 119°0E **227** F10
Dajin Chuan → *China* 31°16N 101°59E **228** B3
Dak Dam *Cambodia* 12°20N 107°21E **236** F6
Dak Nhe *Vietnam* 15°28N 107°48E **236** E6
Dak Pek *Vietnam* 15°4N 107°44E **236** E6
Dak Song *Vietnam* 12°19N 107°35E **237** F6
Dak Sui *Vietnam* 14°55N 107°43E **236** E6
Dakar *Senegal* 14°34N 17°29W **262** C1
Dakar □ *Senegal* 14°45N 17°20W **262** C1
Dakhal, W. el → *Egypt* 28°48N 32°47E **251** K3
Dakhin *Bangla.* 22°30N 90°45E **241** D3
Dakhla *W. Sahara* 23°50N 15°53W **260** D1
Dakhla, El Wâhât el- *Egypt* 25°30N 28°50E **256** B2
Dakhnoye *Russia* 59°49N 30°15E **137** C1
Dakingari *Nigeria* 11°37N 4°1E **263** C5
Dakoank *India* 7°2N 93°43E **245** L11
Dakor *India* 22°45N 73°11E **242** H5
Dakoro *Niger* 14°31N 6°46E **263** C6
Dakota City *Iowa, U.S.A.* 42°43N 94°12W **310** B2
Dakota City *Nebr., U.S.A.* 42°25N 96°25W **308** D5
Đakovica *Serbia* 42°22N 20°26E **202** D4
Đakovo *Croatia* 45°19N 18°24E **182** E3
Dal *Norway* 59°53N 8°40E **164** E5
Dala *Lunda Sul, Angola* 11°3S 20°17E **265** E4
Dala *Uige, Angola* 8°5S 15°49E **265** D3
Dala *Solomon Is.* 8°30S 160°41E **287** M11
Dala-Cachibo *Angola* 10°30S 14°41E **265** E2
Dalaba *Guinea* 10°47N 12°12W **262** C2
Dalachi *China* 36°48N 105°0E **226** F3
Dalagan = San Antonio *Phil.* 14°57N 120°5E **232** D3
Dalaguete *Phil.* 9°46N 123°32E **233** G4
Dalai Nur *China* 43°20N 116°45E **226** C9
Dālakī *Iran* 29°26N 51°17E **247** D6
Dalälven → *Sweden* 60°12N 16°43E **162** D10
Dalaman *Turkey* 36°48N 28°47E **205** E10
Dalaman → *Turkey* 36°41N 28°43E **205** E10
Dalandzadgad *Mongolia* 43°27N 104°30E **226** C3
Dalanganem Is. *Phil.* 10°40N 120°17E **233** F3
Dalap-Uliga-Darrit = Majuro *Marshall Is.* 7°9N 171°12E **288** G9
Dalarna *Sweden* 61°0N 14°0E **162** D8
Dalarnas län □ *Sweden* 61°0N 14°0E **162** C8
Dalasýsla □ *Iceland* 65°15N 22°0W **155** B4
Dalat *Malaysia* 2°44N 111°56E **235** B4
Dālbandīn *Pakistan* 29°0N 64°23E **240** C2
Dalbeattie *U.K.* 54°56N 3°50W **167** G5
Dalbeg *Australia* 20°16S 147°18E **280** C4
Dalbosjön *Sweden* 58°40N 12°45E **163** F6
Dalby *Queens., Australia* 27°10S 151°17E **281** D5
Dalby *Skåne, Sweden* 55°40N 13°22E **163** J7
Dalby Söderskog △ *Sweden* 55°41N 13°21E **163** J7
Dale *Sogn og Fjordane, Norway* 61°22N 5°23E **164** C2
Dale *Ind., U.S.A.* 38°10N 86°59W **311** F9
Dale City *U.S.A.* 38°38N 77°19W **309** F15
Dale Hollow L. *U.S.A.* 36°32N 85°27W **315** C12
Dalejsky potok → *Czech Rep.* 50°2N 14°24E **135** B2
Dalen *Norway* 59°26N 8°0E **164** E4
Dalet *Burma* 19°59N 93°51E **241** F4
Daletme *Burma* 21°36N 92°46E **241** E4
Daleville *Ala., U.S.A.* 31°19N 85°43W **316** D4
Daleville *Ind., U.S.A.* 40°7N 85°33W **311** D11
Dalgā *Egypt* 27°39N 30°41E **256** B3
Dalgān *Iran* 27°31N 59°19E **247** E8
Dalgety Bay *U.K.* 56°2N 3°20W **121** A1
Dalhart *U.S.A.* 36°4N 102°31W **314** C3
Dalhousie *N.B., Canada* 48°5N 66°26W **299** C6
Dalhousie *India* 32°38N 75°58E **242** C6
Dali *Shaanxi, China* 34°48N 109°58E **226** G5
Dali *Yunnan, China* 25°40N 100°10E **228** E3
Dalian *China* 38°50N 121°40E **227** E11
Daliang Shan *China* 28°0N 102°45E **228** D4
Daling He → *China* 40°55N 121°40E **227** D11
Dāliyat el Karmel *Israel* 32°43N 35°2E **250** F6
Dalj *Croatia* 45°29N 18°59E **182** E3
Dalkeith *Midloth., U.K.* 55°54N 3°4W **121** B3
Dalkeith *Fla., U.S.A.* 30°0N 85°9W **316** E4
Dalkey *Ireland* 53°16N 6°6W **120** B3
Dalkey I. *Ireland* 53°17N 6°5W **120** B3
Dallas *Ga., U.S.A.* 33°55N 84°51W **316** B5
Dallas *Oreg., U.S.A.* 44°55N 123°19W **304** D2
Dallas *Tex., U.S.A.* 32°47N 96°48W **314** E6
Dallas Center *U.S.A.* 41°41N 93°58W **310** C3
Dallas City *U.S.A.* 40°38N 91°10W **310** D5
Dalle = Yirga Alem *Ethiopia* 6°48N 38°22E **257** F4
Dalles, The *U.S.A.* 45°36N 121°10W **304** D3
Dallgow *Germany* 52°32N 13°3E **115** A1
Dallol *Ethiopia* 14°14N 40°17E **257** E5
Dalmā *U.A.E.* 24°30N 52°20E **247** E7
Dalmacija *Croatia* 43°20N 17°0E **199** E13
Dalmas, L. *Canada* 53°30N 71°50W **299** B5
Dalmatia = Dalmacija *Croatia* 43°20N 17°0E **199** E13
Dalmau *India* 26°4N 81°2E **243** F9
Dalmellington *U.K.* 55°19N 4°23W **167** F4
Dalmeny *N.S.W., Australia* 36°10S 150°8E **283** D9
Dalmeny *Edinburgh, U.K.* 55°59N 3°22W **121** B1
Dalnegorsk *Russia* 44°32N 135°33E **220** B7
Dalnerechensk *Russia* 45°50N 133°40E **220** B6
Dalnevostochnyy □ *Russia* 67°0N 140°0E **215** C14
Dalny = Dalian *China* 38°50N 121°40E **227** E11
Daloa *Ivory C.* 7°0N 6°30W **262** D3
Dalou Shan *China* 28°15N 107°0E **228** C6
Dalry *U.K.* 55°42N 4°43W **167** F4
Dalrymple, L. *Australia* 20°40S 147°0E **280** C4
Dalrymple, Mt. *Australia* 21°1S 148°39E **280** K6
Dals Långed *Sweden* 58°56N 12°18E **163** F6
Dalsætra *Norway* 61°28N 9°26E **164** C6
Dalsjöfors *Sweden* 57°46N 13°5E **163** G7
Dalsland *Sweden* 58°50N 12°15E **163** F6
Dalsmynni *Iceland* 64°48N 21°29W **155** C5
Dalston *U.K.* 51°32N 0°4W **125** A3
Daltenganj *India* 24°0N 84°4E **243** H11
Dalton *Ga., U.S.A.* 34°46N 84°58W **315** D12
Dalton *Mass., U.S.A.* 42°28N 73°11W **313** D11
Dalton *Nebr., U.S.A.* 41°25N 102°58W **308** E2
Dalton, Kap *Greenland* 69°25N 24°3W **154** D8
Dalton-in-Furness *U.K.* 54°10N 3°11W **168** C4
Dalupiri I. *Cagayan, Phil.* 19°5N 121°12E **232** B3
Dalupiri I. *N. Samar, Phil.* 12°25N 124°16E **232** E5
Dalvík *Iceland* 65°58N 18°32W **155** B8
Dálvvadis = Jokkmokk *Sweden* 66°35N 19°50E **160** C18
Dalwallinu *Australia* 30°17S 116°40E **279** F2
Daly → *Australia* 13°35S 130°19E **278** B5
Daly City *U.S.A.* 37°42N 122°27W **136** B2
Daly L. *Canada* 56°32N 105°39W **297** B7
Daly River *Australia* 13°46S 130°42E **278** B5
Daly Waters *Australia* 16°15S 133°24E **280** B1
Dalyan *Turkey* 36°50N 28°39E **205** E10
Dam *Amsterdam, Neths.* **112** b2
Dam Doi *Vietnam* 8°50N 105°12E **237** H5
Dam Ha *Vietnam* 21°21N 107°36E **236** B6
Dam Rak *Amsterdam, Neths.* **112** a2
Damachova *Belarus* 51°45N 23°36E **185** G10
Damaia *Portugal* 38°44N 9°12W **126** A1
Daman *India* 20°25N 72°57E **244** D1
Daman & Diu □ *India* 20°25N 72°58E **244** D1
Dāmaneh *Iran* 33°1N 50°29E **247** C6
Damanganga → *India* 20°25N 72°56E **244** D1
Damanhûr *Egypt* 31°0N 30°30E **256** H7
Damant L. *Canada* 61°45N 105°5W **297** A7
Damanzhuang *China* 38°5N 116°35E **226** E9
Damar *Indonesia* 7°7S 128°40E **231** F7
Damara *C.A.R.* 4°58N 18°42E **264** B3
Damarakia *Greece* 37°58N 23°39E **112** B1
Damaraland *Namibia* 20°0S 15°0E **270** B2
Damascus = Dimashq *Syria* 33°30N 36°18E **250** E7
Damascus *U.S.A.* 31°18N 84°43W **316** D5
Damasi *Greece* 39°43N 22°11E **204** B4
Damaturu *Nigeria* 11°45N 11°55E **263** C7
Damāvand *Iran* 35°47N 52°0E **247** C7
Damāvand, Qolleh-ye *Iran* 35°56N 52°10E **247** C7
Damba *Angola* 6°44S 15°20E **265** D3
Dâmbovița □ *Romania* 45°0N 25°30E **183** F10
Dâmbovița → *Romania* 44°12N 26°26E **183** F11
Dâmbovnic → *Romania* 44°28N 25°18E **183** F10
Dambrowica = Dubrovytsya *Ukraine* 51°31N 26°35E **177** C14
Dambulla *Sri Lanka* 7°51N 80°39E **245** L5
Dame Marie *Haiti* 18°36N 74°26W **321** C5
Dämeritzsee *Germany* 52°34N 13°43E **115** B5
Dāmghān *Iran* 36°10N 54°17E **247** B7
Dămienesti *Romania* 46°44N 26°59E **183** D11
Damietta = Dumyât *Egypt* 31°24N 31°48E **251** G2
Daming *China* 36°15N 115°6E **226** F8
Damīr Qābū *Syria* 36°58N 41°51E **246** B4
Dammai I. *Phil.* 5°47N 120°25E **233** J3
Dammam = Ad Dammām *Si. Arabia* 26°20N 50°5E **247** E6
Dammarie-les-Lys *France* 48°31N 2°39E **173** D9
Dammartin-en-Goële *France* 49°3N 2°41E **173** C9
Damme *Germany* 52°32N 8°11E **178** C4
Damodar → *India* 23°17N 87°35E **243** H12
Damoh *India* 23°50N 79°28E **243** H8
Damous *Algeria* 36°31N 1°42E **261** A5
Dampier *Australia* 20°41S 116°42E **278** D2
Dampier, Selat *Indonesia* 0°40S 131°0E **231** E8
Dampier Arch. *Australia* 20°38S 116°32E **278** D2
Dampier Str. *Papua N. G.* 5°50S 148°0E **286** C5
Damqawt *Yemen* 16°34N 52°50E **249** C6
Damrani *Algeria* 27°45N 2°56W **260** C4
Damrei, Chuor Phnum *Cambodia* 11°30N 103°0E **237** G4
Damroh *India* 28°26N 95°14E **241** A5
Damvillers *France* 49°20N 5°21E **173** C12
Damyang *S. Korea* 35°19N 126°59E **224** E3
Dan-Gulbi *Nigeria* 11°40N 6°15E **263** C6
Dan Ryan Woods *U.S.A.* 41°44N 87°40W **119** C2
Dana *Indonesia* 11°0S 122°52E **231** F6
Dana, L. *Canada* 50°53N 77°20W **298** B4
Dana, Mt. *U.S.A.* 37°54N 119°12W **306** H7
Danakil Depression *Ethiopia* 13°0N 41°0E **267** B5
Danakil Desert *Ethiopia* 12°45N 41°0E **257** E5
Danan *Ethiopia* 6°31N 43°30E **267** C5
Danané *Ivory C.* 7°16N 8°9W **262** D3
Danao *Phil.* 10°31N 124°1E **233** F5
Danau Poso *Indonesia* 1°52S 120°35E **231** E6
Danba *China* 30°54N 101°48E **228** B3
Danbury *U.S.A.* 41°24N 73°28W **313** E11
Danby L. *U.S.A.* 34°13N 115°5W **305** J6
Dand *Afghan.* 31°28N 65°32E **242** D1
Dande → *Angola* 6°15S 15°34E **265** D2
Dande → *Zimbabwe* 15°56S 30°16E **269** F3
Dandeldhura *Nepal* 29°20N 80°35E **243** E9
Dandeli *India* 15°5N 74°30E **245** G2
Dandenong *Australia* 38°0S 145°15E **283** E6
Danderhall *U.K.* 55°55N 3°7W **121** B3
Danderyd *Sweden* 59°24N 18°1E **139** A2
Dandīl *Egypt* 29°10N 31°2E **256** J7
Dandong *China* 40°10N 124°20E **224** B2
Danfeng *China* 33°45N 110°25E **226** H6
Danforth *Canada* 43°43N 79°16W **141** A3
Dangan Liedao *China* 22°2N 114°8E **229** F10
Dange *Angola* 7°56S 15°3E **265** D3
Dangé-St-Romain *France* 46°56N 0°36E **174** B4
Dângeni *Romania* 47°51N 26°58E **183** C11
Danger Is. = Pukapuka *Cook Is.* 10°53S 165°49W **289** J11
Danger Pt. *S. Africa* 34°40S 19°17E **270** D2
Danginpuri *Indonesia* 8°40S 115°13E **231** K18
Dangjin *S. Korea* 36°53N 126°37E **224** D3
Dangla *Ethiopia* 11°18N 36°56E **257** E4
Dangla Shan = Tanggula Shan *China* 32°40N 92°10E **218** C4
Dangora *Nigeria* 11°30N 8°7E **263** C6
Dangouadougou *Burkina Faso* 10°9N 4°56W **262** D4
Dangrek, Phnom *Thailand* 14°15N 105°0E **236** E5
Dangriga *Belize* 17°0N 88°13W **319** D7
Dangshan *China* 34°27N 116°22E **226** G9
Dangtu *China* 31°32N 118°25E **229** B12
Dangyang *China* 30°52N 111°44E **229** B8
Dani *Burkina Faso* 13°43N 0°10W **263** C4
Daniel *U.S.A.* 42°52N 110°4W **304** E8
Daniel's Harbour *Canada* 50°13N 57°35W **299** B8
Danielskuil *S. Africa* 28°11S 23°33E **270** C3
Danielson *U.S.A.* 41°48N 71°53W **313** E13
Danielsville *U.S.A.* 34°8N 83°13W **316** A6
Danilov *Russia* 58°16N 40°13E **188** C11
Danilovgrad *Montenegro* 42°38N 19°4E **202** D3
Danilovka *Russia* 50°25N 44°12E **190** E7
Daning *China* 36°28N 110°45E **226** F6
Danish West Indies = Virgin Is. (U.S.) ☒ *W. Indies* 18°20N 65°0W **321** C7
Danissa *Kenya* 3°17N 40°59E **267** D5
Danja *Nigeria* 11°21N 7°30E **263** C6
Danje-la-Menha *Angola* 9°32S 14°39E **265** D2
Danjiangkou *China* 32°31N 111°30E **229** A8
Danjiangkou Shuiku *China* 32°37N 111°30E **229** A8
Ḍank *Oman* 23°33N 56°16E **247** F8
Dankalwa *Nigeria* 11°52N 12°12E **263** C7
Dankama *Nigeria* 13°20N 7°44E **263** C6
Dankhar Gompa *India* 32°10N 78°10E **242** C8
Dankov *Russia* 53°20N 39°5E **188** F10
Danleng *China* 30°1N 103°31E **228** B4
Danlí *Honduras* 14°4N 86°35W **320** D2
Danmark = Denmark ■ *Europe* 55°45N 10°0E **163** J3
Danmark Fjord *Greenland* 81°30N 22°0W **154** A8
Danmarkshavn *Greenland* 76°45N 18°50W **154** B9
Dannemora *U.S.A.* 44°43N 73°44W **313** B11
Dannenberg *Germany* 53°6N 11°5E **178** B7
Dannevirke *N.Z.* 40°12S 176°8E **284** G5
Dannhauser *S. Africa* 28°0S 30°3E **271** C5
Danot *Ethiopia* 7°33N 45°17E **267** C6
Dansalan = Marawi City *Phil.* 8°0N 124°21E **233** G5
Dansville *U.S.A.* 42°34N 77°42W **312** D7
Danta *India* 24°11N 72°46E **242** G5
Dantan *India* 21°57N 87°20E **243** J12
Dantewara *India* 18°54N 81°21E **244** E5
Danube = Dunărea → *Europe* 45°20N 29°40E **183** E14
Danubyu *Burma* 17°15N 95°35E **241** G5
Danvers *U.S.A.* 42°34N 70°56W **313** D14
Danville *Ga., U.S.A.* 32°37N 83°15W **316** C6
Danville *Ill., U.S.A.* 40°8N 87°37W **311** D9
Danville *Ind., U.S.A.* 39°46N 86°32W **311** E10
Danville *Ky., U.S.A.* 37°39N 84°46W **311** G12
Danville *Pa., U.S.A.* 40°58N 76°37W **313** F8
Danville *Va., U.S.A.* 36°36N 79°23W **309** G14
Danville *Vt., U.S.A.* 44°25N 72°9W **313** B12
Danyang *China* 32°0N 119°31E **229** B12
Danzhai *China* 26°11N 107°48E **228** D6
Danzhou *China* 19°31N 109°33E **236** C7
Danzig = Gdańsk *Poland* 54°22N 18°40E **184** D5
Dao = Tobias Fornier *Phil.* 10°30N 121°57E **233** F3
Dao *Phil.* 11°24N 122°41E **233** F4
Dão → *Portugal* 40°20N 8°11W **194** E2
Dao Xian *China* 25°36N 111°31E **229** E8
Daocheng *China* 29°0N 100°10E **228** C3
Daora *W. Sahara* 27°25N 12°59W **260** C2
Daoud = Aïn Beïda *Algeria* 35°50N 7°29E **261** A6
Daoukro *Ivory C.* 7°10N 3°58W **262** D4
Dapa *Phil.* 9°46N 126°3E **233** G6
Dapaong *Togo* 10°55N 0°16E **263** C5
Dapchi *Nigeria* 12°32N 11°31E **263** C7
Dapiak, Mt. *Phil.* 8°13N 123°28E **233** G4
Dapitan *Phil.* 8°39N 123°25E **233** G4
Dapoli *India* 17°46N 73°11E **244** F1
Daqahlîya □ *Egypt* 30°55N 31°30E **251** H2
Daqing Shan *China* 40°40N 111°0E **226** D6
Daqu Shan *China* 30°25N 122°20E **229** B14
Dar Banda *Africa* 8°0N 23°0E **256** F5
Dar el Beida = Casablanca *Morocco* 33°36N 7°36W **260** B3
Dar es Salaam *Tanzania* 6°50S 39°12E **268** D4
Dar Mazār *Iran* 29°14N 57°20E **247** D8
Dar Rounga *C.A.R.* 0°45N 22°20E **264** A4
Dār Ta'izzah *Syria* 36°20N 36°52E **250** B7
Dar'ā *Syria* 32°36N 36°7E **250** C5
Dar'ā □ *Syria* 32°55N 36°10E **250** F7
Dara Dere = Zlatograd *Bulgaria* 41°22N 25°7E **203** E9
Dārāb *Iran* 28°50N 54°30E **247** D7
Daraban *Pakistan* 31°44N 70°20E **242** D4
Darabani *Romania* 48°10N 26°39E **183** B11
Darai Hills *Papua N. G.* 7°8S 143°33E **286** D2
Daraina *Madag.* 13°12S 49°40E **272** A2
Daraj *Libya* 30°10N 10°28E **258** B2
Darakeh *Iran* 35°49N 51°22E **141** A2
Daram *Phil.* 11°38N 124°48E **233** F5
Dārān *Iran* 32°59N 50°24E **247** C6
Daravica *Serbia* 42°32N 20°8E **202** D4
Daraw *Egypt* 24°22N 32°51E **256** C3
Darayyā *Syria* 33°28N 36°15E **250** E7
Darazo *Nigeria* 11°1N 10°24E **263** C7
Darband *Tehrān, Iran* 35°49N 51°27E **141** A2
Darband *Pakistan* 34°20N 72°50E **242** B5
Darband, Kūh-e *Iran* 31°34N 57°8E **247** D8
Darbhanga *India* 26°15N 85°55E **243** F11
Darburruk *Somali Rep.* 9°44N 44°31E **267** C5
Darby, C. *U.S.A.* 64°19N 162°47W **303** D7
D'Arcy *Canada* 50°33N 122°29W **296** C4
Darda *Croatia* 45°40N 18°41E **182** E3
Dardanelle *Ark., U.S.A.* 35°13N 93°9W **314** D8
Dardanelle *Calif., U.S.A.* 38°20N 119°50W **306** G7
Dardanelles = Çanakkale Boğazı *Turkey* 40°17N 26°32E **203** F10
Dare → *Ethiopia* 7°20N 42°11E **257** F5
Darende *Turkey* 38°31N 37°30E **212** C7
Dārestān *Iran* 29°9N 58°42E **247** D8
Darfield *N.Z.* 43°29S 172°7E **285** D7
Darfo *Italy* 45°53N 10°11E **198** C7
Dârfûr *Sudan* 13°40N 24°0E **254** E6
Dargai *Pakistan* 34°25N 71°55E **242** B4
Dargaville *N.Z.* 35°57S 173°52E **284** B2
Dargol *Niger* 13°54N 1°22E **263** C5
Darhan *Mongolia* 49°37N 106°21E **218** B5
Darhan Muminggan Lianheqi *China* 41°40N 110°28E **226** D6
Dari *Sudan* 5°48N 30°26E **257** F3
Darıca *Turkey* 40°45N 29°23E **212** B3
Darien *U.S.A.* 31°23N 81°26W **316** D8
Darién, G. del *Colombia* 9°0N 77°0W **328** B2
Darién, Serranía del *Colombia* 8°30N 77°30W **320** E4
Darién △ *Panama* 7°36N 77°57W **320** E4
Dariganga = Ovoot *Mongolia* 45°21N 113°45E **226** B7
Daringbadi *India* 19°54N 84°8E **244** E7
Darinskoye *Kazakhstan* 51°20N 51°44E **190** E10
Darjeeling = Darjiling *India* 27°3N 88°18E **241** B2
Darjiling *India* 27°3N 88°18E **241** B2
Darkan *Australia* 33°20S 116°43E **279** F2
Darke Peak *Australia* 33°27S 136°12E **282** B2
Darkhana *Pakistan* 30°39N 72°11E **242** D5
Darkhazīneh *Iran* 31°54N 48°39E **247** D6
Darkot Pass *Pakistan* 36°45N 73°26E **243** A5
Darling → *Australia* 34°4S 141°54E **282** C4
Darling Downs *Australia* 27°30S 150°30E **281** D5
Darling Harbour *Sydney, Australia* **139** b1
Darling Point *Australia* 33°52S 151°15E **139** B2
Darling Ra. *Australia* 32°30S 116°20E **279** F2
Darlington *Durham, U.K.* 54°32N 1°33W **168** C6
Darlington *Fla., U.S.A.* 30°57N 86°3W **316** E3
Darlington *S.C., U.S.A.* 34°18N 79°52W **315** D15
Darlington *Wis., U.S.A.* 42°41N 90°7W **310** B6
Darlington □ *U.K.* 54°32N 1°33W **168** C6
Darlington, L. *S. Africa* 33°10S 25°9E **270** D4
Darlington Point *Australia* 34°37S 146°1E **283** C7
Darlot, L. *Australia* 27°48S 121°35E **279** E3
Darłowo *Poland* 54°25N 16°25E **184** D3
Dărmănești *Bacău, Romania* 46°21N 26°33E **183** D11
Dărmănești *Suceava, Romania* 47°44N 26°9E **183** C11
Darmstadt *Germany* 49°51N 8°39E **179** F4
Darnah *Libya* 32°45N 22°45E **258** B4
Darnah □ *Libya* 31°0N 23°40E **258** B4
Darnall *S. Africa* 29°23S 31°18E **271** C5
Darndale *Ireland* 53°23N 6°12W **120** A2
Darney *France* 48°5N 6°2E **173** D13
Darnick *Australia* 32°48S 143°38E **282** B5
Darnley, C. *Antarctica* 68°0S 69°0E **151** C6
Darnley B. *Canada* 69°30N 123°30W **294** C7
Daroca *Spain* 41°9N 1°25W **196** D3
Daror *Ethiopia* 8°14N 44°52E **267** C5
Darou-Mousti *Senegal* 15°3N 16°3W **262** B1
Darr → *Australia* 23°39S 143°50E **280** C3
Darra Pezu *Pakistan* 32°19N 70°44E **242** C4
Darran Mts. *N.Z.* 44°37S 167°59E **285** E2
Darrequeira *Argentina* 37°42S 63°10W **334** D3
Darrington *U.S.A.* 48°15N 121°36W **304** B3
Darrūs *Iran* 35°46N 51°27E **141** A2
Darsana *Bangla.* 23°35N 88°48E **241** D2
Darsi *India* 15°46N 79°44E **245** G4
Darsser Ort *Germany* 54°28N 12°32E **178** A8
Dart → *U.K.* 50°24N 3°39W **169** G4
Dart, C. *Antarctica* 73°6S 126°20W **151** D14
Dartford *U.K.* 51°26N 0°13E **125** B5
Dartmoor *Vic., Australia* 37°56S 141°19E **282** D4
Dartmoor *Devon, U.K.* 50°38N 3°57W **169** G4
Dartmoor △ *U.K.* 50°37N 3°59W **169** G4
Dartmouth *N.S., Canada* 44°40N 63°30W **299** D7
Dartmouth *Torbay, U.K.* 50°21N 3°36W **169** G4
Dartmouth, L. *Australia* 26°4S 145°18E **281** D4
Dartmouth Res. *Australia* 36°34S 147°32E **283** D7
Dartuch, C. = Artrutx, C. de *Spain* 39°55N 3°49E **206** B4
Daru *Papua N. G.* 9°3S 143°13E **286** E2
Daruvar *Croatia* 45°35N 17°14E **182** E2
Darvaza *Turkmenistan* 40°11N 58°24E **216** D5
Darvel, Teluk = Lahad Datu, Telok *Malaysia* 4°50N 118°20E **235** B5
Darvi *Mongolia* 46°27N 94°7E **217** C12
Darwen *U.K.* 53°42N 2°29W **168** D5
Darwendale *Zimbabwe* 17°41S 30°33E **271** A5
Darwha *India* 20°15N 77°45E **244** D3
Darwin *N. Terr., Australia* 12°25S 130°51E **278** B5
Darwin *Calif., U.S.A.* 36°15N 117°35W **307** J9
Darwin, Mt. *Chile* 54°47S 69°55W **336** D3
Darwin, Volcán *Ecuador* 0°10S 91°18W **330** a
Darya Ganj *Delhi, India* **120** a3
Darya Khan *Pakistan* 31°48N 71°6E **242** D4
Daryapur *India* 20°55N 77°20E **244** D3
Daryoi Amu = Amudarya → *Uzbekistan* 43°58N 59°34E **216** D5
Dās *U.A.E.* 25°20N 53°30E **247** E7
Dashahe *China* 42°44N 128°10E **224** A4
Dashen, Ras *Ethiopia* 13°8N 38°26E **257** E4
Dasher *U.S.A.* 30°45N 83°13W **316** E6
Dashetai *China* 41°0N 109°5E **226** D5
Dashi *China* 23°1N 113°17E **121** B2
Dashkesan = Daşkäsän *Azerbaijan* 40°25N 46°0E **191** K7
Dashköpri *Turkmenistan* 36°16N 62°8E **247** B9
Dashoguz *Turkmenistan* 41°49N 59°58E **216** D5
Dasht *Iran* 37°17N 56°7E **247** B8
Dasht → *Pakistan* 25°10N 61°40E **240** D1
Dasht-i-Tahlab *Pakistan* 28°40N 62°25E **240** C1
Daska *Pakistan* 32°20N 74°20E **242** C6
Daşkäsän *Azerbaijan* 40°25N 46°0E **191** K7
Dasmariñas *Phil.* 14°20N 120°56E **232** D3
Dassa *Benin* 7°46N 2°14E **263** D5
Dasuya *India* 31°49N 75°38E **242** D6
Datansha *China* 23°8N 113°12E **121** B2
Datça *Turkey* 36°46N 27°40E **205** E9
Datia *India* 25°39N 78°27E **243** G8
Datian *China* 25°40N 117°50E **229** E11
Datong *Anhui, China* 30°48N 117°44E **229** B11
Datong *Shanxi, China* 40°6N 113°18E **226** D7
Dattakhel *Pakistan* 32°54N 69°46E **242** C3
Dattapur = Dhamangaon *India* 20°48N 78°9E **244** D4
Datteln *Germany* 51°39N 7°21E **178** D3
Datu, Tanjung *Indonesia* 2°5N 109°39E **235** B3
Datu Piang *Phil.* 7°2N 124°30E **233** H5
Datuk, Tanjong = Datu, Tanjung *Indonesia* 2°5N 109°39E **235** B3
Datun *China* 40°10N 116°23E **114** B2
Daua = Dawa → *Africa* 4°11N 42°6E **257** G5
Daud Khel *Pakistan* 32°53N 71°34E **242** C4
Daudnagar *India* 25°2N 84°24E **243** G11
Daugava → *Latvia* 57°4N 24°3E **188** D3
Daugavpils *Latvia* 55°53N 26°32E **188** E4
Daulatabad *India* 19°57N 75°15E **244** E2
Daulatpur *India* 28°44N 77°6E **120** A1
Daule *Ecuador* 1°56S 79°56W **328** D2
Daule → *Ecuador* 2°10S 79°52W **328** D2
Daulpur *India* 26°45N 77°59E **242** F7
Daun *Germany* 50°11N 6°49E **179** E2
Daund *India* 18°26N 74°40E **244** E2
Dauphin *Man., Canada* 51°9N 100°5W **297** C8
Dauphin *Pa., U.S.A.* 40°22N 76°56W **312** F8
Dauphin L. *Canada* 51°20N 99°45W **297** C9
Dauphiné *France* 45°15N 5°25E **175** C9
Daura *Borno, Nigeria* 11°31N 11°24E **263** C7
Daura *Katsina, Nigeria* 13°2N 8°21E **263** C6
Dausa *India* 26°52N 76°20E **242** F7
Däväçi *Azerbaijan* 41°15N 48°57E **191** K9
Davangere *India* 14°25N 75°55E **245** G2
Davao *Phil.* 7°0N 125°40E **233** H5
Davao □ *Phil.* 7°0N 125°55E **233** H5
Davao del Sur □ *Phil.* 6°30N 125°25E **233** H5
Davao G. *Phil.* 6°30N 125°48E **233** H5
Davao Oriental □ *Phil.* 7°10N 126°30E **233** H6
Dāvar Panāh = Sarāvān *Iran* 27°25N 62°15E **247** E9
Davenport *Calif., U.S.A.* 37°1N 122°12W **306** H4
Davenport *Fla., U.S.A.* 28°10N 81°36W **317** G8
Davenport *Iowa, U.S.A.* 41°32N 90°35W **310** C6
Davenport *Wash., U.S.A.* 47°39N 118°9W **304** C4
Davenport Ra. *Australia* 20°28S 134°0E **280** C1
Daventry *U.K.* 52°16N 1°10W **169** E6
David *Panama* 8°30N 82°30W **320** E3
David City *U.S.A.* 41°15N 97°8W **308** E5
David Glacier *Antarctica* 75°20S 162°0E **151** D21
David Gorodok = Davyd Haradok *Belarus* 52°4N 27°8E **177** B14
David's Citadel *Jerusalem* **123** b3
David's Tomb *Jerusalem* **123** b3
Davidson *Canada* 51°16N 105°59W **297** C7
Davidson, Mt. *U.S.A.* 37°44N 122°27W **136** B2
Davidson Mts. *U.S.A.* 68°41N 142°22W **303** B12
Davidson's Mains *U.K.* 55°58N 3°16W **121** B2
Davie *U.S.A.* 26°3N 80°13W **317** J9
Davis *Antarctica* 68°34S 77°55E **151** C6
Davis *Calif., U.S.A.* 38°33N 121°44W **306** G5
Davis Dam *U.S.A.* 35°12N 114°34W **307** K12
Davis Inlet *Canada* 55°50N 60°59W **299** A7
Davis Mts. *U.S.A.* 30°50N 103°55W **314** F3
Davis Sea *Antarctica* 66°0S 92°0E **151** C7
Davis Str. *N. Amer.* 65°0N 58°0W **292** C14
Davisboro *U.S.A.* 32°59N 82°36W **316** C7
Davison *U.S.A.* 43°2N 83°31W **311** A13
Davo → *Ivory C.* 5°0N 6°10W **262** D3
Davos *Switz.* 46°48N 9°49E **179** J5
Dāvūdiyeh *Iran* 35°45N 51°25E **141** A2
Davutlar *Turkey* 37°43N 27°17E **205** D9
Davy L. *Canada* 58°53N 108°18W **297** B7
Davyd Haradok *Belarus* 52°4N 27°8E **177** B14
Davydkovo *Russia* 55°43N 37°29E **129** B2
Dawa → *Africa* 4°11N 42°6E **257** G5
Dawaki *Bauchi, Nigeria* 9°25N 9°33E **263** D6
Dawaki *Kano, Nigeria* 12°5N 8°23E **263** C6
Dawei = Tavoy *Burma* 14°2N 98°12E **236** E2
Dawes Ra. *Australia* 24°40S 150°40E **280** C5
Dawidy *Poland* 52°8N 20°58E **142** C1
Dawkah *Oman* 18°39N 54°5E **249** C6
Dawley = Telford *U.K.* 52°40N 2°27W **169** E5
Dawlish *U.K.* 50°35N 3°28W **169** G4
Dawna Ra. *Burma* 16°30N 98°30E **236** D2
Dawnyein *Burma* 15°54N 95°36E **241** G5
Dawqah *Si. Arabia* 19°36N 40°54E **248** C3
Dawros Hd. *Ireland* 54°50N 8°33W **166** B3
Dawson *Yukon, Canada* 64°10N 139°30W **294** C6
Dawson *Ga., U.S.A.* 31°46N 84°27W **316** D5
Dawson, I. *Chile* 53°50S 70°50W **336** D2
Dawson B. *Canada* 52°53N 100°49W **297** C8
Dawson Creek *Canada* 55°45N 120°15W **296** B4
Dawson Inlet *Canada* 61°50N 93°25W **297** A10
Dawson Ra. *Australia* 24°30S 149°48E **280** C4
Dawu *Hubei, China* 31°34N 114°7E **229** B9
Dawu *Sichuan, China* 30°55N 101°10E **228** B3
Dawuhan *Oman* 20°30N 58°48E **249** B7
Dawwara, Ras id- *Malta* 35°52N 14°21E **206** F7
Dax *France* 43°44N 1°3W **174** E2
Daxian *China* 31°15N 107°23E **228** B6
Daxin *China* 22°50N 107°11E **228** F6
Daxindian *China* 37°30N 120°50E **227** F11
Daxinggou *China* 43°25N 129°40E **227** C15
Daxue Shan *Sichuan, China* 30°30N 101°30E **228** B3
Daxue Shan *Yunnan, China* 23°42N 99°48E **228** F2
Day *U.S.A.* 30°12N 83°17W **316** E6
Day Kundī □ *Afghan.* 34°0N 66°0E **240** B2
Daya el Khadra *Mauritania* 25°14N 6°2W **260** C3
Dayang He → *China* 39°51N 123°38E **224** C1
Dayao *China* 25°43N 101°20E **228** E3
Daye *China* 30°6N 114°58E **229** B10
Dayet en Naharat *Mali* 17°39N 3°10W **262** B4
Dayi *China* 30°41N 103°29E **228** B4
Daylesford *Australia* 37°21S 144°9E **282** D6
Dayong *China* 29°11N 110°30E **229** C8
Dayr az Zawr *Syria* 35°20N 40°5E **213** E9
Dayr az Zawr □ *Syria* 34°50N 40°10E **213** E9
Days Bay *N.Z.* 41°17S 174°54E **143** B2
Daysland *Canada* 52°50N 112°20W **296** C6
Dayton *Iowa, U.S.A.* 42°16N 94°4W **310** B2
Dayton *Nev., U.S.A.* 39°14N 119°36W **306** F7
Dayton *Ohio, U.S.A.* 39°45N 84°12W **311** E12
Dayton *Pa., U.S.A.* 40°53N 79°15W **312** F5
Dayton *Tenn., U.S.A.* 35°30N 85°1W **315** D12
Dayton *Wash., U.S.A.* 46°19N 117°59W **304** C5
Dayton *Wyo., U.S.A.* 44°53N 107°16W **304** D10
Daytona Beach *U.S.A.* 29°13N 81°1W **317** F8
Dayu *China* 25°24N 114°22E **229** E10
Dayville *U.S.A.* 44°28N 119°32W **304** D4
Dazaifu *Japan* 33°32N 130°32E **222** D2
Dazhu *China* 30°41N 107°15E **228** B6
Dazkırı *Turkey* 37°57N 29°52E **205** D11
Dazu *China* 29°40N 105°42E **228** C5
De Aar *S. Africa* 30°39S 24°0E **270** D3
De Armanville *U.S.A.* 33°38N 85°45W **316** B4
De Bary *U.S.A.* 28°54N 81°18W **317** G8
De Biesbosch △ *Neths.* 51°45N 4°48E **170** C4
De Forest *U.S.A.* 43°15N 89°20W **310** A7
De Funiak Springs *U.S.A.* 30°43N 86°7W **316** E3
De Grey → *Australia* 20°12S 119°13E **278** D2
De Haan *Belgium* 51°16N 3°2E **170** C3
De Hoge Veluwe △ *Neths.* 52°5N 5°46E **170** B5
De Hoop △ *S. Africa* 34°30S 20°28E **270** D3
De Kennemerduinen △ *Neths.* 52°27N 4°33E **170** B4
De Land *U.S.A.* 29°2N 81°18W **317** F8
De Leon *U.S.A.* 32°7N 98°32W **314** E5
De Leon Springs *U.S.A.* 29°7N 81°21W **317** F8
De Long Mts. *U.S.A.* 68°10N 163°30W **303** B7
De Panne *Belgium* 51°6N 2°34E **170** C2
De Pere *U.S.A.* 44°27N 88°4W **308** C9
De Queen *U.S.A.* 34°2N 94°21W **314** D7
De Quincy *U.S.A.* 30°27N 93°26W **314** F8
De Smet *U.S.A.* 44°23N 97°33W **308** C5
De Soto *U.S.A.* 38°8N 90°34W **310** F6
De Tour Village *U.S.A.* 46°0N 83°56W **309** B12
De Waag *Amsterdam, Neths.* **112** b2

De Witt Ark., U.S.A. 34°18N 91°20W 314 D9
De Witt Iowa, U.S.A. 41°49N 90°33W 310 C6
De Witt Mich., U.S.A. 42°51N 84°34W 311 B12
Dead L. U.S.A. 30°10N 85°10W 316 E4
Dead Sea Asia 31°30N 35°30E 251 G6
Deadhorse U.S.A. 70°11N 148°27W 303 A10
Deadman B. U.S.A. 29°30N 83°30W 317 F6
Deadwood U.S.A. 44°23N 103°44W 308 C2
Deadwood L. Canada 59°10N 128°30W 296 B3
Deal U.K. 51°13N 1°25E 169 F9
Deal I. Australia 39°30S 147°20E 281 F4
Dealesville S. Africa 28°41S 25°44E 270 C4
De'an China 29°21N 115°46E 229 C10
Dean → Canada 52°49N 126°58W 296 C3
Dean, Forest of U.K. 51°45N 2°33W 169 F5
Dean Chan. Canada 52°30N 127°15W 296 C3
Deán Funes Argentina 30°20S 64°20W 334 C3
Dearborn Mich., U.S.A. 42°19N 83°10W 311 B13
Dearborn Mo., U.S.A. 39°32N 94°46W 310 E2
Dease → Canada 59°56N 128°32W 296 B3
Dease Inlet U.S.A. 71°2N 155°26W 303 A9
Dease L. Canada 58°40N 130°5W 296 B2
Dease Lake Canada 58°25N 130°6W 296 B2
Death Valley U.S.A. 36°15N 116°50W 307 J10
Death Valley △ U.S.A. 36°29N 117°6W 307 J9
Death Valley Junction U.S.A. 36°20N 116°25W 307 J10
Deauville France 49°23N 0°2E 172 C7
Deba Spain 43°18N 2°21W 196 B2
Deba Habe Nigeria 10°14N 11°20E 263 C7
Debak Malaysia 1°34N 111°25E 235 B4
Debaltsevo Ukraine 48°22N 38°26E 189 H10
Debao China 23°21N 106°46E 228 F6
Debar Macedonia 41°31N 20°30E 202 E4
Debark Ethiopia 13°1N 37°48E 257 E4
Debden Canada 53°30N 106°50W 297 C7
Debdou Morocco 33°59N 3°0W 261 B4
Debe Trin. & Tob. 10°22N 61°27W 323 t
Dębica Poland 50°2N 21°25E 185 H8
Dęblin Poland 51°34N 21°50E 185 G8
Dębno Poland 52°44N 14°41E 185 F1
Débo, L. Mali 15°14N 4°15W 262 B4
DeBolt Canada 55°12N 118°1W 296 B5
Deborah East, L. Australia 30°45S 119°30E 279 F2
Deborah West, L. Australia 30°45S 119°5E 279 F2
Deboyne Is. Papua N. G. 10°43S 152°22E 286 F7
Debrc Serbia 44°38N 19°53E 202 B3
Debre Birhan Ethiopia 9°41N 39°31E 257 F4
Debre Markos Ethiopia 10°20N 37°40E 257 E4
Debre May Ethiopia 11°20N 37°25E 257 E4
Debre Sina Ethiopia 9°51N 39°50E 257 F4
Debre Tabor Ethiopia 11°50N 38°26E 257 E4
Debre Zebit Ethiopia 11°48N 38°30E 257 E4
Debre Zevit Ethiopia 8°50N 39°0E 257 F4
Debrecen Hungary 47°33N 21°42E 182 C6
Debrzno Poland 53°31N 17°14E 184 E4
Dečani Serbia 42°30N 20°18E 202 D4
Decatur Ala., U.S.A. 34°36N 86°59W 315 D11
Decatur Ga., U.S.A. 33°46N 84°16W 113 B3
Decatur Ill., U.S.A. 39°51N 88°57W 310 E8
Decatur Ind., U.S.A. 40°50N 84°56W 311 D12
Decatur Mich., U.S.A. 42°7N 85°58W 311 B11
Decatur Tex., U.S.A. 33°14N 97°35W 314 E6
Decazeville France 44°34N 2°15E 174 D6
Deccan India 18°0N 79°0E 244 F4
Deception, Mt. Australia 30°42S 138°16E 282 A3
Deception B. Papua N. G. 7°45S 144°40E 286 D3
Deception Bay Australia 27°10S 153°5E 281 D5
Deception I. Antarctica 63°0S 60°15W 151 C17
Deception L. Canada 56°33N 104°13W 297 B8
Dechang China 27°25N 102°11E 228 D4
Dechhu India 26°46N 72°20E 242 F5
Děčín Czech Rep. 50°47N 14°12E 180 A7
Decize France 46°50N 3°28E 173 F10
Deckerville U.S.A. 43°32N 82°44W 312 C2
Decollatura Italy 39°3N 16°21E 201 C9
Decorah U.S.A. 43°18N 91°48W 308 D8
Deda Romania 46°56N 24°50E 183 D9
Dedaye Burma 16°24N 95°53E 241 G5
Dedéagach = Alexandroupoli Greece 40°50N 25°54E 203 F9
Dededo Guam 13°31N 144°50E 302 d
Deder Ethiopia 9°19N 41°27E 257 F5
Dedham U.S.A. 42°15N 71°10W 116 B1
Dédougou Burkina Faso 12°30N 3°25W 262 C4
Dedovichi Russia 57°32N 29°56E 188 D5
Dedza Malawi 14°20S 34°20E 269 E3
Dee → Aberds., U.K. 57°9N 2°5W 167 D6
Dee → Dumf. & Gall., U.K. 54°51N 4°3W 167 G4
Dee → Wales, U.K. 53°22N 3°17W 168 D4
Deep B. Canada 61°15N 116°35W 296 A5
Deep Bay = Chilumba Malawi 10°28S 34°12E 269 E3
Deep Bay = Shenzhen Wan China 22°27N 113°55E 219 G10
Deep Lead Australia 37°0S 142°43E 282 D5
Deepwater N.S.W., Australia 29°25S 151°51E 281 D5
Deepwater Mo., U.S.A. 38°16N 93°47W 310 F3
Deer → Canada 58°23N 94°13W 297 B10
Deer I. U.S.A. 54°55N 162°18W 303 J7
Deer L. Canada 52°40N 94°20W 297 C10
Deer Lake Nfld. & L., Canada 49°11N 57°27W 299 C8
Deer Lake Ont., Canada 52°36N 94°20W 297 C10
Deer Lodge U.S.A. 46°24N 112°44W 304 C7
Deer Park Fla., U.S.A. 28°6N 80°54W 317 G9
Deer Park Ohio, U.S.A. 39°12N 84°23W 311 E7
Deer Park Wash., U.S.A. 47°57N 117°28W 304 C5
Deer River U.S.A. 47°20N 93°48W 308 B7
Deeragun Australia 19°16S 146°33E 280 B4
Deerdepoort S. Africa 24°37S 26°27E 270 B4
Deerfield Ill., U.S.A. 42°10N 87°51W 311 B9
Deerfield Mo., U.S.A. 37°50N 94°30W 310 G2
Deerfield Beach U.S.A. 26°19N 80°6W 317 J9
Deering U.S.A. 66°4N 162°42W 303 C7
Defensores del Chaco △ Paraguay 20°13S 60°27W 331 E5
Deferiet U.S.A. 44°2N 75°41W 313 B9
Defiance U.S.A. 41°17N 84°22W 311 C12
Dega Medo Ethiopia 7°59N 43°1E 267 C5
Degana India 26°50N 74°20E 242 F6
Dêgê China 31°44N 98°39E 228 B2
Degebe → Portugal 38°13N 7°29W 195 G3
Degeberga Sweden 55°51N 14°5E 163 J8
Degeh Bur Ethiopia 8°11N 43°31E 267 C5
Dégelis Canada 47°30N 68°35W 299 C6
Degema Nigeria 4°50N 6°48E 263 E6
Degerfors Sweden 59°15N 14°27E 162 E8
Degerhamn Sweden 56°20N 16°24E 163 H10
Deggendorf Germany 48°50N 12°57E 179 G8
Degh → Pakistan 31°3N 73°21E 242 D5
Değirmendere Turkey 40°42N 29°47E 203 F13
Degunino Russia 55°52N 37°33E 129 A3
Deh Bīd Iran 30°39N 53°11E 247 D7
Deh-e Shīr Iran 31°29N 53°45E 247 D7
Deh Nugaled = Nugaaleed, Dooxo Somali Rep. 8°35N 48°35E 267 C6
Dehaj Iran 30°42N 54°53E 247 D7
Dehak Iran 27°11N 62°37E 240 D1
Déhane Cameroon 3°30N 10°5E 264 B2
Dehdez Iran 31°43N 50°17E 247 D6
Dehej India 21°44N 72°40E 242 J5
Dehestān Iran 28°30N 55°35E 247 D7
Dehgolān Iran 35°17N 47°25E 213 E12
Dehibat Tunisia 32°0N 10°47E 258 B2
Dehiwala Sri Lanka 6°50N 79°51E 245 L4
Dehlorān Iran 32°41N 47°16E 213 F12
Dehnow-e Kūhestān Iran 27°58N 58°32E 247 E8
Dehra Dun India 30°20N 78°4E 242 D8
Dehri India 24°50N 84°15E 243 G11
Dehua China 25°26N 118°14E 229 E12
Dehui China 44°30N 125°40E 227 B13
Deim Zubeir Sudan 7°49N 26°16E 257 F2
Deinze Belgium 50°59N 3°32E 170 D3
Deir Dibwan West Bank 31°55N 35°16E 123 A2
Deir Ibzi'e West Bank 31°55N 35°7E 123 A1
Dej Romania 47°10N 23°52E 183 C8
Deje Sweden 59°35N 13°29E 162 E7
Dejiang China 28°18N 108°7E 228 C7
Dejvice Czech Rep. 50°6N 14°23E 135 B2
Deka → Zimbabwe 18°4S 26°42E 270 A4
Dekabristov, Ostrov Russia 59°56N 30°15E 137 B1
DeKalb U.S.A. 41°56N 88°46W 311 C8
Dekemhare Eritrea 15°6N 39°0E 257 D4
Dekese Dem. Rep. of the Congo 3°24S 21°24E 264 C4
Dekoa C.A.R. 6°19N 19°4E 264 A3
Del Caño Rise Ind. Oc. 45°15S 44°15E 273 J3
Del Carmen Phil. 9°50N 126°0E 233 G6
Del Mar U.S.A. 32°58N 117°16W 307 N9
Del Norte U.S.A. 37°41N 106°21W 305 H10
Del Rio U.S.A. 29°22N 100°54W 314 G4
Delai Sudan 17°21N 36°6E 256 D4
Delambre I. Australia 20°26S 117°5E 278 D2
Delami Sudan 11°38N 30°23E 257 E3
Delano U.S.A. 35°46N 119°15W 307 K7
Delano Peak U.S.A. 38°22N 112°22W 304 G7
Delārām Afghan. 32°9N 63°25E 240 B1
Delareyville S. Africa 26°41S 25°26E 270 C4
Delaronde L. Canada 54°3N 107°3W 297 C7
Delavan Ill., U.S.A. 40°22N 89°33W 310 D7
Delavan Wis., U.S.A. 42°38N 88°39W 311 B8
Delaware U.S.A. 40°18N 83°4W 311 D13
Delaware □ U.S.A. 39°0N 75°20W 309 F16
Delaware → U.S.A. 39°15N 75°20W 313 G9
Delaware B. U.S.A. 39°0N 75°10W 309 F16
Delaware Water Gap ⌂ U.S.A. 41°10N 74°55W 313 E10
Delay → Canada 56°56N 71°28W 299 A5
Delbrück Germany 51°46N 8°34E 178 D4
Delčevo Macedonia 41°58N 22°46E 202 E6
Delegate Australia 37°4S 148°56E 283 D8
Delémont Switz. 47°22N 7°20E 179 H3
Delevan U.S.A. 42°29N 78°29W 312 D6
Delft Neths. 52°1N 4°22E 170 B4
Delft I. Sri Lanka 9°30N 79°40E 245 K4
Delfzijl Neths. 53°20N 6°55E 170 A6
Delgada, Punta Chile 52°28S 69°32W 336 D3
Delgado, C. Mozam. 10°45S 40°40E 269 E5
Delgerhet Mongolia 45°50N 110°30E 226 B6
Delgo Sudan 20°6N 30°40E 256 C3
Delhi Ont., Canada 42°51N 80°30W 312 D4
Delhi India 28°39N 77°13E 120 B2
Delhi La., U.S.A. 32°28N 91°30W 314 E9
Delhi N.Y., U.S.A. 42°17N 74°55W 313 D10
Delhi Gate Delhi, India 120 b3
Delhi Indira Gandhi Int. ✕ (DEL) India 28°34N 77°5E 120 B1
Deli Jovan Serbia 44°13N 22°9E 202 B6
Delia Canada 51°38N 112°23W 296 C6
Delice Turkey 39°54N 34°2E 212 C6
Délices Dominica 15°17N 61°17W 323 k
Delicias Mexico 28°13N 105°28W 318 B3
Delījān Iran 33°59N 50°40E 247 C6
Delimara Point Malta 35°49N 14°34E 206 F8
Déline Canada 65°11N 123°25W 294 C7
Delisle Canada 51°55N 107°8W 297 C7
Delitzsch Germany 51°31N 12°20E 178 D8
Dell City U.S.A. 31°56N 105°12W 314 F2
Dell Rapids U.S.A. 43°50N 96°43W 308 D5
Delle France 47°30N 7°2E 173 E14
Dellys Algeria 36°57N 3°57E 261 A5
Delmar Iowa, U.S.A. 42°0N 90°37W 310 C6
Delmar N.Y., U.S.A. 42°37N 73°47W 313 D11
Delmenhorst Germany 53°3N 8°37E 178 B4
Delmiro Gouveia Brazil 9°24S 38°6W 332 C4
Delnice Croatia 45°23N 14°50E 199 C11
Delonga, Ostrova Russia 76°40N 149°20E 215 B15
Deloraine Tas., Australia 41°30S 146°40E 281 G4
Deloraine Man., Canada 49°15N 100°29W 297 D8
Delphi Greece 38°28N 22°30E 204 C4
Delphi Ind., U.S.A. 40°36N 86°41W 311 D10
Delphos U.S.A. 40°51N 84°21W 311 D12
Delportshoop S. Africa 28°22S 24°20E 270 C3
Delray Beach U.S.A. 26°28N 80°4W 317 J9
Delsbo Sweden 61°48N 16°32E 162 C10
Delta Ala., U.S.A. 33°26N 85°42W 316 B4
Delta Colo., U.S.A. 38°44N 108°4W 304 G9
Delta Utah, U.S.A. 39°21N 112°35W 304 G7
Delta □ Nigeria 5°30N 6°0E 263 D6
Delta Amacuro □ Venezuela 8°30N 61°30W 329 B5
Delta del Ebro ⌂ Spain 40°43N 0°43E 196 E5
Delta del Po ⌂ Italy 44°50N 12°15E 199 D9
Delta du Saloum △ Senegal 13°42N 16°43W 262 C1
Delta Dunărea ⌂ Romania 45°15N 29°25E 183 E14
Delta Junction U.S.A. 64°2N 145°44W 303 D11
Deltona U.S.A. 28°54N 81°16W 317 G8
Delungra Australia 29°39S 150°51E 281 D5
Delvada India 20°46N 71°2E 242 J4
Delvinaki Greece 39°57N 20°32E 204 B2
Delvinë Albania 39°59N 20°6E 202 G4
Delyatyn Ukraine 48°32N 24°38E 183 B9
Demagiri India 22°55N 92°28E 241 D4
Demak Indonesia 6°53S 110°38E 235 D4
Demanda, Sierra de la Spain 42°15N 3°0W 196 C2
Demarcation Pt. U.S.A. 69°41N 141°18W 303 B12
Demarest U.S.A. 40°57N 73°57W 132 A2
Demavend = Damāvand, Qolleh-ye Iran 35°56N 52°10E 247 C7
Demba Dem. Rep. of the Congo 5°28S 22°15E 265 D4
Demba Chio Angola 9°41S 13°41E 265 D2
Dembecha Ethiopia 10°32N 37°30E 257 E4
Dembéni Comoros Is. 11°52S 43°23E 272 a
Dembéni Mayotte 12°50S 45°11E 272 b
Dembi Ethiopia 8°5N 36°25E 257 F4
Dembia Dem. Rep. of the Congo 3°33N 25°48E 268 B2
Dembica = Dębica Poland 50°2N 21°25E 185 H8
Dembidolo Ethiopia 8°34N 34°50E 257 F3
Demchok India 32°42N 79°29E 243 C8
Demer → Belgium 50°57N 4°42E 170 D4
Demerara Abyssal Plain Atl. Oc. 10°0N 48°0W 152 F7
Demetrias Greece 39°22N 23°1E 204 B5
Demidov Russia 55°16N 31°30E 188 E6
Deming N. Mex., U.S.A. 32°16N 107°46W 305 K10
Deming Wash., U.S.A. 48°50N 122°13W 306 B4
Demini → Brazil 0°46S 62°56W 329 D5
Demirci Turkey 39°2N 28°38E 205 B10
Demirköprü Barajı Turkey 38°42N 28°25E 205 C10
Demirköy Turkey 41°49N 27°45E 203 E11
Demirtas Turkey 36°25N 32°11E 250 B3
Demmin Germany 53°54N 13°2E 178 B9
Demnate Morocco 31°44N 6°59W 260 B3
Democracia Brazil 5°48S 61°26W 331 B5
Demonte Italy 44°19N 7°17E 198 D4
Demopolis U.S.A. 32°31N 87°50W 315 E11
Dempo Indonesia 4°2S 103°15E 234 C2
Demyansk Russia 57°40N 32°27E 188 D7
Den Bosch = 's-Hertogenbosch Neths. 51°42N 5°17E 170 C5
Den Burg Neths. 53°3N 4°47E 170 A4
Den Chai Thailand 17°59N 100°4E 236 D3
Den Haag = 's-Gravenhage Neths. 52°7N 4°17E 170 B4
Den Helder Neths. 52°57N 4°45E 170 B4
Den Ilp Neths. 52°27N 4°55E 112 A2
Den Lille Havfrue Copenhagen, Denmark 118 a3
Den Oever Neths. 52°56N 5°2E 170 B5
Denain France 50°20N 3°22E 173 B10
Denair U.S.A. 37°32N 120°48W 306 H6
Denali = McKinley, Mt. U.S.A. 63°4N 151°0W 303 E10
Denali △ U.S.A. 63°30N 152°0W 303 E10
Denau Uzbekistan 38°16N 67°54E 217 E7
Denbigh Ont., Canada 45°8N 77°15W 312 A7
Denbigh Denbs., U.K. 53°12N 3°25W 168 D4
Denbigh, C. U.S.A. 64°23N 161°32W 303 D7
Denbighshire □ U.K. 53°8N 3°22W 168 D4
Dendang Indonesia 3°7S 107°56E 235 C3
Dendé = Ndindi Gabon 3°46S 11°9E 264 C2
Dendermonde Belgium 51°2N 4°5E 170 C4
Deneba Ethiopia 9°47N 39°10E 257 F4
Deng Deng Cameroon 5°12N 13°31E 264 A2
Dengchuan China 25°59N 100°3E 228 E3
Denge Nigeria 12°52N 5°21E 263 C6
Dengfeng China 34°25N 113°2E 226 G7
Dengi Nigeria 9°25N 9°55E 263 D6
Dengkou China 40°18N 106°55E 226 D4
Dengzhou China 32°34N 112°4E 229 A9
Denham Australia 25°56S 113°31E 279 E1
Denham, Mt. Jamaica 18°13N 77°32W 320 a
Denham Ra. Australia 21°55S 147°46E 280 C4
Denham Sd. Australia 25°45S 113°15E 279 E1
Denholm Canada 52°39N 108°1W 297 C7
Denia Spain 38°49N 0°8E 197 G5
Denial B. Australia 32°14S 133°32E 281 E1
Deniliquin Australia 35°30S 144°58E 283 C6
Denis Gabon 0°19N 9°22E 264 B1
Denison Iowa, U.S.A. 42°1N 95°21W 308 D6
Denison Tex., U.S.A. 33°45N 96°33W 314 E6
Denison Plains Australia 18°35S 128°0E 278 C4
Denisovka = Ordzhonikīdze Kazakhstan 52°27N 61°39E 216 B6
Denistone Heights Australia 33°48S 151°8E 139 A1
Deniyaya Sri Lanka 6°21N 80°33E 245 L5
Denizli Turkey 37°42N 29°2E 205 D11
Denizli □ Turkey 37°45N 29°5E 205 D11
Denman Australia 32°24S 150°42E 283 B9
Denman Glacier Antarctica 66°45S 99°25E 151 C7
Denmark W. Austral., Australia 34°59S 117°25E 279 F2
Denmark S.C., U.S.A. 33°19N 81°9W 316 B8
Denmark ■ Europe 55°45N 10°0E 163 J3
Denmark Str. Atl. Oc. 66°0N 30°0W 292 C17
Dennery St. Lucia 13°55N 60°54W 323 m
Dennison U.S.A. 40°24N 81°19W 312 F3
Denny U.K. 56°1N 3°55W 167 E5
Denpasar Indonesia 8°39S 115°13E 231 K18
Denpasar ✕ (DPS) Indonesia 8°44S 115°10E 231 K18
Denton Ga., U.S.A. 31°44N 82°42W 316 D7
Denton Mont., U.S.A. 47°19N 109°57W 304 C9
Denton Tex., U.S.A. 33°13N 97°8W 314 E6
Denton Park Canada 43°42N 79°17W 141 A3
D'Entrecasteaux, Pt. Australia 34°50S 115°57E 279 F2
D'Entrecasteaux △ Australia 34°20S 115°33E 279 F2
D'Entrecasteaux Is. Papua N. G. 9°0S 151°0E 286 E6
Dentsville U.S.A. 34°4N 80°58W 316 A9
Denu Ghana 6°4N 1°8E 263 D5
Denver Colo., U.S.A. 39°42N 104°59W 304 G11
Denver Ind., U.S.A. 40°52N 86°5W 311 D10
Denver Iowa, U.S.A. 42°40N 92°20W 310 B4
Denver Pa., U.S.A. 40°14N 76°8W 313 F8
Denver City U.S.A. 32°58N 102°50W 314 E3
Denwood = Wainwright Canada 52°50N 110°50W 297 C6
Deoband India 29°42N 77°43E 242 E7
Deobhog India 19°53N 82°44E 244 E6
Deodrug India 16°26N 76°55E 245 F3
Deogarh Orissa, India 21°32N 84°45E 244 D7
Deogarh Raj., India 25°32N 73°54E 242 G5
Deoghar India 24°30N 86°42E 243 G12
Deogyusan △ S. Korea 35°45N 127°40E 224 E3
Deokjeokdo S. Korea 37°13N 126°7E 224 D3
Deolali India 19°58N 73°50E 244 E1
Deoli = Devli India 25°50N 75°20E 242 G6
Déols France 46°50N 1°43E 173 F8
Deora India 26°22N 70°55E 242 F4
Deorha = Jubbal India 31°5N 77°40E 242 D7
Deori India 23°24N 79°1E 243 H8
Deoria India 26°31N 83°48E 243 F10
Deosai Mts. Pakistan 35°40N 75°0E 243 B6
Deosri India 26°46N 90°29E 241 B3
Depalpur India 22°51N 75°33E 242 H6
Department of the Interior Washington, D.C., U.S.A. 143 b1
DePaul University U.S.A. 41°55N 87°39W 119 B3
Deping China 37°25N 116°58E 227 F9
Deposit U.S.A. 42°4N 75°25W 313 D9
Deptford U.K. 51°28N 0°1W 125 B3
Depuch I. Australia 20°37S 117°44E 278 D2
Deputati, Camera dei Rome, Italy 136 b2
Deputatskiy Russia 69°18N 139°54E 215 C14
Deqên China 28°34N 98°51E 228 C2
Deqing China 23°8N 111°42E 229 F8
Deqing China 30°31N 119°58E 229 B12
Dera, Lach → Somali Rep. 0°15N 42°17E 267 D5
Dera Ghazi Khan Pakistan 30°5N 70°43E 242 D4
Dera Ismail Khan Pakistan 31°50N 70°50E 242 D4
Derabugti Pakistan 29°2N 69°9E 242 E3
Derawar Fort Pakistan 28°46N 71°20E 242 E4
Derbent Russia 42°5N 48°15E 191 J9
Derbent Turkey 38°11N 28°33E 205 C10
Derby W. Austral., Australia 17°18S 123°38E 278 C3
Derby Derby City, U.K. 52°56N 1°28W 168 E6
Derby Conn., U.S.A. 41°19N 73°5W 313 E11
Derby Kans., U.S.A. 37°33N 97°16W 308 G5
Derby N.Y., U.S.A. 42°41N 78°58W 312 D6
Derby City □ U.K. 52°56N 1°28W 168 E6
Derby Line U.S.A. 45°0N 72°6W 313 B12
Derbyshire □ U.K. 53°11N 1°38W 168 D6
Derdap △ Serbia 44°40N 22°23E 202 B6
Derdepoort S. Africa 24°38S 26°24E 270 B4
Derecske Hungary 47°20N 21°33E 182 C6
Dereham U.K. 52°41N 0°57E 169 E8
Dereköy Turkey 41°55N 27°21E 203 E11
Dereli Turkey 40°44N 38°26E 213 B8
Derg → U.K. 54°44N 7°26W 166 B4
Derg, L. Ireland 53°0N 8°20W 166 D3
Dergachi = Derhaci Ukraine 50°9N 36°11E 189 G9
Derhaci Ukraine 50°9N 36°11E 189 G9
Deridder U.S.A. 30°51N 93°17W 314 F8
Derik Turkey 37°21N 40°18E 213 D9
Derinkuyu Turkey 38°22N 34°45E 212 C6
Dermantsi Bulgaria 43°8N 24°17E 203 C8
Dermott U.S.A. 33°32N 91°26W 314 E9
Dernière Rivière St. Lucia 13°57N 60°55W 323 m
Dêrong China 28°44N 99°9E 228 C2
Derrinallum Australia 37°57S 143°15E 282 D5
Derry = Londonderry U.K. 55°0N 7°20W 166 B4
Derry = Londonderry □ U.K. 55°0N 7°20W 166 B4
Derry N.H., U.S.A. 42°53N 71°19W 313 D13
Derry Pa., U.S.A. 40°20N 79°18W 312 F5
Derryveagh Mts. Ireland 54°56N 8°11W 166 B3
Derudub Sudan 17°31N 36°7E 256 D4
Derval France 47°40N 1°41W 172 E5
Derveni Greece 38°8N 22°25E 204 C4
Derventa Bos.-H. 44°59N 17°55E 182 F2
Derwent → Cumb., U.K. 54°39N 3°33W 168 C4
Derwent → Derby, U.K. 52°57N 1°28W 168 E6
Derwent → N. Yorks., U.K. 53°45N 0°58W 168 D7
Derwent Water U.K. 54°35N 3°9W 168 C4
Derzhavīnsk Kazakhstan 51°6N 66°19E 217 B7
Des Moines Iowa, U.S.A. 41°35N 93°37W 310 C3
Des Moines N. Mex., U.S.A. 36°46N 103°50W 305 H12
Des Moines Wash., U.S.A. 47°24N 122°19W 306 C4
Des Moines → U.S.A. 40°23N 91°25W 310 D5
Des Moines ✕ (DSM) U.S.A. 41°32N 93°40W 310 C3
Des Plaines U.S.A. 42°2N 87°54W 119 A1
Des Plaines → U.S.A. 41°23N 88°15W 311 C8
Desa Romania 43°52N 23°2E 182 G8
Desaguadero Peru 16°34S 69°3W 330 D4
Desaguadero → Argentina 34°30S 66°46W 334 C2
Desaguadero → Bolivia 16°35S 69°5W 330 D4
Desantne Ukraine 45°34N 29°32E 183 E14
Désappointement, Is. du French Polynesia 14°10S 141°20W 289 f
Desar Malaysia 1°31N 104°17E 237 d
Descanso, Pta. Mexico 32°21N 117°3W 307 N9
Descartes France 46°59N 0°42E 174 B4
Deschaillons-sur-St-Laurent Canada 46°32N 72°7W 299 C5
Deschambault L. Canada 54°50N 103°30W 297 C8
Deschutes → U.S.A. 45°38N 120°54W 304 D3
Dese Ethiopia 11°5N 39°40E 257 E4
Deseado, C. Chile 52°45S 74°42W 336 D2
Desenzano del Garda Italy 45°28N 10°32E 198 C7
Desert Center U.S.A. 33°43N 115°24W 307 M11
Desert Hot Springs U.S.A. 33°58N 116°30W 307 M10
Desert Wetlands Park U.S.A. 36°7N 115°2W 124 B2
Desertas, Ilhas Madeira 32°30N 16°30W 260 B1
Deset Norway 61°20N 11°26E 164 C8
Desfina Greece 38°25N 22°31E 204 C4
Deshaies Guadeloupe 16°18N 61°47W 322 e
Deshauteur Guadeloupe 16°15N 61°25W 322 e
Deshengmen China 39°56N 116°21E 114 B2
Deshnok India 27°48N 73°21E 242 F5
Desierto Central de Baja California ⌂ Mexico 29°40N 114°50W 318 B2
Desjardins, Complexe Montréal, Canada 130 b2
Deskati Greece 39°55N 21°49E 202 G5
Desna → Ukraine 50°33N 30°32E 177 C16
Desnătui → Romania 43°53N 23°35E 183 G8
Desolación, I. Chile 53°0S 74°0W 336 D2
Despeñaperros, Paso Spain 38°24N 3°30W 195 G7
Despeñaperros ⌂ Spain 38°23N 3°32W 195 G7
Despotiko Greece 36°57N 24°58E 204 E6
Despotovac Serbia 44°6N 21°30E 202 B5
Dessau Germany 51°51N 12°14E 178 D8
Dessye = Dese Ethiopia 11°5N 39°40E 257 E4
Destin U.S.A. 30°24N 86°30W 317 E3
D'Estrees B. Australia 35°55S 137°45E 282 C2
Desuri India 25°18N 73°35E 242 G5
Desvres France 50°40N 1°48E 173 B8
Det Udom Thailand 14°54N 105°5E 236 E5
Deta Romania 45°24N 21°13E 182 E6
Dete Zimbabwe 18°38S 26°50E 270 A4
Detinja → Serbia 43°51N 20°5E 202 C4
Detmold Germany 51°56N 8°52E 178 D4
Detour, Pt. U.S.A. 45°40N 86°40W 308 C10
Detroit U.S.A. 42°19N 83°12W 312 D1
Detroit Lakes U.S.A. 46°49N 95°51W 308 B6
Detroit Metropolitan Wayne County ✕ (DTW) U.S.A. 42°13N 83°21W 311 B13
Detskoye Selo = Pushkin Russia 59°45N 30°25E 188 C6
Dettifoss Iceland 65°48N 16°24W 155 B10
Detva Slovak Rep. 48°34N 19°25E 181 C12
Deua △ Australia 35°32S 149°46E 283 C8
Deurne Neths. 51°27N 5°49E 170 C5
Deutsch = Przemyśl Poland 49°50N 22°45E 185 J9
Deutsch Brod = Havlíčkův Brod Czech Rep. 49°36N 15°33E 180 B8
Deutsch-Eylau = Iława Poland 53°36N 19°34E 184 E6
Deutsch Krone = Wałcz Poland 53°17N 16°27E 185 E3
Deutsch-Luxemburgischer ⌂ Germany 49°58N 6°12E 179 F2
Deutsch-Wagram Austria 48°17N 16°33E 142 A3
Deutsche Bucht Germany 54°15N 8°0E 178 A4
Deutsche Oper Germany 52°30N 13°19E 115 A2
Deutsches Museum Germany 48°7N 11°35E 131 B2
Deutschland = Germany ■ Europe 51°0N 10°0E 178 E6
Deutschlandsberg Austria 46°49N 15°14E 180 E8
Deux-Sèvres □ France 46°35N 0°20W 172 F6
Deva Romania 45°53N 22°55E 182 E7
Devakottai India 9°55N 78°45E 245 K4
Devaprayag India 30°13N 78°35E 243 D8
Devarkonda India 16°42N 78°56E 244 F4
Dévaványa Hungary 47°2N 20°59E 182 C5
Deveci Dağları Turkey 40°6N 36°15E 212 B7
Devecikonağı Turkey 39°55N 28°34E 203 G12
Devecser Hungary 47°6N 17°26E 182 C2
Develi Turkey 38°23N 35°29E 212 C6
Deventer Neths. 52°15N 6°10E 170 B6
Devereux U.S.A. 33°13N 83°5W 316 B6
Deveron → U.K. 57°41N 2°32W 167 D6
Devesel Romania 44°28N 22°41E 182 F7
Devgad I. India 14°48N 74°5E 245 G2
Devgadh Bariya India 22°40N 73°55E 242 H5
Devgarh India 16°23N 73°23E 245 F1
Devi → India 19°59N 86°24E 244 E8
Devikot India 26°42N 71°12E 242 F4
Devil River Pk. N.Z. 40°56S 172°37E 285 A7
Devil's Bridge Antigua & B. 17°6N 61°41W 322 b
Devils Den U.S.A. 35°46N 119°58W 306 K7
Devils Hole = Death Valley △ U.S.A. 36°29N 117°6W 307 J9
Devils Island, I. = Diable, Île du Fr. Guiana 5°16N 52°34W 329 B7
Devils Lake U.S.A. 48°7N 98°52W 308 A4
Devils Paw Canada 58°47N 134°0W 296 B2
Devil's Peak S. Africa 33°57S 18°27E 118 A1
Devils Postpile ⌂ U.S.A. 37°37N 119°5W 306 H7
Devil's Pt. Sri Lanka 9°26N 80°6E 245 K5
Devils Tower U.S.A. 44°35N 104°42W 304 D11
Devils Tower △ U.S.A. 44°48N 104°55W 304 D11
Devil's Woodyard Mud Volcano Trin. & Tob. 10°16N 61°22W 323 t
Devin Bulgaria 41°44N 24°24E 203 E8
Devine U.S.A. 29°8N 98°54W 314 G5
Devipattinam India 9°29N 78°54E 245 K4
Devizes U.K. 51°22N 1°58W 169 F6
Devli India 25°50N 75°20E 242 G6
Devnya Bulgaria 43°13N 27°33E 203 C11
Devoll → Albania 40°57N 20°15E 202 F4
Devon Canada 53°24N 113°44W 296 C6
Devon □ U.K. 50°50N 3°40W 169 G4
Devon I. Canada 75°10N 85°0W 295 B11
Devonport Australia 41°10S 146°22E 281 G4
Devrek Turkey 41°13N 31°57E 212 B4
Devrekâni Turkey 41°36N 33°50E 212 B5
Devrez → Turkey 41°6N 34°25E 212 B6
Devrukh India 17°3N 73°37E 244 F1
Dewas India 22°59N 76°3E 242 H7
Dewetsdorp S. Africa 29°33S 26°39E 270 C4
Dewey Puerto Rico 18°18N 65°18W 321 b
Dexing China 28°46N 117°30E 229 C11
Dexter Maine, U.S.A. 45°1N 69°18W 309 C19
Dexter Mich., U.S.A. 42°20N 83°53W 311 B13
Dexter Mo., U.S.A. 36°48N 89°57W 308 G9
Dexter N. Mex., U.S.A. 33°12N 104°22W 305 K11
Dey-Dey, L. Australia 29°12S 131°4E 279 E5
Deyang China 31°3N 104°27E 228 B5
Deyhūk Iran 33°15N 57°30E 247 C8
Deyyer Iran 27°55N 51°55E 247 E6
Dezadeash L. Canada 60°28N 136°58W 296 A1
Dezfūl Iran 32°20N 48°30E 213 F13
Dezhneva, Mys Russia 66°5N 169°40W 215 C19
Dezhou China 37°26N 116°18E 226 F9
Dhadhar → India 24°56N 85°24E 243 G11
Dhahabān Si. Arabia 21°58N 39°3E 248 B2
Dhahiriya = Aẓ Ẓāhirīyah West Bank 31°25N 34°58E 251 G5
Dhahran = Aẓ Ẓahrān Si. Arabia 26°10N 50°7E 247 E6
Dhak Pakistan 32°25N 72°33E 242 C5
Dhaka Bangla. 23°43N 90°26E 241 D3
Dhaka □ Bangla. 24°25N 90°25E 241 C3
Dhakuria India 22°30N 88°22E 124 B2
Dhali Cyprus 35°1N 33°25E 207 E9
Dhamangaon India 20°48N 78°9E 244 D4
Dhamār Yemen 14°30N 44°20E 248 D4
Dhampur India 29°19N 78°33E 243 E8
Dhamra → India 20°47N 86°58E 244 D8
Dhamtari India 20°42N 81°35E 244 D5
Dhanbad India 23°50N 86°30E 243 H12
Dhangarhi Nepal 28°55N 80°40E 243 E9
Dhankuta Nepal 26°55N 87°40E 243 F12
Dhanora India 20°20N 80°22E 244 D5
Dhanushkodi India 9°11N 79°24E 245 K4
Dhar India 22°35N 75°26E 242 H6
Dharampur Gujarat, India 20°32N 73°17E 244 D1
Dharampur Mad. P., India 22°13N 75°18E 242 H6
Dharamsala = Dharmsala India 32°16N 76°23E 242 C7
Dharangaon India 21°1N 75°16E 244 D2
Dharapuram India 10°45N 77°34E 245 J3
Dharavi India 19°1N 72°51E 130 A2
Dhariwal India 31°57N 75°19E 242 D6
Dharla → Bangla. 25°46N 89°42E 243 G13
Dharmapuri India 12°10N 78°10E 245 H4
Dharmavaram India 14°29N 77°44E 245 G3
Dharmjaygarh India 22°28N 83°13E 243 H10
Dharmsala India 32°16N 76°23E 242 C7
Dharni India 21°33N 76°53E 242 J7
Dharug △ Australia 33°20S 151°2E 283 B9
Dharur India 18°3N 76°8E 244 E3
Dharwad India 15°30N 75°4E 245 G2
Dhasan → India 25°48N 79°24E 243 G8
Dhaulagiri Nepal 28°39N 83°28E 243 E10
Dhebar, L. India 24°10N 74°0E 242 G6
Dheftera Cyprus 35°5N 33°16E 207 E9
Dhenkanal India 20°45N 85°35E 244 D7
Dherinia Cyprus 35°3N 33°57E 207 E9
Dheskáti = Deskati Greece 39°55N 21°49E 202 G5
Dhī Qār □ Iraq 31°0N 46°15E 246 D5
Dhiarrizos → Cyprus 34°41N 32°34E 207 F8
Dhībān Jordan 31°30N 35°46E 251 D4
Dhilwan India 31°31N 75°21E 242 D6
Dhimarkhera India 23°28N 80°22E 243 H9
Dhodhekánisos = Dodecanese Greece 36°35N 27°0E 205 E8
Dholka India 22°44N 72°29E 242 H5
Dhomokós = Domokos Greece 39°10N 22°18E 204 B4
Dhone India 15°25N 77°53E 245 G3
Dhoraji India 21°45N 70°37E 242 J4
Dhragonísi = Tragonhsi Greece 37°27N 25°29E 205 D7
Dhrangadhra India 22°59N 71°31E 242 H4
Dhrol India 22°33N 70°25E 242 H4
Dhubāb Yemen 12°56N 43°25E 248 D3
Dhubri India 26°2N 89°59E 241 B2
Dhulasar Bangla. 21°52N 90°14E 241 E3
Dhule India 20°58N 74°50E 244 D2
Dhupdhara India 26°10N 91°4E 241 B3
Dhuusa Marreeb = Dusa Mareb Somali Rep. 5°30N 46°15E 267 C6
Di-ib, W. → Sudan 22°38N 36°6E 256 C4
Di Linh Vietnam 11°35N 108°4E 237 G7
Di Linh, Cao Nguyen Vietnam 11°30N 108°0E 237 G7
Dia Greece 35°28N 25°14E 207 E6
Diabakania Guinea 10°38N 10°58W 262 C2
Diable, Île du Fr. Guiana 5°16N 52°34W 329 B7
Diable, Pte. du Martinique 14°46N 60°53W 322 j
Diables, Morne aux Dominica 15°37N 61°27W 323 k
Diablo Pt. N. Marianas 15°0N 145°35E 302 e
Diablo Range U.S.A. 37°20N 121°25W 306 J5
Diablotins, Morne Dominica 15°30N 61°24W 323 k
Diadema Brazil 23°41S 46°37W 137 C2
Diafarabé Mali 14°9N 4°57W 262 C4
Diala Mali 14°10N 9°58W 262 C3
Dialakoro Mali 12°18N 7°54W 262 C3
Dialakoto Senegal 13°21N 13°19W 262 C2
Diallassagou Mali 13°47N 3°41W 262 C4
Diamant, Pte. du Martinique 14°27N 61°3W 322 j
Diamant, Rocher du Martinique 14°27N 61°2W 322 j
Diamante Argentina 32°5S 60°40W 334 C3
Diamante Italy 39°41N 15°49E 201 C8
Diamante → Argentina 34°30S 66°46W 334 C2
Diamantina Brazil 18°17S 43°40W 333 E3
Diamantina → Australia 26°45S 139°10E 281 D2
Diamantina △ Australia 23°33S 141°23E 280 C3
Diamantino Brazil 14°30S 56°30W 331 C6
Diamond Bar U.S.A. 34°1N 117°48W 307 L9
Diamond Harbour India 22°11N 88°14E 243 H13
Diamond Head U.S.A. 21°16N 157°49W 302 K14
Diamond I. Grenada 12°20N 61°35W 323 q
Diamond Is. Australia 17°25S 151°5E 280 B5
Diamond Mts. U.S.A. 39°40N 115°50W 304 G6
Diamond Springs U.S.A. 38°42N 120°49W 306 G6
Dian Chi China 24°50N 102°43E 228 E4
Dianalund Denmark 55°32N 11°30E 163 J5
Dianbai China 21°33N 111°0E 229 G8
Diancheng China 21°30N 111°4E 229 G8
Dianjiang China 30°24N 107°20E 228 B6
Diano Marina Italy 43°54N 8°5E 198 E5
Dianópolis Brazil 11°38S 46°50W 333 D2
Dianra Ivory C. 8°45N 6°14W 262 D3
Diaoyu Tai = Senkaku-Shotō E. China Sea 25°45N 123°30E 221 M1
Diapaga Burkina Faso 12°5N 1°46E 263 C5
Diapangou Burkina Faso 12°5N 0°10E 263 C5
Diariguila Guinea 10°35N 10°2W 262 C2
Diavolo, Mt. India 12°40N 92°56E 245 H11
Dībā U.A.E. 25°45N 56°16E 247 E8
Dibai India 28°13N 78°15E 242 E8
Dibaya Dem. Rep. of the Congo 6°30S 22°57E 265 D4
Dibaya-Lubue Dem. Rep. of the Congo 4°12S 19°54E 265 C3
Dibbeen △ Jordan 32°20N 35°45E 251 F6
Dibella Niger 17°32N 13°6E 259 E2
Dibete Botswana 23°45S 26°32E 270 B4
Dibru-Saikhowa △ India 27°40N 95°27E 241 B5
Dibrugarh India 27°29N 94°55E 241 B5
Diciosânmartin = Târnăveni Romania 46°19N 24°13E 183 D9
Dickens U.S.A. 33°37N 100°50W 314 E4
Dickeyville U.S.A. 42°38N 90°36W 310 B6
Dickinson U.S.A. 46°53N 102°47W 308 B2
Dickinson B. Antigua & B. 17°10N 61°51W 322 b
Dick's Pt. Bahamas 25°4N 77°18W 153 D6
Dickson = Dikson Russia 73°40N 80°5E 214 B9
Dickson U.S.A. 36°5N 87°23W 315 C11
Dickson City U.S.A. 41°28N 75°36W 313 E9
Dicle Barajı Turkey 38°20N 40°11E 213 C9
Dicle Nehri → Turkey 37°44N 41°10E 213 D9
Dicomano Italy 43°53N 11°31E 199 E8
Didesa, W. → Ethiopia 10°2N 35°32E 257 E4
Didi Sudan 6°18N 34°29E 257 F3
Didiéni Mali 13°53N 8°6W 262 C3
Didimbo Angola 17°30S 21°45E 265 F4
Didimoticho Greece 41°22N 26°29E 203 E10
Didsbury Canada 51°35N 114°10W 296 C6
Didwana India 27°23N 74°36E 242 F6
Die France 44°47N 5°22E 175 D9
Diébougou Burkina Faso 11°0N 3°15W 262 C4
Diecke Guinea 7°27N 8°54W 262 D3
Diedenhofen = Thionville France 49°20N 6°10E 173 C13
Diefenbaker, L. Canada 51°0N 106°55W 297 C7
Diegen Belgium 50°53N 4°26E 116 A2
Diego de Almagro Chile 26°22S 70°3W 334 B1
Diego Garcia Ind. Oc. 7°50S 72°50E 273 E6
Diego Martin Trin. & Tob. 10°43N 61°34W 323 t
Diego Ramírez, Islas Chile 56°30S 68°44W 336 E3
Diego Suarez = Antsiranana Madag. 12°25S 49°20E 272 A2
Diekirch Lux. 49°52N 6°10E 170 E6
Diéma Mali 14°32N 9°12W 262 C3
Diembéring Senegal 12°29N 16°47W 262 C1
Diemelsee ⌂ Germany 51°20N 8°40E 178 D4
Diemen Neths. 52°21N 4°58E 112 A2
Dien Ban Vietnam 15°53N 108°16E 236 E7
Dien Bien Vietnam 21°20N 103°0E 228 G4
Dien Khanh Vietnam 12°15N 109°6E 237 F7
Diepholz Germany 52°37N 8°22E 178 C4
Diepkloof S. Africa 26°14S 27°57E 123 B1
Dieppe France 49°54N 1°4E 172 C8
Dieppe Bay Town St. Kitts & Nevis 17°25N 62°48W 322 d
Dieprivier S. Africa 34°2S 18°27E 118 B1
Dierks U.S.A. 34°7N 94°1W 314 D7
Diest Belgium 50°58N 5°4E 170 D5
Dieterich U.S.A. 39°4N 88°23W 311 E8
Dietikon Switz. 47°24N 8°24E 179 H4
Dieulefit France 44°32N 5°4E 175 D9
Dieuze France 48°49N 6°43E 173 D13
Dievenow = Dziwnów Poland 54°2N 14°45E 184 D1
Dif Somali Rep. 0°59N 40°58E 267 D5
Diffa □ Niger 16°0N 13°30E 263 B7
Differdange Lux. 49°31N 5°54E 170 E5
Difficult Run → U.S.A. 38°55N 77°15W 143 B1
Diffun Phil. 16°36N 121°33E 232 C3
Dig India 27°28N 77°20E 242 F7
Digba Dem. Rep. of the Congo 4°25N 25°48E 268 B2
Digboi India 27°23N 95°38E 241 B5
Digby Canada 44°38N 65°50W 299 D6
Diggi India 26°22N 75°26E 242 F6
Dighinala Bangla. 23°15N 92°5E 241 D4
Dighton U.S.A. 38°29N 100°28W 308 F3
Digity Mud Volcanoes Trin. & Tob. 10°12N 61°25W 323 t
Diglur India 18°34N 77°33E 244 E3
Digna Mali 14°48N 8°10W 262 C3
Digne-les-Bains France 44°5N 6°12E 175 D10
Digoin France 46°29N 3°58E 173 F11
Digor Turkey 40°22N 43°25E 213 B10
Digos Phil. 6°45N 125°20E 233 H5
Digranes Iceland 66°4N 14°44W 155 A12
Digras India 20°6N 77°45E 244 D3
Digul → Indonesia 7°7S 138°42E 231 F9
Digya △ Ghana 7°15N 0°5E 263 D5
Dihang = Brahmaputra → Asia 23°40N 90°35E 241 D3
Dijlah, Nahr → Asia 31°0N 47°25E 246 D5
Dijon France 47°20N 5°3E 173 E12
Dikhil Djibouti 11°8N 42°20E 257 E5
Dikili Turkey 39°4N 26°53E 205 B8
Dikirnis Egypt 31°6N 31°35E 256 H7
Dikkil = Dikhil Djibouti 11°8N 42°20E 257 E5

Dikodougou Ivory C. 9°4N 5°45W 262 D3
Diksmuide Belgium 51°2N 2°52E 170 C2
Dikson Russia 73°40N 80°5E 214 B9
Dikti Oros Greece 35°8N 25°30E 207 E6
Dikwa Nigeria 12°4N 13°30E 263 C7
Dila Ethiopia 6°21N 38°22E 257 F4
Dilasag Phil. 16°25N 122°11E 232 C4
Dilbeek Belgium 50°51N 4°17E 116 A1
Dilek Yarimadisi △ Turkey 37°40N 27°10E 205 D9
Dili E. Timor 8°39S 125°34E 231 F7
Diligent Strait India 12°11N 92°57E 245 H11
Dilijan Armenia 40°46N 44°57E 191 K7
Dilinata Greece 38°13N 20°31E 207 C2
Dilizhan = Dilijan Armenia 40°46N 44°57E 191 K7
Dilj Croatia 45°29N 18°1E 182 E3
Dillenburg Germany 50°43N 8°17E 178 E4
Dilley U.S.A. 28°40N 99°10W 314 G5
Dilli = Delhi India 28°39N 77°13E 120 B2
Dillia ➔ Niger 14°9N 12°50E 259 F2
Dilling Sudan 12°3N 29°35E 257 E2
Dillingen Bayern, Germany 48°36N 10°30E 179 G6
Dillingen Saarland, Germany 49°22N 6°43E 179 F2
Dillingham U.S.A. 59°3N 158°28W 303 G8
Dillon Sask., Canada 55°56N 108°35W 297 B7
Dillon Mont., U.S.A. 45°13N 112°38W 304 D7
Dillon S.C., U.S.A. 34°25N 79°22W 315 D15
Dillon ➔ Canada 55°56N 108°56W 297 B7
Dillsboro U.S.A. 39°1N 85°4W 311 E11
Dillsburg U.S.A. 40°7N 77°2W 312 F7
Dilly Mali 15°1N 7°40W 262 C3
Dilolo Dem. Rep. of the Congo 10°28S 22°18E 265 E4
Dilos Greece 37°23N 25°15E 205 D7
Dilove Ukraine 47°56N 24°11E 183 C9
Dimapur India 25°54N 93°45E 241 C4
Dimas Mexico 23°43N 106°47W 318 C3
Dimasalang Phil. 12°12N 123°51E 232 E4
Dimashq Syria 33°30N 36°18E 250 E7
Dimashq □ Syria 33°30N 36°30E 250 E7
Dimbaza S. Africa 32°50S 27°14E 271 D4
Dimbelenge Dem. Rep. of the Congo 5°33S 23°7E 265 D4
Dimbokro Ivory C. 6°45N 4°46W 262 D4
Dimboola Australia 36°28S 142°7E 282 D5
Dîmboviţa = Dâmboviţa ➔ Romania 44°12N 26°26E 183 F11
Dimbulah Australia 17°8S 145°4E 280 B4
Dimitrovgrad Bulgaria 42°5N 25°35E 203 D9
Dimitrovgrad Russia 54°14N 49°39E 190 C9
Dimitrovgrad Serbia 43°2N 22°48E 202 C6
Dimitrovo = Pernik Bulgaria 42°35N 23°2E 202 D7
Dimitsana Greece 37°36N 22°3E 204 D4
Dimmitt U.S.A. 34°33N 102°19W 314 D3
Dimo Sudan 5°19N 29°10E 257 F2
Dimona Israel 31°2N 35°1E 251 G6
Dimonika ⌓ Congo 4°13S 12°21E 264 C2
Dimovo Bulgaria 43°43N 22°50E 202 C6
Dinagat Phil. 10°10N 125°40E 233 F5
Dinaig Phil. 7°11N 124°10E 233 H5
Dinajpur Bangla. 25°33N 88°43E 241 C2
Dinalupihan Phil. 14°52N 120°28E 232 D3
Dinan France 48°28N 2°2W 172 D4
Dīnān Āb Iran 32°4N 56°49E 247 C8
Dinant Belgium 50°16N 4°55E 170 D4
Dinapur India 25°38N 85°5E 243 G11
Dinar Turkey 38°5N 30°10E 205 C12
Dīnār, Kūh-e Iran 30°42N 51°46E 247 D6
Dinara Planina Croatia 44°0N 16°30E 199 D13
Dinard France 48°38N 2°6W 172 D4
Dinaric Alps = Dinara Planina Croatia 44°0N 16°30E 199 D13
Dinas Phil. 7°38N 123°20E 233 H4
Dindanko Mali 14°8N 9°30W 262 C3
Dinde Angola 14°17S 13°42E 265 E2
Dinder, Nahr ed ➔ Sudan 14°6N 33°40E 257 E3
Dinder ⌓ Sudan 12°30N 35°10E 257 E4
Dindi ➔ India 16°24N 78°15E 245 F4
Dindigul India 10°25N 78°0E 245 J4
Dindori India 22°57N 81°5E 243 H9
Ding Xian = Dingzhou China 38°30N 114°59E 226 E8
Dinga Dem. Rep. of the Congo 5°17S 16°42E 265 D3
Dinga Pakistan 25°26N 67°10E 242 G2
Dingalan Phil. 15°18N 121°25E 232 D3
Dingalan Bay Phil. 15°18N 121°25E 232 D3
Ding'an China 19°42N 110°19E 236 C8
Dingbian China 37°35N 107°32E 226 F4
Dingelstädt Germany 51°18N 10°19E 178 D6
Dingle Kerry, Ireland 52°9N 10°17W 166 D1
Dingle Sweden 58°32N 11°35E 163 F5
Dingle B. Ireland 52°3N 10°20W 166 D1
Dingli Malta 35°52N 14°23E 206 F7
Dingmans Ferry U.S.A. 41°13N 74°55W 313 E10
Dingnan China 24°45N 115°0E 229 E10
Dingo Australia 23°38S 149°19E 280 C4
Dingolfing Germany 48°37N 12°30E 179 G8
Dingras Phil. 18°6N 120°42E 232 B3
Dingtao China 35°5N 115°35E 226 G8
Dinguira Mali 14°11N 11°16W 262 C2
Dinguiraye Guinea 11°18N 10°49W 262 C2
Dingwall U.K. 57°36N 4°26W 167 D4
Dingxi China 35°30N 104°33E 226 G3
Dingxiang China 38°30N 112°58E 226 E7
Dingyuan China 32°32N 117°41E 229 A11
Dingzhou China 38°30N 114°59E 226 E8
Dinh, Mui Vietnam 11°22N 109°1E 237 G7
Dinh Lap Vietnam 21°33N 107°6E 228 G6
Dinhata India 26°8N 89°27E 241 B2
Dinin ➔ Ireland 52°43N 7°18W 166 D4
Dinokwe Botswana 23°29S 26°37E 270 B4
Dinorwic Canada 49°41N 92°30W 297 D10
Dinosaur ⌓ Alta., Canada 50°47N 111°30W 296 C6
Dinosaur ⌓ Colo., U.S.A. 40°30N 108°45W 304 F9
Dinsor Somali Rep. 2°24N 42°59E 267 D5
Dinuba U.S.A. 36°32N 119°23W 306 J7
Diö Sweden 56°37N 14°15E 163 H8
Dioïla Mali 12°23N 6°50W 262 C3
Dioka Mali 14°57N 10°4W 262 C2
Diomede U.S.A. 65°47N 169°0W 303 D5
Diona Chad 17°51N 22°36E 259 E4
Diongoï Mali 14°38N 8°34W 262 C3
Dionisades Greece 35°20N 26°10E 207 E7
Dionisos, Theatro Athens, Greece 112 c2
Diósgyör Hungary 48°7N 20°43E 182 B5
Diosig Romania 47°18N 22°2E 182 C7
Diougani Mali 14°19N 2°44W 262 C4
Diouloulou Senegal 13°5N 16°38W 262 C1
Dioura Mali 14°59N 5°12W 262 C3
Diourbel Senegal 14°39N 16°12W 262 C1
Diourbel □ Senegal 14°45N 16°15W 262 C1
Dipaculao Phil. 15°51N 121°32E 232 D3
Dipalpur Pakistan 30°40N 73°39E 242 D5
Diplo Pakistan 24°35N 69°35E 242 G3
Dipolog Phil. 8°36N 123°20E 233 G4
Dipperu △ Australia 21°56S 148°42E 280 C4
Dipton N.Z. 45°54S 168°22E 285 F3
Dir Pakistan 35°8N 71°59E 240 B3
Diré Mali 16°20N 3°25W 262 B4
Dire Dawa Ethiopia 9°35N 41°45E 257 F5
Dirfis Oros Greece 38°40N 23°54E 204 C5
Diriamba Nic. 11°51N 86°19W 320 D2
Dirico Angola 17°50S 20°42E 265 F4
Dirk Hartog I. Australia 25°50S 113°5E 279 E1
Dirkou Niger 19°1N 12°53E 259 E2
Dirnismaning Germany 48°13N 11°38E 131 A2
Dirranbandi Australia 28°33S 148°17E 281 D4
Dirri Somali Rep. 4°20N 46°37E 267 D6
Dirs Si. Arabia 18°32N 42°5E 248 C3
Dirschau = Tczew Poland 54°8N 18°50E 184 D5
Disa India 24°18N 72°10E 242 G5
Disa Sudan 12°5N 34°15E 257 E3
Disappointment, C. U.S.A. 46°18N 124°5W 304 C1
Disappointment, L. Australia 23°20S 122°40E 278 D3
Disaster B. Australia 37°15S 149°58E 283 D8
Discovery B. Vic., Australia 38°10S 140°40E 282 E4
Discovery B. China 22°18N 114°1E 219 G11
Discovery Bay △ Australia 38°9S 141°16E 282 E4
Discovery Seamount Atl. Oc. 42°0S 0°10E 152 L12
Disentis Muster Switz. 46°42N 8°50E 179 J4
Dishna Egypt 26°9N 32°32E 256 B3
Dishna Nigeria 11°35N 9°50E 263 C6
Disko = Qeqertarsuaq Greenland 69°45N 53°30W 154 D5
Disko Bugt Greenland 69°10N 52°0W 154 D5
Disna = Dzisna ➔ Belarus 55°34N 28°12E 188 E5
Disney Reef Tonga 19°17S 174°7W 287 P13
Disney Studios U.S.A. 34°9N 118°19W 126 B3
Dispur India 26°3N 91°52E 241 B3
Diss U.K. 52°23N 1°7E 169 E9
Disteghil Sar Pakistan 36°20N 75°12E 243 A6
District Heights U.S.A. 38°51N 76°53W 143 B4
District of Columbia □ U.S.A. 38°55N 77°0W 309 F15
Distrito Federal □ Brazil 15°45S 47°45W 333 E2
Distrito Federal □ Mexico 19°15N 99°10W 319 D5
Distrito Federal □ Venezuela 10°30N 66°55W 328 A4
Disûq Egypt 31°8N 30°35E 256 H7
Ditan Park Beijing, China 114 a2
Diu India 20°45N 70°58E 242 J4
Diuata Mts. Phil. 9°0N 125°50E 233 G5
Dīvāndarreh Iran 35°55N 47°2E 213 E12
Divarata Greece 38°20N 20°33E 207 C2
Divenié Congo 2°43S 12°4E 264 C2
Dives ➔ France 49°18N 0°7W 172 C6
Dives-sur-Mer France 49°18N 0°8W 172 C6
Divi Pt. India 15°59N 81°9E 245 G5
Divichi = Däväçi Azerbaijan 41°15N 48°57E 191 K9
Divide U.S.A. 45°45N 112°45W 304 D7
Dividing Ra. Australia 27°45S 116°0E 279 E2
Divinópolis Brazil 20°10S 44°54W 333 F3
Divisões, Serra dos Brazil 17°0S 51°0W 333 E1
Divjake Albania 41°0N 19°32E 202 F3
Divnoye Russia 45°55N 43°21E 191 H6
Divo Ivory C. 5°48N 5°15W 262 D3
Divriği Turkey 39°22N 38°7E 213 C8
Dīwāl Kol Afghan. 34°23N 67°52E 242 B2
Dix ➔ U.S.A. 37°49N 84°43W 311 G12
Dixie Mt. U.S.A. 39°55N 120°16W 306 F6
Dixie Union U.S.A. 31°20N 82°28W 316 D7
Dixon Calif., U.S.A. 38°27N 121°49W 306 G5
Dixon Ill., U.S.A. 41°50N 89°29W 310 C7
Dixon Mo., U.S.A. 37°59N 92°6W 310 G4
Dixon Entrance U.S.A. 54°30N 132°0W 303 J14
Dixville Canada 45°4N 71°46W 313 A13
Diyadin Turkey 39°33N 43°40E 213 C10
Diyālá □ Iraq 33°45N 44°50E 246 C5
Diyālá ➔ Iraq 33°13N 44°30E 213 F11
Diyarb Nigm Egypt 30°45N 31°26E 251 H2
Diyarbakır Turkey 37°55N 40°18E 213 D9
Diyarbakır □ Turkey 38°0N 40°10E 213 D9
Diyodar India 24°8N 71°50E 242 G4
Dja ⌓ Cameroon 3°10N 12°58E 264 B2
Djadié ➔ Gabon 0°46N 12°58E 264 B2
Djado Niger 21°4N 12°14E 259 D2
Djado, Plateau du Niger 21°29N 12°21E 259 D2
Djakarta = Jakarta Indonesia 6°9S 106°52E 122 A2
Djalma Dutra = Miguel Calmon Brazil 11°26S 40°36W 332 D3
Djalma Dutra = Poções Brazil 14°31S 40°21W 333 D3
Djamâa Algeria 33°32N 5°59E 261 B6
Djamba Angola 16°45S 13°58E 265 F2
Djambala Congo 2°32S 14°30E 264 C2
Djanet Algeria 24°35N 9°32E 261 D6
Djaul I. Papua N. G. 2°58S 150°57E 286 B6
Djawa = Jawa Indonesia 7°0S 110°0E 235 D4
Djebiniana Tunisia 35°1N 11°0E 258 A2
Djédaa Chad 13°31N 18°34E 259 F3
Djelfa Algeria 34°40N 3°15E 261 B5
Djelfa □ Algeria 34°20N 3°40E 261 B5
Djema C.A.R. 6°3N 25°15E 264 A5
Djember Chad 10°25N 17°50E 259 F3
Djembo Dem. Rep. of the Congo 9°54S 22°18E 265 D4
Djendel Algeria 36°15N 2°25E 261 A5
Djenné Mali 14°0N 4°30W 262 C4
Djenoun, Garet el Algeria 25°4N 5°31E 261 C6
Djerba Tunisia 33°48N 10°54E 258 B2
Djerba, Î. de Tunisia 33°50N 10°48E 258 B2
Djeréme ➔ Cameroon 5°20N 13°24E 264 A2
Djerid, Chott Tunisia 33°42N 8°30E 258 B1
Djiba Gabon 1°20S 13°9E 264 C2
Djibo Burkina Faso 14°9N 1°35W 263 C4
Djibouti Djibouti 11°30N 43°5E 257 E5
Djibouti ■ Africa 12°0N 43°0E 257 E5
Djohong Cameroon 6°47N 14°20E 264 A2
Djolu Dem. Rep. of the Congo 0°35N 22°5E 264 B4
Djouab ➔ Gabon 1°13N 13°12E 264 B2
Djougou Benin 9°40N 1°45E 263 D5
Djoum Cameroon 2°41N 12°35E 264 B2
Djouna Chad 10°27N 20°4E 259 F4
Djourab, Erg du Chad 16°40N 18°50E 259 E3
Djugu Dem. Rep. of the Congo 1°55N 30°35E 268 B3
Djukbinj △ Australia 12°11S 131°2E 278 B5
Djúpivík Iceland 65°57N 21°34W 155 B5
Djúpivogur Iceland 64°39N 14°17W 155 C12
Djupvasshytta Norway 62°2N 7°16E 164 B4
Djurås Sweden 60°34N 15°8E 162 D9
Djurdjura △ Algeria 35°20N 4°15E 261 A5
Djurö △ Sweden 58°52N 13°28E 163 F7
Djursholm Sweden 59°24N 18°5E 139 A2
Djursland Denmark 56°27N 10°45E 163 H4
Dmitriya Lapteva, Proliv Russia 73°0N 140°0E 215 B15
Dmitriyev Lgovskiy Russia 52°10N 35°0E 189 F8
Dmitriyevsk = Makiyivka Ukraine 48°0N 38°0E 189 H9
Dmitriyevskoye = Talas Kyrgyzstan 42°30N 72°13E 217 D8
Dmitrov Russia 56°25N 37°32E 188 D9
Dmitrovsk-Orlovskiy Russia 52°29N 35°10E 189 F8
Dnepr = Dnipro ➔ Ukraine 46°30N 32°18E 189 J7
Dneprodzerzhinsk = Dniprodzerzhynsk Ukraine 48°32N 34°37E 189 H8
Dneprodzerzhinskoye Vdkhr. = Dniprodzerzhynske Vdskh. Ukraine 48°49N 34°8E 189 H8
Dnepropetrovsk = Dnipropetrovsk Ukraine 48°30N 35°0E 189 H8
Dneprorudnoye = Dniprorudne Ukraine 47°21N 34°58E 189 J8
Dnestr = Dnister ➔ Europe 46°18N 30°17E 177 E16
Dnestrovski = Belgorod Russia 50°35N 36°35E 189 G9
Dnieper = Dnipro ➔ Ukraine 46°30N 32°18E 189 J7
Dniester = Dnister ➔ Europe 46°18N 30°17E 177 E16
Dnipro ➔ Ukraine 46°30N 32°18E 189 J7
Dniprodzerzhynsk Ukraine 48°32N 34°37E 189 H8
Dniprodzerzhynske Vdskh. Ukraine 48°49N 34°8E 189 H8
Dnipropetrovsk Ukraine 48°30N 35°0E 189 H8
Dnipropetrovsk □ Ukraine 48°15N 34°50E 189 H8
Dniprorudne Ukraine 47°21N 34°58E 189 J8
Dnister ➔ Europe 46°18N 30°17E 177 E16
Dnistrovskyy Lyman Ukraine 46°15N 30°17E 189 J6
Dno Russia 57°50N 29°58E 188 D5
Dnyapro = Dnipro ➔ Ukraine 46°30N 32°18E 189 J7
Doabi Afghan. 36°1N 69°32E 240 A3
Doaktown Canada 46°33N 66°8W 299 C6
Doan Hung Vietnam 21°30N 105°10E 228 G5
Doany Madag. 14°21S 49°30E 272 A2
Doba Chad 8°40N 16°50E 259 G3
Dobandi Pakistan 31°13N 66°50E 242 D2
Dobbiaco Italy 46°44N 12°14E 199 B9
Dobbyn Australia 19°44S 140°2E 280 B3
Dobczyce Poland 49°52N 20°5E 185 J7
Dobele Latvia 56°37N 23°16E 184 B10
Dobele □ Latvia 56°35N 23°5E 184 B10
Döbeln Germany 51°6N 13°7E 178 D9
Doberai, Jazirah Indonesia 1°25S 133°0E 231 E8
Döberitz Germany 52°32N 13°3E 115 A1
Dobiegniew Poland 52°59N 15°45E 185 F2
Doblas Argentina 37°5S 64°0W 334 D3
Döbling Austria 48°14N 16°20E 142 A2
Dobo Dem. Rep. of the Congo 2°20N 22°11E 264 B4
Dobo Indonesia 5°45S 134°15E 231 F8
Doboj Bos.-H. 44°46N 18°4E 182 F3
Dobong S. Korea 37°39N 127°2E 137 B2
Dobongsan S. Korea 37°40N 127°0E 137 A2
Dobra Wielkopolskie, Poland 51°55N 18°37E 185 G5
Dobra Zachodnio-Pomorskie, Poland 53°34N 15°20E 184 E2
Dobra Dâmbovita, Romania 44°52N 25°40E 183 F10
Dobra Hunedoara, Romania 45°54N 22°36E 182 E7
Dobre Miasto Poland 53°58N 20°26E 184 E7
Dobreşti Romania 46°51N 22°18E 182 D7
Dobrich Bulgaria 43°37N 27°49E 203 C11
Dobrinishta Bulgaria 41°49N 23°34E 202 E7
Dobříš Czech Rep. 49°46N 14°10E 180 B7
Dobrodzień Poland 50°45N 18°25E 185 H5
Dobromyl Ukraine 49°34N 22°46E 185 J9
Dobron Ukraine 48°25N 22°23E 182 B7
Dobropole Ukraine 48°25N 37°2E 189 H9
Dobrovolsk Russia 54°46N 22°31E 184 D9
Dobruja Europe 44°30N 28°15E 183 F13
Dobrush Belarus 52°25N 31°22E 177 B16
Dobrzany Poland 53°22N 15°25E 184 E2
Dobrzyń nad Wisłą Poland 52°39N 19°22E 185 F6
Doc, Mui Vietnam 17°58N 106°30E 236 D6
Doc Can I. Phil. 5°55N 119°56E 233 J2
Doce ➔ Brazil 19°37S 39°49W 333 E4
Docker River = Kaltukatjara Australia 24°52S 129°5E 279 D4
Docklands U.K. 51°30N 0°1W 125 A3
Docksta Sweden 63°3N 18°18E 162 A12
Doctor Arroyo Mexico 23°40N 100°11W 318 C4
Doctor Phillips U.S.A. 28°26N 81°29W 133 B2
Doctors Inlet U.S.A. 30°6N 81°47W 316 E8
Doda India 33°10N 75°34E 243 C6
Doda, L. Canada 49°25N 75°13W 298 C4
Doda Betta India 11°24N 76°44E 245 J3
Dodballapur India 13°18N 77°32E 245 H3
Dodder ➔ Ireland 53°20N 6°13W 120 B1
Dodecanese Greece 36°35N 27°0E 205 E8
Dodekanisa = Dodecanese Greece 36°35N 27°0E 205 E8
Dodekanisa □ Greece 36°35N 27°0E 205 E8
Dodge City U.S.A. 37°45N 100°1W 308 G3
Dodge L. Canada 59°50N 105°36W 297 B7
Dodger Stadium U.S.A. 34°4N 118°14W 126 B3
Dodgeville U.S.A. 42°58N 90°8W 310 B6
Dodo Cameroon 7°30N 12°3E 263 D7
Dodo Sudan 5°10N 29°57E 257 F2
Dodola Ethiopia 6°59N 39°11E 257 F4
Dodoma Tanzania 6°8S 35°45E 268 D4
Dodoma □ Tanzania 6°0S 36°0E 268 D4
Dodoni Greece 39°40N 20°46E 204 B2
Dodori ⌓ Kenya 1°55S 41°7E 268 C5
Dodsland Canada 51°50N 108°45W 297 C7
Dodson U.S.A. 48°24N 108°15W 304 B9
Dodurga Turkey 39°49N 29°57E 205 B11
Doerun U.S.A. 31°19N 83°55W 316 D6
Doesburg Neths. 52°1N 6°9E 170 B6
Doetinchem Neths. 51°59N 6°18E 170 C6
Dog Creek Canada 51°35N 122°14W 296 C4
Dog I. U.S.A. 29°48N 84°36W 316 F5
Dog L. Man., Canada 51°2N 98°31W 297 C9
Dog L. Ont., Canada 48°48N 89°30W 298 C2
Doğankent Turkey 36°52N 35°18E 250 B6
Doğanşehir Turkey 38°5N 37°53E 212 C7
Dogliani Italy 44°32N 7°56E 198 D4
Dōgo Japan 36°15N 133°16E 222 A5
Dōgo-San Japan 35°2N 133°13E 222 B5
Dogondoutchi Niger 13°38N 4°2E 263 C5
Dogran Pakistan 31°48N 73°35E 242 D5
Dogs, Isle of U.K. 51°29N 0°1W 125 B3
Doğubayazıt Turkey 39°31N 44°5E 213 C11
Doguéraoua Niger 14°0N 5°31E 263 C6
Dogura Papua N. G. 10°6S 150°5E 286 F6
Doha = Ad Dawḩah Qatar 25°15N 51°35E 247 E6
Dohazari Bangla. 22°10N 92°5E 241 D4
Dohinog = Manukan Phil. 8°32N 123°12E 233 G4
Dohrighat India 26°16N 83°31E 243 F10
Dohrn Banke Greenland 65°55N 25°50W 154 D8
Doi Indonesia 2°14N 127°49E 231 D7
Doi Inthanon △ Thailand 18°33N 98°34E 236 C2
Doi Khuntan △ Thailand 18°33N 99°14E 236 C2
Doi Luang Thailand 18°30N 101°0E 236 C3
Doi Luang △ Thailand 19°22N 99°35E 236 C2
Doi Saket Thailand 18°52N 99°9E 236 C2
Doi Suthep △ Thailand 18°49N 98°53E 236 C2
Dois Irmãos, Sa. Brazil 9°0S 42°30W 332 C3
Dojransko Jezero Macedonia 41°13N 22°44E 202 E6
Dokka Norway 60°49N 10°7E 164 D7
Dokka ➔ Norway 60°49N 10°7E 164 D7
Dokkum Neths. 53°20N 5°59E 170 A5
Dokos Greece 37°20N 23°20E 204 D5
Dokri Pakistan 27°25N 68°7E 242 F3
Dokshukino = Nartkala Russia 43°33N 43°51E 191 J6
Dokuchayevsk Ukraine 47°44N 37°40E 189 J9
Dol-de-Bretagne France 48°34N 1°47W 172 D5
Dolac Serbia 42°36N 20°36E 202 D4
Dolak, Pulau Indonesia 8°0S 138°30E 231 F9
Dolban = Liman Russia 45°45N 47°12E 191 H8
Dolbeau-Mistassini Canada 48°53N 72°14W 299 C5
Dole France 47°7N 5°31E 173 E12
Doleib, Wadi ➔ Sudan 12°10N 33°15E 257 E3
Dolenji Logatec Slovenia 45°56N 14°15E 199 C11
Dolgellau U.K. 52°45N 3°53W 168 E4
Dolgelley = Dolgellau U.K. 52°45N 3°53W 168 E4
Dolgoe Ozero Russia 60°0N 30°15E 137 A1
Dolhasca Romania 47°26N 26°36E 183 C11
Doliana Greece 39°54N 20°32E 204 B2
Dolianova Italy 39°22N 9°10E 200 C2
Dolinskaya = Dolynska Ukraine 48°6N 32°46E 189 H7
Dolj □ Romania 44°10N 23°30E 183 F8
Doll Museum Delhi, India 120 b3
Dollard Neths. 53°20N 7°10E 170 A7
Dollis Hill U.K. 51°33N 0°13W 125 A2
Dollymount Ireland 53°22N 6°11W 120 A2
Dolna Banya Bulgaria 42°18N 23°44E 202 D7
Dolni Czech Rep. 50°2N 14°33E 135 B3
Dolni Chabry Czech Rep. 50°8N 14°26E 135 B2
Dolni Chiflik Bulgaria 42°59N 27°43E 203 D11
Dolni Dŭbnik Bulgaria 43°24N 24°26E 203 C8
Dolni Počernice Czech Rep. 50°5N 14°34E 135 B3
Dolnośląskie □ Poland 51°10N 16°30E 185 G3
Dolný Kubín Slovak Rep. 49°12N 19°18E 181 B12
Dolo Ethiopia 4°11N 42°3E 257 G5
Dolo Italy 45°25N 12°5E 199 C9
Dolomites = Dolomiti Italy 46°23N 11°51E 199 B8
Dolomiti Italy 46°23N 11°51E 199 B8
Dolomiti Bellunesi △ Italy 46°10N 12°5E 199 B9
Dolores Argentina 36°20S 57°40W 334 D4
Dolores Phil. 12°2N 125°29E 232 E5
Dolores Uruguay 33°34S 58°15W 334 C4
Dolores Colo., U.S.A. 37°28N 108°30W 305 H9
Dolores ➔ U.S.A. 38°49N 109°17W 304 G9
Dolovo Serbia 44°55N 20°52E 182 F5
Dolphin, C. Falk. Is. 51°10S 59°0W 153 f
Dolphin and Union Str. Canada 69°5N 114°45W 294 C8
Dolphin Head Jamaica 18°22N 78°10W 320 a
Dolphin I. Jamaica 17°48N 77°10W 320 a
Dolphins Barn Ireland 53°20N 6°17W 120 B2
Dolsk Poland 51°59N 17°3E 185 G4
Dolton U.S.A. 41°38N 87°36W 311 C9
Dolungmukh India 27°30N 94°18E 241 B5
Dolyna Ukraine 48°58N 24°1E 183 B9
Dolynska Ukraine 48°6N 32°46E 189 H7
Dolynske Ukraine 47°32N 29°55E 183 C14
Dolzhanskaya Russia 46°37N 37°48E 189 J9
Dom Joaquim Brazil 18°57S 43°16W 333 E3
Dom Pedrito Brazil 31°0S 54°40W 335 C5
Dom Pedro Brazil 4°59S 44°27W 332 B3
Dom Pedro II, Parque Brazil 23°33S 46°36W 137 B2
Doma = Gombe Nigeria 10°19N 11°2E 263 C7
Doma Nigeria 8°25N 8°18E 263 D6
Doma ⌓ Zimbabwe 16°28S 30°12E 269 F3
Domadare Somali Rep. 1°52N 41°15E 267 D5
Domain, The Sydney, Australia 139 b2
Domaniç Turkey 39°48N 29°36E 205 B11
Domar, E. ➔ Chad 18°11N 18°4E 259 E3
Domariaganj ➔ India 26°17N 83°44E 243 F10
Domasi Malawi 15°15S 35°22E 269 F4
Domažlice Czech Rep. 49°28N 12°58E 180 B5
Dombarovka = Dombarovskiy Russia 50°46N 59°32E 214 D6
Dombarovskiy Russia 50°46N 59°32E 214 D6
Dombås Norway 62°4N 9°8E 164 B6
Dombasle-sur-Meurthe France 48°38N 6°21E 173 D13
Dombes France 45°58N 5°0E 175 C9
Dombóvár Hungary 46°21N 18°9E 182 D3
Dombrád Hungary 48°13N 21°54E 182 B6
Dombrova = Dąbrowa Górnicza Poland 50°15N 19°10E 185 H6
Dombrowitsa = Dubrovytsya Ukraine 51°31N 26°35E 177 C14
Dome Argus Antarctica 80°50S 76°30E 151 E12
Dome C. Antarctica 75°12S 123°37E 151 D17
Dome Fuji Antarctica 77°20S 39°45E 151 D5
Dome of the Rock Jerusalem 123 b3
Domel I. = Letsôk-aw Kyun Burma 11°30N 98°25E 237 G2
Domérat France 46°21N 2°32E 173 F9
Domett N.Z. 42°53S 173°12E 285 C8
Domeyko Chile 29°0S 71°0W 334 B1
Domeyko, Cordillera Chile 24°30S 69°0W 334 A2
Domfront France 48°37N 0°40W 172 D6
Dominador Chile 24°21S 69°20W 334 A2
Dominica ■ W. Indies 15°20N 61°20W 321 C7
Dominica Passage W. Indies 15°10N 61°20W 321 C7
Dominican Rep. ■ W. Indies 19°0N 70°30W 321 C5
Dominion Centre Toronto, Canada 141 b2
Domiongo Dem. Rep. of the Congo 4°37S 21°15E 265 C4
Dömitz Germany 53°8N 11°15E 178 B7
Domme France 44°48N 1°12E 174 D5
Domneşti Romania 45°12N 24°50E 183 E9
Domo Ethiopia 7°50N 47°10E 267 C6
Domodóssola Italy 46°7N 8°17E 198 B5
Domogled-Valea Cernei △ Romania 44°52N 22°27E 182 F7
Domokos Greece 39°10N 22°18E 204 B4
Domoni Comoros Is. 12°15S 44°32E 272 a
Dompaire France 48°14N 6°14E 173 D13
Dompierre-sur-Besbre France 46°31N 3°41E 173 F10
Dompim Ghana 5°10N 2°5W 262 D4
Dompu Indonesia 8°32S 118°28E 235 F5
Domrémy-la-Pucelle France 48°26N 5°40E 173 D12
Domvena Greece 38°15N 22°59E 204 C4
Domville, Mt. Australia 28°1S 151°15E 281 D5
Domžale Slovenia 46°9N 14°35E 199 B11
Don ➔ India 16°20N 76°15E 245 F3
Don ➔ Russia 47°4N 39°18E 189 J10
Don ➔ Aberds., U.K. 57°11N 2°5W 167 D6
Don ➔ S. Yorks., U.K. 53°41N 0°52W 168 D7
Don, C. Australia 11°18S 131°46E 278 B5
Don Benito Spain 38°53N 5°51W 195 G5
Don Mills Canada 43°44N 79°21W 141 A2
Don Muang Int. ✈ (BKK) Thailand 13°53N 100°36E 113 A2
Don Sak Thailand 9°18N 99°41E 237 b
Dona Ana = Nhamaabué Mozam. 17°25S 35°5E 269 F4
Doña Mencía Spain 37°33N 4°21W 195 H6
Donaghadee U.K. 54°39N 5°33W 166 B6
Donaghmede Ireland 53°23N 6°9W 120 A3
Donaghmore Ireland 52°52N 7°36W 166 D4
Donald Australia 36°23S 143°0E 282 D5
Donaldsonville U.S.A. 30°6N 90°59W 314 F9
Donalsonville U.S.A. 31°3N 84°53W 316 D5
Doñana △ Spain 36°59N 6°23W 195 J4
Donau = Dunărea ➔ Europe 45°20N 29°40E 183 E14
Donau ➔ Austria 48°10N 17°0E 181 C10
Donau Auen △ Austria 48°8N 16°44E 181 C9
Donau-Oder Kanal Austria 48°12N 16°32E 142 A3
Donaueschingen Germany 47°56N 8°29E 179 H4
Donaufeld Austria 48°15N 16°24E 142 A2
Donaupark Austria 48°14N 16°24E 142 A2
Donaustadt Austria 48°13N 16°29E 142 A2
Donauwörth Germany 48°43N 10°47E 179 G6
Doncaster U.K. 53°32N 1°6W 168 D6
Dondo Angola 9°45S 14°25E 265 D2
Dondo Dem. Rep. of the Congo 4°11N 21°39E 264 B4
Dondo Mozam. 19°33S 34°46E 269 F3
Dondo, Teluk Indonesia 0°50N 120°30E 231 D6
Dondra Head Sri Lanka 5°55N 80°40E 245 M5
Donduşeni Moldova 48°14N 27°36E 183 B12
Donegal Ireland 54°39N 8°5W 166 B3
Donegal □ Ireland 54°53N 8°0W 166 B4
Donegal B. Ireland 54°31N 8°49W 166 B3
Donets ➔ Russia 47°33N 40°55E 191 G5
Donets Basin Ukraine 49°0N 38°0E 158 F13
Donetsk Ukraine 48°0N 37°45E 189 J9
Donetsk □ Ukraine 47°30N 37°50E 189 J9
Dong Ba Thin Vietnam 12°8N 109°13E 237 F7
Dong Dang Vietnam 21°54N 106°42E 228 G6
Dong Giam Vietnam 19°25N 105°31E 236 C5
Dong Ha Vietnam 16°55N 107°8E 236 D6
Dong Hene Laos 16°40N 105°18E 236 D5
Dong Hoi Vietnam 17°29N 106°36E 236 D6
Dong Jiang ➔ China 23°6N 114°0E 229 F10
Dong Khe Vietnam 22°26N 106°27E 236 A6
Dong Ujimqin Qi China 45°32N 116°55E 226 B9
Dong Van Vietnam 23°16N 105°22E 236 A5
Dong Xoai Vietnam 11°32N 106°55E 237 G6
Donga Nigeria 7°45N 10°2E 263 D7
Donga ➔ Nigeria 8°20N 9°58E 263 D7
Dong'an China 26°23N 111°12E 229 D8
Dongan Hills U.S.A. 40°35N 74°5W 132 C1
Dongara Australia 29°14S 114°57E 279 E1
Dongargarh India 21°10N 80°40E 244 D5
Dongbei China 45°0N 125°0E 227 D13
Dongcheng China 39°54N 116°23E 114 B2
Dongchuan China 26°8N 103°1E 228 D4
Dongdaemung S. Korea 37°34N 127°2E 137 B2
Dongducheon S. Korea 37°54N 127°3E 224 F7
Donges France 47°18N 2°4W 172 E4
Dongfang China 18°50N 108°33E 236 C7
Dongfeng China 42°40N 125°34E 224 C2
Donggala Indonesia 0°30S 119°40E 231 E5
Donggan China 23°22N 105°9E 228 F5
Donggou China 39°52N 124°10E 227 E13
Dongguan China 22°58N 113°44E 229 F9
Dongguang China 37°50N 116°30E 226 F9
Donghae S. Korea 37°29N 129°7E 224 D4
Donghai Dao China 21°0N 110°15E 229 G8
Dongjak S. Korea 37°30N 126°56E 137 B1
Dongjiao China 23°5N 113°12E 121 B2
Dongjingcheng China 44°5N 129°10E 227 B15
Dongkou China 27°6N 110°35E 229 D8
Donglan China 24°30N 107°21E 228 E6
Dongliu China 30°13N 116°55E 229 B11
Dongmen China 22°20N 107°48E 228 F6
Dongnae S. Korea 35°12N 129°5E 224 E4
Dongning China 44°2N 131°5E 227 B16
Dongnyi China 28°3N 100°15E 228 C3
Dongo Angola 14°36S 15°48E 265 E3
Dongobe Dem. Rep. of the Congo 4°35N 23°13E 264 B4
Dongola Sudan 19°9N 30°22E 256 D3
Dongou Congo 2°0N 18°5E 264 B3
Dongping China 35°55N 116°20E 226 G9
Dongri India 18°53N 72°57E 130 B2
Dongsha Dao China 20°45N 116°43E 229 G11
Dongshan China 23°43N 117°30E 229 F11
Dongshanhu Park China 23°7N 113°17E 121 B2
Dongsheng China 39°50N 110°0E 226 E6
Dongtai China 32°51N 120°21E 227 H11
Dongting Hu China 29°18N 112°45E 229 C9
Dongtou China 27°51N 121°10E 229 D13
Dongwe ➔ Zambia 13°59S 23°53E 265 E4
Dongxiang China 28°11N 116°34E 229 C11
Dongxing China 21°34N 108°0E 228 G7
Dongyang China 29°13N 120°15E 229 C13
Dongzhi China 30°9N 117°0E 229 B11
Dongzhimen China 39°56N 116°25E 114 B2
Donington, C. Australia 34°45S 136°0E 282 C2
Doniphan U.S.A. 36°37N 90°50W 308 G8
Donja Stubica Croatia 45°59N 15°59E 199 C12
Donji Dušnik Serbia 43°12N 22°5E 202 C6
Donji Miholjac Croatia 45°45N 18°10E 182 E3
Donji Milanovac Serbia 44°28N 22°6E 202 B6
Donji Vakuf Bos.-H. 44°8N 17°24E 182 F2
Dønna Nordland, Norway 66°6N 12°30E 160 C15
Donna Tex., U.S.A. 26°9N 98°4W 314 H5
Donnacona Canada 46°41N 71°41W 299 C5
Donnelly's Crossing N.Z. 35°42S 173°38E 284 B2
Donnybrook W. Austral., Australia 33°34S 115°48E 279 F2
Donnybrook Dublin, Ireland 53°19N 6°14W 120 B2
Donnybrook KwaZulu Natal, S. Africa 29°59S 29°48E 271 C4
Donora U.S.A. 40°11N 79°52W 312 F5
Donostia = Donostia-San Sebastián Spain 43°17N 1°58W 196 B3
Donostia-San Sebastián Spain 43°17N 1°58W 196 B3
Donousa Greece 37°8N 25°48E 205 D7
Donovan U.S.A. 40°53N 87°37W 311 D9
Donque Angola 15°28S 14°6E 265 F2
Donskoy Russia 53°55N 38°15E 188 F10
Donsol Phil. 12°54N 123°36E 232 E4
Donzère France 44°28N 4°43E 175 D8
Donzy France 47°20N 3°6E 173 E10
Dookie Australia 36°20S 145°41E 283 D6
Doon ➔ U.K. 55°27N 4°39W 167 F4
Doornfontein S. Africa 26°11S 28°3E 123 B2
Doornik = Tournai Belgium 50°35N 3°25E 170 D3
Dora, L. Australia 22°0S 123°0E 278 D3
Dora Báltea ➔ Italy 45°11N 8°3E 198 C5
Dora Ripária ➔ Italy 45°5N 7°44E 198 C4
Doran L. Canada 61°13N 108°6W 297 A7
Doraville U.S.A. 33°54N 84°17W 316 B5
Dorchester Dorset, U.K. 50°42N 2°27W 169 G5
Dorchester Mass., U.S.A. 42°17N 71°4W 116 B2
Dorchester, C. Canada 65°27N 77°27W 295 C12
Dorchester B. U.S.A. 42°18N 71°1W 116 B2
Dorchester Heights Nat. Historical Site ⌓ U.S.A. 42°20N 71°2W 116 B2
Dordabis Namibia 22°52S 17°38E 270 B2
Dordogne □ France 45°5N 0°40E 174 C4
Dordogne ➔ France 45°2N 0°36W 174 C3
Dordrecht Neths. 51°48N 4°39E 170 C4
Dordrecht Eastern Cape, S. Africa 31°20S 27°3E 270 D4
Dore ➔ France 45°50N 3°35E 174 C7
Dore, Mts. France 45°32N 2°50E 174 C6
Doré L. Canada 54°46N 107°17W 297 C7
Dorée ➔ St. Lucia 13°46N 61°3W 323 m
Dores da Boa Esperança = Boa Esperança Brazil 3°21N 61°23W 329 C5
Dores do Indaiá Brazil 19°27S 45°36W 333 E2
Dorfen Germany 48°15N 12°8E 179 G8
Dorgali Italy 40°17N 9°35E 200 B2
Dori Burkina Faso 14°3N 0°2W 263 C4
Doring ➔ S. Africa 31°54S 18°39E 270 D2
Doringbos S. Africa 31°59S 19°16E 270 D2
Dorking U.K. 51°14N 0°19W 169 F7
Dormaa-Ahenkro Ghana 7°15N 2°52W 262 D4
Dormans France 49°4N 3°38E 173 C10
Dormo, Ras Eritrea 13°14N 42°35E 257 E5
Dornach Germany 48°9N 11°41E 131 B3
Dornakal India 17°27N 80°10E 244 F5
Dornbirn Austria 47°25N 9°45E 180 D2
Dornes France 46°48N 3°18E 173 F10
Dorneşti Romania 47°52N 26°1E 183 C11
Dornie U.K. 57°17N 5°31W 167 D3
Dornoch U.K. 57°53N 4°2W 167 D4
Dornoch Firth U.K. 57°51N 4°4W 167 D4
Dornogovĭ □ Mongolia 44°0N 110°0E 226 C6
Doro Mali 16°9N 0°51W 263 B4
Doro, Kavo Greece 38°9N 24°38E 204 C6
Dorog Hungary 47°42N 18°45E 182 C3
Dorogobuzh Russia 54°50N 33°18E 188 E7
Dorohoi Romania 47°56N 26°23E 183 C11
Döröö Nuur Mongolia 48°0N 93°0E 217 C12
Dorpat = Tartu Estonia 58°20N 26°44E 188 C4
Dorr Iran 33°17N 50°38E 247 C6
Dorre I. Australia 25°13S 113°12E 279 E1
Dorrigo Australia 30°20S 152°44E 283 A10
Dorrigo △ Australia 30°22S 152°47E 283 A10
Dorris U.S.A. 41°58N 121°55W 304 F3
Dorset Ont., Canada 45°14N 78°54W 312 A6
Dorset Ohio, U.S.A. 41°40N 80°40W 312 E4
Dorset □ U.K. 50°45N 2°26W 169 G5
Dorsten Germany 51°40N 6°58E 178 D2
Dortmund Germany 51°30N 7°28E 178 D3
Dortmund-Ems-Kanal ➔ Germany 51°50N 7°26E 178 D3
Dörtyol Turkey 36°50N 36°13E 250 B7
Doruk Turkey 36°53N 35°45E 250 B6
Dorum Germany 53°41N 8°34E 178 B4
Doruma Dem. Rep. of the Congo 4°42N 27°33E 268 B2
Dorūneh Iran 35°10N 57°18E 247 C8
Dorval Int., Montréal ✈ (YUL) Canada 45°28N 73°44W 130 B1
Dos Bahías, C. Argentina 44°58S 65°32W 336 B3
Dos Couros ➔ Brazil 23°37S 46°34W 137 C2
Dos d'Âne Réunion 20°58S 55°23E 272 f
Dos Hermanas Spain 37°16N 5°55W 195 H5
Dos Moninos ➔ Brazil 23°40S 46°33W 137 C2
Dos Palos U.S.A. 36°59N 120°37W 306 J6
Döşemealtı Turkey 37°4N 30°36E 205 D12
Dosso Niger 13°0N 3°13E 263 C5
Dosso □ Niger 13°30N 3°30E 263 C5
Dosso ⌓ Niger 12°36N 2°36E 263 C5
Dot Lake U.S.A. 63°40N 144°4W 303 E11
Dothan U.S.A. 31°13N 85°24W 316 D4
Doty U.S.A. 46°38N 123°17W 306 D3
Douai France 50°21N 3°4E 173 B10
Douako Guinea 9°45N 10°8W 262 D2
Douala Cameroon 4°0N 9°45E 263 E6
Douala-Édéa ⌓ Cameroon 3°20N 9°41E 264 B1
Douamenog, C. Mayotte 12°38S 45°8E 272 b
Douaouir Mali 20°45N 3°0W 260 D4
Douarnenez France 48°6N 4°21W 172 D2
Doubabougou Mali 14°13N 7°59W 262 C3
Double Cone N.Z. 45°4S 168°49E 285 F3
Double Island Pt. Australia 25°56S 153°11E 281 D5
Double Mountain Fork ➔ U.S.A. 33°16N 100°0W 314 E4
Doubrava ➔ Czech Rep. 50°2N 15°20E 180 A8
Doubs □ France 47°10N 6°20E 173 E13
Doubs ➔ France 46°53N 5°1E 173 F12
Doubtful Sd. N.Z. 45°20S 166°49E 285 F1
Doubtless B. N.Z. 34°55S 173°26E 284 A2
Doudeville France 49°43N 0°47E 172 C7
Doué-la-Fontaine France 47°11N 0°16W 172 E6
Douentza Mali 14°58N 2°48W 262 C4
Douentza ⌓ Mali 15°40N 2°25W 262 B4
Dougga Tunisia 36°25N 9°13E 258 A1
Doughboy B. N.Z. 47°2S 167°40E 285 H2
Douglas I. of Man 54°10N 4°28W 168 C3
Douglas Northern Cape, S. Africa 29°4S 23°46E 270 C3
Douglas Alaska, U.S.A. 58°17N 134°24W 303 G14
Douglas Ariz., U.S.A. 31°21N 109°33W 305 L9
Douglas Ga., U.S.A. 31°31N 82°51W 316 D7
Douglas Mich., U.S.A. 42°39N 86°14W 311 B10
Douglas Wyo., U.S.A. 42°45N 105°24W 304 E11
Douglas Apsley △ Australia 41°45S 148°11E 281 G4
Douglas B. Dominica 15°36N 61°29W 323 k
Douglas C. U.S.A. 58°51N 153°15W 303 G9
Douglas Chan. Canada 53°40N 129°20W 296 C3
Douglas Park U.S.A. 41°51N 87°42W 119 B2
Douglas Pt. Canada 44°19N 81°37W 312 B3
Douglasville U.S.A. 33°45N 84°45W 316 B5
Douirat Morocco 33°2N 4°11W 260 B4
Doukaton, Akra Greece 38°34N 20°33E 207 B2
Doukoula Cameroon 10°10N 15°0E 259 F2
Doulevant-le-Château France 48°23N 4°55E 173 D11
Doullens France 50°10N 2°20E 173 B9
Doumé Cameroon 4°15N 13°25E 264 B2
Doumen China 22°10N 113°18E 229 F9
Douna Mali 13°13N 6°0W 262 C3
Dounguila Congo 2°53S 11°58E 264 C2
Dounreay U.K. 58°35N 3°44W 167 C5
Dourada, Serra Brazil 13°10S 48°45W 333 D2
Dourados Brazil 22°9S 54°50W 335 A5
Dourados ➔ Brazil 21°58S 54°18W 335 A5
Dourados, Serra dos Brazil 23°30S 53°30W 335 A5
Dourbali Chad 11°49N 15°52E 259 F3
Dourdan France 48°30N 2°1E 173 D9
Douro ➔ Europe 41°8N 8°40W 194 D2
Douvaine France 46°19N 6°16E 173 F13
Douville Guadeloupe 16°15N 61°22W 322 e
Douvres-la-Délivrande France 49°17N 0°23W 172 C6

Douz *Tunisia* 33°25N 9°0E **258** B1
Douze → *France* 43°54N 0°30W **174** E3
Dove → *U.K.* 52°51N 1°36W **168** E6
Dove Creek *U.S.A.* 37°46N 108°54W **305** H9
Dover *Tas., Australia* 43°18S 147°2E **281** G4
Dover *Kent, U.K.* 51°7N 1°19E **169** F9
Dover *Del., U.S.A.* 39°10N 75°32W **309** F16
Dover *Ky., U.S.A.* 38°43N 83°52W **311** F13
Dover *N.H., U.S.A.* 43°12N 70°56W **313** C14
Dover *N.J., U.S.A.* 40°53N 74°34W **313** F10
Dover *Ohio, U.S.A.* 40°32N 81°29W **312** F3
Dover, Pt. *Australia* 32°32S 125°32E **279** F4
Dover, Str. of *Europe* 51°0N 1°30E **169** G9
Dover-Foxcroft *U.S.A.* 45°11N 69°13W **309** C19
Dover Heights *Australia* 33°52S 151°16E **139** B2
Dover Plains *U.S.A.* 41°43N 73°35W **313** E11
Dovey = Dyfi → *U.K.* 52°32N 4°3W **169** E3
Dovhe *Ukraine* 48°22N 23°17E **183** B8
Dovlen = Devin *Bulgaria* 41°44N 24°24E **203** E8
Dovre *Norway* 61°58N 9°15E **164** C6
Dovrefjell *Norway* 62°15N 9°33E **164** B6
Dovrefjell △ *Norway* 62°20N 9°25E **164** B6
Dow Rūd *Iran* 33°28N 49°4E **247** C6
Dowa *Malawi* 13°38S 33°58E **269** E3
Dowagiac *U.S.A.* 41°59N 86°6W **311** C10
Dowerin *Australia* 31°12S 117°2E **279** F2
Dowgha'i *Iran* 36°54N 58°32E **247** B8
Dowlat Yār *Afghan.* 34°30N 65°45E **240** B2
Dowlatābād *Farāh, Afghan.* 32°47N 62°40E **240** B1
Dowlatābād *Fāryāb, Afghan.* 36°26N 64°55E **240** A2
Dowlatābād *Kermān, Iran* 28°20N 56°40E **247** D8
Dowlatābād *Tehrān, Iran* 35°38N 51°27E **141** B2
Dowling Park *U.S.A.* 30°15N 83°15W **316** E6
Down □ *U.K.* 54°23N 6°2W **166** B5
Down, L. *U.S.A.* 28°30N 81°31W **133** A1
Downers Grove *U.S.A.* 41°48N 88°1W **311** C8
Downey *Calif., U.S.A.* 33°56N 118°9W **126** C4
Downey *Idaho, U.S.A.* 42°26N 112°7W **304** E7
Downham Market *U.K.* 52°37N 0°23E **169** E8
Downieville *U.S.A.* 39°34N 120°50W **306** F6
Downing *U.S.A.* 40°29N 92°22W **310** D4
Downpatrick *U.K.* 54°20N 5°43W **166** B6
Downpatrick Hd. *Ireland* 54°20N 9°21W **166** B2
Downsview *Canada* 43°43N 79°30W **141** A1
Downsview C.A.F.B. ✈ *Canada* 43°43N 79°29W **141** A2
Downsville *U.S.A.* 42°5N 75°0W **313** D10
Downton, Mt. *Canada* 52°42N 124°52W **296** C4
Downtown *Montréal, Canada* **130** c2
Downtown *Toronto, Canada* **141** b3
Dowsārī *Iran* 28°25N 57°59E **247** D8
Dowshī *Afghan.* 35°35N 68°43E **240** B3
Doxato *Greece* 41°9N 24°16E **203** E8
Doyle *U.S.A.* 40°2N 120°6W **306** E6
Doylestown *U.S.A.* 40°21N 75°10W **313** F9
Dōzen *Japan* 36°5N 133°5E **222** A5
Dozois, Rés. *Canada* 47°30N 77°5W **298** C4
Dra Khel *Pakistan* 27°58N 66°45E **242** F2
Drâa, C. *Morocco* 28°47N 11°0W **260** C2
Drâa, Hamada du *Algeria* 28°0N 7°0W **260** C3
Drâa, Oued → *Morocco* 28°40N 11°10W **260** C2
Drac → *France* 45°12N 5°42E **175** C9
Dračevo *Macedonia* 41°56N 21°31E **202** E5
Drachten *Neths.* 53°7N 6°5E **170** A6
Drăgănești *Moldova* 47°43N 28°15E **183** C13
Drăgănești-Olt *Romania* 44°9N 24°32E **183** F9
Drăgănești-Vlașca *Romania* 44°5N 25°33E **183** F10
Dragaš *Serbia* 42°5N 20°41E **202** D4
Drăgășani *Romania* 44°39N 24°17E **183** F9
Dragichyn *Belarus* 52°15N 25°8E **177** B13
Dragocvet *Serbia* 43°58N 21°15E **202** C5
Dragon's Mouths = Boca de Drago *Venezuela* 11°0N 61°50W **323** t
Dragør *Denmark* 55°35N 12°38E **118** B3
Dragovishtitsa *Bulgaria* 42°22N 22°39E **202** D6
Draguignan *France* 43°32N 6°27E **175** E10
Drahove *Ukraine* 48°14N 23°33E **183** B8
Drain *U.S.A.* 43°40N 123°19W **304** E2
Drake *U.S.A.* 47°55N 100°23W **308** B3
Drake Passage *S. Ocean* 58°0S 68°0W **151** B17
Drakensberg *S. Africa* 31°0S 28°0E **271** D4
Drama *Greece* 41°9N 24°10E **203** E8
Drama □ *Greece* 41°20N 24°0E **203** E8
Dramburg = Drawsko Pomorskie *Poland* 53°35N 15°50E **184** E2
Drammen *Norway* 59°42N 10°12E **164** E7
Drancy *France* 48°55N 2°26E **134** A3
Dranesville *U.S.A.* 39°0N 77°20W **143** A1
Drangajökull *Iceland* 66°9N 22°15W **155** A4
Drangedal *Norway* 59°6N 9°3E **164** E6
Drangsnes *Iceland* 65°41N 21°27W **155** B5
Dranov, Ostrov *Romania* 44°55N 29°30E **183** F14
Drapetsona *Greece* 37°56N 23°37E **112** B1
Dras *India* 34°25N 75°48E **243** B6
Drastis, Akra *Greece* 39°48N 19°40E **206** B9
Drau = Drava → *Croatia* 45°33N 18°55E **182** E3
Drava → *Croatia* 45°33N 18°55E **182** E3
Dravograd *Slovenia* 46°36N 15°5E **199** B12
Drawa → *Poland* 52°52N 15°59E **185** F2
Drawieński △ *Poland* 53°6N 15°58E **185** E2
Drawno *Poland* 53°13N 15°46E **185** E2
Drawsko Pomorskie *Poland* 53°35N 15°50E **184** E2
Drayton Plains *U.S.A.* 42°41N 83°23W **311** B13
Drayton Valley *Canada* 53°12N 114°58W **296** C6
Dreieich *Germany* 50°1N 8°41E **179** E4
Dreikikir *Papua N. G.* 3°35S 142°46E **286** B2
Dreilinden *Germany* 52°24N 13°10E **115** B2
Dren *Serbia* 43°8N 20°46E **202** C4
Drenthe □ *Neths.* 52°52N 6°40E **170** B6
Drepano, Akra *Greece* 35°28N 24°14E **207** E5
Drepanum, C. *Cyprus* 34°54N 32°19E **207** F8
Dresden *Ont., Canada* 42°35N 82°11W **312** D2
Dresden *Sachsen, Germany* 51°3N 13°44E **178** D9
Dreux *France* 48°44N 1°23E **172** D8
Drevsjø *Norway* 61°53N 12°1E **164** C9
Drewnica *Poland* 52°18N 21°6E **142** B2
Drexel *U.S.A.* 39°45N 84°18W **311** E12
Drezdenko *Poland* 52°50N 15°49E **185** F2
Driesen = Drezdenko *Poland* 52°50N 15°49E **185** F2
Driffield *U.K.* 54°0N 0°26W **168** C7
Driftwood *U.S.A.* 41°20N 78°8W **312** E6
Driggs *U.S.A.* 43°44N 111°6W **304** E8
Drigh Road *Pakistan* 24°52N 67°7E **123** A2
Drimnagh *Ireland* 53°19N 6°19W **120** B2
Drin → *Albania* 42°1N 19°38E **202** D3
Drin i Zi → *Albania* 41°37N 20°28E **202** E4
Drina → *Bos.-H.* 44°53N 19°21E **202** B3
Drincea → *Romania* 44°20N 22°55E **182** F7
Drinjača → *Bos.-H.* 44°15N 19°8E **182** F4
Driopida *Greece* 37°25N 24°26E **204** D6
Drissa = Vyerkhnyadzvinsk *Belarus* 55°45N 27°58E **188** E4
Driva → *Norway* 62°41N 9°31E **164** B6
Drivstoggo *Norway* 62°26N 9°47E **164** B6
Drniš *Croatia* 43°51N 16°10E **199** E13
Drøbak *Norway* 59°39N 10°39E **164** E7
Drobeta-Turnu Severin *Romania* 44°39N 22°41E **182** F7
Drobin *Poland* 52°42N 19°58E **185** F6
Drochia *Moldova* 48°2N 27°48E **183** B12
Drogenbos *Belgium* 50°47N 4°19E **116** B1
Drogheda *Ireland* 53°43N 6°22W **166** C5
Drogichin = Dragichyn *Belarus* 52°15N 25°8E **177** B13
Drogobych = Drohobych *Ukraine* 49°20N 23°30E **185** J10
Drohiczyn *Poland* 52°24N 22°39E **185** F9
Drohobych *Ukraine* 49°20N 23°30E **185** J10
Droichead Atha = Drogheda *Ireland* 53°43N 6°22W **166** C5
Droichead Nua *Ireland* 53°11N 6°48W **166** C5
Droitwich *U.K.* 52°16N 2°8W **169** E5
Drôme □ *France* 44°38N 5°15E **175** D9
Drôme → *France* 44°46N 4°46E **175** D8
Dromedary, C. *Australia* 36°17S 150°10E **283** D9
Drómling ⌂ *Germany* 52°29N 11°5E **178** C7
Dromore *U.K.* 54°31N 7°28W **166** B4
Dromore West *Ireland* 54°15N 8°52W **166** B3
Dronero *Italy* 44°28N 7°22E **198** D4
Dronfield *U.K.* 53°19N 1°27W **168** D6
Dronne → *France* 45°2N 0°9W **174** C3
Dronning Ingrid Land *Greenland* 66°25N 52°5W **154** D5
Dronning Maud Land *Antarctica* 72°30S 12°0E **151** D3
Dronninglund *Denmark* 57°10N 10°19E **163** G4
Dronten *Neths.* 52°32N 5°43E **170** B5
Dropt → *France* 44°35N 0°6W **174** D3
Drosendorf *Austria* 48°52N 15°37E **180** C8
Drosh *Pakistan* 35°33N 71°48E **240** B3
Droué *France* 48°3N 1°6E **172** D8
Drouin *Australia* 38°10S 145°53E **283** E6
Druid Hills *U.S.A.* 33°47N 84°21W **113** B2
Drujba *Uzbekistan* 41°13N 61°18E **216** D6
Druk Yul = Bhutan ■ *Asia* 27°25N 90°30E **241** B3
Drum Towwer *Beijing, China* **114** a2
Drumbo *Canada* 43°16N 80°35W **312** C4
Drumcliff *Ireland* 54°20N 8°29W **166** B3
Drumcondra *Ireland* 53°21N 6°16W **120** A2
Drumheller *Canada* 51°25N 112°40W **296** C6
Drummond *U.S.A.* 46°40N 113°9W **304** C7
Drummond I. *U.S.A.* 46°1N 83°39W **309** B12
Drummond Pt. *Australia* 34°9S 135°16E **281** E2
Drummond Ra. *Australia* 23°45S 147°10E **280** C4
Drummondville *Canada* 45°55N 72°25W **298** C5
Drummoyne *Australia* 33°51S 151°8E **139** B1
Drumright *U.S.A.* 35°59N 96°36W **314** D6
Druskeniki = Druskininkai *Lithuania* 54°3N 23°58E **188** E2
Druskininkai *Lithuania* 54°3N 23°58E **188** E2
Drut → *Belarus* 53°8N 30°5E **177** B16
Druya *Belarus* 55°45N 27°28E **188** E4
Druzhba *Bulgaria* 43°15N 28°1E **203** C12
Druzhina *Russia* 68°14N 145°18E **215** C15
Drvar *Bos.-H.* 44°21N 16°23E **199** D13
Drvenik *Croatia* 43°27N 16°3E **199** E13
Drwęca → *Poland* 53°0N 18°42E **185** E5
Dry Harbour Mts. *Jamaica* 18°19N 77°24W **320** a
Dry Tortugas *U.S.A.* 24°38N 82°55W **315** F13
Dryanovo *Bulgaria* 42°59N 25°28E **203** D9
Dryden *Ont., Canada* 49°47N 92°50W **297** D10
Dryden *N.Y., U.S.A.* 42°30N 76°18W **313** D8
Drygalski I. *Antarctica* 66°0S 92°0E **151** C7
Drygalski Ice Tongue *Antarctica* 75°24S 163°30E **151** D21
Drylaw *U.K.* 55°58N 3°15W **121** B2
Drysdale → *Australia* 13°59S 126°51E **278** B4
Drysdale I. *Australia* 11°41S 136°0E **280** A2
Drysdale River △ *Australia* 14°56S 127°2E **278** B4
Drzewica *Poland* 51°27N 20°29E **185** G7
Drzewiczka → *Poland* 51°36N 20°36E **185** G7
Dschang *Cameroon* 5°32N 10°3E **263** D7
Du Gué → *Canada* 57°21N 70°45W **298** A5
Du He *China* 32°48N 110°40E **229** A8
Du Quoin *U.S.A.* 38°1N 89°14W **310** G7
Du'an *China* 23°59N 108°3E **228** F7
Duanesburg *U.S.A.* 42°45N 74°11W **313** D10
Duaringa *Australia* 23°42S 149°42E **280** C4
Duarte, Pico *Dom. Rep.* 19°2N 70°59W **321** C5
Ḍubā *Si. Arabia* 27°10N 35°40E **246** E2
Dubai = Dubayy *U.A.E.* 25°18N 55°20E **247** E7
Dubăsari *Moldova* 47°15N 29°10E **183** C14
Dubăsari Vdkhr. *Moldova* 47°30N 29°0E **183** C13
Dubawnt → *Canada* 64°33N 100°6W **297** A8
Dubawnt L. *Canada* 63°8N 101°28W **297** A8
Dubayy *U.A.E.* 25°18N 55°20E **247** E7
Dubbo *Australia* 32°11S 148°35E **283** B8
Dubeč *Czech Rep.* 50°3N 14°35E **135** B3
Dubele *Dem. Rep. of the Congo* 2°56N 29°35E **268** B2
Dübendorf *Switz.* 47°24N 8°37E **179** H4
Dubica *Croatia* 45°11N 16°48E **199** C13
Dublanc *Dominica* 15°31N 61°28W **323** k
Dublin *Dublin, Ireland* 53°21N 6°15W **120** A2
Dublin *Ga., U.S.A.* 32°32N 82°54W **316** C7
Dublin *Ohio, U.S.A.* 40°5N 83°7W **311** D13
Dublin *Tex., U.S.A.* 32°5N 98°21W **314** E5
Dublin □ *Ireland* 53°24N 6°20W **166** C5
Dublin ✈ (DUB) *Ireland* 53°26N 6°15W **120** A2
Dublin B. *Ireland* 53°19N 6°7W **120** B3
Dublin Castle *Dublin, Ireland* **120** c2
Dublin Harbour *Ireland* 53°21N 6°11W **120** A2
Dubna *Russia* 56°44N 37°10E **188** D9
Dubnica nad Váhom *Slovak Rep.* 48°58N 18°11E **181** C11
Dubno *Ukraine* 50°25N 25°45E **177** C13
Dubois *Idaho, U.S.A.* 44°10N 112°14W **304** D7
Dubois *Ind., U.S.A.* 38°27N 86°48W **311** F10
Dubois *Pa., U.S.A.* 41°7N 78°46W **312** E6
Dubossary = Dubăsari *Moldova* 47°15N 29°10E **183** C14
Dubossary Vdkhr. = Dubăsari Vdkhr. *Moldova* 47°30N 29°0E **183** C13
Dubove *Ukraine* 48°10N 23°53E **183** B8
Dubovka *Russia* 49°5N 44°50E **191** F7
Dubovskoye *Russia* 47°28N 42°46E **191** G6
Dubrajpur *India* 23°48N 87°25E **243** H12
Dubréka *Guinea* 9°46N 13°31W **262** D2
Dubrovitsa = Dubrovytsya *Ukraine* 51°31N 26°35E **177** C14
Dubrovnik *Croatia* 42°39N 18°6E **202** D2
Dubrovytsya *Ukraine* 51°31N 26°35E **177** C14
Dubulu *Dem. Rep. of the Congo* 4°18N 20°16E **264** B4
Dubuque *U.S.A.* 42°30N 90°41W **310** B6
Dubysa → *Lithuania* 55°5N 23°26E **184** C10
Duc de Gloucester, Îs. *French Polynesia* 20°38S 143°20W **289** f
Ducassous, Pte. *Martinique* 14°32N 60°50W **322** j
Duchang *China* 29°18N 116°12E **229** C11
Duchesne *U.S.A.* 40°10N 110°24W **304** F8
Duchess *Australia* 21°20S 139°50E **280** C2
Ducie I. *Pac. Oc.* 24°40S 124°48W **289** K15
Duck → *U.S.A.* 36°2N 87°52W **315** C11
Duck Cr. → *Australia* 22°37S 116°53E **278** D2
Duck Lake *Canada* 52°50N 106°16W **297** C7
Duck Mountain ⌂ *Canada* 51°45N 101°0W **297** C8
Duckwall, Mt. *U.S.A.* 37°58N 120°7W **306** H6
Ducos *Martinique* 14°33N 60°59W **322** j
Duda → *Colombia* 2°34N 74°3W **328** C3
Duddingston *U.K.* 55°56N 3°8W **121** B3
Duderstadt *Germany* 51°31N 10°15E **178** D6
Dudhi *India* 24°15N 83°10E **243** G10
Dudhnai *India* 25°59N 90°47E **241** C3
Dudinka *Russia* 69°30N 86°13E **215** C9
Dudley *W. Mids., U.K.* 52°31N 2°5W **169** E5
Dudley *Ga., U.S.A.* 32°32N 83°5W **316** C6
Dudna → *India* 19°17N 76°54E **244** E3
Dudo *Somali Rep.* 9°20N 50°12E **267** C7
Dudo, W. → *Somali Rep.* 9°14N 50°40E **267** C7
Dudub *Ethiopia* 6°55N 46°43E **267** C6
Dudwa *India* 28°30N 80°41E **243** E9
Dudwa △ *India* 28°30N 80°40E **243** E9
Duékoué *Ivory C.* 6°40N 7°15W **262** D3
Duenas *Phil.* 11°4N 122°37E **233** F4
Dueñas *Spain* 41°52N 4°33W **194** D6
Dueré *Brazil* 11°20S 49°17W **333** D2
Duero = Douro → *Europe* 41°8N 8°40W **194** D2
Duff Is. *Pac. Oc.* 9°50S 167°10E **277** B12
Dufftown *U.K.* 57°27N 3°8W **167** D5
Dufourspitz *Switz.* 45°56N 7°52E **179** K3
Dugger *U.S.A.* 39°4N 87°18W **311** E9
Dugi Otok *Croatia* 44°0N 15°3E **199** D11
Dugiuma *Somali Rep.* 1°15N 42°34E **267** D5
Dugnano *Italy* 45°33N 9°11E **129** A2
Dugo Selo *Croatia* 45°51N 16°18E **199** C13
Duida-Marahuaca △ *Venezuela* 3°33N 65°33W **328** C4
Duisburg *Germany* 51°26N 6°45E **178** D2
Duitama *Colombia* 5°50N 73°2W **328** B3
Duivendrecht *Neths.* 52°20N 4°55E **112** B2
Duiwelskloof = Modjadjiskloof *S. Africa* 23°42S 30°10E **271** B5
Dujiangyan *China* 31°2N 103°38E **228** B4
Duk Fadiat *Sudan* 7°45N 31°25E **257** F3
Duk Faiwil *Sudan* 7°30N 31°29E **257** F3
Dukat *Albania* 40°16N 19°32E **202** F3
Dūkdamīn *Iran* 35°59N 57°43E **247** C8
Dukelský Průsmyk *Slovak Rep.* 49°25N 21°42E **181** B14
Dukhān *Qatar* 25°25N 50°50E **247** E6
Dukhovshchina *Russia* 55°15N 32°27E **188** E7
Duki *Pakistan* 30°14N 68°25E **240** C3
Dukla *Poland* 49°30N 21°35E **185** J8
Duku *Bauchi, Nigeria* 10°43N 10°43E **263** C7
Duku *Sokoto, Nigeria* 11°11N 4°55E **263** C5
Dula *Dem. Rep. of the Congo* 4°40N 20°21E **264** B4
Dūlāb *Iran* 35°39N 51°27E **141** B2
Dulag *Phil.* 10°57N 125°2E **233** F5
Dulawan = Datu Piang *Phil.* 7°2N 124°30E **233** H5
Dulce *U.S.A.* 36°56N 107°0W **305** H10
Dulce → *Argentina* 30°32S 62°33W **334** C3
Dulce, G. *Costa Rica* 8°40N 83°20W **320** E3
Dulcina *Antigua & B.* 17°35N 61°49W **322** c
Dulf *Iraq* 35°7N 45°51E **246** C5
Dŭlgopol *Bulgaria* 43°3N 27°22E **203** C11
Duliu *China* 39°2N 116°55E **226** E9
Dullabchara *India* 24°30N 92°26E **241** C4
Dulles Int. ✈ (IAD) *Washington, D.C., U.S.A.* **143** B1
Dullewala *Pakistan* 31°50N 71°25E **242** D4
Dullstroom *S. Africa* 25°27S 30°7E **271** C5
Dülmen *Germany* 51°49N 7°17E **178** D3
Dulovo *Bulgaria* 43°48N 27°9E **203** C11
Dulpetorpet *Norway* 60°34N 12°19E **164** D9
Dulq Maghār *Syria* 36°22N 38°39E **213** D8
Duluth *Ga., U.S.A.* 34°0N 84°9W **316** A5
Duluth *Minn., U.S.A.* 46°47N 92°6W **308** B7
Dulwich *U.K.* 51°27N 0°5W **125** B3
Dum Dum *India* 22°39N 88°26E **124** B2
Dum Dum Int. ✈ (CCU) *India* 22°38N 88°26E **124** B2
Dum Duma *India* 27°40N 95°40E **241** B5
Dūmā *Syria* 33°34N 36°24E **250** E7
Dumaguete *Phil.* 9°17N 123°15E **233** G4
Dumai *Indonesia* 1°35N 101°28E **234** B2
Dumalinao *Phil.* 7°49N 123°23E **233** H4
Dumanguilas Bay *Phil.* 7°34N 123°4E **233** H4
Dumanjug *Phil.* 10°4N 123°26E **233** F4
Dumaran *Phil.* 10°33N 119°50E **233** F2
Dumaran I. *Phil.* 10°33N 119°51E **233** F2
Dumarao *Phil.* 11°16N 122°41E **233** F4
Dumas *Ark., U.S.A.* 33°53N 91°29W **314** E9
Dumas *Tex., U.S.A.* 35°52N 101°58W **314** D4
Ḍumayr *Syria* 33°39N 36°42E **250** E7
Dumbarton *U.K.* 55°57N 4°33W **167** F4
Dumbéa *N. Cal.* 22°10S 166°27E **288** d
Ďumbier *Slovak Rep.* 48°56N 19°38E **181** C12
Dumbleyung *Australia* 33°17S 117°42E **279** F2
Dumbo *Angola* 14°6S 17°24E **265** E3
Dumboa *Nigeria* 11°15N 12°55E **263** C7
Dumbrăveni *Romania* 46°14N 24°34E **183** D9
Dumfries *U.K.* 55°4N 3°37W **167** F5
Dumfries & Galloway □ *U.K.* 55°9N 3°58W **167** F5
Dumingag *Phil.* 8°20N 123°20E **233** G4
Dumitrești *Romania* 45°33N 26°55E **183** E11
Dumka *India* 24°12N 87°15E **243** G12
Dumlupınar *Turkey* 38°53N 30°0E **205** C12
Dümmer *Germany* 52°31N 8°20E **178** C4
Dümmer ⌂ *Germany* 52°31N 8°21E **178** C4
Dumoine → *Canada* 46°13N 77°51W **298** C4
Dumoine, L. *Canada* 46°55N 77°55W **298** C4
Dumont *U.S.A.* 40°56N 73°59W **132** A2
Dumont d'Urville *Antarctica* 67°0S 110°0E **151** C10
Dumoulin Is. *Papua N. G.* 10°54S 150°46E **286** F6
Dumpu *Papua N. G.* 5°53S 145°44E **286** C3
Dumraon *India* 25°33N 84°8E **243** G11
Dumyât *Egypt* 31°24N 31°48E **251** G2
Dumyât, Far → *Egypt* 31°32N 31°51E **251** G2
Dumyât, Masabb *Egypt* 31°28N 31°51E **251** G2
Dún Dealgan = Dundalk *Ireland* 54°1N 6°24W **166** B5
Dún Laoghaire *Ireland* 53°17N 6°8W **120** B3
Dun-le-Palestel *France* 46°18N 1°39E **173** F8
Dun-sur-Auron *France* 46°53N 2°33E **173** F9
Dun-sur-Meuse *France* 49°23N 5°11E **173** C12
Duna = Dunărea → *Europe* 45°20N 29°40E **183** E14
Duna-Drava △ *Hungary* 46°15N 18°50E **182** D3
Duna-völgyi-főcsatorna *Hungary* 46°40N 19°14E **182** D4
Dünaburg = Daugavpils *Latvia* 55°53N 26°32E **188** E4
Dunaföldvár *Hungary* 46°50N 18°57E **182** D3
Dunagiri *India* 30°31N 79°52E **243** D8
Dunaj = Dunărea → *Europe* 45°20N 29°40E **183** E14
Dunajec → *Poland* 50°15N 20°44E **185** H7
Dunajská Streda *Slovak Rep.* 48°0N 17°37E **181** C10
Dunakeszi *Hungary* 47°37N 19°8E **182** C4
Dunapataj *Hungary* 46°39N 19°4E **182** D4
Dunărea → *Europe* 45°20N 29°40E **183** E14
Dunaszekcső *Hungary* 46°6N 18°45E **182** D3
Dunaújváros *Hungary* 46°58N 18°57E **182** D3
Dunav = Dunărea → *Europe* 45°20N 29°40E **183** E14
Dunavațu de Jos *Romania* 44°59N 29°13E **183** F14
Dunavtsi *Bulgaria* 43°57N 22°53E **202** C6
Dunay *Russia* 42°52N 132°22E **220** C6
Dunayivtsi *Ukraine* 48°54N 26°50E **183** B11
Dunback *N.Z.* 45°23S 170°36E **285** F5
Dunbar *U.K.* 56°0N 2°31W **167** E6
Dunblane *U.K.* 56°11N 3°58W **167** E5
Duncan *B.C., Canada* 48°45N 123°40W **306** B3
Duncan *Ariz., U.S.A.* 32°43N 109°6W **305** K9
Duncan *Okla., U.S.A.* 34°30N 97°57W **314** D6
Duncan, L. *Canada* 53°29N 77°58W **298** B4
Duncan Dock *Cape Town, S. Africa* **118** a3
Duncan L. *Canada* 62°51N 113°58W **296** A6
Duncan Passage *India* 11°0N 92°0E **245** J11
Duncan Town *Bahamas* 22°15N 75°45W **320** B4
Duncannon *U.S.A.* 40°23N 77°2W **312** F7
Duncans *Jamaica* 18°27N 77°32W **320** a
Duncansby Head *U.K.* 58°38N 3°1W **167** C5
Duncansville *U.S.A.* 40°25N 78°26W **312** F6
Dund-Us *Mongolia* 48°1N 91°38E **217** C12
Dundaga *Latvia* 57°31N 22°21E **184** A9
Dundalk *Ont., Canada* 44°10N 80°24W **312** B4
Dundalk *Louth, Ireland* 54°1N 6°24W **166** B5
Dundalk *Md., U.S.A.* 39°15N 76°31W **309** F15
Dundalk Bay *Ireland* 53°55N 6°15W **166** C5
Dundas = Uummannaq *Greenland* 77°28N 69°13W **154** B4
Dundas *Canada* 43°17N 79°59W **312** C5
Dundas, L. *Australia* 32°35S 121°50E **279** F3
Dundas I. *Canada* 54°30N 130°50W **296** C2
Dundas Str. *Australia* 11°15S 131°35E **278** B5
Dundee *KwaZulu Natal, S. Africa* 28°11S 30°15E **271** C5
Dundee *Dundee C., U.K.* 56°28N 2°59W **167** E6
Dundee *Mich., U.S.A.* 41°57N 83°40W **311** C13
Dundee *N.Y., U.S.A.* 42°32N 76°59W **312** D8
Dundee City □ *U.K.* 56°30N 2°58W **167** E6
Dundgovĭ □ *Mongolia* 45°10N 106°0E **226** B4
Dundrum *Dublin, Ireland* 53°18N 6°14W **120** B2
Dundrum *Down, U.K.* 54°16N 5°52W **166** B6
Dundrum B. *U.K.* 54°13N 5°47W **166** B6
Dunearn *Singapore* 1°19N 103°49E **138** B2
Dunedin *N.Z.* 45°50S 170°33E **285** F5
Dunedin *Fla., U.S.A.* 28°1N 82°46W **317** G7
Dunedoo *Australia* 32°0S 149°25E **283** A8
Dunfanaghy *Ireland* 55°11N 7°58W **166** A4
Dunfermline *U.K.* 56°5N 3°27W **167** E5
Dungannon *Ont., Canada* 43°51N 81°36W **312** C3
Dungannon *Tyrone, U.K.* 54°31N 6°46W **166** B5
Dungarpur *India* 23°52N 73°45E **242** H5
Dungarvan *Ireland* 52°5N 7°37W **166** D4
Dungarvan Harbour *Ireland* 52°4N 7°35W **166** D4
Dungeness *U.K.* 50°54N 0°59E **169** G8
Dunglow *Ireland* 54°57N 8°21W **166** B3
Dungo, L. do *Angola* 17°15S 19°0E **265** F3
Dungog *Australia* 32°22S 151°46E **283** B9
Dungu *Dem. Rep. of the Congo* 3°40N 28°32E **268** B2
Dungun *Malaysia* 4°45N 103°25E **237** K4
Dungunâb *Sudan* 21°10N 37°9E **256** C4
Dungunâb, Khalîg *Sudan* 21°5N 37°12E **256** C4
Dunhua *China* 43°20N 128°14E **227** C15
Dunhuang *China* 40°8N 94°36E **218** B4
Dunk I. *Australia* 17°59S 146°29E **280** B4
Dunkassa *Benin* 10°21N 3°10E **263** C5
Dunkeld *Queens., Australia* 33°25S 149°29E **281** E4
Dunkeld *Vic., Australia* 37°40S 142°22E **282** D5
Dunkeld *Perth & Kinr., U.K.* 56°34N 3°35W **167** E5
Dunkerque *France* 51°2N 2°20E **173** A9
Dunkery Beacon *U.K.* 51°9N 3°36W **169** F4
Dunkirk = Dunkerque *France* 51°2N 2°20E **173** A9
Dunkirk *U.S.A.* 42°29N 79°20W **312** D5
Dunkuj *Sudan* 12°50N 32°49E **257** E3
Dunkwa *Central, Ghana* 6°0N 1°47W **262** D4
Dunkwa *Central, Ghana* 5°30N 1°0W **263** D4
Dúnleary = Dún Laoghaire *Ireland* 53°17N 6°8W **120** B3
Dunleer *Ireland* 53°50N 6°24W **166** C5
Dunmanus B. *Ireland* 51°31N 9°50W **166** E2
Dunmanway *Ireland* 51°43N 9°6W **166** E2
Dunmarra *Australia* 16°42S 133°25E **280** B1
Dunmore *U.S.A.* 41°25N 75°38W **313** E9
Dunmore East *Ireland* 52°9N 7°0W **166** D5
Dunmore Hd. *Ireland* 52°10N 10°35W **166** D1
Dunmore Town *Bahamas* 25°30N 76°39W **320** A4
Dunn *U.S.A.* 35°19N 78°37W **315** D15
Dunn Loring *U.S.A.* 38°54N 77°13W **143** B2
Dunnellon *U.S.A.* 29°3N 82°28W **317** F7
Dunnet Hd. *U.K.* 58°40N 3°21W **167** C5
Dunning *Ill., U.S.A.* 41°56N 87°48W **119** B2
Dunning *Nebr., U.S.A.* 41°50N 100°6W **308** E3
Dunn's River Falls *Jamaica* 18°25N 77°8W **320** a
Dunnville *Canada* 42°54N 79°36W **312** D5
Dunolly *Australia* 36°51S 143°44E **282** D5
Dunoon *U.K.* 55°57N 4°56W **167** F4
Dunqul *Egypt* 23°26N 31°37E **256** C3
Duns *U.K.* 55°47N 2°20W **167** F6
Dunseith *U.S.A.* 48°50N 100°3W **308** A3
Dunshaughlin *Ireland* 53°31N 6°33W **166** C5
Dunsmuir *U.S.A.* 41°13N 122°16W **304** F2
Dunstable *U.K.* 51°53N 0°32W **169** F7
Dunstan Mts. *N.Z.* 44°53S 169°35E **285** E4
Dunster *Canada* 53°8N 119°50W **296** C5
Duntroon *N.Z.* 44°51S 170°40E **285** E5
Dunvegan *Gauteng, S. Africa* 26°9S 28°8E **123** A2
Dunvegan *Highl., U.K.* 57°27N 6°35W **167** D2
Dunvegan L. *Canada* 60°8N 107°10W **297** A7
Duolun *China* 42°12N 116°28E **226** C9
Duomo *Italy* 45°28N 9°11E **129** B2
Duomula *China* 34°8N 82°29E **217** F10
Duong Dong *Vietnam* 10°13N 103°58E **237** G4
Dupax *Phil.* 16°17N 121°5E **232** C3
Dupree *U.S.A.* 45°4N 101°35W **308** C3
Dupuyer *U.S.A.* 48°13N 112°30W **304** B7
Duqm *Oman* 19°39N 57°42E **249** C7
Duque de Caxias *Brazil* 22°46S 43°18W **135** A1
Duque de York, I. *Chile* 50°37S 75°25W **336** D1
Durack → *Australia* 15°33S 127°52E **278** C4
Durack Ra. *Australia* 16°50S 127°40E **278** C4
Durağan *Turkey* 41°25N 35°3E **212** B6
Durak *Turkey* 39°42N 28°17E **205** B10
Ðurakovac *Serbia* 42°43N 20°29E **202** D4
Durance → *France* 43°55N 4°45E **175** E8
Durand *Ga., U.S.A.* 32°55N 84°46W **316** C5
Durand *Ill., U.S.A.* 42°26N 89°20W **310** B7
Durand *Mich., U.S.A.* 42°55N 83°59W **311** B13
Durand *Wis., U.S.A.* 44°38N 91°58W **308** C8
Durandeau *St. Lucia* 13°56N 60°59W **323** m
Durango *Mexico* 24°3N 104°39W **318** C4
Durango *Colo., U.S.A.* 37°16N 107°53W **305** H10
Durango □ *Mexico* 24°50N 105°20W **318** C4
Durankulak *Bulgaria* 43°41N 28°32E **203** C12
Durant *Iowa, U.S.A.* 41°36N 90°54W **310** C6
Durant *Miss., U.S.A.* 33°4N 89°51W **315** E10
Durant *Okla., U.S.A.* 33°59N 96°25W **314** E6
Duratón → *Spain* 41°37N 4°7W **194** D6
Durazno *Uruguay* 33°25S 56°31W **334** C4
Durazzo = Durrës *Albania* 41°19N 19°28E **202** E3
Durban *Aude, France* 42°59N 2°49E **174** F6
Durban *KwaZulu Natal, S. Africa* 29°49S 31°1E **271** C5
Durbo *Somali Rep.* 11°37N 50°20E **267** B7
Durbuy *Belgium* 50°21N 5°28E **170** D5
Dúrcal *Spain* 36°59N 3°34W **195** J7
Ðurđevac *Croatia* 46°2N 17°3E **182** D2
Düren *Germany* 50°48N 6°29E **178** E2
Duren Sawit *Indonesia* 6°13S 106°54E **122** A2
Durg = Bhilainagar-Durg *India* 21°13N 81°26E **244** D5
Durgapur *India* 23°30N 87°20E **243** H12
Durham *Ont., Canada* 44°10N 80°49W **312** B4
Durham *Darlington, U.K.* 54°47N 1°34W **168** C6
Durham *Calif., U.S.A.* 39°39N 121°48W **306** F5
Durham *N.C., U.S.A.* 35°59N 78°54W **315** D15
Durham *N.H., U.S.A.* 43°8N 70°56W **313** C14
Durham □ *U.K.* 54°42N 1°45W **168** C6
Durlești *Moldova* 47°1N 28°46E **183** C13
Ḍurmā *Si. Arabia* 24°37N 46°8E **246** E5
Durmitor *Montenegro* 43°10N 19°0E **202** C2
Durmitor △ *Serbia* 43°15N 19°5E **202** C3
Durness *U.K.* 58°34N 4°45W **167** C4
Durnford, Pta. *W. Sahara* 23°37N 16°0W **260** D1
Durrës *Albania* 41°19N 19°28E **202** E3
Durrow *Ireland* 52°51N 7°24W **166** D4
Dursey I. *Ireland* 51°36N 10°12W **166** E1
Dursley *U.K.* 51°40N 2°21W **169** F5
Dursunbey *Turkey* 39°35N 28°37E **205** B10
Durtal *France* 47°40N 0°18W **172** E6
Duru *Dem. Rep. of the Congo* 4°14N 28°50E **268** B2
Duru Gölü *Turkey* 41°20N 28°35E **203** E12
Durukhsi *Ethiopia* 8°31N 45°28E **267** C6
Durusu *Turkey* 41°17N 28°41E **203** E12
Durūz, Jabal ad *Jordan* 32°35N 36°40E **250** F7
D'Urville, Tanjung *Indonesia* 1°28S 137°54E **231** E9
D'Urville I. *N.Z.* 40°50S 173°55E **285** A8
Duryea *U.S.A.* 41°20N 75°45W **313** E9
Dusa Mareb *Somali Rep.* 5°30N 46°15E **267** C6
Dûsh *Egypt* 24°35N 30°41E **256** C3
Dushak *Turkmenistan* 37°13N 60°1E **247** B9
Dushan *China* 25°48N 107°30E **228** E6
Dushanbe *Tajikistan* 38°33N 68°48E **217** E7
Dusheti *Georgia* 42°10N 44°42E **191** J7
Dushore *U.S.A.* 41°31N 76°24W **313** E8
Dusit *Thailand* 13°47N 100°31E **113** B2
Dusit Zoo *Bangkok, Thailand* **113** a2
Dusky Sd. *N.Z.* 45°47S 166°30E **285** F1
Dussejour, C. *Australia* 14°45S 128°13E **278** B4
Düsseldorf *Germany* 51°14N 6°47E **178** D2
Düsseldorf Rhein-Ruhr ✈ (DUS) *Germany* 51°17N 6°46E **178** D2
Dusti *Tajikistan* 37°20N 68°40E **217** E7
Duszniki-Zdrój *Poland* 50°24N 16°24E **185** H3
Dutch East Indies = Indonesia ■ *Asia* 5°0S 115°0E **235** C4
Dutch Guiana = Suriname ■ *S. Amer.* 4°0N 56°0W **329** C6
Dutch Harbor *U.S.A.* 53°53N 166°32W **303** K6
Dutlwe *Botswana* 23°58S 23°46E **270** B3
Dutsan Wai *Nigeria* 10°50N 8°10E **263** C6
Dutton *Canada* 42°39N 81°30W **312** D3
Dutton → *Australia* 20°44S 143°10E **280** C3
Dutywa *S. Africa* 32°8S 28°18E **271** D4
Duved *Sweden* 63°23N 12°55E **162** A6
Düvertepe *Turkey* 39°14N 28°27E **205** B10
Dúvida = Roosevelt → *Brazil* 7°35S 60°20W **331** B5
Duwayhin, Khawr *U.A.E.* 24°20N 51°25E **247** E6
Duyfken Pt. *Australia* 12°33S 141°38E **280** A3
Duyun *China* 26°18N 107°29E **228** D6
Düzağac *Turkey* 38°48N 30°10E **205** C12
Düzce *Turkey* 40°50N 31°10E **212** B4
Düzce □ *Turkey* 40°50N 31°10E **212** B4
Duzdab = Zāhedān *Iran* 29°30N 60°50E **247** D9
Duzer *Guadeloupe* 16°20N 61°44W **322** e
Dve Mogili *Bulgaria* 43°35N 25°55E **203** C9
Dvigatelstroy = Kaspiysk *Russia* 42°52N 47°40E **191** J8
Dvina, Severnaya → *Russia* 64°32N 40°30E **186** B7
Dvinsk = Daugavpils *Latvia* 55°53N 26°32E **188** E4
Dvinskaya Guba *Russia* 65°0N 39°0E **186** B6
Dvor *Croatia* 45°4N 16°22E **199** C13
Dvůr Králové nad Labem *Czech Rep.* 50°27N 15°50E **180** A8
Dwarka *India* 22°18N 69°8E **242** H3
Dwellingup *Australia* 32°43S 116°4E **279** F2
Dwight *Ont., Canada* 45°20N 79°1W **312** A5
Dwight *Ill., U.S.A.* 41°5N 88°26W **311** C8
Dworp *Belgium* 50°44N 4°18E **116** B1
Dyakove *Ukraine* 48°1N 23°0E **182** B7
Dyakovo *Russia* 55°40N 37°39E **129** B3
Dyatkovo *Russia* 53°40N 34°27E **188** F8
Dyatlovo = Dzyatlava *Belarus* 53°28N 25°28E **177** B13
Dyce *U.K.* 57°13N 2°12W **167** D6
Dyer, C. *Canada* 66°37N 61°16W **295** C13
Dyer Bay *Canada* 45°10N 81°20W **312** A3
Dyer Plateau *Antarctica* 70°45S 65°30W **151** D17
Dyersburg *U.S.A.* 36°3N 89°23W **315** C10
Dyersville *U.S.A.* 42°29N 91°8W **310** B5
Dyfi → *U.K.* 52°32N 4°3W **169** E3
Dyhernfurth = Brzeg Dolny *Poland* 51°16N 16°41E **185** G3
Dyje → *Czech Rep.* 48°37N 16°56E **181** C9
Dyke Ackland B. *Papua N. G.* 9°0S 148°45E **286** E5
Dyker Beach Park *U.S.A.* 40°36N 74°1W **132** C1
Dymer *Ukraine* 50°47N 30°18E **177** C16
Dynów *Poland* 49°50N 22°11E **185** J9
Dyranut *Norway* 60°22N 7°31E **164** D4
Dyrhólaey *Iceland* 63°24N 19°8W **155** D7
Dyrnes *Norway* 63°25N 7°52E **164** A4
Dysart *Queens., Australia* 22°32S 148°23E **280** C4
Dysart *Iowa, U.S.A.* 42°10N 92°18W **310** B4
Dyushambe = Dushanbe *Tajikistan* 38°33N 68°48E **217** E7
Dyviziya 45°55N 29°59E **183** E14
Dzamin Üüd = Borhoyn Tal *Mongolia* 43°50N 111°58E **226** C6
Dzaoudzi *Mayotte* 12°47S 45°16E **272** b
Dzaoudzi ✈ (DZA) *Mayotte* 12°48S 45°18E **272** b
Dzaudzhikau = Vladikavkaz *Russia* 43°0N 44°35E **191** J7
Dzavhan □ *Mongolia* 48°0N 96°0E **217** C13
Dzavhan Gol *Mongolia* 48°54N 93°23E **218** B4
Dzerzhinsk *Russia* 56°14N 43°30E **190** B6
Dzerzhinskiy *Moskva, Russia* 55°38N 37°51E **129** C5
Dzerzhinskiy *Moskva, Russia* 55°47N 37°37E **129** B3
Dzerzhinskiy Park *Russia* 55°50N 37°37E **129** B3
Dzhalal-Abad = Jalal-Abad *Kyrgyzstan* 40°56N 73°0E **217** D8
Dzhalal-Ogly = Stepanavan *Armenia* 41°1N 44°23E **191** K7
Dzhalinda *Russia* 53°26N 124°0E **215** D13
Dzhambeyty = Zhympīty *Kazakhstan* 50°16N 52°35E **216** B4
Dzhambul = Taraz *Kazakhstan* 42°54N 71°22E **217** D8
Dzhankoy *Ukraine* 45°40N 34°20E **189** K8
Dzhanybek = Zhänibek *Kazakhstan* 49°25N 46°50E **190** F8
Dzhargalantu = Hovd □ *Mongolia* 48°2N 91°37E **217** C12
Dzharkent = Zharkent *Kazakhstan* 44°10N 80°0E **217** D10
Dzharylhach, Ostriv *Ukraine* 46°2N 32°55E **189** J7
Dzhezkazgan = Zhezqazghan *Kazakhstan* 47°44N 67°40E **217** C7
Dzhibkhalantu = Uliastay *Mongolia* 47°56N 97°28E **218** B4
Dzhizak = Jizzakh *Uzbekistan* 40°6N 67°50E **217** D7
Dzhugdzur, Khrebet *Russia* 57°30N 138°0E **215** D14
Dzhulynk *Ukraine* 48°26N 29°45E **183** B14
Dzhumgoltau, Khrebet *Kyrgyzstan* 42°15N 74°30E **217** D8
Dzhungarskiye Vorota = Dzungarian Gate *Asia* 45°10N 82°0E **217** C10
Dzhuryn *Ukraine* 48°41N 28°18E **183** B13
Dzhvari = Jvari *Georgia* 42°42N 42°4E **191** J6
Działdowo *Poland* 53°15N 20°15E **185** E7
Działoszyce *Poland* 50°22N 20°20E **185** H7
Działoszyn *Poland* 51°6N 18°50E **185** G5
Dzibilchaltún *Mexico* 21°10N 89°35W **319** C7
Dzierzgoń *Poland* 53°58N 19°20E **184** E6
Dzierżoniów *Poland* 50°45N 16°39E **185** H3
Dzilam de Bravo *Mexico* 21°24N 88°53W **319** C7
Dzioua *Algeria* 33°14N 5°14E **261** B6
Dzisna *Belarus* 55°34N 28°12E **188** E5
Dzisna → *Belarus* 55°34N 28°12E **188** E5
Dziwnów *Poland* 54°2N 14°45E **184** D1
Dzūkija △ *Lithuania* 54°10N 24°30E **161** J21
Dzungaria = Junggar Pendi *China* 44°30N 86°0E **217** D11
Dzungarian Basin = Junggar Pendi *China* 44°30N 86°0E **217** D11
Dzungarian Gate *Asia* 45°10N 82°0E **217** C10
Dzur *Mongolia* 49°39N 95°46E **217** C13
Dzüünharaa *Mongolia* 48°52N 106°28E **218** B5
Dzüünmod *Mongolia* 47°45N 106°58E **218** B5
Dzyarzhynsk *Belarus* 53°40N 27°1E **177** B14
Dzyatlava *Belarus* 53°28N 25°28E **177** B13

E

E.C. Manning ⌂ *Canada* 49°5N 120°45W **296** D4
E.T. Joshua ✈ (SVD) *St. Vincent* 13°8N 61°13W **323** n
E.U.R. = Esposizione Universale di Roma *Italy* 41°49N 12°28E **136** C1
Eabamet L. *Canada* 51°30N 87°46W **298** B2
Eads *U.S.A.* 38°29N 102°47W **304** G12
Eagar *U.S.A.* 34°6N 109°17W **305** J9
Eagle *Alaska, U.S.A.* 64°47N 141°12W **303** D12
Eagle *Colo., U.S.A.* 39°39N 106°50W **304** G10
Eagle → *Canada* 53°36N 57°26W **299** B8
Eagle, Mt. *U.S. Virgin Is.* 17°46N 64°49W **321** b
Eagle Beach *Aruba* 12°32N 70°3W **322** f
Eagle Butte *U.S.A.* 45°0N 101°10W **308** C3
Eagle Cr. → *U.S.A.* 38°36N 85°4W **311** F11
Eagle Grove *U.S.A.* 42°40N 93°54W **310** B3
Eagle L. *Ont., Canada* 49°42N 93°13W **297** D10
Eagle L. *Calif., U.S.A.* 40°39N 120°45W **304** F3
Eagle L. *Maine, U.S.A.* 46°20N 69°22W **309** B19
Eagle Lake *Ont., Canada* 45°8N 78°29W **312** A6
Eagle Lake *Maine, U.S.A.* 47°3N 68°36W **309** B19
Eagle Lake *Tex., U.S.A.* 29°35N 96°20W **314** G6
Eagle Mountain *U.S.A.* 33°49N 115°27W **307** M11
Eagle Nest *U.S.A.* 36°33N 105°16W **305** H11
Eagle Pass *U.S.A.* 28°43N 100°30W **314** G4
Eagle Pk. *U.S.A.* 38°10N 119°25W **306** G7
Eagle Pt. *Australia* 16°11S 124°23E **278** C3
Eagle River *Mich., U.S.A.* 47°25N 88°18W **308** B9
Eagle River *Wis., U.S.A.* 45°55N 89°15W **308** C9
Eagle Rock *U.S.A.* 34°8N 118°12W **126** B3
Eaglehawk *Australia* 36°44S 144°15E **282** D6
Eagles Mere *U.S.A.* 41°25N 76°33W **313** E8
Eagleville *U.S.A.* 40°28N 93°59W **310** D3
Ealing □ *U.K.* 51°31N 0°20W **125** A2
Ear Falls *Canada* 50°38N 93°13W **297** C10
Earle *U.S.A.* 35°16N 90°28W **315** D9
Earlimart *U.S.A.* 35°53N 119°16W **307** K7
Earl's Court *London, U.K.* **125** c1
Earlsfield *U.K.* 51°26N 0°10W **125** B2
Earlville *U.S.A.* 41°35N 88°55W **311** C8
Earlwood *Australia* 33°55S 151°8E **139** B1
Early Branch *U.S.A.* 32°45N 80°55W **316** C9
Earn → *U.K.* 56°21N 3°18W **167** E5
Earn, L. *U.K.* 56°23N 4°13W **167** E4
Earnslaw, Mt. *N.Z.* 44°32S 168°27E **285** E3
Earth *U.S.A.* 34°14N 102°24W **314** D3
Eas *Vanuatu* 16°20S 168°15E **287** F6
Easley *U.S.A.* 34°50N 82°36W **315** D13
East Anglia *U.K.* 52°30N 1°0E **168** E9
East Angus *Canada* 45°30N 71°40W **299** C5
East Antarctica *Antarctica* 80°0S 90°0E **151** D7
East Arlington *Mass., U.S.A.* 42°24N 71°8W **116** A2
East Arlington *Va., U.S.A.* 38°51N 77°4W **143** B3
East Aurora *U.S.A.* 42°46N 78°37W **312** D6
East Ayrshire □ *U.K.* 55°26N 4°11W **167** F4
East Bedfont *U.K.* 51°26N 0°28W **125** B1
East Beskids = Vychodné Beskydy *Europe* 49°20N 22°0E **181** B15
East Boston *U.S.A.* 42°22N 71°1W **116** A2
East Brady *U.S.A.* 40°59N 79°37W **312** F5
East C. = Dezhneva, Mys *Russia* 66°5N 169°40W **215** C19
East C. *N.Z.* 37°42S 178°35E **284** D7
East C. *Papua N. G.* 10°13S 150°53E **286** F6
East Caroline Basin *Pac. Oc.* 4°0N 146°45E **288** G6
East Chicago *U.S.A.* 41°38N 87°27W **311** C9
East China Sea *Asia* 30°0N 126°0E **219** D7
East Coulee *Canada* 51°23N 112°27W **296** C6
East Dereham = Dereham *U.K.* 52°41N 0°57E **169** E8
East Don → *Canada* 43°48N 79°25W **141** A2
East Don Parkland *Canada* 43°47N 79°22W **141** A2
East Dublin *U.S.A.* 32°32N 82°52W **316** C7
East Dubuque *U.S.A.* 42°30N 90°39W **310** B6
East Dunbartonshire □ *U.K.* 55°57N 4°13W **167** F4
East Elmhurst *U.S.A.* 40°45N 73°52W **132** B2
East End Pt. *Bahamas* 25°3N 77°16W **153** b
East Falkland *Falk. Is.* 51°30S 58°30W **153** f
East Finchley *U.K.* 51°35N 0°10W **125** A2
East Flatbush *U.S.A.* 40°39N 73°55W **132** C2
East Fork White → *U.S.A.* 38°33N 87°14W **311** F9
East Grand Forks *U.S.A.* 47°56N 97°1W **308** B5

East Grand Rapids U.S.A. 42°58N 85°37W 311 B11
East Greenwich U.S.A. 41°40N 71°27W 313 E13
East Grinstead U.K. 51°7N 0°0 169 F8
East Ham U.K. 51°32N 0°3E 125 A4
East Hartford U.S.A. 41°46N 72°39W 313 E12
East Helena U.S.A. 46°35N 111°56W 304 C8
East Humber → Canada 43°47N 79°35W 141 A1
East Indies Asia 0°0 120°0E 210 J14
East Kilbride U.K. 55°47N 4°11W 167 F4
East Lamma Channel China 22°14N 114°9E 122 B1
East Lansing U.S.A. 42°44N 84°29W 311 B12
East Las Vegas = Whitney U.S.A. 36°4N 115°5W 124 B2
East Lexington U.S.A. 42°25N 71°12W 116 A1
East Livermore = Livermore Falls U.S.A. 44°29N 70°11W 309 C18
East Liverpool U.S.A. 40°37N 80°35W 312 F4
East London S. Africa 33°0S 27°55E 271 D4
East Los Angeles U.S.A. 34°1N 118°10W 126 B3
East Lothian ☐ U.K. 55°58N 2°44W 167 F6
East Main = Eastmain Canada 52°10N 78°30W 298 B4
East Mariana Basin Pac. Oc. 12°0N 153°0E 288 F7
East Milwaukee = Shorewood U.S.A. 43°5N 87°53W 311 A9
East Molesey U.K. 51°24N 0°21W 125 B1
East Moline U.S.A. 41°32N 90°26W 310 C6
East Naples U.S.A. 26°8N 81°46W 317 J8
East New Britain ☐ Papua N. G. 6°30S 152°30E 286 D7
East New York U.S.A. 40°40N 73°53W 132 B2
East Northport U.S.A. 40°53N 73°20W 313 F11
East Orange U.S.A. 40°46N 74°12W 313 F10
East Pacific Rise Pac. Oc. 15°0S 110°0W 289 J17
East Pakistan = Bangladesh ■ Asia 24°0N 90°0E 241 D3
East Palatka U.S.A. 29°39N 81°36W 316 F8
East Palestine U.S.A. 40°50N 80°33W 312 F4
East Peoria U.S.A. 40°40N 89°34W 310 D7
East Pine Canada 55°48N 120°12W 296 B4
East Pines U.S.A. 38°57N 76°54W 143 B4
East Point U.S.A. 33°41N 84°25W 113 B2
East Potomac Park Washington, D.C., U.S.A. 143 c1
East Providence U.S.A. 41°49N 71°23W 313 E13
East Pt. Br. Virgin Is. 18°40N 64°18W 321 b
East Pt. N.S., Canada 46°27N 61°58W 299 C7
East Pt. U.S. Virgin Is. 17°45N 64°34W 321 b
East Renfrewshire ☐ U.K. 55°46N 4°21W 167 F4
East Retford = Retford U.K. 53°19N 0°56W 168 D7
East Riding of Yorkshire ☐ U.K. 53°55N 0°30W 168 D7
East River → New York, U.S.A. 132 e3
East Rochester U.S.A. 43°7N 77°29W 312 C7
East Rutherford U.S.A. 40°50N 74°5W 132 A1
East St. Louis U.S.A. 38°37N 90°9W 310 F6
East Schelde = Oosterschelde → Neths. 51°33N 4°0E 170 C4
East Sea = Japan, Sea of Asia 40°0N 135°0E 220 E7
East Sepik ☐ Papua N. G. 4°0S 143°45E 286 C2
East Sheen U.K. 51°27N 0°16W 125 B2
East Siberian Sea Russia 73°0N 160°0E 215 B17
East Stroudsburg U.S.A. 41°1N 75°11W 313 E9
East Sussex ☐ U.K. 50°56N 0°19E 169 G8
East Talpiyot West Bank 31°45N 35°13E 123 B2
East Tasman Plateau Pac. Oc. 43°30S 152°0E 288 M7
East Tawas U.S.A. 44°17N 83°29W 309 C12
East Timor ■ Asia 8°50S 126°0E 231 F7
East Toorale Australia 30°27S 145°28E 281 E4
East Troy U.S.A. 42°47N 88°24W 311 B8
East Village New York, U.S.A. 132 e2
East Walker → U.S.A. 38°52N 119°10W 306 G7
East Wickham U.K. 51°28N 0°5E 125 B4
East Windsor U.S.A. 40°17N 74°34W 313 F10
East York Canada 43°40N 79°22W 141 A2
East Youngstown = Campbell U.S.A. 41°5N 80°37W 312 E4
Eastbourne N.Z. 41°19S 174°55E 143 B2
Eastbourne E. Sussex, U.K. 50°46N 0°18E 169 G8
Eastcote U.K. 51°34N 0°23W 125 A1
Eastend Canada 49°32N 108°50W 297 D7
Easter Fracture Zone Pac. Oc. 25°0S 115°0W 289 K16
Easter Howgate U.K. 55°52N 3°12W 121 B2
Easter I. = Pascua, I. de Chile 27°7S 109°23W 330 b
Eastern ☐ Ghana 6°30N 0°30W 263 D4
Eastern ☐ Kenya 0°0 38°30E 268 C4
Eastern ☐ S. Leone 8°15N 11°0W 262 D2
Eastern Cape ☐ S. Africa 32°0S 26°0E 270 D4
Eastern Cr. → Australia 20°40S 141°35E 280 C3
Eastern Ghats India 14°0N 78°50E 245 H4
Eastern Group = Lau Group Fiji 17°0S 178°30W 287 A3
Eastern Group Australia 33°30S 124°30E 279 F3
Eastern Highlands ☐ Papua N. G. 6°30S 145°35E 286 D3
Eastern I. Midway Is. 28°12N 177°19W 302 c
Eastern Samar ☐ Phil. 11°40N 125°40E 233 F5
Eastern Transvaal = Mpumalanga ☐ S. Africa 26°0S 30°0E 271 C5
Easterville Canada 53°8N 99°49W 297 C9
Easthampton U.S.A. 42°16N 72°40W 313 D12
Eastlake U.S.A. 41°40N 81°26W 312 E3
Eastland U.S.A. 32°24N 98°49W 314 E5
Eastleigh U.K. 50°58N 1°21W 169 G6
Eastmain Canada 52°10N 78°30W 298 B4
Eastmain → Canada 52°27N 78°26W 298 B4
Eastman Qué., Canada 45°18N 72°19W 313 A12
Eastman Ga., U.S.A. 32°12N 83°11W 316 C6
Eastman Wis., U.S.A. 43°10N 91°1W 310 A5
Easton Md., U.S.A. 38°47N 76°5W 309 F15
Easton Pa., U.S.A. 40°41N 75°13W 313 F9
Easton Wash., U.S.A. 47°14N 121°11W 306 C5
Eastover U.S.A. 33°52N 80°41W 316 B9
Eastpoint U.S.A. 29°44N 84°53W 316 F5
Eastpoint Park Canada 43°46N 79°10W 141 A4
Eastport U.S.A. 44°56N 67°0W 309 C20
Eastsound U.S.A. 48°42N 122°55W 306 B4
Eastwood Australia 33°47S 151°4E 139 A1
Eaton Colo., U.S.A. 40°32N 104°42W 304 F11
Eaton Ohio, U.S.A. 39°45N 84°38W 311 E12
Eaton Canyon Park U.S.A. 34°10N 118°7W 126 A4
Eaton Centre Toronto, Canada 141 a3
Eaton Rapids U.S.A. 42°31N 84°39W 311 B12
Eatonia Canada 51°13N 109°25W 297 C7
Eatonton U.S.A. 33°20N 83°23W 316 B6
Eatontown U.S.A. 40°19N 74°4W 313 F10
Eatonville U.S.A. 46°52N 122°16W 306 D4
Eau Claire Fr. Guiana 3°30N 53°40W 329 C7
Eau Claire Wis., U.S.A. 44°49N 91°30W 308 C8
Eau Claire, L. à l' Canada 56°10N 74°25W 298 A5
Eauripik Rise Pac. Oc. 2°0N 142°0E 288 G6
Eauze France 43°53N 0°7E 174 E4
Eban Nigeria 9°40N 4°50E 263 D5
Ebanga Angola 12°45S 14°45E 265 E2
Ebangalakata Dem. Rep. of the Congo 0°29S 21°29E 264 C4
Ebano Mexico 22°13N 98°24W 319 C5
Ebara Japan 35°35N 139°42E 140 B3
Ebbegebirge ⌓ Germany 51°10N 7°55E 178 D3
Ebbw Vale U.K. 51°46N 3°12W 169 F4
Ebebiyín Eq. Guin. 2°9N 11°20E 264 B2
Ebeggui Algeria 26°2N 6°0E 261 C6
Ebel Gabon 0°7N 11°5E 264 B2
Ebeltoft Denmark 56°12N 10°41E 163 H4
Ebeltoft Vig Denmark 56°10N 10°35E 163 H4
Ebensburg U.S.A. 40°29N 78°44W 312 F6
Ebensee Austria 47°48N 13°46E 180 D6
Eber Gölü Turkey 38°38N 31°11E 212 C4
Eberbach Germany 49°28N 8°59E 179 F4
Eberswalde-Finow Germany 52°50N 13°49E 178 C9
Ebetsu Japan 43°7N 141°34E 220 C10
Ebey's Landing ⌓ U.S.A. 48°12N 122°41W 306 B4
Ebian China 29°11N 103°13E 228 C4
Ebingen Germany 48°13N 9°1E 179 G5
Ebino Japan 32°2N 130°48E 222 E2
Ebinur Hu China 44°55N 82°55E 217 D10
Ebisu Japan 35°38N 139°42E 140 B3
Ebla Syria 35°50N 36°48E 250 C7
Ebo Angola 11°40S 14°40E 265 E2
Ebola → Dem. Rep. of the Congo 3°20N 20°57E 264 B4
Éboli Italy 40°39N 15°2E 201 B8
Ebolowa Cameroon 2°55N 11°10E 263 E7
Ebonda Dem. Rep. of the Congo 2°12N 22°21E 264 B4
Ebonyi ☐ Nigeria 6°20N 8°0E 263 D6
Eboy Dem. Rep. of the Congo 2°50N 23°11E 264 B4
Ebrach Germany 49°51N 10°29E 179 F6
Ébrié, Lagune Ivory C. 5°12N 4°26W 262 D4
Ebro → Spain 40°43N 0°54E 196 E5
Ebro, Embalse del Spain 43°0N 3°58W 194 C7
Ebstorf Germany 53°2N 10°24E 178 B6
Ebute-Ikorodu Nigeria 6°35N 3°29E 124 A2
Ebute-Metta Nigeria 6°28N 3°23E 124 B2
Ecatepec de Morelos Mexico 19°36N 99°3W 319 D5
Ecclesville Trin. & Tob. 10°19N 61°8W 323 t
Eceabat Turkey 40°11N 26°21E 203 F10
Ech Chéliff Algeria 36°10N 1°20E 261 A5
Ech Chéliff ☐ Algeria 36°15N 1°30E 261 A5
Echechonnee → U.S.A. 32°39N 83°36W 316 C6
Echigo-Sammyaku Japan 36°50N 139°50E 221 F9
Echinades Greece 38°25N 21°2E 207 C3
Echinos Greece 41°16N 25°1E 203 E9
Échirolles France 45°8N 5°44E 175 C9
Echizen-Misaki Japan 35°59N 135°57E 223 B7
Echmiadzin = Yejmiadzin Armenia 40°12N 44°19E 191 K7
Echo U.S.A. 31°29N 85°28W 316 D4
Echo Bay N.W.T., Canada 66°5N 117°55W 294 C8
Echo Bay Ont., Canada 46°29N 84°4W 298 C3
Echo Park Los Angeles, U.S.A. 127 a1
Echoing → Canada 55°51N 92°5W 298 B1
Echterdingen, Stuttgart ✈ (STR) Germany 48°42N 9°11E 179 G5
Echternach Lux. 49°49N 6°25E 170 E6
Echuca Australia 36°10S 144°45E 283 D6
Ecija Spain 37°30N 5°10W 195 H5
Eckental Germany 49°35N 11°12E 179 F7
Eckernförde Germany 54°28N 9°50E 178 A5
Eclectic U.S.A. 32°38N 86°2W 316 C3
Eclipse I. Australia 35°5S 117°58E 279 G2
Eclipse Is. Australia 13°54S 126°19E 278 B4
Eclipse Sd. Canada 72°38N 79°0W 295 B12
Écommoy France 47°50N 0°17E 172 E7
Economy = Ambridge U.S.A. 40°36N 80°14W 312 F4
Ecoporanga Brazil 18°23S 40°50W 333 E3
Écouché France 48°42N 0°10W 172 D6
Ecrins △ France 44°54N 6°18E 175 D10
Ecuador ■ S. Amer. 2°0S 78°0W 328 D2
Ecuador, Volcán Ecuador 1°1S 91°32W 330 a
Écueillé France 47°5N 1°21E 172 E8
Ed Sweden 58°55N 11°55E 163 F5
Ed Dabbura Sudan 17°40N 34°15E 256 D3
Ed Da'ein Sudan 11°26N 26°9E 257 E2
Ed Damazin Sudan 11°46N 34°21E 266 B3
Ed Dâmer Sudan 17°27N 34°0E 256 D3
Ed Dar el Beida = Casablanca Morocco 33°36N 7°36W 260 B3
Ed Debba Sudan 18°0N 30°51E 256 D3
Ed Déffa Egypt 30°40N 26°30E 256 A2
Ed Deim Sudan 10°10N 28°20E 257 E2
Ed Dibeikir Sudan 10°23N 29°9E 266 B2
Ed Dueim Sudan 14°0N 32°10E 257 E3
Eda Japan 35°33N 139°33E 140 B2
Edam Sask., Canada 53°11N 108°46W 297 C7
Edam Neths. 52°31N 5°3E 170 B5
Edane Sweden 59°38N 12°49E 162 E6
Edapally India 11°19N 78°3E 245 J4
Eday U.K. 59°11N 2°47W 167 B6
Edchera W. Sahara 27°2N 13°4W 260 C2
Edd Eritrea 14°0N 41°38E 257 E5
Eddrachillis B. U.K. 58°17N 5°14W 167 C3
Eddystone U.K. 50°11N 4°16W 169 G3
Eddystone Pt. Australia 40°59S 148°20E 281 G4
Eddyville U.S.A. 41°9N 92°38W 310 C4
Ede Neths. 52°4N 5°40E 170 B5
Ede Nigeria 7°45N 4°29E 263 D5
Édéa Cameroon 3°51N 10°9E 263 E7
Edebäck Sweden 60°4N 13°32E 162 D7
Edehon L. Canada 60°25N 97°15W 297 A9
Edekel, Adrar Algeria 23°56N 6°47E 261 D6
Edelény Hungary 48°18N 20°44E 182 B5
Eden = Bar Harbor U.S.A. 44°23N 68°13W 309 C19
Eden N.S.W., Australia 37°3S 149°55E 283 D8
Eden N.C., U.S.A. 36°29N 79°53W 315 C15
Eden N.Y., U.S.A. 42°39N 78°55W 312 D6
Eden Tex., U.S.A. 31°13N 99°51W 314 F5
Eden → U.K. 54°57N 3°1W 168 C4
Edenburg S. Africa 29°43S 25°58E 270 C4
Edendale N.Z. 46°19S 168°48E 285 G3
Edendale Gauteng, S. Africa 26°8S 28°9E 123 A2
Edendale KwaZulu Natal, S. Africa 29°39S 30°18E 271 C5
Edenderry Ireland 53°21N 7°4W 166 C4
Edenhope Australia 37°4S 141°19E 282 D4
Edenmore Ireland 53°22N 6°11W 120 A2
Edenton U.S.A. 36°4N 76°39W 315 C16
Edenville S. Africa 27°37S 27°34E 271 C4
Eder → Germany 51°12N 9°28E 178 D5
Eder-Stausee Germany 51°10N 8°57E 178 D4
Edessa Greece 40°48N 22°5E 202 F6
Edewecht Germany 53°8N 7°58E 178 B3
Edgar U.S.A. 40°22N 97°58W 308 E5
Edgars Cr. → Australia 37°43S 144°58E 128 A1
Edgartown U.S.A. 41°23N 70°31W 313 E14
Edge Hill U.K. 52°8N 1°26W 169 E6
Edgecumbe N.Z. 37°59S 176°47E 284 D5
Edgefield U.S.A. 33°47N 81°56W 316 B8
Edgeley Ont., Canada 43°47N 79°31W 141 A1
Edgeley N. Dak., U.S.A. 46°22N 98°43W 308 B4
Edgemar U.S.A. 37°39N 122°29W 136 C2
Edgemont U.S.A. 43°18N 103°50W 308 D2
Edgeøya Svalbard 77°45N 22°30E 150 B9
Edgerton Ohio, U.S.A. 41°27N 84°45W 311 C12
Edgerton Wis., U.S.A. 42°50N 89°4W 310 B7
Edgewater Fla., U.S.A. 28°59N 80°54W 317 G9
Edgewater N.J., U.S.A. 40°49N 73°58W 132 B2
Edgewood Fla., U.S.A. 28°29N 81°22W 133 B2
Edgewood Ill., U.S.A. 38°55N 88°40W 311 F8
Édhessa = Edessa Greece 40°48N 22°5E 202 F6
Edievale N.Z. 45°49S 169°22E 285 F4
Edina Liberia 6°0N 10°10W 262 D2
Edina Mo., U.S.A. 40°10N 92°11W 310 D4
Edinboro U.S.A. 41°52N 80°8W 312 E4
Edinburg Ill., U.S.A. 39°39N 89°23W 310 E7
Edinburg Tex., U.S.A. 26°18N 98°10W 314 H5
Edinburgh Edinburgh, U.K. 55°57N 3°13W 121 B2
Edinburgh Ind., U.S.A. 39°21N 85°58W 311 E11
Edinburgh ✈ (EDI) U.K. 55°54N 3°22W 121 B1
Edinburgh, City of ☐ U.K. 55°57N 3°17W 167 F5
Edinburgh Castle Edinburgh, U.K. 121 b2
Edineț Moldova 48°9N 27°18E 183 B12
Edirne Turkey 41°40N 26°34E 203 E10
Edirne ☐ Turkey 41°12N 26°30E 203 E10
Edison Ga., U.S.A. 31°34N 84°44W 316 D5
Edison Wash., U.S.A. 48°33N 122°27W 306 B4
Edison Park U.S.A. 42°1N 87°48W 119 A2
Edisto → U.S.A. 32°29N 80°21W 316 C9
Edisto Beach U.S.A. 32°29N 80°20W 316 C9
Edisto I. U.S.A. 32°35N 80°20W 316 C9
Edithburgh Australia 35°5S 137°43E 282 C2
Edjeleh Algeria 28°38N 9°50E 261 C6
Edmeston U.S.A. 42°42N 75°15W 313 D9
Edmond U.S.A. 35°39N 97°29W 314 D6
Edmonds U.S.A. 47°48N 122°22W 306 C4
Edmondston U.S.A. 38°56N 76°54W 143 B4
Edmondstown Ireland 53°17N 6°18W 120 B2
Edmonton Queens., Australia 17°2S 145°46E 280 B4
Edmonton Alta., Canada 53°30N 113°30W 296 C6
Edmund L. Canada 54°45N 93°17W 298 B1
Edmundston Canada 47°23N 68°20W 299 C6
Edna U.S.A. 28°59N 96°39W 314 G6
Edo ☐ Nigeria 6°30N 6°0E 263 D6
Edo → Japan 35°38N 139°52E 140 B4
Edogawa Japan 35°43N 139°52E 140 A4
Edolo Italy 46°10N 10°21E 198 B7
Edøya Norway 63°18N 8°10E 164 A5
Edremit Turkey 39°34N 27°0E 205 B9
Edremit Körfezi Turkey 39°30N 26°45E 205 B8
Edsberg Sweden 59°26N 17°57E 139 A1
Edsbro Sweden 59°54N 18°29E 162 E12
Edsbyn Sweden 61°23N 15°49E 162 C9
Edson Canada 53°35N 116°28W 296 C5
Eduardo Castex Argentina 35°50S 64°18W 334 D3
Edward → Australia 35°5S 143°30E 282 C5
Edward, L. Africa 0°25S 29°40E 268 C2
Edward VII Land Antarctica 80°0S 150°0W 151 E13
Edwardesabad = Bannu Pakistan 33°0N 70°18E 240 B3
Edwards Calif., U.S.A. 34°50N 117°40W 307 L9
Edwards N.Y., U.S.A. 44°20N 75°15W 313 B9
Edwards → U.S.A. 41°9N 90°59W 310 C6
Edwards L. Australia 37°42S 144°59E 128 A1
Edwards Plateau U.S.A. 30°45N 101°20W 314 F4
Edwardsburg U.S.A. 41°48N 86°6W 311 C10
Edwardsville Ill., U.S.A. 38°49N 89°58W 310 F7
Edwardsville Pa., U.S.A. 41°15N 75°56W 313 E9
Edzná Mexico 19°39N 90°19W 319 D6
Edzo Canada 62°49N 116°4W 296 A5
Eek U.S.A. 60°14N 162°2W 303 F7
Eeklo Belgium 51°11N 3°33E 170 C3
Eel → Ind., U.S.A. 39°7N 86°57W 311 E10
Eel → Ind., U.S.A. 40°45N 86°22W 311 D10
Eesti = Estonia ■ Europe 58°30N 25°30E 188 C3
Efate, I. Vanuatu 17°40S 168°25E 287 G6
Eferding Austria 48°18N 14°1E 180 C7
Eferi Algeria 24°30N 9°28E 261 D6
Effigy Mounds ⌓ U.S.A. 43°5N 91°11W 310 A5
Effingham U.S.A. 39°7N 88°33W 311 E8
Eforie Romania 44°1N 28°37E 183 F13
Efoulen Cameroon 2°46N 10°43E 264 B2
Efteløt Norway 59°33N 9°49E 164 E6
Efxinoupoli Greece 39°12N 22°42E 204 B4
Efzonos Greece 37°55N 23°49E 112 B2
Ega → Spain 42°19N 1°55W 196 C3
Égadi, Ísole Italy 37°55N 12°16E 200 E5
Egaleo Greece 37°59N 23°40E 112 B2
Egaleo, Oros Greece 38°0N 23°36E 112 B1
Egan Range U.S.A. 39°35N 114°55W 304 G6
Eganville Canada 45°32N 77°5W 312 A7
Egedesminde = Aasiaat Greenland 68°43N 52°56W 154 D5
Egegik U.S.A. 58°13N 157°22W 303 G8
Eger = Cheb Czech Rep. 50°9N 12°28E 180 A5
Eger Hungary 47°53N 20°27E 182 C5
Eger → Hungary 47°38N 20°50E 182 C5
Egersund Norway 58°26N 6°1E 164 F3
Egg I. St. Helena 15°58S 5°47W 153 h
Egg L. Canada 55°5N 105°30W 297 B7
Eggedal Norway 60°14N 9°22E 164 D6
Eggegebirge Südlicher Teutoburger Wald ⌓ Germany 51°40N 8°59E 178 D4
Eggenburg Austria 48°38N 15°50E 180 C8
Eggenfelden Germany 48°23N 12°46E 179 G8
Egherta Somali Rep. 2°4N 43°11E 267 D5
Éghezée Belgium 50°35N 4°55E 170 D4
Egholo Solomon Is. 8°25S 157°25E 287 M9
Egilsstaðir Iceland 65°16N 14°25W 155 B12
Egina Greece 37°45N 23°26E 204 D5
Eginio Greece 40°28N 22°28E 202 F6
Egio Greece 38°15N 22°5E 204 C4
Egito Angola 12°4S 13°58E 265 E2
Égletons France 45°24N 2°3E 174 C6
Eglinton I. Canada 75°48N 118°30W 295 B8
Egmont Canada 49°45N 123°56W 296 D4
Egmont, C. N.Z. 39°16S 173°45E 284 F2
Egmont, Mt. = Taranaki, Mt. N.Z. 39°17S 174°5E 284 F3
Egmont △ N.Z. 39°17S 174°4E 284 F3
Egra India 21°54N 87°32E 243 J12
Eğridir Turkey 37°52N 30°51E 212 D4
Eğridir Gölü Turkey 37°53N 30°50E 212 D4
Egtved Denmark 55°38N 9°18E 163 J3
Éguas → Brazil 13°26S 44°14W 333 D3
Egum Atoll Papua N. G. 9°25S 152°0E 286 E7
Egume Nigeria 7°30N 7°14E 263 D6
Éguzon-Chantôme France 46°27N 1°33E 173 F8
Egvekinot Russia 66°19N 179°50W 215 C19
Egyek Hungary 47°39N 20°52E 182 C5
Egypt ■ Africa 28°0N 31°0E 256 B3
Eha Amufu Nigeria 6°30N 7°46E 263 D6
Eheli Algeria 22°26N 4°40E 261 D5
Ehime ☐ Japan 33°30N 132°40E 222 D4
Ehingen Germany 48°16N 9°43E 179 G5
Ehrenberg U.S.A. 33°36N 114°31W 307 M12
Ehrhardt U.S.A. 33°6N 81°1W 316 B8
Ehrwald Austria 47°24N 10°56E 180 D3
Eiao French Polynesia 8°0S 140°40W 289 f
Eibar Spain 43°11N 2°28W 196 B2
Eibenschitz = Ivančice Czech Rep. 49°6N 16°23E 181 B9
Eiche Germany 52°33N 13°35E 115 A4
Eiche Sud Germany 52°33N 13°35E 115 A4
Eichstätt Germany 48°54N 11°11E 179 G7
Eide Hordaland, Norway 60°31N 6°44E 164 D3
Eide Møre og Romsdal, Norway 62°55N 7°27E 164 B4
Eider → Germany 54°19N 8°57E 178 A4
Eidsbugarden Norway 61°23N 8°16E 164 C5
Eidsbygda Norway 62°36N 7°30E 164 B4
Eidsdalen Norway 62°16N 7°10E 164 B4
Eidsvåg Norway 62°46N 8°2E 164 B5
Eidsvold Australia 25°25S 151°12E 281 D5
Eidsvoll Norway 60°19N 11°14E 164 D8
Eielson U.S.A. 64°40N 147°4W 303 D11
Eifel Germany 50°15N 6°50E 179 E2
Eiffel, Tour Paris, France 134 c2
Eiffel Flats Zimbabwe 18°20S 30°0E 269 F3
Eiger Switz. 46°34N 8°1E 198 B5
Eigg U.K. 56°54N 6°10W 167 E2
Eighty Mile Beach Australia 19°30S 120°40E 278 C3
Eikefjord Norway 61°35N 5°27E 164 C2
Eikelandsosen Norway 60°15N 5°43E 164 D2
Eiken Norway 58°29N 7°14E 164 F4
Eikeren Norway 59°38N 9°58E 164 E6
Eikesdalen Norway 62°28N 8°12E 164 B5
Eil Somali Rep. 8°0N 49°50E 267 C6
Eil, L. U.K. 56°51N 5°16W 167 E3
Eil Malk Palau 7°10N 134°23E 288 c
Eildon Australia 37°14S 145°55E 283 D6
Eildon, L. Australia 37°10S 146°0E 283 D7
Eildon △ Australia 37°10S 145°56E 283 D6
Eilean Sar = Western Isles ☐ U.K. 57°30N 7°10W 167 D1
Eilenburg Germany 51°27N 12°36E 178 D8
Ein Arik West Bank 31°54N 35°8E 123 A1
Ein el Luweiqa Sudan 14°5N 33°50E 257 E3
Ein Naquba Israel 31°47N 35°7E 123 B1
Ein Rafa Israel 31°47N 35°7E 123 B1
Eina Norway 60°38N 10°35E 164 D7
Einarsstaðir Iceland 65°44N 17°24W 155 B9
Einasleigh Australia 18°32S 144°5E 280 B3
Einasleigh → Australia 17°30S 142°17E 280 B3
Einbeck Germany 51°49N 9°53E 178 D5
Eindhoven Neths. 51°26N 5°28E 170 C5
Einsiedeln Switz. 47°7N 8°46E 179 H4
Eire = Ireland ■ Europe 53°50N 7°52W 166 C4
Eiríksjökull Iceland 64°46N 20°24W 155 C6
Eiríksstaðir Iceland 65°7N 15°25W 155 B11
Eirunepé Brazil 6°35S 69°53W 330 B4
Eiseb → Namibia 20°33S 20°59E 270 B2
Eisenach Germany 50°58N 10°19E 178 E6
Eisenberg Germany 50°58N 11°54E 178 E7
Eisenerz Austria 47°32N 14°54E 180 D7
Eisenhüttenstadt Germany 52°9N 14°38E 178 C10
Eisenkappel Austria 46°29N 14°36E 180 E7
Eisenstadt Austria 47°51N 16°31E 181 D9
Eisenstein = Železná Ruda Czech Rep. 49°8N 13°15E 180 B6
Eisfeld Germany 50°25N 10°54E 179 E6
Eisleben Germany 51°32N 11°32E 178 D7
Eislingen Germany 48°41N 9°42E 179 G5
Eivindvik Norway 60°59N 5°5E 164 D2
Eivissa Spain 38°54N 1°26E 206 D1
Eixe, Serra do Spain 42°24N 6°54W 194 C4
Eizariya West Bank 31°46N 35°16E 123 B2
Ejby Denmark 55°41N 12°24E 118 A2
Ejea de los Caballeros Spain 42°7N 1°9W 196 C3
Ejeda Madag. 24°20S 44°31E 272 C1
Ejigbo Nigeria 6°33N 3°18E 124 A1
Ejura Ghana 7°23N 1°15W 263 D4
Ejutla Mexico 16°34N 96°44W 319 D5
Ekalaka U.S.A. 45°53N 104°33W 304 D11
Ekalla Gabon 1°27S 14°0E 264 C2
Ekanga Dem. Rep. of the Congo 2°23S 23°14E 264 C4
Ekaterinburg = Yekaterinburg Russia 56°50N 60°30E 214 D7
Ekeberg Norway 59°53N 10°46E 133 A3
Ekenäs = Tammisaari Finland 60°0N 23°26E 188 B2
Ekenässjön Sweden 57°28N 15°1E 163 G9
Ekerö Sweden 59°16N 17°45E 162 E11
Eket Nigeria 4°38N 7°56E 263 E6
Eketahuna N.Z. 40°38S 175°43E 284 G4
Ekibastuz Kazakhstan 51°50N 75°10E 217 B9
Ekiti ☐ Nigeria 7°25N 5°20E 263 D6
Eklutna U.S.A. 61°27N 149°22W 303 F10
Eknäs Sweden 59°18N 18°13E 139 B3
Ekoli Dem. Rep. of the Congo 0°23S 24°13E 264 C4
Ekoln Sweden 59°45N 17°37E 162 E11
Ekouamou Congo 0°8N 16°31E 264 B3
Ekoungounou Congo 1°10S 15°52E 264 C3
Ekshärad Sweden 60°10N 13°30E 162 D7
Eksjö Sweden 57°40N 14°58E 163 G8
Ekukola Dem. Rep. of the Congo 0°31S 18°56E 264 C3
Ekuku Dem. Rep. of the Congo 0°41S 21°42E 264 C4
Ekukula Dem. Rep. of the Congo 0°15N 21°30E 264 B4
Ekuma → Namibia 18°40S 16°2E 270 A2
Ekuta Dem. Rep. of the Congo 3°0N 18°50E 264 B3
Ekwan → Canada 53°12N 82°15W 298 B3
Ekwan Pt. Canada 53°16N 82°7W 298 B3
Ekwok U.S.A. 59°22N 157°30W 303 G8
El Aaiún W. Sahara 27°9N 13°12W 260 C2
El Aargub Mauritania 23°37N 15°52W 260 D1
El Abanico Chile 37°20S 71°31W 334 D1
El 'Abbasiya El Qâhira, Egypt 30°3N 31°16E 117 A2
El Abbasiya Sudan 12°10N 31°18E 257 E3
El Abiodh-Sidi-Cheikh Algeria 32°53N 0°31E 261 B5
El Adde Somali Rep. 2°35N 46°9E 267 D6
El Adeb Larache Algeria 27°22N 8°52E 261 C6
El 'Agrûd Egypt 30°14N 34°24E 251 H5
El Agustino Peru 12°2S 77°0W 124 B2
El Agustino, Cerro Peru 12°3S 76°59W 124 B3
El Aïoun Morocco 34°33N 2°30W 261 B4
El Ait Sudan 12°22N 27°27E 257 E2
El 'Aiyat Egypt 29°36N 31°15E 256 J7
El 'Alamein Egypt 30°48N 28°58E 256 A2
El Alto Peru 4°15S 81°14W 330 A1
El Aouj Mauritania 22°53N 12°49W 260 D2
El 'Aqaba, W. → Egypt 30°7N 33°54E 251 H4
El 'Arag Egypt 28°40N 26°20E 256 B2
El Arahal Spain 37°15N 5°33W 195 H5
El Aricha Algeria 34°13N 1°10W 261 B4
El Arīḥā West Bank 31°52N 35°27E 251 G6
El 'Arîsh Egypt 31°8N 33°50E 251 G4
El 'Arîsh, W. → Egypt 31°8N 33°47E 251 G4
El Arrouch Algeria 36°37N 6°53E 261 A6
El Asnam = Ech Chéliff Algeria 36°10N 1°20E 261 A5
El Astillero Spain 43°24N 3°49W 194 B7
El Avagi Somali Rep. 3°36N 46°57E 267 D6
El Badâri Egypt 27°4N 31°25E 256 B3
El Badrshein Egypt 29°51N 31°16E 251 J2
El Bagur Egypt 30°25N 31°2E 251 H2
El Bahrein Egypt 28°30N 26°25E 256 B2
El Ballâs Egypt 26°2N 32°43E 256 B3
El Balyana Egypt 26°10N 32°3E 256 B3
El Banco Colombia 9°0N 73°58W 328 B3
El Baqeir Sudan 18°40N 33°40E 256 D3
El Baragil Egypt 30°4N 31°9E 117 A1
El Barco de Ávila Spain 40°21N 5°31W 194 E5
El Barco de Valdeorras = O Barco Spain 42°23N 6°58W 194 C4
El Basâlîn Egypt 29°58N 31°16E 117 B2
El Bauga Sudan 18°18N 33°52E 256 D3
El Baúl Venezuela 8°57N 68°17W 328 B4
El Bawiti Egypt 28°25N 28°45E 256 B2
El Bayadh Algeria 33°40N 1°1E 261 B5
El Bayadh ☐ Algeria 32°30N 1°10E 261 B5
El Bierzo Spain 42°45N 6°30W 194 C4
El Bira West Bank 31°54N 35°13E 123 A2
El Bluff Nic. 11°59N 83°40W 320 D3
El Bolsón Argentina 41°55S 71°30W 336 B2
El Bonillo Spain 38°57N 2°35W 197 G2
El Bosque Chile 33°32S 70°40W 137 C2
El Buheirat ☐ Sudan 7°0N 30°0E 257 F3
El Bur Somali Rep. 4°40N 46°37E 267 D6
El Burgo de Osma Spain 41°35N 3°4W 196 D1
El Caín Argentina 41°38S 68°19W 336 B3
El Cajon U.S.A. 32°48N 116°58W 307 N10
El Callao Venezuela 7°18N 61°50W 329 B5
El Campo U.S.A. 29°12N 96°16W 314 G6
El Capitan U.S.A. 37°44N 119°38E 306 H7
El Carmen Bolivia 13°40S 63°55W 331 C5
El Carmen Santiago, Chile 33°22S 70°43W 137 B1
El Centro U.S.A. 32°48N 115°34W 307 N11
El Cerro Bolivia 17°30S 61°40W 331 D5
El Cerro de Andévalo Spain 37°45N 6°57W 195 H4
El Cocuy Colombia 6°25N 72°27W 328 B3
El Cocuy △ Colombia 6°33N 72°5W 328 B3
El Compadre Mexico 32°20N 116°14W 307 N10
El Corcovado Argentina 43°25S 71°35W 336 B2
El Coronil Spain 37°5N 5°38W 195 H5
El Cortijo Chile 33°22S 70°42W 137 B1
El Cristo, Vaso Regulador Mexico 19°30N 99°5W 128 B1
El Cuy Argentina 39°55S 68°25W 336 A3
El Cuyo Mexico 21°31N 87°41W 319 C7
El Dab'a Egypt 31°0N 28°27E 256 H6
El Daheir Egypt 31°13N 34°10E 251 G5
El Dambahaddo Somali Rep. 3°17N 46°40E 267 D6
El Deir Egypt 25°25N 32°20E 256 B3
El Dere Ethiopia 5°6N 43°5E 267 C5
El Dere Somali Rep. 3°50N 47°8E 267 D6
El Dere Somali Rep. 5°22N 46°11E 267 C6
El Descanso Mexico 32°12N 116°58W 307 N10
El Desemboque Mexico 30°33N 113°1W 318 A2
El Dilingat Egypt 30°50N 30°31E 256 H7
El Diviso Colombia 1°22N 78°14W 328 C2
El Djouf Africa 21°25N 6°40W 260 D3
El Djouf Mauritania 20°0N 9°0W 260 C3
El Dorado Sinaloa, Mexico 24°17N 107°21W 318 C3
El Dorado Ark., U.S.A. 33°12N 92°40W 314 E8
El Dorado Kans., U.S.A. 37°49N 96°52W 308 G5
El Dorado Venezuela 6°55N 61°37W 329 B5
El Dorado Springs U.S.A. 37°52N 94°1W 310 G2
El Duqqi Egypt 30°1N 31°12E 117 A2
El Eglab Algeria 26°20N 4°30W 260 C4
El 'Ein Sudan 16°35N 29°22E 257 D2
El Ejido Spain 36°47N 2°49W 195 J8
El Encinar de los Reyes Spain 40°30N 3°39W 127 A2
El Escorial Spain 40°35N 4°7W 194 E6
El Espinar Spain 41°43N 4°15W 194 D6
El Eulma Algeria 36°9N 5°42E 261 A6
El Faiyûm Egypt 29°19N 30°50E 256 J7
El Fâsher Sudan 13°33N 25°26E 257 E2
El Fashn Egypt 28°50N 30°54E 256 J7
El Ferrol = Ferrol Spain 43°29N 8°15W 194 B2
El Fifi Sudan 10°4N 25°0E 257 E2
El Fud Ethiopia 7°15N 42°52E 267 C5
El Fuerte Mexico 26°25N 108°39W 318 B3
El Ga'a Sudan 14°16N 29°59E 257 E2
El Gal Somali Rep. 10°58N 50°20E 267 B7
El Gamâlîya Egypt 31°10N 31°52E 251 G2
El Garef Sudan 12°3N 34°19E 257 E3
El Gebir Sudan 13°40N 29°40E 257 E2
El Gedida Egypt 25°40N 28°30E 256 B2
El Geneina = Al Junaynah Sudan 13°27N 22°45E 259 F4
El Geteina Sudan 14°50N 32°27E 257 E3
El Gezira Egypt 30°2N 31°13E 117 A2
El Gezira ☐ Sudan 15°0N 33°0E 257 E3
El Gharbîya ☐ Egypt 30°50N 31°0E 251 H2
El Ghurîya Egypt 30°2N 31°15E 117 A2
El Gir Sudan 19°50N 28°18E 256 D2
El Gîza Egypt 30°0N 31°12E 117 A2
El Gîza ☐ Egypt 29°46N 31°18E 251 J2
El Gogorrón △ Mexico 21°49N 100°57W 318 C4
El Goléa Algeria 30°30N 2°50E 261 B5
El Golfo de Santa Clara Mexico 31°42N 114°30W 318 A2
El Grau Spain 39°0N 0°7W 197 G4
El Hadeb W. Sahara 25°51N 13°0W 260 C2
El Hadjira Algeria 32°36N 5°30E 261 B6
El Hagiz Sudan 15°15N 35°50E 257 D4
El Hâi Egypt 29°39N 31°18E 256 J7
El Hajeb Morocco 33°43N 5°13W 260 B3
El Hamma Tunisia 33°54N 9°48E 258 B1
El Hammam Egypt 30°52N 29°25E 256 A2
El Hammâmi Mauritania 23°3N 11°30W 260 D2
El Hâmûl Egypt 31°18N 31°9E 251 G2
El Hamurre Somali Rep. 7°13N 48°54E 267 C6
El Hank Mauritania 24°30N 7°0W 260 D3
El Hasian W. Sahara 26°20N 14°0W 260 C2
El Hawata Sudan 13°25N 34°42E 257 E3
El Heiz Egypt 27°50N 28°40E 256 B2
El Hideib Sudan 13°0N 32°50E 257 E3
El Hilla Sudan 13°24N 27°2E 257 E2
El Homeur Algeria 29°43N 1°45E 261 C5
El 'Idisât Egypt 25°30N 32°35E 256 B3
El Iskandarîya Egypt 31°13N 29°58E 256 H7
El Jadida Morocco 33°11N 8°17W 260 B3
El Jadida ☐ Morocco 32°45N 8°30W 260 B3
El Jardal Honduras 14°54N 88°50W 320 D2
El Jebelein Sudan 12°40N 32°55E 257 E3
El Jebha Morocco 35°11N 4°43W 260 A4
El Jem Tunisia 35°19N 10°41E 258 A2
El Kab Sudan 19°27N 32°46E 256 D3
El Kafr el Sharqi Egypt 31°16N 31°10E 256 H7
El Kala Algeria 36°53N 8°26E 261 A6
El Kamlin Sudan 15°3N 33°11E 257 D3
El Kantara Algeria 35°14N 5°45E 261 A6
El Kantara Tunisia 33°45N 10°58E 258 B2
El Karaba Sudan 18°32N 33°41E 256 D3
El Kef Tunisia 36°12N 8°47E 258 A1
El Kef ☐ Tunisia 36°0N 9°0E 261 A6
El Kelâa de Srahna Morocco 32°4N 7°27W 260 B3
El Kelâa de Srahna ☐ Morocco 32°10N 7°45W 260 B3
El Kere Ethiopia 5°50N 42°5E 257 F5
El Khadr West Bank 31°42N 35°10E 123 B1
El Khalîfa Egypt 30°0N 31°15E 117 A2
El Khandaq Sudan 18°30N 30°30E 256 D3
El Khânka Egypt 30°13N 31°21E 251 H2
El Khârga Egypt 25°30N 30°33E 256 B3
El Khartûm Sudan 15°31N 32°35E 257 D3
El Khartûm ☐ Sudan 16°0N 33°0E 257 D3
El Khartûm Bahrî Sudan 15°40N 32°31E 257 D3
El Khroub Algeria 36°10N 6°55E 261 A6
El Kôm el Ahmar Egypt 30°6N 31°10E 117 A2
El Kseur Algeria 36°46N 4°49E 261 A5
El Ksiba Morocco 32°45N 6°1W 260 B3
El Kuntilla Egypt 30°1N 34°45E 251 H5
El Laqâwa Sudan 11°25N 29°1E 257 E2
El Leh Ethiopia 3°46N 39°13E 257 G4
El Leiya Sudan 16°15N 35°28E 257 D4
El Lucero Mexico 30°37N 106°31W 318 A3
El Ma'âdi Egypt 29°57N 31°15E 117 B2
El Maestrazgo Spain 40°30N 0°25W 196 E4
El Mafâza Sudan 13°38N 34°30E 257 E3
El Maghra Egypt 30°15N 28°55E 256 A2
El Mahalla el Kubra Egypt 31°0N 31°0E 256 H7
El Mahârîq Egypt 25°35N 30°35E 256 B3
El Maîmûn Egypt 29°14N 31°12E 256 J7
El Maitén Argentina 42°3S 71°10W 336 B2
El Maiz Algeria 28°19N 0°9W 261 C4
El Maks el Bahari Egypt 24°30N 30°40E 256 C3
El Malpais ⌓ U.S.A. 34°53N 108°0W 305 J10
El Manshâh Egypt 26°26N 31°50E 256 B3
El Mansour Algeria 27°47N 0°14W 261 C4
El Mansûra Egypt 31°0N 31°19E 256 H7
El Manteco Venezuela 7°38N 62°45W 329 B5
El Manzala Egypt 31°10N 31°50E 256 H7
El Marâgha Egypt 26°35N 31°10E 256 B3
El Masid Sudan 15°15N 33°0E 257 D3
El Masnou Spain 41°28N 2°20E 196 D7
El Matarîya El Mansûra, Egypt 31°15N 32°0E 256 H8
El Matarîya El Qâhira, Egypt 30°7N 31°18E 117 A2
El Meda Ethiopia 5°39N 41°47E 257 F5
El Medano Canary Is. 28°3N 16°32W 153 e1
El Meghaier Algeria 33°55N 5°58E 261 B6
El Meraguen Algeria 28°0N 0°7W 261 C4
El Metemma Sudan 16°50N 33°10E 257 D3
El Miamo Venezuela 7°39N 61°46W 329 B5
El Milagro Argentina 30°59S 65°59W 334 C2
El Milia Algeria 36°51N 6°13E 261 A6
El Minufîya ☐ Egypt 30°30N 31°0E 251 H2
El Minyâ Egypt 28°7N 30°33E 256 B3
El Mohandessin Egypt 30°2N 31°11E 117 A2
El Monte U.S.A. 34°4N 118°1W 126 B4
El Montseny Spain 41°55N 2°25E 196 D7
El Mreyye Mauritania 18°0N 6°0W 262 B3
El Muqattam Egypt 30°1N 31°17E 117 A2
El Mûskî Egypt 30°3N 31°15E 117 A2
El Nido Phil. 11°10N 119°25E 233 F2
El Niybo Ethiopia 4°40N 39°55E 257 G4
El Obeid Sudan 13°8N 30°10E 257 E3
El Odaiya Sudan 12°8N 28°12E 257 E2
El Oro Mexico 19°51N 100°7W 319 D4
El Oro ☐ Ecuador 3°30S 79°50W 328 D2
El Oued Algeria 33°20N 6°58E 261 B6
El Oued ☐ Algeria 33°10N 7°15E 261 B6
El Palmar Bolivia 17°50S 63°9W 331 D5
El Palmar Venezuela 7°58N 61°53W 329 B5
El Palmar △ Argentina 32°10S 58°31W 334 C4
El Palmito, Presa Mexico 25°40N 105°30W 318 B3
El Pardo Spain 40°30N 3°46W 127 A1
El Paso = Derby U.S.A. 37°33N 97°16W 308 G5
El Paso Ill., U.S.A. 40°44N 89°1W 310 D7
El Paso Tex., U.S.A. 31°45N 106°29W 314 F1
El Pedernoso Spain 39°29N 2°45W 197 F2
El Pedroso Spain 37°51N 5°45W 195 H5
El Pilar Venezuela 10°32N 63°9W 329 A5
El Pinacate y Gran Desierto de Altar = Gran Desierto del Pinacate ⌓ Mexico 31°51N 113°32W 318 A2
El Pobo de Dueñas Spain 40°46N 1°39W 196 E3
El Portal Calif., U.S.A. 37°41N 119°47W 306 H7
El Portal Fla., U.S.A. 25°51N 80°11W 128 A2
El Porvenir Mexico 31°15N 105°51W 318 A3
El Prat de Llobregat Spain 41°19N 2°5E 114 B1
El Progreso Galápagos Is., Ecuador 0°54S 89°33W 330 a
El Progreso Honduras 15°26N 87°51W 320 C2
El Pueblito Mexico 29°6N 105°7W 318 B3
El Pueblo Canary Is. 28°36N 17°47W 153 e1
El Pueblo de Los Angeles Historic Park Los Angeles, U.S.A. 127 b2
El Puente del Arzobispo Spain 39°48N 5°10W 194 F5
El Puerto de Santa María Spain 36°36N 6°13W 195 J4
El Qâhira Egypt 30°2N 31°13E 117 A2
El Qâhira ☐ Egypt 30°2N 31°13E 251 H2
El Qanâyat Egypt 30°37N 31°27E 251 H2
El Qantara Egypt 30°51N 32°20E 251 H3
El Qasr Egypt 25°44N 28°42E 256 B2
El Qassâsîn Egypt 30°33N 31°55E 251 H2
El Qubâbât Egypt 29°28N 31°16E 256 J7
El Qubba Egypt 30°4N 31°16E 117 A2
El Quseima Egypt 30°40N 34°15E 251 H5
El Qusîya Egypt 27°29N 30°44E 256 B3
El Râshda Egypt 25°36N 28°57E 256 B2
El Reloj Mexico 19°19N 99°9W 128 C2
El Reno U.S.A. 35°32N 97°57W 300 C7
El Retiro Spain 40°25N 3°41W 127 B1
El Rey △ Argentina 24°40S 64°34W 334 A3
El Rîdisiya Egypt 24°56N 32°51E 256 C3
El Rio U.S.A. 34°14N 119°10W 307 L7
El Ronquillo Spain 37°44N 6°10W 195 H4
El Roque, Pta. Canary Is. 28°10N 15°25W 153 e1
El Rosarito Mexico 28°38N 114°4W 318 B2
El Rubio Spain 37°22N 5°0W 195 H5
El Saff Egypt 29°34N 31°16E 256 J7
El Salto Santiago, Chile 33°22S 70°38W 137 B2
El Salto Durango, Mexico 23°47N 105°22W 318 C3
El Salvador ■ Cent. Amer. 13°50N 89°0W 320 D2
El Sauce Nic. 13°0N 86°40W 320 D2
El Saucejo Spain 37°4N 5°6W 195 H5
El Sereno U.S.A. 34°6N 118°10W 126 B3
El Shallal Egypt 24°0N 32°53E 256 C3
El Simbillawein Egypt 30°48N 31°13E 256 H7
El Sombrero Venezuela 9°23N 67°3W 328 B4
El Sueco Mexico 29°54N 106°24W 318 B3
El Suweis Egypt 29°58N 32°31E 256 J8
El Suweis ☐ Egypt 29°30N 32°15E 251 J3
El Tabbîn Egypt 29°47N 31°18E 256 J7
El Talibîya Egypt 29°59N 31°10E 117 B2
El Tamá △ S. Amer. 7°25N 72°25W 328 B3
El Tamarâni, W. → Egypt 30°7N 34°43E 251 H5
El Tarf Algeria 36°46N 8°19E 261 A6
El Tarf ☐ Algeria 36°45N 8°10E 261 A6
El Thamad Egypt 29°40N 34°28E 251 J5
El Tigre Venezuela 8°44N 64°15W 329 B5
El Tîh, Gebel Egypt 29°40N 33°50E 251 J4
El Tîna Egypt 31°3N 32°22E 256 H8
El Tocuyo Venezuela 9°47N 69°48W 328 B4
El Tofo Chile 29°22S 71°18W 334 B1
El Tránsito Chile 28°52S 70°17W 334 B1
El Tucuche Trin. & Tob. 10°43N 61°25W 323 t
El Tuparro △ Colombia 5°19N 68°28W 328 B4
El Tûr Egypt 28°14N 33°36E 251 K4
El Turbio Argentina 51°45S 72°5W 336 D2
El Uarre Somali Rep. 3°4N 45°20E 267 D6

El Uinle Somali Rep. 3°4N 41°42E 267 D5
El Uqsur Egypt 25°41N 32°38E 256 B3
El Valle ⌓ Spain 37°56N 1°6W 197 H3
El Vendrell Spain 41°10N 1°30E 196 D6
El Vergel Chihuahua, Mexico 26°28N 106°22W 318 B3
El Vergel Distrito Federal, Mexico 19°18N 99°5W 128 C2
El Vigía Venezuela 8°38N 71°39W 328 B3
El Viso del Alcor Spain 37°23N 5°43W 195 H5
El Wabeira Egypt 29°34N 33°6E 251 J4
El Wâhli Egypt 30°3N 31°16E 117 A2
El Wak North Eastern, Kenya 2°49N 40°56E 268 B5
El Wak Somali Rep. 2°44N 41°1E 267 D5
El Waqf Egypt 25°45N 32°15E 256 B3
El Weguet Ethiopia 5°28N 42°17E 257 F5
El Wuz Sudan 15°5N 30°7E 257 D3
El Yunque Puerto Rico 18°19N 65°48W 321 b
El Zamâlik Egypt 30°3N 31°12E 117 A2
El Zeitûn Egypt 30°6N 31°18E 117 A2
Elafonisos Greece 36°29N 22°56E 204 E4
Elamanchili India 17°33N 82°50E 244 F6
Élancourt France 48°47N 1°58E 173 D8
Elands Australia 31°37S 152°20E 283 A10
Elandsfontein Junc. = Germiston S. Africa 26°13S 28°10E 123 B2
Elasa Greece 35°18N 26°21E 205 F8
Elassona Greece 39°53N 22°12E 204 B4
Elat Israel 29°30N 34°56E 251 J5
Elati Oros Greece 38°43N 20°39E 207 B2
Elatia Greece 38°37N 22°46E 204 C4
Elâzığ Turkey 38°37N 39°14E 213 C8
Elâzığ ☐ Turkey 38°40N 39°15E 213 C8
Elba Italy 42°46N 10°17E 198 F7
Elba Ala., U.S.A. 31°25N 86°4W 316 D3
Elbasan Albania 41°9N 20°9E 202 E4
Elbe U.S.A. 46°45N 122°10W 306 D4
Elbe → Europe 53°50N 9°0E 178 B4
Elbe-Seitenkanal Germany 52°45N 10°32E 178 C6
Elberfeld U.S.A. 38°10N 87°27W 311 F9
Elbert, Mt. U.S.A. 39°7N 106°27W 304 G10
Elberton U.S.A. 34°7N 82°52W 316 A7
Elbeuf France 49°17N 1°2E 172 C8
Elbeyli Turkey 36°40N 37°27E 250 B8
Elbing = Elbląg Poland 54°10N 19°25E 184 D6
Elbistan Turkey 38°13N 37°15E 212 C7
Elbląg Poland 54°10N 19°25E 184 D6
Elbow Canada 51°7N 106°35W 297 C7
Elbrus Russia 43°21N 42°30E 191 J6
Elbufer-Drawehn ⌓ Germany 53°8N 10°58E 178 B6
Elburn U.S.A. 41°54N 88°28W 311 C8
Elburz Mts. = Alborz, Reshteh-ye Kūhhā-ye Iran 36°0N 52°0E 247 C7
Elche Spain 38°15N 0°42W 197 G4
Elche de la Sierra Spain 38°27N 2°3W 197 G2
Elcho I. Australia 11°55S 135°45E 280 A2
Elda Spain 38°29N 0°47W 197 G4
Eldama Ravine Kenya 0°3N 35°43E 268 B4
Elde → Germany 53°7N 11°15E 178 B7
Eldey Iceland 63°45N 22°55W 155 D4
Eldon Iowa, U.S.A. 40°55N 92°13W 310 D4
Eldon Mo., U.S.A. 38°21N 92°35W 310 F4
Eldon Wash., U.S.A. 47°33N 123°3W 306 C3
Eldora U.S.A. 42°22N 93°5W 310 B3
Eldorado = Echo Bay Canada 66°5N 117°55W 294 C8
Eldorado Argentina 26°28S 54°43W 335 B5
Eldorado Ont., Canada 44°35N 77°31W 312 B7
Eldorado Ill., U.S.A. 37°49N 88°26W 311 G8
Eldorado Tex., U.S.A. 30°52N 100°36W 314 F4
Eldorendo U.S.A. 31°3N 84°39W 316 D5
Eldoret Kenya 0°30N 35°17E 268 B4
Eldred U.S.A. 41°58N 78°23W 312 E6
Eldridge U.S.A. 41°39N 90°35W 310 C6
Elea, C. Cyprus 35°19N 34°4E 207 E10
Eleanora, Pk. Australia 32°57S 121°9E 279 F3
Eleao U.S.A. 21°27N 157°52W 302 K14
Elefantes → Africa 24°10S 32°40E 271 B5
Elefantes, B. das Angola 13°13S 12°44E 265 E2
Elefantes, G. Chile 46°28S 73°49W 336 C2
Elefsina Greece 38°4N 23°26E 204 C5
Eleftherios Venizelos ✈ (ATH) Greece 37°56N 23°56E 112 A3
Elektrogorsk Russia 55°56N 38°50E 188 E10
Elektroperedacha = Elektrogorsk Russia 55°56N 38°50E 188 E10
Elektrostal Russia 55°41N 38°32E 188 E10
Elektrovoz = Stupino Russia 54°57N 38°2E 188 E10
Elele Nigeria 5°5N 6°50E 263 D6
Elemi Triangle Africa 5°0N 35°20E 257 G4
Elena Bulgaria 42°55N 25°53E 203 D9
Elephant Butte Res. U.S.A. 33°9N 107°11W 305 K10
Elephant I. Antarctica 61°0S 55°0W 151 C18
Elephant Pass Sri Lanka 9°35N 80°25E 245 K5
Elephanta Caves India 18°57N 72°57E 130 B2
Elephanta I. India 18°57N 72°56E 130 B2
Elesbão Veloso Brazil 6°13S 42°8W 332 C3
Eleshnitsa Bulgaria 41°52N 23°36E 202 E7
Eleşkirt Turkey 39°50N 42°50E 213 C10
Eleuthera Bahamas 25°0N 76°20W 320 B4
Eleutheroupoli Greece 40°52N 24°20E 203 F8
Elfin Cove U.S.A. 58°12N 136°22W 303 G13
Elgå Norway 62°10N 11°56E 164 B8
Elgin Ont., Canada 44°36N 76°13W 313 B8
Elgin Moray, U.K. 57°39N 3°19W 167 D5
Elgin Ill., U.S.A. 42°2N 88°17W 311 B8
Elgin N. Dak., U.S.A. 46°24N 101°51W 308 B3
Elgin Oreg., U.S.A. 45°34N 117°55W 304 D5
Elgin S.C., U.S.A. 34°10N 80°48W 316 A9
Elgin Tex., U.S.A. 30°21N 97°22W 314 F6
Elgoibar Spain 43°13N 2°24W 196 B2
Elgon, Mt. Africa 1°10N 34°30E 268 B3
Elgspiggen Norway 62°10N 11°21E 164 B8
Eliase Indonesia 8°21S 130°48E 231 F8
Elikonos Oros Greece 38°18N 22°45E 204 C4
Elim Namibia 17°48S 15°31E 270 A2
Elim Western Cape, S. Africa 34°35S 19°45E 270 D2
Elim Alaska, U.S.A. 64°37N 162°15W 303 D7
Elin Pelin Bulgaria 42°40N 23°36E 202 D7
Elingampangu Dem. Rep. of the Congo 2°0S 24°4E 264 C4
Elipa Dem. Rep. of the Congo 1°3S 24°20E 264 C4
Eliseu Martins Brazil 8°13S 43°42W 332 C3
Elista Russia 46°16N 44°14E 191 G7
Eliza, L. Australia 37°15S 139°50E 282 D3
Elizabeth S. Austral., Australia 34°42S 138°41E 282 C3
Elizabeth Ill., U.S.A. 42°19N 90°13W 310 B6
Elizabeth N.J., U.S.A. 40°39N 74°12W 313 F10
Elizabeth, B. Ecuador 0°36S 91°12W 330 a
Elizabeth City U.S.A. 36°18N 76°14W 315 C16
Elizabethton U.S.A. 36°21N 82°13W 315 C13
Elizabethtown Ky., U.S.A. 37°42N 85°52W 311 G11
Elizabethtown N.Y., U.S.A. 44°13N 73°36W 313 B11
Elizabethtown Pa., U.S.A. 40°9N 76°36W 313 F8
Elizabethville = Lubumbashi Dem. Rep. of the Congo 11°40S 27°28E 269 E2
Elizondo Spain 43°12N 1°30W 196 B3
Ełk Poland 53°50N 22°21E 184 E9
Elk → B.C., Canada 49°11N 115°14W 296 C5
Ełk → Poland 53°41N 22°28E 184 E9
Elk → Ala., U.S.A. 34°46N 87°16W 315 D11
Elk City U.S.A. 35°25N 99°25W 314 D5
Elk Creek U.S.A. 39°36N 122°32W 306 F4
Elk Grove U.S.A. 38°25N 121°22W 306 G5
Elk Island △ Canada 53°35N 112°59W 296 C6
Elk Lake Canada 47°40N 80°25W 298 C3
Elk Point Canada 53°54N 110°55W 297 C6
Elk River Idaho, U.S.A. 46°47N 116°11W 304 C5
Elk River Minn., U.S.A. 45°18N 93°35W 308 C7
Elkader U.S.A. 42°51N 91°24W 310 B5
Elkedra → Australia 21°8S 136°22E 280 C2
Elkhart Ind., U.S.A. 41°41N 85°58W 311 C11
Elkhart Kans., U.S.A. 37°0N 101°54W 308 G3
Elkhart → U.S.A. 41°41N 85°58W 311 C11
Elkhorn Man., Canada 49°59N 101°14W 297 D8
Elkhorn Wis., U.S.A. 42°40N 88°33W 311 B8
Elkhorn → U.S.A. 41°8N 96°19W 308 E5
Elkhovo Bulgaria 42°10N 26°35E 203 D10
Elkin U.S.A. 36°15N 80°51W 315 C14
Elkins U.S.A. 38°55N 79°51W 309 F14
Elkland U.S.A. 41°59N 77°19W 312 E7
Elko B.C., Canada 49°20N 115°10W 296 D5
Elko Nev., U.S.A. 40°50N 115°46W 304 F6
Elkton U.S.A. 43°49N 83°11W 312 C1
Ellas = Greece ■ Europe 40°0N 23°0E 204 B3
Ellaville Fla., U.S.A. 30°23N 83°10W 316 E6
Ellaville Ga., U.S.A. 32°14N 84°19W 316 C5
Ellboda Sweden 59°24N 18°15E 139 A3
Ellef Ringnes I. Canada 78°30N 102°2W 295 B9
Ellen, Mt. U.S.A. 44°9N 72°56W 313 B12
Ellenburg U.S.A. 44°54N 73°48W 313 B11
Ellendale U.S.A. 46°0N 98°32W 308 B4
Ellenor, L. U.S.A. 28°28N 81°25W 133 B2
Ellensburg U.S.A. 46°59N 120°34W 304 C3
Ellenville U.S.A. 41°43N 74°24W 313 E10
Ellerton Barbados 13°7N 59°33W 323 r
Ellery, Mt. Australia 37°28S 148°47E 283 D8
Ellesmere = Scottsdale Australia 41°9S 147°31E 281 G4
Ellesmere, L. N.Z. 43°47S 172°28E 285 H7
Ellesmere I. Canada 79°30N 80°0W 295 B12
Ellesmere Port U.K. 53°17N 2°54W 168 D5
Ellettsville U.S.A. 39°14N 86°38W 311 E10
Ellice Is. = Tuvalu ■ Pac. Oc. 8°0S 178°0E 277 B14
Ellicottville U.S.A. 42°17N 78°40W 312 D6
Elliniko Olympic Complex Greece 37°50N 23°45E 112 B2
Elliot N. Terr., Australia 17°33S 133°32E 280 B1
Elliot Eastern Cape, S. Africa 31°22S 27°48E 271 D4
Elliot Lake Canada 46°25N 82°35W 298 C3
Elliotdale = Xhora S. Africa 31°55S 28°38E 271 D4
Elliott U.S.A. 34°6N 80°10W 316 A9
Elliott Key U.S.A. 25°27N 80°12W 317 K9
Ellipse, The Washington, D.C., U.S.A. 143 b1
Ellis U.S.A. 38°56N 99°34W 308 F4
Ellis I. U.S.A. 40°41N 74°2W 132 B1
Elliston Australia 33°39S 134°53E 281 E1
Ellisville U.S.A. 31°36N 89°12W 315 F10
Ellon U.K. 57°22N 2°4W 167 D6
Ellora India 20°1N 75°10E 244 D2
Ellore = Eluru India 16°48N 81°8E 244 F5
Elloree U.S.A. 33°32N 80°34W 316 B9
Ellsworth Kans., U.S.A. 38°44N 98°14W 308 F4
Ellsworth Maine, U.S.A. 44°33N 68°25W 309 C19
Ellsworth Land Antarctica 76°0S 89°0W 151 D16
Ellsworth Mts. Antarctica 78°30S 85°0W 151 D16
Ellwangen Germany 48°57N 10°8E 179 G6
Ellwood City U.S.A. 40°52N 80°17W 312 F4
Ellzey U.S.A. 29°19N 82°48W 317 F7
Elm Switz. 46°54N 9°10E 179 J5
Elm-Lappwald ⌓ Germany 52°15N 10°50E 178 C6
Elm Park U.K. 51°32N 0°12E 125 A5
Elma Man., Canada 49°52N 95°55W 297 D9
Elma Wash., U.S.A. 47°0N 123°25W 306 D3
Elmadağ Turkey 39°55N 33°14E 212 C5
Elmalı Turkey 36°44N 29°56E 205 E11
Elmers End U.K. 51°23N 0°2W 125 B3
Elmhurst Ill., U.S.A. 41°53N 87°56W 311 C9
Elmhurst N.Y., U.S.A. 40°44N 73°53W 132 B2
Elmina Ghana 5°5N 1°21W 263 D4
Elmira Ont., Canada 43°36N 80°33W 312 C4
Elmira N.Y., U.S.A. 42°6N 76°48W 312 D8
Elmira Heights U.S.A. 42°8N 76°50W 312 D8
Elmodel U.S.A. 31°21N 84°29W 316 D5
Elmore Vic., Australia 36°30S 144°37E 282 D6
Elmore Ala., U.S.A. 32°32N 86°19W 316 C3
Elmore Ohio, U.S.A. 41°29N 83°18W 311 C13
Elmshorn Germany 53°43N 9°40E 178 B5
Elmstead U.K. 51°24N 0°2E 125 B4
Elmvale Canada 44°35N 79°52W 312 B5
Elmwood U.S.A. 40°47N 89°58W 310 D7
Elmwood Park Ill., U.S.A. 41°55N 87°48W 119 B2
Elmwood Park N.J., U.S.A. 40°54N 74°7W 132 A1
Elne France 42°36N 2°58E 174 F6
Elnesvågen Norway 62°52N 7°10E 164 B4
Elnora U.S.A. 38°53N 87°5W 311 F9
Eloaua I. Papua N. G. 1°38S 149°40E 286 A5
Elobey, Is. Eq. Guin. 1°1N 9°29E 264 B1
Elongo Dem. Rep. of the Congo 0°19S 21°39E 264 C4
Elora Canada 43°41N 80°26W 312 C4
Elorza Venezuela 7°3N 69°31W 328 B4
Elos Greece 36°46N 22°43E 204 E4
Elounda Greece 35°16N 25°42E 207 E6
Eloy U.S.A. 32°45N 111°33W 305 K8
Éloyes France 48°6N 6°36E 173 D13
Elpitiya Sri Lanka 6°17N 80°10E 245 L5
Elrose Canada 51°12N 108°0W 297 C7
Elsberry U.S.A. 39°10N 90°47W 310 E6
Elsdon N.Z. 41°8S 174°50E 143 A1
Elsdorf Germany 50°55N 6°34E 178 E2
Elsie Mich., U.S.A. 43°5N 84°23W 311 A12
Elsie Oreg., U.S.A. 45°52N 123°36W 306 E3
Elsiesrivier S. Africa 33°55S 18°35E 118 A2
Elsinore = Helsingør Denmark 56°2N 12°35E 163 H6
Elster → Germany 51°25N 11°57E 178 D7
Elsternwick Australia 37°52S 145°0E 128 B2
Elsterwerda Germany 51°27N 13°31E 178 D9
Eltanin Fracture Zone System S. Ocean 54°0S 130°0W 151 B14
Eltham N.Z. 39°26S 174°19E 284 F3
Eltham London, U.K. 51°27N 0°3E 125 B4
Elton Russia 49°5N 46°52E 191 F8
Elton, Ozero Russia 49°5N 46°42E 191 F8
Eltville Germany 50°2N 8°7E 179 E4
Eluru India 16°48N 81°8E 244 F5
Elvas Portugal 38°50N 7°10W 195 G3
Elven France 47°44N 2°36W 172 E4
Elverum Norway 60°53N 11°34E 164 D8
Elvire → Australia 17°51S 128°11E 278 C4
Elvire, Mt. Australia 29°22S 119°36E 279 E2
Elvo → Italy 45°23N 8°21E 198 C5
Elwell, L. = Tiber Res. U.S.A. 48°19N 111°6W 304 B8
Elwood Vic., Australia 37°53S 144°59E 128 B1
Elwood Ill., U.S.A. 41°24N 88°7W 311 C8
Elwood Ind., U.S.A. 40°17N 85°50W 311 D11
Elwood Nebr., U.S.A. 40°36N 99°52W 308 E4
Elx = Elche Spain 38°15N 0°42W 197 G4
Ely Cambs., U.K. 52°24N 0°16E 169 E8
Ely Minn., U.S.A. 47°55N 91°51W 308 B8
Ely Nev., U.S.A. 39°15N 114°54W 304 G6
Elyria U.S.A. 41°22N 82°7W 312 E2
Elyros Greece 35°15N 23°45E 204 F5
Élysée France 48°52N 2°19E 134 A2
Elysian Park Los Angeles, U.S.A. 127 a3
Elz → Germany 48°18N 7°44E 179 G3
Emådalen Sweden 61°20N 14°44E 162 C8
Émaé Vanuatu 17°4S 168°24E 287 G6
eMalahleni S. Africa 25°51S 29°14E 271 C4
Emāmrūd Iran 36°30N 55°0E 247 B7
Emāmzādeh Sāleh Iran 35°48N 51°26E 141 A2
Emån → Sweden 57°8N 16°30E 163 G10
Emao Vanuatu 17°29S 168°30E 287 G6
Emas △ Brazil 18°2S 52°50W 331 D7
Emateloa Dem. Rep. of the Congo 1°16N 18°42E 264 B3
Embajadores Madrid, Spain 127 c2
Embarcación Argentina 23°10S 64°0W 334 A3
Embarcadero, The San Francisco, U.S.A. 136 b3
Embarras → U.S.A. 38°39N 87°37W 311 F9
Embarras Portage Canada 58°27N 111°28W 297 B6
Embetsu Japan 44°44N 141°47E 220 B10
Embi Kazakhstan 48°50N 58°8E 216 C5
Embi → Kazakhstan 46°55N 53°28E 187 E9
Embira → Brazil 7°19S 70°15W 330 B3
Embonas Greece 36°13N 27°51E 206 E11
Embrun France 44°34N 6°30E 175 D10
Embu Kenya 0°32S 37°38E 268 C4
Emden Germany 53°21N 7°12E 178 B3
Emecik Turkey 36°46N 27°49E 205 E9
Emek Refa'im Jerusalem 123 c2
Émerainville France 48°48N 2°37E 134 B4
Emerald Queens., Australia 23°32S 148°10E 280 C4
Emerald Vic., Australia 37°56S 145°29E 276 E8
Emerson Man., Canada 49°0N 97°10W 297 D9
Emerson Ga., U.S.A. 34°8N 84°45W 316 A5
Emeryville U.S.A. 37°49N 122°17W 136 A3
Emet Turkey 39°20N 29°15E 205 B11
Emeti Papua N. G. 7°53S 143°15E 286 D2
Emi Koussi Chad 19°45N 18°55E 259 E3
Emília-Romagna ☐ Italy 44°45N 11°0E 198 D8
Emilius, Mte. Italy 45°45N 7°20E 198 C4
Eminabad Pakistan 32°2N 74°8E 242 C6
Emine, Nos Bulgaria 42°40N 27°56E 203 D11
Eminence U.S.A. 38°22N 85°11W 311 F11
Eminönü Turkey 41°0N 28°57E 122 B1
Emirau I. Papua N. G. 1°40S 150°0E 286 A6
Emirdağ Turkey 39°2N 31°8E 212 C4
Emirgan Turkey 41°6N 29°2E 122 B2
Emissi, Tarso Chad 21°27N 18°36E 259 D3
Emlenton U.S.A. 41°11N 79°43W 312 E5
Emlichheim Germany 52°37N 6°51E 178 C2
Emmaboda Sweden 56°37N 15°32E 163 H9
Emmalane U.S.A. 32°46N 82°0W 316 C7
Emmarentia S. Africa 26°9S 28°0E 123 A2
Emmastad Neth. Ant. 12°8N 68°55W 322 g
Emmaus S. Africa 29°2S 25°15E 270 C4
Emmaus Pa., U.S.A. 40°32N 75°30W 313 F9
Emme → Switz. 47°14N 7°32E 179 H3
Emmeloord Neths. 52°44N 5°46E 170 B5
Emmen Neths. 52°48N 6°57E 170 B6
Emmen Switz. 47°5N 8°18E 179 H4
Emmendingen Germany 48°6N 7°51E 179 G3
Emmental Switz. 46°55N 7°40E 179 J3
Emmerich Germany 51°50N 6°14E 178 D2
Emmet Australia 24°45S 144°30E 280 C3
Emmetsburg U.S.A. 43°7N 94°41W 310 A2
Emmett Idaho, U.S.A. 43°52N 116°30W 304 E5
Emmett Mich., U.S.A. 42°59N 82°46W 312 D2
Emmiganuru India 15°44N 77°29E 245 G3
Emmonak U.S.A. 62°47N 164°31W 303 E6
Emo Canada 48°38N 93°50W 297 D10
Emőd Hungary 47°57N 20°47E 182 C5
Emona Bulgaria 42°43N 27°53E 203 D11
Empalme Mexico 27°58N 110°51W 318 B2
Empangeni S. Africa 28°50S 31°52E 271 C5
Empedrado Argentina 28°0S 58°46W 334 B4
Emperor Seamount Chain Pac. Oc. 40°0N 170°0E 288 D9
Emperor Trough Pac. Oc. 43°0N 175°30E 288 C9
Empingham Res. = Rutland Water U.K. 52°39N 0°38W 169 E7
Empire U.S.A. 32°21N 83°18W 316 C6
Empire State Building New York, U.S.A. 132 c2
Empoli Italy 43°43N 10°57E 198 E7
Emporia Kans., U.S.A. 38°25N 96°11W 308 F5
Emporia Va., U.S.A. 36°42N 77°32W 309 G15
Emporium U.S.A. 41°31N 78°14W 312 E6
Empress Canada 50°57N 110°0W 297 C7
Empty Quarter = Rub' al Khālī Si. Arabia 19°0N 48°0E 249 C5
Ems → Germany 53°20N 7°12E 178 B3
Emsdale Canada 45°32N 79°19W 312 A5
Emsdetten Germany 52°10N 7°32E 178 C3
Emu China 43°40N 128°6E 227 C15
Emu Park Australia 23°13S 150°50E 280 C5
eMuziwezinto S. Africa 30°15S 30°45E 271 D5
'En 'Avrona Israel 29°43N 35°0E 251 J6
'En Boqeq Israel 31°12N 35°21E 251 G6
En Gannim = Ramat Gan Israel 32°4N 34°48E 251 F5
'En Gedi Israel 31°28N 35°25E 251 G6
En Na'am Sudan 10°21N 27°58E 266 B2
En Nahrat Mali 22°55N 3°36W 260 D4
En Nahud Sudan 12°45N 28°25E 257 E2
En Nofalab Sudan 15°52N 32°32E 257 D3
En Nuqra Sudan 10°4N 28°10E 266 B2
Ena Japan 35°25N 137°25E 223 B9
Ena-San Japan 35°26N 137°36E 223 B9
Enambú Colombia 1°1N 70°17W 328 C3
Enana Namibia 17°30S 16°23E 270 A2
Enånger Sweden 61°30N 17°9E 162 C11
Enard B. U.K. 58°5N 5°20W 167 C3
Enare = Inarijärvi Finland 69°0N 28°0E 160 B23
Enarotali Indonesia 3°55S 136°21E 231 E9
Encampment U.S.A. 41°12N 106°47W 304 F10
Encantadas, Serra Brazil 30°40S 53°0W 335 C5
Encantado Brazil 22°53S 43°19W 135 B1
Encarnación Paraguay 27°15S 55°50W 335 B4
Encarnación de Díaz Mexico 21°31N 102°14W 318 C4
Enchi Ghana 5°53N 2°48W 262 D4
Encinitas U.S.A. 33°3N 117°17W 307 M9
Encino Calif., U.S.A. 34°9N 118°28W 126 B2
Encino N. Mex., U.S.A. 34°39N 105°28W 305 J11
Encino Res. U.S.A. 34°8N 118°30W 126 B1
Encontrados Venezuela 9°3N 72°14W 328 B3
Encounter B. Australia 35°45S 138°45E 282 C3
Encruzilhada Brazil 15°31S 40°54W 333 E3
Encs Hungary 48°20N 21°8E 182 B6
Endako Canada 54°6N 125°2W 296 C3
Endau Kenya 1°18S 38°31E 268 C4
Endau Rompin △ Malaysia 2°27N 103°45E 234 B2
Ende Indonesia 8°45S 121°40E 231 F6
Endeavour Str. Australia 10°45S 142°0E 286 F2
Endelave Denmark 55°46N 10°18E 163 J4
Enden Norway 61°47N 10°15E 164 C7
Enderbury I. Kiribati 3°8S 171°5W 277 A16
Enderby Canada 50°35N 119°10W 296 C5
Enderby Abyssal Plain S. Ocean 60°0S 40°0E 151 C5
Enderby I. Australia 20°35S 116°30E 278 D2
Enderby Land Antarctica 66°0S 53°0E 151 C5
Enderlin U.S.A. 46°38N 97°36W 308 B5
Endicott U.S.A. 42°6N 76°4W 313 D8
Endicott Mts. U.S.A. 68°0N 152°0W 303 C9
Endimari → Brazil 8°46S 66°7W 330 B4
Endwell U.S.A. 42°6N 76°2W 313 D8
Endyalgout I. Australia 11°40S 132°35E 278 B5
Ene → Peru 11°10S 74°18W 330 C3
Eneabba Australia 29°49S 115°16E 279 E2
Enebyberg Sweden 59°25N 17°59E 139 A1
Enewetak Atoll Marshall Is. 11°30N 162°15E 288 F8
Enez Turkey 40°45N 26°5E 203 F10
Enfer, Pte. d' Martinique 14°22N 60°54W 322 j
Enfield N.S.W., Australia 33°53S 151°6E 139 B1
Enfield N.S., Canada 44°56N 63°32W 299 D7
Enfield Conn., U.S.A. 41°58N 72°36W 313 E12
Enfield Ill., U.S.A. 38°6N 88°20W 311 F8
Enfield N.C., U.S.A. 36°11N 77°41W 315 C16
Enfield N.H., U.S.A. 43°39N 72°9W 313 C12
Enga ☐ Papua N. G. 5°30S 143°30E 286 C2
Engadin Switz. 46°45N 10°10E 179 J6
Engan Norway 63°8N 8°31E 164 A5
Engaño, C. Dom. Rep. 18°30N 68°20W 321 C6
Engaño, C. Phil. 18°35N 122°23E 232 B4
Engaru Japan 44°3N 143°31E 220 B11
Engcobo = Ngcobo S. Africa 31°37S 28°0E 271 D4
Engelberg Switz. 46°48N 8°26E 179 J4
Engels Russia 51°28N 46°6E 190 E8
Engemann L. Canada 58°0N 106°55W 297 B7
Engenho, I. do Brazil 22°50S 43°6W 135 B2
Engerdal Norway 61°45N 11°58E 164 C8
Engershatu Eritrea 16°7N 38°34E 257 D4
Enggano Indonesia 5°20S 102°40E 234 D2
Engineer Group Papua N. G. 10°35S 151°20E 286 F6
Engkilili Malaysia 1°3N 111°42E 235 B4
England U.S.A. 34°33N 91°58W 314 D9
England ☐ U.K. 53°0N 2°0W 169 E5
Englee Canada 50°45N 56°5W 299 B8
Englehart Canada 47°49N 79°52W 298 C4
Englewood Colo., U.S.A. 39°38N 104°59W 304 G11
Englewood Fla., U.S.A. 26°58N 82°21W 317 J7
Englewood Ill., U.S.A. 41°46N 87°38W 119 C3
Englewood N.J., U.S.A. 40°54N 73°58W 132 A2
Englewood Ohio, U.S.A. 39°53N 84°18W 311 E12
Englewood Cliffs U.S.A. 40°53N 73°59W 132 A2
English U.S.A. 38°20N 86°28W 311 F10
English → Ont., Canada 49°12N 91°5W 297 C10
English → Iowa, U.S.A. 41°29N 91°32W 310 C5
English B. Ascension I. 7°54S 14°23W 153 g
English Bazar = Ingraj Bazar India 24°58N 88°10E 243 G13
English Channel Europe 50°0N 2°0W 169 G6
English Company's Is., The Australia 11°50S 136°32E 280 A2
English Harbour Town Antigua & B. 17°1N 61°46W 322 b
English River Canada 49°14N 91°0W 298 C1
Engures ezers Latvia 57°16N 23°6E 184 A10
Enguri → Georgia 42°27N 41°38E 191 J5
Enid U.S.A. 36°24N 97°53W 314 C6
Enipeas → Greece 39°22N 22°17E 204 B4
Enkhuizen Neths. 52°42N 5°17E 170 B5
Enköping Sweden 59°37N 17°4E 162 E11
Enle China 24°0N 101°9E 228 F3
Enmore Australia 33°54S 151°10E 139 B2
Enna Italy 37°34N 14°16E 201 E7
Ennadai Canada 61°8N 100°53W 297 A8
Ennadai L. Canada 60°58N 101°20W 297 A8
Enné, O. → Chad 14°24N 18°45E 259 F4
Ennedi Chad 17°15N 22°0E 259 E4
Enneri Achelouma → Niger 21°55N 13°35E 261 D7
Enngonia Australia 29°21S 145°50E 281 D4
Ennigerloh Germany 51°50N 8°2E 178 D4
Ennis Clare, Ireland 52°51N 8°59W 166 D3
Ennis Mont., U.S.A. 45°21N 111°44W 304 D8
Ennis Tex., U.S.A. 32°20N 96°38W 314 E6
Enniscorthy Ireland 52°30N 6°34W 166 D5
Enniskillen U.K. 54°21N 7°39W 166 B4
Ennistimon Ireland 52°57N 9°17W 166 D2
Enns Austria 48°12N 14°28E 180 C7
Enns → Austria 48°14N 14°32E 180 C7
Eno Finland 62°47N 30°10E 160 E24
Enontekiö Finland 68°23N 23°37E 160 B20
Enosburg Falls U.S.A. 44°55N 72°48W 313 B12
Enping China 22°16N 112°21E 229 F9
Enrile Phil. 17°34N 121°42E 232 C3
Enriquillo, L. Dom. Rep. 18°20N 72°5W 321 C5
Enschede Neths. 52°13N 6°53E 170 B6
Ensenada Argentina 34°55S 57°55W 334 C4
Ensenada Baja Calif., Mexico 31°52N 116°37W 318 A1
Ensenada de los Muertos Mexico 23°59N 109°51W 318 C2
Enshi China 30°18N 109°29E 228 B7
Enshū-Nada Japan 34°27N 137°38E 223 C9
Ensiola, Pta. de n' Spain 39°7N 2°55E 206 B3
Ensisheim France 47°50N 7°20E 173 E14
Enskede Sweden 59°17N 18°4E 139 B2
Ensley U.S.A. 30°31N 87°16W 317 E2
Entebbe Uganda 0°4N 32°28E 268 B3
Enterprise N.W.T., Canada 60°47N 115°45W 296 A5
Enterprise Ala., U.S.A. 31°19N 85°51W 316 D4
Enterprise Nev., U.S.A. 36°13N 115°14W 124 B1
Enterprise Oreg., U.S.A. 45°25N 117°17W 304 D5
Entorno de Doñana ⌓ Spain 37°0N 6°26W 195 J4
Entrance, The Australia 33°21S 151°30E 283 B9
Entraygues-sur-Truyère France 44°38N 2°35E 174 D6
Entre-Deux Réunion 21°14S 55°28E 272 f
Entre Rios = Rio Brilhante Brazil 21°48S 54°33W 335 A5
Entre Rios = Três Rios Brazil 22°6S 43°15W 333 F3
Entre Ríos Bolivia 21°30S 64°25W 334 A3
Entre Rios Bahia, Brazil 11°56S 38°5W 333 D4
Entre Rios Pará, Brazil 5°24S 54°21W 331 B7
Entre Ríos ☐ Argentina 30°30S 58°30W 334 C4
Entrepeñas, Embalse de Spain 40°34N 2°42W 196 E2
Entrevias Spain 40°22N 3°40W 127 B1
Entroncamento Portugal 39°28N 8°28W 195 F2
Enugu Nigeria 6°30N 7°30E 263 D6
Enugu ☐ Nigeria 6°30N 7°45E 263 D6
Enugu Ezike Nigeria 7°0N 7°29E 263 D6
Enumclaw U.S.A. 47°12N 121°59W 306 C5
Envalira, Port d' Europe 42°33N 1°43E 196 C6
Envermeu France 49°53N 1°15E 172 C8
Envigado Colombia 6°10N 75°35W 328 B2
Enviken Sweden 60°49N 15°46E 162 D9
Envira Brazil 7°18S 70°13W 330 B3
Enying Hungary 46°56N 18°15E 182 D3
Enyonga Gabon 0°59S 9°22E 264 C1
Enza → Italy 44°54N 10°31E 198 D7
Enzan Japan 35°42N 138°44E 223 B10
Eólie, Ís. Italy 38°30N 14°57E 201 D7
Eot I. Micronesia 7°23N 151°44E 287 T17
Epanomi Greece 40°25N 22°59E 202 F6
Epe Neths. 52°21N 5°59E 170 B5
Epe Nigeria 6°36N 3°59E 263 D5
Epéna Congo 1°22N 17°29E 264 B3
Épernay France 49°3N 3°56E 173 C10
Épernon France 48°35N 1°40E 173 D8
Ephesus Turkey 37°55N 27°22E 205 D9
Ephraim U.S.A. 39°22N 111°35W 304 G8
Ephrata Pa., U.S.A. 40°11N 76°11W 313 F8
Ephrata Wash., U.S.A. 47°19N 119°33W 304 C4
Epi Vanuatu 16°43S 168°15E 287 F6
Epidavros Limira Greece 36°46N 23°0E 204 E5
Épila Spain 41°36N 1°17W 196 D3
Épinac France 46°59N 4°31E 173 F11
Épinal France 48°10N 6°27E 173 D13
Epira Guyana 5°5N 57°20W 329 B6
Epiros ☐ Greece 39°30N 20°30E 204 B2
Episkopi Cyprus 34°40N 32°54E 207 F8
Episkopi Kriti, Greece 35°20N 24°20E 207 E5
Episkopi Bay Cyprus 34°35N 32°50E 207 F8
Epitalio Greece 37°37N 21°30E 204 D3
Eppalock, L. Australia 36°52S 144°34E 282 D6
Eppan = Appiano Italy 46°28N 11°15E 199 B8
Epping Australia 33°46S 151°5E 139 A1
Eppingen Germany 49°8N 8°53E 179 F4
Epsom U.K. 51°19N 0°16W 169 F7
Epukiro Namibia 21°40S 19°9E 270 B2
Equality U.S.A. 37°44N 88°20W 311 G8
Équateur ☐ Dem. Rep. of the Congo 2°0N 21°0E 264 B4
Equatorial Channel Maldives 0°0 73°10E 272 d
Equatorial Guinea ■ Africa 2°0N 8°0E 264 B1
Equeipa Venezuela 5°22N 62°43W 329 B5
Er Hai China 25°48N 100°11E 228 E3
Er Rachidia Morocco 31°58N 4°20W 260 B4
Er Rachidia ☐ Morocco 31°45N 4°30W 260 B4
Er Rahad Sudan 12°45N 30°32E 257 E3
Er Rif Morocco 35°1N 4°1W 261 A4
Er Rogel Sudan 18°10N 35°25E 256 D4
Er Roseires Sudan 11°55N 34°30E 257 E3
Er Rua'at Sudan 12°21N 32°17E 257 E3
Eraclea Italy 45°35N 12°40E 199 C9
Eran Phil. 9°4N 117°42E 233 G1
Erandol India 20°56N 75°20E 244 D2
Eranga Dem. Rep. of the Congo 1°52S 18°56E 264 C3
Erap Papua N. G. 6°37S 146°51E 286 D4
Erasmus = Bronkhorstspruit S. Africa 25°46S 28°45E 271 C4
Erave Papua N. G. 6°39S 144°0E 286 D2
Erave → Papua N. G. 6°54S 144°47E 286 D3
Erāwadī Myit = Irrawaddy → Burma 15°50N 95°6E 241 G5
Erāwadī Myitwanya = Irrawaddy, Mouths of the Burma 15°30N 95°0E 241 H5
Erawan Shrine Bangkok, Thailand 113 c3
Erba Italy 45°48N 9°15E 198 C6
Erba Sudan 19°5N 36°51E 256 D4
Erba, J. Sudan 20°48N 36°47E 256 C4
Erbaa Turkey 40°42N 36°36E 212 B7
Erbeng Shan China 42°50N 84°59E 217 D10
Erbeskopf Germany 49°44N 7°2E 179 F3
Erbil = Arbīl Iraq 36°15N 44°5E 213 D11
Erbu Ethiopia 6°44N 34°53E 257 E3
Ercan, Nicosia ✈ (ECN) Cyprus 35°10N 33°30E 207 E9
Erçek Turkey 38°39N 43°36E 246 B4
Erçis Turkey 39°2N 43°21E 213 C10
Erciyaş Dağı Turkey 38°30N 35°30E 246 B2
Érd Hungary 47°22N 18°56E 182 C3
Erdao Jiang → China 42°37N 128°0E 224 A3
Erdek Turkey 40°23N 27°47E 203 F11
Erdély = Transilvania Romania 46°30N 24°0E 183 D9
Erdemli Turkey 36°36N 34°19E 250 B5
Erdene = Ulaan-Uul Mongolia 44°13N 111°10E 226 B6
Erdenet Mongolia 49°2N 104°5E 218 B5
Erdenetsogt Mongolia 42°55N 106°5E 226 C4
Erding Germany 48°18N 11°54E 179 G7
Erdre → France 47°13N 1°32W 172 E5
Erebato → Venezuela 5°54N 64°16W 329 B5
Erebus, Mt. Antarctica 77°35S 167°0E 151 D11
Erechim Brazil 27°35S 52°15W 335 B5
Ereğli Konya, Turkey 37°31N 34°4E 212 D6
Ereğli Zonguldak, Turkey 41°15N 31°24E 212 B4
Eregun Nigeria 6°35N 3°22E 124 A2
Erei, Monti Italy 37°20N 14°20E 201 E7
Erenhot China 43°48N 112°2E 226 C7
Erenköy = Kokkina Cyprus 35°11N 32°36E 207 E8
Erenköy Turkey 40°58N 29°3E 122 C2
Eresfjord Norway 62°40N 8°8E 164 B5
Eresma → Spain 41°26N 4°45W 194 D6
Eresos Greece 39°11N 25°57E 205 B7
Ereymentaū Kazakhstan 51°37N 73°6E 217 B8
Erfenisdam S. Africa 28°30S 26°50E 270 C4
Erfjord Norway 59°20N 6°14E 164 E3
Erfoud Morocco 31°30N 4°15W 260 B4
Erfstadt Germany 50°50N 6°50E 178 E2
Erft → Germany 51°11N 6°44E 178 D2
Erfurt Germany 50°58N 11°2E 178 E7
Ergani Turkey 38°17N 39°49E 213 C8
Ergel Mongolia 43°8N 109°5E 226 C5
Ergene → Turkey 41°1N 26°22E 203 E10
Ergeni Vozvyshennost Russia 47°0N 44°0E 191 G7
Ērgli Latvia 56°54N 25°38E 188 D3
Erhlin Taiwan 23°54N 120°22E 225 C2
Erhshui Taiwan 23°45N 120°37E 225 C2
Eria → Spain 42°3N 5°44W 194 C5
Eriba Sudan 16°40N 36°10E 257 D4
Eriboll, L. U.K. 58°30N 4°42W 167 C4
Érice Italy 38°2N 12°35E 200 D5
Eridu U.S.A. 30°18N 83°45W 316 E6
Erie Mich., U.S.A. 41°47N 83°31W 311 C13
Erie Pa., U.S.A. 42°8N 80°5W 312 D4
Erie, L. N. Amer. 42°15N 81°0W 312 D4
Erie Canal U.S.A. 43°5N 78°43W 312 C7
Erieau Canada 42°16N 81°57W 312 D3
Erigavo Somali Rep. 10°35N 47°20E 267 B6
Erikoussa Greece 39°53N 19°34E 206 B9
Eriksdale Canada 50°52N 98°7W 297 C9
Erimanthos Greece 37°57N 21°50E 204 D3
Erimo-misaki Japan 41°50N 143°15E 220 D11
Erin Trin. & Tob. 10°5N 61°39W 323 t
Erin B. Trin. & Tob. 10°4N 61°43W 323 t
Erin Pt. Trin. & Tob. 10°3N 61°39W 323 t
Erinpura India 25°9N 73°3E 242 G5
Eriskay U.K. 57°4N 7°18W 167 D1
Erith U.K. 51°28N 0°11E 125 B5
Erithres Greece 38°13N 23°20E 204 C5
Eritrea ■ Africa 14°0N 38°30E 257 E4
Erivan = Yerevan Armenia 40°10N 44°31E 191 K7
Erjas → Portugal 39°40N 7°1W 194 F3
Erkech-Tam Pass Asia 39°46N 74°2E 217 E8
Erkelenz Germany 51°4N 6°19E 178 D2
Erkner Germany 52°25N 13°44E 178 C9
Erlaa Austria 48°9N 16°19E 142 B1
Erlangen Germany 49°36N 11°0E 179 F6
Erlanger U.S.A. 39°1N 84°36W 311 E12
Erldunda Australia 25°14S 133°12E 280 D1
Ermelo Neths. 52°18N 5°35E 170 B5
Ermelo Mpumalanga, S. Africa 26°31S 29°59E 271 C4
Ermenek Turkey 36°38N 33°0E 250 B4
Ermenek → Turkey 36°35N 33°23E 250 B4
Ermil Sudan 13°35N 27°40E 257 E2
Ermington Australia 33°48S 151°4E 139 A1
Ermioni Greece 37°23N 23°15E 204 D5
Ermita Phil. 14°35N 120°59E 127 B1
Ermones Greece 39°37N 19°46E 206 B9
Ermoúpolis = Syros Greece 37°28N 24°57E 204 D6
Ernakulam India 9°59N 76°22E 245 K3
Erne → Ireland 54°30N 8°16W 166 B3
Erne, Lower L. U.K. 54°28N 7°47W 166 B4
Erne, Upper L. U.K. 54°14N 7°32W 166 B4
Ernée France 48°18N 0°56W 172 D6
Ernest Giles Ra. Australia 27°0S 123°45E 279 E3
Ernest N. Morial Convention Center New Orleans, U.S.A. 131 c3
Ernstberg Germany 50°13N 6°47E 179 E2
Erode India 11°24N 77°45E 245 J3
Eromanga Australia 26°40S 143°11E 281 D3
Erongo Namibia 21°39S 15°58E 270 B2
Erquy France 48°38N 2°29W 172 D4
Erramala Hills India 15°30N 78°15E 245 G4
Errer → Ethiopia 7°32N 42°35E 257 F5
Erri-Nundra △ Australia 37°28S 148°5E 281 F4
Errigal Ireland 55°2N 8°6W 166 A3
Errinundra △ Australia 37°20S 148°47E 283 D8
Erris Hd. Ireland 54°19N 10°0W 166 B1
Erromango Vanuatu 18°45S 169°5E 287 H7
Ersekë Albania 40°22N 20°40E 202 F4
Ersekújvár = Nové Zámky Slovak Rep. 48°2N 18°8E 181 C11
Ershatou China 23°6N 113°18E 121 B2
Erskine U.S.A. 47°40N 96°0W 308 B6
Erskineville Australia 33°54S 151°12E 139 B2
Erstein France 48°25N 7°38E 173 D14
Ertai China 46°3N 90°5E 217 C12
Ertholmene Denmark 55°19N 15°11E 163 J9
Ertil Russia 51°55N 40°50E 190 E5
Ertis = Irtysh → Russia 61°4N 68°52E 214 C7
Ertis Kazakhstan 53°20N 75°27E 217 B9
Ertis → Kazakhstan 47°52N 84°16E 217 C10
Ertvågøy Norway 63°13N 8°26E 164 A5
Eruh Turkey 37°46N 42°13E 213 D10
Erunkan Nigeria 6°36N 3°23E 124 A2
Eruwa Nigeria 7°33N 3°26E 263 D5
Ervy-le-Châtel France 48°2N 3°55E 173 D10
Erwin U.S.A. 36°9N 82°25W 315 C13
Eryuan China 26°7N 99°57E 228 D2
Erzgebirge Germany 50°27N 12°55E 178 E8
Erzin Russia 50°15N 95°10E 217 B13
Erzin Turkey 36°57N 36°11E 250 B7
Erzincan Turkey 39°46N 39°30E 213 C8
Erzincan ☐ Turkey 39°45N 39°30E 213 C8
Erzsébet-Telep Hungary 47°27N 19°10E 117 B3
Erzurum Turkey 39°57N 41°15E 213 C9
Erzurum ☐ Turkey 39°55N 41°15E 213 C9
Es Caló Spain 38°40N 1°30E 206 D2
Es Canar Spain 39°2N 1°36E 206 C2
Es Mercadal Spain 39°59N 4°5E 206 B5
Es Migjorn Gran Spain 39°57N 4°3E 206 B5
Es Safiya Sudan 15°31N 30°7E 257 D3
Es Sahrâ' Esh Sharqîya Egypt 27°30N 32°30E 256 B3
Es Sînâ' Egypt 29°0N 34°0E 246 D2
Es Sûkî Sudan 13°20N 33°58E 257 E3
Es Vedrà Spain 38°52N 1°12E 206 D1
Esa'ala Papua N. G. 9°45S 150°49E 286 E6
Esambo Dem. Rep. of the Congo 3°48S 23°30E 264 C4
Esan-Misaki Japan 41°40N 141°10E 220 D10
Esashi Hokkaidō, Japan 44°56N 142°35E 220 B11
Esashi Hokkaidō, Japan 41°52N 140°7E 220 D10
Esbjerg Denmark 55°29N 8°29E 163 J2
Esbo = Espoo Finland 60°12N 24°40E 188 B3
Escada Brazil 8°22S 35°8W 332 C4
Escalante U.S.A. 37°47N 111°36W 305 H8
Escalante → U.S.A. 37°24N 110°57W 305 H8
Escalente Phil. 10°50N 123°33E 233 F4
Escalón Mexico 26°45N 104°20W 318 B4
Escambia → U.S.A. 30°32N 87°11W 317 E2
Escanaba U.S.A. 45°45N 87°4W 308 C10
Escarparda Pt. Phil. 18°31N 122°13E 232 B4
Escarpé, C. N. Cal. 20°41S 167°13E 288 d
Escaut = Schelde → Belgium 51°15N 4°16E 170 C4
Esch-sur-Alzette Lux. 49°32N 6°0E 170 E6
Eschede Germany 52°44N 10°14E 178 C6
Eschenried Germany 48°13N 11°24E 131 A1
Eschwege Germany 51°11N 10°2E 178 D6
Eschweiler Germany 50°49N 6°15E 178 E2
Escoma Bolivia 15°40S 69°8W 330 D4
Escondido U.S.A. 33°7N 117°5W 307 M9
Escravos → Nigeria 5°35N 5°10E 263 D6
Escuinapa de Hidalgo Mexico 22°50N 105°50W 318 C3
Escuintla Guatemala 14°20N 90°48W 320 D1
Eséka Cameroon 3°41N 10°44E 263 E7
Eşen → Turkey 36°27N 29°16E 205 E11
Esenguly Turkmenistan 37°37N 53°59E 216 E4
Esenler Turkey 41°1N 28°52E 122 B1
Esens Germany 53°38N 7°36E 178 B3
Esenyurt Turkey 41°3N 28°48E 203 E12
Esera → Spain 42°6N 0°15E 196 C5
Eşfahān Iran 32°39N 51°43E 247 C6
Eşfahān ☐ Iran 32°50N 51°50E 247 C6
Esfarāyen Iran 37°4N 57°30E 247 B8
Esfideh Iran 33°39N 59°46E 247 C8
Esgueva → Spain 41°40N 4°43W 194 D6
Esh Sham = Dimashq Syria 33°30N 36°18E 250 E7
Esh Shamâlîya ☐ Sudan 19°0N 29°0E 256 D2
Esha Ness U.K. 60°29N 1°38W 167 A7
Eshan China 24°11N 102°24E 228 E4
Esher U.K. 51°21N 0°20W 125 B1
Eshkāshem = Ishkashim Tajikistan 36°44N 71°37E 217 E8
Eshkol △ Israel 31°20N 34°30E 251 G5
Eshowe S. Africa 28°50S 31°30E 271 C5
Esiama Ghana 4°56N 2°25W 262 E4
Esigodini Zimbabwe 20°18S 28°56E 271 B4
Esil = Ishim → Russia 57°45N 71°10E 214 D8
Esil Kazakhstan 51°57N 66°24E 217 B7
Esino → Italy 43°39N 13°22E 199 E10
Esira Madag. 24°20S 46°42E 272 C2
Esk → Dumf. & Gall., U.K. 54°58N 3°2W 167 G5
Esk → N. Yorks., U.K. 54°30N 0°37W 168 C7

Fayaoué N. Cal. 20°38S 166°33E 288 d
Fayd Si. Arabia 27°1N 42°52E 246 E4
Fayence France 43°38N 6°42E 175 E10
Fayette Ala., U.S.A. 33°41N 87°50W 315 E11
Fayette Iowa, U.S.A. 42°51N 91°48W 310 B5
Fayette Mo., U.S.A. 39°9N 92°41W 310 E4
Fayette Ohio, U.S.A. 41°40N 84°20W 311 C12
Fayetteville Ark., U.S.A. 36°4N 94°10W 314 C7
Fayetteville Ga., U.S.A. 33°27N 84°27W 316 B5
Fayetteville N.C., U.S.A. 35°3N 78°53W 315 D15
Fayetteville Tenn., U.S.A. 35°9N 86°34W 315 D11
Fayied Egypt 30°18N 32°16E 256 H8
Fayón Spain 41°15N 0°20E 196 D5
Fazao-Malfakassa △ Togo 8°45N 0°50E 263 D5
Fazenda Libongo Angola 8°24S 13°24E 265 D2
Fazenda Nova Brazil 16°11S 50°48W 333 E1
Fazilka India 30°27N 74°2E 242 D6
Fazilpur Pakistan 29°18N 70°29E 242 E4
Fdérik Mauritania 22°40N 12°45W 260 D2
Feakle Ireland 52°56N 8°40W 166 D3
Feale → Ireland 52°27N 9°37W 166 D2
Fear, C. U.S.A. 33°50N 77°58W 315 E16
Feather → U.S.A. 38°47N 121°36W 304 G3
Feather Falls U.S.A. 39°36N 121°16W 306 F5
Featherston N.Z. 41°6S 175°20E 284 H4
Featherstone Zimbabwe 18°42S 30°55E 269 F3
Fécamp France 49°45N 0°22E 172 C7
Feda Norway 58°17N 6°50E 164 F3
Fedala = Mohammedia Morocco 33°44N 7°21W 260 B3
Federación Argentina 31°0S 57°55W 334 C4
Federal Capital Terr. □ Nigeria 9°0N 7°10E 263 D6
Federal Way U.S.A. 47°18N 122°19W 306 C4
Fedeshküh Iran 28°49N 53°50E 247 D7
FedEx Stadium U.S.A. 38°54N 76°51W 143 B4
Fedje Norway 60°47N 4°43E 164 D1
Fedorovka Kazakhstan 53°37N 62°42E 216 B6
Fefan I. Pac. Oc. 7°21N 151°51E 287 T18
Fehérgyarmat Hungary 47°58N 22°30E 182 C7
Fehmarn Germany 54°27N 11°7E 178 A7
Fehmarn Bælt Europe 54°35N 11°20E 163 K5
Fehmarn Belt = Fehmarn Bælt Europe 54°35N 11°20E 163 K5
Fei Xian China 35°18N 117°59E 227 G9
Feijó Brazil 8°9S 70°21W 330 B3
Feijó Lisboa, Portugal 38°39N 9°9W 126 B2
Feilding N.Z. 40°13S 175°35E 284 G4
Feira de Santana Brazil 12°15S 38°57W 333 D4
Feirān, W. → Egypt 28°39N 33°12E 251 K4
Feirân, G. Egypt 28°31N 34°19E 251 K3
Feiring Norway 60°30N 11°10E 164 D8
Feixi China 31°43N 117°59E 229 B11
Feixiang China 36°30N 114°45E 226 F8
Fejaj, Chott el Tunisia 33°52N 9°14E 258 B1
Fejér □ Hungary 47°9N 18°30E 182 C3
Fejø Denmark 54°55N 11°30E 163 K5
Feke Turkey 37°48N 35°56E 212 D6
Fekete → Hungary 45°47N 18°15E 182 E3
Felanitx Spain 39°28N 3°9E 206 B10
Felda U.S.A. 26°34N 81°26W 317 J8
Feldbach Austria 46°57N 15°52E 180 E8
Feldberg Baden-W., Germany 47°52N 8°0E 179 H3
Feldberg Mecklenburg-Vorpommern, Germany 53°20N 13°25E 178 B9
Feldkirch Austria 47°15N 9°37E 180 D2
Feldkirchen Austria 46°44N 14°6E 180 E7
Feldkirchen Oberbayern, Germany 48°8N 11°43E 131 B3
Feldmoching Germany 48°14N 11°32E 131 A2
Félicité Seychelles 4°19S 55°52E 272 c
Felicity U.S.A. 38°51N 84°6W 311 F12
Felidhoo Maldives 3°29N 73°29E 272 d
Felidu Atoll Maldives 3°29N 73°29E 272 d
Felipe Carrillo Puerto Mexico 19°38N 88°3W 319 D7
Felixburg Zimbabwe 19°29S 30°51E 271 A5
Felixlândia Brazil 18°47S 44°55W 333 E3
Felixstowe U.K. 51°58N 1°23E 169 F9
Felletin France 45°53N 2°11E 174 C6
Fellingsbro Sweden 59°26N 15°37E 162 E9
Fellsmere U.S.A. 27°46N 80°36W 317 H9
Felshtin = Gvardeyskoye Ukraine 45°7N 34°1E 189 K8
Felsogalla = Tatabánya Hungary 47°32N 18°25E 182 C3
Feltham U.K. 51°26N 0°24W 125 B1
Felton U.S.A. 37°3N 122°4W 306 H4
Feltre Italy 46°1N 11°54E 199 B8
Femer Bælt = Fehmarn Bælt Europe 54°35N 11°20E 163 K5
Femø Denmark 54°58N 11°35E 163 K5
Femunden Norway 62°10N 11°53E 164 B8
Femundsmarka △ Norway 62°18N 12°6E 164 B9
Fen He → China 35°36N 110°42E 226 G6
Fenchih Taiwan 23°30N 120°40E 225 C2
Fene Spain 43°27N 8°9W 194 B2
Fenelon Falls Canada 44°32N 78°45W 312 B6
Fener Turkey 41°1N 28°56E 122 B1
Fener Burnu Turkey 36°58N 27°18E 205 E9
Fenerbahçe Turkey 40°58N 29°2E 122 C2
Feneroa Ethiopia 13°5N 39°3E 257 E4
Feng Xian Jiangsu, China 34°43N 116°35E 226 G9
Feng Xian Shaanxi, China 33°54N 106°40E 226 H4
Fengari Greece 40°25N 25°32E 203 F9
Fengcheng Jiangxi, China 28°12N 115°48E 229 C10
Fengcheng Liaoning, China 40°28N 124°5E 224 B2
Fengfeng China 36°28N 114°8E 226 F8
Fenggang China 27°57N 107°47E 228 D6
Fenghua China 29°40N 121°25E 229 C13
Fenghuang China 27°57N 109°29E 228 D7
Fengkai China 23°24N 111°30E 229 F8
Fengkang Taiwan 22°12N 120°41E 225 D2
Fengle China 31°29N 112°29E 229 B9
Fenglin Taiwan 23°45N 121°26E 225 C3
Fengning China 41°10N 116°33E 226 D9
Fengpin Taiwan 23°36N 121°31E 225 C3
Fengqing China 24°38N 99°55E 228 E2
Fengqiu China 35°2N 114°25E 226 G8
Fengrun China 39°48N 118°8E 227 E10
Fengshan Guangxi Zhuangzu, China 24°39N 109°15E 228 E7
Fengshan Guangxi Zhuangzu, China 24°31N 107°3E 228 E6
Fengshan Taiwan 22°38N 120°21E 225 D2
Fengshun China 23°46N 116°10E 229 F11
Fengtai Anhui, China 32°50N 116°40E 229 A11
Fengtai Beijing, China 39°49N 116°14E 114 C1
Fengxian China 30°55N 121°26E 229 B13
Fengxiang China 34°29N 107°25E 226 G4
Fengxin China 28°41N 115°18E 229 C10
Fengyang China 32°51N 117°29E 227 H9
Fengyi China 25°37N 100°20E 228 E3
Fengyüan Taiwan 24°15N 120°35E 225 B2
Fengzhen China 40°25N 113°2E 226 D7
Feni Is. Papua N. G. 4°0S 153°40E 286 C7
Fenino Russia 55°43N 37°56E 129 B5
Fennimore U.S.A. 42°59N 90°39W 310 B6
Fenny Bangla. 22°55N 91°32E 241 D3
Feno, C. de France 41°58N 8°33E 175 G12
Fenoarivo Fianarantsoa, Madag. 21°43S 46°24E 272 C2
Fenoarivo Fianarantsoa, Madag. 20°52S 46°53E 272 C2
Fenoarivo Afovoany Madag. 18°26S 46°34E 272 B2
Fenoarivo Atsinanana Madag. 17°22S 49°25E 272 B2
Fens, The U.K. 52°38N 0°2W 168 E7
Fensmark Denmark 55°17N 11°48E 163 J5
Fenton U.S.A. 42°48N 83°42W 311 B13
Fenxi China 36°40N 111°31E 226 F6
Fenyang China 37°18N 111°48E 226 F6
Fenyi China 27°45N 114°47E 229 D10
Fenyuan Taiwan 24°1N 120°37E 225 B2
Feodosiya Ukraine 45°2N 35°16E 189 K8
Fer, C. de Algeria 37°3N 7°10E 261 A6
Fera Solomon Is. 8°6S 159°37E 287 M10
Ferbane Ireland 53°16N 7°50W 166 C4
Ferdows Iran 33°58N 58°2E 247 C8
Fère-Champenoise France 48°45N 3°59E 173 D10
Fère-en-Tardenois France 49°10N 3°30E 173 C10
Ferencváros Hungary 47°29N 19°5E 117 B2
Ferentino Italy 41°42N 13°15E 199 G10
Feres Greece 40°53N 26°10E 203 F10
Ferfer Somali Rep. 5°4N 45°9E 267 C6
Fergana = Farghona Uzbekistan 40°23N 71°19E 217 D8
Fergana Range Asia 41°0N 73°50E 217 D8
Fergus Canada 43°43N 80°24W 312 C4
Fergus Falls U.S.A. 46°17N 96°4W 308 B5
Ferguson U.S.A. 38°44N 90°18W 310 F6
Fergusson I. Papua N. G. 9°30S 150°45E 286 E6
Fériana Tunisia 34°59N 8°33E 258 B1
Feričanci Croatia 45°32N 18°0E 182 E2
Ferihegy, Budapest ✕ (BUD) Hungary 47°26N 19°14E 117 B3
Ferkane Algeria 34°37N 7°26E 261 B6
Ferkéssédougou Ivory C. 9°35N 5°6W 262 D3
Ferlach Austria 46°32N 14°18E 180 E7
Ferland Canada 50°19N 88°27W 298 B2
Ferlo, Vallée du Senegal 15°15N 14°15W 262 B2
Ferlo-Nord ⌂ Senegal 15°43N 14°30W 262 B2
Ferlo-Sud ⌂ Senegal 15°43N 14°0W 262 B2
Fermanagh □ U.K. 54°21N 7°40W 166 B4
Fermo Italy 43°9N 13°43E 199 E10
Fermont Canada 52°47N 67°5W 299 B6
Fermoselle Spain 41°19N 6°27W 194 D4
Fermoy Ireland 52°9N 8°16W 166 D3
Fern Creek U.S.A. 38°9N 85°36W 311 G11
Fern Gully Jamaica 18°22N 77°5W 320 a
Fernán Núñez Spain 37°40N 4°44W 195 H6
Fernández Argentina 27°55S 63°50W 334 B3
Fernandina, I. Ecuador 0°25S 91°30W 330 a
Fernandina Beach U.S.A. 30°40N 81°27W 316 E8
Fernando de Noronha Brazil 4°0S 33°10W 152 G8
Fernando Póo = Bioko Eq. Guin. 3°30N 8°40E 263 E6
Fernandópolis Brazil 20°16S 50°14W 333 F1
Ferndale Gauteng, S. Africa 26°5S 28°0E 123 A2
Ferndale Wash., U.S.A. 48°51N 122°36W 306 B4
Fernie Canada 49°30N 115°5W 296 D5
Fernlees Australia 23°51S 148°7E 280 C4
Fernley U.S.A. 39°36N 119°15W 304 G4
Feroke India 11°9N 75°46E 245 J2
Férolles-Attilly France 48°44N 2°37E 134 B4
Ferozepore = Firozpur India 30°55N 74°40E 242 D6
Ferrandina Italy 40°29N 16°27E 201 B9
Ferrara Italy 44°50N 11°35E 199 D8
Ferrato, C. Italy 39°18N 9°38E 200 C2
Ferré, C. Martinique 14°27N 60°49W 322 j
Ferreira do Alentejo Portugal 38°4N 8°6W 195 G2
Ferreira Gomes Brazil 0°48N 51°8W 332 A1
Ferreñafe Peru 6°42S 79°50W 330 B2
Ferrerías Spain 39°59N 4°1E 206 B5
Ferret, C. France 44°38N 1°15W 174 D2
Ferrette France 47°30N 7°20E 173 E14
Ferriday U.S.A. 31°38N 91°33W 314 F9
Ferriere Italy 44°40N 9°30E 198 D6
Ferrières France 48°5N 2°48E 173 D9
Ferro, Capo Italy 41°9N 9°31E 200 A2
Ferrol Spain 43°29N 8°15W 194 B2
Ferrol, Pen. de Peru 9°10S 78°35W 330 B2
Ferron U.S.A. 39°5N 111°8W 304 G8
Ferros Brazil 19°14S 43°2W 333 E3
Ferrutx, C. Spain 39°47N 3°21E 206 B4
Ferry Pass U.S.A. 30°31N 87°13W 317 E2
Ferryland Canada 47°2N 52°53W 299 C9
Ferrysburg U.S.A. 43°5N 86°13W 311 A10
Ferryville = Menzel-Bourguiba Tunisia 37°9N 9°49E 258 A1
Fertile U.S.A. 47°32N 96°17W 308 B5
Fertőszentmiklós Hungary 47°35N 16°53E 182 C1
Fertotavi △ Hungary 47°25N 16°50E 182 C1
Fès Morocco 34°0N 5°0W 260 B4
Fès □ Morocco 34°1N 5°0W 260 B4
Feshi Dem. Rep. of the Congo 6°8S 18°10E 265 D3
Fessenden U.S.A. 47°39N 99°38W 308 B4
Festenberg = Twardogóra Poland 51°23N 17°28E 185 G4
Festøya Norway 62°22N 6°19E 164 B3
Festus U.S.A. 38°13N 90°24W 310 F6
Feté Bowé Senegal 14°56N 13°30W 262 C2
Fetești Romania 44°22N 27°51E 183 F12
Fethiye Turkey 36°36N 29°6E 205 E11
Fethiye Körfezi Turkey 36°40N 29°0E 205 E11
Fetlar U.K. 60°36N 0°52W 167 A8
Fetsund Norway 59°56N 11°10E 164 E8
Feuilles → Canada 58°47N 70°4W 295 D12
Feurs France 45°45N 4°13E 175 C8
Fevik Norway 58°22N 8°39E 164 F5
Fevzipaşa Turkey 37°6N 36°37E 250 A7
Feyzābād Badakhshān, Afghan. 37°7N 70°33E 240 A3
Feyzābād Fāryāb, Afghan. 36°17N 64°52E 240 A2
Fez = Fès Morocco 34°0N 5°0W 260 B4
Fezzan Libya 27°0N 13°0E 258 C2
Fia Congo 3°25S 14°49E 264 C2
Fiambalá Argentina 27°45S 67°37W 334 B2
Fianarantsoa Madag. 21°26S 47°5E 272 C2
Fianarantsoa □ Madag. 19°30S 47°0E 272 B2
Fianga Cameroon 9°55N 15°9E 259 G2
Fiche Ethiopia 9°50N 38°46E 257 F4
Fichtelgebirge Germany 50°2N 11°55E 179 E7
Fichtelgebirge ⌂ Germany 50°8N 12°0E 179 E8
Fichtenau Germany 52°27N 13°42E 115 B5
Ficksburg S. Africa 28°51S 27°53E 271 C4
Fidenza Italy 44°52N 10°3E 198 D7
Fiditi Nigeria 7°45N 3°53E 263 D5
Fidjeland Norway 58°57N 6°54E 164 F3
Field → Australia 23°48S 138°0E 280 C2
Field I. Australia 12°5S 132°23E 278 B5
Field Museum of Natural History Chicago, U.S.A. 119 e2
Fields Corner U.S.A. 42°18N 71°3W 116 B2
Fieni Romania 45°8N 25°25E 183 E10
Fier Albania 40°43N 19°33E 202 F3
Fiera Camp Italy 45°28N 9°9E 129 B1
Fierzë Albania 42°15N 20°1E 202 D4
Fife □ U.K. 56°16N 3°1W 167 E5
Fife ⌂ U.K. 56°15N 3°15W 167 E5
Fife Ness U.K. 56°17N 2°35W 167 E6
Fifth Cataract Sudan 18°22N 33°50E 256 D3
Fig Tree St. Kitts & Nevis 17°8N 62°35W 322 d
Figari France 41°29N 9°7E 175 G13
Figeac France 44°37N 2°2E 174 D6
Figeholm Sweden 57°22N 16°33E 163 G10
Figino Italy 45°29N 9°4E 129 B1
Figline Valdarno Italy 43°37N 11°28E 199 E8
Figtree Zimbabwe 20°22S 28°20E 269 G2
Figueira = Governador Valadares Brazil 18°15S 41°57W 333 E3
Figueira Castelo Rodrigo Portugal 40°57N 6°58W 194 E4
Figueira da Foz Portugal 40°7N 8°54W 194 E2
Figueiró dos Vinhos Portugal 39°55N 8°16W 194 F2
Figueres Spain 42°18N 2°58E 196 C7
Figuig Morocco 32°5N 1°11W 261 B4
Figuig □ Morocco 32°50N 2°15E 261 B5
Fihaonana Madag. 18°36S 47°12E 272 B2
Fiherenana Madag. 18°29S 48°24E 272 B2
Fiherenana → Madag. 23°19S 43°37E 272 C1
Fiji ■ Pac. Oc. 17°20S 179°0E 287 A2
Fijir Iraq 33°21N 44°21E 244 C2
Fik Ethiopia 8°10N 42°19E 257 F5
Fika Nigeria 11°15N 11°13E 263 C7
Filabres, Sierra de los Spain 37°13N 2°20W 195 H8
Filabusi Zimbabwe 20°34S 29°20E 271 B4
Filadelfia Bolivia 11°20S 68°46W 330 C4
Filadélfia Brazil 7°21S 47°30W 332 C2
Filadelfia Athina, Greece 38°2N 23°43E 112 A2
Filadélfia Italy 38°47N 16°17E 201 D9
Fil'akovo Slovak Rep. 48°17N 19°50E 181 C12
Filchner Ice Shelf Antarctica 79°0S 40°0W 151 D1
Filefjell Norway 61°8N 8°10E 164 C5
Filey U.K. 54°12N 0°18W 168 C7
Filey B. U.K. 54°12N 0°15W 168 C7
Filfla Malta 35°47N 14°24E 206 F7
Fili-Mazilovo Russia 55°44N 37°29E 129 B2
Filiaşi Romania 44°32N 23°31E 183 F8
Filiates Greece 39°38N 20°16E 206 B10
Filiatra Greece 37°9N 21°35E 204 D3
Filicudi Italy 38°35N 14°33E 201 D7
Filim Oman 20°37N 58°12E 249 B7
Filingué Niger 14°21N 3°22E 263 C5
Filiouri = Lissos → Greece 41°15N 25°40E 203 E9
Filipada Greece 39°12N 20°53E 204 B2
Filipstad Sweden 59°43N 14°9E 162 E8
Filisur Switz. 46°41N 9°40E 179 J5
Fillmore Calif., U.S.A. 34°24N 118°55W 307 L8
Fillmore Utah, U.S.A. 38°58N 112°20W 304 G7
Filothei Greece 38°2N 23°46E 112 A2
Filotio Greece 37°3N 25°30E 205 D7
Filottrano Italy 43°26N 13°21E 199 E10
Filtu Ethiopia 5°8N 40°35E 257 F5
Fimi → Dem. Rep. of the Congo 3°1S 16°58E 264 C3
Fina ⌂ Mali 13°15N 8°46W 262 C3
Finale Emilia Italy 44°50N 11°18E 199 D8
Finale Ligure Italy 44°10N 8°20E 198 D5
Finalmarina = Finale Ligure Italy 44°10N 8°20E 198 D5
Fiñana Spain 37°10N 2°50W 195 H8
Financial District San Francisco, U.S.A. 136 b3
Finch Canada 45°11N 75°7W 313 A9
Finch Hatton Australia 20°25S 148°39E 280 B4
Finchley U.K. 51°36N 0°11W 125 A2
Findhorn → U.K. 57°38N 3°38W 167 D5
Findlay U.S.A. 41°2N 83°39W 311 C13
Fine Art, Museum of = Kunsthistorischesmuseum Vienna, Austria 142 b1
Fine Arts, Museum of U.S.A. 42°20N 71°5W 116 B2
Finger L. Canada 53°33N 93°30W 298 B1
Finger Lakes U.S.A. 42°40N 76°30W 313 D8
Finglas Ireland 53°23N 6°19W 120 A2
Fingoè Mozam. 14°55S 31°50E 269 E3
Finike Turkey 36°21N 30°10E 205 E12
Finike Körfezi Turkey 36°17N 30°16E 205 E12
Finiq Albania 39°54N 20°3E 202 G4
Finistère □ France 48°20N 4°0W 172 D3
Finisterre = Fisterra Spain 42°54N 9°16W 194 C1
Finisterre, C. = Fisterra, C. Spain 42°50N 9°19W 194 C1
Finisterre Ra. Papua N. G. 6°0S 146°30E 286 D4
Finke Australia 25°34S 134°35E 280 D1
Finke Gorge △ Australia 24°8S 132°49E 278 D5
Finland ■ Europe 63°0N 27°0E 160 E22
Finland, G. of Europe 60°0N 26°0E 188 C3
Finlay → Canada 57°0N 125°10W 296 B3
Finley N.S.W., Australia 35°38S 145°35E 283 C6
Finley N. Dak., U.S.A. 47°31N 97°50W 308 B5
Finn → Ireland 54°51N 7°28W 166 B4
Finnerödja Sweden 58°57N 14°24E 163 F8
Finnigan, Mt. Australia 15°49S 145°17E 280 B4
Finniss, C. Australia 33°8S 134°51E 281 E1
Finnmark Norway 69°37N 23°57E 160 B20
Finnsnes Norway 69°14N 18°0E 160 B18
Finsbury U.K. 51°31N 0°6W 125 A3
Finsbury Park U.K. 51°34N 0°6W 125 A3
Finschhafen Papua N. G. 6°33S 147°50E 286 D4
Finse Norway 60°36N 7°30E 164 D4
Finspång Sweden 58°43N 15°47E 163 F9
Finsteraarhorn Switz. 46°31N 8°10E 179 J4
Finsterwalde Germany 51°37N 13°42E 178 D9
Fiora → Italy 42°20N 11°34E 199 F8
Fiordland △ N.Z. 45°46S 167°0E 285 F2
Fiorenzuola d'Arda Italy 44°56N 9°55E 198 D6
Fiorito Argentina 34°42S 58°26W 117 C2
Fiq Syria 32°46N 35°41E 250 F6
Firat = Furāt, Nahr al → Asia 31°0N 47°25E 246 D5
Fire Island ⌂ U.S.A. 40°38N 73°8W 313 F11
Firebag → Canada 57°45N 111°21W 297 B6
Firebaugh U.S.A. 36°52N 120°27W 306 J6
Firedrake L. Canada 61°25N 104°30W 297 A8
Firenze Italy 43°46N 11°15E 199 E8
Firenze Amerigo Vespucci ✕ (FLR) Italy 43°49N 11°13E 199 E8
Firenze Pisa ✕ (PSA) Italy 43°40N 10°22E 198 E7
Firenzuola Italy 44°7N 11°23E 199 D8
Firhouse Ireland 53°17N 6°20W 120 B2
Firk, Sha'ib → Iraq 30°59N 44°34E 246 D5
Firkachi Niger 15°40N 14°20E 259 E2
Firmi France 44°33N 2°19E 174 D6
Firminy France 45°23N 4°18E 175 C8
Firozabad India 27°10N 78°25E 243 F8
Firozpur India 30°55N 74°40E 242 D6
Firozpur-Jhirka India 27°48N 76°57E 242 F7
Fīrūzābād Iran 28°52N 52°35E 247 D7
Fīrūzkūh Iran 35°50N 52°50E 247 C7
Firvale Canada 52°27N 126°13W 296 C3
Fischerhäuser Germany 48°14N 11°41E 131 A3
Fish → Namibia 28°7S 17°10E 270 C2
Fish → Northern Cape, S. Africa 31°30S 20°16E 270 D3
Fish River Canyon Namibia 27°40S 17°35E 270 C2
Fisheating Cr. → U.S.A. 26°57N 81°7W 317 J8
Fisher B. Canada 51°35N 97°13W 297 C9
Fisher Island U.S.A. 25°45N 80°8W 128 B2
Fishermans Bend Australia 37°49S 144°55E 128 A1
Fisherman's Wharf San Francisco, U.S.A. 136 a1
Fishers I. U.S.A. 41°15N 72°0W 313 E13
Fisherville Canada 43°46N 79°28W 141 A2
Fishguard U.K. 52°0N 4°58W 169 E3
Fishing L. Canada 52°10N 95°24W 297 C9
Fishkill U.S.A. 41°32N 73°54W 313 E11
Fiskardo Greece 38°28N 20°35E 207 C2
Fiskenæsset = Qeqertarsuatsiaat Greenland 63°5N 50°45W 154 E5
Fisksätra Sweden 59°17N 18°13E 139 B3
Fismes France 49°20N 3°40E 173 C10
Fisterra Spain 42°54N 9°16W 194 C1
Fisterra, C. Spain 42°50N 9°19W 194 C1
Fitchburg Mass., U.S.A. 42°35N 71°48W 313 D13
Fitchburg Wis., U.S.A. 42°58N 89°28W 310 B7
Fitjar Iceland 64°28N 21°18W 155 C5
Fitjar Hordaland, Norway 59°55N 5°17E 164 E2
Fitri, L. Chad 12°50N 17°28E 259 F3
Fitz Roy Argentina 47°0S 67°0W 336 C3
Fitz Roy, Cerro Argentina 49°17S 73°5W 336 C2
Fitzgerald Alta., Canada 59°51N 111°36W 296 B6
Fitzgerald Ga., U.S.A. 31°43N 83°15W 316 D6
Fitzgerald River △ Australia 33°53S 119°55E 279 F3
Fitzmaurice → Australia 14°45S 130°5E 278 B5
Fitzroy → Queens., Australia 23°32S 150°52E 280 C5
Fitzroy → W. Austral., Australia 17°31S 123°35E 278 C3
Fitzroy Crossing Australia 18°9S 125°38E 278 C4
Fitzroy Gardens Australia 37°48S 144°58E 128 A1
Fitzwilliam I. Canada 45°30N 81°45W 312 A3
Fiuggi Italy 41°48N 13°13E 199 G10
Fiume = Rijeka Croatia 45°20N 14°21E 199 C11
Fiumicino, Roma ✕ (FCO) Italy 41°48N 12°15E 199 G9
Five Dock Australia 33°52S 151°8E 139 B1
Five Island Harbour Antigua & B. 17°6N 61°54W 322 b
Five Points U.S.A. 36°26N 120°6W 306 J6
Fivizzano Italy 44°14N 10°8E 198 D7
Fizi Dem. Rep. of the Congo 4°17S 28°55E 268 C2
Fjæra Norway 59°52N 6°22E 164 E3
Fjærland Norway 61°24N 6°43E 164 C3
Fjærlandsfjorden Norway 61°17N 6°40E 164 C3
Fjällbacka Sweden 58°36N 11°17E 163 F5
Fjärdhundra Sweden 59°47N 16°56E 162 E10
Fjellerup Denmark 56°29N 10°34E 163 H4
Fjellstrand Norway 59°47N 10°36E 133 B2
Fjerritslev Denmark 57°5N 9°15E 163 G3
Fjugesta Sweden 59°11N 14°52E 162 E8
Fkih ben Salah Morocco 32°32N 6°45W 260 B3
Flå Norway 60°25N 9°28E 164 D6
Flacq Plain Mauritius 20°13S 57°43E 272 e
Flagler Beach U.S.A. 29°29N 81°8W 317 F8
Flagstaff U.S.A. 35°12N 111°39W 305 J8
Flagstaff B. St. Helena 15°54S 5°41W 153 h
Flagstaff L. U.S.A. 45°12N 70°18W 313 A14
Flaherty I. Canada 56°15N 79°15W 298 A4
Flåm Norway 60°50N 7°7E 164 D4
Flamands St.-Martin 17°55N 62°51W 322 a
Flambeau → U.S.A. 45°18N 91°14W 308 C8
Flamborough Hd. U.K. 54°7N 0°5W 168 C7
Flamengo Brazil 22°56S 43°11W 135 B1
Flamengos Azores 38°33N 28°39W 153 d1
Fläming Germany 52°6N 12°23E 178 C8
Flaming Gorge ⌂ U.S.A. 41°10N 109°25W 304 F9
Flaming Gorge Res. U.S.A. 41°10N 109°25W 304 F9
Flamingo Fla., U.S.A. 28°22N 81°22W 133 B2
Flamingo Fla., U.S.A. 25°8N 80°57W 317 K9
Flamingo, Teluk Indonesia 5°30S 138°0E 231 F9
Flaminio Italy 41°55N 12°28E 136 B1
Flanagan U.S.A. 40°53N 88°52W 311 D8
Flanagin Town Trin. & Tob. 10°25N 61°19W 323 t
Flanders = Flandre Europe 50°50N 2°30E 173 B9
Flandre Europe 50°50N 2°30E 173 B9
Flandre-Occidentale = West-Vlaanderen □ Belgium 51°0N 3°0E 170 D2
Flandre-Orientale = Oost-Vlaanderen □ Belgium 51°5N 3°50E 170 C3
Flandreau U.S.A. 44°3N 96°36W 308 C5
Flanigan U.S.A. 40°10N 119°53W 306 E7
Flannan Is. U.K. 58°9N 7°52W 167 C1
Flåsjön Sweden 64°5N 15°40E 160 D16
Flaskebekk Norway 59°51N 10°39E 133 A2
Flat U.S.A. 62°28N 158°1W 303 E8
Flat → N.W.T., Canada 61°33N 125°18W 296 A3
Flat → Mich., U.S.A. 42°56N 85°20W 311 B11
Flat Pt. N.Z. 41°14S 175°57E 284 H4
Flat Rock U.S.A. 42°6N 83°17W 311 B13
Flatbush U.S.A. 40°39N 73°56W 132 C2
Flateby Norway 59°50N 11°10E 164 E8
Flaten Sweden 59°15N 18°9E 139 B2
Flatey Iceland 66°10N 17°52W 155 A9
Flateyri Iceland 66°3N 23°31W 155 A3
Flathead L. U.S.A. 47°51N 114°8W 304 C6
Flatiron Building New York, U.S.A. 132 d2
Flatlands U.S.A. 40°37N 73°56W 132 C2
Flatow = Złotów Poland 53°22N 17°2E 184 E4
Flatrock → U.S.A. 39°12N 85°56W 311 F10
Flattery, C. Queens., Australia 14°58S 145°21E 280 A4
Flattery, C. Wash., U.S.A. 48°23N 124°29W 306 B2
Flatts Village Bermuda 32°18N 64°43W 153 a
Flatwoods U.S.A. 38°31N 82°43W 309 F12
Flecha Pt. Phil. 7°22N 123°24E 233 H4
Flechas Pt. Phil. 10°22N 119°34E 233 F2
Fleet Center Boston, U.S.A. 116 a2
Fleetwood Lancs., U.K. 53°55N 3°1W 168 D4
Fleetwood Pa., U.S.A. 40°27N 75°49W 313 F9
Flekke Norway 61°19N 5°20E 164 C2
Flekkefjord Norway 58°18N 6°39E 164 F3
Flemingsburg U.S.A. 38°25N 83°45W 311 F13
Flemington U.S.A. 41°7N 77°28W 312 E7
Flemington Racecourse Australia 37°47S 144°54E 128 A1
Flemish Cap Atl. Oc. 47°0N 45°0W 152 B7
Flen Sweden 59°4N 16°35E 162 E10
Flensburg Germany 54°47N 9°27E 178 A5
Flers France 48°47N 0°33W 172 D6
Flesberg Norway 59°51N 9°27E 164 E6
Flesherton Canada 44°16N 80°33W 312 B4
Flesko, Tanjung Indonesia 0°29N 124°30E 231 D6
Fletcher = Aurora U.S.A. 39°43N 104°49W 304 G11
Fleurance France 43°52N 0°40E 174 E4
Fleurier Switz. 46°54N 6°35E 179 J2
Fleurieu Pen. Australia 35°40S 138°5E 282 C3
Flevoland □ Neths. 52°30N 5°30E 170 B5
Flin Flon Canada 54°46N 101°53W 297 C8
Flinders → Australia 17°36S 140°36E 280 B3
Flinders B. Australia 34°19S 115°19E 279 F2
Flinders Chase △ Australia 35°50S 136°42E 282 C2
Flinders Group Australia 14°11S 144°15E 280 A3
Flinders I. S. Austral., Australia 33°44S 134°41E 281 E1
Flinders I. Tas., Australia 40°0S 148°0E 281 G4
Flinders Ranges Australia 31°30S 138°30E 282 A3
Flinders Ranges △ Australia 31°30S 138°40E 282 A3
Flinders Reefs Australia 17°37S 148°31E 280 B4
Flint Flints., U.K. 53°15N 3°8W 168 D4
Flint Mich., U.S.A. 43°1N 83°41W 311 A13
Flint → U.S.A. 30°57N 84°34W 316 E5
Flint I. Kiribati 11°26S 151°48W 289 f
Flint Pk. U.S.A. 34°9N 118°11W 126 B3
Flintshire □ U.K. 53°17N 3°17W 168 D4
Flipper Pt. Wake I. 19°18N 166°37E 302 b
Flisa Norway 60°37N 12°6E 164 D9
Flisa → Norway 60°37N 12°6E 164 D9
Fliseryd Sweden 57°6N 16°15E 163 G10
Flix Spain 41°14N 0°32E 196 D5
Flixecourt France 50°1N 2°5E 173 B9
Floby Sweden 58°8N 13°20E 163 F7
Floda Sweden 57°49N 12°22E 163 G6
Flodden U.K. 55°37N 2°8W 168 B5
Flogny-la-Chapelle France 47°57N 3°57E 173 E10
Floodplains △ Sri Lanka 8°10N 81°10E 245 K5
Floodwood U.S.A. 46°56N 92°55W 308 B7
Flora Apayao, Phil. 18°14N 121°5E 232 B3
Flora Ill., U.S.A. 38°40N 88°29W 310 F8
Flora Ind., U.S.A. 40°33N 86°31W 311 D10
Florac France 44°20N 3°37E 174 D7
Florahome U.S.A. 29°44N 81°54W 316 F8
Floral City U.S.A. 28°45N 82°17W 317 G7
Florala U.S.A. 31°0N 86°20W 315 F11
Florânia Brazil 6°8S 36°49W 332 C4
Floreana, I. = Santa María, I. Ecuador 1°17S 90°26W 330 a
Florence = Firenze Italy 43°46N 11°15E 199 E8
Florence Ala., U.S.A. 34°48N 87°41W 315 D11
Florence Ariz., U.S.A. 33°2N 111°23W 305 K8
Florence Calif., U.S.A. 33°57N 118°13W 126 C3
Florence Colo., U.S.A. 38°23N 105°8W 304 G11
Florence Oreg., U.S.A. 43°58N 124°7W 304 D1
Florence S.C., U.S.A. 34°12N 79°46W 315 D15
Florence, L. Australia 28°53S 138°9E 281 D2
Florence Bay = Chtimba Malawi 10°35S 34°13E 269 E3
Florence Bloom Bird Sanctuary ⌂ S. Africa 26°7S 28°0E 123 A2
Florencia Colombia 1°36N 75°36W 328 C2
Florennes Belgium 50°15N 4°35E 170 D4
Florensac France 43°23N 3°28E 174 E7
Florentia S. Africa 26°16S 28°8E 123 B2
Florenville Belgium 49°40N 5°19E 170 E5
Flores = Florânia Brazil 6°8S 36°49W 332 C4
Flores = Timon Brazil 5°8S 42°52W 332 C3
Flores B. Aires, Argentina 34°38S 58°27W 117 B2
Flores Azores 39°26N 31°13W 153 d2
Flores Brazil 7°51S 37°59W 332 C4
Flores Guatemala 16°59N 89°50W 320 C2
Flores Indonesia 8°35S 121°0E 231 F6
Flores, Mercado de Mexico 19°19N 99°5W 128 C2
Flores I. Canada 49°20N 126°10W 296 D3
Flores Sea Indonesia 6°30S 120°0E 231 F6
Floresta B. Aires, Argentina 34°37S 58°27W 117 B2
Floresta Brazil 8°40S 37°26W 332 C4
Florești Moldova 47°53N 28°17E 183 C13
Floresville U.S.A. 29°8N 98°10W 314 G5
Floriano Brazil 6°50S 43°0W 332 C3
Florianópolis Brazil 27°30S 48°30W 335 B6
Florida B. Aires, Argentina 34°31S 58°28W 117 B2
Florida Cuba 21°32N 78°14W 320 B4
Florida Puerto Rico 18°22N 66°34W 321 b
Florida Gauteng, S. Africa 26°10S 27°55E 123 B1
Florida Uruguay 34°7S 56°10W 335 C4
Florida □ U.S.A. 28°0N 82°0W 315 G14
Florida, Straits of U.S.A. 25°0N 80°0W 320 B4
Florida B. U.S.A. 25°0N 80°45W 320 B3
Florida City U.S.A. 25°27N 80°29W 317 K9
Florida Is. Solomon Is. 9°5S 160°15E 287 M11
Florida Keys U.S.A. 24°40N 81°0W 317 L8
Floridablanca Phil. 14°59N 120°31E 232 D3
Florídia Italy 37°5N 15°9E 201 E8
Floridsdorf Austria 48°15N 16°26E 142 A2
Florin U.S.A. 38°30N 121°24W 306 G5
Florina Greece 40°48N 21°26E 202 F5
Florina □ Greece 40°45N 21°20E 202 F5
Florissant U.S.A. 38°47N 90°19W 310 F6
Florø Norway 61°35N 5°1E 164 C2
Flotte, C. de N. Cal. 21°10S 167°25E 288 d
Flower Station Canada 45°10N 76°41W 313 A8
Flowerpot I. Canada 45°18N 81°38W 312 A3
Floydada U.S.A. 33°59N 101°20W 314 E4
Fludir Iceland 64°7N 20°6W 155 C6
Flugumyri Iceland 65°34N 19°19W 155 B7
Fluk Indonesia 1°42S 127°44E 231 E7
Flúmen → Spain 41°43N 0°9W 196 D4
Flumendosa → Italy 39°26N 9°37E 200 C2
Fluminimaggiore Italy 39°26N 8°30E 200 C1
Flushing = Vlissingen Neths. 51°26N 3°34E 170 C3
Flushing Mich., U.S.A. 43°4N 83°51W 311 A13
Flushing N.Y., U.S.A. 40°45N 73°49W 132 B3
Flushing Meadows Corona Park U.S.A. 40°44N 73°50W 132 B2
Fluviá → Spain 42°12N 3°7E 196 C8
Fly → Papua N. G. 8°25S 143°0E 286 E2
Flying Fish, C. Antarctica 72°6S 102°29W 151 D15
Flysta Sweden 59°22N 17°54E 139 A1
Fo Tan China 22°23N 114°11E 122 A2
Foa Tonga 19°45S 174°18W 287 P13
Foam Lake Canada 51°40N 103°32W 297 C8
Foča Bos.-H. 43°31N 18°47E 202 C2
Foça Turkey 38°39N 26°46E 205 C8
Fochabers U.K. 57°37N 3°6W 167 D5
Focşani Romania 45°41N 27°15E 183 E12
Fodé C.A.R. 5°29N 23°18E 264 A4
Fodécontéa Guinea 10°50N 14°22W 262 C2
Fogang China 23°52N 113°30E 229 F9
Foggaret el Arab Algeria 27°13N 2°49E 261 C5
Foggaret ez Zoua Algeria 27°20N 2°53E 261 C5
Fóggia Italy 41°27N 15°34E 201 A8
Foggo Nigeria 11°21N 9°57E 263 C6
Foglia → Italy 43°55N 12°54E 199 E9
Fogo Nfld. & L., Canada 49°43N 54°17W 299 C9
Fogo C. Verde Is. 15°5N 24°20W 153 j
Fogo I. Canada 49°40N 54°5W 299 C9
Fohnsdorf Austria 47°12N 14°40E 180 D7
Föhr Germany 54°43N 8°30E 178 A4
Föhrenhain Austria 48°19N 16°26E 142 A2
Foia Portugal 37°19N 8°37W 195 H2
Foix France 42°58N 1°38E 174 F5
Fojnica Bos.-H. 43°59N 17°51E 182 G2
Fokida □ Greece 38°30N 22°15E 204 C4
Fokino Russia 53°30N 34°22E 188 F8
Fokku Nigeria 11°36N 4°32E 263 C5
Fokstugu Norway 62°7N 9°17E 164 B6
Folda Nord-Trøndelag, Norway 64°32N 10°30E 160 D14
Folda Nordland, Norway 67°38N 14°50E 160 C16
Földeák Hungary 46°19N 20°30E 182 D5
Folegandros Greece 36°40N 24°55E 204 E6
Foley Botswana 21°34S 27°21E 270 B4
Foley Ala., U.S.A. 30°24N 87°41W 315 F11
Foley Fla., U.S.A. 30°4N 83°32W 316 E6
Foleyet Canada 48°15N 82°25W 298 C3
Folgefonna Norway 60°3N 6°23E 164 D3
Foligno Italy 42°57N 12°42E 199 F9
Folkestad Norway 62°7N 6°1E 164 B3
Folkestone U.K. 51°5N 1°12E 169 F9
Folkestone Underwater Park Barbados 13°11N 59°38W 323 r
Folkston U.S.A. 30°50N 82°0W 316 E7
Folla → Norway 62°7N 10°37E 164 B7
Follansbee U.S.A. 40°19N 80°35W 312 F4
Folldal Norway 62°8N 10°0E 164 B6
Folle Anse, Pte. de Guadeloupe 15°56N 61°19W 322 e
Follebu Norway 61°13N 10°16E 164 C7
Follónica Italy 42°55N 10°45E 198 F7
Follónica, G. di Italy 42°54N 10°43E 198 F7
Folsom L. U.S.A. 38°42N 121°9W 306 G5
Folteşti Romania 45°45N 28°3E 183 E13
Fomboni Comoros Is. 12°18S 43°46E 272 a
Fomm ir-Rih Bay Malta 35°54N 14°20E 206 F7
Fond-du-Lac Sask., Canada 59°19N 107°12W 297 B7
Fond du Lac Wis., U.S.A. 43°47N 88°27W 308 D9
Fond-du-Lac → Canada 59°17N 106°0W 297 B7
Fond Rousseau Martinique 14°38N 61°6W 322 j
Fond St. Jacques St. Lucia 13°50N 61°1W 323 m
Fonda Iowa, U.S.A. 42°35N 94°51W 310 B2
Fonda N.Y., U.S.A. 42°57N 74°22W 313 D10
Fondi Italy 41°21N 13°25E 200 A6
Fonds-St-Denis Martinique 14°44N 61°8W 322 j
Fonfría Spain 41°37N 6°9W 194 D4
Fongafale Tuvalu 8°31S 179°13E 277 B14
Fongen Norway 63°11N 11°38E 164 A8
Fonni Italy 40°7N 9°15E 200 B2
Fonsagrada = A Fonsagrada Spain 43°8N 7°4W 194 B3
Fonseca, G. de Cent. Amer. 13°10N 87°40W 320 D2
Font-Romeu-Odeillo-Via France 42°31N 2°3E 174 F5
Fontaine-Française France 47°32N 5°21E 173 E12
Fontainebleau Seine-et-Marne, France 48°24N 2°40E 173 D9
Fontainebleau Gauteng, S. Africa 26°6S 27°57E 123 A1
Fontana U.S.A. 34°6N 117°26W 307 L9
Fontana, L. Argentina 44°55S 71°30W 336 B2
Fontas → Canada 58°14N 121°48W 296 B4
Fonte Boa Brazil 2°33S 66°0W 328 D4
Fontem Cameroon 5°32N 9°52E 263 D6
Fontenay-aux-Roses France 48°47N 2°17E 134 B2
Fontenay-le-Comte France 46°28N 0°48W 174 B3
Fontenay-le-Fleury France 48°48N 2°2E 134 B1
Fontenay-sous-Bois France 48°51N 2°28E 134 A3
Fontenelle Res. U.S.A. 42°1N 110°3W 304 E8
Fontur Iceland 66°23N 14°32W 155 A12
Fonuafo'ou Tonga 20°19S 175°25W 287 Q13
Fonuakula Cook Is. 19°2S 169°55W 289 g
Fonualei Tonga 18°1S 174°19W 287 P13
Fonyód Hungary 46°44N 17°33E 182 D2
Foochow = Fuzhou China 26°5N 119°16E 229 D12
Foots Cray U.K. 51°24N 0°7E 125 B4
Footscray Australia 37°48S 144°56E 128 A1
Foping China 33°41N 108°0E 226 H5
Foraker, Mt. U.S.A. 62°58N 151°24W 303 E10
Forari Vanuatu 17°40S 168°31E 287 G6
Forbach France 49°10N 6°52E 173 C13
Forbes Australia 33°22S 148°5E 283 B8
Forbesganj India 26°17N 87°18E 243 F12
Forbidden City = Imperial Palace Museum Beijing, China 114 b2
Forcados Nigeria 5°26N 5°26E 263 D6
Forcados → Nigeria 5°25N 5°19E 263 D6
Forcalquier France 43°58N 5°47E 175 E9
Forchheim Germany 49°43N 11°2E 179 F7
Ford City Calif., U.S.A. 35°9N 119°27W 307 K7
Ford City Pa., U.S.A. 40°46N 79°32W 312 F5
Ford d'Or B. St. Lucia 13°56N 60°54W 323 m
Ford I. U.S.A. 21°22N 157°58W 302 K14
Forda → Norway 62°57N 10°40E 164 B7
Førde Hordaland, Norway 59°36N 5°27E 164 E2
Førde Sogn og Fjordane, Norway 61°27N 5°53E 164 C2
Førdefjorden Norway 61°29N 5°18E 164 C2
Fords Bridge Australia 29°41S 145°29E 281 D4
Ford's Theater Washington, D.C., U.S.A. 143 b2
Fordyce U.S.A. 33°49N 92°25W 314 E8
Forécariah Guinea 9°28N 13°10W 262 D2
Forel, Mt. Greenland 66°52N 36°55W 154 D7
Foremost Canada 49°26N 111°34W 296 D6
Foreshore Cape Town, S. Africa 118 a3
Forest Belgium 50°49N 4°20E 116 B1
Forest Ont., Canada 43°6N 82°0W 312 C3
Forest Miss., U.S.A. 32°22N 89°29W 315 E10
Forest Acres U.S.A. 34°1N 80°58W 316 A9
Forest City Iowa, U.S.A. 43°16N 93°39W 308 D7
Forest City N.C., U.S.A. 35°20N 81°52W 315 D14
Forest City Pa., U.S.A. 41°39N 75°28W 313 E9
Forest Gate U.K. 51°32N 0°1E 125 A4
Forest Grove U.S.A. 45°31N 123°7W 306 E3
Forest Heights U.S.A. 38°48N 77°0W 143 C3
Forest Hill Ont., Canada 43°41N 79°25W 141 A2
Forest Hill London, U.K. 51°26N 0°2W 125 B3
Forest Hills U.S.A. 40°42N 73°51W 132 B2
Forest Park Ga., U.S.A. 33°37N 84°22W 316 B5
Forest Park Ill., U.S.A. 41°51N 87°47W 119 B2
Forest Park N.Y., U.S.A. 40°42N 73°51W 132 B2
Forest Park Ohio, U.S.A. 39°17N 84°30W 311 E12
Forest View U.S.A. 41°48N 87°47W 119 C2
Forestburg Canada 52°35N 112°1W 296 C6
Foreste Casentinesi-Monte Falterona-Campigna △ Italy 43°50N 11°48E 199 E8
Foresthill U.S.A. 39°1N 120°49W 306 F6
Forestier Pen. Australia 43°0S 148°0E 281 G4
Forestville Qué., Canada 48°48N 69°2W 299 C6
Forestville Calif., U.S.A. 38°28N 122°54W 306 G4
Forestville Md., U.S.A. 38°50N 76°52W 143 B4
Forestville N.Y., U.S.A. 42°28N 79°10W 312 D5
Forêt d'Orient ⌂ France 48°16N 4°25E 173 D11
Forêt du Day △ Djibouti 11°56N 42°40E 267 B5
Forez, Mts. du France 45°40N 3°50E 174 C7
Forfar U.K. 56°39N 2°53W 167 E6
Forillon △ Canada 48°46N 64°12W 299 C7

Forks U.S.A. 47°57N 124°23W 306 C2
Forks, The = Merritt Canada 50°10N 120°45W 296 C4
Forksville U.S.A. 41°29N 76°35W 313 E8
Forlì Italy 44°13N 12°3E 199 D9
Forman U.S.A. 46°7N 97°38W 308 B5
Formazza Italy 46°22N 8°26E 198 B5
Formby Pt. U.K. 53°33N 3°6W 168 D4
Formentera Spain 38°43N 1°27E 206 D1
Formentor, C. de Spain 39°58N 3°13E 206 B4
Former Yugoslav Republic of Macedonia = Macedonia ■ Europe 41°53N 21°40E 202 E5
Fórmia Italy 41°15N 13°37E 200 A6
Formiga Brazil 20°27S 45°25W 333 F2
Formigine Italy 44°37N 10°51E 198 D7
Formosa = Taiwan ■ Asia 23°30N 121°0E 225 C3
Formosa Argentina 26°15S 58°10W 334 B4
Formosa Brazil 15°32S 47°20W 333 E2
Formosa □ Argentina 25°0S 60°0W 334 B4
Formosa, Serra Brazil 12°0S 55°0W 331 C7
Formosa B. = Ungwana B. Kenya 2°45S 40°20E 268 C5
Formosa Strait = Taiwan Strait Asia 24°40N 120°0E 229 E12
Formoso → Brazil 10°34S 49°56W 333 D2
Fornebu Norway 59°53N 10°36E 133 A2
Fornells Spain 40°3N 4°7E 206 A5
Fornos de Algodres Portugal 40°38N 7°32W 194 E3
Fornovo di Taro Italy 44°42N 10°6E 198 D7
Foro Romano Rome, Italy 136 c3
Føroyar ⊠ Atl. Oc. 62°0N 7°0W 160 F9
Førre Norway 59°25N 5°20E 164 E2
Forres U.K. 57°37N 3°37W 167 D5
Forrest Vic., Australia 38°33S 143°47E 282 E5
Forrest W. Austral., Australia 30°51S 128°6E 279 F4
Forrest, Mt. Australia 24°48S 127°45E 279 D4
Forreston U.S.A. 42°8N 89°35W 310 B7
Fors Sweden 60°14N 16°20E 162 D10
Forsand Norway 58°54N 6°5E 164 F3
Forsayth Australia 18°33S 143°34E 280 B3
Forshaga Sweden 59°33N 13°29E 162 E7
Förslöv Sweden 56°21N 12°48E 163 H6
Forsmo Sweden 63°16N 17°11E 162 A11
Forssa Finland 60°49N 23°38E 188 B2
Forst Germany 51°45N 14°37E 178 D10
Forstenried Germany 48°5N 11°29E 131 B1
Forstenrieder Park Germany 48°3N 11°27E 131 B1
Forster Australia 32°12S 152°31E 283 B10
Forsvik Sweden 58°35N 14°26E 163 F8
Forsyth Ga., U.S.A. 33°2N 83°56W 316 B6
Forsyth Mont., U.S.A. 46°16N 106°41W 304 C10
Forsyth I. N.Z. 40°58S 174°5E 285 A9
Fort Mumbai, India 130 c2
Fort Abbas Pakistan 29°12N 72°52E 242 E5
Fort Albany Canada 52°15N 81°35W 298 B3
Fort-Aleksandrovsky = Fort Shevchenko Kazakhstan 44°35N 50°23E 191 H10
Fort Ann U.S.A. 43°25N 73°29W 313 C11
Fort Archambault = Sarh Chad 9°5N 18°23E 259 G3
Fort Assiniboine Canada 54°20N 114°45W 296 C6
Fort Atkinson U.S.A. 42°56N 88°50W 311 B8
Fort Augustus U.K. 57°9N 4°42W 167 D4
Fort Bay Neth. Ant. 17°37N 63°15W 322 a
Fort Bayard = Zhanjiang China 21°15N 110°20E 229 G8
Fort Beaufort S. Africa 32°46S 26°40E 270 D4
Fort Benton U.S.A. 47°49N 110°40W 304 C8
Fort Bragg U.S.A. 39°26N 123°48W 304 G2
Fort Bridger U.S.A. 41°19N 110°23W 304 F8
Fort Canning Park Singapore 138 b2
Fort Caroline ⌓ U.S.A. 30°23N 81°30W 316 E8
Fort Charles Jamaica 17°55N 76°50W 320 a
Fort Charlotte St. Lucia 13°59N 61°0W 323 m
Fort Chipewyan Canada 58°42N 111°8W 297 B6
Fort Clatsop ⌓ U.S.A. 46°8N 123°53W 306 D3
Fort Collins U.S.A. 40°35N 105°5W 304 F11
Fort-Coulonge Canada 45°50N 76°45W 298 C4
Fort Covington U.S.A. 44°59N 74°29W 313 B10
Fort Dauphin = Taolanaro Madag. 25°2S 47°0E 272 D2
Fort Davis Ala., U.S.A. 32°15N 85°43W 316 C4
Fort Davis Tex., U.S.A. 30°35N 103°54W 314 F3
Fort-de-France Martinique 14°36N 61°2W 322 j
Fort-de-France, B. de Martinique 14°34N 61°4W 322 j
Fort de Kock = Bukittinggi Indonesia 0°20S 100°20E 234 C2
Fort de Polignac = Illizi Algeria 26°31N 8°32E 261 C6
Fort de Possel = Possel C.A.R. 5°5N 19°10E 264 A3
Fort Defiance U.S.A. 35°45N 109°5W 305 J9
Fort Dodge U.S.A. 42°30N 94°11W 310 B2
Fort Drum U.S.A. 27°32N 80°48W 317 H9
Fort Dupont Park U.S.A. 38°52N 76°56W 143 B4
Fort Edward U.S.A. 43°16N 73°35W 313 C11
Fort Erie Canada 42°54N 78°56W 312 D6
Fort Fairfield U.S.A. 46°46N 67°50W 309 B20
Fort Flatters = Bordj Omar Driss Algeria 28°10N 6°40E 261 C6
Fort Foote Village U.S.A. 38°46N 77°1W 143 C3
Fort-Foureau = Kousseri Cameroon 12°0N 14°55E 259 F2
Fort Frances Canada 48°36N 93°24W 297 D10
Fort Franklin = Déline Canada 65°11N 123°25W 294 C7
Fort Frederica ⌓ U.S.A. 31°13N 81°23W 316 D8
Fort Gaines U.S.A. 31°36N 85°3W 316 D4
Fort Garland U.S.A. 37°26N 105°26W 305 H11
Fort George = Chisasibi Canada 53°50N 79°0W 298 B4
Fort George = Prince George Canada 53°55N 122°50W 296 C4
Fort George Grenada 12°3N 61°45W 323 q
Fort Good Hope Canada 66°14N 128°40W 294 C7
Fort Gouraud = Fdérik Mauritania 22°40N 12°45W 260 D2
Fort Hancock U.S.A. 31°18N 105°51W 314 F2
Fort Hertz = Putao Burma 27°28N 97°30E 241 B6
Fort Hill = Chitipa Malawi 9°41S 33°19E 269 D3
Fort Hope Canada 51°30N 88°0W 298 B2
Fort Irwin U.S.A. 35°16N 116°41W 307 K10
Fort Jameson = Chipata Zambia 13°38S 32°28E 269 E3
Fort Jeudy, Pt. of Grenada 11°59N 61°42W 323 q
Fort Johnston = Mangoche Malawi 14°25S 35°16E 269 E4
Fort Kent U.S.A. 47°15N 68°36W 309 B19
Fort Klamath U.S.A. 42°42N 122°0W 304 D3
Fort Lamy = Ndjamena Chad 12°10N 14°59E 259 F2
Fort-Laperrine = Tamanrasset Algeria 22°50N 5°30E 261 D6
Fort Laramie U.S.A. 42°13N 104°31W 304 E11
Fort Lauderdale U.S.A. 26°7N 80°8W 317 J9
Fort Lee U.S.A. 40°50N 73°58W 132 A2
Fort Liard Canada 60°14N 123°30W 296 A4
Fort Liberté Haiti 19°42N 71°51W 321 C5
Fort Lupton U.S.A. 40°5N 104°49W 304 F11
Fort MacKay Canada 57°12N 111°41W 296 B6
Fort Macleod Canada 49°45N 113°30W 296 D6
Fort MacMahon = El Homeur Algeria 29°43N 1°45E 261 C5
Fort McMurray Canada 56°44N 111°7W 296 B6
Fort McPherson Canada 67°30N 134°55W 294 C6
Fort Madison U.S.A. 40°38N 91°27W 310 D5
Fort Manning = Mchinji Malawi 13°47S 32°58E 269 E3
Fort Mason Center San Francisco, U.S.A. 136 a1
Fort Matanzas ⌓ U.S.A. 29°43N 81°14W 316 F8
Fort Meade U.S.A. 27°45N 81°48W 317 H8
Fort Mitchell U.S.A. 32°20N 85°1W 316 C4
Fort Morgan U.S.A. 40°15N 103°48W 304 F12
Fort Myers U.S.A. 26°39N 81°52W 317 J8
Fort Myers Beach U.S.A. 26°26N 81°52W 317 J8
Fort Myers Villas U.S.A. 26°33N 81°52W 317 J8
Fort Napoléon Guadeloupe 15°52N 61°35W 322 e
Fort Nelson Canada 58°50N 122°44W 296 B4
Fort Nelson → Canada 59°32N 124°0W 296 B4
Fort Norman = Tulita Canada 64°57N 125°30W 294 C7
Fort Ogden U.S.A. 27°5N 81°57W 317 H8
Fort Payne U.S.A. 34°26N 85°43W 315 D12
Fort Peck U.S.A. 48°1N 106°27W 304 B10
Fort Peck Dam U.S.A. 48°0N 106°26W 304 C10
Fort Peck L. U.S.A. 48°0N 106°26W 304 C10
Fort Pierce U.S.A. 27°27N 80°20W 317 H9
Fort Pierre U.S.A. 44°21N 100°22W 308 C3
Fort Pierre Bordes = Ti-n-Zaouatene Algeria 19°55N 2°55E 261 E5
Fort Plain U.S.A. 42°56N 74°37W 313 D10
Fort Portal Uganda 0°40N 30°20E 268 B3
Fort Providence Canada 61°3N 117°40W 296 A5
Fort Pulaski ⌓ U.S.A. 32°2N 80°56W 316 C9
Fort Qu'Appelle Canada 50°45N 103°50W 297 C8
Fort Recovery U.S.A. 40°25N 84°47W 311 D12
Fort Resolution Canada 61°10N 113°40W 296 A6
Fort Rixon Zimbabwe 20°2S 29°17E 269 G2
Fort Rosebery = Mansa Zambia 11°13S 28°55E 269 E2
Fort Ross U.S.A. 38°32N 123°13W 306 G3
Fort-Rousset = Owando Congo 0°29S 15°55E 264 C3
Fort Rupert = Waskaganish Canada 51°30N 78°40W 298 B4
Fort St. James Canada 54°30N 124°10W 296 C4
Fort St. John Canada 56°15N 120°50W 296 B4
Fort Sandeman = Zhob Pakistan 31°20N 69°31E 242 D3
Fort Saskatchewan Canada 53°40N 113°15W 296 C6
Fort Scott U.S.A. 37°50N 94°42W 308 G6
Fort Severn Canada 56°0N 87°40W 298 A2
Fort Shevchenko Kazakhstan 44°35N 50°23E 191 H10
Fort Simpson Canada 61°45N 121°15W 296 A4
Fort Smith Alta., Canada 60°0N 111°51W 296 B6
Fort Smith Ark., U.S.A. 35°23N 94°25W 314 D7
Fort Stockton U.S.A. 30°53N 102°53W 314 F3
Fort Sumner U.S.A. 34°28N 104°15W 305 J11
Fort Thomas U.S.A. 39°4N 84°26W 311 E12
Fort Thompson U.S.A. 44°3N 99°26W 308 C4
Fort Trinquet = Bir Mogreïn Mauritania 25°10N 11°25W 260 C2
Fort Union ⌓ U.S.A. 35°54N 105°1W 305 J11
Fort Uritskogo = Fort Shevchenko Kazakhstan 44°35N 50°23E 191 H10
Fort Valley U.S.A. 32°33N 83°53W 316 C6
Fort Vermilion Canada 58°24N 116°0W 296 B5
Fort Walton Beach U.S.A. 30°25N 86°36W 317 E3
Fort Wayne U.S.A. 41°4N 85°9W 311 C11
Fort White U.S.A. 29°55N 82°43W 316 F7
Fort William U.K. 56°49N 5°7W 167 E3
Fort Worth U.S.A. 32°43N 97°19W 314 E6
Fort Yates U.S.A. 46°5N 100°38W 308 B3
Fort Yukon U.S.A. 66°34N 145°16W 303 C11
Fortaleza = Pedra Azul Brazil 16°2S 41°17W 333 E3
Fortaleza Bolivia 12°6S 66°49W 330 C4
Fortaleza Brazil 3°45S 38°35W 332 B4
Forteau Canada 51°28N 56°58W 299 B8
Fortescue → Australia 21°0S 116°4E 278 D2
Forth → U.K. 56°9N 3°50W 167 E5
Forth, Firth of U.K. 56°5N 2°55W 121 A3
Forth Rail Bridge U.K. 56°0N 3°23W 121 A1
Forth Road Bridge U.K. 56°0N 3°24W 121 A1
Forthassa Rharbia Algeria 32°52N 1°18W 261 B4
Fortín Garrapatal Paraguay 21°27S 61°30W 331 E5
Fortín General Pando Paraguay 19°45S 59°47W 331 D6
Fortín Ingavi Paraguay 19°55S 60°47W 331 D5
Fortín Madrejón Paraguay 20°45S 59°52W 331 E6
Fortín Uno Argentina 38°50S 65°18W 336 A3
Fortore → Italy 41°55N 15°17E 199 G12
Fortrose N.Z. 46°38S 168°45E 285 G3
Fortrose Highl., U.K. 57°35N 4°9W 167 D4
Fortuna Spain 38°11N 1°7W 197 G3
Fortuna Calif., U.S.A. 40°36N 124°9W 304 F1
Fortuna N. Dak., U.S.A. 48°55N 103°47W 308 A2
Fortuna Ledge = Marshall U.S.A. 61°53N 162°5W 303 F7
Fortune Canada 47°4N 55°50W 299 C8
Fortune B. Canada 47°30N 55°22W 299 C8
Forūr Iran 26°17N 54°32E 247 E7
Fos-sur-Mer France 43°26N 4°56E 175 E8
Fosen Norway 63°50N 10°20E 160 E14
Foshan China 23°4N 113°5E 229 F9
Fosnavåg Norway 62°22N 5°38E 164 B2
Foso Ghana 5°43N 1°15W 263 D4
Foss Iceland 63°51N 17°52W 155 D9
Fossano Italy 44°33N 7°43E 198 D4
Fossil U.S.A. 45°0N 120°9W 304 D3
Fossil Butte ⌓ U.S.A. 41°50N 110°27W 304 F8
Fossombrone Italy 43°41N 12°48E 199 E9
Fossvellir Iceland 65°27N 14°37W 155 B12
Foster Vic., Australia 38°40S 146°15E 283 E7
Foster Qué., Canada 45°17N 72°30W 313 A12
Foster Ky., U.S.A. 38°48N 84°13W 311 F12
Foster → Canada 55°47N 105°49W 297 B7
Foster Village U.S.A. 21°21N 157°55W 302 K14
Fosters Ra. Australia 21°35S 133°48E 280 C1
Fostoria U.S.A. 41°10N 83°25W 311 C13
Fót Hungary 47°35N 19°11E 117 A3
Fotadrevo Madag. 24°3S 45°1E 272 C2
Fouesnant France 47°53N 4°1W 172 E2
Fougamou Gabon 1°16S 10°30E 264 C2
Fougères France 48°21N 1°14W 172 D5
Foul Pt. Sri Lanka 8°35N 81°18E 245 K5
Foula U.K. 60°10N 2°5W 167 A6
Foulalaba Mali 10°40N 7°20W 262 C3
Foulness I. U.K. 51°36N 0°55E 169 F8
Foulpointe Madag. 17°41S 49°31E 272 B2
Foulwind, C. N.Z. 41°45S 171°28E 285 B6
Foum Assaka Morocco 29°8N 10°24W 260 C2
Foum Zguid Morocco 30°2N 6°59W 260 B3
Foumban Cameroon 5°45N 10°50E 263 D7
Foumbot Cameroon 5°31N 10°38E 263 D7
Foumbouni Comoros Is. 11°51S 43°29E 272 a
Foumirate Algeria 27°30N 3°12W 260 C4
Foundiougne Senegal 14°5N 16°32W 262 C1
Fountain Colo., U.S.A. 38°41N 104°42W 304 G11
Fountain Fla., U.S.A. 30°29N 85°25W 316 E4
Fountain Hills U.S.A. 33°37N 111°43W 305 K8
Fountain Springs U.S.A. 35°54N 118°51W 307 K8
Four Mountains, Is. of U.S.A. 53°0N 170°0W 303 K5
Four Roads Trin. & Tob. 10°41N 61°33W 323 t
Fourchambault France 47°2N 3°3E 173 E10
Fourche, Île St.-Martin 17°58N 62°54W 322 a
Fouriesburg S. Africa 28°38S 28°14E 270 C4
Fourmies France 50°1N 4°2E 173 B11
Fournás Greece 39°3N 21°52E 204 B3
Fournaise, Piton de la Réunion 21°14S 55°43E 272 f
Fourni Greece 37°36N 26°32E 205 D8
Fourqueux France 48°53N 2°3E 134 A1
Fours France 46°50N 3°42E 173 F10
Fous, Pte. de Dominica 15°12N 61°20W 323 k
Fousinshin = Fuxin China 42°5N 121°48E 227 C11
Fouta Djallon Guinea 11°20N 12°10W 262 C2
Foux, Cap-à- Haiti 19°43N 73°27W 321 C5
Foveaux Str. N.Z. 46°42S 168°10E 285 G3
Fowey U.K. 50°20N 4°39W 169 G3
Fowler Calif., U.S.A. 36°38N 119°41W 306 J7
Fowler Colo., U.S.A. 38°8N 104°2W 304 G11
Fowler Ind., U.S.A. 40°37N 87°19W 311 D9
Fowler Mich., U.S.A. 43°0N 84°45W 311 B12
Fowler, Pt. Australia 32°2S 132°3E 279 F5
Fowlers B. Australia 31°59S 132°34E 279 F5
Fowlerville U.S.A. 42°40N 84°4W 311 B12
Fowman Iran 37°13N 49°19E 213 D13
Fox → Canada 56°3N 93°18W 297 B10
Fox Creek Canada 54°24N 116°48W 296 C5
Fox Is. U.S.A. 53°0N 168°0W 303 K6
Fox Lake Alta., Canada 58°28N 114°31W 296 B6
Fox Lake Ill., U.S.A. 42°24N 88°11W 311 B8
Fox Valley Canada 50°30N 109°25W 297 C7
Foxboro U.S.A. 42°4N 71°16W 313 D13
Foxdale Australia 20°22S 148°35E 280 J6
Foxe Basin Canada 66°0N 77°0W 295 C12
Foxe Chan. Canada 65°0N 80°0W 295 C12
Foxe Pen. Canada 65°0N 76°0W 295 C12
Foxen Sweden 59°25N 11°55E 162 E5
Foxford Ireland 53°59N 9°7W 166 C2
Foxrock Ireland 53°17N 6°11W 120 B2
Foxton N.Z. 40°29S 175°18E 284 G4
Foyle, Lough U.K. 55°7N 7°4W 166 A4
Foynes Ireland 52°37N 9°7W 166 D2
Foz Spain 43°33N 7°20W 194 B3
Foz do Copeá Brazil 3°52S 63°19W 329 D5
Foz do Cunene Angola 17°15S 11°48E 265 F2
Foz do Gregório Brazil 6°47S 70°44W 330 B3
Foz do Iguaçu Brazil 25°30S 54°30W 335 B5
Foz do Mamoriá Brazil 2°27S 66°32W 328 D4
Foz do Riosinho Brazil 7°11S 71°50W 330 B3
Frackville U.S.A. 40°47N 76°14W 313 F8
Fraga Spain 41°32N 0°21E 196 D5
Fraile Muerto Uruguay 32°31S 54°32W 335 C5
Framingham U.S.A. 42°18N 71°24W 313 D13
Framnes Iceland 66°1N 20°26W 155 A6
Frampol Poland 50°41N 22°40E 185 H9
Franca Brazil 20°33S 47°30W 333 F2
Francavilla al Mare Italy 42°25N 14°17E 199 F11
Francavilla Fontana Italy 40°32N 17°35E 201 B10
France ■ Europe 47°0N 3°0E 171 C5
Frances Australia 36°41S 140°55E 282 D4
Frances → Canada 60°16N 129°10W 296 A3
Frances L. Canada 61°23N 129°30W 296 A3
Francesville U.S.A. 40°59N 86°53W 311 D10
Franceville Gabon 1°40S 13°32E 264 C2
Franche-Comté □ France 46°50N 5°55E 173 F12
Francis Case, L. U.S.A. 43°4N 98°34W 308 D4
Francisco Beltrão Brazil 26°5S 53°4W 335 B5
Francisco de Orellana Ecuador 0°28S 76°58W 328 D2
Francisco Ignacio Madero Coahuila, Mexico 25°48N 103°18W 318 B4
Francisco Ignacio Madero Durango, Mexico 24°26N 104°18W 318 C4
Francisco Ignacio Madero, Presa Mexico 28°10N 105°37W 318 B3
Francisco Sá Brazil 16°28S 43°30W 333 E3
Francistown Botswana 21°7S 27°33E 271 B4
Francofonte Italy 37°14N 14°53E 201 E7
François Canada 47°35N 56°45W 299 C8
François, B. du Martinique 14°38N 60°54W 322 j
François-Joseph, Chutes Dem. Rep. of the Congo 7°37S 17°17E 265 D3
François L. Canada 54°0N 125°30W 296 C3
Francois Peron △ Australia 25°42S 113°33E 279 E1
Franconia U.S.A. 38°47N 77°7W 143 C3
Francs Pk. U.S.A. 43°58N 109°20W 304 E9
Franeker Neths. 53°12N 5°33E 170 A5
Frank Hann △ Australia 32°52S 120°19E 279 F3
Frank Lloyd Wright Home U.S.A. 41°53N 87°47W 119 B2
Frankado Djibouti 12°30N 43°12E 257 E5
Frankel Singapore 1°18N 103°55E 138 B3
Frankenberg Germany 51°3N 8°48E 178 D4
Frankenhöhe ⌓ Germany 49°20N 10°25E 179 F6
Frankenstein = Ząbkowice Śląskie Poland 50°35N 16°50E 185 H3
Frankenwald Germany 50°20N 11°30E 179 E7
Frankenwald ⌓ Germany 50°15N 11°30E 179 E7
Frankfield Jamaica 18°8N 77°22W 320 a
Frankford Ont., Canada 44°12N 77°36W 312 B7
Frankford U.S.A. 39°29N 91°19W 310 E5
Frankfort Free State, S. Africa 27°17S 28°30E 271 C4
Frankfort Ind., U.S.A. 40°17N 86°31W 311 D10
Frankfort Kans., U.S.A. 39°42N 96°25W 308 F5
Frankfort Ky., U.S.A. 38°12N 84°52W 311 F12
Frankfort N.Y., U.S.A. 43°2N 75°4W 313 C9
Frankfort Ohio, U.S.A. 39°24N 83°11W 311 E13
Frankfurt Brandenburg, Germany 52°20N 14°32E 178 C10
Frankfurt Hessen, Germany 50°7N 8°41E 179 E4
Frankfurt ✈ (FRA) Germany 50°1N 8°34E 179 E4
Fränkische Alb Germany 49°10N 11°23E 179 F7
Fränkische Rezat → Germany 49°11N 11°1E 179 F7
Fränkische Saale → Germany 50°3N 9°42E 179 E5
Fränkische Schweiz Germany 49°50N 11°16E 179 F7
Fränkische Schweiz-Veldensteiner Forst ⌓ Germany 49°45N 11°22E 179 F7
Frankland → Australia 35°0S 116°48E 279 G2
Franklin Ga., U.S.A. 33°17N 85°6W 316 B4
Franklin Ind., U.S.A. 39°29N 86°3W 311 E10
Franklin Ky., U.S.A. 36°43N 86°35W 308 G10
Franklin La., U.S.A. 29°48N 91°30W 314 G9
Franklin Mass., U.S.A. 42°5N 71°24W 313 D13
Franklin N.H., U.S.A. 43°27N 71°39W 313 C13
Franklin Nebr., U.S.A. 40°6N 98°57W 308 E4
Franklin Ohio, U.S.A. 39°34N 84°18W 311 E12
Franklin Pa., U.S.A. 41°24N 79°50W 312 E5
Franklin Va., U.S.A. 36°41N 76°56W 309 G15
Franklin W. Va., U.S.A. 38°39N 79°20W 309 F14
Franklin B. Canada 69°45N 126°0W 294 C7
Franklin D. Roosevelt L. U.S.A. 48°18N 118°9W 304 B4
Franklin-Gordon Wild Rivers △ Australia 42°19S 145°51E 281 G4
Franklin Harb. Australia 33°43S 136°55E 282 B2
Franklin I. Antarctica 76°10S 168°30E 151 D11
Franklin L. U.S.A. 40°25N 115°22W 304 F6
Franklin Mts. N.W.T., Canada 65°0N 125°0W 294 C7
Franklin Mts. N.Z. 44°55S 167°45E 285 E2
Franklin Park Ill., U.S.A. 41°55N 87°52W 119 B1
Franklin Park Mass., U.S.A. 42°18N 71°5W 116 B2
Franklin Park Va., U.S.A. 38°55N 77°9W 143 B3
Franklin Res. U.S.A. 34°5N 118°24W 126 B2
Franklin Str. Canada 72°0N 96°0W 294 B10
Franklinton U.S.A. 30°51N 90°9W 315 F9
Franklinville U.S.A. 42°20N 78°27W 312 D6
Franklyn Mt. N.Z. 42°4S 172°42E 285 C7
Frankston Australia 38°8S 145°8E 283 E6
Fränö Sweden 62°55N 17°50E 162 B11
Fransfontein Namibia 20°12S 15°1E 270 B2
Fränsta Sweden 62°30N 16°11E 162 B10
Frantsa Iosifa, Zemlya Russia 82°0N 55°0E 214 A6
Franz Canada 48°25N 84°30W 298 C3
Franz Josef Land = Frantsa Iosifa, Zemlya Russia 82°0N 55°0E 214 A6
Franz Josef Strauss ✈ (MUC) Germany 48°21N 11°47E 131 A2
Franzburg Germany 54°11N 12°51E 178 A8
Frascati Italy 41°48N 12°41E 199 G9
Fraser U.S.A. 42°32N 82°57W 312 D2
Fraser → B.C., Canada 49°7N 123°11W 306 A3
Fraser → Nfld. & L., Canada 56°39N 62°10W 299 A7
Fraser, Mt. Australia 25°35S 118°20E 279 E2
Fraser I. Australia 25°15S 153°10E 281 D5
Fraser Lake Canada 54°0N 124°50W 296 C4
Fraserburg S. Africa 31°55S 21°30E 270 D3
Fraserburg Road = Leeu Gamka S. Africa 32°47S 21°59E 270 D3
Fraserburgh U.K. 57°42N 2°1W 167 D6
Fraserdale Canada 49°55N 81°37W 298 C3
Fraserpet = Kushalnagar India 12°14N 75°57E 245 H2
Frasertown N.Z. 38°58S 177°28E 284 E6
Fraserville = Rivière-du-Loup Canada 47°50N 69°30W 299 C6
Frashër Albania 40°23N 20°26E 202 F4
Frasne France 46°50N 6°10E 173 F13
Frătești Romania 43°58N 25°58E 183 G10
Frauenfeld Switz. 47°34N 8°54E 179 H4
Frauenkirche Munich, Germany 131 b2
Frauenstadt = Wadowice Poland 49°52N 19°30E 185 J6
Fraustadt = Wschowa Poland 51°48N 16°20E 185 G3
Fray Bentos Uruguay 33°10S 58°15W 334 C4
Fray Jorge △ Chile 30°42S 71°40W 334 C1
Frechilla Spain 42°8N 4°50W 194 C6
Fredericia Denmark 55°34N 9°45E 163 J3
Frederick Md., U.S.A. 39°25N 77°25W 309 F15
Frederick Okla., U.S.A. 34°23N 99°1W 314 D5
Frederick S. Dak., U.S.A. 45°50N 98°31W 308 C4
Frederick E. Hyde Fjord Greenland 83°25N 29°0W 154 A8
Fredericksburg Pa., U.S.A. 40°27N 76°26W 313 F8
Fredericksburg Tex., U.S.A. 30°16N 98°52W 314 F5
Fredericksburg Va., U.S.A. 38°18N 77°28W 309 F15
Fredericktown Mo., U.S.A. 37°34N 90°18W 310 G7
Fredericktown Ohio, U.S.A. 40°29N 82°33W 312 F2
Frederico Westphalen Brazil 27°22S 53°24W 335 B5
Fredericton Canada 45°57N 66°40W 299 C6
Fredericton Junction Canada 45°41N 66°40W 299 C6
Frederiksberg Denmark 55°40N 12°33E 118 A3
Frederiksdal Denmark 55°46N 12°25E 118 A2
Frederikshåb = Paamiut Greenland 62°0N 49°43W 154 E6
Frederikshald = Halden Norway 59°9N 11°23E 164 E8
Frederikshamn = Hamina Finland 60°34N 27°12E 188 B4
Frederikshavn Denmark 57°28N 10°31E 163 G4
Frederikssund Denmark 55°50N 12°3E 163 J6
Frederiksted U.S. Virgin Is. 17°43N 64°53W 321 C7
Frederiksværk Denmark 55°58N 12°4E 163 J6
Fredersdorf Germany 52°31N 13°45E 115 A5
Fredonia Ariz., U.S.A. 36°57N 112°32W 305 H7
Fredonia Kans., U.S.A. 37°32N 95°49W 308 G6
Fredonia N.Y., U.S.A. 42°26N 79°20W 312 D5
Fredrica, L. U.S.A. 28°30N 81°18W 133 A3
Fredriksberg Sweden 60°8N 14°23E 162 D8
Fredrikstad Norway 59°13N 10°57E 164 F7
Fredriksvern = Stavern Norway 59°0N 10°1E 164 F7
Free State □ S. Africa 28°30S 27°0E 270 C4
Freeburg U.S.A. 38°19N 91°56W 310 F5
Freehold U.S.A. 40°16N 74°17W 313 F10
Freeland U.S.A. 41°1N 75°54W 313 E9
Freels, C. Canada 49°15N 53°30W 299 C9
Freeman Calif., U.S.A. 35°35N 117°53W 307 K9
Freeman Mo., U.S.A. 38°37N 94°30W 310 F2
Freeman S. Dak., U.S.A. 43°21N 97°26W 308 D5
Freeport Bahamas 26°30N 78°47W 320 A4
Freeport Trin. & Tob. 10°27N 61°25W 323 t
Freeport Fla., U.S.A. 30°30N 86°8W 316 E3
Freeport Ill., U.S.A. 42°17N 89°36W 310 B7
Freeport N.Y., U.S.A. 40°39N 73°35W 313 F11
Freeport Ohio, U.S.A. 40°12N 81°15W 312 F3
Freeport Pa., U.S.A. 40°41N 79°41W 312 F5
Freeport Tex., U.S.A. 28°57N 95°21W 314 G7
Freetown Antigua & B. 17°3N 61°42W 322 b
Freetown S. Leone 8°30N 13°17W 262 D2
Frégate, L. de la Canada 53°15N 74°45W 298 B5
Fregate Island Nature Reserve St. Lucia 13°52N 60°53W 323 m
Fregenal de la Sierra Spain 38°10N 6°39W 195 G4
Fregene Italy 41°51N 12°12E 199 G9
Freguesia Brazil 22°48S 43°10W 135 A1
Fréhel, C. France 48°40N 2°20W 172 D4
Freiberg Germany 50°55N 13°20E 178 E9
Freibourg = Fribourg Switz. 46°49N 7°9E 179 J3
Freiburg Baden-W., Germany 47°59N 7°51E 179 H3
Freiburg Niedersachsen, Germany 53°49N 9°16E 178 B5
Freiburg in Schlesien = Świebodzice Poland 50°51N 16°20E 185 H3
Freidrichshain, Volkspark Germany 52°31N 13°25E 115 A3
Freienwalde = Chociwel Poland 53°29N 15°21E 184 E2
Freiham Germany 48°8N 11°25E 131 B1
Freilassing Germany 47°50N 12°58E 179 H8
Freimann Germany 48°11N 11°37E 131 A2
Freire Chile 38°54S 72°38W 336 A2
Freirina Chile 28°30S 71°10W 334 B1
Freising Germany 48°24N 11°45E 179 G7
Freistadt Austria 48°30N 14°30E 180 C7
Freital Germany 51°1N 13°39E 178 D9
Freiwaldau = Jeseník Czech Rep. 50°14N 17°8E 181 A10
Fréjus France 43°25N 6°44E 175 E10
Fremantle Australia 32°7S 115°47E 279 F2
Fremont Calif., U.S.A. 37°32N 121°57W 306 H4
Fremont Ind., U.S.A. 41°44N 84°56W 311 C12
Fremont Iowa, U.S.A. 41°13N 92°26W 310 C4
Fremont Mich., U.S.A. 43°28N 85°57W 309 D11
Fremont Nebr., U.S.A. 41°26N 96°30W 308 E5
Fremont Ohio, U.S.A. 41°21N 83°7W 311 C13
Fremont → U.S.A. 38°24N 110°42W 304 G8
Fremont Camp U.S.A. 37°53N 121°16W 306 H5
French Cays = Plana Cays Bahamas 22°38N 73°30W 321 B5
French Creek → U.S.A. 41°24N 79°50W 312 E5
French Frigate Shoals U.S.A. 23°45N 166°10W 302 G10
French Guiana ⊠ S. Amer. 4°0N 53°0W 329 C7
French Guinea = Guinea ■ W. Afr. 10°20N 11°30W 262 C2
French I. Australia 38°20S 145°22E 283 E6
French Island △ Australia 38°20S 145°22E 283 E6
French Lick U.S.A. 38°33N 86°37W 311 F10
French Market New Orleans, U.S.A. 131 a3
French Pass N.Z. 40°55S 173°55E 285 A8
French Polynesia ⊠ Pac. Oc. 20°0S 145°0W 289 f
French Quarter New Orleans, U.S.A. 131 a2
French Sudan = Mali ■ Africa 17°0N 3°0W 262 B4
French Territory of the Afars and Issas = Djibouti ■ Africa 12°0N 43°0E 257 E5
French Togoland = Togo ■ W. Afr. 8°30N 1°35E 263 D5
Frenchburg U.S.A. 37°57N 83°38W 311 G13
Frenchman → N. Amer. 48°31N 107°10W 304 B10
Frenchman Cr. → U.S.A. 40°14N 100°50W 308 E3
Frenda Algeria 35°2N 1°1E 261 A5
Frenštát pod Radhoštěm Czech Rep. 49°33N 18°13E 181 B11
Fresco Ivory C. 5°3N 5°31W 262 D3
Fresco → Brazil 7°15S 51°30W 331 B7
Fresh Pond U.S.A. 42°22N 71°8W 116 A2
Freshfield, C. Antarctica 68°25S 151°10E 151 C10
Fresnay-sur-Sarthe France 48°17N 0°1E 172 D7
Fresnes France 48°45N 2°18E 134 B2
Fresnillo Mexico 23°10N 102°53W 318 C4
Fresno U.S.A. 36°44N 119°47W 306 J7
Fresno Alhandiga Spain 40°42N 5°37W 194 E5
Fresno Res. U.S.A. 48°36N 109°57W 304 B9
Fresvik Norway 61°4N 6°55E 164 C3
Freudenau Austria 48°11N 16°25E 142 A2
Freudenstadt Germany 48°27N 8°24E 179 G4
Freudenthal = Bruntál Czech Rep. 49°59N 17°27E 181 B10
Frévent France 50°15N 2°17E 173 B9
Frew → Australia 20°0S 135°38E 280 C2
Frewsburg U.S.A. 42°3N 79°10W 312 D5
Freycinet △ Australia 42°11S 148°19E 281 G4
Freycinet Pen. Australia 42°10S 148°25E 281 G4
Freyming-Merlebach France 49°8N 6°48E 173 C13
Freystadt = Kisielice Poland 53°36N 19°16E 184 E6
Freystadt = Kożuchów Poland 51°45N 15°31E 185 G2
Freyung Germany 48°48N 13°31E 179 G9
Fria Guinea 10°27N 13°38W 262 C2
Fria, C. Namibia 18°0S 12°0E 270 A1
Friant U.S.A. 36°59N 119°43W 306 J7
Friar's B. St. Kitts & Nevis 17°16N 62°40W 322 d
Friarstown Ireland 53°15N 6°21W 120 B1
Frías Argentina 28°40S 65°5W 334 B2
Fribourg Switz. 46°49N 7°9E 179 J3
Fribourg □ Switz. 46°40N 7°0E 179 J3
Frick Collection New York, U.S.A. 132 b3
Fridafors Sweden 56°25N 14°39E 163 H8
Friday Harbor U.S.A. 48°32N 123°1W 306 B3
Friedberg Bayern, Germany 48°21N 10°59E 179 G6
Friedberg Hessen, Germany 50°19N 8°45E 179 E4
Friedeberg = Mirsk Poland 50°58N 15°23E 185 H2
Friedeberg in Neumark = Strzelce Krajeńskie Poland 52°52N 15°33E 185 F2
Friedenau Germany 52°28N 13°22E 115 B3
Friedens U.S.A. 40°3N 78°59W 312 F6
Friedland = Mieroszów Poland 50°40N 16°11E 185 H3
Friedland = Pravdinsk Russia 56°29N 43°28E 190 B6
Friedland Germany 53°40N 13°33E 178 B9
Friedrichsfelde Germany 52°29N 13°33E 115 B4
Friedrichshafen Germany 47°39N 9°30E 179 H5
Friedrichshagen Germany 52°27N 13°37E 115 B4
Friedrichshain Germany 52°31N 13°25E 115 A3
Friedrichskoog Germany 54°1N 8°53E 178 A4
Friedrichslust Germany 52°31N 13°31E 115 A5
Friedrichstadt Germany 54°23N 9°6E 178 A5
Friendly Is. = Tonga ■ Pac. Oc. 19°50S 174°30W 287 P13
Friendship U.S.A. 42°12N 78°8W 312 D6
Friesach Austria 46°57N 14°24E 180 E7
Friesack Germany 52°44N 12°34E 178 C8
Friesland □ Neths. 53°5N 5°50E 170 A5
Friesoythe Germany 53°1N 7°51E 178 B3
Frigate Seychelles 4°35S 55°56E 272 c
Frigate Bay St. Kitts & Nevis 17°16N 62°41W 322 d
Frigate I. Grenada 12°25N 61°29W 323 q
Friggesund Sweden 61°54N 16°33E 162 C10
Friherrs Finland 60°16N 24°49E 121 B1
Frillesås Sweden 57°20N 12°12E 163 G6
Frilufts Museum Finland 60°11N 24°52E 121 B2
Frinnaryd Sweden 57°55N 14°50E 163 G8
Frio → U.S.A. 28°26N 98°11W 314 G5
Frio, C. Brazil 22°50S 41°50W 326 F6
Friol Spain 43°2N 7°47W 194 B3
Friona U.S.A. 34°38N 102°43W 314 D3
Frisches Haff = Zalew Wiślany Poland 54°20N 19°50E 184 D6
Fristad Sweden 57°50N 13°0E 163 G6
Fritch U.S.A. 35°38N 101°36W 314 D4
Fritsla Sweden 57°33N 12°47E 163 G6
Fritzlar Germany 51°7N 9°16E 178 D5
Friuli-Venézia Giulia □ Italy 46°0N 13°0E 199 B9
Frobisher B. Canada 62°30N 66°0W 295 C13
Frobisher Bay = Iqaluit Canada 63°44N 68°31W 295 C13
Frobisher L. Canada 56°20N 108°15W 297 B7
Frohavet Norway 64°0N 9°30E 160 E13
Frohenbruck = Veselí nad Lužnicí Czech Rep. 49°12N 14°43E 180 B7
Frohnleiten Austria 47°16N 15°19E 180 D8
Frolovo Russia 49°45N 43°40E 190 F6
Frombork Poland 54°21N 19°41E 184 D6
Frome U.K. 51°14N 2°19W 169 F5
Frome → U.K. 50°41N 2°6W 169 G5
Frome, L. Australia 30°45S 139°45E 282 A3
Frome Downs Australia 31°13S 139°45E 282 A3
Frómista Spain 42°16N 4°25W 194 C6
Front Range U.S.A. 40°25N 105°45W 300 C5
Front Royal U.S.A. 38°55N 78°12W 309 F14
Fronteira Portugal 39°3N 7°39W 195 F3
Fronteiras Brazil 7°5S 40°37W 332 C3
Frontera Canary Is. 27°47N 17°59W 153 e1
Frontera Tabasco, Mexico 18°32N 92°38W 319 D6
Fronteras Mexico 30°56N 109°31W 318 A3
Frontignan France 43°27N 3°45E 174 E7
Frontón, I. Peru 12°7S 77°11W 124 B1
Frosinone Italy 41°38N 13°19E 200 A6
Frostburg U.S.A. 39°39N 78°56W 309 F14
Frostisen Norway 68°14N 17°10E 160 B17
Frostproof U.S.A. 27°45N 81°32W 317 H8
Frouard France 48°47N 6°8E 173 D13
Frövi Sweden 59°28N 15°24E 162 E9
Frøya Norway 63°43N 8°40E 160 E13
Fruithurst U.S.A. 33°44N 85°26W 316 B4
Fruitland Park U.S.A. 28°51N 81°54W 317 G8
Frumoasa Romania 46°28N 25°48E 183 D10
Frunze = Bishkek Kyrgyzstan 42°54N 74°46E 214 E8
Frunze Russia 55°47N 37°33E 129 B3
Frunzivka Ukraine 47°20N 29°45E 183 C14
Fruška Gora Serbia 45°7N 19°30E 182 E4
Fruška Gora △ Serbia 45°8N 19°40E 202 A3
Frutal Brazil 20°0S 49°0W 333 F2
Frutigen Switz. 46°35N 7°38E 179 J3
Frýdek-Místek Czech Rep. 49°40N 18°20E 181 B11
Frýdlant Czech Rep. 50°56N 15°9E 180 A8
Fryeburg U.S.A. 44°1N 70°59W 313 B14
Fryvaldov = Jeseník Czech Rep. 50°14N 17°8E 181 A10
Fthiotida □ Greece 38°50N 22°25E 204 C4
Fu Jiang → China 30°0N 106°16E 228 C6
Fu Xian = Wafangdian China 39°38N 121°58E 227 E11
Fu Xian China 36°0N 109°20E 226 G5
Fua Mulaku Maldives 0°17S 73°26E 272 d
Fu'an China 27°11N 119°36E 229 D12
Fubian China 31°17N 102°22E 228 B4
Fucécchio Italy 43°44N 10°48E 198 E7
Fucheng China 37°50N 116°10E 226 F9
Fuchou = Fuzhou China 26°5N 119°16E 229 D12
Fuchū Hiroshima, Japan 34°34N 133°14E 222 C5
Fuchū Tōkyō, Japan 35°40N 139°29E 140 A1
Fuchuan China 24°50N 111°5E 229 E8
Fuchun Jiang → China 30°5N 120°5E 229 B13
Fúcino, Piana del Italy 42°1N 13°31E 199 F10
Fuding China 27°20N 120°12E 229 D13
Fuencaliente Canary Is. 28°28N 17°50W 153 e1
Fuencaliente Spain 38°25N 4°18W 195 G6
Fuencaliente, Pta. Canary Is. 28°27N 17°51W 153 e1
Fuencarral Spain 40°29N 3°42W 127 B1
Fuengirola Spain 36°32N 4°41W 195 J6
Fuenlabrada Spain 40°17N 3°48W 127 C1
Fuensalida Spain 40°3N 4°12W 194 E6
Fuente-Álamo Spain 38°44N 1°24W 197 G3
Fuente-Álamo de Murcia Spain 37°42N 1°6W 197 H3
Fuente de Cantos Spain 38°15N 6°18W 195 G4
Fuente del Maestre Spain 38°31N 6°28W 195 G4
Fuente el Fresno Spain 39°14N 3°46W 195 F7
Fuente Obejuna Spain 38°15N 5°25W 195 G5
Fuente Palmera Spain 37°42N 5°6W 195 H5
Fuentes de Andalucía Spain 37°28N 5°20W 195 H5
Fuentes de Ebro Spain 41°31N 0°38W 196 D4
Fuentes de León Spain 38°5N 6°32W 195 G4
Fuentes de Oñoro Spain 40°33N 6°52W 194 E4
Fuentesaúco Spain 41°15N 5°30W 194 D5
Fuerte → Mexico 25°54N 109°22W 318 B3
Fuerte Olimpo Paraguay 21°0S 57°51W 334 A4
Fuerteventura Canary Is. 28°30N 14°0W 153 e2
Fuerteventura ✈ (FUE) Canary Is. 28°24N 13°52W 153 e2
Fufeng China 34°22N 108°0E 226 G5
Fuga I. Phil. 18°52N 121°20E 232 B3
Fughmah Yemen 16°9N 49°26E 249 C5
Fugong China 27°5N 98°47E 228 D2
Fugou China 34°3N 114°25E 226 G8
Fugu China 39°2N 111°3E 226 E6
Fuhai China 47°2N 87°25E 217 C11
Fuḩaymī Iraq 34°16N 42°10E 213 E10
Fuhlsbüttel, Hamburg ✈ (HAM) Germany 53°35N 9°59E 178 B5
Fuhsien = Fu Xian China 36°0N 109°20E 226 G5
Fuhsing Changhua, Taiwan 24°3N 120°25E 225 B2
Fuhsing Kaohsung, Taiwan 23°13N 120°48E 225 C2
Fuhsing Taoyüan, Taiwan 24°49N 121°21E 225 B3
Fuji Japan 35°9N 138°39E 223 B10
Fuji-Hakone-Izu △ Japan 35°15N 138°45E 223 B10
Fuji-San Japan 35°22N 138°44E 223 B10
Fuji-Yoshida Japan 35°30N 138°46E 223 B10
Fujian □ China 26°0N 118°0E 229 E12
Fujieda Japan 34°52N 138°16E 223 C10
Fujinomiya Japan 35°10N 138°40E 223 B10
Fujioka Japan 36°15N 139°5E 223 A11
Fujisawa Japan 35°22N 139°29E 223 B11
Fujiyama, Mt. = Fuji-San Japan 35°22N 138°44E 223 B10
Fukagawa Hokkaidō, Japan 43°43N 142°2E 220 C11
Fukagawa Tōkyō, Japan 35°39N 139°48E 140 B3
Fukang China 44°10N 87°59E 217 D11
Fukaya Japan 36°12N 139°12E 223 A11
Fukiage Japan 31°27N 130°17E 222 F2
Fukiage Imperial Garden Tokyo, Japan 140 a4
Fukien = Fujian □ China 26°0N 118°0E 229 E12
Fukuchiyama Japan 35°19N 135°9E 223 B7
Fukue-Shima Japan 32°40N 128°45E 221 H4
Fukuei Chiao Taiwan 25°17N 121°32E 225 A3
Fukui Japan 36°5N 136°10E 223 A8
Fukui □ Japan 36°0N 136°12E 223 B8
Fukuma Japan 33°46N 130°28E 222 D2
Fukuoka Japan 33°39N 130°21E 222 D2
Fukuoka □ Japan 33°30N 131°0E 222 D3
Fukuoka Int. ✈ (FUK) Japan 33°34N 130°28E 222 D2
Fukuroi Japan 34°45N 137°55E 223 C9

372 Fukushima
INDEX

Fukushima Fukushima, Japan 37°44N 140°28E 220 F10
Fukushima Ōsaka, Japan 34°41N 135°28E 133 A1
Fukushima □ Japan 37°30N 140°15E 220 F10
Fukuyama Japan 34°35N 133°20E 222 C5
Fulacunda Guinea-Biss. 11°44N 15°3W 262 C1
Fulaga Fiji 19°8S 178°33W 287 B3
Fulda Germany 50°32N 9°40E 178 E5
Fulda → Germany 51°25N 9°39E 178 D5
Fulford = North Miami Beach U.S.A. 25°55N 80°9W 128 A2
Fulford Harbour Canada 48°47N 123°27W 306 B3
Fulham U.K. 51°28N 0°12W 125 B2
Fuli Taiwan 23°11N 121°14E 225 C3
Fuliang China 29°23N 117°14E 229 C11
Fullarton Trin. & Tob. 10°5N 61°54W 323 t
Fullerton Calif., U.S.A. 33°53N 117°56W 307 M9
Fullerton Nebr., U.S.A. 41°22N 97°58W 308 E5
Fulongquan China 44°20N 124°42E 227 B13
Fülöpszállás Hungary 46°49N 19°15E 182 D4
Fulton Ill., U.S.A. 41°52N 90°11W 310 C6
Fulton Ind., U.S.A. 40°57N 86°16W 311 D10
Fulton Mo., U.S.A. 38°52N 91°57W 310 F5
Fulton N.Y., U.S.A. 43°19N 76°25W 313 C8
Fuluälven → Sweden 61°18N 13°4E 162 C7
Fulufjället Sweden 61°32N 12°41E 162 C6
Fumay France 49°58N 4°40E 173 C11
Fumel France 44°30N 0°58E 174 D4
Fumin China 25°10N 102°20E 228 E4
Funabashi Japan 35°45N 140°0E 223 B12
Funabori Japan 35°41N 139°52E 140 A4
Funafuti = Fongafale Tuvalu 8°31S 179°13E 277 B14
Funafuti Pac. Oc. 8°31S 179°13E 277 B14
Funäsdalen Sweden 62°33N 12°32E 162 B6
Funchal Madeira 32°38N 16°54W 153 c
Funchal ✕ (FNC) Madeira 32°42N 16°45W 153 c
Fundación Colombia 10°31N 74°11W 328 A3
Fundão Brazil 19°55S 40°24W 333 E3
Fundão Portugal 40°8N 7°30W 194 E3
Fundão, I. do Brazil 22°51S 43°13W 135 B1
Fundu Moldovei Romania 47°32N 25°24E 183 C10
Fundulea Romania 44°28N 26°31E 183 F11
Fundy, B. of Canada 45°0N 66°0W 299 D6
Fundy △ Canada 45°35N 65°10W 299 C6
Fünfhaus Austria 48°11N 16°20E 142 A2
Fünfkirchen = Pécs Hungary 46°5N 18°15E 182 D3
Funhalouro Mozam. 23°3S 34°25E 271 B5
Funing Hebei, China 39°53N 119°12E 227 E10
Funing Jiangsu, China 33°45N 119°50E 227 H10
Funing Yunnan, China 23°35N 105°45E 228 F5
Funiu Shan China 33°30N 112°20E 226 H7
Funsi Ghana 10°21N 1°54W 262 C4
Funtua Nigeria 11°30N 7°18E 263 C6
Fuping Hebei, China 38°48N 114°12E 226 E8
Fuping Shaanxi, China 34°42N 109°10E 226 G5
Fuqing China 25°41N 119°21E 229 E12
Fuquan China 26°40N 107°27E 228 D6
Furano Japan 43°21N 142°23E 220 C11
Furāt, Nahr al → Asia 31°0N 47°25E 246 D5
Fureso Denmark 55°47N 12°25E 118 A2
Fürg Iran 28°18N 55°13E 247 D7
Furkating India 26°28N 93°59E 241 B4
Furman U.S.A. 32°41N 81°11W 316 C8
Furmanov Russia 57°10N 41°9E 190 B5
Furmanovo Kazakhstan 49°42N 49°25E 190 F9
Furnas Azores 37°46N 25°19W 153 d3
Furnás Spain 39°3N 1°32E 206 C2
Furnas, Reprêsa de Brazil 20°50S 45°30W 333 F2
Furneaux Group Australia 40°10S 147°50E 281 G4
Furqlus Syria 34°36N 37°8E 250 D8
Fürstenau Germany 52°31N 7°40E 178 C3
Fürstenberg = Eisenhüttenstadt Germany 52°9N 14°38E 178 C10
Fürstenberg Germany 53°10N 13°8E 178 B9
Fürstenfeld Austria 47°3N 16°3E 180 D9
Fürstenfeldbruck Germany 48°11N 11°15E 179 G7
Fürstenwalde Germany 52°22N 14°3E 178 C10
Fürth Mittelfranken, Germany 49°28N 10°59E 179 F6
Fürth Oberbayern, Germany 48°2N 11°35E 131 B2
Fürth im Wald Germany 49°18N 12°50E 179 F8
Furtwangen Germany 48°2N 8°12E 179 G4
Furudal Sweden 61°10N 15°11E 162 C9
Furukawa Gifu, Japan 36°14N 137°11E 223 A9
Furukawa Miyagi, Japan 38°34N 140°58E 220 E10
Furulund Sweden 55°46N 13°6E 163 J7
Fury and Hecla Str. Canada 69°56N 84°0W 295 C11
Fusagasuga Colombia 4°21N 74°22W 328 C3
Fuscaldo Italy 39°25N 16°2E 201 C9
Fushan Shandong, China 37°30N 121°15E 227 F11
Fushan Shanxi, China 35°58N 111°51E 226 G6
Fushë Arrëz Albania 42°4N 20°2E 202 D4
Fushë Krujë Albania 41°29N 19°43E 202 E3
Fushun Liaoning, China 41°50N 123°56E 224 B1
Fushun Sichuan, China 29°13N 104°52E 228 C5
Fusong China 42°20N 127°15E 224 A3
Füssen Germany 47°34N 10°42E 179 H6
Fusui China 22°40N 107°56E 228 F6
Futago-tamagawaen Japan 35°36N 139°39E 140 B2
Futago-Yama Japan 33°35N 131°36E 222 D3
Futian China 22°32N 114°4E 219 F11
Futiga Amer. Samoa 14°21S 170°45W 302 f
Futog Serbia 45°15N 19°42E 182 E4
Futrono Chile 40°8S 72°24W 336 B2
Futtsu Japan 35°13N 139°49E 223 B10
Fuwa Egypt 31°12N 30°33E 256 H7
Fuxian Hu China 24°30N 102°53E 228 E4
Fuxin China 42°5N 121°48E 227 C11
Fuxing Dao China 31°16N 121°33E 138 B2
Fuxing Park China 31°13N 121°27E 138 B1
Fuxinglu China 39°52N 116°16E 114 B1
Fuyang Anhui, China 33°0N 115°48E 226 H8
Fuyang Zhejiang, China 30°5N 119°57E 229 B12
Fuyang He → China 38°12N 117°0E 226 E9
Fuying Dao China 26°34N 120°9E 229 D13
Fuyong China 22°40N 113°49E 219 F10
Fuyu Heilongjiang, China 47°49N 124°27E 217 B7
Fuyu Jilin, China 45°12N 124°43E 227 B13
Fuyuan China 25°40N 104°16E 228 E5
Fuyun China 47°0N 89°28E 217 C11
Füzesgyarmat Hungary 47°6N 21°14E 182 C6
Fuzhou China 26°5N 119°16E 229 D12
Fylde U.K. 53°50N 2°58W 168 D5
Fyn Denmark 55°20N 10°30E 163 J4
Fyne, L. U.K. 55°59N 5°23W 167 F3
Fynshav Denmark 55°0N 9°59E 163 K3
Fyresdal Norway 59°11N 8°5E 164 E5
Fyresvatn Norway 59°6N 8°10E 164 E5
Fyzabad = Faizabad India 26°45N 82°10E 243 F10
Fyzabad Trin. & Tob. 10°11N 61°33W 323 t

G

G. Ross Lord Park Canada 43°47N 79°28W 141 A2
Ga Ghana 9°47N 2°30W 262 D4
Ga-eun S. Korea 36°38N 128°5E 224 D4
Gaa Faru Atoll Maldives 4°45N 73°26E 272 d
Gaanda Nigeria 10°10N 12°27E 263 C7
Gabarin Nigeria 11°8N 10°27E 263 C7
Gabas → France 43°46N 0°42W 174 E3
Gabela Angola 11°0S 14°24E 265 E2
Gaberones = Gaborone Botswana 24°45S 25°57E 270 B4
Gabès Tunisia 33°53N 10°2E 258 B2
Gabès □ Tunisia 33°35N 9°30E 261 B6
Gabès, G. de Tunisia 34°0N 10°30E 258 B2
Gabgaba, W. → Egypt 22°10N 33°5E 256 C3
Gabia Dem. Rep. of the Congo 4°37S 17°14E 265 C3
Gąbin Poland 52°23N 19°41E 185 F6
Gablonz = Jablonec nad Nisou Czech Rep. 50°43N 15°10E 180 A8
Gabon ■ Africa 0°10S 10°0E 264 C2
Gabon → Gabon 0°25N 9°20E 264 B1
Gaborone Botswana 24°45S 25°57E 270 B4
Gabrat Sai'd Sudan 16°6N 31°50E 266 A3
Gabriels U.S.A. 44°26N 74°12W 313 B10
Gābrīk Iran 25°44N 58°28E 247 E8
Gabro Ethiopia 6°18N 43°16E 267 C5
Gabrovo Bulgaria 42°52N 25°19E 203 D9
Gabú = Nova Lamego Guinea-Biss. 12°19N 14°11W 262 C2
Gacé France 48°49N 0°20E 172 D7
Gāch Sār Iran 36°7N 51°19E 247 B6
Gachsārān Iran 30°15N 50°45E 247 D6
Gacko Bos.-H. 43°10N 18°33E 202 C2
Gad Hinglaj India 16°14N 74°21E 245 F2
Gadag India 15°30N 75°45E 245 G2
Gadaisu Papua N. G. 10°22S 149°46E 286 F5
Gadamai Sudan 17°11N 36°10E 257 D4
Gadap Pakistan 25°5N 67°28E 242 G2
Gadarwara India 22°50N 78°50E 243 H8
Gadebusch Germany 53°42N 11°7E 178 B7
Gadein Sudan 8°10N 28°45E 257 F2
Gadhada India 22°0N 71°35E 242 J4
Gádor, Sierra de Spain 36°57N 2°45W 195 J8
Gadra Pakistan 25°40N 70°38E 242 G4
Gadsden Ala., U.S.A. 34°1N 86°1W 316 A3
Gadsden S.C., U.S.A. 33°51N 80°46W 316 B9
Gadwal India 16°10N 77°50E 245 F3
Gadyach = Hadyach Ukraine 50°21N 34°0E 189 G8
Gadzi C.A.R. 4°47N 16°42E 264 B3
Gaebong S. Korea 37°29N 126°52E 137 C1
Găeşti Romania 44°48N 25°19E 183 F10
Gaeta Italy 41°12N 13°35E 200 A6
Gaeta, G. di Italy 41°6N 13°30E 200 A6
Gaffney U.S.A. 35°5N 81°39W 315 D14
Gafsa Tunisia 34°24N 8°43E 258 B1
Gafsa □ Tunisia 34°30N 8°48E 261 B6
Gagarawa Nigeria 12°25N 9°32E 263 C6
Gagaria India 25°43N 70°46E 242 G4
Gagarin Russia 55°38N 35°0E 188 E8
Găgăuzia □ Moldova 46°10N 28°40E 183 D13
Gage Park U.S.A. 41°47N 87°42W 119 C2
Gaggenau Germany 48°48N 8°18E 179 G4
Gaghamni Sudan 11°41N 28°19E 257 E2
Gagil-Tomil, I. Pac. Oc. 9°31N 138°12E 287 R16
Gagino Russia 55°15N 45°1E 190 C7
Gagliano del Capo Italy 39°50N 18°22E 201 C11
Gagnef Sweden 60°36N 15°5E 162 D9
Gagnoa Ivory C. 6°56N 5°16W 262 D3
Gagnon Canada 51°50N 68°5W 299 B6
Gagnon, L. Canada 62°3N 110°27W 297 A6
Gagny France 48°53N 2°32E 134 A4
Gago Coutinho São Tomé & Príncipe 0°1S 6°32E 265 a
Gagra Georgia 43°20N 40°10E 191 J5
Gahini Rwanda 1°50S 30°30E 268 C3
Gahmar India 25°27N 83°49E 243 G10
Gai Xian = Gaizhou China 40°22N 122°20E 224 B1
Gaibanda Bangla. 25°20N 89°36E 241 C2
Gaidouronisi Greece 34°53N 25°41E 207 F6
Gail U.S.A. 32°46N 101°27W 314 E4
Gail → Austria 46°36N 13°53E 180 E6
Gaillac France 43°54N 1°54E 174 E5
Gaillimh = Galway Ireland 53°17N 9°3W 166 C2
Gaillon France 49°10N 1°20E 172 C8
Gaimán Argentina 43°10S 65°25W 336 B3
Gaines U.S.A. 41°46N 77°35W 312 E7
Gainesville Fla., U.S.A. 29°40N 82°20W 317 F7
Gainesville Ga., U.S.A. 34°18N 83°50W 315 D13
Gainesville Mo., U.S.A. 36°36N 92°26W 308 G7
Gainesville Tex., U.S.A. 33°38N 97°8W 314 E6
Gainsborough U.K. 53°24N 0°46W 168 D7
Gairdner, L. Australia 31°30S 136°0E 282 A2
Gairloch U.K. 57°43N 5°41W 167 D3
Gairloch, L. U.K. 57°43N 5°45W 167 D3
Gaizhou China 40°22N 122°20E 224 B1
Gaj Croatia 45°28N 17°3E 182 E2
Gaj → Pakistan 26°26N 67°21E 242 F2
Gajendragarh India 15°44N 75°59E 245 G2
Gakona U.S.A. 62°18N 145°18W 303 E11
Gakuch Pakistan 36°7N 73°45E 243 A5
Gal Laghet Somali Rep. 4°9N 47°10E 267 D6
Gal Oya △ Sri Lanka 7°0N 81°20E 245 L5
Gal Oya Res. Sri Lanka 7°5N 81°30E 245 L5
Gal Tardo Somali Rep. 3°34N 45°58E 267 D6
Galachipa Bangla. 22°8N 90°26E 241 D3
Galâla, Gebel el Egypt 29°21N 32°22E 256 J8
Galâla el Baharîya, G. el Egypt 29°22N 32°23E 251 J3
Galâla el Qiblîya, G. el Egypt 28°42N 32°22E 251 K3
Galán, Cerro Argentina 25°55S 66°52W 334 B2
Galana → Kenya 3°9S 40°8E 268 C5
Galangue Angola 13°42S 16°9E 265 E3
Galangue, Serra Angola 14°18S 15°52E 265 E3
Galanta Slovak Rep. 48°11N 17°45E 181 C10
Galapagar Spain 40°36N 3°58W 194 E7
Galápagos = Colón, Arch. de Ecuador 0°0 91°0W 330 a
Galapagos Fracture Zone Pac. Oc. 3°0N 110°0W 289 G17
Galapagos Rise Pac. Oc. 15°0S 95°0W 289 J18
Galashiels U.K. 55°37N 2°49W 167 F6
Galata Turkey 41°1N 28°58E 122 B1
Galata Tower Turkey 41°1N 28°59E 122 B1
Galatas Greece 37°30N 23°26E 204 D5
Galatea N.Z. 38°24S 176°45E 284 E5
Galaţi Romania 45°27N 28°2E 183 E13
Galaţi □ Romania 45°45N 27°30E 183 E12
Galatia Turkey 39°30N 33°0E 212 C5
Galatina Italy 40°10N 18°10E 201 B11
Galátone Italy 40°9N 18°4E 201 B11
Galatsi Greece 38°1N 23°45E 112 A2
Galax U.S.A. 36°40N 80°56W 309 G13
Galaxidi Greece 38°22N 22°23E 204 C4
Galcaio Somali Rep. 6°30N 47°30E 267 C6
Gáldar Canary Is. 28°9N 15°39W 153 e1
Galdhøpiggen Norway 61°38N 8°18E 164 C5
Galeana Chihuahua, Mexico 30°7N 107°38W 318 A3
Galeana Nuevo León, Mexico 24°50N 100°4W 318 A3
Galeão, Int. de ✕ (GIG) Brazil 22°49S 43°15W 135 A1
Galegu Sudan 12°36N 35°2E 257 E4
Galela Indonesia 1°50N 127°49E 231 D7
Galena Alaska, U.S.A. 64°44N 156°56W 303 D8
Galena Ill., U.S.A. 42°25N 90°26W 310 B6
Galeota Pt. Trin. & Tob. 10°8N 60°59W 323 t
Galera Spain 37°45N 2°33W 197 H2
Galera, Pta. Chile 39°59S 73°43W 336 A2
Galera, Pta. da Azores 37°42N 25°30W 153 d3
Galera Pt. Trin. & Tob. 10°49N 60°54W 323 t
Galesburg Ill., U.S.A. 40°57N 90°22W 310 D6
Galesburg Mich., U.S.A. 42°17N 85°26W 311 B11
Galestan △ Iran 37°30N 56°0E 247 B8
Galeton U.S.A. 41°44N 77°39W 312 E7
Galets → Réunion 20°56S 55°17E 272 f
Galga Ethiopia 6°39N 37°47E 257 F4
Galgasc Somali Rep. 0°11N 41°38E 267 D5
Galheirão → Brazil 12°23S 45°5W 333 D2
Galheiros Brazil 13°18S 46°25W 333 D2
Gali Georgia 42°37N 41°46E 191 J5
Galicea Mare Romania 44°4N 23°19E 183 F8
Galich Russia 58°22N 42°24E 190 A6
Galiche Bulgaria 43°34N 23°53E 202 C7
Galicia □ Spain 42°43N 7°45W 194 C3
Galičica △ Macedonia 41°2N 20°55E 202 E4
Galien U.S.A. 41°48N 86°30W 311 C10
Galilee = Hagalil Israel 32°53N 35°18E 250 F6
Galilee, L. Australia 22°20S 145°50E 280 C4
Galilee, Sea of = Yam Kinneret Israel 32°45N 35°35E 250 F6
Galim Cameroon 7°6N 12°25E 263 D7
Galina Pt. Jamaica 18°24N 76°58W 320 a
Galinoporni Cyprus 35°31N 34°18E 207 E10
Galion U.S.A. 40°44N 82°47W 312 F2
Galion, B. du Martinique 14°44N 60°56W 322 j
Galite, Îs. de la Tunisia 37°30N 8°59E 261 A6
Galiuro Mts. U.S.A. 32°30N 110°20W 305 K8
Galiwinku Australia 12°2S 135°34E 280 A2
Gallâbât Sudan 12°58N 36°11E 257 E4
Gallan Hd. U.K. 58°15N 7°2W 167 C1
Gallarate Italy 45°40N 8°48E 198 C5
Gallatin Mo., U.S.A. 39°55N 93°58W 310 E3
Gallatin Tenn., U.S.A. 36°24N 86°27W 315 C11
Galle Sri Lanka 6°5N 80°10E 245 L5
Gállego → Spain 41°39N 0°51W 196 D4
Gallegos → Argentina 51°35S 69°0W 336 D3
Gallery of Inuit Art = Dominion Centre Toronto, Canada 141 b2
Galletti → Ethiopia 8°46N 41°10E 257 F5
Galley Hd. Ireland 51°32N 8°55W 166 E3
Galliate Italy 45°29N 8°42E 198 C5
Gallinas, Pta. Colombia 12°28N 71°40W 328 A3
Gallipoli = Gelibolu Turkey 40°28N 26°43E 203 F10
Gallipoli Italy 40°3N 17°58E 201 B10
Gallipolis U.S.A. 38°49N 82°12W 309 F12
Gällivare Sweden 67°9N 20°40E 160 C19
Gallneukirchen Austria 48°21N 14°25E 180 C7
Gällö Sweden 62°55N 15°13E 162 B9
Gallo, C. Italy 38°13N 13°19E 200 D6
Gallocanta, L. de Spain 40°58N 1°30W 196 D3
Galloo I. U.S.A. 43°55N 76°25W 313 C8
Galloway U.K. 55°1N 4°29W 167 F4
Galloway, Mull of U.K. 54°39N 4°52W 167 G4
Galloway ⌂ U.K. 55°3N 4°20W 167 F4
Gallup U.S.A. 35°32N 108°45W 305 J9
Gallur Spain 41°52N 1°19W 196 D3
Galma Galla Kenya 1°11S 40°47E 267 E5
Galong Australia 34°37S 148°34E 283 C8
Galoya Sri Lanka 8°10N 80°55E 245 K5
Galt Calif., U.S.A. 38°15N 121°18W 306 G5
Galt Mo., U.S.A. 40°8N 93°23W 310 D3
Galten Denmark 56°9N 9°54E 163 H3
Galtür Austria 46°58N 10°11E 180 E3
Galty Mts. Ireland 52°22N 8°10W 166 D3
Galtymore Ireland 52°21N 8°11W 166 D3
Galva U.S.A. 41°10N 90°3W 310 C6
Galvarino Chile 38°24S 72°47W 336 A2
Galve de Sorbe Spain 41°13N 3°10W 196 D1
Galveston Ind., U.S.A. 40°35N 86°11W 311 D10
Galveston Tex., U.S.A. 29°18N 94°48W 314 G7
Galveston B. U.S.A. 29°36N 94°50W 314 G7
Gálvez Argentina 32°0S 61°14W 334 C3
Galway Ireland 53°17N 9°3W 166 C2
Galway □ Ireland 53°22N 9°1W 166 C2
Galway B. Ireland 53°13N 9°10W 166 C2
Galyanovo Russia 55°48N 37°47E 129 B4
Gam → Vietnam 21°55N 105°12E 236 B5
Gamagōri Japan 34°50N 137°14E 223 C9
Gamari, L. Ethiopia 11°32N 41°40E 257 E5
Gamawa Nigeria 12°10N 10°31E 263 C7
Gamay Phil. 12°23N 125°18E 232 E5
Gamay Bay Phil. 12°21N 125°21E 232 E5
Gamba Angola 11°42S 17°14E 265 E3
Gambaga Ghana 10°30N 0°28W 263 C4
Gambat Pakistan 27°17N 68°26E 242 F3
Gambela Ethiopia 8°14N 34°38E 257 F3
Gambela △ Ethiopia 8°0N 34°0E 257 F3
Gambela Hizboch □ Ethiopia 8°0N 34°0E 257 F3
Gambell U.S.A. 63°47N 171°45W 303 E5
Gambhir → India 26°58N 77°27E 242 F6
Gambia ■ W. Afr. 13°25N 16°0W 262 C1
Gambia → W. Afr. 13°28N 16°34W 262 C1
Gambier U.S.A. 40°22N 82°23W 312 F2
Gambier, C. Australia 11°56S 130°57E 278 B5
Gambier, Îs. French Polynesia 23°8S 134°58W 289 f
Gambier Is. Australia 35°3S 136°30E 282 C2
Gambier Village Bahamas 25°4N 77°30W 153 b
Gambir Indonesia 6°9S 106°48E 122 A1
Gambo C.A.R. 4°39N 22°16E 264 B4
Gambo Canada 48°47N 54°13W 299 C9
Gamboa Brazil 22°53S 43°11W 135 B1
Gamboli Pakistan 29°53N 68°24E 242 E3
Gambolòita Italy 45°26N 9°13E 129 B2
Gamboma Congo 1°55S 15°52E 264 C3
Gamboula C.A.R. 4°8N 15°9E 264 B3
Gamka → S. Africa 33°18S 21°39E 270 D3
Gamkab → Namibia 28°4S 17°54E 270 C2
Gamla Stan Stockholm, Sweden 139 c2
Gamla Uppsala Sweden 59°54N 17°40E 162 E11
Gamlakarleby = Kokkola Finland 63°50N 23°8E 160 E20
Gamleby Sweden 57°54N 16°24E 163 G10
Gamlebyen Norway 59°54N 10°46E 133 A3
Gammon → Canada 51°24N 95°44W 297 C9
Gammon Ranges △ Australia 30°38S 139°8E 281 E2
Gammouda Tunisia 35°3N 9°39E 258 A1
Gamo-Gofa Ethiopia 5°40N 36°40E 257 F4
Gamoda-Saki Japan 33°50N 134°45E 222 D6
Gamou Niger 14°20N 9°55E 259 F1
Gampaha Sri Lanka 7°5N 79°59E 245 L4
Gampo S. Korea 35°48N 129°31E 224 E4
Gampola Sri Lanka 7°10N 80°34E 245 L5
Gamtoos → S. Africa 33°58S 25°1E 270 D4
Gan France 43°12N 0°27W 174 E3
Gan Gan Argentina 42°30S 68°10W 336 B3
Gan Goriama, Mts. Cameroon 7°44N 12°45E 263 D7
Gan Jiang → China 29°15N 116°0E 229 C11
Ganado U.S.A. 35°43N 109°33W 305 J9
Gananita Sudan 18°22N 33°50E 256 D3
Gananoque Canada 44°20N 76°10W 313 B8
Ganassi Phil. 7°49N 124°6E 233 H5
Ganāveh Iran 29°35N 50°35E 247 D6
Gäncä Azerbaijan 40°45N 46°20E 191 K8
Gancheng China 18°51N 108°37E 236 C7
Gand = Gent Belgium 51°2N 3°42E 170 C3
Ganda Angola 13°3S 14°35E 265 E2
Gandajika Dem. Rep. of the Congo 6°46S 23°58E 265 D4
Gandak → India 25°39N 85°13E 243 G11
Gandara Phil. 12°1N 124°49E 232 E5
Gandava Pakistan 28°32N 67°32E 242 E2
Gander Canada 48°58N 54°35W 299 C9
Gander L. Canada 48°58N 54°35W 299 C9
Ganderkesee Germany 53°2N 8°32E 178 B4
Ganderowe Falls Zimbabwe 17°20S 29°10E 269 F2
Gandesa Spain 41°3N 0°26E 196 D5
Gandhi Sagar India 24°40N 75°40E 242 G6
Gandhinagar India 23°15N 72°45E 242 H5
Gandi Nigeria 12°55N 5°49E 263 C6
Gandia Spain 38°58N 0°9W 197 G4
Gandino Italy 45°49N 9°54E 198 C6
Gando, Pta. Canary Is. 27°55N 15°22W 153 e1
Gandole Nigeria 8°28N 11°35E 263 D7
Gandou Congo 2°25N 17°25E 264 B3
Gandu Brazil 13°45S 39°30W 333 D4
Gâneb Mauritania 18°29N 10°8W 262 B2
Ganedidalem = Gani Indonesia 0°48S 128°14E 231 E7
Ganetti Sudan 18°0N 31°10E 256 D3
Ganga → India 23°20N 90°30E 243 H14
Ganga Sagar India 21°38N 88°5E 243 J13
Gangafani Mali 14°20N 2°20W 262 C4
Gangakher India 18°57N 76°45E 244 E3
Gangan → India 28°38N 78°58E 243 E8
Ganganagar India 29°56N 73°56E 242 E5
Gangapur Maharashtra, India 19°41N 75°1E 244 E2
Gangapur Raj., India 26°32N 76°49E 242 F7
Gangara Niger 14°35N 8°29E 259 F1
Gangaw Burma 22°5N 94°5E 241 D5
Gangaw Taungdan Burma 24°55N 96°35E 241 C6
Gangawati India 15°30N 76°36E 245 G3
Gangdisê Shan China 31°20N 81°0E 243 D9
Gangdong S. Korea 37°30N 127°5E 137 B2
Ganges = Ganga → India 23°20N 90°30E 243 H14
Ganges Canada 48°51N 123°31W 296 D4
Ganges Hérault, France 43°56N 3°42E 174 E7
Ganges, Mouths of the India 21°30N 90°0E 241 E3
Ganggyeong S. Korea 36°10N 127°0E 224 D3
Gånghester Sweden 57°42N 13°1E 163 G7
Ganghwa S. Korea 37°45N 126°30E 224 D3
Gangi Italy 37°48N 14°12E 201 E7
Gângiova Romania 43°54N 23°50E 183 G8
Gangnam S. Korea 37°30N 126°59E 137 B1
Gangneung S. Korea 37°45N 128°54E 224 D4
Gangoh India 29°46N 77°18E 242 E7
Gangotri India 30°50N 79°10E 243 D8
Gangotri △ India 30°50N 79°10E 243 D8
Gangseo S. Korea 37°32N 126°51E 137 B1
Gangseong S. Korea 38°24N 128°30E 224 C4
Gangtok India 27°20N 88°37E 241 B2
Gangtou China 23°12N 113°8E 121 A1
Gangu China 34°40N 105°15E 226 G3
Gangwa Dem. Rep. of the Congo 3°30S 20°54E 264 C4
Gangwei China 23°4N 113°11E 121 B2
Gangwon-do □ S. Korea 37°45N 128°15E 224 D4
Gangyao China 44°12N 126°37E 227 B14
Gani Indonesia 0°48S 128°14E 231 E7
Ganj India 27°45N 78°57E 243 F8
Ganjam India 19°23N 85°4E 244 E7
Ganjiakou China 39°54N 116°16E 114 B1
Ganluc China 28°58N 102°59E 228 C4
Ganmain Australia 34°47S 147°1E 283 C7
Ganna Sudan 7°30N 28°0E 266 C2
Gannat France 46°7N 3°11E 173 F10
Gannett Peak U.S.A. 43°11N 109°39W 304 E9
Ganquan China 36°20N 109°20E 226 F5
Gänserdorf Austria 48°20N 16°43E 181 C9
Ganshoren Belgium 50°52N 4°18E 116 A1
Ganshui China 28°40N 106°40E 228 C6
Gansu □ China 36°0N 104°0E 226 G3
Ganta Liberia 7°15N 8°59W 262 D3
Gantheaume, C. Australia 36°4S 137°32E 282 D2
Gantheaume B. Australia 27°40S 114°10E 279 E1
Gants Hill U.K. 51°34N 0°4E 125 A4
Gantsevichi = Hantsavichy Belarus 52°49N 26°30E 177 B14
Ganye Nigeria 8°25N 12°4E 263 D7
Ganyem = Genyem Indonesia 2°46S 140°12E 231 E10
Ganyu China 34°50N 119°8E 227 G10
Ganyushkino Kazakhstan 46°35N 49°20E 191 G9
Ganzhou China 25°51N 114°56E 229 E10
Gao Mali 16°15N 0°5W 263 B4
Gao Xian China 28°21N 104°32E 228 C5
Gao'an China 28°26N 115°17E 229 C10
Gaochun China 31°20N 118°49E 229 B12
Gaohe China 22°46N 112°57E 229 F9
Gaohebu China 30°43N 116°49E 229 B11
Gaokeng China 27°40N 113°58E 229 D9
Gaolan Dao China 21°55N 113°10E 229 G9
Gaoligong Shan China 24°45N 98°45E 228 E2
Gaomi China 36°20N 119°42E 227 F10
Gaoping China 35°45N 112°55E 226 G7
Gaoqiao China 31°21N 121°34E 138 A2
Gaotang China 36°50N 116°15E 226 F9
Gaoua Burkina Faso 10°20N 3°8W 262 C4
Gaoual Guinea 11°45N 13°25W 262 C2
Gaoxiong = Kaohsiung Taiwan 22°35N 120°16E 225 D2
Gaoyang China 38°40N 115°45E 226 E8
Gaoyao China 23°3N 112°27E 229 F9
Gaoyou China 32°47N 119°26E 229 A12
Gaoyou Hu China 32°45N 119°20E 227 H10
Gaoyuan China 37°8N 117°58E 227 F9
Gaozhou China 21°58N 110°50E 229 G8
Gap France 44°33N 6°5E 175 D10
Gapan Phil. 15°19N 120°57E 232 D3
Gapat → India 24°30N 82°28E 243 G10
Gapuwiyak Australia 12°25S 135°43E 280 A2
Gar China 32°10N 79°58E 218 C2
Gara, L. Ireland 53°57N 8°26W 166 C3
Garabogazköl Aylagy Turkmenistan 41°0N 53°30E 187 F9
Garachico Canary Is. 28°22N 16°46W 153 e1
Garachiné Panama 8°0N 78°12W 320 E4
Garad Somali Rep. 6°57N 49°24E 267 C6
Garafia Canary Is. 28°48N 17°57W 153 e1
Garagum Turkmenistan 39°30N 60°0E 247 B8
Garah Australia 29°5S 149°38E 281 D4
Garaina Papua N. G. 7°53S 147°8E 286 D4
Garajonay Canary Is. 28°7N 17°14W 153 e1
Garamba △ Dem. Rep. of the Congo 4°10N 29°40E 268 B2
Garango Burkina Faso 11°48N 0°34W 263 C4
Garanhuns Brazil 8°50S 36°30W 332 C4
Garapan N. Marianas 15°12N 145°43E 302 e
Garautha India 25°34N 79°18E 243 G8
Garawe Liberia 4°35N 8°0W 262 E3
Garba Harre Somali Rep. 3°19N 42°13E 267 D5
Garba Tula Kenya 0°30N 38°32E 268 B4
Garbagnate Milanese Italy 45°34N 9°4E 129 A1
Garbagududu Ethiopia 6°12N 43°50E 267 C5
Garbahaarrey = Garba Harre Somali Rep. 3°19N 42°13E 267 D5
Garbatella Italy 41°51N 12°30E 136 B2
Garberville U.S.A. 40°6N 123°48W 304 F2
Garbiyang India 30°8N 80°54E 243 D9
Garbsen Germany 52°26N 9°31E 178 C5
Garça Brazil 22°14S 49°37W 333 F2
Garças → Mato Grosso, Brazil 15°54S 52°16W 331 D7
Garças → Pernambuco, Brazil 8°43S 39°41W 332 C4
Garches France 48°50N 2°11E 134 A2
Garching Germany 48°14N 11°39E 131 A3
Garchitorena Phil. 13°52N 123°40E 232 E4
Garcia Hernandez Phil. 9°37N 124°18E 233 G5
Garcias Brazil 20°34S 52°13W 331 E7
Gard □ France 44°2N 4°10E 175 D8
Gard → France 43°51N 4°37E 175 E8
Garda, L. di Italy 45°40N 10°41E 198 C7
Gardanne France 43°27N 5°27E 175 E9
Gårdby Sweden 56°36N 16°38E 163 H10
Garde L. Canada 62°50N 106°13W 297 A7
Gardelegen Germany 52°32N 11°24E 178 C7
Garden City El Qâhira, Egypt 30°2N 31°14E 117 A2
Garden City Ga., U.S.A. 32°6N 81°9W 316 C8
Garden City Kans., U.S.A. 37°58N 100°53W 308 G3
Garden City Mo., U.S.A. 38°34N 94°12W 310 F2
Garden City Tex., U.S.A. 31°52N 101°29W 314 F4
Garden Grove U.S.A. 33°47N 117°55W 307 M9
Garden Reach India 22°33N 88°15E 124 B1
Gardens of Stone △ Australia 33°14S 150°11E 283 B9
Garder Norway 59°45N 10°38E 133 B2
Gardēz Afghan. 33°37N 69°9E 242 C3
Garðabær Iceland 64°5N 21°55W 155 C5
Garðskagi Iceland 64°5N 22°43W 155 C4
Garður Iceland 66°4N 16°46W 155 A10
Gardiki Greece 38°50N 21°55E 204 C3
Gardiner Maine, U.S.A. 44°14N 69°47W 309 C19
Gardiner Mont., U.S.A. 45°2N 110°22W 304 D8
Gardiners I. U.S.A. 41°6N 72°6W 313 E12
Gardner Fla., U.S.A. 27°21N 81°48W 317 H8
Gardner Ill., U.S.A. 41°12N 88°17W 311 C8
Gardner Mass., U.S.A. 42°34N 71°59W 313 D13
Gardner Canal Canada 53°27N 128°8W 296 C3
Gardner Pinnacles U.S.A. 25°0N 167°55W 302 F10
Gardnerville U.S.A. 38°56N 119°45W 306 G7
Gardno, Jezioro Poland 54°40N 17°7E 184 D4
Gardo Somali Rep. 9°30N 49°6E 267 C6
Gardone Val Trómpia Italy 45°41N 10°11E 198 C7
Gárdony Hungary 47°12N 18°39E 182 C3
Gare Tigre Fr. Guiana 4°58N 53°9W 329 C7
Gareloi I. U.S.A. 51°48N 178°48W 303 L3
Garešnica Croatia 45°36N 16°56E 199 C13
Garéssio Italy 44°12N 8°2E 198 D5
Garey U.S.A. 34°53N 120°19W 307 L6
Garfield N.J., U.S.A. 40°52N 74°7W 132 A1
Garfield Wash., U.S.A. 47°1N 117°9W 304 C5
Garfield Park U.S.A. 41°52N 87°42W 119 B2
Garforth U.K. 53°47N 1°24W 168 D6
Gargaliani Greece 37°4N 21°38E 204 D3
Gargan, Mt. France 45°37N 1°39E 174 C5
Gargano △ Italy 41°43N 15°52E 199 G12
Gargantua, C. Canada 47°36N 85°2W 309 B11
Gargareta Greece 37°57N 23°43E 112 B2
Gargett Australia 21°9S 148°46E 280 K6
Gargouna Mali 15°56N 0°13E 263 B5
Gargždai Lithuania 55°43N 21°24E 184 C8
Garhchiroli India 20°10N 80°0E 244 D5
Garibaldi ⌂ Canada 49°50N 122°40W 296 D4
Garibong S. Korea 37°29N 126°54E 137 C1
Gariep, L. S. Africa 30°40S 25°40E 270 D4
Garies S. Africa 30°32S 17°59E 270 D2
Garigliano → Italy 41°13N 13°45E 200 A6
Garissa Kenya 0°25S 39°40E 268 C4
Garkida Nigeria 10°27N 12°36E 263 C7
Garko Nigeria 11°45N 8°35E 263 C6
Garland Tex., U.S.A. 32°54N 96°38W 314 E6
Garland Utah, U.S.A. 41°45N 112°10W 304 F7
Garlasco Italy 45°12N 8°55E 198 C5
Garliava Lithuania 54°49N 23°52E 184 D10
Garlin France 43°33N 0°16W 174 E3
Garm Tajikistan 39°0N 70°20E 214 F8
Garmāb Iran 35°25N 56°45E 247 C8
Garmisch-Partenkirchen Germany 47°30N 11°6E 179 H7
Garmo, Qullai = imeni Ismail Samani, Pik Tajikistan 39°0N 72°2E 217 E8
Garmsār Iran 35°20N 52°25E 247 C7
Garner U.S.A. 43°6N 93°36W 310 A3
Garnett U.S.A. 38°17N 95°14W 308 F6
Garnpung L. Australia 33°25S 143°10E 282 B5
Garo Hills India 25°30N 90°30E 241 C3
Garoe Somali Rep. 8°25N 48°33E 267 C6
Garonne → France 45°2N 0°36W 174 C3
Garonne, Canal Latéral à la France 44°15N 0°18E 174 D4
Garoowe = Garoe Somali Rep. 8°25N 48°33E 267 C6
Garorimman S. Korea 36°54N 126°21E 224 D3
Garot India 24°19N 75°41E 242 G6
Garoua Cameroon 9°19N 13°21E 263 D7
Garove I. Papua N. G. 4°42S 149°30E 286 C5
Garpenberg Sweden 60°19N 16°12E 162 D10
Garphyttan Sweden 59°18N 14°56E 162 E8
Garrauli India 25°5N 79°22E 243 G8
Garrel Germany 52°57N 8°1E 178 C4
Garreru Palau 7°19N 134°32E 288 c
Garrett U.S.A. 41°21N 85°8W 311 C11
Garrigues France 43°40N 3°55E 174 E7
Garrison Ky., U.S.A. 38°36N 83°10W 311 F13
Garrison Mont., U.S.A. 46°31N 112°49W 304 C7
Garrison N. Dak., U.S.A. 47°40N 101°25W 308 B3
Garrison Res. = Sakakawea, L. U.S.A. 47°30N 101°25W 308 B3
Garron Pt. U.K. 55°3N 5°59W 166 A6
Garrovillas Spain 39°40N 6°33W 195 F4
Garrucha Spain 37°11N 1°49W 197 H3
Garry → U.K. 56°44N 3°47W 167 E5
Garry, L. Canada 65°58N 100°18W 294 C9
Garrygala Turkmenistan 38°31N 56°29E 247 B8
Garsen Kenya 2°20S 40°5E 268 C5
Gärsnäs Sweden 55°32N 14°10E 163 J8
Garson L. Canada 56°19N 110°2W 297 B6
Garstang U.K. 53°55N 2°46W 168 D5
Gartempe → France 46°47N 0°49E 174 B4
Gartz Germany 53°13N 14°22E 178 B10
Garu Ghana 10°55N 0°11W 263 C4
Garu India 23°40N 84°14E 243 H11
Garub Namibia 26°37S 16°0E 270 C2
Garusuun Palau 7°21N 134°31E 288 c
Garut Indonesia 7°14S 107°53E 235 D3
Garvanza U.S.A. 34°6N 118°11W 126 B3
Garvão Portugal 37°42N 8°21W 195 H2
Garvie Mts. N.Z. 45°30S 168°50E 285 F3
Garwa = Garoua Cameroon 9°19N 13°21E 263 D7
Garwa India 24°11N 83°47E 243 G10
Garwolin Poland 51°55N 21°38E 185 G8
Gary U.S.A. 41°36N 87°20W 311 C9
Garz Germany 54°19N 13°20E 178 A9
Garzê China 31°38N 100°1E 228 B3
Garzón Colombia 2°10N 75°40W 328 C2
Gas City U.S.A. 40°29N 85°37W 311 D11
Gas-San Japan 38°32N 140°1E 220 E10
Gasa Bhutan 27°55N 89°44E 241 B2
Gasan Phil. 13°19N 121°51E 232 E3
Gasan Kuli = Esenguly Turkmenistan 37°37N 53°59E 216 E4
Gascogne France 43°45N 0°20E 174 E4
Gascogne, G. de Europe 44°0N 2°0W 174 E2
Gasconade U.S.A. 38°40N 91°34W 310 F5
Gasconade → U.S.A. 38°41N 91°33W 310 F5
Gascony = Gascogne France 43°45N 0°20E 174 E4
Gascoyne → Australia 24°52S 113°37E 279 D1
Gascoyne Junction Australia 25°2S 115°17E 279 E2
Gascueña Spain 40°18N 2°31W 196 E2
Gash, Wadi → Ethiopia 16°48N 35°51E 257 D4
Gash Setit ⌂ Eritrea 15°12N 36°58E 257 D4
Gåshaga Sweden 59°21N 18°13E 139 A3
Gashagar Nigeria 13°22N 12°47E 263 C7
Gashaka Nigeria 7°20N 11°29E 263 D7
Gashaka-Gumti △ Nigeria 7°23N 11°34E 263 D7
Gasherbrum Pakistan 35°40N 76°40E 243 B7
Gashua Nigeria 12°54N 11°0E 263 C7
Gasmata Papua N. G. 6°17S 150°20E 286 D6
Gasparilla I. U.S.A. 26°46N 82°16W 317 J7
Gasparillo Trin. & Tob. 10°18N 61°26W 323 t
Gasparito Neth. Ant. 12°8N 68°56W 322 g
Gaspé Canada 48°52N 64°30W 299 C7
Gaspé, C. Canada 48°48N 64°7W 299 C7
Gaspé Pen. = Gaspésie, Pén. de la Canada 48°45N 65°40W 299 C6
Gasper Grande Trin. & Tob. 10°40N 61°39W 323 t
Gaspésie, Pén. de la Canada 48°45N 65°40W 299 C6
Gaspésie ⌂ Canada 48°55N 66°10W 299 C6
Gassan Burkina Faso 12°49N 3°12W 262 C4
Gassen = Jasień Poland 51°46N 15°0E 185 G2
Gassol Nigeria 8°34N 10°25E 263 D7
Gasteiz = Vitoria-Gasteiz Spain 42°50N 2°41W 196 C2
Gaston U.S.A. 33°49N 81°5W 316 B8
Gastonia U.S.A. 35°16N 81°11W 315 D14
Gastouni Greece 37°51N 21°15E 204 D3
Gastouri Greece 39°34N 19°54E 206 B9
Gastre Argentina 42°20S 69°15W 336 B3
Gästrikland Sweden 60°45N 16°40E 162 D10
Gata, C. Cyprus 34°34N 33°2E 207 F9
Gata, C. de Spain 36°41N 2°13W 197 J2
Gata, Sierra de Spain 40°20N 6°45W 194 E4
Gataga → Canada 58°35N 126°59W 296 B3
Gătaia Romania 45°26N 21°30E 182 E6
Gatchina Russia 59°35N 30°9E 188 C6
Gatehouse of Fleet U.K. 54°53N 4°12W 167 G4
Gates U.S.A. 43°9N 77°42W 312 C7
Gates of the Arctic ⌂ U.S.A. 67°45N 153°15W 303 C9
Gateshead U.K. 54°57N 1°35W 168 C6
Gatesville U.S.A. 31°26N 97°45W 314 F6
Gateway ⌂ U.S.A. 40°38N 73°51W 132 C2
Gateway of India India 18°55N 72°50E 130 B2
Gaths Zimbabwe 20°2S 30°32E 269 G3
Gatico Chile 22°29S 70°20W 334 A1
Gâtinais France 48°5N 2°40E 173 D9
Gâtine, Hauteurs de France 46°35N 0°45W 174 B3
Gatineau Canada 45°29N 75°39W 313 A9
Gatineau → Canada 45°27N 75°42W 298 C4
Gatineau △ Canada 45°40N 76°0W 298 C4
Gatow Germany 52°29N 13°11E 115 B1
Gattaran Phil. 18°4N 121°38E 232 B3
Gattinara Italy 45°37N 8°22E 198 C5
Gatton Australia 27°32S 152°17E 281 D5
Gatun, L. Panama 9°7N 79°56W 320 E4
Gatwick, London ✕ (LGW) U.K. 51°10N 0°11W 169 F7
Gatyana S. Africa 32°16S 28°31E 271 D4
Gau Fiji 18°2S 179°18E 287 B2
Gaua Vanuatu 14°15S 167°30E 287 D5
Gaucín Spain 36°31N 5°19W 195 J5
Gauer L. Canada 57°0N 97°50W 297 B9
Gauhati = Guwahati India 26°10N 91°45E 241 B3
Gauja → Latvia 57°10N 24°16E 184 A11
Gaujas △ Latvia 57°10N 24°50E 161 H21
Gaula → Norway 63°21N 10°14E 164 A7
Gaupne Norway 61°25N 7°18E 164 C4
Gaurdak = Gowurdak Turkmenistan 37°50N 66°4E 217 E7
Gauri Phanta India 28°41N 80°36E 243 E9
Gauribidanur India 13°37N 77°32E 245 H3
Gaustatoppen Norway 59°48N 8°40E 164 E5
Gauteng □ S. Africa 26°0S 28°0E 271 C4
Gāv Koshī Iran 28°38N 57°12E 247 D8
Gavà Spain 41°18N 2°1W 114 B1
Gāvakān Iran 29°37N 53°10E 247 D7
Gavallai △ Liberia 5°8N 7°20W 262 D3
Gavarnie France 42°44N 0°1W 174 F3
Gavāter Iran 25°10N 61°31E 247 E9
Gāvbandī Iran 27°12N 53°4E 247 E7
Gavdopoula Greece 34°56N 24°0E 207 F5
Gavdos Greece 34°50N 24°5E 207 F5
Gávea Brazil 22°58S 43°13W 135 B1
Gávea, Pedra da Brazil 22°59S 43°18W 135 B1
Gavi Italy 44°41N 8°49E 198 D5
Gavião Portugal 39°28N 7°56W 195 F3
Gaviota U.S.A. 34°29N 120°13W 307 L6
Gāvkhūnī, Bāţlāq-e Iran 32°6N 52°52E 247 C7
Gävle Sweden 60°40N 17°9E 162 D11
Gävleborgs län □ Sweden 61°30N 16°15E 162 C10
Gävlebukten Sweden 60°40N 17°20E 162 D11
Gavorrano Italy 42°55N 10°54E 198 F7
Gavray France 48°55N 1°20W 172 D5
Gavrilov Yam Russia 57°18N 39°49E 188 D10
Gavrio Greece 37°54N 24°44E 204 D6
Gawachab Namibia 27°4S 17°55E 270 C2
Gawai Burma 27°56N 97°30E 241 B6
Gawilgarh Hills India 21°15N 76°45E 244 D3
Gawler Australia 34°30S 138°42E 282 C3
Gawler Ranges Australia 32°30S 135°45E 281 E2
Gawler Ranges S. Australi., Australia 32°20S 136°0E 282 B2
Gawu Nigeria 9°14N 6°52E 263 D6
Gaxun Nur China 42°22N 100°30E 218 B5
Gay Russia 51°27N 58°27E 186 D10
Gay Ga., U.S.A. 33°6N 84°35W 316 B5

Gaya India 24°47N 85°4E 243 G11
Gaya Niger 11°52N 3°28E 263 C5
Gaya Nigeria 11°57N 9°0E 263 C6
Gayasan △ S. Korea 35°45N 128°10E 224 E4
Gayéri Burkina Faso 12°39N 0°29E 263 C5
Gaylord U.S.A. 45°2N 84°41W 309 C11
Gayndah Australia 25°35S 151°32E 281 D5
Gaysin = Haysyn Ukraine 48°57N 29°25E 183 B14
Gayvoron = Hayvoron Ukraine 48°22N 29°52E 183 B14
Gaza Gaza Strip 31°30N 34°28E 251 G5
Gaza □ Mozam. 23°10S 32°45E 271 B5
Gaza Strip ■ Asia 31°29N 34°25E 251 G5
Gazanjyk = Bereket Turkmenistan 39°16N 55°32E 247 B7
Gazaoua Niger 13°32N 7°55E 263 C6
Gāzbor Iran 28°5N 58°51E 247 D8
Gazdagrét Hungary 47°29N 19°0E 117 B1
Gazelle Pen. Papua N. G. 4°40S 152°0E 286 C7
Gazi Dem. Rep. of the Congo 1°3N 24°30E 264 B4
Gaziantep Turkey 37°6N 37°23E 250 A8
Gaziantep □ Turkey 37°0N 37°0E 250 B8
Gazimağosa = Famagusta Cyprus 35°8N 33°55E 207 E9
Gaziosmanpaşa Turkey 41°5N 28°50E 122 B1
Gazipaşa Turkey 36°16N 32°18E 250 B3
Gazli Uzbekistan 40°8N 63°27E 216 D6
Gbarnga Liberia 7°19N 9°13W 262 D3
Gbekebo Nigeria 6°20N 4°56E 263 D5
Gboko Nigeria 7°17N 9°4E 263 D6
Gbongan Nigeria 7°28N 4°20E 263 D5
Gcoverega Botswana 19°8S 24°18E 270 A3
Gcuwa S. Africa 32°20S 28°11E 271 D4
Gdańsk Poland 54°22N 18°40E 184 D5
Gdańsk ✈ (GDN) Poland 54°22N 18°30E 184 D5
Gdańska, Zatoka Poland 54°30N 19°20E 184 D6
Gdingen = Gdynia Poland 54°35N 18°33E 184 D5
Gdov Russia 58°48N 27°55E 188 C4
Gdynia Poland 54°35N 18°33E 184 D5
Geba ➞ Guinea-Biss. 11°46N 15°36W 262 C1
Gebe Indonesia 0°5N 129°25E 231 D7
Gebeciler Turkey 38°46N 30°46E 205 C12
Gebeit Mine Sudan 21°3N 36°29E 256 C4
Gebel Abyad Sudan 19°0N 28°0E 256 D2
Gebel el Ahmar Egypt 30°2N 31°21E 117 A3
Gebel el Muqattam Egypt 30°1N 31°17E 117 A2
Gebel el Tura Egypt 29°56N 31°15E 117 B2
Gebel Iweibid Egypt 30°8N 32°13E 256 H8
Gebze Turkey 40°47N 29°25E 203 F13
Gecha Ethiopia 7°30N 35°18E 257 F4
Gedaref Sudan 14°2N 35°28E 257 E4
Gedaref □ Sudan 14°0N 35°0E 257 E4
Gede, Tanjung Indonesia 6°46S 105°12E 234 D3
Gediz Turkey 39°1N 29°24E 205 B11
Gediz ➞ Turkey 38°35N 26°48E 205 C8
Gedo Ethiopia 9°2N 37°25E 257 F4
Gèdre France 42°47N 0°2E 174 F4
Gedser Denmark 54°35N 11°55E 163 K5
Gedung, Pulau Malaysia 5°17N 100°23E 237 c
Geegully Cr. ➞ Australia 18°32S 123°41E 278 C3
Geel Belgium 51°10N 4°59E 170 C4
Geelong Australia 38°10S 144°22E 282 E6
Geelvink B. = Cenderwasih, Teluk Indonesia 3°0S 135°20E 231 E9
Geelvink Chan. Australia 28°30S 114°0E 279 E1
Geesthacht Germany 53°26N 10°22E 178 B6
Geidam Nigeria 12°57N 11°57E 263 C7
Geikie ➞ Canada 57°45N 103°52W 297 B8
Geikie Gorge △ Australia 18°3S 125°41E 278 C4
Geilenkirchen Germany 50°57N 6°8E 178 E2
Geili Sudan 16°1N 32°37E 257 D3
Geilo Norway 60°32N 8°14E 164 D5
Geiselgasteig Germany 48°3N 11°33E 131 B2
Geisingen Germany 47°54N 8°38E 179 H4
Geislingen Germany 48°37N 9°50E 179 G5
Geistown U.S.A. 40°18N 78°52W 312 F6
Geita Tanzania 2°48S 32°12E 268 C3
Geitastrand Norway 63°22N 9°56E 164 A6
Geithus Norway 59°57N 9°59E 164 E6
Gejiu China 23°20N 103°10E 228 F4
Gel ➞ Sudan 7°5N 29°10E 257 F2
Gel, Meydān-e Iran 29°4N 54°50E 247 D7
Gel River Sudan 7°5N 29°10E 257 F2
Gela Italy 37°4N 14°15E 201 F7
Gela, G. di Italy 37°0N 14°20E 201 F7
Geladi Ethiopia 6°59N 46°30E 267 C6
Gelahun Liberia 7°55N 10°28W 262 D2
Gelang Patah Malaysia 1°27N 103°35E 237 d
Gelderland □ Neths. 52°5N 6°10E 170 B6
Geldern Germany 51°31N 6°20E 178 D2
Geldrop Neths. 51°25N 5°32E 170 C5
Geleen Neths. 50°57N 5°49E 170 D5
Gelehun S. Leone 8°20N 11°40W 262 D2
Gelembe Turkey 39°10N 27°50E 205 B9
Gelemso Ethiopia 8°49N 40°31E 257 F5
Gelendost Turkey 38°7N 31°1E 212 C4
Gelendzhik Russia 44°33N 38°10E 189 K10
Gelib Somali Rep. 0°29N 42°46E 267 D5
Gelibolu Turkey 40°28N 26°43E 203 F10
Gelibolu Yarımadası Turkey 40°20N 26°30E 203 F10
Gelidonya Burnu Turkey 36°12N 30°24E 212 D4
Gelnhausen Germany 50°11N 9°11E 179 E5
Gelnica Slovak Rep. 48°51N 20°55E 181 C13
Gelsenkirchen Germany 51°32N 7°6E 178 D3
Gelting Germany 54°45N 9°53E 178 A5
Gelugur Malaysia 5°22N 100°18E 237 c
Gemas Malaysia 2°37N 102°36E 237 L4
Gembloux Belgium 50°34N 4°43E 170 D4
Gembu Nigeria 6°42N 11°10E 263 D7
Gemena Dem. Rep. of the Congo 3°13N 19°48E 264 B3
Gemerek Turkey 39°15N 36°10E 212 C7
Gemla Sweden 56°52N 14°39E 163 H8
Gemlik Turkey 40°26N 29°9E 203 F13
Gemlik Körfezi Turkey 40°25N 28°55E 203 F12
Gemona del Friuli Italy 46°16N 13°9E 199 B10
Gemsa Egypt 27°39N 33°35E 256 B3
Gemsbok △ Botswana 25°5S 21°1E 270 C3
Gemünden Germany 50°3N 9°42E 179 E5
Genadi Greece 36°2N 27°56E 206 E11
Genale Somali Rep. 1°48N 44°42E 267 D5
Genale ➞ Ethiopia 6°2N 39°1E 257 F4
Genç Turkey 38°44N 40°34E 213 C9
Gençay France 46°23N 0°23E 174 B4
Geneina, Gebel Egypt 29°2N 33°55E 256 B3
General Acha Argentina 37°20S 64°38W 334 D3
General Alvear B. Aires, Argentina 36°0S 60°0W 334 D4
General Alvear Mendoza, Argentina 35°0S 67°40W 334 D2
General Artigas Paraguay 26°52S 56°16W 334 B4
General Belgrano Argentina 36°35S 58°47W 334 D4
General Bernardo O'Higgins Antarctica 63°0S 58°3W 151 C18
General Cabrera Argentina 32°53S 63°52W 334 C3
General Carrera, L. Chile 46°35S 72°0W 336 C2
General Cepeda Mexico 25°21N 101°22W 318 B4
General Conesa Argentina 40°6S 64°25W 336 B4
General Eugenio A. Garay Paraguay 20°31S 62°8W 331 E5
General Germán Busch = Villa Abecia Bolivia 21°0S 68°18W 334 A2
General Guido Argentina 36°40S 57°50W 334 D4
General Juan Madariaga Argentina 37°0S 57°0W 334 D4
General La Madrid Argentina 37°17S 61°20W 334 D3
General Lorenzo Vintter Argentina 40°45S 64°26W 336 B4
General Luna Phil. 13°41N 122°10E 232 E4
General MacArthur Phil. 11°18N 125°28E 233 F5
General Martin Miguel de Güemes Argentina 24°50S 65°0W 334 A3
General Paz Argentina 27°45S 57°36W 334 B4
General Pico Argentina 35°45S 63°50W 334 D3
General Pinedo Argentina 27°15S 61°20W 334 B3
General Pinto Argentina 34°45S 61°50W 334 C3
General Sampaio Brazil 4°2S 39°29W 332 B4
General San Martín Argentina 34°35S 58°32W 117 B1
General Santos Phil. 6°5N 125°14E 233 H5
General Tinio Phil. 15°39N 121°10E 232 D3
General Toshevo Bulgaria 43°42N 28°6E 203 C12
General Treviño Mexico 26°14N 99°29W 319 B5
General Trías Mexico 28°21N 106°22W 318 B3
General Uriburu = Zárate Argentina 34°7S 59°0W 334 C4
General Viamonte Argentina 35°1S 61°3W 334 D3
General Villegas Argentina 35°5S 63°0W 334 D3
General Vintter, L. Argentina 43°55S 71°40W 336 B2
Generoso Ponce = Jaciparaná Brazil 9°15S 64°23W 331 B5
Genesee Idaho, U.S.A. 46°33N 116°56W 304 C5
Genesee Pa., U.S.A. 41°59N 77°54W 312 E7
Genesee ➞ U.S.A. 43°16N 77°36W 312 C7
Geneseo Ill., U.S.A. 41°27N 90°9W 310 C6
Geneseo N.Y., U.S.A. 42°48N 77°49W 312 D7
Geneva = Genève Switz. 46°12N 6°9E 179 J2
Geneva Ala., U.S.A. 31°2N 85°52W 316 D4
Geneva Ga., U.S.A. 32°35N 84°33W 316 C5
Geneva Ill., U.S.A. 41°53N 88°18W 311 C8
Geneva Ind., U.S.A. 40°36N 84°58W 311 D12
Geneva N.Y., U.S.A. 42°52N 76°59W 312 D8
Geneva Nebr., U.S.A. 40°32N 97°36W 308 E5
Geneva Ohio, U.S.A. 41°48N 80°57W 312 E4
Geneva, L. = Léman, L. Europe 46°26N 6°30E 173 F13
Geneva, L. U.S.A. 42°38N 88°30W 311 B8
Genève Switz. 46°12N 6°9E 179 J2
Geng Afghan. 31°22N 61°28E 240 C1
Gengenbach Germany 48°24N 8°1E 179 G4
Gengma China 23°32N 99°20E 228 F2
Genichesk = Henichesk Ukraine 46°12N 34°50E 189 J8
Genil ➞ Spain 37°42N 5°19W 195 H5
Génipa, B. de Martinique 14°33N 61°0W 322 j
Genisea Greece 41°1N 24°57E 203 E8
Genk Belgium 50°58N 5°32E 170 D5
Genkai-Nada Japan 34°0N 130°0E 222 D2
Genlis France 47°11N 5°12E 173 E12
Gennargentu, Mti. del Italy 40°1N 9°19E 200 B2
Gennes France 47°20N 0°17W 172 E6
Gennevilliers France 48°56N 2°17E 134 A2
Genoa = Génova Italy 44°25N 8°57E 198 D5
Genoa Vic., Australia 37°29S 149°35E 283 D8
Genoa Ill., U.S.A. 42°6N 88°42W 311 B8
Genoa N.Y., U.S.A. 42°40N 76°32W 313 D8
Genoa Nebr., U.S.A. 41°27N 97°44W 308 E5
Genoa Nev., U.S.A. 39°2N 119°50W 306 F7
Genoa ➞ Argentina 44°55S 70°5W 336 C2
Genoa City U.S.A. 42°30N 88°20W 311 B8
Génova Italy 44°25N 8°57E 198 D5
Génova ✈ (GOA) Italy 44°25N 8°56E 198 D5
Génova, G. di Italy 44°0N 9°0E 198 E6
Genovesa, I. Ecuador 0°20N 89°58W 330 a
Genriyetty, Ostrov Russia 77°6N 156°30E 215 B16
Gent Belgium 51°2N 3°42E 170 C3
Genteng Bali, Indonesia 8°22S 114°9E 231 J17
Genteng Jawa Barat, Indonesia 7°22S 106°24E 231 G12
Genthin Germany 52°25N 12°9E 178 C8
Gentilly France 48°48N 2°21E 134 B3
Gentio do Ouro Brazil 11°25S 42°30W 332 D3
Gentofte Denmark 55°44N 12°32E 118 A3
Gentryville U.S.A. 38°6N 87°2W 311 F9
Genval Belgium 50°43N 4°29E 116 B2
Genyem Indonesia 2°46S 140°12E 231 E10
Genzano di Lucánia Italy 40°51N 16°2E 201 B9
Genzano di Roma Italy 41°42N 12°41E 199 G9
Geoagiu Romania 45°55N 23°12E 183 E8
Geochang S. Korea 35°41N 127°55E 224 E3
Geogeumdo S. Korea 34°27N 127°10E 224 E3
Geographe B. Australia 33°30S 115°15E 279 F2
Geographe Chan. Australia 24°30S 113°0E 279 D1
Geoje S. Korea 34°51N 128°35E 224 E4
Geojedo S. Korea 34°51N 128°38E 224 E4
Geokchay = Göyçay Azerbaijan 40°42N 47°43E 191 K8
Georga, Zemlya Russia 80°30N 49°0E 214 A5
George S. Africa 33°58S 22°29E 270 D3
George ➞ Canada 58°49N 66°10W 299 A6
George, L. N.S.W., Australia 35°10S 149°25E 283 C8
George, L. S. Austral., Australia 37°25S 140°0E 282 D4
George, L. W. Austral., Australia 22°45S 123°40E 278 D3
George, L. Uganda 0°5N 30°10E 268 B3
George, L. Fla., U.S.A. 29°17N 81°36W 317 G8
George, L. N.Y., U.S.A. 43°37N 73°33W 313 C11
George Gill Ra. Australia 24°22S 131°45E 278 D5
George I. Hong Kong, China 22°13N 114°7E 122 B1
George I. St. Helena 15°58S 5°38W 153 h
George Pt. Australia 20°6S 148°36E 280 J6
George River = Kangiqsualujjuaq Canada 58°30N 65°59W 295 D13
George Rogers Clark Nat. Memorial △ U.S.A. 38°41N 87°32W 311 F9
George Sound N.Z. 44°52S 167°25E 285 E2
George Town Tas., Australia 41°6S 146°49E 281 G4
George Town Bahamas 23°33N 75°47W 320 B4
George Town Cayman Is. 19°20N 81°24W 320 C3
George Town Malaysia 5°25N 100°20E 237 c
George V Land Antarctica 69°0S 148°0E 151 C10
George VI Sound Antarctica 71°0S 68°0W 151 D17
George West U.S.A. 28°20N 98°7W 314 G5
Georges River Bridge Australia 34°0S 151°6E 139 C1
Georgetown = Janjanbureh Gambia 13°30N 14°47W 262 C2
Georgetown Ascension I. 7°56S 14°25W 153 g
Georgetown Queens., Australia 18°17S 143°33E 280 B3
Georgetown Ont., Canada 43°40N 79°56W 312 C5
Georgetown P.E.I., Canada 46°13N 62°24W 299 C7
Georgetown Guyana 6°50N 58°12W 329 B6
Georgetown St. Vincent 13°16N 61°7W 323 n
Georgetown Calif., U.S.A. 38°54N 120°50W 306 G6
Georgetown Colo., U.S.A. 39°42N 105°42W 304 G11
Georgetown D.C., U.S.A. 38°54N 77°3W 143 B3
Georgetown Fla., U.S.A. 29°23N 81°38W 317 F8
Georgetown Ga., U.S.A. 31°53N 85°6W 316 D4
Georgetown Ill., U.S.A. 39°59N 87°38W 311 E9
Georgetown Ky., U.S.A. 38°13N 84°33W 311 F12
Georgetown N.Y., U.S.A. 42°46N 75°44W 313 D9
Georgetown Ohio, U.S.A. 38°52N 83°54W 311 F13
Georgetown S.C., U.S.A. 33°23N 79°17W 315 E15
Georgetown Tex., U.S.A. 30°38N 97°41W 314 F6
Georgia □ U.S.A. 32°50N 83°15W 316 C6
Georgia ■ Asia 42°0N 43°0E 191 J6
Georgia, Str. of N. Amer. 49°25N 124°0W 306 A3
Georgia Basin S. Ocean 50°45S 35°30W 151 B1
Georgia Dome U.S.A. 33°45N 84°23W 113 B2
Georgian B. Canada 45°15N 81°0W 312 A4
Georgian Bay Islands △ Canada 44°53N 79°52W 312 B5
Georgievka Kazakhstan 49°19N 84°34E 217 C10
Georgina ➞ Australia 23°30S 139°47E 280 C2
Georgina I. Canada 44°22N 79°17W 312 B5
Georgioupoli Greece 35°20N 24°15E 207 E5
Georgiu-Dezh = Liski Russia 51°3N 39°30E 189 G10
Georgiyevsk Russia 44°12N 43°28E 191 H6
Georgsmarienhütte Germany 52°13N 8°3E 178 C4
Gera Germany 50°53N 12°4E 178 E8
Geraardsbergen Belgium 50°45N 3°53E 170 D3
Geraki Greece 37°0N 22°42E 204 D4
Geraki, Akra Greece 37°42N 20°59E 207 D2
Geral, Serra Bahia, Brazil 14°0S 41°0W 333 D3
Geral, Serra Goiás, Brazil 11°15S 46°30W 332 D2
Geral, Serra Sta. Catarina, Brazil 26°25S 50°0W 335 B6
Geral de Goiás, Serra Brazil 12°0S 46°0W 333 D2
Geral do Paraná, Serra Brazil 15°0S 47°30W 333 E2
Gerald U.S.A. 38°24N 91°20W 310 F5
Geraldine N.Z. 44°5S 171°15E 285 E6
Geraldine Mont., U.S.A. 47°36N 110°16W 304 C8
Geraldton = Innisfail Australia 17°33S 146°5E 280 B4
Geraldton W. Austral., Australia 28°48S 114°32E 279 E1
Geraldton Ont., Canada 49°44N 86°59W 298 C2
Geranium Australia 35°23S 140°11E 282 C4
Gérardmer France 48°3N 6°50E 173 D13
Gerasdorf bei Wien Austria 48°17N 16°28E 142 A2
Gerberau Germany 48°12N 11°23E 131 A1
Gercüş Turkey 37°34N 41°23E 213 D9
Gerdine, Mt. U.S.A. 61°35N 152°27W 303 F9
Gerede Turkey 40°45N 32°10E 212 B5
Gerês, Sierra do Portugal 41°48N 8°0W 194 D3
Gereshk Afghan. 31°47N 64°35E 240 C2
Geretsried Germany 47°51N 11°28E 179 H7
Gérgal Spain 37°7N 2°31W 197 H2
Gerik Malaysia 5°50N 101°15E 237 K3
Gering U.S.A. 41°50N 103°40W 308 E2
Geriş Turkey 36°57N 31°43E 250 B2
Gerlach U.S.A. 40°39N 119°21W 304 F4
Gerlachovský štít Slovak Rep. 49°11N 20°7E 181 B13
Gerli Argentina 34°41S 58°22W 117 C2
Gerlogubi Ethiopia 6°53N 45°3E 267 C6
German East Africa = Tanzania ■ Africa 6°0S 34°0E 268 D3
German Planina Macedonia 42°20N 22°0E 202 D6
German South West Africa = Namibia ■ Africa 22°0S 18°9E 270 B2
Germania Land Greenland 77°5N 19°30W 154 B9
Germansen Landing Canada 55°43N 124°40W 296 B4
Germantown Ohio, U.S.A. 39°38N 84°22W 311 E12
Germantown Tenn., U.S.A. 35°5N 89°49W 315 D10
Germantown Wis., U.S.A. 43°14N 88°6W 311 A8
Germany ■ Europe 51°0N 10°0E 178 E6
Germencik Turkey 37°52N 27°37E 205 D9
Germering Germany 48°8N 11°22E 179 G7
Germersheim Germany 49°12N 8°22E 179 F4
Germī Iran 39°1N 48°3E 213 C13
Germiston S. Africa 26°13S 28°10E 123 B2
Gern Germany 48°10N 11°32E 131 B2
Gernene Algeria 21°40N 2°24E 261 D5
Gernika-Lumo Spain 43°19N 2°40W 196 B2
Gernsheim Germany 49°45N 8°30E 179 F4
Gero Japan 35°48N 137°14E 223 B9
Gerogery Australia 35°50S 147°1E 283 C7
Gerokgak Indonesia 8°11S 114°27E 231 J17
Gerolzhofen Germany 49°54N 10°21E 179 F6
Gerona = Girona Spain 41°58N 2°46E 196 D7
Geropotamos ➞ Greece 35°3N 24°50E 207 E5
Gerrard Canada 50°30N 117°17W 296 C5
Gerringong Australia 34°46S 150°47E 283 C9
Gers □ France 43°35N 0°30E 174 E4
Gers ➞ France 44°9N 0°39E 174 D4
Gersfeld Germany 50°27N 9°56E 178 E5
Gersoppa Falls India 14°12N 74°46E 245 G2
Gersthofen Germany 48°25N 10°53E 179 G6
Gertak Sanggul Malaysia 5°17N 100°12E 237 c
Gertak Sanggul, Tanjung Malaysia 5°16N 100°11E 237 c
Gerung Indonesia 8°43S 116°7E 231 K19
Géryville = El Bayadh Algeria 33°40N 1°1E 261 B5
Gerzat France 45°48N 3°8E 174 C7
Gerze Turkey 41°48N 35°12E 212 B6
Geseke Germany 51°38N 8°31E 178 D4
Geser Indonesia 3°50S 130°54E 231 E8
Gesira △ Somali Rep. 1°58N 44°59E 267 D5
Gesso ➞ Italy 44°24N 7°33E 198 D4
Gestro, Wabi ➞ Ethiopia 4°12N 42°2E 257 G5
Getafe Spain 40°18N 3°43W 127 C1
Getinge Sweden 56°49N 12°44E 163 H6
Getty Center, The U.S.A. 34°4N 118°29W 126 B2
Gettysburg Pa., U.S.A. 39°50N 77°14W 309 F15
Gettysburg S. Dak., U.S.A. 45°1N 99°57W 308 C4
Getxo Spain 43°21N 2°59W 196 B2
Getz Ice Shelf Antarctica 75°0S 130°0W 151 D14
Geumodo S. Korea 34°31N 127°45E 224 E3
Geunjeong S. Korea 37°28N 126°54E 137 C1
Geureudong, Gunong Indonesia 4°13N 96°42E 234 B1
Geurie Australia 32°22S 148°50E 283 B8
Geva Binyamin West Bank 31°51N 35°17E 123 A2
Gevaş Turkey 38°15N 43°6E 213 C10
Gévaudan France 44°40N 3°40E 174 D7
Gevgelija Macedonia 41°9N 22°30E 202 E6
Gévora ➞ Spain 38°53N 6°57W 195 G4
Gevrai India 19°16N 75°45E 244 E2
Gewani Ethiopia 10°12N 40°40E 257 E5
Gex France 46°21N 6°3E 173 F13
Geyikli Turkey 39°48N 26°12E 205 B8
Geylang Serai Singapore 1°19N 103°53E 138 B3
Geyser U.S.A. 47°16N 110°30W 304 C8
Geyserville U.S.A. 38°42N 122°54W 306 G4
Geysir Iceland 64°19N 20°18W 155 C6
Geyve Turkey 40°30N 30°18E 212 B4
Ghâbat el Arab = Wang Kai Sudan 9°3N 29°23E 257 F2
Ghabeish Sudan 12°9N 27°21E 257 E2
Ghadāmis Libya 30°11N 9°29E 258 B1
Ghadāmis □ Libya 30°25N 10°25E 258 B2
Ghaddūwah Libya 26°26N 14°19E 258 C2
Ghaggar ➞ India 29°30N 74°53E 242 E6
Ghaghara ➞ India 25°45N 84°40E 243 G11
Ghaghat ➞ Bangla. 25°19N 89°38E 241 C2
Ghaghe Solomon Is. 7°24S 158°15E 287 L10
Ghagra India 23°17N 84°33E 243 H11
Ghagra ➞ India 27°29N 81°9E 243 F9
Ghajn Tuffieha Bay Malta 35°56N 14°21E 206 F7
Ghajnsielem Malta 36°2N 14°17E 206 E7
Ghalla, Wadi el ➞ Sudan 10°25N 27°32E 257 E2
Ghallamane Mauritania 23°15N 10°0W 260 D3
Ghamid az Zenad Si. Arabia 19°35N 41°24E 248 C3
Ghana ■ W. Afr. 8°0N 1°0W 263 D4
Ghansor India 22°39N 80°1E 243 H9
Ghanzi Botswana 21°50S 21°34E 270 B3
Gharapuri India 18°57N 72°57E 130 B2
Gharb = Shahrak-e Qods Iran 35°47N 51°22E 141 A2
Gharb Malta 36°4N 14°13E 206 E6
Gharb Bahr el Ghazâl □ Sudan 7°30N 27°30E 257 F2
Gharb Dârfûr □ Sudan 13°0N 23°0E 259 F4
Gharb el Istiwa'iya □ Sudan 5°0N 30°0E 257 G3
Gharb Kordofân □ Sudan 12°0N 28°0E 257 E2
Gharbîya, Es Sahrâ el Egypt 27°40N 26°30E 256 B2
Ghardaïa Algeria 32°20N 3°37E 261 B5
Ghardaïa □ Algeria 31°5N 3°10E 261 B5
Ghârib, G. Egypt 28°6N 32°54E 256 B3
Gharig Sudan 10°47N 27°33E 257 E2
Gharm, W. ➞ Oman 19°57N 57°38E 249 C7
Gharyān Libya 32°10N 13°0E 258 B2
Gharyān □ Libya 30°35N 13°0E 258 C2
Ghat Libya 24°59N 10°11E 258 D2
Ghatal India 22°40N 87°46E 243 H12
Ghatampur India 26°8N 80°13E 243 F9
Ghatgaon India 21°24N 85°53E 244 D7
Ghatkopar India 19°4N 72°54E 130 A2
Ghatprabha ➞ India 16°15N 75°20E 245 F2
Ghats, Eastern India 14°0N 78°50E 245 H4
Ghats, Western India 14°0N 75°0E 245 H2
Ghatsila India 22°36N 86°29E 243 H12
Ghaţţī Si. Arabia 31°16N 37°31E 246 D3
Ghawdex = Gozo Malta 36°3N 14°15E 206 E7
Ghayl Si. Arabia 21°40N 46°20E 248 B4
Ghazal, Bahr el ➞ Chad 13°0N 15°47E 259 F3
Ghazâl, Bahr el ➞ Sudan 9°31N 30°25E 257 F3
Ghazaouet Algeria 35°8N 1°50W 261 A4
Ghaziabad India 28°42N 77°26E 242 E7
Ghazipur Delhi, India 28°37N 77°19E 120 B2
Ghazipur Ut. P., India 25°38N 83°35E 243 G10
Ghaznī Afghan. 33°30N 68°28E 242 C3
Ghaznī □ Afghan. 32°10N 68°20E 240 B3
Ghedi Italy 45°24N 10°16E 198 C7
Ghelari Romania 45°38N 22°45E 182 E7
Ghèlinsor Somali Rep. 6°28N 46°39E 267 C6
Ghent = Gent Belgium 51°2N 3°42E 170 C3
Gheorghe Gheorghiu-Dej = Oneşti Romania 46°17N 26°47E 183 D11
Gheorgheni Romania 46°43N 25°41E 183 D10
Gherla Romania 47°2N 23°57E 183 C8
Ghidigeni Romania 46°3N 27°30E 183 D12
Ghilarza Italy 40°7N 8°50E 200 B1
Ghimeş-Făget Romania 46°35N 26°2E 183 D11
Ghīnah, Wādī al ➞ Si. Arabia 30°27N 38°14E 246 D3
Ghirardelli Square San Francisco, U.S.A. 136 a1
Ghisonaccia France 42°1N 9°26E 175 F13
Ghisoni France 42°7N 9°12E 175 F13
Ghizar ➞ Pakistan 36°15N 73°43E 243 A5
Ghizri Pakistan 24°49N 67°2E 123 B2
Ghizri Cr. ➞ Pakistan 24°47N 67°5E 123 B2
Ghod ➞ India 18°30N 74°35E 244 E2
Ghogha India 21°40N 72°20E 244 D1
Ghonda India 28°41N 77°16E 120 A2
Ghot Ogrein Egypt 31°10N 25°20E 256 A2
Ghotaru India 27°20N 70°1E 242 F4
Ghotki Pakistan 28°5N 69°21E 242 E3
Ghowr □ Afghan. 34°0N 64°20E 240 B2
Ghubbet el Bûs Egypt 29°35N 32°21E 251 J3
Ghudaf, W. al ➞ Iraq 32°56N 43°30E 213 F10
Ghughri India 22°39N 80°41E 243 H9
Ghugus India 19°58N 79°12E 244 E4
Ghulam Mohammad Barrage Pakistan 25°30N 68°20E 242 G3
Ghurayrah Si. Arabia 18°37N 42°41E 248 C3
Ghūrīān Afghan. 34°17N 61°25E 240 B1
Ghusuri India 22°37N 88°21E 124 B2
Ghuzzayil, Sabkhat Libya 29°30N 19°30E 258 C3
Gia Dinh Vietnam 10°49N 106°42E 237 G6
Gia Lai = Plei Ku Vietnam 13°57N 108°0E 236 F7
Gia Nghia Vietnam 11°58N 107°42E 237 G6
Gia Ngoc Vietnam 14°50N 108°58E 236 E7
Gia Vuc Vietnam 14°42N 108°34E 236 E7
Giali Greece 36°41N 27°11E 205 E9
Gialtra Greece 38°51N 22°59E 204 C4
Giamama Somali Rep. 0°4N 42°44E 267 D5
Gianicolense Italy 41°53N 12°28E 136 B1
Gianicolo Rome, Italy 136 c1
Giannitsa Greece 40°46N 22°24E 202 F6
Giannutri Italy 42°15N 11°6E 198 F8
Giant Forest U.S.A. 36°36N 118°43W 306 J8
Giant Mts. = Krkonoše Czech Rep. 50°50N 15°35E 180 A8
Giant Sequoia △ U.S.A. 36°10N 118°35W 306 K8
Giant Wheel = Riesenrad Austria 48°14N 16°23E 142 A2
Giants Causeway U.K. 55°16N 6°29W 166 A5
Giant's Tank Sri Lanka 8°51N 80°2E 245 K5
Gianyar Indonesia 8°32S 115°20E 231 K18
Giarabub = Al Jaghbūb Libya 29°42N 24°38E 258 C4
Giarre Italy 37°43N 15°11E 201 E8
Giaros Greece 37°32N 24°40E 204 D6
Giaveno Italy 45°2N 7°21E 198 C4
Gibara Cuba 21°9N 76°11W 320 B4
Gibb River Australia 16°26S 126°26E 278 C4
Gibbon U.S.A. 40°45N 98°51W 308 E4
Gibe ➞ Ethiopia 7°20N 37°36E 257 F4
Gibellina Nuova Italy 37°47N 12°58E 200 E5
Gibeon Namibia 25°9S 17°43E 270 C2
Gibraleón Spain 37°23N 6°58W 195 H4
Gibraltar □ Europe 36°7N 5°22W 195 J5
Gibraltar, Str. of Medit. S. 35°55N 5°40W 195 K5
Gibraltar Pt. Canada 43°36N 79°23W 141 B2
Gibraltar Range △ Australia 29°31S 152°19E 281 D5
Gibson U.S.A. 33°14N 82°36W 316 B7
Gibson City U.S.A. 40°28N 88°22W 311 D8
Gibson Desert Australia 24°0S 126°0E 278 D4
Gibsonburg U.S.A. 41°23N 83°19W 311 C13
Gibsons Canada 49°24N 123°32W 296 D4
Gibsonton U.S.A. 27°51N 82°23W 317 H7
Gibsonville U.S.A. 39°46N 120°54W 306 F6
Gidami Ethiopia 8°59N 34°37E 266 C3
Giddalur India 15°20N 78°57E 245 G4
Giddings U.S.A. 30°11N 96°56W 314 F6
Gidea Park U.K. 51°35N 0°11E 125 A5
Gidole Ethiopia 5°40N 37°25E 257 F4
Giebnegáisi = Kebnekaise Sweden 67°53N 18°33E 160 C18
Gien France 47°40N 2°36E 173 E9
Giengen Germany 48°37N 10°14E 179 G6
Giesing Germany 48°6N 11°35E 131 B2
Giessen Germany 50°34N 8°41E 178 E4
Gīfān Iran 37°54N 57°28E 247 B8
Gifatin, Geziret Egypt 27°10N 33°50E 256 B3
Gifford U.S.A. 27°40N 80°25W 317 H9
Gifhorn Germany 52°30N 10°33E 178 C6
Gift Lake Canada 55°53N 115°49W 296 B5
Gifu Japan 35°30N 136°45E 223 B8
Gifu □ Japan 35°40N 137°0E 223 B9
Gigant Russia 46°28N 41°20E 191 G5
Giganta, Sa. de la Mexico 26°0N 111°39W 318 B2
Gigen Bulgaria 43°40N 24°28E 203 C8
Gigha U.K. 55°42N 5°44W 167 F3
Giglei Somali Rep. 5°25N 45°20E 267 C6
Giglio Italy 42°20N 10°52E 198 F7
Gignac France 43°39N 3°32E 174 E7
Gigüela ➞ Spain 39°8N 3°44W 195 F7
Gijang S. Korea 35°14N 129°12E 224 E4
Gijón Spain 43°32N 5°42W 194 B5
Gil I. Canada 53°12N 129°15W 296 C3
Gila ➞ U.S.A. 32°43N 114°33W 305 K6
Gila Bend U.S.A. 32°57N 112°43W 305 K7
Gila Bend Mts. U.S.A. 33°10N 113°0W 305 K7
Gila Cliff Dwellings △ U.S.A. 33°12N 108°16W 305 K9
Gīlān □ Iran 37°0N 50°0E 247 B6
Gilău Romania 46°45N 23°23E 183 D8
Gilbert ➞ Australia 16°35S 141°15E 280 B3
Gilbert Is. Kiribati 1°0N 172°0E 277 A14
Gilbert River Australia 18°9S 142°52E 280 B3
Gilbert Seamounts Pac. Oc. 52°50N 150°10W 150 D18
Gilbués Brazil 9°50S 45°21W 332 C2
Gilead U.S.A. 44°24N 70°59W 313 B14
Gilf el Kebîr, Hadabat el Egypt 23°50N 25°50E 256 C2
Gilford I. Canada 50°40N 126°30W 296 C3
Gilgandra Australia 31°43S 148°39E 283 A8
Gilgil Kenya 0°30S 36°20E 268 C4
Gilgit India 35°50N 74°15E 243 B6
Gilgit ➞ Pakistan 35°44N 74°37E 243 B6
Gilgunnia Australia 32°26S 146°2E 283 B7
Gili △ Mozam. 16°39S 38°27E 269 F4
Gilimanuk Indonesia 8°10S 114°26E 231 J17
Giljeva Planina Europe 43°9N 20°0E 202 C3
Gill Pt. St. Helena 15°58S 5°38W 153 h
Gillam Canada 56°20N 94°40W 297 B10
Gilleleje Denmark 56°8N 12°19E 163 H6
Gillen, L. Australia 26°11S 124°38E 279 E3
Gilles, L. Australia 32°50S 136°45E 282 B2
Gillespie U.S.A. 39°8N 89°49W 310 F7
Gillespies Pt. N.Z. 43°24S 169°49E 285 D4
Gillette U.S.A. 44°18N 105°30W 304 D11
Gilliat Australia 20°40S 141°28E 280 C3
Gillingham U.K. 51°23N 0°33E 169 F8
Gilman U.S.A. 40°46N 88°0W 311 D9
Gilman City U.S.A. 40°8N 93°53W 310 D3
Gilmer U.S.A. 32°44N 94°57W 314 E7
Gilmerton U.K. 55°54N 3°7W 121 B3
Gilmore, L. Australia 32°29S 121°37E 279 F3
Gilo West Bank 31°44N 35°11E 123 B2
Gilo ➞ Ethiopia 8°10N 33°15E 257 F3
Gilort ➞ Romania 44°38N 23°32E 183 F8
Gilroy U.S.A. 37°1N 121°34W 306 H5
Giluwe, Mt. Papua N. G. 6°8S 143°52E 286 D2
Gimbi Ethiopia 9°3N 35°42E 257 F4
Gimcheon S. Korea 36°11N 128°4E 224 D4
Gimhae S. Korea 35°14N 128°53E 224 E4
Gimhwa S. Korea 38°17N 127°28E 224 C3
Gimie, Mt St. Lucia 13°54N 61°0W 323 m
Gimje S. Korea 35°48N 126°45E 224 E3
Gimli Canada 50°40N 97°0W 297 C9
Gimmersta Sweden 59°14N 18°14E 139 B3
Gimo Sweden 60°11N 18°12E 162 D12
Gimone ➞ France 44°0N 1°6E 174 E5
Gimont France 43°38N 0°52E 174 E4
Gin ➞ Sri Lanka 6°5N 80°7E 245 L5
Gin Gin Australia 25°0S 151°58E 281 D5
Ginâh Egypt 25°21N 30°30E 256 B3
Ginatilan Phil. 9°34N 123°19E 233 G4
Gineifa Egypt 30°12N 32°25E 256 H8
Gingee India 12°15N 79°25E 245 H4
Gingin Australia 31°22S 115°54E 279 F2
Gingindlovu S. Africa 29°2S 31°30E 271 C5
Gingoog Phil. 8°50N 125°7E 233 G5
Ginir Ethiopia 7°6N 40°40E 257 F5
Ginosa Italy 40°35N 16°45E 201 B9
Ginowan Japan 26°15N 127°45E 288 a
Ginza Tokyo, Japan 140 b5
Ginzo de Limia = Xinzo de Limia Spain 42°3N 7°47W 194 C3
Giofyros ➞ Greece 35°20N 25°6E 207 E6
Giohar Somali Rep. 2°48N 45°30E 267 D6
Gióia, G. di Italy 38°30N 15°45E 201 D8
Gióia del Colle Italy 40°48N 16°55E 201 B9
Gióia Táuro Italy 38°25N 15°54E 201 D8
Gioiosa Iónica Italy 38°20N 16°18E 201 D9
Gioiosa Marea Italy 38°10N 14°54E 201 D7
Giona, Oros Greece 38°38N 22°14E 204 C4
Giovi, Passo dei Italy 44°33N 8°57E 198 D5
Giovinazzo Italy 41°11N 16°40E 201 A9
Gippsland Australia 37°52S 147°0E 283 D7
Gir △ India 21°0N 71°0E 242 J4
Gir Hills India 21°0N 71°0E 242 J4
Girab India 26°2N 70°38E 242 F4
Girâfi, W. ➞ Egypt 29°58N 34°39E 251 J5
Giraltovce Slovak Rep. 49°7N 21°32E 181 B14
Girapetra, Akra Greece 38°51N 20°41E 207 B2
Girard St. Lucia 13°59N 60°57W 323 m
Girard Ga., U.S.A. 33°3N 81°43W 316 B8
Girard Ill., U.S.A. 39°27N 89°47W 310 E7
Girard Kans., U.S.A. 37°31N 94°51W 308 G6
Girard Ohio, U.S.A. 41°9N 80°42W 312 E4
Girard Pa., U.S.A. 42°0N 80°19W 312 E4
Girardot Colombia 4°18N 74°48W 328 C3
Giraud, Pte. Dominica 15°20N 61°15W 323 k
Girdle Ness U.K. 57°9N 2°3W 167 D6
Giresun Turkey 40°55N 38°30E 213 B8
Giresun □ Turkey 40°30N 38°30E 213 B8
Girga Egypt 26°17N 31°55E 256 B3
Girgaum Mumbai, India 130 b2
Girgenti = Agrigento Italy 37°19N 13°34E 200 E6
Girgir, C. Papua N. G. 3°50S 144°35E 286 B3
Giri ➞ Dem. Rep. of the Congo 0°28N 17°59E 264 B3
Giri ➞ India 30°28N 77°41E 242 D7
Giridih India 24°10N 86°21E 243 G12
Girifalco Italy 38°49N 16°25E 201 D9
Giriftu Kenya 1°59N 39°46E 268 B4
Girilambone Australia 31°16S 146°57E 283 A7
Girne = Kyrenia Cyprus 35°20N 33°20E 207 E9
Giro Nigeria 11°7N 4°42E 263 C5
Giromagny France 47°45N 6°50E 173 E13
Giron = Kiruna Sweden 67°52N 20°15E 160 C19
Girona Spain 41°58N 2°46E 196 D7
Girona □ Spain 42°11N 2°30E 196 C7
Gironde □ France 44°45N 0°30W 174 D3
Gironde ➞ France 45°32N 1°7W 174 C2
Gironella Spain 42°2N 1°53E 196 C6
Girraween △ Australia 28°46S 151°54E 281 D5
Giru Australia 19°30S 147°5E 280 B4
Girvan U.K. 55°14N 4°51W 167 F4
Gisborne Vic., Australia 37°29S 144°36E 282 D6
Gisborne N.Z. 38°39S 178°5E 284 E7
Gisborne □ N.Z. 38°30S 178°2E 284 E6
Gisenyi Rwanda 1°41S 29°15E 268 C2
Gislaved Sweden 57°19N 13°32E 163 G7
Gisors France 49°15N 1°47E 173 C8
Gitega Burundi 3°26S 29°56E 268 C2
Githio Greece 36°46N 22°34E 204 E4
Gitschin = Jičín Czech Rep. 50°25N 15°28E 180 A8
Giuba ➞ Somali Rep. 1°30N 42°35E 267 D5
Giugliano in Campania Italy 40°56N 14°12E 201 B7
Giulianova Italy 42°45N 13°57E 199 F10
Giura Greece 39°23N 24°10E 204 B6
Giurgeni Romania 44°45N 27°48E 183 F12
Giurgiu Romania 43°52N 25°57E 183 G10
Giurgiu □ Romania 44°20N 26°0E 183 F10
Giurgiuleşti Moldova 45°29N 28°12E 183 E13
Giv'at Ram Israel 31°47N 35°12E 123 B2
Giv'at Ye'arim Israel 31°47N 35°5E 123 B1
Giv'at Ze'ev West Bank 31°52N 35°10E 123 A2
Give Denmark 55°51N 9°13E 163 J3
Givet France 50°8N 4°49E 173 B11
Giv'on West Bank 31°51N 35°10E 123 A1
Givors France 45°35N 4°45E 175 C8
Givry France 46°41N 4°46E 173 F11
Giyon Ethiopia 8°33N 38°1E 257 F4
Giza = El Giza Egypt 30°0N 31°12E 117 A2
Giza Pyramids Egypt 29°58N 31°9E 117 B1
Gizab Afghan. 33°22N 66°17E 242 C1
Gizhiga Russia 62°3N 160°30E 215 C17
Gizhiginskaya Guba Russia 61°0N 158°0E 215 C16
Gizo Solomon Is. 8°7S 156°50E 287 M9
Giżycko Poland 54°2N 21°48E 184 D8
Gizzeria Italy 38°59N 16°12E 201 D9
Gjalicë e Lumës, Mal. Albania 42°2N 20°25E 202 D4
Gjegjan Albania 41°58N 20°3E 202 E4
Gjendesheim Norway 61°30N 8°48E 164 C5
Gjermundshamn Norway 60°4N 5°55E 164 D2
Gjersjøen Norway 59°47N 10°47E 133 B3
Gjerstad Norway 58°54N 9°1E 164 F6
Gjevillvatnet Norway 62°43N 9°23E 164 B6
Gjirokastër Albania 40°7N 20°10E 202 F4
Gjoa Haven Canada 68°38N 95°53W 294 C10
Gjøra Norway 62°33N 9°4E 164 B6
Gjøvik Norway 60°47N 10°43E 164 D7
Gjuhës, Kep i Albania 40°28N 19°15E 202 F3
Glace Bay Canada 46°11N 59°58W 299 C8
Glacier △ B.C., Canada 51°15N 117°30W 296 C5
Glacier △ Mont., U.S.A. 48°42N 113°48W 304 B7
Glacier Bay U.S.A. 58°40N 136°0W 303 G14
Glacier Bay △ U.S.A. 58°45N 136°30W 296 B1
Glacier Peak U.S.A. 48°7N 121°7W 304 B3
Gladesville Australia 33°50S 151°8E 139 B1
Gladewater U.S.A. 32°33N 94°56W 314 E7
Gladsakse Denmark 55°45N 12°25E 118 A2
Gladstone Queens., Australia 23°52S 151°16E 280 C5
Gladstone S. Austral., Australia 33°15S 138°22E 282 B3
Gladstone Man., Canada 50°13N 98°57W 297 C9
Gladstone Ill., U.S.A. 40°52N 90°57W 310 D6
Gladstone Mich., U.S.A. 45°51N 87°1W 308 C10
Gladstone Mo., U.S.A. 39°13N 94°35W 310 E2
Gladwin U.S.A. 43°59N 84°29W 309 D11
Glafsfjorden Sweden 59°30N 12°37E 162 E6
Glagah Indonesia 8°13S 114°18E 231 J17
Glagów Małapolski Poland 50°10N 21°56E 185 H8
Glåma = Glomma ➞ Norway 59°12N 10°57E 164 E7
Gláma Iceland 65°48N 23°0W 155 B4
Glamis U.S.A. 32°55N 115°5W 307 N11
Glamoč Bos.-H. 44°3N 16°51E 199 D13
Glamorgan, Vale of □ U.K. 51°28N 3°25W 169 F4
Glåmos Norway 62°41N 11°25E 164 B8
Glamsbjerg Denmark 55°17N 10°6E 163 J4
Glanvillia Dominica 15°34N 61°28W 323 k
Glarus Switz. 47°3N 9°4E 179 H5
Glarus □ Switz. 47°0N 9°5E 179 J5
Glasco Kans., U.S.A. 39°22N 97°50W 308 F5
Glasco N.Y., U.S.A. 42°3N 73°57W 313 D11
Glasgow C. of Glasg., U.K. 55°51N 4°15W 167 F4
Glasgow Ky., U.S.A. 37°0N 85°55W 309 G11
Glasgow Mo., U.S.A. 39°14N 92°51W 310 E4
Glasgow Mont., U.S.A. 48°12N 106°38W 304 B10
Glasgow, City of □ U.K. 55°51N 4°12W 167 F4
Glasgow Int. ✈ (GLA) U.K. 55°51N 4°21W 167 F4
Glaslyn Canada 53°22N 108°21W 297 C7
Glasnevin Ireland 53°22N 6°15W 120 A2
Glassmanor U.S.A. 38°49N 77°0W 143 C4
Glasthule Ireland 53°17N 6°7W 120 B3
Glastonbury Somst., U.K. 51°9N 2°43W 169 F5
Glastonbury Conn., U.S.A. 41°43N 72°37W 313 E12
Glatz = Kłodzko Poland 50°28N 16°38E 185 H3
Glauchau Germany 50°49N 12°31E 178 E8
Glava Sweden 59°33N 12°35E 162 E6
Glavice Croatia 43°43N 16°41E 199 E13
Glazov Russia 58°9N 52°40E 190 A11
Gleichen Canada 50°52N 113°3W 296 C6
Gleisdorf Austria 47°6N 15°44E 180 D8
Gleiwitz = Gliwice Poland 50°22N 18°41E 185 H5
Glen U.S.A. 44°7N 71°11W 313 B13
Glen Affric U.K. 57°17N 5°1W 167 D3
Glen Afton N.Z. 37°37S 175°4E 284 D4
Glen Canyon U.S.A. 37°30N 110°40W 305 H8
Glen Canyon △ U.S.A. 37°15N 111°0W 305 H8
Glen Canyon Dam U.S.A. 36°57N 111°29W 305 H8
Glen Coe U.K. 56°40N 5°0W 167 E3
Glen Cove U.S.A. 40°51N 73°38W 313 F11
Glen Garry U.K. 57°3N 5°7W 167 D3
Glen Innes Australia 29°44S 151°44E 281 D5
Glen Iris Australia 37°51S 145°3E 128 B2
Glen Lyon U.S.A. 41°10N 76°5W 313 E8
Glen Mar Park U.S.A. 38°57N 77°7W 143 B3
Glen Massey N.Z. 37°38S 175°2E 284 D4

374 Glen Mor INDEX

Glen Mor U.K. 57°9N 4°37W 167 D4
Glen More ⌂ U.K. 57°8N 3°40W 167 D5
Glen Moriston U.K. 57°11N 4°52W 167 D4
Glen Robertson Canada 45°22N 74°30W 313 A10
Glen Rock U.S.A. 40°57N 74°7W 132 A1
Glen Rouge Park Canada 43°49N 79°10W 141 A4
Glen Spean U.K. 56°53N 4°40W 167 E4
Glen Ullin U.S.A. 46°49N 101°50W 308 B3
Glenallen U.S.A. 62°7N 145°33W 303 E11
Glénan, Îs. de France 47°42N 4°0W 172 E3
Glenarden U.S.A. 38°56N 76°51W 143 B4
Glenariff △ Ireland 55°2N 6°10W 166 A5
Glenasmole Reservoirs Ireland 53°15N 6°21W 120 B1
Glenavy N.Z. 44°54S 171°7E 285 E6
Glenbeigh Ireland 52°3N 9°58W 166 D2
Glenburn Australia 37°27S 145°26E 283 D6
Glencoe Ont., Canada 42°45N 81°43W 312 D3
Glencoe KwaZulu Natal, S. Africa 28°11S 30°11E 271 C5
Glencoe Ala., U.S.A. 33°57N 85°56W 316 B4
Glencoe Minn., U.S.A. 44°46N 94°9W 308 C6
Glencolumbkille Ireland 54°43N 8°42W 166 B3
Glencorse Res. U.K. 55°51N 3°15W 121 B2
Glencullen Ireland 53°14N 6°12W 120 B2
Glendale Ariz., U.S.A. 33°32N 112°11W 305 K7
Glendale Calif., U.S.A. 34°9N 118°15W 126 B3
Glendale Fla., U.S.A. 30°52N 86°7W 316 E3
Glendale Zimbabwe 17°22S 31°5E 269 F3
Glendive U.S.A. 47°7N 104°43W 304 C11
Glendo U.S.A. 42°30N 105°2W 304 E11
Glendoo Mt. Ireland 53°14N 6°16W 120 B2
Glenelg Australia 34°58S 138°31E 282 C3
Glenelg ➔ Australia 38°4S 140°59E 282 E4
Glenfield U.S.A. 43°43N 75°24W 313 C9
Glengad Hd. Ireland 55°20N 7°10W 166 A4
Glengarriff Ireland 51°45N 9°34W 166 E2
Glengoffe Jamaica 18°10N 76°53W 320 a
Glenham N.Z. 46°26S 168°52E 285 G3
Glenhope N.Z. 41°40S 172°39E 285 B7
Glenhuntly Australia 37°52S 145°1E 128 B2
Glenmary, Mt. N.Z. 43°55S 169°55E 285 D4
Glenmont U.S.A. 40°31N 82°6W 312 F2
Glenmorgan Australia 27°14S 149°42E 281 D4
Glenn U.S.A. 39°31N 122°1W 306 F4
Glennamaddy Ireland 53°37N 8°33W 166 C3
Glenns Ferry U.S.A. 42°57N 115°18W 304 E6
Glennville U.S.A. 31°56N 81°56W 316 D8
Glenorchy Tas., Australia 42°49S 147°18E 281 G4
Glenorchy Vic., Australia 36°55S 142°41E 282 D5
Glenorchy N.Z. 44°51S 168°24E 285 E3
Glenore Australia 17°50S 141°12E 280 B3
Glenreagh Australia 30°2S 153°1E 281 E5
Glenrock U.S.A. 42°52N 105°52W 304 E11
Glenrothes U.K. 56°12N 3°10W 167 E5
Glenrowan Australia 36°29S 146°13E 283 D7
Glens Falls U.S.A. 43°19N 73°39W 313 C11
Glenside Wellington, N.Z. 41°12S 174°48E 143 B1
Glenside Pa., U.S.A. 40°6N 75°9W 313 F9
Glenthompson Australia 37°38S 142°38E 282 D5
Glenties Ireland 54°49N 8°16W 166 B3
Glenveagh △ Ireland 55°3N 8°1W 166 A3
Glenview U.S.A. 42°3N 87°48W 119 A2
Glenview Countryside U.S.A. 42°3N 87°49W 119 A2
Glenville U.S.A. 38°56N 80°50W 309 F13
Glenvista S. Africa 26°17S 28°3E 123 B2
Glenwood Nfld. & L., Canada 49°0N 54°58W 299 C9
Glenwood Ark., U.S.A. 34°20N 93°33W 314 D8
Glenwood Ga., U.S.A. 32°11N 82°40W 316 C7
Glenwood Hawai'i, U.S.A. 19°29N 155°9W 302 D6
Glenwood Iowa, U.S.A. 41°3N 95°45W 308 E6
Glenwood Minn., U.S.A. 45°39N 95°23W 308 C6
Glenwood Wash., U.S.A. 46°1N 121°17W 306 D5
Glenwood Springs U.S.A. 39°33N 107°19W 304 G10
Glettinganes Iceland 65°30N 13°37W 155 B13
Glidden U.S.A. 42°4N 94°44W 310 B2
Glifada Greece 37°52N 23°45E 112 B2
Glimåkra Sweden 56°19N 14°7E 163 H8
Glin Ireland 52°34N 9°17W 166 D2
Glina Croatia 45°20N 16°6E 199 C13
Glinojeck Poland 52°49N 20°21E 185 F7
Glittertind Norway 61°40N 8°32E 164 C5
Gliwice Poland 50°22N 18°41E 185 H5
Globe U.S.A. 33°24N 110°47W 305 K8
Glodeanu Siliştea Romania 44°50N 26°48E 183 F11
Glodeni Moldova 47°45N 27°31E 183 C12
Glödnitz Austria 46°53N 14°7E 180 E7
Glogau = Głogów Poland 51°37N 16°5E 185 G3
Gloggnitz Austria 47°41N 15°56E 180 D8
Głogów Poland 51°37N 16°5E 185 G3
Głogówek Poland 50°21N 17°53E 185 H4
Glomma ➔ Norway 59°12N 10°57E 164 E7
Glömsta Sweden 59°14N 17°55E 139 B1
Glória Phil. 12°59N 121°30E 232 E3
Glorieuses, Îs. Ind. Oc. 11°30S 47°20E 272 A2
Glosa Greece 39°10N 23°45E 204 B5
Glossop U.K. 53°27N 1°56W 168 D6
Glostrup Denmark 55°39N 12°23E 118 B2
Gloucester N.S.W., Australia 32°0S 151°59E 283 B9
Gloucester Papua N. G. 5°31S 148°31E 286 C5
Gloucester Gloucs., U.K. 51°53N 2°15W 169 F5
Gloucester Mass., U.S.A. 42°37N 70°40W 313 D14
Gloucester, C. Papua N. G. 5°26S 148°21E 286 C5
Gloucester I. Australia 20°0S 148°30E 280 J6
Gloucester Island △ Australia 20°2S 148°30E 280 J6
Gloucester Point U.S.A. 37°15N 76°30W 309 G15
Gloucestershire □ U.K. 51°46N 2°15W 169 F5
Glover I. Grenada 11°59N 61°47W 323 q
Gloversville U.S.A. 43°3N 74°21W 313 C10
Glovertown Canada 48°40N 54°3W 299 C9
Gloverville = Warrenville U.S.A. 33°33N 81°48W 316 B8
Głowno Poland 51°59N 19°42E 185 G6
Głubczyce Poland 50°13N 17°52E 185 H4
Glubokiy Russia 48°35N 40°25E 191 F5
Glubokoe Kazakhstan 50°8N 82°18E 217 B10
Glubokoye = Hlybokaye Belarus 55°10N 27°45E 188 E4
Głuchołazy Poland 50°19N 17°24E 185 H4
Glücksburg Germany 54°50N 9°33E 178 A5
Glückstadt Germany 53°45N 9°25E 178 B5
Glukhov = Hlukhiv Ukraine 51°40N 33°58E 189 G7
Glusk Belarus 52°53N 28°41E 177 B15
Głuszyca Poland 50°41N 16°23E 185 H3
Glyngøre Denmark 56°46N 8°52E 163 H2
Gmünd Kärnten, Austria 46°54N 13°31E 180 E6
Gmünd Niederösterreich, Austria 48°45N 15°0E 180 C8
Gmunden Austria 47°55N 13°48E 180 D6
Gnali Gabon 2°34S 11°18E 264 C2
Gnarp Sweden 62°3N 17°16E 162 B11
Gnesen = Gniezno Poland 52°30N 17°35E 185 F4
Gnesta Sweden 59°3N 17°17E 162 E11
Gniew Poland 53°50N 18°50E 184 E5
Gniewkowo Poland 52°54N 18°25E 185 F5
Gniezno Poland 52°30N 17°35E 185 F4
Gnjilane Serbia 42°28N 21°29E 202 D5
Gnoien Germany 53°58N 12°41E 178 B8
Gnosjö Sweden 57°22N 13°43E 163 G7
Gnowangerup Australia 33°58S 117°59E 279 F2
Go Cong Vietnam 10°22N 106°40E 237 G6
Gō-Gawa ➔ Japan 35°2N 132°13E 222 B4
Gō-no-ura Japan 33°44N 129°40E 222 D1
Goa India 15°33N 73°59E 245 G1
Goa Phil. 13°42N 123°29E 232 E4
Goa □ India 15°33N 73°59E 245 G1
Goalen Hd. Australia 36°33S 150°4E 283 D9
Goalpara India 26°10N 90°40E 241 B3
Goaltor India 22°43N 87°10E 243 H12
Goalundo Ghat Bangla. 23°50N 89°47E 243 H13
Goaso Ghana 6°48N 2°30W 262 D4
Goat Fell U.K. 55°38N 5°11W 167 F3
Goat I. Antigua & B. 17°43N 61°51W 322 c
Goat Pt. Antigua & B. 17°44N 61°51W 322 c
Goba Ethiopia 7°1N 39°59E 257 F4
Goba Mozam. 26°15S 32°13E 271 C5
Gobabis Namibia 22°30S 19°0E 270 B2
Gobe Papua N. G. 9°4S 149°0E 286 E5
Göbel Turkey 40°0N 28°9E 203 F12
Gobernador Gregores Argentina 48°46S 70°15W 336 C2
Gobi Asia 44°0N 110°0E 226 C6
Gobichettipalayam India 11°31N 77°21E 245 J3
Gobles U.S.A. 42°22N 85°53W 311 B11
Gobō Japan 33°53N 135°10E 223 D7
Gobo Sudan 5°40N 31°10E 257 F3
Göçbeyli Turkey 39°13N 27°25E 205 B9
Goch Germany 51°41N 6°9E 178 D2
Gochang S. Korea 35°26N 126°42E 224 E3
Gochas Namibia 24°59S 18°55E 270 B2
God Dere Ethiopia 5°12N 44°1E 267 C5
Godalming U.K. 51°11N 0°36W 169 F7
Godavari ➔ India 16°25N 82°18E 244 F6
Godavari Pt. India 17°0N 82°20E 244 F6
Godbout Canada 49°20N 67°38W 299 C6
Godda India 24°50N 87°13E 243 G12
Godech Bulgaria 43°1N 23°4E 202 C7
Goderich Canada 43°45N 81°41W 312 C3
Goderville France 49°38N 0°22E 172 C7
Godfrey U.S.A. 38°58N 90°11W 310 F6
Godfrey Ra. Australia 24°0S 117°0E 279 D2
Goðafoss Iceland 65°41N 17°33W 155 B9
Godhavn = Qeqertarsuaq Greenland 69°15N 53°38W 154 D5
Goðdalir Iceland 65°20N 19°6W 155 B7
Godhra India 22°49N 73°40E 242 H5
Godinlave Somali Rep. 5°54N 46°38E 267 C6
Gödöllő Hungary 47°38N 19°25E 182 C4
Godoy Cruz Argentina 32°56S 68°52W 334 C2
Gods ➔ Canada 56°22N 92°51W 298 A1
Gods L. Canada 54°40N 94°15W 298 B1
Gods River Canada 54°50N 94°5W 297 C10
Godthåb = Nuuk Greenland 64°10N 51°35W 154 E5
Godwin Austen = K2 Pakistan 35°58N 76°32E 243 B7
Goeie Hoop, Kaap die = Good Hope, C. of S. Africa 34°24S 18°30E 270 D2
Goéland, L. au Canada 49°50N 76°48W 298 C4
Goélands, L. aux Canada 55°27N 64°17W 299 A7
Goeree Neths. 51°50N 4°0E 170 C3
Goes Neths. 51°30N 3°55E 170 C3
Gofca ➔ Somali Rep. 1°10N 43°43E 267 D5
Goffstown U.S.A. 43°1N 71°36W 313 C13
Gogama Canada 47°35N 81°43W 298 C3
Gogar U.K. 55°56N 3°20W 121 B2
Gogebic, L. U.S.A. 46°30N 89°35W 308 B9
Goggetti Ethiopia 8°11N 38°35E 257 F4
Gogolin Poland 50°30N 18°0E 185 H5
Gogounou Benin 10°50N 2°50E 263 C5
Gogra = Ghaghara ➔ India 25°45N 84°40E 243 G11
Gogriâl Sudan 8°30N 28°8E 257 F2
Gogti Ethiopia 10°7N 42°51E 257 E5
Gohana India 29°8N 76°42E 242 E7
Goharganj India 23°1N 77°41E 242 H7
Goheung S. Korea 34°36N 127°17E 224 E3
Goi ➔ India 22°4N 74°46E 242 H6
Goiana Brazil 7°33S 34°59W 332 C5
Goianésia Brazil 15°18S 49°7W 333 E2
Goiânia Brazil 16°43S 49°20W 333 E2
Goiás Brazil 15°55S 50°10W 333 E1
Goiás □ Brazil 12°10S 48°0W 332 D2
Goiatuba Brazil 18°1S 49°23W 333 E2
Goidu Atoll Maldives 4°53N 72°54E 272 d
Goio-Erê Brazil 24°12S 53°1W 335 A5
Góis Portugal 40°10N 8°6W 194 E2
Gojam Ethiopia 10°55N 36°30E 257 E4
Gojeb, Wabi ➔ Ethiopia 7°12N 36°40E 257 F4
Gojō Japan 34°21N 135°42E 223 C7
Gojra Pakistan 31°10N 72°40E 242 D5
Gokak India 16°11N 74°52E 245 F2
Gokarn India 14°33N 74°17E 245 G2
Gökçe = Sevana Lich Armenia 40°30N 45°20E 191 K7
Gökçeada Turkey 40°10N 25°50E 203 F9
Gökçedağ Turkey 39°33N 28°56E 205 B10
Gökçen Turkey 38°7N 27°53E 205 C9
Gökçeören Turkey 38°37N 28°35E 205 C10
Gökçeyazı Turkey 39°40N 27°40E 205 B9
Gökırmak ➔ Turkey 41°25N 35°8E 212 B6
Gökova Turkey 37°1N 28°17E 205 D10
Gökova Körfezi Turkey 36°55N 27°50E 205 E9
Göksu ➔ Turkey 36°19N 34°5E 250 B5
Göksun Turkey 38°2N 36°30E 212 C7
Gokteik Burma 22°26N 97°0E 241 D6
Göktepe Karaman, Turkey 36°37N 32°37E 250 B3
Göktepe Muğla, Turkey 37°25N 28°34E 205 D10
Göktürk Turkey 41°10N 28°53E 122 A1
Gokurt Pakistan 29°40N 67°26E 242 E2
Gokwe Zimbabwe 18°7S 28°58E 271 A4
Gol Norway 60°42N 8°55E 164 D5
Gol Gol Australia 34°12S 142°14E 282 C5
Gola India 28°30N 80°32E 243 E9
Golabari India 22°35N 88°20E 124 B2
Golabki Poland 52°12N 20°52E 142 B1
Golaghat India 26°30N 94°0E 241 B5
Golakganj India 26°8N 89°52E 241 B2
Golan Heights = Hagolan Syria 33°0N 35°45E 250 F6
Gołańcz Poland 52°57N 17°18E 185 F4
Golāshkerd Iran 27°59N 57°16E 247 E8
Golaya Pristen = Hola Pristan Ukraine 46°29N 32°32E 189 J7
Gölbaşı Adiyaman, Turkey 37°43N 37°25E 212 D7
Gölbaşı Ankara, Turkey 39°47N 32°49E 212 C5
Golchikha Russia 71°45N 83°30E 150 B12
Golconda India 17°24N 78°23E 244 F4
Golconda Nev., U.S.A. 40°58N 117°30W 304 F5
Gölcük Kocaeli, Turkey 40°42N 29°48E 203 F13
Gölcük Niğde, Turkey 38°14N 34°47E 212 C6
Gold U.S.A. 41°52N 77°50W 312 E7
Gold Beach U.S.A. 42°25N 124°25W 304 E1
Gold Coast = Ghana ■ W. Afr. 8°0N 1°0W 263 D4
Gold Coast Queens., Australia 28°0S 153°25E 276 F9
Gold Coast Chicago, U.S.A. 4°0N 1°40W 119 a2
Gold Coast W. Afr. 4°0N 1°40W 263 E4
Gold Creek U.S.A. 62°46N 149°41W 303 E10
Gold Hill U.S.A. 42°26N 123°3W 304 E2
Gold River Canada 49°46N 126°3W 296 D3
Gołdap Poland 54°19N 22°18E 184 D9
Goldberg = Złotoryja Poland 51°8N 15°55E 185 G2
Goldberg Germany 53°35N 12°4E 178 B8
Golden B.C., Canada 51°20N 116°59W 296 C5
Golden Ill., U.S.A. 40°7N 91°1W 310 D5
Golden B. N.Z. 40°40S 172°50E 285 A7
Golden Gate U.S.A. 37°48N 122°29W 136 B2
Golden Gate ⌂ U.S.A. 37°49N 122°31W 136 A2
Golden Gate Bridge U.S.A. 37°49N 122°28W 136 B2
Golden Gate Highlands △ S. Africa 28°40S 28°40E 271 C4
Golden Gate Park U.S.A. 37°46N 122°28W 136 B2
Golden Grove Middlesex, Jamaica 18°19N 77°9W 320 a
Golden Grove Surrey, Jamaica 17°55N 76°16W 320 a
Golden Hinde Canada 49°40N 125°44W 296 D3
Golden Horn = Haliç Turkey 41°1N 28°57E 122 B1
Golden Lake Canada 45°34N 77°21W 312 A7
Golden Rock India 10°45N 78°48E 245 J4
Golden Spike ⌂ U.S.A. 41°37N 112°33W 304 F7
Golden Vale Ireland 52°33N 8°17W 166 D3
Goldendale U.S.A. 45°49N 120°50W 304 D3
Golders Green U.K. 51°34N 0°11W 125 A2
Goldfield U.S.A. 37°42N 117°14W 305 H5
Goldingen = Kuldīga Latvia 56°58N 21°59E 184 B8
Goldsand L. Canada 57°2N 101°8W 297 B8
Goldsboro U.S.A. 35°23N 77°59W 315 D16
Goldsmith U.S.A. 31°59N 102°37W 314 F3
Goldthwaite U.S.A. 31°27N 98°34W 314 F5
Golegã Portugal 39°24N 8°29W 195 F2
Goleniów Poland 53°35N 14°50E 184 E1
Golestān □ Iran 37°20N 55°25E 247 B7
Golestan Palace Iran 35°41N 51°25E 141 A2
Golestānak Iran 30°36N 54°14E 247 D7
Goleta U.S.A. 34°27N 119°50W 307 L7
Golfito Costa Rica 8°41N 83°5W 320 E3
Golfo Aranci Italy 40°59N 9°38E 200 B2
Golfo di Orosei e del Gennargentu △ Italy 40°5N 9°15E 200 B2
Gölgeli Dağları Turkey 37°10N 28°55E 205 D10
Gölhisar Turkey 37°8N 29°31E 205 D11
Goliad U.S.A. 28°40N 97°23W 314 G6
Golija Montenegro 43°5N 18°45E 202 C2
Golija Serbia 43°22N 20°15E 202 C4
Golina Poland 52°15N 18°4E 185 F5
Goljam Bratan = Morozov Bulgaria 42°30N 25°10E 203 D9
Gölköy Turkey 40°41N 37°37E 212 B7
Gollans Stream ➔ N.Z. 41°22S 174°52E 143 B2
Gollel = Lavumisa Swaziland 27°20S 31°55E 271 C5
Göllersdorf Austria 48°29N 16°7E 180 C9
Gollnow = Goleniów Poland 53°35N 14°50E 184 E1
Gölmarmara Turkey 38°42N 27°55E 205 C9
Golo ➔ France 42°31N 9°32E 175 F13
Golol Somali Rep. 3°38N 43°49E 267 D5
Gölova Turkey 36°48N 30°5E 205 E12
Golovin U.S.A. 64°33N 163°2W 303 D7
Golpāyegān Iran 33°27N 50°18E 247 C6
Gölpazarı Turkey 40°16N 30°18E 212 B4
Golra Pakistan 33°37N 72°56E 242 C5
Golspie U.K. 57°58N 3°59W 167 D5
Golub-Dobrzyń Poland 53°7N 19°2E 185 E6
Golubac Serbia 44°38N 21°38E 202 B5
Golungo Alto Angola 9°8S 14°46E 265 D2
Golyam Perelik Bulgaria 41°36N 24°33E 203 E8
Golyama Kamchiya ➔ Bulgaria 43°10N 27°55E 203 C11
Golyevo Russia 55°48N 37°18E 129 B1
Golyshi = Vetluzhskiy Russia 58°23N 45°26E 190 A7
Goma Dem. Rep. of the Congo 1°37S 29°10E 268 C2
Gomal Pass Pakistan 31°56N 69°20E 242 D3
Gomati ➔ India 25°32N 83°11E 243 G10
Gombari Dem. Rep. of the Congo 2°45N 29°3E 268 B2
Gombe Dem. Rep. of the Congo 0°45S 17°36E 264 C3
Gombe Nigeria 10°19N 11°2E 263 C7
Gombe Turkey 36°33N 29°38E 205 E11
Gombe □ Nigeria 10°0N 11°0E 263 C7
Gombe ➔ Tanzania 4°38S 31°40E 268 C3
Gombi Nigeria 10°12N 12°30E 263 C7
Gomel = Homyel Belarus 52°28N 31°0E 177 B16
Gomera Canary Is. 28°7N 17°14W 153 e1
Gómez Palacio Mexico 25°34N 103°30W 318 B4
Gomfi Greece 39°26N 21°36E 204 B3
Gomīshān Iran 37°4N 54°6E 247 B7
Gommern Germany 52°4N 11°50E 178 C7
Gomogomo Indonesia 6°39S 134°43E 231 F8
Gomoh India 23°52N 86°10E 243 H12
Gomotartsi Bulgaria 44°6N 22°57E 202 B6
Gompa = Ganta Liberia 7°15N 8°59W 262 D3
Gonābād Iran 34°15N 58°45E 247 C8
Gonaïves Haiti 19°20N 72°42W 321 C5
Gonarezhou △ Zimbabwe 21°32S 31°55E 269 G3
Gonâve, G. de la Haiti 19°29N 72°42W 321 C5
Gonâve, Île de la Haiti 18°51N 73°3W 321 C5
Gonbad-e Kāvūs Iran 37°20N 55°25E 247 B7
Gönc Hungary 48°28N 21°14E 182 B6
Gonda India 27°9N 81°58E 243 F9
Gondal India 21°58N 70°52E 242 J4
Gonder Ethiopia 12°39N 37°30E 257 E4
Gondia India 21°23N 80°10E 244 D5
Gondola Mozam. 19°10S 33°37E 269 F3
Gondomar Portugal 41°10N 8°35W 194 D2
Gondrecourt-le-Château France 48°31N 5°30E 173 D12
Gonen Israel 31°46N 35°13E 123 B2
Gönen Balıkesir, Turkey 40°6N 27°39E 203 F11
Gönen Isparta, Turkey 37°57N 30°31E 205 D12
Gönen ➔ Turkey 40°6N 27°39E 203 F11
Gong Xian China 28°23N 104°47E 228 C5
Gong'an China 30°7N 112°12E 229 B9
Gongbei China 22°12N 113°32E 219 G10
Gongchangling China 41°7N 123°27E 224 B1
Gongcheng China 24°50N 110°49E 229 E8
Gongga Shan China 29°40N 101°55E 228 C3
Gongguan China 21°48N 109°36E 228 G7
Gonghe China 36°18N 100°32E 218 C5
Gongju S. Korea 36°27N 127°7E 224 D3
Gongliu China 43°28N 82°8E 217 D10
Gongming China 22°47N 113°53E 219 F10
Gongneung S. Korea 37°36N 127°3E 128 D2
Gongo Yembe Dem. Rep. of the Congo 1°58S 18°40E 264 C3
Gongola ➔ Nigeria 9°30N 12°4E 263 D7
Gongolgon Australia 30°21S 146°54E 281 E4
Gongoué Gabon 0°31S 9°13E 264 C1
Gongshan China 27°43N 98°29E 228 D2
Gongtan China 28°55N 108°20E 228 C7
Gongzhuling China 43°30N 124°40E 227 C13
Goni Greece 39°52N 22°29E 204 B4
Goniadz Poland 53°30N 22°44E 184 E9
Goniri Nigeria 11°30N 12°15E 263 C7
Gonjo China 30°52N 98°17E 228 B2
Gonnesa Italy 39°16N 8°28E 200 C1
Gonnosfanádiga Italy 39°29N 8°39E 200 C1
Gonzaga Phil. 18°16N 122°0E 232 B4
Gonzales Calif., U.S.A. 36°30N 121°26W 306 J5
Gonzales Tex., U.S.A. 29°30N 97°27W 314 G6
González Mexico 22°48N 98°25W 319 C5
González Chaves Argentina 38°2S 60°5W 334 D3
Goobang △ Australia 33°0S 148°32E 283 B8
Good Hope, C. of S. Africa 34°24S 18°30E 270 D2
Good Hope Plantation Jamaica 18°25N 77°41W 320 a
Goodenough I. Papua N. G. 9°20S 150°15E 286 E6
Gooderham Canada 44°54N 78°21W 312 B6
Goodhouse S. Africa 28°57S 18°13E 270 C2
Gooding U.S.A. 42°56N 114°43W 304 E6
Goodland U.S.A. 39°21N 101°43W 308 F3
Goodlands Mauritius 20°2S 57°39E 272 e
Goodlow Canada 56°20N 120°8W 296 B4
Goodmayes U.K. 51°33N 0°6E 125 A4
Goodnews Bay U.S.A. 59°7N 161°35W 303 G7
Goodooga Australia 29°3S 147°28E 281 D4
Goodsprings U.S.A. 35°49N 115°27W 307 K11
Goodwater U.S.A. 33°4N 86°3W 316 B3
Goodwood S. Africa 33°55S 18°32E 118 A2
Goole U.K. 53°42N 0°53W 168 D7
Goolgowi Australia 33°58S 145°41E 283 B6
Goolwa Australia 35°30S 138°47E 282 C3
Goomalling Australia 31°15S 116°49E 279 F2
Goomeri Australia 26°12S 152°6E 281 D5
Goonda Mozam. 19°48S 33°57E 269 F3
Goondiwindi Australia 28°30S 150°21E 281 D5
Goongarrie, L. Australia 30°3S 121°9E 279 F3
Goongarrie △ Australia 30°7S 121°30E 279 F3
Goonyella Australia 21°47S 147°58E 280 C4
Goose ➔ Canada 53°20N 60°35W 299 B7
Goose Creek U.S.A. 32°59N 80°2W 316 C9
Goose L. U.S.A. 41°56N 120°26W 304 F3
Gooty India 15°7N 77°41E 245 G3
Gop India 22°5N 69°50E 242 H3
Gopalganj Bangla. 23°1N 89°50E 241 D2
Gopalganj India 26°28N 84°30E 243 F11
Gopalpur India 22°38N 88°22E 124 B2
Göppingen Germany 48°42N 9°39E 179 G5
Gor Spain 37°23N 2°58W 195 H8
Góra Dolnośląskie, Poland 51°40N 16°31E 185 G3
Góra Mazowieckie, Poland 52°39N 20°6E 185 F7
Góra Kalwaria Poland 51°59N 21°14E 185 G8
Gorakhpur India 26°47N 83°23E 243 F10
Goražde Bos.-H. 43°38N 18°58E 182 G3
Gorbatov Russia 56°12N 43°2E 190 B6
Gorbea, Peña Spain 43°1N 2°50W 196 B2
Górce Poland 52°15N 20°55E 142 B1
Gorczański △ Poland 49°30N 20°10E 185 J7
Gorda, Banco W. Indies 15°40N 80°27W 320 C3
Gorda, Pta. Canary Is. 28°45N 18°0W 153 e1
Gorda, Pta. Nic. 14°20N 83°10W 320 D3
Gordan B. Australia 11°35S 130°10E 278 B5
Gördes Turkey 38°54N 28°17E 205 C10
Gordon Ga., U.S.A. 32°54N 83°20W 316 C6
Gordon Nebr., U.S.A. 42°48N 102°12W 308 D2
Gordon ➔ Australia 42°27S 145°30E 281 G4
Gordon, I. Chile 54°55S 69°30W 336 D3
Gordon L. Alta., Canada 56°30N 110°25W 297 B6
Gordon L. N.W.T., Canada 63°5N 113°11W 296 A6
Gordonvale Australia 17°5S 145°50E 280 B4
Goré Chad 7°59N 16°31E 259 G3
Gore Ethiopia 8°12N 35°32E 257 F4
Gore N.Z. 46°5S 168°58E 285 G3
Gore Bay Canada 45°57N 82°28W 298 C3
Gore Hill Australia 33°49S 151°10E 139 A2
Görele Turkey 41°2N 39°0E 213 B8
Gorelyy ➔ Russia 60°1N 30°30E 137 A3
Goreme Turkey 38°35N 34°52E 212 C6
Gorenki Russia 55°47N 37°53E 129 B5
Gorey Ireland 52°41N 6°18W 166 D5
Gorg Iran 29°29N 59°43E 247 D8
Gorgān Iran 36°55N 54°30E 247 B7
Gorgie U.K. 55°56N 3°14W 121 B2
Gorgol □ Mauritania 15°45N 13°0W 262 B2
Gorgona Italy 43°26N 9°54E 198 E6
Gorgora Ethiopia 12°15N 37°17E 257 E4
Gorgoram Nigeria 12°40N 10°45E 263 C7
Gorham U.S.A. 44°23N 71°10W 313 B13
Gori Georgia 42°0N 44°7E 191 J7
Goribidnur = Gauribidanur India 13°37N 77°32E 245 H3
Goriganga ➔ India 29°45N 80°23E 243 E9
Gorinchem Neths. 51°50N 4°59E 170 C4
Gorinhatã Brazil 19°15S 49°45W 333 E2
Goris Armenia 39°31N 46°22E 213 C12
Goritsy Russia 57°4N 36°43E 188 D9
Gorízia Italy 45°56N 13°37E 199 C10
Gorj □ Romania 45°5N 23°25E 183 E8
Gorki = Horki Belarus 54°17N 30°59E 188 E6
Gorkiy = Nizhniy Novgorod Russia 56°20N 44°0E 190 B7
Gorkovskoye Vdkhr. Russia 57°2N 43°4E 190 B6
Gorky Park Russia 55°43N 37°36E 129 B3
Gorleston U.K. 52°35N 1°44E 169 E9
Gorlice Poland 49°35N 21°11E 185 J8
Görlitz Germany 51°9N 14°58E 178 D10
Gorlovka = Horlivka Ukraine 48°19N 38°5E 189 H10
Gorman U.S.A. 34°47N 118°51W 307 L8
Gorna Djumaya = Blagoevgrad Bulgaria 42°2N 23°5E 202 D7
Gorna Dzhumayo = Blagoevgrad Bulgaria 42°2N 23°5E 202 D7
Gorna Oryakhovitsa Bulgaria 43°7N 25°40E 203 C9
Gornja Radgona Slovenia 46°40N 16°2E 199 B13
Gornja Tuzla Bos.-H. 44°35N 18°46E 182 F3
Gornji Grad Slovenia 46°20N 14°52E 199 B11
Gornji Milanovac Serbia 44°3N 20°29E 202 B4
Gornji Vakuf Bos.-H. 43°57N 17°34E 182 G2
Gorno Ablanovo Bulgaria 43°37N 25°43E 203 C9
Gorno-Altay □ Russia 51°0N 86°0E 217 B11
Gorno-Altaysk Russia 51°50N 86°5E 217 B11
Gorno-Badakhshan = Kŭhiston-Badakhshon □ Tajikistan 38°30N 73°0E 217 E8
Gornyak Russia 50°59N 81°27E 217 B10
Gornyatski Russia 67°32N 64°3E 186 A11
Gornyatskiy Russia 48°18N 40°56E 191 F5
Gornyy Saratov, Russia 51°50N 48°30E 190 E9
Gornyy Sib., Russia 44°57N 133°59E 220 B6
Goro ➔ C.A.R. 9°14N 21°16E 264 A4
Gorodenka = Horodenka Ukraine 48°41N 25°29E 183 B10
Gorodets Russia 56°38N 43°28E 190 B6
Gorodishche = Horodyshche Ukraine 49°17N 31°27E 189 H6
Gorodishche Russia 53°13N 45°40E 190 D7
Gorodnya = Horodnya Ukraine 51°55N 31°33E 189 G6
Gorodok = Haradok Belarus 55°30N 30°3E 188 E6
Gorodok = Horodok Ukraine 49°46N 23°32E 177 D12
Gorodok = Zakamensk Russia 50°23N 103°17E 215 D11
Gorodovikovsk Russia 46°8N 41°58E 191 G5
Goroka Papua N. G. 6°7S 145°25E 286 D3
Goroke Australia 36°43S 141°29E 282 D4
Gorokhov = Horokhiv Ukraine 50°30N 24°45E 177 C13
Gorokhovets Russia 56°13N 42°39E 190 B6
Gorom Gorom Burkina Faso 14°26N 0°14W 263 C4
Goromonzi Zimbabwe 17°52S 31°22E 269 F3
Gorong, Kepulauan Indonesia 3°59S 131°25E 231 E8
Gorongosa △ Mozam. 18°50S 34°29E 271 A5
Gorongose ➔ Mozam. 20°30S 34°40E 271 B5
Gorongoza Mozam. 18°44S 34°2E 269 F3
Gorongoza, Sa. da Mozam. 18°27S 34°2E 269 F3
Gorontalo Indonesia 0°35N 123°5E 231 D6
Gorontalo □ Indonesia 0°50N 122°20E 231 D6
Goronyo Nigeria 13°29N 5°39E 263 C6
Górowo Iławeckie Poland 54°17N 20°30E 184 D7
Gorron France 48°25N 0°50W 172 D6
Gorror Micronesia 9°26N 138°4E 287 S16
Gorshechnoye Russia 51°31N 38°2E 189 G10
Gort Ireland 53°3N 8°49W 166 C3
Gortis Greece 35°4N 24°58E 207 E5
Gorumahisani India 22°20N 86°24E 244 C8
Góry Bystrzyckie Poland 50°16N 16°33E 185 H3
Goryachiy Klyuch Russia 44°38N 39°8E 191 H4
Goryeong S. Korea 35°44N 128°15E 224 E4
Gorzkowice Poland 51°13N 19°36E 185 G6
Górzno Poland 53°12N 19°38E 185 E6
Gorzów Śląski Poland 51°3N 18°22E 185 G5
Gorzów Wielkopolski Poland 52°43N 15°15E 185 F2
Gose Japan 34°27N 135°44E 223 C7
Gosen Germany 52°23N 13°43E 115 B5
Gosener kanal Germany 52°24N 13°42E 115 B5
Goseong S. Korea 34°58N 128°19E 224 E4
Gosford Australia 33°23S 151°18E 283 B9
Goshen Calif., U.S.A. 36°21N 119°25W 306 J7
Goshen Ind., U.S.A. 41°35N 85°50W 311 C11
Goshen N.Y., U.S.A. 41°24N 74°20W 313 E10
Goshogawara Japan 40°48N 140°27E 220 D10
Goskopi = Kopeysk Russia 55°7N 61°37E 216 A6
Goslar Germany 51°54N 10°25E 178 D6
Gospel Oak U.K. 51°32N 0°9W 125 A3
Gospić Croatia 44°35N 15°23E 199 D12
Gosport Hants., U.K. 50°48N 1°9W 169 G6
Gosport Ind., U.S.A. 39°21N 86°40W 311 E10
Gossa Norway 62°52N 6°50E 164 B3
Gossas Senegal 14°28N 16°0W 262 C1
Gosse ➔ Australia 19°32S 134°37E 280 B1
Gossi Mali 15°48N 1°20W 263 B4
Gossinga Sudan 8°36N 25°59E 257 F2
Gostingen = Gostyń Poland 51°50N 17°3E 185 G4
Gostinopolye = Volkhov Russia 59°55N 32°15E 188 C7
Gostivar Macedonia 41°48N 20°57E 202 E4
Gostyń Poland 51°50N 17°3E 185 G4
Gostynin Poland 52°26N 19°29E 185 F6
Göta älv ➔ Sweden 57°42N 11°54E 163 G5
Göta kanal Sweden 58°30N 15°58E 163 F9
Götaland Sweden 57°30N 14°30E 163 G8
Gotanda Japan 35°37N 139°43E 140 B3
Göteborg Sweden 57°43N 11°59E 163 G5
Gotemba Japan 35°18N 138°56E 223 B10
Götene Sweden 58°32N 13°30E 163 F7
Gotenhafen = Gdynia Poland 54°35N 18°33E 184 D5
Goteşti Moldova 46°9N 28°10E 183 D13
Goth Goli Mar Pakistan 24°53N 67°1E 123 A2
Goth Sher Shah Pakistan 24°53N 66°59E 123 A1
Gotha Thüringen, Germany 50°56N 10°42E 178 E6
Gotha Fla., U.S.A. 28°31N 81°31W 133 A1
Gothenburg = Göteborg Sweden 57°43N 11°59E 163 G5
Gothenburg U.S.A. 40°56N 100°10W 308 E3
Gothèye Niger 13°52N 1°34E 263 C5
Gotland Sweden 57°30N 18°33E 163 G12
Gotlands län □ Sweden 57°15N 18°30E 163 G12
Goto Meer Neth. Ant. 12°14N 68°22W 322 h
Gotō-Rettō Japan 32°55N 129°5E 221 H4
Gotse Delchev Bulgaria 41°36N 23°46E 202 E7
Gotska Sandön Sweden 58°24N 19°15E 161 G18
Gōtsu Japan 35°0N 132°14E 222 C4
Gott Pk. Canada 50°18N 122°16W 296 C4
Góttero, Monte Italy 44°22N 9°42E 198 D6
Gottesberg = Boguszów-Gorce Poland 50°45N 16°12E 185 H3
Göttingen Germany 51°31N 9°55E 178 D5
Gottschee = Kočevje Slovenia 45°39N 14°50E 199 C11
Gottwald = Zmiyev Ukraine 49°39N 36°27E 189 H9
Gottwaldov = Zlín Czech Rep. 49°14N 17°40E 181 B10
Goubangzi China 41°20N 121°52E 227 D11
Gouda Neths. 52°1N 4°42E 170 B4
Goudiry Senegal 14°15N 12°45W 262 C2
Goudoumaria Niger 13°40N 11°10E 259 F2
Goudouras, Akra Greece 34°59N 26°6E 207 F7
Gouéké Guinea 8°2N 8°43W 262 D3
Gough I. Atl. Oc. 40°10S 9°45W 152 L11
Gouin, Rés. Canada 48°35N 74°40W 298 C5
Gouitafla Ivory C. 7°30N 5°53W 262 D3
Goulburn Australia 34°44S 149°44E 283 C8
Goulburn Is. Australia 11°40S 133°20E 280 A1
Goulburn River △ Australia 32°19S 150°10E 283 B9
Goulds U.S.A. 25°33N 80°23W 317 K9
Goulia Ivory C. 10°1N 7°11W 262 C3
Goulimine Morocco 28°56N 10°0W 260 C3
Goulimine □ Morocco 29°8N 9°2W 260 C3
Goulmima Morocco 31°41N 4°57W 260 B4
Goumbou Mali 15°2N 7°25W 262 B3
Goumenissa Greece 40°56N 22°37E 202 F6
Gounatolo Solomon Is. 8°25S 160°52E 287 M11
Goundam Mali 16°27N 3°40W 262 B4
Goundi Chad 9°22N 17°21E 259 G3
Gounou-Gaya Chad 9°38N 15°31E 259 G3
Goura Greece 37°56N 22°20E 204 D4
Gouraya Algeria 36°31N 1°56E 261 A5
Gourbassi Mali 13°24N 11°38W 262 C2
Gourbeyre Guadeloupe 16°0N 61°41W 322 e
Gourde, Pt. Trin. & Tob. 10°40N 61°38W 323 t
Gourdon France 44°44N 1°23E 174 D5
Gouré Niger 14°0N 10°10E 259 F2
Gouri Chad 18°50N 16°49E 259 E3
Gourin France 48°8N 3°37W 172 D3
Gourits ➔ S. Africa 34°21S 21°52E 270 D3
Gourma-Rharous Mali 16°55N 1°50W 263 B4
Gournay-en-Bray France 49°29N 1°44E 173 C8
Gournay-sur-Marne France 48°51N 2°34E 134 A4
Gournes Greece 35°19N 25°16E 207 E6
Gouro Chad 19°36N 19°36E 259 E3
Gourock U.K. 55°57N 4°49W 167 F4
Gourock Ra. Australia 36°0S 149°25E 283 D8
Goursi Burkina Faso 12°42N 2°37W 262 C4
Gouvêa Brazil 18°27S 43°44W 333 E3
Gouverneur U.S.A. 44°20N 75°28W 313 B9
Gouvia Greece 39°39N 19°50E 206 B9
Gouyave Grenada 12°10N 61°44W 323 q
Gouzon France 46°12N 2°14E 173 F9
Governador, I. do Brazil 22°48S 43°13W 135 A1
Governador Valadares Brazil 18°15S 41°57W 333 E3
Governor Generoso Phil. 6°39N 126°5E 233 H6
Governor's Harbour Bahamas 25°10N 76°14W 320 A4
Governors I. New York, U.S.A. 132 f1
Govĭaltay □ Mongolia 45°30N 96°0E 217 C13
Govindgarh India 24°23N 81°18E 243 G9
Gowan Ra. Australia 25°0S 145°0E 280 D4
Gowanda U.S.A. 42°28N 78°56W 312 D6
Gower U.K. 51°35N 4°10W 169 F3
Gowers Corner U.S.A. 28°20N 82°30W 317 G7
Gowna, L. Ireland 53°51N 7°34W 166 C4
Gowrie U.S.A. 42°17N 94°17W 310 B2
Gowurdak Turkmenistan 37°50N 66°4E 217 E7
Goya Argentina 29°10S 59°10W 334 B4
Goyang S. Korea 37°39N 126°50E 224 D3
Goyave Guadeloupe 16°8N 61°34W 322 e
Goyaves, Grande Rivière ➔ Guadeloupe 16°18N 61°36W 322 e
Göyçay Azerbaijan 40°42N 47°43E 191 K8
Goyder Lagoon Australia 27°3S 138°58E 281 D2
Goyllarisquisga Peru 10°31S 76°24W 330 C2
Göynük Antalya, Turkey 36°41N 30°33E 205 E12
Göynük Bolu, Turkey 40°24N 30°48E 212 B4
Goz Beïda Chad 12°10N 21°20E 259 F4
Goz Regeb Sudan 16°3N 35°33E 257 D4
Gozdnica Poland 51°28N 15°4E 185 G2
Gözneköy Turkey 36°58N 34°33E 250 B5
Gozo Malta 36°3N 14°15E 206 E7
Graaff-Reinet S. Africa 32°13S 24°32E 270 D3
Graben Vienna, Austria 142 b2
Grabill U.S.A. 41°13N 84°57W 311 C12
Grabo Ivory C. 4°57N 7°30W 262 D3
Grabow Mecklenburg-Vorpommern, Germany 53°17N 11°34E 178 B7
Grabów Warszawa, Poland 52°8N 20°59E 142 C1
Grabów nad Prosną Poland 51°31N 18°7E 185 G5
Graça Lisbon, Portugal 126 b3
Gračac Croatia 44°18N 15°57E 199 D12
Gračanica Bos.-H. 44°43N 18°18E 182 F3
Graçay France 47°10N 1°50E 173 E8
Grace, Mt. N.Z. 41°20S 174°55E 143 B2
Grace Cathedral San Francisco, U.S.A. 136 b2
Gracefield N.Z. 41°14S 174°55E 143 B2
Graceville U.S.A. 30°58N 85°31W 316 E4
Gracewood U.S.A. 33°22N 82°2W 316 B7
Gracia Spain 41°24N 2°10E 114 A2
Gracias a Dios, C. Honduras 15°0N 83°10W 320 D3
Graciosa Azores 39°4N 28°0W 153 d1
Graciosa, I. Canary Is. 29°15N 13°32W 153 e2
Grad Sofiya □ Bulgaria 42°35N 23°20E 202 D7
Gradac Montenegro 43°23N 19°9E 202 C3
Gradačac Bos.-H. 44°52N 18°26E 182 F3
Gradaús Brazil 7°43S 51°11W 332 C1
Gradaús, Serra dos Brazil 8°0S 50°45W 332 C1
Gradeška Planina Macedonia 41°30N 22°15E 202 E6
Gradets Bulgaria 42°46N 26°30E 203 D10
Gradišće Slovenia 46°37N 15°50E 199 B12
Grădiştea de Munte Romania 45°37N 23°13E 183 E8
Grado Italy 45°40N 13°23E 199 C10
Grado Spain 43°23N 6°4W 194 B4
Grady U.S.A. 34°49N 103°19W 305 J12
Graeca, Lacul Romania 44°5N 26°10E 183 F11
Grafarnes Iceland 64°55N 23°16W 155 C3
Gräfelfing Germany 48°7N 11°25E 131 B1
Grafenau Germany 48°51N 13°22E 179 G9
Gräfenberg Germany 49°39N 11°14E 179 F7
Grafham Water U.K. 52°19N 0°18W 169 E7
Grafton N.S.W., Australia 29°38S 152°58E 281 D5
Grafton Ill., U.S.A. 38°58N 90°26W 310 F6
Grafton N. Dak., U.S.A. 48°25N 97°25W 308 A5
Grafton W. Va., U.S.A. 39°21N 80°2W 309 F13
Grafton Caledonia Wildlife Estate Trin. & Tob. 11°11N 60°47W 323 s
Grafton's Pt. Anguilla 18°20N 62°54W 322 a
Gragoatá Brazil 22°53S 43°8W 135 B2
Graham Ont., Canada 49°20N 90°30W 298 C1
Graham Ga., U.S.A. 31°50N 82°30W 316 D7
Graham Tex., U.S.A. 33°6N 98°35W 314 E5
Graham, Mt. U.S.A. 32°42N 109°52W 305 K9
Graham Bell, Ostrov = Greem-Bell, Ostrov Russia 81°0N 62°0E 214 A7
Graham I. Canada 53°40N 132°30W 296 C2
Graham Land Antarctica 65°0S 64°0W 151 C17
Grahamstown S. Africa 33°19S 26°31E 270 D4
Grahamsville U.S.A. 41°51N 74°33W 313 E10
Grahovo Montenegro 42°40N 18°40E 202 D2
Graïba Tunisia 34°30N 10°13E 258 B2
Graie, Alpi Europe 45°30N 7°10E 175 C11
Grain Coast W. Afr. 4°20N 10°0W 262 E3
Grajagan Indonesia 8°35S 114°13E 231 K17
Grajagan, Teluk Indonesia 8°40S 114°18E 231 K17
Grajaú Brazil 5°50S 46°4W 332 C2
Grajaú ➔ Brazil 3°41S 44°48W 332 B3
Grajewo Poland 53°39N 22°30E 184 E9
Gramada Bulgaria 43°49N 22°39E 202 C6
Gramat France 44°48N 1°43E 174 D5
Grammichele Italy 37°13N 14°38E 201 E7
Grámmos, Óros Greece 40°18N 20°47E 202 F4
Grampian U.S.A. 40°58N 78°37W 312 F6
Grampian Highlands = Grampian Mts. U.K. 56°50N 4°0W 167 E5
Grampian Mts. U.K. 56°50N 4°0W 167 E5
Grampians, The Australia 37°15S 142°20E 282 D5
Grampians △ Australia 37°15S 142°28E 282 D5
Gramsh Albania 40°52N 20°12E 202 F4
Gran Norway 60°23N 10°31E 164 D7
Gran ➔ Suriname 4°1N 55°30W 329 C6
Gran Altiplanicie Central Argentina 49°0S 69°30W 336 C3
Gran Canaria Canary Is. 27°55N 15°35W 153 e1
Gran Chaco S. Amer. 25°0S 61°0W 334 B3
Gran Couva Trin. & Tob. 10°24N 61°22W 323 t
Gran Desierto del Pinacate △ Mexico 31°51N 113°32W 318 A2
Gran Laguna Salada Argentina 44°24S 67°23W 336 B3
Gran Pajonal Peru 10°45S 74°30W 330 C3
Gran Paradiso Italy 45°33N 7°17E 198 C4
Gran Sasso d'Itàlia Italy 42°27N 13°42E 199 F10
Gran Sasso e Monti Della Laga △ Italy 42°32N 13°22E 199 F10
Granada Nic. 11°58N 86°0W 320 D2
Granada Spain 37°10N 3°35W 195 H7
Granada Colo., U.S.A. 38°4N 102°19W 304 G12
Granada □ Spain 37°18N 3°0W 195 H7
Granadilla de Abona Canary Is. 28°7N 16°33W 153 e1

Granard Ireland 53°47N 7°30W 166 C4
Granbury U.S.A. 32°27N 97°47W 314 E6
Granby Qué., Canada 45°25N 72°45W 313 A12
Granby Colo., U.S.A. 40°5N 105°56W 304 F11
Grand → Ont., Canada 42°51N 79°34W 312 D5
Grand → Mich., U.S.A. 43°4N 86°15W 311 A10
Grand → Mo., U.S.A. 39°23N 93°7W 310 E3
Grand → S. Dak., U.S.A. 45°40N 100°45W 308 C3
Grand Abaque, Pte.du Guadeloupe 16°21N 61°0W 322 e
Grand Anse Grenada 12°1N 61°45W 323 q
Grand Anse B. Grenada 12°2N 61°45W 323 q
Grand B. Dominica 15°14N 61°18W 323 k
Grand Bahama I. Bahamas 26°40N 78°30W 320 A4
Grand Baie Mauritius 20°0S 57°35E 272 e
Grand Bank Canada 47°6N 55°48W 299 C8
Grand Banks of Newfoundland Atl. Oc. 45°0N 52°0W 152 B6
Grand Bassam Ivory C. 5°10N 3°49W 262 D4
Grand Bassin Réunion 21°10S 55°32E 272 f
Grand Batanga Cameroon 2°50N 9°55E 264 B1
Grand Bazaar = Kapali Carsi Turkey 41°1N 28°58E 122 B1
Grand Bénare Réunion 21°6S 55°25E 272 f
Grand Béréby Ivory C. 4°38N 6°55W 262 E3
Grand Blanc U.S.A. 42°56N 83°38W 311 B13
Grand Bois Mauritius 20°25S 57°32E 272 e
Grand-Bourg Guadeloupe 15°53N 61°19W 322 e
Grand Canal = Da Yunhe → China 39°10N 117°10E 227 E9
Grand Canyon U.S.A. 36°3N 112°9W 305 H7
Grand Canyon △ U.S.A. 36°15N 112°30W 305 H7
Grand Canyon-Parashant △ U.S.A. 36°30N 113°45W 305 H7
Grand Case St.-Martin 18°6N 63°4W 322 a
Grand Cayman Cayman Is. 19°20N 81°20W 320 C3
Grand Central Station New York, U.S.A. 132 c2
Grand Centre Canada 54°25N 110°13W 297 C6
Grand Cess Liberia 4°40N 8°12W 262 E3
Grand Coulee U.S.A. 47°57N 119°0W 304 C4
Grand Coulee Dam U.S.A. 47°57N 118°59W 304 C4
Grand Cul-de-Sac Marin Guadeloupe 16°20N 61°35W 322 e
Grand Erg de Bilma Niger 18°30N 14°0E 259 E2
Grand Étang △ Grenada 12°5N 61°42W 323 q
Grand Falls Canada 47°3N 67°44W 299 C6
Grand Falls-Windsor Canada 48°56N 55°40W 299 C8
Grand Fond St.-Martin 17°53N 62°48W 322 a
Grand Forks B.C., Canada 49°0N 118°30W 296 D5
Grand Forks N. Dak., U.S.A. 47°55N 97°3W 308 B5
Grand Galet Réunion 21°17S 55°38E 272 f
Grand Gaube Mauritius 20°0S 57°39E 272 e
Grand Gorge U.S.A. 42°21N 74°29W 313 D10
Grand Haven U.S.A. 43°4N 86°13W 311 A10
Grand I. Mich., U.S.A. 46°31N 86°40W 308 B10
Grand I. N.Y., U.S.A. 43°0N 78°58W 312 D6
Grand Îlet Guadeloupe 15°50N 61°35W 322 e
Grand Îlet Réunion 21°1S 55°29E 272 f
Grand Island U.S.A. 40°55N 98°21W 308 E4
Grand Isle La., U.S.A. 29°14N 90°0W 315 G9
Grand Isle Vt., U.S.A. 44°43N 73°18W 313 B11
Grand Junction Colo., U.S.A. 39°4N 108°33W 304 G9
Grand Junction Iowa, U.S.A. 42°2N 94°14W 310 B2
Grand L. N.B., Canada 45°57N 66°7W 299 C6
Grand L. Nfld. & L., Canada 49°0N 57°30W 299 C8
Grand L. Nfld. & L., Canada 53°40N 60°30W 299 B7
Grand L. La., U.S.A. 29°55N 92°47W 314 G8
Grand L. Ohio, U.S.A. 40°32N 84°25W 311 D12
Grand Lahou Ivory C. 5°10N 5°5W 262 D3
Grand Lake U.S.A. 40°15N 105°49W 304 F11
Grand Ledge U.S.A. 42°45N 84°45W 311 B12
Grand-Lieu, L. de France 47°6N 1°40W 172 E5
Grand Mal B. Grenada 12°4N 61°45W 323 q
Grand Manan I. Canada 44°45N 66°52W 299 D6
Grand Marais Mich., U.S.A. 46°40N 85°59W 309 B11
Grand Marais Minn., U.S.A. 47°45N 90°25W 298 C1
Grand Marigot B. Dominica 15°25N 61°16W 323 k
Grand-Mère Canada 46°36N 72°40W 298 C5
Grand Palace Bangkok, Thailand 113 b1
Grand Popo Benin 6°15N 1°57E 263 D5
Grand Portage U.S.A. 47°58N 89°41W 308 B9
Grand Prairie U.S.A. 32°44N 96°59W 314 E6
Grand Rapids = Wisconsin Rapids U.S.A. 44°23N 89°49W 308 C9
Grand Rapids Man., Canada 53°12N 99°19W 297 C9
Grand Rapids Mich., U.S.A. 42°58N 85°40W 311 B10
Grand Rapids Minn., U.S.A. 47°14N 93°31W 308 B7
Grand Rapids ✕ (GRR) U.S.A. 42°53N 85°31W 311 B11
Grand Récif Sud N. Cal. 22°47S 166°55E 288 d
Grand Ridge U.S.A. 30°43N 85°1W 316 E4
Grand River U.S.A. 40°49N 93°58W 310 D3
Grand River Bay Mauritius 20°9S 57°27E 272 e
Grand River South East → Mauritius 20°17S 57°46E 272 e
Grand' Rivière Martinique 14°52N 61°11W 322 j
Grand Roy Grenada 12°8N 61°45W 323 q
Grand St-Bernard, Col du Europe 45°50N 7°10E 179 K3
Grand Santi Fr. Guiana 4°20N 54°24W 329 C7
Grand Staircase-Escalante △ U.S.A. 37°25N 111°33W 305 H8
Grand Teton U.S.A. 43°54N 110°50W 304 E8
Grand Teton △ U.S.A. 43°50N 110°50W 304 E8
Grand Union Canal U.K. 52°7N 0°53W 169 E7
Grandas de Salime Spain 43°13N 6°53W 194 B4
Grande → Jujuy, Argentina 24°20S 65°2W 334 A2
Grande → Mendoza, Argentina 36°52S 69°45W 334 D2
Grande → Bolivia 15°51S 64°39W 331 D5
Grande → Bahia, Brazil 11°30S 44°30W 332 D3
Grande → Minas Gerais, Brazil 20°6S 51°4W 333 F1
Grande → Venezuela 8°36N 61°39W 329 B5
Grande, B. Argentina 50°30S 68°20W 336 D3
Grande, I. Brazil 23°9S 44°14W 333 F3
Grande, Rio → N. Amer. 25°58N 97°9W 314 J6
Grande, Serra Piauí, Brazil 8°0S 45°10W 332 C2
Grande, Serra Tocantins, Brazil 11°15S 46°30W 332 D2
Grande Anse = Beauséjour Guadeloupe 16°18N 61°4W 322 e
Grande Anse Guadeloupe 16°19N 61°47W 322 e
Grande Anse Martinique 14°30N 61°5W 322 j
Grande Anse St. Lucia 14°1N 60°54W 323 m
Grande Anse Seychelles 4°18S 55°45E 272 c
Grande Baleine, R. de la → Canada 55°16N 77°47W 298 A4
Grande Cache Canada 53°53N 119°8W 296 C5
Grande Casse, Pte. de la France 45°24N 6°49E 175 C10
Grande Comore Comoros Is. 11°35S 43°20E 272 a
Grand Cul de Sac B St. Lucia 13°59N 61°2W 323 m
Grande-Entrée Canada 47°30N 61°40W 299 C7
Grande Matelot Pt. Trin. & Tob. 10°49N 61°9W 323 t
Grande Place Brussels, Belgium 116 b2
Grande Prairie Canada 55°10N 118°50W 296 B5
Grande Pte. Guadeloupe 15°58N 61°37W 322 e
Grande-Rivière Qué., Canada 48°26N 64°30W 299 C7
Grande Riviere Trin. & Tob. 10°50N 61°3W 323 t
Grande Rivière, Pte. de la Guadeloupe 16°18N 61°36W 322 e
Grande Rivière Noire Mauritius 20°21S 57°21E 272 e
Grande Rivière Sud Est Mauritius 20°17S 57°46E 272 e
Grande Sertão Veredas △ Brazil 15°10S 45°40W 333 E2
Grande-Terre Guadeloupe 16°20N 61°25W 322 e
Grande Terre Mayotte 12°46S 45°7E 272 b
Grande-Vallée Canada 49°14N 65°8W 299 C6
Grande Vigie, Pte. de la Guadeloupe 16°32N 61°27W 322 e
Grandfalls U.S.A. 31°20N 102°51W 314 F3
Grândola Portugal 38°12N 8°35W 195 G2
Grandpré France 49°20N 4°50E 173 C11
Grands Causses △ France 44°5N 2°58E 174 D6
Grands-Jardins △ Canada 47°41N 70°51W 299 C5
Grandview Man., Canada 51°10N 100°42W 297 C8
Grandview Mo., U.S.A. 38°53N 94°32W 310 F2
Grandview Wash., U.S.A. 46°15N 119°54W 304 C4
Grandview Heights U.S.A. 39°58N 83°2W 311 E13
Grandvilliers France 49°40N 1°57E 173 C8
Graneros Chile 34°5S 70°45W 334 C1
Grange Hill Jamaica 18°18N 78°11W 320 a
Grangemouth U.K. 56°1N 3°42W 167 E5
Granger U.S.A. 41°35N 109°58W 304 F9
Grängesberg Sweden 60°6N 15°1E 162 D9
Grangeville U.S.A. 45°56N 116°7W 304 D5
Granisle Canada 54°53N 126°13W 296 C3
Granite City U.S.A. 38°42N 90°8W 310 F6
Granite Falls U.S.A. 44°49N 95°33W 308 C6
Granite L. Canada 48°8N 57°5W 299 C8
Granite Mt. U.S.A. 33°5N 116°28W 307 M10
Granite Pk. U.S.A. 45°10N 109°48W 304 D9
Graniteville S.C., U.S.A. 33°34N 81°49W 316 B8
Graniteville Vt., U.S.A. 44°8N 72°29W 313 B12
Granitola, C. Italy 37°34N 12°39E 200 E5
Granity N.Z. 41°39S 171°51E 285 B6
Granja Brazil 3°7S 40°50W 332 B3
Granja de Moreruela Spain 41°48N 5°44W 194 D5
Granja de Torrehermosa Spain 38°19N 5°35W 195 G5
Grankulla = Kauniainen Finland 60°13N 24°44E 121 B1
Gränna Sweden 58°1N 14°28E 163 F8
Granollers Spain 41°39N 2°18E 196 D7
Gransee Germany 53°1N 13°8E 178 B9
Grant Fla., U.S.A. 27°56N 80°32W 317 H9
Grant Nebr., U.S.A. 40°50N 101°43W 308 E3
Grant, Mt. U.S.A. 38°34N 118°48W 304 G4
Grant City U.S.A. 40°29N 94°25W 310 D2
Grant I. Australia 11°10S 132°52E 278 B5
Grant Park Chicago, U.S.A. 119 c2
Grant Range U.S.A. 38°30N 115°25W 304 G6
Grantham U.K. 52°55N 0°38W 168 E7
Grantley Adams Int. ✕ (BGI) Barbados 13°4N 59°29W 323 r
Granton U.K. 55°58N 3°14W 121 B2
Grantown-on-Spey U.K. 57°20N 3°36W 167 D5
Grants U.S.A. 35°9N 107°52W 305 J10
Grants Pass U.S.A. 42°26N 123°19W 304 E2
Grantsville U.S.A. 40°36N 112°28W 304 F7
Grantville U.S.A. 33°14N 84°50W 316 B5
Granville France 48°50N 1°35W 172 D5
Granville Trin. & Tob. 10°7N 61°48W 323 t
Granville Ill., U.S.A. 41°16N 89°14W 310 C7
Granville N. Dak., U.S.A. 48°16N 100°47W 308 A3
Granville N.Y., U.S.A. 43°24N 73°16W 313 C11
Granville Ohio, U.S.A. 40°4N 82°31W 312 F2
Granville L. Canada 56°18N 100°30W 297 B8
Granvin Norway 60°33N 6°45E 164 D3
Graskop S. Africa 24°56S 30°49E 271 B5
Gräsö Sweden 60°28N 18°35E 162 D12
Grass → Canada 56°3N 96°33W 297 B9
Grass Range U.S.A. 47°2N 108°48W 304 C9
Grass River △ Canada 54°40N 100°50W 297 C8
Grass Valley Calif., U.S.A. 39°13N 121°4W 306 F6
Grass Valley Oreg., U.S.A. 45°22N 120°47W 304 D3
Grassano Italy 40°38N 16°17E 201 B9
Grasse France 43°38N 6°56E 175 E10
Grassflat U.S.A. 41°0N 78°6W 312 E6
Grasslands △ Canada 49°11N 107°38W 297 D7
Grassy Australia 40°3S 144°5E 281 G3
Grassy Park S. Africa 34°3S 18°30E 118 B2
Gråsten Denmark 54°55N 9°35E 163 K3
Grästorp Sweden 58°20N 12°40E 163 F6
Gratis U.S.A. 39°38N 84°32W 311 E12
Gratkorn Austria 47°8N 15°21E 180 D8
Gratosóglio Italy 45°24N 9°1E 129 B2
Gratz U.S.A. 38°28N 84°57W 311 F12
Gratzwalde Germany 52°28N 13°42E 115 B5
Graubünden ☐ Switz. 46°45N 9°30E 179 J5
Graudenz = Grudziądz Poland 53°30N 18°47E 184 E5
Graulhet France 43°45N 1°59E 174 E5
Graus Spain 42°11N 0°20E 196 C5
Gravatá Brazil 8°10S 35°29W 332 C4
Gravberget Norway 60°53N 12°14E 164 D9
Grave, Pte. de France 45°34N 1°4W 174 C2
Gravelbourg Canada 49°50N 106°35W 297 D7
Gravelines France 51°1N 2°10E 173 A9
's-Gravenhage Neths. 52°7N 4°17E 170 B4
Gravenhurst Canada 44°52N 79°20W 312 B5
Gravesend N.S.W., Australia 29°35S 150°20E 281 D5
Gravesend Kent, U.K. 51°26N 0°22E 169 F8
Gravesend N.Y., U.S.A. 40°36N 73°56W 132 C2
Gravina in Púglia Italy 40°49N 16°25E 201 B9
Gravois, Pointe-à- Haiti 18°15N 73°56W 321 C5
Gravone → France 41°58N 8°45E 175 G12
Gray Haute-Saône, France 47°22N 5°35E 173 E12
Gray Ga., U.S.A. 33°1N 83°32W 316 B6
Grayling Alaska, U.S.A. 62°57N 160°3W 303 E7
Grayling Mich., U.S.A. 44°40N 84°43W 309 C11
Grays U.K. 51°28N 0°21E 169 F8
Grays Harbor U.S.A. 46°59N 124°1W 304 C1
Grays L. U.S.A. 43°4N 111°26W 304 E8
Grays River U.S.A. 46°21N 123°37W 306 D3
Grayville U.S.A. 38°16N 88°0W 311 F9
Grayvoron Russia 50°29N 35°41E 189 G8
Graz Austria 47°4N 15°27E 180 D8
Grazhdanka Russia 59°59N 30°24E 137 B2
Grdelica Serbia 42°55N 22°3E 202 D6
Greåker Norway 59°16N 11°12E 164 E8
Greasy L. Canada 62°55N 122°12W 296 A4
Great Abaco I. = Abaco I. Bahamas 26°25N 77°10W 320 A4
Great Artesian Basin Australia 23°0S 144°0E 280 C3
Great Australian Bight Australia 33°30S 130°0E 279 F5
Great Bacolet Bay Grenada 12°4N 61°37W 323 q
Great Bahama Bank Bahamas 23°15N 78°0W 320 B4
Great Barrier I. N.Z. 36°11S 175°25E 284 C4
Great Barrier Reef Australia 18°0S 146°50E 280 B4
Great Barrier Reef △ Australia 20°0S 150°0E 280 B4
Great Barrington U.S.A. 42°12N 73°22W 313 D11
Great Basalt Wall △ Australia 19°52S 145°43E 280 B4
Great Basin U.S.A. 40°0N 117°0W 304 G5
Great Basin △ U.S.A. 38°56N 114°15W 304 G6
Great Basses Sri Lanka 6°11N 81°29E 245 L5
Great Bear → Canada 65°0N 124°0W 294 C7
Great Bear L. Canada 65°30N 120°0W 294 C8
Great Belt = Store Bælt Denmark 55°20N 11°0E 163 J4
Great Bend Kans., U.S.A. 38°22N 98°46W 308 F4
Great Bend Pa., U.S.A. 41°58N 75°45W 313 E9
Great Blasket I. Ireland 52°6N 10°32W 166 D1
Great Britain Europe 54°0N 2°15W 158 E5
Great Camanoe Br. Virgin Is. 18°30N 64°35W 321 b
Great Channel Asia 6°0N 94°0E 245 L11
Great Coco I. Burma 14°7N 93°22E 245 G11
Great Codroy Canada 47°51N 59°16W 299 C8
Great Divide, The = Great Dividing Ra. Australia 23°0S 146°0E 280 C4
Great Divide Basin U.S.A. 42°0N 108°0W 304 E9
Great Dividing Ra. Australia 23°0S 146°0E 280 C4
Great Driffield = Driffield U.K. 54°0N 0°26W 168 C7
Great Exuma I. Bahamas 23°30N 75°50W 320 B4
Great Falls Guyana 5°35N 61°0W 329 B5
Great Falls Mont., U.S.A. 47°30N 111°17W 304 C8
Great Falls Va., U.S.A. 38°59N 77°17W 143 B2
Great Falls Park U.S.A. 38°59N 77°14W 143 B2
Great Fish = Groot-Vis → S. Africa 33°28S 27°5E 270 D4
Great Goat I. Jamaica 17°52N 77°3W 320 a
Great Guana Cay Bahamas 24°0N 76°20W 320 B4
Great Hall of the People Beijing, China 114 b2
Great Harbour Deep Canada 50°25N 56°32W 299 B8
Great Himalayan △ India 31°30N 77°30E 242 D7
Great Inagua I. Bahamas 21°0N 73°20W 321 B5
Great Indian Desert = Thar Desert India 28°0N 72°0E 242 F5
Great Karoo S. Africa 31°55S 21°0E 270 D3
Great Khingan Mts. = Da Hinggan Ling China 48°0N 121°0E 219 B7
Great Lake Australia 41°50S 146°40E 281 G4
Great Lakes N. Amer. 46°0N 84°0W 292 E11
Great Malvern U.K. 52°7N 2°18W 169 E5
Great Miami → U.S.A. 39°7N 84°49W 309 F11
Great Nicobar India 7°0N 93°50E 245 L11
Great Ormes Head U.K. 53°20N 3°52W 168 D4
Great Otway △ Australia 38°50S 143°50E 282 E5
Great Ouse → U.K. 52°48N 0°21E 168 E8
Great Palm I. Australia 18°45S 146°40E 280 B4
Great Pedro Bluff Jamaica 17°51N 77°44W 320 a
Great Pee Dee → U.S.A. 33°21N 79°10W 315 E15
Great Plains N. Amer. 47°0N 105°0W 292 E9
Great Ruaha → Tanzania 7°56S 37°52E 268 D4
Great Sacandaga L. U.S.A. 43°6N 74°16W 313 C10
Great Saint Bernard Pass = Grand St-Bernard, Col du Europe 45°50N 7°10E 179 K3
Great Salt Desert = Kavīr, Dasht-e Iran 34°30N 55°0E 247 C7
Great Salt L. U.S.A. 41°15N 112°40W 304 F7
Great Salt Lake Desert U.S.A. 40°50N 113°30W 304 F7
Great Salt Plains L. U.S.A. 36°45N 98°8W 314 C5
Great Salt Pond St. Kitts & Nevis 17°14N 62°40W 322 d
Great Sand Dunes △ U.S.A. 37°48N 105°45W 305 H11
Great Sand Sea Libya 29°0N 24°0E 258 C4
Great Sandy △ Australia 26°13S 153°2E 281 D5
Great Sandy Desert W. Austral., Australia 21°0S 124°0E 278 D3
Great Sandy Desert Oreg., U.S.A. 43°35N 120°15W 300 B2
Great Sangi = Sangihe, Pulau Indonesia 3°35N 125°30E 231 D7
Great Scarcies → S. Leone 9°0N 13°0W 262 D2
Great Sd. Bermuda 32°17N 64°51W 153 a
Great Sea Reef Fiji 16°15S 179°0E 287 A2
Great Sitkin I. U.S.A. 52°3N 176°6W 303 K3
Great Skellig Ireland 51°47N 10°33W 166 E1
Great Slave L. Canada 61°23N 115°38W 296 A5
Great Smoky Mts. △ U.S.A. 35°40N 83°40W 315 D13
Great Snow Mt. Canada 57°26N 124°0W 296 B4
Great Stour = Stour → U.K. 51°18N 1°22E 169 F9
Great Victoria Desert Australia 29°30S 126°30E 279 E4
Great Wall Antarctica 62°30S 58°0W 151 C18
Great Wall China 38°30N 109°30E 226 E5
Great Western Forum U.S.A. 33°57N 118°20W 126 C2
Great Whale River = Kuujjuarapik Canada 55°20N 77°35W 298 A4
Great Whernside U.K. 54°10N 1°58W 168 C6
Great Yarmouth U.K. 52°37N 1°44E 169 E9
Great Zab = Zāb al Kabīr → Iraq 36°1N 43°24E 213 D10
Great Zimbabwe Zimbabwe 20°16S 30°54E 269 G3
Greater Antilles W. Indies 17°40N 74°0W 321 C5
Greater London ☐ U.K. 51°31N 0°6W 169 F7
Greater Manchester ☐ U.K. 53°30N 2°15W 168 D5
Greater St. Lucia Wetlands △ S. Africa 28°6S 32°27E 271 C5
Greater Sudbury = Sudbury Canada 46°30N 81°0W 298 C3
Greater Sunda Is. Indonesia 7°0S 112°0E 230 F4
Grebbestad Sweden 58°42N 11°15E 163 F5
Grebenka = Hrebenka Ukraine 50°9N 32°22E 189 G7
Greco Italy 45°30N 9°12E 129 A2
Greco, C. Cyprus 34°57N 34°5E 207 F10
Greco, Mte. Italy 41°48N 13°58E 199 G10
Gredos, Sierra de Spain 40°20N 5°0W 194 E6
Greece U.S.A. 43°13N 77°41W 312 C7
Greece ■ Europe 40°0N 23°0E 204 B3
Greeley Colo., U.S.A. 40°25N 104°42W 304 F11
Greeley Nebr., U.S.A. 41°33N 98°32W 308 E4
Greeleyville U.S.A. 33°40N 79°59W 316 B10
Greely Fd. Canada 80°30N 85°0W 295 A11
Greem-Bell, Ostrov Russia 81°0N 62°0E 214 A7
Green → Ky., U.S.A. 37°54N 87°30W 308 G10
Green → Utah, U.S.A. 38°11N 109°53W 304 G9
Green B. U.S.A. 45°0N 87°30W 308 C10
Green Bay U.S.A. 44°31N 88°0W 308 C9
Green C. Australia 37°13S 150°1E 283 D9
Green City U.S.A. 40°16N 92°57W 310 D4
Green Cove Springs U.S.A. 29°59N 81°42W 316 F8
Green I. = Lü Tao Taiwan 22°40N 121°30E 225 D3
Green I. Antigua & B. 17°2N 61°40W 322 b
Green I. Hong Kong, China 22°17N 114°6E 122 B1
Green I. Grenada 12°13N 61°35W 323 q
Green Is. Papua N. G. 4°35S 154°10E 286 C8
Green Island Jamaica 18°23N 78°17W 320 a
Green Island Bay Phil. 10°12N 119°22E 233 F2
Green Lake Canada 54°17N 107°47W 297 C7
Green Mts. U.S.A. 43°45N 72°45W 313 C12
Green Point S. Africa 33°54S 18°25E 118 A1
Green Pond U.S.A. 32°44N 80°37W 316 C9
Green River Papua N. G. 3°54S 141°11E 286 B1
Green River Utah, U.S.A. 38°59N 110°10W 304 G8
Green River Wyo., U.S.A. 41°32N 109°28W 304 F9
Green Valley U.S.A. 31°52N 110°56W 305 L8
Greenacres U.S.A. 26°38N 80°7W 317 J9
Greenbank U.S.A. 48°6N 122°34W 306 B4
Greenbelt U.S.A. 39°0N 76°53W 143 A4
Greenbelt Park U.S.A. 38°58N 76°53W 143 B4
Greenbush Mich., U.S.A. 44°35N 83°19W 312 B1
Greenbush Minn., U.S.A. 48°42N 96°11W 308 A5
Greencastle U.S.A. 39°38N 86°52W 311 E10
Greene Iowa, U.S.A. 42°54N 92°48W 310 B4
Greene N.Y., U.S.A. 42°20N 75°46W 313 D9
Greeneville U.S.A. 36°10N 82°50W 315 C13
Greenfield Calif., U.S.A. 36°19N 121°15W 306 J5
Greenfield Calif., U.S.A. 35°15N 119°0W 307 K8
Greenfield Ill., U.S.A. 39°21N 90°12W 310 E6
Greenfield Ind., U.S.A. 39°47N 85°46W 311 E11
Greenfield Iowa, U.S.A. 41°18N 94°28W 310 C2
Greenfield Mass., U.S.A. 42°35N 72°36W 313 D12
Greenfield Mo., U.S.A. 37°25N 93°51W 308 G7
Greenfield Ohio, U.S.A. 39°21N 83°23W 311 E13
Greenfield Park Canada 45°29N 73°28W 130 B3
Greenford U.K. 51°31N 0°21W 125 A1
Greenhill U.K. 51°35N 0°18W 125 A2
Greenhills Ireland 53°18N 6°20W 120 B1
Greenland ☑ N. Amer. 66°0N 45°0W 154 D6
Greenland Sea Arctic 73°0N 10°0W 154 B10
Greenmarket Square Cape Town, S. Africa 118 c2
Greenock U.K. 55°57N 4°46W 167 F4
Greenore Ireland 54°2N 6°8W 166 B5
Greenore Pt. Ireland 52°14N 6°19W 166 D5
Greenough Australia 28°58S 114°43E 279 E1
Greenough → Australia 28°51S 114°38E 279 E1
Greenough Pt. Canada 44°58N 81°26W 312 B3
Greenpoint N.Y., U.S.A. 40°43N 73°57W 132 B2
Greenpoint New York, U.S.A. 132 e3
Greenport U.S.A. 41°6N 72°22W 313 E12
Greensboro Fla., U.S.A. 30°34N 84°45W 316 E5
Greensboro Ga., U.S.A. 33°35N 83°11W 316 B6
Greensboro N.C., U.S.A. 36°4N 79°48W 315 C15
Greensboro Vt., U.S.A. 44°36N 72°18W 313 B12
Greensburg Ind., U.S.A. 39°20N 85°29W 311 E11
Greensburg Kans., U.S.A. 37°36N 99°18W 308 G4
Greensburg Pa., U.S.A. 40°18N 79°33W 312 F5
Greenstone Pt. U.K. 57°55N 5°37W 167 D3
Greentown U.S.A. 40°29N 85°58W 311 D11
Greenup U.S.A. 39°15N 88°10W 311 E8
Greenvale Australia 18°59S 145°7E 280 B4
Greenville Liberia 5°1N 9°6W 262 D3
Greenville Ala., U.S.A. 31°50N 86°38W 315 F11
Greenville Calif., U.S.A. 40°8N 120°57W 306 E6
Greenville Fla., U.S.A. 30°28N 83°38W 316 E6
Greenville Ga., U.S.A. 33°2N 84°43W 316 B5
Greenville Ill., U.S.A. 38°53N 89°25W 310 F7
Greenville Ind., U.S.A. 38°22N 85°59W 311 F11
Greenville Maine, U.S.A. 45°28N 69°35W 309 C19
Greenville Mich., U.S.A. 43°11N 85°15W 311 A11
Greenville Mo., U.S.A. 37°8N 90°27W 308 G8
Greenville N.C., U.S.A. 35°37N 77°23W 315 D16
Greenville N.H., U.S.A. 42°46N 71°49W 313 D13
Greenville N.Y., U.S.A. 42°25N 74°1W 313 D10
Greenville Ohio, U.S.A. 40°6N 84°38W 311 D12
Greenville Pa., U.S.A. 41°24N 80°23W 312 E4
Greenville S.C., U.S.A. 34°51N 82°24W 315 D13
Greenville Tex., U.S.A. 33°8N 96°7W 314 E6
Greenwater Lake △ Canada 52°32N 103°30W 297 C8
Greenwich Conn., U.S.A. 41°2N 73°38W 313 E11
Greenwich N.Y., U.S.A. 43°5N 73°30W 313 C11
Greenwich Ohio, U.S.A. 41°2N 82°31W 312 E2
Greenwich ☐ U.K. 51°29N 0°1E 125 B3
Greenwich Observatory U.K. 51°28N 0°0 125 B3
Greenwich Village New York, U.S.A. 132 d1
Greenwood B.C., Canada 49°10N 118°40W 296 D5
Greenwood Ark., U.S.A. 35°13N 94°16W 314 D7
Greenwood Fla., U.S.A. 30°52N 85°10W 316 E4
Greenwood Ind., U.S.A. 39°37N 86°7W 311 E10
Greenwood Mass., U.S.A. 42°29N 71°2W 116 A2
Greenwood Miss., U.S.A. 33°31N 90°11W 315 E9
Greenwood S.C., U.S.A. 34°12N 82°10W 315 D13
Greenwood, Mt. Australia 13°48S 130°4E 278 B5
Greenwood Great House Jamaica 18°29N 77°44W 320 a
Grefsen Norway 59°56N 10°47E 133 A3
Gregbe Ivory C. 6°48N 6°43W 262 D3
Gregório → Brazil 6°50S 70°46W 330 B3
Gregory U.S.A. 43°14N 99°26W 308 D4
Gregory → Australia 17°53S 139°17E 280 B2
Gregory, L. S. Austral., Australia 28°55S 139°0E 281 D2
Gregory, L. W. Austral., Australia 20°0S 127°40E 278 D4
Gregory, L. W. Austral., Australia 25°38S 119°58E 279 E2
Gregory △ Australia 15°38S 131°15E 278 C5
Gregory Downs Australia 18°35S 138°45E 280 B2
Gregory Ra. Queens., Australia 19°30S 143°40E 280 B3
Gregory Ra. W. Austral., Australia 21°20S 121°12E 278 D3
Greifenberg = Gryfice Poland 53°55N 15°13E 184 E2
Greifenhagen = Gryfino Poland 53°16N 14°29E 185 E1
Greiffenberg = Gryfów Śląski Poland 51°2N 15°24E 185 G2
Greiffenberg Germany 53°5N 13°57E 178 B9
Greifswald Germany 54°5N 13°23E 178 A9
Greifswalder Bodden Germany 54°12N 13°35E 178 A9
Grein Austria 48°14N 14°51E 180 C7
Greiz Germany 50°39N 12°10E 178 E8
Gremikha Russia 67°59N 39°47E 186 A6
Grenaa Denmark 56°25N 10°53E 163 H4
Grenada U.S.A. 33°47N 89°49W 315 E10
Grenada ■ W. Indies 12°10N 61°40W 323 q
Grenade France 43°47N 1°17E 174 E5
Grenadier I. U.S.A. 44°3N 76°22W 313 B8
Grenadines, The St. Vincent 12°40N 61°20W 323 n
Grenchen Switz. 47°12N 7°24E 179 H3
Grenen Denmark 57°44N 10°40E 163 G4
Grenfell N.S.W., Australia 33°52S 148°8E 283 B8
Grenfell Sask., Canada 50°30N 102°56W 297 C8
Grenivík Iceland 65°57N 18°11W 155 B8
Grenjaðarstaður Iceland 65°49N 17°21W 155 B9
Grenoble France 45°12N 5°42E 175 C9
Grenville Grenada 12°7N 61°37W 323 q
Grenville, C. Australia 12°0S 143°13E 286 F2
Grenville Chan. Canada 53°40N 129°46W 296 C3
Gréoux-les-Bains France 43°45N 5°52E 175 E9
Gresham U.S.A. 45°30N 122°25W 306 E4
Gresham Park U.S.A. 33°43N 84°20W 113 B2
Gresik Indonesia 7°13S 112°38E 235 D4
Gretna Dumf. & Gall., U.K. 55°0N 3°3W 167 F5
Gretna Fla., U.S.A. 30°37N 84°40W 316 E5
Gretna La., U.S.A. 29°54N 90°3W 131 B2
Gretna City Park U.S.A. 29°54N 90°3W 131 B2
Greve Strand Denmark 55°36N 12°19E 163 J6
Greve Strand København, Denmark 55°34N 12°18E 118 B1
Greven Germany 52°6N 7°37E 178 C3
Grevena Greece 40°4N 21°25E 202 F5
Grevena ☐ Greece 40°2N 21°25E 202 F5
Grevenbroich Germany 51°5N 6°35E 178 D2
Grevenmacher Lux. 49°41N 6°26E 170 E6
Grevesmühlen Germany 53°52N 11°12E 178 B7
Grey → Nfld. & L., Canada 47°34N 57°6W 299 C8
Grey → N.Z. 42°27S 171°12E 285 C6
Grey, C. Australia 13°0S 136°35E 280 A2
Grey Ra. Australia 27°0S 143°30E 281 D3
Greybull U.S.A. 44°30N 108°3W 304 D9
Greyfriars Kirk Edinburgh, U.K. 121 c2
Greymouth N.Z. 42°29S 171°13E 285 C6
Greystones Ireland 53°9N 6°5W 166 C5
Greytown N.Z. 41°5S 175°29E 284 H4
Greytown KwaZulu Natal, S. Africa 29°1S 30°36E 271 C5
Gribanovskiy Russia 51°28N 41°50E 190 E5
Gribbell I. Canada 53°23N 129°0W 296 C3
Gribës, Mal i Albania 40°17N 19°45E 202 F3
Gribingui → C.A.R. 8°33N 19°5E 264 A3
Gribingui-Bamingui △ C.A.R. 7°45N 19°17E 264 A3
Gridley U.S.A. 39°22N 121°42W 306 F5
Griebeg, Ras il- Malta 35°58N 14°23E 206 F7
Griebnitzsee Germany 52°23N 13°8E 115 B1
Griekwastad S. Africa 28°49S 23°15E 270 C3
Griesheim Germany 49°51N 8°33E 179 F4
Grieskirchen Austria 48°16N 13°48E 180 C6
Griffin U.S.A. 33°15N 84°16W 316 B5
Griffin, L. U.S.A. 28°52N 81°51W 317 G8
Griffith N.S.W., Australia 34°18S 146°2E 283 C7
Griffith Ont., Canada 45°15N 77°10W 312 A7
Griffith I. Canada 44°50N 80°55W 312 B4
Griffith Park U.S.A. 34°8N 118°17W 126 B3
Griggsville U.S.A. 39°43N 90°43W 310 E6
Grignols France 44°23N 0°2W 174 D3
Grigoriopol Moldova 47°9N 29°18E 183 C14
Grimari C.A.R. 5°43N 20°6E 264 A4
Grimaylov = Hrymayliv Ukraine 49°20N 26°5E 177 D14
Grimbergen Belgium 50°56N 4°22E 116 A2
Grimes U.S.A. 39°4N 121°54W 306 F5
Grimm = Kamenskiy Russia 50°48N 45°25E 190 E7
Grimma Germany 51°14N 12°43E 178 D8
Grimmen Germany 54°7N 13°3E 178 A9
Grimsay U.K. 57°29N 7°14W 167 D1
Grimsby Ont., Canada 43°12N 79°34W 312 C5
Grimsby N.E. Lincs., U.K. 53°34N 0°5W 168 D7
Grímsey Iceland 66°33N 17°58W 155 A9
Grimshaw Canada 56°10N 117°40W 296 B5
Grimslöv Sweden 56°44N 14°34E 163 H8
Grímsstaðir Iceland 65°39N 16°7W 155 B10
Grimstad Norway 58°20N 8°35E 164 F5
Grímsvötn Iceland 64°26N 17°22W 155 C9
Grindavík Iceland 63°50N 22°26W 155 D4
Grindelwald Switz. 46°38N 8°2E 179 J4
Grindsted Denmark 55°46N 8°55E 163 J2
Grindstone I. Canada 44°43N 76°14W 313 B8
Grindu Romania 44°44N 26°50E 183 F11
Grinnell U.S.A. 41°45N 92°43W 310 C4
Grintavec Slovenia 46°22N 14°32E 199 B11
Grinzing Austria 48°15N 16°20E 142 A2
Gris-Nez, C. France 50°52N 1°35E 173 B8
Grise Fiord Canada 76°25N 82°57W 295 B11
Grishino = Krasnoarmeisk Ukraine 48°18N 37°11E 189 H9
Grisolles France 43°49N 1°19E 174 E5
Grisons = Graubünden ☐ Switz. 46°45N 9°30E 179 J5
Grisslehamn Sweden 60°5N 18°49E 162 D12
Grmeč Planina Bos.-H. 44°43N 16°16E 199 D13
Groais I. Canada 50°55N 55°35W 299 B8
Gröbenried Germany 48°13N 11°25E 131 A1
Grobiņa Latvia 56°33N 21°10E 184 B8
Groblersdal S. Africa 25°15S 29°25E 271 C4
Grobming Austria 47°27N 13°54E 180 D6
Grochów Poland 52°15N 21°5E 142 B2
Grocka Serbia 44°40N 20°42E 202 B4
Gródek Poland 53°6N 23°40E 185 E10
Gródek Jagielloński = Horodok Ukraine 49°46N 23°32E 177 D12
Grodekovo = Pogranichnyy Russia 44°25N 131°24E 220 B5
Grodków Poland 50°43N 17°21E 185 H4
Grodno = Hrodna Belarus 53°42N 23°52E 184 E10
Grodzisk Poland 52°19N 21°4E 142 B2
Grodzisk Mazowiecki Poland 52°7N 20°37E 185 F7
Grodzisk Wielkopolski Poland 52°15N 16°22E 185 F3
Grodzyanka = Hrodzyanka Belarus 53°31N 28°42E 177 B15
Groenendaal Belgium 50°46N 4°26E 116 B2
Groesbeck U.S.A. 31°31N 96°32W 314 F6
Grogol Petamburin Indonesia 6°9S 106°46E 122 A1
Groix France 47°38N 3°29W 172 E3
Groix, Î. de France 47°38N 3°28W 172 E3
Grójec Poland 51°50N 20°58E 185 G7
Gronau Niedersachsen, Germany 52°5N 9°47E 178 C5
Gronau Nordrhein-Westfalen, Germany 52°12N 7°2E 178 C3
Grong Norway 64°25N 12°8E 160 D15
Grönhögen Sweden 56°16N 16°24E 163 H10
Groningen Neths. 53°15N 6°35E 170 A6
Groningen Suriname 5°48N 55°28W 329 B6
Groningen ☐ Neths. 53°16N 6°40E 170 A6
Gronnedal = Kangilinnguit Greenland 61°20N 47°57W 154 E6
Gronsdorf Germany 48°7N 11°42E 131 B3
Groom U.S.A. 35°12N 101°6W 314 D4
Groot → S. Africa 33°45S 24°36E 270 D3
Groot-Berg → S. Africa 32°47S 18°8E 270 D2
Groot-Brakrivier S. Africa 34°2S 22°18E 270 D3
Groot Karasberge Namibia 27°20S 18°40E 270 C2
Groot-Kei → S. Africa 32°41S 28°22E 271 D4
Groot-Vis → S. Africa 33°28S 27°5E 270 D4
Grootdrink S. Africa 28°33S 21°42E 270 C3
Groote Eylandt Australia 14°0S 136°40E 280 A2
Grootfontein Namibia 19°31S 18°6E 270 A2
Grootlaagte → Africa 20°55S 21°27E 270 B3
Grootvloer → S. Africa 30°0S 20°40E 270 D3
Grorud Norway 59°57N 10°52E 133 A4
Gros C. Canada 61°59N 113°32W 296 A6
Gros Cap Guadeloupe 16°24N 61°25W 322 e
Gros Islet St. Lucia 14°5N 60°58W 323 m
Gros-Morne Martinique 14°43N 61°2W 322 j
Gros Morne △ Canada 49°40N 57°50W 299 C8
Gros Piton St. Lucia 13°49N 61°5W 323 m
Grosio Italy 46°18N 10°16E 198 B7
Grosne → France 46°42N 4°56E 173 F11
Gross-Glienicke Germany 52°28N 13°6E 115 B1
Gross-Hadern Germany 48°6N 11°29E 131 B1
Gross-Lappen Germany 48°11N 11°35E 131 A2
Gross-Meseritsch = Velké Meziříčí Czech Rep. 49°21N 16°1E 180 B9
Gross-Strehlitz = Strzelce Opolskie Poland 50°31N 18°18E 185 H5
Gross Wartenberg = Syców Poland 51°19N 17°40E 185 G4
Grossa, Pta. Spain 39°6N 1°36E 206 C2
Grosse I. U.S.A. 42°8N 83°9W 311 B13
Grosse Krampe Germany 52°23N 13°40E 115 B5
Grosse Müggelsee Germany 52°26N 13°38E 115 B4
Grosse Point Lighthouse U.S.A. 42°2N 87°41W 119 A2
Grosse Pte. Guadeloupe 16°1N 61°17W 322 e
Grossenbrode Germany 54°21N 11°4E 178 A7
Grossenhain Germany 51°17N 13°32E 178 D9
Grossenzersdorf Austria 48°12N 16°33E 142 A3
Grossenzersdorfer Arm → Austria 48°12N 16°31E 142 A3
Grosser Arber Germany 49°6N 13°8E 179 F9
Grosser Biberhaufen Austria 48°12N 16°28E 142 A2
Grosser Plöner See Germany 54°10N 10°22E 178 A6
Grosser Wannsee Germany 52°25N 13°10E 115 B2
Grosseto Italy 42°46N 11°8E 199 F8
Grossfeld-Siedlung Austria 48°16N 16°26E 142 A2
Grossgerungs Austria 48°34N 14°57E 180 C7
Grossglockner Austria 47°5N 12°40E 180 D5
Grosshesselohe Germany 48°3N 11°32E 131 B2
Grossjedlersdorf Austria 48°16N 16°23E 142 A2
Grosswardein = Oradea Romania 47°2N 21°58E 182 C6
Grossziethen Germany 52°23N 13°26E 115 B3
Groswater B. Canada 54°20N 57°40W 299 B8
Grotli Norway 62°2N 7°42E 164 B4
Groton Conn., U.S.A. 41°21N 72°5W 313 E12
Groton N.Y., U.S.A. 42°36N 76°22W 313 D8
Groton S. Dak., U.S.A. 45°27N 98°6W 308 C4
Grottáglie Italy 40°32N 17°26E 201 B10
Grottaminarda Italy 41°4N 15°2E 201 A8
Grottammare Italy 42°59N 13°52E 199 F10
Grottkau = Grodków Poland 50°43N 17°21E 185 H4
Grouard Mission Canada 55°33N 116°9W 296 B5
Grouin, Pte. du France 48°43N 1°51W 172 D5
Ground Zero New York, U.S.A. 132 e1
Groundhog → Canada 48°45N 82°58W 298 C3
Grouw Neths. 53°5N 5°51E 170 A5
Grove, The U.S.A. 42°5N 87°52W 119 A1
Grove City Fla., U.S.A. 26°56N 82°19W 317 J7
Grove City Ohio, U.S.A. 39°53N 83°6W 311 E13
Grove City Pa., U.S.A. 41°10N 80°5W 312 E4
Grove Hall U.S.A. 42°18N 71°4W 116 B2
Grove Hill U.S.A. 31°42N 87°47W 315 F11
Grove Park Hounslow, U.K. 51°28N 0°15W 125 B2
Grove Park Lewisham, U.K. 51°25N 0°1E 125 B4
Grove Park Georgia, U.S.A. 33°46N 84°26W 113 B2
Groveland Calif., U.S.A. 37°50N 120°14W 306 H6
Groveland Fla., U.S.A. 28°34N 81°51W 317 G8
Grover = Tiltonsville U.S.A. 40°10N 80°41W 312 F4
Grover Beach U.S.A. 35°7N 120°37W 307 K6
Groves U.S.A. 29°57N 93°54W 314 G8
Groveton N.H., U.S.A. 44°36N 71°31W 313 B13
Groveton Va., U.S.A. 38°46N 77°6W 143 C3
Grovetown U.S.A. 33°27N 82°12W 316 B7
Grožnjan Croatia 45°22N 13°43E 199 C10
Groznyy Russia 43°20N 45°45E 191 J7
Grua Norway 60°16N 10°40E 164 D7
Grubišno Polje Croatia 45°44N 17°12E 182 E2
Grudovo Bulgaria 42°21N 27°10E 203 D11
Grudusk Poland 53°3N 20°38E 185 E7
Grudziądz Poland 53°30N 18°47E 184 E5
Gruinard B. U.K. 57°56N 5°35W 167 D3
Gruissan France 43°8N 3°7E 174 E7
Grumo Áppula Italy 41°1N 16°42E 201 A9
Grums Sweden 59°22N 13°5E 162 E7
Grünau Germany 52°25N 13°34E 115 B4
Grünberg Germany 50°35N 8°58E 178 E4
Grünberg in Schlesien = Zielona Góra Poland 51°57N 15°31E 185 G2
Grund Iceland 65°31N 18°9W 155 B8
Gründau Germany 50°10N 9°9E 179 E5
Grundy Center U.S.A. 42°22N 92°47W 310 B4
Grunewald Germany 52°28N 13°13E 115 B2
Grungedal Norway 59°44N 7°43E 164 E4
Grünstadt Germany 49°34N 8°9E 179 F4
Grünwald Germany 48°2N 11°31E 131 B2
Grünwalder Forst Germany 48°2N 11°33E 131 B2
Gruppo di Tessa △ Italy 46°47N 11°0E 198 B8
Gruvberget Sweden 61°6N 16°10E 162 C10
Gruver U.S.A. 36°16N 101°24W 314 C4
Gruyères Switz. 46°35N 7°4E 179 J3
Gruža Serbia 43°54N 20°46E 202 C4
Gryazi Russia 52°30N 39°58E 189 F10
Gryazliv = Borovichi Russia 58°25N 33°55E 188 C7
Gryazovets Russia 58°50N 40°10E 188 C11
Grybów Poland 49°36N 20°55E 185 J7
Grycksbo Sweden 60°40N 15°29E 162 D9
Gryfice Poland 53°55N 15°13E 184 E2
Gryfino Poland 53°16N 14°29E 185 E1
Gryfów Śląski Poland 51°2N 15°24E 185 G2
Grymes Hill U.S.A. 40°36N 74°6W 132 C1

Grythyttan *Sweden* 59°41N 14°32E **162** E8
Gstaad *Switz.* 46°28N 7°18E **179** J3
Gua *India* 22°18N 85°20E **243** H11
Gua Musang *Malaysia* 4°53N 101°58E **237** K3
Guacanayabo, G. de *Cuba* 20°40N 77°20W **320** B4
Guacara *Venezuela* 10°14N 67°53W **328** A4
Guachípas → *Argentina* 25°40S 65°30W **334** B2
Guachiría → *Colombia* 5°27N 70°36W **328** B3
Guadajoz → *Spain* 37°50N 4°51W **195** H6
Guadalajara *Jalisco, Mexico* 20°40N 103°20W **318** C4
Guadalajara *Spain* 40°37N 3°12W **196** E1
Guadalajara □ *Spain* 40°47N 2°30W **196** E2
Guadalcanal *Solomon Is.* 9°32S 160°12E **287** M11
Guadalcanal *Spain* 38°5N 5°52W **195** G5
Guadalén → *Spain* 38°5N 3°32W **195** G7
Guadales *Argentina* 34°30S 67°55W **334** C2
Guadalete → *Spain* 36°35N 6°13W **195** J4
Guadalimar → *Spain* 38°5N 3°28W **195** G7
Guadalmena → *Spain* 38°19N 2°56W **195** G8
Guadalmez → *Spain* 38°46N 5°4W **195** G5
Guadalope → *Spain* 41°15N 0°3W **196** D4
Guadalquivir → *Spain* 36°47N 6°22W **195** J4
Guadalupe = Guadeloupe ☑ *W. Indies* 16°20N 61°40W **322** e
Guadalupe *Brazil* 6°44S 43°47W **332** C3
Guadalupe *Mexico* 32°4N 116°32W **307** N10
Guadalupe *Zacatecas, Mexico* 22°45N 102°31W **318** C4
Guadalupe *Manila, Phil.* 14°34N 121°2E **127** B2
Guadalupe *Spain* 39°27N 5°17W **195** F5
Guadalupe *Calif., U.S.A.* 34°58N 120°34W **307** L6
Guadalupe → *Mexico* 32°6N 116°51W **307** N10
Guadalupe → *Tex., U.S.A.* 28°27N 96°47W **314** G6
Guadalupe, Basilica de *Mexico* 19°29N 99°7W **128** B2
Guadalupe, Sierra de *Spain* 39°28N 5°30W **195** F5
Guadalupe Bravos *Mexico* 31°20N 106°10W **318** A3
Guadalupe I. *Pac. Oc.* 29°0N 118°50W **292** G8
Guadalupe Mts. △ *U.S.A.* 31°40N 104°30W **314** F2
Guadalupe Peak *U.S.A.* 31°50N 104°52W **314** F2
Guadalupe y Calvo *Mexico* 26°6N 106°58W **318** B3
Guadarrama, Sierra de *Spain* 41°0N 4°0W **194** E7
Guadauta *Georgia* 43°7N 40°32E **191** J5
Guadeloupe ☑ *W. Indies* 16°20N 61°40W **322** e
Guadeloupe △ *Guadeloupe* 16°10N 61°40W **322** e
Guadeloupe Passage *W. Indies* 16°50N 62°15W **322** e
Guadelupe *Peru* 7°15S 79°29W **330** B2
Guadiamar → *Spain* 36°55N 6°24W **195** J4
Guadiana → *Portugal* 37°14N 7°22W **195** H3
Guadiana Menor → *Spain* 37°56N 3°15W **195** H7
Guadiaro → *Spain* 36°17N 5°17W **195** J5
Guadiato → *Spain* 37°48N 5°5W **195** H5
Guadiela → *Spain* 40°22N 2°49W **196** E2
Guadix *Spain* 37°18N 3°11W **195** H7
Guafo, Boca del *Chile* 43°35S 74°0W **336** B2
Guafo, I. *Chile* 43°35S 74°50W **336** B2
Guaico *Trin. & Tob.* 10°35N 61°9W **323** t
Guainía □ *Colombia* 2°30N 69°0W **328** C4
Guainía → *Colombia* 2°1N 67°7W **328** C4
Guaíra *Brazil* 24°5S 54°10W **335** A5
Guaíra □ *Paraguay* 25°45S 56°30W **334** B4
Guaitecas, Is. *Chile* 44°0S 74°30W **336** B2
Guajará-Mirim *Brazil* 10°50S 65°20W **331** C4
Guajira □ *Colombia* 11°30N 72°30W **328** A3
Guajira, Pen. de la *Colombia* 12°0N 72°0W **328** A3
Gualaceo *Ecuador* 2°54S 78°47W **328** D2
Gualán *Guatemala* 15°8N 89°22W **320** C2
Gualdo Tadino *Italy* 43°14N 12°47E **199** E9
Gualeguay *Argentina* 33°10S 59°14W **334** C4
Gualeguaychú *Argentina* 33°3S 59°31W **334** C4
Gualequay → *Argentina* 33°19S 59°39W **334** C4
Gualicho, Salina *Argentina* 40°25S 65°20W **336** B3
Gualjaina *Argentina* 42°45S 70°30W **336** B2
Guam ☑ *Pac. Oc.* 13°27N 144°45E **302** d
Guamá *Brazil* 1°37S 47°29W **332** B2
Guamá → *Brazil* 1°29S 48°30W **332** B2
Guamblin, I. *Chile* 44°50S 75°0W **336** B2
Guamini *Argentina* 37°1S 62°28W **334** D3
Guamote *Ecuador* 1°56S 78°43W **328** D2
Guampí, Sierra de *Venezuela* 6°0N 65°35W **329** B4
Guamúchil *Mexico* 25°28N 108°6W **318** B3
Guana I. *Br. Virgin Is.* 18°30N 64°30W **321** b
Guanabacoa *Cuba* 23°8N 82°18W **320** B3
Guanabara, B. de *Brazil* 22°52S 43°10W **135** B1
Guanabara, Jardim *Brazil* 22°48S 43°11W **135** A1
Guanabara, Palácio da *Brazil* 22°56S 43°11W **135** B1
Guanacaste, Cordillera del *Costa Rica* 10°40N 85°4W **320** D2
Guanacaste △ *Costa Rica* 10°57N 85°30W **320** D2
Guanaceví *Mexico* 25°56N 105°57W **318** B3
Guanahani = San Salvador I. *Bahamas* 24°0N 74°40W **321** B5
Guanajay *Cuba* 22°56N 82°42W **320** B3
Guanajuato *Mexico* 21°1N 101°15W **318** C4
Guanajuato □ *Mexico* 21°0N 101°0W **318** C4
Guanambi *Brazil* 14°13S 42°47W **333** D3
Guanapo *Trin. & Tob.* 10°36N 61°15W **323** t
Guanare *Venezuela* 8°42N 69°12W **328** B4
Guanare → *Venezuela* 8°13N 67°46W **328** B4
Guandacol *Argentina* 29°30S 68°40W **334** B2
Guane *Cuba* 22°10N 84°7W **320** B3
Guang'an *China* 30°28N 106°35E **228** B6
Guang'anmen *China* 39°51N 116°18E **114** B1
Guangchang *China* 26°50N 116°21E **229** D11
Guangde *China* 30°54N 119°25E **229** B12
Guangdong □ *China* 23°0N 113°0E **229** F9
Guangfeng *China* 28°20N 118°15E **229** C12
Guanghan *China* 30°58N 104°17E **228** B5
Guangling *China* 39°47N 114°22E **226** E8
Guangnan *China* 24°5N 105°4E **228** E5
Guangning *China* 23°40N 112°22E **229** F9
Guangqumen *China* 39°52N 116°25E **114** B2
Guangrao *China* 37°5N 118°25E **227** F10
Guangshui *China* 31°37N 114°0E **229** B9
Guangshun *China* 26°8N 106°21E **228** D6
Guangwu *China* 37°48N 105°57E **226** F3
Guangxi Zhuangzu Zizhiqu □ *China* 24°0N 109°0E **228** F7
Guangyuan *China* 32°26N 105°51E **228** A5
Guangze *China* 27°30N 117°12E **229** D11
Guangzhou *China* 23°6N 113°13E **121** B2
Guangzhou Baiyun Int. ✕ (CAN) *China* 23°10N 113°15E **121** A2
Guanhães *Brazil* 18°47S 42°57W **333** E3
Guanica *Puerto Rico* 17°58N 66°55W **321** b
Guanipa → *Venezuela* 9°56N 62°26W **329** B5
Guanling *China* 25°56N 105°35E **228** E5
Guannan *China* 34°8N 119°21E **227** G10
Guanshuo *China* 23°4N 113°22E **121** B3
Guanta *Venezuela* 10°14N 64°36W **329** A5
Guantánamo *Cuba* 20°10N 75°14W **321** B4
Guantánamo B. *Cuba* 19°59N 75°10W **321** C4
Guantao *China* 36°42N 115°25E **226** F8
Guanyang *China* 25°30N 111°8E **229** E8
Guanyun *China* 34°20N 119°18E **227** G10
Guapí *Colombia* 2°36N 77°54W **328** C2
Guápiles *Costa Rica* 10°10N 83°46W **320** D3
Guapo → *Trin. & Tob.* 10°11N 61°40W **323** t
Guapo B. *Trin. & Tob.* 10°12N 61°41W **323** t
Guaporé = Rondônia □ *Brazil* 10°52S 61°57W **331** C5
Guaporé *Brazil* 28°51S 51°54W **335** B5
Guaporé → *Brazil* 11°55S 65°4W **331** C4
Guaqui *Bolivia* 16°41S 68°54W **330** D4
Guara, Sierra de *Spain* 42°19N 0°15W **196** C4
Guarabira *Brazil* 6°51S 35°29W **332** C4
Guaracara → *Trin. & Tob.* 10°18N 61°28W **323** t
Guaranda *Ecuador* 1°36S 79°0W **328** D2
Guarani = Pacajus *Brazil* 4°10S 38°31W **332** B4
Guarapari *Brazil* 20°40S 40°30W **333** F3
Guarapuava *Brazil* 25°20S 51°30W **333** G1
Guaratinguetá *Brazil* 22°49S 45°9W **335** A6
Guaratuba *Brazil* 25°53S 48°38W **335** B6
Guarda *Portugal* 40°32N 7°20W **194** E3
Guarda □ *Portugal* 40°40N 7°20W **194** E3
Guardafui, C. = Asir, Ras *Somali Rep.* 11°55N 51°10E **267** B7
Guardamar del Segura *Spain* 38°5N 0°39W **197** G4
Guardavalle *Italy* 38°30N 16°30E **201** D9
Guárdia Sanframondi *Italy* 41°15N 14°36E **201** A7
Guardiagrele *Italy* 42°11N 14°13E **199** F11
Guardo *Spain* 42°47N 4°50W **194** C6
Guareña *Spain* 38°51N 6°6W **195** G4
Guareña → *Spain* 41°29N 5°23W **194** D5
Guari *Papua N. G.* 8°3S 146°52E **286** E4
Guárico □ *Venezuela* 8°40N 66°35W **328** B4
Guaripo → *Colombia* 4°6N 70°42W **328** C3
Guarujá *Brazil* 24°2S 46°25W **335** A6
Guarulhos = Guarus *Brazil* 21°44S 41°20W **333** F3
Guarulhos *Brazil* 23°29S 46°33W **335** A6
Guarus *Brazil* 21°44S 41°20W **333** F3
Guasave *Mexico* 25°34N 108°27W **318** B3
Guascama, Pta. *Colombia* 2°32N 78°24W **328** C2
Guasdualito *Venezuela* 7°15N 70°44W **328** B3
Guasipati *Venezuela* 7°28N 61°54W **329** B5
Guasopa *Papua N. G.* 9°12S 152°56E **286** E7
Guastalla *Italy* 44°55N 10°39E **198** D7
Guatemala *Guatemala* 14°40N 90°22W **320** D1
Guatemala ■ *Cent. Amer.* 15°40N 90°30W **320** C1
Guatemala Basin *Pac. Oc.* 11°0N 95°0W **289** F18
Guatemala Trench *Pac. Oc.* 14°0N 95°0W **292** H10
Guatire *Venezuela* 10°28N 66°32W **328** A4
Guatopo △ *Venezuela* 10°5N 66°30W **328** A4
Guaturaro Pt. *Trin. & Tob.* 10°19N 60°59W **323** t
Guavi → *Papua N. G.* 7°48S 143°16E **286** D2
Guaviare □ *Colombia* 2°0N 72°30W **328** C3
Guaviare → *Colombia* 4°3N 67°44W **328** C4
Guaxupé *Brazil* 21°10S 47°5W **335** A6
Guayabero → *Colombia* 2°36N 72°47W **328** C3
Guayaguayare *Trin. & Tob.* 10°8N 61°2W **323** t
Guayaguayare B. *Trin. & Tob.* 10°7N 61°2W **323** t
Guayama *Puerto Rico* 17°59N 66°7W **321** C6
Guayaneco, Arch. *Chile* 47°45S 75°10W **336** C1
Guayanilla *Puerto Rico* 18°1N 66°47W **321** b
Guayaquil *Ecuador* 2°15S 79°52W **328** D2
Guayaquil *Baja Calif., Mexico* 29°59N 115°4W **318** B1
Guayaquil, G. de *Ecuador* 3°10S 81°0W **328** D1
Guayaramerín *Bolivia* 10°48S 65°23W **331** C4
Guayas → *Ecuador* 2°36S 79°52W **328** D2
Guaymas *Mexico* 27°56N 110°54W **318** B2
Guaynabo *Puerto Rico* 18°22N 66°7W **321** b
Guba *Dem. Rep. of the Congo* 10°38S 26°27E **269** E2
Guba *Ethiopia* 11°17N 35°20E **257** E4
Gûbâl, Madîq *Egypt* 27°30N 34°0E **256** B3
Gubam *Papua N. G.* 8°39S 141°53E **286** E1
Guban *Somali Rep.* 10°30N 44°0E **267** B5
Gubat *Phil.* 12°55N 124°7E **232** E5
Gubbi *India* 13°19N 76°56E **245** H3
Gúbbio *Italy* 43°21N 12°35E **199** E9
Guben *Germany* 51°57N 14°42E **178** D10
Gubin *Poland* 51°57N 14°43E **185** G1
Gubio *Nigeria* 12°30N 12°42E **263** C7
Gubkin *Russia* 51°17N 37°32E **189** G9
Guča *Serbia* 43°46N 20°15E **202** C4
Gucheng *China* 32°20N 111°30E **229** A8
Gudå *Norway* 63°27N 11°36E **164** A8
Gudalur *India* 11°30N 76°29E **245** J3
Gudata = Guadauta *Georgia* 43°7N 40°32E **191** J5
Gudbrandsdalen *Norway* 61°33N 10°10E **164** C7
Guddu Barrage *Pakistan* 28°30N 69°50E **242** E3
Gudenå → *Denmark* 56°29N 10°13E **163** H4
Gudermes *Russia* 43°24N 46°5E **191** J8
Gudhjem *Denmark* 55°12N 14°58E **163** J8
Gudivada *India* 16°30N 81°3E **245** F5
Gudiyattam *India* 12°57N 78°55E **245** H4
Gudö *Sweden* 59°12N 18°12E **139** B3
Gudur *India* 14°12N 79°55E **245** G4
Gudvangen *Norway* 60°52N 6°49E **164** D3
Guebwiller *France* 47°55N 7°12E **173** E14
Guecho = Getxo *Spain* 43°21N 2°59W **196** B2
Guékédou *Guinea* 8°40N 10°5W **262** D2
Guelb er Rîchât *Mauritania* 21°7N 11°24W **260** D2
Guéle Mendouka *Cameroon* 4°23N 12°55E **263** E7
Guélengdeng *Chad* 10°55N 15°31E **259** F3
Güell, Parque de *Spain* 41°24N 2°10E **114** A2
Guelma *Algeria* 36°25N 7°29E **261** A6
Guelma □ *Algeria* 36°25N 7°25E **261** A6
Guelmine = Goulimine *Morocco* 28°56N 10°0W **260** C3
Guelph *Canada* 43°35N 80°20W **312** C4
Guelta Zemmur *W. Sahara* 25°8N 12°22W **260** C3
Guemar *Algeria* 33°30N 6°49E **261** B6
Guéméné-Penfao *France* 47°38N 1°50W **172** E5
Guéméné-sur-Scorff *France* 48°4N 3°13W **172** D3
Guéné *Benin* 11°44N 3°16E **263** C5
Güeppí *Peru* 0°7S 75°15W **328** D2
Guer *France* 47°54N 2°8W **172** E4
Güer Aike *Argentina* 51°39S 69°35W **336** D3
Guera *Chad* 11°55N 18°12E **259** F3
Guéra □ *Chad* 11°30N 18°30E **259** F3
Guérande *France* 47°20N 2°26W **172** E4
Guerara *Algeria* 32°51N 4°22E **261** B5
Guercif *Morocco* 34°14N 3°21W **260** B4
Guéréda *Chad* 14°31N 22°5E **259** F4
Guéret *France* 46°11N 1°51E **173** F8
Guérigny *France* 47°6N 3°10E **173** E10
Guerneville *U.S.A.* 38°30N 123°0W **306** G4
Guernica = Gernika-Lumo *Spain* 43°19N 2°40W **196** B2
Guernsey *Chan. Is., U.K.* 49°26N 2°35W **169** H5
Guernsey *Wyo., U.S.A.* 42°16N 104°45W **304** E11
Guerrara *Algeria* 28°5N 0°8W **261** C4
Guerrero *Mexico City, Mexico* **128** a1
Guerrero □ *Mexico* 17°40N 100°0W **319** D5
Guerzim *Algeria* 29°39N 1°40W **261** C4
Guessou-Sud *Benin* 10°3N 2°38E **263** C5
Gueugnon *France* 46°36N 4°4E **173** F11
Guéyo *Ivory C.* 5°25N 6°5W **262** D3
Gufuðalur *Iceland* 65°34N 22°15W **155** B4
Guggenheim Museum *New York, U.S.A.* **132** b3
Gughe *Ethiopia* 6°12N 37°30E **257** F4
Gügher *Iran* 29°28N 56°27E **247** D8
Guglionesi *Italy* 41°55N 14°55E **199** G11
Guguan *N. Marianas* 17°18N 145°51E **302** a
Guhakolak, Tanjung *Indonesia* 6°50S 105°14E **231** G11
Guhrau = Góra *Poland* 51°40N 16°31E **185** G3
Gui Jiang → *China* 23°30N 111°15E **229** F8
Guia *Canary Is.* 28°8N 15°38W **153** e1
Guia de Isora *Canary Is.* 28°12N 16°46W **153** e1
Guia Lopes da Laguna *Brazil* 21°26S 56°7W **335** A4
Guiana *Venezuela* 5°9N 63°36W **329** B5
Guiana Highlands *S. Amer.* 5°10N 60°40W **326** C4
Guiana I. *Antigua & B.* 17°6N 61°44W **322** b
Guibéroua *Ivory C.* 6°14N 6°10W **262** D3
Guichen B. *Australia* 37°10S 139°45E **282** D3
Guichi *China* 30°39N 117°27E **229** B11
Guider *Cameroon* 9°56N 13°57E **263** D7
Guidiguir *Niger* 13°40N 9°50E **259** F1
Guidimaka □ *Mauritania* 15°20N 12°0W **262** B2
Guidimouni *Niger* 13°42N 9°31E **259** F1
Guiding *China* 26°34N 107°11E **228** D6
Guidong *China* 26°7N 113°57E **229** D9
Guidónia-Montecélio *Italy* 42°1N 12°45E **199** F9
Guiers, L. de *Senegal* 16°10N 15°50W **262** B1
Guigang *China* 23°8N 109°35E **228** F7
Guiglo *Ivory C.* 6°45N 7°30W **262** D3
Guihulñgan *Phil.* 10°7N 123°16E **233** F4
Guijá *Mozam.* 24°27S 33°0E **271** B5
Guijuelo *Spain* 40°33N 5°40W **194** E5
Guildford *U.K.* 51°14N 0°34W **169** F7
Guilford *U.S.A.* 41°17N 72°41W **313** E12
Guilin *China* 25°18N 110°15E **229** E8
Guillaume-Delisle, L. *Canada* 56°15N 76°17W **298** A4
Guillaumes *France* 44°5N 6°52E **175** D10
Guillestre *France* 44°39N 6°40E **175** D10
Guilvinec *France* 47°48N 4°17W **172** E2
Güimar *Canary Is.* 28°18N 16°24W **153** e1
Guimarães *Brazil* 2°9S 44°42W **332** B3
Guimarães *Portugal* 41°28N 8°24W **194** D2
Guimaras □ *Phil.* 10°35N 122°37E **233** F4
Guimba *Phil.* 15°40N 120°46E **232** D3
Guinardó *Spain* 41°24N 2°10E **114** A2
Guinayangan *Phil.* 13°54N 122°27E **232** E4
Guinda *U.S.A.* 38°50N 122°12W **306** G4
Guindulman *Phil.* 9°46N 124°29E **233** G5
Guinea *Africa* 8°0N 8°0E **254** F4
Guinea ■ *W. Afr.* 10°20N 11°30W **262** C2
Guinea, Gulf of *Atl. Oc.* 3°0N 2°30E **263** E5
Guinea Basin *Atl. Oc.* 0°0 5°0W **152** G11
Guinea-Bissau ■ *Africa* 12°0N 15°0W **262** C2
Güines *Cuba* 22°50N 82°0W **320** B3
Guingamp *France* 48°34N 3°10W **172** D3
Guinguinéo *Senegal* 14°20N 15°57W **262** C1
Guinobatan *Phil.* 13°11N 123°36E **232** E4
Guipavas *France* 48°26N 4°29W **172** D2
Guiping *China* 23°21N 110°2E **229** F8
Guipúzcoa □ *Spain* 43°12N 2°15W **196** B2
Guir *Mali* 18°52N 2°52W **262** B4
Guir, O. → *Algeria* 31°29N 2°17W **261** B4
Guiratinga *Brazil* 16°21S 53°45W **331** D7
Guirel *Mauritania* 15°30N 7°3W **262** B3
Güiria *Venezuela* 10°32N 62°18W **329** F8
Guiscard *France* 49°40N 3°1E **173** C10
Guise *France* 49°52N 3°35E **173** C10
Guita-Koulouba *C.A.R.* 5°58N 23°21E **264** A4
Guitiriz *Spain* 43°11N 7°50W **194** B3
Guitri *Ivory C.* 5°30N 5°14W **262** D3
Guiuan *Phil.* 11°5N 125°55E **233** F5
Guixi *China* 28°16N 117°15E **229** C11
Guiyang *Guizhou, China* 26°32N 106°40E **228** D6
Guiyang *Hunan, China* 25°46N 112°42E **229** E9
Guizhou □ *China* 27°0N 107°0E **228** D6
Gujan-Mestras *France* 44°38N 1°4W **174** D2
Gujar Khan *Pakistan* 33°16N 73°19E **242** C5
Gujarat □ *India* 23°20N 71°0E **242** H4
Gujiang *China* 27°11N 114°47E **229** D10
Gujranwala *Pakistan* 32°10N 74°12E **242** C6
Gujrat *Pakistan* 32°40N 74°2E **242** C6
Gukovo *Russia* 48°1N 39°58E **191** F5
Gulargambone *Australia* 31°20S 148°30E **283** A8
Gulbai *Pakistan* 24°52N 66°58E **123** A1
Gulbarga *India* 17°20N 76°50E **244** F3
Gulbene *Latvia* 57°8N 26°52E **188** D4
Gülchö *Kyrgyzstan* 40°19N 73°26E **217** D8
Guledagudda *India* 16°3N 75°48E **245** F2
Gülek *Turkey* 37°12N 34°48E **250** A5
Gulf □ *Papua N. G.* 8°0S 145°0E **286** D3
Gulf, The = Persian Gulf *Asia* 27°0N 50°0E **247** E6
Gulf Breeze *U.S.A.* 30°21N 87°9W **317** E2
Gulf Hammock *U.S.A.* 29°15N 82°43W **317** F7
Gulf Islands △ *U.S.A.* 30°10N 87°10W **317** K2
Gulfport *Fla., U.S.A.* 27°44N 82°42W **317** H7
Gulfport *Miss., U.S.A.* 30°22N 89°6W **315** F10
Gulgong *Australia* 32°20S 149°49E **283** B8
Gulin *China* 28°1N 105°50E **228** C5
Gulistan *Pakistan* 30°30N 66°35E **242** D2
Guliston *Uzbekistan* 40°29N 68°46E **217** D7
Gulkana *U.S.A.* 62°16N 145°23W **303** E11
Gull Lake *Canada* 50°10N 108°29W **297** C7
Gullbrå *Norway* 60°50N 6°17E **164** D3
Gullbrandstorp *Sweden* 56°42N 12°43E **163** H6
Gullbringusýsla □ *Iceland* 64°0N 22°0W **155** D4
Gullfoss *Iceland* 64°20N 20°8W **155** D6
Gullhaug *Norway* 59°30N 10°15E **164** E7
Gullivan B. *U.S.A.* 25°45N 81°40W **317** K8
Gullspång *Sweden* 58°59N 14°6E **163** F8
Gullstein *Norway* 63°13N 8°9E **164** A5
Güllük *Turkey* 37°14N 27°35E **205** D9
Güllük Dağı △ *Turkey* 37°0N 30°30E **205** E12
Güllük Korfezi *Turkey* 37°12N 27°30E **205** D9
Gulma *Nigeria* 12°40N 4°23E **263** C5
Gulmarg *India* 34°3N 74°25E **243** B6
Gülnar *Turkey* 36°19N 33°24E **250** B5
Gulnare *Australia* 33°27S 138°27E **282** B3
Gülpınar *Turkey* 39°32N 26°7E **205** B8
Gülşehir *Turkey* 38°44N 34°37E **212** C6
Gulshat *Kazakhstan* 46°38N 74°21E **217** C8
Gulsvik *Norway* 60°24N 9°38E **164** D6
Gulu *Uganda* 2°48N 32°17E **268** B3
Gŭlŭbovo *Bulgaria* 42°8N 25°55E **203** D9
Gulud, J. *Sudan* 11°41N 29°31E **257** E2
Gulwe *Tanzania* 6°30S 36°25E **268** D4
Gulyaypole = Hulyaypole *Ukraine* 47°45N 36°21E **189** J9
Gum Lake *Australia* 32°42S 143°9E **282** B5
Gumaca *Phil.* 13°55N 122°6E **232** E4
Gumal → *Pakistan* 31°40N 71°50E **242** D4
Gumbaz *Pakistan* 30°2N 69°0E **242** D3
Gumbinnen = Gusev *Russia* 54°35N 22°10E **184** D9
Gumdag *Turkmenistan* 39°9N 54°56E **216** E4
Gumel *Nigeria* 12°39N 9°22E **263** C6
Gumi *S. Korea* 36°10N 128°12E **224** D4
Gumiel de Hizán *Spain* 41°46N 3°41W **194** D7
Gumla *India* 23°3N 84°33E **243** H11
Gumlu *Australia* 19°53S 147°41E **280** B4
Gumma □ *Japan* 36°30N 138°20E **223** A10
Gummersbach *Germany* 51°1N 7°34E **178** D3
Gummi *Nigeria* 12°4N 5°9E **263** C6
Gümüldür *Turkey* 38°6N 27°0E **205** C9
Gumuljina = Komotini *Greece* 41°9N 25°26E **203** E9
Gümüşçay *Turkey* 40°16N 27°17E **203** F11
Gümüşhaciköy *Turkey* 40°50N 35°18E **212** B6
Gümüşhane *Turkey* 40°30N 39°30E **213** B8
Gümüşsu *Turkey* 38°14N 29°1E **205** C11
Gumzai *Indonesia* 5°28S 134°42E **231** F8
Gun Hill Tower *Barbados* 13°8N 59°33W **323** r
Gun Pt. *Grenada* 12°32N 61°37W **323** q
Guna *Amara, Ethiopia* 11°43N 38°14E **266** B4
Guna *Oromiya, Ethiopia* 8°18N 39°52E **257** F4
Guna *India* 24°40N 77°19E **242** G7
Gunbalanya *Australia* 12°20S 133°4E **278** B5
Gundabooka △ *Australia* 30°30S 145°20E **281** E4
Gundagai *Australia* 35°3S 148°6E **283** C8
Gundarehi *India* 20°57N 81°17E **244** D5
Gundelfingen *Germany* 48°34N 10°22E **179** G6
Gundih *Indonesia* 7°10S 110°56E **235** D4
Gundlakamma → *India* 15°30N 80°15E **245** G5
Gundlupet *India* 11°48N 76°41E **245** J3
Gündoğmuş *Turkey* 36°48N 32°0E **250** B3
Gunebang *Australia* 33°1S 146°38E **283** B7
Güney *Burdur, Turkey* 37°29N 29°34E **205** D11
Güney *Denizli, Turkey* 38°10N 29°4E **205** C11
Güneydoğu Toroslar *Turkey* 38°20N 40°30E **213** C9
Gungal *Australia* 32°17S 150°32E **283** B9
Gungo *Angola* 10°58S 15°30E **265** E2
Güngören *Turkey* 41°1N 28°52E **122** B1
Gungu *Dem. Rep. of the Congo* 5°43S 19°20E **265** D3
Gunisao → *Canada* 53°56N 97°53W **297** C9
Gunisao L. *Canada* 53°33N 96°15W **297** C9
Gunjyal *Pakistan* 32°20N 71°55E **242** C4
Günlüce *Turkey* 36°50N 28°20E **205** E10
Gunnarskog *Sweden* 59°49N 12°34E **162** E6
Gunnbjørn Fjeld *Greenland* 68°55N 29°47W **154** D8
Gunnebo *Sweden* 57°44N 16°32E **163** G10
Gunnedah *Australia* 30°59S 150°15E **283** A9
Gunnersbury *U.K.* 51°29N 0°17W **125** B2
Gunnewin *Australia* 25°59S 148°33E **281** D4
Gunningbar Cr. → *Australia* 31°14S 147°6E **283** A7
Gunnison *Colo., U.S.A.* 38°33N 106°56W **304** G10
Gunnison *Utah, U.S.A.* 39°9N 111°49W **304** G8
Gunnison → *U.S.A.* 39°4N 108°35W **304** G9
Gunpowder *Australia* 19°42S 139°22E **280** B2
Gunsan *S. Korea* 35°59N 126°45E **224** E3
Guntakal *India* 15°11N 77°27E **245** G3
Guntersville *U.S.A.* 34°21N 86°18W **315** D11
Guntong *Malaysia* 4°36N 101°3E **237** K3
Guntur *India* 16°23N 80°30E **245** F5
Gunung Buda △ *Malaysia* 4°11N 114°58E **235** B4
Gunung Leuser △ *Indonesia* 3°39N 97°32E **234** B1
Gunung Mulu △ *Malaysia* 4°6N 114°53E **235** B4
Gunung Palung △ *Indonesia* 1°9S 110°13E **235** C4
Gunungapi *Indonesia* 6°45S 126°30E **231** F7
Gunungsitoli *Indonesia* 1°15N 97°30E **234** B1
Gunupur *India* 19°5N 83°50E **244** E6
Günz → *Germany* 48°27N 10°16E **179** G6
Gunza *Angola* 10°50S 13°50E **265** E2
Günzburg *Germany* 48°26N 10°17E **179** G6
Gunzenhausen *Germany* 49°7N 10°44E **179** F6
Guo He → *China* 32°59N 117°10E **227** H9
Guoyang *China* 33°32N 116°12E **226** H9
Gupis *Pakistan* 36°15N 73°20E **243** A5
Gura Humorului *Romania* 47°35N 25°53E **183** C10
Gura-Teghii *Romania* 45°30N 26°25E **183** E11
Gurabo *Puerto Rico* 18°16N 65°58W **321** b
Gurag *Ethiopia* 8°20N 38°20E **257** F4
Gurahonț *Romania* 46°16N 22°21E **182** D7
Gurbantünggüt Shamo *China* 45°8N 87°20E **217** C11
Gurdaspur *India* 32°5N 75°31E **242** C6
Gurdon *U.S.A.* 33°55N 93°9W **314** E8
Güre *Balıkesir, Turkey* 39°36N 26°54E **205** B8
Güre *Uşak, Turkey* 38°39N 29°10E **205** C11
Gurgaon *India* 28°27N 77°1E **242** E7
Gürgentepe *Turkey* 40°51N 37°50E **212** B7
Gurghiu, Munţii *Romania* 46°41N 25°15E **183** D10
Gurgueia → *Brazil* 6°50S 43°24W **332** C3
Gurha *India* 25°12N 71°39E **242** G4
Guri, Embalse de *Venezuela* 7°50N 62°52W **329** B5
Gurig △ *Australia* 11°36S 132°7E **278** B5
Gurimatu *Papua N. G.* 6°45S 144°45E **286** D3
Gurin *Nigeria* 9°5N 12°54E **263** D7
Gurinhatã *Brazil* 19°14S 49°48W **333** E2
Gurjaani *Georgia* 41°43N 45°52E **191** K7
Gurk → *Austria* 46°35N 14°31E **180** E7
Gurkfeld = Krško *Slovenia* 45°57N 15°30E **199** C12
Gurkha *Nepal* 28°5N 84°40E **243** E11
Gurley *Australia* 29°45S 149°48E **281** D4
Gurnee *U.S.A.* 42°22N 87°55W **311** B9
Gurnet Point *U.S.A.* 42°1N 70°34W **313** D14
Guro *Mozam.* 17°26S 32°30E **269** F3
Gürpınar *İstanbul, Turkey* 40°59N 28°37E **203** F12
Gürpınar *Van, Turkey* 38°18N 43°25E **213** C10
Gürsu *Turkey* 40°13N 29°11E **203** F13
Guruê *Mozam.* 15°25S 36°58E **269** F4
Gurun *Malaysia* 5°49N 100°27E **237** K3
Gürün *Turkey* 38°43N 37°15E **212** C7
Gurupá *Brazil* 1°25S 51°35W **329** D7
Gurupá, I. Grande de *Brazil* 1°25S 51°45W **329** D7
Gurupi *Brazil* 11°43S 49°4W **333** D2
Gurupi → *Brazil* 1°13S 46°6W **332** B2
Gurupi, Serra do *Brazil* 5°0S 47°50W **332** C2
Guruwe *Zimbabwe* 16°40S 30°42E **271** A5
Gurvan Sayhan Uul *Mongolia* 43°50N 104°0E **218** B5
Guryev = Atyraū *Kazakhstan* 47°5N 52°0E **187** E9
Guryevsk *Russia* 54°47N 20°38E **184** D7
Gus-Khrustalnyy *Russia* 55°42N 40°44E **190** C5
Gusau *Nigeria* 12°12N 6°40E **263** C6
Gusev *Russia* 54°35N 22°10E **184** D9
Gushan *China* 39°50N 123°35E **224** C1
Gushgy = Serhetabat *Turkmenistan* 35°20N 62°18E **247** C9
Gushi *China* 32°11N 115°41E **229** A10
Gushiago *Ghana* 9°55N 0°15W **263** D4
Gushikami *Japan* 26°7N 127°44E **288** a
Gushikawa *Japan* 26°21N 127°52E **288** a
Gusinje *Montenegro* 42°35N 19°50E **202** D3
Gusinoozersk *Russia* 51°16N 106°27E **215** D11
Gúspini *Italy* 39°32N 8°37E **200** C1
Güssing *Austria* 47°3N 16°20E **181** D9
Gustav Holm, Kap *Greenland* 66°36N 34°15W **154** D7
Gustavia *St.-Martin* 17°53N 62°51W **322** a
Gustavo A. Madero *Mexico* 19°29N 99°8W **128** B2
Gustavsberg *Sweden* 59°19N 18°23E **162** E12
Gustavus *U.S.A.* 58°25N 135°44W **296** B1
Gustine *U.S.A.* 37°16N 121°0W **306** H6
Güstrow *Germany* 53°47N 12°10E **178** B8
Gusum *Sweden* 58°16N 16°30E **163** F10
Guta = Kolárovo *Slovak Rep.* 47°54N 18°0E **181** D10
Gütersloh *Germany* 51°54N 8°24E **178** D4
Gutha *Australia* 28°58S 115°55E **279** E2
Guthalungra *Australia* 19°52S 147°50E **280** B4
Guthrie *Okla., U.S.A.* 35°53N 97°25W **314** D6
Guthrie *Tex., U.S.A.* 33°37N 100°19W **314** E4
Guthrie Center *U.S.A.* 41°41N 94°30W **310** C2
Gutian *China* 26°32N 118°43E **229** D12
Gutiérrez *Bolivia* 19°25S 63°34W **331** D5
Guttenberg *Iowa, U.S.A.* 42°47N 91°6W **310** B5
Guttenberg *New York, U.S.A.* **132** a1
Guttentag = Dobrodzień *Poland* 50°45N 18°25E **185** H5
Guttstadt = Dobre Miasto *Poland* 53°58N 20°26E **184** E7
Gutu *Zimbabwe* 19°41S 31°9E **271** A5
Gutulia △ *Norway* 62°2N 12°11E **164** B9
Gutuyevskiy, Ostrov *Russia* 59°53N 30°15E **137** B1
Guwahati *India* 26°10N 91°45E **241** B3
Guy Fawkes River △ *Australia* 30°0S 152°20E **281** D5
Guy-Fayreau, Complexe *Montréal, Canada* **130** b2
Guyana ■ *S. Amer.* 5°0N 59°0W **329** C6
Guyancourt *France* 48°46N 2°4E **134** B1
Guyane française = French Guiana ☑ *S. Amer.* 4°0N 53°0W **329** C7
Guyang *China* 41°0N 110°5E **226** D6
Guyenne *France* 44°30N 0°40E **174** D4
Guymon *U.S.A.* 36°41N 101°29W **314** C4
Guyotville = Aïn Benian *Algeria* 36°48N 2°55E **261** A5
Guyra *Australia* 30°15S 151°40E **281** E5
Guyton *U.S.A.* 32°20N 81°24W **316** C8
Guyuan *Hebei, China* 41°37N 115°40E **226** D8
Guyuan *Ningxia Huizu, China* 36°0N 106°20E **226** G4
Guzar *Uzbekistan* 38°36N 66°15E **217** E7
Güzelbağ *Turkey* 36°44N 31°53E **250** B2
Güzelbahçe *Turkey* 38°21N 26°54E **205** C8
Güzeloluk *Turkey* 36°47N 34°4E **250** B5
Güzelsu *Turkey* 36°53N 31°51E **250** B2
Güzelyurt = Morphou *Cyprus* 35°12N 32°59E **207** E8
Guzhang *China* 28°42N 109°58E **228** C7
Guzhen *China* 33°22N 117°18E **227** H9
Guzmán, L. de *Mexico* 31°20N 107°30W **318** A3
Gvardeysk *Russia* 54°39N 21°5E **184** D8
Gvardeyskoye *Ukraine* 45°7N 34°1E **189** K8
Gvarv *Norway* 59°23N 9°9E **164** E6
Gwa *Burma* 17°36N 94°34E **241** G5
Gwaai *Zimbabwe* 19°15S 27°45E **269** F2
Gwaai → *Zimbabwe* 17°59S 26°52E **269** F2
Gwabegar *Australia* 30°37S 148°59E **283** A8
Gwadabawa *Nigeria* 13°28N 5°15E **263** C6
Gwādar *Pakistan* 25°10N 62°18E **240** D1
Gwagwada *Nigeria* 10°15N 7°15E **263** C6
Gwaii Haanas △ *Canada* 52°21N 131°26W **296** C2
Gwalior *India* 26°12N 78°10E **242** F8
Gwanak *S. Korea* 37°29N 126°57E **137** C1
Gwanaksan *S. Korea* 37°27N 126°58E **137** C1
Gwanara *Nigeria* 8°55N 3°9E **263** D5
Gwanda *Zimbabwe* 20°55S 29°0E **269** G2
Gwandu *Nigeria* 12°30N 4°41E **263** C5
Gwane *Dem. Rep. of the Congo* 4°45N 25°48E **268** B2
Gwang-yang *S. Korea* 34°58N 127°35E **224** E3
Gwangju *S. Korea* 35°9N 126°54E **224** E3
Gwangju □ *S. Korea* 35°10N 126°45E **224** E3
Gwanju = Gwangju *S. Korea* 35°9N 126°54E **224** E3
Gwaram *Nigeria* 10°15N 10°25E **263** C7
Gwarzo *Nigeria* 12°20N 8°55E **263** C6
Gwasero *Nigeria* 9°29N 3°30E **263** D5
Gwda → *Poland* 53°3N 16°44E **185** E3
Gweebarra B. *Ireland* 54°51N 8°23W **166** B3
Gweedore *Ireland* 55°3N 8°13W **166** A3
Gweru *Zimbabwe* 19°28S 29°45E **269** F2
Gwi *Nigeria* 9°0N 7°10E **263** D6
Gwinn *U.S.A.* 46°19N 87°27W **308** B10
Gwio Kura *Nigeria* 12°40N 11°2E **263** C7
Gwoza *Nigeria* 11°5N 13°40E **263** C7
Gwydir → *Australia* 29°27S 149°48E **281** D4
Gwynedd □ *U.K.* 52°52N 4°10W **168** E3
Gyál *Hungary* 47°23N 19°13E **117** B3
Gyáli-patak → *Hungary* 47°23N 19°7E **117** B2
Gyandzha = Gäncä *Azerbaijan* 40°45N 46°20E **191** K8
Gyaring Hu *China* 34°50N 97°40E **218** C4
Gydanskiy Poluostrov *Russia* 70°0N 78°0E **214** C8
Gyeonggi-do □ *S. Korea* 36°37N 127°15E **224** D3
Gyeongju *S. Korea* 35°51N 129°14E **224** E4
Gyeongsan *S. Korea* 35°49N 128°44E **224** E4
Gyeongsangbuk-do □ *S. Korea* 36°20N 128°45E **224** D4
Gyeongsangnam-do □ *S. Korea* 35°15N 128°15E **224** E4
Gyeryongsan △ *S. Korea* 36°20N 127°15E **224** D3
Gyl *Norway* 62°57N 8°7E **164** B5
Gyldenløve Fjord *Greenland* 64°15N 40°30W **154** E6
Gympie *Australia* 26°11S 152°38E **281** D5
Gyobingauk *Burma* 18°13N 95°39E **241** F5
Gyōda *Japan* 36°10N 139°30E **223** A11
Gyodongdo *S. Korea* 37°47N 126°15E **224** D3
Gyomaendrőd *Hungary* 46°56N 20°50E **182** D5
Gyöngyös *Hungary* 47°48N 19°56E **182** C4
Győr *Hungary* 47°41N 17°40E **182** C2
Győr-Moson-Sopron □ *Hungary* 47°40N 17°20E **182** C2
Gypsum Pt. *Canada* 61°53N 114°35W **296** A6
Gypsumville *Canada* 51°45N 98°40W **297** C9
Gyueshevo *Bulgaria* 42°14N 22°28E **202** D6
Gyula *Hungary* 46°38N 21°17E **182** D6
Gyumri *Armenia* 40°47N 43°50E **191** K6
Gyzylarbat = Serdar *Turkmenistan* 39°4N 56°23E **247** B8
Gyzyletrek = Etrek *Turkmenistan* 37°36N 54°46E **247** B7
Gzhatsk = Gagarin *Russia* 55°38N 35°0E **188** E8
Gzira *Malta* 35°54N 14°29E **206** F7

H

H. Neely Henry L. *U.S.A.* 33°55N 86°2W **316** B3
Ha 'Arava → *Israel* 30°50N 35°20E **251** H6
Ha Coi *Vietnam* 21°26N 107°46E **228** G6
Ha Dong *Vietnam* 20°58N 105°46E **228** G5
Ha Giang *Vietnam* 22°50N 104°59E **228** F5
Ha Karmel △ *Israel* 32°45N 35°5E **250** F6
Ha Long, Vinh *Vietnam* 20°56N 107°3E **236** B6
Ha Tien *Vietnam* 10°23N 104°29E **237** G5
Ha Tinh *Vietnam* 18°20N 105°54E **236** C5
Ha Trung *Vietnam* 19°58N 105°50E **236** C5
Ha Yaek Chalong *Thailand* 7°50N 98°22E **237** a
Haaga *Finland* 60°13N 24°53E **121** B2
Haakon VII Topp *Norway* 71°0N 8°20W **154** C10
Haaksbergen *Neths.* 52°9N 6°45E **170** B6
Ha'ano *Tonga* 19°41S 174°18W **287** P13
Ha'apai Group *Tonga* 19°47S 174°27W **287** P13
Haapiti *Moorea* 17°34S 149°52W **289** e
Haapsalu *Estonia* 58°56N 23°30E **188** C2
Haar *Germany* 48°6N 11°43E **131** B3
Haarby *Denmark* 55°13N 10°7E **163** J4
Haarlem *Neths.* 52°23N 4°39E **170** B4
Haas-Lilienthal House *San Francisco, U.S.A.* **136** b1
Haast *N.Z.* 43°51S 169°1E **285** D4
Haast → *N.Z.* 43°50S 169°2E **285** D4
Haast Bluff *Australia* 23°22S 132°0E **278** D5
Haast Pass *N.Z.* 44°6S 169°21E **285** E4
Hab → *Pakistan* 24°53N 66°41E **242** G3
Hab Nadi Chauki *Pakistan* 25°0N 66°50E **242** G2
Habahe *China* 48°3N 86°23E **217** C11
Ḩabarūt *Yemen* 17°18N 52°44E **249** C6
Habaswein *Kenya* 1°2N 39°30E **268** B4
Ḩabawnah, W. → *Si. Arabia* 17°57N 44°58E **248** C4
Habay *Alta., Canada* 58°50N 118°44W **296** B5
Habay *Manila, Phil.* 14°27N 120°56E **127** C1
Ḩabbān *Yemen* 14°21N 47°5E **248** D4
Ḩabbānīyah *Iraq* 33°17N 43°29E **213** F10
Ḩabbānīyah, Hawr al *Iraq* 33°17N 43°29E **213** F10
Habelschwerdt = Bystrzyca Kłodzka *Poland* 50°19N 16°39E **185** H3
Habichtswald △ *Germany* 51°15N 9°15E **178** D5
Habiganj *Bangla.* 24°24N 91°30E **241** C3
Habisa *Sudan* 15°38N 31°36E **266** A3
Habo *Sweden* 57°55N 14°6E **163** G8
Haboro *Japan* 44°22N 141°42E **220** B10
Ḩabshān *U.A.E.* 23°50N 53°37E **247** F7
Hachenburg *Germany* 50°40N 7°49E **178** E3
Hachi *India* 27°48N 94°2E **241** B5
Hachijō-Jima *Japan* 33°5N 139°45E **223** D11
Hachiman *Japan* 35°45N 136°57E **223** B8
Hachinohe *Japan* 40°30N 141°29E **220** D10
Hachiōji *Japan* 35°40N 139°20E **223** B11
Hacıbektaş *Turkey* 38°56N 34°33E **212** C6
Hacılar *Turkey* 38°38N 35°26E **212** C6
Hack, Mt. *Australia* 30°45S 138°55E **282** A3
Hackås *Sweden* 62°56N 14°30E **162** B8
Hackbridge *U.K.* 51°23N 0°9W **125** B3
Hackensack *U.S.A.* 40°52N 74°4W **132** A1
Hackensack → *U.S.A.* 40°42N 74°7W **132** B1
Hackettstown *U.S.A.* 40°51N 74°50W **313** F10
Hackney □ *U.K.* 51°33N 0°3W **125** A3
Hackney Wick *U.K.* 51°32N 0°1W **125** A3
Haco *Angola* 10°15S 15°44E **265** E3
Hadali *Pakistan* 32°16N 72°11E **242** C5
Hadano *Japan* 35°22N 139°14E **223** B11
Hadarba, Ras *Sudan* 22°4N 36°51E **256** C4
Hadarom □ *Israel* 31°0N 35°0E **251** H6
Ḩadbaram *Oman* 17°27N 55°15E **249** C6
Ḩadd, Ra's al *Oman* 22°35N 59°50E **249** B7
Ḩaddā *Si. Arabia* 21°27N 39°34E **248** B2
Haddington *U.K.* 55°57N 2°47W **167** F6
Haddock *U.S.A.* 33°2N 83°25W **316** B6
Haddummati Atoll *Maldives* 2°0N 73°0E **272** d
Haded Plain = Xadded *Somali Rep.* 9°46N 48°2E **267** C6
Hadejia *Nigeria* 12°30N 10°5E **263** C7
Hadejia → *Nigeria* 12°50N 10°51E **263** C7
Ḩadera *Israel* 32°27N 34°55E **251** F5
Hadersleben = Haderslev *Denmark* 55°15N 9°30E **163** J3
Haderslev *Denmark* 55°15N 9°30E **163** J3
Hadgaon *India* 19°30N 77°40E **244** E3
Hadhramaut = Ḩaḑramawt *Yemen* 15°30N 49°30E **249** D5
Hadīboh *Yemen* 12°39N 54°2E **249** D6
Hadilik *China* 37°56N 86°6E **217** E11
Hadım *Turkey* 36°58N 32°26E **250** B3
Hadithah *Si. Arabia* 31°27N 37°9E **251** G8
Hadjadj, O. el → *Algeria* 28°18N 5°20E **261** C6
Hadjeb el Aïoun *Tunisia* 35°21N 9°32E **258** A1
Hadjer Kamaran *Chad* 12°41N 21°46E **259** F4
Hadjer Mornou *Chad* 17°12N 23°8E **259** E4
Hadlaskar *Norway* 60°15N 7°9E **164** D4
Hadong *S. Korea* 35°5N 127°44E **224** E3
Hadr, Warrāq el *Egypt* 30°5N 31°12E **117** A2
Ḩaḑramawt *Yemen* 15°30N 49°30E **249** D5
Ḩaḑramawt, W. → *Yemen* 15°10N 51°8E **249** D5
Ḩadrānīyah *Iraq* 35°38N 43°14E **246** C4
Hadrian's Wall *U.K.* 55°0N 2°30W **168** B5
Hadsten *Denmark* 56°19N 10°3E **163** H4
Hadsund *Denmark* 56°44N 10°8E **163** H4
Hadyach *Ukraine* 50°21N 34°0E **189** G8
Hægeland *Norway* 58°22N 7°45E **164** F4
Haeju *N. Korea* 38°3N 125°45E **224** C2
Haeju-man *N. Korea* 37°54N 125°18E **224** D2
Hä'ena *U.S.A.* 22°14N 159°34W **302** A2
Haenam *S. Korea* 34°34N 126°35E **224** E3
Haenertsburg *S. Africa* 24°0S 29°50E **271** B4
Haerhpin = Harbin *China* 45°48N 126°40E **227** B14
Hafar al Bāţin *Si. Arabia* 28°32N 45°52E **246** D5
Hafik *Turkey* 39°51N 37°23E **212** C7
Ḩafīrat al 'Aydā *Si. Arabia* 26°26N 39°12E **246** E3
Ḩafit *Oman* 23°59N 55°49E **247** F7
Hafizabad *Pakistan* 32°5N 73°40E **242** C5
Haflong *India* 25°10N 93°5E **241** C4
Hafnarfjörður *Iceland* 64°4N 21°57W **155** C5
Hafnir *Iceland* 63°56N 22°41W **155** D4
Hafslo *Norway* 61°19N 7°10E **164** C4
Haft Gel *Iran* 31°30N 49°32E **247** D6
Haga *Sweden* 59°21N 18°1E **139** A2
Hagalil *Israel* 32°53N 35°18E **250** F6
Hagari → *India* 15°40N 77°0E **245** G3
Hagby *Sweden* 56°34N 16°11E **163** H10
Hagemeister I. *U.S.A.* 58°39N 160°54W **303** G7
Hagen *Germany* 51°21N 7°27E **178** D3
Hagenbrunn *Austria* 48°19N 16°27E **142** A2
Hagenow *Germany* 53°26N 11°12E **178** B7
Hagerman *U.S.A.* 33°7N 104°20W **305** K11
Hagerman Fossil Beds △ *U.S.A.* 42°48N 114°57W **304** E6
Hägersten *Sweden* 59°18N 17°59E **139** B1
Hagerstown *Ind., U.S.A.* 39°55N 85°10W **311** E11
Hagerstown *Md., U.S.A.* 39°39N 77°43W **309** F15
Hagersville *Canada* 42°58N 80°3W **312** D4
Hagetmau *France* 43°39N 0°37W **174** E3

INDEX
Hatchet L. 377

Hagfors Sweden 60°3N 13°45E 162 D7
Häggvik Sweden 59°26N 17°56E 139 A1
Hagi Iceland 65°28N 23°25W 155 B3
Hagi Japan 34°30N 131°22E 222 C3
Hagolan Syria 33°0N 35°45E 250 F6
Hagondange France 49°16N 6°11E 173 C13
Hagonoy Phil. 14°50N 120°44E 232 D3
Hagonoy Manila, Phil. 14°31N 121°3E 127 B2
Hags Hd. Ireland 52°57N 9°28W 166 D2
Hague, C. de la France 49°44N 1°56W 172 C5
Hague, The = 's-Gravenhage Neths. 52°7N 4°17E 170 B4
Hague Park Canada 43°45N 79°14W 141 A3
Haguenau France 48°49N 7°47E 173 D14
Hagunia W. Sahara 27°26N 12°24W 260 C2
Hahira U.S.A. 30°59N 83°22W 316 E6
Hai Duong Vietnam 20°56N 106°19E 228 G6
Hai'an Guangdong, China 20°18N 110°11E 229 G8
Hai'an Jiangsu, China 32°37N 120°27E 229 A13
Haian Shanmo Taiwan 23°25N 121°25E 225 C3
Haicheng Fujian, China 24°23N 117°48E 229 E11
Haicheng Liaoning, China 40°50N 122°45E 224 B1
Haidan China 39°59N 116°16E 114 B1
Haidar Khel Afghan. 33°58N 68°38E 242 C3
Haidarâbâd = Hyderabad India 17°22N 78°29E 244 F4
Haidargarh India 26°37N 81°22E 243 F9
Haidari Greece 38°2N 23°38E 112 A1
Haidarpur India 28°43N 77°8E 120 A1
Haidhausen Germany 48°7N 11°36E 131 B2
Haifa = Hefa Israel 32°46N 35°0E 250 F6
Haifeng China 22°58N 115°10E 229 F10
Haiger Germany 50°43N 8°12E 178 E4
Haight-Ashbury U.S.A. 37°46N 122°26W 136 B2
Haikou China 20°1N 110°16E 236 B8
Haiku-Pauwela U.S.A. 20°56N 156°19W 302 C5
Ḥā'il Si. Arabia 27°28N 41°45E 246 E4
Ḥā'il □ Si. Arabia 26°40N 41°40E 246 E4
Hailakandi India 24°42N 92°34E 241 C4
Hailar China 49°10N 119°38E 219 B6
Hailey U.S.A. 43°31N 114°19W 304 E6
Haileybury Canada 47°30N 79°38W 298 C4
Hailin China 44°37N 129°30E 227 B15
Hailing Dao China 21°35N 111°47E 229 G8
Hailuoto Finland 65°3N 24°45E 160 D21
Haimen Guangdong, China 23°15N 116°38E 229 F11
Haimen Jiangsu, China 31°52N 121°10E 229 B13
Hainan □ China 19°0N 109°30E 236 C7
Hainan Dao China 19°0N 109°30E 236 C7
Hainan Str. = Qiongzhou Haixia China 20°10N 110°15E 236 B8
Hainault U.K. 51°36N 0°6E 125 A4
Hainaut □ Belgium 50°30N 4°0E 170 D4
Hainburg Austria 48°9N 16°56E 181 C9
Haines Alaska, U.S.A. 59°14N 135°26W 296 B1
Haines Oreg., U.S.A. 44°55N 117°56W 304 D5
Haines City U.S.A. 28°7N 81°38W 317 G8
Haines Junction Canada 60°45N 137°30W 296 A1
Hainfeld Austria 48°3N 15°48E 180 C8
Haining China 30°28N 120°40E 229 B13
Haiphong Vietnam 20°47N 106°41E 228 G6
Haitan Dao China 25°30N 119°45E 229 E12
Haiti ■ W. Indies 19°0N 72°30W 321 C5
Haiya Sudan 18°20N 36°21E 256 D4
Haiyan China 36°53N 100°59E 218 C5
Haiyan Zhejiang, China 30°28N 120°58E 229 B13
Haiyang China 36°47N 121°9E 227 F11
Haiyang Dao China 39°2N 123°10E 224 C1
Haiyuan Guangxi Zhuangzu, China 22°8N 107°35E 228 F6
Haiyuan Ningxia Huizu, China 36°35N 105°52E 226 F3
Haizhou China 34°37N 119°7E 227 G10
Haizhou Wan China 34°50N 119°20E 227 G10
Haizhu Guangchang China 23°6N 113°14E 121 B2
Hajar Bangar Sudan 10°40N 22°45E 259 F4
Hajdú-Bihar □ Hungary 47°30N 21°30E 182 C6
Hajdúböszörmény Hungary 47°40N 21°30E 182 C6
Hajdúdorog Hungary 47°48N 21°30E 182 C6
Hajdúhadház Hungary 47°40N 21°40E 182 C6
Hajdúnánás Hungary 47°50N 21°26E 182 C6
Hajdúsámson Hungary 47°37N 21°42E 182 C6
Hajdúszoboszló Hungary 47°27N 21°22E 182 C6
Haji Ibrahim Iraq 36°40N 44°30E 213 D11
Hajiganj Bangla. 23°15N 90°50E 241 D3
Hajipur India 25°45N 85°13E 243 G11
Ḥajjah Yemen 15°42N 43°36E 248 D3
Ḥājjī Muḥsin Iraq 32°35N 45°29E 246 C5
Ḥājjīābād Iran 28°19N 55°55E 247 D7
Ḥājjīābād-e Zarrīn Iran 33°9N 54°51E 247 C7
Hajnówka Poland 52°47N 23°35E 185 F10
Hajodo S. Korea 34°17N 126°3E 224 E3
Ḥajrah Si. Arabia 20°14N 41°3E 248 B3
Haka Burma 22°39N 93°37E 241 D4
Hakansson, Mts. Dem. Rep. of the Congo 8°40S 25°45E 265 D5
Hakataramea N.Z. 44°43S 170°30E 285 E5
Hakkâri Turkey 37°34N 43°44E 213 D10
Hakkâri □ Turkey 37°30N 44°0E 213 D10
Hakkâri Dağları Turkey 38°2N 42°58E 213 C10
Hakken-Zan Japan 34°10N 135°54E 223 C7
Hakodate Japan 41°45N 140°44E 220 D10
Hakos Namibia 23°13S 16°21E 270 B2
Hakota Japan 36°5N 140°30E 223 A12
Håksberg Sweden 60°11N 15°12E 162 D9
Haku-San Japan 36°9N 136°46E 223 A8
Haku-San △ Japan 36°15N 136°45E 223 A8
Hakuba Japan 36°42N 137°51E 223 A9
Hakui Japan 36°53N 136°47E 221 F8
Hakun Burma 26°46N 95°42E 241 B5
Hakunila Finland 60°16N 25°6E 121 B3
Hakupu Cook Is. 19°6S 169°50W 289 g
Hala Pakistan 25°43N 68°20E 240 D3
Ḥalab Syria 36°10N 37°15E 250 B8
Ḥalab □ Syria 36°10N 37°30E 250 B8
Ḥalaban Si. Arabia 23°29N 44°23E 248 B4
Ḥalabjah Iraq 35°10N 45°58E 213 E11
Halaib Sudan 22°12N 36°30E 256 C4
Halaib Triangle Africa 22°30N 35°20E 256 C4
Halandri Greece 38°3N 23°48E 112 A2
Halangingie Pt. Cook Is. 19°2S 169°58W 289 g
Halasa Sudan 14°26N 30°39E 257 E3
Halásztelek Hungary 47°22N 19°0E 117 B1
Hālat 'Ammār Si. Arabia 29°10N 36°4E 246 D3
Hālawa, C. U.S.A. 21°10N 156°43W 302 B5
Hālawa Heights U.S.A. 21°23N 157°55W 302 K14
Halbā Lebanon 34°34N 36°6E 250 D7
Halberstadt Germany 51°54N 11°3E 178 D7
Halcombe N.Z. 40°8S 175°30E 284 G4
Halcon Phil. 13°0N 121°30E 231 B6
Halcon, Mt. Phil. 13°16N 121°0E 232 E3
Halde Fjäll = Haltiatunturi Finland 69°17N 21°18E 160 B19
Halden Norway 59°9N 11°23E 164 E8
Haldensleben Germany 52°17N 11°24E 178 C7
Haldimand Canada 42°59N 79°52W 312 D5
Haldwani India 29°31N 79°30E 243 E8
Hale U.S.A. 39°36N 93°20W 310 E3
Hale → Australia 24°56S 135°53E 280 C2
Haleakalā △ U.S.A. 20°40N 156°15W 302 C5
Hale'iwa U.S.A. 21°36N 158°6W 302 J13
Halesowen U.K. 52°27N 2°3W 169 E5
Halesworth U.K. 52°20N 1°31E 169 E9
Haleyville U.S.A. 34°14N 87°37W 315 D11
Half Assini Ghana 5°1N 2°50W 262 D4
Half Dome U.S.A. 37°44N 119°32W 306 H7
Halfmoon Bay N.Z. 46°50S 168°5E 285 G3
Halfway → Canada 56°12N 121°32W 296 B4
Halfway Tree Jamaica 18°0N 76°48W 320 a
Halia India 24°50N 82°19E 243 G10
Haliburton Canada 45°3N 78°30W 312 A6
Haliç Turkey 41°1N 28°57E 122 B1
Halifax Queens., Australia 18°32S 146°22E 280 B4
Halifax N.S., Canada 44°38N 63°35W 299 D7
Halifax W. Yorks., U.K. 53°43N 1°52W 168 D6
Halifax Pa., U.S.A. 40°25N 76°55W 312 F8
Halifax B. Australia 18°50S 147°0E 280 B4
Halifax Harbour Grenada 12°6N 61°45W 323 q
Halifax I. Namibia 26°38S 15°4E 270 C2
Halik Shan China 42°20N 81°22E 217 D10
Halīl → Iran 27°40N 58°30E 247 E8
Halim Perdana Kusuma Int. ✕ (HLP) Indonesia 6°16S 106°53E 122 B2
Halin Somali Rep. 9°6N 48°37E 267 C6
Halkett, C. U.S.A. 70°48N 152°11W 303 A9
Halki Greece 36°17N 27°35E 205 E9
Halkida Greece 38°27N 23°42E 204 C5
Halkidiki □ Greece 40°25N 23°20E 202 F7
Halkirk U.K. 58°30N 3°29W 167 C5
Hall Beach = Sanirajak Canada 68°46N 81°12W 295 C11
Hall I. U.S.A. 60°40N 173°6W 303 F4
Hall in Tirol Austria 47°17N 11°30E 180 D4
Hall Pen. Canada 63°30N 66°0W 295 C13
Hall Pt. Australia 15°40S 124°23E 278 C3
Hallabro Sweden 56°22N 15°5E 163 H9
Halland Sweden 57°8N 12°47E 161 H15
Hallandale U.S.A. 25°58N 80°8W 317 K9
Hallands län □ Sweden 57°0N 12°40E 163 H6
Hallands Väderö Sweden 56°27N 12°34E 163 H6
Hallandsås Sweden 56°22N 13°0E 163 H7
Hallāniyat, Ghubbat al Oman 17°40N 55°45E 249 C6
Hallāniyat, Jazā'ir al Oman 17°30N 55°58E 249 C6
Hallasan S. Korea 33°22N 126°32E 224 a
Hallasan △ S. Korea 33°20N 126°30E 224 a
Hällbybrunn Sweden 59°24N 16°25E 162 E10
Halle Belgium 50°44N 4°13E 116 B1
Halle Nordrhein-Westfalen, Germany 52°3N 8°22E 178 C4
Halle Sachsen-Anhalt, Germany 51°30N 11°56E 178 D7
Hällefors Sweden 59°47N 14°31E 162 E8
Hälleforsnäs Sweden 59°10N 16°30E 162 E10
Hallein Austria 47°40N 13°5E 180 D6
Hällekis Sweden 58°38N 13°27E 163 F7
Hallen Sweden 63°11N 14°4E 162 A8
Hallett Australia 33°25S 138°55E 282 B3
Hallettsville U.S.A. 29°27N 96°57W 314 G6
Hallia → India 16°55N 79°20E 244 F4
Hallim S. Korea 33°24N 126°15E 224 a
Hallingby Norway 60°7N 10°10E 164 D7
Hallingdal Norway 60°40N 9°8E 164 D6
Hallingdalselva → Norway 60°23N 9°35E 164 D6
Hallingskarvet Norway 60°36N 7°47E 164 D4
Hallingskeid Norway 60°40N 7°17E 164 D4
Hallock U.S.A. 48°47N 96°57W 308 A5
Hallormsstaður Iceland 65°6N 14°45W 155 B12
Halls Creek Australia 18°16S 127°38E 278 C4
Halls Gap Australia 37°8S 142°34E 281 F3
Hallsberg Sweden 59°5N 15°7E 162 E9
Hallstahammar Sweden 59°38N 16°15E 162 E10
Hallstatt Austria 47°33N 13°38E 180 D6
Hallstavik Sweden 60°5N 18°37E 162 D12
Hallstead U.S.A. 41°58N 75°45W 313 E9
Hallyeo Maritime National Park △ S. Korea 34°45N 128°25E 224 E4
Halmahera Indonesia 0°40N 128°0E 231 D7
Halmeu Romania 47°57N 23°2E 182 C8
Halmstad Sweden 56°41N 12°52E 163 H6
Halq el Oued Tunisia 36°53N 10°18E 258 A2
Hals Denmark 57°0N 10°18E 163 H4
Halsa Norway 63°3N 8°14E 164 A5
Halsafjorden Norway 63°5N 8°10E 164 A5
Hälsingborg = Helsingborg Sweden 56°3N 12°42E 163 H6
Hälsingland Sweden 61°40N 16°5E 162 C10
Halstead U.K. 51°57N 0°40E 169 F8
Haltdalen Norway 62°56N 11°8E 164 B8
Haltern Germany 51°44N 7°11E 178 D3
Haltiala Finland 60°16N 24°57E 121 B2
Haltiatunturi Finland 69°17N 21°18E 160 B19
Haltiavuori Finland 60°16N 24°56E 121 B2
Halton □ U.K. 53°22N 2°45W 168 D5
Haltwhistle U.K. 54°58N 2°26W 168 C5
Ḥālūl Qatar 25°40N 52°40E 247 E7
Halvad India 23°1N 71°11E 242 H4
Halvān Iran 33°57N 56°15E 247 C8
Halve Dag, Pt. Neth. Ant. 12°14N 69°7W 322 g
Ham Chad 10°1N 15°35E 259 F3
Ham Somme, France 49°45N 3°4E 173 C10
Ham London, U.K. 51°25N 0°18W 125 B2
Ham Tan Vietnam 10°40N 107°45E 237 G6
Ham Yen Vietnam 22°4N 105°3E 236 A5
Hamab Namibia 28°7S 19°16E 270 C2
Hamad Sudan 15°20N 33°32E 257 D3
Hamada Japan 34°56N 132°4E 222 C4
Hamadān Iran 34°52N 48°32E 213 E13
Hamadān □ Iran 35°0N 49°0E 247 C6
Hamadia Algeria 35°28N 1°57E 261 A5
Ḥamāh Syria 35°5N 36°40E 250 C7
Ḥamāh □ Syria 35°10N 37°0E 250 C8
Hamakita Japan 34°45N 137°47E 223 C9
Hamamatsu Japan 34°45N 137°45E 223 C9
Haman S. Korea 35°14N 128°28E 224 E4
Hamar Norway 60°48N 11°7E 164 D8
Hamâta, Gebel Egypt 24°17N 35°0E 246 E2
Hambantota Sri Lanka 6°10N 81°10E 245 L5
Hamber △ Canada 52°20N 118°0W 296 C5
Hamburg Hamburg, Germany 53°33N 9°59E 178 B5
Hamburg Ark., U.S.A. 33°14N 91°48W 314 E9
Hamburg N.Y., U.S.A. 42°43N 78°50W 312 D6
Hamburg Pa., U.S.A. 40°33N 75°59W 313 F9
Hamburg □ Germany 53°30N 10°0E 178 B5
Hamburg Fuhlsbüttel ✕ (HAM) Germany 53°35N 9°59E 178 B5
Ḥamḍ, W. al → Si. Arabia 24°55N 36°20E 246 E3
Ḥamḍah Si. Arabia 19°2N 43°36E 248 C3
Ḥamḍānah Si. Arabia 19°59N 40°34E 248 C3
Hamden U.S.A. 41°23N 72°54W 313 E12
Hamdibey Turkey 39°50N 27°15E 205 B9
Häme Finland 61°38N 25°10E 188 B2
Hämeenkylä Finland 60°16N 24°48E 121 B1
Hämeenlinna Finland 61°0N 24°28E 188 B3
Hamélé Ghana 10°56N 2°45W 262 C4
Hamelin Pool Australia 26°22S 114°20E 279 E1
Hameln Germany 52°6N 9°21E 178 C5
Hamerkaz □ Israel 32°15N 34°55E 251 F5
Hamersley Ra. Australia 22°0S 117°45E 278 D2
Hamgyŏng-sanmaek N. Korea 41°35N 129°15E 224 B4
Hamgyŏngbuk-do □ N. Korea 41°50N 129°25E 224 B4
Hamgyŏngnam-do □ N. Korea 40°0N 127°30E 224 C3
Hamhŭng N. Korea 39°54N 127°30E 224 C3
Hamhŭng-man N. Korea 39°48N 127°37E 224 C3
Hami China 42°55N 93°25E 218 B4
Hamili Greece 35°50N 26°15E 205 F8
Hamilton = Churchill → Canada 53°19N 60°10W 299 B7
Hamilton Vic., Australia 37°45S 142°2E 282 D5
Hamilton Bermuda 32°17N 64°47W 153 a
Hamilton Ont., Canada 43°15N 79°50W 312 C5
Hamilton N.Z. 37°47S 175°19E 284 D4
Hamilton S. Lanarks., U.K. 55°46N 4°2W 167 F4
Hamilton Ala., U.S.A. 34°9N 87°59W 315 D11
Hamilton Alaska, U.S.A. 62°54N 163°53W 303 E7
Hamilton Ga., U.S.A. 32°45N 84°53W 316 C5
Hamilton Ill., U.S.A. 40°24N 91°21W 310 D5
Hamilton Ind., U.S.A. 41°33N 84°56W 311 C12
Hamilton Mo., U.S.A. 39°45N 94°0W 310 E2
Hamilton Mont., U.S.A. 46°15N 114°10W 304 C6
Hamilton N.Y., U.S.A. 42°50N 75°33W 313 D9
Hamilton Ohio, U.S.A. 39°24N 84°34W 311 E12
Hamilton Tex., U.S.A. 31°42N 98°7W 314 F5
Hamilton → Queens., Australia 23°30S 139°47E 280 C2
Hamilton → S. Austral., Australia 26°40S 135°19E 281 D2
Hamilton City U.S.A. 39°45N 122°1W 306 F4
Hamilton I. Australia 20°21S 148°56E 280 J6
Hamilton Inlet Canada 54°0N 57°30W 299 B8
Hamilton Mt. U.S.A. 43°25N 74°22W 313 C10
Hamina Finland 60°34N 27°12E 188 B4
Hamirpur H.P., India 31°41N 76°31E 242 D7
Hamirpur Ut. P., India 25°57N 80°9E 243 G9
Hamitabat Turkey 41°30N 27°17E 203 E11
Hamju N. Korea 39°51N 127°26E 224 C3
Hamlet U.S.A. 34°53N 79°42W 315 D15
Hamley Bridge Australia 34°17S 138°35E 282 C3
Hamlin = Hameln Germany 52°6N 9°21E 178 C5
Hamlin N.Y., U.S.A. 43°17N 77°55W 312 C7
Hamlin Tex., U.S.A. 32°53N 100°8W 314 E4
Hamm Germany 51°40N 7°50E 178 D3
Hammam Bouhadjar Algeria 35°23N 0°58W 261 A4
Hammamet Tunisia 36°24N 10°38E 258 A2
Hammamet, G. de Tunisia 36°10N 10°48E 258 A2
Ḥammār, Hawr al Iraq 30°50N 47°10E 246 D5
Hammarby Sweden 59°17N 18°5E 139 B2
Hammarstrand Sweden 63°7N 16°20E 162 A10
Hamme Belgium 50°55N 4°17E 116 A1
Hammelburg Germany 50°6N 9°53E 179 E5
Hammeren Denmark 55°18N 14°47E 163 J8
Hammerfest Norway 70°39N 23°41E 160 A20
Hammersmith U.K. 51°29N 0°14W 125 B2
Hammerstein = Czarne Poland 53°42N 16°58E 184 E3
Hammerum Denmark 56°8N 9°3E 163 H3
Hamminkeln Germany 51°43N 6°35E 178 D2
Hammond Ind., U.S.A. 41°38N 87°30W 311 C9
Hammond La., U.S.A. 30°30N 90°28W 315 F9
Hammond N.Y., U.S.A. 44°27N 75°42W 313 B9
Hammondsport U.S.A. 42°25N 77°13W 312 D7
Hammonton U.S.A. 39°39N 74°48W 309 F16
Hamneda Sweden 56°41N 13°51E 163 H7
Hamoyet, Jebel Sudan 17°33N 38°2E 256 D4
Hampden N.Z. 45°18S 170°50E 285 F5
Hampshire □ U.K. 51°7N 1°23W 169 F6
Hampshire Downs U.K. 51°15N 1°10W 169 F6
Hampstead Qué., Canada 45°28N 73°37W 130 B2
Hampstead Dominica 15°36N 61°23W 323 k
Hampstead London, U.K. 51°33N 0°10W 125 A2
Hampstead Garden Suburb U.K. 51°34N 0°11W 125 A2
Hampstead Heath U.K. 51°33N 0°10W 125 A2
Hampton N.B., Canada 45°32N 65°51W 299 C6
Hampton Ont., Canada 43°58N 78°45W 312 C6
Hampton London, U.K. 51°24N 0°21W 125 B1
Hampton Ark., U.S.A. 33°32N 92°28W 314 E8
Hampton Ga., U.S.A. 33°23N 84°17W 316 B5
Hampton Iowa, U.S.A. 42°45N 93°13W 310 B3
Hampton N.H., U.S.A. 42°57N 70°50W 313 D14
Hampton S.C., U.S.A. 32°52N 81°7W 316 C8
Hampton Va., U.S.A. 37°2N 76°21W 309 G15
Hampton Bays U.S.A. 40°53N 72°30W 313 F12
Hampton Court Palace U.K. 51°24N 0°20W 125 B1
Hampton Springs U.S.A. 30°5N 83°40W 316 E6
Hampton Tableland Australia 32°0S 127°0E 279 F4
Hampton Wick U.K. 51°24N 0°18W 125 B2
Hampyeong S. Korea 35°3N 126°31E 224 E3
Hampyeongman S. Korea 35°6N 126°23E 224 E3
Ḥamrā' Baghdād, Iraq 33°18N 44°18E 113 B1
Hamra Gävleborg, Sweden 61°39N 14°59E 162 C8
Hamra → Chad 12°52N 21°15E 259 F4
Hamrat esh Sheykh Sudan 14°38N 27°55E 257 E2
Hamrun Malta 35°53N 14°29E 206 F8
Hamtik Phil. 10°42N 121°59E 233 F3
Hamur Turkey 39°37N 43°3E 213 C10
Hamyang S. Korea 35°32N 127°42E 224 E3
Hamzalar Turkey 37°7N 32°33E 250 A3
Han i Hotit Albania 42°19N 19°27E 202 D3
Han Jiang → China 23°25N 116°40E 229 F11
Han Shui → China 30°34N 114°17E 229 B10
Hāna U.S.A. 20°45N 155°59W 302 C6
Hanahan U.S.A. 32°55N 80°0W 316 C10
Hanak Si. Arabia 25°32N 37°0E 246 E3
Hanala Finland 60°20N 25°4E 121 A3
Hanalei U.S.A. 22°12N 159°30W 302 A2
Hanamaki Japan 39°23N 141°7E 220 E10
Hanang Tanzania 4°30S 35°25E 268 C4
Hanapēpē U.S.A. 21°55N 159°35W 302 B2
Hanare Iwa Iwo Jima 24°48N 141°21E 288 b
Hanau Germany 50°7N 8°56E 179 E4
Hanauma B. U.S.A. 21°15N 157°40W 302 K14
Hanbogd = Ihbulag Mongolia 43°11N 107°10E 226 C4
Hançalar Turkey 38°8N 29°24E 205 C11
Hânceşti Moldova 46°50N 28°36E 183 D13
Hancheng China 35°31N 110°25E 226 G6
Hanchuan China 30°40N 113°50E 229 B9
Hanchung = Hanzhong China 33°10N 107°1E 226 H4
Hancock Mich., U.S.A. 47°8N 88°35W 308 B9
Hancock N.Y., U.S.A. 41°57N 75°17W 313 E9
Handa Japan 34°53N 136°55E 223 C8
Handa Somali Rep. 10°37N 51°2E 267 B7
Handa I. U.K. 58°23N 5°11W 167 C3
Handan China 36°35N 114°28E 226 F8
Handeni Tanzania 5°25S 38°2E 268 D4
Handlová Slovak Rep. 48°45N 18°35E 181 C11
Handub Sudan 19°15N 37°16E 256 D4
Handwara India 34°21N 74°20E 243 B6
Haneda Japan 35°32N 139°44E 140 B3
Haneda, Tōkyō ✕ (HND) Japan 35°33N 139°46E 140 B3
Hanegev Israel 30°50N 35°0E 251 H6
Hanford U.S.A. 36°20N 119°39W 306 J7
Hanford Reach △ U.S.A. 46°40N 119°30W 304 C4
Hang Chat Thailand 18°20N 99°21E 236 C2
Hang Dong Thailand 18°41N 98°55E 236 C2
Hang Hau China 22°19N 114°16E 122 B2
Hanga Roa Chile 27°8S 109°26W 330 b
Hangang → S. Korea 37°50N 126°30E 227 F14
Hangayn Nuruu Mongolia 47°30N 99°0E 218 B4
Hangchou = Hangzhou China 30°18N 120°11E 229 B13
Hanggin Houqi China 40°58N 107°4E 226 D4
Hanggin Qi China 39°52N 108°50E 226 E5
Hanging Gardens Mumbai, India 130 b1
Hangkow = Wuhan China 30°31N 114°18E 229 B10
Hangku = Hangu China 39°18N 117°53E 227 E9
Hangu China 39°18N 117°53E 227 E9
Hangzhou China 30°18N 120°11E 229 B13
Hangzhou Wan China 30°15N 120°45E 229 B13
Hanhöhiy Uul Mongolia 49°30N 94°30E 217 C12
Hanhongor Mongolia 43°55N 104°28E 226 C3
Hania = Chania Greece 35°30N 24°4E 207 E5
Ḥanīdh Si. Arabia 26°35N 48°38E 247 E6
Ḥanīsh Yemen 13°45N 42°46E 248 D3
Haniska Slovak Rep. 48°37N 21°15E 181 C14
Hanjiang China 25°26N 119°6E 229 E12
Hankinson U.S.A. 46°4N 96°54W 308 B5
Hankö Finland 59°50N 22°57E 188 C2
Hankou China 30°35N 114°30E 229 B10
Hanksville U.S.A. 38°22N 110°43W 304 G8
Hanle India 32°42N 79°4E 243 C8
Hanlon Canada 43°38N 79°39W 141 B1
Hanmer Springs N.Z. 42°32S 172°50E 285 C7
Hann → Australia 17°26S 126°17E 278 C4
Hann, Mt. Australia 15°45S 126°0E 278 C4
Hanna Alta., Canada 51°40N 111°54W 296 C6
Hanna Wyo., U.S.A. 41°52N 106°34W 304 F10
Hannah B. Canada 51°40N 80°0W 298 B4
Hannibal Mo., U.S.A. 39°42N 91°22W 310 E5
Hannibal N.Y., U.S.A. 43°19N 76°35W 313 C8
Hannik Sudan 18°12N 32°20E 256 D3
Hannover Germany 52°22N 9°46E 178 C5
Hanö Sweden 56°1N 14°50E 163 H8
Hanöbukten Sweden 55°35N 14°30E 163 J8
Hanoi Vietnam 21°5N 105°55E 228 G5
Hanover = Hannover Germany 52°22N 9°46E 178 C5
Hanover Ont., Canada 44°9N 81°2W 312 B3
Hanover Northern Cape, S. Africa 31°4S 24°29E 270 D3
Hanover Ind., U.S.A. 38°43N 85°28W 311 F11
Hanover N.H., U.S.A. 43°42N 72°17W 313 C12
Hanover Ohio, U.S.A. 40°4N 82°16W 312 F2
Hanover Pa., U.S.A. 39°48N 76°59W 309 F15
Hanover, I. Chile 51°0S 74°50W 336 D2
Hanpan, C. Papua N. G. 5°0S 154°35E 286 C8
Hans Lollik I. U.S. Virgin Is. 18°24N 64°53W 321 b
Hans Meyer Ra. Papua N. G. 4°20S 152°55E 286 C7
Hansdiha India 24°36N 87°5E 243 G12
Hanshou China 28°56N 111°50E 229 C8
Hansi India 29°10N 75°57E 242 E6
Hanson, L. Australia 31°0S 136°15E 282 A2
Hanstholm Denmark 57°7N 8°36E 163 G2
Hantan = Handan China 36°35N 114°28E 226 F8
Hantsavichy Belarus 52°49N 26°30E 177 B14
Hanumangarh India 29°35N 74°19E 242 E6
Hanwell U.K. 51°30N 0°20W 125 A1
Hanworth U.K. 51°26N 0°23W 125 B1
Hanyin China 32°54N 108°28E 228 A7
Hanyū Japan 36°10N 139°32E 223 A11
Hanyuan China 29°21N 102°40E 228 C4
Hanzhong China 33°10N 107°1E 226 H4
Hanzhuang China 34°33N 117°23E 227 G9
Hao French Polynesia 18°15S 140°54W 289 f
Haora India 22°34N 88°18E 124 B1
Haouach, O. → Chad 16°45N 19°35E 259 E4
Haoxue China 30°3N 112°24E 229 B9
Haparanda Sweden 65°52N 24°8E 160 D21
Hapdeok S. Korea 36°48N 126°46E 224 D3
Hapeville U.S.A. 33°39N 84°24W 113 C2
Happy U.S.A. 34°45N 101°52W 314 D4
Happy Camp U.S.A. 41°48N 123°23W 304 F2
Happy Valley China 22°16N 114°10E 122 B2
Happy Valley-Goose Bay Canada 53°15N 60°20W 299 B7
Hapsu N. Korea 41°13N 128°51E 224 B4
Hapur India 28°45N 77°45E 242 E7
Ḥaql Si. Arabia 29°10N 34°58E 251 J5
Haquira Peru 14°14S 72°12W 330 C3
Har Indonesia 5°16S 133°14E 231 F8
Har Adar West Bank 31°49N 35°8E 123 B1
Har-Ayrag Mongolia 45°47N 109°16E 226 B5
Har Gilo West Bank 31°43N 35°10E 123 B2
Har Homa West Bank 31°44N 35°12E 123 B2
Har Hu China 38°20N 97°38E 218 C4
Har Nof Israel 31°47N 35°11E 123 B2
Har Tsiyon Jerusalem 123 b3
Har Us Nuur Mongolia 48°0N 92°0E 217 C12
Har Yehuda Israel 31°35N 34°57E 251 G5
Ḥaraḍ Si. Arabia 24°22N 49°0E 249 A5
Ḥaraḍ Yemen 16°26N 43°5E 248 D3
Haradok Belarus 55°30N 30°3E 188 E6
Häradsbäck Sweden 56°32N 14°26E 163 H8
Harahan U.S.A. 29°56N 90°12W 131 B1
Haraiki French Polynesia 17°38S 143°27W 289 f
Haranomachi Japan 37°38N 140°58E 220 F10
Harardera Somali Rep. 4°33N 47°38E 267 D6
Harare Zimbabwe 17°43S 31°2E 269 F3
Ḥarāsīs, Jiddat al Oman 19°30N 56°0E 249 C7
Harat Eritrea 16°5N 39°26E 257 D4
Haraz Chad 14°20N 19°12E 259 F3
Harazé Chad 9°57N 20°48E 259 G4
Harbhanga India 20°38N 84°36E 244 D7
Harbin China 45°48N 126°40E 227 B14
Harbiye Turkey 36°10N 36°8E 250 B7
Harbo Sweden 60°7N 17°12E 162 D11
Harboøre Denmark 56°38N 8°10E 163 H2
Harbor Beach U.S.A. 43°51N 82°39W 312 C2
Harbour Breton Canada 47°29N 55°50W 299 C8
Harbour View Jamaica 17°59N 76°50W 320 a
Harburg Germany 53°27N 9°58E 178 B5
Harburger Berge △ Germany 53°26N 9°51E 178 B5
Harda India 22°27N 77°5E 242 H7
Hardangerfjorden Norway 60°5N 6°0E 164 D3
Hardangerjøkulen Norway 60°30N 7°27E 164 D4
Hardangervidda Norway 60°7N 7°20E 164 D4
Hardangervidda △ Norway 60°10N 7°25E 164 D4
Hardap △ Namibia 24°29S 17°45E 270 B2
Hardap Dam Namibia 24°32S 17°50E 270 B2
Hardeeville U.S.A. 32°17N 81°5W 316 C8
Harden Australia 34°32S 148°24E 283 C8
Hardenberg Neths. 52°34N 6°37E 170 B6
Harderwijk Neths. 52°21N 5°38E 170 B5
Hardey → Australia 22°45S 116°8E 278 D2
Hardin Ill., U.S.A. 39°10N 90°37W 310 E6
Hardin Mont., U.S.A. 45°44N 107°37W 304 D10
Harding S. Africa 30°35S 29°55E 271 D4
Harding, L. U.S.A. 32°40N 85°5W 316 C4
Harding Ra. Australia 16°17S 124°55E 278 C3
Hardinsburg U.S.A. 37°47N 86°28W 311 G10
Hardisty Canada 52°40N 111°18W 296 C6
Hardoi India 27°26N 80°6E 243 F9
Hardwar = Haridwar India 29°58N 78°9E 242 E8
Hardwick Ga., U.S.A. 33°4N 83°14W 316 B6
Hardwick Vt., U.S.A. 44°30N 72°22W 313 B12
Hardwicke B. Australia 34°55S 137°20E 282 C2
Hardy, Pen. Chile 55°30S 68°20W 336 E3
Hardy, Pte. St. Lucia 14°6N 60°56W 323 m
Hare B. Canada 51°15N 55°45W 299 B8
Hareid Norway 62°22N 6°1E 164 B3
Haren Brussels, Belgium 50°53N 4°25E 116 A2
Haren Niedersachsen, Germany 52°47N 7°13E 178 C3
Harer Ethiopia 9°20N 42°8E 257 F5
Harerge Ethiopia 7°12N 42°0E 257 F5
Hareskovby Denmark 55°45N 12°23E 118 A2
Harestua Norway 60°11N 10°42E 164 D7
Hareto Ethiopia 9°23N 37°6E 257 F4
Harfleur France 49°30N 0°10E 172 C7
Hargeisa Somali Rep. 9°30N 44°2E 267 C5
Hargeisa △ Somali Rep. 10°2N 44°2E 267 B5
Harghita □ Romania 46°30N 25°30E 183 D10
Harghita, Munții Romania 46°25N 25°35E 183 D10
Hargshamn Sweden 60°12N 18°30E 162 D12
Hari → Indonesia 1°16S 104°5E 234 C2
Haría Canary Is. 29°8N 13°32W 153 E2
Ḥarīb Yemen 14°56N 45°30E 248 D4
Haricha, Hamada el Mali 22°40N 3°15W 260 D4
Haridwar India 29°58N 78°9E 242 E8
Harihar India 14°32N 75°44E 245 G2
Harihari N.Z. 43°9S 170°33E 285 D5
Hārim Syria 36°14N 36°29E 250 B7
Harim, Jabal al Oman 25°58N 56°14E 247 E8
Harima-Nada Japan 34°30N 134°35E 222 C6
Haringey □ U.K. 51°34N 0°5W 125 A3
Haringhata → Bangla. 22°0N 89°58E 241 E2
Haripad India 9°14N 76°28E 245 K3
Harīr, W. al → Syria 32°44N 35°59E 250 F6
Harīrūd → Asia 37°24N 60°38E 240 A1
Härjedalen Sweden 62°22N 13°5E 162 B7
Harjusuo Finland 60°19N 25°0E 121 B3
Harlaching Germany 48°5N 11°33E 131 B2
Harlan Iowa, U.S.A. 41°39N 95°19W 308 E6
Harlan Ky., U.S.A. 36°51N 83°19W 309 G12
Hârlău Romania 47°23N 26°55E 183 C11
Harlaw Res. U.K. 55°52N 3°18W 121 B2
Harlech U.K. 52°52N 4°6W 168 E3
Harlem Ga., U.S.A. 33°25N 82°19W 316 B7
Harlem Mont., U.S.A. 48°32N 108°47W 304 B9
Harlem New York, U.S.A. 132 a3
Harlesden U.K. 51°32N 0°14W 125 A2
Hårlev Denmark 55°21N 12°14E 163 J6
Harleyville U.S.A. 33°13N 80°27W 316 B9
Harlingen Neths. 53°11N 5°25E 170 A5
Harlingen Tex., U.S.A. 26°12N 97°42W 314 H6
Harlington U.K. 51°29N 0°25W 125 B1
Harlow U.K. 51°46N 0°8E 169 F8
Harlowton U.S.A. 46°26N 109°50W 304 C9
Harmaja Finland 60°6N 24°58E 121 C2
Harmancık Turkey 39°41N 29°9E 205 B11
Harmånger Sweden 61°55N 17°20E 162 C11
Harmashatar hegy Hungary 47°33N 19°0E 117 A2
Harmil Eritrea 16°30N 40°10E 257 D5
Harnai India 17°48N 73°6E 244 F1
Harnai Pakistan 30°6N 67°56E 242 D2
Harney, L. U.S.A. 28°45N 81°3W 317 G8
Harney Basin U.S.A. 43°0N 119°30W 304 E4
Harney L. U.S.A. 43°14N 119°8W 304 E4
Harney Peak U.S.A. 43°52N 103°32W 308 D2
Härnön Sweden 62°36N 18°0E 162 B12
Härnösand Sweden 62°38N 17°55E 162 B11
Haro Spain 42°35N 2°55W 192 C2
Harold U.S.A. 30°40N 86°53W 317 E3
Harold Pond Bahamas 25°2N 77°22W 153 b
Harolds Cross Ireland 53°19N 6°16W 120 B2
Haroldswick U.K. 60°48N 0°50W 167 A8
Háros Hungary 47°23N 19°2E 117 B2
Harp L. Canada 55°5N 61°50W 299 A7
Harpanahalli India 14°47N 76°2E 245 G3
Harper = Costa Mesa U.S.A. 33°38N 117°55W 307 M9
Harper Liberia 4°25N 7°43W 262 E3
Harper, Mt. U.S.A. 64°14N 143°51W 303 D12
Harperrig Res. U.K. 55°50N 3°26W 121 B1
Harplinge Sweden 56°45N 12°45E 163 H6
Harr Mauritania 15°20N 12°28W 262 B2
Harrai India 22°37N 79°13E 243 H8
Harrand Pakistan 29°28N 70°3E 242 E4
Ḥarrat Khaybar Si. Arabia 25°30N 39°45E 256 B5
Ḥarrat Nawāṣīf Si. Arabia 21°20N 42°10E 256 C5
Harricana → Canada 50°56N 79°32W 298 B4
Harriman U.S.A. 35°56N 84°33W 315 D12
Harrington Australia 31°52S 152°42E 283 A10
Harrington Harbour Canada 50°31N 59°30W 299 B8
Harrington Sd. Bermuda 32°20N 64°44W 153 a
Harris Montserrat 16°44N 62°11W 323 p
Harris W. Isles, U.K. 57°50N 6°55W 167 D2
Harris, L. S. Austral., Australia 31°10S 135°10E 281 E2
Harris, L. Fla., U.S.A. 28°47N 81°49W 317 G8
Harris, Sd. of U.K. 57°44N 7°6W 167 D1
Harris Mts. N.Z. 44°49S 168°49E 285 E3
Harris Pt. Canada 43°6N 82°9W 312 C2
Harrisburg Ill., U.S.A. 37°44N 88°32W 311 G8
Harrisburg Nebr., U.S.A. 41°33N 103°44W 308 E2
Harrisburg Pa., U.S.A. 40°16N 76°53W 312 F8
Harrismith S. Africa 28°15S 29°8E 271 C4
Harrison Ark., U.S.A. 36°14N 93°7W 314 C8
Harrison Maine, U.S.A. 44°7N 70°39W 313 B14
Harrison Nebr., U.S.A. 42°41N 103°53W 308 D2
Harrison, C. Canada 54°55N 57°55W 299 B8
Harrison Bay U.S.A. 70°40N 151°0W 303 A10
Harrison L. Canada 49°33N 121°50W 296 D4
Harrisonburg U.S.A. 38°27N 78°52W 309 F14
Harrison's Cave Barbados 13°11N 59°34W 323 r
Harrisonville U.S.A. 38°39N 94°21W 310 F2
Harriston Canada 43°57N 80°53W 312 C4
Harrisville Mich., U.S.A. 44°39N 83°17W 312 B1
Harrisville N.Y., U.S.A. 44°9N 75°19W 313 B9
Harrisville Pa., U.S.A. 41°8N 80°0W 312 E5
Harrodsburg Ind., U.S.A. 39°1N 86°33W 311 F10
Harrodsburg Ky., U.S.A. 37°46N 84°51W 311 G12
Harrogate U.K. 54°0N 1°33W 168 C6
Harrow Vic., Australia 37°9S 141°35E 282 D4
Harrow Ont., Canada 42°2N 82°55W 311 B14
Harrow □ U.K. 51°35N 0°21W 125 A1
Harrow on the Hill U.K. 51°34N 0°21W 125 A1
Harrow School U.K. 51°34N 0°20W 125 A1
Harrow Weald U.K. 51°36N 0°20W 125 A1
Harrowsmith Canada 44°24N 76°40W 313 B8
Harry S. Truman Res. U.S.A. 38°16N 93°24W 310 F3
Harsefeld Germany 53°27N 9°30E 178 B5
Harsewinkel Germany 51°56N 8°14E 178 D4
Harsīn Iran 34°18N 47°33E 213 E12
Hârşova Romania 44°40N 27°59E 183 F12
Harstad Norway 68°48N 16°30E 160 B17
Harsud India 22°6N 76°44E 242 H7
Hart U.S.A. 43°42N 86°22W 308 D10
Hart, L. Australia 31°10S 136°25E 282 A2
Hartbees → S. Africa 28°45S 20°32E 270 C3
Hartberg Austria 47°17N 15°58E 180 D8
Hårteigen Norway 60°11N 7°3E 164 D4
Hartford Ala., U.S.A. 31°6N 85°42W 316 D4
Hartford Conn., U.S.A. 41°46N 72°41W 313 E12
Hartford Ky., U.S.A. 37°27N 86°55W 308 G10
Hartford Mich., U.S.A. 42°13N 86°10W 311 B10
Hartford S. Dak., U.S.A. 43°38N 96°57W 308 D5
Hartford Vt., U.S.A. 43°40N 72°20W 313 C12
Hartford Wis., U.S.A. 43°19N 88°22W 308 D9
Hartford City U.S.A. 40°27N 85°22W 311 D11
Hartingsburg = Bela Bela S. Africa 24°51S 28°19E 271 B4
Hartland N.B., Canada 46°20N 67°32W 299 C6
Hartland Wis., U.S.A. 43°6N 88°21W 311 A8
Hartland Pt. U.K. 51°1N 4°32W 169 F3
Hartlepool U.K. 54°42N 1°13W 168 C6
Hartlepool □ U.K. 54°42N 1°17W 168 C6
Hartley Bay Canada 53°25N 129°15W 296 C3
Hartmannberge Namibia 17°0S 13°0E 270 A1
Hartney Canada 49°30N 100°35W 297 D8
Hârtop Moldova 46°39N 28°40E 183 D13
Harts → S. Africa 28°24S 24°17E 270 C3
Hartselle U.S.A. 34°27N 86°56W 315 D11
Hartsfield-Atlanta Int. ✕ (ATL) U.S.A. 33°38N 84°26W 113 C2
Hartshorne U.S.A. 34°51N 95°34W 314 D7
Hartstown U.S.A. 41°33N 80°23W 312 E4
Hartsville U.S.A. 34°23N 80°4W 315 D14
Hartswater S. Africa 27°34S 24°43E 270 C3
Hartwell U.S.A. 34°21N 82°56W 315 D13
Harumi Tokyo, Japan 140 c5
Harunabad Pakistan 29°35N 73°8E 242 E5
Harur India 12°3N 78°29E 245 H4
Hārūt → Afghan. 31°29N 61°24E 240 C1
Harvand Iran 28°25N 55°43E 247 D7
Harvard U.S.A. 42°25N 88°37W 311 B8
Harvard University U.S.A. 42°22N 71°7W 116 A2
Harvey W. Austral., Australia 33°5S 115°54E 279 F2
Harvey Ill., U.S.A. 41°36N 87°50W 311 C9
Harvey La., U.S.A. 29°54N 90°4W 131 B2
Harvey N. Dak., U.S.A. 47°47N 99°56W 308 B4
Harwich U.K. 51°56N 1°17E 169 F9
Harwood Heights U.S.A. 41°57N 87°46W 119 B2
Haryana □ India 29°0N 76°10E 242 E7
Haryn → Belarus 52°7N 27°17E 177 B14
Harz Germany 51°38N 10°44E 178 D6
Harz △ Germany 51°40N 10°18E 178 D6
Harzgerode Germany 51°38N 11°8E 178 D7
Hasa Si. Arabia 25°50N 49°0E 247 E6
Ḥasā, W. al → Jordan 31°4N 35°29E 251 G6
Hasaheisa Sudan 14°44N 33°20E 257 E3
Ḥasanābād Esfahan, Iran 32°8N 52°44E 247 C7
Ḥasanābād Tehrān, Iran 35°44N 51°16E 141 A1
Hasankeyf Turkey 37°42N 41°24E 213 D9
Hasanparti India 18°4N 79°32E 244 E4
Ḥasb, W. → Iraq 31°45N 44°17E 246 D5
Hasbrouck Heights U.S.A. 40°51N 74°6W 132 A1
Hasdo → India 21°44N 82°44E 243 J10
Haselhorst Germany 52°33N 13°14E 115 A2
Haselünne Germany 52°40N 7°29E 178 C3
Hashima Japan 35°20N 136°40E 223 B8
Hashimoto Japan 34°19N 135°37E 223 C7
Hashtjerd Iran 35°52N 50°40E 247 C6
Hasi Nueifed W. Sahara 24°54N 14°49W 260 D2
Hasi Tafraut W. Sahara 27°24N 13°15W 260 C2
Ḥāsik Oman 17°22N 55°17E 249 D7
Haskell U.S.A. 33°10N 99°44W 314 E5
Haskovo = Khaskovo Bulgaria 41°56N 25°30E 203 E9
Hasköy Edirne, Turkey 41°38N 26°52E 203 E10
Hasköy İstanbul, Turkey 41°2N 28°57E 122 B1
Haslach Germany 48°16N 8°5E 179 G4
Hasle Denmark 55°11N 14°44E 163 J8
Hasle Oslo, Norway 59°46N 10°38E 133 B2
Haslemere U.K. 51°5N 0°43W 169 F7
Haslev Denmark 55°18N 11°57E 163 J5
Haslum Norway 59°55N 10°34E 133 A2
Hasparren France 43°24N 1°18W 174 E2
Hassa Turkey 36°48N 36°29E 250 B7
Hassan India 13°0N 76°5E 245 H3
Hassberge △ Germany 50°8N 10°45E 179 E6
Hassela Sweden 62°7N 16°42E 162 B10
Hasselt Belgium 50°56N 5°21E 170 D5
Hassene, Adrar Algeria 21°0N 4°0E 261 D5
Hassfurt Germany 50°2N 10°30E 179 E6
Hassi bel Guebbour Algeria 28°30N 6°41E 261 C6
Hassi bou Khelala Algeria 30°17N 0°18W 261 B4
Hassi Bourarchet Algeria 27°26N 9°19E 261 C6
Hassi Djafou Algeria 30°55N 3°35E 261 B5
Hassi el Abiod Algeria 31°47N 3°37E 261 B5
Hassi el Biod Algeria 28°30N 6°0E 261 C6
Hassi el Hadjar Algeria 31°28N 4°45E 261 B5
Hassi Imoulaye Algeria 29°54N 9°10E 261 C6
Hassi Inifeg Algeria 28°15N 1°30W 261 C4
Hassi Inifel Algeria 29°50N 3°41E 261 C5
Hassi Mana Algeria 28°48N 2°37W 261 C4
Hassi Marroket Algeria 30°10N 3°0E 261 B5
Hassi Messaoud Algeria 31°51N 6°1E 261 B6
Hassi Sougoued Algeria 26°50N 9°28E 261 C6
Hassi Tartrat Algeria 30°5N 6°28E 261 B6
Hassi Zerzour Morocco 30°51N 3°56W 260 B4
Hassi Zguilma Algeria 30°19N 6°30E 260 B4
Hässleholm Sweden 56°10N 13°46E 163 H7
Hassloch Germany 49°22N 8°16E 179 F4
Hästhagen Sweden 59°18N 18°9E 139 B2
Hästholmen Sweden 58°17N 14°38E 163 F8
Hastings Vic., Australia 38°18S 145°12E 283 E6
Hastings Barbados 13°4N 59°36W 323 r
Hastings N.Z. 39°39S 176°52E 284 F5
Hastings U.K. 50°51N 0°35E 169 G8
Hastings Fla., U.S.A. 29°43N 81°31W 316 F8
Hastings Mich., U.S.A. 42°39N 85°17W 311 B11
Hastings Minn., U.S.A. 44°44N 92°51W 308 C7
Hastings Nebr., U.S.A. 40°35N 98°23W 308 E4
Hastings Ra. Australia 31°15S 152°14E 283 A10
Hästveda Sweden 56°17N 13°55E 163 H7
Ḥasy 'Aṭshān Libya 27°20N 10°25E 258 C2
Hat Ukraine 48°19N 22°38E 182 B7
Hat Head △ Australia 31°3S 153°1E 283 A10
Hat Yai Thailand 7°1N 100°27E 237 J3
Hataitai N.Z. 41°18S 174°48E 143 B1
Hatanbulag = Ergel Mongolia 43°8N 109°5E 226 C5
Hatay Turkey 36°14N 36°10E 250 B7
Hatay □ Turkey 36°25N 36°15E 250 B7
Hatch U.S.A. 32°40N 107°9W 305 K10
Hatch End U.K. 51°36N 0°22W 125 A1
Hatchet L. Canada 58°36N 103°40W 297 B8

Haţeg *Romania* 45°36N 22°55E 182 E7
Hateruma-Shima *Japan* 24°3N 123°47E 221 M1
Hatfield P.O. *Australia* 33°54S 143°49E 282 B5
Hatgal *Mongolia* 50°26N 100°9E 218 A5
Hathras *India* 27°36N 78°6E 242 F8
Hatia *Bangla.* 22°30N 91°5E 241 D3
Hatia Is. *Bangla.* 22°30N 91°0E 241 D3
Hatiara *India* 22°36N 88°26E 124 B2
Ḩāţibah, Ra's *Si. Arabia* 21°55N 38°57E 256 C4
Hatid *India* 17°17N 75°3E 244 F2
Hatillo *Puerto Rico* 18°29N 66°50W 321 b
Hato *Bonaire, Neth. Ant.* 12°11N 68°17W 322 h
Hato *Curaçao, Neth. Ant.* 12°11N 68°57W 322 g
Hato Caves *Neth. Ant.* 12°11N 68°57W 322 g
Hato Corozal *Colombia* 6°11N 71°45W 328 B3
Hato Mayor *Dom. Rep.* 18°46N 69°15W 321 C6
Hatsukaichi *Japan* 34°22N 132°22E 222 C4
Hatta *India* 24°7N 79°36E 243 G8
Hatta *U.A.E.* 24°45N 56°4E 247 E8
Hattah *Australia* 34°48S 142°17E 282 C5
Hattah Kulkyne △ *Australia* 34°16S 142°33E 282 C5
Hatteras, C. *U.S.A.* 35°14N 75°32W 315 D17
Hatteras Abyssal Plain *Atl. Oc.* 28°0N 72°0W 152 D4
Hattiesburg *U.S.A.* 31°20N 89°17W 315 F10
Hatutu *French Polynesia* 7°56S 140°38W 289 f
Hatvan *Hungary* 47°40N 19°45E 182 C4
Hau Duc *Vietnam* 15°20N 108°13E 236 E7
Haubstadt *U.S.A.* 38°12N 87°34W 311 F9
Haud *Ethiopia* 8°0N 45°0E 267 C6
Hauganes *Iceland* 65°56N 18°27W 155 B8
Haugastøl *Norway* 60°30N 7°50E 164 D4
Hauge *Norway* 58°20N 6°15E 164 F3
Haugesund *Norway* 59°23N 5°13E 164 E2
Hauhui *Solomon Is.* 9°10S 160°59E 287 M11
Hauhungaroa Ra. *N.Z.* 38°42S 175°40E 284 E4
Haukeligrend *Norway* 59°44N 7°33E 164 E4
Hauketo *Norway* 59°50N 10°48E 133 A3
Haukipudas *Finland* 65°12N 25°20E 160 D21
Haultain → *Canada* 55°51N 106°46W 297 B7
Haungpa *Burma* 25°29N 96°7E 241 C6
Hauraha *Solomon Is.* 10°46S 161°59E 287 N11
Hauraki G. *N.Z.* 36°35S 175°5E 284 C4
Hauroko L. *N.Z.* 45°59S 167°21E 285 F2
Hausruck *Austria* 48°6N 13°30E 180 C6
Haut Atlas *Morocco* 32°30N 5°0W 260 B4
Haut de la Montagne *Guadeloupe* 16°26N 61°28W 322 e
Haut-Jura ⌂ *France* 46°23N 2°23E 173 F9
Haut-Languedoc ⌂ *France* 43°30N 2°43E 174 E6
Haut-Niger △ *Guinea* 10°20N 10°20W 262 C2
Haut-Rhin □ *France* 48°0N 7°15E 173 E14
Haut-Zaïre = Orientale □ *Dem. Rep. of the Congo* 2°20N 26°0E 268 B2
Haute-Corse □ *France* 42°30N 9°30E 175 F13
Haute-Garonne □ *France* 43°30N 1°30E 174 E5
Haute-Loire □ *France* 45°5N 3°50E 174 C7
Haute-Marne □ *France* 48°10N 5°20E 173 D12
Haute-Normandie □ *France* 49°20N 1°0E 172 C7
Haute-Saône □ *France* 47°45N 6°10E 173 E13
Haute-Savoie □ *France* 46°0N 6°20E 175 C10
Haute-Vienne □ *France* 45°50N 1°10E 174 C5
Hautes-Alpes □ *France* 44°42N 6°20E 175 D10
Hautes Fagnes = Hohes Venn *Belgium* 50°30N 6°5E 170 D6
Hautes-Pyrénées □ *France* 43°0N 0°10E 174 F4
Hauteville-Lompnès *France* 45°58N 5°36E 175 C9
Hautmont *France* 50°15N 3°55E 173 B10
Hauts-de-Seine □ *France* 48°52N 2°15E 173 D9
Hauts Plateaux *Algeria* 35°0N 1°0E 261 B5
Hau'ula *U.S.A.* 21°37N 157°55W 302 J14
Hauz Khas *India* 28°33N 77°11E 120 B2
Hauzenberg *Germany* 48°40N 13°37E 179 G9
Havana = La Habana *Cuba* 23°8N 82°22W 320 B3
Havana *Fla., U.S.A.* 30°37N 84°25W 316 E5
Havana *Ill., U.S.A.* 40°18N 90°4W 310 D6
Havant *U.K.* 50°51N 0°58W 169 G7
Havârna *Romania* 48°4N 26°43E 183 B11
Havasor = Kığzı *Turkey* 38°18N 43°25E 246 B4
Havasu, L. *U.S.A.* 34°18N 114°28W 307 L12
Havdata *Greece* 38°12N 20°23E 207 D1
Havdhem *Sweden* 57°10N 18°20E 163 G12
Havel → *Berlin, Germany* 52°37N 13°11E 115 A2
Havel → *Brandenburg, Germany* 52°50N 12°3E 178 C8
Havelian *Pakistan* 34°2N 73°10E 242 B5
Havelkanal *Germany* 52°36N 13°10E 115 A2
Havelock *Ont., Canada* 44°26N 77°53W 312 B7
Havelock *N.Z.* 41°17S 173°48E 285 B8
Havelock *N.C., U.S.A.* 34°53N 76°54W 315 D16
Havelock I. *India* 11°58N 93°0E 245 J11
Havelock North *N.Z.* 39°40S 176°53E 284 F5
Haverfordwest *U.K.* 51°48N 4°58W 169 F3
Haverhill *Suffolk, U.K.* 52°5N 0°28E 169 E8
Haverhill *Fla., U.S.A.* 26°42N 80°7W 317 J9
Haverhill *Mass., U.S.A.* 42°47N 71°5W 313 D13
Haveri *India* 14°53N 75°24E 245 G2
Havering □ *U.K.* 51°34N 0°13E 125 A5
Havering-atte-Bower *U.K.* 51°37N 0°11E 125 A5
Haverstraw *U.S.A.* 41°12N 73°58W 313 E11
Håverud *Sweden* 58°50N 12°28E 163 F6
Havirga *Mongolia* 45°41N 113°5E 226 B7
Havířov *Czech Rep.* 49°46N 18°20E 181 B11
Havlíčkův Brod *Czech Rep.* 49°36N 15°33E 180 B8
Havneby *Denmark* 55°5N 8°34E 163 J2
Havran *Turkey* 39°33N 27°6E 205 B9
Havre *U.S.A.* 48°33N 109°41W 304 B9
Havre-Aubert *Canada* 47°12N 61°56W 299 C7
Havre-St.-Pierre *Canada* 50°18N 63°33W 299 B7
Havsa *Turkey* 41°31N 26°48E 203 E10
Havza *Turkey* 41°0N 35°35E 212 B6
Haw → *U.S.A.* 35°36N 79°3W 315 D15
Hawai'i *U.S.A.* 19°30N 155°30W 302 D6
Hawai'i □ *U.S.A.* 19°30N 156°30W 302 D5
Hawai'i County *U.S.A.* 19°30N 155°30W 302 D6
Hawai'i Volcanoes △ *U.S.A.* 19°25N 155°18W 302 D6
Hawaiian Is. *Pac. Oc.* 20°30N 156°0W 302 G12
Hawaiian Ridge *Pac. Oc.* 24°0N 165°0W 289 E11
Hawarden *U.S.A.* 43°0N 96°29W 308 D5
Hawashîyah, W. *Egypt* 28°31N 32°58E 251 K3
Hawea, L. *N.Z.* 44°28S 169°19E 285 E4
Hawea Flat *N.Z.* 44°40S 169°19E 285 E4
Hawera *N.Z.* 39°35S 174°19E 284 F3
Hawesville *U.S.A.* 37°54N 86°45W 311 G10
Hawi *U.S.A.* 20°14N 155°50W 302 C6
Hawick *U.K.* 55°26N 2°47W 167 F6
Hawk Junction *Canada* 48°5N 84°38W 298 C3
Hawk Point *U.S.A.* 38°58N 91°8W 310 F5
Hawkdun Ra. *N.Z.* 44°53S 170°5E 285 E5
Hawke B. *N.Z.* 39°25S 177°20E 284 F6
Hawker *Australia* 31°59S 138°22E 282 A3
Hawke's Bay *Canada* 50°36N 57°10W 299 B8
Hawke's Bay □ *N.Z.* 39°45S 176°35E 284 F5
Hawkesbury *Canada* 45°37N 74°37W 298 C5
Hawkesbury I. *Canada* 53°37N 129°3W 296 C3
Hawkesbury Pt. *Australia* 11°55S 134°5E 280 A1
Hawkinsville *U.S.A.* 32°17N 83°28W 316 C6
Hawks Nest *Australia* 32°41S 152°11E 283 B10
Hawley *Minn., U.S.A.* 46°53N 96°19W 308 B5
Hawley *Pa., U.S.A.* 41°28N 75°11W 313 E9
Haworth *U.S.A.* 40°57N 73°59W 132 A2
Ḩawrān, W. → *Iraq* 33°58N 42°34E 213 F10
Hawsh Mūssá *Lebanon* 33°45N 35°55E 250 E6
Hawthorne *Fla., U.S.A.* 29°36N 82°5W 317 F7
Hawthorne *Nev., U.S.A.* 38°32N 118°38W 304 G4
Hawthorne Racecourse *U.S.A.* 41°49N 87°44W 119 C2
Hay *Australia* 34°30S 144°51E 283 C6
Hay → *N. Terr., Australia* 24°50S 138°0E 280 C2
Hay → *Alta., Canada* 60°50N 116°26W 296 A5
Hay, C. *Australia* 14°5S 129°29E 278 B4
Hay I. *Canada* 44°53N 80°58W 312 B4
Hay L. *Canada* 58°50N 118°50W 296 B5
Hay-on-Wye *U.K.* 52°5N 3°8W 169 E4
Hay River *Canada* 60°51N 115°44W 296 A5
Hay Springs *U.S.A.* 42°41N 102°41W 308 D2
Haya = Tehoru *Indonesia* 3°23S 129°30E 231 E7
Hayachine-San *Japan* 39°34N 141°29E 220 E10
Hayange *France* 49°20N 6°2E 173 C13
Hayastan = Armenia ■ *Asia* 40°20N 45°0E 191 K7
Hayato *Japan* 31°40N 130°43E 222 F2
Haydān, W. al → *Jordan* 31°29N 35°34E 251 G6
Haydarlı *Turkey* 38°16N 30°23E 205 C12
Hayden *U.S.A.* 40°30N 107°16W 304 F10
Haydon *Australia* 18°0S 141°30E 280 B3
Hayes *Jamaica* 17°52N 77°14W 320 a
Hayes *Kent, U.K.* 51°22N 0°0 125 B4
Hayes *Middlesex, U.K.* 51°30N 0°25W 125 A1
Hayes *S. Dak., U.S.A.* 44°23N 101°1W 308 C3
Hayes → *Canada* 57°3N 92°12W 298 A1
Hayes, Mt. *U.S.A.* 63°37N 146°43W 303 E11
Hayes Creek *Australia* 13°43S 131°22E 278 B5
Hayes End *U.K.* 51°31N 0°25W 125 A1
Hayford *U.S.A.* 41°45N 87°42W 119 C2
Hayle *U.K.* 50°11N 5°26W 169 G2
Hayling I. *U.K.* 50°48N 0°59W 169 G7
Haymā' *Oman* 19°56N 56°19E 249 C7
Haymana *Turkey* 39°26N 32°31E 212 C5
Haymen I. *Australia* 20°3S 148°52E 280 J6
Haynan *Yemen* 15°50N 48°18E 249 D5
Haynau = Chojnów *Poland* 51°18N 15°58E 185 G2
Hayneville *U.S.A.* 32°23N 83°37W 316 C6
Hayrabolu *Turkey* 41°12N 27°5E 203 E11
Hays *Alta., Canada* 50°6N 111°48W 296 C6
Hays *Kans., U.S.A.* 38°53N 99°20W 308 F4
Ḩays *Yemen* 13°56N 43°29E 248 D3
Haysville *U.S.A.* 38°28N 86°55W 311 F10
Haysyn *Ukraine* 48°57N 29°25E 183 B14
Hayvoron *Ukraine* 48°22N 29°52E 183 B14
Hayward *Calif., U.S.A.* 37°40N 122°4W 306 H4
Hayward *Wis., U.S.A.* 46°1N 91°29W 308 B8
Haywards *N.Z.* 41°9S 174°59E 143 A2
Haywards Heath *U.K.* 51°0N 0°5W 169 G7
Hazafon □ *Israel* 32°40N 35°20E 250 F6
Hazar *Turkmenistan* 39°34N 53°16E 187 G9
Hazārān, Kūh-e *Iran* 29°35N 57°20E 247 D8
Hazard *U.S.A.* 37°15N 83°12W 309 G12
Hazaribag *India* 23°58N 85°26E 243 H11
Hazaribag Road *India* 24°12N 85°57E 243 G11
Hazebrouck *France* 50°42N 2°31E 173 B9
Hazelton *B.C., Canada* 55°20N 127°42W 296 B3
Hazelton *N. Dak., U.S.A.* 46°29N 100°17W 308 B3
Hazen *U.S.A.* 47°18N 101°38W 308 B3
Hazlehurst *Ga., U.S.A.* 31°52N 82°36W 316 D7
Hazlehurst *Miss., U.S.A.* 31°52N 90°24W 315 F9
Hazlet *U.S.A.* 40°25N 74°12W 313 F10
Hazleton *Ind., U.S.A.* 38°29N 87°33W 311 F9
Hazleton *Pa., U.S.A.* 40°57N 75°59W 313 F9
Hazlett, L. *Australia* 21°30S 128°48E 278 D4
Hazro *Turkey* 38°15N 40°47E 246 B4
He Xian *Anhui, China* 31°45N 118°20E 229 B12
He Xian *Guangxi Zhuangzu, China* 24°27N 111°30E 229 E8
Head of Bight *Australia* 31°30S 131°25E 279 F5
Headland *U.S.A.* 31°21N 85°21W 316 D4
Headlands *Zimbabwe* 18°15S 32°2E 269 F3
Healdsburg *U.S.A.* 38°37N 122°52W 306 G4
Healdton *U.S.A.* 34°14N 97°29W 314 D6
Healesville *Australia* 37°35S 145°30E 283 D6
Healy *U.S.A.* 63°52N 148°58W 303 E10
Heany Junction *Zimbabwe* 20°6S 28°54E 271 B4
Heanza-shima *Japan* 26°20N 127°57E 288 a
Heard I. *Ind. Oc.* 53°0S 74°0E 273 K6
Hearne *U.S.A.* 30°53N 96°36W 314 F6
Hearst *Canada* 49°40N 83°41W 298 C3
Heart → *U.S.A.* 46°46N 100°50W 308 B3
Heart's Content *Canada* 47°54N 53°27W 299 C9
Heath → *Bolivia* 12°31S 68°38W 330 C4
Heath, Pte. *Canada* 49°8N 61°40W 299 C7
Heath Mts. *N.Z.* 45°39S 167°9E 285 F2
Heathcote *Australia* 36°56S 144°45E 283 D6
Heatherwood = Edson *Canada* 53°35N 116°28W 296 C5
Heathfield *S. Africa* 34°3S 18°27E 118 B1
Heathrow, London ✈ (LHR) *U.K.* 51°28N 0°27W 125 B1
Heavener *U.S.A.* 34°53N 94°36W 314 D7
Hebbronville *U.S.A.* 27°18N 98°41W 314 H5
Hebe Haven *China* 22°21N 114°15E 122 A2
Hebei □ *China* 39°0N 116°0E 226 E9
Hebel *Australia* 28°58S 147°47E 281 D4
Heber *U.S.A.* 32°44N 115°32W 307 N11
Heber Springs *U.S.A.* 35°30N 92°2W 314 D8
Hebgen L. *U.S.A.* 44°52N 111°20W 304 D8
Hebi *China* 35°57N 114°7E 226 G8
Hebrides *U.K.* 57°30N 7°0W 158 D4
Hebrides, Sea of the *U.K.* 57°5N 7°0W 167 D2
Hebron = Al Khalīl *West Bank* 31°32N 35°6E 251 G6
Hebron *Nfld. & L., Canada* 58°5N 62°30W 295 D13
Hebron *N. Dak., U.S.A.* 46°54N 102°3W 308 B2
Hebron *Nebr., U.S.A.* 40°10N 97°35W 308 E5
Heby *Sweden* 59°56N 16°53E 162 E10
Hecate Str. *Canada* 53°10N 130°30W 296 C2
Heceta I. *U.S.A.* 55°46N 133°40W 296 B2
Hechi *China* 24°40N 108°2E 228 E7
Hechingen *Germany* 48°21N 8°57E 179 G4
Hechuan *China* 30°2N 106°12E 228 B6
Hecla *U.S.A.* 45°53N 98°9W 308 C4
Hecla I. *Canada* 51°10N 96°43W 297 C9
Hedal *Norway* 60°37N 9°41E 162 D3
Heddal *Norway* 59°36N 9°9E 164 E6
Hédé *Ille-et-Vilaine, France* 48°18N 1°49W 172 D5
Hede *Jämtland, Sweden* 62°23N 13°30E 162 B7
Hedemora *Sweden* 60°18N 15°58E 162 D9
Hedensted *Denmark* 55°46N 9°42E 163 J3
Hedesunda *Sweden* 60°24N 17°0E 162 D10
Hedgehope *N.Z.* 46°12S 168°34E 285 G3
Hedmark □ *Norway* 61°17N 11°40E 164 C8
Hedo *Japan* 26°52N 128°15E 288 a
Hedo-misaki *Japan* 26°52N 128°16E 288 a
Hedong *China* 23°5N 113°14E 121 B2
Hedrick *U.S.A.* 41°11N 92°19W 310 C4
He'eia *U.S.A.* 21°25N 157°48W 302 K14
Heel Pt. *Wake I.* 19°18N 166°38E 302 b
Heerde *Neths.* 52°24N 6°2E 170 B6
Heerenveen *Neths.* 52°57N 5°55E 170 B5
Heerhugowaard *Neths.* 52°40N 4°51E 170 B4
Heerlen *Neths.* 50°55N 5°58E 170 D5
Heerwegen = Polkowice *Poland* 51°29N 16°3E 185 G3
Hefa *Israel* 32°46N 35°0E 250 F6
Hefa □ *Israel* 32°40N 35°0E 250 F6
Hefei *China* 31°52N 117°18E 229 B11
Hefeng *China* 29°55N 109°52E 229 C8
Heflin *U.S.A.* 33°39N 85°35W 316 B4
Hegalig *Sudan* 14°36N 31°54E 257 E3
Hegang *China* 47°20N 130°19E 219 B8
Heggenes *Norway* 61°9N 9°4E 164 C6
Hegra *Norway* 63°27N 11°8E 164 A8
Hei Ling Chau *China* 22°15N 114°2E 219 G11
Heiban *Sudan* 11°13N 30°31E 257 E3
Heichengzhen *China* 36°24N 106°3E 226 F4
Heidal *Norway* 61°45N 9°19E 164 C6
Heide *Germany* 54°11N 9°6E 178 A5
Heidelberg *Baden-W., Germany* 49°24N 8°42E 179 F4
Heidelberg *Western Cape, S. Africa* 34°6S 20°59E 270 D3
Heidelberg Heights *Australia* 37°45S 145°4E 128 A2
Heidelberg West *Australia* 37°43S 145°2E 128 A2
Heidemühle *Germany* 52°29N 13°40E 115 B5
Heidenau *Germany* 50°57N 13°52E 178 E9
Heidenheim *Germany* 48°41N 10°9E 179 G6
Heideveld *S. Africa* 33°58S 18°32E 118 A2
Heigun-Tō *Japan* 33°47N 132°14E 222 D4
Heihe *China* 50°10N 127°30E 219 A7
Heijing *China* 25°22N 101°44E 228 E3
Heijo = P'yŏngyang *N. Korea* 39°0N 125°30E 224 C2
Heilbad Heiligenstadt *Germany* 51°22N 10°8E 178 D6
Heilbron *S. Africa* 27°16S 27°59E 271 C4
Heilbronn *Germany* 49°9N 9°13E 179 F5
Heiligenblut *Austria* 47°2N 12°51E 180 D5
Heiligenhafen *Germany* 54°22N 10°59E 178 A6
Heiligensee *Germany* 52°36N 13°13E 115 A2
Heiligenstadt *Austria* 48°14N 16°21E 142 A2
Heilongjiang □ *China* 48°0N 126°0E 219 B7
Heilprin Land *Greenland* 82°5N 33°0W 154 A7
Heilsberg = Lidzbark Warmiński *Poland* 54°7N 20°34E 184 D7
Heilunkiang = Heilongjiang □ *China* 48°0N 126°0E 219 B7
Heim *Norway* 63°26N 9°5E 164 A6
Heimaey *Iceland* 63°26N 20°17W 155 D6
Heimdal *Norway* 63°21N 10°22E 164 A7
Heinersdorf *Germany* 52°34N 13°26E 115 A3
Heinola *Finland* 61°13N 26°2E 188 B4
Heinsberg *Germany* 51°3N 6°5E 178 D2
Heinsun *Burma* 25°52N 95°35E 241 C5
Heinze Kyun *Burma* 14°25N 97°45E 236 E1
Heirnkut *Burma* 25°14N 94°44E 241 C5
Heishan *China* 41°40N 122°5E 227 D12
Heishui *Liaoning, China* 42°8N 119°30E 227 C10
Heishui *Sichuan, China* 32°4N 103°2E 228 A4
Hejaz = Ḩijāz *Si. Arabia* 24°0N 40°0E 246 E3
Hejian *China* 38°25N 116°5E 226 E9
Hejiang *China* 28°43N 105°46E 228 C5
Hejin *China* 35°35N 110°42E 226 G6
Hejing *China* 42°18N 86°22E 217 D11
Hekımhan *Turkey* 38°50N 37°55E 212 C7
Hekinan *Japan* 34°52N 137°0E 223 C9
Hekla *Iceland* 63°56N 19°35W 155 D7
Hekou *Guangdong, China* 23°13N 112°45E 229 F9
Hekou *Yunnan, China* 22°30N 103°59E 228 F4
Hel *Poland* 54°37N 18°47E 184 D5
Helagsfjället *Sweden* 62°54N 12°25E 162 B6
Helan Shan *China* 38°30N 105°55E 226 E3
Heldenplatz *Vienna, Austria* 142 b1
Helden's Pt. *St. Kitts & Nevis* 17°25N 62°51W 322 d
Helechosa *Spain* 39°22N 4°53W 195 F6
Helemano → *U.S.A.* 21°35N 158°7W 302 J13
Helen Atoll *Pac. Oc.* 2°40N 132°0E 231 D8
Helena *Ark., U.S.A.* 34°32N 90°36W 315 D9
Helena *Ga., U.S.A.* 32°5N 82°55W 316 C7
Helena *Mont., U.S.A.* 46°36N 112°2W 304 C7
Helendale *U.S.A.* 34°44N 117°19W 307 L9
Hélène de Champlain, Parc ⌂ *Canada* 45°31N 73°32W 130 A2
Helenelund *Sweden* 59°24N 17°58E 139 A1
Helensburgh *N.S.W., Australia* 34°11S 151°1E 283 C9
Helensburgh *Argyll & Bute, U.K.* 56°1N 4°43W 167 E4
Helensville *N.Z.* 36°41S 174°29E 284 C3
Helenvale *Australia* 15°43S 145°14E 280 B4
Helgasjön *Sweden* 56°55N 14°50E 163 H8
Helgeland *Norway* 66°7N 13°29E 160 C15
Helgoland *Germany* 54°10N 7°53E 178 A3
Heligoland = Helgoland *Germany* 54°10N 7°53E 178 A3
Heligoland B. = Deutsche Bucht *Germany* 54°15N 8°0E 178 A4
Heliopolis = Masr el Gedida *Egypt* 30°5N 31°21E 117 A2
Hell *Norway* 63°26N 10°54E 164 A7
Hell-Bourg *Réunion* 21°3S 55°32E 272 f
Hell Hole Gorge △ *Australia* 25°31S 144°12E 280 D3
Hella *Iceland* 63°50N 20°24W 155 D6
Hellas = Greece ■ *Europe* 40°0N 23°0E 204 B3
Helleland *Norway* 58°33N 6°7E 164 F3
Hellersdorf *Germany* 52°32N 13°35E 115 A4
Hellertown *U.S.A.* 40°35N 75°21W 313 F9
Hellerup *Denmark* 55°44N 12°33E 118 A3
Hellespont = Çanakkale Boğazı *Turkey* 40°17N 26°32E 203 F10
Hellesylt *Norway* 62°6N 6°51E 164 B3
Hellevoetsluis *Neths.* 51°50N 4°8E 170 C4
Hellín *Spain* 38°31N 1°40W 197 G3
Hellissandur *Iceland* 64°55N 23°54W 155 C3
Hells Canyon ⌂ *U.S.A.* 45°30N 117°45W 304 D5
Hells Gate *Neth. Ant.* 17°39N 63°14W 322 a
Hell's Gate △ *Kenya* 0°54S 36°19E 268 C4
Hellvik *Norway* 58°29N 5°52E 164 F2
Helmahof *Austria* 48°18N 16°34E 142 A3
Helmand □ *Afghan.* 31°20N 64°0E 240 C2
Helmand → *Afghan.* 31°12N 61°34E 240 C1
Helme → *Germany* 51°20N 11°21E 178 D7
Helmeringhausen *Namibia* 25°54S 16°57E 270 C2
Helmond *Neths.* 51°29N 5°41E 170 C5
Helmsdale *U.K.* 58°7N 3°39W 167 C5
Helmsdale → *U.K.* 58°8N 3°43W 167 C5
Helmstedt *Germany* 52°12N 11°0E 178 C7
Helong *China* 42°40N 129°0E 224 A4
Helper *U.S.A.* 39°41N 110°51W 304 G8
Helsingborg *Sweden* 56°3N 12°42E 163 H6
Helsinge *Denmark* 56°2N 12°12E 163 H6
Helsingfors = Helsinki *Finland* 60°10N 24°55E 121 B2
Helsingør *Denmark* 56°2N 12°35E 163 H6
Helsinki *Finland* 60°10N 24°55E 121 B2
Helsinki-Vantaa ✈ (HEL) *Finland* 60°18N 24°58E 121 B2
Helska, Mierzeja *Poland* 54°45N 18°40E 184 D5
Helston *U.K.* 50°6N 5°17W 169 G2
Helvellyn *U.K.* 54°32N 3°1W 168 C4
Helwân *Egypt* 29°50N 31°20E 256 J7
Hemavati → *India* 12°30N 76°20E 245 H3
Hemel Hempstead *U.K.* 51°44N 0°28W 169 F7
Hemet *U.S.A.* 33°45N 116°58W 307 M10
Hemingford *U.S.A.* 42°19N 103°4W 308 D2
Hemis △ *India* 34°10N 77°15E 242 B7
Hemmingford *Canada* 45°3N 73°35W 313 A11
Hempe *Dem. Rep. of the Congo* 1°54N 22°42E 264 B4
Hempstead *N.Y., U.S.A.* 40°42N 73°37W 313 F11
Hempstead *Tex., U.S.A.* 30°6N 96°5W 314 F6
Hemse *Sweden* 57°15N 18°22E 163 G12
Hemsedal *Norway* 60°53N 8°30E 164 D5
Hemsön *Sweden* 62°42N 18°5E 162 B12
Hen *Norway* 60°13N 10°14E 164 D7
Hen and Chickens Is. *N.Z.* 35°58S 174°45E 284 B3
Henån *Sweden* 58°14N 11°40E 163 F5
Henan □ *China* 34°0N 114°0E 226 H8
Henares → *Spain* 40°24N 3°30W 194 E7
Henashi-Misaki *Japan* 40°37N 139°51E 220 D9
Hendaye *France* 43°23N 1°47W 174 E2
Hendek *Turkey* 40°48N 30°44E 212 B4
Henderson *Argentina* 36°18S 61°43W 334 D3
Henderson *Ga., U.S.A.* 32°21N 83°47W 316 C6
Henderson *Ky., U.S.A.* 37°50N 87°35W 311 G9
Henderson *N.C., U.S.A.* 36°20N 78°25W 315 C15
Henderson *Nev., U.S.A.* 36°2N 114°58W 124 B2
Henderson *Tenn., U.S.A.* 35°26N 88°38W 315 D10
Henderson *Tex., U.S.A.* 32°9N 94°48W 314 E7
Henderson I. *Pac. Oc.* 24°22S 128°19W 289 K15
Hendersonville *N.C., U.S.A.* 35°19N 82°28W 315 D13
Hendersonville *Tenn., U.S.A.* 36°18N 86°37W 315 C11
Hendījān *Iran* 30°14N 49°43E 247 D6
Hendon *U.K.* 51°35N 0°14W 125 A2
Hendorābī *Iran* 26°40N 53°37E 247 E7
Heng Jiang *China* 28°40N 104°25E 228 C5
Heng Xian *China* 22°40N 109°17E 228 F7
Henganofi *Papua N. G.* 6°15S 145°38E 286 D3
Hengcheng *China* 38°18N 106°28E 226 E4
Hëngch'un *Taiwan* 22°0N 120°44E 225 D2
Hengdaohezi *China* 44°52N 129°0E 227 B15
Hengduan Shan *China* 27°30N 99°0E 218 D4
Hengelo *Neths.* 52°16N 6°48E 170 B6
Hengfeng *China* 28°12N 115°48E 229 C10
Henggang *China* 22°39N 114°12E 219 F11
Hengmen *China* 22°33N 113°35E 219 F10
Hengqin Dao *China* 22°7N 113°34E 219 G10
Hengsha *China* 23°9N 113°12E 121 B2
Hengshan *Hunan, China* 27°16N 112°45E 229 D9
Hengshan *Shaanxi, China* 37°58N 109°5E 226 F5
Hengshui *China* 37°41N 115°40E 226 F8
Hengyang *China* 26°59N 112°22E 229 D9
Henichesk *Ukraine* 46°12N 34°50E 189 J8
Henima *India* 25°22N 93°36E 241 C4
Hénin-Beaumont *France* 50°25N 2°58E 173 B9
Hénin-Liétard = Hénin-Beaumont *France* 50°25N 2°58E 173 B9
Henley-on-Thames *U.K.* 51°32N 0°54W 169 F7
Henlopen, C. *U.S.A.* 38°48N 75°6W 309 F16
Henna *Japan* 26°19N 127°53E 288 a
Hennan *Sweden* 62°2N 15°54E 162 B9
Hennebont *France* 47°49N 3°19W 172 E3
Hennenman *S. Africa* 27°59S 27°1E 270 C4
Hennepin *U.S.A.* 41°15N 89°21W 310 C7
Hennessey *U.S.A.* 36°6N 97°54W 314 C6
Hennigsdorf *Germany* 52°38N 13°12E 115 A2
Henrietta *U.S.A.* 33°49N 98°12W 314 E5
Henrietta, Ostrov = Genriyetty, Ostrov *Russia* 77°6N 156°30E 215 B16
Henrietta Maria, C. *Canada* 55°9N 82°20W 298 A3
Henry *U.S.A.* 41°7N 89°22W 310 C7
Henry Lawrence I. *India* 12°9N 93°5E 245 H11
Henryetta *U.S.A.* 35°27N 95°59W 314 D7
Henryków *Poland* 52°19N 20°58E 142 B1
Henryville *Canada* 45°8N 73°11W 313 A11
Hensall *Canada* 43°26N 81°30W 312 C3
Henson Cr. → *U.S.A.* 38°47N 76°58W 143 C4
Henstedt-Ulzburg *Germany* 53°47N 10°0E 178 B6
Hentiesbaai *Namibia* 22°8S 14°18E 270 B1
Hentiyn Nuruu *Mongolia* 48°30N 108°30E 219 B5
Henttaa *Finland* 60°11N 24°45E 121 B1
Henty *Australia* 35°30S 147°3E 283 C7
Henzada *Burma* 17°38N 95°26E 241 G5
Hephaestia *Greece* 39°55N 25°14E 205 B7
Hephzibah *U.S.A.* 33°19N 82°6W 316 B7
Heping *China* 24°29N 115°0E 229 E10
Heping Park *China* 31°16N 121°30E 138 B2
Hepingli *China* 39°57N 116°23E 114 B2
Heppner *U.S.A.* 45°21N 119°33W 304 D4
Hepu *China* 21°40N 109°12E 228 G7
Hepworth *Canada* 44°37N 81°9W 312 B3
Heqing *China* 26°37N 100°11E 228 D3
Hequ *China* 39°20N 111°15E 226 E6
Héraðsflói *Iceland* 65°42N 14°12W 155 B12
Héraðsvötn → *Iceland* 65°45N 19°25W 155 B7
Heradsbygd *Norway* 60°49N 11°39E 164 D8
Heraklion = Iraklio *Greece* 35°20N 25°12E 207 E6
Herald Cays *Australia* 16°58S 149°9E 280 B4
Herand *Norway* 60°20N 6°22E 164 D3
Herāt *Afghan.* 34°20N 62°7E 240 B1
Herāt □ *Afghan.* 35°0N 62°0E 240 B1
Hérault □ *France* 43°34N 3°15E 174 E7
Hérault → *France* 43°17N 3°26E 174 E7
Herbault *France* 47°36N 1°8E 172 E8
Herbert *Canada* 50°30N 107°10W 297 C7
Herbert → *Australia* 18°31S 146°17E 280 B4
Herbert Hoover Nat. Historic Site ⌂ *U.S.A.* 41°40N 91°21W 310 C5
Herbert I. *U.S.A.* 52°45N 170°7W 303 K5
Herbertabad *India* 11°43N 92°37E 245 J11
Herberton *Australia* 17°20S 145°25E 280 B4
Herbertsdale *S. Africa* 34°1S 21°46E 270 D3
Herbertville *N.Z.* 40°30S 176°33E 284 G5
Herbignac *France* 47°27N 2°18W 172 E4
Herborn *Germany* 50°40N 8°18E 178 E4
Herby *Poland* 50°45N 18°50E 185 H5
Herceg-Novi *Montenegro* 42°30N 18°33E 202 D2
Hercegfalva = Mezőfalva *Hungary* 46°55N 18°49E 182 D3
Herchmer *Canada* 57°22N 94°10W 297 B10
Herculânia = Coxim *Brazil* 18°30S 54°55W 331 D7
Herðubreið *Iceland* 65°11N 16°21W 155 B10
Hereford *Hereford, U.K.* 52°4N 2°43W 169 E5
Hereford *Tex., U.S.A.* 34°49N 102°24W 314 D3
Herefordshire □ *U.K.* 52°8N 2°40W 169 E5
Herefoss *Norway* 58°32N 8°23E 164 F5
Héréhérétué *French Polynesia* 19°45S 144°58W 289 f
Herehogna *Sweden* 61°44N 12°8E 164 C9
Hereke *Turkey* 40°47N 29°38E 203 F13
Herekino *N.Z.* 35°18S 173°11E 284 B2
Herencia *Spain* 39°21N 3°22W 195 F7
Herentals *Belgium* 51°12N 4°51E 170 C4
Herford *Germany* 52°7N 8°39E 178 C4
Héricourt *France* 47°32N 6°45E 173 E13
Herington *U.S.A.* 38°40N 96°57W 308 F5
Herisau *Switz.* 47°22N 9°17E 179 H5
Hérisson *France* 46°32N 2°42E 173 F9
Herkimer *U.S.A.* 43°2N 74°59W 313 D10
Herlev *Denmark* 55°43N 12°27E 118 A2
Herlong *U.S.A.* 40°8N 120°8W 306 E6
Herm *U.K.* 49°30N 2°28W 169 H5
Hermakivka *Ukraine* 48°42N 26°11E 183 B11
Herman Eckstein Park *S. Africa* 26°9S 28°1E 123 A2
Hermann *U.S.A.* 38°42N 91°27W 310 F5
Hermannsbad = Ciechocinek *Poland* 52°53N 18°45E 185 F5
Hermannsburg *N. Terr., Australia* 23°57S 132°45E 278 D5
Hermannsburg *Niedersachsen, Germany* 52°50N 10°5E 178 C6
Hermannskogel *Austria* 48°16N 16°17E 142 A1
Hermannstadt = Sibiu *Romania* 45°45N 24°9E 183 E9
Hermansverk *Norway* 61°11N 6°52E 164 C3
Hermanus *S. Africa* 34°27S 19°12E 270 D2
Herment *France* 45°45N 2°24E 174 C6
Hermidale *Australia* 31°30S 146°42E 283 A7
Hermiston *Edinburgh, U.K.* 55°55N 3°19W 121 B2
Hermiston *Oreg., U.S.A.* 45°51N 119°17W 304 D4
Hermit Is. *Papua N. G.* 1°32S 145°5E 286 A3
Hermitage *Grenada* 12°27N 61°28W 323 q
Hermitage *Mo., U.S.A.* 37°56N 93°19W 310 G3
Hermitage and Winter Palace *Russia* 59°55N 30°19E 137 B1
Hermite, I. *Chile* 55°50S 68°0W 336 E3
Hermon *U.S.A.* 44°28N 75°14W 313 B9
Hermon, Mt. = Shaykh, J. ash *Lebanon* 33°25N 35°50E 250 E6
Hermosillo *Mexico* 29°10N 111°0W 318 B2
Hermsdorf *Germany* 52°37N 13°18E 115 A2
Hernád → *Hungary* 47°56N 21°8E 182 C6
Hernals *Austria* 48°13N 16°20E 142 A2
Hernandarias *Paraguay* 25°20S 54°40W 335 B5
Hernandez *U.S.A.* 36°24N 120°46W 306 J6
Hernando *Argentina* 32°28S 63°40W 334 C3
Hernando *Fla., U.S.A.* 28°54N 82°23W 317 G7
Hernando *Miss., U.S.A.* 34°50N 90°0W 315 D10
Hernani *Spain* 43°16N 1°58W 196 B3
Herndon *U.S.A.* 40°43N 76°51W 312 F8
Herne *Germany* 51°32N 7°14E 170 C7
Herne Bay *U.K.* 51°21N 1°8E 169 F9
Herne Hill *U.K.* 51°27N 0°6W 125 B3
Herning *Denmark* 56°8N 8°58E 163 H2
Herod *U.S.A.* 31°42N 84°26W 316 D5
Héroes de Churubusco *Mexico* 19°21N 99°6W 128 B2
Heroica Caborca = Caborca *Mexico* 30°37N 112°6W 318 A2
Heroica Nogales = Nogales *Mexico* 31°19N 110°56W 318 A2
Heron Bay *Canada* 48°40N 86°25W 298 C2
Heron I. *Australia* 23°27S 151°55E 280 C5
Herons, Î. aux *Canada* 45°25N 73°34W 130 B2
Herradura, Pta. de la *Canary Is.* 28°26N 14°8W 153 e2
Herre *Norway* 59°6N 9°34E 164 E6
Herreid *U.S.A.* 45°50N 100°4W 308 C3
Herrenberg *Germany* 48°35N 8°52E 179 G4
Herrera *Spain* 37°26N 4°55W 195 H6
Herrera de Alcántara *Spain* 39°39N 7°25W 195 F3
Herrera de Pisuerga *Spain* 42°35N 4°20W 194 C6
Herrera del Duque *Spain* 39°10N 5°3W 195 F5
Herrestad *Sweden* 58°21N 11°50E 163 F5
Herrin *U.S.A.* 37°48N 89°2W 310 G7
Herriot *Canada* 56°22N 101°16W 297 B8
Herrljunga *Sweden* 58°5N 13°1E 163 F7
Hersbruck *Germany* 49°30N 11°26E 179 F7
Herschel I. *Canada* 69°35N 139°5W 150 C1
Hershey *U.S.A.* 40°17N 76°39W 313 F8
Herso *Greece* 41°5N 22°47E 202 E6
Herstal *Belgium* 50°40N 5°38E 170 D5
Herstedøster *Denmark* 55°40N 12°22E 118 A2
Hertford *U.K.* 51°48N 0°4W 169 F7
Hertfordshire □ *U.K.* 51°51N 0°5W 169 F7
's-Hertogenbosch *Neths.* 51°42N 5°17E 170 C5
Hertsa *Ukraine* 48°9N 26°15E 183 B11
Herttoniemi *Finland* 60°12N 25°2E 121 B3
Hertzogville *S. Africa* 28°9S 25°30E 270 C4
Hervás *Spain* 40°16N 5°52W 194 E5
Hervey B. *Australia* 25°0S 152°52E 280 C5
Herzberg *Brandenburg, Germany* 51°41N 13°14E 178 D9
Herzberg *Niedersachsen, Germany* 51°38N 10°20E 178 D6
Herzliyya *Israel* 32°10N 34°50E 251 F5
Herzogenburg *Austria* 48°17N 15°41E 180 C8
Ḩeşār *Fārs, Iran* 29°52N 50°16E 247 D6
Ḩeşār *Markazī, Iran* 35°50N 49°12E 247 C6
Ḩeşārak *Iran* 35°47N 51°18E 141 A1
Hesdin *France* 50°21N 2°2E 173 B9
Heshan *China* 23°50N 108°53E 228 F7
Heshui *China* 35°48N 108°0E 226 G5
Heshun *China* 37°22N 113°32E 226 F7
Heskestad *Norway* 58°28N 6°22E 164 F3
Hesperia *U.S.A.* 34°25N 117°18W 307 L9
Hessdalen *Norway* 62°48N 11°10E 164 B8
Hesse = Hessen □ *Germany* 50°30N 9°0E 178 E4
Hessen □ *Germany* 50°30N 9°0E 178 E4
Hessenreuther und Manteler Wald ⌂ *Germany* 49°45N 12°1E 179 F8
Hesso *Australia* 32°8S 137°27E 282 B2
Hesteyri *Iceland* 66°20N 22°53W 155 A4
Heston *U.K.* 51°28N 0°22W 125 B1
Hestra *Sweden* 57°26N 13°35E 163 G7
Hetauda *Nepal* 27°25N 85°2E 242 F11
Hetch Hetchy Aqueduct *U.S.A.* 37°29N 122°19W 306 H5
Hettinger *U.S.A.* 46°0N 102°42W 308 B2
Hettstedt *Germany* 51°39N 11°31E 178 D7
Hetzendorf *Austria* 48°9N 16°17E 142 B1
Heuksando *S. Korea* 34°40N 125°30E 224 E2
Heunghae *S. Korea* 36°12N 129°21E 224 D4
Heuvelton *U.S.A.* 44°37N 75°25W 313 B9
Hevelândia *Brazil* 5°12S 61°50W 329 E5
Heves *Hungary* 47°36N 20°17E 182 C5
Heves □ *Hungary* 47°50N 20°0E 182 C5
Hewitt *U.S.A.* 31°28N 97°12W 314 F6
Hexham *U.K.* 54°58N 2°4W 168 C5
Hexi *Yunnan, China* 24°9N 102°38E 228 E4
Hexi *Zhejiang, China* 27°58N 119°38E 229 D12
Hexigten Qi *China* 43°18N 117°30E 227 C9
Hextable *U.K.* 51°24N 0°10E 125 B5
Ḩeydarābād *Iran* 30°33N 55°38E 247 D7
Heydebreck = Kędzierzyn-Koźle *Poland* 50°20N 18°12E 185 H5
Heyfield *Australia* 37°59S 146°47E 283 D7
Heysham *U.K.* 54°3N 2°53W 168 C5
Heyuan *China* 23°39N 114°40E 229 F10
Heywood *Australia* 38°8S 141°37E 282 E4
Heyworth *U.S.A.* 40°19N 88°59W 310 D8
Heze *China* 35°14N 115°20E 226 G8
Hezhang *China* 27°8N 104°41E 228 D5
Hi, Ko *Thailand* 7°44N 98°22E 237 a
Hi-no-Misaki *Japan* 35°26N 132°38E 222 B4
Hi Vista *U.S.A.* 34°45N 117°46W 307 L9
Hialeah *U.S.A.* 25°51N 80°16W 128 A1
Hiawassa, L. *U.S.A.* 28°33N 81°28W 133 A2
Hiawatha *U.S.A.* 39°51N 95°32W 308 F6
Hibbing *U.S.A.* 47°25N 92°56W 308 B7
Hibbs B. *Australia* 42°35S 145°15E 281 G4
Hibernia Reef *Australia* 12°0S 123°23E 278 B3
Hibiki-Nada *Japan* 34°0N 130°0E 222 D2
Hickam Air Force Base *U.S.A.* 21°20N 157°56W 302 K14
Hickam Housing *U.S.A.* 21°21N 157°57W 302 K14
Hickman *U.S.A.* 36°34N 89°11W 308 G9
Hickory *U.S.A.* 35°44N 81°21W 315 D14
Hickory Hills *U.S.A.* 41°43N 87°49W 119 C2
Hicks, Pt. *Australia* 37°49S 149°17E 283 D8
Hicks Bay *N.Z.* 37°34S 178°21E 284 D7
Hicks L. *Canada* 61°25N 100°0W 297 A9
Hicksville *N.Y., U.S.A.* 40°46N 73°32W 313 F11
Hicksville *Ohio, U.S.A.* 41°18N 84°46W 311 C12
Hida *Romania* 47°10N 23°19E 183 C8
Hida-Gawa → *Japan* 35°26N 137°3E 223 B9
Hida-Sammyaku *Japan* 36°30N 137°40E 223 A9
Hida-Sanchi *Japan* 36°10N 137°0E 223 A9
Hidaka *Japan* 35°30N 134°44E 222 B6
Hidaka-Sammyaku *Japan* 42°35N 142°45E 220 C11
Hidalgo □ *Mexico* 20°30N 99°0W 319 C5
Hidalgo, Presa M. *Mexico* 26°30N 108°35W 318 B3
Hidalgo del Parral *Mexico* 26°56N 105°40W 318 B3
Hiddensee *Germany* 54°32N 13°6E 178 A9
Hidrolândia *Brazil* 17°0S 49°15W 333 E2
Hieflau *Austria* 47°36N 14°46E 180 D7
Hiekkaharju *Finland* 60°18N 25°2E 121 B3
Hiendelaencina *Spain* 41°5N 3°0W 196 D2
Hienghène *N. Cal.* 20°41S 164°56E 288 d
Hierro *Canary Is.* 27°44N 18°0W 153 e1
Hietaniemi *Finland* 60°10N 24°54E 121 B2
Hietzing *Austria* 48°10N 16°17E 142 A1
Higashi *Japan* 34°41N 135°30E 133 A2
Higashi-Hiroshima *Japan* 34°25N 132°45E 222 C4
Higashi-Matsuyama *Japan* 36°2N 139°25E 223 A11
Higashiajima-San *Japan* 37°40N 140°10E 220 F10
Higashimurayama *Japan* 35°45N 139°26E 140 A1
Higashinari *Japan* 34°40N 135°32E 133 A2
Higashiōsaka *Japan* 34°39N 135°37E 223 C7
Higashisumiyoshi *Japan* 34°37N 135°31E 133 B2
Higashiyodogawa *Japan* 34°44N 135°28E 133 A1
Higasi-Suidō *Japan* 34°0N 129°30E 222 D1
Higbee *U.S.A.* 39°19N 92°31W 310 E4
Higgins *U.S.A.* 36°7N 100°2W 314 C4
Higgins Corner *U.S.A.* 39°2N 121°5W 306 F5
Higginsville *U.S.A.* 39°4N 93°43W 310 E3
High Bridge *U.S.A.* 40°40N 74°54W 313 F10
High Island Res. *China* 22°22N 114°21E 219 G11
High Level *Canada* 58°31N 117°8W 296 B5
High Park *Canada* 43°38N 79°27W 141 B2
High Peak *Phil.* 15°29N 120°7E 232 D3
High Pk. *St. Helena* 15°58S 5°44W 153 h
High Point *U.S.A.* 35°57N 80°0W 315 D15
High Prairie *Canada* 55°30N 116°30W 296 B5
High River *Canada* 50°30N 113°50W 296 C6
High Springs *U.S.A.* 29°50N 82°36W 316 F7
High Tatra = Tatry *Slovak Rep.* 49°20N 20°0E 181 B13
High Veld *Africa* 27°0S 27°0E 254 J6
High Wycombe *U.K.* 51°37N 0°45W 169 F7
Highbank *N.Z.* 43°37S 171°45E 285 D6
Highbury *U.K.* 51°33N 0°6W 125 A3
Highgate *Jamaica* 18°5N 76°57W 320 a
Highgate *London, U.K.* 51°34N 0°8W 125 A3
Highland *Ill., U.S.A.* 38°44N 89°41W 310 F7
Highland *Ind., U.S.A.* 41°33N 87°28W 311 C9
Highland *Wis., U.S.A.* 43°5N 90°22W 310 A6
Highland □ *U.K.* 57°17N 4°21W 167 D4
Highland City *U.S.A.* 27°58N 81°53W 317 H8
Highland Cr. → *Canada* 43°45N 79°13W 141 A3
Highland Creek *Canada* 43°46N 79°8W 141 A3
Highland Home *U.S.A.* 31°57N 86°19W 316 D3
Highland Mills *U.S.A.* 33°17N 84°17W 316 B5
Highland Park *Calif., U.S.A.* 34°7N 118°13W 126 B3
Highland Park *Ill., U.S.A.* 42°11N 87°48W 311 B9
Highland View *U.S.A.* 29°50N 85°19W 316 F4
Highlands = Fort Thomas *U.S.A.* 39°4N 84°26W 311 E12
Highlands, The *Antigua & B.* 17°38N 61°47W 322 c
Highlands North *S. Africa* 26°8S 28°5E 123 A2
Highmore *U.S.A.* 44°31N 99°27W 308 C4
Highrock L. *Man., Canada* 55°45N 100°30W 297 B8
Highrock L. *Sask., Canada* 57°5N 105°32W 297 B7
Higuero, Pta. *Puerto Rico* 18°22N 67°16W 321 b
Higüey *Dom. Rep.* 18°37N 68°42W 321 C6
Hihya *Egypt* 30°40N 31°36E 256 H7
Hiiumaa *Estonia* 58°50N 22°45E 188 C2
Híjar *Spain* 41°10N 0°27W 196 D4
Ḩijāz *Si. Arabia* 24°0N 40°0E 246 E3
Hiji *Japan* 33°22N 131°32E 222 D3
Hijo = Tagum *Phil.* 7°33N 125°53E 233 H5
Hikari *Japan* 33°58N 131°58E 222 D3
Hiketa *Japan* 34°13N 134°24E 222 C6
Hikkaduwa *Sri Lanka* 6°8N 80°6E 245 L5
Hikmak, Ras el *Egypt* 31°15N 27°51E 256 A2
Hiko *U.S.A.* 37°32N 115°14W 306 H11
Hikone *Japan* 35°15N 136°10E 223 B8
Hikurangi *Gisborne, N.Z.* 37°55S 178°4E 284 E5
Hikurangi *Northland, N.Z.* 35°36S 174°17E 284 B3
Hikutavake *Cook Is.* 18°56S 169°53W 289 g
Hiland Park *U.S.A.* 30°12N 85°33W 316 E4
Hilawng *Burma* 21°23N 93°48E 241 E4
Hildburghausen *Germany* 50°25N 10°42E 178 E6
Hildesheim *Germany* 52°9N 9°56E 178 C5
Hilðarendi *Iceland* 63°44N 19°57W 155 D7
Hill → *Australia* 30°23S 115°3E 279 F2
Hill City *Idaho, U.S.A.* 43°18N 115°3W 304 E6
Hill City *Kans., U.S.A.* 39°22N 99°51W 308 F4
Hill City *Minn., U.S.A.* 46°59N 93°36W 308 B7
Hill City *S. Dak., U.S.A.* 43°56N 103°35W 308 D2
Hill Island L. *Canada* 60°30N 109°50W 297 A7
Hillaby, Mt. *Barbados* 13°12N 59°35W 323 r
Hillared *Sweden* 57°37N 13°10E 163 G7
Hillcrest Center *U.S.A.* 35°23N 118°57W 307 K8
Hillcrest Heights *U.S.A.* 38°49N 76°57W 143 C4
Hillegom *Neths.* 52°18N 4°35E 170 B4
Hillend *U.K.* 56°2N 3°22W 121 A1
Hillerød *Denmark* 55°56N 12°19E 163 J6
Hillerstorp *Sweden* 57°20N 13°52E 163 G7
Hilli *Bangla.* 25°17N 89°1E 241 C2
Hilliard *U.S.A.* 30°41N 81°55W 316 E8
Hillingdon □ *U.K.* 51°32N 0°27W 125 A1
Hillsboro = Deerfield Beach *U.S.A.* 26°19N 80°6W 317 J9
Hillsboro *Ga., U.S.A.* 33°11N 83°38W 316 B6

Hillsboro Ill., U.S.A. 39°9N 89°29W 310 E7
Hillsboro Kans., U.S.A. 38°21N 97°12W 308 F5
Hillsboro Mo., U.S.A. 38°14N 90°34W 310 F6
Hillsboro N. Dak., U.S.A. 47°26N 97°3W 308 B5
Hillsboro Ohio, U.S.A. 39°12N 83°37W 311 E13
Hillsboro Oreg., U.S.A. 45°31N 122°59W 306 E4
Hillsboro Tex., U.S.A. 32°1N 97°8W 314 E6
Hillsboro Canal U.S.A. 26°30N 80°15W 317 J9
Hillsborough Grenada 12°28N 61°28W 323 q
Hillsborough N.H., U.S.A. 43°7N 71°54W 313 C13
Hillsborough Channel Australia 20°56S 149°15E 280 J7
Hillsborough Dam Trin. & Tob. 11°13N 60°40W 323 s
Hillsborough Land = Belle Glade U.S.A. 26°41N 80°40W 317 J9
Hillsdale Mich., U.S.A. 41°56N 84°38W 311 C12
Hillsdale N.Y., U.S.A. 42°11N 73°32W 313 D11
Hillsport Canada 49°27N 85°34W 298 C2
Hillston Australia 33°30S 145°31E 283 B6
Hilltonia U.S.A. 32°53N 81°40W 316 C8
Hillwood U.S.A. 38°52N 77°9W 143 B3
Hilmīya Egypt 30°6N 31°19E 117 A2
Hilo U.S.A. 19°44N 155°5W 302 D6
Hilo ✕ (ITO) U.S.A. 19°43N 155°2W 302 D6
Hilo B. U.S.A. 19°45N 155°5W 302 D6
Hilton U.S.A. 43°17N 77°48W 312 C7
Hilton Head Island U.S.A. 32°13N 80°45W 316 C9
Hilvan Turkey 37°34N 38°58E 213 D8
Hilversum Neths. 52°14N 5°10E 170 B5
Himachal Pradesh □ India 31°30N 77°0E 242 D7
Himalaya Asia 29°0N 84°0E 243 E11
Himamaylan Phil. 10°6N 122°52E 233 F4
Himarë Albania 40°8N 19°43E 202 F3
Himatnagar India 23°37N 72°57E 242 H5
Hime-Jima Japan 33°43N 131°40E 222 D3
Himeji Japan 34°50N 134°40E 222 C6
Himi Japan 36°50N 136°55E 223 A8
Himmerland Denmark 56°45N 9°30E 163 H3
Ḩimş Syria 34°40N 36°45E 250 D7
Ḩimş □ Syria 34°30N 37°0E 250 D8
Hin Keng China 22°22N 114°10E 122 A2
Hinatuan Phil. 8°23N 126°20E 233 G6
Hinatuan Passage Phil. 9°45N 125°47E 233 G5
Hinche Haiti 19°9N 72°1W 321 C5
Hinchinbrook I. Australia 18°20S 146°15E 280 B4
Hinchinbrook Island △ Australia 18°14S 146°6E 280 B4
Hinckley Leics., U.K. 52°33N 1°22W 169 E6
Hinckley Minn., U.S.A. 46°1N 92°56W 308 B7
Hindaun India 26°44N 77°5E 242 F7
Hindenburg = Zabrze Poland 50°18N 18°50E 185 H5
Hindmarsh, L. Australia 36°5S 141°55E 282 D4
Hindol India 20°40N 85°10E 244 D7
Hinds N.Z. 43°59S 171°36E 285 D6
Hindsholm Denmark 55°30N 10°40E 163 J4
Hindu Bagh Pakistan 30°56N 67°50E 242 D2
Hindu Kush Asia 36°0N 71°0E 240 B3
Hindupur India 13°49N 77°32E 245 H3
Hines Creek Canada 56°20N 118°40W 296 B5
Hinesville U.S.A. 31°51N 81°36W 316 D8
Hinganghat India 20°30N 78°52E 244 D4
Hingham U.S.A. 48°33N 110°25W 304 B8
Hinghwa = Xinghua China 32°58N 119°48E 227 H10
Hingir India 21°57N 83°41E 243 J10
Hingoli India 19°41N 77°15E 244 E3
Hinigaran Phil. 10°16N 122°50E 233 F4
Hinis Turkey 39°22N 41°43E 213 C9
Hinna = Imi Ethiopia 6°28N 42°10E 257 F5
Hinna Nigeria 10°25N 11°35E 263 C7
Hinnerup Denmark 56°16N 10°4E 163 H4
Hinnøya Norway 68°35N 15°50E 160 B16
Hino Japan 35°0N 136°15E 223 C8
Hinoba-an Phil. 9°35N 122°28E 233 G4
Hinojosa del Duque Spain 38°30N 5°9W 195 G5
Hinokage Japan 32°39N 131°24E 222 E3
Hinsdale U.S.A. 42°47N 72°29W 313 D12
Hinterrhein ➔ Switz. 46°40N 9°25E 179 J5
Hinthada = Henzada Burma 17°38N 95°26E 241 G5
Hinton Alta., Canada 53°26N 117°34W 296 C5
Hinton W. Va., U.S.A. 37°40N 80°54W 309 G13
Hinuangan Phil. 10°25N 125°12E 233 F5
Hinubuan = Antipolo Phil. 14°35N 121°10E 232 D3
Hios Greece 38°27N 26°9E 205 C8
Hios □ Greece 38°27N 26°9E 205 C8
Hirado Japan 33°22N 129°33E 222 D1
Hirado-Shima Japan 33°20N 129°30E 222 D1
Hirakata Japan 34°48N 135°38E 223 C7
Hirakud India 21°32N 83°51E 244 D6
Hirakud Dam India 21°32N 83°45E 244 D6
Hiran ➔ India 23°6N 79°21E 243 H8
Hirapur India 24°22N 79°13E 243 G8
Hirara Japan 24°48N 125°17E 221 M2
Hirata Japan 35°24N 132°49E 222 B4
Hiratsuka Japan 35°19N 139°21E 223 B11
Hirekerur India 14°28N 75°23E 245 G2
Hirfanlı Barajı Turkey 39°18N 33°31E 212 C5
Hirhafok Algeria 23°49N 5°45E 261 D6
Hiromi Japan 33°13N 132°36E 222 D4
Hiroo Japan 42°17N 143°19E 220 C11
Hirosaki Japan 40°34N 140°28E 220 D10
Hiroshima Japan 34°24N 132°30E 222 C4
Hiroshima □ Japan 34°50N 133°0E 222 C5
Hiroshima-Wan Japan 34°5N 132°20E 222 C4
Hirota Japan 34°45N 135°20E 133 A1
Hirschberg = Jelenia Góra Poland 50°50N 15°45E 185 H2
Hirschstetten Austria 48°14N 16°27E 142 A2
Hirson France 49°55N 4°4E 173 C11
Hirtshals Denmark 57°36N 9°57E 163 G3
Hisai Japan 34°40N 136°28E 223 C8
Hisar India 29°12N 75°45E 242 E6
Hisarcık Turkey 39°15N 29°14E 205 B11
Hisaria Bulgaria 42°30N 24°44E 203 D8
Hisb, Sha'ib = Ḩasb, W. ➔ Iraq 31°45N 44°17E 246 D5
Ḩismá Si. Arabia 28°30N 36°0E 251 K7
Ḩisn al 'Abr Yemen 16°8N 47°14E 248 C4
Hispaniola W. Indies 19°0N 71°0W 321 C5
Histórico Nacional, Museu Rio de J., Brazil 135 b3
History Center U.S.A. 33°45N 84°22W 113 B2
Hīt Iraq 33°38N 42°49E 213 F10
Hita Japan 33°20N 130°58E 222 D2
Hitachi Japan 36°36N 140°39E 223 A12
Hitachi-Ōta Japan 36°30N 140°30E 223 A12
Hitchin U.K. 51°58N 0°16W 169 F7
Hithadhoo Maldives 0°36S 73°5E 272 d
Hither Green U.K. 51°26N 0°0 125 B3
Hitiaa Tahiti 17°36S 149°18W 289 e
Hitoyoshi Japan 32°13N 130°45E 222 E2
Hitra Norway 63°30N 8°45E 164 A5
Hitzacker Germany 53°9N 11°2E 178 B7
Hiu Vanuatu 13°10S 166°35E 287 C4
Hiuchi-Nada Japan 34°5N 133°20E 222 C5
Hiva Oa French Polynesia 9°45S 139°0W 289 f
Hixon Canada 53°25N 122°35W 296 C4
Hiyoshi Japan 35°32N 139°38E 140 B2
Ḩiyyon, N. ➔ Israel 30°25N 35°10E 251 H6
Hizma West Bank 31°50N 35°16E 123 B2
Hjalmar L. Canada 61°33N 109°25W 297 A7
Hjälmaren Sweden 59°18N 15°40E 162 E9
Hjalteyri Iceland 65°55N 18°18W 155 B8
Hjältevad Sweden 57°38N 15°20E 163 G9
Hjartdal Norway 59°37N 8°41E 164 E5
Hjelmelandsvågen Norway 59°14N 6°10E 164 E3
Hjelset Norway 62°48N 7°30E 164 B4
Hjerkinn Norway 62°13N 9°33E 164 B6
Hjo Sweden 58°22N 14°17E 163 F8
Hjørring Denmark 57°29N 9°59E 163 G3
Hjörsey Iceland 64°32N 22°21W 155 C4
Hjort Trench S. Ocean 58°0S 157°30E 151 B10
Hjortekær Denmark 55°47N 12°32E 118 A3
Hjortespring Denmark 55°44N 12°25E 118 A2
Hjortkvarn Sweden 58°54N 15°26E 163 F9
Hjukse Norway 59°31N 9°19E 164 E6
Hkakabo Razi Burma 28°25N 97°23E 241 B6
Hkakaborazi △ Burma 28°0N 97°55E 241 A6
Hko-lam Burma 21°7N 98°5E 241 E7
Hko-ut Burma 20°58N 98°2E 241 E7
Hkyenhpa Burma 27°43N 97°25E 241 B6
Hlaingbwe Burma 17°8N 97°50E 241 G6
Hlinsko Czech Rep. 49°45N 15°54E 180 B8
Hlobane S. Africa 27°42S 31°0E 271 C5
Hlohovec Slovak Rep. 48°26N 17°49E 181 C10
Hlubočepy Czech Rep. 50°2N 14°23E 135 B2
Hlučín Czech Rep. 49°54N 18°11E 181 B11
Hluhluwe S. Africa 28°1S 32°15E 271 C5
Hluhluwe △ S. Africa 22°10S 32°5E 271 B5
Hlukhiv Ukraine 51°40N 33°58E 189 G7
Hlwaze Burma 18°54N 96°37E 241 F6
Hlyboka Ukraine 48°5N 25°56E 183 B10
Hlybokaye Belarus 55°10N 27°45E 188 E4
Hnappadalssýsla □ Iceland 64°50N 22°30W 155 C4
Hnífsdalur Iceland 66°7N 23°8W 155 A3
Hnúšťa Slovak Rep. 48°35N 19°58E 181 C12
Ho Ghana 6°37N 0°27E 263 D5
Ho Chi Minh City = Thanh Pho Ho Chi Minh Vietnam 10°58N 106°40E 237 G6
Ho Chung China 22°21N 114°14E 122 A2
Ho Man Tin China 22°18N 114°11E 122 B2
Ho Thuong Vietnam 19°32N 105°48E 236 C5
Hoa Binh Vietnam 20°50N 105°20E 228 G5
Hoa Da Vietnam 11°16N 108°40E 237 G7
Hoa Hiep Vietnam 11°34N 105°51E 237 G5
Hoai Nhon Vietnam 14°28N 109°1E 236 E7
Hoang Lien Son Vietnam 22°0N 104°0E 228 F4
Hoanib ➔ Namibia 19°27S 12°46E 270 A2
Hoare B. Canada 65°17N 62°30W 295 C13
Hoarusib ➔ Namibia 19°3S 12°36E 270 A2
Hobart Tas., Australia 42°50S 147°21E 281 G4
Hobart Ind., U.S.A. 41°32N 87°15W 311 C9
Hobart Okla., U.S.A. 35°1N 99°6W 314 D5
Hobbs U.S.A. 32°42N 103°8W 305 K12
Hobbs Coast Antarctica 74°50S 131°0W 151 D14
Hobe Sound U.S.A. 27°4N 80°8W 317 H9
Hobo Colombia 2°35N 75°30W 328 C2
Hoboken Ga., U.S.A. 31°11N 82°8W 316 D7
Hoboken New York, U.S.A. 132 d1
Hobro Denmark 56°39N 9°46E 163 H3
Hobsons B. Australia 37°51S 144°55E 128 B1
Hoburgen Sweden 56°55N 18°7E 163 H12
Hocalar Turkey 38°36N 30°0E 205 C11
Hochbrück Germany 48°14N 11°37E 131 A2
Hochelaga Canada 45°32N 73°33W 130 A2
Hochfeld Namibia 21°28S 17°58E 270 B2
Hochharz △ Germany 51°48N 10°38E 178 D6
Hochschwab Austria 47°35N 15°0E 180 D8
Höchstadt Germany 49°42N 10°47E 179 F6
Hochtaunus △ Germany 50°20N 8°30E 179 E4
Hoch'uan = Hechuan China 30°2N 106°12E 228 B6
Hochwan = Hechuan China 30°2N 106°12E 228 B6
Hockenheim Germany 49°19N 8°32E 179 F4
Hockey Hall of Fame Toronto, Canada 141 b3
Hockley = Levelland U.S.A. 33°35N 102°23W 314 E3
Hodaka-Dake Japan 36°17N 137°39E 223 A9
Hodeida = Al Ḩudaydah Yemen 14°50N 43°0E 248 D3
Hodgeville Canada 50°7N 106°58W 297 C7
Hodgkins U.S.A. 41°46N 87°53W 119 C1
Hodgson Canada 51°13N 97°36W 297 C9
Hodh El Gharbi □ Mauritania 16°30N 10°0W 262 B3
Hódmezővásárhely Hungary 46°28N 20°22E 182 D5
Hodna, Chott el Algeria 35°26N 4°43E 261 A6
Hodo-dan N. Korea 39°23N 127°32E 224 C3
Hodonín Czech Rep. 48°50N 17°10E 181 C10
Hœdic, Î. de France 47°20N 2°53W 172 E4
Hoegi S. Korea 37°35N 127°3E 127 B2
Hoeilaart Belgium 50°46N 4°28E 116 B2
Hoek van Holland Neths. 52°0N 4°7E 170 C4
Hoengseong S. Korea 37°29N 127°59E 224 D3
Hoeryong N. Korea 42°30N 129°45E 224 A4
Hoeyang N. Korea 38°43N 127°36E 224 C3
Hof Bayern, Germany 50°19N 11°55E 179 E7
Hof Norður-Múlasýsla, Iceland 65°39N 15°0W 155 B11
Hof Suður-Múlasýsla, Iceland 64°33N 14°40W 155 C12
Hof Vestfold, Norway 59°32N 10°5E 164 E7
Hofburg Vienna, Austria 142 b1
Hofei = Hefei China 31°52N 117°18E 229 B11
Hoffell Iceland 64°23N 15°20W 155 C11
Hoffman I. U.S.A. 40°34N 74°3W 132 C1
Hofgarten Munich, Germany 131 a3
Hofgeismar Germany 51°29N 9°23E 178 D5
Hofheim Germany 50°5N 8°26E 179 E4
Hofmeyr S. Africa 31°39S 25°50E 270 D4
Höfn Iceland 64°15N 15°13W 155 C11
Hofors Sweden 60°31N 16°15E 162 D10
Hofsjökull Iceland 64°49N 18°48W 155 C8
Hofsós Iceland 65°53N 19°26W 155 B7
Hōfu Japan 34°3N 131°34E 222 C3
Hog Harbour Vanuatu 15°8S 167°6E 287 E5
Hog I. = Paradise I. Bahamas 25°6N 77°19W 153 b
Hog I. Grenada 12°0N 61°44W 323 q
Hog Pt. Antigua & B. 17°41N 61°47W 322 c
Hogan Group Australia 39°13S 147°1E 281 F4
Höganäs Sweden 56°12N 12°33E 163 H6
Hogansville U.S.A. 33°10N 84°55W 316 B5
Hogarth, Mt. Australia 21°48S 136°58E 280 C2
Hoge Kempen △ Belgium 51°6N 5°35E 170 C5
Høgeloft Norway 61°3N 8°12E 164 C5
Hogenakai Falls India 12°6N 77°50E 245 H3
Högsäter Sweden 58°38N 12°5E 163 F6
Högsby Sweden 57°10N 16°1E 163 G10
Högsjö Sweden 59°4N 15°44E 162 E9
Hogsty Reef Bahamas 21°41N 73°48W 321 B5
Hoh ➔ U.S.A. 47°45N 124°29W 306 C2
Hoh Xil Shan China 35°0N 89°0E 218 C3
Hohd ech Chargui □ Mauritania 19°0N 7°15W 260 E3
Hohe Acht Germany 50°22N 7°0E 179 E3
Hohe Tauern Austria 47°11N 12°40E 180 D5
Hohe Tauern △ Austria 47°5N 12°20E 180 D5
Hohenau Austria 48°36N 16°55E 181 C9
Hohenbrunn Germany 48°2N 11°42E 131 B3
Hohenelbe = Vrchlabí Czech Rep. 50°38N 15°37E 180 A8
Hohenems Austria 47°22N 9°42E 180 D2
Hohenloher Ebene Germany 49°14N 9°36E 179 F5
Hohenmauth = Vysoké Mýto Czech Rep. 49°58N 16°10E 181 B9
Hohensalza = Inowrocław Poland 52°50N 18°12E 185 F5
Hohensalzburg = Lunino Russia 53°38N 45°18E 190 D7
Hohenschönhausen Germany 52°33N 13°30E 115 A4
Hohenstadt = Zábřeh Czech Rep. 49°53N 16°52E 181 B9
Hohenstein = Olsztynek Poland 53°34N 20°19E 184 E7
Hohenwald U.S.A. 35°33N 87°33W 315 D11
Hohenwestedt Germany 54°5N 9°40E 178 A5
Hoher Rhön = Rhön Germany 50°24N 9°58E 178 E5
Hoher Vogelsberg △ Germany 51°45N 9°35E 178 D5
Hohes Venn Belgium 50°30N 6°5E 170 D6
Hohes Venn-Eifel △ Europe 50°30N 6°10E 178 E2
Hohhot China 40°52N 111°40E 226 D6
Hohoe Ghana 7°8N 0°32E 263 D5
Hoi An Vietnam 15°30N 108°19E 236 E7
Hoi Xuan Vietnam 20°25N 105°9E 228 G5
Hoihow = Haikou China 20°1N 110°16E 236 B8
Hoisington U.S.A. 38°31N 98°47W 308 F4
Hojai India 26°2N 92°54E 241 B4
Hojambaz Turkmenistan 38°7N 65°0E 216 E6
Højer Denmark 54°58N 8°42E 163 K2
Hōjō Japan 33°58N 132°46E 222 D4
Hok Sweden 57°31N 14°16E 163 G8
Hokang = Hegang China 47°20N 130°19E 219 B8
Hökensås Sweden 58°0N 14°5E 163 G8
Hökerum Sweden 57°51N 13°16E 163 G7
Hokianga Harbour N.Z. 35°31S 173°22E 284 B2
Hokitika N.Z. 42°42S 171°0E 285 C6
Hokkaidō □ Japan 43°30N 143°0E 220 C11
Hokksund Norway 59°48N 9°54E 164 E6
Hol-Hol Djibouti 11°20N 42°50E 257 E5
Hola Kenya 1°29S 40°2E 268 B4
Hola Pristan Ukraine 46°29N 32°32E 189 J7
Holakas Greece 35°57N 27°53E 206 F11
Holalkere India 14°2N 76°11E 245 G3
Hólar Iceland 65°44N 19°8W 155 B7
Holargos Greece 37°59N 23°48E 112 B2
Holbæk Denmark 55°43N 11°43E 163 J5
Holborn London, U.K. 125 a4
Holbrook N.S.W., Australia 35°42S 147°18E 283 C7
Holbrook Ariz., U.S.A. 34°54N 110°10W 305 J8
Holden Mo., U.S.A. 38°43N 94°0W 310 F3
Holden Utah, U.S.A. 39°6N 112°16W 304 G7
Holden, L. U.S.A. 28°30N 81°23W 133 B2
Holdenville U.S.A. 35°5N 96°24W 314 D6
Holdich Argentina 45°57S 68°13W 336 C3
Holdrege U.S.A. 40°26N 99°23W 308 E4
Hole-Narsipur India 12°48N 76°16E 245 H3
Holešov Czech Rep. 49°20N 17°35E 181 B10
Holešovice Czech Rep. 50°6N 14°28E 135 B2
Holetown Barbados 13°11N 59°38W 323 g
Holgate U.S.A. 41°15N 84°8W 311 C12
Holguín Cuba 20°50N 76°20W 320 B4
Holíč Slovak Rep. 48°49N 17°10E 181 C10
Holice Czech Rep. 50°5N 16°0E 180 A8
Holiday U.S.A. 28°11N 82°44W 317 G7
Höljes Sweden 60°50N 12°35E 162 D6
Hollabrunn Austria 48°34N 16°5E 180 C9
Hollams Bird I. Namibia 24°40S 14°30E 270 B1
Holland Mich., U.S.A. 42°47N 86°7W 311 B10
Holland N.Y., U.S.A. 42°38N 78°32W 312 D6
Holland B. Jamaica 17°57N 76°13W 320 a
Holland Tunnel New York, U.S.A. 132 d1
Holland Village Singapore 1°18N 103°47E 138 B2
Hollandia = Jayapura Indonesia 2°28S 140°38E 231 E10
Holley U.S.A. 43°14N 78°2W 312 C6
Hollfeld Germany 49°56N 11°18E 179 F7
Hollidaysburg U.S.A. 40°26N 78°24W 312 F6
Hollis U.S.A. 34°41N 99°55W 314 D5
Hollis Reservoir Trin. & Tob. 10°40N 61°10W 323 t
Hollister Calif., U.S.A. 36°51N 121°24W 306 J5
Hollister Idaho, U.S.A. 42°21N 114°35W 304 E6
Höllriegelskreuth Germany 48°2N 11°30E 131 B1
Höllviken = Höllviksnäs Sweden 55°26N 12°58E 163 J6
Höllviksnäs Sweden 55°26N 12°58E 163 J6
Holly U.S.A. 42°48N 83°38W 311 B13
Holly Hill Fla., U.S.A. 29°16N 81°3W 317 F8
Holly Hill S.C., U.S.A. 33°19N 80°25W 316 B9
Holly Springs Ga., U.S.A. 34°10N 84°30W 316 A5
Holly Springs Miss., U.S.A. 34°46N 89°27W 315 D10
Hollywood Calif., U.S.A. 34°5N 118°19W 126 B3
Hollywood Fla., U.S.A. 26°0N 80°8W 317 J9
Hollywood Bowl U.S.A. 34°7N 118°20W 126 B2
Holman Canada 70°44N 117°44W 294 B8
Hólmavík Iceland 65°42N 21°40W 155 B5
Holmen Oppland, Norway 60°40N 10°22E 164 D7
Holmen Wis., U.S.A. 43°58N 91°15W 308 D8
Holmenkollen Norway 59°57N 10°41E 133 A3
Holmes Beach U.S.A. 27°31N 82°43W 317 H7
Holmes Cr. ➔ U.S.A. 30°30N 85°50W 316 E4
Holmes Reefs Australia 16°27S 148°0E 280 B4
Holmes Run Acres U.S.A. 38°51N 77°13W 143 B2
Holmestrand Norway 59°31N 10°14E 164 E7
Holmgärd Sweden 59°14N 18°0E 139 B1
Holmlia Norway 59°49N 10°46E 133 B3
Holmsjö Sweden 56°25N 15°32E 163 H9
Holmsjön Västernorrland, Sweden 62°41N 16°33E 162 B10
Holmsjön Västernorrland, Sweden 62°26N 15°20E 162 B9
Holmsland Klit Denmark 56°0N 8°5E 163 J2
Holmsund Sweden 63°41N 20°20E 160 E19
Holocaust Memorial Israel 31°47N 35°11E 123 B2
Holocaust Memorial Park Boston, U.S.A. 116 b2
Holod Romania 46°49N 22°8E 182 D7
Holon Israel 32°0N 34°46E 251 G5
Holopaw U.S.A. 28°8N 81°5W 317 G8
Holovne Ukraine 51°20N 24°5E 185 G11
Holøydal Norway 62°18N 11°27E 164 B8
Holozubyntsi Ukraine 48°50N 26°55E 183 B11
Holroyd ➔ Australia 14°10S 141°36E 280 A3
Holstebro Denmark 56°22N 8°37E 163 H2
Holsteinische Schweiz △ Germany 54°8N 10°30E 178 A6
Holsteinsborg = Sisimiut Greenland 66°40N 53°30W 154 D5
Holsworthy U.K. 50°48N 4°22W 169 G3
Holt Iceland 63°33N 19°48W 155 D7
Holt Fla., U.S.A. 30°43N 86°45W 317 E3
Holt Mich., U.S.A. 42°39N 84°31W 311 B12
Holton Nfld. & L., Canada 54°31N 57°12W 299 B8
Holton Kans., U.S.A. 39°28N 95°44W 308 F6
Holts Summit U.S.A. 38°38N 92°7W 310 F4
Holtville U.S.A. 32°49N 115°23W 307 N11
Holualoa U.S.A. 19°37N 155°57W 302 D6
Holum Norway 58°6N 7°32E 164 F4
Holwerd Neths. 53°22N 5°54E 170 A5
Holy Cross U.S.A. 62°12N 159°46W 303 E8
Holy I. Anglesey, U.K. 53°17N 4°37W 168 D3
Holy I. Northumberland, U.K. 55°40N 1°47W 168 B6
Holyhead U.K. 53°18N 4°38W 168 D3
Holyoke Colo., U.S.A. 40°35N 102°18W 304 F12
Holyoke Mass., U.S.A. 42°12N 72°37W 313 D12
Holyrood Canada 47°27N 53°8W 299 C9
Holyrood House, Palace of U.K. 55°57N 3°10W 121 B3
Holysloot Neths. 52°25N 5°2E 112 A3
Holzkirchen Germany 47°52N 11°42E 179 H7
Holzminden Germany 51°50N 9°28E 178 D5
Homa Bay Kenya 0°36S 34°30E 268 C3
Homalin Burma 24°55N 95°0E 241 C5
Homand Iran 32°28N 59°37E 247 C8
Homathko ➔ Canada 51°0N 124°56W 296 C4
Homberg Germany 51°2N 9°25E 178 D5
Hombori Mali 15°20N 1°38W 263 B4
Hombori Tondo Mali 15°16N 1°40W 263 B4
Homburg Germany 49°28N 7°18E 179 F3
Home B. Canada 68°40N 67°10W 295 C13
Home Hill Australia 19°43S 147°25E 280 B4
Home Reef Tonga 18°59S 174°47W 287 P13
Homedale U.S.A. 43°37N 116°56W 304 E5
Homei Taiwan 24°7N 120°29E 225 B2
Homeland U.S.A. 30°51N 82°1W 316 E7
Homer Alaska, U.S.A. 59°39N 151°33W 303 G10
Homer La., U.S.A. 32°48N 93°4W 314 E8
Homer Mich., U.S.A. 42°9N 84°49W 311 B12
Homer City U.S.A. 40°32N 79°10W 312 F5
Homert △ Germany 51°15N 8°0E 178 D4
Homerton U.K. 51°32N 0°2W 125 A3
Homerville U.S.A. 31°2N 82°45W 316 D7
Homestead Queens., Australia 20°20S 145°40E 280 C4
Homestead Fla., U.S.A. 25°28N 80°29W 317 K9
Homestead △ U.S.A. 40°17N 96°50W 308 E5
Hometown U.S.A. 41°44N 87°42W 119 C2
Homewood U.S.A. 41°34N 87°40W 311 C9
Hommelvik Norway 63°25N 10°48E 164 A7
Hommersåk Norway 58°56N 5°50E 164 F2
Homnabad India 17°45N 77°11E 244 F3
Homoine Mozam. 23°55S 35°8E 271 B6
Homoljske Planina Serbia 44°10N 21°45E 202 B5
Homonhon I. Phil. 10°44N 125°43E 233 F5
Homorod Romania 46°5N 25°15E 183 D10
Homosassa Springs U.S.A. 28°48N 82°35W 317 G7
Homs = Al Khums Libya 32°40N 14°17E 258 B2
Homs = Ḩimş Syria 34°40N 36°45E 250 D7
Homyel Belarus 52°28N 31°0E 177 B16
Homyel □ Belarus 52°40N 30°10E 189 F6
Hon Chong Vietnam 10°25N 104°30E 237 G5
Hon Hai Vietnam 10°0N 109°0E 237 H7
Hon Me Vietnam 19°23N 105°56E 236 C5
Honan = Henan □ China 34°0N 114°0E 226 H8
Hōnanchō Japan 35°40N 139°39E 140 A2
Hōnaunau U.S.A. 19°26N 155°55W 302 D6
Honavar India 14°17N 74°27E 245 G2
Honaz Turkey 37°46N 29°18E 205 D11
Honbetsu Japan 43°7N 143°37E 220 C11
Honcho Japan 35°40N 139°41E 140 A3
Honcut U.S.A. 39°20N 121°32W 306 F5
Honda Colombia 5°12N 74°45W 328 B3
Honda, Bahía Cuba 22°54N 83°10W 320 B3
Honda Bay Phil. 9°53N 118°49E 233 G2
Hondarribia Spain 43°22N 1°47W 196 B3
Hondeklipbaai S. Africa 30°19S 17°17E 270 D2
Honden Japan 35°43N 139°50E 140 A4
Hondo Japan 32°27N 130°12E 222 E2
Hondo Tex., U.S.A. 29°21N 99°9W 314 G5
Hondo, Río ➔ Belize 18°25N 88°21W 319 D7
Hondo, Rio ➔ Calif., U.S.A. 34°2N 118°15W 126 B4
Honduras ■ Cent. Amer. 14°40N 86°30W 320 D2
Honduras, G. de Caribbean 16°50N 87°0W 320 C2
Hønefoss Norway 60°10N 10°18E 164 D7
Honesdale U.S.A. 41°34N 75°16W 313 E9
Honey L. U.S.A. 40°15N 120°19W 306 E6
Honfleur France 49°25N 0°13E 172 C7
Høng Denmark 55°31N 11°18E 163 J5
Hong Gai Vietnam 20°57N 107°5E 228 G6
Hong He ➔ China 32°25N 115°35E 226 H8
Hong Hu China 29°54N 113°24E 229 C9
Hong Kong China 22°17N 114°11E 122 B1
Hong Kong □ China 22°11N 114°14E 219 G11
Hong Kong, Univ. of China 22°16N 114°8E 122 B1
Hong Kong I. China 22°16N 114°12E 122 B2
Hong Kong Int. ✕ (HKG) China 22°19N 113°57E 219 G10
Hong Kong Park Hong Kong, China 122 c1
Honga Angola 15°9S 15°12E 265 F3
Hong'an China 31°20N 114°40E 229 B10
Hongcheon S. Korea 37°44N 127°53E 224 D3
Hongdo S. Korea 34°41N 125°12E 224 E2
Honghai Wan China 22°40N 115°0E 229 F10
Honghe China 23°25N 102°25E 228 F4
Honghu China 29°50N 113°30E 229 C9
Hongje S. Korea 37°35N 126°56E 137 B1
Hongjiang China 27°7N 109°59E 228 D7
Hongjimun Tunnel S. Korea 37°37N 126°58E 137 B1
Hongkou China 31°16N 121°29E 138 B1
Hongliu He ➔ China 38°0N 109°50E 226 F5
Hongmiao China 39°54N 116°26E 114 B2
Hongor Mongolia 45°45N 112°50E 226 B7
Hongqiao China 31°11N 121°22E 138 B1
Hongsa Laos 19°43N 101°20E 236 C3
Hongseong S. Korea 36°37N 126°38E 224 D3
Hongshui He ➔ China 23°48N 109°30E 228 F7
Hongtong China 36°16N 111°40E 226 F6
Honguedo, Détroit d' Canada 49°15N 64°0W 299 C7
Hongwon N. Korea 40°0N 127°56E 224 C3
Hongya China 29°57N 103°22E 228 C4
Hongyuan China 32°51N 102°40E 228 A4
Hongze Hu China 33°15N 118°35E 227 H10
Honiara Solomon Is. 9°27S 159°57E 287 M10
Honiton U.K. 50°47N 3°11W 169 G4
Honjō Akita, Japan 39°23N 140°3E 220 E10
Honjō Gumma, Japan 36°14N 139°11E 223 A11
Honjyo Japan 35°41N 139°48E 140 A3
Honkawane Japan 35°5N 138°5E 223 B10
Honkorâb, Ras Egypt 24°35N 35°10E 256 C4
Honnali India 14°15N 75°40E 245 G2
Honningsvåg Norway 70°59N 25°59E 160 A21
Hönö Sweden 57°41N 11°39E 163 G5
Honoka'a U.S.A. 20°5N 155°28W 302 C6
Honokahua U.S.A. 21°0N 156°40W 302 B5
Honokai Hale U.S.A. 21°20N 158°6W 302 K13
Honolulu U.S.A. 21°19N 157°52W 302 K14
Honolulu District U.S.A. 21°19N 157°46W 302 K14
Honolulu Int. ✕ (HNL) U.S.A. 21°19N 157°55W 302 K14
Honolulu Watershed Forest Reserve U.S.A. 21°21N 157°48W 302 K14
Honomu U.S.A. 19°52N 155°7W 302 D6
Honoré Mercier, Pont Canada 45°24N 73°39W 130 B1
Honouliuli U.S.A. 21°22N 158°2W 302 K13
Honouliuli Forest Reserve U.S.A. 21°25N 158°4W 302 K13
Hönow Germany 52°32N 13°38E 115 A4
Honshū Japan 36°0N 138°0E 223 A8
Hontoria del Pinar Spain 41°50N 3°10W 196 D1
Honu'apo B. U.S.A. 19°5N 155°33W 302 D6
Hood, I. = Española, I. Ecuador 1°23S 89°39W 330 a
Hood, Mt. U.S.A. 45°23N 121°42W 304 D3
Hood, Pt. Australia 34°23S 119°34E 279 F2
Hood Pt. Papua N. G. 10°4S 147°45E 286 F4
Hood River U.S.A. 45°43N 121°31W 304 D3
Hoodsport U.S.A. 47°24N 123°9W 306 C3
Hooge Germany 54°34N 8°33E 178 A4
Hoogeveen Neths. 52°44N 6°28E 170 B6
Hoogezand-Sappemeer Neths. 53°9N 6°45E 170 A6
Hooghly = Hugli ➔ India 21°56N 88°4E 243 J13
Hooghly-Chinsura = Chunchura India 22°53N 88°27E 243 H13
Hook U.K. 51°22N 0°17W 125 B2
Hook Hd. Ireland 52°7N 6°56W 166 D5
Hook I. Australia 20°4S 149°0E 280 J6
Hook of Holland = Hoek van Holland Neths. 52°0N 4°7E 170 C4
Hooker U.S.A. 36°52N 101°13W 314 C4
Hooker Creek = Lajamanu Australia 18°23S 130°38E 278 C5
Ho'olehua U.S.A. 21°10N 157°5W 302 B4
Hoonah U.S.A. 58°7N 135°27W 296 B1
Hoop Neth. Ant. 12°7N 68°17W 322 h
Hooper Bay U.S.A. 61°32N 166°6W 303 F6
Hoopeston U.S.A. 40°28N 87°40W 311 D9
Hoopstad S. Africa 27°50S 25°55E 270 C4
Höör Sweden 55°56N 13°33E 163 J7
Hoorn Neths. 52°38N 5°4E 170 B5
Hoover U.S.A. 33°24N 86°49W 315 E11
Hoover Dam U.S.A. 36°1N 114°44W 307 K12
Hooversville U.S.A. 40°9N 78°55W 312 F6
Hop Bottom U.S.A. 41°42N 75°46W 313 E9
Hopa Turkey 41°28N 41°30E 213 B9
Hope B.C., Canada 49°25N 121°25W 296 D4
Hope Ariz., U.S.A. 33°43N 113°42W 307 M13
Hope Ark., U.S.A. 33°40N 93°36W 314 E8
Hope Ind., U.S.A. 39°18N 85°46W 311 E11
Hope, L. S. Austral., Australia 28°24S 139°18E 281 D2
Hope, L. W. Austral., Australia 32°35S 120°15E 279 F3
Hope, Pt. U.S.A. 68°21N 166°47W 303 B6
Hope Bay Jamaica 18°12N 76°34W 320 a
Hope I. Canada 44°55N 80°11W 312 B4
Hope Town Bahamas 26°35N 76°57W 320 A4
Hope Vale Australia 15°16S 145°20E 280 B4
Hopedale Nfld. & L., Canada 55°28N 60°13W 299 A7
Hopedale Mass., U.S.A. 42°8N 71°33W 313 D13
Hopefield S. Africa 33°3S 18°22E 270 D2
Hopei = Hebei □ China 39°0N 116°0E 226 E9
Hopelchén Mexico 19°46N 89°51W 319 D7
Hopetoun Vic., Australia 35°42S 142°22E 282 C5
Hopetoun W. Austral., Australia 33°57S 120°7E 279 F3
Hopetown S. Africa 29°34S 24°3E 270 C3
Hopewell U.S.A. 37°18N 77°17W 309 G15
Hopfgarten Austria 47°27N 12°10E 180 D5
Hopin Burma 24°58N 96°30E 241 C6
Hoping Changhua, Taiwan 24°10N 120°56E 225 B2
Hoping T'aitung, Taiwan 23°4N 121°20E 225 C3
Hopkins U.S.A. 40°33N 94°49W 310 D2
Hopkins, L. Australia 24°15S 128°35E 278 D4
Hopkinsville U.S.A. 36°52N 87°29W 308 G10
Hopland U.S.A. 38°58N 123°7W 306 G3
Hopong Burma 20°47N 97°11E 241 E6
Hopwood's Ferry = Echuca Australia 36°10S 144°45E 283 D6
Hoque Angola 14°40S 13°55E 265 E2
Hoquiam U.S.A. 46°59N 123°53W 306 D3
Hora Hoverla Ukraine 48°7N 24°41E 183 B9
Hora Sfakion = Chora Sfakion Greece 35°15N 24°9E 207 E5
Hōrai Japan 34°58N 137°32E 223 C9
Horana Sri Lanka 6°43N 80°4E 245 L5
Horasan Turkey 40°3N 42°11E 213 B10
Horažďovice Czech Rep. 49°19N 13°42E 180 B6
Horb Germany 48°26N 8°47E 179 G4
Hörby Sweden 55°51N 13°40E 163 J7
Horcajo de Santiago Spain 39°50N 3°1W 196 F1
Hordabø Norway 60°42N 4°54E 164 D1
Hordaland □ Norway 60°25N 6°15E 164 D3
Hordern Hills Australia 20°15S 130°0E 278 D5
Hordio Somali Rep. 10°33N 51°6E 267 B7
Horezu Romania 45°6N 24°0E 183 E8
Horgen Switz. 47°15N 8°35E 179 H4
Horgoš Serbia 46°10N 20°0E 182 D4
Hořice Czech Rep. 50°21N 15°39E 180 A8
Horikiri Japan 35°44N 139°50E 140 A4
Horinchove Ukraine 48°16N 23°26E 183 B8
Horinger China 40°28N 111°48E 226 D6
Horki Belarus 54°17N 30°59E 188 E6
Horlick Mts. Antarctica 84°0S 102°0W 151 E15
Horlivka Ukraine 48°19N 38°5E 189 H10
Hormak Iran 29°58N 60°51E 247 D9
Hormigueros Puerto Rico 18°8N 67°8W 321 b
Hormoz Iran 27°35N 55°0E 247 E7
Hormoz, Jaz.-ye Iran 27°8N 56°28E 247 E8
Hormozgān □ Iran 27°30N 56°0E 247 E8
Hormuz, Kūh-e Iran 27°27N 55°10E 247 E7
Hormuz, Str. of The Gulf 26°30N 56°30E 247 E8
Horn Austria 48°39N 15°40E 180 C8
Horn Iceland 66°28N 22°28W 155 A4
Horn Sweden 57°54N 15°51E 163 G9
Horn ➔ Canada 61°30N 118°1W 296 A5
Horn, Cape = Hornos, C. de Chile 55°50S 67°30W 336 E3
Horn, Is. Wall. & F. Is. 14°16S 178°6W 277 C15
Horn Head Ireland 55°14N 8°0W 166 A3
Horn I. Australia 10°37S 142°17E 286 F2
Horn Plateau Canada 62°15N 119°15W 296 A5
Horn Pond U.S.A. 42°28N 71°9W 116 A1
Hornachuelos Spain 37°50N 5°14W 195 H5
Hornavan Sweden 66°15N 17°30E 160 C17
Hornbeck U.S.A. 31°20N 93°24W 314 F8
Hornbrook U.S.A. 41°55N 122°33W 304 F2
Hornburg Germany 52°2N 10°37E 178 C6
Hornby N.Z. 43°33S 172°33E 285 D7
Horncastle U.K. 53°13N 0°7W 168 D7
Hornchurch U.K. 51°33N 0°14E 125 A5
Horndal Sweden 60°18N 16°23E 162 D10
Hornell U.S.A. 42°20N 77°40W 312 D7
Hornell L. Canada 62°20N 119°25W 296 A5
Hornepayne Canada 49°14N 84°48W 298 C3
Horni Czech Rep. 50°2N 14°33E 135 B3
Horní Planá Czech Rep. 48°46N 14°2E 180 C7
Horni Počernice Czech Rep. 50°6N 14°36E 135 B3
Hornindal Norway 61°58N 6°30E 164 C3
Hornings Mills Canada 44°9N 80°12W 312 B4
Hornitos U.S.A. 37°30N 120°14W 306 H6
Hornopirén △ Chile 41°58S 72°17W 336 B2
Hornos, C. de Chile 55°50S 67°30W 336 E3
Hornos Is. Papua N. G. 2°12S 147°45E 286 B4
Hornoy-le-Bourg France 49°50N 1°54E 173 C8
Hornsby Australia 33°42S 151°2E 283 B9
Hornsea U.K. 53°55N 0°11W 168 D7
Hornsey U.K. 51°35N 0°7W 125 A3
Hornsjø Norway 61°19N 10°38E 164 C7
Hornslandet Sweden 61°35N 17°37E 162 C11
Hörnum Germany 54°45N 8°17E 178 A4
Horobetsu = Noboribetsu Japan 42°24N 141°6E 220 C10
Horodenka Ukraine 48°41N 25°29E 183 B10
Horodnya Ukraine 51°55N 31°33E 189 G6
Horodok Khmelnytskyy, Ukraine 49°10N 26°34E 177 D14
Horodok Lviv, Ukraine 49°46N 23°32E 177 D12
Horodyshche Ukraine 49°17N 31°27E 189 H6
Horokhiv Ukraine 50°30N 24°45E 177 C13
Horoměřice Czech Rep. 50°8N 14°20E 135 B1
Horovice Czech Rep. 49°48N 13°53E 180 B6
Horqin Youyi Qianqi China 46°5N 122°3E 227 A12
Horqueta Paraguay 23°15S 56°55W 334 A4
Horred Sweden 57°22N 12°28E 163 G6
Horse Cr. ➔ U.S.A. 41°57N 103°58W 304 F12
Horse I. Canada 53°20N 99°6W 297 C9
Horse Is. Canada 50°15N 55°50W 299 B8
Horsefly L. Canada 52°25N 121°0W 296 C4
Horseheads U.S.A. 42°10N 76°49W 312 D8
Horsens Denmark 55°52N 9°51E 163 J3
Horseshoe Bend △ U.S.A. 32°59N 85°44W 316 C4
Horsham Vic., Australia 36°44S 142°13E 282 D5
Horsham W. Susx., U.K. 51°4N 0°20W 169 F7
Horšovský Týn Czech Rep. 49°31N 12°58E 180 B5
Horta Azores 38°32N 28°38W 153 d1
Hortaleza Spain 40°28N 3°38W 127 B2
Horten Norway 59°25N 10°32E 164 E7
Hortense U.S.A. 31°20N 81°57W 316 D8
Horti India 17°7N 75°47E 244 F2
Hortobágy ➔ Hungary 47°30N 21°6E 182 C6
Hortobágyi △ Hungary 47°36N 21°10E 182 C6
Horton Kans., U.S.A. 39°40N 95°32W 308 F6
Horton Mo., U.S.A. 37°58N 94°22W 310 G2
Horton ➔ Canada 69°56N 126°52W 294 C7
Horwood L. Canada 48°5N 82°20W 298 C3
Hosaina Ethiopia 7°30N 37°47E 257 F4
Hosdurga India 13°49N 76°17E 245 H3
Hosenofu Libya 23°41N 21°4E 258 D4
Ḩoseynābād Khuzestān, Iran 32°45N 48°20E 247 C6
Ḩoseynābād Kordestān, Iran 35°33N 47°8E 213 E12
Hosford U.S.A. 30°23N 84°48W 316 E5
Hoshangabad India 22°45N 77°45E 242 H7
Hoshiarpur India 31°30N 75°58E 242 D6
Hoskins Papua N. G. 5°29S 150°27E 286 C6
Hoskote India 13°4N 77°48E 245 H3
Hosoyama Japan 35°36N 139°31E 140 B2
Hospet India 15°15N 76°20E 245 G3
Hostafrancs Spain 41°21N 2°8E 114 A1
Hoste, I. Chile 55°0S 69°0W 336 E3
Hostens France 44°30N 0°40W 174 D3
Hostivař Czech Rep. 50°3N 14°31E 135 B3
Hosur India 12°43N 77°49E 245 H3
Hot Thailand 18°8N 98°29E 236 C2
Hot Creek Range U.S.A. 38°40N 116°20W 304 G5
Hot Springs = Truth or Consequences U.S.A. 33°8N 107°15W 305 K10
Hot Springs Ark., U.S.A. 34°31N 93°3W 314 D8
Hot Springs S. Dak., U.S.A. 43°26N 103°29W 308 D2
Hot Springs △ U.S.A. 34°31N 93°3W 314 D8
Hotagen Sweden 63°59N 14°12E 160 E16
Hotan China 37°25N 79°55E 217 E9
Hotan He ➔ China 40°22N 80°56E 217 D10
Hotazel S. Africa 27°17S 22°58E 270 C3
Hotchkiss U.S.A. 38°48N 107°43W 304 G10
Hôtel des Invalides Paris, France 134 c2
Hotham, C. Australia 12°2S 131°18E 278 B5
Hoting Sweden 64°8N 16°15E 160 D17
Hotolisht Albania 41°10N 20°25E 202 E4
Hotspur Seamount Atl. Oc. 17°55S 35°55W 152 H8
Hotte, Massif de la Haiti 18°30N 73°45W 321 C5
Hottentotsbaai Namibia 26°8S 14°59E 270 C1
Hou Hai China 22°32N 113°56E 219 F10
Houailou N. Cal. 21°17S 165°38E 288 d
Houat, Î. de France 47°24N 2°58W 172 E4
Houbětin Czech Rep. 50°6N 14°33E 135 B3
Houdan France 48°48N 1°35E 173 D8
Houei Sai Laos 20°18N 100°26E 228 G3
Houeillès France 44°12N 0°2E 174 D4
Houffalize Belgium 50°8N 5°48E 170 D5
Houghton Gauteng, S. Africa 26°10S 28°3E 123 B2
Houghton Mich., U.S.A. 47°7N 88°34W 308 B9
Houghton N.Y., U.S.A. 42°25N 78°10W 312 D6
Houghton L. U.S.A. 44°21N 84°44W 309 C11
Houghton-le-Spring U.K. 54°51N 1°28W 168 C6
Houhora Heads N.Z. 34°49S 173°9E 284 A2
Houilles France 48°56N 2°11E 134 A2
Houli Taiwan 24°19N 120°44E 225 B2
Houlton U.S.A. 46°8N 67°51W 309 B20
Houlung Taiwan 24°37N 120°47E 225 B2
Houma U.S.A. 29°36N 90°43W 315 G9
Houmt Souk = Djerba Tunisia 33°48N 10°54E 258 B2
Houndé Burkina Faso 11°34N 3°31W 262 C4
Hounslow □ U.K. 51°28N 0°21W 125 B2
Houpi Taiwan 23°22N 120°21E 225 C2
Hourtin France 45°11N 1°4W 174 C2
Hourtin-Carcans, Étang d' France 45°10N 1°6W 174 C2
Housatonic ➔ U.S.A. 41°10N 73°7W 313 E11
House of Nobility = Riddarhuset Stockholm, Sweden 139 c2
House of Parliament = Riksdagshuset Stockholm, Sweden 139 b2
Houses of Parliament London, U.K. 125 c3
Houston B.C., Canada 54°25N 126°39W 296 C3
Houston Fla., U.S.A. 30°15N 82°54W 316 E7
Houston Mo., U.S.A. 37°22N 91°58W 308 G8
Houston Tex., U.S.A. 29°45N 95°21W 314 G7
Hout = Mogwadi ➔ S. Africa 23°4S 29°36E 271 B4
Hout Bay S. Africa 34°2S 18°23E 118 B1

Houtkraal S. Africa 30°23S 24°5E 270 D3
Houtman Abrolhos Australia 28°43S 113°48E 279 E1
Hov Norway 60°42N 10°20E 164 D7
Hovd □ Mongolia 48°2N 91°37E 217 C12
Hovda Norway 60°53N 9°11E 164 D6
Hovden Aust-Agder, Norway 59°33N 7°22E 164 E4
Hovden Sogn og Fjordane, Norway 61°41N 4°52E 164 C1
Hove U.K. 50°50N 0°10W 169 G7
Hove Å → Denmark 55°43N 12°7E 118 B2
Hovedøya Norway 59°53N 10°43E 133 A3
Hovedstaden □ Denmark 56°0N 10°0E 163 J6
Hovenweep ⌓ U.S.A. 37°20N 109°0W 305 H9
Hovet Norway 60°38N 8°8E 164 D5
Hoveyzeh Iran 31°27N 48°4E 247 D6
Hovgaard Ø Greenland 79°55N 18°50W 154 B9
Høvik Norway 59°54N 10°34E 133 A2
Hovin Norway 59°51N 9°0E 164 E6
Hovmantorp Sweden 56°47N 15°7E 163 H9
Hovorčovice Czech Rep. 50°10N 14°31E 135 A3
Hövsgöl Mongolia 43°37N 109°39E 226 C5
Hövsgöl Nuur Mongolia 51°0N 100°30E 218 A5
Hovsta Sweden 59°22N 15°15E 162 E9
Howakil Eritrea 15°10N 40°16E 257 D5
Howar, Wadi → Sudan 17°30N 27°8E 257 D2
Howard Queens., Australia 25°16S 152°32E 281 D5
Howard Pa., U.S.A. 41°1N 77°40W 312 F7
Howard S. Dak., U.S.A. 44°1N 97°32W 308 C5
Howard Beach U.S.A. 40°39N 73°50W 132 C2
Howe U.S.A. 43°48N 113°0W 304 E7
Howe, C. Australia 37°30S 150°0E 283 D9
Howe, West Cape Australia 35°8S 117°36E 279 G2
Howe I. Canada 44°16N 76°17W 313 B8
Howell U.S.A. 42°36N 83°56W 311 B13
Howick Qué., Canada 45°11N 73°51W 313 A11
Howick N.Z. 36°54S 174°56E 284 C3
Howick KwaZulu Natal, S. Africa 29°28S 30°14E 271 C5
Howick Group Australia 14°20S 145°30E 280 A4
Howitt, L. Australia 27°40S 138°40E 281 D2
Howland I. Pac. Oc. 0°48N 176°38W 288 G10
Howlong Australia 35°59S 146°38E 283 C7
Howrah = Haora India 22°34N 88°18E 124 B1
Howth Ireland 53°23N 6°6W 120 A3
Howth Hd. Ireland 53°22N 6°4W 120 A3
Höxter Germany 51°46N 9°22E 178 D5
Hoxtolgay China 46°35N 85°59E 217 C11
Hoxton London, U.K. 125 a5
Hoxud China 42°15N 86°51E 217 D11
Hoy U.K. 58°50N 3°15W 167 C5
Hoya Niedersachsen, Germany 52°49N 9°8E 178 C5
Hōya Tōkyō, Japan 35°44N 139°34E 140 A2
Høyanger Norway 61°13N 6°4E 164 C3
Hoyerswerda Germany 51°26N 14°14E 178 D10
Hoylake U.K. 53°24N 3°10W 168 D4
Hōyo-Kaikyō Japan 33°20N 131°58E 222 D3
Hoyos Spain 40°9N 6°45W 194 E4
Hpa-an = Pa-an Burma 16°51N 97°40E 241 G6
Hpawlum Burma 27°12N 98°12E 241 B7
Hpettintha Burma 24°14N 95°23E 241 C5
Hpizow Burma 26°57N 98°24E 241 B7
Hpunan Pass Burma 27°30N 96°55E 241 A6
Hradčany Czech Rep. 50°5N 14°24E 135 B2
Hradec Králové Czech Rep. 50°15N 15°50E 180 A8
Hrádek Czech Rep. 48°46N 16°16E 181 C9
Hrafnseyri Iceland 65°46N 23°28W 155 B3
Hranice Czech Rep. 49°34N 17°45E 181 B10
Hrazdan Armenia 40°30N 44°46E 191 K7
Hrebenka Ukraine 50°9N 32°22E 189 G7
Hrífunes Iceland 63°38N 18°30W 155 D8
Hrísey Iceland 66°0N 18°23W 155 B8
Hrisoupoli Greece 40°58N 24°42E 203 F8
Hristiana Greece 36°14N 25°13E 205 E7
Hrodna Belarus 53°42N 23°52E 184 E10
Hrodna □ Belarus 53°20N 24°45E 188 F3
Hrodzyanka Belarus 53°31N 28°42E 177 B15
Hron → Slovak Rep. 47°49N 18°45E 181 D11
Hrubieszów Poland 50°49N 23°51E 185 H10
Hrubý Jeseník Czech Rep. 50°5N 17°10E 181 A10
Hrvatska = Croatia ■ Europe 45°20N 16°0E 199 C13
Hrymayliv Ukraine 49°20N 26°5E 177 D14
Hrynyava Ukraine 47°59N 24°53E 183 C9
Hsa-paw Burma 19°1N 97°30E 241 F6
Hsenwi Burma 23°22N 97°55E 241 D6
Hsi-hkip Burma 20°25N 96°42E 241 E6
Hsiafu Taiwan 25°7N 121°17E 225 A3
Hsiamen = Xiamen China 24°25N 118°4E 229 E12
Hsian = Xi'an China 34°15N 109°0E 226 G5
Hsiangshan Taiwan 24°48N 120°54E 225 B2
Hsiaochinmen Tao Taiwan 24°26N 118°14E 225 a
Hsiaohungt'ou Hsü Taiwan 21°57N 121°36E 225 E3
Hsiaokang Taiwan 22°34N 120°20E 225 D2
Hsiatahsi Taiwan 22°28N 120°56E 225 D2
Hsiaying Taiwan 23°14N 120°15E 225 C2
Hsichih Taiwan 25°4N 121°39E 225 A3
Hsikang Taiwan 23°7N 120°12E 225 C2
Hsilo Taiwan 23°48N 120°27E 225 C2
Hsinche Taiwan 24°10N 120°50E 225 B2
Hsinch'eng Taiwan 24°8N 121°39E 225 B3
Hsinchu Taiwan 24°48N 120°58E 225 B2
Hsinchu □ Taiwan 24°45N 121°10E 225 B3
Hsinchuang Kaohsung, Taiwan 22°34N 120°29E 225 D2
Hsinchuang T'aipei, Taiwan 25°2N 121°27E 225 A3
Hsinfa Taiwan 23°1N 120°39E 225 C2
Hsinfeng Taiwan 24°54N 120°59E 225 B2
Hsinhailien = Lianyungang China 34°40N 119°11E 227 G10
Hsinhua Taiwan 23°2N 120°18E 225 C2
Hsini Taiwan 23°41N 120°51E 225 C2
Hsinking = Changchun China 43°57N 125°17E 227 C13
Hsinpi Taiwan 22°28N 120°33E 225 D2
Hsinshih Taiwan 23°4N 120°17E 225 C2
Hsintien Taiwan 24°57N 121°32E 225 B3
Hsinwu Taiwan 24°59N 121°6E 225 B3
Hsinying Taiwan 23°21N 120°17E 225 C2
Hsinyuan Taiwan 22°32N 120°27E 225 D2
Hsipaw Burma 22°37N 97°18E 241 D6
Hsiukuluan Hsi → Taiwan 23°28N 121°30E 225 C3
Hsiushui Taiwan 24°3N 120°30E 225 B2
Hsiyu Taiwan 23°36N 119°30E 225 C1
Hsopket Burma 23°11N 98°26E 228 F2
Hsüchou = Xuzhou China 34°18N 117°10E 227 G9
Hsüeh Pa △ Taiwan 24°36N 121°22E 225 B3
Hsüeh Shan China 24°24N 121°12E 225 B3
Hsüehchia Taiwan 23°14N 120°10E 225 C2
Hsühaitsun Taiwan 22°12N 120°52E 225 D2
Htapodia Greece 37°24N 25°34E 205 D7
Htawgaw Burma 25°57N 98°23E 241 C7
Hu Xian China 34°8N 108°42E 226 G5
Hua Hin Thailand 12°34N 99°58E 236 F2
Hua Xian Henan, China 35°30N 114°30E 226 G8
Hua Xian Shaanxi, China 34°30N 109°48E 226 G5
Hua Yü Taiwan 23°24N 119°19E 225 C1
Hua'an China 25°1N 117°32E 229 E11
Huab → Namibia 20°52S 13°25E 270 A2
Huacaya Bolivia 20°45S 63°43W 331 E5
Huachacalla Bolivia 18°45S 68°17W 330 D4
Huacheng China 24°4N 115°37E 229 E10
Huachinera Mexico 30°9N 108°55W 318 A3
Huacho Peru 11°10S 77°35W 330 C2
Huachón Peru 10°35S 76°0W 330 C2
Huade China 41°55N 113°59E 226 D7
Huadian China 43°0N 126°40E 227 C14
Huadu China 23°22N 113°12E 229 F9
Huahine, Î. French Polynesia 16°46S 150°58W 289 f
Huai Had △ Thailand 16°52N 104°17E 236 D5
Huai He → China 33°0N 118°30E 229 A12
Huai Nam Dang △ Thailand 19°30N 98°30E 236 C2
Huai Yot Thailand 7°45N 99°37E 237 J2
Huai'an Hebei, China 40°30N 114°20E 226 D8
Huai'an Jiangsu, China 33°30N 119°10E 227 H10
Huaibei China 34°0N 116°48E 226 G9
Huaibin China 32°32N 115°27E 229 A10
Huaicho = Puerto Acosta Bolivia 15°32S 69°15W 330 D4
Huaide = Gongzhuling China 43°30N 124°40E 227 C13
Huaidezhen China 43°48N 124°50E 227 C13
Huaihua China 27°32N 109°57E 228 D7
Huaiji China 23°55N 112°12E 229 F9
Huainan China 32°38N 116°58E 229 A11
Huaining China 30°24N 116°40E 229 B11
Huairen China 39°48N 113°20E 226 E7
Huairou China 40°20N 116°35E 226 D9
Huaiyang China 33°40N 114°52E 226 H8
Huaiyin China 33°30N 119°2E 227 H10
Huaiyuan Anhui, China 32°55N 117°10E 227 H9
Huaiyuan Guangxi Zhuangzu, China 24°31N 108°22E 228 E7
Huajuapán de León Mexico 17°48N 97°46W 319 D5
Hualālai U.S.A. 19°42N 155°52W 302 D6
Hualapai Peak U.S.A. 35°5N 113°54W 305 J7
Hualien Taiwan 23°59N 121°36E 225 C3
Hualien □ Taiwan 23°45N 121°25E 225 C3
Huallaga → Peru 5°15S 75°30W 330 B2
Huallanca Peru 8°50S 77°56W 330 B2
Huamachuco Peru 7°50S 78°5W 330 B2
Huambo Angola 12°42S 15°54E 265 E3
Huambo □ Angola 13°0S 16°0E 265 E3
Huan Jiang → China 34°28N 109°0E 226 G5
Huan Xian China 36°33N 107°7E 226 F4
Huancabamba Peru 5°10S 79°15W 330 B2
Huancane Peru 15°10S 69°44W 330 D4
Huancapi Peru 13°40S 74°0W 330 C3
Huancavelica Peru 12°50S 75°5W 330 C2
Huancavelica □ Peru 13°0S 75°0W 330 C3
Huancayo Peru 12°5S 75°12W 330 C2
Huanchaca Bolivia 20°15S 66°40W 330 E4
Huanchaca, Serranía de Bolivia 14°30S 60°39W 331 C5
Huang Hai = Yellow Sea China 35°0N 123°0E 227 G12
Huang He → China 37°55N 118°50E 227 F10
Huang Xian China 37°38N 120°30E 227 F11
Huangchuan China 32°15N 115°10E 229 A10
Huanggang China 30°29N 114°52E 229 B10
Huangguoshu China 26°0N 105°40E 228 E5
Huanghuagang Mausoleum China 23°9N 113°17E 121 B2
Huangling China 35°34N 109°15E 226 G5
Huanglong China 35°30N 109°59E 226 G5
Huanglongtan China 32°40N 110°33E 229 A8
Huangmei China 30°5N 115°56E 229 B10
Huangpi China 30°50N 114°22E 229 B10
Huangping China 26°52N 107°54E 228 D6
Huangpu China 31°14N 121°30E 138 B2
Huangpu Jiang → China 31°11N 121°29E 138 B1
Huangpu Park China 31°14N 121°29E 138 B1
Huangshan Anhui, China 30°8N 118°9E 229 B12
Huangshan Anhui, China 29°42N 118°25E 229 C12
Huangshi China 30°10N 115°3E 229 B10
Huangsongdian China 43°45N 127°25E 227 C14
Huangtugang China 39°49N 116°15E 114 C1
Huangyan China 28°38N 121°19E 229 C13
Huangyangsi China 26°33N 111°39E 229 D8
Huaning China 24°17N 102°56E 228 E4
Huanjiang China 24°50N 108°18E 228 E7
Huanren China 41°23N 125°20E 224 B2
Huanren Shuiku China 41°17N 125°34E 224 B2
Huanta Peru 12°55S 74°20W 330 C3
Huantai China 36°58N 117°56E 227 F9
Huánuco Peru 9°55S 76°15W 330 B2
Huánuco □ Peru 9°55S 76°14W 330 B2
Huanuni Bolivia 18°16S 66°51W 330 D4
Huanzo, Cordillera de Peru 14°35S 73°20W 330 C3
Huaping China 26°46N 101°25E 228 D3
Huara Chile 19°59S 69°47W 330 D4
Huaral Peru 11°32S 77°13W 330 C2
Huaraz Peru 9°30S 77°32W 330 B2
Huari Peru 9°14S 77°14W 330 B2
Huarmey Peru 10°5S 78°5W 330 C2
Huarochiri Peru 12°9S 76°15W 330 C2
Huarocondo Peru 13°26S 72°14W 330 C3
Huarong China 29°29N 112°30E 229 C9
Huascar Peru 11°59S 77°1W 124 A2
Huascarán, Nevado Peru 9°7S 77°37W 330 B2
Huasco Chile 28°30S 71°15W 334 B1
Huasco → Chile 28°27S 71°13W 334 B1
Huasna U.S.A. 35°6N 120°24W 307 K6
Huatabampo Mexico 26°50N 109°38W 318 B3
Huauchinango Mexico 20°12N 98°3W 319 C5
Huautla de Jiménez Mexico 18°8N 96°51W 319 D5
Huaxi China 26°25N 106°40E 228 D6
Huay Khwang Thailand 13°47N 100°33E 113 B2
Huayhuash, Cordillera Peru 10°30S 76°45W 330 B2
Huayin China 34°35N 110°5E 226 G6
Huayllay Peru 11°3S 76°21W 330 C2
Huayuan China 28°37N 109°29E 228 C7
Huayun China 30°14N 106°40E 228 B6
Huazhou China 21°33N 110°33E 229 G8
Hubbard Iowa, U.S.A. 42°18N 93°18W 310 B3
Hubbard Ohio, U.S.A. 41°9N 80°34W 312 E4
Hubbard Tex., U.S.A. 31°51N 96°48W 314 F6
Hubbard, Mt. N. Amer. 60°19N 139°4W 303 F13
Hubbart Pt. Canada 59°21N 94°41W 297 B10
Hubei □ China 31°0N 112°0E 229 B9
Hubli India 15°22N 75°15E 245 G2
Huch'ang N. Korea 41°25N 127°2E 224 B3
Huchow = Huzhou China 30°51N 120°8E 229 B13
Hucknall U.K. 53°3N 1°13W 168 D6
Huddersfield U.K. 53°39N 1°47W 168 D6
Huddinge Sweden 59°14N 18°0E 139 B2
Hude Germany 53°7N 8°26E 178 B4
Hudi Sudan 17°43N 34°18E 256 D3
Hudiksvall Sweden 61°43N 17°10E 162 C11
Hudson Ont., Canada 50°6N 92°9W 298 B1
Hudson Fla., U.S.A. 28°22N 82°42W 317 G7
Hudson Mass., U.S.A. 42°23N 71°34W 313 D13
Hudson Mich., U.S.A. 41°51N 84°21W 311 C12
Hudson N.Y., U.S.A. 42°15N 73°46W 313 D11
Hudson Wis., U.S.A. 44°58N 92°45W 308 C7
Hudson Wyo., U.S.A. 42°54N 108°35W 304 E9
Hudson → U.S.A. 40°42N 74°2W 313 F10
Hudson, C. Antarctica 68°21S 153°45E 151 C20
Hudson Bay Nunavut, Canada 60°0N 86°0W 295 D11
Hudson Bay Sask., Canada 52°51N 102°23W 297 C8
Hudson Falls U.S.A. 43°18N 73°35W 313 C11
Hudson Mts. Antarctica 74°32S 99°20W 151 D16
Hudson Str. Canada 62°0N 70°0W 295 C13
Hudson's Hope Canada 56°0N 121°54W 296 B4
Hudsonville U.S.A. 42°52N 85°52W 311 B11
Hue Vietnam 16°30N 107°35E 236 D6
Huebra → Spain 41°2N 6°48W 194 D4
Huechucuicui, Pta. Chile 41°48S 74°2W 336 B2
Huechuraba Chile 33°22S 70°39W 137 B1
Huedin Romania 46°52N 23°2E 182 D8
Huehuetenango Guatemala 15°20N 91°28W 320 C1
Huejúcar Mexico 22°21N 103°13W 318 C4
Huélamo Spain 40°17N 1°48W 196 E3
Huelgoat France 48°22N 3°46W 172 D3
Huelma Spain 37°39N 3°28W 195 H7
Huelva Spain 37°18N 6°57W 195 H4
Huelva □ Spain 37°40N 7°0W 195 H4
Huelva → Spain 37°27N 6°0W 195 H5
Hueneme = Port Hueneme U.S.A. 34°7N 119°12W 307 L7
Huentelauquén Chile 31°38S 71°33W 334 C1
Huércal-Overa Spain 37°23N 1°57W 197 H3
Huerquehue △ Chile 39°6S 71°42W 336 A2
Huerta, Sa. de la Argentina 31°10S 67°30W 334 C2
Huertas, C. de las Spain 38°21N 0°24W 197 G4
Huertas de San Beltran Spain 41°22N 2°9E 114 A1
Huerva → Spain 41°39N 0°52W 196 D4
Huesca Spain 42°8N 0°25W 196 C4
Huesca □ Spain 42°20N 0°1E 196 C5
Huéscar Spain 37°44N 2°35W 197 H2
Huetamo Mexico 18°35N 100°53W 318 D4
Huete Spain 40°10N 2°43W 196 E2
Huevos I. Trin. & Tob. 10°42N 61°43W 323 t
Huger U.S.A. 33°6N 79°48W 316 B10
Hugh → Australia 25°1S 134°1E 280 D1
Hughenden Australia 20°52S 144°10E 280 C3
Hughes U.S.A. 66°3N 154°15W 303 C9
Hughesville U.S.A. 41°14N 76°44W 313 E8
Hugli → India 21°56N 88°4E 243 J13
Hugo Colo., U.S.A. 39°8N 103°28W 304 G12
Hugo Okla., U.S.A. 34°1N 95°31W 314 D7
Hugoton U.S.A. 37°11N 101°21W 308 G3
Huhehaote = Hohhot China 40°52N 111°40E 226 D6
Huhsi Taiwan 23°35N 119°39E 225 C1
Hui Xian = Huixian China 35°27N 113°12E 226 G7
Hui Xian China 33°50N 106°4E 226 H4
Hui'an China 25°1N 118°43E 229 E12
Hui'anbu China 37°28N 106°38E 226 F4
Huiarau Ra. N.Z. 38°45S 176°55E 284 E5
Huichang China 25°32N 115°45E 229 E10
Huichapan Mexico 20°23N 99°39W 319 C5
Huichon N. Korea 40°10N 126°16E 224 B3
Huidong Guangdong, China 22°58N 114°43E 229 F10
Huidong Sichuan, China 26°34N 102°35E 228 D4
Huifa He → China 43°0N 127°50E 227 C14
Huíla Angola 15°4S 13°32E 265 F2
Huíla □ Angola 14°0S 15°0E 265 E2
Huila □ Colombia 2°30N 75°45W 328 C2
Huila, Nevado del Colombia 3°0N 76°0W 328 C2
Huilai China 23°0N 116°18E 229 F11
Huili China 26°35N 102°17E 228 D4
Huimin China 37°27N 117°28E 227 F9
Huinan China 42°40N 126°2E 224 A3
Huinca Renancó Argentina 34°51S 64°22W 334 C3
Huining China 35°38N 105°0E 226 G3
Huinong China 39°5N 106°35E 226 E4
Huiroa N.Z. 39°15S 174°30E 284 F3
Huishui China 26°7N 106°38E 228 D6
Huisne → France 47°59N 0°11E 172 E7
Huiting China 34°5N 116°5E 226 G9
Huitong China 26°51N 109°45E 228 D7
Huixian China 35°27N 113°12E 226 G7
Huixtla Mexico 15°9N 92°28W 319 D6
Huize China 26°24N 103°15E 228 D4
Huizhou China 23°0N 114°23E 229 F10
Huizingen Belgium 50°45N 4°17E 116 B1
Hukawng Valley Burma 26°30N 96°30E 241 B6
Hukeri India 16°14N 74°36E 245 F2
Hukou Jiangxi, China 29°45N 116°21E 229 C11
Huk'ou Taiwan 24°54N 121°2E 225 B3
Hukuntsi Botswana 23°58S 21°45E 270 B3
Hula Papua N. G. 10°5S 147°43E 286 F4
Ḩulayfā' Si. Arabia 25°58N 40°45E 246 E4
Huld = Ulaanjirem Mongolia 45°5N 105°30E 226 B3
Hulin He → China 45°0N 122°10E 227 B12
Hull = Kingston upon Hull U.K. 53°45N 0°21W 168 D7
Hull Canada 45°26N 75°43W 313 A9
Hull → U.K. 53°44N 0°20W 168 D7
Hulst Neths. 51°17N 4°2E 170 C4
Hultschin = Hlučín Czech Rep. 49°54N 18°11E 181 B11
Hultsfred Sweden 57°30N 15°52E 163 G9
Hulun = Hailar China 49°10N 119°38E 219 B6
Hulun Nur China 49°0N 117°30E 219 B6
Hulyaypole Ukraine 47°45N 36°21E 189 J9
Huma, Tanjung Malaysia 5°29N 100°16E 237 c
Humacao Puerto Rico 18°9N 65°50W 321 b
Humahuaca Argentina 23°10S 65°25W 334 A2
Humaíta = Pôrto Válter Brazil 8°15S 72°40W 330 B3
Humaitá Brazil 7°35S 63°1W 331 B5
Humaitá Paraguay 27°2S 58°31W 334 B4
Humansdorp S. Africa 34°2S 24°46E 270 D3
Humansville U.S.A. 37°48N 93°35W 310 G3
Humara, J. Sudan 16°16N 30°59E 257 D3
Humayun's Tomb India 28°35N 77°15E 120 B2
Humbe Angola 16°40S 14°55E 265 F2
Humbe, Serra do Angola 12°10S 15°25E 265 E2
Humber → Ont., Canada 43°47N 79°38W 141 A1
Humber → England, U.K. 53°42N 0°27W 168 D7
Humber B. Canada 43°37N 79°27W 141 B2
Humber Bay Canada 43°38N 79°29W 141 B2
Humber Bay Park Canada 43°37N 79°28W 141 B2
Humber College Canada 43°35N 79°30W 141 B1
Humber Summit Canada 43°45N 79°32W 141 A1
Humber Valley Village Canada 43°40N 79°31W 141 A1
Humberlea Canada 43°43N 79°31W 141 A1
Humberwood Park Canada 43°44N 79°37W 141 A1
Humboldt Sask., Canada 52°15N 105°9W 297 C7
Humboldt Iowa, U.S.A. 42°44N 94°13W 310 B2
Humboldt Tenn., U.S.A. 35°50N 88°55W 315 D10
Humboldt → U.S.A. 39°59N 118°36W 304 G4
Humboldt Gletscher = Sermersuaq Greenland 79°30N 62°0W 154 B4
Humboldt Mts. N.Z. 44°30S 168°15E 285 E3
Humboldt Park U.S.A. 41°54N 87°42W 119 B2
Humbolt, Mt. N. Cal. 21°53S 166°25E 288 d
Hume U.S.A. 36°48N 118°54W 306 J8
Hume, L. Australia 36°0S 147°5E 283 D7
Humen China 22°50N 113°40E 219 F10
Humenné Slovak Rep. 48°55N 21°50E 181 C14
Humera Spain 40°25N 3°46W 127 B1
Humeston U.S.A. 40°52N 93°30W 310 D3
Hummelsta Sweden 59°34N 16°58E 162 E10
Hummelvika Norway 63°29N 8°19E 164 A5
Hummingbird Centre Toronto, Canada 141 b3
Hummock Hill = Whyalla Australia 33°2S 137°30E 282 B2
Humpata Angola 15°2S 13°24E 265 F2
Humphreys, Mt. U.S.A. 37°17N 118°40W 306 H8
Humphreys Peak U.S.A. 35°21N 111°41W 305 J8
Humpolec Czech Rep. 49°31N 15°20E 180 B8
Humptulips U.S.A. 47°14N 123°57W 306 C3
Humula Australia 35°30S 147°46E 283 C7
Hūn Libya 29°2N 16°0E 258 C3
Hun He → China 40°41N 122°8E 224 B1
Hun Jiang → China 40°50N 125°38E 227 D13
Húnaflói Iceland 65°50N 20°50W 155 B6
Hunan □ China 27°30N 112°0E 229 D9
Húnavatnssýsla □ Iceland 65°30N 20°25W 155 B6
Hunaydī Iraq 33°18N 44°29E 113 B2
Hunchun China 42°52N 130°28E 227 C16
Hundested Denmark 55°58N 11°52E 163 J5
Hundewali Pakistan 31°55N 72°38E 242 D5
Hundige Denmark 55°35N 12°18E 118 B1
Hundige Strand Denmark 55°35N 12°20E 118 B2
Hundorp Norway 61°33N 9°59E 164 C7
Hundred Islands △ Phil. 16°10N 120°2E 232 C3
Hundred Mile House Canada 51°38N 121°18W 296 C4
Hundvåg Norway 59°0N 5°43E 164 E2
Hunedoara Romania 45°40N 22°50E 182 E7
Hunedoara □ Romania 45°50N 22°54E 182 E7
Hunei Taiwan 22°53N 120°14E 225 D2
Hünfeld Germany 50°39N 9°46E 178 E5
Hung Hom China 22°18N 114°11E 122 B2
Hung Yen Vietnam 20°39N 106°4E 228 G6
Hunga Ha'apai Tonga 20°41S 175°7W 287 Q13
Hungary ■ Europe 47°20N 19°20E 181 D12
Hungary, Plain of Europe 47°0N 20°0E 158 F10
Hungerford Australia 28°58S 144°24E 281 D3
Hŭngnam N. Korea 39°49N 127°45E 224 C3
Hungt'ou Hsü = Lan Yü Taiwan 22°4N 121°25E 225 D3
Hungund India 16°4N 76°3E 245 F3
Huni Valley Ghana 5°33N 1°56W 262 D4
Hunjiang China 41°54N 126°26E 224 B3
Hunneberg Sweden 58°18N 12°30E 163 F6
Hunnebostrand Sweden 58°27N 11°18E 163 F5
Hunsberge Namibia 27°45S 17°12E 270 C2
Hunsrück Germany 49°56N 7°27E 179 F3
Hunstanton U.K. 52°56N 0°29E 168 E8
Hunsur India 12°16N 76°16E 245 H3
Hunte → Germany 53°14N 8°28E 178 B4
Hunter N.Z. 44°36S 171°2E 285 E6
Hunter N.Y., U.S.A. 42°13N 74°13W 313 D10
Hunter → N.S.W., Australia 32°52S 151°46E 283 B9
Hunter → N.Z. 44°21S 169°27E 285 E4
Hunter, C. Solomon Is. 9°48S 159°50E 287 M10
Hunter Hills, The N.Z. 44°26S 170°46E 285 E5
Hunter I. Tas., Australia 40°30S 144°45E 281 G3
Hunter I. B.C., Canada 51°55N 128°0W 296 C3
Hunter Mts. N.Z. 45°43S 167°25E 285 F2
Hunter Ra. Australia 32°45S 150°15E 283 B9
Hunters Hill Australia 33°50S 151°9E 139 B1
Hunters Pt. U.S.A. 37°43N 122°21W 136 B2
Hunters Road Zimbabwe 19°9S 29°49E 269 F2
Hunters Valley U.S.A. 38°54N 77°17W 143 B2
Hunterville N.Z. 39°56S 175°35E 284 F4
Huntingburg U.S.A. 38°18N 86°57W 311 F10
Huntingdon Qué., Canada 45°6N 74°10W 298 C5
Huntingdon Cambs., U.K. 52°20N 0°11W 169 E7
Huntingdon Pa., U.S.A. 40°30N 78°1W 312 F6
Huntington = Shelton U.S.A. 41°19N 73°5W 313 E11
Huntington Ind., U.S.A. 40°53N 85°30W 311 D11
Huntington N.Y., U.S.A. 40°52N 73°26W 313 F11
Huntington Oreg., U.S.A. 44°21N 117°16W 304 D5
Huntington Utah, U.S.A. 39°20N 110°58W 304 G8
Huntington Va., U.S.A. 38°47N 77°4W 143 C3
Huntington W. Va., U.S.A. 38°25N 82°27W 309 F12
Huntington Beach U.S.A. 33°40N 118°5W 307 M9
Huntington Park U.S.A. 33°58N 118°13W 126 C3
Huntley Jamaica 18°4N 77°35W 320 a
Huntley Ill., U.S.A. 42°10N 88°26W 311 B8
Huntly N.Z. 37°34S 175°11E 284 D4
Huntly Aberds., U.K. 57°27N 2°47W 167 D6
Huntsville Ont., Canada 45°20N 79°14W 312 A5
Huntsville Ala., U.S.A. 34°44N 86°35W 315 D11
Huntsville Mo., U.S.A. 39°26N 92°33W 310 E4
Huntsville Tex., U.S.A. 30°43N 95°33W 314 F7
Hunyani → Zimbabwe 15°57S 30°39E 269 F3
Hunyuan China 39°42N 113°42E 226 E7
Hunza → India 35°54N 74°20E 243 B6
Huo Xian = Huozhou China 36°36N 111°42E 226 F6
Huocheng China 44°0N 80°48E 217 D10
Huon G. Papua N. G. 7°0S 147°30E 286 D4
Huon Pen. Papua N. G. 6°20S 147°30E 286 D4
Huong Khe Vietnam 18°13N 105°41E 236 C5
Huonville Australia 43°0S 147°5E 281 G4
Huoqiu China 32°20N 116°12E 229 A11
Huoshan Anhui, China 32°28N 118°30E 229 A12
Huoshan Anhui, China 31°25N 116°20E 229 B11
Huoshao Dao = Lü Tao Taiwan 22°40N 121°30E 225 D3
Huozhou China 36°36N 111°42E 226 F6
Hupeh = Hubei □ China 31°0N 112°0E 229 B9
Ḩūr Iran 30°50N 57°7E 247 D8
Ḩuraymīla Si. Arabia 25°8N 46°8E 246 E5
Hurbanovo Slovak Rep. 47°51N 18°11E 181 D11
Hurd, C. Canada 45°13N 81°44W 312 A3
Hure Qi China 42°45N 121°45E 227 C11
Hurezani Romania 44°49N 23°40E 183 F8
Hurghada Egypt 27°15N 33°50E 256 B3
Hurīya Iraq 33°21N 44°19E 113 A1
Hurley N. Mex., U.S.A. 32°42N 108°8W 305 K9
Hurley Wis., U.S.A. 46°27N 90°11W 308 B8
Huron Calif., U.S.A. 36°12N 120°6W 306 J6
Huron Ohio, U.S.A. 41°24N 82°33W 312 E2
Huron S. Dak., U.S.A. 44°22N 98°13W 308 C4
Huron, L. U.S.A. 44°30N 82°40W 312 B2
Huron East Canada 43°37N 81°18W 312 C3
Hurricane U.S.A. 37°11N 113°17W 305 H7
Hurso Ethiopia 9°35N 41°33E 257 F5
Hurstville Australia 33°57S 151°6E 139 B1
Hurtsboro U.S.A. 32°15N 85°25W 316 C4
Hurungwe ⌓ Zimbabwe 16°7S 29°5E 269 F2
Hurunui → N.Z. 42°54S 173°18E 285 C8
Hurup Denmark 56°46N 8°25E 163 H2
Húsafell Iceland 64°42N 20°53W 155 C6
Husan West Bank 31°42N 35°8E 123 B1
Húsavík Iceland 66°3N 17°21W 155 A9
Husby Sweden 59°24N 17°56E 139 A1
Huşi Romania 46°41N 28°7E 183 D13
Huskisson Australia 35°2S 150°41E 283 C9
Huskvarna Sweden 57°47N 14°15E 163 G8
Huslia U.S.A. 65°41N 156°24W 303 D8
Husnes Norway 59°52N 5°45E 164 E2
Hustad Norway 62°57N 7°6E 164 B4
Hustadvika Norway 63°0N 7°0E 164 A3
Hustontown U.S.A. 40°3N 78°2W 312 F6
Hustopeče Czech Rep. 48°57N 16°43E 181 C9
Husum København, Denmark 55°42N 12°27E 118 A2
Husum Schleswig-Holstein, Germany 54°28N 9°4E 178 A5
Husum Sweden 63°21N 19°12E 162 A13
Huszt = Khust Ukraine 48°10N 23°18E 183 B8
Hutchinson Kans., U.S.A. 38°5N 97°56W 308 F5
Hutchinson Minn., U.S.A. 44°54N 94°22W 308 C6
Ḩūth Yemen 16°14N 43°58E 248 C3
Hutjena Papua N. G. 5°23S 154°42E 286 C8
Hutsonville U.S.A. 39°7N 87°40W 311 E9
Hutt → N.Z. 41°14S 174°54E 143 B2
Hutte Sauvage, L. de la Canada 56°15N 64°45W 299 A7
Hütteldorf Austria 48°12N 16°15E 142 A1
Hüttenberg Austria 46°56N 14°33E 180 E7
Hüttener Berge ⌓ Germany 54°24N 9°40E 178 A5
Hutton, Mt. Australia 25°51S 148°20E 281 D4
Huvadu Atoll Maldives 0°30N 73°15E 272 d
Hüvösvölgy Hungary 47°32N 19°0E 117 A2
Huwei Taiwan 23°42N 120°26E 225 C2
Huwei Hsi → Taiwan 23°37N 120°22E 225 C2
Huwon Secret Garden S. Korea 37°34N 126°59E 137 B1
Huwun Ethiopia 4°23N 40°6E 257 G5
Huy Belgium 50°31N 5°15E 170 D5
Huzhou China 30°51N 120°8E 229 B13
Huzurabad India 18°12N 79°25E 244 E4
Huzurnagar India 16°54N 79°53E 244 F4
Hvalpsund Denmark 56°42N 9°11E 163 H3
Hvalstad Norway 59°51N 10°27E 133 A1
Hvalstrand Norway 59°50N 10°30E 133 A2
Hvammsfjörður Iceland 65°4N 22°5W 155 B4
Hvammstangi Iceland 65°24N 20°57W 155 B6
Hvammur Mýrasýsla, Iceland 64°50N 21°21W 155 C5
Hvammur Skagafjarðarsýsla, Iceland 65°53N 19°51W 155 B7
Hvannadalshnúkur Iceland 64°1N 16°41W 155 C10
Hvanneyri Iceland 64°34N 21°36W 155 C5
Hvar Croatia 43°11N 16°28E 199 E13
Hvarski Kanal Croatia 43°15N 16°35E 199 E13
Hveragerði Iceland 64°0N 21°12W 155 C5
Hvidovre Denmark 55°38N 12°27E 118 B2
Hvítá → Iceland 64°30N 21°58W 155 C5
Hvítárvatn Iceland 64°37N 19°50W 155 C7
Hvittingfoss Norway 59°29N 10°0E 164 E7
Hvizdets Ukraine 48°35N 25°17E 183 B10
Hvolsvöllur Iceland 63°45N 20°14W 155 D6
Hwacheon-Cheosuji S. Korea 38°5N 127°50E 224 C3
Hwagok S. Korea 37°32N 126°51E 137 B1
Hwainan = Huainan China 32°38N 116°58E 229 A11
Hwaiyin = Huaiyin China 33°30N 119°2E 227 H10
Hwang Ho = Huang He → China 37°55N 118°50E 227 F10
Hwange Zimbabwe 18°18S 26°30E 269 F2
Hwange △ Zimbabwe 19°0S 26°30E 270 A4
Hwanghaebuk-do □ N. Korea 38°30N 126°25E 224 C3
Hwanghaenam-do □ N. Korea 38°15N 125°30E 224 C2
Hwangju N. Korea 38°40N 125°46E 224 C2
Hwangshih = Huangshi China 30°10N 115°3E 229 B10
Hwaseong S. Korea 37°12N 126°48E 224 D3
Hwasun S. Korea 35°3N 126°59E 224 E3
Hwekum Burma 26°7N 95°22E 241 B5
Hyaing Burma 22°39N 94°44E 241 D5
Hyannis Mass., U.S.A. 41°39N 70°17W 309 E18
Hyannis Nebr., U.S.A. 42°0N 101°46W 308 E3
Hyargas Nuur Mongolia 49°0N 93°0E 217 C12
Hyattsville U.S.A. 38°57N 76°57W 143 B4
Hybo Sweden 61°49N 16°15E 162 C10
Hydaburg U.S.A. 55°15N 132°50W 296 B2
Hyde N.Z. 45°18S 170°16E 285 F5
Hyde Park N.S.W., Australia 33°52S 151°12E 139 B2
Hyde Park Guyana 6°30N 58°16W 329 B6
Hyde Park Gauteng, S. Africa 26°6S 28°2E 123 A2
Hyde Park London, U.K. 51°30N 0°10W 125 A2
Hyde Park Ill., U.S.A. 41°47N 87°35W 119 C3
Hyde Park Mass., U.S.A. 42°15N 71°7W 116 B2
Hyde Park N.Y., U.S.A. 41°47N 73°56W 313 E11
Hyden Australia 32°24S 118°53E 279 F2
Hyder U.S.A. 55°55N 130°5W 296 B2
Hyderabad India 17°22N 78°29E 244 F4
Hyderabad Pakistan 25°23N 68°24E 242 G3
Hydra Greece 37°20N 23°28E 204 D5
Hyen Norway 61°44N 5°56E 164 C2
Hyères France 43°8N 6°9E 175 E10
Hyères, Îs. d' France 43°0N 6°20E 175 F10
Hyesan N. Korea 41°20N 128°10E 224 B4
Hyland → Canada 59°52N 128°12W 296 B3
Hylestad Norway 59°6N 7°29E 164 E4
Hyllestad Norway 61°10N 5°17E 164 C2
Hyltebruk Sweden 56°59N 13°15E 163 H7
Hymia India 33°40N 78°2E 243 C8
Hyndman Peak U.S.A. 43°45N 114°8W 304 E6
Hynnekleiv Norway 58°36N 8°25E 164 F5
Hyōgo □ Japan 35°15N 134°50E 222 B6
Hyrra Banda C.A.R. 5°58N 22°1E 264 A4
Hyrum U.S.A. 41°38N 111°51W 304 F8
Hysham U.S.A. 46°18N 107°14W 304 C10
Hythe U.K. 51°4N 1°5E 169 F9
Hyūga Japan 32°25N 131°35E 222 E3
Hyvinge = Hyvinkää Finland 60°38N 24°50E 188 B3
Hyvinkää Finland 60°38N 24°50E 188 B3

I

I-n-Azaoua Illizi, Algeria 25°42N 6°54E 261 C6
I-n-Azaoua Tamanrasset, Algeria 20°46N 7°32E 261 D6
I-n-Échaï Mali 20°10N 2°5W 260 D4
I-n-Gall Niger 16°51N 7°1E 263 B6
I-n-Kelemet Algeria 26°57N 5°47E 261 C6
I-n-Oudad Algeria 20°17N 4°38E 261 D5
I-n-Ouzzal Algeria 20°41N 2°34E 261 D5
I-n-Tadreft Niger 19°5N 6°38E 263 B6
Iabès, Erg Algeria 27°30N 2°2W 261 C4
Iablaniţa Romania 44°57N 22°19E 182 F7
Iaco → Brazil 9°3S 68°34W 330 B4
Iacobeni Romania 47°25N 25°20E 183 C10
Iaçu Brazil 12°45S 40°13W 333 D3
Iakora Madag. 23°6S 46°40E 272 C2
Ialibu Papua N. G. 6°17S 143°59E 286 D2
Ialomiţa □ Romania 44°30N 27°30E 183 F12
Ialomiţa → Romania 44°42N 27°51E 183 F12
Ialoveni Moldova 46°56N 28°47E 183 D13
Ialpug → Moldova 45°41N 28°35E 183 E13
Iamonia L. U.S.A. 30°38N 84°14W 316 E5
Ianca Romania 45°6N 27°29E 183 E12
Iara Romania 46°31N 23°35E 183 D8
Iarda Ethiopia 11°9N 35°53E 257 E4
Iargara Moldova 46°24N 28°23E 183 D13
Iaşi Romania 47°10N 27°40E 183 C12
Iaşi □ Romania 47°20N 27°0E 183 C12
Iasmos Greece 41°8N 25°11E 203 E9
Iauaretê Colombia 0°36N 69°12W 328 C4
Ib → India 21°34N 83°48E 243 J10
Iba Phil. 15°22N 120°0E 232 D2
Ibadan Nigeria 7°22N 3°58E 263 D5
Ibagué Colombia 4°20N 75°20W 328 C2
Ibaiti Brazil 23°50S 50°10W 333 F1
Ibajay Phil. 11°49N 122°10E 233 F4
Iballë Albania 42°12N 20°2E 202 D4
Ibăneşti Botoşani, Romania 48°4N 26°22E 183 B11
Ibăneşti Mureş, Romania 46°45N 24°57E 183 D9
Ibanshe Dem. Rep. of the Congo 4°58S 21°30E 265 C4
Ibar → Serbia 43°43N 20°45E 202 C4
Ibara Japan 34°36N 133°28E 222 C5
Ibaraki Japan 34°49N 135°34E 223 C7
Ibaraki □ Japan 36°10N 140°10E 223 A12
Ibarra Ecuador 0°21N 78°7W 328 C2
Ibb Yemen 14°2N 44°10E 248 D4
Ibba Sudan 4°49N 29°2E 257 G2
Ibba, Bahr el → Sudan 5°30N 28°55E 257 F2
Ibbenbüren Germany 52°16N 7°43E 178 C3
Ibeke Gembo Dem. Rep. of the Congo 1°24S 18°51E 264 C3
Ibembo Dem. Rep. of the Congo 2°35N 23°35E 264 B4
Ibenga → Congo 2°19N 18°9E 264 B3
Ibera, L. Argentina 28°30S 57°9W 334 B4
Iberia U.S.A. 38°5N 92°18W 310 F4
Iberian Peninsula Europe 40°0N 5°0W 158 H5
Iberville Canada 45°19N 73°17W 313 A11
Iberville, Lac d' Canada 55°55N 73°15W 298 A5
Ibese Nigeria 6°33N 3°28E 124 A2
Ibi Nigeria 8°15N 9°44E 263 D6
Ibi Spain 38°38N 0°34W 197 G4
Ibiá Brazil 19°30S 46°30W 333 E2
Ibiapaba, Sa. da Brazil 4°0S 41°30W 332 B3
Ibicaraí Brazil 14°51S 39°36W 333 D4
Ibicuí Brazil 14°51S 39°59W 333 D4
Ibicuí → Brazil 29°25S 56°47W 335 B4
Ibicuy Argentina 33°55S 59°10W 334 C4
Ibipetuba Brazil 11°0S 44°32W 332 D3
Ibirapuera Brazil 23°36S 46°40W 137 B1
Ibirapuera, Parque do Brazil 23°35S 46°38W 137 B2
Ibitiara Brazil 12°39S 42°13W 333 D3
Ibiza = Eivissa Spain 38°54N 1°26E 206 D1
Ibiza ✈ (IBZ) Spain 38°53N 1°22E 197 G6
Íblei, Monti Italy 37°15N 14°45E 201 E7
Ibn Hāni', Ra's Syria 35°35N 35°43E 250 C6
Ibo Mozam. 12°22S 40°40E 269 E5
Ibonma Indonesia 3°29S 133°31E 231 E8
Ibotirama Brazil 12°13S 43°12W 333 D3
İbradı Turkey 37°4N 31°35E 250 A2
Ibrāhīm → Lebanon 34°4N 35°38E 250 D6
'Ibrī Oman 23°14N 56°30E 247 F8
İbriktepe Turkey 41°0N 26°30E 203 E10
Ibshawâi Egypt 29°21N 30°40E 256 J7
Ibu Indonesia 1°35N 127°33E 231 D7
Ibuki-Sanchi Japan 35°25N 136°18E 223 B8
Ibusuki Japan 31°12N 130°40E 222 F2
Ica Peru 14°0S 75°48W 330 C2
Ica □ Peru 14°20S 75°30W 330 C2
Iça → Brazil 2°55S 67°58W 330 A4
Icabarú Venezuela 4°20N 61°45W 329 C5
Icabarú → Venezuela 4°45N 62°15W 329 C5
Icacos Trin. & Tob. 10°3N 61°54W 323 t
Icacos Pt. Trin. & Tob. 10°3N 61°57W 323 t
Içana Brazil 0°21N 67°19W 328 C4
Içana → Brazil 0°26N 67°19W 328 C4
Icarai Brazil 22°54S 43°6W 135 B2
Icatu Brazil 2°46S 44°4W 332 B3
Icaturama = Santa Rosa de Viterbo Colombia 5°53N 72°59W 328 B3
İçel Turkey 36°51N 34°36E 250 B5
İcel □ Turkey 36°45N 34°0E 250 B5
Iceland ■ Europe 64°45N 19°0W 155 C8
Iceland Basin Atl. Oc. 61°0N 19°0W 150 C7
Icelandic Plateau Arctic 64°0N 10°0W 150 C7
Içerenköy Turkey 40°58N 29°6E 122 C2
Ichalkaranji India 16°40N 74°33E 244 F2
Ich'ang = Yichang China 30°40N 111°20E 229 B8
Ichchapuram India 19°10N 84°40E 244 E7
Icheon S. Korea 37°17N 127°27E 224 D3
Ichgao Japan 35°32N 139°32E 140 B2
Ichhawar India 23°1N 77°1E 242 H7
Ichigaya Tokyo, Japan 140 a3
Ichihara Japan 35°28N 140°5E 223 B12
Ichikawa Japan 35°43N 139°54E 140 A4
Ichilo → Bolivia 15°57S 64°50W 331 D5
Ichinohe Japan 40°13N 141°17E 220 D10
Ichinomiya Gifu, Japan 35°18N 136°48E 223 B8
Ichinomiya Kumamoto, Japan 32°58N 131°5E 222 E3
Ichinoseki Japan 38°55N 141°8E 220 E10
Ichkeul △ Tunisia 37°5N 9°37E 258 A1
Ichnya Ukraine 50°52N 32°24E 189 G7
Icht Morocco 29°6N 8°54W 260 C3
Ichu Taiwan 23°20N 120°14E 225 C2
Ichun = Yichun China 47°44N 128°52E 219 B7
Ickenham U.K. 51°33N 0°26W 125 A1
Icó Brazil 6°24S 38°51W 332 C4
Icoca Angola 6°12S 16°20E 265 D3
Icod Canary Is. 28°22N 16°43W 153 e1
Iconi Comoros Is. 12°21S 43°51E 272 a
Icoraci Brazil 1°18S 48°28W 332 B2
Icy C. U.S.A. 70°20N 161°52W 303 A7
Ida Grove U.S.A. 42°21N 95°28W 308 D6
Idabel U.S.A. 33°54N 94°50W 314 E7
Idaga Hamus Ethiopia 14°13N 39°48E 257 E4
Idah Nigeria 7°5N 6°40E 263 D6
Idaho □ U.S.A. 45°0N 115°0W 304 D6
Idaho City U.S.A. 43°50N 115°50W 304 E6
Idaho Falls U.S.A. 43°30N 112°2W 304 E7
Idalia △ Australia 24°49S 144°36E 280 C3
Idanha-a-Nova Portugal 39°50N 7°15W 194 F3
Idar-Oberstein Germany 49°43N 7°16E 179 F3
Iday Niger 14°54N 11°33E 259 F2
'Idd el Ghanam Sudan 11°30N 24°19E 259 F4
Iddan Somali Rep. 6°10N 48°55E 267 C6

Iddo Nigeria 6°28N 3°22E 124 B2
Idelès Algeria 23°50N 5°53E 261 D6
Idensalmi = Iisalmi Finland 63°32N 27°10E 160 E22
Idfû Egypt 24°55N 32°49E 256 C3
Ídhra = Hydra Greece 37°20N 23°28E 204 D5
Idi Indonesia 5°2N 97°37E 234 A1
Idi, Oros = Psiloritis, Oros Greece 35°15N 24°45E 207 E5
Idi Amin Dada, L. = Edward, L. Africa 0°25S 29°40E 268 C2
Idi-Oro Nigeria 6°31N 3°21E 124 A2
Idiofa Dem. Rep. of the Congo 4°55S 19°42E 265 C3
Idjil = Fdérik Mauritania 22°40N 12°45W 260 D2
Idkerberget Sweden 60°22N 15°15E 162 D9
Idku, Bahra el Egypt 31°18N 30°18E 256 H7
Idlib Syria 35°55N 36°36E 250 C7
Idlib □ Syria 35°45N 36°45E 250 C7
Idre Sweden 61°52N 12°42E 162 C6
Idria U.S.A. 36°25N 120°41W 306 J6
Idrija Slovenia 46°0N 14°5E 199 C11
Idritsa Russia 56°17N 28°53E 188 D5
Idutywa = Dutywa S. Africa 32°8S 28°18E 271 D4
Ie Shima Japan 26°43N 127°48E 288 a
Ie Suido Japan 26°42N 127°51E 288 a
Ieper Belgium 50°51N 2°53E 170 D2
Ierapetra Greece 35°1N 25°44E 207 F6
Ierissos Greece 40°22N 23°52E 202 F7
Ierissos Kolpos Greece 40°27N 23°57E 202 F7
Iernut Romania 46°27N 24°15E 183 D9
Ieshima-Shotō Japan 34°40N 134°32E 222 C6
Iesi Italy 43°31N 13°14E 199 E10
Iésolo Italy 45°32N 12°38E 199 C9
Iet Ethiopia 4°33N 43°1E 267 D5
Ifach, Peñón de Spain 38°38N 0°5E 197 G5
'Ifâl, W. al → Si. Arabia 28°7N 35°3E 251 K6
Ifanadiana Madag. 21°19S 47°39E 272 C2
Ife Nigeria 7°30N 4°31E 263 D5
Iférouâne Niger 19°5N 8°24E 259 E1
Ifetesene Algeria 25°30N 4°33E 261 C5
Iffley Australia 18°53S 141°12E 280 B3
Ifon Nigeria 6°58N 5°40E 263 D6
Iforas, Adrar des Africa 19°40N 1°40E 261 D5
Ifould, L. Australia 30°52S 132°6E 279 F5
Ifrane Morocco 33°33N 5°7W 260 B3
Ifrane □ Morocco 33°20N 5°15W 260 B3
Ifugao □ Phil. 16°40N 121°10E 232 C3
Iga Japan 34°45N 136°10E 223 C8
Igalo Montenegro 42°28N 18°30E 202 D2
Iganga Uganda 0°37N 33°28E 268 B3
Iganmu Nigeria 6°28N 3°22E 124 B2
Igara Paraná → Colombia 2°9S 71°47W 328 D3
Igarapava Brazil 20°3S 47°47W 333 F2
Igarapé Açu Brazil 1°4S 47°33W 332 B2
Igarapé-Mirim Brazil 1°59S 48°58W 332 B2
Igarka Russia 67°30N 86°33E 214 C9
Igatimi Paraguay 24°5S 55°40W 335 A4
Igatpuri India 19°40N 73°35E 244 E1
Igbetti Nigeria 8°44N 4°8E 263 D5
Igbo-Ora Nigeria 7°29N 3°15E 263 D5
Igbobi Nigeria 6°31N 3°22E 124 A2
Igboho Nigeria 8°53N 3°50E 263 D5
Igbologun Nigeria 6°24N 3°19E 124 B1
Igbor Nigeria 7°27N 8°34E 263 D6
Iğdır Turkey 39°55N 44°2E 213 C11
Igelfors Sweden 58°52N 15°41E 163 F9
Iggesund Sweden 61°39N 17°10E 162 C11
Ighil Izane = Relizane Algeria 35°44N 0°31E 261 A5
Igiugig U.S.A. 59°20N 155°55W 303 G9
Iglau = Jihlava Czech Rep. 49°28N 15°35E 180 B8
Iglésias Italy 39°19N 8°32E 200 C1
Igli Algeria 30°25N 2°19W 261 B4
Igloolik Canada 69°20N 81°49W 295 C11
Igluligaarjuk = Chesterfield Inlet Canada 63°30N 90°45W 294 C10
Iglulik = Igloolik Canada 69°20N 81°49W 295 C11
'Igma, G. el Egypt 29°10N 34°0E 251 J5
'Igma, Gebel el Egypt 28°55N 34°0E 256 B3
Ignace Canada 49°30N 91°40W 298 C1
İğneada Turkey 41°52N 27°59E 203 E12
İğneada Burnu Turkey 41°53N 28°2E 203 E12
Igny France 48°44N 2°13E 134 B2
Igoumenitsa Greece 39°32N 20°18E 206 B10
Igra Russia 57°33N 53°7E 190 B11
Iguaçu → Brazil 25°36S 54°36W 335 B5
Iguaçu, Cat. del Brazil 25°41S 54°26W 335 B5
Iguaçu △ Brazil 25°30S 54°0W 335 B5
Iguaçu Falls = Iguaçu, Cat. del Brazil 25°41S 54°26W 335 B5
Iguala Mexico 18°21N 99°32W 319 D5
Igualada Spain 41°37N 1°37E 196 D6
Iguape Brazil 24°43S 47°33W 333 F2
Iguaratinga = São Francisco do Maranhão Brazil 6°15S 42°52W 332 C3
Iguassu = Iguaçu → Brazil 25°36S 54°36W 335 B5
Iguatu Brazil 6°20S 39°18W 332 C4
Iguazú △ Argentina 25°42S 54°22W 335 B5
Iguéla Gabon 2°0S 9°16E 264 C1
Iguéla, Lagune Gabon 1°48S 9°16E 264 C2
Iguetti, Sebkhet Mauritania 25°5N 9°50W 260 C3
Iguidi, Erg Africa 27°0N 6°0W 260 C3
Iguig Phil. 17°45N 121°44E 232 C3
Igumen = Cherven Belarus 53°45N 28°28E 177 B15
Iharana Madag. 13°25S 50°0E 272 A3
Ihavandiffulu Atoll Maldives 7°0N 72°50E 272 d
Ihbulag Mongolia 43°11N 107°10E 226 C4
Iheya-Shima Japan 27°4N 127°58E 221 L3
Ihiala Nigeria 5°51N 6°55E 263 D6
Ihirene → Algeria 20°28N 4°37E 261 D5
Ihosy Madag. 22°24S 46°8E 272 C2
Ihotry, Farihy Madag. 21°56S 43°41E 272 C1
Ihu Papua N. G. 7°55S 145°24E 286 D3
Ihugh Nigeria 7°2N 9°0E 263 D6
Ii Finland 65°19N 25°22E 160 D21
Ii-Shima Japan 26°43N 127°47E 221 L3
Iida Japan 35°35N 137°50E 223 B9
Iijoki → Finland 65°20N 25°20E 160 D21
Iisalmi Finland 63°32N 27°10E 160 E22
Iiyama Japan 36°51N 138°22E 221 F9
Iizuka Japan 33°38N 130°42E 222 D2
IJ, Het → Neths. 52°23N 4°54E 112 A2
IJ-meer Neths. 52°23N 4°54E 112 A2
Ijâfene Mauritania 20°40N 8°0W 260 D3
Ijebu-Igbo Nigeria 6°56N 4°1E 263 D5
Ijebu-Ode Nigeria 6°47N 3°58E 263 D5
Ijesa-Tedo Nigeria 6°29N 3°19E 124 B1
Ijill, Sebkhet Mauritania 22°47N 12°53W 260 D2
IJmuiden Neths. 52°28N 4°35E 170 B4
Ijo älv = Iijoki → Finland 65°20N 25°20E 160 D21
Ijora Nigeria 6°27N 3°22E 124 B2
IJssel → Neths. 52°35N 5°50E 170 B5
IJsselmeer Neths. 52°45N 5°20E 170 B5
IJtunnel Amsterdam, Neths. 112 a3
Ijuí Brazil 28°23S 53°55W 335 B5
Ijuí → Brazil 27°58S 55°20W 335 B4
Ijūin Japan 31°37N 130°24E 222 F2
Ikalamavony Madag. 21°9S 46°35E 272 C2
Ikale Nigeria 7°40N 5°37E 263 D6
Ikali Dem. Rep. of the Congo 2°2S 21°4E 264 C4
Ikaluktutiak Canada 69°10N 105°0W 294 C9
Ikamatua N.Z. 42°16S 171°41E 285 C6
Ikang Nigeria 4°49N 8°30E 263 E6
Ikanga Kenya 1°42S 38°4E 268 C4
Ikara Nigeria 11°12N 8°15E 263 C6
Ikare Nigeria 7°32N 5°40E 263 D6
Ikaria Greece 37°35N 26°10E 205 D8
Ikast Denmark 56°8N 9°10E 163 H3
Ikebe Japan 35°31N 139°34E 140 B2
Ikebukuro Japan 35°43N 139°42E 140 A3
Ikeda Japan 34°1N 133°48E 222 C5
Ikegami Japan 35°33N 139°42E 140 B3
Ikei-shima Japan 26°23N 127°59E 288 a
Ikeja Nigeria 6°35N 3°20E 124 A2
Ikela Dem. Rep. of the Congo 1°6S 23°6E 264 C4
Ikélemba Congo 1°12N 16°38E 264 B3
Ikélemba → Dem. Rep. of the Congo 0°7N 18°17E 264 B3
Ikengo Dem. Rep. of the Congo 0°8S 18°8E 264 C3
Ikerre-Ekiti Nigeria 7°25N 5°19E 263 D6
Ikeuchi Japan 34°35N 135°32E 133 B2
Ikhtiman Bulgaria 42°27N 23°48E 202 D7
Iki Japan 33°45N 129°42E 222 D1
Iki-Kaikyō Japan 33°40N 129°45E 222 D1
Ikimba L. Tanzania 1°30S 31°20E 268 C3
Ikire Nigeria 7°23N 4°15E 263 D5
Ikitsuki-Shima Japan 33°23N 129°26E 222 D1
İkizdere Turkey 40°46N 40°32E 213 B9
Iko Congo 0°35S 16°0E 264 C3
Ikom Nigeria 6°0N 8°42E 263 D6
Ikomu Dem. Rep. of the Congo 1°54S 19°40E 264 C3
Ikongo Madag. 21°52S 47°27E 272 C2
Ikopa → Madag. 16°45S 46°40E 272 B2
Ikorongo △ Tanzania 1°50S 34°53E 268 C3
Ikot Ekpene Nigeria 5°12N 7°40E 263 D6
Ikoyi Nigeria 6°27N 3°26E 124 B2
Ikparjuk = Arctic Bay Canada 73°1N 85°7W 295 B11
Iksan S. Korea 35°59N 127°0E 224 E3
Ikuata Nigeria 6°24N 3°21E 124 B2
Ikungu Tanzania 1°33S 33°42E 268 C3
Ikuno Hyōgo, Japan 35°10N 134°48E 222 B6
Ikuno Ōsaka, Japan 34°40N 135°30E 133 A2
Ikuntji = Haast Bluff Australia 23°22S 132°0E 278 D5
Ikurun Nigeria 7°54N 4°40E 263 D5
Ikuta Japan 35°36N 139°32E 140 B2
Il-Kullana Malta 35°50N 14°24E 206 F7
Il-Munxar Malta 35°51N 14°34E 206 F8
Ila Dem. Rep. of the Congo 2°53S 21°7E 264 C4
Ila Nigeria 8°0N 4°39E 263 D5
Ila Oslo, Norway 59°57N 10°35E 133 A2
Ilafer Algeria 21°40N 1°58E 261 D5
Ilagan Phil. 17°7N 121°53E 232 C3
Ilaka Madag. 19°33S 48°52E 272 B2
Īlām Iran 33°36N 46°36E 250 E12
Ilam Nepal 26°58N 87°58E 243 F12
Īlām □ Iran 33°0N 47°0E 246 C5
Ilan Taiwan 24°45N 121°44E 225 B3
Ilan □ Taiwan 24°30N 121°35E 225 B3
Ilanskiy Russia 56°14N 96°3E 215 D10
Ilaro Nigeria 6°53N 3°3E 263 D5
Ilatane Niger 16°30N 4°45E 263 B5
Ilave Peru 16°5S 69°40W 330 D4
Iława Poland 53°36N 19°34E 184 E6
Ilayangudi India 9°34N 78°37E 245 K4
Ile → Kazakhstan 45°53N 77°10E 217 C9
Île-à-la-Crosse Canada 55°27N 107°53W 297 B7
Île-à-la-Crosse, Lac Canada 55°40N 107°45W 297 B7
Île-de-France □ France 49°0N 2°20E 173 D9
Ileanda Romania 47°20N 23°38E 183 C8
Ilebo Dem. Rep. of the Congo 4°17S 20°55E 265 C4
Ilek Russia 51°32N 53°21E 216 B4
Ilek → Russia 51°30N 53°22E 186 D9
Iler Algeria 20°57N 3°21E 261 D5
Iler, O. → Algeria 20°59N 3°14E 261 D5
Ilero Nigeria 8°0N 3°20E 263 D5
Ilesha Kwara, Nigeria 8°57N 3°28E 263 D5
Ilesha Oyo, Nigeria 7°37N 4°40E 263 D5
Ilet = Krasnogorskiy Russia 56°10N 48°28E 190 B9
Iletskaya = Sol Iletsk Russia 51°10N 55°0E 186 D10
Iletsky Gorodok = Ilek Russia 51°32N 53°21E 216 B4
Ilford Man., Canada 56°4N 95°35W 297 B9
Ilford London, U.K. 51°33N 0°4E 125 A4
Ilfracombe Queens., Australia 23°30S 144°30E 280 C3
Ilfracombe Devon, U.K. 51°12N 4°8W 169 F3
Ilgaz Turkey 40°55N 33°37E 212 B5
Ilgaz Dağları Turkey 41°10N 33°50E 212 B5
Ilgın Turkey 38°16N 31°55E 212 C4
Ilha, Pta. da Azores 38°25N 28°3W 153 d1
Ilha de Moçambique Mozam. 15°4S 40°52E 269 F5
Ilha Grande Brazil 0°27S 65°2W 329 D4
Ilha Grande, B. da Brazil 23°9S 44°30W 333 F3
Ílhavo Portugal 40°33N 8°43W 194 E2
Ilhéus Brazil 14°49S 39°2W 333 D4
Ili = Ile → Kazakhstan 45°53N 77°10E 217 C9
Ilia Romania 45°57N 22°40E 182 E7
Ilia □ Greece 37°45N 21°35E 204 D3
Iliamna U.S.A. 59°45N 154°55W 303 G9
Iliamna L. U.S.A. 59°30N 155°0W 303 G9
Ilich Kazakhstan 40°50N 68°27E 217 E7
Iligan Phil. 8°12N 124°13E 233 G5
Iligan Bay Phil. 8°25N 124°5E 233 G5
Iligan Pt. Phil. 18°25N 122°25E 232 B4
Ilin I. Phil. 12°14N 121°5E 232 E3
'Ilio Pt. U.S.A. 21°13N 157°16W 302 B4
Ilion U.S.A. 43°1N 75°2W 311 D9
Ilioupoli Greece 37°54N 23°47E 112 B2
Ilirska-Bistrica Slovenia 45°34N 14°14E 199 C11
Ilisyk = Qapshaghay Kazakhstan 43°51N 77°14E 217 D9
Ilkal India 15°57N 76°8E 245 G3
Ilkenau = Olkusz Poland 50°18N 19°33E 185 H6
Ilkeston U.K. 52°58N 1°19W 168 E6
Ilkley U.K. 53°56N 1°48W 168 D6
Illampu = Ancohuma, Nevado Bolivia 16°0S 68°50W 330 D4
Illana B. Phil. 7°35N 123°45E 233 H4
Illapel Chile 32°0S 71°10W 334 C1
Ille-et-Vilaine □ France 48°10N 1°30W 172 D5
Ille-sur-Têt France 42°40N 2°38E 174 F6
Illéla Niger 14°32N 5°20E 263 C6
Iller → Germany 48°23N 9°58E 179 G5
Illertissen Germany 48°12N 10°7E 179 G6
Illescas Spain 40°8N 3°51W 194 E7
Illetas Spain 39°32N 2°35E 206 B3
Illichivsk Ukraine 46°20N 30°35E 189 J6
Illiers-Combray France 48°18N 1°15E 172 D8
Illimani, Nevado Bolivia 16°30S 67°50W 330 D4
Illinois □ U.S.A. 40°15N 89°30W 310 D7
Illinois → U.S.A. 38°58N 90°28W 310 F6
Illinois at Chicago, University of U.S.A. 41°52N 87°38W 119 B3
Illinois Institute of Technology U.S.A. 41°50N 87°37W 119 B3
Illiopolis U.S.A. 39°51N 89°15W 310 E7
Illium = Troy Turkey 39°57N 26°12E 205 B8
Illizi Algeria 26°31N 8°32E 261 C6
Illizi □ Algeria 26°50N 8°10E 261 C6
Illkirch-Graffenstaden France 48°34N 7°42E 173 D14
Íllora Spain 37°17N 3°53W 195 H7
Ilulissat Greenland 69°12N 51°10W 154 D5
Ilm → Germany 51°6N 11°40E 178 D7
Ilma, L. Australia 29°13S 127°46E 279 E4
Ilmajoki Finland 62°44N 22°34E 160 E20
Ilmen, Ozero Russia 58°15N 31°10E 188 C6
Ilmenau = Jordanów Poland 49°41N 19°49E 185 J6
Ilmenau = Limanowa Poland 49°42N 20°22E 185 J7
Ilmenau Germany 50°41N 10°54E 178 E6
Ilnytsya Ukraine 48°21N 23°5E 182 B8
Ilo Peru 17°40S 71°20W 330 D3
Ilobu Nigeria 7°45N 4°25E 263 D5
Ilocos Norte □ Phil. 18°10N 120°45E 232 B3
Ilocos Sur □ Phil. 17°20N 120°35E 232 C3
Iloilo Phil. 10°45N 122°33E 233 F4
Iloilo □ Phil. 11°0N 122°40E 233 F4
Ilomantsi Finland 62°38N 30°57E 160 E24
Ilora Nigeria 7°45N 3°50E 263 D5
Ilorin Nigeria 8°30N 4°35E 263 D5
Ilovatka Russia 50°30N 45°50E 190 E7
Ilovlya Russia 49°15N 44°2E 191 F7
Ilovlya → Russia 49°14N 44°0E 191 F7
Iłowa Poland 51°30N 15°10E 185 G2
Ilpendam Neths. 52°28N 4°57E 112 A2
Ilsos → Greece 37°55N 23°41E 112 B2
Ilubabor Ethiopia 7°25N 35°0E 257 F4
Ilva Mică Romania 47°17N 24°40E 183 C9
Ilwaco U.S.A. 46°19N 124°3W 306 D2
Ilwaki Indonesia 7°55S 126°30E 231 F7
Ilyichevsk = Illichivsk Ukraine 46°20N 30°35E 189 J6
Iłża Poland 51°10N 21°15E 185 G8
Iłżanka → Poland 51°14N 21°48E 185 G8
Imabari Japan 34°4N 133°0E 222 C5
Imagem e do Som, Museu da Rio de J., Brazil 135 b3
Imaichi Japan 36°43N 139°46E 223 A11
Imaloto → Madag. 23°27S 45°13E 272 C2
İmamoğlu Turkey 37°15N 35°38E 212 D6
Iman = Dalnerechensk Russia 45°50N 133°40E 220 B6
Imandra, Ozero Russia 67°30N 33°0E 160 C25
Imanombo Madag. 24°26S 45°49E 272 C2
Imari Japan 33°15N 129°52E 222 D1
Imasa Sudan 18°0N 36°12E 256 D4
Imathia □ Greece 40°30N 22°15E 202 F6
Imatra Finland 61°12N 28°48E 188 B5
Imazu Japan 35°24N 136°2E 223 B8
Imbâbah Egypt 30°3N 31°12E 117 A2
Imbabura □ Ecuador 0°30N 78°45W 328 C2
Imbaimadai Guyana 5°44N 60°17W 329 B5
Imbonga Dem. Rep. of the Congo 0°43S 19°44E 264 C3
Imdahane Morocco 32°8N 7°0W 260 B3
Iménas Mali 16°20N 0°40E 263 B5
imeni 26 Bakinskikh Komissarov = Neftçala Azerbaijan 39°19N 49°12E 213 C13
imeni 26 Bakinskikh Komissarov Turkmenistan 39°22N 54°10E 247 B7
imeni Dvadtsati Shesti Bakinskikh Komissarov = Neftçala Azerbaijan 39°19N 49°12E 213 C13
imeni Dzerzhinskogo = Naryan-Mar Russia 67°42N 53°12E 186 A9
imeni Ismail Samani, Pik Tajikistan 39°0N 72°2E 217 E8
imeni Mikoyana = Kara-Balta Kyrgyzstan 42°50N 73°49E 217 D8
imeni Petrovskogo G.I. = Horodyshche Ukraine 49°17N 31°27E 189 H6
imeni Sverdlova = Sverdlovsk Ukraine 48°5N 39°47E 189 H10
imeni Tovarishcha Khateyevicha = Synelnykove Ukraine 48°25N 35°30E 189 H8
imeni Tretyego Internatsionala = Novoshakhtinsk Russia 47°46N 39°58E 189 J10
Imeri, Serra Brazil 0°50N 65°25W 328 C4
Imerimandroso Madag. 17°26S 48°35E 272 B2
Imesan Mauritania 22°54N 15°30W 260 D1
Imese Dem. Rep. of the Congo 2°6N 18°6E 264 B3
Imfolozi △ S. Africa 28°18S 31°50E 271 C5
Imi Ethiopia 6°28N 42°10E 257 F5
Imielin Poland 52°9N 21°0E 142 C2
Imirim Brazil 23°29S 46°39W 137 A2
Imishly = İmişli Azerbaijan 39°55N 48°4E 191 L9
İmişli Azerbaijan 39°55N 48°4E 191 L9
Imitek Morocco 29°43N 8°10W 260 C3
Imitos Greece 37°55N 23°45E 112 B2
Imitos, Oros Greece 37°53N 23°48E 112 B2
Imjado S. Korea 35°5N 126°5E 224 E3
Imjin-gang → N. Korea 37°47N 126°39E 224 E3
Imlay U.S.A. 40°40N 118°9W 304 F4
Imlay City U.S.A. 43°2N 83°5W 312 D1
Immaseri Sudan 15°40N 25°31E 257 D2
Immenstadt Germany 47°33N 10°13E 179 H6
Immingham U.K. 53°37N 0°13W 168 D7
Immokalee U.S.A. 26°25N 81°25W 317 J8
Imo □ Nigeria 5°30N 7°10E 263 D6
Imo → Nigeria 4°36N 7°35E 263 E6
Ímola Italy 44°20N 11°42E 199 D8
Imotski Croatia 43°27N 17°12E 199 E14
Impé Congo 2°45S 15°16E 264 C3
Imperatorskaya Gavan = Vanino Russia 48°50N 140°5E 215 E15
Imperatriz Amazonas, Brazil 5°18S 67°11W 330 B4
Imperatriz Maranhão, Brazil 5°30S 47°29W 332 C2
Impéria Italy 43°53N 8°3E 198 E5
Imperial Sask., Canada 51°21N 105°28W 297 C7
Imperial Peru 13°4S 76°21W 330 C2
Imperial Calif., U.S.A. 32°51N 115°34W 307 N11
Imperial Nebr., U.S.A. 40°31N 101°39W 308 E3
Imperial Beach U.S.A. 32°35N 117°6W 307 N9
Imperial Dam U.S.A. 32°55N 114°25W 307 N12
Imperial Palace = Paco Imperial Rio de J., Brazil 135 a2
Imperial Palace Museum Beijing, China 114 b2
Imperial Res. U.S.A. 32°53N 114°28W 307 N12
Imperial Valley U.S.A. 33°0N 115°30W 307 N11
Imperieuse Reef Australia 17°36S 118°50E 278 C2
Impfondo Congo 1°40N 18°0E 264 B3
Imphal India 24°48N 93°56E 241 C4
Imphy France 46°55N 3°16E 173 F10
Impulo Angola 13°51S 13°39E 265 E2
Imranlı Turkey 39°54N 38°7E 213 C8
İmroz = Gökçeada Turkey 40°10N 25°50E 203 F9
İmroz Turkey 40°10N 25°55E 203 F9
Imst Austria 47°15N 10°44E 180 D3
Imuris Mexico 30°47N 110°52W 318 A2
Imuruan B. Phil. 10°40N 119°10E 233 F2
Imus Phil. 14°26N 120°56E 232 D3
In Akhmed Mali 19°49N 0°56W 261 E4
In Alei Mali 17°42N 2°30W 262 B4
In Amenas Algeria 28°5N 9°33E 261 C6
In Atei Algeria 20°33N 6°4E 261 D6
In Belbel Algeria 27°55N 1°12E 261 C5
In Delimane Mali 15°52N 1°31E 263 B5
In Guezzam Algeria 19°37N 5°52E 261 E6
In Koufi Mali 19°11N 1°25E 263 B5
In Rhar Algeria 27°10N 1°59E 261 C5
In Salah Algeria 27°10N 2°32E 261 C5
In Tallak Mali 16°19N 3°15E 263 B5
In Tebezas Mali 17°49N 1°53E 263 B5
Ina Japan 35°50N 137°55E 223 B9
Ina Ill., U.S.A. 38°9N 88°54W 311 F8
Ina-Bonchi Japan 35°45N 137°58E 223 B9
Inabanga Phil. 10°2N 124°4E 233 F5
Inaguan Phil. 9°33N 118°39E 233 G2
Inagi Japan 35°38N 139°31E 140 B2
Inajá Brazil 8°54S 37°49W 332 C4
Inambari → Peru 12°41S 69°44W 330 C4
Inangahua N.Z. 41°52S 171°59E 285 B6
Inanwatan Indonesia 2°8S 132°10E 231 E8
Iñapari Peru 11°0S 69°40W 330 C4
Inarajan Guam 13°16N 144°45E 302 d
Inari Finland 68°54N 27°1E 160 B22
Inarijärvi Finland 69°0N 28°0E 160 B23
Inawashiro-Ko Japan 37°29N 140°6E 220 F10
Inazawa Japan 35°15N 136°47E 223 B8
Inbin Burma 18°6N 95°16E 241 F5
Inca Spain 39°43N 2°54E 206 B3
Inca de Oro Chile 26°45S 69°54W 334 B2
Incaguasi Chile 29°12S 71°5W 334 B1
Incahuasi Argentina 27°2S 68°18W 334 B2
İnce Burun Turkey 42°7N 34°56E 212 A6
İncekum Burnu Turkey 36°13N 33°57E 250 B4
İncesu Turkey 38°38N 35°11E 246 B2
Inchcolm U.K. 56°2N 3°18W 121 A2
Incheon S. Korea 37°27N 126°40E 224 D3
Inchicore Ireland 53°20N 6°20W 120 A1
Inchiri □ Mauritania 20°0N 15°0W 260 E2
Inchkeith U.K. 56°2N 3°8W 121 A3
Inchmickery U.K. 56°0N 3°16W 121 A2
Incio = Cruz de Incio Spain 42°39N 7°21W 194 C3
Incirano Italy 45°34N 9°9E 129 A1
İncirliova Turkey 37°50N 27°41E 205 D9
Incline Village U.S.A. 39°10N 119°58W 304 G4
Incomáti → Mozam. 25°46S 32°43E 271 C5
Incudine, Mte. France 41°50N 9°12E 175 G13
Inda Silase Ethiopia 14°10N 38°15E 257 E4
Indal Sweden 62°35N 17°5E 162 B11
Indalsälven → Sweden 62°36N 17°30E 162 B11
Indaw Burma 24°15N 96°5E 241 C6
Indawgyi In Burma 25°8N 96°20E 241 C6
Indbir Ethiopia 8°7N 37°52E 257 F4
Indefatigable, I. = Santa Cruz, I. Ecuador 0°38S 90°23W 330 a
Independence Calif., U.S.A. 36°48N 118°12W 306 J8
Independence Iowa, U.S.A. 42°28N 91°54W 310 B5
Independence Kans., U.S.A. 37°14N 95°42W 308 G6
Independence Ky., U.S.A. 38°57N 84°33W 311 F12
Independence Mo., U.S.A. 39°6N 94°25W 310 E2
Independence Avenue Washington, D.C., U.S.A. 143 c2
Independence Fjord Greenland 82°10N 29°0W 154 A8
Independence Mts. U.S.A. 41°20N 116°0W 304 F5
Independência Brazil 5°23S 40°19W 332 C3
Independencia Santiago, Chile 33°25S 70°39W 137 B2
Independencia Lima, Peru 11°59S 77°3W 124 A2
Independenţa Romania 45°25N 27°42E 183 E12
Inderbor Kazakhstan 48°33N 51°47E 216 C4
Index U.S.A. 47°50N 121°33W 306 C5
Indi India 17°10N 75°58E 244 F2
India ■ Asia 20°0N 78°0E 239 F11
India Gate Delhi, India 120 c2
Indialantic U.S.A. 28°6N 80°34W 317 G9
Indian → U.S.A. 27°59N 80°34W 317 G9
Indian Cabins Canada 59°52N 117°40W 296 B5
Indian Creek Village U.S.A. 25°52N 80°8W 128 A2
Indian Harbour Canada 54°27N 57°13W 299 B8
Indian Harbour Beach U.S.A. 28°10N 80°35W 317 G9
Indian Head Canada 50°30N 103°41W 297 C8
Indian Lake U.S.A. 43°47N 74°16W 313 C10
Indian Ocean 5°0S 75°0E 273 E6
Indian Rocks Beach U.S.A. 27°52N 82°51W 317 H7
Indian Springs U.S.A. 36°35N 115°40W 307 J11
Indian Town Pt. Antigua & B. 17°6N 61°40W 322 b
Indian Walk Trin. & Tob. 10°16N 61°20W 323 t
Indiana U.S.A. 40°37N 79°9W 312 F5
Indiana □ U.S.A. 40°0N 86°0W 311 E11
Indiana Dunes △ U.S.A. 41°40N 87°0W 311 C9
Indianapolis U.S.A. 39°46N 86°9W 311 E10
Indianapolis Int. ✕ (IND) U.S.A. 39°43N 86°17W 311 E10
Indianola Iowa, U.S.A. 41°22N 93°34W 310 C3
Indianola Miss., U.S.A. 33°27N 90°39W 315 E9
Indianópolis Brazil 23°35S 46°38W 137 B2
Indiantown U.S.A. 27°1N 80°28W 317 H9
Indiapora Brazil 19°57S 50°17W 333 E1
Indiga Russia 67°38N 49°9E 186 A8
Indigirka → Russia 70°48N 148°54E 215 B15
Inđija Serbia 45°6N 20°7E 182 E5
Indio U.S.A. 33°43N 116°13W 307 M10
Indira Gandhi Canal India 28°0N 72°0E 242 F5
Indira Gandhi Int. ✕ (DEL) India 28°33N 77°6E 120 B1
Indira Pt. India 6°44N 93°49E 245 L11
Indira Sagar India 22°15N 76°40E 242 H7
Indispensable Strait Solomon Is. 9°0S 160°30E 287 M11
Indo-China Asia 15°0N 102°0E 210 G12
Indonesia ■ Asia 5°0S 115°0E 235 C4
Indore India 22°42N 75°53E 242 H6
Indramayu Indonesia 6°20S 108°19E 235 D3
Indrapura = Kerinci Indonesia 1°40S 101°15E 234 C2
Indravati → India 19°20N 80°20E 244 E5
Indre □ France 46°50N 1°39E 173 F8
Indre → France 47°16N 0°11E 172 E7
Indre Ålvik Norway 60°26N 6°26E 164 D3
Indre Arna Norway 60°26N 5°30E 164 D2
Indre-et-Loire □ France 47°20N 0°40E 172 E7
Indulkana Australia 26°58S 133°5E 281 D1
Indungo Angola 14°48S 16°17E 265 E3
Indura Belarus 53°26N 23°53E 184 E10
Indus → Pakistan 24°20N 67°47E 242 G2
Indus, Mouths of the Pakistan 24°0N 68°0E 242 H3
Industria S. Africa 26°11S 27°58E 123 B1
Industrial Canal U.S.A. 30°4N 90°4W 131 A2
Industry U.S.A. 40°20N 90°36W 310 D6
İnebolu Turkey 41°55N 33°40E 212 B5
İnecik Turkey 40°56N 27°16E 203 F11
İnegöl Turkey 40°5N 29°31E 203 F13
Inés, Mt. Argentina 48°30S 69°40W 336 C3
Ineu Romania 46°26N 21°51E 182 D6
Inezgane Morocco 30°25N 9°29W 260 B3
Infanta Phil. 14°45N 121°39E 232 D3
Infantes = Villanueva de los Infantes Spain 38°43N 3°1W 195 G7
Infiernillo, Presa del Mexico 18°35N 101°50W 318 D4
Infiesto Spain 43°21N 5°21W 194 B5
Inga, Barrage d' Dem. Rep. of the Congo 5°39S 13°39E 265 D2
Ingabu Burma 17°37N 95°20E 241 G5
Inganda Dem. Rep. of the Congo 0°5S 20°57E 264 C4
Ingapirca Ecuador 2°38S 78°56W 328 D2
Ingelstad Sweden 56°45N 14°56E 163 H8
Ingende Dem. Rep. of the Congo 0°12S 18°57E 264 C3
Ingeniero Jacobacci Argentina 41°20S 69°36W 336 B3
Ingenio Canary Is. 27°55N 15°26W 153 e1
Ingenio Santa Ana Argentina 27°25S 65°40W 334 B2
Ingersoll Canada 43°4N 80°55W 312 C4
Ingham Australia 18°43S 146°10E 280 B4
Ingierstrand Norway 59°49N 10°46E 133 B3
Ingleborough U.K. 54°10N 2°22W 168 C5
Inglefield Land Greenland 78°30N 70°0W 154 B4
Inglewood Queens., Australia 28°25S 151°2E 281 D5
Inglewood Vic., Australia 36°29S 143°53E 282 D5
Inglewood N.Z. 39°9S 174°14E 284 F3
Inglewood Calif., U.S.A. 33°58N 118°21W 126 C3
Inglis U.S.A. 29°2N 82°40W 317 F7
Ingliston U.K. 55°56N 3°23W 121 B1
Ingolf Fjord Greenland 80°35N 17°30W 154 A9
Ingólfshöfði Iceland 63°48N 16°39W 155 D10
Ingolstadt Germany 48°46N 11°26E 179 G7
Ingomar U.S.A. 46°35N 107°23W 304 C10
Ingonish Canada 46°42N 60°18W 299 C7
Ingore Guinea-Biss. 12°24N 15°48W 262 C1
Ingraj Bazar India 24°58N 88°10E 243 G13
Ingrid Christensen Coast Antarctica 69°30S 76°0E 151 C6
Ingul = Inhul → Ukraine 46°50N 32°0E 189 J7
Ingulec = Inhulec Ukraine 47°42N 33°14E 189 J7
Ingulets = Inhulets → Ukraine 46°46N 32°47E 189 J7
Inguri = Enguri → Georgia 42°27N 41°38E 191 J5
Ingushetia □ Russia 43°20N 44°50E 191 J7
Ingwavuma S. Africa 27°9S 31°59E 271 C5
Inhaca Mozam. 26°1S 32°57E 271 C5
Inhafenga Mozam. 20°36S 33°53E 271 B5
Inhambane Mozam. 23°54S 35°30E 271 B6
Inhambane □ Mozam. 22°30S 34°20E 271 B5
Inhambupe Brazil 11°47S 38°21W 333 D4
Inhaminga Mozam. 18°26S 35°0E 269 F4
Inharrime Mozam. 24°30S 35°0E 271 B6
Inharrime → Mozam. 24°30S 35°0E 271 B6
Inhaúma Brazil 22°51S 43°17W 135 B1
Inhisar Turkey 40°3N 30°23E 205 A12
Inhul → Ukraine 46°50N 32°0E 189 J7
Inhulec Ukraine 47°42N 33°14E 189 J7
Inhulets → Ukraine 46°46N 32°47E 189 J7
Inhuma Brazil 6°40S 41°42W 332 C3
Inhumas Brazil 16°22S 49°30W 333 E2
Iniesta Spain 39°27N 1°45W 197 F3
Ining = Yining China 43°58N 81°10E 217 D10
Inini □ Fr. Guiana 4°0N 53°0W 329 C7
Inírida → Colombia 3°55N 67°52W 328 C4
Inishbofin Ireland 53°37N 10°13W 166 C1
Inisheer Ireland 53°3N 9°32W 166 C2
Inishfree B. Ireland 55°4N 8°23W 166 A3
Inishkea North Ireland 54°9N 10°11W 166 B1
Inishkea South Ireland 54°7N 10°12W 166 B1
Inishmaan Ireland 53°5N 9°35W 166 C2
Inishmore Ireland 53°8N 9°45W 166 C2
Inishmurray I. Ireland 54°26N 8°39W 166 B3
Inishowen Pen. Ireland 55°14N 7°15W 166 A4
Inishshark Ireland 53°37N 10°16W 166 C1
Inishturk Ireland 53°42N 10°7W 166 C1
Inishvickillane Ireland 52°3N 10°37W 166 D1
Injibara Ethiopia 10°59N 37°0E 257 E4
Injune Australia 25°53S 148°32E 281 D4
Inkisi → Dem. Rep. of the Congo 4°46S 14°52E 265 D3
Inklin → N. Amer. 58°50N 133°10W 296 B2
Inland Kaikoura Ra. N.Z. 41°59S 173°41E 285 B8
Inland Sea = Setonaikai Japan 34°20N 133°30E 222 C5
Inle L. Burma 20°30N 96°58E 241 D6
Inlet U.S.A. 43°45N 74°48W 313 C10
Inn → Austria 48°35N 13°28E 180 C6
Innamincka Australia 27°44S 140°46E 281 D3
Innbygda Norway 61°19N 12°17E 164 C9
Inner Hebrides U.K. 57°0N 6°30W 167 E2
Inner Mongolia = Nei Monggol Zizhiqu □ China 42°0N 112°0E 226 D7
Inner Port Shelter China 22°22N 114°17E 122 A2
Inner Sound U.K. 57°30N 5°55W 167 D3
Innerkip Canada 43°13N 80°42W 312 C4
Innes △ Australia 35°52S 136°53E 282 C2
Innetalling I. Canada 56°0N 79°0W 298 A4
Innisfail Queens., Australia 17°33S 146°5E 280 B4
Innisfail Alta., Canada 52°2N 113°57W 296 C6
Innoko Nat. Wildlife Refuge △ U.S.A. 63°20N 158°25W 303 E8
In'noshima Japan 34°19N 133°10E 222 C5
Innsbruck Austria 47°16N 11°23E 180 D4
Innviertel Austria 48°15N 13°15E 180 C6
Innvik Norway 61°51N 6°37E 164 C3
Inny → Ireland 53°30N 7°50W 166 C4
Ino Japan 33°33N 133°26E 222 D5
Inocência Brazil 19°47S 51°48W 333 E1
Inongo Dem. Rep. of the Congo 1°55S 18°30E 264 C3
Inoni Congo 3°4S 15°39E 264 C3
İnönü Turkey 39°48N 30°9E 205 B12
Inoucdjouac = Inukjuak Canada 58°25N 78°15W 295 D12
Inousses Greece 38°33N 26°14E 205 C8
Inowrocław Poland 52°50N 18°12E 185 F5
Inquisivi Bolivia 16°50S 67°10W 330 D4
Inscription, C. Australia 25°29S 112°59E 279 E1
Insein Burma 16°50N 96°5E 241 G6
Insjön Sweden 60°41N 15°6E 162 D9
Ińsko Poland 53°25N 15°32E 184 E2
Insterburg = Chernyakhovsk Russia 54°36N 21°48E 184 D8
Însurăţei Romania 44°50N 27°40E 183 F12
Inta Russia 66°5N 60°8E 186 A11
Intendente Alvear Argentina 35°12S 63°32W 334 D3
İntepe Turkey 40°1N 26°20E 205 A8
Interlachen U.S.A. 29°37N 81°53W 317 F8
Interlagos Brazil 23°41S 46°42W 137 C1
Interlaken Switz. 46°41N 7°50E 179 J3
Interlaken N.Y., U.S.A. 42°37N 76°44W 313 D8
International Falls U.S.A. 48°36N 93°25W 308 A7
Interview I. India 12°55N 92°43E 245 H11
Intiyaco Argentina 28°43S 60°5W 334 B3
Întorsura Buzăului Romania 45°41N 26°2E 183 E11
Intramuros Phil. 14°35N 120°57E 127 B1
Intrepid Air and Space Museum New York, U.S.A. 132 b1
Intutu Peru 3°32S 74°48W 328 D3
Inubō-Zaki Japan 35°42N 140°52E 223 B12
Inukjuak Canada 58°25N 78°15W 295 D12
Inútil, B. Chile 53°30S 70°15W 336 D2
Inuvik Canada 68°16N 133°40W 294 C6
Inuyama Japan 35°23N 136°56E 223 B8
Invalides France 48°51N 2°18E 134 A2
Inveraray U.K. 56°14N 5°5W 167 E3
Inverbervie U.K. 56°51N 2°17W 167 E6
Invercargill N.Z. 46°24S 168°24E 285 G3
Inverclyde □ U.K. 55°55N 4°49W 167 F4
Inverell Australia 29°45S 151°8E 281 D5
Invergordon U.K. 57°41N 4°10W 167 D4
Inverkeithing U.K. 56°2N 3°24W 121 A1
Inverleigh Australia 38°6S 144°3E 282 E6
Inverloch Australia 38°38S 145°45E 281 F4
Invermere Canada 50°30N 116°2W 296 C5
Inverness N.S., Canada 46°15N 61°19W 299 C7
Inverness Highl., U.K. 57°29N 4°13W 167 D4
Inverness Ala., U.S.A. 32°1N 85°45W 316 C4
Inverness Fla., U.S.A. 28°50N 82°20W 317 G7
Inverurie U.K. 57°17N 2°23W 167 D6
Investigator Group Australia 34°45S 134°20E 281 E1
Investigator Ridge Ind. Oc. 11°30S 98°10E 273 F8
Investigator Str. Australia 35°30S 137°0E 282 C2
Inya Russia 50°28N 86°37E 217 B11
Inyanga Zimbabwe 18°12S 32°40E 269 F3
Inyangani Zimbabwe 18°5S 32°50E 269 F3
Inyantue Zimbabwe 18°33S 26°39E 270 A4
Inyo Mts. U.S.A. 36°40N 118°0W 306 J9
Inyokern U.S.A. 35°39N 117°49W 307 K9
Inywa Burma 23°56N 96°17E 241 D6
Inza Russia 53°55N 46°25E 190 D8
Inzersdorf Austria 48°8N 16°21E 142 B2
Inzhavino Russia 52°22N 42°30E 190 D6
Inzia → Dem. Rep. of the Congo 3°45S 17°57E 265 C3
Iō-Jima Japan 30°48N 130°18E 221 J5
Ioannina Greece 39°42N 20°47E 204 B2
Ioannina □ Greece 39°39N 20°57E 204 B2
Iokea Papua N. G. 8°25S 146°16E 286 E4
Iola U.S.A. 37°55N 95°24W 308 G6
Iolani Palace U.S.A. 21°18N 157°51W 302 K14
Ioma Papua N. G. 8°19S 147°52E 286 E4
Ion Corvin Romania 44°7N 27°50E 183 F12
Iona Angola 16°54S 12°34E 265 F2
Iona Argyll & Bute, U.K. 56°20N 6°25W 167 E2
Iona △ Angola 16°47S 12°20E 265 F2
Ione U.S.A. 38°21N 120°56W 306 G6
Iongo Angola 9°11S 17°45E 265 D3
Ionia U.S.A. 42°59N 85°4W 311 B11
Ionian Is. = Ionioi Nisoi Greece 38°40N 20°0E 204 C2
Ionian Sea Medit. S. 37°30N 17°30E 193 D7
Ionioi Nisoi Greece 38°40N 20°0E 204 C2
Ionioi Nisoi □ Greece 38°40N 20°0E 207 B2
Ios Greece 36°41N 25°20E 205 E7
Iowa □ U.S.A. 42°18N 93°30W 310 C3
Iowa → U.S.A. 41°10N 91°1W 310 C5
Iowa City U.S.A. 41°40N 91°32W 310 C5
Iowa Falls U.S.A. 42°31N 93°16W 310 B3
Iowa Park U.S.A. 33°57N 98°40W 314 E5
Ipala Tanzania 4°30S 32°52E 268 C3
Ipameri Brazil 17°44S 48°9W 333 E2
Ipanema Minas Gerais, Brazil 19°47S 41°44W 333 E3
Ipanema Rio de J., Brazil 22°59S 43°12W 135 B1
Iparía Peru 9°17S 74°29W 330 B3
Ipati Greece 38°52N 22°14E 204 C4
Ipatinga Brazil 19°32S 42°30W 333 E3
Ipatovo Russia 45°45N 42°50E 191 H6
Ipek = Peć Serbia 42°40N 20°17E 202 D4
Ipel' → Europe 47°48N 18°53E 181 D11
Ipiales Colombia 0°50N 77°37W 328 C2
Ipiaú Brazil 14°8S 39°44W 333 D4
Ipil Phil. 7°47N 122°35E 233 H4
Ipin = Yibin China 28°45N 104°32E 228 C5
Ipirá Brazil 12°10S 39°44W 333 D4
Ipiranga Brazil 23°35S 46°36W 137 B2
Ipiranga → Brazil 23°37S 46°47W 137 B2
Ipixuna Brazil 7°0S 71°40W 330 B3
Ipixuna → Amazonas, Brazil 7°11S 71°51W 330 B3
Ipixuna → Amazonas, Brazil 5°45S 63°2W 331 B5
Ipoh Malaysia 4°35N 101°5E 237 K3
Iponri Nigeria 6°28N 3°22E 124 B2
Iporá Brazil 16°28S 51°7W 331 D7
Ipota Vanuatu 18°52S 169°20E 287 H7
Ippy C.A.R. 6°5N 21°7E 264 A4
İpsala Turkey 40°55N 26°23E 203 F10
Ipsario, Oros Greece 40°40N 24°40E 203 F8
Ipsos Greece 39°43N 19°48E 206 B9
Ipswich Queens., Australia 27°35S 152°40E 281 D5
Ipswich Suffolk, U.K. 52°4N 1°10E 169 E9
Ipswich Mass., U.S.A. 42°41N 70°50W 313 D14
Ipswich S. Dak., U.S.A. 45°27N 99°2W 308 C4
Ipu Brazil 4°23S 40°44W 332 B3
Ipueiras Brazil 4°33S 40°43W 332 B3
Ipupiara Brazil 11°49S 42°37W 333 D3
Iqaluit Canada 63°44N 68°31W 295 C13
Iquique Chile 20°19S 70°5W 330 E3
Iquitos Peru 3°45S 73°10W 328 D3
Ir Gannim = Bat Yam Israel 32°2N 34°44E 251 F5
Irabu-Jima Japan 24°50N 125°10E 221 M2
Iracoubo Fr. Guiana 5°30N 53°10W 329 B7
Īrafshān Iran 26°42N 61°56E 247 E9
Irahuan Phil. 9°48N 118°41E 233 G2
Iraklia Cyclades, Greece 36°50N 25°28E 205 E7
Iraklia Serres, Greece 41°10N 23°16E 202 E7
Iraklio Greece 35°20N 25°12E 207 E6
Iraklio □ Greece 35°10N 25°10E 207 E6
Iraklio ✕ (HER) Greece 35°20N 25°15E 207 E6
Iráklion = Iraklio Greece 35°20N 25°12E 207 E6
Irako-Zaki Japan 34°35N 137°1E 223 C9
Irala Paraguay 25°55S 54°35W 335 B5
Iran ■ Asia 33°0N 53°0E 247 C7
Iran, Pegunungan Malaysia 2°20N 114°50E 235 B4
Iran Ra. = Iran, Pegunungan Malaysia 2°20N 114°50E 235 B4
Iranamadu Tank Sri Lanka 9°23N 80°29E 245 K5

Īrānshahr Iran 27°15N 60°40E 247 E9
Irapa Venezuela 10°34N 62°35W 329 A5
Irapuato Mexico 20°41N 101°28W 318 C4
Iraq ■ Asia 33°0N 44°0E 213 F10
Irarrar, O. → Mali 20°0N 1°30E 261 E5
Irarrarene Algeria 27°37N 7°30E 261 C6
Irati Brazil 25°25S 50°38W 335 B5
Irbes saurums Latvia 57°45N 22°5E 184 A9
Irbid Jordan 32°35N 35°48E 251 F6
Irbid □ Jordan 32°30N 35°50E 250 F6
Irebu Dem. Rep. of the Congo 0°40S 17°46E 264 C3
Irecê Brazil 11°18S 41°52W 332 D3
Iregua → Spain 42°27N 2°24E 196 C7
Ireland ■ Europe 53°50N 7°52W 166 C4
Ireland I. Bermuda 32°19N 64°50W 153 a
Ireland Island Bermuda 32°19N 64°50W 153 a
Ireland's Eye Ireland 53°24N 6°4W 120 A3
Irele Nigeria 7°40N 5°40E 263 D6
Ireng → Brazil 3°33N 59°51W 329 C6
Irerrer, O. → Algeria 19°25N 5°47E 261 E6
Irgiz = Yrghyz Kazakhstan 48°37N 61°16E 216 C6
Irgiz = Yrghyz → Kazakhstan 48°6N 62°30E 216 C6
Irgiz, Bolshaya → Russia 52°10N 49°10E 190 D9
Irharrhar, O. → Algeria 28°3N 6°15E 261 C6
Irherm Morocco 30°7N 8°18W 260 B3
Irhil M'Goun Morocco 31°30N 6°28W 260 B3
Iri = Iksan S. Korea 35°59N 127°0E 224 E3
Irian Barat = Papua □ Indonesia 4°0S 137°0E 231 E9
Irian Jaya = Papua □ Indonesia 4°0S 137°0E 231 E9
Irian Jaya Barat □ Indonesia 2°5S 132°50E 231 E8
Iriba Chad 15°7N 22°15E 259 E4
Irié Guinea 8°15N 9°10W 262 D3
Iriga Phil. 13°25N 123°25E 232 E4
Iriklinskoye Vdkhr. Russia 52°0N 59°0E 216 B5
Iringa Tanzania 7°48S 35°43E 268 D4
Iringa □ Tanzania 7°48S 35°43E 268 D4
Irinjalakuda India 10°21N 76°14E 245 J3
Iriomote △ Japan 24°29N 123°53E 221 M1
Iriomote-Jima Japan 24°19N 123°48E 221 M1
Iriona Honduras 15°57N 85°11W 320 C2
Iriri → Brazil 3°52S 52°37W 329 D7
Iriri Novo → Brazil 8°46S 53°22W 331 B7
Irish Republic ■ Europe 53°50N 7°52W 166 C4
Irish Sea Europe 53°38N 4°48W 168 D3
Irkutsk Russia 52°18N 104°20E 215 D11
Irlığanlı Turkey 37°53N 29°12E 205 D11
Irma Canada 52°55N 111°14W 297 C6
Irma, L. U.S.A. 28°35N 81°16W 133 A3
Irō-Zaki Japan 34°36N 138°51E 223 C10
Irois B. Trin. & Tob. 10°9N 61°45W 323 t
Iroise, Mer d' France 48°15N 4°45W 172 D2
Iron Baron Australia 32°58S 137°11E 282 B2
Iron Gate = Portile de Fier Europe 44°44N 22°30E 182 F7
Iron Knob Australia 32°46S 137°8E 282 B2
Iron Mountain U.S.A. 45°49N 88°4W 308 C9
Iron Range △ Australia 12°34S 143°18E 280 A3
Iron River U.S.A. 46°6N 88°39W 308 B9
Irondequoit U.S.A. 43°13N 77°35W 312 C7
Ironton Mo., U.S.A. 37°36N 90°38W 308 G8
Ironton Ohio, U.S.A. 38°32N 82°41W 309 F12
Ironwood U.S.A. 46°27N 90°9W 308 B8
Ironwood Forest ⌂ U.S.A. 32°32N 111°28W 305 K8
Iroquois Canada 44°51N 75°19W 313 B9
Iroquois → U.S.A. 41°5N 87°49W 311 C9
Iroquois Falls Canada 48°46N 80°41W 298 C3
Iroquois Point U.S.A. 21°19N 157°58W 302 K14
Irosin Phil. 12°42N 124°2E 232 E5
Irpin Ukraine 50°30N 30°15E 177 C16
Irqieqa, Ras I- Malta 35°56N 14°29E 206 F7
Irrara Cr. → Australia 29°35S 145°31E 281 D4
Irrawaddy □ Burma 17°0N 95°0E 241 G5
Irrawaddy → Burma 15°50N 95°6E 241 G5
Irrawaddy, Mouths of the Burma 15°30N 95°0E 241 H5
Irricana Canada 51°19N 113°37W 296 C6
Irshava Ukraine 48°19N 23°3E 182 B8
Irsina Italy 40°45N 16°14E 201 B9
Irtysh → Russia 61°4N 68°52E 214 C7
Irumu Dem. Rep. of the Congo 1°32N 29°53E 268 B2
Irún Spain 43°20N 1°52W 196 B3
Irunea = Pamplona Spain 42°48N 1°38W 196 C3
Irurzun Spain 42°55N 1°50W 196 C3
Irvine Alta., Canada 49°57N 110°16W 297 D6
Irvine N. Ayrs., U.K. 55°37N 4°41W 167 F4
Irvine Calif., U.S.A. 33°41N 117°46W 307 M9
Irvine Ky., U.S.A. 37°42N 83°58W 311 G13
Irvinestown U.K. 54°28N 7°39W 166 B4
Irving U.S.A. 32°48N 96°56W 314 E6
Irving Park U.S.A. 41°57N 87°42W 119 B2
Irvington U.S.A. 37°53N 86°17W 311 G10
Irvona U.S.A. 40°46N 78°33W 312 F6
Irwin → Australia 29°15S 114°54E 279 E1
Irwinton U.S.A. 32°49N 83°10W 316 C6
Irwinville U.S.A. 31°39N 83°23W 316 D6
Irymple Australia 34°14S 142°8E 282 C5
Is, Jebel Sudan 22°3N 35°28E 256 C4
Is-sur-Tille France 47°30N 5°8E 173 E12
Isa Nigeria 13°14N 6°24E 263 C6
Isa Khel Pakistan 32°41N 71°17E 242 C4
Isaac → Australia 22°55S 149°20E 280 C4
Isabel Rio de J., Brazil 22°55S 43°14W 135 B1
Isabel S. Dak., U.S.A. 45°24N 101°26W 308 C3
Isabel, I. Mexico 21°51N 105°55W 318 C3
Isabel Segunda Puerto Rico 18°9N 65°27W 321 b
Isabela Basilan, Phil. 6°40N 121°59E 233 H3
Isabela Negros, Phil. 10°12N 122°59E 233 F4
Isabela Puerto Rico 18°30N 67°2W 321 b
Isabela □ Phil. 17°0N 122°0E 232 C4
Isabela, Canal Ecuador 0°20S 90°55W 330 a
Isabela, I. Ecuador 0°30S 91°4W 330 a
Isabella, Cord. Nic. 13°30N 85°25W 320 D2
Isabella Ra. Australia 21°0S 121°4E 278 D3
Isaccea Romania 45°16N 28°28E 183 E13
Ísafjarðardjúp Iceland 66°10N 23°0W 155 A3
Ísafjarðarsýsla □ Iceland 66°0N 23°0W 155 B3
Ísafjörður Iceland 66°5N 23°9W 155 A3
Isagarh India 24°48N 77°51E 242 G7
Isagatedo Nigeria 6°31N 3°19E 124 A1
Isahaya Japan 32°52N 130°2E 222 E2
Isaka Dem. Rep. of the Congo 2°33S 18°54E 264 C3
Isaka Tanzania 3°56S 32°59E 268 C3
Işalniţa Romania 44°24N 23°44E 183 F8
Isalo △ Madag. 22°23S 45°16E 272 C2
Isan → India 26°51N 80°7E 243 F9
Isana = Içana → Brazil 0°26N 67°19W 328 C4
Isandja Dem. Rep. of the Congo 2°59S 21°59E 264 C4
Isangano △ Zambia 11°8S 30°35E 269 E3
Isangi Dem. Rep. of the Congo 0°52N 24°10E 264 B4
Isanlu Makutu Nigeria 8°20N 5°50E 263 D6
Isar → Bayern, Germany 48°48N 12°57E 179 G8
Isar → Oberbayern, Germany 48°15N 11°41E 131 A3
Isarco → Italy 46°27N 11°18E 199 B8
Isaris Greece 37°22N 22°0E 204 D3
Isarog, Mt. Phil. 13°39N 123°23E 232 E4
Íscar Spain 41°22N 4°32W 194 D6
Iscayachi Bolivia 21°31S 65°3W 331 E4
İscehisar Turkey 38°51N 30°45E 205 C12
Íschia Italy 40°44N 13°57E 200 B6
Iscuandé Colombia 2°28N 77°59W 328 C2
Isdell → Australia 16°27S 124°51E 278 C3
Ise Japan 34°25N 136°45E 223 C8
Ise-Shima △ Japan 34°25N 136°48E 223 C8
Ise-Wan Japan 34°43N 136°43E 223 C8
Isefjord Denmark 55°53N 11°50E 163 J5
Isel → Austria 46°50N 12°47E 180 E5
Iseo Italy 45°39N 10°3E 198 C7
Iseo, L. d' Italy 45°43N 10°4E 198 C7
Iseramagazi Tanzania 4°37S 32°10E 268 C3
Isère □ France 45°15N 5°40E 175 C9
Isère → France 44°59N 4°51E 175 D8
Iserlohn Germany 51°22N 7°41E 178 D3
Isérnia Italy 41°36N 14°14E 201 A7
Isesaki Japan 36°19N 139°12E 223 A11
Iseyin Nigeria 8°0N 3°36E 263 D5
Isfahan = Eşfahān Iran 32°39N 51°43E 247 C6
Isfjorden Norway 62°35N 7°49E 164 B4
Ishbīlīya Iraq 33°21N 44°26E 113 A2
Ishëm Albania 41°33N 19°34E 202 E3
Ishenga Oshwe Dem. Rep. of the Congo 3°57S 22°33E 264 C4
Isherton Guyana 2°20N 59°25W 329 C6
Ishigaki Japan 24°26N 124°10E 221 M2
Ishigaki-Shima Japan 24°20N 124°10E 221 M2
Ishikari-Gawa → Japan 43°15N 141°23E 220 C10
Ishikari-Sammyaku Japan 43°30N 143°0E 220 C11
Ishikari-Wan Japan 43°25N 141°1E 220 C10
Ishikawa Japan 26°25N 127°49E 288 a
Ishikawa □ Japan 36°30N 136°30E 223 A8
Ishim Russia 56°10N 69°30E 214 D7
Ishim → Russia 57°45N 71°10E 214 D8
Ishimbay Russia 53°28N 56°2E 216 B5
Ishinomaki Japan 38°32N 141°20E 220 E10
Ishioka Japan 36°11N 140°16E 223 A12
Ishizuchi-Yama Japan 33°45N 133°6E 222 D5
Ishkashim Tajikistan 36°44N 71°37E 217 E8
Ishkuman Pakistan 36°30N 73°50E 243 A5
Ishøj Strand Denmark 55°36N 12°20E 118 B2
Ishpeming U.S.A. 46°29N 87°40W 308 B10
Ishurdi Bangla. 24°9N 89°3E 241 C2
Isiboro Sécure △ Bolivia 16°15S 65°50W 331 D4
Isigny-sur-Mer France 49°19N 1°6W 172 C5
Isıklar Dağı Turkey 40°45N 27°15E 203 F11
Işıklı Turkey 38°19N 29°51E 205 C11
Isil Kul Russia 54°55N 71°16E 217 B8
Ísili Italy 39°44N 9°6E 200 C2
Isiolo Kenya 0°24N 37°33E 268 B4
Isiro Dem. Rep. of the Congo 2°53N 27°40E 268 B2
Isisford Australia 24°15S 144°21E 280 C3
İskenderun Turkey 36°32N 36°10E 250 B7
İskenderun Körfezi Turkey 36°40N 35°50E 250 B6
İskilip Turkey 40°45N 34°29E 212 B6
Iskitim Russia 54°38N 83°18E 217 B10
Iskŭr → Bulgaria 43°45N 24°25E 203 C8
Iskŭr, Yazovir Bulgaria 42°23N 23°30E 202 D7
Iskut → Canada 56°45N 131°49W 296 B2
Isla → U.K. 56°32N 3°20W 167 E5
Isla Coiba △ Panama 7°33N 81°36W 320 E4
Isla Cristina Spain 37°13N 7°17W 195 H3
Isla Gorge △ Australia 25°10S 149°57E 280 D4
Isla Gorgona △ Colombia 2°59N 78°10W 328 C2
Isla Guamblin △ Chile 44°50S 75°4W 336 B1
Isla Isabel △ Mexico 21°54N 105°58W 318 C3
Isla Magdalena △ Chile 44°20S 73°13W 336 B2
Isla Tiburón y San Estebán ⌂ Mexico 29°0N 112°27W 318 B2
Isla Vista U.S.A. 34°25N 119°53W 307 L7
İslâhiye Turkey 37°0N 36°35E 250 B7
Islam Headworks Pakistan 29°49N 72°33E 242 E5
Islamabad Pakistan 33°40N 73°10E 242 C5
Islamgarh Pakistan 27°51N 70°48E 242 F4
Islamkot Pakistan 24°42N 70°13E 242 G4
Islamorada U.S.A. 24°56N 80°37W 317 L9
Islampur Bihar, India 25°9N 85°12E 243 G11
Islampur Maharashtra, India 17°2N 74°20E 244 F2
Island = Iceland ■ Europe 64°45N 19°0W 155 C8
Island Bay N.Z. 41°20S 174°46E 143 B1
Island Bay Phil. 9°6N 118°10E 233 G2
Island Harbour Anguilla 18°12N 63°0W 322 a
Island L. Canada 53°47N 94°25W 297 C10
Island Lagoon Australia 31°30S 136°40E 282 A2
Island Park Canada 43°37N 79°22W 141 B2
Island Pond U.S.A. 44°49N 71°53W 313 B13
Islands, B. of Nfld. & L., Canada 49°11N 58°15W 299 C8
Islands, B. of N.Z. 35°15S 174°6E 284 B3
Islay U.K. 55°46N 6°10W 167 F2
Isle → France 44°55N 0°15W 174 D3
Isle aux Morts Canada 47°35N 59°0W 299 C8
Isle of Hope U.S.A. 31°58N 81°5W 316 D8
Isle of Wight □ U.K. 50°41N 1°17W 169 G6
Isle Royale △ U.S.A. 48°0N 88°55W 308 B9
Isleton U.S.A. 38°10N 121°37W 306 G5
Islev Denmark 55°41N 12°27E 118 A2
Isleworth U.K. 51°28N 0°19W 125 B2
Islington Canada 43°38N 79°30W 141 B1
Islington □ U.K. 51°33N 0°5W 125 A3
Islote Pt. Trin. & Tob. 10°4N 61°47W 323 t
Ismail = Izmayil Ukraine 45°22N 28°46E 183 E13
Ismâ'ilîya Egypt 30°37N 32°18E 251 H3
Ismâ'ilîya □ Egypt 30°35N 32°16E 251 H3
Ismâ'ilîya, Tir'at el → Egypt 30°4N 31°16E 251 H2
Ismaning Germany 48°13N 11°40E 131 A3
Ismayloskiy Park Russia 55°46N 37°46E 129 B4
Isna Egypt 25°17N 32°30E 256 B3
Isoanala Madag. 23°50S 45°44E 272 C2
Isogstalo India 34°15N 78°46E 243 B8
Ísola del Liri Italy 41°41N 13°34E 199 G10
Ísola della Scala Italy 45°16N 11°0E 198 C7
Ísola di Capo Rizzuto Italy 38°58N 17°6E 201 D10
Isolo Nigeria 6°31N 3°19E 124 A1
İsparta Turkey 37°47N 30°30E 205 D12
İsparta □ Turkey 38°0N 31°0E 212 D4
Isperikh Bulgaria 43°43N 26°50E 203 C10
Íspica Italy 36°47N 14°55E 201 F7
Israel ■ Asia 32°0N 34°50E 251 G5
Isratu Eritrea 16°20N 39°53E 257 D4
Issakly Russia 54°8N 51°32E 190 C10
Issano Guyana 5°49N 59°26W 329 B6
Issia Ivory C. 6°33N 6°33W 262 D3
Issoire France 45°32N 3°15E 174 C7
Issoudun France 46°57N 1°59E 173 F8
Issy-les-Moulineaux France 48°49N 2°15E 134 B2
Issyk-Kul = Balykchy Kyrgyzstan 42°26N 76°12E 217 D9
Issyk-Kul, Ozero = Ysyk-Köl Kyrgyzstan 42°25N 77°15E 217 D9
Ist Croatia 44°17N 14°47E 199 D11
Istaihah U.A.E. 23°19N 54°4E 249 B6
Istállós-kő Hungary 48°4N 20°26E 182 B5
İstanbul Turkey 41°0N 28°58E 122 C1
İstanbul □ Turkey 41°0N 29°0E 203 E12
İstanbul ✈ (IST) Turkey 40°59N 28°49E 203 F12
İstanbul Boğazı Turkey 41°5N 29°3E 122 B2
Isteren Norway 61°58N 11°47E 164 B8
Istiea Greece 38°57N 23°9E 204 C5
Istinye Turkey 41°6N 29°3E 122 B2
Istmina Colombia 5°10N 76°39W 328 B2
Isto, Mt. U.S.A. 69°12N 143°48W 303 B12
Istok Serbia 42°45N 20°24E 202 D4
Istokpoga, L. U.S.A. 27°23N 81°17W 317 H8
Istra Croatia 45°10N 14°0E 199 C10
Istres France 43°31N 4°59E 175 E8
Istria = Istra Croatia 45°10N 14°0E 199 C10
Isugod Phil. 9°19N 118°5E 233 G2
Isulan Phil. 6°30N 124°29E 233 H5
Itá Paraguay 25°29S 57°21W 334 B4
Itä Hakkila Finland 60°17N 25°7E 121 B3
Itabaiana Paraíba, Brazil 7°18S 35°19W 332 C4
Itabaiana Sergipe, Brazil 10°41S 37°37W 332 D4
Itabaianinha Brazil 11°16S 37°47W 332 D4
Itaberaba Brazil 12°32S 40°18W 333 D3
Itaberaí Brazil 16°2S 49°48W 333 E2
Itabira Brazil 19°37S 43°13W 333 E3
Itabirito Brazil 20°15S 43°48W 333 F3
Itaboca Brazil 4°50S 62°40W 329 D5
Itabuna Brazil 14°48S 39°16W 333 D4
Itacajá Brazil 8°19S 47°46W 332 C2
Itacaunas → Brazil 5°21S 49°8W 332 C2
Itacuaí → Brazil 4°20S 70°12W 330 A3
Itaewon S. Korea 37°32N 126°58E 137 B1
Itaguaçu Brazil 19°48S 40°51W 333 E3
Itaguari → Brazil 14°11S 44°40W 333 D3
Itaguatins Brazil 5°47S 47°29W 332 C2
Itaim → Brazil 7°2S 42°2W 332 C3
Itainópolis Brazil 7°24S 41°31W 332 C3
Itaipú, Represa de Brazil 25°30S 54°30W 335 B5
Itaituba Brazil 4°10S 55°50W 329 D6
Itajaí Brazil 27°50S 48°39W 335 B6
Itajany do Sul = Rio do Sul Brazil 27°13S 49°37W 335 B6
Itajubá Brazil 22°24S 45°30W 333 F2
Itajuípe Brazil 14°41S 39°22W 333 D4
Itaka Tanzania 8°50S 32°49E 269 D3
Itako Japan 35°56N 140°33E 223 B12
Itala ⌂ S. Africa 27°30S 31°7E 271 C5
Italy ■ Europe 42°0N 13°0E 192 C6
Itamaraju Brazil 17°4S 39°32W 333 E4
Itamarati Brazil 6°24S 68°15W 330 B4
Itamataré Brazil 2°16S 46°24W 332 B2
Itambacuri Brazil 18°1S 41°42W 333 E3
Itambé Brazil 15°15S 40°37W 333 E3
Itami Japan 34°46N 135°24E 133 A1
Itampolo Madag. 24°41S 43°57E 272 C1
Itanagar India 27°6N 93°37E 241 B4
Itandrano Madag. 21°47S 45°17E 272 C2
Itanhaém Brazil 24°11S 46°47W 333 F2
Itanhanga Brazil 22°59S 43°19W 135 B1
Itanhauã → Brazil 4°45S 63°48W 329 D5
Itanhém Brazil 17°9S 40°20W 333 E3
Itano Japan 34°7N 134°28E 222 C6
Itapaci Brazil 14°57S 49°34W 333 D2
Itapagé Brazil 3°41S 39°34W 332 B4
Itaparica = Petrolândia Brazil 9°5S 38°20W 332 C4
Itaparica, I. de Brazil 12°54S 38°42W 333 D4
Itapebi Brazil 15°56S 39°32W 333 E4
Itapecuru-Mirim Brazil 3°24S 44°20W 332 B3
Itaperuna Brazil 21°10S 41°54W 333 F3
Itapetinga Brazil 15°15S 40°15W 333 E3
Itapetininga Brazil 23°36S 48°7W 335 A6
Itapeva Brazil 23°59S 48°59W 335 A6
Itapicuru → Bahia, Brazil 11°47S 37°32W 332 D4
Itapicuru → Maranhão, Brazil 2°52S 44°12W 332 B3
Itapinima Brazil 5°25S 60°44W 331 B5
Itapipoca Brazil 3°30S 39°35W 332 B4
Itapira = Ubaitaba Brazil 14°18S 39°20W 333 D4
Itapiranga Brazil 2°45S 58°1W 329 D6
Itapiúna Brazil 4°33S 38°57W 332 B4
Itaporanga Paraíba, Brazil 7°18S 38°0W 332 C4
Itaporanga São Paulo, Brazil 23°42S 49°29W 333 F2
Itapuá □ Paraguay 26°40S 55°40W 335 B4
Itapuranga Brazil 15°40S 49°59W 333 E2
Itaquari Brazil 20°20S 40°25W 333 F3
Itaquatiara Brazil 2°58S 58°30W 329 D6
Itaquí Brazil 29°8S 56°30W 334 B4
Itararé Brazil 24°6S 49°23W 335 A6
Itarsi India 22°36N 77°51E 242 H7
Itarumã Brazil 18°42S 51°25W 333 E1
Itatí Argentina 27°16S 58°15W 334 B4
Itatiaia △ Brazil 22°22S 44°38W 335 A7
Itatira Brazil 4°30S 39°37W 332 B4
Itatuba Brazil 5°46S 63°20W 331 B5
Itatupa Brazil 0°37S 51°12W 329 D7
Itaueira Brazil 7°36S 43°2W 332 C3
Itaueira → Brazil 6°41S 42°55W 332 C3
Itaúna Brazil 20°4S 44°34W 333 F3
Itbayat Phil. 20°47N 121°51E 232 A3
Itbayat I. Phil. 20°45N 121°50E 232 A3
Itchen → U.K. 50°55N 1°22W 169 G6
Itchouma Niger 20°14N 13°32E 261 D7
Ite Peru 17°55S 70°57W 330 D3
Itea Greece 38°25N 22°25E 204 C4
Itezhi Tezhi, L. Zambia 15°30S 25°30E 269 F2
Ithaca = Ithaki Greece 38°25N 20°40E 207 C2
Ithaca U.S.A. 42°27N 76°30W 313 D8
Ithaki Greece 38°25N 20°40E 207 C2
Ithakis, Stenon Greece 38°22N 20°39E 207 C2
Iti △ Greece 38°50N 22°15E 204 C4
Itinga Brazil 16°36S 41°47W 333 E3
Itiquira Brazil 17°12S 54°7W 331 D7
Itiquira → Brazil 17°18S 56°44W 331 D6
Itiruçu Brazil 13°31S 40°9W 333 D3
Itiúba Brazil 10°43S 39°51W 332 D4
Itkilik → U.S.A. 70°9N 150°56W 303 A10
Itō Japan 34°58N 139°5E 223 C11
Itogon Phil. 16°22N 120°41E 232 C3
Itoigawa Japan 37°2N 137°51E 221 F8
Itoko Dem. Rep. of the Congo 1°0S 21°48E 264 C4
Itoman Japan 26°7N 127°40E 288 a
Iton → France 49°9N 1°12E 172 C8
Itonamas → Bolivia 12°28S 64°24W 331 C5
Itri Italy 41°17N 13°32E 200 A6
Itsa Egypt 29°15N 30°47E 256 J7
Itsamia Comoros Is. 12°21S 43°52E 272 a
Itsandra Comoros Is. 11°40S 43°15E 272 a
Itsuki Japan 32°24N 130°50E 222 E2
Íttiri Italy 40°36N 8°34E 200 B1
Ittoqqortoormiit Greenland 70°20N 23°0W 154 C8
Itu Brazil 23°17S 47°15W 335 A6
Itu Nigeria 5°10N 7°58E 263 D6
Itu Aba I. S. China Sea 10°23N 114°21E 230 B4
Ituaçu Brazil 13°50S 41°18W 333 D3
Ituango Colombia 7°4N 75°45W 328 B2
Ituí → Brazil 4°38S 70°19W 328 D3
Ituiutaba Brazil 19°0S 49°25W 333 E2
Itumbiara Brazil 18°20S 49°10W 333 E2
Ituna Canada 51°10N 103°24W 297 C8
Itunge Port Tanzania 9°40S 33°55E 269 D3
Ituni Guyana 5°28N 58°15W 329 B6
Itupiranga Brazil 5°9S 49°20W 332 C2
Iturama Brazil 19°44S 50°11W 333 E1
Iturbe Argentina 23°0S 65°25W 334 A2
Ituri → Dem. Rep. of the Congo 1°40N 27°1E 268 B2
Iturup, Ostrov Russia 45°0N 148°0E 215 E15
Ituverava Brazil 20°20S 47°47W 333 F2
Ituxi → Brazil 7°18S 64°51W 331 B5
Ituyuro → Argentina 22°40S 63°50W 334 A3
Itzehoe Germany 53°55N 9°31E 178 B5
Iuka U.S.A. 38°37N 88°47W 311 F8
Iungsdalshytta Norway 60°49N 7°55E 164 D4
Ivahona Madag. 23°27S 46°10E 272 C2
Ivaí → Brazil 23°18S 53°42W 335 A5
Ivalo Finland 68°38N 27°35E 160 B22
Ivalojoki → Finland 68°40N 27°40E 160 B22
Ivanava Belarus 52°7N 25°29E 177 B13
Ivančice Czech Rep. 49°6N 16°23E 181 B9
Ivane-Puste Ukraine 48°39N 26°10E 183 B11
Ivăneşti Romania 46°39N 27°27E 183 D12
Ivangorod = Dęblin Poland 51°34N 21°50E 185 G8
Ivangorod Russia 59°27N 28°13E 188 C5
Ivanhoe N.S.W., Australia 32°56S 144°20E 282 B6
Ivanhoe Vic., Australia 37°45S 145°3E 128 A2
Ivanhoe Calif., U.S.A. 36°23N 119°13W 306 J7
Ivanhoe Minn., U.S.A. 44°28N 96°15W 308 C5
Ivanhorod Ukraine 48°48N 29°50E 183 B14
Ivanić Grad Croatia 45°41N 16°25E 199 C13
Ivanjica Serbia 43°35N 20°12E 202 C4
Ivanjska Bos.-H. 44°55N 17°4E 182 F2
Ivankoyskoye Vdkhr. Russia 56°37N 36°32E 188 D9
Ivano-Frankivsk Ukraine 48°40N 24°40E 183 B9
Ivano-Frankivsk □ Ukraine 48°45N 24°30E 183 B9
Ivanof Bay U.S.A. 55°54N 159°29W 303 J8
Ivanovo = Ivanava Belarus 52°7N 25°29E 177 B13
Ivanovo Russia 57°5N 41°0E 188 D11
Ivanovo □ Russia 57°10N 41°50E 190 B5
Ivanšćica Croatia 46°12N 16°13E 199 B13
Ivashchenkovo = Chapayevsk Russia 53°0N 49°40E 190 D9
Ivato Madag. 20°37S 47°10E 272 C2
Ivatsevichy Belarus 52°43N 25°21E 177 B13
Ivaylovgrad Bulgaria 41°32N 26°8E 203 E10
Ivdel Russia 60°42N 60°24E 186 B11
Ivgres = Komsomolsk Russia 57°2N 40°20E 188 D11
Ivindo → Gabon 0°9S 12°9E 264 C2
Ivinheima → Brazil 23°14S 53°42W 335 A5
Ivinhema Brazil 22°10S 53°37W 335 A5
Ivittuut Greenland 61°14N 48°12W 154 E6
Iviza = Eivissa Spain 38°54N 1°26E 206 D1
Ivohibe Madag. 22°31S 46°57E 272 C2
Ivolândia Brazil 16°34S 50°51W 333 E1
Ivory Coast W. Afr. 4°20N 5°0W 262 E4
Ivory Coast ■ Africa 7°30N 5°0W 262 D4
Ivösjön Sweden 56°8N 14°25E 163 H8
Ivrea Italy 45°28N 7°52E 198 C4
İvrindi Turkey 39°34N 27°30E 205 B9
Ivry-sur-Seine France 48°49N 2°22E 134 B3
Ivujivik Canada 62°24N 77°55W 295 C12
Ivybridge U.K. 50°23N 3°56W 169 G4
Iwai-Jima Japan 33°47N 131°58E 222 D3
Iwaizumi Japan 39°50N 141°45E 220 E10
Iwaki Japan 37°3N 140°55E 221 F10
Iwakuni Japan 34°15N 132°8E 222 C4
Iwami Japan 35°32N 134°15E 222 B6
Iwamizawa Japan 43°12N 141°46E 220 C10
Iwanai Japan 42°58N 140°30E 220 C10
Iwase Japan 36°21N 140°6E 223 A12
Iwata Japan 34°42N 137°51E 223 C9
Iwate □ Japan 39°30N 141°30E 220 E10
Iwate-San Japan 39°51N 141°0E 220 E10
Iwo Nigeria 7°39N 4°9E 263 D5
Iwo Jima Pac. Oc. 24°47N 141°20E 288 b
Iwŏn N. Korea 40°19N 128°39E 224 B4
Iwonicz-Zdrój Poland 49°37N 21°47E 185 J8
Iwungu Dem. Rep. of the Congo 5°16S 19°17E 265 D3
Ixelles Belgium 50°50N 4°22E 116 B2
Ixiamas Bolivia 13°50S 68°5W 330 C4
Ixopo S. Africa 30°11S 30°5E 271 D5
Ixtepec Mexico 16°34N 95°6W 319 D5
Ixtlán del Río Mexico 21°2N 104°22W 318 C4
'Iyādh Yemen 14°59N 46°51E 248 D4
Iyal Bakhit Sudan 13°20N 28°39E 257 E2
Iyo Japan 33°45N 132°45E 222 D4
Iyo-Mishima Japan 33°58N 133°30E 222 D5
Iyo-Nada Japan 33°40N 132°20E 222 D4
Izabal, L. de Guatemala 15°30N 89°10W 320 C2
Izamal Mexico 20°56N 89°1W 319 C7
Izberbash Russia 42°35N 47°52E 191 J8
Izbica Poland 50°53N 23°10E 185 H10
Izbica Kujawska Poland 52°25N 18°40E 185 F5
Izbiceni Romania 43°45N 24°40E 183 G9
Izembek Nat. Wildlife Refuge ⌂ U.S.A. 55°15N 162°45W 303 J7
Izena-Shima Japan 26°56N 127°56E 221 L3
Izgrev Bulgaria 43°36N 26°58E 203 C10
Izhevsk Russia 56°51N 53°14E 186 C9
Izhma = Sosnogorsk Russia 63°37N 53°51E 186 B9
Izhma → Russia 65°19N 52°54E 186 A9
Izileg Algeria 20°20N 6°4E 261 D6
Izkī Oman 22°56N 57°46E 249 B7
Izmayil Ukraine 45°22N 28°46E 183 E13
Izmaylovo Russia 55°47N 37°47E 129 B4
İzmir Turkey 38°25N 27°8E 205 C9
İzmir □ Turkey 38°15N 27°40E 205 C9
İzmir Adnan Menderes ✈ (ADB) Turkey 38°23N 27°6E 205 C9
İzmir Körfezi Turkey 38°30N 26°50E 205 C8
İzmit = Kocaeli Turkey 40°45N 29°50E 203 F13
Iznájar Spain 37°15N 4°19W 195 H6
Iznalloz Spain 37°24N 3°30W 195 H7
İznik Turkey 40°23N 29°46E 212 B3
İznik Gölü Turkey 40°27N 29°30E 203 F13
Izobilno-Tishchenskoye = Izobil'nyy Russia 45°25N 41°44E 191 H5
Izobil'nyy Russia 45°25N 41°44E 191 H5
Izola Slovenia 45°32N 13°39E 199 C10
Izozog, Bañados de Bolivia 18°48S 62°10W 331 D5
Izra Syria 32°51N 36°15E 250 F7
Iztacalco Mexico 19°23N 99°5W 128 B2
Iztapalapa Mexico 19°21N 99°6W 128 B2
Iztochni Rodopi Bulgaria 41°45N 25°30E 203 E9
Izu-Hantō Japan 34°45N 139°0E 223 C11
Izu-Shotō Japan 34°30N 140°0E 221 G10
Izúcar de Matamoros Mexico 18°36N 98°28W 319 D5
Izuhara Japan 34°12N 129°17E 222 C1
Izumi Kagoshima, Japan 32°5N 130°22E 222 E2
Izumi Ōsaka, Japan 34°28N 135°24E 223 C7
Izumi-Sano Japan 34°23N 135°18E 223 C7
Izumo Japan 35°20N 132°46E 222 B4
Izyaslav Ukraine 50°5N 26°50E 177 C14
Izyum Ukraine 49°12N 37°19E 189 H9

J

J.F.K. Int. ✈ (JFK) U.S.A. 40°38N 73°47W 313 F11
J.F. Rodrigues Brazil 2°55S 50°20W 332 B1
J.P. Koch Fjord Greenland 82°45N 44°0W 154 A6
J. Strom Thurmond L. U.S.A. 33°40N 82°12W 316 B7
Ja-ela Sri Lanka 7°5N 79°53E 245 L4
Ja-eundo S. Korea 34°53N 126°2E 224 E3
Jaba Ethiopia 6°20N 35°7E 257 F4
Jaba West Bank 31°51N 35°16E 123 A2
Jabal al Awliya' Sudan 15°14N 32°29E 266 A3
Jabal at Ţā'ir Red Sea 15°35N 41°52E 257 D5
Jabalón → Spain 38°53N 4°5W 195 G6
Jabalpur India 23°9N 79°58E 243 H8
Jabbūl Syria 36°4N 37°30E 246 B3
Jabiru Australia 12°40S 132°53E 278 B5
Jablah Syria 35°20N 36°0E 250 C7
Jablanac Croatia 44°42N 14°56E 199 D11
Jablanica Bos.-H. 43°40N 17°45E 182 G2
Jablonec nad Nisou Czech Rep. 50°43N 15°10E 180 A8
Jablonica Slovak Rep. 48°37N 17°26E 181 C10
Jabłonowo Pomorskie Poland 53°23N 19°10E 184 E6
Jablunkov Czech Rep. 49°35N 18°46E 181 B11
Jaboatão Brazil 8°7S 35°1W 332 C4
Jabonga Phil. 9°20N 125°32E 233 G5
Jaboticabal Brazil 21°15S 48°17W 335 A6
Jabukovac Serbia 44°22N 22°21E 202 B6
Jaburu Brazil 5°30S 64°0W 331 B5
Jaca Spain 42°35N 0°33W 196 C4
Jacaré Brazil 22°53S 43°14W 135 B1
Jacaré → Brazil 10°3S 42°13W 332 D3
Jacareí Brazil 23°20S 46°0W 335 A6
Jacarèzinho Brazil 23°5S 49°58W 335 A6
Jaciara Brazil 15°59S 54°57W 331 D7
Jacinto Brazil 16°10S 40°17W 333 E3
Jaciparaná Brazil 9°15S 64°23W 331 B5
Jackman U.S.A. 45°37N 70°15W 309 C18
Jacksboro U.S.A. 33°13N 98°10W 314 E5
Jackson Barbados 13°7N 59°36W 323 r
Jackson Ala., U.S.A. 31°31N 87°53W 315 F11
Jackson Calif., U.S.A. 38°21N 120°46W 306 G6
Jackson Ga., U.S.A. 33°20N 83°57W 316 B6
Jackson Ky., U.S.A. 37°33N 83°23W 309 G12
Jackson Mich., U.S.A. 42°15N 84°24W 311 B12
Jackson Minn., U.S.A. 43°37N 95°1W 308 D6
Jackson Miss., U.S.A. 32°18N 90°12W 315 E9
Jackson Mo., U.S.A. 37°23N 89°40W 308 G9
Jackson N.H., U.S.A. 44°10N 71°11W 313 B13
Jackson Ohio, U.S.A. 39°3N 82°39W 309 F12
Jackson S.C., U.S.A. 33°20N 81°47W 316 B8
Jackson Tenn., U.S.A. 35°37N 88°49W 315 D10
Jackson Wyo., U.S.A. 43°29N 110°46W 304 E8
Jackson, C. N.Z. 40°59S 174°20E 285 A9
Jackson B. N.Z. 43°58S 168°42E 285 D3
Jackson Center U.S.A. 40°27N 84°4W 311 D12
Jackson Hd. N.Z. 43°58S 168°37E 285 D3
Jackson Heights U.S.A. 40°44N 73°53W 132 B2
Jackson L. Fla., U.S.A. 30°30N 84°17W 316 E5
Jackson L. Ga., U.S.A. 33°19N 83°50W 316 B6
Jackson L. Wyo., U.S.A. 43°52N 110°36W 304 E8
Jackson Park U.S.A. 41°46N 87°34W 119 C3
Jacksons N.Z. 42°46S 171°32E 285 C6
Jackson's Arm Canada 49°52N 56°47W 299 C8
Jacksonville Ala., U.S.A. 33°49N 85°46W 316 B4
Jacksonville Ark., U.S.A. 34°52N 92°7W 314 D8
Jacksonville Calif., U.S.A. 37°52N 120°24W 306 H6
Jacksonville Fla., U.S.A. 30°20N 81°39W 316 E8
Jacksonville Ga., U.S.A. 31°49N 82°59W 316 D7
Jacksonville Ill., U.S.A. 39°44N 90°14W 310 E6
Jacksonville N.C., U.S.A. 34°45N 77°26W 315 D16
Jacksonville Tex., U.S.A. 31°58N 95°17W 314 F7
Jacksonville Beach U.S.A. 30°17N 81°24W 316 E8
Jacksonville Int. ✈ (JAX) U.S.A. 30°30N 81°41W 316 E8
Jacmel Haiti 18°14N 72°32W 321 C5
Jaco, Pte. Dominica 15°39N 61°24W 323 k
Jacob Lake U.S.A. 36°43N 112°13W 305 H7
Jacobabad Pakistan 28°20N 68°29E 242 E3
Jacobina Brazil 11°11S 40°30W 332 D3
Jacobshagen = Dobrzany Poland 53°22N 15°25E 184 E2
Jacon Javits Convention Center New York, U.S.A. 132 c1
Jacotet, B. Mauritius 20°30S 57°26E 272 e
Jacqueline Kennedy Onassis Res. New York, U.S.A. 132 a3
Jacques-Cartier Canada 45°31N 73°27W 130 A3
Jacques-Cartier, Dét. de Canada 50°0N 63°30W 299 C7
Jacques-Cartier, Mt. Canada 48°57N 66°0W 299 C6
Jacques-Cartier, Pont Canada 45°31N 73°32W 130 A2
Jacques-Cartier ⌂ Canada 47°15N 71°33W 299 C5
Jacqueville Ivory C. 5°12N 4°25W 262 D4
Jacuí → Brazil 30°2S 51°15W 335 C5
Jacumba U.S.A. 32°37N 116°11W 307 N10
Jacundá → Brazil 1°57S 50°26W 332 B1
Jadavpur India 22°28N 88°22E 124 C2
Jadcherla India 16°46N 78°9E 244 F4
Jade Germany 53°20N 8°14E 178 B4
Jade Buddha Temple China 31°15N 121°25E 138 B1
Jade Mt. = Yü Shan Taiwan 23°25N 120°52E 225 C2
Jadebusen Germany 53°29N 8°12E 178 B4
Jadotville = Likasi Dem. Rep. of the Congo 10°55S 26°48E 269 E2
Jadovnik Serbia 43°20N 19°45E 202 C3
Jadraque Spain 40°55N 2°55W 196 E2
Jādū Libya 32°0N 12°0E 258 B2
Jægersborg Denmark 55°45N 12°31E 118 A3
Jægersborg Dyrehave Denmark 55°46N 12°33E 118 A3
Jaén Peru 5°25S 78°40W 330 B2
Jaén Spain 37°44N 3°43W 195 H7
Jaén □ Spain 37°50N 3°30W 195 H7
Jæren Norway 58°42N 5°47E 164 F2
Jærens Rev Norway 58°45N 5°45E 164 F2
Jafarabad India 20°52N 71°22E 242 J4
Jaffa = Tel Aviv-Yafo Israel 32°4N 34°48E 251 F5
Jaffa, C. Australia 36°58S 139°40E 282 D3
Jaffna Sri Lanka 9°45N 80°2E 245 K5
Jaffray Canada 49°47N 94°26W 297 D10
Jaffrey U.S.A. 42°49N 72°2W 313 D12
Jagadhri India 30°10N 77°20E 242 D7
Jagadishpur Bihar, India 25°30N 84°21E 243 G11
Jagadishpur W. Bengal, India 22°39N 88°17E 124 B1
Jagatpur India 28°44N 77°13E 120 A2
Jagdalpur India 19°3N 82°0E 244 E6
Jagersfontein S. Africa 29°44S 25°27E 270 C4
Jaghīn → Iran 27°17N 57°13E 247 E8
Jagna Phil. 9°39N 124°22E 233 G5
Jagodina Serbia 44°5N 21°15E 202 B5
Jagraon India 30°50N 75°25E 242 D6
Jagst → Germany 49°14N 9°10E 179 F5
Jagtial India 18°50N 79°0E 244 E4
Jaguaquara Brazil 13°32S 39°58W 333 D4
Jaguaré, Rib. do → Brazil 23°32S 46°45W 137 B1
Jaguariaíva Brazil 24°10S 49°50W 335 A6
Jaguaribe Brazil 5°53S 38°37W 332 C4
Jaguaribe → Brazil 4°25S 37°45W 332 B4
Jaguaruana Brazil 4°50S 37°47W 332 B4
Jagüey Grande Cuba 22°35N 81°7W 320 B3
Jagungal, Mt. Australia 36°8S 148°22E 283 D8
Jahanabad India 25°13N 84°59E 243 G11
Jahangirpur India 28°43N 77°12E 120 A2
Jahazpur India 25°37N 75°17E 242 G6
Jahrom Iran 28°30N 53°31E 247 D7
Jaicós Brazil 7°21S 41°8W 332 C3
Jaigarh India 17°17N 73°13E 244 F1
Jaijon India 31°21N 76°9E 242 D7
Jailolo Indonesia 1°5N 127°30E 231 D7
Jailolo, Selat Indonesia 0°5N 129°5E 231 D7
Jaintiapur Bangla. 25°8N 92°7E 241 C4
Jaipur Assam, India 27°16N 95°24E 241 B5
Jaipur Raj., India 27°0N 75°50E 242 F6
Jais India 26°15N 81°32E 243 F9
Jaisalmer India 26°55N 70°54E 242 F4
Jaisinghnagar India 23°38N 78°34E 243 H8
Jaitaran India 26°12N 73°56E 242 F5
Jaithari India 23°14N 78°37E 243 H8
Jājarm Iran 36°58N 56°27E 247 B8
Jajce Bos.-H. 44°19N 17°17E 182 F2
Jajpur India 20°53N 86°22E 244 D8
Jakam → India 23°54N 74°13E 242 H6
Jakar Dzong Bhutan 27°33N 90°43E 241 B3
Jakarta Indonesia 6°9S 106°52E 122 A2
Jakarta, Teluk Indonesia 6°5S 106°50E 122 A1
Jakarta Halim Perdana Kusuma Int. ✈ (HLP) Indonesia 6°16S 106°53E 122 B2
Jakhal India 29°48N 75°50E 242 E6
Jakhau India 23°13N 68°43E 242 H3
Jakobshavn = Illulissat Greenland 69°12N 51°10W 154 D5
Jakobstad = Pietarsaari Finland 63°40N 22°43E 160 E20
Jakupica Macedonia 41°45N 21°22E 202 E5
Jal U.S.A. 32°7N 103°12W 305 K12
Jalaihai Pt. Guam 13°18N 144°46E 302 d
Jalal-Abad Kyrgyzstan 40°56N 73°0E 217 D8
Jalal-Abad □ Kyrgyzstan 41°30N 72°30E 217 D8
Jalālābād Afghan. 34°30N 70°29E 242 B4
Jalalabad India 27°41N 79°42E 243 F8
Jalalpur Jattan Pakistan 32°38N 74°11E 242 C6
Jalama U.S.A. 34°29N 120°29W 307 L6
Jalan Kayu Singapore 1°24N 103°52E 138 A3
Jalapa Guatemala 14°39N 89°59W 320 D2
Jalapa Enríquez = Xalapa Mexico 19°32N 96°55W 319 D5
Jalasjärvi Finland 62°29N 22°47E 160 E20
Jalaun India 26°8N 79°25E 243 F8
Jalāzīn Afghan. 37°2N 64°49E 240 A2
Jaldak Afghan. 31°58N 66°43E 240 C2
Jaldhaka → Bangla. 26°16N 89°16E 241 B2
Jales Brazil 20°10S 50°33W 333 F1
Jalesar India 27°29N 78°19E 242 F8
Jaleswar Nepal 26°38N 85°48E 243 F11
Jalgaon India 21°0N 75°42E 244 D2
Jalībah Iraq 30°35N 46°32E 246 D5
Jalingo Nigeria 8°55N 11°25E 263 D7
Jalisco □ Mexico 20°20N 103°40W 318 D4
Jalkot Pakistan 35°14N 73°24E 243 B5
Jallas → Spain 42°54N 9°8W 194 C1
Jalna India 19°48N 75°38E 244 E2
Jalón → Spain 41°47N 1°4W 196 D3
Jalor India 25°21N 72°37E 242 G5
Jalpa Mexico 21°38N 102°58W 318 C4
Jalpaiguri India 26°32N 88°46E 241 B2
Jalpan Mexico 21°14N 99°29W 319 C5
Jālq Iran 27°35N 62°46E 240 D1
Jālū Libya 29°2N 21°33E 258 C4
Jaluit I. Marshall Is. 6°0N 169°30E 288 G8
Jalūlā Iraq 34°16N 45°10E 213 E11
Jamaane = Giamama Somali Rep. 0°4N 42°44E 267 D5
Jamaari Nigeria 11°44N 9°53E 263 C6
Jamaica ■ W. Indies 18°10N 77°30W 293 H12
Jamaica B. U.S.A. 40°36N 73°50W 132 C3
Jamaica Channel Jamaica 17°0N 76°0W 321 C4
Jamaica Plain U.S.A. 42°18N 71°6W 116 B2
Jamakpuri India 28°37N 77°5E 120 B1
Jamalpur Bangla. 24°52N 89°56E 241 C2
Jamalpur India 25°18N 86°28E 243 G12
Jamalpurganj India 23°2N 87°59E 243 H13
Jamanota Aruba 12°29N 69°57W 322 f
Jamanxim → Brazil 4°43S 56°18W 331 A6
Jamari Brazil 8°45S 63°27W 331 B5
Jamari → Brazil 8°27S 63°30W 331 B5
Jamba Angola 14°40S 16°2E 265 E3
Jambewangi Indonesia 8°17S 114°7E 231 J17
Jambi Indonesia 1°38S 103°30E 234 C2
Jambi □ Indonesia 1°30S 102°30E 234 C2
Jambongan, Pulau Malaysia 6°45N 117°20E 235 A5
Jambusar India 22°3N 72°51E 242 H5
James U.S.A. 32°58N 83°29W 316 C6
James → S. Dak., U.S.A. 42°52N 97°18W 308 D5
James → Va., U.S.A. 36°56N 76°27W 309 G15
James, I. = San Salvador, I. Ecuador 0°16S 90°42W 330 a
James B. Canada 54°0N 80°0W 298 B3
James Island U.S.A. 32°45N 79°55W 316 C10
James Ranges Australia 24°10S 132°30E 278 D5
James Ross I. Antarctica 63°58S 57°50W 151 C18
Jamesabad Pakistan 25°17N 69°15E 242 G3
Jameson Land Greenland 71°0N 23°30W 154 C8
Jamesport U.S.A. 39°58N 93°48W 310 E3
Jamestown = Wawa Canada 47°59N 84°47W 298 C3
Jamestown S. Austral., Australia 33°10S 138°32E 282 B3
Jamestown St. Helena 15°55S 5°43W 153 h
Jamestown Eastern Cape, S. Africa 31°6S 26°45E 270 D4
Jamestown Ind., U.S.A. 39°56N 86°38W 311 E10
Jamestown Mo., U.S.A. 38°48N 92°30W 310 F4
Jamestown N. Dak., U.S.A. 46°54N 98°42W 308 B4
Jamestown N.Y., U.S.A. 42°6N 79°14W 312 D5
Jamestown Ohio, U.S.A. 39°39N 83°33W 311 E13
Jamestown Pa., U.S.A. 41°29N 80°27W 312 E4
Jamestown S.C., U.S.A. 33°17N 79°42W 316 B10
Jamīlābād Iran 34°24N 48°28E 247 C6
Jamira → India 21°35N 88°28E 243 J13
Jämjö Sweden 56°12N 15°49E 163 H9
Jamkhandi India 16°30N 75°15E 244 F2
Jamkhed India 18°43N 75°19E 244 E2
Jammalamadugu India 14°51N 78°25E 245 G4
Jammerbugten Denmark 57°15N 9°20E 163 G3
Jammu India 32°43N 74°54E 242 C6
Jammu & Kashmir □ India 34°25N 77°0E 243 B7

Jamnagar India 22°30N 70°6E 242 H4
Jamner India 20°45N 75°52E 244 D2
Jamni → India 25°13N 78°35E 243 G8
Jampur Pakistan 29°39N 70°40E 242 E4
Jamrud Pakistan 33°59N 71°24E 242 C4
Jämsä Finland 61°53N 25°10E 188 B3
Jamshedpur India 22°44N 86°12E 243 H12
Jamshīdīyeh Iran 35°42N 51°22E 141 A2
Jamsil S. Korea 37°30N 127°4E 137 B2
Jamtara India 23°59N 86°49E 243 H12
Jämtland Sweden 63°31N 14°0E 160 E16
Jämtlands län □ Sweden 63°0N 14°40E 162 B7
Jamuna → Bangla. 23°51N 89°45E 241 D2
Jamunamukh India 26°6N 92°44E 241 B4
Jamurki Bangla. 24°9N 90°2E 241 C3
Jamwon S. Korea 37°30N 127°0E 137 B2
Jan L. Canada 54°56N 102°55W 297 C8
Jan Mayen Arctic 71°0N 9°0W 150 B7
Janakkala Finland 60°54N 24°36E 188 B3
Janaúba Brazil 15°48S 43°19W 333 E3
Janaucu, I. Brazil 0°30N 50°10W 332 A1
Jand Pakistan 33°30N 72°6E 242 C5
Jandaia Brazil 17°6S 50°7W 333 E1
Jandaq Iran 34°3N 54°22E 247 C7
Jandia Canary Is. 28°6N 14°21W 153 e2
Jandia, Pta. de Canary Is. 28°3N 14°31W 153 e2
Jandia △ Canary Is. 28°4N 14°19W 153 e2
Jandiatuba → Brazil 3°28S 68°42W 328 D4
Jandola Pakistan 32°20N 70°9E 242 C4
Jandowae Australia 26°45S 151°7E 281 D5
Jándula → Spain 38°3N 4°6W 195 G6
Jane Pk. N.Z. 45°15S 168°20E 285 F3
Janesville U.S.A. 42°41N 89°1W 310 B7
Janga Ghana 10°5N 1°0W 263 C4
Jangamo Mozam. 24°6S 35°21E 271 B6
Janghai India 25°33N 82°19E 243 G10
Jangheung S. Korea 34°41N 126°52E 224 E3
Janghowon S. Korea 37°7N 127°37E 224 D3
Jango Brazil 20°27S 55°29W 331 E6
Jangoon India 17°44N 79°5E 244 F4
Jangsu S. Korea 35°38N 127°31E 224 E3
Janhtang Ga Burma 26°32N 96°38E 241 B6
Jani Khel Afghan. 32°46N 68°24E 240 B3
Janikowo Poland 52°45N 18°7E 185 F5
Janin, Sabkhat al Libya 30°10N 21°0E 258 B3
Janinà = Ioannina □ Greece 39°39N 20°57E 204 B2
Janiuay Phil. 10°58N 122°30E 233 F4
Janja Bos.-H. 44°40N 19°14E 182 F4
Janjanbureh Gambia 13°30N 14°47W 262 C2
Janjevo Serbia 42°35N 21°19E 202 D5
Janjgir India 22°1N 82°34E 243 J10
Janjina Croatia 42°58N 17°25E 199 F14
Janjina Madag. 20°30S 45°50E 272 C2
Jankau = Janikowo Poland 52°45N 18°7E 185 F5
Janki Poland 52°8N 20°52E 142 C1
Jannali Australia 34°0S 151°4E 139 C1
Janos Mexico 30°54N 108°10W 318 A3
Jánoshalma Hungary 46°18N 19°21E 182 D4
Jánosháza Hungary 47°8N 17°12E 182 C2
Jánossomorja Hungary 47°47N 17°11E 182 C2
Janów Poland 50°44N 19°27E 185 H6
Janów Lubelski Poland 50°48N 22°23E 185 H9
Janów Podlaski Poland 52°11N 23°11E 185 F10
Janowiec Wielkopolski Poland 52°45N 17°30E 185 F4
Januária Brazil 15°25S 44°25W 333 E3
Janub △ Sudan 6°50N 28°45E 257 F2
Janub Dārfūr □ Sudan 11°0N 25°0E 257 E2
Janub Kordofān □ Sudan 12°0N 30°0E 257 E3
Janūb Sīnī □ Egypt 29°30N 33°50E 251 J4
Janubio Canary Is. 28°56N 13°50W 153 e2
Janville France 48°10N 1°50E 173 D8
Janwada India 18°0N 77°29E 244 E3
Janzé France 47°55N 1°28W 172 E5
Jaora India 23°40N 75°10E 242 H6
Japan ■ Asia 36°0N 136°0E 221 G8
Japan, Sea of Asia 40°0N 135°0E 220 E7
Japan Center San Francisco, U.S.A. 136 b
Japan Trench Pac. Oc. 32°0N 142°0E 288 D6
Japen = Yapen Indonesia 1°50S 136°0E 231 E9
Japiim Brazil 7°37S 72°54W 330 B3
Japla India 24°33N 84°1E 243 G11
Japurá Brazil 1°48S 66°34W 328 D4
Japurá → Brazil 3°8S 65°46W 328 D4
Jaquarão Brazil 32°34S 53°23W 335 C5
Jaqué Panama 7°27N 78°8W 328 B2
Jarābulus Syria 36°49N 38°1E 213 D8
Jaraguá Goiás, Brazil 15°45S 49°20W 333 E2
Jaraguá São Paulo, Brazil 23°27S 46°44W 137 A1
Jaraguá, Pico de Brazil 23°27S 46°46W 137 A1
Jaraguari Brazil 20°9S 54°35W 331 E7
Jaraicejo Spain 39°40N 5°49W 195 F5
Jaraíz de la Vera Spain 40°4N 5°45W 194 E5
Jarama → Spain 40°24N 3°32W 194 E7
Jaramānah Syria 33°29N 36°21E 250 E7
Jaramillo Argentina 47°10S 67°7W 336 C3
Jarandilla Spain 40°8N 5°39W 194 E5
Jaranwala Pakistan 31°15N 73°26E 242 D5
Jarash Jordan 32°17N 35°54E 251 F6
Jarash □ Jordan 32°17N 35°54E 251 F6
Jaraucu → Brazil 1°48S 52°22W 329 D7
Järbo Sweden 60°43N 16°36E 162 D10
Jarboesville = Lexington Park U.S.A. 38°16N 76°27W 309 F15
Jardas al 'Abīd Libya 32°18N 20°59E 258 B4
Jardim Brazil 21°28S 56°2W 334 A4
Jardim Paulista Brazil 23°34S 46°41W 137 B1
Jardín → Spain 38°50N 2°10W 197 G2
Jardin Botanique Brussels, Belgium 116 a3
Jardine River △ Australia 11°9S 142°21E 280 A3
Jardines de la Reina, Arch. de los Cuba 20°50N 78°50W 320 B4
Jargalang China 43°5N 122°55E 227 C12
Jargalant = Hovd □ Mongolia 48°2N 91°37E 217 C12
Jari → Brazil 1°9S 51°54W 329 D7
Jaria Janjail Bangla. 25°0N 90°40E 241 C3
Jarīr, W. al → Si. Arabia 25°38N 42°30E 246 E4
Järlåsa Sweden 59°53N 17°12E 162 E11
Jarlsberg og Larvik = Vestfold □ Norway 59°15N 10°0E 164 E7
Jarmen Germany 53°54N 13°20E 178 B9
Järna Dalarna, Sweden 60°33N 14°26E 162 D8
Järna Stockholm, Sweden 59°6N 17°34E 162 E11
Jarnac France 45°40N 0°11W 174 C3
Jarny France 49°9N 5°53E 173 C12
Jaro Phil. 11°11N 124°47E 233 F6
Jarocin Poland 51°59N 17°29E 185 G4
Jaroměř Czech Rep. 50°22N 15°52E 180 A8
Jarosław Poland 50°2N 22°42E 185 H9
Järpås Sweden 58°23N 12°57E 163 F6
Järpen Sweden 63°21N 13°26E 162 A7
Jarrahdale Australia 32°24S 116°5E 279 F2
Jarrahi → Iran 30°49N 48°48E 247 D6
Jarres, Plaine des Laos 19°27N 103°10E 236 C4
Jarso Ethiopia 5°15N 37°30E 257 F4
Jartai China 39°45N 105°48E 226 E3
Jaru Brazil 10°26S 62°27W 331 C5
Jaru → Brazil 10°5S 61°59W 331 C5
Jarud Qi China 44°28N 120°50E 227 B11
Järvatältet Sweden 59°25N 17°54E 139 A1
Järvenpää Finland 60°29N 25°5E 188 B3
Jarvis Canada 42°53N 80°6W 312 D4
Jarvis I. Pac. Oc. 0°15S 160°5W 289 H12
Jarvorník Czech Rep. 50°23N 17°2E 181 A10
Järvsö Sweden 61°43N 16°10E 162 C10
Jarwa India 27°38N 82°30E 243 F10
Jaša Tomić Serbia 45°26N 20°50E 182 E5
Jasaan Phil. 8°39N 124°45E 233 G5
Jasdan India 22°2N 71°12E 242 H4
Jashpurnagar India 22°54N 84°9E 243 H11
Jasidih India 24°31N 86°39E 243 G12
Jasień Poland 51°46N 15°0E 185 G2
Jāsimīyah Iraq 33°45N 44°41E 213 F11
Jasin Malaysia 2°20N 102°26E 237 L4
Jāsk Iran 25°38N 57°45E 247 E8
Jaskhar India 18°54N 72°58E 130 B2
Jasło Poland 49°45N 21°30E 185 J8
Jasmund Germany 54°32N 13°35E 178 A9
Jasmund △ Germany 54°31N 13°38E 178 A9
Jaso India 24°30N 80°29E 243 G9
Jason Is. Falk. Is. 51°0S 61°0W 153 f
Jasonville U.S.A. 39°10N 87°12W 311 E9
Jasper Alta., Canada 52°55N 118°5W 296 C5
Jasper Ont., Canada 44°52N 75°57W 313 B9
Jasper Ala., U.S.A. 33°50N 87°17W 315 E11
Jasper Fla., U.S.A. 30°31N 82°57W 316 E7
Jasper Ind., U.S.A. 38°24N 86°56W 311 F10
Jasper Tex., U.S.A. 30°56N 94°1W 314 F7
Jasper △ Canada 52°50N 118°8W 296 C5
Jasrasar India 27°43N 73°49E 242 F5
Jassy = Iaşi Romania 47°10N 27°40E 183 C12
Jastarnia Poland 54°42N 18°40E 184 D5
Jastrebarsko Croatia 45°41N 15°39E 199 C12
Jastrow = Jastrowie Poland 53°26N 16°49E 184 E3
Jastrowie Poland 53°26N 16°49E 184 E3
Jastrzębie Zdrój Poland 49°57N 18°35E 185 J5
Jász-Nagykun-Szolnok □ Hungary 47°15N 20°30E 182 C5
Jászapáti Hungary 47°32N 20°10E 182 C5
Jászárokszállás Hungary 47°39N 19°58E 182 C4
Jászberény Hungary 47°30N 19°55E 182 C4
Jászkisér Hungary 47°27N 20°20E 182 C5
Jászladány Hungary 47°23N 20°10E 182 C5
Jataí Brazil 17°58S 51°48W 333 E1
Jatapu → Brazil 2°13S 58°17W 329 D6
Jath India 17°3N 75°13E 244 F2
Jati Pakistan 24°20N 68°19E 242 G3
Jatibarang Indonesia 6°28S 108°18E 235 D3
Jatiluwih Indonesia 8°23S 115°8E 231 J18
Jatinegara Indonesia 6°13S 106°52E 122 B2
Játiva = Xátiva Spain 38°59N 0°32W 197 G4
Jatobá = Petrolândia Brazil 9°5S 38°20W 332 C4
Jättendal Sweden 61°58N 17°15E 162 C11
Jaú Angola 15°12S 13°31E 265 F2
Jaú Brazil 22°10S 48°30W 335 A6
Jaú → Brazil 1°54S 61°26W 329 D5
Jauaperí → Brazil 1°26S 61°35W 329 D5
Jauer = Jawor Poland 51°4N 16°11E 185 G3
Jauja Peru 11°45S 75°15W 330 C2
Jaunpur India 25°46N 82°44E 243 G10
Jauru → Brazil 16°22S 57°46W 331 D6
Java = Jawa Indonesia 7°0S 110°0E 235 D4
Java Sea Indonesia 4°35S 107°15E 235 C3
Java Trench Ind. Oc. 9°0S 105°0E 234 D2
Javadi Hills India 12°40N 78°40E 245 H4
Jāvadīyeh Iran 35°39N 51°22E 141 B2
Javalambre, Sa. de Spain 40°6N 1°0W 196 E4
Jávea Spain 38°48N 0°10E 197 G5
Javhlant = Uliastay Mongolia 47°56N 97°28E 218 B4
Javier, I. Chile 47°5S 74°25W 336 C2
Javla India 17°18N 75°9E 244 F2
Jawa Indonesia 7°0S 110°0E 235 D4
Jawa Barat □ Indonesia 7°0S 107°0E 231 G12
Jawa Tengah □ Indonesia 7°0S 110°0E 231 G14
Jawa Timur □ Indonesia 8°0S 113°0E 231 G15
Jawad India 24°36N 74°51E 242 G6
Jawf, W. al → Yemen 15°50N 45°30E 248 D4
Jawhar India 19°55N 73°14E 244 E1
Jawor Poland 51°4N 16°11E 185 G3
Jaworowa Poland 52°9N 20°56E 142 C1
Jaworzno Poland 50°13N 19°11E 185 H6
Jaworzyna Śląska Poland 50°55N 16°28E 185 H3
Jay U.S.A. 30°57N 87°9W 317 E2
Jay Peak U.S.A. 44°55N 72°32W 313 B12
Jaya, Puncak Indonesia 3°57S 137°17E 231 E9
Jayanca Peru 6°24S 79°50W 330 B2
Jayanti India 26°45N 89°40E 241 B2
Jayapura Indonesia 2°28S 140°38E 231 E10
Jayawijaya, Pegunungan Indonesia 5°0S 139°0E 231 F9
Jaynagar India 26°43N 86°9E 243 F12
Jayrūd Syria 33°49N 36°44E 250 E7
Jayton U.S.A. 33°15N 100°34W 314 E4
Jāz Mūrīān, Hāmūn-e Iran 27°20N 58°55E 247 E8
Jazīreh-ye Shīf Iran 29°4N 50°54E 247 D6
Jazminal Mexico 24°52N 101°24W 318 C4
Jazz Museum New Orleans, U.S.A. 131 a3
Jazzīn Lebanon 33°31N 35°35E 250 E6
Jean U.S.A. 35°47N 115°20W 307 K11
Jean Lafitte Nat. Historical Park ⌂ U.S.A. 29°51N 90°9W 131 B1
Jean Marie River Canada 61°32N 120°38W 296 A4
Jean-Rabel Haiti 19°50N 73°5W 321 C5
Jeanerette U.S.A. 29°55N 91°40W 314 G9
Jeanette, Ostrov = Zhannetty, Ostrov Russia 76°43N 158°0E 215 B16
Jeanne-Mance, Parc Montréal, Canada 130 b1
Jeanneton, Morne Guadeloupe 16°14N 61°43W 322 e
Jeannette U.S.A. 40°20N 79°36W 312 F5
Jebāl Bārez, Kūh-e Iran 28°30N 58°20E 247 D8
Jebba Nigeria 9°9N 4°48E 263 D5
Jebel, Bahr el → Sudan 9°30N 30°25E 257 F3
Jebel Ali = Minā' Jabal 'Alī U.A.E. 25°2N 55°8E 247 E7
Jebel Dud Sudan 13°25N 33°9E 257 E3
Jebel Qerri Sudan 16°16N 32°50E 257 D3
Jeberos Peru 5°15S 76°10W 330 B2
Jecheon S. Korea 37°8N 128°12E 224 D4
Jedburgh U.K. 55°29N 2°33W 167 F6
Jedda = Jiddah Si. Arabia 21°29N 39°10E 248 B2
Jeddore L. Canada 48°3N 55°55W 299 C8
Jedlesee Austria 48°15N 16°23E 142 A2
Jedlicze Poland 49°43N 21°40E 185 J8
Jędrzejów Poland 50°35N 20°15E 185 H7
Jedwabne Poland 53°17N 22°18E 185 E9
Jeetzel → Germany 53°9N 11°3E 178 B7
Jefferson Ga., U.S.A. 34°7N 83°35W 316 A6
Jefferson Iowa, U.S.A. 42°1N 94°23W 310 B2
Jefferson La., U.S.A. 29°57N 90°9W 131 B2
Jefferson Ohio, U.S.A. 41°44N 80°46W 312 E4
Jefferson Tex., U.S.A. 32°46N 94°21W 314 E7
Jefferson Wis., U.S.A. 43°0N 88°48W 311 B8
Jefferson, Mt. Nev., U.S.A. 38°47N 116°56W 304 G5
Jefferson, Mt. Oreg., U.S.A. 44°41N 121°48W 304 D3
Jefferson City Mo., U.S.A. 38°34N 92°10W 310 F4
Jefferson City Tenn., U.S.A. 36°7N 83°30W 315 C13
Jefferson Memorial Washington, D.C., U.S.A. 143 c1
Jefferson Park U.S.A. 41°58N 87°46W 119 B2
Jeffersontown U.S.A. 38°12N 85°35W 311 F11
Jeffersonville Ga., U.S.A. 32°41N 83°20W 316 C6
Jeffersonville Ind., U.S.A. 38°17N 85°44W 311 F11
Jeffersonville Ohio, U.S.A. 39°39N 83°34W 311 E13
Jeffrey City U.S.A. 42°30N 107°49W 304 E10
Jega Nigeria 12°15N 4°23E 263 C5
Jegi S. Korea 37°34N 127°1E 137 B2
Jejevo Solomon Is. 8°6S 159°8E 287 M10
Jeju S. Korea 33°31N 126°32E 224 a
Jeju-do S. Korea 33°29N 126°34E 224 a
Jeju-do □ S. Korea 33°25N 126°30E 224 a
Jēkabpils Latvia 56°29N 25°57E 188 D3
Jekyll I. U.S.A. 31°4N 81°25W 316 D8
Jelambar Indonesia 6°9S 106°47E 122 A1
Jelcz-Laskowice Poland 51°2N 17°19E 185 G4
Jelenia Góra Poland 50°50N 15°45E 185 H2
Jelgava Latvia 56°41N 23°49E 184 B10
Jelgava □ Latvia 56°35N 23°45E 184 B10
Jelica Serbia 43°50N 20°17E 202 C4
Jelli Sudan 5°25N 31°45E 257 F3
Jelonki Poland 52°14N 20°54E 142 B1
Jelšava Slovak Rep. 48°37N 20°15E 181 C13
Jema'a Mallam = Kafanchan Nigeria 9°40N 8°20E 263 D6
Jemaja Indonesia 3°5N 105°45E 237 L5
Jemaluang Malaysia 2°16N 103°52E 237 L4
Jember Indonesia 8°11S 113°41E 235 D4
Jena Thüringen, Germany 50°54N 11°35E 178 E7
Jena La., U.S.A. 31°41N 92°8W 314 F8
Jenai Taiwan 24°2N 121°8E 225 B3
Jenbach Austria 47°24N 11°47E 180 D4
Jendouba Tunisia 36°29N 8°47E 258 A1
Jendouba □ Tunisia 36°34N 8°52E 261 A6
Jenho Taiwan 23°54N 121°36E 225 C3
Jenin West Bank 32°28N 35°18E 251 F6
Jenison U.S.A. 42°54N 85°47W 311 B11
Jenkins U.S.A. 37°10N 82°38W 309 G12
Jenner U.S.A. 38°27N 123°7W 306 G3
Jennings Fla., U.S.A. 30°36N 83°6W 316 E6
Jennings La., U.S.A. 30°13N 92°40W 314 F8
Jennings Mo., U.S.A. 38°43N 90°15W 310 F6
Jenny Pt. Dominica 15°28N 61°15W 323 k
Jensen Beach U.S.A. 27°15N 80°14W 317 H9
Jente Taiwan 22°58N 120°16E 225 D2
Jenwu Taiwan 22°42N 120°20E 225 D2
Jeollabuk-do □ S. Korea 35°45N 127°15E 224 E3
Jeollanam-do □ S. Korea 34°45N 127°0E 224 E3
Jeong-eup S. Korea 35°35N 126°50E 224 E3
Jeonju S. Korea 35°50N 127°4E 224 E3
Jepara Indonesia 7°40S 109°14E 235 D3
Jeparit Australia 36°8S 142°1E 282 D5
Jequié Brazil 13°51S 40°5W 333 D3
Jequitaí → Brazil 17°4S 44°50W 333 E3
Jequitinhonha Brazil 16°30S 41°0W 333 E3
Jequitinhonha → Brazil 15°51S 38°53W 333 E4
Jerada Morocco 34°17N 2°10W 261 B4
Jerantut Malaysia 3°56N 102°22E 237 L4
Jerejak, Pulau Malaysia 5°19N 100°19E 237 c
Jérémie Haiti 18°40N 74°10W 321 C5
Jeremoabo Brazil 10°4S 38°21W 332 D4
Jerez, Pta. Mexico 22°58N 97°40W 319 C5
Jerez de García Salinas Mexico 22°39N 103°0W 318 C4
Jerez de la Frontera Spain 36°41N 6°7W 195 J4
Jerez de los Caballeros Spain 38°20N 6°45W 195 G4
Jericho = El Arīḥā West Bank 31°52N 35°27E 251 G6
Jericho Australia 23°38S 146°6E 280 C4
Jerichow Germany 52°30N 12°1E 178 C8
Jerico Springs U.S.A. 37°37N 94°1W 310 G2
Jerid, Chott el = Djerid, Chott Tunisia 33°42N 8°30E 258 B1
Jerilderie Australia 35°20S 145°41E 283 C6
Jermyn U.S.A. 41°32N 75°33W 313 E9
Jerningham Junction Trin. & Tob. 10°33N 61°23W 323 t
Jerome U.S.A. 42°44N 114°31W 304 E6
Jerónimos, Mosteiro dos Portugal 38°41N 9°11W 126 A1
Jerramungup Australia 33°55S 118°55E 279 F2
Jersey U.K. 49°11N 2°7W 169 H5
Jersey City U.S.A. 40°42N 74°4W 132 B1
Jersey Shore U.S.A. 41°12N 77°15W 312 E7
Jerseyville U.S.A. 39°7N 90°20W 310 E6
Jerumenha Brazil 7°5S 43°30W 332 C3
Jerusalem Israel/West Bank 31°47N 35°10E 123 B2
Jervis B. Australia 35°8S 150°46E 283 C9
Jervis Inlet Canada 50°0N 123°57W 296 C4
Jerzu Italy 39°47N 9°31E 200 C2
Jesenice Slovenia 46°28N 14°3E 199 B11
Jeseník Czech Rep. 50°14N 17°8E 181 A10
Jesenské Slovak Rep. 48°20N 20°10E 181 C13
Jesi = Iesi Italy 43°31N 13°14E 199 E10
Jessamine, L. U.S.A. 28°28N 81°23W 133 B2
Jessel = Jasło Poland 49°45N 21°30E 185 J8
Jesselton = Kota Kinabalu Malaysia 6°0N 116°4E 235 A5
Jessheim Norway 60°9N 11°10E 164 D8
Jessnitz Germany 51°40N 12°18E 178 D8
Jessore Bangla. 23°10N 89°10E 241 D2
Jesup Ga., U.S.A. 31°36N 81°53W 316 D8
Jesup Iowa, U.S.A. 42°29N 92°4W 310 B4
Jesup, L. U.S.A. 28°43N 81°14W 317 G8
Jesús Peru 7°15S 78°25W 330 B2
Jésus, Î. Canada 45°36N 73°44W 130 A1
Jesús Carranza Mexico 17°26N 95°2W 319 D5
Jesús María Argentina 30°59S 64°5W 334 C3
Jesús María Lima, Peru 12°4S 77°3W 124 B2
Jetmore U.S.A. 38°4N 99°54W 308 F4
Jetpur India 21°45N 70°10E 242 J4
Jette Belgium 50°53N 4°20E 116 A1
Jeumont France 50°18N 4°6E 173 B11
Jeungdo S. Korea 34°56N 126°9E 224 E3
Jeungpyeong S. Korea 36°47N 127°34E 224 D3
Jevnaker Norway 60°15N 10°26E 164 D7
Jewell U.S.A. 42°20N 93°39W 310 B3
Jewett U.S.A. 40°22N 81°2W 312 F3
Jewett City U.S.A. 41°36N 71°59W 313 E13
Jewish Quarter Jerusalem 123 b3
Jey Iran 35°41N 51°20E 141 B2
Jeyḩūnābād Iran 34°58N 48°59E 247 C6
Jeypore India 18°50N 82°38E 244 E6
Jeziorak, Jezioro Poland 53°40N 19°35E 184 E6
Jeziorany Poland 53°58N 20°46E 184 E7
Jeziorka → Poland 52°8N 21°9E 185 F8
Jha Jha India 24°46N 86°22E 243 G12
Jhaarkand = Jharkhand □ India 24°0N 85°50E 243 H11
Jhabua India 22°46N 74°36E 242 H6
Jhajjar India 28°37N 76°42E 242 E7
Jhal Pakistan 28°17N 67°27E 242 E2
Jhal Jhao Pakistan 26°20N 65°35E 240 D2
Jhalakati Bangla. 22°39N 90°12E 241 D3
Jhalawar India 24°40N 76°10E 242 G7
Jhalida India 23°22N 85°58E 243 H11
Jhalrapatan India 24°33N 76°10E 242 G7
Jhang Maghiana Pakistan 31°15N 72°22E 242 D5
Jhansi India 25°30N 78°36E 243 G8
Jhargram India 22°27N 86°59E 243 H12
Jharia India 23°45N 86°26E 243 H12
Jharkhand □ India 24°0N 85°50E 243 H11
Jharsuguda India 21°56N 84°5E 244 D7
Jhelum Pakistan 33°0N 73°45E 242 C5
Jhelum → Pakistan 31°20N 72°10E 242 D5
Jhenaidah Bangla. 23°33N 89°10E 241 D2
Jhilimili India 23°24N 82°51E 243 H10
Jhudo Pakistan 24°58N 69°18E 242 G3
Jhunjhunu India 28°10N 75°30E 242 E6
Ji-Paraná Brazil 10°50S 61°58W 331 C5
Ji Xian Hebei, China 37°35N 115°30E 226 F8
Ji Xian Henan, China 35°22N 114°5E 226 G8
Ji Xian Shanxi, China 36°7N 110°40E 226 F6
Jia Xian Henan, China 33°59N 113°12E 226 H7
Jia Xian Shaanxi, China 38°12N 110°28E 226 E6
Jiading China 31°22N 121°15E 229 B13
Jiahe China 25°38N 112°19E 229 E9
Jiaji = Qionghai China 19°15N 110°26E 236 C8
Jialing Jiang → China 29°30N 106°20E 228 C6
Jiamusi China 46°40N 130°26E 219 B8
Ji'an Jiangxi, China 27°6N 114°59E 229 D10
Ji'an Jilin, China 41°5N 126°10E 227 D14
Jianchang China 40°55N 120°35E 227 D11
Jianchangying China 40°10N 118°50E 227 D10
Jianchuan China 26°38N 99°55E 228 D2
Jiande China 29°23N 119°15E 229 C12
Jiang'an China 28°40N 105°3E 228 C5
Jiangbei China 29°40N 106°34E 228 C6
Jiangcheng China 22°36N 101°52E 228 F3
Jiangchuan China 24°8N 102°39E 228 E4
Jiangdi China 26°57N 103°37E 228 D4
Jiangdu China 32°27N 119°36E 229 A12
Jiange China 32°4N 105°32E 228 A5
Jianghua China 25°0N 111°47E 229 E8
Jiangjin China 29°14N 106°14E 228 C6
Jiangkou China 27°40N 108°49E 228 D7
Jiangle China 26°42N 117°23E 229 D11
Jiangling China 30°25N 112°12E 229 B9
Jiangmen China 22°32N 113°0E 229 F9
Jiangning China 31°55N 118°50E 229 B12
Jiangshan China 28°40N 118°37E 229 C12
Jiangsu □ China 33°0N 120°0E 227 H11
Jianguomen China 39°53N 116°24E 114 B2
Jiangwan China 31°18N 121°28E 138 B1
Jiangxi □ China 27°30N 116°0E 229 D11
Jiangyan China 32°30N 120°7E 229 A13
Jiangyin China 31°54N 120°17E 229 B13
Jiangyong China 25°20N 111°22E 229 E8
Jiangyou China 31°44N 104°43E 228 B5
Jianhe China 26°37N 108°31E 228 D7
Jianli China 29°46N 112°56E 229 C9
Jianning China 26°50N 116°50E 229 D11
Jian'ou China 27°3N 118°17E 229 D12
Jianshi China 30°37N 109°38E 228 B7
Jianshui China 23°36N 102°43E 228 F4
Jianyang Fujian, China 27°20N 118°5E 229 D12
Jianyang Sichuan, China 30°24N 104°33E 228 B5
Jiao Xian = Jiaozhou China 36°18N 120°1E 227 F11
Jiaohe Hebei, China 38°2N 116°20E 226 E9
Jiaohe Jilin, China 43°40N 127°22E 227 C14
Jiaojiang China 28°40N 121°24E 229 C13
Jiaoling China 24°41N 116°12E 229 E11
Jiaozhou China 36°18N 120°1E 227 F11
Jiaozhou Wan China 36°5N 120°10E 227 F11
Jiaozuo China 35°16N 113°12E 226 G7
Jiashan China 30°55N 120°55E 229 B13
Jiawang China 34°28N 117°26E 227 G9
Jiaxiang China 35°25N 116°20E 226 G9
Jiaxing China 30°49N 120°45E 229 B13
Jiayi = Chiai Taiwan 23°29N 120°25E 225 C2
Jiayu China 29°55N 113°55E 229 C9
Jib West Bank 31°51N 35°11E 123 A2
Jibão, Serra do Brazil 14°48S 45°0W 333 D3
Jibiya Nigeria 13°5N 7°12E 263 C6
Jibou Romania 47°15N 23°17E 183 C8
Jibuti = Djibouti ■ Africa 12°0N 43°0E 257 E5
Jicarón, I. Panama 7°10N 81°50W 320 E3
Jičín Czech Rep. 50°25N 15°28E 180 A8
Jiddah Si. Arabia 21°29N 39°10E 248 B2
Jido India 29°2N 94°58E 241 A5
Jido S. Korea 35°4N 126°14E 224 E3
Jieshou China 33°18N 115°22E 226 H8
Jiexiu China 37°2N 111°55E 226 F6
Jieyang China 23°35N 116°21E 229 F11
Jigalong Australia 23°21S 120°47E 278 D3
Jigawa □ Nigeria 12°0N 9°45E 263 C6
Jigme Dorje △ Bhutan 28°0N 89°40E 241 B2
Jigme Singye Wangchuck Bhutan 27°20N 90°25E 241 B3
Jigni India 25°45N 79°25E 243 G8
Jihād Iraq 33°17N 44°19E 113 B1
Jihlava Czech Rep. 49°28N 15°35E 180 B8
Jihlava → Czech Rep. 48°55N 16°36E 181 C9
Jihlavský □ Czech Rep. 49°30N 15°30E 180 B8
Jihnan Taiwan 24°22N 120°39E 225 B2
Jihočeský □ Czech Rep. 49°8N 14°35E 180 B7
Jihomoravský □ Czech Rep. 49°5N 16°30E 181 B9
Jijel Algeria 36°52N 5°50E 261 A6
Jijel □ Algeria 36°45N 6°0E 261 A6
Jijiga Ethiopia 9°20N 42°50E 267 C5
Jikamshi Nigeria 12°12N 7°45E 263 C6
Jikau Sudan 8°28N 33°47E 257 F3
Jilib = Gelib Somali Rep. 0°29N 42°46E 267 D5
Jilin China 43°44N 126°30E 227 C14
Jilin □ China 44°0N 127°0E 227 C13
Jiloca → Spain 41°21N 1°39W 196 D3
Jilong = Chilung Taiwan 25°3N 121°45E 225 A3
Jim Thompson's House Bangkok, Thailand 113 b3
Jim Thorpe U.S.A. 40°52N 75°44W 313 F9
Jima Ethiopia 7°40N 36°47E 257 F4
Jimbaran, Teluk Indonesia 8°46S 115°9E 231 K18
Jimbōchō Tokyo, Japan 140 a4
Jimbolia Romania 45°47N 20°43E 182 E5
Jimena de la Frontera Spain 36°27N 5°24W 195 J5
Jiménez Chihuahua, Mexico 27°8N 104°54W 318 B4
Jimenez Phil. 8°20N 123°50E 233 G5
Jimo China 36°23N 120°30E 227 F11
Jimsar China 44°3N 89°2E 217 C11
Jin Jiang → China 28°24N 115°48E 229 C10
Jin Xian = Jinzhou Hebei, China 38°2N 115°2E 226 E8
Jin Xian = Jinzhou Liaoning, China 38°55N 121°42E 227 E11
Jinan China 36°38N 117°1E 226 F9
Jinchang China 38°30N 102°10E 218 C5
Jincheng China 35°29N 112°50E 226 G7
Jinchuan China 31°30N 102°3E 228 B4
Jind India 29°19N 76°22E 242 E7
Jindabyne Australia 36°25S 148°35E 283 D8
Jinding China 22°22N 113°33E 219 G10
Jindo S. Korea 34°28N 126°15E 224 F3
Jindřichův Hradec Czech Rep. 49°10N 15°2E 180 B8
Jing He → China 34°27N 109°4E 226 G5
Jing Shan China 31°20N 111°35E 229 B8
Jing Xian China 30°38N 118°25E 229 B12
Jing'an Jiangxi, China 28°50N 115°17E 229 C10
Jingan Shanghai, China 31°14N 121°25E 138 B1
Jingbian China 37°20N 108°30E 226 F5
Jingchuan China 35°20N 107°20E 226 G4
Jingde China 30°15N 118°27E 229 B12
Jingdezhen China 29°20N 117°11E 229 C11
Jingdong China 24°23N 100°47E 228 E3
Jinggangshan China 26°58N 114°15E 229 D10
Jinggu China 23°35N 100°41E 228 F3
Jinghai China 38°55N 116°55E 226 E9
Jinghong China 22°0N 100°45E 228 G3
Jingjiang China 32°2N 120°16E 229 A13
Jingle China 38°20N 111°55E 226 E6
Jingmen China 31°0N 112°10E 229 B9
Jingning China 35°30N 105°43E 226 G3
Jingpo Hu China 43°55N 128°55E 227 C15
Jingshan China 31°1N 113°7E 229 B9
Jingtai China 37°10N 104°6E 226 F3
Jingu Outer Garden Tokyo, Japan 140 b2
Jingxi China 23°8N 106°27E 228 F6
Jingxing China 38°2N 114°8E 226 E8
Jingyang China 34°30N 108°50E 226 G5
Jingyu China 42°25N 126°45E 224 A3
Jingyuan China 36°30N 104°40E 226 F3
Jingzhou China 26°33N 109°40E 228 D7
Jingziguan China 33°15N 111°0E 226 H6
Jinhua China 29°8N 119°38E 229 C12
Jining Nei Monggol Zizhiqu, China 41°5N 113°0E 226 D7
Jining Shandong, China 35°22N 116°34E 226 G9
Jinja Uganda 0°25N 33°12E 268 B3
Jinjang Malaysia 3°13N 101°39E 237 L3
Jinji China 37°58N 106°8E 226 F4
Jinjiang Fujian, China 24°43N 118°33E 229 E12
Jinjiang Yunnan, China 26°14N 100°34E 228 D3
Jinjini Ghana 7°26N 2°42W 262 D4
Jinju S. Korea 35°12N 128°2E 224 E4
Jinkou China 30°20N 114°8E 229 B10
Jinkouhe China 29°18N 103°4E 228 C4
Jinmen Dao China 24°25N 118°25E 229 E12
Jinnah Barrage Pakistan 32°58N 71°33E 242 C4
Jinning China 24°38N 102°38E 228 E4
Jinočany Czech Rep. 50°2N 14°16E 135 B1
Jinonice Czech Rep. 50°3N 14°22E 135 B2
Jinotega Nic. 13°6N 85°59W 320 D2
Jinotepe Nic. 11°50N 86°10W 320 D2
Jinping Guizhou, China 26°41N 109°10E 228 D7
Jinping Yunnan, China 22°45N 103°18E 228 F4
Jinsha China 27°29N 106°12E 228 D6
Jinsha Jiang → China 28°50N 104°36E 228 C5
Jinshan China 30°54N 121°10E 229 B13
Jinshi China 29°40N 111°50E 229 C8
Jintan China 31°42N 119°36E 229 B12
Jintotolo Channel Phil. 11°48N 123°5E 233 F4
Jintur India 19°37N 76°42E 244 E3
Jinxi Jiangxi, China 27°56N 116°45E 229 D11
Jinxi Liaoning, China 40°52N 120°50E 227 D11
Jinxian China 28°26N 116°17E 229 C11
Jinxiang China 35°5N 116°22E 226 G9
Jinyang China 27°28N 103°5E 228 D4
Jinyun China 28°35N 120°5E 229 C13
Jinzhai China 31°40N 115°53E 229 B10
Jinzhou Hebei, China 38°2N 115°2E 226 E8
Jinzhou Liaoning, China 38°55N 121°42E 227 E11
Jinzhou Liaoning, China 41°5N 121°3E 227 D11
Jiparaná → Brazil 8°3S 62°52W 331 B5
Jipijapa Ecuador 1°0S 80°40W 328 D1
Jiquilpan Mexico 19°59N 102°43W 318 D4
Jirisan S. Korea 35°20N 127°44E 224 E3
Jirisan △ S. Korea 35°15N 127°30E 224 E3
Jishan China 35°34N 110°58E 226 G6
Jishou China 28°21N 109°43E 228 C7
Jishui China 27°12N 115°8E 229 D10
Jisr ash Shughūr Syria 35°49N 36°18E 250 C7
Jitarning Australia 32°48S 117°57E 279 F2
Jitra Malaysia 6°16N 100°25E 237 J3
Jiu → Romania 43°47N 23°48E 183 G8
Jiudengkou China 39°56N 106°40E 226 E4
Jiujiang Guangdong, China 22°50N 113°0E 229 F9
Jiujiang Jiangxi, China 29°42N 115°58E 229 C10
Jiuling Shan China 28°40N 114°40E 229 C10
Jiulong = Kowloon China 22°19N 114°11E 122 B1
Jiulong China 28°57N 101°31E 228 C3
Jiutai China 44°10N 125°50E 227 B13
Jiuxincheng China 39°17N 115°59E 226 E8
Jiuyuhang China 30°18N 119°56E 229 B12
Jiwa U.A.E. 23°0N 54°10E 249 B6
Jiwani Pakistan 25°1N 61°44E 240 D1
Jiwani, Ras Pakistan 25°1N 61°44E 240 D1
Jixi Anhui, China 30°5N 118°34E 229 B12
Jixi Heilongjiang, China 45°20N 130°50E 227 B16
Jiyang China 37°0N 117°12E 227 F9
Jiyuan China 35°7N 112°57E 226 G7
Jiyūgaoka Japan 35°35N 139°40E 140 B3
Jīz', W. → Yemen 16°12N 52°14E 249 C6
Jīzā'ir Iraq 33°15N 44°23E 113 B2
Jīzān Si. Arabia 17°0N 42°20E 248 C3
Jize China 36°54N 114°56E 226 F8
Jizera → Czech Rep. 50°10N 14°43E 180 A7
Jizīra Iraq 33°15N 44°25E 113 B2
Jizl, Wādī al → Si. Arabia 25°39N 38°25E 246 E3
Jizō-Zaki Japan 35°34N 133°20E 222 B5
Jizzakh Uzbekistan 40°6N 67°50E 217 D7
Jizzakh □ Uzbekistan 40°20N 67°40E 217 D7
Joaçaba Brazil 27°5S 51°31W 335 B5
Joaíma Brazil 16°39S 41°2W 333 E3
Joal Fadiout Senegal 14°9N 16°50W 262 C1
João Amaro Brazil 12°46S 40°22W 333 D3
João Belo = Xai-Xai Mozam. 25°6S 33°31E 271 C5
João Câmara Brazil 5°32S 35°48W 332 C4
João Pessoa = Eirunepé Brazil 6°35S 69°53W 330 B4
João Pessoa = Pôrto Brazil 3°54S 42°42W 332 B3
João Pessoa Brazil 7°10S 34°52W 332 C5
João Pinheiro Brazil 17°45S 46°10W 333 E2
Joaquim Távora Brazil 23°30S 49°58W 335 A6
Joaquín V. González Argentina 25°10S 64°0W 334 B3
Jobat India 22°25N 74°34E 242 H6
Jobourg, Nez de France 49°41N 1°57W 172 C5
Jódar Spain 37°50N 3°21W 195 H7
Jodhpur India 26°23N 73°8E 242 F5
Jodiya India 22°42N 70°18E 242 H4
Joensuu Finland 62°37N 29°49E 160 E23
Jōetsu Japan 37°12N 138°10E 221 F9
Jœuf France 49°12N 6°1E 173 C12
Jofane Mozam. 21°15S 34°18E 271 B5
Joffre, Morne = Moustique, Morne Guadeloupe 16°7N 61°44W 322 e
Jogbani India 26°25N 87°15E 243 F12
Jõgeva Estonia 58°45N 26°24E 188 C4
Jogjakarta = Yogyakarta Indonesia 7°49S 110°22E 235 D4
Joglo Indonesia 6°13S 106°45E 122 B1
Jōhana Japan 36°30N 136°57E 223 A8
Johannesburg Gauteng, S. Africa 26°11S 28°2E 123 B2
Johannesburg Calif., U.S.A. 35°22N 117°38W 307 K9
Johannesburg, Univ. of S. Africa 26°11S 28°0E 123 B2
Johannesburg Int. ✕ (GCJ) S. Africa 27°7S 29°16E 123 A2
Johanneskirchen Germany 48°10N 11°38E 131 A2
Johannesstift Germany 52°34N 13°12E 115 A2
Johannisburg = Pisz Poland 53°38N 21°49E 184 E8
Johannisthal Germany 52°26N 13°30E 115 B4
Johansfors Sweden 56°42N 15°32E 163 H9
Johilla → India 23°37N 81°14E 243 H9
John Crow Mts. Jamaica 18°5N 76°25W 320 a
John Day U.S.A. 44°25N 118°57W 304 D4
John Day → U.S.A. 45°44N 120°39W 304 D3
John Day Fossil Beds ⌂ U.S.A. 44°33N 119°38W 304 D4
John D'Or Prairie Canada 58°30N 115°8W 296 B5
John F. Kennedy Nat. Historic Site ⌂ U.S.A. 42°20N 71°7W 116 A2
John F. Kennedy Space Center U.S.A. 28°40N 80°42W 317 G9
John H. Kerr Res. U.S.A. 36°36N 78°18W 315 C15
John Hancock Center Chicago, U.S.A. 119 a2
John McLaren Park U.S.A. 37°43N 122°24W 136 B2
John o' Groats U.K. 58°38N 3°4W 167 C5
Johnnie U.S.A. 36°25N 116°5W 307 J10
John's Ra. Australia 21°55S 133°23E 280 C1
Johns I. U.S.A. 32°47N 80°7W 316 C9
Johnson U.S.A. 44°38N 72°41W 313 B12
Johnson City Kans., U.S.A. 37°34N 101°45W 308 G3
Johnson City N.Y., U.S.A. 42°7N 75°58W 313 D9
Johnson City Tenn., U.S.A. 36°19N 82°21W 315 C13
Johnson City Tex., U.S.A. 30°17N 98°25W 314 F5
Johnsonburg U.S.A. 41°29N 78°41W 312 E6
Johnsondale U.S.A. 35°58N 118°32W 307 K8
Johnsons Crossing Canada 60°29N 133°18W 296 A2
Johnsons Pt. Antigua & B. 17°2N 61°53W 322 b
Johnsonville N.Z. 41°13S 174°48E 143 B1
Johnston U.S.A. 33°50N 81°48W 316 B8
Johnston, L. Australia 32°25S 120°30E 279 F3
Johnston City U.S.A. 37°49N 88°56W 310 G8
Johnston Falls = Mambilima Falls Zambia 10°31S 28°45E 269 E2
Johnston I. Pac. Oc. 17°10N 169°8W 289 F11
Johnstone Str. Canada 50°28N 126°0W 296 C3
Johnstown Kilkenny, Ireland 52°45N 7°33W 166 D4
Johnstown N.Y., U.S.A. 43°0N 74°22W 313 C10
Johnstown Ohio, U.S.A. 40°9N 82°41W 312 F2
Johnstown Pa., U.S.A. 40°20N 78°55W 312 F6
Johor □ Malaysia 2°5N 103°20E 234 B2
Johor, Selat Asia 1°28N 103°47E 237 d
Johor Bahru Malaysia 1°28N 103°46E 237 d
Jõhvi Estonia 59°22N 27°27E 188 C4
Joigny France 47°58N 3°20E 173 E10
Joinville Brazil 26°15S 48°55W 335 B6
Joinville Haute-Marne, France 48°27N 5°10E 173 D12
Joinville I. Antarctica 65°0S 55°30W 151 C18
Joinville-le-Pont France 48°49N 2°27E 134 B3
Jojutla Mexico 18°37N 99°11W 319 D5
Jokkmokk Sweden 66°35N 19°50E 160 C18
Jökulsá á Bru → Iceland 65°40N 14°16W 155 B12
Jökulsá á Fjöllum → Iceland 66°10N 16°30W 155 A10
Jökulsárgljúfur △ Iceland 65°56N 16°31W 155 B10
Jolfā Āzarbājān-e Sharqī, Iran 38°57N 45°38E 213 C11
Jolfā Eşfahan, Iran 32°58N 51°37E 247 C6
Joli-Bois Belgium 50°42N 4°24E 116 B2
Joliet U.S.A. 41°32N 88°5W 311 C8
Joliette Canada 46°3N 73°24W 298 C5
Jollas Finland 60°10N 25°5E 121 B3
Jolo Phil. 6°0N 121°0E 233 H3
Jolo Group Phil. 6°0N 121°9E 233 J3
Jolon U.S.A. 35°58N 121°9W 306 K5
Jølstravatnet Norway 61°32N 6°23E 164 C3
Jomalig I. Phil. 14°42N 122°22E 232 D4
Jombang Indonesia 7°33S 112°14E 235 D4
Jomda China 31°28N 98°12E 228 B2
Jonava Lithuania 55°8N 24°12E 188 E3
Jondal Norway 60°16N 6°15E 164 D3
Jones Phil. 16°33N 121°42E 232 C3
Jones Sound Canada 76°0N 85°0W 295 B11
Jonesboro Ark., U.S.A. 35°50N 90°42W 315 D9
Jonesboro Ga., U.S.A. 33°31N 84°22W 316 B5
Jonesboro La., U.S.A. 32°15N 92°43W 314 E8
Jonesburg U.S.A. 38°51N 91°18W 310 F5
Jonesville Ind., U.S.A. 39°5N 85°54W 311 E11
Jonesville Mich., U.S.A. 41°59N 84°40W 311 C12
Jong → S. Leone 7°32N 12°23W 262 D2
Jonglei Sudan 6°25N 30°50E 257 F3
Jonglei □ Sudan 7°30N 32°30E 257 F3
Jonglei Canal Sudan 9°20N 31°39E 267 C3
Jongmyo Royal Shrine S. Korea 37°34N 126°59E 137 B1
Jongno S. Korea 37°35N 126°59E 137 B1
Joniškis Lithuania 56°13N 23°35E 184 B10
Jönköping Sweden 57°45N 14°8E 163 G8
Jönköpings län □ Sweden 57°30N 14°30E 163 G8
Jonquière Canada 48°27N 71°14W 299 C5
Jonsered Sweden 57°45N 12°10E 163 G6
Jonstrup Denmark 55°45N 12°20E 118 A2
Jonzac France 45°27N 0°28W 174 C3
Joplin U.S.A. 37°6N 94°31W 308 G6
Joppa U.K. 55°57N 3°6W 121 B3
Jora India 26°20N 77°49E 242 F6
Jordan Guimaras, Phil. 10°40N 122°35E 233 F4
Jordan Mont., U.S.A. 47°19N 106°55W 304 C10
Jordan N.Y., U.S.A. 43°4N 76°29W 313 C8
Jordan ■ Asia 31°0N 36°0E 251 H7
Jordan → Asia 31°48N 35°32E 251 G6
Jordan Valley U.S.A. 42°59N 117°3W 304 E5
Jordânia Brazil 15°55S 40°11W 333 E3
Jordanów Poland 49°41N 19°49E 185 J6
Jordet Norway 61°25N 12°8E 164 C9
Jorge, C. Chile 51°40S 75°35W 336 D1
Jorge Chavez, Int. ✕ (LIM) Peru 12°2S 77°8W 124 B2
Jorge Newbery ✕ Argentina 34°34S 58°25W 117 B2
Jorgen Brønlund Fjord Greenland 82°30N 29°0W 154 A8
Jorhat India 26°45N 94°12E 241 B5
Jori → Norway 62°4N 9°5E 162 B3
Jorm Afghan. 36°50N 70°52E 240 A3
Jörn Sweden 65°4N 20°1E 160 D19
Jorong Indonesia 3°58S 114°56E 235 C4
Jørpeland Norway 59°3N 6°1E 164 E3
Jorquera → Chile 28°3S 69°58W 334 B2

Jos Nigeria 9°53N 8°51E 263 D6
Jos Plateau Nigeria 9°55N 9°0E 263 D6
Jošanička Banja Serbia 43°24N 20°47E 202 C4
Jose Abad Santos Phil. 5°55N 125°39E 233 J5
José Batlle y Ordóñez Uruguay 33°20S 55°10W 335 C4
José Bonifácio = Erechim Brazil 27°35S 52°15W 335 B5
José de San Martín Argentina 44°4S 70°26W 336 B2
Jose Panganiban Phil. 14°17N 122°41E 232 D4
Józefa Piłsudskiego Park Poland 52°15N 21°2E 142 B1
Joseni Romania 46°42N 25°29E 183 D10
Joseph, L. Nfld. & L., Canada 52°45N 65°18W 299 B6
Joseph, L. Ont., Canada 45°10N 79°44W 312 A5
Joseph Banks Group Australia 34°36S 136°16E 282 C2
Joseph Bonaparte G. Australia 14°35S 128°50E 278 B4
Joshinath India 30°34N 79°34E 243 D8
Joshinetsu-Kōgen △ Japan 36°42N 138°32E 223 A10
Joshua Tree U.S.A. 34°8N 116°19W 307 L10
Joshua Tree △ U.S.A. 33°55N 116°0W 307 M10
Josselin France 47°57N 2°33W 172 E4
Jost Van Dyke I. Br. Virgin Is. 18°29N 64°47W 321 b
Jostedal Norway 61°35N 7°15E 164 C4
Jostedalsbreen Norway 61°40N 6°59E 164 C3
Jōtō Japan 34°42N 135°33E 133 A2
Jotunheimen Norway 61°35N 8°25E 164 C5
Jotunheimen △ Norway 61°32N 8°25E 164 C5
Joubertberge Namibia 18°30S 14°0E 270 A1
Joué-lès-Tours France 47°21N 0°40E 172 E7
Jourdanton U.S.A. 28°55N 98°33W 314 G5
Joutseno Finland 61°7N 28°31E 188 B5
Jouy-en-Josas France 48°46N 2°10E 134 B2
Jovellanos Cuba 22°40N 81°10W 320 B3
Jovellar Phil. 13°4N 123°36E 232 E4
Jowai India 25°26N 92°12E 241 C4
Jowhar = Giohar Somali Rep. 2°48N 45°30E 267 D6
Jowzjān □ Afghan. 36°10N 66°0E 240 A2
Joyeuse France 44°29N 4°16E 175 D8
Jōyō Japan 34°50N 135°47E 223 C7
Józefów Lubelskie, Poland 50°28N 23°2E 185 H10
Józefów Mazowieckie, Poland 52°10N 21°11E 185 F8
Ju Xian China 36°35N 118°20E 227 F10
Juan Aldama Mexico 24°19N 103°21W 318 C4
Juan Anchorena Argentina 34°30S 58°29W 117 A2
Juan Bautista Alberdi Argentina 34°26S 61°48W 334 C3
Juan de Bolas Jamaica 18°5N 77°9W 320 a
Juan de Fuca, Str of. N. Amer. 48°15N 124°0W 306 B3
Juán de Nova Ind. Oc. 17°3S 43°45E 271 A7
Juan Fernández, Arch. de Pac. Oc. 33°50S 80°0W 326 G2
Juan González Romero Mexico 19°30N 99°3W 128 A2
Juan José Castelli Argentina 25°27S 60°57W 334 B3
Juan L. Lacaze Uruguay 34°26S 57°25W 334 C4
Juana Díaz Puerto Rico 18°3N 66°31W 321 b
Juanjuí Peru 7°10S 76°45W 330 B2
Juankoski Finland 63°3N 28°19E 160 E23
Juara Brazil 11°20S 57°25W 331 C6
Juárez Argentina 37°40S 59°43W 334 D4
Juárez Mexico 32°20N 115°57W 307 N11
Juárez Coahuila, Mexico 27°37N 100°44W 318 B4
Juárez, Sierra de Mexico 32°0N 116°0W 318 A1
Juárez Int. ✈ (MEX) Mexico 19°25N 99°5W 128 B2
Juatinga, Ponta de Brazil 23°17S 44°30W 333 F3
Juàzeiro Brazil 9°30S 40°30W 332 C3
Juàzeiro do Norte Brazil 7°10S 39°18W 332 C4
Juba = Giuba → Somali Rep. 1°30N 42°35E 267 D5
Jûbâ Sudan 4°50N 31°35E 257 G3
Jubany Antarctica 62°30S 58°0W 151 C18
Jubayl Lebanon 34°5N 35°39E 250 D6
Jubbah Si. Arabia 28°2N 40°56E 246 D4
Jubbal India 31°5N 77°40E 242 D7
Jubbulpore = Jabalpur India 23°9N 79°58E 243 H8
Jübek Germany 54°33N 9°22E 178 A5
Jubga Russia 44°19N 38°48E 191 H4
Jubilee L. Australia 29°0S 126°50E 279 E4
Juby, C. Morocco 28°0N 12°59W 260 C2
Júcar = Xúquer → Spain 39°5N 0°10W 197 F4
Júcaro Cuba 21°37N 78°51W 320 B4
Juchitán de Zaragoza Mexico 16°26N 95°1W 319 D5
Judaberg Norway 59°10N 5°51E 164 E2
Judea = Har Yehuda Israel 31°35N 34°57E 251 G5
Judeira West Bank 31°52N 35°12E 123 A2
Judenburg Austria 47°12N 14°38E 180 D7
Judith → U.S.A. 47°44N 109°39W 304 C9
Judith, Pt. U.S.A. 41°22N 71°29W 313 E13
Judith Gap U.S.A. 46°41N 109°45W 304 C9
Juelsminde Denmark 55°43N 10°1E 163 J4
Jufari → Brazil 1°13S 62°0W 329 D5
Jugoslavia = Serbia ■ Europe 43°20N 20°0E 202 C4
Juhdum West Bank 31°42N 35°15E 123 B2
Juhu India 19°5N 73°0E 130 A2
Juifang Taiwan 25°7N 121°48E 225 A3
Juigalpa Nic. 12°6N 85°26W 320 D2
Juillac France 45°20N 1°19E 174 C5
Juist Germany 53°40N 6°59E 178 B2
Juisui Taiwan 23°30N 121°22E 225 C3
Juiz de Fora Brazil 21°43S 43°19W 333 F3
Jūjā Japan 35°45N 139°43E 140 A3
Jujuy □ Argentina 23°20S 65°40W 334 A2
Jukao = Rugao China 32°23N 120°31E 229 A13
Jukskeirivier → S. Africa 26°5S 28°6E 123 A2
Julesburg U.S.A. 40°59N 102°16W 304 F12
Juli Peru 16°10S 69°25W 330 D4
Julia Cr. → Australia 20°0S 141°11E 280 C3
Julia Creek Australia 20°39S 141°44E 280 C3
Juliaca Peru 15°25S 70°10W 330 D3
Julian U.S.A. 33°4N 116°38W 307 M10
Julian, L. Canada 54°25N 77°57W 298 B4
Julian Alps = Julijske Alpe Slovenia 46°15N 14°1E 199 B11
Juliana Top = Mandala, Puncak Indonesia 4°44S 140°20E 231 E10
Julianadorp Neth. Ant. 12°9N 68°57W 322 g
Julianatop Suriname 3°40N 56°30W 329 C6
Julianehåb = Qaqortoq Greenland 60°43N 46°0W 154 E6
Julianów Poland 52°10N 21°9E 142 B2
Jülich Germany 50°55N 6°22E 178 E2
Juliette, L. U.S.A. 33°2N 83°50W 316 B6
Julijske Alpe Slovenia 46°15N 14°1E 199 B11
Julimes Mexico 28°25N 105°27W 318 B3
Jullundur India 31°20N 75°40E 242 D6
Julu China 37°15N 115°2E 226 F8
Jumbo Zimbabwe 17°30S 30°58E 269 F3
Jumbo Pk. U.S.A. 36°12N 114°11W 307 J12
Jumentos Cays Bahamas 23°0N 75°40W 320 B4
Jumilla Spain 38°28N 1°19W 197 G3
Jumla Nepal 29°15N 82°13E 243 E10
Jumna = Yamuna → India 25°30N 81°53E 243 G9
Jumunjin S. Korea 37°55N 128°54E 224 D4
Junagadh India 21°30N 70°30E 242 J4
Juncos Puerto Rico 18°14N 65°55W 321 b
Junction Tex., U.S.A. 30°29N 99°46W 314 F5
Junction Utah, U.S.A. 38°14N 112°13W 305 G7
Junction B. Australia 11°52S 133°55E 280 A1
Junction City Ga., U.S.A. 32°36N 84°28W 316 C5
Junction City Kans., U.S.A. 39°2N 96°50W 308 F5
Junction City Oreg., U.S.A. 44°13N 123°12W 304 D2
Junction Pt. Australia 11°45S 133°50E 280 A1
Jundah Australia 24°46S 143°2E 280 C3
Jundiaí Brazil 24°30S 47°0W 335 A6
Juneau U.S.A. 58°18N 134°25W 296 B2
Junee Australia 34°53S 147°35E 283 C7
Jung S. Korea 37°33N 126°59E 137 B1
Jungbunzlau = Mladá Boleslav Czech Rep. 50°27N 14°53E 180 A7
Jungfernheide, Volkspark Germany 52°32N 13°18E 115 A2
Jungfernsee Germany 52°25N 13°6E 115 B1
Jungfrau Switz. 46°32N 7°58E 179 J3
Junggar Pendi China 44°30N 86°0E 217 D11
Junghwa S. Korea 37°35N 127°3E 137 B2
Jungnang S. Korea 37°36N 127°5E 137 B2
Jungnangcheon → S. Korea 37°32N 126°55E 137 B1
Jungsdalshytta = Iungsdalshytta Norway 60°49N 7°55E 164 D4
Jungshahi Pakistan 24°52N 67°44E 242 G2
Juniata → U.S.A. 40°24N 77°1W 312 F7
Junín Argentina 34°33S 60°57W 334 C3
Junín Peru 11°12S 76°0W 330 C2
Junín □ Peru 11°30S 75°0W 330 C3
Junín de los Andes Argentina 39°45S 71°0W 336 A2
Juniper Green U.K. 55°54N 3°16W 121 B2
Jūniyah Lebanon 33°59N 35°38E 250 E6
Junk B. China 22°17N 114°15E 122 B2
Junlian China 28°8N 104°29E 228 C5
Junnar India 19°12N 73°58E 244 E1
Juno Beach U.S.A. 26°52N 80°3W 317 J9
Juntas Chile 28°24S 69°58W 334 B2
Juntura U.S.A. 43°45N 118°5W 304 E4
Juparanã, L. Brazil 19°16S 40°8W 333 E3
Jupiter U.S.A. 26°57N 80°6W 317 J9
Juquiá Brazil 24°19S 47°38W 333 F2
Jur, Nahr el → Sudan 8°45N 29°15E 257 F2
Jura = Jura, Mts. du Europe 46°40N 6°5E 173 F13
Jura = Schwäbische Alb Germany 48°20N 9°30E 179 G5
Jura U.K. 56°0N 5°50W 167 F3
Jura □ France 46°47N 5°45E 173 F12
Jura □ Switz. 47°20N 7°20E 179 H3
Jūra → Lithuania 55°3N 22°9E 184 C9
Jura, Mts. du Europe 46°40N 6°5E 173 F13
Jura, Sd. of U.K. 55°57N 5°45W 167 F3
Jurado Colombia 7°7N 77°46W 328 B2
Jurbarkas Lithuania 55°4N 22°46E 184 C9
Jurien Australia 30°18S 115°2E 279 F2
Jurilovca Romania 44°46N 28°52E 183 F13
Jūrmala Latvia 56°58N 23°34E 184 B10
Jurong Jiangsu, China 31°57N 119°9E 229 B12
Jurong Singapore 1°19N 103°42E 138 B2
Jurong, Selat Singapore 1°17N 103°42E 138 B2
Jurong Industrial Estate Singapore 1°19N 103°40E 138 B1
Juruá Brazil 3°27S 66°3W 328 D4
Juruá → Brazil 2°37S 65°44W 328 D4
Juruena Brazil 13°0S 58°10W 331 C6
Juruena → Brazil 7°20S 58°3W 331 B6
Jurujuba, Enseada de Brazil 22°54S 43°6W 135 B2
Juruti Brazil 2°9S 56°4W 329 D6
Jūsō Japan 34°42N 135°27E 133 A1
Jussey France 47°50N 5°55E 173 E12
Justice U.S.A. 41°44N 87°49W 119 C2
Justicia Madrid, Spain 127 a3
Justo Daract Argentina 33°52S 65°12W 334 C2
Jutaí Amazonas, Brazil 2°44S 66°57W 328 D4
Jutaí Amazonas, Brazil 5°11S 68°54W 330 B4
Jutaí → Brazil 2°43S 66°57W 328 D4
Jüterbog Germany 51°59N 13°5E 178 D9
Juticalpa Honduras 14°40N 86°12W 320 D2
Jutland = Jylland Denmark 56°25N 9°30E 163 H3
Juuka Finland 63°13N 29°17E 160 E23
Juventud, I. de la Cuba 21°40N 82°40W 320 B3
Juvigny-sous-Andaine France 48°32N 0°30W 172 D6
Juwangsan △ S. Korea 36°20N 129°15E 224 D4
Jūy Zar Iran 33°50N 46°18E 213 F12
Juye China 35°22N 116°5E 226 G9
Juzennecourt France 48°10N 4°58E 173 D11
Južni Brod = Brod Macedonia 41°32N 21°17E 202 E5
Jvari Georgia 42°42N 42°4E 191 J6
Jwalahari India 28°40N 77°6E 120 B1
Jyderup Denmark 55°40N 11°26E 163 J5
Jylland Denmark 56°25N 9°30E 163 H3
Jyväskylä Finland 62°14N 25°50E 188 A3

K

K2 Pakistan 35°58N 76°32E 243 B7
Ka → Nigeria 11°40N 4°10E 263 C5
Kaa-Iya △ Bolivia 18°35S 61°40W 331 D5
Kaaawa U.S.A. 21°33N 157°51W 302 J14
Kaakha = Kaka Turkmenistan 37°21N 59°36E 247 B8
Ka'ala U.S.A. 21°31N 158°9W 302 J13
Kaala-Gomén N. Cal. 20°40S 164°25E 288 d
Ka'alu'alu B. U.S.A. 18°58N 155°37W 302 E6
Kaap Plateau S. Africa 28°30S 24°0E 270 C3
Kaapkruis Namibia 21°55S 13°57E 270 B1
Kaapstad = Cape Town S. Africa 33°55S 18°22E 118 A1
Kaashidhoo Atoll Maldives 4°58N 73°28E 272 d
Kaashidhoo Channel Maldives 5°1N 73°28E 272 d
Kaataon, Mt. Phil. 8°10N 124°52E 233 G5
Kaba Guinea 10°9N 11°40W 262 C2
Kabacan Phil. 7°8N 124°49E 233 H5
Kabachishche = Zelenodolsk Russia 55°55N 48°30E 190 C9
Kabaena Indonesia 5°15S 122°0E 231 F6
Kabala S. Leone 9°38N 11°37W 262 D2
Kabale Uganda 1°15S 30°0E 268 C3
Kabalebostuwmeer Suriname 4°45N 57°30W 329 C6
Kabalo Dem. Rep. of the Congo 6°0S 27°0E 265 D5
Kabambare Dem. Rep. of the Congo 4°41S 27°39E 268 C2
Kabango Dem. Rep. of the Congo 8°35S 28°30E 269 D2
Kabanjahe Indonesia 3°6N 98°30E 234 B1
Kabankalan Phil. 9°59N 122°49E 233 G4
Kabara Fiji 18°59S 178°56W 287 B3
Kabara Mali 16°40N 2°50W 262 B4
Kabardinka Russia 44°40N 37°57E 189 K10
Kabardino-Balkar Republic = Kabardino-Balkaria □ Russia 43°30N 43°30E 191 J6
Kabardino-Balkaria □ Russia 43°30N 43°30E 191 J6
Kabarega Falls = Murchison Falls Uganda 2°15N 31°30E 268 B3
Kabarnet Kenya 0°30N 35°45E 268 B4
Kabasalan Phil. 7°47N 122°44E 233 H4
Kabat Indonesia 8°16S 114°19E 231 J17
Kabaty Poland 52°8N 21°4E 142 C2
Kabba Nigeria 7°50N 6°3E 263 D6
Kabbani → India 12°13N 76°54E 245 H3
Kabi Niger 13°30N 12°35E 259 F2
Kabin Buri Thailand 13°57N 101°43E 236 F3
Kabinakagami L. Canada 48°54N 84°25W 298 C3
Kabinda Dem. Rep. of the Congo 6°10S 24°29E 265 D4
Kabkabīyah Sudan 13°50N 24°0E 259 F4
Kablungu, C. Papua N. G. 6°20S 150°1E 286 D6
Kabna Sudan 19°6N 32°40E 256 D3
Kabo C.A.R. 7°35N 18°38E 264 A3
Kabompo Zambia 13°36S 24°14E 265 E4
Kabompo → Zambia 14°11S 23°11E 265 E4
Kabondo Dem. Rep. of the Congo 8°58S 25°40E 265 D5
Kabongo Dem. Rep. of the Congo 7°22S 25°33E 265 D5
Kabot Guinea 10°48N 14°57W 262 C2
Kabou Togo 9°28N 0°55E 263 D5
Kaboudia, Rass Tunisia 35°13N 11°10E 258 A2
Kabr Sudan 10°54N 26°50E 257 E2
Kabrît, G. el Egypt 29°42N 33°16E 251 J4
Kabrousse Senegal 12°25N 16°45W 262 C1
Kabubu Dem. Rep. of the Congo 9°42S 24°40E 265 D4
Kabūd Gonbad Iran 37°5N 59°45E 247 B8
Kabugao Phil. 18°2N 121°11E 232 B3
Kābul Afghan. 34°28N 69°11E 242 B3
Kābul □ Afghan. 34°30N 69°0E 240 B3
Kābul → Pakistan 33°55N 72°14E 242 C5
Kabuli Papua N. G. 2°7S 146°40E 286 B4
Kabunga Dem. Rep. of the Congo 1°38S 28°3E 268 C2
Kaburuang Indonesia 3°50N 126°30E 231 D7
Kabushiya Sudan 16°54N 33°41E 257 D3
Kabwanga Dem. Rep. of the Congo 7°2S 22°36E 265 D4
Kabwe Zambia 14°30S 28°29E 269 E2
Kabwum Papua N. G. 6°11S 147°15E 286 D4
Kačanik Serbia 42°13N 21°12E 202 D5
Kačerginė Lithuania 54°56N 23°42E 184 D10
Kachar Kazakhstan 53°23N 62°55E 216 B6
Kachchh, Gulf of India 22°50N 69°15E 242 H3
Kachchh, Rann of India 24°0N 70°0E 242 H4
Kachchhidhana India 21°44N 78°46E 243 J8
Kachebera Zambia 13°50S 32°50E 269 E3
Kachia Nigeria 9°50N 7°55E 263 D6
Kachikau Botswana 18°8S 24°26E 270 A3
Kachin □ Burma 26°0N 97°30E 228 D1
Kachira, L. Uganda 0°40S 31°7E 268 C3
Kachiry Kazakhstan 53°10N 75°50E 217 B9
Kachisi Ethiopia 9°40N 37°50E 257 F4
Kachnara India 23°50N 75°6E 242 H6
Kachot Cambodia 11°30N 103°3E 237 G4
Kaçkar Turkey 40°45N 41°10E 213 B9
Kada Chad 19°20N 19°39E 259 E3
Kadaingti Burma 17°37N 97°32E 241 G6
Kadaiyanallur India 9°3N 77°22E 245 K3
Kadan Czech Rep. 50°23N 13°16E 180 A6
Kadan Kyun Burma 12°30N 98°20E 236 F2
Kadanai → Afghan. 31°22N 65°45E 242 D1
Kadarkút Hungary 46°13N 17°39E 182 D2
Kadavu Fiji 19°0S 178°15E 287 B2
Kadavu Passage Fiji 18°45S 178°0E 287 B2
Kade Ghana 6°7N 0°56W 263 D4
Kadei → C.A.R. 3°31N 16°3E 264 B3
Kademlija = Triglav Slovenia 46°21N 13°50E 199 B10
Kadena Japan 26°22N 127°45E 288 a
Kadhimain = Al Kāẓimīyah Iraq 33°22N 44°18E 213 F11
Kadi India 23°18N 72°23E 242 H5
Kadiak I. = Kodiak I. U.S.A. 57°30N 152°45W 303 H9
Kadıköy Turkey 40°59N 29°1E 122 C2
Kadina Australia 33°55S 137°43E 282 B2
Kadınhanı Turkey 38°14N 32°13E 212 C5
Kadiolo Mali 10°35N 7°41W 262 C3
Kadipur India 26°10N 82°23E 243 F10
Kadirabad India 19°51N 75°54E 244 E2
Kadiri India 14°12N 78°13E 245 G4
Kadirli Turkey 37°23N 36°5E 212 D7
Kadiyevka = Stakhanov Ukraine 48°35N 38°40E 189 H10
Kadja, O. → Chad 12°2N 22°28E 259 F4
Kadmat I. India 11°14N 72°47E 245 J1
Kadodo Sudan 11°4N 29°31E 257 E2
Kadoka U.S.A. 43°50N 101°31W 308 D3
Kadom Russia 54°37N 42°30E 190 C6
Kadoma Ōsaka, Japan 34°44N 135°35E 133 A2
Kadoma Zimbabwe 18°20S 29°52E 269 F2
Kâdugli Sudan 11°0N 29°45E 257 E2
Kaduna Nigeria 10°30N 7°21E 263 C6
Kaduna □ Nigeria 11°0N 7°30E 263 C6
Kadur India 13°34N 76°1E 245 H3
Kaduy Russia 59°12N 37°9E 188 C9
Kaédi Mauritania 16°9N 13°28W 262 B2
Kaélé Cameroon 10°7N 14°27E 259 F2
Ka'ena U.S.A. 21°34N 158°14W 302 J13
Ka'ena Pt. U.S.A. 21°35N 158°17W 302 J13
Kaeng Khoï Thailand 14°35N 101°0E 236 E3
Kaeng Kra Chan △ Thailand 12°57N 99°23E 236 F2
Kaeng Tana △ Thailand 15°25N 105°32E 236 E5
Kaeo N.Z. 35°6S 173°49E 284 B2
Kaesŏng N. Korea 37°58N 126°35E 224 D3
Kaesŏng □ N. Korea 38°0N 126°37E 224 D3
Kāf Si. Arabia 31°25N 37°29E 246 D3
Kafakumba Dem. Rep. of the Congo 9°38S 23°46E 265 D4
Kafan = Kapan Armenia 39°18N 46°27E 213 C12
Kafanchan Nigeria 9°40N 8°20E 263 D6
Kafareti Nigeria 10°25N 11°12E 263 C7
Kaffrine Senegal 14°8N 15°36W 262 C1
Kafia Kingi Sudan 9°20N 24°25E 264 A4
Kafin Nigeria 9°30N 7°4E 263 D6
Kafin Madaki Nigeria 10°41N 9°46E 263 C6
Kafinda Zambia 12°32S 30°20E 269 E3
Kafr 'Aqab West Bank 31°52N 35°13E 123 A2
Kafr el Battikh Egypt 31°25N 31°44E 256 H7
Kafr el Dauwâr Egypt 31°8N 30°8E 256 H7
Kafr el Sheikh Egypt 31°15N 30°50E 251 G1
Kafr el Sheikh □ Egypt 31°15N 30°55E 251 G1
Kafue Zambia 15°46S 28°9E 269 F2
Kafue △ Zambia 15°12S 25°38E 269 F2
Kafue Flats Zambia 15°40S 27°25E 269 F2
Kafulwe Zambia 9°0S 29°1E 269 D2
Kafumba Dem. Rep. of the Congo 5°23S 18°55E 265 D3
Kaga Afghan. 34°14N 70°10E 242 B4
Kaga Japan 36°16N 136°15E 223 A8
Kaga Bandoro C.A.R. 7°0N 19°10E 264 A3
Kagamil I. U.S.A. 53°0N 169°43W 303 K5
Kagan Uzbekistan 39°43N 64°33E 216 E6
Kaganovich = Tovarkovskiy Russia 53°40N 38°14E 188 F10
Kagarko Nigeria 9°28N 7°36E 263 D6
Kagawa □ Japan 34°15N 134°0E 222 C6
Kagera □ Tanzania 2°0S 31°30E 268 C3
Kagera → Uganda 0°57S 31°47E 268 C3
Kâğıthane Turkey 41°4N 28°58E 122 B1
Kâğıthane → Turkey 41°9N 28°56E 122 B1
Kağızman Turkey 40°5N 43°10E 213 B10
Kagmar Sudan 14°24N 30°25E 257 E3
Kagopal Chad 8°16N 16°23E 259 G3
Kagoshima Japan 31°35N 130°33E 222 F2
Kagoshima □ Japan 31°30N 130°30E 222 F2
Kagoshima-Wan Japan 31°25N 130°40E 222 F2
Kagran Austria 48°14N 16°26E 142 A2
Kagua Papua N. G. 6°26S 143°48E 286 D2
Kagul = Cahul Moldova 45°50N 28°15E 183 E13
Kahak Iran 36°6N 49°46E 247 B6
Kahalu'u U.S.A. 21°27N 157°50W 302 K14
Kahama Tanzania 4°8S 32°30E 268 C3
Kahan Pakistan 29°18N 68°54E 242 E3
Kahana U.S.A. 21°34N 157°53W 302 J14
Kahana B. U.S.A. 21°35N 157°50W 302 J14
Kahana Valley State Park ⌂ U.S.A. 21°32N 157°53W 302 J14
Kahang Malaysia 2°12N 103°32E 237 L4
Kahayan → Indonesia 3°40S 114°0E 235 C4
Kahe Tanzania 3°30S 37°25E 268 C4
Kahemba Dem. Rep. of the Congo 7°18S 18°55E 265 D3
Kaherekoau Mts. N.Z. 45°45S 167°15E 285 F2
Kahil, Djebel bou Algeria 34°26N 4°0E 261 B5
Kahnawake Canada 45°24N 73°40W 130 B1
Kahnūj Iran 27°55N 57°40E 247 E8
Kahoka U.S.A. 40°25N 91°44W 310 D5
Kaho'olawe U.S.A. 20°33N 156°37W 302 C5
Kahouanne Guadeloupe 16°15N 61°12W 322 e
Kahouanne, Îlet à Guadeloupe 16°22N 61°46W 322 e
Kahramanmaraş Turkey 37°37N 36°53E 212 D7
Kahramanmaraş □ Turkey 37°35N 36°33E 212 D7
Kâhta Turkey 37°46N 38°36E 213 D8
Kahuku U.S.A. 21°41N 157°57W 302 J14
Kahuku Pt. U.S.A. 21°43N 157°59W 302 J14
Kahul, Ozero Ukraine 45°24N 28°24E 183 E13
Kahului U.S.A. 20°54N 156°28W 302 C5
Kahului ✈ (OGG) U.S.A. 20°54N 156°26W 302 C5
Kahurangi △ N.Z. 41°10S 172°32E 285 B7
Kahurangi Pt. N.Z. 40°50S 172°10E 285 A7
Kahuta Pakistan 33°35N 73°24E 242 C5
Kahuzi-Biega △ Dem. Rep. of the Congo 1°50S 27°55E 268 C2
Kai, Kepulauan Indonesia 5°55S 132°45E 231 F8
Kai Besar Indonesia 5°35S 133°0E 231 F8
Kai Is. = Kai, Kepulauan Indonesia 5°55S 132°45E 231 F8
Kai Kecil Indonesia 5°45S 132°40E 231 F8
Kai Xian China 31°11N 108°21E 228 B7
Kaiama Nigeria 9°36N 4°1E 263 D5
Kaiapit Papua N. G. 6°18S 146°18E 286 D4
Kaiapoi N.Z. 43°24S 172°40E 285 D7
Kaidu He → China 41°46N 86°31E 218 B3
Kaieteur Falls Guyana 5°1N 59°10W 329 B6
Kaifeng China 34°48N 114°21E 226 G8
Kaihua China 29°12N 118°20E 229 C12
Kaijiang China 31°7N 107°55E 228 B6
Kaikohe N.Z. 35°25S 173°49E 284 B2
Kaikoura N.Z. 42°25S 173°43E 285 C8
Kaikoura Pen. N.Z. 42°25S 173°43E 285 C8
Kailahun S. Leone 8°18N 10°39W 262 D2
Kailash = Kangrinboqe Feng China 31°0N 81°25E 243 D9
Kailashahar India 24°19N 92°0E 241 C4
Kaileuna I. Papua N. G. 8°32S 150°57E 286 E6
Kaili China 26°33N 107°59E 228 D6
Kailu China 43°38N 121°18E 227 C11
Kailua Hawai'i, U.S.A. 19°39N 155°59W 302 D6
Kailua Hawai'i, U.S.A. 21°24N 157°44W 302 K14
Kailua B. U.S.A. 21°25N 157°40W 302 K14
Kaim → Papua N. G. 6°55S 141°33E 286 D1
Kaimaktsalan Oros = Voras Oros Greece 40°57N 21°45E 202 F5
Kaimana Indonesia 3°39S 133°45E 231 E8
Kaimanawa Mts. N.Z. 39°15S 175°56E 284 F4
Kaimata N.Z. 42°34S 171°28E 285 C6
Kaimes U.K. 55°54N 3°10W 121 B2
Kaimganj India 27°33N 79°24E 243 F8
Kaimon-Dake Japan 31°11N 130°32E 222 F2
Kaimur Hills India 24°30N 82°0E 243 G10
Kainab → Namibia 28°32S 19°34E 270 C2
Kainan Japan 34°9N 135°12E 223 C7
Kainantu Papua N. G. 6°18S 145°52E 286 D3
Kainji Dam Nigeria 9°55N 4°35E 263 D5
Kainji Lake △ Nigeria 10°5N 4°6E 263 C5
Kainji Res. Nigeria 10°1N 4°40E 263 C5
Kainsk = Samara Russia 53°8N 50°6E 190 D10
Kainuu Finland 64°30N 29°7E 160 D23
Kaipara Harbour N.Z. 36°25S 174°14E 284 C3
Kaiping China 22°23N 112°42E 229 F9
Kaipokok B. Canada 54°54N 59°47W 299 B8
Kaira India 22°45N 72°50E 242 H5
Kairana India 29°24N 77°15E 242 E7
Kairiru I. Papua N. G. 3°21S 143°34E 286 B2
Kaironi Indonesia 0°47S 133°40E 231 E8
Kairouan Tunisia 35°45N 10°5E 258 A2
Kairouan □ Tunisia 35°30N 9°46E 261 A6
Kairuku Papua N. G. 8°51S 146°35E 286 E4
Kaiser Wilhelm Kanal = Nord-Ostsee-Kanal Germany 54°12N 9°32E 178 A5
Kaiser Wilhelm Kirche Berlin, Germany 115 b2
Kaiser-Wilhelmsland = Papua □ Indonesia 4°0S 137°0E 231 E9
Kaiserebersdorf Austria 48°9N 16°26E 142 B2
Kaiserslautern Germany 49°26N 7°45E 179 F3
Kaiserstuhl Germany 48°4N 7°40E 179 G3
Kaita Japan 34°22N 132°32E 222 C4
Kaitaia N.Z. 35°8S 173°17E 284 B2
Kaitangata N.Z. 46°17S 169°51E 285 G4
Kaithal India 29°48N 76°26E 242 E7
Kaitu → Pakistan 33°10N 70°30E 242 C4
Kaivoksela Finland 60°15N 24°53E 121 B2
Kaiwi Channel U.S.A. 21°15N 157°30W 302 K14
Kaiyang China 27°4N 106°59E 228 D6
Kaiyuan Liaoning, China 42°28N 124°1E 224 A2
Kaiyuan Yunnan, China 23°40N 103°12E 228 F4
Kaiyuh Mts. U.S.A. 64°30N 158°0W 303 D8
Kajaani Finland 64°17N 27°46E 160 D22
Kajabbi Australia 20°0S 140°1E 280 C3
Kajana = Kajaani Finland 64°17N 27°46E 160 D22
Kajang Malaysia 2°59N 101°48E 237 L3
Kajaran Armenia 39°10N 46°7E 213 C12
Kajiado Kenya 1°53S 36°48E 268 C4
Kajo Kaji Sudan 3°58N 31°40E 257 G3
Kajuru Nigeria 10°15N 7°34E 263 C6
Kaka Sudan 10°38N 32°10E 257 E3
Kaka Turkmenistan 37°21N 59°36E 247 B8
Kakabeka Falls Canada 48°24N 89°37W 298 C2
Kakadu △ Australia 12°0S 132°3E 278 B5
Kakamas S. Africa 28°45S 20°33E 270 C3
Kakamega Kenya 0°20N 34°46E 268 B3
Kakamigahara Japan 35°28N 136°48E 223 B8
Kakana India 9°7N 92°48E 245 K11
Kakanj Bos.-H. 44°4N 18°4E 182 F3
Kakanui Mts. N.Z. 45°10S 170°30E 285 F5
Kakata Liberia 6°35N 10°20W 262 D2
Kakdwip India 21°53N 88°11E 243 J13
Kake Japan 34°36N 132°19E 222 C4
Kake Alaska, U.S.A. 56°59N 133°57W 296 B2
Kakegawa Japan 34°45N 138°1E 223 C10
Kakeroma-Jima Japan 28°8N 129°14E 221 K4
Kakhib Russia 42°28N 46°34E 191 J8
Kakhonak U.S.A. 59°26N 154°51W 303 G9
Kakhovka Ukraine 46°45N 33°30E 189 J7
Kakhovske Vdskh. Ukraine 47°5N 34°0E 189 J7
Kakinada India 16°57N 82°11E 244 F6
Kakisa → Canada 61°3N 118°10W 296 A5
Kakisa L. Canada 60°56N 117°43W 296 A5
Käkisalmi = Priozersk Russia 61°2N 30°7E 188 B6
Kakogawa Japan 34°46N 134°51E 222 C6
Kaktovik U.S.A. 70°8N 143°38W 303 A12
Kakum △ Ghana 5°24N 1°20W 263 D4
Kakuma Kenya 3°43N 34°52E 268 B3
Kakwa → Canada 54°37N 118°28W 296 C5
Kāl Gūsheh Iran 30°59N 58°12E 247 D8
Kal Safīd Iran 34°52N 47°23E 213 E12
Kala Nigeria 12°2N 14°40E 263 C7
Kala Oya → Sri Lanka 8°20N 79°45E 245 K4
Kalaa-Kebira Tunisia 35°59N 10°32E 258 A2
Kalaallit Nunaat = Greenland ⊠ N. Amer. 66°0N 45°0W 154 D6
Kalabagh Pakistan 33°0N 71°28E 242 C4
Kalabahi Indonesia 8°13S 124°31E 231 F6
Kalabak = Radomir Bulgaria 42°37N 22°59E 202 D6
Kalabakan Malaysia 4°25N 117°29E 235 B5
Kalabana Mali 14°10N 8°35W 262 C3
Kalabo Zambia 14°58S 22°40E 265 E4
Kalach Russia 50°22N 41°0E 190 E5
Kalach na Donu Russia 48°43N 43°32E 191 F6
Kalachinsk Russia 55°3N 74°33E 217 A8
Kaladan → Burma 20°20N 93°5E 241 E4
Kaladar Canada 44°37N 77°5W 312 B7
Kalae U.S.A. 18°55N 155°41W 302 E6
Kalahari Africa 24°0S 21°30E 270 B3
Kalahari Gemsbok △ S. Africa 25°30S 20°30E 270 C3
Kalaheo U.S.A. 21°56N 159°32W 302 B2
Kalaikhum Tajikistan 38°28N 70°46E 217 E8
Kalajoki Finland 64°12N 24°10E 160 D21
Kalakamati Botswana 20°40S 27°25E 271 B4
Kalakan Russia 55°15N 116°45E 215 D12
Kalakol Kenya 3°33N 35°54E 266 D4
K'alak'unlun Shank'ou = Karakoram Pass Asia 35°33N 77°50E 243 B7
Kalam Pakistan 35°34N 72°30E 243 B5
Kalama Dem. Rep. of the Congo 2°52S 28°35E 268 C2
Kalama Wash., U.S.A. 46°1N 122°51W 306 E4
Kalamaki Greece 37°52N 23°43E 112 B2
Kalamaloué △ Cameroon 12°9N 14°58E 259 F2
Kalamansig Phil. 6°33N 124°3E 233 H5
Kalamaria Greece 40°33N 22°55E 202 F6
Kalamata Greece 37°3N 22°10E 204 D4
Kalamazoo U.S.A. 42°17N 85°35W 311 B11
Kalamazoo → U.S.A. 42°40N 86°10W 311 B10
Kalamb India 18°3N 74°48E 244 E2
Kalambaka Greece 39°42N 21°39E 204 B3
Kalambo Falls Tanzania 8°37S 31°35E 269 D3
Kalamitsi Greece 38°45N 20°36E 207 B2
Kalamnuri India 19°40N 77°20E 244 E3
Kalamos Attiki, Greece 38°17N 23°52E 204 C5
Kalamos Lefkada, Greece 38°37N 20°55E 207 B2
Kalan Turkey 39°7N 39°32E 246 B3
Kalangadoo Australia 37°34S 140°41E 282 D4
Kalankalan Guinea 10°7N 8°54W 262 C3
Kalannie Australia 30°22S 117°5E 279 F2
Kalāntarī Iran 32°10N 54°8E 247 C7
Kalao Indonesia 7°21S 121°0E 231 F6
Kalaoa U.S.A. 19°43N 155°58W 302 D6
Kalaotoa Indonesia 7°20S 121°50E 231 F6
Kälarne Sweden 62°59N 16°5E 162 B10
Kalasin Thailand 16°26N 103°30E 236 D4
Kālat Iran 25°29N 59°22E 247 E8
Kalat Pakistan 29°8N 66°31E 240 C2
Kalāteh Iran 36°33N 55°41E 247 B7
Kalāteh-ye Ganj Iran 27°31N 57°55E 247 E8
Kalathos Greece 36°9N 28°8E 206 E12
Kalatungan Mt. Phil. 7°54N 124°50E 233 H5
Kalaupapa U.S.A. 21°12N 156°59W 302 B5
Kalaupapa ⌂ U.S.A. 21°10N 156°59W 302 B5
Kalaus → Russia 45°40N 44°7E 191 H7
Kalavrita Greece 38°3N 22°8E 204 C4
Kalaw Burma 20°38N 96°34E 241 E6
Kalawao County U.S.A. 21°11N 156°58W 302 B5
Kalbā U.A.E. 25°5N 56°22E 247 E8
Kalbadevi Mumbai, India 130 b2
Kalbān Oman 20°18N 58°38E 249 B7
Kalbarri Australia 27°40S 114°10E 279 E1
Kalbarri △ Australia 27°51S 114°30E 279 E1
Kalce Slovenia 45°54N 14°13E 176 F8
Kaldrananes Iceland 65°45N 21°25W 155 B5
Kale Antalya, Turkey 36°14N 30°0E 205 E12
Kale Denizli, Turkey 37°27N 28°49E 205 D10
Kalecik Turkey 40°4N 33°26E 212 B5
Kalegauk Kyun Burma 15°33N 97°35E 236 E1
Kalehe Dem. Rep. of the Congo 2°6S 28°50E 268 C2
Kalema Tanzania 1°12S 31°55E 268 C3
Kalemie Dem. Rep. of the Congo 5°55S 29°9E 268 D2
Kalemyo Burma 23°11N 94°4E 241 D5
Kalety Poland 50°35N 18°52E 185 H5
Kalewa Burma 23°10N 94°15E 241 D5
Kaleybar Iran 38°47N 47°2E 246 B5
Kálfafell Iceland 63°57N 17°41W 155 D9
Kalgan = Zhangjiakou China 40°48N 114°55E 226 D8
Kalghatgi India 15°11N 74°58E 245 G2
Kalgoorlie-Boulder Australia 30°40S 121°22E 279 F3
Kalhovd Norway 60°4N 8°21E 164 D5
Kali → India 27°6N 79°55E 243 F8
Kali Sindh → India 25°32N 76°17E 242 G6
Kaliakra, Nos Bulgaria 43°21N 28°30E 203 C12
Kalianda Indonesia 5°50S 105°45E 234 D3
Kalibo Phil. 11°43N 122°22E 233 F4
Kaliganj Bangla. 22°25N 89°8E 241 D2
Kalihi U.S.A. 21°20N 157°53W 302 K14
Kalihi Valley U.S.A. 21°20N 157°52W 302 K14
Kalima Dem. Rep. of the Congo 2°33S 26°32E 268 C2
Kalimantan Indonesia 0°0 114°0E 235 C4
Kalimantan Barat □ Indonesia 0°0 110°30E 235 C4
Kalimantan Selatan □ Indonesia 2°30S 115°30E 235 C5
Kalimantan Tengah □ Indonesia 2°0S 113°30E 235 C4
Kalimantan Timur □ Indonesia 1°30N 116°30E 235 B5
Kálimnos Greece 37°0N 27°0E 205 D8
Kalimpong India 27°4N 88°35E 241 B2
Kalinadi → India 14°50N 74°7E 245 G2
Kalinga □ Phil. 17°30N 121°20E 232 C3
Kalinikinsk Russia 51°29N 44°28E 216 B2
Kalinin = Tver Russia 56°55N 35°55E 188 D8
Kaliningrad Russia 54°42N 20°32E 184 D7
Kaliningrad ✈ (KGD) Russia 54°45N 20°33E 184 D7
Kalininsk = Petrozavodsk Russia 61°41N 34°20E 188 B8
Kalininsk Russia 51°30N 44°40E 190 E7
Kalinkavichy Belarus 52°12N 29°20E 177 B15
Kalinkovichi = Kalinkavichy Belarus 52°12N 29°20E 177 B15
Kalinovik Bos.-H. 43°31N 18°25E 202 C2
Kalipetrovo Bulgaria 44°5N 27°14E 203 B11
Kalipur India 22°40N 88°17E 124 A1
Kalirachi Greece 40°40N 24°35E 203 F8
Kaliro Uganda 0°56N 33°30E 268 B3
Kalispell U.S.A. 48°12N 114°19W 304 B6
Kalisz Poland 51°45N 18°8E 185 G5
Kalisz Pomorski Poland 53°17N 15°55E 185 E2
Kalithea Greece 37°56N 23°43E 112 B2
Kaliua Tanzania 5°5S 31°48E 268 D3
Kaliveli Tank India 12°5N 79°50E 245 H4
Kalivia Thorikou Greece 37°50N 23°55E 204 D5
Kalix = Kalixälven → Sweden 65°50N 23°11E 160 D20
Kalix Sweden 65°53N 23°12E 160 D20
Kalixälven → Sweden 65°50N 23°11E 160 D20
Kalka India 30°46N 76°57E 242 D7
Kalkaji India 28°32N 77°12E 120 B2
Kalkali Ghat India 24°36N 92°20E 241 C4
Kalkan Turkey 36°15N 29°23E 205 E11
Kalkarindji Australia 17°30S 130°47E 278 C5
Kalkaska U.S.A. 44°44N 85°11W 309 C11
Kalkfeld Namibia 20°57S 16°14E 270 B2
Kalkfontein Botswana 22°4S 20°57E 270 B3
Kalkım Turkey 39°48N 27°13E 205 B9
Kalkrand Namibia 24°1S 17°35E 270 B2
Kallakkurichchi India 11°44N 79°1E 245 J4
Kallam India 18°36N 76°2E 244 E3
Kållandsö Sweden 58°40N 13°5E 163 F7
Kallavesi Finland 62°58N 27°30E 160 E22
Källby Sweden 58°30N 13°8E 163 F7
Kållered Sweden 57°32N 12°4E 163 G6
Kallidaikurichi India 8°38N 77°31E 245 K3
Kallies = Kalisz Pomorski Poland 53°17N 15°55E 185 E2
Kallimasia Greece 38°18N 26°6E 205 C8
Kallinge Sweden 56°15N 15°18E 163 H9
Kallmet Albania 41°51N 19°41E 202 E3
Kallsjön Sweden 63°38N 13°0E 160 E15
Kalmalo Nigeria 13°40N 5°20E 263 C6
Kalmanstunga Iceland 64°44N 20°48W 155 C6
Kalmar Sweden 56°40N 16°20E 163 H10
Kalmar län □ Sweden 57°25N 16°0E 163 G10
Kalmarsund Sweden 56°40N 16°25E 163 H10
Kalmunai Sri Lanka 7°25N 81°49E 245 L5
Kalmyk Republic = Kalmykia □ Russia 46°5N 46°1E 191 G8
Kalmykia □ Russia 46°5N 46°1E 191 G8
Kalmykovo Kazakhstan 49°0N 51°47E 187 E9
Kalna India 23°13N 88°25E 243 H13
Kalnai India 22°46N 83°30E 243 H10
Kalni → Bangla. 24°21N 91°13E 241 C3
Kalo Papua N. G. 10°1S 147°48E 286 F4
Kalo Nero Greece 37°20N 21°38E 204 D3
Kalocsa Hungary 46°32N 19°0E 182 D4
Kalofer Bulgaria 42°37N 24°59E 203 D8
Kalohi Channel U.S.A. 21°0N 157°0W 302 C5
Kalokhorio Cyprus 34°51N 33°2E 207 F9
Kaloko Dem. Rep. of the Congo 6°47S 25°48E 265 D5
Kaloko-Honokōhau ⌂ U.S.A. 19°40N 156°1W 302 D5
Kalol Gujarat, India 22°37N 73°31E 242 H5
Kalol Gujarat, India 23°15N 72°33E 242 H5
Kalolimnos Greece 37°4N 27°5E 205 D9
Kalomo Zambia 17°0S 26°30E 269 F2
Kalona U.S.A. 41°29N 91°43W 310 C5
Kaloni Greece 39°14N 26°12E 205 B8
Kaloni, Kolpos Greece 39°10N 26°10E 205 B8
Kalpeni I. India 10°5N 73°38E 245 J1
Kalpi India 26°8N 79°47E 243 F8
Kalpitiya Sri Lanka 8°14N 79°46E 245 K4
Kalputhi I. India 10°49N 72°10E 245 J1
Kalrayan Hills India 11°45N 78°40E 245 J4
Kalsubai India 19°35N 73°45E 244 E1
Kaltag U.S.A. 64°20N 158°43W 303 D8
Kaltern = Caldaro Italy 46°25N 11°14E 199 B8
Kaltukatjara Australia 24°52S 129°5E 279 D4
Kaltungo Nigeria 9°48N 11°19E 263 D7
Kalu Pakistan 25°5N 67°39E 242 G2
Kaluga Russia 54°35N 36°10E 188 E9
Kaluga □ Russia 54°15N 34°50E 188 E8
Kalulong, Bukit Malaysia 3°14N 114°39E 235 B4
Kalulushi Zambia 12°50S 28°3E 269 E2
Kalumburu Australia 13°55S 126°35E 278 B4
Kalundborg Denmark 55°41N 11°5E 163 J5
Kalush Ukraine 49°3N 24°23E 177 D13
Kałuszyn Poland 52°13N 21°52E 185 F8
Kalutara Sri Lanka 6°35N 80°0E 245 L5
Kalvåg Norway 61°46N 4°51E 164 C1
Kalvarija Lithuania 54°24N 23°14E 184 D10
Kalvebod Fælled Denmark 55°35S 12°33E 118 B3
Kalveboderne Denmark 55°37N 12°31E 118 B3
Kalwakurti India 16°41N 78°30E 244 F4
Kalya Russia 60°15N 59°59E 186 B10
Kalyan Maharashtra, India 20°30N 74°3E 244 D2
Kalyan Maharashtra, India 19°15N 73°9E 244 E1
Kalyandurg India 14°33N 77°6E 245 G3
Kalyani India 17°52N 76°57E 244 F3
Kalyansingapuram India 19°30N 83°19E 244 E6
Kalyazin Russia 57°15N 37°55E 188 D9
Kam Albania 42°17N 20°18E 202 D4
Kam → Nigeria 8°15N 1°10E 263 D7
Kama Burma 19°1N 95°4E 241 F5
Kama Dem. Rep. of the Congo 3°30S 27°5E 268 C2
Kama → Russia 55°45N 52°0E 186 C9
Kama Iwa Iwo Jima 24°47N 141°17E 288 b
Kamachumu Tanzania 1°37S 31°37E 268 C3
Kamae Japan 32°48N 131°56E 222 E3
Kamaing Burma 25°26N 96°35E 241 C6
Kamaishi Japan 39°16N 141°53E 220 E10
Kamakou U.S.A. 21°7N 156°52W 302 B5
Kamakura Japan 35°19N 139°33E 223 B11
Kamalapurum India 14°35N 78°39E 245 G4
Kamaléte Gabon 0°43S 11°49E 264 C2
Kamalia Pakistan 30°44N 72°42E 242 D5
Kamalō U.S.A. 21°3N 156°52W 302 B5
Kaman India 27°39N 77°16E 242 F6
Kaman Turkey 39°22N 33°44E 212 C5

Kamana Dem. Rep. of the Congo 5°59S 24°58E 265 D4
Kamananui → U.S.A. 21°38N 158°4W 302 J13
Kamanjab Namibia 19°35S 14°51E 270 A2
Kamapanda Zambia 12°5S 24°0E 269 E1
Kamarān Yemen 15°21N 42°35E 248 D3
Kamareddi India 18°19N 78°21E 244 E4
Kamarhati India 22°40N 88°23E 124 A2
Kamata Japan 35°33N 139°43E 140 B3
Kamativi Zimbabwe 18°20S 27°6E 270 A4
Kamba Dem. Rep. of the Congo 4°0S 22°22E 265 C4
Kamba Nigeria 11°50N 3°45E 263 C5
Kambalda West Australia 31°10S 121°37E 279 F3
Kambam India 9°45N 77°16E 245 K3
Kambar Pakistan 27°37N 68°1E 242 F3
Kambarka Russia 56°15N 54°11E 186 C9
Kambia S. Leone 9°3N 12°53W 262 D2
Kambolé Togo 8°43N 1°39E 263 D5
Kambolé Zambia 8°47S 30°48E 269 D3
Kambos Cyprus 35°2N 32°44E 207 E8
Kambove Dem. Rep. of the Congo 10°51S 26°33E 269 E2
Kambuie Dem. Rep. of the Congo 6°59S 22°19E 265 D4
Kambwata Zambia 14°3S 23°43E 265 E4
Kamchatka, Poluostrov Russia 57°0N 160°0E 215 D17
Kamchatka Pen. = Kamchatka, Poluostrov Russia 57°0N 160°0E 215 D17
Kamchiya → Bulgaria 43°4N 27°44E 203 C11
Kame Ruins Zimbabwe 20°7S 28°25E 269 G2
Kameari Japan 35°45N 139°50E 140 A4
Kameido Japan 35°42N 139°50E 140 A4
Kamen Russia 53°50N 81°30E 217 B10
Kamen-Rybolov Russia 44°46N 132°2E 220 B6
Kamende Dem. Rep. of the Congo 6°26S 24°35E 265 D4
Kamenica Serbia 43°27N 22°27E 202 C6
Kamenica Serbia 44°25N 19°45E 202 B3
Kamenice nad Lipou Czech Rep. 49°18N 15°2E 180 B8
Kamenjak, Rt Croatia 44°47N 13°55E 199 D10
Kamenka = Kaminka Ukraine 49°3N 32°6E 189 H7
Kamenka Kazakhstan 51°7N 50°19E 190 E10
Kamenka Arkhangelsk, Russia 65°58N 44°0E 186 A7
Kamenka Penza, Russia 53°10N 44°5E 190 D6
Kamenka Voronezh, Russia 50°47N 39°20E 189 G10
Kamenka Bugskaya = Kamyanka-Buzka Ukraine 50°8N 24°16E 177 C13
Kamenka Dneprovskaya = Kamyanka-Dniprovska Ukraine 47°29N 34°28E 189 J8
Kamenka-Shevchenkovskaya = Kamyanka-Buzka Ukraine 50°8N 24°16E 177 C13
Kamennomostskiy Russia 44°18N 40°13E 191 H5
Kameno Bulgaria 42°34N 27°18E 203 D11
Kamenolomini Russia 47°40N 40°14E 191 G5
Kamensk-Shakhtinskiy Russia 48°23N 40°20E 191 F5
Kamensk Uralskiy Russia 56°25N 62°2E 214 D7
Kamenskaya = Kamensk-Shakhtinskiy Russia 48°23N 40°20E 191 F5
Kamenskiy Russia 50°48N 45°25E 190 E7
Kamenskoye = Dniprodzerzhynsk Ukraine 48°32N 34°37E 189 H8
Kamenskoye Russia 62°45N 165°30E 215 C17
Kamenyak Bulgaria 43°24N 26°57E 203 C10
Kamenz Germany 51°15N 14°5E 178 D10
Kameoka Japan 35°0N 135°35E 223 C7
Kamet India 30°55N 79°35E 243 D8
Kameyama Japan 34°51N 136°27E 223 C8
Kami-Itabashi Japan 35°45N 139°40E 140 A3
Kami-Jima Japan 32°27N 130°20E 222 E2
Kami-Koshiki-Jima Japan 31°50N 129°52E 222 F1
Kamiagata Japan 34°47N 129°24E 222 C1
Kamiah U.S.A. 46°14N 116°2W 304 C5
Kamień Krajeński Poland 53°32N 17°32E 184 E4
Kamień Pomorski Poland 53°57N 14°43E 184 E1
Kamienna → Poland 51°6N 21°47E 185 G8
Kamienna Góra Poland 50°47N 16°2E 185 H3
Kamieńsk Poland 51°12N 19°29E 185 G6
Kamieskroon S. Africa 30°9S 17°56E 270 D2
Kamikitazawa Japan 35°39N 139°36E 140 B2
Kamilukuak L. Canada 62°22N 101°40W 297 A8
Kamin-Kashyrskyy Ukraine 51°39N 24°56E 177 C13
Kamina Dem. Rep. of the Congo 8°45S 25°0E 265 D5
Kaminak L. Canada 62°10N 95°0W 297 A10
Kaministiquia Canada 48°32N 89°35W 298 C1
Kaminka Ukraine 49°3N 32°6E 189 H7
Kaminoyama Japan 38°9N 140°17E 220 E10
Kamioka Japan 36°25N 137°15E 223 A9
Kamiros Greece 36°20N 27°56E 206 E11
Kamishak Bay U.S.A. 59°15N 153°45W 303 G9
Kamitsuruma Japan 35°30N 139°26E 140 B1
Kamitsushima Japan 34°50N 129°28E 222 C1
Kamituga Dem. Rep. of the Congo 3°2S 28°10E 268 C2
Kamla → India 25°35N 86°36E 243 G12
Kamloops Canada 50°40N 120°20W 296 C4
Kamnik Slovenia 46°14N 14°37E 199 B11
Kamo Armenia 40°21N 45°7E 191 K7
Kamo Japan 37°39N 139°3E 220 F9
Kamo N.Z. 35°42S 174°20E 284 B3
Kamoa Mts. Guyana 1°30N 59°0W 329 C6
Kamogawa Japan 35°5N 140°5E 223 B12
Kamojima Japan 34°4N 134°21E 222 C6
Kamoke Pakistan 32°4N 74°4E 242 C6
Kamo'oloa U.S.A. 21°34N 158°7W 302 J13
Kamoshida Japan 35°33N 139°31E 140 B2
Kamp → Austria 48°23N 15°42E 180 C8
Kampala Uganda 0°20N 32°30E 268 B3
Kampar Malaysia 4°18N 101°9E 237 K3
Kampar → Indonesia 0°30N 103°8E 234 B2
Kampen Neths. 52°33N 5°53E 170 B5
Kamphaeng Phet Thailand 16°28N 99°30E 236 D2
Kampinoski △ Poland 52°21N 20°40E 185 F7
Kampolombo, L. Zambia 11°37S 29°42E 269 E2
Kampong Chhnang Cambodia 12°20N 104°35E 237 F5
Kampong Landang Singapore 1°20N 103°55E 138 A3
Kampong Pengerang Malaysia 1°22N 104°7E 237 d
Kampong Punggai Malaysia 1°27N 104°18E 237 d
Kampong Saom Cambodia 10°38N 103°30E 237 G4
Kampong Saom, Chaak Cambodia 10°50N 103°32E 237 G4
Kampong Tanjong Langsat Malaysia 1°28N 104°1E 237 d
Kampong Tanjong Penjuru Singapore 1°18N 103°45E 138 B2
Kampong Telok Ramunia Malaysia 1°22N 104°15E 237 d
Kampong To Thailand 6°3N 101°13E 237 J3
Kampot Cambodia 10°36N 104°10E 237 G5
Kampsville U.S.A. 39°18N 90°37W 310 E6
Kampti Burkina Faso 10°7N 3°25W 262 C4
Kampuchea = Cambodia ■ Asia 12°15N 105°0E 236 F5
Kampung Air Putih Malaysia 4°15N 103°10E 237 K4
Kampung Bali Indonesia 6°11S 106°48E 122 B1
Kampung Jerangau Malaysia 4°50N 103°10E 237 K4
Kampung Raja Malaysia 5°45N 102°35E 237 K4
Kampungbaru = Tolitoli Indonesia 1°5N 120°50E 231 D6
Kamrau, Teluk Indonesia 3°30S 133°36E 231 E8
Kamsack Canada 51°34N 101°54W 297 C8
Kamsai Guinea 10°40N 14°36W 262 C2
Kamskoye Ustye Russia 55°10N 49°20E 190 C9
Kamskoye Vdkhr. Russia 58°41N 56°7E 186 C10
Kamthi India 21°9N 79°19E 244 D4
Kamuchawie L. Canada 56°18N 101°59W 297 B8
Kamuela U.S.A. 20°1N 155°41W 302 C6
Kamui-Misaki Japan 43°20N 140°21E 220 C10
Kamyanets-Podilskyy Ukraine 48°45N 26°40E 183 B11
Kamyanka-Buzka Ukraine 50°8N 24°16E 177 C13
Kamyanka-Dniprovska Ukraine 47°29N 34°28E 189 J8
Kamyanyets Belarus 52°23N 23°49E 185 F10
Kamyanyuki Belarus 52°32N 23°49E 185 F10
Kāmyārān Iran 34°47N 46°56E 213 E12
Kamyshin Russia 50°10N 45°24E 190 E7
Kamyzyak Russia 46°4N 48°10E 191 G9
Kan = Gan Jiang → China 29°15N 116°0E 229 C11
Kan Burma 22°25N 94°5E 241 D5
Kan Sudan 9°1N 31°47E 257 F3
Kanaaupscow Canada 53°39N 77°9W 295 D12
Kanaaupscow → Canada 54°2N 76°30W 298 B4
Kanab U.S.A. 37°3N 112°32W 305 H7
Kanab Cr. → U.S.A. 36°24N 112°38W 305 H7
Kanacea Lau Group, Fiji 17°15S 179°6W 287 A3
Kanacea Taveuni, Fiji 16°59S 179°56E 287 A2
Kanaga I. U.S.A. 51°45N 177°22W 303 L3
Kanagawa □ Japan 35°20N 139°20E 223 B11
Kanagi Japan 40°54N 140°27E 220 D10
Kanairiktok → Canada 55°2N 60°18W 299 A7
Kanakanak U.S.A. 59°0N 158°32W 303 G8
Kanakapura India 12°33N 77°28E 245 H3
Kanalia Greece 39°30N 22°53E 204 B4
Kanamori Japan 35°31N 139°27E 140 B1
Kananga Dem. Rep. of the Congo 5°55S 22°18E 265 D4
Kanangra-Boyd △ Australia 33°57S 150°15E 283 B9
Kanash Russia 55°30N 47°32E 190 C8
Kanaskat U.S.A. 47°19N 121°54W 306 C5
Kanastraíon, Ákra = Paliouri, Akra Greece 39°57N 23°45E 202 G7
Kanawha → U.S.A. 38°50N 82°9W 309 F12
Kanazawa Japan 36°30N 136°38E 223 A8
Kanbalu Burma 23°12N 95°31E 241 D5
Kanchanaburi Thailand 14°2N 99°31E 236 E2
Kanchenjunga Nepal 27°50N 88°10E 243 F13
Kanchipuram India 12°52N 79°45E 245 H4
Kanchow = Ganzhou China 25°51N 114°56E 229 E10
Kańczuga Poland 49°59N 22°25E 185 J9
Kanda Tokyo, Japan 140 a5
Kanda Kanda Dem. Rep. of the Congo 6°52S 23°48E 265 D4
Kandagach = Oktyabrsk Kazakhstan 49°28N 57°25E 187 E10
Kandaghat India 30°59N 77°7E 242 D7
Kandahār Kandahār, Afghan. 31°32N 65°43E 240 C2
Kandahar India 18°52N 77°12E 244 E3
Kandahār □ Afghan. 31°0N 65°0E 240 C2
Kandala Dem. Rep. of the Congo 6°20S 19°40E 265 D3
Kandalaksha Russia 67°9N 32°30E 160 C25
Kandalakshskiy Zaliv Russia 66°0N 35°0E 186 A6
Kandangan Indonesia 2°50S 115°20E 235 C5
Kandanghaur Indonesia 6°21S 108°6E 231 G13
Kandanos Greece 35°19N 23°44E 207 E4
Kandava Latvia 57°2N 22°46E 184 A9
Kandavu = Kadavu Fiji 19°0S 178°15E 287 B2
Kandavu Passage = Kadavu Passage Fiji 18°45S 178°0E 287 B2
Kandep Papua N. G. 5°54S 143°32E 286 C2
Kandhkot Pakistan 28°16N 69°8E 242 E3
Kandhla India 29°18N 77°19E 242 E7
Kandi Benin 11°7N 2°55E 263 C5
Kandi India 23°58N 88°5E 243 H13
Kandiaro Pakistan 27°4N 68°13E 242 F3
Kandila Arkadia, Greece 37°46N 22°22E 204 D4
Kandila Etoloakarnania, Greece 38°42N 20°56E 207 B2
Kandilli Turkey 41°4N 29°3E 122 B2
Kandira Turkey 41°4N 30°9E 212 B4
Kandla India 23°0N 70°10E 242 H4
Kandor, O. → Chad 17°13N 20°52E 259 E4
Kandos Australia 32°45S 149°58E 283 B8
Kandreho Madag. 17°29S 46°6E 272 B2
Kandrian Papua N. G. 6°14S 149°37E 286 D5
Kandy Sri Lanka 7°18N 80°43E 245 L5
Kane U.S.A. 41°40N 78°49W 312 E6
Kane Basin Greenland 79°1N 70°0W 154 B4
Kaneilio Pt. U.S.A. 21°27N 158°12W 302 K13
Kanel Senegal 15°30N 13°18W 262 B2
Kanem □ Chad 15°0N 16°0E 259 E3
Kāne'ohe U.S.A. 21°25N 157°48W 302 K14
Kāne'ohe B. U.S.A. 21°30N 157°50W 302 K14
Kaneohe Marine Corps Air Station U.S.A. 21°27N 157°46W 302 K14
Kanevskaya Russia 46°3N 38°57E 191 G4
Kanfanar Croatia 45°7N 13°50E 199 C10
Kang Botswana 23°41S 22°50E 270 B3
Kang Krung △ Thailand 9°30N 98°50E 237 H2
Kangaamiut Greenland 65°50N 53°20W 154 D5
Kangaba Mali 11°56N 8°25W 262 C3
Kangal Turkey 39°14N 37°23E 212 C7
Kangān Fārs, Iran 27°50N 52°3E 247 E7
Kangān Hormozgān, Iran 25°48N 57°28E 247 E8
Kangar Malaysia 6°27N 100°12E 237 J3
Kangaré Mali 11°36N 8°4W 262 C3
Kangaroo I. Australia 35°45S 137°0E 282 C2
Kangaroo Mts. Australia 23°29S 141°51E 280 C3
Kangasala Finland 61°28N 24°4E 188 B3
Kangāvar Iran 34°40N 48°0E 213 E12
Kangding China 30°2N 101°57E 228 B3
Kangdong N. Korea 39°9N 126°5E 224 C3
Kangean, Kepulauan Indonesia 6°55S 115°23E 235 D5
Kangean Is. = Kangean, Kepulauan Indonesia 6°55S 115°23E 235 D5
Kangen → Sudan 6°47N 33°9E 257 F3
Kangerdlugssuak Greenland 68°10N 32°20W 154 D7
Kangerluarsoruseq Greenland 63°45N 51°27W 154 E5
Kangerluarsoruset = Kangerluarsoruseq Greenland 63°45N 51°27W 154 E5
Kangerlussuaq Greenland 66°59N 50°40W 154 D5
Kanggye N. Korea 41°0N 126°35E 224 B3
Kanghsi Taiwan 23°34N 120°8E 225 C2
Kangikajik Greenland 70°7N 22°0W 154 C8
Kangilinnguit Greenland 61°20N 47°57W 154 E6
Kangiqliniq = Rankin Inlet Canada 62°30N 93°0W 294 C10
Kangiqsualujjuaq Canada 58°30N 65°59W 295 D13
Kangiqsujuaq Canada 61°30N 72°0W 295 C12
Kangiqtugaapik = Clyde River Canada 70°30N 68°30W 295 B13
Kangirsuk Canada 60°0N 70°0W 295 D13
Kangkar Chemaran Malaysia 1°34N 104°12E 237 d
Kangkar Sungai Tiram Malaysia 1°35N 103°55E 237 d
Kangkar Teberau Malaysia 1°32N 103°51E 237 d
Kango Gabon 0°11N 10°5E 264 B2
Kangoku Iwa Iwo Jima 24°48N 141°17E 288 b
Kangoya Dem. Rep. of the Congo 9°55S 22°48E 265 D4
Kangping China 42°43N 123°18E 227 C12
Kangpokpi India 25°8N 93°58E 241 C4
Kangra India 32°6N 76°16E 242 C7
Kangrinboqe Feng China 31°0N 81°25E 243 D9
Kangshan Taiwan 22°48N 120°17E 225 D2
Kangto China 27°50N 92°35E 241 B4
Kangtzu Taiwan 22°8N 120°52E 225 D2
Kangwon-do □ N. Korea 38°47N 127°35E 224 C3
Kangyidaung Burma 16°56N 94°54E 241 G5
Kanha △ India 22°15N 80°40E 243 H9
Kanhan → India 21°4N 79°34E 244 D4
Kanhangad India 12°21N 74°58E 245 H2
Kanhar → India 24°28N 83°8E 243 G10
Kanheri India 19°13N 72°50E 244 E1
Kani Sagaing, Burma 23°52N 95°22E 241 D5
Kani Sagaing, Burma 22°26N 94°51E 241 D5
Kani Ivory C. 8°29N 6°36W 262 D3
Kani-Keli Mayotte 12°57S 45°6E 272 b
Kaniama Dem. Rep. of the Congo 7°30S 24°12E 265 D4
Kaniapiskau = Caniapiscau → Canada 56°40N 69°30W 299 A6
Kaniapiskau, L. = Caniapiscau, L. Canada 54°10N 69°55W 299 B6
Kaniere, L. N.Z. 42°50S 171°10E 285 C6
Kanif Micronesia 9°31N 138°5E 287 R16
Kanigiri India 15°24N 79°31E 245 G4
Kanin, Poluostrov Russia 68°0N 45°0E 186 A8
Kanin Nos, Mys Russia 68°39N 43°32E 186 A7
Kanin Pen. = Kanin, Poluostrov Russia 68°0N 45°0E 186 A8
Kaninë Albania 40°23N 19°30E 202 F3
Kaniva Australia 36°22S 141°18E 282 D4
Kanjiža Serbia 46°3N 20°4E 182 D5
Kanjut Sar Pakistan 36°7N 75°25E 243 A6
Kankaanpää Finland 61°44N 22°50E 188 B2
Kankakee U.S.A. 41°7N 87°52W 311 C9
Kankakee → U.S.A. 41°23N 88°15W 311 C8
Kankan Guinea 10°23N 9°15W 262 C3
Kankendy = Xankändi Azerbaijan 39°52N 46°49E 213 C12
Kanker India 20°10N 81°40E 244 D5
Kankesanturai Sri Lanka 9°49N 80°2E 245 K5
Kankossa Mauritania 15°54N 11°31W 262 B2
Kankroli India 25°4N 73°53E 242 G5
Kankurgachi India 22°34N 88°23E 124 B2
Kanlıca Turkey 41°5N 29°3E 122 B2
Kanmuri-Yama Japan 34°30N 132°4E 222 C4
Kannabe Japan 34°32N 133°23E 222 C5
Kannapolis U.S.A. 35°30N 80°37W 315 D14
Kannauj India 27°3N 79°56E 243 F8
Kanniyakumari India 8°5N 77°34E 245 K3
Kano Nigeria 12°2N 8°30E 263 C6
Kano □ Nigeria 11°30N 8°30E 263 C6
Kanonerskiy, Ostrov Russia 59°53N 30°13E 137 B1
Kan'onji Japan 34°7N 133°39E 222 C5
Kanoroba Ivory C. 9°7N 6°8W 262 D3
Kanowha U.S.A. 42°57N 93°47W 310 B3
Kanowit Malaysia 2°14N 112°20E 235 B4
Kanoya Japan 31°25N 130°50E 222 F2
Kanpetlet Burma 21°10N 93°59E 241 E4
Kanpur India 26°28N 80°20E 243 F9
Kansai Int. ✕ (KIX) Japan 34°27N 135°12E 133 B2
Kansas U.S.A. 39°33N 87°56W 311 E9
Kansas □ U.S.A. 38°30N 99°0W 308 F4
Kansas → U.S.A. 39°7N 94°37W 308 F6
Kansas City Kans., U.S.A. 39°7N 94°38W 310 E2
Kansas City Mo., U.S.A. 39°6N 94°35W 310 E2
Kansas City Int. ✕ (MCI) U.S.A. 39°18N 94°43W 310 E2
Kansenia Dem. Rep. of the Congo 10°20S 26°0E 269 E2
Kansk Russia 56°20N 95°37E 215 D10
Kansu = Gansu □ China 36°0N 104°0E 226 G3
Kantaphor India 22°35N 76°34E 242 H7
Kantchari Burkina Faso 12°37N 1°37E 263 C5
Kantché Niger 13°31N 8°30E 259 F1
Kanté Togo 9°57N 1°3E 263 D5
Kantemirovka Russia 49°43N 39°55E 189 H10
Kanth = Kąty Wrocławskie Poland 51°2N 16°45E 185 G3
Kantharalak Thailand 14°39N 104°39E 236 E5
Kantishna U.S.A. 63°31N 150°57W 303 E10
Kantishna → U.S.A. 64°45N 149°58W 303 D10
Kantli → India 28°20N 75°30E 242 E6
Kantō □ Japan 36°15N 139°30E 223 A11
Kantō-Sanchi Japan 35°59N 138°50E 223 B10
Kantu-long Burma 19°57N 97°36E 241 F6
Kanturk Ireland 52°11N 8°54W 166 D3
Kanuma Japan 36°34N 139°42E 223 A11
Kanus Namibia 27°50S 18°39E 270 C2
Kanuti Nat. Wildlife Refuge ⌂ U.S.A. 66°25N 151°50W 303 C10
Kanyakumari India 8°3N 77°40E 245 K3
Kanye Botswana 24°55S 25°28E 270 B4
Kanzaki → Japan 34°41N 135°24E 133 A1
Kanzenze Dem. Rep. of the Congo 10°30S 25°12E 265 E5
Kanzi, Ras Tanzania 7°1S 39°33E 268 D4
Kanzoni, Chissioua Comoros Is. 12°23S 43°40E 272 a
Kao Tonga 19°40S 175°1W 287 P13
Kao Phara Thailand 8°3N 98°22E 237 a
Kaohsiung Taiwan 22°35N 120°16E 225 D2
Kaohsiung □ Taiwan 23°0N 120°35E 225 D2
Kaoka Solomon Is. 9°42S 160°43E 287 M11
Kaokaona Solomon Is. 10°27S 161°56E 287 N11
Kaokoveld Namibia 19°15S 14°30E 270 A1
Kaolack Senegal 14°5N 16°8W 262 C1
Kaolack □ Senegal 14°0N 15°15W 262 C1
Kaolan = Lanzhou China 36°1N 103°52E 226 F2
Kaolo Solomon Is. 8°24S 159°38E 287 M10
Kaoma Zambia 14°47S 24°48E 265 E4
Kaoshan China 44°38N 124°50E 227 B13
Kaoshu Taiwan 22°49N 120°36E 225 D2
Kaouar Niger 19°5N 12°52E 259 E2
Kaoyao = Zhaoqing China 23°0N 112°20E 229 F9
Kapaa U.S.A. 22°5N 159°19W 302 A2
Kapadvanj India 23°5N 73°0E 242 H5
Kapagere Papua N. G. 9°46S 147°42E 286 E4
Kapahulu U.S.A. 21°16N 157°49W 302 K14
Kapaklı Turkey 41°19N 27°59E 203 E11
Kapali Carsi Turkey 41°1N 28°58E 122 B1
Kapan Armenia 39°18N 46°27E 213 C12
Kapanga Bandundu, Dem. Rep. of the Congo 5°4S 16°58E 265 D3
Kapanga Katanga, Dem. Rep. of the Congo 8°30S 22°40E 265 D4
Kapapa I. U.S.A. 21°29N 157°48W 302 K14
Kapatagan Phil. 7°52N 123°44E 233 H4
Kapchagai = Qapshaghay Kazakhstan 43°51N 77°14E 217 D9
Kapchagaiskoye Vdkhr. = Qapshaghay Bögeni Kazakhstan 43°45N 77°50E 217 D9
Kapedo Kenya 1°10N 36°6E 268 B4
Kapela = Velika Kapela Croatia 45°10N 15°5E 199 C12
Kapellerfeld Austria 48°18N 16°29E 142 A2
Kapelo, Akra Greece 36°9N 23°3E 204 E5
Kapema Dem. Rep. of the Congo 10°45S 28°22E 269 E2
Kapenguria Kenya 1°14N 35°7E 268 B4
Kapfenberg Austria 47°26N 15°18E 180 D8
Kapı Dağı Turkey 40°28N 27°50E 203 F11
Kapia Dem. Rep. of the Congo 4°17S 19°46E 265 C3
Kapiri Mposhi Zambia 13°59S 28°43E 269 E2
Kāpīsā □ Afghan. 35°0N 69°20E 240 B3
Kapiskau → Canada 52°47N 81°55W 298 B3
Kapit Malaysia 2°0N 112°55E 235 B4
Kapiti I. N.Z. 40°50S 174°56E 284 G3
Kapka, Massif du Chad 15°7N 21°45E 259 E4
Kaplan U.S.A. 30°0N 92°17W 314 F8
Kaplice Czech Rep. 48°42N 14°30E 180 C7
Kapoe Thailand 9°34N 98°32E 237 H2
Kapoeta Sudan 4°50N 33°35E 257 G3
Kapoho U.S.A. 19°30N 154°50W 302 D7
Kápolnásnyék Hungary 47°16N 18°41E 182 C3
Kapombo Dem. Rep. of the Congo 10°40S 23°30E 265 E4
Kaponga N.Z. 39°29S 174°9E 284 F3
Kapos → Hungary 46°44N 18°30E 182 D3
Kaposvár Hungary 46°25N 17°47E 182 D2
Káposztásmegyer Hungary 47°35N 19°6E 117 A2
Kapotnya Russia 55°39N 37°48E 129 C4
Kapowsin U.S.A. 46°59N 122°13W 306 D4
Kapp Norway 60°43N 10°52E 164 D7
Käppala Sweden 59°21N 18°13E 139 A3
Kappeln Germany 54°40N 9°55E 178 A5
Kappelshamn Sweden 57°52N 18°47E 163 G12
Kapps Namibia 22°32S 17°18E 270 B2
Kaprije Croatia 43°42N 15°43E 199 E12
Kapsabet Kenya 0°12N 35°6E 268 B4
Kapsan N. Korea 41°4N 128°19E 224 B4
Kapsukas = Marijampolė Lithuania 54°33N 23°19E 184 D10
Kaptai Bangla. 22°21N 92°17E 241 D4
Kaptai L. Bangla. 22°40N 92°20E 241 D4
Kapuas Indonesia 3°10S 114°5E 235 C4
Kapuas → Indonesia 0°25S 109°20E 235 C3
Kapuas Hulu, Pegunungan Malaysia 1°30N 113°30E 235 B4
Kapuas Hulu Ra. = Kapuas Hulu, Pegunungan Malaysia 1°30N 113°30E 235 B4
Kapuk Indonesia 6°7S 106°44E 122 A1
Kapulo Dem. Rep. of the Congo 8°18S 29°15E 269 D2
Kapunda Australia 34°20S 138°56E 282 C3
Kapuni N.Z. 39°29S 174°8E 284 F3
Kapurthala India 31°23N 75°25E 242 D6
Kapuskasing Canada 49°25N 82°30W 298 C3
Kapuskasing → Canada 49°49N 82°0W 298 C3
Kapustin Yar Russia 48°37N 45°40E 191 F7
Kaputar, Mt. Australia 30°15S 150°10E 281 E5
Kaputir Kenya 2°5N 35°28E 268 B4
Kapuvár Hungary 47°36N 17°1E 182 C2
Käpylä Finland 60°13N 24°57E 121 B2
Kara Russia 69°10N 65°0E 214 C7
Karā, W. → Si. Arabia 20°45N 41°42E 256 C5
Kara Ada Turkey 36°58N 27°28E 205 E9
Kara-Balta Kyrgyzstan 42°50N 73°49E 217 D8
Kara Bogaz Gol, Zaliv = Garabogazköl Aylagy Turkmenistan 41°0N 53°30E 187 F9
Kara Burun Turkey 36°32N 27°58E 205 E9
Kara-Kala = Garrygala Turkmenistan 38°31N 56°29E 247 B8
Kara Kalpak Republic = Qoraqalpoghistan □ Uzbekistan 43°0N 58°0E 216 D5
Kara-Köl Kyrgyzstan 41°40N 72°43E 217 D8
Kara Kum = Garagum Turkmenistan 39°30N 60°0E 247 B8
Kara-Saki Japan 34°41N 129°30E 222 C1
Kara Sea Russia 75°0N 70°0E 214 B8
Karaadilli Turkey 38°18N 30°37E 205 C12
Karabiğa Turkey 40°23N 27°17E 203 F11
Karabük Turkey 41°12N 32°37E 212 B5
Karabük □ Turkey 41°10N 32°30E 212 B5
Karaburun Albania 40°25N 19°20E 202 F3
Karaburun Turkey 38°41N 26°28E 205 C8
Karabutak = Qarabutaq Kazakhstan 49°59N 60°14E 216 C6
Karacabey Turkey 40°12N 28°21E 203 F12
Karacakılavuz Turkey 41°8N 27°21E 203 E11
Karacaköy Turkey 41°24N 28°22E 203 E12
Karaçal Tepesi Turkey 36°21N 32°38E 250 B3
Karacasu Turkey 37°43N 28°35E 205 D10
Karachala = Qaraçala Azerbaijan 39°45N 48°53E 191 L9
Karachayevsk Russia 43°50N 41°55E 191 J5
Karachev Russia 53°10N 35°5E 189 F8
Karachey-Cherkessia □ Russia 43°40N 41°30E 191 J5
Karachi Pakistan 24°50N 67°0E 123 A2
Karachi Int. ✕ (KHI) Pakistan 24°53N 67°9E 123 A2
Karad India 17°15N 74°10E 244 F2
Karadirek Turkey 38°34N 30°11E 205 C12
Karaga Ghana 9°58N 0°28W 263 D4
Karaganda = Qaraghandy Kazakhstan 49°50N 73°10E 217 C8
Karagayly = Qaraghayly Kazakhstan 49°26N 76°0E 214 E8
Karaginskiy, Ostrov Russia 58°45N 164°0E 215 D17
Karagiye, Vpadina Kazakhstan 43°27N 51°45E 187 F9
Karagiye Depression = Karagiye, Vpadina Kazakhstan 43°27N 51°45E 187 F9
Karagola Road India 25°29N 87°23E 243 G12
Karagüney Dağları Turkey 40°30N 34°40E 212 B6
Karahallı Turkey 38°21N 29°33E 205 C11
Karaikal India 10°59N 79°50E 245 J4
Karaikkudi India 10°5N 78°45E 245 J4
Karaisali Turkey 37°16N 35°2E 212 D6
Karaitivu I. Sri Lanka 9°45N 79°52E 245 K4
Karaiskakis Greece 38°35N 21°4E 207 B3
Karaj Iran 35°48N 51°0E 247 C6
Karak Malaysia 3°25N 102°2E 237 L4
Karakalpakstan = Qoraqalpoghistan □ Uzbekistan 43°0N 58°0E 216 D5
Karakaya Barajı Turkey 38°31N 38°23E 213 C8
Karakelong Indonesia 4°35N 126°50E 231 D7
Karakitang Indonesia 3°14N 125°28E 231 D7
Karaklis = Vanadzor Armenia 40°48N 44°30E 191 K7
Karakoçan Turkey 38°57N 40°2E 213 C9
Karakol Kyrgyzstan 42°30N 78°20E 217 D9
Karakoram Pass Asia 35°33N 77°50E 243 B7
Karakoram Ra. Pakistan 35°30N 77°0E 243 B7
Karakul Tajikistan 39°2N 73°33E 217 E8
Karakul Uzbekistan 39°32N 63°50E 216 E6
Karakul, Ozero Tajikistan 39°5N 73°25E 217 E8
Karakurt Turkey 40°10N 42°37E 213 B10
Karakuwisa Namibia 18°56S 19°40E 270 A2
Karal Chad 12°50N 14°46E 259 F2
Karalon Russia 57°5N 115°50E 215 D12
Karama Jordan 31°57N 35°35E 251 G6
Karaman Balıkesir, Turkey 39°39N 28°0E 205 B9
Karaman Konya, Turkey 37°14N 33°13E 212 D5
Karaman □ Turkey 37°5N 33°15E 250 A4
Karamanlı Turkey 37°23N 29°47E 205 D11
Karamay China 45°30N 84°58E 217 C10
Karambu Indonesia 3°53S 116°6E 235 C5
Karamea N.Z. 41°14S 172°6E 285 B7
Karamea → N.Z. 41°13S 172°26E 285 B7
Karamea Bight N.Z. 41°22S 171°40E 285 B6
Karamnasa → India 25°31N 83°52E 243 G10
Karamürsel Turkey 40°41N 29°36E 203 F13
Karān Si. Arabia 27°43N 49°49E 247 E6
Karand Iran 34°16N 46°15E 213 E12
Karangana Mali 12°15N 5°4W 262 C3
Karanganyar Indonesia 7°38S 109°37E 235 D3
Karangasem Indonesia 8°27S 115°37E 231 J18
Karanja Maharashtra, India 21°11N 78°24E 244 D4
Karanja Maharashtra, India 20°29N 77°31E 244 D3
Karanjia India 21°47N 85°58E 243 J11
Karankasso Burkina Faso 10°50N 3°53W 262 C4
Karaova Turkey 37°5N 27°40E 205 D9
Karapınar Turkey 37°41N 33°30E 212 D5
Karapiro N.Z. 37°53S 175°32E 284 D4
Karasburg Namibia 28°0S 18°44E 270 C2
Karasino Russia 66°50N 86°50E 214 C9
Karasjok Norway 69°27N 25°30E 160 B21
Karasu Turkey 41°4N 30°46E 212 B4
Karasu → Antalya, Turkey 36°18N 30°10E 205 E12
Karasu → Hatay, Turkey 36°20N 36°20E 250 B7
Karasubazar = Bilohirsk Ukraine 45°3N 34°35E 189 K8
Karasuk Russia 53°44N 78°2E 217 B9
Karasuyama Japan 36°39N 140°9E 223 A12
Karataş Adana, Turkey 36°36N 35°21E 250 B6
Karataş Manisa, Turkey 38°35N 28°16E 205 C10
Karataş Burnu Turkey 36°31N 35°24E 250 B6
Karatau, Khrebet = Qarataū Kazakhstan 43°30N 69°30E 217 D7
Karatax Shan China 35°57N 81°0E 217 E10
Karateki Shan China 40°40N 77°50E 217 D9
Karativu Sri Lanka 8°22N 79°47E 245 K4
Karatoprak Turkey 37°2N 27°15E 205 D9
Karatoya → India 24°7N 89°36E 241 C2
Karatsu Japan 33°26N 129°58E 222 D1
Karaul Russia 70°6N 82°15E 214 B9
Karauli India 26°30N 77°4E 242 F7
Karavastasë, L. e Albania 40°55N 19°30E 202 F3
Karavia Greece 36°49N 23°37E 204 E5
Karavostasi Cyprus 35°8N 32°50E 207 E8
Karawa Dem. Rep. of the Congo 3°18N 20°17E 264 B4
Karawang Indonesia 6°30S 107°15E 235 D3
Karawanken Europe 46°30N 14°40E 180 E7
Karayazı Turkey 39°41N 42°9E 213 C10
Karazhal = Qarazhal Kazakhstan 48°2N 70°49E 214 E8
Karbalā' Iraq 32°36N 44°3E 213 F11
Karbalā' □ Iraq 32°30N 43°50E 213 F10
Kårböle Sweden 61°59N 15°22E 162 C9
Karcag Hungary 47°19N 20°57E 182 C5
Karcha → Pakistan 34°45N 76°10E 243 B7
Karchana India 25°17N 81°56E 243 G9
Karczew Poland 52°5N 21°15E 185 F8
Kardakata Greece 38°17N 20°28E 207 C1
Kardam Bulgaria 43°45N 28°6E 203 C12
Kardamila Greece 38°35N 26°5E 205 C8
Kardamili Greece 36°53N 22°13E 204 E4
Kardeljovo = Ploče Croatia 43°4N 17°26E 199 E14
Karditsa Greece 39°23N 21°54E 204 B3
Karditsa □ Greece 39°15N 21°50E 204 B3
Kärdla Estonia 59°0N 22°45E 188 C2
Kareeberge S. Africa 30°59S 21°50E 270 D3
Kareha → India 25°44N 86°21E 243 G12
Kareima Sudan 18°30N 31°49E 256 D3
Karelia □ Russia 65°30N 32°30E 160 D25
Karelian Republic = Karelia □ Russia 65°30N 32°30E 160 D25
Karelo-Finnish S.S.R. = Karelia □ Russia 65°30N 32°30E 160 D25
Karema Papua N. G. 9°12S 147°18E 286 E4
Karen = Kayin □ Burma 18°0N 97°30E 241 G6
Karenni = Kayah □ Burma 19°15N 97°15E 241 F6
Karera India 25°32N 78°9E 242 G8
Karevāndar Iran 27°53N 60°44E 247 E9
Kargasok Russia 59°3N 80°53E 214 D9
Kargat Russia 55°10N 80°15E 214 D9
Kargi Eastern, Kenya 2°31N 37°34E 268 B4
Kargı Turkey 41°11N 34°30E 212 B6
Kargil India 34°32N 76°12E 243 B7
Kargopol Russia 61°30N 38°58E 188 B10
Kargowa Poland 52°5N 15°51E 185 F2
Karguéri Niger 13°27N 10°30E 259 F2
Karhal India 27°1N 78°57E 243 F8
Karia Greece 38°45N 20°39E 207 B2
Karia ba Mohammed Morocco 34°22N 5°12W 260 B3
Karīān Iran 26°57N 57°14E 247 E8
Karianga Madag. 22°25S 47°22E 272 C2
Kariba Zimbabwe 16°28S 28°50E 269 F2
Kariba, L. Zimbabwe 16°40S 28°25E 269 F2
Kariba Dam Zimbabwe 16°30S 28°35E 269 F2
Kariba Gorge Zambia 16°30S 28°50E 269 F2
Karibib Namibia 22°0S 15°56E 270 B2
Karies Greece 40°14N 24°19E 203 F8
Karijini △ Australia 23°8S 118°15E 278 D2
Karikari, C. N.Z. 34°46S 173°24E 284 A2
Karimata, Kepulauan Indonesia 1°25S 109°0E 235 C3
Karimata, Selat Indonesia 2°0S 108°40E 235 C3
Karimata Is. = Karimata, Kepulauan Indonesia 1°25S 109°0E 235 C3
Karimganj India 24°52N 92°20E 241 C4
Karimnagar India 18°26N 79°10E 244 E4
Karimun Kecil, Pulau Indonesia 1°8N 103°22E 237 d
Karimunjawa, Kepulauan Indonesia 5°50S 110°30E 235 D4
Karin Somali Rep. 10°50N 45°52E 267 B6
Karistos Greece 38°1N 24°29E 204 C6
Karit Iran 33°29N 56°55E 247 C8
Kariya Japan 34°58N 137°1E 223 C9
Kariyangwe Zimbabwe 18°0S 27°38E 271 A4
Karjala Finland 62°0N 30°25E 188 A5
Karjat Maharashtra, India 18°33N 75°0E 244 E2
Karjat Maharashtra, India 18°55N 73°20E 244 E1
Karkal India 13°15N 74°56E 245 H2
Karkar Papua N. G. 4°32S 145°57E 286 C3
Karkar I. Papua N. G. 4°40S 146°0E 286 C4
Karkaralinsk = Qarqaraly Kazakhstan 49°26N 75°30E 217 C9
Karkh Iraq 33°20N 44°22E 113 A2
Karkheh → Iran 31°2N 47°29E 246 D5
Karkinitska Zatoka Ukraine 45°56N 33°0E 189 K7
Karkinitskiy Zaliv = Karkinitska Zatoka Ukraine 45°56N 33°0E 189 K7
Karkuk = Kirkūk Iraq 35°30N 44°21E 213 E11
Karkur Tohl Egypt 22°5N 25°5E 256 C2
Karl Liebknecht Russia 51°40N 35°35E 189 G8
Karl-Marx-Stadt = Chemnitz Germany 50°51N 12°54E 178 E8
Karla, L. = Volvi, L. Greece 40°40N 23°34E 202 F7
Karleby = Kokkola Finland 63°50N 23°8E 160 E20
Karlholmsbruk Sweden 60°31N 17°37E 162 D11
Karlin Czech Rep. 50°5N 14°26E 135 B2
Karlino Poland 54°3N 15°53E 184 D2
Karlivka Ukraine 49°29N 35°8E 189 H8
Karlobag Croatia 44°32N 15°5E 199 D12
Karlovac Croatia 45°31N 15°36E 199 C12
Karlovarský □ Czech Rep. 50°10N 12°50E 180 A5
Karlovasi Greece 37°45N 26°42E 205 D8
Karlovka = Karlivka Ukraine 49°29N 35°8E 189 H8
Karlovo Bulgaria 42°38N 24°47E 203 D8
Karlovo náměstí Prague, Czech Rep. 135 c1
Karlovy Vary Czech Rep. 50°13N 12°51E 180 A5
Karlowitz = Sremski Karlovci Serbia 45°12N 19°56E 182 E4
Karlowitz = Velké Karlovice Czech Rep. 49°20N 18°17E 181 B11
Karlsbad = Karlovy Vary Czech Rep. 50°13N 12°51E 180 A5
Karlsborg Sweden 58°33N 14°33E 163 F8
Karlsburg = Alba-Iulia Romania 46°8N 23°39E 183 D8
Karlsfeld Germany 48°13N 11°28E 131 A1
Karlshamn Sweden 56°10N 14°51E 163 H8
Karlshorst Germany 52°29N 13°31E 115 B4
Karlsnus Norway 59°21N 10°52E 164 E7
Karlskoga Sweden 59°28N 14°33E 162 E8
Karlskrona Sweden 56°10N 15°35E 163 H9
Karlsplatz Munich, Germany 131 b1
Karlsruhe Germany 49°0N 8°23E 179 F4
Karlstad = Karlovac Croatia 45°31N 15°36E 199 C12
Karlstad Sweden 59°23N 13°30E 162 E7
Karlstad Minn., U.S.A. 48°35N 96°31W 308 A5
Karlstadt Germany 49°57N 9°47E 179 F5
Karluk U.S.A. 57°34N 154°28W 303 H9
Karlův most Prague, Czech Rep. 135 b1
Karma Niger 13°38N 1°52E 263 C5
Karmala India 18°25N 75°12E 244 E2
Karmėlava Lithuania 54°58N 24°4E 184 D11
Karmi'el Israel 32°55N 35°18E 250 F6
Karmøy Norway 59°15N 5°15E 164 E2
Karnak Egypt 25°43N 32°39E 256 B3
Karnal India 29°42N 77°2E 242 E7
Karnali → Nepal 28°45N 81°16E 243 E9
Karnaphuli Res. = Kaptai L. Bangla. 22°40N 92°20E 241 D4
Karnaprayag India 30°16N 79°15E 243 D8
Karnataka □ India 13°15N 77°0E 245 H3
Karnes City U.S.A. 28°53N 97°54W 314 G6
Karnische Alpen Europe 46°36N 13°0E 180 E6
Karnobat Bulgaria 42°39N 26°59E 203 D10
Kärnten □ Austria 46°52N 13°30E 180 E6
Karntner Strasse Vienna, Austria 142 b2
Karo Mali 12°16N 3°18W 262 C4
Karoi Zimbabwe 16°48S 29°45E 269 F2
Karol Bagh India 28°39N 77°11E 120 B2
Karolinenhof Germany 52°23N 13°38E 115 B4
Karomatan Phil. 7°55N 123°44E 233 H4
Karon, Ao Thailand 7°51N 98°17E 237 a
Karonga Malawi 9°57S 33°55E 269 D3
Karoo △ S. Africa 32°18S 22°27E 270 D3
Karoonda Australia 35°1S 139°59E 282 C3
Karor Pakistan 31°15N 70°59E 242 D4
Karora Sudan 17°44N 38°15E 256 D4
Karori N.Z. 41°17S 174°44E 143 B1
Karounga Mali 15°20N 7°35W 262 B3
Karousades Greece 39°47N 19°45E 206 B9
Karow Germany 52°36N 13°29E 115 A3
Karpacz Poland 50°46N 15°46E 185 H2
Karpasia Cyprus 35°32N 34°15E 207 E10
Karpathos Greece 35°37N 27°10E 205 F9
Karpathos, Stenon Greece 36°0N 27°30E 205 F9
Karpatsky △ Ukraine 48°20N 24°35E 183 B9
Karpenisi Greece 38°55N 21°40E 204 C3
Karpilovka = Aktsyabrski Belarus 52°38N 28°53E 177 B15
Karpinsk Russia 59°45N 60°1E 186 C11
Karpogory Russia 64°0N 44°27E 186 B7
Karpuz Burnu = Apostolos Andreas, C. Cyprus 35°42N 34°35E 207 E10
Karpuzlu Turkey 37°33N 27°51E 205 D9
Karrādah Iraq 33°17N 44°23E 113 B2
Karratha Australia 20°53S 116°40E 278 D2
Kars Turkey 40°40N 43°5E 213 B10
Kars □ Turkey 40°40N 43°0E 213 B10
Karsakpay Kazakhstan 47°55N 66°40E 217 C7
Karsha Kazakhstan 49°45N 51°35E 190 F10
Karshi = Qarshi Uzbekistan 38°53N 65°48E 217 E7
Karsiyang India 26°56N 88°18E 241 B2
Karsog India 31°23N 77°12E 242 D7
Kärsön Sweden 59°19N 17°54E 139 B1
Karst = Kras Croatia 45°35N 14°0E 199 C10
Kartal Turkey 40°53N 29°11E 203 F13
Kartal Dağları Turkey 37°4N 36°55E 250 A7
Kartala Comoros Is. 11°45S 43°21E 272 a
Kartaly Russia 53°3N 60°40E 216 B6
Kartapur India 31°27N 75°32E 242 D6
Karthaus U.S.A. 41°8N 78°9W 312 E6
Kartuzy Poland 54°22N 18°10E 184 D5
Karuah Australia 32°37S 151°56E 283 B9
Karufa Indonesia 3°50S 133°20E 231 E8
Karuma △ Uganda 2°5N 32°15E 268 B3
Karumba Australia 17°31S 140°50E 280 B3
Karumo Tanzania 2°25S 32°50E 268 C3
Karumwa Tanzania 3°12S 32°38E 268 C3
Kārūn → Iran 30°26N 48°10E 247 D6
Karungu Kenya 0°50S 34°10E 268 C3

Karup Denmark 56°19N 9°10E 163 H3
Karur India 10°59N 78°2E 245 J4
Karviná Czech Rep. 49°53N 18°31E 181 B11
Karwan → India 27°26N 78°4E 242 F8
Karwar India 14°55N 74°13E 245 G2
Karwendel ⌓ Austria 47°25N 11°30E 180 D4
Karwi India 25°12N 80°57E 243 G9
Kaş Turkey 36°11N 29°37E 205 E11
Kasaan U.S.A. 55°32N 132°24W 303 J14
Kasaba Turkey 36°18N 29°44E 205 E11
Kasabi Zambia 14°52S 23°45E 265 E4
Kasache Malawi 13°25S 34°20E 269 E3
Kasai Hyōgo, Japan 34°55N 134°52E 222 C6
Kasai Tōkyō, Japan 35°39N 139°52E 140 B4
Kasai → Dem. Rep. of the Congo 3°30S 16°10E 265 C3
Kasai-Occidental □ Dem. Rep. of the Congo 6°0S 22°0E 265 D4
Kasai-Oriental □ Dem. Rep. of the Congo 5°0S 24°30E 265 D4
Kasaji Dem. Rep. of the Congo 10°25S 23°27E 265 E4
Kasama Japan 36°23N 140°16E 223 A12
Kasama Zambia 10°16S 31°9E 269 E3
Kasan N. Korea 41°18N 126°55E 224 B3
Kasandra Greece 40°0N 23°30E 202 F7
Kasandra Kolpos Greece 40°5N 23°30E 202 F7
Kasandras, Akra Greece 39°57N 23°30E 202 G7
Kasane Namibia 17°34S 24°50E 270 A3
Kasanga Tanzania 8°30S 31°10E 269 D3
Kasangaie Dem. Rep. of the Congo 6°20S 22°42E 265 D4
Kasangulu Dem. Rep. of the Congo 4°33S 15°15E 265 C3
Kasanka △ Zambia 11°34S 30°15E 269 E3
Kasaoka Japan 34°30N 133°30E 222 C5
Kasar, Ras Sudan 18°2N 38°36E 256 D4
Kasaragod India 12°30N 74°58E 245 H2
Kasat Burma 15°56N 98°13E 241 G7
Kasba Bangla. 23°45N 91°2E 241 D3
Kasba L. Canada 60°20N 102°10W 297 A8
Kasba Tadla Morocco 32°36N 6°17W 260 B3
Kaschau = Košice Slovak Rep. 48°42N 21°15E 181 C14
Kaseda Japan 31°25N 130°19E 222 F2
Kāseh Garān Iran 34°5N 46°2E 246 C5
Kasempa Zambia 13°30S 25°44E 269 E2
Kasenga Dem. Rep. of the Congo 10°20S 28°45E 269 E2
Kasese Uganda 0°13N 30°3E 268 B3
Kasewa Zambia 14°28S 28°53E 269 E2
Kasganj India 27°48N 78°42E 243 F8
Kashabowie Canada 48°40N 90°26W 298 C1
Kashaf Iran 35°58N 61°7E 247 C9
Kāshān Iran 34°5N 51°30E 247 C6
Kashechewan Canada 52°18N 81°37W 298 B3
Kashgar = Kashi China 39°30N 76°2E 217 E9
Kashi China 39°30N 76°2E 217 E9
Kashihara Japan 34°27N 135°46E 223 C7
Kashiji Plain Zambia 13°12S 22°20E 265 E4
Kashima Ibaraki, Japan 35°58N 140°38E 223 B12
Kashima Saga, Japan 33°7N 130°6E 222 D2
Kashima-Nada Japan 36°0N 140°45E 223 B12
Kashimbo Dem. Rep. of the Congo 11°12S 26°19E 269 E2
Kashin Russia 57°20N 37°36E 188 D9
Kashing = Jiaxing China 30°49N 120°45E 229 B13
Kashipur Orissa, India 19°16N 83°3E 244 E6
Kashipur Uttaranchal, India 29°15N 79°0E 243 E8
Kashira Russia 54°45N 38°10E 188 E10
Kashiwa Japan 35°52N 139°59E 223 B11
Kashiwabara = Severo-Kurilsk Russia 50°40N 156°8E 215 D16
Kashiwazaki Japan 37°22N 138°33E 221 F9
Kashk-e Kohneh Afghan. 34°55N 62°30E 240 B1
Kashkū'īyeh Iran 30°31N 55°40E 247 D7
Kāshmar Iran 35°16N 58°26E 247 C8
Kashmir Asia 34°0N 76°0E 243 C7
Kashmor Pakistan 28°28N 69°32E 242 E3
Kashpirovka Russia 53°0N 48°30E 190 D9
Kashun Noerh = Gaxun Nur China 42°22N 100°30E 218 B5
Kasiari India 22°8N 87°14E 243 H12
Kasilof U.S.A. 60°23N 151°18W 303 F10
Kasimov Russia 54°55N 41°20E 190 C5
Kasinge Dem. Rep. of the Congo 6°15S 26°58E 268 D2
Kasipur India 22°37N 88°22E 124 B2
Kasiruta Indonesia 0°25S 127°12E 231 E7
Kaskaskia → U.S.A. 37°58N 89°57W 310 G7
Kaskattama → Canada 57°3N 90°4W 297 B10
Kaskinen Finland 62°22N 21°15E 160 E19
Kaskö = Kaskinen Finland 62°22N 21°15E 160 E19
Kaslo Canada 49°55N 116°55W 296 D5
Kasmere L. Canada 59°34N 101°10W 297 B8
Kasongan Indonesia 2°0S 113°23E 235 C4
Kasongo Dem. Rep. of the Congo 4°30S 26°33E 268 C2
Kasongo Lunda Dem. Rep. of the Congo 6°35S 16°49E 265 D3
Kasos Greece 35°20N 26°55E 205 F8
Kasos, Stenon Greece 35°30N 26°30E 205 F8
Kaspi Georgia 41°59N 44°26E 191 K7
Kaspichan Bulgaria 43°18N 27°11E 203 C11
Kaspiysk Russia 42°52N 47°40E 191 J8
Kaspiyskiy Russia 45°22N 47°23E 191 H8
Kassab Syria 35°55N 35°59E 250 C6
Kassab ed Doleib Sudan 13°30N 33°35E 257 E3
Kassaba Egypt 22°40N 29°55E 256 C2
Kassalâ Sudan 15°30N 36°0E 257 D4
Kassalâ □ Sudan 15°20N 36°26E 257 D4
Kassandrino Greece 40°1N 23°27E 202 F7
Kassel Germany 51°18N 9°26E 178 D5
Kasserine □ Tunisia 35°15N 9°0E 261 A6
Kassinger Sudan 18°46N 31°51E 256 D3
Kassiopi Greece 39°48N 19°53E 206 B9
Kasson U.S.A. 44°2N 92°45W 308 C7
Kastamonu Turkey 41°25N 33°43E 212 B5
Kastamonu □ Turkey 41°20N 34°0E 212 B5
Kastav Croatia 45°22N 14°20E 199 C11
Kasteli Greece 35°29N 23°38E 207 E4
Kastellet Copenhagen, Denmark 118 a3
Kastelli Greece 35°12N 25°20E 207 E6
Kastellórizon = Megisti Greece 36°8N 29°34E 205 E11
Kastelo, Akra Greece 35°30N 27°15E 205 F9
Kasterlee Belgium 51°15N 4°59E 170 C4
Kastlösa Sweden 56°26N 16°25E 163 H10
Kastoria Greece 40°30N 21°19E 202 F5
Kastoria □ Greece 40°30N 21°15E 202 F5
Kastorias, L. Greece 40°30N 21°20E 202 F5
Kastorio Greece 37°10N 22°17E 204 D4
Kastornoye Russia 51°55N 38°2E 189 G10
Kastos Greece 38°35N 20°55E 207 B2
Kastrosikia Greece 39°6N 20°38E 207 A2
Kastrup Denmark 55°38N 12°39E 118 B3
Kastrup, København ✈ (CPH) Denmark 55°37N 12°39E 118 B3
Kastsyukovichy Belarus 53°20N 32°4E 188 F7
Kasuga Fukuoka, Japan 33°32N 130°26E 222 D2
Kasuga Tōkyō, Japan 35°45N 139°38E 140 A2
Kasugai Japan 35°12N 136°59E 223 B8
Kasuge Japan 35°45N 139°49E 140 A3
Kasukabe Japan 35°58N 139°49E 223 B11
Kasulu Tanzania 4°37S 30°5E 268 C3
Kasumi Japan 35°38N 134°38E 222 B6
Kasumiga-Ura Japan 36°0N 140°25E 223 B12
Kasumigaseki Tokyo, Japan 140 b4
Kasumkent Russia 41°47N 48°15E 191 K9
Kasungu Malawi 13°0S 33°29E 269 E3
Kasungu △ Malawi 12°53S 33°9E 269 E3
Kasur Pakistan 31°5N 74°25E 242 D6
Kata Archanes Greece 35°15N 25°10E 207 E6
Kata Tjuta Australia 25°20S 130°50E 279 E5
Kataba Zambia 16°5S 25°10E 269 F2
Katagum Nigeria 12°18N 10°21E 263 C7
Katahdin, Mt. U.S.A. 45°54N 68°56W 309 C19
Katako Kombe Dem. Rep. of the Congo 3°25S 24°20E 264 C4
Katakolo Greece 37°38N 21°19E 204 D3
Katale Tanzania 4°52S 31°7E 268 C3
Katalla U.S.A. 60°12N 144°31W 303 F11
Katamatite Australia 36°6S 145°41E 283 D6
Katanda Katanga, Dem. Rep. of the Congo 7°52S 24°13E 265 D4
Katanda Nord-Kivu, Dem. Rep. of the Congo 0°55S 29°21E 268 C2
Katanga □ Dem. Rep. of the Congo 8°0S 25°0E 268 D2
Katangi India 21°56N 79°50E 244 D4
Katanning Australia 33°40S 117°33E 279 F2
Katapakishi Dem. Rep. of the Congo 8°15S 22°49E 265 D4
Katastari Greece 37°50N 20°45E 207 D2
Katavi △ Tanzania 6°51S 31°3E 268 D3
Katavi Swamp Tanzania 6°50S 31°10E 268 D3
Katchall India 7°57N 93°22E 245 L11
Katchiungo Angola 12°35S 16°13E 265 E3
Katerini Greece 40°18N 22°37E 202 F6
Katghora India 22°30N 82°33E 243 H10
Katha Burma 24°10N 96°30E 241 C6
Kathapa △ Burma 22°20N 94°30E 241 D5
Katherîna, Gebel Egypt 28°30N 33°57E 251 K4
Katherine Australia 14°27S 132°20E 278 B5
Katherine Gorge Australia 14°18S 132°28E 278 B5
Kathi India 21°47N 74°3E 242 J6
Kathiawar India 22°20N 71°0E 242 H4
Kathikas Cyprus 34°55N 32°25E 207 F8
Kathleen U.S.A. 28°7N 82°2W 317 G7
Kathmandu = Katmandu Nepal 27°45N 85°20E 243 F11
Kathua India 32°23N 75°34E 242 C6
Kati Mali 12°41N 8°4W 262 C3
Katihar India 25°34N 87°36E 243 G12
Katikati N.Z. 37°32S 175°57E 284 D4
Katima Mulilo Zambia 17°28S 24°13E 270 A3
Katimbira Malawi 12°40S 34°0E 269 E3
Katingan = Mendawai → Indonesia 3°30S 113°0E 235 C4
Katiola Ivory C. 8°10N 5°10W 262 D3
Katipunan Phil. 8°31N 123°17E 233 G4
Katla Iceland 63°36N 19°7W 155 D7
Katlabukh, Ozero Ukraine 45°28N 29°0E 183 E14
Katlanovo Macedonia 41°52N 21°40E 202 E5
Katmai △ U.S.A. 58°20N 155°0W 303 G9
Katmandu Nepal 27°45N 85°20E 243 F11
Katni India 23°51N 80°24E 243 H9
Kato Achaia Greece 38°8N 21°33E 204 C3
Kato Chorio Greece 35°3N 25°47E 207 E6
Kato Korakiana Greece 39°42N 19°45E 206 B9
Káto Pyrgos Cyprus 35°11N 32°41E 207 E8
Katochi Greece 38°26N 21°15E 204 C3
Katol India 21°17N 78°38E 244 D4
Katompe Dem. Rep. of the Congo 6°2S 26°23E 265 D5
Katong Singapore 1°18N 103°53E 138 B3
Katonga → Uganda 0°34N 31°50E 268 B3
Katoomba Australia 33°41S 150°19E 283 B9
Katouna Greece 38°47N 21°7E 204 C3
Katowice Poland 50°17N 19°5E 185 H6
Katrancı Dağı Turkey 37°27N 30°25E 205 D12
Katrine, L. U.K. 56°15N 4°30W 167 E4
Katrineberg Sweden 59°13N 17°54E 139 B1
Katrineholm Sweden 59°9N 16°12E 162 E10
Katsepe Madag. 15°45S 46°15E 272 B2
Katsina Nigeria 13°0N 7°32E 263 C6
Katsina □ Nigeria 12°30N 7°30E 263 C6
Katsina Ala Nigeria 7°10N 9°30E 263 D6
Katsina Ala → Nigeria 7°10N 9°20E 263 D6
Katsumoto Japan 33°51N 129°42E 222 D1
Katsushika Japan 35°44N 139°51E 140 A4
Katsuta Japan 36°25N 140°31E 223 A12
Katsuura Japan 35°10N 140°20E 223 B12
Katsuyama Fukui, Japan 36°3N 136°30E 223 A8
Katsuyama Okayama, Japan 35°5N 133°41E 222 B5
Kattaqŭrghon Uzbekistan 39°55N 66°15E 217 E7
Kattavia Greece 35°57N 27°46E 206 F11
Kattegat Denmark 56°40N 11°20E 163 H5
Katthammarsvik Sweden 57°26N 18°51E 163 G12
Kattowitz = Katowice Poland 50°17N 19°5E 185 H6
Katul, J. Sudan 14°12N 29°25E 257 E2
Katumba Dem. Rep. of the Congo 7°40S 25°17E 265 D5
Katwa India 23°30N 88°5E 243 H13
Katwijk Neths. 52°12N 4°24E 170 B4
Kąty Wrocławskie Poland 51°2N 16°45E 185 G3
Ka'ū Desert U.S.A. 19°21N 155°19W 302 D6
Kau Pai Chau China 22°12N 114°15E 122 B2
Kau Yi Chau China 22°17N 114°4E 122 B1
Kaua'i U.S.A. 22°3N 159°30W 302 A2
Kauai Channel U.S.A. 21°45N 158°50W 302 B3
Kauai Island Lihue Municipal ✈ (LIH) U.S.A. 21°58N 159°20W 302 B2
Kaub Germany 50°5N 7°46E 179 E3
Kaudom ⌓ Namibia 18°45S 20°51E 270 A3
Kauehi French Polynesia 15°49S 145°10W 289 f
Kaufbeuren Germany 47°53N 10°37E 179 H6
Kaufman U.S.A. 32°35N 96°19W 314 E6
Kauhajoki Finland 62°25N 22°10E 160 E20
Kauhola Pt. U.S.A. 20°15N 155°47W 302 C6
Kaukauna U.S.A. 44°17N 88°17W 308 C9
Kaukauveld Namibia 20°0S 20°15E 270 B3
Kaukonahua → U.S.A. 21°35N 158°7W 302 J13
Ka'ula I. U.S.A. 21°40N 160°33W 302 B1
Kaulakahi Channel U.S.A. 22°0N 159°55W 302 B2
Kaulsdorf Germany 52°29N 13°34E 115 B4
Kaumalapau U.S.A. 20°47N 156°59W 302 C5
Kaunä Pt. U.S.A. 19°2N 155°53W 302 D6
Kaunakakai U.S.A. 21°6N 157°1W 302 B4
Kaunas Lithuania 54°54N 23°54E 184 D10
Kaunas ✈ (KUN) Lithuania 54°57N 24°3E 184 D11
Kaunchi = Yangiyul Uzbekistan 41°0N 69°3E 217 D7
Kaunghein Burma 25°41N 95°26E 241 C5
Kaunia Bangla. 25°46N 89°26E 241 C2
Kauniainen Finland 60°13N 24°44E 121 B1
Kaunos Turkey 36°49N 28°39E 205 E10
Kaupangur Iceland 65°38N 18°2W 155 B8
Kaupō U.S.A. 20°38N 156°8W 302 C5
Kaura Namoda Nigeria 12°37N 6°33E 263 C6
Kauru Nigeria 10°33N 8°12E 263 C6
Kautokeino Norway 69°0N 23°4E 160 B20
Kauwapur India 27°31N 82°18E 243 F10
Kavacha Russia 60°16N 169°51E 215 C17
Kavadarci Macedonia 41°26N 22°3E 202 E6
Kavajë Albania 41°11N 19°33E 202 E3
Kavak Turkey 41°4N 36°3E 212 B7
Kavak Dağı Turkey 37°10N 28°2E 205 D10
Kavaklı Turkey 41°39N 27°10E 203 E11
Kavaklıdere Turkey 37°27N 28°21E 205 D10
Kavaklii = Topolovgrad Bulgaria 42°5N 26°20E 203 D10
Kavala Greece 40°57N 24°28E 203 F8
Kavala □ Greece 41°5N 24°30E 203 E8
Kavala Kolpos Greece 40°50N 24°25E 203 F8
Kavalerovo Russia 44°15N 135°4E 220 B7
Kavali India 14°55N 80°1E 245 G5
Kavār Iran 29°11N 52°44E 247 D7
Kavaratti India 10°34N 72°37E 245 J1
Kavaratti I. India 10°33N 72°38E 245 J1
Kavarna Bulgaria 43°26N 28°22E 203 C12
Kavava Dem. Rep. of the Congo 8°52S 22°19E 265 D4
Kavi India 22°12N 72°38E 242 H5
Kavieng Papua N. G. 2°36S 150°51E 286 B6
Kavimba Botswana 18°2S 24°38E 270 A3
Kavīr, Dasht-e Iran 34°30N 55°0E 247 C7
Kavīr △ Iran 34°40N 52°0E 247 C7
Kavirondo G. = Winam G. Kenya 0°20S 34°15E 268 C3
Kavkaz Russia 45°20N 36°40E 189 K9
Kävlinge Sweden 55°47N 13°9E 163 J7
Kavos Greece 39°23N 20°3E 206 C10
Kavousi Greece 35°7N 25°51E 207 E6
Kavungo Angola 11°31S 23°3E 265 E4
Kaw Fr. Guiana 4°30N 52°15W 329 C7
Kawa Sudan 13°42N 32°34E 257 E3
Kawachi-Nagano Japan 34°28N 135°31E 223 C7
Kawagama L. Canada 45°18N 78°45W 312 A6
Kawagoe Japan 35°55N 139°29E 223 B11
Kawaguchi Japan 35°52N 139°45E 223 B11
Kawaihae B. U.S.A. 20°0N 155°50W 302 C6
Kawaihoa Pt. U.S.A. 21°47N 160°12W 302 B1
Kawaikini U.S.A. 22°5N 159°29W 302 A2
Kawailoa U.S.A. 21°36N 158°3W 302 J13
Kawailoa Beach U.S.A. 21°37N 158°5W 302 J13
Kawailoa Forest Reserve U.S.A. 21°37N 158°0W 302 J14
Kawakawa N.Z. 35°23S 174°6E 284 B3
Kawambwa Zambia 9°48S 29°3E 269 D2
Kawanabe Japan 31°23N 130°24E 222 F2
Kawanoe Japan 34°1N 133°34E 222 C5
Kawardha India 22°0N 81°17E 243 J9
Kawasaki Japan 35°31N 139°43E 140 B3
Kawasi Indonesia 1°38S 127°28E 231 E7
Kawau I. N.Z. 36°25S 174°52E 284 C3
Kawawa Japan 35°31N 139°33E 140 B2
Kawawachikamach Canada 54°48N 66°50W 299 B6
Kawęczyn Poland 52°16N 21°5E 142 B2
Kaweka Ra. N.Z. 39°17S 176°19E 284 F5
Kawela U.S.A. 21°42N 158°1W 302 J13
Kawerau N.Z. 38°7S 176°42E 284 E5
Kawhia N.Z. 38°4S 174°49E 284 E3
Kawhia Harbour N.Z. 38°5S 174°51E 284 E3
Kawio, Kepulauan Indonesia 4°30N 125°30E 231 D7
Kawkareik Burma 16°33N 98°14E 241 G7
Kawlin Burma 23°47N 95°41E 241 D5
Kawthaung Burma 10°5N 98°36E 237 H2
Kawthoolei = Kayin □ Burma 18°0N 97°30E 241 G6
Kawthule = Kayin □ Burma 18°0N 97°30E 241 G6
Kawya Burma 24°50N 94°58E 241 C5
Kaxholmen Sweden 57°51N 14°19E 163 G8
Kaya Burkina Faso 13°4N 1°10W 263 C4
Kayah □ Burma 19°15N 97°15E 241 F6
Kayak I. U.S.A. 59°56N 144°23W 303 G11
Kayalıköy Barajı Turkey 41°50N 27°5E 203 E11
Kayan Burma 16°54N 96°34E 241 G6
Kayan → Indonesia 2°55N 117°35E 235 B5
Kayan Mentarang △ Indonesia 2°25N 115°0E 235 B5
Kayankulam India 9°10N 76°33E 245 K3
Kaycee U.S.A. 43°43N 106°38W 304 E10
Kayeli Indonesia 3°20S 127°10E 231 E7
Kayenda Dem. Rep. of the Congo 10°48S 23°6E 265 E4
Kayenta U.S.A. 36°44N 110°15W 305 H8
Kayes Congo 4°25S 11°41E 265 C2
Kayes Mali 14°25N 11°30W 262 C2
Kayes □ Mali 14°0N 11°0W 262 C2
Kayı Turkey 39°12N 30°46E 205 B12
Kayima S. Leone 8°54N 11°15W 262 D2
Kayin □ Burma 18°0N 97°30E 241 G6
Kaymakçı Turkey 38°10N 28°8E 205 C10
Kayoa Indonesia 0°1N 127°28E 231 D7
Kayomba Zambia 13°11S 24°2E 269 E1
Kayombo Zambia 13°3S 23°51E 265 E4
Kaysatskoye Russia 49°47N 46°49E 190 F8
Kayseri Turkey 38°45N 35°30E 212 C6
Kayseri □ Turkey 38°40N 36°0E 212 C7
Kaysville U.S.A. 41°2N 111°56W 304 F8
Kayts Sri Lanka 9°42N 79°51E 245 K4
Kayu Putih Indonesia 6°10S 106°53E 122 B2
Kayuagung Indonesia 3°24S 104°50E 234 C2
Kaz Dağı Turkey 39°42N 26°50E 205 B8
Kazachye Russia 70°52N 135°58E 215 B14
Kazakhstan ■ Asia 50°0N 70°0E 217 C8
Kazan Russia 55°50N 49°10E 190 C9
Kazan → Canada 64°2N 95°29W 297 A9
Kazan-Rettō Pac. Oc. 25°0N 141°0E 288 E6
Kazancı Turkey 36°29N 32°51E 250 B3
Kazanlı Turkey 36°49N 34°43E 250 B5
Kazanlŭk Bulgaria 42°38N 25°20E 203 D9
Kazanskaya Russia 49°50N 41°10E 190 F5
Kazatin = Kozyatyn Ukraine 49°45N 28°50E 177 D15
Kazaure Nigeria 12°42N 8°28E 263 C6
Kazbek Russia 42°42N 44°30E 191 J7
Kāzerūn Iran 29°38N 51°40E 247 D6
Kazi Magomed = Qazimämmäd Azerbaijan 40°3N 49°0E 191 K9
Kazimierz Dolny Poland 51°19N 21°57E 185 G8
Kazimierza Wielka Poland 50°15N 20°30E 185 H7
Kazincbarcika Hungary 48°17N 20°36E 182 B5
Kazipet India 17°58N 79°30E 244 F4
Kaziranga △ India 26°40N 93°30E 241 B4
Kaziza Dem. Rep. of the Congo 10°42S 23°52E 265 E4
Kazlų Rūda Lithuania 54°46N 23°30E 184 D10
Kazo Japan 36°7N 139°36E 223 A11
Kaztalovka Kazakhstan 49°47N 48°43E 190 F9
Kazu Burma 25°27N 97°46E 241 C6
Kazuma Pan △ Zimbabwe 18°20S 25°48E 269 F2
Kazumba Dem. Rep. of the Congo 6°25S 22°5E 265 D4
Kazungula Zambia 17°35S 25°15E 265 F5
Kazuno Japan 40°10N 140°45E 220 D10
Kazym → Russia 63°54N 65°50E 214 C7
Kbely Czech Rep. 50°8N 14°32E 135 B3
Kcynia Poland 53°0N 17°30E 185 F4
Ke-hsi Mansam Burma 21°56N 97°50E 241 E6
Ké-Macina Mali 13°58N 5°22W 262 C3
Kea Greece 37°35N 24°22E 204 D6
Kea'au U.S.A. 19°37N 155°2W 302 D6
Keady U.K. 54°15N 6°42W 166 B5
Keahi Pt. U.S.A. 21°19N 157°59W 302 K14
Keahole Pt. U.S.A. 19°44N 156°4W 302 D5
Kealaikahiki Channel U.S.A. 20°35N 156°50W 302 C5
Kealakekua U.S.A. 19°31N 155°55W 302 D6
Kealia U.S.A. 19°24N 155°53W 302 D6
Kearney Mo., U.S.A. 39°22N 94°22W 310 E2
Kearney Nebr., U.S.A. 40°42N 99°5W 308 E4
Kearny U.S.A. 33°3N 110°55W 305 K8
Kearsarge, Mt. U.S.A. 43°22N 71°50W 313 C13
Keawakapu U.S.A. 20°43N 156°27W 302 C5
Keban Turkey 38°50N 38°50E 213 C8
Keban Barajı Turkey 38°41N 38°33E 213 C8
Kebara Congo 2°27S 14°25E 264 C2
Kebayoran Baru Indonesia 6°14S 106°47E 122 B1
Kebayoran Lama Indonesia 6°13S 106°46E 122 B1
Kebbi □ Nigeria 11°35N 4°0E 263 C5
Kébi Ivory C. 9°18N 6°37W 262 D3
Kebi, Mayo → Cameroon 9°18N 13°33E 264 A2
Kebili Tunisia 33°47N 9°0E 258 B1
Kebili □ Tunisia 33°30N 8°50E 261 B6
Kebnekaise Sweden 67°53N 18°33E 160 C18
Kebon Jeruk Indonesia 6°11S 106°46E 122 B1
Kebri Dehar Ethiopia 6°45N 44°17E 267 C5
Kebumen Indonesia 7°42S 109°40E 235 D3
Kecel Hungary 46°31N 19°16E 182 D4
Kechika → Canada 59°41N 127°12W 296 B3
Keçiborlu Turkey 37°57N 30°18E 205 D12
Kecskemét Hungary 46°57N 19°42E 182 D4
Kedada Ethiopia 5°25N 35°58E 257 F4
Kedah □ Malaysia 5°50N 100°40E 234 A2
Kėdainiai Lithuania 55°15N 24°2E 184 C11
Kedar West Bank 31°44N 35°18E 123 B2
Kedarnath India 30°44N 79°4E 243 D8
Kedgwick Canada 47°40N 67°20W 299 C6
Kediet Ijill Mauritania 22°38N 12°33W 260 D2
Kediri Indonesia 7°51S 112°1E 235 D4
Kedja Dem. Rep. of the Congo 4°50N 19°16E 264 B3
Kedjebi Ghana 8°12N 0°25E 263 D5
Kédougou Senegal 12°35N 12°10W 262 C2
Kedoya Indonesia 6°10S 106°45E 122 B1
Kedros Oros Greece 35°11N 24°37E 207 E5
Kędzierzyn-Koźle Poland 50°20N 18°12E 185 H5
Ke'ehi Lagoon U.S.A. 21°20N 157°54W 302 K14
Keeler U.S.A. 36°29N 117°52W 306 J9
Keeley L. Canada 54°54N 108°8W 297 C7
Keeling Is. = Cocos Is. Ind. Oc. 12°10S 96°55E 273 F8
Keelung = Chilung Taiwan 25°3N 121°45E 225 A3
Keenapusan Phil. 6°50N 118°50E 233 H2
Keene Ont., Canada 44°15N 78°10W 312 B6
Keene Calif., U.S.A. 35°13N 118°33W 307 K8
Keene N.H., U.S.A. 42°56N 72°17W 313 D12
Keene N.Y., U.S.A. 44°16N 73°46W 313 B11
Keep River △ Australia 15°49S 129°8E 278 C4
Keeper Hill Ireland 52°45N 8°16W 166 D3
Keepit, L. Australia 30°50S 150°30E 283 A9
Keerweer, C. Australia 14°0S 141°32E 280 A3
Keeseville U.S.A. 44°29N 73°30W 313 B11
Keetmanshoop Namibia 26°35S 18°8E 270 C2
Keewatin Canada 49°46N 94°34W 297 D10
Keewatin → Canada 56°29N 100°46W 297 B8
Kefa Ethiopia 6°55N 36°30E 257 F4
Kefalonia Greece 38°15N 20°30E 207 C2
Kefalonia □ Greece 38°15N 20°30E 207 C2
Kefalonia ✈ (EFL) Greece 38°10N 20°30E 207 C1
Kefalos Greece 36°45N 26°59E 205 E8
Kefamenanu Indonesia 9°28S 124°29E 231 F6
Kefar Sava Israel 32°11N 34°54E 251 F5
Keffi Nigeria 8°55N 7°43E 263 D6
Keffin Hausa Nigeria 12°13N 9°59E 263 C6
Keflavík Iceland 64°2N 22°35W 155 C4
Keflavík ✈ (KEF) Iceland 64°0N 22°45W 155 C4
Keftya Ethiopia 13°54N 37°7E 257 E4
Keg River Canada 57°54N 117°55W 296 B5
Kegalla Sri Lanka 7°15N 80°21E 245 L5
Kegaska Canada 50°9N 61°18W 299 B7
Kehancha Kenya 1°11S 34°37E 268 C3
Keheili Sudan 19°25N 32°50E 256 D3
Kehena U.S.A. 19°23N 154°55W 302 D7
Kehl Germany 48°34N 7°50E 179 G3
Keibul Lamjao △ India 24°30N 93°55E 241 C4
Keighley U.K. 53°52N 1°54W 168 D6
Keijo = Seoul S. Korea 37°31N 126°58E 137 B2
Keikiwaha Pt. U.S.A. 19°31N 155°58W 302 D6
Keila Estonia 59°18N 24°25E 188 C3
Keilor Australia 37°42S 144°50E 128 A1
Keilor North Australia 37°44S 144°51E 128 A1
Keimoes S. Africa 28°41S 20°59E 270 C3
Keimola Finland 60°20N 24°49E 121 A1
Keita Niger 14°46N 5°56E 263 C6
Keïta, B. → Chad 9°14N 18°21E 259 G3
Keitele Finland 63°10N 26°20E 160 E22
Keith S. Austral., Australia 36°6S 140°20E 282 D4
Keith Moray, U.K. 57°32N 2°57W 167 D6
Keithsburg U.S.A. 41°6N 90°56W 310 C6
Keiyasi Fiji 17°53S 177°46E 287 A1
Keizer U.S.A. 44°57N 123°1W 304 D2
Kejimkujik △ Canada 44°25N 65°25W 299 D6
Kejserr Franz Joseph Fd. Greenland 73°30N 24°30W 154 C8
Kekaha U.S.A. 21°58N 159°43W 302 B2
Kekri India 26°0N 75°10E 242 G6
Keksgolm = Priozersk Russia 61°2N 30°7E 188 B6
Kelafo Ethiopia 5°37N 44°8E 267 C5
Kelam Ethiopia 4°48N 35°58E 257 G4
Kelamet Eritrea 16°0N 38°30E 257 D4
Kelan China 38°43N 111°31E 226 E6
Kelang = Klang Malaysia 3°2N 101°26E 237 L3
Kelani Ganga → Sri Lanka 6°58N 79°50E 245 L4
Kelantan □ Malaysia 5°10N 102°0E 234 A2
Kelantan → Malaysia 6°13N 102°14E 237 J4
Kelapa Gading Indonesia 6°9S 106°52E 122 A2
Këlcyrë Albania 40°20N 20°12E 202 F4
Kelekçi Turkey 37°15N 29°20E 205 D11
Kelenföld Hungary 47°27N 19°2E 117 B2
Keles Turkey 39°54N 29°14E 203 G13
Keleti-főcsatorna Hungary 47°45N 21°20E 182 C6
Kelheim Germany 48°54N 11°52E 179 G7
Kelibia Tunisia 36°50N 11°3E 258 A2
Kelkit Turkey 40°7N 39°16E 213 B8
Kelkit → Turkey 40°45N 36°32E 212 B7
Kellé Congo 0°8S 14°38E 264 C2
Keller U.S.A. 31°50N 81°15W 316 D8
Kellerberrin Australia 31°36S 117°38E 279 F2
Kellett, C. Canada 72°0N 126°0W 295 B7
Kelleys I. U.S.A. 41°36N 82°42W 312 E2
Kellogg U.S.A. 47°32N 116°7W 304 C5
Kells = Ceanannus Mor Ireland 53°44N 6°53W 166 C5
Kelmė Lithuania 55°38N 22°56E 184 C9
Kelmentsi Ukraine 48°28N 26°50E 183 B11
Kélo Chad 9°10N 15°45E 259 G3
Kelokedhara Cyprus 34°48N 32°39E 207 F8
Kelowna Canada 49°50N 119°25W 296 D5
Kelsey Creek Australia 20°26S 148°31E 280 J6
Kelseyville U.S.A. 38°59N 122°50W 306 G4
Kelso N.Z. 45°54S 169°15E 285 F4
Kelso Borders, U.K. 55°36N 2°26W 167 F6
Kelso Wash., U.S.A. 46°9N 122°54W 306 D4
Keluang = Kluang Malaysia 2°3N 103°18E 237 L4
Kelvin S. Africa 26°4S 28°5E 123 A2
Kelvington Canada 52°10N 103°30W 297 C8
Kem Russia 65°0N 34°38E 186 B5
Kem → Russia 64°57N 34°41E 186 B5
Kem-Kem Morocco 30°40N 4°30W 260 B4
Kema Indonesia 1°22N 125°8E 231 D7
Kemah Turkey 39°32N 39°5E 213 C8
Kemaliye Erzincan, Turkey 39°16N 38°29E 213 C8
Kemaliye Manisa, Turkey 38°27N 28°25E 205 C10
Kemalpaşa Turkey 38°25N 27°27E 205 C9
Kemaman Malaysia 4°12N 103°18E 237 K4
Kemang Indonesia 6°15S 106°48E 122 B1
Kemano Canada 53°35N 128°0W 296 C3
Kemapyu Burma 18°49N 97°19E 241 F6
Kemasik Malaysia 4°25N 103°27E 237 K4
Kemayoran Indonesia 6°10S 106°51E 122 B2
Kembé C.A.R. 4°36N 21°54E 264 B4
Kembolcha Ethiopia 11°2N 39°42E 257 E4
Kemer Antalya, Turkey 36°36N 30°34E 205 E12
Kemer Burdur, Turkey 37°21N 30°4E 205 D12
Kemer Muğla, Turkey 36°40N 29°22E 205 E11
Kemer Barajı Turkey 37°30N 28°37E 205 D10
Kemerburgaz Turkey 41°9N 28°54E 122 B1
Kemerovo Russia 55°20N 86°5E 214 D9
Kemerovo □ Russia 55°0N 86°0E 217 B11
Ķemeru △ Latvia 56°58N 23°25E 184 B10
Kemi Finland 65°44N 24°34E 160 D21
Kemi älv = Kemijoki → Finland 65°47N 24°32E 160 D21
Kemi träsk = Kemijärvi Finland 66°43N 27°22E 160 C22
Kemijärvi Finland 66°43N 27°22E 160 C22
Kemijoki → Finland 65°47N 24°32E 160 D21
Kemmerer U.S.A. 41°48N 110°32W 304 F8
Kemmuna = Comino Malta 36°1N 14°20E 206 E7
Kemp, L. U.S.A. 33°46N 99°9W 314 E5
Kemp Land Antarctica 69°0S 55°0E 151 C5
Kempas Malaysia 1°33N 103°42E 237 d
Kempen = Kępno Poland 51°18N 17°58E 185 G4
Kempsey Australia 31°1S 152°50E 283 A10
Kempt, L. Canada 47°25N 74°22W 298 C5
Kempten Germany 47°45N 10°17E 179 H6
Kempton Tas., Australia 42°31S 147°12E 281 G4
Kempton Ind., U.S.A. 40°17N 86°14W 311 D10
Kempton Park Races U.K. 51°24N 0°23W 125 B1
Kemptville Canada 45°0N 75°38W 313 B9
Ken → India 25°13N 80°27E 243 G9
Kenadsa Algeria 31°48N 2°26W 261 B4
Kenai U.S.A. 60°33N 151°16W 303 F10
Kenai Fjords △ U.S.A. 59°40N 149°50W 303 G10
Kenai Mts. U.S.A. 60°0N 150°0W 303 G10
Kenai Nat. Wildlife Refuge ⌓ U.S.A. 60°20N 150°30W 303 F10
Kenansville U.S.A. 27°53N 80°59W 317 H9
Kendai India 22°45N 82°37E 243 H10
Kendal Indonesia 6°56S 110°14E 235 D4
Kendal Cumb., U.K. 54°20N 2°44W 168 C5
Kendall N.S.W., Australia 31°35S 152°44E 283 A10
Kendall Fla., U.S.A. 25°40N 80°19W 317 K9
Kendall → Australia 14°4S 141°35E 280 A3
Kendallville U.S.A. 41°27N 85°16W 311 C11
Kendari Indonesia 3°50S 122°30E 231 E6
Kendawangan Indonesia 2°32S 110°17E 235 C4
Kende Nigeria 11°30N 4°12E 263 C5
Kendi, Pulau Malaysia 5°13N 100°11E 237 c
Kendigué Chad 10°0N 18°36E 259 F3
Kendrapara India 20°35N 86°30E 244 D8
Këndrevicës, Maja e Albania 40°15N 19°52E 202 F3
Kendrew S. Africa 32°32S 24°30E 270 D3
Kendrick U.S.A. 29°15N 82°10W 317 F7
Kene Thao Laos 17°44N 101°10E 236 D3
Kenedy U.S.A. 28°49N 97°51W 314 G6
Kenema S. Leone 7°50N 11°14W 262 D2
Keng Kok Laos 16°26N 105°12E 236 D5
Keng Tawng Burma 20°45N 98°18E 241 E7
Keng Tung Burma 21°0N 99°30E 228 G2
Kengani Dem. Rep. of the Congo 2°59S 17°36E 264 C3
Kenge Dem. Rep. of the Congo 4°50S 17°4E 265 C3
Kengeja Tanzania 5°26S 39°45E 268 D4
Kenhardt S. Africa 29°19S 21°12E 270 C3
Kéniéba Mali 12°54N 11°17W 262 C2
Kenilworth S. Africa 33°59S 18°27E 118 A1
Kenitra Morocco 34°15N 6°40W 260 B3
Kenitra □ Morocco 34°18N 6°25W 260 B3
Kenli China 37°30N 118°20E 227 F10
Kenmare Kerry, Ireland 51°53N 9°36W 166 E2
Kenmare N. Dak., U.S.A. 48°41N 102°5W 308 A2
Kenmare River Ireland 51°48N 9°51W 166 E2
Kennebago Lake U.S.A. 45°4N 70°40W 313 A14
Kennebec U.S.A. 43°54N 99°52W 308 D4
Kennebec → U.S.A. 43°45N 69°46W 309 D19
Kennebunk U.S.A. 43°23N 70°33W 313 C14
Kennedy Zimbabwe 18°52S 27°10E 270 A4
Kennedy, C. = Canaveral, C. U.S.A. 28°27N 80°32W 317 G9
Kennedy Entrance U.S.A. 59°1N 152°0W 303 G10
Kennedy Kanal Arctic 80°50N 66°0W 154 A4
Kennedy Ra. Australia 24°45S 115°10E 279 D2
Kennedy Range △ Australia 24°34S 115°2E 279 D2
Kennedy Space Center U.S.A. 28°40N 80°42W 317 G9
Kennedy Town China 22°16N 114°6E 122 B1
Kenner U.S.A. 29°59N 90°14W 131 A1
Kennesaw U.S.A. 34°1N 84°37W 316 A5
Kennet → U.K. 51°27N 0°57W 169 F7
Kenneth Ra. Australia 23°50S 117°8E 279 D2
Kennett U.S.A. 36°14N 90°3W 308 G8
Kennewick U.S.A. 46°12N 119°7W 304 C4
Kennington London, U.K. 125 c4
Kenogami → Canada 51°6N 84°28W 298 B3
Kenora Canada 49°47N 94°29W 297 D10
Kenosha U.S.A. 42°35N 87°49W 311 B9
Kensal Green U.K. 51°32N 0°13W 125 A2
Kensal Rise London, U.K. 125 a1
Kensington N.S.W., Australia 33°54S 151°13E 139 B2
Kensington P.E.I., Canada 46°28N 63°34W 299 C7
Kensington Gauteng, S. Africa 26°11S 28°6E 123 B2
Kensington London, U.K. 51°29N 0°10W 125 B2
Kensington N.Y., U.S.A. 40°38N 73°57W 132 C2
Kensington Palace U.K. 51°30N 0°11W 125 A2
Kent Ohio, U.S.A. 41°9N 81°22W 312 E3
Kent Tex., U.S.A. 31°4N 104°13W 314 F2
Kent Wash., U.S.A. 47°22N 122°14W 306 C4
Kent □ U.K. 51°12N 0°40E 169 F8
Kent Group Australia 39°30S 147°20E 281 F4
Kent Pen. Canada 68°30N 107°0W 294 C9
Kent Village U.S.A. 38°55N 76°53W 143 B4
Kentaū Kazakhstan 43°32N 68°36E 217 D7
K'enting △ Taiwan 21°57N 120°48E 225 E2
Kentish Town U.K. 51°32N 0°8W 125 A3
Kentland U.S.A. 40°46N 87°27W 311 D9
Kenton London, U.K. 51°34N 0°17W 125 A2
Kenton Ohio, U.S.A. 40°39N 83°37W 311 D13
Kentucky □ U.S.A. 37°0N 84°0W 309 G11
Kentucky → U.S.A. 38°41N 85°11W 311 F11
Kentucky L. U.S.A. 37°1N 88°16W 308 G9
Kentville Canada 45°6N 64°29W 299 C7
Kentwood La., U.S.A. 30°56N 90°31W 315 F9
Kentwood Mich., U.S.A. 42°52N 85°39W 311 B11
Kenwood House U.K. 51°34N 0°9W 125 A3
Kenya ■ Africa 1°0N 38°0E 268 B4
Kenya, Mt. Kenya 0°10S 37°18E 268 C4
Kenzou Cameroon 4°10N 15°2E 264 B3
Keo Neua, Deo Vietnam 18°23N 105°10E 236 C5
Keokuk U.S.A. 40°24N 91°24W 310 D5
Keoladeo △ India 27°0N 77°20E 242 F7
Keonjhargarh India 21°28N 85°35E 243 J11
Keosauqua U.S.A. 40°44N 91°58W 310 D5
Keota U.S.A. 41°22N 91°57W 310 C5
Kep Cambodia 10°29N 104°19E 237 G5
Kep Vietnam 21°24N 106°16E 236 B6
Kepa Poland 52°13N 21°3E 142 B2
Kepala Batas Malaysia 5°31N 100°26E 237 c
Kepez Turkey 40°5N 26°24E 203 F10
Kepi Indonesia 6°32S 139°19E 231 F9
Kępice Poland 54°16N 16°51E 184 D3
Kepler Mts. N.Z. 45°25S 167°20E 285 F2
Kępno Poland 51°18N 17°58E 185 G4
Keppel Harbour Singapore 1°15N 103°49E 138 B2
Keppel Pt. Papua N. G. 10°10S 147°58E 286 F4
Kepsut Turkey 39°40N 28°9E 205 B10
Kepuhi Pt. U.S.A. 21°29N 158°14W 302 K13
Kerala □ India 11°0N 76°15E 245 J3
Keram → Papua N. G. 4°7S 144°5E 286 C3
Kerama-Rettō Japan 26°5N 127°15E 221 L3
Keramikos Athens, Greece 112 b1
Keran Pakistan 34°35N 73°59E 243 B5
Keran △ Togo 10°9N 0°41E 263 C5
Kerang Australia 35°40S 143°55E 282 C5
Keranyo Ethiopia 5°3N 38°18E 257 F4
Kerao → Sudan 11°0N 32°41E 257 E3
Keratea Greece 37°48N 23°58E 204 D5
Keraudren, C. Australia 19°58S 119°45E 278 C2
Kerava Finland 60°25N 25°5E 188 B3
Keravat Papua N. G. 4°17S 152°2E 286 C7
Kerch Ukraine 45°20N 36°20E 189 K9
Kerchenskiy Proliv Black Sea 45°10N 36°30E 189 K9
Kerchoual Mali 17°12N 0°20E 263 B5
Kerema Papua N. G. 7°58S 145°50E 286 D3
Kerempe Burnu Turkey 42°2N 33°20E 212 A5
Keren Eritrea 15°45N 38°28E 257 D4
Kerewan Gambia 13°29N 16°10W 262 C1
Kerguelen Ind. Oc. 49°15S 69°10E 273 J5
Kerguelen Plateau S. Ocean 55°0S 75°0E 273 K6
Keri Greece 37°40N 20°49E 207 D2
Keri Kera Sudan 12°21N 32°42E 257 E3
Kericho Kenya 0°22S 35°15E 268 C4
Kerikeri N.Z. 35°12S 173°59E 284 B2
Kerinci Indonesia 1°40S 101°15E 234 C2
Kerinci Seblat △ Indonesia 1°46S 98°45E 234 C1
Kerintji = Kerinci Indonesia 1°40S 101°15E 234 C2
Keriya He → China 38°30N 82°10E 217 E10
Kerkenna, Îs. Tunisia 34°48N 11°11E 258 B2
Kerki = Atamyrat Turkmenistan 37°50N 65°12E 217 E7
Kerkini, L. Greece 41°12N 23°10E 202 E7
Kerkouane Tunisia 36°58N 11°2E 200 F4
Kerkrade Neths. 50°53N 6°4E 170 D6
Kerkyra Greece 39°38N 19°50E 206 B9
Kerkyra □ Greece 39°37N 19°50E 206 B9
Kerkyra ✈ (CFU) Greece 39°35N 19°54E 204 B1
Kerkyras, Notio Steno Greece 39°34N 20°0E 206 B10
Kerma Sudan 19°33N 30°32E 256 D3
Kermadec Is. Pac. Oc. 30°0S 178°15W 277 G15
Kermadec Trench Pac. Oc. 30°30S 176°0W 277 G15
Kermān Iran 30°15N 57°1E 247 D8
Kerman Calif., U.S.A. 36°43N 120°4W 306 J6
Kermān □ Iran 30°0N 57°0E 247 D8
Kermān, Bīābān-e Iran 28°45N 59°45E 247 D8
Kermānshāh Iran 34°23N 47°0E 213 E12
Kermānshāh □ Iran 34°0N 46°30E 246 C5
Kermen Bulgaria 42°30N 26°16E 203 D10
Kermine = Nawoiy Uzbekistan 40°9N 65°22E 217 D7
Kermit U.S.A. 31°52N 103°6W 314 F3
Kern → U.S.A. 35°16N 119°18W 307 K7
Kernhof Austria 47°49N 15°32E 180 D8
Kernow = Cornwall □ U.K. 50°26N 4°40W 169 G3
Kernville U.S.A. 35°45N 118°26W 307 K8
Keroh Malaysia 5°43N 101°1E 237 K3
Keros Greece 36°54N 25°40E 205 E7
Kérou Benin 10°50N 2°5E 263 C5
Kérouane Guinea 9°15N 9°0W 262 D3
Kerowagi Papua N. G. 5°51S 144°51E 286 C3
Kerpen Germany 50°51N 6°41E 178 E2
Kerrera U.K. 56°24N 5°33W 167 E3
Kerrobert Canada 51°56N 109°8W 297 C7
Kerrville U.S.A. 30°3N 99°8W 314 F5
Kerry □ Ireland 52°7N 9°35W 166 D2
Kerry Hd. Ireland 52°25N 9°56W 166 D2
Kersa Ethiopia 9°28N 41°48E 257 F5
Kertosono Indonesia 7°38S 112°9E 235 D4
Kerulen → Asia 48°48N 117°0E 219 B6
Kervo = Kerava Finland 60°25N 25°5E 188 B3
Kerzaz Algeria 29°29N 1°37W 261 C4
Kesagami → Canada 51°40N 79°45W 298 B4
Kesagami L. Canada 50°23N 80°15W 298 B3
Keşan Turkey 40°49N 26°38E 203 F10
Kesariani Greece 37°57N 23°46E 112 B2
Kesennuma Japan 38°54N 141°35E 220 E10
Keshit Iran 29°43N 58°17E 247 D8
Kesigi = Kosgi India 15°51N 77°16E 245 G3
Keşiş Dağ Turkey 39°47N 39°46E 213 C8
Keskal India 20°5N 81°35E 244 D5
Keskin Turkey 39°40N 33°36E 212 C5
Kestell S. Africa 28°17S 28°42E 271 C4
Kestenga Russia 65°50N 31°45E 160 D24
Keswick U.K. 54°36N 3°8W 168 C4
Keszthely Hungary 46°50N 17°15E 182 D2
Ket → Russia 58°55N 81°32E 214 D9
Keta Ghana 5°49N 1°0E 263 D5
Keta Lagoon Ghana 5°55N 1°0E 263 D5
Ketapang Bali, Indonesia 8°9S 114°23E 231 J17
Ketapang Kalimantan, Indonesia 1°55S 110°0E 235 C4
Ketchenery Russia 47°18N 44°32E 191 G7

Ketchikan U.S.A. 55°21N 131°39W 296 B2
Ketchum U.S.A. 43°41N 114°22W 304 E6
Kete Krachi Ghana 7°46N 0°1W 263 D4
Ketef, Khalîg Umm el Egypt 23°40N 35°35E 246 F2
Keti Bandar Pakistan 24°8N 67°27E 242 G2
Kétou Benin 7°25N 2°45E 263 D5
Ketri India 28°1N 75°50E 242 E6
Kętrzyn Poland 54°7N 21°22E 184 D8
Kettering Northants., U.K. 52°24N 0°43W 169 E7
Kettering Md., U.S.A. 38°53N 76°49W 143 B5
Kettering Ohio, U.S.A. 39°41N 84°10W 311 E12
Kettle → Canada 56°40N 89°34W 297 B11
Kettle Falls U.S.A. 48°37N 118°3W 304 B4
Kettle Pt. Canada 43°13N 82°1W 312 C2
Kettleman City U.S.A. 36°1N 119°58W 306 J7
Kęty Poland 49°51N 19°16E 185 J6
Keuka L. U.S.A. 42°30N 77°9W 312 D7
Keuruu Finland 62°16N 24°41E 188 A3
Kevelaer Germany 51°36N 6°15E 178 D2
Kew Vic., Australia 37°48S 145°2E 128 A2
Kew London, U.K. 51°28N 0°17W 125 B2
Kew Gardens Ont., Canada 43°39N 79°18W 141 A3
Kew Gardens London, U.K. 51°28N 0°17W 125 B2
Kewanee U.S.A. 41°14N 89°56W 310 C7
Kewanna U.S.A. 41°1N 86°25W 311 C10
Kewaunee U.S.A. 44°27N 87°31W 308 C10
Keweenaw B. U.S.A. 47°0N 88°15W 308 B9
Keweenaw Pen. U.S.A. 47°15N 88°15W 308 B9
Keweenaw Pt. U.S.A. 47°25N 87°43W 308 B10
Kexholm = Priozersk Russia 61°2N 30°7E 188 B6
Key, L. Ireland 54°0N 8°15W 166 C3
Key Biscayne U.S.A. 25°41N 80°9W 128 B2
Key Colony Beach U.S.A. 24°45N 80°57W 317 L9
Key Largo U.S.A. 25°5N 80°27W 317 K9
Key West U.S.A. 24°33N 81°48W 317 L8
Keyala Sudan 4°27N 32°52E 257 G3
Keynsham U.K. 51°24N 2°29W 169 F5
Keyser U.S.A. 39°26N 78°59W 309 F14
Keystone Heights U.S.A. 29°47N 82°2W 316 F7
Keytesville U.S.A. 39°26N 92°56W 310 E4
Kezhma Russia 58°59N 101°9E 215 D11
Kezi Zimbabwe 20°58S 28°32E 271 B4
Kežmarok Slovak Rep. 49°10N 20°28E 181 B13
Kgalagadi Transfrontier ⌓ Africa 25°10S 21°0E 270 C3
Khabarovsk Russia 48°30N 135°5E 215 E14
Khabr Iran 28°51N 56°22E 247 D8
Khābūr → Syria 35°17N 40°35E 213 E9
Khachmas = Xaçmaz Azerbaijan 41°31N 48°42E 191 K9
Khachrod India 23°25N 75°20E 242 H6
Khadari, W. el → Sudan 10°29N 27°15E 257 E2
Khadro Pakistan 26°11N 68°50E 242 F3
Khadyzhensk Russia 44°26N 39°32E 191 H4
Khadzhilyangar = Dahongliutan China 35°45N 79°20E 243 B8
Khaga India 25°47N 81°7E 243 G9
Khagaria India 25°30N 86°32E 243 G12
Khaipur Pakistan 29°34N 72°17E 242 E5
Khair India 27°57N 77°46E 242 F7
Khairabad India 27°33N 80°47E 243 F9
Khairagarh India 21°27N 81°2E 243 J9
Khairpur Pakistan 27°32N 68°49E 242 F3
Khairpur Nathan Shah Pakistan 27°6N 67°44E 242 F2
Khairwara India 23°58N 73°38E 242 H5
Khaisor → Pakistan 31°17N 68°59E 242 D3
Khajuri Kach Pakistan 32°4N 69°51E 242 C3
Khāk Dow Afghan. 34°57N 67°16E 240 B2
Khakassia □ Russia 53°0N 90°0E 217 B12
Khakhea Botswana 24°48S 23°22E 270 B3
Khalafābād Iran 30°54N 49°24E 247 D6
Khalfallah Algeria 34°20N 0°16E 261 B5
Khalfūt Yemen 15°52N 52°10E 249 D6
Khalīj Iraq 33°18N 44°28E 113 B2
Khalilabad India 26°48N 83°5E 243 F10
Khalīlī Iran 27°38N 53°17E 247 E7
Khalkhāl Iran 37°37N 48°32E 213 D13
Khalkís = Halkida Greece 38°27N 23°42E 204 C5
Khalmer-Sede = Tazovskiy Russia 67°30N 78°44E 214 C8
Khalmer Yu Russia 67°58N 65°1E 214 C7
Khalturin Russia 58°40N 48°50E 186 C8
Kham Keut Laos 18°15N 104°43E 236 C5
Khamaria India 23°5N 80°48E 243 H9
Khambhaliya India 22°14N 69°41E 242 H3
Khambhat India 22°23N 72°33E 242 H5
Khambhat, G. of India 20°45N 72°30E 239 E10
Khamgaon India 20°42N 76°37E 244 D3
Khamīr Iran 26°57N 55°36E 247 E7
Khamir Yemen 16°2N 44°0E 248 C4
Khamīs Mushayṭ Si. Arabia 18°18N 42°44E 248 C3
Khammam India 17°11N 80°6E 244 F5
Khamsa Egypt 30°27N 32°23E 251 H3
Khan → Namibia 22°37S 14°56E 270 B2
Khān Abū Shāmat Syria 33°39N 36°53E 250 E7
Khān Azād Iraq 33°7N 44°22E 246 C5
Khān Mujiddah Iraq 32°21N 43°48E 246 C4
Khān Shaykhūn Syria 35°26N 36°38E 212 E7
Khan Tengri, Pik Asia 42°12N 80°10E 217 D10
Khān Yūnis Gaza Strip 31°21N 34°18E 251 G5
Khānābād Afghan. 36°45N 69°5E 240 A3
Khanai Pakistan 30°30N 67°8E 242 D2
Khānaqīn Iraq 34°23N 45°25E 213 E11
Khānaṣir Syria 35°45N 37°30E 250 C8
Khānbāghī Iran 36°10N 55°25E 247 B7
Khandallah N.Z. 41°15S 174°47E 143 B1
Khandwa India 21°49N 76°22E 244 D3
Khandyga Russia 62°42N 135°35E 215 C14
Khāneh Iran 36°41N 45°8E 246 B5
Khanewal Pakistan 30°20N 71°55E 242 D4
Khangah Dogran Pakistan 31°50N 73°37E 242 D5
Khanh Duong Vietnam 12°44N 108°44E 236 F7
Khaniá = Chania Greece 35°30N 24°4E 207 E5
Khaniadhana India 25°1N 78°8E 242 G8
Khanka, L. Asia 45°0N 132°24E 220 B6
Khankendy = Xankändi Azerbaijan 39°52N 46°49E 213 C12
Khanna India 30°42N 76°16E 242 D7
Khanozai Pakistan 30°37N 67°19E 242 D2
Khanpur Pakistan 28°42N 70°35E 242 E4
Khansā' Iraq 33°21N 44°28E 113 A2
Khanty-Mansiysk Russia 61°0N 69°0E 214 C7
Khanzira, Ras Somali Rep. 10°52N 45°48E 267 B6
Khao Laem △ Thailand 14°56N 98°31E 236 E2
Khao Laem Res. Thailand 14°50N 98°30E 236 E2
Khao Luang △ Thailand 8°34N 99°42E 237 H2
Khao Phlu Thailand 9°29N 99°59E 237 b
Khao Pu-Khao Ya △ Thailand 7°26N 99°57E 237 J2
Khao Sam Roi Yot △ Thailand 12°13N 99°57E 237 F2
Khao Sok △ Thailand 8°55N 98°38E 237 H2
Khao Yai △ Thailand 14°21N 101°29E 236 E3
Khaoen Si Nakarin △ Thailand 14°47N 99°0E 236 E2
Khapalu Pakistan 35°10N 76°20E 243 B7
Khapcheranga Russia 49°42N 112°24E 215 E12
Khaptao △ Nepal 29°20N 81°10E 243 E9
Kharabali Russia 47°25N 47°15E 191 G8
Kharaghoda India 23°11N 71°46E 242 H4
Kharagpur India 22°20N 87°25E 243 H12
Kharan Kalat Pakistan 28°34N 65°21E 240 C2
Kharānaq Iran 32°20N 54°45E 247 C7
Kharavli India 18°54N 72°55E 130 B2
Kharda India 18°40N 75°34E 244 E2
Khardung La India 34°20N 77°43E 243 B7
Kharg = Khārk, Jazīreh-ye Iran 29°15N 50°28E 247 D6
Khârga, El Wâhât-el Egypt 25°10N 30°35E 256 B3
Khargon India 21°45N 75°40E 244 D2
Khari → India 25°54N 74°31E 242 G6
Kharian Pakistan 32°49N 73°52E 242 C5
Khariar India 20°17N 82°46E 244 D6
Kharit, Wadi el → Egypt 24°26N 33°3E 256 C3
Khārk, Jazīreh-ye Iran 29°15N 50°28E 247 D6
Kharkiv Ukraine 49°58N 36°20E 189 H9
Kharkiv □ Ukraine 48°20N 36°20E 189 H9
Kharkov = Kharkiv Ukraine 49°58N 36°20E 189 H9
Kharmanli Bulgaria 41°55N 25°55E 203 E9
Kharovsk Russia 59°56N 40°13E 188 C11
Kharsawangarh India 22°48N 85°50E 243 H11
Kharta Turkey 40°55N 29°7E 212 B3
Khartoum = El Khartûm Sudan 15°31N 32°35E 257 D3
Khasan Russia 42°25N 130°40E 220 C5
Khasavyurt Russia 43°16N 46°40E 191 J8
Khāsh Iran 28°15N 61°15E 240 C1
Khāsh, Dasht-e Afghan. 31°50N 62°30E 240 C1
Khashm el Girba Sudan 14°59N 35°58E 257 E4
Khashum Sudan 12°27N 28°2E 257 E2
Khashuri Georgia 42°3N 43°35E 191 J6
Khasi Hills India 25°30N 91°30E 241 C3
Khaskovo Bulgaria 41°56N 25°30E 203 E9
Khaskovo □ Bulgaria 42°0N 25°40E 203 E9
Khatanga Russia 72°0N 102°20E 215 B11
Khatanga → Russia 72°55N 106°0E 215 B11
Khatauli India 29°17N 77°43E 242 E7
Khatlon □ Tajikistan 37°50N 69°0E 217 E7
Khatra India 22°59N 86°51E 243 H12
Khātūnābād Iran 30°1N 55°25E 247 D7
Khatyrka Russia 62°3N 175°15E 215 C18
Khavda India 23°51N 69°43E 242 H3
Khawlaf, Ra's Yemen 12°40N 54°7E 249 D6
Khawr Fakkān U.A.E. 25°21N 56°22E 247 E8
Khay' Si. Arabia 18°45N 41°24E 248 C3
Khaybar, Ḥarrat Si. Arabia 25°45N 40°0E 246 E4
Khāzimiyah Iraq 34°46N 43°37E 246 C4
Khazzān Jabal al Awliyā Sudan 15°24N 32°20E 257 D3
Khe Bo Vietnam 19°8N 104°41E 236 C5
Khe Long Vietnam 21°29N 104°46E 236 B5
Khe Sanh Vietnam 16°37N 106°45E 236 D6
Khed Maharashtra, India 17°43N 73°27E 244 F1
Khed Maharashtra, India 18°51N 73°56E 244 E1
Khed Brahma India 24°7N 73°5E 242 G5
Khefren Egypt 29°58N 31°8E 117 B1
Khekra India 28°52N 77°20E 242 E7
Khem-Beldyr = Kyzyl Russia 51°50N 94°30E 217 B12
Khemarak Phouminville = Krong Kaoh Kong Cambodia 11°37N 102°59E 237 G4
Khemisset Morocco 33°50N 6°1W 260 B3
Khemisset □ Morocco 33°40N 6°15W 260 B3
Khemmarat Thailand 16°10N 105°15E 236 D5
Khenāmān Iran 30°27N 56°29E 247 D8
Khenchela Algeria 35°28N 7°11E 261 A6
Khenchela □ Algeria 35°0N 7°0E 261 B6
Khénifra Morocco 32°58N 5°46W 260 B3
Kherrata Algeria 36°27N 5°13E 261 A6
Khersān → Iran 31°33N 50°22E 247 D6
Kherson Ukraine 46°35N 32°35E 189 J7
Kherson □ Ukraine 46°30N 33°0E 189 J7
Kheta → Russia 71°54N 102°6E 215 B11
Khewari Pakistan 26°36N 68°52E 242 F3
Khibinogorsk = Kirovsk Russia 67°32N 33°41E 186 A5
Khichripur India 28°37N 77°18E 120 B2
Khidirpur India 22°32N 88°19E 124 B1
Khilchipur India 24°2N 76°34E 242 G7
Khilok Russia 51°30N 110°45E 215 D12
Khimki Russia 55°50N 37°20E 188 E9
Khimki-Khovrino Russia 55°51N 37°31E 129 A3
Khíos = Hios Greece 38°27N 26°9E 205 C8
Khirbet Batin Abu Lihyah West Bank 31°50N 35°6E 123 A1
Khirbet el-Misbah West Bank 31°53N 35°4E 123 A1
Khirbet Jub e-Rum West Bank 31°44N 35°16E 123 B2
Khirsadoh India 22°11N 78°47E 243 H8
Khiuma = Hiiumaa Estonia 58°50N 22°45E 188 C2
Khiva Uzbekistan 41°30N 60°18E 216 D6
Khīyāv Iran 38°30N 47°45E 246 B5
Khlebarovo Bulgaria 43°37N 26°15E 203 C10
Khlong Khlung Thailand 16°12N 99°43E 236 D2
Khlong San Thailand 13°43N 100°29E 113 B2
Khlong Toey Thailand 13°43N 100°33E 113 B2
Khmelnik Ukraine 49°33N 27°58E 177 D14
Khmelnitskiy = Khmelnytskyy Ukraine 49°23N 27°0E 177 D14
Khmelnytskyy Ukraine 49°23N 27°0E 177 D14
Khmelnytskyy □ Ukraine 49°50N 26°40E 189 H4
Khmer Rep. = Cambodia ■ Asia 12°15N 105°0E 236 F5
Khoai, Hon Vietnam 8°26N 104°50E 237 H5
Khodoriv Ukraine 49°24N 24°19E 177 D13
Khodzent = Khŭjand Tajikistan 40°17N 69°37E 217 D7
Khodzheyli = Khŭjayli Uzbekistan 42°29N 59°31E 216 D5
Khojak Pass Afghan. 30°51N 66°34E 242 D2
Khok Kloi Thailand 8°17N 98°19E 237 a
Khok Pho Thailand 6°43N 101°6E 237 J3
Khokhropār Pakistan 25°42N 70°12E 240 D3
Kholm Afghan. 36°45N 67°40E 240 A2
Kholm Russia 57°10N 31°15E 188 D6
Kholmsk Russia 47°40N 142°5E 215 E15
Khomas Hochland Namibia 22°40S 16°0E 270 B2
Khombole Senegal 14°43N 16°42W 262 C1
Khomeyn Iran 33°40N 50°7E 247 C6
Khomeynī Shahr Iran 32°41N 51°31E 247 C6
Khomodino Botswana 22°46S 23°52E 270 B3
Khon Kaen Thailand 16°30N 102°47E 236 D4
Khong → Cambodia 13°32N 105°58E 236 F5
Khong Sedone Laos 15°34N 105°49E 236 E5
Khonuu Russia 66°30N 143°12E 215 C15
Khoper → Russia 49°30N 42°20E 190 F6
Khor el 'Atash Sudan 13°20N 34°15E 257 E3
Khorāsān □ Iran 34°0N 58°0E 247 C8
Khorāsān-e Razavī □ Iran 35°0N 59°0E 216 F5
Khorāsān-e Shemālī □ Iran 37°0N 57°0E 216 E5
Khorat = Nakhon Ratchasima Thailand 14°59N 102°12E 236 E4
Khorat, Cao Nguyen Thailand 15°30N 102°50E 236 E4
Khorazm □ Uzbekistan 43°0N 60°0E 216 D6
Khorb el Ethel Algeria 28°30N 6°17W 260 C3
Khorel India 22°41N 88°18E 124 A1
Khorixas Namibia 20°16S 14°59E 270 B1
Khorol Ukraine 49°48N 33°15E 189 H7
Khorosovo Russia 55°46N 37°27E 129 B2
Khorramābād Khorāsān, Iran 35°6N 57°57E 247 C8
Khorramābād Lorestān, Iran 33°30N 48°25E 213 F13
Khorrāmshahr Iran 30°29N 48°15E 247 D6
Khorugh Tajikistan 37°30N 71°36E 240 A3
Khosravī Iran 30°48N 51°28E 247 D6
Khosrowābād Khuzestān, Iran 30°10N 48°25E 247 D6
Khosrowābād Kordestān, Iran 35°31N 47°38E 213 E12
Khost Pakistan 30°13N 67°35E 242 D2
Khosūyeh Iran 28°32N 54°26E 247 D7
Khotan = Hotan China 37°25N 79°55E 217 E9
Khotyn Ukraine 48°31N 26°27E 183 B11
Khouribga Morocco 32°58N 6°57W 260 B3
Khouribga □ Morocco 32°56N 6°36W 260 B3
Khowai Bangla. 24°5N 91°40E 241 C3
Khowst Afghan. 33°22N 69°58E 242 C3
Khowst □ Afghan. 33°20N 70°0E 240 B3
Khoyniki Belarus 51°54N 29°55E 177 C15
Khrami → Georgia 41°25N 45°0E 191 K7
Khrenovoye Russia 51°4N 40°16E 190 E5
Khromtau Kazakhstan 50°17N 58°27E 216 B5
Khrysokhou B. Cyprus 35°6N 32°25E 207 E8
Khu Khan Thailand 14°42N 104°12E 236 E5
Khuan Wa Thailand 7°53N 98°17E 237 a
Khudrah, W. → Yemen 18°10N 50°20E 249 C5
Khudzhand = Khŭjand Tajikistan 40°17N 69°37E 217 D7
Khuff Si. Arabia 24°55N 44°53E 246 E5
Khūgīānī Afghan. 31°34N 66°32E 242 D2
Khuis Botswana 26°40S 21°49E 270 C3
Khuiyala India 27°9N 70°25E 242 F4
Khŭjand Tajikistan 40°17N 69°37E 217 D7
Khŭjayli Uzbekistan 42°29N 59°31E 216 D5
Khujner India 23°47N 76°36E 242 H7
Khulayṣ Si. Arabia 22°9N 39°19E 248 B2
Khulna Bangla. 22°45N 89°34E 241 D2
Khulna □ Bangla. 22°25N 89°35E 241 D2
Khulo Georgia 41°33N 42°19E 191 K6
Khumago Botswana 20°26S 24°32E 270 B3
Khumrah Si. Arabia 21°22N 39°13E 248 B2
Khunjerab △ Pakistan 36°40N 75°30E 243 A6
Khunjerab Pass = Kinjirap Daban Asia 36°40N 75°25E 240 A4
Khūnsorkh Iran 27°9N 56°7E 247 E8
Khunti India 23°5N 85°17E 243 H11
Khūr Iran 32°55N 58°18E 247 C8
Khurai India 24°3N 78°23E 242 G8
Khuraydah Yemen 15°33N 48°18E 249 D5
Khurayṣ Si. Arabia 25°6N 48°2E 247 E6
Khurda India 20°11N 85°37E 244 D7
Khureit Sudan 13°59N 26°33E 257 E2
Khurja India 28°15N 77°58E 242 E7
Khūrmāl Iraq 35°18N 46°2E 246 C5
Khurr, Wādī al Iraq 32°3N 43°52E 246 C4
Khūsf Iran 32°46N 58°53E 247 C8
Khushab Pakistan 32°20N 72°20E 242 C5
Khust Ukraine 48°10N 23°18E 183 B8
Khutse ⌓ Botswana 23°31S 24°12E 270 B3
Khuzdar Pakistan 27°52N 66°30E 242 F2
Khūzestān □ Iran 31°0N 49°0E 247 D6
Khvāf Iran 34°33N 60°8E 247 C9
Khvājeh Iran 38°9N 46°35E 246 B5
Khvājeh Moḥammad, Kūh-e Afghan. 36°22N 70°17E 240 A3
Khvalynsk Russia 52°30N 48°2E 190 D9
Khvānsār Iran 29°56N 54°8E 247 D7
Khvatovka Russia 52°24N 46°32E 190 D8
Khvor Iran 33°45N 55°0E 247 C7
Khvorgū Iran 27°34N 56°27E 247 E8
Khvormūj Iran 28°40N 51°30E 247 D6
Khvoy Iran 38°35N 45°0E 213 C11
Khvoynaya Russia 58°58N 34°28E 188 C8
Khyber Pass Afghan. 34°10N 71°8E 242 B4
Khyriv Ukraine 49°32N 22°50E 185 J9
Kia Fiji 16°16S 179°8E 287 A2
Kia Solomon Is. 7°32S 158°26E 287 L10
Kiabukwa Dem. Rep. of the Congo 8°40S 24°48E 265 D4
Kiadho → India 19°37N 77°40E 244 E3
Kiama N.S.W., Australia 34°40S 150°50E 283 C9
Kiama Dem. Rep. of the Congo 7°19S 17°49E 265 D3
Kiamari Pakistan 24°49N 66°58E 123 B1
Kiamba Phil. 6°2N 124°46E 233 H5
Kiambi Dem. Rep. of the Congo 7°15S 28°0E 268 D2
Kiambu Kenya 1°8S 36°50E 268 C4
Kiamusze = Jiamusi China 46°40N 130°26E 219 B8
Kian = Ji'an China 41°5N 126°10E 227 D14
Kiana U.S.A. 66°58N 160°26W 303 C7
Kiang West △ Gambia 13°25N 15°50W 262 C1
Kiangara Madag. 17°58S 47°2E 273 B8
Kiangsi = Jiangxi □ China 27°30N 116°0E 229 D11
Kiangsu = Jiangsu □ China 33°0N 120°0E 227 H11
Kiato Greece 38°1N 22°45E 204 C4
Kibæk Denmark 56°2N 8°51E 163 H2
Kibale △ Uganda 0°16N 30°18E 268 B3
Kibanga Port Uganda 0°10N 32°58E 268 B3
Kibangou Congo 3°26S 12°22E 264 C2
Kibara Tanzania 2°8S 33°30E 268 C3
Kibare, Mts. Dem. Rep. of the Congo 8°25S 27°10E 268 D2
Kibawe Phil. 7°34N 125°0E 233 H5
Kibenga Dem. Rep. of the Congo 7°56S 17°30E 265 D3
Kibira △ Burundi 3°6S 30°24E 268 C3
Kibombo Dem. Rep. of the Congo 3°57S 25°53E 265 C5
Kibondo Tanzania 3°35S 30°45E 268 C3
Kibre Mengist Ethiopia 5°54N 38°59E 257 F4
Kıbrıs = Cyprus ■ Asia 35°0N 33°0E 207 F9
Kibumbu Burundi 3°32S 29°45E 268 C2
Kibungo Rwanda 2°10S 30°32E 268 C3
Kibuye Burundi 3°39S 29°59E 268 C2
Kibuye Rwanda 2°3S 29°21E 268 C2
Kibwesa Tanzania 6°30S 29°58E 268 D2
Kibwezi Kenya 2°27S 37°57E 268 C4
Kicasalih Turkey 41°23N 26°48E 203 E10
Kičevo Macedonia 41°34N 20°59E 202 E4
Kichha India 28°53N 79°30E 243 E8
Kichha → India 28°41N 79°18E 243 E8
Kichmengskiy Gorodok Russia 59°59N 45°48E 186 B8
Kicking Horse Pass Canada 51°28N 116°16W 296 C5
Kid, W. → Egypt 28°9N 34°27E 251 K5
Kid I. Antigua & B. 17°42N 61°49W 322 c
Kidal Mali 18°26N 1°22E 263 B5
Kidal □ Mali 19°55N 1°5E 261 E5
Kidapawan Phil. 7°1N 125°3E 233 H5
Kidderminster U.K. 52°24N 2°15W 169 E5
Kidepo Valley △ Uganda 3°52N 33°50E 268 B3
Kidete Tanzania 6°25S 37°17E 268 D4
Kidira Senegal 14°28N 12°13W 262 C2
Kidnappers, C. N.Z. 39°38S 177°5E 284 F6
Kidsgrove U.K. 53°5N 2°14W 168 D5
Kidston Australia 18°52S 144°8E 280 B3
Kidugallo Tanzania 6°49S 38°15E 268 D4
Kidurong, Tanjong Malaysia 3°16N 113°3E 235 B4
Kiel Germany 54°19N 10°8E 178 A6
Kiel Canal = Nord-Ostsee-Kanal Germany 54°12N 9°32E 178 A5
Kiel-Kanal = Nord-Ostsee-Kanal Germany 54°12N 9°32E 178 A5
Kielce Poland 50°52N 20°42E 185 H7
Kielder Water U.K. 55°11N 2°31W 168 B5
Kieler Bucht Germany 54°35N 10°25E 178 A6
Kiembara Burkina Faso 13°15N 2°44W 262 C4
Kien Binh Vietnam 9°55N 105°19E 237 H5
Kien Tan Vietnam 10°7N 105°17E 237 G5
Kienge Dem. Rep. of the Congo 10°30S 27°30E 269 E2
Kierling Austria 48°18N 16°16E 142 A1
Kierlingbach → Austria 48°18N 16°19E 142 A1
Kiessé Niger 13°29N 4°1E 263 C5
Kieta Papua N. G. 6°12S 155°36E 286 D8
Kiev = Kyyiv Ukraine 50°30N 30°28E 177 C16
Kifaya Guinea 12°10N 13°4W 262 C2
Kiffa Mauritania 16°37N 11°24W 262 B2
Kifisos → Athina, Greece 37°58N 23°42E 112 B2
Kifisos → Voiotia, Greece 38°35N 23°20E 204 C5
Kifissia Greece 38°4N 23°49E 204 C5
Kifrī Iraq 34°45N 45°0E 213 E11
Kigali Rwanda 1°59S 30°4E 268 C3
Kigarama Tanzania 1°1S 31°50E 268 C3
Kigelle Sudan 8°40N 34°2E 257 F3
Kigezi ⌓ Uganda 0°34S 29°55E 268 C2
Kigoma □ Tanzania 5°0S 30°0E 268 D3
Kigoma-Ujiji Tanzania 4°55S 29°36E 268 C2
Kigomasha, Ras Tanzania 4°58S 38°58E 268 C4
Kiğzı Turkey 38°18N 43°25E 246 B4
Kihei U.S.A. 20°47N 156°28W 302 C5
Kihikihi N.Z. 38°2S 175°22E 284 E4
Kihnu Estonia 58°9N 24°1E 188 C3
Kīholo B. U.S.A. 19°50N 155°55W 302 D6
Kii-Hantō Japan 34°0N 135°45E 223 D7
Kii-Nagashima Japan 34°12N 136°20E 223 C8
Kii-Sanchi Japan 34°20N 136°0E 223 C8
Kii-Suidō Japan 33°40N 134°45E 222 D6
Kiira Dam Uganda 0°25N 33°0E 268 B3
Kiire Japan 31°22N 130°33E 222 F2
Kijik U.S.A. 60°20N 154°20W 303 F9
Kikaiga-Shima Japan 28°19N 129°59E 221 K4
Kikinda Serbia 45°50N 20°30E 182 E5
Kikládhes = Cyclades Greece 37°0N 24°30E 204 E6
Kikoira Australia 33°39S 146°40E 283 B7
Kikombo Bandundu, Dem. Rep. of the Congo 5°37S 18°50E 265 D3
Kikombo Bandundu, Dem. Rep. of the Congo 5°49S 17°45E 265 D3
Kikongo Dem. Rep. of the Congo 4°16S 17°17E 265 C3
Kikori Papua N. G. 7°25S 144°15E 286 D3
Kikori → Papua N. G. 7°38S 144°20E 286 D3
Kikuchi Japan 32°59N 130°47E 222 E2
Kikuna Japan 35°30N 139°37E 140 B2
Kikwit Dem. Rep. of the Congo 5°0S 18°45E 265 D3
Kil Sweden 59°30N 13°20E 162 E7
Kilafors Sweden 61°14N 16°36E 162 C10
Kilakkarai India 9°12N 78°47E 245 K4
Kilar India 33°6N 76°25E 242 C7
Kilauea U.S.A. 22°13N 159°25W 302 A2
Kīlauea Caldera U.S.A. 19°25N 155°17W 302 D6
Kilbarrack Ireland 53°23N 6°9W 120 A3
Kilbeggan Ireland 53°22N 7°30W 166 C4
Kilbirnie N.Z. 41°19S 174°48E 143 B1
Kilbrannan Sd. U.K. 55°37N 5°26W 167 F3
Kilbuck Mts. U.S.A. 60°36N 159°53W 303 F8
Kilburn U.K. 51°32N 0°11W 125 A2
Kilchu N. Korea 40°57N 129°25E 224 B4
Kilcoy Australia 26°59S 152°30E 281 D5
Kildare Ireland 53°9N 6°55W 166 C5
Kildare □ Ireland 53°10N 6°50W 166 C5
Kildinstroy Russia 68°48N 33°6E 160 B25
Kileikli Sudan 11°25N 25°31E 257 E2
Kilembe Dem. Rep. of the Congo 5°42S 19°55E 265 D3
Kilen Norway 59°20N 8°49E 164 E5
Kilfinnane Ireland 52°21N 8°28W 166 D3
Kilgarvan Ireland 51°54N 9°27W 166 E2
Kilgore U.S.A. 32°23N 94°53W 314 E7
Kilgoris Kenya 1°0S 34°53E 268 C3
Kilibo Benin 8°32N 2°38E 263 D5
Kilifi Kenya 3°40S 39°48E 268 C4
Kilimanjaro Tanzania 3°7S 37°20E 268 C4
Kilimanjaro □ Tanzania 4°0S 38°0E 268 C4
Kilimli Turkey 41°28N 31°50E 212 B4
Kilinailau Is. Papua N. G. 4°45S 155°20E 286 C8
Kilindini Kenya 4°4S 39°40E 268 C4
Kilis Turkey 36°42N 37°6E 250 B8
Kilis □ Turkey 36°50N 37°10E 212 D7
Kiliya Ukraine 45°28N 29°16E 183 E14
Kilkee Ireland 52°41N 9°39W 166 D2
Kilkeel U.K. 54°4N 6°0W 166 B5
Kilkenny Ireland 52°39N 7°15W 166 D4
Kilkenny □ Ireland 52°35N 7°15W 166 D4
Kilkieran B. Ireland 53°20N 9°41W 166 C2
Kilkis Greece 40°58N 22°57E 202 F6
Kilkis □ Greece 41°5N 22°50E 202 E6
Killakee Ireland 53°15N 6°19W 120 B2
Killala Ireland 54°13N 9°12W 166 B2
Killala B. Ireland 54°16N 9°8W 166 B2
Killaloe Ont., Canada 45°33N 77°25W 312 A7
Killaloe Clare, Ireland 52°48N 8°28W 166 D3
Killarney Queens., Australia 28°20S 152°18E 281 D5
Killarney Man., Canada 49°10N 99°40W 297 D9
Killarney Kerry, Ireland 52°4N 9°30W 166 D2
Killarney, L. Bahamas 25°3N 77°27W 153 b
Killarney △ Ireland 52°0N 9°33W 166 D2
Killary Harbour Ireland 53°38N 9°52W 166 C2
Killdeer U.S.A. 47°22N 102°45W 308 B2
Killeberg Sweden 56°29N 14°5E 163 H8
Killeen U.S.A. 31°7N 97°44W 314 F6
Killester Ireland 53°22N 6°11W 120 A2
Killin U.K. 56°28N 4°19W 167 E4
Killiney Ireland 53°15N 6°7W 120 B3
Killiney B. Ireland 53°16N 6°5W 120 B3
Killington Pk. U.S.A. 43°36N 72°49W 313 C12
Killíni = Kyllini Greece 37°55N 21°8E 207 D3
Killíni Greece 37°54N 22°25E 204 D4
Killorglin Ireland 52°6N 9°47W 166 D2
Killybegs Ireland 54°38N 8°26W 166 B3
Kilmacud Ireland 53°17N 6°13W 120 B2
Kilmainham Ireland 53°20N 6°17W 120 A2
Kilmainham Gaol Ireland 53°21N 6°19W 120 A2
Kilmarnock U.K. 55°37N 4°29W 167 F4
Kilmashogue Mt. Ireland 53°15N 6°15W 120 B2
Kilmez Russia 56°58N 50°55E 190 B10
Kilmez → Russia 56°58N 50°28E 190 B10
Kilmore Vic., Australia 37°25S 144°53E 283 D6
Kilmore Dublin, Ireland 53°23N 6°13W 120 A2
Kilmore Quay Ireland 52°10N 6°36W 166 D5
Kilnamanagh Ireland 53°18N 6°22W 120 B2
Kilo Finland 60°13N 24°47E 121 B1
Kilokri India 28°34N 77°15E 120 B2
Kilómetro 1082 = Joaquín V. González Argentina 25°10S 64°0W 334 B3
Kilondo Tanzania 9°45S 34°20E 269 D3
Kilosa Tanzania 6°48S 37°0E 268 D4
Kilrush Ireland 52°38N 9°29W 166 D2
Kiltan I. India 11°29N 73°0E 245 J1
Kiltiernan Ireland 53°15N 6°11W 120 B2
Kilwa Kisiwani Tanzania 8°58S 39°32E 269 D4
Kilwa Kivinje Tanzania 8°45S 39°25E 269 D4
Kilwa Masoko Tanzania 8°55S 39°30E 269 D4
Kilwinning U.K. 55°39N 4°43W 167 F4
Kim U.S.A. 37°15N 103°21W 305 H12
Kim → Cameroon 5°28N 11°7E 263 D7
Kimaam Indonesia 7°58S 138°53E 231 F9
Kimamba Tanzania 6°45S 37°10E 268 D4
Kimba Australia 33°8S 136°23E 282 B2
Kimball Nebr., U.S.A. 41°14N 103°40W 308 E2
Kimball S. Dak., U.S.A. 43°45N 98°57W 308 D4
Kimbanda Dem. Rep. of the Congo 4°16S 18°30E 265 C3
Kimbe Papua N. G. 5°33S 150°11E 286 C6
Kimbe B. Papua N. G. 5°15S 150°30E 286 C6
Kimberley W. Austral., Australia 16°20S 127°0E 278 C4
Kimberley B.C., Canada 49°40N 115°59W 296 D5
Kimberley Northern Cape, S. Africa 28°43S 24°46E 270 C3
Kimberly U.S.A. 42°32N 114°22W 304 E6
Kimbongo Dem. Rep. of the Congo 6°8S 18°1E 265 D3
Kimch'aek N. Korea 40°40N 129°10E 224 B4
Kimhae = Gimhae S. Korea 35°14N 128°53E 224 E4
Kimhwa N. Korea 38°25N 127°36E 224 C3
Kimi Greece 38°38N 24°6E 204 C6
Kimitsu Japan 35°19N 139°54E 223 B10
Kimjŏngsugŭp N. Korea 41°24N 127°45E 224 B3
Kimmage Ireland 53°18N 6°17W 120 B2
Kimmirut Canada 62°50N 69°50W 295 C13
Kimolos Greece 36°48N 24°37E 204 E6
Kimongo Congo 4°27S 12°53E 265 C2
Kimovsk Moskva, Russia 55°21N 37°28E 188 E9
Kimovsk Tula, Russia 54°0N 38°29E 188 E10
Kimpangu Dem. Rep. of the Congo 5°52S 15°5E 265 D3
Kimparana Mali 12°48N 5°0W 262 C4
Kimry Russia 56°55N 37°15E 188 D9
Kimstad Sweden 58°35N 15°58E 163 F9
Kimvula Dem. Rep. of the Congo 5°44S 15°58E 265 D3
Kin Burma 22°46N 94°22E 241 D5
Kin-u Burma 22°46N 95°37E 241 D5
Kin-wan Japan 26°23N 127°55E 288 a
Kinabalu, Gunung Malaysia 6°3N 116°14E 235 A5
Kinabalu △ Malaysia 6°0N 116°30E 235 A5
Kinango Kenya 4°8S 39°19E 268 C4
Kinard U.S.A. 30°16N 85°15W 316 E4
Kinaros Greece 36°59N 26°15E 205 E8
Kinaskan L. Canada 57°38N 130°8W 296 B2
Kinbasket L. Canada 52°0N 118°10W 296 C5
Kincaid U.S.A. 39°35N 89°25W 310 E7
Kincardine Canada 44°10N 81°40W 312 B3
Kinchafoonee Cr. → U.S.A. 31°38N 84°10W 316 D5
Kinchega △ Australia 32°27S 142°15E 282 B5
Kincolith Canada 55°0N 129°57W 296 C3
Kinda Kasai-Or., Dem. Rep. of the Congo 9°18S 25°4E 265 D5
Kinda Katanga, Dem. Rep. of the Congo 4°47S 21°48E 265 C4
Kindambi Dem. Rep. of the Congo 5°6S 18°14E 265 D4
Kindberg Austria 47°30N 15°27E 180 D8
Kinde U.S.A. 43°56N 83°0W 312 C2
Kindele Dem. Rep. of the Congo 8°39S 24°10E 265 D4
Kinder Scout U.K. 53°24N 1°52W 168 D6
Kinderhook U.S.A. 39°42N 91°10W 310 E5
Kindersley Canada 51°30N 109°10W 297 C7
Kindi Iraq 33°18N 44°22E 113 B2
Kindia Guinea 10°0N 12°52W 262 D2
Kindongo Dem. Rep. of the Congo 3°58S 17°30E 264 C3
Kindu Dem. Rep. of the Congo 2°55S 25°50E 264 C5
Kinel Russia 53°15N 50°40E 190 D10
Kineshma Russia 57°30N 42°5E 190 B6
Kinesi Tanzania 1°25S 33°50E 268 C3
King, L. Australia 33°10S 119°35E 279 F2
King, Mt. Australia 25°10S 147°30E 280 D4
King City Calif., U.S.A. 36°13N 121°8W 306 J5
King City Mo., U.S.A. 40°3N 94°31W 310 D2
King Cove U.S.A. 55°3N 162°19W 303 J7
King Cr. → Australia 24°35S 139°30E 280 C2
King Edward → Australia 14°14S 126°35E 278 B4
King Frederick VI Land = Kong Frederik VI Kyst Greenland 63°0N 43°0W 154 E6
King George B. Falk. Is. 51°30S 60°30W 153 f
King George I. Antarctica 60°0S 60°0W 151 C18
King George Is. Canada 57°20N 80°30W 295 D11
King George VI Falls Guyana 5°42N 61°5W 329 B5
King I. = Kadan Kyun Burma 12°30N 98°20E 236 F2
King I. Tas., Australia 39°50S 144°0E 281 F3
King I. B.C., Canada 52°10N 127°40W 296 C3
King Leopold Ranges Australia 17°30S 125°45E 278 C4
King of Prussia U.S.A. 40°5N 75°23W 313 F9
King Salmon U.S.A. 58°42N 156°40W 303 G8
King Sd. Australia 16°50S 123°20E 278 C3
King Sejong Antarctica 62°30S 58°0W 151 C18
King William I. Canada 69°10N 97°25W 294 C10
King William's Town S. Africa 32°51S 27°22E 270 D4
Kingait = Cape Dorset Canada 64°14N 76°32W 295 C12
Kingaok = Bathurst Inlet Canada 66°50N 108°1W 294 C9
Kingaroy Australia 26°32S 151°51E 281 D5
Kingdom City U.S.A. 38°56N 91°56W 310 F5
Kingfisher U.S.A. 35°52N 97°56W 314 D6
Kinghorn U.K. 56°5N 3°10W 121 A2
Kingirbān Iraq 34°40N 44°54E 246 C5
Kingisepp = Kuressaare Estonia 58°15N 22°30E 188 C2
Kingisepp Russia 59°25N 28°40E 188 C5
Kingking = Pantukan Phil. 7°9N 125°54E 233 H5
Kinglake △ Australia 37°30S 145°22E 283 D6
Kingman Ariz., U.S.A. 35°12N 114°4W 307 K12
Kingman Ind., U.S.A. 39°58N 87°18W 311 E9
Kingman Kans., U.S.A. 37°39N 98°7W 308 G4
Kingoonya Australia 30°55S 135°19E 281 E2
Kingri Pakistan 30°27N 69°49E 242 D3
Kings → U.S.A. 36°3N 119°50W 306 J7
Kings Canyon △ U.S.A. 36°50N 118°40W 306 J8
Kings County = Offaly □ Ireland 53°15N 7°30W 166 C4
Kings Cross Sydney, Australia 139 c3
King's Cross London, U.K. 125 a4
Kings Domain Australia 37°49S 144°58E 128 A1
Kings Forest = Kongelunden Denmark 55°34N 12°34E 118 B3
King's Lynn U.K. 52°45N 0°24E 168 E8
Kings Park N.Y., U.S.A. 40°53N 73°16W 313 F11
Kings Park Va., U.S.A. 38°48N 77°17W 143 C2
Kings Park West U.S.A. 38°48N 77°18W 143 C2
Kings Peak U.S.A. 40°46N 110°23W 304 F8
King's Trough Atl. Oc. 43°48N 22°0W 152 B9
Kingsbridge U.K. 50°17N 3°47W 169 G4
Kingsburg U.S.A. 36°31N 119°33W 306 J7
Kingsbury Vic., Australia 37°43S 145°2E 128 A2
Kingsbury London, U.K. 51°34N 0°15W 125 A2
Kingscote Australia 35°40S 137°38E 282 C2
Kingscourt Ireland 53°55N 6°48W 166 C5
Kingsford N.S.W., Australia 33°56S 151°14E 139 B2
Kingsford Mich., U.S.A. 45°48N 88°4W 308 C9
Kingsford Smith, Sydney ✕ (SYD) Australia 33°57S 151°11E 139 B2
Kingsland U.S.A. 30°48N 81°41W 316 E8
Kingsport U.S.A. 36°33N 82°33W 315 C13
Kingston Ont., Canada 44°14N 76°30W 313 B8
Kingston Jamaica 18°0N 76°50W 293 H12
Kingston N.Z. 45°20S 168°43E 285 F3
Kingston N.H., U.S.A. 42°56N 71°3W 313 D13
Kingston N.Y., U.S.A. 41°56N 73°59W 313 E11
Kingston Pa., U.S.A. 41°16N 75°54W 313 E9
Kingston R.I., U.S.A. 41°29N 71°30W 313 E13
Kingston Pk. U.S.A. 35°44N 115°55W 307 K11
Kingston South East Australia 36°51S 139°55E 282 D3
Kingston upon Hull U.K. 53°45N 0°21W 168 D7
Kingston upon Hull □ U.K. 53°45N 0°21W 168 D7
Kingston-upon-Thames □ U.K. 51°24N 0°17W 125 B2
Kingston Vale U.K. 51°25N 0°25W 125 B2
Kingstown = Dún Laoghaire Ireland 53°17N 6°8W 120 B3
Kingstown N.S.W., Australia 30°29S 151°6E 283 A9
Kingstown St. Vincent 13°10N 61°10W 323 n
Kingstree U.S.A. 33°40N 79°50W 316 B10
Kingsville Ont., Canada 42°2N 82°45W 312 D2
Kingsville Tex., U.S.A. 27°31N 97°52W 314 H6
Kingsway Canada 43°38N 79°32W 141 B1
Kingtechen = Jingdezhen China 29°20N 117°11E 229 C11
Kingunda Dem. Rep. of the Congo 6°36S 16°58E 265 D3
Kingussie U.K. 57°6N 4°2W 167 D4
Kingwood U.S.A. 30°2N 95°16W 314 F7
Kinhwa = Jinhua China 29°8N 119°38E 229 C12
Kınık Antalya, Turkey 36°20N 29°20E 205 E11
Kınık İzmir, Turkey 39°6N 27°24E 205 B9
Kinistino Canada 52°57N 105°2W 297 C7
Kinjirap Daban Asia 36°40N 75°25E 240 A4
Kinkala Congo 4°18S 14°49E 265 C2
Kinki □ Japan 33°45N 136°0E 223 D8
Kinleith N.Z. 38°20S 175°56E 284 E4
Kinlochleven U.K. 56°43N 5°0W 167 E4
Kinmount Canada 44°48N 78°45W 312 B6
Kinmundy U.S.A. 38°46N 88°51W 311 F8
Kinn Norway 61°34N 4°45E 164 C1
Kinna Sweden 57°32N 12°42E 163 G6
Kinnairds Hd. U.K. 57°43N 2°1W 167 D6
Kinnared Sweden 57°2N 13°7E 163 G7
Kinnarp Sweden 58°5N 13°32E 163 F7
Kinneviken Sweden 58°35N 13°15E 163 F7
Kino Nuevo Mexico 28°52N 112°3W 318 B2
Kinogitan Phil. 9°0N 124°48E 233 G5
Kinoje → Canada 52°8N 81°25W 298 B3
Kinomoto Japan 35°30N 136°13E 223 B8
Kinoni Uganda 0°41S 30°28E 268 C3
Kinoosao Canada 57°5N 102°1W 297 B8
Kinross U.K. 56°13N 3°25W 167 E5
Kinsale Cork, Ireland 51°42N 8°31W 166 E3
Kinsale Montserrat 16°42N 62°13W 323 p
Kinsale, Old Hd. of Ireland 51°37N 8°33W 166 E3
Kinsaley Ireland 53°24N 6°11W 120 A2
Kinsarvik Norway 60°22N 6°43E 164 D3
Kinsha = Chang Jiang → China 31°48N 121°10E 229 B13
Kinshasa Dem. Rep. of the Congo 4°20S 15°15E 265 C3
Kinsley U.S.A. 37°55N 99°25W 308 G4
Kinsman U.S.A. 41°26N 80°35W 312 E4
Kinston Ala., U.S.A. 31°13N 86°10W 316 D3
Kinston N.C., U.S.A. 35°16N 77°35W 315 D16
Kintamani Indonesia 8°14S 115°19E 231 J18
Kintampo Ghana 8°5N 1°41W 263 D4
Kintap Indonesia 3°51S 115°13E 235 C5
Kintore U.K. 57°14N 2°20W 167 D6
Kintore Ra. Australia 23°15S 128°47E 278 D4
Kintshua Dem. Rep. of the Congo 4°27S 19°38E 265 C3
Kintyre U.K. 55°30N 5°35W 167 F3
Kintyre, Mull of U.K. 55°17N 5°47W 167 F3
Kinu-Gawa → Japan 35°36N 139°57E 223 B11
Kinushseo → Canada 55°15N 83°45W 298 A3
Kinuso Canada 55°20N 115°25W 296 B5
Kinvarra Ireland 53°8N 8°56W 166 C3
Kinwat India 19°38N 78°12E 244 E4
Kinyangiri Tanzania 4°25S 34°37E 268 C3
Kinyeti Sudan 3°57N 32°54E 257 G3
Kinzia Dem. Rep. of the Congo 3°36S 18°26E 264 C3
Kinzig → Germany 48°36N 7°49E 179 G3
Kinzua U.S.A. 41°52N 78°58W 312 E6
Kioni Greece 38°27N 20°41E 207 C2
Kiosk Canada 46°6N 78°53W 298 C4
Kiowa Kans., U.S.A. 37°1N 98°29W 308 G4
Kiowa Okla., U.S.A. 34°43N 95°54W 314 D7
Kipahigan L. Canada 55°20N 101°55W 297 B8
Kipanga Tanzania 6°15S 35°20E 268 D4
Kipapa → U.S.A. 21°24N 158°1W 302 K13
Kiparissia Greece 37°15N 21°40E 204 D3
Kiparissiakos Kolpos Greece 37°25N 21°25E 204 D3
Kipawa, L. Canada 46°50N 79°0W 298 C4
Kipembawe Tanzania 7°38S 33°27E 268 D3
Kipengere Ra. Tanzania 9°12S 34°15E 269 D3
Kipili Tanzania 7°28S 30°32E 268 D2
Kipini Kenya 2°30S 40°32E 268 C5
Kipling Canada 50°6N 102°38W 297 C8
Kipling Heights Canada 43°43N 79°34W 141 A1
Kipnuk U.S.A. 59°56N 164°3W 303 G6
Kippure Ireland 53°11N 6°23W 166 C5
Kipseli Greece 37°59N 23°45E 112 B2
Kipushi Dem. Rep. of the Congo 11°48S 27°12E 269 E2
Kira Panagia Greece 39°17N 24°6E 204 B6
Kirandul India 18°33N 81°10E 244 E5
Kirane Mali 15°20N 10°20W 262 B2

388 Kiranomena INDEX

Kiranomena Madag. 18°17S 46°2E 272 B2
Kiraz Turkey 38°14N 28°13E 205 C10
Kirazlı Turkey 40°2N 26°41E 203 F10
Kirchhain Germany 50°47N 8°56E 178 E4
Kirchheim Germany 48°39N 9°27E 179 G5
Kirchheimbolanden Germany 49°40N 8°0E 179 F3
Kirchschlag Austria 47°30N 16°19E 181 D9
Kirchstockbach Germany 48°1N 11°40E 131 B3
Kirchtrudering Germany 48°7N 11°40E 131 B3
Kirdâsa Egypt 30°2N 31°6E 251 H2
Kirdimi Chad 18°11N 18°31E 259 E3
Kireç Turkey 39°33N 28°22E 205 B10
Kirensk Russia 57°50N 107°55E 215 D11
Kirghiz Range Asia 42°40N 73°40E 217 D8
Kirghizia = Kyrgyzstan ■ Asia 42°0N 75°0E 217 D9
Kirgiz-Kulak = Chirchiq Uzbekistan 41°29N 69°35E 217 D7
Kirgiziya Steppe Eurasia 50°0N 55°0E 187 E10
Kiri Dem. Rep. of the Congo 1°29S 19°0E 264 C3
Kiri Buru India 22°0N 85°0E 244 D7
Kiribati ■ Pac. Oc. 3°0S 180°0E 277 A15
Kırıkhan Turkey 36°31N 36°21E 250 B7
Kirikiri Nigeria 6°26N 3°18E 124 B1
Kırıkkale Turkey 39°51N 33°32E 212 C5
Kirikopuni N.Z. 35°50S 174°1E 284 B3
Kirillov Russia 59°49N 38°24E 188 C10
Kirin = Jilin China 43°44N 126°30E 227 C14
Kirindi Oya → Sri Lanka 6°15N 81°20E 245 L5
Kirinyaga = Kenya, Mt. Kenya 0°10S 37°18E 268 C4
Kirishi Russia 59°28N 31°59E 188 C7
Kirishima Yaku △ Japan 31°24N 130°50E 221 J5
Kirishima-Yama Japan 31°58N 130°55E 222 F2
Kiritimati Kiribati 1°58N 157°27W 289 G12
Kiriwina I. Papua N. G. 8°40S 151°6E 286 E6
Kırka Turkey 39°17N 30°33E 205 B12
Kırkağaç Turkey 39°8N 27°40E 205 B9
Kirkby U.K. 53°30N 2°54W 168 D5
Kirkby-in-Ashfield U.K. 53°6N 1°14W 168 D6
Kirkby Lonsdale U.K. 54°12N 2°36W 168 C5
Kirkby Stephen U.K. 54°29N 2°21W 168 C5
Kirkcaldy U.K. 56°7N 3°9W 167 E5
Kirkcudbright U.K. 54°50N 4°2W 167 G4
Kirke Værløse Denmark 55°47N 12°19E 118 A1
Kirkee India 18°34N 73°56E 244 E1
Kirkehamn Norway 58°14N 6°31E 164 F3
Kirkenær Norway 60°27N 12°3E 164 D9
Kirkenes Norway 69°40N 30°5E 160 B24
Kirkfield Canada 44°34N 78°59W 312 B6
Kirkhill U.K. 55°50N 3°13W 121 B2
Kirkintilloch U.K. 55°56N 4°8W 167 F4
Kirkjubæjarklaustur Iceland 63°47N 18°4W 155 D8
Kirkkonummi Finland 60°8N 24°26E 188 B3
Kirkland Ill., U.S.A. 42°6N 88°51W 311 B8
Kirkland Wash., U.S.A. 47°40N 122°12W 306 C4
Kirkland Lake Canada 48°9N 80°2W 298 C3
Kırklareli Turkey 41°44N 27°15E 203 E11
Kırklareli □ Turkey 41°45N 27°15E 203 E11
Kirklin U.S.A. 40°12N 86°22W 311 D10
Kirkliston U.K. 55°57N 3°24W 121 B1
Kirkliston Ra. N.Z. 44°25S 170°34E 285 E5
Kirknewton U.K. 55°53N 3°25W 121 B1
Kirknitz = Cerknica Slovenia 45°48N 14°21E 199 C11
Kirksville U.S.A. 40°12N 92°35W 310 D4
Kirkūk Iraq 35°30N 44°21E 213 E11
Kirkwall U.K. 58°59N 2°58W 167 C6
Kirkwood Eastern Cape, S. Africa 33°22S 25°15E 270 D4
Kirkwood Mo., U.S.A. 38°35N 90°24W 310 F6
Kirlampudi India 17°12N 82°12E 244 F6
Kirmasti = Mustafakemalpaşa Turkey 40°2N 28°24E 203 F12
Kirn Germany 49°47N 7°26E 179 F3
Kirobası Turkey 36°43N 33°52E 250 B4
Kirov Kaluga, Russia 54°3N 34°20E 188 E8
Kirov Kirov, Russia 58°35N 49°40E 186 C8
Kirov Palace of Culture Russia 59°55N 30°16E 137 B1
Kirovabad = Gäncä Azerbaijan 40°45N 46°20E 191 K8
Kirovakan = Vanadzor Armenia 40°48N 44°30E 191 K7
Kirovo = Kirovohrad Ukraine 48°35N 32°20E 189 H7
Kirovograd = Kirovohrad Ukraine 48°35N 32°20E 189 H7
Kirovohrad Ukraine 48°35N 32°20E 189 H7
Kirovohrad □ Ukraine 48°30N 31°30E 189 H6
Kirovsk Russia 67°32N 33°41E 186 A5
Kirovskiy = Balpyq Bī Kazakhstan 44°52N 78°12E 217 D9
Kirovskiy Astrakhan, Russia 45°51N 48°11E 191 H9
Kirovskiy Kamchatka, Russia 54°27N 155°42E 215 D16
Kirovskiy Primorsk, Russia 45°7N 133°30E 220 B6
Kirriemuir U.K. 56°41N 3°1W 167 E5
Kirsanov Russia 52°35N 42°40E 190 D6
Kırşehir Turkey 39°14N 34°5E 212 C6
Kirtachi Niger 12°52N 2°30E 263 C5
Kīrteh Afghan. 32°15N 63°0E 240 B1
Kirthar △ Pakistan 25°45N 67°30E 242 F2
Kirthar Range Pakistan 27°0N 67°0E 242 F2
Kirtland U.S.A. 36°44N 108°21W 305 H9
Kiruna Sweden 67°52N 20°15E 160 C19
Kirundu Dem. Rep. of the Congo 0°50S 25°35E 264 C5
Kirya Russia 55°8N 46°55E 190 C8
Kiryat Anavim Israel 31°49N 35°6E 123 B1
Kiryat Ha Yovel Israel 31°46N 35°10E 123 B1
Kiryū Japan 36°24N 139°20E 223 A11
Kisa Sweden 58°0N 15°39E 163 G9
Kisaga Tanzania 4°30S 34°23E 268 C3
Kisalaya Nic. 14°40N 84°3W 320 D3
Kisalföld Hungary 47°30N 17°0E 182 C2
Kisambo Dem. Rep. of the Congo 6°25S 18°14E 265 D3
Kisandji Dem. Rep. of the Congo 6°18S 19°16E 265 D3
Kisanga Dem. Rep. of the Congo 2°30N 26°35E 268 B2
Kisangani Dem. Rep. of the Congo 0°35N 25°15E 268 B2
Kisantu Dem. Rep. of the Congo 5°7S 15°5E 265 D3
Kisar Indonesia 8°5S 127°10E 231 F7
Kisaran Indonesia 3°0N 99°37E 234 B1
Kisarawe Tanzania 6°53S 39°0E 268 D4
Kisarazu Japan 35°23N 139°55E 223 B11
Kisbér Hungary 47°30N 18°2E 182 C3
Kiselevsk Russia 54°0N 86°39E 217 B11
Kishanganga → Pakistan 34°18N 73°28E 243 B5
Kishanganj India 26°3N 88°14E 241 B2
Kishangarh Raj., India 26°34N 74°52E 242 F6
Kishangarh Raj., India 27°50N 70°30E 242 F4
Kishb, Ḩarrat al Si. Arabia 22°30N 40°15E 248 B3
Kishi Nigeria 9°1N 3°52E 263 D5
Kishinev = Chişinău Moldova 47°2N 28°50E 183 C13
Kishiwada Japan 34°28N 135°22E 223 C7
Kishkareny = Lazo Moldova 47°33N 28°2E 183 C13
Kishkenekol Kazakhstan 53°38N 72°20E 217 B8
Kishorganj Bangla. 24°26N 90°40E 241 C3
Kishtwar India 33°20N 75°48E 242 C6
Kishwaukee → U.S.A. 42°12N 89°8W 310 B7
Kisielice Poland 53°36N 19°16E 184 E6
Kisigo ⌂ Tanzania 6°27S 34°17E 268 D3
Kisii Kenya 0°40S 34°45E 268 C3
Kisiju Tanzania 7°23S 39°19E 268 D4
Kısıklı Turkey 41°1N 29°2E 122 B2
Kisir Turkey 41°0N 43°5E 213 B10
Kisizi Uganda 1°0S 29°58E 268 C2
Kiska I. U.S.A. 51°59N 177°30E 303 L2
Kiskomárom = Zalakomár Hungary 46°33N 17°10E 182 D2
Kiskörei-víztároló Hungary 47°31N 20°36E 182 C5
Kiskőrös Hungary 46°37N 19°20E 182 D4
Kiskundorozsma Hungary 46°16N 20°5E 182 D5
Kiskunfélegyháza Hungary 46°42N 19°53E 182 D4
Kiskunhalas Hungary 46°28N 19°37E 182 D4
Kiskunmajsa Hungary 46°30N 19°48E 182 D4
Kiskunsági △ Hungary 46°39N 19°30E 182 D4
Kislovodsk Russia 43°50N 42°45E 191 J6
Kismayu = Chisimaio Somali Rep. 0°22S 42°32E 267 E5
Kismayu △ Somali Rep. 1°25N 41°30E 267 D5
Kiso-Gawa → Japan 35°20N 136°45E 223 B8
Kiso-Sammyaku Japan 35°45N 137°45E 223 B9
Kisofukushima Japan 35°52N 137°43E 223 B9
Kisoro Uganda 1°17S 29°48E 268 C2
Kispest Hungary 47°27N 19°8E 117 B2
Kissamos = Kasteli Greece 35°29N 23°38E 207 E4
Kissamos, Kolpos Greece 35°30N 23°38E 207 E4
Kissidougou Guinea 9°5N 10°5W 262 D2
Kissimmee U.S.A. 28°18N 81°24W 317 G8
Kissimmee → U.S.A. 27°9N 80°52W 317 H8
Kissimmee, L. U.S.A. 27°55N 81°17W 317 H8
Kississing L. Canada 55°10N 101°20W 297 B8
Kissónerga Cyprus 34°49N 32°24E 207 F8
Kissu, J. Sudan 21°37N 25°10E 256 C2
Kista Sweden 59°24N 17°57E 139 A1
Kistanje Croatia 43°58N 15°55E 199 E12
Kistna = Krishna → India 15°57N 80°59E 245 G5
Kisújszállás Hungary 47°12N 20°50E 182 C5
Kisuki Japan 35°17N 132°54E 222 B4
Kisumu Kenya 0°3S 34°45E 268 C3
Kisvárda Hungary 48°14N 22°4E 182 B7
Kiswani Tanzania 4°5S 37°57E 268 C4
Kiswere Tanzania 9°27S 39°30E 269 D4
Kit Carson U.S.A. 38°46N 102°48W 304 G12
Kita Ōsaka, Japan 34°41N 135°30E 133 A2
Kita Tōkyō, Japan 35°44N 139°44E 140 A3
Kita Mali 13°5N 9°25W 262 C3
Kita-Ura Japan 36°0N 140°34E 223 B12
Kitaa □ Greenland 70°0N 47°0W 154 C6
Kitaibaraki Japan 36°50N 140°45E 221 F10
Kitakami Japan 39°20N 141°10E 220 E10
Kitakami-Gawa → Japan 38°25N 141°19E 220 E10
Kitakami-Sammyaku Japan 39°30N 141°30E 220 E10
Kitakata Japan 37°39N 139°52E 220 F9
Kitakyūshū Japan 33°50N 130°50E 222 D2
Kitale Kenya 1°0N 35°0E 268 B4
Kitami Japan 43°48N 143°54E 220 C11
Kitami-Sammyaku Japan 44°22N 142°43E 220 B11
Kitangiri, L. Tanzania 4°5S 34°20E 268 C3
Kitano Hana Iwo Jima 24°49N 141°20E 288 b
Kitano-Kaikyō Japan 34°17N 134°58E 222 C6
Kitaotao Phil. 7°40N 125°1E 233 H5
Kitava I. Papua N. G. 8°40S 151°20E 286 E6
Kitaya Tanzania 10°38S 40°8E 269 E5
Kitazawa Japan 35°39N 139°40E 140 B3
Kitcharao Phil. 9°27N 125°36E 233 G5
Kitchener Canada 43°27N 80°29W 312 C4
Kitee Finland 62°5N 30°8E 188 A6
Kitega = Gitega Burundi 3°26S 29°56E 268 C2
Kitengo Dem. Rep. of the Congo 7°26S 24°8E 265 D4
Kitgum Uganda 3°17N 32°52E 268 B3
Kíthira = Kythira Greece 36°8N 23°0E 204 E5
Kíthnos Greece 37°26N 24°27E 204 D6
Kiti Cyprus 34°50N 33°34E 207 F9
Kiti, C. Cyprus 34°48N 33°36E 207 F9
Kitimat Canada 54°3N 128°38W 296 C3
Kitinen → Finland 67°14N 27°27E 160 C22
Kitiyab Sudan 17°13N 33°35E 257 D3
Kitombe Dem. Rep. of the Congo 5°22S 18°59E 265 D3
Kitridge Pt. Barbados 13°9N 59°25W 323 r
Kitros Greece 40°22N 22°34E 202 F6
Kitsman Ukraine 48°26N 25°46E 183 B10
Kitsuki Japan 33°25N 131°37E 222 D3
Kittakittaooloo, L. Australia 28°3S 138°14E 281 D2
Kittanning U.S.A. 40°49N 79°31W 312 F5
Kittatinny Mt. U.S.A. 41°19N 74°39W 313 F10
Kittery U.S.A. 43°5N 70°45W 313 C14
Kittilä Finland 67°40N 24°51E 160 C21
Kitui Kenya 1°17S 38°0E 268 C4
Kitwanga Canada 55°6N 128°4W 296 B3
Kitwe Zambia 12°54S 28°13E 269 E2
Kityang = Jieyang China 23°35N 116°21E 229 F11
Kitzbühel Austria 47°27N 12°24E 180 D5
Kitzbühler Alpen Austria 47°20N 12°20E 180 D5
Kitzingen Germany 49°44N 10°9E 179 F6
Kiu Tsiu China 22°22N 114°17E 122 A2
Kiukiang = Jiujiang China 29°42N 115°58E 229 C10
Kiunga Papua N. G. 6°7S 141°18E 286 D1
Kivalina U.S.A. 67°44N 164°33W 303 C6
Kivarli India 24°33N 72°46E 242 G5
Kivertsi Ukraine 50°50N 25°28E 177 C13
Kividhes Cyprus 34°46N 32°51E 207 F8
Kivik Sweden 55°41N 14°13E 163 J8
Kivistö Finland 60°18N 24°50E 121 B2
Kivotos Greece 40°13N 21°26E 202 F5
Kivu, L. Dem. Rep. of the Congo 1°48S 29°0E 268 C2
Kiwai I. Papua N. G. 8°35S 143°30E 286 E2
Kiyev = Kyyiv Ukraine 50°30N 30°28E 177 C16
Kiyevskoye Vdkhr. = Kyyivske Vdskh. Ukraine 51°0N 30°25E 177 C16
Kıyıköy Turkey 41°38N 28°5E 203 E12
Kizel Russia 59°3N 57°40E 186 C10
Kizhi, Ostrov Russia 65°12N 35°28E 188 A8
Kiziguru Rwanda 1°46S 30°23E 268 C3
Kızıl Adalar Turkey 40°52N 29°5E 203 F13
Kızıl Dağ Turkey 36°19N 35°57E 250 B6
Kızıl Irmak → Turkey 41°44N 35°58E 212 B6
Kizil Jilga China 35°26N 78°50E 243 B8
Kizil Yurt Russia 43°13N 46°54E 191 J8
Kızılcabölük Turkey 37°37N 29°1E 205 D11
Kızılcadağ Turkey 37°1N 29°58E 205 D11
Kızılcahamam Turkey 40°30N 32°30E 212 B5
Kızıldağ △ Turkey 38°5N 31°20E 246 B1
Kızılhisar Turkey 37°32N 29°17E 212 D3
Kızılırmak Turkey 40°21N 33°59E 212 B5
Kızılkaya Turkey 37°18N 30°27E 205 D12
Kızılören Turkey 38°15N 30°10E 205 C12
Kızıltepe Turkey 37°12N 40°35E 213 D9
Kızıltoprak Turkey 40°58N 29°3E 122 C2
Kizimkazi Tanzania 6°28S 39°30E 268 D4
Kizlyar Russia 43°51N 46°40E 191 J8
Kizuri Japan 34°38N 135°34E 133 B2
Kizyl-Arvat = Serdar Turkmenistan 39°4N 56°23E 247 B8
Kjellerup Denmark 56°17N 9°25E 163 H3
Kjellmyra Norway 60°39N 12°1E 164 D9
Kjelsås Norway 59°57N 10°47E 133 A3
Kjølen Norway 62°3N 8°45E 164 C5
Kjölur Iceland 64°50N 19°25W 155 C7
Kjósarsýsla □ Iceland 64°15N 21°30W 155 C5
Kladanj Bos.-H. 44°14N 18°42E 182 F3
Kladnica Serbia 43°23N 20°2E 202 C4
Kladno Czech Rep. 50°10N 14°7E 180 A7
Kladovo Serbia 44°36N 22°33E 202 B6
Kladow Germany 52°27N 13°9E 115 B1
Klæbu Norway 63°18N 10°29E 164 A7
Klaeng Thailand 12°47N 101°39E 236 F3
Klagan Malaysia 5°58N 117°27E 235 A5
Klagenfurt Austria 46°38N 14°20E 180 E7
Klaipėda Lithuania 55°43N 21°10E 184 C8
Klaipėda □ Lithuania 55°43N 21°7E 184 C8
Klaksvík Færoe Is. 62°14N 6°35W 160 E9
Klamath → U.S.A. 41°33N 124°5W 304 F1
Klamath Falls U.S.A. 42°13N 121°46W 304 E3
Klamath Mts. U.S.A. 41°50N 123°20W 304 F2
Klamono Indonesia 1°8S 131°30E 231 E8
Klampenborg Denmark 55°46N 12°35E 118 A3
Klang Malaysia 3°2N 101°26E 237 L3
Klangklang Burma 22°41N 93°26E 241 D4
Klanjec Croatia 46°3N 15°45E 199 B12
Klappan → Canada 58°0N 129°43W 296 B3
Klara = Trysilelva → Norway 61°2N 12°35E 164 C9
Klarälven → Sweden 59°23N 13°32E 162 E7
Klässbol Sweden 59°33N 12°45E 162 E6
Klaten Indonesia 7°43S 110°36E 235 D4
Klatovy Czech Rep. 49°23N 13°18E 180 B6
Klaudyń Poland 52°17N 20°50E 142 B1
Klausenburg = Cluj-Napoca Romania 46°47N 23°38E 183 D8
Klawer S. Africa 31°44S 18°36E 270 D2
Klawock U.S.A. 55°33N 133°6W 303 J14
Klazienaveen Neths. 52°44N 7°0E 170 B6
Klé Mali 12°0N 6°28W 262 C3
Klečany Czech Rep. 50°10N 14°24E 135 A2
Kłecko Poland 52°38N 17°25E 185 F4
Kleczew Poland 52°22N 18°9E 185 F5
Kledering Austria 48°8N 16°26E 142 B2
Kleena Kleene Canada 52°0N 124°59W 296 C4
Klein Bonaire Neth. Ant. 12°9N 68°18W 322 h
Klein Jukskei → S. Africa 26°6S 27°57E 123 A1
Klein-Karas Namibia 27°33S 18°7E 270 C2
Klein-Schlatten = Zlatna Romania 46°8N 23°11E 183 D8
Kleinmachnow Germany 52°24N 13°14E 115 B2
Kleinschönebeck Germany 52°29N 13°42E 115 B5
Klekovača Bos.-H. 44°25N 16°32E 199 D13
Klembivka Ukraine 48°23N 28°25E 183 B13
Klemetsrud Norway 59°50N 10°51E 133 A4
Klender Indonesia 6°12S 106°54E 122 A2
Klenoec Macedonia 41°32N 20°49E 202 E4
Klenovec Slovak Rep. 48°36N 19°54E 181 C12
Klerksdorp S. Africa 26°53S 26°38E 270 C4
Kleszczele Poland 52°35N 23°19E 185 F10
Kletnya Russia 53°23N 33°12E 188 F7
Kletsk = Klyetsk Belarus 53°5N 26°45E 177 B14
Kletskiy Russia 49°16N 43°11E 191 F6
Kleve Germany 51°47N 6°7E 178 D2
Kličany Czech Rep. 50°11N 14°25E 135 A2
Klickitat U.S.A. 45°49N 121°9W 304 D3
Klickitat → U.S.A. 45°42N 121°17W 306 E5
Klidhes Cyprus 35°42N 34°36E 207 E10
Klimovichi Belarus 53°36N 32°0E 188 F6
Klin Russia 56°20N 36°48E 188 D9
Klina Serbia 42°37N 20°35E 202 D4
Klinaklini → Canada 51°21N 125°40W 296 C3
Klintehamn Sweden 57°24N 18°12E 163 G12
Klintsy Russia 52°50N 32°10E 189 F7
Klip → S. Africa 27°3S 29°3E 271 C4
Klipdale S. Africa 34°19S 19°57E 270 D2
Klippan Sweden 56°8N 13°10E 163 H7
Klipplaat S. Africa 33°1S 24°22E 270 D3
Klipriviersberg Nature Reserve S. Africa 26°16S 28°2E 123 B2
Klishkivtsi Ukraine 48°26N 26°16E 183 B11
Klisura Bulgaria 42°40N 24°28E 203 D8
Kljajićevo Serbia 45°45N 19°17E 182 E4
Ključ Bos.-H. 44°32N 16°48E 199 D13
Kłobuck Poland 50°55N 18°55E 185 H5
Klockestrand Sweden 62°53N 17°55E 162 B11
Kłodawa Poland 52°15N 18°55E 185 F5
Kłodzko Poland 50°28N 16°38E 185 H3
Kløfta Norway 60°4N 11°10E 164 D8
Klondike Goldrush ⌂ U.S.A. 59°27N 135°19W 303 G14
Klong Wang Chao △ Thailand 16°20N 99°9E 236 D2
Klos Albania 41°28N 20°10E 202 E4
Klosterneuburg Austria 48°18N 16°19E 142 A1
Klosters Switz. 46°52N 9°52E 179 J5
Klötze Germany 52°37N 11°10E 178 C7
Klouto Togo 6°57N 0°44E 263 D5
Kluane △ Canada 60°45N 139°30W 296 A1
Kluane L. Canada 61°15N 138°40W 294 C6
Kluang Malaysia 2°3N 103°18E 237 L4
Kluczbork Poland 50°58N 18°12E 185 H5
Klukhori = Karachayevsk Russia 43°50N 41°55E 191 J5
Klukwan U.S.A. 59°24N 135°54W 296 B1
Klungkung Indonesia 8°32S 115°24E 231 K18
Klyetsk Belarus 53°5N 26°45E 177 B14
Klyuchevskaya, Gora Russia 55°50N 160°30E 215 D17
Knaben Norway 58°40N 7°4E 164 F4
Knappavellir Iceland 63°54N 16°36W 155 D10
Knäred Sweden 56°31N 13°19E 163 H7
Knaresborough U.K. 54°1N 1°28W 168 C6
Knarvik Norway 60°32N 5°19E 164 D2
Knee L. Man., Canada 55°3N 94°45W 298 A1
Knee L. Sask., Canada 55°51N 107°0W 297 B7
Kneïss, Îs. Tunisia 34°22N 10°18E 258 B2
Knesset Jerusalem 123 b1
Knezha Bulgaria 43°30N 24°5E 203 C8
Knight I. U.S.A. 60°21N 147°45W 303 F11
Knight Inlet Canada 50°45N 125°40W 296 C3
Knighton U.K. 52°21N 3°3W 169 E4
Knights Ferry U.S.A. 37°50N 120°40W 306 H6
Knights Landing U.S.A. 38°48N 121°43W 306 G5
Knightsbridge London, U.K. 125 c2
Knightstown U.S.A. 39°48N 85°32W 311 E11
Knin Croatia 44°3N 16°17E 199 D13
Knislinge Sweden 56°12N 14°5E 163 H8
Knittelfeld Austria 47°13N 14°51E 180 D7
Knivsta Sweden 59°43N 17°48E 162 E11
Knjaževac Serbia 43°35N 22°18E 202 C6
Knob, C. Australia 34°32S 119°16E 279 F2
Knob Lake = Kawawachikamach Canada 54°48N 66°50W 299 B6
Knob Noster U.S.A. 38°46N 93°33W 310 F3
Knock Ireland 53°48N 8°55W 166 C3
Knockmealdown Mts. Ireland 52°14N 7°56W 166 D4
Knokke-Heist Belgium 51°21N 3°17E 170 C3
Knossos Greece 35°16N 25°10E 207 E6
Knowlton Canada 45°13N 72°31W 313 A12
Knox U.S.A. 41°18N 86°37W 311 C10
Knox Coast Antarctica 66°30S 108°0E 151 C8
Knoxville Ga., U.S.A. 32°47N 83°59W 316 C6
Knoxville Ill., U.S.A. 40°55N 90°17W 310 D6
Knoxville Iowa, U.S.A. 41°19N 93°6W 310 C4
Knoxville Pa., U.S.A. 41°57N 77°27W 312 E7
Knoxville Tenn., U.S.A. 35°58N 83°55W 315 D13
Knud Rasmussen Land Greenland 78°0N 60°0W 154 B4
Knysna S. Africa 34°2S 23°2E 270 D3
Knyszyn Poland 53°20N 22°56E 184 E9
Ko Kha Thailand 18°11N 99°24E 236 C2
Kō-Saki Japan 34°5N 129°13E 222 C1
Ko Tarutao △ Thailand 6°31N 99°26E 237 J2
Ko Yao Thailand 8°7N 98°35E 237 a
Koartac = Quaqtaq Canada 60°55N 69°40W 295 C13
Koba Aru, Indonesia 6°37S 134°37E 231 F8
Koba Bangka, Indonesia 2°26S 106°14E 234 C3
Kőbánya Hungary 47°28N 19°9E 117 B2
Kobarid Slovenia 46°15N 13°30E 199 B10
Kobayashi Japan 31°56N 130°59E 222 F2
Kobbegem Belgium 50°55N 4°15E 116 A1
Kobdo = Hovd □ Mongolia 48°2N 91°37E 217 C12
Kōbe Japan 34°41N 135°13E 223 C7
Kobelyaky Ukraine 49°11N 34°9E 189 H8
København Denmark 55°40N 12°26E 118 A2
København ✈ (CPH) Denmark 55°37N 12°39E 118 B3
Kobenni Mauritania 15°58N 9°24W 262 B3
Kōbi-Sho Japan 25°56N 123°41E 221 M1
Koblenz Germany 50°21N 7°36E 179 E3
Kobo Dem. Rep. of the Congo 4°54S 17°9E 265 C3
Kobo Ethiopia 12°2N 39°56E 257 E4
Kobryn Belarus 52°15N 24°22E 177 B13
Kobuchizawa Japan 35°52N 138°19E 223 B10
Kobuk U.S.A. 66°55N 156°52W 303 C8
Kobuk → U.S.A. 66°54N 160°38W 303 C7
Kobuk Valley △ U.S.A. 67°0N 160°0W 303 C7
Kobuleti Georgia 41°55N 41°45E 191 K5
Kobyletska Polyana Ukraine 48°3N 24°4E 183 B9
Kobylin Poland 51°43N 17°12E 185 G4
Kobylisy Czech Rep. 50°7N 14°26E 135 B2
Kobyłka Poland 52°20N 21°10E 142 A3
Kobylkino Russia 54°8N 43°56E 190 C6
Koca → Turkey 40°8N 27°57E 203 F11
Kocabaş Turkey 37°49N 29°20E 205 D11
Kocaeli Turkey 40°45N 29°50E 203 F13
Kocaeli □ Turkey 40°45N 29°55E 203 F13
Kočane Serbia 43°12N 21°52E 202 C5
Kočani Macedonia 41°55N 22°25E 202 E6
Koçarlı Turkey 37°45N 27°43E 205 D9
Koceljevo Serbia 44°28N 19°50E 202 B3
Kočevje Slovenia 45°39N 14°50E 199 C11
Kocgiri = Zara Turkey 39°58N 37°43E 212 C7
Koch Bihar India 26°22N 89°29E 241 B2
Kochas India 25°15N 83°56E 243 G10
Kocher → Germany 49°13N 9°12E 179 F5
Kochi = Cochin India 9°58N 76°20E 245 K3
Kōchi Japan 33°30N 133°35E 222 D5
Kōchi □ Japan 33°40N 133°30E 222 D5
Kochiu = Gejiu China 23°20N 103°10E 228 F4
Kochkor Kyrgyzstan 42°13N 75°46E 217 D9
Kock Poland 51°38N 22°27E 185 G9
Kodaira Japan 35°43N 139°28E 140 A1
Kodala India 19°38N 84°57E 244 E7
Kodanaka Japan 35°34N 139°37E 140 B2
Kodarma India 24°28N 85°36E 243 G11
Koddiyar B. Sri Lanka 8°33N 81°15E 245 K5
Kode Sweden 57°57N 11°51E 163 G5
Kodenmacho Tokyo, Japan 140 a5
Kodi Dem. Rep. of the Congo 3°34S 22°12E 264 C4
Kodiak U.S.A. 57°47N 152°24W 303 H9
Kodiak I. U.S.A. 57°30N 152°45W 303 H9
Kodinar India 20°46N 70°46E 242 J4
Kodlipet India 12°48N 75°53E 245 H2
Kodok Sudan 9°53N 32°7E 257 F3
Kodori → Georgia 42°47N 41°10E 191 J5
Kodoro Dem. Rep. of the Congo 1°16N 20°6E 264 B4
Kodyma Ukraine 48°6N 29°7E 183 B14
Koedoesberge S. Africa 32°40S 20°11E 270 D3
Koekelberg Belgium 50°52N 4°20E 116 A1
Koes Namibia 26°0S 19°15E 270 C2
Kofçaz Turkey 41°58N 27°12E 203 E11
Koffiefontein S. Africa 29°30S 25°0E 270 C4
Kofiau Indonesia 1°11S 129°50E 231 E7
Köflach Austria 47°4N 15°5E 180 D8
Koforidua Ghana 6°3N 0°17W 263 D4
Kōfu Japan 35°40N 138°30E 223 B10
Koga Japan 36°11N 139°43E 223 A11
Kogaluc → Canada 56°12N 61°44W 299 A7
Koganei Japan 35°42N 139°31E 140 A2
Kogarah Australia 33°57S 151°8E 139 B1
Køge Denmark 55°27N 12°11E 163 J6
Køge Bugt Denmark 55°34N 12°24E 163 J6
Kogi □ Nigeria 7°45N 6°45E 263 D6
Kogin Baba Nigeria 7°55N 11°35E 263 D7
Kogo Eq. Guin. 1°5N 9°42E 264 B1
Koh-i-Khurd Afghan. 33°30N 65°59E 242 C1
Koh-i-Maran Pakistan 29°18N 66°50E 242 E2
Kohala Forest Reserve U.S.A. 20°9N 155°4W 302 C6
Kohala Mts. U.S.A. 20°5N 155°45W 302 C6
Kohat Pakistan 33°40N 71°29E 242 C4
Kohima India 25°35N 94°10E 241 C5
Kohkīlūyeh va Būyer Aḩmadi □ Iran 31°30N 50°30E 247 D6
Kohler Ra. Antarctica 77°0S 110°0W 151 D15
Kohlfurt = Węgliniec Poland 51°18N 15°10E 185 G2
Kohlu Pakistan 29°54N 69°15E 242 E3
Kohtla-Järve Estonia 59°20N 27°20E 188 C4
Kohukohu N.Z. 35°22S 173°38E 284 B2
Kohylnyk → Ukraine 45°49N 29°40E 183 E14
Koi Sanjaq Iraq 36°5N 44°38E 213 D11
Koihoa India 8°12N 93°29E 245 K11
Koilkuntla India 15°14N 78°19E 245 G4
Koillismaa Finland 65°44N 28°36E 160 D23
Koimbani Comoros Is. 11°37S 43°21E 272 a
Koin N. Korea 40°28N 126°18E 224 B3
Koinare Bulgaria 43°21N 24°8E 203 C8
Koindu S. Leone 8°26N 10°19W 262 D2
Koivisto = Primorsk Russia 60°22N 28°37E 188 B5
Koivupää Finland 60°18N 24°53E 121 B2
Koja Indonesia 6°8S 106°52E 122 A2
Koja Utara Indonesia 6°5S 106°53E 122 A2
Kojetín Czech Rep. 49°21N 17°20E 181 B10
Kojŏ N. Korea 38°58N 127°58E 224 C3
Kojonup Australia 33°48S 117°10E 279 F2
Kojūr Iran 36°23N 51°43E 247 B6
Koka Sudan 20°5N 30°35E 256 C3
Kokand = Qŭqon Uzbekistan 40°31N 70°56E 217 D8
Kokas Indonesia 2°42S 132°26E 231 E8
Kokava Slovak Rep. 48°35N 19°50E 181 C12
Kokcha → Afghan. 37°9N 69°24E 240 A3
Kokchetav = Kökshetaū Kazakhstan 53°20N 69°25E 217 B7
Köke'e State Park ⌂ U.S.A. 22°6N 159°40W 302 A2
Kokemäenjoki → Finland 61°32N 21°44E 188 B1
Kokerite Guyana 7°12N 59°35W 329 B6
Kokhav Ya'akov West Bank 31°53N 35°14E 123 A2
Kokhma Russia 56°57N 41°8E 190 B5
Koki Senegal 15°30N 15°59W 262 B1
Kokiu = Gejiu China 23°20N 103°10E 228 F4
Kokkilai Sri Lanka 9°0N 80°57E 245 K5
Kokkina Cyprus 35°11N 32°36E 207 E8
Kokkola Finland 63°50N 23°8E 160 E20
Koko Nigeria 11°28N 4°29E 263 C5
Koko Head U.S.A. 21°16N 157°43W 302 K14
Kokobunji Japan 35°42N 139°27E 140 A1
Kokobunji-Temple Japan 35°44N 139°55E 140 A4
Kokoda Papua N. G. 8°54S 147°47E 286 E4
Kokolopozo Ivory C. 5°8N 6°5W 262 D3
Kokomo U.S.A. 40°29N 86°8W 311 D10
Kokopo Papua N. G. 4°22S 152°19E 286 C7
Kokoro Niger 14°12N 0°55E 263 C5
Koksan N. Korea 38°46N 126°40E 224 C3
Kökshetaū Kazakhstan 53°20N 69°25E 217 B7
Koksoak → Canada 58°30N 68°10W 295 D13
Kokstad S. Africa 30°32S 29°29E 271 D4
Köktal Kazakhstan 44°8N 79°48E 217 D9
Kokubu Japan 31°44N 130°46E 222 F2
Kokyar China 37°23N 77°10E 217 E9
Kola Indonesia 5°35S 134°30E 231 F8
Kola Russia 68°45N 33°8E 160 B25
Kola Pen. = Kolskiy Poluostrov Russia 67°30N 38°0E 186 A6
Kolachel India 8°10N 77°15E 245 K3
Kolachi → Pakistan 27°8N 67°2E 242 F2
Kolahoi India 34°12N 75°22E 243 B6
Kolahun Liberia 8°15N 10°4W 262 D2
Kolaka Indonesia 4°3S 121°46E 231 E6
Kolar India 13°12N 78°15E 245 H4
Kolar Gold Fields India 12°58N 78°16E 245 H4
Kolarängen Sweden 59°16N 18°10E 139 B3
Kolaras India 25°14N 77°36E 242 G6
Kolari Finland 67°20N 23°48E 160 C20
Kolarovgrad = Shumen Bulgaria 43°18N 26°55E 203 C10
Kolárovo Slovak Rep. 47°54N 18°0E 181 D10
Kolašin Montenegro 42°50N 19°31E 202 D3
Kolayat India 27°50N 72°50E 242 F5
Kolbäck Sweden 59°34N 16°15E 162 E10
Kolbäcksån → Sweden 59°36N 16°16E 162 E10
Kolbeinsstaðir Iceland 64°59N 22°16W 155 C4
Kolberg = Kołobrzeg Poland 54°10N 15°35E 184 D2
Kolbermoor Germany 47°51N 12°4E 179 H8
Kolbio Kenya 1°8S 41°12E 267 E5
Kolbotn Norway 59°48N 10°48E 133 B3
Kolbu Norway 60°39N 10°45E 164 D7
Kolbuszowa Poland 50°15N 21°46E 185 H8
Kolchugino = Leninsk-Kuznetskiy Russia 54°44N 86°10E 217 B11
Kolchugino Russia 56°17N 39°22E 188 D10
Kolda Senegal 12°55N 14°57W 262 C2
Kolda □ Senegal 13°5N 14°50W 262 C2
Koldegi Sudan 12°3N 30°16E 257 E3
Kolding Denmark 55°30N 9°29E 163 J3
Kole Dem. Rep. of the Congo 3°16S 22°42E 264 C4
Koléa Algeria 36°38N 2°46E 261 A5
Kolepom = Dolak, Pulau Indonesia 8°0S 138°30E 231 F9
Kolguyev, Ostrov Russia 69°20N 48°30E 186 A8
Kolhapur India 16°43N 74°15E 244 F2
Kolia Ivory C. 9°46N 6°28W 262 D3
Koliganek U.S.A. 59°48N 157°25W 303 G8
Kolín Czech Rep. 50°2N 15°9E 180 A8
Kolind Denmark 56°21N 10°34E 163 H4
Kolkas rags Latvia 57°46N 22°37E 184 A9
Kolkata India 22°34N 88°21E 124 B2
Kolkata Dum Dum Int. ✈ (CCU) India 22°38N 88°26E 124 B2
Kolkata Maidan India 22°33N 88°21E 124 B1
Kollam = Quilon India 8°50N 76°38E 245 K3
Kölleda Germany 51°11N 11°15E 178 D7
Kollegal India 12°9N 77°9E 245 H3
Kolleru L. India 16°40N 81°10E 244 F5
Kollum Neths. 53°17N 6°10E 170 A6
Kolmanskop Namibia 26°45S 15°14E 270 C2
Köln Germany 50°56N 6°57E 178 E2
Kolno Poland 53°25N 21°56E 184 E8
Koło Warszawa, Poland 52°14N 20°56E 142 B1
Koło Wielkopolskie, Poland 52°14N 18°40E 185 F5
Koloa U.S.A. 21°55N 159°28W 302 B2
Kołobrzeg Poland 54°10N 15°35E 184 D2
Kolochava Ukraine 48°26N 23°41E 183 B8
Kolokani Mali 13°35N 7°45W 262 C3
Kolokinthou Greece 38°0N 23°42E 112 B2
Koloko Burkina Faso 11°5N 5°19W 262 C3
Kololo Ethiopia 7°29N 41°58E 257 F5
Kolombangara Solomon Is. 8°0S 157°5E 287 M9
Kolomna Russia 55°8N 38°45E 188 E10
Kolomyagi Russia 60°0N 30°19E 137 A1
Kolomyya Ukraine 48°31N 25°2E 183 B10
Kolondiéba Mali 11°5N 6°54W 262 C3
Kolonodale Indonesia 2°0S 121°19E 231 E6
Kolonos Greece 37°59N 23°43E 112 B2
Kolonowskie Poland 50°39N 18°22E 185 H5
Kolosib India 24°15N 92°45E 241 C4
Kolpashevo Russia 58°20N 83°5E 214 D9
Kolpino Russia 59°44N 30°39E 188 C6
Kolpny Russia 52°17N 37°1E 189 F9
Kolsås Norway 59°55N 10°30E 133 A2
Kolskiy Poluostrov Russia 67°30N 38°0E 186 A6
Kolskiy Zaliv Russia 69°23N 34°0E 160 B26
Kolsva Sweden 59°36N 15°51E 162 E9
Kolubara → Serbia 44°35N 20°15E 202 B4
Kolumadulu Atoll Maldives 2°22N 73°7E 272 d
Koluszki Poland 51°45N 19°46E 185 G6
Kolwezi Dem. Rep. of the Congo 10°40S 25°25E 269 E2
Kolyma → Russia 69°30N 161°0E 215 C17
Kolymskoye Nagorye Russia 63°0N 157°0E 215 C16
Kôm Hamâda Egypt 30°46N 30°41E 256 H7
Kôm Ombo Egypt 24°25N 32°52E 256 C3
Komadugu Gana → Nigeria 13°5N 12°24E 263 C7
Komae Japan 35°37N 139°34E 140 B2
Komagane Japan 35°44N 137°58E 223 B9
Komagome Japan 35°43N 139°45E 140 A3
Komaki Japan 35°17N 136°55E 223 B8
Komandorskiye Is. = Komandorskiye Ostrova Russia 55°0N 167°0E 215 D17
Komandorskiye Ostrova Russia 55°0N 167°0E 215 D17
Komárno Slovak Rep. 47°49N 18°5E 181 D11
Komarnyky Ukraine 48°59N 23°3E 182 B8
Komárom Hungary 47°43N 18°7E 182 C3
Komárom-Esztergom □ Hungary 47°35N 18°20E 182 C3
Komáromújváros = Komárom Hungary 47°43N 18°7E 182 C3
Komatipoort S. Africa 25°25S 31°55E 271 C5
Komatou Yialou Cyprus 35°25N 34°8E 207 E10
Komatsu Japan 36°25N 136°30E 223 A8
Komatsushima Japan 34°0N 134°35E 222 D6
Komavangard = Sobinka Russia 56°0N 40°0E 188 E11
Komazawa Japan 35°37N 139°40E 140 B3
Komba Dem. Rep. of the Congo 2°52N 24°3E 264 B4
Kombissiri Burkina Faso 12°4N 1°20W 263 C4
Kombo Gabon 0°20S 12°22E 264 C2
Kombong India 28°7N 94°51E 241 A5
Kombori Burkina Faso 13°26N 3°56W 262 C4
Komboti Greece 39°6N 21°5E 204 B3
Komebail Lagoon Palau 7°25N 134°25E 288 c
Komen Slovenia 45°49N 13°45E 199 C10
Komenda Ghana 5°4N 1°28W 263 D4
Komi □ Russia 64°0N 55°0E 186 B10
Kominter = Novoshakhtinsk Russia 47°46N 39°58E 189 J10
Komintern = Marhanets Ukraine 47°40N 34°40E 189 J8
Komiža Croatia 43°3N 16°11E 199 E13
Komló Hungary 46°15N 18°16E 182 D3
Kommamur Canal India 16°0N 80°25E 245 G5
Kommunarsk = Alchevsk Ukraine 48°30N 38°45E 189 H10
Kommunizma, Pik = imeni Ismail Samani, Pik Tajikistan 39°0N 72°2E 217 E8
Komodo Indonesia 8°37S 119°20E 231 F5
Komoé → Ivory C. 5°12N 3°44W 262 D4
Komono Congo 3°10S 13°20E 264 C2
Komoran, Pulau Indonesia 8°18S 138°45E 231 F9
Komoro Japan 36°19N 138°26E 223 A10
Komotau = Chomutov Czech Rep. 50°28N 13°23E 180 A6
Komotini Greece 41°9N 25°26E 203 E9
Komovi Montenegro 42°41N 19°39E 202 D3
Kompasberg S. Africa 31°45S 24°32E 270 D3
Kompong Bang Cambodia 12°24N 104°40E 237 F5
Kompong Cham Cambodia 12°0N 105°30E 237 G5
Kompong Chhnang = Kampong Chhnang Cambodia 12°20N 104°35E 237 F5
Kompong Chikreng Cambodia 13°5N 104°18E 236 F5
Kompong Kleang Cambodia 13°6N 104°8E 236 F5
Kompong Luong Cambodia 11°49N 104°48E 237 G5
Kompong Pranak Cambodia 13°35N 104°55E 236 F5
Kompong Som = Kampong Saom Cambodia 10°38N 103°30E 237 G4
Kompong Som, Chhung = Kampong Saom, Chaak Cambodia 10°50N 103°32E 237 G4
Kompong Speu Cambodia 11°26N 104°32E 237 G5
Kompong Sralau Cambodia 14°5N 105°46E 236 E5
Kompong Thom Cambodia 12°35N 104°51E 236 F5
Kompong Trabeck Cambodia 13°6N 105°14E 236 F5
Kompong Trabeck Cambodia 11°9N 105°28E 237 G5
Kompong Trach Cambodia 11°25N 105°48E 237 G5
Kompong Tralach Cambodia 11°54N 104°47E 237 G5
Komrat = Comrat Moldova 46°18N 28°40E 183 D13
Komsberg S. Africa 32°40S 20°45E 270 D3
Komsomolets, Ostrov Russia 80°30N 95°0E 215 A10
Komsomolsk Amur, Russia 50°30N 137°0E 215 D14
Komsomolsk Ivanovo, Russia 57°2N 40°20E 188 D11
Komsomolskiy Russia 54°27N 45°33E 190 C7
Komsomolskoe Kazakhstan 50°25N 60°5E 216 B6
Komsomolsky = Chirchiq Uzbekistan 41°29N 69°35E 217 D7
Kömür Burnu Turkey 38°39N 26°12E 205 C8
Kon Tum Vietnam 14°24N 108°0E 236 E7
Kon Tum, Plateau du Vietnam 14°30N 108°30E 236 E7
Kona W. Bengal, India 22°37N 88°18E 124 B1
Kona Mali 14°57N 3°53W 262 C4
Kona ✈ (KOA) U.S.A. 19°44N 156°3W 302 D5
Kōnāhuanui U.S.A. 21°21N 157°47W 302 K14
Konakovo Russia 56°40N 36°51E 188 D9
Konala Finland 60°14N 24°52E 121 B2
Konar □ Afghan. 34°30N 71°3E 240 B3
Konarak India 19°54N 86°7E 244 E8
Konārī Iran 28°13N 51°36E 247 D6
Konch India 26°0N 79°10E 243 G8
Kondagaon India 19°35N 81°35E 244 E5
Konde Tanzania 4°57S 39°45E 268 C4
Kondias Greece 39°49N 25°10E 205 B7
Kondinin Australia 32°34S 118°8E 279 F2
Kondli India 28°36N 77°19E 120 B2
Kondo Dem. Rep. of the Congo 5°35S 13°0E 265 D2
Kondoa Tanzania 4°55S 35°50E 268 C4
Kondopaga Russia 62°12N 34°17E 188 A8
Kondoz Afghan. 36°50N 68°50E 240 A3
Kondoz □ Afghan. 36°50N 68°50E 240 A3
Kondratyevo Russia 57°22N 98°15E 215 D10
Kondrovo Russia 54°48N 35°56E 188 E8
Konduga Nigeria 11°35N 13°26E 263 C7
Kondukur India 15°12N 79°57E 245 G4
Koné Cameroon 8°50N 13°17E 264 A2
Koné N. Cal. 21°4S 164°52E 288 d
Köneürgench Turkmenistan 42°19N 59°10E 216 D5
Konevo Russia 62°8N 39°20E 188 A10
Kong = Khong → Cambodia 13°32N 105°58E 236 F5
Kong Ivory C. 8°54N 4°36W 262 D4
Kong, Koh Cambodia 11°20N 103°0E 237 G4
Kong Christian IX Land Greenland 68°0N 36°0W 154 D7
Kong Christian X Land Greenland 74°0N 29°0W 154 C8
Kong Frederik IX Land Greenland 67°0N 52°0W 154 D5

Kong Frederik VI Kyst Greenland 63°0N 43°0W 154 E6
Kong Frederik VIII Land Greenland 78°30N 26°0W 154 B8
Kong Karls Land Svalbard 79°0N 28°0E 154 B13
Kong Oscar Fjord Greenland 72°20N 24°0W 154 C8
Kongauru I. Palau 7°3N 134°16E 288 c
Kongbo C.A.R. 4°44N 21°23E 264 B4
Kongeå → Denmark 55°23N 8°39E 163 J2
Kongelunden Denmark 55°34N 12°34E 118 B3
Kongens Lyngby Denmark 55°46N 12°30E 118 A3
Kongerslev Denmark 56°54N 10°6E 163 H4
Kongkemul Indonesia 1°52N 112°11E 235 B4
Konglu Burma 27°13N 97°57E 241 B6
Kongmoon = Jiangmen China 22°32N 113°0E 229 F9
Kongo Finland 60°20N 24°47E 121 A1
Kongola Namibia 17°45S 23°20E 270 A3
Kongolo Kasai-Or., Dem. Rep. of the Congo 5°26S 24°49E 265 D4
Kongolo Katanga, Dem. Rep. of the Congo 5°22S 27°0E 268 D2
Kongor Sudan 7°1N 31°27E 257 F3
Kongoulou Cameroon 2°59N 11°7E 264 B2
Kongoussi Burkina Faso 13°19N 1°32W 263 C4
Kongsberg Norway 59°39N 9°39E 164 E6
Kongsvinger Norway 60°12N 12°2E 164 D9
Kongur Shan China 38°34N 75°18E 217 E9
Kongwa Tanzania 6°11S 36°26E 268 D4
Koni Dem. Rep. of the Congo 10°40S 27°11E 269 E2
Koni, Mts. Dem. Rep. of the Congo 10°36S 27°10E 269 E2
Koniakari Mali 14°35N 10°50W 262 C2
Koniecpol Poland 50°46N 19°40E 185 H6
Königgrätz = Hradec Králové Czech Rep. 50°15N 15°50E 180 A8
Königs Wusterhausen Germany 52°19N 13°38E 178 C9
Königsberg = Chojna Poland 52°58N 14°25E 185 F1
Königsberg = Kaliningrad Russia 54°42N 20°32E 184 D7
Königsbrunn Germany 48°16N 10°54E 179 G6
Königshütte = Chorzów Poland 50°18N 18°57E 185 H5
Königslutter Germany 52°15N 10°49E 178 C6
Konin Poland 52°12N 18°15E 185 F5
Köninginhof an der Elbe = Dvůr Králové nad Labem Czech Rep. 50°27N 15°50E 180 A8
Koninklijk Paleis Amsterdam, Neths. 112 b2
Konispol Albania 39°42N 20°10E 206 B10
Konitsa Greece 40°5N 20°48E 204 A2
Konjic Bos.-H. 43°42N 17°58E 182 G2
Konkiep Namibia 26°49S 17°15E 270 C2
Konkō Japan 34°33N 133°36E 222 C4
Konkouré → Guinea 9°50N 13°42W 262 D2
Konnagar India 22°42N 88°21E 124 A2
Könnern Germany 51°41N 11°47E 178 D7
Konnur India 16°14N 74°49E 245 F2
Kono S. Leone 8°30N 11°5W 262 D2
Konogogo Papua N. G. 3°29S 152°10E 286 B7
Konohana Japan 34°40N 135°26E 133 A1
Konongo Ghana 6°40N 1°15W 263 D4
Konos Papua N. G. 3°10S 151°44E 286 B6
Konosha Russia 61°0N 40°5E 188 B11
Kōnosu Japan 36°3N 139°31E 223 A11
Konotop Ukraine 51°12N 33°7E 189 G7
Konqi He → China 41°0N 86°0E 217 D11
Konradshof = Skawina Poland 49°59N 19°50E 185 J6
Konradshöhe Germany 52°35N 13°13E 115 A2
Konrei Palau 7°43N 134°36E 288 c
Konsankoro Guinea 9°2N 9°0W 262 D3
Końskie Poland 51°15N 20°23E 185 G7
Konsmo Norway 58°16N 7°23E 164 F4
Konstadt = Wołczyn Poland 51°1N 18°3E 185 G5
Konstancin-Jeziorna Poland 52°5N 21°7E 185 F8
Konstantinograd = Krasnohrad Ukraine 49°27N 35°27E 189 H8
Konstantinovka = Kostyantynivka Ukraine 48°32N 37°39E 189 H9
Konstantinovsk Russia 47°33N 41°10E 191 G5
Konstantynów Łódźki Poland 51°45N 19°20E 185 G6
Konstanz Germany 47°40N 9°10E 179 H5
Kont Iran 26°55N 61°50E 247 E9
Konta India 17°48N 81°23E 244 F5
Kontagora Nigeria 10°23N 5°27E 263 C6
Kontcha Cameroon 7°59N 12°15E 263 D7
Kontiolahti Finland 62°46N 29°50E 160 E23
Kontokali Greece 39°38N 19°51E 206 B9
Konya Turkey 37°52N 32°35E 212 D5
Konya □ Turkey 37°46N 32°20E 250 A3
Konya Ovası Turkey 38°9N 33°5E 212 C5
Konyin Burma 22°58N 94°42E 241 D5
Konz Germany 49°42N 6°34E 179 F2
Konza Kenya 1°45S 37°7E 268 C4
Koo-wee-rup Australia 38°13S 145°28E 283 E6
Koocanusa, L. Canada 49°20N 115°15W 304 B6
Kookynie Australia 29°17S 121°22E 279 E3
Ko'olau Range U.S.A. 21°35N 157°50W 302 J14
Ko'olauloa District U.S.A. 21°35N 157°55W 302 J14
Ko'olaupoko District U.S.A. 21°25N 157°50W 302 K14
Koolyanobbing Australia 30°48S 119°36E 279 F2
Koondrook Australia 35°33S 144°8E 282 C6
Koonibba Australia 31°54S 133°25E 281 E1
Koorawatha Australia 34°2S 148°33E 283 C8
Koorda Australia 30°48S 117°35E 279 F2
Kooskia U.S.A. 46°9N 115°59W 304 C6
Kootenay → U.S.A. 49°19N 117°39W 296 D5
Kootenay △ Canada 51°0N 116°0W 296 C5
Kootenay L. Canada 49°45N 116°50W 304 B5
Kootingal Australia 31°3S 151°4E 283 A9
Kootjieskolk S. Africa 31°15S 20°21E 270 D3
Kopanina Czech Rep. 50°3N 14°17E 135 B1
Kopanovka Russia 47°28N 46°50E 191 G8
Kopaonik Serbia 43°10N 20°50E 202 C4
Kopaonik △ Serbia 43°20N 20°50E 202 C4
Kopargaon India 19°51N 74°28E 244 E2
Koparkhairna India 19°6N 72°59E 130 A2
Kópasker Iceland 66°18N 16°27W 155 A10
Kópavogur Iceland 64°6N 21°55W 155 C5
Kopayhorod Ukraine 48°52N 27°47E 183 B12
Köpenick Germany 52°26N 13°35E 115 B4
Koper Slovenia 45°31N 13°44E 199 C10
Kopervik Norway 59°17N 5°17E 164 E2
Kopet Dagh Asia 38°0N 58°0E 247 B8
Kopeysk Russia 55°7N 61°37E 216 A6
Kopi Australia 33°24S 135°40E 281 E2
Köping Sweden 59°31N 16°3E 162 E10
Köpingsvik Sweden 56°53N 16°43E 163 H10
Kopište Croatia 42°48N 16°42E 199 F13
Koplik Albania 42°15N 19°25E 202 D3
Köpmanholmen Sweden 63°10N 18°35E 162 A12
Koppa India 13°33N 75°21E 245 H2
Koppal India 15°23N 76°5E 245 G3
Koppang Norway 61°34N 11°3E 164 C8
Kopparberg Sweden 59°52N 15°0E 162 E9
Koppeh Dāgh = Kopet Dagh Asia 38°0N 58°0E 247 B8
Kopperå Norway 63°24N 11°50E 164 A8
Koppies S. Africa 27°20S 27°30E 271 C4
Koppom Sweden 59°43N 12°10E 162 E6
Koprivlen Bulgaria 41°31N 23°53E 202 E7
Koprivnica Croatia 46°12N 16°45E 199 B13
Kopřivnice Czech Rep. 49°36N 18°9E 181 B11
Koprivshtitsa Bulgaria 42°40N 24°19E 203 D8
Köprü → Turkey 36°48N 31°11E 250 B2
Köprübaşı Turkey 38°43N 28°23E 205 C10
Köprülü Turkey 36°43N 32°10E 250 B3
Köprülü △ Turkey 37°20N 31°5E 246 B1
Kopychyntsi Ukraine 49°7N 25°58E 177 D13
Kora △ Kenya 0°14S 38°44E 268 C4
Korab Macedonia 41°44N 20°40E 202 E4
Koral India 21°50N 73°12E 242 J5
Korangal India 17°6N 77°38E 244 E3
Korangi Pakistan 24°47N 67°8E 123 B2
Koraput India 18°50N 82°40E 244 E6
Korarou, L. Mali 15°15N 3°15W 262 B4
Korba India 22°20N 82°45E 243 H10
Korbach Germany 51°16N 8°52E 178 D4
Korbu, G. Malaysia 4°41N 101°18E 237 K3
Korçë Albania 40°37N 20°50E 202 F4
Korčula Croatia 42°56N 16°57E 199 F13
Korčulanski Kanal Croatia 43°3N 16°40E 199 E13
Kord Kūy Iran 36°48N 54°7E 247 B7
Kord Sheykh Iran 28°31N 52°53E 247 D7
Kordestan = Kurdistan Asia 37°20N 43°30E 213 D10
Kordestān □ Iran 36°0N 47°0E 246 C5
Koré Mayroua Niger 13°18N 3°55E 263 C5
Korea, North ■ Asia 40°0N 127°0E 227 E14
Korea, South ■ Asia 36°0N 128°0E 227 G15
Korea Bay Korea 39°0N 124°0E 224 C2
Korea Strait Asia 34°0N 129°30E 227 H15
Koregaon India 17°40N 74°10E 244 F2
Korem Ethiopia 12°30N 39°32E 257 E4
Koremasa Japan 35°39N 139°29E 140 B1
Korenevo Kursk, Russia 51°27N 34°55E 189 G8
Korenevo Moskva, Russia 55°40N 38°0E 129 B6
Korenica = Titova Korenica Croatia 44°45N 15°41E 199 D12
Korenovsk Russia 45°30N 39°22E 191 H4
Korets Ukraine 50°40N 27°5E 177 C14
Korfantów Poland 50°29N 17°36E 185 H4
Korgan Turkey 40°44N 37°13E 212 B7
Korgus Sudan 19°16N 33°29E 256 D3
Korhogo Ivory C. 9°29N 5°28W 262 D3
Koribundu S. Leone 7°41N 11°46W 262 D2
Koridalos Greece 37°59N 23°39E 112 B1
Korienzé Mali 15°22N 3°50W 262 B4
Korinthia □ Greece 37°50N 22°35E 204 D4
Korinthiakos Kolpos Greece 38°16N 22°30E 204 C4
Korinthos Greece 37°56N 22°55E 204 D4
Korioumé Mali 16°35N 3°0W 262 B4
Korissa, L. Greece 39°27N 19°53E 206 C9
Korithi Greece 37°55N 20°42E 207 D2
Kōriyama Japan 37°24N 140°23E 220 F10
Korkino Russia 54°54N 61°23E 216 B6
Korkuteli Turkey 37°4N 30°13E 205 D12
Korla China 41°45N 86°4E 217 D11
Kormakiti, C. Cyprus 35°23N 32°56E 207 E8
Körmend Hungary 47°5N 16°35E 182 C1
Kornat Croatia 43°50N 15°20E 199 E12
Kornat △ Croatia 43°50N 15°12E 199 E12
Korneshty = Corneşti Moldova 47°21N 28°1E 183 C13
Korneuburg Austria 48°20N 16°20E 181 C9
Kórnik Poland 52°15N 17°6E 185 F4
Kornsjø Norway 58°57N 11°39E 164 F8
Koro Fiji 17°19S 179°23E 287 A2
Koro Ivory C. 8°32N 7°30W 262 D3
Koro Mali 14°1N 2°58W 262 C4
Koro Sea Fiji 17°30S 179°45W 287 A3
Koro Toro Chad 16°5N 18°30E 259 E3
Koroba Papua N. G. 5°44S 142°47E 286 C2
Korobkovo = Gubkin Russia 51°17N 37°32E 189 G9
Korocha Russia 50°54N 37°19E 189 G9
Köroğlu Dağları Turkey 40°38N 33°0E 212 B5
Korogwe Tanzania 5°5S 38°25E 268 D4
Koroit Australia 38°18S 142°24E 282 E5
Korokoro N.Z. 41°13S 174°52E 143 B2
Korokoro Stream → N.Z. 41°14S 174°52E 143 B2
Koroleve Ukraine 48°9N 23°8E 183 B8
Korolevu Fiji 18°12S 177°46E 287 B1
Koromiri Cook Is. 21°15S 159°43W 289 h
Korona U.S.A. 29°25N 81°12W 317 F8
Koronadal Phil. 6°12N 125°1E 233 H5
Korong Vale Australia 36°22S 143°45E 282 D5
Koroni Greece 36°48N 21°57E 204 E3
Koronia, L. Greece 40°47N 23°10E 202 F7
Koronos Greece 37°12N 25°35E 205 D7
Koronowo Poland 53°19N 17°55E 185 E4
Koropelé C.A.R. 4°44N 17°11E 264 B3
Koropets Ukraine 48°56N 25°10E 183 B10
Koror Palau 7°20N 134°28E 288 c
Körös → Hungary 46°43N 20°12E 182 D5
Körös Maros △ Hungary 47°8N 20°52E 182 C5
Köröstarcsa Hungary 46°53N 21°3E 182 D6
Korosten Ukraine 50°54N 28°36E 177 C15
Korostyshev Ukraine 50°19N 29°4E 177 C15
Korotoyak Russia 51°1N 39°2E 189 G10
Korovou Fiji 17°47S 178°32E 287 A2
Koroyanitu △ Fiji 17°40S 177°35E 287 A1
Korraraika, Helodranon' i Madag. 17°45S 43°57E 272 B1
Korror I. Palau 7°20N 134°29E 288 c
Korsakov Russia 46°36N 142°42E 215 E15
Korsberga Sweden 57°19N 15°7E 163 G9
Korshiv Ukraine 48°39N 25°1E 183 B10
Korshunovo Russia 58°37N 110°10E 215 D12
Korsør Denmark 55°20N 11°9E 163 J5
Korsun Shevchenkovskiy Ukraine 49°26N 31°16E 189 H6
Korsze Poland 54°11N 21°9E 184 D8
Korti Sudan 18°6N 31°33E 256 D3
Kortrijk Belgium 50°50N 3°17E 170 D3
Korucu Turkey 39°28N 27°22E 205 B9
Korumburra Australia 38°26S 145°50E 283 E6
Korup △ Cameroon 5°15N 9°2E 264 A1
Korwai India 24°7N 78°5E 242 G8
Koryakskoye Nagorye Russia 61°0N 171°0E 215 C18
Koryukovka Ukraine 51°46N 32°16E 189 G7
Kos Greece 36°50N 27°15E 205 E9
Kosa Ethiopia 7°50N 36°50E 257 F4
Kosai Japan 34°42N 137°32E 223 C9
Kosan N. Korea 38°52N 127°25E 224 C3
Kosaya Gora Russia 54°10N 37°30E 188 E9
Koschagyl Kazakhstan 46°40N 54°0E 187 E9
Kościan Poland 52°5N 16°40E 185 F3
Kościerzyna Poland 54°8N 17°59E 184 D4
Kosciusko U.S.A. 33°4N 89°35W 315 E10
Kosciuszko, Mt. Australia 36°27S 148°16E 283 D8
Kosciuszko △ Australia 36°30S 148°20E 283 D8
Kösély → Hungary 47°25N 21°5E 182 C6
Kosgi Andhra Pradesh, India 16°58N 77°43E 244 F3
Kosgi Andhra Pradesh, India 15°51N 77°16E 245 G3
Kosha Sudan 20°50N 30°30E 256 C3
Koshava Bulgaria 44°4N 23°2E 202 B7
Koshigaya Japan 35°54N 139°48E 223 B11
K'oshih = Kashi China 39°30N 76°2E 217 E9
Koshiki-Rettō Japan 31°45N 129°49E 222 F1
Koshkonong L. U.S.A. 42°52N 88°58W 311 B8
Kōshoku Japan 36°38N 138°6E 223 A10
Koshu-Kavak = Krumovgrad Bulgaria 41°29N 25°38E 203 E9
Kosi India 27°48N 77°29E 242 F7
Kosi → India 28°41N 78°57E 243 E8
Košice Slovak Rep. 48°42N 21°15E 181 C14
Košický □ Slovak Rep. 48°45N 21°0E 181 C14
Kosino Russia 55°43N 37°50E 129 B5
Kosiv Ukraine 48°19N 25°6E 183 B10
Kosjerić Serbia 44°0N 19°55E 202 B3
Köşk Turkey 37°50N 28°3E 205 D10
Koskinou Greece 36°23N 28°13E 206 E12
Koslan Russia 63°34N 49°14E 186 B8
Köslin = Koszalin Poland 54°11N 16°8E 184 D3
Kosmach Ukraine 48°20N 24°50E 183 B9
Kosŏng N. Korea 38°40N 128°22E 224 C4
Kosovo □ Serbia 42°30N 21°0E 202 D4
Kosovo Polje Serbia 42°40N 21°5E 202 D5
Kosovska Kamenica Serbia 42°35N 21°35E 202 D5
Kosovska Mitrovica Serbia 42°54N 20°52E 202 D4
Kossou, L. de Ivory C. 6°59N 5°31W 262 D3
Kosta Sweden 56°50N 15°24E 163 H9
Kostajnica Croatia 45°17N 16°30E 199 C13
Kostanjevica Slovenia 45°51N 15°27E 199 C12
Kostenets = Pernik Bulgaria 42°35N 23°2E 202 D7
Kostenets Bulgaria 42°15N 23°52E 202 D7
Koster S. Africa 25°52S 26°54E 270 C4
Kôstî Sudan 13°8N 32°43E 257 E3
Kostinbrod Bulgaria 42°49N 23°13E 202 D7
Kostolac Serbia 44°37N 21°15E 202 B5
Kostopil Ukraine 50°51N 26°22E 177 C14
Kostroma Russia 57°50N 40°58E 188 D11
Kostromo □ Russia 58°10N 42°50E 190 A6
Kostromskoye Vdkhr. Russia 57°52N 40°49E 188 D11
Kostryzhivka Ukraine 48°39N 25°43E 183 B10
Kostrzyn Lubuskie, Poland 52°35N 14°39E 185 F1
Kostrzyn Wielkopolskie, Poland 52°24N 17°14E 185 F4
Kostyantynivka Ukraine 48°32N 37°39E 189 H9
Kostyukovichi = Kastsyukovichy Belarus 53°20N 32°4E 188 F7
Kosugi Japan 35°34N 139°39E 140 B2
Koszalin Poland 54°11N 16°8E 184 D3
Kőszeg Hungary 47°23N 16°33E 182 C1
Kot Addu Pakistan 30°30N 71°0E 242 D4
Kot Kapura India 30°35N 74°50E 242 D6
Kot Moman Pakistan 32°13N 73°0E 242 C5
Kot Sultan Pakistan 30°46N 70°56E 242 D4
Kota India 25°14N 75°49E 242 G6
Kota Jakarta, Indonesia 6°7S 106°48E 122 A1
Kota Barrage India 25°6N 75°51E 242 G6
Kota Belud Malaysia 6°21N 116°26E 235 A5
Kota Bharu Malaysia 6°7N 102°14E 237 J4
Kota Kinabalu Malaysia 6°0N 116°4E 235 A5
Kota Kubu Bharu Malaysia 3°34N 101°39E 237 L3
Kota Tinggi Malaysia 1°44N 103°53E 237 M4
Kotaagung Indonesia 5°38S 104°29E 234 D2
Kotabaru Indonesia 3°20S 116°20E 235 C5
Kotabumi Indonesia 4°49S 104°54E 234 C2
Kotagede Indonesia 7°54S 110°26E 235 D4
Kotamobagu Indonesia 0°57N 124°31E 231 D6
Kotapad India 19°9N 82°21E 244 E6
Kotawaringin Indonesia 2°28S 111°27E 235 C4
Kotchandpur Bangla. 23°24N 89°1E 241 D2
Kotcho L. Canada 59°7N 121°12W 296 B4
Kotdwara India 29°45N 78°32E 243 E8
Kotel Bulgaria 42°52N 26°26E 203 D10
Kotelnich Russia 58°22N 48°24E 190 A9
Kotelnikovo Russia 47°38N 43°8E 191 G6
Kotelnyy, Ostrov Russia 75°10N 139°0E 215 B14
Kotelyniki Russia 55°39N 37°52E 129 C5
Kothagudam India 17°30N 80°40E 244 F5
Kothapet India 19°21N 79°28E 244 E4
Kothari → India 25°20N 75°4E 242 G6
Köthen Germany 51°45N 11°59E 178 D7
Kothi Chhattisgarh, India 23°21N 82°3E 243 H10
Kothi Mad. P., India 24°45N 80°40E 243 G9
Kotiro Pakistan 26°17N 67°13E 242 F2
Kotka Finland 60°28N 26°58E 188 B4
Kotlas Russia 61°17N 46°43E 186 B8
Kotlenska Planina Bulgaria 42°56N 26°30E 203 D10
Kotli Pakistan 33°30N 73°55E 242 C5
Kotlik U.S.A. 63°2N 163°33W 303 E7
Kotma India 23°12N 81°58E 243 H9
Kotmul Pakistan 35°32N 75°10E 243 B6
Kōtō Japan 35°40N 139°48E 140 A3
Kotohira Japan 34°11N 133°49E 222 C5
Koton-Karifi Nigeria 8°0N 6°48E 263 D6
Kotonkoro Nigeria 11°3N 5°58E 263 C6
Kotor Montenegro 42°25N 18°47E 202 D2
Kotor Varoš Bos.-H. 44°38N 17°22E 182 F2
Kotoriba Croatia 46°23N 16°48E 199 B13
Kotovo Russia 50°22N 44°45E 190 E7
Kotovsk Russia 52°36N 41°32E 190 D5
Kotovsk Ukraine 47°45N 29°35E 177 E15
Kotputli India 27°43N 76°12E 242 F7
Kotri Pakistan 25°22N 68°22E 242 G3
Kotri → India 19°15N 80°35E 244 E5
Kotronas Greece 36°38N 22°29E 204 E4
Kotrung India 22°41N 88°20E 124 A2
Kötschach-Mauthen Austria 46°41N 13°1E 180 E6
Kottayam India 9°35N 76°33E 245 K3
Kotto → C.A.R. 4°14N 22°2E 264 B4
Kottur India 10°34N 76°56E 245 J3
Kotturu India 14°45N 76°10E 245 G3
Kotu Group Tonga 20°0S 174°45W 287 Q13
Kotuy → Russia 71°54N 102°6E 215 B11
Kotyuzhany Ukraine 48°48N 27°42E 183 B12
Kotzebue U.S.A. 66°53N 162°39W 303 C7
Kotzebue Sound U.S.A. 66°20N 163°0W 303 C7
Kotzenau = Chocianów Poland 51°27N 15°55E 185 G2
Kouango C.A.R. 5°0N 20°10E 264 B4
Kouchibouguac △ Canada 46°50N 65°0W 299 C6
Koudougou Burkina Faso 12°10N 2°20W 262 C4
Koufonisi Iraklio, Greece 34°56N 26°8E 207 F7
Koufonisi Notio Aigaio, Greece 36°57N 25°35E 205 E7
Kougaberge S. Africa 33°48S 23°50E 270 D3
K'ouhu Taiwan 23°35N 120°11E 225 C2
Kouibli Ivory C. 7°15N 7°14W 262 D3
Kouilou → Congo 4°10S 12°5E 265 C2
Kouki C.A.R. 7°22N 17°3E 264 A3
Koukoulé, Mt. Comoros Is. 12°18S 43°41E 272 a
Koula Greece 41°23N 24°44E 203 E8
Koula Moutou Gabon 1°15S 12°25E 264 C2
Koulen = Kulen Cambodia 13°50N 104°40E 236 F5
Koulikoro Mali 12°40N 7°50W 262 C3
Koulikoro □ Mali 14°0N 7°45W 262 C3
Kouloura Greece 39°42N 19°54E 206 B9
Koumac N. Cal. 20°33S 164°17E 288 d
Koumala Australia 21°38S 149°15E 280 C4
Koumameveng Gabon 0°11N 11°51E 264 B2
Koumankou Mali 11°58N 6°6W 262 C3
Koumbia Burkina Faso 11°10N 3°50W 262 C4
Koumbia Guinea 11°48N 13°29W 262 C2
Koumboum Guinea 10°25N 13°0W 262 C2
Koumpenntoum Senegal 13°59N 14°34W 262 C2
Koumra Chad 8°50N 17°35E 259 G3
Koun-Fao Ivory C. 7°30N 3°15W 262 D4
Koundara Guinea 12°29N 13°18W 262 C2
Koundé C.A.R. 6°7N 14°38E 264 A2
Koundian Guinea 13°10N 10°35W 262 C3
Koungheul Senegal 14°0N 14°50W 262 C2
Koungou Mayotte 12°43S 45°12E 272 b
Koungoulou Congo 3°31S 13°20E 264 C2
Kountze U.S.A. 30°22N 94°19W 314 F7
Koupéla Burkina Faso 12°11N 0°21W 263 C4
Kouponia Greece 37°57N 23°47E 112 B2
Kourémalé Mali 11°59N 8°42W 262 C3
Kouri-shima Japan 26°42N 128°1E 288 a
Kouris → Cyprus 34°38N 32°54E 207 F8
Kourizo, P. de Chad 22°28N 15°27E 258 D3
Kourou Fr. Guiana 5°9N 52°39W 329 B7
Kourouba Mali 13°22N 10°57W 262 C2
Kouroukoto Mali 12°35N 10°5W 262 C2
Kourouma Burkina Faso 11°35N 4°50W 262 C4
Kourouninkoto Mali 13°52N 9°35W 262 C3
Kouroussa Guinea 10°45N 9°45W 262 C3
Koussanar Senegal 13°52N 14°5W 262 C2
Koussané Mali 14°53N 11°14W 262 C2
Koussane Senegal 14°10N 12°22W 262 C2
Kousseri Cameroon 12°0N 14°55E 259 F2
Koutiala Mali 12°25N 5°23W 262 C3
Kouto Ivory C. 9°53N 6°25W 262 D3
Kouts U.S.A. 41°19N 87°2W 311 C9
Kouvé Togo 6°25N 1°25E 263 D5
Kouvola Finland 60°52N 26°43E 188 B4
Kouyi Congo 2°29S 12°25E 264 C2
Kouyou → Congo 0°44S 16°38E 264 C3
Kovačica Serbia 45°5N 20°38E 182 E5
Kovdor Russia 67°34N 30°24E 160 C24
Kovel Ukraine 51°11N 24°38E 177 C13
Kovilpatti India 9°10N 77°50E 245 K3
Kovin Serbia 44°44N 20°59E 182 F5
Kovno = Kaunas Lithuania 54°54N 23°54E 184 D10
Kovrov Russia 56°25N 41°25E 190 B5
Kovur Andhra Pradesh, India 17°3N 81°39E 244 F5
Kovur Andhra Pradesh, India 14°30N 80°1E 245 G5
Kowal Poland 52°32N 19°7E 185 F6
Kowalewo Pomorskie Poland 53°10N 18°52E 185 E5
Kowanyama Australia 15°29S 141°44E 280 B3
Kowlīnī Afghan. 37°39N 65°58E 240 A2
Kowloon China 22°19N 114°11E 122 B1
Kowloon Park Hong Kong, China 122 a2
Kowloon Peak China 22°20N 114°13E 122 A2
Kowloon Res. China 22°21N 114°9E 122 A1
Kowloon Tong China 22°20N 114°10E 122 A2
Kowŏn N. Korea 39°26N 127°14E 224 C3
Kōyama Japan 31°20N 130°56E 222 F2
Koyampattur = Coimbatore India 11°2N 76°59E 245 J3
Köyceğiz Turkey 36°57N 28°40E 205 E10
Köyceğiz Gölü Turkey 36°56N 28°42E 205 E10
Köýtendag Turkmenistan 37°30N 66°1E 240 A2
Koyuk U.S.A. 64°56N 161°9W 303 D7
Koyukuk U.S.A. 64°53N 157°42W 303 D8
Koyukuk → U.S.A. 64°55N 157°32W 303 D8
Koyukuk Nat. Wildlife Refuge ⌓ U.S.A. 65°35N 156°30W 303 D8
Koyulhisar Turkey 40°20N 37°52E 212 B7
Koyunyeri Turkey 40°50N 26°26E 203 F10
Koza = Okinawa Japan 26°19N 127°46E 288 a
Kozak Turkey 39°15N 27°6E 205 B9
Kozan Turkey 37°26N 35°50E 212 D6
Kozani Greece 40°19N 21°47E 202 F5
Kozani □ Greece 40°18N 21°45E 202 F5
Kozara Bos.-H. 45°0N 17°0E 199 D14
Kozara △ Bos.-H. 45°0N 17°0E 182 F2
Kozarac Bos.-H. 44°58N 16°48E 199 D13
Kozelets Ukraine 50°55N 31°7E 189 G6
Kozelsk Russia 54°2N 35°48E 188 E8
Kozhikode = Calicut India 11°15N 75°43E 245 J2
Kozhukhovo Russia 55°43N 37°53E 129 B5
Kozhva Russia 65°10N 57°0E 186 A10
Koziegłowy Poland 50°37N 19°8E 185 H6
Kozienice Poland 51°35N 21°34E 185 G8
Kozje Slovenia 46°5N 15°35E 199 B12
Kozloduy Bulgaria 43°45N 23°42E 202 C7
Kozlov = Michurinsk Russia 52°58N 40°27E 190 D5
Kozlovets Bulgaria 43°30N 25°20E 203 C9
Kozlovka Russia 55°52N 48°14E 190 C9
Kozlu Turkey 41°26N 31°45E 212 B4
Kozluk Turkey 38°11N 41°31E 213 C9
Koźmin Poland 51°48N 17°27E 185 G4
Kozmodemyansk Russia 56°20N 46°36E 190 B8
Kōzu-Shima Japan 34°13N 139°10E 223 C11
Kożuchów Poland 51°45N 15°31E 185 G2
Kozyatyn Ukraine 49°45N 28°50E 177 D15
Kpabia Ghana 9°10N 0°20W 263 D4
Kpalimé Togo 6°57N 0°44E 263 D5
Kpandae Ghana 8°30N 0°2W 263 D4
Kpessi Togo 8°4N 1°16E 263 D5
Kra, Isthmus of = Kra, Kho Khot Thailand 10°15N 99°30E 237 G2
Kra, Kho Khot Thailand 10°15N 99°30E 237 G2
Kra Buri Thailand 10°22N 98°46E 237 G2
Kraai → S. Africa 30°40S 26°45E 270 D4
Kraainem Belgium 50°52N 4°28E 116 A2
Krabi Thailand 8°4N 98°55E 237 H2
Kracheh Cambodia 12°32N 106°10E 236 F6
Kragan Indonesia 6°43S 111°38E 235 D4
Kragerø Norway 58°52N 9°25E 164 F6
Kragujevac Serbia 44°2N 20°56E 202 B4
Krailling Germany 48°5N 11°25E 131 B1
Krainburg = Kranj Slovenia 46°16N 14°22E 199 B11
Krajenka Poland 53°18N 16°59E 185 E3
Krakatau = Rakata, Pulau Indonesia 6°10S 105°20E 234 D3
Krakatoa = Rakata, Pulau Indonesia 6°10S 105°20E 234 D3
Krakau = Kraków Poland 50°4N 19°57E 185 H6
Krakor Cambodia 12°32N 104°12E 236 F5
Kraków Poland 50°4N 19°57E 185 H6
Kraków ✈ (KRK) Poland 50°5N 19°52E 185 H6
Kraksaan Indonesia 7°43S 113°23E 235 D4
Kralanh Cambodia 13°35N 103°25E 236 F4
Kralendijk Neth. Ant. 12°9N 68°16W 322 h
Králíky Czech Rep. 50°6N 16°45E 181 A9
Kraljevo Serbia 43°44N 20°41E 202 C4
Kralovéhradecký □ Czech Rep. 50°25N 15°50E 180 A8
Královský Chlmec Slovak Rep. 48°27N 22°0E 181 C14
Kralupy nad Vltavou Czech Rep. 50°13N 14°20E 180 A7
Kramatorsk Ukraine 48°50N 37°30E 189 H9
Kramfors Sweden 62°55N 17°48E 162 B11
Kramis, C. Algeria 36°26N 0°45E 261 A5
Krampnitz Germany 52°27N 13°3E 115 B1
Krampnitzsee Germany 52°27N 13°3E 115 B1
Krania Greece 39°53N 21°18E 202 G5
Krania Elasonas Greece 39°57N 22°2E 204 B4
Kranidi Greece 37°20N 23°10E 204 D5
Kranj Slovenia 46°16N 14°22E 199 B11
Kranji, Sungei → Singapore 1°26N 103°44E 138 A2
Kranji Industrial Estate Singapore 1°26N 103°45E 138 A2
Kranjska Gora Slovenia 46°29N 13°48E 199 B10
Krankskop S. Africa 28°0S 30°47E 271 C5
Kranz = Zelenogradsk Russia 54°53N 20°29E 184 D7
Krapina Croatia 46°10N 15°52E 199 B12
Krapina → Croatia 45°50N 15°50E 199 C12
Krapkowice Poland 50°29N 17°56E 185 H4
Krappitz = Krapkowice Poland 50°29N 17°56E 185 H4
Kras Croatia 45°35N 14°0E 199 C10
Krasavino Russia 60°58N 46°29E 186 B8
Kraskino Russia 42°44N 130°48E 220 C5
Kraskovo Russia 55°39N 37°58E 129 C5
Krāslava Latvia 55°54N 27°10E 188 E4
Kraslice Czech Rep. 50°19N 12°31E 180 A5
Krasnaya Gorbatka Russia 55°52N 41°45E 190 C5
Krasnaya Polyana Russia 43°40N 40°13E 191 J5
Krasnaya Sloboda = Krasnoslobodsk Russia 48°42N 44°33E 191 F7
Krasne Ukraine 46°7N 29°15E 183 D14
Krasni Okny Ukraine 47°32N 29°27E 183 C14
Kraśnik Poland 50°55N 22°15E 185 H9
Krasno-Presnenskaya Russia 55°45N 37°32E 129 B3
Krasnoarmeisk Ukraine 48°18N 37°11E 189 H9
Krasnoarmeysk = Tayynsha Kazakhstan 53°50N 69°45E 217 B7
Krasnoarmeysk Russia 51°0N 45°42E 190 E7
Krasnoarmeyskiy Russia 47°0N 42°12E 191 G6
Krasnoarmeyskoye = Volnansk Ukraine 48°2N 35°29E 189 H8
Krasnoarmeysky Rudnik = Dobropole Ukraine 48°25N 37°2E 189 H9
Krasnobrod Poland 50°33N 23°12E 185 H10
Krasnodar Russia 45°5N 39°0E 191 H4
Krasnodar □ Russia 46°30N 39°30E 191 G4
Krasnodon Ukraine 48°17N 39°44E 189 H10
Krasnogorsk Russia 55°49N 37°18E 129 B1
Krasnogorskiy Russia 56°10N 48°28E 190 B9
Krasnograd = Krasnohrad Ukraine 49°27N 35°27E 189 H8
Krasnogvardeysk = Gatchina Russia 59°35N 30°9E 188 C6
Krasnogvardeysk Ukraine 45°32N 34°16E 189 K8
Krasnogvardeyskoye Russia 45°52N 41°33E 191 H5
Krasnohrad Ukraine 49°27N 35°27E 189 H8
Krasnokamsk Russia 58°4N 55°48E 186 C10
Krasnokokshaysk = Yoshkar Ola Russia 56°38N 47°55E 190 B8
Krasnokutsk Ukraine 50°10N 34°50E 189 G8
Krasnolesnyy Russia 51°53N 39°35E 189 G10
Krasnoperekopsk Ukraine 46°0N 33°54E 189 J7
Krasnorechenskiy Russia 44°41N 135°14E 220 B7
Krasnoselkup Russia 65°20N 82°10E 214 C9
Krasnoslobodsk Mordvinia, Russia 54°25N 43°45E 190 C6
Krasnoslobodsk Volgograd, Russia 48°42N 44°33E 191 F7
Krasnoturinsk Russia 59°46N 60°12E 186 C11
Krasnoufimsk Russia 56°36N 57°38E 186 C10
Krasnouralsk Russia 58°21N 60°3E 186 C11
Krasnovishersk Russia 60°23N 57°3E 186 B10
Krasnovodsk = Türkmenbashi Turkmenistan 40°5N 53°5E 247 A7
Krasnoyarsk Russia 56°8N 93°0E 215 D10
Krasnoyarskoye Russia 54°31N 21°56E 184 D8
Krasnoye = Krasnyy Russia 54°25N 31°30E 188 E6
Krasnoye = Ulan Erge Russia 46°19N 44°53E 191 G7
Krasnoyilsk 47°59N 25°38E 183 C10
Krasnozavodsk Russia 56°27N 38°25E 188 D10
Krasnoznamensk Russia 54°57N 22°30E 184 D9
Krasny = Kyzyl Russia 51°50N 94°30E 217 B12
Krasny = Mozhga Russia 56°26N 52°15E 190 B11
Krasny Boyevik = Kotovsk Russia 52°36N 41°32E 190 D5
Krasny Sulin Russia 47°52N 40°8E 189 J11
Krasnystaw Poland 50°57N 23°5E 185 H10
Krasnyy Russia 54°25N 31°30E 188 E6
Krasnyy Kholm Russia 58°10N 37°10E 188 C9
Krasnyy Kut Russia 50°50N 47°0E 190 E8
Krasnyy Liman Ukraine 48°58N 37°50E 189 H9
Krasnyy Luch Ukraine 48°13N 39°0E 189 H10
Krasnyy Profintern Russia 57°45N 40°27E 188 D11
Krasnyy Yar Astrakhan, Russia 46°43N 48°23E 191 G9
Krasnyy Yar Samara, Russia 53°30N 50°22E 190 D10
Krasnyy Yar Volgograd, Russia 50°42N 44°45E 190 E7
Krasnyye Baki Russia 57°8N 45°10E 190 B7
Krasnyyoskolske Vdskh. Ukraine 49°27N 37°40E 189 H9
Kraszna → Hungary 48°4N 22°20E 182 B7
Kratie = Kracheh Cambodia 12°32N 106°10E 236 F6
Kratke Ra. Papua N. G. 6°45S 146°0E 286 D4
Kratovo Macedonia 42°6N 22°10E 202 D6
Krau Indonesia 3°19S 140°5E 231 E10
Kraulshavn = Nuussauq Greenland 74°8N 57°3W 154 C5
Kravanh, Chuor Phnum Cambodia 12°0N 103°32E 237 G4
Krč Czech Rep. 50°2N 14°26E 135 B2
Kreb es Sefia Algeria 27°12N 7°11W 260 C3
Kreb n-Naga Algeria 27°3N 7°9W 260 C3
Kreb n-Neggar Algeria 27°20N 7°15W 260 C3
Krefeld Germany 51°20N 6°33E 178 D2
Kremaston, L. Greece 38°52N 21°30E 204 C3
Kremen Croatia 44°28N 15°53E 199 D12
Kremenchuk Ukraine 49°5N 33°25E 189 H7
Kremenchuksk Vdskh. Ukraine 49°20N 32°30E 189 H7
Kremenets Ukraine 50°8N 25°43E 177 C13
Kremennaya Ukraine 49°1N 38°10E 189 H10
Kremges = Svitlovodsk Ukraine 49°2N 33°13E 189 H7
Kremlin Moscow, Russia 129 c2
Kremmen Germany 52°45N 13°1E 178 C9
Kremmling U.S.A. 40°4N 106°24W 304 F10
Kremnica Slovak Rep. 48°45N 18°50E 181 C11
Krems Austria 48°25N 15°36E 180 C8
Kremsmünster Austria 48°3N 14°8E 180 C7
Krenau = Chrzanów Poland 50°10N 19°21E 185 H6
Krestena Greece 37°35N 21°37E 204 D3
Krestovskiye, Ostrov Russia 59°57N 30°14E 137 B1
Kretinga Lithuania 55°53N 21°15E 184 C8
Krettamia Algeria 28°47N 3°27W 260 C4
Krettsy Russia 58°15N 32°30E 188 C7
Kreuzberg Bayern, Germany 50°22N 9°58E 179 E5
Kreuzberg Berlin, Germany 52°30N 13°24E 115 A3
Kreuzburg = Kluczbork Poland 50°58N 18°12E 185 H5
Kreuztal Germany 50°57N 8°0E 178 E4
Kria Vrisi Greece 40°41N 22°18E 202 F6
Kribi Cameroon 2°57N 9°56E 263 E6
Krichem Bulgaria 42°8N 24°28E 203 D8
Krichev = Krychaw Belarus 53°40N 31°41E 177 B16
Krim Slovenia 45°53N 14°30E 199 C11
Krim-Krim Chad 9°0N 15°24E 259 G3
Krindachyovka = Krasnyy Luch Ukraine 48°13N 39°0E 189 H10
Krios, Akra Greece 35°13N 23°34E 207 E4
Krishna → India 15°57N 80°59E 245 G5
Krishnagiri India 12°32N 78°16E 245 H4
Krishnanagar India 23°24N 88°33E 243 H13
Krishnaraja Sagara India 12°20N 76°30E 245 H3
Kristdala Sweden 57°24N 16°13E 163 G10
Kristians = Oppland □ Norway 61°15N 9°40E 164 C6
Kristiansand Norway 58°8N 8°1E 164 F5
Kristianstad Sweden 56°2N 14°9E 163 H8
Kristiansund Norway 63°7N 7°45E 164 A4
Kristiinankaupunki Finland 62°16N 21°21E 160 E19
Kristinehamn Sweden 59°18N 14°7E 162 E8
Kristinestad = Kristiinankaupunki Finland 62°16N 21°21E 160 E19
Kristinopol = Chervonohrad Ukraine 50°25N 24°10E 177 C13
Krithoti, Akra Greece 38°30N 21°2E 207 B3
Kriti Greece 35°15N 25°0E 207 E6
Kritsa Greece 35°10N 25°41E 207 E6
Kritzendorf Austria 48°19N 16°18E 142 A1
Kriva → Macedonia 42°5N 21°47E 202 D5
Kriva Palanka Macedonia 42°11N 22°19E 202 D6
Krivaja → Bos.-H. 44°27N 18°9E 182 F3
Krivelj Serbia 44°10N 22°5E 202 B6
Křivoklátsko ⌓ Czech Rep. 50°1N 13°51E 180 A6
Krivoy Rog = Kryvyy Rih Ukraine 47°51N 33°20E 189 J7
Križevci Croatia 46°3N 16°32E 199 B13
Krk Croatia 45°8N 14°40E 199 C11
Krka → Slovenia 45°50N 15°30E 199 C12
Krka △ Croatia 43°53N 15°56E 199 E12
Krkonoše Czech Rep. 50°50N 15°35E 180 A8
Krkonoše △ Czech Rep. 50°43N 15°39E 180 A8
Krnjaja = Kljajićevo Serbia 45°45N 19°17E 182 E4
Krnov Czech Rep. 50°5N 17°40E 181 A10
Krobia Poland 51°47N 16°59E 185 G3
Krøderen Norway 60°9N 9°49E 164 D6
Krokees Greece 36°53N 22°32E 204 E4
Krokek Sweden 58°40N 16°24E 163 F10
Krokodil = Umgwenya → Mozam. 25°14S 32°18E 271 C5
Krokom Sweden 63°20N 14°30E 162 A8
Krokowa Poland 54°47N 18°9E 184 D5
Króksfjarðarnes Iceland 65°27N 21°56W 155 B5
Krokstadelva Norway 59°56N 10°1E 164 E7
Krolevets Ukraine 51°35N 33°20E 189 G7
Królewska Huta = Chorzów Poland 50°18N 18°57E 185 H5
Kroměříž Czech Rep. 49°18N 17°21E 181 B10
Krompachy Slovak Rep. 48°54N 20°52E 181 C13
Kromy Russia 52°48N 35°48E 189 F8
Kronach Germany 50°14N 11°19E 179 E7
Kronau = Kranjska Gora Slovenia 46°29N 13°48E 199 B10
Krong Kaoh Kong Cambodia 11°37N 102°59E 237 G4
Kronobergs län □ Sweden 56°45N 14°30E 163 H8
Kronprins Christian Land Greenland 80°30N 22°0W 154 A8
Kronprins Frederik Land Greenland 79°0N 55°0W 154 B5
Kronprins Olav Kyst Antarctica 69°0S 42°0E 151 C5
Kronprinsesse Märtha Kyst Antarctica 73°30S 10°0W 151 D2
Kronshtadt Russia 59°57N 29°51E 188 C5
Kronstadt = Braşov Romania 45°38N 25°35E 183 E10
Kroonstad S. Africa 27°43S 27°19E 270 C4
Kröpelin Germany 54°4N 11°47E 178 A7
Kropotkin Russia 45°28N 40°28E 191 H5
Kropp Germany 54°24N 9°31E 178 A5
Krosna Lithuania 54°23N 23°33E 184 D10
Krośniewice Poland 52°15N 19°11E 185 F6
Krosno Poland 49°42N 21°46E 185 J8
Krosno Odrzańskie Poland 52°3N 15°7E 185 F2
Krotoszyn Poland 51°42N 17°23E 185 G4
Krotovka Russia 53°18N 51°10E 190 D10
Krousonas Greece 35°13N 24°59E 207 E5
Krrabë Albania 41°13N 20°0E 202 E3
Krško Slovenia 45°57N 15°30E 199 C12
Krstača Serbia 42°57N 20°8E 202 D4
Kruger △ S. Africa 24°50S 26°10E 271 B4
Krugersdorp S. Africa 26°5S 27°46E 271 C4
Kruisfontein S. Africa 33°59S 24°43E 270 D3
Krujë Albania 41°32N 19°46E 202 E3
Krulevshchina = Krulyewshchyna Belarus 55°5N 27°45E 188 E4
Krulyewshchyna Belarus 55°5N 27°45E 188 E4
Krumbach Germany 48°13N 10°22E 179 G6
Krumë Albania 42°14N 20°28E 202 D4
Krummau = Český Krumlov Czech Rep. 48°43N 14°21E 180 C7
Krumme Lanke Germany 52°27N 13°14E 115 B2
Krummensee Germany 52°35N 13°41E 115 A5
Krummhübel = Karpacz Poland 50°46N 15°46E 185 H2
Krumovgrad Bulgaria 41°29N 25°38E 203 E9
Krung Thep = Bangkok Thailand 13°45N 100°35E 113 B2
Krupanj Serbia 44°25N 19°22E 202 B3
Krupina Slovak Rep. 48°22N 19°5E 181 C12
Krupinica → Slovak Rep. 48°4N 18°55E 181 C11
Krupki Belarus 54°19N 29°8E 177 A15
Krusboda Sweden 59°13N 18°14E 139 B3
Krusenstern, C. U.S.A. 67°8N 163°45W 303 C7
Kruševac Serbia 43°35N 21°28E 202 C5

Kruševo Macedonia 41°23N 21°19E 202 E5
Krushchyov = Svitlovodsk Ukraine 49°2N 33°13E 189 H7
Krushelnyksya Ukraine 49°7N 23°29E 185 J10
Kruszwica Poland 52°40N 18°20E 185 F5
Krychaw Belarus 53°40N 31°41E 177 B16
Krylatskoye Russia 55°44N 37°23E 129 B2
Krymsk Russia 44°50N 38°0E 189 K10
Krymskiy Poluostrov = Krymskyy Pivostriv Ukraine 45°0N 34°0E 189 K8
Krymskyy Pivostriv Ukraine 45°0N 34°0E 189 K8
Krynica Poland 49°25N 20°57E 185 J7
Krynica Morska Poland 54°23N 19°28E 184 D6
Krynki Poland 53°17N 23°43E 185 E10
Krynychne Ukraine 45°32N 28°40E 183 E13
Kryvyy Rih Ukraine 47°51N 33°20E 189 J7
Kryzhopil Ukraine 48°23N 28°53E 183 B13
Krzemieniec = Kremenets Ukraine 50°8N 25°43E 177 C13
Krzepice Poland 50°58N 18°50E 185 H5
Krzeszów Poland 50°24N 22°21E 185 H9
Krzna → Poland 52°8N 23°32E 185 F10
Krzywiń Poland 51°58N 16°50E 185 G3
Krzyż Wielkopolski Poland 52°52N 16°0E 185 F2
Ksabi Morocco 32°51N 4°13W 260 B4
Ksar Chellala Algeria 35°13N 2°19E 261 A5
Ksar el Boukhari Algeria 35°51N 2°52E 261 A5
Ksar el Kebir Morocco 35°0N 6°0W 260 B3
Ksar es Souk = Er Rachidia Morocco 31°58N 4°20W 260 B4
Ksar Rhilane Tunisia 33°0N 9°39E 258 B1
Ksiąz Wielkopolski Poland 52°4N 17°14E 185 F4
Ksour, Mts. des Algeria 32°45N 0°30W 261 B4
Kstovo Russia 56°12N 44°13E 190 B7
Ku, W. el → Sudan 13°37N 25°15E 257 E2
Ku-Ring-Gai Chase △ Australia 33°39S 151°14E 283 B9
Ku Tree Res. U.S.A. 21°30N 157°59W 302 J14
Kuah Malaysia 6°19N 99°51E 237 J2
Kuala Indonesia 2°55N 105°47E 234 B3
Kuala Belait Malaysia 4°35N 114°11E 235 B4
Kuala Berang Malaysia 5°5N 103°1E 237 K4
Kuala Dungun = Dungun Malaysia 4°45N 103°25E 237 K4
Kuala Kangsar Malaysia 4°46N 100°56E 237 K3
Kuala Kelawang Malaysia 2°56N 102°5E 237 L4
Kuala Kerai Malaysia 5°30N 102°12E 237 K4
Kuala Kerian Malaysia 5°10N 100°25E 237 c
Kuala Lipis Malaysia 4°10N 102°3E 237 K4
Kuala Lumpur Malaysia 3°9N 101°41E 237 L3
Kuala Nerang Malaysia 6°16N 100°37E 237 J3
Kuala Pilah Malaysia 2°45N 102°15E 237 L4
Kuala Rompin Malaysia 2°49N 103°29E 237 L4
Kuala Selangor Malaysia 3°20N 101°15E 237 L3
Kuala Sepetang Malaysia 4°49N 100°28E 237 K3
Kuala Terengganu Malaysia 5°20N 103°8E 237 K4
Kualajelai Indonesia 2°58S 110°46E 235 C4
Kualakapuas Indonesia 2°55S 114°20E 235 C4
Kualakurun Indonesia 1°10S 113°50E 235 C4
Kualapembuang Indonesia 3°14S 112°38E 235 C4
Kualapu'u U.S.A. 21°9N 157°2W 302 B4
Kualasimpang Indonesia 4°17N 98°3E 234 B1
Kualoa Pt. U.S.A. 21°31N 157°50W 302 J14
Kuamat Malaysia 5°13N 117°30E 235 A5
Kuan Shan Taiwan 23°14N 120°54E 225 C2
Kuanao Taiwan 24°31N 118°24E 225 a
Kuancheng China 40°37N 118°30E 227 D10
Kuandang Indonesia 0°56N 123°1E 231 D6
Kuandian China 40°45N 124°45E 224 B2
Kuangchou = Guangzhou China 23°6N 113°13E 121 B2
Kuangfu Taiwan 23°40N 121°25E 225 C3
Kuanhsi Taiwan 24°48N 121°10E 225 B3
Kuanmiao Taiwan 22°58N 120°19E 225 D2
Kuanshan Taiwan 23°3N 121°9E 225 C3
Kuantan Malaysia 3°49N 103°20E 237 L4
Kuanyin Ilan, Taiwan 24°23N 121°46E 225 B3
Kuanyin Taoyüan, Taiwan 25°2N 121°4E 225 A3
Kuapä Pond U.S.A. 21°17N 157°43W 302 K14
Kuba = Quba Azerbaijan 41°21N 48°32E 191 K9
Kubah △ Malaysia 1°35N 110°9E 235 B4
Kuban → Russia 45°20N 37°30E 189 K9
Kuban Depression = Prikubanskaya Nizmennost Russia 45°39N 38°33E 191 H4
Kubenskoye, Ozero Russia 59°40N 39°25E 188 C10
Kuberle = Krasnoarmeyskiy Russia 47°0N 42°12E 191 G6
Kubokawa Japan 33°12N 133°8E 222 D5
Kubor, Mt. Papua N. G. 6°10S 144°44E 286 D3
Kubrat Bulgaria 43°49N 26°31E 203 C10
Kubu Indonesia 8°16S 115°35E 231 J18
Kubutambahan Indonesia 8°5S 115°10E 231 J18
Kucar, Tanjung Indonesia 8°39S 114°34E 231 K18
Kučevo Serbia 44°30N 21°40E 202 B5
Kucha Gompa India 34°25N 76°56E 243 B7
Kuchaman India 27°13N 74°47E 242 F6
Kuchchaveli Sri Lanka 8°49N 81°6E 245 K5
Kuchenspitze Austria 47°7N 10°12E 180 D3
Kuchinda India 21°44N 84°21E 243 J11
Kuching Malaysia 1°33N 110°25E 235 B4
Kuchino-eruba-Jima Japan 30°28N 130°12E 221 J5
Kuchino-Shima Japan 29°57N 129°55E 221 K4
Kuchinotsu Japan 32°36N 130°11E 222 E2
Kuchl Austria 47°37N 13°9E 180 D6
Kūchnay Darvīshān Afghan. 30°59N 64°10E 240 C2
Kuchurhan → Ukraine 46°33N 29°57E 183 D14
Kucing = Kuching Malaysia 1°33N 110°25E 235 B4
Kuçovë Albania 40°47N 19°57E 202 F3
Küçükbahçe Turkey 38°33N 26°24E 205 C8
Küçükköy Balıkesir, Turkey 39°16N 26°42E 205 B8
Küçükköy İstanbul, Turkey 41°3N 28°52E 122 B1
Küçükkuyu Turkey 39°32N 26°36E 205 B8
Küçükmenderes → Turkey 37°57N 27°16E 205 D9
Küçüksu Turkey 41°5N 29°5E 122 B2
Kud → Pakistan 26°5N 66°20E 242 F2
Kuda India 23°10N 71°15E 242 H4
Kudahuvadhoo Maldives 2°40N 72°54E 272 d
Kudahuvadhoo Channel Maldives 2°40N 73°0E 272 d
Kudaka-shima Japan 26°9N 127°53E 288 a
Kudal India 16°2N 73°41E 245 F1
Kudalier → India 18°35N 79°48E 244 E4
Kudamatsu Japan 34°0N 131°52E 222 D3
Kudankita Tokyo, Japan 140 a3
Kudarebe Aruba 12°37N 70°4W 322 f
Kudat Malaysia 6°55N 116°55E 235 A5
Kudirkos Naumiestis Lithuania 54°46N 22°53E 184 D9
Kudowa-Zdrój Poland 50°27N 16°15E 185 H3
Kudremukh India 13°15N 75°20E 245 H2
Kudrovo Russia 59°54N 30°30E 137 B3
Kudus Indonesia 6°48S 110°51E 235 D4
Kudymkar Russia 59°1N 54°39E 186 C9
Kueishan Tao Taiwan 24°51N 121°57E 225 B3
Kueiyang = Guiyang China 26°32N 106°40E 228 D6
Kufra Oasis = Al Kufrah Libya 24°17N 23°15E 258 D4
Kufstein Austria 47°35N 12°11E 180 D5
Kugaaruk = Pelly Bay Canada 68°38N 89°50W 295 C11
Kugluktuk Canada 67°50N 115°5W 294 C8
Kugong I. Canada 56°18N 79°50W 298 A4
Kūh-e-Jebāl Bārez Iran 29°0N 58°0E 247 D8
Kūh-e Sorkh Iran 35°30N 58°45E 216 E5
Kūhak Iran 27°12N 63°10E 240 D1
Kuhan Pakistan 28°19N 67°14E 242 E2
Kūhbonān Iran 31°23N 56°19E 247 D8
Kūhestak Iran 26°47N 57°2E 247 E8
Kūhestān Afghan. 34°39N 61°12E 240 B1
Kuhin Iran 36°22N 49°40E 247 B6
Kūhīrī Iran 26°55N 61°2E 247 E9
Kūhiston-Badakhshon □ Tajikistan 38°30N 73°0E 217 E8
Kuhmo Finland 64°7N 29°31E 160 D23
Kuhnsdorf Austria 46°37N 14°38E 180 E7
Kūhpāyeh Eşfahan, Iran 32°44N 52°20E 247 C7
Kūhpāyeh Kermān, Iran 30°35N 57°15E 247 D8
Kūhrān, Kūh-e Iran 26°46N 58°12E 247 E8
Kui Buri Thailand 12°3N 99°52E 237 F2
Kuichong China 22°38N 114°25E 219 F11
Kuiseb → Namibia 22°59S 14°31E 270 B1
Kuito Angola 12°22S 16°55E 265 E3
Kuiu I. U.S.A. 57°45N 134°10W 296 B2
Kujang N. Korea 39°57N 126°1E 224 C3
Kujawsko-Pomorskie □ Poland 53°20N 18°30E 184 E5
Kuji Japan 40°11N 141°46E 220 D10
Kujū-San Japan 33°5N 131°15E 222 D3
Kukarka = Sovetsk Russia 57°38N 48°53E 190 B9
Kukava Ukraine 48°37N 27°43E 183 B12
Kukavica Serbia 42°48N 21°57E 202 D5
Kukawa Nigeria 12°58N 13°27E 263 C7
Kuk'eng Taiwan 23°38N 120°33E 225 C2
Kukës Albania 42°5N 20°27E 202 D4
Kuki Japan 36°4N 139°40E 223 A11
Kukipi Papua N. G. 8°10S 146°6E 286 E4
Kukmor Russia 56°11N 50°54E 190 B10
Kükong = Shaoguan China 24°48N 113°35E 229 E9
Kuku Pt. Wake I. 19°18N 166°34E 302 b
Kukuan Taiwan 24°17N 121°2E 225 B3
Kukuihaele U.S.A. 20°5N 155°35W 302 C6
Kukup Malaysia 1°20N 103°27E 237 d
Kukup, Pulau Malaysia 1°18N 103°25E 237 d
Kukvidze Russia 50°40N 43°0E 190 E6
Kula Bulgaria 43°52N 22°36E 202 C6
Kula Serbia 45°37N 19°32E 182 E4
Kula Turkey 38°32N 28°40E 205 C10
Kula Gulf Solomon Is. 8°5S 157°18E 287 M9
K'ula Shan Bhutan 28°14N 90°36E 218 C4
Kulachi Pakistan 31°56N 70°27E 242 D4
Kulai Malaysia 1°44N 103°35E 237 M4
Kulal, Mt. Kenya 2°43N 36°56E 266 D4
Kulaly, Ostrov = Kulaly Aral Kazakhstan 45°0N 50°0E 191 H10
Kulaly Aral Kazakhstan 45°0N 50°0E 191 H10
Kulasekarappattinam India 8°20N 78°5E 245 K4
Kulassein I. Phil. 6°25N 120°41E 233 H3
Kulaura Bangla. 24°32N 92°3E 241 C4
Kulautuva Lithuania 54°56N 23°36E 184 D10
Kuldīga Latvia 56°58N 21°59E 184 B8
Kuldīga □ Latvia 56°55N 22°0E 184 B8
Kuldja = Yining China 43°58N 81°10E 217 D10
Kuldu Sudan 12°50N 28°30E 257 E2
Kulebaki Russia 55°22N 42°25E 190 C6
Kulen Cambodia 13°50N 104°40E 236 F5
Kulen Vakuf Bos.-H. 44°35N 16°2E 199 D13
Kulgam India 33°36N 75°2E 243 C6
Kulgera Australia 25°50S 133°18E 280 D1
Kulhudhuffushi Maldives 6°37N 73°3E 272 d
Kulim Malaysia 5°22N 100°34E 237 K3
Kulin Australia 32°40S 118°2E 279 F2
Kulittalai India 10°55N 78°25E 245 J4
Kulkayu = Hartley Bay Canada 53°25N 129°15W 296 C3
Kullen Sweden 56°18N 12°26E 163 H6
Kulmbach Germany 50°6N 11°26E 179 E7
Kŭlob Tajikistan 37°55N 69°50E 217 E7
Kulosaari Finland 60°11N 25°0E 121 B3
Kulp Turkey 38°29N 41°2E 213 C9
Kulpawn → Ghana 10°20N 1°5W 263 D4
Kulsary Kazakhstan 46°59N 54°1E 187 E9
Kulti India 23°43N 86°50E 243 H12
Kulturforum Berlin, Germany 115 b3
Kulu India 31°58N 77°6E 242 D7
Kulu Turkey 39°5N 33°4E 212 C5
Kulumadau Papua N. G. 9°3S 152°43E 286 E7
Kulunda Russia 52°35N 78°57E 217 B9
Kulundinskoye, Ozero Russia 53°0N 79°36E 217 B9
Kulungar Afghan. 34°0N 69°2E 242 C3
Kūlvand Iran 31°21N 54°35E 247 D7
Kulwin Australia 35°2S 142°42E 282 C5
Kulyab = Kŭlob Tajikistan 37°55N 69°50E 217 E7
Kuma Japan 33°39N 132°54E 222 D4
Kuma → Russia 44°55N 47°0E 191 H8
Kumafşarı Turkey 37°19N 29°32E 205 D11
Kumaganum Nigeria 13°8N 10°38E 263 C7
Kumagaya Japan 36°9N 139°22E 223 A11
Kumai Indonesia 2°44S 111°43E 235 C4
Kumalar Dağı Turkey 38°15N 30°20E 205 C12
Kumamba, Kepulauan Indonesia 1°36S 138°45E 231 E9
Kumamoto Japan 32°45N 130°45E 222 E2
Kumamoto □ Japan 32°55N 130°55E 222 E2
Kumano Japan 33°54N 136°5E 223 D8
Kumano-Nada Japan 33°47N 136°20E 223 D8
Kumanovo Macedonia 42°9N 21°42E 202 D5
Kumar → Afghan. 34°30N 70°28E 240 B3
Kumara N.Z. 42°37S 171°12E 285 C6
Kumarina Roadhouse Australia 24°41S 119°32E 279 D2
Kumarkhali Bangla. 23°51N 89°15E 241 D2
Kumasi Ghana 6°41N 1°38W 262 D4
Kumba Cameroon 4°36N 9°24E 263 E6
Kumbağ Turkey 40°51N 27°27E 203 F11
Kumbakonam India 10°58N 79°25E 245 J4
Kumbarilla Australia 27°15S 150°55E 281 D5
Kumbatine △ Australia 31°8S 152°35E 283 A10
Kumbhraj India 24°22N 77°3E 242 G7
Kumbia Australia 26°41S 151°39E 281 D5
Kumbo Cameroon 6°15N 10°36E 263 D7
Kumbukkan Oya → Sri Lanka 6°35N 81°40E 245 L5
Kŭmch'ŏn N. Korea 38°10N 126°29E 224 C3
Kumdah Si. Arabia 20°23N 45°5E 248 B4
Kumdok India 33°32N 78°10E 243 C8
Kume-Shima Japan 26°20N 126°47E 221 L3
Kumeny Russia 58°10N 49°47E 190 A9
Kumertau Russia 52°45N 55°57E 186 D10
Kumharsain India 31°19N 77°27E 242 D7
Kumi Uganda 1°30N 33°58E 268 B3
Kumkale Turkey 39°59N 26°11E 203 G10
Kumla Örebro, Sweden 59°8N 15°10E 162 E9
Kumla Stockholm, Sweden 59°13N 18°11E 139 B3
Kumlu Turkey 36°21N 36°27E 250 B7
Kumluca Turkey 36°22N 30°20E 205 E12
Kummerower See Germany 53°49N 12°51E 178 B8
Kumo Nigeria 10°1N 11°12E 263 C7
Kumo älv = Kokemäenjoki → Finland 61°32N 21°44E 188 B1
Kumon Bum Burma 26°30N 97°15E 241 B6
Kumotori-Yama Japan 35°51N 138°57E 223 B10
Kumta India 14°29N 74°25E 245 G2
Kumtag Shamo China 39°40N 92°0E 218 C4
Kumukahi, C. U.S.A. 19°31N 154°49W 302 D7
Kumusi → Papua N. G. 8°16S 148°13E 286 E5
Kumylzhenskaya Russia 49°51N 42°38E 190 F6
Kunágota Hungary 46°26N 21°3E 182 D6
Kunak Malaysia 4°41N 118°15E 235 B5
Kunashir, Ostrov Russia 44°0N 146°0E 215 E15
Kunchaung Burma 23°50N 96°35E 241 D6
Kunda Estonia 59°30N 26°34E 188 C4
Kunda India 25°43N 81°31E 243 G9
Kundar → Pakistan 31°56N 69°19E 242 D3
Kundelungu △ Dem. Rep. of the Congo 10°30S 27°40E 269 E2
Kundelungu Ouest △ Dem. Rep. of the Congo 9°55S 27°17E 269 D2
Kundian Pakistan 32°27N 71°28E 242 C4
Kundiawa Papua N. G. 6°2S 145°1E 286 D3
Kundla India 21°21N 71°25E 242 J4
Kundur Indonesia 3°8S 107°48E 234 C3
Kung, Ao Thailand 8°5N 98°24E 237 a
Kunga → Bangla. 21°46N 89°30E 241 E2
Kungälv Sweden 57°53N 11°59E 163 G5
Kungens kurva Sweden 59°15N 17°53E 139 B1
Kunghit I. Canada 52°6N 131°3W 296 C2
Kungkuan Taiwan 24°35N 120°44E 225 B2
Kungliao Taiwan 25°1N 121°54E 225 A3
Kungliga Slottet Stockholm, Sweden 139 b2
Kungrad = Qŭnghirot Uzbekistan 43°2N 58°50E 216 D5
Kungsängen Sweden 59°29N 17°45E 162 E11
Kungsbacka Sweden 57°30N 12°5E 163 G6
Kungsgården Sweden 60°37N 16°35E 162 D10
Kungshamn Sweden 58°22N 11°15E 163 F5
Kungshatt Sweden 59°17N 17°53E 139 B1
Kungsholmen Sweden 59°20N 18°2E 139 A2
Kungsör Sweden 59°25N 16°5E 162 E10
Kungssuliao Taiwan 24°37N 120°45E 225 B2
Kungu Dem. Rep. of the Congo 2°47N 19°12E 264 B3
Kungur Russia 57°25N 56°57E 186 C10
Kungurri Australia 21°4S 148°45E 280 K6
Kungyangon Burma 16°27N 96°20E 241 G6
Kunhar → Pakistan 34°20N 73°30E 243 B5
Kunhegyes Hungary 47°22N 20°36E 182 C5
Kunia U.S.A. 21°28N 158°4W 302 K13
Kunigami Japan 26°46N 128°12E 288 a
Kunimi-Dake Japan 32°33N 131°1E 222 E3
Kuningan Jakarta, Indonesia 6°13S 106°49E 122 B1
Kuningan Jawa Barat, Indonesia 6°59S 108°29E 235 D3
Kunisaki Japan 33°33N 131°45E 222 D3
Kunitachi Japan 35°41N 139°27E 140 A1
Kunjirap Daban Pakistan 36°52N 75°27E 240 A4
Kunlara Australia 34°54S 139°55E 282 C3
Kunlong Burma 23°20N 98°50E 228 F2
Kunlun Shan Asia 36°0N 86°30E 217 E11
Kunmadaras Hungary 47°28N 20°45E 182 C5
Kunming China 25°1N 102°41E 228 E4
Kunming Hu China 39°59N 116°13E 114 B1
Kunnamkulam India 10°38N 76°7E 245 J3
Kunów Poland 50°57N 21°17E 185 H8
Kunratice Czech Rep. 50°0N 14°28E 135 B2
Kunshan China 31°22N 120°58E 229 B13
Kunsthistorischesmuseum Vienna, Austria 142 b1
Kunszentmárton Hungary 46°50N 20°20E 182 D5
Kunszentmiklós Hungary 47°2N 19°8E 182 C4
Kuntaur Senegal 13°40N 14°48W 262 C2
Kuntsevo Russia 55°43N 37°23E 129 B2
Kunua Papua N. G. 5°46S 154°43E 286 C8
Kununurra Australia 15°40S 128°50E 278 C4
Kunwari → India 26°26N 79°11E 243 F8
Kunya-Urgench = Köneürgench Turkmenistan 42°19N 59°10E 216 D5
Künzelsau Germany 49°17N 9°42E 179 F5
Kunzulu Dem. Rep. of the Congo 3°28S 16°12E 264 C3
Kuohsing Taiwan 24°2N 120°51E 225 B2
Kuopio Finland 62°53N 27°35E 160 E22
Kupa → Croatia 45°28N 16°24E 199 C13
Kupang Indonesia 10°19S 123°39E 231 F6
Kupchino Russia 59°50N 30°23E 137 B2
Kupiano Papua N. G. 10°4S 148°14E 286 F5
Küpikipiki'ö Pt. U.S.A. 21°15N 157°47W 302 K14
Kupino Russia 54°21N 77°16E 217 B9
Kupreanof I. U.S.A. 56°50N 133°30W 296 B2
Kupres Bos.-H. 43°56N 17°15E 182 G2
Kupyansk Ukraine 49°52N 37°35E 189 H9
Kupyansk-Uzlovoi Ukraine 49°40N 37°43E 189 H9
Kuqa China 41°35N 82°30E 217 D10
Kür → Azerbaijan 39°29N 49°15E 213 C13
Kur → Bhutan 26°50N 91°0E 241 B3
Kür Dili Azerbaijan 39°3N 49°13E 213 C13
Kura = Kür → Azerbaijan 39°29N 49°15E 213 C13
Kurahashi-Jima Japan 34°8N 132°31E 222 C4
Kuranda Australia 16°48S 145°35E 280 B4
Kuranga India 22°4N 69°10E 242 H3
Kurashiki Japan 34°40N 133°50E 222 C5
Kurayn Si. Arabia 27°39N 49°50E 247 E6
Kurayoshi Japan 35°26N 133°50E 222 B5
Kurbağalı → Turkey 40°58N 29°1E 122 C2
Kūrchatov Kazakhstan 50°45N 78°32E 217 B9
Kürdämir Azerbaijan 40°25N 48°3E 191 K9
Kurdistan Asia 37°20N 43°30E 213 D10
Kurduvadi India 18°8N 75°29E 244 E2
Kŭrdzhali Bulgaria 41°38N 25°21E 203 E9
Kure Japan 34°14N 132°32E 222 C4
Küre Turkey 41°48N 33°43E 212 B5
Küre Dağları Turkey 41°50N 34°10E 212 B6
Kure I. U.S.A. 28°25N 178°25W 302 F8
Kuressaare Estonia 58°15N 22°30E 188 C2
Kurgan Russia 55°26N 65°18E 216 A7
Kurgan-Tyube = Qŭrghonteppa Tajikistan 37°50N 68°47E 217 E7
Kurganinsk Russia 44°54N 40°34E 191 H5
Kurgannaya = Kurganinsk Russia 44°54N 40°34E 191 H5
Kuri India 26°37N 70°43E 242 F4
Kuria Maria Is. = Hallāniyat, Jazā'ir al Oman 17°30N 55°58E 249 C6
Kurichchi India 11°36N 77°35E 245 J3
Kuridala Australia 21°16S 140°29E 280 C3
Kurigram Bangla. 25°49N 89°39E 241 C2
Kurihara Japan 35°45N 139°34E 140 A2
Kurikka Finland 62°36N 22°24E 160 E20
Kuril Basin Pac. Oc. 47°0N 150°0E 150 E15
Kuril Is. = Kurilskiye Ostrova Russia 45°0N 150°0E 215 E16
Kuril-Kamchatka Trench Pac. Oc. 44°0N 153°0E 288 C7
Kurilsk Russia 45°14N 147°53E 215 E15
Kurilskiye Ostrova Russia 45°0N 150°0E 215 E16
Kurino Japan 31°57N 130°43E 222 F2
Kurinskaya Kosa = Kür Dili Azerbaijan 39°3N 49°13E 213 C13
Kurisches Haff = Kurshskiy Zaliv Russia 55°9N 21°6E 184 C8
Kürkçü Turkey 36°34N 33°39E 250 B4
Kurkheda India 20°37N 80°12E 244 D5
Kurkur Egypt 23°50N 32°0E 256 C3
Kurla India 19°4N 72°52E 130 A2
Kurlovskiy Russia 55°25N 40°40E 190 C5
Kurmuk Sudan 10°33N 34°21E 257 E3
Kurmuri India 19°4N 72°53E 130 A2
Kurnool India 15°45N 78°0E 245 G4
Kuro-Shima Kagoshima, Japan 30°50N 129°57E 221 J4
Kuro-Shima Okinawa, Japan 24°14N 124°1E 221 M2
Kurobe-Gawe → Japan 36°55N 137°25E 223 A9
Kurogi Japan 33°12N 130°40E 222 D2
Kuror, J. Sudan 20°27N 31°30E 256 C3
Kurow N.Z. 44°44S 170°29E 285 E5
Kurów Poland 51°23N 22°12E 185 G9
Kurrajong Australia 33°33S 150°42E 283 B9
Kurram → Pakistan 32°36N 71°20E 242 C4
Kurri Kurri Australia 32°50S 151°28E 283 B9
Kurrimine Australia 17°47S 146°6E 280 B4
Kursavka Russia 44°29N 42°32E 191 H6
Kurse Korhi India 20°14N 80°46E 244 D5
Kürshim Kazakhstan 48°34N 83°39E 217 C10
Kurshskaya Kosa ⌓ Russia 55°7N 20°45E 184 C7
Kurshskiy Zaliv Russia 55°9N 21°6E 184 C8
Kuršių Nerijos △ Lithuania 55°30N 21°6E 184 C8
Kursk Russia 51°42N 36°11E 189 G9
Kursk □ Russia 51°50N 36°10E 189 G9
Kursu = Salla Finland 66°50N 28°49E 160 C23
Kuršumlija Serbia 43°9N 21°19E 202 C5
Kuršumlijska Banja Serbia 43°3N 21°11E 202 C5
Kurşunlu Bursa, Turkey 40°3N 29°40E 203 F13
Kurşunlu Çankırı, Turkey 40°51N 33°15E 212 B5
Kurtalan Turkey 37°56N 41°44E 213 D9
Kurtbey Turkey 41°9N 26°35E 203 E10
Kurtistown U.S.A. 19°36N 155°4W 302 D6
Kuru Sudan 7°43N 26°31E 257 F2
Kuru, Bahr el → Sudan 8°10N 26°50E 257 F2
Kurucaşile Turkey 41°49N 32°42E 212 B5
Kuruçay Turkey 39°39N 38°29E 246 B3
Kuruktag China 41°0N 89°0E 217 D11
Kuruman S. Africa 27°28S 23°28E 270 C3
Kuruman → S. Africa 26°56S 20°39E 270 C3
Kurume Fukuoka, Japan 33°15N 130°30E 222 D2
Kurume Tōkyō, Japan 35°45N 139°31E 140 A2
Kurun → Sudan 5°30N 34°17E 257 F3
Kurunegala Sri Lanka 7°30N 80°23E 245 L5
Kurupukari Guyana 4°43N 58°37W 329 C6
Kurya Russia 61°42N 57°9E 186 B10
Kuryanovo Russia 55°39N 37°42E 129 C4
Kus Gölü Turkey 40°10N 27°55E 203 F11
Kuşadası Turkey 37°52N 27°15E 212 D2
Kuşadası Körfezı Turkey 37°56N 27°0E 205 D8
Kusamba Indonesia 8°34S 115°27E 231 K18
Kusatsu Gumma, Japan 36°37N 138°36E 223 A10
Kusatsu Shiga, Japan 34°58N 135°57E 223 C7
Kusawa L. Canada 60°20N 136°13W 296 A1
Kusel Germany 49°32N 7°24E 179 F3
Kushaka Nigeria 10°32N 6°48E 263 C6
Kushalgarh India 23°10N 74°27E 242 H6
Kushalnagar India 12°14N 75°57E 245 H2
Kushchevskaya Russia 46°33N 39°35E 191 G4
Kusheriki Nigeria 10°33N 6°28E 263 C6
Kushikino Japan 31°44N 130°16E 222 F2
Kushima Japan 31°29N 131°14E 222 F3
Kushimoto Japan 33°28N 135°47E 223 D7
Kushiro Japan 43°0N 144°25E 220 C12
Kushiro-Gawa → Japan 42°59N 144°23E 220 C12
Kushiro Shitsugen △ Japan 43°9N 144°26E 220 C12
Kūshk Iran 28°46N 56°51E 247 D8
Kushka = Serhetabat Turkmenistan 35°20N 62°18E 247 C9
Kūshkī Iran 33°31N 47°13E 246 C5
Kushmurun = Qusmuryn Kazakhstan 52°27N 64°36E 216 B6
Kushnytsya Ukraine 48°27N 23°15E 183 B8
Kushol India 33°40N 76°36E 243 C7
Kushtia Bangla. 23°55N 89°5E 241 D2
Kushum → Kazakhstan 49°20N 50°30E 190 F10
Kushva Russia 58°18N 59°45E 186 C10
Kuskan Turkey 36°29N 33°17E 250 B4
Kuskokwim → U.S.A. 60°5N 162°25W 303 F7
Kuskokwim B. U.S.A. 59°45N 162°25W 303 G7
Kuskokwim Mts. U.S.A. 62°30N 156°0W 303 E9
Kuskovo Russia 55°44N 37°48E 129 B4
Kusmi India 23°17N 83°55E 243 H10
Kusŏng N. Korea 39°59N 125°15E 224 C2
Kussharo-Ko Japan 43°38N 144°21E 220 C12
Kustanay = Qostanay Kazakhstan 53°10N 63°35E 216 B6
Küstenje = Constanţa Romania 44°14N 28°38E 183 F13
Kustia India 22°31N 88°23E 124 B2
Küstrin = Kostrzyn Poland 52°35N 14°39E 185 F1
Kusu Japan 33°16N 131°9E 222 D3
Kut, Ko Thailand 11°40N 102°35E 237 G4
Kuta Indonesia 8°43S 115°11E 231 K18
Kutacane Indonesia 3°50N 97°50E 234 B1
Kütahya Turkey 39°30N 30°2E 205 B12
Kütahya □ Turkey 39°10N 29°30E 205 B11
Kutai △ Indonesia 0°23N 117°16E 235 B5
Kutaisi Georgia 42°19N 42°40E 191 J6
Kutaraja = Banda Aceh Indonesia 5°35N 95°20E 234 A1
Kutch, Gulf of = Kachchh, Gulf of India 22°50N 69°15E 242 H3
Kutch, Rann of = Kachchh, Rann of India 24°0N 70°0E 242 H4
Kutina Croatia 45°29N 16°48E 199 C13
Kutiyana India 21°36N 70°2E 242 J4
Kutjevo Croatia 45°23N 17°55E 182 E2
Kutkai Burma 23°27N 97°56E 241 D6
Kutkashen Azerbaijan 40°58N 47°47E 191 K8
Kutná Hora Czech Rep. 49°57N 15°16E 180 B8
Kutno Poland 52°15N 19°23E 185 F6
Kutru India 19°5N 80°46E 244 E5
Kutse Botswana 21°7S 22°16E 270 B3
Kutsino Russia 55°44N 37°55E 129 B5
Kuttabul Australia 21°1S 148°54E 280 K6
Kutu Dem. Rep. of the Congo 2°40S 18°11E 264 C3
Kutu Moke Dem. Rep. of the Congo 3°12S 17°21E 264 C3
Kutum Sudan 14°10N 24°40E 257 E1
Kúty Slovak Rep. 48°40N 17°3E 181 C10
Kuty Ukraine 48°16N 25°11E 183 B10
Kuujjuaq Canada 58°6N 68°15W 295 D13
Kuujjuarapik Canada 55°20N 77°35W 298 A4
Kuusamo Finland 65°57N 29°8E 160 D23
Kuusankoski Finland 60°55N 26°38E 188 B4
Kuvango Angola 14°28S 16°20E 265 E3
Kuvshinovo Russia 57°2N 34°11E 188 D8
Kuwait = Al Kuwayt Kuwait 29°30N 48°0E 246 D5
Kuwait ■ Asia 29°30N 47°30E 246 D5
Kuwana Japan 35°5N 136°43E 223 B8
Kuwana → India 26°25N 83°15E 243 F10
Kuwol-san N. Korea 38°30N 125°15E 224 C2
Kuybyshev = Samara Russia 53°8N 50°6E 190 D10
Kuybyshev Russia 55°27N 78°19E 214 D8
Kuybyshevka-Vostochnaya = Belogorsk Russia 51°0N 128°20E 215 D13
Kuybyshevo Ukraine 47°25N 36°40E 189 J9
Kuybyshevskoye Vdkhr. Russia 55°2N 49°30E 190 C9
Kuye He → China 38°23N 110°46E 226 E6
Kūyeh Iran 38°45N 47°57E 246 B5
Kuyto, Ozero Russia 65°6N 31°20E 160 D24
Kuytun China 44°25N 85°0E 217 D11
Kuyucak Turkey 37°55N 28°28E 205 D10
Kuyumba Russia 60°58N 96°59E 215 C10
Kuzey Anadolu Dağları Turkey 41°0N 36°45E 212 B7
Kuzguncuk Turkey 41°2N 29°2E 122 B2
Kuzhitturai India 8°18N 77°11E 245 K3
Kuzitrin → U.S.A. 65°10N 165°25W 303 D6
Kuzmin Serbia 45°2N 19°25E 182 E4
Kuznetsk Russia 53°12N 46°40E 190 D8
Kuznetsovo = Konakovo Russia 56°40N 36°51E 188 D9
Kuzomen Russia 66°22N 36°50E 186 A6
Kuzucubelen Turkey 36°51N 34°27E 250 B5
Kuzyminki Russia 55°42N 37°46E 129 B4
Kvænangen Norway 70°5N 21°15E 160 A19
Kværndrup Denmark 55°10N 10°31E 163 J4
Kvaløya Norway 69°40N 18°30E 160 B18
Kvam Norway 61°40N 9°42E 164 C6
Kvänum Sweden 58°18N 13°11E 163 F7
Kvareli = Qvareli Georgia 41°57N 45°47E 191 K7
Kvarner Croatia 44°50N 14°10E 199 D11
Kvarnerič Croatia 44°43N 14°37E 199 D11
Kvås Norway 58°16N 7°14E 164 F4
Kvernaland Norway 58°47N 5°45E 164 F2
Kvichak B. U.S.A. 58°48N 157°30W 303 G8
Kvicksund Sweden 59°27N 16°19E 162 E10
Kvikne Norway 62°35N 10°16E 164 B7
Kvillsfors Sweden 57°24N 15°29E 163 G9
Kvina → Norway 58°19N 6°55E 164 F3
Kvinlog Norway 58°31N 6°55E 164 F3
Kvirily = Zestaponi Georgia 42°6N 43°0E 191 J6
Kvismare kanal Sweden 59°11N 15°35E 162 E9
Kvissleby Sweden 62°18N 17°22E 162 B11
Kviteseid Norway 59°24N 8°29E 164 E5
Kvitøya Svalbard 80°8N 32°35E 154 A14
Kwabhaca S. Africa 30°51S 29°0E 271 D4
Kwai Chung China 22°22N 114°7E 122 A1
Kwajalein Marshall Is. 9°5N 167°20E 288 G8
Kwakhanai Botswana 21°39S 21°16E 270 B3
Kwakoegron Suriname 5°12N 55°25W 329 B6
Kwale Coast, Kenya 4°15S 39°31E 268 C4
Kwale Nigeria 5°46N 6°26E 263 D6
Kwamalasamutu Suriname 2°20N 56°47W 329 C6
KwaMashu S. Africa 29°45S 30°58E 271 C5
Kwamouth Dem. Rep. of the Congo 3°9S 16°12E 264 C3
Kwando → Africa 18°27S 23°32E 265 F4
Kwangchow = Guangzhou China 23°6N 113°13E 121 B2
Kwango → Dem. Rep. of the Congo 3°14S 17°22E 264 C3
Kwangsi-Chuang = Guangxi Zhuangzu Zizhiqu □ China 24°0N 109°0E 228 F7
Kwangtung = Guangdong □ China 23°0N 113°0E 229 F9
Kwara □ Nigeria 8°45N 4°30E 263 D6
Kwataboahegan → Canada 51°9N 80°50W 298 B3
Kwatisore Indonesia 3°18S 134°50E 231 E8
KwaZulu Natal □ S. Africa 29°0S 30°0E 271 C5
Kweichow = Guizhou □ China 27°0N 107°0E 228 D6
Kweilin = Guilin China 25°18N 110°15E 229 E8
Kweisui = Hohhot China 40°52N 111°40E 226 D6
Kweiyang = Guiyang China 26°32N 106°40E 228 D6
Kwekwe Zimbabwe 18°58S 29°48E 269 F2
Kwenge → Dem. Rep. of the Congo 4°50S 18°44E 265 C3
Kwethluk U.S.A. 60°49N 161°26W 303 F7
Kwidzyn Poland 53°44N 18°55E 184 E5
Kwigillingok U.S.A. 59°51N 163°8W 303 G7
Kwiha Ethiopia 13°29N 39°32E 257 E4
Kwikila Papua N. G. 9°49S 147°38E 286 E4
Kwilu → Dem. Rep. of the Congo 3°22S 17°22E 265 C3
Kwinana Australia 32°15S 115°47E 279 F2
Kwinbet Burma 16°20N 94°14E 241 G5
Kwisa → Poland 51°34N 15°24E 185 G2
Kwoka Indonesia 0°31S 132°27E 231 E8
Kwolla Nigeria 9°0N 9°15E 263 D6
Kwun Tong China 22°19N 114°13E 219 G11
Kwun Tong Hong Kong, China 22°19N 114°13E 122 B2
Kya-in-Seikkyi Burma 16°2N 98°8E 241 G7
Kyabé Chad 9°30N 19°0E 259 G3
Kyabra Cr. → Australia 25°36S 142°55E 281 D3
Kyabram Australia 36°19S 145°4E 283 D6
Kyaikkami Burma 16°4N 97°34E 241 G6
Kyaiklat Burma 16°25N 95°40E 241 G5
Kyaikmaraw Burma 16°23N 97°44E 241 G6
Kyaikthin Burma 23°32N 95°40E 241 D5
Kyaikto Burma 17°20N 97°3E 236 D1
Kyakhta Russia 50°30N 106°25E 215 D11
Kyambura ⌓ Uganda 0°7S 30°9E 268 C3
Kyan-zaki Japan 26°5N 127°39E 288 a
Kyancutta Australia 33°8S 135°33E 281 E2
Kyangin Burma 18°20N 95°20E 241 F5
Kyaukhnyat Burma 18°15N 97°31E 241 F6
Kyaukki Burma 18°27N 96°56E 241 F6
Kyaukkyi Burma 18°15N 94°29E 241 F5
Kyaukme Burma 22°32N 97°2E 241 D6
Kyaukpadaung Burma 20°52N 95°8E 241 E5
Kyaukpyu Burma 19°28N 93°30E 241 F4
Kyaukse Burma 21°36N 96°10E 241 E6
Kyauktaga Burma 18°10N 96°37E 241 F6
Kyauktan Burma 16°38N 96°19E 241 G6
Kyauktaw Burma 20°51N 92°59E 241 E4
Kyaunggon Burma 17°6N 95°11E 241 G5
Kyawkku Burma 21°48N 96°56E 241 E6
Kybartai Lithuania 54°39N 22°45E 184 D9
Kyburz U.S.A. 38°47N 120°18W 306 G6
Kyeintali Burma 18°0N 94°29E 241 G5
Kyelang India 32°35N 77°2E 242 C7
Kyenjojo Uganda 0°40N 30°37E 268 B3
Kyidaunggan Burma 19°53N 96°12E 241 F6
Kyje Czech Rep. 50°6N 14°33E 135 B3
Kyjov Czech Rep. 49°1N 17°7E 181 B10
Kyle Canada 50°50N 108°2W 297 C7
Kyle Dam Zimbabwe 20°15S 31°0E 269 G3
Kyle of Lochalsh U.K. 57°17N 5°44W 167 D3
Kyll → Germany 49°48N 6°41E 179 F2
Kyllburg Germany 50°2N 6°34E 179 E2
Kyllini Greece 37°55N 21°8E 207 D3
Kyllini, Akra Greece 37°57N 21°8E 207 D3
Kymijoki → Finland 60°30N 26°55E 188 B4
Kymmene älv = Kymijoki → Finland 60°30N 26°55E 188 B4
Kyneton Australia 37°10S 144°29E 282 D6
Kynuna Australia 21°37S 141°55E 280 C3
Kyō-ga-Saki Japan 35°45N 135°15E 223 B7
Kyoga, L. Uganda 1°35N 33°0E 268 B3
Kyogle Australia 28°40S 153°0E 281 D5
Kyom → Sudan 8°58N 28°13E 257 F2
Kyŏngju = Gyeongju S. Korea 35°51N 129°14E 224 E4
Kyŏngsŏng N. Korea 41°35N 129°36E 224 B4
Kyōto Japan 35°0N 135°45E 223 C7
Kyōto □ Japan 35°15N 135°45E 223 B7
Kyparissovouno Cyprus 35°19N 33°10E 207 E9
Kyperounda Cyprus 34°56N 32°58E 207 F8
Kypros = Cyprus ■ Asia 35°0N 33°0E 207 F9
Kyrenia Cyprus 35°20N 33°20E 207 E9
Kyrgyzstan ■ Asia 42°0N 75°0E 217 D9
Kyritz Germany 52°56N 12°24E 178 C8
Kyrkhult Sweden 56°22N 14°34E 163 H8
Kyrksæterøra Norway 63°18N 9°5E 164 A6
Kyrnasivka Ukraine 48°35N 28°58E 183 B13
Kyrnychky Ukraine 45°42N 29°4E 183 E14
Kyro älv = Kyrönjoki → Finland 63°14N 21°45E 160 E19
Kyrönjoki → Finland 63°14N 21°45E 160 E19
Kystatyam Russia 67°20N 123°10E 215 C13
Kysucké Nové Mesto Slovak Rep. 49°18N 18°47E 181 B11
Kytay, Ozero Ukraine 45°40N 29°13E 183 E14
Kythira Greece 36°8N 23°0E 204 E5
Kythréa Cyprus 35°15N 33°29E 207 E9
Kyu-hkok Burma 24°4N 98°4E 241 C7
Kyūhōji Japan 34°38N 135°33E 133 B2
Kyunhla Burma 23°25N 95°15E 241 D5
Kyuquot Sound Canada 50°2N 127°22W 296 D3
Kyurdamir = Kürdämir Azerbaijan 40°25N 48°3E 191 K9
Kyūshū Japan 33°0N 131°0E 222 E3
Kyūshū □ Japan 33°0N 131°0E 222 E3
Kyushu-Palau Ridge Pac. Oc. 20°0N 136°0E 288 E5
Kyūshū-Sanchi Japan 32°35N 131°17E 222 E3
Kyustendil Bulgaria 42°16N 22°41E 202 D6
Kyusyur Russia 70°19N 127°30E 215 B13
Kywong Australia 34°58S 146°44E 283 C7
Kyyiv Ukraine 50°30N 30°28E 177 C16
Kyyiv □ Ukraine 50°5N 30°45E 189 G6
Kyyivske Vdskh. Ukraine 51°0N 30°25E 177 C16
Kyzyl Russia 51°50N 94°30E 217 B12
Kyzyl-Adyr Kyrgyzstan 42°39N 71°35E 217 D8
Kyzyl-Burun = Siyäzän Azerbaijan 41°3N 49°10E 191 K9
Kyzyl-Khoto = Kyzyl Russia 51°50N 94°30E 217 B12
Kyzyl Kum Tajikistan 42°0N 65°0E 238 A9
Kyzyl Kum Uzbekistan 42°30N 65°0E 217 D7
Kyzyl-Kyya Kyrgyzstan 40°16N 72°8E 217 D8
Kyzyl-Orda = Qyzylorda Kazakhstan 44°48N 65°28E 217 D7
Kyzyl-Suu Kyrgyzstan 42°20N 78°0E 217 D9

L

La Albuera Spain 38°45N 6°49W 195 G4
La Alcarria Spain 40°31N 2°45W 196 E2
La Almarcha Spain 39°41N 2°24W 196 F2
La Almunia de Doña Godina Spain 41°29N 1°23W 196 D3
La Amistad △ Cent. Amer. 9°28N 83°18W 320 E3
La Asunción Venezuela 11°2N 63°53W 329 A5
La Baie Canada 48°19N 70°53W 299 C5
La Banda Argentina 27°45S 64°10W 334 B3
La Bañeza Spain 42°17N 5°54W 194 C5
La Barca Mexico 20°17N 102°34W 318 C4
La Barge U.S.A. 42°16N 110°12W 304 E8
La Bastide-Puylaurent France 44°35N 3°55E 174 D7
La Baule France 47°17N 2°24W 172 E4
La Belle Fla., U.S.A. 26°46N 81°26W 317 J8
La Belle Mo., U.S.A. 40°7N 91°55W 310 D5
La Biche → Canada 59°57N 123°50W 296 B4
La Biche, L. Canada 54°50N 112°3W 296 C6
La Bisbal d'Empordà Spain 41°58N 3°2E 196 D8
La Blanca Chile 33°30S 70°40W 137 C2
La Boca Argentina 34°38S 58°22W 117 B2
La Brea Trin. & Tob. 10°15N 61°37W 323 t
La Brède France 44°41N 0°32W 174 D3
La Bresse France 48°2N 6°53E 173 D13
La Bretèche France 48°51N 2°1E 134 A1
La Bureba Spain 42°36N 3°24W 194 C7
La Cal → Bolivia 17°27S 58°15W 331 D6
La Calera Chile 32°50S 71°10W 334 C1
La Calle = El Kala Algeria 36°53N 8°26E 261 A6
La Campana △ Chile 32°58S 71°14W 334 C1
La Campiña Lima, Peru 12°11S 77°0W 124 C2
La Campiña Spain 37°45N 4°45W 195 H6
La Canal = Sa Canal Spain 38°51N 1°23E 206 D1
La Cañiza = A Cañiza Spain 42°13N 8°16W 194 C2
La Canourgue France 44°26N 3°13E 174 D7
La Capelle France 49°59N 3°50E 173 C10
La Carlota Argentina 33°30S 63°20W 334 C3
La Carlota Phil. 10°25N 122°55E 233 F4
La Carlota Spain 37°40N 4°56W 195 H6
La Carolina Spain 38°17N 3°38W 195 G7
La Castellana Phil. 10°20N 123°3E 233 F4
La Cavalerie France 44°1N 3°10E 174 D7
La Ceiba Honduras 15°40N 86°50W 320 C2
La Ceiba Venezuela 9°28N 71°4W 328 C3
La Celle-St-Cloud France 48°50N 2°9E 134 A1
La Chaise-Dieu France 45°18N 3°42E 174 C7
La Chapelle d'Angillon France 47°21N 2°25E 173 E9
La Chapelle-St-Luc France 48°20N 4°3E 173 D11
La Chapelle-sur-Erdre France 47°18N 1°34W 172 E5
La Charité-sur-Loire France 47°10N 3°1E 173 E10
La Chartre-sur-le-Loir France 47°44N 0°34E 172 E7
La Châtaigneraie France 46°39N 0°44W 174 B3
La Châtre France 46°35N 2°0E 173 F9
La Chaux → Mauritius 20°23S 57°41E 272 e
La Chaux-de-Fonds Switz. 47°7N 6°50E 179 H2
La Chorrera Colombia 0°44S 73°1W 328 D3
La Chorrera Panama 8°53N 79°47W 320 E4
La Ciotat France 43°10N 5°37E 175 E9
La Cisterna Chile 33°32S 70°39W 137 C2
La Ciudadela Mexico City, Mexico 128 c2

La Clayette France 46°17N 4°19E 173 F11
La Cocha Argentina 27°50S 65°40W 334 B2
La Concepción = Ri-Aba Eq. Guin. 3°28N 8°40E 263 E6
La Concepción Panama 8°31N 82°37W 320 E3
La Concepción Venezuela 10°30N 71°50W 328 A3
La Concordia Mexico 16°5N 92°38W 319 D6
La Constitución, Plaza de = Zócalo Mexico City, Mexico 128 b3
La Coruña = A Coruña Spain 43°20N 8°25W 194 B2
La Coruña □ Spain 43°10N 8°30W 194 B2
La Côte-St-André France 45°24N 5°15E 175 C9
La Courneuve France 48°55N 2°22E 134 A3
La Courtine France 45°41N 2°15E 174 C6
La Crau Bouches-du-Rhône, France 43°32N 4°40E 175 E8
La Crau Var, France 43°9N 6°4E 175 E10
La Crescent U.S.A. 43°50N 91°18W 308 D8
La Crete Canada 58°11N 116°24W 296 B5
La Crosse Fla., U.S.A. 29°51N 82°24W 316 F7
La Crosse Kans., U.S.A. 38°32N 99°18W 308 F4
La Crosse Wis., U.S.A. 43°48N 91°15W 308 D8
La Cruz Costa Rica 11°4N 85°39W 320 D2
La Cruz Sinaloa, Mexico 23°55N 106°54W 318 C3
La Cumbre, Volcán Ecuador 0°21S 91°32W 330 a
La Dehesa Chile 33°21S 70°33W 137 B2
La Désirade Guadeloupe 16°18N 61°3W 322 e
La Digue Seychelles 4°20S 55°51E 272 c
La Dorada Colombia 5°30N 74°40W 328 B3
La Encantada Peru 12°13S 77°1W 124 C2
La Ensenada Chile 41°12S 72°33W 336 B2
La Esmeralda Paraguay 22°16S 62°33W 334 A3
La Esperanza Argentina 40°26S 68°32W 336 B3
La Esperanza Cuba 22°46N 83°44W 320 B3
La Esperanza Honduras 14°15N 88°10W 320 D2
La Estación Spain 40°27N 3°48W 127 B1
La Estrada = A Estrada Spain 42°43N 8°27W 194 C2
La Falaise, Gorges de Martinique 14°49N 61°10W 322 j
La Faouët France 48°2N 3°30W 172 D3
La Fayette U.S.A. 34°42N 85°17W 315 D12
La Fé Cuba 22°2N 84°15W 320 B3
La Fère France 49°39N 3°21E 173 C10
La Ferté-Bernard France 48°10N 0°40E 172 D7
La Ferté-Gaucher France 48°47N 3°19E 173 D10
La Ferté-Macé France 48°35N 0°22W 172 D6
La Ferté-St-Aubin France 47°42N 1°57E 173 E8
La Ferté-sous-Jouarre France 48°56N 3°8E 173 D10
La Ferté-Vidame France 48°37N 0°53E 172 D7
La Flèche France 47°42N 0°4W 172 E6
La Floresta Spain 41°26N 2°3E 114 A1
La Florida Chile 33°33S 70°34W 137 C2
La Foa N. Cal. 21°43S 165°50E 288 d
La Follette U.S.A. 36°23N 84°7W 315 C12
La Fontaine U.S.A. 40°40N 85°43W 311 D11
La Fortuna Spain 40°21N 3°46W 127 B1
La Fransa Spain 41°22N 2°9E 114 A1
La Fregeneda Spain 40°58N 6°54W 194 E4
La Fría Venezuela 8°13N 72°15W 328 B3
La Fuente de San Esteban Spain 40°49N 6°15W 194 E4
La Gacilly France 47°45N 2°8W 172 E4
La Garenne-Colombes France 48°54N 2°15E 134 A2
La Gineta Spain 39°8N 2°1W 197 F2
La Giustiniana Italy 41°59N 12°24E 136 B1
La Gloria Colombia 8°37N 73°48W 328 B3
La Goulette = Halq el Oued Tunisia 36°53N 10°18E 258 A2
La Gran Sabana Venezuela 5°30N 61°30W 329 B5
La Grand'Combe France 44°13N 4°2E 175 D8
La Grande U.S.A. 45°20N 118°5W 304 D4
La Grande → Canada 53°50N 79°0W 298 B5
La Grande Deux, Rés. Canada 53°40N 76°55W 298 B4
La Grande-Motte France 43°23N 4°5E 175 E8
La Grande Quatre, Rés. Canada 54°0N 73°15W 298 B5
La Grande Trois, Rés. Canada 53°40N 75°10W 298 B4
La Grange Calif., U.S.A. 37°42N 120°27W 306 H6
La Grange Ga., U.S.A. 33°2N 85°2W 316 B4
La Grange Ill., U.S.A. 41°48N 87°53W 119 C1
La Grange Ky., U.S.A. 38°24N 85°22W 311 F11
La Grange Mo., U.S.A. 40°3N 91°35W 310 D5
La Grange Tex., U.S.A. 29°54N 96°52W 314 G6
La Grange Park U.S.A. 41°49N 87°51W 119 C1
La Granja Chile 33°31S 70°38W 137 C2
La Grave France 45°3N 6°18E 175 C10
La Grita Venezuela 8°8N 71°59W 328 B3
La Guaira Venezuela 10°36N 66°56W 328 A4
La Guardia = A Guarda Spain 41°56N 8°52W 194 D2
La Guardia, New York ✈ (LGA) U.S.A. 40°46N 73°52W 132 B2
La Gudiña = A Gudiña Spain 42°4N 7°8W 194 C3
La Güera Mauritania 20°51N 17°0W 260 D1
La Guerche-de-Bretagne France 47°57N 1°16W 172 E5
La Guerche-sur-l'Aubois France 46°58N 2°56E 173 F9
La Habana Cuba 23°8N 82°22W 320 B3
La Harpe U.S.A. 40°35N 90°58W 310 D6
La Haute Vallée de Chevreuse ⌓ France 48°35N 1°58E 173 D8
La Haye-du-Puits France 49°17N 1°33W 172 C5
La Horqueta Venezuela 7°55N 60°20W 329 B5
La Horra Spain 41°44N 3°53W 194 D7
La Hulpe Belgium 50°43N 4°30E 116 B2
La Independencia Mexico 16°15N 92°1W 319 D6
La Isabela Dom. Rep. 19°58N 71°2W 321 C5
La Jonquera Spain 42°25N 2°53E 196 C7
La Joya Peru 16°43S 71°52W 330 D3
La Junta U.S.A. 37°59N 103°33W 304 H12
La Laguna Canary Is. 28°28N 16°18W 153 e1
La Lézarde → Martinique 14°35N 61°1W 322 j
La Libertad = Puerto Libertad Mexico 29°55N 112°43W 318 B2
La Libertad Guatemala 16°47N 90°7W 320 C1
La Libertad □ Peru 8°0S 78°30W 330 B2
La Ligua Chile 32°30S 71°16W 334 C1
La Línea de la Concepción Spain 36°15N 5°23W 195 J5
La Llacuna Spain 41°24N 2°12E 114 A2
La Loche Canada 56°29N 109°26W 297 B7
La Loma Mexico 19°31N 99°11W 128 A1
La Londe-les-Maures France 43°8N 6°14E 175 E10
La Lora Spain 42°45N 4°0W 194 C7
La Loupe France 48°29N 1°0E 172 D8
La Louvière Belgium 50°27N 4°10E 170 D4
La Lucila Argentina 34°30S 58°29W 117 B2
La Lune Trin. & Tob. 10°3N 61°22W 323 t
La Machine France 46°54N 3°27E 173 F10
La Maddalena Italy 41°13N 9°24E 200 A2
La Maladrerie France 48°54N 2°1E 134 A1
La Malbaie Canada 47°40N 70°10W 299 C5
La Malinche △ Mexico 19°15N 98°3W 319 D5
La Mancha Spain 39°10N 2°54W 197 F2
La Manche → Martinique 14°33N 61°0W 322 j
La Mariña Spain 43°30N 7°40W 194 B3
La Martre, L. Canada 63°15N 117°55W 296 A5
La Mesa Baja Calif., Mexico 32°30N 116°57W 307 N10
La Mesa Calif., U.S.A. 32°46N 117°1W 307 N9
La Mesilla U.S.A. 32°16N 106°48W 305 K10
La Milla, Cerro Peru 12°2S 77°5W 124 B2
La Misión Mexico 32°6N 116°53W 318 A1
La Moille U.S.A. 41°32N 89°17W 310 C7
La Moine → U.S.A. 39°59N 90°31W 310 E6
La Monachina Italy 41°53N 12°21E 136 B1
La Montagne Réunion 20°53S 55°26E 272 f
La Monte U.S.A. 38°46N 93°26W 310 F3
La Moraleja Spain 40°30N 3°38W 127 A2
La Mothe-Achard France 46°37N 1°40W 172 F5
La Motte-Chalançon France 44°30N 5°21E 175 D9
La Motte-du-Caire France 44°20N 6°3E 175 D10
La Motte-Servolex France 45°35N 5°53E 175 C9
La Moure U.S.A. 46°21N 98°18W 308 B4
La Moustique → Guadeloupe 16°10N 61°34W 322 e
La Muela Spain 41°36N 1°7W 196 D3
La Mure France 44°55N 5°48E 175 D9
La Negra Chile 23°46S 70°18W 334 A1
La Nopalera Mexico 19°18N 99°5W 128 C2
La Oliva Canary Is. 28°36N 13°57W 153 e2
La Oraya Peru 11°32S 75°54W 330 C2
La Orotava Canary Is. 28°22N 16°31W 153 e1
La Oroya Peru 11°32S 75°54W 330 C2
La Pacaudière France 46°11N 3°52E 173 F10
La Pagerie Martinique 14°32N 61°3W 322 j
La Palma Canary Is. 28°40N 17°50W 153 e1
La Palma Panama 8°15N 78°0W 320 E4
La Palma del Condado Spain 37°21N 6°38W 195 H4
La Paloma Chile 30°35S 71°0W 334 C1
La Pampa □ Argentina 36°50S 66°0W 334 D2
La Paragua Venezuela 6°50N 63°20W 329 B5
La Pastora Trin. & Tob. 10°42N 61°19W 323 t
La Paternal Argentina 34°35S 58°26W 117 B2
La Paya △ Colombia 0°0 75°5W 328 C2
La Paz Entre Ríos, Argentina 30°50S 59°45W 334 C4
La Paz San Luis, Argentina 33°30S 67°20W 334 C2
La Paz Bolivia 16°20S 68°10W 330 D4
La Paz Honduras 14°20N 87°47W 320 D2
La Paz Baja Calif. S., Mexico 24°10N 110°18W 318 C2
La Paz Abra, Phil. 17°40N 120°41E 232 C3
La Paz Tarlac, Phil. 15°26N 120°45E 232 D3
La Paz □ Bolivia 15°30S 68°0W 330 D4
La Paz Centro Nic. 12°20N 86°41W 320 D2
La Pedrera Colombia 1°18S 69°43W 328 D4
La Pérade Canada 46°35N 72°12W 299 C5
La Perla Chihuahua, Mexico 28°18N 104°32W 318 B4
La Perla Lima, Peru 12°4S 77°7W 124 B2
La Perouse Australia 33°59S 151°14E 139 B2
La Perouse, Bahia Chile 27°5S 109°18W 330 b
La Perouse Str. Asia 45°40N 142°0E 220 B11
La Pesca Mexico 23°46N 97°47W 319 C5
La Piedad Mexico 20°21N 102°0W 318 C4
La Pine U.S.A. 43°40N 121°30W 304 E3
La Pineda Spain 41°15N 2°1E 114 B1
La Pisana Italy 41°51N 12°23E 136 B1
La Plaine Dominica 15°20N 61°15W 323 k
La Plaine des Cafres Réunion 21°13S 55°33E 272 f
La Plaine des Palmistes Réunion 21°7S 55°38E 272 f
La Plata Argentina 35°0S 57°55W 334 D4
La Plata Colombia 2°23N 75°53W 328 C2
La Plata Mo., U.S.A. 40°2N 92°29W 310 D4
La Plata, L. Argentina 44°55S 71°50W 336 B2
La Pobla de Lillet Spain 42°16N 1°59E 196 C6
La Pocatière Canada 47°22N 70°2W 299 C5
La Pola de Gordón Spain 42°51N 5°41W 194 C5
La Porta France 42°25N 9°21E 175 F13
La Porte U.S.A. 29°40N 95°1W 314 G7
La Porte City U.S.A. 42°19N 92°12W 310 B4
La Possession Réunion 20°55S 55°20E 272 f
La Prairie Canada 45°25N 73°29W 130 B3
La Presanella Italy 46°13N 10°40E 198 B7
La Puebla = Sa Pobla Spain 39°46N 3°1E 206 B4
La Puebla de Cazalla Spain 37°10N 5°20W 195 H5
La Puebla de los Infantes Spain 37°47N 5°24W 195 H5
La Puebla de Montalbán Spain 39°52N 4°22W 194 F6
La Puebla del Río Spain 37°16N 6°3W 195 H4
La Puerta de Segura Spain 38°22N 2°45W 195 G8
La Punta Peru 12°4S 77°10W 124 B1
La Puntigala Spain 41°27N 2°13E 114 A2
La Purísima Mexico 26°10N 112°4W 318 B2
La Push U.S.A. 47°55N 124°38W 306 C2
La Queue-en-Brie France 48°47N 2°34E 134 B4
La Quiaca Argentina 22°5S 65°35W 334 A2
La Reina Chile 33°26S 70°33W 137 B2
La Réole France 44°35N 0°1W 174 D3
La Republica, Plaza de Mexico City, Mexico 128 b1
La Restinga Canary Is. 27°38N 17°59W 153 e1
La Ribera Spain 41°21N 2°4E 114 A1
La Rioja Argentina 29°20S 67°0W 334 B2
La Rioja □ Argentina 29°30S 67°0W 334 B2
La Rioja □ Spain 42°20N 2°20W 196 C2
La Rivière des Pluies Réunion 20°54S 55°31E 272 f
La Robla Spain 42°50N 5°41W 194 C5
La Roche N. Cal. 21°26S 168°2E 288 d
La Roche-Bernard France 47°31N 2°19W 172 E4
La Roche-Canillac France 45°12N 1°57E 174 C5
La Roche-en-Ardenne Belgium 50°11N 5°35E 170 D5
La Roche-sur-Foron France 46°4N 6°19E 173 F13
La Roche-sur-Yon France 46°40N 1°25W 172 F5
La Rochefoucauld France 45°44N 0°24E 174 C4
La Rochelle France 46°10N 1°9W 174 B2
La Roda Spain 39°13N 2°15W 197 F2
La Roda de Andalucía Spain 37°12N 4°46W 195 H6
La Romaine Canada 50°13N 60°40W 299 B7
La Romana Dom. Rep. 18°27N 68°57W 321 C6
La Ronge Canada 55°5N 105°20W 297 B7
La Rue U.S.A. 40°35N 83°23W 311 D13
La Rumorosa Mexico 32°34N 116°6W 307 N10
La Sabina = Sa Savina Spain 38°44N 1°25E 206 D1
La Sagra Spain 37°57N 2°35W 197 H2
La Sagrera Spain 41°25N 2°11E 114 A2
La Salada Argentina 34°43S 58°28W 117 C2
La Saline Réunion 21°4S 55°16E 272 f
La Salle U.S.A. 41°20N 89°6W 310 C7
La Sanabria Spain 42°0N 6°30W 194 C4
La Santa Canary Is. 29°5N 13°40W 153 e2
La Sarre Canada 48°45N 79°15W 298 C4
La Scala Italy 45°28N 9°11E 129 B2
La Scie Canada 49°57N 55°36W 299 C8
La Selva Spain 42°0N 2°45E 196 C7
La Selva Beach U.S.A. 36°56N 121°51W 306 J5
La Selva del Camp Spain 41°13N 1°8E 196 D6
La Serena Chile 29°55S 71°10W 334 B1
La Serena Spain 38°45N 5°40W 195 G5
La Seu d'Urgell Spain 42°22N 1°23E 196 C6
La Seyne-sur-Mer France 43°7N 5°52E 175 E9
La Sila Italy 39°15N 16°35E 201 C9
La Solana Spain 38°59N 3°14W 195 G7
La Soufrière St. Vincent 13°20N 61°11W 323 n
La Souterraine France 46°15N 1°30E 173 F8
La Spézia Italy 44°7N 9°50E 198 D6
La Storta Italy 41°59N 12°20E 136 A1
La Suze-sur-Sarthe France 47°53N 0°2E 172 E7
La Tagua Colombia 0°3N 74°40W 328 C3
La Taxonera Spain 41°25N 2°10E 114 A2
La Teste-de-Buch France 44°37N 1°8W 174 D2
La Tortuga Venezuela 11°0N 65°22W 329 A4
La Tour-du-Pin France 45°33N 5°27E 175 C9
La Tranche-sur-Mer France 46°20N 1°27W 172 F5
La Tremblade France 45°46N 1°8W 174 C2
La Trinidad Phil. 16°28N 120°35E 232 C3
La Trinité Martinique 14°43N 60°58W 322 j
La Tuque Canada 47°30N 72°50W 298 C5
La Unión Chile 40°10S 73°0W 336 B2
La Unión Colombia 1°35N 77°5W 328 C2
La Unión El Salv. 13°20N 87°50W 320 D2
La Unión Guerrero, Mexico 17°58N 101°49W 318 D4
La Unión Peru 9°43S 76°45W 330 B2
La Unión Spain 37°38N 0°53W 197 H4
La Union □ Phil. 16°30N 120°25E 232 C3
La Urbana Venezuela 7°8N 66°56W 328 B4
La Vache B. Trin. & Tob. 10°45N 61°29W 323 t
La Vache Pt. Trin. & Tob. 10°47N 61°28W 323 t
La Vall d'Uixó Spain 39°49N 0°15W 196 F4
La Vecilla de Curveño Spain 42°51N 5°27W 194 C5
La Vega Dom. Rep. 19°20N 70°30W 321 C5
La Vega Peru 10°41S 77°44W 330 C2
La Vela de Coro Venezuela 11°27N 69°34W 328 A4
La Veleta Spain 37°1N 3°22W 195 H7
La Venta Mexico 18°5N 94°3W 319 D6
La Venturosa Colombia 6°8N 68°48W 328 B4
La Vergne U.S.A. 36°1N 86°35W 315 C11
La Veronica Trin. & Tob. 10°42N 61°21W 323 t
La Victoria Lima, Peru 12°3S 77°2W 124 B2
La Victoria Venezuela 10°14N 67°20W 328 A4
La Voulte-sur-Rhône France 44°48N 4°46E 175 D8
Laa an der Thaya Austria 48°43N 16°23E 181 C9
Laaber, Grosse → Germany 48°55N 12°30E 179 G8
Laage Germany 53°55N 12°21E 178 B8
Laajalahti Finland 60°11N 24°48E 121 B1
Laajasalo Finland 60°10N 25°1E 121 B3
Laaksolahti Finland 60°14N 24°45E 121 B1
Laas Caanood = Las Anod Somali Rep. 8°26N 47°19E 267 C6
Laatzen Germany 52°19N 9°48E 178 C5
Lä'au Pt. U.S.A. 21°6N 157°19W 302 B4
Laba → Russia 45°11N 39°42E 191 H4
Laban Burma 25°52N 96°40E 241 C6
Labasa Fiji 16°30S 179°27E 287 A2
Labason Phil. 8°4N 122°31E 233 G4
Labastide-Murat France 44°39N 1°33E 174 D5
Labastide-Rouairoux France 43°28N 2°39E 174 E6
Labbézenga Mali 15°2N 0°48E 263 B5
Labdah = Leptis Magna Libya 32°40N 14°12E 258 B2
Labe = Elbe → Europe 53°50N 9°0E 178 B4
Labé Guinea 11°24N 12°16W 262 C2
Laberge, L. Canada 61°11N 135°12W 296 A1
Labes = Łobez Poland 53°38N 15°39E 184 E2
Labian, Tanjong Malaysia 5°9N 119°13E 235 A5
Labiau = Polessk Russia 54°50N 21°8E 184 D8
Labig Pt. = Iligan Pt. Phil. 18°25N 122°25E 232 B4
Labin Croatia 45°5N 14°8E 199 C11
Labinsk Russia 44°40N 40°48E 191 H5
Labis Malaysia 2°22N 103°2E 237 L4
Łabiszyn Poland 52°57N 17°54E 185 F4
Lablâba, W. el → Egypt 30°1N 31°19E 117 A2
Labo Phil. 14°9N 122°51E 232 D4
Laboe Germany 54°24N 10°13E 178 A6
Laboka Gabon 0°19N 11°32E 264 B2
Laborec → Slovak Rep. 48°37N 21°58E 181 C14
Laborie St. Lucia 13°45N 61°2W 323 m
Labouheyre France 44°13N 0°55W 174 D3
Laboulaye Argentina 34°10S 63°30W 334 C3
Labrador Canada 53°20N 61°0W 299 B7
Labrador City Canada 52°57N 66°55W 299 B6
Labrador Sea Atl. Oc. 57°0N 54°0W 295 D14
Lábrea Brazil 7°15S 64°51W 331 B5
Labruguière France 43°31N 2°16E 174 E6
Labuan Malaysia 5°20N 115°14E 235 A5
Labuan, Pulau Malaysia 5°21N 115°13E 235 A5
Labuha Indonesia 0°30S 127°30E 231 E7
Labuhan Indonesia 6°22S 105°50E 234 D3
Labuhanbajo Indonesia 8°28S 119°54E 231 F6
Labuk, Telok Malaysia 6°10N 117°50E 235 A5
Labutta Burma 16°9N 94°46E 241 G5
Labyrinth, L. Australia 30°40S 135°11E 281 E2
Labytnangi Russia 66°39N 66°21E 214 C7
Laç Albania 41°38N 19°43E 202 E3
Lac □ Chad 13°30N 14°30E 259 F2
Lac Bay Neth. Ant. 12°6N 68°13W 322 h
Lac-Bouchette Canada 48°16N 72°11W 299 C5
Lac Édouard Canada 47°40N 72°16W 298 C5
Lac La Biche Canada 54°45N 111°58W 296 C6
Lac la Martre = Wha Ti Canada 63°8N 117°16W 294 C8
Lac La Ronge ⌓ Canada 55°9N 104°41W 297 B7
Lac-Mégantic Canada 45°35N 70°53W 299 C5
Lac Thien Vietnam 12°25N 108°11E 236 F7
Lacanau France 44°58N 1°5W 174 D2
Lacanau, Étang de France 44°58N 1°7W 174 D2
Lacantún → Mexico 16°36N 90°39W 319 D6
Lacara → Spain 38°55N 6°25W 195 G4
Lacaune France 43°43N 2°40E 174 E6
Lacaune, Mts. de France 43°43N 2°50E 174 E6
Laccadive Is. = Lakshadweep Is. India 10°0N 72°30E 245 J1
Lacepede B. Australia 36°40S 139°40E 282 D3
Lacepede Is. Australia 16°55S 122°0E 278 C3
Lacerdónia Mozam. 18°3S 35°35E 269 F4
Lacey U.S.A. 47°7N 122°49W 306 C4
Lachania Greece 35°58N 27°54E 206 F11
Lachay, Pta. Peru 11°17S 77°44W 330 C2
Lachen India 27°46N 88°36E 241 B2
Lachhmangarh India 27°50N 75°4E 242 F6
Lachi Pakistan 33°25N 71°20E 242 C4
Lachia Taiwan 22°43N 120°53E 225 D2
Lachine Canada 45°26N 73°42W 130 B1
Lachine, Canal de Canada 45°26N 73°38W 130 B2
Lachlan → Australia 34°22S 143°55E 282 C5
Lachoc Peru 12°50S 75°6W 330 C2
Lachute Canada 45°39N 74°21W 298 C5
Lackagh Hills Ireland 54°16N 8°10W 166 B3
Lackawanna U.S.A. 42°50N 78°50W 312 D6
Lackawaxen U.S.A. 41°29N 74°59W 313 E10
Lacolle Canada 45°5N 73°22W 313 A11
Lacombe Canada 52°30N 113°44W 296 C6
Lacon U.S.A. 41°2N 89°24W 310 C7
Lacona Iowa, U.S.A. 41°12N 93°23W 310 C3
Lacona N.Y., U.S.A. 43°39N 76°10W 313 C8
Láconi Italy 39°54N 9°4E 200 C2
Laconia U.S.A. 43°32N 71°28W 313 C13
Lacoochee U.S.A. 28°28N 82°11W 317 G7
Lacq France 43°25N 0°35W 174 E3
Lacre Punt Neth. Ant. 12°1N 68°14W 322 h
Lad Phrao Thailand 13°47N 100°35E 113 B2
Ladakh Ra. India 34°0N 78°0E 243 C8
Ladário Brazil 19°1S 57°35W 331 D6
Ladd U.S.A. 41°23N 89°13W 310 C7
Laddonia U.S.A. 39°15N 91°39W 310 E5
Lądek-Zdrój Poland 50°21N 16°53E 185 H3
Ladera Heights U.S.A. 33°59N 118°22W 126 C2
Ladik Turkey 40°57N 35°58E 212 B6
Ladismith S. Africa 33°28S 21°15E 270 D3
Ladíspoli Italy 41°56N 12°5E 199 G9
Lādīz Iran 28°55N 61°15E 247 D9
Ladnun India 27°38N 74°25E 242 F6
Ladoga, L. = Ladozhskoye Ozero Russia 61°15N 30°30E 188 B6
Ladonas → Greece 37°40N 21°50E 204 D3
Ladozhskoye Ozero Russia 61°15N 30°30E 188 B6
Ladrillero, G. Chile 49°20S 75°35W 336 C1
Ladson U.S.A. 32°59N 80°6W 316 C9
Ladushkin Russia 54°34N 20°10E 184 D7
Ládví Czech Rep. 50°8N 14°27E 135 B2
Lady Poland 52°8N 20°57E 142 C1
Lady Elliott I. Australia 24°7S 152°42E 280 C5
Lady Grey S. Africa 30°43S 27°13E 270 D4
Lady Lake U.S.A. 28°55N 81°55W 317 G8
Ladybrand S. Africa 29°9S 27°29E 270 C4
Ladysmith B.C., Canada 49°0N 123°49W 306 B3
Ladysmith KwaZulu Natal, S. Africa 28°32S 29°46E 271 C4
Ladysmith Wis., U.S.A. 45°28N 91°12W 308 C8
Ladyzhyn Ukraine 48°40N 29°15E 183 B14
Lae Papua N. G. 6°40S 147°2E 286 D4
Lae 'o Kākā U.S.A. 20°31N 156°33W 302 C5
Lae 'o Kealaikahiki U.S.A. 20°32N 156°42W 302 C5
Laem Hin Khom Thailand 9°25N 99°56E 237 b
Laem Khat Thailand 8°6N 98°26E 237 a
Laem Nga Thailand 7°55N 98°27E 237 a
Laem Ngop Thailand 12°10N 102°26E 237 F4
Laem Phan Wa Thailand 7°47N 98°25E 237 a
Laem Pho Thailand 6°55N 101°19E 237 J3
Laem Phrom Thep Thailand 7°45N 98°19E 237 a
Laem Riang Thailand 8°7N 98°27E 237 a
Laem Sam Rong Thailand 9°35N 100°4E 237 b
Laem Son Thailand 7°59N 98°16E 237 a
Laem Yamu Thailand 7°59N 98°26E 237 a
Lærdalsøyri Norway 61°6N 7°28E 164 C4
Laerma Greece 36°9N 27°57E 206 E11
Læsø Denmark 57°15N 11°5E 163 G5
Læsø Rende Denmark 57°20N 10°45E 163 G4
Lafayette Ala., U.S.A. 32°54N 85°24W 316 C4
Lafayette Ind., U.S.A. 40°25N 86°54W 311 D10
Lafayette La., U.S.A. 30°14N 92°1W 314 F8
Lafayette Tenn., U.S.A. 36°31N 86°2W 315 C11
Lafayette Park San Francisco, U.S.A. 136 b1
Lafayette Square New Orleans, U.S.A. 131 b2
Laferte → Canada 61°53N 117°44W 296 A5
Lafia Nigeria 8°30N 8°34E 263 D6
Lafiagi Nigeria 8°52N 5°20E 263 D6
Lafkos Greece 39°9N 23°14E 204 B5
Lafleche Canada 49°45N 106°40W 297 D7
Lafon Sudan 5°5N 32°29E 257 F3
Lafontaine Montréal, Canada 130 a1
Lafontaine, Parc Canada 45°33N 73°34W 130 A2
Laful India 7°10N 93°52E 245 L11
Lagaip → Papua N. G. 5°4S 142°52E 286 C2
Lagan = Kaspiyskiy Russia 45°22N 47°23E 191 H8
Lagan Sweden 56°56N 13°58E 163 H7
Lagan → Sweden 56°30N 12°58E 163 H6
Lagan → Antrim, U.K. 54°36N 5°55W 166 B6
Lagana, Kolpas Greece 37°42N 20°53E 207 D2
Laganas Greece 37°44N 20°53E 207 D2
Lagangilang Phil. 17°37N 120°44E 232 C3
Lagarfljót → Iceland 65°40N 14°18W 155 B12
Lagarto Brazil 10°54S 37°41W 332 D4
Lagawe Phil. 16°49N 121°6E 232 C3
Lagdo, Rés. de Cameroon 8°40N 14°0E 264 A2
Lage Germany 51°59N 8°48E 178 D4
Lågen → Oppland, Norway 61°8N 10°25E 164 C7
Lågen → Vestfold, Norway 59°3N 10°3E 164 E7
Lägerdorf Germany 53°53N 9°34E 178 B5
Laggan = Lake Louise Canada 51°30N 116°10W 296 C5
Lagh Badana △ Somali Rep. 1°16S 41°49E 267 E5
Laghmān □ Afghan. 34°20N 70°0E 242 B4
Laghouat Algeria 33°50N 2°59E 261 B5
Laghouat □ Algeria 33°35N 2°40E 261 B5
Lagnieu France 45°55N 5°20E 175 C9
Lagny-sur-Marne France 48°52N 2°44E 173 D9
Lago = Niassa □ Mozam. 13°30S 36°0E 269 E4
Lago Italy 39°10N 16°9E 201 C9
Lago de Sanabria y Entorno ⌓ Spain 42°9N 6°45W 194 C4
Lago Posadas Argentina 47°30S 71°40W 336 C2
Lago Puelo △ Argentina 42°30S 71°55W 336 B2
Lago Ranco Chile 40°19S 72°30W 336 B2
Lagoa Azores 37°45N 25°20W 153 d3
Lagoa Rio de J., Brazil 22°58S 43°11W 135 B1
Lagôa Portugal 37°8N 8°27W 195 H2
Lagoa do Peixe △ Brazil 31°12S 50°55W 335 C5
Lagoa Vermelha Brazil 28°13S 51°32W 335 B5
Lagoaça Portugal 41°11N 6°44W 194 D4
Lagodekhi Georgia 41°50N 46°22E 191 K8
Lagona = Laguna Beach U.S.A. 33°33N 117°47W 307 M9
Lagónegro Italy 40°8N 15°45E 201 B8
Lagonoy G. Phil. 13°35N 123°50E 232 E4
Lagos Angola 16°3S 16°35E 265 F3
Lagos Greece 41°1N 25°6E 203 E9
Lagos Nigeria 6°25N 3°27E 263 D5
Lagos Portugal 37°5N 8°41W 195 H2
Lagos □ Nigeria 6°28N 3°25E 263 D5
Lagos de Moreno Mexico 21°21N 101°55W 318 C4
Lagos Harbour Nigeria 6°26N 3°23E 124 B2
Lagos-Ikeja ✈ (LOS) Nigeria 6°34N 3°19E 124 A1
Lagos Island Nigeria 6°26N 3°23E 124 B2
Lagos Lagoon Nigeria 6°30N 3°28E 124 B2
Lagrange = Bidyadanga Australia 18°45S 121°43E 278 C3
Lagrange U.S.A. 41°39N 85°25W 311 C11
Lagrange B. Australia 18°38S 121°42E 278 C3
Laguardia Spain 42°33N 2°35W 196 C2
Laguépie France 44°8N 1°57E 174 D5
Lagún Neth. Ant. 12°19N 69°10W 322 g
Laguna = Padilla Bolivia 19°19S 64°20W 331 D5
Laguna Brazil 28°30S 48°50W 335 B6
Laguna N. Mex., U.S.A. 35°2N 107°25W 305 J10
Laguna □ Phil. 14°10N 121°20E 232 D3
Laguna, Sa. de la Mexico 23°35N 109°55W 318 C3
Laguna Beach U.S.A. 33°33N 117°47W 307 M9
Laguna Blanca △ Argentina 39°0S 70°5W 336 A2
Laguna de B. Phil. 14°29N 121°6E 127 C2
Laguna de Duera Spain 41°35N 4°43W 194 D6
Laguna de Tacarigua △ Venezuela 10°59N 64°7W 328 A4
Laguna del Laja △ Chile 37°27S 71°20W 334 D1
Laguna del Tigre △ Guatemala 17°32N 90°56W 320 C1
Laguna Limpia Argentina 26°32S 59°45W 334 B4
Laguna San Rafael △ Chile 46°54S 73°31W 336 C2
Lagunas Chile 21°0S 69°45W 334 A2
Lagunas Peru 5°10S 75°35W 330 B2
Lagunas de Chacahua △ Mexico 16°0N 97°43W 319 D5
Lagunas de Montebello △ Mexico 16°4N 91°42W 319 D6
Lagunas de Ruidera ⌓ Spain 38°57N 2°52W 197 G2
Lagunillas Bolivia 19°38S 63°43W 331 D5
Lahad Datu Malaysia 5°0N 118°20E 235 A5
Lahad Datu, Telok Malaysia 4°50N 118°20E 235 B5
Lahaina U.S.A. 20°53N 156°41W 302 C5
Lahan Sai Thailand 14°25N 102°52E 236 E4
Lahanam Laos 16°16N 105°16E 236 D5
Lahar India 26°12N 78°57E 243 F8
Laharpur India 27°43N 80°56E 243 F9
Lahat Indonesia 3°45S 103°30E 234 C2
Lahe Burma 26°20N 95°26E 241 B5
Lahewa Indonesia 1°22N 97°12E 234 B1
Laḥij Yemen 13°4N 44°53E 248 D4
Lāhījān Iran 37°10N 50°6E 247 B6
Lahilahi Pt. U.S.A. 21°28N 158°13W 302 K13
Lähn = Wleń Poland 51°2N 15°39E 185 G2
Lahn → Germany 50°19N 7°37E 179 E3
Lahnstein Germany 50°19N 7°37E 179 E3
Laholm Sweden 56°30N 13°2E 163 H7
Laholmsbukten Sweden 56°30N 12°45E 163 H6
Lahore Pakistan 31°32N 74°22E 242 D6
Lahpongsel Burma 27°7N 98°25E 241 B7
Lahr Germany 48°20N 7°53E 179 G3
Lahri Pakistan 29°11N 68°13E 242 E3
Lahti Finland 60°58N 25°40E 188 B3
Lahtis = Lahti Finland 60°58N 25°40E 188 B3
Lahugala Kitulana △ Sri Lanka 6°50N 81°40E 245 L5
Laï Chad 9°25N 16°18E 259 G3
Lai Chau Vietnam 22°5N 103°3E 228 F4
Lai-hka Burma 21°16N 97°40E 241 E6
Laiagam Papua N. G. 5°33S 143°30E 286 C2
Lai'an China 32°28N 118°30E 229 A12
Laibach = Ljubljana Slovenia 46°4N 14°33E 199 B11
Laibin China 23°42N 109°14E 228 F7
Lā'ie U.S.A. 21°39N 157°56W 302 J14
Laifeng China 29°27N 109°20E 228 C7
L'Aigle France 48°46N 0°38E 172 D7
Laignes France 47°50N 4°20E 173 E11
L'Aiguillon-sur-Mer France 46°20N 1°18W 174 B2
Laila = Layla Si. Arabia 22°10N 46°40E 248 B4
Laim Germany 48°7N 11°30E 131 B2
Laimbach Italy 45°34N 9°1E 129 A1
Lainate Italy 45°34N 9°1E 129 A1
Laingsburg S. Africa 33°9S 20°52E 270 D3
Lainioälven → Sweden 67°35N 22°40E 160 C20
Lainz Austria 48°10N 16°16E 142 B1
Lair U.K. 58°2N 4°24W 167 C4
Laïri, B. de Chad 12°28N 16°45E 259 F3
Lais Phil. 6°20N 125°39E 233 H5
Laisamis Kenya 1°36N 37°48E 268 B4
Laishui China 39°23N 115°45E 226 E8
Laissac France 44°23N 2°50E 174 D6
Láives Italy 46°26N 11°20E 199 B8
Laiwu China 36°15N 117°40E 227 F9
Laixi China 36°50N 120°31E 227 F11
Laiyang China 36°59N 120°45E 227 F11
Laiyuan China 39°20N 114°40E 226 E8
Laizhou China 37°8N 119°57E 227 F10
Laizhou Wan China 37°30N 119°30E 227 F10
Laja → Mexico 20°55N 100°46W 318 C4
Lajamanu Australia 18°23S 130°38E 278 C5
Lajeado = Guiratinga Brazil 16°21S 53°45W 331 D7
Lajedo Azores 39°23N 31°15W 153 d2
Lajere Nigeria 12°10N 11°25E 263 C7
Lajes Azores 38°46N 27°6W 153 d1
Lajes Rio Grande do N., Brazil 5°41S 36°14W 332 C4
Lajes Sta. Catarina, Brazil 27°48S 50°20W 335 B5
Lajes das Flores Azores 39°23N 31°10W 153 d2
Lajes do Pico Azores 38°23N 28°16W 153 d1
Lajinha Brazil 20°9S 41°37W 333 F3
Lajkovac Serbia 44°27N 20°14E 202 B4
Lajosmizse Hungary 47°3N 19°32E 182 C4
Lak Sao Laos 18°11N 104°59E 236 C5
Lakaband Pakistan 31°2N 69°15E 242 D3
Lakamané Mali 14°35N 9°44W 262 C3
Lakatoro Vanuatu 16°6S 167°25E 287 F5
Lake U.S.A. 44°33N 110°24W 304 D8
Lake Alfred U.S.A. 28°6N 81°44W 317 G8
Lake Alpine U.S.A. 38°29N 120°0W 306 G7
Lake Andes U.S.A. 43°9N 98°32W 308 D4
Lake Arthur U.S.A. 30°5N 92°41W 314 F8
Lake Bindegolly ⌓ Australia 28°0S 144°12E 281 D3
Lake Boga Australia 35°26S 143°38E 282 C5
Lake Buena Vista U.S.A. 28°23N 81°32W 133 B1
Lake Butler U.S.A. 30°1N 82°21W 316 E7
Lake Cain Hills U.S.A. 28°29N 81°28W 133 B2
Lake Cargelligo Australia 33°15S 146°22E 283 B7
Lake Charles U.S.A. 30°14N 93°13W 314 F8
Lake City Colo., U.S.A. 38°2N 107°19W 304 G10
Lake City Fla., U.S.A. 30°11N 82°38W 316 E7
Lake City Iowa, U.S.A. 42°16N 94°44W 310 B2
Lake City Mich., U.S.A. 44°20N 85°13W 309 C11
Lake City Minn., U.S.A. 44°27N 92°16W 308 C7
Lake City Pa., U.S.A. 42°1N 80°21W 312 D4
Lake City S.C., U.S.A. 33°52N 79°45W 316 B10
Lake Clark △ U.S.A. 61°0N 154°0W 303 F9
Lake Clarke Shores U.S.A. 26°39N 80°5W 317 J9
Lake Coleridge N.Z. 43°17S 171°30E 285 D6
Lake Cowichan Canada 48°49N 124°3W 296 D4
Lake District △ U.K. 54°30N 3°21W 168 C4
Lake Elsinore U.S.A. 33°38N 117°20W 307 M9
Lake Eyre △ Australia 28°40S 137°31E 281 D2
Lake Fairfax Park U.S.A. 38°57N 77°19W 143 B2
Lake Forest U.S.A. 42°15N 87°50W 311 B9
Lake Gairdner △ Australia 31°41S 135°51E 281 E2
Lake Geneva U.S.A. 42°36N 88°26W 311 B8
Lake George U.S.A. 43°26N 73°43W 313 C11
Lake Grace Australia 33°7S 118°28E 279 F2
Lake Harbor U.S.A. 26°42N 80°48W 317 J9
Lake Harbour = Kimmirut Canada 62°50N 69°50W 295 C13
Lake Havasu City U.S.A. 34°27N 114°22W 307 L12
Lake Helen U.S.A. 28°59N 81°14W 317 G8
Lake Hughes U.S.A. 34°41N 118°26W 307 L8
Lake Isabella U.S.A. 35°38N 118°28W 307 K8
Lake Jackson U.S.A. 29°3N 95°27W 314 G7
Lake King Australia 33°5S 119°45E 279 F2
Lake Kopiago Papua N. G. 5°23S 142°31E 286 C2
Lake Kutubu Papua N. G. 6°20S 143°18E 286 D2
Lake Lenore Canada 52°24N 104°59W 297 C8
Lake Louise Canada 51°30N 116°10W 296 C5
Lake Malawi △ Malawi 14°2S 34°53E 269 E3
Lake Mburo △ Uganda 0°33S 30°56E 268 C3
Lake Mead ⌓ U.S.A. 36°30N 114°22W 307 K12
Lake Meredith ⌓ U.S.A. 35°50N 101°50W 314 D4
Lake Mills Iowa, U.S.A. 43°25N 93°32W 308 D7
Lake Mills Wis., U.S.A. 43°5N 88°55W 311 A8
Lake Murray Papua N. G. 6°48S 141°29E 286 D1
Lake Nakura △ Kenya 0°21S 36°8E 268 C4
Lake Naujan △ Phil. 13°9N 121°20E 232 E3
Lake Odessa U.S.A. 42°47N 85°8W 311 B11
Lake Orion U.S.A. 42°47N 83°14W 311 B13
Lake Park Fla., U.S.A. 26°48N 80°3W 317 J9
Lake Park Ga., U.S.A. 30°41N 83°11W 316 E6
Lake Placid Fla., U.S.A. 27°18N 81°22W 317 H8
Lake Placid N.Y., U.S.A. 44°17N 73°59W 313 B11
Lake Pleasant U.S.A. 43°28N 74°25W 313 C10
Lake Point Tower Chicago, U.S.A. 119 b3
Lake Providence U.S.A. 32°48N 91°10W 314 E9
Lake Pukaki N.Z. 44°11S 170°8E 285 E5
Lake Roosevelt ⌓ U.S.A. 48°5N 118°14W 304 B4
Lake St. Peter Canada 45°18N 78°2W 312 A6
Lake Shore Drive Chicago, U.S.A. 119 a2
Lake Shore Park Chicago, U.S.A. 119 a2
Lake Superior ⌓ Canada 47°45N 84°45W 298 C3
Lake Tekapo N.Z. 44°0S 170°30E 285 E5
Lake Torrens △ Australia 30°55S 137°40E 281 E2
Lake View U.S.A. 42°18N 95°3W 310 B1
Lake Villa U.S.A. 42°25N 88°5W 311 B8
Lake Village U.S.A. 33°20N 91°17W 314 E9
Lake Wales U.S.A. 27°54N 81°35W 317 H8
Lake Worth U.S.A. 26°37N 80°3W 317 J9
Lake Zurich U.S.A. 42°12N 88°5W 311 B8
Lakeba Fiji 18°13S 178°47W 287 B3
Lakeba Passage Fiji 18°0S 178°45W 287 B3
Lakefield Canada 44°25N 78°16W 312 B6
Lakefield △ Australia 15°24S 144°26E 280 B3
Lakehurst U.S.A. 40°1N 74°19W 313 F10
Lakeland Queens., Australia 15°49S 144°57E 280 B3
Lakeland Fla., U.S.A. 28°3N 81°57W 317 G8
Lakeland Ga., U.S.A. 31°2N 83°4W 316 D6
Lakemba = Lakeba Fiji 18°13S 178°47W 287 B3
Lakemba Australia 33°55S 151°5E 139 B1
Lakepa Cook Is. 18°59S 169°48W 289 g
Lakeport Calif., U.S.A. 39°3N 122°55W 306 F4
Lakeport Mich., U.S.A. 43°7N 82°30W 312 C2
Lakes Entrance Australia 37°50S 148°0E 283 D8
Lakeside Gauteng, S. Africa 26°5S 28°8E 123 A2
Lakeside Western Cape, S. Africa 34°5S 18°27E 118 B1
Lakeside Calif., U.S.A. 32°52N 116°55W 307 N10
Lakeside Nebr., U.S.A. 42°3N 102°26W 308 D2
Lakeside Ohio, U.S.A. 41°32N 82°46W 312 E2
Lakeside Center Chicago, U.S.A. 119 f3
Lakeview Ill., U.S.A. 41°56N 87°38W 119 B3
Lakeview Oreg., U.S.A. 42°11N 120°21W 304 E3
Lakeville U.S.A. 44°39N 93°14W 308 C7
Lakewood Colo., U.S.A. 39°42N 105°4W 304 G11
Lakewood N.J., U.S.A. 40°6N 74°13W 313 F10
Lakewood N.Y., U.S.A. 42°6N 79°19W 312 D5
Lakewood Ohio, U.S.A. 41°28N 81°47W 312 E3
Lakewood Wash., U.S.A. 47°11N 122°32W 306 C4
Lakewood Park Fla., U.S.A. 27°33N 80°24W 317 H9
Lakewood Park Georgia, U.S.A. 33°43N 84°24W 113 B2
Lakha India 26°9N 70°54E 242 F4
Lakhimpur India 27°57N 80°46E 243 F9
Lakhipur Assam, India 24°48N 93°0E 241 C4
Lakhipur Assam, India 26°2N 90°18E 241 B3
Lakhnadon India 22°36N 79°36E 243 H8
Lakhnau = Lucknow India 26°50N 81°0E 243 F9
Lakhonpheng Laos 15°54N 105°34E 236 E5
Lakhpat India 23°48N 68°47E 242 H3
Lakhtinskiy Russia 59°59N 30°9E 137 B1
Lakhtinskiy Razliv, Oz. Russia 59°59N 30°12E 137 B1
Läki Azerbaijan 40°34N 47°22E 191 K8
Laki Iceland 64°4N 18°14W 155 C8
Lakin U.S.A. 37°57N 101°15W 308 G3
Lakitusaki → Canada 54°21N 82°25W 298 B3
Lakka Greece 39°17N 20°9E 206 C10
Lakki Greece 35°24N 23°57E 207 E4
Lakki Pakistan 32°36N 70°55E 242 C4
Lakonia □ Greece 36°55N 22°30E 204 E4
Lakonikos Kolpos Greece 36°40N 22°40E 204 E4
Lakor Indonesia 8°15S 128°17E 231 F7
Lakota Ivory C. 5°50N 5°30W 262 D3
Lakota N. Dak., U.S.A. 48°2N 98°21W 308 A4
Laksar India 29°46N 78°3E 242 E8
Laksefjorden Norway 70°45N 26°50E 160 A22
Lakselv Norway 70°2N 25°0E 160 A21
Laksettipet India 18°52N 79°13E 244 E4
Lakshadweep □ India 10°0N 72°30E 245 J1
Lakshadweep Is. India 10°0N 72°30E 245 J1
Laksham Bangla. 23°14N 91°8E 241 D3
Lakshimpur Bangla. 22°58N 90°50E 241 D3
Lakshmanpur Chhattisgarh, India 22°58N 83°3E 243 H10
Lakshmanpur W. Bengal, India 22°38N 88°16E 124 B1
Lakshmeshwar India 15°9N 75°28E 245 G2
Lakshmikantapur India 22°5N 88°20E 243 H13
Laksi Thailand 13°53N 100°35E 113 A2
Lakuramau Papua N. G. 2°54S 151°15E 286 B6
Lal-lo Phil. 18°12N 121°40E 232 B3
Lal Qila Delhi, India 120 a3
Lala Dem. Rep. of the Congo 4°10S 20°20E 265 C4
Lala Phil. 7°59N 123°46E 233 H4
Lala Musa Pakistan 32°40N 73°57E 242 C5
Lalaghat India 24°30N 92°40E 241 C4
Lalago Tanzania 3°28S 33°58E 268 C3
Lalapanzi Zimbabwe 19°20S 30°15E 269 F3
Lalapaşa Turkey 41°49N 26°44E 203 E10
L'Albenque France 44°19N 1°34E 174 D5
Lalbert Australia 35°38S 143°20E 282 C5
L'Albufera Spain 39°20N 0°27W 197 F4
Lalganj India 25°52N 85°13E 243 G11
Lalgola India 24°25N 88°15E 243 G13
Lālī Iran 32°21N 49°6E 247 C6
Lalibela Ethiopia 12°3N 39°0E 257 E4
Lalin Heilongjiang, China 45°12N 127°0E 227 B14
Lalín Spain 42°40N 8°5W 194 C2
Lalin He → China 45°32N 125°40E 227 B13
Lalinde France 44°50N 0°44E 174 D4
Lalitapur Nepal 27°40N 85°20E 243 F11

Lalitpur India 24°42N 78°28E 243 G8
Lalkua India 29°5N 79°31E 243 E8
Lalm Norway 61°50N 9°17E 164 C6
Lalsot India 26°34N 76°20E 242 F7
Lam Vietnam 21°21N 106°31E 236 B6
Lam Pao Res. Thailand 16°50N 103°15E 236 D4
Lam Tin China 22°18N 114°14E 122 B2
Lama Kara Togo 9°30N 1°15E 263 D5
Lamag Malaysia 5°29N 117°49E 235 A5
Lamaing Burma 15°25N 97°53E 236 E1
Lamaipum Burma 25°40N 97°57E 241 C6
Lamap Vanuatu 16°26S 167°43E 287 F5
Lamar Colo., U.S.A. 38°5N 102°37W 304 G12
Lamar Mo., U.S.A. 37°30N 94°16W 308 G6
Lamarque Argentina 39°24S 65°40W 336 A3
Lamas Peru 6°28S 76°31W 330 B2
Lamastre France 44°59N 4°35E 175 D8
Lambach Austria 48°6N 13°51E 180 C6
Lamballe France 48°29N 2°31W 172 D4
Lambaréné Gabon 0°41S 10°12E 264 C2
Lambasa = Labasa Fiji 16°30S 179°27E 287 A2
Lambay I. Ireland 53°29N 6°1W 166 C5
Lambayeque □ Peru 6°45S 80°0W 330 B2
Lambert Norway 59°52N 10°48E 133 A3
Lambert, C. Papua N. G. 4°11S 151°31E 286 C6
Lambert-St. Louis Int. ✈ (STL) U.S.A. 38°45N 90°22W 310 F6
Lambert's Bay S. Africa 32°5S 18°17E 270 D2
Lambertville U.S.A. 41°46N 83°35W 311 C13
Lambesc France 43°39N 5°16E 175 E9
Lambèse = Tazoult Algeria 35°29N 6°11E 261 A6
Lambeth Canada 42°54N 81°18W 312 D3
Lambeth □ U.K. 51°28N 0°6W 125 B3
Lambi Solomon Is. 9°22S 159°39E 287 M10
Lambia Greece 37°52N 21°53E 204 D3
Lambir Hills △ Malaysia 4°12N 114°1E 235 B4
Lambomakondro Madag. 22°41S 44°44E 272 C1
Lambon Papua N. G. 4°45S 152°48E 286 C7
Lambrate Italy 45°28N 9°16E 129 B2
Lambro ➜ Italy 45°8N 9°32E 198 C6
Lambro, Parco Italy 45°29N 9°14E 129 B2
Lambton Mills Canada 43°39N 79°30W 141 B1
Lambton Shores Canada 43°10N 81°56W 312 C3
Lambu Papua N. G. 3°18S 151°43E 286 B6
Lambunao Phil. 11°3N 122°29E 233 F4
Lamé Chad 9°15N 14°32E 259 G2
Lame Nigeria 10°30N 9°20E 263 C6
Lame Deer U.S.A. 45°37N 106°40W 304 D10
Lamego Portugal 41°5N 7°52W 194 D3
Lamentin Guadeloupe 16°16N 61°38W 322 e
Lamèque Canada 47°45N 64°38W 299 C7
Lameroo Australia 35°19S 140°33E 282 C4
Lamesa U.S.A. 32°44N 101°58W 314 E4
Lamia Greece 38°55N 22°26E 204 C4
Lamigan Pt. Phil. 6°48N 126°21E 233 H6
Lamine ➜ U.S.A. 38°59N 92°51W 310 F4
Lamington △ Australia 28°13S 153°12E 281 D5
Lamitan Phil. 6°39N 122°8E 233 H4
Lamlam, Mt. Guam 13°22N 144°41E 302 d
Lamma I. China 22°12N 114°7E 122 B1
Lammermuir Hills U.K. 55°50N 2°40W 167 F6
Lammhult Sweden 57°10N 14°35E 163 G8
Lamoille ➜ U.S.A. 44°38N 73°13W 313 B11
Lamon B. Phil. 14°30N 122°20E 232 D4
Lamongan Indonesia 7°7S 112°25E 235 D4
Lamoni U.S.A. 40°37N 93°56W 310 D3
Lamont Alta., Canada 53°46N 112°50W 296 C6
Lamont Calif., U.S.A. 35°15N 118°55W 307 K8
Lamont Fla., U.S.A. 30°23N 83°49W 316 E6
Lamont Iowa, U.S.A. 42°36N 91°39W 310 B5
Lamont Wyo., U.S.A. 42°13N 107°29W 304 E10
Lamotte-Beuvron France 47°36N 2°2E 173 E9
Lampa Peru 15°22S 70°22W 330 D3
Lampang Thailand 18°16N 99°32E 236 C2
Lampasas U.S.A. 31°4N 98°11W 314 F5
Lampazos de Naranjo Mexico 27°1N 100°31W 318 B4
Lampedusa Medit. S. 35°36N 12°40E 261 A7
Lampertheim Germany 49°35N 8°27E 179 F4
Lampeter U.K. 52°7N 4°4W 169 E3
Lampione Medit. S. 35°33N 12°20E 258 A2
Lampman Canada 49°25N 102°50W 297 D8
Lamprechtshausen Austria 48°0N 12°58E 180 D5
Lampung □ Indonesia 5°30S 104°30E 234 D2
Lamta India 22°8N 80°7E 243 H9
Lamu Burma 19°14N 94°10E 241 F5
Lamu Coast, Kenya 2°16S 40°55E 268 C5
Lamud Peru 6°10S 77°57W 330 B2
Lamy U.S.A. 35°29N 105°53W 305 J11
Lan Xian China 38°15N 111°35E 226 E6
Lan Yü Taiwan 22°4N 121°25E 225 D3
Lāna'i U.S.A. 20°50N 156°55W 302 C5
Lāna'i City U.S.A. 20°50N 156°55W 302 C5
Lāna'ihale U.S.A. 20°49N 156°53W 302 C5
Lanak La China 34°27N 79°32E 243 B8
Lanak'o Shank'ou = Lanak La China 34°27N 79°32E 243 B8
Lanao, L. Phil. 7°52N 124°15E 233 H5
Lanao del Norte □ Phil. 8°0N 124°10E 233 H5
Lanao del Sur □ Phil. 7°40N 124°15E 233 H5
Lanark Ont., Canada 45°1N 76°22W 313 A8
Lanark S. Lanarks., U.K. 55°40N 3°47W 167 F5
Lanark Ill., U.S.A. 42°6N 89°50W 310 B7
Lanbi Kyun Burma 10°50N 98°20E 237 G2
Lancang China 22°36N 99°58E 228 F2
Lancang Jiang ➜ China 21°40N 101°10E 228 G3
Lancashire □ U.K. 53°50N 2°48W 168 D5
Lancaster Ont., Canada 45°10N 74°30W 313 A10
Lancaster Lancs., U.K. 54°3N 2°48W 168 C5
Lancaster Calif., U.S.A. 34°42N 118°8W 307 L8
Lancaster Ky., U.S.A. 37°37N 84°35W 309 G11
Lancaster Mo., U.S.A. 40°31N 92°32W 310 D4
Lancaster N.H., U.S.A. 44°29N 71°34W 313 B13
Lancaster N.Y., U.S.A. 42°54N 78°40W 312 D6
Lancaster Ohio, U.S.A. 39°43N 82°36W 309 F12
Lancaster Pa., U.S.A. 40°2N 76°19W 313 F8
Lancaster S.C., U.S.A. 34°43N 80°46W 315 D14
Lancaster Wis., U.S.A. 42°51N 90°43W 310 B6
Lancaster, Récif = Neilson, Récif Pac. Oc. 27°1S 146°2W 289 f
Lancaster Sd. Canada 74°13N 84°0W 295 B11
Lancelin Australia 31°0S 115°18E 279 F2
Lanchow = Lanzhou China 36°1N 103°52E 226 F2
Lanchyn Ukraine 48°33N 24°45E 183 B9
Lanciano Italy 42°14N 14°23E 199 F11
Lanco Chile 39°24S 72°46W 336 A2
Lancones Peru 4°30S 80°30W 330 A1
Lancun China 36°25N 120°10E 227 F11
Łańcut Poland 50°10N 22°13E 185 H9
Land Between the Lakes ⌂ U.S.A. 36°25N 88°0W 315 C11
Landau Bayern, Germany 48°40N 12°41E 179 G8
Landau Rhld-Pfz., Germany 49°12N 8°7E 179 F4
Landay Afghan. 30°31N 63°47E 240 C1
Landeck Austria 47°9N 10°34E 180 D3
Lander U.S.A. 42°50N 108°44W 304 E9
Lander ➜ Australia 22°0S 132°0E 278 D5
Landerneau France 48°28N 4°17W 172 D2
Landeryd Sweden 57°7N 13°15E 163 G7
Landes France 44°0N 1°0W 174 D2
Landes □ France 43°57N 0°48W 174 E3
Landes de Gascogne ⌂ France 44°23N 0°50W 174 D3
Landeshut = Kamienna Góra Poland 50°47N 16°2E 185 H3
Landete Spain 39°56N 1°25W 196 F3
Landfall I. India 13°40N 93°2E 245 H11
Landi Kotal Pakistan 34°7N 71°6E 242 B4
Landisburg U.S.A. 40°21N 77°19W 312 F7
Landivisiau France 48°31N 4°6W 172 D2
Landmannalaugar Iceland 63°59N 19°4W 155 D7
Landover Hills U.S.A. 38°56N 76°54W 143 B4
Landquart Switz. 46°58N 9°32E 179 J5
Landrecies France 50°7N 3°40E 173 B10
Land's End U.K. 50°4N 5°44W 169 G2
Landsberg = Górowo Iławeckie Poland 54°17N 20°30E 184 D7
Landsberg Germany 48°2N 10°53E 179 G6
Landsberg an der Warthe = Gorzów Wielkopolski Poland 52°43N 15°15E 185 F2
Landsberg in Oberschlesien = Gorzów Śląski Poland 51°3N 18°22E 185 G5
Landsborough Cr. ➜ Australia 22°28S 144°35E 280 C3
Landsbro Sweden 57°24N 14°56E 163 G8
Landshut Germany 48°34N 12°8E 179 G8
Landskrona Sweden 55°53N 12°50E 163 J6
Landsmeer Neths. 52°26N 4°55E 112 A2
Landstrasse Austria 48°12N 16°23E 142 A2
Landstuhl Germany 49°24N 7°33E 179 F3
Landvetter Sweden 57°41N 12°17E 163 G6
Landwehr kanal Germany 52°29N 13°24E 115 B3
Lane U.S.A. 33°32N 79°53W 316 B10
Lane Cove Australia 33°48S 151°9E 139 A1
Lane Cove National Park △ Australia 33°47S 151°8E 139 A1
Lanesboro U.S.A. 41°57N 75°34W 313 E9
Lanester France 47°46N 3°22W 172 E3
Lanett U.S.A. 32°52N 85°12W 316 C4
Lang Qua Vietnam 22°16N 104°27E 236 A5
Lang Shan China 41°0N 106°30E 226 D4
Lang Son Vietnam 21°52N 106°42E 228 G6
Lang Suan Thailand 9°57N 99°4E 237 H2
Langå Midtjylland, Denmark 56°23N 9°54E 163 H3
Langa Western Cape, S. Africa 33°57S 18°31E 118 A2
La'nga Co China 30°45N 81°15E 243 D9
Langa-Langa Dem. Rep. of the Congo 3°50S 15°59E 264 C3
Langadas Greece 40°46N 23°6E 202 F7
Langadia Greece 37°43N 22°1E 204 D4
Långan ➜ Sweden 63°19N 14°44E 162 A8
Langanes Iceland 66°20N 14°53W 155 A12
Langano, L. Ethiopia 7°36N 38°43E 257 F4
Langar Afghan. 37°2N 73°47E 240 A4
Langar Iran 35°23N 60°25E 247 C9
Langara I. Canada 54°14N 133°1W 296 C2
Långås Sweden 56°58N 12°26E 163 H6
Langatabbetje Suriname 4°59N 54°28W 329 C7
Langdai China 26°6N 105°21E 228 D5
Langdon U.S.A. 48°45N 98°22W 308 A4
Långe Jan = Ölands södra udde Sweden 56°12N 16°23E 163 H10
Langeac France 45°7N 3°29E 174 C7
Langeais France 47°20N 0°24E 172 E7
Langeb Baraka ➜ Sudan 17°28N 36°50E 256 D4
Langeberg S. Africa 33°55S 21°0E 270 D3
Langeberge S. Africa 28°15S 22°33E 270 C3
Langeland Denmark 54°56N 10°48E 163 K4
Langelands Bælt Denmark 54°50N 10°55E 163 K4
Langen Hessen, Germany 49°59N 8°40E 179 F4
Langen Niedersachsen, Germany 53°36N 8°36E 178 B4
Langenbielau = Bielawa Poland 50°43N 16°37E 185 H3
Langenburg Canada 50°51N 101°43W 297 C8
Langeneß Germany 54°38N 8°36E 178 A4
Langenlois Austria 48°29N 15°40E 180 C8
Langenzersdorf Austria 48°18N 16°21E 142 A2
Langeoog Germany 53°45N 7°32E 178 B3
Langer See Germany 52°24N 13°37E 115 B4
Langeskov Denmark 55°22N 10°35E 163 J4
Langesund Norway 59°0N 9°45E 164 F6
Langevåg Norway 62°26N 6°13E 164 B3
Länghem Sweden 57°36N 13°14E 163 G7
Langhirano Italy 44°37N 10°16E 198 D7
Langholm U.K. 55°9N 3°0W 167 F5
Langisjór Iceland 64°11N 18°15W 155 C8
Langjökull Iceland 64°39N 20°12W 155 C6
Langkawi, Pulau Malaysia 6°25N 99°45E 237 J2
Langklip S. Africa 28°12S 20°20E 270 C3
Langkon Malaysia 6°30N 116°40E 235 A5
Langlade St-P. & M. 46°50N 56°20W 299 C8
Langley B.C., Canada 49°7N 122°39W 306 A4
Langley Va., U.S.A. 38°57N 77°11W 143 B2
Langley Park U.S.A. 38°59N 76°58W 143 B4
Langnau Switz. 46°56N 7°47E 179 J3
Langogne France 44°43N 3°50E 174 D7
Langøya Norway 68°45N 14°50E 160 B16
Langreo Spain 43°18N 5°40W 194 B5
Langres France 47°52N 5°20E 173 E12
Langres, Plateau de France 47°45N 5°3E 173 E12
Langsa Indonesia 4°30N 97°57E 234 B1
Långsele Sweden 63°12N 17°4E 162 A11
Långshyttan Sweden 60°27N 16°2E 162 D10
Langtang △ Nepal 28°10N 85°30E 243 E11
Langtao Burma 27°15N 97°34E 241 B6
Langting India 25°31N 93°7E 241 C4
Langtry U.S.A. 29°49N 101°34W 314 G4
Langu Thailand 6°53N 99°47E 237 J2
Langue de Barbarie △ Senegal 14°54N 16°30W 262 C1
Languedoc France 43°58N 3°55E 174 E7
Languedoc-Roussillon □ France 43°25N 3°0E 174 E6
Langwald Germany 48°10N 11°25E 131 A1
Langwang China 22°38N 113°27E 219 F9
Langxi China 31°10N 119°12E 229 B12
Langxiangzhen China 39°43N 116°8E 226 E9
Langzhong China 31°38N 105°58E 228 B5
Lanham U.S.A. 38°59N 76°51W 143 B4
Lanigan Canada 51°51N 105°2W 297 C7
Lanín △ Argentina 40°0S 71°58W 336 A2
Lanjigarh India 19°43N 83°23E 244 E6
Lankao China 34°48N 114°50E 226 G8
Länkäran Azerbaijan 38°48N 48°52E 213 C13
Lankwitz Germany 52°25N 13°21E 115 B2
Lanmeur France 48°39N 3°43W 172 D3
Lannemezan France 43°8N 0°23E 174 E4
Lannilis France 48°35N 4°32W 172 D2
Lannion France 48°46N 3°29W 172 D3
L'Annonciation Canada 46°25N 74°55W 298 C5
L'Annunziatella Italy 41°49N 12°33E 136 C2
Lanouaille France 45°24N 1°9E 174 C5
Lanping China 26°28N 99°15E 228 D2
Lansdale U.S.A. 40°14N 75°17W 313 F9
Lansdowne N.S.W., Australia 31°48S 152°30E 283 A10
Lansdowne Ont., Canada 44°24N 76°1W 313 B8
Lansdowne India 29°50N 78°41E 243 E8
Lansdowne Western Cape, S. Africa 33°59S 18°30E 118 A2
Lansdowne House Canada 52°14N 87°53W 298 B2
L'Anse U.S.A. 46°45N 88°27W 308 B9
L'Anse à l'Âne Martinique 14°32N 61°4W 322 j
L'Anse au Loup Canada 51°32N 56°50W 299 B8
L'Anse aux Epines Grenada 11°59N 61°45W 323 q
L'Anse aux Meadows Canada 51°36N 55°32W 299 B8
L'Anse la Raye St. Lucia 13°55N 61°3W 323 m
L'Anse Mitan Martinique 14°32N 61°3W 322 j
Lansford U.S.A. 40°50N 75°53W 313 F9
Lanshan China 25°24N 112°10E 229 E9
Lansing Ont., Canada 43°45N 79°24W 141 A2
Lansing Mich., U.S.A. 42°44N 84°33W 311 B12
Lanslebourg-Mont-Cenis France 45°17N 6°52E 175 C10
Lanta Yai, Ko Thailand 7°35N 99°3E 237 J2
Lantana U.S.A. 26°35N 80°3W 317 J9
Lantau I. China 22°15N 113°56E 219 G10
Lantewa Nigeria 12°16N 11°44E 263 C7
Lantian China 34°11N 109°20E 226 G5
Lanus Argentina 34°42S 58°23W 117 C2
Lanusei Italy 39°52N 9°34E 200 C2
Lanuza Phil. 9°14N 126°4E 233 G6
Lanxi China 29°13N 119°28E 229 C12
Lanyang Hsi ➜ Taiwan 24°43N 121°49E 225 B3
Lanyü Taiwan 22°2N 121°33E 225 D3
Lanzarote Canary Is. 29°0N 13°40W 153 e2
Lanzarote ✈ (ACE) Canary Is. 28°57N 13°40W 153 e2
Lanzhou China 36°1N 103°52E 226 F2
Lanzo Torinese Italy 45°16N 7°28E 198 C4
Lao ➜ Italy 39°47N 15°48E 201 C8
Lao Bao Laos 16°35N 106°30E 236 D6
Lao Cai Vietnam 22°30N 103°57E 228 F4
Laoag Phil. 18°7N 120°34E 232 B3
Laoang Phil. 12°32N 125°8E 232 E5
Laoha He ➜ China 43°25N 120°35E 227 C11
Laohekou China 32°22N 111°38E 229 A8
Laois □ Ireland 52°57N 7°36W 166 D4
Laon France 49°33N 3°35E 173 C10
Laona U.S.A. 45°34N 88°40W 308 C9
Laonung Hsi ➜ Taiwan 22°47N 120°27E 225 D2
Laos ■ Asia 17°45N 105°0E 236 D5
Lapa Paraná, Brazil 25°46S 49°44W 335 B6
Lapa Rio de J., Brazil 22°54S 43°10W 135 B1
Lapac I. Phil. 5°32N 120°47E 233 J3
Lapai Nigeria 9°5N 6°32E 263 D6
Lapalisse France 46°15N 3°38E 173 F10
Lapara I. Phil. 5°57N 120°0E 233 J2
Lapeer U.S.A. 43°3N 83°19W 311 A13
Lapeyrade France 44°4N 0°3W 174 D3
Lapithos Cyprus 35°21N 33°11E 207 E9
Lapland = Lappland Europe 68°7N 24°0E 160 B21
LaPorte Ind., U.S.A. 41°36N 86°43W 311 C10
Laporte Pa., U.S.A. 41°25N 76°30W 313 E8
Lapovo Serbia 44°10N 21°2E 202 B5
Lappeenranta Finland 61°3N 28°12E 188 B5
Lappland Europe 68°7N 24°0E 160 B21
Lappo = Lapua Finland 62°58N 23°0E 160 E20
Laprida Argentina 37°34S 60°45W 334 D3
Lapseki Turkey 40°20N 26°41E 203 F10
Laptev Sea Russia 76°0N 125°0E 215 B13
Lapu-Lapu Phil. 10°20N 123°55E 233 F4
Lapua Finland 62°58N 23°0E 160 E20
Lăpuş ➜ Romania 47°25N 23°40E 183 C8
Lapuş, Munţii Romania 47°20N 23°50E 183 C8
Lăpuşna Moldova 46°53N 28°25E 183 D13
Łapy Poland 52°59N 22°52E 185 F9
Laqiya Arba'in Sudan 20°1N 28°1E 256 C2
Laqiya Umran Sudan 19°55N 28°18E 256 D2
L'Áquila Italy 42°22N 13°22E 199 F10
Lār Āzarbājān-e Sharqī, Iran 38°30N 47°52E 246 B5
Lār Fārs, Iran 27°40N 54°14E 247 E7
Lara Australia 38°2S 144°26E 282 E6
Lara □ Venezuela 10°10N 69°50W 328 A4
Larabanga Ghana 9°16N 1°56W 262 D4
Larache Morocco 35°10N 6°5W 260 A3
Larache □ Morocco 35°10N 5°50W 260 A3
Laragaran = Plaridel Phil. 8°37N 123°43E 233 G4
Laragne-Montéglin France 44°18N 5°49E 175 D9
Laramie U.S.A. 41°19N 105°35W 304 F11
Laramie Mts. U.S.A. 42°0N 105°30W 304 F11
Laranjeiras Rio de J., Brazil 22°55S 43°10W 135 B1
Laranjeiras Sergipe, Brazil 10°48S 37°10W 332 D4
Laranjeiras do Sul Brazil 25°23S 52°23W 335 B5
Larantuka Indonesia 8°21S 122°55E 231 F6
Larat Indonesia 7°0S 132°0E 231 F8
L'Arbresle France 45°50N 4°36E 175 C8
Lärbro Sweden 57°47N 18°50E 163 G12
Lårdal Norway 59°25N 8°10E 164 E5
Larde Mozam. 16°28S 39°43E 269 F4
Larder Lake Canada 48°5N 79°40W 298 C4
Lardos, Akra = Lindos, Akra Greece 36°4N 28°10E 206 E12
Lardos, Ormos Greece 36°4N 28°2E 206 E12
Lare Kenya 0°20N 37°56E 268 C4
Laredo Spain 43°26N 3°28W 194 B7
Laredo Tex., U.S.A. 27°30N 99°30W 314 H5
Laredo Sd. Canada 52°30N 128°53W 296 C3
Larena Phil. 9°15N 123°35E 233 G4
Lares Puerto Rico 18°18N 66°53W 321 b
Large I. Grenada 12°24N 61°30W 323 q
Largentière France 44°34N 4°18E 175 D8
L'Argentière-la-Bessée France 44°47N 6°33E 175 D10
Largo U.S.A. 27°54N 82°47W 317 H7
Largo, Key U.S.A. 25°15N 80°15W 317 K9
Largs U.K. 55°47N 4°52W 167 F4
Lari Italy 43°34N 10°35E 198 E7
Lariang Indonesia 1°26S 119°17E 231 E5
Larimore U.S.A. 47°54N 97°38W 308 B5
Larino Italy 41°48N 14°54E 199 G11
Larisa Greece 39°36N 22°27E 204 B4
Larisis Station Athens, Greece 112 a1
Larissa = Larisa Greece 39°36N 22°27E 204 B4
Larissas □ Greece 39°39N 22°24E 204 B4
Larkana Pakistan 27°32N 68°18E 242 F3
Larkins = South Miami U.S.A. 25°42N 80°17W 128 B1
Larnaca Cyprus 34°55N 33°38E 207 F9
Larnaca ✈ (LCA) Cyprus 34°50N 33°34E 207 F9
Larnaca Bay Cyprus 34°53N 33°45E 207 F9
Larnare, Pte. Martinique 14°47N 61°13W 322 j
Larne U.K. 54°51N 5°51W 166 B6
Larned U.S.A. 38°11N 99°6W 308 F4
Laroquebrou France 44°58N 2°12E 174 D6
Larose U.S.A. 29°34N 90°23W 315 G9
Larose, Pte. Martinique 14°39N 60°53W 322 j
Larrimah Australia 15°35S 133°12E 278 C5
Larsen Bay U.S.A. 57°32N 153°59W 303 H9
Larsen Ice Shelf Antarctica 67°0S 62°0W 151 C17
Laruns France 43°0N 0°26W 174 F3
Larvik Norway 59°4N 10°2E 164 F7
Larzac, Causse du France 43°50N 3°17E 174 E7
Las Poland 52°13N 21°6E 142 B2
Las Alpujarras Spain 36°55N 3°20W 197 J1
Las Animas U.S.A. 38°4N 103°13W 304 G12
Las Anod Somali Rep. 8°26N 47°19E 267 C6
Las Arenas Spain 43°17N 4°50W 194 B6
Las Batuecas ⌂ Spain 40°32N 6°5W 194 E4
Las Bonitas Venezuela 7°52N 65°40W 328 B4
Las Brenãs Argentina 27°5S 61°7W 334 B3
Las Cabezas de San Juan Spain 36°57N 5°58W 195 J5
Las Cañadas del Teide △ Canary Is. 28°15N 16°37W 153 e1
Las Chimeneas Mexico 32°8N 116°5W 307 N10
Las Coloradas Argentina 39°34S 70°36W 336 A2
Las Corts Spain 41°23N 2°9E 114 A1
Las Cruces U.S.A. 32°19N 106°47W 305 K10
Las Dawa'o Somali Rep. 10°28N 49°0E 267 B6
Las Flores Argentina 36°10S 59°7W 334 D4
Las Heras Argentina 32°51S 68°49W 334 C2
Las Hermosas △ Colombia 3°48N 75°51W 328 C2
Las Horquetas Argentina 48°14S 71°11W 336 C2
Las Kabacki Poland 52°7N 21°2E 142 C2
Las Khoreh Somali Rep. 11°10N 48°20E 267 B6
Las Lajas Argentina 38°30S 70°25W 336 A2
Las Lomas Peru 4°40S 80°10W 330 A1
Las Lomitas Argentina 24°43S 60°35W 334 A3
Las Marismas Spain 37°5N 6°20W 195 H4
Las Mercedes Venezuela 9°7N 66°24W 328 B4
Las Minas Spain 38°20N 1°41W 197 G3
Las Navas de la Concepción Spain 37°56N 5°30W 195 H5
Las Navas del Marqués Spain 40°36N 4°20W 194 E6
Las Nieves Phil. 8°46N 125°34E 233 G5
Las Orquídeas △ Colombia 6°36N 76°16W 328 B2
Las Palmas Argentina 27°8S 58°45W 334 B4
Las Palmas Canary Is. 28°7N 15°26W 153 e1
Las Palmas ➜ Mexico 32°31N 116°58W 307 N10
Las Palmas ✈ (LPA) Canary Is. 27°55N 15°25W 153 e1
Las Palmas de Cocalán △ Chile 34°18S 71°4W 334 C1
Las Pedroñas Spain 39°26N 2°40W 197 F2
Las Piedras Puerto Rico 18°11N 65°52W 321 b
Las Piedras Uruguay 34°44S 56°14W 335 C4
Las Pinas Phil. 14°29N 120°58E 127 C1
Las Pipinas Argentina 35°30S 57°19W 334 D4
Las Plumas Argentina 43°40S 67°15W 336 B3
Las Rejas Chile 33°27S 70°42W 137 B1
Las Rosas Argentina 32°30S 61°35W 334 C3
Las Rozas Spain 40°29N 3°52W 194 E7
Las Tablas Panama 7°49N 80°14W 320 E3
Las Termas Argentina 27°29S 64°52W 334 B3
Las Toscas Argentina 28°21S 59°18W 334 B4
Las Truchas Mexico 17°57N 102°13W 318 D4
Las Tunas Cuba 20°58N 76°59W 320 B4
Las Varillas Argentina 31°50S 62°50W 334 C3
Las Vegas N. Mex., U.S.A. 35°36N 105°13W 305 J11
Las Vegas Nev., U.S.A. 36°10N 115°8W 124 A2
Las Vegas McCarran Int. ✈ (LAS) U.S.A. 36°5N 115°9W 124 B2
Lasa = Lhasa China 29°25N 90°58E 218 D4
Lasalle Canada 45°26N 73°38W 130 B2
LaSalle Street Chicago, U.S.A. 119 a1
LaSalle Street Station Chicago, U.S.A. 119 d1
Lasanga I. Papua N. G. 7°25S 147°15E 286 D4
Lasarte Spain 43°16N 2°1W 196 B2
Lascano Uruguay 33°35S 54°12W 335 C5
Lascelles Australia 35°34S 142°34E 282 C5
Lasek Bielański Poland 52°17N 20°57E 142 B1
Lasek Na Kole Poland 52°15N 20°56E 142 B1
Lash-e Joveyn Afghan. 31°45N 61°30E 240 D1
Lashburn Canada 53°10N 109°40W 297 C7
Lashio Burma 22°56N 97°45E 241 D6
Lashkar India 26°10N 78°10E 242 F8
Lashkar Gāh Afghan. 31°35N 64°21E 240 C2
Lasin Poland 53°30N 19°2E 184 E6
Lasithi Greece 35°11N 25°31E 207 E6
Lasithi □ Greece 35°5N 25°50E 207 E7
Läsjerd Iran 35°24N 53°4E 247 C7
Lask Poland 51°34N 19°8E 185 G6
Laskarzew Poland 51°48N 21°36E 185 G8
Laski Poland 52°18N 20°50E 142 B1
Laško Slovenia 46°10N 15°16E 199 B12
Lassance Brazil 17°54S 44°34W 333 E3
Lassay-les-Châteaux France 48°27N 0°30W 172 D6
Lassen Pk. U.S.A. 40°29N 121°30W 304 F3
Lassen Volcanic △ U.S.A. 40°30N 121°20W 304 F3
Lassongo Angola 12°55S 22°46E 265 E4
Last Mountain L. Canada 51°5N 105°14W 297 C7
Lastchance Cr. ➜ U.S.A. 40°2N 121°15W 306 E5
Lastoursville Gabon 0°55S 12°38E 264 C2
Lastovo Croatia 42°46N 16°55E 199 F13
Lastovski Kanal Croatia 42°50N 17°0E 199 F14
Lat Yao Thailand 15°45N 99°48E 236 E2
Lata Mt. Amer. Samoa 14°14S 169°27W 302 f
Latacunga Ecuador 0°50S 78°35W 328 D2
Latakia = Al Lādhiqīyah Syria 35°30N 35°45E 250 C6
Latchford Canada 47°20N 79°50W 298 C4
Late Tonga 18°48S 174°39W 287 P13
Latehar India 23°45N 84°30E 243 H11
Laterza Italy 40°37N 16°48E 201 B9
Latham Australia 29°44S 116°20E 279 E2
Lathen Germany 52°52N 7°19E 178 C3
Lathi India 27°43N 71°23E 242 F4
Lathi Vanuatu 14°57S 167°8E 287 D5
Lathrop U.S.A. 39°33N 94°20W 310 E2
Lathrop Wells U.S.A. 36°39N 116°24W 307 J10
Latiano Italy 40°33N 17°43E 201 B10
Latin, Quartier Montréal, Canada 130 b2
Latina Italy 41°28N 12°52E 200 A5
Latina Madrid, Spain 40°24N 3°44W 127 B1
Latisana Italy 45°47N 13°0E 199 C10
Latium = Lazio □ Italy 42°10N 12°30E 199 F9
Laton U.S.A. 36°26N 119°41W 306 J7
Latorytsya ➜ Slovak Rep. 48°28N 21°50E 181 C14
Latouche Treville, C. Australia 18°27S 121°49E 278 C3
Latouma Niger 22°10N 14°50E 259 D2
Látrar Iceland 66°24N 23°2W 155 A3
Latrobe Tas., Australia 41°14S 146°30E 281 G4
Latrobe Pa., U.S.A. 40°19N 79°23W 312 F5
Latrónico Italy 40°5N 16°1E 201 B9
Latur India 18°25N 76°40E 244 E3
Latvia ■ Europe 56°50N 24°0E 188 D2
Lau Nigeria 9°11N 11°19E 263 D7
Lau Basin Pac. Oc. 20°0S 177°0W 277 E15
Lau Fau Shan China 22°28N 113°59E 219 G10
Lau Group Fiji 17°0S 178°30W 287 A3
Lau Ridge Pac. Oc. 21°0S 178°30W 277 E15
Lauban = Lubań Poland 51°5N 15°15E 185 G2
Lauca ➜ Bolivia 19°9S 68°10W 330 D4
Lauchhammer Germany 51°29N 13°47E 178 D9
Lauda-Königshofen Germany 49°33N 9°42E 179 F5
Laudal Norway 58°15N 7°30E 164 F4
Laudat Dominica 15°20N 61°21W 323 k
Lauenburg = Lębork Poland 54°33N 17°46E 184 D4
Lauenburg Germany 53°22N 10°32E 178 B6
Lauenburgische Seen ⌂ Germany 53°38N 10°45E 178 B6
Lauf Germany 49°30N 11°16E 179 F7
Laufás Iceland 65°53N 18°4W 155 B8
Laugar Iceland 65°15N 21°48W 155 B5
Laugarás Iceland 64°7N 20°30W 155 C6
Laugarbakki Iceland 65°20N 20°55W 155 B6
Laugarvatn Iceland 64°13N 20°44W 155 C6
Laughlin U.S.A. 35°10N 114°34W 305 J6
Laujar de Andarax Spain 37°0N 2°54W 197 H2
Laukaa Finland 62°24N 25°56E 160 E21
Laulau, Bahia N. Marianas 15°8N 145°45E 302 e
Launceston Tas., Australia 41°24S 147°8E 281 G4
Launceston Corn., U.K. 50°38N 4°22W 169 G3
Laune ➜ Ireland 52°7N 9°47W 166 D2
Launglon Bok Burma 13°50N 97°54E 236 F1
Laupheim Germany 48°14N 9°52E 179 G5
Laura Queens., Australia 15°32S 144°32E 280 B3
Laura S. Austral., Australia 33°10S 138°18E 282 B3
Laureana di Borrello Italy 38°30N 16°5E 201 D9
Laurel Fla., U.S.A. 27°8N 82°27W 317 H7
Laurel Ind., U.S.A. 39°30N 85°11W 311 E11
Laurel Miss., U.S.A. 31°41N 89°8W 315 F10
Laurel Mont., U.S.A. 45°40N 108°46W 304 D9
Laurel Bay U.S.A. 32°27N 80°47W 316 C9
Laurel Hill U.S.A. 40°14N 79°6W 312 F5
Laurencekirk U.K. 56°50N 2°28W 167 E6
Laurens Iowa, U.S.A. 42°51N 94°52W 310 B2
Laurens S.C., U.S.A. 34°30N 82°1W 315 D13
Laurentian Plateau Canada 52°0N 70°0W 299 B6
Lauria Italy 40°3N 15°50E 201 B8
Laurie L. Canada 56°35N 101°57W 297 B8
Laurinburg U.S.A. 34°47N 79°28W 315 D15
Laurium U.S.A. 47°14N 88°27W 308 B9
Lausanne Switz. 46°32N 6°38E 179 J2
Laut Indonesia 4°45N 108°0E 235 B3
Laut, Pulau Indonesia 3°40S 116°10E 235 C5
Laut Kecil, Kepulauan Indonesia 4°45S 115°40E 235 C5
Lautaro Chile 38°31S 72°27W 336 A2
Lauterbach Germany 50°37N 9°24E 178 E5
Lauterecken Germany 49°38N 7°35E 179 F3
Lautoka Fiji 17°37S 177°27E 287 A1
L'Autre Bord Guadeloupe 16°20N 61°20W 322 e
Lauttasaari Finland 60°9N 24°53E 121 C2
Lauzès France 44°34N 1°35E 174 D5
Lava ➜ Russia 54°37N 21°14E 184 D8
Lava Beds ⌂ U.S.A. 41°40N 121°30W 304 F3
Lavagh More Ireland 54°46N 8°6W 166 B3
Lavagna Italy 44°18N 9°20E 198 D6
Laval France 48°4N 0°48W 172 D6
Laval-des-Rapides Canada 45°33N 73°42W 130 A1
Lavalle Argentina 28°15S 65°15W 334 B2
Lavanggu Solomon Is. 11°36S 160°16E 287 N11
Lavant Station Canada 45°3N 76°42W 313 A8
Lāvar Meydān Iran 30°20N 54°30E 247 D7
Lávara Greece 41°19N 26°22E 203 E10
Lavardac France 44°12N 0°20E 174 D4
Lavaur France 43°40N 1°49E 174 E5
Lavelanet France 42°57N 1°51E 174 F5
Lavello Italy 41°3N 15°48E 201 A8
L'Averdy, C. Papua N. G. 5°33S 155°4E 286 C8
Lavers Hill Australia 38°40S 143°25E 282 E5
Laverton Australia 28°44S 122°29E 279 E3
Lavik Norway 61°6N 5°25E 164 C2
Lavis Italy 46°8N 11°7E 198 B8
Lavīzān Iran 35°47N 51°30E 141 A2
Lavos Portugal 40°6N 8°49W 194 E2
Lavoutte, Anse St. Lucia 14°5N 60°55W 323 m
Lavradio Portugal 38°40N 9°2W 126 A2
Lavras Brazil 21°20S 45°0W 333 F3
Lavre Portugal 38°46N 8°22W 195 G2
Lavrio Greece 37°40N 24°4E 204 D6
Lavris Greece 35°25N 24°40E 207 E5
Lavumisa Swaziland 27°20S 31°55E 271 C5
Lavushi Manda △ Zambia 12°46S 31°0E 269 E3
Lawa Phil. 6°12N 125°41E 233 H5
Lawa-an Phil. 11°51N 125°5E 233 F5
Lawaki Fiji 17°40S 178°35E 287 A2
Lawas Malaysia 4°55N 115°25E 235 B5
Lawdar Yemen 13°53N 45°52E 248 D4
Lawele Indonesia 5°13S 122°57E 231 F6
Lawksawk Burma 21°15N 96°52E 241 E6
Lawn Hill △ Australia 18°15S 138°6E 280 B2
Lawndale U.S.A. 41°50N 87°42W 119 B2
Lawne L. U.S.A. 28°33N 81°26W 133 A2
Lawqah Si. Arabia 29°49N 42°45E 246 D4
Lawra Ghana 10°39N 2°51W 262 C4
Lawrence N.Z. 45°55S 169°41E 285 F4
Lawrence Ind., U.S.A. 39°50N 86°2W 311 E10
Lawrence Kans., U.S.A. 38°58N 95°14W 308 F6
Lawrence Mass., U.S.A. 42°43N 71°10W 313 D13
Lawrence Heights Canada 43°43N 79°25W 141 A2
Lawrenceburg Ind., U.S.A. 39°6N 84°52W 311 E12
Lawrenceburg Ky., U.S.A. 38°2N 84°54W 311 F12
Lawrenceburg Tenn., U.S.A. 35°14N 87°20W 315 D11
Lawrenceville Ga., U.S.A. 33°57N 83°59W 316 B6
Lawrenceville Ill., U.S.A. 38°44N 87°41W 311 F9
Lawrenceville Pa., U.S.A. 41°59N 77°8W 312 E7
Laws U.S.A. 37°24N 118°20W 306 H8
Lawson U.S.A. 39°26N 94°12W 310 E2
Lawtey U.S.A. 30°3N 82°5W 316 E7
Lawton Mich., U.S.A. 42°10N 85°50W 311 B11
Lawton Okla., U.S.A. 34°37N 98°25W 314 D5
Lawu Indonesia 7°40S 111°13E 235 D4
Lawz, J. al Si. Arabia 28°39N 35°18E 251 K6
Laxå Sweden 58°59N 14°37E 163 F8
Laxamýri Iceland 65°58N 17°24W 155 B9
Laxford, L. U.K. 58°24N 5°6W 167 C3
Laxou France 48°41N 6°8E 173 D13
Lay ➜ France 46°18N 1°17W 174 B2
Layari Pakistan 24°52N 67°0E 123 A2
Layari ➜ Pakistan 24°52N 66°58E 123 A1
Layla Si. Arabia 22°10N 46°40E 248 B4
Laylān Iraq 35°18N 44°31E 246 C5
Layon ➜ France 47°20N 0°45W 172 E6
Layou St. Vincent 13°12N 61°17W 323 n
Layou ➜ Dominica 15°23N 61°21W 323 k
Laysan I. U.S.A. 25°50N 171°50W 302 F9
Layton Fla., U.S.A. 24°50N 80°47W 317 L9
Layton Utah, U.S.A. 41°4N 111°58W 304 F8
Laytonville U.S.A. 39°41N 123°29W 304 G2
Laza Burma 26°30N 97°38E 241 B6
Lazarata Greece 38°47N 20°40E 207 B2
Lazarevac Serbia 44°23N 20°17E 202 B4
Lazarevskoye Russia 43°55N 39°21E 191 J4
Lazarivo Madag. 23°54S 44°59E 272 C1
Lázaro Cárdenas Mexico 17°55N 102°11W 318 D4
Lazdijai Lithuania 54°14N 23°31E 184 D10
Lazhuglung China 34°52N 81°24E 217 F10
Lazi Phil. 9°8N 123°38E 233 G4
Lazienki Palace Warsaw, Poland 142 c3
Lazienkowski Park Poland 52°13N 21°1E 142 B2
Lazio □ Italy 42°10N 12°30E 199 F9
Lazo Moldova 47°33N 28°2E 183 C13
Lazo Russia 43°25N 133°55E 220 C6
Lbishchensk = Chapayev Kazakhstan 50°25N 51°10E 190 E10
Le Beausset France 43°12N 5°48E 175 E9
Le Bélier Réunion 21°2S 55°28E 272 f
Le Bic Canada 48°20N 68°41W 299 C6
Le Blanc France 46°37N 1°3E 174 B5
Le Blanc-Mesnil France 48°56N 2°27E 134 A3
Le Bleymard France 44°30N 3°42E 174 D7
Le Bourget France 48°56N 2°25E 134 A3
Le Bourgneuf-la-Fôret France 48°10N 0°59W 172 D6
Le Bugue France 44°55N 0°56E 174 D4
Le Carbet Martinique 14°42N 61°11W 322 j
Le Cateau Cambrésis France 50°7N 3°32E 173 B10
Le Caylar France 43°51N 3°19E 174 E7
Le Chambon-Feugerolles France 45°24N 4°19E 175 C8
Le Chameau Guadeloupe 15°51N 61°35W 322 e
Le Châtelet France 46°38N 2°16E 173 F9
Le Chenoi Belgium 50°41N 4°18E 116 B2
Le Chesnay France 48°49N 2°8E 134 B1
Le Chesne France 49°30N 4°45E 173 C11
Le Cheylard France 44°55N 4°25E 175 D8
Le Christ de Saclay France 48°43N 2°9E 134 B2
Le Claire U.S.A. 41°36N 90°21W 310 C6
Le Conquet France 48°21N 4°46W 172 D2
Le Creusot France 46°48N 4°24E 173 F11
Le Croisic France 47°18N 2°30W 172 E4
Le Diamant Martinique 14°28N 61°2W 322 j
Le Donjon France 46°22N 3°48E 173 F10
Le Dorat France 46°14N 1°5E 174 B5
Le François Martinique 14°38N 60°57W 322 j
Le Gosier Guadeloupe 16°14N 61°29W 322 e
Le Grand Brûlé Réunion 21°14S 55°47E 272 f
Le Grand-Lucé France 47°52N 0°28E 172 E7
Le Grand-Pressigny France 46°55N 0°48E 172 F7
Le Grand-Quevilly France 49°24N 1°3E 172 C8
Le Gris Gris Mauritius 20°31S 57°32E 272 e
Le Gros Morne Réunion 21°5S 55°28E 272 f
Le Havre France 49°30N 0°5E 172 C7
Le Kremlin-Bicêtre France 48°48N 2°21E 134 B3
Le Lamentin Martinique 14°35N 61°2W 322 j
Le Lavandou France 43°8N 6°22E 175 E10
Le Lion-d'Angers France 47°37N 0°43W 172 E6
Le Lorrain Martinique 14°48N 61°3W 322 j
Le Louroux-Béconnais France 47°30N 0°55W 172 E6
Le Luc France 43°23N 6°21E 175 E10
Le Lude France 47°39N 0°9E 172 E7
Le Maire, Estr. de Argentina 54°50S 65°0W 336 D4
Le Mans France 48°0N 0°10E 172 E7
Le Marigot Martinique 14°50N 61°4W 322 j
Le Marin Martinique 14°27N 60°55W 322 j
Le Mars U.S.A. 42°47N 96°10W 308 D5
Le Mayet-de-Montagne France 46°4N 3°40E 173 F10
Le Mêle-sur-Sarthe France 48°31N 0°22E 172 D7
Le Mesnil-le-Roi France 48°56N 2°7E 134 A1
Le Monastier-sur-Gazeille France 44°57N 3°59E 174 D7
Le Monêtier-les-Bains France 44°58N 6°30E 175 D10
Le Mont-Dore France 45°35N 2°49E 174 C6
Le Mont-St-Michel France 48°40N 1°30W 172 D5
Le Morne Brabant Mauritius 20°27S 57°19E 272 e
Le Morne Rouge Martinique 14°47N 61°8W 322 j
Le Morne-Vert Martinique 14°42N 61°8W 322 j
Le Moule Guadeloupe 16°20N 61°22W 322 e
Le Muy France 43°28N 6°34E 175 E10
Le Palais France 47°20N 3°10W 172 E3
Le Pecq France 48°53N 2°6E 134 A1
Le Perreux France 48°50N 2°29E 134 A3
Le Perthus France 42°30N 2°53E 174 F6
Le Pin France 48°54N 2°37E 134 A4
Le Plessis-Robinson France 48°47N 2°15E 134 B2
Le Plessis-Trévise France 48°48N 2°34E 134 B4
Le Port Réunion 20°56S 55°18E 272 f
Le Port-Marly France 48°52N 2°6E 134 A1
Le Pré-St-Gervais France 48°53N 2°23E 134 A3
Le Prêcheur Martinique 14°50N 61°12W 322 j
Le Puy-en-Velay France 45°3N 3°52E 174 C7
Le Raincy France 48°53N 2°31E 134 A4
Le Robert Martinique 14°40N 60°56W 322 j
Le Roy U.S.A. 40°21N 88°46W 311 D8
Le St-Esprit Martinique 14°34N 60°56W 322 j
Le Souffleur Guadeloupe 16°19N 61°29W 322 e
Le Sueur U.S.A. 44°28N 93°55W 308 C7
Le Tampon Réunion 21°16S 55°32E 272 f
Le Teil France 44°33N 4°40E 175 D8
Le Teilleul France 48°32N 0°53W 172 D6
Le Theil France 48°16N 0°42E 172 D7
Le Thillot France 47°53N 6°46E 173 E13
Le Thuy Vietnam 17°14N 106°49E 236 D6
Le Touquet-Paris-Plage France 50°30N 1°36E 173 B8
Le Tréport France 50°3N 1°20E 172 B8
Le Trou à Diable Guadeloupe 15°57N 61°14W 322 e
Le Val-d'Ajol France 47°55N 6°30E 173 E13
Le Val Nature Park Mauritius 20°22S 57°37E 272 e
Le Vauclin Martinique 14°33N 60°52W 322 j
Le Verdon-sur-Mer France 45°33N 1°4W 174 C2
Le Vésinet France 48°54N 2°8E 134 A1
Le Vigan France 43°59N 3°36E 174 E7
Lea ➜ U.K. 51°31N 0°1E 169 F8
Lea Bridge U.K. 51°33N 0°2W 125 A3
Lea Lea Papua N. G. 9°17S 146°59E 286 E4
Leach Cambodia 12°21N 103°46E 237 F4
Lead U.S.A. 44°21N 103°46W 308 C2
Leader Canada 50°50N 109°30W 297 C7
Leadville U.S.A. 39°15N 106°18W 304 G10
Leaf ➜ U.S.A. 30°59N 88°44W 315 F10
Leaf Rapids Canada 56°30N 99°59W 297 B9
Leaghur, L. Australia 33°35S 143°3E 282 B5
Leaksville = Eden U.S.A. 36°29N 79°53W 315 C15
Lealui Zambia 15°10S 23°2E 265 F4
Leamington Ont., Canada 42°3N 82°36W 312 D2
Leamington N.Z. 37°55S 175°30E 284 D4
Leamington Utah, U.S.A. 39°32N 112°17W 304 G7
Leamington Spa = Royal Leamington Spa U.K. 52°18N 1°31W 169 E6
Le'an China 27°22N 115°48E 229 D10
Leandro Norte Alem Argentina 27°34S 55°15W 335 B4
Leane, L. Ireland 52°2N 9°32W 166 D2
Learmonth Australia 22°13S 114°10E 278 D1
Leary U.S.A. 31°29N 84°31W 316 D5
Leaside Canada 43°42N 79°22W 141 A2

Leask Canada 53°5N 106°45W 297 C7
Leatherhead U.K. 51°18N 0°20W 169 F7
Leavenworth Ind., U.S.A. 38°12N 86°21W 311 F10
Leavenworth Kans., U.S.A. 39°19N 94°55W 308 F6
Leavenworth Wash., U.S.A. 47°36N 120°40W 304 C3
Leawood U.S.A. 38°58N 94°37W 310 F2
Łeba Poland 54°45N 17°32E 184 D4
Łeba → Poland 54°46N 17°33E 184 D4
Lebach Germany 49°25N 6°54E 179 F2
Lebak Phil. 6°32N 124°5E 233 H5
Lebam U.S.A. 46°34N 123°33W 306 D3
Lebane Serbia 42°56N 21°44E 202 D5
Lebango Congo 0°39N 14°21E 264 B2
Lebango → Congo 0°2N 14°52E 264 B2
Lebanon Ill., U.S.A. 38°38N 89°49W 310 F7
Lebanon Ind., U.S.A. 40°3N 86°28W 311 D10
Lebanon Kans., U.S.A. 39°49N 98°33W 308 F4
Lebanon Ky., U.S.A. 37°34N 85°15W 309 G11
Lebanon Mo., U.S.A. 37°41N 92°40W 310 G4
Lebanon N.H., U.S.A. 43°39N 72°15W 313 C12
Lebanon Ohio, U.S.A. 39°26N 84°13W 311 E12
Lebanon Oreg., U.S.A. 44°32N 122°55W 304 D2
Lebanon Pa., U.S.A. 40°20N 76°26W 313 F8
Lebanon Tenn., U.S.A. 36°12N 86°18W 315 C11
Lebanon ■ Asia 34°0N 36°0E 250 E7
Lebanon Junction U.S.A. 37°50N 85°44W 311 G11
Lebanon Station U.S.A. 29°10N 82°37W 317 F7
Lebap □ Turkmenistan 40°0N 63°0E 216 D6
Lebec U.S.A. 34°51N 118°52W 307 L8
Lebedyan Russia 53°0N 39°10E 189 F10
Lebedyn Ukraine 50°35N 34°30E 189 G8
Lebel-sur-Quévillon Canada 49°3N 76°59W 298 C4
Leblon Brazil 22°59S 43°14W 135 B1
Lebo Dem. Rep. of the Congo 4°30N 23°58E 264 B4
Lebomboberge S. Africa 24°30S 32°0E 271 B5
Lębork Poland 54°33N 17°46E 184 D4
Lebrija Spain 36°53N 6°5W 195 J4
Łebsko, Jezioro Poland 54°40N 17°25E 184 D4
Lebu Chile 37°40S 73°47W 334 D1
Leca da Palmeira Portugal 41°12N 8°42W 194 D2
Lecce Italy 40°23N 18°11E 201 B11
Lecco Italy 45°51N 9°23E 198 C6
Lecco, L. di Italy 45°55N 9°19E 198 C6
Lécera Spain 41°13N 0°43W 196 D4
Lech Austria 47°13N 10°9E 180 D3
Lech → Germany 48°43N 10°56E 179 G6
Lechang China 25°10N 113°20E 229 E9
Lechena Greece 37°57N 21°16E 204 D3
Lechtaler Alpen Austria 47°15N 10°30E 180 D3
Léconi Gabon 1°35S 14°14E 264 C2
Léconi → Gabon 1°11S 13°16E 264 C2
Lecontes Mills U.S.A. 41°5N 78°17W 312 E6
Lectoure France 43°56N 0°38E 174 E4
Łęczna Poland 51°18N 22°53E 185 G9
Łęczyca Poland 52°5N 19°15E 185 F6
Ledang, Gunung Malaysia 2°22N 102°37E 234 B2
Ledesma Spain 41°6N 5°59W 194 D5
Lediba Dem. Rep. of the Congo 3°1S 16°34E 264 C3
Lédo, Cabo Angola 9°43S 13°12E 265 D2
Ledong China 18°41N 109°5E 236 C7
Leduc Canada 53°15N 113°30W 296 C6
Lee London, U.K. 51°27N 0°0 125 B4
Lee Fla., U.S.A. 30°25N 83°18W 316 E6
Lee Mass., U.S.A. 42°19N 73°15W 313 D11
Lee → Ireland 51°53N 8°56W 166 E3
Lee Vining U.S.A. 37°58N 119°7W 306 H7
Leech L. U.S.A. 47°10N 94°24W 308 B6
Leechburg U.S.A. 40°37N 79°36W 312 F5
Leeds W. Yorks., U.K. 53°48N 1°33W 168 D6
Leeds Ala., U.S.A. 33°33N 86°33W 315 E11
Leek Neths. 53°10N 6°24E 170 A6
Leek Staffs., U.K. 53°7N 2°1W 168 D5
Leeman Australia 29°57S 114°58E 279 E1
Leeper U.S.A. 41°22N 79°18W 312 E5
Leer Germany 53°13N 7°26E 178 B3
Lee's Summit U.S.A. 38°55N 94°23W 310 F2
Leesburg Fla., U.S.A. 28°49N 81°53W 317 G8
Leesburg Ga., U.S.A. 31°44N 84°10W 316 D5
Leesburg Ohio, U.S.A. 39°21N 83°33W 311 E13
Leeston N.Z. 43°45S 172°19E 285 D7
Leesville U.S.A. 31°8N 93°16W 314 F8
Leeton Australia 34°33S 146°23E 283 C7
Leetonia U.S.A. 40°53N 80°45W 312 F4
Leeu Gamka S. Africa 32°47S 21°59E 270 D3
Leeuwarden Neths. 53°15N 5°48E 170 A5
Leeuwin, C. Australia 34°20S 115°9E 279 F2
Leeuwin Naturaliste △ Australia 34°6S 115°3E 279 F2
Leeward Is. Atl. Oc. 16°30N 63°30W 321 C7
Léfini Congo 2°55S 15°39E 264 C3
Léfini → Congo 2°56S 16°9E 264 C3
Léfini ⌓ Congo 2°55S 15°20E 264 C3
Lefka Cyprus 35°6N 32°51E 207 E8
Lefkada Greece 38°40N 20°43E 207 B2
Lefkimis Greece 39°25N 20°3E 206 C10
Lefkimis, Akra Greece 39°29N 20°4E 206 C10
Lefkímmi = Lefkimis Greece 39°25N 20°3E 206 C10
Lefkoniko Cyprus 35°18N 33°44E 207 E9
Lefroy Canada 44°16N 79°34W 312 B5
Lefroy, L. Australia 31°21S 121°40E 279 F3
Łeg → Poland 50°42N 21°50E 185 H8
Leganés Spain 40°19N 3°45W 127 C1
Legazpi Phil. 13°10N 123°45E 232 E4
Legazpi Madrid, Spain 40°23N 3°41W 127 B1
Lège-Cap-Ferret France 44°48N 1°9W 174 D2
Lege Hida Ethiopia 7°56N 41°4E 257 F5
Legendre I. Australia 20°22S 116°55E 278 D2
Leghorn = Livorno Italy 43°33N 10°19E 198 E7
Legionowo Poland 52°25N 20°50E 185 F7
Legnago Italy 45°11N 11°18E 199 C8
Legnano Italy 45°36N 8°54E 198 C5
Legnica Poland 51°12N 16°10E 185 G3
Legrad Croatia 46°17N 16°51E 199 B13
Leh India 34°9N 77°35E 243 B7
Lehigh Acres U.S.A. 26°36N 81°39W 317 J8
Lehighton U.S.A. 40°50N 75°43W 313 F9
Lehliu Romania 44°29N 26°50E 183 F11
Leho Sudan 7°7N 33°52E 257 F3
Lehrte Germany 52°22N 9°58E 178 C5
Lehtisaari Finland 60°10N 24°51E 121 B2
Lehua I. U.S.A. 22°1N 160°6W 302 A1
Lehututu Botswana 23°54S 21°55E 270 B3
Lei Shui → China 26°55N 112°35E 229 D9
Lei Yue Mun China 22°17N 114°14E 122 B2
Leiah Pakistan 30°58N 70°58E 242 D4
Leião Portugal 38°43N 9°17W 126 A1
Leibnitz Austria 46°47N 15°34E 180 E8
Leibo China 28°11N 103°34E 228 C4
Leicester U.K. 52°38N 1°8W 169 E6
Leicester City □ U.K. 52°38N 1°8W 169 E6
Leicester Square London, U.K. 125 b3
Leicestershire □ U.K. 52°41N 1°17W 169 E6
Leichhardt Australia 33°53S 151°9E 139 B1
Leichhardt → Australia 17°35S 139°48E 280 B2
Leichhardt Ra. Australia 20°46S 147°40E 280 C4
Leiden Neths. 52°9N 4°30E 170 B4
Leie → Belgium 51°2N 3°45E 170 C3
Leifers = Láives Italy 46°26N 11°20E 199 B8
Leigh → Australia 38°18S 144°30E 282 E6
Leigh Creek Australia 30°38S 138°26E 282 A3
Leikang Norway 62°15N 5°47E 164 B2
Leikanger Sogn og Fjordane, Norway 62°8N 5°18E 164 B2
Leikanger Sogn og Fjordane, Norway 61°10N 6°51E 164 C3
Leiktho Burma 19°13N 96°35E 241 F6
Leimen Germany 49°21N 8°41E 179 F4
Leine → Germany 52°43N 9°36E 178 C5
Leinefelde Germany 51°23N 10°19E 178 D6
Leinster Australia 27°51S 120°36E 279 E3
Leinster □ Ireland 53°3N 7°8W 166 C4
Leinster, Mt. Ireland 52°37N 6°46W 166 D5
Leipalingis Lithuania 54°5N 23°51E 184 D10
Leipe = Lipno Poland 52°49N 19°15E 185 F6
Leipzig Germany 51°18N 12°22E 178 D8
Leira Norway 60°58N 9°17E 164 D6
Leiria Portugal 39°46N 8°53W 194 F2
Leiria □ Portugal 39°46N 8°53W 194 F2
Leirvassbu Norway 61°33N 8°13E 164 C5
Leirvik Norway 59°47N 5°28E 164 E2
Leishan China 26°15N 108°20E 228 D7
Leisler, Mt. Australia 23°23S 129°20E 278 D4
Leisure City U.S.A. 25°30N 80°26W 317 K9
Leith U.K. 55°59N 3°11W 121 B3
Leith Hill U.K. 51°11N 0°22W 169 F7
Leitha → Europe 47°50N 17°15E 181 D10
Leitrim Ireland 54°0N 8°5W 166 B3
Leitrim □ Ireland 54°8N 8°0W 166 B4
Leitza Spain 43°5N 1°55W 196 B3
Leiyang China 26°27N 112°45E 229 D9
Leizhou China 20°52N 110°8E 229 G8
Leizhou Bandao China 21°0N 110°0E 228 G7
Leizhou Wan China 20°50N 110°20E 229 G8
Lek → Neths. 51°54N 4°35E 170 C4
Leka Norway 65°5N 11°35E 160 D14
Lekani Greece 41°10N 24°35E 203 E8
Lekbibaj Albania 42°17N 19°56E 202 D3
Lekeitio Spain 43°20N 2°32W 196 B2
Lékéti, Mt. Congo 2°34S 14°17E 264 C2
Lékoli-Pandaka ⌓ Congo 0°41N 14°50E 264 B2
Lekoui Burkina Faso 12°37N 3°40W 262 C4
Leksand Sweden 60°44N 15°1E 162 D9
Leksura = Lentekhi Georgia 42°47N 42°45E 191 J6
Leland U.S.A. 45°1N 85°45W 309 C11
Lelång Sweden 59°10N 12°5E 162 E6
Leleiwi Pt. U.S.A. 19°44N 155°0W 302 D7
Lelepa Vanuatu 17°35S 168°11E 287 G6
Leleque Argentina 42°28S 71°0W 336 B2
Leli Solomon Is. 8°42S 161°4E 287 M11
Lelu Burma 19°4N 95°30E 241 F5
Lelydorp Suriname 5°42N 55°14W 329 B6
Lelystad Neths. 52°30N 5°25E 170 B5
Lem Denmark 56°1N 8°24E 163 H2
Lema Nigeria 12°58N 4°13E 263 C5
Lema Shilindi Ethiopia 4°50N 42°6E 257 G5
Léman, L. Europe 46°26N 6°30E 173 F13
Lemankoa Papua N. G. 5°3S 154°34E 286 C8
Lembar Indonesia 8°45S 116°4E 231 K19
Lemberg = Lviv Ukraine 49°50N 24°0E 177 D13
Lembuak Indonesia 8°36S 116°11E 231 K19
Leme Brazil 22°58S 43°10W 135 B1
Lemera Dem. Rep. of the Congo 3°0S 28°55E 268 C2
Lemery Phil. 13°51N 120°56E 232 E3
Lemfu Dem. Rep. of the Congo 5°18S 15°13E 265 D3
Lemhi Ra. U.S.A. 44°0N 113°0W 304 D7
Lemmer Neths. 52°51N 5°43E 170 B5
Lemmon U.S.A. 45°57N 102°10W 308 C2
Lemon Grove U.S.A. 32°44N 117°1W 307 N9
Lemoore U.S.A. 36°18N 119°46W 306 J7
Lemotol B. Micronesia 7°21N 151°35E 287 T17
Lemoyne Canada 45°29N 73°29W 130 B3
Lempdes France 45°22N 3°17E 174 C7
Lemsid W. Sahara 26°33N 13°51W 260 C2
Lemvig Denmark 56°33N 8°20E 163 H2
Lemyethna Burma 17°36N 95°9E 241 G5
Lena U.S.A. 42°23N 89°49W 310 B7
Lena → Russia 72°52N 126°40E 215 B13
Lenadoon Pt. Ireland 54°18N 9°3W 166 B2
Lenakel Vanuatu 19°38S 169°16E 287 J7
Lenart Slovenia 46°36N 15°48E 199 B12
Lenartovce Slovak Rep. 48°18N 20°19E 181 C13
Lencloître France 46°50N 0°20E 172 F7
Lençóis Brazil 12°35S 41°24W 333 D3
Lençóis Maranhenses △ Brazil 2°30S 43°0W 332 B3
Lendava Slovenia 46°35N 16°25E 199 B13
Lendeh Iran 30°58N 50°25E 247 D6
Lendinara Italy 45°5N 11°36E 199 C8
Lenger Kazakhstan 42°12N 69°54E 217 D7
Lengerich Germany 52°11N 7°52E 178 C3
Lenggong Malaysia 5°6N 100°58E 237 K3
Lenggries Germany 47°41N 11°35E 179 H7
Léngoué Congo 1°15N 15°38E 264 B3
Lengshuijiang China 27°40N 111°26E 229 D8
Lengshuitan China 26°27N 111°35E 229 D8
Lengua de Vaca, Pta. Chile 30°14S 71°38W 334 C1
Lengwe △ Malawi 16°14S 34°45E 269 F3
Lengwethen = Lunino Russia 53°38N 45°18E 190 D7
Lengyeltóti Hungary 46°40N 17°40E 182 D2
Lengyeltótihács = Lengyeltóti Hungary 46°40N 17°40E 182 D2
Lenhovda Sweden 57°0N 15°16E 163 G9
Lenin Russia 55°43N 37°34E 129 B3
Lenin Mausoleum Moscow, Russia 129 b2
Lenina, Kanal → Russia 43°44N 45°17E 191 J7
Leninabad = Khŭjand Tajikistan 40°17N 69°37E 217 D7
Leninakan = Gyumri Armenia 40°47N 43°50E 191 K6
Leningrad = Sankt-Peterburg Russia 59°55N 30°20E 137 B1
Leningrad □ Russia 59°40N 32°0E 188 C7
Lenino = Leninsk-Kuznetskiy Russia 54°44N 86°10E 217 B11
Lenino Moskva, Russia 55°38N 37°39E 129 C3
Lenino Ukraine 45°17N 35°46E 189 K8
Leninogorsk Kazakhstan 50°20N 83°30E 217 B10
Leninogorsk Russia 54°36N 52°30E 216 B4
Leninsk = Petrodvorets Russia 59°52N 29°54E 188 C5
Leninsk Russia 48°40N 45°15E 191 F7
Leninsk-Kuznetskiy Russia 54°44N 86°10E 217 B11
Leninsk-Turkmensky = Türkmenabat Turkmenistan 39°6N 63°34E 247 B9
Leninskiye Gory Russia 55°41N 37°32E 129 B3
Leninskoye Russia 58°23N 47°3E 190 A8
Lenk Switz. 46°27N 7°28E 179 J3
Lenkoran = Länkäran Azerbaijan 38°48N 48°52E 213 C13
Lenmalu Indonesia 1°45S 130°15E 231 E8
Lenne → Germany 51°25N 7°29E 178 D3
Lennestadt Germany 51°8N 8°2E 178 D4
Lennox Calif., U.S.A. 33°56N 118°20W 126 C2
Lennox S. Dak., U.S.A. 43°21N 96°53W 308 D5
Lennox, I. Chile 55°18S 66°50W 336 E3
Lennoxville Canada 45°22N 71°51W 313 A13
Leno Italy 45°22N 10°13E 198 C7
Lenoir U.S.A. 35°55N 81°32W 315 D14
Lenoir City U.S.A. 35°48N 84°16W 315 D12
Lenore L. Canada 52°30N 104°59W 297 C8
Lenox Ga., U.S.A. 31°16N 83°28W 316 D6
Lenox Iowa, U.S.A. 40°53N 94°34W 310 D2
Lenox Mass., U.S.A. 42°22N 73°17W 313 D11
Lens France 50°26N 2°50E 173 B9
Lensahn Germany 54°13N 10°53E 178 A6
Lensk Russia 60°48N 114°55E 215 C12
Lensvik Norway 63°31N 9°48E 164 A6
Lentas Greece 34°56N 24°56E 207 F5
Lentekhi Georgia 42°47N 42°45E 191 J6
Lenti Hungary 46°37N 16°33E 182 D1
Lentini Italy 37°17N 15°0E 201 E8
Lentschütz = Łęczyca Poland 52°5N 19°15E 185 F6
Lenwood U.S.A. 34°53N 117°7W 307 L9
Lenya Burma 11°33N 98°57E 237 G2
Lenzen Germany 53°5N 11°29E 178 B7
Léo Burkina Faso 11°3N 2°2W 262 C4
Leoben Austria 47°22N 15°5E 180 D8
Leobschütz = Głubczyce Poland 50°13N 17°52E 185 H4
Leodhas = Lewis U.K. 58°9N 6°40W 167 C2
Leola U.S.A. 45°43N 98°56W 308 C4
Leominster Hereford, U.K. 52°14N 2°43W 169 E5
Leominster Mass., U.S.A. 42°32N 71°46W 313 D13
León = Cotopaxi □ Ecuador 0°5S 78°55W 328 D2
Léon Landes, France 43°53N 1°18W 174 E2
León Guanajuato, Mexico 21°6N 101°41W 318 C4
León Nic. 12°20N 86°51W 320 D2
León Spain 42°38N 5°34W 194 C5
Leon Iowa, U.S.A. 40°44N 93°45W 310 D3
León □ Spain 42°40N 5°55W 194 C5
Leon → U.S.A. 31°14N 97°28W 314 F6
León, Montes de Spain 42°30N 6°18W 194 C4
Leonardo da Vinci, Roma ✈ (FCO) Italy 41°48N 12°15E 199 G9
Leonardtown U.S.A. 38°17N 76°38W 309 F15
Leonardville Namibia 23°29S 18°49E 270 B2
Leonberg Germany 48°48N 9°1E 179 G5
Leonding Austria 48°16N 14°15E 180 C7
Leone Amer. Samoa 14°23S 170°48W 302 f
Leonessa Italy 42°34N 12°58E 199 F9
Leonforte Italy 37°38N 14°23E 201 E7
Leongatha Australia 38°30S 145°58E 283 E6
Leonia Fla., U.S.A. 30°55N 86°1W 316 E3
Leonia N.J., U.S.A. 40°51N 73°59W 132 A2
Leonidio Greece 37°9N 22°52E 204 D4
Leonora Australia 28°49S 121°19E 279 E3
Leopardstown Ireland 53°16N 6°11W 120 B2
Leopold II, L. = Mai-Ndombe, L. Dem. Rep. of the Congo 2°0S 18°20E 264 C3
Leopoldau Austria 48°15N 16°26E 142 A2
Leopoldina = Aruanã Brazil 14°54S 51°10W 333 D1
Leopoldina = Parnamirim Brazil 8°5S 39°34W 332 C4
Leopoldina Brazil 21°28S 42°40W 333 F3
Leopoldo Bulhões Brazil 16°37S 48°46W 333 E2
Leopoldsburg Belgium 51°7N 5°13E 170 C5
Leopoldsdorf Austria 48°7N 16°23E 142 B2
Leopoldstadt Austria 48°13N 16°22E 142 A2
Leopoldville = Kinshasa Dem. Rep. of the Congo 4°20S 15°15E 265 C3
Leoti U.S.A. 38°29N 101°21W 308 F3
Leova Moldova 46°28N 28°15E 183 D13
Leoville Canada 53°39N 107°33W 297 C7
Lepe Spain 37°15N 7°12W 195 H3
Lepel = Lyepyel Belarus 54°50N 28°40E 188 E5
Lepenou Greece 38°42N 21°17E 204 C3
Leping China 28°47N 117°7E 229 C11
Lépo, L. do Angola 17°0S 19°0E 265 F3
Lepontine, Alpi Italy 46°22N 8°27E 198 B5
Leportovo Russia 55°46N 37°43E 129 B4
Leppävaara Finland 60°13N 24°49E 121 B1
Leppävirta Finland 62°29N 27°46E 160 E22
Lepsény Hungary 47°0N 18°15E 182 D3
Leptis Magna Libya 32°40N 14°12E 258 B2
Lequeitio = Lekeitio Spain 43°20N 2°32W 196 B2
Lercara Friddi Italy 37°45N 13°36E 200 E6
Léré C.A.R. 6°46N 17°25E 264 A3
Léré Chad 9°39N 14°13E 259 G2
Léré Mali 15°45N 4°55W 262 B4
Lere Bauchi, Nigeria 9°43N 9°18E 263 D6
Lere Kaduna, Nigeria 10°23N 8°35E 263 C6
Leribe Lesotho 28°51S 28°3E 271 C4
Lérici Italy 44°4N 9°55E 198 D6
Lérida = Lleida Spain 41°37N 0°39E 196 D5
Lérins, Îs. de France 43°31N 7°3E 175 E11
Lerma Spain 42°0N 3°47W 194 C7
Leros Greece 37°10N 26°50E 205 D8
Lérouville France 48°44N 5°30E 173 D12
Lerum Sweden 57°46N 12°16E 163 G6
Lerwick U.K. 60°9N 1°9W 167 A7
Leş Romania 46°58N 21°50E 182 D6
Les Abrets France 45°32N 5°35E 175 C9
Les Abymes Guadeloupe 16°17N 61°32W 322 e
Les Andelys France 49°15N 1°25E 172 C8
Les Anses-d'Arlets Martinique 14°28N 61°6W 322 j
Les Avirons Réunion 21°14S 55°20E 272 f
Les Borges Blanques Spain 41°31N 0°52E 196 D5
Les Cayes Haiti 18°15N 73°46W 321 C5
Les Coteaux Canada 45°15N 74°13W 313 A10
Les Escoumins Canada 48°21N 69°24W 299 C6
Les Essarts France 46°47N 1°12W 172 F5
Les Grands Fonds Guadeloupe 16°16N 61°26W 322 e
Les Herbiers France 46°52N 1°1W 172 F5
Les Lilas France 48°52N 2°25E 134 A3
Les Loges-en-Josas France 48°45N 2°8E 134 B1
Les Mangles Guadeloupe 16°23N 61°27W 322 e
Les Minquiers, Plateau des Chan. Is. 48°58N 2°8W 172 D4
Les Moroubas C.A.R. 6°11N 20°13E 264 A4
Les Pavillons-sous-Bois France 48°54N 2°30E 134 A4
Les Pieux France 49°30N 1°48W 172 C5
Les Ponts-de-Cé France 47°25N 0°30W 172 E6
Les Riceys France 47°59N 4°22E 173 E11
Les Sables-d'Olonne France 46°30N 1°45W 174 B2
Les Tantes Grenada 12°19N 61°33W 323 q
Les Trois-Bassins Réunion 21°5S 55°18E 272 f
Les Trois-Îlets Martinique 14°32N 61°2W 322 j
Les Vans France 44°25N 4°7E 175 D8
Lesbos Greece 39°10N 26°20E 205 B8
L'Escala Spain 42°7N 3°8E 196 C8
L'Escalier Mauritius 20°28S 57°36E 272 e
Leschnitz = Leśnica Poland 50°26N 18°11E 185 H5
Leshan China 29°33N 103°41E 228 C4
Leshukonskoye Russia 64°54N 45°46E 186 B8
Leshwe ⌓ Dem. Rep. of the Congo 12°45S 29°30E 269 E2
Lésigny France 48°44N 2°37E 134 B4
Lésina Italy 41°52N 15°21E 199 G12
Lésina, L. di Italy 41°53N 15°26E 199 G12
Lesjaskog Norway 62°14N 8°22E 164 B5
Lesjaverk Norway 62°12N 8°34E 164 B5
Lesjöfors Sweden 59°58N 14°11E 162 E8
Leskhimstroy = Syeverodonetsk Ukraine 48°58N 38°35E 189 H10
Lesko Poland 49°30N 22°23E 185 J9
Leskov I. Antarctica 56°0S 28°0W 151 B1
Leskovac Serbia 43°0N 21°58E 202 C5
Leskovik Albania 40°10N 20°34E 202 F4
Leslau = Włocławek Poland 52°40N 19°3E 185 F6
Leslie Ga., U.S.A. 31°57N 84°5W 316 D5
Leslie Mich., U.S.A. 42°27N 84°26W 311 B12
Leśna Poland 51°1N 15°15E 185 G2
Lesneven France 48°35N 4°20W 172 D2
Leśnica Poland 50°26N 18°11E 185 H5
Lešnica Serbia 44°39N 19°20E 202 B3
Lesnoi = Umba Russia 66°42N 34°11E 186 A5
Lesnoye Russia 58°15N 35°18E 188 C8
Lesnozavodskaya Russia 59°51N 30°29E 137 B2
Lesopilnoye Russia 46°44N 134°20E 220 A7
Lesotho ■ Africa 29°40S 28°0E 271 C4
Lesozavodsk Russia 45°30N 133°29E 220 B6
Lesparre-Médoc France 45°18N 0°57W 174 C3
Lessay France 49°14N 1°30W 172 C5
Lesse → Belgium 50°15N 4°54E 170 D4
Lesse et Lomme ⌓ Belgium 50°8N 5°9E 170 D5
Lessebo Sweden 56°45N 15°16E 163 H9
Lesser Antilles W. Indies 15°0N 61°0W 321 D7
Lesser Slave L. Canada 55°30N 115°25W 296 B5
Lesser Sunda Is. Indonesia 8°0S 120°0E 235 D5
Lessines Belgium 50°42N 3°50E 170 D3
Lester B. Pearson Int., Toronto ✈ (YYZ) Canada 43°46N 79°35W 141 A1
L'Esterre Grenada 12°28N 61°29W 323 q
Lestershire = Johnson City U.S.A. 42°7N 75°58W 313 D9
Lestock Canada 51°19N 103°59W 297 C8
Lesuer I. Australia 13°50S 127°17E 278 B4
Lesueur △ Australia 30°11S 115°10E 279 F2
Lésvos = Lesbos Greece 39°10N 26°20E 205 B8
Leszno Poland 51°50N 16°30E 185 G3
Letaba S. Africa 23°59S 31°50E 271 B5
Letälven → Sweden 59°5N 14°20E 162 E8
L'Étang-la-Ville France 48°52N 2°4E 134 A1
L'Étang-Salé Réunion 21°15S 55°23E 272 f
Létavértes Hungary 47°23N 21°55E 182 C6
Letchworth U.K. 51°59N 0°13W 169 F7
Letea, Ostrov Romania 45°18N 29°20E 183 E14
Lethbridge Canada 49°45N 112°45W 296 D6
Lethem Guyana 3°20N 59°50W 329 C6
Leti, Kepulauan Indonesia 8°10S 128°0E 231 F7
Leti Is. = Leti, Kepulauan Indonesia 8°10S 128°0E 231 F7
Letiahau → Botswana 21°16S 24°0E 270 B3
Leticia Colombia 4°9S 70°0W 328 D4
Leting China 39°23N 118°55E 227 E10
Letjiesbos S. Africa 32°34S 22°16E 270 D3
Letlhakane Botswana 21°27S 25°30E 270 B4
Letlhakeng Botswana 24°0S 24°59E 270 B3
Letná Prague, Czech Rep. 135 a1
Letňany Czech Rep. 50°8N 14°30E 135 B3
Letopolis = Ausîm Egypt 30°7N 31°8E 117 A1
Letpadan Burma 17°45N 95°45E 241 G5
Letpan Burma 19°28N 94°10E 241 F5
Letsôk-aw Kyun Burma 11°30N 98°25E 237 G2
Letterkenny Ireland 54°57N 7°45W 166 B4
Leu Romania 44°10N 24°0E 183 F9
Léua Angola 11°34S 20°32E 265 E4
Leucadia U.S.A. 33°4N 117°18W 307 M9
Leucate France 42°56N 3°3E 174 F7
Leucate, Étang de France 42°50N 3°0E 174 F7
Leuchars U.K. 56°24N 2°53W 167 E6
Leuk Switz. 46°19N 7°37E 179 J3
Leuşeni Moldova 46°49N 28°12E 183 D13
Leuser, G. Indonesia 3°46N 97°12E 234 B1
Leusoalii Amer. Samoa 14°14S 169°25W 302 f
Leutkirch Germany 47°49N 10°1E 179 H6
Leutschau = Levoča Slovak Rep. 49°2N 20°35E 181 B13
Leuven Belgium 50°52N 4°42E 170 D4
Leuze-en-Hainaut Belgium 50°36N 3°37E 170 D3
Lev Tolstoy Russia 53°13N 39°29E 188 F10
Levallois-Perret France 48°53N 2°16E 134 A2
Levan Albania 40°40N 19°28E 202 F3
Levanger Norway 63°45N 11°19E 160 E14
Levant, Î. du France 43°3N 6°28E 175 E10
Lévanto Italy 44°10N 9°38E 198 D6
Lévanzo Italy 38°0N 12°20E 200 D5
Leveld Norway 60°44N 8°33E 164 D5
Levelland U.S.A. 33°35N 102°23W 314 E3
Levelock U.S.A. 59°7N 156°51W 303 G8
Leven U.K. 56°12N 3°0W 167 E6
Leven, L. U.K. 56°12N 3°22W 167 E5
Leven, Toraka Madag. 12°30S 47°45E 272 A2
Levent Turkey 41°5N 29°0E 122 B2
Leveque C. Australia 16°20S 123°0E 278 C3
Levera △ Grenada 12°13N 61°38W 323 q
Leverano Italy 40°17N 18°0E 201 B10
Leverger = Santo Antônio do Leverger Brazil 15°52S 56°5W 331 D6
Leverkusen Germany 51°1N 7°1E 178 D3
Levice Slovak Rep. 48°13N 18°35E 181 C11
Lévico Terme Italy 46°0N 11°18E 199 C8
Levie France 41°40N 9°7E 175 G13
Levier France 46°58N 6°8E 173 F13
Levin N.Z. 40°37S 175°18E 284 G4
Lévis Canada 46°48N 71°9W 299 C5
Levis, L. Canada 62°37N 117°58W 296 A5
Levitha Greece 37°0N 26°28E 205 D8
Levittown N.Y., U.S.A. 40°44N 73°31W 313 F11
Levittown Pa., U.S.A. 40°9N 74°51W 313 F10
Levka Bulgaria 41°52N 26°15E 203 E10
Levka Oros Greece 35°18N 24°3E 207 E5
Levkada □ Greece 38°45N 20°40E 207 B2
Levkás = Lefkada Greece 38°40N 20°43E 207 B2
Levkôsia = Nicosia Cyprus 35°10N 33°25E 207 E9
Levoča Slovak Rep. 49°2N 20°35E 181 B13
Levroux France 46°59N 1°38E 173 F8
Levski Bulgaria 43°21N 25°10E 203 C9
Levskigrad = Karlovo Bulgaria 42°38N 24°47E 203 D8
Levuka Fiji 17°34S 179°0E 287 A2
Lewe Burma 19°38N 96°7E 241 F6
Lewes E. Sussex, U.K. 50°52N 0°1E 169 G8
Lewes Del., U.S.A. 38°46N 75°9W 309 F16
Lewin Brzeski Poland 50°45N 17°37E 185 H4
Lewis U.K. 58°9N 6°40W 167 C2
Lewis → U.S.A. 45°51N 122°48W 306 E4
Lewis, Butt of U.K. 58°31N 6°16W 167 C2
Lewis Pass N.Z. 42°31S 172°11E 285 C7
Lewis Ra. Australia 20°3S 128°50E 278 D4
Lewis Range U.S.A. 48°5N 113°5W 304 B7
Lewis Run U.S.A. 41°52N 78°40W 312 E6
Lewisburg Ohio, U.S.A. 39°51N 84°33W 311 E12
Lewisburg Pa., U.S.A. 40°58N 76°54W 312 F8
Lewisburg Tenn., U.S.A. 35°27N 86°48W 315 D11
Lewisburg W. Va., U.S.A. 37°48N 80°27W 309 G13
Lewisdale U.S.A. 38°58N 76°59W 143 B4
Lewisham □ U.K. 51°27N 0°1W 125 B3
Lewisport U.S.A. 37°56N 86°54W 311 G10
Lewisporte Canada 49°15N 55°3W 299 C8
Lewiston Idaho, U.S.A. 46°25N 117°1W 304 C5
Lewiston Maine, U.S.A. 44°6N 70°13W 309 C18
Lewiston N.Y., U.S.A. 43°11N 79°3W 312 C5
Lewistown Ill., U.S.A. 40°24N 90°9W 310 D6
Lewistown Mo., U.S.A. 40°5N 91°49W 310 D5
Lewistown Mont., U.S.A. 47°4N 109°26W 304 C9
Lewistown Pa., U.S.A. 40°36N 77°34W 312 F7
Lexington Ga., U.S.A. 33°52N 83°7W 316 B6
Lexington Ill., U.S.A. 40°39N 88°47W 311 D8
Lexington Ky., U.S.A. 38°3N 84°30W 311 F12
Lexington Mass., U.S.A. 42°25N 71°12W 116 A1
Lexington Mich., U.S.A. 43°16N 82°32W 312 C2
Lexington Mo., U.S.A. 39°11N 93°52W 310 E3
Lexington N.C., U.S.A. 35°49N 80°15W 315 D14
Lexington N.Y., U.S.A. 42°15N 74°22W 313 D10
Lexington Nebr., U.S.A. 40°47N 99°45W 308 E4
Lexington Ohio, U.S.A. 40°41N 82°35W 312 F2
Lexington S.C., U.S.A. 33°59N 81°11W 316 B8
Lexington Tenn., U.S.A. 35°39N 88°24W 315 D10
Lexington Va., U.S.A. 37°47N 79°27W 309 G14
Lexington Park U.S.A. 38°16N 76°27W 309 F15
Leyburn U.K. 54°19N 1°48W 168 C6
Leye China 24°48N 106°29E 228 E6
Leyeh Taiwan 23°28N 120°42E 225 C2
Leyland U.K. 53°42N 2°43W 168 D5
Leyre → France 44°39N 1°1W 174 D2
Leyte Phil. 10°30N 125°0E 233 F5
Leyte □ Phil. 11°0N 125°0E 233 F5
Leyte Gulf Phil. 10°50N 125°25E 233 F5
Leyton U.K. 51°33N 0°1W 125 A3
Leytonstone U.K. 51°34N 0°0 125 A4
Leżajsk Poland 50°16N 22°25E 185 H9
Lezay France 46°15N 0°1W 174 B3
Lezhë Albania 41°47N 19°39E 202 E3
Lezhi China 30°19N 104°58E 228 B5
Lézignan-Corbières France 43°13N 2°43E 174 E6
Lezoux France 45°49N 3°21E 174 C7
Lgov Russia 51°42N 35°16E 189 G8
Lhasa China 29°25N 90°58E 218 D4
L'Haÿ-les-Roses France 48°46N 2°20E 134 B3
Lhazê China 29°5N 87°38E 218 D3
Lhokkruet Indonesia 4°55N 95°24E 234 B1
Lhokseumawe Indonesia 5°10N 97°10E 234 A1
L'Hospitalet de Llobregat Spain 41°21N 2°6E 114 A1
Lhotka Czech Rep. 50°1N 14°26E 135 B2
Lhuntsi Dzong Bhutan 27°39N 91°10E 241 B3
Lhut, W. → Somali Rep. 10°17N 50°9E 267 B7
Li Thailand 17°48N 98°57E 236 D2
Li Jiang → China 24°40N 110°40E 229 E8
Li Shui → China 29°24N 112°1E 229 C9
Li Xian Gansu, China 34°10N 105°5E 226 G3
Li Xian Hebei, China 38°30N 115°35E 226 E8
Li Xian Hunan, China 29°36N 111°42E 229 C8
Lia-Moya C.A.R. 6°54N 16°17E 264 A3
Liadi Greece 36°50N 26°11E 205 E8
Liamuiga, Mt. St. Kitts & Nevis 17°22N 62°48W 322 d
Lian Phil. 14°3N 120°39E 232 D3
Liancheng China 25°42N 116°40E 229 E11
Liancourt Rocks = Tok-do Asia 37°15N 131°52E 221 F5
Liang Tao Taiwan 26°23N 128°28E 225 b
Lianga Phil. 8°38N 126°6E 233 G6
Lianga Bay Phil. 8°37N 126°12E 233 G6
Liangcheng Nei Monggol Zizhiqu, China 40°28N 112°25E 226 D7
Liangcheng Shandong, China 35°32N 119°37E 227 G10
Liangdang China 33°56N 106°18E 226 H4
Lianghe China 24°50N 98°20E 228 E2
Lianghekou China 29°11N 108°44E 228 C7
Liangping China 30°38N 107°47E 228 B6
Liangpran Indonesia 1°4N 114°23E 235 B4
Liangshui He → China 39°48N 116°23E 114 C2
Lianhua China 27°3N 113°54E 229 D9
Lianhua Chi China 39°52N 116°16E 114 B1
Lianhua He → China 39°52N 116°13E 114 B1
Lianjiang Fujian, China 26°12N 119°27E 229 D12
Lianjiang Guangdong, China 21°40N 110°20E 229 G8
Lianping China 24°26N 114°30E 229 E10
Lianshan China 24°38N 112°8E 229 E9
Lianshanguan China 40°53N 123°43E 224 B1
Lianshui China 33°42N 119°20E 227 H10
Lianyuan China 27°40N 111°38E 229 D8
Lianyungang China 34°40N 119°11E 227 G10
Lianzhou China 24°51N 112°22E 229 E9
Liao He → China 41°0N 121°50E 227 D11
Liaocheng China 36°28N 115°58E 226 F8
Liaodong Bandao China 40°0N 122°30E 227 E12
Liaodong Wan China 40°20N 121°10E 227 D11
Liaoning □ China 41°40N 122°30E 224 B1
Liaotung, G. of = Liaodong Wan China 40°20N 121°10E 227 D11
Liaoyang China 41°15N 122°58E 224 B1
Liaoyuan China 42°58N 125°2E 227 C13
Liaozhong China 41°23N 122°50E 224 B1
Liard → Canada 61°51N 121°18W 296 A4
Liard River Canada 59°25N 126°5W 296 B3
Liari Pakistan 25°37N 66°30E 242 G2
Líbano Colombia 4°55N 75°4W 328 C2
Libau = Liepāja Latvia 56°30N 21°0E 184 B8
Libby U.S.A. 48°23N 115°33W 304 B6
Libčice nad Vitavou Czech Rep. 50°11N 14°22E 135 A2
Libeň Czech Rep. 50°6N 14°27E 135 B2
Libenge Dem. Rep. of the Congo 3°40N 18°55E 264 B3
Liberal U.S.A. 37°3N 100°55W 308 G3
Liberdade Acre, Brazil 10°5S 70°20W 330 C3
Liberdade São Paulo, Brazil 23°33S 46°37W 137 B2
Liberdade → Brazil 9°40S 52°17W 331 B7
Liberdade, Avenida da Lisbon, Portugal 126 b1
Liberec Czech Rep. 50°47N 15°7E 180 A8
Liberecký □ Czech Rep. 50°45N 15°0E 180 A8
Liberia Costa Rica 10°40N 85°30W 320 D2
Liberia ■ W. Afr. 6°30N 9°30W 262 D3
Libertad Antique, Phil. 11°46N 121°55E 233 F3
Libertad Venezuela 8°20N 69°37W 328 B4
Liberton U.K. 55°54N 3°9W 121 B3
Liberty Ind., U.S.A. 39°38N 84°56W 311 E12
Liberty Mo., U.S.A. 39°15N 94°25W 310 E2
Liberty N.Y., U.S.A. 41°48N 74°45W 313 E10
Liberty Pa., U.S.A. 41°34N 77°6W 312 E7
Liberty Tex., U.S.A. 30°3N 94°48W 314 F7
Liberty Center U.S.A. 41°27N 84°1W 311 C12
Liberty I. U.S.A. 40°41N 74°2W 132 B1
Liberty-Newark Int. ✈ (EWR) U.S.A. 40°42N 74°10W 313 F10
Liberty Osaka Museum Japan 34°38N 135°29E 133 B1
Liberty State Park ⌓ U.S.A. 40°42N 74°2W 132 B1
Libertyville U.S.A. 42°18N 87°57W 311 B9
Libeznice Czech Rep. 50°11N 14°29E 135 A2
Libiąż Poland 50°7N 19°21E 185 H6
Libibi Angola 14°42S 17°44E 265 E3
Lîbîya, Sahrâ' Africa 25°0N 25°0E 258 C4
Libjo Phil. 10°12N 125°32E 233 F5
Libmanan Phil. 13°42N 123°4E 232 E4
Libo China 25°22N 107°53E 228 E6
Libobo, Tanjung Indonesia 0°54S 128°28E 231 E7
Libode S. Africa 31°33S 29°2E 271 D4
Libohovë Albania 40°3N 20°10E 202 F4
Liboi Kenya 0°24N 40°57E 267 D5
Libona Phil. 8°20N 124°44E 233 G5
Libonda Zambia 14°28S 23°12E 265 E4
Libourne France 44°55N 0°14W 174 D3
Libramont Belgium 49°55N 5°23E 170 E5
Library of Congress Washington, D.C., U.S.A. 143 b3
Librazhd Albania 41°12N 20°22E 202 E4
Libreville Gabon 0°25N 9°26E 264 B1
Libuš Czech Rep. 50°0N 14°27E 135 B2
Libya ■ N. Afr. 27°0N 17°0E 258 C3
Libyan Desert = Lîbîya, Sahrâ' Africa 25°0N 25°0E 258 C4
Libyan Plateau = Ed Déffa Egypt 30°40N 26°30E 256 A2
Licantén Chile 35°55S 72°0W 334 D1
Licata Italy 37°6N 13°56E 200 E6
Lice Turkey 38°27N 40°39E 213 C9
Licheng China 36°28N 113°20E 226 F7
Lichfield U.K. 52°41N 1°49W 169 E6
Lichia Taiwan 22°47N 121°3E 225 D3
Lichiao China 23°3N 113°18E 121 B2
Lichinga Mozam. 13°13S 35°11E 269 E4
Lichtenburg Berlin, Germany 52°31N 13°30E 115 A4
Lichtenburg North West, S. Africa 26°8S 26°8E 270 C4
Lichtenfels Germany 50°8N 11°4E 179 E7
Lichterfelde Germany 52°25N 13°19E 115 B2
Lichuan Hubei, China 30°18N 108°57E 228 B7
Lichuan Jiangxi, China 27°18N 116°55E 229 D11
Licking → U.S.A. 39°6N 84°30W 311 F12
Licosa, Punta Italy 40°15N 14°54E 201 B7
Licungo → Mozam. 17°40S 37°15E 269 F4
Lida Belarus 53°53N 25°15E 177 B13
Liden Sweden 62°42N 16°48E 162 B10
Lidhult Sweden 56°50N 13°27E 163 H7
Lidingö Sweden 59°21N 18°8E 139 A2
Lidköping Sweden 58°31N 13°7E 163 F7
Lido Italy 45°25N 12°22E 199 C9
Lido Niger 12°54N 3°44E 263 C5
Lido di Roma = Óstia, Lido di Italy 41°43N 12°17E 199 G9
Lidoriki Greece 38°32N 22°12E 204 C4
Lidzbark Poland 53°15N 19°49E 185 E6
Lidzbark Warmiński Poland 54°7N 20°34E 184 D7
Liebenthal = Lubomierz Poland 51°1N 15°31E 185 G2
Liebenwalde Germany 52°52N 13°24E 178 C9
Lieberose Germany 51°59N 14°17E 178 D10
Liebig, Mt. Australia 23°18S 131°22E 278 D5
Liebling Romania 45°36N 21°20E 182 E6
Liechtenstein ■ Europe 47°8N 9°35E 179 H5
Liège Belgium 50°38N 5°35E 170 D5
Liège □ Belgium 50°32N 5°35E 170 D5
Liegnitz = Legnica Poland 51°12N 16°10E 185 G3
Lieksa Finland 63°18N 30°2E 160 E24
Lienart Dem. Rep. of the Congo 3°3N 25°31E 268 B2
Lienyünchiangshih = Lianyungang China 34°40N 119°11E 227 G10
Lienz Austria 46°50N 12°46E 180 E5
Liepāja Latvia 56°30N 21°0E 184 B8
Liepāja □ Latvia 56°30N 21°30E 184 B8
Liepājas ezers Latvia 56°27N 21°3E 184 B8
Lier Belgium 51°7N 4°34E 170 C4
Liernais France 47°13N 4°16E 173 E11
Lieshi Lingyuan China 23°7N 113°16E 121 B2
Liesing Austria 48°8N 16°17E 142 B1
Liesing → Austria 48°8N 16°28E 142 B2
Lieşti Romania 45°38N 27°34E 183 E12
Lietuva = Lithuania ■ Europe 55°30N 24°0E 188 E2
Liévin France 50°24N 2°47E 173 B9
Lièvre → Canada 45°31N 75°26W 298 C4
Liezen Austria 47°34N 14°15E 180 D7
Liffey → Ireland 53°21N 6°13W 166 C5
Lifford Ireland 54°51N 7°29W 166 B4
Liffré France 48°12N 1°30W 172 D5
Lifjell Norway 59°27N 8°45E 164 E5
Lifou, Î. N. Cal. 20°53S 167°13E 288 d
Lifudzin Russia 44°21N 134°58E 220 B7
Lifuka Tonga 19°48S 174°21W 287 P13
Ligao Phil. 13°14N 123°32E 232 E4
Ligasa Dem. Rep. of the Congo 0°44N 23°49E 264 B4
Lighthouse Point U.S.A. 26°15N 80°7W 317 J9
Lighthouse Pt. U.S.A. 29°54N 84°21W 316 F5
Lightning Ridge Australia 29°22S 148°0E 281 D4
Lignano Sabbiadoro Italy 45°42N 13°9E 199 C10
Ligny-en-Barrois France 48°36N 5°20E 173 D12
Ligonha → Mozam. 16°54S 39°9E 269 F4
Ligonier Ind., U.S.A. 41°28N 85°35W 311 C11
Ligonier Pa., U.S.A. 40°15N 79°14W 312 F5
Ligourio Greece 37°37N 23°4E 204 D5
Ligovo Russia 59°49N 30°10E 137 C1
Ligueil France 47°2N 0°49E 172 E7
Liguria □ Italy 44°30N 8°50E 198 D5
Ligurian Sea Medit. S. 43°20N 9°0E 198 E5
Lihir Group Papua N. G. 3°0S 152°35E 286 B7
Lihir I. Papua N. G. 3°5S 152°35E 286 B7
Lihou Reefs and Cays Australia 17°25S 151°40E 280 B5
Lihue U.S.A. 21°59N 159°23W 302 B2
Lihué Calel △ Argentina 38°0S 65°10W 334 D2
Lijiang China 26°55N 100°20E 228 D3
Lijordet Norway 59°56N 10°36E 133 A2
Likang Taiwan 22°47N 120°29E 225 D2
Likasi Dem. Rep. of the Congo 10°55S 26°48E 269 E2
Likati Dem. Rep. of the Congo 3°20N 24°0E 264 B4
Likati → Dem. Rep. of the Congo 2°53N 24°3E 264 B4
Likenäs Sweden 60°37N 13°3E 162 D7
Likete Dem. Rep. of the Congo 0°48S 21°31E 264 C4
Likhaya = Likhovskoy Russia 48°10N 40°10E 189 H11
Likhoborka → Russia 55°50N 37°37E 129 A3
Likhoslavl Russia 57°12N 35°30E 188 D8
Likhovskoy Russia 48°10N 40°10E 189 H11
Likhvin = Chekalin Russia 54°10N 36°10E 188 E9
Likimi Dem. Rep. of the Congo 2°44N 20°47E 264 B4
Likita Dem. Rep. of the Congo 4°15N 23°36E 264 B4
Liknes Norway 58°19N 6°59E 164 F3
Likokou Gabon 0°12S 12°48E 264 C2
Likoma I. Malawi 12°3S 34°45E 269 E3
Likouala → Congo 0°2N 14°53E 264 C3
Likouala aux Herbes → Congo 0°52S 17°8E 264 C3
Liku Cook Is. 19°2S 168°47W 289 g

Likumburu *Tanzania* 9°43S 35°8E **269** D4
Lilanga
  Dem. Rep. of the Congo 0°34S 23°56E **264** C4
L'Île-Bouchard *France* 47°7N 0°26E **172** E7
L'Île-Rousse *France* 42°38N 8°57E **175** F12
Lilenga *Dem. Rep. of the Congo* 1°4N 22°2E **264** B4
Liling *China* 27°42N 113°29E **229** D9
Lilla Edet *Sweden* 58°8N 12°8E **163** F6
Lilla Värtan *Sweden* 59°20N 18°11E **139** A3
Lille *France* 50°38N 3°3E **173** B10
Lille Bælt *Denmark* 55°20N 9°45E **163** J3
Lille Værlose *Denmark* 55°47N 12°22E **118** A2
Lillebonne *France* 49°30N 0°32E **172** C7
Lillesand *Norway* 58°15N 8°23E **163** G2
Lillesand *Norway* 58°15N 8°23E **164** C7
Lillestrom *Norway* 59°58N 11°5E **164** E8
Lillhärdal *Sweden* 61°51N 14°5E **162** C8
Lillo *Spain* 39°45N 3°20W **194** F7
Lillooet *Canada* 50°44N 121°57W **296** C4
Lillooet → *Canada* 49°15N 121°57W **296** C4
Lilongwe *Malawi* 14°0S 33°48E **269** E3
Liloy *Phil.* 8°4N 122°39E **233** G4
Liluah *India* 22°37N 88°19E **124** B1
Lim → *Europe* 43°45N 19°15E **202** C2
Lima *Brazil* 4°36S 63°40W **329** D5
Lima *Indonesia* 3°39S 127°58E **231** E7
Lima *Peru* 12°3S 77°2W **324** B2
Lima *Ill., U.S.A.* 40°11N 91°23W **310** D5
Lima *Mont., U.S.A.* 44°38N 112°36W **304** D7
Lima *Ohio, U.S.A.* 40°44N 84°6W **311** D12
Lima → *Peru* 12°3S 77°3W **324** D2
Lima → *Portugal* 41°41N 8°50W **194** D2
Lima Jorge Chavez, Int. ✈ (LIM)
  Peru 12°2S 77°8W **324** D2
Liman = Krasnyy Liman
  Ukraine 48°58N 37°50E **189** H9
Liman *Indonesia* 7°48S 111°45E **231** G14
Liman *Russia* 45°45N 47°12E **191** H8
Limanowa *Poland* 49°42N 20°22E **185** J7
Limassol *Cyprus* 34°42N 33°1E **207** F9
Limavady *U.K.* 55°3N 6°56W **166** A5
Limay → *Argentina* 39°0S 68°0W **336** A3
Limay Mahuida
  Argentina 37°10S 66°45W **334** D2
Limbach-Oberfrohna
  Germany 50°52N 12°43E **178** E8
Limbang *Brunei* 4°42N 115°6E **235** B5
Limbara, Mte. *Italy* 40°51N 9°10E **200** B2
Limbaži *Latvia* 57°31N 24°42E **188** B4
Limbdi *India* 22°34N 71°51E **142** H4
Limbe *Cameroon* 4°1N 9°10E **263** E6
Limbiate *Italy* 45°35N 9°7E **129** A1
Limbueta *Angola* 12°30S 18°42E **265** H3
Limbuhan = Pio V. Corpuz
  Phil. 11°55N 124°2E **233** F3
Limburg
  Germany 50°22N 8°4E **179** E4
Limburg □ *Belgium* 51°2N 5°25E **170** C5
Limburg □ *Neths.* 51°20N 5°55E **170** C5
Lime Village *U.S.A.* 61°21N 155°28W **303** F9
Limedsforsen *Sweden* 60°52N 13°26E **162** C6
Limehouse *U.S.A.* 51°30N 0°1W **125** A3
Limeil-Brévannes *France* 48°44N 2°29E **134** B3
Limeira = Joaçaba *Brazil* 57°3S 51°31W **335** B5
Limeira *Brazil* 22°35S 47°28W **335** E6
Limenaria *Greece* 40°38N 24°32E **203** F8
Limenas Chersonisou
  Greece 35°18N 25°21E **207** E6
Limerick *Limerick, Ireland* 52°40N 8°37W **166** D3
Limerick *Maine, U.S.A.* 43°41N 70°48W **313** C14
Limerick □ *Ireland* 52°30N 8°50W **166** D3
Limestone → *Canada* 42°2N 78°38W **312** D6
Limestone → *Canada* 56°31N 94°7W **297** B10
Limestone Hill = Lackawanna
  U.S.A. 42°50N 78°50W **312** D6
Limfjorden *Denmark* 56°55N 9°0E **163** H3
Limia = Lima → *Portugal* 41°41N 8°50W **194** D2
Limingen *Norway* 64°48N 13°35E **160** D15
Limmared *Sweden* 57°34N 13°20E **163** G7
Limmen Bight *Australia* 14°40S 135°35E **280** A2
Limmen Bight →
  Australia 15°7S 135°44E **280** A2
Limni *Greece* 38°43N 23°18E **204** C5
Limnos *Greece* 39°50N 25°5E **205** B7
Limoeiro *Brazil* 7°52S 35°27W **332** C4
Limoeiro do Norte *Brazil* 5°5S 38°0W **332** C4
Limoges *Ont., Canada* 45°20N 75°16W **313** A9
Limoges *Haute-Vienne,*
  France 45°50N 1°15E **174** C5
Limón *Costa Rica* 10°0N 83°2W **320** E3
Limon *Colo., U.S.A.* 39°16N 103°41W **304** G12
Limone Piemonte *Italy* 44°12N 7°34E **198** D4
Limonlu *Turkey* 36°34N 34°15E **206** D5
Limousin □ *France* 45°30N 1°30E **174** C5
Limousin, Plateaux du
  France 45°45N 1°15E **174** C5
Limoux *France* 43°4N 2°12E **174** E6
Limpopo → *S. Africa* 24°5S 29°0E **271** A4
Limpopo → *Africa* 25°5S 33°30E **271** D5
Limuru *Kenya* 1°2S 36°35E **268** C4
Lin Xian *China* 37°57N 110°58E **226** F6
Lin'an *China* 30°15N 119°42E **229** B12
Linao Pt. *Phil.* 6°46N 123°58E **233** H4
Linapacan *Phil.* 11°30N 119°52E **233** F2
Linapacan I. *Phil.* 11°27N 119°49E **233** F2
Linapacan Str. *Phil.* 11°37N 119°56E **233** F2
Linares *Chile* 35°50S 71°40W **334** D1
Linares *Colombia* 1°23N 77°31W **328** C2
Linares *Nuevo León,*
  Mexico 24°52N 99°34W **319** C5
Linares *Spain* 38°10N 3°40W **195** G7
Linaro, Capo *Italy* 42°2N 11°53E **198** F5
Linas Mte. *Italy* 39°25N 8°38E **200** C1
Linate, Milano ✈ (LIN)
  Italy 45°27N 9°16E **129** B2
Linbropark *S. Africa* 26°5S 28°7E **123** A2
Lincang *China* 23°58N 100°1E **228** F3
Lincheng *China* 37°25N 114°30E **226** F8
Linchuan *China* 27°57N 116°15E **229** D11
Lincoln *Argentina* 34°55S 61°30W **334** C3
Lincoln *Ont., Canada* 43°12N 79°28W **312** C6
Lincoln *N.Z.* 43°38S 172°30E **285** D7
Lincoln *Lincs., U.K.* 53°14N 0°32W **168** D7
Lincoln *Calif., U.S.A.* 38°54N 121°17W **306** G5
Lincoln *Ill., U.S.A.* 40°9N 89°22W **310** D7
Lincoln *Kans., U.S.A.* 39°3N 98°9W **308** F5
Lincoln *Maine, U.S.A.* 45°22N 68°30W **309** C19
Lincoln *N.H., U.S.A.* 44°3N 71°40W **313** C13
Lincoln *N. Mex., U.S.A.* 33°30N 105°23W **305** K11
Lincoln *Nebr., U.S.A.* 40°49N 96°41W **308** E5
Lincoln Boyhood △
  U.S.A. 38°7N 86°25W **311** F10
Lincoln Center for Performing Arts
  New York, U.S.A. **132** B2
Lincoln City *U.S.A.* 44°57N 124°1W **304** D1
Lincoln Hav = Lincoln Sea
  Arctic 84°0N 55°0W **154** A5
Lincoln Heights *U.S.A.* 34°4N 118°12W **126** B3
Lincoln Memorial *U.S.A.* 38°52N 77°4W **143** B3
Lincoln Park *Calif.,*
  U.S.A. 37°47N 122°30W **136** B1
Lincoln Park *Ga., U.S.A.* 32°52N 84°20W **316** C5

Lincoln Park *Ill., U.S.A.* 41°57N 87°38W **119** B3
Lincoln Park *Mich.,*
  U.S.A. 42°15N 83°11W **311** B13
Lincoln Park *N.J., U.S.A.* 40°55N 74°18W **132** B1
Lincoln Park Zoo *U.S.A.* 41°55N 87°38W **119** B3
Lincoln Sea *Arctic* 84°0N 55°0W **154** A5
Lincoln Tunnel *New York, U.S.A.* **132** C1
Lincolnshire □ *U.K.* 53°14N 0°32W **168** D7
Lincolnshire Wolds *U.K.* 53°26N 0°13W **168** D7
Lincolnton *U.S.A.* 33°48N 82°29W **316** B7
Lincolnton *N.C., U.S.A.* 35°29N 81°16W **315** D14
Lincolnwood *U.S.A.* 42°1N 87°43W **119** A2
Lind *U.S.A.* 46°58N 118°37W **304** C4
Linda *U.S.A.* 39°8N 121°34W **306** F5
Linda-a-Pastora *Portugal* 38°42N 9°15E **196** A1
Lindale *U.S.A.* 34°11N 85°11W **316** A4
Lindås *Norway* 60°44N 5°9E **164** D2
Lindau *Germany* 47°33N 9°41E **179** H5
Lindeman I. *Australia* 20°27S 149°3E **280** J7
Linden = Gladstone
  U.S.A. 39°13N 94°35W **310** E2
Linden *Guyana* 6°0N 58°10W **329** B6
Linden *Wellington, N.Z.* 41°10S 174°58E **143** A1
Linden *Gauteng, S. Africa* 26°8S 28°0E **123** A2
Linden *Ala., U.S.A.* 32°18N 87°48W **315** E11
Linden *Ind., U.S.A.* 40°11N 86°54W **311** D10
Linden *Mich., U.S.A.* 42°49N 83°47W **311** B13
Linden *Tex., U.S.A.* 33°1N 94°22W **314** E7
Lindenhurst *U.S.A.* 40°41N 73°23W **313** F11
Lindenow Fjord
  Greenland 60°30N 43°25W **154** D6
Lindesberg *Sweden* 59°36N 15°15E **162** E9
Lindesnes *Norway* 57°58N 7°3E **164** G4
Lindi *Tanzania* 9°58S 39°38E **269** D4
Lindi □ *Tanzania* 9°40S 38°30E **269** D4
Lindi →
  Dem. Rep. of the Congo 0°33N 25°5E **268** B2
Lindö *Sweden* 58°37N 16°15E **163** F10
Lindome *Sweden* 57°35N 12°5E **163** G6
Lindos *Greece* 36°6N 28°4E **206** E12
Lindos, Akra *Greece* 36°4N 28°10E **206** E12
Lindoso *Portugal* 41°52N 8°11W **194** D2
Lindow *Germany* 52°58N 12°59E **178** C8
Lindøya *Norway* 59°53N 10°42E **133** A3
Lindsay *Ont., Canada* 44°22N 78°43W **312** B6
Lindsay *Calif., U.S.A.* 36°12N 119°5W **306** J7
Lindsay *Okla., U.S.A.* 34°50N 97°38W **314** D6
Lindsborg *U.S.A.* 38°35N 97°40W **308** F6
Lindsdal *Sweden* 56°44N 16°18E **163** H10
Line Islands *Pac. Oc.* 7°0N 160°0W **289** H12
Linesville *U.S.A.* 41°39N 80°26W **312** E4
Lineville *Ala., U.S.A.* 33°19N 85°45W **316** B4
Lineville *Iowa, U.S.A.* 40°35N 93°32W **310** D3
Linfen *China* 36°3N 111°30E **226** F6
Ling Xian *Hunan, China* 26°29N 113°48E **229** D9
Ling Xian *Shandong,*
  China 37°22N 116°30E **226** F9
Lingal *India* 16°17N 78°31E **245** F4
Lingao *China* 19°56N 109°42E **236** C7
Lingayen *Phil.* 16°1N 120°14E **232** C3
Lingayen G. *Phil.* 16°10N 120°15E **232** C3
Lingbi *China* 33°33N 117°33E **227** H9
Lingbo *Sweden* 61°3N 16°41E **162** C10
Lingchuan *Guangxi Zhuangzu,*
  China 25°26N 110°21E **229** E8
Lingchuan *Shanxi, China* 35°45N 113°12E **226** G7
Lingding Yang *China* 22°25N 113°44E **219** G10
Lingen *Germany* 52°31N 7°19E **178** C3
Lingga *Indonesia* 0°12S 104°37E **234** C2
Lingga, Kepulauan
  Indonesia 0°10S 104°30E **234** C2
Lingga Arch. = Lingga, Kepulauan
  Indonesia 0°10S 104°30E **234** C2
Linghem *Sweden* 58°26N 15°47E **163** F9
Lingig *Phil.* 8°2N 126°24E **233** G6
Lingle *U.S.A.* 42°8N 104°21W **304** E11
Lingomo
  Dem. Rep. of the Congo 0°38N 22°3E **264** B4
Lingqiu *China* 39°28N 114°22E **226** E8
Lingshan *China* 22°25N 109°18E **228** F7
Lingshi *China* 36°48N 111°48E **226** F6
Lingshou *China* 38°20N 114°20E **226** E8
Lingshui *China* 18°27N 110°0E **236** C8
Lingsugur *India* 16°10N 76°31E **245** F3
Lingtai *China* 35°0N 107°40E **226** G4
Linguère *Senegal* 15°25N 15°5W **262** B1
Lingui *China* 25°12N 110°2E **229** E8
Lingunda
  Dem. Rep. of the Congo 0°49N 21°8E **264** C3
Lingwu *China* 38°6N 106°20E **226** E4
Lingyuan *China* 41°10N 119°15E **227** D10
Lingyun *China* 25°2N 106°35E **228** E6
Linhai *China* 28°50N 121°8E **229** C13
Linhares *Brazil* 19°25S 40°4W **333** E3
Linhe *China* 40°48N 107°20E **226** D4
Liniers *Argentina* 34°39S 58°30W **117** B1
Linjiang *China* 41°50N 127°0E **224** B3
Linkebeek *Belgium* 50°46N 4°20E **116** B2
Linköping *Sweden* 58°28N 15°36E **163** F9
Linkou *China* 45°15N 130°18E **227** B16
Linksfield *S. Africa* 26°9S 28°6E **123** A2
Linli *China* 29°31N 111°30E **229** C8
Linlithgow = West Lothian □
  U.K. 55°54N 3°36W **167** F5
Linmeyer *S. Africa* 26°16S 28°4E **123** B2
Linn *U.S.A.* 38°29N 91°51W **310** F5
Linna *Finland* 60°20N 24°50E **121** A2
Linnei *Taiwan* 23°45N 120°36E **225** C2
Linneus *U.S.A.* 39°53N 93°11W **310** E3
Linnhe, L. *U.K.* 56°36N 5°25W **167** E3
Linosa, Medit. *S.* 35°51N 12°50E **258** A2
Linpien *Taiwan* 22°26N 120°30E **225** D2
Linqing *China* 36°50N 115°42E **226** F8
Linqu *China* 36°25N 118°30E **227** F10
Linru *China* 34°11N 112°52E **226** G7
Linshui *China* 30°21N 106°57E **228** B6
Linsia = Linxia *China* 35°36N 103°0E **226** G2
Linstead *Jamaica* 18°8N 77°2W **320** a
Linta → *Madag.* 25°2S 44°5E **272** D1
Linth → *Switz.* 47°7N 9°7E **179** H5
Linthal *Switz.* 46°54N 9°0E **179** H5
Linton *U.S.A.* 39°2N 87°10W **311** F9
Linton *N. Dak., U.S.A.* 46°16N 100°14W **308** B4
Linton *U.S.A.* 34°20N 109°10E **226** G5
Lintong *China* 34°20N 109°10E **226** G5
Lintuvaara *Finland* 43°35N 80°43W **312** C4
Linville *Canada* 25°19N 121°33E **118** G7
Linwu *China* 25°11N 112°31E **229** E9
Linxi *China* 43°36N 118°2E **227** C10
Linxia *China* 35°36N 103°0E **226** G2
Linxiang *China* 29°28N 113°23E **229** C9
Linyi *China* 35°5N 118°21E **227** G10
Linyuan *Taiwan* 22°29N 120°25E **225** D2
Linz *Austria* 48°18N 14°18E **180** D7
Linz *Rhld-Pfz., Germany* 50°34N 7°17E **178** E3
Linzhenzhen *China* 36°30N 109°59E **226** F5
Linzi *China* 36°50N 118°20E **227** F10
Lioko *Équateur,*
  Dem. Rep. of the Congo 0°2N 22°4E **264** B4

Lioko *Orientale,*
  Dem. Rep. of the Congo 1°25N 23°7E **264** B4
Liomseter *Norway* 61°15N 9°35E **164** C6
Lion, G. du *France* 43°10N 4°0E **174** E7
Lion Rock Country Park △
  China 22°21N 114°11E **122** A2
Lionárisso *Cyprus* 35°28N 34°8E **207** E10
Lionel Town *Jamaica* 17°50N 77°15W **320** a
Lions, G. of = Lion, G. du
  France 43°10N 4°0E **174** E7
Lion's Den *Zimbabwe* 17°15S 30°5E **269** F3
Lion's Head *Canada* 44°58N 81°15W **312** B3
Lion's Head *Western Cape,*
  S. Africa 33°56S 18°23E **118** A1
Liouesso *Congo* 1°2N 15°43E **264** B3
Lioumi *Greece* 38°0N 23°54E **112** B2
Liozno = Lyozna *Belarus* 55°0N 30°50E **188** E6
Lipa *Phil.* 13°57N 121°10E **232** E3
Lipali *Mozam.* 15°50S 35°50E **269** F4
Lipany *Slovak Rep.* 49°9N 20°58E **181** B13
Lipari *Italy* 38°26N 14°58E **201** E7
Lipari, I. *Italy* 38°29N 14°56E **201** D7
Lipari, Ís. = Eólie, Ís.
  Italy 38°30N 14°57E **201** D7
Lipcani *Moldova* 48°14N 26°48E **183** B11
Liperi *Finland* 62°31N 29°24E **160** E23
Lipetsk *Russia* 52°37N 39°35E **189** F10
Lipetsk □ *Russia* 52°50N 38°50E **190** D4
Lipiany *Poland* 53°2N 14°58E **185** B1
Liping *China* 26°15N 109°7E **228** D7
Lipin *Russia* 57°19N 26°50E **205** D8
Lipkany = Lipcani
  Moldova 48°14N 26°48E **183** B11
Lipljan *Serbia* 42°31N 21°7E **202** D5
Lipnik nad Bečvou
  Czech Rep. 49°32N 17°36E **181** B10
Lipno *Poland* 52°49N 19°15E **185** F6
Lipova *Romania* 46°8N 21°42E **182** D2
Lipovets *Ukraine* 49°12N 29°1E **177** D15
Lippe → *Germany* 51°39N 6°36E **178** D2
Lippehne = Lipiany *Poland* 52°3N 14°58E **185** B1
Lippstadt *Germany* 51°41N 8°25E **178** D4
Lipscomb *U.S.A.* 36°14N 100°16W **314** C4
Lipsk *Poland* 53°44N 23°24E **184** E10
Lipsko *Poland* 51°9N 21°24E **185** G9
Liptovský Hrádok
  Slovak Rep. 49°2N 19°44E **181** B12
Liptrap, C. *Australia* 38°50S 145°55E **283** G6
Lipu *China* 24°30N 110°22E **229** E8
Lira *Uganda* 2°17N 32°57E **268** B3
Liranga *Congo* 0°43S 17°32E **264** C3
Lirí → *Italy* 41°25N 13°52E **200** A6
Liria = Llíria *Spain* 39°37N 0°35W **197** F4
Lisakovsk *Kazakhstan* 52°33N 62°37E **216** B6
Lisala
  Dem. Rep. of the Congo 2°12N 21°38E **264** B4
Lisboa *Portugal* 38°42N 9°8W **196** A1
Lisboa □ *Portugal* 39°0N 9°12W **195** F1
Lisboa ✈ (LIS) *Portugal* 38°46N 9°8W **126** A2
Lisbon = Lisboa *Portugal* 38°42N 9°8W **196** A1
Lisbon *N. Dak., U.S.A.* 46°27N 97°41W **308** B5
Lisbon *N.H., U.S.A.* 44°13N 71°55W **313** B13
Lisbon *Ohio, U.S.A.* 40°46N 80°46W **312** F4
Lisbon Falls *U.S.A.* 44°0N 70°4W **309** D18
Lisburn *U.K.* 54°31N 6°3W **166** B5
Lisburn, C. *Vanuatu* 15°39S 166°46E **287** E4
Lisburne, C. *U.S.A.* 68°53N 166°13W **303** B6
Liscannor B. *Ireland* 52°55N 9°24W **166** D2
Liscia → *Italy* 41°11N 9°9E **200** A2
Lisdoonvarna *Ireland* 53°2N 9°18W **166** C2
Lishan *Taiwan* 24°16N 121°14E **225** B3
Lishe Jiang → *China* 24°15N 101°35E **228** E3
Lishi *China* 37°31N 111°8E **226** F6
Lishu *China* 43°20N 124°18E **227** C13
Lishui *Guangdong, China* 23°12N 113°9E **121** A1
Lishui *Jiangsu, China* 31°38N 119°2E **229** B12
Lishui *Zhejiang, China* 28°28N 119°54E **229** C12
Lisianski I. *U.S.A.* 26°2N 174°0W **302** F9
Lisichansk = Lysychansk
  Ukraine 48°55N 38°30E **189** H10
Lisieux *France* 49°10N 0°12E **172** C7
Liski *Russia* 51°3N 39°30E **189** G10
L'Isle-Jourdain *Gers, France* 43°36N 1°5E **174** E4
L'Isle-Jourdain *Vienne,*
  France 46°13N 0°31E **174** B4
L'Isle-sur-la-Sorgue *France* 43°54N 5°2E **175** E9
Lisle-sur-Tarn *France* 43°52N 1°49E **174** E5
Lismore *N.S.W.,*
  Australia 28°44S 153°21E **281** D5
Lismore *Waterford, Ireland* 52°8N 7°55W **166** D4
Lissa = Leszno *Poland* 51°50N 16°30E **185** G3
Lista *Norway* 58°7N 6°39E **164** G3
Lister, Mt. *Antarctica* 78°0S 162°0E **151** D11

Little Churchill →
  Canada 57°30N 95°22W **297** B9
Little Coco I. *Burma* 61°15N 93°18E **245** H11
Little Colorado →
  U.S.A. 36°12N 111°48W **305** H8
Little Current *Canada* 45°55N 82°0W **298** C3
Little Current → *Canada* 50°57N 84°36W **298** B3
Little Desert △ *Australia* 37°25S 141°30E **282** D4
Little Diomede I. *U.S.A.* 65°45N 168°56W **303** D5
Little Falls *Minn., U.S.A.* 45°59N 94°22W **308** C7
Little Falls *N.Y., U.S.A.* 43°3N 74°51W **313** C10
Little Ferry *U.S.A.* 40°50N 74°2W **132** A1
Little Fork → *U.S.A.* 48°31N 93°35W **308** A7
Little Grand Rapids
  Canada 52°10N 95°29W **297** C9
Little Humboldt →
  U.S.A. 41°1N 117°43W **304** F5
Little Inagua I. *Bahamas* 21°40N 73°50W **321** B5
Little Italy *New York, U.S.A.* **132** e2
Little Karoo *S. Africa* 33°45S 21°0E **270** D3
Little Khingan Mts. = Xiao
  Hinggan Ling *China* 49°0N 127°0E **219** B7
Little Lake *U.S.A.* 35°56N 117°55W **307** K9
Little Lake Conway
  U.S.A. 28°29N 81°21W **133** B2
Little Laut Is. = Laut Kecil,
  Kepulauan *Indonesia* 4°45S 115°40E **235** D5
Little London *Jamaica* 18°15N 78°13W **320** a
Little Mecatina = Petit-
  Mécatina → *Canada* 50°40N 59°30W **299** B8
Little Mermaid = Den Lille Havfrue
  Copenhagen, Denmark **118** a3
Little Minch *U.K.* 57°35N 6°45W **167** D2
Little Missouri →
  U.S.A. 47°36N 102°25W **308** B3
Little Nicobar *India* 7°20N 93°40E **245** L11
Little Ouse → *U.K.* 52°22N 1°12E **169** E9
Little Rann *India* 23°25N 71°25E **242** H4
Little Red → *U.S.A.* 35°11N 91°27W **314** D9
Little Red School House Nature
  Center *U.S.A.* 41°42N 87°51W **119** C1
Little River *N.Z.* 43°45S 172°49E **285** D7
Little Rock *U.S.A.* 34°45N 92°17W **314** D8
Little Rouge → *Canada* 43°45N 79°11W **141** A4
Little Ruaha → *Tanzania* 7°57S 37°53E **268** D4
Little Sable Pt. *U.S.A.* 43°38N 86°33W **308** D10
Little Scarcies → *S. Leone* 8°50N 13°10W **262** D2
Little Sioux → *U.S.A.* 41°48N 96°4W **308** E5
Little Sitkin I. *U.S.A.* 51°57N 178°31E **303** L2
Little Smoky → *Canada* 54°44N 117°11W **296** C5
Little Snake → *U.S.A.* 40°27N 108°26W **304** F9
Little Sound *Bermuda* 32°15N 64°50W **153** a
Little Tokyo *Los Angeles, U.S.A.* **127** C2
Little Valley *U.S.A.* 42°15N 78°48W **312** D6
Little Wabash → *U.S.A.* 37°55N 88°5W **311** G8
Little White → *U.S.A.* 43°40N 100°40W **308** D3
Little York *U.S.A.* 41°0N 90°45W **310** D6
Little Zab = Zāb as Şaghīr →
  Iraq 35°17N 43°29E **213** E10
Littlefield *U.S.A.* 33°55N 102°20W **314** D3
Littlehampton *U.K.* 50°49N 0°32W **169** G7
Littleton *U.S.A.* 44°18N 71°46W **313** B13
Littoral □ *Cameroon* 4°0N 10°0E **263** E7
Littoria = Latina *Italy* 41°28N 12°52E **200** A5
Litunga *Angola* 13°19S 16°48E **265** H3
Litvínov *Czech Rep.* 50°36N 13°37E **180** A6
Liu He → *Jilin, China* 42°46N 126°13E **224** A3
Liu He → *Liaoning,*
  China 40°55N 121°35E **227** D11
Liu Jiang → *China* 23°55N 109°30E **228** F7
Liuba *China* 33°38N 106°55E **226** H4
Liucheng *China* 24°38N 109°14E **228** E7
Liuchia *Taiwan* 23°13N 120°21E **225** C2
Liuch'iu Yü *Taiwan* 22°21N 120°23E **225** D2
Liugou *China* 40°57N 118°15E **227** D10
Liuhang *China* 31°21N 121°21E **138** A4
Liuheng Dao *China* 29°40N 122°5E **229** C14
Liujiang *China* 24°22N 109°13E **228** E7
Liukang Tenggaja = Sabalana,
  Kepulauan *Indonesia* 6°45S 118°50E **231** F5
Liuli *Tanzania* 11°3S 34°38E **269** E3
Liupanshui *China* 26°38N 104°48E **228** D5
Liurong Temple *China* 23°8N 113°15E **121** B2
Liuwa Plain *Zambia* 14°20S 22°30E **265** H4
Liuwa Plain △ *Zambia* 14°45S 22°35E **265** H4
Liuyang *China* 28°10N 113°37E **229** C9
Liuying *Taiwan* 23°17N 120°18E **225** C2
Liuzhou *China* 24°22N 109°22E **228** E7
Liuzhuang *China* 33°12N 120°18E **227** H11
Livada *Romania* 47°52N 23°5E **182** C8
Livadero *Greece* 40°2N 21°57E **202** F5
Livadhia *Cyprus* 34°57N 33°38E **207** F9
Livadhje *Albania* 39°40N 20°7E **206** B8
Livadi *Greece* 39°50N 23°37E **206** B7
Livadia *Greece* 38°27N 22°54E **204** C4
Livarot *France* 49°0N 0°9E **172** D7
Live Oak *Calif., U.S.A.* 39°17N 121°40W **306** F5
Live Oak *Fla., U.S.A.* 30°18N 82°59W **316** E7
Lively *Canada* 46°26N 81°9W **309** B13
Livengood *U.S.A.* 65°32N 148°33W **303** D10
Liveras *Cyprus* 35°23N 32°57E **207** E8
Livermore *Calif., U.S.A.* 37°41N 121°47W **306** H5
Livermore, Mt. *U.S.A.* 30°38N 104°11W **314** F2
Livermore Falls *U.S.A.* 44°29N 70°11W **309** C18
Liverpool *N.S.W.,*
  Australia 33°54S 150°58E **283** B9
Liverpool *N.S., Canada* 44°5N 64°41W **299** D7
Liverpool *U.K.* 53°25N 3°0W **168** D4
Liverpool Bay *U.K.* 53°30N 3°20W **168** D4
Liverpool Plains
  Australia 31°15S 150°15E **283** A9
Liverpool Ra. *Australia* 31°50S 150°30E **283** A9
Liverpool Street *London, U.K.* **125** a5
Livigno *Italy* 46°35N 10°12E **198** B7
Livingston *Guatemala* 15°50N 88°50W **320** C2
Livingston *W. Loth., U.K.* 55°54N 3°30W **167** F5
Livingston *Ala., U.S.A.* 32°35N 88°11W **315** E10
Livingston *Calif., U.S.A.* 37°23N 120°43W **306** H6
Livingston *Mont.,*
  U.S.A. 45°40N 110°34W **304** D8
Livingston *S.C., U.S.A.* 33°38N 81°7W **315** C14
Livingston *Tenn., U.S.A.* 36°23N 85°19W **315** C12
Livingston *Tex., U.S.A.* 30°43N 94°56W **314** F7
Livingston *Wis., U.S.A.* 42°54N 90°26W **310** B6
Livingston, L. *U.S.A.* 30°50N 95°10W **314** F7
Livingston Manor
  U.S.A. 41°54N 74°50W **313** E10
Livingstone *Zambia* 17°46S 25°52E **269** F2
Livingstone △ *Australia* 32°25S 147°22E **283** B7
Livingstone Mts. *N.Z.* 45°15S 168°9E **285** E3
Livingstone Mts. *Tanzania* 9°40S 34°20E **269** D3
Livingstonia *Malawi* 10°38S 34°5E **269** E3
Livny *Russia* 52°30N 37°30E **189** F10
Livonia *Mich., U.S.A.* 42°23N 83°23W **311** B13
Livonia *N.Y., U.S.A.* 42°49N 77°40W **312** D7
Livorno *Italy* 43°33N 10°19E **198** E7
Livradois-Forez △ *France* 45°25N 3°40E **174** C7
Livramento = Nossa Senhora do
  Livramento *Brazil* 15°48S 56°22W **331** D6

Livramento *Brazil* 30°55S 55°30W **335** C4
Livramento do Brumado
  Brazil 13°39S 41°50W **333** D3
Loche, L. La *Canada* 56°30N 109°30W **297** B7
Loches *France* 47°7N 1°0E **172** E7
Lochem *Neths.* 52°9N 6°26E **170** B6
Lochaber *U.K.* 56°57N 5°0W **167** E3
Lochboisdale *U.K.* 57°9N 7°20W **167** D1
Locharbriggs *U.K.* 55°7N 3°35W **167** F5
Lochboisdale *U.K.* 57°9N 7°20W **167** D1
Lochaber *Queens.,*
  Australia 23°33S 145°38E **280** C4
Lochnagar *Aberds., U.K.* 56°57N 3°15W **167** E5
Lochów *Poland* 52°33N 21°42E **185** F8
Lochy, L. *U.K.* 57°0N 4°53W **167** E4
Lock *Australia* 33°34S 135°46E **281** E2
Lock Haven *U.S.A.* 41°8N 77°28W **312** E7
Lockeford *U.S.A.* 38°10N 121°9W **306** G5
Lockeport *Canada* 43°47N 65°4W **299** D6
Lockerbie *U.K.* 55°7N 3°21W **167** F5
Lockhart *N.S.W.,*
  Australia 35°14S 146°40E **283** C7
Lockhart *Tex., U.S.A.* 29°53N 97°40W **314** G6
Lockhart, L. *Australia* 33°15S 119°3E **279** F2
Lockhart River *Australia* 12°58S 143°30E **280** A3
Lockhausen *Germany* 52°4N 8°31E **179** A4
Lockney *U.S.A.* 34°7N 101°27W **314** D4
Lockport *Ill., U.S.A.* 41°35N 88°3W **311** C8
Lockport *N.Y., U.S.A.* 43°10N 78°42W **312** C6
Locminé *France* 47°54N 2°51W **172** E4
Locri *Italy* 38°14N 16°16E **201** D9
Locronan *France* 48°7N 4°15W **172** D2
Locust Cr. → *U.S.A.* 39°40N 93°17W **310** E3
Locust Grove *U.S.A.* 33°21N 84°7W **316** B5
Lod *Israel* 31°57N 34°54E **251** G5
Lodalskåpa *Norway* 61°47N 7°13E **164** C4
Lodeinoye Pole *Russia* 60°44N 33°33E **188** B7
Lodève *France* 43°44N 3°19E **174** E7
Lodge Bay *Canada* 52°14N 55°51W **299** B8
Lodge Grass *U.S.A.* 45°19N 107°22W **304** D10
Lodhran *Pakistan* 29°32N 71°30E **242** E4
Lodi *Italy* 45°19N 9°30E **198** C6
Lodi *Calif., U.S.A.* 38°8N 121°16W **306** G5
Lodi *N.J., U.S.A.* 40°52N 74°5W **132** A1
Lodi *Ohio, U.S.A.* 41°2N 82°1W **312** E3
Lodi Estate *India* 28°36N 77°15E **120** B2
Lodja *Dem. Rep. of the Congo* 3°30S 23°23E **264** C4
Lodosa *Spain* 42°25N 2°4W **196** C2
Lödöse *Sweden* 58°2N 12°9E **163** F6
Lodwar *Kenya* 3°7N 35°36E **268** B4
Łódź *Poland* 51°45N 19°27E **185** G6
Łódzkie □ *Poland* 51°30N 19°30E **185** G6
Loei *Thailand* 17°29N 101°35E **238** D3
Loengo
  Dem. Rep. of the Congo 4°48S 26°30E **265** C5
Loeriesfontein *S. Africa* 31°0S 19°26E **270** C2
Lofa □ *Liberia* 6°35N 11°30E **262** D2
Lofa → *Liberia* 7°55N 10°25W **262** D2
Lofer *Austria* 47°35N 12°41E **180** D5
Lofoten *Norway* 68°30N 14°0E **160** B16
Lofsdalen *Sweden* 62°7N 13°57E **162** B7
Lofsen → *Sweden* 62°7N 13°57E **162** B7
Loftahammar *Sweden* 57°54N 16°41E **163** G10
Loga *Niger* 13°40N 3°15E **263** C5
Logan *Iowa, U.S.A.* 41°39N 95°47W **308** E6
Logan *Ohio, U.S.A.* 39°32N 82°25W **309** F12
Logan *Utah, U.S.A.* 41°44N 111°50W **304** F8
Logan *W. Va., U.S.A.* 37°51N 81°59W **309** G13
Logan, Mt. *Canada* 60°34N 140°23W **294** C5
Logan Int., Boston ✈ (BOS)
  U.S.A. 42°22N 71°1W **116** A2
Logan Martin L. *U.S.A.* 33°26N 86°20W **316** B3
Logan Square *U.S.A.* 41°55N 87°42W **119** B2
Logandale *U.S.A.* 36°36N 114°29W **307** J12
Logansport *Ind., U.S.A.* 40°45N 86°22W **311** D10
Logansport *La., U.S.A.* 31°58N 94°0W **314** F8
Logirim *Sudan* 4°43N 33°14E **257** G3
Lognes-Émerainville ✈
  France 48°49N 2°37E **134** B4
Logo *Sudan* 12°6N 15°2E **257** F9
Logone → *Chad* 12°6N 15°2E **259** F9
Logone Gana *Chad* 11°36N 15°4E **259** F9
Logone Occidental □ *Chad* 8°30N 16°0E **259** G3
Logone Occidental →
  Chad 8°50N 16°0E **259** G3
Logone Oriental □ *Chad* 8°30N 16°30E **259** G3
Logone Orientale → *Chad* 8°30N 16°30E **259** G3
Logroño *Spain* 42°28N 2°27W **196** C2
Logrosán *Spain* 39°20N 5°32W **195** F5
Løgstør *Denmark* 56°58N 9°14E **163** H3
Logtak L. *India* 24°39N 93°50E **243** G9
Logumkloster *Denmark* 55°4N 8°57E **163** J2
Loh *Germany* 13°21S 166°38E **287** E4
Lohals *Denmark* 55°8N 10°55E **163** J4
Lohardaga *India* 23°27N 84°45E **243** H11
Loharia *India* 23°45N 74°14E **242** H6
Loharu *India* 28°27N 75°49E **242** E6
Lohja *Finland* 60°12N 24°5E **163** B8
Löhme *Germany* 52°37N 13°40E **115** A5
Lohne *Germany* 52°40N 8°13E **178** C4
Lohne → *Germany* 51°49N 8°54E **115** A5
Loho = Luohe *China* 33°32N 114°2E **226** H8
Loho *Phil.* 4°39N 99°37E **238** D1
Lohri Wah → *Pakistan* 27°27N 67°37E **242** F2
Loi-kaw *Burma* 19°40N 97°17E **241** F6
Loi-lem *Burma* 20°58N 97°40E **241** G6
Loimaa *Finland* 60°50N 23°5E **163** B8
Loir → *France* 47°33N 0°32W **172** E6
Loir-et-Cher □ *France* 47°40N 1°20E **172** E8
Loire □ *France* 45°40N 4°5E **175** C8
Loire → *France* 47°16N 2°10W **172** E4
Loire Anjou Touraine △
  France 47°14N 0°5W **172** E6
Loire-Atlantique □ *France* 47°25N 1°40W **172** E5
Loire Inférieure = Loire-
  Atlantique □ *France* 47°25N 1°40W **172** E5
Loiret □ *France* 47°55N 2°30E **173** E9
Loitz *Germany* 53°58N 13°8E **178** B9
Loja *Ecuador* 3°59S 79°16W **330** D2
Loja *Spain* 37°10N 4°9W **195** H6
Loja □ *Ecuador* 4°0S 79°30W **328** D2
Loji = Kawasi *Indonesia* 1°38S 127°28E **231** E7
Løjt Kirkeby *Denmark* 55°7N 9°26E **163** J3
Lojung *China* 24°27N 109°36E **228** E7
Loka *Sudan* 4°13N 31°0E **257** H3
Lokako
  Dem. Rep. of the Congo 0°20N 21°38E **264** B4
Lokandu
  Dem. Rep. of the Congo 2°30S 25°45E **264** C5
Lokawa
  Dem. Rep. of the Congo 2°30S 25°45E **264** C5
Loken *Norway* 59°48N 11°29E **164** E8
Lokeren *Belgium* 51°6N 3°59E **170** C3
Lokgwabe *Botswana* 24°10S 21°50E **270** B3
Lokhvitsa *Ukraine* 50°25N 33°18E **189** G7
Lokichar *Kenya* 2°23N 35°39E **268** B4
Lokichokio *Kenya* 4°19N 34°13E **268** B3

Lokitaung *Kenya* 4°12N 35°48E **268** B4
Lokkan tekojärvi
Finland 67°55N 27°35E **160** C22
Løkken *Denmark* 57°22N 9°41E **163** G3
Løkken *Sør-Trøndelag, Norway* 63°9N 9°41E **164** A6
Loknya *Russia* 56°49N 30°4E **188** D6
Loko *C.A.R.* 3°38N 18°2E **264** B3
Loko *Nigeria* 8°1N 7°53E **263** D6
Lokoja *Nigeria* 7°47N 6°45E **263** D6
Lokolama
Dem. Rep. of the Congo 2°35S 19°50E **264** C3
Lokolenge
Dem. Rep. of the Congo 1°12N 22°38E **264** B4
Lokolo →
Dem. Rep. of the Congo 0°43S 19°40E **264** C3
Lokoro →
Dem. Rep. of the Congo 1°43S 18°23E **264** C3
Lokot *Russia* 52°34N 34°36E **189** F8
Loktak L. = Logtak L.
India 24°33N 93°50E **241** C4
Lokuru *Solomon Is.* 8°20S 157°0E **287** M9
Lol → *Sudan* 9°13N 26°30E **257** F2
Lola *Angola* 14°19S 13°37E **265** E2
Lola *Guinea* 7°52N 8°29W **262** D3
Lola, Mt. *U.S.A.* 39°26N 120°22W **306** F6
Lolgorien *Kenya* 1°14S 34°48E **268** C3
Lolibai, Gebel *Sudan* 3°50N 33°0E **257** G3
Lolimi *Sudan* 4°35N 34°0E **257** G3
Loliondo *Tanzania* 2°2S 35°39E **268** C4
Lolland *Denmark* 54°45N 11°30E **163** K5
Lollar *Germany* 50°37N 8°43E **178** E4
Lolo *U.S.A.* 46°45N 114°5W **304** C6
Lolo → *Eq. Guin.* 1°36N 9°37E **264** B1
Lolo → *Gabon* 0°18S 12°18E **264** C2
Lolobau I. *Papua N. G.* 4°55S 151°10E **286** C6
Lolodorf *Cameroon* 3°16N 10°49E **263** E7
Lolokhet *Pakistan* 24°54N 67°2E **123** A2
Loloma *Zambia* 13°24S 24°21E **265** E4
Loltong *Vanuatu* 15°32S 168°10E **287** E6
Lom *Bulgaria* 43°48N 23°12E **202** C7
Lom *Oppland, Norway* 61°50N 8°34E **164** C5
Lom → *Bulgaria* 43°45N 23°15E **202** C7
Lom → *Cameroon* 5°20N 13°24E **264** A2
Lom Kao *Thailand* 16°53N 101°14E **236** D3
Lom Sak *Thailand* 16°47N 101°15E **236** D3
Loma *U.S.A.* 47°56N 110°30W **304** C8
Loma Linda *U.S.A.* 34°3N 117°16W **307** L9
Loma Mansa *S. Leone* 9°13N 11°7W **262** D2
Lomako →
Dem. Rep. of the Congo 0°50N 20°50E **264** B4
Lomaloma *Fiji* 17°17S 178°59W **287** A3
Lomami →
Dem. Rep. of the Congo 0°46N 24°16E **264** B4
Lomas Chapultepec
Mexico 19°25N 99°12W **128** B1
Lomas de San Angel Inn
Mexico 19°20N 99°13W **128** B1
Lomas de Zamóra
Argentina 34°45S 58°24W **334** C4
Lombadina *Australia* 16°31S 122°54E **278** C3
Lombard *U.S.A.* 41°53N 88°1W **311** C8
Lombárdia □ *Italy* 45°40N 9°30E **198** C6
Lombardy = Lombárdia □
Italy 45°40N 9°30E **198** C6
Lombardy East *S. Africa* 26°6S 28°7E **123** A2
Lombe *Angola* 9°27S 16°13E **265** D3
Lombez *France* 43°29N 0°55E **174** E4
Lomblen *Indonesia* 8°30S 123°32E **231** F6
Lombok *Indonesia* 8°45S 116°30E **235** D5
Lombok, Selat *Indonesia* 8°30S 115°50E **231** K18
Lomé *Togo* 6°9N 1°20E **263** D5
Lomela
Dem. Rep. of the Congo 2°19S 23°15E **264** C4
Lomela →
Dem. Rep. of the Congo 0°15S 20°40E **264** C4
Lomianki *Poland* 52°21N 20°54E **142** A1
Lomié *Cameroon* 3°13N 13°38E **264** B2
Lomma *Sweden* 55°43N 13°6E **163** J7
Lommel *Belgium* 51°14N 5°19E **170** C5
Lomond *Canada* 50°24N 112°36W **296** C6
Lomond, L. *U.K.* 56°8N 4°38W **167** E4
Lomonosov Ridge *Arctic* 88°0N 140°0E **150** A
Lomphat *Cambodia* 13°30N 106°59E **236** F6
Lompobatang *Indonesia* 5°24S 119°56E **231** F5
Lompoc *U.S.A.* 34°38N 120°28W **307** L6
Lomsegga *Norway* 61°49N 8°21E **164** C5
Lomus Reforma *Mexico* 19°24N 99°14W **128** B1
Łomża *Poland* 53°10N 22°2E **185** E9
Lon, Ko *Thailand* 7°47N 98°23E **237** a
Lonavale *India* 18°46N 73°29E **244** E1
Loncoche *Chile* 39°20S 72°50W **336** A2
Loncopuè *Argentina* 38°4S 70°37W **336** A2
Londa *India* 15°30N 74°30E **245** G2
Londiani *Kenya* 0°10S 35°33E **268** C4
Londinières *France* 49°50N 1°25E **172** C8
London *Ont., Canada* 42°59N 81°15W **312** D3
London *London, U.K.* 51°30N 0°3W **125** B3
London *Ky., U.S.A.* 37°8N 84°5W **309** G11
London *Ohio, U.S.A.* 39°53N 83°27W **311** E13
London, Greater □ *U.K.* 51°36N 0°5W **169** F7
London Avenue Canal
U.S.A. 30°3N 90°6W **131** A2
London Bridge *Grenada* 12°15N 61°35W **323** q
London Bridge *London, U.K.* **125** b5
London City ✈ (LCY) *U.K.* 51°30N 0°3E **125** A4
London Gatwick ✈ (LGW)
U.K. 51°10N 0°11W **169** F7
London Heathrow ✈ (LHR)
U.K. 51°28N 0°27W **125** B1
London Mills *U.S.A.* 40°43N 90°11W **310** D6
London Stansted ✈ (STN)
U.K. 51°54N 0°14E **169** F8
London Zoo *U.K.* 51°31N 0°9W **125** A3
Londonderry *U.K.* 55°0N 7°20W **166** B4
Londonderry □ *U.K.* 55°0N 7°20W **166** B4
Londonderry, C.
Australia 13°45S 126°55E **278** B4
Londonderry, I. *Chile* 55°0S 71°0W **336** E2
Londrina *Brazil* 23°18S 51°10W **335** A5
Londuimbale *Angola* 12°15S 15°19E **265** E3
Lone Pine *U.S.A.* 36°36N 118°4W **306** J8
Lonely Mine *Zimbabwe* 19°30S 28°49E **271** A4
Long, Î. *Martinique* 14°36N 60°51W **322** j
Long Akah *Malaysia* 3°19N 114°47E **235** B4
Long B. *N.S.W., Australia* 33°59S 151°15E **139** B2
Long B. *Cornwall, Jamaica* 18°20N 78°20W **320** a
Long B. *S.C., U.S.A.* 33°35N 78°45W **315** E15
Long Beach *Calif., U.S.A.* 33°46N 118°11W **307** M8
Long Beach *N.Y., U.S.A.* 40°35N 73°39W **313** F11
Long Beach *Wash., U.S.A.* 46°21N 124°3W **306** D2
Long Branch *Ont., Canada* 43°35N 79°31W **141** B1
Long Branch *N.J., U.S.A.* 40°18N 74°0W **313** F11
Long Brook → *U.S.A.* 38°49N 77°15W **143** C2
Long Cay *Bahamas* 25°6N 77°22W **153** b
Long Creek *U.S.A.* 44°43N 119°6W **304** D4
Long Ditton *U.K.* 51°22N 0°19W **125** B2
Long Eaton *U.K.* 52°53N 1°15W **168** E6
Long I. *Antigua & B.* 17°8N 61°45W **322** b
Long I. *Queens., Australia* 20°22S 148°51E **280** J6
Long I. *Bahamas* 23°20N 75°10W **321** B4
Long I. *Nunavut, Canada* 54°50N 79°20W **298** B4
Long I. *Cork, Ireland* 51°30N 9°34W **166** E2
Long I. *Papua N. G.* 5°20S 147°5E **286** C4
Long I. *N.Y., U.S.A.* 40°45N 73°30W **313** F11
Long Island City *U.S.A.* 40°45N 73°56W **132** B2
Long Island Sd. *U.S.A.* 41°10N 73°0W **313** E12
Long L. *Canada* 49°30N 86°50W **298** C2
Long Lake *U.S.A.* 43°58N 74°25W **313** C10
Long Mountain *Mauritius* 20°8S 57°33E **272** e
Long Point B. *Canada* 42°40N 80°10W **312** D4
Long Prairie *U.S.A.* 45°59N 94°52W **308** C6
Long Prairie → *U.S.A.* 46°20N 94°36W **308** B6
Long Pt. *Bahamas* 25°1N 77°20W **153** b
Long Pt. *Ont., Canada* 42°35N 80°2W **312** D4
Long Pt. *Otago, N.Z.* 46°34S 169°36E **285** G4
Long Range Mts. *Canada* 49°30N 57°30W **299** C8
Long Reef *Australia* 14°1S 125°48E **278** B4
Long Spruce *Canada* 56°24N 94°21W **297** B10
Long Str. = Longa, Proliv
Russia 70°0N 175°0E **150** C16
Long Street *Cape Town, S. Africa* **118** c2
Long Thanh *Vietnam* 10°47N 106°57E **237** G6
Long Xian *China* 34°55N 106°55E **226** G4
Long Xuyen *Vietnam* 10°19N 105°28E **237** G5
Longa *Angola* 14°42S 18°32E **265** E3
Longa *Greece* 36°53N 21°55E **204** E3
Longa → *Angola* 10°15S 13°29E **265** E2
Longa, Proliv *Russia* 70°0N 175°0E **150** C16
Long'an *China* 23°10N 107°40E **228** F6
Longana *Vanuatu* 15°18S 168°0E **287** E5
Longarone *Italy* 46°16N 12°18E **199** B9
Longbenton *U.K.* 55°1N 1°31W **168** B6
Longboat Key *U.S.A.* 27°23N 82°39W **317** H7
Longburn *N.Z.* 40°23S 175°35E **284** G4
Longchamp, Hippodrome de
France 48°51N 2°13E **134** A2
Longchang *China* 29°18N 105°15E **228** C5
Longchi *China* 29°25N 103°24E **228** C4
Longchuan *Guangdong, China* 24°5N 115°17E **229** E10
Longchuan *Yunnan, China* 24°23N 97°58E **228** E1
Longde *China* 35°30N 106°20E **226** G4
Longdenville *Trin. & Tob.* 10°31N 61°23W **323** t
Longeau *France* 47°47N 5°20E **173** E12
Longford *Tas., Australia* 41°32S 147°3E **281** G4
Longford *Longf., Ireland* 53°43N 7°49W **166** C4
Longford □ *Ireland* 53°42N 7°45W **166** C4
Longgan Shan *China* 42°19N 126°30E **224** A3
Longhai *China* 24°25N 117°46E **229** E11
Longhua *Guangdong, China* 22°39N 114°0E **219** F11
Longhua *Hebei, China* 41°18N 117°45E **227** D9
Longhua Pagoda *China* 31°10N 121°26E **138** B1
Longhua Park *China* 31°10N 121°26E **138** B1
Longhui *China* 27°7N 111°2E **229** D8
Longido *Tanzania* 2°43S 36°42E **268** C4
Longiram *Indonesia* 0°5S 115°45E **235** C5
Longjohn Slough *U.S.A.* 41°42N 87°52W **119** C1
Longkou *Jiangxi, China* 26°8N 115°10E **229** D10
Longkou *Shandong, China* 37°40N 120°18E **227** F11
Longlac *Canada* 49°45N 86°25W **298** C2
Longli *China* 26°25N 106°58E **228** D6
Longlin *China* 24°47N 105°20E **228** E5
Longling *China* 24°37N 98°39E **228** E2
Longmeadow *U.S.A.* 42°3N 72°34W **313** D12
Longmen *China* 23°40N 114°18E **229** F10
Longming *China* 22°59N 107°7E **228** F6
Longmont *U.S.A.* 40°10N 105°6W **304** F11
Longnan *China* 24°55N 114°47E **229** E10
Longnawan *Indonesia* 1°51N 114°55E **235** B4
Longobucco *Italy* 39°27N 16°37E **201** C9
Longoni, B. de *Mayotte* 12°41S 45°8E **272** b
Longonot △ *Kenya* 0°55S 36°28E **266** E4
Longos *Greece* 39°16N 20°7E **206** C10
Longquan *China* 28°7N 119°10E **229** C12
Longreach *Australia* 23°28S 144°14E **280** C3
Longshan *China* 29°29N 109°25E **228** C7
Longsheng *China* 25°48N 110°0E **229** E8
Longtan Hu → *China* 39°51N 116°24E **114** B2
Longué-Jumelles *France* 47°22N 0°8W **172** E6
Longue-Pointe *Canada* 45°35N 73°31W **130** A2
Longueau *France* 49°52N 2°21E **173** C9
Longueuil *Canada* 45°31N 73°29W **130** A3
Longueuil-St-Hubert = St-Hubert
Canada 45°29N 73°25W **130** B3
Longuy *Cameroon* 3°5N 9°58E **264** B1
Longuyon *France* 49°27N 5°35E **173** C12
Longvic *France* 47°17N 5°4E **173** E12
Longview *Tex., U.S.A.* 32°30N 94°44W **314** E7
Longview *Wash., U.S.A.* 46°8N 122°57W **306** D4
Longwood *St. Helena* 15°57S 5°41W **153** h
Longwood *Fla., U.S.A.* 28°42N 81°21W **317** G8
Longwy *France* 49°30N 5°46E **172** C12
Longxi *China* 34°53N 104°40E **226** G3
Longxue Dao *China* 22°41N 113°38E **219** F10
Longyan *China* 25°10N 117°0E **229** E11
Longyearbyen *Svalbard* 78°13N 15°40E **150** B8
Longyou *China* 29°1N 119°8E **229** C12
Longzhou *China* 22°22N 106°50E **228** F6
Loni *India* 28°45N 77°17E **120** A2
Lonigo *Italy* 45°23N 11°23E **199** C8
Löningen *Germany* 52°44N 7°46E **178** C3
Lonja → *Croatia* 45°22N 16°40E **199** C13
Lonkala
Dem. Rep. of the Congo 4°37S 23°14E **265** C4
Lonkin *Burma* 25°39N 96°22E **241** C6
Lonoke *U.S.A.* 34°47N 91°54W **314** D9
Lonquimay *Chile* 38°26S 71°14W **336** A2
Lons-le-Saunier *France* 46°40N 5°31E **173** F12
Lönsboda *Sweden* 56°24N 14°20E **163** H8
Lønset *Norway* 62°46N 7°24E **164** B4
Lonton *Burma* 25°6N 96°17E **241** C6
Looe *U.K.* 50°22N 4°28W **169** G3
Loogootee *U.S.A.* 38°41N 86°55W **311** F10
Lookout, C. *Canada* 55°18N 83°56W **298** A3
Lookout, C. *N.C., U.S.A.* 34°35N 76°32W **315** D16
Loolmalasin *Tanzania* 3°0S 35°53E **268** C4
Loon → *Alta., Canada* 57°8N 115°3W **296** B5
Loon → *Man., Canada* 55°53N 101°59W **297** B8
Loon Lake *Canada* 54°2N 109°10W **297** C7
Loongana *Australia* 30°52S 127°5E **279** F4
Loop, The *Chicago, U.S.A.* **119** c1
Loop Hd. *Ireland* 52°34N 9°56W **166** D2
Lop *China* 37°3N 80°11E **217** E10
Lop Buri *Thailand* 14°48N 100°37E **236** E3
Lop Nor = Lop Nur
China 40°20N 90°10E **217** D12
Lop Nur *China* 40°20N 90°10E **217** D12
Lopare *Bos.-H.* 44°39N 18°46E **182** F3
Lopatin *Russia* 43°50N 47°35E **191** J8
Lopatina, Gora *Russia* 50°47N 143°10E **215** D15
Lopatino = Volzhsk
Russia 55°57N 48°23E **190** C9
Lopaye *Sudan* 6°37N 33°40E **257** F3
Lopé-Okanda △ *Gabon* 0°45S 11°34E **264** C2
Lopevi *Vanuatu* 16°30S 168°21E **287** F6
Lopez *Phil.* 13°53N 122°15E **232** E4
Lopez *Pa., U.S.A.* 41°27N 76°20W **313** E8
Lopez, C. *Gabon* 0°47S 8°40E **264** C1
López de Filippis = Mariscal
Estigarribia *Paraguay* 22°3S 60°40W **334** A3
Lopinot *Trin. & Tob.* 10°41N 61°19W **323** t
Lopori →
Dem. Rep. of the Congo 1°14N 19°49E **264** B3
Lopphavet *Norway* 70°27N 21°15E **160** A19
Lora *Norway* 62°8N 8°45E **164** B5
Lora → *Afghan.* 31°35N 66°32E **240** C2
Lora → *Oppland, Norway* 62°8N 8°42E **164** B5
Lora, Hāmūn-i- *Pakistan* 29°38N 64°58E **240** C2
Lora Cr. → *Australia* 28°10S 135°22E **281** D2
Lora del Río *Spain* 37°39N 5°33W **195** H5
Lorain *U.S.A.* 41°28N 82°11W **312** E2
Loraine *U.S.A.* 40°9N 91°13W **310** D5
Loralai *Pakistan* 30°20N 68°41E **242** D3
Lorca *Spain* 37°41N 1°42W **197** H3
Lord Howe I. *Pac. Oc.* 31°33S 159°6E **277** G10
Lord Howe Rise *Pac. Oc.* 30°0S 162°30E **277** H12
Lord Howe Seamount Chain
Pac. Oc. 28°0S 159°0E **277** F10
Lord's Cricket Ground
U.K. 51°31N 0°10W **125** A2
Lordsburg *U.S.A.* 32°21N 108°43W **305** K9
Lorengau *Papua N. G.* 2°1S 147°15E **286** B4
Lorestān □ *Iran* 33°30N 48°40E **247** C6
Loreto *Bolivia* 15°13S 64°40W **331** D5
Loreto *Brazil* 7°5S 45°10W **332** C2
Loreto *Marche, Italy* 43°26N 13°36E **199** E10
Loreto *Piemonte, Italy* 45°29N 9°12E **129** B2
Loreto *Baja Calif. S., Mexico* 26°0N 111°21W **318** B2
Loreto *Surigao N., Phil.* 10°21N 125°34E **233** F5
Loreto □ *Peru* 5°0S 75°0W **328** E3
Lorgues *France* 43°28N 6°22E **175** E10
Lorhosso *Burkina Faso* 10°17N 3°38W **262** C4
Lorian Swamp *Kenya* 0°40N 39°35E **267** D4
Lorica *Colombia* 9°14N 75°49W **328** B2
Lorient *Morbihan, France* 47°45N 3°23W **172** E3
Lorient *St.-Martin* 17°54N 62°49W **322** a
Lorimor *U.S.A.* 41°8N 94°3W **310** C2
Lőrinci *Hungary* 47°44N 19°41E **182** C4
Lormi *India* 22°17N 81°41E **243** H9
Lorn *U.K.* 56°26N 5°10W **167** E3
Lorn, Firth of *U.K.* 56°20N 5°40W **167** E3
Lorne *Australia* 38°33S 143°59E **282** E5
Loronyo *Sudan* 4°38N 32°38E **257** G3
Lorovouno *Cyprus* 35°8N 32°36E **207** E8
Lörrach *Germany* 47°36N 7°40E **179** H3
Lorrain → *Martinique* 14°50N 61°3W **322** j
Lorraine = Baker
U.S.A. 46°22N 104°17W **304** C11
Lorraine □ *France* 48°53N 6°0E **173** D13
Lorraine △ *France* 48°55N 5°50E **173** D12
Los *Sweden* 61°45N 15°10E **162** C9
Los, Îles de *Guinea* 9°30N 13°50W **262** D2
Los Alamos *Calif., U.S.A.* 34°44N 120°17W **307** L6
Los Alamos *N. Mex., U.S.A.* 35°53N 106°19W **305** J10
Los Alcornocales △ *Spain* 36°21N 5°32W **195** J5
Los Alerces △ *Argentina* 42°55S 71°55W **336** B2
Los Altos *U.S.A.* 37°23N 122°7W **306** H4
Los Andes *Chile* 32°50S 70°40W **334** C1
Los Angeles *Chile* 37°28S 72°23W **334** D1
Los Angeles *Calif., U.S.A.* 34°4N 118°15W **126** B3
Los Angeles, Bahia de
Mexico 28°56N 113°34W **318** B2
Los Angeles Aqueduct
U.S.A. 35°22N 118°5W **307** K9
Los Angeles Int. ✈ (LAX)
U.S.A. 33°57N 118°25W **126** C2
Los Antiguos *Argentina* 46°35S 71°40W **336** C2
Los Banos *U.S.A.* 37°4N 120°51W **306** H6
Los Barrios *Spain* 36°11N 5°30W **195** J5
Los Blancos *Argentina* 23°40S 62°30W **334** A3
Los Cardones △ *Argentina* 25°8S 65°55W **334** B2
Los Cerrillos ✈ (ULC)
Chile 33°29S 70°42W **137** B1
Los Chiles *Costa Rica* 11°2N 84°43W **320** D3
Los Corrales de Buelna
Spain 43°16N 4°4W **194** B6
Los Cristianos *Canary Is.* 28°3N 16°42W **153** e1
Los Gallardos *Spain* 37°10N 1°57W **197** H3
Los Gallos Pt. *Trin. & Tob.* 10°5N 61°55W **323** t
Los Gatos *U.S.A.* 37°14N 121°59W **306** H5
Los Glaciares △ *Argentina* 50°0S 73°55W **336** C2
Los Haïtises △ *Dom. Rep.* 19°4N 69°36W **321** C6
Los Hermanos Is.
Venezuela 11°45N 64°25W **329** A5
Los Islotes *Canary Is.* 29°4N 13°44W **153** e2
Los Katios △ *Colombia* 7°50N 77°10W **328** B2
Los Lagos *Chile* 39°51S 72°50W **336** A2
Los Llanos de Aridane
Canary Is. 28°38N 17°54W **153** e1
Los Lomas *Peru* 4°40S 80°10W **330** A1
Los Loros *Chile* 27°50S 70°6W **334** B1
Los Lunas *U.S.A.* 34°48N 106°44W **305** J10
Los Menucos *Argentina* 40°50S 68°10W **336** B3
Los Mochis *Mexico* 25°45N 108°57W **318** B3
Los Monegros *Spain* 41°29N 0°13W **196** D4
Los Monos *Argentina* 46°1S 69°36W **336** C3
Los Muermos *Chile* 41°24S 73°29W **336** B2
Los Nevados △ *Colombia* 4°41N 75°21W **328** C2
Los Nietos *Spain* 37°39N 0°47W **197** H4
Los Nietos *Calif., U.S.A.* 33°57N 118°4W **126** C4
Los Olivos *Lima, Peru* 11°59S 77°5W **124** A2
Los Olivos *Calif., U.S.A.* 34°40N 120°7W **307** L6
Los Palacios *Cuba* 22°35N 83°15W **320** B3
Los Palacios y Villafranca
Spain 37°10N 5°55W **195** H5
Los Reyes *Mexico* 19°21N 99°6W **128** B2
Los Reyes de Salgado
Mexico 19°35N 102°29W **318** D4
Los Ríos □ *Ecuador* 1°30S 79°25W **328** D2
Los Roques Is. *Venezuela* 11°50N 66°45W **328** A4
Los Santos de Maimona
Spain 38°27N 6°22W **195** G4
Los Teques *Venezuela* 10°21N 67°2W **328** A4
Los Testigos, Is. *Venezuela* 11°23N 63°6W **329** A5
Los Vilos *Chile* 32°10S 71°30W **334** C1
Los Yébenes *Spain* 39°36N 3°55W **195** F7
Loshan = Leshan *China* 29°33N 103°41E **228** C4
Losice *Poland* 52°13N 22°43E **185** F9
Lošinj *Croatia* 44°30N 14°30E **199** D11
Loskop Dam *S. Africa* 25°23S 29°20E **271** C4
Løsning *Denmark* 55°48N 9°42E **163** J3
Losombo
Dem. Rep. of the Congo 1°2N 19°4E **264** B3
Lossiemouth *U.K.* 57°42N 3°17W **167** D5
Lossnen △ *Sweden* 62°26N 12°45E **162** B6
Lostwithiel *U.K.* 50°24N 4°41W **169** G3
Losuia *Papua N. G.* 8°30S 151°4E **286** E6
Lot *Belgium* 50°46N 4°16E **170** D4
Lot □ *France* 44°39N 1°40E **174** D5
Lot → *France* 44°18N 0°20E **174** D4
Lot-et-Garonne □ *France* 44°22N 0°30E **174** D4
Lota *Chile* 37°5S 73°10W **334** D1
Lotagipi Swamp *Sudan* 4°36N 34°55E **257** G3
Løten *Norway* 60°51N 11°21E **164** D8
Loṭfābād *Iran* 37°32N 59°20E **247** B8
Lothair *S. Africa* 26°22S 30°27E **271** C5
Loto *Dem. Rep. of the Congo* 2°48S 22°3E **264** C4
Lotoi →
Dem. Rep. of the Congo 1°35S 18°30E **264** C3
Lotorp *Sweden* 58°44N 15°50E **163** F9
Lötschbergtunnel *Switz.* 46°26N 7°43E **179** J3
Lotta → *Europe* 68°42N 31°6E **160** B24
Lottorp *Sweden* 57°10N 17°0E **163** G11
Lotung *Taiwan* 24°41N 121°46E **225** B3
Lotus River *S. Africa* 34°4S 18°31E **118** B2
Lotus Temple *India* 28°33N 77°15E **120** B2
Lötzen = Giżycko *Poland* 54°2N 21°48E **184** D8
Lou I. *Papua N. G.* 2°25S 147°22E **286** B4
Loubière *Dominica* 15°16N 61°23W **323** k
Loubomo *Congo* 4°9S 12°47E **264** C2
Loudéac *France* 48°11N 2°47W **172** D4
Loudi *China* 27°42N 111°59E **229** D8
Loudima *Congo* 4°6S 13°5E **264** C2
Loudonville *U.S.A.* 40°38N 82°14W **312** F2
Loudun *France* 47°3N 0°5E **172** E7
Loue → *France* 47°1N 5°28E **173** E12
Louga *Senegal* 15°45N 16°5W **262** B1
Louga □ *Senegal* 15°20N 15°35W **262** B1
Loughborough *U.K.* 52°47N 1°11W **168** E6
Lougheed I. *Canada* 77°26N 105°6W **295** B9
Loughlinstown *Ireland* 53°15N 6°7W **120** B3
Loughman *U.S.A.* 28°14N 81°34W **317** G8
Loughrea *Ireland* 53°12N 8°33W **166** C3
Loughros More B. *Ireland* 54°48N 8°32W **166** B3
Louhans *France* 46°38N 5°12E **173** F12
Louis Armstrong New Orleans
Int. ✈ (MSY) *U.S.A.* 30°0N 90°15W **131** A1
Louis Armstrong Park
New Orleans, U.S.A. **131** a2
Louis-Gentil = Youssoufia
Morocco 32°16N 8°31W **260** B3
Louis Trichardt *S. Africa* 23°1S 29°43E **271** B4
Louis XIV, Pte. *Canada* 54°37N 79°45W **298** B4
Louisa *U.S.A.* 38°7N 82°36W **309** F12
Louisbourg *Canada* 45°55N 60°0W **299** C8
Louisburg *U.S.A.* 38°37N 94°41W **310** F2
Louisburgh *Ireland* 53°46N 9°49W **166** C2
Louise, L. *U.S.A.* 28°28N 81°32W **133** B1
Louise I. *Canada* 52°55N 131°50W **296** C2
Louiseville *Canada* 46°20N 72°56W **298** C5
Louisiade Arch.
Papua N. G. 11°10S 153°0E **286** F7
Louisiana *U.S.A.* 39°27N 91°3W **310** E6
Louisiana □ *U.S.A.* 30°50N 92°0W **314** F9
Louisiana Superdome
New Orleans, U.S.A. **131** b1
Louisville *Ala., U.S.A.* 31°47N 85°33W **316** D4
Louisville *Ga., U.S.A.* 33°0N 82°25W **316** B7
Louisville *Ill., U.S.A.* 38°46N 88°30W **311** F8
Louisville *Ky., U.S.A.* 38°15N 85°46W **311** F11
Louisville *Miss., U.S.A.* 33°7N 89°3W **315** E10
Louisville *Ohio, U.S.A.* 40°50N 81°16W **312** F3
Louisville Ridge *Pac. Oc.* 31°0S 172°30W **288** L10
Loukoléla *Congo* 1°4S 17°10E **264** C3
Loukouo *Congo* 3°38S 14°39E **264** C2
Loulay *France* 46°3N 0°30W **174** B3
Loulé *Portugal* 37°9N 8°0W **195** H3
Louny *Czech Rep.* 50°20N 13°48E **180** A6
Loup City *U.S.A.* 41°17N 98°58W **308** E4
Loups Marins, Lacs des
Canada 56°30N 73°45W **298** A5
Lourdes *France* 43°6N 0°3W **174** E3
Lourdes-de-Blanc-Sablon
Canada 51°24N 57°12W **299** B8
Lourenço *Brazil* 2°30N 51°40W **329** C7
Lourenço Marques = Maputo
Mozam. 25°58S 32°32E **271** C5
Loures *Portugal* 38°49N 9°10W **126** A1
Lourinhã *Portugal* 39°14N 9°17W **195** F1
Louros *Greece* 39°3N 20°47E **207** A2
Lousã *Portugal* 40°7N 8°14W **194** E2
Louta *Burkina Faso* 13°30N 3°10W **262** C4
Louth *N.S.W., Australia* 30°30S 145°8E **283** A6
Louth *Louth, Ireland* 53°58N 6°32W **166** C5
Louth *Lincs., U.K.* 53°22N 0°1W **168** D7
Louth □ *Ireland* 53°56N 6°34W **166** C5
Louth B. *Australia* 34°33S 135°56E **282** C1
Loutra Edipsou *Greece* 38°54N 23°2E **204** C5
Loutra Kyllinis *Greece* 37°52N 21°7E **207** D3
Loutraki *Greece* 37°58N 22°57E **204** D4
Loutropoli Thermis
Greece 39°11N 26°29E **205** B8
Louvain = Leuven
Belgium 50°52N 4°42E **170** D4
Louvale *U.S.A.* 32°10N 84°50W **316** C5
Louveciennes *France* 48°51N 2°8E **134** A1
Louviers *France* 49°12N 1°10E **172** C8
Louvre, Musée du *Paris, France* **134** b4
Louvre, Palais du *Paris, France* **134** b4
Louwsburg *S. Africa* 27°37S 31°7E **271** C5
Lovat → *Russia* 58°14N 31°28E **188** C6
Lovćen *Montenegro* 42°23N 18°51E **202** D2
Lovćen △ *Serbia* 42°20N 18°50E **202** D2
Lovech *Bulgaria* 43°8N 24°42E **203** C8
Lovech □ *Bulgaria* 43°15N 24°45E **203** C8
Loveland *Colo., U.S.A.* 40°24N 105°5W **304** F11
Loveland *Ohio, U.S.A.* 39°16N 84°16W **311** E12
Lovell *U.S.A.* 44°50N 108°24W **304** D9
Lovelock *U.S.A.* 40°11N 118°28W **304** F4
Lóvere *Italy* 45°49N 10°4E **198** C7
Lovers Leap *Jamaica* 17°52N 77°39W **320** a
Loves Park *U.S.A.* 42°19N 89°3W **310** B7
Lövestad *Sweden* 55°40N 13°54E **163** J7
Loviisa *Finland* 60°28N 26°12E **188** B4
Lovilia *U.S.A.* 41°8N 92°55W **310** C4
Loving *U.S.A.* 32°17N 104°6W **305** K11
Lovington *Ill., U.S.A.* 39°43N 88°38W **311** E8
Lovington *N. Mex., U.S.A.* 32°57N 103°21W **305** K12
Lovisa = Loviisa *Finland* 60°28N 26°12E **188** B4
Lovosice *Czech Rep.* 50°30N 14°2E **180** A7
Lovran *Croatia* 45°18N 14°15E **199** C11
Lovrin *Romania* 45°58N 20°48E **182** E5
Lövstabruk *Sweden* 60°25N 17°53E **162** D11
Lövstabukten *Sweden* 60°35N 17°45E **162** D11
Lóvua *Lunda Norte, Angola* 7°19S 20°12E **265** D4
Lóvua *Moxico, Angola* 11°33S 23°33E **265** E4
Lóvua →
Dem. Rep. of the Congo 6°6S 20°37E **265** D4
Low, L. *Canada* 52°29N 76°17W **298** B4
Low Bd. *Antigua & B.* 17°39N 61°51W **322** b
Low Pt. *Australia* 32°25S 127°25E **279** F4
Low Tatra = Nízke Tatry
Slovak Rep. 48°55N 19°30E **181** C12
Lowa *Dem. Rep. of the Congo* 1°25S 25°47E **268** C2
Lowa →
Dem. Rep. of the Congo 1°24S 25°51E **268** C2
Lowden *U.S.A.* 41°52N 90°56W **310** C6
Lowell *Ind., U.S.A.* 41°18N 87°25W **311** C9
Lowell *Mass., U.S.A.* 42°38N 71°19W **313** D13
Lowell *Mich., U.S.A.* 42°56N 85°20W **311** B11
Lowellville *U.S.A.* 41°2N 80°32W **312** E4
Löwen = Lewin Brzeski
Poland 50°45N 17°37E **185** H4
Löwen → *Namibia* 26°51S 18°17E **270** C2
Löwenberg = Lwówek Śląski
Poland 51°7N 15°38E **185** G2
Löwenstadt = Brzeziny
Poland 51°49N 19°42E **185** G6
Lower Alkali L. *U.S.A.* 41°16N 120°2W **304** F3
Lower Arrow L. *Canada* 49°40N 118°5W **296** D5
Lower Austria =
Niederösterreich □
Austria 48°25N 15°40E **180** C8
Lower B. *U.S.A.* 40°32N 74°5W **132** C1
Lower California = Baja California
Mexico 31°10N 115°12W **318** A1
Lower East Side *New York, U.S.A.* **132** e2
Lower Glenelg △
Australia 38°4S 141°41E **282** E4
Lower Hutt *N.Z.* 41°10S 174°55E **143** B2
Lower Kalskag *U.S.A.* 61°31N 160°22W **303** F7
Lower Lake *U.S.A.* 38°55N 122°37W **306** G4
Lower Manhattan *New York, U.S.A.* **132** e1
Lower Manitou L.
Canada 49°15N 93°0W **297** D10
Lower Manzanilla
Trin. & Tob. 10°31N 61°3W **323** t
Lower New York B. = Lower B.
U.S.A. 40°32N 74°5W **132** C1
Lower Paia *U.S.A.* 20°55N 156°23W **302** C5
Lower Post *Canada* 59°58N 128°30W **296** B3
Lower Red L. *U.S.A.* 47°58N 95°0W **308** B6
Lower Saxony = Niedersachsen □
Germany 52°50N 9°0E **178** C4
Lower Shing Mun Res.
China 22°22N 114°9E **122** A1
Lower Tunguska = Tunguska,
Nizhnyaya → *Russia* 65°48N 88°4E **215** C9
Lower Zambezi △ *Zambia* 15°25S 29°40E **269** F2
Lowestoft *U.K.* 52°29N 1°45E **169** E9
Lowgar □ *Afghan.* 34°0N 69°0E **240** B3
Łowicz *Poland* 52°6N 19°55E **185** F6
Lowly, Pt. *Australia* 33°0S 137°46E **282** B2
Lowry Bay *N.Z.* 41°15S 174°55E **143** B2
Lowry City *U.S.A.* 38°8N 93°44W **310** F3
Lowville *U.S.A.* 43°47N 75°29W **313** C9
Loxton *S. Austral., Australia* 34°28S 140°31E **282** C4
Loxton *Northern Cape, S. Africa* 31°30S 22°22E **270** D3
Loyalton *U.S.A.* 39°41N 120°14W **306** F6
Loyalty Is. = Loyauté, Îs.
N. Cal. 20°50S 166°30E **288** d
Loyang = Luoyang
China 34°40N 112°26E **226** G7
Loyauté, Îs. *N. Cal.* 20°50S 166°30E **288** d
Loyev = Loyew *Belarus* 51°56N 30°46E **177** C16
Loyew *Belarus* 51°56N 30°46E **177** C16
Loyola University *U.S.A.* 42°0N 87°39W **119** B3
Loyoro *Uganda* 3°22N 34°14E **268** B3
Lož *Slovenia* 45°43N 14°30E **199** C11
Lozère □ *France* 44°35N 3°30E **174** D7
Loznica *Serbia* 44°32N 19°12E **202** B3
Lozova *Ukraine* 49°0N 36°20E **189** H9
Lu *India* 26°58N 95°14E **241** B5
Lü Shan *China* 29°30N 115°55E **229** C11
Lü Tao *Taiwan* 22°40N 121°30E **225** D3
Lu Verne *U.S.A.* 42°55N 94°5W **310** B2
Lu Wo *China* 22°33N 114°6E **219** F11
Lu Xun, Tomb of *China* 31°17N 121°29E **138** B1
Lu Xun Museum *Beijing, China* **114** b1
Lu Xun Park *China* 31°17N 121°28E **138** B1
Lua →
Dem. Rep. of the Congo 2°46N 18°26E **264** B3
Lua Makiki *U.S.A.* 20°33N 156°37W **302** C5
Luachimo *Angola* 7°23S 20°48E **265** D4
Luacono *Angola* 11°15S 21°37E **265** E4
Luajan → *India* 24°44N 85°1E **243** G11
Lualaba →
Dem. Rep. of the Congo 0°26N 25°20E **264** B5
Luale *Dem. Rep. of the Congo* 1°9N 23°5E **264** B4
Lualualei Naval Reserve
U.S.A. 21°27N 158°6W **302** K13
Luampa *Zambia* 15°4S 24°20E **265** F4
Lu'an *China* 31°45N 116°29E **229** B11
Luan Chau *Vietnam* 21°38N 103°24E **228** G4
Luan He → *China* 39°20N 119°5E **227** E10
Luan Xian *China* 39°40N 118°40E **227** E10
Luancheng *Guangxi Zhuangzu, China* 22°48N 108°55E **228** F7
Luancheng *Hebei, China* 37°53N 114°40E **226** F8
Luanco *Spain* 43°37N 5°48W **194** B5
Luanda *Angola* 8°50S 13°15E **265** D2
Luando △ *Angola* 11°0S 17°32E **265** E3
Luang, Thale *Thailand* 7°30N 100°15E **237** J3
Luang Prabang *Laos* 19°52N 102°10E **228** H4
Luanginga → *Zambia* 15°11S 22°55E **265** F4
Luangwa *Zambia* 15°35S 30°16E **269** F3
Luangwa → *Zambia* 14°25S 30°25E **269** E3
Luangwa Valley *Zambia* 13°30S 31°30E **269** E3
Luania-Bubi
Dem. Rep. of the Congo 7°28S 24°49E **265** D4
Luanne *China* 40°55N 117°40E **227** D9
Luanping *China* 40°53N 117°23E **227** D9
Luanshya *Zambia* 13°3S 28°28E **269** E2
Luapula □ *Zambia* 11°0S 29°0E **269** E2
Luapula → *Africa* 9°26S 28°33E **269** D2
Luarca *Spain* 43°32N 6°32W **194** B4
Luashi
Dem. Rep. of the Congo 10°50S 23°36E **265** E4
Luatamba *Angola* 12°6S 20°19E **265** F4
Luatira *Angola* 12°52S 17°14E **265** E3
Luau *Angola* 10°40S 22°10E **265** E4
Luba *Phil.* 17°19N 120°42E **232** C3
Lubaczów *Poland* 50°10N 23°8E **185** H10
Lubalo *Angola* 9°10S 19°15E **265** D3
Lubamiti
Dem. Rep. of the Congo 2°28S 17°47E **264** C3
Lubań *Poland* 51°5N 15°15E **185** G2
Lubana, Ozero = Lubānas Ezers
Latvia 56°45N 27°0E **188** D4
Lubānas Ezers *Latvia* 56°45N 27°0E **188** D4
Lubang *Phil.* 13°52N 120°7E **232** E3
Lubang Is. *Phil.* 13°50N 120°12E **232** E3
Lubango *Angola* 14°55S 13°30E **265** E2
Lubao
Dem. Rep. of the Congo 5°17S 25°42E **265** D5
Lübars *Germany* 52°37N 13°21E **115** A3
Lubartów *Poland* 51°28N 22°42E **185** G9
Lubawa *Poland* 53°30N 19°48E **184** E6
Lübbecke *Germany* 52°18N 8°37E **178** C4
Lübben *Germany* 51°56N 13°54E **178** D9
Lübbenau *Germany* 51°52N 13°57E **178** D9
Lubbock *U.S.A.* 33°35N 101°51W **314** E4
Lübeck *Germany* 53°52N 10°40E **178** B6
Lübecker Bucht *Germany* 54°3N 10°54E **178** A6
Lubefu
Dem. Rep. of the Congo 4°47S 24°27E **265** C4
Lubefu →
Dem. Rep. of the Congo 4°10S 23°0E **265** C4
Lubelskie □ *Poland* 51°20N 22°50E **185** G9
Lüben = Lubin *Poland* 51°24N 16°11E **185** G3
Lubero = Luofu
Dem. Rep. of the Congo 0°10S 29°15E **268** C2
Luberon △ *France* 43°52N 5°25E **175** E9
Lubersac *France* 45°26N 1°23E **174** C5
Lubicon L. *Canada* 56°23N 115°56W **296** B5
Lubień Kujawski *Poland* 52°23N 19°9E **185** F6
Lubilash →
Dem. Rep. of the Congo 6°2S 23°45E **265** D4
Lubin *Poland* 51°24N 16°11E **185** G3
Lublin *Poland* 51°12N 22°38E **185** G9
Lubliniec *Poland* 50°43N 18°45E **185** H5
Lubnān = Lebanon ■ *Asia* 34°0N 36°0E **250** E7
Lubnān, Jabal *Lebanon* 33°45N 35°40E **250** E6
Lubniewice *Poland* 52°31N 15°15E **185** F2
Lubny *Ukraine* 50°3N 32°58E **189** G7
Lubomierz *Poland* 51°1N 15°31E **185** G2
Luboń *Poland* 52°21N 16°51E **185** F3
Lubondaie
Dem. Rep. of the Congo 8°1S 26°32E **265** D4
Lubongola
Dem. Rep. of the Congo 2°35S 27°50E **268** C2
L'ubotin *Slovak Rep.* 49°17N 20°53E **181** B13
Lubraniec *Poland* 52°33N 18°50E **185** F5
Lubsko *Poland* 51°45N 14°57E **185** G1
Lübtheen *Germany* 53°18N 11°5E **178** B7
Lubuagan *Phil.* 17°21N 121°10E **232** C3
Lubudi
Dem. Rep. of the Congo 6°51S 21°18E **265** D4
Lubudi → *Kasai-Occ.,*
Dem. Rep. of the Congo 4°19S 20°23E **265** C4
Lubudi → *Katanga,*
Dem. Rep. of the Congo 9°0S 25°35E **265** D5
Lubuklinggau *Indonesia* 3°15S 102°55E **234** C2
Lubuksikaping *Indonesia* 0°10N 100°15E **234** B2
Lubumbashi
Dem. Rep. of the Congo 11°40S 27°28E **269** E2
Lubunda
Dem. Rep. of the Congo 5°12S 26°41E **265** D5
Lubungu *Zambia* 14°35S 26°24E **269** E2
Lubuskie □ *Poland* 52°10N 15°20E **185** F2
Lubutu
Dem. Rep. of the Congo 0°45S 26°30E **268** C2
Luc An Chau *Vietnam* 22°6N 104°43E **236** A5
Luc-en-Diois *France* 44°36N 5°28E **175** D9
Lucala *Angola* 9°7S 15°58E **265** D3
Lucala → *Angola* 9°38S 14°14E **265** D2
Lucan *Canada* 43°11N 81°24W **312** C3
Lucania, Mt. *Canada* 61°1N 140°27W **294** C5
Lucapa *Angola* 8°25S 20°45E **265** D4
Lucas *U.S.A.* 41°2N 93°29W **310** C3
Lucas Channel *Canada* 45°21N 81°45W **312** A3
Lucban *Phil.* 14°6N 121°33E **232** D3
Lucca *Italy* 43°50N 10°29E **198** E7
Lucé *France* 48°26N 1°27E **172** D8
Luce Bay *U.K.* 54°45N 4°48W **167** G4
Lucedale *U.S.A.* 30°56N 88°35W **315** F10
Lucena *Phil.* 13°56N 121°37E **232** E3
Lucena *Spain* 37°27N 4°31W **195** H6
Lučenec *Slovak Rep.* 48°18N 19°42E **181** C12
Lucera *Italy* 41°30N 15°20E **201** A8
Lucerne = Lake Worth
U.S.A. 26°37N 80°3W **317** J9
Lucerne = Luzern *Switz.* 47°3N 8°18E **179** H4
Lucerne *U.S.A.* 39°6N 122°48W **306** F4
Lucerne Valley *U.S.A.* 34°27N 116°57W **307** L10
Lucero *Mexico* 30°49N 106°30W **318** A3
Luchena → *Spain* 37°44N 1°50W **197** H3
Lucheng *China* 36°20N 113°11E **226** F7
Lucheringo → *Mozam.* 11°43S 36°17E **269** E4
Luchow = Luzhou
China 28°52N 105°20E **228** C5
Lüchow *Germany* 52°58N 11°8E **178** C7
Luchu *Taiwan* 22°52N 120°15E **225** D2
Luchuan *China* 22°21N 110°12E **229** F8
Lucia *U.S.A.* 36°2N 121°33W **306** J5
Lucie → *Suriname* 3°35N 57°38W **329** C6
Lucinda *Australia* 18°32S 146°20E **280** B4
Lucindale *Australia* 36°58S 140°26E **282** D4
Lucira *Angola* 14°0S 12°35E **265** E2
Luciras, B. das *Angola* 13°52S 12°31E **265** E2
Luckau *Germany* 51°50N 13°42E **178** D9
Luckenwalde *Germany* 52°5N 13°10E **178** C9
Luckey *U.S.A.* 41°27N 83°29W **311** C13
Luckhoff *S. Africa* 29°44S 24°43E **270** C3
Lucknow *Ont., Canada* 43°57N 81°31W **312** C3
Lucknow *India* 26°50N 81°0E **243** F9
Luçon *France* 46°28N 1°10W **174** B2
Lucusse *Angola* 12°32S 20°48E **265** E4
Lucy, L. *U.S.A.* 28°34N 81°29W **133** A2
Lüda = Dalian *China* 38°50N 121°40E **227** E11
Luda Kamchiya →
Bulgaria 43°3N 27°29E **203** C11
Ludbreg *Croatia* 46°15N 16°38E **199** B13
Lüdenscheid *Germany* 51°13N 7°37E **178** D3
Lüderitz *Namibia* 26°41S 15°8E **270** C2
Lüderitzbaai *Namibia* 26°36S 15°8E **270** C2
Ludhiana *India* 30°57N 75°56E **242** D6
Ludian *China* 27°10N 103°33E **228** D4
Luding Qiao *China* 29°53N 102°12E **228** C4
Lüdinghausen *Germany* 51°46N 7°26E **178** D3
Ludington *U.S.A.* 43°57N 86°27W **308** D10
Ludlow *Shrops., U.K.* 52°22N 2°42W **169** E5
Ludlow *Calif., U.S.A.* 34°43N 116°10W **307** L10
Ludlow *Pa., U.S.A.* 41°43N 78°56W **312** E6
Ludlow *Vt., U.S.A.* 43°24N 72°42W **313** C12
Ludowici *U.S.A.* 31°43N 81°45W **316** D8
Ludus *Romania* 46°29N 24°5E **183** D9
Ludvika *Sweden* 60°8N 15°14E **162** D9
Ludwigsburg *Germany* 48°53N 9°11E **179** G5
Ludwigsfeld *Germany* 48°12N 11°27E **131** A1
Ludwigsfelde *Germany* 52°17N 13°17E **178** C9
Ludwigshafen *Germany* 49°29N 8°26E **179** F4
Ludwigslust *Germany* 53°19N 11°30E **178** B7
Ludza *Latvia* 56°32N 27°43E **188** D4
Lue *Australia* 32°38S 149°50E **283** B8
Luebo
Dem. Rep. of the Congo 5°21S 21°23E **265** D4
Lueki *Dem. Rep. of the Congo* 3°20S 25°48E **264** C5
Luena *Angola* 12°13S 19°51E **265** E3
Luena
Dem. Rep. of the Congo 9°28S 25°43E **269** D2
Luena *Zambia* 10°40S 30°25E **269** E3
Luena → *Angola* 12°30S 22°34E **265** E4
Luena → *Zambia* 14°46S 23°30E **265** E4
Luena Flats *Zambia* 14°47S 23°17E **265** E4
Luengué △ *Angola* 16°55S 19°55E **265** F3
Luenha = Ruenya →
Africa 16°24S 33°48E **269** F3
Luepa *Venezuela* 5°43N 61°31W **329** B5
Lueta →
Dem. Rep. of the Congo 7°4S 21°40E **265** D4
Luete → *Zambia* 15°46S 23°10E **265** F4
Lüeyang *China* 33°22N 106°10E **226** H4
Lufeng *Guangdong, China* 22°57N 115°38E **229** F10
Lufeng *Yunnan, China* 25°0N 102°5E **228** E4
Lufico *Angola* 6°24S 13°23E **265** D2
Lufira →
Dem. Rep. of the Congo 9°30S 27°0E **269** D2
Lufkin *U.S.A.* 31°21N 94°44W **314** F7
Lufupa
Dem. Rep. of the Congo 10°37S 24°56E **265** E4
Luga *Russia* 58°40N 29°55E **188** C5
Luga → *Russia* 59°40N 28°18E **188** C5
Lugano *Switz.* 46°1N 8°57E **179** J4
Lugano, L. di *Switz.* 46°0N 9°0E **198** C6
Lugansk = Luhansk
Ukraine 48°38N 39°15E **189** H10
Luganville *Vanuatu* 15°27S 167°10E **287** E5
Lugard's Falls *Kenya* 3°6S 38°41E **268** C4
Lugela *Mozam.* 16°25S 36°43E **269** F4
Lugenda → *Mozam.* 11°25S 38°33E **269** E4
Lugh Ganana *Somali Rep.* 3°48N 42°34E **267** D5
Lugnaquilla *Ireland* 52°58N 6°28W **166** D5
Lugo *Italy* 44°25N 11°54E **199** D8
Lugo *Spain* 43°2N 7°35W **194** B3
Lugo □ *Spain* 43°0N 7°30W **194** C3

Lugoj Romania 45°42N 21°57E 182 E6
Lugovoy = Qulan Kazakhstan 42°55N 72°43E 214 E8
Lugus I. Phil. 5°41N 120°50E 233 J3
Luhansk Ukraine 48°38N 39°15E 189 H10
Luhansk □ Ukraine 49°10N 38°40E 189 H10
Luhe China 32°19N 118°50E 229 A12
Luhe → Germany 53°23N 10°13E 178 B6
Luhit → India 27°48N 95°28E 241 B5
Luhu China 23°59N 113°16E 121 B2
Luhuo China 31°21N 100°48E 228 B3
Lui → Angola 8°21S 17°33E 265 D3
Lui → Zambia 16°18S 23°17E 265 F4
Luia Angola 8°10S 21°32E 265 D4
Luia → Angola 8°32S 21°47E 265 D4
Luiana Angola 17°25S 22°59E 265 F4
Luiana → Angola 17°24S 23°3E 265 F4
Luiana △ Angola 16°55S 22°20E 265 F4
Luichow = Liuzhou China 24°22N 109°22E 228 E7
Luichow Pen. = Leizhou Bandao China 21°0N 110°0E 228 G7
Luikuei Taiwan 23°0N 120°38E 225 D2
Luilaka → Dem. Rep. of the Congo 0°52S 20°12E 264 C4
Luimneach = Limerick Ireland 52°40N 8°37W 166 D3
Luing U.K. 56°14N 5°39W 167 E3
Luino Italy 45°59N 8°44E 198 C5
Luio → Angola 13°17S 21°37E 265 E4
Luís Correia Brazil 3°0S 41°35W 332 B3
Luís Gonçalves Brazil 5°37S 50°25W 332 C1
Luitpold Coast Antarctica 78°30S 32°0W 151 D1
Luiza Dem. Rep. of the Congo 7°40S 22°30E 265 D4
Luizi Dem. Rep. of the Congo 6°0S 27°25E 268 D2
Luján Argentina 34°45S 59°5W 334 C4
Lujiang China 31°20N 117°15E 229 B11
Lukala Dem. Rep. of the Congo 5°31S 14°32E 265 D2
Lukang Taiwan 24°1N 120°22E 225 B2
Lukanga Bandundu, Dem. Rep. of the Congo 1°41S 18°9E 264 C3
Lukanga Équateur, Dem. Rep. of the Congo 1°0S 18°8E 264 C3
Lukanga Swamp Zambia 14°30S 27°40E 269 E2
Lukavac Bos.-H. 44°33N 18°32E 182 F3
Lukenie → Dem. Rep. of the Congo 3°0S 18°50E 264 C3
Lukhisaral India 25°11N 86°5E 243 G12
Lŭki Bulgaria 41°50N 24°43E 203 E8
Lukk Libya 32°1N 24°46E 258 B4
Lukolela Équateur, Dem. Rep. of the Congo 1°10S 17°12E 264 C3
Lukolela Kasai-Or., Dem. Rep. of the Congo 5°23S 24°32E 265 D4
Lukosi Zimbabwe 18°30S 26°30E 269 F2
Lukovë Albania 39°59N 19°54E 202 G3
Lukovit Bulgaria 43°13N 24°11E 203 C8
Łuków Poland 51°55N 22°23E 185 G9
Lukoyanov Russia 55°2N 44°29E 190 C7
Luksefjell Norway 59°23N 9°34E 164 E6
Luku Taiwan 23°44N 120°45E 225 C2
Lukuni Dem. Rep. of the Congo 5°50S 17°16E 265 D3
Lukusuzi △ Zambia 12°43S 32°36E 269 E3
Lula Dem. Rep. of the Congo 5°22S 16°52E 265 D3
Luleå Sweden 65°35N 22°10E 160 D20
Luleälven → Sweden 65°35N 22°10E 160 D20
Lüleburgaz Turkey 41°23N 27°22E 203 E11
Luliang China 25°0N 103°40E 228 E4
Luling U.S.A. 29°41N 97°39W 314 G6
Lulong China 39°53N 118°51E 227 E10
Lulonga → Dem. Rep. of the Congo 1°0N 18°10E 264 B3
Lulu U.S.A. 30°7N 82°29W 316 E7
Lulu → Dem. Rep. of the Congo 1°18N 23°42E 264 B4
Lulua → Dem. Rep. of the Congo 4°30S 20°30E 265 C4
Luluabourg = Kananga Dem. Rep. of the Congo 5°55S 22°18E 265 D4
Luma Amer. Samoa 14°16S 169°33W 302 f
Lumai Angola 13°13S 21°25E 265 E4
Lumajang Indonesia 8°8S 113°13E 235 D4
Lumaku, Gunong Malaysia 4°52N 115°38E 235 B5
Lumbala → Angola 12°39S 22°35E 265 E4
Lumbala Kaquengue Angola 12°39S 22°34E 265 E4
Lumbala N'guimbo Angola 14°18S 21°18E 265 E4
Lumbe → Zambia 16°44S 23°41E 265 F4
Lumber City U.S.A. 31°56N 82°41W 316 D7
Lumberton U.S.A. 34°37N 79°0W 315 D15
Lumding India 25°46N 93°10E 241 C4
Lumholtz △ Australia 18°15S 145°32E 280 B4
Lumi Papua N. G. 3°30S 142°2E 286 B2
Lumiar Portugal 38°46N 9°10W 126 A2
Lumphini Park Bangkok, Thailand 113 c3
Lumpkin U.S.A. 32°3N 84°48W 316 C5
Lumsden Sask., Canada 50°39N 104°52W 297 C8
Lumsden N.Z. 45°44S 168°27E 285 F3
Lumut Malaysia 4°13N 100°37E 237 K3
Lumut, Tanjung Indonesia 3°50S 105°58E 234 C3
Luna India 23°43N 69°16E 242 H3
Luna Apayao, Phil. 18°18N 121°21E 232 B3
Lunan China 24°40N 103°18E 228 E4
Lunavada India 23°8N 73°37E 242 H5
Lunca Romania 47°22N 25°1E 183 C10
Lunca Corbului Romania 44°42N 24°45E 183 F9
Lund Sweden 55°44N 13°12E 163 J7
Lunda Norte □ Angola 8°0S 20°0E 265 D4
Lunda Sul □ Angola 10°0S 20°0E 265 E4
Lundamo Norway 63°9N 10°19E 164 A7
Lundazi Zambia 12°20S 33°7E 269 E3
Lundenburg = Břeclav Czech Rep. 48°46N 16°53E 181 C9
Lunderskov Denmark 55°29N 9°19E 163 J3
Lundi → Zimbabwe 21°43S 32°34E 269 G3
Lundtofte Denmark 55°47N 12°32E 118 A3
Lundu Malaysia 1°40N 109°50E 235 B3
Lundy U.K. 51°10N 4°41W 169 F3
Lune → U.K. 54°0N 2°51W 168 C5
Lüneburg Germany 53°15N 10°24E 178 B6
Lüneburg Heath = Lüneburger Heide Germany 53°10N 10°12E 178 B6
Lüneburger Heide Germany 53°10N 10°12E 178 B6
Lunel France 43°39N 4°9E 175 E8
Lünen Germany 51°37N 7°32E 178 D3
Lunenburg Canada 44°22N 64°18W 299 D7
Lunéville France 48°36N 6°30E 173 D13
Lung Mei China 22°23N 114°15E 122 A2
Lunga Dem. Rep. of the Congo 5°46S 12°14E 265 C4
Lunga → Zambia 14°34S 26°25E 269 E2
Lunga Lunga Kenya 4°33S 39°7E 268 C4
Lungchin Taiwan 24°12N 120°31E 225 B2
Lunge Angola 12°13S 16°7E 265 E3
Lungga Solomon Is. 9°25S 160°3E 287 M11
Lungi Airport S. Leone 8°40N 13°17W 262 D2
Lunglei India 22°55N 92°45E 241 D4
Lungngo Burma 21°57N 93°36E 241 E4
Lung'tan Taiwan 24°52N 121°12E 225 B3
Lungwebungu → Zambia 14°19S 23°14E 265 E4
Luni India 26°0N 73°6E 242 G5
Luni → India 24°41N 71°14E 242 G4
Luninets = Luninyets Belarus 52°15N 26°50E 177 B14
Luning U.S.A. 38°30N 118°11W 304 G4
Lunino Russia 53°38N 45°18E 190 D7
Luninyets Belarus 52°15N 26°50E 177 B14
Lunkaransar India 28°29N 73°44E 242 E5
Lunner Norway 60°19N 10°35E 164 D7
Lunpei Taiwan 24°45N 120°21E 225 C2
Lunsemfwa → Zambia 14°54S 30°12E 269 E3
Lunsemfwa Falls Zambia 14°30S 29°6E 269 E2
Luntai China 41°46N 84°14E 217 D10
Luo He → China 34°35N 110°20E 226 G6
Luocheng China 24°48N 108°53E 228 E7
Luochuan China 35°45N 109°26E 226 G5
Luoci China 25°19N 102°18E 228 E4
Luodian China 25°24N 106°43E 228 E6
Luoding China 22°45N 111°40E 229 F8
Luofu Dem. Rep. of the Congo 0°10S 29°15E 268 C2
Luohe China 33°32N 114°2E 226 H8
Luojiang Guangdong, China 23°5N 113°17E 121 B2
Luojiang Sichuan, China 31°18N 104°33E 228 B5
Luonan China 34°5N 110°10E 226 G6
Luoning China 34°35N 111°40E 226 G6
Luoshan China 32°13N 114°30E 229 A10
Luotian China 30°46N 115°22E 229 B10
Luoxiao Shan China 26°30N 114°1E 229 D10
Luoyang China 34°40N 112°26E 226 G7
Luoyuan China 26°28N 119°30E 229 D12
Luozi Dem. Rep. of the Congo 4°54S 14°0E 265 C2
Luozigou China 43°42N 130°18E 227 C16
Lupeni Romania 45°21N 23°13E 183 E8
Lupilichi Mozam. 11°47S 35°13E 269 E4
Lupire Angola 14°36S 19°29E 265 E3
Łupków Poland 49°15N 22°4E 185 J9
Lupoing China 24°53N 104°21E 228 E5
Lupon Phil. 6°54N 126°0E 233 H6
Luputa Dem. Rep. of the Congo 7°7S 23°43E 265 D4
Luqa Malta 35°52N 14°29E 206 F7
Luquan China 25°35N 102°25E 228 E4
Luque Paraguay 25°19S 57°25W 334 B4
Luquembo Angola 10°44S 17°43E 265 E3
Luquillo Puerto Rico 18°23N 65°43W 321 b
Luquillo, Sierra de Puerto Rico 18°20N 65°47W 321 b
Lúras Italy 40°56N 9°10E 200 B2
Luray U.S.A. 38°40N 78°28W 309 F14
Lure France 47°40N 6°30E 173 E13
Luremo Angola 8°30S 17°50E 265 D3
Lurgan U.K. 54°28N 6°19W 166 B5
Luribay Bolivia 17°6S 67°39W 330 D4
Lurin Peru 12°17S 76°52W 330 C2
Lusaka Zambia 15°28S 28°16E 269 F2
Lusaka □ Zambia 15°30S 29°0E 269 F2
Lusambo Dem. Rep. of the Congo 4°58S 23°28E 265 C4
Lusancay Is. and Reefs Papua N. G. 8°30S 150°30E 286 E6
Lusangaye Dem. Rep. of the Congo 4°54S 26°0E 265 C5
Luseland Canada 52°5N 109°24W 297 C7
Lusenga Plain △ Zambia 9°22S 29°14E 269 D2
Lusengo Dem. Rep. of the Congo 1°47N 19°31E 264 B3
Lushan Henan, China 33°45N 112°55E 226 H7
Lushan Sichuan, China 30°12N 102°52E 228 B4
Lushi China 34°3N 111°3E 226 G6
Lushnjë Albania 40°55N 19°41E 202 F3
Lushoto Tanzania 4°47S 38°20E 268 C4
Lushui China 25°58N 98°44E 228 E2
Lushuihe China 42°31N 127°47E 224 A3
Lüshun China 38°45N 121°15E 227 E11
Lusignan France 46°26N 0°8E 174 B4
Lusigny-sur-Barse France 48°16N 4°15E 173 D11
Lusiye Zambia 15°30S 23°57E 265 F4
Lusk U.S.A. 42°46N 104°27W 304 E11
Lussac-les-Châteaux France 46°24N 0°43E 174 B4
Lustenau Austria 47°26N 9°39E 180 D2
Lustheim Germany 48°14N 11°34E 131 A2
Lustrafjorden Norway 61°23N 7°25E 164 C4
Lūt, Dasht-e Iran 31°30N 58°0E 247 D8
Luta = Dalian China 38°50N 121°40E 227 E11
Lütao Taiwan 22°40N 121°29E 225 D3
Lutembo Angola 13°26S 21°16E 265 E4
Lutherstadt Wittenberg Germany 51°53N 12°39E 178 D8
Luthersville U.S.A. 33°13N 84°45W 316 B5
Luti Solomon Is. 7°14S 157°0E 287 L9
Luton U.K. 51°53N 0°24W 169 F7
Luton □ U.K. 51°53N 0°24W 169 F7
Lutong Malaysia 4°28N 114°0E 235 B4
Lutsel K'e Canada 62°24N 110°44W 297 A6
Lutshima → Dem. Rep. of the Congo 5°22S 18°59E 265 D3
Lutsk Ukraine 50°50N 25°15E 177 C13
Luttenberg = Ljutomer Slovenia 46°31N 16°11E 199 B13
Lutto = Lotta → Europe 68°42N 31°6E 160 B24
Lutuai Angola 12°41S 20°7E 265 E4
Lutz U.S.A. 28°9N 82°28W 317 G7
Lützow Holmbukta Antarctica 69°10S 37°30E 151 C4
Lutzputs S. Africa 28°3S 20°40E 270 C3
Luuk Phil. 5°58N 121°18E 233 J3
Luuq = Lugh Ganana Somali Rep. 3°48N 42°34E 267 D5
Luverne Ala., U.S.A. 31°43N 86°16W 316 D3
Luverne Minn., U.S.A. 43°39N 96°13W 308 D5
Luvo Angola 5°51S 14°5E 265 D2
Luvua Dem. Rep. of the Congo 8°48S 25°17E 265 D5
Luvua → Dem. Rep. of the Congo 6°50S 27°30E 268 D2
Luvuvhu → S. Africa 22°25S 31°18E 271 B5
Luwan China 31°12N 121°27E 138 B1
Luwegu → Tanzania 8°31S 37°23E 269 D4
Luwuk Indonesia 0°56S 122°47E 231 E6
Luxembourg Lux. 49°37N 6°9E 170 E6
Luxembourg □ Belgium 49°58N 5°30E 170 E5
Luxembourg ■ Europe 49°45N 6°0E 170 E5
Luxembourg ✕ (LUX) Lux. 49°37N 6°10E 170 E6
Luxembourg, Palais du Paris, France 134 c4
Luxemburg U.S.A. 42°36N 91°5W 310 B5
Luxeuil-les-Bains France 47°49N 6°24E 173 E13
Luxi Hunan, China 28°20N 110°7E 229 C8
Luxi Yunnan, China 24°40N 103°55E 228 E4
Luxi Yunnan, China 24°27N 98°36E 228 E2
Luxor = El Uqsur Egypt 25°41N 32°38E 256 B3
Luy-de-Béarn → France 43°39N 0°48W 174 E3
Luy-de-France → France 43°39N 0°48W 174 E3
Luyeh Hualien, Taiwan 23°35N 121°32E 225 C3
Luyeh T'aitung, Taiwan 22°55N 121°8E 225 D3
Luyi China 33°50N 115°35E 226 H8
Luz Azores 39°1N 28°0W 153 d1
Luz-St-Sauveur France 42°53N 0°0 174 F4
Luza Russia 60°39N 47°10E 186 B8
Luzern Switz. 47°3N 8°18E 179 H4
Luzern □ Switz. 47°2N 7°55E 179 H3
Luzhai China 24°29N 109°42E 228 E7
Luzhany Ukraine 48°22N 25°47E 183 B10
Luzhi China 26°21N 105°16E 228 D5
Luzhniki Sports Centre Russia 55°43N 37°31E 129 B3
Luzhou China 28°52N 105°20E 228 C5
Luziânia Brazil 16°20S 48°0W 333 E2
Luzilândia Brazil 3°28S 42°22W 332 B3
Lužnice → Czech Rep. 49°14N 14°23E 180 B7
Luzon Phil. 16°0N 121°0E 232 C3
Luzon Strait Asia 21°0N 120°40E 229 G13
Luzy France 46°47N 3°58E 173 F10
Luzzi Italy 39°27N 16°17E 201 C9
Lviv Ukraine 49°50N 24°0E 177 D13
Lviv □ Ukraine 49°30N 23°45E 189 H2
Lvov = Lviv Ukraine 49°50N 24°0E 177 D13
Lwówek Poland 52°28N 16°10E 185 F3
Lwówek Śląski Poland 51°7N 15°38E 185 G2
Lyakhavichy Belarus 53°2N 26°32E 177 B14
Lyakhovskiye, Ostrova Russia 73°40N 141°0E 215 B15
Lyaki = Läki Azerbaijan 40°34N 47°22E 191 K8
Lyal I. Canada 44°57N 81°24W 312 B3
Lyall Mt. N.Z. 45°16S 167°32E 285 F2
Lyallpur = Faisalabad Pakistan 31°30N 73°5E 242 D5
Lyaskovets Bulgaria 43°6N 25°44E 203 C9
Lyasnaya Belarus 52°9N 23°31E 185 F10
Lybster U.K. 58°18N 3°15W 167 C5
Lycabettus Athens, Greece 112 b3
Lycaonia Turkey 38°0N 33°0E 212 D5
Lychen Germany 53°12N 13°18E 178 B9
Lychkova Russia 57°55N 32°24E 188 D7
Lycia Turkey 36°30N 29°30E 205 E11
Lyck = Ełk Poland 53°50N 22°21E 184 E9
Lyckebyån → Sweden 56°12N 15°39E 163 H9
Lycksele Sweden 64°38N 18°40E 160 D18
Lycosura Greece 37°20N 22°3E 204 D4
Lydda = Lod Israel 31°57N 34°54E 251 G5
Lyddan I. Antarctica 74°0S 21°0W 151 D2
Lydenburg S. Africa 25°10S 30°29E 271 C5
Lydia Turkey 38°48N 28°19E 205 C10
Łydynia → Poland 52°43N 20°26E 185 F7
Lyell N.Z. 41°48S 172°4E 285 B7
Lyell I. Canada 52°40N 131°35W 296 C2
Lyepyel Belarus 54°50N 28°40E 188 E5
Lyford Cay Bahamas 25°2N 77°33W 153 b
Lygnern Sweden 57°30N 12°15E 163 G6
Lykavittos Hill = Lycabettus Athens, Greece 112 b3
Lykens U.S.A. 40°34N 76°42W 313 F8
Lyman Ukraine 45°41N 29°45E 183 E14
Lyman Wyo., U.S.A. 41°20N 110°18W 304 F8
Lymanske Ukraine 46°40N 29°58E 183 D14
Lyme B. U.K. 50°42N 2°53W 169 G4
Lyme Regis U.K. 50°43N 2°57W 169 G5
Lymington U.K. 50°45N 1°32W 169 G6
Łyna → Poland 54°37N 21°14E 184 D8
Lynchburg Ohio, U.S.A. 39°15N 83°48W 311 E13
Lynchburg S.C., U.S.A. 34°3N 80°4W 316 A9
Lynchburg Va., U.S.A. 37°25N 79°9W 309 G14
Lynd → Australia 16°28S 143°18E 280 B3
Lynd Ra. Australia 25°30S 149°20E 281 D4
Lynden Ont., Canada 43°14N 80°9W 312 C4
Lynden Wash., U.S.A. 48°57N 122°27W 306 B4
Lyndhurst S. Austral., Australia 30°15S 138°18E 281 E2
Lyndhurst N.J., U.S.A. 40°49N 74°7W 132 B1
Lyndon → Australia 23°29S 114°6E 279 D1
Lyndonville N.Y., U.S.A. 43°20N 78°23W 312 C6
Lyndonville Vt., U.S.A. 44°31N 72°1W 313 B12
Lyngdal Buskerud, Norway 59°54N 9°32E 164 E6
Lyngdal Vest-Agder, Norway 58°8N 7°7E 164 F4
Lyngen Norway 69°45N 20°30E 160 B19
Lyngør Norway 58°38N 9°8E 164 F6
Lynher Reef Australia 15°27S 121°55E 278 C3
Lynn Ind., U.S.A. 40°3N 84°56W 311 D12
Lynn Mass., U.S.A. 42°28N 70°57W 313 D14
Lynn Canal U.S.A. 58°50N 135°15W 303 G14
Lynn Haven U.S.A. 30°15N 85°39W 316 E4
Lynn Lake Canada 56°51N 101°3W 297 B8
Lynn Woods Res. U.S.A. 42°29N 71°0W 116 A2
Lynne U.S.A. 29°12N 81°55W 317 F8
Lynnville U.S.A. 38°12N 87°18W 311 F9
Lynnwood U.S.A. 47°49N 122°18W 306 C4
Lynton U.K. 51°13N 3°50W 169 F4
Lyntupy Belarus 55°4N 26°23E 188 E4
Lynx L. Canada 62°25N 106°15W 297 A7
Lyon France 45°46N 4°50E 175 C8
Lyon, Gare de Paris, France 134 c5
Lyon St-Exupery ✕ (LYS) France 45°44N 5°2E 175 C9
Lyonnais France 45°45N 4°15E 175 C8
Lyons = Lyon France 45°46N 4°50E 175 C8
Lyons Ga., U.S.A. 32°12N 82°19W 316 C7
Lyons Ill., U.S.A. 41°48N 87°49W 119 C2
Lyons Kans., U.S.A. 38°21N 98°12W 308 F4
Lyons N.Y., U.S.A. 43°5N 77°0W 312 C8
Lyons → Australia 25°2S 115°9E 279 E2
Lyons Falls U.S.A. 43°37N 75°22W 313 C9
Lyozna Belarus 55°0N 30°50E 188 E6
Lyra Reef Papua N. G. 1°50S 153°35E 286 A7
Lys = Leie → Belgium 51°2N 3°45E 170 C3
Lysá nad Labem Czech Rep. 50°11N 14°51E 180 A7
Lysaker Norway 59°54N 10°38E 133 A2
Lysakerselva → Norway 59°54N 10°38E 133 A2
Lysebotn Norway 59°3N 6°37E 164 E3
Lysefjorden Norway 59°0N 6°23E 164 E3
Lysekil Sweden 58°17N 11°26E 163 F5
Lyskovo Russia 56°0N 45°3E 190 B7
Lysolaje Czech Rep. 50°8N 14°22E 135 B2
Lystrup Denmark 56°14N 10°14E 163 H4
Lysva Russia 58°7N 57°49E 186 C10
Lysvik Sweden 60°1N 13°9E 162 D7
Lysychansk Ukraine 48°55N 38°30E 189 H10
Lytham St. Anne's U.K. 53°45N 3°0W 168 D4
Lyttelton N.Z. 43°35S 172°44E 285 D7
Lytton Canada 50°13N 121°31W 296 C4
Lyuban Russia 59°16N 31°18E 188 C6
Lyubertsy Russia 55°40N 37°51E 129 B5
Lyubim Russia 58°20N 40°39E 188 C11
Lyubimets Bulgaria 41°50N 26°5E 203 E10
Lyublino Russia 55°41N 37°44E 129 B4
Lyuboml Ukraine 51°11N 24°4E 185 G11
Lyubotyn Ukraine 50°0N 36°0E 189 H8
Lyubytino Russia 58°50N 33°16E 188 C7
Lyudinovo Russia 53°52N 34°28E 188 F8

M

M.R. Stefanik, Bratislava ✕ (BTS) Slovak Rep. 48°11N 17°9E 181 C10
Ma → Vietnam 19°47N 105°56E 228 H5
Ma, O. el → Algeria 27°45N 7°52W 260 C3
Ma Nam Wat China 22°21N 114°16E 122 A2
Ma On Shan Country Park △ China 22°22N 114°14E 122 A2
Ma'adaba Jordan 30°43N 35°47E 251 H6
Maafushi Maldives 3°59N 73°27E 272 d
Ma'ale Adumim West Bank 31°49N 35°17E 123 B2
Ma'ale Ha Khamisha Israel 31°49N 35°7E 123 B1
Ma'ale Mikhmas West Bank 31°52N 35°18E 123 A2
Maamba Zambia 17°17S 26°28E 270 A4
Ma'ān Jordan 30°12N 35°44E 251 H6
Ma'ān □ Jordan 30°0N 36°0E 251 J7
Maana'oba Solomon Is. 8°17S 160°50E 287 M11
Maanselkä Finland 63°52N 28°32E 160 E23
Ma'anshan China 31°44N 118°29E 229 B12
Maantiekylä Finland 60°20N 25°0E 121 A3
Maarianhamina = Mariehamn Finland 60°5N 19°55E 161 F18
Maarifa Iraq 33°15N 44°21E 113 B2
Maarmorilik Greenland 71°3N 51°0W 154 C5
Ma'arrat an Nu'mān Syria 35°43N 36°43E 250 C7
Maas → Neths. 51°45N 4°32E 170 C4
Maaseik Belgium 51°6N 5°45E 170 C5
Maasim Phil. 5°52N 125°0E 233 J5
Maasin Phil. 10°8N 124°50E 233 F5
Maastricht Neths. 50°50N 5°40E 170 D5
Maasupa Solomon Is. 9°16S 161°17E 287 M11
Maave Mozam. 21°4S 34°47E 271 B5
Mababe Depression Botswana 18°50S 24°15E 270 A3
Mabaia Angola 7°12S 14°2E 265 D2
Mabalane Mozam. 23°37S 32°31E 271 B5
Mabanga Dem. Rep. of the Congo 1°30N 19°6E 264 B3
Ma'bar Yemen 14°48N 44°17E 248 D4
Mabaruma Guyana 8°10N 59°50W 329 B6
Mabato Pt. Phil. 14°29N 121°5E 127 C2
Mabein Burma 23°29N 96°37E 241 D6
Mabel L. U.S.A. 28°25N 81°33W 133 B1
Mabel L. Canada 50°35N 118°43W 296 C5
Mabenga Dem. Rep. of the Congo 3°39S 18°40E 264 C3
Mabenge Dem. Rep. of the Congo 4°15N 24°12E 264 B4
Maberly Canada 44°50N 76°32W 313 B8
Mabian China 28°47N 103°37E 228 C4
Mabil Ethiopia 10°26N 36°52E 257 E4
Mabinay Phil. 9°48N 122°54E 233 G4
Mabirou Congo 1°3S 15°42E 264 C3
Mablethorpe U.K. 53°20N 0°15E 168 D8
Mableton U.S.A. 33°49N 84°35W 316 B5
Mably France 46°5N 4°4E 173 F11
Maboma Dem. Rep. of the Congo 2°30N 28°10E 268 B2
Mabonto S. Leone 8°53N 11°50W 262 D2
Maboukou Congo 3°39S 12°31E 264 C2
Mabouya I. Grenada 12°29N 61°30W 323 q
Mabroük Mali 19°29N 1°15W 261 E4
Mabrous Niger 21°14N 13°35E 259 D2
Mabuasehube △ Botswana 25°5S 21°10E 270 C3
Mabungo Somali Rep. 0°49N 42°35E 267 D5
Mac Bac Vietnam 9°46N 106°7E 237 H6
Macachín Argentina 37°10S 63°43W 334 D3
Macaco, Morro do Brazil 22°56S 43°6W 135 B2
Macaé Brazil 22°20S 41°43W 333 F3
Macael Spain 37°20N 2°18W 197 H2
Macaíba Brazil 5°51S 35°21W 332 C4
Macajuba Brazil 12°9S 40°22W 333 D3
McAlester U.S.A. 34°56N 95°46W 314 D7
McAllen U.S.A. 26°12N 98°14W 314 H5
McAlpin U.S.A. 30°8N 82°57W 316 E7
McAlpine L. Canada 66°32N 102°45W 294 C9
Macamic Canada 48°45N 79°0W 298 C4
Macao = Macau China 22°12N 113°33E 219 G10
Macão Portugal 39°35N 7°59W 195 F3
Macapá Brazil 0°5N 51°4W 329 C7
Macaque, Morne Dominica 15°20N 61°20W 323 k
Macará Ecuador 4°23S 79°57W 328 D2
Macarani Brazil 15°33S 40°24W 333 E3
Macarena, Serranía de la Colombia 2°45N 73°55W 328 C3
Macareo, Caño → Venezuela 9°47N 61°36W 329 B5
Macarthur Australia 38°5S 142°0E 282 E5
McArthur → Australia 15°54S 136°40E 280 B2
McArthur, Port Australia 16°4S 136°23E 280 B2
Macas Ecuador 2°19S 78°7W 328 D2
Macate Peru 8°48S 78°7W 330 B2
Macau Brazil 5°15S 36°40W 332 C4
Macau China 22°12N 113°33E 219 G10
Macaúbas Brazil 13°2S 42°42W 333 D3
Macauley I. Pac. Oc. 30°12S 178°28W 277 G15
Macaya → Colombia 0°59N 72°20W 328 C3
McBride Canada 53°20N 120°19W 296 C4
McCall U.S.A. 44°55N 116°6W 304 D5
McCamey U.S.A. 31°8N 102°14W 314 F3
McCammon U.S.A. 42°39N 112°12W 304 E7
McCarran Int., Las Vegas ✕ (LAS) U.S.A. 36°5N 115°9W 124 B2
McCarthy U.S.A. 61°26N 142°56W 303 F12
McCauley I. Canada 53°40N 130°15W 296 C2
McCleary U.S.A. 47°3N 123°16W 306 C3
Macclenny U.S.A. 30°17N 82°7W 316 E7
Macclesfield U.K. 53°15N 2°8W 168 D5
M'Clintock Chan. Canada 72°0N 102°0W 294 B9
McClintock Ra. Australia 18°44S 127°38E 278 C4
McCloud U.S.A. 41°15N 122°8W 304 F2
McCluer I. Australia 11°5S 133°0E 278 B5
McClure U.S.A. 40°42N 77°19W 312 F7
McClure, L. U.S.A. 37°35N 120°16W 306 H6
M'Clure Str. Canada 75°0N 119°0W 295 B8
McClusky U.S.A. 47°29N 100°27W 308 B3
McComb U.S.A. 31°15N 90°27W 315 F9
McCook Ill., U.S.A. 41°47N 87°49W 119 C2
McCook Nebr., U.S.A. 40°12N 100°38W 308 E3
McCormick U.S.A. 33°55N 82°17W 316 B7
McCreary Canada 50°47N 99°29W 297 C9
McCullough Mt. U.S.A. 35°35N 115°13W 307 K11
McCusker → Canada 55°32N 108°39W 297 B7
McDame Canada 59°44N 128°59W 296 B3
McDavid U.S.A. 30°52N 87°19W 317 E2
McDermitt U.S.A. 41°59N 117°43W 304 F5
McDonald U.S.A. 40°22N 80°14W 312 F4
Macdonald, L. Australia 23°30S 129°0E 278 D4
Macdonald, Mt. Vanuatu 17°36S 168°23E 287 G6
McDonald Is. Ind. Oc. 53°0S 73°0E 273 K6
MacDonnell Ranges Australia 23°40S 133°0E 278 D5
McDonough U.S.A. 33°27N 84°9W 316 B5
McDougalls Well Australia 31°8S 141°15E 282 A4
MacDowell L. Canada 52°15N 92°45W 298 B1
Macduff U.K. 57°40N 2°31W 167 D6
Maceda Spain 42°16N 7°39W 194 C3
Macedonia U.S.A. 41°19N 81°31W 312 E3
Macedonia ■ Europe 41°53N 21°40E 202 E5
Maceió Brazil 9°40S 35°41W 332 C4
Maceira Portugal 39°41N 8°55W 194 F2
Macenta Guinea 8°35N 9°32W 262 D3
Macerata Italy 43°18N 13°27E 199 E10
McFarland U.S.A. 35°41N 119°14W 307 K7
McFarlane → Canada 59°12N 107°58W 297 B7
Macfarlane, L. Australia 32°0S 136°40E 282 B2
McGehee U.S.A. 33°38N 91°24W 314 E9
McGill U.S.A. 39°23N 114°47W 304 G6
McGill University Montréal, Canada 130 b1
Macgillycuddy's Reeks Ireland 51°58N 9°45W 166 E2
McGrath U.S.A. 62°58N 155°36W 303 E9
McGraw U.S.A. 42°36N 76°8W 313 D8
McGregor U.S.A. 43°1N 91°11W 310 A5
McGregor Ra. Australia 27°0S 142°45E 281 D3
McGuire, Mt. Australia 20°18S 148°23E 280 J6
Mach Pakistan 29°50N 67°20E 242 E2
Māch Kowr Iran 25°48N 61°28E 247 E9
Machacalis Brazil 17°5S 40°45W 333 E3
Machado = Jiparaná → Brazil 8°3S 62°52W 331 B5
Machagai Argentina 26°56S 60°2W 334 B3
Machakos Kenya 1°30S 37°15E 268 C4
Machala Ecuador 3°20S 79°57W 328 D2
Machalilla △ Ecuador 1°24S 80°42W 328 D1
Machanga Mozam. 20°59S 35°0E 271 B6
Machattie, L. Australia 24°50S 139°48E 280 C2
Machault France 49°21N 4°29E 173 C11
Machava Mozam. 25°54S 32°28E 271 C5
Machece Mozam. 19°15S 35°32E 269 F4
Machecoul France 47°0N 1°49W 172 F5
Macheke Zimbabwe 18°5S 31°51E 271 A5
Machelen Belgium 50°55N 4°26E 116 A2
Macheng China 31°12N 115°2E 229 B10
McHenry U.S.A. 42°21N 88°16W 311 B8
Macherado Greece 37°46N 20°49E 207 D2
Macherla India 16°29N 79°26E 244 F4
Machero Spain 39°21N 4°20W 195 F6
Machgaon India 20°5N 86°17E 244 D8
Machhu → India 23°6N 70°46E 242 H4
Machiara △ Pakistan 34°40N 73°30E 242 B5
Machias Maine, U.S.A. 44°43N 67°28W 309 C20
Machias N.Y., U.S.A. 42°25N 78°29W 312 D6
Machichi → Canada 57°3N 92°6W 297 B10
Machico Madeira 32°43N 16°44W 153 c
Machida Japan 35°32N 139°26E 140 B1
Machilipatnam India 16°12N 81°8E 245 F5
Machiques Venezuela 10°4N 72°34W 328 A3
Machupicchu Peru 13°8S 72°30W 330 C3
Machynlleth U.K. 52°35N 3°50W 169 E4
Macia Mozam. 25°2S 33°8E 271 C5
Macias Nguema Biyoga = Bioko Eq. Guin. 3°30N 8°40E 263 E6
Maciejowice Poland 51°36N 21°26E 185 G8
McIlwraith Ra. Australia 13°50S 143°20E 280 A3
Măcin Romania 45°16N 28°8E 183 E13
Macina Mali 14°50N 5°0W 262 C4
McInnes L. Canada 52°13N 93°45W 297 C10
McIntosh U.S.A. 45°55N 101°21W 308 C3
McIntosh L. Canada 55°45N 105°0W 297 B8
Macintosh Ra. Australia 27°39S 125°32E 279 E4
Macintyre → Australia 28°37S 150°47E 281 D5
Maciołki Poland 52°19N 21°9E 142 B2
Macizo Galaico Spain 42°30N 7°30W 194 C3
Mackay Queens., Australia 21°8S 149°11E 280 K7
Mackay Idaho, U.S.A. 43°55N 113°37W 304 E7
MacKay → Canada 57°10N 111°38W 296 B6
Mackay, L. Australia 22°30S 129°0E 278 D4
McKay Ra. Australia 23°0S 122°30E 278 D3
McKeesport U.S.A. 40°20N 79°51W 312 F5
McKellar Canada 45°30N 79°55W 312 A5
McKenna U.S.A. 46°56N 122°33W 306 D4
Mackenzie Canada 55°20N 123°5W 296 B4
McKenzie U.S.A. 36°8N 88°31W 315 C10
Mackenzie → Queens., Australia 23°38S 149°46E 280 C4
Mackenzie → N.W.T., Canada 69°10N 134°20W 294 C6
McKenzie → U.S.A. 44°7N 123°6W 304 D2
Mackenzie Bay Canada 69°0N 137°30W 292 C6
Mackenzie City = Linden Guyana 6°0N 58°10W 329 B6
Mackenzie King I. Canada 77°45N 111°0W 295 B8
Mackenzie Mts. Canada 64°0N 130°0W 294 C7
Mackenzie Plains N.Z. 44°10S 170°25E 285 E5
McKerrow, L. N.Z. 44°25S 168°5E 285 E3
McKerrow, Mt. N.Z. 41°19S 174°58E 143 B2
Mackheim = Maków Mazowiecki Poland 52°52N 21°6E 185 F8
Mackinaw U.S.A. 40°32N 89°21W 310 D7
Mackinaw → U.S.A. 40°33N 89°44W 310 D7
Mackinaw City U.S.A. 45°47N 84°44W 309 C11
McKinlay Australia 21°16S 141°18E 280 C3
McKinlay → Australia 20°50S 141°28E 280 C3
McKinley, Mt. U.S.A. 63°4N 151°0W 303 E10
McKinley Park Alaska, U.S.A. 63°44N 148°55W 303 E10
McKinley Park Ill., U.S.A. 41°49N 87°40W 119 C2
McKinley Sea Arctic 82°0N 0°0 154 A11
McKinney U.S.A. 33°12N 96°37W 314 E6
Mackinnon Road Kenya 3°40S 39°1E 268 C4
McKittrick Calif., U.S.A. 35°18N 119°37W 307 K7
McKittrick Mo., U.S.A. 38°44N 91°27W 310 F5
Macklin Canada 52°20N 109°56W 297 C7
Macksville Australia 30°40S 152°56E 283 A10
McLaren Vale Australia 35°13S 138°31E 282 C3
McLaughlin U.S.A. 45°49N 100°49W 308 C3
Maclean Australia 29°26S 153°16E 281 D5
McLean Ill., U.S.A. 40°19N 89°10W 310 D7
McLean Tex., U.S.A. 35°14N 100°36W 314 D4
McLean Va., U.S.A. 38°56N 77°10W 143 B2
McLeansboro U.S.A. 38°6N 88°32W 311 F8
Maclear S. Africa 31°2S 28°23E 271 D4
Maclear, C. Malawi 13°58S 34°49E 269 E3
Macleay → Australia 30°56S 153°0E 283 A10
McLennan Canada 55°42N 116°50W 296 B5
MacLeod = Fort Macleod Canada 49°45N 113°30W 296 D6
McLeod → Canada 54°9N 115°44W 296 C5
McLeod, L. Australia 24°9S 113°47E 279 D1
McLeod B. Canada 62°53N 110°0W 297 A7
McLeod Lake Canada 54°58N 123°0W 296 C4
McLoughlin, Mt. U.S.A. 42°27N 122°19W 304 E2
MacMahon = Aïn Touta Algeria 35°26N 5°54E 261 A6
McMechen U.S.A. 39°57N 80°44W 312 G4
McMinnville Oreg., U.S.A. 45°13N 123°12W 304 D2
McMinnville Tenn., U.S.A. 35°41N 85°46W 315 D12
McMurdo Antarctica 77°0S 140°0E 151 D11
McMurdo Sd. Antarctica 77°0S 170°0E 151 D11
McMurray = Fort McMurray Canada 56°44N 111°7W 296 B6
McMurray U.S.A. 48°19N 122°14W 306 B4
Maco Phil. 7°20N 125°50E 233 H5
Macocolo Angola 6°47S 16°8E 265 D3
Macodoene Mozam. 23°32S 35°5E 271 B6
Macolo Angola 7°5S 16°42E 265 D3
Macomb U.S.A. 40°27N 90°40W 310 D6
Macomer Italy 40°16N 8°47E 200 B1
Mâcon Saône-et-Loire, France 46°19N 4°50E 173 F11
Macon Ga., U.S.A. 32°51N 83°38W 316 C6
Macon Ill., U.S.A. 39°43N 89°0W 310 E8
Macon Miss., U.S.A. 33°7N 88°34W 315 E10
Macon Mo., U.S.A. 39°44N 92°28W 310 E4
Macondo Angola 12°37S 23°46E 265 E4
Macopocho → Chile 33°24S 70°40W 137 B1
Macossa Mozam. 17°55S 33°56E 269 F3
Macou → Dominica 15°25N 61°27W 323 k
Macou, Pte. Guadeloupe 16°21N 61°31W 322 e
Macouba Martinique 14°52N 61°9W 322 j
Macoun L. Canada 56°32N 103°40W 297 B8
Macoupin Cr. → U.S.A. 39°11N 90°38W 310 E6
Macovane Mozam. 21°30S 35°2E 271 B6
MacPherson = Kapuskasing Canada 49°25N 82°30W 298 C3
McPherson U.S.A. 38°22N 97°40W 308 F5
McPherson Pk. U.S.A. 34°53N 119°53W 307 L7
McPherson Ra. Australia 28°15S 153°15E 281 D5
Macquarie → Australia 30°7S 147°24E 283 A7
Macquarie Harbour Australia 42°15S 145°23E 281 G4
Macquarie Is. Pac. Oc. 54°36S 158°55E 288 N7
Macquarie Ridge S. Ocean 57°0S 159°0E 151 B10
Macqueripe B. Trin. & Tob. 10°44N 61°37W 323 t
McRae U.S.A. 32°4N 82°54W 316 C7
MacRitchie Res. Singapore 1°20N 103°49E 138 A2
MacRobertson Land Antarctica 71°0S 64°0E 151 D6
Macroom Ireland 51°54N 8°57W 166 E3
MacTier Canada 45°8N 79°47W 312 A5
Macubela Mozam. 16°53S 37°49E 269 F4
Macugnaga Italy 45°58N 7°58E 198 C4
Macuira △ Colombia 12°9N 71°21W 328 A3
Macuiza Mozam. 18°7S 34°29E 269 F3
Macujer Colombia 0°24N 73°10W 328 C3
Macul Chile 33°30S 70°35W 137 C2
Macumba → Australia 27°52S 137°12E 281 D2
Macuro Venezuela 10°42N 61°55W 329 F9
Macusani Peru 14°4S 70°29W 330 C3
Macuse Mozam. 17°45S 37°10E 269 F4
Macuspana Mexico 17°46N 92°36W 319 D6
Macusse Angola 17°48S 20°23E 265 F4
Mada → Nigeria 7°59N 7°55E 263 D6
Ma'dabā □ Jordan 31°43N 35°47E 251 G6
Madadeni S. Africa 27°43S 30°3E 271 C5
Madadi Chad 18°28N 20°45E 259 E4
Madagali Nigeria 10°56N 13°33E 263 C7
Madagascar ■ Africa 20°0S 47°0E 272 B2
Madagoi → Somali Rep. 0°49N 42°58E 267 D5
Madā'in Sālih Si. Arabia 26°46N 37°57E 246 E3
Madakasira India 13°56N 77°16E 245 H3
Madalena Azores 38°32N 28°32W 153 d1
Madama Niger 22°0N 13°40E 259 D2
Madamarodi Somali Rep. 2°39N 44°36E 267 D5
Madame, I. Canada 45°30N 60°58W 299 C7
Madame Tussaud's London, U.K. 125 a3
Madan Bulgaria 41°30N 24°57E 203 E8
Madanapalle India 13°33N 78°28E 245 H4
Madang Papua N. G. 5°12S 145°49E 286 C3
Madang □ Papua N. G. 5°0S 145°30E 286 C3
Madaoua Niger 14°5N 6°27E 263 C6
Madara Nigeria 11°45N 10°35E 263 C7
Madaripur Bangla. 23°19N 90°15E 241 D3
Madau I. Papua N. G. 8°58S 152°28E 286 E7
Madauk Burma 17°56N 96°52E 241 G6
Madawaska Canada 45°30N 78°0W 312 A7
Madawaska → Canada 45°27N 76°21W 312 A7
Madaya Burma 22°12N 96°10E 241 D6
Madbar Sudan 6°17N 30°45E 257 F3
Maddalena Italy 41°16N 9°23E 200 A2
Maddaloni Italy 41°2N 14°23E 201 A7
Maddela Phil. 16°21N 121°41E 232 C3
Maddur India 12°36N 77°4E 245 H3
Madeira Atl. Oc. 32°50N 17°0W 153 c
Madeira Ohio, U.S.A. 39°11N 84°21W 311 E12
Madeira → Brazil 3°22S 58°45W 329 D6
Madeleine, Îs. de la Canada 47°30N 61°40W 299 C7
Maden Turkey 38°23N 39°40E 213 C8
Madera Chihuahua, Mexico 29°12N 108°7W 318 B3
Madera Calif., U.S.A. 36°57N 120°3W 306 J6
Madera Pa., U.S.A. 40°49N 78°26W 312 F6
Madgaon India 15°12N 73°58E 245 G1
Madha India 18°0N 75°30E 244 F2
Madhavpur India 21°15N 69°58E 242 J3
Madhepura India 26°11N 86°23E 243 F12
Madhira India 16°55N 80°22E 244 F5
Madhubani India 26°21N 86°7E 243 F12
Madhugiri India 13°40N 77°12E 245 H3
Madhumati → Bangla. 22°53N 89°52E 241 D2
Madhupur Bangla. 24°37N 90°2E 241 C3
Madhupur India 24°16N 86°39E 243 G12
Madhya Pradesh □ India 22°50N 78°0E 242 J8
Madhyamgram India 22°41N 88°26E 124 A2
Madidi → Bolivia 12°32S 66°52W 330 C4
Madikeri India 12°30N 75°45E 245 H2
Madikwe △ S. Africa 27°38S 32°15E 271 C5
Madill U.S.A. 34°6N 96°46W 314 D6
Madimba Angola 6°36S 14°23E 265 D2
Madimba Dem. Rep. of the Congo 4°58S 15°5E 265 C3
Madín México, Mexico 19°32N 99°16W 128 A1
Ma'din Syria 35°45N 39°36E 213 E8
Madín, L. Mexico 19°31N 99°16W 128 A1
Madina Mali 13°25N 8°50W 262 C3
Madīnah Al Manṣūr Iraq 33°18N 44°20E 113 B2
Madinani Ivory C. 9°37N 6°57W 262 D3
Madīnat ash Shaʻb Yemen 12°50N 45°0E 248 D4
Madînet Nasr Egypt 30°4N 31°18E 117 A2
Madingo Congo 4°5S 11°24E 264 C2
Madingou Congo 4°10S 13°33E 264 C2
Madîq Gûbâl Egypt 27°47N 33°55E 251 L4
Madîq Tirân Egypt 27°55N 34°30E 251 L5
Madirovalo Madag. 16°26S 46°32E 272 B2
Madison Calif., U.S.A. 38°41N 121°59W 306 G5
Madison Fla., U.S.A. 30°28N 83°25W 316 E6
Madison Ga., U.S.A. 33°36N 83°28W 316 B6
Madison Ind., U.S.A. 38°44N 85°23W 311 F11
Madison Mo., U.S.A. 39°28N 92°13W 310 E4
Madison Nebr., U.S.A. 41°50N 97°27W 308 E5
Madison Ohio, U.S.A. 41°46N 81°3W 312 E3
Madison S. Dak., U.S.A. 44°0N 97°7W 308 C5
Madison Wis., U.S.A. 43°4N 89°24W 310 A7
Madison → U.S.A. 45°56N 111°31W 304 D8
Madison Avenue New York, U.S.A. 132 c2
Madison Heights U.S.A. 37°25N 79°8W 309 G14
Madison Square New York, U.S.A. 132 d2
Madison Square Garden New York, U.S.A. 132 c2
Madisonville Ky., U.S.A. 37°20N 87°30W 308 G10
Madisonville Tex., U.S.A. 30°57N 95°55W 314 F7
Madista Botswana 21°15S 25°6E 270 B4
Madiun Indonesia 7°38S 111°32E 235 D4
Madjingo Gabon 1°20N 14°4E 264 B2
Mado Gashi Kenya 0°44N 39°10E 268 B4
Madoc Canada 44°30N 77°28W 312 B7
Madol Sudan 9°3N 27°45E 257 F2

Madon → France 48°36N 6°6E 173 D13
Madona Latvia 56°53N 26°5E 188 D4
Madonie Italy 37°50N 13°50E 200 E6
Madonna di Campíglio Italy 46°14N 10°49E 198 B7
Madra Dağı Turkey 39°23N 27°12E 205 B9
Madrakah, Ra's al Oman 19°0N 57°50E 249 C7
Madras = Chennai India 13°8N 80°19E 245 H5
Madras = Tamil Nadu □ India 11°0N 77°0E 245 J3
Madras U.S.A. 44°38N 121°8W 304 D3
Madre, L. U.S.A. 25°15N 97°30W 314 J6
Madre, Sierra Phil. 17°0N 122°0E 232 C4
Madre de Dios □ Peru 12°0S 70°15W 330 C3
Madre de Dios → Bolivia 10°59S 66°8W 330 C4
Madre de Dios, I. Chile 50°20S 75°10W 336 D1
Madre del Sur, Sierra Mexico 17°30N 100°0W 319 D5
Madre Occidental, Sierra Mexico 27°0N 107°0W 318 B3
Madre Oriental, Sierra Mexico 25°0N 100°0W 318 C5
Madri India 24°16N 73°32E 242 G5
Madrid Spain 40°24N 3°42W 127 B1
Madrid Ala., U.S.A. 31°2N 85°24W 316 D4
Madrid Iowa, U.S.A. 41°53N 93°49W 310 C3
Madrid N.Y., U.S.A. 44°45N 75°8W 313 B9
Madrid □ Spain 40°30N 3°45W 194 E7
Madrid Barajas ✈ (MAD) Spain 40°26N 3°34W 127 B2
Madridejos Spain 39°28N 3°33W 195 F7
Madrigal de las Altas Torres Spain 41°5N 5°0W 194 D6
Madrona Spain 41°27N 2°1E 114 A1
Madrona, Sierra Spain 38°27N 4°16W 195 G6
Madroñera Spain 39°26N 5°42W 195 F5
Madrusah Libya 24°48N 14°32E 258 D2
Madu Sudan 14°37N 26°4E 257 E2
Maduo Dem. Rep. of the Congo 1°24S 20°44E 264 C4
Madura W. Austral., Australia 31°55S 127°0E 279 F4
Madura Indonesia 7°30S 114°0E 231 G15
Madura, Selat Indonesia 7°30S 113°20E 235 D4
Madura Oya △ Sri Lanka 7°20N 81°10E 245 L5
Madurai India 9°55N 78°10E 245 K4
Madurantakam India 12°30N 79°50E 245 H4
Madzhalis Russia 42°9N 47°47E 191 J8
Mae Chan Thailand 20°9N 99°52E 236 B2
Mae Hong Son Thailand 19°16N 97°56E 236 C2
Mae Khlong → Thailand 13°24N 100°0E 236 F3
Mae Phrik Thailand 17°27N 99°7E 236 D2
Mae Ping △ Thailand 17°37N 98°51E 236 D2
Mae Ramat Thailand 16°58N 98°31E 236 D2
Mae Rim Thailand 18°54N 98°57E 236 C2
Mae Sot Thailand 16°43N 98°34E 236 D2
Mae Suai Thailand 19°39N 99°33E 228 H2
Mae Tha Thailand 18°28N 99°8E 236 C2
Mae Wong △ Thailand 15°54N 99°12E 236 E2
Mae Yom △ Thailand 18°43N 100°15E 236 C3
Maebaru Japan 33°33N 130°12E 222 D2
Maebashi Japan 36°24N 139°4E 223 A11
Maella Spain 41°8N 0°7E 196 D5
Maesawa Japan 35°44N 139°31E 140 A2
Maesteg U.K. 51°36N 3°40W 169 F4
Maestra, Sierra Cuba 20°15N 77°0W 320 B4
Maestre de Campo I. Phil. 12°56N 121°42E 232 E3
Maetambe, Mt. Solomon Is. 7°3S 157°1E 287 L9
Maevatanana Madag. 16°56S 46°49E 272 B2
Maéwo Vanuatu 15°10S 168°10E 287 E6
Ma'fan Libya 25°56N 14°29E 258 C2
Mafate, Cirque de Réunion 21°3S 55°25E 272 f
Mafeking = Mafikeng S. Africa 25°50S 25°38E 270 C4
Mafeking Canada 52°40N 101°10W 297 C8
Maféré Ivory C. 5°30N 3°2W 262 D4
Mafeteng Lesotho 29°51S 27°15E 270 C4
Maffra Australia 37°53S 146°58E 283 D7
Mafia I. Tanzania 7°45S 39°50E 268 D4
Mafikeng S. Africa 25°50S 25°38E 270 C4
Mafra Brazil 26°10S 49°55W 335 B6
Mafra Portugal 38°55N 9°20W 195 G1
Mafungabusi Plateau Zimbabwe 18°30S 29°8E 269 F2
Magadan Russia 59°38N 150°50E 215 D16
Magadi India 12°58N 77°14E 245 H3
Magadi Rift Valley, Kenya 1°54S 36°19E 268 C4
Magadi, L. Kenya 1°54S 36°19E 268 C4
Magaliesburg S. Africa 26°0S 27°32E 271 C4
Magallanes = Punta Arenas Chile 53°10S 71°0W 336 D2
Magallanes Phil. 12°50N 123°50E 232 E4
Magallanes □ Chile 52°0S 72°0W 336 D2
Magallanes, Estrecho de Chile 52°30S 75°0W 336 D2
Magaluf Spain 39°29N 2°32E 206 B3
Magangué Colombia 9°14N 74°45W 328 B3
Maganoy Phil. 6°51N 124°31E 233 H5
Magaria Niger 13°4N 9°5E 259 F1
Magarida Papua N. G. 10°18S 149°20E 286 F5
Magburaka S. Leone 8°47N 12°0W 262 D2
Magdalen Is. = Madeleine, Îs. de la Canada 47°30N 61°40W 299 C7
Magdalena Argentina 35°5S 57°30W 334 D4
Magdalena Bolivia 13°13S 63°57W 331 C5
Magdalena Lima, Peru 12°5S 77°5W 124 B2
Magdalena N. Mex., U.S.A. 34°7N 107°15W 305 J10
Magdalena □ Colombia 10°0N 74°0W 328 B3
Magdalena → Colombia 11°6N 74°51W 328 A3
Magdalena → Mexico 30°40N 112°25W 318 A2
Magdalena, B. Mexico 24°35N 112°0W 318 C2
Magdalena, I. Chile 44°40S 73°0W 336 B2
Magdalena, I. Mexico 24°40N 112°15W 318 C2
Magdalena, Llano de Mexico 25°0N 111°25W 318 C2
Magdalena Contreras Mexico 19°20N 99°13W 128 C1
Magdalena de Kino Mexico 30°38N 110°57W 318 A2
Magdeburg Germany 52°7N 11°38E 178 C7
Magdelaine Cays Australia 16°33S 150°18E 280 B5
Magdub Sudan 13°42N 25°5E 257 E2
Magee U.S.A. 31°52N 89°44W 315 F10
Magelang Indonesia 7°29S 110°13E 235 D4
Magellan's Str. = Magallanes, Estrecho de Chile 52°30S 75°0W 336 D2
Magenta Italy 45°28N 8°53E 198 C5
Magenta, L. Australia 33°30S 119°2E 279 F2
Magerøya Norway 71°3N 25°40E 160 A21
Maggea Australia 34°28S 140°2E 282 C4
Maggia → Switz. 46°18N 8°36E 179 J4
Maggiorasca, Mte. Italy 44°33N 9°29E 198 D6
Maggiore, Lago Italy 45°57N 8°39E 198 B5
Maggotty Jamaica 18°9N 77°46W 320 a
Maghâgha Egypt 28°38N 30°50E 256 B3
Maghama Mauritania 15°32N 12°57W 262 B2
Magherafelt U.K. 54°45N 6°37W 166 B5
Maghnia Algeria 34°50N 1°43W 261 B4
Maghreb Baghdād, Iraq 33°23N 44°22E 113 A2
Maghreb N. Afr. 32°0N 4°0W 254 C3
Maginu Japan 35°34N 139°34E 140 B2
Magione Italy 43°8N 12°12E 199 E9
Magistralnyy Russia 56°16N 107°36E 215 D11
Maglaj Bos.-H. 44°33N 18°7E 182 F3
Magliana Italy 41°50N 12°26E 136 B1
Magliano in Toscana Italy 42°36N 11°17E 199 F8
Máglie Italy 40°7N 18°18E 201 B11
Magnac-Laval France 46°13N 1°11E 174 B5
Magnetic Pole (North) Canada 82°42N 114°24W 295 B9
Magnetic Pole (South) Antarctica 64°8S 138°8E 151 C9
Magnisia □ Greece 39°15N 23°0E 204 B5
Magnitogorsk Russia 53°27N 59°4E 186 D10
Magnolia Ark., U.S.A. 33°16N 93°14W 314 E8
Magnolia Miss., U.S.A. 31°9N 90°28W 315 F9
Magnor Norway 59°56N 12°15E 164 E9
Magny-en-Vexin France 49°9N 1°47E 173 C8
Magny-les-Hameaux France 48°44N 2°3E 134 B1
Mago Fiji 17°26S 179°8W 287 A3
Mago △ Ethiopia 5°40N 36°18E 257 F4
Magog Canada 45°18N 72°9W 313 A12
Magoro Uganda 1°45N 34°12E 268 B3
Magoša = Famagusta Cyprus 35°8N 33°55E 207 E9
Magoulades Greece 39°45N 19°42E 206 B9
Magoye Zambia 16°1S 27°30E 269 F2
Magpie, L. Canada 51°0N 64°41W 299 B7
Magrath Canada 49°25N 112°50W 296 D6
Magre → Spain 39°11N 0°25W 197 F4
Magrur Sudan 14°1N 30°27E 257 E3
Magrur, Wadi → Sudan 16°5N 26°30E 257 D2
Magsingal Phil. 17°41N 120°25E 232 C3
Magta Lahjar Mauritania 17°28N 13°17W 262 B2
Maguan China 23°0N 104°21E 228 F5
Maguarinho, C. Brazil 0°15S 48°30W 332 B2
Magude Mozam. 25°2S 32°40E 271 C5
Maguindanao □ Phil. 7°5N 124°0E 233 H5
Magurski △ Poland 49°30N 21°30E 185 J8
Mağusa = Famagusta Cyprus 35°8N 33°55E 207 E9
Maguse L. Canada 61°37N 95°10W 297 A9
Maguse Pt. Canada 61°20N 93°50W 297 A10
Magvana India 23°13N 69°22E 242 H3
Magwe Burma 20°10N 95°0E 241 E5
Magwe Sudan 4°8N 32°17E 257 G3
Magwe □ Burma 20°0N 95°0E 241 F5
Magyarorszag = Hungary ■ Europe 47°20N 19°20E 181 D12
Maha Oya Sri Lanka 7°31N 81°22E 245 L5
Maha Sarakham Thailand 16°12N 103°16E 236 D4
Mahābād Iran 36°50N 45°45E 213 D11
Mahabaleshwar India 17°58N 73°43E 244 F1
Mahabharat Lekh Nepal 28°30N 82°0E 243 E10
Mahabo Madag. 20°23S 44°40E 272 C1
Mahad India 18°6N 73°29E 244 E1
Mahaddei Uen Somali Rep. 2°58N 45°32E 267 D6
Mahadeo Hills India 22°20N 78°30E 243 H8
Mahadeopur India 18°48N 80°0E 244 E5
Mahaffey U.S.A. 40°53N 78°44W 312 F6
Mahagi Dem. Rep. of the Congo 2°20N 31°0E 268 B3
Mahaicony Guyana 6°36N 57°48W 329 B6
Mahajamba → Madag. 15°33S 47°8E 272 B2
Mahajamba, Helodranon' i Madag. 15°24S 47°5E 272 B2
Mahajan India 28°48N 73°56E 242 E5
Mahajanga Madag. 15°40S 46°25E 272 B2
Mahajanga □ Madag. 17°0S 47°0E 272 B2
Mahajilo → Madag. 19°42S 45°22E 272 B2
Mahakam → Indonesia 0°35S 117°17E 235 C5
Mahalapye Botswana 23°1S 26°51E 270 B4
Mahalaxmi Mumbai, India 130 a1
Mahalchhar Bangla. 22°55N 92°2E 241 D4
Mahale Mts. Tanzania 6°20S 30°0E 268 D3
Mahale Mts. △ Tanzania 6°10S 29°50E 268 D2
Maḩallāt Iran 33°55N 50°30E 247 C6
Māhān Iran 30°5N 57°18E 247 D8
Mahan → India 23°30N 82°50E 243 H10
Mahanadi → India 20°20N 86°25E 244 D8
Mahananda → India 25°12N 87°52E 243 G12
Mahanoro Madag. 19°54S 48°48E 272 B2
Mahanoy City U.S.A. 40°49N 76°9W 313 F8
Mahaplag Phil. 10°35N 124°57E 233 F5
Maharashtra □ India 20°30N 75°30E 244 D2
Maharès Tunisia 34°32N 10°29E 258 B2
Mahasamund India 21°6N 82°6E 244 D6
Mahasham, W. → Egypt 30°15N 34°10E 251 H5
Mahasoa Madag. 23°23S 45°41E 272 C2
Mahasolo Madag. 19°7S 46°22E 272 B2
Mahattat ash Shīdīyah Jordan 29°55N 35°55E 251 J6
Mahattat 'Unayzah Jordan 30°30N 35°47E 251 H6
Mahaut Dominica 15°21N 61°24W 323 k
Mahaut Guadeloupe 16°11N 61°46W 322 e
Mahavavy → Madag. 15°57S 45°54E 272 B2
Mahaweli Ganga → Sri Lanka 8°27N 81°13E 245 K5
Mahaxay Laos 17°22N 105°12E 236 D5
Mahbubabad India 17°42N 80°2E 244 F5
Mahbubnagar India 16°45N 77°59E 244 F3
Mahd adh Dhahab Si. Arabia 23°30N 40°52E 248 B3
Maḩḑah Oman 24°24N 55°59E 247 E7
Mahdia Guyana 5°13N 59°8W 329 B6
Mahdia Tunisia 35°28N 11°0E 258 A2
Mahdia □ Tunisia 35°20N 10°35E 261 A7
Mahe Jammu & Kashmir, India 33°10N 78°32E 243 C8
Mahé Pondicherry, India 11°42N 75°34E 245 J2
Mahé Seychelles 5°0S 55°30E 272 c
Mahé ✈ (SEZ) Seychelles 4°40S 55°31E 272 c
Mahébourg Mauritius 20°24S 57°42E 272 e
Mahendra Giri India 8°20N 77°30E 245 K3
Mahendraganj India 25°20N 89°45E 241 C2
Mahendragarh India 28°17N 76°14E 242 E7
Mahendranagar Nepal 28°55N 80°20E 243 E9
Mahenge Tanzania 8°45S 36°41E 269 D4
Maheno N.Z. 45°10S 170°50E 285 F5
Mahesana India 23°39N 72°26E 242 H5
Maheshtala India 22°29N 88°15E 124 C1
Maheshwar India 22°11N 75°35E 242 H6
Mahgawan India 26°29N 78°37E 243 F8
Mahi → India 22°15N 72°55E 242 H5
Mahia Pen. N.Z. 39°9S 177°55E 284 F6
Mahibadhoo Maldives 3°47N 72°58E 272 d
Mahighe Solomon Is. 8°30S 159°58E 287 M10
Mahilyow Belarus 53°55N 30°18E 177 B16
Mahilyow □ Belarus 54°10N 30°50E 188 E6
Mahim Maharashtra, India 19°2N 72°50E 130 A2
Mahim Maharashtra, India 19°39N 72°44E 244 E1
Mahim B. India 19°2N 72°49E 130 A1
Mahina Tahiti 17°30S 149°27W 289 e
Mahirija Morocco 34°0N 3°16W 261 B4
Mahlaing Burma 21°6N 95°39E 241 E5
Mahlsdorf Germany 52°30N 13°37E 115 A4
Mahmiya Sudan 17°12N 33°43E 257 D3
Mahmoodabad Pakistan 24°51N 67°4E 123 A2
Mahmud Kot Pakistan 30°16N 71°0E 242 D4
Mahmudia Romania 45°5N 29°5E 183 E14
Mahmudiye Turkey 39°48N 30°15E 205 B12
Mahmutbey Turkey 41°3N 28°49E 203 E12
Mahmutlar Turkey 36°29N 32°5E 250 B3
Mahnomen U.S.A. 47°19N 95°58W 308 B6
Maho Sri Lanka 7°49N 80°16E 245 L5
Mahoba India 25°15N 79°55E 243 G8
Mahomet U.S.A. 40°12N 88°24W 311 D8
Mahón = Maó Spain 39°53N 4°16E 206 B5
Mahon, Menorca ✈ (MAH) Spain 39°50N 4°16E 196 F9
Mahone Bay Canada 44°27N 64°23W 299 D7
Mahopac U.S.A. 41°22N 73°45W 313 E11
Mahoua Chad 11°49N 18°26E 259 F3
Mahrauli India 28°31N 77°10E 120 B2
Mährisch-Budwitz = Moravské Budějovice Czech Rep. 49°4N 15°49E 180 B8
Mährisch-Schönberg = Šumperk Czech Rep. 49°59N 16°59E 181 B9
Mährisch-Trubau = Moravská Třebová Czech Rep. 49°45N 16°40E 181 B9
Mahul India 19°0N 72°53E 130 A2
Mahuta Nigeria 11°32N 4°58E 263 C5
Mahuva India 21°5N 71°48E 242 J4
Mahya Daği Turkey 41°47N 27°36E 203 E11
Mai-Ndombe, L. Dem. Rep. of the Congo 2°0S 18°20E 264 C3
Mai-Sai Thailand 20°20N 99°55E 228 G2
Mai Thon, Ko Thailand 7°40N 98°28E 237 a
Maia Amer. Samoa 14°13S 169°25W 302 g
Maia Azores 36°56N 25°1W 153 d4
Maia Portugal 41°14N 8°37W 194 D2
Maia Spain 43°12N 1°29W 196 B3
Maials Spain 41°22N 0°30E 196 D5
Maibong India 25°18N 93°10E 241 C4
Maicao Colombia 11°23N 72°13W 328 A3
Maîche France 47°16N 6°48E 173 E13
Maici → Brazil 6°30S 61°43W 331 B5
Maicurú → Brazil 2°14S 54°17W 329 D7
Máida Italy 38°51N 16°22E 201 D9
Maida Vale London, U.K. 125 a1
Maidan Khula Afghan. 33°36N 69°50E 242 C3
Maidenhead U.K. 51°31N 0°42W 169 F7
Maidstone Vic., Australia 37°47S 144°52E 128 A1
Maidstone Sask., Canada 53°5N 109°20W 297 C7
Maidstone Kent, U.K. 51°16N 0°32E 169 F8
Maiduguri Nigeria 12°0N 13°20E 263 C7
Maiella △ Italy 42°5N 14°5E 199 F11
Măieruș Romania 45°53N 25°31E 183 E10
Maigatari Nigeria 12°46N 9°27E 263 C6
Maignelay Montigny France 49°32N 2°30E 173 C9
Maigo Phil. 8°10N 123°57E 233 G4
Maigualida, Sierra Venezuela 5°30N 65°10W 329 B4
Maigudo Ethiopia 7°30N 37°8E 257 F4
Maihar India 24°16N 80°45E 243 G9
Maihara Japan 35°19N 136°17E 223 B8
Maijdi Bangla. 22°48N 91°10E 241 D3
Maikala Ra. India 22°0N 81°0E 244 D5
Maiko △ Dem. Rep. of the Congo 0°30S 27°50E 268 C2
Mailani India 28°17N 80°21E 243 E9
Mä'ili U.S.A. 21°25N 158°11W 302 K13
Mä'ili Pt. U.S.A. 21°24N 158°11W 302 K13
Maillezais France 46°22N 0°45W 174 B3
Mailsi Pakistan 29°48N 72°15E 242 E5
Maimbung Phil. 5°56N 121°2E 233 J3
Main → Bayern, Germany 50°0N 8°18E 179 F4
Main → Antrim, U.K. 54°48N 6°18W 166 B5
Main Range △ Australia 28°11S 152°27E 281 D5
Main Ridge Trin. & Tob. 11°16N 60°40W 323 s
Mainburg Germany 48°38N 11°47E 179 G7
Maindargi India 17°28N 76°18E 244 F3
Maine France 48°20N 0°15W 172 D6
Maine □ U.S.A. 45°20N 69°0W 309 C19
Maine → Ireland 52°9N 9°45W 166 D2
Maine, G. of U.S.A. 43°0N 68°30W 309 D19
Maine-et-Loire □ France 47°31N 0°30W 172 E6
Maïne-Soroa Niger 13°13N 12°2E 263 C7
Maingkaing Burma 24°48N 95°16E 241 C5
Maingkwan Burma 26°15N 96°37E 241 B6
Mainit Phil. 9°32N 125°32E 233 G5
Mainit, L. Phil. 9°31N 125°30E 233 G5
Mainland Orkney, U.K. 58°59N 3°8W 167 C5
Mainland Shet., U.K. 60°15N 1°22W 167 A7
Mainoru Australia 14°0S 134°6E 280 A1
Mainpuri India 27°18N 79°4E 243 F8
Maintal Germany 50°7N 8°52E 179 E4
Maintenon France 48°35N 1°35E 173 D8
Maintirano Madag. 18°3S 44°1E 272 B1
Mainz Germany 50°1N 8°14E 179 E4
Maio C. Verde Is. 15°10N 23°10W 153 j
Maipú Argentina 36°52S 57°50W 334 D4
Maipú Santiago, Chile 33°30S 70°45W 137 C1
Maiquetía Venezuela 10°36N 66°57W 328 A4
Máira → Italy 44°49N 7°38E 198 D4
Mairabari India 26°30N 92°22E 241 B4
Mairipotaba Brazil 17°18S 49°28W 333 E2
Maisi Cuba 20°17N 74°9W 321 B5
Maisi, Pta. de Cuba 20°10N 74°10W 321 B5
Maiskhal I. Bangla. 21°36N 91°56E 241 E3
Maison Coloniale Guadeloupe 16°18N 61°16W 322 e
Maisonneuve, Parc Canada 45°32N 73°33W 130 A2
Maisons-Alfort France 48°48N 2°26E 134 B3
Maisons-Laffitte France 48°57N 2°8E 134 A1
Maissoneuve Canada 45°32N 73°33W 130 A2
Maitland N.S.W., Australia 32°33S 151°36E 283 B9
Maitland S. Austral., Australia 34°23S 137°40E 282 C2
Maitland Western Cape, S. Africa 33°53S 18°29E 118 A1
Maitland → Canada 43°45N 81°43W 312 C3
Maitland, Banjaran Malaysia 4°55N 116°37E 235 B5
Maitri Antarctica 70°0S 3°0W 151 D3
Maitum Phil. 6°2N 124°30E 233 H5
Maiyema Nigeria 12°5N 4°25E 263 C5
Maiyuan China 25°34N 117°28E 229 E11
Maiz, Is. del Nic. 12°15N 83°4W 320 D3
Maizuru Japan 35°25N 135°22E 223 B7
Majagual Colombia 8°33N 74°38W 328 B3
Majalengka Indonesia 6°50S 108°13E 235 D3
Majari → Brazil 3°29N 60°58W 329 C5
Majdūl Libya 25°51N 15°7E 258 C3
Majene Indonesia 3°38S 118°57E 231 E5
Majes → Peru 16°40S 72°44W 330 D3
Majete ⌓ Malawi 15°54S 34°34E 269 F3
Majevica Bos.-H. 44°45N 18°50E 182 F3
Maji Ethiopia 6°12N 35°30E 257 F4
Majiang China 26°28N 107°32E 228 D6
Majorca = Mallorca Spain 39°30N 3°0E 206 B4
Majors Creek Australia 35°33S 149°45E 283 C8
Majuriã Brazil 7°30S 64°55W 331 B5
Majuro Marshall Is. 7°9N 171°12E 288 G9
Maka Senegal 13°40N 14°10W 262 C2
Mäkaha Hawai'i, U.S.A. 21°29N 158°13W 302 K13
Makaha Zimbabwe 17°20S 32°39E 271 A5
Makahoa Pt. U.S.A. 21°41N 157°56W 302 J14
Makahuena Pt. U.S.A. 21°52N 159°27W 302 B2
Makak Cameroon 3°36N 11°0E 263 E7
Makakilo City U.S.A. 21°22N 158°5W 302 K13
Makakou Gabon 0°11S 12°12E 264 C2
Makalamabedi Botswana 20°19S 23°51E 270 B3
Makale Indonesia 3°6S 119°51E 231 E5
Makalu-Barun △ Nepal 27°45N 87°10E 243 F12
Makamba Burundi 4°8S 29°49E 268 C2
Makapu'u Pt. U.S.A. 21°19N 157°39W 302 K14
Makarewa Junction N.Z. 46°20S 168°21E 285 G3
Makari Cameroon 12°35N 10°27E 259 F2
Makarikari = Makgadikgadi Salt Pans Botswana 20°40S 25°45E 270 B4
Makarov Basin Arctic 87°0N 150°0W 150 A
Makarovo Russia 57°40N 107°45E 215 D11
Makarska Croatia 43°20N 17°2E 199 E14
Makaryev Russia 57°52N 43°50E 190 B6
Makasar = Ujung Pandang Indonesia 5°10S 119°20E 231 F5
Makasar Indonesia 6°17S 106°52E 122 A2
Makasar, Selat Indonesia 1°0S 118°20E 235 C5
Makasar, Str. of = Makasar, Selat Indonesia 1°0S 118°20E 235 C5
Makat = Maqat Kazakhstan 47°39N 53°19E 187 E9
Makati Phil. 14°33N 121°7E 127 B2
Makaw Dem. Rep. of the Congo 3°29S 18°20E 264 C3
Makawao U.S.A. 20°52N 156°17W 302 C5
Makaya Dem. Rep. of the Congo 3°21S 18°1E 264 C3
Makedonija = Macedonia ■ Europe 41°53N 21°40E 202 E5
Makefu Cook Is. 18°59S 169°55W 289 g
Makemo French Polynesia 16°35S 143°40W 289 f
Makeni S. Leone 8°55N 12°5W 262 D2
Makeyevka = Makiyivka Ukraine 48°0N 38°0E 189 H9
Makgadikgadi △ Botswana 20°27S 24°47E 270 B3
Makgadikgadi Salt Pans Botswana 20°40S 25°45E 270 B4
Makhachkala Russia 43°0N 47°30E 191 J8
Makhado = Louis Trichardt S. Africa 23°1S 29°43E 271 B4
Makharadze = Ozurgeti Georgia 41°55N 42°0E 191 K5
Makhfar al Buşayyah Iraq 30°0N 46°10E 246 D5
Makhmūr Iraq 35°46N 43°35E 213 E10
Makhtal India 16°30N 77°31E 245 E3
Makhyah, W. → Yemen 17°40N 49°1E 249 C5
Makian Indonesia 0°20N 127°20E 231 D7
Makina Solomon Is. 9°50S 160°50E 287 M11
Makindu Kenya 2°18S 37°50E 268 C4
Mäkiniitty Finland 60°20N 24°58E 121 A2
Makinka = Makīnsk Kazakhstan 52°37N 70°26E 217 B8
Makīnsk Kazakhstan 52°37N 70°26E 217 B8
Makira = San Cristóbal Solomon Is. 10°30S 161°0E 287 N11
Makiv Ukraine 48°48N 26°43E 183 B11
Makiyivka Ukraine 48°0N 38°0E 189 H9
Makkah Si. Arabia 21°30N 39°54E 248 B2
Makkah □ Si. Arabia 21°30N 42°30E 248 B3
Makkovik Canada 55°10N 59°10W 299 A8
Makó Hungary 46°14N 20°33E 182 D5
Mako Senegal 12°52N 12°20W 262 C2
Makogai Fiji 17°28S 179°0E 287 A2
Makok Gabon 0°1S 9°35E 264 C1
Makokou Gabon 0°40N 12°50E 264 B2
Makongo Dem. Rep. of the Congo 3°25N 26°17E 268 B2
Makoro Dem. Rep. of the Congo 3°10N 29°59E 268 B2
Makoua Congo 0°5S 15°50E 264 C3
Maków Mazowiecki Poland 52°52N 21°6E 185 F8
Maków Podhalański Poland 49°43N 19°45E 185 J6
Makra Greece 36°15N 25°54E 205 E7
Makrai India 22°2N 77°0E 242 H7
Makran Asia 26°13N 61°30E 240 D1
Makran Coast Range Pakistan 25°40N 64°0E 240 D2
Makrana India 27°2N 74°46E 242 F6
Makrany Belarus 51°48N 24°17E 185 G11
Makri Greece 40°52N 25°40E 203 F9
Makri India 19°46N 81°55E 244 E5
Makrigialos Greece 35°2N 25°59E 207 E6
Makthar Tunisia 35°48N 9°12E 258 A1
Mākū Iran 39°15N 44°31E 213 C11
Mäkua U.S.A. 21°32N 158°13W 302 J13
Mäkua Kea'au Forest Reserve U.S.A. 21°30N 158°12W 302 J13
Makua Military Reservation U.S.A. 21°32N 158°14W 302 J13
Makum India 27°30N 95°23E 241 B5
Makumbi Dem. Rep. of the Congo 5°50S 20°43E 265 D4
Makunda Botswana 22°30S 20°7E 270 B3
Makung Taiwan 23°34N 119°34E 225 C1
Makunudu Atoll Maldives 6°20N 72°35E 272 d
Makunza Dem. Rep. of the Congo 8°52S 24°19E 265 D4
Makurazaki Japan 31°15N 130°20E 222 F2
Makurdi Nigeria 7°43N 8°35E 263 D6
Makushin Volcano U.S.A. 53°53N 166°55W 303 K6
Makūyeh Iran 28°7N 53°9E 247 D7
Makwassie S. Africa 27°17S 26°0E 270 C4
Maķwiro Zimbabwe 17°58S 30°25E 271 A5
Mal India 26°51N 88°45E 241 B2
Mâl Mauritania 16°58N 13°23W 262 B2
Mal B. Ireland 52°50N 9°30W 166 D2
Mala Peru 12°40S 76°38W 330 C2
Mala, Pta. Panama 7°28N 80°2W 320 E3
Mala Belozërka Ukraine 47°12N 34°56E 189 J8
Malá Fatra △ Slovak Rep. 49°10N 19°0E 181 B12
Mala Kapela Croatia 44°45N 15°30E 199 D12
Mała Panew → Poland 50°43N 17°54E 185 H4
Malá Strana Czech Rep. 50°4N 14°24E 135 B2
Mala Vyska Ukraine 48°39N 31°36E 189 H6
Malabang Phil. 7°36N 124°3E 233 H5
Malabar N.S.W., Australia 33°58S 151°14E 139 B2
Malabar Fla., U.S.A. 28°0N 80°34W 317 H9
Malabar Coast India 11°0N 75°0E 245 J2
Malabar Hill India 18°57N 72°48E 130 B1
Malabar Pt. India 18°56N 72°48E 130 B1
Malabo = Rey Malabo Eq. Guin. 3°45N 8°50E 263 E6
Malabon Phil. 14°39N 120°56E 127 B1
Malabrigo = Puerto Chicama Peru 7°45S 79°20W 330 B2
Malabrigo Pt. Phil. 13°36N 121°15E 232 E3
Malabu Nigeria 9°32N 12°48E 263 D7
Malabuñgan Phil. 9°3N 117°38E 233 G1
Malacañang Palace Phil. 14°35N 120°59E 127 B1
Malacca, Straits of Indonesia 3°0N 101°0E 237 L3
Malacky Slovak Rep. 48°27N 17°0E 181 C10
Malad City U.S.A. 42°12N 112°15W 304 E7
Maladeta Spain 42°39N 0°39E 196 C5
Maladzyechna Belarus 54°20N 26°50E 177 A14
Malae Pt. U.S.A. 20°7N 155°53W 302 C6
Málaga Colombia 6°42N 72°44W 328 B3
Málaga Spain 36°43N 4°23W 195 J6
Málaga □ Spain 36°38N 4°58W 195 J6
Malagarasi Tanzania 5°5S 30°50E 268 D3
Malagarasi → Tanzania 5°12S 29°47E 268 D2
Malagasy Rep. = Madagascar ■ Africa 20°0S 47°0E 272 B2
Malagón Spain 39°11N 3°52W 195 F7
Malagón → Spain 37°35N 7°29W 195 H3
Malah Syria 32°33N 36°54E 251 F7
Malahide Ireland 53°26N 6°9W 120 A3
Malaimbandy Madag. 20°20S 45°36E 272 C2
Malaita Solomon Is. 9°0S 161°0E 287 M11
Malakâl Sudan 9°33N 31°40E 257 F3
Malakal Harb. Palau 7°19N 134°27E 288 c
Malakanagiri India 18°21N 81°54E 244 E5
Malakand Pakistan 34°40N 71°55E 242 B4
Malakhovka Russia 55°39N 38°0E 129 C6
Malakoff France 48°49N 2°18E 134 B2
Malakula Vanuatu 16°15S 167°30E 287 F5
Malakwal Pakistan 32°34N 73°13E 242 C5
Malalag Phil. 6°36N 125°24E 233 H5
Malalaua Papua N. G. 8°4S 146°10E 286 E4
Malam Chad 11°27N 20°59E 259 F4
Malamala Indonesia 3°21S 120°55E 231 E6
Malanda Australia 17°22S 145°35E 280 B4
Malang Indonesia 7°59S 112°45E 235 D4
Malangas Phil. 7°37N 123°1E 233 H4
Malange □ Angola 9°30S 16°0E 265 D3
Malangen Norway 69°24N 18°37E 160 B18
Malanje Angola 9°36S 16°17E 265 D3
Malapatan Phil. 5°59N 125°18E 233 J5
Mälaren Sweden 59°30N 17°10E 162 E11
Malargüe Argentina 35°32S 69°30W 334 D2
Mälarhöjaen Sweden 59°18N 17°58E 139 B1
Malartic Canada 48°9N 78°9W 298 C4
Malaryta Belarus 51°50N 24°3E 185 G11
Malaspina Glacier U.S.A. 59°50N 140°30W 303 G12
Malate Phil. 14°34N 120°59E 127 B1
Malatya Turkey 38°25N 38°20E 213 C8
Malatya □ Turkey 38°15N 38°0E 212 C7
Malawali Malaysia 7°3N 117°18E 235 A5
Malawi ■ Africa 11°55S 34°0E 269 E3
Malawi, L. Africa 12°30S 34°30E 269 E3
Malay Phil. 11°54N 121°55E 233 F3
Malay Pen. Asia 7°25N 100°0E 237 J3
Malay Quarter Cape Town, S. Africa 118 c2
Malaya Belozërka = Mala Belozërka Ukraine 47°12N 34°56E 189 J8
Malaya Neva Russia 59°56N 30°16E 137 B1
Malaya Okhta Russia 59°55N 30°25E 137 B2
Malaya Vishera Russia 58°55N 32°25E 188 C7
Malaya Viska = Mala Vyska Ukraine 48°39N 31°36E 189 H6
Malaybalay Phil. 8°5N 125°7E 233 G5
Malāyer Iran 34°19N 48°51E 213 E13
Malaysia ■ Asia 5°0N 110°0E 237 K4
Malazgirt Turkey 39°10N 42°33E 213 C10
Malbaza Niger 13°59N 5°38E 263 C6
Malbon Australia 21°5S 140°17E 280 C3
Malbooma Australia 30°41S 134°11E 281 E1
Malbork Poland 54°3N 19°1E 184 D6
Malca Dube Ethiopia 6°47N 42°4E 267 C5
Malcésine Italy 45°46N 10°48E 198 C7
Malchin Germany 53°44N 12°44E 178 B8
Malchow Berlin, Germany 52°34N 13°29E 115 A3
Malchow Mecklenburg-Vorpommern, Germany 53°28N 12°25E 178 B8
Malcolm Australia 28°51S 121°25E 279 E3
Malcolm, Pt. Australia 33°48S 123°45E 279 F3
Malczyce Poland 51°14N 16°29E 185 G3
Maldah India 25°2N 88°9E 243 G13
Maldegem Belgium 51°14N 3°26E 170 C3
Malden London, U.K. 51°23N 0°15W 125 B2
Malden Mass., U.S.A. 42°26N 71°3W 116 A2
Malden Mo., U.S.A. 36°34N 89°57W 308 G9
Malden I. Kiribati 4°3S 155°1W 289 H12
Maldives ■ Ind. Oc. 5°0N 73°0E 272 d
Maldon Vic., Australia 37°0S 144°6E 282 D6
Maldon Essex, U.K. 51°44N 0°42E 169 F8
Maldonado Uruguay 34°59S 55°0W 335 C5
Maldonado, Pta. Mexico 16°20N 98°33W 319 D5
Malè Italy 46°21N 10°55E 198 B7
Malé Maldives 4°10N 73°28E 272 d
Malé ✈ (MLE) Maldives 4°11N 73°28E 272 d
Malé Atoll Maldives 4°45N 73°15E 272 d
Malé Karpaty Slovak Rep. 48°30N 17°20E 181 C10
Maleas, Akra Greece 36°28N 23°7E 204 E5
Malebo, Pool Africa 4°17S 15°20E 265 C3
Malegaon India 20°30N 74°38E 244 D2
Malei Mozam. 17°12S 36°58E 269 F4
Maleizen Belgium 50°45N 4°31E 116 B3
Malek Sudan 6°4N 31°36E 257 F3
Malek Kandī Iran 37°9N 46°6E 213 D12
Malela Bas-Congo, Dem. Rep. of the Congo 5°59S 12°37E 265 D2
Malela Maniema, Dem. Rep. of the Congo 4°22S 26°8E 265 C5
Malema Mozam. 14°57S 37°20E 269 E4
Maleme Greece 35°31N 23°49E 207 E4
Malendok I. Papua N. G. 3°28S 153°13E 286 B7
Målerås Sweden 56°54N 15°34E 163 H9
Malerkotla India 30°32N 75°58E 242 D6
Males Greece 35°6N 25°35E 207 E6
Malesherbes France 48°15N 2°24E 173 D9
Maleshevska Planina Europe 41°38N 23°7E 202 E7
Malešice Czech Rep. 50°5N 14°30E 135 B3
Malesina Greece 38°37N 23°14E 204 C5
Malestroit France 47°49N 2°25W 172 E4
Malfa Italy 38°35N 14°50E 201 D7
Malgobek Russia 43°30N 44°34E 191 J7
Malgomaj Sweden 64°40N 16°30E 160 D17
Malgrat de Mar Spain 41°39N 2°46E 196 D7
Malha Sudan 15°8N 25°10E 257 D2
Malhada Brazil 14°21S 43°47W 333 D3
Malhargarh India 24°17N 74°59E 242 G6
Malheur → U.S.A. 44°4N 116°59W 304 D5
Malheur L. U.S.A. 43°20N 118°48W 304 E4
Mali Guinea 12°10N 12°20W 262 C2
Mali ■ Africa 17°0N 3°0W 262 B4
Mali → Burma 25°42N 97°30E 241 C6
Mali Kanal Serbia 45°36N 19°24E 182 E4
Mali Kyun Burma 13°0N 98°20E 236 F2
Malia Greece 35°17N 25°32E 207 E6
Malia, Kolpos Greece 35°19N 25°27E 207 E6
Maliao Taiwan 23°48N 120°13E 225 C2
Malibu U.S.A. 34°2N 118°41W 307 L8
Maligaya = Gloria Phil. 12°59N 121°30E 232 E3
Maliku Indonesia 0°39S 123°16E 231 E6
Malili Indonesia 2°42S 121°6E 231 E6
Målilla Sweden 57°23N 15°48E 163 G9
Malimba, Mts. Dem. Rep. of the Congo 7°30S 29°30E 268 D2
Malin Hd. Ireland 55°23N 7°23W 166 A4
Malin Pen. Ireland 55°20N 7°17W 166 A4
Malindang, Mt. Phil. 8°13N 123°38E 233 G4
Malindi Kenya 3°12S 40°5E 268 C5
Malines = Mechelen Belgium 51°2N 4°29E 170 C4
Malino Indonesia 1°0N 121°0E 231 D6
Malinyi Tanzania 8°56S 36°0E 269 D4
Malipo China 23°7N 104°42E 228 F5
Maliq Albania 40°45N 20°48E 202 F4
Malir → Pakistan 24°49N 67°4E 123 B2
Malita Phil. 6°19N 125°39E 233 H5
Maliwun Burma 10°17N 98°40E 237 G2
Maliya India 23°5N 70°46E 242 H4
Maljenik Serbia 43°54N 21°43E 202 C5
Malka Mari △ Kenya 4°11N 40°46E 268 B5
Malkapur India 20°53N 73°58E 244 D1
Malkara Turkey 40°53N 26°53E 203 F10
Malkhangiri = Malakanagiri India 18°21N 81°54E 244 E5
Małkinia Górna Poland 52°42N 22°5E 185 F9
Malko Tŭrnovo Bulgaria 41°59N 27°31E 203 E11
Mall, The Washington, D.C., U.S.A. 143 b2
Mallacoota Australia 37°40S 149°40E 283 D8
Mallacoota Inlet Australia 37°34S 149°40E 283 D8
Mallaig U.K. 57°0N 5°50W 167 D3
Mallala Australia 34°26S 138°30E 282 C3
Mallaoua Niger 13°2N 9°36E 263 C6
Mallard U.S.A. 42°56N 94°41W 310 B2
Mallawan India 27°4N 80°12E 243 F9
Mallawi Egypt 27°44N 30°44E 256 B3
Mallee Cliffs △ Australia 34°16S 142°32E 282 C5
Mallembe Gabon 3°34S 10°53E 264 C2
Mallemort France 43°43N 5°11E 175 E9
Malleny Mills U.K. 55°52N 3°20W 121 B2
Málles Venosta Italy 46°41N 10°32E 198 B7
Mallicolo = Malakula Vanuatu 16°15S 167°30E 287 F5
Mallorca Spain 39°30N 3°0E 206 B4
Mallorytown Canada 44°29N 75°53W 313 B9
Mallow Ireland 52°8N 8°39W 166 D3
Malmbäck Sweden 57°34N 14°28E 163 G8
Malmberget Sweden 67°11N 20°40E 160 C19
Malmédy Belgium 50°25N 6°2E 170 D6
Malmesbury S. Africa 33°28S 18°41E 270 D2
Malmi Finland 60°15N 24°59E 121 B2
Malmivaara = Malmberget Sweden 67°11N 20°40E 160 C19
Malmköping Sweden 59°8N 16°44E 162 E10
Malmö Sweden 55°36N 12°59E 163 J7
Malmok Aruba 12°36N 70°4W 322 f
Malmøya Norway 59°52N 10°45E 133 A3
Malmslätt Sweden 58°27N 15°33E 163 F9
Malmyzh Russia 56°31N 50°41E 190 B10
Malnaş Romania 46°2N 25°49E 183 D10
Malo Vanuatu 15°40S 167°11E 287 E5
Malo Konare Bulgaria 42°12N 24°24E 203 D8
Maloarkhangelsk Russia 52°28N 36°30E 189 F9
Maloca Brazil 0°43N 55°57W 329 C6
Malolo Fiji 17°45S 177°11E 287 A1
Malolos Phil. 14°50N 120°49E 232 D3
Malolotja ⌓ Swaziland 26°4S 31°6E 271 C5
Malombe L. Malawi 14°40S 35°15E 269 E4
Małomice Poland 51°34N 15°29E 185 G2
Malomir Bulgaria 42°16N 26°32E 203 D10
Malone Fla., U.S.A. 30°57N 85°10W 316 E4
Malone N.Y., U.S.A. 44°51N 74°18W 313 B10
Malong China 25°24N 103°34E 228 E4
Malonga Dem. Rep. of the Congo 10°24S 23°10E 265 E4
Małopolskie □ Poland 49°50N 20°20E 185 J7
Malorad Bulgaria 43°28N 23°41E 202 C7
Måløv Denmark 55°44N 12°20E 118 A2
Måløy Norway 61°57N 5°6E 164 C2
Maloyaroslovets Russia 55°2N 36°20E 188 E9
Malpartida Spain 39°26N 6°30W 195 F4
Malpaso Canary Is. 27°43N 18°3W 153 e1
Malpaso, Presa = Netzahualcóyotl, Presa Mexico 17°8N 93°35W 319 D6
Malpelo, I. de Colombia 4°3N 81°35W 289 G19
Malpica de Bergantiños Spain 43°19N 8°50W 194 B2
Malprabha → India 16°20N 76°5E 245 F3
Malpur India 23°21N 73°27E 242 H5
Malpura India 26°17N 75°23E 242 F6
Mals = Málles Venosta Italy 46°41N 10°32E 198 B7
Malsiras India 17°52N 74°55E 244 F2
Malta Brazil 6°54S 37°31W 332 C4
Malta Idaho, U.S.A. 42°18N 113°22W 304 E7
Malta Mont., U.S.A. 48°21N 107°52W 304 B10
Malta ■ Europe 35°55N 14°26E 206 F7
Malta ✈ (MLA) Malta 35°52N 14°29E 206 F7
Maltahöhe Namibia 24°55S 17°0E 270 B2
Maltepe Turkey 40°55N 29°8E 203 F13
Malton Ont., Canada 43°42N 79°38W 141 A1
Malton N. Yorks., U.K. 54°8N 0°49W 168 C7
Malu'a Solomon Is. 8°20S 160°38E 287 M11
Maludam △ Malaysia 1°39N 111°2E 235 B4
Maluko = Manolo Fortich Phil. 8°28N 124°50E 233 G5
Maluku Indonesia 1°0S 127°0E 231 E7
Maluku □ Indonesia 3°0S 128°0E 231 E7
Maluku Sea = Molucca Sea Indonesia 0°0 125°0E 231 E6
Malumfashi Nigeria 11°48N 7°39E 263 C6
Malundo Angola 14°51S 22°0E 265 E4
Malung Sweden 60°42N 13°44E 162 D7
Malungon Phil. 6°16N 125°14E 233 H5
Malungsfors Sweden 60°44N 13°33E 162 D7
Malur India 13°0N 77°55E 245 H3
Maluso Phil. 6°33N 121°53E 233 H3
Maluwe Ghana 8°40N 2°17W 262 D4
Malvalli India 12°28N 77°8E 245 H3
Malvan India 16°2N 73°30E 245 F1
Malvern Vic., Australia 37°50S 145°2E 128 B2
Malvern Ont., Canada 43°47N 79°13W 141 A3
Malvern Gauteng, S. Africa 26°11S 28°5E 123 B2
Malvern Ark., U.S.A. 34°22N 92°49W 314 D8
Malvern Hills U.K. 52°0N 2°19W 169 E5
Malvik Norway 63°25N 10°40E 164 A7
Malvinas, Is. = Falkland Is. ☑ Atl. Oc. 51°30S 59°0W 153 f
Malý Dunaj → Slovak Rep. 47°45N 18°9E 181 D11
Malya Tanzania 3°5S 33°38E 268 C3
Malye Derbety Russia 47°57N 44°42E 191 G7
Malyn Ukraine 50°46N 29°3E 177 C15
Malyy Lyakhovskiy, Ostrov Russia 74°7N 140°36E 215 B15
Mama Russia 58°18N 112°54E 215 D12
Mamadysh Russia 55°44N 51°23E 190 C10
Mamaku N.Z. 38°5S 176°8E 284 E5
Mämala B. U.S.A. 21°15N 157°55W 302 K14
Mamanguape Brazil 6°50S 35°4W 332 C4
Mamanuca Group Fiji 17°35S 177°5E 287 A1
Mamarr Mitlā Egypt 30°2N 32°54E 251 H3
Mamasa Indonesia 2°55S 119°20E 231 E5
Mambajao Phil. 9°15N 124°43E 233 G5
Mambasa Dem. Rep. of the Congo 1°22N 29°3E 268 B2
Mamberamo → Indonesia 2°0S 137°50E 231 E9
Mambéré → C.A.R. 3°31N 16°3E 264 B3
Mambili → Congo 0°6N 16°5E 264 B3

398 Mambilima Falls INDEX

Mambilima Falls *Zambia* 10°31S 28°45E **269** E2
Mambirima *Dem. Rep. of the Congo* 11°25S 27°33E **269** E2
Mambo *Tanzania* 4°52S 38°22E **268** C4
Mambrui *Kenya* 3°5S 40°5E **268** C5
Mamburao *Phil.* 13°13N 120°39E **232** E3
Mameigwess L. *Canada* 52°35N 87°50W **298** B2
Mamers *France* 48°21N 0°22E **172** D7
Mamfé *Cameroon* 5°50N 9°15E **263** D6
Māmī, Ra's *Yemen* 12°32N 54°30E **249** D6
Mamiña *Chile* 20°5S 69°14W **330** E4
Mamlyutka *Kazakhstan* 54°56N 68°32E **217** B7
Mammoth *U.S.A.* 32°43N 110°39W **305** K8
Mammoth Cave △ *U.S.A.* 37°8N 86°13W **308** G10
Mamonovo *Kaliningrad, Russia* 54°28N 19°55E **184** D6
Mamonovo *Moskva, Russia* 55°41N 37°18E **129** B2
Mamoré → *Bolivia* 10°23S 65°53W **331** C4
Mamou *Guinea* 10°15N 12°0W **262** C2
Mamoudzou *Mayotte* 12°48S 45°14E **272** b
Mampang Prapatan *Indonesia* 6°15S 106°49E **122** B1
Mampatá *Guinea-Biss.* 11°54N 14°53W **262** C2
Mampikony *Madag.* 16°6S 47°38E **272** B2
Mampoko *Dem. Rep. of the Congo* 0°51N 18°42E **264** B3
Mampong *Ghana* 7°6N 1°26W **263** D4
Mampukuji *Japan* 35°36N 139°31E **140** B2
Mamry, Jezioro *Poland* 54°5N 21°50E **184** D8
Mamuil Malal, Paso *S. Amer.* 39°35S 71°28W **336** A2
Mamuju *Indonesia* 2°41S 118°50E **231** E5
Ma'mūl *Oman* 18°8N 55°16E **249** C6
Mamuno *Botswana* 22°16S 20°1E **270** B3
Mamuras *Albania* 41°34N 19°41E **202** E3
Man *Ivory C.* 7°30N 7°40W **262** D3
Man → *India* 17°31N 75°32E **244** F2
Man, I. of *India* 8°28N 93°36E **245** K11
Man, I. of *U.K.* 54°15N 4°30W **168** C3
Man-Bazar *India* 23°4N 86°39E **243** H12
Man Budrukh *India* 19°2N 72°55E **130** A2
Man Kat *Burma* 22°5N 98°1E **241** D7
Man Khurd *India* 19°3N 72°55E **130** A2
Man Na *Burma* 23°27N 97°19E **241** D7
Man-of-War B. *Trin. & Tob.* 11°19N 60°34W **323** s
Man Tun *Burma* 23°52N 98°38E **241** D7
Mana *Fr. Guiana* 5°45N 53°55W **329** B7
Mānā *Hawai'i, U.S.A.* 22°2N 159°47W **302** A2
Mana → *Fr. Guiana* 5°45N 53°55W **329** B7
Mana Pools △ *Zimbabwe* 15°56S 29°25E **269** F2
Manaar, G. of = Mannar, G. of *Asia* 8°30N 79°0E **245** K4
Manabí □ *Ecuador* 0°40S 80°5W **328** D1
Manacacías → *Colombia* 4°23N 72°4W **328** C3
Manacapuru *Brazil* 3°16S 60°37W **329** D5
Manacapuru → *Brazil* 3°18S 60°37W **329** D5
Manacor *Spain* 39°34N 3°13E **206** B4
Manadas *Azores* 38°38N 28°6W **153** d1
Manado *Indonesia* 1°29N 124°51E **231** D6
Managua *Nic.* 12°6N 86°20W **320** D2
Managua, L. de *Nic.* 12°20N 86°30W **320** D2
Manaia *N.Z.* 39°33S 174°8E **284** F3
Manakara *Madag.* 22°8S 48°1E **272** C2
Manakau *N.Z.* 42°15S 173°42E **285** C8
Manākhah *Yemen* 15°5N 43°44E **248** D3
Manakhat *Israel* 31°45N 35°11E **123** B2
Manali *India* 32°16N 77°10E **242** C7
Manam I. *Papua N. G.* 4°5S 145°0E **286** C3
Manama = Al Manāmah *Bahrain* 26°10N 50°30E **247** E6
Manambao → *Madag.* 17°35S 44°0E **272** B1
Manambato *Madag.* 13°43S 49°7E **272** A2
Manambolo → *Madag.* 19°18S 44°22E **272** B1
Manambolosy *Madag.* 16°2S 49°40E **272** B2
Mánamo, Caño → *Venezuela* 9°55N 62°16W **329** B5
Mānana I. *U.S.A.* 21°20N 157°40W **302** K14
Mananara *Madag.* 16°10S 49°46E **272** B2
Mananara → *Madag.* 23°21S 47°42E **272** C2
Mananara ⌓ *Madag.* 16°14S 49°45E **272** B2
Manangatang *Australia* 35°5S 142°54E **282** C5
Mananjary *Madag.* 21°13S 48°20E **272** C2
Manankoro *Mali* 10°28N 7°25W **262** C3
Manantavadi *India* 11°49N 76°1E **245** J3
Manantenina *Madag.* 24°17S 47°19E **272** C2
Manaos = Manaus *Brazil* 3°0S 60°0W **329** D6
Manapala *Phil.* 10°58N 123°5E **233** F4
Manapire → *Venezuela* 7°42N 66°7W **328** B4
Manapouri *N.Z.* 45°34S 167°39E **285** F2
Manapouri, L. *N.Z.* 45°32S 167°32E **285** F2
Manapparai *India* 10°36N 78°25E **245** J4
Manaqil *Sudan* 14°15N 32°59E **257** E3
Manar → *India* 18°50N 77°20E **244** E3
Manār, Jabal *Yemen* 14°2N 44°17E **248** D4
Manaravolo *Madag.* 23°59S 45°39E **272** C2
Manas *Xinjiang Uygur, China* 44°17N 85°56E **217** D11
Manas *Somali Rep.* 2°57N 43°28E **267** D5
Manas → *India* 26°12N 90°40E **241** B3
Manas △ *India* 26°40N 91°0E **241** B3
Manas He → *China* 45°38N 85°12E **218** B3
Manas Hu *China* 45°45N 85°55E **217** C11
Manaslu *Nepal* 28°33N 84°33E **243** E11
Manasquan *U.S.A.* 40°8N 74°3W **313** F10
Manassa *U.S.A.* 37°11N 105°56W **305** H11
Manatí *Puerto Rico* 18°26N 66°29W **321** b
Manati B. *St. Helena* 16°0S 5°46W **153** h
Manau *Papua N. G.* 8°4S 148°0E **286** E4
Manaung *Burma* 18°45N 93°40E **241** F4
Manaus *Brazil* 3°0S 60°0W **329** D6
Manavgat *Turkey* 36°47N 31°26E **250** B2
Manavgat → *Turkey* 36°43N 31°27E **250** B2
Manawan = Rizal *Phil.* 17°51N 121°21E **232** C3
Manawan L. *Canada* 55°24N 103°14W **297** B8
Manawatu → *N.Z.* 40°28S 175°12E **284** G4
Manawatu-Wanganui □ *N.Z.* 39°50S 175°30E **284** F4
Manay *Phil.* 7°17N 126°33E **233** H6
Manbij *Syria* 36°31N 37°57E **212** D7
Mancha Real *Spain* 37°48N 3°39W **195** H7
Manche □ *France* 49°10N 1°20W **172** C5
Manchegorsk *Russia* 67°54N 32°58E **214** C4
Manchester *Gt. Man., U.K.* 53°29N 2°12W **168** D5
Manchester *Calif., U.S.A.* 38°58N 123°41W **306** G3
Manchester *Conn., U.S.A.* 41°47N 72°31W **313** E12
Manchester *Ga., U.S.A.* 32°51N 84°37W **316** C5
Manchester *Iowa, U.S.A.* 42°29N 91°27W **310** D5
Manchester *Ky., U.S.A.* 37°9N 83°46W **309** G12
Manchester *Mich., U.S.A.* 42°9N 84°2W **311** B12
Manchester *N.H., U.S.A.* 42°59N 71°28W **313** D13
Manchester *N.Y., U.S.A.* 42°56N 77°16W **312** D7
Manchester *Ohio, U.S.A.* 38°41N 83°36W **311** F13
Manchester *Pa., U.S.A.* 40°4N 76°43W **313** F8
Manchester *Tenn., U.S.A.* 35°29N 86°5W **315** D11
Manchester *Vt., U.S.A.* 43°10N 73°5W **313** C11
Manchester Int. ✈ (MAN) *U.K.* 53°21N 2°17W **168** D5
Manchester L. *Canada* 61°28N 107°29W **297** A7
Manchhar L. *Pakistan* 26°25N 67°39E **242** F2
Manchineel Bay *Grenada* 12°26N 61°29W **323** q
Manchou *Taiwan* 22°1N 120°50E **225** D2
Manchuria = Dongbei *China* 45°0N 125°0E **227** D13
Manchurian Plain *China* 47°0N 124°0E **210** D14
Manciano *Italy* 42°35N 11°31E **199** F8
Mancifa *Ethiopia* 6°53N 41°50E **257** F5
Mancora *Peru* 4°9S 81°1W **330** A1
Mand → *India* 21°42N 83°15E **243** J10
Mand → *Iran* 28°20N 52°30E **247** D7
Manda *Ludewe, Tanzania* 10°30S 34°40E **269** E3
Manda *Mbeya, Tanzania* 7°58S 32°29E **268** D3
Manda *Mbeya, Tanzania* 8°30S 32°49E **269** D3
Manda △ *Chad* 9°45N 17°52E **259** G3
Mandabé *Madag.* 21°0S 44°55E **272** C1
Mandaguari *Brazil* 23°32S 51°42W **335** A5
Mandah = Töhöm *Mongolia* 44°27N 108°2E **226** B5
Mandal *Norway* 58°2N 7°25E **164** F4
Mandala, Puncak *Indonesia* 4°44S 140°20E **231** E10
Mandalay *Burma* 22°0N 96°4E **241** E6
Mandalay □ *Burma* 22°0N 96°5E **241** E5
Mandale = Mandalay *Burma* 22°0N 96°4E **241** E6
Mandalgarh *India* 25°12N 75°6E **242** G6
Mandalgovĭ *Mongolia* 45°45N 106°10E **226** B4
Mandalī *Iraq* 33°43N 45°28E **213** F11
Mandalselva → *Norway* 58°2N 7°28E **164** F4
Mandaluyong *Phil.* 14°35N 121°1E **127** B2
Mandan *U.S.A.* 46°50N 100°54W **308** B3
Mandaoli *India* 28°37N 77°17E **120** B2
Mandaon *Phil.* 12°13N 123°17E **232** E4
Mandaqui → *Brazil* 23°30S 46°40W **137** A2
Mandar, Teluk *Indonesia* 3°35S 119°15E **231** E5
Mandara Mts. *Nigeria* 10°40N 13°40E **259** F2
Mándas *Italy* 39°40N 9°8E **200** C2
Mandasor = Mandsaur *India* 24°3N 75°8E **242** G6
Mandaue *Phil.* 10°20N 123°56E **233** F4
Mandelieu-la-Napoule *France* 43°34N 6°57E **175** E10
Mandera *Kenya* 3°55N 41°53E **268** B5
Mandeville *Jamaica* 18°2N 77°31W **320** a
Mandi *India* 31°39N 76°58E **242** D7
Mandi Dabwali *India* 29°58N 74°42E **242** E6
Mandiana *Guinea* 10°37N 8°39W **262** C3
Mandigos = Manica *Mozam.* 18°58S 32°59E **271** A5
Mandimba *Mozam.* 14°20S 35°40E **269** E4
Mandioli *Indonesia* 0°40S 127°20E **231** E7
Mandioré, L. *S. Amer.* 18°8S 57°33W **331** D6
Mandla *India* 22°39N 80°30E **243** H9
Mandø *Denmark* 55°18N 8°33E **163** J2
Mandoli *India* 28°41N 77°18E **120** A2
Mandorah *Australia* 12°32S 130°42E **278** B5
Mandoto *Madag.* 19°34S 46°17E **272** B2
Mandoudi *Greece* 38°48N 23°29E **204** C5
Mandra *Greece* 38°4N 23°30E **204** C5
Mandra *Pakistan* 33°23N 73°12E **242** C5
Mandraki *Greece* 36°36N 27°11E **205** E9
Mandrare → *Madag.* 25°10S 46°30E **272** D2
Mandritsara *Madag.* 15°50S 48°49E **272** B2
Mandronarivo *Madag.* 21°7S 45°38E **272** C2
Mandsaur *India* 24°3N 75°8E **242** G6
Mandurah *Australia* 32°36S 115°48E **279** F2
Mandúria *Italy* 40°24N 17°38E **201** B10
Mandvi *Gujarat, India* 22°51N 69°22E **242** H3
Mandvi *Maharashtra, India* 18°56N 72°50E **130** B2
Mandya *India* 12°30N 77°0E **245** H3
Mandzai *Pakistan* 30°55N 67°6E **242** D2
Mané *Burkina Faso* 12°59N 1°21W **263** C4
Maneh *Iran* 37°39N 57°7E **247** B8
Manenberg *S. Africa* 33°58S 18°33E **118** A2
Manengouba, Mts. *Cameroon* 5°0N 9°50E **263** E6
Maner → *India* 18°30N 79°40E **244** E4
Manera *Madag.* 22°55S 44°20E **272** C1
Manérbio *Italy* 45°21N 10°8E **198** C7
Maneroo Cr. → *Australia* 23°21S 143°53E **280** C3
Manfalût *Egypt* 27°20N 30°52E **256** B3
Manfred *Australia* 33°19S 143°45E **282** B5
Manfredónia *Italy* 41°38N 15°55E **199** G12
Manfredónia, G. di *Italy* 41°35N 16°5E **199** G13
Mang Kung Uk *China* 22°18N 114°16E **122** B2
Mang-won *S. Korea* 37°33N 126°55E **137** B1
Manga *Brazil* 14°46S 43°56W **333** D3
Manga *Burkina Faso* 11°40N 1°4W **263** C4
Manga *Congo* 0°13S 16°5E **264** C3
Manga *Niger* 15°0N 14°0E **259** F2
Mangabeiras, Chapada das *Brazil* 10°0S 46°30W **332** D2
Mangai *Dem. Rep. of the Congo* 4°2S 19°33E **265** C3
Mangaia *Cook Is.* 21°55S 157°55W **289** K12
Mangakino *N.Z.* 38°22S 175°47E **284** E4
Mangal *Phil.* 6°25N 121°58E **233** H3
Mangalagiri *India* 16°26N 80°36E **245** F5
Mangaldai *India* 26°26N 92°2E **241** B4
Mangaldan *Phil.* 16°4N 120°24E **232** C3
Mangalia *Romania* 43°50N 28°35E **183** G13
Mangalmé *Chad* 12°26N 19°37E **259** F3
Mangalore *India* 12°55N 74°47E **245** H2
Mangalvedha *India* 17°31N 75°28E **244** F2
Mangan *India* 27°31N 88°32E **241** B2
Mangaon *India* 18°15N 73°20E **244** E1
Mangawan *India* 24°41N 81°33E **243** G9
Mangaweka *N.Z.* 39°48S 175°47E **284** F4
Mangaweka, Mt. *N.Z.* 39°49S 176°5E **284** F5
Mange *Dem. Rep. of the Congo* 0°54N 20°30E **264** B4
Manger *Norway* 60°38N 5°3E **164** D2
Manggar *Indonesia* 2°50S 108°10E **235** C3
Manggawitu *Indonesia* 4°8S 133°32E **231** E8
Mangghystaū □ *Kazakhstan* 45°0N 53°0E **216** D4
Mangghystaū Tübegi *Kazakhstan* 44°30N 52°30E **216** D4
Manggis *Indonesia* 8°29S 115°31E **231** J18
Mangin Taungdan *Burma* 24°15N 95°45E **241** C5
Mangindrano *Madag.* 14°17S 48°58E **272** A2
Mangkalihat, Tanjung *Indonesia* 1°2N 118°59E **235** B5
Mangla *Pakistan* 33°7N 73°39E **242** C5
Mangla Dam *Pakistan* 33°9N 73°44E **243** C5
Manglares, C. *Colombia* 1°36N 79°2W **328** C2
Manglaur *India* 29°44N 77°49E **242** E7
Mangnai *China* 37°52N 91°43E **218** C4
Mangnai Zhen *China* 38°24N 90°14E **217** E12
Mango *Togo* 10°20N 0°30E **263** C5
Mango *Tonga* 20°17S 174°29W **287** O13
Mangoche *Malawi* 14°25S 35°16E **269** E4
Mangoky → *Madag.* 21°29S 43°41E **272** C1
Mangole *Indonesia* 1°50S 125°55E **231** E6
Mangolpuri *India* 28°41N 77°6E **120** A1
Mangombe *Dem. Rep. of the Congo* 1°20S 26°48E **268** C2
Mangonui *N.Z.* 35°1S 173°32E **284** B2
Mangoro → *Madag.* 20°0S 48°45E **272** C2
Mangrol *Mad. P., India* 21°7N 70°7E **242** J4
Mangrol *Raj., India* 25°20N 76°31E **242** G6
Mangrul Pir *India* 20°19N 77°21E **244** D3
Manguaba = Pilar *Brazil* 9°36S 35°56W **332** C4
Mangualde *Portugal* 40°38N 7°48W **194** E3
Mangueigne *Chad* 10°30N 21°15E **259** F4
Mangueira, L. da *Brazil* 33°0S 52°50W **335** C5
Manguéni, Hamada *Niger* 22°35N 12°40E **258** D2
Manguinhos ✈ *Brazil* 22°52S 43°14W **135** B1
Mangum *U.S.A.* 34°53N 99°30W **314** D5
Mangungu *Dem. Rep. of the Congo* 5°16S 19°36E **265** D3
Mangyshlak, Poluostrov = Mangghystaū Tübegi *Kazakhstan* 44°30N 52°30E **216** D4
Manhattan *Kans., U.S.A.* 39°11N 96°35W **308** F5
Manhattan *New York, U.S.A.* **132** d2
Manhattan Beach *U.S.A.* 40°34N 73°56W **132** C2
Manhattan Bridge *New York, U.S.A.* **132** f2
Manhatten *U.S.A.* 41°26N 87°59W **311** C9
Manhiça *Mozam.* 25°23S 32°49E **271** C5
Manhuaçu *Brazil* 20°15S 42°2W **333** F3
Manhumirim *Brazil* 20°22S 41°57W **333** F3
Mani *Colombia* 4°49N 72°17W **328** C3
Mania → *Madag.* 19°42S 45°22E **272** B2
Maniago *Italy* 46°10N 12°43E **199** B9
Manica *Mozam.* 18°58S 32°59E **271** A5
Manica □ *Mozam.* 19°10S 33°45E **271** A5
Manicaland □ *Zimbabwe* 19°0S 32°30E **269** F3
Manicoré *Brazil* 5°48S 61°16W **331** B5
Manicoré → *Brazil* 5°51S 61°19W **331** B5
Manicouagan → *Canada* 49°30N 68°30W **299** C6
Manicouagan, Rés. *Canada* 51°5N 68°40W **299** B6
Maniema □ *Dem. Rep. of the Congo* 3°0S 26°0E **268** C2
Manīfah *Si. Arabia* 27°44N 49°0E **247** E6
Manifold, C. *Australia* 22°41S 150°50E **280** C5
Maniganggo *China* 31°56N 99°10E **228** B2
Manigotagan *Canada* 51°6N 96°18W **297** C9
Manigotagan → *Canada* 51°7N 96°20W **297** C9
Manihari *India* 25°21N 87°38E **243** G12
Manihi *French Polynesia* 14°24S 145°56W **289** f
Manihiki *Cook Is.* 10°24S 161°1W **289** J11
Manihiki Plateau *Pac. Oc.* 11°0S 164°0W **289** J11
Maniitsoq *Greenland* 65°26N 52°55W **154** D5
Manika, Plateau de la *Dem. Rep. of the Congo* 10°0S 25°5E **269** E2
Manikchhari *Bangla.* 22°51N 91°50E **241** D3
Manikganj *Bangla.* 23°52N 90°0E **241** D3
Manikpur *India* 25°4N 81°7E **243** G9
Manila *Phil.* 14°35N 120°58E **127** B1
Manila *U.S.A.* 40°59N 109°43W **304** F9
Manila B. *Phil.* 14°40N 120°35E **232** D3
Manila Ninoy Aquino Int. ✈ (MNL) *Phil.* 14°31N 121°0E **127** B2
Manildra *Australia* 33°11S 148°41E **283** B8
Manilla *Australia* 30°45S 150°43E **283** A9
Manimpé *Mali* 14°11N 5°28W **262** C3
Maningrida *Australia* 12°3S 134°13E **280** A1
Maninian *Ivory C.* 10°3N 7°52W **262** C3
Manipur □ *India* 25°0N 94°0E **241** C5
Manipur → *Burma* 23°45N 94°20E **241** D5
Manisa *Turkey* 38°38N 27°30E **205** C9
Manisa □ *Turkey* 38°40N 28°0E **205** C9
Manistee *U.S.A.* 44°15N 86°19W **308** C10
Manistee → *U.S.A.* 44°15N 86°21W **308** C10
Manistique *U.S.A.* 45°57N 86°15W **308** C10
Manito *U.S.A.* 40°26N 89°47W **310** D7
Manitoba □ *Canada* 53°30N 97°0W **297** B9
Manitoba, L. *Canada* 51°0N 98°45W **297** C9
Manitou *Canada* 49°15N 98°32W **297** D9
Manitou, L. *Canada* 50°55N 65°17W **299** B6
Manitou Beach *U.S.A.* 41°58N 84°19W **311** C12
Manitou Is. *U.S.A.* 45°8N 86°0W **309** C10
Manitou L. *Canada* 52°43N 109°43W **297** C7
Manitou Springs *U.S.A.* 38°52N 104°55W **304** G11
Manitoulin I. *Canada* 45°40N 82°30W **298** C3
Manitouwadge *Canada* 49°8N 85°48W **298** C2
Manitowoc *U.S.A.* 44°5N 87°40W **308** C10
Manitsauá-Missu → *Brazil* 10°58S 53°20W **331** C7
Maniyachi *India* 8°51N 77°55E **245** K3
Manizales *Colombia* 5°5N 75°32W **328** B2
Manja *Madag.* 21°26S 44°20E **272** C1
Manjacaze *Mozam.* 24°45S 34°0E **271** B5
Manjakandriana *Madag.* 18°55S 47°47E **272** B2
Manjeri *India* 11°7N 76°11E **245** J3
Manjhand *Pakistan* 25°50N 68°10E **242** G3
Manjiang *China* 41°56N 127°35E **224** B3
Manjil *Iran* 36°46N 49°30E **247** B6
Manjimup *Australia* 34°15S 116°6E **279** F2
Manjlegaon *India* 19°9N 76°14E **244** E3
Manjra → *India* 18°49N 77°52E **244** E3
Mankato *Kans., U.S.A.* 39°47N 98°13W **308** F4
Mankato *Minn., U.S.A.* 44°10N 94°0W **308** C6
Mankayan *Phil.* 16°52N 120°47E **232** C3
Mankayane *Swaziland* 26°40S 31°4E **271** C5
Mankera *Pakistan* 31°23N 71°26E **242** D4
Mankim *Cameroon* 5°6N 12°3E **263** D7
Mankkaa *Finland* 60°11N 24°47E **121** B1
Mankono *Ivory C.* 8°1N 6°10W **262** D3
Mankota *Canada* 49°25N 107°5W **297** D7
Mankulam *Sri Lanka* 9°8N 80°26E **245** K5
Manlay = Üydzin *Mongolia* 44°9N 107°0E **226** B4
Manley Hot Springs *U.S.A.* 65°0N 150°38W **303** D10
Manlleu *Spain* 42°2N 2°17E **196** C7
Manly *Australia* 33°47S 151°17E **139** A2
Manmad *India* 20°18N 74°28E **244** D2
Mann, L. *U.S.A.* 28°32N 81°35W **133** A2
Mann Ranges *Australia* 26°6S 130°5E **279** E5
Manna *Indonesia* 4°25S 102°55E **234** C2
Mannahill *Australia* 32°25S 140°0E **282** B4
Mannar *Sri Lanka* 9°1N 79°54E **245** K4
Mannar, G. of *Asia* 8°30N 79°0E **245** K4
Mannar I. *Sri Lanka* 9°5N 79°45E **245** K4
Mannargudi *India* 10°45N 79°51E **245** J4
Mannheim *Germany* 49°29N 8°29E **179** F4
Manning *Alta., Canada* 56°53N 117°39W **296** B5
Manning *Oreg., U.S.A.* 45°45N 123°13W **306** E3
Manning *S.C., U.S.A.* 33°42N 80°13W **316** B9
Manning △ *Canada* 49°5N 120°45W **296** D4
Manning Str. *Solomon Is.* 7°30S 158°0E **287** L10
Mann's Chinese Theatre *U.S.A.* 34°6N 118°20W **126** B2
Mannswörth *Austria* 48°8N 16°30E **142** B3
Mannu → *Italy* 39°16N 9°0E **200** C2
Mannu, C. *Italy* 40°3N 8°21E **200** B1
Mannum *Australia* 34°50S 139°20E **282** C3
Mano *S. Leone* 8°3N 12°2W **262** D2
Mano → *Liberia* 6°56N 11°30W **262** D2
Mano River *Liberia* 7°20N 11°6W **262** D2
Manoa *Bolivia* 9°40S 65°27W **331** B4
Manoharpur *India* 22°23N 85°12E **243** H11
Manokotak *U.S.A.* 58°58N 159°3W **303** G8
Manokwari *Indonesia* 0°54S 134°0E **231** E8
Manolada *Greece* 38°4N 21°21E **204** C3
Manolo Fortich *Phil.* 8°28N 124°50E **233** G5
Manombo *Madag.* 22°57S 43°28E **272** C1
Manono *Dem. Rep. of the Congo* 7°15S 27°25E **268** D2
Manono *Samoa* 13°50S 172°5W **287** V19
Manoppello *Italy* 42°15N 14°3E **199** F11
Manor Park *Wellington, N.Z.* 41°10S 174°59E **143** A2
Manor Park *London, U.K.* 51°32N 0°1E **125** A4
Manora *Pakistan* 24°47N 66°58E **123** B1
Manora Pt. *Pakistan* 24°47N 66°58E **123** B1
Manorhamilton *Ireland* 54°18N 8°9W **166** B3
Manosque *France* 43°49N 5°47E **175** E9
Manotick *Canada* 45°13N 75°41W **313** A9
Manouane → *Canada* 49°30N 71°10W **299** C5
Manouane, L. *Canada* 50°45N 70°45W **299** B5
Manovo-Gounda Saint Floris △ *C.A.R.* 9°30N 21°25E **264** A4
Manp'o *N. Korea* 41°6N 126°24E **224** B3
Manpojin = Manp'o *N. Korea* 41°6N 126°24E **224** B3
Manpur *Chhattisgarh, India* 23°17N 83°35E **243** H10
Manpur *Chhattisgarh, India* 20°22N 80°43E **244** D5
Manpur *Mad. P., India* 22°26N 75°37E **242** H6
Manquehue, Cerro *Chile* 33°21S 70°35W **137** B2
Manra *Kiribati* 4°27S 171°15W **277** A16
Manresa *Spain* 41°48N 1°50E **196** D6
Mansa *Gujarat, India* 23°27N 72°45E **242** H5
Mansa *Punjab, India* 30°0N 75°27E **242** E6
Mansa *Zambia* 11°13S 28°55E **269** E2
Mansalay *Phil.* 12°31N 121°26E **232** E3
Månsåsen *Sweden* 63°5N 14°18E **162** A8
Mansehra *Pakistan* 34°20N 73°15E **242** B5
Mansel I. *Canada* 62°0N 80°0W **295** C12
Mansfield *Vic., Australia* 37°4S 146°6E **283** D7
Mansfield *Notts., U.K.* 53°9N 1°11W **168** D6
Mansfield *Ga., U.S.A.* 33°31N 83°44W **316** B6
Mansfield *La., U.S.A.* 32°2N 93°43W **314** E8
Mansfield *Mass., U.S.A.* 42°2N 71°13W **313** D13
Mansfield *Ohio, U.S.A.* 40°45N 82°31W **312** F2
Mansfield *Pa., U.S.A.* 41°48N 77°5W **312** E7
Mansfield *Tex., U.S.A.* 32°33N 97°8W **314** E6
Mansfield, Mt. *U.S.A.* 44°33N 72°49W **313** B12
Mansi *Burma* 24°48N 95°52E **241** C5
Mansidão *Brazil* 10°43S 44°2W **332** D3
Mansilla de las Mulas *Spain* 42°30N 5°25W **194** C5
Mansle *France* 45°52N 0°12E **174** C4
Manso → *Brazil* 13°50S 47°0W **333** D2
Mansoa *Guinea-Biss.* 12°0N 15°20W **262** C1
Manson *U.S.A.* 42°32N 94°32W **310** B2
Manson Creek *Canada* 55°37N 124°32W **296** B4
Mansoura *Algeria* 36°1N 4°31E **261** A5
Manta *Ecuador* 1°0S 80°40W **328** D1
Manta, B. de *Ecuador* 0°54S 80°44W **328** D1
Mantadia △ *Madag.* 18°54S 48°21E **272** B2
Mantalingajan, Mt. *Phil.* 8°55N 117°45E **233** G1
Mantantale *Dem. Rep. of the Congo* 2°10S 20°11E **264** C4
Mantare *Tanzania* 2°42S 33°13E **268** C3
Mantaro → *Peru* 12°16S 73°57W **330** C3
Manteca *U.S.A.* 37°48N 121°13W **306** H5
Mantecal *Venezuela* 7°34N 69°17W **328** B4
Mantena *Brazil* 18°47S 40°59W **333** E3
Manteno *U.S.A.* 41°15N 87°50W **311** C9
Manteo *U.S.A.* 35°55N 75°40W **315** D17
Mantes-la-Jolie *France* 48°58N 1°41E **173** D8
Mantha *India* 19°40N 76°23E **244** E3
Manthani *India* 18°40N 79°35E **244** E4
Manti *U.S.A.* 39°16N 111°38W **304** G8
Mantiqueira, Serra da *Brazil* 22°0S 44°0W **333** F3
Manton *U.S.A.* 44°25N 85°24W **309** C11
Mantorp *Sweden* 58°21N 15°20E **163** F9
Mántova *Italy* 45°9N 10°48E **198** C7
Mänttä *Finland* 62°3N 24°40E **188** A3
Mantua = Mántova *Italy* 45°9N 10°48E **198** C7
Mantung *Australia* 34°35S 140°3E **282** C4
Manturovo *Russia* 58°23N 44°45E **190** A7
Manu *Peru* 12°10S 70°51W **330** C3
Manu → *Peru* 12°16S 70°55W **330** C3
Manu'a Is. *Amer. Samoa* 14°13S 169°35W **287** W21
Manuel Alves → *Brazil* 11°19S 48°28W **333** D2
Manuel Alves Grande → *Brazil* 7°27S 47°35W **332** C2
Manuel Urbano *Brazil* 8°53S 69°18W **330** B4
Manui *Indonesia* 3°35S 123°5E **231** E6
Manukan *Phil.* 8°32N 123°22E **233** G4
Manukau *N.Z.* 37°0S 174°52E **284** D3
Manukau Harbour *N.Z.* 37°3S 174°45E **284** D3
Manunui *N.Z.* 38°54S 175°21E **284** E4
Manuoha *N.Z.* 38°39S 177°7E **284** E6
Manuripi → *Bolivia* 11°6S 67°36W **330** C4
Manus □ *Papua N. G.* 2°0S 147°0E **286** B4
Manus I. *Papua N. G.* 2°0S 147°0E **286** B4
Manvi *India* 15°57N 76°59E **245** G3
Manwath *India* 19°19N 76°32E **244** E3
Many *U.S.A.* 31°34N 93°29W **314** F8
Manyani *Kenya* 3°5S 38°30E **268** C4
Manyara, L. *Tanzania* 3°40S 35°50E **268** C4
Manyas *Turkey* 40°2N 27°59E **203** F11
Manyas Gölü = Kus Gölü *Turkey* 40°10N 27°55E **203** F11
Manyava *Ukraine* 48°39N 24°21E **183** B9
Manych → *Russia* 47°15N 40°0E **191** G5
Manych-Gudilo, Ozero *Russia* 46°24N 42°38E **191** G6
Manyonga → *Tanzania* 4°10S 34°15E **268** C3
Manyoni *Tanzania* 5°45S 34°55E **268** D3
Manzai *Pakistan* 32°12N 70°15E **242** C4
Manzala, Bahra el *Egypt* 31°10N 31°56E **256** H7
Manzanar ⌓ *U.S.A.* 36°44N 118°9W **306** J7
Manzanares *Spain* 39°2N 3°22W **195** F7
Manzanares, Canal de *Spain* 40°19N 3°38W **127** C2
Manzaneda *Spain* 42°12N 7°15W **194** C3
Manzanilla Pt. *Trin. & Tob.* 10°31N 61°1W **323** t
Manzanillo *Cuba* 20°20N 77°31W **320** B4
Manzanillo *Colima, Mexico* 19°3N 104°20W **318** D4
Manzanillo, Pta. *Panama* 9°30N 79°40W **320** E4
Manzano Mts. *U.S.A.* 34°40N 106°20W **305** J10
Manzarīyeh *Iran* 34°53N 50°50E **247** C6
Manzhouli *China* 49°35N 117°25E **219** B6
Manzini *Swaziland* 26°30S 31°25E **271** C5
Manzur Vadisi △ *Turkey* 39°10N 39°30E **246** B3
Mao *Chad* 14°4N 15°19E **259** F3
Maó *Spain* 39°53N 4°16E **206** B5
Mao Mausoleum *Beijing, China* **114** c2
Maoka = Kholmsk *Russia* 47°40N 142°5E **215** E15
Maoke, Pegunungan *Indonesia* 3°40S 137°30E **231** E9
Maolin *China* 43°58N 123°30E **227** C12
Maoming *China* 21°50N 110°54E **229** G8
Maopi T'ou *China* 21°56N 120°43E **225** E2
Maouri, Dallol → *Niger* 12°5N 3°30E **263** C5
Maoxian *China* 31°41N 103°49E **228** B4
Maoxing *China* 45°28N 124°40E **227** B13
Map *Micronesia* 9°35N 138°10E **287** R16
Mapalma *Dem. Rep. of the Congo* 2°3N 24°30E **264** B4
Mapam Yumco *China* 30°45N 81°28E **243** D9
Mapastepec *Mexico* 15°26N 92°54W **319** D6
Mapfongui *Gabon* 1°15S 12°59E **264** C2
Maphrao, Ko *Thailand* 7°56N 98°26E **237** a
Mapia, Kepulauan *Indonesia* 0°50N 134°20E **231** D8
Mapimí *Mexico* 25°49N 103°51W **318** B4
Mapimí, Bolsón de *Mexico* 27°0N 104°15W **318** B4
Maping *China* 31°34N 113°32E **229** B9
Mapinga *Tanzania* 6°40S 39°12E **268** D4
Mapinhane *Mozam.* 22°20S 35°0E **271** B6
Mapire *Venezuela* 7°45N 64°42W **329** B5
Maple → *U.S.A.* 42°59N 84°57W **311** B12
Maple Creek *Canada* 49°55N 109°29W **297** D7
Maple Valley *U.S.A.* 47°25N 122°3W **306** C4
Mapleton *U.S.A.* 44°2N 123°52W **304** D2
Mapo *S. Korea* 37°32N 126°56E **137** B1
Mapourika, L. *N.Z.* 43°16S 170°12E **285** D5
Maprik *Papua N. G.* 3°44S 143°3E **286** B2
Mapuca *India* 15°36N 73°46E **245** G1
Mapuera → *Brazil* 1°5S 57°2W **329** D6
Mapulanguene *Mozam.* 24°29S 32°6E **271** B5
Mapungubwe △ *S. Africa* 22°12S 29°22E **269** G2
Maputo *Mozam.* 25°58S 32°32E **271** C5
Maputo □ *Mozam.* 26°0S 32°25E **271** C5
Maputo, B. de *Mozam.* 25°50S 32°45E **271** C5
Maputo ⌓ *Mozam.* 26°23S 32°48E **271** C5
Maqanshy *Kazakhstan* 46°47N 82°1E **217** C10
Maqat *Kazakhstan* 47°39N 53°19E **187** E9
Maqên *China* 34°24N 100°6E **218** C5
Maqiaohe *China* 44°40N 130°30E **227** B16
Maqnā *Si. Arabia* 28°25N 34°50E **251** K5
Maqran, W. → *Si. Arabia* 20°55N 47°12E **248** B4
Maqteïr *Mauritania* 21°50N 11°40W **260** D2
Maquan He = Brahmaputra → *Asia* 23°40N 90°35E **241** D3
Maqueda *Spain* 40°4N 4°22W **194** E6
Maqueda Channel *Phil.* 13°42N 124°1E **232** E5
Maquela do Zombo *Angola* 6°0S 15°15E **265** D3
Maquinchao *Argentina* 41°15S 68°50W **336** B3
Maquoketa *U.S.A.* 42°4N 90°40W **310** B6
Mar, Serra do *Brazil* 25°30S 49°0W **335** B6
Mar Chiquita, L. *Argentina* 30°40S 62°50W **334** C3
Mar del Plata *Argentina* 38°0S 57°30W **334** D4
Mar Menor *Spain* 37°40N 0°45W **197** H4
Mara *Guyana* 6°0N 57°36W **329** B6
Mara *India* 28°11N 94°14E **241** A5
Mara *Tanzania* 1°30S 34°32E **268** C3
Mara □ *Tanzania* 1°45S 34°20E **268** C3
Maraã *Brazil* 1°52S 65°25W **328** D4
Maraa *Tahiti* 17°46S 149°34W **289** e
Marabá *Brazil* 5°20S 49°5W **332** C2
Maracá, I. de *Brazil* 2°10N 50°30W **329** C7
Maracaibo *Venezuela* 10°40N 71°37W **328** A3
Maracaibo, L. de *Venezuela* 9°40N 71°30W **328** B3
Maracaju *Brazil* 21°38S 55°9W **335** A4
Maracajú, Serra de *Brazil* 20°57S 55°1W **331** E6
Maracanã *Pará, Brazil* 0°46S 47°27W **332** B2
Maracanã *Rio de J., Brazil* 22°54S 43°13W **135** B1
Maracás *Brazil* 13°26S 40°18W **333** D3
Maracas *Trin. & Tob.* 10°41N 61°24W **323** t
Maracas → *Trin. & Tob.* 10°34N 61°25W **323** t
Maracas B. *Trin. & Tob.* 10°45N 61°26W **323** t
Maracas Bay Village *Trin. & Tob.* 10°46N 61°28W **323** t
Maracas Falls *Trin. & Tob.* 10°44N 61°24W **323** t
Maracay *Venezuela* 10°15N 67°28W **328** A4
Maracena *Spain* 37°12N 3°38W **195** H7
Marādah *Libya* 29°15N 19°15E **258** C3
Maradi *Niger* 13°29N 7°20E **263** C6
Maradi □ *Niger* 14°15N 7°15E **263** C6
Marāgheh *Iran* 37°30N 46°12E **213** D12
Maragogipe *Brazil* 12°46S 38°55W **333** D4
Marāh *Si. Arabia* 25°0N 45°35E **246** E5
Marahoue △ *Ivory C.* 8°0N 7°8W **262** D3
Marais du Cotentin et du Bessin ⌓ *France* 49°10N 1°30W **172** C5
Marais Poitevin, Val de Sèvre et Vendée ⌓ *France* 46°18N 0°35W **174** B3
Maraisburg = Hofmeyr *S. Africa* 31°39S 25°50E **270** D4
Marajó, B. de *Brazil* 1°0S 48°30W **332** B2
Marajó, I. de *Brazil* 1°0S 49°30W **332** B2
Marākand *Iran* 38°51N 45°16E **246** B5
Marakele △ *S. Africa* 32°14S 25°27E **271** D4
Maralal *Kenya* 1°0N 36°38E **268** B4
Maralinga *Australia* 30°13S 131°32E **279** F5
Maram *India* 25°25N 94°6E **241** C5
Marama *Australia* 35°10S 140°10E **282** C4
Maramag *Phil.* 7°46N 125°0E **233** H5
Maramaraereğlisi *Turkey* 40°57N 27°57E **203** F11
Maramasike *Solomon Is.* 9°30S 161°25E **287** M11
Marambio *Antarctica* 64°0S 56°0W **151** C18
Marampa *S. Leone* 8°45N 12°28W **262** D2
Maramureş □ *Romania* 47°45N 24°0E **183** C9
Maran *Malaysia* 3°35N 102°45E **237** L4
Marana *U.S.A.* 32°27N 111°13W **305** K8
Maranboy *Australia* 14°40S 132°39E **278** B5
Maranchón *Spain* 41°6N 2°15W **196** D2
Marand *Iran* 38°30N 45°45E **213** C11
Marandochori *Greece* 38°38N 20°39E **207** B2
Marang *Malaysia* 5°12N 103°13E **237** K4
Maranguape *Brazil* 3°55S 38°50W **332** B4
Maranhão = São Luís *Brazil* 2°39S 44°15W **332** B3
Maranhão □ *Brazil* 5°0S 46°0W **332** C3
Marano, L. di *Italy* 45°44N 13°10E **199** C10
Maranoa → *Australia* 27°50S 148°37E **281** D4
Marañón → *Peru* 4°30S 73°35W **330** A3
Marão *Mozam.* 24°18S 34°2E **271** B5
Maraoli *India* 19°2N 72°53E **130** A2
Marapi → *Brazil* 0°37N 55°58W **329** C6
Marari *Brazil* 5°43S 67°47W **330** B4
Maraş = Kahramanmaraş *Turkey* 37°37N 36°53E **212** D7
Mărăşeşti *Romania* 45°52N 27°14E **183** E12
Maratea *Italy* 39°59N 15°43E **201** C8
Marateca *Portugal* 38°34N 8°40W **195** G2
Marathasa *Cyprus* 34°59N 32°51E **207** F8
Marathia, Akra *Greece* 37°39N 20°49E **207** C5
Marathokambos *Greece* 37°43N 26°42E **205** D8
Marathon *Queens., Australia* 20°51S 143°32E **280** C3
Marathon *Ont., Canada* 48°44N 86°23W **298** C2
Marathon *Fla., U.S.A.* 24°43N 81°5W **317** L8
Marathon *N.Y., U.S.A.* 42°27N 76°2W **313** D8
Marathon *Tex., U.S.A.* 30°12N 103°15W **314** F3
Marathonas *Greece* 38°11N 23°58E **204** C5
Marathóvouno *Cyprus* 35°13N 33°37E **207** E9
Maratua *Indonesia* 2°10N 118°35E **235** B5
Maraú *Brazil* 14°6S 39°0W **333** D4
Marau *Solomon Is.* 10°31S 161°31E **287** N11
Maraval *Trin. & Tob.* 10°42N 61°31W **323** t
Maraval → *Trin. & Tob.* 10°39N 61°32W **323** t
Maravari *Solomon Is.* 7°50S 156°42E **287** L9
Maravatío *Mexico* 19°54N 100°27W **318** D4
Marawi City *Phil.* 8°0N 124°21E **233** G5
Marāwih *U.A.E.* 24°18N 53°18E **247** E7
Marazliyivka 46°8N 30°3E **183** D15
Marbella *Spain* 36°30N 4°57W **195** J6
Marble Bar *Australia* 21°9S 119°44E **278** D2
Marble Falls *U.S.A.* 30°35N 98°16W **314** F5
Marblehead *U.S.A.* 42°29N 70°51W **313** D14
Mårbu *Norway* 60°11N 8°9E **164** D5
Marburg = Maribor *Slovenia* 46°36N 15°40E **199** B12
Marburg *Germany* 50°47N 8°46E **178** E4
Marca, Pta. Da *Angola* 16°31S 11°43E **265** F2
Marcal → *Hungary* 47°41N 17°40E **182** C2
Marcali *Hungary* 46°35N 17°25E **182** D2
Marcapata *Peru* 13°31S 70°52W **330** C3
Marcaria *Italy* 45°7N 10°32E **198** C7
Mărcăuţi *Moldova* 48°20N 27°14E **183** B12
Marcelin *Poland* 52°19N 20°59E **142** B1
Marceline *U.S.A.* 39°43N 92°57W **310** E4
March *U.K.* 52°33N 0°5E **169** E8
Marchal *Dem. Rep. of the Congo* 5°16S 14°58E **265** D2
Marchand = Rommani *Morocco* 33°31N 6°40W **260** B3
Marche *France* 46°5N 1°20E **174** B5
Marche □ *Italy* 43°30N 13°15E **199** E10
Marché Bonsecours *Montréal, Canada* **130** b3
Marche-en-Famenne *Belgium* 50°14N 5°19E **170** D5
Marchena *Spain* 37°18N 5°23W **195** H5
Marchena, Canal de *Ecuador* 0°19N 90°12W **330** a
Marchena, I. *Ecuador* 0°19N 90°29W **330** a
Marches = Marche □ *Italy* 43°30N 13°15E **199** E10
Marchesale ⌓ *Italy* 38°32N 16°13E **201** D9
Marciana Marina *Italy* 42°48N 10°12E **198** F7
Marcianise *Italy* 41°2N 14°17E **201** A7
Marcigny *France* 46°17N 4°2E **173** F11
Marcillat-en-Combraille *France* 46°12N 2°38E **173** F9
Marck *France* 50°57N 1°57E **173** B8
Marckolsheim *France* 48°10N 7°30E **173** D14
Marco Island *U.S.A.* 25°58N 81°44W **317** K8
Marco Rondon *Brazil* 12°0S 60°56W **331** C5
Marcona *Peru* 15°10S 75°0W **330** D3
Marcos Juárez *Argentina* 32°42S 62°5W **334** C3
Mărculeşti *Moldova* 47°52N 28°14E **183** C13
Marcus Baker, Mt. *U.S.A.* 61°26N 147°45W **303** F11
Marcus I. = Minami-Tori-Shima *Pac. Oc.* 24°20N 153°58E **288** E7
Marcy, Mt. *U.S.A.* 44°7N 73°56W **313** B11
Mardan *Pakistan* 34°20N 72°0E **242** B5
Mardarivka *Ukraine* 47°32N 29°44E **183** C14
Mardin *Turkey* 37°20N 40°43E **213** D9
Mårdsjö *Sweden* 63°18N 15°35E **162** A9
Maré, Î. *N. Cal.* 21°30S 168°0E **277** E12
Marécchia → *Italy* 44°4N 12°34E **199** D9
Marechal Deodoro *Brazil* 9°43S 35°54W **332** C4
Marechal Floriano = Piranhas *Brazil* 9°27S 37°46W **332** C4
Maree, L. *U.K.* 57°40N 5°26W **167** D3
Mareeba *Australia* 16°59S 145°28E **280** B4
Mareetsane *S. Africa* 26°9S 25°25E **270** C4
Mareil-Marly *France* 48°52N 2°4E **134** A1
Maremma *Italy* 42°30N 11°30E **199** F8
Maremma ⌓ *Italy* 42°35N 11°8E **198** F8
Maréna *Kayes, Mali* 14°36N 10°45W **262** C2
Maréna *Koulikoro, Mali* 13°55N 7°20W **262** C3
Marengo *Ind., U.S.A.* 38°22N 86°21W **311** F10
Marengo *Iowa, U.S.A.* 41°48N 92°4W **310** C4
Marennes *France* 45°49N 1°7W **174** C2
Marerano *Madag.* 21°23S 44°52E **272** C1
Maréttimo *Italy* 37°58N 12°4E **200** E5
Mareuil *France* 45°26N 0°29E **174** C4
Marfa *U.S.A.* 30°19N 104°1W **314** F2
Marganets = Marhanets *Ukraine* 47°40N 34°40E **189** J8
Margaret → *Australia* 18°9S 125°41E **278** C4
Margaret Bay *Canada* 51°20N 127°35W **296** C3
Margaret L. *Canada* 58°56N 115°25W **296** B5
Margaret River *Australia* 33°57S 115°4E **279** F2
Margareten *Austria* 48°11N 16°20E **142** A2
Margarita, I. de *Venezuela* 11°0N 64°0W **329** A5
Margariti *Greece* 39°22N 20°26E **204** B2
Margaritovo *Russia* 43°25N 134°45E **220** C7
Margate *KwaZulu Natal, S. Africa* 30°50S 30°20E **271** D5
Margate *Kent, U.K.* 51°23N 1°23E **169** F9
Margate *Fla., U.S.A.* 26°15N 80°12W **317** J9
Margeride, Mts. de la *France* 44°43N 3°38E **174** D7
Marggrabowa = Olecko *Poland* 54°2N 22°31E **184** D9
Margherita *India* 27°16N 95°40E **241** B5
Margherita di Savóia *Italy* 41°22N 16°9E **201** A9
Margherita Pk. *Uganda* 0°22N 29°51E **268** B3
Marghilon *Uzbekistan* 40°27N 71°42E **217** D8
Marghita *Romania* 47°22N 22°22E **182** C7
Margonin *Poland* 52°58N 17°5E **185** F4
Margosatubig *Phil.* 7°34N 123°10E **233** H4
Margow, Dasht-e *Afghan.* 30°40N 62°30E **240** C1
Marguerite *Canada* 52°30N 122°25W **296** C4
Marhanets *Ukraine* 47°40N 34°40E **189** J8
Marhoum *Algeria* 34°27N 0°11W **261** B4
Mari *Papua N. G.* 9°11S 141°42E **286** E1
Mārī *Syria* 36°29N 37°10E **250** B3
Mari El □ *Russia* 56°30N 48°0E **190** B8
Mari Indus *Pakistan* 32°57N 71°34E **242** C4
Mari Republic = Mari El □ *Russia* 56°30N 48°0E **190** B8
Maria *Austria* 48°11N 16°21E **142** A2
Maria, Îs. *French Polynesia* 21°48S 154°41W **289** f
María, Sa. de *Spain* 37°39N 2°14W **197** H2
Maria Aurora *Phil.* 15°48N 121°28E **232** D3
María Elena *Chile* 22°18S 69°40W **334** A2
María Grande *Argentina* 31°45S 59°55W **334** C4
Maria I. *N. Terr., Australia* 14°52S 135°45E **280** A2
Maria I. *Tas., Australia* 42°35S 148°0E **281** G4
Maria Is. *St. Lucia* 13°44N 60°56W **323** m
Maria Island △ *Australia* 42°38S 148°5E **281** G4
Maria Pereira = Mombaça *Brazil* 5°43S 39°45W **332** C4
Maria Theresiopel = Subotica *Serbia* 46°6N 19°39E **182** D4
Maria van Diemen, C. *N.Z.* 34°29S 172°40E **284** A1
Mariager *Denmark* 56°40N 9°59E **163** H3
Mariager Fjord *Denmark* 56°42N 10°19E **163** H4
Mariahilferstrasse *Vienna, Austria* **142** b1
Mariakani *Kenya* 3°50S 39°27E **268** C4
Mariala △ *Australia* 25°57S 145°2E **281** D4
Marian *Australia* 21°9S 148°57E **280** K6
Marian L. *Canada* 63°0N 116°15W **296** A5
Mariana Islands *N. Marianas* 15°15N 145°48E **302** a
Mariana Trench *Pac. Oc.* 13°0N 145°0E **302** a
Mariani *India* 26°39N 94°19E **241** B5

Marianica, Cord. = Morena, Sierra *Spain* 38°20N 4°0W **195** G7
Marianna *U.S.A.* 30°46N 85°14W **316** E4
Mariannelund *Sweden* 57°37N 15°35E **163** G9
Mariánské Lázně *Czech Rep.* 49°58N 12°41E **180** B5
Marias → *U.S.A.* 47°56N 110°30W **304** C8
Marías, Islas *Mexico* 21°25N 106°28W **318** C3
Mariato, Punta *Panama* 7°12N 80°52W **320** E3
Mariazell *Austria* 47°47N 15°19E **180** D8
Ma'rib *Yemen* 15°25N 45°21E **248** D4
Maribo *Denmark* 54°48N 11°30E **163** K5
Maribor *Slovenia* 46°36N 15°40E **199** B12
Maricaban I. *Phil.* 13°39N 120°53E **232** E3
Maricao *Puerto Rico* 18°11N 66°59W **321** b
Marico → *Africa* 23°35S 26°57E **270** B4
Maricopa *Ariz., U.S.A.* 33°4N 112°3W **305** K7
Maricopa *Calif., U.S.A.* 35°4N 119°24W **307** K7
Maridalen *Norway* 59°59N 10°45E **133** A3
Maridalsvatnet *Norway* 59°59N 10°46E **133** A3
Marîdî *Sudan* 4°55N 29°25E **257** G2
Marîdî, Wadi → *Sudan* 6°15N 29°21E **257** F2
Marié → *Brazil* 0°27S 66°26W **328** D4
Marie Byrd Land *Antarctica* 79°30S 125°0W **151** D14
Marie-Galante *Guadeloupe* 15°56N 61°16W **322** e
Marie-Galante, Canal de *Guadeloupe* 16°0N 61°25W **322** e
Mariecourt = Kangiqsujuaq *Canada* 61°30N 72°0W **295** C12
Mariefred *Sweden* 59°15N 17°12E **162** E11
Mariehamn *Finland* 60°5N 19°55E **161** F18
Marieholm *Sweden* 55°53N 13°10E **163** J7
Mariembourg *Belgium* 50°6N 4°31E **170** D4
Marienbad = Mariánské Lázně *Czech Rep.* 49°58N 12°41E **180** B5
Marienberg *Germany* 50°39N 13°9E **178** E9
Marienburg = Malbork *Poland* 54°3N 19°1E **184** D6
Mariendorf *Germany* 52°26N 13°23E **115** B3
Marienfelde *Germany* 52°24N 13°23E **115** B3
Marienplatz *Munich, Germany* **131** b2
Mariental *Namibia* 24°36S 18°0E **270** B2
Marienville *U.S.A.* 41°28N 79°8W **312** E5
Mariestad *Sweden* 58°43N 13°50E **163** F7
Marietta *Ga., U.S.A.* 33°57N 84°33W **316** B5
Marietta *Ohio, U.S.A.* 39°25N 81°27W **309** F13
Marieville *Canada* 45°26N 73°10W **313** A11
Mariga → *Nigeria* 9°40N 5°55E **263** C6
Marignane *France* 43°25N 5°13E **175** E9
Marigot *Dominica* 15°33N 61°18W **323** k
Marigot *Guadeloupe* 16°5N 61°46W **322** e
Marigot *St.-Martin* 18°4N 63°5W **322** a
Marigot Bay *St. Lucia* 13°58N 61°1W **323** m
Marihatag *Phil.* 8°48N 126°18E **233** G6
Mariinsk *Russia* 56°10N 87°20E **214** D9
Mariinsk Water = Volgo-Baltiyskiy Kanal *Russia* 60°0N 38°0E **188** B9
Mariinskiy Posad *Russia* 56°10N 47°45E **190** B8
Marijampolė *Lithuania* 54°33N 23°19E **184** D10
Marijampolės □ *Lithuania* 54°34N 23°21E **184** D10
Marikina *Phil.* 14°37N 121°5E **127** B2
Marikina → *Phil.* 14°33N 121°3E **127** B2
Marília *Brazil* 22°13S 50°0W **335** A6
Marimba *Angola* 8°28S 17°8E **265** D3
Marín *Spain* 42°23N 8°42W **194** C2
Marin, Cul-de-Sac du *Martinique* 14°27N 60°53W **322** j
Marin City *U.S.A.* 37°52N 122°30W **136** A1
Marin Pen. *U.S.A.* 37°50N 122°30W **136** A1
Marina *U.S.A.* 36°41N 121°48W **306** J5
Marina del Rey *U.S.A.* 33°58N 118°27W **126** C2
Marinduque *Phil.* 13°25N 122°0E **231** B6
Marinduque □ *Phil.* 13°18N 122°0E **232** E4
Marine City *U.S.A.* 42°43N 82°30W **312** D2
Marine Drive *Mumbai, India* **130** b1
Marineland *U.S.A.* 29°40N 81°13W **316** F8
Marineo *Italy* 37°57N 13°25E **200** E6
Marinette *U.S.A.* 45°6N 87°38W **308** C10
Maringá *Brazil* 23°26S 52°2W **335** A5
Maringa → *Dem. Rep. of the Congo* 1°14N 19°48E **264** B3
Marinha Grande *Portugal* 39°45N 8°56W **194** F2
Marinho dos Abrolhos △ *Brazil* 17°50S 39°0W **333** E4
Marino *Dublin, Ireland* 53°22N 6°14W **120** A2
Marino *Italy* 41°46N 12°39E **199** G9
Marion *Ala., U.S.A.* 32°38N 87°19W **315** E11
Marion *Ill., U.S.A.* 37°44N 88°56W **310** G8
Marion *Ind., U.S.A.* 40°32N 85°40W **311** D11
Marion *Iowa, U.S.A.* 42°2N 91°36W **310** B5
Marion *Kans., U.S.A.* 38°21N 97°1W **308** F5
Marion *N.C., U.S.A.* 35°41N 82°1W **315** D13
Marion *Ohio, U.S.A.* 40°35N 83°8W **311** D13
Marion *S.C., U.S.A.* 34°11N 79°24W **315** D15
Marion *Va., U.S.A.* 36°50N 81°31W **309** G13
Marion, L. *U.S.A.* 33°28N 80°10W **316** B9
Marion Bay *Australia* 35°12S 136°59E **282** C2
Marion I. *Ind. Oc.* 47°0S 38°0E **273** J2
Maripa *Venezuela* 7°26N 65°9W **329** B4
Maripasoula *Fr. Guiana* 3°40N 54°4W **329** C7
Mariposa *U.S.A.* 37°29N 119°58W **306** H7
Mariscal Estigarribia *Paraguay* 22°3S 60°40W **334** A3
Marisco, Ponta do *Brazil* 23°1S 43°18W **135** C1
Maritim, Museu *Barcelona, Spain* **114** c2
Maritime Alps = Maritimes, Alpes *Europe* 44°10N 7°10E **175** D11
Maritimes, Alpes *Europe* 44°10N 7°10E **175** D11
Maritsa = Evros → *Greece* 41°40N 26°34E **212** B2
Maritsa *Greece* 36°22N 28°8E **206** E12
Marium, Mt. *Vanuatu* 16°15S 168°7E **287** F6
Mariupol *Ukraine* 47°5N 37°31E **189** J9
Marīvān *Iran* 35°30N 46°25E **213** E12
Mariveles *Phil.* 14°26N 120°29E **232** D3
Marj 'Uyūn *Lebanon* 33°21N 35°34E **250** E6
Marjan = Wazikhwah *Afghan.* 32°11N 68°21E **240** B3
Mark Twain L. *U.S.A.* 39°28N 91°55W **310** E5
Marka = Merca *Somali Rep.* 1°48N 44°50E **267** D5
Marka *Si. Arabia* 18°14N 41°19E **256** D5
Markam *China* 29°42N 98°38E **228** C2
Markapur *India* 15°44N 79°19E **245** G4
Markaryd *Sweden* 56°28N 13°35E **163** H7
Markat *Albania* 39°44N 20°12E **206** B10
Markazī □ *Iran* 35°0N 49°30E **216** F3
Markdale *Canada* 44°19N 80°39W **312** B4
Marked Tree *U.S.A.* 35°32N 90°25W **315** D9
Markelsdorfer Huk *Germany* 54°33N 11°4E **178** A7
Market Drayton *U.K.* 52°54N 2°29W **168** E5
Market Harborough *U.K.* 52°29N 0°55W **169** E7
Market Rasen *U.K.* 53°24N 0°20W **168** D7
Markham *Canada* 43°52N 79°16W **141** A2
Markham → *Papua N. G.* 6°41S 147°2E **286** D4
Markham, Mt. *Antarctica* 83°0S 164°0E **151** E11
Marki *Poland* 52°19N 21°6E **142** B2
Märkisch Friedland = Mirosławiec *Poland* 53°20N 16°5E **184** E3
Märkische Schweiz ⌓ *Germany* 52°34N 14°2E **178** C10
Markit *China* 38°54N 77°40E **217** E9
Markkleeberg *Germany* 51°16N 12°23E **178** D8
Markland Wood *Canada* 43°38N 79°34W **141** B1
Markleeville *U.S.A.* 38°42N 119°47W **306** G7
Markopoulo *Greece* 37°53N 23°57E **204** D5
Markounda *C.A.R.* 7°39N 16°55E **264** A3
Markovac *Serbia* 44°14N 21°7E **202** B5
Markovo *Russia* 64°40N 170°24E **215** C17
Markoye *Burkina Faso* 14°39N 0°2E **263** C5
Marks *Russia* 51°45N 46°50E **190** E8
Marksshtadt = Marks *Russia* 51°45N 46°50E **190** E8
Marksville *U.S.A.* 31°8N 92°4W **314** F8
Markt Schwaben *Germany* 48°11N 11°52E **179** G7
Marktoberdorf *Germany* 47°45N 10°37E **179** H6
Marktredwitz *Germany* 50°1N 12°6E **179** E8
Marl *Germany* 51°39N 7°4E **178** D3
Marla *Australia* 27°19S 133°33E **281** D1
Marlbank *Canada* 44°26N 77°6W **312** B7
Marlboro *U.S.A.* 41°36N 73°59W **313** E11
Marlborough *Queens., Australia* 22°46S 149°52E **280** C4
Marlborough *Wilts., U.K.* 51°25N 1°43W **169** F6
Marlborough *Mass., U.S.A.* 42°21N 71°33W **313** D13
Marlborough □ *N.Z.* 41°40S 173°50E **285** B8
Marlborough Downs *U.K.* 51°27N 1°53W **169** F6
Marle *France* 49°43N 3°47E **173** C10
Marlin *U.S.A.* 31°18N 96°54W **314** F6
Marlow *Mecklenburg-Vorpommern, Germany* 54°9N 12°33E **178** A8
Marlow *Bucks., U.K.* 51°34N 0°46W **169** F7
Marlow *Okla., U.S.A.* 34°39N 97°58W **314** D6
Marly, Forêt de *France* 48°52N 2°2E **134** A1
Marly-le-Roi *France* 48°52N 2°5E **134** A1
Marmagao *India* 15°25N 73°56E **245** G1
Marmande *France* 44°30N 0°10E **174** D4
Marmara *Turkey* 40°35N 27°34E **203** F11
Marmara, Sea of = Marmara Denizi *Turkey* 40°45N 28°15E **203** F12
Marmara Denizi *Turkey* 40°45N 28°15E **203** F12
Marmara Gölü *Turkey* 38°37N 28°2E **205** C10
Marmaris *Turkey* 36°50N 28°14E **205** E10
Marmaris Limanı *Turkey* 36°50N 28°19E **205** E10
Marmelos → *Brazil* 6°6S 61°46W **331** B5
Marmion, Mt. *Australia* 29°16S 119°50E **279** E2
Marmion L. *Canada* 48°55N 91°20W **298** C1
Marmolada, Mte. *Italy* 46°26N 11°51E **199** B8
Marmolejo *Spain* 38°3N 4°13W **195** G6
Marmora *Canada* 44°28N 77°41W **312** B7
Mármora, La *Italy* 39°59N 9°20E **200** C2
Marnay *France* 47°16N 5°48E **173** E12
Marne *Germany* 53°56N 9°2E **178** B5
Marne □ *France* 48°50N 4°10E **173** D11
Marne → *France* 48°47N 2°29E **173** D9
Marne-la-Vallée *France* 48°50N 2°37E **134** A4
Marneuli *Georgia* 41°30N 44°48E **191** K7
Marnia = Maghnia *Algeria* 34°50N 1°43W **261** B4
Marnoo *Australia* 36°40S 142°52E **282** D5
Maro *Chad* 8°30N 19°0E **259** G3
Maro Reef *U.S.A.* 25°25N 170°35W **302** F9
Maroa *Ill., U.S.A.* 40°2N 88°57W **310** D8
Maroa *Venezuela* 2°43N 67°33W **328** C4
Maroala *Madag.* 15°23S 47°59E **272** B2
Maroantsetra *Madag.* 15°26S 49°44E **272** B2
Maroelaboom *Namibia* 19°15S 18°53E **270** A2
Marofandilia *Madag.* 20°7S 44°34E **272** C1
Marojejy ⌓ *Madag.* 14°26S 49°21E **272** A2
Marokau *French Polynesia* 18°2S 142°17W **289** f
Marolambo *Madag.* 20°2S 48°7E **272** C2
Marolles-en-Brie *France* 48°44N 2°33E **134** B4
Maromandia *Madag.* 14°13S 48°5E **272** A2
Maromokotro *Madag.* 14°0S 49°0E **272** A2
Marondera *Zimbabwe* 18°5S 31°42E **269** F3
Maroni → *Fr. Guiana* 5°30N 54°0W **329** B7
Maronia *Greece* 40°53N 25°30E **203** F9
Maronne → *France* 45°5N 1°56E **174** C5
Maroochydore *Australia* 26°29S 153°5E **281** D5
Maroon Town *Jamaica* 18°22N 77°48W **320** a
Maroona *Australia* 37°27S 142°54E **282** D5
Maros → *Hungary* 46°15N 20°13E **182** D5
Marosakoa *Madag.* 15°26S 46°38E **272** B2
Maroseranana *Madag.* 18°32S 48°51E **272** B2
Maróstica *Italy* 45°44N 11°40E **199** C8
Marotandrano *Madag.* 16°10S 48°50E **272** B2
Marotaolano *Madag.* 12°47S 49°15E **272** A2
Marotiri, Îs. = Bass, Îs. de *French Polynesia* 27°55S 143°26W **289** f
Maroua *Cameroon* 10°40N 14°20E **259** F2
Maroubra *Australia* 33°56S 151°16E **139** B2
Marovato *Madag.* 15°48S 48°5E **272** B2
Marovoay *Madag.* 16°6S 46°39E **272** B2
Marowijne □ *Suriname* 4°0N 55°0W **329** C7
Marowijne → *Suriname* 5°45N 53°58W **329** B7
Marquard *S. Africa* 28°40S 27°28E **270** C4
Marquesas Fracture Zone *Pac. Oc.* 9°0S 125°0W **289** H15
Marquesas Is. = Marquises, Îs. *French Polynesia* 9°30S 140°0W **289** f
Marquesas Keys *U.S.A.* 24°35N 82°10W **317** L7
Marquette *U.S.A.* 46°33N 87°24W **308** B10
Marquette Park *U.S.A.* 41°46N 87°42W **119** C2
Marquis *St. Lucia* 14°2N 60°54W **323** m
Marquis, C. *St. Lucia* 14°3N 60°54W **323** m
Marquis I. *Grenada* 12°5N 61°37W **323** q
Marquise *France* 50°50N 1°40E **173** B8
Marquises, Îs. *French Polynesia* 9°30S 140°0W **289** f
Marra, Gebel *Sudan* 7°20N 27°35E **257** F2
Marra, Pta. da *Angola* 16°31S 11°43E **265** F2
Marra Cr. → *Australia* 30°8S 147°15E **283** A7
Marra-Marra △ *Australia* 33°30S 151°4E **283** B9
Marracuene *Mozam.* 25°45S 32°35E **271** C5
Marradi *Italy* 44°4N 11°37E **199** D8
Marrakech *Morocco* 31°9N 8°0W **260** B3
Marrakech □ *Morocco* 31°30N 7°30W **260** B3
Marratxi *Spain* 39°39N 2°48E **206** B3
Marrawah *Australia* 40°55S 144°42E **281** G3
Marrecas, Serra das *Brazil* 9°0S 41°0W **332** C3
Marree *Australia* 29°39S 138°1E **281** D2
Marrero *U.S.A.* 29°53N 90°6W **131** B2
Marrickville *Australia* 33°54S 151°9E **139** B1
Marrimane *Mozam.* 22°58S 33°34E **271** B5
Marromeu *Mozam.* 18°15S 36°25E **271** A6
Marromeu ⌓ *Mozam.* 19°0S 36°0E **271** A6
Marroquí, Punta *Spain* 36°0N 5°37W **195** K5
Marrowie Cr. → *Australia* 33°23S 145°40E **283** B6
Marruás = Pôrto *Brazil* 3°54S 42°42W **332** B3
Marrubane *Mozam.* 18°0S 37°0E **269** F4
Marrúbiu *Italy* 39°40N 8°35E **200** C1
Marrupa *Mozam.* 13°8S 37°30E **269** E4
Mars B. *Ascension I.* 7°59S 14°24W **153** g
Mars Hill *U.S.A.* 46°31N 67°52W **309** B20
Marsá al Burayqah *Libya* 30°24N 19°37E **258** B3
Marsá 'Alam *Egypt* 25°5N 34°54E **256** B3
Marsá Matrûh *Egypt* 31°19N 27°9E **256** A2
Marsá Sha'b *Sudan* 22°52N 35°47E **256** C4
Marsá Susah *Libya* 32°52N 21°59E **258** B4
Marsabit *Kenya* 2°18N 38°0E **268** B4
Marsabit △ *Kenya* 2°23N 37°56E **268** B4
Marsala *Italy* 37°48N 12°26E **200** E5
Marsalforn *Malta* 36°4N 14°16E **206** E7
Mârşani *Romania* 44°1N 24°1E **183** F9
Marsaskala *Malta* 35°52N 14°34E **206** F8
Marsaxlokk *Malta* 35°51N 14°33E **206** F8
Marsaxlokk Bay *Malta* 35°49N 14°33E **206** F8
Marsberg *Germany* 51°28N 8°52E **178** D4
Marsciano *Italy* 42°54N 12°20E **199** F9
Marsden *Australia* 33°47S 147°32E **283** B7
Marseillan *France* 43°23N 3°31E **174** E7
Marseille *France* 43°18N 5°23E **175** E9
Marseille-Marignane ✈ **(MRS)** *France* 43°26N 5°14E **175** E9
Marseilles = Marseille *France* 43°18N 5°23E **175** E9
Marseilles *U.S.A.* 41°20N 88°43W **311** C8
Marsfield *Australia* 33°46S 151°7E **139** A1
Marsh I. *U.S.A.* 29°34N 91°53W **314** G9
Marsha, L. *U.S.A.* 28°29N 81°29W **133** B2
Marshall *Liberia* 6°8N 10°22W **262** D2
Marshall *Alaska, U.S.A.* 61°53N 162°5W **303** F7
Marshall *Ark., U.S.A.* 35°55N 92°38W **314** D8
Marshall *Ill., U.S.A.* 39°23N 87°42W **311** E9
Marshall *Mich., U.S.A.* 42°16N 84°58W **311** B12
Marshall *Minn., U.S.A.* 44°27N 95°47W **308** C6
Marshall *Mo., U.S.A.* 39°7N 93°12W **310** E3
Marshall *Tex., U.S.A.* 32°33N 94°23W **314** E7
Marshall → *Australia* 22°59S 136°59E **280** C2
Marshall, C. *Ecuador* 0°1S 91°12W **330** a
Marshall Bennett Is. *Papua N. G.* 8°50S 151°55E **286** E6
Marshall Field's *Chicago, U.S.A.* **119** c2
Marshall Is. ■ *Pac. Oc.* 9°0N 171°0E **288** G9
Marshalltown *U.S.A.* 42°3N 92°55W **310** B4
Marshallville = Lewisporte *Canada* 49°15N 55°3W **299** C8
Marshallville *U.S.A.* 32°27N 83°56W **316** C6
Marshbrook *Zimbabwe* 18°33S 31°9E **271** A5
Marshfield = Coos Bay *U.S.A.* 43°22N 124°13W **304** E1
Marshfield *Mo., U.S.A.* 37°15N 92°54W **308** G7
Marshfield *Vt., U.S.A.* 44°20N 72°20W **313** B12
Marshfield *Wis., U.S.A.* 44°40N 90°10W **308** C8
Marshūn *Iran* 36°19N 49°23E **247** B6
Mársico Nuovo *Italy* 40°25N 15°44E **201** B8
Marsouins, R. des → *Réunion* 21°1S 55°44E **272** f
Märsta *Sweden* 59°37N 17°52E **162** E11
Marstal *Denmark* 54°51N 10°30E **163** K4
Marstrand *Sweden* 57°53N 11°35E **163** G5
Mart *U.S.A.* 31°33N 96°50W **314** F6
Marta → *Italy* 42°14N 11°42E **199** F8
Martaban *Burma* 16°30N 97°35E **241** G6
Martaban, G. of *Burma* 16°5N 96°30E **241** G6
Martano *Italy* 40°12N 18°18E **201** B11
Martapura *Kalimantan, Indonesia* 3°22S 114°47E **235** C4
Martapura *Sumatera, Indonesia* 4°19S 104°22E **234** C2
Marte *Nigeria* 12°23N 13°46E **263** C7
Marte, Campo de *Brazil* 23°30S 46°38W **137** B2
Marte R. Gómez, Presa *Mexico* 26°10N 99°0W **319** B5
Martel *France* 44°57N 1°37E **174** D5
Martelange *Belgium* 49°49N 5°43E **170** E5
Martellago *Italy* 45°33N 12°9E **199** C9
Martés, Sierra *Spain* 39°20N 1°0W **197** F4
Martesana, Navíglio della *Italy* 45°31N 9°17E **129** A2
Martfű *Hungary* 47°1N 20°17E **182** C5
Marthaguy Cr. → *Australia* 30°16S 147°35E **283** A7
Marthapal *India* 19°24N 81°37E **244** E5
Martha's Vineyard *U.S.A.* 41°25N 70°38W **313** E14
Martigné-Ferchaud *France* 47°50N 1°20W **172** E5
Martigny *Switz.* 46°6N 7°3E **179** J3
Martigues *France* 43°24N 5°4E **175** E9
Martil *Morocco* 35°36N 5°15W **260** A3
Martin *Slovak Rep.* 49°6N 18°58E **181** B11
Martin *S. Dak., U.S.A.* 43°11N 101°44W **308** D3
Martin *Tenn., U.S.A.* 36°21N 88°51W **315** C10
Martín → *Spain* 41°18N 0°19W **196** D4
Martin L. *U.S.A.* 32°41N 85°55W **316** C4
Martin Luther King Nat. Historic Site ⌓ *U.S.A.* 33°45N 84°22W **113** B2
Martin Pt. *U.S.A.* 70°8N 143°16W **303** A12
Martin Vaz *Atl. Oc.* 20°30S 28°51W **152** J9
Martina Franca *Italy* 40°42N 17°20E **201** B10
Martinborough *N.Z.* 41°14S 175°29E **284** H4
Martinez *B. Aires, Argentina* 34°29S 58°31W **117** A1
Martinez *Calif., U.S.A.* 38°1N 122°8W **306** G4
Martinez *Ga., U.S.A.* 33°31N 82°5W **315** E13
Martinho Campos *Brazil* 19°20S 45°13W **333** E2
Martinique ☒ *W. Indies* 14°40N 61°0W **322** j
Martinique Channel *St. Vincent* 12°34N 61°25W **323** n
Martinique Passage *W. Indies* 15°15N 61°0W **321** C7
Martinkylä *Finland* 60°17N 24°51E **121** B2
Martino *Greece* 38°35N 23°12E **204** C5
Martinópolis *Brazil* 22°11S 51°12W **335** A5
Martins Ferry *U.S.A.* 40°6N 80°44W **312** F4
Martinsberg *Austria* 48°22N 15°9E **180** C8
Martinsburg *Pa., U.S.A.* 40°19N 78°20W **312** F6
Martinsburg *W. Va., U.S.A.* 39°27N 77°58W **309** F15
Martinsicuro *Italy* 42°54N 13°54E **199** F10
Martinsried *Germany* 48°6N 11°27E **131** B1
Martinsville *Ill., U.S.A.* 39°20N 87°53W **311** E9
Martinsville *Ind., U.S.A.* 39°26N 86°25W **311** E10
Martinsville *Va., U.S.A.* 36°41N 79°52W **309** G14
Marton *N.Z.* 40°4S 175°23E **284** G4
Martorell *Spain* 41°28N 1°56E **196** D6
Martos *Spain* 37°44N 3°58W **195** H7
Martūbah *Libya* 32°35N 22°46E **258** B4
Martuni *Armenia* 40°8N 45°20E **191** K7
Maru *Nigeria* 12°22N 6°22E **263** C6
Marudi *Malaysia* 4°11N 114°19E **235** B4
Maruf *Afghan.* 31°30N 67°6E **240** C2
Marugame *Japan* 34°15N 133°40E **222** C5
Marui = Pagwi *Papua N. G.* 4°4S 143°2E **286** C2
Maruia → *N.Z.* 41°47S 172°13E **285** B7
Maruim *Brazil* 10°45S 37°5W **332** D4
Maruko *Japan* 35°33N 139°40E **140** B3
Marulan *Australia* 34°43S 150°3E **283** C9
Marunga *Angola* 17°28S 20°2E **265** F4
Marungu, Mts. *Dem. Rep. of the Congo* 7°30S 30°0E **268** D3
Marunouchi *Tokyo, Japan* **140** b4
Maruoka *Japan* 36°9N 136°16E **223** A8
Marusino *Russia* 55°41N 37°58E **129** B5
Marv Dasht *Iran* 29°50N 52°40E **247** D7
Marvão = Castelo do Piauí *Brazil* 5°20S 41°33W **332** C3
Marvast *Iran* 30°30N 54°15E **247** D7
Marvejols *France* 44°33N 3°19E **174** D7
Marvel Loch *Australia* 31°28S 119°29E **279** F2
Marwar *India* 25°43N 73°45E **242** G5
Mary *Turkmenistan* 37°40N 61°50E **247** B9
Mary Esther *U.S.A.* 30°25N 86°40W **317** E3
Maryborough = Port Laoise *Ireland* 53°2N 7°18W **166** C4
Maryborough *Queens., Australia* 25°31S 152°37E **281** D5
Maryborough *Vic., Australia* 37°3S 143°44E **282** D5
Maryfield *Canada* 49°50N 101°35W **297** D8
Maryino = Pristen *Russia* 51°15N 36°44E **189** G9
Maryino *Russia* 55°40N 37°45E **129** B4
Maryland *Singapore* 1°19N 103°47E **138** B2
Maryland □ *U.S.A.* 39°0N 76°30W **309** F15
Maryland Junction *Zimbabwe* 17°45S 30°31E **269** F3
Marylebone *London, U.K.* **125** a2
Marymont *Poland* 52°16N 20°58E **142** B1
Maryport *U.K.* 54°44N 3°28W **168** C4
Mary's Harbour *Canada* 52°18N 55°51W **299** B8
Marysin Wawerski *Poland* 52°14N 21°9E **142** B2
Marystown *Canada* 47°10N 55°10W **299** C8
Marysville *B.C., Canada* 49°35N 116°0W **296** D5
Marysville *Calif., U.S.A.* 39°9N 121°35W **306** F5
Marysville *Kans., U.S.A.* 39°51N 96°39W **308** F5
Marysville *Mich., U.S.A.* 42°54N 82°29W **312** D2
Marysville *Ohio, U.S.A.* 40°14N 83°22W **311** D13
Marysville *Wash., U.S.A.* 48°3N 122°11W **306** B4
Maryville *Mo., U.S.A.* 40°21N 94°52W **310** D2
Maryville *Tenn., U.S.A.* 35°46N 83°58W **315** D13
Marzahn *Germany* 52°32N 13°34E **115** A4
Marzo, Punta *Colombia* 6°50N 77°42W **328** B2
Marzūq *Libya* 25°53N 13°57E **258** C2
Marzūq □ *Libya* 25°0N 16°0E **258** D3
Marzūq, Idehān *Libya* 24°50N 13°51E **258** D2
Masada = Mesada *Israel* 31°20N 35°19E **251** G6
Mas'ada *Syria* 33°13N 35°45E **250** E6
Masahunga *Tanzania* 2°6S 33°18E **268** C3
Masai *Malaysia* 1°29N 103°55E **237** d
Masai Mara △ *Kenya* 1°25S 35°5E **268** C4
Masai Steppe *Tanzania* 4°30S 36°30E **268** C4
Masaka *Uganda* 0°21S 31°45E **268** C3
Masalembo, Kepulauan *Indonesia* 5°35S 114°30E **235** D4
Masalima, Kepulauan *Indonesia* 5°4S 117°5E **235** D5
Masallı *Azerbaijan* 39°3N 48°40E **213** C13
Masalog Pt. *N. Marianas* 15°1N 145°40E **302** e
Masamba *Indonesia* 2°30S 120°15E **231** E6
Masan *S. Korea* 35°11N 128°32E **224** E4
Masandam, Ra's *Oman* 26°30N 56°30E **247** E8
Masasi *Tanzania* 10°45S 38°52E **269** E4
Masaya *Nic.* 12°0N 86°7W **320** D2
Masba *Nigeria* 11°35N 13°1E **263** C7
Masbate *Phil.* 12°21N 123°36E **232** E4
Masbate □ *Phil.* 12°20N 123°30E **232** E4
Masbate Pass *Phil.* 12°30N 123°35E **232** E4
Máscali *Italy* 37°45N 15°12E **201** E8
Mascara *Algeria* 35°26N 0°6E **261** A5
Mascara □ *Algeria* 35°25N 0°10E **261** A5
Mascarene Is. *Ind. Oc.* 22°0S 55°0E **273** G4
Mascot *Australia* 33°55S 151°12E **139** B2
Mascota *Mexico* 20°32N 104°49W **318** C4
Mascoutah *U.S.A.* 38°29N 89°48W **310** F7
Masefau B. *Amer. Samoa* 14°15S 170°37W **302** f
Masein *Burma* 23°22N 94°21E **241** D5
Masela *Indonesia* 8°9S 129°51E **231** F7
Maseru *Lesotho* 29°18S 27°30E **270** C4
Masfjorden *Norway* 60°48N 5°18E **164** D2
Mashaba *Zimbabwe* 20°2S 30°29E **269** G3
Mashābih *Si. Arabia* 25°35N 36°30E **246** E3
Mashan *China* 23°40N 108°11E **228** F7
Mashar *Sudan* 9°16N 26°51E **257** F2
Mashatu ⌓ *Botswana* 22°5S 29°5E **271** B4
Mashegu *Nigeria* 10°0N 5°35E **263** D6
Masherbrum *Pakistan* 35°38N 76°18E **243** B7
Mashhad *Iran* 36°20N 59°35E **247** B8
Mashi *Nigeria* 13°0N 7°54E **263** C6
Mashiki *Japan* 32°51N 130°53E **222** E2
Mashīz *Iran* 29°56N 56°37E **247** D8
Mashkal → *Pakistan* 26°2N 65°19E **240** D2
Māshkel, Hāmūn-i- *Pakistan* 28°20N 62°56E **240** C1
Mashki Chāh *Pakistan* 29°5N 62°30E **240** C1
Mashonaland Central □ *Zimbabwe* 17°30S 31°0E **271** A5
Mashonaland East □ *Zimbabwe* 18°0S 32°0E **271** A5
Mashonaland West □ *Zimbabwe* 17°30S 29°30E **271** A4
Mashrakh *India* 26°7N 84°48E **243** F11
Mashtaga = Maştağa *Azerbaijan* 40°35N 50°1E **191** K10
Masi Manimba *Dem. Rep. of the Congo* 4°40S 17°54E **265** C3
Masibi *Angola* 11°6S 22°41E **265** E4
Masindi *Uganda* 1°40N 31°43E **268** B3
Masindi Port *Uganda* 1°43N 32°2E **268** B3
Masinloc *Phil.* 15°32N 119°57E **232** D2
Maşīrah *Oman* 21°0N 58°50E **249** B7
Maşīrah, Khalīj *Oman* 20°10N 58°10E **249** B7
Maşīrah, Tur'at *Oman* 20°30N 58°40E **249** B7
Masisea *Peru* 8°35S 74°22W **330** B3
Masisi *Dem. Rep. of the Congo* 1°23S 28°49E **268** C2
Masjed Soleyman *Iran* 31°55N 49°18E **247** D6
Mask, L. *Ireland* 53°36N 9°22W **166** C2
Maskelyne Is. *Vanuatu* 16°32S 167°49E **287** F5
Maski *India* 15°56N 76°46E **245** G3
Maskin *Oman* 23°44N 56°52E **247** F8
Maslen Nos *Bulgaria* 42°18N 27°48E **203** D11
Maslinica *Croatia* 43°24N 16°13E **199** E13
Masmo *Sweden* 59°15N 17°53E **139** B1
Maşna'ah *Yemen* 14°27N 48°17E **249** D5
Masnou = El Masnou *Spain* 41°28N 2°20E **196** D7
Masoala, Tanjon' i *Madag.* 15°59S 50°13E **272** B3
Masoala △ *Madag.* 15°30S 50°12E **272** B3
Masoarivo *Madag.* 19°3S 44°19E **272** B1
Masohi = Amahai *Indonesia* 3°20S 128°55E **231** E7
Masomeloka *Madag.* 20°17S 48°37E **272** C2
Mason *Mich., U.S.A.* 42°35N 84°27W **311** B12
Mason *Nev., U.S.A.* 38°56N 119°8W **306** G7
Mason *Ohio, U.S.A.* 39°22N 84°19W **311** E12
Mason *Tex., U.S.A.* 30°45N 99°14W **314** F5
Mason B. *N.Z.* 46°55S 167°45E **285** G2
Mason City *Ill., U.S.A.* 40°12N 89°42W **310** D7
Mason City *Iowa, U.S.A.* 43°9N 93°12W **310** A3
Mason Hall *Trin. & Tob.* 11°13N 60°43W **323** s
Maspalomas *Canary Is.* 27°46N 15°35W **153** e1
Maspalomas, Pta. *Canary Is.* 27°43N 15°36W **153** e1
Maspeth *U.S.A.* 40°43N 73°55W **132** B2
Masqat *Oman* 23°37N 58°36E **249** B7
Masr el Gedida *Egypt* 30°5N 31°21E **117** A2
Masr el Qadîma *Egypt* 30°0N 31°14E **117** A2
Massa *Congo* 3°45S 15°29E **264** C3
Massa *Italy* 44°1N 10°9E **198** D7
Massa, O. → *Morocco* 30°2N 9°40W **260** B3
Massa Maríttima *Italy* 43°3N 10°52E **198** E7
Massachusetts □ *U.S.A.* 42°30N 72°0W **313** D13
Massachusetts Avenue *Washington, D.C., U.S.A.* **143** a2
Massachusetts B. *U.S.A.* 42°25N 70°50W **313** D14
Massachusetts Inst. of Tech. *U.S.A.* 42°21N 71°5W **116** A2
Massacre *Dominica* 15°20N 61°25W **323** k
Massafra *Italy* 40°35N 17°7E **201** B10
Massaguet *Chad* 12°28N 15°26E **259** F3
Massakory *Chad* 13°0N 15°49E **259** F3
Massamá *Portugal* 38°45N 9°16W **126** A1
Massanella *Spain* 39°48N 2°51E **206** B3
Massangano *Angola* 9°40S 14°13E **265** D2
Massangena *Mozam.* 21°34S 33°0E **271** B5
Massango *Angola* 8°1S 16°10E **265** D3
Massapê *Brazil* 3°31S 40°19W **332** B3
Massat *France* 42°53N 1°21E **174** F5
Massawa = Mitsiwa *Eritrea* 15°35N 39°25E **257** D4
Massena *U.S.A.* 44°56N 74°54W **313** B10
Massénya *Chad* 11°21N 16°9E **259** F3
Masset *Canada* 54°2N 132°10W **296** C2
Masseube *France* 43°25N 0°34E **174** E4
Massey → *Canada* 43°42N 79°19W **141** A3
Massey Hall *Toronto, Canada* **141** a3
Massiac *France* 45°15N 3°11E **174** C7
Massif Central *France* 44°55N 3°0E **174** D7
Massif des Bauges ⌓ *France* 45°40N 6°10E **173** G13
Massigui *Mali* 11°48N 6°50W **262** C3
Massillon *U.S.A.* 40°48N 81°32W **312** F3
Massima *Gabon* 1°27S 11°33E **264** C2
Massine, O. → *Algeria* 36°13N 2°12E **261** A5
Massinga *Mozam.* 23°15S 35°22E **271** B6
Massingir *Mozam.* 23°51S 32°4E **271** B5
Masson-Angers *Canada* 45°32N 75°25W **313** A9
Masson I. *Antarctica* 66°10S 93°20E **151** C7
Massouka *Gabon* 1°37S 9°56E **264** C1
Massow = Maszewo *Poland* 53°29N 15°3E **184** E2
Massy *France* 48°43N 2°16E **134** B2
Mastābah *Si. Arabia* 20°49N 39°26E **248** B2
Maştağa *Azerbaijan* 40°35N 50°1E **191** K10
Mastanli = Momchilgrad *Bulgaria* 41°33N 25°23E **203** E9
Masterton *N.Z.* 40°56S 175°39E **284** G4
Mastic *U.S.A.* 40°47N 72°54W **313** F12
Mastuj *Pakistan* 36°20N 72°36E **243** A5
Mastung *Pakistan* 29°50N 66°56E **240** C2
Mastūrah *Si. Arabia* 23°7N 38°52E **248** B2
Masty *Belarus* 53°27N 24°38E **177** B13
Masuda *Japan* 34°40N 131°51E **222** C3
Masuika *Dem. Rep. of the Congo* 7°37S 22°32E **265** D4
Masvingo *Zimbabwe* 20°8S 30°49E **269** G3
Masvingo □ *Zimbabwe* 21°0S 31°30E **269** G3
Maswa ⌓ *Tanzania* 2°58S 34°19E **268** C3
Maşyāf *Syria* 35°4N 36°20E **250** C7
Maszewo *Poland* 53°29N 15°3E **184** E2
Mat → *Albania* 41°40N 19°35E **202** E3
Mât → *Réunion* 20°57S 55°42E **272** f
Mata *Israel* 31°43N 35°4E **123** B1
Mata-au = Clutha → *N.Z.* 46°20S 169°49E **285** G4
Mata de São João *Brazil* 12°31S 38°17W **333** D4
Mata-Utu *Wall. & F. Is.* 13°17S 176°8W **277** C15
Matabele Plain *Zambia* 16°20S 23°10E **265** F4
Matabeleland North □ *Zimbabwe* 19°0S 28°0E **269** F2
Matabeleland South □ *Zimbabwe* 21°0S 29°0E **269** G2
Matachel → *Spain* 38°50N 6°17W **195** G4
Matachewan *Canada* 47°56N 80°39W **298** C3
Matacuni → *Venezuela* 3°2N 65°16W **329** C4
Matadi *Dem. Rep. of the Congo* 5°52S 13°31E **265** D2
Matafao, Mt. *Amer. Samoa* 14°17S 170°42W **302** f
Matagalpa *Nic.* 13°0N 85°58W **320** D2
Matagami *Canada* 49°45N 77°34W **298** C4
Matagami, L. *Canada* 49°50N 77°40W **298** C4
Matagorda B. *U.S.A.* 28°40N 96°12W **314** G6
Matagorda I. *U.S.A.* 28°15N 96°30W **314** G6
Mataguinao *Phil.* 12°5N 124°55E **232** E5
Matahiva *French Polynesia* 17°32S 149°20W **289** f
Mataiea *Tahiti* 17°46S 149°25W **289** e
Matak *Indonesia* 3°18N 106°16E **234** B3
Matakana *N.S.W., Australia* 32°59S 145°54E **283** B6
Matakana *N.Z.* 36°21S 174°43E **284** C3
Matala *Angola* 14°46S 15°4E **265** E3
Matala *Kriti, Greece* 34°59N 24°45E **207** F5
Matalaque *Peru* 16°26S 70°49W **330** D3
Matale *Sri Lanka* 7°30N 80°37E **245** L5
Matam *Senegal* 15°34N 13°17W **262** B2
Matamata *N.Z.* 37°48S 175°47E **284** D4
Matameye *Niger* 13°26N 8°28E **259** F1
Matamoros *Campeche, Mexico* 18°50N 90°50W **319** D6
Matamoros *Coahuila, Mexico* 25°32N 103°15W **318** B4
Matamoros *Tamaulipas, Mexico* 25°53N 97°30W **319** B5
Ma'ţan as Sarra *Libya* 21°45N 22°0E **259** D4
Ma'ţan Bishārah *Libya* 23°0N 22°32E **258** D4
Matandu → *Tanzania* 8°45S 34°19E **269** D3
Matane *Canada* 48°50N 67°33W **299** C6
Matang *China* 23°30N 104°7E **228** F5
Matankari *Niger* 13°46N 4°1E **263** C5
Matanomadh *India* 23°33N 68°57E **242** H3
Matanzas *Cuba* 23°0N 81°40W **320** B3
Matapa *Botswana* 23°11S 24°39E **270** B3
Matapan, C. = Tenaro, Akra *Greece* 36°22N 22°27E **204** E4
Matapédia *Canada* 48°0N 66°59W **299** C6
Matapo △ *Zimbabwe* 20°30S 29°40E **269** G2
Matara *Sri Lanka* 5°58N 80°30E **245** M5
Mataram *Indonesia* 8°35S 116°7E **231** K19
Matarani *Peru* 17°0S 72°10W **330** D3
Mataranka *Australia* 14°55S 133°4E **278** B5
Matarma, Râs *Egypt* 30°27N 32°44E **251** H3
Mataró *Spain* 41°32N 2°29E **196** D7
Matarraña → *Spain* 41°14N 0°22E **196** D5
Mataruška Banja *Serbia* 43°40N 20°40E **202** C4
Mataso *Vanuatu* 17°14S 168°26E **287** G6
Matata *N.Z.* 37°54S 176°48E **284** D5
Matatiele *S. Africa* 30°20S 28°49E **271** D4
Matatula, C. *Amer. Samoa* 14°15S 170°33W **302** f
Mataura *N.Z.* 46°11S 168°51E **285** G3
Mataura → *N.Z.* 46°34S 168°44E **285** G3
Matavai, B. de *Tahiti* 17°30S 149°23W **289** e
Matavera *Cook Is.* 21°13S 159°44W **289** h
Mataveri *Chile* 27°9S 109°27W **330** b
Mategua *Bolivia* 13°1S 62°48W **331** C5
Matehuala *Mexico* 23°39N 100°39W **318** C4
Mateira *Brazil* 18°54S 50°30W **333** E1
Mateke *Dem. Rep. of the Congo* 4°52S 24°25E **264** C3
Mateke Hills *Zimbabwe* 21°48S 31°0E **269** G3
Matelot *Trin. & Tob.* 10°50N 61°7W **323** t
Matera *Italy* 40°40N 16°36E **201** B9
Matese, Monti del *Italy* 41°27N 14°22E **201** A7
Matese ⌓ *Italy* 41°24N 14°23E **201** A7
Mátészalka *Hungary* 47°58N 22°20E **182** C7
Matetsi *Zimbabwe* 18°12S 26°0E **269** F2
Mateur *Tunisia* 37°0N 9°40E **258** A1
Matfors *Sweden* 62°21N 17°2E **162** B11
Matha *France* 45°52N 0°20W **174** C3
Matheniko ⌓ *Uganda* 2°49N 34°27E **268** B3
Mathis *U.S.A.* 28°6N 97°50W **314** G6
Mathoura *Australia* 35°50S 144°55E **283** C6
Mathraki *Greece* 39°48N 19°31E **206** B9
Mathura *India* 27°30N 77°40E **242** F7
Mati *Phil.* 6°55N 126°15E **233** H6
Matiakoali *Burkina Faso* 12°28N 1°2E **263** C5
Matiali *India* 26°56N 88°49E **243** F13
Matías Romero *Mexico* 16°53N 95°2W **319** D5
Matibane *Mozam.* 14°49S 40°45E **269** E5
Matihutong *China* 39°56N 116°19E **114** B1
Matinha *Portugal* 38°45N 9°5W **126** A2
Matinhos *Brazil* 25°49S 48°32W **333** G2
Matiri Ra. *N.Z.* 41°38S 172°20E **285** B7
Matjiesfontein *S. Africa* 33°14S 20°35E **270** D3
Matla → *India* 21°40N 88°40E **243** J13
Matlamanyane *Botswana* 19°33S 25°57E **270** A4
Matli *Pakistan* 25°2N 68°39E **242** G3
Matlock *U.K.* 53°9N 1°33W **168** D6
Matmata *Tunisia* 33°37N 9°59E **258** B1
Matna *Sudan* 13°49N 35°10E **257** E4
Matnog *Phil.* 12°35N 124°5E **232** E5
Mato *Dem. Rep. of the Congo* 8°1S 24°24E **265** D4
Mato → *Venezuela* 7°9N 65°7W **329** B4
Mato, Serrania de *Venezuela* 6°25N 65°25W **328** B4
Mato Grosso □ *Brazil* 14°0S 55°0W **331** C7
Mato Grosso, Planalto do *Brazil* 15°0S 55°0W **331** D7
Mato Grosso do Sul □ *Brazil* 18°0S 55°0W **331** D7
Mato Verde *Brazil* 11°13S 50°40W **333** D1
Matobo = Matapo △ *Zimbabwe* 20°30S 29°40E **269** G2
Matochkin Shar *Russia* 73°10N 56°40E **214** B6
Matong *Papua N. G.* 5°36S 151°50E **286** C6
Matopo Hills *Zimbabwe* 20°36S 28°20E **269** G2
Matopos *Zimbabwe* 20°20S 28°29E **269** G2
Matosinhos *Portugal* 41°11N 8°42W **194** D2
Matou *Taiwan* 23°11N 120°15E **225** C2
Matouba *Guadeloupe* 16°2N 61°41W **322** e
Matour *France* 46°19N 4°29E **173** F11
Matramam *Indonesia* 6°12S 106°51E **122** B2
Matroosberg *S. Africa* 33°23S 19°40E **270** D2
Maţruḩ *Oman* 23°37N 58°30E **249** B7
Matsena *Nigeria* 13°5N 10°5E **263** C7
Matsesta *Russia* 43°34N 39°51E **191** J4
Matsu Tao *Taiwan* 26°8N 119°56E **225** b
Matsubara = Takahagi *Japan* 36°43N 140°45E **221** F10
Matsubara *Japan* 34°34N 135°33E **133** B2
Matsudo *Japan* 35°47N 139°54E **223** B11
Matsue *Japan* 35°25N 133°10E **222** B5
Matsum, Ko *Thailand* 9°22N 99°59E **237** b
Matsumae *Japan* 41°26N 140°7E **220** D10
Matsumoto *Japan* 36°15N 138°0E **223** A10
Matsusaka *Japan* 34°34N 136°32E **223** C8
Matsushima *Japan* 32°30N 130°25E **222** E2
Matsuura *Japan* 33°20N 129°49E **222** D1
Matsuyama *Japan* 33°45N 132°45E **222** D4
Matsuzaki *Japan* 34°43N 138°50E **223** C10
Mattagami → *Canada* 50°43N 81°29W **298** B3
Mattancheri *India* 9°50N 76°15E **245** K3
Mattapan *U.S.A.* 42°16N 71°6W **116** B2
Mattawa *Canada* 46°20N 78°45W **298** C4
Matterhorn *Switz.* 45°58N 7°39E **179** K3
Mattersburg *Austria* 47°44N 16°24E **181** D9
Matteson *U.S.A.* 41°30N 87°42W **311** C9
Matthew, Î. *N. Cal.* 22°29S 171°15E **277** E13
Matthew Town *Bahamas* 20°57N 73°40W **321** B5
Matthews *U.S.A.* 40°23N 85°30W **311** D11
Matthews Ridge *Guyana* 7°37N 60°10W **329** B5
Mattias Church *Budapest, Hungary* **117** b1
Mattice *Canada* 49°40N 83°20W **298** C3
Mattili *India* 18°33N 82°12E **244** E6
Mattituck *U.S.A.* 40°59N 72°32W **313** F12
Mattō *Japan* 36°31N 136°34E **223** A8
Mattoon *U.S.A.* 39°29N 88°23W **311** E8
Matuba *Mozam.* 24°28S 32°49E **271** B5
Matucana *Peru* 11°55S 76°25W **330** C2
Matugama *Sri Lanka* 6°31N 80°7E **245** L5
Matuka *Papua N. G.* 4°54S 145°47E **286** C3
Matuku *Fiji* 19°10S 179°44E **287** B2
Matūn = Khowst *Afghan.* 33°22N 69°58E **242** C3
Matura *Trin. & Tob.* 10°40N 61°4W **323** t
Matura B. *Trin. & Tob.* 10°39N 61°1W **323** t
Maturín *Venezuela* 9°45N 63°11W **329** B5
Matusadona △ *Zimbabwe* 16°58S 28°42E **269** F2
Matutum, Mt. *Phil.* 6°22N 125°5E **233** H5
Matveyev Kurgan *Russia* 47°35N 38°57E **189** J10
Matxitxako, C. *Spain* 43°28N 2°47W **196** B2
Mátyásföld *Hungary* 47°30N 19°12E **117** A3
Mau *Mad. P., India* 26°17N 78°41E **243** F8
Mau *Ut. P., India* 25°56N 83°33E **243** G10
Mau *Ut. P., India* 25°17N 81°23E **243** G9
Mau Escarpment *Kenya* 0°40S 36°0E **268** C4
Mau Ranipur *India* 25°16N 79°8E **243** G8
Mau Tso Ngam *China* 22°22N 114°13E **122** A2
Maua *Kenya* 0°14N 37°56E **268** C4
Mauban *Phil.* 14°12N 121°44E **232** D3
Maubeuge *France* 50°17N 3°57E **173** B10
Maubin *Burma* 16°44N 95°39E **241** G5
Maubourguet *France* 43°29N 0°1E **174** E4
Maud, Pt. *Australia* 23°6S 113°45E **278** D1
Maud Rise *S. Ocean* 66°0S 3°0E **151** C3
Maude *Australia* 34°29S 144°18E **282** C6
Maudin Sun *Burma* 16°0N 94°30E **241** G5
Mauer *Austria* 48°9N 16°16E **142** B1
Maués *Brazil* 3°20S 57°45W **329** D6
Maués-Acu → *Brazil* 3°22S 57°44W **329** D6
Maug Is. *N. Marianas* 20°1N 145°13E **302** a
Mauganj *India* 24°50N 81°55E **243** G9
Maughold Hd. *I. of Man* 54°18N 4°18W **168** C3
Mauguio *France* 43°37N 4°1E **174** E7
Maui *U.S.A.* 20°48N 156°20W **302** C5
Maulamyaing = Moulmein *Burma* 16°30N 97°40E **241** G6
Maule □ *Chile* 36°5S 72°30W **334** D1
Mauléon-Licharre *France* 43°14N 0°54W **174** E3
Maullín *Chile* 41°38S 73°37W **336** B2
Maulvibazar *Bangla.* 24°29N 91°42E **241** C3
Maumee *U.S.A.* 41°34N 83°39W **311** C13
Maumee → *U.S.A.* 41°42N 83°28W **311** C13
Maumere *Indonesia* 8°38S 122°13E **231** F6
Maumusson, Pertuis de *France* 45°48N 1°14W **174** C2
Maun *Botswana* 20°0S 23°26E **270** B3
Mauna Kea *U.S.A.* 19°50N 155°28W **302** D6
Mauna Kea Forest Reserve *U.S.A.* 19°52N 155°26W **302** D6
Mauna Loa *U.S.A.* 19°30N 155°35W **302** D6
Mauna Loa Forest Reserve *U.S.A.* 19°35N 155°33W **302** D6
Maunabo *Puerto Rico* 18°1N 65°54W **321** b
Maunaloa *U.S.A.* 21°8N 157°13W **302** B4
Maunalua B. *U.S.A.* 21°15N 157°45W **302** K14

Maunawili U.S.A. 21°23N 157°46W **302** K14
Maunga Orito Chile 27°10S 109°25W **330** b
Maunga Puakatiki Chile 27°6S 109°15W **330** b
Maunga Terevaka Chile 27°5S 109°23W **330** b
Maungaroa Cook Is. 21°13S 159°48W **289** h
Maungaturoto N.Z. 36°6S 174°23E **284** C3
Maungdaw Burma 20°50N 92°21E **241** E4
Maungmagan Kyunzu Burma 14°0N 97°48E **236** E1
Maungu Kenya 3°33S 38°45E **268** C4
Maupihaa French Polynesia 16°50S 153°55W **289** f
Maupin U.S.A. 45°11N 121°5W **304** D3
Maupiti French Polynesia 16°27S 152°15W **289** f
Maure-de-Bretagne France 47°59N 1°58W **172** E5
Maurepas, L. U.S.A. 30°15N 90°30W **315** F9
Maures France 43°15N 6°15E **175** E10
Mauriac France 45°13N 2°19E **174** C6
Maurice, L. Australia 29°30S 131°0E **279** E5
Mauriceville N.Z. 40°45S 175°42E **284** G4
Mauricie △ Canada 46°45N 73°0W **298** C5
Maurienne France 45°11N 6°30E **175** C10
Mauripur Pakistan 24°52N 66°55E **123** A1
Mauritania ■ Africa 20°50N 10°0W **260** D3
Mauritius ■ Ind. Oc. 20°0S 57°0E **272** e
Mauritius ✈ (MRU) Mauritius 20°25S 57°40E **272** e
Mauron France 48°9N 2°18W **172** D4
Maurs France 44°43N 2°12E **174** C6
Mauston U.S.A. 43°48N 90°5W **308** D8
Mauterndorf Austria 47°9N 13°40E **180** D6
Mauthen Austria 46°40N 13°0E **180** E6
Mauvezin France 43°44N 0°53E **174** E4
Mauzé-sur-le-Mignon France 46°12N 0°41W **174** B3
Mavaca → Venezuela 2°31N 65°11W **329** C4
Mavinga Angola 15°50S 20°21E **269** H6
Mavli India 24°45N 73°55E **242** G5
Mavrata Greece 38°40N 20°45E **202** F3
Mavrové Albania 40°26N 19°32E **202** F3
Mavrovo △ Macedonia 41°36N 20°45E **202** E4
Mavuradonha Mts. Zimbabwe 16°30S 31°30E **269** F3
Mawa Dem. Rep. of the Congo 2°45N 26°40E **268** B2
Mawai India 23°20N 81°4E **243** H9
Mawana India 29°6N 77°58E **242** E7
Mawand Pakistan 29°33N 68°38E **242** E3
Mawjib, W. al → Jordan 31°28N 35°36E **251** G6
Mawk Mai Burma 20°14N 97°37E **241** G6
Mawlaik Burma 23°40N 94°26E **241** D5
Mawlamyine = Moulmein Burma 16°30N 97°40E **241** G6
Mawlawkho Burma 17°50N 97°38E **241** G6
Mawqaq Si. Arabia 27°25N 41°8E **246** E4
Mawshij Yemen 13°43N 43°17E **248** D3
Mawson Base Antarctica 67°30S 62°53E **151** C6
Mawson Coast Antarctica 68°30S 63°0E **151** C6
Mawsynram India 25°15N 91°30E **241** C3
Max U.S.A. 47°49N 101°18W **308** B3
Maxambamba = Nova Iguaçu Brazil 22°45S 43°28W **333** F3
Maxcanú Mexico 20°35N 90°0W **319** C6
Maxesibeni S. Africa 30°49S 29°23E **271** D4
Maxeys U.S.A. 33°45N 83°11W **316** B6
Maxhamish L. Canada 59°50N 123°17W **296** B4
Maxhof Germany 48°4N 11°29E **131** B1
Maxixe Mozam. 23°54S 35°17E **271** B6
Maxville Canada 45°17N 74°51W **313** A10
Maxwell N.Z. 39°51S 174°49E **284** F3
Maxwell Calif., U.S.A. 39°17N 122°11W **306** E4
Maxwelton Australia 20°43S 142°41E **280** C3
May, C. U.S.A. 38°56N 74°58W **309** F16
May Jirrui Niger 12°34N 8°9E **259** f1
May River Papua N. G. 4°19S 141°58E **286** C1
Maya Indonesia 1°10S 109°35E **235** C3
Maya Mts. Belize 16°30N 89°0W **319** D7
Maya → Russia 60°28N 134°28E **215** D14
Mayabandar India 12°56N 92°56E **245** H11
Mayaguana Bahamas 22°30N 72°44W **321** B5
Mayagüez Puerto Rico 18°12N 67°9W **321** d
Mayahi Niger 13°58N 7°40E **263** C6
Mayaky Ukraine 47°26N 29°38E **183** C14
Mayals = Maials Spain 41°22N 0°30E **196** D5
Mayama Congo 3°51S 14°54E **264** C2
Mayâmey Iran 36°24N 55°42E **247** B7
Mayang China 27°53N 109°49E **228** D7
Mayanup Australia 33°57S 116°27E **279** F2
Mayapán Mexico 20°29N 89°11W **319** C7
Mayarí Cuba 20°40N 75°41W **321** B4
Mayaro Trin. & Tob. 10°12N 61°1W **323** t
Mayaro □ Trin. & Tob. 10°10N 61°5W **323** t
Mayaro B. Trin. & Tob. 10°14N 60°59W **323** t
Mayavaram = Mayuram India 11°3N 79°42E **245** J4
Maybell U.S.A. 40°31N 108°5W **304** F9
Maybole U.K. 55°21N 4°42W **167** F4
Maychew Ethiopia 12°50N 39°31E **257** E4
Maydan Iraq 34°55N 45°37E **213** E11
Maydan Ukraine 48°36N 23°29E **183** B8
Maydena Australia 42°45S 146°30E **281** G4
Maydī Yemen 16°19N 42°48E **248** C3
Mayen Germany 50°19N 7°13E **179** E3
Mayenne France 48°20N 0°38W **172** D6
Mayenne □ France 48°10N 0°40W **172** D6
Mayenne → France 47°30N 0°32W **172** E6
Mayer U.S.A. 34°24N 112°14W **305** J7
Mayerthorpe Canada 53°57N 115°8W **296** C5
Mayesville U.S.A. 34°0N 80°12W **316** A9
Mayfair Gauteng, S. Africa 26°11S 28°0E **123** B2
Mayfair London, U.K. **125** b3
Mayfield Ky., U.S.A. 36°44N 88°38W **310** C3
Mayfield N.Y., U.S.A. 43°6N 74°16W **313** C10
Mayhill U.S.A. 32°53N 105°29W **305** K11
Mayma Russia 44°35N 85°55E **217** B11
Maymyo Burma 22°2N 96°28E **241** D6
Maynard Mass., U.S.A. 42°26N 71°27W **313** D13
Maynard Wash., U.S.A. 47°59N 122°55W **306** C4
Maynard Hills Australia 28°28S 119°49E **279** E2
Mayne → Australia 23°40S 141°55E **280** C3
Maynooth Ireland 53°23N 6°34W **166** C5
Mayo Yukon, Canada 63°38N 135°57W **294** C6
Mayo Fla., U.S.A. 30°3N 83°10W **317** F6
Mayo □ Ireland 53°53N 9°3W **166** C2
Mayo → Argentina 45°45S 69°45W **330** B2
Mayo → Peru 6°38S 76°15W **330** B2
Mayo Bay Phil. 6°56N 126°22E **233** H6
Mayo Daga Nigeria 6°59N 11°25E **263** D7
Mayo Faran Nigeria 9°59N 10°51E **259** G3
Mayo-Kébbi □ Chad 10°0N 15°0E **259** G3
Mayoko Congo 2°18S 12°49E **264** C2
Mayoko Dem. Rep. of the Congo 1°6S 23°10E **264** C4
Mayo Volcano Phil. 13°15N 123°41E **232** E4
Mayor Buratovich Argentina 39°15S 62°37W **336** A4
Mayor I. N.Z. 37°16S 176°17E **284** D5
Mayorga Spain 42°10N 5°16W **194** C5
Mayotte ☑ Ind. Oc. 12°50S 45°10E **272** b

Mayoyao Phil. 16°59N 121°14E **232** C3
Mayqayyng Kazakhstan 51°27N 75°47E **217** B9
Mayraira Pt. Phil. 18°39N 120°51E **232** B3
Mayreau St. Vincent 12°39N 61°23W **323** n
Maysān □ Iraq 31°55N 47°15E **246** D5
Mayskiy Russia 43°47N 44°2E **191** J7
Maysville Ky., U.S.A. 38°39N 83°46W **311** F13
Maysville Mo., U.S.A. 39°53N 94°22W **310** E2
Mayu Indonesia 1°30N 126°30E **231** D7
Mayumba Gabon 3°25S 10°39E **264** C2
Mayuram India 11°3N 79°42E **245** J4
Mayville N. Dak., U.S.A. 47°30N 97°20W **308** B5
Mayville N.Y., U.S.A. 42°15N 79°30W **312** D5
Maywood Calif., U.S.A. 33°59N 118°12W **126** C3
Maywood Ill., U.S.A. 41°52N 87°51W **119** B8
Maywood N.J., U.S.A. 40°53N 74°3W **132** A1
Maywood Park Race Track U.S.A. 41°54N 87°50W **119** B1
Mayya Russia 61°44N 130°18E **215** C14
Mazabuka Zambia 15°52S 27°44E **269** F2
Mazagán = El Jadida Morocco 33°11N 8°17W **260** B3
Mazagão Brazil 0°7S 51°16W **329** D7
Mazamet France 43°30N 2°20E **174** E6
Mazamari Peru 3°30S 73°0W **328** D3
Mäzandarän □ Iran 36°30N 52°0E **247** B7
Mazapil Mexico 24°38N 101°34W **318** C4
Mazar China 36°32N 77°1E **217** E9
Mazar, O. → Algeria 31°50N 1°36E **261** B5
Mazâr-e Sharif Afghan. 36°41N 67°0E **240** A2
Mazarredo Argentina 47°10S 66°50W **330** C3
Mazarrón Spain 37°38N 1°19W **197** H3
Mazarrón, G. de Spain 37°27N 1°19W **197** H3
Mazaruni → Guyana 6°25N 58°35W **329** B6
Mazatán Mexico 29°0N 110°8W **318** B2
Mazatenango Guatemala 14°35N 91°30W **320** D1
Mazatlán Mexico 23°10N 106°30W **318** C3
Mazhafa, J. Si. Arabia 28°52N 35°5E **251** K6
Mäzhän Iran 32°30N 59°0E **247** C8
Mazinan Iran 36°19N 56°56E **247** B8
Mazo Cruz Peru 16°45S 69°44W **330** D4
Mazoe Mozam. 16°42S 33°7E **269** F3
Mazoe → Mozam. 16°20S 33°30E **269** F3
Mazomanie U.S.A. 43°11N 89°48W **310** A7
Mazowe Zimbabwe 17°28S 30°58E **269** F3
Mazowieckie □ Poland 52°40N 21°0E **185** F8
Mazu Dao China 26°10N 119°55E **229** D12
Mazurian Lakes = Mazurski, Pojezierze Poland 53°50N 21°0E **184** E7
Mazurski, Pojezierze Poland 53°50N 21°0E **184** E7
Mazyr Belarus 51°59N 29°15E **177** B15
Mba Fiji 17°33S 177°41E **287** A1
Mbaba Senegal 14°59N 16°44W **262** C1
Mbabane Swaziland 26°18S 31°6E **271** C5
Mbaéré → C.A.R. 3°47N 17°31E **264** B3
Mbagne Mauritania 16°6N 14°47W **262** B2
M'bahiakro Ivory C. 7°33N 4°19W **262** D4
Mbaïki C.A.R. 3°53N 18°1E **264** B3
Mbakana, Mt. de Cameroon 7°57N 15°6E **264** A3
Mbala Zambia 8°46S 31°24E **269** D3
Mbalabala Zimbabwe 20°27S 29°3E **271** B4
Mbale Uganda 1°8N 34°12E **268** B3
Mbali → C.A.R. 4°27N 18°20E **264** B3
Mbalmayo Cameroon 3°33N 11°33E **263** E7
Mbam → Cameroon 4°24N 11°17E **263** E7
Mbamba Bay Tanzania 11°13S 34°49E **269** E3
Mbandaka Dem. Rep. of the Congo 0°1N 18°18E **264** B3
Mbanga Cameroon 4°30N 9°33E **263** E6
Mbanika Solomon Is. 9°3S 159°13E **287** M10
M'Banio, Lagune Gabon 3°35S 11°0E **264** C2
Mbanza Congo Angola 6°18S 14°16E **265** D2
Mbanza Ngungu Dem. Rep. of the Congo 5°12S 14°53E **265** D2
Mbarangandu Tanzania 10°11S 36°48E **269** D4
Mbarara Uganda 0°35S 30°40E **268** C3
Mbari → C.A.R. 4°34N 22°43E **264** B4
Mbatto Ivory C. 6°28N 4°22E **262** D4
Mbau Solomon Is. 7°47S 156°33E **287** L9
Mbé Congo 3°14S 15°50E **264** C3
Mbe Eq. Guin. 1°47N 9°56E **264** B1
Mbengga = Beqa Fiji 18°23S 178°8E **287** B2
Mbengui Gabon 2°2S 11°7E **264** C2
Mbengui Gabon 2°3S 10°4E **264** C2
Mbéni Comoros Is. 11°30S 43°22E **272** a
Mbenkuru → Tanzania 9°25S 39°50E **269** D4
Mbéré → Cameroon 7°45N 15°36E **264** A3
Mberengwa Zimbabwe 20°29S 29°57E **269** G2
Mberengwa, Mt. Zimbabwe 20°37S 29°55E **269** G2
Mberubu Nigeria 6°10N 7°38E **263** D6
Mbesuma Zambia 10°0S 32°2E **269** E3
Mbeya Tanzania 8°54S 33°29E **269** D3
Mbeya □ Tanzania 8°15S 33°30E **269** D3
Mbhashe → S. Africa 32°15S 28°54E **271** D4
Mbigou Gabon 1°53S 11°56E **264** C2
M'bili Sudan 7°35N 28°15E **257** F2
Mbinga Tanzania 10°50S 35°0E **269** E4
Mbini = Rio Muni □ Eq. Guin. 1°30N 10°0E **264** B1
Mbini Eq. Guin. 1°35N 9°37E **264** B1
Mboi Dem. Rep. of the Congo 6°57S 21°54E **264** B4
M'bonge Cameroon 4°8N 23°9E **264** B4
Mboro Senegal 15°9N 16°54E **262** C1
Mboua Cameroon 4°25N 14°16E **264** A2
Mboune Cameroon 6°23N 12°50E **263** D7
Mboune Senegal 14°42N 13°34W **262** C2
Mbouanna Congo 0°52S 15°4E **264** C3
Mbour Senegal 14°22N 16°54W **262** C1
Mbout Mauritania 16°1N 12°38W **262** B2
Mbrès C.A.R. 6°40N 19°48E **264** A3
M'Bridge → Angola 7°12S 12°51E **265** D2
Mbuji-Mayi Dem. Rep. of the Congo 6°9S 23°40E **264** B4
Mbulu Tanzania 3°45S 35°30E **268** C4
Mbuma Dem. Rep. of the Congo 3°23N 24°50E **264** B4
Mbumi Tanzania 8°57S 160°7E **287** M11
Mburucuyá Argentina 28°1S 58°14W **334** B4
M'bwat Cameroon 6°23N 10°54E **264** A2
Mchinja Tanzania 9°44S 39°45E **269** D4
Mchinji Malawi 13°47S 32°58E **269** E3
McKean Kiribati 3°36S 174°8W **277** A16
Mdennah Mauritania 24°37N 6°0W **260** D3
Me'a She' Arim Jerusalem **251** J2
Mead, L. U.S.A. 36°0N 114°44W **307** J12
Meade = Atqasuk U.S.A. 70°28N 157°24W **294** A8
Meade U.S.A. 37°17N 100°20W **308** G4
Meade River = Atqasuk U.S.A. 70°28N 157°24W **303** A8

Meadow Lake Canada 54°10N 108°26W **297** C7
Meadow Lake △ Canada 54°27N 109°0W **297** C7
Meadow Valley Wash → U.S.A. 36°40N 114°34W **307** J12
Meadowbank Park Australia 33°49S 151°6E **139** A1
Meadville Mo., U.S.A. 39°47N 93°18W **310** E3
Meadville Pa., U.S.A. 41°39N 80°9W **312** E4
Meaford Canada 44°36N 80°35W **312** B4
Mealhada Portugal 40°22N 8°27W **194** E2
Mealy Mts. Canada 53°10N 58°0W **299** B8
Meander River Canada 59°2N 117°42W **296** B5
Meares, C. U.S.A. 45°37N 124°0W **304** D1
Mearim → Brazil 3°4S 44°35W **332** B3
Meath □ Ireland 53°40N 6°57W **166** C5
Meath Park Canada 53°27N 105°22W **297** C7
Meaulne France 46°36N 2°36E **172** B6
Meaux France 48°58N 2°50E **173** D9
Mebechi-Gawa → Japan 40°31N 141°31E **220** D10
Mebonden Norway 63°13N 11°2E **164** A8
Mebulu, Tanjung Indonesia 8°50S 115°5E **231** K18
Mecanhelas Mozam. 15°12S 35°54E **269** F4
Mecaya → Colombia 0°29N 75°11W **328** C2
Mecca = Makkah Si. Arabia 21°30N 39°54E **248** B2
Mecca U.S.A. 33°34N 116°5W **307** M10
Mechanicsburg Ohio, U.S.A. 40°4N 83°33W **311** D13
Mechanicsburg Pa., U.S.A. 40°13N 77°1W **312** F8
Mechanicsville U.S.A. 41°54N 91°16W **310** E8
Mechanicville U.S.A. 42°54N 73°41W **313** D11
Mechara Ethiopia 8°36N 40°20E **257** F5
Mechelen Belgium 51°2N 4°29E **170** C4
Mecheria Algeria 33°35N 0°18W **261** B4
Mechernich Germany 50°35N 6°39E **178** E2
Mechetinskaya Russia 46°45N 40°32E **191** G5
Mechra Bel Ksiri Morocco 34°34N 5°57W **260** B3
Mechra Benâbbou Morocco 32°39N 7°48W **260** B3
Mêcice Czech Rep. 50°11N 14°31E **135** A3
Mecidiye Turkey 40°38N 26°32E **203** F10
Mecidiyeköy Turkey 41°4N 29°0E **122** B2
Mecitözü Turkey 40°32N 35°17E **212** B6
Mecklenburg Germany 51°2N 8°2E **178** D4
Mecklenburg-Vorpommern □ Germany 53°45N 12°15E **178** B8
Mecklenburger Bucht Germany 54°20N 11°40E **178** A7
Meconta Mozam. 14°59S 39°50E **269** E4
Mecsek Hungary 46°10N 18°18E **182** D3
Medak India 18°1N 78°15E **244** E4
Medan Indonesia 3°40N 98°38E **234** B1
Medanosa, Pta. Argentina 48°8S 66°0W **330** C3
Medart U.S.A. 30°5N 84°23W **316** E5
Medaryville U.S.A. 41°5N 86°55W **311** C10
Medawachchiya Sri Lanka 8°30N 80°30E **245** K5
Mede Italy 45°6N 8°44E **198** C5
Medea Algeria 36°12N 2°50E **261** A5
Médéa □ Algeria 35°0N 3°0E **261** B5
Medéguê Gabon 0°37N 10°8E **264** B2
Medeiros Neto Brazil 17°20S 40°14W **333** E3
Medellín Colombia 6°15N 75°35W **328** B2
Medelpad Sweden 62°33N 16°30E **162** B10
Medemblik Neths. 52°46N 5°8E **170** B5
Médenine Tunisia 33°21N 10°30E **258** B2
Médenine □ Tunisia 32°20N 10°0E **261** B7
Mederdra Mauritania 17°0N 15°38W **262** B1
Medford Mass., U.S.A. 42°25N 71°7W **116** A2
Medford Oreg., U.S.A. 42°19N 122°52W **304** E2
Medford Wis., U.S.A. 45°9N 90°20W **308** C8
Medgidia Romania 44°15N 28°19E **183** F13
Medi Sudan 5°4N 30°42E **257** G3
Media Agua Argentina 31°58S 68°25W **334** C2
Media Luna Argentina 34°45S 66°44W **334** C2
Medianeira Brazil 25°17S 54°5W **335** B5
Mediapolis U.S.A. 41°0N 91°10W **310** D5
Medias Romania 46°9N 24°22E **183** E9
Medicilândia Brazil 3°33S 53°8W **329** D7
Medicina Italy 44°28N 11°38E **199** D8
Medicine Bow U.S.A. 41°54N 106°12W **304** F10
Medicine Bow Mts. U.S.A. 40°40N 106°0W **304** F10
Medicine Bow Pk. U.S.A. 41°21N 106°19W **304** F10
Medicine Hat Canada 50°0N 110°45W **297** D6
Medicine Lake U.S.A. 48°30N 104°30W **304** B11
Medicine Lodge U.S.A. 37°17N 98°35W **308** G4
Medina = Al Madīnah Si. Arabia 24°35N 39°52E **246** E3
Medina Brazil 16°15S 41°29W **333** E3
Medina Colombia 4°30N 73°21W **328** C3
Medina Mis. Or., Phil. 8°55N 125°0E **233** G6
Medina N. Dak., U.S.A. 46°54N 99°18W **308** B4
Medina N.Y., U.S.A. 43°13N 78°23W **312** C6
Medina Ohio, U.S.A. 41°8N 81°52W **312** E3
Medina → U.S.A. 29°16N 98°29W **314** G5
Medina de Pomar Spain 42°56N 3°29W **194** C7
Medina de Rioseco Spain 41°53N 5°3W **194** C5
Medina del Campo Spain 41°18N 4°55W **194** D6
Medina L. U.S.A. 29°32N 98°56W **314** G5
Medina Sidonia Spain 36°28N 5°57W **195** J5
Medinaceli Spain 41°12N 2°30W **196** D2
Mediodia Spain 38°48N 1°0W **196** G2
Mediterranean Sea Europe 35°0N 15°0E **193** D7
Medjerda, O. → Tunisia 37°7N 10°13E **258** A2
Medjerda, Mts. de la Tunisia 37°7N 10°13E **258** A2
Medley Canada 54°25N 110°16W **297** C6
Médoc France 45°10N 0°50W **174** C3
Medora U.S.A. 38°49N 86°10W **311** F10
Medouneu Gabon 1°0N 10°24E **264** B2
Medulin Croatia 44°49N 13°55E **199** D10
Medveda Serbia 42°50N 21°32E **202** C6
Medvedevo Russia 56°37N 47°47E **190** B8
Medvedica → Volgograd, Russia 49°35N 42°41E **191** F7
Medvedok Russia 57°20N 50°1E **190** B10
Medvezhi, Ostrava Russia 71°0N 161°0E **215** B17
Medvezhyegorsk Russia 63°0N 34°25E **186** B5
Medway → U.K. 51°27N 0°46E **169** F8
Medway □ U.K. 51°25N 0°32E **169** F8
Medyn Russia 54°58N 35°52E **190** D8
Medzev Slovak Rep. 48°43N 20°55E **181** C13
Medzilaborce Slovak Rep. 49°17N 21°52E **181** B14
Medžitlija Macedonia 40°56N 21°26E **202** F5

Meekatharra Australia 26°32S 118°29E **279** E2
Meeker U.S.A. 40°2N 107°55W **304** F10
Meelpaeg L. Canada 48°20N 56°30W **299** C8
Meeniyan Australia 38°35S 146°3E **283** E7
Meersburg Germany 47°41N 9°16E **179** H5
Meerut India 29°1N 77°42E **242** E7
Meeteetse U.S.A. 44°9N 108°52W **304** D9
Mega Ethiopia 3°57N 38°19E **257** G4
Megalo Horio Greece 36°27N 27°22E **205** E9
Megalonisos Greece 38°0N 24°15E **204** D6
Megalopoli Greece 37°25N 22°7E **204** D4
Meganisi Greece 38°37N 20°45E **204** C2
Megara Greece 37°58N 23°22E **204** D5
Megasini Greece 21°38N 86°21E **243** J12
Megdovas = Tavropos → Greece 39°10N 21°45E **204** B3
Megève France 45°51N 6°37E **175** C10
Meghalaya □ India 25°50N 91°0E **241** C3
Meghezez Ethiopia 9°18N 39°26E **257** F4
Meghna → Bangla. 22°50N 90°50E **241** D3
Mégiscane, L. Canada 48°35N 75°55W **298** C4
Megisti Greece 36°8N 29°34E **205** E11
Megra Russia 60°11N 37°14E **188** A6
Meguro Japan 35°37N 139°42E **140** B3
Meguro → Japan 35°37N 139°45E **140** B3
Mehadia Romania 44°56N 22°23E **182** F7
Mehaïgueune, O. → Algeria 32°15N 2°59E **261** B5
Meharry, Mt. Australia 22°59S 118°35E **279** D2
Mehedeby Sweden 60°27N 17°25E **162** D11
Mehedinți □ Romania 44°40N 22°45E **182** F7
Meheisa Sudan 19°38N 32°57E **256** D3
Mehekar India 20°9N 76°34E **244** D3
Méhétia French Polynesia 17°52S 148°3W **289** f
Mehlville U.S.A. 38°30N 90°19W **310** f13
Mehndawal India 26°58N 83°5E **243** F10
Mehpalpur India 28°32N 77°7E **126** b2
Mehr Jān Iran 33°50N 55°6E **247** C7
Mehrābād Iran 36°53N 47°55E **246** B5
Mehrābād ✈ (THR) Iran 35°41N 51°18E **141** A1
Mehram Nagar India 28°34N 77°8E **126** B1
Mehrān Iran 33°7N 46°10E **213** F12
Mehrgarh Pakistan 29°30N 67°30E **242** E2
Mehriz Iran 31°35N 54°28E **247** D7
Mehrow Germany 52°34N 13°37E **131** a2
Mehun-sur-Yèvre France 47°10N 2°13E **173** E9
Mei Jiang → China 24°25N 116°35E **229** E11
Mei Lanfang Beijing, China **114** a2
Mei Xian China 34°18N 107°55E **228** H5
Meia Ponte → Brazil 18°35S 49°36W **333** E2
Meicheng China 29°29N 119°16E **229** C12
Meichengzhen China 28°9N 111°40E **229** C8
Meichuan China 30°8N 115°31E **229** B10
Meidling Austria 48°10N 16°20E **142** A2
Méier Brazil 22°52S 43°15W **135** B1
Meiganga Cameroon 6°30N 14°25E **264** A2
Meighen I. Canada 80°0N 99°30W **296** A10
Meigs U.S.A. 31°4N 84°6W **316** D5
Meihekou China 42°32N 125°40E **224** A2
Meiji Shrine Tokyo, Japan **140** b1
Meiktila Burma 20°53N 95°54E **241** E5
Meinerzhagen Germany 51°6N 7°38E **178** D3
Meiningen Germany 50°34N 10°25E **178** E6
Meinung Taiwan 22°54N 120°32E **225** D2
Meio → Brazil 13°36S 44°7W **333** D2
Meira, Serra de Spain 43°15N 7°15W **194** B3
Meiringen Switz. 46°43N 8°12E **179** a4
Meise Belgium 50°55N 4°20E **116** A1
Meishan Sichuan, China 30°3N 103°23E **228** B4
Meishan Taiwan 23°35N 120°33E **225** C2
Meissen Germany 51°9N 13°29E **178** D9
Meissner Germany 51°14N 9°50E **178** D5
Meissner-Kaufunger Wald △ Germany 51°9N 9°45E **178** D5
Meitan China 27°45N 107°29E **228** D6
Meizhou China 24°16N 116°6E **229** E11
Meja China 25°9N 82°7E **243** G10
Mejillones Chile 23°10S 70°30W **334** A1
Mejiro Japan 35°43N 21°10E **140** A3
Mékambo Gabon 1°2N 13°50E **264** B2
Mekdela Ethiopia 11°24N 39°10E **257** E4
Mekele Ethiopia 13°33N 39°30E **257** E4
Mekhtar Pakistan 30°30N 69°15E **242** D3
Meknès Morocco 33°57N 5°33W **260** B3
Meknès □ Morocco 33°30N 5°35W **260** B3
Meko Nigeria 7°27N 2°52E **263** D5
Mekong → Asia 9°30N 106°15E **237** H6
Mekongga Indonesia 3°39S 121°15E **231** E6
Mekoryuk U.S.A. 60°23N 166°11W **303** D6
Mekrou → Benin 12°24N 2°18E **263** C5
Mekvari = Kür → Azerbaijan 39°29N 49°15E **213** C13
Mel Italy 46°4N 12°5E **199** B9
Melagiri Hills India 12°20N 77°30E **245** H3
Melah, Oued el → Algeria 32°20N 2°28E **261** B5
Melaka Malaysia 2°15N 102°15E **237** L4
Melaka □ Malaysia 2°15N 102°15E **234** C2
Melalap Malaysia 5°10N 116°5E **235** A5
Melanesia Pac. Oc. 4°0S 155°0E **277** A10
Melanesian Basin Pac. Oc. 0°5N 160°35E **288** G8
Melapalaiyam India 8°39N 77°44E **245** K3
Melawi → Indonesia 0°5N 111°29E **235** B4
Melaya Indonesia 8°17S 114°30E **231** J17
Melbourne Vic., Australia 37°48S 144°58E **128** A4
Melbourne Fla., U.S.A. 28°5N 80°37W **317** F7
Melbourne Iowa, U.S.A. 41°57N 93°6W **310** D3
Melbourne ✈ (MEL) Australia 37°40S 144°50E **128** B4
Melchor-Dallas U.S.A. 41°14N 93°15W **310** C3
Melchor Múzquiz Mexico 27°53N 101°31W **318** B4
Melchor Ocampo Mexico 24°51N 101°39W **318** C4
Meldal Norway 63°3N 9°42E **164** A6
Meldola Italy 44°7N 12°5E **199** D9
Meldorf Germany 54°5N 9°5E **178** A5
Mélé C.A.R. 9°46N 21°33E **264** A4
Mele, B. Vanuatu 17°44S 168°14E **287** f
Meleda = Mljet Croatia 42°43N 17°30E **199** G14
Melegnano Italy 45°21N 9°19E **198** C6
Melekeok Palau 7°27N 134°38E **288** g
Melekess = Dimitrovgrad Russia 54°25N 49°33E **190** C9
Melenci Serbia 45°32N 20°20E **182** E5
Melenki Russia 55°20N 41°37E **188** C8
Meleuz Russia 52°58N 55°55E **216** D6
Mélèzes → Canada 57°40N 69°29W **298** A5
Melfi Chad 11°0N 17°59E **259** G3
Melfi Italy 41°0N 15°38E **201** B8
Melfort Sask., Canada 52°50N 104°37W **297** C7
Melfort Zimbabwe 18°0S 31°25E **269** F3
Melgaço Portugal 42°7N 8°15W **194** C2
Melgar de Fernamental Spain 42°27N 4°17W **194** C6
Melghir, Chott Algeria 34°13N 6°30E **261** B6
Melhus Norway 63°17N 10°18E **164** A7
Melide Spain 42°55N 8°1W **194** C2
Meligalá Greece 37°15N 21°59E **204** D3
Melilla N. Afr. 35°21N 2°57W **261** A4
Melilli Italy 37°11N 15°7E **201** E8
Melipilla Chile 33°42S 71°15W **334** C1
Melissa, Akra Greece 35°6N 24°33E **207** E5
Melissa Oros Greece 37°32N 26°4E **205** D8
Melissani Cave Greece 38°15N 20°38E **204** C2
Melita Canada 49°15N 101°0W **297** D8
Melitopol Ukraine 46°50N 35°22E **189** J8
Melk Austria 48°13N 15°20E **180** C8
Melkki Finland 60°8N 24°53E **121** C2
Mellan Fryken Sweden 59°45N 13°10E **162** E7
Mellansel Sweden 63°26N 18°19E **160** E18
Mellbystrand Sweden 56°30N 12°56E **163** H6
Melle Deux-Sèvres, France 46°14N 0°10W **174** B3
Melle Niedersachsen, Germany 52°12N 8°20E **178** C4
Mellen U.S.A. 46°20N 90°40W **308** B8
Mellerud Sweden 58°41N 12°28E **163** F6
Mellette U.S.A. 45°9N 98°30W **308** C4
Mellid = Melide Spain 42°55N 8°1W **194** C2
Mellieha Malta 35°57N 14°22E **206** F7
Mellieha Bay Malta 35°59N 14°22E **206** F7
Mellit Sudan 14°7N 25°34E **257** E2
Mellizo Sur, Cerro Chile 48°33S 73°10W **336** C2
Mellrichstadt Germany 50°25N 10°17E **178** E6
Mellunkylä Finland 60°14N 25°6E **121** B3
Mellunmäki Finland 60°14N 25°7E **121** B3
Melnik Bulgaria 41°30N 23°25E **202** E7
Mělník Czech Rep. 50°22N 14°23E **180** A7
Melo Uruguay 32°20S 54°10W **335** C5
Melolo Indonesia 9°53S 120°40E **231** F6
Melouprey Cambodia 13°48N 105°16E **236** F5
Melrhir, Chott Algeria 34°13N 6°30E **261** B6
Melrose N.S.W., Australia 32°42S 146°57E **283** B7
Melrose S. Austral., Australia 32°50S 146°32E **283** B4
Melrose Borders, U.K. 55°36N 2°43W **167** F6
Melrose Minn., U.S.A. 45°40N 94°49W **308** C6
Melrose N. Mex., U.S.A. 34°26N 103°38W **305** J12
Melrose N.Y., U.S.A. 40°49N 73°55W **132** B2
Melrose Park U.S.A. 41°53N 87°50W **119** B1
Mels Switz. 47°3N 9°25E **179** a5
Melsbroek Belgium 50°55N 4°29E **116** A2
Melsisi Vanuatu 15°46S 168°10E **287** E6
Melstone U.S.A. 46°36N 107°52W **304** C10
Melsungen Germany 51°7N 9°32E **178** D5
Melton Australia 37°41S 144°35E **282** D6
Melton Mowbray U.K. 52°47N 0°54W **168** E7
Melun France 48°32N 2°39E **173** D9
Melur India 10°2N 78°23E **245** J4
Melut Sudan 10°30N 32°13E **257** E3
Melville Sask., Canada 50°55N 102°50W **297** C8
Melville, C. Australia 14°11S 144°30E **280** A3
Melville, L. Canada 53°30N 60°0W **299** B8
Melville B. N. Terr., Australia 12°0S 136°45E **280** A2
Melville B. Greenland 75°30N 63°0W **294** B4
Melville I. N. Terr., Australia 11°30S 131°0E **278** A5
Melville I. Canada 75°30N 112°0W **296** B8
Melville Pen. Canada 68°0N 84°0W **295** C11
Melvin, Lough Ireland 54°26N 8°10W **166** B3
Mélykút Hungary 46°11N 19°25E **182** D4
Memaliaj Albania 40°25N 19°58E **202** F3
Memba Mozam. 14°11S 40°30E **269** E5
Memboro Indonesia 9°30S 119°30E **231** F5
Membrilla Spain 38°59N 3°21W **195** G7
Memel = Klaipėda Lithuania 55°43N 21°10E **184** A8
Memel S. Africa 27°38S 29°36E **271** C4
Memmingen Germany 47°58N 10°10E **179** H6
Mempawah Indonesia 0°30N 109°5E **235** B3
Memphis Mich., U.S.A. 42°54N 82°46W **312** D2
Memphis Tenn., U.S.A. 35°8N 90°3W **310** H6
Memphis Tex., U.S.A. 34°44N 100°33W **314** H4
Memphis Egypt 29°52N 31°12E **256** B7
Memphrémagog, L. N. Amer. 45°8N 72°17W **313** C12
Mena Ukraine 51°31N 32°15E **189** G7
Mena Ark., U.S.A. 34°35N 94°15W **314** H7
Mena → Ethiopia 5°40N 40°50E **257** F5
Menan = Chao Phraya → Thailand 13°40N 100°31E **236** F3
Menarandra → Madag. 25°17S 44°30E **273** K7
Menard U.S.A. 30°55N 99°47W **314** F5
Menard Fracture Zone Pac. Oc. 43°0S 97°0W **289** M18
Menate Indonesia 0°12S 113°3E **235** C4
Menawashei Sudan 12°41N 24°59E **257** E1
Mendaña Fracture Zone Pac. Oc. 16°0S 91°0W **289** J18
Mendawai → Indonesia 3°30S 113°0E **235** C4
Mende France 44°31N 3°30E **174** D7
Mendebo Mts. Ethiopia 7°0N 39°22E **257** F4
Mendeleyev Ridge Arctic 80°0N 178°0W **150** B17
Mendenhall, C. U.S.A. 59°45N 166°10W **303** D6
Menderes Turkey 38°14N 27°8E **205** D9
Mendez Mexico 25°7N 98°34W **319** B5
Mendhar India 33°35N 74°10E **243** C6
Mendi Ethiopia 9°47N 35°4E **257** F4
Mendi Papua N. G. 6°11S 143°39E **286** B2
Mendip Hills U.K. 51°17N 2°40W **169** F5
Mendocino U.S.A. 39°19N 123°48W **306** F3
Mendocino, C. U.S.A. 40°26N 124°25W **304** F1
Mendocino Fracture Zone Pac. Oc. 41°0S 140°0W **289** D13
Mendota Calif., U.S.A. 36°45N 120°23W **306** J6
Mendota Ill., U.S.A. 41°33N 89°7W **310** C7
Mendota, L. U.S.A. 43°6N 89°22W **310** A7
Mendoyo Indonesia 8°23S 114°42E **231** J17
Mendoza Argentina 32°50S 68°52W **334** C2
Mendoza □ Argentina 33°0S 69°0W **334** C2
Mene Grande Venezuela 9°49N 70°56W **328** B3
Menemen Turkey 38°34N 27°3E **205** D9
Menen Belgium 50°47N 3°7E **170** D3
Menfi Italy 37°36N 12°58E **201** E5
Mengdingjie China 23°37N 99°10E **228** E1
Mengeš Slovenia 46°10N 14°35E **199** B11
Menggala Indonesia 4°30S 105°15E **234** E3
Menghai China 21°49N 100°15E **228** F3
Mengibar Spain 37°58N 3°48W **195** H7
Mengjin China 34°55N 112°45E **229** B9
Mengla China 21°20N 101°12E **228** F3
Menglian China 22°21N 99°27E **228** F2
Mengshan China 24°14N 110°55E **229** E8
Mengyin China 35°40N 117°58E **227** G9
Mengzhe China 22°2N 100°15E **228** F3
Mengzi China 23°20N 103°22E **228** F5

Menihek Canada 54°28N 56°36W **299** B6
Menihek L. Canada 54°0N 67°0W **298** B6
Menin = Menen Belgium 50°47N 3°7E **170** D3
Menindee Australia 32°20S 142°25E **282** B5
Menindee L. Australia 32°20S 142°25E **282** B5
Meningie Australia 35°50S 139°18E **282** C3
Menjangan, Pulau Indonesia 8°7S 114°31E **231** J17
Menkrour Algeria 26°27N 8°9E **261** C6
Menlo Park U.S.A. 37°27N 122°12W **306** H4
Menominee U.S.A. 45°6N 87°37W **308** C10
Menominee → U.S.A. 45°6N 87°35W **308** C10
Menomonee Falls U.S.A. 43°11N 88°7W **311** A8
Menomonie U.S.A. 44°53N 91°55W **308** C8
Menongue Angola 14°48S 17°52E **265** E3
Menorca Spain 40°0N 4°0E **206** B5
Menorca ✈ (MAH) Spain 39°40N 4°16E **196** F5
Mentakab Malaysia 3°29N 102°21E **237** L4
Mentasta Lake U.S.A. 62°55N 143°45W **303** C12
Mentawai, Kepulauan Indonesia 2°0S 99°0E **234** C1
Menteng Indonesia 6°11S 106°49E **122** B1
Menton France 43°50N 7°29E **175** E11
Mentone U.S.A. 41°10N 86°2W **311** C10
Mentor U.S.A. 41°40N 81°21W **312** E3
Menyamya Papua N. G. 7°10S 145°59E **286** D3
Menzel-Bourguiba Tunisia 37°9N 9°49E **258** A1
Menzel-Chaker Tunisia 35°0N 10°26E **258** A1
Menzel-Temime Tunisia 36°46N 11°0E **258** A2
Menzelinsk Russia 55°47N 53°11E **186** C9
Menzies Australia 29°40S 121°2E **279** E3
Meob B. Namibia 24°25S 14°34E **270** B1
Me'ona Israel 33°1N 35°15E **250** E6
Meoqui Mexico 28°17N 105°29W **318** B3
Mepaco Mozam. 15°57S 30°48E **269** F3
Meppel Neths. 52°42N 6°12E **170** B6
Meppen Germany 52°41N 7°18E **178** C3
Mequinenza Spain 41°22N 0°17E **196** D5
Mequinenza, Embalse de Spain 41°25N 0°15E **196** D5
Mequon U.S.A. 43°14N 87°59W **311** A8
Mer France 47°42N 1°31E **172** E8
Merai Papua N. G. 4°52S 152°9E **287** d
Merak Indonesia 6°10N 106°26E **231** F12
Meråker Norway 63°25N 11°46E **164** A8
Meramangye, L. Australia 28°25S 132°13E **279** E5
Meramec → U.S.A. 38°24N 90°21W **310** F6
Meran = Merano Italy 46°40N 11°9E **199** B8
Merano Italy 46°40N 11°9E **199** B8
Mérantaise → France 48°42N 2°8E **134** B1
Merapi Indonesia 7°32S 110°26E **235** D4
Merate Italy 45°42N 9°25E **198** C6
Merauke Indonesia 8°29S 140°24E **231** F10
Merbabu Indonesia 7°30S 110°40E **235** D4
Merbein Australia 34°10S 142°2E **282** B5
Merbuk, Gunung Indonesia 8°13S 114°39E **231** J17
Merca Somali Rep. 1°48N 44°50E **267** D5
Mercadal Spain 40°21N 3°9W **127** B2
Mercantour △ France 44°10N 6°43E **175** D10
Mercato Saraceno Italy 43°57N 12°12E **199** E9
Merced U.S.A. 37°18N 120°29W **306** H6
Merced → U.S.A. 37°21N 120°59W **306** H6
Merced, L. U.S.A. 37°43N 122°29W **136** B2
Merced Pk. U.S.A. 37°36N 119°24W **306** H7
Mercedes B. Aires, Argentina 34°40S 59°30W **334** C4
Mercedes Corrientes, Argentina 29°10S 58°5W **334** B4
Mercedes San Luis, Argentina 33°40S 65°21W **334** C2
Mercedes Camarines N., Phil. 14°7N 123°1E **232** D4
Mercedes Uruguay 33°12S 58°0W **334** C4
Merceditas Chile 28°20S 70°35W **334** B1
Mercer N.Z. 37°16S 175°5E **284** D4
Mercer Mo., U.S.A. 40°31N 93°32W **310** D3
Mercer Pa., U.S.A. 41°14N 80°15W **312** E4
Mercer Island U.S.A. 47°34N 122°13W **306** D4
Merchandise Mart Chicago, U.S.A. **119** b1
Mercier Bolivia 13°14S **119** b1
Mercury U.S.A. 36°40N 115°59W **307** J11
Mercury B. N.Z. 36°48S 175°45E **284** C4
Mercury Is. N.Z. 36°37S 175°52E **284** C4
Mercy, C. Canada 65°0N 63°30W **295** C13
Merdrignac France 48°11N 2°27W **172** D4
Mere U.K. 51°6N 2°16W **169** F5
Mere Lava Vanuatu 14°25S 168°3E **287** D6
Meredith, C. Falk. Is. 52°15S 60°40W **153** f
Meredith, L. U.S.A. 35°43N 101°33W **305** H12
Meredosia U.S.A. 39°50N 90°34W **310** E6
Merefa Ukraine 49°48N 36°3E **189** H9
Meregh Somali Rep. 3°47N 47°18E **267** B5
Merei Romania 45°7N 26°43E **183** E11
Merga = Nukheila Sudan 19°1N 26°21E **256** D2
Mergui Burma 12°26N 98°34E **236** F2
Mergui Arch. = Myeik Kyunzu Burma 11°30N 97°30E **237** G1
Méribel-les-Allues France 45°25N 6°34E **175** C10
Meriç Turkey 41°11N 26°25E **203** E10
Meriç → Turkey 40°52N 26°12E **203** F10
Mérida Yucatán, Mexico 20°58N 89°37W **319** C7
Mérida Spain 38°55N 6°25W **195** G4
Mérida Venezuela 8°24N 71°8W **328** B3
Mérida □ Venezuela 8°30N 71°10W **328** B3
Mérida, Cord. de Venezuela 9°0N 71°0W **328** B3
Meriden W. Mids., U.K. 52°26N 1°38W **169** E6
Meriden Conn., U.S.A. 41°32N 72°48W **313** E12
Meridian Calif., U.S.A. 39°9N 121°55W **306** F5
Meridian Idaho, U.S.A. 43°37N 116°24W **304** E6
Meridian Miss., U.S.A. 32°22N 88°42W **315** E10
Mérignac France 44°51N 0°39W **174** D3
Merimbula Australia 36°53S 149°54E **283** D8
Merin Gubai Somali Rep. 10°44N 45°16E **267** B6
Mérinaghène Senegal 15°57N 15°15W **262** B1
Merinda Australia 20°3S 148°11E **280** C4
Mering Germany 48°16N 11°0E **179** G6
Meringa Nigeria 10°44N 12°59E **263** C7
Meringur Australia 34°20S 141°19E **282** B5
Merir Pac. Oc. 4°19N 132°18E **288** D3
Merirumã Brazil 1°15N 54°50W **329** C7
Merizo Guam 13°16N 144°40E **302** d
Merke Kazakhstan 42°52N 73°11E **217** C10
Merkel U.S.A. 32°28N 100°1W **314** E4
Merksem Belgium 51°16N 4°25E **116** a
Merkys → Lithuania 54°10N 24°10E **184** B9
Merlimau, Pulau Singapore 1°17N 103°42E **139** B2
Mermaid Reef Australia 17°6S 119°38E **278** C2
Mero → Dominica 15°25N 61°26W **323** f
Meroe Sudan 16°56N 33°10E **256** D3
Merowe Sudan 18°29N 31°46E **256** D3
Merowe Dam Sudan 18°45N 32°3E **256** D3
Merri Cr. → Australia 37°47S 144°59E **128** A4
Merrick U.K. 55°8N 4°28W **167** F4
Merrickville Canada 44°55N 75°50W **313** B9
Merrill Oreg., U.S.A. 42°1N 121°36W **304** E3

Miquelon St-P. & M. 47°8N 56°22W 299 C8
Mir Niger 14°5N 11°59E 259 F2
Mīr Kūh Iran 26°22N 58°55E 247 E8
Mīr Shahdād Iran 26°15N 58°29E 247 E8
Mira Italy 45°26N 12°8E 199 C9
Mira Portugal 40°26N 8°44W 194 E2
Mira → Colombia 1°36N 79°1W 328 C2
Mira → Portugal 37°43N 8°47W 195 H2
Mira por vos Cay Bahamas 22°9N 74°30W 321 B5
Mīrābād Afghan. 30°25N 61°50E 240 C1
Mirabella Eclano Italy 41°2N 14°59E 201 A7
Mirabello, Kolpos Greece 35°10N 25°50E 207 E6
Miracema do Norte Brazil 9°33S 48°24W 332 C2
Mirador Brazil 6°22S 44°22W 332 C3
Mirador-Río Azul △ Guatemala 17°45N 89°50W 320 C1
Miraflores = Rovira Colombia 4°15N 75°20W 328 C2
Miraflores Colombia 1°25N 72°13W 328 C3
Miraflores Lima, Peru 12°7S 77°2W 124 B2
Miraj India 16°50N 74°45E 244 F2
Miram Shah Pakistan 33°0N 70°2E 242 C4
Miramar Argentina 38°15S 57°50W 334 D4
Miramar Mozam. 23°50S 35°35E 271 B6
Miramar N.Z. 41°18S 174°49E 143 B1
Miramas France 43°33N 4°59E 175 E8
Mirambeau France 45°23N 0°35W 174 C3
Miramichi Canada 47°2N 65°28W 299 C6
Miramichi B. Canada 47°15N 65°0W 299 C7
Miramont-de-Guyenne France 44°37N 0°21E 174 D4
Miranda Brazil 20°10S 56°15W 331 E6
Miranda □ Venezuela 10°15N 66°25W 328 A4
Miranda → Brazil 19°25S 57°20W 331 D6
Miranda de Ebro Spain 42°41N 2°57W 196 C2
Miranda do Corvo Portugal 40°6N 8°20W 194 E2
Miranda do Douro Portugal 41°30N 6°16W 194 D4
Mirande France 43°31N 0°25E 174 E4
Mirandela Portugal 41°32N 7°10W 194 D3
Mirándola Italy 44°53N 11°4E 198 D8
Mirandópolis Brazil 21°9S 51°6W 335 A5
Mirango Malawi 13°32S 34°58E 269 E3
Mirani Australia 21°8S 148°53E 280 K6
Mirano Italy 45°30N 12°7E 199 C9
Miras Albania 40°30N 20°56E 202 F4
Mirassol Brazil 20°46S 49°28W 335 A6
Mirbāţ Oman 17°0N 54°45E 249 C6
Mirboo North Australia 38°24S 146°10E 283 F7
Mirear Egypt 23°15N 35°41E 256 C4
Mirebeau France 46°49N 0°10E 172 F7
Mirebeau-sur-Bèze France 47°25N 5°20E 173 E12
Mirecourt France 48°20N 6°10E 173 D13
Mires Greece 35°4N 24°56E 207 E5
Mirgorod = Myrhorod Ukraine 49°58N 33°37E 189 H7
Miri Malaysia 4°23N 113°59E 235 B4
Mirialguda India 16°52N 79°35E 244 F4
Miriam Vale Australia 24°20S 151°33E 280 C5
Miribel France 45°50N 4°57E 173 G11
Mirigama Sri Lanka 7°15N 80°8E 245 L5
Mirim, L. S. Amer. 32°45S 52°50W 335 C5
Mirimire Venezuela 11°10N 68°43W 328 A4
Miringoni Comoros Is. 12°17S 43°38E 272 a
Miriti Brazil 6°15S 59°0W 331 B6
Mīrjāveh Iran 29°1N 61°30E 247 D9
Mirnyy Antarctica 66°50S 92°30E 151 C14
Mirnyy Russia 62°33N 113°53E 215 C12
Miroč Serbia 44°32N 22°16E 202 B6
Mirokhan Pakistan 27°46N 68°6E 242 F3
Mirond L. Canada 55°6N 102°47W 297 B8
Mirosławiec Poland 53°20N 16°5E 184 E3
Mirpur Pakistan 33°32N 73°56E 243 C5
Mirpur Batoro Pakistan 24°44N 68°16E 242 G3
Mirpur Bibiwari Pakistan 28°33N 67°44E 242 E2
Mirpur Khas Pakistan 25°30N 69°0E 242 G3
Mirpur Sakro Pakistan 24°33N 67°41E 242 G2
Mirria Niger 13°43N 9°7E 259 F1
Mirrool Australia 34°19S 147°10E 283 C7
Mirs Bay = Tai Pang Wan China 22°33N 114°24E 219 F11
Mirsk Poland 50°58N 15°23E 185 H2
Mirtağ Turkey 38°23N 41°56E 246 C4
Mirtoo Sea Greece 37°0N 23°20E 204 D5
Mirtou, Kolpos Greece 38°20N 20°27E 207 C1
Miryang S. Korea 35°31N 128°44E 224 E4
Mirzaani Georgia 41°24N 46°5E 191 K8
Mirzachul = Guliston Uzbekistan 40°29N 68°46E 217 D7
Mirzapur India 25°10N 82°34E 243 G10
Mirzapur-cum-Vindhyachal = Mirzapur India 25°10N 82°34E 243 G10
Mirzoyan = Taraz Kazakhstan 42°54N 71°22E 217 D8
Misaki Japan 34°18N 135°9E 223 C7
Misamis = Ozamiz Phil. 8°15N 123°50E 233 G4
Misamis Occidental □ Phil. 8°20N 123°42E 233 G4
Misamis Oriental □ Phil. 8°45N 125°0E 233 G5
Misantla Mexico 19°56N 96°50W 319 D5
Misawa Japan 40°41N 141°24E 220 D10
Miscou I. Canada 47°57N 64°31W 299 C7
Misdroy = Międzyzdroje Poland 53°56N 14°26E 184 E1
Misericordia = Itaporanga Brazil 7°18S 38°0W 332 C4
Misericordia, Sa. da Brazil 22°51S 43°17W 135 B1
Misha India 7°59N 93°20E 245 L10
Mish'āb, Ra's al Si. Arabia 28°15N 48°43E 247 D6
Mishagua → Peru 11°12S 72°58W 330 C3
Mishan China 45°37N 131°48E 219 B8
Mishawaka U.S.A. 41°40N 86°11W 311 C10
Mishbih, Gebel Egypt 22°38N 34°44E 256 C3
Mishima Japan 35°10N 138°52E 223 B10
Mishmi Hills India 29°0N 96°0E 241 A6
Mishō Japan 32°57N 132°35E 222 E4
Misima I. Papua N. G. 10°40S 152°45E 286 F7
Misión Mexico 32°6N 116°53W 307 N10
Misión Fagnano Argentina 54°32S 67°17W 336 D3
Misiones □ Argentina 27°0S 55°0W 335 B5
Misiones □ Paraguay 27°0S 56°0W 334 B4
Miskah Si. Arabia 24°49N 42°56E 246 E4
Miskī, E. → Chad 20°0N 17°55E 259 E3
Miskitos, Cayos Nic. 14°26N 82°50W 320 D3
Miskolc Hungary 48°7N 20°50E 182 B5
Misoke Dem. Rep. of the Congo 0°42S 28°2E 268 C2
Misool Indonesia 1°52S 130°10E 231 E8
Miṣr = Egypt ■ Africa 28°0N 31°0E 256 B3
Miṣrātah Libya 32°24N 15°3E 258 B3
Miṣrātah □ Libya 33°30N 15°0E 258 C3
Missanabie Canada 48°20N 84°6W 298 C3
Missão Catrimani Brazil 2°48N 62°18W 329 C5
Missão Velha Brazil 7°15S 39°10W 332 C4
Missinaibi → Canada 50°43N 81°29W 298 B3
Missinaibi L. Canada 48°23N 83°40W 298 C3
Mission B.C., Canada 49°10N 122°15W 296 D4
Mission Calif., U.S.A. 37°44N 122°25W 136 B2
Mission S. Dak., U.S.A. 43°18N 100°39W 308 D3
Mission Tex., U.S.A. 26°13N 98°20W 314 H5
Mission Beach Australia 17°53S 146°6E 280 B4
Mission Viejo U.S.A. 33°36N 117°40W 307 M9
Missirah Senegal 13°40N 16°30W 262 C1
Missisa L. Canada 52°20N 85°7W 298 B2
Missisicabi → Canada 51°14N 79°31W 298 B4
Missisagi → Canada 46°15N 83°9W 298 C3
Mississauga Canada 43°32N 79°35W 141 B1
Mississinewa L. U.S.A. 40°42N 85°52W 311 D10
Mississippi □ U.S.A. 33°0N 90°0W 315 E10
Mississippi → U.S.A. 29°9N 89°15W 310 E5
Mississippi L. Canada 45°5N 76°10W 313 A8
Mississippi River Delta U.S.A. 29°10N 89°15W 315 G10
Mississippi Sd. U.S.A. 30°20N 89°0W 315 F10
Missoula U.S.A. 46°52N 114°1W 304 C6
Missour Morocco 33°3N 4°0W 260 B4
Missouri □ U.S.A. 38°25N 92°30W 310 E3
Missouri → U.S.A. 38°49N 90°7W 310 F6
Missouri City U.S.A. 29°37N 95°32W 314 G7
Missouri Valley U.S.A. 41°34N 95°53W 308 E6
Mist U.S.A. 45°59N 123°15W 306 E3
Mistassibi → Canada 48°53N 72°13W 299 B5
Mistassini → Canada 48°42N 72°20W 299 C5
Mistassini, L. Canada 51°0N 73°30W 298 B5
Mistastin L. Canada 55°57N 63°20W 299 A7
Mistelbach Austria 48°34N 16°34E 181 C9
Misterbianco Italy 37°31N 15°1E 201 E8
Misteriosa Bank W. Indies 18°50N 83°50W 320 C3
Misti, Volcán Peru 16°18S 71°24W 330 D3
Mistinibi, L. Canada 55°56N 64°17W 299 A7
Mistissini Canada 48°53N 72°12W 299 C5
Mistretta Italy 37°56N 14°22E 201 E7
Misty Fjords Nat. Monument △ U.S.A. 55°40N 130°40W 303 J15
Misty L. Canada 58°53N 101°40W 297 B8
Misugi Japan 34°31N 136°16E 223 C8
Misumi Japan 32°37N 130°27E 222 E2
Misurata = Miṣrātah Libya 32°24N 15°3E 258 B3
Mīt Ghamr Egypt 30°42N 31°12E 256 H7
Mitaka Japan 35°41N 139°34E 140 A2
Mitatib Sudan 15°59N 36°12E 257 D4
Mitau = Jelgava Latvia 56°41N 23°49E 184 B10
Mitava = Jelgava Latvia 56°41N 23°49E 184 B10
Mitcham U.K. 51°23N 0°10W 125 B2
Mitcham Common U.K. 51°23N 0°8W 125 B3
Mitchell Queens., Australia 26°29S 147°58E 281 D4
Mitchell Ont., Canada 43°28N 81°12W 312 C3
Mitchell Ga., U.S.A. 33°13N 82°42W 316 B7
Mitchell Ind., U.S.A. 38°44N 86°28W 311 F10
Mitchell Nebr., U.S.A. 41°57N 103°49W 308 E2
Mitchell Oreg., U.S.A. 44°34N 120°9W 304 D3
Mitchell S. Dak., U.S.A. 43°43N 98°2W 308 D4
Mitchell → Australia 15°12S 141°35E 280 B3
Mitchell, Mt. U.S.A. 35°46N 82°16W 315 D13
Mitchell-Alice Rivers △ Australia 15°28S 142°5E 280 B3
Mitchell Museum of the American Indian U.S.A. 42°4N 87°43W 119 A2
Mitchell Ra. Australia 12°49S 135°36E 280 A2
Mitchell River △ Australia 37°37S 147°22E 283 D7
Mitchell's Plain S. Africa 34°5S 18°35E 118 B2
Mitchelstown Ireland 52°15N 8°16W 166 D3
Mitha Tiwana Pakistan 32°13N 72°6E 242 C5
Mithi Pakistan 24°44N 69°48E 242 G3
Mithimna Greece 39°20N 26°12E 205 B8
Mithrao Pakistan 27°28N 69°40E 242 F3
Mitiamo Australia 36°12S 144°15E 282 D6
Mitikas Etoloakarnania, Greece 38°40N 20°56E 207 B2
Mitikas Preveza, Greece 39°0N 20°42E 207 B2
Mitilini Greece 39°6N 26°35E 205 B8
Mitilinii Greece 37°42N 26°56E 205 D8
Mitino Russia 55°51N 37°20E 129 A2
Mitla Pass = Mamarr Mitlā Egypt 30°2N 32°54E 251 H3
Mito Japan 36°20N 140°30E 223 A12
Mitra, Mt. Eq. Guin. 1°23N 9°19E 264 B1
Mitre, Mt. N.Z. 40°50S 175°30E 284 G4
Mitrofanovka Russia 49°58N 39°42E 189 H10
Mitrovica = Kosovska Mitrovica Serbia 42°54N 20°52E 202 D4
Mitrowitz = Sremska Mitrovica Serbia 44°59N 19°38E 182 F4
Mitsamiouli Comoros Is. 11°20S 43°16E 272 a
Mitsang Gabon 0°42N 12°33E 264 B2
Mitsinjo Madag. 16°1S 45°52E 272 B2
Mitsiwa Eritrea 15°35N 39°25E 257 D4
Mitsiwa Channel Eritrea 15°30N 40°0E 257 D5
Mitsoudjé Comoros Is. 11°48S 43°16E 272 a
Mitsukaidō Japan 36°1N 139°59E 223 A11
Mitsushima Japan 34°15N 129°20E 222 C1
Mittagong Australia 34°28S 150°29E 283 C9
Mitte Germany 52°32N 13°24E 115 A3
Mittel Isarkanal → Germany 48°12N 11°40E 131 A3
Mittel Schreiberhau = Szklarska Poreba Poland 50°50N 15°33E 185 H2
Mittelberg Austria 47°20N 10°10E 180 D3
Mittelfranken □ Germany 49°25N 10°40E 179 F6
Mittellandkanal → Germany 52°20N 8°28E 178 C4
Mittelwalde = Międzylesie Poland 50°8N 16°40E 185 H3
Mittenwalde Germany 52°15N 13°31E 178 C9
Mittersill Austria 47°16N 12°29E 180 D5
Mitterteich Germany 49°57N 12°14E 179 F8
Mittimatalik = Pond Inlet Canada 72°40N 77°0W 295 B12
Mittweida Germany 50°59N 12°59E 178 E8
Mitú Colombia 1°15N 70°13W 328 C3
Mituas Colombia 3°52N 68°49W 328 C4
Mitumba Tanzania 7°8S 31°2E 268 D3
Mitumba, Mts. Dem. Rep. of the Congo 7°0S 27°30E 268 D2
Mitwaba Dem. Rep. of the Congo 8°2S 27°17E 269 D2
Mityana Uganda 0°23N 32°2E 268 B3
Mitzic Gabon 0°45N 11°40E 264 B2
Miura Japan 35°12N 139°40E 223 B11
Mixcoac Mexico 19°23N 99°11W 128 B1
Mixteco → Mexico 18°11N 98°30W 319 D5
Miyagi □ Japan 38°15N 140°45E 220 E10
Miyāh, W. el → Egypt 25°0N 33°23E 256 C3
Miyāh, W. el → Syria 34°44N 39°57E 246 C3
Miyake-Jima Japan 34°5N 139°30E 223 C11
Miyako Japan 39°40N 141°59E 220 E10
Miyako-Jima Japan 24°45N 125°20E 221 M2
Miyako-Rettō Japan 24°24N 125°0E 221 M2
Miyakojima Japan 34°42N 135°31E 133 A2
Miyakonojō Japan 31°40N 131°5E 222 F3
Miyani India 21°50N 69°26E 242 J3
Miyanojō Japan 31°54N 130°27E 222 F2
Miyanoura-Dake Japan 30°20N 130°31E 221 J5
Miyata Japan 33°49N 130°42E 222 D2
Miyazaki Japan 31°56N 131°30E 222 F3
Miyazaki □ Japan 32°30N 131°30E 222 E3
Miyazu Japan 35°35N 135°10E 223 B7
Miyet, Bahr el = Dead Sea Asia 31°30N 35°30E 251 G6
Miyi China 26°47N 102°9E 228 D4
Miyoshi Japan 34°48N 132°51E 222 C4
Miyun China 40°28N 116°50E 226 D9
Miyun Shuiku China 40°30N 117°0E 227 D9
Mizan Teferi Ethiopia 6°57N 35°35E 257 F4
Mizdah Libya 31°30N 13°0E 258 B2
Mizen Hd. Cork, Ireland 51°27N 9°50W 166 E2
Mizen Hd. Wicklow, Ireland 52°51N 6°4W 166 D5
Mizhhirya Ukraine 48°32N 23°30E 183 B8
Mizhi China 37°47N 110°12E 226 F6
Mizil Romania 44°59N 26°29E 183 F11
Mizo Hills = Mizoram □ India 23°30N 92°40E 241 D4
Mizonokuchi Japan 35°35N 139°34E 140 B2
Mizoram □ India 23°30N 92°40E 241 D4
Mizpe Ramon Israel 30°34N 34°49E 251 H5
Mizue Japan 35°41N 139°54E 140 A4
Mizuho Antarctica 70°30S 41°0E 151 D5
Mizuho Japan 35°6N 135°17E 223 B7
Mizunami Japan 35°22N 137°15E 223 B9
Mizusawa Japan 39°8N 141°8E 220 E10
Mjällby Sweden 56°3N 14°40E 163 H8
Mjöbäck Sweden 57°28N 12°53E 163 G6
Mjölby Sweden 58°20N 15°10E 163 F9
Mjølfjell Norway 60°41N 6°55E 164 D3
Mjømna Norway 60°55N 4°55E 164 D1
Mjörn Sweden 57°55N 12°25E 163 G6
Mjøsa Norway 60°40N 11°0E 164 D8
Mkata Tanzania 5°45S 38°20E 268 D4
Mkhaya △ Swaziland 26°34S 31°45E 271 C5
Mkhuze △ S. Africa 29°27S 29°30E 271 C4
Mkokotoni Tanzania 5°55S 39°15E 268 D4
Mkomazi Tanzania 4°40S 38°7E 268 C4
Mkomazi → S. Africa 30°12S 30°50E 271 D5
Mkomazi △ Tanzania 4°4S 30°2E 268 C3
Mkulwe Tanzania 8°37S 32°20E 269 D3
Mkumbi, Ras Tanzania 7°38S 39°55E 268 D4
Mkushi Zambia 14°25S 29°15E 269 E2
Mkushi River Zambia 13°32S 29°45E 269 E2
Mkuze S. Africa 27°10S 32°0E 271 C5
Mladá Boleslav Czech Rep. 50°27N 14°53E 180 A7
Mladenovac Serbia 44°28N 20°44E 202 B4
Mlala Hills Tanzania 6°50S 31°40E 268 D3
Mlange = Mulanje Malawi 16°2S 35°33E 269 F4
Mlava → Serbia 44°45N 21°13E 202 B5
Mława Poland 53°9N 20°25E 185 E7
Mlawula △ Swaziland 26°12S 32°2E 271 C5
Mliniště Bos.-H. 44°15N 16°50E 199 D13
Mljet Croatia 42°43N 17°30E 199 F14
Mljet △ Croatia 42°45N 17°25E 199 F14
Mljetski Kanal Croatia 42°48N 17°35E 199 F14
Mlocinski Park Poland 52°19N 20°57E 142 B1
Młociny Poland 52°18N 20°55E 142 B1
Mlynary Poland 54°12N 19°46E 184 D6
Mmabatho S. Africa 25°49S 25°30E 270 C4
Mme Cameroon 6°18N 10°14E 263 D7
Mnevniki Russia 55°45N 37°28E 129 B2
Mnichovo Hradiště Czech Rep. 50°32N 14°59E 180 A7
Mo Hordaland, Norway 60°49N 5°48E 164 D2
Mo Møre og Romsdal, Norway 63°0N 8°59E 164 A5
Mo Telemark, Norway 59°28N 7°50E 164 E4
Mo i Rana Norway 66°20N 14°7E 160 C16
Moa Cuba 20°40N 74°56W 321 B4
Moa Indonesia 8°0S 128°0E 231 F7
Moa → S. Leone 6°59N 11°36W 262 D2
Moa, I. Papua N. G. 10°10S 142°15E 286 F2
Moab U.S.A. 38°35N 109°33W 304 G9
Moabi Gabon 2°24S 10°59E 264 C2
Moaco → Brazil 7°41S 68°18W 330 B4
Moala Fiji 18°36S 179°53E 287 B2
Moama Australia 36°7S 144°46E 281 F3
Moamba Mozam. 25°36S 32°15E 271 C5
Moapa U.S.A. 36°40N 114°37W 307 J12
Moate Ireland 53°24N 7°44W 166 C4
Moba Dem. Rep. of the Congo 7°0S 29°48E 268 D2
Moba Lagos, Nigeria 6°26N 3°28E 124 B2
Mobara Japan 35°25N 140°18E 223 B12
Mobārakābād Iran 28°24N 53°20E 247 D7
Mobaye C.A.R. 4°25N 21°5E 264 B4
Mobayi Dem. Rep. of the Congo 4°15N 21°8E 264 B4
Mobeka Dem. Rep. of the Congo 1°52N 19°49E 264 B3
Mobenzélé Congo 0°56N 17°50E 264 B3
Moberley Lake Canada 55°50N 121°44W 296 B4
Moberly U.S.A. 39°25N 92°26W 310 E4
Mobile U.S.A. 30°41N 88°3W 315 F10
Mobile B. U.S.A. 30°30N 88°0W 315 F11
Mobridge U.S.A. 45°32N 100°26W 308 C3
Mobutu Sese Seko, L. = Albert, L. Africa 1°30N 31°0E 268 B3
Moc Chau Vietnam 20°50N 104°38E 236 B5
Moc Hoa Vietnam 10°46N 105°56E 237 G5
Moca Puerto Rico 18°24N 67°10W 321 d
Mocaba, Sa. de Angola 7°12S 15°0E 265 D3
Mocabe Kasari Dem. Rep. of the Congo 9°58S 26°12E 269 D2
Mocajuba Brazil 2°35S 49°30W 332 B2
Moçambique = Mozambique ■ Africa 19°0S 35°0E 269 F4
Moçambique Mozam. 15°3S 40°42E 269 F5
Moçâmedes = Namibe Angola 15°7S 12°11E 265 F2
Mocanaqua U.S.A. 41°9N 76°8W 313 E8
Mocapra → Venezuela 7°56N 66°46W 328 B4
Moce Fiji 18°40S 178°29W 287 B3
Mocha = Al Mukhā Yemen 13°18N 43°15E 248 D3
Mocha, I. Chile 38°22S 73°56W 336 A2
Mochos Greece 35°16N 25°27E 207 E6
Mochudi Botswana 24°27S 26°7E 270 B4
Mocimboa da Praia Mozam. 11°25S 40°20E 269 E5
Mociu Romania 46°46N 24°3E 183 D9
Möckeln Sweden 56°40N 14°15E 163 H8
Mockfjärd Sweden 60°30N 14°57E 162 D8
Moclips U.S.A. 47°14N 124°13W 306 C2
Mocoa Colombia 1°7N 76°35W 328 C2
Mococa Brazil 21°28S 47°0W 335 A6
Mocorito Mexico 25°29N 107°55W 318 B3
Moctezuma Mexico 29°48N 109°42W 318 B3
Moctezuma → Mexico 21°59N 98°34W 319 C5
Mocuba Mozam. 16°54S 36°57E 269 F4
Moczydło Poland 52°8N 21°2E 142 C2
Moda Burma 24°22N 96°29E 241 C6
Modane France 45°12N 6°40E 175 C10
Modasa India 23°30N 73°21E 242 H5
Modder → S. Africa 29°2S 24°37E 270 C3
Modderfontein = Niekerkshoop S. Africa 29°19S 22°51E 270 C3
Modderfontein S. Africa 26°5S 28°10E 123 A2
Modderrivier S. Africa 29°2S 24°38E 270 C3
Módena Italy 44°40N 10°55E 198 D7
Modena Utah, U.S.A. 37°48N 113°56W 305 H7
Modernamuseet Stockholm, Sweden 139 b3
Modesto U.S.A. 37°39N 121°0W 306 H6
Möðrudalur Iceland 65°22N 15°53W 155 B11
Möðruvellir Iceland 65°46N 18°15W 155 B8
Módica Italy 36°52N 14°46E 201 F7
Modimolle S. Africa 24°42S 28°22E 271 B4
Modjadjiskloof S. Africa 23°42S 30°10E 271 B5
Modjamboli Dem. Rep. of the Congo 2°28N 22°6E 264 B4
Mödling Austria 48°5N 16°17E 181 C9
Modo Sudan 5°31N 30°33E 257 F3
Modoc U.S.A. 33°44N 82°13W 316 B7
Modra Slovak Rep. 48°19N 17°20E 181 C10
Modřany Czech Rep. 50°0N 14°24E 135 B2
Modriča Bos.-H. 44°57N 18°17E 182 F3
Moe Australia 38°12S 146°19E 283 E7
Moebase Mozam. 17°3S 38°41E 269 F4
Moëlan-sur-Mer France 47°49N 3°38W 172 E3
Moelv Norway 60°56N 10°43E 164 D7
Moen I. = Weno Pac. Oc. 7°27N 151°52E 287 T18
Moengo Suriname 5°45N 54°20W 329 B7
Moerewa N.Z. 35°8S 174°1E 284 B3
Moffat U.K. 55°21N 3°27W 167 F5
Moga India 30°48N 75°8E 242 D6
Mogadishu = Muqdisho Somali Rep. 2°2N 45°25E 267 D6
Mogador = Essaouira Morocco 31°32N 9°42W 260 B3
Mogadouro Portugal 41°22N 6°47W 194 D4
Mogalakwena → S. Africa 22°38S 28°40E 271 B4
Mogami-Gawa → Japan 38°45N 140°0E 220 E10
Mogán Canary Is. 27°53N 15°43W 153 e1
Mogandjo Dem. Rep. of the Congo 1°23N 24°15E 264 B4
Mogaung Burma 25°20N 97°0E 241 C6
Mogen Norway 60°2N 7°52E 164 D4
Mogente = Moixent Spain 38°52N 0°45W 197 G4
Mogho Ethiopia 4°54N 40°16E 257 G5
Mogi das Cruzes Brazil 23°31S 46°11W 335 A6
Mogi-Guaçu → Brazil 20°53S 48°10W 335 A6
Mogi-Mirim Brazil 22°29S 47°0W 335 A6
Mogielnica Poland 51°42N 20°41E 185 G7
Mogige Ethiopia 5°24N 36°14E 257 F4
Mogilev = Mahilyow Belarus 53°55N 30°18E 177 B16
Mogilev-Podolskiy = Mohyliv-Podilskyy Ukraine 48°26N 27°48E 183 B12
Mogilno Poland 52°39N 17°55E 185 F4
Mogincual Mozam. 15°35S 40°25E 269 F5
Mogliano Véneto Italy 45°33N 12°14E 199 C9
Mogocha Russia 53°40N 119°50E 215 D12
Mogok Burma 23°0N 96°40E 241 D6
Mogollon Rim U.S.A. 34°10N 110°50W 305 J8
Mógoro Italy 39°41N 8°47E 200 C1
Mograt Sudan 19°28N 33°16E 256 D3
Mogroum Chad 11°6N 15°25E 259 F3
Moguer Spain 37°15N 6°52W 195 H4
Mogumber Australia 31°2S 116°3E 279 F2
Mogwadi → S. Africa 23°4S 29°36E 271 B4
Mogyoród Hungary 47°35N 19°14E 117 A3
Mohács Hungary 45°58N 18°41E 182 E3
Mohaka → N.Z. 39°7S 177°12E 284 F6
Mohala India 20°35N 80°44E 244 D5
Mohales Hoek Lesotho 30°7S 27°26E 270 D4
Mohali Congo 0°15N 15°29E 264 B3
Mohall U.S.A. 48°46N 101°31W 308 A3
Moḥammadābād Iran 37°52N 59°5E 247 B8
Mohammadia Algeria 35°33N 0°3E 261 A5
Mohammedia Morocco 33°44N 7°21W 260 B3
Mohammerah = Khorrāmshahr Iran 30°29N 48°15E 247 D6
Mohana India 19°27N 84°16E 244 E7
Mohana → India 24°43N 85°0E 243 G11
Mohanganj Bangla. 24°54N 90°59E 241 C3
Mohanlalganj India 26°41N 80°58E 243 F9
Mohave, L. U.S.A. 35°12N 114°34W 307 K12
Mohawk → U.S.A. 42°47N 73°41W 313 D11
Moheda Sweden 57°1N 14°35E 163 G8
Mohéli Comoros Is. 12°20S 43°40E 272 a
Mohéli ✕ (NWA) Comoros Is. 12°19S 43°47E 272 a
Mohenjodaro Pakistan 27°19N 68°7E 242 F3
Moher, Cliffs of Ireland 52°58N 9°27W 166 D2
Mohican, C. U.S.A. 60°12N 167°25W 303 F6
Mohicanville Res. U.S.A. 40°45N 82°9W 312 F2
Möhne → Germany 51°29N 7°57E 178 D3
Mohns Ridge Arctic 72°30N 5°0W 150 B7
Mohnyin Burma 24°47N 96°22E 241 C6
Mohoro Tanzania 8°6S 39°8E 268 D4
Mohrin = Moryń Poland 52°51N 14°22E 185 F1
Mohyliv-Podilskyy Ukraine 48°26N 27°48E 183 B12
Moi Norway 58°27N 6°32E 164 F3
Moia Sudan 5°3N 28°2E 257 F2
Moidart, L. U.K. 56°47N 5°52W 167 E3
Moinabad India 17°44N 77°16E 244 F3
Moineşti Romania 46°28N 26°31E 183 D11
Moinho Velho, Cor. Brazil 23°35S 46°35W 137 B2
Moira → Canada 44°21N 77°24W 312 B7
Moirang India 24°30N 93°46E 241 C4
Moirans France 45°20N 5°33E 175 C9
Moirans-en-Montagne France 46°26N 5°43E 173 F12
Moisaküla Estonia 58°3N 25°12E 188 C3
Moisie Canada 50°12N 66°1W 299 B6
Moisie → Canada 50°14N 66°5W 299 B6
Moissac France 44°7N 1°5E 174 D5
Moïssala Chad 8°21N 17°46E 259 G3
Moita Portugal 38°38N 8°58W 195 G2
Moixent Spain 38°52N 0°45W 197 G4
Mója Sweden 59°26N 18°55E 162 E12
Mojácar Spain 37°6N 1°55W 197 H3
Mojados Spain 41°26N 4°40W 194 D6
Mojave U.S.A. 35°3N 118°10W 307 K8
Mojave → U.S.A. 35°7N 115°32W 307 K11
Mojave Desert U.S.A. 35°0N 116°30W 307 L10
Mojiang China 23°37N 101°35E 228 F3
Mojo → Ethiopia 7°55N 42°0E 257 F5
Mojkovac Montenegro 42°58N 19°35E 202 D3
Mojo Bolivia 21°48S 65°33W 334 A2
Mojo Ethiopia 8°35N 39°5E 257 F4
Mojokerto Indonesia 7°28S 112°26E 235 D4
Mojos, Llanos de Bolivia 15°10S 65°0W 331 D5
Moju Brazil 1°53S 48°46W 332 B2
Moju → Brazil 1°40S 48°25W 332 B2
Mok S. Korea 37°32N 126°52E 137 B1
Moka Mauritius 20°13S 57°29E 272 e
Mokai N.Z. 38°32S 175°56E 284 E4
Mokambo Dem. Rep. of the Congo 12°25S 28°20E 269 E2
Mokameh India 25°24N 85°55E 243 G11
Mokane U.S.A. 38°41N 91°53W 310 F5
Mōkapu Peninsula U.S.A. 21°25N 157°45W 302 K14
Mokau N.Z. 38°42S 174°39E 284 E3
Mokau → N.Z. 38°35S 174°35E 284 E3
Mokelumne → U.S.A. 38°13N 121°28W 306 G5
Mokelumne Hill U.S.A. 38°18N 120°43W 306 G6
Mokhotlong Lesotho 29°22S 29°2E 271 C4
Mokihinui → N.Z. 41°33S 171°58E 285 B6
Möklinta Sweden 60°4N 16°33E 162 D10
Moknine Tunisia 35°35N 10°58E 258 A2
Mokoan, L. Australia 36°27S 146°5E 283 D7
Mokokchung India 26°15N 94°30E 241 B5
Mōkōlea Rock U.S.A. 21°27N 157°44W 302 K14
Mokolo Cameroon 10°49N 13°54E 259 F2
Mokolo Dem. Rep. of the Congo 1°55N 18°6E 264 B3
Mokolo → S. Africa 23°14S 27°43E 271 B4
Mokombe Dem. Rep. of the Congo 0°14S 23°48E 264 C4
Mokopane S. Africa 24°10S 28°55E 271 B4
Mokotów Poland 52°12N 21°0E 142 B2
Mokpalin Burma 17°26N 96°53E 241 G6
Mokpo S. Korea 34°50N 126°25E 224 E3
Mokra Gora Europe 42°50N 20°30E 202 D4
Mokronog Slovenia 45°57N 15°9E 199 C12
Moksha → Russia 54°45N 41°53E 190 C6
Mokshan Russia 53°25N 44°35E 190 D7
Mokuauia I. U.S.A. 21°40N 157°56W 302 J14
Mokulua Is. U.S.A. 21°24N 157°42W 302 K14
Mokumanu U.S.A. 21°28N 157°43W 302 K14
Mokwa Nigeria 9°19N 5°0E 263 D6
Mol Belgium 51°11N 5°5E 170 C5
Mola di Bari Italy 41°4N 17°5E 201 A10
Molai Greece 36°49N 22°56E 204 E4
Molakalmuru India 14°55N 76°50E 245 G3
Molale Ethiopia 10°10N 39°41E 257 E4
Molaly Kazakhstan 45°27N 78°18E 217 C9
Molanda Dem. Rep. of the Congo 2°28N 20°48E 264 B4
Molara Italy 40°52N 9°43E 200 B2
Molat Croatia 44°15N 14°50E 199 D11
Molave Phil. 8°5N 123°30E 233 G4
Molchanovo Russia 57°40N 83°50E 214 D9
Mold U.K. 53°9N 3°8W 168 D4
Moldava nad Bodvou Slovak Rep. 48°38N 21°0E 181 C14
Moldavia = Moldova ■ Europe 47°0N 28°0E 183 C13
Moldavia Romania 46°30N 27°0E 183 D12
Molde Norway 62°45N 7°9E 164 B4
Moldova ■ Europe 47°0N 28°0E 183 C13
Moldova Nouă Romania 44°45N 21°41E 182 F6
Moldoveanu, Vf. Romania 45°36N 24°45E 183 E9
Moldoviţa Romania 47°41N 25°32E 183 C10
Mole → U.K. 51°24N 0°21W 169 F7
Mole △ Ghana 9°43N 1°44W 263 D4
Mole Creek Australia 41°34S 146°24E 281 G4
Molegbwe Dem. Rep. of the Congo 4°12N 20°53E 264 B4
Molenbeek-St-Jean Belgium 50°51N 4°19E 117 A1
Molepolole Botswana 24°28S 25°28E 270 B4
Molesworth N.Z. 42°5S 173°16E 285 C8
Molfetta Italy 41°12N 16°36E 201 A9
Mōli'i Pond U.S.A. 21°31N 157°51W 302 J14
Molina de Aragón Spain 40°46N 1°52W 196 E3
Molina de Segura Spain 38°3N 1°12W 197 G3
Moline U.S.A. 41°30N 90°31W 310 C6
Molinella Italy 44°37N 11°40E 199 D8
Molino U.S.A. 30°43N 87°20W 317 E2
Molino de Rosas Mexico 19°21N 99°14W 128 B1
Molinos Argentina 25°28S 66°15W 334 B2
Moliro Dem. Rep. of the Congo 8°12S 30°30E 268 D3
Moliterno Italy 40°14N 15°52E 201 B8
Molkom Sweden 59°37N 13°44E 162 E7
Mölle Sweden 56°17N 12°31E 163 H6
Molledo Spain 43°8N 4°6W 194 B6
Mollem Belgium 50°56N 4°13E 116 A1
Mollendo Peru 17°0S 72°0W 330 D3
Mollerin, L. Australia 30°30S 117°35E 279 F2
Mollerussa Spain 41°37N 0°54E 196 D5
Mollina Spain 37°8N 4°38W 195 H6
Mollins de Rey Spain 41°24N 2°1E 114 A1
Mölln Germany 53°39N 10°32E 178 B6
Mölltorp Sweden 58°30N 14°26E 163 F8
Mölnlycke Sweden 57°40N 12°8E 163 G6
Molo Burma 23°22N 96°53E 241 D6
Molo Rift Valley, Kenya 0°15S 35°44E 268 C4
Molochansk Ukraine 47°15N 35°35E 189 J8
Molochnoye, Ozero Ukraine 46°30N 35°20E 189 J8
Molodechno = Maladzyechna Belarus 54°20N 26°50E 177 A14
Molodezhnaya Antarctica 67°40S 45°51E 151 C9
Molodove Ukraine 46°13N 29°39E 183 D14
Moloka'i U.S.A. 21°8N 157°0W 302 B4
Molokai Fracture Zone Pac. Oc. 28°0N 125°0W 289 E15
Molokini I. U.S.A. 20°38N 156°30W 302 C5
Molong Australia 33°5S 148°54E 283 B8
Molopo → Africa 28°30S 20°12E 270 C3
Molos Greece 38°47N 22°37E 204 C4
Molotov = Perm Russia 58°0N 56°10E 186 C10
Molotov, Mys = Arktichesky, Mys Russia 81°10N 95°0E 215 A10
Molotovsk = Nolinsk Russia 57°28N 49°57E 190 B9
Molotovsk = Severodvinsk Russia 64°27N 39°58E 186 B6
Molotovskoye = Krasnogvardeyskoye Russia 45°52N 41°33E 191 H5
Moloundou Cameroon 2°8N 15°15E 264 B3
Molowaie Dem. Rep. of the Congo 5°47S 23°18E 265 D4
Molsheim France 48°33N 7°29E 173 D14
Molson L. Canada 54°22N 96°40W 297 C9
Molteno S. Africa 31°22S 26°22E 270 D4
Molu Indonesia 6°45S 131°40E 231 F8
Molucca Sea Indonesia 0°0 125°0E 231 E6
Moluccas = Maluku Indonesia 1°0S 127°0E 231 E7
Molundo Phil. 7°57N 124°23E 233 H5
Moma Dem. Rep. of the Congo 1°35S 23°52E 264 C4
Moma Mozam. 16°47S 39°4E 269 F4
Momba Australia 30°58S 143°30E 282 A5
Mombaça Brazil 5°43S 39°45W 332 C4
Mombango Dem. Rep. of the Congo 1°45N 24°26E 264 B4
Mombasa Kenya 4°3S 39°40E 268 C4
Mombetsu Japan 44°21N 143°22E 220 B11
Mombil Burma 27°46N 98°6E 241 B7
Momboyo → Dem. Rep. of the Congo 0°16S 19°0E 264 C3
Mombuey Spain 42°3N 6°20W 194 C4
Momchilgrad Bulgaria 41°33N 25°23E 203 E9
Momence U.S.A. 41°10N 87°40W 311 C9
Momi Dem. Rep. of the Congo 1°42S 27°0E 268 C2
Momote Papua N. G. 2°4S 147°27E 286 B4
Mompog Pass Phil. 13°34N 122°13E 232 E4
Mompós Colombia 9°14N 74°26W 328 B3
Møn Denmark 54°57N 12°20E 163 K6
Mon Hordaland, Norway 60°39N 6°31E 164 D3
Mon □ Burma 16°0N 97°30E 241 G6
Mona, Canal de la = Mona Passage W. Indies 18°30N 67°45W 321 C6
Mona, Isla Puerto Rico 18°5N 67°54W 321 C6
Mona, Pta. Costa Rica 9°37N 82°36W 320 E3
Mona Passage W. Indies 18°30N 67°45W 321 C6
Mona Quimbundo Angola 9°55S 19°58E 265 D3
Monaca U.S.A. 40°41N 80°17W 312 F4
Monaco ■ Europe 43°46N 7°23E 175 E11
Monadhliath Mts. U.K. 57°10N 4°4W 167 D4
Monadnock, Mt. U.S.A. 42°52N 72°7W 313 D12
Monagas □ Venezuela 9°20N 63°0W 329 B5
Monaghan Ireland 54°15N 6°57W 166 B5
Monaghan □ Ireland 54°11N 6°56W 166 B5
Monahans U.S.A. 31°36N 102°54W 314 F3
Monapo Mozam. 14°56S 40°19E 269 E5
Monar, L. U.K. 57°26N 5°8W 167 D3
Monaragala Sri Lanka 6°52N 81°22E 245 L5
Monarch Mt. Canada 51°55N 125°57W 296 C3
Monashee Mts. Canada 51°0N 118°43W 296 C5
Monasterevin Ireland 53°8N 7°4W 166 C4
Monastir = Bitola Macedonia 41°1N 21°20E 202 E5
Monastir Tunisia 35°50N 10°49E 258 A2
Monastir □ Tunisia 35°37N 10°45E 261 A7
Moncada Phil. 15°44N 120°34E 232 D3
Moncalieri Italy 45°0N 7°41E 198 D4
Moncalvo Italy 45°3N 8°16E 198 C5
Monção Portugal 42°4N 8°27W 194 C2
Moncarapacho Portugal 37°5N 7°46W 195 H3
Moncayo, Sierra del Spain 41°48N 1°50W 196 D3
Moncha-Guba = Monchegorsk Russia 67°54N 32°58E 160 C25
Monchegorsk Russia 67°54N 32°58E 160 C25
Mönchengladbach Germany 51°11N 6°27E 178 D2
Monchique Portugal 37°19N 8°38W 195 H2
Moncks Corner U.S.A. 33°12N 80°1W 316 B9
Monclova Mexico 26°54N 101°25W 318 B4
Moncontour France 48°22N 2°38W 172 D4
Moncton Canada 46°7N 64°51W 299 C7
Mondariz Spain 42°14N 8°27W 194 C2
Mondego → Portugal 40°9N 8°52W 194 E2
Mondego, C. Portugal 40°11N 8°54W 194 E2
Mondeodo Indonesia 3°34S 122°9E 231 E6
Mondeor S. Africa 26°16S 28°0E 123 B2
Mondeville France 49°10N 0°18W 172 C6
Mondimbi Dem. Rep. of the Congo 1°48N 22°46E 264 B4
Mondjuku Dem. Rep. of the Congo 1°41S 21°12E 264 C4
Mondo Chad 13°47N 15°32E 259 F3
Mondolfo Italy 43°45N 13°6E 199 E10
Mondoñedo Spain 43°25N 7°23W 194 B3
Mondovì Italy 44°23N 7°49E 198 D4
Mondragon Phil. 12°31N 124°45E 232 E5
Mondragone Italy 41°7N 13°53E 200 A6
Mondrain I. Australia 34°9S 122°14E 279 F3
Moneague Jamaica 18°16N 77°7W 320 a
Moneda, Palacio de la Chile 33°26S 70°39W 137 B2
Monemvasia Greece 36°41N 23°3E 204 E5
Monerό Brazil 22°48S 43°11W 135 A1
Moneron, Ostrov Russia 46°15N 141°16E 220 A10
Monessen U.S.A. 40°9N 79°54W 312 F5
Monesterio Spain 38°6N 6°15W 195 G4
Monestier-de-Clermont France 44°55N 5°38E 175 D9
Monett U.S.A. 36°55N 93°55W 308 G7
Moneymore U.K. 54°41N 6°40W 166 B5
Monfalcone Italy 45°49N 13°32E 199 C10
Monflanquin France 44°32N 0°47E 174 D4
Monforte Portugal 39°6N 7°25W 195 F3
Monforte de Lemos Spain 42°31N 7°33W 194 C3
Mong Cai Vietnam 21°27N 107°54E 236 B6
Mong Hsu Burma 21°54N 98°30E 228 G2
Mong Hta Burma 19°50N 98°35E 241 F7
Mong Ket Burma 23°8N 98°22E 241 D7
Mong Kok China 22°19N 114°10E 122 B2
Mong Kung Burma 21°35N 97°35E 241 E6
Mong Kyawt Burma 19°56N 98°45E 241 F7
Mong Long Burma 22°47N 96°37E 241 D6
Mong Mit Burma 23°7N 96°41E 241 D6
Mong Nai Burma 20°32N 97°46E 241 E6
Mong Pan Burma 20°19N 98°22E 241 E7
Mong Ping Burma 21°22N 99°2E 228 G2
Mong Pu Burma 20°55N 98°44E 241 E7
Mong Ton Burma 20°17N 98°45E 241 E7
Mong Tung Burma 22°2N 97°41E 241 D6
Mong Yai Burma 22°21N 98°3E 241 D7
Mong Yu Burma 23°30N 97°47E 241 D6
Monga Dem. Rep. of the Congo 4°12N 22°49E 264 B4
Mongala → Dem. Rep. of the Congo 1°53N 19°46E 264 B3
Mongalla Sudan 5°8N 31°42E 257 F3
Mongandia Congo 0°45N 17°11E 264 B3
Mongers, L. Australia 29°25S 117°5E 279 E2
Mongga Solomon Is. 7°52S 157°0E 287 L9
Monghyr = Munger India 25°23N 86°30E 243 G12
Mongibello = Etna Italy 37°50N 14°55E 201 E7
Mongla Bangla. 22°8N 89°35E 241 D2
Mongmong Guam 13°28N 144°45E 302 d
Mongngaw Burma 22°47N 96°59E 241 D6
Mongo Chad 12°14N 18°43E 259 F3
Mongó Eq. Guin. 1°52N 10°10E 264 B2
Mongo → S. Leone 9°35N 12°10W 262 D2
Mongolia ■ Asia 47°0N 103°0E 218 B5
Mongolia, Plateau of Asia 45°0N 105°0E 210 D12
Mongomo Eq. Guin. 1°38N 11°19E 264 B2
Mongonu Nigeria 12°40N 13°32E 263 C7
Mongororo Chad 12°3N 22°26E 259 F4
Mongstad Norway 60°49N 5°2E 164 D2
Mongu Zambia 15°16S 23°12E 265 F4
Mônguá Angola 16°43S 15°20E 265 F3
Moniac U.S.A. 30°31N 82°14W 316 E7
Monifieth U.K. 56°30N 2°48W 167 E6
Monistrol-sur-Loire France 45°17N 4°11E 175 C8
Monkayo Phil. 7°50N 126°5E 233 H6
Monkey Bay Malawi 14°7S 35°1E 269 E4
Monkey Mia Australia 25°48S 113°43E 279 E1
Monkey River Belize 16°22N 88°29W 319 D7
Monkey Town Trin. & Tob. 10°12N 61°25W 323 t
Mońki Poland 53°23N 22°48E 184 E9
Monkoto Dem. Rep. of the Congo 1°38S 20°35E 264 C4
Monkstown Ireland 53°18N 6°10W 120 B3
Monkton Canada 43°35N 81°5W 312 C3
Monmouth Monmouths., U.K. 51°48N 2°42W 169 F5
Monmouth Ill., U.S.A. 40°55N 90°39W 310 D6
Monmouth Oreg., U.S.A. 44°51N 123°14W 304 D2
Monmouthshire □ U.K. 51°48N 2°54W 169 F5
Monnickendam Neths. 52°28N 5°2E 112 A3
Mono Solomon Is. 7°20S 155°35E 287 L8
Mono L. U.S.A. 38°1N 119°1W 306 H7
Monolith U.S.A. 35°7N 118°22W 307 K8
Monolithos Greece 36°7N 27°45E 206 E11
Monon U.S.A. 40°52N 86°53W 311 D10
Monona Iowa, U.S.A. 43°3N 91°23W 310 A5
Monona Wis., U.S.A. 43°4N 89°20W 310 A7
Monongahela U.S.A. 40°12N 79°56W 312 F5
Monópoli Italy 40°57N 17°18E 201 B10
Monor Hungary 47°21N 19°27E 182 C4
Monos I. Trin. & Tob. 10°42N 61°44W 323 t
Monóvar Spain 38°28N 0°53W 197 G4
Monowai N.Z. 45°53S 167°31E 285 F2

Monowai, L. N.Z. 45°53S 167°25E 285 F2
Monqoumba C.A.R. 3°33N 18°40E 264 B3
Monreal del Campo Spain 40°47N 1°20W 196 E3
Monreale Italy 38°5N 13°17E 200 D6
Monroe Ga., U.S.A. 33°47N 83°43W 316 B6
Monroe Iowa, U.S.A. 41°31N 93°6W 310 C3
Monroe La., U.S.A. 32°30N 92°7W 314 E8
Monroe Mich., U.S.A. 41°55N 83°24W 311 C13
Monroe N.C., U.S.A. 34°59N 80°33W 315 D14
Monroe N.Y., U.S.A. 41°20N 74°11W 313 E10
Monroe Ohio, U.S.A. 39°27N 84°22W 311 E12
Monroe Utah, U.S.A. 38°38N 112°7W 304 G7
Monroe Wash., U.S.A. 47°51N 121°58W 306 C5
Monroe Wis., U.S.A. 42°36N 89°38W 310 B7
Monroe, L. U.S.A. 28°50N 81°19W 317 G8
Monroe City Ind., U.S.A. 38°37N 87°20W 311 F9
Monroe City Mo., U.S.A. 39°39N 91°44W 310 E5
Monroe L. U.S.A. 39°1N 86°31W 311 E10
Monroeton U.S.A. 41°43N 76°29W 313 E8
Monroeville Ala., U.S.A. 31°31N 87°20W 315 F11
Monroeville Ind., U.S.A. 40°59N 84°52W 311 D12
Monroeville Pa., U.S.A. 40°26N 79°45W 312 F5
Monrovia Liberia 6°18N 10°47W 262 D2
Monrovia Calif., U.S.A. 34°9N 118°1W 126 B4
Mons Belgium 50°27N 3°58E 170 D3
Mons Klint Denmark 54°57N 12°33E 163 K6
Monsanto Portugal 38°44N 9°12W 126 A1
Monsanto, Parque Florestal de Portugal 38°43N 9°11W 126 A1
Monsaraz Portugal 38°28N 7°22W 195 G3
Monse Indonesia 4°7S 123°15E 231 E6
Monsefú Peru 6°52S 79°52W 330 B2
Monségur France 44°38N 0°4E 174 D4
Monsélice Italy 45°14N 11°45E 199 C8
Mönsterås Sweden 57°3N 16°26E 163 G10
Mont Cenis, Col du France 45°15N 6°55E 175 C10
Mont-de-Marsan France 43°54N 0°31W 174 E3
Mont-Dore N. Cal. 22°16S 166°34E 288 d
Mont Fouari ⌓ Congo 2°52S 11°32E 264 C2
Mont-Joli Canada 48°37N 68°10W 299 C6
Mont-Laurier Canada 46°35N 75°30W 298 C4
Mont-Louis Canada 49°15N 65°44W 299 C6
Mont Peko △ Ivory C. 9°5N 7°15W 262 D3
Mont-roig del Camp Spain 41°5N 0°58E 196 D5
Mont-Royal Canada 45°30N 73°38W 130 A2
Mont-Royal, Parc Canada 45°30N 73°36W 130 A2
Mont-St-Michel, Le France 48°40N 1°30W 172 D5
Mont Sangbe △ Ivory C. 8°0N 7°10W 262 D3
Mont-Tremblant ⌓ Canada 46°30N 74°30W 298 C5
Montabaur Germany 50°25N 7°50E 178 E3
Montagnac = Remchi Algeria 35°2N 1°26W 261 A4
Montagnac France 43°29N 3°28E 174 E7
Montagnana Italy 45°14N 11°28E 199 C8
Montagne Blanche Mauritius 20°16S 57°39E 272 e
Montagne d'Ambre △ Madag. 12°37S 49°8E 272 A2
Montagne de Reims ⌓ France 49°8N 4°0E 173 C11
Montagu S. Africa 33°45S 20°8E 270 D3
Montagu I. Antarctica 58°25S 26°20W 151 B1
Montague Canada 46°10N 62°39W 299 C7
Montague, I. Mexico 31°45N 114°48W 318 A2
Montague I. N.S.W., Australia 36°16S 150°13E 283 D9
Montague I. Alaska, U.S.A. 60°0N 147°30W 303 G11
Montague Ra. Australia 27°15S 119°30E 279 E2
Montague Sd. Australia 14°28S 125°20E 278 B4
Montaigu France 46°59N 1°18W 172 F5
Montalbán Spain 40°50N 0°45W 196 E4
Montalbano Iónico Italy 40°17N 16°34E 201 B9
Montalbo Spain 39°53N 2°42W 196 F2
Montalcino Italy 43°3N 11°29E 199 E8
Montalegre Angola 8°45S 17°4E 265 D3
Montalegre Portugal 41°49N 7°47W 194 D3
Montalto Italy 38°10N 15°55E 201 D8
Montalto di Castro Italy 42°21N 11°37E 199 F8
Montalto Uffugo Italy 39°24N 16°9E 201 C9
Montalvo U.S.A. 34°15N 119°12W 307 L7
Montamarta Spain 41°39N 5°49W 194 D5
Montana Bulgaria 43°27N 23°16E 202 C7
Montaña Peru 6°0S 73°0W 330 B3
Montana ☐ Bulgaria 43°30N 23°20E 202 C7
Montana ☐ U.S.A. 47°0N 110°0W 304 C9
Montaña Clara, I. Canary Is. 29°17N 13°33W 153 e2
Montana de Montjuich Spain 41°21N 2°9E 114 A1
Montañas de Malaga ⌓ Spain 36°48N 4°32W 195 J6
Montánchez Spain 39°15N 6°8W 195 F4
Montanhas do Tumucumaque Brazil 2°5N 53°0W 329 C7
Montañita Colombia 1°22N 75°28W 328 C2
Montargil Portugal 39°5N 8°10W 195 F2
Montargis France 47°59N 2°43E 173 E9
Montauban France 44°2N 1°21E 174 D5
Montauk U.S.A. 41°3N 71°57W 313 E13
Montauk Pt. U.S.A. 41°4N 71°51W 313 E13
Montbard France 47°38N 4°20E 173 E11
Montbarrey France 47°1N 5°39E 173 E12
Montbéliard France 47°31N 6°48E 173 E13
Montblanc Spain 41°23N 1°4E 196 D6
Montbrison France 45°36N 4°3E 175 C8
Montcada i Reixac Spain 41°29N 2°12W 114 A2
Montcalm, Pic de France 42°40N 1°25E 174 F5
Montceau-les-Mines France 46°40N 4°23E 173 F11
Montcenis France 46°47N 4°23E 175 B8
Montclair U.S.A. 40°49N 74°12W 313 F10
Montcornet France 49°40N 4°1E 173 C11
Montcuq France 44°21N 1°13E 174 D5
Montdidier France 49°38N 2°35E 173 C9
Monte Albán Mexico 17°2N 96°46W 319 D5
Monte Alegre Brazil 2°0S 54°0W 329 D7
Monte Alegre de Goiás Brazil 13°14S 47°10W 333 D2
Monte Alegre de Minas Brazil 18°52S 48°52W 333 E2
Monte Alegre do Piauí Brazil 9°46S 45°18W 332 C2
Monte Azul Brazil 15°9S 42°53W 333 E3
Monte-Carlo Monaco 43°44N 7°25E 175 E11
Monte Carmelo Brazil 18°43S 47°29W 333 E2
Monte Caseros Argentina 30°10S 57°50W 334 C4
Monte Chingolo Argentina 34°43S 58°22W 117 C2
Monte Comán Argentina 34°40S 67°53W 334 C2
Monte Cristi Dom. Rep. 19°52N 71°39W 321 C5
Monte Cucco ⌓ Italy 43°22N 12°43E 199 E9
Monte Dinero Argentina 52°18S 68°33W 336 D3
Monte Dourado Brazil 0°52S 52°31W 329 D7
Monte Lindo → Paraguay 23°56S 57°12W 334 A4
Monte Palatino Rome, Italy 136 c3
Monte Pascoal △ Brazil 16°51S 39°21W 333 E4
Monte Patria Chile 30°42S 70°58W 334 C1
Monte Quemado Argentina 25°53S 62°41W 334 B3
Monte Redondo Portugal 39°53N 8°50W 194 F2
Monte Rio U.S.A. 38°28N 123°0W 306 G4
Monte San Giovanni Campano Italy 41°38N 13°31E 200 A6
Monte San Giuliano = Érice Italy 38°2N 12°35E 200 D5
Monte San Savino Italy 43°20N 11°43E 199 E8
Monte Sant' Ángelo Italy 41°42N 15°59E 199 G12
Monte Santu, C. di Italy 40°5N 9°44E 200 B2
Monte Sibillini △ Italy 42°55N 13°15E 199 F10
Monte Subasio ⌓ Italy 43°5N 12°40E 199 E9
Monte Vista U.S.A. 37°35N 106°9W 305 H10
Monteagudo Argentina 27°14S 54°8W 335 B5
Monteagudo Bolivia 19°49S 63°59W 331 D5
Montealegre del Castillo Spain 38°48N 1°17W 197 G3
Montebello Qué., Canada 45°40N 74°55W 298 C5
Montebello Guadeloupe 16°10N 61°36W 322 e
Montebello Calif., U.S.A. 34°1N 118°8W 126 B4
Montebello Iónico Italy 37°59N 15°45E 201 E8
Montebello Is. Australia 20°30S 115°45E 278 D2
Montebelluna Italy 45°47N 12°3E 199 C9
Montebourg France 49°30N 1°20W 172 C5
Montecastrilli Italy 42°39N 12°29E 199 F9
Montecatini Terme Italy 43°53N 10°46E 198 E7
Montecito U.S.A. 34°26N 119°40W 307 L7
Montecristi Ecuador 1°0S 80°40W 328 D1
Montecristo Italy 42°20N 10°19E 198 F7
Montefalco Italy 42°54N 12°39E 199 F9
Montefiascone Italy 42°32N 12°2E 199 F9
Montefrío Spain 37°20N 4°0W 195 H7
Montegiórgio Italy 43°6N 13°33E 199 E10
Montego B. Jamaica 18°28N 77°56W 320 a
Montehermoso Spain 40°5N 6°21W 194 E4
Monteiro Brazil 7°48S 37°2W 332 C4
Montejicar Spain 37°33N 3°30W 195 H7
Monteleone di Calabria = Vibo Valéntia Italy 38°40N 16°6E 201 D9
Montelíbano Colombia 8°5N 75°29W 328 B2
Montélimar France 44°33N 4°45E 175 D8
Montella Italy 40°51N 15°1E 201 B8
Montellano Spain 36°59N 5°29W 195 J5
Montello U.S.A. 43°48N 89°20W 308 D9
Montemayor, Meseta de Argentina 44°20S 66°10W 336 B3
Montemor Portugal 38°49N 9°12W 126 A1
Montemor-o-Novo Portugal 38°40N 8°12W 195 G2
Montemor-o-Velho Portugal 40°11N 8°40W 194 E2
Montemorelos Mexico 25°12N 99°49W 319 B5
Montendre France 45°16N 0°26W 174 C3
Montenegro Brazil 29°39S 51°29W 335 B5
Montenegro ■ Europe 42°40N 19°20E 202 D3
Montenero di Bisáccia Italy 41°57N 14°47E 199 G11
Montepuez Mozam. 13°8S 38°59E 269 E4
Montepuez → Mozam. 12°32S 40°27E 269 E5
Montepulciano Italy 43°5N 11°47E 199 E8
Montereale Italy 42°31N 13°15E 199 F10
Montereau-Faut-Yonne France 48°22N 2°57E 173 D9
Monterey Calif., U.S.A. 36°37N 121°55W 306 J5
Monterey Ind., U.S.A. 41°11N 86°30W 311 C10
Monterey B. U.S.A. 36°45N 122°0W 306 J5
Monterey Park U.S.A. 34°3N 118°7W 126 B4
Montería Colombia 8°46N 75°53W 328 B2
Montero Bolivia 17°20S 63°15W 331 D5
Monteros Argentina 27°11S 65°30W 334 B2
Monterotondo Italy 42°3N 12°37E 199 F9
Monterrey Mexico 25°40N 100°19W 318 B4
Montes Altos Brazil 5°50S 47°4W 332 C2
Montes Azules ⌓ Mexico 16°21N 91°3W 319 D6
Montes Claros Brazil 16°30S 43°50W 333 E3
Montesano U.S.A. 46°59N 123°36W 306 D3
Montesano sulla Marcellana Italy 40°16N 15°42E 201 B8
Montesárchio Italy 41°4N 14°38E 201 A7
Montescaglioso Italy 40°33N 16°40E 201 B9
Montesilvano Italy 42°29N 14°8E 199 F11
Montesinho ⌓ Portugal 41°54N 6°52W 194 D4
Montespaccato Italy 41°54N 12°23E 136 B1
Montesson France 48°54N 2°8E 134 A1
Montevarchi Italy 43°31N 11°34E 199 E8
Monteverde Nuovo Italy 41°52N 12°26E 136 B1
Montevideo Uruguay 34°50S 56°11W 335 C4
Montevideo Minn., U.S.A. 44°57N 95°43W 308 C6
Montezuma Ga., U.S.A. 32°18N 84°2W 316 C5
Montezuma Ind., U.S.A. 39°48N 87°22W 311 E9
Montezuma Iowa, U.S.A. 41°35N 92°32W 310 C4
Montezuma Castle ⌓ U.S.A. 34°39N 111°45W 305 J8
Montfaucon France 47°6N 1°7W 172 E5
Montfaucon-d'Argonne France 49°16N 5°8E 173 C12
Montfaucon-en-Velay France 45°11N 4°20E 175 C8
Montfermeil France 48°54N 2°33E 134 A4
Montfort-le-Gesnois France 48°3N 0°25E 172 D7
Montfort-sur-Meu France 48°9N 1°58W 172 D5
Montfragüe ⌓ Spain 39°48N 5°52W 194 F5
Montgenèvre France 44°56N 6°43E 175 D10
Montgomery = Sahiwal Pakistan 30°45N 73°8E 242 D5
Montgomery Powys, U.K. 52°34N 3°8W 169 E4
Montgomery Ala., U.S.A. 32°23N 86°19W 316 C3
Montgomery Ill., U.S.A. 41°44N 88°21W 311 C8
Montgomery Pa., U.S.A. 41°10N 76°53W 312 E8
Montgomery W. Va., U.S.A. 38°11N 81°19W 309 F13
Montgomery City U.S.A. 38°59N 91°30W 310 F5
Montguyon France 45°12N 0°12W 174 C3
Monthermé France 49°52N 4°44E 173 C11
Monthey Switz. 46°15N 6°56E 179 J2
Monthois France 49°19N 4°43E 173 C11
Monti Italy 40°49N 9°19E 200 B2
Monti Lucrétili ⌓ Italy 42°5N 12°50E 199 F9
Monti Picentini ⌓ Italy 40°45N 15°2E 201 B8
Monti Simbruini ⌓ Italy 41°55N 13°13E 199 G10
Monticelli d'Ongina Italy 45°5N 9°56E 198 C6
Monticello Ark., U.S.A. 33°38N 91°47W 314 E9
Monticello Fla., U.S.A. 30°33N 83°52W 316 E6
Monticello Ga., U.S.A. 33°18N 83°40W 316 B6
Monticello Ill., U.S.A. 40°1N 88°34W 311 D8
Monticello Ind., U.S.A. 40°45N 86°46W 311 D10
Monticello Iowa, U.S.A. 42°15N 91°12W 310 B5
Monticello Ky., U.S.A. 36°50N 84°51W 309 G11
Monticello Minn., U.S.A. 45°18N 93°48W 308 C7
Monticello Miss., U.S.A. 31°33N 90°7W 315 F9
Monticello Mo., U.S.A. 40°7N 91°43W 310 D5
Monticello N.Y., U.S.A. 41°39N 74°42W 313 E10
Monticello Utah, U.S.A. 37°52N 109°21W 305 H9
Montichiari Italy 45°25N 10°23E 198 C7
Montier-en-Der France 48°30N 4°45E 173 D11
Montignac France 45°4N 1°10E 174 C5
Montigny-le-Bretonneux France 48°46N 2°1E 134 B1
Montigny-les-Metz France 49°7N 6°10E 173 C13
Montigny-sur-Aube France 47°57N 4°45E 173 E11
Montijo Portugal 38°41N 8°54W 195 G2
Montijo Spain 38°52N 6°39W 195 G4
Montilla Spain 37°36N 4°40W 195 H6
Montivilliers France 49°33N 0°12E 172 C7
Montjay-la-Tour France 48°54N 2°40E 134 A4
Montjuïc, Parc de Barcelona, Spain 114 c1
Montluçon France 46°22N 2°36E 173 F9
Montmagny Canada 46°58N 70°34W 299 C5
Montmarault France 46°19N 2°57E 173 F9
Montmartre Canada 50°14N 103°27W 297 C8
Montmédy France 49°30N 5°20E 173 C12
Montmélian France 45°30N 6°4E 175 C10
Montmirail France 48°51N 3°30E 173 D10
Montmoreau-St-Cybard France 45°23N 0°8E 174 C4
Montmorillon France 46°26N 0°50E 174 B4
Montmort-Lucy France 48°55N 3°49E 173 D10
Monto Australia 24°52S 151°6E 280 C5
Montoire-sur-le-Loir France 47°45N 0°52E 172 E7
Montongbuwoh Indonesia 8°33S 116°4E 231 K19
Montório al Vomano Italy 42°35N 13°38E 199 F10
Montoro Spain 38°1N 4°27W 195 G6
Montour Falls U.S.A. 42°21N 76°51W 312 D8
Montoursville U.S.A. 41°15N 76°55W 312 E8
Montparnasse, Gare France 48°50N 2°19E 134 A2
Montpelier Idaho, U.S.A. 42°19N 111°18W 304 E8
Montpelier Ind., U.S.A. 40°33N 85°17W 311 D11
Montpelier Ohio, U.S.A. 41°35N 84°37W 311 C12
Montpelier Vt., U.S.A. 44°16N 72°35W 313 B12
Montpellier France 43°37N 3°52E 174 E7
Montpezat-de-Quercy France 44°15N 1°30E 174 D5
Montpon-Ménestérol France 45°0N 0°11E 174 D4
Montréal Qué., Canada 45°30N 73°33W 130 A2
Montréal Aude, France 43°13N 2°8E 174 E6
Montréal Gers, France 43°56N 0°11E 174 E4
Montréal → Canada 47°14N 84°39W 298 C3
Montréal, Î. de Canada 45°30N 73°40W 130 A2
Montréal, Université de Canada 45°29N 73°37W 130 B2
Montréal Est Canada 45°37N 73°31W 130 A2
Montreal L. Canada 54°20N 105°45W 297 C7
Montreal Lake Canada 54°3N 105°46W 297 C7
Montréal-Nord Canada 45°36N 73°36W 130 A2
Montréal-Ouest Canada 45°27N 73°39W 130 B1
Montréal Trudeau Int. ✈ (YUL) Canada 45°28N 73°44W 130 B1
Montredon-Labessonnié France 43°45N 2°18E 174 E6
Montrésor France 47°10N 1°10E 172 E8
Montret France 46°40N 5°7E 173 F12
Montreuil Pas-de-Calais, France 50°27N 1°45E 173 B8
Montreuil Seine-St-Denis, France 48°51N 2°27E 134 A3
Montreuil-Bellay France 47°8N 0°9W 172 E6
Montreux Switz. 46°26N 6°55E 179 J2
Montrevel-en-Bresse France 46°21N 5°8E 173 F12
Montrichard France 47°20N 1°10E 172 E8
Montrose Angus, U.K. 56°44N 2°27W 167 E6
Montrose Colo., U.S.A. 38°29N 107°53W 304 G10
Montrose Pa., U.S.A. 41°50N 75°53W 313 E9
Montrose, L. U.S.A. 38°18N 93°50W 310 F3
Montrouge France 48°48N 2°18E 134 B2
Monts, Pte. des Canada 49°20N 67°12W 299 C6
Montsalvy France 44°41N 2°30E 174 D6
Montsant, Serra de Spain 41°17N 1°0E 196 D6
Montsauche-les-Settons France 47°13N 4°2E 173 E11
Montsec, Serra del Spain 42°5N 0°45E 196 C5
Montseny ⌓ Spain 41°43N 2°22W 196 D7
Montserrat B. Aires, Argentina 34°37S 58°24W 117 B2
Montserrat Spain 41°36N 1°49E 196 D6
Montserrat ☒ W. Indies 16°40N 62°10W 323 p
Montserrat Hills Trin. & Tob. 10°23N 61°21W 323 t
Montuenga Spain 41°3N 4°38W 194 D6
Montuiri Spain 39°34N 2°59E 206 B3
Montvert-les-Bas Réunion 21°19S 55°32E 272 f
Monveda Dem. Rep. of the Congo 2°52N 21°30E 264 B4
Monyo Burma 17°59N 95°30E 241 G5
Monywa Burma 22°7N 95°11E 241 D5
Monza Italy 45°35N 9°16E 129 A2
Monze Zambia 16°17S 27°29E 269 F2
Monze, C. Pakistan 24°47N 66°37E 242 G2
Monzón Spain 41°52N 0°10E 196 D5
Monzoro Italy 45°27N 9°2E 129 B1
Moóca Brazil 23°33S 46°35W 137 B2
Moodyville = North Vancouver Canada 49°19N 123°4W 306 A3
Mooers U.S.A. 44°58N 73°35W 313 B11
Mooi → S. Africa 28°45S 30°34E 271 C5
Mooi River S. Africa 29°13S 29°50E 271 C4
Mo'oka Japan 36°26N 140°1E 223 A12
Mookgophong = Mookgopong S. Africa 24°31S 28°44E 271 B4
Mookgopong S. Africa 24°31S 28°44E 271 B4
Moonachie U.S.A. 40°50N 74°2W 132 B1
Moonah → Australia 22°3S 138°33E 280 C2
Moonda, L. Australia 25°52S 140°25E 280 D3
Moonee Ponds Australia 37°45S 144°53E 128 A1
Moonee Valley Racecourse Australia 37°45S 144°55E 128 A1
Moonie Australia 27°46S 150°20E 281 D5
Moonie → Australia 29°19S 148°43E 281 D4
Moonta Australia 34°6S 137°32E 282 C2
Moora Australia 30°37S 115°58E 279 F2
Moorcroft U.S.A. 44°16N 104°57W 304 D11
Moore → Australia 31°22S 115°30E 279 F2
Moore, L. Australia 29°50S 117°35E 279 E2
Moore Haven U.S.A. 26°50N 81°6W 317 J8
Moore Park Australia 24°43S 152°17E 280 C5
Moore Res. U.S.A. 44°20N 71°53W 313 B13
Moore River △ Australia 31°7S 115°39E 279 F2
Moorea French Polynesia 17°30S 149°50W 289 e
Moorefield U.S.A. 39°4N 78°58W 309 F14
Mooresville U.S.A. 39°37N 86°22W 311 E10
Moorfoot Hills U.K. 55°44N 3°8W 167 F5
Moorhead U.S.A. 46°53N 96°45W 308 B5
Moorland U.S.A. 42°26N 94°18W 310 B2
Moormerland Germany 53°20N 7°20E 178 B3
Moornanyah L. Australia 33°15S 143°42E 282 B5
Mooroopna Australia 36°25S 145°22E 283 D6
Moorpark U.S.A. 34°17N 118°53W 307 L8
Moorreesburg S. Africa 33°6S 18°38E 270 D2
Moorrinya △ Australia 21°42S 144°58E 280 C3
Moosach Germany 48°10N 11°30E 131 A2
Moosburg Germany 48°27N 11°56E 179 G7
Moose → Ont., Canada 51°20N 80°25W 298 B3
Moose → N.Y., U.S.A. 43°38N 75°24W 313 C9
Moose Creek Canada 45°15N 74°58W 313 A10
Moose Factory Canada 51°16N 80°32W 298 B3
Moose Jaw Canada 50°24N 105°30W 297 C7
Moose Jaw → Canada 50°34N 105°18W 297 C7
Moose Lake Man., Canada 53°46N 100°8W 297 C8
Moose Lake Minn., U.S.A. 46°27N 92°46W 308 B7
Moose Mountain ⌓ Canada 49°48N 102°25W 297 D8
Moose Pass U.S.A. 60°29N 149°22W 303 F10
Moosehead L. U.S.A. 45°38N 69°40W 309 C19
Mooselookmeguntic L. U.S.A. 44°55N 70°49W 313 B14
Moosilauke, Mt. U.S.A. 44°3N 71°40W 313 B13
Moosomin Canada 50°9N 101°40W 297 C8
Moosonee Canada 51°17N 80°39W 298 B3
Moosup U.S.A. 41°43N 71°53W 313 E13
Mootwingee ⌓ Australia 31°10S 142°30E 282 A5
Mopane S. Africa 22°37S 29°52E 271 B4
Mopeia Velha Mozam. 17°30S 35°40E 269 F4
Mopipi Botswana 21°6S 24°55E 270 B3
Mopoi C.A.R. 5°6N 26°54E 268 A2
Mopti Mali 14°30N 4°0W 262 C4
Mopti ☐ Mali 14°40N 4°0W 262 C4
Moqatta Sudan 14°38N 35°50E 257 E4
Moqor Afghan. 32°50N 67°42E 242 C2
Moquegua Peru 17°15S 70°46W 330 D3
Moquegua ☐ Peru 16°50S 70°55W 330 D3
Mór Hungary 47°25N 18°12E 182 C3
Mora Cameroon 11°2N 14°7E 259 F2
Mora Maharashtra, India 18°54N 72°55E 130 B2
Móra Portugal 38°55N 8°10W 195 G2
Mora Spain 39°41N 3°46W 195 F7
Mora Sweden 61°2N 14°38E 162 C8
Mora Minn., U.S.A. 45°53N 93°18W 308 C7
Mora N. Mex., U.S.A. 35°58N 105°20W 305 J11
Mora de Rubielos Spain 40°15N 0°45W 196 E4
Mòra d'Ebre Spain 41°6N 0°38E 196 D5
Mòra la Nova Spain 41°7N 0°39E 196 D5
Morača → Montenegro 42°20N 19°9E 202 D3
Morada Nova Brazil 5°7S 38°23W 332 C4
Morada Nova de Minas Brazil 18°37S 45°22W 333 E2
Moradabad India 28°50N 78°50E 243 E8
Morafenobe Madag. 17°50S 44°53E 272 B1
Morąg Poland 53°55N 19°56E 184 E6
Moral de Calatrava Spain 38°51N 3°33W 195 G7
Moraleda, Canal Chile 44°30S 73°30W 336 B2
Moraleja Spain 40°6N 6°43W 194 E4
Morales Bolivar, Colombia 8°16N 73°51W 328 B3
Morales Cauca, Colombia 2°45N 76°38W 328 C2
Moramanga Madag. 18°56S 48°12E 272 B2
Moran Kans., U.S.A. 37°55N 95°10W 308 G6
Moran Wyo., U.S.A. 43°50N 110°31W 304 E8
Moranbah Australia 22°1S 148°6E 280 C4
Morané French Polynesia 23°10S 137°7W 289 f
Moranhat India 27°10N 94°50E 241 B5
Morano Cálabro Italy 39°50N 16°8E 201 C9
Morant Bay Jamaica 17°53N 76°25W 320 a
Morant Cays Jamaica 17°22N 76°0W 320 C4
Morar India 26°14N 78°14E 242 F8
Morar, L. U.K. 56°57N 5°40W 167 E3
Moratalaz Spain 40°24N 3°39W 127 B2
Moratalla Spain 38°14N 1°49W 197 G3
Moratuwa Sri Lanka 6°45N 79°55E 245 L4
Morava → Slovak Rep. 48°10N 16°59E 181 C9
Moravia Iowa, U.S.A. 40°53N 92°49W 310 D4
Moravia N.Y., U.S.A. 42°43N 76°25W 313 D8
Moravian Hts. = Českomoravská Vrchovina Czech Rep. 49°30N 15°40E 180 B8
Moravica → Serbia 43°52N 20°8E 202 C4
Moravița Romania 45°17N 21°14E 182 E6
Moravská Třebová Czech Rep. 49°45N 16°40E 181 B9
Moravské Budějovice Czech Rep. 49°4N 15°49E 180 B8
Morawa Australia 29°13S 116°0E 279 E2
Morawhanna Guyana 8°30N 59°40W 329 B6
Moray ☐ U.K. 57°31N 3°18W 167 D5
Moray Firth U.K. 57°40N 3°52W 167 D5
Morbach Germany 49°48N 7°6E 179 F3
Morbegno Italy 46°8N 9°34E 198 B6
Morbi India 22°50N 70°42E 242 H4
Morbihan ☐ France 47°55N 2°50W 172 E4
Mörbylånga Sweden 56°32N 16°22E 163 H10
Morcenx France 44°3N 0°55W 174 D3
Morcone Italy 41°20N 14°40E 201 A7
Mordelles France 48°5N 1°52W 172 D5
Morden Man., Canada 49°15N 98°10W 297 D9
Morden London, U.K. 51°24N 0°13W 125 B2
Mordoğan Turkey 38°30N 26°37E 205 C8
Mordovian Republic = Mordvinia ☐ Russia 54°20N 44°30E 190 C7
Mordovo Russia 52°6N 40°50E 190 D5
Mordvinia ☐ Russia 54°20N 44°30E 190 C7
Mordy Poland 52°13N 22°31E 185 F9
Møre og Romsdal ☐ Norway 62°30N 8°0E 164 B4
Moreau → U.S.A. 45°18N 100°43W 308 C3
Morebeng S. Africa 23°30S 29°55E 271 B4
Morecambe U.K. 54°5N 2°52W 168 C5
Morecambe B. U.K. 54°7N 3°0W 168 C5
Moree Australia 29°28S 149°54E 281 D4
Morée → France 48°57N 2°25E 134 A3
Morehead Papua N. G. 8°41S 141°41E 286 E1
Morehead Ky., U.S.A. 38°11N 83°26W 311 F13
Morehead City U.S.A. 34°43N 76°43W 315 D16
Morel → India 26°13N 76°36E 242 F7
Moreland U.S.A. 33°17N 84°46W 316 B5
Morelia Mexico 19°42N 101°7W 318 D4
Morella Queens., Australia 23°0S 143°52E 280 C3
Morella Spain 40°35N 0°5W 196 E4
Morelos Mexico 26°42N 107°40W 318 B3
Morelos ☐ Mexico 18°45N 99°0W 319 D5
Moremi ⌓ Botswana 19°18S 23°10E 270 A3
Morena India 26°30N 78°4E 242 F8
Morena, Sierra Spain 38°20N 4°0W 195 G7
Morenci U.S.A. 41°43N 84°13W 311 C12
Moreni Romania 44°59N 25°36E 183 F10
Moreno Valley U.S.A. 33°56N 117°14W 307 M10
Moreno Bolivia 11°9S 66°15W 331 C4
Moreru → Brazil 10°10S 59°15W 331 C6
Moresby I. Canada 52°30N 131°40W 296 C2
Morestel France 45°40N 5°28E 175 C9
Moreton I. Australia 27°10S 153°25E 281 D5
Moreton Island △ Australia 27°2S 153°24E 281 D5
Moreuil France 49°46N 2°30E 173 C9
Morey Spain 39°44N 3°20E 206 B10
Morez France 46°31N 6°2E 173 F13
Morgan S. Austral., Australia 34°2S 139°35E 282 C3
Morgan Ga., U.S.A. 31°32N 84°36W 316 D5
Morgan Utah, U.S.A. 41°2N 111°41W 304 F8
Morgan City U.S.A. 29°42N 91°12W 314 G9
Morgan Hill U.S.A. 37°8N 121°39W 306 H5
Morgan Park U.S.A. 41°41N 87°38W 119 C3
Morganfield U.S.A. 37°41N 87°55W 308 G10
Morganton U.S.A. 35°45N 81°41W 315 D14
Morgantown Ind., U.S.A. 39°22N 86°16W 311 E10
Morgantown W. Va., U.S.A. 39°38N 79°57W 309 F14
Morgenzon S. Africa 26°45S 29°36E 271 C4
Morges Switz. 46°31N 6°29E 179 J2
Morghak Iran 29°7N 57°54E 247 D8
Morgongåva Sweden 59°57N 16°58E 162 E10
Morhange France 48°55N 6°38E 173 D13
Morhar → India 25°29N 85°11E 243 G11
Mori China 43°49N 90°11E 217 D12
Mori Italy 45°51N 10°59E 198 C7
Mori Japan 42°6N 140°35E 220 C10
Moriah Trin. & Tob. 11°15N 60°43W 323 s
Moriarty U.S.A. 34°59N 106°3W 305 J10
Moribaya Guinea 9°53N 9°32W 262 D3
Morice L. Canada 53°50N 127°40W 296 C3
Morichal Colombia 2°10N 70°34W 328 C3
Morichal Largo → Venezuela 9°27N 62°25W 329 B5
Moriguchi Japan 34°43N 135°34E 133 A2
Moriki Nigeria 12°52N 6°30E 263 C6
Morinville Canada 53°49N 113°41W 296 C6
Morioka Japan 39°45N 141°8E 220 E10
Moris Mexico 28°10N 108°32W 318 B3
Morisset Australia 33°6S 151°30E 283 B9
Morivione Italy 45°26N 9°12E 129 B2
Moriyama Japan 35°4N 135°59E 223 B7
Morlaàs France 43°21N 0°18W 174 E3
Morlaix France 48°36N 3°52W 172 D3
Mörlunda Sweden 57°19N 15°52E 163 G9
Mormanno Italy 39°53N 15°59E 201 C8
Mormant France 48°37N 2°52E 173 D9
Morne-à-l'Eau Guadeloupe 16°20N 61°27W 322 e
Morne des Esses Martinique 14°44N 61°1W 322 j
Morne Diablotins Dominica 15°30N 61°24W 323 k
Morne Fendue Grenada 12°12N 61°38W 323 q
Morne Raquette Dominica 15°27N 61°27W 323 k
Morne Trois Pitons △ Dominica 15°22N 61°20W 323 k
Morningside Gauteng, S. Africa 26°4S 28°3E 123 A2
Morningside Edinburgh, U.K. 55°56N 3°12W 121 B2
Morningside Md., U.S.A. 38°49N 76°53W 143 C4
Morningside Park Ont., Canada 43°47N 79°12W 141 A3
Morningside Park Fla., U.S.A. 28°26N 81°24W 133 B2
Mornington Australia 38°15S 145°5E 283 E6
Mornington, I. Chile 49°50S 75°30W 336 C1
Mornington I. Australia 16°30S 139°30E 280 B2
Mornington Peninsula △ Australia 38°28S 144°53E 283 E6
Mornos → Greece 38°25N 21°50E 204 C3
Moro Pakistan 26°40N 68°0E 242 F2
Moro Sudan 10°50N 30°9E 257 E3
Moro → Pakistan 29°42N 67°22E 242 E2
Moro G. Phil. 6°30N 123°0E 233 H4
Morobe Papua N. G. 7°49S 147°38E 286 D4
Morobe ☐ Papua N. G. 7°0S 147°0E 286 D4
Morocco U.S.A. 40°57N 87°27W 311 D9
Morocco ■ N. Afr. 32°0N 5°50W 260 B3
Morococha Peru 11°40S 76°5W 330 C2
Morogoro Tanzania 6°50S 37°40E 268 D4
Morogoro ☐ Tanzania 8°0S 37°0E 268 D4
Moroleón Mexico 20°8N 101°12W 318 C4
Morombe Madag. 21°45S 43°22E 272 C1
Moron = Morong Phil. 14°41N 120°16E 232 D3
Morón Argentina 34°39S 58°37W 334 C4
Morón Cuba 22°8N 78°39W 320 B4
Mörön Mongolia 49°38N 100°9E 218 B4
Morón de Almazán Spain 41°29N 2°27W 196 D2
Morón de la Frontera Spain 37°6N 5°28W 195 H5
Morona → Peru 4°40S 77°10W 328 D2
Morona-Santiago ☐ Ecuador 2°30S 78°0W 328 D2
Morondava Madag. 20°17S 44°17E 272 C1
Morondo Ivory C. 8°57N 6°47W 262 D3
Morong Phil. 14°41N 120°16E 232 D3
Morongo Valley U.S.A. 34°3N 116°37W 307 L10
Moroni Comoros Is. 11°40S 43°16E 272 a
Moroni Utah, U.S.A. 39°32N 111°35W 304 G8
Moroni Iconi ✈ (YVA) Comoros Is. 11°32S 43°15E 272 a
Moronou Ivory C. 6°16N 4°59W 262 D4
Morotai Indonesia 2°10N 128°30E 231 D7
Moroto Uganda 2°28N 34°42E 268 B3
Moroto, Mt. Uganda 2°30N 34°43E 268 B3
Morozov Bulgaria 42°30N 25°10E 203 D9
Morozovsk Russia 48°25N 41°50E 191 F5
Morpeth U.K. 55°10N 1°41W 168 B6
Morphou Cyprus 35°12N 32°59E 207 E8
Morphou Bay Cyprus 35°15N 32°50E 207 E8
Morrelganj Bangla. 22°28N 89°51E 241 D2
Morrilton U.S.A. 35°9N 92°44W 314 D8
Morrinhos Ceará, Brazil 3°14S 40°7W 332 B3
Morrinhos Minas Gerais, Brazil 17°45S 49°10W 333 E2
Morrinsville N.Z. 37°40S 175°32E 284 D4
Morris Man., Canada 49°25N 97°22W 297 D9
Morris Ill., U.S.A. 41°22N 88°26W 311 C8
Morris Minn., U.S.A. 45°35N 95°55W 308 C6
Morris N.Y., U.S.A. 42°33N 75°15W 313 D9
Morris Pa., U.S.A. 41°35N 77°17W 312 E7
Morris, Mt. Australia 26°9S 131°4E 279 E5
Morris Jesup, Kap Greenland 83°40N 34°0W 154 A7
Morrisburg Canada 44°55N 75°7W 313 B9
Morrison U.S.A. 41°49N 89°58W 310 C7
Morrisonville U.S.A. 39°25N 89°27W 310 E7
Morristown Ariz., U.S.A. 33°51N 112°37W 305 K7
Morristown Ind., U.S.A. 39°40N 85°42W 311 E11
Morristown N.J., U.S.A. 40°48N 74°29W 313 F10
Morristown N.Y., U.S.A. 44°35N 75°39W 313 B9
Morristown Tenn., U.S.A. 36°13N 83°18W 315 C13
Morrisville N.Y., U.S.A. 42°53N 75°35W 313 D9
Morrisville Pa., U.S.A. 40°13N 74°47W 313 F10
Morrisville Vt., U.S.A. 44°34N 72°36W 313 B12
Morro, Pta. Chile 27°6S 71°0W 334 B1
Morro Bay U.S.A. 35°22N 120°51W 306 K6
Morro Chico Chile 52°2S 71°26W 336 D2
Morro del Jable Canary Is. 28°3N 14°23W 153 e2
Morro do Chapéu Brazil 11°33S 41°9W 333 D3
Morro Grande = Barão de Cocais Brazil 19°56S 43°28W 333 E3
Morro Jable, Pta. de Canary Is. 28°2N 14°20W 153 e2
Morro Solar, Cerro Peru 12°11S 77°1W 124 C2
Morros Brazil 2°52S 44°3W 332 B3
Morrosquillo, G. de Colombia 9°35N 75°40W 320 E4
Morrow U.S.A. 39°21N 84°8W 311 E12
Mörrum Sweden 56°12N 14°45E 163 H8
Morrumbene Mozam. 23°31S 35°16E 271 B6
Mörrumsån → Sweden 56°10N 14°45E 163 H8
Mors Denmark 56°50N 8°45E 163 H2
Morshansk Russia 53°28N 41°50E 190 D5
Morsi India 21°21N 78°0E 244 D4
Mörsil Sweden 63°19N 13°40E 162 A7
Mortagne → France 48°33N 6°27E 173 D13
Mortagne-au-Perche France 48°31N 0°33E 172 D7
Mortagne-sur-Gironde France 45°28N 0°47W 174 C3
Mortagne-sur-Sèvre France 47°0N 0°59W 172 F6
Mortain France 48°40N 0°57W 172 D6
Mortara Italy 45°15N 8°44E 198 C5
Morteau France 47°3N 6°35E 173 E13
Morteros Argentina 30°50S 62°0W 334 C3
Mortes, R. das → Brazil 11°45S 50°44W 333 D1
Mortlach Canada 50°27N 106°4W 297 C7
Mortlake N.S.W., Australia 33°50S 151°6E 139 B1
Mortlake Vic., Australia 38°5S 142°50E 282 E5
Mortlake London, U.K. 51°27N 0°15W 125 B2
Morton Ill., U.S.A. 40°37N 89°28W 310 D7
Morton Tex., U.S.A. 33°44N 102°46W 314 E3
Morton Wash., U.S.A. 46°34N 122°17W 306 D4
Morton △ Australia 35°0S 150°12E 283 C9
Morton Grove U.S.A. 42°2N 87°46W 119 A2
Moruga Trin. & Tob. 10°4N 61°16W 323 t
Moruga → Trin. & Tob. 10°5N 61°16W 323 t
Morumbi Brazil 23°35S 46°42W 137 B1
Morundah Australia 34°57S 146°19E 283 C7
Morung Sudan 10°32N 31°3E 266 B3
Moruya Australia 35°58S 150°3E 283 C9
Morvan France 47°5N 4°3E 173 E11
Morvan ⌓ France 47°12N 4°3E 173 E11
Morvant Trin. & Tob. 10°40N 61°29W 323 t
Morven Queens., Australia 26°22S 147°5E 281 D4
Morven N.Z. 44°50S 171°6E 285 E6
Morven Ga., U.S.A. 30°57N 83°30W 316 E6
Morvern U.K. 56°38N 5°44W 167 E3
Morwell Australia 38°10S 146°22E 283 E7
Morwell △ Australia 38°14S 146°23E 283 E7
Moryń Poland 52°51N 14°22E 185 F1
Morzhovets, Ostrov Russia 66°44N 42°35E 186 A7
Morzine France 46°11N 6°42E 173 F13
Mosalsk Russia 54°30N 34°55E 188 E8
Mosbach Germany 49°21N 9°9E 179 F5
Mosby Norway 58°12N 7°55E 164 F4
Moscavide Portugal 38°47N 9°6W 126 A2
Mošćenice Croatia 45°17N 14°16E 199 C11
Moschato Greece 37°55N 23°40E 112 B2
Mosciano Sant' Ángelo Italy 42°42N 13°52E 199 F10
Moscone Convention Center San Francisco, U.S.A. 136 c2
Moscos Is. Burma 14°0N 97°30E 236 F1
Moscow = Moskva Russia 55°45N 37°37E 129 B3
Moscow Idaho, U.S.A. 46°44N 117°0W 304 C5
Moscow Mich., U.S.A. 42°3N 84°30W 311 B12
Moscow Pa., U.S.A. 41°20N 75°31W 313 E9
Moscow Mills U.S.A. 38°57N 90°55W 310 F6
Mosel → Europe 50°22N 7°36E 173 B14
Moselle = Mosel → Europe 50°22N 7°36E 173 B14
Moselle ☐ France 48°59N 6°33E 173 D13
Moses Lake U.S.A. 47°8N 119°17W 304 C4
Mosgiel N.Z. 45°53S 170°21E 285 F5
Moshaweng → S. Africa 26°35S 22°50E 270 C3
Moshchnyy, Ostrov Russia 60°1N 27°50E 161 F22
Moshi Tanzania 3°22S 37°18E 268 C4
Moshupa Botswana 24°46S 25°29E 270 B4
Mosina Poland 52°15N 16°50E 185 F3
Mosite Dem. Rep. of the Congo 0°53N 23°40E 264 B4
Mosjøen Norway 65°51N 13°12E 160 D15
Moskenesøya Norway 67°58N 13°0E 160 C15
Moskenstraumen Norway 67°47N 12°45E 160 C15
Moskog Norway 61°26N 6°0E 164 C2
Moskva Russia 55°45N 37°37E 129 B3
Moskva ☐ Russia 56°20N 37°20E 188 D9
Moskva → Russia 55°5N 38°51E 188 E10
Moskvoretskiy Russia 55°42N 37°37E 129 B3
Moslavačka Gora Croatia 45°40N 16°37E 199 C13
Mosman Australia 33°49S 151°15E 139 A2
Moso Vanuatu 17°30S 168°15E 287 G6
Mosomane Botswana 24°2S 26°19E 270 B4
Mosonmagyaróvár Hungary 47°52N 17°18E 182 C2
Mošorin Serbia 45°19N 20°4E 182 E5
Mospino Ukraine 47°52N 38°0E 189 J9
Mosqueiro Brazil 1°10S 48°28W 332 B2
Mosquera Colombia 2°35N 78°24W 328 C2
Mosquero U.S.A. 35°47N 103°58W 305 J12
Mosqueruela Spain 40°21N 0°27W 196 E4
Mosquitia Honduras 15°20N 84°10W 320 C3
Mosquito Coast = Mosquitia Honduras 15°20N 84°10W 320 C3
Mosquito Creek L. U.S.A. 41°18N 80°46W 312 E4
Mosquito L. Canada 62°35N 103°20W 297 A8
Mosquitos, G. de los Panama 9°15N 81°10W 320 E3
Moss Norway 59°27N 10°40E 164 E7
Moss Vale Australia 34°32S 150°25E 283 C9
Mossaka Congo 1°15S 16°45E 264 C3
Mossâmedes Brazil 16°7S 50°11W 333 E1
Mossbank Canada 49°56N 105°56W 297 D7
Mossburn N.Z. 45°41S 168°15E 285 F3
Mosselbaai S. Africa 34°11S 22°8E 270 D3
Mossendjo Congo 2°55S 12°42E 264 C2
Mossfellsbær Iceland 64°11N 21°45W 155 C5
Mossgiel Australia 33°15S 144°5E 282 B6
Mossingen Germany 48°24N 9°4E 179 G5
Mossman Australia 16°21S 145°15E 280 B4
Mossoró Brazil 5°10S 37°15W 332 C4
Mossuril Mozam. 14°58S 40°42E 269 E5
Mossy Head U.S.A. 30°45N 86°19W 317 E3
Mossy Point Australia 35°50S 150°11E 283 C9
Most Czech Rep. 50°31N 13°38E 180 A6
Mosta Malta 35°55N 14°26E 206 F7
Mostaganem Algeria 35°54N 0°5E 261 A5
Mostaganem ☐ Algeria 35°40N 0°15E 261 A5
Mostar Bos.-H. 43°22N 17°50E 182 G2
Mostardas Brazil 31°2S 50°51W 335 C5
Mostefa, Rass Tunisia 36°55N 11°3E 258 A2
Mosteiros Azores 37°53N 25°49W 153 d3
Mosterhamn Norway 59°42N 5°21E 164 E2
Mostiska = Mostyska Ukraine 49°48N 23°4E 185 J10
Móstoles Spain 40°19N 3°53W 127 C1
Mosty = Masty Belarus 53°27N 24°38E 177 B13
Mostyska Ukraine 49°48N 23°4E 185 J10
Mosul = Al Mawşil Iraq 36°15N 43°5E 213 D10
Møsvatnet Norway 59°52N 8°5E 164 E5
Mota Ethiopia 11°5N 37°52E 257 E4
Mota Vanuatu 13°49S 167°42E 287 C5
Mota del Cuervo Spain 39°30N 2°52W 197 F2
Mota del Marqués Spain 41°38N 5°11W 194 D5
Mota Lava Vanuatu 13°40S 167°40E 287 C5
Motaba Congo 2°6N 18°2E 264 B3
Motagua → Guatemala 15°44N 88°14W 320 C2
Motala Sweden 58°32N 15°1E 163 F9
Motaze Mozam. 24°48S 32°52E 271 B5
Moțca Romania 47°15N 26°37E 183 C11
Motegi Japan 36°32N 140°11E 223 A12
Moth India 25°43N 78°57E 243 G8

Motherwell U.K. 55°47N 3°58W 167 F5
Moti Bagh India 28°33N 77°10E 120 B2
Motihari India 26°30N 84°55E 243 F11
Motilla del Palancar Spain 39°34N 1°55W 197 F3
Motiti I. N.Z. 37°38S 176°25E 284 D5
Motnik Slovenia 46°14N 14°54E 199 B11
Motobu Japan 26°39N 127°53E 288 a
Motocurunya Venezuela 4°24N 64°5W 329 C5
Motol Czech Rep. 50°3N 14°19E 135 B1
Motovun Croatia 45°20N 13°50E 199 C10
Motozintla de Mendoza Mexico 15°22N 92°14W 319 D6
Motril Spain 36°31N 3°37W 195 J7
Motru Romania 44°48N 22°59E 182 F7
Motru → Romania 44°32N 23°31E 183 F8
Motsa Israel 31°47N 35°9E 123 B2
Motsa Ilit Israel 31°48N 35°9E 123 B1
Motspur Park U.K. 51°23N 0°14W 125 B2
Mott U.S.A. 46°23N 102°20W 308 B2
Mottingham U.K. 51°26N 0°1E 125 B4
Möttling = Metlika Slovenia 45°40N 15°20E 199 C12
Móttola Italy 40°38N 17°2E 201 B10
Motu → N.Z. 37°52S 177°36E 284 D6
Motu Nui Chile 27°12S 109°28W 330 b
Motu Tapu Cook Is. 21°14S 159°43W 289 h
Motuba Dem. Rep. of the Congo 2°20N 18°34E 264 B3
Motueka N.Z. 41°7S 173°1E 285 B8
Motueka → N.Z. 41°5S 173°1E 285 B8
Motul Mexico 21°6N 89°17W 319 C7
Motupena Pt. Papua N. G. 6°30S 155°10E 286 D8
Mou N. Cal. 21°5S 165°26E 288 d
Mouanda Gabon 1°28S 13°7E 264 C2
Mouchalagane → Canada 50°56N 68°41W 299 B6
Mouchoir Bank W. Indies 20°57N 70°47W 321 B5
Mouding China 25°20N 101°28E 228 E3
Moudjeria Mauritania 17°50N 12°28W 262 B2
Moudon Switz. 46°40N 6°49E 179 J2
Moudros Greece 39°50N 25°18E 205 B7
Mougoundou Congo 2°40S 12°41E 264 C2
Mouila Gabon 1°50S 11°0E 264 C2
Mouka C.A.R. 7°16N 21°52E 264 A4
Moukalaba ⌓ Gabon 2°50S 10°35E 264 C2
Moukambo Gabon 3°5S 11°38E 264 C2
Moul Niger 15°5N 13°11E 259 F2
Moulamein Australia 35°3S 144°1E 282 C6
Moule à Chique, C. St. Lucia 13°43N 60°57W 323 m
Mouliana Greece 35°10N 25°59E 207 E6
Moulin Rouge Paris, France 134 a3
Moulins France 46°35N 3°19E 173 F10
Moulmein Burma 16°30N 97°40E 241 G6
Moulmeingyun Burma 16°23N 95°16E 241 G5
Moulouya, O. → Morocco 35°5N 2°25W 261 A4
Moulton U.S.A. 40°41N 92°41W 310 D4
Moultrie U.S.A. 31°11N 83°47W 316 D6
Moultrie, L. U.S.A. 33°20N 80°5W 316 B9
Mounana Gabon 1°18S 13°13E 264 C2
Mound City Mo., U.S.A. 40°7N 95°14W 308 E6
Mound City S. Dak., U.S.A. 45°44N 100°4W 308 C3
Moundou Chad 8°40N 16°10E 259 G3
Moundsville U.S.A. 39°55N 80°44W 312 G4
Mounembé Congo 3°20S 12°32E 264 C2
Moung Cambodia 12°46N 103°27E 236 F4
Moungoudi Congo 2°45S 11°46E 264 C2
Mount Airy U.S.A. 36°31N 80°37W 315 C14
Mount Albert Canada 44°8N 79°19W 312 B5
Mount Apo △ Phil. 7°0N 125°10E 233 H5
Mount Aspiring △ N.Z. 44°19S 168°47E 285 E3
Mount Ayliff = Maxesibeni S. Africa 30°49S 29°23E 271 D4
Mount Ayr U.S.A. 40°43N 94°14W 310 D2
Mount Barker S. Austral., Australia 35°5S 138°52E 282 C3
Mount Barker W. Austral., Australia 34°38S 117°40E 279 F2
Mount Beauty Australia 36°47S 147°10E 283 D7
Mount Bellew Bridge Ireland 53°28N 8°31W 166 C3
Mount Brydges Canada 42°54N 81°29W 312 D3
Mount Buffalo △ Australia 36°43S 146°46E 283 D7
Mount Burr Australia 37°34S 140°26E 281 F3
Mount Carmel = Ha Karmel △ Israel 32°45N 35°5E 250 F6
Mount Carmel Ill., U.S.A. 38°25N 87°46W 311 F9
Mount Carmel Pa., U.S.A. 40°47N 76°26W 313 F8
Mount Carroll U.S.A. 42°6N 89°59W 310 B7
Mount Clemens U.S.A. 42°35N 82°53W 312 D2
Mount Cook N.Z. 43°44S 170°5E 285 D5
Mount Cook △ N.Z. 43°35S 170°15E 285 D5
Mount Coolon Australia 21°25S 147°25E 280 C4
Mount Darwin Zimbabwe 16°47S 31°38E 269 F3
Mount Dennis Canada 43°40N 79°28W 141 A2
Mount Desert I. U.S.A. 44°21N 68°20W 309 C19
Mount Dora U.S.A. 28°48N 81°38W 317 G8
Mount Eccles △ Australia 38°5S 141°54E 282 E4
Mount Eden U.S.A. 38°3N 85°9W 311 F11
Mount Edziza ⌓ Canada 57°30N 130°45W 296 B2
Mount Elgon △ E. Afr. 1°4N 34°42E 268 B3
Mount Field △ Australia 42°39S 146°35E 281 G4
Mount Fletcher S. Africa 30°40S 28°30E 271 D4
Mount Forest Canada 43°59N 80°43W 312 C4
Mount Frankland △ Australia 31°47S 116°37E 278 F2
Mount Frere = Kwabhaca S. Africa 30°51S 29°0E 271 D4
Mount Gambier Australia 37°50S 140°46E 282 D4
Mount Garnet Australia 17°37S 145°6E 280 B4
Mount Greenwood U.S.A. 41°42N 87°42W 119 C2
Mount Hagen Papua N. G. 5°52S 144°16E 286 C3
Mount Holly U.S.A. 39°59N 74°47W 313 G10
Mount Holly Springs U.S.A. 40°7N 77°12W 312 F7
Mount Hood Memorial Park ⌓ U.S.A. 42°26N 71°1W 116 A2
Mount Hope N.S.W., Australia 32°51S 145°51E 283 B6
Mount Hope S. Austral., Australia 34°7S 135°23E 281 E2
Mount Horeb U.S.A. 43°1N 89°44W 310 B7
Mount Isa Australia 20°42S 139°26E 280 C2
Mount Isarog △ Phil. 13°38N 123°24E 232 E4
Mount Jewett U.S.A. 41°44N 78°39W 312 E6
Mount Ka'ala Nat. Area Reserve ⌓ U.S.A. 21°31N 158°7W 302 J13
Mount Kaputar △ Australia 30°16S 150°10E 281 E5
Mount Kenya △ Kenya 0°7S 37°21E 268 C4
Mount Kilimanjaro △ Tanzania 3°2S 37°19E 268 C4
Mount Kisco U.S.A. 41°12N 73°44W 313 E11
Mount Laguna U.S.A. 32°52N 116°25W 307 N10
Mount Larcom Australia 23°48S 150°59E 280 C5
Mount Lofty Ranges Australia 34°35S 139°5E 282 C3
Mount McKinley = Denali △ U.S.A. 63°30N 152°0W 303 E10
Mount Magnet Australia 28°2S 117°47E 279 E2
Mount Malindang △ Phil. 8°17N 123°32E 233 G4
Mount Manara Australia 32°29S 143°58E 282 B5
Mount Maunganui N.Z. 37°40S 176°14E 284 D5
Mount Merrion Ireland 53°18N 6°12W 120 B2
Mount Molloy Australia 16°42S 145°20E 280 B4
Mount Morgan Australia 23°40S 150°25E 280 C5
Mount Morris Mich., U.S.A. 43°7N 83°42W 311 A13
Mount Morris N.Y., U.S.A. 42°44N 77°52W 312 D7
Mount Olive U.S.A. 39°4N 89°44W 310 E7
Mount Olivet U.S.A. 38°32N 84°2W 311 F12
Mount Orab U.S.A. 39°2N 83°55W 311 E13
Mount Pearl Canada 47°31N 52°47W 299 C9
Mount Penn U.S.A. 40°20N 75°54W 313 F9
Mount Perry Australia 25°13S 151°42E 281 D5
Mount Pleasant Iowa, U.S.A. 40°58N 91°33W 310 D5
Mount Pleasant Mich., U.S.A. 43°36N 84°46W 309 D11
Mount Pleasant Pa., U.S.A. 40°9N 79°33W 312 F5
Mount Pleasant S.C., U.S.A. 32°47N 79°52W 316 C10
Mount Pleasant Tenn., U.S.A. 35°32N 87°12W 315 D11
Mount Pleasant Tex., U.S.A. 33°9N 94°58W 314 E7
Mount Pleasant Utah, U.S.A. 39°33N 111°27W 304 G8
Mount Pocono U.S.A. 41°7N 75°22W 313 E9
Mount Pulaski U.S.A. 40°1N 89°17W 310 D7
Mount Pulog △ Phil. 16°35N 120°57E 232 C3
Mount Rainier U.S.A. 38°56N 76°57W 143 B4
Mount Rainier △ U.S.A. 46°55N 121°50W 306 D5
Mount Remarkable △ Australia 32°47S 138°3E 282 B3
Mount Revelstoke △ Canada 51°5N 118°30W 296 C5
Mount Robson ⌓ Canada 53°0N 119°0W 296 C5
Mount St. Helens ⌓ U.S.A. 46°14N 122°11W 306 D4
Mount Selinda Zimbabwe 20°24S 32°43E 271 B5
Mount Shasta U.S.A. 41°19N 122°19W 304 F2
Mount Signal U.S.A. 32°39N 115°37W 307 N11
Mount Somers N.Z. 43°45S 171°27E 285 D6
Mount Sterling Ill., U.S.A. 39°59N 90°45W 310 E6
Mount Sterling Ky., U.S.A. 38°4N 83°56W 311 F13
Mount Sterling Ohio, U.S.A. 39°43N 83°16W 311 E13
Mount Surprise Australia 18°10S 144°17E 280 B3
Mount Union U.S.A. 40°23N 77°53W 312 F7
Mount Upton U.S.A. 42°26N 75°23W 313 D9
Mount Vernon Ga., U.S.A. 32°11N 82°36W 316 C7
Mount Vernon Ill., U.S.A. 38°19N 88°55W 308 F9
Mount Vernon Ind., U.S.A. 37°56N 87°54W 308 G10
Mount Vernon Iowa, U.S.A. 41°55N 91°23W 310 C5
Mount Vernon N.Y., U.S.A. 40°54N 73°49W 132 A3
Mount Vernon Ohio, U.S.A. 40°23N 82°29W 312 F2
Mount Vernon Wash., U.S.A. 48°25N 122°20W 306 B4
Mount Vernon Square Washington, D.C., U.S.A. 143 a2
Mount Victor Australia 32°11S 139°44E 282 B3
Mount Washington U.S.A. 39°5N 84°24W 311 F11
Mount Wellington N.Z. 36°55S 174°52E 284 C3
Mount William △ Australia 40°56S 148°14E 281 G4
Mount Wynne St. Vincent 13°14N 61°16W 323 n
Mount Zion = Har Tsiyon Jerusalem 123 b3
Mount Zion U.S.A. 39°46N 88°53W 311 E8
Mounta, Akra Greece 38°3N 20°47E 207 C2
Mountain □ Phil. 17°20N 121°10E 232 C3
Mountain Ash U.K. 51°40N 3°23W 169 F4
Mountain Center U.S.A. 33°42N 116°44W 307 M10
Mountain City Nev., U.S.A. 41°50N 115°58W 304 F6
Mountain City Tenn., U.S.A. 36°29N 81°48W 315 C14
Mountain Dale U.S.A. 41°41N 74°32W 313 E10
Mountain Grove U.S.A. 37°8N 92°16W 308 G7
Mountain Home Ark., U.S.A. 36°20N 92°23W 314 C8
Mountain Home Idaho, U.S.A. 43°8N 115°41W 304 E6
Mountain Iron U.S.A. 47°32N 92°37W 308 B7
Mountain Pass U.S.A. 35°29N 115°35W 307 K11
Mountain View Ark., U.S.A. 35°52N 92°7W 314 D8
Mountain View Calif., U.S.A. 37°23N 122°5W 306 H4
Mountain View Hawai'i, U.S.A. 19°33N 155°7W 302 D6
Mountain Village U.S.A. 62°5N 163°43W 303 E7
Mountain Zebra △ S. Africa 32°14S 25°27E 270 D4
Mountainair U.S.A. 34°31N 106°15W 305 J10
Mountlake Terrace U.S.A. 47°47N 122°18W 306 C4
Mountmellick Ireland 53°7N 7°20W 166 C4
Mountrath Ireland 53°0N 7°28W 166 D4
Moura Queens., Australia 24°35S 149°58E 280 C4
Moura Brazil 1°32S 61°38W 329 D5
Moura Portugal 38°7N 7°30W 195 G3
Mourão Portugal 38°22N 7°22W 195 G3
Mourdi, Dépression du Chad 18°10N 23°0E 259 E4
Mourdiah Mali 14°35N 7°25W 262 C3
Mourenx France 43°22N 0°38W 174 E3
Mouri Ghana 5°6N 1°14W 263 D4
Mourilyan Australia 17°35S 146°3E 280 B4
Mourmelon-le-Grand France 49°8N 4°22E 173 C11
Mourne → U.K. 54°52N 7°26W 166 B4
Mourne Mts. U.K. 54°10N 6°0W 166 B5
Mournies Greece 35°29N 24°1E 207 E5
Mouscron Belgium 50°45N 3°12E 170 D3
Mousgougou Chad 10°47N 16°9E 259 F3
Moussoro Chad 13°41N 16°35E 259 F3
Moustique, Morne Guadeloupe 16°7N 61°44W 322 e
Mouthe France 46°44N 6°12E 173 F13
Moutier Switz. 47°16N 7°21E 179 H3
Moûtiers France 45°29N 6°32E 175 C10
Moutong Indonesia 0°28N 121°13E 231 D6
Mouy France 49°18N 2°20E 173 C9
Mouydir, Monts du Algeria 25°30N 4°10E 261 C5
Mouyondzi Congo 4°1S 13°59E 264 C2
Mouzaki Greece 39°25N 21°37E 204 B3
Mouzon France 49°36N 5°3E 173 C12
Movas Mexico 28°10N 109°25W 318 B3
Moville Ireland 55°11N 7°3W 166 A4
Mowandjum Australia 17°22S 123°40E 278 C3
Moweaqua U.S.A. 39°38N 89°1W 310 E7
Moxico □ Angola 12°0S 20°30E 265 E4
Moxotó → Brazil 9°19S 38°14W 332 C4
Moy → Ireland 54°8N 9°8W 166 B2
Moya Comoros Is. 12°18S 44°18E 272 a
Moyale Ethiopia 3°34N 39°5E 266 D4
Moyale Eastern, Kenya 3°30N 39°0E 257 G4
Moyamba S. Leone 8°4N 12°30W 262 D2
Moyen Atlas Morocco 33°0N 5°0W 260 B4
Moyen-Chari □ Chad 9°0N 18°0E 259 G3
Moyne, L. Le Canada 56°45N 68°47W 299 A6
Moyo Indonesia 8°10S 117°40E 235 D5
Moyobamba Peru 6°0S 77°0W 330 B2
Moyto Chad 12°35N 16°33E 259 F3
Moyu China 37°15N 79°44E 217 E9
Moyyero → Russia 68°44N 103°42E 215 C11
Moyynqum Kazakhstan 44°12N 71°0E 217 D8
Moyynqum Zhambyl, Kazakhstan 44°17N 72°57E 217 D8
Moyynty Kazakhstan 47°10N 73°18E 217 C8
Mozambique = Moçambique Mozam. 15°3S 40°42E 269 F5
Mozambique ■ Africa 19°0S 35°0E 269 F4
Mozambique Basin Ind. Oc. 30°0S 40°0E 273 H3
Mozambique Chan. Africa 17°30S 42°30E 271 A7
Mozarthaus Vienna, Austria 142 b2
Mozdok Russia 43°45N 44°48E 191 J7
Mozdūrān Iran 36°9N 60°35E 247 B9
Mozhaysk Russia 55°30N 36°2E 188 E9
Mozhga Russia 56°26N 52°15E 190 B11
Mozhnābād Iran 34°7N 60°6E 247 C9
Mozirje Slovenia 46°22N 14°58E 199 B11
Mozyr = Mazyr Belarus 51°59N 29°15E 177 B15
Mpanda Tanzania 6°23S 31°1E 268 D3
Mpé Congo 2°58S 14°38E 264 C2
Mpese Dem. Rep. of the Congo 5°16S 15°30E 265 D3
Mpésoba Mali 12°31N 5°39W 262 C3
Mphoengs Zimbabwe 21°10S 27°51E 271 B4
Mpika Zambia 11°51S 31°25E 269 E3
Mpoko → C.A.R. 4°19N 18°33E 264 B3
Mpouya Congo 2°38S 16°13E 264 C3
Mpulungu Zambia 8°51S 31°5E 269 D3
Mpumalanga S. Africa 29°50S 30°33E 271 C5
Mpumalanga □ S. Africa 26°0S 30°0E 271 C5
Mpwapwa Tanzania 6°23S 36°30E 268 D4
Mqabba Malta 35°51N 14°28E 206 F7
Mqanduli S. Africa 31°49S 28°45E 271 D4
Mqinvartsveri = Kazbek Russia 42°42N 44°30E 191 J7
Mrągowo Poland 53°52N 21°18E 184 E8
M'ramani Comoros Is. 12°20S 44°31E 272 a
Mramor Serbia 43°20N 21°45E 202 C5
Mrimina Morocco 29°50N 7°9W 260 C3
Mrkonjić Grad Bos.-H. 44°26N 17°4E 182 F2
Mrkopalj Croatia 45°21N 14°52E 199 C11
Mrocza Poland 53°16N 17°35E 185 E4
Msaken Tunisia 35°49N 10°33E 258 A2
Msambansovu Zimbabwe 15°50S 30°3E 269 F3
Msida Malta 35°54N 14°29E 206 F7
M'sila Algeria 35°46N 4°30E 261 A5
M'sila □ Algeria 35°20N 4°20E 261 A5
Msoro Zambia 13°35S 31°50E 269 E3
Msta → Russia 58°25N 31°20E 188 C6
Mstislavl = Mstsislaw Belarus 54°0N 31°50E 177 A16
Mstsislaw Belarus 54°0N 31°50E 177 A16
Mszana Dolna Poland 49°41N 20°5E 185 J7
Mszczonów Poland 51°58N 20°33E 185 G7
Mtama Tanzania 10°17S 39°21E 269 E4
Mtamvuna = Mthamvuna → S. Africa 31°6S 30°12E 271 D5
Mthamvuna → S. Africa 31°6S 30°12E 271 D5
Mthatha S. Africa 31°36S 28°49E 271 D4
Mtilikwe → Zimbabwe 21°9S 31°30E 269 G3
Mtima Congo 3°49S 12°7E 264 C2
Mtito Andei Kenya 2°41S 38°10E 268 C4
Mtsamboro Mayotte 12°42S 45°4E 272 b
Mtsamboro, Î. Mayotte 12°38S 45°2E 272 b
Mtsangamouji Mayotte 12°45S 45°5E 272 b
Mtsapéré Mayotte 12°46S 45°11E 272 b
Mtsensk Russia 53°17N 36°36E 188 F9
Mtskheta Georgia 41°52N 44°45E 191 K7
Mtubatuba S. Africa 28°30S 32°8E 271 C5
Mtwalume S. Africa 30°30S 30°38E 271 D5
Mtwara-Mikindani Tanzania 10°20S 40°20E 269 E5
Mu → Burma 21°56N 95°38E 241 E5
Mu Gia, Deo Vietnam 17°40N 105°47E 236 D5
Mu Ko Chang △ Thailand 11°59N 102°22E 237 G4
Mu Us Shamo China 39°0N 109°0E 226 E5
Muacandala Angola 10°2S 19°40E 265 E3
Muan S. Korea 34°59N 126°28E 224 E3
Muaná Brazil 1°25S 49°15W 332 B2
Muanda Dem. Rep. of the Congo 6°0S 12°20E 265 D2
Muang Chiang Rai = Chiang Rai Thailand 19°52N 99°50E 228 H2
Muang Khong Laos 14°7N 105°51E 236 E5
Muang Lamphun Thailand 18°40N 99°2E 236 C2
Muang Mai Thailand 8°5N 98°21E 237 a
Muang Pak Beng Laos 19°54N 101°8E 228 H3
Muangai Angola 12°32S 19°55E 265 E3
Muar Malaysia 2°3N 102°34E 237 L4
Muarabungo Indonesia 1°28S 102°52E 234 C2
Muaraenim Indonesia 3°40S 103°50E 234 C2
Muarajuloi Indonesia 0°12S 114°3E 235 C4
Muarakaman Indonesia 0°2S 116°45E 235 C5
Muaratebo Indonesia 1°30S 102°26E 234 C2
Muaratembesi Indonesia 1°42S 103°8E 234 C2
Muaratewe Indonesia 0°58S 114°52E 235 C4
Mubarakpur India 26°6N 83°18E 243 F10
Mubarraz = Al Mubarraz Si. Arabia 25°30N 49°40E 247 E6
Mubende Uganda 0°33N 31°22E 268 B3
Mubi Nigeria 10°18N 13°16E 263 C7
Mucajá Brazil 3°57S 57°32W 329 D6
Mucajaí → Brazil 2°25N 60°52W 329 C5
Mucajaí, Serra do Brazil 2°23N 61°10W 329 C5
Mucari Angola 9°30S 16°54E 265 D3
Muchachos, Roque de los Canary Is. 28°44N 17°52W 153 e1
Mücheln Germany 51°17N 11°47E 178 D7
Muchinga Mts. Zambia 11°30S 31°30E 269 E3
Muchkapskiy Russia 51°52N 42°28E 190 E6
Muchuan China 28°57N 103°55E 228 C5
Muck U.K. 56°50N 6°15W 167 E2
Muckadilla Australia 26°35S 148°23E 281 D4
Muckalee Cr. → U.S.A. 31°38N 84°9W 316 D5
Muckle Flugga U.K. 60°51N 0°54W 167 A8
Muco → Colombia 4°15N 70°21W 328 C3
Mucoma Angola 15°18S 13°39E 265 F2
Muconda Angola 10°31S 21°15E 265 E4
Mucope Angola 16°24S 14°52E 265 F2
Mucugê Brazil 13°0S 41°23W 333 D3
Mucuim → Brazil 6°33S 64°18W 331 B5
Mucur Turkey 39°3N 34°22E 212 C6
Mucura Brazil 2°31S 62°43W 329 D5
Mucuri Brazil 18°0S 39°36W 333 E4
Mucurici Brazil 18°6S 40°31W 333 E3
Mucusso Angola 18°1S 21°25E 265 F4
Mucusso ⌓ Angola 17°27S 21°0E 265 F4
Mud L. U.S.A. 28°23N 81°17W 133 B3
Muda Canary Is. 28°34N 13°57W 153 e2
Mudanjiang China 44°38N 129°30E 227 B15
Mudanya Turkey 40°25N 28°50E 203 F12
Muddebihal India 16°20N 76°8E 245 F3
Muddy Cr. → U.S.A. 38°24N 110°42W 304 G8
Mudgee Australia 32°32S 149°31E 283 B8
Mudhol Andhra Pradesh, India 18°58N 77°55E 244 E3
Mudhol Karnataka, India 16°21N 75°17E 245 F2
Mudiata Dem. Rep. of the Congo 7°15S 22°1E 265 D4
Mudigere India 13°8N 75°38E 245 H2
Mudjatik → Canada 56°1N 107°36W 297 B7
Mudon Burma 16°15N 97°44E 241 G6
Mudugh Somali Rep. 7°0N 47°30E 267 C6
Mudukulattur India 9°21N 78°31E 245 K4
Mudurnu Turkey 40°27N 31°12E 212 B4
Muecate Mozam. 14°55S 39°40E 269 E4
Mueda Mozam. 11°36S 39°28E 269 E4
Mueller Ranges Australia 18°18S 126°46E 278 C4
Muende Mozam. 14°28S 33°0E 269 E3
Muerto, Mar Mexico 16°10N 94°10W 319 D6
Mufu Shan China 29°20N 114°30E 229 C10
Mufulira Zambia 12°32S 28°15E 269 E2
Mufuma Angola 9°12S 16°29E 265 D3
Mufumbiro Range Africa 1°25S 29°30E 268 C2
Mugardos Spain 43°27N 8°15W 194 B2
Muge → Portugal 39°8N 8°44W 195 F2
Müggelberge Germany 52°25N 13°37E 115 B4
Müggelheim Germany 52°24N 13°40E 115 B5
Múggia Italy 45°36N 13°46E 199 C10
Muggiò Italy 45°35N 9°13E 129 A2
Mughal Gardens Delhi, India 120 c1
Mughal Sarai India 25°18N 83°7E 243 G10
Mughalzhar Taūy Kazakhstan 49°0N 58°40E 216 C5
Mughayrā' Si. Arabia 29°17N 37°41E 246 D3
Mugi Japan 33°40N 134°25E 222 D6
Mugia = Muxía Spain 43°3N 9°10W 194 B1
Mugila, Mts. Dem. Rep. of the Congo 7°0S 28°50E 268 D2
Muginga Angola 8°21S 17°36E 265 D3
Muğla Turkey 37°15N 28°22E 205 D10
Muğla □ Turkey 37°15N 28°0E 205 D10
Muglad Sudan 11°1N 27°50E 257 E2
Mŭglizh Bulgaria 42°37N 25°32E 203 D9
Mugodzhary = Mughalzhar Taūy Kazakhstan 49°0N 58°40E 216 C5
Mugu Nepal 29°45N 82°30E 243 E10
Muhammad, Râs Egypt 27°44N 34°16E 251 L5
Muhammad Qol Sudan 20°53N 37°9E 256 C4
Muhammadabad India 26°4N 83°25E 243 F10
Muḩayriqah Si. Arabia 23°59N 45°4E 248 B4
Muhesi → Tanzania 7°0S 35°20E 268 D4
Mühlacker Germany 48°57N 8°51E 179 G4
Mühldorf Germany 48°14N 12°32E 179 G8
Mühleiten Austria 48°10N 16°33E 142 A3
Mühlenfliess → Germany 52°32N 13°42E 115 A5
Mühlhausen = Milevsko Czech Rep. 49°27N 14°21E 180 B7
Mühlhausen Germany 51°12N 10°27E 178 D6
Mühlig Hofmann fjell Antarctica 72°30S 5°0E 151 D3
Mühlviertel Austria 48°30N 14°10E 180 C7
Muhoro Kenya 1°1S 34°7E 266 E3
Muhos Finland 64°47N 25°59E 160 D21
Muḩradah Syria 35°15N 36°35E 250 C7
Muhu Estonia 58°36N 23°11E 188 C2
Muhutwe Tanzania 1°35S 31°45E 268 C3
Mui Wo China 22°16N 113°59E 219 G10
Muiden Neths. 52°20N 5°4E 112 A3
Muiderpoort Station Amsterdam, Neths. 112 b3
Muie Angola 14°23S 20°25E 265 E4
Muine Bheag Ireland 52°42N 6°58W 166 D5
Muir, L. Australia 34°30S 116°40E 279 F2
Muir of Ord U.K. 57°32N 4°28W 167 D4
Muisné Ecuador 0°36N 80°2W 328 C1
Muizenberg S. Africa 34°5S 18°27E 118 B1
Mujahidpur India 28°33N 77°14E 120 B2
Mujnak = Muynak Uzbekistan 43°44N 59°10E 216 D5
Mujuí dos Campos Brazil 2°35S 54°41W 329 D7
Muka, Tanjung Malaysia 5°28N 100°11E 237 c
Mukacheve Ukraine 48°27N 22°45E 182 B7
Mukachevo = Mukacheve Ukraine 48°27N 22°45E 182 B7
Mukah Malaysia 2°55N 112°5E 235 B4
Mukandpur India 28°44N 77°11E 120 A2
Mukandwara India 24°49N 75°59E 242 G6
Mukawa Papua N. G. 9°38S 149°59E 286 E5
Mukawwa, Geziret Egypt 23°55N 35°53E 256 C4
Mukawwar Sudan 20°50N 37°17E 256 C4
Mukaylah Si. Arabia 19°16N 41°48E 248 C3
Mukdahan Thailand 16°32N 104°43E 236 D5
Mukden = Shenyang China 41°48N 123°27E 224 B1
Mukerian India 31°57N 75°37E 242 D6
Mukhavyets Belarus 52°5N 23°39E 185 F10
Mukher India 18°42N 77°22E 244 E3
Mukhmas West Bank 31°52N 35°17E 123 A2
Mukhtolovo Russia 55°29N 43°15E 190 C6
Mukhtuya = Lensk Russia 60°48N 114°55E 215 C12
Mukinbudin Australia 30°55S 118°5E 279 F2
Mukishi Kasai-Occ., Dem. Rep. of the Congo 5°39S 21°3E 265 D4
Mukishi Katanga, Dem. Rep. of the Congo 8°30S 24°44E 265 D4
Muko → Japan 34°48N 135°22E 133 A1
Mukojima Japan 35°43N 139°49E 140 A3
Mukomuko Indonesia 2°30S 101°10E 234 C2
Mukomwenze Dem. Rep. of the Congo 6°49S 27°15E 268 D2
Muktsar India 30°30N 74°30E 242 D6
Mukur = Moqor Afghan. 32°50N 67°42E 242 C2
Mukutawa → Canada 53°10N 97°24W 297 C9
Mukwela Zambia 17°0S 26°40E 269 F2
Mukwonago U.S.A. 42°52N 88°20W 311 B8
Mul India 20°4N 79°40E 244 D4
Mula Spain 38°3N 1°33W 197 G3
Mula → India 18°34N 74°21E 244 E2
Mula → Pakistan 27°57N 67°36E 242 F2
Mulaku Atoll Maldives 3°0N 73°30E 272 d
Mulamba Dem. Rep. of the Congo 6°21S 21°13E 265 D4
Mulanay Phil. 13°31N 122°24E 232 E4
Mulange Dem. Rep. of the Congo 3°40S 27°10E 268 C2
Mulanje Malawi 16°2S 35°33E 269 F4
Mulanje, Mt. Malawi 16°0S 35°30E 269 F4
Mulatre, Pte. Dominica 15°17N 61°15W 323 k
Mulatupo Panama 8°57N 77°45W 328 B2
Mulbagal India 13°10N 78°24E 245 H4
Mulbarton S. Africa 26°17S 28°3E 123 B2
Mulberry U.S.A. 27°54N 81°59W 317 H8
Mulberry Grove U.S.A. 38°56N 89°16W 310 F7
Mulchatna → U.S.A. 59°40N 157°7W 303 G8
Mulchén Chile 37°45S 72°20W 334 D1
Mulde → Germany 51°53N 12°15E 178 D8
Muldraugh U.S.A. 37°56N 85°59W 311 G11
Mule Creek Junction U.S.A. 43°23N 104°13W 304 E11
Muleba Tanzania 1°50S 31°37E 268 C3
Mulegé Mexico 26°53N 111°59W 318 B2
Muleshoe U.S.A. 34°13N 102°43W 314 D3
Muletta, Gara Ethiopia 9°15N 41°44E 257 F5
Mulgrave Canada 45°38N 61°31W 299 C7
Mulgrave I. = Badu I. Papua N. G. 10°5S 142°10E 286 F2
Mulhacén Spain 37°4N 3°20W 195 H7
Mülheim Germany 51°25N 6°54E 178 D2
Mulhouse France 47°40N 7°20E 173 E14
Muli Sichuan, China 27°52N 101°8E 228 D3
Muli Maldives 2°55N 73°34E 272 d
Mulifanua Samoa 13°50S 171°59W 287 V20
Muling China 44°35N 130°10E 227 B16
Mulki India 13°6N 74°48E 245 H2
Mull U.K. 56°25N 5°56W 167 E3
Mull, Sound of U.K. 56°30N 5°50W 167 E3
Mullaittivu Sri Lanka 9°15N 80°49E 245 K5
Mullen U.S.A. 42°3N 101°1W 308 D3
Mullens U.S.A. 37°35N 81°23W 309 G13
Muller, Pegunungan Indonesia 0°30N 113°30E 235 B4
Muller Ra. Papua N. G. 5°35S 142°20E 286 C2
Mullet Pen. Ireland 54°13N 10°2W 166 B1
Mulletbaai St.-Maarten 18°4N 63°7W 322 a
Mullewa Australia 28°29S 115°30E 279 E2
Müllheim Germany 47°47N 7°36E 179 H3
Mulligan → Australia 25°0S 139°0E 280 D2
Mullingar Ireland 53°31N 7°21W 166 C4
Mullins U.S.A. 34°12N 79°15W 315 D15
Mullsjö Sweden 57°56N 13°55E 163 G7
Mullumbimby Australia 28°30S 153°30E 281 D5
Mulobezi Zambia 16°45S 25°7E 269 F2
Mulondo Angola 15°41S 15°12E 265 F3
Mulonga Plain Zambia 16°20S 22°40E 265 F4
Mulroy B. Ireland 55°15N 7°46W 166 A4
Mulshi L. India 18°30N 73°48E 244 E1
Multai India 21°50N 78°21E 244 D4
Multan Pakistan 30°15N 71°36E 242 D4
Mulu, Gunung Malaysia 4°3N 114°56E 235 B4
Mulug India 18°11N 79°57E 244 E4
Mulumbe, Mts. Dem. Rep. of the Congo 8°40S 27°30E 269 D2
Mulundu Dem. Rep. of the Congo 6°40S 20°33E 265 D4
Mulungushi Dam Zambia 14°48S 28°48E 269 E2
Mulurulu L. Australia 33°15S 143°20E 282 B5
Mulvane U.S.A. 37°29N 97°15W 308 G5
Mulwad Sudan 18°45N 30°39E 256 D3
Mulwala Australia 35°59S 146°0E 283 C7
Muma Dem. Rep. of the Congo 3°25N 23°21E 264 B4
Mumbai India 18°56N 72°50E 130 B2
Mumbai Chhatrapati Shivaji Int. ✈ (BOM) India 19°5N 72°51E 130 A2
Mumbai Harbour India 18°58N 72°55E 130 B2
Mumbeji Zambia 13°51S 23°39E 265 E4
Mumbondo Angola 10°9S 14°15E 265 E2
Mumbwa Zambia 15°0S 27°0E 269 F2
Mumeng Papua N. G. 7°1S 146°37E 286 D4
Mumias Kenya 0°20N 34°29E 268 C4
Mummel Gulf △ Australia 31°17S 151°51E 283 A9
Mumra Russia 45°45N 47°41E 191 H8
Mun → Thailand 15°19N 105°30E 236 E5
Mun-gyeong S. Korea 36°35N 128°12E 224 D4
Muna Indonesia 5°0S 122°30E 231 F6
Munabao India 25°45N 70°17E 242 G4
Munakata Japan 33°48N 130°38E 222 D2
Munamagi Estonia 57°43N 27°4E 188 D4
Muncan Indonesia 8°34S 115°11E 231 K18
Muncar Indonesia 8°26S 114°20E 231 J17
Munch Museum Norway 59°55N 10°46E 133 A3
Münchberg Germany 50°11N 11°47E 179 E7
Müncheberg Germany 52°30N 14°9E 178 C10
Münchehofe Germany 52°29N 13°40E 115 B5
München Germany 48°8N 11°34E 131 B2
München Franz Josef Strauss Int. ✈ (MUC) Germany 48°21N 11°47E 131 A2
Munchen-Gladbach = Mönchengladbach Germany 51°11N 6°27E 178 D2
Munchique △ Colombia 2°44N 77°1W 328 C2
Muncho Lake Canada 59°0N 125°50W 296 B3
Munch'ŏn N. Korea 39°14N 127°19E 224 C3
Muncie U.S.A. 40°12N 85°23W 311 D11
Muncoonie L. West Australia 25°12S 138°40E 280 D2
Munda Solomon Is. 8°20S 157°16E 287 M9
Mundabbera Australia 25°36S 151°18E 281 D5
Mundakayam India 9°30N 76°50E 245 K3
Mundal Sri Lanka 7°48N 79°48E 245 L4
Munday U.S.A. 33°27N 99°38W 314 E5
Mundelein U.S.A. 42°16N 88°0W 311 B8
Münden Germany 51°25N 9°38E 178 D5
Münden ⌓ Germany 51°28N 9°42E 178 D5
Mundiwindi Australia 23°47S 120°9E 278 D3
Mundo → Spain 38°30N 2°15W 197 G2
Mundo Novo Brazil 11°50S 40°29W 333 D3
Mundo Nuevo Trin. & Tob. 10°28N 61°15W 323 t
Mundra India 22°54N 69°48E 242 H3
Mundrabilla Australia 31°52S 127°51E 279 F4
Munducurus Brazil 4°47S 58°16W 329 D6
Munenga Angola 10°2S 14°41E 265 E2
Munera Spain 39°2N 2°29W 197 F2
Muneru → India 16°45N 80°3E 244 F5
Mungallala Australia 26°28S 147°34E 281 D4
Mungallala Cr. → Australia 28°53S 147°5E 281 D4
Mungana Australia 17°8S 144°27E 280 B3
Mungaoli India 24°24N 78°7E 242 G8
Mungari Mozam. 17°12S 33°30E 269 F3
Mungbere Dem. Rep. of the Congo 2°36N 28°28E 268 B2
Mungeli India 22°4N 81°41E 243 H9
Munger India 25°23N 86°30E 243 G12
Mungkan Kandju △ Australia 13°35S 142°52E 280 A3
Mungo Angola 11°49S 16°16E 265 E3
Mungo, L. Australia 33°45S 143°0E 282 B5
Mungo △ Australia 33°44S 143°6E 282 B5
Munhango Angola 12°10S 18°38E 265 E3
Munhango → Angola 11°17S 19°44E 265 E4
Munich = München Germany 48°8N 11°34E 131 B2
Munirabad India 15°20N 76°20E 245 F3
Munising U.S.A. 46°25N 86°40W 308 B10
Munka-Ljungby Sweden 56°16N 12°58E 163 H6
Munkebo Denmark 55°27N 10°34E 163 J4
Munkedal Sweden 58°28N 11°40E 163 F5
Munkfors Sweden 59°47N 13°30E 162 E7
Munkkiniemi Finland 60°11N 24°52E 121 B2
Munku-Sardyk Russia 51°45N 100°20E 215 D11
Münnerstadt Germany 50°14N 10°12E 179 E6
Munoz Phil. 15°43N 120°54E 232 D3
Muñoz Gamero, Pen. Chile 52°30S 73°5W 336 D2
Munro Argentina 34°31S 58°31W 117 B1
Munroe L. Canada 59°13N 98°35W 297 B9
Munsan S. Korea 37°51N 126°48E 224 D3
Munshiganj Bangla. 23°33N 90°32E 241 D3
Munson U.S.A. 30°52N 86°52W 317 E3
Munster Haut-Rhin, France 48°2N 7°8E 173 D14
Münster Niedersachsen, Germany 52°58N 10°5E 178 C6
Münster Nordrhein-Westfalen, Germany 51°58N 7°37E 178 D3
Munster □ Ireland 52°18N 8°44W 166 D3
Münsterberg = Ziębice Poland 50°37N 17°2E 185 H4
Muntadgin Australia 31°45S 118°33E 279 F2
Muntele Mare, Vf. Romania 46°30N 23°12E 183 D8
Muntinlupa Phil. 14°23N 121°2E 127 C2
Muntok Indonesia 2°5S 105°10E 234 C3
Munyama Zambia 16°5S 28°31E 269 F2
Munzur Dağları Turkey 39°30N 39°10E 213 C8
Muong Beng Laos 20°23N 101°46E 228 G3
Muong Boum Vietnam 22°24N 102°49E 228 F4
Muong Et Laos 20°49N 104°1E 236 B5
Muong Hai Laos 21°3N 101°49E 228 G3
Muong Hiem Laos 20°5N 103°22E 236 B4
Muong Houn Laos 20°8N 101°23E 228 G3
Muong Hung Vietnam 20°56N 103°53E 228 G4
Muong Kau Laos 15°6N 105°47E 236 E5
Muong Khao Laos 19°38N 103°32E 236 C4
Muong Khoua Laos 21°5N 102°31E 228 G4
Muong Liep Laos 18°29N 101°40E 236 C3
Muong May Laos 14°49N 106°56E 236 E6
Muong Ngeun Laos 20°36N 101°3E 228 G3
Muong Ngoi Laos 20°43N 102°41E 228 G4
Muong Nhie Vietnam 22°12N 102°28E 228 F4
Muong Nong Laos 16°22N 106°30E 236 D6
Muong Ou Tay Laos 22°7N 101°48E 228 F3
Muong Oua Laos 18°18N 101°20E 236 C3
Muong Peun Laos 20°13N 103°52E 228 G4
Muong Phalane Laos 16°39N 105°34E 236 D5
Muong Phieng Laos 19°6N 101°32E 236 C3
Muong Phine Laos 16°32N 106°2E 236 D6
Muong Sai Laos 20°42N 101°59E 228 G3
Muong Saiapoun Laos 18°24N 101°31E 236 C3
Muong Sen Vietnam 19°24N 104°8E 236 C5
Muong Sing Laos 21°11N 101°9E 228 G3
Muong Son Laos 20°27N 103°19E 228 G4
Muong Soui Laos 19°33N 102°52E 236 C4
Muong Va Laos 21°53N 102°19E 228 G4
Muong Xia Vietnam 20°19N 104°50E 236 B5
Muonio Finland 67°57N 23°40E 160 C20
Muonio älv = Muonionjoki → Finland 67°11N 23°34E 160 C20
Muonioälven = Muonionjoki → Finland 67°11N 23°34E 160 C20
Muonionjoki → Finland 67°11N 23°34E 160 C20
Mupa Angola 16°5S 15°50E 265 F3
Mupa △ Angola 15°55S 15°35E 265 F3
Muping China 37°22N 121°36E 227 F11
Mupoi Sudan 5°28N 27°40E 257 F2
Muqaddam, Wadi → Sudan 18°4N 31°30E 256 D3
Muqdisho Somali Rep. 2°2N 45°25E 267 D6
Muqshin, W. → Oman 19°44N 55°14E 249 C6
Muquequete Angola 14°50S 14°16E 265 E2
Mur → Austria 46°18N 16°52E 181 E9
Mûr-de-Bretagne France 48°12N 3°0W 172 D4
Muradiye Manisa, Turkey 38°39N 27°21E 205 C9
Muradiye Van, Turkey 39°0N 43°44E 213 C10
Murai Res. Singapore 1°23N 103°40E 138 A2
Murakami Japan 38°14N 139°29E 220 E9
Murallón, Cerro Chile 49°48S 73°30W 336 C2
Muranda Rwanda 1°52S 29°20E 268 C2
Murang'a Kenya 0°45S 37°9E 268 C4
Muranów Poland 52°14N 20°58E 142 B1
Murashi Russia 59°30N 49°0E 186 C8
Murat France 45°7N 2°53E 174 C6
Murat → Turkey 38°46N 40°0E 213 C9
Murat Bay = Ceduna Australia 32°7S 133°46E 281 E1
Murat Dağı Turkey 38°55N 29°43E 205 C11
Muratlı Turkey 41°10N 27°29E 203 E11
Murato France 42°35N 9°20E 175 F13
Murau Austria 47°6N 14°10E 180 D7
Murava Belarus 52°39N 24°15E 185 F11
Muravera Italy 39°25N 9°34E 200 C2
Muravyevo = Mažeikiai Lithuania 56°20N 22°20E 184 B9
Muravyovsky = Korsakov Russia 46°36N 142°42E 215 E15
Murayama Japan 38°30N 140°25E 220 E10
Murça Portugal 41°24N 7°28W 194 D3
Murchison N.Z. 41°49S 172°21E 285 B7
Murchison → Australia 27°45S 114°0E 279 E1
Murchison, Mt. Antarctica 73°25S 166°20E 151 D11
Murchison, Mt. N.Z. 43°0S 171°22E 285 D6
Murchison Falls Uganda 2°15N 31°30E 268 B3
Murchison Falls △ Uganda 2°17N 31°48E 268 B3
Murchison Mts. N.Z. 45°13S 167°23E 285 F2
Murchison Ra. Australia 20°0S 134°10E 280 C1
Murchison Rapids Malawi 15°55S 34°35E 269 F3
Murcia Spain 38°5N 1°10W 197 G3
Murcia □ Spain 37°50N 1°30W 197 H3
Murdo U.S.A. 43°53N 100°43W 308 D3
Murdoch Pt. Australia 14°37S 144°55E 280 A3
Mürefte Turkey 40°40N 27°14E 203 F11
Mureş □ Romania 46°45N 24°40E 183 D9
Mureş → Romania 46°15N 20°13E 182 D5
Mureşul = Mureş → Romania 46°15N 20°13E 182 D5
Muret France 43°30N 1°20E 174 E5
Murewa Zimbabwe 17°39S 31°47E 271 A5
Murfreesboro N.C., U.S.A. 36°27N 77°6W 315 C16
Murfreesboro Tenn., U.S.A. 35°51N 86°24W 315 D11
Murgap Tajikistan 38°10N 74°2E 217 E8
Murgap → Turkmenistan 38°18N 61°12E 247 B9
Murgenella Australia 11°34S 132°56E 278 B5
Murgeni Romania 46°12N 28°1E 183 D13
Murgha Kibzai Pakistan 30°44N 69°25E 242 D3
Murghob = Murgap Tajikistan 38°10N 74°2E 217 E8
Murgon Australia 26°15S 151°54E 281 D5
Muri Cook Is. 21°15S 159°43W 289 h
Muri India 23°22N 85°52E 243 H11
Muria Indonesia 6°36S 110°53E 235 D4
Muriaé Brazil 21°8S 42°23W 333 F3
Murias de Paredes Spain 42°52N 6°11W 194 C4
Murici Brazil 9°19S 35°56W 332 C4
Muriége Angola 9°58S 21°11E 265 D4
Muriel Mine Zimbabwe 17°14S 30°40E 269 F3

Murila Angola 10°44S 20°20E 265 E4
Murino Russia 59°59N 30°29E 137 B2
Müritz Germany 53°25N 12°42E 178 B8
Müritz △ Germany 53°22N 12°55E 178 B8
Muriwai Beach N.Z. 36°50S 174°26E 284 C3
Murkong Selek India 27°44N 95°18E 241 B5
Murliganj India 25°54N 86°59E 243 G12
Murmansk Russia 68°57N 33°10E 160 B25
Murmashi Russia 68°47N 32°42E 160 B25
Murnau Germany 47°40N 11°12E 179 H7
Muro Haute-Corse, France 42°34N 8°54E 175 F12
Muro Spain 39°44N 3°3E 206 B4
Muro, C. de France 41°44N 8°37E 175 G12
Muro de Alcoy Spain 38°46N 0°26W 197 G4
Muro Lucano Italy 40°45N 15°29E 201 B8
Murom Russia 55°35N 42°3E 190 C6
Muroran Japan 42°25N 141°0E 220 C10
Muros Spain 42°45N 9°5W 194 C1
Muros y de Noya, Ría de Spain 42°45N 9°0W 194 C1
Muroto Japan 33°18N 134°9E 222 D6
Muroto-Misaki Japan 33°15N 134°10E 222 D6
Murovani Kurylivtsi Ukraine 48°44N 27°31E 183 B12
Murowana Goślina Poland 52°35N 17°0E 185 F3
Murphy U.S.A. 43°13N 116°33W 304 E5
Murphys U.S.A. 38°8N 120°28W 306 G6
Murphy's Station = Sunnyvale U.S.A. 37°23N 122°2W 306 H4
Murphysboro U.S.A. 37°46N 89°20W 310 G7
Murrat Sudan 18°51N 29°33E 256 D2
Murrat Wells Sudan 21°3N 32°55E 256 C3
Murray Iowa, U.S.A. 41°3N 93°57W 310 C3
Murray Ky., U.S.A. 36°37N 88°19W 308 G9
Murray Utah, U.S.A. 40°40N 111°53W 304 F8
Murray → Australia 35°20S 139°22E 282 C3
Murray, L. Papua N. G. 7°0S 141°35E 286 D1
Murray, L. S.C., U.S.A. 34°3N 81°13W 316 A8
Murray Bridge Australia 35°6S 139°14E 282 C3
Murray Fracture Zone Pac. Oc. 35°0N 130°0W 289 D14
Murray Harbour Canada 46°0N 62°28W 299 C7
Murray River △ Australia 34°23S 140°32E 281 E3
Murray-Sunset △ Australia 34°45S 141°30E 282 C4
Murrayfield U.K. 55°57N 3°15W 121 B2
Murraysburg S. Africa 31°58S 23°47E 270 D3
Murrayville U.S.A. 39°35N 90°15W 310 E6
Murree Pakistan 33°56N 73°28E 242 C5
Murrieta U.S.A. 33°33N 117°13W 307 M9
Murro di Porco, Capo Italy 37°0N 15°20E 201 F8
Murrumbateman Australia 34°58S 149°0E 283 C8
Murrumbidgee → Australia 34°43S 143°12E 282 C5
Murrumburrah Australia 34°32S 148°22E 283 C8
Murrurundi Australia 31°42S 150°51E 283 A9
Murshid Sudan 21°40N 31°10E 256 C3
Murshidabad India 24°11N 88°19E 243 G13
Murska Sobota Slovenia 46°39N 16°12E 199 B13
Murtazapur India 20°40N 77°25E 244 D3
Murtle L. Canada 52°8N 119°38W 296 C5
Murtoa Australia 36°35S 142°28E 282 D5
Murtosa Portugal 40°44N 8°40W 194 E2
Muru → Brazil 8°9S 70°45W 330 B3
Murud India 18°19N 72°58E 244 E1
Murungu Tanzania 4°12S 31°10E 268 C3
Murupara N.Z. 38°28S 176°42E 284 E5
Mururoa French Polynesia 21°52S 138°55W 289 f
Murwara India 23°46N 80°28E 243 H9
Murwillumbah Australia 28°18S 153°27E 281 D5
Mürz → Austria 47°30N 15°25E 180 D8
Mürzzuschlag Austria 47°36N 15°41E 180 D8
Mus India 9°14N 92°47E 245 K11
Muş Turkey 38°45N 41°30E 213 C9
Muş □ Turkey 38°45N 41°30E 213 C9
Musa Dem. Rep. of the Congo 2°40N 19°18E 264 B3
Musa → Papua N. G. 9°3S 148°55E 286 E5
Mûsa, Gebel Egypt 28°33N 33°59E 251 K4
Musa Khel Pakistan 30°59N 69°52E 242 D3
Mūsa Qal'eh Afghan. 32°20N 64°50E 240 B2
Musabeyli Turkey 36°53N 36°55E 250 B7
Musadi Dem. Rep. of the Congo 2°31S 22°50E 264 C4
Musafirkhana India 26°22N 81°48E 243 F9
Musala Bulgaria 42°13N 23°37E 202 D7
Musala Indonesia 1°41N 98°28E 234 B1
Musan N. Korea 42°12N 129°12E 224 A4
Musandam, Ra's Oman 26°20N 56°20E 249 A7
Musangu Dem. Rep. of the Congo 10°28S 23°55E 265 E4
Musasa Tanzania 3°25S 31°30E 268 C3
Musashino Japan 35°42N 139°33E 140 A2
Musay'īd Qatar 25°0N 51°33E 247 E6
Musaymīr Yemen 13°27N 44°37E 248 D4
Muscat = Masqat Oman 23°37N 58°36E 249 B7
Muscat & Oman = Oman ■ Asia 23°0N 58°0E 249 B7
Muscatatuck → U.S.A. 38°46N 86°10W 311 F10
Muscatine U.S.A. 41°25N 91°3W 310 C5
Muschu I. Papua N. G. 3°25S 143°35E 286 B2
Muscle Shoals U.S.A. 34°45N 87°40W 315 D11
Muscoda U.S.A. 43°11N 90°27W 310 A6
Musengezi = Unsengedsi → Zimbabwe 15°43S 31°14E 269 F3
Museu Nacional Brazil 22°59S 43°13W 135 B1
Museum of Contemporary Art Los Angeles, U.S.A. 127 b1
Museum of Modern Art San Francisco, U.S.A. 136 b2
Museum of Science Boston, U.S.A. 116 a1
Museumquartier Vienna, Austria 142 c1
Musgrave Harbour Canada 49°27N 53°58W 299 C9
Musgrave Ranges Australia 26°0S 132°0E 279 E5
Mushie Dem. Rep. of the Congo 2°56S 16°55E 264 C3
Mushima Zambia 14°10S 24°56E 265 E4
Mushin Nigeria 6°31N 3°21E 124 A2
Musi → India 16°41N 79°40E 244 F4
Musi → Indonesia 2°20S 104°56E 234 C2
Music Garden Toronto, Canada 141 c1
Musiektheater Amsterdam, Neths. 112 b2
Musina S. Africa 22°20S 30°5E 271 B5
Musiri India 10°56N 78°27E 245 J4
Muskeg → Canada 60°20N 123°20W 296 A4
Muskego U.S.A. 42°55N 88°8W 311 B8
Muskegon U.S.A. 43°14N 86°16W 311 A10
Muskegon → U.S.A. 43°14N 86°21W 308 D10
Muskegon Heights U.S.A. 43°12N 86°16W 311 A10
Muskogee U.S.A. 35°45N 95°22W 314 D7
Muskoka, L. Canada 45°0N 79°25W 312 B5
Muskwa → Canada 58°47N 122°48W 296 B4
Muslim Quarter Jerusalem 123 a3
Muslimiyah Syria 36°19N 37°12E 246 B3
Musmar Sudan 18°13N 35°40E 256 D4
Musocco Italy 45°29N 9°8E 129 B1
Musofu Zambia 13°30S 29°0E 269 E2
Musoma Tanzania 1°30S 33°48E 268 C3
Musquaro, L. Canada 50°38N 61°5W 299 B7
Musquodoboit Harbour Canada 44°50N 63°9W 299 D7
Mussau I. Papua N. G. 1°30S 149°40E 286 A5
Musselburgh U.K. 55°57N 3°2W 167 F5
Musselshell → U.S.A. 47°21N 107°57W 304 C10
Mussende Angola 10°32S 16°5E 265 E3
Mussidan France 45°2N 0°22E 174 C4
Mussolinea di Sardegna = Arborea Italy 39°46N 8°35E 200 C1
Mussolo Angola 9°59S 17°19E 265 D3
Mussomeli Italy 37°35N 13°45E 200 E6
Mussoorie India 30°27N 78°6E 242 D8
Mussuco Angola 17°2S 19°3E 265 F3
Mustafakemalpaşa Turkey 40°2N 28°24E 203 F12
Mustahil Ethiopia 5°16N 44°45E 267 C5
Mustang Nepal 29°10N 83°55E 243 E10
Mustansirīya Iraq 33°22N 44°24E 113 A2
Musters, L. Argentina 45°20S 69°25W 336 C3
Mustique I. St. Vincent 12°52N 61°11W 323 n
Musturud Egypt 30°8N 31°17E 117 A2
Musudan N. Korea 40°50N 129°43E 224 B4
Muswell Hill U.K. 51°35N 0°8W 125 A3
Muswellbrook Australia 32°16S 150°56E 283 B9
Muszyna Poland 49°22N 20°55E 185 J7
Mût Egypt 25°28N 28°58E 256 B2
Mut Turkey 36°40N 33°28E 250 B4
Mutalau Cook Is. 18°56S 169°50W 289 g
Mutanabi Iraq 33°19N 44°21E 113 B2
Mutanda Dem. Rep. of the Congo 5°17S 16°34E 265 D3
Mutanda Mozam. 21°0S 33°34E 271 B5
Mutanda Zambia 12°24S 26°13E 269 E2
Mutankiang = Mudanjiang China 44°38N 129°30E 227 B15
Mutanshe Taiwan 22°9N 120°48E 225 D2
Mutare Zimbabwe 18°58S 32°38E 269 F3
Mutawintji △ Australia 31°10S 142°30E 281 E3
Mutha Kenya 1°48S 38°26E 268 C4
Muthana Iraq 33°19N 44°27E 113 B2
Muting Indonesia 7°23S 140°20E 231 F10
Mutki = Mirtağ Turkey 38°23N 41°56E 246 B4
Mutoko Zimbabwe 17°24S 32°13E 271 A5
Mutomo Kenya 1°51S 38°12E 268 C4
Mutoray Russia 60°56N 101°0E 215 C11
Mutoto Dem. Rep. of the Congo 5°42S 22°42E 265 D4
Mutoxo Angola 12°17S 21°40E 265 E4
Mutsamudu Comoros Is. 12°10S 44°25E 272 a
Mutshatsha Dem. Rep. of the Congo 10°35S 24°20E 265 E4
Mutsu Japan 41°5N 140°55E 220 D10
Mutsu-Wan Japan 41°5N 140°55E 220 D10
Muttaburra Australia 22°38S 144°29E 280 C3
Muttalip Turkey 39°50N 30°32E 205 B12
Mutton I. Ireland 52°49N 9°32W 166 D2
Muttra = Mathura India 27°30N 77°40E 242 F7
Muttukuru India 14°16N 80°6E 245 G5
Mutuáli Mozam. 14°55S 37°0E 269 E4
Mutum Biyu Nigeria 8°40N 10°50E 263 D7
Mutunópolis Brazil 13°40S 49°15W 333 D2
Mutur Sri Lanka 8°27N 81°16E 245 K5
Muweilih Egypt 30°42N 34°19E 251 H5
Muxaluando Angola 8°8S 14°18E 265 D2
Muxía Spain 43°3N 9°10W 194 B1
Muxima Angola 9°33S 13°58E 265 D2
Muy Muy Nic. 12°39N 85°36W 320 D2
Muyinga Burundi 3°14S 30°33E 268 C3
Muynak Uzbekistan 43°44N 59°10E 216 D5
Muyunkum, Peski = Moyynqum Kazakhstan 44°12N 71°0E 217 D8
Muz Tag China 36°25N 87°25E 217 E11
Muzaffarabad Pakistan 34°25N 73°30E 243 B5
Muzaffargarh Pakistan 30°5N 71°14E 242 D4
Muzaffarnagar India 29°26N 77°40E 242 E7
Muzaffarpur India 26°7N 85°23E 243 F11
Muzafirpur Pakistan 30°58N 69°9E 242 D3
Muzeze Angola 15°3S 17°43E 265 F3
Muzhi Russia 65°25N 64°40E 186 A11
Muzillac France 47°35N 2°30W 172 E4
Muzon, C. U.S.A. 54°40N 132°42W 303 J14
Muztagh-Ata China 38°17N 75°7E 217 E9
Muztor = Toktogul Kyrgyzstan 41°50N 72°50E 217 D8
Muzūra Egypt 28°53N 30°48E 256 J7
Mvadhi-Ousyé Gabon 1°13N 13°12E 264 B2
Mvam Gabon 0°13S 9°39E 264 C1
Mvangan Cameroon 2°17N 11°43E 264 B2
Mvôlô Sudan 6°2N 29°53E 257 F2
Mvuma Zimbabwe 19°16S 30°30E 269 F3
Mvurwi Zimbabwe 17°0S 30°57E 269 F3
Mwabvi △ Malawi 16°42S 35°0E 269 F3
Mwadi-Kalumbu Dem. Rep. of the Congo 7°53S 18°43E 265 D3
Mwadui Tanzania 3°26S 33°32E 268 C3
Mwali = Mohéli Comoros Is. 12°20S 43°40E 272 a
Mwambo Tanzania 10°30S 40°22E 269 E5
Mwandi Zambia 17°30S 24°51E 269 F1
Mwanza Katanga, Dem. Rep. of the Congo 7°55S 26°43E 265 D5
Mwanza Tanzania 2°30S 32°58E 268 C3
Mwanza Zambia 16°58S 24°28E 265 F4
Mwanza □ Tanzania 2°0S 33°0E 268 C3
Mwaya Tanzania 9°32S 33°55E 269 D3
Mweelrea Ireland 53°39N 9°49W 166 C2
Mweka Dem. Rep. of the Congo 4°50S 21°34E 265 C4
Mwendjila Dem. Rep. of the Congo 7°12S 18°51E 265 D3
Mwene-Ditu Dem. Rep. of the Congo 6°35S 22°27E 265 D4
Mwenezi Zimbabwe 21°15S 30°48E 269 G3
Mwenezi → Mozam. 22°40S 31°50E 269 G3
Mwenga Dem. Rep. of the Congo 3°1S 28°28E 268 C2
Mweru, L. Zambia 9°0S 28°40E 269 D2
Mweru Wantipa △ Zambia 8°39S 29°25E 269 D2
Mwetshi Dem. Rep. of the Congo 4°50S 22°38E 265 C4
Mweza Range Zimbabwe 21°0S 30°0E 269 G3
Mwilambwe Dem. Rep. of the Congo 8°7S 25°5E 265 D5
Mwimbi Tanzania 8°38S 31°39E 269 D3
Mwingi Kenya 0°56S 38°4E 268 C4
Mwinilunga Zambia 11°43S 24°25E 265 E4
My Tho Vietnam 10°29N 106°23E 237 G6
Mya, O. → Algeria 30°46N 4°54E 261 B5
Myajlar India 26°15N 70°20E 242 F4
Myakinino Russia 55°48N 37°22E 129 B2
Myakka → U.S.A. 26°56N 82°11W 317 J7
Myall Lakes △ Australia 32°25S 152°30E 283 B10
Myanaung Burma 18°18N 95°22E 241 F5
Myanmar = Burma ■ Asia 21°0N 96°30E 241 E6
Myaung Burma 21°50N 95°25E 241 E5
Myaungmya Burma 16°30N 94°40E 241 G5
Mycenæ = Mikines Greece 37°43N 22°46E 204 D4
Myebon Burma 20°3N 93°22E 241 E4
Myedna Belarus 51°52N 23°48E 185 G10
Myeik Kyunzu Burma 11°30N 97°30E 237 G1
Myerstown U.S.A. 40°22N 76°19W 313 F8
Myingyan Burma 21°30N 95°20E 241 E5
Myitkyina Burma 25°24N 97°26E 241 C6
Myitson Burma 23°16N 96°34E 241 D6
Myittha Burma 21°25N 96°8E 241 E6
Myittha → Burma 23°12N 94°17E 241 D5
Myjava Slovak Rep. 48°41N 17°37E 181 C10
Mykerinos Egypt 29°58N 31°8E 117 B1
Mykhaylivka Ukraine 47°12N 35°15E 189 J8
Mykines Færoe Is. 62°7N 7°35W 160 E9
Myking Norway 60°41N 5°19E 164 D2
Mykolayiv Ukraine 46°58N 32°0E 189 J7
Mykolayiv □ Ukraine 47°20N 31°50E 189 J6
Mykonos Greece 37°30N 25°25E 205 D7
Mylius Erichsen Land Greenland 81°30N 27°0W 154 A8
Myllypuro Finland 60°13N 25°3E 121 B3
Mymensingh Bangla. 24°45N 90°24E 241 C3
Mynydd Du U.K. 51°52N 3°50W 169 F4
Myo-gyi Burma 21°27N 96°22E 241 E6
Myohaung Burma 20°35N 93°11E 241 E4
Myohla Burma 19°16N 95°25E 241 F5
Myotha Burma 21°41N 95°43E 241 E5
Myothit Kachin, Burma 24°24N 97°24E 241 C6
Myothit Magwe, Burma 20°12N 95°27E 241 E5
Myrasýsla □ Iceland 64°45N 21°30W 155 C5
Mýrdalsjökull Iceland 63°40N 19°6W 155 D7
Myrhorod Ukraine 49°58N 33°37E 189 H7
Mýri Iceland 65°23N 17°23W 155 B9
Myrtle Beach U.S.A. 33°42N 78°53W 315 E15
Myrtle Creek U.S.A. 43°1N 123°17W 304 E2
Myrtle Grove U.S.A. 30°23N 87°17W 317 E2
Myrtle Point U.S.A. 43°4N 124°8W 304 E1
Myrtleford Australia 36°34S 146°44E 283 D7
Myrtou Cyprus 35°18N 33°4E 207 E9
Mysen Norway 59°33N 11°20E 164 E8
Mysia Turkey 39°50N 27°0E 203 G11
Myślenice Poland 49°51N 19°57E 185 J6
Myślibórz Poland 52°55N 14°50E 185 F1
Mysłowice Poland 50°15N 19°12E 185 H6
Myslowitz = Mysłowice Poland 50°15N 19°12E 185 H6
Mysore = Karnataka □ India 13°15N 77°0E 245 H3
Mysore India 12°17N 76°41E 245 H3
Mystic Conn., U.S.A. 41°21N 71°58W 313 E13
Mystic Iowa, U.S.A. 40°47N 92°57W 310 D4
Mystic → U.S.A. 42°22N 71°3W 116 A2
Myszków Poland 50°45N 19°22E 185 H6
Myszyniec Poland 53°23N 21°21E 184 E8
Mytishchi Russia 55°50N 37°50E 188 E9
Mývatn Iceland 65°36N 17°0W 155 B10
Mzab, Oued en → Algeria 32°15N 5°0E 261 B6
Mže → Czech Rep. 49°46N 13°24E 180 B6
Mzimba Malawi 11°55S 33°39E 269 E3
Mzimkulu → S. Africa 30°44S 30°28E 271 D5
Mzimvubu → S. Africa 31°38S 29°33E 271 D4
Mzuzu Malawi 11°30S 33°55E 269 E3

N

N.S.W. Jervis Bay △ Australia 35°9S 150°40E 283 C9
Na Hearadh = Harris U.K. 57°50N 6°55W 167 D2
Na-lang Burma 22°42N 97°33E 241 D6
Na Noi Thailand 18°19N 100°43E 236 C3
Na Phao Laos 17°35N 105°44E 236 D5
Na Sam Vietnam 22°3N 106°37E 228 F6
Na San Vietnam 21°12N 104°2E 236 B5
Na Thon Thailand 9°32N 99°56E 237 b
Naab → Germany 49°1N 12°2E 179 F8
Nā'ālehu U.S.A. 19°4N 155°35W 302 D6
Na'am Sudan 9°42N 28°27E 257 F2
Na'am → Sudan 6°48N 29°57E 257 F2
Naama Algeria 33°16N 0°19E 261 B5
Naama □ Algeria 33°15N 0°45E 261 B5
Naantali Finland 60°29N 22°2E 188 B1
Naas Ireland 53°12N 6°40W 166 C5
Nababeep S. Africa 29°36S 17°46E 270 C2
Nabadwip = Navadwip India 23°34N 88°20E 243 H13
Nabari Japan 34°37N 136°5E 223 C8
Nabawa Australia 28°30S 114°48E 279 E1
Nabberu, L. Australia 25°50S 120°30E 279 E3
Nabburg Germany 49°27N 12°11E 179 F8
Naberezhnyye Chelny Russia 55°42N 52°19E 190 C11
Nabesna U.S.A. 62°22N 143°0W 303 E12
Nabeul Tunisia 36°30N 10°44E 258 A2
Nabeul □ Tunisia 36°30N 10°40E 261 A7
Nabha India 30°26N 76°14E 242 D7
Nabi Sālih Egypt 28°37N 33°59E 251 K4
Nabīd Iran 29°40N 57°38E 247 D8
Nabire Indonesia 3°15S 135°26E 231 E9
Nabisar Pakistan 25°8N 69°40E 242 G3
Nabisipi → Canada 50°14N 62°13W 299 B7
Nabiswera Uganda 1°27N 32°15E 268 B3
Nāblus = Nābulus West Bank 32°14N 35°15E 251 F6
Naboomspruit S. Africa 24°32S 28°40E 271 B4
Nabou Burkina Faso 11°25N 2°50W 262 C4
Nabouwalu Fiji 17°0S 178°45E 287 A2
Nabq Egypt 28°6N 34°25E 251 K5
Nabua Phil. 13°24N 123°22E 232 E4
Nābulus West Bank 32°14N 35°15E 251 F6
Nabunturan Phil. 7°35N 125°58E 233 H5
Nacala Mozam. 14°31S 40°34E 269 E5
Nacala-Velha Mozam. 14°32S 40°34E 269 E5
Nacaome Honduras 13°31N 87°30W 320 D2
Nacaroa Mozam. 14°22S 39°56E 269 E4
Naches U.S.A. 46°44N 120°42W 304 C3
Naches → U.S.A. 46°38N 120°31W 306 D6
Nachicapau, L. Canada 56°40N 68°5W 299 A6
Nachikatsuura Japan 33°33N 135°58E 223 D7
Nachingwea Tanzania 10°23S 38°49E 269 E4
Nachna India 27°34N 71°41E 242 F4
Náchod Czech Rep. 50°25N 16°8E 180 A9
Nachuge India 10°47N 92°21E 245 J11
Nacimiento, L. U.S.A. 35°46N 120°53W 306 K6
Nacional, Palacio Mexico City, Mexico 128 b3
Nacka Sweden 59°19N 18°10E 139 B3
Nackara Australia 32°48S 139°12E 282 B3
Naco Mexico 31°19N 109°56W 318 A3
Nacogdoches U.S.A. 31°36N 94°39W 314 F7
Nácori Chico Mexico 29°40N 108°57W 318 B3
Nacozari de García Mexico 30°25N 109°38W 318 A3
Nacula Fiji 16°54S 177°27E 287 A1
Nådendal = Naantali Finland 60°29N 22°2E 188 B1
Nadezhdinsky = Serov Russia 59°29N 60°35E 186 C11
Nadi Fiji 17°42S 177°20E 287 A1
Nadi Sudan 18°40N 33°41E 256 D3
Nadiad India 22°41N 72°56E 242 H5
Nădlac Romania 46°10N 20°50E 182 D5
Nador Morocco 35°14N 2°58W 261 A4
Nadur Malta 35°54N 14°22E 206 F7
Nadur Gozo, Malta 36°2N 14°18E 206 E7
Nadūshan Iran 32°2N 53°35E 247 C7
Nadvirna Ukraine 48°37N 24°30E 183 B9
Nadvoitsy Russia 63°52N 34°14E 186 B5
Nadvornaya = Nadvirna Ukraine 48°37N 24°30E 183 B9
Nadym Russia 65°35N 72°42E 214 C8
Nadym → Russia 66°12N 72°0E 214 C8
Naenae N.Z. 41°12S 174°57E 143 B2
Nærbø Norway 58°40N 5°39E 164 F2
Nærsnes Norway 59°45N 10°27E 133 B1
Næstved Denmark 55°13N 11°44E 163 J5
Nafada Nigeria 11°8N 11°20E 263 C7
Nafpaktos Greece 38°24N 21°50E 204 C3
Nafplio Greece 37°33N 22°50E 204 D4
Naft-e Safīd Iran 31°40N 49°17E 247 D6
Naftan Pt. N. Marianas 15°5N 145°45E 302 e
Naftshahr Iran 34°0N 45°30E 213 E11
Nafud Desert = An Nafūd Si. Arabia 28°15N 41°0E 246 D4
Nafūsah, Jabal Libya 32°12N 12°30E 258 B2
Nag Hammâdi Egypt 26°2N 32°18E 256 B3
Naga Japan 26°34N 127°43E 288 a
Naga Camarines S., Phil. 13°38N 123°15E 232 E4
Naga Cebu, Phil. 10°13N 123°45E 233 F4
Naga Zamboanga del S., Phil. 7°46N 122°45E 233 H4
Naga, Kreb en Africa 24°12N 6°0W 260 D3
Naga Hills = Nagaland □ India 26°0N 94°30E 241 C5
Naga-Shima Kagoshima, Japan 32°10N 130°9E 222 E2
Naga-Shima Yamaguchi, Japan 33°49N 132°5E 222 D4
Nagagami Canada 50°23N 84°20W 298 B3
Nagahama Ehime, Japan 33°36N 132°29E 222 D4
Nagahama Shiga, Japan 35°23N 136°16E 223 B8
Nagai Japan 38°6N 140°2E 220 E10
Nagai I. U.S.A. 55°5N 160°0W 303 J8
Nagaland □ India 26°0N 94°30E 241 C5
Nagambie Australia 36°47S 145°10E 283 D6
Nagano Japan 36°40N 138°10E 223 A10
Nagano □ Japan 36°15N 138°0E 223 A10
Nagaoka Japan 37°27N 138°51E 221 F9
Nagappattinam India 10°46N 79°51E 245 J4
Nagar → Bangla. 24°27N 89°12E 241 C2
Nagar Karnul India 16°29N 78°20E 245 F4
Nagar Parkar Pakistan 24°28N 70°46E 242 G4
Nagara-Gawa → Japan 35°40N 136°43E 223 B8
Nagaram India 18°21N 80°26E 244 E5
Nagarhole △ India 12°0N 76°10E 245 J3
Nagari Hills India 13°3N 79°45E 245 H4
Nagasaki Japan 32°47N 129°50E 222 E1
Nagasaki □ Japan 32°50N 129°40E 222 E1
Nagato Japan 34°19N 131°5E 222 C3
Nagatsuta Japan 35°32N 139°31E 140 B2
Nagaur India 27°15N 73°45E 242 F5
Nagbhir India 20°34N 79°55E 244 D4
Nagda India 23°27N 75°25E 242 H6
Nagercoil India 8°12N 77°26E 245 K3
Nagina India 29°30N 78°30E 243 E8
Nagīneh Iran 34°20N 57°15E 247 C8
Naginimara India 26°49N 94°50E 241 B5
Nagir Pakistan 36°12N 74°42E 243 A6
Naglarby Sweden 60°25N 15°34E 162 D9
Nagles Mts. Ireland 52°8N 8°30W 166 D3
Nago-wan Japan 26°34N 127°57E 288 a
Nagod India 24°34N 80°36E 243 G9
Nagold Germany 48°32N 8°43E 179 G4
Nagold → Germany 48°52N 8°42E 179 G4
Nagoorin Australia 24°17S 151°15E 280 C5
Nagorno-Karabakh □ Azerbaijan 39°55N 46°45E 213 C12
Nagornyy Russia 55°58N 124°57E 215 D13
Nagoya Japan 35°10N 136°50E 223 B8
Nagoya ✕ (NGO) Japan 35°14N 136°57E 223 B8
Nagpartian = Burgos Phil. 18°31N 120°39E 232 B3
Nagpur India 21°8N 79°10E 244 D4
Nags Head St. Kitts & Nevis 17°13N 62°38W 322 d
Nagua Dom. Rep. 19°23N 69°50W 321 C6
Naguabo Puerto Rico 18°13N 65°44W 321 b
Nagyatád Hungary 46°14N 17°22E 182 D2
Nagyecsed Hungary 47°53N 22°24E 182 C7
Nagykálló Hungary 47°53N 21°51E 182 C6
Nagykanizsa Hungary 46°28N 17°0E 182 D2
Nagykáta Hungary 47°25N 19°45E 182 C4
Nagykőrös Hungary 47°5N 19°48E 182 C4
Nagyszombat = Trnava Slovak Rep. 48°23N 17°35E 181 C10
Nagytétény Hungary 47°23N 18°59E 117 B1
Nagyvárad = Oradea Romania 47°2N 21°58E 182 C6
Naha Japan 26°13N 127°42E 288 a
Nahalin West Bank 31°41N 35°7E 123 B1
Nahan India 30°33N 77°18E 242 D7
Nahanni △ Canada 61°36N 125°41W 296 A4
Nahanni Butte Canada 61°2N 123°31W 296 A4
Nahargarh Mad. P., India 24°10N 75°14E 242 G6
Nahargarh Raj., India 24°55N 76°50E 242 G7
Nahariyya Israel 33°1N 35°5E 250 F6
Nahāvand Iran 34°10N 48°22E 213 E13
Nahe → Germany 49°58N 7°54E 179 F3
Nahirne Ukraine 45°26N 28°27E 183 E13
Nahīya, W. → Egypt 28°55N 31°0E 256 B3
Nahuel Huapi, L. Argentina 41°0S 71°32W 336 B2
Nahuel Huapi △ Argentina 41°3S 71°59W 336 B2
Nahuelbuta △ Chile 37°44S 72°57W 334 D1
Nahunta U.S.A. 31°12N 81°59W 316 D8
Nai Yong Thailand 8°14N 98°22E 237 a
Naic Phil. 14°19N 120°46E 232 D3
Naicá Mexico 27°53N 105°31W 318 B3
Naicam Canada 52°30N 104°30W 297 C8
Naifaru Maldives 5°26N 73°20E 272 d
Naikoon △ Canada 53°55N 131°55W 296 C2
Naikul India 21°20N 84°58E 244 D7
Naila Germany 50°19N 11°42E 179 E7
Naimisharanya India 27°21N 80°30E 243 F9
Nain Nfld. & L., Canada 56°34N 61°40W 299 A7
Nā'īn Iran 32°54N 53°0E 247 C7
Nain Jamaica 17°57N 77°38W 320 a
Naini Tal India 29°30N 79°30E 243 E8
Nainpur India 22°30N 80°10E 243 H9
Naintré France 46°46N 0°29E 172 F7
Nainwa India 25°46N 75°51E 242 G6
Naipu Romania 44°12N 25°47E 183 F10
Nairai Fiji 17°49S 179°15E 287 A2
Nairn U.K. 57°35N 3°53W 167 D5
Nairobi Kenya 1°17S 36°48E 268 C4
Nairobi △ Kenya 1°22S 36°50E 268 C4
Naissaar Estonia 59°34N 24°29E 188 C3
Naita, Mt. Ethiopia 5°30N 35°18E 257 F4
Naitaba Fiji 17°0S 179°16W 287 A3
Naivasha Kenya 0°40S 36°30E 268 C4
Naivasha, L. Kenya 0°48S 36°20E 268 C4
Najac France 44°14N 1°58E 174 D5
Najaf = An Najaf Iraq 32°3N 44°15E 213 G11
Najafābād Iran 32°40N 51°15E 247 C6
Najafgarh Drain → India 28°39N 77°4E 120 B1
Najd Si. Arabia 26°30N 42°0E 238 D4
Nájera Spain 42°26N 2°48W 196 C2
Najerilla → Spain 42°32N 2°48W 196 C2
Najibabad India 29°40N 78°20E 242 E8
Najin N. Korea 42°12N 130°15E 224 A5
Najmah Si. Arabia 26°42N 50°6E 247 E6
Najrān Si. Arabia 17°34N 44°18E 248 C4
Najrān □ Si. Arabia 18°30N 45°50E 248 C4
Naju S. Korea 35°3N 126°43E 224 E3
Naka-Gawa → Japan 36°20N 140°36E 223 A12
Nakadōri-Shima Japan 32°57N 129°4E 221 H4
Nakagusuku-wan Japan 26°14N 127°53E 288 a
Nakahara Japan 35°33N 139°37E 140 B2
Nakal = Nakło nad Notecią Poland 53°9N 17°38E 185 E4
Nakalagba Dem. Rep. of the Congo 2°50N 27°58E 268 B2
Nakalele Pt. U.S.A. 21°2N 156°35W 302 B5
Nakama Japan 33°56N 130°43E 222 D2
Nakaminato Japan 36°21N 140°36E 223 A12
Nakamura Japan 32°59N 132°56E 222 E4
Nakanai Mts. Papua N. G. 5°40S 151°0E 286 C6
Nakano Japan 36°45N 138°22E 223 A10
Nakano Tōkyō, Japan 35°42N 139°39E 140 A2
Nakano-Shima Japan 29°51N 129°52E 221 K4
Nakanojō Japan 36°35N 138°51E 223 A10
Nakashibetsu Japan 43°33N 144°59E 220 C12
Nakatsu Japan 33°34N 131°15E 222 D3
Nakatsugawa Japan 35°29N 137°30E 223 B9
Nakfa Eritrea 16°40N 38°32E 257 D4
Nakfa △ Eritrea 17°28N 38°55E 257 D4
Nakha Yai, Ko Thailand 8°3N 98°28E 237 a
Nakhichevan = Naxçıvan Azerbaijan 39°12N 45°15E 213 C11
Nakhichevan Rep. = Naxçıvan □ Azerbaijan 39°25N 45°26E 213 C11
Nakhl Egypt 29°55N 33°43E 251 J4
Nakhl-e Taqī Iran 27°28N 52°36E 247 E7
Nakhodka Russia 42°53N 132°54E 220 C6
Nakhon Nayok Thailand 14°12N 101°13E 236 E3
Nakhon Pathom Thailand 13°49N 100°3E 236 F3
Nakhon Phanom Thailand 17°23N 104°43E 236 D5
Nakhon Ratchasima Thailand 14°59N 102°12E 236 E4
Nakhon Sawan Thailand 15°35N 100°10E 236 E3
Nakhon Si Thammarat Thailand 8°29N 100°0E 237 H3
Nakhon Thai Thailand 17°5N 100°44E 236 D3
Nakhtarana India 23°20N 69°15E 242 H3
Nakijin Japan 26°40N 127°58E 288 a
Nakina Canada 50°10N 86°40W 298 B2
Nakło nad Notecią Poland 53°9N 17°38E 185 E4
Naknek U.S.A. 58°44N 157°1W 303 G8
Nako Burkina Faso 10°40N 3°4W 262 C4
Nakodar India 31°8N 75°31E 242 D6
Nakskov Denmark 54°50N 11°8E 163 K5
Naktong → S. Korea 35°7N 128°57E 227 G15
Nakuru Kenya 0°15S 36°4E 268 C4
Nakuru, L. Kenya 0°23S 36°5E 268 C4
Nakusp Canada 50°20N 117°45W 296 C5
Nal Pakistan 27°40N 66°12E 242 F2
Nal → Pakistan 25°20N 65°30E 242 G1
Nalázi Mozam. 24°3S 33°20E 271 B5
Nalchik Russia 43°30N 43°33E 191 J6
Nałęczów Poland 51°17N 22°9E 185 G9
Nalerigu Ghana 10°35N 0°25W 263 C4
Nalgonda India 17°6N 79°15E 244 F4
Nalhati India 24°17N 87°52E 243 G12
Naliya India 23°16N 68°50E 242 H3
Nallamalai Hills India 15°30N 78°50E 245 G4
Nallıhan Turkey 40°11N 31°20E 212 B4
Nalolo Zambia 15°33S 23°7E 265 F4
Nalón → Spain 43°32N 6°4W 194 B4
Nalong Burma 24°44N 97°28E 241 C6
Nalubaale Dam Uganda 0°30N 33°5E 268 B3
Nālūt Libya 31°54N 11°0E 258 B2
Nam Can Vietnam 8°46N 104°59E 237 H5
Nam-ch'on N. Korea 38°15N 126°26E 224 E3
Nam Co China 30°30N 90°45E 218 C4
Nam Dinh Vietnam 20°25N 106°5E 228 G6
Nam Du, Hon Vietnam 9°41N 104°21E 237 H5
Nam Nao △ Thailand 16°44N 101°32E 236 D3
Nam Ngum Res. Laos 18°35N 102°34E 236 C4
Nam-Phan Vietnam 10°30N 106°0E 237 G6
Nam Phong Thailand 16°42N 102°52E 236 D4
Nam Tha Laos 20°58N 101°30E 228 G3
Nam Tok Thailand 14°21N 99°4E 236 E2
Namachire Angola 11°26S 22°43E 265 E4
Namacunde Angola 17°18S 15°50E 265 F3
Namacurra Mozam. 17°30S 36°50E 271 A6
Namadgi △ Australia 35°42S 149°0E 283 C8
Namai B. Palau 7°31N 134°38E 288 c
Namak, Daryācheh-ye Iran 34°30N 52°0E 247 C7
Namak, Kavir-e Iran 34°30N 57°30E 247 C8
Namakkal India 11°13N 78°13E 245 J4
Namakzār, Daryācheh-ye Iran 34°0N 60°30E 240 B1
Namaland Namibia 26°0S 17°0E 270 B2
Namanga Kenya 2°33S 36°47E 268 C4
Namangan Uzbekistan 41°0N 71°40E 217 D8
Namangan □ Uzbekistan 41°0N 71°15E 217 D8
Namapa Mozam. 13°43S 39°50E 269 E4
Namaqua △ S. Africa 30°0S 17°25E 270 C2
Namaqualand S. Africa 30°0S 17°25E 270 D2
Namasagali Uganda 1°2N 33°0E 268 B3
Namatanai Papua N. G. 3°40S 152°29E 286 B7
Namber Indonesia 1°2S 134°49E 231 E8
Nambour Australia 26°32S 152°58E 281 D5
Nambouwalu = Nabouwalu Fiji 17°0S 178°45E 287 A2
Nambuangongo Angola 8°1S 14°12E 265 D2
Nambucca Heads Australia 30°37S 153°0E 283 A10
Nambung △ Australia 30°30S 115°5E 279 F2
Namcha Barwa China 29°40N 95°10E 218 D4
Namche Bazar Nepal 27°51N 86°47E 243 F12
Namchonjŏm = Nam-ch'on N. Korea 38°15N 126°26E 224 C3
Namdapha △ India 27°30N 96°50E 241 B6
Namecunda Mozam. 14°54S 37°37E 269 E4
Nameh Indonesia 2°34N 116°21E 235 B5
Namen = Namur Belgium 50°27N 4°52E 170 D4
Namenalala Fiji 17°8S 179°9E 287 A2
Nameponda Mozam. 15°50S 39°50E 269 F4
Nameri △ India 26°55N 92°55E 241 B4
Namerikawa Japan 36°46N 137°20E 223 A9
Náměšť nad Oslavou Czech Rep. 49°12N 16°10E 181 B9
Námestovo Slovak Rep. 49°24N 19°25E 181 B12
Nametil Mozam. 15°40S 39°21E 269 F4
Namew L. Canada 54°14N 101°56W 297 C8
Namgia India 31°48N 78°40E 243 D8
Namhkam Burma 23°50N 97°41E 228 E1
Namho Burma 22°49N 99°1E 241 D7
Namhsan Burma 22°48N 97°2E 241 D6
Namib Desert Namibia 22°30S 15°0E 270 B2
Namib-Naukluft ⌂ Namibia 24°40S 15°16E 270 B2
Namibe Angola 15°7S 12°11E 265 F2
Namibe □ Angola 16°35S 12°30E 265 F2
Namibe ⌂ Angola 16°35S 12°20E 265 F2
Namibia ■ Africa 22°0S 18°9E 270 B2
Namibia Abyssal Plain Atl. Oc. 30°0S 5°30E 152 J12
Namibwoestyn = Namib Desert Namibia 22°30S 15°0E 270 B2
Namīn Iran 38°25N 48°30E 213 C13
Namjeju S. Korea 33°14N 126°33E 224 a
Namlan Burma 22°15N 97°24E 241 D6
Namlea Indonesia 3°18S 127°5E 231 E7
Namoi → Australia 30°12S 149°30E 283 A9
Namous, O. en → Algeria 31°0N 0°15W 261 B4
Nampa U.S.A. 43°34N 116°34W 304 E5
Nampala Mali 15°20N 5°30W 262 B3
Namp'o N. Korea 38°52N 125°10E 224 C2
Namp'o □ N. Korea 38°52N 125°25E 224 C2
Nampō-Shotō Japan 32°0N 140°0E 221 J10
Nampula Mozam. 15°6S 39°15E 269 F4
Namrole Indonesia 3°46S 126°46E 231 E7
Namsan Park S. Korea 37°32N 126°59E 137 B1
Namsang Burma 20°53N 97°43E 241 E6
Namse Shankou China 30°0N 82°25E 243 E10
Namsen → Norway 64°28N 11°37E 160 D14
Namslau = Namysłów Poland 51°6N 17°42E 185 G4
Namsos Norway 64°29N 11°30E 160 D14
Namtok Chat Trakan △ Thailand 17°17N 100°40E 236 D3
Namtok Mae Surin △ Thailand 18°55N 98°2E 236 C2
Namtsy Russia 62°43N 129°37E 215 C13
Namtu Burma 23°5N 97°28E 241 D6
Namtumbo Tanzania 10°30S 36°4E 269 E4
Namu Canada 51°52N 127°50W 296 C3
Namuka-i-Lau Fiji 18°53S 178°37W 287 B3
Namukulu Cook Is. 18°57S 169°54W 289 g
Namumea Tuvalu 5°41S 176°9E 277 B14
Namur Belgium 50°27N 4°52E 170 D4
Namur □ Belgium 50°17N 5°0E 170 D4
Namuruputh Kenya 4°34N 35°57E 268 B4
Namutoni Namibia 18°49S 16°55E 270 A2
Namwala Zambia 15°44S 26°30E 269 F2
Namwon Jeju-do, S. Korea 33°16N 126°43E 224 a
Namwon Jeollabuk-do, S. Korea 35°23N 127°23E 224 E3
Namyang N. Korea 42°57N 129°52E 224 A4
Namyangju S. Korea 37°38N 127°12E 224 D3
Namyeong S. Korea 37°32N 126°57E 137 B1
Namysłów Poland 51°6N 17°42E 185 G4
Nan Thailand 18°48N 100°46E 236 C3
Nan → Thailand 15°42N 100°9E 236 E3
Nan-ch'ang = Nanchang China 28°42N 115°55E 229 C10
Nan Ling China 25°0N 112°30E 229 E8
Nan Xian China 29°20N 112°22E 229 C9
Nana C.A.R. 5°0N 15°50E 264 A3
Nana Romania 44°17N 26°34E 183 F11
Nana-Barya ⌂ C.A.R. 7°40N 17°29E 264 A3
Nana Kru Liberia 4°55N 8°45W 262 E3
Nanaimo Canada 49°10N 124°0W 296 D4
Nānākuli U.S.A. 21°24N 158°9W 302 K13
Nanam N. Korea 41°44N 129°40E 224 B4
Nanan China 24°59N 118°21E 229 E12
Nanango Australia 26°40S 152°0E 281 D5
Nan'ao Guangdong, China 23°28N 117°5E 229 F11
Nanao Japan 37°0N 137°0E 221 F8
Nanao Taiwan 24°28N 121°48E 225 B3
Nanbiancun China 23°4N 113°10E 121 B1
Nanbu China 31°18N 106°3E 228 B6
Nanchang China 28°42N 115°55E 229 C10
Nanchang He → China 39°58N 116°14E 114 B1
Nancheng China 27°33N 116°35E 229 D11
Nanching = Nanjing China 32°2N 118°47E 229 A12
Nanchong China 30°43N 106°2E 228 B6
Nanchuan China 29°9N 107°6E 228 C6
Nanchung = Nanchong China 30°43N 106°2E 228 B6
Nancowry India 7°59N 93°32E 245 L11
Nancy France 48°42N 6°12E 173 D13
Nanda Devi India 30°23N 79°59E 243 D8
Nanda Devi △ India 30°30N 79°50E 243 D8
Nanda Kot India 30°17N 80°5E 243 D9
Nandan Guangxi Zhuangzu, China 24°58N 107°29E 228 E6
Nandan Japan 34°10N 134°42E 222 C6
Nandang China 23°6N 113°12E 121 B1
Nanded India 19°10N 77°20E 244 E3
Nandewar Ra. Australia 30°15S 150°35E 281 E5
Nandgaon India 20°19N 74°39E 244 D2
Nandi = Nadi Fiji 17°42S 177°20E 287 A1
Nandigama India 16°47N 80°18E 244 F5
Nandigram India 22°1N 87°58E 243 H12
Nandikotkur India 15°52N 78°18E 245 G4
Nandura India 20°52N 76°25E 244 D3
Nandurbar India 21°20N 74°15E 244 D2
Nandyal India 15°30N 78°30E 245 G4
Nanfeng Guangdong, China 23°45N 111°47E 229 F8
Nanfeng Jiangxi, China 27°12N 116°28E 229 D11
Nanga-Eboko Cameroon 4°41N 12°22E 263 E7
Nanga Parbat Pakistan 35°10N 74°35E 243 B6
Nangade Mozam. 11°5S 39°36E 269 E4
Nangal Dewat India 28°33N 77°5E 120 B1
Nangapinoh Indonesia 0°20S 111°44E 235 C4
Nangar △ Australia 33°23S 148°3E 283 B8
Nangarhār □ Afghan. 34°20N 70°0E 240 B3
Nangatayap Indonesia 1°32S 110°34E 235 C4
Nangeya Mts. Uganda 3°30N 33°30E 268 B3
Nangis France 48°33N 3°1E 173 D10
Nangnim-sanmaek N. Korea 40°13N 126°51E 224 B3
Nangong China 37°23N 115°22E 226 F8
Nangtud, Mt. Phil. 11°17N 122°11E 233 F4
Nanguneri India 8°29N 77°40E 245 K3
Nangwarry Australia 37°33S 140°48E 282 D4
Nanhua Yunnan, China 25°13N 101°21E 228 E3
Nanhua Taiwan 23°2N 120°28E 225 C2
Nanhuang China 36°58N 121°48E 227 F11
Nanhui China 31°5N 121°44E 229 B13
Nanhunan Shan Taiwan 24°21N 121°26E 225 B3
Naniwa Japan 34°39N 135°29E 133 B1
Nanjangud India 12°6N 76°43E 245 H3
Nanjeko Zambia 15°31S 23°30E 269 F1
Nanji Shan China 27°27N 121°4E 229 D13
Nanjian China 25°2N 100°25E 228 E3
Nanjiang China 32°28N 106°51E 228 A6
Nanjing Fujian, China 24°25N 117°20E 229 E11
Nanjing Jiangsu, China 32°2N 118°47E 229 A12
Nanjirinji Tanzania 9°41S 39°5E 269 D4
Nankana Sahib Pakistan 31°27N 73°38E 242 D5
Nankang Jiangxi, China 25°40N 114°45E 229 E10
Nankang Taiwan 25°3N 121°37E 125 B2
Nanking = Nanjing China 32°2N 118°47E 229 A12
Nankoku Japan 33°39N 133°44E 222 D5
Nanlang China 22°30N 113°32E 219 G10
Nanliao Taiwan 24°50N 120°55E 225 B2
Nanling China 30°55N 118°20E 229 B12
Nannial India 19°4N 79°38E 244 E4
Nanning China 22°48N 108°20E 228 F7
Nannup Australia 33°59S 115°48E 279 F2
Nanole India 19°0N 72°55E 130 A2
Nanortalik Greenland 60°10N 45°17W 154 E6
Nanpan Jiang → China 25°10N 106°5E 228 E6

Nanpara India 27°52N 81°33E 243 F9
Nanpi China 38°2N 116°45E 226 E9
Nanping Fujian, China 26°38N 118°10E 229 D12
Nanping Henan, China 29°55N 112°3E 229 C9
Nanpu Bridge China 31°12N 121°30E 138 B2
Nanri Dao China 25°15N 119°25E 229 E12
Nanripe Mozam. 13°52S 38°52E 269 E4
Nansei-Shotō = Ryūkyū-rettō Japan 26°0N 126°0E 221 M3
Nansen Basin Arctic 84°0N 50°0E 150 A10
Nansen Land Greenland 83°0N 43°0W 154 A6
Nansen Sd. Canada 81°0N 91°0W 295 A10
Nansha China 22°45N 113°34E 219 F10
Nanshan I. S. China Sea 10°45N 115°49E 230 B5
Nanshi China 31°12N 121°29E 138 B1
Nansio Tanzania 2°3S 33°4E 268 C3
Nant France 44°1N 3°18E 174 D7
Nanterre France 48°53N 2°12E 134 A2
Nantes France 47°12N 1°33W 172 E5
Nantiat France 46°1N 1°11E 174 B5
Nanticoke U.S.A. 41°12N 76°0W 313 E8
Nanton Canada 50°21N 113°46W 296 C6
Nanton Pt. Antigua & B. 17°0N 61°45W 322 b
Nantong China 32°1N 120°52E 229 A13
Nantou China 22°32N 113°55E 219 F10
Nant'ou Taiwan 23°55N 120°41E 225 C2
Nant'ou □ Taiwan 23°50N 121°0E 225 C3
Nantua France 46°10N 5°35E 173 F12
Nantucket U.S.A. 41°17N 70°6W 309 E18
Nantucket I. U.S.A. 41°16N 70°5W 309 E18
Nantung = Nantong China 32°1N 120°52E 229 A13
Nantwich U.K. 53°4N 2°31W 168 D5
Nanty Glo U.S.A. 40°28N 78°50W 312 F6
Nantzu Taiwan 22°44N 120°19E 225 D2
Nanuku Passage Fiji 16°45S 179°15W 287 A3
Nanumanga Pac. Oc. 6°18S 176°20E 277 B14
Nanuque Brazil 17°50S 40°21W 333 E3
Nanusa, Kepulauan Indonesia 4°45N 127°1E 231 D7
Nanutarra Roadhouse Australia 22°32S 115°30E 278 D2
Nanwan Taiwan 21°57N 120°46E 225 E2
Nanxi China 28°54N 104°59E 228 C5
Nanxiong China 25°6N 114°15E 229 E10
Nanyang China 33°11N 112°30E 226 H7
Nanyi Hu China 31°5N 119°0E 229 B12
Nanyuki Kenya 0°2N 37°4E 268 B4
Nanzhang China 31°45N 111°50E 229 B8
Nao, C. de la Spain 38°44N 0°14E 197 G5
Naoabad India 22°28N 88°26E 124 C2
Naococane, L. Canada 52°50N 70°45W 299 B5
Naogaon Bangla. 24°52N 88°52E 241 C2
Naoné Vanuatu 15°0S 168°8E 287 E6
Naoussa Cyclades, Greece 37°7N 25°14E 205 D7
Naoussa Imathia, Greece 40°42N 22°9E 202 F6
Naozhou Dao China 20°55N 110°20E 229 G8
Napa U.S.A. 38°18N 122°17W 306 G4
Napa → U.S.A. 38°10N 122°19W 306 G4
Napaimiut U.S.A. 61°33N 158°42W 303 F8
Napakiak U.S.A. 60°42N 161°57W 303 F7
Nāpali Coast U.S.A. 22°11N 159°39W 302 A2
Napanee Canada 44°15N 77°0W 312 B8
Napanoch U.S.A. 41°44N 74°22W 313 E10
Napaskiak U.S.A. 60°43N 161°55W 303 F7
Nape Laos 18°18N 105°6E 236 C5
Nape Pass = Keo Neua, Deo Vietnam 18°23N 105°10E 236 C5
Naperville U.S.A. 41°46N 88°9W 311 C8
Napier N.Z. 39°30S 176°56E 284 F5
Napier Broome B. Australia 14°2S 126°37E 278 B4
Napier Mole Pakistan 24°49N 66°58E 123 B1
Napier Pen. Australia 12°4S 135°43E 280 A2
Napierville Canada 45°11N 73°25W 313 A11
Napili-Honokowai U.S.A. 20°58N 156°39W 302 C5
Naples = Nápoli Italy 40°50N 14°15E 201 B7
Naples U.S.A. 26°8N 81°48W 317 J8
Naples Park U.S.A. 26°17N 81°46W 317 J8
Napo China 23°22N 105°50E 228 F5
Napo □ Ecuador 0°30S 77°0W 328 D2
Napo → Peru 3°20S 72°40W 328 D3
Napoleon N. Dak., U.S.A. 46°30N 99°46W 308 B4
Napoleon Ohio, U.S.A. 41°23N 84°8W 311 C12
Napoleon's Tomb St. Helena 15°56S 5°42W 153 h
Nápoli Italy 40°50N 14°15E 201 B7
Nápoli, G. di Italy 40°43N 14°10E 201 B7
Nápoli Capodichino ✈ (NAP) Italy 40°53N 14°16E 201 B7
Napopo Dem. Rep. of the Congo 4°15N 28°0E 268 B2
Nappanee U.S.A. 41°27N 86°0W 311 C11
Napperby Australia 33°9S 138°7E 282 B3
Naqāda Egypt 25°53N 32°42E 256 B3
Naqadeh Iran 36°57N 45°23E 213 D11
Naqb, Ra's an Jordan 29°48N 35°44E 251 J6
Naqqāsh Iran 35°40N 49°6E 247 C6
Nara Japan 34°40N 135°49E 223 G7
Nara Mali 15°10N 7°20W 262 B3
Nara □ Japan 34°30N 136°0E 223 C8
Nara Canal Pakistan 24°30N 69°20E 242 G3
Nara Visa U.S.A. 35°37N 103°6W 305 J12
Naracoorte Australia 36°58S 140°45E 282 D4
Naradhan Australia 33°34S 146°17E 283 B7
Naraina India 28°36N 77°8E 120 B1
Naraini India 25°11N 80°29E 243 G9
Naranjos Mexico 21°21N 97°41W 319 C5
Narasannapeta India 18°25N 84°3E 244 E7
Narasapur India 16°26N 81°40E 245 F5
Narasaropet India 16°14N 80°4E 245 F5
Narathiwat Thailand 6°30N 101°48E 237 J3
Narayanapatnam India 18°53N 83°10E 244 E6
Narayanganj Bangla. 23°40N 90°33E 241 D3
Narayanpet India 16°45N 77°30E 244 F3
Narbada = Narmada → India 21°38N 72°36E 242 J5
Narberth U.K. 51°47N 4°44W 169 F3
Narbonne France 43°11N 3°0E 174 E7
Narborough, I. = Fernandina, I. Ecuador 0°25S 91°30W 330 a
Narbuvoll Norway 62°21N 11°27E 164 B8
Narcea → Spain 43°33N 6°44W 194 B4
Narcondam I. India 13°20N 94°16E 245 H12
Nardīn Iran 37°3N 55°59E 247 B7
Nardò Italy 40°11N 18°2E 201 B11
Narembeen Australia 32°7S 118°24E 279 F2
Narendranagar India 30°10N 78°18E 242 D8
Nares Abyssal Plain Atl. Oc. 22°0N 67°0W 152 D5
Nares Str. Arctic 80°0N 70°0W 154 B3
Naretha Australia 31°0S 124°45E 279 F3
Narew → Poland 52°26N 20°41E 157 F7
Nari → Pakistan 28°0N 67°40E 242 F2
Nariman Point Mumbai, India 18°55N 72°49E 130 c1
Nariman Pt. India 18°55N 72°49E 130 B1
Narin Afghan. 36°5N 69°0E 240 A3
Narindra, Helodranon' i Madag. 14°55S 47°30E 272 A2
Narino □ Colombia 1°30N 78°0W 328 C2
Narita Japan 35°47N 140°19E 223 B12
Narita, Tōkyō ✈ (NRT) Japan 35°45N 140°25E 223 B12
Nariva □ Trin. & Tob. 10°22N 61°10W 323 t
Nariva → Trin. & Tob. 10°24N 61°14W 323 t
Nariva Swamp Trin. & Tob. 10°26N 61°4W 323 t
Närke Sweden 59°10N 15°0E 162 E8
Narmada → India 21°38N 72°36E 242 J5
Narmak Iran 35°42N 51°28E 141 A2
Narman Turkey 40°26N 41°57E 213 B9
Narnaul India 28°5N 76°11E 242 E7
Narni Italy 42°30N 12°30E 199 F9
Naro Ghana 10°22N 2°27W 262 C4
Naro Fominsk Russia 55°23N 36°43E 188 E9
Narodnaya Russia 65°5N 59°58E 186 A10
Narok Kenya 1°55S 35°52E 268 C4
Narón Spain 43°32N 8°9W 194 B2
Narooma Australia 36°14S 150°4E 283 D9
Narowal Pakistan 32°6N 74°52E 242 C6
Narra Phil. 9°18N 118°28E 233 G2
Narrabri Australia 30°19S 149°46E 281 E4
Narragansett U.S.A. 41°26N 71°27W 313 E13
Narran → Australia 28°37S 148°12E 281 D4
Narrandera Australia 34°42S 146°31E 283 C7
Narrogin Australia 32°58S 117°14E 279 F2
Narromine Australia 32°12S 148°12E 283 B8
Narrow Hills ⌓ Canada 54°0N 104°37W 297 C8
Narrows, The St. Kitts & Nevis 17°12N 62°40W 322 d
Narsampet India 17°57N 79°58E 244 F4
Narsaq Greenland 60°57N 46°4W 154 E6
Narsimhapur India 22°54N 79°14E 243 H8
Narsinghgarh India 23°45N 76°40E 242 H7
Narsinghpur India 20°28N 85°5E 244 D7
Narsipatnam India 17°40N 82°37E 244 F6
Nartes, L. e Albania 40°32N 19°25E 202 F3
Nartkala Russia 43°33N 43°51E 191 J6
Naruo Japan 34°43N 135°22E 133 A1
Naruto Kantō, Japan 34°11N 134°37E 222 C6
Narutō Shikoku, Japan 35°36N 140°25E 223 B12
Naruto-Kaikyō Japan 34°14N 134°39E 222 C6
Narva Estonia 59°23N 28°12E 188 C5
Narva → Russia 59°27N 28°2E 188 C4
Narva Bay = Narva Laht Estonia 59°35N 27°35E 161 G22
Narva Laht Estonia 59°35N 27°35E 161 G22
Narvacan Phil. 17°25N 120°28E 232 C3
Narvik Norway 68°28N 17°26E 160 B17
Narvskoye Vdkhr. Russia 59°18N 28°14E 188 C5
Narwana India 29°39N 76°6E 242 E7
Narwiański △ Poland 52°5N 22°53E 185 F9
Naryan-Mar Russia 67°42N 53°12E 186 A9
Narym Russia 59°0N 81°30E 214 D9
Naryn Kyrgyzstan 41°26N 75°58E 217 D9
Naryn □ Kyrgyzstan 41°26N 75°58E 217 D9
Naryn → Uzbekistan 40°52N 71°36E 217 D8
Naryn Qum Kazakhstan 47°30N 49°0E 191 G9
Nasa Norway 66°29N 15°23E 160 C16
Nasau Fiji 17°19S 179°27E 287 A2
Năsăud Romania 47°19N 24°29E 183 C9
Nasawa Vanuatu 15°12S 168°9E 287 E6
Naşb, W. → Egypt 28°29N 34°31E 251 K5
Näsby Sweden 59°25N 18°5E 139 A2
Näsbypark Sweden 59°25N 18°5E 139 A2
Nasca = Nazca Peru 14°50S 74°57W 330 C3
Naseby N.Z. 45°1S 170°10E 285 F5
Naselle U.S.A. 46°22N 123°49W 306 D3
Naser, Buheirat en Egypt 23°0N 32°30E 256 C3
Nashua Iowa, U.S.A. 42°57N 92°32W 310 B4
Nashua Mont., U.S.A. 48°8N 106°22W 304 B10
Nashua N.H., U.S.A. 42°45N 71°28W 313 D13
Nashville Ark., U.S.A. 33°57N 93°51W 314 E8
Nashville Ga., U.S.A. 31°12N 83°15W 316 D6
Nashville Ill., U.S.A. 38°21N 89°23W 310 F7
Nashville Ind., U.S.A. 39°12N 86°15W 311 E10
Nashville Mich., U.S.A. 42°36N 85°5W 311 B11
Nashville Tenn., U.S.A. 36°10N 86°47W 315 C11
Našice Croatia 45°32N 18°4E 182 E3
Nasielsk Poland 52°35N 20°50E 185 F7
Nasik India 19°58N 73°50E 244 E1
Nasipit Phil. 8°57N 125°19E 233 G5
Nasir Sudan 8°36N 33°4E 257 F3
Nasirabad = Mymensingh Bangla. 24°45N 90°24E 241 C3
Nasirabad India 26°15N 74°45E 242 F6
Nasirabad Pakistan 28°23N 68°24E 242 E3
Nasiriyah = An Nāşirīyah Iraq 31°0N 46°15E 246 D5
Naskaupi → Canada 53°47N 60°51W 299 B7
Naso Italy 38°7N 14°47E 201 D7
Naso Pt. Phil. 10°25N 121°57E 233 F3
Naşrābād Iran 34°8N 51°26E 247 C6
Naşrīān-e Pā'īn Iran 32°52N 46°52E 246 C5
Nass → Canada 55°0N 129°40W 296 C3
Nassarawa Nigeria 8°32N 7°41E 263 D6
Nassarawa □ Nigeria 8°30N 8°20E 263 D6
Nassau Bahamas 25°5N 77°20W 153 b
Nassau N.Y., U.S.A. 42°31N 73°37W 313 D11
Nassau, B. Chile 55°20S 68°0W 336 E3
Nassau Int. ✈ (NAS) Bahamas 25°3N 77°28W 153 b
Nasser, L. = Naser, Buheirat en Egypt 23°0N 32°30E 256 C3
Nasser City = Kôm Ombo Egypt 24°25N 32°52E 256 C3
Nassian Ivory C. 8°28N 3°28W 262 D4
Nässjö Sweden 57°39N 14°42E 163 G8
Nastapoka → Canada 56°55N 76°33W 298 A4
Nastapoka, Is. Canada 56°55N 76°50W 298 A4
Nasugbu Phil. 14°5N 120°38E 232 D3
Näsum Sweden 56°10N 14°29E 163 H8
Näsviken Sweden 61°46N 16°52E 162 C10
Nata Botswana 20°12S 26°12E 270 B4
Nata → Botswana 20°14S 26°10E 270 B4
Natagaima Colombia 3°37N 75°6W 328 C2
Natal Brazil 5°47S 35°13W 332 C4
Natal Indonesia 0°35N 99°7E 234 B1
Natal Drakensberg ⌓ S. Africa 29°27S 29°30E 271 C4
Natalinci Serbia 44°15N 20°49E 182 F5
Naṭanz Iran 33°30N 51°55E 247 C6
Natashquan Canada 50°14N 61°46W 299 B7
Natashquan → Canada 50°7N 61°50W 299 B7
Natchez U.S.A. 31°34N 91°24W 314 F9
Natchitoches U.S.A. 31°46N 93°5W 314 F8
Natewa B. Fiji 16°35S 179°40E 287 A2
Nathalia Australia 36°1S 145°13E 283 D6
Nathan Philips Square Toronto, Canada 141 b2
Nathan Road Hong Kong, China 122 a2
Nathdwara India 24°55N 73°50E 242 G5
Nati, Pta. Spain 40°3N 3°50E 206 A4
Natimuk Australia 36°42S 142°0E 282 D5
Nation → Canada 55°30N 123°32W 296 B4
National Air and Space Museum Washington, D.C., U.S.A. 143 b2
National Arboretum U.S.A. 38°54N 76°59W 143 B3
National Archeological Museum Athens, Greece 112 a2
National Capital District □ Papua N. G. 9°25S 147°10E 286 E4
National City U.S.A. 32°40N 117°5W 307 N9
National Fine Arts Museum = Belas Artes, Museu Nacional de Rio de J., Brazil 135 b2
National Gallery Budapest, Hungary 117 b2
National Gallery of Art Washington, D.C., U.S.A. 143 b2
National Library = Biblioteca Nacional Rio de J., Brazil 135 c2
National Maritime Museum San Francisco, U.S.A. 136 a1
National Museum Budapest, Hungary 117 c3
National Museum Bangkok, Thailand 113 b1
National Museum of American Art Washington, D.C., U.S.A. 143 b2
National Museum of American History Washington, D.C., U.S.A. 143 b1
National Museum of Natural History Washington, D.C., U.S.A. 143 b1
National Place Washington, D.C., U.S.A. 143 b2
National Zoological Park U.S.A. 38°55N 77°4W 143 B3
Nationalmuseum Stockholm, Sweden 139 b2
Natitingou Benin 10°20N 1°26E 263 C5
Natividad, I. Mexico 27°52N 115°11W 318 B1
Natividade Brazil 11°43S 47°47W 333 D2
Nativity, Basilica of West Bank 31°42N 35°12E 123 B2
Natkyizin Burma 14°57N 97°59E 236 E1
Natmauk Burma 20°20N 95°24E 241 E5
Natogyi Burma 21°25N 95°39E 241 E5
Natolin Poland 52°8N 21°4E 122 D2
Natonin Phil. 17°6N 121°18E 232 C3
Natron, L. Tanzania 2°20S 36°0E 268 C4
Natrona Heights U.S.A. 40°37N 79°44W 312 F5
Natrûn, W. el → Egypt 30°25N 30°13E 256 H7
Nattai △ Australia 34°12S 150°22E 283 C9
Nättraby Sweden 56°13N 15°31E 163 H9
Natukanaoka Pan Namibia 18°40S 15°45E 270 A2
Natuna Besar, Kepulauan Indonesia 4°0N 108°15E 234 B3
Natuna Is. = Natuna Besar, Kepulauan Indonesia 4°0N 108°15E 234 B3
Natuna Selatan, Kepulauan Indonesia 2°45N 109°0E 235 B3
Natural Bridge U.S.A. 44°5N 75°30W 313 B9
Natural Bridges ⌓ U.S.A. 37°36N 110°0W 305 H9
Naturaliste, C. Australia 40°50S 148°15E 281 G4
Naturaliste Plateau Ind. Oc. 34°0S 112°0E 276 G1
Naturhistorischesmuseum Vienna, Austria 142 b1
Nau Qala Afghan. 34°5N 68°5E 242 B3
Naucalpan de Juárez Mexico 19°28N 99°14W 128 B1
Naucelle France 44°13N 2°20E 174 D6
Nauders Austria 46°54N 10°30E 180 E3
Nauen Germany 52°36N 12°52E 178 C8
Naugard = Nowogard Poland 53°41N 15°10E 184 E2
Naugatuck U.S.A. 41°30N 73°3W 313 E11
Naujaat = Repulse Bay Canada 66°30N 86°30W 295 C11
Naujan Phil. 13°20N 121°18E 232 E3
Naujoji Akmenė Lithuania 56°19N 22°54E 184 B9
Naulila Angola 17°13S 14°39E 265 F2
Naumburg Germany 51°9N 11°47E 178 D7
Naumburg am Queis = Nowogrodziec Poland 51°12N 15°24E 185 G2
Naupada Andhra Pradesh, India 18°34N 84°18E 244 E7
Naupada Maharashtra, India 19°3N 72°50E 130 A2
Nā'ūr Jordan 31°53N 35°50E 251 D4
Nauru ■ Pac. Oc. 1°0S 166°0E 288 H8
Naushahra = Nowshera Pakistan 34°0N 72°0E 240 B4
Naushahro Pakistan 26°50N 68°7E 242 F3
Naushon I. U.S.A. 41°29N 70°45W 313 E14
Nausori Fiji 18°2S 178°32E 287 B2
Naustdal Norway 61°31N 5°43E 164 C2
Nauta Peru 4°31S 73°35W 328 D3
Nautanwa India 27°20N 83°25E 243 F10
Naute ⌓ Namibia 26°55S 17°57E 270 C2
Nautla Mexico 20°13N 96°47W 319 C5
Nauvoo U.S.A. 40°33N 91°23W 310 D5
Nava Coahuila, Mexico 28°25N 100°45W 318 B4
Nava Spain 43°21N 5°31W 194 B5
Nava del Rey Spain 41°22N 5°6W 194 D5
Navadwip India 23°34N 88°20E 243 H13
Navahermosa Spain 39°41N 4°28W 195 F6
Navahrudak Belarus 53°40N 25°50E 177 B13
Navai Fiji 17°36S 177°57E 287 A1
Navajo Res. U.S.A. 36°48N 107°36W 305 H10
Naval Phil. 11°34N 124°23E 233 F5
Navalcarnero Spain 40°17N 4°5W 194 E6
Navalgund India 15°34N 75°22E 245 G2
Navalmoral de la Mata Spain 39°52N 5°33W 194 F5
Navalvillar de Pela Spain 39°9N 5°24W 195 F5
Navan = An Uaimh Ireland 53°39N 6°41W 166 C5
Navanagar = Jamnagar India 22°30N 70°6E 242 H4
Navapolatsk Belarus 55°32N 28°37E 188 E5
Navarin, Mys Russia 62°15N 179°5E 150 C16
Navarino, I. Chile 55°0S 67°40W 336 E3
Navarra □ Spain 42°40N 1°40W 196 C3
Navarre Fla., U.S.A. 30°24N 86°52W 317 E3
Navarre Ohio, U.S.A. 40°43N 81°31W 312 F3
Navarro → U.S.A. 39°11N 123°45W 306 F3
Navas de San Juan Spain 38°30N 3°19W 195 G7
Navasota U.S.A. 30°23N 96°5W 314 F6
Navassa I. W. Indies 18°30N 75°0W 321 C5
Nävekvarn Sweden 58°38N 16°49E 163 F10
Naver → U.K. 58°32N 4°14W 167 C4
Navet Trin. & Tob. 10°21N 61°10W 323 t
Navet → Trin. & Tob. 10°24N 61°5W 323 t
Navet Res. Trin. & Tob. 10°24N 61°15W 323 t
Navi Mumbai India 19°5N 73°0E 130 A2
Navia Spain 43°35N 6°42W 194 B4
Navia → Spain 43°15N 6°50W 194 B4
Navia de Suarna Spain 42°58N 7°3W 194 C4
Navibandar India 21°26N 69°48E 242 J3
Navidad Chile 33°57S 71°50W 334 C1
Navidad Bank W. Indies 20°0N 68°58W 321 B6
Navíglio di Pavia Italy 45°24N 9°9E 129 B1
Navíglio Grande Italy 45°25N 9°5E 129 B1
Naviraí Brazil 23°8S 54°13W 335 A5
Naviti Fiji 17°7S 177°15E 287 A1
Navlakhi India 22°58N 70°28E 242 H4
Navlya Russia 52°53N 34°30E 189 F8
Năvodari Romania 44°19N 28°36E 183 F14
Navoi = Nawoiy Uzbekistan 40°9N 65°22E 217 D7
Navojoa Mexico 27°6N 109°26W 318 B3
Navolato Mexico 24°47N 107°42W 318 C3
Navona, Piazza Rome, Italy 136 b2
Navotas Phil. 14°39N 120°56E 127 B1
Navrongo Ghana 10°51N 1°3W 263 C4
Navsari India 20°57N 72°59E 244 D1
Navua Fiji 18°12S 178°11E 287 B2
Navy Pier Chicago, U.S.A. 119 b3
Nawa Kot Pakistan 28°21N 71°24E 242 E4
Nawab Khan Pakistan 30°17N 69°12E 242 D3
Nawabganj Bangla. 24°35N 88°14E 241 C2
Nawabganj Ut. P., India 26°56N 81°14E 243 F9
Nawabganj Ut. P., India 28°32N 79°40E 243 E8
Nawabshah Pakistan 26°15N 68°25E 242 F3
Nawada India 24°50N 85°33E 243 G11
Nawakot Nepal 27°55N 85°10E 243 F11
Nawalgarh India 27°50N 75°15E 242 F6
Nawanshahr India 32°33N 74°48E 243 C6
Nawapara India 20°46N 82°33E 244 D6
Nawar, Dasht-i- Afghan. 33°52N 68°0E 242 C3
Nawāşīf, Ḩarrat Si. Arabia 21°20N 42°10E 248 B3
Nawi Sudan 18°32N 30°50E 256 D3
Nawng Hpa Burma 22°30N 98°30E 241 D7
Nawoiy Uzbekistan 40°9N 65°22E 217 D7
Naws, Ra's Oman 17°15N 55°16E 249 C6
Naxçıvan Azerbaijan 39°12N 45°15E 213 C11
Naxçıvan □ Azerbaijan 39°25N 45°26E 213 C11
Naxos Greece 37°8N 25°25E 205 D7
Naxxar Malta 35°55N 14°27E 206 F7
Nay France 43°10N 0°18W 174 E3
Nay, Mui Vietnam 12°55N 109°23E 230 B3
Nāy Band Būshehr, Iran 27°20N 52°40E 247 E7
Nāy Band Khorāsān, Iran 32°20N 57°34E 247 C8
Naya → Colombia 3°13N 77°22W 328 C2
Nayagarh India 20°8N 85°6E 244 D7
Nayakhan Russia 61°56N 159°0E 215 C16
Nayarit □ Mexico 22°0N 105°0W 318 C4
Nayé Senegal 14°28N 12°12W 262 C2
Nayong China 26°50N 105°20E 228 D5
Nayoro Japan 44°21N 142°28E 220 B11
Nayudupeta India 13°54N 79°54E 245 H4
Nayyāl, W. → Si. Arabia 28°35N 39°4E 246 D3
Nazal Hikmat Beg Iraq 33°23N 44°25E 113 A2
Nazaré Bahia, Brazil 13°2S 39°0W 333 D4
Nazaré Pará, Brazil 6°25S 52°29W 331 B7
Nazaré Tocantins, Brazil 6°23S 47°40W 332 C2
Nazaré Portugal 39°36N 9°4W 195 F1
Nazareth = Nazerat Israel 32°42N 35°17E 250 F6
Nazareth U.S.A. 40°44N 75°19W 313 F9
Nazas Mexico 25°14N 104°8W 318 B4
Nazas → Mexico 25°12N 104°12W 318 B4
Nazca Peru 14°50S 74°57W 330 C3
Nazca Ridge Pac. Oc. 20°0S 80°0W 289 K19
Naze Japan 28°22N 129°27E 221 K4
Naze, The U.K. 51°53N 1°18E 169 F9
Nazerat Israel 32°42N 35°17E 250 F6
Nāzīk Iran 39°1N 45°4E 213 C11
Nazilli Turkey 37°55N 28°15E 205 D10
Nazimabad Pakistan 24°54N 67°1E 123 A2
Nazir Hat Bangla. 22°35N 91°49E 241 D3
Nazko Canada 53°1N 123°37W 296 C4
Nazko → Canada 53°7N 123°34W 296 C4
Nazlet el Simmân Egypt 29°59N 31°9E 117 B1
Nazret Ethiopia 8°32N 39°22E 257 F4
Nchanga Zambia 12°30S 27°49E 269 E2
Ncheu Malawi 14°50S 34°47E 269 E3
Ndala Tanzania 4°45S 33°15E 268 C3
Ndalatando Angola 9°12S 14°48E 265 D2
Ndali Benin 9°50N 2°46E 263 D5
Ndareda Tanzania 4°12S 35°30E 268 C4
Ndélé C.A.R. 8°25N 20°36E 264 A4
Ndendé Gabon 2°22S 11°23E 264 C2
Ndiael ⌓ Senegal 16°15N 16°0W 262 B1
Ndikinimeki Cameroon 4°46N 10°50E 263 E7
Ndindi Gabon 3°46S 11°9E 264 C2
N'Dioum Senegal 16°31N 14°39W 262 B2
Ndjamena Chad 12°10N 14°59E 259 F2
Ndjolé Gabon 0°10S 10°45E 264 C2
Ndogo, Lagune Gabon 2°35S 10°0E 264 C2
Ndoki-Nouabalé ⌓ Congo 2°32N 16°32E 264 B3
Ndola Zambia 13°0S 28°34E 269 E2
Ndomo ⌓ S. Africa 26°52S 32°15E 271 C5
Ndoto Mts. Kenya 2°0N 37°0E 268 B4
Ndoua, C. N. Cal. 22°24S 166°56E 288 d
Ndouba Congo 0°9S 14°4E 264 C2
Nduguti Tanzania 4°18S 34°41E 268 C3
Nea → Norway 63°15N 11°0E 164 A8
Nea Alexandria Greece 37°52N 23°46E 112 B2
Nea Alikarnassos Greece 35°18N 25°13E 205 F7
Nea Anchialos Greece 39°16N 22°49E 204 B4
Nea Epidavros Greece 37°40N 23°7E 204 D5
Nea Ionia Athina, Greece 38°3N 23°45E 112 A2
Nea Ionia Magnisia, Greece 39°22N 22°56E 204 B4
Nea Kalikratia Greece 40°21N 23°3E 202 F7
Nea Liosia Greece 38°3N 23°43E 112 A2
Nea Makri Greece 38°5N 23°59E 204 C5
Nea Moudania Greece 40°15N 23°17E 202 F7
Nea Peramos Attiki, Greece 38°0N 23°26E 204 C5
Nea Peramos Kavala, Greece 40°50N 24°18E 203 F8
Nea Samsounda Greece 39°5N 20°45E 207 A2
Nea Smirni Greece 37°54N 23°43E 112 B2
Nea Visa Greece 41°34N 26°33E 203 E10
Nea Zichni Greece 41°2N 23°49E 202 E7
Neagari Japan 36°26N 136°25E 223 A8
Neagh, Lough U.K. 54°37N 6°25W 166 B5
Neah Bay U.S.A. 48°22N 124°37W 306 B2
Neale, L. Australia 24°15S 130°0E 278 D5
Neales → Australia 28°8S 136°47E 281 D2
Neamati India 26°50N 94°20E 241 B5
Neamţ □ Romania 47°0N 26°20E 183 C11
Neapoli Athina, Greece 37°58N 23°45E 112 B2
Neapoli Kozani, Greece 40°20N 21°24E 202 F5
Neapoli Kriti, Greece 35°15N 25°37E 207 E6
Neapoli Lakonia, Greece 36°27N 23°8E 204 E5
Near Is. U.S.A. 52°30N 174°0E 303 K1
Near North Chicago, U.S.A. 119 b1
Neath U.K. 51°39N 3°48W 169 F4
Neath Port Talbot □ U.K. 51°42N 3°45W 169 F4
Nebbou Burkina Faso 11°9N 1°51W 263 C4
Nebelat el Hagana Sudan 13°13N 29°2E 257 E2
Nebine Cr. → Australia 29°27S 146°56E 281 D4
Nebitdag = Balkanabat Turkmenistan 39°30N 54°22E 247 B7
Nebka Algeria 27°28N 3°12W 260 C4
Nebo Australia 21°42S 148°42E 280 C4
Nebolchy Russia 59°8N 33°18E 188 C7
Nebraska □ U.S.A. 41°30N 99°30W 308 E4
Nebraska City U.S.A. 40°41N 95°52W 308 E6
Nébrodi, Monti Italy 37°54N 14°35E 201 E7
Nebušice Czech Rep. 50°6N 14°19E 135 B1
Necedah U.S.A. 44°2N 90°4W 308 C8
Nechako → Canada 53°55N 122°42W 296 C4
Neches → U.S.A. 29°58N 93°51W 314 G8
Nechisar △ Ethiopia 5°58N 37°55E 257 F4
Neckar → Germany 49°27N 8°29E 179 F4
Neckartal-Odenwald ⌓ Germany 49°30N 9°5E 179 F5
Necker I. U.S.A. 23°35N 164°42W 302 G11
Necochea Argentina 38°30S 58°50W 334 D4
Nectar Brook Australia 32°43S 137°57E 282 B2
Neda Spain 43°30N 8°9W 194 B2
Neda → Greece 37°25N 21°45E 204 D3
Nedalshytta Norway 62°59N 12°3E 164 B9
Nedelino Bulgaria 41°27N 25°3E 203 E9
Nedelišće Croatia 46°23N 16°22E 199 B13
Nederhorst Neths. 52°16N 5°3E 112 B3
Nederland = Netherlands ■ Europe 52°0N 5°30E 170 C5
Nedlitz Germany 52°25N 13°3E 115 B1
Nedoboyivtsi Ukraine 48°26N 26°21E 183 B11
Nedreberg Norway 60°59N 11°41E 164 D8
Nedroma Algeria 35°1N 1°45W 261 A4
Nedstrand Norway 59°21N 5°49E 164 E2
Nee Soon Singapore 1°24N 103°49E 138 A2
Needham U.S.A. 42°17N 71°14W 116 B1
Needham Heights U.S.A. 42°17N 71°14W 116 B1
Needles B.C., Canada 49°53N 118°7W 296 D5
Needles Calif., U.S.A. 34°51N 114°37W 307 L12
Needles, The U.K. 50°39N 1°35W 169 G6
Needles Pt. N.Z. 36°3S 175°25E 284 C4
Ñeembucú □ Paraguay 27°0S 58°0W 334 B4
Neemuch = Nimach India 24°30N 74°56E 242 G6
Neenah U.S.A. 44°11N 88°28W 308 C9
Neepawa Canada 50°15N 99°30W 297 C9
Neeses U.S.A. 33°33N 81°7W 316 B8
Nefta Tunisia 33°53N 7°50E 258 B1
Neftah Sidi Boubekeur Algeria 35°1N 0°4E 261 A5
Neftçala Azerbaijan 39°19N 49°12E 213 C13
Neftechala = Neftçala Azerbaijan 39°19N 49°12E 213 C13
Neftegorsk Russia 44°25N 39°45E 191 H4
Neftekumsk Russia 44°46N 44°50E 191 H7
Nefyn U.K. 52°56N 4°31W 168 E3
Négala Mali 12°52N 8°30W 262 C3
Negapatam = Nagappattinam India 10°46N 79°51E 245 J4
Negara Indonesia 8°22S 114°37E 231 J17
Negaunee U.S.A. 46°30N 87°36W 308 B10
Negele Ethiopia 5°20N 39°36E 257 F4
Negeri Sembilan □ Malaysia 2°45N 102°10E 234 B2
Negev Desert = Hanegev Israel 30°50N 35°0E 251 H6
Negoiul, Vf. Romania 45°38N 24°35E 183 E9
Negombo Sri Lanka 7°12N 79°50E 245 L4
Negotin Serbia 44°16N 22°37E 182 F7
Negotino Macedonia 41°29N 22°7E 202 E6
Negra, Peña Spain 42°11N 6°30W 194 C4
Negra, Pta. Mauritania 22°54N 16°18W 260 D1
Negra, Pta. Peru 6°6S 81°10W 330 B1
Negra Pt. Phil. 18°40N 120°50E 232 B3
Negra Pt. Trin. & Tob. 10°4N 61°23W 323 t
Negrais, C. = Maudin Sun Burma 16°0N 94°30E 241 G5
Nègres, Pte. des Martinique 14°35N 61°5W 322 j
Negreşti Romania 46°50N 27°30E 183 D12
Negreşti-Oaş Romania 47°52N 23°26E 183 C8
Négrine Algeria 34°30N 7°30E 261 B6
Negro → Argentina 41°2S 62°47W 336 B4
Negro → Bolivia 14°11S 63°7W 331 C5
Negro → Brazil 3°0S 60°0W 329 D6
Negro → Uruguay 33°24S 58°22W 334 C4
Negros Phil. 9°30N 122°40E 233 G4
Negros Occidental □ Phil. 10°0N 122°55E 233 F4
Negros Oriental □ Phil. 9°45N 123°0E 233 G4
Negru Vodă Romania 43°47N 28°21E 183 G13
Neguac Canada 47°15N 65°5W 299 C6
Nehalem → U.S.A. 45°40N 123°56W 306 E3
Nehāvand Iran 35°56N 49°31E 247 C6
Nehbandān Iran 31°35N 60°5E 247 D9
Nehoiu Romania 45°24N 26°20E 183 E11
Nei Monggol Zizhiqu □ China 42°0N 112°0E 226 D7
Neiafu Tonga 18°39S 173°59W 287 P14
Neidenburg = Nidzica Poland 53°25N 20°28E 185 E7
Neiges, Piton des Réunion 21°5S 55°29E 272 f
Neijiang China 29°35N 104°55E 228 C5
Neikiang = Neijiang China 29°35N 104°55E 228 C5
Neilingding Dao China 22°25N 113°48E 219 G10
Neill I. India 11°50N 93°3E 245 J11
Neillsville U.S.A. 44°34N 90°36W 308 C8
Neilson, Récif Pac. Oc. 27°1S 146°2W 289 f
Neilton U.S.A. 47°25N 123°53W 304 C2
Neipu Taiwan 22°37N 120°33E 225 D2
Neiqiu China 37°15N 114°30E 226 F8
Neisse = Nysa → Europe 52°4N 14°46E 178 C10
Neiva Colombia 2°56N 75°18W 328 C2
Neiwan Taiwan 24°42N 121°10E 225 B3
Neixiang China 33°10N 111°52E 226 H6
Nejanilini L. Canada 59°33N 97°48W 297 B9
Nejd = Najd Si. Arabia 26°30N 42°0E 238 D4
Nejo Ethiopia 9°30N 35°28E 257 F4
Nekā Iran 36°39N 53°19E 247 B7
Nekemte Ethiopia 9°4N 36°30E 257 F4
Nĕkheb Egypt 25°10N 32°48E 256 B3
Nekrasovka Russia 55°41N 37°55E 129 B5
Neksø Denmark 55°4N 15°8E 163 J9
Nelamangala India 13°6N 77°24E 245 H3
Nelas Portugal 40°32N 7°52W 194 E3
Nelaug Norway 58°39N 8°40E 164 F5
Nelia Australia 20°39S 142°12E 280 C3
Nelidovo Russia 56°13N 32°49E 188 D7
Neligh U.S.A. 42°8N 98°2W 308 D4
Nelkan Russia 57°40N 136°4E 215 D14
Nellikuppam India 11°46N 79°43E 245 J4
Nellis Air Force Base ✈ U.S.A. 36°14N 115°2W 124 A2
Nellore India 14°27N 79°59E 245 G4
Nelson B.C., Canada 49°30N 117°20W 296 D5
Nelson N.Z. 41°18S 173°16E 285 B8
Nelson Lancs., U.K. 53°50N 2°13W 168 D5
Nelson Ariz., U.S.A. 35°31N 113°19W 305 J7
Nelson Nev., U.S.A. 35°42N 114°49W 307 K12
Nelson □ N.Z. 41°20S 173°20E 285 B8
Nelson → Canada 54°33N 98°2W 297 C9
Nelson, C. Vic., Australia 38°26S 141°32E 282 E4
Nelson, C. Papua N. G. 9°0S 149°20E 286 E5
Nelson, Estrecho Chile 51°30S 75°0W 336 D2
Nelson Bay Australia 32°43S 152°9E 283 B10
Nelson Forks Canada 59°30N 124°0W 296 B4
Nelson House Canada 55°47N 98°51W 297 B9
Nelson L. Canada 55°48N 100°7W 297 B8
Nelson Lakes △ N.Z. 41°55S 172°44E 285 B7
Nelson's Dockyard Antigua & B. 17°1N 61°46W 322 b
Nelspoort S. Africa 32°7S 23°0E 270 D3
Nelspruit S. Africa 25°29S 30°59E 271 C5
Néma Mauritania 16°40N 7°15W 262 B3
Neman = Nemunas → Lithuania 55°25N 21°10E 184 C8
Neman Russia 55°2N 22°2E 184 C9
N'ematābād Iran 35°38N 51°21E 141 B2
Nemchinovka Russia 55°42N 37°23E 129 B3
Nemea Greece 37°49N 22°40E 204 D4
Nemecký Brod = Havlíčkův Brod Czech Rep. 49°36N 15°33E 180 B8
Nemeiben L. Canada 55°20N 105°20W 297 B7
Nemërçkë, Mal Albania 40°15N 20°15E 202 F4
Nemira, Vf. Romania 46°17N 26°19E 183 D11
Nemiscau Canada 51°18N 76°54W 298 B4
Nemiscau, L. Canada 51°25N 76°40W 298 B4
Nemours = Ghazaouet Algeria 35°8N 1°50W 261 A4
Nemours France 48°16N 2°40E 173 D9
Nemšová Slovak Rep. 48°58N 18°7E 181 C11
Nemunas → Lithuania 55°25N 21°10E 184 C8
Nemuro Japan 43°20N 145°35E 220 C12
Nemuro-Kaikyō Japan 43°30N 145°30E 220 C12
Nemyriv Ukraine 50°7N 23°27E 185 H10
Nen Jiang → China 45°28N 124°30E 227 B13
Nenagh Ireland 52°52N 8°11W 166 D3
Nenana U.S.A. 64°34N 149°5W 303 D10
Nenasi Malaysia 3°9N 103°23E 237 L4
Nendo Pac. Oc. 10°45S 165°54E 277 C12
Nene → U.K. 52°49N 0°11E 169 E8
Nengkao Shan Taiwan 23°58N 121°16E 225 C3
Nengonengo French Polynesia 18°47S 141°48W 289 f
Nenita Greece 38°14N 26°6E 205 C8
Nenjiang China 49°10N 125°10E 219 B7
Neno Malawi 15°25S 34°40E 269 F3
Neo Chori Greece 38°25N 21°17E 204 C3
Neochori Greece 39°4N 21°0E 204 B2
Neodesha U.S.A. 37°25N 95°41W 308 G6
Neoga U.S.A. 39°19N 88°27W 311 E8
Neon Petritsi Greece 41°16N 23°15E 202 E7
Neópolis Brazil 10°18S 36°35W 332 D4
Neora Valley △ India 27°0N 88°45E 241 B2
Neosho U.S.A. 36°52N 94°22W 308 G6
Neosho → U.S.A. 36°48N 95°18W 314 C7
Nepal ■ Asia 28°0N 84°30E 243 F11
Nepalganj Nepal 28°5N 81°40E 243 E9
Nepalganj Road India 28°1N 81°41E 243 E9
Nepean B. Australia 35°42S 137°37E 282 C2
Nephi U.S.A. 39°43N 111°50W 304 G8
Nephin Ireland 54°1N 9°22W 166 B2
Nephin Beg Range Ireland 54°0N 9°40W 166 C2
Nepi Italy 42°14N 12°21E 199 F9
Nepomuk Czech Rep. 49°29N 13°35E 180 B6
Neppel = Moses Lake U.S.A. 47°8N 119°17W 304 C4
Neptune U.S.A. 40°13N 74°2W 313 F10
Neptune Is. Australia 35°17S 136°10E 282 C2
Nera → Italy 42°26N 12°24E 199 F9
Nera → Romania 44°48N 21°25E 182 F6
Nérac France 44°8N 0°21E 174 D4
Nerang Australia 27°58S 153°20E 281 D5
Nerastro, Sarīr Libya 24°20N 20°37E 258 D4
Neratovice Czech Rep. 50°16N 14°31E 180 A7
Nerchinsk Russia 52°0N 116°39E 215 D12
Nereju Romania 45°43N 26°43E 183 E11
Nerekhta Russia 57°26N 40°38E 188 D11
Neresnytsya Ukraine 48°7N 23°46E 183 B8
Néret, L. Canada 54°45N 70°44W 299 B5
Neretvanski Kanal Croatia 43°7N 17°10E 199 E14
Nerima Japan 35°44N 139°40E 140 A3
Neringa Lithuania 55°20N 21°5E 184 C8
Neris → Lithuania 55°8N 24°16E 188 E3
Nerja Spain 36°43N 3°55W 195 J7
Nerl → Russia 56°11N 40°34E 188 D11
Nerpio Spain 38°11N 2°16W 197 G2
Nerva Spain 37°42N 6°30W 195 H4
Nervi Italy 44°23N 9°2E 198 D6
Neryungri Russia 57°38N 124°28E 215 D13
Nes Iceland 65°53N 17°24W 155 B9
Nes Buskerud, Norway 60°34N 9°59E 164 D6
Nesbyen Norway 60°34N 9°8E 164 D6
Nescopeck U.S.A. 41°3N 76°12W 313 E8
Nesebŭr Bulgaria 42°41N 27°46E 203 D11
Neset Norway 61°53N 10°7E 164 C7
Nesflaten Norway 59°38N 6°48E 164 E3
Nesjahverfi Iceland 64°20N 15°15W 155 C11
Neskaupstaður Iceland 65°9N 13°42W 155 B13
Nesland Norway 59°31N 7°59E 164 E4
Neslandsvatn Norway 58°57N 9°10E 164 F6
Nesodden Norway 59°48N 10°41E 133 B3
Nesoddtangen Norway 59°48N 10°40E 133 A3
Nesøya Norway 59°52N 10°31E 133 A2
Ness, L. U.K. 57°15N 4°32W 167 D4
Ness City U.S.A. 38°27N 99°54W 308 F4
Nesterov Russia 54°38N 22°41E 184 D9
Nesterov Ukraine 50°4N 23°58E 177 C12
Nestorio Greece 40°24N 21°5E 202 F5
Nestos → Greece 41°20N 24°35E 203 E8
Nesttun Norway 60°19N 5°20E 164 D2
Nesvady Slovak Rep. 47°56N 18°7E 181 D11
Nesvizh = Nyasvizh Belarus 53°14N 26°38E 177 B14
Netanya Israel 32°20N 34°51E 251 F5
Netarhat India 23°29N 84°16E 243 H11
Nete → Belgium 51°7N 4°14E 170 C4
Netherdale Australia 21°10S 148°33E 280 K6
Netherlands ■ Europe 52°0N 5°30E 170 C5
Netherlands Antilles ☒ W. Indies 12°15N 69°0W 328 A4
Netherlands East Indies = Indonesia ■ Asia 5°0S 115°0E 235 C4
Netherlands Guiana = Suriname ■ S. Amer. 4°0N 56°0W 329 C6
Neto → Italy 39°12N 17°9E 201 C10
Netrakona Bangla. 24°53N 90°47E 241 C3
Netrang India 21°39N 73°21E 242 J5
Nettancourt France 48°51N 4°57E 173 D11
Nettetal Germany 51°19N 6°12E 178 D2
Nettilling L. Canada 66°30N 71°0W 295 C12
Nettuno Italy 41°27N 12°39E 200 A5
Netzahualcóyotl, Presa Mexico 17°8N 93°35W 319 D6
Neu Aubing Germany 48°8N 11°25E 131 B1
Neu-Bentschen = Zbąszynek Poland 52°16N 15°51E 185 F2
Neu Buch Germany 52°37N 13°31E 115 A4
Neu Buchhorst Germany 52°24N 13°44E 115 B5
Neu Fahrland Germany 52°26N 13°1E 115 B1
Neu-Isenburg Germany 50°3N 8°42E 179 E4
Neu-Langenburg = Tukuyu Tanzania 9°17S 33°35E 269 D3
Neu Lindenberg Germany 52°36N 13°33E 115 A4
Neu-Mecklenburg = New Ireland Papua N. G. 3°20S 151°50E 286 B6
Neu Pommern = New Britain Papua N. G. 5°50S 150°20E 286 C6
Neu-Sandec = Nowy Sącz Poland 49°40N 20°41E 185 J7
Neu Sandez = Nowy Sącz Poland 49°40N 20°41E 185 J7
Neu-Ulm Germany 48°22N 10°0E 179 G6
Neubiberg Germany 48°4N 11°40E 131 B3
Neubrandenburg Germany 53°33N 13°15E 178 B9
Neubukow Germany 54°2N 11°39E 178 A7
Neuburg Germany 48°44N 11°11E 179 G7
Neuchâtel Switz. 47°0N 6°55E 179 J2
Neuchâtel □ Switz. 47°0N 6°55E 179 J2
Neuchâtel, Lac de Switz. 46°53N 6°50E 179 J2
Neudau Austria 47°11N 16°6E 180 D9
Neuenburg an der Elbe = Nymburk Czech Rep. 50°10N 15°1E 180 A8
Neuenhagen Germany 52°32N 13°38E 115 A4
Neuenhaus Germany 52°30N 6°58E 178 C2
Neuessling Austria 48°15N 16°32E 142 A3
Neuf-Brisach France 48°1N 7°30E 173 D14
Neufahrn Bayern, Germany 48°41N 12°11E 179 G8
Neufahrn Bayern, Germany 48°18N 11°40E 179 G7
Neufchâteau Belgium 49°50N 5°25E 170 E5
Neufchâteau Vosges, France 48°21N 5°40E 173 D12

Neufchâtel-en-Bray *France* 49°44N 1°26E **172** C8
Neufchâtel-sur-Aisne *France* 49°26N 4°1E **173** C11
Neuhaus = Jindřichův Hradec *Czech Rep.* 49°10N 15°2E **180** B8
Neuhaus *Germany* 53°17N 10°56E **178** B6
Neuhäusel = Nové Zámky *Slovak Rep.* 48°2N 18°8E **181** C11
Neuhausen *Germany* 48°9N 11°32E **131** B2
Neuherberg *Germany* 48°13N 11°35E **131** A2
Neuhönow *Germany* 52°34N 13°44E **115** A5
Neuillé-Pont-Pierre *France* 47°33N 0°33E **172** E7
Neuilly-Plaisance *France* 48°51N 2°30E **134** A4
Neuilly-St-Front *France* 49°10N 3°15E **173** C10
Neuilly-sur-Marne *France* 48°51N 2°31E **134** A4
Neuilly-sur-Seine *France* 48°53N 2°15E **134** A2
Neukagran *Austria* 48°14N 16°27E **142** A2
Neukalen *Germany* 53°49N 12°46E **178** B8
Neukettenhof *Austria* 48°7N 16°28E **142** B2
Neukölln *Germany* 52°28N 13°25E **115** B3
Neumarkt = Nowy Targ *Poland* 49°29N 20°2E **185** J7
Neumarkt = Środa Śląska *Poland* 51°10N 16°36E **185** G3
Neumarkt *Germany* 49°26N 11°27E **179** F7
Neumarktl = Tržič *Slovenia* 46°22N 14°18E **199** B11
Neumayer *Antarctica* 71°0S 68°30W **151** D17
Neumittelwalde = Międzybórz *Poland* 51°25N 17°34E **185** G4
Neumünster *Germany* 54°4N 9°58E **178** A5
Neung-sur-Beuvron *France* 47°30N 1°50E **173** E8
Neunkirchen *Austria* 47°43N 16°4E **180** D9
Neunkirchen *Saarland, Germany* 49°20N 7°9E **179** F3
Neuperlach *Germany* 48°6N 11°37E **131** B2
Neuquén *Argentina* 38°55S 68°0W **336** A3
Neuquén □ *Argentina* 38°0S 69°50W **334** D2
Neuquén → *Argentina* 38°59S 68°0W **336** A3
Neuried *Germany* 48°5N 11°27E **131** B1
Neuruppin *Germany* 52°55N 12°48E **178** C8
Neusalz an der Oder = Nowa Sól *Poland* 51°48N 15°44E **185** G2
Neusäss *Germany* 48°24N 10°50E **179** G6
Neusatz = Novi Sad *Serbia* 45°18N 19°52E **182** E4
Neuse → *U.S.A.* 35°6N 76°29W **315** D16
Neusiedl *Austria* 47°57N 16°50E **181** D9
Neusiedler See *Austria* 47°50N 16°47E **181** D9
Neusiedler See-Seewinkel △ *Austria* 47°50N 16°45E **181** D9
Neusohl = Banská Bystrica *Slovak Rep.* 48°46N 19°14E **181** C12
Neuss *Germany* 51°11N 6°42E **178** D2
Neussargues-Moissac *France* 45°9N 3°0E **174** C7
Neustadt = Lwówek *Poland* 52°28N 16°10E **185** F3
Neustadt = Prudnik *Poland* 50°20N 17°38E **185** H4
Neustadt = Wejherowo *Poland* 54°35N 18°12E **184** D5
Neustadt *Bayern, Germany* 49°44N 12°10E **179** F8
Neustadt *Bayern, Germany* 48°48N 11°46E **179** G7
Neustadt *Bayern, Germany* 49°34N 10°37E **179** F6
Neustadt *Bayern, Germany* 50°19N 11°7E **179** E7
Neustadt *Brandenburg, Germany* 52°50N 12°27E **178** C8
Neustadt *Hessen, Germany* 50°51N 9°9E **178** E5
Neustadt *Niedersachsen, Germany* 52°30N 9°30E **178** C5
Neustadt *Rhld-Pfz., Germany* 49°21N 8°10E **179** F4
Neustadt *Sachsen, Germany* 51°2N 14°12E **178** D10
Neustadt *Schleswig-Holstein, Germany* 54°6N 10°49E **178** A6
Neustadt *Thüringen, Germany* 50°45N 11°43E **178** E7
Neustädtel = Nowe Miasteczko *Poland* 51°42N 15°42E **185** G2
Neustädtl = Novo Mesto *Slovenia* 45°47N 15°12E **199** C12
Neustettin = Szczecinek *Poland* 53°43N 16°41E **184** E3
Neustift am Walde *Austria* 48°14N 16°17E **142** A1
Neustrelitz *Germany* 53°21N 13°4E **178** B9
Neusüssenbrunn *Austria* 48°16N 16°29E **142** A2
Neutitschein = Nový Jičín *Czech Rep.* 49°30N 18°2E **181** B11
Neuvic *France* 45°23N 2°16E **174** C6
Neuville-sur-Saône *France* 45°52N 4°51E **175** C8
Neuvy-le-Roi *France* 47°36N 0°36E **172** E7
Neuvy-St-Sépulchre *France* 46°35N 1°48E **173** F8
Neuvy-sur-Barangeon *France* 47°20N 2°15E **173** E9
Neuwaldegg *Austria* 48°14N 16°17E **142** A1
Neuwedell = Drawno *Poland* 53°13N 15°46E **185** E2
Neuwerk *Germany* 53°55N 8°30E **178** B4
Neuwied *Germany* 50°26N 7°29E **178** E3
Neva → *Russia* 59°56N 30°20E **188** C6
Nevada *Iowa, U.S.A.* 42°1N 93°27W **310** B3
Nevada *Mo., U.S.A.* 37°51N 94°22W **310** G2
Nevada □ *U.S.A.* 39°0N 117°0W **304** G5
Nevada City *U.S.A.* 39°16N 121°1W **306** F6
Nevado, Cerro *Argentina* 35°30S 68°32W **334** D2
Nevado de Colima = Volcán de Colima △ *Mexico* 19°30N 103°40W **318** D4
Nevado de Tres Cruces △ *Chile* 27°13S 69°5W **334** B2
Nevado del Huila △ *Colombia* 3°5N 75°58W **328** C2
Nevasa *India* 19°34N 75°0E **244** E2
Neve, Sa. da *Angola* 13°43S 13°10E **265** E2
Neve Ya'akov *West Bank* 31°50N 35°14E **123** A2
Nevel *Russia* 56°0N 29°55E **188** D5
Nevers *France* 47°0N 3°9E **173** F10
Nevertire *Australia* 31°50S 147°44E **283** A7
Neves *Brazil* 22°51S 43°5W **135** B2
Nevesinje *Bos.-H.* 43°14N 18°6E **202** C2
Neville *Canada* 49°58N 107°39W **297** D7
Nevinnomyssk *Russia* 44°40N 42°0E **191** H6
Nevis *St. Kitts & Nevis* 17°0N 62°30W **322** d
Nevis Pk. *St. Kitts & Nevis* 17°9N 62°34W **322** d
Nevlunghavn *Norway* 58°58N 9°53E **164** F6
Nevoso, Mte. = Snežnik *Slovenia* 45°36N 14°35E **199** C11
Nevrokop = Gotse Delchev *Bulgaria* 41°36N 23°46E **202** E7
Nevşehir *Turkey* 38°33N 34°40E **212** C6
Nevşehir □ *Turkey* 38°50N 34°40E **212** C6
Nevskoye *Russia* 54°32N 22°39E **184** D9
Nevyansk *Russia* 57°30N 60°13E **186** C11
New → *Guyana* 3°20N 57°37W **329** C6
New → *W. Va., U.S.A.* 38°10N 81°12W **309** F13
New Aiyansh *Canada* 55°12N 129°4W **296** B3
New Albany *Ind., U.S.A.* 38°18N 85°49W **311** F11
New Albany *Miss., U.S.A.* 34°29N 89°0W **315** D10
New Albany *Pa., U.S.A.* 41°36N 76°27W **313** E8
New Amsterdam *Guyana* 6°15N 57°36W **329** B6
New Angledool *Australia* 29°5S 147°55E **281** D4
New Athens *U.S.A.* 38°19N 89°53W **310** F7
New Baghdād *Iraq* 33°18N 44°28E **113** B2
New Baltimore *U.S.A.* 42°41N 82°44W **312** D2
New Barakpur *India* 22°40N 88°26E **124** A2
New Barbadoes = Hackensack *U.S.A.* 40°52N 74°4W **132** A1
New Bedford *U.S.A.* 41°38N 70°56W **313** E14
New Berlin = North Canton *U.S.A.* 40°53N 81°24W **312** F3
New Berlin *Ill., U.S.A.* 39°44N 89°55W **310** E7
New Berlin *N.Y., U.S.A.* 42°37N 75°20W **313** D9
New Berlin *Pa., U.S.A.* 40°50N 76°57W **312** F8
New Berlin *Wis., U.S.A.* 42°59N 88°6W **311** B8
New Bern *U.S.A.* 35°7N 77°3W **315** D16
New Bethlehem *U.S.A.* 41°0N 79°20W **312** F5
New Bight *Bahamas* 24°19N 75°24W **321** B4
New Bloomfield *U.S.A.* 40°25N 77°11W **312** F7
New Boston *U.S.A.* 33°28N 94°25W **314** E7
New Braunfels *U.S.A.* 29°42N 98°8W **314** G5
New Brighton *N.Z.* 43°29S 172°43E **285** D7
New Brighton *N.Y., U.S.A.* 40°38N 74°5W **132** C1
New Brighton *Pa., U.S.A.* 40°42N 80°19W **312** F4
New Britain *Papua N. G.* 5°50S 150°20E **286** C6
New Britain *Conn., U.S.A.* 41°40N 72°47W **313** E12
New Britain Trench *Pac. Oc.* 6°0S 153°0E **276** J3
New Brockton *U.S.A.* 31°23N 85°56W **316** D4
New Brookland = West Columbia *U.S.A.* 33°59N 81°4W **316** B8
New Brunswick *U.S.A.* 40°30N 74°27W **313** F10
New Brunswick □ *Canada* 46°50N 66°30W **299** C6
New Buffalo *U.S.A.* 41°47N 86°45W **311** C10
New Bussa *Nigeria* 9°53N 4°31E **263** D5
New Caledonia ☒ *Pac. Oc.* 21°0S 165°0E **288** d
New Caledonia Trough *Pac. Oc.* 30°0S 165°0E **288** L8
New Canada *S. Africa* 26°12S 27°56E **123** B1
New Canada Dam *S. Africa* 26°12S 27°56E **123** B1
New Carlisle *Ind., U.S.A.* 41°45N 86°32W **311** C10
New Carlisle *Ohio, U.S.A.* 39°56N 84°2W **311** E12
New Carrollton *U.S.A.* 38°58N 76°53W **143** B4
New Castile = Castilla-La Mancha □ *Spain* 39°30N 3°30W **195** F7
New Castle *Ind., U.S.A.* 39°55N 85°22W **311** E11
New Castle *Ky., U.S.A.* 38°26N 85°10W **311** F11
New Castle *Pa., U.S.A.* 41°0N 80°21W **312** F4
New City *U.S.A.* 41°9N 73°59W **313** E11
New Concord *U.S.A.* 39°59N 81°54W **312** G3
New Cross *U.K.* 51°28N 0°1W **125** B3
New Cumberland *U.S.A.* 40°30N 80°36W **312** F4
New Cuyama *U.S.A.* 34°57N 119°38W **307** L7
New Delhi *India* 28°36N 77°11E **120** B2
New Denver *Canada* 50°0N 117°25W **296** D5
New Don Pedro Res. *U.S.A.* 37°43N 120°24W **306** H6
New Dorp *U.S.A.* 40°34N 74°7W **132** C1
New Dorp Beach *U.S.A.* 40°33N 74°6W **132** C1
New Ellenton *U.S.A.* 33°28N 81°41W **316** B8
New England *U.S.A.* 43°0N 71°0W **301** B12
New England *N. Dak., U.S.A.* 46°32N 102°52W **308** B2
New England △ *Australia* 30°25S 152°30E **283** A10
New England Aquarium *Boston, U.S.A.* **116** b3
New England Ra. *Australia* 30°20S 151°45E **281** E5
New England Seamounts *Atl. Oc.* 38°0N 63°0W **152** C5
New Forest △ *U.K.* 50°53N 1°34W **169** G6
New Franklin *U.S.A.* 39°1N 92°44W **310** E4
New Galloway *U.K.* 55°5N 4°9W **167** F4
New Georgia Is. *Solomon Is.* 8°15S 157°30E **287** M9
New Georgia Sound *Solomon Is.* 8°0S 158°20E **287** L9
New Glarus *U.S.A.* 42°49N 89°38W **310** B7
New Glasgow *Canada* 45°35N 62°36W **299** C7
New Grant *Trin. & Tob.* 10°17N 61°19W **323** t
New Guinea *Oceania* 4°0S 136°0E **286** C1
New Hamburg *Canada* 43°23N 80°42W **312** C4
New Hampshire □ *U.S.A.* 44°0N 71°30W **313** C13
New Hampton *U.S.A.* 43°3N 92°19W **310** A4
New Hanover *Papua N. G.* 2°30S 150°10E **286** B6
New Hanover *KwaZulu Natal, S. Africa* 29°22S 30°31E **271** C5
New Harmony *U.S.A.* 38°8N 87°56W **311** F9
New Hartford *U.S.A.* 43°4N 75°18W **313** C9
New Haven *Conn., U.S.A.* 41°18N 72°55W **313** E12
New Haven *Ill., U.S.A.* 37°55N 88°8W **311** G8
New Haven *Ind., U.S.A.* 41°4N 85°1W **311** C11
New Haven *Mich., U.S.A.* 42°44N 82°48W **312** D2
New Haven *Mo., U.S.A.* 38°37N 91°13W **310** F5
New Hazelton *Canada* 55°20N 127°30W **296** B3
New Hebrides = Vanuatu ■ *Pac. Oc.* 15°0S 168°0E **287** E6
New Holland *U.S.A.* 40°6N 76°5W **313** F8
New Iberia *U.S.A.* 30°1N 91°49W **314** F9
New Ireland *Papua N. G.* 3°20S 151°50E **286** B6
New Ireland □ *Papua N. G.* 3°0S 151°30E **286** B6
New Jersey □ *U.S.A.* 40°0N 74°30W **309** F16
New Kensington *U.S.A.* 40°34N 79°46W **312** F5
New Lexington *U.S.A.* 39°43N 82°13W **309** F12
New Liskeard *Canada* 47°31N 79°41W **298** C4
New London *Conn., U.S.A.* 41°22N 72°6W **313** E12
New London *Iowa, U.S.A.* 40°55N 91°24W **310** D5
New London *Mo., U.S.A.* 39°35N 91°24W **310** E5
New London *Ohio, U.S.A.* 41°5N 82°24W **312** E2
New London *Wis., U.S.A.* 44°23N 88°45W **308** C9
New Madrid *U.S.A.* 36°36N 89°32W **308** G9
New Malden *U.K.* 51°24N 0°15W **125** B2
New Martinsville *U.S.A.* 39°39N 80°52W **309** F13
New Meadows *U.S.A.* 44°58N 116°18W **304** D5
New Melones L. *U.S.A.* 37°57N 120°31W **306** H6
New Mexico □ *U.S.A.* 34°30N 106°0W **305** J11
New Miami *U.S.A.* 39°26N 84°32W **311** E12
New Milford *Conn., U.S.A.* 41°35N 73°25W **313** E11
New Milford *N.Y., U.S.A.* 40°56N 74°0W **132** A1
New Milford *Pa., U.S.A.* 41°52N 75°44W **313** E9
New Mumbai = Navi Mumbai *India* 19°5N 73°0E **130** A2
New Norcia *Australia* 30°57S 116°13E **279** F2
New Norfolk *Australia* 42°46S 147°2E **281** G4
New Orleans *U.S.A.* 29°57N 90°4W **131** B2
New Orleans Int. ✈ (MSY) *U.S.A.* 30°0N 90°15W **131** A1
New Palestine *U.S.A.* 39°45N 85°52W **311** E11
New Panamao *Phil.* 5°59N 121°13E **233** J3
New Paris *U.S.A.* 39°51N 84°48W **311** E12
New Pekin *U.S.A.* 38°30N 86°0W **311** F10
New Philadelphia *U.S.A.* 40°30N 81°27W **312** F3
New Plymouth *N.Z.* 39°4S 174°5E **284** F3
New Plymouth *Idaho, U.S.A.* 43°58N 116°49W **304** E5
New Pomerania = New Britain *Papua N. G.* 5°50S 150°20E **286** C6
New Port Richey *U.S.A.* 28°16N 82°43W **317** G7
New Providence *Bahamas* 25°25N 78°35W **153** b
New Quay *U.K.* 52°13N 4°21W **169** E3
New Radnor *U.K.* 52°15N 3°9W **169** E4
New Richmond *Qué., Canada* 48°15N 65°45W **299** C6
New Richmond *Ohio, U.S.A.* 38°57N 84°17W **311** F12
New Richmond *Wis., U.S.A.* 45°7N 92°32W **308** C7
New River Gorge ⌂ *U.S.A.* 37°53N 81°5W **309** G13
New Roads *U.S.A.* 30°42N 91°26W **314** F9
New Rochelle *U.S.A.* 40°55N 73°46W **313** F11
New Rockford *U.S.A.* 47°41N 99°8W **308** B4
New Romney *U.K.* 50°59N 0°57E **169** G8
New Ross *Ireland* 52°23N 6°57W **166** D5
New Salem *U.S.A.* 46°51N 101°25W **308** B3
New Scone = Scone *U.K.* 56°25N 3°24W **167** E5
New Sharon *U.S.A.* 41°28N 92°39W **310** C4
New Siberian I. = Novaya Sibir, Ostrov *Russia* 75°10N 150°0E **215** B16
New Siberian Is. = Novosibirskiye Ostrova *Russia* 75°0N 142°0E **215** B15
New Smyrna Beach *U.S.A.* 29°1N 80°56W **317** F9
New South Wales □ *Australia* 33°0S 146°0E **283** B7
New Stuyahok *U.S.A.* 59°29N 157°20W **303** G8
New Tecumseth *Canada* 44°9N 79°52W **312** B5
New Territories *China* 22°23N 114°10E **122** A1
New Toronto *Canada* 43°35N 79°30W **141** B1
New Town = Nowe Miasto *Warsaw, Poland* **142** a2
New Town *Edinburgh, U.K.* **121** a2
New Town *N. Dak., U.S.A.* 47°59N 102°30W **308** B2
New Tredegar *U.K.* 51°44N 3°16W **169** F4
New Ulm *U.S.A.* 44°19N 94°28W **308** C6
New Utrecht *U.S.A.* 40°36N 73°59W **132** C2
New Vienna *U.S.A.* 39°19N 83°42W **311** E13
New Washington *Phil.* 11°39N 122°26E **233** F4
New Waterford *Canada* 46°13N 60°4W **299** C7
New-Wes-Valley *Canada* 49°8N 53°36W **299** C9
New Westminster *Canada* 49°13N 122°55W **306** A4
New York *U.S.A.* 40°43N 74°0W **132** B3
New York □ *U.S.A.* 43°0N 75°0W **313** D9
New York Avenue *Washington, D.C., U.S.A.* **143** a2
New York J.F. Kennedy Int. ✈ (JFK) *U.S.A.* 40°38N 73°47W **313** F11
New York La Guardia ✈ (LGA) *U.S.A.* 40°46N 73°52W **132** B2
New York University *New York, U.S.A.* **132** d2
New Zealand ■ *Oceania* 40°0S 176°0E **284** G5
Newaj → *India* 24°24N 76°49E **242** G7
Newala *Tanzania* 10°58S 39°18E **269** E4
Newark *Del., U.S.A.* 39°41N 75°46W **309** F16
Newark *N.J., U.S.A.* 40°44N 74°10W **313** F10
Newark *N.Y., U.S.A.* 43°3N 77°6W **312** C7
Newark *Ohio, U.S.A.* 40°3N 82°24W **312** F2
Newark B. *U.S.A.* 40°40N 74°8W **132** B1
Newark Liberty Int. ✈ (EWR) *U.S.A.* 40°42N 74°10W **313** F10
Newark-on-Trent *U.K.* 53°5N 0°48W **168** D7
Newark Valley *U.S.A.* 42°14N 76°11W **313** D8
Newbattle *U.K.* 55°53N 3°4W **121** B3
Newberg *U.S.A.* 45°18N 122°58W **304** D2
Newberry *Fla., U.S.A.* 29°39N 82°37W **317** F7
Newberry *Mich., U.S.A.* 46°21N 85°30W **309** B11
Newberry *S.C., U.S.A.* 34°17N 81°37W **315** D14
Newberry Springs *U.S.A.* 34°50N 116°41W **307** L10
Newboro L. *Canada* 44°38N 76°20W **313** B8
Newbridge = Droichead Nua *Ireland* 53°11N 6°48W **166** C5
Newburg *U.S.A.* 37°55N 91°54W **310** G5
Newburgh *Ont., Canada* 44°19N 76°52W **312** B8
Newburgh *Ind., U.S.A.* 37°57N 87°24W **311** G9
Newburgh *N.Y., U.S.A.* 41°30N 74°1W **313** E10
Newbury *W. Berkshire, U.K.* 51°24N 1°20W **169** F6
Newbury *N.H., U.S.A.* 43°19N 72°3W **313** B12
Newbury *Vt., U.S.A.* 44°5N 72°4W **313** B12
Newbury Park *U.K.* 51°34N 0°5E **125** A4
Newburyport *U.S.A.* 42°49N 70°53W **313** D14
Newcastle *N.S.W., Australia* 33°0S 151°46E **283** B9
Newcastle *N.B., Canada* 47°1N 65°38W **299** C6
Newcastle *Ont., Canada* 43°55N 78°35W **298** D4
Newcastle *St. Kitts & Nevis* 17°14N 62°42W **322** d
Newcastle *KwaZulu Natal, S. Africa* 27°45S 29°58E **271** C4
Newcastle *Down, U.K.* 54°13N 5°54W **166** B6
Newcastle *Calif., U.S.A.* 38°53N 121°8W **306** G5
Newcastle *Wyo., U.S.A.* 43°50N 104°11W **304** E11
Newcastle Emlyn *U.K.* 52°2N 4°28W **169** E3
Newcastle Ra. *Australia* 15°45S 130°15E **278** C5
Newcastle-under-Lyme *U.K.* 53°1N 2°14W **168** D5
Newcastle-upon-Tyne *U.K.* 54°58N 1°36W **168** C6
Newcastle Waters *Australia* 17°30S 133°28E **280** B1
Newcastle West *Ireland* 52°27N 9°3W **166** D2
Newcomb *U.S.A.* 43°58N 74°10W **313** C10
Newcomerstown *U.S.A.* 40°16N 81°36W **312** F3
Newcraighall *U.K.* 55°56N 3°5W **121** B3
Newdegate *Australia* 33°6S 119°0E **279** F2
Newell *Queens., Australia* 16°20S 145°16E **280** B4
Newell *Iowa, U.S.A.* 42°36N 95°0W **310** B1
Newell *S. Dak., U.S.A.* 44°43N 103°25W **308** C2
Newenham, C. *U.S.A.* 58°39N 162°11W **303** G7
Newfane *U.S.A.* 43°17N 78°43W **312** C6
Newfield *U.S.A.* 42°18N 76°33W **313** D8
Newfound L. *U.S.A.* 43°40N 71°47W **313** C13
Newfoundland *Canada* 49°0N 55°0W **299** C8
Newfoundland *Pa., U.S.A.* 41°18N 75°19W **313** E9
Newfoundland & Labrador □ *Canada* 53°0N 58°0W **299** B8
Newhalen *U.S.A.* 59°43N 154°54W **303** G9
Newham □ *U.K.* 51°31N 0°3E **125** A4
Newhaven *E. Sussex, U.K.* 50°47N 0°3E **169** G8
Newhaven *Edinburgh, U.K.* 55°59N 3°11W **121** B2
Newington *Edinburgh, U.K.* 55°56N 3°10W **121** B2
Newington *London, U.K.* **125** c5
Newington *Ga., U.S.A.* 32°35N 81°30W **316** C8
Newkirk *U.S.A.* 36°53N 97°3W **314** C6
Newlands *Wellington, N.Z.* 41°13S 174°49E **143** B1
Newlands *Gauteng, S. Africa* 26°10S 27°57E **123** B1
Newlyn *U.K.* 50°6N 5°34W **169** G2
Newman *W. Austral., Australia* 23°18S 119°45E **278** D2
Newman *Calif., U.S.A.* 37°19N 121°1W **306** H5
Newman *Ill., U.S.A.* 39°48N 87°59W **311** E9
Newmarket *Ont., Canada* 44°3N 79°28W **312** B5
Newmarket *Cork, Ireland* 52°13N 9°0W **166** D2
Newmarket *Jamaica* 18°9N 77°55W **320** a
Newmarket *Suffolk, U.K.* 52°15N 0°25E **169** E8
Newmarket *N.H., U.S.A.* 43°5N 70°56W **313** C14
Newnan *U.S.A.* 33°23N 84°48W **316** B5
Newport = Nieuwpoort *Neth. Ant.* 12°3N 68°49W **322** g
Newport *Vic., Australia* 37°50S 144°51E **128** B1
Newport *Mayo, Ireland* 53°53N 9°33W **166** C2
Newport *I. of W., U.K.* 50°42N 1°17W **169** G6
Newport *Newport, U.K.* 51°35N 3°0W **169** F5
Newport *Ark., U.S.A.* 35°37N 91°16W **314** D9
Newport *Fla., U.S.A.* 30°11N 84°10W **316** E5
Newport *Ind., U.S.A.* 39°53N 87°25W **311** E9
Newport *Ky., U.S.A.* 39°5N 84°29W **311** E12
Newport *N.H., U.S.A.* 43°22N 72°10W **313** C12
Newport *N.Y., U.S.A.* 43°11N 75°1W **313** C9
Newport *Oreg., U.S.A.* 44°39N 124°3W **304** D1
Newport *Pa., U.S.A.* 40°29N 77°8W **312** F7
Newport *R.I., U.S.A.* 41°29N 71°19W **313** E13
Newport *Tenn., U.S.A.* 35°58N 83°11W **315** D13
Newport *Vt., U.S.A.* 44°56N 72°13W **313** B12
Newport *Wash., U.S.A.* 48°11N 117°3W **304** B5
Newport □ *U.K.* 51°33N 3°1W **169** F4
Newport Beach *U.S.A.* 33°37N 117°56W **307** M9
Newport News *U.S.A.* 36°58N 76°25W **309** G15
Newport Pagnell *U.K.* 52°5N 0°43W **169** E7
Newquay *U.K.* 50°25N 5°6W **169** G2
Newry *U.K.* 54°11N 6°21W **166** B5
Newtok *U.S.A.* 60°56N 164°38W **303** F6
Newton *Ga., U.S.A.* 31°19N 84°20W **316** D5
Newton *Ill., U.S.A.* 38°59N 88°10W **311** F8
Newton *Iowa, U.S.A.* 41°42N 93°3W **310** C3
Newton *Kans., U.S.A.* 38°3N 97°21W **308** F5
Newton *Mass., U.S.A.* 42°21N 71°12W **116** B1
Newton *Miss., U.S.A.* 32°19N 89°10W **315** E10
Newton *N.C., U.S.A.* 35°40N 81°13W **315** D14
Newton *N.J., U.S.A.* 41°3N 74°45W **313** E10
Newton *Tex., U.S.A.* 30°51N 93°46W **314** F8
Newton Abbot *U.K.* 50°32N 3°37W **169** G4
Newton Aycliffe *U.K.* 54°37N 1°34W **168** C6
Newton Falls *U.S.A.* 41°11N 80°59W **312** E4
Newton L. *U.S.A.* 38°55N 88°15W **311** F8
Newton Stewart *U.K.* 54°57N 4°30W **167** G4
Newton Terrace *Barbados* 13°4N 59°32W **323** r
Newtonbrook *Canada* 43°47N 79°24W **141** A2
Newtongrange *U.K.* 55°53N 3°3W **121** B3
Newtonmore *U.K.* 57°4N 4°8W **167** D4
Newtontoppen *Svalbard* 79°0N 17°30E **154** B12
Newtonville *U.S.A.* 42°20N 71°11W **116** A1
Newtown *N.S.W., Australia* 33°54S 151°11E **139** B2
Newtown *Powys, U.K.* 52°31N 3°19W **169** E4
Newtown *Ind., U.S.A.* 40°13N 87°9W **311** D9
Newtown *Mo., U.S.A.* 40°22N 93°20W **310** D3
Newtownabbey *U.K.* 54°40N 5°56W **166** B6
Newtownards *U.K.* 54°36N 5°42W **166** B6
Newtownbarry = Bunclody *Ireland* 52°39N 6°40W **166** D5
Newtownstewart *U.K.* 54°43N 7°23W **166** B4
Newville *U.S.A.* 40°10N 77°24W **312** F7
Nexon *France* 45°41N 1°11E **174** C5
Neya *Russia* 58°21N 43°49E **190** A6
Neyrīz *Iran* 29°15N 54°19E **247** D7
Neyshābūr *Iran* 36°10N 58°50E **247** B8
Neyveli *India* 11°32N 79°29E **245** J4
Neyyattinkara *India* 8°26N 77°5E **245** K3
Nezametny = Aldan *Russia* 58°40N 125°30E **215** D13
Nezhin = Nizhyn *Ukraine* 51°5N 31°55E **189** G6
Nezperce *U.S.A.* 46°14N 116°14W **304** C5
Nezvysko *Ukraine* 48°46N 25°15E **183** B10
Ngabang *Indonesia* 0°23N 109°55E **235** B3
Ngabe *Congo* 3°12S 16°12E **264** C3
Ngabordamlu, Tanjung *Indonesia* 6°56S 134°11E **231** F8
N'Gage *Angola* 7°46S 15°15E **265** D3
Ngaio *N.Z.* 41°15S 174°46E **143** B1
Ngaiphaipi *Burma* 22°14N 93°15E **241** D4
Ngala *Nigeria* 12°20N 14°11E **263** C7
Ngama *Chad* 11°45N 17°6E **259** F3
Ngambé *Centre, Cameroon* 5°48N 11°29E **263** D7
Ngambé *Littoral, Cameroon* 4°21N 10°40E **263** E7
Ngami Depression *Botswana* 20°30S 22°46E **270** B3
Ngamo *Zimbabwe* 19°3S 27°32E **269** F2
Ngangala *Sudan* 4°42N 31°55E **257** G3
Nganglong Kangri *China* 33°0N 81°0E **243** C9
Nganjuk *Indonesia* 7°32S 111°55E **235** D4
Ngao *Thailand* 18°46N 99°59E **236** C2
Ngaoundéré *Cameroon* 7°15N 13°35E **264** A2
Ngapara *N.Z.* 44°57S 170°46E **285** E5
Ngape *Burma* 20°20N 94°28E **241** E5
Ngara *Tanzania* 2°29S 30°40E **268** C3
Ngardmau *Palau* 7°37N 134°34E **288** c
Ngardmau B. *Palau* 7°38N 134°34E **288** c
Ngardololok *Palau* 7°0N 134°14E **288** c
Ngaregur *Palau* 7°45N 134°37E **288** c
Ngaruawahia *N.Z.* 37°42S 175°11E **284** D4
Ngaruroro → *N.Z.* 39°34S 176°55E **284** F5
Ngatangiia *Cook Is.* 21°14S 159°43W **289** h
Ngatapa *N.Z.* 38°32S 177°45E **284** E6
Ngathainggyaung *Burma* 17°24N 95°5E **241** G5
Ngau Chi Wan *China* 22°20N 114°12E **122** A2
Ngau Tau Kok *China* 22°19N 114°12E **122** B2
Ngauranga *N.Z.* 41°15S 174°49E **143** B1
Ngauruhoe, Mt. *N.Z.* 39°13S 175°45E **284** F4
Ngawi *Indonesia* 7°24S 111°26E **235** D4
Ngcobo *S. Africa* 31°37S 28°0E **271** D4
Ngele *Dem. Rep. of the Congo* 0°30S 20°22E **264** C4
Ngelebok *Cameroon* 4°16N 14°3E **264** B2
Ngeregong *Palau* 7°6N 134°21E **288** c
Ngergoi *Palau* 7°5N 134°15E **288** c
Ngesebus I. *Palau* 7°3N 134°15E **288** c
Nggatokae *Solomon Is.* 8°45S 158°15E **287** M10
Nggela Pile *Solomon Is.* 9°5S 160°20E **287** M11
Nggela Sule *Solomon Is.* 9°2S 160°12E **287** M11
Nghia Lo *Vietnam* 21°33N 104°28E **228** G5
Ngidinga *Dem. Rep. of the Congo* 5°37S 15°17E **265** D3
Ngo *Congo* 2°29S 15°45E **264** C3
Ngoap *Cameroon* 4°9N 12°51E **264** B2
Ngobasangel *Palau* 7°16N 134°19E **288** c
Ngoboli *Sudan* 4°57N 32°37E **257** G3
N'Gola *Angola* 14°10S 14°30E **265** E2
Ngoma *Malawi* 13°8S 33°45E **269** E3
Ngomahura *Zimbabwe* 20°26S 30°43E **269** G3
Ngomba *Tanzania* 8°20S 32°53E **269** D3
Ngomeni, Ras *Kenya* 2°59S 40°14E **268** C5
Ngong *Kenya* 1°22S 36°39E **268** C4
Ngong Shuen Chau *China* 22°19N 114°8E **122** B1
Ngongotaha *N.Z.* 38°5S 176°12E **284** E5
Ngonye Falls *Zambia* 16°40S 23°25E **265** F4
Ngop *Sudan* 6°17N 30°9E **257** F3
Ngoring Hu *China* 34°55N 97°5E **218** C4
Ngorkou *Mali* 15°40N 3°41W **262** B4
Ngorongoro *Tanzania* 3°11S 35°32E **268** C4
Ngorongoro ⌂ *Tanzania* 2°40S 35°30E **268** C4
Ngoto *C.A.R.* 3°59N 17°19E **264** B3
Ngouo, Dj. *C.A.R.* 7°55N 24°38E **264** A4
Ngoura *Chad* 12°44N 16°21E **259** F3
Ngouri *Chad* 13°38N 15°22E **259** F3
Ngourti *Niger* 15°19N 13°12E **259** E2
Ngoussou *Gabon* 3°0S 11°7E **264** C2
Ngozi *Burundi* 2°54S 29°50E **268** C2
Ngua Kok Wan *China* 22°21N 114°5E **122** A1
Ngudu *Tanzania* 2°58S 33°25E **268** C3
Nguigmi *Niger* 14°20N 13°20E **259** F2
Nguila *Cameroon* 4°41N 11°43E **263** E7
Nguiu *Australia* 11°46S 130°38E **278** B5
Ngukurr *Australia* 14°44S 134°44E **280** A1
Nguna *Vanuatu* 17°26S 168°22E **287** G6
Ngunga *Tanzania* 3°37S 33°37E **268** C3
Nguru *Nigeria* 12°56N 10°29E **263** C7
Nguru Mts. *Tanzania* 6°0S 37°30E **268** D4
Ngusi *Malawi* 14°0S 34°50E **269** E3
Nguyen Binh *Vietnam* 22°39N 105°56E **228** F5
Ngwedaung *Burma* 19°31N 97°9E **241** F6
Nha Trang *Vietnam* 12°16N 109°10E **237** F7
Nhacoongo *Mozam.* 24°18S 35°14E **271** B6
Nhamaabué *Mozam.* 17°25S 35°5E **269** F4
Nhambiquara *Brazil* 12°50S 59°49W **331** C6
Nhamundá *Brazil* 2°14S 56°43W **329** D6
Nhamundá → *Brazil* 2°12S 56°41W **329** D6
Nhangulaze, L. *Mozam.* 24°0S 34°30E **271** B5
Nharêa *Angola* 11°38S 16°58E **265** E3
Nhecolândia *Brazil* 19°17S 56°58W **331** D6
Nhill *Australia* 36°18S 141°40E **282** D4
Nho Quan *Vietnam* 20°18N 105°45E **228** G5
Nhulunbuy *Australia* 12°10S 137°20E **280** A2
Nhundo *Angola* 14°25S 21°23E **265** E4
Nia-nia *Dem. Rep. of the Congo* 1°30N 27°40E **268** B2
Niafounké *Mali* 16°0N 4°5W **262** B4
Niagara Falls *Ont., Canada* 43°7N 79°5W **312** C5
Niagara Falls *N.Y., U.S.A.* 43°5N 79°4W **312** C6
Niagara-on-the-Lake *Canada* 43°15N 79°4W **312** C5
Niah *Malaysia* 3°58N 113°46E **235** B4
Nialaha'u Pt. *Solomon Is.* 9°47S 161°34E **287** M11
Niamey *Niger* 13°27N 2°6E **263** C5
Niandan-Koro *Guinea* 11°5N 9°15W **262** C3
Nianforando *Guinea* 9°37N 10°36W **262** D2
Niangara *Dem. Rep. of the Congo* 3°42N 27°50E **268** B2
Niangbo *Ivory C.* 8°49N 5°10W **262** D3
Niangoloko *Burkina Faso* 10°15N 4°55W **262** C4
Niangua → *U.S.A.* 38°58N 92°48W **310** G4
Niantic *U.S.A.* 41°20N 72°11W **313** E12
Niari *Congo* 4°9S 14°9E **264** C2
Niaro *Sudan* 10°38N 31°3E **257** E3
Nias *Indonesia* 1°0N 97°30E **234** B1
Niassa □ *Mozam.* 13°30S 36°0E **269** E4
Niassa ⌂ *Mozam.* 12°4S 36°57E **269** E4
Nīāvarān *Iran* 35°47N 51°29E **141** A2
Nibāk *Si. Arabia* 24°25N 50°50E **247** E7
Nibe *Denmark* 56°59N 9°38E **163** H3
Nibra *India* 22°36N 88°15E **124** B1
Nicaragua ■ *Cent. Amer.* 11°40N 85°30W **320** D2
Nicaragua, L. de *Nic.* 12°0N 85°30W **320** D2
Nicastro *Italy* 38°59N 16°19E **201** D9
Nice *France* 43°42N 7°14E **175** E11
Nice-Côte-d'Azur ✈ (NCE) *France* 43°41N 7°12E **175** E11
Niceville *U.S.A.* 30°31N 86°30W **317** E3
Nichicun, L. *Canada* 53°5N 71°0W **299** B5
Nichinan *Japan* 31°38N 131°23E **222** F3
Nicholás, Canal *W. Indies* 23°30N 80°5W **320** B3
Nicholasville *U.S.A.* 37°53N 84°34W **311** G12
Nicholls *U.S.A.* 31°31N 82°38W **316** D7
Nichols *U.S.A.* 42°1N 76°22W **313** D8
Nicholson *W. Austral., Australia* 18°2S 128°54E **278** C4
Nicholson *Pa., U.S.A.* 41°37N 75°47W **313** E9
Nicholson → *Australia* 17°31S 139°36E **280** B2
Nicholson L. *Canada* 62°40N 102°40W **297** A8
Nicholson Ra. *Australia* 27°15S 116°45E **279** E2
Nicholville *U.S.A.* 44°41N 74°39W **313** B10
Nickerie → *Suriname* 5°58N 57°0W **329** B6
Nico Pérez = José Batlle y Ordóñez *Uruguay* 33°20S 55°10W **335** C4
Nicobar Is. *Ind. Oc.* 8°0N 93°30E **245** L11
Nicola *Canada* 50°12N 120°40W **296** C4
Nicolls Town *Bahamas* 25°8N 78°0W **320** A4
Nicosia *Cyprus* 35°10N 33°25E **207** E9
Nicosia *Italy* 37°45N 14°24E **201** E7
Nicótera *Italy* 38°33N 15°56E **201** D8
Nicoya *Costa Rica* 10°9N 85°27W **320** D2
Nicoya, G. de *Costa Rica* 10°0N 85°0W **320** E3
Nicoya, Pen. de *Costa Rica* 9°45N 85°40W **320** E2
Nictheroy = Niterói *Brazil* 22°53S 43°7W **135** B2
Nida *Lithuania* 55°20N 21°4E **184** C8
Nidāl *Iraq* 33°19N 44°25E **113** B2
Nidaros = Trondheim *Norway* 63°36N 10°25E **164** A7
Nidd → *U.K.* 53°59N 1°23W **168** D6
Nidda *Germany* 50°23N 9°1E **179** E5
Nidda → *Germany* 50°17N 8°48E **179** E4
Niddrie *Vic., Australia* 37°44S 144°51E **128** A1
Niddrie *Edinburgh, U.K.* 55°56N 3°7W **121** B3
Nidri *Greece* 38°43N 20°42E **207** B2
Nidwalden □ *Switz.* 46°50N 8°25E **179** J4
Nidzica *Poland* 53°25N 20°28E **185** F7
Niebüll *Germany* 54°46N 8°48E **178** A4
Nied → *Germany* 49°23N 6°40E **173** C13
Nieder Neuendorf *Germany* 52°36N 13°12E **115** A2
Niederaula *Germany* 50°47N 9°36E **178** E5
Niederbayern □ *Germany* 48°40N 12°50E **179** G8
Niederbronn-les-Bains *France* 48°57N 7°39E **173** D14
Niedere Tauern *Austria* 47°20N 14°0E **180** D7
Niederlausitz *Germany* 51°42N 13°59E **178** D9
Niederösterreich □ *Austria* 48°25N 15°40E **180** C8
Niedersachsen □ *Germany* 52°50N 9°0E **178** C4
Niedersächsisches Wattenmeer △ *Germany* 53°45N 7°30E **178** B3
Niederschöneweide *Germany* 52°27N 13°30E **115** B3
Niederschönhausen *Germany* 52°35N 13°25E **115** A3
Niefang *Eq. Guin.* 1°50N 10°14E **264** B2
Niekerkshoop *S. Africa* 29°19S 22°51E **270** C3
Niellé *Ivory C.* 10°5N 5°38W **262** C3
Niellim *Chad* 9°42N 17°49E **259** G3
Niem *C.A.R.* 6°12N 15°14E **264** A3
Niemba *Dem. Rep. of the Congo* 5°58S 28°24E **268** D2
Niemen = Nemunas → *Lithuania* 55°25N 21°10E **184** C8
Niemeyer *Brazil* 22°59S 43°15W **135** B1
Niemodlin *Poland* 50°38N 17°38E **185** H4
Niemur *Australia* 35°17S 144°9E **282** C6
Nienburg *Germany* 52°39N 9°13E **178** C5
Niepołomice *Poland* 50°3N 20°13E **185** H7
Niers → *Germany* 51°43N 5°57E **178** D1
Niesky *Germany* 51°17N 14°49E **178** D10
Nieszawa *Poland* 52°52N 18°50E **185** F5
Nieu Bethesda *S. Africa* 31°51S 24°34E **270** D3
Nieuw Amsterdam *Suriname* 5°53N 55°5W **329** B6
Nieuw Nickerie *Suriname* 6°0N 56°59W **329** B6
Nieuw Zuid *Amsterdam, Neths.* **112** c2
Nieuwe Kerk *Amsterdam, Neths.* **112** b2
Nieuwendam *Neths.* 52°23N 4°57E **112** A2
Nieuwoudtville *S. Africa* 31°23S 19°7E **270** D2
Nieuwpoort *Belgium* 51°8N 2°45E **170** C2
Nieuwpoort *Neth. Ant.* 12°3N 68°49W **322** g
Nieves, Pico de las *Canary Is.* 27°57N 15°35W **153** e1
Nièvre □ *France* 47°10N 3°40E **173** E10
Nif *Micronesia* 9°28N 138°4E **287** S16
Niga *Mali* 13°38N 5°27W **262** C3
Niğde *Turkey* 37°58N 34°40E **212** D6
Niğde □ *Turkey* 38°0N 34°30E **212** D6
Nigel *S. Africa* 26°27S 28°25E **271** C4
Niger □ *Nigeria* 10°0N 5°30E **263** D6
Niger ■ *W. Afr.* 17°30N 10°0E **259** E2
Niger → *W. Afr.* 5°33N 6°33E **263** D6
Niger Delta *Africa* 5°0N 6°0E **263** E6
Nigeria ■ *W. Afr.* 8°30N 8°0E **263** D6
Nighasin *India* 28°14N 80°52E **243** E9
Nightcaps *N.Z.* 45°57S 168°2E **285** F3
Nightmute *U.S.A.* 60°29N 164°44W **303** F6
Nigrita *Greece* 40°56N 23°29E **202** F7
Nihoa *U.S.A.* 23°6N 161°58W **302** G11
Nihon = Japan ■ *Asia* 36°0N 136°0E **221** G8
Nihonbashi *Tokyo, Japan* **140** b5
Nii-Jima *Japan* 34°20N 139°15E **223** C11
Niigata *Japan* 37°58N 139°0E **220** F9
Niigata □ *Japan* 37°15N 138°45E **221** F9
Niihama *Japan* 33°55N 133°16E **222** D5
Ni'ihau *U.S.A.* 21°54N 160°9W **302** B1
Niimi *Japan* 34°59N 133°28E **222** C5
Niipperi *Finland* 60°18N 24°45E **121** B1
Niislel Khureheh = Ulaanbaatar *Mongolia* 47°55N 106°53E **218** B5
Niitsu *Japan* 37°48N 139°7E **220** F9
Nij Laluk *India* 27°7N 93°56E **241** B4
Nijar *Spain* 36°53N 2°15W **197** J2
Nijil *Jordan* 30°32N 35°33E **251** H6
Nijkerk *Neths.* 52°13N 5°30E **170** B5
Nijmegen *Neths.* 51°50N 5°52E **170** C5
Nijverdal *Neths.* 52°22N 6°28E **170** B6
Nīk Pey *Iran* 36°50N 48°10E **213** D13
Nikao *Cook Is.* 21°12S 159°48W **289** h
Nikaweratiya *Sri Lanka* 7°45N 80°7E **245** L5
Nike *Nigeria* 6°26N 7°29E **263** D6
Nikea *Greece* 37°57N 23°38E **112** B1
Nikel *Russia* 69°24N 30°13E **160** B24
Nikiboko *Neth. Ant.* 12°9N 68°16W **322** h
Nikiniki *Indonesia* 9°49S 124°30E **231** F6
Nikisiani *Greece* 40°57N 24°9E **203** F8
Nikiski *U.S.A.* 61°41N 151°18W **303** F10
Nikiti *Greece* 40°13N 23°43E **202** F7
Nikitinskiye promysly = Kirovskiy *Russia* 45°51N 48°11E **191** H9
Nikki *Benin* 9°58N 3°12E **263** D5
Nikkō *Japan* 36°45N 139°35E **223** A11
Nikkō △ *Japan* 36°56N 139°37E **221** F9
Nikolai *U.S.A.* 62°58N 154°10W **303** E9
Nikolainkaupunki = Vaasa *Finland* 63°6N 21°38E **160** E19
Nikolaistad = Vaasa *Finland* 63°6N 21°38E **160** E19
Nikolassee *Germany* 52°25N 13°12E **115** B2
Nikolayev = Mykolayiv *Ukraine* 46°58N 32°0E **189** J7
Nikolayevsk *Russia* 50°0N 45°35E **190** E7
Nikolayevsk-na-Amur *Russia* 53°8N 140°44E **215** D15
Nikolsburg = Mikulov *Czech Rep.* 48°48N 16°39E **181** C9
Nikolsk *Russia* 53°49N 46°4E **190** D8
Nikolsk-Ussuriysky = Ussuriysk *Russia* 43°48N 131°59E **220** C5
Nikolskaya Pestravka = Nikolsk *Russia* 53°49N 46°4E **190** D8
Nikolski *U.S.A.* 52°56N 168°52W **303** K5
Nikolskiy *Russia* 55°49N 37°29E **129** B2
Nikolskoye = Ussuriysk *Russia* 43°48N 131°59E **220** C5
Nikolskoye *Russia* 55°12N 166°0E **215** D17
Nikolsky Khutor = Sursk *Russia* 53°3N 45°40E **190** D7
Nikolyskoye *Russia* 55°46N 37°53E **129** B5
Nikopol *Bulgaria* 43°43N 24°54E **203** C8
Nikopol *Ukraine* 47°35N 34°25E **189** J8
Nikopolis *Greece* 39°5N 20°43E **207** A2
Niksar *Turkey* 40°31N 37°2E **212** B7
Nīkshahr *Iran* 26°15N 60°10E **247** E9
Nikšić *Montenegro* 42°50N 18°57E **202** D2
Nikulino *Russia* 55°40N 37°25E **129** B2
Nikumaroro *Kiribati* 4°40S 174°32W **277** A16
Nikunau *Kiribati* 1°22S 176°28E **277** A14
Nîl, Nahr en → *Africa* 30°10N 31°6E **256** H7
Nîl el Abyad → *Sudan* 15°38N 32°31E **257** D3
Nîl el Azraq → *Sudan* 15°38N 32°31E **257** D3
Nila *Indonesia* 6°44S 129°31E **231** F7
Nilakkottai *India* 10°10N 77°52E **245** J3
Niland *U.S.A.* 33°14N 115°31W **307** M11
Nilanga *India* 18°6N 76°46E **244** E3
Nile = Nîl, Nahr en → *Africa* 30°10N 31°6E **256** H7
Nile Delta *Egypt* 31°40N 31°0E **256** H7
Niles *Ill., U.S.A.* 42°1N 87°48W **119** A2
Niles *Mich., U.S.A.* 41°50N 86°15W **311** C10
Niles *Ohio, U.S.A.* 41°11N 80°46W **312** E4
Niles Center = Skokie *U.S.A.* 42°2N 87°43W **119** A2
Nileshwar *India* 12°15N 75°6E **245** H2
Nilgiri Hills *India* 11°30N 76°30E **245** J3
Nilo Peçanha *Brazil* 13°37S 39°6W **333** D4
Nilsebu *Norway* 59°11N 6°39E **164** E3
Nilüfer → *Turkey* 40°18N 28°27E **203** F12
Nim Ka Thana *India* 27°44N 75°48E **242** F6
Nimach *India* 24°30N 74°56E **242** G6
Nimba, Mt. *Guinea* 7°37N 8°25W **262** D3
Nimbahera *India* 24°37N 74°45E **242** G6
Nîmes *France* 43°50N 4°23E **175** E8
Nimfaion, Ákra = Pines, Akra *Greece* 40°5N 24°20E **203** F8
Nimmitabel *Australia* 36°29S 149°15E **283** D8
Nīmrūz □ *Afghan.* 30°0N 62°0E **240** C1
Nimta *India* 22°40N 88°24E **124** A2
Nimule *Sudan* 3°32N 32°3E **257** G3
Nimule △ *Sudan* 3°38N 32°2E **257** G3
Nin *Croatia* 44°16N 15°12E **199** D12
Nīnawá *Iraq* 36°25N 43°10E **213** D10
Nīnawá □ *Iraq* 36°15N 43°0E **246** B4
Ninda *Angola* 14°47S 21°24E **265** E4
Nindigully *Australia* 28°21S 148°50E **281** D4
Nine Degree Channel *India* 9°0N 73°0E **245** K1
Ninepin Group *China* 22°16N 114°21E **219** G11
Ninety Mile Beach *N.Z.* 34°48S 173°0E **284** A2
Ninety Mile Beach, The *Australia* 38°15S 147°24E **283** E7

Ninety Six U.S.A. 34°11N 82°1W 316 A7
Ninetyeast Ridge Ind. Oc. 1°0S 90°0E 273 E7
Nineveh = Nīnawá Iraq 36°25N 43°10E 213 D10
Ning Xian China 35°30N 107°58E 226 G4
Ningaloo ⌓ Australia 22°23S 113°32E 278 D1
Ning'an China 44°22N 129°20E 227 B15
Ningbo China 29°51N 121°28E 229 C13
Ningcheng China 41°32N 119°53E 227 D10
Ningde China 26°38N 119°23E 229 D12
Ningdu China 26°25N 115°59E 229 D10
Ningerum Papua N. G. 5°41S 141°8E 286 C1
Ninggang China 26°42N 113°55E 229 D9
Ningguo China 30°35N 119°0E 229 B12
Ninghai China 29°15N 121°27E 229 C13
Ninghua China 26°14N 116°45E 229 D11
Ningi Nigeria 10°55N 9°30E 263 C6
Ningjin China 37°35N 114°57E 226 F8
Ningjing Shan China 30°0N 98°20E 228 C2
Ninglang China 27°20N 100°55E 228 D3
Ningling China 34°25N 115°22E 226 G8
Ningming China 22°8N 107°4E 228 F6
Ningnan China 27°5N 102°36E 228 D4
Ningpo = Ningbo China 29°51N 121°28E 229 C13
Ningqiang China 32°47N 106°15E 226 H4
Ningshan China 33°21N 108°21E 226 H5
Ningsia Hui A.R. = Ningxia Huizu Zizhiqu □ China 38°0N 106°0E 226 F4
Ningwu China 39°0N 112°18E 226 E7
Ningxia Huizu Zizhiqu □ China 38°0N 106°0E 226 F4
Ningxiang China 28°15N 112°30E 229 C9
Ningyang China 35°47N 116°45E 226 G9
Ningyuan China 25°37N 111°57E 229 E8
Ninh Binh Vietnam 20°15N 105°55E 228 G5
Ninh Giang Vietnam 20°44N 106°24E 236 B6
Ninh Hoa Vietnam 12°30N 109°7E 236 F7
Ninh Ma Vietnam 12°48N 109°21E 236 F7
Nini-Suhien △ Ghana 5°20N 2°34W 262 D4
Ninigo Group Papua N. G. 1°22S 144°17E 286 A3
Ninini Pt. U.S.A. 21°58N 159°20W 302 B2
Ninove Belgium 50°51N 4°2E 170 D4
Ninoy Aquino Int. ✈ (MNL) Phil. 14°31N 121°0E 127 B2
Nioaque Brazil 21°5S 55°50W 335 A4
Niobrara U.S.A. 42°45N 98°2W 308 D4
Niobrara → U.S.A. 42°46N 98°3W 308 D4
Nioki Dem. Rep. of the Congo 2°47S 17°40E 264 C3
Niokolo-Koba △ Senegal 13°3N 13°2W 262 C2
Niono Mali 14°15N 6°0W 262 C3
Nionsamoridougou Guinea 8°45N 8°50W 262 D3
Nioro du Rip Senegal 13°40N 15°50W 262 C1
Nioro du Sahel Mali 15°15N 9°30W 262 B3
Niort France 46°19N 0°29W 174 B3
Nioumachoua Comoros Is. 12°21S 43°42E 272 a
Nipa Papua N. G. 6°9S 143°29E 286 D2
Nipani India 16°20N 74°25E 245 F2
Nipawin Canada 53°20N 104°0W 297 C8
Nipfjället Sweden 61°59N 12°50E 162 C6
Nipigon Canada 49°0N 88°17W 298 C2
Nipigon, L. Canada 49°50N 88°30W 298 C2
Nipishish L. Canada 54°12N 60°45W 299 B7
Nipissing, L. Canada 46°20N 80°0W 298 C4
Nipomo U.S.A. 35°3N 120°29W 307 K6
Nippa Japan 35°31N 139°36E 140 B2
Nippon = Japan ■ Asia 36°0N 136°0E 221 G8
Nippori Japan 35°43N 139°45E 140 A3
Nipton U.S.A. 35°28N 115°16W 307 K11
Niquelândia Brazil 14°33S 48°23W 333 D2
Nīr Iran 38°2N 47°59E 213 C12
Nira → India 17°58N 75°8E 244 F2
Nirasaki Japan 35°42N 138°27E 223 B10
Nirmal India 19°3N 78°20E 244 E4
Nirmali India 26°20N 86°35E 243 F12
Niš Serbia 43°19N 21°58E 202 C5
Nisa = Nysa → Europe 52°4N 14°46E 178 C10
Nisa Portugal 39°30N 7°41W 195 F3
Nişāb Si. Arabia 29°11N 44°43E 246 D5
Nişāb Yemen 14°25N 46°29E 248 D4
Nišava → Serbia 43°20N 21°46E 202 C5
Niscemi Italy 37°9N 14°23E 201 E7
Nishi Japan 34°40N 135°28E 133 A1
Nishi-Sonogi-Hantō Japan 32°55N 129°45E 222 E1
Nishi-Tosa Japan 33°13N 132°46E 222 D4
Nishinari Japan 34°37N 135°28E 133 B1
Nishinomiya Japan 34°45N 135°20E 133 A1
Nishino'omote Japan 30°43N 130°59E 221 J5
Nishio Japan 34°52N 137°3E 223 C9
Nishiwaki Japan 34°59N 134°58E 222 C6
Nishiyodogawa Japan 34°41N 135°24E 133 A1
Nisibin = Nusaybin Turkey 37°3N 41°10E 213 D9
Niška Banja Serbia 43°18N 22°1E 202 C6
Niskibi → Canada 56°29N 88°9W 298 A2
Nisko Poland 50°35N 22°7E 185 H9
Nisporeni Moldova 47°4N 28°10E 183 C13
Nisqually → U.S.A. 47°7N 122°42W 306 C4
Nissaki Greece 39°43N 19°52E 206 B9
Nissan → Sweden 56°40N 12°51E 163 H6
Nissedal Norway 59°10N 8°30E 164 E5
Nisser Norway 59°7N 8°28E 164 E5
Nissiros Greece 36°35N 27°12E 205 E9
Nissum Bredning Denmark 56°40N 8°20E 163 H2
Nissum Fjord Denmark 56°20N 8°11E 163 H2
Nistru = Dnister → Europe 46°18N 30°17E 177 E16
Nisutlin → Canada 60°14N 132°34W 296 A2
Nitchequon Canada 53°10N 70°58W 299 B5
Niterói Brazil 22°53S 43°7W 135 B2
Nith → Ont., Canada 43°12N 80°23W 312 C4
Nith → Dumf. & Gall., U.K. 55°14N 3°33W 167 F5
Nitmiluk △ Australia 14°6S 132°15E 278 B5
Nitra Slovak Rep. 48°19N 18°4E 181 C11
Nitra → Slovak Rep. 47°46N 18°10E 181 D11
Nitriansky □ Slovak Rep. 48°10N 18°30E 181 C11
Nittenau Germany 49°12N 12°16E 179 F8
Niu Valley U.S.A. 21°19N 157°44W 302 K14
Niua Group Tonga 15°57S 173°45W 277 D16
Niuafo'ou Tonga 15°30S 175°58W 277 D15
Niuatoputapu Tonga 15°57S 173°45W 277 D16
Niue Pac. Oc. 19°2S 169°54W 289 g
Niulakita Pac. Oc. 10°45S 179°30E 277 C14
Niulan Jiang → China 27°30N 103°5E 228 D4
Niulantsun Taiwan 25°1N 121°2E 225 A3
Niut Indonesia 0°55N 110°6E 235 B4
Niutao Pac. Oc. 6°7S 177°18E 277 B14
Niutou Shan China 29°5N 121°59E 229 C13
Niuzhuang China 40°58N 122°28E 224 B1
Nivala Finland 63°56N 24°57E 160 E21
Nivelles Belgium 50°35N 4°20E 170 D4
Nivernais France 47°15N 3°30E 173 E10
Niverville Canada 49°36N 97°3W 297 D9
Niwas India 23°3N 80°26E 243 H9
Nixa U.S.A. 37°3N 93°18W 308 G7
Nixon U.S.A. 29°16N 97°46W 314 G6
Nizam Sagar India 18°10N 77°58E 244 E3
Nizamabad India 18°45N 78°7E 244 E4
Nizamghat India 28°20N 95°45E 241 A5
Nizhne Kolymsk Russia 68°34N 160°55E 215 C17
Nizhneangarsk Russia 55°47N 109°30E 215 D11
Nizhnegorskiy = Nyzhnohirskyy Ukraine 45°27N 34°38E 189 K8
Nizhnekamsk Russia 55°38N 51°49E 190 C10
Nizhneudinsk Russia 54°54N 99°3E 215 D10
Nizhnevartovsk Russia 60°56N 76°38E 214 C8
Nizhniy Chir Russia 48°22N 43°5E 191 F6
Nizhniy Lomov Russia 53°34N 43°38E 190 D6
Nizhniy Novgorod Russia 56°20N 44°0E 190 B7
Nizhniy Novgorod □ Russia 56°30N 44°20E 190 B7
Nizhniy Tagil Russia 57°55N 59°57E 186 C10
Nizhniye Kresty = Cherskiy Russia 68°45N 161°18E 215 C17
Nizhyn Ukraine 51°5N 31°55E 189 G6
Nizina Mazowiecka Poland 52°30N 21°0E 185 F8
Nizip Turkey 37°5N 37°50E 212 D7
Nízké Tatry Slovak Rep. 48°55N 19°30E 181 C12
Nízké Tatry △ Slovak Rep. 48°55N 19°37E 181 C12
Nízký Jeseník Czech Rep. 49°50N 17°30E 181 B10
Nizwá Oman 22°56N 57°32E 249 B7
Nizza Monferrato Italy 44°46N 8°21E 198 D5
Njakwa Malawi 11°1S 33°56E 269 E3
Njanji Zambia 14°25S 31°46E 269 E3
Njarðvíkur Iceland 63°59N 22°32W 155 D4
Njazidja = Grande Comore Comoros Is. 11°35S 43°20E 272 a
Njegoš Montenegro 42°53N 18°45E 202 D2
Njinjo Tanzania 8°48S 38°54E 269 D4
Njoko → Zambia 17°8S 24°4E 265 F4
Njombe Tanzania 9°20S 34°50E 269 D3
Njombe → Tanzania 6°56S 35°6E 268 D4
Njurundabommen Sweden 62°15N 17°25E 162 B11
Nkambe Cameroon 6°35N 10°40E 263 D7
Nkana Zambia 12°50S 28°8E 269 E2
Nkandla S. Africa 28°37S 31°5E 271 C5
Nkawkaw Ghana 6°36N 0°49W 263 D4
Nkayi Zimbabwe 19°41S 29°20E 269 F2
Nkhotakota Malawi 12°56S 34°15E 269 E3
Nkhotakota ⌓ Malawi 12°50S 34°0E 269 E3
Nkolabona Gabon 1°14N 11°43E 264 B2
Nkomi, Lagune Gabon 1°35S 9°17E 264 C1
Nkone Dem. Rep. of the Congo 1°2S 22°20E 264 C4
Nkongsamba Cameroon 4°55N 9°55E 263 E6
Nkunga Dem. Rep. of the Congo 4°41S 18°34E 265 C3
Nkurenkuru Namibia 17°42S 18°32E 270 A2
Nkwanta Ghana 6°10N 2°10W 262 D4
Nmai → Burma 25°30N 97°25E 228 F2
Noakhali = Maijdi Bangla. 22°48N 91°10E 241 D3
Noatak U.S.A. 67°34N 162°58W 303 C7
Noatak ⌓ U.S.A. 68°10N 160°0W 303 B8
Nob Hill San Francisco, U.S.A. 136 b1
Nobel Canada 45°25N 80°6W 312 A4
Nobeoka Japan 32°36N 131°41E 222 E3
Noble U.S.A. 38°42N 88°14W 311 F8
Noblejas Spain 39°58N 3°26W 194 F7
Noblesville U.S.A. 40°3N 86°1W 311 D11
Noboribetsu Japan 42°24N 141°6E 220 C10
Nocatee U.S.A. 27°10N 81°53W 317 H8
Noccundra Australia 27°50S 142°36E 281 D3
Noce → Italy 46°9N 11°4E 198 B8
Nocera Inferiore Italy 40°44N 14°38E 201 B7
Nocera Umbra Italy 43°5N 12°47E 199 E9
Noci Italy 40°48N 17°7E 201 B10
Nockeby Sweden 59°19N 17°56E 139 B1
Nocona U.S.A. 33°47N 97°44W 314 E6
Nocrich Romania 45°55N 24°26E 183 E9
Noda Japan 35°56N 139°52E 223 B11
Nodeland Norway 58°8N 7°51E 164 F4
Noel Kempff Mercado △ Bolivia 14°9S 60°49W 331 C5
Noel Park U.K. 51°35N 0°5W 125 A3
Nogal Valley = Nugaaleed, Dooxo Somali Rep. 8°35N 48°35E 267 C6
Nogales Sonora, Mexico 31°19N 110°56W 318 A2
Nogales Ariz., U.S.A. 31°21N 110°56W 305 L8
Nogaro France 43°45N 0°2W 174 E3
Nogat → Poland 54°17N 19°17E 184 D6
Nōgata Japan 33°48N 130°44E 222 D2
Nogatino Russia 55°41N 37°41E 129 B4
Nogaysk = Primorskoye Ukraine 46°48N 36°20E 189 J9
Nogent France 48°1N 5°20E 173 D12
Nogent-le-Rotrou France 48°20N 0°50E 172 D7
Nogent-sur-Marne France 48°50N 2°28E 134 A3
Nogent-sur-Seine France 48°30N 3°30E 173 D10
Noggerup Australia 33°32S 116°5E 279 F2
Noginsk Moskva, Russia 55°50N 38°25E 188 E10
Noginsk Tunguska, Russia 64°30N 90°50E 215 C10
Nogoa → Australia 23°40S 147°55E 280 C4
Nogoyá Argentina 32°24S 59°48W 334 C4
Nógrád □ Hungary 48°0N 19°30E 182 C4
Noguera Pallaresa → Spain 41°55N 0°55E 196 D5
Noguera Ribagorzana → Spain 41°40N 0°43E 196 D5
Nohar India 29°11N 74°49E 242 E6
Nohfelden Germany 49°35N 7°7E 179 F3
Nohili Pt. U.S.A. 22°4N 159°47W 302 A2
Nohta India 23°40N 79°34E 243 H8
Nohwa S. Korea 34°10N 126°34E 224 E3
Nohwado S. Korea 34°12N 126°35E 224 E3
Noia Spain 42°48N 8°53W 194 C2
Noichi Japan 33°33N 133°42E 222 D5
Noida India 28°36N 77°19E 120 B2
Noing Phil. 5°40N 125°28E 233 J5
Noipuos Papua N. G. 2°25S 150°7E 286 B6
Noire, Montagne France 43°28N 2°18E 174 E6
Noires, Mts. France 48°11N 3°40W 172 D3
Noirétable France 45°48N 3°46E 174 C7
Noirmoutier, Î. de France 46°58N 2°10W 172 F4
Noirmoutier-en-l'Île France 47°0N 2°14W 172 F4
Noiseau France 48°46N 2°32E 134 B4
Noisiel France 48°51N 2°37E 134 A4
Noisy-le-Grand France 48°50N 2°33E 134 A4
Noisy-le-Roi France 48°50N 2°3E 134 A1
Noisy-le-Sec France 48°53N 2°27E 134 A3
Nojane Botswana 23°15S 20°14E 270 B3
Nojima-Zaki Japan 34°54N 139°53E 223 C11
Nok Kundi Pakistan 28°50N 62°45E 240 C1
Nok Ta Phao, Ko Thailand 9°23N 99°40E 237 b
Nokaneng Botswana 19°40S 22°17E 270 A3
Nokia Finland 61°30N 23°30E 188 B2
Nokkala Finland 60°8N 24°45E 121 C1
Nokkeushi = Kitami Japan 43°48N 143°54E 220 C11
Nokomis Sask., Canada 51°35N 105°0W 297 C8
Nokomis Fla., U.S.A. 27°7N 82°27W 317 H7
Nokomis Ill., U.S.A. 39°18N 89°18W 310 E7
Nokomis L. Canada 57°0N 103°0W 297 B8
Nokou Chad 14°35N 14°47E 259 F2
Nokuku Vanuatu 14°54S 166°35E 287 D4
Nola C.A.R. 3°35N 16°4E 264 B3
Nola Italy 40°55N 14°33E 201 B7
Nolay France 46°58N 4°35E 173 F11
Noli, C. di Italy 44°12N 8°25E 198 D5
Nolinsk Russia 57°28N 49°57E 190 B9
Noma U.S.A. 30°59N 85°37W 316 E4
Noma Omuramba → Namibia 18°52S 20°53E 270 A3
Noma-Saki Japan 31°25N 130°7E 222 F2
Nomad Papua N. G. 6°19S 142°13E 286 D2
Nombre de Dios Panama 9°34N 79°28W 320 E4
Nome U.S.A. 64°30N 165°25W 303 D6
Nomentano Italy 41°55N 12°30E 136 B2
Nomo-Zaki Japan 32°35N 129°44E 222 E1
Nomoneas Micronesia 7°24N 151°53E 287 T18
Nomuka Tonga 20°17S 174°48W 287 Q13
Nomuka Group Tonga 20°20S 174°48W 287 Q13
Nona, L. U.S.A. 28°24N 81°16W 133 B3
Nonacho L. Canada 61°42N 109°40W 297 A7
Nonakashinden Japan 35°44N 139°30E 140 A2
Nonancourt France 48°47N 1°11E 172 D8
Nonda Australia 20°40S 142°28E 280 C3
Nondalton U.S.A. 60°0N 154°51W 303 F9
None Italy 44°56N 7°32E 198 D4
Nong Chang Thailand 15°23N 99°51E 236 E2
Nong Het Laos 19°29N 103°59E 236 C4
Nong Khai Thailand 17°50N 102°46E 236 D4
Nong'an China 44°25N 125°5E 227 B13
Nongjrong India 25°29N 92°6E 241 C4
Nongminyundong Jiangxisuo China 23°7N 113°15E 121 B2
Nongoma S. Africa 27°58S 31°35E 271 C5
Nongsa Indonesia 1°11N 104°8E 237 d
Nongstoin India 25°31N 91°16E 241 C3
Nonhyeon S. Korea 37°30N 127°1E 137 B2
Nono Ethiopia 8°32N 37°26E 266 C4
Nonoava Mexico 27°28N 106°44W 318 B3
Nonoc I. Phil. 9°51N 125°37E 233 G5
Nonsan S. Korea 36°12N 127°5E 224 D3
Nonsuch B. Antigua & B. 17°3N 61°42W 322 b
Nonthaburi Thailand 13°50N 100°29E 113 A1
Nontron France 45°31N 0°40E 174 C4
Nonza France 42°47N 9°21E 175 F13
Noon Gun Cape Town, S. Africa 118 b1
Noonamah Australia 12°40S 131°4E 278 B5
Noondie, L. Australia 28°30S 119°30E 279 E2
Noord Aruba 12°34N 70°1W 322 f
Noord Brabant □ Neths. 51°40N 5°0E 170 C5
Noord Holland □ Neths. 52°30N 4°45E 170 B4
Noord Saliña Neth. Ant. 12°11N 68°16W 322 h
Noordbeveland Neths. 51°35N 3°50E 170 C3
Noorder Kerk Amsterdam, Neths. 112 a1
Noordgesig S. Africa 26°13S 27°56E 123 B1
Noordkaap Aruba 12°34N 70°1W 322 f
Noordoostpolder Neths. 52°45N 5°45E 170 B5
Noordpunt Bonaire, Neth. Ant. 12°18N 68°23W 322 h
Noordpunt Curaçao, Neth. Ant. 12°24N 69°10W 322 g
Noordwijk Neths. 52°14N 4°26E 170 B4
Noordzeekanaal Neths. 52°28N 4°37E 112 A1
Noorvik U.S.A. 66°50N 161°3W 303 C7
Noosa Heads Australia 26°25S 153°6E 281 D5
Nootka I. Canada 49°32N 126°42W 296 D3
Nopiming ⌓ Canada 50°30N 95°37W 297 C9
Nóqui Angola 5°55S 13°30E 265 D2
Nor-Bayzzet = Kamo Armenia 40°21N 45°7E 191 K7
Nora Eritrea 16°6N 40°4E 257 D5
Nora Sweden 59°32N 15°2E 162 E9
Nora Springs U.S.A. 43°9N 93°0W 310 A4
Norala Phil. 6°32N 124°40E 233 H5
Noralee Canada 53°59N 126°26W 296 C3
Noranda = Rouyn-Noranda Canada 48°20N 79°0W 298 C4
Norberg Sweden 60°4N 15°56E 162 D9
Norborne U.S.A. 39°18N 93°40W 310 E3
Nórcia Italy 42°48N 13°5E 199 F10
Norco U.S.A. 33°56N 117°33W 307 M9
Norcross U.S.A. 33°56N 84°13W 316 B5
Nord □ Cameroon 8°30N 14°0E 263 D7
Nord □ France 50°15N 3°30E 173 B10
Nord, Gare du Paris, France 134 a4
Nord, Pt. Comoros Is. 11°22S 43°19E 272 a
Nord-Kivu □ Dem. Rep. of the Congo 1°0S 29°0E 268 C2
Nord-og-Østgrønland △ Greenland 75°0N 35°0W 154 C7
Nord-Ostsee-Kanal Germany 54°12N 9°32E 178 A5
Nord-Ouest □ Cameroon 6°20N 10°30E 263 D7
Nord-Pas-de-Calais □ France 50°30N 2°50E 173 B9
Nordagutu Norway 59°25N 9°20E 164 E6
Nordaustlandet Svalbard 79°14N 23°0E 150 B9
Nordberg Norway 61°54N 8°10E 164 C5
Nordborg Denmark 55°5N 9°50E 163 J3
Nordby Denmark 55°27N 8°24E 163 J2
Norddeich Germany 53°36N 7°9E 178 B3
Nordegg Canada 52°29N 116°5W 296 C5
Norden Germany 53°35N 7°12E 178 B3
Nordenham Germany 53°30N 8°30E 178 B4
Nordenskjöld Sea = Laptev Sea Russia 76°0N 125°0E 215 B13
Norderhov Norway 60°7N 10°17E 164 D7
Norderney Germany 53°42N 7°9E 178 B3
Norderstedt Germany 53°42N 10°1E 178 B6
Nordeste Azores 37°50N 25°10W 153 d3
Nordfjord Norway 61°55N 5°30E 164 C2
Nordfjordeid Norway 61°54N 6°0E 164 C2
Nordfriesische Inseln Germany 54°40N 8°20E 178 A4
Nordgrønland = Avannaarsua □ Greenland 80°0N 55°0W 154 B5
Nordhausen Germany 51°30N 10°47E 178 D6
Nordhorn Germany 52°26N 7°4E 178 C3
Norðoyar Færoe Is. 62°17N 6°35W 160 E9
Norðtunga Iceland 64°44N 21°24W 155 C5
Norður-múlasýsla □ Iceland 65°30N 15°0W 155 B11
Norðurbotn Iceland 65°36N 23°46W 155 B3
Nördinge-Nol Sweden 57°56N 12°5E 163 G6
Nordingrå Sweden 62°56N 18°17E 162 B12
Nordjylland □ Denmark 57°0N 9°30E 163 G3
Nordkapp Finnmark, Norway 71°10N 25°50E 160 A21
Nordkapp Svalbard 80°31N 20°0E 150 A9
Nordkinnhalvøya Norway 70°55N 27°40E 160 A22
Nördlicher Teutoburger Wald-Wiehengebirge ⌓ Germany 52°18N 8°10E 178 C4
Nördlingen Germany 48°48N 10°30E 179 G6
Nordmarka Norway 59°58N 10°41E 133 A3
Nordmøre Norway 63°6N 8°15E 164 B4
Nordostrundingen Greenland 81°22N 11°40W 154 A9
Nordøyane Norway 62°40N 6°0E 164 B3
Nordrand-Siedlung Austria 48°16N 16°26E 142 A2
Nordre Bergenhus = Sogn og Fjordane □ Norway 61°40N 6°45E 164 C3
Nørdre Osa Norway 61°18N 11°45E 164 C8
Nordre Strømfjord Greenland 67°10N 53°35W 154 D5
Nordrhein-Westfalen □ Germany 51°45N 7°30E 178 D3
Nordsinni Norway 60°50N 9°57E 164 D6
Nørdstedalssæter Norway 61°40N 7°48E 164 C4
Nordstrand Schleswig-Holstein, Germany 54°30N 8°52E 178 A4
Nordstrand Oslo, Norway 59°52N 10°48E 133 A3
Nordvik Russia 74°2N 111°32E 215 B12
Nore → Ireland 52°25N 6°58W 166 D4
Norefjell Norway 60°16N 9°29E 164 D6
Noresund Norway 60°11N 9°37E 164 D6
Norfolk Ont., Canada 42°50N 80°23W 312 D4
Norfolk Nebr., U.S.A. 42°2N 97°25W 308 D5
Norfolk Va., U.S.A. 36°50N 76°17W 309 G15
Norfolk □ U.K. 52°39N 0°54E 169 E8
Norfolk Basin Pac. Oc. 32°0S 170°0E 277 G13
Norfolk Broads △ U.K. 52°45N 1°30E 169 E9
Norfolk I. Pac. Oc. 28°58S 168°3E 277 F12
Norfolk Ridge Pac. Oc. 29°0S 168°0E 288 K8
Norfork L. U.S.A. 36°15N 92°14W 314 C8
Norge = Norway ■ Europe 63°0N 11°0E 160 E14
Norheimsund Norway 60°23N 6°6E 164 D3
Norilsk Russia 69°20N 88°6E 215 C9
Norma, Mt. Australia 20°55S 140°42E 280 C3
Normal U.S.A. 40°31N 88°59W 310 D8
Norman U.S.A. 35°13N 97°26W 314 D6
Norman → Australia 19°18S 141°51E 280 B3
Norman Manley Int. ✈ (KIN) Jamaica 17°56N 76°47W 320 a
Norman Park U.S.A. 31°16N 83°41W 316 D6
Norman Wells Canada 65°17N 126°51W 294 C7
Normanby N.Z. 39°32S 174°18E 284 F3
Normanby → Australia 14°23S 144°10E 280 A3
Normanby I. Papua N. G. 10°5S 151°5E 286 F6
Normandale N.Z. 41°12S 174°53E 143 B2
Normandie France 48°45N 0°10E 171 B4
Normandie-Maine ⌓ France 48°30N 0°20W 172 D6
Normandin Canada 48°49N 72°31W 298 C5
Normandy = Normandie France 48°45N 0°10E 171 B4
Normanhurst, Mt. Australia 25°4S 122°30E 279 E3
Normanton Australia 17°40S 141°10E 280 B3
Normanville Australia 35°27S 138°18E 282 C3
Normétal Canada 49°0N 79°22W 298 C4
Norquay Canada 51°53N 102°5W 297 C8
Norquinco Argentina 41°51S 70°55W 336 B2
Norra Dellen Sweden 61°53N 16°43E 162 C10
Norra Kvill △ Sweden 57°46N 15°35E 163 G9
Norra Ulvön Sweden 63°3N 18°40E 162 A12
Norrahammar Sweden 57°43N 14°7E 163 G8
Norrbottens län □ Sweden 66°50N 20°0E 160 C19
Nørre Åby Denmark 55°27N 9°52E 163 J3
Nørre Alslev Denmark 54°54N 11°52E 163 K5
Nørrebro Copenhagen, Denmark 118 a1
Nørresundby Denmark 57°5N 9°52E 163 G3
Norrhult-Klavreström Sweden 57°7N 15°10E 163 G9
Norridge U.S.A. 41°57N 87°49W 119 B2
Norris City U.S.A. 37°59N 88°20W 311 G8
Norris Point Canada 49°31N 57°53W 299 C8
Norristown Ga., U.S.A. 32°30N 82°30W 316 C7
Norristown Pa., U.S.A. 40°7N 75°21W 313 F9
Norrköping Sweden 58°37N 16°11E 163 F10
Norrland Sweden 62°15N 15°45E 160 E16
Norrmalm Stockholm, Sweden 139 a1
Norrsundet Sweden 60°56N 17°8E 162 D11
Norrtälje Sweden 59°46N 18°42E 162 E12
Norseman Australia 32°8S 121°43E 279 F3
Norsewood N.Z. 40°3S 176°13E 284 G5
Norsjø Norway 59°18N 9°20E 164 E6
Norsk Russia 52°30N 130°5E 215 D14
Norsup Vanuatu 16°3S 167°24E 287 F5
Norte, C. Chile 27°3S 109°24W 330 b
Norte, Canal do → Brazil 0°40N 50°20W 329 C7
Norte, Pta. Argentina 42°5S 63°46W 336 B4
Norte, Pta. del Canary Is. 27°51N 17°57W 153 e1
Norte, Pta. do Azores 37°1N 25°4W 153 d4
Norte, Serra do Brazil 11°20S 59°0W 331 C6
Norte de Santander □ Colombia 8°0N 73°0W 328 B3
Norte Grande Azores 38°40N 28°4W 153 d1
Nortelândia Brazil 14°25S 56°48W 331 C6
North U.S.A. 33°37N 81°6W 316 B8
North, C. Canada 47°2N 60°20W 299 C7
North Adams U.S.A. 42°42N 73°7W 313 D11
North America 40°0N 100°0W 292 F10
North Andaman I. India 13°15N 92°55E 245 H11
North Arlington U.S.A. 40°47N 74°7W 132 B1
North Arm Canada 62°0N 114°30W 296 A5
North Atlantic Ocean Atl. Oc. 30°0N 50°0W 152 C7
North Augusta U.S.A. 33°30N 81°59W 316 B8
North Australian Basin Ind. Oc. 14°30S 116°30E 276 C2
North Ayrshire □ U.K. 55°45N 4°44W 167 F4
North Baltimore U.S.A. 41°11N 83°41W 311 C13
North Bass I. U.S.A. 41°40N 82°56W 312 E2
North Battleford Canada 52°50N 108°17W 297 C7
North Bay Canada 46°20N 79°30W 298 C4
North Bay Village U.S.A. 25°50N 80°9W 128 A2
North Beach San Francisco, U.S.A. 136 a2
North Belcher Is. Canada 56°50N 79°50W 298 A4
North Bend Oreg., U.S.A. 43°24N 124°14W 304 E1
North Bend Pa., U.S.A. 41°20N 77°42W 312 E7
North Bend Wash., U.S.A. 47°30N 121°47W 306 C5
North Bennington U.S.A. 42°56N 73°15W 313 D11
North Bergen U.S.A. 40°48N 74°0W 132 B1
North Berwick E. Loth., U.K. 56°4N 2°42W 167 E6
North Berwick Maine, U.S.A. 43°18N 70°44W 313 C14
North Borneo = Sabah □ Malaysia 6°0N 117°0E 235 A5
North Breakers Midway Is. 28°13N 177°24W 302 c
North Brother I. India 10°59N 92°40E 245 J11
North Bull I. Ireland 53°22N 6°9W 120 A3
North C. N.B., Canada 47°5N 64°0W 299 C7
North C. N.Z. 34°23S 173°4E 284 A2
North C. Papua N. G. 2°32S 150°50E 286 B6
North Canadian → U.S.A. 35°22N 95°37W 314 D7
North Canton U.S.A. 40°53N 81°24W 312 F3
North Cape = Nordkapp Norway 71°10N 25°50E 160 A21
North Caribou L. Canada 52°50N 90°40W 298 B1
North Carolina □ U.S.A. 35°30N 80°0W 315 D15
North Cascades △ U.S.A. 48°45N 121°10W 304 B3
North Cay Bahamas 25°6N 77°26W 153 b
North Channel Ont., Canada 46°0N 83°0W 298 C3
North Channel U.K. 55°13N 5°52W 167 F3
North Charleston U.S.A. 32°53N 79°58W 316 C10
North Cheam U.K. 51°22N 0°11W 125 B2
North Chicago U.S.A. 42°19N 87°51W 311 B9
North College Hill U.S.A. 39°13N 84°33W 311 E12
North Comino Channel Malta 36°1N 14°20E 206 E7
North Cray U.K. 51°25N 0°8E 125 B4
North Creek U.S.A. 43°42N 73°59W 313 C11
North Dakota □ U.S.A. 47°30N 100°15W 308 B3
North Decatur U.S.A. 33°48N 84°17W 113 B3
North Downs U.K. 51°19N 0°21E 169 F8
North Druid Hills U.S.A. 33°49N 84°17W 113 B3
North East U.S.A. 42°13N 79°50W 312 D5
North East B. Ascension I. 7°55S 14°21W 153 g
North East Frontier Agency = Arunachal Pradesh □ India 28°0N 95°0E 241 B5
North East Lincolnshire □ U.K. 53°34N 0°2W 168 D7
North Eastern □ Kenya 1°30N 40°0E 268 B5
North End Boston, U.S.A. 116 a3
North Esk → Angus, U.K. 56°46N 2°24W 167 E6
North Esk → Midloth., U.K. 55°54N 3°4W 121 B2
North European Plain Europe 55°0N 25°0E 158 E10
North Fabius → U.S.A. 39°54N 91°30W 310 E5
North Foreland U.K. 51°22N 1°28E 169 F9
North Fork U.S.A. 37°14N 119°21W 306 H7
North Fork, Salt → U.S.A. 39°26N 91°53W 310 E5
North Fork American → U.S.A. 38°57N 120°59W 306 G5
North Fork Edisto → U.S.A. 33°16N 80°54W 316 B9
North Fork Feather → U.S.A. 38°33N 121°30W 306 F5
North Fork Grand → U.S.A. 45°47N 102°16W 308 C2
North Fork Red → U.S.A. 34°24N 99°14W 314 D5
North Fort Myers U.S.A. 26°41N 81°53W 317 J8
North Frisian Is. = Nordfriesische Inseln Germany 54°40N 8°20E 178 A4
North Gower Canada 45°8N 75°43W 313 A9
North Greenfield = West Allis U.S.A. 43°1N 88°0W 311 B8
North Gyle U.K. 55°57N 3°19W 121 B2
North Hackensack U.S.A. 40°54N 74°2W 132 A1
North Harbor Phil. 14°37N 120°57E 127 B1
North Hd. N.S.W., Australia 33°49S 151°18E 139 A2
North Hd. W. Austral., Australia 30°14S 114°59E 279 F1
North Henik L. Canada 61°45N 97°40W 297 A9
North Highlands U.S.A. 38°40N 121°23W 306 G5
North Hollywood U.S.A. 34°9N 118°22W 126 B2
North Horr Kenya 3°20N 37°8E 268 B4
North I. India 10°8N 72°20E 245 J1
North I. Rift Valley, Kenya 4°5N 36°5E 268 B4
North I. N.Z. 38°0S 175°0E 284 E4
North I. Seychelles 4°25S 55°13E 272 c
North Judson U.S.A. 41°13N 86°46W 311 C10
North Kingsville U.S.A. 41°54N 80°42W 312 E4
North Kitui ⌓ Kenya 0°15S 38°29E 268 C4
North Knife → Canada 58°53N 94°45W 297 B10
North Koel → India 24°45N 83°50E 243 G10
North Korea ■ Asia 40°0N 127°0E 227 E14
North L. Australia 32°30S 143°5E 282 B5
North Lakhimpur India 27°14N 94°7E 241 B5
North Lanarkshire □ U.K. 55°52N 3°56W 167 F5
North Las Vegas U.S.A. 36°11N 115°7W 124 A1
North Las Vegas ✈ (VGT) U.S.A. 36°12N 115°11W 124 A1
North Lexington U.S.A. 42°27N 71°14W 116 A1
North Liberty U.S.A. 41°32N 86°26W 311 C10
North Lincolnshire □ U.K. 53°36N 0°30W 168 D7
North Little Rock U.S.A. 34°45N 92°16W 314 D8
North Loup → U.S.A. 41°17N 98°24W 308 E4
North Luangwa △ Zambia 11°49S 32°9E 269 E3
North Magnetic Pole Canada 82°42N 114°24W 295 B9
North Malé Atoll Maldives 4°25N 73°30E 272 d
North Malosmadulu Atoll Maldives 5°37N 72°55E 272 d
North Manchester U.S.A. 41°0N 85°46W 311 D11
North Mankato U.S.A. 44°10N 94°2W 308 C6
North Miami U.S.A. 25°53N 80°11W 128 A2
North Miami Beach U.S.A. 25°55N 80°9W 128 A2
North Minch U.K. 58°5N 5°55W 167 C3
North Moose L. Canada 54°4N 100°12W 297 C8
North Myrtle Beach U.S.A. 33°48N 78°42W 315 E15
North Nahanni → Canada 62°15N 123°20W 296 A4
North Naples U.S.A. 26°12N 81°48W 317 J8
North Nazimabad Pakistan 24°55N 67°3E 123 A2
North New River Canal U.S.A. 26°30N 80°30W 317 J9
North Nilandu Atoll Maldives 3°14N 72°56E 272 d
North Olmsted U.S.A. 41°25N 81°56W 312 E3
North Ossetia □ Russia 43°30N 44°30E 191 J7
North Pagai, I. = Pagai Utara, Pulau Indonesia 2°35S 100°0E 234 C2
North Palisade U.S.A. 37°6N 118°31W 306 H8
North Platte U.S.A. 41°8N 100°46W 308 E3
North Platte → U.S.A. 41°7N 100°42W 308 E3
North Point Park Boston, U.S.A. 116 a1
North Pole Arctic 90°0N 0°0 150 A
North Pole Alaska, U.S.A. 64°45N 147°21W 303 D11
North Portal Canada 49°0N 102°33W 297 D8
North Powder U.S.A. 45°2N 117°55W 304 D5
North Pt. Ascension I. 7°53S 14°23W 153 g
North Pt. Barbados 13°20N 59°37W 323 r
North Pt. Hong Kong, China 22°17N 114°12E 122 B2
North Pt. Mich., U.S.A. 45°2N 83°16W 312 A1
North Pt. Vanuatu 14°56S 168°6E 287 D6
North Queensferry U.K. 56°1N 3°24W 121 A1
North Quincy U.S.A. 42°16N 71°1W 116 B2
North Reef I. India 13°5N 92°43E 245 H11
North Res. U.S.A. 42°27N 71°6W 116 A2
North Rhine Westphalia = Nordrhein-Westfalen □ Germany 51°45N 7°30E 178 D3
North River Canada 53°49N 57°6W 299 B8
North Riverside U.S.A. 41°50N 87°48W 119 B2
North Ronaldsay U.K. 59°22N 2°26W 167 B6
North Salem U.S.A. 39°52N 86°39W 311 E10
North Saskatchewan → Canada 53°15N 105°5W 297 C7
North Saugus U.S.A. 42°29N 71°0W 116 A2
North Sea Europe 56°0N 4°0E 158 D6
North Seal → Canada 58°50N 98°7W 297 B9
North Sentinel I. India 11°33N 92°15E 245 J11
North Shields Australia 34°38S 135°52E 282 C1
North Shore U.S.A. 21°39N 158°30W 302 J13
North Shore Channel → U.S.A. 41°58N 87°42W 119 B2
North Solomons □ Papua N. G. 4°0S 155°0E 286 B8
North Somerset □ U.K. 51°24N 2°45W 169 F5
North Springfield U.S.A. 38°48N 77°11W 143 C2
North Station Boston, U.S.A. 116 a2
North Sydney N.S.W., Australia 33°50S 151°13E 139 B2
North Sydney N.S., Canada 46°12N 60°15W 299 C7
North Syracuse U.S.A. 43°8N 76°7W 313 C8
North Taranaki Bight N.Z. 38°50S 174°15E 284 E3
North Thompson → Canada 50°40N 120°20W 296 C4
North Tonawanda U.S.A. 43°2N 78°53W 312 C6
North Troy U.S.A. 45°0N 72°24W 313 B12
North Twin I. Canada 53°20N 80°0W 298 B4
North Tyne → U.K. 55°0N 2°8W 168 B5
North Ubian I. Phil. 6°9N 120°27E 233 H3
North Uist U.K. 57°40N 7°15W 167 D1
North Union = Shaker Heights U.S.A. 41°28N 81°32W 312 E3
North Union St. Vincent 13°13N 61°8W 323 n
North Vancouver Canada 49°19N 123°4W 306 A3
North Vernon U.S.A. 39°0N 85°38W 311 F11
North Wabasca L. Canada 56°0N 113°55W 296 B6
North Walsham U.K. 52°50N 1°22E 168 E9
North Webster U.S.A. 41°25N 85°48W 311 C11
North West = Severo-Zapadnyy □ Russia 65°0N 40°0E 214 C4
North-West □ S. Africa 27°0S 25°0E 270 C4
North West Bluff Montserrat 16°49N 62°12W 323 p
North West C. Australia 21°45S 114°9E 278 D1
North West Frontier □ Pakistan 34°0N 72°0E 242 C4
North West Highlands U.K. 57°33N 4°58W 167 D4
North West Pt. Jamaica 18°27N 78°13W 320 a
North West River Canada 53°30N 60°10W 299 B7
North Western □ Zambia 13°30S 25°30E 269 E2
North-Western Provinces and Oudh = Uttar Pradesh □ India 27°0N 80°0E 243 F9
North Wildwood U.S.A. 39°0N 74°48W 309 F16
North Woolwich U.K. 51°30N 0°3E 125 A4
North Yakima = Yakima U.S.A. 46°36N 120°31W 304 C3
North York Canada 43°45N 79°27W 141 A2
North York Moors U.K. 54°23N 0°53W 168 C7
North York Moors △ U.K. 54°27N 0°51W 168 C7
North Yorkshire □ U.K. 54°15N 1°25W 168 C6
Northallerton U.K. 54°20N 1°26W 168 C6
Northam W. Austral., Australia 31°35S 116°42E 279 F2
Northam Limpopo, S. Africa 24°56S 27°18E 270 B4
Northampton W. Austral., Australia 28°27S 114°33E 279 E1
Northampton Northants., U.K. 52°15N 0°53W 169 E7
Northampton Mass., U.S.A. 42°19N 72°38W 313 D12
Northampton Pa., U.S.A. 40°41N 75°30W 313 F9
Northamptonshire □ U.K. 52°16N 0°55W 169 E7
Northbridge N.S.W., Australia 33°49S 151°15E 139 A2
Northbridge Mass., U.S.A. 42°9N 71°39W 313 D13
Northbridge Park Australia 33°49S 151°15E 139 A2
Northcliff S. Africa 26°8S 27°58E 123 A1
Northcliffe Australia 34°39S 116°7E 279 F2
Northcote Australia 37°46S 145°0E 128 A2
Northeast C. U.S.A. 63°18N 168°42W 303 E5
Northeast Pacific Basin Pac. Oc. 32°0N 145°0W 289 D13
Northeast Providence Chan. W. Indies 26°0N 76°0W 320 A4
Northeastern University U.S.A. 42°20N 71°4W 116 A2
Northeim Germany 51°42N 10°0E 178 D6
Northern = Limpopo □ S. Africa 24°5S 29°0E 271 B4
Northern □ Ghana 9°30N 1°0W 263 D4
Northern □ Malawi 11°0S 34°0E 269 E3
Northern □ Papua N. G. 9°0S 148°30E 286 E5
Northern □ S. Leone 9°15N 11°30W 262 D2
Northern □ Zambia 10°30S 31°0E 269 E3
Northern Areas □ Pakistan 36°30N 73°0E 243 A5
Northern Cape □ S. Africa 30°0S 20°0E 270 C3
Northern Circars India 17°30N 82°30E 244 F6
Northern Indian L. Canada 57°20N 97°20W 297 B9
Northern Ireland □ U.K. 54°45N 7°0W 166 B5
Northern Lau Group Fiji 17°30S 178°59W 287 A3
Northern Light L. Canada 48°15N 90°39W 298 C1
Northern Marianas ⊠ Pac. Oc. 17°0N 145°0E 302 a
Northern Province □ S. Africa 24°0S 29°0E 271 B4
Northern Range Trin. & Tob. 10°46N 61°15W 323 t
Northern Rhodesia = Zambia ■ Africa 15°0S 28°0E 269 F2
Northern Samar □ Phil. 12°30N 124°40E 232 E5
Northern Sporades Greece 39°15N 23°30E 204 B5
Northern Territory □ Australia 20°0S 133°0E 278 D5
Northern Virginia Regional Park ⌓ U.S.A. 38°55N 77°6W 143 B3
Northfield Minn., U.S.A. 44°27N 93°9W 308 C7
Northfield Vt., U.S.A. 44°9N 72°40W 313 B12
Northlake U.S.A. 41°54N 87°53W 119 B1
Northland □ N.Z. 35°30S 173°30E 284 B2
Northmount Canada 43°46N 79°23W 141 A2
Northolt U.K. 51°32N 0°22W 125 A1
Northome U.S.A. 47°52N 94°17W 308 B6
Northport Ala., U.S.A. 33°14N 87°35W 315 E11
Northport Wash., U.S.A. 48°55N 117°48W 304 B5
Northumberland □ U.K. 55°12N 2°0W 168 B6
Northumberland, C. Australia 38°5S 140°40E 282 E4
Northumberland Heath U.K. 51°28N 0°10E 125 B5
Northumberland Is. Australia 21°30S 149°50E 280 C4
Northumberland Str. Canada 46°20N 64°0W 299 C7
Northville U.S.A. 43°13N 74°11W 313 C10
Northway U.S.A. 62°58N 141°56W 303 E12
Northwest Atlantic Mid-Ocean Canyon Atl. Oc. 54°0N 48°0W 152 A7
Northwest Pacific Basin Pac. Oc. 32°0N 165°0E 288 D8

Northwest Providence Channel
W. Indies 26°0N 78°0W **320** A4
Northwest Pt. *Bahamas* 25°4N 77°31W **153** b
Northwest Territories □
Canada 63°0N 118°0W **294** C8
Northwestern Station
U.S.A. 41°52N 87°38W **119** B3
Northwestern University
U.S.A. 42°3N 87°40W **119** A2
Northwich *U.K.* 53°15N 2°31W **168** D5
Northwood *London, U.K.* 51°36N 0°25W **125** A1
Northwood *Iowa, U.S.A.* 43°27N 93°13W **308** D7
Northwood *N. Dak.,*
U.S.A. 47°44N 97°34W **308** B5
Northwood Park *Canada* 43°45N 79°30W **141** A1
Norton *Kans., U.S.A.* 39°50N 99°53W **308** F4
Norton *Zimbabwe* 17°52S 30°40E **269** F3
Norton B. *U.S.A.* 64°45N 161°15W **303** D7
Norton Sd. *U.S.A.* 63°50N 164°0W **303** E7
Norton Shores *U.S.A.* 43°10N 86°16W **311** A10
Nortorf *Germany* 54°10N 9°50E **178** A5
Norwalk *Calif., U.S.A.* 33°54N 118°4W **307** M8
Norwalk *Conn., U.S.A.* 41°7N 73°22W **313** E11
Norwalk *Iowa, U.S.A.* 41°29N 93°41W **310** C3
Norwalk *Ohio, U.S.A.* 41°15N 82°37W **312** E2
Norway *Maine, U.S.A.* 44°13N 70°32W **309** C18
Norway *Mich., U.S.A.* 45°47N 87°55W **308** C10
Norway ■ *Europe* 63°0N 11°0E **160** E14
Norway House *Canada* 53°59N 97°50W **297** C9
Norwegian B. *Canada* 77°30N 90°0W **295** B11
Norwegian Basin *Atl. Oc.* 68°0N 2°0W **150** C7
Norwegian Sea *Atl. Oc.* 66°0N 1°0E **158** B6
Norwich *Ont., Canada* 42°59N 80°36W **312** D4
Norwich *Norfolk, U.K.* 52°38N 1°18E **169** E9
Norwich *Conn., U.S.A.* 41°31N 72°5W **313** E12
Norwich *N.Y., U.S.A.* 42°32N 75°32W **313** D9
Norwood *Ont., Canada* 44°23N 77°59W **312** B7
Norwood *Gauteng, S. Africa* 26°9S 28°4E **123** A2
Norwood *N.Y., U.S.A.* 44°45N 75°0W **313** B10
Norwood *Ohio, U.S.A.* 39°9N 84°27W **311** E12
Norwood Park *U.S.A.* 41°59N 87°48W **119** B2
Noryangjin *S. Korea* 37°30N 126°56E **137** B1
Nosappu-Misaki *Japan* 45°26N 141°39E **220** C12
Noshaq *Pakistan* 36°24N 71°49E **240** A3
Noshiro *Japan* 40°12N 140°0E **220** D10
Nosivka *Ukraine* 50°50N 31°37E **189** G6
Nosovka = Nosivka
Ukraine 50°50N 31°37E **189** G6
Nosratābād *Iran* 29°55N 60°0E **247** D8
Noss Hd. *U.K.* 58°28N 3°3W **167** C5
Nossa Senhora da Glória
Brazil 10°14S 37°25W **332** D4
Nossa Senhora das Dores
Brazil 10°29S 37°13W **332** D4
Nossa Senhora de Candelária
Rio de J., Brazil **135** a2
Nossa Senhora do Livramento
Brazil 15°48S 56°22W **331** D6
Nossa Senhora do Ó
Brazil 23°30S 46°41W **137** B1
Nossebro *Sweden* 58°12N 12°43E **163** F6
Nossegem *Belgium* 50°53N 4°30E **116** A3
Nossob ➛ *S. Africa* 26°55S 20°45E **270** C3
Nossombougou *Mali* 13°5N 7°55W **262** C3
Nosy Barren *Madag.* 18°25S 43°40E **272** B1
Nosy Bé *Madag.* 13°25S 48°15E **272** A2
Nosy Boraha *Madag.* 16°50S 49°55E **272** B2
Nosy Lava *Madag.* 14°33S 47°36E **272** A2
Nosy Mitsio *Madag.* 12°54S 48°36E **272** A2
Nosy Varika *Madag.* 20°35S 48°32E **272** C2
Notasulga *U.S.A.* 32°34N 85°41W **316** C4
Noteć ➛ *Poland* 52°44N 15°26E **185** F2
Notikewin ➛ *Canada* 57°2N 117°38W **296** B5
Notio Aigaio = Notios
Aiyaion □ 36°52N 25°34E **205** E7
Notios Aiyaion □ 36°52N 25°34E **205** E7
Notios Evvoïkos Kólpos
Greece 38°20N 24°0E **204** C5
Noto *Italy* 36°53N 15°4E **201** F8
Noto, G. di *Italy* 36°50N 15°12E **201** F8
Notodden *Norway* 59°35N 9°17E **164** E6
Notre-Dame *Paris, France* **134** c4
Notre-Dame, Basilique
Montréal, Canada **130** c3
Notre-Dame, Bois *France* 48°45N 2°34E **134** B4
Notre Dame B. *Canada* 49°45N 55°30W **299** C8
Notre-Dame-de-Grace
Canada 45°28N 73°38W **130** B2
Notre-Dame-de-Koartac = Quaqtaq
Canada 60°55N 69°40W **295** C13
Notre-Dame-des-Bois
Canada 45°24N 71°4W **313** A13
Notre-Dame-d'Ivugivic = Ivujivik
Canada 62°24N 77°55W **295** C12
Notre-Dame-du-Nord
Canada 47°36N 79°30W **298** C4
Notsé *Togo* 7°0N 1°17E **263** D5
Nottawasaga B. *Canada* 44°35N 80°15W **312** B4
Nottaway = Senneterre
Canada 48°25N 77°15W **298** C4
Nottaway ➛ *Canada* 51°22N 78°55W **298** B4
Notting Hill *London, U.K.* **125** b1
Nottingham *U.K.* 52°58N 1°10W **168** E6
Nottingham, City of □
U.K. 52°58N 1°10W **168** E6
Nottingham I. *Canada* 63°20N 77°55W **295** C12
Nottinghamshire □ *U.K.* 53°10N 1°3W **168** D6
Nottoway ➛ *U.S.A.* 36°33N 76°55W **309** G15
Notwane ➛ *Botswana* 23°35S 26°58E **270** B4
Nouâdhibou *Mauritania* 20°54N 17°0W **260** D1
Nouâdhibou, Dakhlet
Mauritania 20°55N 16°52W **260** D1
Nouâdhibou, Râs
Mauritania 20°50N 17°0W **260** D1
Nouakchott *Mauritania* 18°9N 15°58W **262** B1
Nouâmghâr *Mauritania* 19°20N 16°20W **262** B1
Nouméa *N. Cal.* 22°17S 166°30E **288** d
Nouna *Burkina Faso* 12°45N 3°52W **262** C4
Noupoort *S. Africa* 31°10S 24°57E **270** D3
Nouveau Comptoir = Wemindji
Canada 53°0N 78°49W **298** B4
Nouvelle Amsterdam, Î.
Ind. Oc. 38°30S 77°30E **273** H6
Nouvelle-Calédonie = New
Caledonia ☑ *Pac. Oc.* 21°0S 165°0E **288** d
Nouvelle France *Mauritius* 20°22S 57°33E **272** e
Nouzonville *France* 49°48N 4°44E **173** C11
Nova Aripuanã *Brazil* 5°8S 60°22W **329** E5
Nová Baňa *Slovak Rep.* 48°28N 18°39E **181** C11
Nová Bystřice *Czech Rep.* 49°2N 15°8E **180** B8
Nova Casa Nova *Brazil* 9°25S 41°5W **332** C3
Nova Cruz *Brazil* 6°28S 35°25W **332** C4
Nova Era *Brazil* 19°45S 43°3W **333** E3
Nova Esperança *Brazil* 23°8S 52°24W **335** A5
Nova Fontesvila = Vila Machado
Mozam. 19°15S 34°14E **269** F3
Nova-Freixo = Cuamba
Mozam. 14°45S 36°22E **269** E4
Nova Friburgo *Brazil* 22°16S 42°30W **333** F3
Nova Gaia = Cambundi-Catembo
Angola 10°10S 17°35E **265** E3
Nova Gorica *Slovenia* 45°7N 13°39E **199** C10
Nova Gradiška *Croatia* 45°17N 17°28E **182** E2
Nova Granada *Brazil* 20°30S 49°20W **333** F2
Nova Iguaçu *Brazil* 22°45S 43°28W **333** F3
Nova Iorque *Brazil* 7°0S 44°5W **332** C3
Nova Kakhovka *Ukraine* 46°42N 33°27E **189** J7
Nova Lamego
Guinea-Biss. 12°19N 14°11W **262** C2
Nova Lima *Brazil* 19°59S 43°51W **335** A7
Nova Lisboa = Huambo
Angola 12°42S 15°54E **265** E3
Nova Lusitânia *Mozam.* 19°50S 34°34E **269** F3
Nova Mambone *Mozam.* 21°0S 35°3E **271** B6
Nova Milanese *Italy* 45°35N 9°12E **129** A2
Nova Odesa *Ukraine* 47°19N 31°47E **189** J6
Nova Olinda do Norte
Brazil 3°45S 59°3W **329** D6
Nová Paka *Czech Rep.* 50°29N 15°30E **180** A8
Nova Pavova *Serbia* 44°56N 20°14E **182** F5
Nova Ponte *Brazil* 19°8S 47°41W **333** E2
Nova Scotia □ *Canada* 45°10N 63°0W **299** C7
Nova Siri *Italy* 40°10N 16°35E **201** B9
Nova Sofala *Mozam.* 20°7S 34°42E **271** B5
Nova Ushytsya *Ukraine* 48°50N 27°17E **183** B12
Nova Varoš *Serbia* 43°29N 19°48E **202** C3
Nova Venécia *Brazil* 18°45S 40°24W **333** E3
Nova Vida *Brazil* 10°11S 62°47W **331** C5
Nova Zagora *Bulgaria* 42°32N 26°1E **203** D10
Novaci *Macedonia* 41°5N 21°29E **202** E5
Novaci *Romania* 45°10N 23°42E **183** E8
Novafeltria *Italy* 43°53N 12°17E **199** E9
Novannenskiy = Novoannenskiy
Russia 50°32N 42°39E **190** E6
Novar *Canada* 45°27N 79°15W **312** A5
Novara *Italy* 45°28N 8°38E **198** C5
Novate Milanese *Italy* 45°30N 9°8E **129** A1
Novato *U.S.A.* 38°6N 122°35W **306** G4
Novaya Aleksandriya = Puławy
Poland 51°23N 21°59E **185** G8
Novaya Bukhara = Kagan
Uzbekistan 39°43N 64°33E **216** E6
Novaya Derevnya *Russia* 60°0N 30°19E **137** A1
Novaya Kakhovka = Nova
Kakhovka *Ukraine* 46°42N 33°27E **189** J7
Novaya Kazanka = Zhangaqala
Kazakhstan 48°56N 49°36E **191** F9
Novaya Ladoga *Russia* 60°7N 32°16E **188** B7
Novaya Lyalya *Russia* 59°4N 60°45E **186** C11
Novaya Pismyanka = Leninogorsk
Kazakhstan 50°20N 83°30E **217** B10
Novaya Sibir, Ostrov
Russia 75°10N 150°0E **215** B16
Novaya Zemlya *Russia* 75°0N 56°0E **214** B6
Nové Město *Praha,*
Czech Rep. 50°4N 14°25E **135** B2
Nové Město *Slovak Rep.* 48°45N 17°50E **181** C10
Nové Město na Moravě
Czech Rep. 49°34N 16°5E **180** B9
Nové Město nad Metují
Czech Rep. 50°20N 16°10E **181** A9
Nové Zámky *Slovak Rep.* 48°2N 18°8E **181** C11
Novelda *Spain* 38°24N 0°45W **197** G4
Novellara *Italy* 44°51N 10°44E **198** D7
Novelty *U.S.A.* 40°1N 92°12W **310** D4
Noventa Vicentina *Italy* 45°17N 11°32E **199** C8
Novgorod *Russia* 58°30N 31°25E **188** C6
Novgorod □ *Russia* 58°50N 32°30E **188** C7
Novgorod-Severskiy = Novhorod-
Siverskyy *Ukraine* 52°2N 33°10E **189** G7
Novgradets = Suvorovo
Bulgaria 43°20N 27°35E **203** C11
Novhorod-Siverskyy
Ukraine 52°2N 33°10E **189** G7
Novi Bečej *Serbia* 45°36N 20°10E **182** E5
Novi Iskar *Bulgaria* 42°48N 23°21E **202** D7
Novi Kneževac *Serbia* 46°4N 20°8E **182** D5
Novi Lígure *Italy* 44°46N 8°47E **198** D5
Novi Pazar *Bulgaria* 43°25N 27°15E **203** C11
Novi Pazar *Serbia* 43°12N 20°28E **202** C4
Novi Sad *Serbia* 45°18N 19°52E **182** E4
Novi Slankamen *Serbia* 45°8N 20°15E **182** E5
Novi Travnik *Bos.-H.* 44°10N 17°40E **182** F2
Novi Vinodolski *Croatia* 45°10N 14°48E **199** C11
Novigrad *Istra, Croatia* 45°19N 13°33E **199** C10
Novigrad *Zadar, Croatia* 44°10N 15°32E **199** D12
Novigradsko More
Croatia 44°12N 15°33E **199** D12
Novinger *U.S.A.* 40°14N 92°43W **310** D4
Novo Acôrdo *Brazil* 10°10S 46°48W **332** D2
Novo Airão *Brazil* 2°40S 60°59W **329** D5
Novo Aripuanã *Brazil* 5°8S 60°22W **329** E5
Novo Cruzeiro *Brazil* 17°29S 41°53W **333** E3
Novo Hamburgo *Brazil* 29°37S 51°7W **335** B5
Novo Horizonte *Brazil* 21°25S 49°10W **333** F2
Novo Ivanivka *Ukraine* 45°55N 29°5E **183** E14
Novo-Mariinsk = Anadyr
Russia 64°35N 177°20E **215** C18
Novo Mesto *Slovenia* 45°47N 15°12E **199** C12
Novo Miloševo *Serbia* 45°42N 20°20E **182** E5
Novo Nikolaevsk = Novosibirsk
Russia 55°0N 83°5E **217** B10
Novo Paraiso *Brazil* 1°17N 60°28W **329** C5
Novo Remanso *Brazil* 9°41S 42°4W **332** C3
Novo-Starobinsk = Salihorsk
Belarus 52°51N 27°27E **177** B14
Novo Urgench = Urganch
Uzbekistan 41°40N 60°41E **216** D6
Novoaleksandrovsk = Zarasai
Lithuania 55°40N 26°20E **188** E4
Novoaleksandrovsk
Russia 45°29N 41°17E **191** H5
Novoaleksandrovskaya =
Novoaleksandrovsk
Russia 45°29N 41°17E **191** H5
Novoaleksandrovskoye
Russia 59°50N 30°31E **137** B2
Novoaltaysk *Russia* 53°30N 84°0E **217** B10
Novoannenskiy *Russia* 50°32N 42°39E **190** E6
Novoazovsk *Ukraine* 47°15N 38°4E **189** J10
Novocheboksarsk *Russia* 56°5N 47°27E **190** B8
Novocherkassk *Russia* 47°27N 40°15E **191** G5
Novodevichye *Russia* 53°37N 48°50E **190** D9
Novogireyevo *Russia* 55°45N 37°46E **129** B4
Novogrudok = Navahrudak
Belarus 53°40N 25°50E **177** B13
Novohrad-Volynskyy
Ukraine 50°34N 27°35E **177** C14
Novoivanovskoye *Russia* 55°42N 37°21E **129** B1
Novokachalinsk *Russia* 45°5N 132°0E **220** B5
Novokazalinsk = Zhangaqazaly
Kazakhstan 45°48N 62°6E **216** C6
Novokhopersk *Russia* 51°5N 41°39E **190** E5
Novokiyevskoye = Kraskino
Russia 42°44N 130°48E **220** C5
Novokuybyshevsk *Russia* 53°7N 49°58E **190** D9
Novokuznetsk *Russia* 53°45N 87°10E **217** B11
Novolazarevskaya
Antarctica 71°0S 12°0E **151** D3
Novolyalinsky = Novaya Lyalya
Russia 59°4N 60°45E **186** C11
Novomirgorod *Ukraine* 48°45N 31°33E **189** H6
Novomoskovsk *Russia* 54°5N 38°15E **188** E10
Novomoskovsk *Ukraine* 48°33N 35°17E **189** H8
Novonikolayevka = Novoazovsk
Ukraine 47°15N 38°4E **189** J10
Novonikolyskoye *Russia* 55°50N 37°14E **129** A1
Novopolotsk = Navapolatsk
Belarus 55°32N 28°37E **188** E5
Novorossiysk *Russia* 44°43N 37°46E **189** K9
Novorybnoye *Russia* 72°50N 105°50E **215** B11
Novorzhev *Russia* 57°3N 29°25E **188** D5
Novosaratovka *Russia* 59°50N 30°32E **137** B3
Novosej *Albania* 41°56N 20°35E **202** E4
Novoselytsya *Ukraine* 48°14N 26°15E **183** B11
Novoshakhtinsk *Russia* 47°46N 39°58E **189** J10
Novosibirsk *Russia* 55°0N 83°5E **217** B10
Novosibirskiye Ostrova
Russia 75°0N 142°0E **215** B15
Novosibirskoye Vdkhr.
Russia 54°35N 82°35E **217** B10
Novosil *Russia* 52°59N 37°2E **189** F9
Novosokolniki *Russia* 56°20N 30°2E **188** D6
Novotitarovskaya *Russia* 45°17N 39°2E **191** H4
Novotroitsk *Russia* 51°10N 58°15E **186** D10
Novotroitskoye = Töle Bī
Kazakhstan 43°42N 73°46E **217** D8
Novoukrayinka *Ukraine* 48°25N 31°30E **189** H6
Novouljanovsk *Russia* 54°8N 48°24E **190** C9
Novouzensk *Russia* 50°32N 48°17E **190** E9
Novovolynsk *Ukraine* 50°45N 24°4E **185** H11
Novovoronezhskiy
Russia 51°19N 39°13E **189** G10
Novoyavoriske *Ukraine* 49°53N 23°33E **185** J10
Novozybkov *Russia* 52°30N 32°0E **189** F6
Novska *Croatia* 45°19N 17°0E **199** C14
Novvy Urengoy *Russia* 65°48N 76°52E **214** C8
Nový Bor *Czech Rep.* 50°46N 14°35E **180** A7
Novy Bug = Novyy Buh
Ukraine 47°34N 32°29E **189** J7
Nový Bydžov *Czech Rep.* 50°14N 15°29E **180** A8
Novy Dvor *Belarus* 52°50N 24°21E **185** F11
Novy Dwór Mazowiecki
Poland 52°26N 20°44E **185** F7
Nový Jičín *Czech Rep.* 49°30N 18°2E **181** B11
Novy Margelan = Farghona
Uzbekistan 40°23N 71°19E **217** D8
Novyy Afon *Georgia* 43°7N 40°50E **191** J5
Novyy Bor *Russia* 66°43N 52°19E **186** A9
Novyy Buh *Ukraine* 47°34N 32°29E **189** J7
Novyy Oskol *Russia* 50°44N 37°55E **189** G9
Novyy Port *Russia* 67°40N 72°30E **214** C8
Now Shahr *Iran* 36°40N 51°30E **247** B6
Nowa Deba *Poland* 50°26N 21°41E **185** H8
Nowa Nowa *Australia* 37°44S 148°3E **283** D8
Nowa Ruda *Poland* 50°35N 16°30E **185** H3
Nowa Sarzyna *Poland* 50°21N 22°21E **185** H9
Nowa Sól *Poland* 51°48N 15°44E **185** G2
Nowata *U.S.A.* 36°42N 95°38W **314** C7
Nowbarān *Iran* 35°8N 49°42E **247** C6
Nowe *Poland* 53°41N 18°44E **184** E5
Nowe-Babice *Poland* 52°15N 20°51E **142** B1
Nowe Miasteczko *Poland* 51°42N 15°42E **185** G2
Nowe Miasto *Mazowieckie,*
Poland 51°38N 20°34E **185** G7
Nowe Miasto *Warsaw, Poland* **142** a2
Nowe Miasto Lubawskie
Poland 53°27N 19°33E **184** E6
Nowe Skalmierzyce
Poland 51°43N 18°0E **185** G4
Nowe Warpno *Poland* 53°42N 14°18E **184** E1
Nowendoc *Australia* 31°32S 151°44E **283** A9
Nowendoc △ *Australia* 31°33S 151°45E **283** A9
Nowghāb *Iran* 33°53N 59°4E **247** C8
Nowgong *Assam, India* 26°20N 92°50E **241** B4
Nowgong *Mad. P., India* 25°4N 79°27E **243** G8
Nowitna Nat. Wildlife Refuge ⌂
U.S.A. 64°40N 154°16W **303** D9
Nowogard *Poland* 53°41N 15°10E **184** E2
Nowogród *Poland* 53°14N 21°53E **185** E8
Nowogród Bobrzanski
Poland 51°48N 15°15E **185** G2
Nowogrodziec *Poland* 51°12N 15°24E **185** G2
Noworadomsk = Radomsko
Poland 51°5N 19°28E **185** G6
Nowra *Australia* 34°53S 150°35E **283** C9
Nowrangapur *India* 19°14N 82°33E **244** E6
Nowshāk = Noshaq
Pakistan 36°24N 71°49E **240** A3
Nowshera *Pakistan* 34°0N 72°0E **240** B4
Nowy Dwór Gdański
Poland 54°13N 19°7E **184** D6
Nowy Sącz *Poland* 49°40N 20°41E **185** J7
Nowy Staw *Poland* 54°13N 19°2E **184** D6
Nowy Targ *Poland* 49°29N 20°2E **185** J7
Nowy Tomyśl *Poland* 52°19N 16°10E **185** F3
Nowy Wiśnicz *Poland* 49°55N 20°28E **185** J7
Noxen *U.S.A.* 41°25N 76°4W **313** E8
Noyabr'sk *Russia* 64°34N 76°21E **214** C8
Noyant *France* 47°30N 0°6E **172** E7
Noyers *France* 47°40N 4°0E **173** E10
Nöykkiö *Finland* 60°10N 24°42E **121** B1
Noyon *Oise, France* 49°34N 2°59E **173** C9
Noyon *Mongolia* 43°2N 102°4E **226** C2
Nozay *France* 47°34N 1°38W **172** E5
Nqutu *S. Africa* 28°13S 30°32E **271** C5
Nsa *Congo* 2°22S 15°19E **264** C3
Nsa, O. en ➛ *Algeria* 32°28N 5°24E **261** B6
Nsa, Plateau de *Congo* 2°26S 15°20E **264** C3
Nsanje *Malawi* 16°55S 35°12E **269** F4
Nsawam *Ghana* 5°50N 0°24W **263** D4
Nsok *Eq. Guin.* 1°10N 11°19E **264** B2
Nsomba *Zambia* 10°45S 29°51E **269** E2
Nsontin
Dem. Rep. of the Congo 3°7S 17°56E **264** C3
Nsopzup *Burma* 25°51N 97°30E **241** C6
Nsukka *Nigeria* 6°51N 7°29E **263** D6
Ntem ➛ *Cameroon* 2°21N 9°49E **264** B2
Ntingui, Mt. *Comoros Is.* 12°12S 44°25E **272** a
Ntoum *Gabon* 0°22N 9°47E **264** B1
N'Tsama *Congo* 0°53S 14°44E **264** C2
Ntsaouéni *Comoros Is.* 11°27S 43°15E **272** a
Ntsoudjini *Comoros Is.* 11°39S 43°15E **272** a
Ntui *Cameroon* 4°27N 11°38E **263** E7
Nu Jiang ➛ *China* 29°58N 97°25E **228** E2
Nu Shan *China* 26°0N 99°20E **228** E2
Nuakata I. *Papua N. G.* 10°17S 151°2E **286** F6
Nuba Mts. = Nubah, Jibalan
Sudan 12°0N 31°0E **257** E3
Nubah, Jibalan *Sudan* 12°0N 31°0E **257** E3
Nubia *Africa* 21°0N 32°0E **254** D7
Nubian Desert = Nûbîya, Es Sahrâ
en *Sudan* 21°30N 33°30E **256** C3
Nûbîya, Es Sahrâ en
Sudan 21°30N 33°30E **256** C3
Nubl *Syria* 36°22N 36°59E **250** B7
Nubledo *Spain* 43°31N 5°52W **194** B5
Nuboai *Indonesia* 2°10S 136°30E **231** E9
Nubra ➛ *India* 34°35N 77°35E **243** B7
Nucet *Romania* 46°28N 22°35E **182** D7
Nueces ➛ *U.S.A.* 27°51N 97°30W **314** H6
Nueltin L. *Canada* 60°30N 99°30W **297** A9
Nueva, I. *Chile* 55°13S 66°30W **336** E3
Nueva Antioquia *Colombia* 6°5N 69°26W **328** B4
Nueva Atzacoalco *Mexico* 19°29N 99°4W **128** B2
Nueva Carteya *Spain* 37°35N 4°28W **195** H6
Nueva Ciudad Guerrero
Mexico 26°34N 99°12W **319** B5
Nueva Ecija □ *Phil.* 15°35N 121°0E **232** D3
Nueva Esparta □ *Venezuela* 11°0N 64°0W **329** A5
Nueva Gerona *Cuba* 21°53N 82°49W **320** B3
Nueva Imperial *Chile* 38°45S 72°58W **336** A2
Nueva Palmira *Uruguay* 33°52S 58°20W **334** C4
Nueva Pompeya
Argentina 34°40S 58°25W **117** C2
Nueva Rosita *Mexico* 27°57N 101°13W **318** B4
Nueva San Salvador
El Salv. 13°40N 89°18W **320** D2
Nueva Tabarca *Spain* 38°17N 0°30W **197** G4
Nueva Tenochtitlán
Mexico 19°27N 99°5W **128** B2
Nueva Vizcaya □ *Phil.* 16°20N 121°20E **232** C3
Nuéve de Julio *Argentina* 35°30S 61°0W **334** D3
Nuevitas *Cuba* 21°30N 77°20W **320** B4
Nuevo, G. *Argentina* 43°0S 64°30W **336** B4
Nuevo Casas Grandes
Mexico 30°25N 107°55W **318** A3
Nuevo Laredo *Mexico* 27°30N 99°31W **319** B5
Nuevo León □ *Mexico* 25°20N 100°0W **318** C5
Nuevo Mundo, Cerro
Bolivia 21°55S 66°53W **330** E4
Nuevo Rocafuerte
Ecuador 0°55S 75°27W **328** D2
Nugaaleed, Dooxo
Somali Rep. 8°35N 48°35E **267** C6
Nugget Pt. *N.Z.* 46°27S 169°50E **285** G4
Nugrus, Gebel *Egypt* 24°47N 34°35E **256** C3
Nuguria Is. *Papua N. G.* 3°20S 154°45E **286** B8
Nuhaka *N.Z.* 39°3S 177°45E **284** F6
Nui *Pac. Oc.* 7°15S 177°10E **277** B14
Nuijala *Finland* 60°12N 24°46E **121** B1
Nuits-St-Georges *France* 47°10N 4°56E **173** E11
Nukey Bluff *Australia* 32°26S 135°29E **281** E2
Nukha = Şaki *Azerbaijan* 41°10N 47°5E **191** K8
Nukhayb *Iraq* 32°4N 42°3E **213** F10
Nukheila *Sudan* 19°1N 26°21E **256** D2
Nukiki *Solomon Is.* 6°46S 156°35E **287** L9
Nuku *Papua N. G.* 3°41S 142°28E **286** B2
Nuku Hiva *French Polynesia* 8°54S 140°6W **289** f
Nuku'alofa *Tonga* 21°10S 175°12W **287** Q13
Nukuhu *Papua N. G.* 5°34S 149°22E **286** C5
Nukulaelae *Tuvalu* 9°23S 179°52E **277** B14
Nukunonu *Pac. Oc.* 9°12S 171°54W **277** B16
Nukus *Uzbekistan* 42°27N 59°41E **216** D5
Nulato *U.S.A.* 64°43N 158°6W **303** D8
Nules *Spain* 39°51N 0°9W **196** F4
Nullagine *Australia* 21°53S 120°7E **278** D3
Nullagine ➛ *Australia* 21°20S 120°20E **278** D3
Nullarbor *Australia* 31°28S 130°55E **279** F5
Nullarbor △ *Australia* 32°39S 130°0E **279** F2
Nullarbor Plain *Australia* 31°10S 129°0E **279** F4
Numabukuro *Japan* 35°43N 139°39E **140** A2
Numalla, L. *Australia* 28°43S 144°20E **281** D3
Numan *Nigeria* 9°29N 12°3E **263** D7
Numanuma *Papua N. G.* 9°41S 150°55E **286** E6
Numata *Japan* 36°45N 139°4E **223** A11
Numatinna ➛ *Sudan* 7°38N 27°20E **257** F2
Numaykoos Lake ⌂
Canada 57°52N 95°58W **297** B9
Numazu *Japan* 35°7N 138°51E **223** B10
Numbulwar *Australia* 14°15S 135°45E **280** A2
Numedal *Norway* 60°6N 9°6E **164** D6
Numfoor *Indonesia* 1°0S 134°50E **231** E8
Numurkah *Australia* 36°5S 145°26E **283** D6
Nunaksaluk I. *Canada* 55°49N 60°20W **299** A7
Nunap Isua *Greenland* 59°48N 43°55W **154** F6
Nunavut □ *Canada* 66°0N 85°0W **295** C11
Nunda *U.S.A.* 42°35N 77°56W **312** D7
Nuneaton *U.K.* 52°32N 1°27W **169** E6
Nuñez *Argentina* 34°32S 58°27W **117** B2
Nungarin *Australia* 31°12S 118°6E **279** F2
Nungo *Mozam.* 13°23S 37°43E **269** E4
Nungwe *Tanzania* 2°48S 32°2E **268** C3
Nunhead *U.K.* 51°27N 0°3W **125** B3
Nunivak I. *U.S.A.* 60°10N 166°30W **303** F6
Nunkun *India* 33°57N 76°2E **243** C7
Ñuñoa *Chile* 33°27S 70°35W **137** B2
Núoro *Italy* 40°20N 9°20E **200** B2
Núpur *Iceland* 65°56N 23°36W **155** B3
Nuqayy, Jabal *Libya* 23°11N 19°30E **258** D3
Nuqūb *Yemen* 14°59N 45°48E **248** D4
Nuquí *Colombia* 5°42N 77°17W **328** B2
Nur Dağı *Turkey* 36°54N 35°39E **250** B6
Nur Dağları *Turkey* 36°50N 36°23E **250** B7
Nura ➛ *Kazakhstan* 50°30N 69°59E **217** B7
Nūrābād *Iran* 27°47N 57°12E **247** E8
Nurabad *Uzbekistan* 39°36N 66°17E **217** E7
Nure ➛ *Italy* 45°3N 9°49E **198** C6
Nuremberg = Nürnberg
Germany 49°27N 11°3E **179** F7
Nuri *Sonora, Mexico* 28°5N 109°22W **318** B3
Nuri *Sudan* 18°29N 31°59E **256** D3
Nuriootpa *Australia* 34°27S 139°0E **282** C3
Nuristān □ *Afghan.* 35°20N 71°0E **217** E8
Nurlat *Russia* 54°29N 50°45E **190** C10
Nurmes *Finland* 63°33N 29°10E **160** E23
Nürnberg *Germany* 49°27N 11°3E **179** F7
Nurpur *Pakistan* 31°53N 71°54E **242** D4
Nurra, La *Italy* 40°45N 8°15E **200** B1
Nurran, L. = Terewah, L.
Australia 29°52S 147°35E **281** D4
Nurrari Lakes *Australia* 29°1S 130°5E **279** E5
Nurri *Italy* 39°43N 9°14E **200** C2
Nürtingen *Germany* 48°37N 9°19E **179** G5
Nurzec ➛ *Poland* 52°37N 22°25E **185** F9
Nus *Italy* 45°45N 7°28E **198** C4
Nusa Barung *Indonesia* 8°30S 113°30E **235** D4
Nusa Dua *Indonesia* 8°48S 115°14E **231** K18
Nusa Kambangan
Indonesia 7°40S 108°10E **235** D3
Nusa Tenggara Barat □
Indonesia 8°50S 117°30E **235** D5
Nusa Tenggara Timur □
Indonesia 9°30S 122°0E **231** F6
Nusaybin *Turkey* 37°3N 41°10E **213** D9
Nuşayrīyah, J. an *Syria* 35°20N 36°13E **250** C7
Nushki *Pakistan* 29°35N 66°0E **242** E2
Nusle *Czech Rep.* 50°3N 14°26E **135** B2
Nussdorf *Austria* 48°15N 16°21E **142** A2
Nuuk *Greenland* 64°10N 51°35W **154** E5
Nuupere, Pte. *Moorea* 17°36S 149°47W **289** e
Nuusuatsiaq *Greenland* 74°8N 57°3W **154** C5
Nu'uli *Amer. Samoa* 14°19S 170°42W **302** f
Nuwakot *Nepal* 28°10N 83°55E **243** E10
Nuwara Eliya *Sri Lanka* 6°58N 80°48E **245** L5
Nuwaybi'ī, W. an ➛
Si. Arabia 29°18N 34°57E **251** J5
Nuweiba' *Egypt* 28°59N 34°39E **251** K5
Nuwerus *S. Africa* 31°8S 18°24E **270** D2
Nuweveldberge *S. Africa* 32°10S 21°45E **270** D3
Nuyts, Pt. *Australia* 35°4S 116°38E **279** G2
Nuyts Arch. *Australia* 32°35S 133°20E **281** E1
Nuzvid *India* 16°47N 80°53E **244** F5
N'Vinda *Angola* 13°8S 19°2E **265** E3
Nxai Pan △ *Botswana* 19°50S 24°46E **270** A3
Nxau-Nxau *Botswana* 18°57S 21°4E **270** A3
Nyaake *Liberia* 4°52N 7°37W **262** E3
Nyabessan *Cameroon* 2°28N 10°24E **264** B2
Nyabing *Australia* 33°33S 118°9E **279** F2
Nyack *U.S.A.* 41°5N 73°55W **313** E11
Nyagan *Russia* 62°30N 65°38E **214** C7
Nyah West *Australia* 35°16S 143°21E **282** C5
Nyahanga *Tanzania* 2°20S 33°37E **268** C3
Nyahua *Tanzania* 5°25S 33°23E **268** D3
Nyahururu *Kenya* 0°2N 36°27E **268** B4
Nyainqêntanglha Shan
China 30°0N 90°0E **218** D3
Nyakanazi *Tanzania* 3°2S 31°10E **268** C3
Nyakrom *Ghana* 5°40N 0°50W **263** D4
Nyâlâ *Sudan* 12°2N 24°58E **257** E1
Nyamandhlovu *Zimbabwe* 19°55S 28°16E **269** F2
Nyambiti *Tanzania* 2°48S 33°27E **268** C3
Nyamira *Kenya* 0°36S 34°52E **268** B4
Nyamlell *Sudan* 9°7N 26°59E **257** F2
Nyamwaga *Tanzania* 1°27S 34°33E **268** C3
Nyandekwa *Tanzania* 3°57S 32°32E **268** C3
Nyanding ➛ *Sudan* 8°40N 32°41E **257** F3
Nyandoma *Russia* 61°40N 40°12E **188** B11
Nyanga *S. Africa* 33°59S 18°35E **118** A2
Nyanga ➛ *Gabon* 2°58S 10°15E **264** C2
Nyanga △ *Zimbabwe* 18°17S 32°46E **269** F3
Nyangana *Namibia* 18°0S 20°40E **270** A3
Nyanguge *Tanzania* 2°30S 33°12E **268** C3
Nyankpala *Ghana* 9°21N 0°58W **263** D4
Nyanza *Rwanda* 2°20S 29°42E **268** C2
Nyanza □ *Kenya* 0°10S 34°15E **268** C3
Nyanza-Lac *Burundi* 4°21S 29°36E **268** C2
Nyaponges *Sudan* 5°5N 33°45E **257** F3
Nyasa, L. = Malawi, L.
Africa 12°30S 34°30E **269** E3
Nyasaland = Malawi ■
Africa 11°55S 34°0E **269** E3
Nyasvizh *Belarus* 53°14N 26°38E **177** B14
Nyaunglebin *Burma* 17°52N 96°42E **241** G6
Nyazepetrovsk *Russia* 56°3N 59°36E **186** C10
Nyazura *Zimbabwe* 18°40S 32°16E **269** F3
Nyazwidzi ➛ *Zimbabwe* 20°0S 31°17E **269** G3
Nybergsund *Norway* 61°15N 12°19E **164** C9
Nyborg *Denmark* 55°18N 10°47E **163** J4
Nybro *Sweden* 56°44N 15°55E **163** H9
Nyda *Russia* 66°40N 72°58E **214** C8
Nyeboe Land *Greenland* 82°0N 57°0W **154** A5
Nyengo Swamp *Zambia* 14°51S 22°7E **265** E4
Nyeri *Kenya* 0°23S 36°56E **268** C4
Nyerol *Sudan* 8°41N 32°1E **257** F3
Nyhammar *Sweden* 60°17N 14°58E **162** D8
Nyika △ *Malawi* 10°30S 33°53E **269** E3
Nyinahin *Ghana* 6°43N 2°3W **262** D4
Nyíradony *Hungary* 47°41N 21°55E **182** C6
Nyírbátor *Hungary* 47°49N 22°9E **182** C7
Nyíregyháza *Hungary* 47°58N 21°47E **182** C6
Nyiru, Mt. *Kenya* 2°8N 36°50E **268** B4
Nykarleby = Uusikaarlepyy
Finland 63°32N 22°31E **160** E20
Nykirke *Norway* 60°54N 10°19E **164** D7
Nykøbing *Nordjylland,*
Denmark 56°48N 8°51E **163** H2
Nykøbing *Sjælland,*
Denmark 54°56N 11°52E **163** K5
Nykøbing *Sjælland,*
Denmark 55°55N 11°40E **163** J5
Nyköping *Sweden* 58°45N 17°1E **163** F11
Nykroppa *Sweden* 59°37N 14°18E **162** E8
Nykvarn *Sweden* 59°11N 17°25E **162** E11
Nyland *Sweden* 63°1N 17°45E **162** A11
Nylstroom = Modimolle
S. Africa 24°42S 28°22E **271** B4
Nymagee *Australia* 32°7S 146°20E **283** B7
Nymboida △ *Australia* 29°38S 152°26E **281** D5
Nymburk *Czech Rep.* 50°10N 15°1E **180** A8
Nymphenburg *Germany* 48°9N 11°30E **131** B2
Nymphenburg, Schloss
Germany 48°9N 11°30E **131** B2
Nynäshamn *Sweden* 58°54N 17°57E **163** F11
Nyngan *Australia* 31°30S 147°8E **283** A7
Nyoma Rap *India* 33°10N 78°40E **243** C8
Nyoman = Nemunas ➛
Lithuania 55°25N 21°10E **184** C8
Nyon *Switz.* 46°23N 6°14E **179** J2
Nyong ➛ *Cameroon* 3°17N 9°54E **263** E6
Nyons *France* 44°22N 5°10E **175** D9
Nyou *Burkina Faso* 12°42N 2°1W **263** C4
Nýrsko *Czech Rep.* 49°18N 13°9E **180** B6
Nysa *Poland* 50°30N 17°22E **185** H4
Nysa ➛ *Europe* 52°4N 14°46E **178** C10
Nysa Kłodzka ➛ *Poland* 50°49N 17°40E **185** H4
Nysætre *Norway* 62°2N 8°20E **164** B5
Nysäter *Sweden* 59°17N 12°47E **162** E6
Nyslott = Savonlinna
Finland 61°52N 28°53E **188** B5
Nyssa *U.S.A.* 43°53N 117°0W **304** E5
Nystad = Uusikaupunki
Finland 60°47N 21°25E **188** B1
Nysted *Denmark* 54°40N 11°44E **163** K5
Nyunzu
Dem. Rep. of the Congo 5°57S 27°58E **268** D2
Nyurba *Russia* 63°17N 118°28E **215** C12
Nyzhankovychi *Ukraine* 49°40N 22°49E **185** J9
Nyzhnohirskyy *Ukraine* 45°27N 34°38E **189** K8
Nyzhny Vorota *Ukraine* 48°46N 23°6E **182** B8
Nzébéla *Guinea* 8°9N 9°7W **262** D3
Nzega *Tanzania* 4°10S 33°12E **268** C3
Nzérékoré *Guinea* 7°49N 8°48W **262** D3
Nzeto *Angola* 7°10S 12°52E **265** D2
Nzilo, Chutes de
Dem. Rep. of the Congo 10°18S 25°27E **265** E5
Nzilo, L.
Dem. Rep. of the Congo 10°35S 25°39E **265** E5
N'zo ➛ *Ivory C.* 6°15N 7°34W **262** D3
N'zo ⌂ *Ivory C.* 6°15N 7°15W **262** D3
Nzubuka *Tanzania* 4°45S 32°50E **268** C3
Nzwani = Anjouan
Comoros Is. 12°15S 44°20E **272** a

O

O Barco *Spain* 42°23N 6°58W **194** C4
O Carballiño *Spain* 42°26N 8°5W **194** C2
O Corgo *Spain* 42°56N 7°25W **194** C3
O Le Pupū Pu'e △
Samoa 13°59S 171°43W **287** V20
O Pino *Spain* 42°56N 8°20W **194** C2
O Porriño *Spain* 42°10N 8°37W **194** C2
Ō-Shima *Hokkaidō, Japan* 41°30N 139°22E **220** D9
Ō-Shima *Nagasaki, Japan* 33°29N 129°33E **222** D1
Ō-Shima *Shizuoka,*
Japan 34°44N 139°24E **223** C11
Oa, Mull of *U.K.* 55°35N 6°20W **167** F2
Oacoma *U.S.A.* 43°48N 99°24W **308** D4
Oahe, L. *U.S.A.* 44°27N 100°24W **308** C3
Oahe Dam *U.S.A.* 44°27N 100°24W **308** C3
O'ahu *U.S.A.* 21°28N 157°58W **302** K14
Oak Creek *U.S.A.* 42°52N 87°55W **311** B9
Oak Grove *U.S.A.* 33°50N 84°18W **113** A3
Oak Harbor *U.S.A.* 48°18N 122°39W **306** B4
Oak Hill *Fla., U.S.A.* 28°52N 80°51W **317** G9
Oak Hill *Mass., U.S.A.* 42°18N 71°10W **116** B1
Oak Hill *W. Va., U.S.A.* 37°59N 81°9W **309** G13
Oak Island *U.S.A.* 33°55N 78°10W **315** E15
Oak Lawn *U.S.A.* 41°42N 87°45W **119** C2
Oak Park *Ga., U.S.A.* 32°22N 82°19W **316** C7
Oak Park *Ill., U.S.A.* 41°52N 87°47W **119** B2
Oak Ridge *U.S.A.* 36°1N 84°16W **315** C12
Oak Street Beach *Chicago, U.S.A.* **119** a2
Oak View *Calif., U.S.A.* 34°24N 119°18W **307** L7
Oak View *Md., U.S.A.* 39°1N 76°58W **143** A4
Oakan-Dake *Japan* 43°27N 144°10E **220** C12
Oakbank *Australia* 33°4S 140°33E **282** B4
Oakdale *Calif., U.S.A.* 37°46N 120°51W **306** H6
Oakdale *Georgia, U.S.A.* 33°51N 84°30W **113** A2
Oakdale *La., U.S.A.* 30°49N 92°40W **314** F8
Oakes *U.S.A.* 46°8N 98°6W **308** B4
Oakesdale *U.S.A.* 47°8N 117°15W **304** C5
Oakey *Australia* 27°25S 151°43E **281** D5
Oakfield *Ga., U.S.A.* 31°47N 83°58W **316** D6
Oakfield *N.Y., U.S.A.* 43°4N 78°16W **312** C6
Oakford *U.S.A.* 40°6N 89°58W **310** D7
Oakham *U.K.* 52°40N 0°43W **169** E7
Oakhurst *U.S.A.* 37°19N 119°40W **306** H7
Oakland *Calif., U.S.A.* 37°48N 122°18W **136** B3
Oakland *Ill., U.S.A.* 39°39N 88°2W **311** E8
Oakland *Md., U.S.A.* 38°53N 76°54W **143** B4
Oakland City *U.S.A.* 38°20N 87°21W **310** F9
Oakland Park *U.S.A.* 26°10N 80°7W **317** J9
Oaklands *Australia* 35°34S 146°10E **283** C7
Oaklawn *U.S.A.* 38°46N 76°56W **143** C4
Oakleigh *Australia* 37°54S 145°5E **128** B2
Oakley *Idaho, U.S.A.* 42°15N 113°53W **304** E7
Oakley *Kans., U.S.A.* 39°8N 100°51W **308** F3
Oakover ➛ *Australia* 21°0S 120°40E **278** D3
Oakridge *U.S.A.* 43°45N 122°28W **304** E2
Oaks, The *Australia* 34°3S 150°34E **283** C9
Oakton *U.S.A.* 38°52N 77°18W **143** B2
Oaktown *U.S.A.* 38°52N 87°27W **311** F9
Oakville *Ont., Canada* 43°27N 79°41W **312** C5
Oakville *Wash., U.S.A.* 46°51N 123°14W **306** D3
Oakwood *U.S.A.* 41°6N 84°23W **311** C12
Oakwood Beach *U.S.A.* 40°33N 74°7W **132** C1
Oamaru *N.Z.* 45°5S 170°59E **285** F5
Ōamishirasato *Japan* 35°31N 140°18E **223** B12
Oancea *Romania* 45°21N 27°42E **183** E12
Oarai *Japan* 36°21N 140°34E **223** A12
Oasi Faunistica di Vendicari ⌂
Italy 36°49N 15°6E **201** F8
Oasis *Calif., U.S.A.* 37°29N 117°55W **306** H9
Oasis *Calif., U.S.A.* 33°28N 116°6W **307** M10
Oates Land *Antarctica* 69°0S 160°0E **151** C11
Oatlands *Australia* 42°17S 147°21E **281** G4
Oatley *Australia* 33°59S 151°4E **139** B1
Oatman *U.S.A.* 35°1N 114°19W **307** K12
Oaxaca *Mexico* 17°3N 96°43W **319** D5
Oaxaca □ *Mexico* 17°0N 96°30W **319** D5
Ob ➛ *Russia* 66°45N 69°30E **214** C7
Oba *Canada* 49°4N 84°7W **298** C3
Obala *Cameroon* 4°9N 11°32E **263** E7
Obalende *Nigeria* 6°26N 3°25E **124** B2
Obama *Fukui, Japan* 35°30N 135°45E **223** B7
Obama *Nagasaki, Japan* 32°43N 130°13E **222** E2
Oban *Nigeria* 5°17N 8°33E **263** D6
Oban *Argyll & Bute, U.K.* 56°25N 5°29W **167** E3
Oba's Palace *Nigeria* 6°26N 3°22E **124** B2
Obbia *Somali Rep.* 5°25N 48°30E **267** C6
Obdorsk = Salekhard
Russia 66°30N 66°35E **214** C7
Obera *Argentina* 27°21S 55°2W **335** B4
Oberammergau *Germany* 47°36N 11°4E **179** H7
Oberasbach *Germany* 49°25N 10°57E **179** F6
Oberbayern □ *Germany* 48°5N 11°50E **179** G7
Oberburg = Gornji Grad
Slovenia 46°20N 14°52E **199** B11
Oberdonau = Oberösterreich □
Austria 48°10N 14°0E **180** C7
Oberdrauburg *Austria* 46°44N 12°58E **180** E5
Obere Donau ⌂ *Germany* 48°5N 9°0E **179** G5
Oberer Bayerischer Wald ⌂
Germany 49°15N 12°40E **179** F8
Oberföhring *Germany* 48°10N 11°37E **131** B2
Oberfranken □ *Germany* 50°10N 11°20E **179** E7
Oberglogau = Głogówek
Poland 50°21N 17°53E **185** H4
Oberhaching *Germany* 48°1N 11°35E **131** B2
Oberhausen *Germany* 51°28N 6°51E **178** D2
Oberkirch *Germany* 48°31N 8°4E **179** G4
Oberlaa *Austria* 48°8N 16°24E **142** B2
Oberlaibach = Vrhnika
Slovenia 45°58N 14°15E **199** C11
Oberlausitz *Germany* 51°16N 14°18E **178** D10
Oberlin *Kans., U.S.A.* 39°49N 100°32W **308** F3
Oberlin *La., U.S.A.* 30°37N 92°46W **314** F8
Oberlin *Ohio, U.S.A.* 41°18N 82°13W **312** E2
Oberlisse *Austria* 48°17N 16°27E **142** A2
Obermenzing *Germany* 48°10N 11°28E **131** A1
Obermoos Schwaige
Germany 48°14N 11°27E **131** A1
Obernai *France* 48°28N 7°30E **173** D14
Oberndorf *Germany* 48°17N 8°34E **179** G4
Obernigk = Oborniki Śląskie
Poland 51°17N 16°53E **185** G3
Oberon *Australia* 33°45S 149°52E **283** B8
Oberösterreich □ *Austria* 48°10N 14°0E **180** C7
Oberpfalz □ *Germany* 49°20N 12°10E **179** F8
Oberpfälzer Wald
Germany 49°30N 12°30E **179** F8
Oberpfälzer Wald ⌂
Germany 49°40N 12°20E **179** F8
Oberschleissheim
Germany 48°15N 11°33E **131** A2
Oberschöneweide
Germany 52°27N 13°31E **115** B4
Oberstdorf *Germany* 47°24N 10°15E **179** H6
Oberting *Gabon* 0°22S 9°46E **264** C1
Obertyn *Ukraine* 48°42N 25°10E **183** B10
Oberursel *Germany* 50°11N 8°35E **179** E4
Oberwart *Austria* 47°17N 16°12E **181** D9
Obi, Kepulauan *Indonesia* 1°23S 127°45E **231** E7
Obiaruku *Nigeria* 5°51N 6°9E **263** D6
Óbidos *Brazil* 1°50S 55°30W **329** D6
Óbidos *Portugal* 39°19N 9°10W **195** F1
Obihiro *Japan* 42°56N 143°12E **220** C11
Obilatu *Indonesia* 1°25S 127°20E **231** E7
Obilnoye *Russia* 47°32N 44°30E **191** G7
Obing *Germany* 48°0N 12°24E **179** G8
Objat *France* 45°16N 1°24E **174** C5
Oblong *U.S.A.* 39°0N 87°55W **311** F9
Obluchye *Russia* 49°1N 131°4E **215** E14
Obninsk *Russia* 55°8N 36°37E **188** E9
Obo *C.A.R.* 5°20N 26°32E **264** A5
Oboa, Mt. *Uganda* 1°45N 34°45E **268** B3
Obock *Djibouti* 12°0N 43°20E **257** E5
Obodivka *Ukraine* 48°24N 29°15E **183** B14
Oborniki *Poland* 52°39N 16°50E **185** F3
Oborniki Śląskie *Poland* 51°17N 16°53E **185** G3
Obouya *Congo* 0°56S 15°43E **264** C3
Oboyan *Russia* 51°15N 36°21E **189** G9
Obozerskaya = Obozerskiy
Russia 63°34N 40°21E **186** B7
Obozerskiy *Russia* 63°34N 40°21E **186** B7
Obrenovac *Serbia* 44°40N 20°11E **202** B4
O'Brien *U.S.A.* 30°2N 82°57W **316** E7
Obrovac *Croatia* 44°11N 15°41E **199** D12
Obruk *Turkey* 38°7N 33°12E **212** C5
Obrzycko *Poland* 52°42N 16°32E **185** F3
Observatory *Sydney, Australia* **139** a1
Observatory *Gauteng,*
S. Africa 26°10S 28°4E **123** B2
Observatory Inlet
Canada 55°10N 129°54W **296** B3

Obshchi Syrt Russia 52°0N 53°0E 158 E16
Obskaya Guba Russia 69°0N 73°0E 214 C8
Obuasi Ghana 6°17N 1°40W 263 D4
Obubra Nigeria 6°8N 8°20E 263 D6
Óbuda Hungary 47°33N 19°2E 117 A2
Obudu Nigeria 6°38N 9°5E 263 D6
Obukhovo Russia 59°53N 30°22E 137 B2
Obura Papua N. G. 6°33S 145°58E 286 D3
Obvodnyy Kanal Russia 59°54N 30°20E 137 B1
Obwalden □ Switz. 46°55N 8°15E 179 J4
Obzor Bulgaria 42°50N 27°52E 203 D11
Ocala U.S.A. 29°11N 82°8W 317 F7
Ocamo → Venezuela 2°48N 65°14W 329 C4
Ocampo Chihuahua, Mexico 28°11N 108°23W 318 B3
Ocampo Tamaulipas, Mexico 22°50N 99°20W 319 C5
Ocaña Colombia 8°15N 73°20W 328 B3
Ocaña Spain 39°55N 3°30W 194 F7
Occidental, Cordillera Colombia 5°0N 76°0W 328 C2
Occidental, Cordillera Peru 14°0S 74°0W 330 C3
Occidental, Grand Erg Algeria 30°20N 1°0E 261 B5
Ocean City Md., U.S.A. 38°20N 75°5W 309 F16
Ocean City N.J., U.S.A. 39°17N 74°35W 309 F16
Ocean City Wash., U.S.A. 47°4N 124°10W 306 C2
Ocean Falls Canada 52°18N 127°48W 296 C3
Ocean I. = Banaba Kiribati 0°45S 169°50E 288 H8
Ocean Park Hong Kong, China 22°13N 114°10E 122 B2
Ocean Park Wash., U.S.A. 46°30N 124°3W 306 D2
Oceano U.S.A. 35°6N 120°37W 307 K6
Oceanport U.S.A. 40°19N 74°3W 313 F10
Oceanside U.S.A. 33°12N 117°23W 307 M9
Ochagavía Spain 42°55N 1°5W 196 C3
Ochakiv Ukraine 46°37N 31°33E 189 J6
Ochakovo Russia 55°41N 37°26E 129 B2
Ochamchira Georgia 42°46N 41°32E 191 J5
Ochi, Oros Greece 38°5N 24°25E 204 C6
Ochiai Japan 35°1N 133°45E 222 B5
Ochil Hills U.K. 56°14N 3°40W 167 E5
Ochlocknee U.S.A. 30°58N 84°3W 316 E5
Ochlockonee → U.S.A. 29°59N 84°26W 316 F5
Ocho Rios Jamaica 18°24N 77°6W 320 a
Ochopee U.S.A. 25°54N 81°18W 317 K8
Ochota Poland 52°13N 20°58E 142 B1
Ochsenfurt Germany 49°40N 10°4E 179 F6
Ochsenhausen Germany 48°4N 9°57E 179 G5
Ocilla U.S.A. 31°36N 83°15W 316 D6
Ockelbo Sweden 60°54N 16°45E 162 D10
Ocmulgee → U.S.A. 31°58N 82°33W 316 D7
Ocmulgee ⌓ U.S.A. 32°49N 83°37W 316 C6
Ocna Mureş Romania 46°23N 23°55E 183 D8
Ocna Sibiului Romania 45°52N 24°2E 183 E9
Ocnele Mari Romania 45°8N 24°18E 183 E9
Ocniţa Moldova 48°25N 27°30E 183 B12
Ocoee U.S.A. 28°34N 81°32W 133 A1
Ocoña Peru 16°26S 73°8W 330 D3
Ocoña → Peru 16°28S 73°8W 330 D3
Oconee → U.S.A. 31°58N 82°33W 316 D7
Oconee, L. U.S.A. 33°28N 83°15W 316 B6
O'Connell Street Dublin, Ireland 120 b2
Oconomowoc U.S.A. 43°7N 88°30W 311 A8
Oconto U.S.A. 44°53N 87°52W 308 C10
Oconto Falls U.S.A. 44°52N 88°9W 308 C9
Ocosingo Mexico 16°53N 92°6W 319 D6
Ocotal Nic. 13°41N 86°31W 320 D2
Ocotlán Jalisco, Mexico 20°21N 102°46W 318 C4
Ocotlán Oaxaca, Mexico 16°48N 96°40W 319 D5
Ocreza → Portugal 39°32N 7°50W 195 F3
Ócsa Hungary 47°17N 19°15E 182 C4
Octeville France 49°38N 1°40W 172 C5
Ocumare del Tuy Venezuela 10°7N 66°46W 328 A4
Ocuri Bolivia 18°45S 65°50W 331 D4
Oda Ghana 5°50N 0°51W 263 D4
Ōda Shimane, Japan 35°11N 132°30E 222 B4
Oda, J. Sudan 20°21N 36°39E 256 C4
Ódáðahraun Iceland 65°5N 17°0W 155 B9
Ŏdaejin N. Korea 41°34N 129°40E 224 B4
Odaesan △ S. Korea 37°40N 128°30E 224 D4
Ödåkra Sweden 56°7N 12°45E 163 H6
Ōdana Japan 35°33N 139°35E 140 B2
Odate Japan 40°16N 140°34E 220 D10
Odawara Japan 35°20N 139°6E 223 B11
Odda Norway 60°3N 6°35E 164 D3
Odder Denmark 55°58N 10°10E 163 J4
Oddur Somali Rep. 4°11N 43°52E 267 D5
Odei → Canada 56°6N 96°54W 297 B9
Odell U.S.A. 41°0N 88°31W 311 C8
Odemira Portugal 37°35N 8°40W 195 H2
Ödemiş Turkey 38°15N 28°0E 205 C9
Öden-Stockach Germany 48°5N 11°41E 131 B3
Ödenburg = Sopron Hungary 47°45N 16°32E 182 C1
Odendaalsrus S. Africa 27°48S 26°45E 270 C4
Odensbacken Sweden 59°10N 15°32E 162 E9
Odense Denmark 55°22N 10°23E 163 J4
Odenwald = Neckartal-Odenwald ⌓ Germany 49°30N 9°5E 179 F5
Odenwald Germany 49°35N 9°0E 179 F5
Oder → Europe 53°33N 14°38E 178 B10
Oder-Havel Kanal Germany 52°52N 14°2E 178 C10
Oderzo Italy 45°47N 12°29E 199 C9
Odesa Ukraine 46°30N 30°45E 189 J6
Odesa □ Ukraine 47°20N 29°55E 189 J5
Ödeshög Sweden 58°14N 14°39E 163 F8
Odessa = Odesa Ukraine 46°30N 30°45E 189 J6
Odessa Ont., Canada 44°17N 76°43W 313 B8
Odessa Mo., U.S.A. 39°0N 93°57W 310 F3
Odessa Tex., U.S.A. 31°52N 102°23W 314 F3
Odessa Wash., U.S.A. 47°20N 118°41W 304 C4
Odiakwe Botswana 20°12S 25°17E 270 B4
Odiel → Spain 37°10N 6°55W 195 H4
Odienné Ivory C. 9°30N 7°34W 262 D3
Odilampi Finland 60°18N 24°45E 121 B1
Odimba Gabon 2°2S 9°33E 264 C2
Odintsovo Russia 55°40N 37°16E 129 B1
Odiongan Phil. 12°24N 121°59E 232 E3
Odivelas Portugal 38°47N 9°10W 126 A1
Odobeşti Romania 45°43N 27°4E 183 E12
Odolanów Poland 51°34N 17°40E 185 G4
Odolany Poland 52°13N 20°55E 142 B1
O'Donnell U.S.A. 32°58N 101°50W 314 E4
Odorheiu Secuiesc Romania 46°21N 25°21E 183 D10
Odoyevo Russia 53°56N 36°42E 188 F9
Odra = Oder → Europe 53°33N 14°38E 178 B10
Odra → Spain 42°14N 4°17W 194 C6
Odum U.S.A. 31°40N 82°2W 316 D7
Odweina Somali Rep. 9°25N 45°4E 267 C6
Odžaci Serbia 45°30N 19°17E 182 E4
Odžak Bos.-H. 45°3N 18°18E 182 E3
Odzala Congo 0°37N 14°37E 264 B2
Odzala △ Congo 0°55N 14°55E 264 B2
Odzi Zimbabwe 19°0S 32°20E 271 A5
Odzi → Zimbabwe 19°45S 32°23E 271 A5
Oebisfelde Germany 52°27N 10°57E 178 C6
Oedong S. Korea 35°42N 129°14E 224 E4
Oeiras Brazil 7°0S 42°8W 332 C3
Oeiras Portugal 38°41N 9°18W 126 A1
Oeiras do Para Brazil 1°58S 49°51W 329 D8
Oelrichs U.S.A. 43°11N 103°14W 308 D2
Oels in Schlesien = Oleśnica Poland 51°13N 17°22E 185 G4
Oelsnitz Germany 50°24N 12°10E 179 E8
Oelwein U.S.A. 42°41N 91°55W 310 B5
Oenarodo S. Korea 34°26N 127°30E 224 E3
Oeno I. Pac. Oc. 24°0S 131°0W 289 K14
Oenpelli = Gunbalanya Australia 12°20S 133°4E 278 B5
Oetz Austria 47°13N 10°53E 180 D3
Of Turkey 40°59N 40°23E 213 B9
O'Fallon U.S.A. 38°49N 90°42W 310 F6
Ofanto → Italy 41°22N 16°13E 201 A9
Offa Nigeria 8°13N 4°42E 263 D5
Offaly □ Ireland 53°15N 7°30W 166 C4
Offenbach Germany 50°6N 8°44E 179 E4
Offenburg Germany 48°28N 7°56E 179 G3
Officer Cr. → Australia 27°46S 132°30E 279 E5
Offida Italy 42°56N 13°41E 199 F10
Offoué → Gabon 0°4S 11°44E 264 C2
Ofidousa Greece 36°33N 26°8E 205 E8
Ofin Nigeria 6°32N 3°30E 124 A3
Ofolanga Tonga 19°38S 174°27W 287 P13
Ofotfjorden Norway 68°27N 17°0E 160 B17
Ofte Norway 59°30N 8°12E 164 E5
Ofu Amer. Samoa 14°11S 169°41W 302 g
Ōfunato Japan 39°4N 141°43E 220 E10
Oga Japan 39°55N 139°50E 220 E9
Oga-Hantō Japan 39°58N 139°47E 220 E9
Ogaden Ethiopia 7°30N 45°30E 267 C6
Ōgaki Japan 35°21N 136°37E 223 B8
Ogallala U.S.A. 41°8N 101°43W 308 E3
Ogan → Indonesia 3°1S 104°44E 234 C2
Ogasawara Gunto Pac. Oc. 27°0N 142°0E 288 E6
Ogawa Japan 35°44N 139°28E 140 A1
Ogbomosho Nigeria 8°1N 4°11E 263 D5
Ogden Iowa, U.S.A. 42°2N 94°2W 310 B2
Ogden Utah, U.S.A. 41°13N 111°58W 304 F8
Ogden Park U.S.A. 41°46N 87°39W 119 C2
Ogden Slip Chicago, U.S.A. 119 b3
Ogdensburg U.S.A. 44°42N 75°30W 313 B9
Ogea Driki Fiji 19°12S 178°27W 287 B3
Ogea Levu Fiji 19°8S 178°24W 287 B3
Ogeechee → U.S.A. 31°50N 81°3W 316 D8
Ogikubo Japan 35°42N 139°37E 140 A2
Ogilby U.S.A. 32°49N 114°50W 307 N12
Oglat Beraber Algeria 30°15N 3°34W 260 B4
Oglats de Khenachiche Mali 21°51N 3°58W 260 D4
Oglesby U.S.A. 41°18N 89°4W 310 C7
Oglethorpe U.S.A. 32°18N 84°4W 316 C5
Oglio → Italy 45°2N 10°39E 198 C7
Óglio Nord ⌓ Italy 45°22N 9°54E 198 C6
Óglio Sud ⌓ Italy 45°7N 10°24E 198 C7
Ogmore Australia 22°37S 149°35E 280 C4
Ognon → France 47°16N 5°28E 173 E12
Ogogoro Nigeria 6°25N 3°24E 124 B2
Ogoja Nigeria 6°38N 8°39E 263 D6
Ogoki Canada 51°38N 85°58W 298 B2
Ogoki → Canada 51°38N 85°57W 298 B2
Ogoki L. Canada 50°50N 87°10W 298 B2
Ogoki Res. Canada 50°45N 88°15W 298 B2
Ogooué → Gabon 1°0S 9°0E 264 C1
Ogōri Japan 34°6N 131°24E 222 C3
Ogosta → Bulgaria 43°48N 23°55E 202 C7
Ogoueïleten Nmâdi Mauritania 19°46N 11°1W 260 E2
Ogowe = Ogooué → Gabon 1°0S 9°0E 264 C1
Ogoyo Nigeria 6°25N 3°29E 124 B2
Ogr = Sharafa Sudan 11°59N 27°7E 257 E2
Ograźden Macedonia 41°30N 22°50E 202 E6
Ogre Latvia 56°49N 24°36E 188 D3
Ogrein Sudan 17°55N 34°50E 256 D3
Ogudu Nigeria 6°34N 3°24E 124 A2
Ogulin Croatia 45°16N 15°16E 199 C12
Ogun □ Nigeria 7°0N 3°0E 263 D5
Oguni Japan 33°11N 131°8E 222 D3
Ögur Iceland 66°2N 22°44W 155 A4
Ogurchinskiy, Ostrov Turkmenistan 38°55N 53°2E 247 B7
Oguta Nigeria 5°44N 6°44E 263 D6
Oğuzeli Turkey 36°58N 37°27E 250 B8
Ogwashi-Uku Nigeria 6°15N 6°30E 263 D6
Ogwe Nigeria 5°0N 7°14E 263 E6
Ohai N.Z. 45°55S 168°0E 285 F3
Ohakune N.Z. 39°24S 175°24E 284 F4
Ohanet Algeria 28°44N 8°46E 261 C6
Ōhara Japan 35°15N 140°23E 223 B12
O'Hare Int., Chicago ✈ (ORD) U.S.A. 41°59N 87°54W 119 B1
Ohariu Stream → N.Z. 41°12S 174°47E 143 B1
Ohata Japan 41°24N 141°10E 220 D10
Ohatchee U.S.A. 33°47N 86°0W 316 B4
Ohau, L. N.Z. 44°15S 169°53E 285 E4
Ohaupo N.Z. 37°56S 175°20E 284 D4
O'Higgins, C. Chile 27°5S 109°15W 330 b
O'Higgins, Parque Chile 33°27S 70°40W 137 B2
Ohio □ U.S.A. 40°15N 82°45W 312 F2
Ohio → U.S.A. 36°59N 89°8W 311 G8
Ohio City U.S.A. 40°46N 84°37W 311 D12
Ohiwa Harbour N.Z. 37°59S 177°10E 284 D6
Ohlau = Oława Poland 50°57N 17°20E 185 H4
Ohře → Czech Rep. 50°30N 14°10E 180 A7
Ohre → Sachsen-Anhalt, Germany 52°18N 11°46E 178 C7
Ohrid Macedonia 41°8N 20°52E 202 E4
Ohridsko Jezero Macedonia 41°8N 20°52E 202 E4
Ohrigstad S. Africa 24°39S 30°36E 271 B5
Öhringen Germany 49°12N 9°31E 179 F5
Ohura N.Z. 38°51S 174°59E 284 E3
Oi Qu China 28°37N 98°16E 228 C2
Oiapoque Brazil 3°50N 51°50W 329 C7
Oiapoque → S. Amer. 4°8N 51°40W 329 C7
Oikou China 38°35N 117°42E 227 E9
Oil City U.S.A. 41°26N 79°42W 312 E5
Oil Springs Canada 42°47N 82°7W 312 D2
Oildale U.S.A. 35°25N 119°1W 307 K7
Ōimachi Japan 35°35N 139°43E 140 B3
Oinousa = Inousses Greece 38°33N 26°14E 205 C8
Oise □ France 49°28N 2°30E 173 C9
Oise → France 49°0N 2°4E 173 C9
Oiseaux du Djoudj △ Senegal 16°24N 16°14W 262 B1
Oistins Barbados 13°4N 59°33W 323 r
Ōita Japan 33°14N 131°36E 222 D3
Ōita □ Japan 33°15N 131°30E 222 D3
Oiticica Brazil 5°3S 41°5W 332 C3
Ojai U.S.A. 34°27N 119°15W 307 L7
Ojcowski △ Poland 50°15N 19°50E 185 H6
Ojhar India 20°6N 73°56E 244 D1
Ojinaga Mexico 29°34N 104°25W 318 B4
Ojiya Japan 37°18N 138°48E 221 F9
Ojo Caliente Mexico 21°53N 102°15W 318 C4
Ojos del Salado, Cerro Argentina 27°0S 68°40W 334 B2
Ojota Nigeria 6°35N 3°23E 124 A2
Oka → Russia 56°20N 43°59E 190 B7
Okaba Indonesia 8°6S 139°42E 231 F9
Okahandja Namibia 22°0S 16°59E 270 B2
Okahukura N.Z. 38°48S 175°14E 284 E4
Okaihau N.Z. 35°19S 173°47E 284 B2
Okalataka Congo 0°18S 14°54E 264 C2
Okanagan L. Canada 50°0N 119°30W 296 D5
Okandja Gabon 0°35S 13°45E 264 C2
Okano → Gabon 0°5S 10°57E 264 C2
Okanogan U.S.A. 48°22N 119°35W 304 B4
Okanogan → U.S.A. 48°6N 119°44W 304 B4
Okanogan Range N. Amer. 49°0N 119°55W 296 D5
Okány Hungary 46°52N 21°21E 182 D6
Okapa Papua N. G. 6°38S 145°39E 286 D3
Okapi △ Dem. Rep. of the Congo 2°30N 27°20E 268 B2
Okaputa Namibia 20°5S 17°0E 270 B2
Okara Pakistan 30°50N 73°31E 242 D5
Okarito N.Z. 43°15S 170°9E 285 D5
Okato N.Z. 39°12S 173°53E 284 F2
Okau Micronesia 9°32N 138°6E 287 R16
Okaukuejo Namibia 19°10S 16°0E 270 A2
Okavango Delta Botswana 18°45S 22°45E 270 A3
Okavango Swamp = Okavango Delta Botswana 18°45S 22°45E 270 A3
Ōkawa Japan 33°9N 130°21E 222 D2
Okawville U.S.A. 38°26N 89°33W 310 F7
Okaya Japan 36°5N 138°10E 223 A10
Okayama Japan 34°40N 133°54E 222 C5
Okayama □ Japan 35°0N 133°50E 222 C5
Okazaki Japan 34°57N 137°10E 223 C9
Oke-Iho Nigeria 8°1N 3°18E 263 D5
Okęcie Poland 52°11N 20°56E 142 B1
Okęcie, Warszawa ✈ (WAW) Poland 52°9N 20°59E 142 B1
Okeechobee U.S.A. 27°15N 80°50W 317 H9
Okeechobee, L. U.S.A. 27°0N 80°50W 317 J9
Okefenokee ⌓ U.S.A. 30°45N 82°18W 316 E7
Okefenokee Swamp U.S.A. 30°40N 82°20W 316 E7
Okehampton U.K. 50°44N 4°0W 169 G4
Okelra Nigeria 6°29N 3°22E 124 B2
Okemos U.S.A. 42°43N 84°26W 311 B12
Okene Nigeria 7°32N 6°11E 263 D6
Okeogbe Nigeria 6°24N 3°23E 124 B2
Oker → Germany 52°32N 10°22E 178 C6
Okha Gujarat, India 22°27N 69°4E 242 H3
Okha Russia 53°40N 143°0E 215 D15
Okhla India 28°33N 77°16E 120 B2
Okhotsk Russia 59°20N 143°10E 215 D15
Okhotsk, Sea of Asia 55°0N 145°0E 215 D15
Okhotskiy Perevoz Russia 61°52N 135°35E 215 C14
Okhta → Russia 59°56N 30°25E 137 B2
Okhtyrka Ukraine 50°25N 35°0E 189 G8
Oki-no-Shima Japan 32°44N 132°33E 222 E4
Oki-Shotō Japan 36°5N 133°15E 222 A5
Okiep S. Africa 29°39S 17°53E 270 C2
Okigwi Nigeria 5°52N 7°20E 263 D6
Okija Nigeria 5°54N 6°55E 263 D6
Okinawa Japan 26°19N 127°46E 288 a
Okinawa □ Japan 26°40N 128°0E 288 a
Okinawa-Guntō Japan 26°40N 128°0E 221 L4
Okinawa-Jima Japan 26°32N 128°0E 221 L4
Okino-erabu-Shima Japan 27°21N 128°33E 221 L4
Okitipupa Nigeria 6°31N 4°50E 263 D5
Okkervil → Russia 59°56N 30°30E 137 B2
Oklahoma □ U.S.A. 35°20N 97°30W 314 D6
Oklahoma City U.S.A. 35°30N 97°30W 314 D6
Oklawaha → U.S.A. 29°28N 81°41W 317 F8
Okmulgee U.S.A. 35°37N 95°58W 314 D7
Oknitsa = Ocniţa Moldova 48°25N 27°30E 183 B12
Oko, W. → Sudan 21°15N 35°56E 256 C4
Okolo Uganda 2°37N 31°8E 268 B3
Okolona Ky., U.S.A. 38°8N 85°41W 311 F11
Okolona Miss., U.S.A. 34°0N 88°45W 315 E10
Okombahe Namibia 21°23S 15°22E 270 B2
Okonek Poland 53°32N 16°51E 184 E3
Okotoks Canada 50°43N 113°58W 296 C6
Okoyo Congo 1°28S 15°0E 264 C3
Okrika Nigeria 4°40N 7°10E 263 E6
Okrzeszyn Poland 52°8N 21°8E 142 C2
Oksapmin Papua N. G. 5°17S 142°15E 286 C2
Øksendalsøra Norway 62°42N 8°27E 164 B5
Oksibil Indonesia 4°59S 140°35E 231 E10
Øksna Norway 60°58N 11°27E 164 D8
Oksovskiy Russia 62°33N 39°57E 186 B6
Oksval Norway 59°51N 10°40E 133 A3
Oktabrsk = Oktyabrsk Kazakhstan 49°28N 57°25E 187 E10
Oktwin Burma 18°49N 96°26E 241 F6
Oktyabrsk Kazakhstan 49°28N 57°25E 187 E10
Oktyabrsk Russia 53°11N 48°40E 190 D9
Oktyabrskiy = Aktsyabrski Belarus 52°38N 28°53E 177 B15
Oktyabrskiy Bashkortostan, Russia 54°28N 53°28E 186 D9
Oktyabrskiy Moskva, Russia 55°41N 37°35E 129 B3
Oktyabrskiy Rostov, Russia 47°30N 40°4E 191 G5
Oktyabrskoy Revolyutsii, Ostrov Russia 79°30N 97°0E 215 B10
Oktyabrskoye = Zhovtneve Ukraine 46°54N 32°3E 189 J7
Okubo Tokyo, Japan 140 a2
Ōkuchi Japan 32°4N 130°37E 222 E2
Okulovka Russia 58°25N 33°19E 188 C7
Ōkura Japan 35°35N 139°27E 140 B1
Okuru N.Z. 43°55S 168°55E 285 D3
Okushiri-Tō Japan 42°15N 139°30E 220 C9
Okuta Nigeria 9°14N 3°12E 263 D5
Okwa → Botswana 22°30S 23°0E 270 B3
Ola U.S.A. 35°2N 93°13W 314 D8
Ólafsfjörður Iceland 66°4N 18°39W 155 A8
Ólafsvík Iceland 64°53N 23°43W 155 C3
Olaine Latvia 56°48N 23°59E 184 B10
Olancha U.S.A. 36°17N 118°1W 307 J8
Olancha Pk. U.S.A. 36°16N 118°7W 307 J8
Olanchito Honduras 15°30N 86°30W 320 C2
Öland Sweden 56°45N 16°38E 163 H10
Ölands norra udde Sweden 57°22N 17°5E 163 G11
Ölands södra udde Sweden 56°12N 16°23E 163 H10
Olanta U.S.A. 33°56N 79°56W 316 B10
Olar U.S.A. 33°11N 81°11W 316 B8
Olargues France 43°34N 2°53E 174 E6
Olari Finland 60°10N 24°44E 121 B1
Olaria Brazil 22°50S 43°16W 135 B1
Olary Australia 32°18S 140°19E 282 B4
Olascoaga Argentina 35°15S 60°39W 334 D3
Olathe U.S.A. 38°53N 94°49W 308 F6
Olavarría Argentina 36°55S 60°20W 334 D3
Oława Poland 50°57N 17°20E 185 H4
Olbernhau Germany 50°40N 13°19E 178 E9
Ólbia Italy 40°55N 9°31E 200 B2
Ólbia, G. di Italy 40°55N 9°39E 200 B2
Olching Germany 48°12N 11°21E 179 G7
Olcott U.S.A. 43°20N 78°42W 312 C6
Old Admiralty Russia 59°55N 30°20E 137 B1
Old Bahama Chan. = Bahama, Canal Viejo de W. Indies 22°10N 77°30W 320 B4
Old Baldy Pk. = San Antonio, Mt. U.S.A. 34°17N 117°38W 307 L9
Old Bar Australia 31°58S 152°35E 283 A10
Old Bridge U.S.A. 40°25N 74°22W 313 F10
Old Castile = Castilla y Leon □ Spain 42°0N 5°0W 194 D6
Old City Shanghai, China 31°13N 121°29E 138 B1
Old City Delhi, India 120 a3
Old City Jerusalem 123 b3
Old City Hall Toronto, Canada 141 b2
Old Crow Canada 67°30N 139°55W 294 C6
Old Dale U.S.A. 34°8N 115°47W 307 L11
Old Forge N.Y., U.S.A. 43°43N 74°58W 313 C10
Old Forge Pa., U.S.A. 41°22N 75°45W 313 E9
Old Fort = Purana Qila Delhi, India 120 c3
Old Fort B. Bahamas 25°3N 77°32W 153 b
Old Fort Pt. Montserrat 16°40N 62°11W 323 p
Old Fort York Canada 43°39N 79°24W 141 B2
Old Harbor Alaska, U.S.A. 57°12N 153°18W 303 H9
Old Harbor Mass., U.S.A. 42°19N 71°1W 116 B2
Old Harbour Jamaica 17°56N 77°7W 320 a
Old Harbour Bay Jamaica 17°54N 77°6W 320 a
Old Ironside Boston, U.S.A. 116 a3
Old Perlican Canada 48°5N 53°1W 299 C9
Old Road Bluff Antigua & B. 16°59N 61°50W 322 b
Old Road Town St. Kitts & Nevis 17°17N 62°47W 322 d
Old Roundhouse Toronto, Canada 141 c1
Old Shinyanga Tanzania 3°33S 33°27E 268 C3
Old Speck Mt. U.S.A. 44°34N 70°57W 313 B14
Old Town = Stare Miasto Warsaw, Poland 142 a2
Old Town Edinburgh, U.K. 121 a2
Old Town Fla., U.S.A. 29°36N 82°59W 317 F7
Old Town Ill., U.S.A. 41°54N 87°37W 119 B3
Old Town Maine, U.S.A. 44°56N 68°39W 309 C19
Old Town Hall = Altes Rathaus Munich, Germany 131 b3
Old Town Square Warsaw, Poland 142 a2
Old Washington U.S.A. 40°2N 81°27W 312 F3
Old Wives L. Canada 50°5N 106°0W 297 C7
Oldbawn Ireland 53°17N 6°21W 120 B1
Oldbury U.K. 51°38N 2°33W 169 F5
Oldcastle Ireland 53°46N 7°10W 166 C4
Oldeani Tanzania 3°22S 35°35E 268 C4
Olden Norway 61°49N 6°49E 164 C3
Oldenburg Niedersachsen, Germany 53°9N 8°13E 178 B4
Oldenburg Schleswig-Holstein, Germany 54°17N 10°52E 178 A6
Oldenzaal Neths. 52°19N 6°53E 170 B6
Oldham U.K. 53°33N 2°7W 168 D5
Oldman → Canada 49°57N 111°42W 296 D6
Oldmeldrum U.K. 57°20N 2°19W 167 D6
Olds Canada 51°50N 114°10W 296 C6
Oldsmar U.S.A. 28°2N 82°39W 317 G7
Olduvai Gorge Tanzania 2°57S 35°23E 268 C4
Oldziyt Mongolia 44°40N 109°1E 226 B5
Ole Rømer Land Greenland 74°10N 24°30W 154 C8
Olean U.S.A. 42°5N 78°26W 312 D6
Olecko Poland 54°2N 22°31E 184 D9
Oléggio Italy 45°36N 8°38E 198 C5
Oleiros Portugal 39°56N 7°56W 194 F3
Oleiros Spain 43°20N 8°19W 194 B2
Olekma → Russia 60°22N 120°42E 215 C13
Olekminsk Russia 60°25N 120°30E 215 C13
Oleksandriya Kirovohrad, Ukraine 48°42N 33°3E 189 H7
Oleksandriya Rivne, Ukraine 50°37N 26°19E 177 C14
Oleksandrovka Ukraine 48°55N 32°20E 189 H7
Olema U.S.A. 38°3N 122°47W 306 G4
Ølen Norway 59°36N 5°48E 164 E2
Olenegorsk Russia 68°9N 33°18E 160 B25
Olenek Russia 68°28N 112°18E 215 C12
Olenek → Russia 73°0N 120°10E 215 B13
Olenino Russia 56°15N 33°30E 188 D7
Olenya = Olenegorsk Russia 68°9N 33°18E 160 B25
Oléron, Î. d' France 45°55N 1°15W 174 C2
Olesk Ukraine 51°6N 24°11E 185 G11
Oleśnica Poland 51°13N 17°22E 185 G4
Olesno Poland 50°51N 18°26E 185 H5
Olevsk Ukraine 51°12N 27°39E 177 C14
Olga Russia 43°50N 135°14E 215 E14
Olga, L. Canada 49°47N 77°15W 298 C4
Olgas, The = Kata Tjuta Australia 25°20S 130°50E 279 E5
Olgino Russia 60°0N 30°10E 137 A1
Ölgiy Mongolia 48°56N 89°57E 217 C11
Ølgod Denmark 55°49N 8°36E 163 J2
Olhão Portugal 37°3N 7°48W 195 H3
Olhopil Ukraine 48°12N 29°30E 183 B14
Olhovatka Russia 54°30N 22°18E 184 D9
Olib Croatia 44°23N 14°44E 199 D11
Oliena Italy 40°16N 9°24E 200 B2
Oliete Spain 41°1N 0°41W 196 D4
Olifants = Elefantes → Africa 24°10S 32°40E 271 B5
Olifants → Namibia 25°30S 19°30E 270 B2
Olifantshoek S. Africa 27°57S 22°42E 270 C3
Olimbos Greece 35°44N 27°11E 205 F9
Ólimbos, Óros = Olymbos Oros Greece 40°6N 22°23E 202 F6
Olímpia Brazil 20°44S 48°54W 335 A6
Olimpico, Estadio Mexico 19°20N 99°11W 128 C1
Olimpos-Beydaglari △ Turkey 36°36N 30°30E 205 E12
Olin U.S.A. 42°0N 91°9W 310 B5
Olinda Brazil 8°1S 34°51W 332 C5
Olindiná Brazil 11°22S 38°21W 332 D4
Olite Spain 42°29N 1°40W 196 C3
Oliva Argentina 32°0S 63°38W 334 C3
Oliva Spain 38°58N 0°9W 197 G4
Oliva, Punta del Spain 43°37N 5°28W 194 B5
Oliva de la Frontera Spain 38°17N 6°54W 195 G4
Olivais Portugal 38°45N 9°7W 126 A2
Olivar de los Padres Mexico 19°21N 99°14W 128 B1
Olivar del Conde Mexico 19°22N 99°12W 128 B1
Olivares Spain 39°46N 2°20W 196 F2
Olive Branch U.S.A. 34°57N 89°49W 315 D10
Olive Hill U.S.A. 38°18N 83°13W 311 F13
Olive Park Chicago, U.S.A. 119 b3
Olivehurst U.S.A. 39°6N 121°34W 306 F5
Oliveira Brazil 20°39S 44°50W 333 F3
Oliveira de Azeméis Portugal 40°49N 8°29W 194 E2
Oliveira do Douro Portugal 41°5N 8°2W 194 D2
Oliveira dos Brejinhos Brazil 12°19S 42°54W 333 D3
Olivenza Spain 38°41N 7°9W 195 G3
Oliver Canada 49°13N 119°37W 296 D5
Oliver L. Canada 56°56N 103°22W 297 B8
Olives, Mt. of West Bank 31°46N 35°15E 123 B2
Olivet Loiret, France 47°51N 1°55E 173 E8
Olivet Mich., U.S.A. 42°27N 84°56W 311 B12
Olivia, L. U.S.A. 28°31N 81°31W 133 A1
Olivine Ra. N.Z. 44°15S 168°30E 285 E3
Olivos Argentina 34°30S 58°28W 117 B2
Olkhovka Russia 49°48N 44°32E 190 F7
Olkusz Poland 50°18N 19°33E 185 H6
Ollachea Peru 13°49S 70°29W 330 C3
Ollagüe Chile 21°15S 68°10W 334 A2
Olloua Congo 0°54S 14°34E 264 C2
Olmaliq Uzbekistan 40°50N 69°35E 217 D7
Olmedo Spain 41°20N 4°43W 194 D6
Olmeto France 41°43N 8°55E 175 G12
Olmos Peru 5°59S 79°46W 330 B2
Olmütz = Olomouc Czech Rep. 49°38N 17°12E 181 B10
Olney Ill., U.S.A. 38°44N 88°5W 311 F8
Olney Tex., U.S.A. 33°22N 98°45W 314 E5
Olofström Sweden 56°17N 14°32E 163 H8
Oloitokitok Kenya 2°56S 37°30E 268 C4
Ololi Congo 0°15S 14°36E 264 C2
Oloma Cameroon 3°29N 11°19E 263 E7
Olomane → Canada 50°14N 60°37W 299 B7
Olombo Congo 1°18S 15°53E 264 C3
Olomouc Czech Rep. 49°38N 17°12E 181 B10
Olomoucký □ Czech Rep. 49°45N 17°5E 181 B10
Olona → Italy 45°29N 9°6E 129 B1
Olonets Russia 61°0N 32°54E 188 B7
Olongapo Phil. 14°50N 120°18E 232 D3
Olonne-sur-Mer France 46°32N 1°47W 174 B2
Oloron, Gave d' → France 43°33N 1°5W 174 E2
Oloron-Ste-Marie France 43°11N 0°38W 174 E3
Olosega Amer. Samoa 14°10S 169°37W 302 g
Olosenga = Swains I. Amer. Samoa 11°11S 171°4W 289 J11
Olot Spain 42°11N 2°30E 196 C7
Olovo Bos.-H. 44°8N 18°35E 182 F3
Olovyannaya Russia 50°58N 115°35E 215 D12
Olowalu U.S.A. 20°49N 156°38W 302 C5
Oloy → Russia 66°29N 159°29E 215 C16
Olsberg Germany 51°21N 8°31E 178 D4
Olshammar Sweden 58°45N 14°48E 163 F8
Olshanka Ukraine 48°16N 30°58E 189 H6
Olshany Ukraine 50°3N 35°53E 189 G8
Olsztyn Poland 53°48N 20°29E 184 E7
Olsztynek Poland 53°34N 20°19E 184 E7
Olt □ Romania 44°20N 24°30E 183 F9
Olt → Romania 43°43N 24°51E 183 G9
Oltedal Norway 58°49N 6°2E 164 F3
Olten Switz. 47°21N 7°53E 179 H3
Olteniţa Romania 44°7N 26°42E 183 F11
Olton U.S.A. 34°11N 102°8W 314 D3
Oltu Turkey 40°35N 41°58E 213 B9
Oluan Pi Taiwan 21°53N 120°51E 225 E2
Oluanpi Taiwan 21°54N 120°51E 225 E2
Olula del Rio Spain 37°21N 2°18W 197 H2
Olur Turkey 40°49N 42°8E 213 B10
Olustee U.S.A. 30°12N 82°26W 316 E7
Olutanga Phil. 7°26N 122°54E 233 H4
Olutanga I. Phil. 7°22N 122°52E 233 H4
Olvega Spain 41°47N 2°0W 196 D2
Olvera Spain 36°55N 5°18W 195 J5
Olymbos Cyprus 35°21N 33°45E 207 E9
Olymbos Oros Greece 40°6N 22°23E 202 F6
Olympia Greece 37°39N 21°39E 204 D3
Olympia London, U.K. 125 c1
Olympia Wash., U.S.A. 47°3N 122°53W 306 D4
Olympia, L. U.S.A. 28°34N 81°31W 133 A1
Olympic △ U.S.A. 47°45N 123°43W 306 C3
Olympic Dam Australia 30°30S 136°55E 282 A2
Olympic Mts. U.S.A. 47°55N 123°45W 306 C3
Olympic Stadium = Turner Field U.S.A. 33°44N 84°23W 113 B2
Olympic Stadium Finland 60°11N 24°55E 121 B2
Olympique, Stade Canada 45°33N 73°33W 130 A2
Olympus Cyprus 34°56N 32°52E 207 F8
Olympus, Mt. = Olymbos Oros Greece 40°6N 22°23E 202 F6
Olympus, Mt. = Uludağ Turkey 40°4N 29°13E 203 F13
Olympus, Mt. U.S.A. 47°48N 123°43W 306 C3
Olyphant U.S.A. 41°27N 75°36W 313 E9
Om → Russia 54°59N 73°22E 217 B8
Om Hajer Eritrea 14°20N 36°41E 257 E4
Om Koi Thailand 17°48N 98°22E 236 D2
Ōma Japan 41°45N 141°5E 220 D10
Ōmachi Japan 36°30N 137°50E 223 A9
Omae-Zaki Japan 34°36N 138°14E 223 C10
Ōmagari Japan 39°27N 140°29E 220 E10
Omagh U.K. 54°36N 7°19W 166 B4
Omagh □ U.K. 54°35N 7°15W 166 B4
Omaha U.S.A. 41°17N 95°58W 308 E6
Omak U.S.A. 48°25N 119°31W 304 B4
Omalos Greece 35°19N 23°55E 207 E4
Omalur India 11°44N 78°4E 245 J4
Oman ■ Asia 23°0N 58°0E 249 B7
Oman, G. of Asia 24°30N 58°30E 247 E8
Omapere N.Z. 35°37S 173°25E 284 B2
Omar Combon Somali Rep. 3°10N 45°47E 267 D6
Omaruru Namibia 21°26S 16°0E 270 B2
Omaruru → Namibia 22°7S 14°15E 270 B1
Omate Peru 16°45S 71°0W 330 D3
Ombai, Selat Indonesia 8°30S 124°50E 231 F6
Omboué Gabon 1°35S 9°15E 264 C1
Ombrone → Italy 42°42N 11°5E 198 F8
Omchi Chad 21°22N 17°53E 259 D3
Omdurmân Sudan 15°40N 32°28E 257 D3
Ōme Japan 35°47N 139°15E 223 B11
Omega U.S.A. 31°21N 83°36W 316 D6
Omegna Italy 45°53N 8°24E 198 C5
Omemee Canada 44°18N 78°33W 312 B6
Omeo Australia 37°6S 147°36E 283 D7
Omeonga Dem. Rep. of the Congo 3°40S 24°22E 264 C4
Ometepe, I. de Nic. 11°32N 85°35W 320 D2
Ometepec Mexico 16°41N 98°25W 319 D5
Ōmi-Shima Ehime, Japan 34°15N 133°0E 222 C5
Ōmi-Shima Yamaguchi, Japan 34°25N 131°9E 222 C3
Omihachiman Japan 35°7N 136°3E 223 B8
Omin Micronesia 9°36N 138°9E 287 R16
Ominato Japan 41°17N 141°10E 220 D10
Omineca → Canada 56°3N 124°16W 296 B4
Omineca Mts. Canada 56°30N 125°30W 296 B3
Omiš Croatia 43°28N 16°40E 199 E13
Omišalj Croatia 45°13N 14°32E 199 C11
Omitara Namibia 22°16S 18°2E 270 B2
Ōmiya = Saitama Japan 35°54N 139°38E 223 B11
Ommaney, C. U.S.A. 56°10N 134°40W 303 H14
Omme Å → Denmark 55°56N 8°32E 163 J2
Ommen Neths. 52°31N 6°26E 170 B6
Ömnögovĭ □ Mongolia 43°15N 104°0E 226 C3
Omo → Ethiopia 6°25N 36°10E 257 F4
Omo △ Ethiopia 5°54N 35°55E 257 F4
Omo Valley Ethiopia 5°7N 36°0E 257 F4
Omodeo, L. Italy 40°8N 8°56E 200 B1
Omodhos Cyprus 34°51N 32°48E 207 F8
Omoï Congo 2°56S 13°13E 264 C2
Omoko Nigeria 5°19N 6°40E 263 D6
Omolon → Russia 68°42N 158°36E 215 C16
Omona Solomon Is. 7°30S 158°43E 287 L10
Omonia Square Athens, Greece 112 b1
Omono-Gawa → Japan 39°46N 140°3E 220 E10
Ōmori Japan 35°34N 139°43E 140 B3
Omsk Russia 55°0N 73°12E 217 B8
Omsukchan Russia 62°32N 155°48E 215 C16
Ōmu Japan 44°34N 142°58E 220 B11
Omul, Vf. Romania 45°27N 25°29E 183 E10
Omulew → Poland 53°5N 21°33E 185 E8
Ōmura Japan 32°56N 129°57E 222 E1
Ōmura-Wan Japan 32°57N 129°52E 222 E1
Omuramba Omatako → Namibia 17°45S 20°25E 270 A2
Omuramba Ovambo → Namibia 18°45S 16°59E 270 A2
Omurtag Bulgaria 43°8N 26°26E 203 C10
Ōmuta Japan 33°5N 130°26E 222 D2
On-ma-thi Burma 22°17N 96°41E 241 D6
On-Take Japan 31°35N 130°39E 222 F2
Oña Spain 42°43N 3°25W 194 C7
Ona Fla., U.S.A. 27°29N 81°55W 317 H8
Ona Dikonde Dem. Rep. of the Congo 3°51S 24°11E 264 C4
Onaga U.S.A. 39°29N 96°10W 308 F5
Onalaska U.S.A. 43°53N 91°14W 308 D8
Onancock U.S.A. 37°43N 75°45W 309 G16
Onang Indonesia 3°2S 118°49E 231 E5
Onangue, L. Gabon 0°57S 10°4E 264 C1
Onaping L. Canada 47°3N 81°30W 298 C3
Onarga U.S.A. 40°43N 88°1W 311 D8
Oñati Spain 43°3N 2°25W 196 B2
Onavas Mexico 28°31N 109°35W 318 B3
Onawa U.S.A. 42°2N 96°6W 308 D5
Oncócua Angola 16°30S 13°25E 265 F2
Onda Spain 39°55N 0°17W 196 F4
Ondangwa Namibia 17°57S 16°4E 270 A2
Ondarroa Spain 43°19N 2°25W 196 B2
Ondas → Brazil 12°8S 44°55W 333 D3
Ondava → Slovak Rep. 48°27N 21°48E 181 C14
Ondjiva Angola 16°48S 15°50E 265 F3
Ondo Japan 34°11N 132°32E 222 C4
Ondo Nigeria 7°4N 4°47E 263 D5
Ondo □ Nigeria 6°45N 5°0E 263 D6
Öndörshil Mongolia 45°13N 108°5E 226 B5
Öndverðarnes Iceland 64°52N 24°0W 155 C2
One and a Half Degree Channel Maldives 1°30N 73°20E 272 d
One Tree Australia 34°11S 144°43E 281 E3
Oneata Fiji 18°26S 178°25W 287 B3
Oneco U.S.A. 27°25N 82°31W 317 H7
Onega Russia 64°0N 38°10E 186 B6
Onega → Russia 63°58N 38°2E 186 B6
Onega, G. of = Onezhskaya Guba Russia 64°24N 36°38E 186 B6
Onega, L. = Onezhskoye Ozero Russia 61°44N 35°22E 188 B8
Onehunga N.Z. 36°55S 174°48E 284 C3
Oneida Ill., U.S.A. 41°4N 90°13W 310 C6
Oneida N.Y., U.S.A. 43°6N 75°39W 313 C9
Oneida L. U.S.A. 43°12N 75°54W 313 C9
O'Neill U.S.A. 42°27N 98°39W 308 D4
Onekotan, Ostrov Russia 49°25N 154°45E 215 E16
Onema Dem. Rep. of the Congo 4°35S 24°30E 265 C4
Oneonta U.S.A. 42°27N 75°4W 313 D9
Onerahi N.Z. 35°45S 174°22E 284 B3
Oneroa Cook Is. 21°15S 159°43W 289 h
Oneşti Romania 46°17N 26°47E 183 D11
Onezhskaya Guba Russia 64°24N 36°38E 186 B6
Onezhskoye Ozero Russia 61°44N 35°22E 188 B8
Ongarue N.Z. 38°42S 175°19E 284 E4
Ongea Levu = Ogea Levu Fiji 19°8S 178°24W 287 B3
Ongers → S. Africa 31°4S 23°13E 270 D3
Ongerup Australia 33°58S 118°28E 279 F2
Ongjin N. Korea 37°56N 125°21E 224 D2
Ongkharak Thailand 14°8N 101°1E 236 E3
Ongniud Qi China 43°0N 118°38E 227 C10
Ongoka Dem. Rep. of the Congo 1°20S 26°0E 268 C2
Ongole India 15°33N 80°2E 245 G5
Ongon = Havirga Mongolia 45°41N 113°5E 226 B7
Ongouendjo Gabon 1°23S 9°5E 264 C1
Ongoujou Comoros Is. 12°18S 44°30E 272 a
Ongtüstik Qazaqstan □ Kazakhstan 43°0N 68°0E 217 D7
Oni Georgia 42°33N 43°26E 191 J6
Onida U.S.A. 44°42N 100°4W 308 C3
Onilahy → Madag. 23°34S 43°45E 272 C1
Onima Neth. Ant. 12°15N 68°19W 322 h
Onisigun Nigeria 6°35N 3°24E 124 A2
Onitsha Nigeria 6°6N 6°42E 263 D6
Onna Japan 26°29N 127°51E 288 a
Ono Fiji 18°55S 178°29E 287 B2
Ono Fukui, Japan 35°59N 136°29E 223 B8
Ono Hyōgo, Japan 34°51N 134°56E 222 C6
Onoda Japan 33°59N 131°11E 222 C3
Onohara Japan 34°5N 133°40E 222 C5
Onoke, L. N.Z. 41°22S 175°8E 284 H4
Onomichi Japan 34°25N 133°12E 222 C5
Onotoa Kiribati 1°52S 175°34E 277 A14
Ons, I. de Spain 42°23N 8°55W 194 C2
Onsala Sweden 57°26N 12°0E 163 G6
Onslow Australia 21°40S 115°12E 278 D2
Onslow B. U.S.A. 34°20N 77°15W 315 D16
Ontake-San Japan 35°53N 137°29E 223 B9
Ontar Vanuatu 14°17S 167°27E 287 D5
Ontario Calif., U.S.A. 34°4N 117°39W 307 L9
Ontario Oreg., U.S.A. 44°2N 116°58W 304 D5
Ontario □ Canada 48°0N 83°0W 298 B2
Ontario, L. N. Amer. 43°20N 78°0W 312 C7
Ontario Science Centre Canada 43°43N 79°20W 141 A2
Ontinyent Spain 38°50N 0°35W 197 G4
Ontonagon U.S.A. 46°52N 89°19W 308 B9
Ontong Java Plateau Pac. Oc. 1°0N 157°0E 277 A10
Ontur Spain 38°38N 1°29W 197 G3
Onverwacht Suriname 5°35N 55°11W 329 B6
Onyx U.S.A. 35°41N 118°14W 307 K8
Oodnadatta Australia 27°33S 135°30E 281 D2
'Ō'ōkala U.S.A. 20°1N 155°17W 302 C6
Ōokayama Japan 35°36N 139°40E 140 B3
Ooku = Ōma Japan 41°45N 141°5E 220 D10
Ooldea Australia 30°27S 131°50E 279 F5
Oombulgurri Australia 15°15S 127°45E 278 C4
Oorindi Australia 20°40S 141°1E 280 C3
Oost-Vlaanderen □ Belgium 51°5N 3°50E 170 C3
Oostende Belgium 51°15N 2°54E 170 C2
Oosterhout Neths. 51°39N 4°47E 170 C4
Oosterpark Amsterdam, Neths. 112 b3
Oosterschelde → Neths. 51°33N 4°0E 170 C4
Oosterwolde Neths. 53°0N 6°17E 170 B6
Oostpunt Neth. Ant. 12°2N 68°44W 322 g
Oostzaan Neths. 52°26N 4°52E 112 A2
Ootacamund = Udagamandalam India 11°30N 76°44E 245 J3
Ootha Australia 33°6S 147°29E 283 B7
Ootsa L. Canada 53°50N 126°2W 296 C3
Op Luang △ Thailand 18°12N 98°32E 236 C2
Opa-Locka U.S.A. 25°54N 80°15W 128 A1
Opa-Locka ✈ (OPF) U.S.A. 25°54N 80°16W 128 A1
Opacz Poland 52°10N 20°53E 142 B1

Opaka *Bulgaria* 43°28N 26°10E **203** C10
Opala
Dem. Rep. of the Congo 0°40S 24°20E **264** C4
Opalenica *Poland* 52°18N 16°24E **185** F3
Opan *Bulgaria* 42°13N 25°41E **203** D9
Opanake *Sri Lanka* 6°35N 80°40E **245** L5
Opapa *N.Z.* 39°47S 176°42E **284** F5
Opasatika *Canada* 49°30N 82°50W **298** C3
Opasquia △ *Canada* 53°33N 93°5W **298** B1
Opatija *Croatia* 45°21N 14°17E **199** C11
Opatów *Poland* 50°50N 21°27E **185** H8
Opava *Czech Rep.* 49°57N 17°58E **181** B10
Opelika *U.S.A.* 32°39N 85°23W **316** C4
Opelousas *U.S.A.* 30°32N 92°5W **314** F8
Opémisca, L. *Canada* 49°56N 74°52W **298** C5
Opera House *Sydney, Australia* **139** a2
Opera House *Chicago, U.S.A.* **119** c1
Opera House *San Francisco, U.S.A.* **136** c1
Opheim *U.S.A.* 48°51N 106°24W **304** B10
Ophir *U.S.A.* 63°10N 156°31W **303** E8
Ophirton *S. Africa* 26°13S 28°1E **123** B2
Ophthalmia Ra.
Australia 23°15S 119°30E **278** D2
Opi *Nigeria* 6°36N 7°28E **263** D6
Opihikao *U.S.A.* 19°26N 154°53W **302** D7
Opinaca ➔ *Canada* 52°15N 78°2W **298** B4
Opinaca, Rés. *Canada* 52°39N 76°20W **298** B4
Opinnagau ➔ *Canada* 54°12N 82°25W **298** B3
Opiscotéo, L. *Canada* 53°10N 68°10W **299** B6
Opobo *Nigeria* 4°35N 7°34E **263** E6
Opochka *Russia* 56°42N 28°45E **188** D5
Opoczno *Poland* 51°22N 20°18E **185** G7
Opol *Phil.* 8°31N 124°34E **233** G5
Opole *Poland* 50°42N 17°58E **185** H4
Opole Lubelskie *Poland* 51°9N 21°58E **185** G8
Opolskie □ *Poland* 50°30N 18°0E **185** H5
Opon = **Lapu-Lapu** *Phil.* 10°20N 123°55E **233** F4
Opononо L. *Namibia* 18°8S 15°45E **270** A2
Opornyy *Kazakhstan* 46°11N 54°25E **216** C4
Oporto = **Porto** *Portugal* 41°8N 8°40W **194** D2
Opotiki *N.Z.* 38°1S 177°19E **284** E6
Opp *U.S.A.* 31°17N 86°16W **316** D3
Oppdal *Norway* 62°35N 9°41E **164** B6
Oppegård *Norway* 59°45N 10°49E **133** B3
Oppeln = **Opole** *Poland* 50°42N 17°58E **185** H4
Oppem *Belgium* 50°56N 4°18E **116** A1
Óppido Mamertina *Italy* 38°16N 15°59E **201** D8
Oppland □ *Norway* 61°15N 9°40E **164** C6
Opportunity *U.S.A.* 47°39N 117°15W **304** C5
Oppsal *Norway* 59°53N 10°50E **133** A4
Oprişor *Romania* 44°17N 23°5E **182** F8
Oprtalj *Croatia* 45°23N 13°50E **199** C10
Opua *N.Z.* 35°19S 174°9E **284** B3
Opunake *N.Z.* 39°26S 173°52E **284** F2
Opuwo *Namibia* 18°3S 13°45E **270** A1
Opuzen *Croatia* 43°1N 17°34E **199** E14
Oquawka *U.S.A.* 40°56N 90°57W **310** D6
Or ➔ *Kazakhstan* 51°11N 58°32E **216** B5
Ora *Cyprus* 34°51N 33°12E **207** F9
Ora *Israel* 31°45N 35°9E **123** B1
Oracabessa *Jamaica* 18°24N 76°57W **320** a
Oracle *U.S.A.* 32°37N 110°46W **305** K8
Oracuzar *Peru* 4°42S 78°6W **328** D2
Oradea *Romania* 47°2N 21°58E **182** C6
Oradell *U.S.A.* 40°57N 74°2W **132** A1
Oradell Res. *U.S.A.* 40°57N 74°1W **132** A1
Öræfajökull *Iceland* 64°2N 16°39W **155** C10
Orahovac *Serbia* 42°24N 20°40E **202** D4
Orahovica *Croatia* 45°35N 17°52E **182** E2
Orai *India* 25°58N 79°30E **243** G8
Oraison *France* 43°55N 5°55E **175** E9
Oral = **Zhayyq** ➔
Kazakhstan 47°0N 51°48E **187** E9
Oral *Kazakhstan* 51°20N 51°20E **190** E10
Oran *Algeria* 35°45N 0°39W **261** A4
Oran □ *Algeria* 35°0N 0°45W **261** B4
Orange *N.S.W., Australia* 33°15S 149°7E **283** B8
Orange *Vaucluse, France* 44°8N 4°47E **175** D8
Orange *Calif., U.S.A.* 33°47N 117°51W **307** M9
Orange *Mass., U.S.A.* 42°35N 72°19W **313** D12
Orange *Tex., U.S.A.* 30°6N 93°44W **314** F8
Orange *Va., U.S.A.* 38°15N 78°7W **309** F14
Orange ➔ *S. Africa* 28°41S 16°28E **270** C2
Orange, C. *Brazil* 4°20N 51°30W **329** C7
Orange Bowl Stadium
U.S.A. 25°46N 80°14W **128** B2
Orange City *U.S.A.* 28°57N 81°18W **317** G8
Orange Cove *U.S.A.* 36°38N 119°19W **306** J7
Orange Free State = **Free State** □
S. Africa 28°30S 27°0E **270** C4
Orange Grove *U.S.A.* 27°58N 97°56W **314** H6
Orange Hill *Barbados* 13°12N 59°36W **323** r
Orange Hill *Jamaica* 18°16N 77°59W **320** a
Orange Hill *St. Vincent* 13°19N 61°7W **323** n
Orange L. *U.S.A.* 29°25N 82°13W **317** F7
Orange Park *U.S.A.* 30°10N 81°42W **316** E8
Orange River Colony = **Free State** □ *S. Africa* 28°30S 27°0E **270** C4
Orange Walk *Belize* 18°6N 88°33W **319** D7
Orangeburg *U.S.A.* 33°30N 80°52W **316** B9
Orangeville *Ont., Canada* 43°55N 80°5W **312** C4
Orangeville *Ill., U.S.A.* 42°28N 89°39W **310** B7
Orangi *Pakistan* 24°54N 67°0E **123** A2
Orango *Guinea-Biss.* 11°5N 16°0W **262** C1
Orani *Phil.* 14°49N 120°32E **232** D3
Oranienburg *Germany* 52°45N 13°14E **178** C9
Oranje = **Orange** ➔
S. Africa 28°41S 16°28E **270** C2
Oranjemund *Namibia* 28°38S 16°29E **270** C2
Oranjerivier *S. Africa* 29°40S 24°12E **270** C3
Oranjestad *Aruba* 12°32N 70°2W **322** f
Oranjestad *Neth. Ant.* 17°28N 62°59W **322** a
Orap *Vanuatu* 15°58S 167°20E **287** E5
Orarak *Sudan* 6°15N 32°23E **257** F3
Oras *Phil.* 12°9N 125°28E **232** E5
Orašje *Bos.-H.* 45°1N 18°42E **182** E3
Orăştie *Romania* 45°50N 23°10E **183** E8
Orava ➔ *Slovak Rep.* 49°9N 19°8E **181** B12
Orava, Vodna nádriž
Slovak Rep. 49°25N 19°35E **181** B12
Oravița *Romania* 45°2N 21°43E **182** E6
Orawia *N.Z.* 46°1S 167°50E **285** G2
Orb ➔ *France* 43°15N 3°18E **174** E7
Orba ➔ *Italy* 44°53N 8°37E **198** D5
Ørbæk *Denmark* 55°17N 10°39E **163** J4
Orbe *Switz.* 46°43N 6°32E **179** J2
Orbec *France* 49°1N 0°23E **172** C7
Orbetello *Italy* 42°27N 11°13E **199** F8
Órbigo ➔ *Spain* 42°5N 5°42W **194** C5
Orbisonia *U.S.A.* 40°15N 77°54W **312** F7
Orbost *Australia* 37°40S 148°29E **283** D8
Örbyhus *Sweden* 60°15N 17°43E **162** D11
Orcadas *Antarctica* 60°44S 44°37W **151** C18
Orcas I. *U.S.A.* 48°42N 122°56W **306** B4
Orce *Spain* 37°44N 2°28W **197** H2
Orce ➔ *Spain* 37°44N 2°28W **197** H2
Orchard City *U.S.A.* 38°50N 107°58W **304** G10
Orchard Homes *U.S.A.* 46°55N 114°4W **304** C6
Orchard Road *Singapore* **138** a1
Orchid I. = **Lan Yü**
Taiwan 22°4N 121°25E **225** D3
Orchies *France* 50°28N 3°14E **173** B10
Orchila, I. *Venezuela* 11°48N 66°10W **328** A4
Orchilla, Pta. *Canary Is.* 27°42N 18°10W **153** e1
Òrcia ➔ *Italy* 42°58N 11°21E **199** F8
Orco ➔ *Italy* 45°10N 7°52E **198** C4
Orcopampa *Peru* 15°20S 72°23W **330** D3
Orcutt *U.S.A.* 34°52N 120°27W **307** L6
Ord *U.S.A.* 41°36N 98°56W **308** E4
Ord ➔ *Australia* 15°33S 128°15E **278** C4
Ord, Mt. *Australia* 17°20S 125°34E **278** C4
Ord Mts. *U.S.A.* 34°39N 116°45W **307** L10
Ordenes = **Ordes** *Spain* 43°5N 8°29W **194** B2
Orderville *U.S.A.* 37°17N 112°38W **305** H7
Ordes *Spain* 43°5N 8°29W **194** B2
Ordesa y Monte Perido △
Spain 42°40N 0°10W **196** C4
Ording = **St-Peter-Ording**
Germany 54°20N 8°36E **178** A4
Ordos = **Mu Us Shamo**
China 39°0N 109°0E **226** E5
Ordrup *Denmark* 55°45N 12°34E **118** A3
Ordu *Turkey* 40°55N 37°53E **212** B7
Ordu □ *Turkey* 41°0N 37°50E **212** B7
Ordubad *Azerbaijan* 38°54N 46°1E **213** C12
Orduña *Álava, Spain* 42°58N 2°58W **196** C2
Orduña *Granada, Spain* 37°20N 3°30W **195** H7
Ordway *U.S.A.* 38°13N 103°46W **304** G12
Ordzhonikidze = **Vladikavkaz**
Russia 43°0N 44°35E **191** J7
Ordzhonikidze = **Yenakiyeve**
Ukraine 48°15N 38°15E **189** H10
Ordzhonīkīdze
Kazakhstan 52°27N 61°39E **216** B6
Ordzhonikidze *Ukraine* 47°39N 34°3E **189** J8
Ore *Dem. Rep. of the Congo* 3°17N 29°30E **268** B2
Ore Mts. = **Erzgebirge**
Germany 50°27N 12°55E **178** E8
Orealla *Guyana* 5°15N 57°23W **329** B6
Orebić *Croatia* 43°0N 17°11E **199** F14
Örebro *Sweden* 59°20N 15°18E **162** E9
Örebro län □ *Sweden* 59°27N 15°0E **162** E8
Orecchiella △ *Italy* 44°16N 10°22E **198** D7
Orech *Czech Rep.* 50°1N 14°17E **135** B1
Oregon *Ill., U.S.A.* 42°1N 89°20W **310** B7
Oregon *Ohio, U.S.A.* 41°38N 83°25W **311** C13
Oregon *Wis., U.S.A.* 42°56N 89°23W **310** B7
Oregon □ *U.S.A.* 44°0N 121°0W **304** E3
Oregon City *U.S.A.* 45°21N 122°36W **306** E4
Oregon Dunes △
U.S.A. 43°40N 124°10W **304** E1
Öregrund *Sweden* 60°21N 18°30E **162** D12
Öregrundsgrepen
Sweden 60°25N 18°15E **162** D12
Orekhov = **Orikhiv**
Ukraine 47°30N 35°48E **189** J8
Orekhovo-Zuyevo
Russia 55°50N 38°55E **188** E10
Orel *Russia* 52°57N 36°3E **189** F9
Orel □ *Russia* 52°30N 36°40E **189** F9
Orel ➔ *Ukraine* 48°40N 34°39E **189** H8
Orellana *Spain* 39°1N 5°32W **195** F5
Orellana, Canal de *Spain* 39°2N 6°0W **195** F5
Orellana, Embalse de *Spain* 39°5N 5°10W **195** F5
Orem *U.S.A.* 40°19N 111°42W **304** F8
Ören *Turkey* 37°3N 27°57E **205** D9
Orenburg *Russia* 51°45N 55°6E **186** D10
Örencik *Turkey* 39°16N 29°33E **205** B11
Orense = **Ourense** *Spain* 42°19N 7°55W **194** C3
Orense □ *Spain* 42°15N 7°51W **194** C3
Orepuki *N.Z.* 46°19S 167°46E **285** G2
Orestes Pereyra *Mexico* 26°30N 105°39W **318** B3
Orestiada *Greece* 41°30N 26°33E **203** E10
Øresund *Europe* 55°45N 12°40E **163** J6
Oretana, Cordillera = **Toledo, Montes de** *Spain* 39°33N 4°20W **195** F6
Oreti ➔ *N.Z.* 46°28S 168°14E **285** G3
Orfanos Kolpos *Greece* 40°33N 24°0E **202** F7
Orford Ness *U.K.* 52°5N 1°35E **169** E9
Organ Pipe Cactus △
U.S.A. 32°0N 112°52W **305** K7
Organos, Pta. de los
Canary Is. 28°12N 17°17W **153** e1
Organyà *Spain* 42°13N 1°20E **196** C6
Orgaz *Spain* 39°39N 3°53W **195** F7
Ørgenvika *Norway* 60°17N 9°42E **164** D6
Orgeyev = **Orhei**
Moldova 47°24N 28°50E **183** C13
Orgūn *Afghan.* 32°55N 69°12E **240** B3
Orhaneli *Turkey* 39°54N 28°59E **203** G12
Orhaneli ➔ *Turkey* 39°50N 28°55E **203** G12
Orhangazi *Turkey* 40°29N 29°18E **203** F13
Orhei *Moldova* 47°24N 28°50E **183** C13
Orhon Gol ➔ *Mongolia* 50°21N 106°0E **218** A5
Ória *Italy* 40°30N 17°38E **201** B10
Orida *Niger* 21°20N 12°15E **261** D7
Orient Heights *U.S.A.* 42°23N 70°59W **116** A3
Oriental, Cordillera *Bolivia* 17°0S 66°0W **331** D4
Oriental, Cordillera
Colombia 6°0N 73°0W **328** B3
Oriental, Grand Erg *Algeria* 30°0N 6°30E **261** C6
Orientale □
Dem. Rep. of the Congo 2°20N 26°0E **268** B2
Oriente *Argentina* 38°44S 60°37W **334** D3
Orihuela *Spain* 38°7N 0°55W **197** G4
Orihuela del Tremedal
Spain 40°33N 1°39W **196** E3
Orikhiv *Ukraine* 47°30N 35°48E **189** J8
Orikum *Albania* 40°20N 19°26E **202** F3
Orillia *Canada* 44°40N 79°24W **312** B5
Orinduik *Guyana* 4°40N 60°3W **329** C5
Orinoco ➔ *Venezuela* 9°15N 61°30W **329** B5
Orion *Canada* 49°27N 110°49W **297** D6
Orion *Ala., U.S.A.* 31°58N 86°0W **316** D4
Orion *Ill., U.S.A.* 41°21N 90°23W **310** C6
Oriskany *U.S.A.* 43°10N 75°20W **313** C9
Orissa □ *India* 20°0N 84°0E **244** E7
Orissaare *Estonia* 58°34N 23°5E **188** C2
Oristano *Italy* 39°54N 8°36E **200** C1
Oristano, G. di *Italy* 39°50N 8°29E **200** C1
Orituco ➔ *Venezuela* 8°45N 67°27W **328** B4
Oriximina *Brazil* 1°45S 55°52W **329** D6
Orizaba *Mexico* 18°51N 97°6W **319** D5
Orizaba, Pico de *Mexico* 18°58N 97°15W **319** D5
Orizare *Bulgaria* 42°44N 27°39E **203** D11
Orizona *Brazil* 17°3S 48°18W **333** D6
Ørje *Norway* 59°29N 11°39E **164** E8
Orjen *Bos.-H.* 42°35N 18°34E **202** D2
Orjiva *Spain* 36°53N 3°24W **195** J7
Orkanger *Norway* 63°18N 9°52E **164** A6
Örkelljunga *Sweden* 56°17N 13°17E **163** H7
Örken *Sweden* 57°6N 15°1E **163** G9
Örkény *Hungary* 47°9N 19°26E **182** C4
Orkhaniye = **Botevgrad**
Bulgaria 42°55N 23°47E **202** D7
Orkla ➔ *Norway* 63°18N 9°51E **164** A6
Orkney *S. Africa* 26°58S 26°40E **270** C4
Orkney □ *U.K.* 59°2N 3°13W **167** B5
Orkney Is. *U.K.* 59°0N 3°0W **167** B6
Orland *Calif., U.S.A.* 39°45N 122°12W **306** F4
Orland *Ind., U.S.A.* 41°47N 85°12W **311** C11
Orland Park *U.S.A.* 41°38N 87°52W **311** C8
Orlando *U.S.A.* 28°32N 81°22W **133** A2
Orlando, C. d' *Italy* 38°10N 14°43E **201** D7
Orlando Dam *S. Africa* 26°15S 27°55E **123** B1
Orlando East *S. Africa* 26°14S 27°55E **123** B1
Orlando Executive ✈
U.S.A. 28°32N 81°20W **133** A2
Orlando Int. ✈ **(MCO)**
U.S.A. 28°26N 81°19W **133** B3
Orléanais *France* 48°0N 2°0E **173** E9
Orléans *Loiret, France* 47°54N 1°52E **173** E8
Orleans *Ind., U.S.A.* 38°40N 86°27W **311** F10
Orleans *Vt., U.S.A.* 44°49N 72°12W **313** B12
Orléans, Î. d' *Canada* 46°54N 70°58W **299** C5
Orléansville = **Ech Chéliff**
Algeria 36°10N 1°20E **261** A5
Orlice ➔ *Czech Rep.* 50°13N 15°50E **180** A8
Orlivka *Ukraine* 45°19N 28°27E **183** E13
Orlov = **Khalturin** *Russia* 58°40N 48°50E **186** C8
Orlov *Slovak Rep.* 49°17N 20°51E **181** B13
Orlov Gay *Russia* 50°56N 48°19E **190** E9
Orlová *Czech Rep.* 49°51N 18°26E **181** B11
Orlovat *Serbia* 45°14N 20°33E **182** E5
Orlovista *U.S.A.* 28°32N 81°27W **133** A2
Orlovo *Russia* 55°38N 37°22E **129** C2
Orly *France* 48°45N 2°23E **134** B3
Orly, Paris ✈ **(ORY)**
France 48°44N 2°23E **134** B3
Ormara *Pakistan* 25°16N 64°33E **240** D2
Ormea *Italy* 44°9N 7°54E **198** D4
Ormesson-sur-Marne
France 48°47N 2°32E **134** B4
Ormilia *Greece* 40°16N 23°39E **202** F7
Ormoc *Phil.* 11°0N 124°37E **233** F5
Ormond *Vic., Australia* 37°54S 145°1E **128** B2
Ormond *N.Z.* 38°33S 177°56E **284** E6
Ormond Beach *U.S.A.* 29°17N 81°3W **317** F8
Ormond-by-the-Sea
U.S.A. 29°21N 81°4W **317** F8
Ormondville *N.Z.* 40°5S 176°19E **284** G5
Ormøya *Norway* 59°52N 10°45E **133** A3
Ormož *Slovenia* 46°25N 16°10E **199** B13
Ormskirk *U.K.* 53°35N 2°54W **168** D5
Ormstown *Canada* 45°8N 74°0W **313** A11
Ormtjernkampen △
Norway 61°12N 9°48E **164** C6
Ornans *France* 47°7N 6°10E **173** E13
Orne □ *France* 48°40N 0°5E **172** D7
Orne ➔ *France* 49°18N 0°15W **172** C6
Orneta *Poland* 54°8N 20°9E **184** D7
Ornö *Sweden* 59°4N 18°24E **162** E12
Örnsköldsvik *Sweden* 63°17N 18°40E **162** A12
Oro *N. Korea* 40°1N 127°27E **224** B3
Oro ➔ *Mexico* 25°35N 105°2W **318** B3
Oro Grande *U.S.A.* 34°36N 117°20W **307** L9
Oro Valley *U.S.A.* 32°26N 110°58W **305** K8
Orobie, Alpi *Italy* 46°7N 10°0E **198** B6
Orobie Bergamasche △
Italy 46°0N 9°45E **198** C6
Orobie Valtellinesi △ *Italy* 46°5N 9°45E **198** B6
Orocué *Colombia* 4°48N 71°20W **328** C3
Orodara *Burkina Faso* 11°0N 4°55W **262** C4
Orodo *Nigeria* 5°34N 7°4E **263** D6
Orofino *U.S.A.* 46°29N 116°15W **304** C5
Orohena, Mt. *Tahiti* 17°37S 149°28W **289** e
Orol Dengizi = **Aral Sea**
Asia 44°30N 60°0E **216** C5
Oromiya □ *Ethiopia* 7°0N 40°0E **257** F5
Oromocto *Canada* 45°54N 66°29W **299** C6
Oron *Nigeria* 4°48N 8°14E **263** E6
Orona *Kiribati* 4°31S 172°11W **277** A16
Orongo *Chile* 27°11S 109°27W **330** b
Orono *Ont., Canada* 43°59N 78°37W **312** C6
Orono *Maine, U.S.A.* 44°53N 68°40W **309** C19
Oronsay *U.K.* 56°1N 6°15W **167** E2
Oropesa *Spain* 39°57N 5°10W **194** F5
Oropuche ➔ *Trin. & Tob.* 10°36N 61°6W **323** t
Oropuche Lagoon
Trin. & Tob. 10°14N 61°31W **323** t
Oroqen Zizhiqi *China* 50°34N 123°43E **219** A7
Oroquieta *Phil.* 8°32N 123°44E **233** G4
Orós *Brazil* 6°15S 38°55W **332** C4
Orosei *Italy* 40°23N 9°42E **200** B2
Orosei, G. di *Italy* 40°15N 9°44E **200** B2
Orosháza *Hungary* 46°32N 20°42E **182** D5
Oroszlány *Hungary* 47°29N 18°19E **182** C3
Orote Pen. *Guam* 13°26N 144°38E **302** d
Orotukan *Russia* 62°16N 151°42E **215** C16
Oroville *Calif., U.S.A.* 39°31N 121°33W **306** F5
Oroville *Wash., U.S.A.* 48°56N 119°26W **304** B4
Oroville, L. *U.S.A.* 39°33N 121°29W **306** F5
Orpington *U.K.* 51°22N 0°6E **125** B4
Orrefors *Sweden* 56°50N 15°45E **163** H9
Orrick *U.S.A.* 39°13N 94°7W **310** E2
Orroroo *Australia* 32°43S 138°38E **282** B3
Orrviken *Sweden* 63°6N 14°26E **162** B8
Orrville *U.S.A.* 40°50N 81°46W **312** F3
Orsa *Sweden* 61°7N 14°37E **162** C8
Orsara di Púglia *Italy* 41°17N 15°16E **201** A8
Orsasjön *Sweden* 61°7N 14°37E **162** C8
Orsay, Musée d' *Paris, France* **134** b3
Orsha *Belarus* 54°30N 30°25E **188** E6
Örsjö *Sweden* 56°42N 15°45E **163** H9
Orsk *Russia* 51°12N 58°34E **216** B5
Orşova *Romania* 44°41N 22°25E **182** F7
Ørsta *Norway* 62°13N 6°8E **164** B3
Ørsted *Denmark* 56°30N 10°20E **163** H4
Örsundsbro *Sweden* 59°44N 17°18E **162** E11
Országos Levéltár *Budapest, Hungary* **117** b1
Orta, L. d' *Italy* 45°49N 8°24E **198** C5
Orta Nova *Italy* 41°19N 15°42E **201** A8
Ortaca *Turkey* 36°49N 28°45E **205** E10
Ortakent *Turkey* 37°5N 27°21E **205** D9
Ortaklar *Turkey* 37°53N 27°30E **205** D9
Ortaköy *Çorum, Turkey* 40°16N 35°15E **212** B6
Ortaköy *İstanbul, Turkey* 41°3N 29°1E **122** B2
Ortaköy *Niğde, Turkey* 38°44N 34°3E **212** C6
Orte *Italy* 42°27N 12°23E **199** F9
Ortegal, C. *Spain* 43°43N 7°52W **194** B3
Orteguaza ➔ *Colombia* 0°43N 75°16W **328** C2
Ortelsburg = **Szczytno**
Poland 53°33N 21°0E **184** E7
Orthez *France* 43°29N 0°48W **174** E3
Ortica *Italy* 45°29N 9°16E **129** B2
Ortigueira *Spain* 43°40N 7°50W **194** B3
Orting *U.S.A.* 47°6N 122°12W **306** C4
Ortisei *Italy* 46°34N 11°40E **199** B8
Ortles *Italy* 46°31N 10°33E **198** B7
Ortnevik *Norway* 61°6N 6°7E **164** C3
Orton *U.K.* 54°28N 2°35W **168** C5
Ortona *Italy* 42°21N 14°24E **199** F11
Ortoire ➔ *Trin. & Tob.* 10°20N 61°30W **323** t
Ortón ➔ *Bolivia* 10°50S 67°0W **330** C4
Ortonville *U.S.A.* 45°19N 96°27W **308** C5
Orūmīyeh *Iran* 37°40N 45°0E **213** D11
Orūmīyeh, Daryācheh-ye
Iran 37°50N 45°30E **213** D11
Orune *Italy* 40°24N 9°22E **200** B2
Oruro *Bolivia* 18°0S 67°9W **330** D4
Oruro □ *Bolivia* 18°40S 67°30W **330** D4
Orust *Sweden* 58°10N 11°40E **163** F5
Oruzgān □ *Afghan.* 33°0N 66°0E **240** B2
Orvault *France* 47°17N 1°38W **172** E5
Orvieto *Italy* 42°43N 12°7E **199** F9
Orwell *N.Y., U.S.A.* 43°35N 75°50W **313** C9
Orwell *Ohio, U.S.A.* 41°32N 80°52W **312** E4
Orwell ➔ *U.K.* 51°59N 1°18E **169** F9
Orwigsburg *U.S.A.* 40°38N 76°6W **313** F8
Oryakhovo *Bulgaria* 43°40N 23°57E **202** C7
Orynyn *Ukraine* 48°46N 26°24E **183** B11
Orzinuovi *Italy* 45°24N 9°55E **198** C6
Orzyc ➔ *Poland* 52°46N 21°14E **185** F8
Orzysz *Poland* 53°50N 21°58E **184** E8
Os *Norway* 62°30N 11°14E **164** B8
Osa *Russia* 57°17N 55°26E **186** C10
Osa ➔ *Poland* 53°33N 18°46E **184** E5
Osa, Pen. de *Costa Rica* 8°0N 84°0W **320** E3
Osage *U.S.A.* 43°17N 92°49W **308** D7
Osage ➔ *U.S.A.* 38°36N 91°57W **310** F5
Osage City *U.S.A.* 38°38N 95°50W **308** F6
Ōsaka *Japan* 34°42N 135°30E **133** B2
Ōsaka □ *Japan* 34°30N 135°30E **223** C7
Ōsaka Castle *Japan* 34°41N 135°32E **133** A2
Ōsaka Harbour *Japan* 34°38N 135°25E **133** B1
Ōsaka Itami Int. ✈ **(ITM)**
Japan 34°46N 135°26E **133** A1
Ōsaka Kansai Int. ✈ **(KIX)**
Japan 34°27N 135°12E **133** B2
Ōsaka-Wan *Japan* 34°30N 135°18E **223** C7
Osakarovka *Kazakhstan* 50°33N 72°34E **217** B8
Ōsaki *Kagoshima, Japan* 31°25N 131°2E **222** F3
Ōsaki *Tōkyō, Japan* 35°36N 139°42E **140** B3
Osan *S. Korea* 37°11N 127°4E **224** D3
Osasco *Brazil* 23°31S 46°46W **137** B1
Osawatomie *U.S.A.* 38°31N 94°57W **308** F6
Osborn Plateau *Ind. Oc.* 14°45S 87°0E **273** F7
Osborne *U.S.A.* 39°26N 98°42W **308** F4
Osby *Sweden* 56°23N 13°59E **163** H7
Osceola *Ark., U.S.A.* 35°42N 89°58W **315** D10
Osceola *Iowa, U.S.A.* 41°2N 93°46W **310** C3
Osceola *Mo., U.S.A.* 38°3N 93°42W **310** F3
Oschatz *Germany* 51°17N 13°6E **178** D9
Oschersleben *Germany* 52°2N 11°14E **178** C7
Óschiri *Italy* 40°43N 9°6E **200** B2
Oscoda *U.S.A.* 44°26N 83°20W **312** B1
Osdorf *Germany* 52°24N 13°20E **115** B3
Osdorp *Neths.* 52°22N 4°47E **112** A1
Osečina *Serbia* 44°23N 19°34E **202** B3
Ösel = **Saaremaa** *Estonia* 58°30N 22°30E **188** C2
Osensjøen *Norway* 61°13N 11°50E **164** C8
Osery *Russia* 54°52N 38°28E **188** E10
Osgood *U.S.A.* 39°8N 85°18W **311** E11
Osgoode *Canada* 45°8N 75°36W **313** A9
Osgoode Hall *Toronto, Canada* **141** b2
Osh *Kyrgyzstan* 40°37N 72°49E **217** D8
Osh □ *Kyrgyzstan* 40°0N 73°0E **217** E8
Oshawa *Canada* 43°50N 78°50W **312** C6
Oshigambo *Namibia* 17°45S 16°5E **270** A2
Oshkosh *Nebr., U.S.A.* 41°24N 102°21W **308** E2
Oshkosh *Wis., U.S.A.* 44°1N 88°33W **308** C9
Oshmyany = **Ashmyany**
Belarus 54°26N 25°52E **177** A13
Oshnovīyeh *Iran* 37°2N 45°6E **246** B5
Oshodi *Nigeria* 6°33N 3°21E **124** A2
Oshogbo *Nigeria* 7°48N 4°37E **263** D5
Oshtorīnān *Iran* 34°1N 48°38E **213** E13
Oshwe
Dem. Rep. of the Congo 3°25S 19°28E **264** C3
Osi *Nigeria* 8°8N 5°14E **263** D6
Osieczna *Poland* 51°55N 16°40E **185** G3
Osijek *Croatia* 45°34N 18°41E **182** E3
Ósilo *Italy* 40°45N 8°40E **200** B1
Ósimo *Italy* 43°28N 13°30E **199** E10
Osintorf *Belarus* 54°40N 30°39E **188** E6
Osipenko = **Berdyansk**
Ukraine 46°45N 36°50E **189** J9
Osipovichi = **Asipovichy**
Belarus 53°19N 28°33E **177** B15
Osiyan *India* 26°43N 72°55E **242** F5
Osizweni *S. Africa* 27°49S 30°7E **271** C5
Oskaloosa *U.S.A.* 41°18N 92°39W **310** C4
Oskarshamn *Sweden* 57°15N 16°27E **163** G10
Oskarström *Sweden* 56°48N 12°58E **163** H6
Oskélanéo *Canada* 48°5N 75°15W **298** C4
Öskemen *Kazakhstan* 50°0N 82°36E **217** C10
Oskol ➔ *Ukraine* 49°6N 37°25E **189** H9
Oslo *Norway* 59°54N 10°43E **133** A3
Oslo □ *Norway* 59°54N 10°43E **164** D7
Oslo ✈ **(OSL)** *Norway* 60°11N 11°6E **133** A4
Oslob *Phil.* 9°31N 123°26E **233** G4
Oslofjorden *Norway* 59°20N 10°35E **164** E7
Osmanabad *India* 18°5N 76°10E **244** E3
Osmancık *Turkey* 40°58N 34°47E **212** B6
Osmaniye *Turkey* 37°5N 36°10E **250** A7
Osmanli *Turkey* 41°35N 26°51E **203** E10
Osmannagar *India* 18°32N 79°20E **244** E4
Ösmo *Sweden* 58°58N 17°55E **162** F11
Osnabrück *Germany* 52°17N 8°3E **178** C4
Ośno Lubuskie *Poland* 52°28N 14°51E **185** F1
Osoblaha *Czech Rep.* 50°17N 17°44E **181** A10
Osogovska Planina
Macedonia 42°10N 22°30E **202** D6
Ōsone *Japan* 35°31N 139°37E **140** B2
Osor *Italy* 44°42N 14°24E **199** D11
Osório *Brazil* 29°53S 50°17W **335** B5
Osório da Fonseca *Brazil* 3°52S 58°14W **329** D6
Osorno *Chile* 40°25S 73°0W **336** B2
Osorno *Spain* 42°24N 4°22W **196** C6
Osorno □ *Chile* 40°34S 73°9W **336** B2
Osorno, Vol. *Chile* 41°0S 72°30W **336** B2
Osun *Nigeria* 6°33N 3°29E **124** A2
Osoyoos *Canada* 49°0N 119°30W **296** D5
Osøyro *Norway* 60°9N 5°30E **164** D2
Ospakseyri *Iceland* 65°27N 21°26W **155** B5
Ospiate *Italy* 45°32N 9°6E **129** A1
Ospika ➔ *Canada* 56°20N 124°0W **296** B4
Osprey *U.S.A.* 27°12N 82°29W **317** H7
Osprey Reef *Australia* 13°52S 146°36E **280** A4
Oss *Neths.* 51°46N 5°32E **170** C5
Ossa, Mt. *Australia* 41°52S 146°3E **281** G4
Ossa, Oros *Greece* 39°47N 22°42E **204** B4
Ossa de Montiel *Spain* 38°58N 2°45W **197** G2
Ossabaw I. *U.S.A.* 31°50N 81°5W **316** D8
Ossabaw Sd. *U.S.A.* 31°50N 81°6W **316** D8
Osse ➔ *Lot-et-Garonne, France* 44°7N 0°17E **174** D4
Osse ➔ *Nigeria* 6°10N 5°20E **263** D6
Ossersee = **Zarasai**
Lithuania 55°40N 26°20E **188** E4
Ossi *Italy* 40°40N 8°35E **200** B1
Ossining *U.S.A.* 41°10N 73°55W **313** E11
Ossipee *U.S.A.* 43°41N 71°7W **313** C13
Ossokmanuan L. *Canada* 53°25N 65°0W **299** B7
Ossora *Russia* 59°20N 163°13E **215** D17
Ostankino *Russia* 55°49N 37°37E **129** B3
Ostashkov *Russia* 57°4N 33°2E **188** D7
Östavall *Sweden* 62°26N 15°29E **162** B9
Østby *Norway* 61°15N 12°33E **164** C9
Oste ➔ *Germany* 53°49N 9°2E **178** B5
Ostenburg = **Pułtusk**
Poland 52°43N 21°6E **185** F8
Ostend = **Oostende**
Belgium 51°15N 2°54E **170** C2
Ostend *N.Z.* 36°48S 175°2E **284** C4
Oster *Ukraine* 50°57N 30°53E **177** C16
Österbotten = **Pohjanmaa**
Finland 62°58N 22°50E **160** E20
Østerbro *Copenhagen, Denmark* **118** a1
Osterburg *Sachsen-Anhalt, Germany* 52°47N 11°45E **178** C7
Osterburg *Pa., U.S.A.* 40°16N 78°31W **312** F6
Osterburken *Germany* 49°25N 9°26E **179** F5
Österbybruk *Sweden* 60°13N 17°55E **162** D11
Österbymo *Sweden* 57°49N 15°15E **163** G9
Österdalälven *Sweden* 61°30N 13°45E **162** C7
Østerdalen *Norway* 61°40N 10°50E **162** C4
Österfärnebo *Sweden* 60°19N 16°48E **162** D10
Österforse *Sweden* 63°9N 17°3E **162** A11
Östergötlands län □
Sweden 58°35N 15°45E **163** F9
Osterholz-Scharmbeck
Germany 53°13N 8°47E **178** B4
Østerild *Denmark* 57°2N 8°51E **163** G2
Osterley *U.K.* 51°28N 0°21W **125** B1
Osterley Park *U.K.* 51°29N 0°21W **125** B1
Östermalm *Stockholm, Sweden* 59°20N 18°4E **139** A2
Östermalm *Stockholm, Sweden* **139** a3
Östermyra = **Seinäjoki**
Finland 62°40N 22°51E **160** E20
Osterode *Germany* 51°43N 10°15E **178** D6
Osterode in Ostpreussen = **Ostróda**
Poland 53°42N 19°58E **184** E6
Österreich = **Austria** ■
Europe 47°0N 14°0E **180** E7
Österreich ober der Ems = **Oberösterreich** □
Austria 48°10N 14°0E **180** C7
Österskär *Sweden* 59°26N 18°16E **139** A3
Östersund *Sweden* 63°10N 14°38E **162** A8
Östervåla *Sweden* 60°11N 17°11E **162** D11
Østfold □ *Norway* 59°25N 11°25E **164** E8
Ostfriesische Inseln
Germany 53°42N 7°0E **178** B3
Ostfriesland *Germany* 53°20N 7°30E **178** B3
Østgrønland = **Tunu** □
Greenland 75°0N 30°0W **154** C7
Östhammar *Sweden* 60°16N 18°22E **162** D12
Ostia, Lido di *Italy* 41°43N 12°17E **199** G9
Ostia Malpasso *Italy* 41°47N 12°26E **136** C1
Ostiense *Italy* 41°51N 12°29E **136** B1
Ostiglia *Italy* 45°4N 11°8E **199** C8
Östmark *Sweden* 60°17N 12°45E **162** D6
Østmarkkapellet *Norway* 59°52N 10°51E **133** A4
Østøya *Norway* 59°52N 10°34E **133** A2
Östra Husby *Sweden* 58°35N 16°33E **163** F10
Ostrava *Czech Rep.* 49°51N 18°18E **181** B11
Ostravský □ *Czech Rep.* 49°55N 17°58E **181** B10
Østre Aker *Norway* 59°54N 10°49E **133** A3
Ostróda *Poland* 53°42N 19°58E **184** E6
Ostrogozhsk *Russia* 50°55N 39°7E **189** G10
Ostroh *Ukraine* 50°20N 26°30E **177** C14
Ostrołęka *Poland* 53°4N 21°32E **185** E8
Ostrov *Bulgaria* 43°40N 24°9E **203** C8
Ostrov *Czech Rep.* 50°18N 12°57E **180** A5
Ostrov *Romania* 44°6N 27°24E **183** F12
Ostrov *Russia* 57°25N 28°20E **188** D5
Ostrów Lubelski *Poland* 51°29N 22°51E **185** G9
Ostrów Mazowiecka
Poland 52°50N 21°51E **185** F8
Ostrów Wielkopolski
Poland 51°36N 17°44E **185** G4
Ostrowiec-Świętokrzyski
Poland 50°55N 21°22E **185** H8
Ostrowo = **Ostrów Wielkopolski**
Poland 51°36N 17°44E **185** G4
Ostrožac *Bos.-H.* 43°43N 17°49E **182** G2
Ostrzeszów *Poland* 51°25N 17°52E **185** G4
Ostseebad Kühlungsborn
Germany 54°8N 11°44E **178** A7
Osttirol □ *Austria* 46°50N 12°30E **180** E5
Ostuni *Italy* 40°44N 17°35E **201** B10
Ostyako-Vogulsk = **Khanty-Mansiysk** *Russia* 61°0N 69°0E **214** C7
Osum ➔ *Albania* 40°40N 20°10E **202** F4
Osŭm ➔ *Bulgaria* 43°40N 24°50E **203** C8
Ōsumi-Hantō *Japan* 31°20N 130°55E **222** F2
Ōsumi-Kaikyō *Japan* 30°55N 131°0E **221** J5
Ōsumi-Shotō *Japan* 30°30N 130°0E **221** J5
Osun □ *Nigeria* 7°30N 4°30E **263** D5
Osuna *Spain* 37°14N 5°8W **195** H5
Oswegatchie ➔ *U.S.A.* 44°42N 75°30W **313** B9
Oswego *U.S.A.* 43°27N 76°31W **313** C8
Oswego ➔ *U.S.A.* 43°27N 76°30W **313** C8
Oswestry *U.K.* 52°52N 3°3W **168** E4
Oświęcim *Poland* 50°2N 19°11E **185** H6
Ōta *Fukui, Japan* 35°57N 136°3E **223** B8
Ōta *Gumma, Japan* 36°18N 139°22E **223** A11
Ōta *Tōkyō, Japan* 35°34N 139°41E **140** B3
Ōta-Gawa ➔ *Japan* 34°21N 132°18E **222** C4
Otaci *Moldova* 48°27N 27°47E **183** B12
Otago □ *N.Z.* 45°15S 170°0E **285** F4
Otago Harbour *N.Z.* 45°47S 170°42E **285** F5
Otago Pen. *N.Z.* 45°48S 170°39E **285** F5
Otaheite B. *Trin. & Tob.* 10°15N 61°30W **323** t
Otahuhu *N.Z.* 36°56S 174°51E **284** C3
Ōtake *Japan* 34°12N 132°13E **222** C4
Ōtaki *Japan* 35°17N 140°15E **223** B12
Otaki *N.Z.* 40°45S 175°10E **284** G4
Otane *N.Z.* 39°54S 176°39E **284** F5
Otaniemi *Finland* 60°11N 24°49E **121** B1
Otari Open Air Museum
N.Z. 41°16S 174°46E **143** B1
Otaru *Japan* 43°10N 141°0E **220** C10
Otaru-Wan = **Ishikari-Wan**
Japan 43°25N 141°1E **220** C10
Otautau *N.Z.* 46°9S 168°1E **285** G3
Otava ➔ *Czech Rep.* 49°26N 14°12E **180** B7
Otavalo *Ecuador* 0°13N 78°20W **328** C2
Otavi *Namibia* 19°40S 17°24E **270** A2
Otchinjau *Angola* 16°30S 13°56E **265** F2
Oteiza = **Marihatag** *Phil.* 8°48N 126°18E **233** G6
Otelec *Romania* 45°36N 20°50E **182** E5
Otelnuk, L. *Canada* 56°9N 68°12W **299** A6
Oţelu Roşu *Romania* 45°32N 22°22E **182** E7
Otero de Rey = **Outeiro de Rei**
Spain 43°6N 7°36W **194** B3
Othello *U.S.A.* 46°50N 119°10W **304** C4
Othoni *Greece* 39°52N 19°22E **206** B9
Othris, Oros *Greece* 39°2N 22°37E **204** B4
Oti ➔ *Togo* 10°40N 0°35E **263** C5
Otira *N.Z.* 42°49S 171°35E **285** C6
Otira Gorge *N.Z.* 42°53S 171°33E **285** C6
Otjiwarongo *Namibia* 20°30S 16°33E **270** B2
Otmuchów *Poland* 50°28N 17°10E **185** H4
Oto Tolu Group *Tonga* 20°21S 174°32W **287** Q13
Otočac *Croatia* 44°53N 15°12E **199** D12
Otoineppu *Japan* 44°44N 142°16E **220** B11
Otok *Croatia* 45°10N 18°50E **182** E3
Otomavi = **Korsakov**
Russia 46°36N 142°42E **215** E15
Oton *Phil.* 10°42N 122°29E **233** F4
Otopeni, Bucureşti ✈ **(OTP)**
Romania 44°30N 26°11E **183** F11
Otorohanga *N.Z.* 38°12S 175°14E **284** E4
Otoskwin ➔ *Canada* 52°13N 88°6W **298** B2
Ōtoyo *Japan* 33°43N 133°45E **222** D5
Otpor = **Zabaykalsk**
Russia 49°40N 117°25E **215** E12
Otra ➔ *Norway* 58°9N 8°1E **164** F5
Otradnyy *Russia* 53°22N 51°21E **190** D10
Otranto *Italy* 40°9N 18°28E **201** B11
Otranto, C. d' *Italy* 40°7N 18°30E **201** B11
Otranto, Str. of *Italy* 40°15N 18°40E **201** B11
Otrokovice *Czech Rep.* 49°12N 17°32E **181** B10
Otse *S. Africa* 25°2S 25°45E **270** C4
Otsego *U.S.A.* 42°27N 85°42W **311** B11
Ōtsu *Japan* 35°0N 135°50E **223** C7
Ōtsuka *Japan* 35°43N 139°44E **140** A3
Ōtsuki *Japan* 35°36N 138°57E **223** B10
Otta *Norway* 61°46N 9°32E **164** C6
Otta ➔ *Norway* 61°46N 9°31E **164** C6
Ottakring *Austria* 48°12N 16°18E **142** A1
Ottapalam *India* 10°46N 76°23E **245** J3
Ottávia *Italy* 41°57N 12°24E **136** B1
Ottawa = **Outaouais** ➔
Canada 45°27N 74°8W **298** C5
Ottawa *Ont., Canada* 45°26N 75°42W **313** A9
Ottawa *Ill., U.S.A.* 41°21N 88°51W **311** C8
Ottawa *Kans., U.S.A.* 38°37N 95°16W **308** F6
Ottawa *Ohio, U.S.A.* 41°1N 84°3W **311** C12
Ottawa Is. *Canada* 59°35N 80°10W **295** D11
Ottélé *Cameroon* 3°38N 11°19E **263** E7
Ottensheim *Austria* 48°21N 14°12E **180** C7
Otter Cr. ➔ *U.S.A.* 44°13N 73°17W **313** B11
Otter Creek *U.S.A.* 29°19N 82°46W **317** F7
Otter L. *Canada* 55°35N 104°39W **297** B8
Otterbein *U.S.A.* 40°29N 87°6W **311** D9
Otterndorf *Germany* 53°48N 8°53E **178** B4
Otterøya *Norway* 62°45N 6°50E **164** B3
Otterup *Denmark* 55°30N 10°22E **163** J4
Otterville *Ont., Canada* 42°55N 80°36W **312** D4
Otterville *Mo., U.S.A.* 38°42N 93°0W **310** F4
Ottery *S. Africa* 34°1S 18°32E **118** B2
Ottery St. Mary *U.K.* 50°44N 3°17W **169** G4
Ottilien Reef *Papua N. G.* 4°33S 148°49E **286** C5
Ottmachau = **Otmuchów**
Poland 50°28N 17°10E **185** H4
Otto Beit Bridge *Zimbabwe* 15°59S 28°56E **269** F2
Ottobrunn *Germany* 48°3N 11°40E **131** B3
Ottosdal *S. Africa* 26°46S 25°59E **270** C4
Ottoville *U.S.A.* 40°57N 84°22W **311** D12
Ottumwa *U.S.A.* 41°1N 92°25W **310** D4
Otu *Nigeria* 8°14N 3°22E **263** D5
Otukpa *Nigeria* 7°9N 7°41E **263** D6
Oturkpo *Nigeria* 7°16N 8°8E **263** D6
Otvazhnoye = **Zhigulevsk**
Russia 53°28N 49°30E **190** D9
Otvazhny = **Zhigulevsk**
Russia 53°28N 49°30E **190** D9
Otway, B. *Chile* 53°30S 74°0W **336** D2
Otway, C. *Australia* 38°52S 143°30E **282** E5
Otway, Seno de *Chile* 53°5S 71°30W **336** D2
Otway △ *Australia* 38°47S 143°34E **282** E5
Otwock *Poland* 52°5N 21°20E **185** F8
Otyniya *Ukraine* 48°44N 24°51E **183** B9
Ötztaler Ache ➔ *Austria* 47°14N 10°50E **180** D3
Ötztaler Alpen *Austria* 46°56N 11°0E **180** E3
Ou ➔ *Laos* 20°4N 102°13E **236** B4
Ou Neua *Laos* 22°18N 101°48E **228** F3
Ou-Sammyaku *Japan* 39°20N 140°35E **220** E10
Ouachita ➔ *U.S.A.* 31°38N 91°49W **314** F9
Ouachita, L. *U.S.A.* 34°34N 93°12W **314** D8
Ouachita Mts. *U.S.A.* 34°30N 94°30W **314** D7
Ouadâne *Mauritania* 20°50N 11°40W **260** D2
Ouadda *C.A.R.* 8°15N 22°20E **264** A4
Ouaddaï □ *Chad* 13°0N 21°0E **259** F4
Ouagadougou
Burkina Faso 12°25N 1°30W **263** C4
Ouagam *Chad* 14°22N 14°42E **259** F2
Ouaham ➔ *C.A.R.* 6°35N 15°12E **264** A3
Ouahigouya *Burkina Faso* 13°31N 2°25W **262** C4
Ouahila *Algeria* 27°50N 5°0W **260** C4
Ouahran = **Oran** *Algeria* 35°45N 0°39W **261** A4
Oualâta *Mauritania* 17°20N 6°55W **262** B3
Ouallah *Comoros Is.* 12°19S 43°39E **272** a
Ouallam *Niger* 14°23N 2°10E **263** C5
Ouallene *Algeria* 24°41N 1°11E **261** D5
Ouanary *Fr. Guiana* 4°13N 51°40W **329** C7
Ouanda Djallé *C.A.R.* 8°55N 22°53E **264** A4
Ouandago *C.A.R.* 7°13N 18°50E **264** A3
Ouandjia, Bahr ➔ *C.A.R.* 9°35N 21°43E **264** A4
Ouandjia-Vakaga △ *C.A.R.* 9°2N 22°18E **264** A4
Ouangani *Mayotte* 12°50S 45°8E **272** b
Ouango *C.A.R.* 4°19N 22°30E **264** B4
Ouani *Comoros Is.* 12°9S 44°18E **272** a
Ouantonou *C.A.R.* 7°19N 15°18E **264** A3
Ouarâne *Mauritania* 21°0N 10°30W **260** D2
Ouargaye *Burkina Faso* 11°40N 0°5E **263** C5
Ouargla *Algeria* 31°59N 5°16E **261** B6
Ouargla □ *Algeria* 30°30N 6°10E **261** B6
Ouarkoye *Burkina Faso* 12°5N 3°40W **262** C4
Ouarkziz, Jebel *Algeria* 28°50N 8°0W **260** C3
Ouarra ➔ *C.A.R.* 5°5N 24°26E **264** A4
Ouarzazate *Morocco* 30°55N 6°50W **260** B3
Ouarzazate □ *Morocco* 31°0N 6°30W **260** B3
Ouassouas *Mali* 16°10N 1°23E **263** B5
Ouatagouna *Mali* 15°11N 0°43E **263** B5
Ouatere *C.A.R.* 5°30N 19°8E **264** A3
Oubangi ➔
Dem. Rep. of the Congo 0°30S 17°50E **264** C3
Oubarakai, O. ➔ *Algeria* 27°20N 9°0E **261** C6
Ouche ➔ *France* 47°6N 5°16E **173** E12
Oud Zuid *Amsterdam, Neths.* **112** b1
Ouddorp *Neths.* 51°50N 3°57E **170** C3
Oude Kerk *Amsterdam, Neths.* **112** b2
Oude Rijn ➔ *Neths.* 52°12N 4°24E **170** B4
Oudeïka *Mali* 17°30N 1°40W **263** B4
Oudenaarde *Belgium* 50°50N 3°37E **170** D3
Ouderkerk *Neths.* 52°18N 4°55E **112** B2
Oudon ➔ *France* 47°41N 0°53W **172** E6
Oudtshoorn *S. Africa* 33°35S 22°14E **270** D3
Oued Zem *Morocco* 32°52N 6°34W **260** B3
Ouégoa *N. Cal.* 20°20S 164°26E **288** d
Oueita *Chad* 17°47N 20°39E **259** E4
Ouellé *Ivory C.* 7°26N 4°1W **262** D4
Ouéme ➔ *Benin* 6°30N 2°30E **263** D5
Ouenza *Algeria* 35°57N 8°4E **261** A6
Ouessa *Burkina Faso* 11°4N 2°47W **262** C4
Ouessant, Î. d' *France* 48°28N 5°6W **172** D1
Ouesso *Congo* 1°37N 16°5E **264** B3
Ouest □ *Cameroon* 5°30N 10°30E **263** D7
Ouest, Pte. de l' *Canada* 49°52N 64°40W **299** C7
Ouezzane *Morocco* 34°51N 5°35W **260** B3
Ougarou *Burkina Faso* 12°10N 0°58E **263** C5
Oughter, L. *Ireland* 54°1N 7°28W **166** B4
Oughterard *Ireland* 53°26N 9°18W **166** C2
Ouhan ➔ *Chad* 9°18N 18°14E **259** G3
Ouidah *Benin* 6°25N 2°0E **263** D5
Ouidi *Niger* 14°10N 13°0E **259** F2
Ouissongo *Angola* 7°40S 15°41E **265** E3
Ouistreham *France* 49°17N 0°18W **172** C6
Oujda *Morocco* 34°41N 1°55W **261** B4
Oujda □ *Morocco* 33°18N 2°24W **260** B4
Oujeft *Mauritania* 20°2N 13°0W **260** D2
Oulainen *Finland* 64°17N 24°47E **160** D21
Ould Yenjé *Mauritania* 15°38N 12°16W **262** B2
Ouled Djellal *Algeria* 34°28N 5°2E **261** B6
Ouled Naïl, Mts. des
Algeria 34°30N 3°30E **261** B5
Ouli *Cameroon* 5°12N 14°33E **264** A2
Oullins *France* 45°43N 4°49E **175** C8
Oulmès *Morocco* 33°17N 6°0W **260** B3
Oulou, Bahr ➔ *C.A.R.* 9°48N 21°32E **264** A4
Oulu *Finland* 65°1N 25°29E **160** D21

Oulujärvi Finland 64°25N 27°15E 160 D22
Oulujoki → Finland 65°1N 25°30E 160 D21
Oulunkylä Finland 60°13N 24°58E 121 B2
Oulx Italy 45°2N 6°50E 198 C3
Oum Chalouba Chad 15°48N 20°46E 259 E4
Oum-el-Bouaghi Algeria 35°55N 7°6E 261 A6
Oum-el-Bouaghi □ Algeria 35°50N 7°5E 261 A6
Oum el Ksi Algeria 29°4N 6°59W 260 C3
Oum-er-Rbia, O. → Morocco 33°19N 8°21W 260 B3
Oum Hadjer Chad 13°18N 19°41E 259 F3
Oum Hadjer, O. → Chad 16°38N 20°14E 259 E4
Oumé Ivory C. 6°21N 5°27W 262 D3
Oumm ed Droûs Guebli, Sebkhet Mauritania 24°3N 11°45W 260 D2
Oumm ed Droûs Telli, Sebkhet Mauritania 24°20N 11°30W 260 D2
Ounane, Dj. Algeria 25°4N 7°19E 261 C6
Ounasjoki → Finland 66°31N 25°40E 160 C21
Ounguati Namibia 22°0S 15°46E 270 B2
Ounianga Kébir Chad 19°4N 20°29E 259 E4
Ounianga Sérir Chad 18°54N 20°51E 259 E4
Ounissoui Niger 17°34N 12°13E 259 E2
Our → Lux. 49°55N 6°5E 170 E6
Oura, Akra Greece 38°10N 26°2E 205 C8
Oura-wan Japan 26°32N 128°4E 288 a
Ouranoupoli Greece 40°20N 23°59E 202 F7
Ourârene Niger 19°30N 7°10E 263 B6
Ourari, Tarso Chad 21°27N 17°27E 259 D3
Ouray U.S.A. 38°1N 107°40W 305 G10
Ourcq → France 49°1N 3°1E 173 C10
Ourcq, Canal de l' France 48°54N 2°28E 134 A3
Ourém Brazil 1°33S 47°6W 332 B2
Ourense Spain 42°19N 7°55W 194 C3
Ouricuri Brazil 7°53S 40°5W 332 C3
Ourinhos Brazil 23°0S 49°54W 335 A6
Ourique Portugal 37°38N 8°16W 195 H2
Ouro Fino Brazil 22°16S 46°25W 335 A6
Ouro-Ndia Mali 15°8N 4°35W 262 B4
Ouro Prêto Brazil 20°20S 43°30W 333 F3
Ouro Prêto do Oeste Brazil 10°40S 62°18W 331 C5
Ouro Sogui Senegal 15°36N 13°19W 262 B2
Oursi Burkina Faso 14°41N 0°27W 263 C4
Ourthe → Belgium 50°29N 5°35E 170 D5
Ouse → E. Sussex, U.K. 50°47N 0°4E 169 G8
Ouse → N. Yorks., U.K. 53°44N 0°55W 168 D7
Oust France 42°52N 1°13E 174 F5
Oust → France 47°35N 2°6W 172 E4
Outamba-Kilimi △ S. Leone 9°50N 12°40W 262 D2
Outaouais → Canada 45°27N 74°8W 298 C5
Outardes → Canada 49°24N 69°30W 299 C6
Outat Oulad el Haj Morocco 33°22N 3°42W 261 B4
Outeiro de Rei Spain 43°6N 7°36W 194 B3
Outer Hebrides U.K. 57°30N 7°40W 167 D1
Outer Mission U.S.A. 37°43N 122°26W 136 B2
Outes = Serra de Outes Spain 42°52N 8°55W 194 C2
Outjo Namibia 20°5S 16°7E 270 B2
Outlook Canada 51°30N 107°0W 297 C7
Outokumpu Finland 62°43N 29°1E 160 E23
Outreau France 50°40N 1°36E 173 B8
Outremont Canada 45°31N 73°36W 130 A2
Ouvéa, Î. N. Cal. 20°35S 166°35E 288 d
Ouvèze → France 43°59N 4°51E 175 E8
Ouyen Australia 35°1S 142°22E 282 C5
Ouzinkie U.S.A. 57°56N 152°30W 303 H9
Ouzouer-le-Marché France 47°54N 1°32E 173 E8
Ovacık Turkey 36°11N 33°40E 250 B4
Ovada Italy 44°38N 8°38E 198 D5
Ovahe Chile 27°5S 109°19W 330 b
Ovalau Fiji 17°40S 178°48E 287 A2
Ovalle Chile 30°33S 71°18W 334 C1
Ovamboland Namibia 18°30S 16°0E 270 A2
Ovar Portugal 40°51N 8°40W 194 E2
Ovau Solomon Is. 6°40S 156°8E 287 L9
Overath Germany 50°56N 7°17E 178 E3
Overflakkee Neths. 51°44N 4°10E 170 C4
Overijse Belgium 50°47N 4°32E 116 B3
Overijssel □ Neths. 52°25N 6°35E 170 B6
Overland U.S.A. 38°42N 90°21W 310 F6
Overland Park U.S.A. 38°58N 94°40W 308 F6
Overton U.S.A. 36°33N 114°27W 307 J12
Övertorneå Sweden 66°23N 23°38E 160 C20
Överum Sweden 58°0N 16°20E 163 F10
Ovid Mich., U.S.A. 43°1N 84°22W 311 A12
Ovid N.Y., U.S.A. 42°41N 76°49W 313 D8
Ovidiopol Ukraine 46°15N 30°30E 189 J6
Ovidiu Romania 44°16N 28°34E 183 F13
Oviedo Spain 43°25N 5°50W 194 B5
Oviedo Fla., U.S.A. 28°40N 81°13W 317 G8
Oviksfjällen Sweden 63°0N 13°49E 162 A7
Ovišī Latvia 57°33N 21°44E 184 A8
Ovoot Mongolia 45°21N 113°45E 226 B7
Övör Hangay □ Mongolia 45°0N 102°30E 226 B2
Ovoro Nigeria 5°26N 7°16E 263 D6
Øvre Årdal Norway 61°19N 7°48E 164 C4
Övre Fryken Sweden 60°0N 13°7E 162 E7
Øvre Rendal Norway 61°54N 11°4E 164 C8
Øvre Rindal Norway 63°6N 9°10E 164 A6
Øvre Sirdal Norway 58°48N 6°43E 164 F3
Ovruch Ukraine 51°25N 28°45E 177 C15
Owaka N.Z. 46°27S 169°40E 285 G4
Owambo = Ovamboland Namibia 18°30S 16°0E 270 A2
Owando Congo 0°29S 15°55E 264 C3
Owasco L. U.S.A. 42°50N 76°31W 313 D8
Owase Japan 34°7N 136°12E 223 C8
Owatonna U.S.A. 44°5N 93°14W 308 C7
Owbeh Afghan. 34°28N 63°10E 240 B1
Owego U.S.A. 42°6N 76°16W 313 D8
Owen Australia 34°15S 138°32E 282 C3
Owen, Mt. N.Z. 41°35S 172°33E 285 B7
Owen Falls Dam = Nalubaale Dam Uganda 0°30N 33°5E 268 B3
Owen Sound Canada 44°35N 80°55W 312 B4
Owen Stanley Ra. Papua N. G. 8°30S 147°0E 286 E4
Owendo Gabon 0°17N 9°30E 264 B1
Oweniny → Ireland 54°8N 9°34W 166 B2
Owens → U.S.A. 36°32N 117°59W 306 J9
Owens L. U.S.A. 36°26N 117°57W 307 J9
Owensboro U.S.A. 37°46N 87°7W 311 G9
Owensville Ind., U.S.A. 38°16N 87°41W 311 F9
Owensville Mo., U.S.A. 38°21N 91°30W 310 F5
Owenteik Guyana 4°27N 59°35W 329 C6
Owenton U.S.A. 38°32N 84°50W 311 F12
Owerri Nigeria 5°29N 7°0E 263 D6
Owhango N.Z. 39°0S 175°23E 284 F4
Owhiro Bay N.Z. 41°21S 174°45E 143 C1
Owingsville U.S.A. 38°9N 83°46W 311 F13
Owl → Canada 57°51N 92°44W 297 B10
Owo Nigeria 7°10N 5°39E 263 D6
Oworonsoki Nigeria 6°32N 3°24E 124 A2
Owosso U.S.A. 43°0N 84°10W 311 B12
Owyhee U.S.A. 41°57N 116°6W 304 F5
Owyhee → U.S.A. 43°49N 117°2W 304 E5
Owyhee, L. U.S.A. 43°38N 117°14W 304 E5
Ox Mts. = Slieve Gamph Ireland 54°6N 9°0W 166 B3
Oxapampa Peru 10°33S 75°26W 330 C2
Öxarfjörður Iceland 66°15N 16°45W 155 A10
Oxbow Canada 49°14N 102°10W 297 D8
Oxelösund Sweden 58°43N 17°5E 163 F11
Oxford N.Z. 43°18S 172°11E 285 D7
Oxford Oxon., U.K. 51°46N 1°15W 169 F6
Oxford Ala., U.S.A. 33°36N 85°51W 316 B4
Oxford Iowa, U.S.A. 41°43N 91°47W 310 C5
Oxford Mass., U.S.A. 42°7N 71°52W 313 D13
Oxford Mich., U.S.A. 42°49N 83°16W 311 B13
Oxford Miss., U.S.A. 34°22N 89°31W 315 D10
Oxford N.C., U.S.A. 36°19N 78°35W 315 C15
Oxford N.Y., U.S.A. 42°27N 75°36W 313 D9
Oxford Ohio, U.S.A. 39°31N 84°45W 311 E12
Oxford L. Canada 54°51N 95°37W 297 C9
Oxford Street London, U.K. 125 b3
Oxfordshire □ U.K. 51°48N 1°16W 169 F6
Oxgangs U.K. 55°54N 3°13W 121 B2
Oxia Greece 38°18N 21°6E 207 C3
Oxie Sweden 55°33N 13°6E 163 J7
Oxilithos Greece 38°35N 24°7E 204 C6
Oxley Australia 34°11S 144°6E 282 C6
Oxley Wild Rivers △ Australia 30°57S 152°12E 283 A10
Oxnard U.S.A. 34°12N 119°11W 307 L7
Oxon Hill U.S.A. 38°48N 76°59W 143 C4
Oxsjövålen Sweden 62°34N 13°57E 162 B7
Oxus = Amudarya → Uzbekistan 43°58N 59°34E 216 D5
Oya Malaysia 2°55N 111°55E 235 B4
Oyabe Japan 36°47N 136°56E 223 A8
Oyama Japan 36°18N 139°48E 223 A11
Oyambre ⌓ Spain 43°22N 4°21W 194 B6
Oyapock → Fr. Guiana 4°8N 51°40W 329 C7
Øye Norway 58°16N 6°49E 164 F3
Oyem Gabon 1°34N 11°31E 264 B2
Oyen Canada 51°22N 110°28W 297 C6
Øyer Norway 61°16N 10°25E 164 C7
Øyeren Norway 59°50N 11°15E 164 E8
Oykel → U.K. 57°56N 4°26W 167 D4
Oymyakon Russia 63°25N 142°44E 215 C15
Oyo Nigeria 7°46N 3°56E 263 D5
Oyo □ Nigeria 8°15N 3°30E 263 D5
Oyodo Japan 34°42N 135°29E 133 A1
Oyón Peru 10°37S 76°47W 330 C2
Oyonnax France 46°16N 5°40E 173 F12
Oyrot = Gorno-Altay □ Russia 51°0N 86°0E 217 B11
Oyrot-Tura = Gorno-Altaysk Russia 51°50N 86°5E 217 B11
Øyslebø Norway 58°9N 7°34E 164 F4
Oyster B. Australia 34°0S 151°5E 139 C1
Oyster Bay U.S.A. 40°52N 73°32W 313 F11
Oyster Harbour = Ladysmith Canada 49°0N 123°49W 306 B3
Oyster Rock India 18°54N 72°49E 130 B1
Oyster Rocks Pakistan 24°48N 66°59E 123 B2
Øystese Norway 60°22N 6°9E 164 D3
Öyübari Japan 43°1N 142°5E 220 C11
Oyyl → Kazakhstan 49°4N 54°40E 216 C4
Özalp Turkey 38°39N 43°59E 213 C10
Ozamiz Phil. 8°15N 123°50E 233 G4
Ozark Ala., U.S.A. 31°28N 85°39W 316 D4
Ozark Ark., U.S.A. 35°29N 93°50W 314 D8
Ozark Mo., U.S.A. 37°1N 93°12W 308 G7
Ozark Plateau U.S.A. 37°20N 91°40W 308 G8
Ozarks, L. of the U.S.A. 38°12N 92°38W 310 F4
Ożarów Poland 50°53N 21°40E 185 H8
Ózd Hungary 48°14N 20°15E 182 B5
Ozernoye Russia 51°46N 51°28E 190 E10
Ozero Svityaz Ukraine 51°30N 23°50E 185 G10
Ozersk Russia 54°25N 22°0E 184 D8
Ozette, L. U.S.A. 48°6N 124°38W 306 B2
Ozieri Italy 40°35N 9°0E 200 B2
Ozimek Poland 50°41N 18°11E 185 H5
Ozinki Russia 51°12N 49°44E 190 E9
Ozoir-la-Ferrière France 48°46N 2°40E 134 B4
Ozona U.S.A. 30°43N 101°12W 314 F4
Ozone Park U.S.A. 40°40N 73°50W 132 B2
Ozorków Poland 51°57N 19°16E 185 G6
Ozren Bos.-H. 43°55N 18°29E 182 G3
Ōzu Ehime, Japan 33°30N 132°33E 222 D4
Ōzu Kumamoto, Japan 32°52N 130°52E 222 E2
Ozuluama Mexico 21°40N 97°51W 319 C5
Ozun Romania 45°47N 25°50E 183 E10
Ozurgeti Georgia 41°55N 42°0E 191 K5

P

Pa Burkina Faso 11°33N 3°19W 262 C4
Pa-an Burma 16°51N 97°40E 241 G6
Pa Mong Dam Thailand 18°0N 102°22E 236 D4
Pa Sak → Thailand 15°30N 101°0E 236 E3
Paama Vanuatu 16°28S 168°14E 287 F6
Paamiut Greenland 62°0N 49°43W 154 E6
Paar → Germany 48°46N 11°36E 179 G7
Paarl S. Africa 33°45S 18°56E 270 D2
Pa'auilo U.S.A. 20°2N 155°22W 302 C6
Pab Hills Pakistan 26°30N 66°45E 242 F2
Pabbay U.K. 57°46N 7°14W 167 D1
Pabianice Poland 51°40N 19°20E 185 G6
Pabna Bangla. 24°1N 89°18E 241 C2
Pabo Uganda 3°1N 32°10E 268 B3
Pacaás Novos, Serra dos Brazil 10°45S 64°15W 331 C5
Pacaás Novos △ Brazil 11°0S 63°0W 331 C5
Pacaipampa Peru 5°35S 79°39W 330 B2
Pacaja → Brazil 1°56S 50°50W 332 B1
Pacajus Brazil 4°10S 38°31W 332 B4
Pacaraima, Sa. S. Amer. 4°0N 62°30W 329 C5
Pacarán Peru 12°50S 76°3W 330 C2
Pacaraos Peru 11°12S 76°42W 330 C2
Pacasmayo Peru 7°20S 79°35W 330 B2
Pace U.S.A. 30°36N 87°10W 317 E2
Paceco Italy 37°59N 12°33E 200 E5
Pachacamac Peru 12°14S 77°53W 330 C2
Pachang Hsi → Taiwan 23°20N 120°7E 225 C2
Pachao Yü Taiwan 23°22N 119°29E 225 C1
Pachhar India 24°40N 77°42E 242 G7
Pachia Greece 36°17N 25°50E 205 E7
Pachino Italy 36°43N 15°5E 201 F8
Pachitea → Peru 8°46S 74°33W 330 B3
Pachiza Peru 7°16S 76°46W 330 B2
Pachmarhi India 22°28N 78°26E 243 H8
Pachnai India 26°57N 92°19E 241 B4
Pachnes Greece 35°16N 24°4E 207 E5
Pacho Colombia 5°8N 74°10W 328 B3
Pachora India 20°38N 75°29E 244 D2
Pachpadra India 25°58N 72°10E 242 G5
Pachuca Mexico 20°7N 98°44W 319 C5
Pacific U.S.A. 38°29N 90°45W 310 F6
Pacific Antarctic Ridge Pac. Oc. 43°0S 115°0W 151 B13
Pacific City = Huntington Beach U.S.A. 33°40N 118°5W 307 M9
Pacific Grove U.S.A. 36°38N 121°56W 306 J5
Pacific Heights U.S.A. 37°47N 122°26W 136 B2
Pacific Manor U.S.A. 37°38N 122°27W 136 C2
Pacific Ocean 10°0N 140°0W 289 G14
Pacific Palisades Calif., U.S.A. 34°2N 118°32W 126 B1
Pacific Palisades Hawai'i, U.S.A. 21°25N 157°58W 302 K14
Pacific Rim △ Canada 48°40N 124°45W 306 B2
Pacifica U.S.A. 37°37N 122°27W 136 C2
Pacitan Indonesia 8°12S 111°7E 235 D4
Packsaddle Australia 30°36S 141°58E 282 A4
Packwood U.S.A. 46°36N 121°40W 306 D5
Paco Phil. 14°35N 120°59E 127 B1
Paco de Arcos Portugal 38°41N 9°17W 126 A1
Paco Imperial Rio de J., Brazil 135 a2
Pacov Czech Rep. 49°27N 15°0E 180 B8
Pacoval Brazil 2°40S 54°11W 329 D7
Pacuí → Brazil 16°46S 45°1W 333 E2
Pacy-sur-Eure France 49°1N 1°23E 172 C8
Padaido, Kepulauan Indonesia 1°15S 136°30E 231 E9
Padali = Amursk Russia 50°14N 136°54E 215 D14
Padampur India 20°59N 83°4E 244 D6
Padang Indonesia 1°0S 100°20E 234 C2
Padang Endau Malaysia 2°40N 103°38E 237 L4
Padangpanjang Indonesia 0°40S 100°20E 234 C2
Padangsidempuan Indonesia 1°30N 99°15E 234 B1
Padangtikar Indonesia 0°44S 109°15E 235 C3
Padatchaung Burma 19°46N 94°48E 241 F5
Padauari → Brazil 0°15S 64°5W 329 D5
Padaung Burma 18°43N 95°9E 241 F5
Padborg Denmark 54°49N 9°21E 163 K3
Padcaya Bolivia 21°52S 64°48W 331 E5
Paddington N.S.W., Australia 33°53S 151°14E 139 B2
Paddington London, U.K. 125 b2
Paddle Prairie Canada 57°57N 117°29W 296 B5
Paddockwood Canada 53°30N 105°30W 297 C7
Paderborn Germany 51°42N 8°45E 178 D4
Paderno Italy 45°33N 9°9E 129 A1
Paderoo India 18°5N 82°40E 244 E6
Padeş, Vf. Romania 45°40N 22°22E 182 E7
Padilla Bolivia 19°19S 64°20W 331 D5
Padina Romania 44°50N 27°8E 183 F12
Padma India 24°12N 85°22E 243 G11
Padma → Bangla. 23°22N 90°32E 241 D3
Pádova Italy 45°25N 11°53E 199 C8
Padra India 22°15N 73°7E 242 H5
Padrauna India 26°54N 83°59E 243 F10
Padre Burgos Phil. 10°1N 125°0E 233 F5
Padre I. U.S.A. 27°10N 97°25W 314 H6
Padre Island ⌓ U.S.A. 27°0N 97°25W 314 H6
Padrón Spain 42°41N 8°39W 194 C2
Padstow U.K. 50°33N 4°58W 169 G3
Padthaway Australia 36°36S 140°31E 282 D4
Padua = Pádova Italy 45°25N 11°53E 199 C8
Paducah Ky., U.S.A. 37°5N 88°37W 308 G9
Paducah Tex., U.S.A. 34°1N 100°18W 314 D4
Padukka Sri Lanka 6°50N 80°5E 245 L5
Padul Spain 37°1N 3°38W 195 H7
Padwa India 18°27N 82°47E 244 E6
Paea Tahiti 17°41S 149°35W 289 e
Paekakariki N.Z. 40°59S 174°58E 284 G3
Paektu-san N. Korea 41°59N 128°4E 224 B4
Paengaroa N.Z. 37°49S 176°29E 284 D5
Paeroa N.Z. 37°23S 175°41E 284 D4
Paesana Italy 44°41N 7°16E 198 D4
Paete Phil. 14°23N 121°29E 232 D3
Pafúri Mozam. 22°28S 31°17E 271 B5
Pag Croatia 44°25N 15°3E 199 D12
Paga Gabon 0°45S 10°21E 264 C2
Paga Ghana 11°1N 1°8W 263 C4
Pagadian Phil. 7°55N 123°30E 233 H4
Pagai Selatan, Pulau Indonesia 3°0S 100°15E 234 C2
Pagai Utara, Pulau Indonesia 2°35S 100°0E 234 C2
Pagalu = Annobón Atl. Oc. 1°25S 5°36E 255 G4
Pagalungan Phil. 7°4N 124°41E 233 H5
Pagan Burma 21°10N 94°52E 241 E5
Pagan N. Marianas 18°7N 145°46E 302 a
Pagara India 24°22N 80°1E 243 G9
Pagastikos Kolpos Greece 39°15N 23°0E 204 B5
Pagatan Indonesia 3°33S 115°59E 235 C5
Page U.S.A. 36°57N 111°27W 305 H8
Pagėgiai Lithuania 55°9N 21°54E 184 C8
Pagei Papua N. G. 3°2S 141°10E 286 B1
Paget I. India 13°26N 92°50E 245 H11
Pagewood Australia 33°56S 151°14E 139 B2
Pago B. Guam 13°25N 144°47E 302 d
Pago Pago Amer. Samoa 14°16S 170°43W 302 f
Pago Pago Harbor Amer. Samoa 14°17S 170°40W 302 f
Pagosa Springs U.S.A. 37°16N 107°1W 305 H10
Pagote India 18°53N 72°59E 130 B2
Pagua B. Dominica 15°32N 61°17W 323 k
Pagudpud Phil. 18°34N 120°47E 232 B3
Pagwa River Canada 50°2N 85°14W 298 B2
Pagwi Papua N. G. 4°4S 143°2E 286 C2
Pāhala U.S.A. 19°12N 155°29W 302 D6
Pahang □ Malaysia 3°30N 102°45E 234 B2
Pahang → Malaysia 3°30N 103°9E 237 L4
Paharpur Bangla. 24°51N 88°44E 241 C2
Pahia Pt. N.Z. 46°20S 167°41E 285 G2
Pahiatua N.Z. 40°27S 175°50E 284 G4
Pāhoa U.S.A. 19°30N 154°57W 302 D7
Pahokee U.S.A. 26°50N 80°40W 317 J9
Pahrump U.S.A. 36°12N 115°59W 307 J11
Pahute Mesa U.S.A. 37°20N 116°45W 306 H10
Pai Thailand 19°19N 98°27E 236 C2
Pai, I. do Brazil 22°59S 43°5W 135 B2
Paia U.S.A. 20°54N 156°22W 302 C5
Paichuan Liehtao Taiwan 25°58N 119°57E 225 b
Paicines U.S.A. 36°44N 121°17W 306 J5
Paide Estonia 58°53N 25°33E 188 C3
Paignton U.K. 50°26N 3°35W 169 G4
Paihia N.Z. 35°17S 174°6E 284 B3
Paiho Taiwan 23°21N 120°25E 225 C2
Paiján Peru 7°42S 79°20W 330 B2
Päijänne Finland 61°30N 25°30E 188 B3
Pailani India 25°45N 80°26E 243 G9
Pailin Cambodia 12°46N 102°36E 236 F4
Pailolo Channel U.S.A. 21°0N 156°40W 302 B5
Paimpol France 48°48N 3°4W 172 D3
Painan Indonesia 1°21S 100°34E 234 C2
Paine, Cerro Chile 50°59S 73°4W 336 D2
Painesville U.S.A. 41°43N 81°15W 312 E3
Paint Hills = Wemindji Canada 53°0N 78°49W 298 B4
Paint L. Canada 55°28N 97°57W 297 B9
Painted Desert U.S.A. 36°0N 111°0W 305 H8
Paintsville U.S.A. 37°49N 82°48W 309 G12
País Vasco □ Spain 42°50N 2°45W 196 C2
Paisha Taiwan 23°40N 119°35E 225 C1
Paisley Ont., Canada 44°18N 81°16W 312 B3
Paisley Renf., U.K. 55°50N 4°25W 167 F4
Paisley Oreg., U.S.A. 42°42N 120°32W 304 E3
Païta N. Cal. 22°8S 166°22E 288 d
Paita Peru 5°11S 81°9W 330 B1
Paithan India 19°29N 75°23E 244 E2
Paiva → Portugal 41°4N 8°16W 194 D2
Paizhou China 30°12N 113°55E 229 B9
Paja, Cerro Ecuador 1°17S 90°26W 330 a
Pájara Canary Is. 28°21N 14°6W 153 e2
Pajares Spain 43°1N 5°46W 194 B5
Pajares, Puerto de Spain 42°58N 5°46W 194 C5
Pajarito Colombia 5°17N 72°43W 328 B3
Pajęczno Poland 51°10N 19°0E 185 G5
Paju S. Korea 37°45N 126°46E 224 D3
Pak Kok China 22°14N 114°7E 122 B1
Pak Kong China 22°22N 114°15E 122 A2
Pak Lay Laos 18°15N 101°27E 236 C3
Pak Phanang Thailand 8°21N 100°12E 237 H3
Pak Sane Laos 18°22N 103°39E 236 C4
Pak Song Laos 15°11N 106°14E 236 E6
Pak Suong Laos 19°58N 102°15E 228 H4
Pak Tam Chung China 22°24N 114°19E 219 G11
Pakala India 13°29N 79°8E 245 H4
Pakaraima Mts. Guyana 6°0N 60°0W 329 B6
Pakaur India 24°38N 87°51E 243 G12
Pakch'ŏn N. Korea 39°44N 125°35E 224 C2
Pakenham Vic., Australia 38°6S 145°30E 283 E6
Pakenham Ont., Canada 45°18N 76°18W 313 A8
Pakhoi = Beihai China 21°28N 109°6E 228 G7
Pakhuis S. Africa 32°9S 19°5E 270 D2
Pakila Finland 60°15N 24°55E 121 B2
Pakistan ■ Asia 30°0N 70°0E 242 E4
Pakkading Laos 18°19N 103°59E 236 C4
Paklay = Sayaboury Laos 19°15N 101°45E 236 C3
Paklenica △ Croatia 44°20N 15°39E 199 D12
Pakokku Burma 21°20N 95°0E 241 E5
Pakość Poland 52°48N 18°6E 185 F5
Pakowki L. Canada 49°20N 111°0W 297 D6
Pakpattan Pakistan 30°25N 73°27E 242 D5
Pakrac Croatia 45°27N 17°12E 182 E2
Pakruojis Lithuania 55°58N 23°52E 184 C10
Paks Hungary 46°38N 18°55E 182 D3
Paktīā □ Afghan. 33°30N 69°15E 240 B3
Paktīkā □ Afghan. 32°30N 69°0E 240 B3
Pakwach Uganda 2°28N 31°27E 268 B3
Pakxe Laos 15°5N 105°52E 236 E5
Pal Lahara India 21°27N 85°11E 243 J11
Pala Chad 9°25N 15°5E 259 G3
Pala Dem. Rep. of the Congo 6°45S 29°30E 268 D2
Pala Calif., U.S.A. 33°22N 117°5W 307 M9
Palabek Uganda 3°22N 32°33E 268 B3
Palacio de Communicaciones Madrid, Spain 127 a3
Palacio Real Barcelona, Spain 114 b3
Palacio Real Madrid, Spain 127 b1
Palacios U.S.A. 28°42N 96°13W 314 G6
Palafrugell Spain 41°55N 3°10E 196 D8
Palagiano Italy 40°35N 17°2E 201 B10
Palagonía Italy 37°19N 14°45E 201 E7
Palagruža Croatia 42°24N 16°15E 199 F13
Palais de Justice Brussels, Belgium 116 c2
Palais Royal Brussels, Belgium 116 b3
Palais Royal Paris, France 134 b4
Palaiseau France 48°42N 2°14E 134 B2
Palakol India 16°31N 81°46E 245 F5
Palalankwe India 10°52N 92°29E 245 J11
Palam India 19°0N 77°0E 244 E3
Palamas Greece 39°26N 22°4E 204 B4
Palamòs Spain 41°50N 3°10E 196 D8
Palampur India 32°10N 76°30E 242 C7
Palamut Turkey 38°59N 27°41E 205 C9
Palana Tas., Australia 39°45S 147°55E 281 F4
Palana Russia 59°10N 159°59E 215 D16
Palanan Phil. 17°8N 122°29E 232 C4
Palanan Bay Phil. 17°9N 122°27E 232 C4
Palanan Pt. Phil. 17°17N 122°30E 232 C4
Palandri Pakistan 33°42N 73°40E 243 C5
Palanga Lithuania 55°58N 21°3E 184 C8
Palanganene Dem. Rep. of the Congo 6°32S 18°52E 265 D3
Palangkaraya Indonesia 2°16S 113°56E 235 C4
Palani India 10°30N 77°30E 245 J3
Palani Hills India 10°14N 77°33E 245 J3
Palanpur India 24°10N 72°25E 242 G5
Palaoa Pt. U.S.A. 20°44N 156°58W 302 C5
Palapag Phil. 12°33N 125°7E 232 E5
Palapye Botswana 22°30S 27°7E 270 B4
Palar → India 12°27N 80°13E 245 H5
Palas Pakistan 35°4N 73°14E 243 B5
Palas de Rei Spain 42°52N 7°52W 194 C3
Palashi India 23°47N 88°15E 243 H13
Palasponga India 21°47N 85°34E 243 J11
Palatine U.S.A. 42°7N 88°3W 311 B8
Palatka Russia 60°6N 150°54E 215 C16
Palatka Fla., U.S.A. 29°39N 81°38W 316 F8
Palau Italy 41°11N 9°23E 200 A2
Palau ■ Palau 7°30N 134°30E 288 c
Palau Nacional Museu d'Art Barcelona, Spain 114 c1
Palauk Burma 13°10N 98°40E 236 F2
Palawan Phil. 9°30N 118°30E 233 G2
Palawan □ Phil. 10°0N 119°0E 233 G2
Palawan Passage Phil. 10°0N 118°0E 233 G2
Palayan Phil. 15°36N 121°8E 232 D3
Palayankottai India 8°45N 77°45E 245 K3
Palazzo, Pte. France 42°28N 8°30E 175 F12
Palazzo San Gervásio Italy 40°56N 15°59E 201 B8
Palazzolo Italy 45°34N 9°9E 129 A1
Palazzolo Acréide Italy 37°4N 14°54E 201 E7
Palca Chile 19°7S 69°9W 330 D4
Paldiski Estonia 59°23N 24°9E 188 C3
Pale Bos.-H. 43°50N 18°38E 182 G3
Palekastro Greece 35°12N 26°15E 207 E7
Palel India 24°27N 94°2E 241 C5
Paleleh Indonesia 1°10N 121°50E 231 D6
Palembang Indonesia 3°0S 104°50E 234 C2
Palena → Chile 43°50S 73°50W 336 B2
Palena, L. Chile 43°55S 71°40W 336 B2
Palencia Spain 42°1N 4°34W 194 C6
Palencia □ Spain 42°31N 4°33W 194 C6
Paleng Taiwan 24°41N 121°23E 225 B3
Palenque Mexico 17°29N 92°1W 319 D6
Paleo Faliro Greece 37°53N 23°42E 112 B2
Paleochora Greece 35°16N 23°39E 207 E4
Paleokastritsa Greece 39°40N 19°41E 206 B9
Paleometokho Cyprus 35°7N 33°11E 207 E9
Palermo B. Aires, Argentina 34°35S 58°24W 117 B2
Palermo Colombia 2°54N 75°26W 328 C2
Palermo Italy 38°7N 13°22E 200 D6
Palermo Calif., U.S.A. 39°26N 121°33W 304 G3
Palermo ✕ (PMO) Italy 38°11N 13°5E 200 D6
Paleros Greece 38°47N 20°53E 207 B2
Palestina = Jordânia Brazil 15°55S 40°11W 333 E3
Palestine Asia 32°0N 35°0E 251 G6
Palestine Ill., U.S.A. 39°0N 87°37W 311 F9
Palestine Tex., U.S.A. 31°46N 95°38W 314 F7
Palestrina Italy 41°50N 12°53E 199 G9
Paletwa Burma 21°10N 92°50E 241 E4
Palghat India 10°46N 76°42E 245 J3
Palgrave, Mt. Australia 23°22S 115°58E 278 D2
Palhais Portugal 38°37N 9°2W 126 B2
Pali India 25°50N 73°20E 242 G5
Pali Taiwan 25°8N 121°23E 225 A3
Pali-Aike △ Chile 52°6S 69°44W 336 D3
Palikea U.S.A. 21°26N 158°6W 302 K13
Palikir Micronesia 6°55N 158°9E 288 G7
Palimbang Phil. 6°12N 124°12E 233 H5
Palin, Mt. Malaysia 6°10N 117°10E 235 A5
Palinuro Italy 40°2N 15°17E 201 B8
Palinuro, C. Italy 40°2N 15°16E 201 B8
Paliouri, Akra Greece 39°57N 23°45E 202 G7
Palisades Park U.S.A. 40°50N 74°1W 132 A1
Palisades Res. U.S.A. 43°20N 111°12W 304 E8
Palisadoes, The Jamaica 17°57N 76°48W 320 a
Paliseul Belgium 49°54N 5°8E 170 E5
Palitana India 21°32N 71°49E 242 J4
Palizada Mexico 18°15N 92°5W 319 D6
Palk Bay Asia 9°30N 79°15E 245 K4
Palk Strait Asia 10°0N 79°45E 245 K4
Palkānah Iraq 35°49N 44°26E 246 C5
Palkonda India 18°36N 83°48E 244 E6
Palkonda Ra. India 13°50N 79°20E 245 H4
Palkot India 22°53N 84°39E 243 H11
Palla Road = Dinokwe Botswana 23°29S 26°37E 270 B4
Pallanza = Verbánia Italy 45°56N 8°33E 198 C5
Pallarenda Australia 19°12S 146°46E 280 B4
Pallasovka Russia 50°4N 47°0E 190 E8
Palleru → India 16°45N 80°2E 244 F5
Pallës, Bishti i Albania 41°24N 19°24E 202 E3
Pallinup → Australia 34°27S 118°50E 279 F2
Pallisa Uganda 1°12N 33°43E 268 B3
Palliser, C. N.Z. 41°37S 175°14E 284 H4
Palliser, Îs. French Polynesia 15°30S 146°30W 289 f
Palliser B. N.Z. 41°26S 175°5E 284 H4
Pallu India 28°59N 74°14E 242 E6
Palm Bay U.S.A. 28°2N 80°35W 317 G9
Palm Beach Aruba 12°34N 70°2W 322 f
Palm Beach Fla., U.S.A. 26°43N 80°2W 317 J9
Palm Coast U.S.A. 29°35N 81°12W 317 F8
Palm Desert U.S.A. 33°43N 116°22W 307 M10
Palm Harbor U.S.A. 28°5N 82°46W 317 G7
Palm Is. Australia 18°40S 146°35E 280 B4
Palm Springs U.S.A. 33°50N 116°33W 307 M10
Palm Valley U.S.A. 30°11N 81°23W 316 E8
Palma = Paraná Brazil 12°30S 47°48W 333 D2
Palma Mozam. 10°46S 40°29E 269 E5
Palma → Brazil 12°33S 47°52W 333 D2
Palma, B. de Spain 39°30N 2°39E 206 B3
Palma de Mallorca Spain 39°35N 2°39E 206 B3
Palma de Mallorca ✕ (PMI) Spain 39°34N 2°43E 197 F7
Palma del Río Spain 37°43N 5°17W 195 H5
Palma di Montechiaro Italy 37°11N 13°46E 200 E6
Palma Nova Spain 39°32N 2°34E 206 B3
Palma Soriano Cuba 20°15N 76°0W 320 B4
Palmaner India 13°12N 78°45E 245 H4
Palmares Brazil 8°41S 35°28W 332 C4
Palmarito Venezuela 7°37N 70°10W 328 B3
Palmarola Italy 40°56N 12°51E 200 B5
Palmas Brazil 26°29S 52°0W 335 B5
Palmas, C. Liberia 4°27N 7°46W 262 E3
Pálmas, G. di Italy 39°0N 8°30E 200 D1
Palmas de Monte Alto Brazil 14°16S 43°10W 333 D3
Palmdale Calif., U.S.A. 34°35N 118°7W 307 L8
Palmdale Fla., U.S.A. 26°57N 81°19W 317 J8
Palmeira Brazil 25°25S 50°0W 333 G2
Palmeira das Missões Brazil 27°55S 53°17W 335 B5
Palmeira dos Índios Brazil 9°25S 36°37W 332 C4
Palmeirais Brazil 6°0S 43°0W 332 C3
Palmeiras Brazil 12°31S 41°34W 333 D3
Palmeiras → Brazil 12°22S 47°8W 333 D2
Palmeirinhas, Pta. das Angola 9°2S 12°57E 265 D2
Palmela Portugal 38°32N 8°57W 195 G2
Palmelo Brazil 17°20S 48°27W 333 E2
Palmer Antarctica 64°35S 65°0W 151 C17
Palmer Alaska, U.S.A. 61°36N 149°7W 303 F10
Palmer → Australia 16°0S 142°26E 280 B3
Palmer Arch. Antarctica 64°15S 65°0W 151 C17
Palmer Lake U.S.A. 39°7N 104°55W 304 G11
Palmer Land Antarctica 73°0S 63°0W 151 D18
Palmer Park U.S.A. 38°55N 76°52W 143 B4
Palmerston = Darwin Australia 12°25S 130°51E 278 B5
Palmerston N. Terr., Australia 12°31S 130°59E 278 B5
Palmerston Ont., Canada 43°50N 80°51W 312 C4
Palmerston Dublin, Ireland 53°20N 6°22W 120 A1
Palmerston N.Z. 45°29S 170°43E 285 F5
Palmerston North N.Z. 40°21S 175°39E 284 G4
Palmerton U.S.A. 40°48N 75°37W 313 F9
Palmetto Fla., U.S.A. 27°31N 82°34W 317 H7
Palmetto Ga., U.S.A. 33°31N 84°40W 316 B5
Palmetto Pt. Antigua & B. 17°37N 61°51W 322 c
Palmetto Pt. St. Kitts & Nevis 17°18N 62°46W 322 d
Palmi Italy 38°21N 15°51E 201 D8
Palmira Argentina 32°59S 68°34W 334 C2
Palmira Colombia 3°32N 76°16W 328 C2
Palmyra = Tudmur Syria 34°36N 38°15E 213 E8
Palmyra Ill., U.S.A. 39°26N 90°0W 310 E7
Palmyra Mo., U.S.A. 39°48N 91°32W 310 E5
Palmyra N.J., U.S.A. 40°0N 75°1W 313 F9
Palmyra N.Y., U.S.A. 43°5N 77°18W 312 C7
Palmyra Pa., U.S.A. 40°18N 76°36W 313 F8
Palmyra Wis., U.S.A. 42°52N 88°36W 311 B8
Palmyra Is. Pac. Oc. 5°52N 162°5W 289 G11
Palmyras = Santos Dumont Brazil 22°55S 43°10W 333 F3
Palmyras Pt. India 20°46N 87°1E 244 D8
Palo Phil. 11°10N 124°59E 233 F5
Palo Alto U.S.A. 37°27N 122°10W 306 H4
Palo Seco Trin. & Tob. 10°4N 61°36W 323 t
Palo Verde U.S.A. 33°26N 114°44W 307 M12
Palo Verde △ Costa Rica 10°21N 85°21W 320 D2
Paloheinä Finland 60°15N 24°56E 121 B2
Paloich Sudan 10°28N 32°32E 257 E3
Palomar Mt. U.S.A. 33°22N 116°50W 307 M10
Palomeras Spain 40°22N 3°39W 127 B2
Palompon Phil. 11°3N 124°23E 233 F5
Palopo Indonesia 3°0S 120°16E 231 E6
Palos, C. de Spain 37°38N 0°40W 197 H4
Palos de la Frontera Spain 37°14N 6°53W 195 H4
Palos Heights U.S.A. 41°39N 87°47W 119 D2
Palos Hills U.S.A. 41°42N 87°49W 119 C2
Palos Hills Forest U.S.A. 41°40N 87°52W 119 C1
Palos Park U.S.A. 41°40N 87°50W 119 C1
Palos Verdes, Pt. U.S.A. 33°46N 118°25W 307 M8
Palos Verdes Estates U.S.A. 33°48N 118°23W 307 M8
Palpa Peru 14°30S 75°15W 330 C2
Palpara India 22°38N 88°22E 124 B2
Pålsboda Sweden 59°3N 15°22E 162 E9
Palu Indonesia 1°0S 119°52E 231 E5
Palu Turkey 38°45N 40°0E 213 C9
Paluan Phil. 13°26N 120°29E 232 E3
Paluke Liberia 5°2N 8°5W 262 D3
Paluzza Italy 46°32N 13°1E 199 B10
Palwal India 28°8N 77°19E 242 E7
Pama Burkina Faso 11°19N 0°44E 263 C5
Pama → C.A.R. 4°23N 18°43E 264 B3
Pama ⌓ Burkina Faso 11°27N 0°40E 263 C5
Pamandzi Mayotte 12°47S 45°16E 272 b
Pamanukan Indonesia 6°16S 107°49E 235 D3
Pamban I. India 9°15N 79°20E 245 K4
Pamekasan Indonesia 7°10S 113°28E 235 D4
Pamenang Indonesia 8°24S 116°6E 231 J19
Pamiers France 43°7N 1°39E 174 E5
Pamir Tajikistan 37°40N 73°0E 239 B10
Pamirsky Post = Murgap Tajikistan 38°10N 74°2E 217 E8
Pamlico → U.S.A. 35°20N 76°28W 315 D16
Pamlico Sd. U.S.A. 35°20N 76°0W 315 D17
Pampa U.S.A. 35°32N 100°58W 314 D4
Pampa de Agma Argentina 43°45S 69°40W 336 B3
Pampa de las Salinas Argentina 32°1S 66°58W 334 C2
Pampa Grande Bolivia 18°5S 64°6W 331 D5
Pampa Hermosa Peru 7°7S 75°4W 330 B2
Pampanga □ Phil. 15°4N 120°40E 232 D3
Pampanua Indonesia 4°16S 120°8E 231 E6
Pampas Argentina 35°0S 63°0W 334 D3
Pampas Peru 12°20S 74°50W 330 C3
Pampas → Peru 13°24S 73°12W 330 C3
Pamphylia Turkey 37°0N 31°20E 250 B2
Pamplemousses Mauritius 20°6S 57°34E 272 e
Pamplona Colombia 7°23N 72°39W 328 B3
Pamplona Phil. 18°31N 121°20E 232 B3
Pamplona Spain 42°48N 1°38W 196 C3
Pampoenpoort S. Africa 31°3S 22°40E 270 D3
Pamuk → Turkey 37°2N 34°49E 250 A5
Pamukçu Turkey 39°30N 27°54E 205 B9
Pamukkale Turkey 37°55N 29°8E 205 D11
Pan de Azúcar △ Chile 26°0S 70°40W 334 B1
Pan Xian China 25°46N 104°38E 228 E5
Pana U.S.A. 39°23N 89°5W 310 E7
Panabo Phil. 7°19N 125°42E 233 H5
Panaca U.S.A. 37°47N 114°23W 305 H6
Panacea U.S.A. 30°2N 84°23W 316 E5
Panagyurishte Bulgaria 42°30N 24°15E 203 D8
Panaitan Indonesia 6°36S 105°12E 234 D3
Panaji India 15°25N 73°50E 245 G1
Panamá Panama 9°0N 79°25W 320 E4
Panama Sri Lanka 6°45N 81°48E 245 L5
Panama ■ Cent. Amer. 8°48N 79°55W 320 E4
Panamá, G. de Panama 8°4N 79°20W 320 E4
Panama, Isthmus of Cent. Amer. 9°0N 79°0W 320 E4
Panama Basin Pac. Oc. 5°0N 83°30W 289 G19
Panama Canal Panama 9°10N 79°37W 320 E4
Panama City U.S.A. 30°10N 85°40W 316 E4
Panama City Beach U.S.A. 30°11N 85°48W 316 E4
Panamint Range U.S.A. 36°20N 117°20W 307 J9
Panamint Springs U.S.A. 36°20N 117°28W 307 J9
Panão Peru 9°55S 75°55W 330 B2
Panaon I. Phil. 10°3N 125°13E 233 F5
Panare Thailand 6°51N 101°30E 237 J3
Panarea Italy 38°38N 15°4E 201 D8
Panaro → Italy 44°55N 11°25E 199 D8
Panarukan Indonesia 7°42S 113°56E 235 D4
Panay Phil. 11°10N 122°30E 233 F4
Panay G. Phil. 11°0N 122°30E 233 F4
Pančevo Serbia 44°52N 20°41E 182 F5
Panch'iao Taiwan 25°1N 121°27E 225 A3
Panchur India 22°32N 88°16E 124 B1
Panciu Romania 45°54N 27°8E 183 E12
Pancol Phil. 10°52N 119°25E 233 F2
Pancorbo, Desfiladero Spain 42°32N 3°5W 194 C7
Pâncota Romania 46°20N 21°45E 182 D6
Panda Mozam. 24°2S 34°45E 271 B5
Pandacan Phil. 14°35N 121°0E 127 B2
Pandan Malaysia 1°32N 103°46E 237 d
Pandan Antique, Phil. 11°45N 122°10E 233 F4
Pandan Catanduanes, Phil. 14°3N 124°10E 232 D5
Pandan, Selat Singapore 1°15N 103°44E 138 B2
Pandan Bay Phil. 11°43N 122°0E 233 F4
Pandan Res. Singapore 1°18N 103°44E 138 B2
Pandan Tampoi = Tampoi Malaysia 1°30N 103°39E 237 d
Pandegelang Indonesia 6°25S 106°5E 234 D3
Pandhana India 21°42N 76°13E 242 J7
Pandharkawada India 20°1N 78°32E 244 D4
Pandharpur India 17°41N 75°20E 244 F2
Pandhurna India 21°36N 78°35E 244 D4
Pando Uruguay 34°44S 56°0W 335 C4
Pando □ Bolivia 11°20S 67°40W 330 C4
Pando, L. = Hope, L. Australia 28°24S 139°18E 281 D2
Pandokratoras Greece 39°45N 19°50E 206 B9
Pandora Costa Rica 9°43N 83°3W 320 E3
Pandrup Denmark 57°14N 9°40E 163 G3
Pandu Dem. Rep. of the Congo 4°59N 19°16E 264 B3
Panepistimio Athens, Greece 112 b2
Panevéggio-Pale di San Martino ⌓ Italy 46°14N 11°46E 199 B8
Panevėžys Lithuania 55°42N 24°25E 188 E3
Panfilov = Zharkent Kazakhstan 44°10N 80°0E 217 D10
Panfilovo Russia 50°25N 42°46E 190 E6
Pang Sida △ Thailand 14°5N 102°17E 236 E4
Panga Dem. Rep. of the Congo 1°52N 26°18E 268 B2
Pangaíon Óros Greece 40°50N 24°0E 203 F8
Pangala Congo 3°16S 14°34E 264 C2
Pangalanes, Canal des = Ampangalana, Lakandranon' Madag. 22°48S 47°50E 272 C2
Pangani Tanzania 5°25S 38°58E 268 D4
Pangani → Tanzania 5°26S 38°58E 268 D4
Pangantocan Phil. 7°50N 124°49E 233 H5
Pangar Djérem ⌓ Cameroon 5°50N 13°10E 264 A2
Pangasinan □ Phil. 15°55N 120°20E 232 D3
Pangfou = Bengbu China 32°58N 117°20E 227 H9
Pangil Dem. Rep. of the Congo 3°10S 26°35E 268 C2
Pangkah, Tanjung Indonesia 6°51S 112°33E 235 D4
Pangkai Burma 22°40N 98°40E 241 D7
Pangkajene Indonesia 4°46S 119°34E 231 E5
Pangkalanbrandan Indonesia 4°1N 98°20E 234 B1
Pangkalanbuun Indonesia 2°41S 111°37E 235 C4
Pangkalansusu Indonesia 4°2N 98°13E 234 B1
Pangkalpinang Indonesia 2°0S 106°0E 234 C3
Pangkoh Indonesia 3°5S 114°8E 235 C4
Panglao Phil. 9°35N 123°45E 233 G4
Panglao I. Phil. 9°35N 123°48E 233 G4
Pangnirtung Canada 66°8N 65°43W 295 C13
Pango Alucuem Angola 8°43S 14°33E 265 D2
Pangong Tso India 34°40N 78°40E 242 B8
Pangrango Indonesia 6°46S 107°1E 234 D3
Pangrati Greece 37°56N 23°45E 112 B2
Pangsau Pass Burma 27°15N 96°10E 241 B6
Pangsua, Sungei → Singapore 1°25N 103°45E 138 A2
Pangtara Burma 20°57N 96°40E 241 E6
Panguipulli Chile 39°38S 72°20W 336 A2
Panguitch U.S.A. 37°50N 112°26W 305 H7
Panguna Papua N. G. 6°21S 155°25E 286 D8
Pangutaran Phil. 6°18N 120°35E 233 H3
Pangutaran Group Phil. 6°18N 120°34E 233 H3
Panhala India 16°49N 74°7E 244 F2
Panhandle U.S.A. 35°21N 101°23W 314 D4

Pani Mines India 22°29N 73°50E 242 H5
Pania-Mutombo Dem. Rep. of the Congo 5°11S 23°51E 265 D4
Pänï'au U.S.A. 21°56N 160°5W 302 B1
Panié, Mt. N. Cal. 20°36S 164°46E 288 d
Panihati India 22°41N 88°22E 124 A2
Panikota I. India 20°46N 71°21E 242 J4
Panipat India 29°25N 77°2E 242 E7
Panitan Phil. 11°28N 122°46E 233 F4
Panj = Pyandzh → Asia 37°6N 68°20E 240 A2
Panjab Afghan. 34°23N 67°1E 240 B2
Panjakent = Pendzhikent Tajikistan 39°29N 67°37E 217 E7
Panjal Range = Pir Panjal Range India 32°30N 76°50E 242 C7
Panjang, Bukit Singapore 1°22N 103°45E 138 A2
Panjang, Hon Vietnam 9°20N 103°28E 237 H4
Panjgur Pakistan 27°0N 64°5E 240 D2
Panjhra → India 21°13N 74°57E 244 D2
Panjim = Panaji India 15°25N 73°50E 245 G1
Panjin China 41°3N 122°2E 227 D12
Panjnad → Pakistan 28°57N 70°30E 242 E4
Panjnad Barrage Pakistan 29°22N 71°15E 242 E4
Panjsher □ Afghan. 35°50N 69°45E 240 B3
Panjwai Afghan. 31°26N 65°27E 242 D1
Panke → Germany 52°31N 13°22E 115 A3
Pankow Germany 52°34N 13°23E 115 A3
Pankshin Nigeria 9°16N 9°25E 263 D6
Panmunjŏm N. Korea 37°59N 126°38E 224 D3
Panna India 24°40N 80°15E 243 G9
Panna △ India 24°40N 80°0E 243 G8
Panna Hills India 24°40N 81°15E 243 G9
Pannawonica Australia 21°39S 116°19E 278 D2
Pannga, Tanjung Indonesia 8°54S 116°2E 231 K19
Panngi Vanuatu 15°58S 168°12E 287 E6
Pannirtuuq = Pangnirtung Canada 66°8N 65°43W 295 C13
Pano Akil Pakistan 27°51N 69°7E 242 F3
Pano Lefkara Cyprus 34°53N 33°20E 207 F9
Pano Panayia Cyprus 34°55N 32°38E 207 F8
Panora U.S.A. 41°42N 94°22W 310 C2
Panorama Brazil 21°21S 51°51W 335 A5
Panormos Greece 35°25N 24°41E 207 E5
Panruti India 11°46N 79°35E 245 J4
Pansemal India 21°39N 74°42E 242 J6
Panshan = Panjin China 41°3N 122°2E 227 D12
Panshi China 42°58N 126°5E 227 C14
Pantanal Matogrossense △ Brazil 17°35S 57°27W 331 D6
Pantanaw Burma 16°59N 95°28E 241 G5
Pantanos de Centla ⌓ Mexico 18°25N 92°25W 319 D6
Pantar Indonesia 8°28S 124°10E 231 F6
Pante Macassar E. Timor 9°30S 123°58E 231 F6
Pante Makasar = Pante Macassar E. Timor 9°30S 123°58E 231 F6
Pantelleria Italy 36°50N 11°57E 200 F4
Panthéon Paris, France 134 c4
Pantheon Rome, Italy 136 b2
Panthersville U.S.A. 33°43N 84°16W 113 B3
Pantin France 48°53N 2°24E 134 A3
Pantin Sakan Burma 18°38N 97°33E 241 F6
Pantitlán Mexico 19°24N 99°4W 128 B2
Pantoja Peru 0°58S 75°10W 328 D2
Pantón Spain 42°31N 7°37W 194 C3
Pantukan Phil. 7°9N 125°54E 233 H5
Panu Dem. Rep. of the Congo 3°50S 19°10E 264 C3
Pánuco Mexico 22°3N 98°10W 319 C5
Panukulan Phil. 14°56N 121°49E 232 D3
Panvel India 18°59N 73°4E 244 E1
Panvel Cr. → India 18°59N 73°0E 130 B2
Panyam Nigeria 9°27N 9°8E 263 D6
Panyu = Guangzhou China 23°6N 113°13E 121 B2
Panyu China 22°51N 113°20E 229 F9
Panzhihua China 26°33N 101°44E 228 D3
Panzi Dem. Rep. of the Congo 7°17S 18°1E 265 D3
Pao → Anzoátegui, Venezuela 8°6N 64°17W 329 B5
Pao → Apure, Venezuela 8°33N 68°1W 328 B4
Paochi = Baoji China 34°20N 107°5E 226 G4
Paoki = Baoji China 34°20N 107°5E 226 G4
Páola Italy 39°21N 16°2E 201 C9
Paola Malta 35°52N 14°30E 206 F8
Paola Kans., U.S.A. 38°35N 94°53W 308 F6
Paoli U.S.A. 38°33N 86°28W 311 F10
Paonia U.S.A. 38°52N 107°36W 304 G10
Paopao Moorea 17°30S 149°49W 289 e
Paoting = Baoding China 38°50N 115°28E 226 E8
Paot'ou = Baotou China 40°32N 110°2E 226 D6
Paoua C.A.R. 7°9N 16°20E 264 A3
Pápa Hungary 47°22N 17°30E 182 C2
Päpä Hawai'i, U.S.A. 19°13N 155°52W 302 D6
Papa Stour U.K. 60°20N 1°42W 167 A7
Papa Westray U.K. 59°20N 2°55W 167 B6
Päpa'aloa U.S.A. 19°59N 155°13W 302 D6
Papagayo → Mexico 16°46N 99°43W 319 D5
Papagayo, G. de Costa Rica 10°30N 85°50W 320 D2
Papagni → India 15°35N 77°45E 245 G3
Papaïchton Fr. Guiana 3°48N 54°10W 329 C7
Päpa'ikou U.S.A. 19°47N 155°6W 302 D6
Papakura N.Z. 37°4S 174°59E 284 D3
Papantla Mexico 20°27N 97°19W 319 C5
Papar Malaysia 5°45N 116°0E 235 A5
Papara Tahiti 17°43S 149°31W 289 e
Paparangi N.Z. 41°12S 174°48E 143 B1
Paparoa N.Z. 36°6S 174°16E 284 C3
Paparoa △ N.Z. 42°7S 171°26E 285 C6
Paparoa Ra. N.Z. 42°5S 171°35E 285 C6
Papas, Akra Greece 38°13N 21°20E 204 C3
Papatoetoe N.Z. 36°59S 174°51E 284 C3
Papatura Solomon Is. 7°32S 158°47E 287 L10
Papawai Pt. U.S.A. 20°47N 156°32W 302 C5
Papeete Tahiti 17°32S 149°34W 289 e
Papenburg Germany 53°5N 7°23E 178 B3
Papenoo Tahiti 17°30S 149°25W 289 e
Papenoo → Tahiti 17°30S 149°25W 289 e
Papetoai Moorea 17°29S 149°52W 289 e
Paphlagonia Turkey 41°30N 33°0E 212 B5
Paphos Cyprus 34°46N 32°25E 207 F8
Paphos ✈ (PFO) Cyprus 34°43N 32°30E 207 F8
Papien Chiang = Da → Vietnam 21°15N 105°20E 228 G5
Papikio Oros Greece 41°15N 25°13E 203 E9
Papiol Spain 41°25N 2°0E 114 A1
Paposo Chile 25°0S 70°30W 334 B1
Papoutsa Cyprus 34°54N 33°4E 207 F9
Papua □ Indonesia 4°0S 137°0E 231 E9
Papua, G. of Papua N. G. 9°0S 144°50E 286 E3
Papua New Guinea ■ Oceania 8°0S 145°0E 286 E3
Papudo Chile 32°29S 71°27W 334 C1
Papuk Croatia 45°30N 17°30E 182 E2
Papun Burma 18°2N 97°30E 241 F6
Papunya Australia 23°15S 131°54E 278 D5
Pará = Belém Brazil 1°20S 48°30W 332 B2
Pará □ Brazil 3°20S 52°0W 331 A7
Paraburdoo Australia 23°14S 117°32E 278 D2
Paracale Phil. 14°17N 122°48E 232 D4
Paracas, Pen. Peru 13°53S 76°20W 330 C2
Paracatu Brazil 17°10S 46°50W 333 E2
Paracatu → Brazil 16°30S 45°4W 333 E2
Paracel Is. S. China Sea 15°50N 112°0E 230 A4
Parachilna Australia 31°10S 138°21E 282 A3
Parachinar Pakistan 33°55N 70°5E 242 C4
Paraćin Serbia 43°54N 21°27E 202 C5
Paracuru Brazil 3°24S 39°4W 332 B4
Parada, Punta Peru 15°22S 75°11W 330 D2
Paradas Spain 37°18N 5°29W 195 H5
Paradela Spain 42°44N 7°37W 194 C3
Paradera Aruba 12°32N 70°0W 322 f
Paradip India 20°15N 86°35E 244 D8
Paradise Calif., U.S.A. 39°46N 121°37W 306 F5
Paradise Nev., U.S.A. 36°5N 115°8W 124 B2
Paradise → Canada 53°27N 57°19W 299 B8
Paradise Hill Canada 53°32N 109°28W 297 C7
Paradise I. Bahamas 25°6N 77°19W 153 b
Paradise River Canada 53°27N 57°17W 299 B8
Paradise Valley U.S.A. 41°30N 117°32W 304 F5
Paradisi Greece 36°18N 28°7E 206 E12
Parado Indonesia 8°42S 118°30E 235 D5
Paragould U.S.A. 36°3N 90°29W 315 C9
Paragua = Palawan Phil. 9°30N 118°30E 233 G2
Paraguá → Bolivia 13°34S 61°53W 331 C5
Paragua → Venezuela 6°55N 62°55W 329 B5
Paraguaçu = Paraguaçu Paulista Brazil 22°22S 50°35W 335 A5
Paraguaçu → Brazil 12°45S 38°54W 333 D4
Paraguaçu Paulista Brazil 22°22S 50°35W 335 A5
Paraguaipoa Venezuela 11°21N 71°57W 328 A3
Paraguaná, Pen. de Venezuela 12°0N 70°0W 328 A4
Paraguarí Paraguay 25°36S 57°0W 334 B4
Paraguarí □ Paraguay 26°0S 57°10W 334 B4
Paraguay ■ S. Amer. 23°0S 57°0W 334 A4
Paraguay → Paraguay 27°18S 58°38W 334 B4
Paraíba = João Pessoa Brazil 7°10S 34°52W 332 C5
Paraíba □ Brazil 7°0S 36°0W 332 C4
Paraíba do Sul → Brazil 21°37S 41°3W 333 F3
Parainen Finland 60°18N 22°18E 188 B2
Paraiso Brazil 19°3S 52°59W 331 D7
Paraíso Tabasco, Mexico 18°24N 93°14W 319 D6
Parak Iran 27°38N 52°25E 247 E7
Parakhino Paddubye Russia 58°26N 33°10E 188 C7
Parakou Benin 9°25N 2°40E 263 D5
Parakylia Australia 30°24S 136°25E 282 A2
Paralimni Cyprus 35°2N 33°58E 207 E9
Paralio Astros Greece 37°25N 22°45E 204 D4
Paralkote India 19°47N 80°41E 244 E5
Param I. Micronesia 7°21N 151°47E 287 T18
Parama I. Papua N. G. 9°0S 143°25E 286 E2
Paramaribo Suriname 5°50N 55°10W 329 B6
Parambu Brazil 6°13S 40°43W 332 C3
Paramillo, Nudo del Colombia 7°4N 75°55W 328 B2
Paramillo △ Colombia 7°37N 76°13W 328 B2
Paramirim Brazil 13°26S 42°15W 333 D3
Paramirim → Brazil 11°34S 43°18W 333 D3
Paramithia Greece 39°30N 20°35E 204 B2
Paramount Studios U.S.A. 34°5N 118°19W 126 B3
Paramus U.S.A. 40°56N 74°2W 132 A1
Paramushir, Ostrov Russia 50°24N 156°0E 215 D16
Paran → Israel 30°20N 35°10E 251 H6
Paraná Argentina 31°45S 60°30W 334 C3
Paraná Brazil 12°30S 47°48W 333 D2
Paraná □ Brazil 24°30S 51°0W 335 A5
Paraná → Argentina 33°43S 59°15W 334 C4
Paraná → Brazil 12°30S 48°14W 333 D2
Paranaguá Brazil 25°30S 48°30W 335 B6
Paranaíba Brazil 19°40S 51°11W 331 D7
Paranaíba → Brazil 20°6S 51°4W 333 F1
Paranapanema → Brazil 22°40S 53°9W 335 A5
Paranapiacaba, Serra do Brazil 24°31S 48°35W 335 A6
Paranaque Phil. 14°30N 120°59E 127 B1
Paranas Phil. 11°42N 125°2E 233 F5
Paranavaí Brazil 23°4S 52°56W 335 A5
Parang Maguindanao, Phil. 7°23N 124°16E 233 H5
Parang Sulu, Phil. 5°55N 120°54E 233 J3
Parangaba Brazil 3°45S 38°33W 332 B4
Parangippettai India 11°30N 79°38E 245 J4
Parângul Mare, Vf. Romania 45°20N 23°37E 183 E8
Paranthan Sri Lanka 9°26N 80°24E 245 K5
Paraoa French Polynesia 19°9S 140°43W 289 f
Paraparaumu N.Z. 40°57S 175°3E 284 G4
Parapetí → Bolivia 18°58S 62°21W 331 D5
Paraspori, Akra Greece 35°55N 27°15E 205 F9
Paratinga Brazil 12°40S 43°10W 333 D3
Paratoo Australia 32°42S 139°20E 282 B3
Paraúna Brazil 16°55S 50°26W 333 E1
Paray-le-Monial France 46°27N 4°7E 173 F11
Paray-Vieille-Poste France 48°42N 2°20E 134 B3
Parbati → Mad. P., India 25°50N 76°30E 242 G7
Parbati → Raj., India 26°54N 77°53E 242 F7
Parbatipur Bangla. 25°39N 88°55E 241 C2
Parbhani India 19°8N 76°52E 244 E3
Parchim Germany 53°26N 11°52E 178 B7
Parchwitz = Prochowice Poland 51°17N 16°20E 185 G3
Parco = Sinclair U.S.A. 41°47N 107°7W 304 F10
Parczew Poland 51°40N 22°52E 185 G9
Pardes Hanna-Karkur Israel 32°28N 34°57E 251 F5
Pardilla Spain 41°33N 3°43W 194 D7
Pardisān Nature Park Iran 35°44N 51°22E 141 A2
Pardo → Bahia, Brazil 15°40S 39°0W 333 E4
Pardo → Mato Grosso, Brazil 21°46S 52°9W 335 A5
Pardo → Minas Gerais, Brazil 15°48S 44°48W 333 E3
Pardo → São Paulo, Brazil 20°10S 48°38W 333 F2
Pardoo Roadhouse Australia 20°6S 119°3E 278 D2
Pardubice Czech Rep. 50°3N 15°45E 180 A8
Pardubický □ Czech Rep. 49°50N 16°0E 180 B8
Pardubitz = Pardubice Czech Rep. 50°3N 15°45E 180 A8
Pare Indonesia 7°43S 112°12E 235 D4
Pare Mts. Tanzania 4°0S 37°45E 268 C4
Parecis, Serra dos Brazil 13°0S 60°0W 331 C6
Paredes de Nava Spain 42°9N 4°42W 194 C6
Parel India 18°59N 72°49E 130 B1
Parelhas Brazil 6°41S 36°39W 332 C4
Paren Russia 62°30N 163°15E 215 C17
Parenda India 18°16N 75°28E 244 E2
Parengarenga Harbour N.Z. 34°31S 173°0E 284 A2
Parent Canada 47°55N 74°35W 298 C5
Parent, L. Canada 48°31N 77°1W 298 C4
Parentis-en-Born France 44°21N 1°4W 174 D2
Parepare Indonesia 4°0S 119°40E 231 E5
Parfino Russia 57°59N 31°34E 188 D6
Parga Greece 39°15N 20°29E 204 B2
Pargas = Parainen Finland 60°18N 22°18E 188 B2
Pargi India 17°11N 77°53E 244 E3
Pargo, Pta. do Madeira 32°49N 17°17W 153 c
Parguera Puerto Rico 17°59N 67°3W 321 b
Pari Brazil 23°32S 46°36W 137 B2
Paria → U.S.A. 36°52N 111°36W 305 H8
Paria, G. de Venezuela 10°20N 62°0W 323 t
Paria, Pen. de Venezuela 10°50N 62°30W 329 A5
Pariaguán Venezuela 8°51N 64°34W 329 B5
Pariaman Indonesia 0°47S 100°11E 234 C2
Paricatuba Brazil 4°26S 61°53W 329 D5
Paricutín, Cerro Mexico 19°28N 102°15W 318 D4
Parigi Java, Indonesia 7°42S 108°29E 235 D3
Parigi Sulawesi, Indonesia 0°50S 120°5E 231 E6
Parika Guyana 6°50N 58°20W 329 B6
Parikia Greece 37°6N 25°11E 205 D7
Parikkala Finland 61°33N 29°31E 188 B5
Parima, Serra Brazil 2°30N 64°0W 329 C5
Parinari Peru 4°35S 74°25W 330 A3
Pariñas, Pta. S. Amer. 4°30S 82°0W 326 D2
Parincea Romania 46°27N 27°9E 183 D12
Paringa Australia 34°10S 140°46E 282 C4
Parintins Brazil 2°40S 56°50W 329 D6
Parioli Italy 41°55N 12°29E 136 B1
Paris Ont., Canada 43°12N 80°25W 312 C4
Paris Paris, France 48°53N 2°20E 134 A3
Paris Idaho, U.S.A. 42°14N 111°24W 304 E8
Paris Ill., U.S.A. 39°36N 87°42W 311 E9
Paris Ky., U.S.A. 38°13N 84°15W 311 F12
Paris Mo., U.S.A. 39°29N 92°0W 310 E5
Paris Tenn., U.S.A. 36°18N 88°19W 315 C10
Paris Tex., U.S.A. 33°40N 95°33W 314 E7
Paris, Ville de □ France 48°50N 2°20E 173 D9
Paris Charles de Gaulle ✈ (CDG) France 49°0N 2°32E 173 D9
Paris Orly ✈ (ORY) France 48°44N 2°23E 134 B3
Parish U.S.A. 43°25N 76°8W 313 C8
Parishville U.S.A. 44°38N 74°49W 313 B10
Parje India 18°54N 72°57E 130 B2
Park U.S.A. 48°45N 122°18W 306 B4
Park City U.S.A. 37°48N 97°20W 308 G5
Pārk-e Āzādegān Iran 35°37N 51°28E 141 B2
Pārk-e Mellat Iran 35°47N 51°24E 141 A2
Park Falls U.S.A. 45°56N 90°27W 308 C8
Park Forest U.S.A. 41°29N 87°40W 311 C9
Park Head Canada 44°36N 81°9W 312 B3
Park Hills U.S.A. 37°51N 90°51W 310 G6
Park Range U.S.A. 40°41N 106°41W 304 F10
Park Rapids U.S.A. 46°55N 95°4W 308 B6
Park Ridge U.S.A. 42°2N 87°51W 119 A1
Park River U.S.A. 48°24N 97°45W 308 A5
Park Royal U.K. 51°31N 0°16W 125 A2
Park Rynie S. Africa 30°25S 30°45E 271 D5
Parkā Bandar Iran 25°55N 59°35E 247 E8
Parkal India 18°12N 79°43E 244 E4
Parkán = Štúrovo Slovak Rep. 47°48N 18°41E 181 D11
Parkano Finland 62°1N 23°0E 188 A2
Parkchester U.S.A. 40°49N 73°50W 132 B2
Parkdale Canada 43°38N 79°25W 141 B2
Parkent Uzbekistan 41°18N 69°40E 217 D7
Parker Ariz., U.S.A. 34°9N 114°17W 307 L12
Parker Pa., U.S.A. 41°5N 79°41W 312 E5
Parker Center Los Angeles, U.S.A. 127 b2
Parker Dam U.S.A. 34°18N 114°8W 307 L12
Parkersburg Iowa, U.S.A. 42°35N 92°47W 310 B4
Parkersburg W. Va., U.S.A. 39°16N 81°34W 309 F13
Parkes Australia 33°9S 148°11E 283 B8
Parkfield U.S.A. 35°54N 120°26W 306 K6
Parkhill Canada 43°15N 81°38W 312 C3
Parkhurst S. Africa 26°8S 28°1E 123 A2
Parkland U.S.A. 47°9N 122°26W 306 C4
Parklawn U.S.A. 38°50N 77°7W 143 B3
Parkmore S. Africa 26°5S 28°2E 123 A2
Parkside U.S.A. 37°44N 122°29W 136 B2
Parkston U.S.A. 43°24N 97°59W 308 D5
Parksville Canada 49°20N 124°21W 296 D4
Parktown S. Africa 26°10S 28°2E 123 B2
Parkview S. Africa 26°9S 28°1E 123 A2
Parkville U.S.A. 40°38N 73°57W 132 C2
Parkway U.S.A. 38°32N 121°26W 306 G5
Parkwood Gauteng, S. Africa 26°9S 28°2E 123 A2
Parkwood Western Cape, S. Africa 34°2S 18°30E 118 B1
Parla Spain 40°14N 3°46W 194 E7
Parlakimidi India 18°45N 84°5E 244 E7
Parlatuvier Trin. & Tob. 11°18N 60°39W 323 s
Parli India 18°50N 76°35E 244 E3
Parliament Budapest, Hungary 117 b2
Pârliţa Moldova 47°19N 27°52E 183 C12
Parma Italy 44°48N 10°20E 198 D7
Parma Idaho, U.S.A. 43°47N 116°57W 304 E5
Parma Ohio, U.S.A. 41°24N 81°43W 312 E3
Parma → Italy 44°56N 10°26E 198 D7
Parnaguá Brazil 10°10S 44°38W 332 D3
Parnaíba Brazil 2°54S 41°47W 332 B3
Parnaíba → Brazil 3°0S 41°50W 332 B3
Parnamirim Brazil 8°5S 39°34W 332 C4
Parnarama Brazil 5°31S 43°6W 332 C3
Parnassos Greece 38°35N 22°30E 204 C4
Parnassus N.Z. 42°42S 173°23E 285 C8
Parndana Australia 35°48S 137°12E 282 C2
Parner India 19°0N 74°26E 244 E2
Parnitha Greece 38°14N 23°45E 204 C5
Parnitha △ Greece 38°12N 23°44E 204 C5
Parnonas Oros Greece 37°15N 22°45E 204 D4
Pärnu Estonia 58°28N 24°33E 188 C3
Paro Dzong Bhutan 27°32N 89°53E 241 B2
Parola India 20°47N 75°7E 244 D2
Paroo → Australia 31°28S 143°32E 282 A5
Paroo-Darling △ Australia 31°32S 144°0E 281 E3
Paros Greece 37°5N 25°12E 205 D7
Parow S. Africa 33°53S 18°37E 118 A2
Parowan U.S.A. 37°51N 112°50W 305 H7
Parpaillon France 44°30N 6°40E 175 D10
Parque Chacabuco Argentina 34°39S 58°26W 117 B2
Parque Patricios Argentina 34°39S 58°23W 117 B2
Parral Chile 36°10S 71°52W 334 D1
Parramatta Australia 33°48S 151°1E 283 B9
Parramatta → Australia 33°49S 151°3E 139 A1
Parras Mexico 25°25N 102°11W 318 B4
Parrett → U.K. 51°12N 3°1W 169 F4
Parris I. U.S.A. 32°20N 80°41W 316 C9
Parrish U.S.A. 27°35N 82°26W 317 H7
Parrott U.S.A. 31°54N 84°31W 316 D5
Parrsboro Canada 45°30N 64°25W 299 C7
Parry I. Canada 45°18N 80°10W 312 A4
Parry Is. Canada 77°0N 110°0W 295 B9
Parry Sound Canada 45°20N 80°0W 312 A5
Parsaloi Kenya 1°16N 36°51E 268 B4
Parsberg Germany 49°10N 11°43E 179 F7
Parsęta → Poland 54°11N 15°34E 184 D2
Parsnip → Canada 55°10N 123°2W 296 B4
Parsons U.S.A. 37°20N 95°16W 308 G6
Parsons Ra. Australia 13°30S 135°15E 280 A2
Partabpur India 20°0N 80°42E 244 E5
Partanna Italy 37°43N 12°53E 200 E5
Partenio ⌓ Italy 40°56N 14°38E 201 B7
Parthenay France 46°38N 0°16W 172 F6
Parthenon Athens, Greece 112 c2
Partinico Italy 38°3N 13°7E 200 D6
Partizansk Russia 43°8N 133°9E 220 C6
Partizánske Slovak Rep. 48°38N 18°23E 181 C11
Partridge I. Canada 55°59N 87°37W 298 A2
Partry Mts. Ireland 53°40N 9°28W 166 C2
Partur India 19°40N 76°14E 244 E3
Paru → Brazil 1°33S 52°38W 329 D7
Parú → Venezuela 4°20N 66°27W 328 C4
Paru de Oeste → Brazil 1°30N 56°0W 329 C6
Parucito → Venezuela 5°18N 65°59W 328 B4
Parur India 10°13N 76°14E 245 J3
Paruro Peru 13°45S 71°50W 330 C3
Parvān □ Afghan. 35°0N 69°0E 240 B3
Parvatipuram India 18°50N 83°25E 244 E6
Parvatsar India 26°52N 74°49E 242 F6
Påryd Sweden 56°34N 15°55E 163 H9
Parys S. Africa 26°52S 27°29E 270 C4
Pas, Pta. des Spain 38°46N 1°26E 206 D1
Pas, The Canada 53°45N 101°15W 297 C8
Pas-de-Calais □ France 50°30N 2°10E 173 B9
Paşabahçe Turkey 41°6N 29°5E 122 B2
Pasada Spain 43°23N 5°40W 194 B5
Pasadena Nfld. & L., Canada 49°1N 57°36W 299 C8
Pasadena Calif., U.S.A. 34°9N 118°8W 126 B4
Pasadena Tex., U.S.A. 29°43N 95°13W 314 G7
Pasaje Ecuador 3°23S 79°50W 328 D2
Pasaje → Argentina 25°39S 63°56W 334 B3
Paşalimanı Turkey 40°29N 27°36E 203 F11
Pasar Indonesia 8°27S 114°54E 231 J17
Pasar Minggu Indonesia 6°16S 106°49E 122 B1
Pasay Phil. 14°32N 120°59E 127 B1
Pascagoula U.S.A. 30°21N 88°33W 315 F10
Pascagoula → U.S.A. 30°23N 88°37W 315 F10
Paşcani Romania 47°14N 26°45E 183 C11
Pasco U.S.A. 46°14N 119°6W 304 C4
Pasco □ Peru 10°40S 75°0W 330 C3
Pasco, Cerro de Peru 10°45S 76°10W 330 C2
Pasco I. Australia 20°57S 115°20E 278 D2
Pascoag U.S.A. 41°57N 71°42W 313 E13
Pascoe Vale Australia 37°43S 144°55E 128 A1
Pascua, I. de Chile 27°7S 109°23W 330 b
Paseo de la Reforma Mexico City, Mexico 128 b2
Pasewalk Germany 53°30N 13°58E 178 B9
Pasfield L. Canada 58°24N 105°20W 297 B7
Pasha → Russia 60°29N 32°55E 188 B7
Pashmakli = Smolyan Bulgaria 41°36N 24°38E 203 E8
Pasig Phil. 14°33N 121°4E 127 B2
Pasig → Phil. 14°31N 121°6E 127 B2
Pasighat India 28°4N 95°21E 241 A5
Pasila Finland 60°12N 24°56E 121 B2
Pasing Germany 48°8N 11°28E 131 B1
Pasinler Turkey 39°59N 41°41E 213 C9
Pasir Mas Malaysia 6°2N 102°8E 237 J4
Pasir Panjang Singapore 1°18N 103°46E 138 B2
Pasir Putih Malaysia 5°50N 102°24E 237 K4
Pasir Ris Singapore 1°22N 103°56E 138 A3
Pasirian Indonesia 8°13S 113°8E 235 D4
Pasirkuning Indonesia 0°30S 104°33E 234 C2
Påskallavik Sweden 57°10N 16°26E 163 G10
Paskūh Iran 27°34N 61°39E 247 E9
Pasłęk Poland 54°3N 19°41E 184 D6
Pasłęka → Poland 54°26N 19°46E 184 D6
Pasley, C. Australia 33°52S 123°35E 279 F3
Pašman Croatia 43°58N 15°20E 199 E12
Pasmore → Australia 31°5S 139°49E 282 A3
Pasni Pakistan 25°15N 63°27E 240 D1
Paso Cantinela Mexico 32°33N 115°47W 307 N11
Paso de Indios Argentina 43°55S 69°0W 336 B3
Paso de los Indios Argentina 38°32S 69°25W 336 A3
Paso de los Libres Argentina 29°44S 57°10W 334 B4
Paso de los Toros Uruguay 32°45S 56°30W 334 C4
Paso Flores Argentina 40°35S 70°38W 336 B2
Paso Robles U.S.A. 35°38N 120°41W 306 K6
Pasorapa Bolivia 18°16S 64°37W 331 D5
Paspébiac Canada 48°3N 65°17W 299 C6
Pasrur Pakistan 32°16N 74°43E 242 C6
Passage East Ireland 52°14N 7°0W 166 D5
Passage West Ireland 51°52N 8°21W 166 E3
Passaic U.S.A. 40°51N 74°7W 132 A1
Passaic → U.S.A. 40°42N 74°10W 132 B1
Passam Papua N. G. 3°41S 143°38E 286 B2
Passau Germany 48°34N 13°28E 179 G9
Passenheim = Pasym Poland 53°48N 20°49E 184 E7
Passero, C. Italy 36°41N 15°10E 201 F8
Passi Phil. 11°6N 122°38E 233 F4
Passirana Italy 45°32N 9°2E 129 A1
Passo Fundo Brazil 28°10S 52°20W 335 B5
Passos Brazil 20°45S 46°37W 333 F2
Passow Germany 53°8N 14°6E 178 B10
Passy France 45°55N 6°41E 175 C10
Pastavy Belarus 55°4N 26°50E 188 E4
Pastaza □ Ecuador 2°0S 77°0W 328 D2
Pastaza → Peru 4°50S 76°52W 328 D2
Pasto Colombia 1°13N 77°17W 328 C2
Pastol B. U.S.A. 63°7N 163°15W 303 E7
Pastos Bons Brazil 6°36S 44°5W 332 C3
Pastrana Spain 40°27N 2°53W 196 E2
Pasuquin Phil. 18°20N 120°37E 232 B3
Pasuruan Indonesia 7°40S 112°44E 235 D4
Pasym Poland 53°48N 20°49E 184 E7
Pásztó Hungary 47°52N 19°43E 182 C4
Pata Phil. 5°51N 121°10E 233 J3
Pata I. Phil. 5°49N 121°10E 233 J3
Patagonia Argentina 45°0S 69°0W 336 C3
Patagonia Ariz., U.S.A. 31°33N 110°45W 305 L8
Patambar Iran 29°45N 60°17E 247 D9
Patan = Lalitapur Nepal 27°40N 85°20E 243 F11
Patan Gujarat, India 23°54N 72°14E 242 H5
Patan Gujarat, India 17°22N 73°57E 244 F1
Patani Indonesia 0°20N 128°50E 231 D7
Pătârlagele Romania 45°19N 26°21E 183 E11
Pataudi India 28°18N 76°48E 242 E7
Patchewollock Australia 35°22S 142°12E 282 C5
Patchogue U.S.A. 40°46N 73°1W 313 F11
Pate Coast, Kenya 2°10S 41°0E 268 C5
Pate Taiwan 24°56N 121°17E 225 B3
Patea N.Z. 39°45S 174°30E 284 F3
Pategi Nigeria 8°50N 5°45E 263 D6
Patel Nagar India 28°39N 77°10E 120 B1
Patensie S. Africa 33°46S 24°49E 270 D3
Paterna Spain 39°30N 0°26W 197 F4
Paternion Austria 46°43N 13°38E 180 E6
Paternò Italy 37°34N 14°54E 201 E7
Pateros Manila, Phil. 14°32N 121°3E 127 B2
Pateros Wash., U.S.A. 48°3N 119°54W 304 B4
Paterson N.S.W., Australia 32°35S 151°36E 283 B9
Paterson N.J., U.S.A. 40°54N 74°9W 313 F10
Paterson Inlet N.Z. 46°56S 168°12E 285 G3
Paterson Ra. Australia 21°45S 122°10E 278 D3
Pathankot India 32°18N 75°45E 242 C6
Pathardi India 19°10N 75°11E 244 E2
Patharghata Bangla. 22°2N 89°58E 241 D2
Pathein = Bassein Burma 16°45N 94°30E 241 G5
Pathfinder Res. U.S.A. 42°28N 106°51W 304 E10
Pathiu Thailand 10°42N 99°19E 237 G2
Pathri India 19°15N 76°27E 244 E3
Pathum Thani Thailand 14°1N 100°32E 236 E3
Pathumwan Thailand 13°44N 100°31E 113 B2
Pati Indonesia 6°45S 111°1E 235 D4
Pati Pt. Guam 13°35N 144°57E 302 d
Patía Colombia 2°4N 77°4W 328 C2
Patía → Colombia 2°13N 78°40W 328 C2
Patiala Punjab, India 30°23N 76°26E 242 D7
Patiala Ut. P., India 27°43N 79°1E 243 F8
Patine Kouka Senegal 12°45N 13°45W 262 C2
Patipukur India 22°36N 88°24E 124 B2
Patisia Greece 38°2N 23°45E 112 A2
Patitiri Greece 39°8N 23°50E 204 B5
Pativilca Peru 10°42S 77°48W 330 C2
Patkai Bum India 27°0N 95°30E 241 B5
Patmos Greece 37°21N 26°36E 205 D8
Patna India 25°35N 85°12E 243 G11
Patnagarh India 20°43N 83°9E 244 D6
Patnanongan I. Phil. 14°48N 122°11E 232 D4
Patnongon Phil. 10°55N 122°0E 233 F4
Patnos Turkey 39°13N 42°51E 213 C10
Pato Branco Brazil 26°13S 52°40W 335 B5
Patoka L. U.S.A. 38°20N 86°40W 311 F10
Patong, Ao Thailand 7°54N 98°17E 237 a
Patonga Uganda 2°45N 33°15E 268 B3
Patos Albania 40°42N 19°38E 202 F3
Patos Brazil 6°55S 37°16W 332 C4
Patos, L. dos Brazil 31°20S 51°0W 335 C5
Patos, Río de los → Argentina 31°18S 69°25W 334 C2
Patos de Minas Brazil 18°35S 46°32W 333 E2
Patquía Argentina 30°2S 66°55W 334 C2
Patra Greece 38°14N 21°47E 204 C3
Patraikos Kolpos Greece 38°17N 21°30E 204 C3
Patras = Patra Greece 38°14N 21°47E 204 C3
Patreksfjörður Iceland 65°35N 24°0W 155 B2
Patriarsheye = Donskoy Russia 53°55N 38°15E 188 F10
Patricio Lynch, I. Chile 48°35S 75°30W 336 C1
Patriot Hills Antarctica 82°20S 81°25W 151 E16
Patrocínio Brazil 18°57S 47°0W 333 E2
Pattada Italy 40°35N 9°6E 200 B2
Pattani Thailand 6°48N 101°15E 237 J3
Pattaya Thailand 12°52N 100°55E 236 F3
Patten U.S.A. 46°0N 68°38W 309 B19
Patterson Calif., U.S.A. 37°28N 121°8W 306 H5
Patterson Ga., U.S.A. 31°23N 82°8W 316 D7
Patterson La., U.S.A. 29°42N 91°18W 314 G9
Patterson, Mt. U.S.A. 38°29N 119°20W 306 G7
Patteson, Passage Vanuatu 15°26S 168°12E 287 E6
Patti Punjab, India 31°17N 74°54E 242 D6
Patti Ut. P., India 25°55N 82°12E 243 G10
Patti Italy 38°8N 14°58E 201 D7
Pattoki Pakistan 31°5N 73°52E 242 D5
Patton = Monroeville U.S.A. 40°26N 79°45W 312 F5
Patton U.S.A. 40°38N 78°39W 312 F6
Pattonsburg U.S.A. 40°3N 94°8W 310 D2
Pattukkattai India 10°25N 79°20E 245 J4
Patu Brazil 6°6S 37°38W 332 C4
Patuakhali Bangla. 22°20N 90°25E 241 D3
Patuanak Canada 55°55N 107°43W 297 B7
Patuca → Honduras 15°50N 84°18W 320 C3
Patuca, Punta Honduras 15°49N 84°14W 320 C3
Patuca △ Honduras 14°30N 85°30W 320 D2
Pătulele Romania 44°21N 22°47E 182 F7
Patur India 20°27N 76°56E 244 D3
Patvinsuo △ Finland 63°7N 30°45E 160 E24
Pátzcuaro Mexico 19°31N 101°38W 318 D4
Pau France 43°19N 0°25W 174 E3
Pau, Gave de → France 43°33N 1°12W 174 E2
Pau d' Arco Brazil 7°30S 49°22W 332 C2
Pau dos Ferros Brazil 6°7S 38°10W 332 C4
Pauanui N.Z. 37°1S 175°52E 284 D4
Paucartambo Peru 13°19S 71°35W 330 C3
Pauillac France 45°11N 0°46W 174 C3
Pauini Brazil 7°40S 66°58W 330 B4
Pauini → Brazil 1°42S 62°50W 329 D5
Pauk Burma 21°27N 94°30E 241 E5
Paukkaung Burma 18°54N 95°33E 241 F5
Pauktaw Burma 20°11N 93°4E 241 E4
Paul I. Canada 56°30N 61°20W 299 A7
Paul Isnard Fr. Guiana 4°47N 54°1W 329 C7
Paul Revere Park Boston, U.S.A. 116 a2
Paul Smiths U.S.A. 44°26N 74°15W 313 B10
Paulatuk Canada 69°25N 124°0W 294 C7
Paulding U.S.A. 41°8N 84°35W 311 C12
Paulhan France 43°33N 3°28E 174 E7
Paulis = Isiro Dem. Rep. of the Congo 2°53N 27°40E 268 B2
Paulista = Paulistana Brazil 8°9S 41°9W 332 C3
Paulista Brazil 7°57S 34°53W 332 C5
Paulistana Brazil 8°9S 41°9W 332 C3
Paulo Afonso Brazil 9°21S 38°15W 332 C4
Paulo de Faria Brazil 20°2S 49°24W 333 F2
Paulo E. Virginia, Gruta Brazil 22°56S 43°16W 135 B1
Paulpietersburg S. Africa 27°23S 30°50E 271 C5
Pauls Valley U.S.A. 34°44N 97°13W 314 D6
Paulshof Germany 52°34N 13°42E 115 A5
Pauma Valley U.S.A. 33°16N 116°58W 307 M10
Paung Burma 16°37N 94°28E 241 G5
Paungde Burma 18°29N 95°30E 241 F5
Pauni India 20°48N 79°40E 244 D4
Pauri India 30°9N 78°47E 243 D8
Pausa Peru 15°16S 73°22W 330 D3
Pauto → Colombia 5°9N 70°55W 328 B3
Pavagada India 14°6N 77°16E 245 G3
Pāveh Iran 35°3N 46°22E 213 E12
Pavelets Russia 53°49N 39°14E 188 F10
Pavia Italy 45°7N 9°8E 198 C6
Pavilion U.S.A. 42°52N 78°1W 312 D6
Pavilly France 49°34N 0°57E 172 C7
Pāvilosta Latvia 56°53N 21°14E 184 B8
Pavlikeni Bulgaria 43°14N 25°20E 203 C9
Pavlodar Kazakhstan 52°33N 77°0E 217 B9
Pavlograd = Pavlohrad Ukraine 48°30N 35°52E 189 H8
Pavlohrad Ukraine 48°30N 35°52E 189 H8
Pavlovo Russia 55°58N 43°5E 190 C6
Pavlovsk Russia 50°26N 40°5E 190 E5
Pavlovskaya Russia 46°17N 39°47E 191 G4
Pavlovskiy-Posad Russia 55°47N 38°42E 188 E10
Pavo U.S.A. 30°58N 83°45W 316 E6
Pavshino Russia 55°49N 37°20E 129 B1
Pavullo nel Frignano Italy 44°20N 10°50E 198 D7
Pavuvu Solomon Is. 9°4S 159°8E 287 M10
Paw Paw Ill., U.S.A. 41°41N 88°59W 310 C8
Paw Paw Mich., U.S.A. 42°13N 85°53W 311 B11
Pawahku Burma 26°11N 98°40E 241 B7
Pawai, Pulau Singapore 1°11N 103°44E 237 d
Pawan → Indonesia 1°55S 110°0E 235 C4
Pawayan India 28°4N 80°6E 243 E9
Pawhuska U.S.A. 36°40N 96°20W 314 C6
Pawling U.S.A. 41°34N 73°36W 313 E11
Pawnee Ill., U.S.A. 39°36N 89°35W 310 E7
Pawnee Okla., U.S.A. 36°20N 96°48W 314 C6
Pawnee City U.S.A. 40°7N 96°9W 308 E5
Pawtucket U.S.A. 41°53N 71°23W 313 E13
Paxi Greece 39°14N 20°12E 206 C10
Paximadia Greece 35°0N 24°35E 207 F5
Paxson U.S.A. 63°2N 145°30W 303 E11
Paxton U.S.A. 40°27N 88°6W 311 D8
Paya Lebar Singapore 1°21N 103°52E 138 A3
Payagyi Burma 17°29N 96°32E 241 G6
Payakumbuh Indonesia 0°20S 100°35E 234 C2
Payapa = General Tinio Phil. 15°39N 121°10E 232 D3
Payas = Yakacık Turkey 36°46N 36°11E 250 B7
Payerne Switz. 46°49N 6°56E 179 J2
Payette U.S.A. 44°5N 116°56W 304 D5
Paymogo Spain 37°44N 7°21W 195 H3
Payne U.S.A. 41°5N 84°44W 311 C12
Payne Bay = Kangirsuk Canada 60°0N 70°0W 295 D13
Payne L. Canada 59°30N 74°30W 295 D12
Payne Pt. Ascension I. 7°57S 14°25W 153 g
Paynes Find Australia 29°15S 117°42E 279 E2
Paynesville Liberia 6°20N 10°45W 262 D2
Paynesville Minn., U.S.A. 45°23N 94°43W 308 C6
Payo Obispo = Chetumal Mexico 18°30N 88°20W 319 D7
Pays de la Loire □ France 47°45N 0°25W 172 E6
Paysandú Uruguay 32°19S 58°8W 334 C4
Payson Ariz., U.S.A. 34°14N 111°20W 305 J8
Payson Utah, U.S.A. 40°3N 111°44W 304 F8
Paz → Guatemala 13°44N 90°10W 320 D1
Paz, B. de la Mexico 24°9N 110°25W 318 C2
Pāzanān Iran 30°35N 49°59E 247 D6
Pazar Turkey 41°10N 40°50E 213 B9
Pazarcık Turkey 37°30N 37°17E 212 D7
Pazardzhik Bulgaria 42°12N 24°20E 203 D8
Pazarköy Turkey 39°51N 27°24E 205 B9
Pazarlar Turkey 39°0N 29°7E 205 C11
Pazaryeri Turkey 40°0N 29°56E 205 B11
Pazaryolu Turkey 40°21N 40°47E 213 B9
Pazin Croatia 45°14N 13°56E 199 C10
Pazña Bolivia 18°36S 66°55W 330 D4
Pčinja → Macedonia 41°50N 21°45E 202 E5
Pe Ell U.S.A. 46°34N 123°18W 306 D3
Pea → U.S.A. 31°1N 85°51W 316 D4
Peabody U.S.A. 42°31N 70°56W 313 D14
Peace → Alta., Canada 59°0N 111°25W 296 B6
Peace → Fla., U.S.A. 26°56N 82°6W 317 J7
Peace Point Canada 59°7N 112°27W 296 B6
Peace River Canada 56°15N 117°18W 296 B5
Peach Springs U.S.A. 35°32N 113°25W 305 J7
Peachland Canada 49°47N 119°45W 296 D5
Peachtree City U.S.A. 33°25N 84°35W 316 B5
Peacock Pt. Wake I. 19°16N 166°37E 302 b
Peak, The = Kinder Scout U.K. 53°24N 1°52W 168 D6
Peak, The Ascension I. 7°57S 14°20W 153 g
Peak Charles △ Australia 32°42S 121°10E 279 F3
Peak District △ U.K. 53°24N 1°46W 168 D6
Peak Hill N.S.W., Australia 32°47S 148°11E 283 B8
Peak Hill W. Austral., Australia 25°35S 118°43E 279 E2
Peak Ra. Australia 22°50S 148°20E 280 C4
Peake Australia 35°25S 139°55E 282 C3
Peake Cr. → Australia 28°2S 136°7E 281 D2
Peakhurst Australia 33°57S 151°3E 139 B1
Peal de Becerro Spain 37°55N 3°7W 195 H7
Peale, Mt. U.S.A. 38°26N 109°14W 304 G9
Peale I. Wake I. 19°18N 166°37E 302 b
Peania Greece 37°56N 23°50E 112 B3
Pearblossom U.S.A. 34°30N 117°55W 307 L9
Pearl U.S.A. 39°28N 90°38W 310 E6
Pearl → U.S.A. 30°11N 89°32W 315 F10
Pearl and Hermes Reef U.S.A. 27°55N 175°45W 302 F8
Pearl Banks Sri Lanka 8°45N 79°45E 245 K4
Pearl City U.S.A. 21°24N 157°59W 302 K14
Pearl Harbor U.S.A. 21°21N 157°57W 302 K14
Pearl Harbor Nat. Wildlife Refuge ⌓ U.S.A. 21°23N 157°59W 302 K14
Pearl River = Zhu Jiang → China 22°45N 113°37E 229 F9
Pearl River U.S.A. 41°4N 74°2W 313 E10
Pearls Grenada 12°9N 61°37W 323 q
Pearls Rock Grenada 12°9N 61°36W 323 q
Pearsall U.S.A. 28°54N 99°6W 314 G5
Pearson U.S.A. 31°18N 82°51W 316 D7
Pearson Int. Toronto ✈ (YYZ) Canada 43°46N 79°35W 141 A1
Peary Land Greenland 82°40N 33°0W 154 A7
Pease → U.S.A. 34°12N 99°2W 314 D5
Peawanuck Canada 55°15N 85°12W 295 D11
Pebane Mozam. 17°10S 38°8E 269 F4
Pebas Peru 3°10S 71°46W 328 D3
Pebble, I. Falk. Is. 51°20S 59°40W 153 f
Pebble Beach U.S.A. 36°34N 121°57W 306 J5
Peć Serbia 42°40N 20°17E 202 D4
Peçanha Brazil 18°33S 42°34W 333 E3
Pecatonica U.S.A. 42°19N 89°22W 310 B7
Pecatonica → U.S.A. 42°26N 89°12W 310 B7
Péccioli Italy 43°33N 10°43E 198 E7
Pechea Romania 45°36N 27°49E 183 E12
Pechenga Russia 69°29N 31°4E 160 B24
Pechenizhyn Ukraine 48°30N 24°48E 183 B9
Pechiguera, Pta. Canary Is. 28°51N 13°53W 153 e2
Pechnezhskoye Vdkhr. Ukraine 50°5N 36°54E 189 G9
Pechora Russia 65°10N 57°11E 186 A10
Pechora → Russia 68°13N 54°15E 186 A9
Pechorskaya Guba Russia 68°40N 54°0E 186 A9
Pechory Russia 57°48N 27°40E 188 D4
Pecica Romania 46°10N 21°3E 182 D6
Pecka Serbia 44°18N 19°33E 202 B3
Peckham U.K. 51°28N 0°3W 125 B3
Pécora, C. Italy 39°27N 8°23E 200 C1
Pecos N. Mex., U.S.A. 35°35N 105°41W 305 J11
Pecos Tex., U.S.A. 31°26N 103°30W 314 F3
Pecos → U.S.A. 29°42N 101°22W 314 G4
Pécs Hungary 46°5N 18°15E 182 D3
Pedda Bellala India 19°4N 78°49E 244 E4
Peddapalli India 18°40N 79°24E 244 E4
Peddapuram India 17°6N 82°8E 244 F6
Pedder, L. Australia 42°55S 146°10E 281 G4
Peddie S. Africa 33°14S 27°7E 271 D4
Pedernales Dom. Rep. 18°2N 71°44W 321 C5
Pedernales Ecuador 0°5N 80°3W 328 C1
Pederstrup Denmark 55°44N 12°20E 118 A2
Pedieos → Cyprus 35°10N 33°54E 207 E9
Pedirka Australia 26°40S 135°14E 281 D2
Pedra Azul Brazil 16°2S 41°17W 333 E3
Pedra Branca Brazil 0°51N 51°58W 329 C7
Pedra Grande, Recifes de Brazil 17°45S 38°58W 333 E4
Pedra Lume C. Verde Is. 16°40N 22°52W 153 j
Pedralbes Spain 41°23N 2°7E 114 A1
Pedras Negras Brazil 12°51S 62°54W 331 C5
Pedras Tinhosas, I. São Tomé & Príncipe 1°22N 7°17E 265 a
Pedregal de San Angel, Jardines del Mexico 19°19N 99°12W 128 C1
Pedreguer Spain 38°48N 0°3E 197 G5
Pedreiras Brazil 4°32S 44°40W 332 B3
Pedro Afonso Brazil 9°0S 48°10W 332 C2
Pedro Bank W. Indies 17°5N 78°20W 320 C4

Pedro Bay U.S.A. 59°47N 154°7W 303 G9
Pedro Cays Jamaica 17°5N 77°48W 320 C4
Pedro Chico Colombia 1°4N 70°25W 328 C3
Pedro de Valdivia Chile 22°55S 69°38W 334 A2
Pedro Dorado Colombia 1°0N 70°14W 328 C3
Pedro Juan Caballero Paraguay 22°30S 55°40W 335 A4
Pedro Muñoz Spain 39°25N 2°56W 195 F8
Pedro Pt. = North West Pt. Jamaica 18°27N 78°13W 320 a
Pedrógão Grande Portugal 39°55N 8°9W 194 F2
Pee Dee = Great Pee Dee → U.S.A. 33°21N 79°10W 315 E15
Peebinga Australia 34°52S 140°57E 282 C4
Peebles Borders, U.K. 55°40N 3°11W 167 F5
Peebles Ohio, U.S.A. 38°57N 83°24W 311 F13
Peekskill U.S.A. 41°17N 73°55W 313 E11
Peel I. of Man 54°13N 4°40W 168 C3
Peel → N.S.W., Australia 30°50S 150°29E 283 A9
Peel → Canada 67°0N 135°0W 294 C6
Peel Sd. Canada 73°0N 96°0W 294 B10
Peene → Germany 54°9N 13°46E 178 A9
Peera Peera Poolanna L. Australia 26°30S 138°0E 281 D2
Peerless Lake Canada 56°37N 114°40W 296 B6
Peers Canada 53°40N 116°0W 296 C5
Peery L. Australia 30°45S 143°35E 282 A5
Pegasus Bay N.Z. 43°20S 173°10E 285 D8
Peggau Austria 47°12N 15°21E 180 D8
Pegnitz Germany 49°44N 11°31E 179 F7
Pegnitz → Germany 49°30N 10°59E 179 F6
Pego Spain 38°51N 0°8W 197 G4
Pegu Burma 17°20N 96°29E 241 G6
Pegu □ Burma 17°30N 96°30E 241 G6
Pegu Yoma Burma 19°0N 96°0E 241 F6
Pehčevo Macedonia 41°41N 22°55E 202 E6
Pehlivanköy Turkey 41°20N 26°55E 203 E10
Pehuajó Argentina 35°45S 62°0W 334 D3
Pei Xian = Pizhou China 34°44N 116°55E 226 G9
Peian = Bei'an China 48°10N 126°20E 219 B7
Peibei = Beihai China 21°28N 109°6E 228 G7
Peikang Taiwan 23°34N 120°18E 225 C2
Peikang Hsi → Taiwan 24°2N 120°50E 225 B2
Peikant'ang Taiwan 26°13N 120°0E 225 b
Peimen Taiwan 23°16N 120°7E 225 C2
Peinan Taiwan 22°47N 121°7E 225 D3
Peinan Hsi → Taiwan 22°46N 121°10E 225 D3
Peinanchu Shan Taiwan 23°3N 120°52E 225 C2
Peine Chile 23°45S 68°8W 334 A2
Peine Niedersachsen, Germany 52°19N 10°14E 178 C6
Peip'ing = Beijing China 39°53N 116°21E 114 B1
Peipu Taiwan 24°2N 121°36E 225 B3
Peipus, L. = Chudskoye, Ozero Russia 58°13N 27°30E 188 C4
Peissenberg Germany 47°48N 11°4E 179 H7
Peitawu Shan Taiwan 22°38N 120°46E 225 D2
Peitou Changhua, Taiwan 23°52N 120°30E 225 C2
Peitou T'aipei, Taiwan 25°11N 121°27E 225 A3
Peitun Taiwan 24°10N 120°41E 225 B2
Peitz Germany 51°51N 14°24E 178 D10
Peixe Brazil 12°0S 48°40W 333 D2
Peixe → Brazil 21°31S 51°58W 333 F1
Peixoto de Azeredo → Brazil 10°6S 55°31W 331 C6
Pek → Serbia 44°45N 21°29E 202 B5
Pekalongan Indonesia 6°53S 109°40E 235 D3
Pekan Malaysia 3°30N 103°25E 237 L4
Pekan Nenas Malaysia 1°31N 103°31E 237 d
Pekanbaru Indonesia 0°30N 101°15E 234 B2
Pekhorka → Russia 55°37N 38°2E 129 C6
Pekhra-Pokrovskoye Russia 55°50N 37°56E 129 A5
Pekhra-Yakovlevskaya Russia 55°47N 37°57E 129 B5
Pekin U.S.A. 40°35N 89°40W 310 D7
Peking = Beijing China 39°53N 116°21E 114 B1
Pekutatan Indonesia 8°25S 114°49E 231 J17
Pela Greece 40°46N 22°23E 202 F6
Pêla Guinea 7°37N 9°7W 262 D3
Pelabuhan Klang Malaysia 3°0N 101°23E 237 L3
Pelabuhan Ratu, Teluk Indonesia 7°5S 106°30E 234 D3
Pelabuhanratu Indonesia 7°0S 106°32E 234 D3
Pélagos = Kira Panagia Greece 39°17N 24°4E 204 B6
Pelaihari Indonesia 3°55S 114°45E 235 C4
Pelat, Mt. France 44°16N 6°42E 175 D10
Pelcowizna Poland 52°17N 21°0E 142 B2
Pelczyce Poland 53°3N 15°16E 185 E2
Peleaga, Vf. Romania 45°22N 22°55E 182 E7
Pelechuco Bolivia 14°48S 69°4W 330 C4
Pelée, Mt. Martinique 14°48N 61°10W 322 j
Pelee, Pt. Canada 41°54N 82°31W 298 D3
Pelee I. Canada 41°47N 82°40W 312 E2
Pelejo Peru 6°10S 75°49W 330 B2
Pelekech Kenya 3°52N 35°8E 268 B4
Peleliu I. Palau 7°1N 134°15E 288 c
Peleng Indonesia 1°20S 123°30E 231 E6
Pelenge Dem. Rep. of the Congo 2°44S 22°39E 264 C4
Pelentong Malaysia 1°32N 103°49E 237 d
Pélézi Ivory C. 7°17N 6°54W 262 D3
Pelham U.S.A. 31°8N 84°9W 316 D5
Pelhřimov Czech Rep. 49°24N 15°12E 180 B8
Pelican U.S.A. 57°58N 136°14W 296 B1
Pelican L. Canada 52°28N 100°20W 297 C8
Pelican Narrows Canada 55°10N 102°56W 297 B8
Pelion U.S.A. 33°46N 81°15W 316 B8
Pelister △ Macedonia 41°0N 21°10E 202 F5
Pelješac Croatia 42°55N 17°25E 199 F14
Pelkosenniemi Finland 67°6N 27°28E 160 C22
Pell City U.S.A. 33°35N 86°17W 316 B3
Pella Northern Cape, S. Africa 29°1S 19°6E 270 C2
Pella Iowa, U.S.A. 41°25N 92°55W 310 C4
Pella □ Greece 40°52N 22°0E 202 F6
Pello Finland 66°47N 23°59E 160 C20
Pellworm Germany 54°31N 8°39E 178 A4
Pelly → Canada 62°47N 137°19W 296 A1
Pelly Bay Canada 68°38N 89°50W 295 C11
Peloponnese □ Greece 37°10N 22°0E 204 D4
Peloponnisos Station Athens, Greece 112 a1
Peloritani, Monti Italy 38°3N 15°20E 201 D8
Pelorus → N.Z. 41°16S 173°45E 285 B8
Pelorus Sd. N.Z. 40°59S 173°59E 285 A8
Pelotas Brazil 31°42S 52°23W 335 C5
Pelotas → Brazil 27°28S 51°55W 335 B5
Pelovo Bulgaria 43°26N 24°17E 203 C8
Pelplin Poland 53°55N 18°42E 184 E5
Pelvoux, Massif du France 44°52N 6°20E 175 D10
Pemalang Indonesia 6°53S 109°23E 235 D3
Pemanggil, Pulau Malaysia 2°37N 104°21E 237 L5
Pematangsiantar Indonesia 2°57N 99°5E 234 B1
Pemba Mozam. 12°58S 40°30E 269 E5
Pemba Zambia 16°30S 27°28E 269 F2
Pemba Channel Tanzania 5°0S 39°37E 268 D4
Pemba I. Tanzania 5°0S 39°45E 268 D4
Pemberton W. Austral., Australia 34°30S 116°0E 279 F2
Pemberton B.C., Canada 50°25N 122°50W 296 C4
Pembina → Canada 54°45N 114°17W 296 C6
Pembroke Ont., Canada 45°50N 77°7W 298 C4
Pembroke Pembs., U.K. 51°41N 4°55W 169 F3
Pembroke Trin. & Tob. 11°13N 60°37W 323 s
Pembroke Ga., U.S.A. 32°8N 81°37W 316 C8
Pembroke Pines U.S.A. 26°0N 80°13W 317 J9
Pembrokeshire □ U.K. 51°52N 4°56W 169 F3
Pembrokeshire Coast △ U.K. 51°50N 5°2W 169 F2
Pembuang → Indonesia 3°24S 112°33E 235 C4
Pen India 18°45N 73°5E 244 E1
Pen-y-Ghent U.K. 54°10N 2°14W 168 C5
Peña, Sierra de la Spain 42°32N 0°45W 196 C4
Peña de Francia, Sierra de la Spain 40°32N 6°10W 194 E4
Penafiel Portugal 41°12N 8°17W 194 D2
Peñafiel Spain 41°35N 4°7W 194 D6
Peñaflor Spain 37°43N 5°21W 195 H5
Penal Trin. & Tob. 10°9N 61°29W 323 t
Peñalara Spain 40°51N 3°57W 194 E7
Peñalolén Chile 33°28S 70°32W 137 B2
Penalva Brazil 3°18S 45°10W 332 B2
Penamacôr Portugal 40°10N 7°10W 194 E3
Penang = Pinang Malaysia 5°25N 100°15E 237 c
Penápolis Brazil 21°30S 50°0W 335 A6
Peñaranda de Bracamonte Spain 40°53N 5°13W 194 E5
Peñarroya Spain 40°25N 0°40W 196 E4
Peñarroya-Pueblonuevo Spain 38°19N 5°16W 195 G5
Penarth U.K. 51°26N 3°11W 169 F4
Peñas, C. de Spain 43°42N 5°52W 194 B5
Peñas, G. de Chile 47°0S 75°0W 336 C2
Peñas, Pta. Venezuela 11°17N 62°0W 329 A5
Peñas de San Pedro Spain 38°44N 2°0W 197 G3
Peñas del Chache Canary Is. 29°6N 13°33W 153 e2
Peñausende Spain 41°17N 5°52W 194 D5
Pencarrow Hd. N.Z. 41°22S 174°51E 143 C2
Pench → India 21°17N 79°10E 244 D4
Pench △ India 21°45N 79°20E 243 J8
Pench'i = Benxi China 41°20N 123°48E 224 B1
Pend Oreille → U.S.A. 49°4N 117°37W 304 B5
Pend Oreille, L. U.S.A. 48°10N 116°21W 304 B5
Pendalofos Greece 40°14N 21°12E 202 F5
Pendé → C.A.R. 7°55N 16°36E 264 A3
Pendembu Eastern, S. Leone 8°10N 10°42W 262 D2
Pendembu Northern, S. Leone 9°7N 11°14W 262 D2
Pendências Brazil 5°15S 36°43W 332 C4
Pender B. Australia 16°45S 122°42E 278 C3
Pendik Turkey 40°53N 29°13E 203 F13
Pendjari → Benin 10°55N 0°50E 263 C5
Pendjari △ Benin 11°15N 1°32E 263 C5
Pendleton Ind., U.S.A. 40°0N 85°45W 311 E11
Pendleton Oreg., U.S.A. 45°40N 118°47W 304 D4
Pendra India 22°46N 81°57E 243 H9
Pendzhikent Tajikistan 39°29N 67°37E 217 E7
Peneda-Gerês △ Portugal 41°57N 8°15W 194 D2
Penedo Brazil 10°15S 36°36W 332 D4
Penelokan Indonesia 8°17S 115°22E 231 J18
Penetanguishene Canada 44°50N 79°55W 312 B5
Penfield U.S.A. 41°13N 78°35W 312 E6
Peng Chau China 22°17N 114°2E 219 G11
Peng Siang → Singapore 1°24N 103°43E 138 A2
Pengalengan Indonesia 7°9S 107°30E 235 D3
Penganga → India 19°53N 79°9E 244 E4
Penge Kasai-Or., Dem. Rep. of the Congo 5°30S 24°33E 265 D4
Penge Sud-Kivu, Dem. Rep. of the Congo 4°27S 28°25E 268 C2
Penge London, U.K. 51°24N 0°3W 125 B3
P'enghu □ Taiwan 23°30N 119°30E 225 C1
P'enghu Ch'üntou Taiwan 23°34N 119°30E 225 C1
P'enghu Tao Taiwan 23°34N 119°37E 225 C1
Penglai China 37°48N 120°42E 227 F11
Pengshan China 30°14N 103°58E 228 B4
Pengshui China 29°17N 108°12E 228 C7
Penguin Australia 41°8S 146°6E 281 G4
Pengxi China 30°44N 105°45E 228 B5
Pengze China 29°52N 116°32E 229 C11
Penha Brazil 22°49S 43°17W 135 A1
Penhalonga Zimbabwe 18°52S 32°40E 269 F3
Peniche Portugal 39°19N 9°22W 195 F1
Penicuik U.K. 55°50N 3°13W 121 B2
Penida, Nusa Indonesia 8°45S 115°30E 231 K18
Peninnes, Alpes = Pennine, Alpi Alps 46°4N 7°30E 179 J3
Peninsular Malaysia □ Malaysia 4°0N 102°0E 237 L4
Peñíscola Spain 40°22N 0°24E 196 E5
Penitente, Serra do Brazil 8°45S 46°20W 332 C2
Penjaringan Indonesia 6°7S 106°48E 122 A1
Penki = Benxi China 41°20N 123°48E 224 B1
Penkridge U.K. 52°44N 2°6W 168 E5
Penmarch France 47°49N 4°21W 172 E2
Penmarch, Pte. de France 47°48N 4°22W 172 E2
Penn = Penn Hills U.S.A. 40°28N 79°52W 312 F5
Penn Hills U.S.A. 40°28N 79°52W 312 F5
Penn Station New York, U.S.A. 132 c2
Penn Yan U.S.A. 42°40N 77°3W 312 D7
Penna, Punta della Italy 42°10N 14°43E 199 F11
Pennant Canada 50°32N 108°14W 297 C7
Penne Italy 42°27N 13°55E 199 F10
Penner → India 14°35N 80°10E 245 G5
Penneshaw Australia 35°44S 137°56E 282 C2
Pennine, Alpi Alps 46°4N 7°30E 179 J3
Pennines U.K. 54°45N 2°27W 168 C5
Pennington U.S.A. 39°15N 121°47W 306 F5
Pennington → Nigeria 4°45N 5°35E 263 E6
Pennino, Mte. Italy 43°6N 12°53E 199 E9
Pennsburg U.S.A. 40°23N 75°29W 313 F9
Pennsylvania □ U.S.A. 40°45N 77°30W 309 E15
Pennsylvania Avenue Washington, D.C., U.S.A. 143 b2
Pennville U.S.A. 40°30N 85°9W 311 D11
Penny Canada 53°51N 121°20W 296 C4
Penny Str. Canada 76°30N 97°0W 295 B8
Peno Russia 57°2N 32°49E 188 D7
Penobscot → U.S.A. 44°30N 68°48W 309 C19
Penobscot B. U.S.A. 44°35N 68°50W 309 C19
Penola Australia 37°25S 140°48E 282 D4
Penong Australia 31°56S 133°1E 279 F5
Penonomé Panama 8°31N 80°21W 320 E3
Penot, Mt. Vanuatu 16°20S 167°31E 287 F5
Penrhyn Cook Is. 9°0S 158°0W 289 H12
Penrith N.S.W., Australia 33°43S 150°38E 283 B9
Penrith Cumb., U.K. 54°40N 2°45W 168 C5
Penryn U.K. 50°9N 5°7W 169 G2
Pensacola U.S.A. 30°25N 87°13W 317 E2
Pensacola B. U.S.A. 30°25N 87°5W 317 E2
Pensacola Mts. Antarctica 84°0S 40°0W 151 E1
Pense Canada 50°25N 104°59W 297 C8
Penshurst Australia 37°49S 142°20E 282 D5
Pensiangan Malaysia 4°33N 116°19E 235 B5
Pentagon U.S.A. 38°53N 77°3W 143 B3
Pentecost = Pentecôte Vanuatu 15°42S 168°10E 287 E6
Pentecoste Brazil 3°48S 39°17W 332 B4
Pentecôte Vanuatu 15°42S 168°10E 287 E6
Penticton Canada 49°30N 119°38W 296 D5
Pentland Australia 20°32S 145°25E 280 C4
Pentland Firth U.K. 58°43N 3°10W 167 C5
Pentland Hills U.K. 55°48N 3°25W 167 F5
Pentland Hills ⌂ U.K. 55°50N 3°20W 167 F5
Penukonda India 14°5N 77°38E 245 G3
Penyagino Russia 55°50N 37°20E 129 A2
Penza Russia 53°15N 45°5E 190 D7
Penza □ Russia 52°50N 44°50E 190 D7
Penzance U.K. 50°7N 5°33W 169 G2
Penzberg Germany 47°45N 11°22E 179 H7
Penzhino Russia 63°30N 167°55E 215 C17
Penzhinskaya Guba Russia 61°30N 163°0E 215 C17
Penzhou China 31°4N 103°32E 228 B4
Penzing Austria 48°11N 16°18E 142 A1
Penzlin Germany 53°30N 13°5E 178 B9
People's Park China 31°13N 121°28E 138 B1
People's Square China 31°13N 121°28E 138 B1
Peoria Ariz., U.S.A. 33°43N 112°14W 305 K7
Peoria Ill., U.S.A. 40°42N 89°36W 310 D7
Peoria Heights U.S.A. 40°45N 89°35W 310 D7
Peotone U.S.A. 41°20N 87°48W 311 C9
Pepacton Res. U.S.A. 42°5N 74°58W 313 D10
Pepani → S. Africa 25°49S 22°47E 270 C3
Pepeekeo U.S.A. 19°51N 155°6W 302 D6
Pepel S. Leone 8°40N 13°5W 262 D2
Peqin Albania 41°3N 19°44E 202 E3
Pera Hd. Australia 12°55S 141°37E 280 A3
Perabumulih Indonesia 3°27S 104°15E 234 C2
Perachora Greece 38°2N 22°56E 204 C4
Perachori Greece 38°21N 20°43E 207 C2
Perak □ Malaysia 5°0N 101°0E 234 A2
Perak → Malaysia 4°0N 100°50E 237 K3
Perales de Alfambra Spain 40°38N 1°0W 196 E4
Perales del Puerto Spain 40°10N 6°40W 194 E4
Perales del Rio Spain 40°18N 3°38W 127 C2
Perama Kerkyra, Greece 39°34N 19°54E 206 B9
Perama Kriti, Greece 35°20N 24°40E 207 E5
Perancak Indonesia 8°24S 114°37E 231 J17
Peräpohjola Finland 66°16N 26°10E 160 C22
Perast Montenegro 42°31N 18°47E 202 D2
Peratia Greece 38°49N 20°45E 207 B2
Peravillo Mexico City, Mexico 128 a3
Percé Canada 48°31N 64°13W 299 C7
Perche France 48°31N 1°1E 172 D8
Perche, Collines du France 48°30N 0°40E 171 B4
Perche ⌂ France 48°24N 0°46E 172 D7
Perchtoldsdorf Austria 48°7N 16°17E 142 B1
Percival Lakes Australia 21°25S 125°0E 278 D4
Percy Manche, France 48°55N 1°11W 172 D5
Percy Ill., U.S.A. 38°5N 89°41W 310 F7
Percy Is. Australia 21°39S 150°16E 280 C5
Perdido → Argentina 42°55S 67°0W 336 B3
Perdido, Mte. Spain 42°40N 0°5E 196 C5
Perdizes Brazil 23°32S 46°39W 137 B2
Perdu, Mt. = Perdido, Mte. Spain 42°40N 0°5E 196 C5
Perechyn Ukraine 48°44N 22°28E 182 B7
Peredelkino Russia 55°38N 37°20E 129 C2
Perehinske Ukraine 48°49N 24°11E 183 B9
Pereira Colombia 4°49N 75°43W 328 C2
Perelazovskiy Russia 49°8N 42°35E 191 F6
Peremul Par India 11°10N 72°4E 245 J1
Peremyshl = Przemyśl Poland 49°50N 22°45E 185 J9
Perené → Peru 11°9S 74°14W 330 C3
Perenjori Australia 29°26S 116°16E 279 E2
Peresecina Moldova 47°16N 28°46E 183 C13
Pereslavl-Zalesskiy Russia 56°45N 38°50E 188 D10
Peretu Romania 44°3N 25°5E 183 F10
Pereyaslav-Khmelnytskyy Ukraine 50°3N 31°28E 189 G6
Pereyma Ukraine 48°4N 29°30E 183 B14
Pérez, I. Mexico 22°24N 89°42W 319 C7
Perg Austria 48°15N 14°38E 180 C7
Pergamino Argentina 33°52S 60°30W 334 C3
Pergamon Museum Berlin, Germany 115 a4
Pergau → Malaysia 5°23N 102°2E 237 K3
Perge Turkey 37°3N 30°56E 250 A1
Pérgine Valsugana Italy 46°4N 11°14E 199 B8
Pérgola Italy 43°34N 12°50E 199 E9
Perham U.S.A. 46°36N 95°34W 308 B6
Perhentian, Kepulauan Malaysia 5°54N 102°42E 237 K4
Peri → Turkey 38°53N 39°52E 213 C8
Periam Romania 46°2N 20°52E 182 D5
Péribonka → Canada 48°45N 72°5W 299 C5
Péribonka, L. Canada 50°1N 71°10W 299 B5
Perico Argentina 24°20S 65°5W 334 A2
Pericos Mexico 25°3N 107°42W 318 B3
Périers France 49°11N 1°25W 172 C5
Périgord France 45°0N 0°40E 174 D4
Périgord-Limousin ⌂ France 45°40N 0°50E 174 C4
Périgueux France 45°10N 0°42E 174 C4
Perijá, Sierra de Colombia 9°30N 73°3W 328 B3
Perijá △ Venezuela 9°30N 72°55W 328 B3
Perisher Valley Australia 36°27S 148°25E 283 D8
Peristera Greece 39°15N 23°58E 204 B5
Peristeri Greece 38°1N 23°42E 112 A2
Peristerona → Cyprus 35°8N 33°5E 207 E9
Perito Moreno Argentina 46°36S 70°56W 336 C2
Perito Moreno △ Argentina 47°49S 72°17W 336 C2
Peritoró Brazil 4°20S 44°18W 332 B3
Perivale U.K. 51°31N 0°18W 125 A2
Perivol = Dragovishtitsa Bulgaria 42°22N 22°39E 202 D6
Periyakulam India 10°5N 77°30E 245 J3
Periyar → India 10°15N 76°10E 245 J3
Periyar, L. India 9°25N 77°10E 245 K3
Periyar △ India 9°25N 77°10E 245 K3
Perk Belgium 50°56N 4°30E 116 A2
Perkasie U.S.A. 40°22N 75°18W 313 F9
Perković Croatia 43°41N 16°10E 199 E13
Perlach Germany 48°5N 11°37E 131 B2
Perlacher Forst Germany 48°4N 11°34E 131 B2
Perlas, Arch. de las Panama 8°41N 79°7W 320 E4
Perlas, Punta de Nic. 12°30N 83°30W 320 D3
Perleberg Germany 53°5N 11°52E 178 B7
Perlez Serbia 45°11N 20°22E 182 E5
Perlis □ Malaysia 6°30N 100°15E 234 A2
Perm Russia 58°0N 56°10E 186 C10
Përmet Albania 40°15N 20°21E 202 F4
Permskoye = Komsomolsk Russia 50°30N 137°0E 215 D14
Pernambuco = Recife Brazil 8°0S 35°0W 332 C5
Pernambuco □ Brazil 8°0S 37°0W 332 C4
Pernambuco Abyssal Plain Atl. Oc. 5°0S 24°0W 152 G9
Pernatty Lagoon Australia 31°30S 137°12E 282 A2
Pernik Bulgaria 42°35N 23°2E 202 D7
Pernov = Pärnu Estonia 58°28N 24°33E 188 C3
Pero Italy 45°30N 9°5E 129 A1
Peron Is. Australia 13°9S 130°4E 278 B5
Peron Pen. Australia 26°0S 113°10E 279 E1
Péronne France 49°55N 2°57E 173 C9
Peropok, Bukit Singapore 1°19N 103°42E 138 B2
Perosa Argentina Italy 44°58N 7°10E 198 D4
Perovo Russia 55°44N 37°45E 129 B4
Perovsk = Qyzylorda Kazakhstan 44°48N 65°28E 217 D7
Perow Canada 54°35N 126°10W 296 C3
Perparim = Pogradec Albania 40°54N 20°37E 202 F4
Perpignan France 42°42N 2°53E 174 F6
Perrégaux = Mohammadia Algeria 35°33N 0°3E 261 A5
Perrine U.S.A. 25°36N 80°21W 317 K9
Perris U.S.A. 33°47N 117°14W 307 M9
Perros-Guirec France 48°49N 3°28W 172 D3
Perry Fla., U.S.A. 30°7N 83°35W 316 E6
Perry Ga., U.S.A. 32°28N 83°44W 316 C6
Perry Iowa, U.S.A. 41°51N 94°6W 310 C2
Perry Mich., U.S.A. 42°50N 84°13W 311 B12
Perry Mo., U.S.A. 39°26N 91°40W 310 E5
Perry Okla., U.S.A. 36°17N 97°14W 314 C6
Perrysburg U.S.A. 41°34N 83°38W 311 C13
Perryton U.S.A. 36°24N 100°48W 314 C4
Perryville Alaska, U.S.A. 55°55N 159°9W 303 J8
Perryville Mo., U.S.A. 37°43N 89°52W 310 G7
Persan France 49°9N 2°16E 173 C9
Persberg Sweden 59°47N 14°15E 162 E8
Perşembe Turkey 41°5N 37°46E 212 B7
Persepolis Iran 29°55N 52°50E 247 D7
Perseverancia Bolivia 14°44S 62°48W 331 C5
Pershing Square Los Angeles, U.S.A. 127 c1
Pershotravensk Ukraine 50°13N 27°40E 177 C14
Pershotravnevoye = Pershotravensk Ukraine 50°13N 27°40E 177 C14
Persia = Iran ■ Asia 33°0N 53°0E 247 C7
Persian Gulf Asia 27°0N 50°0E 247 E6
Perstorp Sweden 56°10N 13°25E 163 H7
Pertek Turkey 38°51N 39°19E 213 C8
Perth W. Austral., Australia 31°57S 115°52E 279 F2
Perth Ont., Canada 44°55N 76°15W 313 B8
Perth Perth & Kinr., U.K. 56°24N 3°26W 167 E5
Perth & Kinross □ U.K. 56°45N 3°55W 167 E5
Perth Amboy U.S.A. 40°30N 74°15W 313 F10
Perth-Andover Canada 46°44N 67°42W 299 C6
Pertuis France 43°42N 5°30E 175 E9
Pertusato, C. France 41°21N 9°11E 175 G13
Pertusella Italy 45°35N 9°3E 129 A1
Peru Ill., U.S.A. 41°20N 89°8W 310 C7
Peru Ind., U.S.A. 40°45N 86°4W 311 D10
Peru N.Y., U.S.A. 44°35N 73°32W 313 B11
Peru ■ S. Amer. 4°0S 75°0W 328 D3
Peru Basin Pac. Oc. 20°0S 95°0W 289 J18
Peru-Chile Trench Pac. Oc. 20°0S 72°0W 326 E3
Perúgia Italy 43°7N 12°23E 199 E9
Perušić Croatia 44°40N 15°22E 199 D12
Peruvian Vale St. Vincent 13°13N 61°12W 323 n
Pervomaysk Russia 54°56N 43°58E 190 C6
Pervomaysk Ukraine 48°10N 30°46E 189 H6
Pervouralsk Russia 56°59N 59°59E 186 C10
Pervouralsky = Pervouralsk Russia 56°59N 59°59E 186 C10
Pesada Greece 38°7N 20°35E 207 C2
Pesagot West Bank 31°54N 35°13E 123 A2
Pesanggrahag, Kali → Indonesia 6°10S 106°44E 122 B1
Pésaro Italy 43°54N 12°55E 199 E9
Pescadores = P'enghu Ch'üntou Taiwan 23°34N 119°30E 225 C1
Pescara Italy 42°28N 14°13E 199 F11
Pescara → Italy 42°28N 14°13E 199 F11
Peschanokopskoye Russia 46°14N 41°4E 191 G5
Peschanoye = Yashkul Russia 46°11N 45°21E 191 G7
Peschiera Borromeo Italy 45°26N 9°19E 129 B2
Péscia Italy 43°54N 10°41E 198 E7
Pescina Italy 42°2N 13°39E 199 F10
Pesek, Pulau Singapore 1°17N 103°41E 138 B2
Peshawar Pakistan 34°2N 71°37E 242 B4
Peshkopi Albania 41°41N 20°25E 202 E4
Peshtera Bulgaria 42°2N 24°18E 203 D8
Peshtigo U.S.A. 45°3N 87°45W 308 C10
Peski Russia 51°14N 42°29E 190 E6
Peski Turkmenistan 38°11N 62°59E 216 E6
Pêso da Régua Portugal 41°10N 7°47W 194 D3
Pesochnya = Kirov Russia 54°3N 34°20E 188 E8
Pesqueira Brazil 8°20S 36°42W 332 C4
Pessac France 44°48N 0°37W 174 D3
Pest Hungary 47°29N 19°4E 117 B2
Pest □ Hungary 47°29N 19°5E 182 C4
Pesterzsébet Hungary 47°26N 19°6E 117 B2
Pesthidegkút Hungary 47°33N 18°57E 117 A1
Pestimre Hungary 47°24N 19°11E 117 B3
Pestlörinc Hungary 47°26N 19°11E 117 B3
Pestovo = Zavolzhye Russia 56°37N 43°26E 190 B6
Pestovo Russia 58°33N 35°42E 188 C8
Pestravka Russia 52°28N 49°57E 190 D9
Pestújhely Hungary 47°32N 19°7E 117 A2
Petah Tiqwa Israel 32°6N 34°53E 251 F5
Petalas Greece 38°25N 21°5E 207 C3
Petalidi Greece 36°57N 21°55E 204 E3
Petaling Jaya Malaysia 3°4N 101°42E 237 L3
Petaloudes Greece 36°18N 28°5E 206 E12
Petaluma U.S.A. 38°14N 122°39W 306 G4
Pétange Lux. 49°33N 5°55E 170 E5
Petaro Pakistan 25°31N 68°18E 242 G3
Petas Helsinki, Finland 60°15N 24°50E 121 B2
Petas Greece 39°10N 21°2E 204 B3
Petatlán Mexico 17°31N 101°16W 318 D4
Petauke Zambia 14°14S 31°20E 269 E3
Petawawa Canada 45°54N 77°17W 298 C4
Petén Itzá, L. Guatemala 16°58N 89°50W 320 C2
Peter I. Br. Virgin Is. 18°22N 64°35W 321 b
Peter I. Øy Antarctica 69°0S 91°0W 151 C16
Peter Pond L. Canada 55°55N 108°44W 297 B7
Peterbell Canada 48°36N 83°21W 298 C3
Peterborough S. Austral., Australia 32°58S 138°51E 282 B3
Peterborough Ont., Canada 44°20N 78°20W 312 B6
Peterborough Peterborough, U.K. 52°35N 0°15W 169 E7
Peterborough N.H., U.S.A. 42°53N 71°57W 313 D13
Peterborough □ U.K. 52°35N 0°15W 169 E7
Peterculter U.K. 57°6N 2°16W 167 D6
Peterhead U.K. 57°31N 1°48W 167 D7
Peterhof = Petrodvorets Russia 59°52N 29°54E 188 C5
Peterlee U.K. 54°47N 1°20W 168 C6
Petermann Bjerg Greenland 73°7N 28°25W 154 C8
Petermann Gletscher Greenland 80°30N 60°0W 154 A4
Petermann Ranges Australia 26°0S 130°30E 279 E5
Peter's Mine Guyana 6°14N 59°20W 329 B6
Petersburg = Peterborough Australia 32°58S 138°51E 282 B3
Petersburg Alaska, U.S.A. 56°48N 132°58W 303 H14
Petersburg Ill., U.S.A. 40°1N 89°51W 310 D7
Petersburg Ind., U.S.A. 38°30N 87°17W 311 F9
Petersburg Mich., U.S.A. 41°54N 83°43W 311 C13
Petersburg Pa., U.S.A. 40°34N 78°3W 312 F6
Petersburg Va., U.S.A. 37°14N 77°24W 309 G15
Petersburg W. Va., U.S.A. 39°1N 79°5W 309 F14
Petersfield U.K. 51°1N 0°56W 169 F7
Petershagen Germany 52°23N 8°58E 178 C4
Petília Policastro Italy 39°7N 16°48E 201 C9
Petit Batanga Cameroon 3°15N 9°54E 264 B1
Petit-Bourg Guadeloupe 16°11N 61°37W 322 e
Petit-Canal Guadeloupe 16°25N 61°31W 322 e
Petit Cul-de-Sac Marin Guadeloupe 16°12N 61°33W 322 e
Petit Dominique Grenada 12°30N 61°24W 323 q
Petit Goâve Haiti 18°27N 72°51W 321 C5
Petit Jardin Canada 48°28N 59°14W 299 C8
Petit Lac Manicouagan Canada 51°25N 67°40W 299 B6
Petit-Mécatina → Canada 50°40N 59°30W 299 B8
Petit-Mécatina, Î. du Canada 50°30N 59°25W 299 B8
Petit Piton St. Lucia 13°51N 61°5W 323 m
Petit Raffray Mauritius 20°0S 57°36E 272 e
Petit-Saguenay Canada 48°15N 70°4W 299 C5
Petit Saint Bernard, Col du Italy 45°40N 6°52E 175 C10
Petit Soufrière B. Dominica 15°23N 61°15W 323 k
Petitcodiac Canada 45°57N 65°11W 299 C6
Petite Anse Martinique 14°28N 61°4W 322 j
Petite-Île Réunion 21°20S 55°35E 272 f
Petite Martinique Grenada 12°31N 61°23W 323 q
Petite Rivière Mauritius 20°11S 57°26E 272 e
Petite Savane Dominica 15°15N 61°17W 323 k
Petite Terre = Pamandzi Mayotte 12°47S 45°16E 272 b
Petite Terre, Îles de la Guadeloupe 16°13N 61°9W 322 e
Petites-Anses Guadeloupe 15°51N 61°38W 322 e
Petitjean = Sidi Kacem Morocco 34°12N 5°42W 260 B3
Petitot → Canada 60°14N 123°29W 296 A4
Petitsikapau L. Canada 54°37N 66°25W 299 B6
Petlad India 22°30N 72°45E 242 H5
Peto Mexico 20°8N 88°55W 319 C7
Petone N.Z. 41°13S 174°53E 143 B2
Petorca Chile 32°15S 70°56W 334 C1
Petoskey U.S.A. 45°22N 84°57W 309 C11
Petra Jordan 30°20N 35°22E 251 H6
Petra Spain 39°37N 3°6E 206 B4
Petra, Ostrova Russia 76°15N 118°30E 150 B13
Petra Velikogo, Zaliv Russia 42°40N 132°0E 220 C6
Petrel = Petrer Spain 38°30N 0°46W 197 G4
Petrella, Monte Italy 41°18N 13°40E 200 A6
Petrer Spain 38°30N 0°46W 197 G4
Petreto-Bicchisano France 41°47N 8°58E 175 G12
Petrich Bulgaria 41°24N 23°13E 202 E7
Petrified Forest △ U.S.A. 35°0N 109°30W 305 J9
Petrijanec Croatia 46°23N 16°17E 199 B13
Petrikov = Pyetrikaw Belarus 52°11N 28°29E 177 B15
Petrila Romania 45°29N 23°29E 183 E8
Petrinja Croatia 45°28N 16°18E 199 C13
Petrodvorets Russia 59°52N 29°54E 188 C5
Petrograd = Sankt-Peterburg Russia 59°55N 30°20E 137 B1
Petrogradskaya Storona Russia 59°56N 30°20E 137 B2
Petrolândia Brazil 9°5S 38°20W 332 C4
Petrolia Canada 42°54N 82°9W 312 D2
Petrolina Brazil 9°24S 40°30W 332 C3
Petromaryevka = Pervomaysk Ukraine 48°10N 30°46E 189 H6
Petropavl Kazakhstan 54°53N 69°13E 217 B7
Petropavlovsk = Petropavl Kazakhstan 54°53N 69°13E 217 B7
Petropavlovsk-Kamchatskiy Russia 53°3N 158°43E 215 D16
Petropavlovskiy = Akhtubinsk Russia 48°13N 46°7E 191 F8
Petropavlovsky = Severouralsk Russia 60°9N 59°57E 186 B10
Petrópolis Brazil 22°33S 43°9W 333 F3
Petroşani Romania 45°28N 23°20E 183 E8
Petroupoli Greece 38°3N 23°40E 112 A2
Petrova Gora Croatia 45°15N 15°45E 199 C12
Petrovac Montenegro 42°13N 18°57E 202 D2
Petrovac Serbia 44°22N 21°26E 202 B5
Petrovaradin Serbia 45°16N 19°55E 182 E4
Petrovgrad = Zrenjanin Serbia 45°22N 20°23E 182 E5
Petrovice Czech Rep. 50°2N 14°33E 135 B3
Petrovsk Russia 52°22N 45°19E 190 D7
Petrovsk-Port = Makhachkala Russia 43°0N 47°30E 191 J8
Petrovsk-Zabaykalskiy Russia 51°20N 108°55E 215 D11
Petrovskaya Russia 45°25N 37°58E 189 K9
Petrovskiy Park Russia 55°47N 37°34E 129 B3
Petrovsko-Razumovskoye Russia 55°49N 37°34E 129 B3
Petrovskoye = Svetlograd Russia 45°25N 42°58E 191 H6
Petrovsky Zavod = Petrovsk-Zabaykalskiy Russia 51°20N 108°55E 215 D11
Petrozavodsk Russia 61°41N 34°20E 188 B8
Petrus Steyn S. Africa 27°38S 28°8E 271 C4
Petrusburg S. Africa 29°4S 25°26E 270 C4
Petsamo = Pechenga Russia 69°29N 31°4E 160 B24
Pettycur U.K. 56°4N 3°10W 121 A2
Petukhovo Russia 55°6N 67°58E 217 A7
Petuna = Fuyu China 45°12N 124°43E 227 B13
Petzeck Austria 46°57N 12°48E 180 E5
Peumo Chile 34°21S 71°12W 334 C1
Peureulak Indonesia 4°48N 97°45E 234 B1
Peusangan → Indonesia 5°16N 96°51E 234 A1
Peutie Belgium 50°56N 4°27E 116 A2
Pevek Russia 69°41N 171°19E 215 C18
Pevely U.S.A. 38°17N 90°24W 310 F6
Peveragno Italy 44°20N 7°37E 198 D4
Peyrehorade France 43°34N 1°7W 174 E2
Peyruis France 44°1N 5°56E 175 D9
Pézenas France 43°28N 3°24E 174 E7
Pezinok Slovak Rep. 48°17N 17°17E 181 C10
Pfaffenhofen Germany 48°31N 11°31E 179 G7
Pfälzerwald ⌂ Germany 49°18N 9°55E 179 F5
Pfarrkirchen Germany 48°25N 12°56E 179 G8
Pfaueninsel Germany 52°26N 13°7E 115 B1
Pfeffenhausen Germany 48°39N 11°58E 179 G7
Pforzheim Germany 48°52N 8°41E 179 G4
Pfullendorf Germany 47°55N 9°15E 179 H5
Pfungstadt Germany 49°48N 8°35E 179 F4
Pha Taem △ Thailand 15°32N 105°30E 236 E5
Phaestos Greece 35°2N 24°50E 207 E5
Phagwara India 31°10N 75°40E 242 D6
Phala Botswana 23°45S 26°50E 270 B4
Phalera = Phulera India 26°52N 75°16E 242 F6
Phalodi India 27°12N 72°24E 242 F5
Phalsbourg France 48°46N 7°15E 173 D14
Phaltan India 17°59N 74°26E 244 F2
Phaluai, Ko Thailand 9°32N 99°41E 237 b
Phan Thailand 19°28N 99°43E 236 C2
Phan Rang Vietnam 11°34N 109°0E 237 G7
Phan Ri = Hoa Da Vietnam 11°16N 108°40E 237 G7
Phan Thiet Vietnam 11°1N 108°9E 237 G7
Phanae Greece 38°8N 25°57E 205 C7
Phanat Nikhom Thailand 13°27N 101°11E 236 F3
Phangan, Ko Thailand 9°45N 100°0E 237 H3
Phangnga Thailand 8°28N 98°30E 237 H2
Phangnga, Ao Thailand 8°16N 98°33E 237 a
Phanom Sarakham Thailand 13°45N 101°21E 236 F3
Phaphund India 26°36N 79°28E 243 F8
Pharenda India 27°5N 83°17E 243 F10
Pharr U.S.A. 26°12N 98°11W 314 H5
Phatthalung Thailand 7°39N 100°6E 237 J3
Phaya Thai Bangkok, Thailand 113 a3
Phayao Thailand 19°11N 99°55E 236 C2
Phelps U.S.A. 42°58N 77°3W 312 D7
Phelps L. Canada 59°15N 103°15W 297 B8
Phenix City U.S.A. 32°28N 85°0W 315 E12
Phet Buri Thailand 13°1N 99°55E 236 F2
Phetchabun Thailand 16°25N 101°8E 236 D3
Phetchabun, Thiu Khao Thailand 16°0N 101°20E 236 E3
Phetchaburi = Phet Buri Thailand 13°1N 99°55E 236 F2
Phi Phi, Ko Thailand 7°45N 98°46E 237 J2
Phiafay Laos 14°48N 106°0E 236 E6
Phibun Mangsahan Thailand 15°14N 105°14E 236 E5
Phichai Thailand 17°22N 100°10E 236 D3
Phichit Thailand 16°26N 100°22E 236 D3
Phihai Pakistan 24°50N 67°8E 123 A2
Philadelphia Miss., U.S.A. 32°46N 89°7W 315 E10
Philadelphia N.Y., U.S.A. 44°9N 75°43W 313 B9
Philadelphia Pa., U.S.A. 39°57N 75°9W 313 G9
Philip U.S.A. 44°2N 101°40W 308 C3
Philip Smith Mts. U.S.A. 68°0N 148°0W 303 C10
Philipi Greece 41°1N 24°16E 203 E8
Philippeville = Skikda Algeria 36°50N 6°58E 261 A6
Philippeville Belgium 50°12N 4°33E 170 D4
Philippi U.S.A. 39°9N 80°3W 309 F13
Philippi L. Australia 24°20S 138°55E 280 C2
Philippine Basin Pac. Oc. 17°0N 132°0E 288 F5
Philippine Sea Pac. Oc. 18°0N 125°0E 288 F4
Philippine Trench = Mindanao Trench Pac. Oc. 12°0N 126°6E 232 E5
Philippines ■ Asia 12°0N 123°0E 232 E4
Philippolis S. Africa 30°15S 25°16E 270 D4
Philippopolis = Plovdiv Bulgaria 42°8N 24°44E 203 D8
Philipsburg Qué., Canada 45°2N 73°5W 313 A11
Philipsburg St.-Maarten 18°3N 63°5W 322 a
Philipsburg Mont., U.S.A. 46°20N 113°18W 304 C7
Philipsburg Pa., U.S.A. 40°54N 78°13W 312 F6
Philipstown = Daingean Ireland 53°18N 7°17W 166 C4
Philipstown S. Africa 30°28S 24°30E 270 D3
Phillip B. Australia 33°58S 151°14E 139 B2
Phillip I. Australia 38°30S 145°12E 283 E6
Phillips U.S.A. 45°42N 90°24W 308 C8
Phillipsburg Ga., U.S.A. 31°25N 83°30W 316 D6
Phillipsburg Kans., U.S.A. 39°45N 99°19W 308 F4
Phillipsburg N.J., U.S.A. 40°42N 75°12W 313 F9
Philmont U.S.A. 42°15N 73°39W 313 D11
Philomath Ga., U.S.A. 33°44N 82°59W 316 B7
Philomath Oreg., U.S.A. 44°32N 123°22W 304 D2
Phimai Thailand 15°13N 102°30E 236 E4
Phitsanulok Thailand 16°50N 100°12E 236 D3
Phnom Dangrek Thailand 14°20N 104°0E 236 E5
Phnom Penh Cambodia 11°33N 104°55E 237 G5
Phnum Penh = Phnom Penh Cambodia 11°33N 104°55E 237 G5
Phoenicia U.S.A. 42°5N 74°14W 313 D10
Phoenix Mauritius 20°17S 57°30E 272 e
Phoenix Ariz., U.S.A. 33°26N 112°4W 305 K7
Phoenix N.Y., U.S.A. 43°14N 76°18W 313 C8
Phoenix Is. Kiribati 3°30S 172°0W 277 A16
Phoenix Park Ireland 53°21N 6°20W 120 A2
Phoenixville U.S.A. 40°8N 75°31W 313 F9
Phon Thailand 15°49N 102°36E 236 E4
Phon Tiou Laos 17°53N 104°37E 236 D5
Phong → Thailand 16°23N 102°56E 236 D4
Phong Saly Laos 21°42N 102°9E 228 G4
Phong Tho Vietnam 22°32N 103°21E 236 A4
Phonhong Laos 18°30N 102°25E 236 C4
Phonum Thailand 8°49N 98°48E 237 H2
Phosphate Hill Australia 21°53S 139°58E 280 C2
Photharam Thailand 13°41N 99°51E 236 F2
Phra Khanong Thailand 13°40N 100°36E 113 B2
Phra Nakhon Thailand 13°45N 100°30E 113 B2
Phra Nakhon Si Ayutthaya Thailand 14°25N 100°30E 236 E3
Phra Pradaeng Thailand 13°39N 100°33E 113 C2
Phra Thong, Ko Thailand 9°5N 98°17E 237 H2
Phrae Thailand 18°7N 100°9E 236 C3
Phranakhon Thailand 13°44N 100°29E 113 B1
Phrom Phiram Thailand 17°2N 100°12E 236 D3
Phrygia Turkey 38°40N 30°0E 212 C4
Phu Bia Laos 19°10N 103°0E 236 C4
Phu Chong-Na Yoi △ Thailand 14°25N 105°30E 236 E5
Phu Dien Vietnam 18°58N 105°31E 236 C5
Phu Hin Rang Kla △ Thailand 17°0N 100°59E 236 D3
Phu Kradung △ Thailand 17°2N 101°44E 236 D3
Phu Loi Laos 20°14N 103°14E 236 B4
Phu Luang △ Thailand 17°15N 101°29E 236 D3
Phu Ly Vietnam 20°35N 105°50E 228 G5
Phu Phan △ Thailand 17°0N 103°56E 236 D4
Phu Quoc, Dao Vietnam 10°20N 104°0E 237 G4
Phu Tho Vietnam 21°24N 105°13E 228 G5
Phuc Yen Vietnam 21°16N 105°45E 228 G5
Phuket Thailand 7°53N 98°24E 237 a
Phuket, Ko Thailand 8°0N 98°22E 237 a
Phul India 30°19N 75°14E 242 D6
Phulad India 25°38N 73°49E 242 G5
Phulbani India 20°28N 84°14E 244 D7
Phulbari India 25°55N 90°2E 241 C3
Phulchari Bangla. 25°11N 89°37E 241 C2
Phulera India 26°52N 75°16E 242 F6
Phulpur India 25°31N 82°49E 243 G10
Phun Phin Thailand 9°7N 99°12E 237 H2
Piacá Brazil 7°42S 47°18W 332 C2
Piacenza Italy 45°1N 9°40E 198 C6
Piaçubaçu Brazil 10°24S 36°25W 332 D4
Piai, Tanjung Malaysia 1°17N 103°30E 237 d
Piako → N.Z. 37°12S 175°30E 284 D4
Pian Cr. → Australia 30°2S 148°12E 281 E4
Pian-Upe ⌂ Uganda 1°44N 34°20E 268 B3
Piana France 42°15N 8°34E 175 F12
Pianella Italy 42°24N 14°2E 199 F11
Piangil Australia 35°5S 143°20E 282 C5
Pianosa Puglia, Italy 42°12N 15°44E 199 F12

Poiana Stampei Romania 47°19N 25°8E 183 C10
Poike, Peninsula Chile 27°6S 109°15W 330 b
Poindimié N. Cal. 20°56S 165°20E 288 d
Poinsett, C. Antarctica 65°42S 113°18E 151 C8
Point Arena U.S.A. 38°55N 123°41W 306 G3
Point Baker U.S.A. 56°21N 133°37W 296 B2
Point Calimere India 10°17N 79°49E 245 J4
Point Edward Canada 43°0N 82°30W 298 D3
Point Fortin Trin. & Tob. 10°10N 61°42W 323 t
Point Hope U.S.A. 68°21N 166°47W 303 B6
Point L. Canada 65°15N 113°4W 294 C8
Point Lay U.S.A. 69°46N 163°3W 303 B7
Point Lisas Industrial Estate
  Trin. & Tob. 10°24N 61°29W 323 t
Point Pedro Sri Lanka 9°50N 80°15E 245 K5
Point Pelee △ Canada 41°57N 82°31W 312 E2
Point Pleasant N.J., U.S.A. 40°5N 74°4W 313 F10
Point Pleasant W. Va.,
  U.S.A. 38°51N 82°8W 309 F12
Point Reyes △ U.S.A. 38°10N 122°55W 306 G2
Point Salines Int. ✈ (GND)
  Grenada 12°0N 61°46W 323 q
Pointe-à-Pierre
  Trin. & Tob. 10°19N 61°28W 323 t
Pointe-à-Pitre Guadeloupe 16°10N 61°32W 322 e
Pointe-au-Pic = La Malbaie
  Canada 47°40N 70°10W 299 C5
Pointe-aux-Trembles
  Canada 45°38N 73°30W 130 A2
Pointe-Claire Canada 45°26N 73°50W 313 A11
Pointe-Gatineau Canada 45°27N 75°41W 313 A9
Pointe Michel Dominica 15°15N 61°23W 323 k
Pointe-Noire Congo 4°48S 11°53E 265 C2
Pointe-Noire Guadeloupe 16°14N 61°47W 322 e
Poio Spain 42°28N 8°41W 194 C2
Poirino Italy 44°56N 7°48E 198 D4
Poisonbush Ra.
  Australia 22°30S 121°30E 278 D3
Poissonnier Pt. Australia 19°57S 119°10E 278 C2
Poissy France 48°55N 2°2E 134 A1
Poitiers France 46°35N 0°20E 172 F7
Poitou France 46°40N 0°10W 172 F5
Poitou-Charentes □
  France 46°10N 0°15E 174 B4
Poix-de-Picardie France 49°47N 1°58E 173 C8
Poix-Terron France 49°38N 4°38E 173 C11
Pojoaque U.S.A. 35°54N 106°1W 305 J10
Pok Fu Lam China 22°16N 114°7E 122 B1
Pōka'ī B. U.S.A. 21°27N 158°12W 302 K13
Pokaran India 27°0N 71°50E 242 F4
Pokataroo Australia 29°30S 148°36E 281 D4
Pokcheong S. Korea 39°28N 127°8E 137 G2
Pokhara Nepal 28°14N 83°58E 243 E10
Pokhvistnevo Russia 53°36N 52°0E 190 D11
Pokigron Suriname 4°30N 55°22W 329 C6
Poko Dem. Rep. of the Congo 3°7N 26°52E 268 B2
Poko Sudan 5°41N 31°55E 257 F3
Pokrov Russia 55°55N 39°7E 188 C10
Pokrovka = Kyzyl-Suu
  Kyrgyzstan 42°20N 78°0E 217 D9
Pokrovsk = Engels Russia 51°28N 46°6E 190 E8
Pokrovsk Russia 61°29N 129°0E 215 C13
Pokrovsko-Sresnevo
  Russia 55°49N 37°27E 129 B2
Pokrovskoy = Priazovskoye
  Ukraine 46°44N 35°40E 189 J8
Pokrovskoye Ukraine 47°25N 38°54E 189 J10
Pol-e Khomri Afghan. 35°56N 68°42E 240 B3
Pola = Istra Croatia 45°10N 14°0E 199 C10
Pola = Pula Croatia 44°54N 13°57E 199 D10
Pola Russia 57°55N 32°0E 188 C7
Pola de Allande Spain 43°16N 6°37W 194 B4
Pola de Lena Spain 43°10N 5°49W 194 B5
Pola de Siero Spain 43°24N 5°39W 194 B5
Pola de Somiedo Spain 43°5N 6°15W 194 B4
Pola I. Amer. Samoa 14°14S 170°40W 302 t
Polacca U.S.A. 35°50N 110°23W 305 J8
Polan Iran 25°30N 61°10E 247 E9
Pol'ana Slovak Rep. 48°38N 19°29E 181 C12
Poland ■ Europe 52°0N 20°0E 185 G3
Polanica-Zdrój Poland 50°24N 16°32E 185 H4
Polaniec Poland 50°28N 21°17E 185 H8
Polanów Poland 54°7N 16°41E 184 D3
Polar Bear △ Canada 54°30N 83°45W 298 A2
Polath Turkey 39°36N 32°9E 212 C5
Polatsk Belarus 55°30N 28°50E 188 E5
Polavaram India 17°15N 81°38E 244 F5
Polcura Chile 37°17S 71°43W 334 D1
Polczyn-Zdrój Poland 53°47N 16°5E 184 E3
Poleski △ Poland 51°29N 23°5E 185 G10
Polessk Russia 54°50N 21°8E 184 D8
Polesye = Pripet Marshes
  Europe 52°10N 28°10E 177 B15
Polevskoy Russia 56°26N 60°11E 186 C11
Polgar Hungary 47°54N 21°6E 182 C6
Poli Cameroon 8°34N 13°15E 263 C7
Policastro, G. di Italy 40°0N 15°35E 201 C8
Police Poland 53°33N 14°33E 184 E1
Police, Pte. Seychelles 4°51S 55°32E 272 c
Polichnitos Greece 39°6N 26°10E 205 B8
Poličká Czech Rep. 49°43N 16°15E 181 B9
Policoro Italy 40°13N 16°41E 201 C9
Poliegos Greece 36°45N 24°38E 206 F7
Poligiros Greece 40°23N 23°25E 202 F7
Polignano a Mare Italy 41°0N 17°13E 201 A10
Poligny France 46°50N 5°42E 173 F12
Polillo Is. Phil. 14°43N 121°56E 232 D4
Polillo Is. Phil. 14°56N 122°0E 232 D4
Polillo Strait Phil. 14°44N 121°51E 232 D4
Polis Cyprus 35°2N 32°26E 207 E8
Polistena Italy 38°24N 16°4E 201 D8
Pölitz = Police Poland 53°33N 14°33E 184 E1
Polk U.S.A. 41°22N 79°56W 312 F5
Polkowice Poland 51°29N 16°3E 185 G3
Polkwitz = Polkowice
  Poland 51°29N 16°3E 185 G3
Polla Italy 40°31N 15°29E 201 B8
Pollachi India 10°35N 77°0E 245 J3
Pollença Spain 39°54N 3°1E 206 B4
Pollença, B. de Spain 39°53N 3°8E 206 B4
Pollfoss Norway 61°58N 7°54E 164 C4
Pollica Italy 40°11N 15°0E 201 B8
Pollino, Mte. Italy 39°55N 16°11E 201 C9
Pollino △ Italy 39°54N 16°13E 201 C9
Polna Russia 58°31N 28°5E 188 C5
Polo Ill., U.S.A. 41°59N 89°35W 310 C7
Polo Mo., U.S.A. 39°33N 94°3W 310 E7
Pology Ukraine 47°29N 36°15E 189 J9
Polokwane S. Africa 23°54S 29°25E 271 A4
Polokwane → S. Africa 23°56S 30°55E 271 B5
Polonne Ukraine 50°6N 27°30E 177 C14
Polonnoye = Polonne
  Ukraine 50°6N 27°30E 177 C14
Polski Trümbesh
  Bulgaria 43°20N 25°38E 203 C9
Polsko Kosovo Bulgaria 43°23N 25°38E 203 C9
Polson U.S.A. 47°41N 114°9W 304 C6
Poltár Slovak Rep. 48°26N 19°48E 181 C12
Poltava Ukraine 49°35N 34°35E 189 H8
Poltava □ Ukraine 49°35N 34°35E 189 H8
Polton U.K. 55°52N 3°7W 121 B3

Poltoratsk = Ashgabat
  Turkmenistan 38°0N 57°50E 247 B8
Põltsamaa Estonia 58°39N 25°58E 188 C3
Polunochnoye Russia 60°52N 60°25E 214 C7
Polur India 12°32N 79°11E 245 H4
Põlva Estonia 58°3N 27°3E 188 C4
Polvoranca, Parque de
  Spain 40°19N 3°48W 127 C1
Polyana Ukraine 48°38N 22°58E 187 D2
Polyarny Russia 69°8N 33°20E 160 B25
Polyarnyye Zori Russia 67°22N 32°30E 160 C25
Polynesia Pac. Oc. 10°0S 162°0W 289 F11
Polynesian Cultural Center
  U.S.A. 21°38N 157°55W 302 J14
Polynésie française = French
  Polynesia ☒ Pac. Oc. 20°0S 145°0W 289 f
Polyustrovo Russia 59°57N 30°25E 137 B2
Pomabamba = Azurduy
  Bolivia 19°59S 64°29W 331 D5
Pomabamba Peru 8°50S 77°28W 330 B2
Pomarance Italy 43°18N 10°52E 198 E7
Pombal Brazil 6°45S 37°50W 332 C4
Pombal Portugal 39°55N 8°40W 194 F2
Pombia Greece 35°0N 24°51E 207 F5
Pombos, B. dos Angola 11°40S 13°47E 265 E2
Pomene Mozam. 22°53S 35°33E 271 B6
Pomeroy Ohio, U.S.A. 39°2N 82°2W 309 F12
Pomeroy Wash., U.S.A. 46°28N 117°36W 304 C5
Pomézia Italy 41°40N 12°30E 200 A5
Pomichna Ukraine 48°13N 31°36E 189 H6
Pomio Papua N. G. 5°32S 151°33E 286 C6
Pomme de Terre L.
  U.S.A. 37°54N 93°19W 310 G3
Pomme Rose Grenada 12°3N 61°39W 323 q
Pomona Queens.,
  Australia 26°22S 152°52E 281 D5
Pomona Calif., U.S.A. 34°4N 117°45W 307 L9
Pomona Park U.S.A. 29°30N 81°36W 317 F8
Pomorie Bulgaria 42°32N 27°41E 203 D11
Pomorskie □ Poland 54°30N 18°0E 184 D5
Pomorskie, Pojezierze
  Poland 53°40N 16°37E 184 E3
Pomos Cyprus 35°9N 32°33E 207 E8
Pomos, C. Cyprus 35°10N 32°33E 207 E8
Pompano Beach U.S.A. 26°14N 80°7W 317 J9
Pompei Italy 40°45N 14°30E 201 B7
Pompey France 48°46N 6°6E 173 D13
Pompeys Pillar U.S.A. 45°59N 107°57W 304 D10
Pompeys Pillar △ U.S.A. 46°0N 108°0W 304 D10
Pomprap Thailand 13°44N 100°30E 113 B2
Pompton Lakes U.S.A. 41°0N 74°17W 313 F10
Ponape = Pohnpei
  Micronesia 6°55N 158°10E 288 G7
Ponask L. Canada 54°0N 92°41W 298 B1
Ponca U.S.A. 42°34N 96°43W 308 D5
Ponca City U.S.A. 36°42N 97°5W 314 C6
Ponce Puerto Rico 18°1N 66°37W 321 C6
Ponce de Leon U.S.A. 30°44N 85°56W 316 E4
Ponce de Leon B. U.S.A. 25°15N 81°10W 317 K8
Ponchatoula U.S.A. 30°26N 90°26W 315 F9
Poncheville, L. Canada 50°10N 76°55W 298 B4
Pond U.S.A. 35°43N 119°20W 307 K7
Pond Inlet Canada 72°40N 77°0W 295 B12
Pondicherry = Puducherry
  India 11°59N 79°50E 245 J4
Pondo Papua N. G. 4°33S 151°33E 286 C6
Pondok Gede Indonesia 6°20S 106°55E 122 A2
Pondok Indah Indonesia 6°16S 106°46E 122 B1
Ponds, I. of Canada 53°27N 55°52W 299 B9
Ponérihouen N. Cal. 21°5S 165°24E 288 d
Ponferrada Spain 42°32N 6°35W 194 C4
Pongo, Wadi → Sudan 8°42N 27°40E 257 F2
Poniatowa Poland 51°11N 22°3E 185 G9
Poniec Poland 51°48N 16°50E 185 G3
Ponikva Slovenia 46°16N 15°26E 199 B12
Ponizovkin = Krasny Profintern
  Russia 57°45N 40°27E 188 D11
Ponnaiyar → India 11°50N 79°45E 245 J4
Ponnani India 10°45N 75°59E 245 J2
Ponnuru India 13°20N 80°15E 245 H5
Ponnyadaung Burma 16°5N 80°34E 245 F5
Ponoka Canada 52°42N 113°40W 296 C6
Ponorogo Indonesia 7°52S 111°27E 235 D4
Ponot Phil. 8°25N 123°0E 233 G4
Ponoy Russia 67°0N 41°13E 186 A7
Ponoy → Russia 66°59N 41°17E 186 A7
Pons France 45°35N 0°34W 174 C3
Pons = Ponts Spain 41°55N 1°12E 196 D6
Ponsul → Portugal 39°40N 7°31W 194 F3
Pont-à-Mousson France 48°54N 6°1E 173 D13
Pont-Audemer France 49°21N 0°25E 172 C7
Pont-Aven France 47°51N 3°47W 172 E3
Pont Canavese Italy 45°25N 7°36E 198 C4
Pont-de-Roide France 47°23N 6°45E 173 E13
Pont-de-Salars France 44°18N 2°44E 174 D6
Pont-de-Veyle France 46°17N 4°53E 173 F11
Pont-du-Château France 45°47N 3°15E 174 D6
Pont-l'Abbé France 47°52N 4°15W 172 E2
Pont-l'Évêque France 49°18N 0°11E 172 C7
Pont-St-Esprit France 44°16N 4°40E 175 D8
Pont-St-Martin Italy 45°36N 7°48E 198 C4
Pont-Ste-Maxence France 49°18N 2°36E 173 C9
Pont-sur-Yonne France 48°18N 3°10E 173 D10
Pont-Viau Canada 45°35N 73°41W 130 A1
Ponta de Pedras Brazil 1°23S 48°52W 332 B2
Ponta Delgada Flores,
  Azores 39°31N 31°13W 153 d2
Ponta Delgada São Miguel,
  Azores 37°44N 25°40W 153 d3
Ponta do Sol Madeira 32°42N 17°7W 153 c
Ponta Grossa Brazil 25°7S 50°10W 335 B5
Ponta Pora Brazil 22°20S 55°35W 335 A4
Pontacq France 43°11N 0°8W 174 E3
Pontal Brazil 17°42S 47°40W 333 E2
Ponta Alta, Serra do
  Brazil 19°42S 47°40W 333 E2
Ponta Alta do Norte
  Brazil 10°45S 47°34W 332 D2
Ponte Branca Brazil 16°27S 52°40W 333 E7
Ponte da Barca Portugal 41°48N 8°25W 194 D2
Ponte dell'Ólio Italy 44°52N 9°39E 198 D6
Ponte di Legno Italy 46°15N 10°31E 198 B7
Ponte de Lima Portugal 41°46N 8°35W 194 D2
Ponte de Pungué Mozam. 19°30S 34°33E 269 F3
Ponte-Leccia France 42°28N 9°13E 175 F13

Ponte nelle Alpi Italy 46°11N 12°16E 199 B9
Ponte Nova Brazil 20°25S 42°54W 333 F3
Ponte Vedra Beach
  U.S.A. 30°15N 81°23W 316 E8
Pontearaes Spain 42°10N 8°28W 194 C2
Pontebba Italy 46°30N 13°18E 199 B10
Ponteceso Spain 43°15N 8°54W 194 B2
Pontecorvo Italy 41°27N 13°40E 200 A6
Pontedera Italy 43°24N 10°38E 198 E7
Ponteix Canada 49°46N 107°29W 297 D7
Pontes e Lacerda Brazil 15°12S 59°22W 331 D6
Pontevedra Capiz, Phil. 11°29N 122°50E 233 F4
Pontevedra Neg. Occ.,
  Phil. 10°22N 122°52E 233 F4
Pontevedra Spain 42°26N 8°40W 194 C2
Pontevedra □ Spain 42°26N 8°39W 194 C2
Pontevedra, R. de →
  Spain 42°22N 8°45W 194 C2
Pontevico Italy 45°16N 10°5E 198 C7
Ponthierville = Ubundu
  Dem. Rep. of the Congo 0°22S 25°30E 268 C2
Pontiac Ill., U.S.A. 40°53N 88°38W 311 D8
Pontiac Mich., U.S.A. 42°38N 83°18W 312 D1
Pontian Kechil Malaysia 1°29N 103°23E 237 d
Pontianak Indonesia 0°3S 109°15E 235 C3
Pontine Is. = Ponziane, Ísole
  Italy 40°55N 12°57E 200 B5
Pontine Mts. = Kuzey Anadolu
  Dağları Turkey 41°0N 36°45E 212 B7
Pontinha Portugal 38°45N 9°11W 126 A1
Pontínia Italy 41°25N 13°2E 200 A6
Pontivy France 48°5N 2°58W 172 D4
Pontoise France 49°3N 2°5E 173 C9
Ponton → Canada 58°27N 116°11W 296 B5
Pontorson France 48°34N 1°30W 172 D5
Pontrémoli Italy 44°22N 9°53E 198 D6
Pontrieux France 48°42N 3°10W 172 D3
Ponts Spain 41°55N 1°12E 196 D6
Pontypool Ont., Canada 44°6N 78°38W 312 B6
Pontypool Torf., U.K. 51°42N 3°2W 169 F4
Ponza Italy 40°54N 12°58E 200 B5
Ponziane, Ísole Italy 40°55N 12°57E 200 B5
Poochera Australia 32°43S 134°51E 281 E1
Poole Poole, U.K. 50°43N 1°59W 169 G6
Poole □ U.K. 50°43N 1°59W 169 G6
Poole → Trin. & Tob. 10°15N 61°5W 323 t
Pooler U.S.A. 32°7N 81°15W 316 D8
Poona = Pune India 18°29N 73°57E 244 E1
Poonamallee India 13°3N 80°10E 245 H5
Pooncarie Australia 33°22S 142°31E 282 B5
Poopelloe L. Australia 31°40S 144°0E 282 A6
Poopó Bolivia 18°35S 66°59W 330 D4
Poopó, L. de Bolivia 18°30S 67°35W 330 D4
Poor Knights Is. N.Z. 35°29S 174°43E 284 B3
Poorman U.S.A. 64°5N 155°33W 303 D9
Popa Gabon 1°35S 12°32E 264 C2
Popa, Mt. Burma 20°50N 95°20E 241 E5
Popayán Colombia 2°27N 76°36W 328 C2
Poperinge Belgium 50°51N 2°42E 170 D2
Popilta L. Australia 33°10S 141°42E 282 B4
Popina Bulgaria 44°7N 26°57E 203 B10
Popio L. Australia 33°10S 141°52E 282 B4
Poplar U.K. 51°30N 0°0 125 A3
Poplar Mont., U.S.A. 48°7N 105°12W 304 B11
Poplar → Canada 53°0N 97°19W 297 C9
Poplar Bluff U.S.A. 36°46N 90°24W 308 G8
Poplar Head = Dothan
  U.S.A. 31°13N 85°24W 316 D4
Poplarville U.S.A. 30°51N 89°32W 315 F10
Popocatépetl, Volcán
  Mexico 19°2N 98°38W 319 D5
Popokabaka
  Dem. Rep. of the Congo 5°41S 16°40E 265 D3
Pópoli Italy 42°9N 13°50E 199 F10
Popolo
  Dem. Rep. of the Congo 2°22N 21°8E 264 B4
Popolo, Porta del Rome, Italy 136 a2
Popomanaseu, Mt.
  Solomon Is. 9°40S 160°1E 287 M11
Popondetta Papua N. G. 8°48S 148°17E 286 E5
Popovača Croatia 45°30N 16°41E 199 C13
Popovo Bulgaria 43°21N 26°18E 203 C10
Poppberg Germany 49°26N 11°37E 179 F7
Poppi Italy 43°43N 11°46E 199 E9
Poppintree Ireland 53°23N 6°17W 120 A2
Poprad Slovak Rep. 49°3N 20°18E 181 B13
Poprad → Slovak Rep. 49°38N 20°42E 181 B13
Poradaha Bangla. 23°51N 89°1E 241 D2
Porali → Pakistan 25°58N 66°26E 242 G2
Porangaba Brazil 8°48S 70°36W 330 B4
Porangahau N.Z. 40°17S 176°37E 284 H6
Porangatu Brazil 13°26S 49°10W 333 D2
Porbandar India 21°44N 69°43E 242 J3
Porce → Colombia 7°28N 74°53W 328 B3
Porcher I. Canada 53°50N 130°30W 296 C2
Porco Bolivia 19°50S 65°59W 331 D4
Porcos → Brazil 12°42S 45°7W 333 D3
Porcuna Spain 37°52N 4°11W 195 H6
Porcupine → Canada 59°11N 104°46W 297 B8
Porcupine → Alaska,
  U.S.A. 66°34N 145°19W 303 C11
Porcupine Abyssal Plain
  Atl. Oc. 48°0N 8°0W 152 B7
Porcupine Gorge △
  Australia 20°22S 144°26E 280 C3
Pordenone Italy 45°57N 12°39E 199 C9
Pordim Bulgaria 43°23N 24°51E 203 C8
Pore Colombia 5°43N 72°0W 328 B3
Poreč Croatia 45°14N 13°36E 199 C10
Porecatu Brazil 22°43S 51°24W 333 F1
Porechye = Demidov
  Russia 55°16N 31°30E 188 E6
Poretskoye Russia 55°9N 46°21E 190 C8
Porgera Papua N. G. 5°28S 143°12E 286 C2
Pori Finland 61°29N 21°48E 188 B1
Pori Greece 35°58N 23°13E 204 F5
Porirua N.Z. 41°8S 174°52E 143 A2
Porirua East N.Z. 41°8S 174°52E 143 A2
Porkhov Russia 57°45N 29°38E 188 C6
Porlamar Venezuela 10°57N 63°51W 329 A5
Porlezza Italy 46°2N 9°7E 198 B6
Porma → Spain 42°49N 5°28W 194 C5
Pornic France 47°7N 2°5W 172 E4
Poronaysk Russia 49°13N 143°0E 215 D15
Poros Attiki, Greece 37°30N 23°30E 206 D5
Poros Kefalonia, Greece 38°9N 20°47E 207 C2
Poros Lefkada, Greece 38°38N 20°44E 207 C2
Poroshiri-Dake Japan 42°41N 142°52E 220 C11
Poroszló Hungary 47°39N 20°40E 182 C5
Poroto Mts. Tanzania 9°0S 33°30E 269 D3
Porpoise B. Antarctica 66°0S 128°0E 151 C9
Porpoise Pt. Ascension I. 7°54S 14°21W 153 g
Porquerolles, Î. de France 43°0N 6°13E 175 F10
Porrentruy Switz. 47°25N 7°6E 179 H3
Porreres Spain 39°31N 3°2E 206 B10
Porretta, Passo di Italy 44°2N 10°56E 198 D8
Porsangerfjorden
  Norway 70°40N 25°40E 160 A21
Porsgrunn Norway 59°10N 9°40E 164 E3
Port Adelaide Australia 34°46S 138°30E 283 B2
Port Alberni Canada 49°14N 124°50W 296 D4
Port Albert Australia 38°42S 146°42E 283 C7
Port Alexander U.S.A. 56°15N 134°38W 303 E14

Port Alfred S. Africa 33°36S 26°55E 270 D4
Port Alice Canada 50°20N 127°25W 296 C3
Port Allegany U.S.A. 41°48N 78°17W 312 E6
Port Allen U.S.A. 30°27N 91°12W 314 F9
Port Alma Australia 23°38S 150°53E 280 C5
Port Angeles U.S.A. 48°7N 123°27W 306 B3
Port Aransas U.S.A. 27°50N 97°4W 314 H6
Port Arthur = Lüshun
  China 38°45N 121°15E 135 H11
Port Arthur Tas.,
  Australia 43°7S 147°50E 281 G4
Port Arthur Tex., U.S.A. 29°54N 93°56W 314 G8
Port au Choix Canada 50°43N 57°22W 299 B8
Port au Port B. Canada 48°40N 58°50W 299 C8
Port-au-Prince Haiti 18°40N 72°20W 321 C5
Port Augusta Australia 32°30S 137°50E 282 B2
Port Austin U.S.A. 44°3N 83°1W 312 B2
Port Authority Bus Terminal
  New York, U.S.A. 132 c2
Port Bell Uganda 0°18N 32°35E 268 B3
Port Bergé Vaovao
  Madag. 15°33S 47°40E 272 B2
Port Blair India 11°40N 92°45E 245 J11
Port Blandford Canada 48°20N 54°10W 299 C9
Port Bradshaw Australia 12°30S 137°20E 280 A2
Port Broughton
  Australia 33°37S 137°56E 282 B2
Port Burwell Canada 42°40N 80°48W 312 D4
Port Byron U.S.A. 41°36N 90°20W 310 C8
Port Campbell Vic.,
  Australia 38°37S 143°1E 282 E5
Port Campbell △ Australia 38°38S 143°6E 282 E5
Port Canning India 22°23N 88°40E 243 H13
Port-Cartier Canada 50°2N 66°50W 299 B6
Port Chalmers N.Z. 45°49S 170°30E 285 F5
Port Charles N.Z. 36°33S 175°30E 284 C4
Port Charlotte U.S.A. 26°59N 82°6W 317 J7
Port Chester U.S.A. 41°0N 73°40W 313 F11
Port Clements Canada 53°40N 132°10W 296 C2
Port Clinton U.S.A. 41°31N 82°56W 311 C14
Port Colborne Canada 42°50N 79°10W 312 D5
Port Coquitlam Canada 49°15N 122°45W 306 A3
Port Cornwallis India 13°17N 93°5E 245 H11
Port Credit Canada 43°33N 79°35W 312 C5
Port-Cros △ France 43°0N 6°24E 175 F10
Port Curtis Australia 23°57S 151°20E 280 C5
Port d'Alcúdia Spain 39°50N 3°7E 206 B4
Port Dalhousie Canada 43°13N 79°16W 312 C5
Port d'Andratx Spain 39°32N 2°23E 206 B3
Port Darwin N. Terr.,
  Australia 12°24S 130°45E 278 B5
Port Darwin Falk. Is. 51°50S 59°0W 153 f
Port Davey Australia 43°16S 145°55E 281 G4
Port-de-Bouc France 43°24N 4°59E 175 E8
Port-de-Paix Haiti 19°50N 72°50W 321 C5
Port de Pollença Spain 39°54N 3°4E 206 B4
Port de Sóller Spain 39°48N 2°42E 206 B3
Port Dickson Malaysia 2°30N 101°49E 237 L3
Port Douglas Australia 16°30S 145°30E 280 B4
Port Dover Canada 42°47N 80°12W 312 D4
Port Edward Canada 54°12N 130°10W 296 C2
Port Elgin Canada 44°25N 81°25W 312 B3
Port Elizabeth S. Africa 33°58S 25°40E 270 D4
Port Ellen U.K. 55°38N 6°11W 167 F2
Port Elliot Australia 35°32S 138°41E 282 C3
Port Erin I. of Man 54°5N 4°45W 168 C3
Port Essington Australia 11°15S 132°10E 278 B5
Port Etienne = Nouâdhibou
  Mauritania 20°54N 17°0W 260 D1
Port Ewen U.S.A. 41°54N 73°59W 313 E11
Port Fairy Australia 38°22S 142°12E 282 E5
Port Fitzroy N.Z. 36°8S 175°20E 284 C4
Port Florence = Kisumu
  Kenya 0°3S 34°45E 268 C3
Port Fouâd = Bûr Fuad
  Egypt 31°15N 32°20E 256 H8
Port Francqui = Ilebo
  Dem. Rep. of the Congo 4°17S 20°55E 265 C4
Port Gamble U.S.A. 47°51N 122°34W 306 C4
Port-Gentil Gabon 0°40S 8°50E 264 C1
Port Germein Australia 33°1S 138°1E 282 B2
Port Gibson U.S.A. 31°58N 90°59W 314 F9
Port Glasgow U.K. 55°56N 4°41W 167 F4
Port-Gueydon = Azeffoun
  Algeria 36°51N 4°22E 261 A5
Port Harcourt Nigeria 4°40N 7°10E 263 E6
Port Hardy Canada 50°41N 127°30W 296 C3
Port Harrison = Inukjuak
  Canada 58°25N 78°15W 295 D12
Port Hawkesbury
  Canada 45°36N 61°22W 299 C7
Port Hedland Australia 20°25S 118°35E 278 D2
Port Heiden U.S.A. 56°55N 158°41W 303 H8
Port Henry U.S.A. 44°3N 73°28W 313 B11
Port Hood Canada 46°0N 61°32W 299 C7
Port Hope Ont., Canada 43°56N 78°20W 312 C6
Port Hope Mich., U.S.A. 43°57N 82°43W 312 C2
Port Hope Simpson
  Canada 52°33N 56°18W 299 B8
Port Hueneme U.S.A. 34°7N 119°12W 307 L7
Port Huron U.S.A. 42°58N 82°26W 312 D2
Port Iilic Azerbaijan 38°53N 48°47E 213 C13
Port Jefferson U.S.A. 40°57N 73°3W 313 F11
Port Jervis U.S.A. 41°22N 74°41W 313 E10
Port Katon Russia 46°52N 38°46E 189 J10
Port Kelang = Pelabuhan Klang
  Malaysia 3°0N 101°23E 237 L3
Port Kembla Australia 34°52S 150°49E 283 C9
Port Kenny Australia 33°10S 134°41E 281 E1
Port-la-Nouvelle France 43°1N 3°3E 174 E7
Port Laoise Ireland 53°2N 7°18W 166 D4
Port Lavaca U.S.A. 28°37N 96°38W 314 G6
Port Leyden U.S.A. 43°35N 75°21W 313 D10
Port Lincoln Australia 34°42S 135°52E 282 C1
Port Loko S. Leone 8°48N 12°46W 262 D2
Port Louis Guadeloupe 16°28N 61°32W 322 d
Port Louis Mauritius 20°10S 57°30E 272 e
Port Lyautey = Kenitra
  Morocco 34°15N 6°40W 260 B3
Port MacDonnell
  Australia 38°5S 140°48E 282 E4
Port McNeill Canada 50°35N 127°6W 296 C3
Port Macquarie
  Australia 31°25S 152°25E 283 B5
Port Matilda U.S.A. 40°48N 78°3W 312 F6
Port Maria Jamaica 18°22N 76°54W 320 a
Port Mellon Canada 49°32N 123°31W 306 A3
Port-Menier Canada 49°51N 64°15W 299 C7
Port Moller U.S.A. 55°59N 160°34W 303 J7
Port Moody Canada 49°17N 122°51W 306 A3
Port Moresby Papua N. G. 9°24S 147°8E 286 E6

Port Mourant Guyana 6°15N 57°20W 329 B6
Port Musgrave Australia 11°55S 141°50E 280 A3
Port Narevin Vanuatu 18°45S 169°10E 287 H7
Port-Navalo France 47°34N 2°54W 172 E4
Port Neches U.S.A. 30°0N 93°59W 314 G8
Port Nicholson N.Z. 41°20S 174°52E 143 B2
Port Nolloth S. Africa 29°17S 16°52E 270 C2
Port of Spain Trin. & Tob. 10°40N 61°31W 323 t
Port Olry Vanuatu 15°1S 167°4E 287 E6
Port Orange U.S.A. 29°9N 80°59W 317 F9
Port Orchard U.S.A. 47°32N 122°38W 306 C4
Port Orford U.S.A. 42°45N 124°30W 304 E1
Port Pegasus N.Z. 47°12S 167°41E 285 H2
Port Perry Canada 44°6N 78°56W 312 B6
Port Phillip B. Australia 38°10S 144°50E 283 E6
Port Pirie Australia 33°10S 138°1E 282 B2
Port Renfrew Canada 48°30N 124°20W 306 B2
Port Richmond U.S.A. 39°58N 75°7W 123 a
Port Roper Australia 14°45S 135°25E 280 A2
Port Rowan Canada 42°40N 80°30W 312 D4
Port Royal Jamaica 17°56N 76°51W 320 a
Port Royal Sd. U.S.A. 32°15N 80°40W 316 D9
Port Safaga = Bûr Safaga
  Egypt 26°43N 33°57E 246 E2
Port Said = Bûr Sa'id
  Egypt 31°16N 32°18E 256 H8
Port St. Joe U.S.A. 29°49N 85°18W 316 F4
Port St. John U.S.A. 11°56N 92°37E 245 J11
Port St. Johns = Umzimvubu
  S. Africa 31°38S 29°33E 271 D4
Port-St-Louis-du-Rhône
  France 43°23N 4°49E 175 E8
Port St. Lucie U.S.A. 27°18N 80°21W 317 H10
Port-Ste-Marie France 44°15N 0°25E 174 D4
Port Salerno U.S.A. 27°9N 80°12W 317 H10
Port Sanilac U.S.A. 43°26N 82°33W 312 C2
Port Severn Canada 44°48N 79°43W 312 B5
Port Shelter China 22°20N 114°17E 122 A2
Port Shepstone S. Africa 30°44S 30°28E 271 D5
Port Simpson Canada 54°30N 130°20W 296 C2
Port Stanley = Stanley
  Falk. Is. 51°40S 59°51W 153 f
Port Stanley Canada 42°40N 81°10W 312 D3
Port Sudan = Bûr Sûdân
  Sudan 19°32N 37°9E 256 D4
Port Sulphur U.S.A. 29°29N 89°42W 315 G10
Port-sur-Saône France 47°42N 6°2E 173 E13
Port Swettenham = Pelabuhan
  Klang Malaysia 3°0N 101°23E 237 L3
Port Talbot U.K. 51°35N 3°47W 169 F4
Port Taufiq = Bûr Taufiq
  Egypt 29°54N 32°32E 256 J8
Port Townsend U.S.A. 48°7N 122°45W 306 B4
Port Union Canada 43°47N 79°7W 141 A4
Port-Vato Vanuatu 16°20S 168°1E 287 G6
Port-Vendres France 42°32N 3°8E 174 F7
Port Victoria Australia 34°30S 137°29E 282 C2
Port Vila Vanuatu 17°45S 168°18E 287 G6
Port Vladimir Russia 69°25N 33°6E 160 B25
Port Wakefield Australia 34°12S 138°10E 282 B2
Port Washington
  U.S.A. 43°23N 87°53W 308 D10

Pôrto Acre Brazil 9°34S 67°31W 330 B4
Pôrto Alegre = Luzilândia
  Brazil 3°28S 42°22W 332 B3
Pôrto Alegre Pará, Brazil 4°22S 52°44W 329 D7
Pôrto Alegre Rio Grande do S.,
  Brazil 30°5S 51°10W 335 C5
Porto Alegre
  São Tomé & Príncipe 0°2N 6°32E 265 a
Pôrto Amboim = Gunza
  Angola 10°50S 13°50E 265 E2
Pôrto Amélia = Pemba
  Mozam. 12°58S 40°30E 269 E5
Pôrto Azzurro Italy 42°46N 10°24E 198 E7
Pôrto Brandão Portugal 38°40N 9°12W 126 A1
Pôrto Cajueiro Brazil 11°3S 55°55W 331 C6
Pôrto Cristo Spain 39°33N 3°20E 206 B4
Pôrto de Móz Brazil 1°41S 52°13W 329 D7
Pôrto de Pedras Brazil 9°55S 37°17E 332 C4
Pôrto dos Gaúchos
  Brazil 11°32S 57°16W 331 C6
Pôrto Esperança Brazil 19°37S 57°29W 331 D6
Pôrto Esperidão Brazil 15°51S 58°28W 331 D6
Pôrto Formoso Azores 37°49N 25°25W 153 d3
Pôrto Franco Brazil 6°20S 47°24W 332 C2
Pôrto Grande Brazil 0°42S 51°24W 329 C7
Porto Inglês C. Verde Is. 15°21N 23°10W 153 j
Pôrto Jofre Brazil 17°20S 56°48W 331 D6
Pôrto Lengone = Porto Azzurro
  Italy 42°46N 10°24E 198 E7
Porto Maurizio = Impéria
  Italy 43°53N 8°3E 198 E5
Pôrto Mendes Brazil 24°30S 54°15W 335 A5
Pôrto Moniz Madeira 32°52N 17°11W 153 c
Pôrto Murtinho Brazil 21°45S 57°55W 331 E6
Pôrto Nacional Brazil 10°40S 48°30W 332 D2
Porto-Novo Benin 6°23N 2°42E 263 D5
Pôrto Novo Rio de J., Brazil 22°50S 43°7W 135 A2
Porto Novo → Nigeria 6°23N 2°48E 124 B2
Pôrto Petro Spain 39°22N 3°13E 206 B4
Pôrto San Giórgio Italy 43°11N 13°48E 199 E10
Porto Sant' Elpídio Italy 43°15N 13°43E 199 E10
Pôrto Santana Brazil 0°3S 51°11W 329 D7
Pôrto Santo, I. de
  Madeira 33°45N 16°25W 260 B1
Porto Santo Stéfano Italy 42°26N 11°7E 198 F8
Pôrto São José Brazil 22°43S 53°10W 335 A5
Porto Seguro Brazil 16°26S 39°5W 333 E4
Porto Tolle Italy 44°56N 12°22E 199 D9
Pôrto Tôrres Italy 40°50N 8°24E 200 B1
Pôrto União Brazil 26°10S 51°10W 335 B5
Pôrto Válter Brazil 8°15S 72°40W 330 B3
Porto-Vecchio France 41°35N 9°16E 175 G13
Pôrto Velho Brazil 8°46S 63°54W 331 B5
Portobelo Panama 9°35N 79°42W 320 E4
Portoferráio Italy 42°48N 10°20E 198 E7
Portogruaro Italy 45°47N 12°50E 199 C9
Portola U.S.A. 39°49N 120°28W 306 F6
Portomaggiore Italy 44°42N 11°48E 199 D8
Portoscuso Italy 39°12N 8°24E 200 C1
Portovénere Italy 44°3N 9°51E 198 D6
Portoviejo Ecuador 1°7S 80°28W 328 D1
Portpatrick U.K. 54°51N 5°7W 167 G3
Portree U.K. 57°25N 6°12W 167 D2
Portreath U.K. 50°15N 5°17W 169 G2
Portrush U.K. 55°12N 6°40W 166 A5
Portsmouth Dominica 15°34N 61°27W 323 k
Portsmouth Portsmouth,
  U.K. 50°48N 1°6W 169 G6
Portsmouth N.H., U.S.A. 43°5N 70°45W 313 C14
Portsmouth Ohio,
  U.S.A. 38°44N 82°57W 309 F12
Portsmouth R.I., U.S.A. 41°36N 71°15W 313 E13
Portsmouth Va., U.S.A. 36°58N 76°23W 309 G15
Portsmouth □ U.K. 50°48N 1°6W 169 G6
Portsoy U.K. 57°41N 2°41W 167 D6
Portstewart U.K. 55°11N 6°43W 166 A5
Porttipahdan tekojärvi
  Finland 68°5N 26°40E 160 B22
Portugal ■ Europe 40°0N 8°0W 194 F3
Portugalete Spain 43°19N 3°4W 196 B1
Portuguesa □ Venezuela 9°10N 69°15W 328 B4
Portuguese East Africa =
  Mozambique ■ Africa 19°0S 35°0E 269 F4
Portuguese Guinea =
  Guinea-Bissau ■ Africa 12°0N 15°0W 262 C2
Portuguese Timor = East Timor
  ■ Asia 8°50S 126°0E 231 F7
Portuguese West Africa =
  Angola ■ Africa 12°0S 18°0E 265 E3
Portumna Ireland 53°6N 8°14W 166 D3
Portville U.S.A. 42°3N 78°20W 312 D6
Porus Jamaica 18°2N 77°25W 320 a
Porvenir Bolivia 11°10S 68°50W 330 C4
Porvenir Chile 53°10S 70°16W 336 D2
Porvoo Finland 60°24N 25°40E 188 B3
Porzuna Spain 39°9N 4°9W 195 F6
Pos Chiquito Aruba 12°27N 69°57W 322 f
Posada Italy 40°38N 9°43E 200 B2
Posada → Italy 40°39N 9°45E 200 B2
Posadas Argentina 27°30S 55°50W 335 B4
Posadas Spain 37°47N 5°11W 195 H5
Poschiavo Switz. 46°19N 10°4E 179 J6
Posets Spain 42°39N 0°25E 196 D5
Poseyville U.S.A. 38°10N 87°47W 311 F9
Poshan = Boshan China 36°28N 117°49E 227 F9
Posht-e Badam Iran 33°2N 55°23E 247 C7
Posidium Greece 35°30N 27°10E 205 D9
Poso Indonesia 1°20S 120°55E 231 E6
Posoegroenoe Suriname 4°15N 56°0W 329 C7
Posse Brazil 14°4S 46°18W 333 D2
Possession I. Antarctica 72°4S 172°0E 151 D11
Possneck Germany 50°42N 11°58E 178 E6
Possum Kingdom L.
  U.S.A. 32°52N 98°26W 314 E5
Post U.S.A. 33°12N 101°23W 314 E4
Post Falls U.S.A. 47°43N 116°57W 304 C5
Postavy = Pastavy Belarus 55°4N 26°50E 188 E4
Poste de Flacq Mauritius 20°9S 57°43E 272 e
Poste Maurice Cortier
  Algeria 22°14N 1°2E 261 D5
Postmasburg S. Africa 28°18S 23°5E 270 C3
Postojna Slovenia 45°46N 14°12E 199 C11
Poston U.S.A. 34°0N 114°24W 307 M12
Postumia = Postojna
  Slovenia 45°46N 14°12E 199 C11
Postville Nfld. & L.,
  Canada 55°20N 59°10W 298 A4
Postville U.S.A. 54°54N 59°47W 299 B8

Pulai *Malaysia* 1°20N 103°31E **237** d
Pulandian *China* 39°25N 121°58E **227** E11
Pulaski *N.Y., U.S.A.* 43°34N 76°8W **313** C8
Pulaski *Tenn., U.S.A.* 35°12N 87°2W **315** D11
Pulaski *Va., U.S.A.* 37°3N 80°47W **309** G13
Pulau → *Indonesia* 5°50S 138°15E **231** F9
Pulau Miangas *Indonesia* 5°35N 126°34E **233** J6
Puławy *Poland* 51°23N 21°59E **185** G8
Pulga *U.S.A.* 39°48N 121°29W **306** F5
Pulgaon *India* 20°44N 78°21E **244** D4
Puli *Taiwan* 23°58N 120°57E **225** C2
Pulicat *India* 13°25N 80°19E **245** H5
Pulicat L. *India* 13°40N 80°15E **245** H5
Pulivendla *India* 14°25N 78°14E **245** G4
Puliyangudi *India* 9°11N 77°24E **245** K3
Pulkovo Int. ✕ (LED) *Russia* 59°48N 30°18E **137** C1
Pullach *Germany* 48°3N 11°31E **131** B1
Pullman *U.S.A.* 46°44N 117°10W **304** C5
Pullman Historic District *U.S.A.* 41°41N 87°36W **119** C3
Pulo Gadung *Indonesia* 6°11S 106°54E **122** B2
Pulog, Mt. *Phil.* 16°40N 120°50E **232** C3
Púlpito do Sul *Angola* 15°46S 12°0E **265** F2
Pułtusk *Poland* 52°43N 21°6E **185** F8
Pülümür *Turkey* 39°30N 39°51E **213** C8
Pumlumon Fawr *U.K.* 52°28N 3°46W **169** E4
Puna *Bolivia* 19°45S 65°28W **331** D4
Puná, I. *Ecuador* 2°55S 80°5W **328** D1
Puna Forest Reserve *U.S.A.* 19°26N 154°59W **302** D7
Punaauia *Tahiti* 17°37S 149°34W **289** e
Pūnak *Iran* 35°46N 51°20E **141** A2
Punakha Dzong *Bhutan* 27°42N 89°52E **241** B2
Punalur *India* 9°0N 76°56E **245** K3
Punalu'u *U.S.A.* 21°35N 157°53W **302** J14
Punasar *India* 27°6N 73°6E **242** F5
Punata *Bolivia* 17°32S 65°50W **331** D4
Punch *India* 33°48N 74°4E **243** C6
Punch → *Pakistan* 33°12N 73°40E **242** C5
Punchbowl *Australia* 33°55S 151°3E **139** B1
Punda *Neth. Ant.* 12°6N 68°55W **322** g
Punda Maria *S. Africa* 22°40S 31°5E **271** B5
Punde *India* 18°53N 72°57E **130** B2
Pune *India* 18°29N 73°57E **244** E1
Punggol *Singapore* 1°23N 103°54E **138** A3
Punggol, Sungei → *Singapore* 1°24N 103°54E **138** A3
Punggol Pt. *Singapore* 1°24N 103°54E **138** A3
Pungo Andongo *Angola* 9°44S 15°35E **265** D3
P'ungsan *N. Korea* 40°50N 128°9E **224** B4
Pungsan *S. Korea* 36°34N 128°34E **224** D4
Pungue, Ponte de *Mozam.* 19°0S 34°0E **269** F3
Puning *China* 23°20N 116°12E **229** F11
Punjab □ *India* 31°0N 76°0E **242** D7
Punjab □ *Pakistan* 32°0N 72°30E **242** E6
Punjabi Bagh *India* 28°40N 77°6E **120** A1
Puno *Peru* 15°55S 70°3W **330** D3
Punpun → *India* 25°31N 85°18E **243** G11
Punta, Cerro de *Puerto Rico* 18°10N 66°37W **321** b
Punta Alta *Argentina* 38°53S 62°4W **336** A4
Punta Arenas *Chile* 53°10S 71°0W **336** D2
Punta Cardón *Venezuela* 11°38N 70°14W **328** A3
Punta Coles *Peru* 17°43S 71°23W **330** D3
Punta de Bombón *Peru* 17°10S 71°48W **330** D3
Punta de Díaz *Chile* 28°0S 70°45W **334** B1
Punta del Hidalgo *Canary Is.* 28°33N 16°19W **153** e1
Punta Delgado *Argentina* 42°43S 63°38W **336** B4
Punta Gorda *Belize* 16°10N 88°45W **319** D7
Punta Gorda *Fla., U.S.A.* 26°56N 82°3W **317** J7
Punta Prieta *Mexico* 28°58N 114°17W **318** B2
Punta Prima *Spain* 39°48N 4°16E **206** B5
Punta Umbría *Spain* 37°10N 6°56W **195** H4
Puntarenas *Costa Rica* 10°0N 84°50W **320** E3
Puntland *Somali Rep.* 8°0N 49°0E **267** C6
Punto Fijo *Venezuela* 11°50N 70°13W **328** A3
Punxsatawney *U.S.A.* 40°57N 78°59W **312** F6
Punyu = Guangzhou *China* 23°6N 113°13E **121** B2
Puolo Pt. *U.S.A.* 21°54N 159°36W **302** B2
Puotila *Finland* 60°13N 25°6E **121** B3
Pupuan *Indonesia* 8°19S 115°0E **231** J18
Pūpūkea *U.S.A.* 21°40N 158°3W **302** J13
Puqi *China* 29°40N 113°50E **229** C9
Puquio *Peru* 14°45S 74°10W **330** C3
Pur → *Russia* 67°31N 77°55E **216** C8
Puracé, Vol. *Colombia* 2°21N 76°23W **328** C2
Puracé △ *Colombia* 2°10N 76°21W **328** C2
Puračić *Bos.-H.* 44°33N 18°28E **182** F3
Puralia = Puruliya *India* 23°17N 86°24E **243** H12
Purana Qila *Delhi, India* **120** c3
Puranpur *India* 28°31N 80°9E **243** E9
Purari → *Papua N. G.* 7°49S 145°0E **286** D3
Purbeck, Isle of *U.K.* 50°39N 1°59W **169** G5
Purcell *U.S.A.* 35°1N 97°22W **314** D6
Purcell Mts. *Canada* 49°55N 116°15W **296** D5
Puri *India* 19°50N 85°58E **244** E7
Purificación *Colombia* 3°51N 74°55W **328** C3
Purmerend *Neths.* 52°32N 4°58E **170** B4
Purna → *India* 19°6N 77°2E **244** E3
Purnia *India* 25°45N 87°31E **243** G12
Purnululu △ *Australia* 17°20S 128°20E **278** C4
Pursat = Pouthisat *Cambodia* 12°34N 103°50E **236** F4
Purukcahu *Indonesia* 0°35S 114°35E **235** C4
Puruliya *India* 23°17N 86°24E **243** H12
Purus → *Brazil* 3°42S 61°28W **329** D5
Purutu I. *Papua N. G.* 8°24S 143°27E **286** E2
Puruvesi *Finland* 61°50N 29°30E **188** B5
Purvis *U.S.A.* 31°9N 89°25W **315** F10
Pŭrvomay *Bulgaria* 42°8N 25°17E **203** D9
Purwa *India* 26°28N 80°47E **243** F9
Purwakarta *Indonesia* 6°35S 107°29E **235** D3
Purwo, Tanjung *Indonesia* 8°44S 114°21E **231** K18
Purwodadi *Indonesia* 7°7S 110°55E **235** D4
Purwokerto *Indonesia* 7°25S 109°14E **235** D3
Purworejo *Indonesia* 7°43S 110°2E **235** D4
Puryŏng *N. Korea* 42°5N 129°43E **224** A4
Pus → *India* 19°55N 77°55E **244** E3
Pusa *India* 25°59N 85°41E **243** G11
Pusad *India* 19°56N 77°36E **244** E3
Pusan = Busan *S. Korea* 35°5N 129°0E **224** E4
Pushkin *Russia* 59°45N 30°25E **188** C6
Pushkino *Moskva, Russia* 56°2N 37°49E **188** D9
Pushkino *Saratov, Russia* 51°16N 47°0E **190** E8
Püspökladány *Hungary* 47°19N 21°6E **182** C6
Pustoshka *Russia* 56°20N 29°30E **188** D5
Puszczykowo *Poland* 52°18N 16°49E **185** F3
Putahow L. *Canada* 59°54N 100°40W **297** B8
Putai *Taiwan* 23°23N 120°9E **225** C2
Putao *Burma* 27°28N 97°30E **241** B6
Putaruru *N.Z.* 38°2S 175°50E **284** E4
Putbus *Germany* 54°22N 13°28E **178** A9
Puteaux *France* 48°53N 2°14E **134** A2
Putian *China* 25°23N 119°0E **229** E12
Putignano *Italy* 40°51N 17°7E **201** B10
Putilkovo *Russia* 55°51N 37°22E **129** A2
Putina *Peru* 14°55S 69°55W **330** C4
Puting, Tanjung *Indonesia* 3°31S 111°46E **235** C4
Putlitz *Germany* 53°15N 12°2E **178** B8
Putna *Romania* 47°50N 25°33E **183** C10
Putna → *Romania* 45°42N 27°26E **183** E12
Putnam *U.S.A.* 41°55N 71°55W **313** E13
Putney *London, U.K.* 51°27N 0°13W **125** B2
Putney *Ga., U.S.A.* 31°29N 84°8W **316** D5
Putnok *Hungary* 48°18N 20°26E **182** B5
Putorana, Gory *Russia* 69°0N 95°0E **215** C10
Putorino *N.Z.* 39°4S 176°58E **284** F5
Putrajaya *Malaysia* 2°55N 101°40E **237** L3
Putre *Chile* 18°12S 69°35W **330** D4
Puttalam *Sri Lanka* 8°1N 79°55E **245** K5
Puttalam Lagoon *Sri Lanka* 8°15N 79°45E **245** K4
Puttegga *Norway* 62°13N 7°42E **164** B4
Puttgarden *Germany* 54°30N 11°10E **178** A7
Püttlingen *Germany* 49°17N 6°53E **179** F2
Puttur *Andhra Pradesh, India* 13°27N 79°33E **245** H4
Puttur *Karnataka, India* 12°46N 75°12E **245** H2
Putty *Australia* 32°57S 150°42E **283** B9
Putumayo → *S. Amer.* 3°7S 67°58W **328** D4
Putuo *Shanghai, China* 31°15N 121°24E **138** B1
Putuo *Zhejiang, China* 29°56N 122°20E **229** C14
Putussibau *Indonesia* 0°50N 112°56E **235** B4
Pututahi *N.Z.* 38°39S 177°53E **284** E6
Putxet *Spain* 41°24N 2°8E **134** A1
Putyla *Ukraine* 48°0N 25°5E **183** B10
Pu'uanahulu *U.S.A.* 19°49N 155°51W **302** D6
Pu'uhonua o Hōnaunau ⌂ *U.S.A.* 19°25N 155°54W **302** D6
Pu'uka'aumakua *U.S.A.* 21°30N 157°54W **302** J14
Pu'ukeahiakahoe *U.S.A.* 21°23N 157°49W **302** K14
Pu'ukoholā Heiau ⌂ *U.S.A.* 20°1N 155°49W **302** C6
P'u'ula'ula *U.S.A.* 20°42N 156°15W **302** C5
Puunene *U.S.A.* 20°53N 156°23W **302** C5
Pu'u'oke'oke'o *U.S.A.* 19°13N 155°44W **302** D6
Pu'uwai *U.S.A.* 21°54N 160°12W **302** B1
Puvirnituq *Canada* 60°2N 77°10W **295** C12
Puxi *China* 31°12N 121°30E **138** B1
Puy-de-Dôme *France* 45°46N 2°57E **174** C6
Puy-de-Dôme □ *France* 45°40N 3°5E **174** C7
Puy-l'Évêque *France* 44°31N 1°9E **174** D5
Puyallup *U.S.A.* 47°12N 122°18W **306** C4
Puyang *China* 35°40N 115°1E **226** G8
Puyehue *Chile* 40°40S 72°37W **336** B2
Puyehue △ *Chile* 40°27S 72°6W **336** B2
Puylaurens *France* 43°35N 2°0E **174** E6
Puyo *Ecuador* 1°28S 77°59W **328** D2
Pūzeh Rīg *Iran* 27°20N 58°40E **247** E8
Puzhaykove *Ukraine* 48°7N 29°50E **183** B14
Pwani □ *Tanzania* 7°0S 39°0E **268** D4
Pweto *Dem. Rep. of the Congo* 8°25S 28°51E **269** D2
Pwinbyu *Burma* 20°23N 94°40E **241** E5
Pwllheli *U.K.* 52°53N 4°25W **168** E3
Pya-ozero *Russia* 66°5N 30°58E **160** C24
Pyana → *Russia* 55°43N 46°1E **190** C8
Pyandzh = Dusti *Tajikistan* 37°20N 68°40E **217** E7
Pyandzh → *Asia* 37°6N 68°20E **240** A2
Pyapon *Burma* 16°20N 95°40E **241** G5
Pyasina → *Russia* 73°30N 87°0E **215** B9
Pyatigorsk *Russia* 44°2N 43°6E **191** H6
Pyatykhatky *Ukraine* 48°28N 33°38E **189** H7
Pyawbwe *Burma* 20°35N 96°4E **241** E6
Pyaye *Burma* 19°12N 95°10E **241** F5
Pydhuni *Mumbai, India* **130** b2
Pydna *Greece* 40°20N 22°34E **202** F6
Pyè = Prome *Burma* 18°49N 95°13E **241** F5
Pyeonghae *S. Korea* 36°43N 129°26E **224** D4
Pyeongtaek *S. Korea* 37°1N 127°4E **224** D3
Pyetrikaw *Belarus* 52°11N 28°29E **177** B15
Pyhäjoki *Finland* 64°28N 24°14E **160** D21
Pyinbauk *Burma* 19°10N 95°12E **241** F5
Pyingaing *Burma* 23°9N 94°50E **241** D5
Pyinkayaing *Burma* 15°58N 94°24E **241** H5
Pyinmana *Burma* 19°45N 96°12E **241** F6
Pyinyaung *Burma* 20°49N 96°25E **241** E6
Pyla *Cyprus* 35°1N 33°41E **250** C4
Pyla, C. *Cyprus* 34°56N 33°51E **207** F9
Pymatuning Res. *U.S.A.* 41°30N 80°28W **312** E4
Pyŏktong *N. Korea* 40°50N 125°50E **224** B2
P'yŏngan-bukdo □ *N. Korea* 40°0N 125°15E **224** C2
P'yŏngannam-do □ *N. Korea* 39°30N 126°24E **224** C3
Pyŏnggang *N. Korea* 38°24N 127°17E **224** C3
P'yŏngsong *N. Korea* 39°14N 125°52E **224** C2
P'yŏngyang *N. Korea* 39°0N 125°30E **224** C2
P'yŏngyang □ *N. Korea* 39°4N 125°50E **224** C2
Pyote *U.S.A.* 31°32N 103°8W **314** F3
Pyramid L. *U.S.A.* 40°1N 119°35W **304** F4
Pyramid Pk. *U.S.A.* 36°25N 116°37W **307** J10
Pyramid Pt. *Ascension I.* 7°55S 14°24W **153** g
Pyramids *Egypt* 29°58N 31°9E **117** B1
Pyrénées *Europe* 42°45N 0°18E **174** F4
Pyrénées △ *France* 42°52N 0°10W **174** F3
Pyrénées-Atlantiques □ *France* 43°10N 0°50W **174** E3
Pyrénées-Orientales □ *France* 42°35N 2°26E **174** F6
Pyry *Poland* 52°8N 21°0E **142** C1
Pyryatyn *Ukraine* 50°15N 32°25E **189** G7
Pyrzyce *Poland* 53°10N 14°55E **185** E1
Pyskowice *Poland* 50°24N 18°38E **185** H5
Pytalovo *Russia* 57°5N 27°55E **188** D4
Pyttegga = Puttegga *Norway* 62°13N 7°42E **164** B4
Pyu *Burma* 18°30N 96°28E **241** F6
Pyzdry *Poland* 52°11N 17°42E **185** F4

Q

Qaanaaq *Greenland* 77°40N 69°0W **154** B4
Qabanbay *Kazakhstan* 45°50N 80°37E **217** C10
Qabirri → *Azerbaijan* 41°3N 46°17E **191** K8
Qabr Hūd *Yemen* 16°9N 49°34E **249** C5
Qachasnek *S. Africa* 30°6S 28°42E **271** D4
Qādub *Yemen* 12°37N 53°57E **249** D6
Qa'el Jafr *Jordan* 30°20N 36°25E **251** H7
Qā'emābād *Iran* 31°44N 60°2E **247** D9
Qā'emshahr *Iran* 36°30N 52°53E **247** B7
Qagan Nur *China* 43°30N 114°55E **226** C8
Qahar Youyi Zhongqi *China* 41°12N 112°40E **226** D7
Qahremānshahr = Kermānshāh *Iran* 34°23N 47°0E **213** E12
Qaidam Pendi *China* 37°0N 95°0E **218** C4
Qajarīyeh *Iran* 31°1N 48°22E **247** D6
Qala *Malta* 36°2N 14°19E **206** E7
Qala, Ras il *Malta* 36°2N 14°20E **206** E7
Qala-i-Jadid = Spīn Būldak *Afghan.* 31°1N 66°25E **242** D2
Qala Point = Qala, Ras il *Malta* 36°2N 14°20E **206** E7
Qala Viala *Pakistan* 30°49N 67°17E **242** D2
Qala Yangi *Afghan.* 34°20N 66°30E **242** B2
Qalācheh *Afghan.* 35°30N 67°43E **240** B2
Qalaikhum = Kalaikhum *Tajikistan* 38°28N 70°46E **217** E8
Qalandiya *West Bank* 31°52N 35°12E **123** A2
Qalansīyah *Yemen* 12°41N 53°29E **249** D6
Qal'at al Akhḍar *Si. Arabia* 28°4N 37°9E **251** K8
Qal'at Bīshah *Si. Arabia* 20°0N 42°36E **248** C3
Qal'at Dīzah *Iraq* 36°11N 45°7E **213** D11
Qalāt-i-Ghilzai *Afghan.* 32°15N 66°58E **240** B2
Qal'at Şāliḩ *Iraq* 31°31N 47°16E **246** D5
Qal'at Sukkar *Iraq* 31°51N 46°5E **213** G12
Qal'eh Morghī *Iran* 35°38N 51°22E **141** B2
Qal'eh-ye Bost *Afghan.* 31°30N 64°21E **240** C2
Qal'eh-ye Now *Afghan.* 35°0N 63°5E **240** B1
Qal'eh-ye Panjeh *Afghan.* 37°0N 72°35E **240** A4
Qal'eh-ye Sarkari *Afghan.* 35°54N 67°17E **240** B2
Qal'eh-ye Valī *Afghan.* 35°46N 63°45E **240** B1
Qalyûb *Egypt* 30°12N 31°11E **251** H2
Qalyûbîya □ *Egypt* 30°18N 31°18E **251** H2
Qamani'tuaq = Baker Lake *Canada* 64°20N 96°3W **294** C10
Qamar, Ghubbat al *Yemen* 16°20N 52°30E **249** C6
Qamar, Jabal al *Oman* 16°48N 53°15E **249** C6
Qamdo *China* 31°15N 97°6E **228** B1
Qamea *Fiji* 16°45S 179°45W **287** A3
Qamīnis *Libya* 31°40N 20°1E **258** B4
Qammieh Point *Malta* 35°58N 14°19E **206** F7
Qamruddin Karez *Pakistan* 31°45N 68°20E **242** D3
Qanâ el Ismâ'ilîya *Egypt* 30°7N 31°17E **117** A2
Qandahār = Kandahār *Afghan.* 31°32N 65°43E **240** C2
Qandahār = Kandahār □ *Afghan.* 31°0N 65°0E **240** C2
Qapān *Iran* 37°40N 55°47E **247** B7
Qapqal *China* 43°48N 81°5E **217** D10
Qapshaghay *Kazakhstan* 43°51N 77°14E **217** D9
Qapshaghay Bögeni *Kazakhstan* 43°45N 77°50E **217** D9
Qaqortoq *Greenland* 60°43N 46°0W **154** E6
Qâra *Egypt* 29°38N 26°30E **256** B2
Qarā', Jabal al *Oman* 17°15N 54°15E **249** C6
Qara Qash → *China* 35°0N 78°30E **243** B8
Qarabutaq *Kazakhstan* 49°59N 60°14E **216** C6
Qaraçala *Azerbaijan* 39°45N 48°53E **191** L9
Qaraghandy *Kazakhstan* 49°50N 73°10E **217** C8
Qaraghayly *Kazakhstan* 49°26N 76°0E **214** E8
Qārah *Si. Arabia* 29°55N 40°3E **246** D4
Qaraoba *Kazakhstan* 47°6N 56°15E **216** C5
Qarataū *Kazakhstan* 43°30N 69°30E **217** D7
Qarataū *Zhambyl, Kazakhstan* 43°10N 70°28E **217** D8
Qarāvol *Afghan.* 37°14N 68°46E **240** A3
Qarazhal *Kazakhstan* 48°2N 70°49E **214** E8
Qardho = Gardo *Somali Rep.* 9°30N 49°6E **267** C6
Qardud *Sudan* 10°20N 29°56E **257** E2
Qareh → *Iran* 39°25N 47°22E **213** C12
Qareh Tekān *Iran* 36°38N 49°29E **247** B6
Qarnein *U.A.E.* 24°56N 52°52E **247** E7
Qarqan He → *China* 39°30N 88°30E **217** E11
Qarqaraly *Kazakhstan* 49°26N 75°30E **217** C9
Qarqin *Afghan.* 37°24N 66°4E **240** A2
Qarrasa *Sudan* 14°38N 32°5E **257** E3
Qarshi *Uzbekistan* 38°53N 65°48E **217** E7
Qartabā *Lebanon* 34°4N 35°50E **250** D6
Qaryat al Gharab *Iraq* 31°27N 44°48E **246** D5
Qaryat al 'Ulyā *Si. Arabia* 27°33N 47°42E **246** E5
Qarynzharyq Oyysy *Kazakhstan* 42°55N 54°25E **216** D4
Qasbah, Râs al *Si. Arabia* 28°2N 34°38E **251** K5
Qāsemābād *Iran* 35°46N 51°30E **141** A3
Qashqadaryo □ *Uzbekistan* 38°35N 66°0E **217** E7
Qasigiannguit *Greenland* 68°50N 51°18W **154** D5
Qasr 'Amra *Jordan* 31°48N 36°35E **246** D3
Qaşr Bū Hadi *Libya* 31°1N 16°45E **258** B3
Qaşr-e Fīrūzeh *Iran* 35°29N 51°31E **141** B3
Qaşr-e Qand *Iran* 26°15N 60°45E **247** E9
Qaşr-e Shīrīn *Iran* 34°31N 45°35E **246** C5
Qasr Farâfra *Egypt* 27°0N 28°1E **256** B2
Qasr Larocu *Libya* 26°32N 13°19E **258** C2
Qa'taba *Yemen* 13°51N 44°42E **248** D3
Qatanā *Syria* 33°26N 36°4E **250** E7
Qaţānan, Ra's *Yemen* 12°21N 53°33E **249** D6
Qatane *West Bank* 31°50N 35°6E **123** B1
Qatar ■ *Asia* 25°30N 51°15E **247** E6
Qatlīsh *Iran* 37°50N 57°19E **247** B8
Qattâra *Egypt* 30°12N 27°3E **256** A2
Qattâra, Munkhafed el *Egypt* 29°30N 27°30E **256** B2
Qattâra Depression = Qattâra, Munkhafed el *Egypt* 29°30N 27°30E **256** B2
Qausiuittuq = Resolute *Canada* 74°42N 94°54W **295** B10
Qawām al Ḩamzah = Al Ḩamzah *Iraq* 31°43N 44°58E **246** D5
Qawra Point *Malta* 35°58N 14°26E **206** F7
Qāyen *Iran* 33°40N 59°10E **247** C8
Qaynar *Kazakhstan* 49°12N 77°22E **217** C9
Qazaly *Kazakhstan* 45°45N 62°6E **216** C6
Qazaqstan = Kazakhstan ■ *Asia* 50°0N 70°0E **217** C8
Qazaqtyng Usaqshogylyghy *Kazakhstan* 50°0N 72°0E **217** C8
Qazimämmäd *Azerbaijan* 40°3N 49°0E **191** K9
Qazvīn *Iran* 36°15N 50°0E **247** B6
Qazvīn □ *Iran* 36°20N 50°0E **247** B6
Qazyghurt *Kazakhstan* 41°45N 69°23E **217** D7
Qeisari = Caesarea *Israel* 32°30N 34°53E **251** F5
Qeissan *Sudan* 11°4N 34°40E **257** E3
Qena *Egypt* 26°10N 32°43E **256** B3
Qena, W. → *Egypt* 26°12N 32°44E **256** B3
Qeqertarsuaq *Greenland* 69°45N 53°30W **154** D5
Qeqertarsuaq *Greenland* 69°15N 53°38W **154** D5
Qeqertarsuatsiaat *Greenland* 63°5N 50°45W **154** E5
Qeshlāq *Iran* 34°55N 46°28E **213** E12
Qeshm *Iran* 26°55N 56°10E **247** E8
Qeys *Iran* 26°32N 53°58E **247** E7
Qezel Owzen → *Iran* 36°45N 49°22E **247** B6
Qezi'ot *Israel* 30°52N 34°26E **251** H5
Qi Xian *China* 34°40N 114°48E **226** G8
Qian Gorlos *China* 45°5N 124°42E **227** B13
Qian Hai *China* 22°32N 113°54E **219** F10
Qian Xian *China* 34°31N 108°15E **226** G5
Qiancheng *China* 27°12N 109°50E **228** D7
Qianjiang *Guangxi Zhuangzu, China* 23°38N 108°58E **228** F7
Qianjiang *Hubei, China* 30°24N 112°55E **229** B9
Qianjiang *Sichuan, China* 29°33N 108°47E **228** C7
Qianmen *China* 39°51N 116°21E **114** B2
Qianshan *Anhui, China* 30°37N 116°35E **229** B11
Qianshan *Guangdong, China* 22°15N 113°31E **219** G10
Qianwei *China* 29°13N 103°56E **228** C4
Qianxi *China* 27°3N 106°3E **228** D6
Qianyang *Hunan, China* 27°18N 110°10E **229** D8
Qianyang *Shaanxi, China* 34°40N 107°8E **226** G4
Qianyang *Zhejiang, China* 30°11N 119°25E **229** B12
Qi'ao *China* 22°25N 113°39E **219** G10
Qi'ao Dao *China* 22°25N 113°38E **219** G10
Qiaojia *China* 26°56N 102°58E **228** D4
Qichun *China* 30°18N 115°25E **229** B10
Qidong *Hunan, China* 26°49N 112°7E **229** D9
Qidong *Jiangsu, China* 31°48N 121°38E **229** B13
Qiemo *China* 38°8N 85°32E **217** E11
Qijiang *China* 28°57N 106°35E **228** C6
Qijiaojing *China* 43°28N 91°36E **218** B4
Qikiqtarjuaq *Canada* 67°33N 63°0W **295** C13
Qila Saifullāh *Pakistan* 30°45N 68°17E **242** D3
Qilian Shan *China* 38°30N 96°0E **218** C4
Qimen *China* 29°50N 117°42E **229** C11
Qin He → *China* 35°1N 113°22E **226** G7
Qin Jiang → *Guangxi Zhuangzu, China* 21°53N 108°35E **228** F7
Qin Jiang → *Jiangxi, China* 26°15N 115°55E **229** D10
Qin Ling = Qinling Shandi *China* 33°50N 108°10E **226** H5
Qināb, W. → *Yemen* 17°55N 49°59E **249** C5
Qin'an *China* 34°48N 105°40E **226** G3
Qing Xian *China* 38°35N 116°45E **226** E9
Qingcheng *China* 37°15N 117°40E **227** F9
Qingdao *China* 36°5N 120°20E **227** F11
Qingfeng *China* 35°52N 115°8E **226** G8
Qinghai □ *China* 36°0N 98°0E **218** C4
Qinghai Hu *China* 36°40N 100°10E **218** C5
Qinghe *China* 46°37N 90°25E **217** C12
Qinghecheng *China* 41°28N 124°15E **227** D13
Qinghemen *China* 41°48N 121°25E **227** D11
Qinghuayuan *China* 39°59N 116°19E **114** B1
Qingjian *China* 37°8N 110°8E **226** F6
Qingjiang = Huaiyin *China* 33°30N 119°2E **227** H10
Qingliu *China* 26°11N 116°48E **229** D11
Qinglong *China* 25°49N 105°12E **228** E5
Qingningsi *China* 31°16N 121°33E **138** B2
Qingping *China* 26°39N 107°47E **228** D6
Qingpu *China* 31°10N 121°6E **229** B13
Qingshui *China* 34°48N 106°8E **226** G4
Qingshuihe *China* 39°55N 111°35E **226** E6
Qingtian *China* 28°12N 120°15E **229** C13
Qingtongxia Shuiku *China* 37°50N 105°58E **226** F3
Qingxi *China* 27°8N 108°43E **228** D7
Qingxu *China* 37°34N 112°22E **226** F7
Qingyang *Anhui, China* 30°38N 117°50E **229** B11
Qingyang *Gansu, China* 36°2N 107°55E **226** F4
Qingyi Jiang → *China* 29°32N 103°44E **228** C4
Qingyuan *Guangdong, China* 23°40N 112°59E **229** F9
Qingyuan *Liaoning, China* 42°10N 124°55E **224** A2
Qingyuan *Zhejiang, China* 27°36N 119°3E **229** D12
Qingyun *China* 37°45N 117°20E **227** F9
Qingzhen *China* 26°31N 106°25E **228** D6
Qinhuangdao *China* 39°56N 119°30E **227** E10
Qinling Shandi *China* 33°50N 108°10E **226** H5
Qinshui *China* 35°40N 112°8E **226** G7
Qinyang = Jiyuan *China* 35°7N 112°57E **226** G7
Qinyuan *China* 36°29N 112°20E **226** F7
Qinzhou *China* 21°58N 108°38E **228** G7
Qionghai *China* 19°15N 110°26E **236** C8
Qionglai *China* 30°25N 103°31E **228** B4
Qionglai Shan *China* 31°0N 102°30E **228** B4
Qiongzhou Haixia *China* 20°10N 110°15E **236** B8
Qiqihar *China* 47°26N 124°0E **219** B7
Qira *China* 37°0N 80°48E **217** E10
Qirāya, W. → *Egypt* 30°27N 34°0E **251** H5
Qiryat Ata *Israel* 32°47N 35°6E **250** F6
Qiryat Gat *Israel* 31°32N 34°46E **251** G5
Qiryat Mal'akhi *Israel* 31°44N 34°44E **251** G5
Qiryat Shemona *Israel* 33°13N 35°35E **250** E6
Qiryat Yam *Israel* 32°51N 35°4E **250** F6
Qirzah, W. → *Libya* 30°56N 14°31E **258** B2
Qishan *China* 34°25N 107°38E **226** G4
Qishn *Yemen* 15°26N 51°40E **249** D5
Qitai *China* 44°2N 89°35E **217** D11
Qitbīt, W. → *Oman* 19°15N 54°23E **249** C6
Qiubei *China* 24°2N 104°12E **228** E5
Qixia *China* 37°17N 120°52E **227** F11
Qiyang *China* 26°35N 111°50E **229** D8
Qızılağac Körfäzi *Azerbaijan* 39°9N 49°0E **213** C13
Qobda *Kazakhstan* 50°55N 54°31E **216** B4
Qojūr *Iran* 36°12N 47°55E **246** B5
Qolhak *Iran* 35°45N 51°26E **141** A2
Qom *Iran* 34°40N 51°0E **247** C6
Qom □ *Iran* 34°40N 51°0E **247** C6
Qomolangma Feng = Everest, Mt. *Nepal* 28°5N 86°58E **243** E12
Qomsheh *Iran* 32°0N 51°55E **247** D6
Qondūz = Kondoz *Afghan.* 36°50N 68°50E **240** A3
Qondūz = Kondoz □ *Afghan.* 36°50N 68°50E **240** A3
Qondūz → *Afghan.* 37°0N 68°16E **240** A3
Qong Muztag *China* 35°42N 82°22E **217** E10
Qoqon = Qŭqon *Uzbekistan* 40°31N 70°56E **217** D8
Qorakūl = Karakul *Uzbekistan* 39°32N 63°50E **216** E6
Qoraqalpoghistan □ *Uzbekistan* 43°0N 58°0E **216** D5
Qormi *Malta* 35°53N 14°28E **206** F7
Qorveh *Iran* 35°10N 47°48E **213** E12
Qostanay *Kazakhstan* 53°10N 63°35E **216** B6
Qoţūr *Iran* 38°28N 44°25E **213** C11
Qoz Salsilgo *C.A.R.* 10°45N 22°54E **264** A4
Qrejten Point *Malta* 35°57N 14°27E **206** F7
Qu Jiang → *China* 30°1N 106°24E **228** B6
Qu Xian *China* 30°48N 106°58E **228** B6
Quabbin Res. *U.S.A.* 42°20N 72°20W **313** D12
Quadraro *Italy* 41°51N 12°33E **136** B2
Quaid-i-Azam *Pakistan* 24°50N 66°59E **123** A1
Quairading *Australia* 32°0S 117°21E **279** F2
Quakenbrück *Germany* 52°41N 7°57E **178** C3
Quakertown *U.S.A.* 40°26N 75°21W **313** F9
Qualicum Beach *Canada* 49°22N 124°26W **296** D4
Quambatook *Australia* 35°49S 143°34E **282** C5
Quambone *Australia* 30°57S 147°53E **283** A7
Quamby *Australia* 20°22S 140°17E **280** C3
Quan Long = Ca Mau *Vietnam* 9°7N 105°8E **237** H5
Quanah *U.S.A.* 34°18N 99°44W **314** D5
Quandialla *Australia* 34°1S 147°47E **283** C7
Quang Ngai *Vietnam* 15°13N 108°58E **236** E7
Quang Tri *Vietnam* 16°45N 107°13E **236** D6
Quang Yen *Vietnam* 20°56N 106°52E **228** G6
Quanjiao *China* 32°45N 118°18E **229** A12
Quannan *China* 24°45N 114°33E **229** E10
Quantock Hills *U.K.* 51°8N 3°10W **169** F4
Quanzhou *Fujian, China* 24°55N 118°34E **229** E12
Quanzhou *Guangxi Zhuangzu, China* 25°57N 111°5E **229** E8
Qu'Appelle → *Canada* 50°33N 103°53W **297** C8
Quaqtaq *Canada* 60°55N 69°40W **295** C13
Quaraí *Brazil* 30°15S 56°20W **334** C4
Quarré-les-Tombes *France* 47°21N 4°0E **173** E11
Quarteira *Portugal* 37°4N 8°6W **195** H2
Quarter, The *Anguilla* 18°13N 63°3W **322** a
Quartier D'Orléans *St.-Martin* 18°5N 63°2W **322** a
Quartier Militaire *Mauritius* 20°14S 57°35E **272** e
Quartiere Zingone *Italy* 45°25N 9°3E **129** B1
Quartu Sant'Élena *Italy* 39°15N 9°10E **200** C2
Quartzsite *U.S.A.* 33°40N 114°13W **307** M12
Quatre Cocos, I. à *St. Vincent* 12°59N 61°15W **323** n
Quatre Bornes *Mauritius* 20°15S 57°28E **272** e
Quatsino Sd. *Canada* 50°25N 127°58W **296** C3
Quba *Azerbaijan* 41°21N 48°32E **191** K9
Qubeiba *West Bank* 31°50N 35°8E **123** A1
Qūchān *Iran* 37°10N 58°27E **247** B8
Quds *Iraq* 33°23N 44°24E **113** A2
Queanbeyan *Australia* 35°17S 149°14E **283** C8
Québec *Canada* 46°52N 71°13W **299** C5
Québec □ *Canada* 48°0N 74°0W **299** C6
Quebrada del Condorito △ *Argentina* 31°49S 64°40W **334** C3
Quebradillas *Puerto Rico* 18°29N 66°56W **321** b
Quedlinburg *Germany* 51°47N 11°8E **178** D7
Queen Alexandra Ra. *Antarctica* 85°0S 170°0E **151** E11
Queen Charlotte I. *Falk. Is.* 51°50S 60°40W **153** f
Queen Charlotte City *Canada* 53°15N 132°2W **296** C2
Queen Charlotte Is. *Canada* 53°20N 132°10W **296** C2
Queen Charlotte Sd. *B.C., Canada* 51°0N 128°0W **296** C3
Queen Charlotte Sd. *N.Z.* 41°10S 174°15E **285** B9
Queen Charlotte Strait *Canada* 50°45N 127°10W **296** C3
Queen City *U.S.A.* 40°25N 92°34W **310** D4
Queen Elizabeth △ *Uganda* 0°0 30°0E **268** C3
Queen Elizabeth ⌂ *U.K.* 56°7N 4°30W **167** E4
Queen Elizabeth Is. *Canada* 76°0N 95°0W **295** B10
Queen Elizabeth Nat. Park = Ruwenzori △ *Uganda* 0°20N 30°0E **268** B2
Queen Mary Land *Antarctica* 70°0S 95°0E **151** D7
Queen Mary Res. *U.K.* 51°24N 0°27W **125** B1
Queen Maud G. *Canada* 68°15N 102°30W **294** C9
Queen Maud Land = Dronning Maud Land *Antarctica* 72°30S 12°0E **151** D3
Queen Maud Mts. *Antarctica* 86°0S 160°0W **151** E13
Queen Street *Edinburgh, U.K.* **121** a1
Queen Victoria Market *Australia* 37°47S 144°57W **128** A1
Queens Channel *Australia* 15°0S 129°30E **278** C4
Queens-Midtown Tunnel *New York, U.S.A.* **132** d2
Queen's Quay Terminal *Toronto, Canada* **141** c2
Queensboro Bridge *New York, U.S.A.* **132** c3
Queensbury *U.K.* 51°35N 0°16W **125** A2
Queenscliff *Australia* 38°16S 144°39E **282** E6
Queenscliffe *Australia* 33°47S 151°17E **139** A2
Queensferry *U.K.* 55°59N 3°23W **121** B1
Queensland *U.S.A.* 31°46N 83°14W **316** D6
Queensland □ *Australia* 22°0S 142°0E **280** C3
Queensland Plateau *Pac. Oc.* 17°0S 150°0E **276** D8
Queenstown = Cóbh *Ireland* 51°51N 8°17W **166** E3
Queenstown *Tas., Australia* 42°4S 145°35E **281** G4
Queenstown *N.Z.* 45°1S 168°40E **285** F3
Queenstown *Singapore* 1°18N 103°48E **138** B2
Queenstown *Eastern Cape, S. Africa* 31°52S 26°52E **270** D4
Queets *U.S.A.* 47°32N 124°19W **306** C2
Queguay Grande → *Uruguay* 32°9S 58°9W **334** C4
Queimada, Pta. da *Azores* 38°23N 28°14W **153** d1
Queimadas *Brazil* 11°0S 39°38W **332** D4
Queiros, C. *Vanuatu* 14°55S 167°1E **287** D5
Quela *Angola* 9°10S 16°56E **265** D3
Quelimane *Mozam.* 17°53S 36°58E **269** F4
Quellerina *S. Africa* 26°9S 27°56E **123** A1
Quellón *Chile* 43°7S 73°37W **336** B2
Quelo *Angola* 6°29S 12°36E **265** D2
Quelpart = Jeju-do *S. Korea* 33°29N 126°34E **224** a
Queluz *Portugal* 38°45N 9°14W **126** A1
Quemado *N. Mex., U.S.A.* 34°20N 108°30W **305** J9
Quemado *Tex., U.S.A.* 28°56N 100°37W **314** G4
Quemoy = Chinmen *Taiwan* 24°26N 118°19E **225** a
Quemú-Quemú *Argentina* 36°3S 63°36W **334** D3
Quepem *India* 15°13N 74°3E **245** G2
Quequén *Argentina* 38°30S 58°30W **334** D4
Querco *Peru* 13°50S 74°52W **330** C3
Querétaro *Mexico* 20°36N 100°23W **318** C4
Querétaro □ *Mexico* 21°0N 99°55W **318** C5
Querfurt *Germany* 51°23N 11°35E **178** D7
Quérigut *France* 42°42N 2°6E **174** F6
Querqueville *France* 49°40N 1°42W **172** C5
Quesada *Spain* 37°51N 3°4W **195** H7
Queshan *China* 32°55N 114°2E **226** H8
Quesnel *Canada* 53°0N 122°30W **296** C4
Quesnel → *Canada* 52°58N 122°29W **296** C4
Quesnel L. *Canada* 52°30N 121°20W **296** C4
Questa *U.S.A.* 36°42N 105°36W **305** H11
Questembert *France* 47°40N 2°28W **172** E4
Quetena *Bolivia* 22°10S 67°25W **330** E4
Quetico ⌂ *Canada* 48°30N 91°45W **298** C1
Quetrequile *Argentina* 41°33S 69°22W **336** B3
Quetta *Pakistan* 30°15N 66°55E **242** D2
Queulat △ *Chile* 44°29S 72°34W **336** B2
Quevedo *Ecuador* 1°2S 79°29W **328** D2
Queyras ⌂ *France* 44°45N 6°50E **175** D10
Quezaltenango *Guatemala* 14°50N 91°30W **320** D1
Quezon *Phil.* 9°15N 117°59E **233** G1
Quezon □ *Phil.* 14°40N 121°30E **232** D3
Quezon △ *Phil.* 14°0N 121°55E **232** D3
Quezon City *Phil.* 14°38N 121°0E **232** D3
Qufār *Si. Arabia* 27°26N 41°37E **246** E4
Qui Nhon *Vietnam* 13°40N 109°13E **236** F7
Quibala *Angola* 10°46S 14°59E **265** E2
Quibaxe *Angola* 8°24S 14°27E **265** D2
Quibdó *Colombia* 5°42N 76°40W **328** B2
Quiberon *France* 47°29N 3°9W **172** E3
Quiberon, Presqu'île de *France* 47°30N 3°8W **172** E3
Quiçama △ *Angola* 9°41S 13°35E **265** D2
Quickborn *Germany* 53°42N 9°52E **178** B5
Quiet L. *Canada* 61°5N 133°5W **296** A2
Quiindy *Paraguay* 25°58S 57°14W **334** B4
Quilá *México* 24°23N 107°13W **318** C3
Quilán, C. *Chile* 43°15S 74°30W **336** B2
Quilcene *U.S.A.* 47°49N 122°53W **306** C4
Quilenda *Angola* 10°39S 14°23E **265** E2
Quilengues *Angola* 14°12S 14°12E **265** E2
Quilicura *Chile* 33°22S 70°43W **137** B1
Quilimarí *Chile* 32°5S 71°30W **334** C1
Quilino *Argentina* 30°14S 64°29W **334** C3
Quill, The *Neth. Ant.* 17°28N 62°57W **322** a
Quill Lakes *Canada* 51°55N 104°13W **297** C8
Quillabamba *Peru* 12°50S 72°50W **330** C3
Quillacollo *Bolivia* 17°26S 66°17W **330** D4
Quillagua *Chile* 21°40S 69°40W **334** A2
Quillaicillo *Chile* 31°17S 71°40W **334** C1
Quillan *France* 42°53N 2°10E **174** F6
Quillota *Chile* 32°54S 71°16W **334** C1
Quilmes *Argentina* 34°43S 58°15W **334** C4
Quilon *India* 8°50N 76°38E **245** K3
Quilpie *Australia* 26°35S 144°11E **281** D3
Quilpué *Chile* 33°5S 71°33W **334** C1
Quilua *Mozam.* 16°17S 39°54E **269** F4
Quimbele *Angola* 6°17S 16°41E **265** D3
Quimbo *Angola* 14°4S 16°11E **265** E3
Quimbonge *Angola* 8°36S 18°30E **265** D3
Quime *Bolivia* 17°2S 67°15W **330** D4
Quimilí *Argentina* 27°40S 62°30W **334** B3
Quimper *France* 48°0N 4°9W **172** E2
Quimperlé *France* 47°53N 3°33W **172** E3
Quinam B. *Trin. & Tob.* 10°4N 61°30W **323** t
Quinault → *U.S.A.* 47°21N 124°18W **306** C2
Quincemil *Peru* 13°15S 70°40W **330** C3
Quincy *Calif., U.S.A.* 39°56N 120°57W **306** F6
Quincy *Fla., U.S.A.* 30°35N 84°34W **316** E5
Quincy *Ill., U.S.A.* 39°56N 91°23W **310** E5
Quincy *Mass., U.S.A.* 42°14N 71°0W **116** B2
Quincy *Mich., U.S.A.* 41°57N 84°53W **311** C12
Quincy *Wash., U.S.A.* 47°14N 119°51W **304** C4
Quincy B. *U.S.A.* 42°16N 70°59W **116** B3
Quines *Argentina* 32°13S 65°48W **334** C2
Quinga *Mozam.* 15°49S 40°15E **269** F5
Quingey *France* 47°7N 5°52E **173** E12
Quingombe *Angola* 6°38S 13°1E **265** D2
Quinhagak *U.S.A.* 59°45N 161°54W **303** G7
Quiniluban Group *Phil.* 11°27N 120°48E **233** F3
Quinta Normal *Chile* 33°26S 70°42W **137** B1
Quintana de la Serena *Spain* 38°45N 5°40W **195** G5
Quintana Roo □ *Mexico* 19°40N 88°30W **319** D7
Quintanar de la Orden *Spain* 39°36N 3°5W **195** F7
Quintanar de la Sierra *Spain* 41°57N 2°55W **196** D2
Quintanar del Rey *Spain* 39°21N 1°56W **197** F3
Quinte West *Canada* 44°10N 77°34W **312** B7
Quintero *Chile* 32°45S 71°30W **334** C1
Quintin *France* 48°26N 2°56W **172** D4
Quinto *Spain* 41°25N 0°32W **196** D4
Quinto de Stampi *Italy* 45°24N 9°10E **129** B2
Quinto Romano *Italy* 45°28N 9°7E **129** B1
Quinzáu *Angola* 6°51S 12°44E **265** D2
Quípar → *Spain* 38°15N 1°40W **197** G3
Quipeio *Angola* 12°27S 15°30E **265** E3
Quirihue *Chile* 36°15S 72°35W **334** D1
Quirima *Angola* 10°47S 18°6E **265** E3
Quirimbo *Angola* 10°36S 14°12E **265** E2
Quirinale *Italy* 41°53N 12°29E **136** B1
Quirinale, Palazzo dei *Rome, Italy* **136** b3
Quirindi *Australia* 31°28S 150°40E **283** A9
Quirino □ *Phil.* 16°15N 121°40E **232** C3
Quirinópolis *Brazil* 18°32S 50°30W **333** E1
Quiroga *Spain* 42°28N 7°18W **194** C3
Quiruvilca *Peru* 8°1S 78°19W **330** B2
Quissac *France* 43°55N 4°0E **175** E8
Quissanga *Mozam.* 12°24S 40°28E **269** E5
Quissico *Mozam.* 24°42S 34°44E **271** B5
Quitapa *Angola* 10°20S 18°19E **265** E3
Quitilipi *Argentina* 26°50S 60°13W **334** B3
Quitman *U.S.A.* 30°47N 83°34W **316** E6
Quito *Ecuador* 0°15S 78°35W **328** D2
Quixadá *Brazil* 4°55S 39°0W **332** B4
Quixaxe *Mozam.* 15°17S 40°4E **269** F5
Quixeramobim *Brazil* 5°12S 39°17W **332** C4
Quixico *Angola* 7°59S 14°25E **265** D2
Quixinge *Angola* 9°52S 14°23E **265** D2
Quizenga *Angola* 9°21S 15°28E **265** D3
Qujing *China* 25°32N 103°41E **228** E4
Qulan *Kazakhstan* 42°55N 72°43E **214** E8
Qul'ân, Jazâ'ir *Egypt* 24°22N 35°31E **246** E2
Qumbu *S. Africa* 31°10S 28°48E **271** D4
Qunayyin, Sabkhat al *Libya* 30°10N 21°0E **258** B4
Qŭnghirot *Uzbekistan* 43°2N 58°50E **216** D5
Qu'nyido *China* 31°15N 98°6E **228** B2
Quoin I. *Australia* 14°54S 129°32E **278** B4
Quoin Pt. *S. Africa* 34°46S 19°37E **270** D2
Quorn *Australia* 32°25S 138°5E **282** B3
Qŭqon *Uzbekistan* 40°31N 70°56E **217** D8
Qurein *Sudan* 13°30N 34°50E **257** E3
Qŭrghonteppa *Tajikistan* 37°50N 68°47E **217** E7
Qurnat as Sawdā' *Lebanon* 34°18N 36°6E **250** D7
Quryq *Kazakhstan* 43°12N 51°39E **216** D4
Qûs *Egypt* 25°55N 32°50E **256** B3
Qusar *Azerbaijan* 41°25N 48°26E **191** K9
Quşaybā' *Si. Arabia* 26°53N 43°35E **246** E4
Qusaybah *Iraq* 34°24N 40°59E **213** E9
Quşay'ir *Yemen* 14°55N 50°20E **249** D5
Quseir *Egypt* 26°7N 34°16E **246** E2
Qūshchī *Iran* 37°59N 45°3E **213** D11
Qusmuryn *Kazakhstan* 52°27N 64°36E **216** B6
Qusmuryn Köli *Kazakhstan* 52°41N 64°48E **216** B6
Quthing *Lesotho* 30°25S 27°36E **271** D4
Qūţīābād *Iran* 35°47N 48°30E **213** E13
Quwayq → *Syria* 36°20N 37°10E **250** B8
Quweisna *Egypt* 30°34N 31°9E **251** H2
Quwo *China* 35°38N 111°25E **226** G6
Quyang *China* 38°35N 114°40E **226** E8
Quynh Nhai *Vietnam* 21°49N 103°33E **236** B4
Quyon *Canada* 45°31N 76°14W **313** A8
Quzhou *China* 28°57N 118°54E **229** C12
Quzi *China* 36°20N 107°20E **226** F4
Qvareli *Georgia* 41°57N 45°47E **191** K7
Qytet Stalin = Kuçovë *Albania* 40°47N 19°57E **202** F3
Qyzylorda *Kazakhstan* 44°48N 65°28E **217** D7
Qyzylorda □ *Kazakhstan* 45°0N 65°0E **216** D6
Qyzylzhar *Kazakhstan* 48°17N 69°38E **217** C7

R

R.F.K. Memorial Stadium *U.S.A.* 38°52N 76°58W **143** B4
Ra, Ko *Thailand* 9°13N 98°16E **237** H2
Raab *Austria* 48°21N 13°39E **180** C6
Raahe *Finland* 64°40N 24°28E **160** D21
Raalte *Neths.* 52°23N 6°16E **170** B6
Ra'ananna *Israel* 32°10N 34°52E **251** F5
Raasay *U.K.* 57°25N 6°4W **167** D2
Raasay, Sd. of *U.K.* 57°30N 6°8W **167** D2
Raasdorf *Austria* 48°14N 16°33E **142** A3
Rab *Croatia* 44°45N 14°45E **199** D11
Raba *Indonesia* 8°36S 118°55E **235** D5
Rába → *Hungary* 47°38N 17°38E **182** C2
Raba → *Poland* 50°8N 20°30E **185** H7
Rabaçal → *Portugal* 41°30N 7°12W **194** D3
Rabah *Nigeria* 13°5N 5°30E **263** C6
Rabai *Kenya* 3°50S 39°31E **268** C4
Rabak *Sudan* 13°9N 32°44E **257** E3

Rabaraba *Papua N. G.* 9°58S 149°49E **286** E5
Rabastens *France* 43°50N 1°43E **174** E5
Rabastens-de-Bigorre
  France 43°23N 0°9E **174** E4
Rabat = Victoria *Malta* 36°3N 14°14E **206** G6
Rabat *Malta* 35°53N 14°24E **206** F6
Rabat *Morocco* 34°2N 6°48W **260** B3
Rabat □ *Morocco* 34°10N 6°45W **260** B3
Rabaul *Papua N. G.* 4°24S 152°18E **286** C7
Rabi *Fiji* 16°30S 179°59W **287** A3
Rābigh *Si. Arabia* 22°50N 39°5E **248** B2
Rabka *Poland* 49°37N 19°59E **185** A6
Râbniţa *Moldova* 47°45N 29°0E **183** C14
Rābor *Iran* 29°17N 56°55E **247** D8
Rabyānah *Libya* 24°15N 22°0E **258** D4
Rača *Serbia* 44°14N 21°0E **202** B4
Răcăciuni *Romania* 46°20N 26°59E **183** D11
Răcășdia *Romania* 44°59N 21°36E **182** F6
Racconigi *Italy* 44°46N 7°46E **198** D4
Raccoon → *U.S.A.* 41°35N 93°37W **310** C3
Raccoon Cr. → *U.S.A.* 39°47N 87°23W **311** E9
Race, C. *Canada* 46°40N 53°5W **299** C9
Race Course *Jamaica* 17°51N 77°20W **320** a
Racepond *U.S.A.* 31°1N 82°8W **316** D7
Rach Gia *Vietnam* 10°5N 105°5E **237** G5
Rachid *Mauritania* 18°45N 11°35W **262** B2
Raciąż *Poland* 52°46N 20°10E **185** F7
Racibórz *Poland* 50°7N 18°18E **185** H5
Racine *U.S.A.* 42°44N 87°47W **311** D9
Račišdorf = Rača *Serbia* 44°14N 21°0E **202** B4
Rackerby *U.S.A.* 39°26N 121°22W **306** F5
Radama, Nosy *Madag.* 14°0S 47°47E **272** A2
Radama, Saikanosy
  Madag. 14°16S 47°53E **272** A2
Radan *Serbia* 42°59N 21°29E **203** D5
Rădăuţi *Romania* 47°50N 25°59E **183** C10
Rădăuţi-Prut *Romania* 48°14N 26°48E **183** B11
Radbuza → *Czech Rep.* 49°45N 13°22E **180** B6
Radcliff *U.S.A.* 37°51N 85°57W **311** G11
Radcliffe College *U.S.A.* 42°22N 71°7W **116** A2
Radeberg *Germany* 51°7N 13°55E **178** D9
Radebeul *Germany* 51°6N 13°39E **178** D9
Radeče *Slovenia* 46°5N 15°14E **199** B12
Radekhiv *Ukraine* 50°25N 24°32E **177** C13
Radekhov = Radekhiv
  Ukraine 50°25N 24°32E **177** C13
Radenthein *Austria* 46°48N 13°43E **180** E6
Radew → *Poland* 54°2N 15°52E **184** D2
Radford *U.S.A.* 37°8N 80°34W **309** G13
Radhanpur *India* 23°50N 71°38E **242** H4
Rădhus *Oslo, Norway* **133** b1
Radhwa, Jabal *Si. Arabia* 24°34N 38°18E **246** D3
Radika → *Macedonia* 41°38N 20°37E **202** E4
Radisson *Qué., Canada* 53°47N 77°37W **298** B4
Radisson *Sask., Canada* 52°30N 107°20W **297** C7
Radium Hot Springs
  Canada 50°35N 116°2W **296** C5
Radlice *Czech Rep.* 50°3N 14°23E **135** B2
Radlje ob Dravi *Slovenia* 46°38N 15°13E **199** B12
Radmannsdorf = Radovljica
  Slovenia 46°22N 14°12E **199** B11
Radnevo *Bulgaria* 42°17N 25°58E **203** D9
Radnice *Czech Rep.* 49°51N 13°35E **180** B6
Radnor Forest *U.K.* 52°17N 3°10W **169** E4
Radolfzell *Germany* 47°39N 8°58E **179** H4
Radom *Poland* 51°23N 21°12E **185** G8
Radom *Sudan* 9°20N 23°50E **266** A4
Radom △ *Sudan* 9°20N 23°50E **266** A4
Radomir *Bulgaria* 42°37N 22°59E **202** D6
Radomka → *Poland* 51°43N 21°28E **185** G8
Radomsko *Poland* 51°5N 19°28E **185** H6
Radomyshl *Ukraine* 50°30N 29°12E **177** C15
Radomyśl Wielki *Poland* 50°14N 21°15E **185** E8
Radość *Poland* 52°11N 21°11E **142** B3
Radoszyce *Poland* 51°4N 20°15E **185** G7
Radotín *Czech Rep.* 49°59N 14°21E **135** C2
Radoviš *Macedonia* 41°38N 22°28E **202** E6
Radovljica *Slovenia* 46°22N 14°12E **199** B11
Radstadt *Austria* 47°24N 13°28E **180** D6
Radstock, C. *Australia* 33°12S 134°20E **281** E1
Răducăneni *Romania* 46°58N 27°54E **183** D12
Raduša *Macedonia* 42°7N 21°15E **202** E5
Radvanichy *Belarus* 52°1N 24°0E **185** F11
Radviliškis *Lithuania* 55°49N 23°33E **184** C10
Radville *Canada* 49°30N 104°15W **297** D8
Raḍwā, J. *Si. Arabia* 24°34N 38°18E **256** C4
Radymno *Poland* 49°59N 22°52E **185** J9
Radzanów *Poland* 52°56N 20°8E **185** F7
Radziejów *Poland* 52°40N 18°30E **185** F5
Radzyń Chełmiński
  Poland 53°23N 18°55E **184** E5
Radzyń Podlaski *Poland* 51°47N 22°37E **185** G9
Rae *Canada* 62°50N 116°3W **296** A5
Rae Bareli *India* 26°18N 81°20E **243** F9
Rae Isthmus *Canada* 66°40N 87°30W **295** C11
Raeren *U.S.A.* 50°41N 6°7E **170** D6
Raeside, L. *Australia* 29°20S 122°0E **279** E3
Raetihi *N.Z.* 39°25S 175°17E **284** F4
Rafaela *Argentina* 31°10S 61°30W **334** C3
Rafah *Gaza Strip* 31°18N 34°14E **251** G5
Rafai *C.A.R.* 4°59N 23°58E **264** B4
Rafat *West Bank* 31°52N 35°11E **123** A2
Raffadali *Italy* 37°24N 13°32E **200** E6
Raffili *Sudan* 6°50N 28°0E **257** F2
Raffles Hotel *Singapore* **138** b3
Raffles Park *Singapore* 1°19N 103°48E **138** B2
Rafḩā *Si. Arabia* 29°35N 43°35E **246** D4
Rafsanjān *Iran* 30°30N 56°5E **247** D8
Raft Pt. *Australia* 16°4S 124°26E **278** C3
Râga *Sudan* 8°28N 25°41E **257** F2
Raga → *Sudan* 8°41N 25°52E **257** F2
Ragachev *Belarus* 53°8N 30°5E **177** B16
Ragag *Sudan* 10°59N 24°40E **257** E1
Ragang, Mt. *Phil.* 7°43N 124°32E **233** H5
Ragay *Phil.* 13°49N 122°47E **232** E4
Ragay G. *Phil.* 13°30N 122°45E **232** E4
Ragged, Mt. *Australia* 33°27S 123°25E **279** F3
Rāgh *Afghan.* 37°32N 70°27E **240** A3
Raghunathpalli *India* 22°14N 84°48E **243** H11
Raghunathpur *India* 23°33N 86°40E **243** H12
Raglan *U.S.A.* 37°55S 174°55E **284** D3
Raglan Harbour *N.Z.* 37°47S 174°50E **284** D3
Ragland *U.S.A.* 33°45N 86°9W **316** B3
Raguda *India* 55°2N 22°2E **184** C9
Ragusa = Dubrovnik
  Croatia 42°39N 18°6E **202** D2
Ragusa *Italy* 36°55N 14°44E **201** F7
Raha *Indonesia* 4°55S 123°0E **231** E6
Rahad, Nahr ed →
  Sudan 14°28N 33°31E **257** E3
Rahad al Bardī *Sudan* 11°20N 23°40E **259** F4
Rahaeng = Tak *Thailand* 16°52N 99°8E **236** D2
Rahatgarh *India* 23°47N 78°22E **243** H8
Rahden *Germany* 52°26N 8°36E **178** C4
Raheb, Ras ir- *Malta* 35°54N 14°20E **206** F7
Raheita *Eritrea* 12°46N 43°4E **257** E3
Raheng = Tak *Thailand* 16°52N 99°8E **236** D2
Raheny *Ireland* 53°22N 6°10W **120** A3
Rahimyar Khan *Pakistan* 28°30N 70°25E **242** E4
Rāhjerd *Iran* 34°22N 50°8E **247** C6
Rahnsdorf *Germany* 52°25N 13°41E **115** D5

Rahole △ *Kenya* 0°5N 38°57E **268** B4
Râhoti *Norway* 60°16N 11°11E **164** D8
Rahon *India* 31°3N 76°7E **242** D7
Rahotu *N.Z.* 39°20S 173°49E **284** F2
Rahuri *India* 19°23N 74°39E **244** E2
Raiatéa, Î.
  French Polynesia 16°50S 151°25W **289** f
Raichur *India* 16°10N 77°20E **245** F3
Raiford *U.S.A.* 30°4N 82°14W **316** E7
Raiganj *India* 25°37N 88°10E **243** G13
Raigarh *India* 21°56N 83°25E **244** D6
Raighar *India* 19°51N 82°6E **244** E6
Raijua *Indonesia* 10°37S 121°36E **231** F6
Raikot *India* 30°41N 75°42E **242** D6
Railton *Australia* 41°25S 146°28E **281** G4
Rainbow Bridge △
  U.S.A. 37°5N 110°58W **305** H8
Rainbow City *U.S.A.* 33°57N 86°5W **316** B3
Rainbow Lake *Canada* 58°30N 119°23W **296** B5
Rainham *U.K.* 51°31N 0°11E **125** A5
Rainier *U.S.A.* 46°53N 122°41W **306** D4
Rainier, Mt. *U.S.A.* 46°52N 121°46W **306** D5
Rainy → *Canada* 48°42N 93°10W **297** D10
Rainy River *Canada* 48°43N 94°29W **297** D10
Raippaluoto *Finland* 63°13N 21°14E **160** E19
Raipur *India* 21°17N 81°45E **244** D5
Rairakhol *India* 21°4N 84°21E **244** D7
Ra'is *Si. Arabia* 23°33N 38°43E **256** C4
Raisen *India* 23°20N 77°48E **242** H8
Raisio *Finland* 60°28N 22°11E **188** D2
Raivavae *French Polynesia* 23°52S 147°40W **289** f
Raj Ghat *Delhi, India* **120** b3
Raj Nandgaon *India* 21°5N 81°5E **244** D5
Raj Nilgiri *India* 21°28N 86°46E **243** J12
Raja, Ujung *Indonesia* 3°40N 96°25E **234** D1
Raja Ampat, Kepulauan
  Indonesia 0°30S 130°0E **231** E8
Rajah Sikatuna △ *Phil.* 9°40N 124°20E **233** G5
Rajahmundry *India* 17°1N 81°48E **244** F5
Rajaji △ *India* 30°10N 78°20E **242** D8
Rajakylä *Finland* 60°15N 25°5E **121** B3
Rajampet *India* 14°11N 79°10E **245** G4
Rajang → *Malaysia* 2°30N 112°0E **235** B4
Rajanpur *Pakistan* 29°6N 70°19E **242** E4
Rajapalaiyam *India* 9°25N 77°35E **245** K3
Rajapur *India* 16°40N 73°31E **244** F1
Rajasthan □ *India* 26°45N 73°30E **242** F5
Rajasthan Canal = Indira Gandhi
  Canal *India* 28°0N 72°0E **242** F5
Rajauri *India* 33°25N 74°21E **243** C6
Rajbari *Bangla.* 23°47N 89°41E **241** D2
Rajgarh *Mad. P., India* 24°2N 76°45E **242** G7
Rajgarh *Raj., India* 27°14N 76°38E **242** F7
Rajgarh *Raj., India* 28°40N 75°25E **242** E6
Rajgir *India* 25°2N 85°25E **243** G11
Rajgród *Poland* 53°42N 22°42E **184** E9
Rajkot *India* 22°15N 70°56E **242** H4
Rajmahal Hills *India* 24°30N 87°30E **243** G12
Rajpipla *India* 21°50N 73°30E **244** D1
Rajpura *India* 22°18N 74°21E **242** H6
Rajpura *Delhi, India* 28°41N 77°12E **120** A2
Rajpura *Punjab, India* 30°25N 76°32E **242** D7
Rajputana = Rajasthan □
  India 26°45N 73°30E **242** F5
Rajshahi *Bangla.* 24°22N 88°39E **241** C2
Rajshahi □ *Bangla.* 25°0N 89°0E **241** C2
Rājū *Syria* 36°40N 36°40E **250** B7
Rajula *India* 21°3N 71°26E **242** J4
Rajur *India* 20°7N 78°55E **244** E4
Rajura *India* 19°47N 79°22E **244** E4
Rakaia *N.Z.* 43°45S 172°1E **285** D7
Rakaia → *N.Z.* 43°36S 172°15E **285** D7
Rakan, Ra's *Qatar* 26°10N 51°20E **247** E6
Rakaposhi *Pakistan* 36°10N 74°25E **243** A6
Rakata, Pulau *Indonesia* 6°10S 105°20E **234** D3
Rakhiv *Ukraine* 48°3N 24°12E **183** B9
Rakhni *Pakistan* 30°4N 69°56E **242** D3
Rakhni → *Pakistan* 29°31N 69°36E **242** E3
Rakhyūt *Oman* 16°44N 53°20E **249** D5
Rakitnoye *Russia* 45°36N 134°17E **220** B7
Rakitovo *Bulgaria* 41°59N 24°5E **203** E8
Rakkestad *Norway* 59°25N 11°21E **164** E8
Rakoniewice *Poland* 52°10N 16°16E **185** F3
Rakops *Botswana* 21°1S 24°28E **270** B3
Rákos-patak → *Hungary* 47°29N 19°12E **117** B3
Rákoshegy *Hungary* 47°27N 19°14E **117** B3
Rákoskeresztúr *Hungary* 47°29N 19°11E **117** B3
Rákoskert *Hungary* 47°29N 19°16E **117** B3
Rákosliget *Hungary* 47°29N 19°17E **117** B3
Rákospalota *Hungary* 47°34N 19°9E **117** B3
Rákosszentmihály
  Hungary 47°31N 19°8E **117** A2
Rakovica *Croatia* 44°59N 15°38E **199** D12
Rakovník *Czech Rep.* 50°6N 13°42E **180** A6
Rakovski *Bulgaria* 42°21N 24°57E **203** D8
Rakshan → *Pakistan* 27°10N 63°25E **240** D1
Rakvere *Estonia* 59°20N 26°25E **188** C4
Raleigh *Fla., U.S.A.* 29°25N 82°32W **317** F7
Raleigh *N.C., U.S.A.* 35°47N 78°39W **315** D15
Rali Salem *Algeria* 21°3N 1°9E **261** D5
Ralik Chain *Pac. Oc.* 8°0N 168°0E **288** G8
Ralja *Serbia* 44°33N 20°34E **202** B4
Ralls *U.S.A.* 33°41N 101°24W **314** E4
Ralston *U.S.A.* 41°30N 76°57W **312** E8
Ram → *Canada* 31°5N 35°14E **123** A2
Ram West Bank 31°5N 35°14E **123** A2
Ram → *Canada* 62°1N 123°41W **296** A4
Rām Allāh *West Bank* 31°55N 35°10E **123** A2
Rama *Nic.* 12°9N 84°15W **320** D3
Ramacca *Italy* 37°23N 14°42E **201** E7
Ramachandrapuram
  India 16°50N 82°4E **244** F6
Ramadān *Iraq* 33°19N 44°0E **256** C5
Ramagiri Udayagiri *India* 19°5N 84°18E **244** E7
Ramakona *India* 21°43N 78°50E **243** J8
Ramakrishna Puram
  India 28°32N 77°12E **120** B1
Ramales de la Victoria
  Spain 43°3N 3°28W **194** B7
Ramalho, Serra do *Brazil* 13°45S 44°0W **333** D3
Rāmallāh = Rām Allāh
  West Bank 31°55N 35°10E **123** A2
Raman *Thailand* 6°29N 101°18E **237** J3
Ramanathapuram *India* 9°25N 78°55E **245** K4
Ramanetaka, B. de *Madag.* 14°13S 47°52E **272** A2
Ramanuj Ganj *India* 23°48N 83°42E **243** H10
Ramas C. *India* 15°5N 73°55E **245** G1
Ramat Allon *West Bank* 31°55N 35°16E **123** B2
Ramat Eshkol *West Bank* 31°47N 35°14E **123** B2
Ramat Gan *Israel* 32°4N 34°48E **251** F5
Ramat Razi'el *Israel* 31°46N 35°4E **123** B1
Ramat Shafet *West Bank* 31°46N 35°12E **123** B2
Ramatlhabama *S. Africa* 25°37S 25°33E **270** D4
Ramban *India* 33°14N 75°12E **243** C6
Rambervilliers *France* 48°20N 6°38E **173** D7
Rambi = Rabi *Fiji* 16°30S 179°59W **287** A3
Rambipuji *Indonesia* 8°12S 113°37E **235** D4
Rambla, La *Spain* 37°36N 4°45W **195** D6
Rambla, La *Barcelona, Spain* **114** b2
Rambler Channel *China* 22°21N 114°6E **122** A1

Rambouillet *France* 48°39N 1°50E **173** D8
Rambrai *India* 25°40N 91°19E **241** C3
Rambutyo I. *Papua N. G.* 2°18S 147°49E **286** B4
Ramdurg *India* 15°58N 75°22E **245** G2
Rame Hd. *Australia* 37°47S 149°30E **283** D8
Ramenki *Russia* 55°41N 37°28E **129** B2
Ramenskoye *Russia* 55°32N 38°15E **188** E10
Ramer *U.S.A.* 32°3N 86°13W **316** C3
Ramersdorf *Germany* 48°6N 11°35E **131** B2
Rameses Station *Egypt* 30°3N 31°15E **117** A2
Rameswaram *India* 9°17N 79°18E **245** K4
Ramganga → *India* 27°5N 79°58E **243** F8
Ramgarh *Bangla.* 22°59N 91°44E **241** D3
Ramgarh *Jharkhand,*
  India 23°40N 85°35E **243** H11
Ramgarh *Raj., India* 27°16N 75°14E **242** F6
Ramgarh *Raj., India* 27°30N 70°36E **242** F4
Ramhormoz *Iran* 31°15N 49°35E **247** D6
Ramīān *Iran* 37°3N 55°16E **247** B7
Ramingining *Australia* 12°19S 135°3E **280** A2
Ramla *Israel* 31°55N 34°52E **251** G5
Ramlat Zalṭan *Libya* 28°30N 19°30E **258** C3
Ramnā *Eritrea* 13°32N 41°40E **257** E5
Ramna → *India* 26°36N 27°3E **183** E12
Ramnad = Ramanathapuram
  India 9°25N 78°55E **245** K4
Ramnagar *Jammu & Kashmir,*
  India 32°47N 75°18E **243** C6
Ramnagar *Uttaranchal,*
  India 29°24N 79°7E **243** E8
Ramnäs *Sweden* 59°46N 16°12E **162** E10
Râmnicu Sărat *Romania* 45°26N 27°3E **183** E12
Râmnicu Vâlcea *Romania* 45°9N 24°21E **183** E9
Ramnous *Greece* 38°12N 24°3E **204** C6
Ramon *Isabela, Phil.* 16°50N 121°31E **232** C3
Ramon *Russia* 51°55N 39°21E **189** G10
Ramona *U.S.A.* 33°2N 116°52W **307** M10
Ramore *Canada* 48°30N 80°25W **298** C3
Ramos *Brazil* 22°50S 43°14W **135** B1
Ramos → *Nigeria* 5°8N 5°22E **263** D6
Ramos Mejía *Argentina* 34°39S 58°33W **117** B1
Ramot *West Bank* 31°48N 35°13E **123** B2
Ramotswa *Botswana* 24°50S 25°52E **270** B4
Rampanalgas *Trin. & Tob.* 10°44N 60°59W **323** t
Rampart *U.S.A.* 65°30N 150°10W **303** D10
Rampur *H.P., India* 31°26N 77°43E **242** D7
Rampur *Mad. P., India* 23°25N 73°53E **242** H5
Rampur *Orissa, India* 21°48N 83°58E **244** D6
Rampur *Ut. P., India* 28°44N 77°18E **120** A2
Rampur *Ut. P., India* 28°50N 79°5E **243** E8
Rampur Hat *India* 24°10N 87°50E **243** G12
Ramrama Tola *India* 21°52N 79°55E **243** J8
Ramree I. *Burma* 19°0N 93°40E **241** F5
Ramsar *Iran* 36°53N 50°41E **247** B6
Ramsey *I. of Man* 54°20N 4°22W **168** C3
Ramsey *Ill., U.S.A.* 39°8N 89°7W **310** E7
Ramsey *N.J., U.S.A.* 41°4N 74°9W **313** E10
Ramsey L. *Canada* 47°13N 82°15W **298** C3
Ramsgate *N.S.W.,*
  Australia 33°58S 151°8E **139** B1
Ramsgate *Kent, U.K.* 51°20N 1°25E **169** F9
Ramshai *India* 26°44N 88°31E **241** C2
Ramsjö *Sweden* 62°11N 15°37E **162** B9
Ramsund *Germany* 49°27N 7°32E **179** F3
Ramtek *India* 21°20N 79°15E **244** D4
Ramu *Kenya* 3°55N 41°10E **268** B5
Ramu → *Papua N. G.* 4°0S 144°41E **286** C3
Ramvik *Sweden* 62°49N 17°51E **162** B11
Ramville, Î. = Chancel, Î.
  Martinique 14°41N 60°53W **322** j
Rana Pratap Sagar Dam
  India 24°58N 75°38E **242** G6
Ranaghat *India* 23°15N 88°35E **243** H13
Ranahu *Pakistan* 25°55N 69°45E **242** G3
Ranau *Malaysia* 6°2N 116°40E **234** A5
Rancagua *Chile* 34°10S 70°50W **334** C1
Rance → *France* 48°34N 1°59E **172** D5
Rancharia *Brazil* 22°15S 50°55W **333** F1
Ranchester *U.S.A.* 44°54N 107°10W **304** D10
Ranchi *India* 23°19N 85°27E **243** H11
Rancho Cordova *U.S.A.* 38°36N 121°18W **306** G5
Rancho Cucamonga
  U.S.A. 34°10N 117°30W **307** L9
Ranco, L. *Chile* 40°15S 72°10W **338** B2
Rand *Australia* 35°33S 146°32E **283** C7
Rand ✕ (QRA) *S. Africa* 26°14S 28°8E **123** B2
Randaberg *Norway* 59°1N 5°36E **164** E2
Randalstown *U.K.* 54°45N 6°19W **166** B5
Randan *France* 46°2N 3°21E **173** F10
Randazzo *Italy* 37°53N 14°57E **201** E7
Randburg *S. Africa* 26°5S 27°57E **123** A1
Rander *India* 21°14N 72°47E **244** D1
Randers *Denmark* 56°29N 10°1E **163** H4
Randers Fjord *Denmark* 56°37N 10°20E **163** H4
Randfontein *S. Africa* 26°8S 27°45E **271** C4
Randhart *S. Africa* 26°16S 28°7E **123** B2
Randle *U.S.A.* 46°32N 121°57W **306** D5
Randolph *Mass., U.S.A.* 42°10N 71°2W **313** D13
Randolph *N.Y., U.S.A.* 42°10N 78°59W **312** D6
Randolph *Utah, U.S.A.* 41°40N 111°11W **304** F8
Randsburg *U.S.A.* 35°22N 117°39W **307** K9
Randsfjorden *Norway* 60°25N 10°24E **164** D7
Randsjö *Norway* 61°44N 9°3E **164** C6
Randwick *Australia* 33°54S 151°14E **139** B2
Råneälven → *Sweden* 65°50N 22°20E **160** D20
Ranelagh *Ireland* 53°20N 6°15W **120** A2
Ranenburg = Chaplygin
  Russia 53°15N 40°0E **188** F11
Ranfurly *N.Z.* 45°7S 170°6E **285** F5
Rangae *Thailand* 6°19N 101°44E **237** J3
Rangamati *Bangla.* 22°38N 92°21E **241** D4
Rangapara *India* 26°49N 92°39E **241** B4
Rangārdhálsysla □
  Iceland 63°55N 20°0W **155** D7
Rangataua *N.Z.* 39°26N 175°15E **284** F4
Rangaunu B. *N.Z.* 34°51S 173°15E **284** A4
Range, The *Zimbabwe* 19°2S 31°2E **269** F3
Rangeley *U.S.A.* 44°58N 70°39W **313** B14
Rangely *U.S.A.* 40°5N 108°48W **304** F9
Ranger *U.S.A.* 32°28N 98°41W **314** E5
Rangia *India* 26°28N 91°38E **241** B3
Rangiora *N.Z.* 43°19S 172°36E **285** D8
Rangiroa *French Polynesia* 15°10S 147°35W **289** f
Rangitaiki → *N.Z.* 37°54S 176°49E **284** E5
Rangitaiki *N.Z.* 38°52S 176°25E **284** F5
Rangitata → *N.Z.* 44°15S 171°15E **285** E6
Rangitikei → *N.Z.* 40°17S 175°15E **284** G4
Rangitoto ki te tonga = D'Urville I.
  N.Z. 40°50S 173°55E **285** A8
Rangitoto Ra. *N.Z.* 38°20S 175°31E **284** F4
Rangkasbitung *Indonesia* 6°21S 106°15E **234** D3
Rangoon *Burma* 16°45N 96°20E **241** G6

Rangoon □ *Burma* 17°0N 96°10E **241** G6
Rangpur *Bangla.* 25°42N 89°22E **241** C2
Rangpuri *India* 28°32N 77°8E **120** B1
Rangsang *Indonesia* 1°20N 103°30E **234** B2
Rangsit *Thailand* 13°59N 100°37E **236** F3
Rangwe *Kenya* 0°36S 34°35E **266** E3
Ranheim *Norway* 63°26N 10°23E **164** A7
Ranibennur *India* 14°35N 75°30E **245** G2
Raniganj *India* 27°3N 82°13E **243** F9
Ranikhet *India* 29°39N 79°25E **243** E8
Ranipettai *India* 12°56N 79°23E **245** H4
Raniwara *India* 24°50N 72°10E **242** G5
Rāniyah *Iraq* 36°15N 44°53E **246** B5
Ranjang Mangroves △
  Malaysia 2°21N 112°12E **235** B4
Ranka *India* 23°59N 83°47E **243** H10
Ranken → *Australia* 20°31S 137°36E **280** C2
Rankin □ *U.S.A.* 40°28N 87°54W **311** D9
Rankin *Tex., U.S.A.* 31°13N 101°56W **314** F4
Rankin Inlet *Canada* 62°30N 93°0W **294** C10
Rankins Springs
  Australia 33°49S 146°14E **283** B7
Rankovicevo = Kraljevo
  Serbia 43°44N 20°41E **202** C4
Rankweil *Austria* 47°17N 9°39E **180** D2
Rannersdorf *Austria* 48°7N 16°27E **142** B2
Rannoch, L. *U.K.* 56°41N 4°20W **167** E4
Rannoch Moor *U.K.* 56°38N 4°48W **167** E4
Rano Kau *Chile* 27°11S 109°26W **330** b
Rano Raraku, Volcán
  Chile 27°7S 109°17W **330** b
Ranobe, Helodranon' i
  Madag. 23°3S 43°33E **272** C1
Ranohira *Madag.* 22°29S 45°24E **272** C2
Ranomafana *Toamasina,*
  Madag. 18°57S 48°50E **272** B2
Ranomafana △ *Madag.* 24°34S 47°0E **272** C2
Ranomafana *Madag.* 21°16S 47°25E **272** C2
Ranon *Vanuatu* 16°8S 168°7E **287** F6
Ranong *Thailand* 9°56N 98°40E **237** H2
Ranongga Solomon Is. 8°5S 156°35E **287** M9
Ranotsara Nord *Madag.* 22°48S 46°36E **272** C2
Ranpur *India* 20°5N 85°20E **244** D7
Rānsa *Iran* 33°39N 48°18E **247** C6
Ransbèche *Belgium* 50°56N 4°27E **116** D4
Ransdorp *Neths.* 52°24N 5°0E **116** A2
Ranski *Indonesia* 1°30S 134°10E **231** E8
Ransom → *Australia* 41°9N 88°39W **311** C8
Rantabe *Madag.* 15°42S 49°39E **272** B2
Rantau *Indonesia* 2°56S 115°9E **235** C5
Rantauprapat *Indonesia* 2°15N 99°50E **234** B1
Rantemario *Indonesia* 3°15S 119°57E **231** E5
Ranthambore △ *India* 26°10N 76°30E **242** F7
Rantoul *U.S.A.* 40°19N 88°9W **311** D8
Ranum *Denmark* 56°54N 9°14E **163** H3
Ranvad *India* 18°53N 72°58E **130** B2
Raŋah, W. = Si. Arabia 21°18N 43°20E **248** B3
Raon l'Étape *France* 48°24N 6°50E **173** D3
Raoping *China* 23°42N 117°1E **229** F11
Raoui, Erg er *Algeria* 29°0N 2°0W **261** C4
Raoul I. *Pac. Oc.* 29°16S 177°54W **277** F15
Raoyang *China* 38°15N 115°45E **226** E8
Rap, Ko *Thailand* 9°19N 99°58E **237** b
Rapa *French Polynesia* 27°35S 144°20W **289** f
Rapa Nui = Pascua, I. de
  Chile 27°7S 109°23W **330** b
Rapallo *Italy* 44°21N 9°14E **198** D6
Rapar *India* 23°34N 70°38E **242** H4
Rāpch *Iran* 25°40N 59°15E **247** E8
Raper, C. *Canada* 69°44N 67°6W **295** C13
Rapid City *U.S.A.* 44°5N 103°14W **308** C2
Rapid River *U.S.A.* 45°55N 86°58W **308** C10
Rapla *Estonia* 59°1N 24°52E **188** C3
Raposo *Portugal* 38°40N 9°11W **126** A1
Rapti → *India* 26°18N 83°41E **243** F10
Rapu Rapu I. *Phil.* 13°12N 124°9E **232** E5
Raqaba ez Zarqa → *Sudan* 9°14N 29°44E **257** F2
Rāqūbah *Libya* 28°58N 19°2E **258** C3
Raquette → *U.S.A.* 45°0N 74°42W **313** B10
Raquette Lake *U.S.A.* 43°49N 74°40W **313** C10
Rara → *Nepal* 29°30N 82°10E **243** E10
Raraka *French Polynesia* 16°10S 144°54W **289** f
Raroia *French Polynesia* 16°1S 142°27W **289** f
Rarotonga *Cook Is.* 21°30S 160°0W **289** h
Ra's al 'Ayn *Syria* 36°45N 40°12E **213** D9
Ra's al Hadd *Oman* 22°39N 59°52E **249** C6
Ra's al Khaymah *U.A.E.* 25°50N 55°59E **247** E7
Ra's an Naqb *Jordan* 30°0N 35°29E **251** F4
Râs Ghârib *Egypt* 28°6N 33°18E **256** C3
Râs Mallap *Egypt* 29°18N 32°50E **256** C3
Râs Muhammad △
  Egypt 27°45N 34°16E **256** B3
Ra's Shamrah *Syria* 35°35N 35°45E **250** B6
Ras'a, Punta *Argentina* 40°50S 62°15W **336** B4
Rasca, Pta. de la
  Canary Is. 27°59N 16°41W **153** e1
Rāşcani *Moldova* 47°58N 27°33E **183** C12
Rasdhoo *Maldives* 4°17N 72°58E **272** d
Rasdu Atoll *Maldives* 4°18N 72°58E **272** d
Raseiniai *Lithuania* 55°25N 23°5E **184** C10
Rashad *Sudan* 11°55N 31°0E **257** E3
Rashid *Egypt* 31°21N 30°22E **256** H7
Rashid, Masabb *Egypt* 31°22N 30°0E **256** H7
Rashm *Iran* 35°21N 52°55E **247** C7
Rashmi *India* 25°4N 74°22E **242** G6
Rasht *Iran* 37°20N 49°40E **213** D13
Rashtrapati Bhawan *Delhi, India* **120** c1
Rasi Salai *Thailand* 15°20N 104°9E **236** E5
Rasipuram *India* 11°30N 78°15E **245** J4
Raska *Serbia* 43°19N 20°39E **202** C4
Râsnov *Romania* 45°35N 25°27E **183** E10
Rason L. *Australia* 28°45S 124°25E **279** E3
Rasova *Bulgaria* 44°24N 27°4E **183** E10
Rasra *India* 25°50N 83°50E **243** G10
Rass el Oued *Algeria* 35°57N 5°2E **261** A6
Rasskazovka *Russia* 55°38N 37°20E **129** C2
Rasskazovo *Russia* 52°35N 41°50E **190** D5
Rastatt *Germany* 48°50N 8°12E **179** G4
Rastede *Germany* 53°15N 8°12E **178** B4
Rastān *Syria* 34°52N 36°50E **250** C6
Raszyn *Poland* 52°9N 20°54E **142** C1
Rat → *U.S.A.* 48°35N 97°46E **299** D9
Rat Buri *Thailand* 13°30N 99°54E **236** F2
Rat I. *St. Lucia* 14°1N 60°57W **323** u
Rat I. *Alaska, U.S.A.* 51°48N 178°15E **303** L1
Rat Islands *U.S.A.* 52°0N 178°0E **303** L2
Rat L. *Canada* 56°10N 99°40W **297** B9
Ratak Chain *Pac. Oc.* 1°0N 170°0E **288** G8

Rätan *Sweden* 62°29N 14°33E **162** B8
Ratangarh *India* 28°5N 74°35E **242** E6
Razim, Lacul *Romania* 44°50N 29°0E **183** F14
Razlog *Bulgaria* 41°53N 23°28E **202** E7
Razmak *Pakistan* 32°45N 69°50E **242** C3
Ré, Î. de *France* 46°12N 1°30W **174** B2
Reach Falls *Jamaica* 18°2N 76°18W **320** a
Reading *Reading, U.K.* 51°27N 0°58W **169** F7
Reading *Mich., U.S.A.* 41°50N 84°45W **311** C12
Reading *Ohio, U.S.A.* 39°13N 84°26W **311** E12
Reading *Pa., U.S.A.* 40°20N 75°56W **313** F9
Reading □ *U.K.* 51°27N 0°58W **169** F7
Real, Cordillera *Bolivia* 17°0S 67°10W **330** D4
Real Felipe, Fuerte *Peru* 12°4S 77°9W **124** B2
Realejo Alto *Canary Is.* 28°22N 16°34W **153** e1
Realicó *Argentina* 35°0S 64°15W **334** D3
Réalmont *France* 43°48N 2°10E **174** E6
Ream *Cambodia* 10°34N 103°39E **237** G4
Reams, L. *U.S.A.* 28°26N 81°34W **133** B1
Réao *French Polynesia* 18°31S 136°23W **289** f
Reay Forest *U.K.* 58°22N 4°55W **167** C4
Rebais *France* 48°50N 3°10E **173** D10
Rebi *Indonesia* 6°57N 7°18E **244** F11
Rebiana *Libya* 24°12N 22°10E **258** D3
Rebiana, Sahrâ' *Libya* 24°30N 21°0E **258** D3
Reboly *Russia* 63°49N 30°47E **160** E24
Rebun-Tō *Japan* 45°23N 141°2E **220** B10
Recanati *Italy* 43°24N 13°32E **199** E10
Recaş *Romania* 45°46N 21°30E **182** E6
Recco *Italy* 44°22N 9°9E **198** D6
Recherche, Arch. of the
  Australia 34°15S 122°50E **279** F3
Rechna Doab *Pakistan* 31°35N 73°30E **242** D5
Rechytsa *Belarus* 52°21N 30°24E **177** B16
Recife *Brazil* 8°0S 35°0W **332** D5
Recife *Seychelles* 4°36S 55°42E **272** c
Recklinghausen *Germany* 51°37N 7°12E **170** C7
Recoleta B. Aires,
  Argentina 34°36S 58°24W **117** B2
Recoleta *Santiago, Chile* 33°25S 70°40W **137** B2
Reconquista *Argentina* 29°10S 59°45W **334** B4
Recreio *Brazil* 8°0S 58°25W **331** B6
Recta Argentina 29°25S 65°10W **334** B2
Recuay *Peru* 9°43S 77°29W **330** B2
Raukumara Ra. *N.Z.* 38°5S 177°55E **284** E6
Raul Soares *Brazil* 20°5S 42°22W **333** F3
Rauma *Finland* 61°10N 21°30E **188** B1
Rauma → *Norway* 62°34N 7°43E **164** B4
Raumo = Rauma *Finland* 61°10N 21°30E **188** B1
Raung, Gunung *Indonesia* 8°8S 114°3E **231** J17
Raurkela *India* 22°14N 84°50E **243** H11
Rausu-Dake *Japan* 44°4N 145°7E **220** B12
Rāut → *Moldova* 47°15N 29°9E **183** C14
Rava-Ruska *Ukraine* 50°15N 23°42E **185** H10
Rava Russkaya = Rava-Ruska
  Ukraine 50°15N 23°42E **185** H10
Ravahere *French Polynesia* 18°14S 142°9W **289** f
Ravalli *U.S.A.* 47°17N 114°11W **304** C6
Ravānsar *Iran* 34°43N 46°40E **213** E12
Rāvar *Iran* 31°20N 56°51E **247** D8
Ravelston *U.K.* 55°57N 3°14W **121** B2
Ravena *U.S.A.* 42°28N 73°49W **313** D11
Ravenel *U.S.A.* 32°46N 80°15W **316** D9
Ravenna *Italy* 44°25N 12°12E **199** D9
Ravenna *Ky., U.S.A.* 37°41N 83°57W **311** G13
Ravenna *Nebr., U.S.A.* 41°1N 98°55W **308** E4
Ravenna *Ohio, U.S.A.* 41°9N 81°15W **312** E3
Ravensburg *Germany* 47°46N 9°36E **179** H5
Ravenshoe *Australia* 17°37S 145°29E **280** B4
Ravensthorpe *Australia* 33°35S 120°2E **279** F3
Ravenswood *Queens.,*
  Australia 20°6S 146°54E **280** C4
Ravenswood *W. Va.,*
  U.S.A. 38°57N 81°46W **309** F13
Ravensworth *Australia* 32°26S 151°4E **283** B9
Ravenwood *U.S.A.* 40°22N 94°41W **310** D2
Raver *India* 21°15N 76°2E **244** D3
Ravi → *Pakistan* 30°35N 71°49E **242** D4
Ravine Chaude
  Guadeloupe 16°14N 61°40W **322** a
Ravna Gora *Croatia* 45°24N 14°50E **199** C11
Ravna Reka *Serbia* 44°1N 21°35E **202** B5
Ravne na Koroškem
  Slovenia 46°36N 14°59E **199** B11
Rawa Mazowiecka
  Poland 51°46N 20°12E **185** G7
Rawaki *Kiribati* 3°43S 170°43W **277** A16
Rawalpindi *Pakistan* 33°38N 73°8E **242** C5
Rawamangun *Indonesia* 6°11S 106°52E **122** B2
Rawang *Malaysia* 3°20N 101°35E **237** L3
Rawene *N.Z.* 35°25S 173°32E **284** B4
Rawicz *Poland* 51°36N 16°52E **185** G3
Rawitsch = Rawicz
  Poland 51°36N 16°52E **185** G3
Rawka → *Poland* 52°9N 20°8E **185** F7
Rawlinna *Australia* 30°58S 125°28E **279** F4
Rawlins *U.S.A.* 41°47N 107°14W **304** F10
Rawlinson Ra. *Australia* 24°40S 128°30E **279** D4
Rawson *Argentina* 43°15S 65°5W **336** B3
Raxaul *India* 26°59N 84°51E **243** F11
Ray, C. *Canada* 47°33N 59°15W **299** C8
Ray, C. *U.S.A.* 47°33N 59°15W **299** C8
Ray City *U.S.A.* 31°4N 83°12W **317** E7
Ray Mts. *U.S.A.* 66°0N 152°0W **303** D9
Raya Ring, Ko *Thailand* 8°18N 98°29E **237** a
Rayachoti *India* 14°4N 78°50E **245** G4
Rayadurg *India* 14°40N 76°50E **245** G3
Rayagada *India* 19°15N 83°20E **244** E6
Raychikhinsk *Russia* 49°46N 129°25E **215** E13
Rāyen *Iran* 29°34N 57°26E **247** D8
Rayle *U.S.A.* 33°48N 82°54W **316** B7
Rayleigh *U.K.* 51°36N 0°37E **169** F8
Raymond *Alta., Canada* 49°30N 112°35W **296** D6
Raymond *Calif., U.S.A.* 37°13N 119°54W **306** H7
Raymond *Ill., U.S.A.* 39°19N 89°34W **310** F7
Raymond *N.H., U.S.A.* 43°2N 71°11W **313** C13
Raymond *Wash., U.S.A.* 46°41N 123°44W **306** D3
Raymond Terrace
  Australia 32°45S 151°44E **283** B9
Raymondville *U.S.A.* 26°29N 97°47W **314** H6
Raymore *Canada* 51°25N 104°31W **297** C8
Rayners Lane *U.K.* 51°34N 0°23W **125** A2
Rayón *Mexico* 29°43N 110°35W **318** B2
Rayong *Thailand* 12°40N 101°20E **236** F3
Raypur *India* 22°28N 82°22E **244** D6
Raytown *U.S.A.* 39°1N 94°28W **314** A7
Rayville *U.S.A.* 32°29N 91°46W **314** E9
Raz, Pte. du *France* 48°2N 4°47W **172** D2
Razan *Iran* 35°23N 49°2E **213** E13
Razan *Serbia* 43°40N 21°31E **202** C5
Razāni *Serbia* 43°40N 21°31E **202** C5
Razāzah, Buḩayrat ar
  Iraq 32°40N 43°35E **213** F10
Razazah, L. = Razāzah, Buḩayrat ar
  Iraq 32°40N 43°35E **213** F10
Razdel'naya = Rozdilna
  Ukraine 46°50N 30°2E **183** C16
Razdolnoye *Russia* 43°30N 131°52E **220** C5
Razdolnoye *Ukraine* 45°46N 33°29E **189** K7
Razdory *Russia* 55°44N 37°17E **129** B1

Razeh *Iran* 32°47N 48°9E **247** C6
Razgrad *Bulgaria* 43°33N 26°34E **203** C10
Razim, Lacul *Romania* 44°50N 29°0E **183** F14
Razlog *Bulgaria* 41°53N 23°28E **202** E7
Razmak *Pakistan* 32°45N 69°50E **242** C3
Ratcatchers L. *Australia* 32°30S 143°12E **282** A5
Ratcha Thewi *Bangkok, Thailand* **113** b3
Rath *India* 25°36N 79°37E **243** G8
Rath Luirc *Ireland* 52°21N 8°40W **166** D3
Rathangan *Ireland* 53°13N 7°1W **166** C4
Rathdrum *Ireland* 52°56N 6°14W **166** D5
Rathdrum *U.S.A.* 47°49N 116°54W **304** C5
Rathenow *Germany* 52°37N 12°19E **178** C8
Rathkeale *Ireland* 52°32N 8°56W **166** D3
Rathlin I. *U.K.* 55°18N 6°14W **166** A5
Rathmelton *Ireland* 55°2N 7°38W **166** A4
Rathmolton *Ireland* 55°2N 7°38W **166** A4
Ratho Station *U.K.* 55°55N 3°23W **121** B1
Ratho *U.K.* 55°55N 3°24W **121** B1
Ratibor = Racibórz *Poland* 50°7N 18°18E **185** H5
Rätikon *Austria* 47°0N 9°55E **180** D2
Ratingen *Germany* 51°18N 6°52E **178** D2
Ratlam *India* 23°20N 75°0E **242** H6
Ratnagiri *India* 16°57N 73°18E **244** F1
Ratnapura *Sri Lanka* 6°40N 80°20E **245** L5
Rato *Portugal* 38°43N 9°9W **126** A2
Ratodero *Pakistan* 27°48N 68°18E **242** F3
Raton *U.S.A.* 36°54N 104°24W **305** H11
Rattaphum *Thailand* 7°8N 100°16E **237** J3
Ratten *Austria* 47°28N 15°44E **180** D8
Rattray Hd. *U.K.* 57°38N 1°50W **167** D7
Rättvik *Sweden* 60°52N 15°7E **162** B9
Ratz, Mt. *Canada* 57°23N 132°12W **296** B2
Ratzeburg = Okonek
  Poland 53°32N 16°51E **184** E3
Ratzeburg *Germany* 53°40N 10°46E **178** B6
Raub *Malaysia* 3°47N 101°52E **237** L3
Rauch *Argentina* 36°45S 59°5W **334** D4
Raudeberg *Norway* 61°59N 5°7E **164** C2
Raufarhöfn *Iceland* 66°27N 15°57W **155** A11
Raufoss *Norway* 60°44N 10°37E **164** D7
Rauhellern *Norway* 60°15N 7°50E **164** D4

Reflecting Pool *Washington, D.C., U.S.A.* **143** b1

Refshaleøen Denmark 55°41N 12°36E 118 A3
Reftele Sweden 57°11N 13°35E 163 G7
Refugio U.S.A. 28°18N 97°17W 314 G6
Rega → Poland 54°10N 15°18E 184 D2
Regalbuto Italy 37°39N 14°38E 201 E7
Regen Germany 48°58N 13°8E 179 G9
Regen → Germany 49°1N 12°6E 179 F8
Regeneração Brazil 6°15S 42°41W 332 C3
Regensburg Germany 49°1N 12°6E 179 F8
Regenstauf Germany 49°7N 12°8E 179 F8
Regents Park Gauteng, S. Africa 26°14S 28°3E 123 B2
Regent's Park London, U.K. 125 a2
Regenwalde = Resko Poland 53°47N 15°25E 184 E2
Reggâne = Zaouiet Reggâne Algeria 26°32N 0°3E 261 C5
Reggello Italy 43°41N 11°32E 199 E8
Réggio di Calábria Italy 38°6N 15°39E 201 D8
Réggio nell'Emília Italy 44°43N 10°36E 198 D7
Reghin Romania 46°46N 24°42E 183 D9
Regina Sask., Canada 50°27N 104°35W 297 C8
Régina Fr. Guiana 4°19N 52°8W 329 C7
Regina Beach Canada 50°47N 105°0W 297 C8
Register U.S.A. 32°22N 81°53W 316 C8
Registro Brazil 24°29S 47°49W 335 A6
Rego Park U.S.A. 40°43N 73°51W 132 B2
Reguengos de Monsaraz Portugal 38°25N 7°32W 195 G3
Reh, Erg er Algeria 27°48N 4°30E 261 C5
Rehar → India 23°55N 82°40E 243 H10
Rehli India 23°38N 79°5E 243 H8
Rehoboth Namibia 23°15S 17°4E 270 B2
Rehovot Israel 31°54N 34°48E 251 G5
Reïbell = Ksar Chellala Algeria 35°13N 2°19E 261 A5
Reichenau = Rychnov nad Kněžnou Czech Rep. 50°10N 16°17E 181 A9
Reichenbach = Dzierżoniów Poland 50°45N 16°39E 185 H3
Reichenbach Germany 50°37N 12°17E 178 E8
Reichenberg = Liberec Czech Rep. 50°47N 15°7E 180 A8
Reichshof = Rzeszów Poland 50°5N 21°58E 185 H8
Reichstag Berlin, Germany 115 a3
Reid Australia 30°49S 128°26E 279 F4
Reidsville Ga., U.S.A. 32°6N 82°7W 316 C7
Reidsville N.C., U.S.A. 36°21N 79°40W 315 C15
Reifnig = Ribnica Slovenia 45°45N 14°45E 199 C11
Reigate U.K. 51°14N 0°12W 169 F7
Reillo Spain 39°54N 1°53W 196 F3
Reims France 49°15N 4°1E 173 C11
Reina Adelaida, Arch. Chile 52°20S 74°0W 336 D2
Reina Beatrix Int. ✕ (AUA) Aruba 12°30N 70°1W 322 f
Reina Sofía, Centro de Arte Madrid, Spain 127 c3
Reina Sofía, Tenerife ✕ (TFS) Canary Is. 28°3N 16°33W 153 e1
Reinbeck U.S.A. 42°19N 92°36W 310 B4
Reinbek Germany 53°30N 10°16E 178 B6
Reindeer → Canada 55°36N 103°11W 297 B8
Reindeer I. Canada 52°30N 98°0W 297 C9
Reindeer L. Canada 57°15N 102°15W 297 B8
Reinga, C. N.Z. 34°25S 172°43E 284 A1
Reinickendorf Germany 52°34N 13°22E 115 A3
Reinosa Spain 43°2N 4°15W 194 B6
Reinsvoll Norway 60°40N 10°38E 164 D7
Reitan Norway 62°49N 11°22E 164 B8
Reitz S. Africa 27°48S 28°29E 271 C4
Reivilo S. Africa 27°36S 24°8E 270 C3
Rejaf Sudan 4°45N 31°35E 257 G3
Rejmyre Sweden 58°50N 15°55E 163 F9
Rejowiec Fabryczny Poland 51°5N 23°17E 185 G10
Reka → Slovenia 45°40N 14°0E 199 C11
Rekohua = Chatham I. N.Z. 43°50S 176°20W 285 a
Rekola Finland 60°19N 25°4E 121 B3
Rekovac Serbia 43°51N 21°3E 202 C5
Reliance Canada 63°0N 109°20W 297 A7
Relizane Algeria 35°44N 0°31E 261 A5
Relizane ☐ Algeria 35°45N 0°55E 261 A5
Remad, Oued → Algeria 33°28N 1°20W 261 B4
Rémalard France 48°26N 0°47E 172 D7
Remarkable, Mt. Australia 32°48S 138°10E 282 B3
Remarkables, The N.Z. 45°10S 168°50E 285 F3
Rembang Indonesia 6°42S 111°21E 235 D4
Rembau Malaysia 2°35N 102°6E 234 B2
Rembert U.S.A. 34°6N 80°32W 316 A9
Rembertów Poland 52°15N 21°9E 142 B2
Rembrandthuis Amsterdam, Neths. 112 b2
Rembrandtpark Neths. 52°22N 4°51E 112 A2
Rembrandtsplein Amsterdam, Neths. 112 b2
Remchi Algeria 35°2N 1°26W 261 A4
Remedios Colombia 7°2N 74°41W 328 B3
Remedios Panama 8°15N 81°50W 320 E3
Remedios, Parque Nacional de los △ Mexico 19°28N 99°17W 128 B1
Remedios de Escalada Argentina 34°43S 58°24W 117 C2
Remeshk Iran 26°55N 58°50E 247 E8
Remetea Romania 46°45N 25°29E 183 D10
Remich Lux. 49°32N 6°22E 170 E6
Remington U.S.A. 40°46N 87°9W 311 D9
Rémire Fr. Guiana 4°53N 52°17W 329 C7
Remiremont France 48°2N 6°36E 173 D13
Remo Ethiopia 6°48N 41°20E 257 F5
Rémola, Estany del Spain 41°16N 2°4E 114 B1
Remontnoye Russia 46°34N 43°37E 191 G6
Remoulins France 43°55N 4°35E 175 E8
Rempart → Mauritius 20°19S 57°22E 272 e
Remparts → Réunion 21°22S 55°37E 272 f
Remscheid Germany 51°11N 7°12E 170 C7
Ren Xian China 37°8N 114°40E 226 F8
Rena Norway 61°8N 11°20E 164 C8
Rena → Norway 61°8N 11°23E 164 C8
Renascença Brazil 3°50S 66°21W 328 D4
Renca Chile 33°24S 70°42W 137 B1
Rend Lake U.S.A. 38°2N 88°58W 310 F8
Rendang Indonesia 8°26S 115°25E 231 J18
Rende Italy 39°20N 16°11E 201 C9
Rendezvous Barbados 13°4N 59°35W 323 r
Rendina Greece 39°4N 21°58E 204 B3
Rendova Solomon Is. 8°33S 157°17E 287 M10
Rendsburg Germany 54°17N 9°39E 178 A5
Renfrew Canada 45°30N 76°40W 313 A8
Renfrewshire ☐ U.K. 55°49N 4°38W 167 F4
Renfroe U.S.A. 32°14N 84°43W 316 C5
Rengat Indonesia 0°30S 102°45E 234 C2
Rengo Chile 34°24S 70°50W 334 C1
Renhua China 25°5N 113°40E 229 E9
Renhuai China 27°48N 106°24E 228 D6
Reni Ukraine 45°28N 28°15E 183 E13
Renigunta India 13°38N 79°30E 245 H4
Renk Sudan 11°50N 32°50E 257 E3
Renland Greenland 71°10N 26°30W 154 C8
Renmark Australia 34°11S 140°43E 282 C4
Rennebu Norway 62°52N 9°49E 164 B6
Rennell Solomon Is. 11°40S 160°10E 287 N11
Rennell Sd. Canada 53°23N 132°35W 296 C2
Rennemoulin France 48°50N 2°2E 134 A1
Renner Springs Australia 18°20S 133°47E 280 B1
Rennes France 48°7N 1°41W 172 D5
Rennick Glacier Antarctica 70°30S 161°45E 151 D21
Rennie L. Canada 61°32N 105°35W 297 A7
Reno U.S.A. 39°31N 119°48W 306 F7
Reno → Italy 44°38N 12°16E 199 D9
Renovo U.S.A. 41°20N 77°45W 312 E7
Renqiu China 38°43N 116°5E 226 E9
Rens Denmark 54°54N 9°5E 163 K3
Renshou China 30°3N 104°9E 228 C5
Rensselaer Ind., U.S.A. 40°57N 87°9W 311 D9
Rensselaer N.Y., U.S.A. 42°38N 73°45W 313 D11
Rentería Spain 43°19N 1°54W 196 B3
Renton U.S.A. 47°28N 122°12W 306 C4
Renwick N.Z. 41°30S 173°51E 285 B8
Réo Burkina Faso 12°28N 2°35W 262 C4
Reocín Spain 43°21N 4°5W 194 B6
Reotipur India 25°33N 83°45E 243 G10
Repalle India 16°2N 80°45E 245 F5
Répcelak Hungary 47°24N 17°1E 182 C2
Řeporyje Czech Rep. 50°1N 14°18E 135 B1
Reppen = Rzepin Poland 52°20N 14°49E 185 F1
Republic Mo., U.S.A. 37°7N 93°29W 308 G7
Republic Wash., U.S.A. 48°39N 118°44W 304 B4
Republican → U.S.A. 39°4N 96°48W 308 F5
Republiek Suriname 5°30N 55°13W 329 B6
République, Place de la Paris, France 134 b5
Repulse B. Australia 20°35S 148°46E 280 J6
Repulse Bay Nunavut, Canada 66°30N 86°30W 295 C11
Repulse Bay Hong Kong, China 22°13N 114°10E 122 B2
Repy Czech Rep. 50°4N 14°17E 135 B1
Requena Peru 5°5S 73°52W 330 B3
Requena Spain 39°30N 1°4W 197 F3
Requin Bay Grenada 12°2N 61°39W 323 q
Réquista France 44°1N 2°32E 174 D6
Reşadiye = Datça Turkey 36°46N 27°40E 205 E9
Reşadiye Turkey 40°23N 37°20E 212 B7
Reşadiye Yarımadası Turkey 36°40N 27°45E 205 E9
Resavica Serbia 44°4N 21°31E 202 B5
Resen Macedonia 41°5N 21°0E 202 E5
Reserve U.S.A. 33°43N 108°45W 305 K9
Resht = Rasht Iran 37°20N 49°40E 213 D13
Residenz Germany 48°8N 11°34E 131 B2
Residenzmuseum Munich, Germany 131 b3
Resistencia Argentina 27°30S 59°0W 334 B4
Reşiţa Romania 45°18N 21°53E 182 E6
Resko Poland 53°47N 15°25E 184 E2
Reso = Raisio Finland 60°28N 22°11E 188 B2
Resolute Canada 74°42N 94°54W 295 B10
Resolution I. Nunavut, Canada 61°30N 65°0W 295 C13
Resolution I. N.Z. 45°40S 166°40E 285 F1
Resplandes Brazil 6°17S 45°13W 332 C2
Resplendor Brazil 19°20S 41°15W 333 E3
Ressano Garcia Mozam. 25°25S 32°0E 271 C5
Restinga de Jurubatiba △ Brazil 22°55S 41°20W 333 F3
Reston Man., Canada 49°33N 101°6W 297 D8
Reston Va., U.S.A. 38°57N 77°20W 143 B2
Resulayn = Ceylânpınar Turkey 36°50N 40°2E 213 D9
Reszel Poland 54°4N 21°10E 184 D8
Retalhuleu Guatemala 14°33N 91°46W 320 D1
Retenue, L. de Dem. Rep. of the Congo 11°0S 27°0E 269 E2
Retezat, Munţii Romania 45°25N 23°0E 182 E8
Retezat △ Romania 45°23N 22°56E 182 E7
Retford U.K. 53°19N 0°56W 168 D7
Rethel France 49°30N 4°20E 173 C11
Rethem Germany 52°47N 9°22E 178 C5
Rethimno Greece 35°18N 24°30E 207 E5
Rethimno ☐ Greece 35°23N 24°28E 207 E5
Reti Pakistan 28°5N 69°48E 242 E3
Retiche, Alpi Switz. 46°30N 10°0E 179 J6
Retiers France 47°55N 1°23W 172 E5
Retiro B. Aires, Argentina 34°35S 58°23W 117 B2
Retiro Madrid, Spain 40°24N 3°40W 127 B1
Retiro, Puerto Argentina 34°36S 58°21W 117 B2
Retortillo Spain 40°48N 6°21W 194 E4
Retournac France 45°12N 4°2E 175 C8
Retreat S. Africa 34°4S 18°28E 118 B1
Rétság Hungary 47°58N 19°10E 182 C4
Réunion ☑ Ind. Oc. 21°0S 56°0E 272 f
Reus Spain 41°10N 1°5E 196 D6
Reuterstadt Stavenhagen Germany 53°42N 12°54E 178 B8
Reutlingen Germany 48°29N 9°12E 179 G5
Reutov Russia 55°45N 37°50E 129 B5
Reutte Austria 47°29N 10°42E 180 D3
Reval = Tallinn Estonia 59°22N 24°48E 188 C3
Revda Russia 56°48N 59°57E 186 C10
Réveillon → France 48°42N 2°32E 134 B4
Revel = Tallinn Estonia 59°22N 24°48E 188 C3
Revel France 43°28N 2°1E 174 E6
Revelganj India 25°50N 84°40E 243 G11
Revelstoke Canada 51°0N 118°10W 296 C5
Reventazón Peru 6°10S 80°58W 330 B1
Revere U.S.A. 42°25N 71°0W 116 A2
Revere House Boston, U.S.A. 116 b3
Revigny-sur-Ornain France 48°49N 4°59E 173 D11
Revillagigedo, Is. de Pac. Oc. 18°40N 112°0W 318 D2
Revin France 49°55N 4°39E 173 C11
Revúca Slovak Rep. 48°41N 20°7E 181 C13
Revuè → Mozam. 19°50S 34°0E 269 F3
Rewa India 24°33N 81°25E 243 G9
Rewa → Guyana 3°19N 58°42W 329 C6
Rewari India 28°15N 76°40E 242 E7
Rexburg U.S.A. 43°49N 111°47W 304 E8
Rexford U.S.A. 43°43N 79°35W 141 A1
Rey Iran 35°35N 51°25E 247 C6
Rey, I. del Panama 8°20N 78°30W 320 E4
Rey, L. del Mexico 27°1N 103°26W 318 B4
Rey, Mayo → Cameroon 8°47N 14°1E 264 A2
Rey, Rio-del- → Cameroon 4°31N 8°45E 264 B1
Rey Bouba Cameroon 8°40N 14°15E 264 A2
Rey Malabo Eq. Guin. 3°45N 8°50E 263 E6
Reyðarfjörður Iceland 65°2N 14°13W 155 B12
Reyes Bolivia 14°19S 67°23W 330 C4
Reyes, Pt. U.S.A. 38°0N 123°0W 306 H3
Reyhanlı Turkey 36°16N 36°35E 250 B7
Reykhólar Iceland 65°27N 22°12W 155 B4
Reykholt Árnessýsla, Iceland 64°40N 21°18W 155 C5
Reykholt Borgarfjarðarsýsla, Iceland 64°10N 20°25W 155 C6
Reykjahlíð Iceland 65°40N 16°55W 155 B10
Reykjanes Iceland 63°48N 22°40W 155 D4
Reykjanes Ridge Atl. Oc. 59°0N 31°0W 152 A8
Reykjavík Iceland 64°10N 21°57W 155 C5
Reykjavík Keflavík ✕ (KEF) Iceland 64°0N 22°45W 155 C4
Reynolds Ga., U.S.A. 32°33N 84°6W 316 C5
Reynolds Ill., U.S.A. 41°20N 90°40W 310 C6
Reynolds Ra. Australia 22°30S 133°0E 278 D5
Reynoldsville Ga., U.S.A. 30°51N 84°47W 316 E5
Reynoldsville Pa., U.S.A. 41°6N 78°53W 312 E6
Reynosa Mexico 26°7N 98°18W 319 B5
Reynosa Tamaulipas Mexico 19°30N 99°10W 128 A1
Reza'iyeh = Orūmīyeh Iran 37°40N 45°0E 213 D11
Reza'iyeh, L. = Orūmīyeh, Daryācheh-ye Iran 37°50N 45°30E 213 D11
Rēzekne Latvia 56°30N 27°17E 188 D4
Rezhitsa = Rēzekne Latvia 56°30N 27°17E 188 D4
Rezina Moldova 47°45N 28°58E 183 C13
Rezovo Bulgaria 42°0N 28°0E 203 D12
Rezvān Iran 27°34N 56°6E 247 E8
Rgotina Serbia 44°1N 22°17E 202 B6
Rharbi, Zahrez Algeria 34°50N 2°55E 261 B5
Rharis, O. → Algeria 26°0N 5°4E 261 C6
Rhayader U.K. 52°18N 3°29W 169 E4
Rheda-Wiedenbrück Germany 51°50N 8°20E 178 D4
Rhede Germany 51°50N 6°42E 178 D2
Rhein → Europe 51°52N 6°2E 170 C6
Rhein-Main-Donau-Kanal Germany 49°1N 11°27E 179 F7
Rhein-Ruhr, Düsseldorf ✕ (DUS) Germany 51°17N 6°46E 178 D2
Rhein-Taunus ⌂ Germany 50°10N 8°10E 179 E4
Rhein-Westerwald ⌂ Germany 50°32N 7°20E 178 E3
Rheinbach Germany 50°38N 6°57E 178 E2
Rheine Germany 52°17N 7°26E 178 C3
Rheinfelden Germany 47°33N 7°47E 179 H3
Rheinhessen-Pfalz ☐ Germany 49°20N 8°0E 179 F3
Rheinland-Pfalz ☐ Germany 50°0N 7°0E 179 E2
Rheinsberg Germany 53°6N 12°54E 178 B8
Rheris, Oued → Morocco 30°50N 4°34W 260 B4
Rhin = Rhein → Europe 51°52N 6°2E 170 C6
Rhine = Rhein → Europe 51°52N 6°2E 170 C6
Rhine U.S.A. 31°59N 83°12W 316 D6
Rhinebeck U.S.A. 41°56N 73°55W 313 E11
Rhineland-Palatinate = Rheinland-Pfalz ☐ Germany 50°0N 7°0E 179 E2
Rhinelander U.S.A. 45°38N 89°25W 308 C9
Rhinns Pt. U.K. 55°40N 6°29W 167 F2
Rhino Camp Uganda 3°0N 31°22E 268 B3
Rhîr, Cap Morocco 30°38N 9°54W 260 B3
Rho Italy 45°31N 9°2E 129 A1
Rhode Island ☐ U.S.A. 41°40N 71°30W 313 E13
Rhodes N.S.W., Australia 33°49S 151°6E 139 A1
Rhodes Greece 36°15N 28°10E 206 E12
Rhodes ✕ (RHO) Greece 36°23N 28°12E 205 E10
Rhodesia = Zimbabwe ■ Africa 19°0S 30°0E 269 F3
Rhodon France 48°42N 2°3E 134 B1
Rhodon → France 48°42N 2°4E 134 B1
Rhodope Mts. = Rhodopi Planina Bulgaria 41°40N 24°20E 203 E8
Rhodopi Planina Bulgaria 41°40N 24°20E 203 E8
Rhön Germany 50°24N 9°58E 178 E5
Rhondda U.K. 51°39N 3°31W 169 F4
Rhondda Cynon Taff ☐ U.K. 51°42N 3°27W 169 F4
Rhône ☐ France 45°54N 4°35E 175 C8
Rhône → France 43°28N 4°42E 175 E8
Rhône-Alpes ☐ France 45°40N 6°0E 175 C9
Rhum U.K. 57°0N 6°20W 167 E2
Rhyl U.K. 53°20N 3°29W 168 D4
Ri-Aba Eq. Guin. 3°28N 8°40E 263 E6
Ria Formosa ⌂ Portugal 37°1N 7°48W 195 H3
Riachão Brazil 7°20S 46°37W 332 C2
Riacho de Santana Brazil 13°37S 42°57W 333 D3
Rialma Brazil 15°18S 49°34W 333 E2
Rialto Towers Australia 37°49S 144°57W 128 A1
Riang India 27°31N 92°56E 241 B4
Riangnom Sudan 9°55N 30°1E 257 F3
Riaño Spain 42°59N 4°59W 194 C6
Rians France 43°37N 5°44E 175 E9
Riansáres → Spain 39°32N 3°18W 195 F7
Riasi India 33°10N 74°50E 243 C6
Riau ☐ Indonesia 0°0 102°35E 234 B2
Riau, Kepulauan Indonesia 0°30N 104°20E 234 B2
Riau Arch. = Riau, Kepulauan Indonesia 0°30N 104°20E 234 B2
Riaza Spain 41°18N 3°30W 194 D7
Riaza → Spain 41°42N 3°55W 194 D7
Riba de Saelices Spain 40°55N 2°17W 196 E2
Riba-Roja de Turia Spain 39°33N 0°34W 197 F4
Ribadavia Spain 42°17N 8°8W 194 C2
Ribadeo Spain 43°35N 7°5W 194 B3
Ribadesella Spain 43°30N 5°7W 194 B5
Ribado Nigeria 9°16N 12°47E 263 D7
Ribamar Brazil 2°33S 44°3W 332 B3
Ribao Cameroon 6°32N 11°30E 263 D7
Ribas = Ribes de Freser Spain 42°19N 2°15E 196 C7
Ribas do Rio Pardo Brazil 20°27S 53°46W 331 E7
Ribauè Mozam. 14°57S 38°17E 269 E4
Ribble → U.K. 53°52N 2°25W 168 D5
Ribe Denmark 55°19N 8°44E 163 J2
Ribeauvillé France 48°10N 7°20E 173 D14
Ribécourt-Dreslincourt France 49°30N 2°55E 173 C9
Ribeira = Santa Uxía Spain 42°36N 8°58W 194 C2
Ribeira Brazil 22°49S 43°10W 135 A1
Ribeira Brava Madeira 32°41N 17°4W 153 c
Ribeira do Pombal Brazil 10°50S 38°32W 332 D4
Ribeira Grande Azores 37°49N 25°31W 153 d3
Ribeira Grande C. Verde Is. 17°0N 25°4W 153 j
Ribeirão Brazil 8°31S 35°23W 332 C4
Ribeirão Prêto Brazil 21°10S 47°50W 335 A6
Ribeiro Gonçalves Brazil 7°32S 45°14W 332 C2
Ribemont France 49°47N 3°27E 173 C10
Ribera Italy 37°30N 13°16E 200 E6
Ribérac France 45°15N 0°20E 174 C4
Riberalta Bolivia 11°0S 66°0W 331 C4
Ribes de Freser Spain 42°19N 2°15E 196 C7
Ribnica Slovenia 45°45N 14°45E 199 C11
Ribnitz-Damgarten Germany 54°15N 12°27E 178 A8
Ričany Czech Rep. 50°0N 14°40E 180 B7
Ricarda, Estany de la Spain 41°17N 2°6E 114 B1
Riccarton N.Z. 43°32S 172°37E 285 D7
Riccia Italy 41°30N 14°50E 201 A7
Riccione Italy 43°59N 12°39E 199 E9
Rice U.S.A. 34°5N 114°51W 307 L12
Rice L. Canada 44°12N 78°10W 312 B6
Rice Lake U.S.A. 45°30N 91°44W 308 C8
Riceboro U.S.A. 31°44N 81°26W 316 D8
Rich Morocco 32°16N 4°30W 260 B4
Rich, C. Canada 44°43N 80°38W 312 B4
Richard Toll Senegal 16°25N 15°42W 262 B1
Richards Bay S. Africa 28°48S 32°6E 271 C5
Richardson → Canada 58°25N 111°14W 297 B6
Richardson Lakes U.S.A. 44°46N 70°58W 309 C18
Richardson Mts. N.Z. 44°49S 168°34E 285 E3
Richardson Springs U.S.A. 39°51N 121°46W 306 F5
Riche, C. Australia 34°36S 118°47E 279 F2
Richelieu France 47°1N 0°20E 172 E7
Richey U.S.A. 47°39N 105°4W 304 C11
Richfield U.S.A. 38°46N 112°5W 304 G7
Richfield Springs U.S.A. 42°51N 74°59W 313 D10
Richford U.S.A. 45°0N 72°40W 313 B12
Richibucto Canada 46°42N 64°54W 299 C7
Richland Ga., U.S.A. 32°5N 84°40W 316 C5
Richland Iowa, U.S.A. 41°13N 92°0W 310 C5
Richland Mo., U.S.A. 37°51N 92°26W 310 G4
Richland Wash., U.S.A. 46°17N 119°18W 304 C4
Richland Center U.S.A. 43°21N 90°23W 308 D8
Richlands U.S.A. 37°6N 81°48W 309 G13
Richmond N.S.W., Australia 33°35S 150°42E 283 B9
Richmond Queens., Australia 20°43S 143°8E 280 C3
Richmond Vic., Australia 37°48S 145°0E 128 A2
Richmond Nelson-Marlborough, N.Z. 41°20S 173°12E 285 B8
Richmond N. Yorks., U.K. 54°25N 1°43W 168 C6
Richmond Calif., U.S.A. 37°46N 122°27W 136 B2
Richmond Calif., U.S.A. 37°56N 122°21W 306 H4
Richmond Ind., U.S.A. 39°50N 84°53W 311 E12
Richmond Ky., U.S.A. 37°45N 84°18W 311 G12
Richmond Mich., U.S.A. 42°49N 82°45W 312 D2
Richmond Mo., U.S.A. 39°17N 93°58W 310 E3
Richmond Tex., U.S.A. 29°35N 95°46W 314 G7
Richmond Utah, U.S.A. 41°56N 111°48W 304 F8
Richmond Va., U.S.A. 37°33N 77°27W 309 G15
Richmond Vt., U.S.A. 44°24N 72°59W 313 B12
Richmond, Mt. N.Z. 41°32S 173°22E 285 B8
Richmond Hill Ont., Canada 43°52N 79°27W 312 C5
Richmond Hill Ga., U.S.A. 31°56N 81°18W 316 D8
Richmond Hill N.Y., U.S.A. 40°41N 73°51W 132 B2
Richmond Park U.K. 51°26N 0°16W 125 B2
Richmond Peak St. Vincent 13°17N 61°13W 323 n
Richmond Ra. N.S.W., Australia 29°0S 152°45E 281 D5
Richmond Ra. N.Z. 41°32S 173°22E 285 B8
Richmond-upon-Thames ☐ U.K. 51°27N 0°17W 125 B2
Richtersveld △ S. Africa 28°15S 17°10E 270 C2
Richwood Ohio, U.S.A. 40°26N 83°18W 311 D13
Richwood W. Va., U.S.A. 38°14N 80°32W 309 F13
Ricla Spain 41°31N 1°24W 196 D3
Ricupe Angola 14°37S 21°25E 265 E4
Ridā' Yemen 14°25N 44°50E 248 D4
Riddarholmen Stockholm, Sweden 139 c1
Riddarhuset Stockholm, Sweden 139 c2
Ridder = Leninogorsk Kazakhstan 50°20N 83°30E 217 B10
Riddlesburg U.S.A. 40°9N 78°15W 312 F6
Ridge, The India 28°37N 77°10E 120 B2
Ridge Farm U.S.A. 39°54N 87°39W 311 E9
Ridge Spring U.S.A. 33°51N 81°40W 316 B8
Ridgecrest U.S.A. 35°38N 117°40W 307 K9
Ridgefield Conn., U.S.A. 41°17N 73°30W 313 E11
Ridgefield N.J., U.S.A. 40°49N 74°0W 132 B1
Ridgefield Wash., U.S.A. 45°49N 122°45W 306 E4
Ridgefield Park U.S.A. 40°52N 74°1W 132 A1
Ridgeland Miss., U.S.A. 32°26N 90°8W 315 E9
Ridgeland S.C., U.S.A. 32°29N 80°59W 316 C9
Ridgetown Canada 42°26N 81°52W 312 D3
Ridgeville Ind., U.S.A. 40°18N 85°2W 311 D11
Ridgeville S.C., U.S.A. 33°6N 80°19W 316 B9
Ridgewood N.J., U.S.A. 40°59N 74°7W 313 F10
Ridgewood N.Y., U.S.A. 40°42N 73°53W 132 B2
Ridgway Ill., U.S.A. 37°48N 88°16W 311 G8
Ridgway Pa., U.S.A. 41°25N 78°44W 312 E6
Riding Mountain △ Canada 50°50N 100°0W 297 C9
Ridley, Mt. Australia 33°12S 122°7E 279 F3
Riebeek-Oos S. Africa 33°10S 26°10E 270 D4
Ried Austria 48°14N 13°30E 180 C6
Riedlingen Germany 48°9N 9°28E 179 G5
Riedstadt Germany 49°45N 8°30E 179 F4
Riem Germany 48°8N 11°41E 131 B3
Rienza → Italy 46°49N 11°47E 199 B8
Riesa Germany 51°17N 13°17E 178 D9
Riesco, I. Chile 52°55S 72°40W 336 D2
Riesenburg = Prabuty Poland 53°47N 19°15E 184 E6
Riesenrad Austria 48°14N 16°23E 142 A2
Riesi Italy 37°17N 14°5E 201 E7
Riet → S. Africa 29°0S 23°54E 270 C3
Rietavas Lithuania 55°44N 21°56E 184 C8
Rietbron S. Africa 32°54S 23°10E 270 D3
Rietfontein Namibia 21°58S 20°58E 270 B3
Rieti Italy 42°24N 12°51E 199 F9
Rieupeyroux France 44°19N 2°12E 174 D6
Riez France 43°49N 6°6E 175 E10
Rif = Er Rif Morocco 35°1N 4°1W 261 A4
Rif Iceland 64°56N 23°49W 155 C3
Riffe L. U.S.A. 46°32N 122°26W 306 D4
Rifle U.S.A. 39°32N 107°47W 304 G10
Rifstangi Iceland 66°32N 16°12W 155 A10
Rift Valley Africa 7°0N 30°0E 254 G7
Rift Valley ☐ Kenya 0°20N 36°0E 268 B4
Rig Rig Chad 14°13N 14°25E 259 F2
Riga India 26°39N 85°2E 241 A5
Rīga Latvia 56°53N 24°8E 184 B11
Rīga ✕ (RIX) Latvia 56°54N 23°59E 184 B10
Riga, G. of Latvia 57°40N 23°45E 184 A10
Rigacikun Nigeria 10°40N 7°28E 263 C6
Rīgān Iran 28°37N 58°58E 247 D8
Rīgas Jūras Līcis = Riga, G. of Latvia 57°40N 23°45E 184 A10
Rigaud Canada 45°29N 74°18W 313 A10
Rigby U.S.A. 43°40N 111°55W 304 E8
Rīgestān Afghan. 30°15N 65°0E 240 C2
Riggins U.S.A. 45°25N 116°19W 304 D5
Rignac France 44°25N 2°16E 174 D6
Rigolet Canada 54°10N 58°23W 299 B8
Rihand Dam India 24°9N 83°2E 243 G10
Riihimäki Finland 60°45N 24°48E 188 B3
Riiser-Larsen-halvøya Antarctica 68°0S 35°0E 151 C4
Rijau Nigeria 11°8N 5°17E 263 C6
Rijeka Croatia 45°20N 14°21E 199 C11
Rijeka Crnojevića Montenegro 42°24N 19°1E 202 D3
Rijksmuseum Amsterdam, Neths. 112 b1
Rijssen Neths. 52°19N 6°31E 170 B6
Rika → Ukraine 48°11N 23°16E 183 B8
Rikā', W. ar → Si. Arabia 22°25N 44°50E 248 B4
Rike Ethiopia 10°50N 39°53E 257 E4
Rikers I. U.S.A. 40°47N 73°53W 132 B2
Riksdagshuset Stockholm, Sweden 139 b2
Rikuchū-Kaigan △ Japan 39°20N 142°0E 220 E11
Rikuzentakada Japan 39°0N 141°40E 220 E10
Rila Bulgaria 42°7N 23°7E 202 D7
Rila Planina Bulgaria 42°10N 23°20E 202 D7
Riley U.S.A. 43°32N 119°28W 304 E4
Rima → Nigeria 13°4N 5°10E 263 C6
Rimac Peru 12°2S 77°2W 124 B2
Rimah, Wadi ar → Si. Arabia 26°5N 41°30E 246 E4
Rimatara French Polynesia 22°38S 152°51W 289 f
Rimau, Pulau Malaysia 5°15N 100°16E 237 c
Rimavská Sobota Slovak Rep. 48°22N 20°2E 181 C13
Rimbey Canada 52°35N 114°15W 296 C6
Rimbo Sweden 59°44N 18°21E 162 E12
Rimersburg U.S.A. 41°3N 79°30W 312 E5
Rimforsa Sweden 58°6N 15°43E 163 F9
Rimi Nigeria 12°58N 7°43E 263 C6
Rìmini Italy 44°3N 12°33E 199 D9
Rimouski Canada 48°27N 68°30W 299 C6
Rimrock U.S.A. 46°40N 121°7W 306 D5
Rinca Indonesia 8°45S 119°35E 231 F5
Rincon Neth. Ant. 12°14N 68°20W 322 h
Rincon Puerto Rico 18°20N 67°15W 321 b
Rincon Ga., U.S.A. 32°18N 81°14W 316 C8
Rincón de la Victoria Spain 36°43N 4°18W 195 J6
Rincón de Romos Mexico 22°14N 102°18W 318 C4
Rincon Falls Trin. & Tob. 10°46N 61°24W 323 t
Rinconada Argentina 22°26S 66°10W 334 A2
Rind → India 25°53N 80°33E 243 G9
Rindal Norway 63°3N 9°13E 164 A6
Ringarum Sweden 58°21N 16°26E 163 F10
Ringas India 27°21N 75°34E 242 F6
Ringdove Vanuatu 16°40S 168°10E 287 F6
Ringe Denmark 55°13N 10°28E 163 J4
Ringebu Norway 61°32N 10°7E 164 C7
Ringgi Solomon Is. 8°5S 157°10E 287 M9
Ringgold Is. Fiji 16°15S 179°25W 287 A3
Ringim Nigeria 12°13N 9°10E 263 C6
Ringkøbing Denmark 56°5N 8°15E 163 H2
Ringkøbing Fjord Denmark 56°0N 8°15E 163 H2
Ringoma Angola 12°25S 17°32E 265 E3
Ringsaker Norway 60°54N 10°45E 164 D7
Ringsend Ireland 53°20N 6°12W 120 A2
Ringsjön Sweden 55°55N 13°30E 163 J7
Ringsted Denmark 55°25N 11°46E 163 J5
Ringvassøya Norway 69°56N 19°15E 160 B18
Ringwood U.S.A. 41°7N 74°15W 313 E10
Rinia Greece 37°23N 25°13E 205 D7
Rinjani Indonesia 8°24S 116°28E 235 D5
Rinkeby Sweden 59°23N 17°55E 139 A1
Rinteln Germany 52°10N 9°8E 178 C5
Río, Punta del Spain 36°49N 2°24W 197 J2
Rio Bonito = Caiapônia Brazil 16°57S 51°49W 331 D7
Rio Branco = Arcoverde Brazil 8°25S 37°4W 332 C4
Rio Branco = Paratinga Brazil 12°40S 43°10W 333 D3
Rio Branco = Roraima ☐ Brazil 2°0N 61°30W 329 C5
Rio Branco Brazil 9°58S 67°49W 330 B4
Río Branco Uruguay 32°40S 53°40W 335 C5
Río Bravo Mexico 25°59N 98°6W 319 B5
Río Bravo ⌂ N. Amer. 29°2N 102°45W 318 B4
Río Bravo del Norte → Mexico 25°57N 97°9W 319 B5
Rio Brilhante Brazil 21°48S 54°33W 335 A5
Río Bueno Chile 40°19S 72°58W 336 B2
Rio Bueno Jamaica 18°28N 77°28W 320 a
Río Caribe Venezuela 10°42N 63°7W 329 A5
Río Chico Venezuela 10°19N 65°59W 328 A4
Rio Claro Brazil 22°19S 47°35W 335 A6
Rio Claro Trin. & Tob. 10°20N 61°25W 323 t
Rio Cobre → Jamaica 17°59N 76°52W 320 a
Río Colorado Argentina 39°0S 64°0W 336 A4
Rio Comprido Brazil 22°55S 43°13W 135 B1
Río Cuarto Argentina 33°10S 64°25W 334 C3
Rio das Pedras Mozam. 23°8S 35°28E 271 B6
Rio de Contas Brazil 13°36S 41°48W 333 D3
Rio de Janeiro Brazil 22°54S 43°12W 135 B1
Rio de Janeiro ☐ Brazil 22°50S 43°0W 333 F3
Rio de Janeiro Galeão ✕ (GIG) Brazil 22°49S 43°15W 135 A1
Rio de Mouro Portugal 38°46N 9°15W 126 A1
Río de Oro, B. de W. Sahara 23°45N 15°50W 260 D1
Rio do Prado Brazil 16°35S 40°34W 333 E3
Rio do Sul Brazil 27°13S 49°37W 335 B6
Río Dulce △ Guatemala 15°43N 88°50W 320 C2
Río Gallegos Argentina 51°35S 69°15W 336 D3
Río Grande Argentina 53°50S 67°45W 336 D3
Río Grande Bolivia 20°51S 67°17W 330 E4
Rio Grande Brazil 32°0S 52°20W 335 C5
Río Grande Zacatecas, Mexico 23°50N 103°2W 318 C4
Río Grande Nic. 12°54N 83°33W 320 D3
Río Grande Puerto Rico 18°23N 65°50W 321 b
Rio Grande → N. Amer. 25°58N 97°9W 314 J6
Rio Grande City U.S.A. 26°23N 98°49W 314 H5
Río Grande de Santiago → Mexico 21°36N 105°26W 318 C3
Rio Grande do Norte ☐ Brazil 5°40S 36°0W 332 C4
Rio Grande do Sul ☐ Brazil 30°0S 53°0W 335 C5
Rio Grande Rise Atl. Oc. 31°0S 35°0W 152 K8
Río Hato Panama 8°22N 80°10W 320 E3
Río Lagartos Mexico 21°36N 88°10W 319 C7
Rio Largo Brazil 9°28S 35°50W 332 C4
Rio Maior Portugal 39°19N 8°57W 195 F2
Rio Marina Italy 42°49N 10°25E 198 F7
Río Mayo Argentina 45°40S 70°15W 336 C2
Río Mulatos Bolivia 19°40S 66°50W 330 D4
Río Muni ☐ Eq. Guin. 1°30N 10°0E 264 B2
Rio Negro Brazil 26°0S 49°55W 335 B6
Río Negro Chile 40°47S 73°14W 336 B2
Rio Negro, Pantanal do Brazil 19°0S 56°0W 331 D6
Rio Novo = Ipiaú Brazil 14°8S 39°44W 333 D4
Rio Pardo = Ribas do Rio Pardo Brazil 20°27S 53°46W 331 E7
Rio Pardo Brazil 30°0S 52°30W 335 C5
Río Pico Argentina 44°0S 70°22W 336 B2
Río Pilcomayo △ Argentina 25°5S 58°5W 334 B4
Río Platano △ Honduras 15°45N 85°0W 320 C2
Rio Prêto = Ibipetuba Brazil 11°0S 44°32W 332 D3
Rio Preto da Eva Brazil 2°46S 59°41W 329 D6
Rio Rancho U.S.A. 35°14N 106°41W 305 J10
Rio Real Brazil 11°28S 37°56W 333 D4
Río Seco = Villa de María Argentina 29°55S 63°43W 334 B3
Río Segundo Argentina 31°40S 63°59W 334 C3
Río Simpson △ Chile 45°27S 73°30W 336 C2
Río Tercero Argentina 32°15S 64°8W 334 C3
Rio Tinto Brazil 6°48S 35°5W 332 C4
Rio Tinto Portugal 41°11N 8°34W 194 D2
Río Turbio Argentina 51°32S 72°18W 336 D2
Rio Verde Brazil 17°50S 51°0W 333 E1
Río Verde San Luis Potosí, Mexico 21°56N 99°59W 319 C5
Rio Verde de Mato Grosso Brazil 18°56S 54°52W 331 D7
Río Viejo △ Venezuela 7°15N 71°20W 328 B3
Rio Vista U.S.A. 38°10N 121°42W 306 G5
Ríobamba Ecuador 1°50S 78°45W 328 D2
Ríohacha Colombia 11°33N 72°55W 328 A3
Rioja Peru 6°11S 77°5W 330 B2
Riom France 45°54N 3°7E 174 C7
Riom-ès-Montagnes France 45°17N 2°39E 174 C6
Rion-des-Landes France 43°55N 0°56W 174 E3
Rionegro Antioquia, Colombia 6°9N 75°22W 328 B2
Rionegro Santander, Colombia 7°15N 73°9W 328 B3
Rionero in Vúlture Italy 40°55N 15°40E 201 B8
Rioni → Georgia 42°14N 41°44E 191 J5
Rios Spain 41°58N 7°16W 194 D3
Riosinho → Brazil 7°7S 51°39W 331 B7
Ríosucio Caldas, Colombia 5°30N 75°40W 328 B2
Ríosucio Choco, Colombia 7°27N 77°7W 328 B2
Riou L. Canada 59°7N 106°25W 297 B7
Rioz France 47°26N 6°5E 173 E13
Riozinho → Brazil 2°55S 67°7W 328 D4
Ripatransone Italy 42°59N 13°46E 199 F10
Ripley Ont., Canada 44°4N 81°35W 312 B3
Ripley Calif., U.S.A. 33°32N 114°39W 307 M12
Ripley N.Y., U.S.A. 42°16N 79°43W 312 D5
Ripley Ohio, U.S.A. 38°45N 83°51W 311 F13
Ripley Tenn., U.S.A. 35°45N 89°32W 315 D10
Ripley W. Va., U.S.A. 38°49N 81°43W 309 F13
Ripoll Spain 42°15N 2°13E 196 C7
Ripollet Spain 41°26N 2°10E 114 A1
Ripon N. Yorks., U.K. 54°9N 1°31W 168 C6
Ripon Calif., U.S.A. 37°44N 121°7W 306 H5
Ripon Wis., U.S.A. 43°51N 88°50W 308 D9
Riposto Italy 37°44N 15°12E 201 E8
Rippin = Rypin Poland 53°3N 19°25E 185 E6
Ris Norway 59°56N 10°41E 133 A3
Risan Montenegro 42°32N 18°42E 202 D2
Risaralda ☐ Colombia 5°0N 76°10W 328 C2
Risby Denmark 55°41N 12°19E 118 A1
Riscle France 43°39N 0°5W 174 E3
Rishā', W. ar → Si. Arabia 25°33N 44°5E 246 E5
Rishiri-Rebun-Sarobetsu △ Japan 45°26N 141°30E 220 B10
Rishiri-Tō Japan 45°11N 141°15E 220 B10
Rishon le Ẕiyyon Israel 31°58N 34°48E 251 G5
Rishra India 22°42N 88°20E 124 A2
Rising Sun U.S.A. 38°57N 84°51W 311 F12
Risle → France 49°26N 0°23E 172 C7
Risnjak △ Croatia 45°25N 14°36E 199 C11
Rison U.S.A. 33°58N 92°11W 314 E8
Risør Norway 58°43N 9°13E 164 F6
Rissani Morocco 31°18N 4°12W 260 B4
Rita Blanca Cr. → U.S.A. 35°40N 102°29W 314 D3
Ritchie U.S.A. 38°52N 76°51W 143 B4
Ritchie's Arch. India 12°14N 93°10E 245 H11
Rithala India 28°43N 77°6E 120 A1
Riti Nigeria 7°57N 9°41E 263 D6
Ritidian Pt. Guam 13°39N 144°51E 302 d
Ritter, Mt. U.S.A. 37°41N 119°12W 306 H7
Rittman U.S.A. 40°58N 81°47W 312 F3
Ritzville U.S.A. 47°8N 118°23W 304 C4
Riu India 28°19N 95°3E 241 A5
Riva del Garda Italy 45°53N 10°50E 198 C7
Riva Lígure Italy 43°50N 7°50E 198 E4
Rivadavia B. Aires, Argentina 35°29S 62°59W 334 D3
Rivadavia Mendoza, Argentina 33°13S 68°30W 334 C2
Rivadavia Salta, Argentina 24°5S 62°54W 334 A3
Rivadavia Chile 29°57S 70°35W 334 B1
Rivarolo Canavese Italy 45°19N 7°43E 198 C4
Rivas Nic. 11°30N 85°50W 320 D2
Rive-de-Gier France 45°32N 4°37E 175 C8
Rive Sud, Canal de la Canada 45°24N 73°31W 130 B2
River Cess Liberia 5°30N 9°32W 262 D3
River Edge U.S.A. 40°56N 74°1W 132 A1
River Estate & Waterwheel Trin. & Tob. 10°41N 61°33W 323 t
River Forest U.S.A. 41°53N 87°49W 119 B2
River Grove U.S.A. 41°55N 87°50W 119 B1
River Jordan Canada 48°26N 124°3W 306 B2
River North Chicago, U.S.A. 119 b1
River Ridge U.S.A. 29°57N 90°12W 131 B1
Rivera Argentina 37°12S 63°14W 334 D3
Rivera Uruguay 31°0S 55°50W 335 C4
Riverbank U.S.A. 37°44N 120°56W 306 H6
Riverdale Calif., U.S.A. 36°26N 119°52W 306 J7
Riverdale Ga., U.S.A. 33°34N 84°25W 316 B5
Riverdale Md., U.S.A. 38°57N 76°54W 143 B4
Riverdale N.Y., U.S.A. 40°59N 74°17W 132 A2
Riverdale Park Canada 43°40N 79°21W 141 A2
Riverhead U.S.A. 40°55N 72°40W 313 F12
Riverhurst Canada 50°55N 106°50W 297 C7
Riverlea S. Africa 26°12S 27°58E 123 B1
Rivers Canada 50°2N 100°14W 297 C8
Rivers ☐ Nigeria 4°30N 7°10E 263 E6
Rivers Inlet Canada 51°42N 127°15W 296 C3
Riversdale N.Z. 45°54S 168°44E 285 F3
Riversdale Western Cape, S. Africa 34°7S 21°15E 270 D3
Riverside Calif., U.S.A. 33°59N 117°22W 307 M9
Riverside Ill., U.S.A. 41°49N 87°49W 119 C2
Riverton S. Austral., Australia 34°10S 138°46E 282 C3
Riverton Man., Canada 51°1N 97°0W 297 C9
Riverton N.Z. 46°21S 168°0E 285 G3
Riverton Ill., U.S.A. 39°51N 89°33W 310 E7
Riverton Wyo., U.S.A. 43°2N 108°23W 304 E9
Riverview Fla., U.S.A. 27°52N 82°20W 317 H7
Riverview Fla., U.S.A. 30°32N 87°12W 317 E2
Riverwood Australia 33°57S 151°3E 139 B1
Rives France 45°21N 5°31E 175 C9
Rivesaltes France 42°47N 2°50E 174 F6
Riviera U.S.A. 35°4N 114°35W 307 K12
Riviera Beach U.S.A. 26°47N 80°3W 317 J9
Riviera di Levante Italy 44°15N 9°30E 198 D6
Riviera di Ponente Italy 44°10N 8°20E 198 D5
Rivière à Goyave, Pte. de la Guadeloupe 16°8N 61°33W 322 e
Rivière-au-Renard Canada 48°59N 64°23W 299 C7
Rivière des Anguilles Mauritius 20°29S 57°33E 272 e
Rivière-des-Prairies Canada 45°38N 73°34W 130 A2
Rivière-du-Loup Canada 47°50N 69°30W 299 C6
Rivière du Rempart Mauritius 20°6S 57°41E 272 e
Rivière-Pentecôte Canada 49°57N 67°1W 299 C6
Rivière-Pilote Martinique 14°26N 60°53W 322 j
Rivière St-Paul Canada 51°28N 57°45W 299 B8
Rivière-Salée Martinique 14°31N 61°0W 322 j
Rivne Odesa, Ukraine 46°1N 29°10E 183 D14
Rivne Rivne, Ukraine 50°40N 26°10E 177 C14
Rivne ☐ Ukraine 51°15N 26°30E 189 G4
Rívoli Italy 45°3N 7°31E 198 C4
Rivoli B. Australia 37°32S 140°3E 282 D4
Riwaka N.Z. 41°5S 172°59E 285 B7
Rixensart Belgium 50°43N 4°32E 116 B3
Rixheim France 47°40N 7°24E 173 E14
Riyad Iraq 33°18N 44°27E 113 B2
Riyadh = Ar Riyāḍ Si. Arabia 24°41N 46°42E 246 E5

Riyadh al Khabrā' Si. Arabia 26°2N 43°33E 246 E4
Riza Greece 40°31N 23°15E 202 F7
Rizal Cagayan, Phil. 17°51N 121°21E 232 C3
Rizal Nueva Ecija, Phil. 15°43N 121°6E 232 D3
Rizal Zamboanga del N., Phil. 8°35N 123°26E 233 G4
Rizal Park Phil. 14°35N 120°58E 127 B1
Rizal Stadium Phil. 14°34N 120°59E 127 B1
Rize Turkey 41°0N 40°30E 213 B9
Rize □ Turkey 41°0N 40°30E 213 B9
Rizhao China 35°25N 119°30E 227 G10
Rizokarpaso Cyprus 35°36N 34°23E 207 E10
Rizzuto, C. Italy 38°53N 17°5E 201 D10
Rjukan Norway 59°54N 8°33E 164 E5
Rjuven Norway 59°9N 7°8E 164 E4
Ro Greece 36°9N 29°33E 205 E11
Roa Dem. Rep. of the Congo 3°49N 24°56E 264 B4
Roa Oppland, Norway 60°17N 10°37E 164 D7
Røa Oslo, Norway 59°57N 10°39E 133 A2
Roa Spain 41°41N 3°56W 194 D7
Roachdale U.S.A. 39°51N 86°48W 311 E10
Road Town Br. Virgin Is. 18°27N 64°37W 321 C7
Roan Plateau U.S.A. 39°20N 109°20W 304 G9
Roanne France 46°3N 4°4E 173 F11
Roanoke Ala., U.S.A. 33°9N 85°22W 316 B4
Roanoke Ind., U.S.A. 40°58N 85°22W 311 D11
Roanoke Va., U.S.A. 37°16N 79°56W 309 G14
Roanoke → U.S.A. 35°57N 76°42W 315 D16
Roanoke I. U.S.A. 35°53N 75°39W 315 D17
Roanoke Rapids U.S.A. 36°28N 77°40W 315 C16
Roatán Honduras 16°18N 86°35W 320 C2
Rob Roy Solomon Is. 7°23S 157°36E 287 L9
Robāt Sang Iran 35°35N 59°10E 247 C8
Robāṭkarīm Iran 35°25N 50°59E 247 C6
Robāṭkarīm □ Iran 35°26N 50°59E 247 B6
Robbins U.S.A. 41°38N 87°42W 119 D2
Robbins I. Australia 40°42S 145°0E 281 G4
Róbbio Italy 45°17N 8°35E 198 C5
Robe Australia 37°11S 139°45E 282 D3
Robe → Australia 21°42S 116°15E 278 D2
Röbel Germany 53°22N 12°35E 178 B8
Robert, Havre du Martinique 14°40N 60°55W 322 j
Robert Lee U.S.A. 31°54N 100°29W 314 F4
Roberta U.S.A. 32°43N 84°1W 316 C5
Roberts U.S.A. 40°37N 88°11W 311 D8
Roberts, Mt. Trin. & Tob. 10°47N 61°10W 323 t
Roberts, Mt. Alaska, U.S.A. 60°2N 166°16W 303 F6
Robertsdale U.S.A. 40°11N 78°6W 312 F6
Robertsganj India 24°44N 83°4E 243 G10
Robertsham S. Africa 26°15S 28°1E 123 B2
Robertson S. Africa 33°46S 19°50E 270 D2
Robertson I. Antarctica 65°15S 59°30W 151 C18
Robertson Ra. Australia 23°15S 121°0E 278 D3
Robertsport Liberia 6°45N 11°26W 262 D2
Robertstown Australia 33°58S 139°5E 282 B3
Roberval Canada 48°32N 72°15W 299 C5
Robeson Chan. N. Amer. 82°0N 61°30W 154 A4
Robesonia U.S.A. 40°21N 76°8W 313 F8
Robi Ethiopia 7°52N 39°38E 257 F4
Robinson U.S.A. 39°0N 87°44W 311 F9
Robinson → Australia 16°3S 137°16E 280 B2
Robinson Ra. Australia 25°40S 119°0E 279 E2
Robinvale Australia 34°40S 142°45E 282 C5
Robledo Spain 38°46N 2°26W 197 G2
Roblin Canada 51°14N 101°21W 297 C8
Roboré Bolivia 18°10S 59°45W 331 D6
Robson Canada 49°20N 117°41W 296 D5
Robson, Mt. Canada 53°10N 119°10W 296 C5
Robstown U.S.A. 27°47N 97°40W 314 H6
Roca, C. da Portugal 38°40N 9°31W 195 G1
Roca Partida, I. Mexico 19°1N 112°2W 318 D2
Rocamadour France 44°48N 1°37E 174 D5
Rocca San Casciano Italy 44°3N 11°50E 199 D8
Roccadáspide Italy 40°27N 15°10E 201 B8
Roccastrada Italy 43°0N 11°10E 199 F8
Roccella Iónica Italy 38°19N 16°24E 201 D9
Rocciamelone, Monte = Roche Melon Italy 45°12N 7°5E 175 C11
Rocha Uruguay 34°30S 54°25W 335 C5
Rochdale U.K. 53°38N 2°9W 168 D5
Roche Melon Italy 45°12N 7°5E 175 C11
Rochechouart France 45°50N 0°49E 174 C4
Rochedo Brazil 19°57S 54°52W 331 D7
Rochefort Belgium 50°9N 5°12E 170 D5
Rochefort Charente-Maritime, France 45°56N 0°57W 174 C3
Rochefort-en-Terre France 47°42N 2°22W 172 E4
Rochelle Ga., U.S.A. 31°57N 83°27W 316 D6
Rochelle Ill., U.S.A. 41°56N 89°4W 310 C7
Rochelle Park U.S.A. 40°54N 74°4W 132 A1
Rocher River Canada 61°23N 112°44W 296 A6
Roches, R. des → Réunion 21°0S 55°42E 272 f
Roche's Bluff Montserrat 16°42N 62°9W 323 p
Roches Noires Mauritius 20°6S 57°42E 272 e
Rocheservière France 46°57N 1°30W 172 F5
Rochester Vic., Australia 36°22S 144°41E 282 D6
Rochester Medway, U.K. 51°23N 0°31E 169 F8
Rochester Ind., U.S.A. 41°4N 86°13W 311 C10
Rochester Minn., U.S.A. 44°1N 92°28W 308 C7
Rochester N.H., U.S.A. 43°18N 70°59W 313 C14
Rochester N.Y., U.S.A. 43°10N 77°37W 312 C7
Rochester Hills U.S.A. 42°41N 83°8W 311 B13
Rociu Romania 44°43N 25°2E 183 F10
Rock → Yukon, Canada 60°7N 127°7W 296 A3
Rock → Ill., U.S.A. 41°29N 90°37W 310 C6
Rock, The Australia 35°15S 147°2E 283 C7
Rock Cr. → U.S.A. 38°54N 77°3W 143 B3
Rock Creek U.S.A. 41°40N 80°52W 312 E4
Rock Creek Park U.S.A. 38°56N 77°2W 143 B3
Rock Falls U.S.A. 41°47N 89°41W 310 C7
Rock Flat Australia 36°21S 149°13E 283 D8
Rock Hall Barbados 13°11N 59°36W 323 r
Rock Hill U.S.A. 34°56N 81°1W 315 D14
Rock Island U.S.A. 41°30N 90°34W 310 C6
Rock Port U.S.A. 40°25N 95°31W 308 E6
Rock Pt. N.Z. 41°8S 174°47E 143 A1
Rock Rapids U.S.A. 43°26N 96°10W 308 D5
Rock Sound Bahamas 24°54N 76°12W 320 B4
Rock Springs Mont., U.S.A. 46°49N 106°15W 304 C10
Rock Springs Wyo., U.S.A. 41°35N 109°14W 304 F9
Rock Valley U.S.A. 43°12N 96°18W 308 D5
Rockall Atl. Oc. 57°37N 13°42W 158 D3
Rockall Trough Atl. Oc. 57°0N 12°0W 152 A10
Rockaway Beach U.S.A. 40°34N 73°49W 132 C3
Rockaway Pt. U.S.A. 40°33N 73°54W 132 C2
Rockdale N.S.W., Australia 33°57S 151°8E 139 B1
Rockdale Tex., U.S.A. 30°39N 97°0W 314 F6
Rockdale Wash., U.S.A. 47°22N 121°28W 306 C5
Rockeby = Mungkan Kandju △ Australia 13°35S 142°52E 280 A3
Rockefeller Center New York, U.S.A. 132 c2
Rockefeller Plateau Antarctica 76°0S 130°0W 151 E14
Rockford Ala., U.S.A. 32°53N 86°13W 316 C3
Rockford Ill., U.S.A. 42°16N 89°6W 310 B7
Rockford Iowa, U.S.A. 43°3N 92°57W 310 A4
Rockford Mich., U.S.A. 43°7N 85°34W 311 A11
Rockford Ohio, U.S.A. 40°41N 84°39W 311 D12
Rockglen Canada 49°11N 105°57W 297 D7
Rockhampton Australia 23°22S 150°32E 280 C5
Rockingham W. Austral., Australia 32°15S 115°38E 279 F2
Rockingham N.C., U.S.A. 34°57N 79°46W 315 D15
Rockingham Vt., U.S.A. 43°11N 72°29W 313 C12
Rockingham B. Australia 18°5S 146°10E 280 B4
Rocklake U.S.A. 48°47N 99°15W 308 A4
Rockland Ont., Canada 45°33N 75°17W 313 A9
Rockland Idaho, U.S.A. 42°34N 112°53W 304 E7
Rockland Maine, U.S.A. 44°6N 69°7W 309 C19
Rockland Mich., U.S.A. 46°44N 89°11W 308 B9
Rocklands Bird Sanctuary Jamaica 18°24N 77°55W 320 a
Rocklands Reservoir Australia 37°15S 142°5E 282 D5
Rockledge U.S.A. 28°20N 80°43W 317 G9
Rocklin U.S.A. 38°48N 121°14W 306 G5
Rockly B. Trin. & Tob. 11°9N 60°46W 323 s
Rockmart U.S.A. 34°0N 85°3W 315 D12
Rockport Ind., U.S.A. 37°53N 87°3W 311 G9
Rockport Mass., U.S.A. 42°39N 70°37W 313 D14
Rockport Tex., U.S.A. 28°2N 97°3W 314 G6
Rocksprings U.S.A. 30°1N 100°13W 314 F4
Rockstone Guyana 5°59N 58°33W 329 B6
Rockville Conn., U.S.A. 41°52N 72°28W 313 E12
Rockville Ind., U.S.A. 39°46N 87°14W 311 E9
Rockville Md., U.S.A. 39°5N 77°9W 309 F15
Rockwall U.S.A. 32°56N 96°28W 314 E6
Rockwell City U.S.A. 42°24N 94°38W 310 B2
Rockwood Ont., Canada 43°37N 80°8W 312 C4
Rockwood Maine, U.S.A. 45°41N 69°45W 309 C19
Rockwood Tenn., U.S.A. 35°52N 84°41W 315 D12
Rocky Ford U.S.A. 38°3N 103°43W 304 G12
Rocky Fork L. U.S.A. 39°11N 83°26W 311 E13
Rocky Gully Australia 34°30S 116°57E 279 F2
Rocky Harbour Canada 49°36N 57°55W 299 C8
Rocky Island L. Canada 46°55N 83°0W 298 C3
Rocky Lane Canada 58°31N 116°22W 296 B5
Rocky Mount U.S.A. 35°57N 77°48W 315 D16
Rocky Mountain △ U.S.A. 40°25N 105°45W 304 F11
Rocky Mountain House Canada 52°22N 114°55W 296 C6
Rocky Mts. N. Amer. 49°0N 115°0W 304 B6
Rocky Point Namibia 19°3S 12°30E 270 A2
Rocky Run → U.S.A. 38°58N 77°14W 143 B2
Rocroi France 49°55N 4°30E 173 C11
Rod Pakistan 28°10N 63°5E 240 C1
Roda = Stadtroda Germany 50°52N 11°44E 178 E7
Roda Greece 39°48N 19°46E 206 B9
Roda, Gezîret el Egypt 30°1N 31°13E 117 A2
Roda I. = Roda, Gezîret el Egypt 30°1N 31°13E 117 A2
Rodaon Austria 48°8N 16°16E 142 B1
Rødberg Norway 60°17N 8°56E 164 D5
Rødby Denmark 54°41N 11°23E 163 K5
Rødbyhavn Denmark 54°39N 11°22E 163 K5
Roddickton Canada 50°51N 56°8W 299 B8
Rødding Denmark 55°23N 9°3E 163 J3
Rödeby Sweden 56°15N 15°37E 163 H9
Rødekro Denmark 55°4N 9°20E 163 J3
Rodenkirchen Germany 53°23N 8°26E 178 B4
Rodez France 44°21N 2°33E 174 D6
Ródhos = Rhodes Greece 36°15N 28°10E 206 E12
Rodi Gargánico Italy 41°55N 15°53E 199 G12
Rodia Greece 35°22N 25°1E 207 D7
Rodina Kazakhstan 50°16N 66°53E 217 B7
Rodna Romania 47°25N 24°50E 183 C9
Rodnei, Munții Romania 47°35N 24°35E 183 C9
Rodney Canada 42°34N 81°41W 312 D3
Rodney, C. N.Z. 36°17S 174°50E 284 C3
Rodney B. St. Lucia 14°5N 60°58W 323 m
Rodniki Russia 57°7N 41°47E 190 B5
Rodolivos Greece 40°55N 24°0E 202 F7
Rodonit, Kepi i Albania 41°35N 19°27E 202 E3
Rodopi □ Greece 41°5N 25°30E 203 E9
Rodopos Greece 35°34N 23°45E 207 E4
Rødovre Denmark 55°40N 12°26E 118 A2
Rodrigo de Freitas, L. Brazil 22°58S 43°12W 135 B1
Rodriguez Ind. Oc. 19°45S 63°20E 273 F5
Roe → U.K. 55°6N 6°59W 166 A5
Roebling U.S.A. 40°7N 74°47W 313 F10
Roebourne Australia 20°44S 117°9E 278 D2
Roebuck B. Australia 18°5S 122°20E 278 C3
Roehampton U.K. 51°27N 0°15W 125 B2
Roermond Neths. 51°12N 6°0E 170 C6
Roes Welcome Sd. Canada 65°0N 87°0W 295 C11
Roeselare Belgium 50°57N 3°7E 170 D3
Rogachev = Ragachow Belarus 53°8N 30°5E 177 B16
Rogačica Serbia 44°4N 19°40E 202 B3
Rogagua, L. Bolivia 13°43S 66°50W 330 C4
Rogaland □ Norway 59°12N 6°20E 164 E3
Rogaška Slatina Slovenia 46°15N 15°42E 199 B12
Rogatec Slovenia 46°15N 15°46E 199 B12
Rogatica Bos.-H. 43°47N 19°0E 182 G4
Rogatyn Ukraine 49°24N 24°36E 177 D13
Rogdhia Greece 35°22N 25°1E 207 D7
Rogers U.S.A. 36°20N 94°7W 314 C7
Rogers City U.S.A. 45°25N 83°49W 309 C12
Rogers Park U.S.A. 42°0N 87°40W 119 A3
Rogersville Canada 46°44N 65°26W 299 C6
Roggan → Canada 54°24N 79°25W 298 B4
Roggan L. Canada 54°8N 77°50W 298 B4
Roggeveen Basin Pac. Oc. 31°30S 95°30W 289 L18
Roggeveldberge S. Africa 32°10S 20°10E 270 D3
Roggiano Gravina Italy 39°37N 16°9E 201 C9
Rogliano Haute-Corse, France 42°57N 9°30E 175 F13
Rogliano Italy 39°10N 16°19E 201 C9
Rogoaguado, L. Bolivia 13°0S 65°30W 331 C4
Rogojampi Indonesia 8°19S 114°17E 231 J17
Rogoźno Poland 52°45N 16°59E 185 F3
Rogue → U.S.A. 42°26N 124°26W 304 E1
Roha India 18°26N 73°7E 244 E1
Rohan France 48°4N 2°45W 172 D4
Rohnert Park U.S.A. 38°16N 122°40W 306 G4
Rohri Pakistan 27°45N 68°51E 242 F3
Rohri Canal Pakistan 26°15N 68°27E 242 F3
Rohtak India 28°55N 76°43E 242 E7
Rohtisch-Sauerbrunn = Rogaška Slatina Slovenia 46°15N 15°42E 199 B12
Roi Et Thailand 16°4N 103°40E 236 D4
Roi-Georges, Îs. du French Polynesia 14°32S 145°8W 289 f
Roihuvuori Finland 60°11N 25°2E 121 B3
Roissy-en-Brie France 48°48N 2°39E 134 B4
Roja Latvia 57°29N 22°43E 184 A9
Rojas Argentina 34°10S 60°45W 334 C3
Roješte Romania 44°4N 23°59E 183 F8
Rojo, C. Mexico 21°33N 97°20W 319 C5
Rokan → Indonesia 2°0N 100°50E 234 B2
Rokel → S. Leone 8°30N 12°48W 262 D2
Rokin Amsterdam, Neths. 112 b2
Rokiškis Lithuania 55°55N 25°35E 188 E3
Rokitno Russia 50°57N 35°56E 189 G8
Rokycany Czech Rep. 49°43N 13°35E 180 B6
Rokytka → Czech Rep. 50°6N 14°27E 135 B3
Rolândia Brazil 23°18S 51°23W 335 A5
Røldal Norway 59°47N 6°50E 164 E3
Rolfe U.S.A. 42°49N 94°31W 310 B2
Rolla Mo., U.S.A. 37°57N 91°46W 310 G5
Rolla N. Dak., U.S.A. 48°52N 99°37W 308 A4
Rolleston Queens., Australia 24°28S 148°35E 280 C4
Rolleston N.Z. 43°35S 172°24E 285 D7
Rolling Fork → U.S.A. 37°55N 85°50W 311 G11
Rollingstone Australia 19°2S 146°24E 280 B4
Rom Vest-Agder, Norway 58°8N 7°5E 164 F4
Rom Sudan 9°54N 32°16E 257 F3
Roma Queens., Australia 26°32S 148°49E 281 D4
Roma Italy 41°54N 12°28E 136 B1
Roma Sweden 57°32N 18°26E 163 G12
Roma Fiumicino ✕ (FCO) Italy 41°48N 12°15E 199 G9
Roma-Los Saenz U.S.A. 26°24N 99°1W 314 H5
Roma Urbe ✕ Italy 41°57N 12°30E 136 B2
Római-Fürdö Hungary 47°34N 19°4E 117 A2
Romain, C. U.S.A. 33°0N 79°22W 315 E15
Romaine → Canada 50°18N 63°47W 299 B7
Romainville France 48°52N 2°26E 134 A3
Roman Bulgaria 43°8N 23°57E 202 C7
Roman Romania 46°57N 26°55E 183 D11
Roman Forum = Foro Romano Rome, Italy 136 c3
Roman-Kosh, Gora Ukraine 44°37N 34°15E 189 K8
Romanche → France 45°5N 5°43E 175 C9
Romang Indonesia 7°30S 127°20E 231 F7
Români Egypt 30°59N 32°38E 251 H3
Romania ■ Europe 46°0N 25°0E 183 D10
Romanija Bos.-H. 43°50N 18°45E 182 G3
Romano, C. U.S.A. 25°51N 81°41W 317 K8
Romano, Cayo Cuba 22°0N 77°30W 320 B4
Romano Banco Italy 45°25N 9°6E 129 B1
Romanov-Borisoglebsk = Tutayev Russia 57°53N 39°32E 188 D10
Romanovka = Basarabeasca Moldova 46°21N 28°58E 183 D13
Romanovna-Murmane = Murmansk Russia 68°57N 33°10E 160 B25
Romanovsk = Kropotkin Russia 45°28N 40°28E 191 H5
Romanovskiy Khutor = Kropotkin Russia 45°28N 40°28E 191 H5
Romans-sur-Isère France 45°3N 5°3E 175 C9
Romanshorn Switz. 47°33N 9°22E 179 H5
Romanzof C. U.S.A. 61°49N 166°6W 303 F6
Romashkovo Russia 55°43N 37°19E 129 B1
Rombari Sudan 4°33N 31°2E 257 G3
Romblon Phil. 12°33N 122°17E 232 E4
Romblon □ Phil. 12°30N 122°15E 232 E4
Romblon Pass Phil. 12°27N 122°12E 232 E4
Rome = Roma Italy 41°54N 12°28E 136 B1
Rome Ga., U.S.A. 34°15N 85°10W 315 D12
Rome N.Y., U.S.A. 43°13N 75°27W 313 C9
Rome Pa., U.S.A. 41°51N 76°21W 313 E8
Romema Israel 31°48N 35°12E 123 B2
Romeoville U.S.A. 41°39N 88°3W 311 C8
Rometta Italy 38°10N 15°25E 201 D8
Romford U.K. 51°34N 0°11E 125 A5
Romilly-sur-Seine France 48°31N 3°44E 173 D10
Romiton Uzbekistan 39°56N 64°23E 216 E6
Rommani Morocco 33°31N 6°40W 260 B3
Romney U.S.A. 39°21N 78°45W 309 F14
Romney Marsh U.K. 51°2N 0°54E 169 F8
Romny Ukraine 50°48N 33°28E 189 G7
Rømø Denmark 55°10N 8°30E 163 J2
Romodan Ukraine 49°55N 33°15E 189 G7
Romodanovo Russia 54°26N 45°23E 190 C7
Romont Switz. 46°42N 6°54E 179 J2
Romorantin-Lanthenay France 47°21N 1°45E 173 E8
Rompin → Malaysia 2°49N 103°29E 234 B2
Romsdalen Norway 62°25N 7°52E 164 B4
Romsdalsfjorden Norway 62°38N 7°20E 164 B4
Romsey U.K. 51°0N 1°29W 169 G6
Ron India 15°40N 75°44E 245 G2
Ron Vietnam 17°53N 106°27E 236 D6
Rona U.K. 57°34N 5°59W 167 D3
Ronald Reagan National, Washington ✕ (DCA) U.S.A. 38°51N 77°2W 143 B3
Ronan U.S.A. 47°32N 114°6W 304 C6
Roncador, Cayos Colombia 13°32N 80°4W 320 D3
Roncador, Serra do Brazil 12°30S 52°30W 333 D1
Ronciglione Italy 42°17N 12°13E 199 F9
Ronco → Italy 44°24N 12°12E 199 D9
Ronda Spain 36°46N 5°12W 195 J5
Ronda, Serranía de Spain 36°44N 5°3W 195 J5
Rondane Norway 61°57N 9°50E 164 C6
Rondane △ Norway 61°55N 9°44E 164 C6
Ronde, Pt. Dominica 15°33N 61°29W 323 k
Ronde I. Grenada 12°29N 61°36W 323 q
Rondebosch S. Africa 33°58S 18°28E 118 A1
Rondón Colombia 6°17N 71°6W 328 B3
Rondônia Brazil 10°52S 61°57W 331 C5
Rondônia □ Brazil 11°0S 63°0W 331 C5
Rondonópolis Brazil 16°28S 54°38W 331 D7
Rondslottet Norway 61°55N 9°45E 164 C6
Rong, Koh Cambodia 10°45N 103°15E 237 G4
Rong Jiang → China 24°35N 109°20E 228 E7
Rong Xian Guangxi Zhuangzu, China 22°50N 110°31E 229 F8
Rong Xian Sichuan, China 29°23N 104°22E 228 C5
Rong'an China 25°14N 109°22E 228 E7
Rongchang China 29°20N 105°32E 228 C5
Ronge, L. la Canada 55°6N 105°17W 297 B7
Rongjiang China 25°57N 108°28E 228 E7
Rongotea N.Z. 40°19S 175°25E 284 G4
Rongshui China 25°5N 109°12E 228 E7
Rønne Denmark 55°6N 14°43E 163 J8
Ronne Ice Shelf Antarctica 77°30S 60°0W 151 D18
Ronneby Sweden 56°12N 15°17E 163 H9
Ronnebyån → Sweden 56°11N 15°18E 163 H9
Rönneshytta Sweden 58°56N 15°2E 163 F9
Ronsard, C. Australia 24°46S 113°10E 279 D1
Ronse Belgium 50°45N 3°35E 170 D3
Ronuro → Brazil 11°56S 53°33W 331 C7
Roodepoort S. Africa 26°11S 27°54E 271 C4
Roodhouse U.S.A. 39°29N 90°24W 310 E6
Roof Butte U.S.A. 36°28N 109°5W 305 H9
Rooiboklaagte → Namibia 20°50S 21°0E 270 B3
Rooniu, Mt. Tahiti 17°49S 149°12W 289 e
Roopville U.S.A. 33°27N 85°8W 316 B4
Roorkee India 29°52N 77°59E 242 E7
Roosendaal Neths. 51°32N 4°29E 170 C4
Roosevelt U.S.A. 40°18N 109°59W 304 F9
Roosevelt → Brazil 7°35S 60°20W 331 B5
Roosevelt, Mt. Canada 58°26N 125°20W 296 B3
Roosevelt I. Antarctica 79°30S 162°0W 151 D12
Roosevelt Island New York, U.S.A. 132 c3
Ropczyce Poland 50°4N 21°38E 185 H8
Roper → Australia 14°43S 135°27E 280 A2
Roper Bar Australia 14°44S 134°44E 280 A1
Roppongi Tokyo, Japan 140 c3
Roque Pérez Argentina 35°25S 59°24W 334 D4
Roquefort France 44°2N 0°20W 174 D3
Roquemaure France 44°3N 4°48E 175 D8
Roquetas de Mar Spain 36°46N 2°36W 197 J2
Roquetes Spain 40°50N 0°30E 196 E5
Roquevaire France 43°20N 5°36E 175 E9
Roraima □ Brazil 2°0N 61°30W 329 C5
Roraima, Mt. Venezuela 5°10N 60°40W 329 B5
Røros Norway 62°35N 11°23E 164 B8
Rorschach Switz. 47°28N 9°28E 179 H5
Rosa Zambia 9°33S 31°15E 269 D6
Rosa, C. Algeria 37°0N 8°16E 261 A6
Rosa, C. Galápagos Is., Ecuador 1°4S 91°10W 330 a
Rosa, Monte Europe 45°57N 7°53E 198 C4
Rosais, Pta. dos Azores 38°45N 28°19W 153 d1
Rosal de la Frontera Spain 37°59N 7°13W 195 H3
Rosales Phil. 15°54N 120°38E 232 D3
Rosalia U.S.A. 47°14N 117°22W 304 C5
Rosalie Dominica 15°22N 61°16W 323 k
Rosalie → Dominica 15°22N 61°15W 323 k
Rosalind Bank W. Indies 16°30N 80°30W 320 C3
Rosamond U.S.A. 34°52N 118°10W 307 L8
Rosans France 44°24N 5°29E 175 D9
Rosario Argentina 33°0S 60°40W 334 C3
Rosário Maranhão, Brazil 3°0S 44°15W 332 B3
Rosario Baja Calif., Mexico 30°0N 115°50W 318 B1
Rosario Sinaloa, Mexico 22°58N 105°53W 318 C3
Rosario Paraguay 24°30S 57°35W 334 A4
Rosario Phil. 8°24N 125°59E 233 G5
Rosario, Villa del Venezuela 10°19N 72°19W 328 A3
Rosario de la Frontera Argentina 25°50S 65°0W 334 B3
Rosario de Lerma Argentina 24°59S 65°35W 334 A2
Rosario del Tala Argentina 32°20S 59°10W 334 C4
Rosário do Sul Brazil 30°15S 54°55W 335 C5
Rosário Oeste Brazil 14°50S 56°25W 331 C6
Rosarito Mexico 32°20N 117°2W 307 N9
Rosarno Italy 38°29N 15°58E 201 D8
Rosas = Roses Spain 42°19N 3°10E 196 C8
Roscoe Mo., U.S.A. 37°58N 93°48W 310 G3
Roscoe N.Y., U.S.A. 41°56N 74°55W 313 E10
Roscoff France 48°44N 3°58W 172 D3
Roscommon Ireland 53°38N 8°11W 166 C3
Roscommon □ Ireland 53°49N 8°23W 166 C3
Roscrea Ireland 52°57N 7°49W 166 D4
Rose → Australia 14°16S 135°45E 280 A2
Rose, L. Bahamas 21°0N 73°30W 321 B5
Rose, L. Fla., U.S.A. 28°32N 81°30W 133 A1
Rose Belle Mauritius 20°24S 57°36E 272 e
Rose Blanche-Harbour Le Cou Canada 47°38N 58°45W 299 C8
Rose Bowl U.S.A. 34°9N 118°10W 126 B4
Rose Hall Great House Jamaica 18°31N 77°49W 320 a
Rose Hill = Port Mourant Guyana 6°15N 57°20W 329 B6
Rose Hill Mauritius 20°14S 57°27E 272 e
Rose Hill Va., U.S.A. 38°47N 77°6W 143 C3
Rose Pt. Canada 54°11N 131°39W 296 C2
Rose Rock Grenada 12°24N 61°28W 323 q
Rose Valley Canada 52°19N 103°49W 297 C8
Roseau Dominica 15°17N 61°24W 323 k
Roseau Minn., U.S.A. 48°51N 95°46W 308 A6
Rosebank Gauteng, S. Africa 26°8S 28°2E 123 A2
Rosebank N.Y., U.S.A. 40°36N 74°4W 132 C1
Rosebery N.S.W., Australia 33°55S 151°12E 139 B2
Rosebery Tas., Australia 41°46S 145°33E 281 G4
Rosebud Vic., Australia 38°21S 144°54E 282 E6
Rosebud S. Dak., U.S.A. 43°14N 100°51W 308 D3
Rosebud Tex., U.S.A. 31°4N 96°59W 314 F6
Roseburg U.S.A. 43°13N 123°20W 304 E2
Rosedal La Candelaria Mexico 19°20N 99°10W 128 B2
Rosehearty U.K. 57°42N 2°7W 167 D6
Roseires Res. Sudan 11°51N 34°23E 266 B3
Roseland Calif., U.S.A. 38°25N 122°43W 306 G4
Roseland Ill., U.S.A. 41°42N 87°37W 119 C3
Rosemary Canada 50°46N 112°5W 296 C6
Rosemead U.S.A. 34°4N 118°4W 126 B4
Rosemont Qué., Canada 45°34N 73°33W 130 A2
Rosemont Ill., U.S.A. 41°59N 87°53W 119 B1
Rosenberg = Olesno Poland 50°51N 18°26E 185 H5
Rosenberg = Susz Poland 53°44N 19°20E 184 E6
Rosenberg U.S.A. 29°34N 95°49W 314 G7
Rosenborg Slot Copenhagen, Denmark 118 b3
Rosendaël France 51°3N 2°24E 173 A9
Rosendal Norway 59°59N 6°0E 164 E3
Rosendale U.S.A. 40°4N 94°51W 310 D2
Rosenheim Germany 47°51N 12°7E 179 H8
Rosenthal Germany 52°35N 13°22E 115 A3
Roses Spain 42°19N 3°10E 196 C8
Roses, G. de Spain 42°10N 3°15E 196 C8
Roseto degli Abruzzi Italy 42°41N 14°1E 199 F11
Rosetown Canada 51°35N 107°59W 297 C7
Rosetta = Rashîd Egypt 31°21N 30°22E 256 H7
Rosettenville S. Africa 26°15S 28°3E 123 B2
Roseville Calif., U.S.A. 38°45N 121°17W 306 G5
Roseville Ill., U.S.A. 40°44N 90°40W 310 D6
Roseville Mich., U.S.A. 42°30N 82°56W 312 D2
Rosewell U.K. 55°51N 3°8W 121 B3
Rosewood Australia 27°38S 152°36E 281 D5
Rosherville Dam S. Africa 26°13S 28°6E 123 B2
Roshkhvār Iran 34°58N 59°37E 247 C8
Rosières-en-Santerre France 49°49N 2°42E 173 C9
Rosignano Maríttimo Italy 43°24N 10°28E 198 E7
Rosignol Guyana 6°15N 57°30W 329 B6
Roşiori de Vede Romania 44°9N 25°0E 183 F10
Rositsa Bulgaria 43°57N 27°57E 203 C11
Rositsa → Bulgaria 43°10N 25°30E 203 C9
Rösjön Sweden 59°26N 18°0E 139 A2
Roskilde Denmark 55°38N 12°3E 163 J6
Roskovec Albania 40°44N 19°43E 202 F3
Roslags-Näsby Sweden 59°25N 18°2E 139 A2
Roslavl Russia 53°57N 32°55E 188 F7
Roslin U.K. 55°51N 3°11W 121 B3
Roslindale U.S.A. 42°17N 71°7W 116 B2
Rosmaninhal Portugal 39°44N 7°5W 194 F3
Rosmead S. Africa 31°29S 25°8E 270 D4
Røsnæs Denmark 55°44N 10°55E 163 J4
Rosny-sous-Bois France 48°52N 2°30E 134 A4
Rosolini Italy 36°49N 14°57E 201 F7
Rosporden France 47°57N 3°50W 172 E3
Ross Tas., Australia 42°2S 147°30E 281 G4
Ross N.Z. 42°53S 170°49E 285 D5
Ross Béthio Mauritania 16°15N 16°8W 262 B1
Ross Dependency Antarctica 76°0S 170°0W 151 D12
Ross I. Antarctica 77°30S 168°0E 151 D11
Ross Ice Shelf Antarctica 80°0S 180°0E 151 E12
Ross L. U.S.A. 48°44N 121°4W 304 B3
Ross-on-Wye U.K. 51°54N 2°34W 169 F5
Ross River N. Terr., Australia 23°44S 134°30E 280 C1
Ross River Yukon, Canada 62°30N 131°30W 296 A2
Ross Sea Antarctica 74°0S 178°0E 151 D11
Rossall Pt. U.K. 53°55N 3°3W 168 D4
Rossan Pt. Ireland 54°42N 8°47W 166 B3
Rossano Italy 39°36N 16°39E 201 C9
Rossburn Canada 50°40N 100°49W 297 C8
Rosseau Canada 45°16N 79°39W 312 A5
Rosseau, L. Canada 45°10N 79°35W 312 A5
Rössel = Reszel Poland 54°4N 21°10E 184 D8
Rossel I. Papua N. G. 11°21S 154°9E 286 F8
Rosses, The Ireland 55°2N 8°20W 166 A3
Rossford U.S.A. 41°36N 83°34W 311 C13
Rossignol, L. Canada 52°43N 73°40W 298 B5
Rossignol L. Canada 44°12N 65°10W 299 D6
Rossiya = Russia ■ Eurasia 62°0N 105°0E 215 C11
Rosskreppfjorden Norway 59°4N 7°10E 164 E4
Rossland Canada 49°6N 117°50W 296 D5
Rosslare Ireland 52°17N 6°24W 166 D5
Rosslare Harbour Ireland 52°15N 6°20W 166 D5
Rosslau Germany 51°52N 12°15E 178 D8
Rosslyn U.S.A. 38°53N 77°4W 143 B3
Rosso Mauritania 16°40N 15°45W 262 B1
Rosso, C. France 42°13N 8°32E 175 F12
Rossosh Russia 50°15N 39°28E 189 G10
Røssvatnet Norway 65°45N 14°5E 160 D16
Rossville Ill., U.S.A. 40°23N 87°40W 311 D9
Rossville Ind., U.S.A. 40°25N 86°36W 311 D10
Røst Norway 67°32N 12°0E 160 C15
Rostāq Afghan. 37°7N 69°49E 240 A3
Rosthern Canada 52°40N 106°20W 297 C7
Rostock Germany 54°5N 12°8E 178 A8
Rostov Don, Russia 47°15N 39°45E 189 J10
Rostov Sverdlovsk, Russia 57°14N 39°25E 188 D10
Rostov □ Russia 48°50N 41°10E 191 F5
Rostrenen France 48°14N 3°21W 172 D3
Roswell Ga., U.S.A. 34°2N 84°22W 316 A5
Roswell N. Mex., U.S.A. 33°24N 104°32W 305 K11
Rosyth U.K. 56°2N 3°25W 121 A1
Rot-Front = Dobropole Ukraine 48°25N 37°2E 189 H9
Rota N. Marianas 14°9N 145°12E 302 a
Rota Spain 36°37N 6°20W 195 J4
Rotan U.S.A. 32°51N 100°28W 314 E4
Rotenburg Hessen, Germany 50°59N 9°44E 178 E5
Rotenburg Niedersachsen, Germany 53°6N 9°25E 178 B5
Roth Germany 49°15N 11°5E 179 F7
Rothaargebirge Germany 51°6N 8°13E 178 D4
Rothaargebirge △ Germany 51°0N 8°15E 178 E4
Rothenburg ob der Tauber Germany 49°23N 10°11E 179 F6
Rother → U.K. 50°59N 0°45E 169 G8
Rothera Antarctica 67°0S 63°0W 151 C17
Rotherham U.K. 53°26N 1°20W 168 D6
Rotherhithe U.K. 51°29N 0°2W 125 B3
Rothes U.K. 57°32N 3°13W 167 D5
Rothesay N.B., Canada 45°23N 66°0W 299 C6
Rothesay Argyll & Bute, U.K. 55°50N 5°3W 167 F3
Rothneusiedl Austria 48°8N 16°23E 142 B2
Rothschmaige Germany 48°14N 11°27E 131 A1
Roti Indonesia 10°50S 123°0E 231 F6
Rotja, Pta. Spain 38°38N 1°35E 206 D2
Rotnes Norway 60°3N 10°51E 164 D7
Roto Australia 33°0S 145°30E 283 B6
Rotoaira, L. N.Z. 39°3S 175°45E 284 F4
Rotoehu, L. N.Z. 38°1S 176°32E 284 E5
Rotoiti, L. Bay of Plenty, N.Z. 38°2S 176°26E 284 E5
Rotoiti, L. W. Coast, N.Z. 41°51S 172°49E 285 B7
Rotoma, L. N.Z. 38°2S 176°35E 284 E5
Rotondo, Mte. France 42°14N 9°8E 175 F13
Rotoroa, L. N.Z. 41°55S 172°39E 285 B7
Rotorua N.Z. 38°9S 176°16E 284 E5
Rotorua, L. N.Z. 38°5S 176°18E 284 E5
Rott → Germany 48°27N 13°25E 179 G9
Rottenburg Germany 48°28N 8°55E 179 G4
Rottenmann Austria 47°31N 14°22E 180 D7
Rotterdam Neths. 51°55N 4°30E 170 C4
Rotterdam N.Y., U.S.A. 42°48N 74°1W 313 D10
Rottne Sweden 57°1N 14°54E 163 G8
Rottnest I. Australia 32°0S 115°27E 279 F2
Rottumeroog Neths. 53°33N 6°34E 170 A6
Rottweil Germany 48°9N 8°37E 179 G4
Rotuma Fiji 12°25S 177°5E 277 C14
Roubaix France 50°40N 3°10E 173 B10
Rouche Island St. Lucia 13°57N 60°52W 323 m
Roudnice nad Labem Czech Rep. 50°25N 14°15E 180 A7
Rouen France 49°27N 1°4E 172 C8
Rouergue France 44°15N 2°0E 174 D5
Rouge Hill Canada 43°48N 79°6W 141 A4
Rough Ridge N.Z. 45°10S 169°55E 285 F4
Rouillac France 45°47N 0°4W 174 C3
Rouleau Canada 50°10N 104°56W 297 C8
Roulers = Roeselare Belgium 50°57N 3°7E 170 D3
Round Hill Jamaica 17°50N 77°23W 320 a
Round Hill St. Kitts & Nevis 17°11N 62°36W 322 d
Round I. China 22°13N 114°11E 122 B2
Round Mountain U.S.A. 38°43N 117°4W 304 G5
Round Mt. Australia 30°26S 152°16E 283 A10
Round Rock U.S.A. 30°31N 97°41W 314 F6
Roundhouse Park Toronto, Canada 141 c2
Roundup U.S.A. 46°27N 108°33W 304 C9
Roura Fr. Guiana 4°44N 52°20W 329 C7
Rousay U.K. 59°10N 3°2W 167 B5
Rouses Point U.S.A. 44°59N 73°22W 313 B11
Rouseville U.S.A. 41°28N 79°42W 312 E5
Rousse = Ruse Bulgaria 43°48N 25°59E 203 C9
Roussenski Lom △ Bulgaria 43°40N 26°10E 203 C10
Roussillac Swamp Trin. & Tob. 10°14N 61°35W 323 t
Roussillon Isère, France 45°24N 4°49E 175 C8
Roussillon Pyrénées-Or., France 42°30N 2°35E 174 F6
Rouxville S. Africa 30°25S 26°50E 270 D4
Rouyn-Noranda Canada 48°20N 79°0W 298 C4
Rovaniemi Finland 66°29N 25°41E 160 C21
Rovato Italy 45°34N 10°0E 198 C7
Rovenki Ukraine 48°5N 39°21E 189 H10
Rovereto Italy 45°53N 11°3E 198 C8
Roverud Norway 60°15N 12°3E 164 D9
Rovigo Italy 45°4N 11°47E 199 C8
Rovinj Croatia 45°5N 13°40E 199 C10
Rovira Colombia 4°15N 75°20W 328 C2
Rovno = Rivne Ukraine 50°40N 26°10E 177 C14
Rovnoye Russia 50°52N 46°3E 190 E8
Rovuma = Ruvuma → Tanzania 10°29S 40°28E 269 E5
Row'ān Iran 35°8N 48°51E 247 C6
Rowena Australia 29°48S 148°55E 281 D4
Rowley Shoals Australia 17°30S 119°0E 278 C2
Roxa Guinea-Biss. 11°15N 15°45W 262 C1
Roxas Capiz, Phil. 11°36N 122°49E 233 F4
Roxas Isabela, Phil. 17°8N 121°36E 232 C3
Roxas Mind. Or., Phil. 12°35N 121°31E 232 E3
Roxas Palawan, Phil. 10°20N 119°21E 233 F2
Roxboro U.S.A. 36°24N 78°59W 315 C15
Roxborough Trin. & Tob. 11°15N 60°35W 323 s
Roxburgh N.Z. 45°33S 169°19E 285 F4
Roxbury Mass., U.S.A. 42°19N 71°5W 116 B2
Roxbury Pa., U.S.A. 40°6N 77°39W 312 F7
Roxby Downs Australia 30°43S 136°46E 281 E2
Roxen Sweden 58°30N 15°40E 163 F9
Roxeth U.K. 51°33N 0°20W 125 A1
Roy Mont., U.S.A. 47°20N 108°58W 304 C9
Roy N. Mex., U.S.A. 35°57N 104°12W 305 J11
Roy Utah, U.S.A. 41°10N 112°2W 304 F7
Roy Thomson Hall Toronto, Canada 141 b2
Royal △ Australia 34°5S 151°5E 283 C9
Royal Bardia △ Nepal 28°20N 81°20E 243 E9
Royal Botanic Gardens Sydney, Australia 139 b2
Royal Botanic Gardens Edinburgh, U.K. 55°58N 3°12W 121 B2
Royal Canal Ireland 53°30N 7°13W 166 C4
Royal Center U.S.A. 40°52N 86°30W 311 D10
Royal Chitawan △ Nepal 26°30N 84°30E 243 F11
Royal Leamington Spa U.K. 52°18N 1°31W 169 E6
Royal Manas △ Bhutan 26°45N 90°50E 241 B3
Royal Natal △ S. Africa 28°43S 28°51E 271 C4
Royal Oak U.S.A. 42°30N 83°9W 311 B13
Royal Observatory U.K. 55°55N 3°12W 121 B2
Royal Palace = Koninklijk Paleis Amsterdam, Neths. 112 b2
Royal Palace = Kungliga Slottet Stockholm, Sweden 139 b2
Royal Palace = Palacio Real Barcelona, Spain 114 b3
Royal Palace = Palacio Real Madrid, Spain 127 b1
Royal Palace = Palais Royal Brussels, Belgium 116 b3
Royal Palace = Slottet Oslo, Norway 133 a1
Royal Palm Beach U.S.A. 26°42N 80°14W 317 J9
Royal Park Australia 37°46S 144°57E 128 A1
Royal Tunbridge Wells U.K. 51°7N 0°16E 169 F8
Royal Turf Club Bangkok, Thailand 113 b2
Royale, Isle U.S.A. 48°0N 88°54W 308 B9
Royalla Australia 35°30S 149°9E 283 C8
Royan France 45°37N 1°2W 174 C2
Roye France 49°42N 2°48E 173 C9
Röylä Finland 60°18N 24°42E 121 B1
Royston U.K. 52°3N 0°0 169 E7
Rožaj Montenegro 42°50N 20°11E 202 D4
Różan Poland 52°52N 21°25E 185 F8
Rozas, Portilleros de las Spain 40°29N 3°49W 127 B1
Rozay-en-Brie France 48°41N 2°58E 173 D9
Rozdilna Ukraine 46°50N 30°2E 183 D15
Rozhnyativ Ukraine 48°56N 24°9E 183 B9
Rozhyshche Ukraine 50°54N 25°15E 177 C13
Rožmitál pod Třemšínem Czech Rep. 49°36N 13°53E 180 B6
Rožňava Slovak Rep. 48°37N 20°35E 181 C13
Rozogi Poland 53°28N 21°19E 184 E8
Rozoy-sur-Serre France 49°40N 4°8E 173 C11
Roztoczański △ Poland 50°37N 23°0E 185 H10
Roztoky Czech Rep. 50°9N 14°23E 135 B2
Rozzano Italy 45°22N 9°10E 129 B1
Rrëshen Albania 41°47N 19°49E 202 E3
Rrogozhine Albania 41°4N 19°50E 202 E3
Rtanj Serbia 43°45N 21°50E 202 C5
Rtem, O. el → Algeria 33°29N 5°38E 261 B6
Rtishchevo Russia 52°18N 43°46E 190 D6
Rúa = A Rúa Spain 42°24N 7°6W 194 C3
Ruacaná Namibia 17°27S 14°21E 265 F2
Ruaha △ Tanzania 7°41S 34°30E 268 D3
Ruahine Ra. N.Z. 39°55S 176°2E 284 F5
Ruamahanga → N.Z. 41°24S 175°8E 284 H4
Ruapehu N.Z. 39°17S 175°35E 284 F4
Ruapuke I. N.Z. 46°46S 168°31E 285 G3
Ruâq, W. → Egypt 30°0N 33°49E 251 J4
Ruatoria N.Z. 37°55S 178°20E 284 D7
Ruavatu Solomon Is. 9°26S 160°26E 287 M11
Ruawai N.Z. 36°8S 173°59E 284 C2
Rub' al Khālī Si. Arabia 19°0N 48°0E 249 C5
Rubeho Mts. Tanzania 6°50S 36°25E 268 D4
Rubezhnoye = Rubizhne Ukraine 49°6N 38°25E 189 H10
Rubh a' Mhail U.K. 55°56N 6°8W 167 F2
Rubha Hunish U.K. 57°42N 6°20W 167 D2
Rubha Robhanais = Lewis, Butt of U.K. 58°31N 6°16W 167 C2
Rubi Spain 41°29N 2°2E 196 D7
Rubí → Spain 41°26N 2°0E 114 A1
Rubiataba Brazil 15°8S 49°48W 333 E2
Rubicon → U.S.A. 38°53N 121°4W 306 G5
Rubicone → Italy 44°8N 12°28E 199 D9
Rubik Albania 41°46N 19°47E 202 E3
Rubinéia Brazil 20°13S 51°2W 333 F1
Rubino Ivory C. 6°4N 4°18W 262 D4
Rubio Venezuela 7°43N 72°22W 328 B3
Rubizhne Ukraine 49°6N 38°25E 189 H10
Rublovo Russia 55°47N 37°21E 129 B2
Rubondo △ Tanzania 2°18S 31°58E 268 C3
Rubtsovsk Russia 51°30N 81°10E 217 B10
Ruby U.S.A. 64°45N 155°30W 303 D9
Ruby Beach = Jacksonville Beach U.S.A. 30°17N 81°24W 316 E8
Ruby L. U.S.A. 40°10N 115°28W 304 F6
Ruby Mts. U.S.A. 40°30N 115°20W 304 F6
Rubyvale Australia 23°25S 147°42E 280 C4
Rucheng China 25°33N 113°38E 229 E9
Ruciane-Nida Poland 53°40N 21°32E 184 E8
Rūd Sar Iran 37°8N 50°18E 247 B6
Ruda Sweden 57°6N 16°7E 163 G10
Ruda Śląska Poland 50°16N 18°50E 185 H5
Rudall Australia 33°43S 136°17E 282 B2
Rudall → Australia 22°34S 122°13E 278 D3
Rudall River △ Australia 22°38S 122°30E 278 D3
Rūdbār Afghan. 30°9N 62°36E 240 C1
Rüdersdorf Germany 52°27N 13°47E 178 C9
Rudewa Tanzania 10°7S 34°40E 269 E3
Rudkøbing Denmark 54°56N 10°41E 163 K4
Rudky Ukraine 49°38N 23°29E 185 J10
Rudna Poland 51°30N 16°17E 185 G3
Rudnevka → Russia 55°43N 37°56E 129 B5
Rudnik Bulgaria 42°36N 27°30E 203 D11
Rudnik Poland 50°26N 22°15E 185 H9
Rudnik Serbia 44°7N 20°35E 202 B4
Rudnya Russia 54°55N 31°7E 188 E6
Rudnytsa Ukraine 48°16N 28°54E 183 B13
Rudnyy Kazakhstan 52°57N 63°7E 216 B6
Rudo Bos.-H. 43°41N 19°23E 182 G4
Rudolfa, Ostrov Russia 81°45N 58°30E 214 A6
Rudolfsheim Austria 48°12N 16°20E 142 A2
Rudolfshöhe Germany 52°37N 13°44E 115 A5
Rudolstadt Germany 50°44N 11°19E 178 E7
Rudong China 32°20N 121°12E 229 A13
Rudow Germany 52°24N 13°29E 115 B2
Rudozem Bulgaria 41°29N 24°51E 203 E8

422 Rudyard INDEX

Rudyard U.S.A. 46°14N 84°36W 309 B11
Rue France 50°15N 1°40E 173 B8
Rueil-Malmaison France 48°52N 2°11E 134 A2
Ruenya → Africa 16°24S 33°48E 269 F3
Rufa'a Sudan 14°44N 33°22E 257 E3
Rufflin U.S.A. 33°00N 80°49W 316 B9
Ruffling Pt. Br. Virgin Is. 18°44N 64°27W 321 b
Rufiji → Tanzania 7°50S 39°15E 268 D4
Rufino Argentina 34°20S 62°50W 334 C3
Rufisque Senegal 14°40N 17°15W 262 C1
Rufunsa Zambia 15°4S 29°34E 269 F2
Rugao China 32°23N 120°31E 229 A13
Rugby Warks., U.K. 52°23N 1°16W 169 E6
Rugby N. Dak., U.S.A. 48°22N 100°0W 308 A4
Rügen Germany 54°22N 13°24E 178 A9
Rügen ⌓ Germany 54°25N 13°25E 178 A9
Rugles France 48°50N 0°40E 172 D7
Ruhea Bangla. 26°10N 88°25E 241 B2
Ruhengeri Rwanda 1°30S 29°36E 268 C2
Ruhla Germany 50°54N 10°23E 178 E6
Ruhland Germany 51°27N 13°51E 178 D9
Ruhnu Estonia 57°48N 23°15E 184 A10
Ruhr → Germany 51°27N 6°43E 178 D2
Ruhuhu → Tanzania 10°31S 34°34E 269 E3
Rui Barbosa Brazil 12°18S 40°27W 333 D3
Rui'an China 27°47N 120°40E 229 D13
Ruichang China 29°40N 115°39E 229 C10
Ruidoso U.S.A. 33°20N 105°41W 305 K11
Ruijin China 25°48N 116°0E 229 E10
Ruili China 24°1N 97°43E 228 E1
Ruisbroek Belgium 50°47N 4°18E 116 B1
Ruislip U.K. 51°34N 0°24W 125 A1
Ruivo, Pico Madeira 32°45N 16°56W 153 c
Ruj Bulgaria 42°52N 22°34E 202 D6
Rujen Macedonia 42°9N 22°30E 202 D6
Rujm Tal'at al Jamā'ah Jordan 30°24N 35°30E 251 H6
Ruk Pakistan 27°50N 68°42E 242 F3
Rukan-sho Japan 26°6N 127°32E 288 a
Rukhla Pakistan 32°27N 71°57E 242 C4
Rukwa □ Tanzania 7°0S 31°30E 268 D3
Rukwa, L. Tanzania 8°0S 32°20E 268 D3
Rulhieres, C. Australia 13°56S 127°22E 278 B4
Rum = Rhum U.K. 57°0N 6°20W 167 E2
Rum Jordan 29°39N 35°26E 251 J6
Rum Cay Bahamas 23°40N 74°58W 321 B5
Rum Jungle Australia 13°0S 130°59E 278 B5
Ruma Serbia 45°0N 19°50E 182 E4
Ruma △ Kenya 0°39S 34°18E 268 C3
Rumāḥ Si. Arabia 25°29N 47°10E 246 E5
Rumania = Romania ■ Europe 46°0N 25°0E 183 D10
Rumaylah Iraq 30°47N 47°37E 246 D5
Rumaylah, 'Urūq ar Si. Arabia 22°0N 48°30E 249 B5
Rumbêk Sudan 6°54N 29°37E 257 F2
Rumburk Czech Rep. 50°57N 14°32E 180 A7
Rumelihisarı Turkey 41°4N 29°2E 122 B2
Rumford U.S.A. 44°33N 70°33W 313 B14
Rumia Poland 54°37N 18°25E 184 D5
Rumilly France 45°53N 5°56E 175 C9
Rummelsburg = Miastko Poland 54°0N 16°58E 184 E3
Rumoi Japan 43°56N 141°39E 220 C10
Rumonge Burundi 3°59S 29°26E 268 C2
Rumson U.S.A. 40°23N 74°0W 313 F11
Rumung Micronesia 9°37N 138°9E 287 R16
Rumuruti Kenya 0°17N 36°32E 268 B4
Rumyantsevo Russia 55°38N 37°25E 129 C2
Runan China 33°0N 114°30E 226 H8
Runanga N.Z. 42°25S 171°15E 285 C6
Runaway, C. N.Z. 37°32S 177°59E 284 D6
Runaway B. Antigua & B. 17°9N 61°51W 322 b
Runaway Bay Jamaica 18°27N 77°20W 320 a
Runcorn U.K. 53°21N 2°44W 168 D5
Rundu Namibia 17°52S 19°43E 270 A2
Rungis France 48°44N 2°20E 134 B3
Rungwa Tanzania 6°55S 33°32E 268 D3
Rungwa → Tanzania 7°36S 31°50E 268 D3
Rungwa ⌓ Tanzania 6°53S 34°2E 268 D3
Rungwe Tanzania 9°11S 33°32E 269 D3
Runka Nigeria 12°28N 7°20E 263 C6
Runn Sweden 60°30N 15°40E 162 D9
Runton Ra. Australia 23°31S 123°6E 278 D3
Runu Micronesia 9°35N 138°8E 287 R16
Ruo Shui → China 41°0N 100°16E 218 B5
Ruokolahti Finland 61°17N 28°50E 188 B5
Ruoqiang China 38°55N 88°10E 217 E11
Rupa India 27°15N 92°21E 241 B4
Rupar India 31°2N 76°38E 242 D7
Rupat Indonesia 1°45N 101°40E 234 B2
Rupea Romania 46°2N 25°13E 183 D10
Rupen → India 23°28N 71°31E 242 H4
Rupert U.S.A. 42°37N 113°41W 304 E7
Rupert → Canada 51°29N 78°45W 298 B4
Rupert B. Canada 51°35N 79°0W 298 B4
Rupert House = Waskaganish Canada 51°30N 78°40W 298 B4
Rupsa India 21°37N 87°1E 243 J12
Rupununi → Guyana 4°3N 58°35W 329 C6
Rur → Germany 51°11N 5°59E 178 D1
Rurópolis Brazil 4°3S 54°59W 329 D7
Rurrenabaque Bolivia 14°30S 67°32W 330 C4
Rurutu French Polynesia 22°26S 151°20W 289 f
Rus → Spain 39°30N 2°30W 197 F2
Rusāfa Iraq 33°21N 44°23E 113 A2
Rusambo Zimbabwe 16°30S 32°4E 269 F3
Rusape Zimbabwe 18°35S 32°8E 269 F3
Ruschuk = Ruse Bulgaria 43°48N 25°59E 203 C9
Ruse Bulgaria 43°48N 25°59E 203 C9
Ruse □ Bulgaria 43°35N 26°20E 203 C10
Ruşeţu Romania 44°57N 27°14E 183 F12
Rush Ireland 53°31N 6°6W 166 C5
Rush Green U.K. 51°33N 0°10E 125 A5
Rushan China 36°56N 121°30E 227 F11
Rushden U.K. 52°18N 0°35W 169 E7
Rushikulya → India 19°23N 85°5E 244 E7
Rushmore, Mt. U.S.A. 43°53N 103°28W 308 D2
Rushville Ill., U.S.A. 40°7N 90°34W 310 D6
Rushville Ind., U.S.A. 39°37N 85°27W 311 E11
Rushville Nebr., U.S.A. 42°43N 102°28W 308 D2
Rushworth Australia 36°32S 145°1E 283 D6
Ruskin U.S.A. 27°43N 82°26W 317 H7
Russa India 22°29N 88°21E 124 C2
Russas Brazil 4°55S 37°50W 332 B4
Russell Man., Canada 50°50N 101°20W 297 C8
Russell N.Z. 35°16S 174°10E 284 B3
Russell Fla., U.S.A. 30°3N 81°45W 316 E8
Russell Kans., U.S.A. 38°54N 98°52W 308 F4
Russell N.Y., U.S.A. 44°27N 75°9W 313 B9
Russell Pa., U.S.A. 41°56N 79°8W 312 E5
Russell Cave ⌓ U.S.A. 34°59N 85°49W 315 D12
Russell Is. Solomon Is. 9°4S 159°12E 287 M10
Russell L. Man., Canada 56°15N 101°30W 297 B8
Russell L. N.W.T., Canada 63°5N 115°44W 296 A5
Russellkonda India 19°57N 84°42E 244 E7
Russells Point U.S.A. 40°28N 83°54W 311 D13
Russellville Ala., U.S.A. 34°30N 87°44W 315 D11
Russellville Ark., U.S.A. 35°17N 93°8W 314 D8
Russellville Ky., U.S.A. 36°51N 86°53W 308 G10
Rüsselsheim Germany 49°59N 8°23E 179 F4
Russi Italy 44°22N 12°2E 199 D9
Russia ■ Eurasia 62°0N 105°0E 215 C11
Russian → U.S.A. 38°27N 123°8W 306 G3
Russian Hill San Francisco, U.S.A. 136 a1
Russian Mission U.S.A. 61°47N 161°19W 303 F7
Russiaville U.S.A. 40°25N 86°16W 311 D10
Russkoye Ustie Russia 71°0N 149°0E 150 B15
Rust Austria 47°49N 16°42E 181 D9
Rustam Pakistan 34°25N 72°13E 242 B5
Rustam Shahr Pakistan 26°58N 66°6E 242 F2
Rustavi Georgia 41°30N 45°0E 191 K7
Rustenburg S. Africa 25°41S 27°14E 270 C4
Ruston U.S.A. 32°32N 92°38W 314 E8
Rutana Burundi 3°55S 30°0E 268 C3
Rute Spain 37°19N 4°23W 195 H6
Ruteng Indonesia 8°35S 120°30E 231 F6
Ruth U.S.A. 43°42N 82°45W 312 C2
Rutherford Calif., U.S.A. 38°26N 122°24W 306 G4
Rutherford N.J., U.S.A. 40°49N 74°6W 132 B1
Rutherglen Australia 36°5S 146°29E 283 D7
Rutland U.S.A. 43°37N 72°58W 313 C12
Rutland □ U.K. 52°38N 0°40W 169 E7
Rutland I. India 11°25N 92°10E 245 J11
Rutland Water U.K. 52°39N 0°38W 169 E7
Rutledalen Norway 61°4N 5°10E 164 C2
Rutledge U.S.A. 33°38N 83°37W 316 B6
Rutledge → Canada 61°4N 112°0W 297 A6
Rutledge L. Canada 61°33N 110°47W 297 A6
Rutog China 33°27N 79°42E 217 F9
Rutqa, W. → Syria 34°30N 41°3E 213 E9
Rutshuru Dem. Rep. of the Congo 1°13S 29°25E 268 C2
Ruvo di Púglia Italy 41°7N 16°29E 201 A9
Ruvu Tanzania 6°49S 38°43E 268 D4
Ruvu → Tanzania 6°23S 38°52E 268 D4
Ruvuba △ Burundi 3°3S 29°33E 268 C2
Ruvuma □ Tanzania 10°20S 36°0E 269 E4
Ruvuma → Tanzania 10°29S 40°28E 269 E5
Ruwais U.A.E. 24°5N 52°50E 247 E7
Ruwenzori Africa 0°30N 29°55E 268 B2
Ruwenzori △ Uganda 0°20N 30°0E 268 B2
Ruya → Zimbabwe 16°27S 32°5E 271 A5
Ruyigi Burundi 3°29S 30°15E 268 C3
Ruyuan China 24°46N 113°16E 229 E9
Ruzaevka Kazakhstan 52°49N 66°56E 217 B7
Ruzayevka Russia 54°4N 45°0E 190 C7
Rŭzhevo Konare Bulgaria 42°23N 24°46E 203 D8
Ružomberok Slovak Rep. 49°3N 19°17E 181 B12
Ruzyně Czech Rep. 50°5N 14°17E 135 B1
Ruzyne, Praha ✕ (PRG) Czech Rep. 50°6N 14°16E 135 B1
Rwanda ■ Africa 2°0S 30°0E 268 C3
Ryakhovo Bulgaria 43°58N 26°18E 203 C10
Ryan, L. U.K. 55°0N 5°2W 167 G3
Ryazan Russia 54°40N 39°40E 188 E10
Ryazan □ Russia 54°5N 39°30E 190 C4
Ryazhsk Russia 53°45N 40°3E 188 F11
Rybachiy Russia 55°10N 20°50E 184 C7
Rybachiy Poluostrov Russia 69°43N 32°0E 160 B25
Rybachye = Balykchy Kyrgyzstan 42°26N 76°12E 217 D9
Rybatskaya Russia 59°59N 30°29E 137 B2
Rybinsk Russia 58°5N 38°50E 188 C10
Rybinskoye Vdkhr. Russia 58°30N 38°25E 188 C10
Rybnik Poland 50°6N 18°32E 185 H5
Rybnitsa = Râbniţa Moldova 47°45N 29°0E 183 C14
Rybnoye Russia 54°45N 39°30E 188 E10
Rychnov nad Kněžnou Czech Rep. 50°10N 16°17E 181 A9
Rychwał Poland 52°4N 18°10E 185 F5
Rycroft Canada 55°45N 118°40W 296 B5
Ryd Sweden 56°27N 14°42E 163 H8
Rydaholm Sweden 56°59N 14°18E 163 H8
Rydboholm Sweden 59°26N 18°12E 139 A3
Ryde N.S.W., Australia 33°48S 151°6E 139 A1
Ryde I. of W., U.K. 50°43N 1°9W 169 G6
Ryderwood U.S.A. 46°23N 123°3W 306 D3
Rydzyna Poland 51°47N 16°39E 185 G3
Rye U.K. 50°57N 0°45E 169 G8
Rye → U.K. 54°11N 0°44W 168 C7
Rye Bay U.K. 50°52N 0°49E 169 G8
Rye Patch Res. U.S.A. 40°28N 118°19W 304 F4
Ryegate U.S.A. 46°18N 109°15W 304 C9
Ryerson Polytechnic University Toronto, Canada 141 a3
Ryfylke Norway 59°25N 6°25E 164 E3
Rykene Norway 58°24N 8°37E 164 F5
Ryki Poland 51°38N 21°56E 185 G8
Rykovo = Yenakiyeve Ukraine 48°15N 38°15E 189 H10
Ryley Canada 53°17N 112°26W 296 C6
Rylsk Russia 51°36N 34°43E 189 G8
Rylstone Australia 32°46S 149°58E 283 B8
Rymanów Poland 49°35N 21°51E 185 J8
Ryn Poland 53°57N 21°34E 184 E8
Ryn Peski = Naryn Qum Kazakhstan 47°30N 49°0E 191 G9
Ryōgoku Japan 35°40N 139°48E 140 A3
Ryōhaku-Sanchi Japan 36°9N 136°49E 223 A8
Ryojun = Lüshun China 38°45N 121°15E 227 E11
Ryōtsu Japan 38°5N 138°26E 220 E9
Rypin Poland 53°3N 19°25E 185 E6
Ryssby Sweden 56°52N 14°10E 163 H8
Rysy Europe 49°10N 20°4E 181 B13
Ryūgasaki Japan 35°54N 140°11E 223 B12
Ryukyu Is. = Ryūkyū-rettō Japan 26°0N 126°0E 221 M3
Ryūkyū-rettō Japan 26°0N 126°0E 221 M3
Rzepin Poland 52°20N 14°49E 185 F1
Rzeszów Poland 50°5N 21°58E 185 H8
Rzhev Russia 56°20N 34°20E 188 D8
Rzhevka Russia 59°59N 30°31E 137 B3

S

Sa Thailand 18°34N 100°45E 236 C3
Sa Canal Spain 38°51N 1°23E 206 D1
Sa Conillera Spain 38°59N 1°13E 206 D1
Sa Dec Vietnam 10°20N 105°46E 237 G5
Sa Dragonera Spain 39°35N 2°19E 206 B3
Sa-koi Burma 19°54N 97°3E 241 F6
Sa Mesquida Spain 39°55N 4°16E 206 B5
Sa Pobla Spain 39°46N 3°1E 206 B4
Sa Savina Spain 38°44N 1°25E 206 D1
Sa'a Solomon Is. 9°43S 161°35E 287 M11
Sa'ādatābād Fārs, Iran 30°10N 53°5E 247 D7
Sa'ādatābād Hormozgān, Iran 28°3N 55°53E 247 D7
Sa'ādatābād Kermān, Iran 29°40N 55°51E 247 D7
Sa'ādatābād Tehrān, Iran 35°47N 51°22E 141 A2
Saādūn Iraq 33°19N 44°25E 113 B2
Saale → Germany 51°56N 11°54E 178 D7
Saaler Bodden Germany 54°20N 12°27E 178 A8
Saalfeld Germany 50°38N 11°21E 178 E7
Saalfelden Austria 47°25N 12°51E 180 D5
Saane → Switz. 47°8N 7°10E 179 H3
Saanich Canada 48°29N 123°26W 306 B3
Saar → Europe 49°41N 6°32E 170 E6
Saar-Hunsrück ⌓ Germany 49°30N 6°50E 179 F2
Saar in Mähren = Žďár nad Sázavou Czech Rep. 49°34N 15°57E 180 B8
Saarbrücken Germany 49°14N 6°59E 179 F2
Saarburg Germany 49°36N 6°32E 179 F2
Saaremaa Estonia 58°30N 22°30E 188 C2
Saarijärvi Finland 62°43N 25°16E 160 E21
Saariselkä Finland 68°16N 28°15E 160 B23
Saarland □ Germany 49°20N 7°0E 179 F2
Saarlautern = Saarlouis Germany 49°18N 6°45E 179 F2
Saarlouis Germany 49°18N 6°45E 179 F2
Saavedra Argentina 34°33S 58°29W 117 B2
Saaz = Žatec Czech Rep. 50°20N 13°32E 180 A6
Sab 'Ābar Syria 33°46N 37°41E 212 F7
Saba W. Indies 17°38N 63°14W 322 a
Šabac Serbia 44°48N 19°42E 202 B3
Sabadell Spain 41°28N 2°7E 196 D7
Sabae Japan 35°57N 136°11E 223 B8
Sabah □ Malaysia 6°0N 117°0E 235 A5
Sabak Bernam Malaysia 3°46N 100°58E 237 L3
Sabalān, Kūhhā-ye Iran 38°15N 47°45E 213 C12
Sabalana, Kepulauan Indonesia 6°45S 118°50E 231 F5
Sabana, Arch. de Cuba 23°0N 80°0W 320 B3
Sábana de la Mar Dom. Rep. 19°7N 69°24W 321 C6
Sabana Grande Puerto Rico 18°5N 66°58W 321 b
Sabana Westpunt = Westpunt Neth. Ant. 12°22N 69°10W 322 g
Sabanalarga Colombia 10°38N 74°55W 328 A3
Sabaneta Pt. N. Marianas 15°17N 145°49E 302 e
Sabang Indonesia 5°50N 95°15E 234 A1
Săbăoani Romania 47°1N 26°51E 183 C11
Sabará Brazil 19°55S 43°46W 333 E3
Sabari → India 17°35N 81°16E 244 F5
Sabarmati → India 22°18N 72°22E 242 H5
Sab'atayn, Ramlat as Yemen 15°30N 46°10E 248 D4
Sabattis U.S.A. 44°6N 74°40W 313 B10
Sabáudia Italy 41°18N 13°1E 200 A6
Sabaya Bolivia 19°1S 68°23W 330 D4
Şabāyā, Jaza'ir Si. Arabia 18°35N 41°3E 248 C3
Saberania Indonesia 2°5S 138°18E 231 E9
Sabhā Libya 27°9N 14°29E 258 C2
Sabhā □ Libya 26°0N 14°0E 258 C2
Sabi → India 28°29N 76°44E 242 E7
Sabi Game Reserve = Kruger △ S. Africa 24°50S 26°10E 271 B4
Sabidana, J. Sudan 18°4N 36°50E 256 D4
Sabie S. Africa 25°10S 30°48E 271 C5
Sabina U.S.A. 39°29N 83°38W 311 E13
Sabinal Chihuahua, Mexico 30°57N 107°30W 318 A3
Sabinal Tex., U.S.A. 29°19N 99°28W 314 G5
Sabiñánigo Spain 42°31N 0°22W 196 C4
Sabinar, Punta del Spain 36°43N 2°44W 197 J2
Sabinas Mexico 27°51N 101°7W 318 B4
Sabinas → Mexico 27°37N 100°42W 318 B4
Sabinas Hidalgo Mexico 26°30N 100°10W 318 B4
Sabine → U.S.A. 29°59N 93°47W 314 G8
Sabine L. U.S.A. 29°53N 93°51W 314 G8
Sabine Pass U.S.A. 29°44N 93°54W 314 G8
Sabinópolis Brazil 18°40S 43°6W 333 E3
Sabinov Slovak Rep. 49°6N 21°5E 181 B14
Sabinsville U.S.A. 41°52N 77°31W 312 E7
Sabirabad Azerbaijan 40°5N 48°30E 191 K9
Sabka Chad 19°15N 16°35E 259 E3
Sablayan Phil. 12°50N 120°50E 232 E3
Sable Canada 55°30N 68°21W 299 A6
Sable, C. N.S., Canada 43°29N 65°38W 299 D6
Sable, C. Fla., U.S.A. 25°9N 81°8W 317 K8
Sable I. Canada 44°0N 60°0W 299 D8
Sable I. Papua N. G. 3°38S 154°42E 286 B8
Sablé-sur-Sarthe France 47°50N 0°20W 172 E6
Saboeiro Brazil 6°32S 39°54W 332 C4
Saboli India 28°42N 77°18E 120 A2
Sabonkafi Niger 14°40N 8°45E 259 F1
Sabor → Portugal 41°10N 7°7W 194 D3
Sabou Burkina Faso 12°1N 2°15W 262 C4
Şabrātah Libya 32°47N 12°29E 258 B2
Sabres France 44°9N 0°43W 174 D3
Sabria Tunisia 33°22N 8°45E 258 B1
Sabrina Coast Antarctica 68°0S 120°0E 151 C9
Sabtang I. Phil. 20°19N 121°52E 232 A3
Sabugal Portugal 40°20N 7°5W 194 E3
Sabugo Portugal 38°49N 9°17W 126 A1
Sabula U.S.A. 42°4N 90°10W 310 B6
Sabulubbek Indonesia 1°36S 98°40E 234 C1
Sabuncu Turkey 39°33N 30°12E 205 B12
Şabyā Si. Arabia 17°9N 42°37E 248 C3
Sabzevār Iran 36°15N 57°40E 247 B8
Sabzi Mand India 28°40N 77°12E 120 A2
Sabzvārān Iran 28°45N 57°50E 247 D8
Sac City U.S.A. 42°25N 95°0W 310 B2
Sacaolo Angola 12°58S 22°28E 265 E4
Sacatengo Angola 13°16S 21°20E 265 E4
Sacavém Portugal 38°47N 9°6W 126 A2
Sacedón Spain 40°29N 2°41W 196 E2
Săcele Romania 45°37N 25°41E 183 E10
Sacheon S. Korea 35°0N 128°6E 224 E4
Sachigo → Canada 55°6N 88°58W 298 A2
Sachigo, L. Canada 53°50N 92°12W 298 B1
Sachimbo Angola 9°14S 20°16E 265 D4
Sachin India 21°5N 72°53E 244 D1
Sachkhere Georgia 42°25N 43°28E 191 J6
Sachsen □ Germany 50°55N 13°10E 178 E9
Sachsen-Anhalt □ Germany 52°0N 12°0E 178 D7
Sächsische Schweiz △ Germany 50°55N 14°10E 178 E10
Sacile Italy 45°57N 12°30E 199 C9
Sackets Harbor U.S.A. 43°57N 76°7W 313 C8
Sackville Canada 45°54N 64°22W 299 C7
Saclay France 48°43N 2°10E 134 B2
Saclay, Étang de France 48°44N 2°9E 134 B1
Saco Maine, U.S.A. 43°30N 70°27W 313 C14
Saco Mont., U.S.A. 48°28N 107°21W 304 B10
Sacomã Brazil 23°36S 46°35W 137 B2
Sacramento = Itatupa Brazil 0°37S 51°12W 329 D7
Sacramento Brazil 19°53S 47°27W 333 E2
Sacramento Calif., U.S.A. 38°35N 121°29W 306 G5
Sacramento → U.S.A. 38°3N 121°56W 306 G5
Sacramento Mts. U.S.A. 32°30N 105°30W 305 K11
Sacramento Valley U.S.A. 39°30N 122°0W 306 G5
Sacratif, C. Spain 36°42N 3°28W 195 J7
Sacré Cœur Paris, France 134 a4
Sacrow Germany 52°25N 13°6E 115 B1
Sacrower See Germany 52°26N 13°6E 115 B1
Săcueni Romania 47°20N 22°5E 182 C7
Sada Mayotte 12°51S 45°6E 271 a
Sada Spain 43°22N 8°15W 194 B2
Sada-Misaki Japan 33°20N 132°5E 222 D4
Sada-Misaki-Hantō Japan 33°22N 132°1E 222 D4
Sădaba Spain 42°19N 1°12W 196 C3
Sadabad India 27°27N 78°3E 242 F8
Şa'dah Yemen 16°15N 43°37E 248 C3
Sadang S. Korea 37°29N 126°58E 137 C1
Sadani Tanzania 5°58S 38°35E 268 D4
Sadao Thailand 6°38N 100°26E 237 J3
Sadar Bazar Delhi, India 120 a1
Sadaseopet India 17°38N 77°59E 244 F3
Sadd el Aali Egypt 23°54N 32°54E 256 C3
Saddle → U.S.A. 40°51N 74°6W 132 A1
Saddle Brook U.S.A. 40°53N 74°5W 132 A1
Saddle Hill St. Kitts & Nevis 17°7N 62°33W 322 d
Saddle Mt. U.S.A. 45°58N 123°41W 306 E3
Saddle Pk. India 13°9N 93°1E 245 H11
Saddle Pt. St. Helena 15°57S 5°38W 153 h
Sade Nigeria 11°22N 10°45E 263 C7
Şadh Oman 17°3N 55°4E 249 C6
Sadhoowa Trin. & Tob. 10°8N 61°27W 323 t
Sadimi Dem. Rep. of the Congo 9°25S 23°32E 265 D4
Sadiola Mali 13°50N 11°40W 262 C2
Sadiya India 27°50N 95°40E 241 B5
Sa'dīyah, Hawr as Iraq 32°15N 46°30E 213 F12
Sadlers St. Kitts & Nevis 17°24N 62°47W 322 d
Sado Japan 38°0N 138°25E 220 F9
Sado → Portugal 38°29N 8°55W 195 G2
Sadon Russia 42°52N 43°58E 191 J6
Sadovoye Russia 47°47N 44°31E 191 G7
Sadowara Japan 32°2N 131°26E 222 E3
Sadr Pakistan 24°51N 67°2E 123 A2
Sadr City Iraq 33°23N 44°27E 113 A2
Sadra India 23°21N 72°43E 242 H5
Sadri India 25°11N 73°26E 242 G5
Sadyba Poland 52°11N 21°3E 142 B2
Sæbøvik Norway 59°47N 5°40E 164 E2
Sæby Denmark 57°21N 10°30E 163 G4
Saegertown U.S.A. 41°43N 80°9W 312 E4
Saelices Spain 39°55N 2°49W 196 F2
Sætre Norway 59°41N 10°33E 164 E7
Sævareid Norway 60°11N 5°46E 164 D2
Safaalan Turkey 41°26N 28°6E 203 E12
Safaga Egypt 26°42N 34°0E 256 B3
Şafājah Si. Arabia 26°25N 39°0E 246 E3
Šafárikovo = Tornal'a Slovak Rep. 48°25N 20°20E 181 C13
Safata B. Samoa 14°0S 171°50W 287 W20
Safdar Jang's Tomb India 28°35N 77°12E 120 B2
Safed Koh Afghan. 34°0N 70°0E 240 B3
Säffle Sweden 59°8N 12°55E 162 E6
Safford U.S.A. 32°50N 109°43W 305 K9
Saffron Walden U.K. 52°1N 0°16E 169 E8
Safi Morocco 32°18N 9°20W 260 B3
Safi □ Morocco 32°10N 8°50W 260 B3
Safia Papua N. G. 9°35S 148°38E 286 E5
Safia, Hamada Mali 23°10N 4°15W 260 D4
Şafīābād Iran 36°45N 57°58E 247 B8
Safīd Dasht Iran 33°27N 48°11E 247 C6
Safīd Kūh Afghan. 34°45N 63°0E 240 B1
Safīd Rūd → Iran 37°23N 50°11E 247 B6
Safipur India 26°44N 80°21E 243 F9
Şāfītā Syria 34°48N 36°7E 250 D7
Safonovo Russia 55°4N 33°16E 188 E7
Safranbolu Turkey 41°15N 32°41E 212 B5
Saft el Laban Egypt 30°1N 31°10E 117 A2
Saft Rashîn Egypt 28°58N 30°55E 256 J7
Safune Samoa 13°25S 172°21W 287 V19
Şafwān Iraq 30°7N 47°43E 246 D5
Sag Harbor U.S.A. 41°0N 72°18W 313 F12
Sag Sag Papua N. G. 5°32S 148°23E 286 C5
Saga Kōchi, Japan 33°5N 133°6E 222 D5
Saga Saga, Japan 33°15N 130°16E 222 D2
Saga □ Japan 33°15N 130°20E 222 D2
Sagae Japan 38°22N 140°17E 220 E10
Sagaing Burma 21°52N 95°59E 241 E5
Sagaing □ Burma 23°55N 95°56E 241 D5
Sagala Mali 14°9N 6°38W 262 C3
Sagami-Nada Japan 34°58N 139°30E 223 C11
Sagami-Wan Japan 35°15N 139°25E 223 B11
Sagamihara Japan 35°33N 139°25E 223 B11
Sagamore U.S.A. 40°46N 79°14W 312 F5
Sagan = Żagań Poland 51°39N 15°22E 185 G2
Saganaga L. Canada 48°14N 90°52W 308 A8
Saganashkee Slough U.S.A. 41°41N 87°53W 119 C1
Saganoseki Japan 33°15N 131°53E 222 D3
Sagar Karnataka, India 16°38N 76°48E 244 F3
Sagar Karnataka, India 14°14N 75°6E 245 G2
Sagar Mad. P., India 23°50N 78°44E 243 H8
Sagara Japan 34°41N 138°12E 223 C10
Sagara, L. Tanzania 5°20S 31°0E 268 D3
Sagarmatha = Everest, Mt. Nepal 28°5N 86°58E 243 E12
Sagarmatha △ Nepal 27°55N 86°45E 243 F12
Sagavanirktok → U.S.A. 70°19N 147°53W 303 A11
Sagay Phil. 10°57N 123°25E 233 F4
Sagene Norway 59°55N 10°46E 133 A3
Saghîr, El Bahr el → Egypt 31°8N 31°54E 251 G2
Sagiada Greece 39°38N 20°12E 206 B10
Saginaw U.S.A. 43°26N 83°56W 309 D12
Saginaw B. U.S.A. 43°50N 83°40W 309 D12
Sagleipie Liberia 7°0N 8°52W 262 D3
Saglouc = Salluit Canada 62°14N 75°38W 295 C12
Sagone France 42°7N 8°42E 175 F12
Sagone, G. de France 42°4N 8°40E 175 F12
Sagrada Familia, Templo de Barcelona, Spain 114 a2
Sagres Portugal 37°0N 8°58W 195 J2
Sagu Burma 20°13N 94°46E 241 E5
Sagua la Grande Cuba 22°50N 80°10W 320 B3
Saguache U.S.A. 38°5N 106°8W 304 G10
Saguaro △ U.S.A. 32°12N 110°38W 305 K8
Saguenay → Canada 48°22N 71°0W 299 C5
Saguia el Hamra → W. Sahara 27°24N 13°43W 260 C2
Sagunt Spain 39°42N 0°18W 196 F4
Sagunto = Sagunt Spain 39°42N 0°18W 196 F4
Sagvag Norway 59°46N 5°25E 164 E2
Sagwara India 23°41N 74°1E 242 H6
Sahaba Sudan 18°57N 30°25E 256 D3
Sahagún Colombia 8°57N 75°27W 328 B2
Sahagún Spain 42°18N 5°2W 194 C5
Saḥam al Jawlān Syria 32°45N 35°55E 250 F6
Sahamandrevo Madag. 23°15S 45°35E 272 C2
Sahand, Kūh-e Iran 37°44N 46°27E 213 D12
Sahar, Mumbai ✕ (BOM) India 19°5N 72°51E 130 A2
Sahara Africa 23°0N 5°0E 254 D4
Sahara, G. Egypt 28°2N 34°8E 251 K5
Saharan Atlas = Saharien, Atlas Algeria 33°30N 1°0E 261 B5
Saharan Seamounts Atl. Oc. 25°30N 19°50W 152 D10
Saharanpur India 29°58N 77°33E 242 E7
Saharien, Atlas Algeria 33°30N 1°0E 261 B5
Saharsa India 25°53N 86°36E 243 G12
Sahasinaka Madag. 21°49S 47°49E 272 C2
Sahaswan India 28°5N 78°45E 243 E8
Saheira, W. el → Egypt 30°5N 33°25E 251 H4
Sahel Africa 16°0N 5°0E 254 E3
Sahel, Canal du Mali 14°20N 6°0W 262 C3
Sahibganj India 25°12N 87°40E 243 G12
Sāḥilīyah Iraq 33°43N 42°42E 213 F10
Sahiwal Pakistan 30°45N 73°8E 242 D5
Şahneh Iran 34°29N 47°41E 213 E12
Sahrawi = Western Sahara ■ Africa 25°0N 13°0W 260 D2
Sahuaripa Mexico 29°3N 109°14W 318 B3
Sahuarita U.S.A. 31°57N 110°58W 305 L8
Sahuayo de Díaz Mexico 20°4N 102°43W 318 C4
Šahy Slovak Rep. 48°4N 18°55E 181 C11
Sai → India 25°39N 82°47E 243 G10
Sai Buri Thailand 6°43N 101°45E 237 J3
Sai-Cinza Brazil 6°17S 57°42W 331 B6
Sai Kung China 22°23N 114°16E 122 A2
Sai Wan Ho China 22°17N 114°12E 122 B2
Sai Ying Pun China 22°17N 114°8E 122 B1
Saibai I. Australia 9°25S 142°40E 286 E2
Sa'id Bundâs Sudan 8°24N 24°48E 259 G4
Saïda Algeria 34°50N 0°11E 261 B5
Saïda □ Algeria 34°40N 0°20E 261 B5
Sa'īdābād = Sīrjān Iran 29°30N 55°45E 247 D7
Sa'īdābād Iran 36°8N 54°11E 247 B7
Saidaiji Japan 34°39N 134°2E 222 C6
Saïdia Morocco 35°5N 2°14W 261 A4
Sa'īdīyeh Iran 36°20N 48°55E 247 B6
Saidor Papua N. G. 5°40S 146°29E 286 C4
Saidpur Bangla. 25°48N 89°0E 241 C2
Saidpur India 25°33N 83°11E 243 G10
Saidu Sharif Pakistan 34°43N 72°24E 243 B5
Saignes France 45°20N 2°31E 174 C6
Saigō Japan 36°12N 133°20E 222 A5
Saigon = Thanh Pho Ho Chi Minh Vietnam 10°58N 106°40E 237 G6
Saijō Japan 33°55N 133°11E 222 D5
Saikai △ Japan 33°12N 129°36E 222 D1
Saikanosy Masoala Madag. 15°45S 50°10E 272 B3
Saikhoa Ghat India 27°50N 95°40E 241 B5
Saiki Japan 32°58N 131°51E 222 E3
Sailana India 23°28N 74°55E 242 H6
Saillans France 44°42N 5°12E 175 D9
Sailolof Indonesia 1°15S 130°46E 231 E8
Sailu India 19°28N 76°28E 244 E3
Saimaa Finland 61°15N 28°15E 188 B5
Saimbeyli Turkey 37°59N 36°6E 212 D7
Saimen = Saimaa Finland 61°15N 28°15E 188 B5
Şa'in Dezh Iran 36°40N 46°25E 213 D12
St. Abb's Head U.K. 55°55N 2°8W 167 F6
St-Affrique France 43°57N 2°53E 174 E6
St-Agrève France 45°0N 4°23E 175 C8
St-Aignan France 47°16N 1°22E 172 E8
St. Alban's Nfld. & L., Canada 47°51N 55°50W 299 C8
St. Albans Herts., U.K. 51°45N 0°19W 169 F7
St. Albans Vt., U.S.A. 44°49N 73°5W 313 B11
St. Albans W. Va., U.S.A. 38°23N 81°50W 309 F13
St. Alban's Head U.K. 50°34N 2°4W 169 G5
St. Albert Canada 53°37N 113°32W 296 C6
St-Amand-en-Puisaye France 47°32N 3°5E 173 E10
St-Amand-les-Eaux France 50°27N 3°25E 173 B10
St-Amand-Montrond France 46°43N 2°30E 173 F9
St-Amarin France 47°54N 7°2E 173 E14
St-Amour France 46°26N 5°21E 173 F12
St-André Montréal, Canada 130 c1
St-André Réunion 20°57S 55°39E 272 f
St-André-de-Cubzac France 44°59N 0°26W 174 D3
St-André-les-Alpes France 43°58N 6°30E 175 E10
St. Andrew □ Trin. & Tob. 10°35N 61°10W 323 t
St. Andrew Sd. U.S.A. 30°58N 81°25W 316 E8
St. Andrew's Nfld. & L., Canada 47°45N 59°15W 299 C8
St. Andrews N.Z. 44°33S 171°10E 285 E6
St. Andrews Fife, U.K. 56°20N 2°47W 167 E6
St. Andrews S.C., U.S.A. 32°47N 80°0W 316 C9
St-Anicet Canada 45°8N 74°22W 313 A10
St. Anne U.S.A. 41°1N 87°43W 311 C9
St. Annes Canada 49°40N 96°39W 297 D9
St. Anns B. Canada 46°22N 60°25W 299 C7
St. Anthony Nfld. & L., Canada 51°22N 55°35W 299 B8
St. Anthony Idaho, U.S.A. 43°58N 111°41W 304 E8
St-Antoine Canada 46°22N 64°45W 299 C7
St-Antonin-Noble-Val France 44°10N 1°45E 174 D5
St. Arnaud = El Eulma Algeria 36°9N 5°42E 261 A6
St. Arnaud Australia 36°40S 143°16E 282 D5
St. Arnaud Ra. N.Z. 42°1S 172°53E 285 C7
St-Astier France 45°8N 0°31E 174 C4
St-Aubin France 48°44N 2°8E 134 B1
St-Aubin-du-Cormier France 48°15N 1°26W 172 D5
St-Augustin Canada 51°13N 58°38W 299 B8
St-Augustin → Canada 51°16N 58°40W 299 B8
St. Augustine U.S.A. 29°54N 81°19W 316 F8
St. Augustine Beach U.S.A. 29°51N 81°16W 316 F8
St-Aulaye France 45°12N 0°9E 174 C4
St. Austell U.K. 50°20N 4°47W 169 G3
St-Avold France 49°6N 6°43E 173 C13
St. Barbe Canada 51°12N 56°46W 299 B8
St-Barthélemy W. Indies 17°50N 62°50W 322 a
St-Barthélemy Channel St.-Martin 18°0N 63°0W 322 a
St. Basil's Cathedral Moscow, Russia 129 b3
St. Bathans N.Z. 44°53S 169°50E 285 E4
St. Bathan's, Mt. N.Z. 44°45S 169°45E 285 E4
St-Béat France 42°55N 0°41E 174 F4
St. Bees Hd. U.K. 54°31N 3°38W 168 C4
St. Bees I. Australia 20°56S 149°26E 280 J7
St-Benoît Réunion 21°2S 55°43E 272 f
St-Benoît-du-Sault France 46°26N 1°24E 174 B5
St-Bonnet-en-Champsaur France 44°40N 6°5E 175 D10
St-Brevin-les-Pins France 47°14N 2°10W 172 E4
St-Brice-en-Coglès France 48°25N 1°22W 172 D5
St. Bride's Canada 46°56N 54°10W 299 C9
St. Brides B. U.K. 51°49N 5°9W 169 F2
St-Brieuc France 48°30N 2°46W 172 D4
St-Calais France 47°55N 0°45E 172 E7
St-Cast-le-Guildo France 48°37N 2°18W 172 D4
St. Catharines Canada 43°10N 79°15W 312 C5
St. Catherine, Mt. Grenada 12°10N 61°40W 323 q
St. Catherine Pt. Bermuda 32°23N 64°40W 153 a
St. Catherines I. U.S.A. 31°40N 81°10W 316 D8
St. Catherine's Monastery Egypt 28°34N 33°58E 251 K4
St. Catherine's Pt. U.K. 50°34N 1°18W 169 G6
St-Céré France 44°51N 1°54E 174 D5
St-Cergue Switz. 46°27N 6°10E 179 J2
St-Cernin France 45°5N 2°25E 174 C6
St-Chamond France 45°28N 4°31E 175 C8
St. Charles Ill., U.S.A. 41°54N 88°19W 311 C8
St. Charles Md., U.S.A. 38°36N 76°56W 309 F15
St. Charles Mo., U.S.A. 38°47N 90°29W 310 F6
St. Charles Va., U.S.A. 36°48N 83°4W 309 G12
St-Chély-d'Apcher France 44°48N 3°17E 174 D7
St-Chinian France 43°25N 2°56E 174 E6
St. Christopher = St. Kitts W. Indies 17°20N 62°40W 322 d
St. Christopher-Nevis = St. Kitts & Nevis ■ W. Indies 17°20N 62°40W 322 d
St-Ciers-sur-Gironde France 45°17N 0°37W 174 C3
St. Clair Ga., U.S.A. 33°9N 82°13W 316 B7
St. Clair Mich., U.S.A. 42°50N 82°30W 312 D2
St. Clair Mo., U.S.A. 38°21N 90°59W 310 F6
St. Clair Pa., U.S.A. 40°43N 76°12W 313 F8
St. Clair → U.S.A. 42°38N 82°31W 312 D2
St. Clair, L. S. Austral., Australia 37°20S 139°55E 282 D3
St. Clair, L. N. Amer. 42°27N 82°39W 312 D2
St. Clair Shores U.S.A. 42°30N 82°53W 311 B14
St. Clairsville U.S.A. 40°5N 80°54W 312 F4
St-Claud France 45°54N 0°28E 174 C4
St. Claude Canada 49°40N 98°20W 297 D9
St-Claude Jura, France 46°22N 5°52E 173 F12
St-Claude Guadeloupe 16°3N 61°42W 322 e
St. Clears U.K. 51°49N 4°31W 169 F3
St-Clet Canada 45°21N 74°13W 313 A10
St. Cloud France 48°50N 2°12E 134 A2
St. Cloud Fla., U.S.A. 28°15N 81°17W 317 G8
St. Cloud Minn., U.S.A. 45°34N 94°10W 308 C6
St. Cricq, C. Australia 25°17S 113°6E 279 E1
St. Croix U.S. Virgin Is. 17°45N 64°45W 321 C7
St. Croix → U.S.A. 44°45N 92°48W 308 C7
St. Croix Falls U.S.A. 45°24N 92°38W 308 C7
St-Cyprien France 42°37N 3°2E 174 F7
St-Cyr-l'École France 48°47N 2°4E 134 B1
St-Cyr-l'École ✕ France 48°48N 2°4E 134 B1
St-Cyr-sur-Mer France 43°11N 5°43E 175 E9
St. David U.S.A. 40°30N 90°3W 310 D6
St. David □ Trin. & Tob. 10°47N 61°3W 323 t
St. David's Nfld. & L., Canada 48°12N 58°52W 299 C8
St. David's Grenada 12°2N 61°40W 323 q
St. David's Pembs., U.K. 51°53N 5°16W 169 F2
St. David's Head U.K. 51°54N 5°19W 169 F2
St. David's I. Bermuda 32°21N 64°39W 153 a
St-Denis = Sig Algeria 35°32N 0°12W 261 A4
St-Denis Seine-St-Denis, France 48°56N 2°20E 134 A3
St-Denis Réunion 20°52S 55°27E 272 f
St-Denis → Réunion 20°52S 55°27E 272 f
St-Denis ✕ (RUN) Réunion 20°53S 55°32E 272 f
St-Dié France 48°17N 6°56E 173 D13
St-Dizier France 48°38N 4°56E 173 D11
St-Égrève France 45°14N 5°41E 175 C9
St. Elias, Mt. U.S.A. 60°18N 140°56W 303 F12
St. Elias Mts. N. Amer. 60°33N 139°28W 296 A1
St-Élie Fr. Guiana 4°49N 53°17W 329 C7
St. Elmo U.S.A. 39°2N 88°51W 311 E8
St-Eloy-les-Mines France 46°10N 2°51E 173 F9
St-Émilion France 44°53N 0°9W 174 D3
St-Étienne France 45°27N 4°22E 175 C8
St-Étienne → Réunion 21°17S 55°25E 272 f
St-Étienne-de-Tinée France 44°16N 6°56E 175 D10
St-Étienne-du-Rouvray France 49°23N 1°6E 172 C8
St. Eugène Canada 45°30N 74°28W 313 A10
St. Eustatius W. Indies 17°20N 63°0W 322 a
St-Exupery, Lyon ✕ (LYS) France 45°44N 5°2E 175 C9
St-Fargeau France 47°39N 3°4E 173 E10
St-Félicien Canada 48°40N 72°25W 298 C5
St. Ferdinand = Florissant U.S.A. 38°47N 90°19W 310 F6
St-Florent France 42°41N 9°18E 175 F13
St-Florent, G. de France 42°47N 9°12E 175 F13
St-Florent-sur-Cher France 46°59N 2°15E 173 F9
St-Florentin France 48°0N 3°45E 173 E10
St-Flour France 45°2N 3°6E 174 C7
St. Francis U.S.A. 39°47N 101°48W 308 F3
St. Francis → U.S.A. 34°38N 90°36W 315 D9
St. Francis, C. S. Africa 34°14S 24°49E 270 D3
St. Francisville Ill., U.S.A. 38°36N 87°39W 311 F9
St. Francisville La., U.S.A. 30°47N 91°23W 314 F9
St-François Guadeloupe 16°16N 61°18W 322 e
St-François, L. Canada 45°10N 74°22W 313 A10
St-Fulgent France 46°50N 1°10W 172 F5
St-Gabriel Canada 46°17N 73°24W 298 C5
St. Gallen = Sankt Gallen Switz. 47°26N 9°22E 179 H5
St-Galmier France 45°35N 4°19E 173 G11
St-Gaudens France 43°6N 0°44E 174 E4
St-Gaultier France 46°39N 1°26E 172 F8
St-Gengoux-le-National France 46°37N 4°40E 173 F11
St-Geniez-d'Olt France 44°27N 2°58E 174 D6
St. George Queens., Australia 28°1S 148°30E 281 D4
St. George Bermuda 32°22N 64°40W 153 a
St. George N.B., Canada 45°11N 66°50W 299 C6
St. George Ga., U.S.A. 30°31N 82°2W 316 E7
St. George S.C., U.S.A. 33°11N 80°35W 316 B9
St. George Utah, U.S.A. 37°6N 113°35W 305 H7
St. George □ Trin. & Tob. 10°40N 61°25W 323 t
St. George, C. Nfld. & L., Canada 48°30N 59°16W 299 C8
St. George, C. Papua N. G. 4°49S 152°53E 286 C7
St. George, C. Fla., U.S.A. 29°40N 85°5W 316 F4
St. George I. Alaska, U.S.A. 56°35N 169°35W 303 H5
St. George I. Fla., U.S.A. 29°35N 84°55W 316 F5
St. George Ra. Australia 18°40S 125°0E 278 C4
St. George's Canada 48°26N 58°31W 299 C8
St-Georges Qué., Canada 46°8N 70°40W 299 C5
St-Georges Fr. Guiana 3°53N 51°50W 329 C7
St. George's Grenada 12°5N 61°43W 323 q
St. George's B. Canada 48°24N 58°53W 299 C8
St. Georges Basin N.S.W., Australia 35°7S 150°36E 283 C9
St. Georges Basin W. Austral., Australia 15°23S 125°2E 278 C4
St. George's Channel Europe 52°0N 6°0W 166 E6
St. George's Channel India 7°15N 93°43E 245 L11
St. George's Channel Papua N. G. 4°10S 152°20E 286 C7
St. Georges Harbour Bermuda 32°33N 64°42W 153 a
St. Georges Hd. Australia 35°12S 150°42E 283 C9
St. Georges I. Bermuda 32°23N 64°40W 153 a
St-Georges-lès-Baillargeaux France 46°41N 0°22E 174 B4
St-Germain, Forêt de France 48°57N 2°5E 134 A1
St-Germain-de-Calberte France 44°13N 3°48E 174 D7
St-Germain-en-Laye France 48°53N 2°4E 134 A1
St-Germain-Lembron France 45°27N 3°14E 174 C7
St-Gervais-d'Auvergne France 46°4N 2°50E 173 F9
St-Gervais-les-Bains France 45°53N 6°42E 175 C10
St-Gildas, Pte. de France 47°8N 2°14W 172 E4
St. Giles Cathedral Edinburgh, U.K. 121 b2
St-Gilles Brussels, Belgium 50°49N 4°20E 116 B2
St-Gilles Gard, France 43°40N 4°26E 175 E8
St-Gilles-les-Bains Réunion 21°2S 55°14E 272 f
St-Gilles-les-Hauts Réunion 21°2S 55°15E 272 f

St-Girons *Ariège, France* 42°59N 1°8E **174** F5
St-Girons *Landes, France* 43°56N 1°18W **174** E2
St. Gotthard P. = San Gottardo, P. del *Switz.* 46°33N 8°33E **179** J4
St. Helena *Atl. Oc.* 15°58S 5°42W **153** h
St. Helena *Calif., U.S.A.* 38°30N 122°28W **304** G2
St. Helena, Mt. *U.S.A.* 38°40N 122°36W **306** G4
St. Helena B. *S. Africa* 32°40S 18°10E **270** D2
St. Helena Sd. *U.S.A.* 32°15N 80°25W **316** C9
St. Helens *Tas., Australia* 41°20S 148°15E **281** G4
St. Helens *Mersey., U.K.* 53°27N 2°44W **168** D5
St. Helens *Oreg., U.S.A.* 45°52N 122°48W **306** E4
St. Helens, Mt. *U.S.A.* 46°12N 122°12W **306** D4
St. Helier *Chan. Is., U.K.* 49°10N 2°7W **169** H5
St. Helier *London, U.K.* 51°23N 0°11W **125** B2
St-Herblain *France* 47°13N 1°40W **172** E5
St-Hilaire-du-Harcouët *France* 48°35N 1°5W **172** D5
St-Hippolyte *France* 47°19N 6°50E **173** E13
St-Hippolyte-du-Fort *France* 43°58N 3°52E **174** E7
St-Honoré-les-Bains *France* 46°54N 3°50E **173** F10
St-Hubert *Belgium* 50°2N 5°23E **170** D5
St-Hubert *Qué., Canada* 45°29N 73°25W **130** B3
St. Hubert, Galeries Royales *Brussels, Belgium* **116** b2
St-Hyacinthe *Canada* 45°40N 72°58W **298** C5
St. Ignace *U.S.A.* 45°52N 84°44W **309** C11
St. Ignace I. *Canada* 48°45N 88°0W **298** C2
St. Ignatius *U.S.A.* 47°19N 114°6W **304** C6
St-Imier *Switz.* 47°9N 6°58E **179** H2
St. Isaac's Cathedral *Russia* 59°55N 30°19E **137** B1
St. Ives *Cambs., U.K.* 52°20N 0°4W **169** E7
St. Ives *Corn., U.K.* 50°12N 5°30W **169** G2
St-Jacques *Montréal, Canada* **130** a2
St-Jacques ➔ *Canada* 45°26N 73°29W **130** B3
St-James *France* 48°31N 1°20W **172** D5
St. James *Minn., U.S.A.* 43°59N 94°38W **308** D6
St. James *Mo., U.S.A.* 38°0N 91°37W **310** G5
St. James Cathedral *Toronto, Canada* **141** b3
St. James's *London, U.K.* **125** b3
St-Jean *St.-Martin* 17°53N 62°50W **322** a
St-Jean ➔ *Canada* 50°17N 64°20W **299** B7
St-Jean, L. *Canada* 48°40N 72°0W **299** C5
St-Jean Baptiste *Montréal, Canada* **130** a1
St-Jean-d'Angély *France* 45°57N 0°31W **174** C3
St-Jean-de-Braye *France* 47°53N 1°58E **173** E8
St-Jean-de-Luz *France* 43°23N 1°39W **174** E2
St-Jean-de-Maurienne *France* 45°16N 6°21E **175** C10
St-Jean-de-Monts *France* 46°47N 2°4W **172** F4
St-Jean-du-Gard *France* 44°7N 3°52E **174** D7
St-Jean-en-Royans *France* 45°1N 5°18E **175** C9
St-Jean-Pied-de-Port *France* 43°10N 1°14W **174** E2
St-Jean-Port-Joli *Canada* 47°15N 70°13W **299** C5
St-Jean-sur-Richelieu *Canada* 45°20N 73°20W **313** A11
St-Jérôme *Canada* 45°47N 74°0W **298** C5
St. Joe *U.S.A.* 41°19N 84°54W **311** C12
St. John *N.B., Canada* 45°20N 66°8W **299** C6
St. John *Kans., U.S.A.* 38°0N 98°46W **308** F4
St. John ➔ *Liberia* 6°40N 9°10W **262** D2
St. John ➔ *N. Amer.* 45°12N 66°5W **309** C20
St. John, C. *Canada* 50°0N 55°32W **299** C8
St. John I. *U.S. Virgin Is.* 18°20N 64°42W **321** b
St. John's *Antigua & B.* 17°6N 61°51W **322** b
St. John's *Nfld. & L., Canada* 47°35N 52°40W **299** C9
St. Johns *Montserrat* 16°46N 62°11W **323** p
St. Johns *Ariz., U.S.A.* 34°30N 109°22W **305** J9
St. Johns *Mich., U.S.A.* 43°0N 84°33W **311** B12
St. Johns ➔ *U.S.A.* 30°24N 81°24W **316** E8
St. John's Cathedral *Hong Kong, China* **122** c1
St. John's Pt. *Ireland* 54°34N 8°27W **166** B3
St. Johnsbury *U.S.A.* 44°25N 72°1W **313** B12
St. Johnston Village *Antigua & B.* 17°7N 61°50W **322** b
St. Johnsville *U.S.A.* 43°0N 74°43W **313** C10
St-Joost-Ten-Node *Belgium* 50°51N 4°21E **116** A2
St. Joseph *Dominica* 15°24N 61°26W **323** k
St-Joseph *Martinique* 14°39N 61°4W **322** j
St-Joseph *Réunion* 21°22S 55°37E **272** f
St. Joseph *Mayaro, Trin. & Tob.* 10°18N 60°59W **323** t
St. Joseph *St. George, Trin. & Tob.* 10°40N 61°25W **323** t
St. Joseph *Ill., U.S.A.* 40°7N 88°2W **311** D8
St. Joseph *La., U.S.A.* 31°55N 91°14W **314** F9
St. Joseph *Mich., U.S.A.* 42°6N 86°29W **311** B10
St. Joseph *Mo., U.S.A.* 39°46N 94°50W **310** E2
St. Joseph ➔ *U.S.A.* 42°7N 86°29W **311** B10
St. Joseph, I. *Canada* 46°12N 83°58W **298** C3
St. Joseph, L. *Canada* 51°10N 90°35W **298** B1
St. Joseph Pt. *U.S.A.* 29°52N 85°24W **316** F4
St-Jovite *Canada* 46°8N 74°38W **298** C5
St-Juéry *France* 43°57N 2°12E **174** E6
St. Julian's *Malta* 35°55N 14°29E **206** F7
St-Julien-Chapteuil *France* 45°2N 4°4E **175** C8
St-Julien-de-Vouvantes *France* 47°38N 1°13W **172** E5
St-Julien-en-Genevois *France* 46°9N 6°5E **173** F13
St-Junien *France* 45°53N 0°55E **174** C4
St-Just-en-Chaussée *France* 49°30N 2°25E **173** C9
St-Just-en-Chevalet *France* 45°55N 3°50E **174** C7
St. Kilda *Vic., Australia* 37°51S 144°58E **128** B1
St. Kilda *N.Z.* 45°53S 170°31E **285** F5
St. Kilda *W. Isles, U.K.* 57°49N 8°34W **165** C2
St. Kitts *W. Indies* 17°20N 62°40W **322** d
St. Kitts & Nevis ■ *W. Indies* 17°20N 62°40W **322** d
St-Lambert *Qué., Canada* 45°30N 73°29W **130** A3
St-Lambert *Yvelines, France* 48°43N 2°1E **134** B1
St. Laurent *Canada* 50°25N 97°58W **297** C9
St-Laurent *Qué., Canada* 45°30N 73°43W **130** A1
St-Laurent *Fr. Guiana* 5°29N 54°3W **329** B7
St-Laurent-de-la-Salanque *France* 42°46N 2°59E **174** F6
St-Laurent-du-Pont *France* 45°23N 5°45E **175** C9
St-Laurent-en-Grandvaux *France* 46°35N 5°58E **173** F12
St-Laurent-Médoc *France* 45°8N 0°49W **174** C3
St. Lawrence *Queens., Australia* 22°16S 149°31E **280** C4
St. Lawrence *Nfld. & L., Canada* 46°54N 55°23W **299** C8
St. Lawrence ➔ *Canada* 49°30N 66°0W **299** C6
St. Lawrence, Gulf of *Canada* 48°25N 62°0W **299** C7
St. Lawrence I. *U.S.A.* 63°30N 170°30W **303** E5
St. Lawrence Islands △ *Canada* 44°27N 75°52W **313** B9
St. Lawrence Market *Toronto, Canada* **141** b3
St-Lazare, Gare *Paris, France* **134** a3
St. Leonard *Canada* 47°12N 67°58W **299** C6
St-Léonard *Canada* 45°35N 73°34W **130** A2
St-Léonard-de-Noblat *France* 45°49N 1°29E **174** C5
St-Leu *Réunion* 21°9S 55°18E **272** f
St. Lewis ➔ *Canada* 52°26N 56°11W **299** B8
St-Lô *France* 49°7N 1°5W **172** C5
St-Louis *Montréal, Canada* **130** b2
St-Louis *Haut-Rhin, France* 47°30N 7°34E **173** E14
St-Louis *Guadeloupe* 15°56N 61°19W **322** e
St-Louis *Réunion* 21°16S 55°25E **272** f
St. Louis *Senegal* 16°8N 16°27W **262** B1
St. Louis *Mo., U.S.A.* 38°37N 90°11W **310** F6
St. Louis □ *Senegal* 16°20N 15°0W **262** B2
St. Louis ➔ *U.S.A.* 46°44N 92°9W **308** B7
St. Louis Lambert Int. ✕ **(STL)** *U.S.A.* 38°45N 90°22W **310** F6
St-Loup-sur-Semouse *France* 47°53N 6°16E **173** E13
St. Lucia ■ *W. Indies* 14°0N 60°57W **323** m
St. Lucia, L. *S. Africa* 28°5S 32°30E **271** C5
St. Lucia Channel *W. Indies* 14°15N 61°0W **321** D7
St. Lucie *U.S.A.* 27°29N 80°20W **317** H9
St. Lucie Canal *U.S.A.* 27°10N 80°18W **317** H9
St. Maarten ☒ *W. Indies* 18°0N 63°5W **322** a
St. Magelungen *Sweden* 59°13N 18°4E **139** B2
St. Magnus B. *U.K.* 60°25N 1°35W **167** A7
St-Maixent-l'École *France* 46°24N 0°12W **174** B3
St-Malo *France* 48°39N 2°1W **172** D4
St-Malo, G. de *France* 48°50N 2°30W **172** D4
St-Mandé *France* 48°50N 2°24E **134** A3
St-Mandrier-sur-Mer *France* 43°4N 5°57E **175** E9
St-Marc *Haiti* 19°10N 72°41W **321** C5
St-Marcellin *France* 45°9N 5°20E **175** C9
St-Marcouf, Îs. *France* 49°30N 1°10W **172** C5
St. Margaret's *Ireland* 53°25N 6°18W **120** A2
St. Maries *U.S.A.* 47°19N 116°35W **304** C5
St. Mark B. *Grenada* 12°11N 61°42W **323** q
St. Marks *U.S.A.* 30°9N 84°12W **316** E5
St-Martin ☒ *W. Indies* 18°0N 63°0W **322** a
St-Martin, Bois *France* 48°48N 2°35E **134** B4
St-Martin, C. *Martinique* 14°52N 61°14W **322** j
St. Martin, L. *Canada* 51°40N 98°30W **297** C9
St-Martin-de-Crau *France* 43°38N 4°48E **175** E8
St-Martin-de-Ré *France* 46°12N 1°21W **174** B2
St-Martin-d'Hères *France* 45°9N 5°45E **175** C9
St-Martin-Vésubie *France* 44°4N 7°15E **175** D11
St-Martory *France* 43°9N 0°56E **174** E4
St. Mary *U.S.A.* 37°53N 89°57W **310** G7
St. Mary, Mt. *Papua N. G.* 8°8S 147°2E **286** E4
St. Mary Cray *U.K.* 51°23N 0°7E **125** B4
St. Mary Is. *India* 13°20N 74°35E **245** H2
St. Mary Pk. *Australia* 31°32S 138°34E **282** A3
St. Marys *Tas., Australia* 41°35S 148°11E **281** G4
St. Marys *Ont., Canada* 43°20N 81°10W **312** C3
St. Mary's *Trin. & Tob.* 10°14N 61°33W **323** t
St. Mary's *Corn., U.K.* 49°55N 6°18W **169** H1
St. Mary's *Orkney, U.K.* 58°54N 2°54W **167** C6
St. Mary's *Alaska, U.S.A.* 62°4N 163°10W **303** E7
St. Marys *Ga., U.S.A.* 30°44N 81°33W **316** E8
St. Marys *Ohio, U.S.A.* 40°33N 84°24W **311** D12
St. Marys *Pa., U.S.A.* 41°26N 78°34W **312** E6
St. Marys ➔ *U.S.A.* 30°43N 81°27W **316** E8
St. Mary's, C. *Canada* 46°50N 54°12W **299** C9
St. Mary's B. *Canada* 46°50N 53°50W **299** C9
St. Marys Bay *Canada* 44°25N 66°10W **299** D6
St. Mary's Cathedral *San Francisco, U.S.A.* **136** c1
St-Mathieu, Pte. *France* 48°20N 4°45W **172** D2
St. Matthew I. *U.S.A.* 60°24N 172°42W **303** F4
St. Matthews *Ky., U.S.A.* 38°15N 85°39W **311** F11
St. Matthews *S.C., U.S.A.* 33°40N 80°46W **316** B9
St. Matthews, I. = Zadetkyi Kyun *Burma* 10°0N 98°25E **237** G2
St. Matthias Group *Papua N. G.* 1°30S 150°0E **286** A6
St-Maur-des-Fossés *France* 48°48N 2°29E **134** B3
St-Maurice *France* 48°49N 2°24E **134** B3
St-Maurice ➔ *Canada* 46°21N 72°31W **298** C5
St. Mawes *U.K.* 50°10N 5°2W **169** G2
St-Maximin-la-Ste-Baume *France* 43°27N 5°52E **175** E9
St-Médard-en-Jalles *France* 44°53N 0°43W **174** D3
St-Méen-le-Grand *France* 48°11N 2°12W **172** D4
St. Meinrad *U.S.A.* 38°10N 86°49W **311** F10
St. Michael *U.S.A.* 63°29N 162°2W **303** E7
St. Michael's Cathedral *Toronto, Canada* **141** a3
St-Michel *Canada* 45°34N 73°37W **130** A2
St-Mihiel *France* 48°54N 5°32E **173** D12
St-Nazaire *France* 47°17N 2°12W **172** E4
St. Neots *U.K.* 52°14N 0°15W **169** E7
St-Nicolas-de-Port *France* 48°38N 6°18E **173** D13
St-Niklaas *Belgium* 51°10N 4°8E **170** C4
St. Nikolaus-Kirken *Czech Rep.* 50°5N 14°23E **135** B2
St-Omer *France* 50°45N 2°15E **173** B9
St-Ouen *France* 48°56N 2°20E **134** A3
St-Palais-sur-Mer *France* 45°38N 1°5W **174** C2
St-Pamphile *Canada* 46°58N 69°48W **299** C6
St-Pardoux-la-Rivière *France* 45°29N 0°45E **174** C4
St. Paris *U.S.A.* 40°8N 83°58W **311** D13
St-Pascal *Canada* 47°32N 69°48W **299** C6
St. Patrick □ *Trin. & Tob.* 10°10N 61°35W **323** t
St. Patricks *Barbados* 13°6N 59°30W **323** r
St. Patrick's Cathedral *Dublin, Ireland* **120** c1
St. Patrick's Cathedral *New York, U.S.A.* **132** c2
St. Patrick's Church *Toronto, Canada* **141** a1
St. Paul *Canada* 54°0N 111°17W **296** C6
St-Paul *Alpes-de-Haute-Provence, France* 44°31N 6°45E **175** D10
St-Paul *Réunion* 20°59S 55°17E **272** f
St. Paul *Alaska, U.S.A.* 57°7N 170°17W **303** H5
St. Paul *Ind., U.S.A.* 39°26N 85°38W **311** E11
St. Paul *Minn., U.S.A.* 44°56N 93°5W **308** C7
St. Paul *Nebr., U.S.A.* 41°13N 98°27W **308** E4
St-Paul ➔ *Canada* 51°27N 57°42W **299** B8
St. Paul ➔ *Liberia* 6°25N 10°48W **262** D2
St. Paul, I. *Ind. Oc.* 38°55S 77°34E **273** H6
St-Paul-de-Fenouillet *France* 42°48N 2°30E **174** F6
St. Paul I. *N.S., Canada* 47°12N 60°9W **299** C7
St. Paul I. *Alaska, U.S.A.* 57°10N 170°15W **303** H5
St-Paul-lès-Dax *France* 43°44N 1°3W **174** E2
St. Paul Subterranean River △ *Phil.* 10°10N 118°55E **233** F2
St. Paul's Bay *Malta* 35°57N 14°24E **206** F7
St. Paul's Cathedral *London, U.K.* **125** b4
St. Paul's Cray *U.K.* 51°23N 0°6E **125** B4
St-Péray *France* 44°57N 4°50E **175** D8
St. Pete Beach *U.S.A.* 27°43N 82°44W **317** H7
St. Peter *U.S.A.* 44°20N 93°57W **308** C7
St. Peter & St. Paul *San Francisco, U.S.A.* **136** a2
St-Peter-Ording *Germany* 54°20N 8°36E **178** A4
St. Peter Port *U.K.* 49°26N 2°33W **169** H5
St. Peters *N.S.W., Australia* 33°55S 151°11E **139** B2
St. Peters *N.S., Canada* 45°40N 60°53W **299** C7
St. Peters *P.E.I., Canada* 46°25N 62°35W **299** C7
St. Peters *Montserrat* 16°43N 62°13W **323** p
St. Peters *Mo., U.S.A.* 38°48N 90°37W **310** F6
St. Peter's Square = San Pietro, Piazza *Rome, Italy* **136** b1
St. Petersburg = Sankt-Peterburg *Russia* 59°55N 30°20E **137** B1
St. Petersburg *U.S.A.* 27°46N 82°40W **317** H7
St. Petersburg Pulkovo Int. ✕ **(LED)** *Russia* 59°48N 30°18E **137** C1
St-Philbert-de-Grand-Lieu *France* 47°2N 1°39W **172** E5
St-Phillippe *Réunion* 21°21S 55°44E **272** f
St-Pie *Canada* 45°30N 72°54W **313** A12
St-Pierre *Qué., Canada* 45°27N 73°38W **130** B2
St-Pierre *Martinique* 14°45N 61°10W **322** j
St. Pierre *Mauritius* 20°13S 57°31E **272** e
St-Pierre *Réunion* 21°19S 55°28E **272** f
St-Pierre *St-P. & M.* 46°46N 56°12W **299** C8
St. Pierre *Seychelles* 9°20S 46°0E **273** E3
St-Pierre, L. *Canada* 46°12N 72°52W **298** C5
St-Pierre, Rade de *Martinique* 14°44N 61°11W **322** j
St-Pierre-de-la-Pointe-aux-Esquimaux = Havre-St.-Pierre *Canada* 50°18N 63°33W **299** B7
St-Pierre-d'Oléron *France* 45°57N 1°19W **174** C2
St-Pierre-en-Port *France* 49°48N 0°30E **172** C7
St-Pierre-et-Miquelon ☒ *N. Amer.* 46°55N 56°10W **299** C8
St-Pierre-le-Moûtier *France* 46°47N 3°7E **173** F10
St-Pierre-sur-Dives *France* 49°2N 0°1W **172** C6
St-Pieters Leew *Belgium* 50°47N 4°16E **116** B1
St-Pol-de-Léon *France* 48°41N 4°0W **172** D3
St-Pol-sur-Mer *France* 51°1N 2°20E **173** A9
St-Pol-sur-Ternoise *France* 50°23N 2°20E **173** B9
St-Pons *France* 43°30N 2°45E **174** E6
St-Pourçain-sur-Sioule *France* 46°18N 3°18E **173** F10
St-Priest *France* 45°42N 4°57E **175** C8
St-Quay-Portrieux *France* 48°39N 2°51W **172** D4
St-Quentin *N.B., Canada* 47°30N 67°23W **299** C6
St-Quentin *Aisne, France* 49°50N 3°16E **173** C10
St-Quentin, Étang de *France* 48°47N 2°0E **134** B1
St-Rambert-d'Albon *France* 45°17N 4°49E **175** C8
St-Raphaël *France* 43°25N 6°46E **175** E10
St. Regis *U.S.A.* 47°18N 115°6W **304** C6
St-Renan *France* 48°26N 4°37W **172** D2
St. Robert *U.S.A.* 37°50N 92°11W **310** G4
St-Saëns *France* 49°41N 1°16E **172** C8
St-Savin *France* 46°34N 0°53E **174** B4
St-Savinien *France* 45°53N 0°42W **174** C3
St. Sebastien, Tanjon' i *Madag.* 12°26S 48°44E **272** A2
St-Seine-l'Abbaye *France* 47°26N 4°47E **173** E11
St-Sernin-sur-Rance *France* 43°54N 2°35E **174** E6
St-Sever *France* 43°45N 0°35W **174** E3
St-Siméon *Canada* 47°51N 69°54W **299** C6
St. Simons I. *U.S.A.* 31°12N 81°15W **316** D8
St. Simons Island *U.S.A.* 31°9N 81°22W **315** F14
St. Stephen *N.B., Canada* 45°16N 67°17W **299** C6
St. Stephen *S.C., U.S.A.* 33°24N 79°55W **316** B10
St. Stephen's Basilica *Budapest, Hungary* **117** b2
St. Stephens Cathedral = Stephansdom *Vienna, Austria* **142** b2
St. Stephen's Green *Dublin, Ireland* **120** c3
St-Stevens-Woluwe *Belgium* 50°52N 4°26E **116** A2
St-Sulpice *France* 43°46N 1°41E **174** E5
St-Sulpice-Laurière *France* 46°3N 1°29E **174** B5
St-Sulpice-les-Feuilles *France* 46°19N 1°21E **174** B5
St-Syprien = St-Cyprien *France* 42°37N 3°2E **174** F7
St. Teresa *U.S.A.* 29°55N 84°27W **316** F5
St-Thégonnec *France* 48°31N 3°57W **172** D3
St. Thomas = Charlotte Amalie *U.S. Virgin Is.* 18°21N 64°56W **321** C7
St. Thomas *Canada* 42°45N 81°10W **312** D3
St. Thomas Bay *Malta* 35°51N 14°34E **206** F8
St. Thomas I. *U.S. Virgin Is.* 18°20N 64°55W **321** C7
St-Tite *Canada* 46°45N 72°34W **298** C5
St-Tropez *France* 43°17N 6°38E **175** E10
St-Troud = St. Truiden *Belgium* 50°48N 5°10E **170** D5
St. Truiden *Belgium* 50°48N 5°10E **170** D5
St-Vaast-la-Hougue *France* 49°35N 1°17W **172** C5
St-Valery-en-Caux *France* 49°52N 0°43E **172** C7
St-Valéry-sur-Somme *France* 50°11N 1°38E **173** B8
St-Vallier *France* 46°38N 4°22E **173** F11
St-Vallier-de-Thiey *France* 43°42N 6°51E **175** E10
St-Varent *France* 46°53N 0°13W **172** F6
St-Vaury *France* 46°12N 1°46E **174** B5
St. Vincent = São Vicente *C. Verde Is.* 17°0N 25°0W **153** j
St. Vincent *Italy* 45°45N 7°39E **198** C4
St. Vincent *W. Indies* 13°10N 61°10W **323** n
St. Vincent, G. *Australia* 35°0S 138°0E **282** C3
St. Vincent & the Grenadines ■ *W. Indies* 13°0N 61°10W **323** n
St-Vincent-de-Paul *Canada* 45°36N 73°39W **130** A2
St-Vincent-de-Tyrosse *France* 43°39N 1°19W **174** E2
St. Vincent I. *U.S.A.* 29°42N 85°3W **317** F4
St. Vincent Passage *W. Indies* 13°30N 61°0W **321** D7
St-Vith *Belgium* 50°17N 6°9E **170** D6
St-Vivien-de-Médoc *France* 45°25N 1°2W **174** C2
St. Walburg *Canada* 53°39N 109°12W **297** C7
St. Xavier University *U.S.A.* 41°42N 87°42W **119** C2
St-Yrieix-la-Perche *France* 45°31N 1°12E **174** C5
Saintala *India* 20°26N 83°20E **244** D6
Ste-Adresse *France* 49°31N 0°5E **172** C7
Ste-Agathe-des-Monts *Canada* 46°3N 74°17W **298** C5
Ste-Anne *Guadeloupe* 16°13N 61°24W **322** e
Ste-Anne *Martinique* 14°25N 60°54W **322** j
Ste-Anne *Réunion* 21°4S 55°45E **272** f
Ste-Anne *Seychelles* 4°36S 55°31E **272** c
Ste-Anne, L. *Canada* 50°0N 67°42W **299** B6
Ste-Anne-des-Monts-Tourelle *Canada* 49°8N 66°30W **299** C6
Ste-Catherine *Canada* 45°24N 73°34W **130** B2
Ste-Croix *Switz.* 46°49N 6°34E **179** J2
Ste-Enimie *France* 44°22N 3°26E **174** D7
Ste-Foy-la-Grande *France* 44°50N 0°13E **174** D4
Ste. Genevieve *U.S.A.* 37°59N 90°2W **310** G6
Ste-Hélène, Î. *Canada* 45°31N 73°32W **130** A2
Ste-Hermine *France* 46°32N 1°4W **174** B2
Ste-Livrade-sur-Lot *France* 44°24N 0°36E **174** D4
Ste-Luce *Martinique* 14°28N 60°55W **322** j
Ste. Madeleine *Trin. & Tob.* 10°16N 61°26W **323** t
Ste-Marguerite *Guadeloupe* 16°23N 61°24W **322** e
Ste-Marguerite ➔ *Canada* 50°9N 66°36W **299** B6
Ste-Marie *Canada* 46°26N 71°0W **299** C5
Ste. Marie *Gabon* 3°48S 11°1E **264** C2
Ste-Marie *Guadeloupe* 16°6N 61°33W **322** e
Ste-Marie *Martinique* 14°48N 61°1W **322** j
Ste-Marie *Réunion* 20°53S 55°33E **272** f
Ste-Marie, Ile = Nosy Boraha *Madag.* 16°50S 49°55E **272** B2
Ste-Marie-aux-Mines *France* 48°15N 7°12E **173** D14
Ste-Marthe *Guadeloupe* 16°15N 61°15W **322** e
Ste-Maure-de-Touraine *France* 47°7N 0°37E **172** E7
Ste-Maxime *France* 43°19N 6°39E **175** E10
Ste-Menehould *France* 49°5N 4°54E **173** C11
Ste-Mère-Église *France* 49°24N 1°19W **172** C5
Ste-Rose *Guadeloupe* 16°20N 61°45W **322** e
Ste-Rose *Réunion* 21°8S 55°45E **272** f
Ste. Rose du Lac *Canada* 51°4N 99°30W **297** C9
Ste-Savine *France* 48°18N 4°3E **173** D11
Ste-Sigolène *France* 45°15N 4°14E **175** C8
Ste-Suzanne *Réunion* 20°54S 55°36E **272** f
Saintes *France* 45°45N 0°37W **174** C3
Saintes, Canal des *Guadeloupe* 15°55N 61°40W **322** e
Saintes, Îs. des *Guadeloupe* 15°50N 61°35W **322** e
Stes-Maries-de-la-Mer *France* 43°26N 4°26E **175** E8
Saintfield *U.K.* 54°28N 5°49W **166** B6
Saintonge *France* 45°40N 0°50W **174** C3
Saipan *N. Marianas* 15°12N 145°45E **302** e
Saipan Channel *N. Marianas* 15°5N 145°41E **302** e
Sairang *India* 23°50N 92°45E **241** D4
Sairecábur, Cerro *Bolivia* 22°43S 67°54W **334** A2
Saitama *Japan* 35°54N 139°38E **223** B11
Saitama □ *Japan* 36°25N 139°30E **223** A11
Saiteli = Kadınhanı *Turkey* 38°14N 32°13E **212** C5
Saiţi *Moldova* 46°30N 29°24E **183** D14
Saito *Japan* 32°3N 131°24E **222** E3
Saiwai *Japan* 35°32N 139°41E **140** B3
Saiyid *Pakistan* 33°7N 73°2E **242** C5
Saja-Besaya ⌓ *Spain* 43°10N 4°9W **194** B6
Sajama *Bolivia* 18°7S 69°0W **330** D4
Sajama, Nevado *Bolivia* 18°6S 68°54W **330** D4
Sajan *Serbia* 45°50N 20°20E **182** E5
Sajó ➔ *Hungary* 47°56N 21°7E **182** C6
Sajókazinc = Kazincbarcika *Hungary* 48°17N 20°36E **182** B5
Sajószentpéter *Hungary* 48°12N 20°44E **182** B5
Sajum *India* 33°20N 79°0E **243** C8
Sak ➔ *S. Africa* 30°52S 20°25E **270** D3
Saka *Kenya* 0°9S 39°20E **268** B4
Saka Kalat *Pakistan* 27°3N 65°3E **240** D2
Sakaba *Nigeria* 11°4N 5°35E **263** C6
Sakai *Japan* 34°34N 135°27E **133** B1
Sakai Harbour *Japan* 34°36N 135°26E **133** B1
Sakaide *Japan* 34°19N 133°50E **222** C5
Sakaiminato *Japan* 35°38N 133°11E **222** B5
Sakākah *Si. Arabia* 30°0N 40°8E **246** D4
Sakakawea, L. *U.S.A.* 47°30N 101°25W **308** B3
Sakami ➔ *Canada* 53°40N 76°40W **298** B4
Sakami, L. *Canada* 53°15N 77°0W **298** B4
Sâkâne, 'Erg i-n *Mali* 20°30N 1°30W **260** D4
Sakania *Dem. Rep. of the Congo* 12°43S 28°30E **269** E2
Sakar I. *Papua N. G.* 5°25S 148°6E **286** C5
Sakaraha *Madag.* 22°55S 44°32E **272** C1
Sakartvelo = Georgia ■ *Asia* 42°0N 43°0E **191** J6
Sakarya *Turkey* 40°48N 30°25E **212** B4
Sakarya □ *Turkey* 40°45N 30°25E **212** B4
Sakarya ➔ *Turkey* 41°7N 30°39E **212** B4
Sakashima-Guntō *Japan* 24°46N 124°0E **221** M2
Sakassou *Ivory C.* 7°29N 5°19W **262** D3
Sakata *Japan* 38°55N 139°50E **220** E9
Sakawa *Japan* 33°28N 133°11E **222** D5
Sakchu *N. Korea* 40°23N 125°2E **224** B2
Sakeny ➔ *Madag.* 20°0S 45°25E **272** C2
Sakété *Benin* 6°40N 2°45E **263** D5
Sakha □ *Russia* 66°0N 130°0E **215** C14
Sakhalin *Russia* 51°0N 143°0E **215** D15
Sakhalinskiy Zaliv *Russia* 54°0N 141°0E **215** D15
Sakhi Gopal *India* 19°58N 85°50E **244** E7
Şaki *Azerbaijan* 41°10N 47°5E **191** K8
Šakiai *Lithuania* 54°59N 23°2E **184** D10
Sakiz-Adasi = Hios *Greece* 38°27N 26°9E **205** C8
Sakmara ➔ *Russia* 51°46N 55°1E **216** B5
Sakoli *India* 21°5N 79°59E **244** D4
Sakon Nakhon *Thailand* 17°10N 104°9E **236** D5
Sakra, Pulau *Singapore* 1°15N 103°41E **138** B2
Sakrand *Pakistan* 26°10N 68°15E **242** F3
Sakri *Maharashtra, India* 26°13N 86°5E **243** F12
Sakri *Maharashtra, India* 21°2N 74°20E **244** D2
Sakrivier *S. Africa* 30°54S 20°28E **270** D3
Sakskøbing *Denmark* 54°49N 11°39E **163** K5
Sakti *India* 22°2N 82°58E **243** H10
Saku *Japan* 36°17N 138°31E **223** A10
Sakuma *Japan* 35°3N 137°49E **223** B9
Sakura *Japan* 35°43N 140°14E **223** B12
Sakurai *Japan* 34°30N 135°51E **223** C7
Saky *Ukraine* 45°9N 33°34E **189** K7
Sal ➔ *Russia* 47°31N 40°45E **191** G5
Sal Rei *C. Verde Is.* 16°11N 22°53W **153** j
Sala *Eritrea* 16°53N 37°36E **257** D4
Šal'a *Slovak Rep.* 48°10N 17°50E **181** C10
Sala *Sweden* 59°58N 16°35E **162** E10
Sala ➔ *Eritrea* 16°53N 37°36E **257** D4
Sala, O. ➔ *Chad* 17°0N 20°53E **259** E4
Sala Consilina *Italy* 40°23N 15°36E **201** B8
Sala-y-Gómez *Pac. Oc.* 26°28S 105°28W **289** K17
Sala y Gómez Ridge *Pac. Oc.* 25°0S 98°0W **289** K18
Salaberry-de-Valleyfield *Canada* 45°15N 74°8W **313** A10
Salacgrīva *Latvia* 57°45N 24°21E **184** A11
Salada, L. *Mexico* 32°20N 115°40W **305** K6
Saladas *Argentina* 28°15S 58°40W **334** B4
Saladillo *Argentina* 35°40S 59°55W **334** D4
Salado ➔ *B. Aires, Argentina* 35°44S 57°22W **334** D4
Salado ➔ *La Pampa, Argentina* 37°30S 67°0W **336** A3
Salado ➔ *Río Negro, Argentina* 41°34S 65°3W **336** B3
Salado ➔ *Santa Fe, Argentina* 31°40S 60°41W **334** C3
Salado ➔ *Tamaulipas, Mexico* 26°52N 99°19W **314** H5
Salaga *Ghana* 8°31N 0°31W **263** D4
Sālah *Syria* 32°40N 36°45E **250** F7
Şalāḩ ad Dīn □ *Iraq* 34°35N 43°35E **246** C4
Salahin *Somali Rep.* 2°57N 46°26E **267** D6
Sălaj □ *Romania* 47°15N 23°0E **182** C8
Salakos *Greece* 36°17N 27°57E **206** E11
Salal *Chad* 14°48N 17°12E **259** F3
Salala *Liberia* 6°42N 10°7W **262** D2
Salala *Sudan* 21°17N 36°16E **256** C4
Salālah *Oman* 16°56N 53°59E **249** C6
Salam *Iraq* 33°20N 44°20E **113** A2
Salamanca *Chile* 31°46S 70°59W **334** C1
Salamanca *Madrid, Spain* 40°25N 3°41W **127** B1
Salamanca *Salamanca, Spain* 40°58N 5°39W **194** E5
Salamanca *N.Y., U.S.A.* 42°10N 78°43W **312** D6
Salamanca □ *Spain* 40°57N 5°40W **194** E5
Salamat □ *Chad* 11°0N 20°30E **259** F4
Salamat, Bahr ➔ *Chad* 9°20N 18°0E **259** G3
Salāmatābād *Iran* 35°39N 47°50E **246** C5
Salamina *Colombia* 5°25N 75°29W **328** B2
Salamina *Greece* 37°56N 23°30E **204** D5
Salamis *Cyprus* 35°11N 33°54E **207** E9
Salamonie L. *U.S.A.* 40°46N 85°37W **311** D11
Salar de Atacama *Chile* 23°30S 68°25W **334** A2
Salar de Uyuni *Bolivia* 20°30S 67°45W **330** E4
Sălard *Romania* 47°12N 22°3E **182** C7
Salas *Spain* 43°25N 6°15W **194** B4
Salas de los Infantes *Spain* 42°2N 3°17W **194** C7
Salatiga *Indonesia* 7°19S 110°30E **235** D4
Salavat *Russia* 53°21N 55°55E **186** D10
Salaverry *Peru* 8°15S 79°0W **330** B2
Salawati *Indonesia* 1°7S 130°52E **231** E8
Salay *Phil.* 8°52N 124°47E **233** G5
Salaya *India* 22°19N 69°35E **242** H3
Salayar *Indonesia* 6°7S 120°30E **231** F6
Salazar ➔ *Spain* 42°40N 1°20W **196** C3
Salazie *Réunion* 21°2S 55°32E **272** f
Salazie, Cirque de *Réunion* 21°3S 55°30E **272** f
Salbris *France* 47°25N 2°3E **173** E9
Salcedo *Phil.* 11°9N 125°40E **233** F5
Salcia *Romania* 43°56N 24°55E **183** G9
Sălciua *Romania* 46°24N 23°26E **183** D8
Salcombe *U.K.* 50°14N 3°47W **169** G4
Saldaña *Spain* 42°32N 4°48W **194** C6
Saldanha *S. Africa* 33°0S 17°58E **270** D2
Saldanha B. *S. Africa* 33°6S 18°0E **270** D2
Saldus *Latvia* 56°38N 22°30E **184** B9
Saldus □ *Latvia* 56°35N 22°30E **184** B9
Sale *Vic., Australia* 38°6S 147°6E **283** E7
Sale *Burma* 20°50N 94°45E **241** E5
Sale *Italy* 44°59N 8°48E **198** D5
Salé *Morocco* 34°3N 6°48W **260** B3
Sale *Gt. Man., U.K.* 53°26N 2°19W **168** D5
Sale City *U.S.A.* 31°16N 84°1W **316** D5
Salée, Rivière *Guadeloupe* 16°17N 61°33W **322** e
Salegard = Salekhard *Russia* 66°30N 66°35E **214** C7
Salekhard *Russia* 66°30N 66°35E **214** C7
Salelologa *Samoa* 13°41S 172°11W **287** V19
Salem *India* 11°40N 78°11E **245** J4
Salem *Montserrat* 16°45N 62°13W **323** p
Salem *Fla., U.S.A.* 29°53N 83°25W **316** F6
Salem *Ill., U.S.A.* 38°38N 88°57W **310** F8
Salem *Ind., U.S.A.* 38°36N 86°6W **311** F10
Salem *Mass., U.S.A.* 42°31N 70°53W **313** D14
Salem *Mo., U.S.A.* 37°39N 91°32W **308** G8
Salem *N.H., U.S.A.* 42°45N 71°12W **313** D13
Salem *N.J., U.S.A.* 39°34N 75°28W **309** F16
Salem *N.Y., U.S.A.* 43°10N 73°20W **313** C11
Salem *Ohio, U.S.A.* 40°54N 80°52W **312** F4
Salem *Oreg., U.S.A.* 44°56N 123°2W **304** D2
Salem *S. Dak., U.S.A.* 43°44N 97°23W **308** D5
Salem *Va., U.S.A.* 37°18N 80°3W **309** G13
Salemi *Italy* 37°49N 12°48E **200** E5
Sälen *Sweden* 61°15N 13°22E **162** C7
Salernes *France* 43°34N 6°15E **175** E10
Salerno *Italy* 40°41N 14°47E **201** B7
Salerno, G. di *Italy* 40°32N 14°42E **201** B7
Sales *Brazil* 4°2S 63°40W **329** D5
Salford *U.K.* 53°30N 2°18W **168** D5
Salgir ➔ *Ukraine* 45°38N 35°1E **189** K8
Salgótarján *Hungary* 48°5N 19°47E **182** B4
Salgueiro *Brazil* 8°4S 39°6W **332** C4
Salher *India* 20°40N 73°55E **244** D1
Salhus *Norway* 60°30N 5°15E **164** D2
Salibabu *Indonesia* 3°51N 126°40E **231** D7
Salibea = Salybia *Trin. & Tob.* 10°43N 61°2W **323** t
Salibia *Dominica* 15°30N 61°16W **323** k
Salida *U.S.A.* 38°32N 106°0W **300** C5
Salies-de-Béarn *France* 43°28N 0°56W **174** E3
Şalif *Yemen* 15°18N 42°41E **248** D3
Salihli *Turkey* 38°28N 28°8E **212** C3
Salihorsk *Belarus* 52°51N 27°27E **177** B14
Salin *Burma* 20°35N 94°40E **241** E5
Salina *Italy* 38°34N 14°50E **201** D7
Salina *Kans., U.S.A.* 38°50N 97°37W **308** F5
Salina *Utah, U.S.A.* 38°58N 111°51W **304** G8
Salina Cruz *Mexico* 16°10N 95°12W **319** D5
Salina di Margherita di Savoia ⌓ *Italy* 41°23N 16°4E **201** A9
Salinas = Salinópolis *Brazil* 0°40S 47°20W **332** B2
Salinas *Brazil* 16°10S 42°10W **333** E3
Salinas *Chile* 23°31S 69°29W **334** A2
Salinas *Ecuador* 2°10S 80°58W **328** D1
Salinas *Calif., U.S.A.* 36°40N 121°39W **306** J5
Salinas ➔ *Guatemala* 16°28N 90°31W **319** D6
Salinas ➔ *Calif., U.S.A.* 36°45N 121°48W **306** J5
Salinas, B. das *Angola* 14°11S 12°21E **265** E2
Salinas, B. de *Nic.* 11°4N 85°45W **320** D2
Salinas, Pampa de las *Argentina* 31°58S 66°42W **334** C2
Salinas Ambargasta *Argentina* 29°0S 65°0W **334** B3
Salinas de Hidalgo *Mexico* 22°38N 101°43W **318** C4
Salinas Grandes *Argentina* 30°0S 65°0W **334** C3
Salinas Pueblo Missions ⌓ *U.S.A.* 34°6N 106°4W **305** J10
Salinas Valley *U.S.A.* 36°15N 121°15W **306** J5
Saline *U.S.A.* 42°10N 83°47W **311** B13
Saline ➔ *Ark., U.S.A.* 33°10N 92°8W **314** E8
Saline ➔ *Kans., U.S.A.* 38°52N 97°30W **308** F5
Saline B. *Trin. & Tob.* 10°42N 61°2W **323** t
Saline di Trapani e Paceco ⌓ *Italy* 37°59N 12°28E **200** E5
Saline I. *Grenada* 12°26N 61°28W **323** q
Salines, C. de ses *Spain* 39°16N 3°4E **206** B4
Salines, Étang des *Martinique* 14°24N 60°52W **322** j
Salines, Pt. *Grenada* 12°0N 61°48W **323** q
Salines, Pte. de *Martinique* 14°23N 60°53W **322** j
Salinópolis *Brazil* 0°40S 47°20W **332** B2
Salins-les-Bains *France* 46°58N 5°52E **173** F12
Salir *Portugal* 37°14N 8°2W **195** H2
Salisbury = Harare *Zimbabwe* 17°43S 31°2E **269** F3
Salisbury *S. Austral., Australia* 34°46S 138°38E **282** C3
Salisbury *Dominica* 15°26N 61°27W **323** k
Salisbury *Wilts., U.K.* 51°4N 1°47W **169** F6
Salisbury *Md., U.S.A.* 38°22N 75°36W **309** F16
Salisbury *Mo., U.S.A.* 39°25N 92°48W **310** E4
Salisbury *N.C., U.S.A.* 35°40N 80°29W **315** D14
Salisbury I. *Canada* 63°30N 77°0W **295** C12
Salisbury Plain *U.K.* 51°14N 1°55W **169** F6
Săliște *Romania* 45°45N 23°56E **183** E8
Salitre ➔ *Brazil* 9°29S 40°39W **332** C3
Salka *Nigeria* 10°20N 4°58E **263** C5
Salkehatchie ➔ *U.S.A.* 32°37N 80°53W **316** C9
Şalkhad *Syria* 32°29N 36°43E **251** F7
Salkove *Ukraine* 48°15N 29°59E **183** B14
Salla *Finland* 66°50N 28°49E **160** C23
Sallanches *France* 45°55N 6°38E **175** C10
Sallent *Spain* 41°49N 1°54E **196** D6
Salles *France* 44°33N 0°52W **174** D3
Salles-Curan *France* 44°11N 2°48E **174** D6
Salling *Denmark* 56°40N 8°55E **163** H2
Salliq = Coral Harbour *Canada* 64°8N 83°10W **295** C11
Sallisaw *U.S.A.* 35°28N 94°47W **314** D7
Sallom *Sudan* 19°17N 37°6E **256** D4
Salluit *Canada* 62°14N 75°38W **295** C12
Sallynoggin *Ireland* 53°17N 6°8W **120** B3
Salmannsdorf *Austria* 48°14N 16°14E **142** A1
Salmās *Iran* 38°11N 44°47E **213** C11
Salmedina *Spain* 40°18N 3°35W **127** C2
Salmerón *Spain* 40°33N 2°29W **196** E2
Salmo *Canada* 49°10N 117°20W **296** D5
Salmon *U.S.A.* 45°11N 113°54W **304** D7
Salmon ➔ *B.C., Canada* 54°3N 122°40W **296** C4
Salmon ➔ *Idaho, U.S.A.* 45°51N 116°47W **304** D5
Salmon Arm *Canada* 50°40N 119°15W **296** C5
Salmon Gums *Australia* 32°59S 121°38E **279** F3
Salmon River Mts. *U.S.A.* 44°50N 115°30W **304** D6
Salo *C.A.R.* 3°10N 16°8E **264** B3
Salo *Finland* 60°22N 23°10E **188** B2
Salò *Italy* 45°36N 10°31E **198** C7
Salobreña *Spain* 36°44N 3°35W **195** J7
Salome *U.S.A.* 33°47N 113°37W **307** M13
Salomea *Poland* 52°11N 20°55E **142** B1
Salomon, C. *Martinique* 14°30N 61°6W **322** j
Salon *India* 26°2N 81°27E **243** F9
Salon-de-Provence *France* 43°39N 5°6E **175** E9
Salonga ➔ *Dem. Rep. of the Congo* 0°10S 19°50E **264** C4
Salonga-Nord △ *Dem. Rep. of the Congo* 1°55S 21°45E **264** C4
Salonga-Sud △ *Dem. Rep. of the Congo* 2°25S 21°0E **264** C4
Salonica = Thessaloniki *Greece* 40°38N 22°58E **202** F6
Salonta *Romania* 46°49N 21°42E **182** D6
Salop = Shropshire □ *U.K.* 52°36N 2°45W **169** E5
Salor ➔ *Spain* 39°39N 7°3W **195** F3
Salou *Spain* 41°4N 1°8E **196** D6
Salou, C. de *Spain* 41°3N 1°10E **196** D6
Saloum ➔ *Senegal* 13°50N 16°45W **262** C1
Salpausselkä *Finland* 61°3N 26°15E **188** B4
Salsacate *Argentina* 31°20S 65°5W **334** C2
Salses *France* 42°50N 2°55E **174** F6
Salsette I. *India* 19°2N 72°53E **130** A2
Salsk *Russia* 46°28N 41°30E **191** G5
Salso ➔ *Italy* 37°6N 13°57E **200** E6
Salsomaggiore Terme *Italy* 44°49N 9°59E **198** D6
Salt *Spain* 41°59N 2°47E **196** D7
Salt ➔ *Alta., Canada* 60°0N 112°25W **296** B6
Salt ➔ *Ariz., U.S.A.* 33°23N 112°19W **305** K7
Salt ➔ *Mo., U.S.A.* 39°28N 91°4W **310** E5
Salt Cay *Bahamas* 25°6N 77°18W **153** b
Salt Flats = Witte Pan *Neth. Ant.* 12°3N 68°17W **322** h
Salt Fork Red ➔ *U.S.A.* 34°27N 99°21W **314** D5
Salt L. *N.S.W., Australia* 30°6S 142°8E **281** E3
Salt L. *Hawai'i, U.S.A.* 21°21N 157°55W **302** K14
Salt Lake City = Bidhan Nagar *India* 22°35N 88°25E **124** B2
Salt Lake City *U.S.A.* 40°45N 111°53W **304** F8
Salt Range *Pakistan* 32°30N 72°25E **242** C5
Salt River *S. Africa* 34°6S 18°28E **118** A1
Salt Springs *U.S.A.* 29°21N 81°44W **317** F8
Salt Water L. *India* 22°33N 88°26E **124** B2
Salta *Argentina* 24°57S 65°25W **334** A2
Salta □ *Argentina* 24°48S 65°30W **334** A2
Saltara *Italy* 43°45N 12°50E **199** E9
Saltash *U.K.* 50°24N 4°14W **169** G3
Saltburn by the Sea *U.K.* 54°35N 0°58W **168** C7
Saltcoats *U.K.* 55°38N 4°47W **167** F4
Saltee Is. *Ireland* 52°7N 6°37W **166** D5
Salters *U.S.A.* 33°36N 79°51W **316** B10
Saltfjellet *Norway* 66°40N 15°15E **160** C16
Saltfjorden *Norway* 67°15N 14°10E **160** C16
Saltholm *Denmark* 55°38N 12°43E **163** J6
Salthólmavík *Iceland* 65°24N 21°57W **155** B5
Saltillo *Mexico* 25°25N 101°0W **318** B4
Salto *Argentina* 34°20S 60°15W **334** C3
Salto *Uruguay* 31°27S 57°50W **334** C4
Salto da Divisa *Brazil* 16°0S 39°57W **333** E4
Salto del Guaíra *Paraguay* 24°3S 54°17W **335** A5
Salton City *U.S.A.* 33°18N 115°57W **307** M11
Salton Sea *U.S.A.* 33°15N 115°45W **307** M11
Saltpond *Ghana* 5°15N 1°3W **263** D4
Saltrød *Norway* 58°30N 8°49E **164** F5
Saltsburg *U.S.A.* 40°29N 79°27W **312** F5
Saltsjö-Duvnäs *Sweden* 59°18N 18°12E **139** B3
Saltsjöbaden *Sweden* 59°15N 18°20E **162** E12
Saltykovka *Russia* 55°45N 37°54E **129** B5
Saluda *U.S.A.* 34°0N 81°46W **316** A8
Saluda ➔ *U.S.A.* 34°1N 81°4W **315** D14
Salug *Phil.* 8°7N 122°47E **233** G4
Salûm *Egypt* 31°31N 25°7E **256** A2
Salûm, Khâlig el *Egypt* 31°35N 25°24E **256** A2
Salur *India* 18°27N 83°18E **244** E6
Salut, Is. du *Fr. Guiana* 5°15N 52°35W **329** B7
Saluzzo *Italy* 44°39N 7°29E **198** D4
Salvación, B. *Chile* 50°50S 75°10W **336** D1
Salvador *Brazil* 13°0S 38°30W **333** D4
Salvador *Sask., Canada* 52°10N 109°32W **297** C7
Salvador, El ■ *Cent. Amer.* 13°50N 89°0W **320** D2
Salvador, L. *U.S.A.* 29°43N 90°15W **315** G9
Salvaterra *Brazil* 0°46S 48°31W **332** B2
Salvaterra de Magos *Portugal* 39°1N 8°47W **195** F2
Salvisa *U.S.A.* 37°54N 84°51W **311** G12
Sálvora, I. de *Spain* 42°30N 8°58W **194** C2
Salween ➔ *Burma* 16°31N 97°37E **241** G6
Salyan *Azerbaijan* 39°33N 48°59E **213** C13
Salybia *Trin. & Tob.* 10°43N 61°2W **323** t
Salza ➔ *Austria* 47°40N 14°43E **180** D7
Salzach ➔ *Austria* 48°12N 12°56E **180** C5
Salzburg *Austria* 47°48N 13°2E **180** D6
Salzburg □ *Austria* 47°15N 13°0E **180** D6
Salzburgen = Château-Salins *France* 48°50N 6°30E **173** D13
Salzgitter *Germany* 52°9N 10°19E **178** C6
Salzkotten *Germany* 51°40N 8°37E **178** D4
Salzwedel *Germany* 52°52N 11°10E **178** C7
Sam *Gabon* 0°58N 11°16E **264** B2
Sam *India* 26°50N 70°31E **242** F4
Sam Neua *Laos* 20°29N 104°5E **228** G5
Sam Ngao *Thailand* 17°18N 99°0E **236** D2
Sam Rayburn Res. *U.S.A.* 31°4N 94°5W **314** F7
Sam Son *Vietnam* 19°44N 105°54E **236** C5
Sam Teu *Laos* 19°59N 104°38E **236** C5
Sama de Langreo = Langreo *Spain* 43°18N 5°40W **194** B5
Samacimbo *Angola* 13°33S 16°59E **265** E3
Şamad *Oman* 22°48N 58°9E **249** B7
Samagaltay *Russia* 50°36N 95°3E **217** B13
Samā'il *Oman* 23°40N 57°50E **249** B7
Samaipata *Bolivia* 18°9S 63°52W **331** D5

Samal *Phil.* 7°5N 125°42E **233** H5
Samal I. *Phil.* 7°3N 125°44E **233** H5
Samales Group *Phil.* 6°0N 122°0E **233** J3
Samalkot *India* 17°3N 82°13E **244** F6
Samâlût *Egypt* 28°20N 30°42E **256** B3
Samana *India* 30°10N 76°13E **242** D7
Samana Cay *Bahamas* 23°3N 73°45W **321** B5
Samandağ *Turkey* 36°5N 35°59E **250** B6
Samandıra *India* 40°59N 29°13E **203** F13
Samanga *Tanzania* 8°2S 39°13E **269** D4
Samangân □ *Afghan.* 36°15N 68°3E **240** A3
Samangwa
  Dem. Rep. of the Congo 4°23S 24°10E **265** C4
Samani *Japan* 42°7N 142°56E **220** C11
Samanlı Dağları *Turkey* 40°32N 29°10E **203** F13
Samannûd *Egypt* 30°57N 31°14E **251** H2
Samar □ *Phil.* 12°0N 125°0E **233** E5
Samar □ *Phil.* 11°50N 125°0E **233** F5
Samar Sea *Phil.* 12°0N 124°15E **232** E5
Samara *Russia* 53°8N 50°6E **190** D10
Samara → *Russia* 53°8N 50°6E **190** D10
Samara → *Ukraine* 48°28N 35°7E **189** H8
Samarai *Papua N. G.* 10°39S 150°41E **286** F6
Samaria = Shōmrōn
  West Bank 32°15N 35°13E **251** F6
Samaria *Kriti, Greece* 35°17N 23°58E **207** E4
Samaria *West Bank* 35°12N 35°17E **251** F6
Samaria △ *Greece* 35°18N 23°57E **204** F5
Samariapo *Venezuela* 5°15N 67°48W **328** B4
Samarinda *Indonesia* 0°30S 117°9E **235** C5
Samarkand = Samarqand
  Uzbekistan 39°40N 66°55E **217** E7
Samarkandsky = Temirtau
  Kazakhstan 50°5N 72°56E **217** B8
Samarqand *Uzbekistan* 39°40N 66°55E **217** E7
Samarqand □ *Uzbekistan* 39°35N 66°35E **217** E7
Sāmarrā′ *Iraq* 34°12N 43°52E **213** H4
Samastipur *India* 25°50N 85°50E **243** G11
Samatya *Turkey* 40°59N 28°55E **122** C1
Samaúma *Brazil* 7°50S 60°2W **331** B5
Şamaxı *Azerbaijan* 40°38N 48°37E **191** K9
Samba *Équateur,*
  Dem. Rep. of the Congo 0°13N 21°25E **264** B4
Samba *Maniema,*
  Dem. Rep. of the Congo 4°38S 26°22E **265** C5
Samba *Jammu & Kashmir,*
  India 32°32N 75°10E **243** C6
Samba Caju *Angola* 8°46S 15°24E **265** D3
Sambaíba *Brazil* 7°8S 45°21W **332** D2
Sambalpur *India* 21°28N 84°4E **244** D7
Sambar, Tanjung
  Indonesia 2°59S 110°19E **235** C4
Sambas *Indonesia* 1°20N 109°20E **235** B3
Sambava *Madag.* 14°16S 50°10E **272** A3
Sambawizi *Zimbabwe* 18°24S 26°13E **269** B2
Sambhal *India* 28°35N 78°37E **243** E8
Sambhar *India* 26°52N 75°6E **242** F6
Sambhar L. *India* 26°55N 75°12E **242** F6
Sambiase *Italy* 38°58N 16°17E **201** D9
Sambir *Ukraine* 49°30N 23°10E **185** J10
Sambo *Angola* 13°3S 16°8E **265** E3
Sambor *Cambodia* 12°46N 106°0E **236** F6
Samborombón, B.
  Argentina 36°5S 57°20W **334** D4
Sambuca di Sicília *Italy* 37°39N 13°7E **200** E6
Samburu □ *Kenya* 0°37N 37°31E **268** B4
Samcheok *S. Korea* 37°30N 129°10E **224** D4
Same *Tanzania* 4°2S 37°38E **268** C4
Samer *France* 50°38N 1°44E **173** B8
Samfya *Zambia* 11°22S 29°31E **269** E2
Samhān, Jabal *Oman* 17°12N 54°55E **249** C6
Sami *Greece* 38°15N 20°39E **207** C2
Samka *Burma* 20°9N 96°57E **241** E6
Sämkir *Azerbaijan* 40°50N 46°0E **191** K8
Sammanturai *Sri Lanka* 7°36N 81°39E **245** E5
Samnah *Si. Arabia* 25°10N 37°15E **246** E3
Samnū □ *Libya* 27°15N 14°55E **262** C8
Samo Alto *Chile* 30°22S 71°0W **334** C1
Samoa ■ *Pac. Oc.* 14°0S 172°0W **287** V20
Samoan Is. *Pac. Oc.* 14°0S 171°0W **287** V20
Samobor *Croatia* 45°47N 15°44E **199** C12
Samoëns *France* 46°5N 6°45E **173** F13
Samokov *Bulgaria* 42°18N 23°35E **202** D7
Šamorín *Slovak Rep.* 48°2N 17°19E **181** C10
Samorogouan
  Burkina Faso 11°21N 4°57W **262** C4
Samos *U.S.A.* 37°45N 26°50E **205** D8
Samoš *Serbia* 45°13N 20°46E **182** E5
Samos *Spain* 42°44N 7°20W **194** C3
Samos □ *Greece* 37°45N 26°50E **205** D8
Samoset *U.S.A.* 27°28N 82°33W **317** H7
Samosir *Indonesia* 2°55N 98°50E **236** D1
Samothráki = Mathráki
  Greece 39°48N 19°31E **206** B9
Samothráki *Greece* 40°28N 25°28E **203** F9
Samoylovka *Russia* 51°12N 43°43E **190** E6
Sampa *Angola* 10°38S 18°56E **265** E3
Sampa *Ghana* 8°0N 2°36W **262** D4
Sampacho *Argentina* 33°20S 64°50W **334** C3
Sampalan *Indonesia* 8°41S 115°34E **231** K18
Sampaloc *Phil.* 14°36N 120°52E **127** B1
Sampang *Indonesia* 7°11S 113°13E **235** D4
Samper de Calanda *Spain* 41°11N 0°28W **198** D4
Sampéyre *Italy* 44°34N 7°11E **198** D4
Samphan Thawong
  Thailand 13°44N 100°31E **113** B2
Sampit *Indonesia* 2°34S 113°0E **235** C4
Sampit → *Indonesia* 2°44S 112°54E **235** C4
Sampit, Teluk *Indonesia* 3°5S 113°3E **235** C4
Sampun *Papua N. G.* 5°21S 152°8E **286** C7
Samrong *Cambodia* 14°15N 103°30E **236** E4
Samrong *Thailand* 15°10N 100°40E **236** E3
Samseon *S. Korea* 37°34N 127°0E **137** B2
Samsø *Denmark* 55°50N 10°35E **163** J4
Samsø Bælt *Denmark* 55°45N 10°45E **163** J4
Samson *U.S.A.* 31°7N 86°3W **316** D10
Samsun *Turkey* 41°15N 36°22E **212** B7
Samsun □ *Turkey* 41°10N 36°10E **212** B7
Samtah *Si. Arabia* 16°36N 42°56E **248** C3
Samtredia *Georgia* 42°7N 42°24E **191** J6
Samuel Smith Park
  Canada 43°35N 79°30W **141** B1
Samui, Ko *Thailand* 9°30N 100°0E **237** b
Samur → *Russia* 41°53N 48°32E **191** K9
Samursky Khrebet
  Russia 41°55N 47°11E **191** K8
Samusole
  Dem. Rep. of the Congo 10°2S 24°0E **265** E4
Samut Prakan *Thailand* 13°32N 100°40E **236** F3
Samut Prakan *Bangkok,*
  Thailand 13°40N 100°36E **113** B2
Samut Songkhram
  Thailand 13°24N 100°1E **236** F3
Samwari *Pakistan* 28°30N 69°8E **242** E2
San *Mali* 13°15N 4°57W **262** C4
San → *Cambodia* 13°32N 105°57E **236** F5
San → *Poland* 50°45N 21°51E **185** H8
San Adrián *Spain* 42°20N 1°55W **194** B3
San Agustin *Colombia* 1°53N 76°16W **328** C2
San Agustín *Romblon,*
  Phil. 12°34N 122°6E **232** E4
San Agustín, C. *Phil.* 6°20N 126°13E **233** H6

San Agustín de Valle Fértil
  Argentina 30°35S 67°30W **334** C2
San Ambrosio *Pac. Oc.* 26°28S 79°53W **326** F3
San Andreas *U.S.A.* 38°12N 120°41W **306** G6
San Andres *Catanduanes,*
  Phil. 13°36N 124°6E **232** E5
San Andres *Romblon,*
  Phil. 13°19N 122°41E **232** E4
San Andrés *Romblon,*
  Phil. 12°31N 122°2E **232** E4
San Andrés *Barcelona,*
  Spain 41°26N 2°11E **114** A2
San Andrès del Rabanedo
  Spain 42°37N 5°36W **194** C5
San Andres Mts. *U.S.A.* 33°0N 106°30E **305** K10
San Andrés Tuxtla
  Mexico 18°27N 95°13W **319** D5
San Angel *Mexico* 19°20N 99°11W **128** B1
San Angelo *U.S.A.* 31°28N 100°30W **314** H4
San Anselmo *U.S.A.* 37°59N 122°34W **306** H4
San Antonio *Belize* 16°15N 89°2W **319** D7
San Antonio *Chile* 33°40S 71°40W **334** C1
San Antonio *Phil.* 14°57N 120°5E **232** D3
San Antonio *N. Mex.,*
  U.S.A. 33°55N 106°52W **305** K10
San Antonio *Tex., U.S.A.* 29°25N 98°29W **314** H5
San Antonio *Venezuela* 3°30N 66°44W **328** C4
San Antonio → *U.S.A.* 28°30N 96°54W **314** G6
San Antonio, C.
  Argentina 36°15S 56°40W **334** D4
San Antonio, C. de *Cuba* 21°50N 84°57W **320** B3
San Antonio, C. de *Spain* 38°48N 0°12E **197** G5
San Antonio, Mt.
  U.S.A. 34°17N 117°38W **307** L9
San Antonio Bay *Phil.* 8°38N 117°35E **233** G1
San Antonio de los Baños
  Cuba 22°54N 82°31W **320** B3
San Antonio de los Cobres
  Argentina 24°10S 66°17W **334** A2
San Antonio Oeste
  Argentina 40°40S 65°0W **336** B4
San Arcángel *Italy* 40°14N 16°14E **201** B9
San Ardo *U.S.A.* 36°1N 120°54W **306** J6
San Augustín *Canary Is.* 27°47N 15°32W **153** e1
San Augustine *U.S.A.* 31°32N 94°7W **314** F7
San Bartolomé *Canary Is.* 28°59N 13°37W **153** e2
San Bartolomé de Tirajana
  Canary Is. 27°54N 15°34W **153** e1
San Bartolomeo in Galdo
  Italy 41°24N 15°1E **201** A8
San Basilio *Italy* 41°56N 12°35E **136** B2
San Benedetto del Tronto
  Italy 42°57N 13°53E **199** F10
San Benedetto Po *Italy* 45°2N 10°55E **198** C7
San Benedicto, I.
  Mexico 19°18N 110°49W **318** D2
San Benito *U.S.A.* 26°8N 97°38W **314** H6
San Benito → *U.S.A.* 36°53N 121°34W **306** J5
San Benito Mt. *U.S.A.* 36°22N 120°37W **306** J6
San Bernardino *U.S.A.* 34°7N 117°19W **307** L9
San Bernardino Mts.
  U.S.A. 34°10N 116°45W **307** L10
San Bernardino Str. *Phil.* 13°0N 125°0E **232** E5
San Bernardo *Chile* 33°40S 70°50W **334** C1
San Bernardo, I. de
  Colombia 9°45N 75°50W **328** B2
San-Beyse = Choybalsan
  Mongolia 48°4N 114°30E **219** B6
San Blas *Mexico* 26°5N 108°46W **318** B3
San Blas, Arch. de
  Panama 9°50N 78°31W **320** E4
San Blas, C. *U.S.A.* 29°40N 85°21W **316** F4
San Bonifacio *Italy* 45°24N 11°16E **199** C8
San Borja *Bolivia* 14°50S 66°52W **330** C4
San Borja *Lima, Peru* 12°6S 76°59W **124** B3
San Bóvio *Italy* 45°27N 9°18E **128** b
San Bruno, Pt. *U.S.A.* 37°37N 122°23W **136** C2
San Bruno Mountain State Park →
  U.S.A. 37°42N 122°26W **136** B2
San Buenaventura = Ventura
  U.S.A. 34°17N 119°18W **307** L7
San Buenaventura
  Bolivia 14°27S 67°35W **330** C4
San Buenaventura *Coahuila,*
  Mexico 27°5N 101°32W **318** B4
San Carlos = Butuku-Luba
  Eq. Guin. 3°29N 8°33E **263** E6
San Carlos = Sant Carles
  Spain 39°3N 1°34E **206** C2
San Carlos *Argentina* 33°50S 69°0W **334** C2
San Carlos *Chile* 36°10S 72°0W **334** D1
San Carlos *Baja Calif. S.,*
  Mexico 24°47N 112°7W **318** C2
San Carlos *Coahuila,*
  Mexico 29°1N 100°51W **318** B4
San Carlos *Nic.* 11°12N 84°50W **320** D3
San Carlos *Neg. Occ.,*
  Phil. 10°29N 123°25E **233** F4
San Carlos *Pangasinan,*
  Phil. 15°55N 120°20E **232** D3
San Carlos *Uruguay* 34°46S 54°58W **335** C5
San Carlos *Amazonas,*
  Venezuela 1°55N 67°4W **328** C4
San Carlos *Cojedes,*
  Venezuela 9°40N 68°36W **328** B4
San Carlos de Bariloche
  Argentina 41°10S 71°25W **336** B2
San Carlos de la Rápita = Sant
  Carles de la Ràpita
  Spain 40°37N 0°35E **196** E5
San Carlos de Río Negro
  Venezuela 1°55N 67°4W **328** C4
San Carlos del Zulia
  Venezuela 9°1N 71°55W **328** B3
San Carlos L. *U.S.A.* 33°11N 110°32W **307** K8
San Carlos Park *U.S.A.* 26°28N 81°49W **317** J8
San Cataldo *Italy* 37°29N 13°59E **200** E6
San Celoni = Sant Celoni
  Spain 41°42N 2°30E **196** D7
San Clemente *Chile* 35°30S 71°29W **334** D1
San Clemente *Spain* 39°24N 2°25W **197** F2
San Clemente *Calif.,*
  U.S.A. 33°26N 117°37W **307** M9
San Clemente I. *U.S.A.* 32°53N 118°29W **307** N8
San Cristóbal = Es Migjorn Gran
  Spain 39°57N 4°3E **206** B5
San Cristóbal *B. Aires,*
  Argentina 34°38S 58°23W **117** B2
San Cristóbal *Santa Fe,*
  Argentina 30°20S 61°10W **334** C3
San Cristóbal *Colombia* 2°18S 73°2W **328** D3
San Cristóbal *Dom. Rep.* 18°25N 70°6W **321** C5
San Cristóbal *Solomon Is.* 10°30S 161°0E **287** N11
San Cristóbal *Madrid,*
  Spain 40°25N 3°35W **127** B2
San Cristóbal *Venezuela* 7°46N 72°14W **328** B3
San Cristóbal, Cerro
  Chile 33°25S 70°38W **137** B2
San Cristóbal, I. *Ecuador* 0°50S 89°26W **330** a

San Cristóbal, Virgen del
  Chile 33°25S 70°38W **137** B2
San Cristóbal de las Casas
  Mexico 16°45N 92°38W **319** D6
San Cristoforo *Italy* 45°26N 9°9E **129** B1
San Damiano d'Asti *Italy* 44°50N 8°4E **198** D5
San Daniele del Friuli
  Italy 46°9N 13°1E **199** B10
San Diego *Calif., U.S.A.* 32°42N 117°9W **307** N9
San Diego *Tex., U.S.A.* 27°46N 98°14W **314** H5
San Diego de la Unión
  Mexico 21°28N 100°52W **318** C4
San Diego Int. ✈ (SAN)
  U.S.A. 32°44N 117°11W **307** N9
San Dimitri, Ras *Malta* 36°4N 14°11E **206** E6
San Dimitri Point = San Dimitri,
  Ras *Malta* 36°4N 14°11E **206** E6
San Donà di Piave *Italy* 45°38N 12°34E **199** C9
San Donato Milanese
  Italy 45°24N 9°16E **129** B2
Sân el Hagar *Egypt* 30°58N 31°52E **251** H2
San Esteban *Venezuela* 10°24N 67°58W **328** A4
San Esteban de Gormaz
  Spain 41°34N 3°13W **196** D1
San Eugenio = Artigas
  Uruguay 30°20S 56°30W **334** C4
San Felice Circeo *Italy* 41°14N 13°5E **200** A6
San Felice sul Panaro
  Italy 44°50N 11°8E **199** D8
San Felipe *Chile* 32°43S 70°42W **334** C1
San Felipe *Colombia* 1°55N 67°6E **328** C4
San Felipe *Baja Calif.,*
  Mexico 31°1N 114°52W **318** A2
San Felipe *Phil.* 15°4N 120°4E **232** D3
San Felipe *Venezuela* 10°20N 68°44W **328** A4
San Felipe → *U.S.A.* 33°10N 115°49W **307** M11
San Félix *Chile* 28°56S 70°28W **334** B1
San Félix *Pac. Oc.* 26°23S 80°0W **326** F2
San Fernando = Sant Ferran
  Spain 38°42N 1°28E **206** C1
San Fernando *Chile* 34°30S 71°0W **334** C1
San Fernando *Tamaulipas,*
  Mexico 24°51N 98°10W **319** C5
San Fernando *Cebu,*
  Phil. 10°10N 123°42E **233** F4
San Fernando *La Union,*
  Phil. 16°40N 120°23E **232** C3
San Fernando *Pampanga,*
  Phil. 15°5N 120°37E **232** D3
San Fernando *Romblon,*
  Phil. 12°19N 122°31E **232** E4
San Fernando *Trin. & Tob.* 10°16N 61°28W **323** t
San Fernando
  U.S.A. 34°17N 118°26W **307** L8
San Fernando de Apure
  Venezuela 7°54N 67°15W **328** B4
San Fernando de Atabapo
  Venezuela 4°3N 67°42W **328** C4
San Fernando di Púglia
  Italy 41°18N 16°5E **201** A9
San Francique = Erin
  Trin. & Tob. 10°5N 61°39W **323** t
San Francisco *Córdoba,*
  Argentina 31°30S 62°5W **334** C3
San Francisco *Bolivia* 15°16S 65°31W **331** D4
San Francisco *Peru* 12°36S 73°49W **330** D3
San Francisco *Agusan del S.,*
  Phil. 8°30N 125°56E **233** G5
San Francisco *Cebu,*
  Phil. 10°39N 124°23E **233** F5
San Francisco *Quezon,*
  Phil. 13°21N 122°31E **232** E4
San Francisco *S. Leyte,*
  Phil. 10°4N 125°9E **233** F5
San Francisco
  U.S.A. 37°46N 122°23W **136** B2
San Francisco, C. de
  Colombia 6°18N 77°29W **328** B2
San Francisco, Paso de
  S. Amer. 27°0S 68°0W **334** B2
San Francisco B. *U.S.A.* 37°30N 122°14W **136** B3
San Francisco Culhuacán
  Mexico 25°N 101°32W **318** B4
San Francisco de Macorís
  Dom. Rep. 19°19N 70°15W **321** C5
San Francisco del Monte de Oro
  Argentina 32°36S 66°8W **334** C2
San Francisco del Oro
  Mexico 26°52N 105°51W **318** B3
San Francisco Int. ✈ (SFO)
  U.S.A. 37°37N 122°22W **306** H4
San Francisco Javier = Sant
  Francesc de Formentera
  Spain 38°42N 1°26E **206** D1
San Fratello *Italy* 38°1N 14°36E **201** D7
San Fruttuoso *Italy* 45°34N 9°14E **129** A2
San Gabriel *Ecuador* 0°36N 77°49W **328** C2
San Gabriel *Calif., U.S.A.* 34°5N 118°5W **126** C4
San Gabriel → *U.S.A.* 33°47N 118°6W **126** C4
San Gabriel Chilac
  Mexico 18°19N 97°21W **319** D5
San Gabriel Mts. *U.S.A.* 34°17N 117°38W **307** L9
San Gavino Monreale
  Italy 39°33N 8°47E **200** C1
San German *Puerto Rico* 18°4N 67°4W **321** b
San Gil *Colombia* 6°33N 73°8W **328** B3
San Giljan = St. Julian's
  Malta 35°55N 14°29E **206** F7
San Gimignano *Italy* 43°28N 11°2E **198** E8
San Giórgio di Nogaro
  Italy 45°50N 13°13E **199** C10
San Giórgio Iónico *Italy* 40°27N 17°23E **201** B10
San Giovanni Bianco *Italy* 45°52N 9°38E **198** C6
San Giovanni in Fiore
  Italy 39°15N 16°42E **201** C9
San Giovanni in Persiceto
  Italy 44°38N 11°11E **199** D8
San Giovanni Rotondo
  Italy 41°42N 15°44E **199** G12
San Giovanni Valdarno
  Italy 43°34N 11°32E **199** E8
San Giuliano Milanese
  Italy 45°24N 9°17E **129** B2
San Giuliano Terme *Italy* 43°46N 10°26E **198** E7
San Gorgonio Mt.
  U.S.A. 34°7N 116°51W **307** L10
San Gottardo, P. del *Switz.* 46°33N 8°33E **179** J4
San Gregorio *Uruguay* 32°37S 55°40W **335** C4
San Gregorio *U.S.A.* 37°20N 122°23W **306** H4
San Giuseppe Jato *Italy* 37°57N 13°11E **200** E6
San Ignacio *Belize* 17°10N 89°5W **319** D7
San Ignacio *Beni, Bolivia* 14°53S 65°36W **331** C4
San Ignacio *Santa Cruz,*
  Bolivia 16°20S 60°55W **331** D5
San Ignacio *Baja Calif.,*
  Mexico 27°27N 112°51W **318** B2
San Ignacio *Paraguay* 26°52S 57°3W **334** B4

San Ignacio *Peru* 5°8S 78°59W **330** B2
San Ignacio, L. *Mexico* 26°54N 113°13W **318** B2
San Ildefonso, C.
  Phil. 16°0N 122°1E **232** C4
San Isidro *Argentina* 34°29S 58°31W **334** C4
San Isidro *Lima, Peru* 12°5S 77°2W **124** B2
San Isidro *Phil.* 6°50N 126°5E **233** H6
San Isidro de Potot = Burgos
  Phil. 16°4N 119°52E **232** C2
San Jacinto *Colombia* 9°50N 75°8W **328** B2
San Jacinto *Phil.* 12°34N 123°44E **232** E4
San Jacinto *Calif.,*
  U.S.A. 33°47N 116°57W **307** M10
San Jaime = Sant Jaume
  Spain 39°54N 4°4E **206** B5
San Javier *Misiones,*
  Argentina 27°55S 55°5W **335** B4
San Javier *Santa Fe,*
  Argentina 30°40S 59°55W **334** C4
San Javier *Beni, Bolivia* 14°34S 64°42W **331** C5
San Javier *Santa Cruz,*
  Bolivia 16°18S 62°30W **331** D5
San Javier *Chile* 35°40S 71°45W **334** D1
San Jerónimo Lídice
  Mexico 19°19N 99°14W **128** C1
San Jerónimo Taviche
  Mexico 16°44N 96°35W **319** D5
San Joaquín *Bolivia* 13°4S 64°49W **331** C5
San Joaquín *Santiago,*
  Chile 33°29S 70°35W **137** B2
San Joaquín *Phil.* 10°35N 122°8E **233** F4
San Joaquín *Calif.,*
  U.S.A. 36°36N 120°11W **306** J6
San Joaquín → *U.S.A.* 38°4N 121°51W **306** G5
San Joaquín → *Bolivia* 13°8S 63°41W **331** C5
San Joaquín → *Calif.,*
  U.S.A. 38°4N 121°51W **306** G5
San Joaquín, Cerro *Ecuador* 0°53S 89°30W **330** a
San Joaquin Valley
  U.S.A. 37°20N 121°0W **306** J6
San Jon *U.S.A.* 35°6N 103°20W **305** J12
San Jordi = Sant Jordi
  Spain 39°33N 2°46E **206** B3
San Jorge *Argentina* 31°54S 61°50W **334** C3
San Jorge *Solomon Is.* 8°28S 159°38E **287** M10
San Jorge, B. *Mexico* 31°20N 113°20W **318** A2
San Jorge, G. *Argentina* 46°0S 66°0W **336** C3
San José = San Josep
  Spain 38°55N 1°18E **206** D1
San José *Costa Rica* 9°55N 84°2W **320** E3
San José *Guatemala* 14°0N 90°50W **320** D1
San Jose *N. Marianas* 14°58N 145°37E **302** e
San Jose *Mind. Occ., Phil.* 12°27N 121°4E **232** E3
San Jose *Nueva Ecija,*
  Phil. 15°45N 120°55E **232** D3
San Jose *Calif., U.S.A.* 37°20N 121°53W **306** H5
San Jose *Ill., U.S.A.* 40°18N 89°36W **312** E8
San Jose → *U.S.A.* 34°25N 106°45W **305** J10
San José, Golfo *Argentina* 42°20S 64°18W **336** B4
San José, I. *Mexico* 25°0N 110°38W **318** C2
San Jose de Buenavista
  Phil. 10°45N 121°56E **233** F3
San José de Chiquitos
  Bolivia 17°53S 60°50W **331** D5
San José de Feliciano
  Argentina 30°26S 58°46W **334** C4
San José de Jáchal
  Argentina 30°15S 68°46W **334** C2
San José de Mayo
  Uruguay 34°27S 56°40W **334** C4
San José de Ocune
  Colombia 4°15N 70°20W **328** C3
San José de Uchapiamonas
  Bolivia 14°13S 68°5W **330** C4
San José del Cabo *Mexico* 23°3N 109°41W **318** C3
San José del Guaviare
  Colombia 2°35N 72°38W **328** C3
San José del Monte *Brazil* 14°49N 121°3E **232** D3
San José Río Hondo
  Mexico 19°26N 99°14W **128** B1
San Josep *Spain* 38°55N 1°18E **206** D1
San Juan *Argentina* 31°30S 68°30W **334** C2
San Juan *Antioquia,*
  Colombia 8°46N 76°32W **328** B2
San Juan *Neth. Ant.* 12°15N 69°6W **322** g
San Juan *Ica, Peru* 15°22S 75°7W **330** D2
San Juan *Puno, Peru* 14°25S 69°19W **124** D4
San Juan *Batangas, Phil.* 13°50N 121°24E **232** E3
San Juan *S. Leyte, Phil.* 10°16N 125°10E **233** F5
San Juan *Puerto Rico* 18°28N 66°7W **321** C6
San Juan *Trin. & Tob.* 10°39N 61°29W **323** t
San Juan □ *Argentina* 31°9S 69°0W **334** C2
San Juan → *Argentina* 32°20S 67°25W **334** C2
San Juan → *Bolivia* 21°9S 64°7W **331** E4
San Juan → *Colombia* 4°3N 77°22W **328** C2
San Juan → *Nic.* 10°56N 83°42W **320** D3
San Juan → *Phil.* 14°35N 121°10E **127** B2
San Juan → *Utah,*
  U.S.A. 37°16N 110°26W **305** H8
San Juan → *Venezuela* 10°14N 62°38W **329** A5
San Juan, C. *Eq. Guin.* 1°0N 9°20W **264** B1
San Juan Bautista = Sant Joan de
  Labritja *Spain* 39°5N 1°31E **206** C2
San Juan Bautista = Villahermosa
  Mexico 17°59N 92°55W **319** D6
San Juan Bautista *Calif.,*
  U.S.A. 36°51N 121°32W **306** J5
San Juan Capistrano
  U.S.A. 33°30N 117°40W **307** M9
San Juan Cr. → *U.S.A.* 35°40N 120°22W **306** J5
San Juan de Alicante
  Spain 38°24N 0°26W **197** G4
San Juan de Aragón
  Mexico 19°28N 99°4W **128** B2
San Juan de Aragón, Parque
  Mexico 19°27N 99°4W **128** B2
San Juan de Guadalupe
  Mexico 24°38N 102°44W **318** B4
San Juan de Guía, Cabo de
  Colombia 11°21N 73°59W **328** A3
San Juan de la Costa
  Mexico 24°20N 110°41W **318** C2
San Juan de los Lagos
  Mexico 21°15N 102°18W **318** C4
San Juan de los Morros
  Venezuela 9°55N 67°21W **328** B4
San Juan de Lurigancho
  Peru 11°59S 77°0W **124** A2
San Juan de Manapiare
  Venezuela 5°15N 66°5W **328** B4
San Juan de Villa Hermosa =
  Villahermosa *Mexico* 17°59N 92°55W **319** D6
San Juan del César
  Colombia 10°46N 73°1W **328** A3
San Juan del Monte *Phil.* 14°36N 121°1E **127** B2
San Juan del Norte *Nic.* 10°58N 83°40W **320** D3
San Juan del Norte, B. de
  Nic. 11°0N 83°40W **320** D3
San Juan del Río *Mexico* 20°23N 100°0W **319** C5
San Juan del Sur *Nic.* 11°20N 85°51W **320** D2
San Juan I. *U.S.A.* 48°32N 123°5W **306** B4

San Juan Island △
  U.S.A. 48°35N 123°8W **306** B4
San Juan Ixtacala
  Mexico 19°31N 99°10W **128** A1
San Juan Mts. *U.S.A.* 37°30N 107°0W **305** H10
San Julián *Argentina* 49°15S 67°45E **336** C3
San Julian *Phil.* 11°45N 125°27E **233** F5
San Just, Sierra de *Spain* 40°45N 0°49W **196** E4
San Just Desvern *Spain* 41°22N 2°4E **114** A1
San Justo *B. Aires,*
  Argentina 34°36S 58°22W **117** C1
San Justo *Santa Fe,*
  Argentina 30°47S 60°30W **334** C4
San Kamphaeng *Thailand* 18°45N 99°8E **236** C2
San Lázaro, C. *Mexico* 24°50N 112°18W **318** C2
San Leandro *U.S.A.* 37°42N 122°9W **306** H4
San Leonardo de Yagüe
  Spain 41°51N 3°5W **196** D1
San Lorenzo = Sant Llorenç des
  Cardassar *Spain* 39°37N 3°17E **206** B4
San Lorenzo *Argentina* 32°45S 60°45W **334** C3
San Lorenzo *Beni, Bolivia* 15°22S 60°45W **331** D5
San Lorenzo *Tarija,*
  Bolivia 21°26S 64°47W **331** E5
San Lorenzo *Ecuador* 1°15N 78°50W **328** C2
San Lorenzo *Paraguay* 25°20S 57°32W **334** B4
San Lorenzo → *Mexico* 24°15N 107°24W **318** C3
San Lorenzo, I. *Baja Calif.,*
  Mexico 28°38N 112°51W **318** B2
San Lorenzo, I. *Peru* 12°7S 77°15W **330** D2
San Lorenzo, Mte.
  Argentina 47°40S 72°20W **336** C2
San Lorenzo de la Parrilla
  Spain 39°51N 2°22W **196** F2
San Lorenzo de Morunys = Sant
  Llorenç de Morunys
  Spain 42°8N 1°35E **196** C6
San Lorenzo Tezonco
  Mexico 19°19N 99°3W **128** C2
San Lucas = Cabo San Lucas
  Mexico 22°53N 109°54W **318** C3
San Lucas *Bolivia* 20°5S 65°7W **331** E4
San Lucas *Baja Calif. S.,*
  Mexico 27°10N 112°14W **318** B2
San Lucas *Calif., U.S.A.* 36°8N 121°1W **306** J5
San Lucas, C. *Mexico* 22°52N 109°53W **318** C3
San Lúcido *Italy* 39°18N 16°3E **201** C9
San Luis = Entre Ríos
  Bolivia 21°30S 64°25W **334** A3
San Luis = Sevilla
  Colombia 4°16N 75°57W **328** C2
San Luis *Argentina* 33°20S 66°20W **334** C2
San Luis *Guatemala* 16°14N 89°27W **320** C2
San Luis *Lima, Peru* 12°4S 77°0W **124** B2
San Luis *Ariz., U.S.A.* 32°29N 114°47W **305** K6
San Luis *Colo., U.S.A.* 37°12N 105°25W **305** H11
San Luis, I. *Mexico* 29°58N 114°26W **318** B2
San Luis, L. de *Bolivia* 13°45S 64°0W **331** C5
San Luis, Sierra de
  Argentina 32°30S 66°10W **334** C2
San Luis de la Paz
  Mexico 21°18N 100°31W **318** C4
San Luis Obispo *U.S.A.* 35°17N 120°40W **307** K6
San Luis Potosí *Mexico* 22°9N 100°59W **318** C4
San Luis Potosí □ *Mexico* 22°10N 101°0W **318** C4
San Luis Res. *U.S.A.* 37°4N 121°5W **306** H5
San Luis Río Colorado
  Mexico 32°29N 114°58W **318** A2
San Manuel *U.S.A.* 32°36N 110°38W **305** K8
San Manuel *Ariz.,*
  U.S.A. 32°36N 110°38W **305** K8
San Marco Argentano
  Italy 39°33N 16°7E **201** C9
San Marco in Lámis
  Italy 41°43N 15°38E **199** G12
San Marcos *Colombia* 8°39N 75°8W **328** B2
San Marcos *Guatemala* 14°59N 91°52W **320** D1
San Marcos *Tex., U.S.A.* 29°53N 97°56W **314** G6
San Marcos, I. *Mexico* 27°13N 112°6W **318** B2
San Mariano *Phil.* 17°0N 122°2E **232** C4
San Marino *San Marino* 43°55N 12°30E **199** E9
San Marino *U.S.A.* 34°7N 118°5W **126** C4
San Marino ■ *Europe* 43°56N 12°25E **199** E9
San Martín *Antarctica* 68°11S 67°0W **151** C17
San Martín *Argentina* 33°5S 68°28W **334** C2
San Martín *Colombia* 3°42N 73°42W **328** C3
San Martín *Barcelona,*
  Spain 41°24N 2°11E **114** A2
San Martín □ *Argentina* 31°9S 69°0W **334** C2
San Martín → *Bolivia* 13°8S 63°43W **331** C5
San Martín, L. *Argentina* 48°50S 72°30W **336** C2
San Martín de los Andes
  Argentina 40°10S 71°20W **336** B2
San Martín de Porras *Peru* 12°1S 77°5W **124** B2
San Martín de Valdeiglesias
  Spain 40°21N 4°24W **194** E6
San Mateo = Sant Mateu *Baleares,*
  Spain 39°3N 1°23E **206** C1
San Mateo = Sant Mateu *Valencia,*
  Spain 40°28N 0°10E **196** E5
San Mateo *Phil.* 16°51N 121°32W **306** H4
San Mateo *Isabela, Phil.* 16°54N 121°33E **232** C3
San Mateo *Calif., U.S.A.* 37°34N 122°19W **306** H4
San Mateo Tlaltenango
  Mexico 19°20N 99°14W **128** B1
San Matías *Bolivia* 16°25S 58°20W **331** D6
San Matías, G. *Argentina* 41°30S 64°0W **336** B4
San Miguel = Sant Miguel
  Spain 39°3N 1°26E **206** C1
San Miguel *Bolivia* 16°42S 61°1W **331** D5
San Miguel *El Salv.* 13°30N 88°12W **320** D2
San Miguel *Panama* 8°27N 78°55W **320** E4
San Miguel *Lima, Peru* 12°5S 77°5W **124** B2
San Miguel *Bulacan, Phil.* 15°9N 120°56E **232** D3
San Miguel *Palawan,*
  Phil. 12°37N 124°52E **232** E5
San Miguel *Spain* 36°17N 5°19W **195** J5
San Miguel → *U.S.A.* 35°45N 120°42W **306** K6
San Miguel → *Bolivia* 13°52S 63°56W **331** C5
San Miguel → *Ecuador* 0°25S 76°30W **328** D2
San Miguel → *Venezuela* 10°58N 71°46W **328** A3
San Miguel Chapama
  Mexico 19°27N 99°15W **128** B1
San Miguel de Huachi
  Bolivia 15°40S 67°15W **330** C4
San Miguel de Tucumán
  Argentina 26°50S 65°20W **334** B2
San Miguel del Monte
  Argentina 35°23S 58°50W **334** D4
San Miguel I. *U.S.A.* 34°2N 120°23W **307** L6

San Miguel Is. *Phil.* 7°45N 118°28E **233** H2
San Miniato *Italy* 43°41N 10°51E **198** E7
San Narciso *Phil.* 13°34N 122°34E **232** E4
San Nicolas = Sint Nicolaas
  Neth. Ant. 12°17N 69°8W **322** g
San Nicolás *B. Aires,*
  Argentina 34°36S 58°22W **117** B2
San Nicolás *Canary Is.* 27°58N 15°47W **153** e1
San Nicolas *Phil.* 18°10N 120°36E **232** B3
San Nicolás de los Arroyas
  Argentina 33°25S 60°10W **334** C3
San Nicolas I. *U.S.A.* 33°15N 119°30W **307** M7
San Onofre *Colombia* 9°44N 75°32W **328** B2
San Onofre *Calif.,*
  U.S.A. 33°22N 117°34W **307** M9
San Onófrio *Italy* 41°57N 12°25E **136** B1
San Pablo *Isabela, Phil.* 17°2N 121°48E **232** C3
San Pablo *Laguna, Phil.* 14°4N 121°7E **232** D3
San Pablo *Calif., U.S.A.* 37°58N 122°21W **306** H4
San Pablo de Manta = Manta
  Ecuador 1°0S 80°40W **328** D1
San Páolo di Civitate
  Italy 41°44N 15°15E **199** G12
San Pascual *Phil.* 13°8N 122°59E **232** E4
San Pedro *B. Aires,*
  Argentina 26°30S 54°10W **335** B5
San Pedro *Chile* 33°54S 71°28W **334** C1
San Pedro *Colombia* 4°56N 71°53W **328** C3
San Pedro *Ivory C.* 4°50N 6°33W **262** E3
San Pedro *Baja Calif. S.,*
  Mexico 23°55N 110°17W **318** C2
San Pedro *Peru* 14°49S 74°5W **330** D3
San Pedro → *Paraguay* 24°0S 57°0W **334** A4
San Pedro → *Chihuahua,*
  Mexico 28°20N 106°10W **318** B3
San Pedro → *Nayarit,*
  Mexico 21°45N 105°30W **318** C3
San Pedro → *Ariz.,*
  U.S.A. 32°59N 110°47W **305** K8
San Pedro, Pta. *Chile* 25°30S 70°38W **334** B1
San Pedro, Sierra de
  Spain 39°18N 6°40W **195** F4
San Pedro Channel
  U.S.A. 33°30N 118°25W **307** M8
San Pedro de Armena
  Colombia 4°37N 71°42W **328** C3
San Pedro de Atacama
  Chile 22°55S 68°15W **334** A2
San Pedro de Jujuy
  Argentina 24°12S 64°55W **334** A3
San Pedro de las Colonias
  Mexico 25°45N 102°59W **318** B4
San Pedro de Lloc *Peru* 7°15S 79°28W **330** B2
San Pedro de Macorís
  Dom. Rep. 18°30N 69°18W **321** C6
San Pedro del Norte *Nic.* 13°4N 84°33W **320** D3
San Pedro del Paraná
  Paraguay 26°43S 56°13W **334** B4
San Pedro del Pinatar
  Spain 37°50N 0°50W **197** H4
San Pedro Mártir *Spain* 41°23N 2°6E **114** A1
San Pedro Mártir, Sierra
  Mexico 31°0N 115°30W **318** A1
San Pedro Mártir △
  Mexico 31°0N 115°21W **318** A1
San Pedro Ocampo = Melchor
  Ocampo *Mexico* 24°51N 101°39W **318** C4
San Pedro Pochutla
  Mexico 15°44N 96°28W **319** D5
San Pedro Sula *Honduras* 15°30N 88°0W **320** C2
San Pedro Tututepec
  Mexico 16°9N 97°38W **319** D5
San Pedro Zacatenco
  Mexico 19°30N 99°6W **128** A2
San Pietro *Italy* 39°8N 8°17E **200** C1
San Pietro, Piazza *Rome, Italy* **136** b1
San Pietro Vernótico
  Italy 40°29N 18°0E **201** B11
San Po Kong *China* 22°20N 114°11E **122** A2
San Rafael *Argentina* 34°40S 68°21W **334** C2
San Rafael *Bolivia* 16°45S 60°43W **331** D5
San Rafael *Trin. & Tob.* 10°34N 61°16W **323** t
San Rafael *Calif., U.S.A.* 37°58N 122°32W **306** H4
San Rafael *N. Mex.,*
  U.S.A. 35°7N 107°53W **305** J10
San Rafael *Venezuela* 10°58N 71°46W **328** A3
San Rafael Chapama
  Mexico 19°27N 99°15W **128** B1
San Rafael Hills *U.S.A.* 34°12N 118°12W **126** B4
San Rafael Mt. *U.S.A.* 34°41N 119°52W **307** L7
San Rafael Mts. *U.S.A.* 34°40N 119°50W **307** L7
San Ramón *Bolivia* 13°17S 64°43W **331** C5
San Ramón *Peru* 11°0S 75°20W **330** C2
San Ramón de la Nueva Orán
  Argentina 23°10S 64°20W **334** A3
San Remo *Vic., Australia* 38°33S 145°22E **283** E6
San Remo *Italy* 43°49N 7°46E **198** E4
San Román, C. *Venezuela* 12°12N 70°0W **328** A4
San Roque *Argentina* 28°25S 58°45W **334** B4
San Roque *Manila, Phil.* 14°37N 121°5E **127** B2
San Roque *N. Samar.,*
  Phil. 12°37N 124°52E **232** E5
San Roque *Spain* 36°17N 5°21W **195** J5
San Rosendo *Chile* 37°16S 72°43W **334** D1
San Saba *U.S.A.* 31°12N 98°43W **314** F5
San Salvador *El Salv.* 13°40N 89°10W **320** D2
San Salvador *Spain* 39°27N 3°11E **206** B4
San Salvador, Canal de
  Ecuador 0°25S 90°30W **330** a
San Salvador, I. *Ecuador* 0°16S 90°42W **330** a
San Salvador de Jujuy
  Argentina 24°10S 64°48W **334** A3
San Salvador I. *Bahamas* 24°0N 74°40W **321** B5
San Salvo *Italy* 42°3N 14°44E **199** F11
Sebastián = Donostia-San
  Sebastián *Spain* 43°17N 1°58W **196** B3
San Sebastián *Argentina* 53°10S 68°30W **336** D3
San Sebastián *Puerto Rico* 18°20N 66°59W **321** b
San Sebastián de la Gomera
  Canary Is. 28°5N 17°7W **153** e1
San Serra = Son Serra
  Spain 39°43N 3°13E **206** B4
San Serverino Marche
  Italy 43°13N 13°10E **199** E10
San Severo *Italy* 41°41N 15°23E **199** G12
San Simeon *U.S.A.* 35°39N 121°11W **306** K5
San Simon *U.S.A.* 32°16N 109°14W **305** K9
San Siro *Italy* 45°58N 9°7E **128** P1
San Souci *Australia* 33°59S 151°8E **138** D4
San Stéfano di Cadore
  Italy 46°34N 12°33E **199** B9
San Stino di Livenza *Italy* 45°44N 12°41E **199** C9
San Telmo = Sant Elm
  Spain 39°35N 2°21E **206** B3
San Telmo *B. Aires,*
  Argentina 34°37S 58°23W **117** C1
San Telmo *Baja Calif.,*
  Mexico 30°58N 116°6W **318** A1
San Teodoro *Phil.* 13°26N 121°1E **232** E3
San Tiburcio *Mexico* 24°8N 101°32W **318** C4
San Valentin, Mte. *Chile* 46°30S 73°30W **336** C2

San Vicenc dels Horts *Spain* 41°23N 2°0E 114 A1
San Vicente de Alcántara *Spain* 39°22N 7°8W 195 F3
San Vicente de la Barquera *Spain* 43°23N 4°29W 194 B6
San Vicente del Caguán *Colombia* 2°7N 74°46W 328 C3
San Vincente del Raspeig *Spain* 38°24N 0°31W 197 G4
San Vincenzo *Italy* 43°6N 10°32E 198 E7
San Vito *Costa Rica* 8°50N 82°58W 320 E3
San Vito *Italy* 39°26N 9°32E 200 C2
San Vito, C. *Italy* 38°11N 12°41E 200 D5
San Vito al Tagliamento *Italy* 45°54N 12°52E 199 C9
San Vito Chietino *Italy* 42°18N 14°27E 199 F11
San Vito dei Normanni *Italy* 40°39N 17°42E 201 B10
San Yanaro *Colombia* 2°47N 69°42W 328 C4
Saña *Peru* 6°54S 79°36W 330 B2
Sana' *Yemen* 15°27N 44°12E 248 D4
Sana → *Bos.-H.* 45°3N 16°23E 199 C13
Sanaba *Burkina Faso* 12°25N 3°47W 262 C4
Sanae IV *Antarctica* 70°20S 9°0W 151 D2
Şanāfīr *Si. Arabia* 27°56N 34°42E 251 L5
Sanaga → *Cameroon* 3°35N 9°38E 263 E6
Sanak I. *U.S.A.* 54°25N 162°40W 303 J7
Sanaloa, Presa *Mexico* 24°50N 107°20W 318 C3
Sanām *Si. Arabia* 23°40N 44°45E 248 B4
Sanana *Indonesia* 2°4S 125°58E 231 E7
Sanand *India* 22°59N 72°25E 242 H5
Sanandaj *Iran* 35°18N 47°1E 213 E12
Sanandita *Bolivia* 21°40S 63°45W 334 A3
Sanaroa I. *Papua N. G.* 9°37S 151°0E 286 E6
Sanary-sur-Mer *France* 43°7N 5°49E 175 E9
Sanāw *Yemen* 17°50N 51°5E 249 C5
Sanawad *India* 22°11N 76°5E 242 H7
Sanbancho *Tokyo, Japan* 140 a3
Sanbe-San *Japan* 35°6N 132°38E 222 B4
Sancellas = Sencelles *Spain* 39°39N 2°54E 206 B3
Sancergues *France* 47°10N 2°54E 173 E9
Sancerre *France* 47°20N 2°50E 173 E9
Sancerrois, Collines du *France* 47°20N 2°40E 173 E9
Sancha He → *China* 26°48N 106°7E 228 D6
Sanchahe *China* 44°50N 126°2E 227 B14
Sánchez *Dom. Rep.* 19°15N 69°36W 321 C6
Sanchez-Mira *Phil.* 18°34N 121°14E 232 B3
Sanchih *Taiwan* 25°15N 121°30E 225 A3
Sanchor *India* 24°45N 71°55E 242 G4
Sanch'ung *Taiwan* 25°4N 121°30E 225 A3
Sanco Pt. *Phil.* 8°15N 126°27E 233 G6
Sancoins *France* 46°47N 2°55E 173 F9
Sancti Spíritus *Cuba* 21°52N 79°33W 320 B4
Sancy, Puy de *France* 45°32N 2°50E 174 C6
Sand = Polokwane → *S. Africa* 22°25S 30°5E 271 B5
Sand *Norway* 59°29N 6°16E 164 E3
Sand Bank B. *St. Kitts & Nevis* 17°15N 62°38W 322 d
Sand Cr. → *U.S.A.* 39°3N 85°51W 311 E11
Sand Hills *Guyana* 6°27N 58°19W 329 B6
Sand Hills *Nebr., U.S.A.* 42°10N 101°30W 308 D3
Sand I. *Midway Is.* 28°12N 177°23W 302 c
Sand I. *Hawai'i, U.S.A.* 21°19N 157°53W 302 K14
Sand Islet *Midway Is.* 28°16N 177°22W 302 c
Sand Lakes △ *Canada* 57°51N 98°32W 297 B9
Sand Point *U.S.A.* 55°20N 160°30W 303 J7
Sand Springs *U.S.A.* 36°9N 96°7W 314 C6
Sanda *Japan* 34°53N 135°14E 223 C7
Sandakan *Malaysia* 5°53N 118°4E 235 A5
Sandalwood *Australia* 34°55S 140°9E 282 C4
Sandan = Sambor *Cambodia* 12°46N 106°0E 236 F6
Sandane *Norway* 61°46N 6°13E 164 C3
Sandanski *Bulgaria* 41°35N 23°16E 202 E7
Sandaré *Mali* 14°40N 10°15W 262 C2
Sandared *Sweden* 57°43N 12°47E 163 G6
Sandarne *Sweden* 61°16N 17°9E 162 C11
Sanday *U.K.* 59°16N 2°31W 167 B6
Sande *Møre og Romsdal, Norway* 62°15N 5°27E 164 B2
Sande *Sogn og Fjordane, Norway* 61°20N 5°47E 164 C2
Sande *Vestfold, Norway* 59°36N 10°12E 162 E4
Sandefjord *Norway* 59°10N 10°15E 164 E7
Sandeid *Norway* 59°33N 5°52E 164 E2
Sanders *Ariz., U.S.A.* 35°13N 109°20W 305 J9
Sanders *Ky., U.S.A.* 38°40N 84°56W 311 F12
Sanderson *Fla., U.S.A.* 30°15N 82°16W 316 E7
Sanderson *Tex., U.S.A.* 30°9N 102°24W 314 F3
Sandersville *U.S.A.* 32°59N 82°48W 316 C7
Sandfire Roadhouse *Australia* 19°45S 121°15E 278 C3
Sandfloegga *Norway* 59°58N 7°10E 164 E4
Sandfly L. *Canada* 55°43N 106°6W 297 B7
Sandfontein *Namibia* 23°48S 19°1E 270 B2
Sandhammaren *Sweden* 55°23N 14°14E 163 J8
Sandheads, The *India* 21°10N 88°20E 241 E2
Sandgerði *Iceland* 64°3N 22°42W 155 C4
Sandia *Peru* 14°10S 69°30W 330 C4
Sandıklı *Turkey* 38°28N 30°17E 205 C12
Sandila *India* 27°5N 80°31E 243 F9
Sandilands *Bahamas* 25°3N 77°19W 153 b
Sandnes *Aust-Agder, Norway* 58°53N 7°45E 164 F4
Sandnes *Rogaland, Norway* 58°50N 5°45E 164 F2
Sandnessjøen *Norway* 66°2N 12°38E 160 C15
Sandoa *Dem. Rep. of the Congo* 9°41S 23°0E 265 D4
Sandomierz *Poland* 50°40N 21°43E 185 H8
Sândominic *Romania* 46°35N 25°47E 183 D10
Sandona *Colombia* 1°17N 77°28W 328 C2
Sandongo *Angola* 15°30S 21°28E 265 F4
Sandoval *U.S.A.* 38°37N 89°7W 310 F7
Sandover → *Australia* 21°43S 136°32E 280 C2
Sandoway = Thandwe *Burma* 18°20N 94°30E 241 F5
Sandown *S. Africa* 26°5S 28°4E 123 A2
Sandown Park Races *U.K.* 51°22N 0°21W 125 B1
Sandoy *Færoe Is.* 61°52N 6°46W 160 F9
Sandpoint *U.S.A.* 48°17N 116°33W 304 B5
Sandray *U.K.* 56°53N 7°31W 167 E1
Sandringham *U.K.* 52°51N 0°31E 168 E8
Sandstone *Australia* 27°59S 119°16E 279 E2
Sandton *S. Africa* 26°5S 28°4E 123 A2
Sandu *China* 26°0N 107°52E 228 E6
Sandumba *Angola* 13°45S 17°34E 265 E3
Sandur *India* 15°6N 76°33E 245 F3
Sandusky *Mich., U.S.A.* 43°25N 82°50W 312 C2
Sandusky *Ohio, U.S.A.* 41°27N 82°42W 312 E2
Sandusky → *U.S.A.* 41°27N 83°0W 311 C14
Sandveld *Namibia* 21°25S 20°0E 270 B3
Sandvig *Denmark* 55°18N 14°47E 163 J8
Sandvika *Norway* 59°54N 10°31E 133 A2
Sandviken *Sweden* 60°38N 16°46E 162 D10
Sandwich *U.S.A.* 41°39N 88°37W 311 C8
Sandwich, C. *Australia* 18°14S 146°18E 280 B4
Sandwich B. *Nfld. & L., Canada* 53°40N 57°15W 299 B8
Sandwich B. *Namibia* 23°25S 14°20E 270 B1
Sandwip I. *Bangla.* 22°30N 91°25E 241 D3
Sandy *Oreg., U.S.A.* 45°24N 122°16W 306 E4
Sandy *Pa., U.S.A.* 41°6N 78°46W 312 E6
Sandy *Utah, U.S.A.* 40°32N 111°50W 304 F8
Sandy B. *St. Helena* 16°0S 5°43W 153 h
Sandy Bay *Canada* 55°31N 102°19W 297 B8
Sandy Bight *Australia* 33°50S 123°20E 279 F3
Sandy C. *Queens., Australia* 24°42S 153°15E 280 C5
Sandy C. *Tas., Australia* 41°25S 144°45E 281 G3
Sandy Cay *Bahamas* 23°13N 75°18W 321 B4
Sandy Cr. → *U.S.A.* 41°51N 109°47W 304 F9
Sandy Ground Village *Anguilla* 18°12N 63°6W 322 a
Sandy Hill Bay *Anguilla* 18°13N 63°1W 322 a
Sandy I. *Anguilla* 18°13N 63°7W 322 a
Sandy I. *Grenada* 12°29N 61°29W 323 q
Sandy I. *Grenada* 12°13N 61°35W 323 q
Sandy L. *Canada* 53°2N 93°0W 298 B1
Sandy Lake *Canada* 53°0N 93°15W 298 B1
Sandy Point *India* 10°32N 92°22E 245 J11
Sandy Point Town *St. Kitts & Nevis* 17°22N 62°51W 322 d
Sandy Springs *U.S.A.* 33°56N 84°23W 316 B5
Sandy Valley *U.S.A.* 35°49N 115°38W 307 K11
Sandyford *Ireland* 53°17N 6°13W 120 B2
Sandymount *Ireland* 53°20N 6°13W 120 B2
Sånfjället △ *Sweden* 62°17N 13°35E 162 B7
Sanford *Fla., U.S.A.* 28°48N 81°16W 317 G8
Sanford *Maine, U.S.A.* 43°27N 70°47W 313 C14
Sanford *N.C., U.S.A.* 35°29N 79°10W 315 D15
Sanford → *Australia* 27°22S 115°53E 279 E2
Sanford, Mt. *U.S.A.* 62°13N 144°8W 303 E11
Sang-i-Masha *Afghan.* 33°8N 67°27E 242 C2
Sanga *Angola* 11°9S 15°21E 265 E3
Sanga *Mozam.* 12°22S 35°21E 269 E4
Sanga → *Congo* 1°5S 17°0E 264 C3
Sangaie *Dem. Rep. of the Congo* 6°48S 22°46E 265 D4
Sangamner *India* 19°37N 74°15E 244 E2
Sangamon → *U.S.A.* 40°1N 90°26W 310 D6
Sanganeb Atoll △ *Sudan* 19°33N 37°11E 256 D4
Sangar *Afghan.* 32°56N 65°30E 242 C1
Sangar *Russia* 64°2N 127°31E 215 C13
Sangar Sarai *Afghan.* 34°27N 70°35E 242 B4
Sangareddi *India* 17°38N 78°7E 244 F4
Sangaredi *Guinea* 11°7N 13°52W 262 C2
Sangarh → *Pakistan* 30°43N 70°44E 242 D4
Sangasangadalam *Indonesia* 0°36S 117°13E 235 C5
Sangasso *Mali* 12°5N 5°35W 262 C3
Sangatte *France* 50°56N 1°44E 173 B8
Sangay *Ecuador* 2°0S 78°20W 328 D2
Sangay △ *Ecuador* 2°15S 78°25W 328 D2
Sangchris L. *U.S.A.* 39°39N 89°29W 310 E7
Sangdong *S. Korea* 37°7N 128°49E 224 D4
Sange *Dem. Rep. of the Congo* 6°58S 28°21E 268 D2
Sangeang *Indonesia* 8°12S 119°6E 235 D5
Sangenjaya *Japan* 35°37N 139°39E 140 B2
Sângeorz-Băi *Romania* 47°22N 24°41E 183 C9
Sanger *U.S.A.* 36°42N 119°33W 306 J7
Săngera *Moldova* 46°55N 28°58E 183 D13
Sangerhausen *Germany* 51°28N 11°18E 178 D7
Sanggan He → *China* 38°12N 117°15E 226 E9
Sanggau *Indonesia* 0°5N 110°30E 235 B4
Sanggye *S. Korea* 37°38N 127°3E 137 B2
Sanghar *Pakistan* 26°2N 68°57E 242 F3
Sangihe, Kepulauan *Indonesia* 3°0N 125°30E 231 D7
Sangihe, Pulau *Indonesia* 3°35N 125°30E 231 D7
Sangju *S. Korea* 36°25N 128°10E 224 D4
Sangkapura *Indonesia* 5°52S 112°40E 235 D4
Sangkhla *Thailand* 14°57N 98°28E 236 E2
Sangkulirang *Indonesia* 0°59N 117°58E 230 D5
Sangla *Pakistan* 31°43N 73°23E 242 D5
Sangley Pt. *Phil.* 14°29N 120°54E 127 C1
Sangli *India* 16°55N 74°33E 244 F2
Sangmélima *Cameroon* 2°57N 12°1E 263 E7
Sango *Angola* 9°51S 15°44E 265 D2
Sangod *India* 24°55N 76°17E 242 G7
Sangole *India* 17°26N 75°12E 244 F2
Sangorodok = Ust-Vorkuta *Russia* 67°24N 64°0E 186 A11
Sangpang Bum *Burma* 26°30N 95°50E 241 B5
Sangre de Cristo Mts. *U.S.A.* 37°30N 105°20W 305 H11
Sangre Grande *Trin. & Tob.* 10°35N 61°8W 323 t
Sangro → *Italy* 42°14N 14°32E 199 F11
Sangrur *India* 30°14N 75°50E 242 D6
Sangudo *Canada* 53°50N 114°54W 296 C6
Sangue → *Brazil* 11°1S 58°39W 331 C6
Sangüesa *Spain* 42°37N 1°17W 196 C3
Sanguinaires, Îs. *France* 41°51N 8°36E 175 G12
Sangzhi *China* 29°25N 110°12E 229 C8
Sanhala *Ivory C.* 10°3N 6°51W 262 C3
Sanhsia *Taiwan* 24°56N 121°22E 225 B3
Sanhsien *Hualien, Taiwan* 23°8N 121°25E 225 C3
Sanhsien *T'aitung, Taiwan* 23°24N 121°19E 225 C3
Sanhsing *Taiwan* 24°40N 121°36E 225 B3
Sani *Taiwan* 24°24N 120°46E 225 B2
Sanibel *U.S.A.* 26°27N 82°1W 317 J7
Sanibel I. *U.S.A.* 26°26N 82°6W 317 J7
Sanikiluaq *Canada* 56°32N 79°14W 298 A4
Sanin-Kaigan △ *Japan* 35°39N 134°37E 222 B6
Sanirajak *Canada* 68°46N 81°12W 295 C11
Sanjawi *Pakistan* 30°17N 68°21E 242 D3
Sanje *Uganda* 0°49S 31°30E 268 C3
Sanjiang *China* 25°48N 109°37E 228 E7
Sanjo *Japan* 37°37N 138°57E 220 F9
Sankarankovil *India* 9°10N 77°35E 245 K3
Sankeshwar *India* 16°23N 74°32E 245 F2
Sankh → *India* 22°15N 84°48E 243 H11
Sankosh → *India* 26°24N 89°47E 241 B2
Sankrail *India* 22°33N 88°13E 124 B1
Sankt Andrä *Austria* 46°46N 14°50E 180 E7
Sankt Anton *Austria* 47°8N 10°16E 179 H6
Sankt Augustin *Germany* 50°45N 7°10E 178 E3
Sankt Blasien *Germany* 47°47N 8°7E 179 H4
Sankt Gallen *Switz.* 47°26N 9°22E 179 H5
Sankt Gallen ☐ *Switz.* 47°25N 9°22E 179 H5
Sankt Goar *Germany* 50°12N 7°43E 179 E3
Sankt Ingbert *Germany* 49°16N 7°6E 179 F3
Sankt Johann im Pongau *Austria* 47°22N 13°12E 180 D6
Sankt Johann in Tirol *Austria* 47°30N 12°25E 180 D5
Sankt Marein = Smarje *Slovenia* 46°15N 15°34E 199 B12
Sankt Michel = Mikkeli *Finland* 61°43N 27°15E 188 B4
Sankt Moritz *Switz.* 46°30N 9°51E 179 J5
Sankt-Peterburg *Russia* 59°55N 30°20E 137 B1
Sankt Pölten *Austria* 48°12N 15°38E 180 C8
Sankt Ulrich = Ortisei *Italy* 46°34N 11°40E 199 B8
Sankt Valentin *Austria* 48°11N 14°33E 180 C7
Sankt Veit *Austria* 48°11N 16°16E 142 A1
Sankt Veit an der Glan *Austria* 46°47N 14°22E 180 E7
Sankt Wendel *Germany* 49°27N 7°9E 179 F3
Sankt Wolfgang *Austria* 47°43N 13°27E 180 D6
Sankuru → *Dem. Rep. of the Congo* 4°17S 20°25E 265 C4
Sanlihe *China* 39°53N 116°18E 114 B1
Sanlintang *China* 31°9N 121°29E 138 C1
Sanliurfa *Turkey* 37°12N 38°50E 213 D8
Sanliurfa ☐ *Turkey* 37°0N 39°0E 213 D8
Sanlúcar de Barrameda *Spain* 36°46N 6°21W 195 J4
Sanluri *Italy* 39°34N 8°54E 200 C1
Sânmartin *Romania* 46°19N 25°58E 183 D10
Sanmen *China* 29°5N 121°35E 229 C13
Sanmenxia *China* 34°47N 111°12E 226 G6
Sanming *China* 26°15N 117°40E 229 D11
Sannan *Japan* 35°2N 135°1E 223 B7
Sannaspos *S. Africa* 29°6S 26°34E 270 C4
Sannat *Malta* 36°1N 14°15E 206 E6
Sannicandro Gargánico *Italy* 41°50N 15°34E 199 G12
Sânnicolau Mare *Romania* 46°5N 20°39E 182 D5
Sannieshof *S. Africa* 26°30S 25°47E 270 C4
Sannîn, J. *Lebanon* 33°57N 35°52E 250 E6
Sanniquellie *Liberia* 7°19N 8°38W 262 D3
Sannûr *Egypt* 28°58N 31°3E 251 K2
Sannûr, W. → *Egypt* 28°59N 31°3E 251 K2
Sano *Japan* 36°19N 139°35E 223 A11
Sanok *Poland* 49°35N 22°10E 185 J9
Sanquhar *U.K.* 55°22N 3°54W 167 F5
Sanquianga △ *Colombia* 2°33N 78°14W 328 C2
Sans *Spain* 41°22N 2°7E 114 A1
Sans Souci *St. Vincent* 13°13N 61°7W 323 n
Sans Souci *Trin. & Tob.* 10°50N 61°0W 323 t
Sansanding *Mali* 13°48N 6°0W 262 C3
Sansepolcro *Italy* 43°34N 12°8E 199 E9
Sansha *China* 26°58N 120°12E 229 D13
Sanshui *China* 23°10N 112°56E 229 F9
Sanski Most *Bos.-H.* 44°46N 16°40E 199 D13
Sanssouci *Germany* 52°23N 13°2E 115 B1
Sansui *China* 26°58N 108°39E 228 D7
Sant Agusti *Barcelona, Spain* 114 c2
Sant Ambrogio, Basilica di *Italy* 45°27N 9°10E 129 B2
Sant Antoni de Portmany *Spain* 38°59N 1°19E 206 D1
Sant Boi de Llobregat *Spain* 41°20N 2°2E 114 A1
Sant Carles *Spain* 39°3N 1°34E 206 C2
Sant Carles de la Ràpita *Spain* 40°37N 0°35E 196 E5
Sant Celoni *Spain* 41°42N 2°30E 196 D7
Sant Cugat *Spain* 41°28N 2°5E 114 A1
Sant Elm *Spain* 39°35N 2°21E 206 B3
Sant Feliu de Guíxols *Spain* 41°45N 3°1E 196 D8
Sant Feliu de Llobregat *Spain* 41°22N 2°2E 114 A1
Sant Ferran *Spain* 38°42N 1°28E 206 D1
Sant Francesc de Formentera *Spain* 38°42N 1°26E 206 D1
Sant Jaume *Spain* 39°54N 4°4E 206 B5
Sant Joan de Labritja *Spain* 39°5N 1°31E 206 C2
Sant Joan Despi *Spain* 41°22N 2°2E 114 A1
Sant Jordi *Ibiza, Spain* 38°53N 1°24E 206 D1
Sant Jordi *Mallorca, Spain* 39°33N 2°46E 206 B3
Sant Jordi, G. de *Spain* 40°53N 1°2E 196 E5
Sant Llorenç de Morunys *Spain* 42°8N 1°35E 196 C6
Sant Llorenç del Munt y l'Obac ⌂ *Spain* 41°39N 1°55W 196 D3
Sant Llorenç des Cardassar *Spain* 39°37N 3°17E 206 B4
Sant Maria del Mar *Barcelona, Spain* 114 b3
Sant Mateu *Baleares, Spain* 39°3N 1°23E 206 C1
Sant Mateu *Valencia, Spain* 40°28N 0°10E 196 E5
Sant Miquel *Spain* 39°3N 1°26E 206 C1
Sant Pau del Camp *Barcelona, Spain* 114 c2
Santa *Peru* 8°59S 78°40W 330 B2
Sant' Ágata Militello *Italy* 38°2N 14°8E 201 D7
Santa Agnés *Spain* 39°3N 1°21E 206 C1
Santa Ana *Beni, Bolivia* 13°50S 65°40W 331 C4
Santa Ana *La Paz, Bolivia* 15°31S 67°30W 330 D4
Santa Ana *Santa Cruz, Bolivia* 18°43S 58°44W 331 D6
Santa Ana *Santa Cruz, Bolivia* 16°37S 60°43W 331 D5
Santa Ana *Ecuador* 1°16S 80°20W 328 D1
Santa Ana *El Salv.* 14°0N 89°31W 320 D2
Santa Ana *Guam* 13°32N 145°46E 302 d
Santa Ana *Sonora, Mexico* 30°33N 111°7W 318 A2
Santa Ana *Cagayan, Phil.* 18°28N 122°20E 232 B4
Santa Ana *Manila, Phil.* 14°34N 121°0E 127 B2
Santa Ana *Solomon Is.* 10°50S 162°30E 287 N12
Santa Ana *Calif., U.S.A.* 33°46N 117°52W 307 M9
Santa Ana → *Venezuela* 9°30N 71°57W 328 B3
Sant' Ángelo Lodigiano *Italy* 45°14N 9°25E 198 C6
Santa Anita Park *U.S.A.* 34°8N 118°5W 126 B4
Sant' Antíoco *Italy* 39°4N 8°27E 200 C1
Santa Bárbara *Santa Maria, Azores* 36°59N 25°4W 153 d4
Santa Bárbara *Terceira, Azores* 38°41N 27°20W 153 d1
Santa Bárbara *Chile* 37°40S 72°1W 334 D1
Santa Bárbara *Colombia* 5°53N 75°35W 328 B2
Santa Bárbara *Honduras* 14°53N 88°14W 320 D2
Santa Bárbara *Chihuahua, Mexico* 26°48N 105°49W 318 B3
Santa Barbara *Neth. Ant.* 12°5N 68°51W 322 g
Santa Barbara *Phil.* 10°50N 122°32E 233 F4
Santa Bárbara *Spain* 40°42N 0°29E 196 E5
Santa Barbara *Calif., U.S.A.* 34°25N 119°42W 307 L7
Santa Bárbara *Amazonas, Venezuela* 3°57N 67°6W 328 C4
Santa Bárbara *Barinas, Venezuela* 7°47N 71°10W 328 B3
Santa Bárbara, Mt. *Spain* 37°23N 2°50W 197 H2
Santa Bárbara, Serra de *Azores* 38°44N 27°19W 153 d1
Santa Barbara Channel *U.S.A.* 34°15N 120°0W 307 L7
Santa Barbara I. *U.S.A.* 33°29N 119°2W 307 M7
Santa Catalina *Colombia* 10°36N 75°17W 328 A2
Santa Catalina *Neg. Or., Phil.* 9°20N 122°52E 233 G4
Santa Catalina *Solomon Is.* 10°53S 162°29E 287 N12
Santa Catalina, Gulf of *U.S.A.* 33°10N 117°50W 307 N9
Santa Catalina, I. *Mexico* 25°40N 110°47W 318 B2
Santa Catalina I. *U.S.A.* 33°23N 118°25W 307 M8
Santa Catarina ☐ *Brazil* 27°25S 48°30W 335 B6
Santa Catarina, I. de *Brazil* 27°30S 48°40W 335 B6
Santa Caterina di Pittinuri *Italy* 40°6N 8°27E 200 B1
Santa Caterina Villarmosa *Italy* 37°35N 14°2E 201 E7
Santa Cecília *Brazil* 26°56S 50°18W 335 B5
Santa Clara *Cuba* 22°20N 80°0W 320 B4
Santa Clara *Calif., U.S.A.* 37°21N 121°57W 306 H5
Santa Clara *Utah, U.S.A.* 37°8N 113°39W 305 H7
Santa Clara de Olimar *Uruguay* 32°50S 54°54W 335 C5
Santa Clara Valley *U.S.A.* 36°50N 121°30W 306 J5
Santa Clarita *U.S.A.* 34°24N 118°33W 307 L8
Santa Clotilde *Peru* 2°33S 73°45W 328 D3
Santa Coloma de Farners *Spain* 41°50N 2°39E 196 D7
Santa Coloma de Gramenet *Spain* 41°27N 2°13E 114 A2
Santa Comba *Spain* 43°2N 8°49W 194 B2
Santa Croce Camerina *Italy* 36°50N 14°31E 201 F7
Santa Croce di Magliano *Italy* 41°42N 14°59E 199 G11
Santa Cruz *Argentina* 50°0S 68°32W 336 D3
Santa Cruz *Aruba* 12°30N 69°59W 322 f
Santa Cruz *Bolivia* 17°43S 63°10W 331 D5
Santa Cruz *Brazil* 6°13S 36°1W 332 C4
Santa Cruz *Chile* 34°38S 71°27W 334 C1
Santa Cruz *Costa Rica* 10°15N 85°35W 320 D2
Santa Cruz *Maharashtra, India* 19°4N 72°51E 130 A1
Santa Cruz *Jamaica* 18°3N 77°43W 320 a
Santa Cruz *Madeira* 32°42N 16°46W 153 c
Santa Cruz *Neth. Ant.* 12°18N 69°7W 322 g
Santa Cruz *Peru* 5°40S 75°56W 330 B2
Santa Cruz *Davao del S., Phil.* 6°50N 125°25E 233 H5
Santa Cruz *Laguna, Phil.* 14°20N 121°24E 232 D3
Santa Cruz *Manila, Phil.* 14°36N 120°58E 127 B1
Santa Cruz *Marinduque, Phil.* 13°28N 122°2E 232 E4
Santa Cruz *Mind. Occ., Phil.* 13°4N 120°43E 232 E3
Santa Cruz *Zambales, Phil.* 15°46N 119°55E 232 D2
Santa Cruz *Calif., U.S.A.* 36°58N 122°1W 306 J4
Santa Cruz *Venezuela* 8°3N 64°27W 329 B5
Santa Cruz ☐ *Argentina* 49°0S 70°0W 336 C3
Santa Cruz ☐ *Bolivia* 17°43S 63°10W 331 D5
Santa Cruz → *Argentina* 50°10S 68°20W 336 D3
Santa Cruz, B. *Neth. Ant.* 12°18N 69°10W 322 g
Santa Cruz, I. *Ecuador* 0°38S 90°23W 330 a
Santa Cruz, I. de *Brazil* 22°51S 43°7W 135 B2
Santa Cruz Cabrália *Brazil* 16°17S 39°2W 333 E4
Santa Cruz da Graciosa *Azores* 39°5N 28°1W 153 d1
Santa Cruz das Flores *Azores* 39°27N 31°7W 153 d2
Santa Cruz de Bravo = Felipe Carrillo Puerto *Mexico* 19°38N 88°3W 319 D7
Santa Cruz de la Palma *Canary Is.* 28°41N 17°46W 153 e1
Santa Cruz de la Palma ✕ (SPC) *Canary Is.* 28°40N 17°45W 153 e1
Santa Cruz de Mudela *Spain* 38°39N 3°28W 195 G7
Santa Cruz de Olorde *Spain* 41°25N 2°3E 114 A1
Santa Cruz de Tenerife *Canary Is.* 28°28N 16°15W 153 e1
Santa Cruz del Norte *Cuba* 23°9N 81°55W 320 B3
Santa Cruz del Retamar *Spain* 40°8N 4°14W 194 E6
Santa Cruz del Sur *Cuba* 20°44N 78°0W 320 B4
Santa Cruz do Rio Pardo *Brazil* 22°54S 49°37W 335 A6
Santa Cruz do Sul *Brazil* 29°42S 52°25W 335 B5
Santa Cruz I. *U.S.A.* 34°1N 119°43W 307 M7
Santa Cruz Is. *Solomon Is.* 10°30S 166°0E 277 C12
Santa Cruz la Vieja △ *Bolivia* 17°55S 60°50W 331 D5
Santa Cruz Mts. *Jamaica* 17°58N 77°43W 320 a
Santa Domingo, Cay *Bahamas* 21°25N 75°15W 320 B4
Santa Efigênia *Brazil* 23°32S 46°38W 137 B2
Sant' Egidio alla Vibrata *Italy* 42°49N 13°42E 199 F10
Santa Elena *Argentina* 30°58S 59°47W 334 C4
Santa Elena *Ecuador* 2°16S 80°52W 328 D1
Santa Elena *Camarines N., Phil.* 14°12N 122°24E 232 D4
Santa Elena *Manila, Phil.* 14°38N 121°5E 127 B2
Santa Elena, C. *Costa Rica* 10°54N 85°56W 320 D2
Santa Elena del Gomero *Chile* 33°28S 70°45W 137 B1
Sant' Eufêmia, G. di *Italy* 38°51N 16°4E 201 D9
Santa Eulalia *Spain* 41°25N 2°10E 114 A2
Santa Eulària des Riu *Spain* 38°59N 1°32E 206 D2
Santa Fé *Argentina* 31°35S 60°41W 334 C3
Santa Fe *Nueva Viscaya, Phil.* 16°10N 120°57E 232 C3
Santa Fe *Romblon, Phil.* 12°10N 122°0E 232 E4
Santa Fé *Spain* 37°11N 3°43W 195 H7
Santa Fe *N. Mex., U.S.A.* 35°41N 105°57W 305 J11
Santa Fé ☐ *Argentina* 31°50S 60°55W 334 C3
Santa Fé, Canal de *Ecuador* 0°48S 89°55W 330 a
Santa Fé, I. *Ecuador* 0°49S 90°5W 330 a
Santa Fé do Sul *Brazil* 20°13S 50°56W 333 F1
Santa Fe Springs *U.S.A.* 33°56N 118°3W 126 C4
Santa Filomena *Brazil* 9°6S 45°50W 332 C2
Santa Fiora *Italy* 42°50N 11°35E 199 F8
Santa Gertrudis *Spain* 39°0N 1°26E 206 C1
Santa Giustina *Italy* 46°10N 12°5E 199 B9
Santa Helena *Brazil* 2°14S 45°18W 332 B2
Santa Helena de Goiás *Brazil* 17°53S 50°35W 333 E1
Santa Inês *Bahia, Brazil* 13°17S 39°48W 333 D4
Santa Inês *Maranhão, Brazil* 3°39S 45°20W 332 B2
Santa Inés *Extremadura, Spain* 38°32N 5°37W 195 G5
Santa Inés, I. *Chile* 54°0S 73°0W 336 D2
Santa Iria da Azóia *Portugal* 38°49N 9°5W 126 A2
Santa Isabel = Rey Malabo *Eq. Guin.* 3°45N 8°50E 263 E6
Santa Isabel *Argentina* 36°10S 66°54W 334 D2
Santa Isabel *Puerto Rico* 17°58N 66°24W 321 b
Santa Isabel *Solomon Is.* 8°0S 159°0E 287 M10
Santa Isabel do Araguaia *Brazil* 6°7S 48°19W 332 C2
Santa Isabel do Morro *Brazil* 11°34S 50°40W 333 D1
Santa Isabel do Río Negro *Brazil* 0°24S 65°2W 329 D4
Santa Julia *Chile* 33°30S 70°35W 137 C2
Santa Lucía *Corrientes, Argentina* 28°58S 59°5W 334 B4
Santa Lucía *San Juan, Argentina* 31°30S 68°30W 334 C2
Santa Lucía *Canary Is.* 27°55N 5°32W 153 e1
Santa Lucía *Phil.* 17°7N 120°27E 232 C3
Santa Lucía *Spain* 37°35N 0°58W 197 H4
Santa Lucía *Uruguay* 34°27S 56°24W 334 C4
Santa Lucia Range *U.S.A.* 36°0N 121°20W 306 K5
Santa Luzia = Luziânia *Brazil* 16°20S 48°0W 333 E2
Santa Luzia *C. Verde Is.* 16°50N 24°35W 153 j
Santa Margalida *Spain* 39°42N 3°6E 206 B4
Santa Margarita *Argentina* 38°28S 61°35W 334 D3
Santa Margarita *Calif., U.S.A.* 35°23N 120°37W 306 K6
Santa Margarita → *U.S.A.* 33°13N 117°23W 307 M9
Santa Margarita, I. *Mexico* 24°27N 111°50W 318 C2
Santa Margherita *Italy* 38°58N 8°58E 200 D1
Santa Margherita Ligure *Italy* 44°20N 9°11E 198 D6
Santa María *Argentina* 26°40S 66°0W 334 B2
Santa Maria *Azores* 36°58N 25°6W 153 d4
Santa Maria *Brazil* 29°40S 53°48W 335 B5
Santa Maria *C. Verde Is.* 16°31N 22°53W 153 j
Santa Maria *Mexico City, Mexico* 128 a1
Santa Maria *Ilocos S., Phil.* 17°22N 120°29E 232 C3
Santa Maria *Isabela, Phil.* 17°28N 121°45E 232 C3
Santa Maria *Calif., U.S.A.* 34°57N 120°26W 307 L6
Santa María → *Mexico* 31°0N 107°14W 318 A3
Santa María, B. de *Mexico* 25°4N 108°6W 318 B3
Santa Maria, C. de *Portugal* 36°58N 7°53W 195 J3
Santa María, I. *Ecuador* 1°17S 90°26W 330 a
Santa Maria Cápua Vétere *Italy* 41°5N 14°15E 201 A7
Santa Maria da Feira *Portugal* 40°55N 8°35W 194 E2
Santa Maria da Vitória *Brazil* 13°24S 44°12W 333 D3
Santa María de Ipire *Venezuela* 8°49N 65°19W 329 B4
Santa Maria del Camí *Spain* 39°38N 2°47E 206 B3
Santa Maria di Léuca, C. *Italy* 39°47N 18°22E 201 C11
Santa Maria do Boiaçu *Brazil* 0°25S 61°48W 329 D5
Santa Maria do Suaçuí *Brazil* 18°12S 42°25W 333 E3
Santa Maria dos Marmelos *Brazil* 6°7S 61°51W 331 B5
Santa María la Real de Nieva *Spain* 41°4N 4°24W 194 D6
Santa Marinella *Italy* 42°2N 11°52E 199 F8
Santa Marta *Colombia* 11°15N 74°13W 328 A3
Santa Marta, Sierra Nevada de *Colombia* 10°55N 73°50W 328 A3
Santa Marta de Tormes *Spain* 40°57N 5°38W 194 E5
Santa Marta Grande, C. *Brazil* 28°43S 48°50W 335 B6
Santa Marta Ortigueira, Ría de *Spain* 43°44N 7°45W 194 B3
Santa Martabaai = Sint Marthabaai *Neth. Ant.* 12°17N 69°8W 322 g
Santa Maura = Lefkada *Greece* 38°40N 20°43E 207 B2
Santa Monica *U.S.A.* 34°1N 118°29W 126 B2
Santa Monica Mts. *U.S.A.* 34°6N 118°29W 126 B2
Santa Monica Mts. ⌂ *U.S.A.* 34°4N 118°44W 307 L8
Santa Olalla *Huelva, Spain* 37°54N 6°14W 195 H4
Santa Olalla *Toledo, Spain* 40°2N 4°25W 194 E6
Santa Paula *U.S.A.* 34°21N 119°4W 307 L7
Santa Pola *Spain* 38°13N 0°35W 197 G4
Santa Ponça *Spain* 39°30N 2°28E 206 B3
Santa Quitéria *Brazil* 4°20S 40°10W 332 B3
Santa Rita = Itumbiara *Brazil* 18°20S 49°10W 333 E2
Santa Rita *Brazil* 3°29S 69°19W 328 D4
Santa Rita *Colombia* 4°53N 68°24W 328 C4
Santa Rita *Guam* 13°23N 144°40E 302 d
Santa Rita *Samar, Phil.* 11°27N 124°56E 233 F5
Santa Rita *Zulia, Venezuela* 10°32N 71°32W 328 A3
Santa Rita do Araguaia = Guiratinga *Brazil* 16°21S 53°45W 331 D7
Santa Rita do Araquaia *Brazil* 17°20S 53°12W 331 D7
Santa Rosa = Bella Unión *Uruguay* 30°15S 57°40W 334 C4
Santa Rosa *La Pampa, Argentina* 36°40S 64°17W 334 D3
Santa Rosa *San Luis, Argentina* 32°21S 65°10W 334 C2
Santa Rosa *Beni, Bolivia* 14°10S 66°53W 330 C4
Santa Rosa *Pando, Bolivia* 10°36S 67°20W 330 C4
Santa Rosa *Santa Cruz, Bolivia* 17°7S 63°35W 331 D5
Santa Rosa *Brazil* 27°52S 54°29W 335 B5
Santa Rosa *Colombia* 3°32N 69°48W 328 C4
Santa Rosa *El Oro, Ecuador* 3°27S 79°58W 328 D2
Santa Rosa *Galápagos Is., Ecuador* 0°40S 90°25W 330 a
Santa Rosa *Neth. Ant.* 12°7N 68°53W 322 g
Santa Rosa *Puno, Peru* 14°30S 70°50W 330 C3
Santa Rosa *San Martín, Peru* 6°41S 76°37W 330 B2
Santa Rosa *Phil.* 15°25N 120°57E 232 D3
Santa Rosa *Calif., U.S.A.* 38°26N 122°43W 306 G4
Santa Rosa *N. Mex., U.S.A.* 34°57N 104°41W 305 J11
Santa Rosa *Amazonas, Venezuela* 1°29N 66°55W 328 C4
Santa Rosa *Mt. Guam* 13°32N 144°55E 302 d
Santa Rosa and San Jacinto Mts. ⌂ *U.S.A.* 33°28N 116°20W 307 M10
Santa Rosa Beach *U.S.A.* 30°22N 86°14W 316 E3
Santa Rosa de Amanadona *Venezuela* 1°29N 66°55W 328 C4
Santa Rosa de Cabal *Colombia* 4°52N 75°38W 328 C2
Santa Rosa de Copán *Honduras* 14°47N 88°46W 320 D2
Santa Rosa de la Roca *Bolivia* 16°3S 61°34W 331 D5
Santa Rosa de Locobe *Chile* 33°25S 70°33W 137 B2
Santa Rosa de Osos *Colombia* 6°39N 75°28W 328 B2
Santa Rosa de Río Primero *Argentina* 31°8S 63°20W 334 C3
Santa Rosa de Viterbo *Colombia* 5°53N 72°59W 328 B3
Santa Rosa del Palmar *Bolivia* 16°54S 62°24W 331 D5
Santa Rosa I. *Calif., U.S.A.* 33°58N 120°6W 307 M6
Santa Rosa I. *Fla., U.S.A.* 30°20N 86°50W 317 E3
Santa Rosa Range *U.S.A.* 41°45N 117°40W 304 F5
Santa Rosalía *Mexico* 27°19N 112°17W 318 B2
Santa Sylvina *Argentina* 27°50S 61°10W 334 B3
Santa Tecla = Nueva San Salvador *El Salv.* 13°40N 89°18W 320 D2
Santa Teresa *Argentina* 33°25S 60°47W 334 C3
Santa Teresa *N. Terr., Australia* 24°8S 134°22E 280 C1
Santa Teresa *Brazil* 19°55S 40°36W 333 E3
Santa Teresa *Tamaulipas, Mexico* 25°17N 97°51W 319 B5
Santa Teresa *Venezuela* 4°43N 61°4W 329 C5
Santa Teresa △ *Uruguay* 33°57S 53°31W 335 C5
Santa Teresa de la Ovalle *Chile* 33°22S 70°44W 137 B1
Santa Teresa di Riva *Italy* 37°57N 15°22E 201 E8
Santa Teresa Gallura *Italy* 41°14N 9°11E 200 A2
Santa Teresinha *Brazil* 10°28S 50°31W 332 D1
Santa Uxía *Spain* 42°36N 8°58W 194 C2
Santa Vitória *Brazil* 18°50S 50°8W 333 E1
Santa Vitória do Palmar *Brazil* 33°32S 53°25W 335 C5
Santa Ynez → *U.S.A.* 34°41N 120°36W 307 L6
Santa Ynez Mts. *U.S.A.* 34°30N 120°0W 307 L6
Santa Ysabel *U.S.A.* 33°7N 116°40W 307 M10
Santadi *Italy* 39°5N 8°43E 200 C1
Santaella *Spain* 37°34N 4°51W 195 H6
Santahamina *Finland* 60°8N 25°2E 121 C3
Santahar *Bangla.* 24°48N 88°59E 241 C2
Santai *China* 31°5N 104°58E 228 B5
Santaluz *Brazil* 11°15S 39°22W 332 D4
Santana = Uruaçu *Brazil* 14°30S 49°10W 333 D2
Santana *Bahia, Brazil* 13°2S 44°5W 333 D3
Santana *São Paulo, Brazil* 23°29S 46°36W 137 A2
Santana *Madeira* 32°48N 16°52W 153 c
Sântana *Romania* 46°20N 21°30E 182 D6
Santana, Coxilha de *Brazil* 30°50S 55°35W 335 C4
Santana do Ipanema *Brazil* 9°22S 37°14W 332 C4
Santana do Livramento *Brazil* 30°55S 55°30W 335 C4
Santana do Paranaíba = Paranaíba *Brazil* 19°40S 51°11W 331 D7
Santander *Colombia* 3°1N 76°28W 328 C2
Santander *Phil.* 9°25N 123°20E 233 G4
Santander *Spain* 43°27N 3°51W 194 B7
Santander ☐ *Colombia* 7°0N 73°15W 328 B3
Santander Jiménez *Mexico* 24°13N 98°28W 319 C5
Santanilla, Is. *Honduras* 17°22N 83°57W 320 C3
Santanyí *Spain* 39°20N 3°5E 206 B4
Santaquin *U.S.A.* 39°59N 111°47W 304 G8
Santarcángelo di Romagna *Italy* 44°4N 12°26E 199 D9
Santarém *Brazil* 2°25S 54°42W 329 D7
Santarém *Portugal* 39°12N 8°42W 195 F2
Santarém ☐ *Portugal* 39°10N 8°40W 195 F2
Santaren Channel *W. Indies* 24°0N 79°30W 320 B4
Santee *U.S.A.* 32°50N 116°58W 307 N10
Santee → *U.S.A.* 33°7N 79°17W 315 E15
Santeny *France* 48°43N 2°34E 134 B4
Santéramo in Colle *Italy* 40°49N 16°45E 201 B9
Santerno → *Italy* 44°34N 11°58E 199 D8
Santhià *Italy* 45°22N 8°10E 198 C5
Santi *Taiwan* 22°43N 120°39E 225 D2
Santi-Quaranta = Sarandë *Albania* 39°52N 19°55E 206 B9
Santiago = Río Grande de Santiago → *Mexico* 21°36N 105°26W 318 C3
Santiago = São Tiago *C. Verde Is.* 15°0N 23°40W 153 j
Santiago *Bolivia* 18°19S 59°34W 331 D6
Santiago *Brazil* 29°11S 54°52W 335 B5
Santiago *Canary Is.* 28°2N 17°12W 153 e1
Santiago *Chile* 33°26S 70°40W 137 B2
Santiago *Panama* 8°0N 81°0W 320 E3
Santiago *Peru* 14°11S 75°43W 330 C2
Santiago *Ilocos S., Phil.* 17°18N 120°27E 232 C3
Santiago *Isabela, Phil.* 16°41N 121°33E 232 C3
Santiago ☐ *Chile* 33°30S 70°50W 334 C1
Santiago → *Peru* 4°27S 77°38W 328 D2
Santiago, C. *Chile* 50°46S 75°27W 336 D1
Santiago, I. = San Salvador, I. *Ecuador* 0°16S 90°42W 330 a
Santiago, Punta de *Eq. Guin.* 3°12N 8°40E 263 E6
Santiago, Serranía de *Bolivia* 18°25S 59°25W 331 D6
Santiago Benítez ✕ (SCL) *Chile* 33°33S 70°42W 137 B1
Santiago de Chuco *Peru* 8°9S 78°11W 330 B2
Santiago de Compostela *Spain* 42°52N 8°37W 194 C2
Santiago de Cuba *Cuba* 20°0N 75°49W 320 C4
Santiago de los Caballeros *Dom. Rep.* 19°30N 70°40W 321 C5
Santiago de Surco *Peru* 12°9S 77°0W 124 B2
Santiago del Estero *Argentina* 27°50S 64°15W 334 B3
Santiago del Estero ☐ *Argentina* 27°40S 63°15W 334 B3
Santiago del Teide *Canary Is.* 28°17N 16°48W 153 e1
Santiago do Boqueirão = Santiago *Brazil* 29°11S 54°52W 335 B5
Santiago do Cacém *Portugal* 38°1N 8°42W 195 G2
Santiago Ixcuintla *Mexico* 21°49N 105°13W 318 C3
Santiago Jamiltepec *Mexico* 16°17N 97°49W 319 D5
Santiago Papasquiaro *Mexico* 25°3N 105°25W 318 C3
Santiago Pinotepa Nacional *Mexico* 16°19N 98°1W 319 D5
Santiaguillo, L. de *Mexico* 24°48N 104°48W 318 C4
Santialing *Taiwan* 25°5N 121°51E 225 A3
Santiao Chiao *Taiwan* 25°1N 122°0E 225 A3
Santiaolun *Taiwan* 23°39N 120°9E 225 C2
Santiguila *Mali* 12°42N 7°25W 262 C3
Santillana *Spain* 43°24N 4°6W 194 B6
Santisteban del Puerto *Spain* 38°17N 3°15W 195 G7
Santo → *Peru* 8°56S 78°37W 330 B2
Santo Amaro *Bahia, Brazil* 12°30S 38°43W 333 D4
Santo Amaro *São Paulo, Brazil* 23°39S 46°42W 137 B1
Santo Amaro *Lisboa, Portugal* 38°42N 9°11W 126 A1
Santo Anastácio *Brazil* 21°58S 51°39W 335 A5
Santo André *Brazil* 23°39S 46°29W 335 A6
Santo André *Lisboa, Portugal* 38°38N 9°3W 126 B2
Santo Ângelo *Brazil* 28°15S 54°15W 335 B5
Santo Antão *C. Verde Is.* 16°52N 25°10W 153 j
Santo Antão do Tojal *Portugal* 38°49N 9°9W 126 A2
Santo António *São Tomé & Principe* 1°37N 7°27E 265 a
Santo Antônio *Brazil* 2°24S 60°58W 329 D5
Santo Antônio, Qta. de *Portugal* 38°39N 9°15W 126 B1

Santo Antônio da Cachoeira = Itaguatins Brazil 5°47S 47°29W 332 C2
Santo Antônio de Jesus Brazil 12°58S 39°16W 333 D4
Santo Antônio do Abaixo = Santo Antônio do Leverger Brazil 15°52S 56°5W 331 D6
Santo Antônio do Içá Brazil 3°5S 67°57W 328 D4
Santo Antônio do Leverger Brazil 15°52S 56°5W 331 D6
Santo Corazón Bolivia 18°0S 58°45W 331 D6
Santo Domingo Dom. Rep. 18°30N 69°59W 321 C6
Santo Domingo Baja Calif., Mexico 30°43N 116°2W 318 A1
Santo Domingo Baja Calif. S., Mexico 25°29N 111°55W 318 B2
Santo Domingo Nic. 12°14N 84°59W 320 D3
Santo Domingo de la Calzada Spain 42°26N 2°57W 196 C2
Santo Domingo de los Colorados Ecuador 0°15S 79°9W 328 D2
Santo Domingo Pueblo U.S.A. 35°31N 106°22W 305 J10
Santo Stéfano di Camastro Italy 38°1N 14°22E 201 D7
Santo Tirso Portugal 41°21N 8°28W 194 D2
Santo Tomás Galápagos Is., Ecuador 0°51S 91°2W 330 a
Santo Tomás Baja Calif., Mexico 31°33N 116°24W 318 A1
Santo Tomás Peru 14°26S 72°8W 330 C3
Santo Tomas, Univ. of Phil. 14°36N 120°59E 127 B1
Santo Tomás, Volcán Ecuador 0°48S 91°7W 330 a
Santo Tomé Argentina 28°40S 56°5W 335 B4
Santo Tomé de Guayana = Ciudad Guayana Venezuela 8°0N 62°30W 329 B5
Santomera Spain 38°4N 1°3W 197 G3
Santoña Spain 43°29N 3°27W 194 B7
Santorini Greece 36°23N 25°27E 205 E7
Santos Brazil 24°0S 46°20W 335 A6
Santos, Sierra de los Spain 38°7N 5°12W 195 G5
Santos Dumont Brazil 22°55S 43°10W 333 F3
Santos Dumont ✕ (SDU) Brazil 22°54S 43°9W 135 B2
Santoshpur India 22°31N 88°16E 124 B1
Santragachi India 22°35N 88°17E 124 B1
Santry Ireland 53°24N 6°15W 120 A2
Sanur Indonesia 8°41S 115°15E 231 K18
Sanwan Taiwan 24°39N 120°57E 225 B2
Sanwer India 22°59N 75°50E 242 H6
Sanxenxo Spain 42°24N 8°49W 194 C2
Sanxiang China 22°21N 113°25E 219 G9
Sanya China 18°14N 109°29E 236 C7
San'yō Japan 34°2N 131°5E 222 C3
Sanyuan China 34°35N 108°58E 226 G5
Sanyuanli China 23°8N 113°14E 121 B2
Sanyuki-Sammyaku Japan 34°5N 134°0E 222 C6
Sanza Pombo Angola 7°18S 15°56E 265 D3
São Bartolomeu de Messines Portugal 37°15N 8°17W 195 H2
São Benedito = Beneditinos Brazil 5°27S 42°22W 332 C3
São Benedito Brazil 4°3S 40°53W 332 B3
São Benedito ➝ Brazil 9°11S 57°2W 331 B6
São Bento Brazil 2°42S 44°50W 332 B3
São Bento do Norte Brazil 5°4S 36°2W 332 C4
São Bernardo do Campo Brazil 23°45S 46°34W 333 F2
São Borja Brazil 28°39S 56°0W 335 B4
São Brás de Alportel Portugal 37°8N 7°37W 195 H3
São Braz, C. de Angola 9°58S 13°19E 265 D2
São Caetano do Sul Brazil 23°37S 46°34W 137 B2
São Caitano Brazil 8°21S 36°6W 332 C4
São Carlos Brazil 22°0S 47°50W 335 A6
São Conrado Brazil 23°5S 43°17W 135 B1
São Cristóvão Rio de J., Brazil 22°53S 43°13W 135 B1
São Cristóvão Sergipe, Brazil 11°1S 37°15W 332 D4
São Domingos Brazil 13°25S 46°19W 333 D2
São Domingos Guinea-Biss. 12°19N 16°13W 262 C1
São Domingos da Boa Vista = Capim Brazil 1°41S 47°47W 332 B2
São Domingos do Capim = Capim Brazil 1°41S 47°47W 332 B2
São Domingos do Maranhão Brazil 5°42S 44°22W 332 C3
São Felipe = Içana Brazil 0°21N 67°19W 328 C4
São Felippe = Eirunepé Brazil 6°35S 69°53W 330 B4
São Félix Brazil 11°36S 50°39W 333 D1
São Félix do Xingu Brazil 6°38S 51°59W 331 B7
São Filipe C. Verde Is. 15°2N 24°30W 153 j
São Francisco = Itapagé Brazil 3°41S 39°34W 332 B4
São Francisco Brazil 16°0S 44°50W 333 E3
São Francisco ➝ Brazil 10°30S 36°24W 332 D4
São Francisco do Maranhão Brazil 6°15S 42°52W 332 C3
São Francisco do Sul Brazil 26°15S 48°36W 335 B6
São Francisco Penitência Rio de J., Brazil 135 b1
São Gabriel Brazil 30°20S 54°20W 335 C5
São Gabriel da Cachoeira Brazil 0°8S 67°5W 328 D4
São Gabriel da Palha Brazil 18°47S 40°39W 333 E3
São Gonçalo = Araripina Brazil 7°33S 40°34W 332 C3
São Gonçalo Brazil 22°48S 43°5W 333 F3
São Gotardo Brazil 19°19S 46°3W 333 E2
Sao Hill Tanzania 8°20S 35°12E 269 D4
São João Guinea-Biss. 11°32N 15°25W 262 C1
São João da Baliza Brazil 0°52N 59°52W 329 C6
São João da Boa Vista Brazil 22°0S 46°52W 335 A6
São João da Madeira Portugal 40°54N 8°30W 194 E2
São João da Pesqueira Portugal 41°8N 7°24W 194 D3
São João da Ponte Brazil 15°56S 44°1W 333 E3
São João de Montenegro = Montenegro Brazil 29°39S 51°29W 335 B5
São João del Rei Brazil 21°8S 44°15W 333 F3
São João do Araguaia Brazil 5°23S 48°46W 332 C2
São João do Paraíso Brazil 15°19S 42°1W 333 E3
São João do Piauí Brazil 8°21S 42°15W 332 C3
São João dos Patos Brazil 6°30S 43°42W 332 C3
São Joaquim Amazonas, Brazil 0°1S 67°16W 328 D4
São Joaquim Sta. Catarina, Brazil 28°18S 49°56W 335 B6
São Joaquim △ Brazil 28°12S 49°37W 335 B6
São Joaquim da Barra Brazil 20°35S 47°53W 333 F2
São Jorge Azores 38°38N 28°3W 153 d1
São Jorge, Canal de Azores 38°30N 28°0W 153 d1
São Jorge, Castelo de Portugal 38°42N 9°8W 126 A2
São Jorge, Pta. de Azores 38°42N 27°3W 153 d1
São Jorge, Pta. de Madeira 32°50N 16°53W 153 c
São José Brazil 27°38S 48°39W 335 B5
São José, B. de Brazil 2°38S 44°4W 332 B3
São José da Lagoa = Nova Era Brazil 19°45S 43°3W 333 E3
São José da Laje Brazil 9°1S 36°3W 332 C4
São José de Mipibu Brazil 6°5S 35°15W 332 C4
São José de Tocantins = Niquelândia Brazil 14°33S 48°23W 333 D2
São José do Norte Brazil 32°1S 52°3W 335 C5
São José do Peixe Brazil 7°24S 42°34W 332 C3
São José do Rio Prêto Brazil 20°50S 49°20W 335 A6
São José dos Campos Brazil 23°7S 45°52W 335 A6
São José dos Cocais = Nossa Senhora do Livramento Brazil 15°48S 56°22W 331 D6
São José dos Matões = Parnarama Brazil 5°31S 43°6W 332 C3
São Juliao do Tojal Portugal 38°49N 9°8W 126 A2
São Leopoldo Brazil 29°50S 51°10W 335 B5
São Lourenço Brazil 22°7S 45°3W 333 F2
São Lourenço ➝ Brazil 17°53S 57°27W 331 D6
São Lourenço, Pantanal do Brazil 17°30S 56°20W 331 D6
São Lourenço, Pta. de Madeira 32°44N 16°39W 153 c
São Lourenço do Sul Brazil 31°22S 51°58W 335 C5
São Luís Brazil 2°39S 44°15W 332 B3
São Luís do Curu Brazil 3°40S 39°14W 332 B4
São Luís do Tapojós Brazil 4°25S 56°12W 329 D6
São Luís Gonzaga = Ipixuna Brazil 7°0S 71°40W 330 B3
São Luís Gonzaga Brazil 28°25S 55°0W 335 B5
São Marcos ➝ Brazil 18°15S 47°37W 333 E2
São Marcos, B. de Brazil 2°0S 44°0W 332 B3
São Martinho da Cortiça Portugal 40°18N 8°8W 194 E2
São Mateus Azores 38°26N 28°27W 153 d1
São Mateus Brazil 18°44S 39°50W 333 E4
São Mateus ➝ Brazil 18°35S 39°44W 333 E4
São Mateus do Sul Brazil 25°52S 50°23W 335 B5
São Miguel Azores 37°47N 25°30W 153 d3
São Miguel do Araguaia Brazil 13°19S 50°13W 333 D1
São Miguel do Guamá = Guamá Brazil 1°37S 47°29W 332 B2
São Miguel do Oeste Brazil 26°45S 53°34W 335 B5
São Miguel dos Campos Brazil 9°47S 36°5W 332 C4
São Nicolau C. Verde Is. 16°20N 24°20W 153 j
São Nicolau ➝ Angola 14°16S 12°22E 265 E2
São Nicolau ➝ Brazil 5°45S 42°2W 332 C3
São Paulo Brazil 23°32S 46°38W 137 B2
São Paulo □ Brazil 22°0S 49°0W 335 A6
São Paulo, I. Atl. Oc. 0°56N 29°22W 152 F9
São Paulo Congonhas ✕ (CGH) Brazil 23°38S 46°39W 137 B2
São Paulo de Olivença Brazil 3°27S 68°48W 328 D4
São Pedro Atl. Oc. 0°56N 29°22W 152 F9
São Pedro do Sul Portugal 40°46N 8°4W 194 E2
São Rafael Brazil 5°47S 36°55W 332 C4
São Raimundo das Mangabeiras Brazil 7°1S 45°29W 332 C2
São Raimundo Nonato Brazil 9°1S 42°42W 332 C3
São Romão Brazil 16°22S 45°4W 333 E2
São Roque Madeira 32°46N 16°48W 153 c
São Roque, C. de Brazil 5°30S 35°16W 332 C4
São Roque do Pico Azores 38°31N 28°19W 153 d1
São Salvador do Congo = Mbanza Congo Angola 6°18S 14°16E 265 D2
São Sebastião Azores 38°39N 27°6W 153 d1
São Sebastião, I. de Brazil 23°50S 45°18W 335 A6
São Sebastião do Paraíso Brazil 20°54S 46°59W 335 A6
São Simão Brazil 18°56S 50°30W 333 E1
São Teotónio Portugal 37°30N 8°42W 195 H2
São Tiago C. Verde Is. 15°0N 23°40W 153 j
São Tomé Brazil 5°58S 36°4W 332 C4
São Tomé São Tomé & Príncipe 0°10N 6°39E 265 a
São Tomé, C. de Brazil 22°0S 40°59W 333 F3
São Tomé, Pico de São Tomé & Príncipe 0°16N 6°33E 265 a
São Tomé & Príncipe ■ Africa 0°12N 6°39E 265 a
São Vicente = Araguatins Brazil 5°38S 48°7W 332 C2
São Vicente Brazil 23°57S 46°23W 335 A6
São Vicente C. Verde Is. 17°0N 25°0W 153 j
São Vicente Madeira 32°48N 17°3W 153 c
São Vicente, C. de Portugal 37°0N 9°0W 195 H1
Saona, I. Dom. Rep. 18°10N 68°40W 321 C6
Saône ➝ France 45°44N 4°50E 173 G11
Saône-et-Loire □ France 46°30N 4°50E 173 F11
Saonek Indonesia 0°22S 130°55E 231 E8
Saoura, O. ➝ Algeria 29°0N 0°55W 261 C4
Sapa India 22°30N 88°15E 124 B1
Sapam, Ao Thailand 8°0N 98°26E 237 a
Sapanca Turkey 40°41N 30°16E 212 B4
Sapão ➝ Brazil 11°1S 45°32W 332 D2
Saparua Indonesia 3°33S 128°40E 231 E7
Sapateiro, Cor. do ➝ Brazil 23°35S 46°41W 137 B1
Sapé Brazil 7°6S 35°13W 332 C4
Sape Indonesia 8°34S 118°59E 235 D5
Sapele Nigeria 5°50N 5°40E 263 D6
Sapelo I. U.S.A. 31°25N 81°12W 316 D8
Sapelo Sound U.S.A. 31°30N 81°10W 316 D8
Sapes Greece 41°2N 25°43E 203 E9
Şaphane Turkey 39°1N 29°13E 205 B11
Sapi ⌂ Zimbabwe 15°48S 29°42E 269 F2
Sapienza Greece 36°45N 21°43E 204 E3
Sapindji Dem. Rep. of the Congo 9°39S 23°12E 265 D4
Sapo △ Liberia 5°15N 8°30W 262 D3
Sapone Burkina Faso 12°3N 1°35W 263 C4
Saposoa Peru 6°55S 76°45W 330 B2
Sapotskina Belarus 53°49N 23°40E 184 E10
Sapouy Burkina Faso 11°34N 1°44W 263 C4
Sapozhok Russia 53°59N 40°41E 190 D5
Sapphire Australia 23°28S 147°43E 280 C4
Sappho U.S.A. 48°4N 124°16W 306 B2
Sapporo Japan 43°0N 141°21E 220 C10
Sapri Italy 40°4N 15°38E 201 B8
Sapu Angola 12°28S 19°26E 265 E3
Sapudi Indonesia 7°6S 114°20E 235 D4
Sapulpa U.S.A. 35°59N 96°5W 314 D6
Saqqez Iran 36°15N 46°20E 213 D12
Sar Dasht Āzarbāyjān-e Gharbī, Iran 36°9N 45°28E 213 D11
Sar Dasht Khuzestān, Iran 32°32N 48°52E 247 C6
Sar-e Pol Afghan. 36°10N 66°0E 240 A2
Sar-e Pol □ Afghan. 36°20N 65°50E 240 A2
Sar Gachīneh = Yāsūj Iran 30°31N 51°31E 247 D6
Sar Passage Palau 7°12N 134°22E 288 c
Sar Planina Macedonia 42°0N 21°0E 202 E4
Sara Burkina Faso 11°40N 3°53W 262 C4
Sara Niger 20°46N 12°35E 259 D2
Sara Phil. 11°16N 123°1E 233 F4
Šara △ Serbia 42°12N 21°0E 202 D5
Sara Buri = Saraburi Thailand 14°30N 100°55E 236 E3
Sarāb Iran 37°55N 47°40E 213 D12
Sarabadi Iraq 33°1N 44°48E 246 C5
Sarabît el Khâdim Egypt 29°2N 33°25E 251 J4
Saraburi Thailand 14°30N 100°55E 236 E3
Saradiya India 21°34N 70°2E 242 J4
Saraféré Mali 15°50N 3°40W 262 B4
Saragossa = Zaragoza Spain 41°39N 0°53W 196 D4
Saraguro Ecuador 3°35S 79°16W 328 D2
Sarahs Turkmenistan 36°32N 61°13E 247 B9
Sarai Naurang Pakistan 32°50N 70°47E 242 C4
Saraikela India 22°42N 85°56E 243 H11
Saraipali India 21°20N 82°59E 244 D6
Saraiu Romania 44°43N 28°10E 183 F13
Sarajevo Bos.-H. 43°52N 18°26E 182 G3
Sarakhs = Sarahs Turkmenistan 36°32N 61°13E 247 B9
Saramacca ➝ Suriname 5°50N 55°55W 329 B6
Saramati Burma 25°44N 95°2E 241 C5
Saran, Gunung Indonesia 0°30S 111°25E 235 C4
Saranac U.S.A. 42°56N 85°13W 311 B11
Saranac Lake U.S.A. 44°20N 74°10W 313 B10
Saranac Lakes U.S.A. 44°20N 74°28W 313 B10
Saranda Tanzania 5°45S 34°59E 268 D3
Sarandë Albania 39°52N 19°55E 206 B9
Sarandi Argentina 34°40S 58°20W 117 C2
Sarandí del Yi Uruguay 33°18S 55°38W 335 C4
Sarandí Grande Uruguay 33°44S 56°20W 334 C4
Sarangani □ Phil. 5°45N 125°20E 233 J5
Sarangani B. Phil. 6°0N 125°13E 233 J5
Sarangani Is. Phil. 5°25N 125°25E 233 J5
Sarangarh India 21°30N 83°5E 244 D6
Saranovo = Septemvri Bulgaria 42°13N 24°6E 203 D8
Saransk Russia 54°10N 45°10E 190 C7
Sarapul Russia 56°28N 53°48E 186 C9
Sarāqib Syria 35°52N 36°47E 250 C7
Sarar Plain = Bannaanka Saraar Somali Rep. 9°25N 46°17E 267 C6
Sarasota U.S.A. 27°20N 82°32W 317 H7
Saraswati ➝ India 22°46N 88°15E 124 A1
Sarata Ukraine 46°1N 29°40E 183 D14
Sarata ➝ Ukraine 45°51N 29°41E 183 E14
Saratoga Calif., U.S.A. 37°16N 122°2W 306 H4
Saratoga Wyo., U.S.A. 41°27N 106°49W 304 F10
Saratoga ⌂ U.S.A. 43°0N 73°38W 313 D11
Saratoga Springs U.S.A. 43°5N 73°47W 313 C11
Saratok Malaysia 1°55N 111°17E 235 B4
Saratov Russia 51°30N 46°2E 190 E7
Saratov □ Russia 51°50N 46°20E 190 E8
Sarāvān Iran 27°25N 62°15E 247 E9
Saravane Laos 15°43N 106°25E 236 E6
Sarawak □ Malaysia 2°0N 113°0E 235 B4
Saray Tekirdağ, Turkey 41°26N 27°55E 203 E11
Saray Van, Turkey 38°38N 44°9E 213 C11
Saraya Senegal 12°50N 11°45W 262 C2
Saraycık Turkey 39°1N 29°49E 205 B11
Sarayköy Turkey 37°55N 28°54E 205 D10
Saraylar Turkey 40°39N 27°40E 203 F11
Sarayönü Turkey 38°16N 32°24E 212 C5
Sarbāz Iran 26°38N 61°19E 247 E9
Sarbīsheh Iran 32°30N 59°40E 247 C8
Sárbogárd Hungary 46°50N 18°40E 182 D3
Sarca ➝ Italy 45°52N 10°52E 198 C7
Sarcelles France 49°1N 2°23E 173 D9
Sarda ➝ India 27°21N 81°23E 243 F9
Sardalas Libya 25°50N 10°34E 258 C2
Sardarshahr India 28°30N 74°29E 242 E6
Sardegna □ Italy 40°0N 9°0E 200 B1
Sardhana India 29°9N 77°39E 242 E7
Sardina, Pta. Canary Is. 28°9N 15°44W 153 e1
Sardinata Colombia 8°5N 72°48W 328 B3
Sardinia = Sardegna □ Italy 40°0N 9°0E 200 B1
Sardinia U.S.A. 39°0N 83°49W 311 F13
Sardis Turkey 38°28N 27°58E 205 C10
Sardis Ga., U.S.A. 32°58N 81°46W 316 C8
Sārdūīyeh = Dar Mazār Iran 29°14N 57°20E 247 D8
Sarecky potok ➝ Czech Rep. 50°7N 14°23E 135 B2
Saren Indonesia 8°26S 115°34E 231 J18
S'Arenal Spain 39°30N 2°45E 206 B3
Sarentino Italy 46°38N 11°21E 199 B8
Saréyamou Mali 16°7N 3°10W 262 B4
Sargasso Sea Atl. Oc. 27°0N 72°0W 292 G13
Sargent U.S.A. 33°26N 84°52W 316 B5
Sargodha Pakistan 32°10N 72°40E 242 C5
Sarh Chad 9°5N 18°23E 259 G3
Sarhala Ivory C. 8°22N 6°8W 262 D3
Sarhro, Jebel Morocco 31°6N 5°0W 260 B4
Sārī Iran 36°30N 53°4E 247 B7
Sari d'Orcino France 42°3N 8°49E 175 F12
Saria Greece 35°54N 27°17E 205 F9
Saria India 21°38N 83°22E 243 J10
Sariab Pakistan 30°6N 66°59E 242 D2
Sarıbeyler Turkey 39°24N 27°35E 205 B9
Saricumbe Angola 12°12S 19°46E 265 E3
Sarigan N. Marianas 16°43N 145°47E 302 a
Sarıgöl Turkey 38°14N 28°41E 212 C3
Sarikamiş Turkey 40°22N 42°35E 213 B10
Sarıkaya Turkey 39°29N 35°22E 212 C6
Sarikei Malaysia 2°8N 111°30E 235 B4
Sarıköy Turkey 40°12N 27°37E 203 F11
Sarila India 25°46N 79°41E 243 G8
Sarimbun Singapore 1°24N 103°40E 138 A2
Sarimbun Res. Singapore 1°25N 103°41E 138 A2
Sarina Australia 21°22S 149°13E 280 C4
Sariñena Spain 41°47N 0°10W 196 D4
Sariri Papua N. G. 9°11S 148°35E 286 E5
Sarita U.S.A. 27°13N 97°47W 314 H6
Sarıveliler Turkey 36°41N 32°37E 250 B3
Sariwŏn N. Korea 38°31N 125°46E 224 C2
Sariyar Barajı Turkey 40°2N 31°33E 212 B4
Sarıyer Turkey 41°10N 29°3E 122 A2
Sarju ➝ India 27°21N 81°23E 243 F9
Sark U.K. 49°25N 2°22W 169 H5
Sarkad Hungary 46°47N 21°23E 182 D6
Sarkari Tala India 27°39N 70°52E 242 F4
Şarkışla Turkey 39°21N 36°25E 212 C7
Şarköy Turkey 40°36N 27°6E 203 F11
Sarlat-la-Canéda France 44°54N 1°13E 174 D5
Sărmăşag Romania 47°21N 22°50E 182 C7
Sărmaşu Romania 46°45N 24°13E 183 D9
Sarmi Indonesia 1°49S 138°44E 231 E9
Sarmiento Argentina 45°35S 69°5W 336 C3
Sarmizegetusa Romania 45°31N 22°47E 182 E7
Särna Sweden 61°41N 13°8E 162 C7
Sarnano Italy 43°2N 13°18E 199 E10
Sarnen Switz. 46°53N 8°13E 179 J4
Sarnia Canada 42°58N 82°23W 312 D2
Sarno Italy 40°49N 14°37E 201 B7
Sarnthein = Sarentino Italy 46°38N 11°21E 199 B8
Särö Sweden 57°31N 11°57E 163 G5
Sarolangun Indonesia 2°19S 102°42E 234 C2
Saronikos Kolpos Greece 37°45N 23°45E 204 D5
Saronno Italy 45°38N 9°2E 198 C6
Saros Körfezi Turkey 40°30N 26°15E 203 F10
Sárospatak Hungary 48°18N 21°33E 182 B6
Sarowbī Afghan. 34°36N 69°44E 240 B3
Sarpsborg Norway 59°16N 11°7E 164 E8
Sarqan Kazakhstan 45°24N 79°55E 217 C9
Sarracín Spain 42°15N 3°45W 194 C7
Sarralbe France 49°0N 7°1E 173 D14
Sarrat Phil. 18°9N 120°39E 232 B3
Sarre = Saar ➝ Europe 49°41N 6°32E 170 E6
Sarre Italy 45°40N 7°15E 198 C4
Sarre-Union France 48°57N 7°4E 173 D14
Sarrebourg France 48°43N 7°3E 173 D14
Sarreguemines France 49°5N 7°4E 173 C14
Sarriá Barcelona, Spain 41°22N 2°8E 114 A1
Sarria Galicia, Spain 42°49N 7°29W 194 C3
Sarrión Spain 40°9N 0°49W 196 E4
Sarro Mali 13°40N 5°15W 262 C3
Sarstedt Germany 52°14N 9°52E 178 C5
Sarsuna India 22°28N 88°17E 124 C1
Sartène France 41°38N 8°58E 175 G12
Sarthe □ France 48°10N 0°10E 172 D7
Sarthe ➝ France 47°33N 0°31W 172 E6
Sartilly France 48°45N 1°28W 172 D5
Sartrouville France 48°56N 2°10E 134 A2
Saruhanlı Turkey 38°44N 27°36E 205 C9
Săruleşti Romania 44°25N 26°39E 183 F11
Saruna ➝ Pakistan 26°31N 67°7E 242 F2
Sarupeta India 26°30N 91°5E 241 B3
Saruwaged Ra. Papua N. G. 6°13S 146°45E 286 D4
Sárvár Hungary 47°15N 16°56E 182 C1
Sarvar India 26°4N 75°0E 242 F6
Sarvestān Iran 29°20N 53°10E 247 D7
Särvfjället Sweden 62°42N 13°30E 162 B7
Sárviz ➝ Hungary 46°24N 18°41E 182 D3
Sary-Tash Kyrgyzstan 39°44N 73°15E 214 F8
Sarych, Mys Ukraine 44°25N 33°45E 189 K7
Saryesik-Atyraū Qumy Kazakhstan 45°30N 76°0E 217 C9
Sarykamyshskoye, Ozero = Saryqamysh Köli Turkmenistan 41°56N 57°25E 216 D5
Sarykemer Kazakhstan 43°0N 71°30E 217 D8
Sarykenggir ➝ Kazakhstan 48°22N 67°59E 217 C7
Saryköl Kazakhstan 53°20N 65°12E 216 B7
Sarykolskiy Khrebet Tajikistan 38°30N 74°30E 217 E8
Saryözek Kazakhstan 44°22N 77°59E 217 D9
Saryqamysh Köli Turkmenistan 41°56N 57°25E 216 D5
Saryshaghan Kazakhstan 46°12N 73°38E 217 C8
Sarysū ➝ Kazakhstan 45°12N 66°36E 217 C7
Sarzana Italy 44°7N 9°58E 198 D6
Sarzeau France 47°31N 2°48W 172 E4
Sasabeneh Ethiopia 7°59N 44°43E 267 C5
Sasad Hungary 47°28N 19°0E 117 B2
Sasamungga Solomon Is. 7°0S 156°50E 287 L9
Sasan Gir India 21°10N 70°36E 242 J4
Sasaram India 24°57N 84°5E 243 G11
Sasari, Mt. Solomon Is. 8°10S 159°30E 287 M10
Sasayama Japan 35°4N 135°13E 223 B7
Sasebo Japan 33°10N 129°43E 222 D1
Saser India 34°50N 77°50E 243 B7
Sashalom Hungary 47°30N 19°10E 117 A3
Saska Poland 52°14N 21°3E 142 B2
Saskatchewan □ Canada 54°40N 106°0W 297 C7
Saskatchewan ➝ Canada 53°37N 100°40W 297 C8
Saskatoon Canada 52°10N 106°38W 297 C7
Saskylakh Russia 71°55N 114°1E 215 B12
Sasolburg S. Africa 26°46S 27°49E 271 C4
Sasovo Russia 54°25N 41°55E 190 C5
Sassandra Ivory C. 4°55N 6°8W 262 E3
Sassandra ➝ Ivory C. 4°58N 6°5W 262 E3
Sássari Italy 40°43N 8°34E 200 B1
Sassnitz Germany 54°29N 13°39E 178 A9
Sasso Marconi Italy 44°24N 11°15E 199 D8
Sassocorvaro Italy 43°47N 12°30E 199 E9
Sassoferrato Italy 43°26N 12°51E 199 E9
Sasstown Liberia 4°45N 8°27W 262 E3
Sassuolo Italy 44°33N 10°47E 198 D7
Sástago Spain 41°19N 0°21W 196 D4
Sasvad India 18°20N 74°2E 244 E2
Sasyk, Ozero Ukraine 45°45N 29°20E 183 E14
Sasyqköl Kazakhstan 46°35N 81°0E 217 C10
Sata-Misaki Japan 31°0N 130°40E 222 F2
Satadougou Mali 12°25N 11°25W 262 C2
Satakunda = Satakunta Finland 61°45N 23°0E 188 B2
Satakunta Finland 61°45N 23°0E 188 B2
Satalice Czech Rep. 50°7N 14°34E 135 B3
Satama-Soukoura Ivory C. 7°55N 4°27W 262 D4
Satara India 17°44N 73°58E 244 F1
Satara S. Africa 24°29S 31°47E 271 B5
Sätbaev Kazakhstan 48°10N 67°31E 217 C7
Satbarwa India 23°55N 84°16E 243 H11
Satellite Beach U.S.A. 28°10N 80°36W 317 G9
Såtenäs Sweden 58°27N 12°41E 163 F6
Säter Sweden 60°21N 15°45E 162 D9
Satevó Mexico 27°57N 106°7W 318 B3
Satgachi India 22°37N 88°25E 124 B2
Sathorn Bangkok, Thailand 113 c3
Satilla ➝ U.S.A. 30°59N 81°29W 316 E8
Satipo Peru 11°15S 74°25W 330 C3
Satka Russia 55°3N 59°1E 186 C10
Satkania Bangla. 22°4N 92°3E 241 D4
Satkhira Bangla. 22°43N 89°8E 241 D2
Satmala Hills Andhra Pradesh, India 19°45N 78°45E 244 E4
Satmala Hills Maharashtra, India 20°15N 74°40E 244 D2
Satna India 24°35N 80°50E 243 G9
Šator Bos.-H. 44°11N 16°37E 199 D13
Sátoraljaújhely Hungary 48°25N 21°41E 182 B6
Satpukur India 22°37N 88°24E 124 B2
Satpura △ India 22°40N 78°15E 242 H8
Satpura Ra. India 21°25N 76°10E 244 D3
Sätra Sweden 59°17N 17°54E 139 B1
Satrup Germany 54°41N 9°36E 178 A5
Satsuma-Hantō Japan 31°25N 130°25E 222 F2
Satsuna-Shotō Japan 30°0N 130°0E 221 K5
Sattahip Thailand 12°41N 100°54E 236 F3
Sattenapalle India 16°25N 80°6E 245 F5
Sattru Pha Bangkok, Thailand 113 b2
Satu Mare Romania 47°46N 22°55E 182 C7
Satu Mare □ Romania 47°45N 23°0E 182 C8
Satui Indonesia 3°50S 115°27E 235 C5
Satun Thailand 6°43N 100°2E 237 J3
Satupa'itea Samoa 13°45S 172°18W 287 V19
Saturnina ➝ Brazil 12°15S 58°10W 331 C6
Sauce = Juan L. Lacaze Uruguay 34°26S 57°25W 334 C4
Sauce Argentina 30°5S 58°46W 334 C4
Sauceda Mexico 25°46N 101°19W 318 B4
Saucillo Mexico 28°1N 105°17W 318 B3
Sauda Norway 59°40N 6°20E 164 E3
Saudasjøen Norway 59°38N 6°17E 164 E3
Saúde Bahia, Brazil 10°56S 40°24W 332 D3
Saúde São Paulo, Brazil 23°36S 46°37W 137 B2
Sauðarkrókur Iceland 65°45N 19°40W 155 B7
Saudi Arabia ■ Asia 26°0N 44°0E 246 B3
Sauerland Germany 51°12N 7°59E 176 C4
Saugatuck U.S.A. 42°40N 86°12W 311 B10
Saugeen ➝ Canada 44°30N 81°22W 312 B3
Saugerties U.S.A. 42°5N 73°57W 313 D11
Saugues France 44°58N 3°32E 174 D7
Saugus Calif., U.S.A. 34°25N 118°32W 307 L8
Saugus Mass., U.S.A. 42°28N 71°0W 116 A2
Saugus ➝ U.S.A. 42°27N 70°58W 116 A2
Saujbulagh = Mahābād Iran 36°50N 45°45E 213 D11
Saujon France 45°41N 0°55W 174 C3
Sauk Centre U.S.A. 45°44N 94°57W 308 C6
Sauk City U.S.A. 43°17N 89°43W 310 A7
Sauk Rapids U.S.A. 45°35N 94°10W 308 C6
Saül Fr. Guiana 3°37N 53°12W 329 C7
Sauland Norway 59°37N 8°56E 164 E5
Saulgau Germany 48°1N 9°29E 179 G5
Saulieu France 47°17N 4°14E 173 E11
Sault France 44°6N 5°24E 175 D9
Sault-au-Récollet Canada 45°35N 73°39W 130 A2
Sault Ste. Marie Ont., Canada 46°30N 84°20W 298 C3
Sault Ste. Marie Mich., U.S.A. 46°30N 84°21W 309 B11
Saūmalkol Kazakhstan 53°17N 68°6E 217 B7
Saumlaki Indonesia 7°55S 131°20E 231 F8
Saumur France 47°15N 0°5W 172 E6
Saundatti India 15°47N 75°7E 245 G2
Saunders, C. N.Z. 45°53S 170°45E 285 F5
Saunders I. Antarctica 57°48S 26°28W 151 B1
Saunders Pt. Australia 27°52S 125°38E 279 E4
Saunemin U.S.A. 40°54N 88°24W 311 D8
Saupite Angola 13°54S 17°43E 265 E3
Saurbær Borgarfjarðarsýsla, Iceland 64°24N 21°35W 155 C5
Saurbær Eyjafjarðarsýsla, Iceland 65°27N 18°13W 155 B8
Sauri Nigeria 11°42N 6°44E 263 C6
Saurimo Angola 9°40S 20°12E 265 D4
Sausalito U.S.A. 37°51N 122°29W 136 A2
Sautatá Colombia 7°50N 77°4W 328 B2
Sauteurs Grenada 12°14N 61°38W 323 q
Sauveterre-de-Béarn France 43°24N 0°57W 174 E3
Sauzé-Vaussais France 46°8N 0°8E 174 B4
Savá Honduras 15°32N 86°15W 320 C2
Sava Italy 40°24N 17°33E 201 B10
Sava ➝ Serbia 44°50N 20°26E 182 F5
Savage U.S.A. 47°27N 104°21W 304 C11
Savage I. = Niue Pac. Oc. 19°2S 169°54W 289 g
Savage River Australia 41°31S 145°14E 281 G4
Savai'i Samoa 13°28S 172°24W 287 V19
Savalou Benin 7°57N 1°58E 263 D5
Savane Mozam. 19°37S 35°8E 269 F4
Savaneta Aruba 12°27N 69°56W 322 f
Savanna U.S.A. 42°5N 90°8W 310 B6
Savannah Ga., U.S.A. 32°5N 81°6W 316 C8
Savannah Mo., U.S.A. 39°56N 94°50W 310 E2
Savannah Tenn., U.S.A. 35°14N 88°15W 315 D10
Savannah ➝ U.S.A. 32°2N 80°53W 316 C9
Savannah Beach = Tybee Island U.S.A. 32°1N 80°51W 316 C9
Savannakhet Laos 16°30N 104°49E 236 D5
Savanne, Piton Mauritius 20°26S 57°29E 272 e
Savannes B. St. Lucia 13°45N 60°56W 323 m
Savant L. Canada 50°16N 90°44W 298 B1
Savant Lake Canada 50°14N 90°40W 298 B1
Savantvadi India 15°55N 73°54E 245 G1
Savanur India 14°59N 75°21E 245 G2
Săvârşin Romania 46°1N 22°14E 182 D7
Savaştepe Turkey 39°22N 27°42E 205 B9
Savda India 21°9N 75°56E 244 D2
Savé Benin 8°2N 2°29E 263 D5
Save ➝ Haute-Garonne, France 43°47N 1°17E 174 E5
Save ➝ Mozam. 21°16S 34°0E 271 B5
Sāveh Iran 35°2N 50°20E 247 C6
Savelugu Ghana 9°38N 0°54W 263 D4
Savenay France 47°20N 1°55W 172 E5
Săveni Romania 47°57N 26°52E 183 C11
Saverdun France 43°14N 1°34E 174 E5
Saverne France 48°43N 7°20E 173 D14
Savigliano Italy 44°38N 7°40E 198 D4
Savigny-sur-Braye France 47°53N 0°49E 172 E7
Sávio ➝ Italy 44°19N 12°20E 199 D9
Šavnik Montenegro 42°59N 19°10E 202 D3
Savo Finland 62°45N 27°30E 160 E22
Savo Solomon Is. 9°8S 159°48E 287 M10
Savoie □ France 45°26N 6°25E 175 C10
Savolax = Savo Finland 62°45N 27°30E 160 E22
Savona Italy 44°17N 8°30E 198 D5
Savona N.Y., U.S.A. 42°17N 77°13W 312 D7
Savonet Neth. Ant. 12°21N 69°7W 322 g
Savonlinna Finland 61°52N 28°53E 188 B5
Savoonga U.S.A. 63°42N 170°29W 303 E5
Savoy = Savoie □ France 45°26N 6°25E 175 C10
Şavşat Turkey 41°15N 42°20E 213 B10
Sävsjö Sweden 57°20N 14°40E 163 G8
Savur Turkey 37°34N 40°53E 246 B4
Savusavu Fiji 16°34S 179°15E 287 A2
Savusavu B. Fiji 16°45S 179°15E 287 A2
Sawah Besar Indonesia 6°8S 106°49E 122 A1
Sawahlunto Indonesia 0°40S 100°52E 234 C2
Sawai Indonesia 3°0S 129°5E 231 E7
Sawai Madhopur India 26°0N 76°25E 242 G7
Sawaleke Fiji 17°59S 179°18E 287 A2
Sawang Daen Din Thailand 17°28N 103°28E 236 D4
Sawankhalok Thailand 17°19N 99°50E 236 D2
Sawara Japan 35°55N 140°30E 223 B12
Sawatch Range U.S.A. 39°0N 106°30W 304 G10
Sawdā', Jabal as Libya 28°51N 15°12E 258 C3
Sawel Mt. U.K. 54°50N 7°2W 166 B4
Sawfajjin □ Libya 31°0N 15°0E 258 B3
Sawfajjin, W. ➝ Libya 31°41N 14°44E 258 B2
Sawi Thailand 10°14N 99°5E 237 G2
Sawla Ghana 9°17N 2°25W 262 D4
Sawmills Zimbabwe 19°30S 28°2E 269 F2
Şawqirah Oman 18°7N 56°32E 249 C7
Şawqirah, Ghubbat Oman 18°35N 57°0E 249 C7
Sawtell Australia 30°19S 153°6E 283 A10
Sawtooth ⌂ U.S.A. 44°0N 114°50W 304 D6
Sawtooth Range U.S.A. 44°3N 114°58W 304 D6
Sawu Indonesia 10°35S 121°50E 231 F6
Sawu Sea Indonesia 9°30S 121°50E 231 F6
Saxby ➝ Australia 18°25S 140°53E 280 B3
Saxmundham U.K. 52°13N 1°30E 169 E9
Saxony = Sachsen □ Germany 50°55N 13°10E 178 E9
Saxony, Lower = Niedersachsen □ Germany 52°50N 9°0E 178 C4
Saxton U.S.A. 40°13N 78°15W 312 F6
Say Mali 13°50N 4°57W 262 C4
Say Niger 13°8N 2°22E 263 C5
Saya Nigeria 9°30N 3°18E 263 D5
Sayabec Canada 48°35N 67°41W 299 C6
Sayaboury Laos 19°15N 101°45E 236 C3
Sayán Peru 11°8S 77°12W 330 C2
Sayan, Vostochnyy Russia 54°0N 96°0E 215 D10
Sayan, Zapadnyy Russia 52°30N 94°0E 217 B12
Saydā Lebanon 33°35N 35°25E 250 E6
Sayghān Afghan. 35°10N 67°55E 240 B2
Sayhandulaan = Oldziyt Mongolia 44°40N 109°1E 226 B5
Sayḩūt Yemen 15°12N 51°10E 249 D5
Saykhin Kazakhstan 48°50N 46°47E 191 F8
Saylac = Zeila Somali Rep. 11°21N 43°30E 267 B5
Saylorville L. U.S.A. 41°48N 93°46W 310 C3
Saynshand = Buyant-Uhaa Mongolia 44°55N 110°11E 219 B6
Sayō Japan 34°59N 134°22E 222 C6
Sayre Okla., U.S.A. 35°18N 99°38W 314 D5
Sayre Pa., U.S.A. 41°59N 76°32W 313 E8
Sayreville U.S.A. 40°28N 74°22W 313 F10
Sayula Mexico 19°52N 103°36W 318 D4
Sayward Canada 50°21N 125°55W 296 C3
Saywūn Yemen 15°56N 48°47E 249 D5
Saza Japan 33°14N 129°39E 222 D1
Sazanit Albania 40°30N 19°20E 202 F3
Sázava ➝ Czech Rep. 49°53N 14°24E 180 B7
Sazin Pakistan 35°35N 73°30E 243 B5
Sazlika ➝ Bulgaria 41°59N 25°50E 203 E9
Sbeïtla Tunisia 35°12N 9°7E 258 A1
Scaër France 48°2N 3°42W 172 D3
Scafell Pike U.K. 54°27N 3°14W 168 C4
Scald Law U.K. 55°50N 3°17W 121 B2
Scalea Italy 39°49N 15°47E 201 C8
Scalloway U.K. 60°9N 1°17W 167 A7
Scalpay U.K. 57°18N 6°0W 167 D3
Scammon Bay U.S.A. 61°51N 165°35W 303 F6
Scandia Canada 50°20N 112°2W 296 C6
Scandiano Italy 44°36N 10°43E 198 D7
Scandicci Italy 43°45N 11°11E 199 E8
Scandinavia Europe 64°0N 12°0E 160 E15
Scansano Italy 42°41N 11°20E 199 F8
Scapa Flow U.K. 58°53N 3°3W 167 C5
Scappoose U.S.A. 45°45N 122°53W 306 E4
Scarámia, Capo Italy 36°47N 14°29E 201 F7
Scarba U.K. 56°11N 5°43W 167 E3
Scarborough Ont., Canada 43°44N 79°14W 141 A3
Scarborough Trin. & Tob. 11°11N 60°42W 323 s
Scarborough N. Yorks., U.K. 54°17N 0°24W 168 C7
Scarborough Bluffs Canada 43°42N 79°14W 141 A3
Scarborough Shoal S. China Sea 15°0N 117°50E 232 D1
Scargill N.Z. 42°56S 172°58E 285 C7
Scariff I. Ireland 51°44N 10°15W 166 E1
Scarp U.K. 58°1N 7°8W 167 C1
Scarpanto = Karpathos Greece 35°37N 27°10E 205 F9
Scarpe-Escaut ⌂ France 50°26N 3°23E 173 B10
Scarsdale Australia 37°41S 143°39E 282 D5
Sceaux France 48°46N 2°17E 134 B2
Scebeli ➝ Ethiopia 7°32N 45°43E 267 C6
Scebeli, Wabi ➝ Somali Rep. 2°0N 44°0E 267 D5
Šćedro Croatia 43°6N 16°43E 199 E13
Scenery, Mt. Neth. Ant. 17°38N 63°14W 322 a
Schaal See Germany 53°36N 10°55E 178 B6
Schaalsee ⌂ Germany 53°40N 10°59E 178 B6
Schaerbeek Belgium 50°52N 4°22E 116 A2
Schaffhausen Switz. 47°42N 8°39E 179 H4
Schagen Neths. 52°49N 4°48E 170 B4
Schaghticoke U.S.A. 42°54N 73°35W 313 D11
Schärding Austria 48°27N 13°27E 180 C6
Scharfenberg Germany 52°35N 13°15E 115 A2
Scharfenwiese = Ostrołęka Poland 53°4N 21°32E 185 E8
Scharhörn Germany 53°57N 8°24E 178 B4
Schässburg = Sighişoara Romania 46°12N 24°50E 183 D9
Scheepvartmuseum Amsterdam, Neths. 112 b3
Scheessel Germany 53°10N 9°29E 178 B5
Schefferville = Kawawachikamach Canada 54°48N 66°50W 299 B6
Scheibbs Austria 48°1N 15°9E 180 C8
Scheidt = Schelde ➝ Belgium 51°15N 4°16E 170 C4
Schelde ➝ Belgium 51°15N 4°16E 170 C4
Schell City U.S.A. 38°1N 94°7W 310 F2
Schell Creek Ra. U.S.A. 39°25N 114°40W 304 G6
Schellsburg U.S.A. 40°3N 78°39W 312 F6
Schemnitz = Banská Štiavnica Slovak Rep. 48°25N 18°55E 181 C11
Schenectady U.S.A. 42°49N 73°57W 313 D11
Schenevus U.S.A. 42°33N 74°50W 313 D10
Scherfede Germany 51°32N 9°2E 178 D5
Schesslitz Germany 49°58N 11°1E 179 F7
Schiedam Neths. 51°55N 4°25E 170 C4
Schieratz = Sieradz Poland 51°37N 18°41E 185 G5
Schiermonnikoog Neths. 53°30N 6°15E 170 A6
Schiller Park U.S.A. 41°56N 87°52W 119 B1
Schiller Woods U.S.A. 41°57N 87°51W 119 B1
Schiltigheim France 48°35N 7°45E 173 D14
Schinousa Greece 36°53N 25°31E 205 E7
Schio Italy 45°43N 11°21E 199 C8
Schiphol, Amsterdam ✕ (AMS) Neths. 52°18N 4°45E 112 B1
Schippenbeil = Sępopol Poland 54°16N 21°2E 184 D8
Schivelbein = Świdwin Poland 53°47N 15°49E 184 E2
Schlachtensee Germany 52°26N 13°13E 115 B2
Schladming Austria 47°23N 13°41E 180 D6
Schlanders = Silandro Italy 46°38N 10°46E 198 B7
Schlawa = Sława Poland 51°52N 16°2E 185 G3
Schlei ➝ Germany 54°40N 10°0E 178 A5
Schleiden Germany 50°31N 6°28E 178 E2
Schleinitz Ra. Papua N. G. 3°0S 151°30E 286 B6
Schleiz Germany 50°35N 11°49E 178 E7
Schlesiersee = Sława Poland 51°52N 16°2E 185 G3
Schleswig Germany 54°31N 9°34E 178 A5
Schleswig-Holstein □ Germany 54°30N 9°30E 178 A5
Schlettstadt = Sélestat France 48°16N 7°26E 173 D14
Schlichtingsheim = Szlichtyngowa Poland 51°42N 16°15E 185 G3
Schlochau = Człuchów Poland 53°41N 17°22E 184 E4
Schloppe = Człopa Poland 53°6N 16°6E 185 E3
Schlossgarten Germany 52°31N 13°18E 115 A2
Schlüchtern Germany 50°20N 9°32E 179 E5
Schmalkalden Germany 50°44N 10°26E 178 E6
Schmargendorf Germany 52°28N 13°17E 115 B2
Schmölln Germany 50°54N 12°19E 178 E8
Schneeberg Austria 47°47N 15°48E 180 D8
Schneeberg Sachsen, Germany 50°35N 12°38E 178 E8
Schneidemühl = Piła Poland 53°10N 16°48E 185 E3
Schneider U.S.A. 41°13N 87°28W 311 C9
Schneverdingen Germany 53°7N 9°48E 178 B5
Schœlcher Martinique 14°36N 61°7W 322 j
Schofield Barracks U.S.A. 21°29N 158°7W 302 K13

Schoharie *U.S.A.* 42°40N 74°19W **313** D10
Schoharie Cr. ➔ *U.S.A.* 42°57N 74°18W **313** D10
Scholls *U.S.A.* 45°24N 122°56W **306** E4
Schönau = Swierzawa *Poland* 51°1N 15°54E **185** G2
Schönberg *Mecklenburg-Vorpommern, Germany* 53°52N 10°56E **178** B6
Schönberg *Schleswig-Holstein, Germany* 54°23N 10°21E **178** A6
Schönblick *Germany* 52°27N 13°43E **115** B5
Schönbrunn *Austria* 48°10N 16°19E **142** A1
Schönbuch ⌂ *Germany* 48°35N 9°2E **179** G5
Schönebeck *Germany* 52°2N 11°44E **178** C7
Schöneberg *Germany* 52°28N 13°20E **115** B3
Schönefeld *Germany* 52°22N 13°33E **115** B4
Schöneiche *Germany* 52°28N 13°41E **115** B5
Schongau *Germany* 47°47N 10°53E **179** H6
Schöningen *Germany* 52°8N 10°56E **178** C6
Schönlanke = Trzcianka *Poland* 53°3N 16°25E **185** E3
Schönstein = Šoštanj *Slovenia* 46°23N 15°4E **199** B12
Schönwalde *Germany* 52°37N 13°7E **115** A1
Schoolcraft *U.S.A.* 42°7N 85°38W **311** B11
Schopfheim *Germany* 47°38N 7°50E **179** H3
Schorndorf *Germany* 48°47N 9°32E **179** G5
Schortens *Germany* 53°31N 7°56E **178** B3
Schotschekloof *Cape Town, S. Africa* **118** b1
Schottegat *Neth. Ant.* 12°7N 68°55W **322** g
Schouten I. *Australia* 42°20S 148°20E **281** G4
Schouten Is. = Supiori *Indonesia* 1°0S 136°0E **231** E9
Schouten Is. *Papua N. G.* 3°30S 144°30E **286** B3
Schouwen *Neths.* 51°43N 3°45E **170** C3
Schramberg *Germany* 48°13N 8°22E **179** G4
Schrankogel *Austria* 47°3N 11°7E **180** D4
Schreiber *Canada* 48°45N 87°20W **298** C2
Schrems *Austria* 48°47N 15°4E **180** C8
Schrobenhausen *Germany* 48°34N 11°16E **179** G7
Schroffenstein *Namibia* 27°11S 18°42E **270** C2
Schroon Lake *U.S.A.* 43°50N 73°46W **313** C11
Schröttersberg = Płock *Poland* 52°32N 19°40E **185** F6
Schruns *Austria* 47°5N 9°56E **180** D2
Schuchye = Shchūchīnsk *Kazakhstan* 52°56N 70°12E **217** B8
Schuler *Canada* 50°20N 110°6W **297** C6
Schulzendorf *Germany* 52°36N 13°16E **115** A2
Schumacher *Canada* 48°30N 81°16W **298** C3
Schurz *U.S.A.* 38°57N 118°49W **304** G4
Schuyler *U.S.A.* 41°27N 97°4W **308** E5
Schuylerville *U.S.A.* 43°6N 73°35W **313** C11
Schuylkill ➔ *U.S.A.* 39°53N 75°12W **313** G9
Schuylkill Haven *U.S.A.* 40°37N 76°11W **313** F8
Schwabach *Germany* 49°19N 11°2E **179** F7
Schwaben □ *Germany* 48°15N 10°30E **179** G6
Schwabing *Germany* 48°10N 11°35E **131** B2
Schwäbisch-Fränkischer Wald ⌂ *Germany* 49°0N 9°30E **179** G5
Schwäbisch Gmünd *Germany* 48°48N 9°47E **179** G5
Schwäbisch Hall *Germany* 49°6N 9°44E **179** F5
Schwäbische Alb *Germany* 48°20N 9°30E **179** G5
Schwabmünchen *Germany* 48°10N 10°46E **179** G6
Schwalmstadt *Germany* 50°55N 9°10E **178** E5
Schwandorf *Germany* 49°20N 12°7E **179** F8
Schwanebeck *Germany* 52°37N 13°32E **115** A4
Schwanenwerder *Germany* 52°26N 13°10E **115** B2
Schwaner, Pegunungan *Indonesia* 1°0S 112°30E **235** C4
Schwanewede *Germany* 53°14N 8°35E **178** B4
Schwarmstedt *Germany* 52°39N 9°38E **178** C5
Schwarze Elster ➔ *Germany* 51°48N 12°50E **178** D8
Schwarzenberg *Germany* 50°32N 12°47E **178** E8
Schwarzlackenau *Austria* 48°16N 16°23E **142** A2
Schwarzrand *Namibia* 25°37S 16°50E **270** C2
Schwarzwald *Germany* 48°30N 8°20E **179** G4
Schwatka Mts. *U.S.A.* 67°20N 156°30W **303** C8
Schwaz *Austria* 47°20N 11°44E **180** D4
Schwechat *Austria* 48°8N 16°28E **142** B2
Schwechat, Wien ✕ (VIE) *Austria* 48°7N 16°35E **142** B3
Schwedt *Germany* 53°3N 14°16E **178** B10
Schweidnitz = Świdnica *Poland* 50°50N 16°30E **185** H3
Schweinfurt *Germany* 50°3N 10°14E **179** E6
Schweiz = Switzerland ■ *Europe* 46°30N 8°0E **179** J4
Schweizer-Reneke *S. Africa* 27°11S 25°18E **270** C4
Schwenningen = Villingen-Schwenningen *Germany* 48°3N 8°26E **179** G4
Schwerin = Skwierzyna *Poland* 52°33N 15°30E **185** F2
Schwerin *Germany* 53°36N 11°22E **178** B7
Schweriner See *Germany* 53°43N 11°28E **178** B7
Schwetzingen *Germany* 49°23N 8°35E **179** F4
Schwiebus = Świebodzin *Poland* 52°15N 15°31E **185** F2
Schwyz *Switz.* 47°2N 8°39E **179** H4
Schwyz □ *Switz.* 47°2N 8°39E **179** H4
Sciacca *Italy* 37°31N 13°3E **200** E6
Sciao *Somali Rep.* 3°26N 45°21E **267** D6
Scicli *Italy* 36°47N 14°42E **201** F7
Science and Industry, Museum of *U.S.A.* 41°47N 87°34W **119** C3
Sciliar ⌂ *Italy* 46°28N 11°35E **199** B8
Scilla *Italy* 38°15N 15°43E **201** D8
Scilly, Isles of *U.K.* 49°56N 6°22W **169** H1
Ścinawa *Poland* 51°25N 16°26E **185** G3
Scione *Greece* 39°57N 23°36E **202** G7
Scioto ➔ *U.S.A.* 38°44N 83°1W **311** D13
Scitrek Museum *U.S.A.* 33°46N 84°22W **113** B2
Scituate *U.S.A.* 42°12N 70°44W **313** D14
Scobey *U.S.A.* 48°47N 105°25W **304** B11
Scone *N.S.W., Australia* 32°5S 150°52E **283** B9
Scone *Perth & Kinr., U.K.* 56°25N 3°24W **167** E5
Scopus, Mt. *West Bank* 31°48N 35°14E **123** B2
Scordia *Italy* 37°18N 14°51E **201** E7
Scoresby Sund *Greenland* 70°28N 21°46W **154** C8
Scoresbysund = Ittoqqortoormiit *Greenland* 70°20N 23°0W **154** C8
Scornicești *Romania* 44°34N 24°33E **183** F9
Scotia *Calif., U.S.A.* 40°29N 124°6W **304** F1
Scotia *N.Y., U.S.A.* 42°50N 73°58W **313** D11
Scotia Sea *Antarctica* 56°5S 56°0W **151** B18
Scotland *Canada* 43°1N 80°22W **312** C4
Scotland □ *U.K.* 57°0N 4°0W **167** E5
Scott *Antarctica* 77°0S 165°0E **151** D11
Scott, C. *Australia* 13°30S 129°49E **278** B4
Scott Circle *Washington, D.C., U.S.A.* **143** a1
Scott City *U.S.A.* 38°29N 100°54W **308** F3
Scott Glacier *Antarctica* 66°15S 100°5E **151** C8
Scott I. *Antarctica* 67°0S 179°0E **151** C11
Scott Is. *Canada* 50°48N 128°40W **296** C3
Scott L. *Canada* 59°55N 106°18W **297** B7
Scott Monument *Edinburgh, U.K.* **121** b2
Scott Reef *Australia* 14°0S 121°50E **278** B3
Scottburgh *S. Africa* 30°15S 30°47E **271** D5
Scottdale *Georgia, U.S.A.* 33°47N 84°16W **113** B3
Scottdale *Pa., U.S.A.* 40°6N 79°35W **312** F5
Scottish Borders □ *U.K.* 55°35N 2°50W **167** F6
Scotts Head *N.S.W., Australia* 30°45S 153°0E **283** A10
Scotts Head *Dominica* 15°13N 61°23W **323** k
Scotts Head Village *Dominica* 15°12N 61°22W **323** k
Scotts Valley *U.S.A.* 37°3N 122°1W **306** H4
Scottsbluff *U.S.A.* 41°52N 103°40W **308** E2
Scottsboro *U.S.A.* 34°40N 86°2W **315** D11
Scottsburg *U.S.A.* 38°41N 85°47W **311** F11
Scottsdale *Tas., Australia* 41°9S 147°31E **281** G4
Scottsdale *Ariz., U.S.A.* 33°40N 111°53W **305** K8
Scottsville *Ky., U.S.A.* 36°45N 86°11W **308** G10
Scottsville *N.Y., U.S.A.* 43°2N 77°47W **312** C7
Scottville *U.S.A.* 43°58N 86°17W **308** D10
Scranton *U.S.A.* 41°25N 75°40W **313** E9
Screven *U.S.A.* 31°29N 82°1W **316** D7
Scrub I. *Anguilla* 18°19N 62°55W **322** a
Scugog, L. *Canada* 44°10N 78°55W **312** B6
Sculeni *Moldova* 47°20N 27°37E **183** C12
Scunthorpe *U.K.* 53°36N 0°39W **168** D7
Scuol Schuls *Switz.* 46°48N 10°17E **179** J6
Scusciuban *Somali Rep.* 10°18N 50°12E **267** B7
Scutari = Shkodër *Albania* 42°4N 19°32E **202** D3
Scutari = Üsküdar *Turkey* 41°1N 29°0E **122** B2
Sea Is. *U.S.A.* 31°30N 81°7W **315** F14
Sea Lake *Australia* 35°28S 142°55E **282** C5
Sea Point *S. Africa* 34°5S 18°23E **118** A1
Seabra = Tarauacá *Brazil* 8°6S 70°48W **330** B3
Seabra *Brazil* 12°25S 41°46W **333** D3
Seabrook *U.S.A.* 38°58N 76°49W **143** B5
Seabrook, L. *Australia* 30°55S 119°40E **279** F2
Seacliff *U.S.A.* 37°47N 122°28W **136** B2
Seaford *E. Sussex, U.K.* 50°47N 0°7E **169** G8
Seaford *Del., U.S.A.* 38°39N 75°37W **309** F16
Seaforth *N.S.W., Australia* 33°48S 151°15E **139** A2
Seaforth *Queens., Australia* 20°55S 148°57E **280** J6
Seaforth *Ont., Canada* 43°35N 81°25W **312** C3
Seaforth, L. *U.K.* 57°52N 6°36W **167** D2
Seagate *U.S.A.* 40°34N 74°0W **132** C1
Seagraves *U.S.A.* 32°57N 102°34W **314** E3
Seaham *U.K.* 54°50N 1°20W **168** C6
Seal ➔ *Canada* 59°4N 94°48W **297** B10
Seal I. *Anguilla* 18°16N 63°9W **322** a
Seal L. *Canada* 54°20N 61°30W **299** B7
Seale *U.S.A.* 32°18N 85°10W **316** C4
Sealy *U.S.A.* 29°47N 96°9W **314** G6
Seaman *U.S.A.* 38°57N 83°34W **311** F13
Searchlight *U.S.A.* 35°28N 114°55W **307** K12
Searcy *U.S.A.* 35°15N 91°44W **314** D9
Searles L. *U.S.A.* 35°44N 117°21W **307** K9
Sears Tower *Chicago, U.S.A.* **119** c1
Seascale *U.K.* 54°24N 3°29W **168** C4
Seaside *Calif., U.S.A.* 36°37N 121°50W **306** J5
Seaside *Oreg., U.S.A.* 46°0N 123°56W **306** E3
Seaspray *Australia* 38°25S 147°15E **283** E7
Seat Pleasant *U.S.A.* 38°53N 76°53W **143** B4
Seattle *U.S.A.* 47°36N 122°19W **306** C4
Seattle-Tacoma Int. ✕ (SEA) *U.S.A.* 47°27N 122°18W **306** C4
Seaview *N.Z.* 41°15S 174°54E **143** B2
Seaview Ra. *Australia* 18°40S 145°45E **280** B4
Seaward Kaikoura Ra. *N.Z.* 42°10S 173°44E **285** C8
Sebago L. *U.S.A.* 43°52N 70°34W **313** C14
Sebago Lake *U.S.A.* 43°51N 70°34W **313** C14
Sebangka *Indonesia* 0°7N 104°36E **234** B2
Sebastian *U.S.A.* 27°49N 80°28W **317** H9
Sebastián Vizcaíno, B. *Mexico* 28°0N 114°30W **318** B2
Sebastopol = Sevastopol *Ukraine* 44°35N 33°30E **189** K7
Sebastopol *U.S.A.* 38°24N 122°49W **306** G4
Sebba *Burkina Faso* 13°35N 0°32E **263** C5
Sebderat *Eritrea* 15°26N 36°42E **257** D4
Sebdou *Algeria* 34°38N 1°19W **261** B4
Sébé ➔ *Gabon* 1°2S 13°6E **264** C2
Sébékoro *Mali* 12°58N 9°0W **262** C3
Seben *Turkey* 40°24N 31°34E **212** B4
Šeberov *Czech Rep.* 50°0N 14°30E **135** B3
Sebeș *Romania* 45°58N 23°34E **183** E8
Sebeșului, Munții *Romania* 45°36N 23°40E **183** E8
Sebewaing *U.S.A.* 43°44N 83°27W **309** D12
Sebezh *Russia* 56°14N 28°22E **188** D5
Sebha = Sabhā *Libya* 27°9N 14°29E **258** C2
Sébi *Mali* 15°50N 4°12W **262** B4
Şebinkarahisar *Turkey* 40°22N 38°28E **213** B8
Sebiș *Romania* 46°23N 22°13E **182** D7
Seblat *Indonesia* 3°14S 101°38E **234** C2
Sebnitz *Germany* 50°58N 14°15E **178** E10
Sebou, Oued ➔ *Morocco* 34°16N 6°40W **260** B3
Sebring *Fla., U.S.A.* 27°30N 81°27W **317** H8
Sebring *Ohio, U.S.A.* 40°55N 81°2W **312** F3
Sebringville *Canada* 43°24N 81°4W **312** C3
Sebta = Ceuta *N. Afr.* 35°52N 5°18W **260** A3
Sebuku *Indonesia* 3°30S 116°25E **235** C5
Sebuku, Teluk *Malaysia* 4°0N 118°10E **235** B5
Sečanj *Serbia* 45°25N 20°47E **182** E5
Secaucus *U.S.A.* 40°47N 74°3W **132** B1
Secchia ➔ *Italy* 45°4N 11°0E **198** C8
Sechelt *Canada* 49°25N 123°42W **296** D4
Sechura *Peru* 5°39S 80°50W **330** B1
Sechura, Desierto de *Peru* 6°0S 80°30W **330** B1
Seclin *France* 50°33N 3°2E **173** B10
Second World War Memorial *Washington, D.C., U.S.A.* **143** b1
Secondigny *France* 46°37N 0°26W **172** F6
Sečovce *Slovak Rep.* 48°42N 21°40E **181** C14
Secretary I. *N.Z.* 45°15S 166°56E **285** F1
Secunderabad *India* 17°28N 78°30E **244** F4
Sécure ➔ *Bolivia* 15°10S 64°52W **331** D5
Security *U.S.A.* 38°45N 104°45W **304** G11
Sedalia *U.S.A.* 38°42N 93°14W **310** F3
Sedam *India* 17°11N 77°17E **244** E3
Sedan *S. Austral., Australia* 34°34S 139°19E **282** C3
Sedan *France* 49°43N 4°57E **173** C11
Sedan *Kans., U.S.A.* 37°8N 96°11W **308** G5
Sedano *Spain* 42°43N 3°49W **194** C7
Sedaw *Burma* 22°19N 96°19E **241** D6
Sedbergh *U.K.* 54°20N 2°31W **168** C5
Seddinsee *Germany* 52°23N 13°41E **115** B5
Seddon *N.Z.* 41°40S 174°7E **285** B7
Seddonville *N.Z.* 41°33S 172°1E **285** B7
Sedé Boqér *Israel* 30°52N 34°47E **251** H5
Sedeh *Fārs, Iran* 30°45N 52°11E **247** D7
Sedeh *Khorāsān, Iran* 33°20N 59°14E **247** C8
Séderon *France* 44°12N 5°32E **175** D9
Sederot *Israel* 31°32N 34°37E **251** G5
Sédhiou *Senegal* 12°44N 15°30W **262** C1
Sedico *Italy* 46°8N 12°6E **199** B9
Sedlčany *Czech Rep.* 49°40N 14°25E **180** B7
Sedley *Canada* 50°10N 104°0W **297** C8
Sedom *Israel* 31°5N 35°20E **251** G6
Sedona *U.S.A.* 34°52N 111°46W **305** J8
Sedova, Pik *Russia* 73°29N 54°58E **214** B6
Sedrata *Algeria* 36°7N 7°31E **261** A6
Sedro-Woolley *U.S.A.* 48°30N 122°14W **306** B4
Šeduva *Lithuania* 55°45N 23°45E **184** C10
Sędziszów *Poland* 50°35N 20°4E **185** H7
Sędziszów Małapolski *Poland* 50°5N 21°45E **185** H8
Seebad Ahlbeck *Germany* 53°56N 14°10E **178** B10
Seeberg *Germany* 52°33N 13°41E **115** A5
Seeburg = Jeziorany *Poland* 53°58N 20°46E **184** E7
Seeburg *Germany* 52°30N 13°7E **115** A1
Seefeld *Germany* 52°37N 13°40E **115** A5
Seefeld in Tirol *Austria* 47°19N 11°13E **180** D4
Seegefeld *Germany* 52°33N 13°5E **115** A1
Seehausen *Germany* 52°54N 11°45E **178** C7
Seeheim *Namibia* 26°50S 17°45E **270** C2
Seeheim-Jugenheim *Germany* 49°49N 8°40E **179** F4
Seehof *Germany* 52°24N 13°17E **115** B2
Seeis *Namibia* 22°29S 17°39E **270** B2
Seekoei ➔ *S. Africa* 30°18S 25°1E **270** D4
Seeley's Bay *Canada* 44°29N 76°14W **313** B8
Seelow *Germany* 52°32N 14°23E **178** C10
Sées *France* 48°38N 0°10E **172** D7
Seesen *Germany* 51°54N 10°10E **178** D6
Seevetal *Germany* 53°26N 10°1E **178** B6
Seewinkel = Neusiedler See-Seewinkel △ *Austria* 47°50N 16°45E **181** D9
Sefadu *S. Leone* 8°35N 10°58W **262** D2
Seferihisar *Turkey* 38°10N 26°50E **205** C8
Séfeto *Mali* 14°8N 9°49W **262** C3
Sefrou *Morocco* 33°52N 4°52W **260** B4
Sefrou □ *Morocco* 33°49N 4°49W **260** B4
Sefton *N.Z.* 43°15S 172°41E **285** D7
Sefuri-San *Japan* 33°28N 130°18E **222** D2
Sefwi Bekwai *Ghana* 6°10N 2°25W **262** D4
Seg-ozero *Russia* 63°20N 33°46E **186** B5
Segag *Ethiopia* 7°39N 42°50E **267** C5
Segamat *Malaysia* 2°30N 102°50E **237** L4
Şegarcea *Romania* 44°6N 23°43E **183** F8
Ségbana *Benin* 10°55N 3°42E **263** C5
Segbwema *S. Leone* 8°0N 11°0W **262** D2
Segeltorp *Sweden* 59°16N 17°56E **139** B1
Segesta *Italy* 37°56N 12°50E **200** E5
Seget *Indonesia* 1°24S 130°58E **231** E8
Segewold = Sigulda *Latvia* 57°10N 24°55E **188** D3
Segezha *Russia* 63°44N 34°19E **186** B5
Seggueur, O. ➔ *Algeria* 32°14N 1°48E **261** B5
Seghe *Solomon Is.* 8°32S 157°54E **287** M9
Segonzac *France* 45°36N 0°14W **174** C3
Segorbe *Spain* 39°50N 0°30W **196** F4
Ségou *Mali* 13°30N 6°16W **262** C3
Ségou □ *Mali* 14°0N 6°0W **262** C3
Segovia = Coco ➔ *Cent. Amer.* 15°0N 83°8W **320** D3
Segovia *Colombia* 7°7N 74°42W **328** B3
Segovia *Spain* 40°57N 4°10W **194** E6
Segovia □ *Spain* 40°55N 4°10W **194** E6
Segrate *Italy* 45°29N 9°17E **129** B2
Segré *France* 47°40N 0°52W **172** E6
Segre ➔ *Spain* 41°40N 0°43E **196** D5
Seguam I. *U.S.A.* 52°19N 172°30W **303** K4
Seguam Pass *U.S.A.* 52°0N 172°30W **303** K4
Séguédine *Niger* 20°9N 12°55E **259** D2
Séguéla *Ivory C.* 7°55N 6°40W **262** D3
Séguénéga *Burkina Faso* 13°25N 1°58W **263** C4
Seguin *U.S.A.* 29°34N 97°58W **314** G6
Segundo ➔ *Argentina* 30°53S 62°44W **334** C3
Segura ➔ *Spain* 38°3N 0°44W **197** G4
Segura, Sierra de *Spain* 38°5N 2°45W **197** G2
Seguro *Italy* 45°28N 9°3E **129** B1
Seh Konj, Kūh-e *Iran* 30°6N 57°30E **247** D8
Seh Qal'eh *Iran* 33°40N 58°24E **247** C8
Sehitwa *Botswana* 20°30S 22°30E **270** B3
Sehlabathebe △ *Lesotho* 29°53S 29°7E **271** C4
Sehore *India* 23°10N 77°5E **242** H7
Sehulea *Papua N. G.* 9°58S 151°10E **286** E6
Sehwan *Pakistan* 26°28N 67°53E **242** F2
Şeica Mare *Romania* 46°1N 24°7E **183** D9
Seikan Tunnel *Japan* 41°28N 140°10E **220** D10
Seikpyu *Burma* 20°54N 94°48E **241** E5
Seil *U.K.* 56°18N 5°38W **167** E3
Seiland *Norway* 70°25N 23°15E **160** A20
Seilhac *France* 45°22N 1°43E **174** C5
Seiling *U.S.A.* 36°9N 98°56W **314** C5
Seille ➔ *Moselle, France* 49°7N 6°11E **173** C13
Seille ➔ *Saône-et-Loire, France* 46°31N 4°57E **173** F11
Sein, Î. de *France* 48°2N 4°52W **172** D2
Seinäjoki *Finland* 62°40N 22°51E **160** E20
Seine ➔ *France* 49°26N 0°26E **172** C7
Seine-et-Marne □ *France* 48°45N 3°0E **173** D10
Seine-Inférieure = Seine-Maritime □ *France* 49°40N 1°0E **172** C7
Seine-Maritime □ *France* 49°40N 1°0E **172** C7
Seine-St-Denis □ *France* 48°58N 2°24E **173** D9
Seini *Romania* 47°44N 23°21E **183** C8
Seirijai *Lithuania* 54°14N 23°49E **184** D10
Seis de Septiembre = Moron *Argentina* 34°39S 58°37W **334** C4
Seistan = Sīstān *Asia* 30°50N 61°0E **247** D9
Seistan, Daryācheh-ye = Sīstān, Daryācheh-ye *Iran* 31°0N 61°0E **247** D9
Seitler = Nyzhnohirskyy *Ukraine* 45°27N 34°38E **189** K8
Seixal *Portugal* 38°38N 9°5W **126** B2
Sejerø *Denmark* 55°54N 11°9E **163** J5
Sejerø Bugt *Denmark* 55°53N 11°15E **163** J5
Sejny *Poland* 54°6N 23°21E **184** D10
Seka *Ethiopia* 8°10N 36°52E **257** F4
Sekayu *Indonesia* 2°51S 103°51E **234** C2
Seke *Tanzania* 3°20S 33°31E **268** C3
Seke-Banza *Dem. Rep. of the Congo* 5°20S 13°16E **265** D2
Sekenke *Tanzania* 4°18S 34°11E **268** C3
Sekhira *Tunisia* 34°20N 10°5E **258** B2
Seki *Japan* 35°29N 136°55E **223** B8
Seki *Turkey* 36°48N 29°33E **205** E11
Sekigahara *Japan* 35°22N 136°28E **223** B8
Sekondi-Takoradi *Ghana* 4°58N 1°45W **262** E4
Sekota *Ethiopia* 12°40N 39°2E **257** E4
Sekseūil *Kazakhstan* 47°5N 61°9E **216** C6
Seksna *Russia* 59°13N 38°30E **188** C10
Sekudai *Malaysia* 1°32N 103°39E **237** d
Sekuma *Botswana* 24°36S 23°50E **270** B3
Selah *U.S.A.* 46°39N 120°32W **304** C3
Selama *Malaysia* 5°12N 100°42E **237** K3
Selangor □ *Malaysia* 3°10N 101°30E **234** B2
Selárgius *Italy* 39°16N 9°10E **200** C2
Selaru *Indonesia* 8°9S 131°0E **231** F8
Selatan, Selat *Malaysia* 5°15N 100°20E **237** c
Selawik *U.S.A.* 66°36N 160°0W **303** C8
Selawik L. *U.S.A.* 66°30N 160°45W **303** C7
Selawik Nat. Wildlife Refuge ⌂ *U.S.A.* 66°35N 159°10W **303** C8
Selb *Germany* 50°10N 12°7E **179** E8
Selbusjøen *Norway* 63°15N 10°50E **164** A7
Selby *Gauteng, S. Africa* 26°12S 28°2E **123** B2
Selby *N. Yorks., U.K.* 53°47N 1°5W **168** D6
Selby *S. Dak., U.S.A.* 45°31N 100°2W **308** C3
Selca *Croatia* 43°20N 16°50E **199** E13
Selçuk *Turkey* 37°56N 27°22E **205** D9
Selden *U.S.A.* 39°33N 100°34W **308** F3
Seldovia *U.S.A.* 59°26N 151°43W **303** G10
Sele ➔ *Italy* 40°29N 14°56E **201** B7
Selebi-Pikwe *Botswana* 21°58S 27°48E **271** B4
Selemdzha ➔ *Russia* 51°42N 128°53E **215** D13
Selendi *Manisa, Turkey* 38°43N 28°50E **205** C10
Selendi *Manisa, Turkey* 38°46N 27°53E **205** C9
Selenga = Selenge Mörön ➔ *Asia* 52°16N 106°16E **218** A5
Selenge *Dem. Rep. of the Congo* 1°58S 18°11E **264** C3
Selenge Mörön ➔ *Asia* 52°16N 106°16E **218** A5
Selenicë *Albania* 40°33N 19°39E **202** F3
Selenter See *Germany* 54°18N 10°26E **178** A6
Sélestat *France* 48°16N 7°26E **173** D14
Seletan, Tanjung *Indonesia* 4°10S 114°40E **235** C4
Seletar, Pulau *Singapore* 1°26N 103°51E **138** A3
Seletar Hills *Singapore* 1°23N 103°52E **138** A3
Seletar Res. *Singapore* 1°24N 103°48E **138** A2
Selevac *Serbia* 44°28N 20°52E **202** B4
Selfoss *Iceland* 63°56N 21°0W **155** D6
Selhurst *U.K.* 51°23N 0°5W **125** B3
Sélibabi *Mauritania* 15°10N 12°15W **262** B2
Seliger, Ozero *Russia* 57°15N 33°0E **188** D7
Seligman *U.S.A.* 35°20N 112°53W **305** J7
Şelim *Turkey* 40°30N 42°46E **213** B10
Selima, El Wâhât el *Sudan* 21°22N 29°19E **256** C2
Selimiye *Turkey* 37°24N 27°40E **205** D9
Selinda Spillway ➔ *Botswana* 18°35S 23°10E **270** A3
Selinsgrove *U.S.A.* 40°48N 76°52W **312** F8
Selizharovo *Russia* 56°51N 33°27E **188** D7
Selje *Norway* 62°3N 5°22E **164** B2
Seljord *Norway* 59°30N 8°40E **164** E5
Selkirk *Man., Canada* 50°10N 96°55W **297** C9
Selkirk *Borders, U.K.* 55°33N 2°50W **167** F6
Selkirk I. = Horse I. *Canada* 53°20N 99°6W **297** C9
Selkirk Mts. *Canada* 51°15N 117°40W **294** D8
Sellafield *U.K.* 54°25N 3°29W **168** C4
Sellama *Sudan* 12°51N 29°46E **257** E2
Sellia *Greece* 35°12N 24°23E **207** E5
Sellières *France* 46°50N 5°32E **173** F12
Sells *U.S.A.* 31°55N 111°53W **305** L8
Sellye *Hungary* 45°52N 17°51E **182** E2
Selma *Ala., U.S.A.* 32°25N 87°1W **315** E11
Selma *Calif., U.S.A.* 36°34N 119°37W **306** J7
Selma *N.C., U.S.A.* 35°32N 78°17W **315** D15
Selmer *U.S.A.* 35°10N 88°36W **315** D10
Selong *Indonesia* 8°39S 116°32E **235** D5
Selongey *France* 47°36N 5°11E **173** E12
Selouane *Morocco* 35°7N 2°57W **261** A4
Selous △ *Tanzania* 8°37S 37°42E **269** D4
Selowandoma Falls *Zimbabwe* 21°15S 31°50E **269** G3
Selpele *Indonesia* 0°1S 130°5E **231** E8
Selsey Bill *U.K.* 50°43N 0°47W **169** G7
Seltso *Russia* 53°22N 34°4E **188** F8
Seltz *France* 48°54N 8°4E **173** D15
Selu *Indonesia* 7°32S 130°55E **231** F8
Sélune ➔ *France* 48°38N 1°22W **172** D5
Selva = La Selva del Camp *Spain* 41°13N 1°8E **196** D6
Selva *Argentina* 29°50S 62°0W **334** B3
Selva Lancandona = Montes Azules △ *Mexico* 16°21N 91°3W **319** D6
Selvagens, Ilhas *Madeira* 30°5N 15°55W **260** B1
Selvas *Brazil* 6°30S 67°0W **330** B4
Selwyn L. *Canada* 60°0N 104°30W **297** B8
Selwyn Mts. *Canada* 63°0N 130°0W **294** C6
Selwyn Passage *Vanuatu* 16°3S 168°12E **287** F6
Selwyn Ra. *Australia* 21°10S 140°0E **280** C3
Selyatyn *Ukraine* 47°50N 25°12E **183** C10
Sem *Norway* 59°14N 10°17E **164** E7
Sem Kolodezey = Lenino *Ukraine* 45°17N 35°46E **189** K8
Semadrek = Samothraki *Greece* 40°28N 25°28E **203** F9
Seman ➔ *Albania* 40°47N 19°30E **202** F3
Semarang *Indonesia* 7°0S 110°26E **235** D4
Sematan *Malaysia* 1°48N 109°46E **235** B3
Sembabule *Uganda* 0°4S 31°25E **268** C3
Sembawang *Singapore* 1°27N 103°50E **138** A2
Sembé *Congo* 1°39N 14°36E **264** B2
Sembung *Indonesia* 8°28S 115°11E **231** J18
Şemdinli *Turkey* 37°18N 44°35E **213** D11
Sémé *Senegal* 15°4N 13°41W **262** B2
Semeih *Sudan* 12°43N 30°53E **257** E3
Semenanjung Blambangan *Indonesia* 8°42S 114°29E **231** K17
Semendua *Dem. Rep. of the Congo* 3°10S 18°6E **264** C3
Semenov *Russia* 56°43N 44°30E **190** B7
Semenovka *Chernihiv, Ukraine* 52°8N 32°36E **189** F7
Semenovka *Kremenchuk, Ukraine* 49°37N 33°10E **189** H7
Semeru *Indonesia* 8°4S 112°55E **235** D4
Semey *Kazakhstan* 50°30N 80°10E **217** B10
Semichi Is. *U.S.A.* 52°42N 174°0E **303** K1
Semikarakorskiy *Russia* 47°31N 40°48E **191** G5
Semiluki *Russia* 51°41N 39°2E **189** G10
Seminoe Res. *U.S.A.* 42°9N 106°55W **304** E10
Seminole *Fla., U.S.A.* 27°50N 82°47W **317** H7
Seminole *Okla., U.S.A.* 35°14N 96°41W **314** D6
Seminole *Tex., U.S.A.* 32°43N 102°39W **314** E3
Seminole, L. *U.S.A.* 30°43N 84°52W **316** E5
Seminole Draw ➔ *U.S.A.* 32°27N 102°20W **314** E3
Semipalatinsk = Semey *Kazakhstan* 50°30N 80°10E **217** B10
Semirara I. *Phil.* 12°4N 121°23E **232** E3
Semirara Is. *Phil.* 12°0N 121°20E **233** F3
Semisopochnoi I. *U.S.A.* 51°55N 179°36E **303** L2
Semitau *Indonesia* 0°29N 111°57E **235** B4
Semiyarka *Kazakhstan* 50°55N 78°23E **214** D8
Semiyarskoye = Semiyarka *Kazakhstan* 50°55N 78°23E **214** D8
Semlin = Zemun *Serbia* 44°51N 20°25E **202** B4
Semmelweis Museum *Budapest, Hungary* **117** c2
Semmering P. *Austria* 47°41N 15°45E **180** D8
Semnān *Iran* 35°40N 53°23E **247** C7
Semnān □ *Iran* 36°0N 54°0E **247** C7
Sempang Mengayou, Tanjong *Malaysia* 7°0N 116°40E **235** A5
Semporna *Malaysia* 4°30N 118°33E **235** B5
Semuda *Indonesia* 2°51S 112°58E **235** C4
Semur-en-Auxois *France* 47°30N 4°20E **173** E11
Semyonovka = Arsenev *Russia* 44°10N 133°15E **220** B6
Semyonovskoye = Bereznik *Russia* 62°51N 42°40E **186** B7
Sen ➔ *Cambodia* 12°32N 104°28E **236** F5
Sena *Bolivia* 11°32S 67°11W **330** C4
Senā *Iran* 28°27N 51°36E **247** D6
Sena *Mozam.* 17°25S 35°0E **269** F4
Sena ➔ *Bolivia* 11°32S 67°11W **330** C4
Sena Madureira *Brazil* 9°5S 68°45W **330** B4
Senachwine L. *U.S.A.* 41°10N 89°18W **310** C7
Senador José Porfírio *Brazil* 2°35S 51°55W **329** D7
Senador Pompeu *Brazil* 5°40S 39°20W **332** C4
Senago *Italy* 45°34N 9°7E **129** A1
Senaja *Malaysia* 6°45N 117°3E **235** A5
Senaki *Georgia* 42°15N 42°7E **191** J6
Senang, Pulau *Singapore* 1°11N 103°52E **237** d
Senanga *Zambia* 16°7S 23°16E **265** F4
Senatobia *U.S.A.* 34°37N 89°58W **315** D10
Sencelles *Spain* 39°39N 2°54E **206** B3
Sendafa *Ethiopia* 9°11N 39°3E **257** F4
Sendai *Kagoshima, Japan* 31°50N 130°20E **222** F2
Sendai *Miyagi, Japan* 38°15N 140°53E **220** E10
Sendai-Wan *Japan* 38°15N 141°0E **220** E10
Senden *Bayern, Germany* 48°19N 10°4E **179** G6
Senden *Nordrhein-Westfalen, Germany* 51°52N 7°22E **178** D3
Sendhwa *India* 21°41N 75°6E **242** J6
Sendling *Germany* 48°7N 11°31E **131** B2
Sendlinger Tor Platz *Munich, Germany* **131** c1
Sendurjana *India* 21°32N 78°17E **244** D4
Sene ➔ *Ghana* 7°30N 0°33W **263** D4
Senec *Slovak Rep.* 48°12N 17°23E **181** C10
Seneca *Ill., U.S.A.* 41°19N 88°37W **310** C8
Seneca *S.C., U.S.A.* 34°41N 82°57W **315** D13
Seneca Falls *U.S.A.* 42°55N 76°48W **313** D8
Seneca L. *U.S.A.* 42°40N 76°54W **312** D8
Senecaville L. *U.S.A.* 39°55N 81°25W **312** G3
Senegal ■ *W. Afr.* 14°30N 14°30W **262** C2
Sénégal ➔ *W. Afr.* 15°48N 16°32W **262** B1
Senegambia *Africa* 12°45N 12°0W **254** E2
Senegambia & Niger = Mali ■ *Africa* 17°0N 3°0W **262** B4
Senekal *S. Africa* 28°20S 27°36E **271** C4
Senftenberg *Germany* 51°32N 14°0E **178** D10
Senga Hill *Zambia* 9°19S 31°11E **269** D3
Senge Khambab = Indus ➔ *Pakistan* 24°20N 67°47E **242** G2
Sengiley *Russia* 53°58N 48°46E **190** D9
Sengua ➔ *Zimbabwe* 17°7S 28°5E **269** F2
Senguerr ➔ *Argentina* 45°35S 68°50W **336** C3
Senhor-do-Bonfim *Brazil* 10°30S 40°10W **332** D3
Senica *Slovak Rep.* 48°41N 17°25E **181** C10
Senigállia *Italy* 43°43N 13°13E **199** E10
Seniku *Burma* 25°32N 97°48E **241** C6
Senio ➔ *Italy* 44°35N 12°15E **199** D9
Senirkent *Turkey* 38°6N 30°33E **205** C12
Senise *Italy* 40°9N 16°17E **201** B9
Senj *Croatia* 45°0N 14°58E **199** D11
Senja *Norway* 69°25N 17°30E **160** B17
Senju *Japan* 35°44N 139°48E **140** A3
Senkaku-Shotō *E. China Sea* 25°45N 123°30E **221** M1
Senkuang *Indonesia* 1°11N 104°2E **237** d
Senlis *France* 49°13N 2°35E **173** C9
Senmonorom *Cambodia* 12°27N 107°12E **236** F6
Sennâr *Sudan* 13°30N 33°35E **257** E3
Sennâr □ *Sudan* 13°0N 34°0E **257** E3
Senneterre *Canada* 48°25N 77°15W **298** C4
Senno *Belarus* 54°45N 29°43E **188** E5
Sènnori *Italy* 40°47N 8°35E **200** B1
Seno *Laos* 16°35N 104°50E **236** D5
Senoia *U.S.A.* 33°18N 84°33W **316** B5
Senonches *France* 48°34N 1°2E **172** D8
Senorbì *Italy* 39°32N 9°8E **200** C2
Senožeče *Slovenia* 45°43N 14°3E **199** C11
Senriyama *Japan* 34°47N 135°30E **133** A2
Sens *France* 48°11N 3°15E **173** D10
Senta *Serbia* 45°55N 20°3E **182** E5
Sentani *Indonesia* 2°36S 140°37E **231** E10
Sentery = Lubao *Dem. Rep. of the Congo* 5°17S 25°42E **265** D5
Sentinel *U.S.A.* 32°52N 113°13W **305** K7
Šentjur *Slovenia* 46°14N 15°24E **199** B12
Sentolo *Indonesia* 7°55S 110°13E **235** D4
Sentosa *Singapore* 1°16N 103°50E **138** B2
Sentry Hill *St.-Maarten* 18°2N 63°4W **322** a
Senwabarana *S. Africa* 23°17S 29°7E **271** B4
Senya Beraku *Ghana* 5°28N 0°31W **263** D4
Seo de Urgel = La Seu d'Urgell *Spain* 42°22N 1°23E **196** C6
Seobinggo *S. Korea* 37°31N 126°58E **137** B1
Seocho *S. Korea* 37°28N 127°0E **137** C1
Seodaemun *S. Korea* 37°34N 126°55E **137** B1
Seogwipo *S. Korea* 33°13N 126°34E **224** a
Seohara *India* 29°15N 78°33E **243** E8
Seokkwan *S. Korea* 37°35N 127°2E **137** B2
Seonath ➔ *India* 21°44N 82°28E **243** J10
Seondha *India* 26°9N 78°48E **243** F8
Seongbuk *S. Korea* 37°35N 127°0E **137** B2
Seongdong *S. Korea* 37°32N 127°3E **137** B2
Seongmodo *S. Korea* 37°41N 126°19E **224** D3
Seongnam *S. Korea* 37°26N 127°8E **224** D3
Seongsu *S. Korea* 37°32N 127°2E **137** B2
Seoni *India* 22°5N 79°30E **243** H8
Seoni Malwa *India* 22°27N 77°28E **242** H8
Seonsan *S. Korea* 36°14N 128°17E **224** D4
Seonyudo *S. Korea* 35°49N 126°24E **224** E3
Seoraksan *S. Korea* 38°7N 128°27E **224** C4
Seoraksan △ *S. Korea* 38°10N 128°25E **224** C4
Seoriarayan *India* 21°45N 82°34E **244** D6
Seosan *S. Korea* 36°47N 126°27E **224** D3
Seoul *S. Korea* 37°31N 126°58E **137** B2
Seoul National University *S. Korea* 37°28N 126°57E **137** C1
Seoul Tower *S. Korea* 37°32N 126°59E **137** B1
Separation Pt. *N.Z.* 40°47S 172°59E **285** A7
Sepatini ➔ *Brazil* 7°36S 65°24W **330** B4
Sepi *Solomon Is.* 8°31S 159°52E **287** M10
Sepīdān *Iran* 30°20N 52°5E **247** D7
Sepik ➔ *Papua N. G.* 3°49S 144°30E **286** B3
Sep'o *N. Korea* 38°57N 127°25E **224** C3
Sepolia *Greece* 38°1N 23°42E **112** A2
Sępólno Krajeńskie *Poland* 53°26N 17°30E **184** E4
Sepone *Laos* 16°45N 106°13E **236** D6
Sępopol *Poland* 54°16N 21°2E **184** D8
Sept-Îles *Canada* 50°13N 66°22W **299** B6
Septemvri *Bulgaria* 42°13N 24°6E **203** D8
Sepúlveda *Spain* 41°18N 3°45W **194** D7
Sepulveda Dam Rec. Area ⌂ *U.S.A.* 34°10N 118°28W **126** A2
Sequeros *Spain* 40°31N 6°2W **194** E4
Sequim *U.S.A.* 48°5N 123°6W **306** B3
Sequoia △ *U.S.A.* 36°30N 118°30W **306** J8
Serafimovich *Russia* 49°36N 42°43E **190** F6
Seraing *Belgium* 50°35N 5°32E **170** D5
Serakhis ➔ *Cyprus* 35°13N 32°55E **207** E8
Seram *Indonesia* 3°10S 129°0E **231** E7
Seram Sea *Indonesia* 2°30S 128°30E **231** E7
Seranantsara *Madag.* 18°30S 49°5E **273** B8
Serang *Indonesia* 6°8S 106°10E **234** D3
Serangoon *Singapore* 1°23N 103°54E **138** A3
Serangoon, Pulau *Singapore* 1°23N 103°55E **138** A3
Serangoon, Sungei ➔ *Singapore* 1°23N 103°55E **138** A3
Serangoon Harbour *Singapore* 1°23N 103°57E **138** A3
Serasan *Indonesia* 2°29N 109°4E **235** B3
Seravezza *Italy* 43°59N 10°13E **198** E7
Seraya, Pulau *Singapore* 1°16N 103°43E **138** B2
Serbāl, G. *Egypt* 28°40N 33°39E **251** K4
Şerbettar *Turkey* 41°27N 26°46E **203** E10
Serbia □ *Serbia* 43°30N 21°0E **202** C5
Serbia ■ *Europe* 43°20N 20°0E **202** C4
Şercaia *Romania* 45°49N 25°9E **183** E10
Serdar *Turkmenistan* 39°4N 56°23E **247** B8
Serdo *Ethiopia* 11°56N 41°14E **257** E5
Serdobol = Sortavala *Russia* 61°42N 30°41E **188** B6
Serdobsk *Russia* 52°28N 44°10E **190** D7
Serebryanka *Russia* 55°44N 37°53E **129** B5
Serebryanka ➔ *Russia* 55°47N 37°44E **129** B4
Serebryansk *Kazakhstan* 49°41N 83°17E **217** C10
Sered' *Slovak Rep.* 48°17N 17°44E **181** C10
Sereda = Furmanov *Russia* 57°10N 41°9E **190** B5
Seredka *Russia* 58°12N 28°10E **188** C5
Serednye *Ukraine* 48°32N 22°30E **182** B7
Şereflikoçhisar *Turkey* 38°56N 33°32E **212** C5
Seregno *Italy* 45°39N 9°12E **198** C6
Seremban *Malaysia* 2°43N 101°53E **237** L3
Serengeti △ *Tanzania* 2°11S 35°0E **268** C3
Serengeti Plain *Tanzania* 2°40S 35°0E **268** C4
Serenje *Zambia* 13°14S 30°15E **269** E3
Serenli *Somali Rep.* 2°22N 42°17E **267** D5
Seret ➔ *Ukraine* 48°37N 25°52E **183** B10
Sereth = Siret ➔ *Romania* 45°24N 28°1E **183** E12
Sergach *Russia* 55°30N 45°30E **190** C7
Sergen *Turkey* 41°41N 27°42E **203** E11
Sergino *Russia* 62°25N 65°12E **214** C7
Sergiopol = Ayaköz *Kazakhstan* 48°10N 80°10E **217** C10
Sergipe □ *Brazil* 10°30S 37°30W **332** D4
Sergiyev Posad *Russia* 56°20N 38°10E **188** D10
Sergo = Stakhanov *Ukraine* 48°35N 38°40E **189** H10
Serhetabat *Turkmenistan* 35°20N 62°18E **247** C9
Seria *Brunei* 4°37N 114°23E **235** B4
Serian *Malaysia* 1°10N 110°31E **235** B4
Seriate *Italy* 45°41N 9°43E **198** C6
Seribu, Kepulauan *Indonesia* 5°36S 106°33E **234** D3
Seribu △ *Indonesia* 5°32S 106°33E **234** D3
Sericho *Kenya* 1°5N 39°5E **268** B4
Sérifontaine *France* 49°20N 1°45E **173** C8
Serifos *Greece* 37°9N 24°30E **204** D6
Sérignan *France* 43°17N 3°17E **174** E7
Sérigny ➔ *Canada* 56°47N 66°0W **299** A6
Serik *Turkey* 36°55N 31°7E **250** B2
Seringapatam Reef *Australia* 13°38S 122°5E **278** B3
Serinhisar *Turkey* 37°36N 29°18E **205** D11
Seririt *Indonesia* 8°12S 114°56E **231** J17
Sermaize-les-Bains *France* 48°47N 4°54E **173** D11
Sermata *Indonesia* 8°15S 128°50E **231** F7
Sermersuaq *Greenland* 79°30N 62°0W **154** B4
Sérmide *Italy* 45°0N 11°18E **199** D8
Sernovodsk *Russia* 53°54N 51°16E **190** D10
Sernur *Russia* 56°52N 49°12E **190** B9
Serock *Poland* 52°31N 21°4E **185** F8
Seroe Colorado *Aruba* 12°25N 69°52W **322** f
Serón *Spain* 37°20N 2°29W **197** H2
Serós *Spain* 41°27N 0°24E **196** D5
Serouenout *Algeria* 24°18N 7°25E **261** D6
Serov *Russia* 59°29N 60°35E **186** C11
Serowe *Botswana* 22°25S 26°43E **270** B4
Serpa *Portugal* 37°57N 7°38W **195** H3
Serpeddì, Punta *Italy* 39°22N 9°18E **200** C2
Serpentara *Italy* 39°8N 9°36E **200** C2
Serpentine Lakes *Australia* 28°30S 129°10E **279** E4
Serpent's Mouth = Sierpe, Bocas de la *Venezuela* 10°0N 61°30W **329** G9
Serpis ➔ *Spain* 38°59N 0°9W **197** G4
Serpneve *Ukraine* 46°18N 29°1E **183** D14
Serpukhov *Russia* 54°55N 37°28E **188** E9
Serra da Bocaina △ *Brazil* 23°0S 44°40W **333** F3
Serra da Canastra △ *Brazil* 20°3S 46°50W **333** F2
Serra da Capivara △ *Brazil* 8°42S 42°15W **332** C3
Serra da Estrela ⌂ *Portugal* 40°27N 7°33W **194** E3
Serra das Confusões △ *Brazil* 8°50S 43°50W **332** C3
Serra de Mesa, Barragem de *Brazil* 14°30S 49°10W **333** D2
Serra de Outes *Spain* 42°52N 8°55W **194** C2
Serra do Cipó △ *Brazil* 19°14S 43°33W **333** E3
Serra do Navio *Brazil* 0°59N 52°3W **329** C7
Serra do Salitre *Brazil* 19°6S 46°41W **333** E2
Serra dos Orgãos △ *Brazil* 22°25S 43°8W **333** F3
Serra San Bruno *Italy* 38°35N 16°20E **201** D9
Serra Talhada *Brazil* 7°59S 38°18W **332** C4
Serradilla *Spain* 39°50N 6°9W **194** F4
Serramanna *Italy* 39°25N 8°55E **200** C1
Serramonte *U.S.A.* 37°39N 122°28W **136** C2
Serranía de la Neblina △ *Venezuela* 1°5N 65°51W **328** C4
Serranía San Luís △ *Paraguay* 22°35S 57°22W **334** A4
Serranilla Bank *W. Indies* 15°50N 80°0W **320** C4
Serranópolis *Brazil* 18°16S 52°0W **331** D7
Serras d'Aire e Candeeiros ⌂ *Portugal* 39°31N 8°48W **195** F2
Serrat, C. *Tunisia* 37°14N 9°10E **258** A1
Serravalle Scrivia *Italy* 44°43N 8°51E **198** D5
Serre-Ponçon, L. de *France* 44°22N 6°20E **175** D10
Serres *Hautes-Alpes, France* 44°26N 5°43E **175** D9
Serres *Greece* 41°5N 23°31E **202** E7
Serres □ *Greece* 41°5N 23°37E **202** E7
Serrezuela *Argentina* 30°40S 65°20W **334** C2
Serrinha *Brazil* 11°39S 39°0W **333** D4
Serrita *Brazil* 7°56S 39°19W **332** C4
Sersale *Italy* 39°1N 16°43E **201** C9
Sertã *Portugal* 39°48N 8°6W **194** F2
Sertânia *Brazil* 8°5S 37°20W **332** C4
Sertanópolis *Brazil* 23°4S 51°2W **335** A5
Sêrtar *China* 32°20N 100°41E **228** A3
Serua *Indonesia* 6°18S 130°1E **231** F8
Serui *Indonesia* 1°53S 136°10E **231** E9
Serule *Botswana* 21°57S 27°20E **270** B4
Servia *Greece* 40°11N 22°0E **202** F6
Serzedelo *Portugal* 41°24N 8°14W **194** D2
Ses Salines *Spain* 39°21N 3°3E **206** B4
Sesayap ➔ *Indonesia* 3°36N 117°15E **235** B5
Sese Is. *Uganda* 0°20S 32°20E **268** C3
Seseko-shima *Japan* 26°39N 127°52E **288** a
Sesepe *Indonesia* 1°30S 127°59E **231** E7
Sesfontein *Namibia* 19°7S 13°39E **270** A1
Sesheke *Zambia* 17°29S 24°13E **270** A3
Sésia ➔ *Italy* 45°5N 8°37E **198** C5
Sesimbra *Portugal* 38°28N 9°6W **195** G1
S'Espalmador *Spain* 38°47N 1°26E **206** D1
S'Espardell *Spain* 38°48N 1°29E **206** D1
Sessa *Angola* 13°56S 20°38E **265** E4
Sessa Aurunca *Italy* 41°14N 13°56E **200** A6
Sesser *U.S.A.* 38°5N 89°1W **310** F7
S'Estanyol *Spain* 39°22N 2°54E **206** B3
Sestao *Spain* 43°18N 3°0W **196** B2
Sesto Calende *Italy* 45°44N 8°37E **198** C5
Sesto San Giovanni *Italy* 45°31N 9°13E **129** A2
Sestri Levante *Italy* 44°16N 9°24E **198** D6
Sestriere *Italy* 44°57N 6°53E **198** D3
Sestroretsk *Russia* 60°5N 29°58E **188** B6

Sestrunj Croatia 44°10N 15°0E 199 D11
Sestu Italy 39°18N 9°5E 200 C2
Setagaya Japan 35°37N 139°36E 140 B2
Setaka Japan 33°9N 130°28E 222 D2
Setana Japan 42°26N 139°51E 220 C9
Sète France 43°25N 3°42E 174 E7
Sete Cidades △ Brazil 4°0S 41°37W 332 B3
Sete Lagôas Brazil 19°27S 44°16W 333 E3
Seter Norway 59°52N 10°47E 133 A3
Setesdalsheiene = Suldalsheiene Norway 59°28N 7°10E 164 E3
Setia Budi Indonesia 6°12S 106°49E 122 B1
Sétif Algeria 36°9N 5°26E 261 A6
Sétif □ Algeria 36°10N 5°0E 261 A6
Seto Japan 35°14N 137°6E 223 B9
Setonaikai Japan 34°20N 133°30E 222 C5
Setonaikai △ Japan 34°15N 133°15E 222 C5
Setsan Burma 16°3N 95°23E 241 G5
Settat Morocco 33°0N 7°40W 260 B3
Settat □ Morocco 33°5N 7°25W 260 B3
Setté-Cama Gabon 2°32S 9°45E 264 C1
Settebagni Italy 42°0N 12°31E 136 A2
Settecamini Italy 41°57N 12°38E 136 B2
Séttimo Milanese Italy 45°28N 9°3E 129 B1
Séttimo Torinese Italy 45°9N 7°46E 198 C4
Setting L. Canada 55°0N 98°38W 297 C9
Settle U.K. 54°5N 2°16W 168 C5
Settlement Wake I. 19°18N 166°38E 302 b
Settlement, The Br. Virgin Is. 18°43N 64°22W 321 b
Settlers S. Africa 25°2S 28°30E 271 C4
Settsu Japan 34°47N 135°33E 133 A2
Setúbal Portugal 38°30N 8°58W 195 G2
Setúbal □ Portugal 38°25N 8°35W 195 G2
Setúbal, B. de Portugal 38°40N 8°56W 195 G2
Setuny → Russia 55°43N 37°21E 129 B2
Seugne → France 45°42N 0°32W 174 C3
Seul, Lac Canada 50°20N 92°30W 298 B1
Seulimeum Indonesia 5°27N 95°15E 234 A1
Seurre France 47°0N 5°8E 173 F12
Seutula Finland 60°20N 24°52E 121 A2
Sevan Armenia 40°33N 44°56E 191 K7
Sevan, Ozero = Sevana Lich Armenia 40°30N 45°20E 191 K7
Sevana Lich Armenia 40°30N 45°20E 191 K7
Sevastopol Ukraine 44°35N 33°30E 189 K7
Seven Corners U.S.A. 38°53N 77°9W 143 B3
Seven Islands = Sept-Îles Canada 50°13N 66°22W 299 B6
Seven Kings U.K. 51°33N 0°5E 125 A4
Seven Sisters Canada 54°56N 128°10W 296 C3
Seventeenth Street Canal U.S.A. 30°3N 90°7W 131 A2
Sever → Spain 39°40N 7°32W 195 F3
Sévérac-le-Château France 44°20N 3°5E 174 D7
Severn → Ont., Canada 56°2N 87°36W 298 A2
Severn → U.K. 51°35N 2°40W 169 F5
Severn L. Canada 53°54N 90°48W 298 B1
Severnaya Zemlya Russia 79°0N 100°0E 215 B11
Severnyye Uvaly Russia 60°0N 50°0E 186 C8
Severo-Kurilsk Russia 50°40N 156°8E 215 D16
Severo-Yeniseyskiy Russia 60°22N 93°1E 215 C10
Severo-Zapadnyy □ Russia 65°0N 40°0E 214 C4
Severočeský □ Czech Rep. 50°30N 14°0E 180 A7
Severodonetsk = Syeverodonetsk Ukraine 48°58N 38°35E 189 H10
Severodvinsk Russia 64°27N 39°58E 186 B6
Severomoravský □ Czech Rep. 49°38N 17°40E 181 B10
Severomorsk Russia 69°5N 33°27E 160 B25
Severouralsk Russia 60°9N 59°57E 186 B10
Sévesco → Italy 45°35N 9°9E 129 A1
Sevier → U.S.A. 39°4N 113°6W 304 G7
Sevier Desert U.S.A. 39°40N 112°45W 304 G7
Sevier L. U.S.A. 38°54N 113°9W 304 G7
Sevilla Colombia 4°16N 75°57W 328 C2
Sevilla Spain 37°23N 5°58W 195 H5
Sevilla □ Spain 37°25N 5°30W 195 H5
Seville = Sevilla Spain 37°23N 5°58W 195 H5
Seville Fla., U.S.A. 29°19N 81°30W 317 F8
Seville Ga., U.S.A. 31°58N 83°36W 316 D6
Sevlievo Bulgaria 43°2N 25°6E 203 C9
Sevnica Slovenia 46°2N 15°19E 199 B12
Sevran France 48°56N 2°31E 134 A4
Sèvre-Nantaise → France 47°12N 1°33W 172 E5
Sèvre-Niortaise → France 46°28N 0°50W 174 B3
Sevsk Russia 52°10N 34°30E 189 F8
Sewa → S. Leone 7°20N 12°10W 262 D2
Sewani India 28°58N 75°39E 242 E6
Seward Alaska, U.S.A. 60°7N 149°27W 303 F10
Seward Nebr., U.S.A. 40°55N 97°6W 308 E5
Seward Pa., U.S.A. 40°25N 79°1W 312 F5
Seward Peninsula U.S.A. 65°30N 166°0W 303 D6
Sewell Chile 34°10S 70°23W 334 C1
Sewer Indonesia 5°53S 134°40E 237 F8
Sewickley U.S.A. 40°32N 80°12W 312 F4
Sewri India 18°59N 72°50E 130 B2
Sexsmith Canada 55°21N 118°47W 296 B5
Seychelles ■ Ind. Oc. 5°0S 56°0E 272 c
Seyðisfjörður Iceland 65°16N 13°57W 155 B13
Seydişehir Turkey 37°25N 31°51E 212 D4
Seydvān Iran 38°34N 45°2E 213 C11
Seyhan → Turkey 36°43N 34°53E 250 B5
Seyhan Barajı Turkey 37°2N 35°18E 212 D6
Seyitgazi Turkey 39°27N 30°43E 205 B12
Seyitömer Turkey 39°34N 29°52E 205 B11
Seym → Ukraine 51°27N 32°34E 189 G7
Seymen Turkey 41°6N 27°57E 203 E11
Seymour Vic., Australia 37°2S 145°10E 283 D6
Seymour Eastern Cape, S. Africa 32°33S 26°46E 271 D4
Seymour Conn., U.S.A. 41°24N 73°4W 313 E11
Seymour Ind., U.S.A. 38°58N 85°53W 311 F11
Seymour Tex., U.S.A. 33°35N 99°16W 314 E5
Seyne France 44°21N 6°22E 175 D10
Seyssel France 45°57N 5°50E 175 C9
Sežana Slovenia 45°43N 13°41E 199 C10
Sézanne France 48°40N 3°40E 173 D10
Sezze Italy 41°30N 13°3E 200 A6
Sfântu Gheorghe Covasna, Romania 45°52N 25°48E 183 E10
Sfântu Gheorghe Tulcea, Romania 44°53N 29°36E 183 F14
Sfântu Gheorghe, Braţul → Romania 44°51N 29°36E 183 F14
Sfax Tunisia 34°49N 10°48E 258 B2
Sfax □ Tunisia 34°40N 10°20E 261 B7
Sforzesso, Castello Italy 45°28N 9°10E 129 B2
Sha Kok Mei China 22°23N 114°16E 122 A2
Sha Tau Kok China 22°33N 114°13E 219 F11
Sha Tin China 22°23N 114°12E 122 A2
Sha Tin Wai China 22°22N 114°11E 122 A2
Sha Xi → China 26°35N 118°0E 229 D12
Sha Xian China 26°23N 117°45E 229 D11
Shaanxi □ China 35°0N 109°0E 226 G5
Sha'ar Binyamin West Bank 31°52N 35°16E 123 A2
Shaba = Katanga □ Dem. Rep. of the Congo 8°0S 25°0E 268 D2
Shaba △ Kenya 0°38N 37°48E 268 B4
Shaballe = Scebeli, Wabi → Somali Rep. 2°0N 44°0E 267 D5
Shabla Bulgaria 43°31N 28°32E 203 C12
Shabogamo L. Canada 53°15N 66°30W 299 B6
Shabrâmant Egypt 29°56N 31°11E 117 B2
Shabunda Dem. Rep. of the Congo 2°40S 27°16E 268 C2
Shabwah Yemen 15°22N 47°1E 248 D4
Shache China 38°20N 77°10E 217 E9
Shackleton Fracture Zone S. Ocean 60°0S 60°0W 151 B18
Shackleton Ice Shelf Antarctica 66°0S 100°0E 151 C8
Shackleton Inlet Antarctica 83°0S 160°0E 151 E11
Shādegān Iran 30°40N 48°38E 247 D6
Shadi Jiangxi, China 26°7N 114°47E 229 D10
Shadi Jammu & Kashmir, India 33°24N 77°14E 243 C7
Shadrinsk Russia 56°5N 63°32E 214 D7
Shady Dale U.S.A. 33°24N 83°36W 316 B6
Shady Grove U.S.A. 30°17N 83°38W 316 E6
Shadyside U.S.A. 39°58N 80°45W 312 G4
Shafer, L. U.S.A. 40°46N 86°46W 311 D10
Shaffa Nigeria 10°30N 12°6E 263 C7
Shafter U.S.A. 35°30N 119°16W 307 K7
Shaftesbury U.K. 51°0N 2°11W 169 F5
Shag Pt. N.Z. 45°29S 170°52E 285 F5
Shag Rocks Atl. Oc. 53°0S 41°0W 152 M7
Shagamu Nigeria 6°51N 3°39E 263 D5
Shageluk U.S.A. 62°41N 159°34W 303 E8
Shagram Pakistan 36°24N 72°20E 243 A5
Shah Alam Malaysia 3°5N 101°30E 234 B2
Shah Alizai Pakistan 29°25N 66°33E 242 E2
Shah Bunder Pakistan 24°13N 67°56E 242 G2
Shāh Jūy Afghan. 32°31N 67°25E 240 B2
Shah Mosque Iran 35°41N 51°25E 141 A2
Shahabad Andhra Pradesh, India 17°10N 78°7E 244 F4
Shahabad Karnataka, India 17°10N 76°54E 244 F3
Shahabad Punjab, India 30°10N 76°55E 242 D7
Shahabad Raj., India 25°15N 77°11E 242 G7
Shahabad Ut. P., India 27°36N 79°56E 243 F8
Shahada India 21°33N 74°30E 244 D2
Shahadpur Pakistan 25°55N 68°35E 242 G3
Shahapur India 15°50N 74°34E 245 G2
Shahbā' Syria 32°52N 36°38E 250 F7
Shahbazpur I. Bangla. 22°30N 90°45E 241 D3
Shahdād Iran 30°30N 57°40E 247 D8
Shahdād, Namakzār-e Iran 30°20N 58°20E 247 D8
Shahdadkot Pakistan 27°50N 67°55E 242 F2
Shahdara India 28°40N 77°18E 120 A2
Shahdol India 23°19N 81°26E 243 H9
Shahe Guangdong, China 23°9N 113°19E 121 B2
Shahe Hebei, China 37°0N 114°32E 226 F8
Shahganj India 26°3N 82°44E 243 F10
Shahgarh India 27°15N 69°50E 242 F3
Shaḥḥāt Libya 32°48N 21°54E 258 B4
Shāhīdān Afghan. 36°42N 67°49E 240 A2
Shahjahanpur India 27°54N 79°57E 243 F8
Shahpur Karnataka, India 16°40N 76°48E 244 F3
Shahpur Mad. P., India 22°12N 77°58E 242 H7
Shahpur Baluchistan, Pakistan 28°46N 68°27E 242 E3
Shahpur Punjab, Pakistan 32°17N 72°26E 242 C5
Shahpur Chakar Pakistan 26°9N 68°39E 242 F3
Shahpura Mad. P., India 23°10N 80°45E 243 H9
Shahpura Raj., India 25°38N 74°56E 242 G6
Shahr-e Bābak Iran 30°7N 55°9E 247 D7
Shahr-e Kord Iran 32°15N 50°55E 247 C6
Shahr-e Rey Iran 35°36N 51°25E 141 B2
Shahrak-e Golshahr Iran 35°37N 51°18E 141 B1
Shahrak-e Qods Iran 35°47N 51°22E 141 A2
Shahrakht Iran 33°38N 60°16E 247 C9
Shahrig Pakistan 30°15N 67°40E 242 D2
Shahrisabz Uzbekistan 39°3N 66°50E 217 E7
Shahukou China 40°20N 112°18E 226 D7
Shaikh Aomar Iraq 33°20N 44°23E 113 A2
Shaikhabad Afghan. 34°2N 68°45E 242 B3
Shajapur India 23°27N 76°21E 242 H7
Shajing China 22°44N 113°48E 219 F10
Shajuwan Taiwan 23°13N 121°23E 225 C3
Shakargarh Pakistan 32°17N 75°10E 242 C6
Shakawe Botswana 18°28S 21°49E 270 A3
Shakenge Dem. Rep. of the Congo 6°14S 18°41E 265 D3
Shaker Heights U.S.A. 41°28N 81°32W 312 E3
Shakhtīnsk Kazakhstan 49°42N 72°35E 217 C8
Shakhty Russia 47°40N 40°16E 191 G5
Shakhtyorskoye = Pershotravensk Ukraine 50°13N 27°40E 177 C14
Shakhunya Russia 57°40N 46°46E 190 B8
Shaki Nigeria 8°41N 3°21E 263 D5
Shākir Egypt 27°30N 33°59E 256 B3
Shaksam Valley Asia 36°0N 76°20E 243 A7
Shaktoolik U.S.A. 64°20N 161°9W 303 D7
Shakurbasti India 28°41N 77°6E 120 A1
Shala, L. Ethiopia 7°30N 38°30E 257 F4
Shali Russia 43°9N 45°55E 191 J7
Shalkiya India 22°36N 88°21E 124 B2
Shallow Lake Canada 44°36N 81°5W 312 B3
Shalqar Kazakhstan 47°48N 59°39E 216 C5
Shalskiy Russia 61°48N 35°58E 188 B8
Shalu Taiwan 24°14N 120°34E 225 B2
Shaluli Shan China 30°40N 99°55E 228 B2
Shām Iran 26°39N 57°21E 247 E8
Shām, Bādiyat ash Asia 32°0N 40°0E 246 C3
Shām, J. ash Oman 23°10N 57°5E 249 B7
Sham Shui Po China 22°19N 114°9E 122 B1
Shamâl Bahr el Ghazal □ Sudan 8°0N 27°30E 257 F2
Shamâl Dârfûr □ Sudan 15°0N 25°0E 257 E2
Shamâl Kordofân □ Sudan 15°0N 30°0E 257 E3
Shamâl Sînî □ Egypt 30°30N 33°30E 251 H4
Shamapur India 28°44N 77°8E 120 A1
Shamattawa Canada 55°51N 92°5W 298 A1
Shamattawa → Canada 55°1N 85°23W 298 A2
Shambe Sudan 7°8N 30°46E 257 F3
Shambe △ Sudan 6°57N 30°50E 257 F3
Shambu Ethiopia 9°32N 37°3E 257 F4
Shamgong Dzong Bhutan 27°13N 90°35E 241 B3
Shamian China 23°6N 113°13E 121 B2
Shamīl Iran 27°30N 56°55E 247 E8
Shamkhor = Şämkir Azerbaijan 40°50N 46°0E 191 K8
Shāmkūh Iran 35°47N 57°50E 247 C8
Shamli India 29°32N 77°18E 242 E7
Shammar, Jabal Si. Arabia 27°40N 41°0E 246 E4
Shamo = Gobi Asia 44°0N 110°0E 226 C6
Shamo, L. Ethiopia 5°45N 37°30E 257 F4
Shamokin U.S.A. 40°47N 76°34W 313 F8
Shamrock U.S.A. 35°13N 100°15W 314 D4
Shamshabad India 17°15N 78°25E 244 F4
Shamva Zimbabwe 17°20S 31°32E 269 F3
Shan □ Burma 21°30N 98°30E 241 E7
Shan Mei China 22°24N 114°10E 122 A2
Shan Shan China 42°52N 90°10E 217 D12
Shan Xian China 34°50N 116°5E 226 G9
Shana = Kurilsk Russia 45°14N 147°53E 215 E15
Shanan → Ethiopia 8°0N 40°20E 257 F5
Shanchengzhen China 42°20N 125°20E 224 A2
Shāndak Iran 28°28N 60°27E 247 D9
Shandon U.S.A. 35°39N 120°23W 306 K6
Shandong □ China 36°0N 118°0E 227 G10
Shandong Bandao China 37°0N 121°0E 227 F11
Shang Xian = Shangzhou China 33°50N 109°58E 226 H5
Shangalowe Dem. Rep. of the Congo 10°50S 26°30E 269 E2
Shangani Zimbabwe 19°41S 29°20E 271 A4
Shangani → Zimbabwe 18°41S 27°10E 269 F2
Shangbancheng China 40°50N 118°1E 227 D10
Shangcheng China 31°47N 115°26E 229 B10
Shangchuan Dao China 21°40N 112°50E 229 G9
Shangdu China 41°30N 113°30E 226 D7
Shanggao China 28°17N 114°55E 229 C10
Shanghai China 31°15N 121°26E 138 B2
Shanghai Hongqiao ✈ (SHA) China 31°12N 121°20E 138 B1
Shanghai Pudong ✈ (PVG) China 31°9N 121°47E 138 B2
Shanghai Shi □ China 31°0N 121°30E 229 B13
Shanghang China 25°2N 116°23E 229 E11
Shanghe China 37°20N 117°10E 227 F9
Shangjao = Shangrao China 28°25N 117°59E 229 C11
Shanglin China 23°27N 108°33E 228 F7
Shangnan China 33°32N 110°50E 226 H6
Shangqiu China 34°26N 115°36E 226 G8
Shangrao China 28°25N 117°59E 229 C11
Shangshui China 33°42N 114°35E 219 C6
Shangsi China 22°8N 107°58E 228 F6
Shangyou China 25°48N 114°32E 229 E10
Shangyu China 30°3N 120°52E 229 B13
Shangzhi China 45°22N 127°56E 227 B14
Shangzhou China 33°50N 109°58E 226 H5
Shanhetun China 44°33N 127°15E 227 B14
Shanhu Tan Taiwan 23°12N 120°23E 225 C2
Shanhua Taiwan 23°8N 120°17E 225 C2
Shani Nigeria 10°14N 12°2E 263 C7
Shankill Ireland 53°14N 6°7W 120 B3
Shanklin U.K. 50°38N 1°11W 169 G6
Shanlin Taiwan 23°0N 120°32E 225 C2
Shannon Greenland 75°10N 18°30W 154 B9
Shannon N.Z. 40°33S 175°25E 284 G4
Shannon → Ireland 52°35N 9°30W 166 D2
Shannon ✈ (SNN) Ireland 52°42N 8°57W 166 D3
Shannon, Mouth of the Ireland 52°30N 9°55W 166 D2
Shannon △ Australia 34°35S 116°25E 279 F2
Shannonbridge Ireland 53°17N 8°3W 166 C3
Shannontown U.S.A. 33°53N 80°21W 316 B9
Shanshang Taiwan 23°6N 120°21E 225 C2
Shansi = Shanxi □ China 37°0N 112°0E 226 F7
Shantar, Ostrov Bolshoy Russia 55°9N 137°40E 215 D14
Shantipur India 23°17N 88°25E 243 H13
Shantou China 23°18N 116°40E 229 F11
Shantung = Shandong □ China 36°0N 118°0E 227 G10
Shanwei China 22°48N 115°22E 229 F10
Shanxi □ China 37°0N 112°0E 226 F7
Shanyang China 33°31N 109°55E 226 H5
Shanyin China 39°25N 112°56E 226 E7
Shaodong China 27°15N 111°43E 229 D8
Shaoguan China 24°48N 113°35E 229 E9
Shaohing = Shaoxing China 30°0N 120°35E 229 C13
Shaoshan China 27°55N 112°33E 229 D9
Shaowu China 27°22N 117°28E 229 D11
Shaoxing China 30°0N 120°35E 229 C13
Shaoyang Hunan, China 26°59N 111°20E 229 D8
Shaoyang Hunan, China 27°14N 111°25E 229 D8
Shap U.K. 54°32N 2°40W 168 C5
Shapinsay U.K. 59°3N 2°51W 167 B6
Shaqq el Gi'eifer → Sudan 15°16N 26°0E 257 D2
Shaqra' Si. Arabia 25°15N 45°16E 246 E5
Shaqrā' Yemen 13°22N 45°44E 248 D4
Shar Kazakhstan 49°35N 81°2E 217 C10
Sharafa Sudan 11°59N 27°7E 257 E2
Sharafkhāneh Iran 38°11N 45°29E 213 C11
Sharashova Belarus 52°34N 24°12E 185 F11
Sharavati → India 14°20N 74°25E 245 G2
Sharbaqty Kazakhstan 51°23N 78°17E 217 B9
Sharbatāt, Ra's ash Oman 17°56N 56°21E 249 C7
Sharbot Lake Canada 44°46N 76°41W 313 B8
Shardara, Step Kazakhstan 42°20N 68°0E 217 D7
Sharhorod Ukraine 48°45N 28°5E 183 B13
Shari Japan 43°55N 144°40E 220 C12
Sharjah = Ash Shāriqah U.A.E. 25°23N 55°26E 247 E7
Shark B. Australia 25°30S 113°32E 279 E1
Shark Bay △ Australia 25°30S 113°32E 279 E1
Sharm el Sheikh Egypt 27°53N 34°18E 251 L5
Sharon Mass., U.S.A. 42°7N 71°11W 313 D13
Sharon Pa., U.S.A. 41°14N 80°31W 312 E4
Sharon Wis., U.S.A. 42°30N 88°44W 311 B8
Sharon Springs Kans., U.S.A. 38°54N 101°45W 308 F3
Sharon Springs N.Y., U.S.A. 42°48N 74°37W 313 D10
Sharonville U.S.A. 39°16N 84°25W 311 E12
Sharp I. China 22°21N 114°17E 122 A2
Sharp Pk. Phil. 5°58N 125°31E 233 J5
Sharp Pt. Australia 10°58S 142°43E 286 F2
Sharpe L. Canada 54°24N 93°40W 298 B1
Sharpes U.S.A. 28°26N 80°46W 317 G9
Sharpsville U.S.A. 41°15N 80°29W 312 E4
Sharq el Istiwa'iya □ Sudan 5°0N 33°0E 257 G3
Sharqi, Al Jabal ash Lebanon 33°40N 36°10E 250 E7
Sharqîya □ Egypt 30°48N 31°48E 251 H2
Sharya Russia 58°22N 45°20E 190 A7
Shasha Ethiopia 6°29N 35°59E 257 F4
Shashemene Ethiopia 7°13N 38°33E 257 F4
Shashi Botswana 21°15S 27°27E 271 B4
Shashi Hubei, China 30°25N 112°14E 229 B9
Shashi → Africa 21°14S 29°20E 269 G2
Shasta, Mt. U.S.A. 41°25N 122°12W 304 F2
Shasta L. U.S.A. 40°43N 122°25W 304 F2
Shastrinagar India 28°40N 77°10E 120 A2
Shatawi Sudan 14°39N 32°26E 257 E3
Shāṭi', Wādī ash → Libya 27°30N 15°0E 258 C3
Shatilki = Svyetlahorsk Belarus 52°38N 29°46E 177 B15
Shatsk Russia 54°5N 41°45E 190 C5
Shatsk Ukraine 51°29N 23°55E 185 G10
Shatsky Rise Pac. Oc. 34°0N 157°0E 288 D7
Shatskyi △ Ukraine 51°30N 23°52E 185 G10
Shatt al Arab Asia 29°57N 48°34E 247 D6
Shatura Russia 55°33N 39°21E 188 E10
Shaturtorf = Shatura Russia 55°33N 39°21E 188 E10
Shau Kei Wan China 22°16N 114°13E 122 B2
Shaumyani = Shulaveri Georgia 41°22N 44°45E 191 K7
Shaunavon Canada 49°35N 108°25W 297 D7
Shaver L. U.S.A. 37°9N 119°18W 306 H7
Shavli = Šiauliai Lithuania 55°56N 23°15E 184 C10
Shaw → Australia 20°21S 119°17E 278 D2
Shaw I. Australia 20°30S 149°2E 280 J7
Shawanaga Canada 45°31N 80°17W 312 A4
Shawangunk Mts. U.S.A. 41°35N 74°30W 313 E10
Shawano U.S.A. 44°47N 88°36W 308 C9
Shawinigan Canada 46°35N 72°50W 298 C5
Shawmari, J. ash Jordan 30°35N 36°35E 251 H7
Shawnee Ga., U.S.A. 32°29N 81°25W 316 C8
Shawnee Kans., U.S.A. 39°1N 94°43W 310 E2
Shawnee Okla., U.S.A. 35°20N 96°55W 314 D6
Shawocun China 39°53N 116°13E 114 B1
Shay Gap Australia 20°30S 120°10E 278 D3
Shayang China 30°42N 112°29E 229 B9
Shaybārā Si. Arabia 25°26N 36°47E 246 E3
Shayib el Banat, Gebel Egypt 26°59N 33°29E 256 B3
Shaykh, J. ash Lebanon 33°25N 35°50E 250 E6
Shaykh Miskīn Syria 32°49N 36°9E 250 F7
Shaykh Sa'īd Iraq 32°34N 46°17E 213 F12
Shaykh 'Uthmān Yemen 12°52N 44°59E 248 D4
Shaytansky Zavod = Pervouralsk Russia 56°59N 59°59E 186 C10
Shayuan China 23°5N 113°15E 121 B2
Shazud Tajikistan 37°45N 72°25E 217 E8
Shcheglovo = Kemerovo Russia 55°20N 86°5E 214 D9
Shchekino Russia 54°1N 37°34E 188 E9
Shcherbakov = Rybinsk Russia 58°5N 38°50E 188 C10
Shchigry Russia 51°55N 36°58E 189 G9
Shchors Ukraine 51°48N 31°56E 189 G6
Shchūchīnsk Kazakhstan 52°56N 70°12E 217 B8
She Xian Anhui, China 29°50N 118°25E 229 C12
She Xian Hebei, China 36°30N 113°40E 226 F7
Shea Guyana 2°48N 59°4W 329 C6
Shebekino Russia 50°28N 36°54E 189 G9
Shebele = Scebeli, Wabi → Somali Rep. 2°0N 44°0E 267 D5
Shebele Ethiopia 8°8N 42°40E 267 C5
Sheberghān Afghan. 36°40N 65°45E 240 A2
Sheboygan U.S.A. 43°46N 87°45W 308 D10
Shebshi Mts. Nigeria 8°30N 12°0E 263 D7
Shedd Aquarium Chicago, U.S.A. 119 e3
Shediac Canada 46°14N 64°32W 299 C7
Sheelin, L. Ireland 53°48N 7°20W 166 C4
Sheen, L. U.S.A. 28°25N 81°31W 133 B1
Sheenjek → U.S.A. 66°45N 144°33W 303 C11
Sheep Haven Ireland 55°11N 7°52W 166 A4
Sheep Range U.S.A. 36°35N 115°15W 307 J11
Sheepshead Bay U.S.A. 40°35N 73°55W 132 C2
Sheerness U.K. 51°26N 0°47E 169 F8
Sheet Harbour Canada 44°56N 62°31W 299 D7
Sheffield N.Z. 43°23S 172°1E 285 D7
Sheffield S. Yorks., U.K. 53°23N 1°28W 168 D6
Sheffield Ala., U.S.A. 34°46N 87°41W 315 D11
Sheffield Ill., U.S.A. 41°21N 89°44W 310 C7
Sheffield Iowa, U.S.A. 42°54N 93°13W 310 B3
Sheffield Mass., U.S.A. 42°5N 73°21W 313 D11
Sheffield Pa., U.S.A. 41°42N 79°3W 312 E5
Shegaon India 20°48N 76°47E 244 D3
Shehojele Ethiopia 10°40N 35°9E 257 E4
Shehong China 30°54N 105°18E 228 B5
Shehuen → Argentina 49°35S 69°34W 336 C3
Sheikh, W. el → Egypt 28°41N 33°41E 251 K4
Sheikh Idris Sudan 11°43N 33°30E 257 E3
Sheikh Zayed Canal Egypt 23°30N 30°15E 256 C3
Sheikhpura India 25°9N 85°53E 243 G11
Shek Hasan Ethiopia 12°5N 35°58E 257 E4
Shek O China 22°13N 114°15E 122 B2
Shekhupura Pakistan 31°42N 73°58E 242 D5
Sheki = Şaki Azerbaijan 41°10N 47°5E 191 K8
Shekki = Zhongshan China 22°26N 113°20E 219 G9
Shekou China 22°30N 113°55E 219 G10
Shelbina U.S.A. 39°47N 92°2W 310 E4
Shelburn U.S.A. 39°11N 87°24W 311 E9
Shelburne N.S., Canada 43°47N 65°20W 299 D6
Shelburne Ont., Canada 44°4N 80°15W 312 B4
Shelburne Vt., U.S.A. 44°23N 73°14W 313 B11
Shelburne B. Australia 11°50S 142°50E 286 F2
Shelburne Falls U.S.A. 42°36N 72°45W 313 D12
Shelby Mich., U.S.A. 43°37N 86°22W 308 D10
Shelby Mont., U.S.A. 48°30N 111°51W 304 B8
Shelby N.C., U.S.A. 35°17N 81°32W 315 D14
Shelby Ohio, U.S.A. 40°53N 82°40W 312 F2
Shelbyville Ill., U.S.A. 39°24N 88°48W 311 E8
Shelbyville Ind., U.S.A. 39°31N 85°47W 311 E11
Shelbyville Ky., U.S.A. 38°13N 85°14W 311 F11
Shelbyville Mo., U.S.A. 39°48N 92°2W 310 E4
Shelbyville Tenn., U.S.A. 35°29N 86°28W 315 D11
Shelbyville, L. U.S.A. 39°26N 88°46W 311 E8
Sheldon Ill., U.S.A. 40°46N 87°34W 311 D9
Sheldon Iowa, U.S.A. 43°11N 95°51W 308 D6
Sheldon Mo., U.S.A. 37°40N 94°18W 310 G2
Sheldon S.C., U.S.A. 32°36N 80°48W 316 C9
Sheldon Point U.S.A. 62°32N 164°52W 303 E6
Sheldrake Canada 50°20N 64°51W 299 B7
Shelek Kazakhstan 43°33N 78°17E 217 D9
Shelengo, Khawr → Sudan 10°33N 28°40E 257 E2
Shelikhova, Zaliv Russia 59°30N 157°0E 215 D16
Shelikof Strait U.S.A. 57°30N 155°0W 303 H9
Shell Beach = Huntington Beach U.S.A. 33°40N 118°5W 307 M9
Shell Lakes Australia 29°20S 127°30E 279 E4
Shellbrook Canada 53°13N 106°24W 297 C7
Shellharbour Australia 34°31S 150°51E 283 C9
Shellman U.S.A. 31°46N 84°37W 316 D5
Shellsburg U.S.A. 42°6N 91°52W 310 B5
Shelon → Russia 58°13N 30°47E 188 C6
Shelter Bay = Port-Cartier Canada 50°2N 66°50W 299 B6
Shelter I. Hong Kong, China 22°19N 114°17E 122 B2
Shelter I. N.Y., U.S.A. 41°4N 72°20W 313 E12
Shelton Conn., U.S.A. 41°19N 73°5W 313 E11
Shelton Wash., U.S.A. 47°13N 123°6W 306 C3
Shemakha = Şamaxi Azerbaijan 40°38N 48°37E 191 K9
Shemonaīkha Kazakhstan 50°37N 81°54E 217 B10
Shëmri Albania 42°7N 20°13E 202 D4
Shemsi Sudan 19°2N 29°57E 256 D2
Shen Xian China 36°15N 115°40E 226 F8
Shenandoah Iowa, U.S.A. 40°46N 95°22W 308 E6
Shenandoah Pa., U.S.A. 40°49N 76°12W 313 F8
Shenandoah Va., U.S.A. 38°29N 78°37W 309 F14
Shenandoah → U.S.A. 39°19N 77°44W 309 F15
Shenandoah △ U.S.A. 38°35N 78°22W 309 F14
Shenchi China 39°8N 112°10E 226 E7
Shencottah India 8°59N 77°18E 245 K3
Shendam Nigeria 8°49N 9°30E 263 D6
Shendī Sudan 16°46N 33°22E 257 D3
Shendurni India 20°39N 75°36E 244 D2
Shenge S. Leone 7°54N 12°55W 262 D2
Shengfang China 39°3N 116°42E 226 E9
Shëngjergj Albania 41°17N 20°10E 202 E4
Shëngjin Albania 41°50N 19°35E 202 E3
Shengzhou China 29°35N 120°50E 229 C13
Shenjingzi China 44°40N 124°30E 227 B13
Shenkang Taiwan 24°9N 120°39E 225 B2
Shenmu China 38°50N 110°29E 226 E6
Shennongjia China 31°43N 110°44E 229 B8
Shenqiu China 33°25N 115°5E 226 H8
Shensi = Shaanxi □ China 35°0N 109°0E 226 G5
Shenyang China 41°48N 123°27E 224 B1
Shenzhen China 22°32N 114°5E 219 F10
Shenzhen ✈ (SZX) China 22°41N 113°49E 219 F10
Shenzhen Shuiku China 22°34N 114°8E 219 F11
Shenzhen Wan China 22°27N 113°55E 219 G10
Sheo India 26°11N 71°15E 242 F4
Sheopur Kalan India 25°40N 76°40E 242 G7
Shepetivka Ukraine 50°10N 27°10E 177 C14
Shepetovka = Shepetivka Ukraine 50°10N 27°10E 177 C14
Shepherd Is. Vanuatu 16°55S 168°36E 287 F6
Shepherds Bush U.K. 51°30N 0°13W 125 A2
Shepherdsville U.S.A. 37°59N 85°43W 311 G11
Shepparton Australia 36°23S 145°26E 283 D6
Shepperton U.K. 51°23N 0°26W 125 B1
Sheppey, I. of U.K. 51°25N 0°48E 169 F8
Shepton Mallet U.K. 51°11N 2°33W 169 F5
Sheqi China 33°12N 112°57E 226 H7
Sher Khan Qala Afghan. 29°53N 66°13E 240 C2
Sher Qila Pakistan 36°7N 74°2E 243 A6
Sherab Sudan 10°44N 24°41E 257 E1
Sherabad Uzbekistan 37°40N 67°1E 217 E7
Sherborne U.K. 50°57N 2°31W 169 G5
Sherbro → S. Leone 7°45N 12°55W 262 D2
Sherbro I. S. Leone 7°30N 12°40W 262 D2
Sherbrooke N.S., Canada 45°8N 61°59W 299 C7
Sherbrooke Qué., Canada 45°28N 71°57W 313 A13
Sherburne U.S.A. 42°41N 75°30W 313 D9
Sherburne Reef Papua N. G. 3°20S 148°0E 286 B5
Sherda Chad 20°7N 16°46E 259 D3
Shereik Sudan 18°44N 33°47E 256 D3
Shergaon India 27°7N 92°16E 241 B4
Shergarh India 26°20N 72°18E 242 F5
Sherghati India 24°34N 84°47E 243 G11
Sheridan Ark., U.S.A. 34°19N 92°24W 314 D8
Sheridan Ill., U.S.A. 41°32N 88°41W 311 C8
Sheridan Ind., U.S.A. 40°8N 86°13W 311 D10
Sheridan Wyo., U.S.A. 44°48N 106°58W 304 D10
Sheringham U.K. 52°56N 1°13E 168 E9
Sherkin I. Ireland 51°28N 9°26W 166 E2
Sherkot India 29°22N 78°35E 243 E8
Sherman U.S.A. 33°38N 96°36W 314 E6
Sherman Oaks U.S.A. 34°8N 118°29W 126 B2
Sherman Park U.S.A. 41°47N 87°39W 119 C2
Sherpur Bangla. 25°0N 90°0E 241 C3
Sherpur India 25°34N 83°47E 243 G10
Sherridon Canada 55°8N 101°5W 297 B8
Sherriffs St. Kitts & Nevis 17°10N 62°32W 322 d
Sherwood U.S.A. 41°17N 84°33W 311 C12
Sherwood, L. U.S.A. 28°33N 81°29W 133 A2
Sherwood Forest U.K. 53°6N 1°7W 168 D6
Sherwood Park Canada 53°31N 113°19W 296 C6
Sheslay → Canada 58°48N 132°5W 296 B2
Shet Bandar India 18°57N 72°55E 130 B2
Shethanei L. Canada 58°48N 97°50W 297 B9
Shetland □ U.K. 60°30N 1°30W 167 A7
Shetland Is. U.K. 60°30N 1°30W 167 A7
Shetou Taiwan 23°53N 120°35E 225 C2
Shetpe Kazakhstan 44°10N 52°7E 216 D4
Shetrunji → India 21°19N 72°7E 242 J5
Sheung Fa Shan China 22°23N 114°5E 122 A1
Sheung Lau Wan China 22°16N 114°16E 122 B2
Sheung Shui China 22°31N 114°7E 219 F11
Sheung Wan China 22°16N 114°9E 122 B1
Sheva India 18°56N 72°57E 130 B2
Sheva Nhava India 18°57N 72°57E 130 B2
Shevaroy Hills India 11°58N 78°12E 245 J4
Shevchenkovo = Dolynska Ukraine 48°6N 32°46E 189 H7
Shevchenkovo Ukraine 45°33N 29°20E 183 E14
Shevgaon India 19°21N 75°14E 244 E2
Shewa Ethiopia 9°33N 38°10E 257 F4
Shewa Gimira Ethiopia 7°4N 35°51E 257 F4
Shey-Phoksundo △ Nepal 29°30N 82°45E 243 E10
Sheyenne → U.S.A. 47°2N 96°50W 308 B5
Shiba Tokyo, Japan 140 c4
Shibām Yemen 15°59N 48°36E 249 D5
Shibata Japan 37°57N 139°20E 220 F9
Shibecha Japan 43°17N 144°36E 220 C12
Shibetsu Japan 44°10N 142°23E 220 B11
Shibîn el Kôm Egypt 30°31N 30°55E 256 H7
Shibîn el Qanâtir Egypt 30°19N 31°19E 256 H7
Shibing China 27°2N 108°7E 228 D7
Shibogama L. Canada 53°35N 88°15W 298 B2
Shibpur India 22°34N 88°19E 124 B1
Shibukawa Japan 36°29N 139°0E 223 A11
Shibushi Japan 31°25N 131°8E 222 F3
Shibushi-Wan Japan 31°24N 131°8E 222 F3
Shibuya Tokyo, Japan 140 c1
Shicheng China 26°22N 116°20E 229 D11
Shicheng Dao China 39°31N 122°59E 227 E12
Shickshinny U.S.A. 41°9N 76°9W 313 E8
Shickshock Mts. = Chic-Chocs, Mts. Canada 48°55N 66°0W 299 C6
Shidād Si. Arabia 21°19N 40°3E 248 B3
Shidao China 36°50N 122°25E 227 F12
Shiderti → Kazakhstan 52°32N 74°50E 217 B8
Shidian China 24°40N 99°5E 228 E2
Shido Japan 34°19N 134°10E 222 C6
Shiel, L. U.K. 56°48N 5°34W 167 E3
Shield, C. Australia 13°20S 136°20E 280 A2
Shīeli Kazakhstan 44°20N 66°15E 217 D7
Shifang China 31°8N 104°10E 228 B5
Shiga □ Japan 35°20N 136°0E 223 B8
Shigaib Sudan 15°5N 23°35E 259 E4
Shigu China 26°51N 99°56E 228 D2
Shiguaigou China 40°52N 110°15E 226 D6
Shihan, W. → Yemen 17°24N 51°26E 249 C5
Shihchiachuangi = Shijiazhuang China 38°2N 114°28E 226 E8
Shihezi China 44°15N 86°2E 217 D11
Shihiu Taiwan 24°38N 121°10E 225 B3
Shihkangkeng Taiwan 24°18N 120°57E 225 B2
Shihmen Taiwan 25°17N 121°33E 225 A3
Shihmen Shuiku Taiwan 24°49N 121°21E 225 B3
Shihtan Taiwan 24°32N 120°55E 225 B2
Shiiba Japan 32°29N 131°4E 222 E3
Shiikh Somali Rep. 9°56N 45°13E 267 C6
Shijak Albania 41°21N 19°33E 202 E3
Shijiazhuang China 38°2N 114°28E 226 E8
Shijiu Hu China 31°25N 118°50E 229 B12
Shikarpur India 28°17N 78°7E 242 E8
Shikarpur Pakistan 27°57N 68°39E 242 F3
Shikhrany = Kanash Russia 55°30N 47°32E 190 C8
Shikine-Jima Japan 34°19N 139°13E 223 C11
Shikohabad India 27°6N 78°36E 243 F8
Shikoku Japan 33°30N 133°30E 222 D5
Shikoku □ Japan 33°30N 133°30E 222 D5
Shikoku-Sanchi Japan 33°30N 133°30E 222 D5
Shikotsu-Ko Japan 42°45N 141°25E 220 C10
Shikotsu-Tōya △ Japan 44°4N 145°8E 220 C10
Shikuka = Poronaysk Russia 49°13N 143°0E 215 E15
Shilabo Ethiopia 6°5N 44°46E 267 C5
Shiliguri India 26°45N 88°25E 241 B2
Shiliu = Changjiang China 19°20N 108°55E 236 C7
Shilka Russia 52°0N 115°55E 215 D12
Shilka → Russia 53°20N 121°26E 215 D13
Shillelagh Ireland 52°45N 6°32W 166 D5
Shillington U.S.A. 40°18N 75°58W 313 F9
Shillong India 25°35N 91°53E 241 C3
Shilo West Bank 32°4N 35°18E 251 F6
Shilong China 23°5N 113°52E 229 F9
Shilou China 37°0N 110°48E 226 F6
Shilovo Russia 54°25N 40°57E 190 C5
Shima-Hantō Japan 34°22N 136°45E 223 C8
Shimabara Japan 32°48N 130°20E 222 E2
Shimada Japan 34°49N 138°10E 223 C10
Shimane □ Japan 35°0N 132°30E 222 C4
Shimane-Hantō Japan 35°30N 133°0E 222 B5
Shimanovsk Russia 52°15N 127°30E 215 D13
Shimba Hills △ Kenya 4°14S 39°25E 268 C4
Shimen China 29°35N 111°20E 229 C8
Shimenjie China 29°29N 116°48E 229 C11
Shimian China 29°17N 102°23E 228 C4
Shimizu Japan 35°0N 138°30E 223 C10
Shimla India 31°2N 77°9E 242 D7
Shimo-Jima Japan 32°15N 130°7E 222 E2
Shimo-Koshiki-Jima Japan 31°40N 129°43E 222 F1
Shimoda Japan 34°40N 138°57E 223 C10
Shimodate Japan 36°20N 139°55E 223 A11
Shimoga India 13°57N 75°32E 245 H2
Shimogawara Japan 35°39N 139°27E 140 B1
Shimoni Kenya 4°38S 39°20E 268 C4
Shimonita Japan 36°13N 138°47E 223 A10
Shimonoseki Japan 33°58N 130°55E 222 D2
Shimosato Japan 35°45N 139°31E 140 A2
Shimoshakujii Japan 35°43N 139°35E 140 A2
Shimotsuma Japan 36°11N 139°58E 223 A11
Shimpuru Rapids Namibia 17°45S 19°55E 265 F3
Shimsha → India 13°15N 77°10E 245 H3
Shimsk Russia 58°15N 30°50E 188 C6
Shin, L. U.K. 58°5N 4°30W 167 C4
Shin-Nan'yō Japan 34°3N 131°49E 222 C3
Shin-Tone-Gawa → Japan 35°44N 140°51E 223 B12
Shinagawa Japan 35°36N 139°44E 140 B3
Shinan China 22°44N 109°53E 228 F7
Shinano-Gawa → Japan 36°50N 138°30E 221 F9
Shināş Oman 24°46N 56°28E 247 E8
Shīndand Afghan. 33°12N 62°8E 240 B1
Shing Mun Res. China 22°23N 114°8E 122 A1
Shingbwiyang Burma 26°41N 96°13E 241 B6
Shinglehouse U.S.A. 41°58N 78°12W 312 E6
Shingū Japan 33°40N 135°55E 223 D7
Shingwidzi S. Africa 23°5S 31°25E 271 B5
Shinji Japan 35°24N 132°54E 222 B4
Shinji-Ko Japan 35°26N 132°57E 222 B4
Shinjō Japan 38°46N 140°18E 220 E10
Shinjuku Tokyo, Japan 140 a1
Shinjuku National Garden Tokyo, Japan 140 a2
Shinkafe Nigeria 13°8N 6°29E 263 C6
Shinkoiwa Japan 35°43N 139°51E 140 A4
Shinminato Japan 36°47N 137°4E 223 A9
Shinnakano Japan 35°41N 139°40E 140 A3
Shinshār Syria 34°36N 36°43E 250 D7
Shinshiro Japan 34°54N 137°30E 223 C9
Shintuya Peru 12°41S 71°15W 330 C3
Shinyanga Tanzania 3°45S 33°27E 268 C3
Shinyanga □ Tanzania 3°50S 34°0E 268 C3
Shio-no-Misaki Japan 33°25N 135°45E 223 D7
Shiogama Japan 38°19N 141°1E 220 E10
Shiojiri Japan 36°6N 137°58E 223 A9
Shipai China 23°8N 113°20E 121 B3
Shipchenski Prokhod Bulgaria 42°45N 25°15E 203 D9
Shiping China 23°45N 102°23E 228 F4
Shippagan Canada 47°45N 64°45W 299 C7
Shippensburg U.S.A. 40°3N 77°31W 312 F7
Shippenville U.S.A. 41°15N 79°28W 312 E5
Shiprock U.S.A. 36°47N 108°41W 305 H9
Shiqian China 27°32N 108°13E 228 D7
Shiqma, N. → Israel 31°37N 34°30E 251 G5
Shiquan China 33°5N 108°15E 226 H5
Shiquan He = Indus → Pakistan 24°20N 67°47E 242 G2
Shīr Khān Afghan. 37°11N 68°36E 240 A3
Shīr Kūh Iran 31°39N 54°3E 247 D7
Shirabad = Sherabad Uzbekistan 37°40N 67°1E 217 E7
Shiragami-Misaki Japan 41°24N 140°12E 220 D10
Shirahama Japan 33°41N 135°20E 223 D7
Shirakawa Fukushima, Japan 37°7N 140°13E 221 F10
Shirakawa Gifu, Japan 36°17N 136°56E 223 A8
Shirane-San Gumma, Japan 36°48N 139°22E 223 A11
Shirane-San Yamanashi, Japan 35°42N 138°9E 223 B10
Shiraoi Japan 42°33N 141°21E 220 C10
Shirati Tanzania 1°8S 33°59E 266 E3
Shīrāz Iran 29°42N 52°30E 247 D7
Shirbīn Egypt 31°11N 31°32E 256 H7
Shire → Africa 17°42S 35°19E 269 F4
Shiretoko-Misaki Japan 44°21N 145°20E 220 B12
Shirinab → Pakistan 30°15N 66°28E 242 D2
Shirinashi → Japan 34°38N 135°27E 133 B1
Shiriya-Zaki Japan 41°25N 141°30E 220 D10
Shirley U.S.A. 39°53N 85°35W 311 E11
Shirogane Japan 35°37N 139°44E 140 B3
Shiroishi Japan 38°0N 140°37E 220 F10
Shirol India 16°47N 74°41E 244 F2
Shirpur India 21°21N 74°57E 244 D2
Shirshov Ridge Pac. Oc. 58°0N 170°0E 288 B8
Shīrvān Iran 37°30N 57°50E 247 B8
Shirwa, L. = Chilwa, L. Malawi 15°15S 35°40E 269 F4
Shishaldin Volcano U.S.A. 54°45N 163°58W 303 J7
Shishi China 24°44N 118°37E 229 E12
Shishmaref U.S.A. 66°15N 166°4W 303 C6
Shishou China 29°38N 112°22E 229 C9
Shitai China 30°12N 117°25E 229 B11
Shitennoji Temple Japan 34°39N 135°31E 133 B2
Shively U.S.A. 38°12N 85°49W 311 F11
Shivpuri India 25°26N 77°42E 242 G7
Shiweitang China 23°6N 113°12E 121 B2
Shixian China 43°5N 129°50E 227 C15
Shixing China 24°46N 114°5E 229 E10
Shiyan Guangdong, China 22°42N 113°52E 219 F10
Shiyan Hubei, China 32°35N 110°45E 229 A8
Shiyan Shuiku China 22°42N 113°54E 219 F10
Shiyata Egypt 29°25N 25°7E 256 B2
Shizhu China 29°58N 108°7E 228 C7
Shizong China 24°50N 104°0E 228 E5
Shizuishan China 39°15N 106°50E 226 E4
Shizuoka Japan 34°57N 138°24E 223 C10
Shizuoka □ Japan 35°15N 138°40E 223 B10
Shkhara Georgia 43°0N 43°8E 213 A10
Shklov = Shklow Belarus 54°16N 30°15E 177 A16
Shklow Belarus 54°16N 30°15E 177 A16
Shkodër Albania 42°4N 19°32E 202 D3
Shkodra = Shkodër Albania 42°4N 19°32E 202 D3

Shkumbini → *Albania* 41°2N 19°31E **202** E3
Shmidta, Ostrov *Russia* 81°0N 91°0E **215** A10
Shō-Gawa → *Japan* 36°47N 137°4E **223** A9
Shoal Cr. → *U.S.A.* 39°44N 93°32W **310** E3
Shoal L. *Canada* 49°33N 95°1W **297** D9
Shoal Lake *Canada* 50°30N 100°35W **297** C8
Shoalhaven → *Australia* 34°54S 150°42E **283** C9
Shoals *U.S.A.* 38°40N 86°47W **311** F10
Shōbara *Japan* 34°51N 133°1E **222** C5
Shōdo-Shima *Japan* 34°30N 134°15E **222** C6
Shogunle *Nigeria* 6°34N 3°20E **124** A2
Sholapur = Solapur *India* 17°43N 75°56E **244** F2
Shomolu *Nigeria* 6°32N 3°22E **124** A2
Shōmrōn *West Bank* 32°15N 35°13E **251** F6
Shonian Harb. *Palau* 7°10N 134°23E **288** c
Shonzhy *Kazakhstan* 43°32N 79°28E **217** D9
Shooters Hill *U.K.* 51°28N 0°4E **125** B4
Shoranur *India* 10°46N 76°19E **245** J3
Shorapur *India* 16°31N 76°48E **245** F3
Shoreditch *London, U.K.* **125** a5
Shoreham by Sea *U.K.* 50°50N 0°16W **169** G7
Shorewood *U.S.A.* 43°5N 87°53W **311** A9
Shori → *Pakistan* 28°29N 69°44E **242** E3
Shorkot Road *Pakistan* 30°47N 72°15E **242** D5
Shorter *U.S.A.* 32°24N 85°57W **316** C4
Shorterville *U.S.A.* 31°34N 85°6W **316** D4
Shortland I. *Solomon Is.* 7°0S 155°45E **287** L8
Shortland Is. *Solomon Is.* 7°0S 156°0E **287** L8
Shortlands *U.K.* 51°23N 0°0 **125** B4
Shortt's I. *India* 20°47N 87°4E **244** D8
Shoshone *Calif., U.S.A.* 35°58N 116°16W **307** K10
Shoshone *Idaho, U.S.A.* 42°56N 114°25W **304** E6
Shoshone L. *U.S.A.* 44°22N 110°43W **304** D8
Shoshone Mts. *U.S.A.* 39°20N 117°25W **304** G5
Shoshong *Botswana* 22°56S 26°31E **270** B4
Shoshoni *U.S.A.* 43°14N 108°7W **304** E9
Shostka *Ukraine* 51°57N 33°32E **189** G7
Shotor Khūn *Afghan.* 34°19N 64°56E **240** B2
Shotover → *N.Z.* 44°59S 168°41E **285** E3
Shou Xian *China* 32°37N 116°42E **229** A11
Shouchang *China* 29°18N 119°12E **229** C12
Shouchia *Taiwan* 22°14N 120°50E **225** D2
Shoufeng *Taiwan* 23°52N 121°30E **225** C3
Shouguang *China* 37°52N 118°45E **227** F10
Shouning *China* 27°27N 119°31E **229** D12
Shouyang *China* 37°54N 113°8E **226** F7
Show Low *U.S.A.* 34°15N 110°2W **305** J8
Showa *Japan* 35°36N 138°29E **223** B10
Shpola *Ukraine* 49°1N 31°30E **189** H6
Shpykiv *Ukraine* 48°47N 28°34E **183** B13
Shqipëria = Albania ■ *Europe* 41°0N 20°0E **202** E4
Shreveport *U.S.A.* 32°31N 93°45W **314** E8
Shrewsbury *U.K.* 52°43N 2°45W **169** E5
Shri Mohangarh *India* 27°17N 71°18E **242** F4
Shrigonda *India* 18°37N 74°41E **244** E2
Shrirampur *India* 22°44N 88°21E **243** H13
Shropshire □ *U.K.* 52°36N 2°45W **169** E5
Shū *Kazakhstan* 43°36N 73°42E **217** D8
Shū → *Kazakhstan* 45°0N 67°44E **217** D7
Shu'afat *West Bank* 31°49N 35°14E **123** B2
Shuangbai *China* 24°42N 101°38E **228** E3
Shuangcheng *China* 45°20N 126°15E **227** B14
Shuangfeng *China* 27°29N 112°11E **229** D9
Shuanggou *China* 34°2N 117°30E **227** G9
Shuangjiang *China* 23°26N 99°58E **228** F2
Shuangliao *China* 43°29N 123°30E **227** C12
Shuangshanzi *China* 40°20N 119°8E **227** D10
Shuangyang *China* 43°28N 125°40E **227** C13
Shuangyashan *China* 46°28N 131°5E **219** B8
Shu'b, Ra's *Yemen* 12°30N 53°25E **249** D6
Shubarqudyq *Kazakhstan* 49°13N 56°34E **216** C5
Shubarshī *Kazakhstan* 48°39N 57°11E **216** C5
Shubrâ *Egypt* 30°5N 31°14E **117** A2
Shubrâ el Kheima *Egypt* 30°4N 31°14E **117** A2
Shubrâ Khit *Egypt* 31°2N 30°42E **256** H7
Shucheng *China* 31°28N 116°57E **229** B11
Shugozero *Russia* 59°54N 34°10E **188** C8
Shuguri Falls *Tanzania* 8°33S 37°22E **269** D4
Shuḥayr *Yemen* 14°41N 49°23E **249** D5
Shuiding = Huocheng *China* 44°0N 80°48E **217** D10
Shuiji *China* 27°13N 118°20E **229** D12
Shuikuo *China* 23°10N 113°10E **121** A2
Shuili *Taiwan* 23°49N 120°51E **225** C2
Shuilien *Taiwan* 23°47N 121°34E **225** C3
Shuishang *Taiwan* 23°25N 120°23E **225** C2
Shuitiliao *Taiwan* 22°23N 120°35E **225** D2
Shuiye *China* 36°7N 114°8E **226** F8
Shujalpur *India* 23°18N 76°46E **242** H7
Shukpa Kunzang *India* 34°22N 78°22E **243** B8
Shulan *China* 44°28N 127°0E **227** B14
Shulaveri *Georgia* 41°22N 44°45E **191** K7
Shule *China* 39°25N 76°3E **217** E9
Shule He → *China* 40°20N 92°50E **218** B4
Shullsburg *U.S.A.* 42°35N 90°13W **310** B6
Shumagin Is. *U.S.A.* 55°7N 160°30W **303** J7
Shumanay *Uzbekistan* 42°38N 58°55E **216** D5
Shumen *Bulgaria* 43°18N 26°55E **203** C10
Shumerlya *Russia* 55°30N 46°25E **190** C8
Shumikha *Russia* 55°10N 63°15E **214** D7
Shûna, W. el → *Egypt* 29°38N 32°6E **251** J3
Shunchang *China* 26°54N 117°48E **229** D11
Shunde *China* 22°42N 113°14E **229** F9
Shungay *Kazakhstan* 48°30N 46°45E **191** F8
Shungnak *U.S.A.* 66°52N 157°9W **303** C8
Shuo Xian = Shuozhou *China* 39°20N 112°33E **226** E7
Shuozhou *China* 39°20N 112°33E **226** E7
Shūr → *Fārs, Iran* 28°30N 55°0E **247** D7
Shūr → *Kermān, Iran* 30°52N 57°37E **247** D8
Shūr → *Yazd, Iran* 31°45N 55°15E **247** D7
Shūr Āb *Iran* 34°23N 51°11E **247** C6
Shūr Gaz *Iran* 29°10N 59°20E **247** D8
Shūrāb *Iran* 33°43N 56°29E **247** C8
Shuri *Japan* 26°13N 127°43E **288** a
Shūrjestān *Iran* 31°24N 52°25E **247** D7
Shurkhua *Burma* 22°15N 93°38E **241** D4
Shurugwi *Zimbabwe* 19°40S 30°0E **269** F3
Shūsf *Iran* 31°50N 60°5E **247** D9
Shūsh *Iran* 32°11N 48°15E **213** F13
Shushenskoye *Russia* 53°19N 91°56E **217** B12
Shūshtar *Iran* 32°0N 48°50E **247** D6
Shuswap L. *Canada* 50°55N 119°3W **296** C5
Shuya *Russia* 56°50N 41°28E **190** B5
Shuyak I. *U.S.A.* 58°31N 152°30W **303** G9
Shuyang *China* 34°10N 118°42E **227** G10
Shuzenji *Japan* 34°58N 138°56E **223** C10
Shūzū *Iran* 29°52N 54°30E **247** D7
Shwangliao = Liaoyuan *China* 42°58N 125°2E **227** C13
Shwebo *Burma* 22°30N 95°45E **241** D5
Shwegu *Burma* 24°15N 96°26E **241** C6
Shwegun *Burma* 17°9N 97°39E **241** G6
Shwegyin *Burma* 17°55N 96°53E **241** G6
Shweli → *Burma* 23°45N 96°45E **241** D6
Shwenyaung *Burma* 20°46N 96°57E **241** E6
Shyamnagar *India* 13°21N 92°57E **245** H11
Shyghanaq *Kazakhstan* 45°6N 73°59E **217** C8
Shyghys Qazaqstan □ *Kazakhstan* 48°30N 82°0E **217** D10
Shymkent *Kazakhstan* 42°18N 69°36E **217** D7
Shyok *India* 34°13N 78°12E **243** B8
Shyok → *Pakistan* 35°13N 75°53E **243** B6
Shyroke *Odesa, Ukraine* 45°59N 30°5E **183** E15
Shyroke *Ternopil, Ukraine* 48°13N 23°6E **182** B8
Si Chon *Thailand* 9°0N 99°54E **237** H2
Si Kiang = Xi Jiang → *China* 22°5N 113°20E **229** F9
Si Lanna △ *Thailand* 19°17N 99°12E **236** C2
Si-ngan = Xi'an *China* 34°15N 109°0E **226** G5
Si Prachan *Thailand* 14°37N 100°9E **236** E3
Si Racha *Thailand* 13°10N 100°48E **236** F3
Si Xian *China* 33°30N 117°50E **227** H9
Siachen Glacier *Asia* 35°20N 77°30E **243** B7
Siahaf → *Pakistan* 29°3N 68°57E **242** E3
Siahan Range *Pakistan* 27°30N 64°40E **240** D2
Siak → *Indonesia* 1°13N 102°9E **234** B2
Siaksriindrapura *Indonesia* 0°51N 102°0E **234** B2
Sialkot *Pakistan* 32°32N 74°30E **242** C6
Sialsuk *India* 23°24N 92°45E **241** D4
Sialum *Papua N. G.* 6°5S 147°36E **286** D4
Siam = Thailand ■ *Asia* 16°0N 102°0E **236** E4
Sian = Xi'an *China* 34°15N 109°0E **226** G5
Sian Ka'an ⌓ *Mexico* 19°35N 87°40W **319** D7
Siangtan = Xiangtan *China* 27°51N 112°54E **229** D9
Sianów *Poland* 54°13N 16°18E **184** D3
Siantan *Indonesia* 3°10N 106°15E **234** B3
Siàpo → *Venezuela* 2°7N 66°28W **328** C4
Sīāreh *Iran* 28°5N 60°14E **247** D9
Siargao I. *Phil.* 9°52N 126°3E **233** G6
Siari *Pakistan* 34°55N 76°40E **243** B7
Siasi *Phil.* 5°34N 120°50E **233** J3
Siasi I. *Phil.* 5°33N 120°51E **233** J3
Siassi *Papua N. G.* 5°40S 147°51E **286** C4
Siatista *Greece* 40°15N 21°33E **202** F5
Siaton *Phil.* 9°4N 123°2E **233** G4
Siau *Indonesia* 2°50N 125°25E **231** D7
Šiauliai *Lithuania* 55°56N 23°15E **184** C10
Šiauliai □ *Lithuania* 55°56N 23°19E **184** C10
Siazan = Siyäzän *Azerbaijan* 41°3N 49°10E **191** K9
Sibâi, Gebel el *Egypt* 25°45N 34°10E **246** E2
Sibang *Gabon* 0°25N 9°31E **264** B1
Sibang *Bali, Indonesia* 8°34S 115°13E **231** K18
Sibay *Russia* 52°42N 58°39E **186** D10
Sibay I. *Phil.* 11°51N 121°29E **233** F3
Sibayi, L. *S. Africa* 27°20S 32°45E **271** C5
Sibdu *Sudan* 10°57N 26°17E **257** E2
Šibenik *Croatia* 43°48N 15°54E **199** E12
Siberia = Sibirskiy □ *Russia* 58°0N 90°0E **215** D10
Siberia *Russia* 60°0N 100°0E **150** D13
Siberië *Neth. Ant.* 12°14N 69°3W **322** g
Siberut *Indonesia* 1°30S 99°0E **234** C1
Siberut △ *Indonesia* 1°17S 98°45E **234** C1
Sibi *Pakistan* 29°30N 67°54E **242** E2
Sibil = Oksibil *Indonesia* 4°59S 140°35E **231** E10
Sibiloi △ *Kenya* 4°0N 36°20E **268** B4
Sibirskiy □ *Russia* 58°0N 90°0E **215** D10
Sibirtsevo *Russia* 44°12N 132°26E **220** B5
Sibiti *Congo* 3°38S 13°19E **264** C2
Sibiu *Romania* 45°45N 24°9E **183** E9
Sibiu □ *Romania* 45°50N 24°15E **183** E9
Sibium Mts. *Papua N. G.* 9°19S 148°25E **286** E5
Sibley *Ill., U.S.A.* 40°35N 88°23W **311** D8
Sibley *Iowa, U.S.A.* 43°24N 95°45W **308** D6
Sibolga *Indonesia* 1°42N 98°45E **234** B1
Sibsagar *India* 27°0N 94°36E **241** B5
Sibu *Malaysia* 2°18N 111°49E **235** B4
Sibuco *Phil.* 7°20N 122°10E **233** H4
Sibuguey B. *Phil.* 7°50N 122°45E **233** H4
Sibut *C.A.R.* 5°46N 19°10E **264** A3
Sibutu *Phil.* 4°45N 119°30E **235** B5
Sibutu Group *Phil.* 4°45N 119°20E **233** J2
Sibutu Passage *E. Indies* 4°50N 120°0E **233** J3
Sibuyan I. *Phil.* 12°25N 122°40E **232** E4
Sibuyan Sea *Phil.* 12°30N 122°20E **232** E4
Sic *Romania* 46°56N 23°53E **183** D8
Sicamous *Canada* 50°49N 119°0W **296** C5
Sicapoo, Mt. *Phil.* 18°1N 120°56E **232** B3
Sicasica *Bolivia* 17°22S 67°45W **330** D4
Siccus → *Australia* 31°55S 139°17E **282** A3
Sichelberg = Sierpc *Poland* 52°55N 19°43E **185** F6
Sichuan □ *China* 30°30N 103°0E **228** B5
Sichuan Pendi *China* 31°0N 105°0E **228** B5
Sicilia *Italy* 37°30N 14°30E **201** E7
Sicily = Sicilia *Italy* 37°30N 14°30E **201** E7
Sicily, Str. of *Medit. S.* 37°35N 11°56E **200** E4
Sicuani *Peru* 14°21S 71°10W **330** C3
Šid *Serbia* 45°8N 19°14E **182** E4
Sidamo *Ethiopia* 5°0N 37°50E **257** G4
Sidaouet *Niger* 18°34N 8°3E **259** E1
Sidari *Greece* 39°47N 19°41E **206** B9
Sidcup *U.K.* 51°25N 0°6E **125** B4
Siddapur *India* 14°20N 74°53E **245** G2
Siddhapur *India* 23°56N 72°25E **242** H5
Siddipet *India* 18°5N 78°51E **244** E4
Side *Turkey* 36°45N 31°23E **250** B2
Sidensjö *Sweden* 63°18N 18°17E **162** A12
Sidéradougou *Burkina Faso* 10°42N 4°12W **262** C4
Siderno *Italy* 38°16N 16°18E **201** D9
Sideros, Akra *Greece* 35°19N 26°19E **207** E7
Sidhauli *India* 27°17N 80°50E **243** F9
Sidhi *India* 24°25N 81°53E **243** G9
Sîdi Abd el Rahmân *Egypt* 30°55N 29°44E **256** A2
Sidi Ahmed Rgueibi *W. Sahara* 27°32N 11°16W **260** C2
Sîdi Barrâni *Egypt* 31°38N 25°58E **256** A2
Sidi-bel-Abbès *Algeria* 35°13N 0°39W **261** A4
Sidi-bel-Abbès □ *Algeria* 34°50N 0°30W **261** B4
Sidi Bennour *Morocco* 32°40N 8°25W **260** B3
Sidi Bou Zid □ *Tunisia* 34°50N 9°30E **261** B6
Sîdi Haneish *Egypt* 31°10N 27°35E **256** A2
Sidi Ifni *Morocco* 29°29N 10°12W **260** C2
Sidi Kacem *Morocco* 34°12N 5°42W **260** B3
Sîdi Omar *Egypt* 31°24N 24°57E **256** A1
Sidi Slimane *Morocco* 34°16N 5°56W **260** B3
Sidi Smaïl *Morocco* 32°50N 8°31W **260** B3
Sīdī 'Uzayz *Libya* 31°41N 24°55E **258** B4
Sidimo *Somali Rep.* 2°27N 41°58E **267** D5
Siding No 14 = Ponoka *Canada* 52°42N 113°40W **296** C6
Sidirokastro *Greece* 41°13N 23°24E **202** E7
Sidlaw Hills *U.K.* 56°32N 3°2W **167** E5
Sidley, Mt. *Antarctica* 77°2S 126°2W **151** D14
Sidmouth *U.K.* 50°40N 3°15W **169** G4
Sidmouth, C. *Australia* 13°25S 143°36E **280** A3
Sidney *B.C., Canada* 48°39N 123°24W **306** B3
Sidney *Mont., U.S.A.* 47°43N 104°9W **304** C11
Sidney *N.Y., U.S.A.* 42°19N 75°24W **313** D9
Sidney *Nebr., U.S.A.* 41°8N 102°59W **308** E2
Sidney *Ohio, U.S.A.* 40°17N 84°9W **311** D12
Sidney Lanier, L. *U.S.A.* 34°10N 84°4W **316** A5
Sido *Mali* 11°37N 7°29W **262** C3
Sidoarjo *Indonesia* 7°27S 112°43E **235** D4
Sidoktaya *Burma* 20°27N 94°15E **241** E5
Sidon = Saydā *Lebanon* 33°35N 35°25E **250** E6
Sidra, G. of = Surt, Khalīj *Libya* 31°40N 18°30E **258** B3
Sidrolândia *Brazil* 20°55S 54°58W **331** E7
Siebenhirten *Austria* 48°8N 16°17E **142** B1
Siedlce *Poland* 52°10N 22°20E **185** F9
Siedlung *Germany* 52°35N 13°7E **115** A1
Sieg → *Germany* 50°46N 7°6E **178** E3
Siegburg *Germany* 50°47N 7°12E **178** E3
Siegen *Germany* 50°51N 8°0E **178** E4
Siekierki *Poland* 52°12N 21°4E **142** B2
Sielce *Poland* 52°12N 21°2E **142** B2
Siem Pang *Cambodia* 14°7N 106°23E **236** E6
Siem Reap = Siemreab *Cambodia* 13°20N 103°52E **236** F4
Siemensstadt *Germany* 52°32N 13°16E **115** A2
Siemiatycze *Poland* 52°27N 22°53E **185** F9
Siemreab *Cambodia* 13°20N 103°52E **236** F4
Siena *Italy* 43°19N 11°21E **199** E8
Sieniawa *Poland* 50°11N 22°38E **185** H9
Sienyang = Xianyang *China* 34°20N 108°40E **226** G5
Sieradz *Poland* 51°37N 18°41E **185** G5
Sieraków *Poland* 52°39N 16°2E **185** F3
Sierck-les-Bains *France* 49°26N 6°20E **173** C13
Sierning *Austria* 48°2N 14°18E **180** C7
Sierpc *Poland* 52°55N 19°43E **185** F6
Sierpe, Bocas de la *Venezuela* 10°0N 61°30W **329** G9
Sierra Blanca *U.S.A.* 31°11N 105°22W **314** F2
Sierra Blanca Peak *U.S.A.* 33°23N 105°49W **305** K11
Sierra City *U.S.A.* 39°34N 120°38W **306** F6
Sierra Colorada *Argentina* 40°35S 67°50W **336** B3
Sierra de Aracena y Picas de Aroche ⌓ *Spain* 37°53N 6°41W **195** H4
Sierra de Bahoruco △ *Dom. Rep.* 18°10N 71°25W **321** C5
Sierra de Baza ⌓ *Spain* 37°20N 2°48W **197** H2
Sierra de Castril ⌓ *Spain* 37°54N 2°50W **197** H2
Sierra de Espuña ⌓ *Spain* 37°50N 1°31W **197** H3
Sierra de Grazalema ⌓ *Spain* 36°31N 5°28W **195** J5
Sierra de Gredos ⌓ *Spain* 40°17N 5°17W **194** E5
Sierra de Hornachuelos ⌓ *Spain* 37°56N 5°14W **195** H5
Sierra de Huétor ⌓ *Spain* 37°14N 3°30W **195** H7
Sierra de la Culata △ *Venezuela* 8°48N 70°56W **328** B3
Sierra de la Macarena △ *Colombia* 11°19N 74°1W **328** A3
Sierra de las Nieves ⌓ *Spain* 36°42N 5°0W **195** J6
Sierra de las Quijadas △ *Argentina* 32°29S 67°5W **334** C2
Sierra de María-Los Vélez ⌓ *Spain* 37°41N 2°10W **197** H2
Sierra de San Luis △ *Venezuela* 11°11N 69°33W **328** A4
Sierra de San Pedro Mártir, Parque Nacional △ *Mexico* 31°10N 115°30W **318** A1
Sierra de Yeguas *Spain* 37°7N 4°52W **195** H6
Sierra del São Mamede ⌓ *Portugal* 39°17N 7°18W **195** F3
Sierra Gorda *Chile* 22°50S 69°15W **334** A2
Sierra Grande *Argentina* 41°36S 65°22W **336** B3
Sierra Leone ■ *W. Afr.* 9°0N 12°0W **262** D2
Sierra Leone Basin *Atl. Oc.* 5°0N 17°0W **152** F10
Sierra Leone Rise *Atl. Oc.* 7°0N 22°0W **152** F9
Sierra Madre *Mexico* 16°0N 93°0W **319** D6
Sierra Madre *Calif., U.S.A.* 34°9N 118°3W **126** B4
Sierra Madre Occidental *Mexico* 27°0N 107°0W **318** B3
Sierra Madre Oriental *Mexico* 25°0N 100°0W **318** C5
Sierra Mágina ⌓ *Spain* 37°44N 3°28W **195** H7
Sierra Mojada *Mexico* 27°18N 103°41W **318** B4
Sierra Nevada *Spain* 37°3N 3°15W **195** H7
Sierra Nevada *Calif., U.S.A.* 39°0N 120°30W **306** H8
Sierra Nevada ⌓ *Spain* 37°4N 3°7W **195** H7
Sierra Norte de Seville ⌓ *Spain* 37°55N 5°46W **195** H5
Sierra Subbéticas ⌓ *Spain* 37°26N 4°18W **195** H6
Sierra Vista *U.S.A.* 31°33N 110°18W **305** L8
Sierras de Cardeña y Montoro ⌓ *Spain* 38°13N 4°15W **195** G6
Sierras de Cazorla, Segura y las Villas ⌓ *Spain* 37°0N 2°45W **197** J2
Sierraville *U.S.A.* 39°36N 120°22W **306** F6
Sierre *Switz.* 46°17N 7°31E **179** J3
Sievering *Austria* 48°15N 16°20E **142** A2
Sifani *Ethiopia* 12°18N 40°19E **257** E5
Sifié *Ivory C.* 8°0N 7°5W **262** D3
Sifnos *Greece* 37°0N 24°45E **204** E6
Sifton *Canada* 51°21N 100°8W **297** C8
Sifton Pass *Canada* 57°52N 126°15W **296** B3
Sig *Algeria* 35°32N 0°12W **261** A4
Sigaboy = Governor Generoso *Phil.* 6°39N 126°5E **233** H6
Sigatoka *Fiji* 18°8S 177°32E **287** B1
Sigdal *Norway* 60°3N 9°38E **164** D6
Sigean *France* 43°2N 2°58E **174** E6
Siggiewi *Malta* 35°51N 14°26E **206** F7
Sighetu-Marmaţiei *Romania* 47°57N 23°52E **183** C8
Sighişoara *Romania* 46°12N 24°50E **183** D9
Sighthill *U.K.* 55°56N 3°17W **121** B2
Sigira *Yemen* 12°37N 54°20E **249** D6
Sigiriya *Sri Lanka* 7°57N 80°45E **245** L5
Sigli *Indonesia* 5°25N 96°0E **234** A1
Siglufjörður *Iceland* 66°12N 18°55W **155** A8
Siglunes *Iceland* 66°12N 18°50W **155** A8
Sigmaringen *Germany* 48°5N 9°12E **179** G5
Signa *Italy* 43°45N 11°10E **198** E8
Signakhi = Tsnori *Georgia* 41°40N 45°57E **191** K7
Signal de Botrang *Belgium* 50°29N 6°4E **170** D6
Signal Hill *S. Africa* 34°5S 18°24E **118** A1
Signal Pk. *U.S.A.* 33°20N 114°2W **307** M12
Signy I. *Antarctica* 60°45S 45°56W **151** C18
Signy-l'Abbaye *France* 49°40N 4°25E **173** C11
Sigourney *U.S.A.* 41°20N 92°12W **310** C4
Sigsbee *U.S.A.* 31°16N 83°52W **316** D6
Sigsbee Deep *Caribbean* 25°0N 92°0W **152** D1
Sigsig *Ecuador* 3°0S 78°50W **328** D2
Sigüenza *Spain* 41°3N 2°40W **196** D2
Siguiri *Guinea* 11°31N 9°10W **262** C3
Sigulda *Latvia* 57°10N 24°55E **188** D3
Sihanoukville = Kampong Saom *Cambodia* 10°38N 103°30E **237** G4
Sihaus *Peru* 8°40S 77°40W **330** B2
Sihawa *India* 20°19N 81°55E **244** D5
Siheung *Gyeonggi-do, S. Korea* 37°25N 126°47E **224** D3
Siheung *Seoul, S. Korea* 37°28N 126°54E **137** C1
Sihora *India* 23°29N 80°6E **243** H9
Sihui *China* 23°20N 112°40E **229** F9
Siikajoki → *Finland* 64°50N 24°43E **160** D21
Siilinjärvi *Finland* 63°4N 27°39E **160** E22
Siirt *Turkey* 37°57N 41°55E **213** D9
Siirt □ *Turkey* 37°55N 41°55E **213** D9
Sijarira Ra. = Chizarira *Zimbabwe* 17°36S 27°45E **269** F2
Sijungjung *Indonesia* 0°42S 100°58E **234** C2
Sika *India* 22°26N 69°47E **242** H3
Sikanni Chief → *Canada* 57°47N 122°15W **296** B4
Sikao *Thailand* 7°34N 99°21E **237** J2
Sikar *India* 27°33N 75°10E **242** F6
Sikasso *Mali* 11°18N 5°35W **262** C3
Sikasso □ *Mali* 10°55N 7°0W **262** C3
Sikátorpuszta *Hungary* 47°34N 19°10E **117** A3
Sikelenge *Zambia* 14°53S 24°14E **265** E4
Sikeston *U.S.A.* 36°53N 89°35W **308** G9
Sikhote Alin, Khrebet *Russia* 45°0N 136°0E **220** B8
Sikhote Alin Ra. = Sikhote Alin, Khrebet *Russia* 45°0N 136°0E **220** B8
Sikia *Greece* 40°2N 23°56E **202** F7
Sikinos *Greece* 36°40N 25°8E **205** E7
Sikkim □ *India* 27°50N 88°30E **241** B2
Siklós *Hungary* 45°50N 18°19E **182** E3
Sil → *Spain* 42°27N 7°43W **194** C3
Silacayoapan *Mexico* 17°30N 98°9W **319** D5
Šilalė *Lithuania* 55°28N 22°12E **184** C9
Silam *Malaysia* 4°59N 118°12E **233** J2
Silampur *India* 28°39N 77°16E **120** B2
Silandro *Italy* 46°38N 10°46E **198** B7
Silang *Phil.* 14°14N 120°58E **232** D3
Silawad *India* 21°54N 74°54E **242** J6
Silay *Phil.* 10°47N 122°58E **233** F4
Silba *Croatia* 44°24N 14°41E **199** D11
Silchar *India* 24°49N 92°48E **241** C4
Sildegapet *Norway* 62°5N 5°0E **164** B2
Şile *Turkey* 41°10N 29°37E **203** E13
Silent Valley △ *India* 11°10N 76°20E **245** J3
Siler City *U.S.A.* 35°44N 79°28W **315** D15
Sileru → *India* 17°49N 81°24E **244** F5
Silesia = Śląsk *Poland* 51°0N 16°30E **176** C9
Silet *Algeria* 22°44N 4°37E **261** D5
Siletitengiz Köli *Kazakhstan* 53°20N 73°10E **217** B8
Silgarhi Doti *Nepal* 29°15N 81°0E **243** E9
Silghat *India* 26°35N 93°0E **241** B4
Silhouette *Seychelles* 4°29S 55°12E **272** c
Sili *Burkina Faso* 11°37N 2°30W **262** C4
Siliana *Tunisia* 36°5N 9°22E **261** A6
Siliana □ *Tunisia* 36°0N 9°20E **261** A6
Silifke *Turkey* 36°22N 33°58E **250** B4
Siliguri = Shiliguri *India* 26°45N 88°25E **241** B2
Silil *Somali Rep.* 11°0N 43°26E **267** B5
Siling Co *China* 31°50N 89°20E **218** C3
Silistea Nouă *Romania* 44°23N 25°1E **183** F10
Silistra *Bulgaria* 44°6N 27°19E **203** B11
Silivri *Turkey* 41°4N 28°14E **203** E12
Siljan *Telemark, Norway* 59°18N 9°42E **164** E6
Siljan *Sweden* 60°55N 14°45E **162** D8
Siljansnäs *Sweden* 60°47N 14°52E **162** D8
Silkeborg *Denmark* 56°10N 9°32E **163** H3
Silkwood *Australia* 17°45S 146°2E **280** B4
Silla *Spain* 39°22N 0°25W **197** F4
Sillajhuay, Cordillera *Chile* 19°46S 68°40W **330** D4
Sillamäe *Estonia* 59°24N 27°45E **188** C4
Sillé-le-Guillaume *France* 48°10N 0°8W **172** D6
Silleda *Spain* 42°42N 8°14W **194** C2
Sillein = Žilina *Slovak Rep.* 49°12N 18°42E **181** B11
Sillim *S. Korea* 37°28N 126°56E **137** C1
Sillod *India* 20°18N 75°39E **244** D2
Silloth *U.K.* 54°52N 3°23W **168** C4
Sillustani *Peru* 15°50S 70°7W **330** D3
Silo *Greece* 41°10N 25°53E **203** E9
Siloam Springs *U.S.A.* 36°11N 94°32W **314** C7
Silopi *Turkey* 37°15N 42°27E **213** D10
Silsbee *U.S.A.* 30°21N 94°11W **314** F7
Siltou *Chad* 16°46N 15°33E **259** E3
Siluko *Nigeria* 6°35N 5°10E **263** D6
Šilutė *Lithuania* 55°21N 21°33E **184** C8
Silva Porto = Kuito *Angola* 12°22S 16°55E **265** E3
Silvan *Turkey* 38°7N 41°2E **213** C9
Silvani *India* 23°18N 78°25E **243** H8
Silver, L. *U.S.A.* 28°35N 81°23W **133** A2
Silver Bank *W. Indies* 20°30N 69°45W **321** B6
Silver Bank Passage *W. Indies* 20°0N 70°0W **321** B5
Silver City *U.S.A.* 32°46N 108°17W **305** K9
Silver Cr. → *U.S.A.* 43°16N 119°13W **304** E4
Silver Creek *U.S.A.* 42°33N 79°10W **312** D5
Silver Grove *U.S.A.* 39°2N 84°23W **311** E12
Silver Hill *Montserrat* 16°49N 62°11W **323** p
Silver Hill *Md., U.S.A.* 38°49N 76°55W **143** C4
Silver L. *U.S.A.* 38°39N 120°6W **306** G6
Silver Lake *Calif., U.S.A.* 35°21N 116°7W **307** K10
Silver Lake *Ind., U.S.A.* 41°4N 85°53W **311** C11
Silver Lake *Oreg., U.S.A.* 43°8N 121°3W **304** E3
Silver Lake *Wis., U.S.A.* 42°33N 88°13W **311** B8
Silver Spring *U.S.A.* 38°59N 77°2W **143** A3
Silver Springs *U.S.A.* 29°13N 82°3W **317** F7
Silverdalen *Sweden* 57°32N 15°45E **163** G9
Silvermine Mts. *Ireland* 52°47N 8°15W **166** D3
Silvermine Nature Reserve *S. Africa* 34°6S 18°27E **118** B1
Silverton *N.S.W., Australia* 31°52S 141°10E **282** A4
Silverton *Colo., U.S.A.* 37°49N 107°40W **305** H10
Silverton *Tex., U.S.A.* 34°28N 101°19W **314** D4
Silves *Brazil* 2°54S 58°27W **329** D6
Silves *Portugal* 37°11N 8°26W **195** H2
Silvi Marina *Italy* 42°34N 14°5E **199** F11
Silvia *Colombia* 2°37N 76°21W **328** C2
Silvies → *U.S.A.* 43°34N 119°2W **304** E4
Silvolantekojärvi *Finland* 60°17N 24°54E **121** B2
Silvrettahorn *Switz.* 46°50N 10°6E **198** B7
Silwa Bahari *Egypt* 24°45N 32°55E **256** C3
Silz *Austria* 47°16N 10°56E **180** D3
Sim, C. *Morocco* 31°26N 9°51W **260** B3
Simakumba *Zambia* 14°12S 23°16E **265** E4
Simaltala *India* 24°43N 86°33E **243** G12
Simaluguri *India* 26°55N 94°46E **241** B5
Sim'ān, J. *Syria* 36°25N 36°53E **250** B7
Simanggang = Sri Aman *Malaysia* 1°15N 111°32E **235** B4
Simao *China* 22°47N 101°5E **228** F3
Simão Dias *Brazil* 10°44S 37°49W **332** D4
Simara I. *Phil.* 12°48N 122°3E **232** E4
Simard, L. *Canada* 47°40N 78°40W **298** C4
Şīmareh → *Iran* 33°9N 47°41E **213** F12
Simav *Turkey* 39°4N 28°58E **205** B10
Simav → *Turkey* 40°23N 28°31E **203** F12
Simav Dağları *Turkey* 39°10N 28°30E **205** B10
Simba *Dem. Rep. of the Congo* 0°38N 22°59E **264** B4
Simba *Tanzania* 2°10S 37°36E **268** C4
Simbach *Germany* 48°16N 13°2E **179** G9
Simberi I. *Papua N. G.* 2°38S 152°0E **286** B7
Simbirsk *Russia* 54°20N 48°25E **190** C9
Simbo *Solomon Is.* 8°16S 156°33E **287** M9
Simbo *Tanzania* 4°51S 29°41E **268** C2
Simcoe *Canada* 42°50N 80°20W **298** D3
Simcoe, L. *Canada* 44°25N 79°20W **312** B5
Simdega *India* 22°37N 84°31E **243** H11
Simei *Singapore* 1°20N 103°47E **138** A3
Simeonovgrad *Bulgaria* 42°1N 25°50E **203** D9
Simeria *Romania* 45°51N 23°1E **182** E8
Simeto → *Italy* 37°24N 15°6E **201** E8
Simeulue *Indonesia* 2°45N 95°45E **234** B1
Simferopol *Ukraine* 44°55N 34°3E **189** K8
Simi *Greece* 36°35N 27°50E **205** E9
Simi Valley *U.S.A.* 34°16N 118°47W **307** L8
Simien Mts. △ *Ethiopia* 13°19N 38°0E **257** E4
Simikot *Nepal* 30°0N 81°50E **243** E9
Similajau △ *Malaysia* 3°27N 113°15E **235** B4
Simití *Colombia* 7°58N 73°57W **328** B3
Simitli *Bulgaria* 41°52N 23°7E **202** E7
Simla = Shimla *India* 31°2N 77°9E **242** D7
Simla *India* 22°35N 88°22E **124** B2
Simlångsdalen *Sweden* 56°43N 13°6E **163** H7
Şimleu-Silvaniei *Romania* 47°17N 22°50E **182** C7
Simlipal △ *India* 21°45N 86°30E **243** J12
Simmering *Austria* 48°10N 16°24E **142** A2
Simmering Heide *Austria* 48°10N 16°26E **142** A2
Simmern *Germany* 49°58N 7°30E **179** F3
Simmie *Canada* 49°56N 108°6W **297** D7
Simmler *U.S.A.* 35°21N 119°59W **307** K7
Simnas *Lithuania* 54°24N 23°39E **184** D10
Simo älv = Simojoki → *Finland* 65°35N 25°1E **160** D21
Simões *Brazil* 7°36S 40°49W **332** C3
Simojoki → *Finland* 65°35N 25°1E **160** D21
Simojovel *Mexico* 17°12N 92°38W **319** D6
Simonette → *Canada* 55°9N 118°15W **296** B5
Simonière, Plaine de la *Guadeloupe* 16°16N 61°19W **322** e
Simonkylä *Finland* 60°18N 25°1E **121** B3
Šimonovany = Partizánske *Slovak Rep.* 48°38N 18°23E **181** C11
Simonstown *S. Africa* 34°14S 18°26E **270** D2
Simontornya *Hungary* 46°45N 18°33E **182** D3
Simpang Empat *Malaysia* 5°27N 100°29E **237** c
Simpangkiri → *Indonesia* 2°50N 97°40E **234** B1
Simplício Mendes *Brazil* 7°51S 41°54W **332** C3
Simplonpass *Switz.* 46°15N 8°3E **179** J4
Simplontunnel *Switz.* 46°15N 8°7E **179** J4
Simpson, Mt. *Papua N. G.* 10°2S 149°34E **286** F5
Simpson Bay Lagoon *St.-Martin* 18°3N 63°6W **322** a
Simpson Desert *Australia* 25°0S 137°0E **280** D2
Simpson Desert △ *Australia* 24°59S 138°21E **280** C2
Simpson Pen. *Canada* 68°34N 88°45W **295** C11
Simrishamn *Sweden* 55°33N 14°22E **163** J8
Simsbury *U.S.A.* 41°53N 72°48W **313** E12
Simsonbaai *St.-Maarten* 18°2N 63°7W **322** a
Simunjan *Malaysia* 1°25N 110°45E **235** B4
Simunul *Phil.* 4°54N 119°51E **233** J2
Simushir, Ostrov *Russia* 46°50N 152°30E **215** E16
Sin Cowe I. *S. China Sea* 9°53N 114°19E **230** C4
Sin-do *N. Korea* 39°52N 124°14E **224** C2
Sina → *India* 17°30N 75°55E **244** F2
Sinabang *Indonesia* 2°30N 96°24E **234** B1
Sinadogo *Somali Rep.* 5°50N 47°0E **267** C6
Sinai = Es Sînâ' *Egypt* 29°0N 34°0E **246** D2
Sinai, Mt. = Mûsa, Gebel *Egypt* 28°33N 33°59E **251** K4
Sinai, Mt. *Grenada* 12°4N 61°42W **323** q
Sinai Peninsula *Egypt* 29°30N 34°0E **251** J5
Sinaia *Romania* 45°21N 25°38E **183** E10
Sinait *Phil.* 17°52N 120°27E **232** C3
Sinako, Mt. *Phil.* 7°30N 125°17E **233** H5
Sinaloa □ *Mexico* 25°0N 107°30W **318** C3
Sinaloa de Leyva *Mexico* 25°50N 108°14W **318** B3
Sinalunga *Italy* 43°12N 11°44E **199** E8
Sinan *China* 27°56N 108°13E **228** D7
Sînandrei *Romania* 45°52N 21°13E **182** E6
Sinarades *Greece* 39°34N 19°51E **206** B9
Sīnāwan *Libya* 31°0N 10°37E **258** B2
Sinbaungwe *Burma* 19°43N 95°10E **241** F5
Sinbo *Burma* 24°46N 97°3E **241** C6
Sincan *Turkey* 40°0N 32°36E **212** B5
Sincanlı *Turkey* 38°45N 30°15E **205** C12
Sincé *Colombia* 9°15N 75°9W **328** B2
Sincelejo *Colombia* 9°18N 75°24W **328** B2
Sinch'ang *N. Korea* 40°7N 128°28E **224** B4
Sincheorwon *S. Korea* 38°8N 127°18E **224** C3
Sinch'ŏn *N. Korea* 38°17N 125°21E **224** C2
Sinchon *Seoul, S. Korea* 37°34N 126°57E **137** B1
Sinclair *U.S.A.* 41°47N 107°7W **304** F10
Sinclair, L. *U.S.A.* 33°8N 83°12W **316** B6
Sinclair Mills *Canada* 54°5N 121°40W **296** C4
Sinclair's B. *U.K.* 58°31N 3°5W **167** C5
Sinclairville *U.S.A.* 42°16N 79°16W **312** D5
Sind = Sindh □ *Pakistan* 26°0N 69°0E **242** G3
Sind *Pakistan* 26°0N 68°30E **242** G3
Sind → *Jammu & Kashmir, India* 34°18N 74°45E **243** B6
Sind → *Mad. P., India* 26°26N 79°13E **243** F8
Sind Sagar Doab *Pakistan* 32°0N 71°30E **242** D4
Sindal *Denmark* 57°28N 10°10E **163** G4
Sindang *S. Korea* 37°35N 127°2E **137** B2
Sindangan *Phil.* 8°10N 123°5E **233** G4
Sindangan Bay *Phil.* 8°11N 122°50E **233** G4
Sindangbarang *Indonesia* 7°27S 107°1E **235** D3
Sindara *Gabon* 1°7S 10°41E **264** C2
Sinde *Zambia* 17°28S 25°51E **269** F2
Sindelfingen *Germany* 48°42N 9°0E **179** G4
Sindewahi *India* 20°17N 79°39E **244** D4
Sindgi *India* 16°55N 76°14E **244** F3
Sindh □ *Pakistan* 26°0N 69°0E **242** G3
Sindhnur *India* 15°47N 76°46E **245** F3
Sindi *India* 20°48N 78°52E **244** D4
Sındırgı *Turkey* 39°13N 28°10E **205** B10
Sindou *Burkina Faso* 10°35N 5°4W **262** C3
Sindri *India* 23°45N 86°42E **243** H12
Sine → *Senegal* 14°10N 16°28W **262** C1
Sinegorskiy *Russia* 47°55N 40°52E **191** G5
Sinekli *Turkey* 41°14N 28°12E **203** E12
Sinelnikovo = Synelnykove *Ukraine* 48°25N 35°30E **189** H8
Sinendé *Benin* 10°20N 2°22E **263** C5
Sines *Portugal* 37°56N 8°51W **195** H2
Sines, C. de *Portugal* 37°58N 8°53W **195** H2
Sineu *Spain* 39°38N 3°1E **206** B4
Sinewit, Mt. *Papua N. G.* 4°44S 152°2E **286** C7
Sinfra *Ivory C.* 6°35N 5°56W **262** D3
Sing Buri *Thailand* 14°53N 100°25E **236** E3
Sing Sing = Ossining *U.S.A.* 41°10N 73°55W **313** E11
Singa *Sudan* 13°10N 33°57E **257** E3
Singako *Chad* 9°50N 19°24E **259** G3
Singalila △ *India* 27°10N 88°5E **243** F13
Singanallur *India* 11°2N 77°1E **245** J3
Singapore ■ *Asia* 1°17N 103°51E **138** B3
Singapore, Straits of *Asia* 1°15N 104°0E **237** d
Singapore, Univ. of *Singapore* 1°19N 103°49E **138** B2
Singapore Changi ✕ **(SIN)** *Singapore* 1°23N 103°59E **138** A3
Singaraja *Indonesia* 8°7S 115°6E **231** J18
Singatoka = Sigatoka *Fiji* 18°8S 177°32E **287** B1
Singen *Germany* 47°45N 8°50E **179** H4
Singida *Tanzania* 4°49S 34°48E **268** C3
Singida □ *Tanzania* 6°0S 34°30E **268** D3
Singkaling Hkamti *Burma* 26°0N 95°39E **241** C5
Singkang *Indonesia* 4°8S 120°1E **231** E6
Singkawang *Indonesia* 1°0N 108°57E **235** B3
Singkep *Indonesia* 0°30S 104°25E **234** C2
Singleton *Australia* 32°33S 151°0E **283** B9
Singleton, Mt. *N. Terr., Australia* 22°0S 130°46E **278** D5
Singleton, Mt. *W. Austral., Australia* 29°27S 117°15E **279** E2
Singö *Sweden* 60°12N 18°45E **162** D12
Singoli *India* 25°0N 75°22E **242** G6
Singora = Songkhla *Thailand* 7°13N 100°37E **237** J3
Singri *India* 26°36N 92°29E **241** B4
Singsås *Norway* 62°56N 10°37E **164** B7
Singu *Burma* 22°33N 96°0E **241** D6
Sinhgarh *India* 18°22N 73°45E **244** E1
Sinhŭng *Hamgyŏngnam-do, N. Korea* 40°11N 127°34E **224** B3
Sinhŭng *Hamgyŏngnam-do, N. Korea* 41°8N 127°31E **224** B3
Sinicka → *Russia* 55°52N 37°18E **129** A1
Siniloan *Phil.* 14°25N 121°27E **232** D3
Sining = Xining *China* 36°34N 101°40E **218** C5
Siniscóla *Italy* 40°34N 9°41E **200** B2
Sinj *Croatia* 43°42N 16°39E **199** E13
Sinjai *Indonesia* 5°7S 120°20E **231** F6
Sinjajevina *Montenegro* 42°57N 19°22E **202** D3
Sinjār *Iraq* 36°19N 41°52E **213** D9
Sinjār *Syria* 35°35N 37°0E **250** C8
Sinkat *Sudan* 18°55N 36°49E **256** D4
Sinki, Selat *Singapore* 1°15N 103°42E **138** B2
Sinkiang = Xinjiang Uygur Zizhiqu □ *China* 42°0N 86°0E **217** D11
Sinlumkaba *Burma* 24°16N 97°31E **241** C6
Sinmak *N. Korea* 38°25N 126°14E **224** C3
Sinmi-do *N. Korea* 39°33N 124°53E **224** C2
Sínnai *Italy* 39°18N 9°13E **200** C2
Sinnar *India* 19°48N 74°0E **244** E2
Sinni → *Italy* 40°8N 16°41E **201** B9
Sinnuris *Egypt* 29°26N 30°31E **256** J7
Sinoie, Lacul *Romania* 44°35N 28°50E **183** F13
Sinop *Turkey* 42°1N 35°11E **212** A6
Sinop □ *Turkey* 42°0N 35°0E **212** B6
Sinor *India* 21°55N 73°20E **242** J5
Sinp'o *N. Korea* 40°0N 128°13E **224** C4
Sinsa *S. Korea* 37°31N 127°0E **137** B2
Sinsang *N. Korea* 39°38N 127°24E **224** C3
Sinsheim *Germany* 49°15N 8°52E **179** F4
Sinsiang = Xinxiang *China* 35°18N 113°50E **226** G7
Sinsk *Russia* 61°8N 126°48E **215** C13
Sint Annabaai *Neth. Ant.* 12°6N 68°55W **322** g
Sint Christoffelberg *Neth. Ant.* 12°20N 69°8W **322** g
Sint-Genesius-Rode *Belgium* 50°45N 4°22E **116** B2
Sint Jorisbaai *Neth. Ant.* 12°7N 68°48W **322** g
Sint Marie, K. *Neth. Ant.* 12°11N 69°3W **322** g
Sint Marthabaai *Neth. Ant.* 12°17N 69°8W **322** g
Sint Michiel *Neth. Ant.* 12°8N 69°0W **322** g
Sint Nicolaas *Aruba* 12°27N 69°54W **322** f
Sint Nicolaas *Neth. Ant.* 12°17N 69°8W **322** g
Sint Wilibrordus *Neth. Ant.* 12°12N 69°4W **322** g
Sintang *Indonesia* 0°5N 111°35E **235** B4
Sinton *U.S.A.* 28°2N 97°31W **314** G6
Sintra *Portugal* 38°47N 9°25W **195** G1
Sintra-Cascais ⌓ *Portugal* 38°50N 9°25W **195** G1
Sinugif *Somali Rep.* 8°33N 48°59E **267** C6
Sinŭiju *N. Korea* 40°5N 124°24E **224** B2
Sinyukha → *Ukraine* 48°3N 30°51E **189** H6
Sinzig *Germany* 50°32N 7°14E **178** E3
Sio → *Hungary* 46°20N 18°53E **182** D3
Siocon *Phil.* 7°40N 122°10E **233** H4
Siófok *Hungary* 46°54N 18°3E **182** D3
Sioma *Zambia* 16°40S 23°32E **265** F4
Sioma Ngwezi △ *Zambia* 17°14S 23°26E **265** F4
Sion *Maharashtra, India* 19°3N 72°52E **130** A2
Sion *Switz.* 46°14N 7°20E **179** J3
Sion Mills *U.K.* 54°48N 7°29W **166** B4
Sioux Center *U.S.A.* 43°5N 96°11W **308** D5
Sioux City *U.S.A.* 42°30N 96°24W **308** D5
Sioux Falls *U.S.A.* 43°33N 96°44W **308** D5
Sioux Lookout *Canada* 50°10N 91°50W **298** B1
Sioux Narrows *Canada* 49°25N 94°10W **297** D10
Sipadan *Malaysia* 7°6N 118°38E **231** D5
Sipalay *Phil.* 9°45N 122°24E **233** G4
Šipan *Croatia* 42°45N 17°52E **202** D1
Sipang, Tanjong *Malaysia* 1°48N 110°20E **235** B4
Siparia *Trin. & Tob.* 10°8N 61°31W **323** t
Sipil Daği △ *Turkey* 38°35N 27°30E **205** C9
Siping *China* 43°8N 124°21E **227** C13
Sipiwesk L. *Canada* 55°5N 97°35W **297** B9
Siple *Antarctica* 75°0S 74°0W **151** D7
Sipocot *Phil.* 13°46N 122°58E **232** E4
Šipovo *Bos.-H.* 44°16N 17°6E **182** F2
Sipra → *India* 23°55N 75°28E **242** H6
Sipson *U.K.* 51°29N 0°26W **125** B1
Sipur *India* 21°11N 85°9E **244** D7
Sipura *Indonesia* 2°18S 99°40E **234** C1
Siqeil *Egypt* 30°7N 31°10E **117** A1
Siquia → *Nic.* 12°10N 84°20W **320** D3
Siquijor *Phil.* 9°12N 123°35E **233** G4
Siquijor □ *Phil.* 9°11N 123°35E **233** G4
Siquirres *Costa Rica* 10°6N 83°30W **320** D3
Siquisique *Venezuela* 10°34N 69°42W **328** A4
Şīr Abu Nu'ayr *U.A.E.* 25°20N 54°20E **247** E7
Şīr Banī Yās *U.A.E.* 24°19N 52°37E **247** E7
Sir Edward Pellew Group *Australia* 15°40S 137°10E **280** B2
Sir Graham Moore Is. *Australia* 13°53S 126°34E **278** B4
Sir James MacBrien, Mt. *Canada* 62°7N 127°41W **294** C7
Sira *India* 13°41N 76°49E **245** H3
Sira *Vest-Agder, Norway* 58°24N 6°40E **164** F3
Sira → *Norway* 58°23N 6°34E **164** F3
Siracusa *Italy* 37°4N 15°17E **201** E8
Sirajganj *Bangla.* 24°25N 89°47E **241** C2
Sirakoro *Mali* 12°41N 9°14W **262** C3
Şiran *Turkey* 40°11N 39°7E **213** B8
Sirasso *Ivory C.* 9°16N 6°6W **262** D3
Sirathu *India* 25°39N 81°19E **243** G9
Sirawai *Phil.* 7°34N 122°8E **233** H4
Sirdalsvatnet *Norway* 58°34N 6°43E **164** F3
Sīrdān *Iran* 36°39N 49°12E **213** D13
Sirdaryo □ *Uzbekistan* 40°30N 68°45E **217** D7
Sire *Ethiopia* 6°55N 35°36E **257** F4
Siren *U.S.A.* 45°47N 92°24W **308** C7
Sirente-Velino ⌓ *Italy* 42°10N 13°32E **199** F10
Sirer *Spain* 38°56N 1°22E **206** D1
Siret *Romania* 47°55N 26°5E **183** C11
Siret → *Romania* 45°24N 28°1E **183** E12
Sirevåg *Norway* 58°30N 5°48E **164** F2
Sirghāyā *Syria* 33°51N 36°8E **250** E7
Şiria *Romania* 46°16N 21°38E **182** D6
Sirik, Tanjong *Malaysia* 2°47N 111°15E **235** B4
Sirinath △ *Thailand* 8°6N 98°17E **237** a
Sirino, Mte. *Italy* 40°7N 15°50E **201** B8
Sīrjān *Iran* 29°30N 55°45E **247** D7
Sirkali = Sirkazhi *India* 11°15N 79°41E **245** J4
Sirkazhi *India* 11°15N 79°41E **245** J4
Sirmans *U.S.A.* 30°21N 83°39W **316** E6
Sirmaur *India* 24°51N 81°23E **243** G9
Sirna *Greece* 36°22N 26°42E **205** E8
Şirnak *Turkey* 37°32N 42°28E **213** D10
Sirohi *India* 24°52N 72°53E **242** G5
Sironj *India* 24°5N 77°39E **242** G7
Síros = Syros *Greece* 37°28N 24°57E **204** D6
Siroz = Serres *Greece* 41°5N 23°31E **202** E7
Sirpur *India* 19°29N 79°36E **244** E4
Sirrayn *Si. Arabia* 19°38N 40°36E **248** C3

Sirretta Pk. *U.S.A.* 35°56N 118°19W **307** K8
Sīrrī *Iran* 25°55N 54°32E **247** E7
Sirsa *India* 29°33N 75°4E **242** E6
Sirsa → *India* 26°51N 79°4E **243** F8
Sirsi *India* 14°40N 74°49E **245** G2
Sirsi *India* 18°23N 78°50E **244** E4
Siruela *Spain* 38°58N 5°3W **195** G5
Sirur *India* 18°50N 74°23E **244** E2
Sisak *Croatia* 45°30N 16°21E **199** C13
Sisaket *Thailand* 15°8N 104°23E **236** E5
Sisante *Spain* 39°25N 2°12W **197** F2
Sisargas, Is. *Spain* 43°21N 8°50W **194** B2
Sishen *S. Africa* 27°47S 22°59E **270** C3
Sishui *Henan, China* 34°48N 113°15E **226** G7
Sishui *Shandong, China* 35°42N 117°18E **227** G9
Sisiga *Solomon Is.* 7°54S 159°1E **287** L10
Sisimiut *Greenland* 66°40N 53°30W **154** D5
Sisipuk L. *Canada* 55°45N 101°50W **297** B8
Sisophon *Cambodia* 13°38N 102°59E **236** F4
Sissano *Papua N. G.* 3°0S 142°3E **286** B2
Sisseton *U.S.A.* 45°40N 97°3W **308** C5
Sisson = Mount Shasta
  U.S.A. 41°19N 122°19W **304** F2
Sissonne *France* 49°34N 3°51E **173** C10
Sīstān *Asia* 30°50N 61°0E **247** D9
Sīstān, Daryācheh-ye *Iran* 31°0N 61°0E **247** D9
Sīstān va Balūchestān □
  Iran 27°0N 62°0E **247** E9
Sisteron *France* 44°12N 5°57E **175** D9
Sisters *U.S.A.* 44°18N 121°33W **304** D3
Sisters, The *Grenada* 12°18N 61°36W **323** q
Sisters, The *Seychelles* 4°16S 55°52E **272** c
Sisters Pk. *Ascension I.* 7°56S 14°22W **153** g
Sisters Rocks *Trin. & Tob.* 11°20N 60°39W **323** s
Siswa Bazar *India* 27°9N 83°46E **243** F10
Sitakili *Mali* 13°7N 11°14W **262** C2
Sitakunda *Bangla.* 22°37N 91°39E **241** D3
Sitamarhi *India* 26°37N 85°30E **243** F11
Sitampiky *Madag.* 16°41S 46°6E **272** B2
Sitapur *India* 27°38N 80°45E **243** F9
Site of Former World Trade Center
  = Ground Zero *New York, U.S.A.* **132** e1
Siteki *Swaziland* 26°32S 31°58E **271** C5
Sitges *Spain* 41°17N 1°47E **196** D6
Sithonia *Greece* 40°0N 23°45E **202** F7
Sitia *Greece* 35°13N 26°6E **207** E7
Sitia ✈ (JSH) *Greece* 35°15N 26°5E **207** E7
Sítio da Abadia *Brazil* 14°48S 46°16W **333** D2
Sítio-Ozima Ridge
  Pac. Oc. 23°0N 143°0E **288** E6
Sitka *U.S.A.* 57°3N 135°20W **296** B1
Sitka □ *U.S.A.* 57°3N 135°19W **303** H14
Sitoti *Botswana* 23°15S 23°40E **270** C3
Sitra *Egypt* 28°40N 26°53E **256** B2
Sittang Myit → *Burma* 17°20N 96°45E **241** G6
Sittard *Neths.* 51°0N 5°52E **170** C5
Sittaung *Burma* 24°10N 94°55E **241** C5
Sittensen *Germany* 53°17N 9°32E **178** B5
Sittingbourne *U.K.* 51°21N 0°45E **169** F8
Sittona *Eritrea* 14°25N 37°23E **257** E4
Sittoung = Sittang Myit →
  Burma 17°20N 96°45E **241** G6
Sittwe *Burma* 20°18N 92°45E **241** E4
Situbondo *Indonesia* 7°42S 114°0E **231** G16
Siufaalete Pt.
  Amer. Samoa 14°17S 169°29W **302** f
Siulagi Pt. *Amer. Samoa* 14°13S 169°30W **302** g
Si'umu *Samoa* 14°1S 171°48W **287** W20
Siuri *India* 23°50N 87°34E **243** H12
Siutghiol, Lacul
  Romania 44°15N 28°35E **183** F13
Sivaganga *India* 9°50N 78°28E **245** K4
Sivagiri *India* 9°16N 77°26E **245** K3
Sivakasi *India* 9°24N 77°47E **245** K3
Sīvand *Iran* 30°5N 52°55E **247** D7
Sivas *Turkey* 39°43N 36°58E **212** C7
Sivas □ *Turkey* 39°45N 37°0E **212** C7
Sivasamudram *India* 12°16N 77°10E **245** H3
Sivash *Turkey* 38°31N 29°42E **205** C11
Siverek *Turkey* 37°50N 39°19E **213** D8
Sivomaskinskiy *Russia* 66°40N 62°35E **188** A11
Sivota *Greece* 39°24N 20°13E **206** C10
Sivrihisar *Turkey* 39°30N 31°35E **212** C4
Sivros *Greece* 38°40N 20°23E **207** B2
Sīwa *Egypt* 29°11N 25°31E **256** B2
Sīwa, El Wâhât es *Egypt* 29°10N 25°30E **256** B2
Siwalik Range *Nepal* 28°0N 83°0E **243** F10
Siwan *India* 25°38N 72°25E **242** G5
Siwana *India* 25°38N 72°25E **242** G5
Six Cross Roads *Barbados* 13°7N 59°28W **323** g
Sixmilebridge *Ireland* 52°44N 8°46W **166** D3
Sixth Cataract *Sudan* 16°20N 32°42E **257** D3
Siyāl, Jazâ'ir *Egypt* 22°49N 36°12E **256** C4
Siyäzän *Azerbaijan* 41°3N 49°10E **191** K9
Siziwang Qi *China* 41°25N 111°40E **226** D6
Sjælland *Denmark* 55°30N 11°30E **163** J5
Sjælland □ *Denmark* 55°30N 11°30E **163** J5
Sjællands Odde *Denmark* 55°58N 11°24E **163** J5
Sjenica *Serbia* 43°16N 20°0E **202** C3
Sjoa *Norway* 61°41N 9°33E **164** C2
Sjöbo *Sweden* 55°37N 13°45E **163** J7
Sjøholt *Norway* 62°27N 6°52E **164** B3
Sjølisand *Norway* 61°29N 11°18E **164** C6
Sjötofta *Sweden* 57°22N 13°17E **163** G7
Sjötorp *Sweden* 58°50N 14°0E **163** F7
Sjumen = Shumen
  Bulgaria 43°18N 26°55E **203** C10
Sjuntorp *Sweden* 58°12N 12°13E **163** F6
Skábu *Norway* 61°32N 9°24E **164** C6
Skadarsko Jezero *Europe* 42°10N 19°20E **202** D3
Skadovsk *Ukraine* 46°17N 32°52E **189** E7
Skælskør *Denmark* 55°16N 11°18E **163** J5
Skærbæk *Denmark* 55°9N 8°45E **163** J3
Skaftafell *Iceland* 64°1N 17°0W **155** D5
Skaftafell △ *Iceland* 64°1N 16°50W **155** C9
Skagafjarðarsýsla □
  Iceland 65°30N 19°0W **155** B7
Skagafjörður *Iceland* 65°54N 19°35W **155** B7
Skagastølstindane
  Norway 61°28N 7°52E **164** C4
Skagaströnd *Iceland* 65°50N 20°19W **155** B6
Skagatá *Iceland* 66°7N 20°6W **155** B4
Skagen *Denmark* 57°43N 10°35E **163** G4
Skagern *Sweden* 59°0N 14°20E **162** E8
Skagerrak *Denmark* 57°30N 9°0E **163** H3
Skagit → *U.S.A.* 48°23N 122°22W **306** B4
Skagway *U.S.A.* 59°28N 135°19W **303** G14
Skala *Greece* 35°28N 26°34E **207** C2
Skala nad Zbruczem = Skala-
  Podilska *Ukraine* 48°50N 26°15E **183** B11
Skala-Podilska *Ukraine* 48°50N 26°15E **183** B11
Skala Podolskaya = Skala-Podilska
  Ukraine 48°50N 26°15E **183** B11

Skálavik *Norway* 58°5N 8°1E **164** F5
Skalica *Slovak Rep.* 48°50N 17°15E **181** C10
Skallingen *Denmark* 55°33N 8°13E **163** J2
Skalni Dol = Kamenyak
  Bulgaria 43°24N 26°57E **203** C10
Skanderborg *Denmark* 56°2N 9°55E **163** H3
Skåne *Sweden* 55°59N 13°30E **163** J7
Skåne län □ *Sweden* 56°15N 14°0E **163** H7
Skaneateles *U.S.A.* 42°57N 76°26W **313** D8
Skaneateles L. *U.S.A.* 42°51N 76°22W **313** D8
Skånevik *Norway* 59°43N 5°53E **164** E2
Skänninge *Sweden* 58°24N 15°5E **163** F9
Skanör med Falsterbo
  Sweden 55°24N 12°50E **163** J6
Skansen *Sweden* 59°19N 18°7E **139** B2
Skantzoura *Greece* 39°5N 24°6E **204** B6
Skara *Sweden* 58°25N 13°30E **163** F7
Skärblacka *Sweden* 58°35N 15°54E **163** F9
Skarð *Iceland* 65°17N 22°19W **155** D1
Skärhamn *Sweden* 57°59N 11°34E **163** G5
Skarnes *Norway* 60°15N 11°41E **164** D8
Skärplinge *Sweden* 60°33N 17°24E **161** B11
Skarpäng *Sweden* 59°26N 18°0E **139** A2
Skarpnäck *Sweden* 59°16N 18°7E **139** B2
Skarszewy *Poland* 54°4N 18°25E **184** D5
Skaryszew *Poland* 51°19N 21°15E **185** G8
Skaryszewski, Park
  Poland 52°15N 21°3E **142** B2
Skarżysko-Kamienna
  Poland 51°7N 20°52E **185** G7
Skattkärr *Sweden* 59°26N 13°40E **162** E7
Skattungbyn *Sweden* 61°10N 14°56E **162** C8
Skawina *Poland* 49°59N 19°50E **185** J6
Skebokvarn *Sweden* 59°58N 16°36E **162** E12
Skeena → *Canada* 54°9N 130°5W **296** C2
Skeena Mts. *Canada* 56°40N 128°30W **296** B3
Skegness *U.K.* 53°9N 0°20E **168** D8
Skei *Norway* 61°34N 6°28E **164** C2
Skeiðarársandur *Iceland* 63°54N 17°14W **155** D9
Skeiðflötur *Iceland* 63°26N 19°11W **155** D7
Skela *Serbia* 44°31N 20°0E **202** C4
Skeldon = Corriverton
  Guyana 5°55N 57°20W **329** B6
Skeleton Coast △ *Namibia* 20°0S 13°20E **270** B1
Skellefteå *Sweden* 64°45N 20°50E **160** D19
Skellefteälven →
  Sweden 64°45N 21°10E **160** D19
Skelleftehamn *Sweden* 64°40N 21°9E **160** D19
Skender Vakuf *Bos.-H.* 44°29N 17°22E **182** F2
Skeppsholmen *Stockholm, Sweden* **139** d3
Skerries, The *U.K.* 53°25N 4°36W **168** D3
Skhidnytsya *Ukraine* 49°13N 23°20E **185** J10
Skhíza *Greece* 36°41N 21°40E **204** E3
Ski *Norway* 59°43N 10°52E **164** E7
Skiathos *Greece* 39°12N 23°30E **204** B5
Skibbereen *Ireland* 51°33N 9°16W **166** E2
Skiddaw *U.K.* 54°39N 3°9W **168** C4
Skidegate *Canada* 53°15N 132°1W **296** C2
Skídra *Greece* 40°46N 22°10E **202** F6
Skien *Norway* 59°12N 9°35E **164** E6
Skierniewice *Poland* 51°58N 20°10E **185** G7
Skíkda *Algeria* 36°50N 6°58E **261** A6
Skíkda □ *Algeria* 36°45N 6°50E **261** A6
Skillet Fork → *U.S.A.* 38°5N 88°5W **311** F8
Skillingaryd *Sweden* 57°27N 14°5E **163** G8
Skillinge *Sweden* 55°30N 14°16E **163** J8
Skilloura *Cyprus* 35°14N 33°10E **207** D12
Skinari, Ákra *Greece* 37°56N 20°42E **207** D2
Skinnastaður *Iceland* 66°4N 16°27W **155** A10
Skinnskatteberg *Sweden* 59°50N 15°42E **162** E9
Skipton *Vic., Australia* 37°39S 143°40E **282** D5
Skipton *N. Yorks., U.K.* 53°58N 2°3W **168** D5
Skiptvet *Norway* 59°28N 11°11E **164** E8
Skírino, C. *Senegal* 16°46W **262** C1
Skíros *Greece* 38°50N 24°21E **204** C6
Skiropoula *Greece* 38°50N 24°21E **204** C6
Skíros *Greece* 38°55N 24°34E **204** C6
Skivarp *Sweden* 55°26N 13°34E **163** J7
Skive *Denmark* 56°33N 9°2E **163** H3
Skjærhallen *Norway* 59°2N 11°2E **164** E8
Skjálfandafljót →
  Iceland 65°59N 17°25W **155** B9
Skjálfandi *Iceland* 66°5N 17°30W **155** A9
Skjeberg *Norway* 59°12N 11°12E **164** E8
Skjern *Denmark* 55°57N 8°30E **163** J2
Skjolden *Norway* 61°31N 5°34E **164** C4
Skjöldólfsstaðir *Iceland* 65°19N 15°7W **155** B11
Skjønhaug *Norway* 59°39N 11°19E **164** E8
Skkobelev = Farghona
  Uzbekistan 40°23N 71°19E **217** D8
Skobeleva, Pik
  Kyrgyzstan 39°48N 72°36E **217** E8
Skoczów *Poland* 49°49N 18°45E **185** J5
Skodje *Norway* 62°30N 6°43E **164** B3
Škofja Loka *Slovenia* 46°9N 14°19E **199** B11
Skógar *Iceland* 63°32N 19°28W **155** D7
Skoghall *Sweden* 59°20N 13°30E **162** E7
Skogstorp *Sweden* 59°19N 16°2E **162** E11
Skoki *Poland* 52°40N 17°11E **185** F4
Skokie → *U.S.A.* 42°2N 87°43W **119** A2
Skokie → *U.S.A.* 42°3N 87°44W **119** A2
Skokie Heritage Museum
  U.S.A. 42°2N 87°44W **119** A2
Skoklefall *Norway* 59°50N 10°40E **164** E7
Skole *Ukraine* 49°3N 23°30E **177** D12
Skollenborg *Norway* 59°38N 9°43E **164** E6
Sköllersta *Sweden* 59°15N 18°6E **139** B2
Skópelos *Greece* 35°11N 26°2E **207** E7
Skopin *Russia* 53°55N 39°32E **188** F10
Skopje *Macedonia* 42°1N 21°26E **202** D5
Skopje ✈ (SKP) *Macedonia* 41°59N 21°29E **202** E5
Skoppum *Norway* 59°23N 10°20E **164** E7
Skórcz *Poland* 53°47N 18°30E **184** E5
Skogstorp *Norway* 59°12N 9°30E **164** E6
Skotfoss *Norway* 59°12N 9°30E **164** E6
Skotterud *Norway* 60°1N 12°7E **164** D9
Skövde *Sweden* 58°24N 13°50E **163** F7
Skovlunde *Denmark* 55°44N 12°23E **118** A2
Skovorodino *Russia* 54°0N 124°0E **215** D13
Skowhegan *U.S.A.* 44°46N 69°43W **309** C19
Skradin *Croatia* 43°52N 15°53E **199** D12
Skreia *Norway* 60°40N 10°56E **164** D7
Skrim *Norway* 59°31N 9°38E **164** E6
Skrunda *Latvia* 56°41N 22°11E **186** B9
Skrwa → *Poland* 52°35N 19°52E **185** F6
Skudeneshavn *Norway* 59°10N 5°10E **164** E1
Skuleskogen △ *Sweden* 63°5N 18°30E **162** A12
Skull *Ireland* 51°32N 9°34W **166** E2
Skultorp *Sweden* 58°24N 13°50E **163** F7
Skultuna *Sweden* 59°43N 16°25E **162** E10
Skuodas *Lithuania* 56°16N 21°33E **184** B8
Skurup *Sweden* 55°28N 13°30E **163** J7
Skútustaðir *Iceland* 65°34N 17°2W **155** B9

Skvyra *Ukraine* 49°44N 29°40E **177** D15
Skwierzyna *Poland* 52°33N 15°30E **185** F2
Sky Dome *Toronto, Canada* **141** e1
Sky Lake *U.S.A.* 28°27N 81°23W **133** B2
Skye *U.K.* 57°15N 6°10W **167** D2
Skykomish *U.S.A.* 47°42N 121°22W **304** C3
Skyland *U.S.A.* 38°34N 119°0W **314** J3
Skyring, Seno *Chile* 52°35S 72°0W **336** D3
Skyros = Skíros *Greece* 38°55N 24°34E **204** C6
Skyttorp *Sweden* 60°5N 17°44E **162** D11
Slade Green *U.K.* 51°27N 0°11E **169** N5
Slade Pt. *Australia* 21°5S 149°13E **280** K7
Slættaratindur *Færoe Is.* 62°18N 7°1W **160** E9
Slagbaai, Boca *Neth. Ant.* 12°18N 68°24W **322** h
Slagelse *Denmark* 55°23N 11°19E **163** J5
Slamet *Indonesia* 7°16S 109°8E **235** D3
Slane *Ireland* 53°42N 6°33W **166** C5
Slaney → *Ireland* 52°26N 6°33W **166** D5
Slangberge *S. Africa* 31°32S 20°48E **270** D3
Slănic *Romania* 45°14N 25°58E **183** E10
Slano *Croatia* 42°48N 17°53E **202** D1
Slantsy *Russia* 59°7N 28°5E **188** C5
Slaný *Czech Rep.* 50°13N 14°6E **180** A7
Śląsk *Poland* 51°0N 16°30E **176** C9
Śląskie □ *Poland* 50°30N 19°0E **185** H6
Slātbaken *Sweden* 58°25N 16°45E **163** F10
Slate Is. *Canada* 48°40N 87°0W **298** C2
Slater *U.S.A.* 39°13N 93°4W **310** E3
Slatina *Croatia* 45°43N 17°37E **199** C14
Slatina *Romania* 44°28N 24°22E **183** F9
Slatina Timiş *Romania* 45°11N 22°16E **183** F9
Slatington *U.S.A.* 40°45N 75°37W **313** F9
Slaton *U.S.A.* 33°26N 101°39W **314** j4
Slave → *Canada* 61°18N 113°39W **296** A6
Slave Coast *W. Afr.* 6°0N 2°30E **263** D5
Slave Lake *Canada* 55°17N 114°43W **296** B6
Slave Pt. *Canada* 61°11N 115°56W **296** A5
Slavgorod *Russia* 53°1N 78°37E **218** D9
Slavinja *Serbia* 43°9N 22°50E **202** C6
Slavkov u Brna
  Czech Rep. 49°10N 16°52E **181** B9
Slavkovský Les △
  Czech Rep. 50°5N 12°44E **180** A5
Slavonija *Europe* 45°20N 17°40E **182** E2
Slavonski Brod *Croatia* 45°11N 18°1E **182** E3
Slavsk *Russia* 55°3N 21°30E **184** C7
Slavuta *Ukraine* 48°51N 23°27E **183** B8
Slavskoye *Russia* 54°30N 20°27E **184** D7
Slavuta *Ukraine* 50°15N 27°2E **177** C14
Slavyanka *Russia* 42°53N 131°21E **220** C5
Slavyanovo *Bulgaria* 43°28N 24°52E **203** C8
Slavyansk = Slovyansk
  Ukraine 48°55N 37°36E **189** H9
Slavyansk-na-Kubani
  Russia 45°15N 38°11E **189** K10
Slawharad *Belarus* 53°27N 31°0E **177** B16
Sławno *Poland* 54°20N 16°41E **184** D3
Sławoborze *Poland* 53°55N 15°42E **184** D2
Sleaford *U.K.* 53°0N 0°24E **168** D7
Sleaford B. *Australia* 34°55S 135°45E **282** E2
Sleat, Sd. of *U.K.* 57°5N 5°47W **167** D3
Sleðbrjótur *Iceland* 65°34N 14°30W **155** B12
Sleeper Is. *Canada* 58°30N 81°0W **295** D11
Sleeping Bear Dunes △
  U.S.A. 44°50N 86°5W **308** C10
Sleepy Eye *U.S.A.* 44°18N 94°43W **308** C6
Sleetmute *U.S.A.* 61°42N 157°10W **303** F8
Sleman *Indonesia* 7°40S 110°20E **235** D4
Slemmestad *Norway* 59°46N 10°29E **133** A2
Slemon L. *Canada* 63°13N 116°4W **296** A5
Slependen *Norway* 59°52N 10°33E **133** A2
Ślesin *Poland* 52°22N 18°14E **185** F5
Slide Mt. *U.S.A.* 42°0N 74°25W **313** E10
Slidell *U.S.A.* 30°17N 89°47W **315** F10
Slidre *Norway* 61°5N 8°58E **164** C5
Sliema *Malta* 35°55N 14°30E **206** F8
Slieve Aughty *Ireland* 53°4N 8°30W **166** C3
Slieve Bloom *Ireland* 53°4N 7°40W **166** C4
Slieve Donard *U.K.* 54°11N 5°55W **166** B6
Slieve Gamph *Ireland* 54°6N 9°0W **166** B3
Slieve Gullion *U.K.* 54°7N 6°26W **166** B5
Slieve League *Ireland* 54°40N 8°42W **166** B3
Slieve Mish *Ireland* 52°12N 9°50W **166** D2
Slievenamon *Ireland* 52°25N 7°34W **166** D4
Sligeach = Sligo *Ireland* 54°16N 8°28W **166** B3
Sligo *Sligo, Ireland* 54°16N 8°28W **166** B3
Sligo *Pa., U.S.A.* 41°6N 79°29W **312** E5
Sligo □ *Ireland* 54°8N 8°42W **166** B3
Sligo B. *Ireland* 54°18N 8°40W **166** B3
Slipi *Indonesia* 6°11S 106°47E **122** B1
Slippery Rock *U.S.A.* 41°4N 80°3W **312** E4
Slite *Sweden* 57°42N 18°48E **163** G12
Sliven *Bulgaria* 42°42N 26°19E **203** D10
Slivenec *Czech Rep.* 50°1N 14°21E **181** B3
Slivnitsa *Bulgaria* 42°50N 23°2E **202** D7
Sloan *U.S.A.* 35°57N 115°12W **307** K11
Sloansville *U.S.A.* 42°45N 74°22W **313** D10
Slobidka *Ukraine* 47°54N 29°21E **183** C14
Slobodskoy *Russia* 58°40N 50°6E **188** C9
Slobozia *Argeş, Romania* 44°34N 25°50E **183** F9
Slobozia *Ialomiţa,*
  Romania 44°34N 27°23E **183** F12
Slocan *Canada* 49°48N 117°28W **296** D5
Slocomb *U.S.A.* 31°7N 85°36W **316** D4
Slomikhino = Furmanovo
  Kazakhstan 49°42N 49°25E **190** F9
Słomniki *Poland* 50°16N 20°4E **185** H7
Slonim *Belarus* 53°4N 25°19E **177** B13
Slot, The = New Georgia Sound
  Solomon Is. 8°0S 158°0E **287** L9
Sloten *Neths.* 52°21N 4°48E **112** A1
Sloterpark *Neths.* 52°22N 4°49E **112** A1
Slotermeer *Neths.* 52°22N 4°49E **112** A1
Slottet *Oslo, Norway* **133** a1
Slough *U.K.* 51°30N 0°36W **169** F7
Slough □ *U.K.* 51°30N 0°36W **169** F7
Sloughhouse *U.S.A.* 38°26N 121°12W **306** G5
Slovak Rep. ■
  Europe 48°30N 20°0E **181** C13
Slovakia = Slovak Rep. ■
  Europe 48°30N 20°0E **181** C13
Slovakian Ore Mts. = Slovenské
  Rudohorie *Slovak Rep.* 48°45N 20°0E **181** C12
Slovenia ■ *Europe* 45°58N 14°30E **199** C11
Slovenija = Slovenia ■
  Europe 45°58N 14°30E **199** C11
Slovenj Gradec *Slovenia* 46°31N 15°5E **199** B12
Slovenska = Slovak Rep. ■
  Europe 48°30N 20°0E **181** C13
Slovenska Bistrica
  Slovenia 46°24N 15°35E **199** B12
Slovenske Konjice
  Slovenia 46°20N 15°28E **199** B12
Slovenské Rudohorie
  Slovak Rep. 48°45N 20°0E **181** C12
Slovenský Raj △
  Slovak Rep. 48°53N 20°25E **181** C13
Slovyansk *Ukraine* 48°55N 37°36E **189** H9
Słowiński △ *Poland* 54°45N 17°0E **184** D4
Słubice *Poland* 52°22N 14°35E **185** F1
Sluch → *Ukraine* 51°37N 26°38E **177** C14

Sluhy *Czech Rep.* 50°11N 14°33E **135** A3
Sluis *Neths.* 51°18N 3°23E **170** C3
Słunchev Bryag
  Bulgaria 42°40N 27°41E **203** D11
Slunj *Croatia* 45°6N 15°33E **199** C12
Slupca *Poland* 52°15N 17°52E **185** F4
Słupia → *Poland* 54°35N 16°51E **184** D3
Słupsk *Poland* 54°30N 17°3E **184** D4
Slurry *S. Africa* 25°49S 25°42E **270** D4
Slutsk *Belarus* 53°2N 27°31E **177** B14
Slutsk = Pavlovsk *Russia* 59°40N 30°45E **190** E5
Slutsk *Belarus* 53°2N 27°31E **177** B14
Slyne Hd. *Ireland* 53°25N 10°10W **166** C1
Slyudyanka *Russia* 51°40N 103°40E **215** D11
Smaalenene = Østfold □
  Norway 59°25N 11°25E **164** E8
Småland *Sweden* 57°15N 15°25E **163** G9
Smålandsfarvandet
  Denmark 55°10N 11°20E **163** J5
Smålandsstenar *Sweden* 57°10N 13°25E **163** H7
Smaldeel = Theunissen
  S. Africa 28°26S 26°43E **270** D4
Smalltree L. *Canada* 61°0N 105°0W **297** A8
Smallwood Res. *Canada* 54°5N 64°30W **299** B7
Smara *W. Sahara* 26°48N 11°41W **260** C2
Smarhon *Belarus* 54°20N 26°24E **177** A14
Smarje *Slovenia* 46°15N 15°34E **199** B12
Smartt Syndicate Dam
  S. Africa 30°45S 23°10E **270** D3
Smartville *U.S.A.* 39°13N 121°18W **306** F5
Smeaton *Canada* 53°30N 104°49W **297** C8
Smedby *Sweden* 56°39N 16°13E **163** H10
Smederevo *Serbia* 44°40N 20°57E **202** B4
Smederevska Palanka
  Serbia 44°22N 20°58E **202** B4
Smedjebacken *Sweden* 60°8N 15°25E **162** D9
Smela = Smila *Ukraine* 49°15N 31°58E **189** H6
Smerwick Harbour
  Ireland 52°12N 10°23W **166** D1
Smethport *U.S.A.* 41°49N 78°27W **312** E6
Smichov *Czech Rep.* 50°4N 14°23E **181** B3
Smidovich *Russia* 48°36N 133°49E **215** E14
Śmigiel *Poland* 52°1N 16°32E **185** F3
Smila *Ukraine* 49°15N 31°58E **189** H6
Smilyan *Bulgaria* 41°29N 24°46E **203** E8
Smith → *U.S.A.* 55°10N 114°0W **296** B6
Smith B. *U.S.A.* 70°30N 154°20W **303** A9
Smith Center *U.S.A.* 39°47N 98°47W **308** F4
Smith Forest Preserve
  U.S.A. 41°59N 87°45W **119** B2
Smith River → *U.S.A.* 41°55N 124°0W **304** F2
Smith Sd. *N. Amer.* 78°25N 74°0W **154** B3
Smithburne → *Australia* 17°3S 140°57E **280** B3
Smithers *Canada* 54°45N 127°10W **296** C3
Smithfield *S. Africa* 30°9S 26°30E **271** D4
Smithfield *N.C., U.S.A.* 35°31N 78°21W **315** D15
Smithfield *Utah, U.S.A.* 41°50N 111°50W **304** F8
Smiths *U.S.A.* 32°32N 85°6W **316** C4
Smiths Falls *Canada* 44°55N 76°0W **313** B9
Smithson B. = Manuae
  Cook Is. 19°15S 158°45W **289** K13
Smithsonian Institution
  Washington, D.C., U.S.A. **143** b2
Smithton *Australia* 40°53S 145°6E **281** G4
Smithton *Ont., Canada* 43°6N 79°33W **312** C5
Smithville *Ga., U.S.A.* 31°54N 84°15W **316** D5
Smithville *Mo., U.S.A.* 39°23N 94°35W **310** E3
Smithville *Tex., U.S.A.* 30°1N 97°10W **314** F6
Smoky → *Canada* 56°10N 117°21W **296** B5
Smoky Bay *Australia* 32°22S 134°13E **281** E1
Smoky Hill → *U.S.A.* 39°4N 96°48W **308** F5
Smoky Hills *U.S.A.* 39°15N 99°30W **308** F4
Smoky Lake *Canada* 54°10N 112°30W **296** C6
Smøla *Norway* 63°23N 8°3E **164** A5
Smolensk *Russia* 54°45N 32°5E **188** E7
Smolensk □ *Russia* 55°20N 33°0E **188** E7
Smolikas, Oros *Greece* 40°9N 20°58E **202** F4
Smolník *Slovak Rep.* 48°43N 20°44E **181** C13
Smolny *Russia* 59°56N 30°25E **137** B2
Smolny Cathedral *Russia* 59°56N 30°24E **137** B2
Smolyan *Bulgaria* 41°36N 24°38E **203** E8
Smooth Rock Falls
  Canada 49°17N 81°37W **298** C3
Smoothstone L. *Canada* 54°40N 106°50W **297** C7
Smorgon = Smarhon
  Belarus 54°20N 26°24E **177** A14
Smotrych *Ukraine* 48°57N 26°33E **183** B11
Smotrych → *Ukraine* 48°37N 26°39E **183** B11
Smulti *Romania* 45°57N 27°44E **183** E12
Smyadovo *Bulgaria* 43°2N 27°1E **203** C11
Smygehamn *Sweden* 55°21N 13°22E **163** J7
Smyrna = İzmir *Turkey* 38°25N 27°8E **205** C9
Smyrna *Del., U.S.A.* 39°18N 75°36W **309** F16
Smyrna *Ga., U.S.A.* 33°53N 84°31W **316** B5
Snæfell *Iceland* 64°48N 15°34W **155** C11
Snaefell *I. of Man* 54°16N 4°27W **168** C3
Snæfellsjökull *Iceland* 64°49N 23°46W **155** D1
Snæfellsnessýsla □ *Iceland* 65°0N 23°0W **155** D1
Snake → *U.S.A.* 46°12N 119°2W **304** C4
Snake Creek Canal
  U.S.A. 25°57N 80°19W **128** A2
Snake I. *Australia* 38°47S 146°33E **283** E7
Snake Pt. *Anguilla* 18°17N 62°58W **322** a
Snake Range *U.S.A.* 39°0N 114°20W **304** G6
Snake River Plain *U.S.A.* 42°50N 114°0W **304** E7
Snakenden Branch →
  U.S.A. 38°55N 77°18W **143** B1
Snaroya *Norway* 59°52N 10°33E **133** A2
Snasahögarna *Sweden* 63°11N 12°10E **162** A5
Snåsavatnet *Norway* 64°12N 12°0E **160** D5
Snåttringe *Sweden* 59°15N 17°58E **139** B1
Snedsted *Denmark* 56°55N 8°32E **163** H2
Sneek *Neths.* 53°2N 5°40E **170** A5
Sneem *Ireland* 51°50N 9°54W **166** E2
Sneeuberge *S. Africa* 31°46S 24°20E **270** D3
Sofara *Mali* 13°59N 4°9W **262** C4
Snežka *Europe* 50°41N 15°50E **180** A8
Snežnik *Slovenia* 45°36N 14°35E **199** C11
Sniadowo *Poland* 53°1N 22°6E **185** E8
Sniardwy, Jezioro *Poland* 53°48N 21°50E **185** E8
Snigirevka *Ukraine* 47°2N 32°49E **189** J7
Snihurivka *Ukraine* 47°2N 32°49E **189** J7
Snizort, L. *U.K.* 57°33N 6°28W **167** D2
Snøhetta *Norway* 62°19N 9°16E **164** B5
Snohomish *U.S.A.* 47°55N 122°6W **306** B4
Snønuten *Norway* 59°31N 6°52E **164** E3
Snoul *Cambodia* 12°4N 106°26E **237** F6
Snovsk = Shchors
  Ukraine 51°48N 31°56E **189** G6
Snow Hill *U.S.A.* 38°11N 75°24W **309** F16
Snow Lake *Canada* 54°52N 100°3W **297** C8

Soh *Iran* 33°26N 51°27E **247** C6
Sohâg *Egypt* 26°33N 31°43E **256** B3
Sohagpur *India* 22°42N 78°12E **242** H8
Sohano *Papua N. G.* 5°22S 154°37E **286** C8
Sohela *India* 21°18N 83°24E **244** D6
Soheuksando *S. Korea* 34°4N 125°7E **224** E2
Sohm Abyssal Plain
  Atl. Oc. 36°0N 55°0W **152** C6
Soho *London, U.K.* **125** b3
Soho *New York, U.S.A.* **132** e1
Soignes, Forêt de *Belgium* 50°47N 4°25E **116** B2
Soignies *Belgium* 50°35N 4°5E **170** D4
Soin *Burkina Faso* 12°47N 3°50W **262** C4
Soira *Eritrea* 14°45N 39°30E **257** E4
Soissons *France* 49°25N 3°19E **173** C10
Söja *Japan* 34°40N 133°45E **222** C5
Sojat *India* 25°55N 73°45E **242** G5
Sok → *Russia* 53°24N 50°8E **190** D10
Sok Kwu Wan *China* 22°13N 114°7E **221** I10
Sokal *Ukraine* 50°31N 24°15E **177** C13
Sokcho *S. Korea* 38°12N 128°36E **224** C4
Söke *Turkey* 37°48N 27°28E **205** D9
Sokelo
  Dem. Rep. of the Congo 9°55S 24°36E **265** D4
Sokhumi *Georgia* 43°0N 41°0E **191** J5
Sokki, Oued In → *Algeria* 29°30N 3°42E **261** C5
Sokna *Norway* 60°13N 9°50E **164** D6
Soknedal *Norway* 62°57N 10°13E **164** B7
Soko Banja *Serbia* 43°40N 21°51E **202** C5
Soko Is. *China* 22°10N 113°54E **219** G10
Sokodé *Togo* 9°0N 1°11E **263** D5
Sokol *Russia* 59°30N 40°5E **188** C11
Sokolac *Bos.-H.* 43°56N 18°48E **182** G3
Sokółka *Poland* 53°25N 23°30E **184** E10
Sokolki *Russia* 55°47N 37°40E **129** B4
Sokolo *Ségou, Mali* 14°53N 6°8W **262** C3
Sokolov *Czech Rep.* 50°12N 12°40E **180** A5
Sokolów Poland 52°9N 20°51E **142** C1
Sokolów Małopolski *Poland* 50°14N 22°7E **185** H9
Sokolów Podlaski *Poland* 52°25N 22°15E **185** F9
Sokoły *Poland* 52°59N 22°42E **185** F9
Sokoto *Nigeria* 13°2N 5°16E **263** C6
Sokoto □ *Nigeria* 12°30N 6°0E **263** C5
Sokoto → *Nigeria* 11°20N 4°10E **263** C5
Sokyrnytsya *Ukraine* 48°7N 23°23E **183** B12
Sokyryany *Ukraine* 48°27N 27°22E **183** B12
Sol Iletsk *Russia* 51°10N 55°0E **186** D10
Sola *Vanuatu* 13°51S 167°37E **287** C5
Sola → *Poland* 50°4N 19°15E **185** H6
Solai *Kenya* 0°2N 36°12E **268** B4
Solalinden *Germany* 48°5N 11°42E **131** B3
Solan *India* 30°55N 77°7E **242** D7
Solana Beach *U.S.A.* `17°39N 121°41E **232** C3
Solana Phil. `17°39N 121°41E **232** C3
Solander I. *N.Z.* 46°34S 166°54E **285** G1
Solapur *India* 17°43N 75°56E **244** F2
Solca *Romania* 47°40N 25°50E **183** C10
Solda Gölü *Turkey* 37°33N 29°42E **205** D11
Söldanleli *Moldova* 47°49N 28°48E **183** C13
Solde u *Andorra* 42°35N 1°40E **196** C6
Soldeu *Andorra* 42°35N 1°40E **196** C6
Soldier Field *Chicago, U.S.A.* **119** a3
Soldier Pt. *Antigua & B.* 17°2N 61°41W **322** b
Soldin = Myślibórz
  Poland 52°55N 14°50E **185** F1
Soldotna *U.S.A.* 60°29N 151°3W **303** F10
Soléa *Cyprus* 35°5N 33°4E **207** E9
Solec Kujawski *Poland* 53°5N 18°14E **185** E5
Soledad *Colombia* 10°55N 74°46W **328** A4
Soledad *Calif., U.S.A.* 36°26N 121°20W **306** J5
Soledad *Venezuela* 8°10N 63°34W **329** B5
Solemint *U.S.A.* 34°26N 118°26W **317** L8
Solen *Norway* 61°53N 11°31E **164** C8
Solent, The *U.K.* 50°45N 1°25W **169** G6
Solenzara *France* 41°53N 9°23E **175** G13
Solesmes *France* 50°10N 3°30E **173** B10
Solfjellsjøen *Norway* 66°22N 12°52E **160** D5
Solfonntaggen *Norway* 60°2N 6°57E **164** D3
Solhan *Turkey* 38°57N 41°3E **213** C9
Solheim *Norway* 60°53N 5°27E **164** D2
Soligalich *Russia* 59°5N 42°10E **188** C12
Soligorsk = Salihorsk
  Belarus 52°51N 27°27E **177** B14
Solihull *U.K.* 52°26N 1°47W **169** E6
Solikamsk *Russia* 59°38N 56°50E **188** C10
Solila *Madag.* 21°25S 46°37E **272** C2
Solimões = Amazonas →
  S. Amer. 0°5S 50°0W **329** D8
Solin *Croatia* 43°33N 16°30E **199** E13
Solingen *Germany* 51°10N 7°5E **178** D3
Söll *Austria* 47°30N 12°11E **179** H8
Sollefteå *Sweden* 63°12N 17°20E **162** A11
Sollentuna *Sweden* 59°26N 17°56E **139** A1
Sóller *Spain* 39°46N 2°43E **196** B3
Sollerön *Sweden* 60°55N 14°37E **162** D8
Solling *Germany* 51°44N 9°36E **178** D5
Solling-Vogler △ *Germany* 51°45N 9°32E **178** D5
Solln *Germany* 48°4N 11°31E **131** B2
Sollsvika *Norway* 60°26N 4°58E **164** D1
Solna *Sweden* 59°21N 17°59E **139** A1
Solnechnogorsk *Russia* 56°10N 36°57E **188** D9
Solntsevo *Russia* 55°38N 37°23E **129** C2
Solo → *Indonesia* 6°47S 112°22E **231** G15
Solofra *Italy* 40°50N 14°51E **201** B7
Sologne *France* 47°40N 1°45E **173** E8
Solok *Indonesia* 0°45S 100°40E **234** D2
Sololá *Guatemala* 14°49N 91°10W **320** D1
Sololo *Kenya* 3°33N 38°39E **268** B4
Solomon, N. Fork →
  U.S.A. 39°29N 98°26W **308** F4
Solomon, S. Fork →
  U.S.A. 39°25N 99°12W **308** F4
Solomon Is. *Papua N. G.* 6°0S 155°0E **286** D8
Solomon Rise *Pac. Oc.* 1°0N 157°0E **288** G7
Solomon Sea *Papua N. G.* 7°0S 150°0E **286** D8
Solon *China* 46°32N 121°10E **219** B7
Solon Springs *U.S.A.* 46°22N 91°49W **308** B8
Solonópole *Brazil* 5°44S 39°1W **332** C4
Solor *Indonesia* 8°27S 123°0E **231** F6
Solotcha *Russia* 54°48N 39°53E **188** E10
Solothurn *Switz.* 47°13N 7°32E **179** H3
Solothurn □ *Switz.* 47°18N 7°40E **179** H3
Solotvyn *Ukraine* 48°42N 24°25E **183** B9
Solsona *Spain* 41°59N 1°31E **196** C6
Solt *Hungary* 46°45N 19°1E **181** E10
Soltau *Germany* 52°59N 9°50E **178** B5
Soltsy *Russia* 58°10N 30°30E **188** C6
Soltüstik Qazaqstan □
  Kazakhstan 54°0N 70°0E **217** D8
Solund *Norway* 61°5N 4°50E **164** C1
Solunska Glava
  Macedonia 41°44N 21°31E **202** E5
Solvang *U.S.A.* 34°36N 120°8W **317** L6
Solvay *U.S.A.* 43°3N 76°13W **313** D8
Sölvesborg *Sweden* 56°5N 14°35E **163** H8
Solvychegodsk *Russia* 61°21N 46°56E **188** B8
Solway Firth *U.K.* 54°49N 3°35W **168** C4
Solwezi *Zambia* 12°11S 26°21E **269** E2

Sõma Japan 37°40N 140°50E 220 F10
Soma Turkey 39°10N 27°35E 205 B9
Somabhula Zimbabwe 19°42S 29°40E 271 A4
Somali = Sumale □ Ethiopia 7°0N 45°0E 267 C6
Somali Pen. Africa 7°0N 46°0E 254 F8
Somali Rep. ■ Africa 7°0N 47°0E 267 C6
Somalia = Somali Rep. ■ Africa 7°0N 47°0E 267 C6
Somaliland □ Somali Rep. 9°0N 46°0E 267 C6
Sombe Dzong Bhutan 27°13N 89°8E 241 B2
Sombernon France 47°20N 4°40E 173 E11
Sombo Angola 8°42S 20°59E 265 D4
Sombor Serbia 45°46N 19°9E 182 E4
Sombra Canada 42°43N 82°29W 312 D2
Sombrerete Mexico 23°38N 103°39W 318 C4
Sombrero Anguilla 18°37N 63°30W 321 C7
Sombrero Channel India 7°41N 93°35E 245 L11
Şomcuta Mare Romania 47°31N 23°28E 183 C8
Somdari India 25°47N 72°38E 242 G5
Someido △ Spain 43°5N 6°11W 194 B4
Somers U.S.A. 48°5N 114°13W 304 B6
Somerset Bermuda 32°17N 64°52W 153 a
Somerset Ky., U.S.A. 37°5N 84°36W 309 G11
Somerset Mass., U.S.A. 41°47N 71°8W 313 E13
Somerset Md., U.S.A. 38°57N 77°5W 143 B3
Somerset Pa., U.S.A. 40°1N 79°5W 312 F5
Somerset □ U.K. 51°9N 3°0W 169 F5
Somerset East S. Africa 32°42S 25°35E 270 D4
Somerset I. Bermuda 32°17N 64°52W 153 a
Somerset I. Nunavut, Canada 73°30N 93°0W 294 B10
Somerset West S. Africa 34°8S 18°50E 270 D2
Somersworth U.S.A. 43°16N 70°52W 313 C14
Somerton U.S.A. 32°36N 114°43W 305 K6
Somerville Mass., U.S.A. 42°22N 71°5W 116 A2
Somerville N.J., U.S.A. 40°35N 74°38W 313 F10
Someş → Romania 47°49N 22°43E 182 C7
Somes I. N.Z. 41°15S 174°52E 143 B2
Someşul Mare → Romania 47°9N 23°55E 183 C8
Somme □ France 49°57N 2°20E 173 C9
Somme → France 50°11N 1°38E 173 B8
Somme, B. de la France 50°14N 1°33E 172 B8
Sommen Jönköping, Sweden 58°12N 14°58E 163 F8
Sommen Östergötland, Sweden 58°0N 15°15E 163 F9
Sommepy-Tahure France 49°15N 4°31E 173 C11
Sömmerda Germany 51°9N 11°7E 178 D7
Sommerfeld = Lubsko Poland 51°45N 14°57E 185 G1
Sommesous France 48°44N 4°12E 173 D11
Sommières France 43°47N 4°6E 175 E8
Somnath India 20°53N 70°22E 242 J4
Somnathpur India 12°19N 76°49E 244 H3
Somogy □ Hungary 46°19N 17°30E 182 D2
Somogyszob Hungary 46°18N 17°20E 182 D2
Somosomo Fiji 16°47S 179°58W 287 A3
Somosomo Str. Fiji 16°0S 180°0E 287 A3
Somoto Nic. 13°28N 86°37W 320 D2
Sompolno Poland 52°26N 18°30E 185 F5
Somport, Puerto de Spain 42°48N 0°31W 196 C4
Somuncurá, Meseta de Argentina 41°30S 67°0W 336 B3
Somvarpet India 12°36N 75°52E 245 H2
Son Norway 59°32N 10°42E 164 E7
Son → India 25°42N 84°52E 243 G11
Son Ha Vietnam 15°3N 108°34E 236 E7
Son Hoa Vietnam 13°2N 108°58E 236 F7
Son La Vietnam 21°20N 103°50E 228 G4
Son Serra Spain 39°43N 3°13E 206 B4
Son Servera Spain 39°37N 3°21E 206 B4
Son Tay Vietnam 21°8N 105°30E 228 G5
Soná Panama 8°0N 81°20W 320 E3
Sonamarg India 34°18N 75°21E 243 B6
Sonamukhi India 23°18N 87°27E 243 H12
Sonamura India 23°29N 91°15E 241 D3
Sonar → India 24°24N 79°56E 243 G8
Sonari India 18°54N 72°59E 130 B2
Sŏnch'ŏn N. Korea 39°48N 124°55E 224 C2
Sondags → S. Africa 33°44S 25°51E 270 D4
Sóndalo Italy 46°20N 10°19E 198 B7
Sondar India 33°28N 75°56E 243 C6
Sondeled Norway 58°46N 9°3E 164 F6
Sønder Felding Denmark 55°57N 8°47E 163 J2
Sønder Omme Denmark 55°50N 8°54E 163 J2
Sønderborg Denmark 54°55N 9°49E 163 K3
Sondershausen Germany 51°22N 10°51E 178 D6
Søndersø Denmark 55°46N 12°21E 118 A2
Søndre Bergenhaus = Hordaland □ Norway 60°25N 6°15E 164 D3
Søndre Strømfjord = Kangerlussuaq Greenland 66°59N 50°40W 154 D5
Søndre Trondhjem = Sør-Trøndelag □ Norway 63°0N 11°0E 164 A7
Sóndrio Italy 46°10N 9°52E 198 B6
Sondur → India 20°40N 82°1E 244 D6
Sone Mozam. 17°23S 34°55E 269 F3
Sonepur India 20°55N 83°50E 244 D6
Sonfim Brazil 6°0S 67°52W 330 B4
Song Nigeria 9°49N 12°39E 263 D7
Song Thailand 18°28N 100°11E 236 C3
Song Cau Vietnam 13°27N 109°18E 236 F7
Song Hong → Vietnam 22°0N 104°0E 228 F5
Song-Köl Kyrgyzstan 41°50N 75°12E 217 D9
Song Xian China 34°12N 112°8E 226 G7
Songadh India 21°9N 73°33E 244 D1
Songan Indonesia 8°13S 115°24E 231 J18
Songavatnet Norway 59°52N 7°32E 164 E4
Songea Tanzania 10°40S 35°40E 269 E4
Songeons France 49°32N 1°50E 173 C8
Sŏnggan N. Korea 40°47N 126°34E 224 B3
Songgang China 22°46N 113°50E 219 F10
Songhua Hu China 43°35N 126°50E 227 C14
Songhua Jiang → China 47°45N 132°30E 219 B8
Songimvelo △ S. Africa 25°50S 31°2E 271 C5
Songjiang Jilin, China 42°34N 128°20E 224 A4
Songjiang Shanghai, China 31°1N 121°12E 229 B13
Songjianghe China 42°10N 127°29E 224 A3
Sŏngjin = Kimch'aek N. Korea 40°40N 129°10E 224 B4
Songkan China 28°35N 106°52E 228 C6
Songkhla Thailand 7°13N 100°37E 237 J3
Songming China 25°12N 103°2E 228 E4
Songnim N. Korea 38°45N 125°39E 224 C2
Songnisan △ S. Korea 36°28N 127°45E 224 D3
Songo Angola 7°22S 14°51E 265 D2
Songololo = Mbanza Ngungu Dem. Rep. of the Congo 5°12S 14°53E 265 D2
Songololo Dem. Rep. of the Congo 5°42S 14°2E 265 D2
Songpa S. Korea 37°30N 127°7E 137 B2
Songpan China 32°40N 103°30E 228 A4
Songtao China 28°11N 109°10E 228 C7
Songwe Dem. Rep. of the Congo 3°20S 26°16E 268 C2
Songwe → Africa 9°44S 33°58E 269 D3
Songxi China 27°31N 118°44E 229 D12
Songzi China 30°12N 111°45E 229 B8
Sonhat India 23°29N 82°31E 243 H10
Sonid Youqi China 42°45N 112°48E 226 C7
Sonipat India 29°0N 77°5E 242 E7
Sonkach India 22°59N 76°21E 242 H7
Sonkovo Russia 57°50N 37°5E 188 D9
Sonmiani Pakistan 25°25N 66°40E 242 G2
Sonmiani B. Pakistan 25°15N 66°30E 242 G2
Sonnino Italy 41°25N 13°14E 200 A6
Sono → Minas Gerais, Brazil 17°2S 45°32W 333 E2
Sono → Tocantins, Brazil 9°58S 48°11W 332 C2
Sonobe Japan 35°6N 135°28E 223 B7
Sonoma U.S.A. 38°18N 122°28W 306 G4
Sonora Calif., U.S.A. 37°59N 120°23W 306 H6
Sonora Tex., U.S.A. 30°34N 100°39W 314 F4
Sonora □ Mexico 29°20N 110°40W 318 B2
Sonora → Mexico 29°5N 110°55W 318 B2
Sonoran Desert U.S.A. 33°40N 113°30W 307 L12
Sonoyta Mexico 31°51N 112°50W 318 A2
Sonqor Iran 34°47N 47°36E 213 E12
Sonseca Spain 39°42N 3°57W 195 F7
Sonsón Colombia 5°43N 75°18W 328 B2
Sonsonate El Salv. 13°43N 89°44W 320 D2
Sonstorp Sweden 58°44N 15°38E 163 F9
Sonthofen Germany 47°30N 10°16E 179 H6
Sony Picture Studio U.S.A. 34°1N 118°4W 126 B2
Soochow = Suzhou China 31°19N 120°38E 229 B13
Sooke Canada 48°13N 123°43W 306 B3
Soomaaliya = Somali Rep. ■ Africa 7°0N 47°0E 267 C6
Soong Qingling, Former Residence of Beijing, China 114 a2
Sop Hao Laos 20°33N 104°27E 228 G5
Sop Prap Thailand 17°53N 99°20E 236 D2
Sopachuy Bolivia 19°29S 64°31W 331 D5
Sopchoppy U.S.A. 30°4N 84°29W 316 E5
Sopelana Spain 43°23N 2°58W 196 B2
Soperton U.S.A. 32°23N 82°35W 316 C7
Sopi Indonesia 2°34N 128°28E 231 D7
Sopo, Nahr → Sudan 8°40N 26°30E 257 F2
Sopot Bulgaria 42°39N 24°45E 203 D8
Sopot Poland 54°27N 18°31E 184 D5
Sopot Serbia 44°29N 20°36E 202 B4
Sopotnica Macedonia 41°18N 21°13E 202 E5
Sopron Hungary 47°45N 16°32E 182 C1
Sopur India 34°18N 74°27E 243 B6
Sør-Rondane Antarctica 72°0S 25°0E 151 D4
Sør-Trøndelag □ Norway 63°0N 11°0E 164 A7
Sora Italy 41°43N 13°37E 199 G10
Sorab India 14°23N 75°6E 245 G2
Sorada India 19°45N 84°26E 244 E7
Sorah Pakistan 27°13N 68°56E 242 F3
Soråker Sweden 62°30N 17°32E 162 B11
Sorang Kazakhstan 49°46N 72°51E 217 C8
Sorano Italy 42°41N 11°43E 199 F8
Soraon India 25°37N 81°51E 243 G9
Sorata Bolivia 15°50S 68°40W 330 D4
Sorbas Spain 37°6N 2°7W 197 H2
Sörbygden Sweden 62°48N 16°12E 162 B10
Sore France 44°18N 0°35W 174 D3
Søre Osa → Norway 61°18N 11°46E 164 C8
Sorel-Tracy Canada 46°0N 73°10W 298 C5
Soresina Italy 45°17N 9°51E 198 C6
Sørfjorden Norway 60°20N 6°37E 164 D3
Sörforsa Sweden 61°43N 16°58E 162 C10
Sórgono Italy 40°1N 9°6E 200 B2
Sorgues France 44°1N 4°53E 175 D8
Sorgun Turkey 39°46N 35°11E 212 C6
Sorgun → Turkey 36°36N 34°20E 250 B5
Sori Papua N. G. 1°58S 146°42E 286 A4
Soria Spain 41°43N 2°32W 196 D2
Soria □ Spain 41°46N 2°28W 196 D2
Soriano Uruguay 33°24S 58°19W 334 C4
Soriano nel Cimino Italy 42°25N 12°14E 199 F9
Sorkh, Kuh-e Iran 35°40N 58°30E 247 C8
Sorø Denmark 55°26N 11°32E 163 J5
Soro Guinea 10°9N 9°48W 262 C3
Soroca Moldova 48°8N 28°12E 183 B13
Sorocaba Brazil 23°31S 47°27W 335 A6
Sorochinsk Russia 52°26N 53°10E 186 D9
Soroka = Belomorsk Russia 64°35N 34°54E 186 B5
Soroki = Soroca Moldova 48°8N 28°12E 183 B13
Sorokino = Krasnodon Ukraine 48°17N 39°44E 189 H10
Soroksár Hungary 47°24N 19°7E 117 B2
Soroksari Duna → Hungary 47°25N 19°5E 117 B2
Sorong Indonesia 0°55S 131°15E 231 E8
Soroni Greece 36°21N 28°1E 206 E12
Soroti Uganda 1°43N 33°35E 268 B3
Sørøya Norway 70°40N 22°30E 160 A20
Sørøyane Norway 62°25N 5°32E 164 B2
Sørøysundet Norway 70°25N 23°0E 160 A20
Sorraia → Portugal 38°55N 8°53W 195 G2
Sorrell Australia 42°47S 147°34E 281 G4
Sorrento Italy 40°37N 14°22E 201 B7
Sorsele Sweden 65°31N 17°30E 160 D17
Sörsjön Sweden 61°24N 13°5E 162 C7
Sorso Italy 40°48N 8°34E 200 B1
Sorsogon Phil. 13°0N 124°0E 232 E5
Sorsogon □ Phil. 12°50N 123°55E 232 E4
Sortavala Russia 61°42N 30°41E 188 B6
Sortino Italy 37°9N 15°2E 201 E8
Sortland Norway 68°42N 15°25E 160 B16
Sørum Norway 60°30N 10°17E 164 D7
Sorvizhi Russia 57°52N 48°32E 190 B9
Sos del Rey Católico Spain 42°30N 1°13W 196 C3
Soscumica, L. Canada 50°15N 77°27W 298 B4
Sösdala Sweden 56°2N 13°41E 163 H7
Sosenka → Russia 55°46N 37°42E 129 B4
Sosna → Russia 52°42N 38°55E 189 F10
Sosnogorsk Russia 63°37N 53°51E 186 B9
Sosnovka Kirov, Russia 56°17N 51°17E 190 B10
Sosnovka St. Petersburg, Russia 60°0N 30°22E 137 B2
Sosnovka Tambov, Russia 53°13N 41°24E 190 D5
Sosnovyy Bor Russia 59°55N 29°6E 188 C5
Sosnowiec Poland 50°20N 19°10E 185 H6
Sosnowitz = Sosnowiec Poland 50°20N 19°10E 185 H6
Soso C.A.R. 3°55N 15°30E 264 B3
Sospel France 43°52N 7°27E 175 E11
Sossus Vlei Namibia 24°40S 15°23E 270 B2
Šoštanj Slovenia 46°23N 15°4E 199 B12
Sŏsura N. Korea 42°16N 130°36E 224 A5
Sot → India 27°27N 79°37E 243 F8
Sotasæter Norway 61°49N 7°43E 164 C4
Sotavento C. Verde Is. 15°0N 25°0W 153 j
Sotik Kenya 0°41S 35°7E 268 C4
Sotkamo Finland 64°8N 28°23E 160 D23
Soto Neth. Ant. 12°16N 69°6W 322 g
Soto del Barco Spain 43°32N 6°4W 194 B4
Soto la Marina Mexico 23°46N 98°13W 319 C5
Soto la Marina → Mexico 23°45N 97°45W 319 C5
Soto y Amio Spain 42°46N 5°53W 194 C5
Sotrondio Spain 43°17N 5°36W 194 B5
Sotuf, Adrar W. Sahara 21°42N 15°36W 260 D1
Sotuta Mexico 20°36N 89°1W 319 C7
Souanké Congo 2°10N 14°3E 264 B2
Soubré Ivory C. 5°50N 6°35W 262 D3
Souda Greece 35°29N 24°4E 207 E6
Soudas, Ormos Greece 35°25N 24°10E 207 E5
Souderton U.S.A. 40°19N 75°19W 313 F9
Soufflay Congo 2°1N 14°54E 264 B2
Soufli Greece 41°12N 26°18E 203 E10
Soufrière Dominica 15°13N 61°22W 323 k
Soufrière Guadeloupe 16°5N 61°40W 322 e
Soufrière St. Lucia 13°51N 61°3W 323 m
Soufrière Bay Dominica 15°13N 61°22W 323 k
Soufrière Bay St. Lucia 13°51N 61°4W 323 m
Soufrière Hills Volcano Montserrat 16°43N 62°10W 323 p
Souillac Lot, France 44°53N 1°29E 174 D5
Souillac Mauritius 20°31S 57°31E 272 e
Souilly France 49°3N 5°17E 173 C12
Souk-Ahras Algeria 36°23N 7°57E 261 A6
Souk-Ahras □ Algeria 36°10N 7°55E 261 A6
Souk el Arba du Rharb Morocco 34°43N 5°59W 260 B3
Soukhouma Laos 14°38N 105°48E 236 E5
Sŏul = Seoul S. Korea 37°31N 126°58E 137 B2
Soulac-sur-Mer France 45°30N 1°7W 174 C2
Soulougou Burkina Faso 13°1N 0°25E 263 C5
Soultz-sous-Forêts France 48°57N 7°52E 173 D14
Sound, The = Øresund Europe 55°45N 12°40E 163 J6
Sound, The U.K. 50°20N 4°10W 169 G3
Sound I. India 12°58N 92°59E 245 H11
Soundview U.S.A. 40°49N 73°53W 132 B2
Sounio, Akra Greece 37°37N 24°1E 204 D6
Sour el Ghozlane Algeria 36°10N 3°45E 261 A5
Sources, Mt. aux Lesotho 28°45S 28°50E 271 C4
Soure Brazil 0°35S 48°30W 332 B2
Soure Portugal 40°4N 8°38W 194 E2
Souris Man., Canada 49°40N 100°20W 297 D8
Souris P.E.I., Canada 46°21N 62°15W 299 C7
Souris → N. Amer. 49°40N 99°34W 308 A4
Sourou → Africa 12°45N 3°25W 262 C4
Sourpi Greece 39°6N 22°54E 204 B4
Sous, O. → Morocco 30°27N 9°31W 260 B3
Sous le Vent, Is. French Polynesia 16°30S 155°30W 289 f
Sous le Vent, Région Réunion 21°12S 55°20E 272 f
Sous-Massa △ Morocco 31°26N 9°35W 260 B3
Sousa Brazil 6°45S 38°10W 332 C4
Sousel Brazil 2°38S 52°29W 332 B1
Sousel Portugal 38°57N 7°40W 195 G3
Sousse Tunisia 35°50N 10°38E 258 A2
Sousse □ Tunisia 35°40N 10°30E 261 A7
Soustons France 43°45N 1°19W 174 E2
Sout → S. Africa 31°35S 18°24E 270 D2
South Africa ■ Africa 32°0S 23°0E 270 D3
South America 10°0S 60°0W 326 E5
South Andaman India 11°45N 92°10E 245 J11
South Atlantic Ocean 20°0S 10°0W 152 J10
South Aulatsivik I. Canada 56°45N 61°30W 299 A7
South Australia □ Australia 32°0S 139°0E 282 B3
South Australian Basin Ind. Oc. 38°0S 126°0E 288 L4
South Ayrshire □ U.K. 55°18N 4°41W 167 F4
South Baldy Pk. U.S.A. 34°6N 107°11W 305 J10
South Bass I. U.S.A. 41°39N 82°49W 312 E2
South Bay U.S.A. 26°40N 80°43W 317 J9
South Beach Bahamas 25°1N 77°20W 153 b
South Beach N.Y., U.S.A. 40°35N 74°4W 132 C1
South Beach Harbor San Francisco, U.S.A. 136 c3
South Beloit U.S.A. 42°29N 89°2W 310 B7
South Bend Ind., U.S.A. 41°41N 86°15W 311 C10
South Bend Wash., U.S.A. 46°40N 123°48W 306 D3
South Bend Park U.S.A. 33°42N 84°23W 113 B2
South Boston Mass., U.S.A. 42°20N 71°2W 116 A2
South Boston Va., U.S.A. 36°42N 78°54W 309 G14
South Branch Canada 47°55N 59°2W 299 C8
South Branch Chicago River → Chicago, U.S.A. 119 d1
South Brook Canada 49°26N 56°5W 299 C8
South Brother I. India 10°56N 92°37E 245 J11
South Bruny I. Australia 43°20S 147°15E 281 G4
South C. = Kalae U.S.A. 18°55N 155°41W 302 E6
South Carolina □ U.S.A. 34°0N 81°0W 315 E14
South Charleston U.S.A. 38°22N 81°44W 309 F13
South China Sea Asia 10°0N 113°0E 232 D2
South Comino Channel Malta 36°0N 14°20E 206 F7
South Congaree U.S.A. 33°53N 81°9W 316 B8
South Cotabato □ Phil. 6°0N 125°0E 233 J5
South Cumberland Is. △ Australia 20°42S 149°11E 280 J7
South Dakota □ U.S.A. 44°15N 100°0W 308 C4
South Daytona U.S.A. 29°10N 81°0W 317 F8
South Decatur U.S.A. 33°44N 84°16W 113 B3
South Deerfield U.S.A. 42°29N 72°37W 313 D12
South Deering U.S.A. 41°42N 87°33W 119 C3
South Downs U.K. 50°52N 0°25W 169 G7
South East B. Ascension I. 7°57S 14°18W 153 g
South East C. Australia 43°40S 146°50E 281 G4
South East Forests △ Australia 37°0S 149°30E 283 D8
South East Is. Australia 34°17S 123°30E 279 F3
South El Monte U.S.A. 34°3N 118°2W 126 B4
South Elgin U.S.A. 42°0N 88°18W 311 C8
South Esk → U.K. 56°43N 2°31W 167 E6
South Fiji Basin Pac. Oc. 26°0S 175°0E 288 K9
South Foreland U.K. 51°8N 1°24E 169 F9
South Fork American → U.S.A. 38°57N 120°59W 306 G5
South Fork Edisto → U.S.A. 33°16N 80°54W 316 B9
South Fork Feather → U.S.A. 39°17N 121°36W 306 F5
South Fork Grand → U.S.A. 45°43N 102°17W 308 C2
South Fork Licking → U.S.A. 38°40N 84°18W 311 F12
South Fork Milk → U.S.A. 48°4N 106°19W 304 B10
South Fork Republican → U.S.A. 40°3N 101°31W 308 E3
South Gate U.S.A. 33°56N 118°12W 126 C3
South Georgia Antarctica 54°30S 37°0W 151 B1
South Gloucestershire □ U.K. 51°32N 2°28W 169 F5
South Grand → U.S.A. 38°17N 93°25W 310 F3
South Hadley U.S.A. 42°16N 72°35W 313 D12
South Harbor Phil. 14°34N 120°58E 127 B1
South Harrow U.K. 51°33N 0°21W 125 A1
South Haven U.S.A. 42°24N 86°16W 311 B10
South Hd. Australia 33°50S 151°16E 139 B2
South Henik L. Canada 61°30N 97°20W 297 A9
South Hill Village Anguilla 18°11N 63°5W 322 a
South Hills S. Africa 26°14S 28°5E 123 B2
South Horr Kenya 2°12N 36°56E 268 B4
South I. India 10°3N 72°17E 245 J1
South I. Eastern, Kenya 2°35N 36°35E 268 B4
South I. N.Z. 44°0S 170°0E 285 E5
South Indian Lake Canada 56°47N 98°56W 297 B9
South Invercargill N.Z. 46°26S 168°23E 285 G3
South Island △ Kenya 2°39N 36°35E 268 B4
South Kensington London, U.K. 51°29N 0°10W 125 c2
South Kitui △ Kenya 1°48S 38°46E 268 C4
South Knife → Canada 58°55N 94°37W 297 B10
South Koel → India 22°32N 85°14E 243 H11
South Korea ■ Asia 36°0N 128°0E 227 G15
South Lake Tahoe U.S.A. 38°57N 119°59W 306 G6
South Lanarkshire □ U.K. 55°37N 3°53W 167 F5
South Lawn U.S.A. 38°47N 77°0W 143 C3
South Loop Chicago, U.S.A. 119 f2
South Loup → U.S.A. 41°4N 98°39W 308 E4
South Luangwa △ Zambia 13°0S 31°20E 269 E3
South Lyon U.S.A. 42°28N 83°39W 311 B13
South Magnetic Pole Antarctica 64°8S 138°8E 151 C9
South Malé Atoll Maldives 4°0N 73°25E 272 d
South Malosmadulu Atoll Maldives 5°12N 73°0E 272 d
South Miami U.S.A. 25°42N 80°17W 128 B1
South Milwaukee U.S.A. 42°55N 87°52W 311 B9
South Molton U.K. 51°1N 3°51W 169 F4
South Monroe U.S.A. 41°54N 83°26W 311 C13
South Moose L. Canada 53°49N 100°1W 297 C8
South Nahanni → Canada 61°3N 123°21W 296 A4
South Nation → Canada 45°34N 75°6W 313 A9
South Natuna Is. = Natuna Selatan, Kepulauan Indonesia 2°45N 109°0E 235 B3
South New Hebrides Trench Pac. Oc. 22°30S 170°0E 277 E13
South Newport U.S.A. 31°38N 81°24W 316 D8
South Nilandu Atoll Maldives 2°52N 72°57E 272 d
South Norwood U.K. 51°23N 0°3W 125 B3
South of Market San Francisco, U.S.A. 136 c2
South Orkney Is. Antarctica 63°0S 45°0W 151 C18
South Ossetia □ Georgia 42°21N 44°2E 191 J7
South Ozone Park U.S.A. 40°41N 73°49W 132 B3
South Pagai, I. = Pagai Selatan, Pulau Indonesia 3°0S 100°15E 234 C2
South Paris U.S.A. 44°14N 70°31W 313 B14
South Pasadena U.S.A. 34°7N 118°8W 126 B4
South Pekin U.S.A. 40°30N 89°39W 310 D7
South Pittsburg U.S.A. 35°1N 85°42W 315 D12
South Platte → U.S.A. 41°7N 100°42W 308 E3
South Pole Antarctica 90°0S 0°0 151 E
South Ponte Vedra Beach U.S.A. 30°3N 81°20W 316 E8
South Porcupine Canada 48°30N 81°12W 298 C3
South Portland U.S.A. 43°38N 70°15W 309 D18
South Pt. Ascension I. 8°0S 14°24W 153 g
South Pt. Barbados 13°2N 59°32W 323 r
South Pt. Mich., U.S.A. 44°52N 83°19W 312 B1
South Res. U.S.A. 42°26N 71°6W 116 A2
South River Ont., Canada 45°52N 79°23W 298 C4
South River N.J., U.S.A. 40°27N 74°23W 313 F10
South Ronaldsay U.K. 58°48N 2°58W 167 C6
South Ruislip U.K. 51°33N 0°24W 125 A1
South San Francisco U.S.A. 37°38N 122°26W 136 C2
South San Gabriel U.S.A. 34°3N 118°6W 126 B4
South Sandwich Is. Antarctica 57°0S 27°0W 151 B1
South Sandwich Trench Atl. Oc. 56°0S 24°0W 151 B1
South Saskatchewan → Canada 53°15N 105°5W 297 C7
South Seal → Canada 58°48N 98°8W 297 B9
South Sentinel I. India 10°59N 92°14E 245 J11
South Shetland Is. Antarctica 62°0S 59°0W 151 C18
South Shields U.K. 55°0N 1°25W 168 C6
South Shore U.S.A. 41°45N 87°34W 119 C3
South Sioux City U.S.A. 42°28N 96°24W 308 D5
South Sister U.S.A. 44°4N 121°51W 304 D3
South Solomon Trench Pac. Oc. 11°0S 164°30E 277 C11
South Soufrière Hills Montserrat 16°41N 62°10W 323 p
South Street Boston, U.S.A. 116 c2
South Taranaki Bight N.Z. 39°40S 174°5E 284 F3
South Tasman Rise S. Ocean 48°0S 146°0E 151 A10
South Thompson → Canada 50°40N 120°20W 296 C4
South Twin I. Canada 53°7N 79°52W 298 B4
South Tyne → U.K. 54°59N 2°8W 168 C5
South Ubian Phil. 5°11N 120°30E 233 J3
South Uist U.K. 57°20N 7°15W 167 D1
South Valley U.S.A. 35°1N 106°41W 305 J10
South Venice U.S.A. 27°3N 82°25W 317 H7
South Wayne U.S.A. 42°34N 89°53W 310 B7
South Wellesley Is. Australia 16°58S 139°17E 280 B2
South West Africa = Namibia ■ Africa 22°0S 18°9E 270 B2
South West B. Ascension I. 7°58S 14°25W 153 g
South West B. Bahamas 25°0N 77°32W 153 b
South West C. Tas., Australia 43°34S 146°3E 281 G4
South West C. N.Z. 47°17S 167°28E 285 H2
South West Pt. Papua N. G. 2°14S 146°34E 286 B4
South West Pt. St. Helena 15°59S 5°48W 153 h
South West Rocks Australia 30°52S 153°3E 283 A10
South Whitley U.S.A. 41°5N 85°38W 311 C11
South Williamsport U.S.A. 41°13N 77°0W 312 E8
South Yemen = Yemen ■ Asia 15°0N 44°0E 248 D4
South Yorkshire □ U.K. 53°27N 1°36W 168 D6
Southall U.K. 51°30N 0°22W 125 A1
Southampton Ont., Canada 44°30N 81°25W 312 B3
Southampton Southampton, U.K. 50°54N 1°23W 169 G6
Southampton N.Y., U.S.A. 40°53N 72°23W 313 F12
Southampton □ U.K. 50°54N 1°23W 169 G6
Southampton I. Canada 64°30N 84°0W 295 C11
Southaven U.S.A. 34°59N 90°0W 315 D9
Southbank Canada 54°2N 125°46W 296 C3
Southborough U.K. 51°23N 0°3E 125 B4
Southbridge N.Z. 43°48S 172°16E 285 D7
Southbridge Mass., U.S.A. 42°5N 72°2W 313 D12
Southeast C. U.S.A. 62°56N 169°39W 303 E5
Southeast Indian Ridge Ind. Oc. 43°0S 80°0E 273 J10
Southend Sask., Canada 56°19N 103°22W 297 B8
Southend London, U.K. 51°25N 0°0 125 B3
Southend-on-Sea U.K. 51°32N 0°44E 169 F8
Southend-on-Sea □ U.K. 51°32N 0°44E 169 F8
Southern = Janub △ Sudan 6°50N 28°45E 257 F2
Southern = Yedebub Biherochch Bihereseboch na Hizboch □ Ethiopia 12°0N 36°0E 257 F4
Southern = Yuzhnyy □ Russia 44°0N 40°0E 191 H5
Southern □ Malawi 15°0S 35°0E 269 F4
Southern □ S. Leone 8°0N 12°30W 262 D2
Southern □ Zambia 16°20S 26°20E 269 F2
Southern Alps N.Z. 43°41S 170°11E 285 D5
Southern California, University of U.S.A. 34°1N 118°17W 126 B3
Southern Cross Australia 31°12S 119°15E 279 F2
Southern Highlands □ Papua N. G. 6°15S 143°25E 286 D2
Southern Indian L. Canada 57°10N 98°30W 297 B9
Southern Lau Group Fiji 18°40S 178°40W 287 B3
Southern Leyte □ Phil. 10°30N 125°10E 233 F5
Southern Ocean Antarctica 62°0S 60°0E 151 C6
Southern Pines U.S.A. 35°11N 79°24W 315 D15
Southern Rhodesia = Zimbabwe ■ Africa 19°0S 30°0E 269 F3
Southern Uplands U.K. 55°28N 3°52W 167 F5
Southfield U.S.A. 42°28N 83°15W 311 B13
Southfields U.K. 51°26N 0°11W 125 B2
Southington U.S.A. 41°36N 72°53W 313 E12
Southland □ N.Z. 45°30S 168°0E 285 F3
Southold U.S.A. 41°4N 72°26W 313 E12
Southport Queens., Australia 27°58S 153°25E 281 D5
Southport Mersey., U.K. 53°39N 3°0W 168 D4
Southport Fla., U.S.A. 30°17N 85°38W 316 E4
Southport N.Y., U.S.A. 42°3N 76°49W 312 D8
Southwark □ U.K. 51°29N 0°6W 125 B3
Southwest △ Australia 43°8S 146°5E 281 G4
Southwest Museum U.S.A. 34°6N 118°13W 126 B3
Southwest Pacific Basin Pac. Oc. 40°0S 140°0W 277 G17
Southwest Pt. U.S. Virgin Is. 17°40N 64°55W 321 b
Southwold U.K. 52°20N 1°41E 169 E9
Southwood △ Australia 27°48S 150°8E 281 D5
Soutpansberg S. Africa 23°0S 29°30E 271 B4
Souvigny France 46°33N 3°10E 173 F10
Søvang Denmark 55°34N 12°37E 118 B3
Sovata Romania 46°35N 25°3E 183 D10
Soverato Italy 38°41N 16°33E 201 D9
Sovetsk Kaliningrad, Russia 55°6N 21°50E 184 C8
Sovetsk Kirov, Russia 57°38N 48°53E 190 B9
Sovetskoye = Zelenokumsk Russia 44°24N 44°0E 191 H6
Sovicille Italy 43°17N 11°13E 199 E8
Søvik Norway 62°33N 6°17E 164 B3
Soweto S. Africa 26°14S 27°52E 123 B1
Sowhānak Iran 35°48N 51°31E 141 A3
Soya Japan 35°44N 139°55E 140 A4
Sōya-Kaikyō = La Perouse Str. Asia 45°40N 142°0E 220 B11
Sōya-Misaki Japan 45°30N 141°55E 220 B10
Soyang-ho S. Korea 37°57N 127°54E 224 D3
Soyaux France 45°39N 0°12E 174 C4
Søyland Norway 58°41N 5°36E 164 F2
Soyo Angola 6°13S 12°20E 265 D2
Sozaq Kazakhstan 44°8N 68°28E 217 D7
Sozh → Belarus 51°57N 30°48E 177 B16
Sozopol Bulgaria 42°23N 27°42E 203 D11
Spa Belgium 50°29N 5°53E 170 D5
Spaans Lagoen Aruba 12°28N 69°58W 322 f
Spaanse Water Neth. Ant. 12°4N 68°51W 322 g
Spaccaforno = Ispica Italy 36°47N 14°55E 201 F7
Spain ■ Europe 39°0N 4°0W 192 D3
Spalato = Split Croatia 43°31N 16°26E 199 E13
Spalding S. Austral., Australia 33°30S 138°37E 282 B3
Spalding Lincs., U.K. 52°48N 0°9W 168 E7
Spanaway U.S.A. 47°6N 122°26W 306 C4
Spandau Germany 52°33N 13°9E 115 A1
Spånga Sweden 59°23N 17°53E 139 A1
Spangler U.S.A. 40°39N 78°48W 312 F6
Spanische Reitschule Vienna, Austria 142 b1
Spanish Canada 46°12N 82°20W 298 C3
Spanish Fork U.S.A. 40°7N 111°39W 304 F8
Spanish Monastery U.S.A. 25°55N 80°11W 128 A2
Spanish Pt. Antigua & B. 17°33N 61°44W 322 c
Spanish Pt. Bermuda 32°18N 64°49W 153 a
Spanish Riding School = Spanische Reitschule Vienna, Austria 142 b1
Spanish Town Br. Virgin Is. 17°43N 64°26W 321 b
Sparks Ga., U.S.A. 31°11N 83°26W 316 D6
Sparks Nev., U.S.A. 39°32N 119°45W 306 F7
Sparreholm Sweden 59°4N 16°49E 162 E10
Sparrow Bay Grenada 12°30N 61°27W 323 q
Sparta = Sparti Greece 37°5N 22°25E 204 D4
Sparta Ga., U.S.A. 33°17N 82°58W 316 B7
Sparta Ill., U.S.A. 38°8N 89°42W 310 F7
Sparta Mich., U.S.A. 43°10N 85°42W 311 A11
Sparta N.J., U.S.A. 41°2N 74°38W 313 E10
Sparta Wis., U.S.A. 43°56N 90°49W 308 D8
Spartanburg U.S.A. 34°56N 81°57W 315 D14
Spartansburg U.S.A. 41°49N 79°41W 312 E5
Spartel, C. Morocco 35°47N 5°56W 260 A3
Sparti Greece 37°5N 22°25E 204 D4
Spartivento, C. Calabria, Italy 37°55N 16°4E 201 E9
Spartivento, C. Sard., Italy 38°53N 8°50E 200 D1
Spartochori Greece 38°40N 20°46E 207 B2
Sparwood Canada 49°44N 114°53W 296 D6
Spas-Demensk Russia 54°20N 34°0E 188 E7
Spas-Klepiki Russia 55°10N 40°10E 188 E11
Spassk = Bednodemyanovsk Russia 53°55N 43°15E 190 D6
Spassk Dalniy Russia 44°40N 132°48E 220 B6
Spassk-Ryazanskiy Russia 54°24N 40°25E 188 E11
Spatha, Akra Greece 35°42N 23°43E 207 E4
Spatsizi → Canada 57°42N 128°7W 296 B3
Spatsizi Plateau Wilderness △ Canada 57°40N 128°0W 296 B3
Spean → U.K. 56°55N 4°59W 167 E4
Spearfish U.S.A. 44°30N 103°52W 308 C2
Spearman U.S.A. 36°12N 101°12W 314 C4
Spectacle I. U.S.A. 42°19N 70°59W 116 A3
Speculator U.S.A. 43°30N 74°22W 313 C10
Speed Australia 35°21S 142°27E 282 C5
Speedway U.S.A. 39°48N 86°16W 311 E10
Speery I. St. Helena 16°1S 5°46W 153 h
Speia Moldova 46°59N 29°19E 183 D14
Speicher-See Germany 48°12N 11°42E 131 A3
Speightstown Barbados 13°15N 59°39W 323 r
Speising Austria 48°10N 16°17E 142 B1
Speke Gulf Tanzania 2°20S 32°50E 268 C3
Spello Italy 42°59N 12°40E 199 F9
Spence Bay = Taloyoak Canada 69°32N 93°32W 294 C10
Spencer Idaho, U.S.A. 44°22N 112°11W 304 D7
Spencer Ind., U.S.A. 39°17N 86°46W 311 E10
Spencer Iowa, U.S.A. 43°9N 95°9W 308 D6
Spencer N.Y., U.S.A. 42°13N 76°30W 313 D8
Spencer Nebr., U.S.A. 42°53N 98°42W 308 D4
Spencer, C. Australia 35°20S 136°53E 282 C2
Spencer B. Namibia 25°30S 14°47E 270 C1
Spencer G. Australia 34°0S 137°20E 282 C2
Spencerville Ont., Canada 44°51N 75°33W 313 B9
Spencerville Ohio, U.S.A. 40°43N 84°21W 311 D12
Spences Bridge Canada 50°25N 121°20W 296 C4
Spennymoor U.K. 54°42N 1°36W 168 C6
Spenser Mts. N.Z. 42°15S 172°45E 285 C7
Spentrup Denmark 56°33N 10°2E 163 H4
Sperchios → Greece 38°57N 22°3E 204 C4
Sperillen Norway 60°28N 10°3E 164 D7
Sperrin Mts. U.K. 54°50N 7°0W 166 B5
Spessart Germany 49°56N 9°18E 179 F5
Spetalen Norway 59°18N 10°45E 164 F7
Spetses Greece 37°15N 23°10E 204 D5
Spey → U.K. 57°40N 3°6W 167 D5
Speyer Germany 49°29N 8°25E 179 F4
Speyside Trin. & Tob. 11°17N 60°32W 323 s
Spezand Pakistan 29°59N 67°0E 242 E2
Spezzano Albanese Italy 39°40N 16°19E 201 C9
Sphinx Egypt 29°58N 31°8E 117 B1
Spickard U.S.A. 40°14N 93°36W 310 D3
Spiddle Ireland 53°15N 9°18W 166 C2
Spiekeroog Germany 53°46N 7°42E 178 B3
Spiez Switz. 46°40N 7°40E 179 J3
Spili Greece 35°13N 24°31E 207 E5
Spilimbergo Italy 46°7N 12°54E 199 B9
Spīn Būldak Afghan. 31°1N 66°25E 242 D2
Spinaceto Italy 41°47N 12°27E 136 C1
Spinalonga Greece 35°18N 25°44E 207 E6
Spinazzola Italy 40°58N 16°5E 201 B9
Spineni Romania 44°43N 24°37E 183 F9
Spirding = Śniardwy, Jezioro Poland 53°48N 21°50E 184 E8
Spirit Lake U.S.A. 46°15N 122°9W 306 D4
Spirit River Canada 55°45N 118°50W 296 B5
Spiritwood Canada 53°24N 107°33W 297 C7
Spišská Nová Ves Slovak Rep. 48°58N 20°34E 181 C13
Spišské Podhradie Slovak Rep. 49°0N 20°48E 181 B13
Spit Junction Australia 33°49S 151°14E 139 A2
Spital Austria 47°42N 14°18E 180 D7
Spithead U.K. 50°45N 1°10W 169 G6
Spittal an der Drau Austria 46°48N 13°31E 180 E6
Spitzbergen = Svalbard Arctic 78°0N 17°0E 150 B8
Spjelkavik Norway 62°28N 6°22E 164 B3
Split Croatia 43°31N 16°26E 199 E13
Split ✕ (SPU) Croatia 43°33N 16°15E 199 E13
Split L. Canada 56°8N 96°15W 297 B9
Split Lake Canada 56°8N 96°15W 297 B9
Splitski Kanal Croatia 43°31N 16°20E 199 E13
Splügenpass Switz. 46°30N 9°20E 179 J5
Spofford U.S.A. 29°10N 100°25W 314 G4
Spokane U.S.A. 47°40N 117°24W 304 C5
Spoleto Italy 42°44N 12°44E 199 F9
Sponvika Norway 59°7N 11°15E 164 E8
Spoon → U.S.A. 40°19N 90°4W 310 D6
Spooner U.S.A. 45°50N 91°53W 308 C8
Spořilov Czech Rep. 50°2N 14°29E 135 B3
Sporyy Navolok, Mys Russia 75°50N 68°40E 214 B7
Spot Pond U.S.A. 42°26N 71°4W 116 A2
Spotswood Australia 37°50S 144°52E 128 B1
Sprague U.S.A. 47°18N 117°59W 304 C5
Spratly I. S. China Sea 8°38N 111°55E 230 C4
Spratly Is. S. China Sea 8°20N 112°0E 230 C4
Spray U.S.A. 44°50N 119°48W 304 D4
Spreča → Bos.-H. 44°44N 18°6E 182 F3
Spree → Germany 52°32N 13°12E 178 C9
Spreewald Germany 51°58N 13°51E 178 D9
Spremberg Germany 51°34N 14°22E 178 D10
Sprengisandur Iceland 64°52N 18°7W 155 C8
Spring City U.S.A. 40°11N 75°33W 313 F9
Spring Cr. → U.S.A. 30°54N 84°45W 316 E5
Spring Creek U.S.A. 40°44N 115°35W 304 F6
Spring Garden Guyana 6°59N 58°31W 329 B6
Spring Garden Calif., U.S.A. 39°52N 120°47W 306 F6
Spring Green U.S.A. 43°11N 90°4W 310 A6
Spring Hill Ala., U.S.A. 31°42N 85°58W 316 D4
Spring Hill Fla., U.S.A. 28°27N 82°41W 317 G7
Spring Mts. U.S.A. 36°0N 115°45W 307 J11
Spring Valley Calif., U.S.A. 32°44N 116°59W 307 N10
Spring Valley Ill., U.S.A. 41°20N 89°12W 310 C7
Spring Valley Nev., U.S.A. 36°6N 115°14W 124 B1
Springbok S. Africa 29°42S 17°54E 270 C2
Springboro U.S.A. 41°48N 80°22W 312 E4
Springdale Nfld. & L., Canada 49°30N 56°6W 299 C8
Springdale Ark., U.S.A. 36°11N 94°8W 314 C7
Springdale Ohio, U.S.A. 39°17N 84°29W 311 E12
Springe Germany 52°13N 9°33E 178 C5
Springeberg Germany 52°26N 13°43E 115 B5
Springer U.S.A. 36°22N 104°36W 305 H11
Springerville U.S.A. 34°8N 109°17W 305 J9
Springfield Ont., Canada 42°50N 80°56W 312 D4
Springfield Dominica 15°21N 61°23W 323 k
Springfield N.Z. 43°19S 171°56E 285 D6
Springfield Colo., U.S.A. 37°24N 102°37W 305 H12
Springfield Fla., U.S.A. 30°10N 85°37W 316 E4
Springfield Ga., U.S.A. 32°22N 81°18W 316 C8
Springfield Ill., U.S.A. 39°48N 89°39W 310 E7
Springfield Ky., U.S.A. 37°41N 85°13W 311 G11
Springfield Mass., U.S.A. 42°6N 72°35W 313 D12
Springfield Mo., U.S.A. 37°13N 93°17W 308 G7
Springfield Ohio, U.S.A. 39°55N 83°49W 311 E13
Springfield Oreg., U.S.A. 44°3N 123°1W 304 D2
Springfield S.C., U.S.A. 33°30N 81°17W 316 B8
Springfield Tenn., U.S.A. 36°31N 86°53W 315 C11
Springfield Va., U.S.A. 38°46N 77°10W 143 C2
Springfield Vt., U.S.A. 43°18N 72°29W 313 C12
Springfield, L. U.S.A. 39°46N 89°36W 310 E7
Springfontein S. Africa 30°15S 25°40E 270 D4
Springhill Canada 45°40N 64°4W 299 C7
Springhill La., U.S.A. 33°0N 93°28W 314 E8
Springhouse Canada 51°56N 122°7W 296 C4
Springs S. Africa 26°13S 28°25E 271 C4
Springsure Australia 24°8S 148°6E 280 C4
Springvale Ga., U.S.A. 31°50N 84°53W 316 D5
Springvale Maine, U.S.A. 43°28N 70°48W 313 C14
Springville Calif., U.S.A. 36°8N 118°49W 306 J8
Springville Iowa, U.S.A. 42°3N 91°27W 310 B5
Springville N.Y., U.S.A. 42°31N 78°40W 312 D6
Springville Utah, U.S.A. 40°10N 111°37W 304 F8
Springwater U.S.A. 42°38N 77°35W 312 D7
Sprottau = Szprotawa Poland 51°33N 15°35E 185 G2
Spruce-Creek U.S.A. 40°36N 78°9W 312 F6
Spruce Knob-Seneca Rocks △ U.S.A. 38°50N 79°30W 309 F14
Spruce Mt. U.S.A. 44°12N 72°19W 313 B12
Spur U.S.A. 33°28N 100°52W 314 E4
Spurn Hd. U.K. 53°35N 0°8E 168 D8
Spuž Montenegro 42°32N 19°10E 202 D3
Spuzzum Canada 49°37N 121°23W 296 D4
Spydeberg Norway 59°36N 11°5E 164 E8

Squam L. U.S.A. 43°45N 71°32W 313 C13
Squamish Canada 49°45N 123°10W 296 D4
Squantum U.S.A. 42°17N 71°0W 116 B2
Square Islands Canada 52°47N 55°47W 299 B8
Squillace, G. di Italy 38°45N 16°50E 201 D9
Squinzano Italy 40°26N 18°2E 201 B11
Squires, Mt. Australia 26°14S 127°28E 279 E4
Sragen Indonesia 7°26S 111°2E 235 D4
Srbac Bos.-H. 45°7N 17°30E 182 E2
Srbica Serbia 42°45N 20°47E 202 D4
Srbija = Serbia ■ Europe 43°20N 20°0E 202 C4
Srbobran Serbia 45°32N 19°48E 182 E4
Sre Ambel Cambodia 11°8N 103°46E 237 G4
Sre Khtum Cambodia 12°10N 106°52E 237 F6
Sre Umbell = Sre Ambel Cambodia 11°8N 103°46E 237 G4
Srebrenica Bos.-H. 44°6N 19°18E 182 F4
Sredinny Ra. = Sredinnyy Khrebet Russia 57°0N 160°0E 215 D17
Sredinnyy Khrebet Russia 57°0N 160°0E 215 D17
Središče Slovenia 46°24N 16°17E 199 B13
Sredna Gora Bulgaria 42°40N 24°20E 203 D8
Srednaya Rogatka Russia 59°49N 30°22E 137 C2
Srednekolymsk Russia 67°27N 153°40E 215 C16
Sredni Rodopi Bulgaria 41°40N 24°45E 203 E8
Srednogorie Bulgaria 42°43N 24°10E 203 D8
Śrem Poland 52°6N 17°2E 185 F4
Sremska Mitrovica Serbia 44°59N 19°38E 182 F4
Sremski Karlovci Serbia 45°12N 19°56E 182 E4
Srepok ➜ Cambodia 13°33N 106°16E 236 F6
Sretensk Russia 52°10N 117°40E 215 D12
Sri Aman Malaysia 1°15N 111°32E 235 B4
Sri Kalahasti India 13°45N 79°44E 245 H4
Sri Lanka ■ Asia 7°30N 80°50E 245 L5
Sriharikota I. India 13°40N 80°20E 245 H5
Srikakulam India 18°14N 83°58E 244 E6
Srinagar India 34°5N 74°50E 243 B6
Srinagarind Res. Thailand 14°35N 99°0E 236 E2
Sripur Bangla. 24°14N 90°30E 241 C3
Srivardhan India 18°4N 73°3E 244 E1
Srivilliputtur India 9°31N 77°40E 245 K3
Środa Śląska Poland 51°10N 16°36E 185 G3
Środa Wielkopolski Poland 52°15N 17°19E 185 F4
Śródmieście Poland 52°13N 21°0E 142 B2
Srono Indonesia 8°24S 114°16E 231 J17
Srpska Crnja Serbia 45°38N 20°44E 182 E5
Srpski Itebej Serbia 45°35N 20°44E 182 E5
Srungavarapukota India 18°7N 83°10E 244 E6
Ssuhu Taiwan 23°38N 120°13E 225 C2
Staaken Germany 52°31N 13°8E 115 A1
Staaten ➜ Australia 16°24S 141°17E 280 B3
Staaten River △ Australia 16°15S 142°40E 280 B3
Stabekk Norway 59°54N 10°36E 133 A2
Staberhuk Germany 54°23N 11°18E 178 A7
Stade Germany 53°35N 9°29E 178 B5
Staðarfell Iceland 65°7N 22°12W 155 B4
Staðarhólskirkja Iceland 65°23N 21°58W 155 B5
Staðastaður Iceland 64°49N 23°1W 155 C3
Stadhavet Norway 62°13N 5°0E 164 B2
Stadhiou Athens, Greece 112 c3
Stadhuis Amsterdam, Neths. 112 b2
Staður Húnavatnssýsla, Iceland 65°9N 21°3W 155 B5
Staður Ísafjarðarsýsla, Iceland 66°15N 22°50W 155 A4
Stadlandet Norway 62°10N 5°10E 164 B2
Stadlau Austria 48°13N 16°27E 142 A2
Stadshuset Stockholm, Sweden 139 b1
Stadskanaal Neths. 53°4N 6°55E 170 A6
Stadtallendorf Germany 50°48N 9°1E 178 E5
Stadthagen Germany 52°19N 9°13E 178 C5
Stadtlohn Germany 51°59N 6°55E 178 D2
Stadtroda Germany 50°52N 11°44E 178 E7
Stafafell Iceland 64°25N 14°52W 155 C12
Staffa U.K. 56°27N 6°21W 167 E2
Staffanstorp Sweden 55°39N 13°13E 163 J7
Stafford Staffs., U.K. 52°49N 2°7W 168 E5
Stafford Kans., U.S.A. 37°58N 98°36W 308 G4
Stafford, L. U.S.A. 29°20N 82°29W 317 F7
Stafford Springs U.S.A. 41°57N 72°18W 313 E12
Staffordshire □ U.K. 52°53N 2°10W 168 E5
Stagnone Italy 37°53N 12°26E 200 E5
Stagnone di Marsala ⌓ Italy 37°52N 12°26E 200 E5
Staines U.K. 51°26N 0°29W 169 F7
Stains France 48°57N 2°22E 134 A3
Stainz Austria 46°53N 15°17E 180 E8
Stakhanov Ukraine 48°35N 38°40E 189 H10
Stalać Serbia 43°43N 21°28E 202 C5
Stalin = Kuçovë Albania 40°47N 19°57E 202 F3
Stalin = Varna Bulgaria 43°13N 27°56E 203 C11
Stalin Pk. = Gerlachovský štit Slovak Rep. 49°11N 20°7E 181 B13
Stalin Pk. = imeni Ismail Samani, Pik Tajikistan 39°0N 72°2E 217 E8
Stalin Pk. = Musala Bulgaria 42°13N 23°37E 202 D7
Stalinabad = Dushanbe Tajikistan 38°33N 68°48E 217 E7
Stalingrad = Volgograd Russia 48°40N 44°25E 191 F7
Staliniri = Tskhinvali Georgia 42°14N 44°1E 191 J7
Stalinogorsk = Novomoskovsk Russia 54°5N 38°15E 188 E10
Stalinogrod = Katowice Poland 50°17N 19°5E 185 H6
Stalinsk = Novokuznetsk Russia 53°45N 87°10E 217 B11
Stalinstadt = Eisenhüttenstadt Germany 52°9N 14°38E 178 C10
Stallarholmen Sweden 59°22N 17°12E 162 E11
Ställdalen Sweden 59°56N 14°56E 162 E8
Stalowa Wola Poland 50°34N 22°3E 185 H9
Stalybridge U.K. 53°28N 2°3W 168 D5
Stamford Queens., Australia 21°15S 143°46E 280 C3
Stamford Lincs., U.K. 52°39N 0°29W 169 E7
Stamford Conn., U.S.A. 41°3N 73°32W 313 E11
Stamford N.Y., U.S.A. 42°25N 74°38W 313 D10
Stamford Tex., U.S.A. 32°57N 99°48W 314 E5
Stamford Hill U.K. 51°34N 0°4W 125 A3
Stammersdorf Austria 48°18N 16°24E 142 A2
Stamnes Norway 60°40N 5°45E 164 D2
Stamping Ground U.S.A. 38°16N 84°41W 311 F12
Stampriet Namibia 24°20S 18°28E 270 B2
Stamps U.S.A. 33°22N 93°30W 314 E8
Stanberry U.S.A. 40°13N 94°35W 310 D2
Stančevo = Kalipetrovo Bulgaria 44°5N 27°14E 203 B11
Standerton S. Africa 26°55S 29°7E 271 C4
Standish U.S.A. 43°59N 83°57W 309 D12
Stanford S. Africa 34°26S 19°29E 270 D2
Stanford Mont., U.S.A. 47°9N 110°13W 304 C8
Stånga Sweden 57°17N 18°29E 163 G12
Stange Norway 60°43N 11°5E 164 D8
Stanger S. Africa 29°27S 31°14E 271 C5
Stängselåsen = Salpausselkä Finland 61°3N 26°15E 188 B4
Stangvik Norway 62°55N 8°28E 164 B5
Stanhope Vic., Australia 36°27S 144°59E 283 D6
Stanhope Iowa, U.S.A. 42°17N 93°48W 310 B3
Stanimaka = Asenovgrad Bulgaria 42°1N 24°51E 203 D8
Stanišić Serbia 45°56N 19°10E 182 E4
Stanislaus ➜ U.S.A. 37°40N 121°14W 306 H5
Stanislav = Ivano-Frankivsk Ukraine 48°40N 24°40E 183 B9
Stanisławów = Ivano-Frankivsk Ukraine 48°40N 24°40E 183 B9
Stanisławów Poland 52°18N 21°33E 185 F8
Stanley Tas., Australia 40°46S 145°19E 281 G4
Stanley Hong Kong, China 22°13N 114°12E 122 B2
Stanley Falk. Is. 51°40S 59°51W 153 f
Stanley Durham, U.K. 54°53N 1°41W 168 C6
Stanley Idaho, U.S.A. 44°13N 114°56W 304 D6
Stanley N. Dak., U.S.A. 48°19N 102°23W 308 A2
Stanley N.Y., U.S.A. 42°48N 77°6W 312 D7
Stanley Falls = Boyoma, Chutes Dem. Rep. of the Congo 0°35N 25°23E 264 B5
Stanley Mission Canada 55°25N 104°33W 297 B8
Stanley Pen. China 22°12N 114°12E 122 B2
Stanley Pool = Malebo, Pool Africa 4°17S 15°20E 265 C3
Stanley Res. India 11°50N 77°40E 245 J3
Stanleyville = Kisangani Dem. Rep. of the Congo 0°35N 25°15E 268 B2
Stanmore U.K. 51°37N 0°18W 125 A2
Stanovoy Khrebet Russia 55°0N 130°0E 215 D14
Stanovoy Ra. = Stanovoy Khrebet Russia 55°0N 130°0E 215 D14
Stansmore Ra. Australia 21°23S 128°33E 278 D4
Stansted, London ✈ (STN) U.K. 51°54N 0°14E 169 F8
Stanthorpe Australia 28°36S 151°59E 281 D5
Stanton Ky., U.S.A. 37°54N 83°52W 311 G13
Stanton Tex., U.S.A. 32°8N 101°48W 314 E4
Stanwood U.S.A. 48°15N 122°23W 306 B4
Staples U.S.A. 46°21N 94°48W 308 B6
Stapleton N.Y., U.S.A. 40°36N 74°5W 132 C1
Stapleton Nebr., U.S.A. 41°29N 100°31W 308 E3
Stąporków Poland 51°9N 20°31E 185 G7
Star City Canada 52°50N 104°20W 297 C8
Star Ferry Hong Kong, China 122 a2
Star Harbour Solomon Is. 10°47S 162°19E 287 N12
Star Lake U.S.A. 44°10N 75°2W 313 B9
Stará Ďala = Hurbanovo Slovak Rep. 47°51N 18°11E 181 D11
Stará L'ubovňa Slovak Rep. 49°18N 20°42E 181 B13
Stara Moravica Serbia 45°50N 19°30E 182 E4
Stara Pazova Serbia 44°58N 20°10E 182 F5
Stara Planina Bulgaria 43°15N 23°0E 202 C7
Stara Sil Ukraine 49°29N 22°58E 185 J9
Stará Turá Slovak Rep. 48°47N 17°42E 181 C10
Stara Ushytsya Ukraine 48°35N 27°8E 183 B12
Stara Zagora Bulgaria 42°26N 25°39E 203 D9
Starachowice Poland 51°3N 21°2E 185 G8
Staraya Derevnya Russia 59°58N 30°15E 137 B1
Staraya Russa Russia 57°58N 31°23E 188 D6
Starbuck I. Kiribati 5°37S 155°55W 289 H12
Starchiojd Romania 45°19N 26°11E 183 E11
Starcke △ Australia 14°56S 145°2E 280 A4
Staré Město Czech Rep. 50°5N 14°25E 135 B2
Stare Miasto Warsaw, Poland 142 a2
Stargard in Pommern = Stargard Szczeciński Poland 53°20N 15°0E 184 E2
Stargard Szczeciński Poland 53°20N 15°0E 184 E2
Stårheim Norway 61°56N 5°40E 164 C2
Stari Bar Montenegro 42°7N 19°10E 202 D3
Stari Bečej = Bečej Serbia 45°36N 20°3E 182 E5
Stari Trg Slovenia 45°29N 15°7E 199 C12
Staritsa Russia 56°33N 34°55E 188 D8
Starke U.S.A. 29°57N 82°7W 316 F7
Starke, L. U.S.A. 28°34N 81°32W 133 A1
Starkville U.S.A. 33°28N 88°49W 315 E10
Starnberg Germany 48°0N 11°21E 179 H7
Starnberger See Germany 47°54N 11°19E 179 H7
Starobilsk Ukraine 49°16N 39°0E 189 H10
Starodub Russia 52°30N 32°50E 189 F7
Starogard Gdański Poland 53°59N 18°30E 184 E5
Starokonstantinov = Starokonstyantyniv Ukraine 49°48N 27°10E 177 D14
Starokonstyantyniv Ukraine 49°48N 27°10E 177 D14
Starokozache Ukraine 46°20N 29°59E 183 D14
Starominskaya Russia 46°33N 39°0E 189 J10
Staroshcherbinovskaya Russia 46°40N 38°53E 189 J10
Starrs Mill U.S.A. 33°19N 84°31W 316 B5
Start Pt. U.K. 50°13N 3°39W 169 G4
Stary Sącz Poland 49°33N 20°35E 185 J7
Staryy Biryuzyak Russia 44°46N 46°50E 191 H8
Staryy Chartoriysk Ukraine 51°15N 25°54E 177 C13
Staryy Krym Ukraine 45°3N 35°8E 189 K8
Staryy Margilan = Marghilon Uzbekistan 40°27N 71°42E 217 D8
Staryy Oskol Russia 51°19N 37°55E 189 G9
Staryy Sambir Ukraine 49°27N 22°59E 185 J9
Stassfurt Germany 51°51N 11°35E 178 D7
Staszów Poland 50°33N 21°10E 185 H8
State Center U.S.A. 42°1N 93°10W 310 B3
State College U.S.A. 40°48N 77°52W 312 F7
Stateline U.S.A. 38°57N 119°56W 306 G7
Staten, I. = Estados, I. de Los Argentina 54°40S 64°30W 336 D4
Staten I. U.S.A. 40°35N 74°9W 313 F10
Staten Island Zoo U.S.A. 40°38N 74°6W 132 C1
Staten Islands Ferry Terminal U.S.A. 40°38N 74°4W 132 C1
Statenice Czech Rep. 50°9N 14°19E 135 B1
Statenville U.S.A. 30°42N 83°2W 316 E6
Statesboro U.S.A. 32°27N 81°47W 316 C8
Statesville U.S.A. 35°47N 80°53W 315 D14
Statham U.S.A. 33°58N 83°35W 316 B6
Stathelle Norway 59°3N 9°41E 164 E6
Statia = St. Eustatius W. Indies 17°20N 63°0W 322 a
Statue Square Hong Kong, China 122 c1
Stauffer U.S.A. 34°45N 119°3W 307 L7
Staunton Ill., U.S.A. 39°1N 89°47W 310 F7
Staunton Va., U.S.A. 38°9N 79°4W 309 F14
Stavanger = Rogaland □ Norway 59°12N 6°20E 164 E3
Stavanger Norway 58°57N 5°40E 164 F2
Stavelot Belgium 50°23N 5°55E 170 D5
Stavern Norway 59°0N 10°1E 164 F7
Stavoren Neths. 52°53N 5°22E 170 B5
Stavropol Russia 45°5N 42°0E 191 H6
Stavropol □ Russia 47°20N 42°50E 191 G6
Stavros Cyprus 35°1N 32°38E 207 E8
Stavros Ithaki, Greece 38°27N 20°39E 207 C2
Stavros Kriti, Greece 35°12N 24°45E 207 E5
Stavros Thessaloniki, Greece 40°39N 23°43E 202 F7
Stavros, Akra Greece 35°26N 24°58E 207 E5
Stavroupoli Greece 41°12N 24°45E 203 E8
Stawell Australia 37°5S 142°47E 282 D5
Stawell ➜ Australia 20°20S 142°55E 280 C3
Stawiski Poland 53°22N 22°9E 184 E9
Stawiszyn Poland 51°56N 18°4E 185 G5
Stayner Canada 44°25N 80°5W 312 B4
Stayton U.S.A. 44°48N 122°48W 304 D2
Steamboat Springs U.S.A. 40°29N 106°50W 304 F10
Stean Norway 59°16N 8°33E 164 E5
Stebbins U.S.A. 63°31N 162°17W 303 E7
Steblevë Albania 41°23N 20°33E 202 E4
Stedelijk Museum Amsterdam, Neths. 112 c1
Steele Ala., U.S.A. 33°56N 86°12W 316 B3
Steele N. Dak., U.S.A. 46°51N 99°55W 308 B4
Steele Creek Australia 37°44S 144°52E 128 A1
Steelton U.S.A. 40°14N 76°50W 312 F8
Steelville U.S.A. 37°58N 91°22W 310 G5
Steen River Canada 59°40N 117°12W 296 B5
Steenkool = Bintuni Indonesia 2°7S 133°32E 231 E8
Steenokkerzeel Belgium 50°55N 4°31E 116 A2
Steens Mt. U.S.A. 42°35N 118°40W 304 E4
Steenstrup Gletscher Greenland 75°15N 57°0W 154 B5
Steenwijk Neths. 52°47N 6°7E 170 B6
Steep Pt. Australia 26°8S 113°8E 279 E1
Steep Rock Canada 51°30N 98°48W 297 C9
Steer, L. U.S.A. 28°31N 81°30W 133 A2
Ştefan Vodă Moldova 46°27N 29°42E 183 D14
Ştefănesti Romania 47°44N 27°15E 183 C12
Stefanie △ Ethiopia 4°55N 36°55E 257 G4
Stefanie L. = Chew Bahir Ethiopia 4°40N 36°50E 257 G4
Stefansson Bay Antarctica 67°20S 59°8E 151 C5
Stege Denmark 54°59N 12°18E 163 K6
Stegi = Siteki Swaziland 26°32S 31°58E 271 C5
Steglitz Germany 52°27N 13°19E 115 B2
Stegman = Artesia U.S.A. 32°51N 104°24W 305 K11
Ştei Romania 46°32N 22°27E 182 D7
Steiermark □ Austria 47°26N 15°0E 180 D8
Steigerwald Germany 49°44N 10°26E 179 F6
Steigerwald ⌓ Germany 49°50N 10°30E 179 F6
Steilacoom U.S.A. 47°10N 122°36W 306 C4
Steilrandberge Namibia 17°45S 13°20E 270 A1
Stein = Kamnik Slovenia 46°14N 14°37E 199 B11
Steinbach Canada 49°32N 96°40W 297 D9
Steinfurt Germany 52°9N 7°20E 178 C3
Steinhatchee U.S.A. 29°40N 83°23W 316 F6
Steinhausen Namibia 21°49S 18°20E 270 B2
Steinheim Germany 51°51N 9°5E 178 D5
Steinhuder Meer Germany 52°29N 9°21E 178 C5
Steinhuder Meer ⌓ Germany 52°30N 9°16E 178 C5
Steinkjer Norway 64°1N 11°31E 160 D14
Steinkopf S. Africa 29°18S 17°43E 270 C2
Steinshamn Norway 62°47N 6°28E 164 B3
Steinwald ⌓ Germany 49°55N 12°8E 179 F8
Stellarton Canada 45°32N 62°30W 299 C7
Stellenbosch S. Africa 33°58S 18°50E 270 D2
Stelvio, Paso dello Italy 46°32N 10°27E 198 B7
Stenay France 49°29N 5°12E 173 C12
Stendal Germany 52°36N 11°53E 178 C7
Stende Latvia 57°11N 22°33E 184 A9
Stenen Koraal Neth. Ant. 12°10N 68°56W 322 g
Stenhamra Sweden 59°20N 17°41E 162 E11
Stenshuvud △ Sweden 55°39N 14°15E 163 J8
Stenstorp Sweden 58°17N 13°45E 163 F7
Stenungsund Sweden 58°6N 11°50E 163 F5
Steornabhaigh = Stornoway U.K. 58°13N 6°23W 167 C2
Stepanakert = Xankändi Azerbaijan 39°52N 46°49E 213 C12
Stepanavan Armenia 41°1N 44°23E 191 K7
Stepaside Ireland 53°15N 6°12W 120 B2
Stephansdom Vienna, Austria 142 b2
Stephens, C. N.Z. 40°42S 173°58E 285 A8
Stephens Creek Australia 31°50S 141°30E 282 A4
Stephens I. B.C., Canada 54°10N 130°45W 296 C2
Stephens I. N.Z. 40°40S 174°1E 285 A9
Stephens L. Canada 56°32N 95°0W 297 B9
Stephenville Nfld. & L., Canada 48°31N 58°35W 299 C8
Stephenville Tex., U.S.A. 32°13N 98°12W 314 E5
Stepney U.K. 51°30N 0°3W 125 A3
Stepnica Poland 53°38N 14°36E 184 E1
Stepnogorsk Kazakhstan 52°21N 71°53E 217 B8
Stepnoi = Elista Russia 46°16N 44°14E 191 G7
Steppe Asia 50°0N 50°0E 210 C7
Steps Pt. Amer. Samoa 14°23S 170°45W 302 f
Sterea Ellas □ Greece 38°50N 23°0E 204 C4
Sterkstroom S. Africa 31°32S 26°32E 270 D4
Sterling Alaska, U.S.A. 60°32N 150°46W 303 F10
Sterling Colo., U.S.A. 40°37N 103°13W 304 F12
Sterling Ga., U.S.A. 31°16N 81°34W 316 D8
Sterling Ill., U.S.A. 41°48N 89°42W 310 C7
Sterling Kans., U.S.A. 38°13N 98°12W 308 F4
Sterling City U.S.A. 31°51N 101°0W 314 F4
Sterling Heights U.S.A. 42°35N 83°2W 311 B13
Sterling Park U.S.A. 37°41N 122°27W 136 B2
Sterling Run U.S.A. 41°25N 78°12W 312 E6
Sterlitamak Russia 53°40N 56°0E 186 D10
Sternberg Germany 53°42N 11°50E 178 B7
Šternberk Czech Rep. 49°45N 17°15E 181 B10
Sternes Greece 35°30N 24°9E 207 E5
Sterzing = Vipiteno Italy 46°54N 11°26E 199 B8
Stettin = Szczecin Poland 53°27N 14°27E 184 E1
Stettiner Haff Germany 53°47N 14°15E 178 B10
Stettler Canada 52°19N 112°40W 296 C6
Steubenville U.S.A. 40°22N 80°37W 312 F4
Stevenage U.K. 51°55N 0°13W 169 F7
Stevens Point U.S.A. 44°31N 89°34W 308 C9
Stevens Pottery U.S.A. 32°57N 83°17W 316 C6
Stevens Village U.S.A. 66°1N 149°6W 303 C10
Stevenson U.S.A. 45°42N 121°53W 306 E5
Stevenson ➜ Australia 27°6S 135°33E 281 D2
Stevenson L. Canada 53°55N 96°0W 297 C9
Stevensville U.S.A. 46°30N 114°5W 304 C6
Stevns Klint Denmark 55°17N 12°28E 163 J6
Steward U.S.A. 41°51N 89°1W 310 C7
Stewardson U.S.A. 39°16N 88°38W 311 E8
Stewart B.C., Canada 55°56N 129°57W 296 B3
Stewart Ga., U.S.A. 33°25N 83°52W 316 B6
Stewart Nev., U.S.A. 39°5N 119°46W 306 F7
Stewart ➜ Canada 63°19N 139°26W 294 C6
Stewart, C. Australia 11°57S 134°56E 280 A1
Stewart, I. Chile 54°50S 71°15W 336 D2
Stewart I. N.Z. 46°58S 167°54E 285 G2
Stewarts Point U.S.A. 38°39N 123°24W 306 G3
Stewartsville U.S.A. 39°45N 94°30W 310 E2
Stewartville U.S.A. 43°51N 92°29W 308 D7
Stewiacke Canada 45°9N 63°22W 299 C7
Steynsburg S. Africa 31°15S 25°49E 270 D4
Steyr Austria 48°3N 14°25E 180 C7
Steyr ➜ Austria 48°3N 14°25E 180 C7
Steytlerville S. Africa 33°17S 24°19E 270 D3
Stia Italy 43°48N 11°42E 199 E8
Sticklinge udde Sweden 59°23N 18°6E 139 A2
Stickney U.S.A. 41°49N 87°46W 119 C2
Stigler U.S.A. 35°15N 95°8W 314 D7
Stigliano Italy 40°24N 16°14E 201 B9
Stigtomta Sweden 58°47N 16°48E 163 F10
Stikine ➜ Canada 56°40N 132°30W 296 B2
Stilfontein S. Africa 26°51S 26°50E 270 C4
Stilida Greece 38°55N 22°47E 204 C4
Stillmore U.S.A. 32°27N 82°13W 316 C7
Stillorgan Ireland 53°17N 6°11W 120 B2
Stillwater N.Y., U.S.A. 42°55N 73°41W 313 D11
Stillwater Okla., U.S.A. 36°7N 97°4W 314 C6
Stillwater Range U.S.A. 39°50N 118°5W 304 G4
Stillwater Res. U.S.A. 43°54N 75°3W 313 C9
Stilo, Pta. Italy 38°25N 16°35E 201 D9
Stilwell U.S.A. 35°49N 94°38W 314 D7
Stînga Nistrului □ Moldova 47°20N 29°15E 183 C14
Štip Macedonia 41°42N 22°10E 202 E6
Stira Greece 38°9N 24°14E 204 C6
Stirling Ont., Canada 44°18N 77°33W 312 B7
Stirling N.Z. 46°14S 169°49E 285 G4
Stirling Stirling, U.K. 56°8N 3°57W 167 E5
Stirling □ U.K. 56°12N 4°18W 167 E4
Stirling Ra. Australia 34°23S 118°0E 279 F2
Stirling Range △ Australia 34°26S 118°20E 279 F2
Stittsville Canada 45°15N 75°55W 313 A9
Stjernøya Norway 70°20N 22°40E 160 A20
Stjørdalshalsen Norway 63°29N 10°51E 164 A7
Stock Island U.S.A. 24°32N 81°34W 317 L8
Stockach Germany 47°50N 9°1E 179 H5
Stockaryd Sweden 57°19N 14°36E 163 G8
Stockbridge Ga., U.S.A. 33°33N 84°14W 316 B5
Stockbridge Mich., U.S.A. 42°27N 84°11W 311 B12
Stockerau Austria 48°24N 16°12E 181 C9
Stockholm Sweden 59°19N 18°4E 139 B2
Stockholm Arlanda ✈ (ARN) Sweden 59°41N 17°56E 139 A1
Stockholms län □ Sweden 59°30N 18°20E 162 E12
Stockport U.K. 53°25N 2°9W 168 D5
Stocksbridge U.K. 53°29N 1°35W 168 D6
Stocksund Sweden 59°23N 18°3E 139 A2
Stockton Calif., U.S.A. 37°58N 121°17W 306 H5
Stockton Ill., U.S.A. 42°21N 90°1W 310 B6
Stockton Kans., U.S.A. 39°26N 99°16W 308 F4
Stockton Mo., U.S.A. 37°42N 93°48W 310 G3
Stockton-on-Tees U.K. 54°35N 1°19W 168 C6
Stockton-on-Tees □ U.K. 54°35N 1°19W 168 C6
Stockton Plateau U.S.A. 30°30N 102°30W 314 F3
Stoczek Łukowski Poland 51°58N 21°58E 185 G8
Stöde Sweden 62°28N 16°35E 162 B10
Stöðvarfjörður Iceland 64°49N 13°52W 155 C13
Stodůlky Czech Rep. 50°3N 14°19E 135 B1
Stoeng Treng Cambodia 13°31N 105°58E 236 F5
Stoer, Pt. of U.K. 58°16N 5°23W 167 C3
Stogovo Macedonia 41°31N 20°38E 202 E4
Stoholm Denmark 56°30N 9°8E 163 H3
Stoke N.Z. 41°19S 173°14E 285 B8
Stoke Newington U.K. 51°33N 0°4W 125 A3
Stoke-on-Trent U.K. 53°1N 2°11W 168 D5
Stoke-on-Trent □ U.K. 53°1N 2°11W 168 D5
Stokes △ Australia 33°45S 121°11E 279 F3
Stokes Pt. Australia 40°10S 143°56E 281 G3
Stokes Ra. Australia 15°50S 130°50E 278 C5
Stokes Valley N.Z. 41°10S 174°59E 143 B2
Stokkseyri Iceland 63°50N 21°2W 155 D5
Stokksnes Iceland 64°14N 14°58W 155 C12
Stokmarknes Norway 68°34N 14°54E 160 B16
Stolac Bos.-H. 43°5N 17°59E 202 C1
Stolberg Germany 50°47N 6°13E 178 E2
Stolbovoy, Ostrov Russia 74°44N 135°14E 215 B14
Stolbtsy = Stowbtsy Belarus 53°30N 26°43E 177 B14
Stolin Belarus 51°53N 26°50E 177 C14
Stöllet Sweden 60°26N 13°15E 162 D7
Stolnici Romania 44°31N 24°48E 183 F9
Stolp = Słupsk Poland 54°30N 17°3E 184 D4
Stolpmünde = Ustka Poland 54°35N 16°55E 184 D3
Stomio Greece 35°21N 23°32E 207 E4
Ston Croatia 42°51N 17°43E 199 F14
Stone U.K. 52°55N 2°9W 168 E5
Stone Canyon Res. U.S.A. 34°6N 118°27W 126 B2
Stone Mountain U.S.A. 33°49N 84°10W 316 B5
Stone Park U.S.A. 41°53N 87°52W 119 B1
Stoneboro U.S.A. 41°20N 80°7W 312 E4
Stonebridge U.K. 51°32N 0°16W 125 A2
Stoneham U.S.A. 42°29N 71°5W 116 A2
Stonehaven U.K. 56°59N 2°12W 167 E6
Stonehenge Queens., Australia 24°22S 143°17E 280 C3
Stonehenge Wilts., U.K. 51°9N 1°45W 169 F6
Stonewall Canada 50°10N 97°19W 297 C9
Stongfjorden Norway 61°26N 5°10E 164 C2
Stonington U.S.A. 39°44N 89°12W 310 E7
Stony Brook Res. U.S.A. 42°15N 71°8W 116 B2
Stony Creek ➜ U.S.A. 41°38N 87°41W 119 C2
Stony Hill Jamaica 18°5N 76°48W 320 a
Stony L. Man., Canada 58°51N 98°40W 297 B9
Stony L. Ont., Canada 44°30N 78°5W 312 B6
Stony Point U.S.A. 41°14N 73°59W 313 E11
Stony Pt. U.S.A. 43°50N 76°18W 313 C8
Stony Rapids Canada 59°16N 105°50W 297 B7
Stony River U.S.A. 61°47N 156°35W 303 F8
Stony Tunguska = Tunguska, Podkamennaya ➜ Russia 61°50N 90°13E 215 C10
Stonyford U.S.A. 39°23N 122°33W 306 F4
Stopnica Poland 50°27N 20°57E 185 H7
Storå Sweden 59°42N 15°6E 162 E9
Storå ➜ Denmark 56°20N 8°19E 163 H2
Stora Gla Sweden 59°30N 12°30E 162 E6
Stora Le Sweden 59°5N 11°55E 162 E5
Stora Lulevatten Sweden 67°10N 19°30E 160 C18
Stora Värtan Sweden 59°25N 18°7E 139 A2
Stóra-Vatnshorn Iceland 65°4N 21°33W 155 B5
Storavan Sweden 65°45N 18°10E 160 D18
Stord Norway 59°52N 5°23E 164 E2
Stordalen Norway 62°23N 7°0E 164 B4
Store Bælt Denmark 55°20N 11°0E 163 J4
Store Hareskov Denmark 55°46N 12°23E 118 A2
Store Heddinge Denmark 55°18N 12°23E 163 J6
Store Jukleggi = Høgeloft Norway 61°3N 8°12E 164 C5
Store Koldewey Greenland 76°30N 19°0W 154 B9
Store Magleby Denmark 55°35N 12°35E 118 B3
Store Mosse △ Sweden 57°18N 13°55E 163 G7
Store Sotra Norway 60°18N 5°4E 164 D1
Storebro Sweden 57°35N 15°52E 163 G9
Støren Norway 63°3N 10°18E 164 A7
Storerikvollen Norway 63°7N 11°58E 164 A8
Storfjellsætra Norway 61°40N 10°30E 164 C7
Storfjorden Norway 62°28N 6°35E 164 B3
Storfors Sweden 59°32N 14°17E 162 E8
Storholmen Sweden 59°23N 18°8E 139 A2
Stóridalur Iceland 63°38N 19°57W 155 D7
Stórinúpur Iceland 64°3N 20°10W 155 C6
Storkyrkan Stockholm, Sweden 139 c2
Storli Norway 62°42N 9°5E 164 B6
Storlien Sweden 63°19N 12°6E 162 A6
Storm B. Australia 43°10S 147°30E 281 G4
Storm Lake U.S.A. 42°39N 95°13W 308 D6
Stormberge S. Africa 31°16S 26°17E 270 D4
Stormsrivier S. Africa 33°59S 23°52E 270 D3
Stornoway U.K. 58°13N 6°23W 167 C2
Storo Italy 45°51N 10°35E 198 C7
Storozhinets = Storozhynets Ukraine 48°14N 25°45E 183 B10
Storozhynets Ukraine 48°14N 25°45E 183 B10
Storrs U.S.A. 41°49N 72°15W 313 E12
Storsjøen Hedmark, Norway 60°20N 11°40E 164 D8
Storsjøen Hedmark, Norway 61°30N 11°14E 164 C8
Storsjön Gävleborg, Sweden 60°35N 16°45E 162 D10
Storsjön Jämtland, Sweden 62°48N 13°7E 162 B7
Storsjön Jämtland, Sweden 63°9N 14°30E 162 A8
Storsølnkletten Norway 61°59N 10°16E 164 C7
Storuman Sweden 65°5N 17°10E 160 D17
Storuman, L. Sweden 65°13N 16°50E 160 D17
Stóruvellir Iceland 65°30N 17°29W 155 B9
Storvätteshågna Sweden 62°6N 12°30E 162 B6
Storviglen Norway 62°32N 12°2E 164 B9
Storvik Sweden 60°35N 16°33E 162 D10
Storvreta Sweden 59°58N 17°44E 162 E11
Story City U.S.A. 42°11N 93°36W 310 B3
Stouffville Canada 43°58N 79°15W 312 C5
Stoughton Sask., Canada 49°40N 103°0W 297 D8
Stoughton Wis., U.S.A. 42°55N 89°13W 310 B8
Stour ➜ Dorset, U.K. 50°43N 1°47W 169 G6
Stour ➜ Kent, U.K. 51°18N 1°22E 169 F9
Stour ➜ Suffolk, U.K. 51°57N 1°4E 169 F9
Stourbridge U.K. 52°28N 2°8W 169 E5
Stout L. Canada 52°0N 94°40W 297 C10
Stove Pipe Wells Village U.S.A. 36°35N 117°11W 307 J9
Støvring Denmark 56°54N 9°50E 163 H3
Stow U.S.A. 41°10N 81°27W 312 E3
Stowbtsy Belarus 53°30N 26°43E 177 B14
Stowmarket U.K. 52°12N 1°0E 169 E9
Stoyka Russia 59°57N 30°25E 137 B2
Strabane U.K. 54°50N 7°27W 166 B4
Stracin Macedonia 42°13N 22°2E 202 D6
Stradella Italy 45°5N 9°18E 198 C6
Strahan Australia 42°9S 145°20E 281 G4
Straiton U.K. 55°53N 3°9W 121 B3
Strajitsa Bulgaria 43°14N 25°58E 203 C9
Strakonice Czech Rep. 49°15N 13°53E 180 B6
Straldzha Bulgaria 42°35N 26°40E 203 D10
Stralsund Germany 54°18N 13°4E 178 A9
Strand Hedmark, Norway 61°17N 11°17E 164 C8
Strand Western Cape, S. Africa 34°9S 18°48E 270 D2
Strand London, U.K. 125 b4
Stranda Møre og Romsdal, Norway 62°19N 6°58E 164 B3
Stranda Nord-Trøndelag, Norway 63°33N 10°14E 160 E14
Strandasýsla □ Iceland 65°45N 21°45W 155 B5
Strandby Denmark 57°30N 10°29E 163 G4
Strandfontein S. Africa 34°4S 18°34E 118 B2
Strangford L. U.K. 54°30N 5°37W 166 B6
Strängnäs Sweden 59°23N 17°2E 162 E11
Stranorlar Ireland 54°48N 7°46W 166 B4
Stranraer U.K. 54°54N 5°1W 167 G3
Strasbourg Sask., Canada 51°4N 104°55W 297 C8
Strasbourg Bas-Rhin, France 48°35N 7°42E 173 D14
Strasburg Germany 53°30N 13°43E 178 B9
Străşeni Moldova 47°8N 28°36E 183 C13
Strašnice Czech Rep. 50°4N 14°28E 135 B2
Stråssa Sweden 59°44N 15°12E 162 E9
Strassburg = Aiud Romania 46°19N 23°44E 183 D8
Strasstrudering Germany 48°6N 11°41E 131 B3
Stratford N.S.W., Australia 32°7S 151°55E 283 B9
Stratford Vic., Australia 37°59S 147°7E 283 D7
Stratford Ont., Canada 43°23N 81°0W 312 C4
Stratford N.Z. 39°20S 174°19E 284 F3
Stratford London, U.K. 51°33N 0°0 125 A4
Stratford Calif., U.S.A. 36°11N 119°49W 306 J7
Stratford Conn., U.S.A. 41°12N 73°8W 313 E11
Stratford Tex., U.S.A. 36°20N 102°4W 314 C3
Stratford-upon-Avon U.K. 52°12N 1°42W 169 E6
Strath Spey U.K. 57°9N 3°49W 167 D5
Strathalbyn Australia 35°13S 138°53E 282 C3
Strathaven U.K. 55°40N 4°5W 167 F4
Strathcona ⌓ Canada 49°38N 125°40W 296 D3
Strathfield Australia 33°52S 151°5E 139 B1
Strathmore Alta., Canada 51°5N 113°18W 296 C6
Strathmore Angus, U.K. 56°37N 3°7W 167 E5
Strathmore Calif., U.S.A. 36°9N 119°4W 306 J7
Strathnaver Canada 53°20N 122°33W 296 C4
Strathpeffer U.K. 57°35N 4°32W 167 D4
Strathroy Canada 42°58N 81°38W 312 D3
Strathy Pt. U.K. 58°36N 4°1W 167 C4
Strattanville U.S.A. 41°12N 79°19W 312 E5
Stratton U.S.A. 45°8N 70°26W 313 A14
Stratton Mt. U.S.A. 43°4N 72°55W 313 C12
Straubing Germany 48°52N 12°34E 179 G8
Straumnes Iceland 66°26N 23°8W 155 A3
Strausberg Germany 52°35N 13°54E 178 C9
Strawberry ➜ U.S.A. 40°10N 110°24W 304 F8
Strawberry Point U.S.A. 42°41N 91°32W 310 B5
Strážnice Czech Rep. 48°54N 17°19E 181 C10
Streaky B. Australia 32°48S 134°13E 281 E1
Streaky Bay Australia 32°51S 134°18E 281 E1
Streatham U.K. 51°25N 0°7W 125 B3
Streatham Vale U.K. 51°24N 0°8W 125 B3
Streator U.S.A. 41°8N 88°50W 311 C8
Strebersdorf Austria 48°17N 16°23E 142 A2
Středočeský □ Czech Rep. 49°55N 14°30E 180 B7
Streetsboro U.S.A. 41°14N 81°21W 312 E3
Streetsville Canada 43°35N 79°42W 312 C5
Strehaia Romania 44°37N 23°10E 183 F8
Strehlen = Strzelin Poland 50°46N 17°2E 185 H4
Strelcha Bulgaria 42°25N 24°19E 203 D8
Strelka Russia 58°5N 93°3E 215 D10
Streng ➜ Cambodia 13°12N 103°37E 236 F4
Stresa Italy 45°52N 8°28E 198 C5
Střešovice Czech Rep. 50°5N 14°23E 135 B2
Streymoy Færoe Is. 62°8N 7°5W 160 E9
Strezhevoy Russia 60°42N 77°34E 214 C8
Stříbro Czech Rep. 49°44N 13°0E 180 A6
Strickland ➜ Papua N. G. 7°35S 141°36E 286 D1
Striegau = Strzegom Poland 50°58N 16°20E 185 H3
Strilky Ukraine 49°20N 22°59E 185 J9
Strimonas ➜ Greece 40°46N 23°51E 202 F7
Strip, The U.S.A. 36°7N 115°10W 124 B2
Střížkov Czech Rep. 50°7N 14°28E 135 B2
Stroeder Argentina 40°12S 62°37W 336 B4
Strofades Greece 37°15N 21°0E 204 D3
Strogino Russia 55°48N 37°24E 129 B2
Strokestown Ireland 53°46N 8°7W 166 C3
Stroma U.K. 58°41N 3°7W 167 C5
Strombeek-Bever Belgium 50°54N 4°21E 116 A2
Stromberg-Heuchelberg ⌓ Germany 49°2N 8°50E 179 F4
Strómboli Italy 38°47N 15°13E 201 D8
Stromeferry U.K. 57°21N 5°33W 167 D3
Strommen Norway 59°57N 11°0E 164 E7
Stromness U.K. 58°58N 3°17W 167 C5
Stromovka Czech Rep. 50°6N 14°25E 135 B2
Strömsbruk Sweden 61°52N 17°18E 162 C11
Stromsburg U.S.A. 41°7N 97°36W 308 E5
Strömsnäsbruk Sweden 56°35N 13°45E 163 H7
Strömstad Sweden 58°56N 11°10E 163 F5
Strömsund Sweden 63°51N 15°33E 160 E16
Stronghurst U.S.A. 40°45N 90°55W 310 D6
Strongili Greece 36°6N 29°42E 205 E11
Stróngoli Italy 39°16N 17°3E 201 C10
Strongsville U.S.A. 41°19N 81°50W 312 E3
Stronie Ślaskie Poland 50°18N 16°53E 185 H3
Stronsay U.K. 59°7N 2°35W 167 B6
Stropkov Slovak Rep. 49°13N 21°39E 181 B14
Stroud U.K. 51°45N 2°13W 169 F5
Stroud Road Australia 32°18S 151°57E 283 B9
Stroudsburg U.S.A. 40°59N 75°12W 313 F9
Stroumbi Cyprus 34°53N 32°29E 207 F8
Struer Denmark 56°30N 8°35E 163 H2
Struga Macedonia 41°11N 20°44E 202 E4
Strugi Krasnyye Russia 58°21N 29°1E 188 C5
Strumica Macedonia 41°28N 22°41E 202 E6
Strumica ➜ Europe 41°20N 23°22E 202 E7
Strumok Ukraine 45°43N 29°27E 183 E14
Struthers Ont., Canada 48°41N 85°51W 298 C2
Struthers Ohio, U.S.A. 41°4N 80°39W 312 E4
Stryama Bulgaria 42°16N 24°54E 203 D8
Stryker U.S.A. 48°41N 114°46W 304 B6
Stryków Poland 51°55N 19°33E 185 G6
Stryn Norway 61°54N 6°43E 164 C3
Stryy Ukraine 49°16N 23°48E 177 D12
Strzegom Poland 50°58N 16°20E 185 H3
Strzelce Krajeńskie Poland 52°52N 15°33E 185 F2
Strzelce Opolskie Poland 50°31N 18°18E 185 H5
Strzelecki Cr. ➜ Australia 29°37S 139°59E 281 D2
Strzelecki Desert Australia 29°30S 140°0E 281 D3
Strzelin Poland 50°46N 17°2E 185 H4
Strzelno Poland 52°35N 18°9E 185 F5
Strzybnica Poland 50°28N 18°48E 185 H5
Strzyżów Poland 49°52N 21°47E 185 J8
Stuart Fla., U.S.A. 27°12N 80°15W 317 H9
Stuart Iowa, U.S.A. 41°30N 94°19W 310 C2
Stuart Nebr., U.S.A. 42°36N 99°8W 308 D4
Stuart ➜ Canada 54°0N 123°35W 296 C4
Stuart Bluff Ra. Australia 22°50S 131°52E 278 D5
Stuart I. U.S.A. 63°35N 162°30W 303 E7
Stuart L. Canada 54°30N 124°30W 296 C4
Stuart Mts. N.Z. 45°2S 167°39E 285 F2
Stuart Ra. Australia 29°10S 134°56E 281 D1
Stubbekøbing Denmark 54°53N 12°9E 163 K6
Stubbs St. Vincent 13°7N 61°9W 323 n
Stuben Austria 47°10N 10°8E 180 D3
Štubnianske Teplice = Turčianske Teplice Slovak Rep. 48°52N 18°52E 181 C11
Studen Kladenets, Yazovir Bulgaria 41°37N 25°30E 203 E9
Studenka Czech Rep. 49°44N 18°5E 181 B11
Studholme N.Z. 44°42S 171°9E 285 E6
Studio City U.S.A. 34°8N 118°24W 126 B2
Studley Park Trin. & Tob. 11°11N 60°40W 323 s
Stugudalen Norway 62°53N 11°53E 164 B8
Stugun Sweden 63°10N 15°40E 162 A9
Stuhlweissenburg = Székesfehérvár Hungary 47°15N 18°25E 182 C3
Stuhm = Sztum Poland 53°55N 19°1E 184 E6
Stuhr Germany 53°5N 8°44E 178 B4
Stull L. Canada 54°24N 92°34W 298 B1
Stung Treng = Stoeng Treng Cambodia 13°31N 105°58E 236 F5
Stupart ➜ Canada 56°0N 93°25W 298 A1
Stupava Slovak Rep. 48°17N 17°2E 181 C10
Stupino Russia 54°57N 38°2E 188 E10
Stureby Sweden 59°15N 18°4E 139 B2
Sturgeon B. Canada 52°0N 97°50W 297 C9
Sturgeon Bay U.S.A. 44°50N 87°23W 308 C10
Sturgeon Falls Canada 46°25N 79°57W 298 C4
Sturgeon L. Alta., Canada 55°6N 117°32W 296 B5
Sturgeon L. Ont., Canada 50°0N 90°45W 298 C1
Sturgeon L. Ont., Canada 44°28N 78°43W 312 B6
Sturgis Sask., Canada 51°56N 102°36W 297 C8
Sturgis Mich., U.S.A. 41°48N 85°25W 311 C11
Sturgis S. Dak., U.S.A. 44°25N 103°31W 308 C2
Sturkö Sweden 56°5N 15°42E 163 H9
Štúrovo Slovak Rep. 47°48N 18°41E 181 D11
Sturt △ Australia 27°17S 141°37E 281 D3
Sturt Cr. ➜ Australia 19°8S 127°50E 278 C4
Sturt Stony Desert Australia 28°30S 141°0E 281 D3
Sturts Meadows Australia 31°18S 141°42E 282 A4
Stutterheim S. Africa 32°33S 27°28E 270 D4
Stuttgart Baden-W., Germany 48°48N 9°11E 179 G5
Stuttgart Ark., U.S.A. 34°30N 91°33W 314 D9
Stuttgart Echterdingen ✈ (STR) Germany 48°42N 9°11E 179 G5
Stutthof = Sztutowo Poland 54°20N 19°15E 184 D6
Stuvsta Sweden 59°15N 18°0E 139 B2
Stuyvesant U.S.A. 42°23N 73°45W 313 D11
Stykkishólmur Iceland 65°2N 22°40W 155 B4
Styria = Steiermark □ Austria 47°26N 15°0E 180 D8
Styrsö Sweden 57°37N 11°46E 163 G5
Su-no-Saki Japan 34°58N 139°45E 223 C11
Su Xian = Suzhou China 33°41N 116°59E 226 H9
Suakin Sudan 19°8N 37°20E 256 D4
Suan N. Korea 38°42N 126°22E 224 C3
Süanhwa = Xuanhua China 40°40N 115°2E 226 D8
Suao Taiwan 24°36N 121°51E 225 B3
Suapure ➜ Venezuela 6°48N 67°1W 328 B4
Suar India 29°2N 79°3E 243 E8
Suatá ➜ Venezuela 7°52N 65°22W 329 B4
Suau Papua N. G. 10°37S 150°2E 286 F6
Suavanao Solomon Is. 7°35S 158°47E 287 L10
Suba Talan Malaysia 6°22N 117°38E 233 H1
Subang Indonesia 6°34S 107°45E 235 D3
Subankhata India 26°48N 91°25E 241 B3
Subansiri ➜ India 26°48N 93°50E 241 B4
Subarnagiri India 19°50N 83°51E 244 E6
Subarnarekha ➜ India 22°34N 87°24E 243 H12
Subayhah Si. Arabia 30°2N 38°50E 246 D3
Subcetate Romania 45°36N 23°0E 182 E8
Subhepur India 28°44N 77°15E 120 A2
Subi Indonesia 2°58N 108°50E 235 B3
Subiaco Italy 41°56N 13°5E 199 G10
Subotica Serbia 46°6N 19°39E 182 D4
Suburban Canal U.S.A. 30°2N 90°11W 131 B1
Suca Ethiopia 6°31N 39°14E 257 F4
Sucat Phil. 14°27N 121°2E 127 C2
Suceava Romania 47°38N 26°16E 183 C11
Suceava □ Romania 47°37N 25°40E 183 C10
Suceava ➜ Romania 47°32N 26°32E 183 C11
Sucesso Brazil 4°56S 40°32W 332 B3
Sucha-Beskidzka Poland 49°44N 19°35E 185 J6
Suchan = Partizansk Russia 43°8N 133°9E 220 C6
Suchań Poland 53°18N 15°18E 185 E2
Suchdol Czech Rep. 50°8N 14°22E 135 B2
Suchedniów Poland 51°3N 20°49E 185 G7
Suchil Mexico 23°38N 103°55W 318 C4
Suchitoto El Salv. 13°56N 89°0W 320 D2
Suchou = Suzhou China 31°19N 120°38E 229 B13

Süchow = Xuzhou
China 34°18N 117°10E 227 G9
Suchowola Poland 53°33N 23°3E 184 E10
Sucio → Colombia 7°27N 77°7W 328 B2
Suck → Ireland 53°17N 8°3W 166 C3
Suckling, Mt. Papua N. G. 9°49S 148°53E 286 E5
Sucre Bolivia 19°0S 65°15W 331 D4
Sucre Colombia 8°49N 74°44W 328 B3
Sucre □ Colombia 8°50N 75°40W 328 B2
Sucre □ Venezuela 10°25N 63°30W 329 A5
Sucuaro Colombia 4°34N 68°50W 328 C4
Sućuraj Croatia 43°10N 17°8E 199 E14
Sucuriju Brazil 1°39N 49°57W 332 A2
Sucuriú → Brazil 20°47S 51°38W 331 E7
Sucy-en-Brie France 48°46N 2°31E 134 B4
Sud □ Cameroon 2°30N 11°45E 263 E7
Sud, Pte. Comoros Is. 11°53S 43°29E 272 a
Sud, Pte. du Canada 49°3N 62°14W 299 C7
Sud-Kivu □
Dem. Rep. of the Congo 3°0S 28°30E 268 C2
Sud-Ouest □ Cameroon 5°25N 9°20E 263 D6
Sud-Ouest, Pte. Qué.,
Canada 49°23N 63°36W 299 C7
Sud Ouest, Pte. Mauritius 20°28S 57°18E 272 e
Suda → Russia 59°0N 37°40E 188 C9
Sudak Ukraine 44°51N 34°57E 189 K8
Sudan U.S.A. 34°4N 102°31W 314 D3
Sudan ■ Africa 15°0N 30°0E 257 E3
Sudauen = Suwalki
Poland 54°8N 22°59E 184 D9
Sudbury Ont., Canada 46°30N 81°0W 298 C3
Sudbury Suffolk, U.K. 52°2N 0°45E 169 E8
Sûdd Sudan 8°20N 30°0E 257 F3
Suddie Guyana 7°8N 58°29W 329 B6
Sudeifel =
Deutsch-Luxemburgischer △
Germany 49°58N 6°12E 179 F2
Süderbrarup Germany 54°38N 9°45E 178 A5
Süderlügum Germany 54°52N 8°54E 178 A4
Süderoogsand Germany 54°27N 8°28E 178 A4
Sudeten Mts. = Sudety
Europe 50°20N 16°45E 181 A9
Sudety Europe 50°20N 16°45E 181 A9
Súðavík Iceland 66°2N 23°0W 155 A3
Südheide △ Germany 52°46N 10°10E 178 C6
Suður-múlasýsla □
Iceland 65°0N 14°30W 155 C12
Suður-þingeyjarsýsla □
Iceland 65°30N 17°0W 155 B9
Suðureyri Iceland 66°7N 23°32W 155 A3
Suðuroy Færoe Is. 61°32N 6°50W 160 F9
Sudi Tanzania 10°11S 39°57E 269 E4
Sudirman, Pegunungan
Indonesia 4°30S 137°0E 231 E9
Sudiţi Romania 44°35N 27°38E 183 F12
Sudogda Russia 55°55N 40°50E 190 C5
Sudong, Pulau Singapore 1°13N 103°44E 237 d
Sudostroy = Severodvinsk
Russia 64°27N 39°58E 186 B6
Sudova Vyshnya
Ukraine 49°46N 23°22E 185 J10
Sudr Egypt 29°40N 32°42E 256 B3
Sudzha Russia 51°14N 35°17E 189 G8
Sue → Sudan 7°41N 28°3E 257 F2
Sue, L. U.S.A. 28°34N 81°21W 133 A2
Sueca Spain 39°12N 0°21W 197 F4
Suedinenie Bulgaria 42°16N 24°33E 203 D8
Suemez I. U.S.A. 55°15N 133°20W 296 B2
Suez = El Suweis Egypt 29°58N 32°31E 256 J8
Suez, G. of = Suweis, Khalîg el
Egypt 28°40N 33°0E 256 J8
Suez Canal = Suweis, Qanâ es
Egypt 31°0N 32°20E 256 H8
Suffield Canada 50°12N 111°10W 296 C6
Suffolk U.S.A. 36°44N 76°35W 309 G15
Suffolk □ U.K. 52°16N 1°0E 169 E9
Suga-no-Sen Japan 35°25N 134°25E 222 B6
Şugag Romania 45°47N 23°37E 183 E8
Sugamo Japan 35°44N 139°43E 140 A3
Sugar → U.S.A. 42°26N 89°12W 310 B7
Sugar Cr. → Ill., U.S.A. 40°9N 89°38W 310 D7
Sugar Cr. → Ind., U.S.A. 39°51N 87°21W 311 E9
Sugar Grove U.S.A. 41°59N 79°20W 312 E5
Sugar Hill U.S.A. 34°6N 84°2W 316 A5
Sugar Loaf Grenada 12°13N 61°36W 323 q
Sugar Loaf Mt. = Açúcar, Pão de
Brazil 22°56S 43°9W 135 B2
Sugar Loaf Pt. St. Helena 15°54S 5°42W 153 h
Sugarive → India 26°16N 86°24E 243 F12
Sugbai Passage Phil. 5°22N 120°33E 233 J3
Suge Japan 35°37N 139°32E 140 B2
Sughd □ Tajikistan 40°0N 69°0E 217 E7
Suginami Japan 35°41N 139°37E 140 A2
Suğla Gölü Turkey 37°20N 32°0E 212 D5
Sugluk = Salluit
Canada 62°14N 75°38W 295 C12
Sugō Japan 35°34N 139°33E 140 B2
Sugun China 39°53N 76°47E 217 E9
Suhaia, Lacul Romania 43°45N 25°15E 183 G10
Şuḩār Oman 24°20N 56°40E 247 E8
Sühbaatar Mongolia 50°17N 106°10E 218 A5
Sühbaatar □ Mongolia 45°30N 114°0E 226 B8
Suheli Par India 10°5N 72°17E 245 J1
Suhl Germany 50°36N 10°42E 178 E6
Şuhut Turkey 38°31N 30°32E 205 C12
Sui Pakistan 28°37N 69°19E 242 E3
Sui Sai Wan China 22°16N 114°14E 122 B1
Sui Xian China 34°25N 115°2E 226 G8
Suiá Missu → Brazil 11°13S 53°15W 331 C7
Šuica Bos.-H. 43°52N 17°11E 182 G2
Suichang China 28°29N 119°15E 229 C12
Suichuan China 26°20N 114°32E 229 D10
Suide China 37°30N 110°12E 226 F6
Suifenhe China 44°25N 131°10E 227 B16
Suihua China 46°32N 126°55E 219 B7
Suijiang China 28°40N 103°59E 228 C4
Suining Hunan, China 26°35N 110°10E 229 D8
Suining Jiangsu, China 33°56N 117°58E 227 H9
Suining Sichuan, China 30°26N 105°35E 228 B5
Suiping China 33°10N 113°59E 226 H7
Suippes France 49°8N 4°30E 173 C11
Suir → Ireland 52°16N 7°9W 166 D4
Suisse = Switzerland ■
Europe 46°30N 8°0E 179 J4
Suisun City U.S.A. 38°15N 122°2W 306 G4
Suita Japan 34°45N 135°30E 133 A2
Suitland U.S.A. 38°50N 76°55W 143 B4
Suixi China 21°19N 110°18E 229 G8
Suiyang Guizhou, China 27°58N 107°18E 228 D6
Suiyang Heilongjiang,
China 44°30N 130°56E 227 B16
Suizhong China 40°21N 120°20E 227 D11
Suizhou China 31°42N 113°24E 229 B9
Sujangarh India 27°42N 74°31E 242 F6
Sukabumi Indonesia 6°56S 106°50E 234 D3
Sukadana Kalimantan,
Indonesia 1°10S 110°0E 235 C4
Sukadana Sumatera,
Indonesia 5°5S 105°33E 234 D3
Sukagawa Japan 37°17N 140°23E 221 F10
Sukaraja Indonesia 2°28S 110°25E 235 C4
Sukarnapura = Jayapura
Indonesia 2°28S 140°38E 231 E10
Sukarno, Puntjak = Jaya, Puncak
Indonesia 3°57S 137°17E 231 E9
Sukawati Indonesia 8°35S 115°17E 231 K18
Sukchar India 22°42N 88°22E 124 A2
Sukch'ŏn N. Korea 39°22N 125°35E 224 C2
Sukhindol Bulgaria 43°11N 25°10E 203 C9
Sukhinichi Russia 54°8N 35°10E 188 E8
Sukhona → Russia 61°15N 46°39E 186 C6
Sukhothai Thailand 17°1N 99°49E 236 D2
Sukhumi = Sokhumi
Georgia 43°0N 41°0E 191 J5
Sukkertoppen = Maniitsoq
Greenland 65°26N 52°55W 154 D5
Sukkur Pakistan 27°42N 68°54E 242 F3
Sukkur Barrage Pakistan 27°40N 68°50E 242 F3
Sukma India 18°24N 81°45E 244 E5
Sukovo Serbia 43°4N 22°37E 202 C6
Sukri → India 25°4N 71°43E 242 G4
Sukumo Japan 32°56N 132°44E 222 E4
Sukunka → Canada 55°45N 121°15W 296 B4
Sul, Canal do Brazil 0°10S 48°30W 332 B2
Sula Norway 61°7N 4°54E 164 C1
Sula → Ukraine 49°40N 32°41E 189 H7
Sula, Kepulauan Indonesia 1°45S 125°0E 231 E7
Sulaco → Honduras 15°2N 87°44W 320 C2
Sulaiman Range Pakistan 30°30N 69°50E 242 D3
Sulak → Russia 43°20N 47°34E 191 J8
Sūlār Iran 31°53N 51°54E 247 D6
Sulawesi Indonesia 2°0S 120°0E 231 E6
Sulawesi Barat □ Indonesia 3°0S 119°0E 231 E5
Sulawesi Sea = Celebes Sea
Indonesia 3°0N 123°0E 231 D6
Sulawesi Selatan □
Indonesia 2°30S 120°0E 231 E6
Sulawesi Tengah □
Indonesia 1°30S 121°0E 231 E6
Sulawesi Tenggara □
Indonesia 3°50S 122°0E 231 E6
Sulawesi Utara □ Indonesia 1°0N 124°0E 231 D6
Suldalsheine Norway 59°28N 7°10E 164 E3
Suldalsosen Norway 59°29N 6°29E 164 E3
Sulechów Poland 52°5N 15°40E 185 F2
Sulęcin Poland 52°26N 15°10E 185 F2
Sulei Solomon Is. 8°3S 159°34E 287 M10
Sulejów Poland 51°26N 19°53E 185 G6
Sulejówek Poland 52°13N 21°17E 185 F8
Süleymanlı Turkey 38°58N 27°47E 205 C9
Sulima S. Leone 6°58N 11°32W 262 D2
Sulina Romania 45°10N 29°40E 183 E14
Sulina, Braţul →
Romania 45°10N 29°40E 183 E14
Sulingen Germany 52°41N 8°48E 178 C4
Suliţa Romania 47°39N 26°59E 183 C11
Sulitjelma Norway 67°9N 16°3E 160 C17
Sułkowice Poland 49°50N 19°49E 185 J6
Sullana Peru 4°52S 80°39W 330 A1
Süller Turkey 38°9N 29°29E 205 C11
Sullivan Ill., U.S.A. 39°36N 88°37W 311 E8
Sullivan Ind., U.S.A. 39°6N 87°24W 311 E9
Sullivan Mo., U.S.A. 38°13N 91°10W 310 F5
Sullivan Bay Canada 50°55N 126°50W 296 C3
Sullivan I. = Lanbi Kyun
Burma 10°50N 98°20E 237 G2
Sullom Voe U.K. 60°27N 1°20W 167 A7
Sully U.S.A. 41°34N 92°50W 310 C4
Sully-sur-Loire France 47°45N 2°20E 173 E9
Sulmierzyce Poland 51°37N 17°32E 185 G4
Sulmona Italy 42°3N 13°55E 199 F10
Sülöğlu Turkey 41°44N 26°53E 203 E10
Sulphur La., U.S.A. 30°14N 93°23W 314 F8
Sulphur Okla., U.S.A. 34°31N 96°58W 314 D6
Sulphur Pt. Canada 60°56N 114°48W 296 A6
Sulphur Springs U.S.A. 33°8N 95°36W 314 E7
Sulsul Ethiopia 5°5N 44°50E 267 C5
Sultan Ont., Canada 47°36N 82°47W 298 C3
Sultan Wash., U.S.A. 47°52N 121°49W 306 C5
Sultan Dağları Turkey 38°20N 31°20E 212 C4
Sultan Hamud Kenya 2°1S 37°22E 268 C4
Sultan Kudarat Phil. 7°16N 124°18E 233 H5
Sultan Kudarat □ Phil. 6°30N 124°10E 233 H5
Sultan Naga Dimaporo
Phil. 7°55N 123°44E 233 H4
Sultan sa Barongis Phil. 6°45N 124°35E 233 H5
Sultanabad = Arāk Iran 34°0N 49°40E 247 C6
Sultanahme Camil Turkey 41°0N 28°58E 122 B1
Sultanhisar Turkey 37°53N 28°9E 205 D10
Sultaniça Turkey 40°37N 26°8E 203 F10
Sultaniye Turkey 40°11N 28°12E 203 F12
Sultanpur Mad. P., India 23°9N 77°56E 242 H8
Sultanpur Punjab, India 31°13N 75°11E 242 D6
Sultanpur Ut. P., India 26°18N 82°4E 243 F10
Sulu □ Phil. 5°30N 120°30E 233 J3
Sulu Arch. Phil. 6°0N 121°0E 233 J3
Sulu Sea E. Indies 8°0N 120°0E 233 G3
Sülüklü Turkey 38°53N 32°20E 212 C5
Sululta Ethiopia 9°10N 38°43E 257 F4
Suluova Turkey 40°46N 35°32E 212 B6
Suluq Libya 31°44N 20°14E 258 B4
Sulur India 13°42N 80°1E 245 H5
Sulzbach Germany 49°18N 7°3E 179 F3
Sulzbach-Rosenberg
Germany 49°30N 11°44E 179 F7
Sulzberger Ice Shelf
Antarctica 78°0S 150°0W 151 E13
Sumaco -Napo Galeras △
Ecuador 0°34S 77°38W 328 D2
Sumalata Indonesia 1°0N 122°31E 231 D6
Sumale □ Ethiopia 7°0N 45°0E 267 C6
Sumampa Argentina 29°25S 63°29W 334 B3
Sumapaz △ Colombia 3°49N 74°13W 328 C3
Sumatera Indonesia 0°40N 100°20E 234 B2
Sumatera Barat □
Indonesia 1°0S 101°0E 234 B1
Sumatera Utara □
Indonesia 2°30N 98°0E 234 B1
Sumatra = Sumatera
Indonesia 0°40N 100°20E 234 B2
Sumatra U.S.A. 30°1N 84°59W 316 E5
Sumava △ Czech Rep. 49°0N 13°49E 180 C6
Sumba Angola 6°15S 12°38E 265 D2
Sumba Indonesia 9°45S 119°35E 231 F5
Sumba, Selat Indonesia 9°0S 118°40E 231 F5
Sumbawa Indonesia 8°26S 117°30E 235 D5
Sumbawa Besar Indonesia 8°30S 117°26E 235 D5
Sumbe Angola 11°10S 13°48E 265 E2
Sumbu △ Zambia 8°43S 30°22E 269 D3
Sumburgh Hd. U.K. 59°52N 1°17W 167 B7
Sumdeo India 31°26N 78°44E 243 D8
Sumdo China 35°6N 78°41E 243 B8
Sumé Brazil 7°39S 36°55W 332 C3
Sumedang Indonesia 6°52S 107°55E 235 D3
Sümeg Hungary 46°59N 17°20E 182 D2
Sumeih Sudan 9°50N 27°39E 257 F2
Šumen = Shumen
Bulgaria 43°18N 26°55E 203 C10
Sumenep Indonesia 7°1S 113°52E 235 D4
Sumgait = Sumqayıt
Azerbaijan 40°34N 49°38E 191 K9
Sumida Japan 35°42N 139°49E 140 A3
Sumida → Japan 35°39N 139°45E 140 A3
Sumisu-Jima Japan 31°27N 140°3E 223 F12
Sumiyoshi Japan 34°36N 135°30E 133 B2
Sumiyoshi Shrine Japan 34°36N 135°30E 133 B1
Summer L. U.S.A. 42°50N 120°45W 304 E3
Summerland Canada 49°32N 119°41W 296 D5
Summerland Key U.S.A. 24°40N 81°27W 317 L8
Summerside Canada 46°24N 63°47W 299 C7
Summersville U.S.A. 38°17N 80°51W 309 F13
Summerton U.S.A. 33°36N 80°20W 316 B9
Summertown U.S.A. 32°45N 82°16W 316 C7
Summerville Ont.,
Canada 43°37N 79°33W 141 B1
Summerville Ga.,
U.S.A. 34°29N 85°21W 315 D12
Summerville S.C., U.S.A. 33°1N 80°11W 316 B9
Summit Alaska, U.S.A. 63°20N 149°7W 303 E10
Summit Ill., U.S.A. 41°47N 87°47W 119 C2
Summit Lake Canada 54°20N 122°40W 296 C4
Summit Peak U.S.A. 37°21N 106°42W 305 H10
Sumner N.Z. 43°35S 172°48E 285 D7
Sumner Ill., U.S.A. 38°42N 87°53W 311 F9
Sumner Iowa, U.S.A. 42°51N 92°6W 310 B4
Sumner Wash., U.S.A. 47°12N 122°14W 306 C4
Sumner, L. N.Z. 42°42S 172°15E 285 C7
Sumner Tunnel Boston, U.S.A. 116 a3
Sumoto Japan 34°21N 134°54E 222 C6
Šumperk Czech Rep. 49°59N 16°59E 181 B9
Sumqayıt Azerbaijan 40°34N 49°38E 191 K9
Sumter U.S.A. 33°55N 80°21W 316 B9
Sumxi China 34°35N 80°22E 217 F10
Sumy Ukraine 50°57N 34°50E 189 G8
Sumy □ Ukraine 50°50N 33°50E 189 G7
Sun City North West,
S. Africa 25°17S 27°3E 270 C4
Sun City Ariz., U.S.A. 33°35N 112°16W 305 K7
Sun City Calif., U.S.A. 33°42N 117°11W 307 M9
Sun City Center U.S.A. 27°43N 82°21W 317 H7
Sun Lakes U.S.A. 33°10N 111°52W 305 K8
Sun Prairie U.S.A. 43°11N 89°13W 310 A7
Sun Valley U.S.A. 43°42N 114°21W 304 E6
Sunagawa Japan 43°29N 141°55E 220 C10
Sunamachi Japan 35°40N 139°50E 140 A4
Sunan N. Korea 39°15N 125°40E 224 C2
Sunart, L. U.K. 56°42N 5°43W 167 E3
Sunburst U.S.A. 48°53N 111°55W 304 B8
Sunbury Vic., Australia 37°35S 144°44E 283 D6
Sunbury Pa., U.S.A. 40°52N 76°48W 313 F8
Sunbury-on-Thames
U.K. 51°25N 0°26W 125 B1
Sunchales Argentina 30°58S 61°35W 334 C3
Suncheon S. Korea 34°52N 127°31E 224 E3
Suncho Corral Argentina 27°55S 63°27W 334 B3
Sunch'on N. Korea 39°25N 125°56E 224 C2
Suncook U.S.A. 43°8N 71°27W 313 C13
Sunda, Selat Indonesia 6°20S 105°30E 234 D3
Sunda Is. Indonesia 5°0S 105°0E 288 H2
Sunda Str. = Sunda, Selat
Indonesia 6°20S 105°30E 234 D3
Sunda Trench = Java Trench
Ind. Oc. 9°0S 105°0E 234 D2
Sundance Man., Canada 56°32N 94°4W 297 B10
Sundance Wyo.,
U.S.A. 44°24N 104°23W 304 D11
Sundar Nagar India 31°32N 76°53E 242 D7
Sundarbans Asia 22°0N 89°0E 241 E2
Sundarbans △ India 22°0N 88°45E 243 J13
Sundargarh India 22°4N 84°5E 244 C7
Sundays = Sondags →
S. Africa 33°44S 25°51E 270 D4
Sundbyberg Sweden 59°22N 17°57E 139 A1
Sundbyerne Denmark 55°39N 12°36E 118 B3
Sunderland Ont., Canada 44°16N 79°4W 312 B5
Sunderland Tyne & W.,
U.K. 54°55N 1°23W 168 C6
Sundi Lutete
Dem. Rep. of the Congo 4°34S 14°14E 265 C2
Sundown △ Australia 28°49S 151°38E 281 D5
Sundre Canada 51°49N 114°38W 296 C6
Sunds Denmark 56°13N 9°1E 163 H3
Sundsvall Sweden 62°23N 17°17E 162 B11
Sundsvallsbukten
Sweden 62°21N 17°25E 162 B11
Sung Hei Vietnam 10°20N 106°2E 237 G6
Sung Kong China 22°11N 114°17E 122 B2
Sungai Acheh Malaysia 5°8N 100°30E 237 c
Sungai Kolok Thailand 6°2N 101°58E 237 J3
Sungai Lembing Malaysia 3°55N 103°3E 237 L4
Sungai Petani Malaysia 5°37N 100°30E 237 K3
Sungaigerong Indonesia 2°59S 104°52E 234 C2
Sungailiat Indonesia 1°51S 106°8E 234 C3
Sungaipenuh Indonesia 2°1S 101°20E 234 C2
Sungaitiram Indonesia 0°45S 117°8E 235 C5
Sungari = Songhua Jiang →
China 47°45N 132°30E 219 B8
Sungei Kadut Industrial Estate
Singapore 1°24N 103°44E 138 A2
Sungei Selatar Res.
Singapore 1°24N 103°51E 138 A3
Sunghua Chiang = Songhua
Jiang → China 47°45N 132°30E 219 B8
Sungikai Sudan 12°20N 29°51E 257 E2
Sungu Dem. Rep. of the Congo 1°5S 17°21E 264 C3
Sungurlu Turkey 40°12N 34°21E 212 B6
Sunja Croatia 45°21N 16°35E 199 C13
Sunland Park U.S.A. 31°50N 106°40W 305 L10
Sunnansjö Sweden 60°13N 14°58E 162 D8
Sunndalsøra Norway 62°40N 8°33E 164 B5
Sunne Sweden 59°52N 13°5E 162 E7
Sunnemo Sweden 59°53N 13°44E 162 E7
Sunnfjord Norway 61°35N 5°45E 164 C2
Sunnmore Norway 62°35N 6°30E 164 B3
Sunnyside U.S.A. 46°20N 120°0W 304 C4
Sunnyvale U.S.A. 37°23N 122°2W 306 H4
Sunrise U.S.A. 26°8N 80°14W 317 J9
Sunrise Manor U.S.A. 36°12N 115°4W 124 A2
Sunrise Mountain Natural Area
U.S.A. 36°12N 114°58W 124 A2
Sunset Beach U.S.A. 21°40N 158°3W 302 J13
Sunset Park N.Y., U.S.A. 40°38N 73°59W 132 C2
Sunset Park Nev., U.S.A. 36°3N 115°6W 124 B2
Sunshine Coast Australia 26°30S 153°0E 276 F9
Suntar Russia 62°15N 117°30E 215 C12
Sunter Indonesia 6°7S 106°51E 122 A2
Sunter, Kali → Indonesia 6°10S 106°53E 122 B2
Suntrana U.S.A. 63°52N 148°51W 303 E10
Sunwi-do N. Korea 37°43N 125°16E 224 D2
Sunyani Ghana 7°21N 2°22W 262 D4
Suō-Nada Japan 33°50N 131°30E 222 D3
Suomenlinna Finland 60°9N 24°59E 121 C2
Suomenselkä Finland 62°52N 24°0E 160 E21
Suomi = Finland ■ Europe 63°0N 27°0E 162 E22
Suomussalmi Finland 64°54N 29°10E 160 D23
Suoyarvi Russia 62°3N 32°20E 188 A7
Supai U.S.A. 36°15N 112°41W 305 H7
Supamo → Venezuela 6°48N 61°50W 329 B5
Supaul India 26°10N 86°40E 243 F12
Supe Peru 11°0S 77°30W 330 C2
Superagüi △ Brazil 25°6S 48°18W 333 G2
Superior Ariz., U.S.A. 33°18N 111°6W 305 K8
Superior Mont., U.S.A. 47°12N 114°53W 304 C6
Superior Nebr., U.S.A. 40°1N 98°4W 308 E4
Superior Wis., U.S.A. 46°44N 92°6W 308 B7
Superior, L. N. Amer. 47°0N 87°0W 298 C2
Supetar Croatia 43°25N 16°32E 199 E13
Suphan Buri Thailand 14°14N 100°10E 236 E3
Suphan Dağı Turkey 38°54N 42°48E 213 C10
Supiori Indonesia 1°0S 136°0E 231 E9
Supraśl Poland 53°13N 23°19E 185 E10
Supraśl → Poland 53°11N 22°57E 185 E9
Supreme Court
Washington, D.C., U.S.A. 143 b3
Supung N. Korea 40°27N 124°54E 224 B2
Supung Shuiku China 40°35N 124°50E 224 B2
Sūq' Abs Yemen 16°0N 43°12E 248 D3
Sūq Suwayq Si. Arabia 24°23N 38°27E 246 E3
Şuqaylabiyah Syria 35°23N 36°23E 250 C7
Suqian China 33°54N 118°8E 227 H10
Suquṭra = Socotra Yemen 12°30N 54°0E 249 D6
Şūr Lebanon 33°19N 35°16E 250 E6
Şūr Oman 22°34N 59°32E 249 B7
Sur, C. Chile 27°12S 109°26W 330 b
Sur, Pt. U.S.A. 36°18N 121°54W 306 J5
Sur Bahr West Bank 31°44N 35°13E 123 B2
Sura India 22°33N 88°24E 124 B2
Sura → Russia 56°6N 46°0E 190 C8
Sura, Ras Somali Rep. 11°10N 47°30E 267 B6
Surab Pakistan 28°25N 66°15E 242 E2
Surabaja = Surabaya
Indonesia 7°17S 112°45E 235 D4
Surabaya Indonesia 7°17S 112°45E 235 D4
Surahammar Sweden 59°43N 16°13E 162 E10
Suraia Romania 45°40N 27°25E 183 E12
Surakarta Indonesia 7°35S 110°48E 235 D4
Surakhany Azerbaijan 40°25N 50°1E 191 K10
Suraksan S. Korea 37°40N 127°4E 137 A2
Šurany Slovak Rep. 48°6N 18°10E 181 C11
Surat Queens., Australia 27°10S 149°6E 281 D4
Surat India 21°12N 72°55E 244 D1
Surat Thani Thailand 9°6N 99°20E 237 H2
Suratgarh India 29°18N 73°55E 242 E5
Suraż Poland 52°57N 22°57E 185 F9
Surazh Belarus 55°25N 30°44E 188 E6
Surazh Russia 53°5N 32°27E 189 F7
Surbiton U.K. 51°23N 0°17W 125 B2
Surduc Romania 47°15N 23°25E 183 C8
Surduc Pasul Romania 45°21N 23°23E 183 E8
Surdulica Serbia 42°41N 22°11E 202 D6
Surendranagar India 22°45N 71°40E 242 H4
Suresnes France 48°52N 2°13E 134 A2
Surf U.S.A. 34°41N 120°36W 307 L6
Surfers Paradise Australia 28°0S 153°25E 281 D5
Surfside U.S.A. 25°52N 80°7W 128 A2
Surgana India 20°34N 73°37E 244 D1
Surgères France 46°7N 0°47W 174 B3
Surgut Russia 61°14N 73°20E 214 C8
Suriapet India 17°10N 79°40E 244 F4
Suribachi Yama Iwo Jima 24°45N 141°17E 288 b
Surigao Phil. 9°47N 125°29E 233 G5
Surigao del Norte □ Phil. 10°0N 125°40E 233 G5
Surigao del Sur □ Phil. 8°45N 126°0E 233 G6
Surigao Strait Phil. 10°15N 125°23E 233 F5
Surin Thailand 14°50N 103°34E 236 E4
Surin Nua, Ko Thailand 9°30N 97°55E 237 H1
Surinam = Suriname ■
S. Amer. 4°0N 56°0W 329 C6
Surinam Mauritius 20°30S 57°30E 272 e
Suriname ■ S. Amer. 4°0N 56°0W 329 C6
Suriname → Suriname 5°50N 55°15W 329 B6
Sürmaq Iran 31°3N 52°48E 247 D7
Surkhandaryo □
Uzbekistan 38°0N 67°30E 217 E7
Surma → Bangla. 24°34N 91°14E 241 C3
Sūrmaq Iran 31°3N 52°48E 247 D7
Sürmene Turkey 41°0N 40°1E 213 B9
Surna → Norway 62°59N 8°40E 164 B5
Surnadalsøra Norway 62°58N 8°40E 164 B5
Surovikino Russia 48°32N 42°55E 191 F6
Surquillo Peru 12°6S 77°1W 124 B2
Surrency U.S.A. 31°44N 82°12W 316 D7
Surrey Canada 49°7N 122°45W 306 A4
Surrey □ Jamaica 18°5N 76°34W 320 a
Surrey □ U.K. 51°15N 0°31W 169 F7
Surrey Hills Australia 33°53S 151°13E 139 B2
Sursand India 26°39N 85°43E 243 F11
Sursar → India 26°14N 87°3E 243 F12
Sursee Switz. 47°11N 8°6E 179 H4
Sursk Russia 53°3N 45°40E 190 D7
Surskoye Russia 54°30N 46°44E 190 C8
Surt Libya 31°11N 16°39E 258 B3
Surt □ Libya 30°0N 17°50E 258 B3
Surt, Al Hammadah al
Libya 30°0N 17°50E 258 C3
Surt, Khalīj Libya 31°40N 18°30E 258 B3
Surtanahu Pakistan 26°22N 70°0E 242 F4
Surte Sweden 57°50N 12°1E 163 G6
Surtsey Iceland 63°20N 20°30W 155 D6
Surubim Brazil 7°50S 35°45W 332 C4
Sürüç Turkey 36°58N 38°25E 213 D8
Surud Ad Somali Rep. 10°42N 47°9E 267 B6
Suruga-Wan Japan 34°45N 138°30E 223 C10
Surumu → Brazil 3°22N 60°19W 329 C5
Susa Iran 32°20N 48°20E 247 C6
Susa = Sousse Tunisia 35°50N 10°38E 258 A2
Susa Italy 45°8N 7°3E 198 C4
Susâ → Denmark 55°12N 11°42E 163 J5
Sušac Croatia 42°46N 16°30E 199 F13
Susaek S. Korea 37°34N 126°54E 137 B1
Susak Croatia 44°30N 14°18E 199 D11
Susaki Japan 33°22N 133°17E 222 D5
Susam-Adasi = Samos
Greece 37°45N 26°50E 205 D8
Susangerd Iran 31°35N 48°6E 213 G13
Susanville U.S.A. 40°25N 120°39W 304 F3
Susch Switz. 46°46N 10°5E 179 J6
Suşehri Turkey 40°10N 38°6E 213 B8
Sušice Czech Rep. 49°17N 13°30E 180 B6
Susleni Moldova 47°25N 28°59E 183 C13
Susner India 23°57N 76°5E 242 H7
Susong China 30°10N 116°5E 229 B11
Susquehanna U.S.A. 41°57N 75°36W 313 E9
Susquehanna → U.S.A. 39°33N 76°5W 313 G8
Susques Argentina 23°35S 66°25W 334 A2
Süssenbrunn Austria 48°16N 16°29E 142 A2
Sussex N.B., Canada 45°45N 65°37W 299 C6
Sussex N.J., U.S.A. 41°13N 74°37W 313 E10
Sussex, E. □ U.K. 51°0N 0°20E 169 G8
Sussex, W. □ U.K. 51°0N 0°30W 169 G7
Sussex Inlet Australia 35°10S 150°36E 283 C9
Sustut → Canada 56°20N 127°30W 296 B3
Susuman Russia 62°47N 148°10E 215 C15
Susunu Indonesia 3°7S 133°39E 231 E8
Susurluk Turkey 39°54N 28°8E 205 B10
Susuz Turkey 40°46N 43°8E 213 B10
Susz Poland 53°44N 19°20E 184 E6
Sutay Uul Asia 46°35N 93°38E 218 B4
Sütçüler Turkey 37°29N 30°57E 212 D4
Şuteşti Romania 45°13N 27°27E 183 E12
Sutherland N.S.W.,
Australia 34°2S 151°4E 283 C9
Sutherland Northern Cape,
S. Africa 32°24S 20°40E 270 D3
Sutherland Highl., U.K. 58°12N 4°50W 167 C4
Sutherland U.S.A. 41°10N 101°8W 308 E3
Sutherland Falls N.Z. 44°48S 167°46E 285 E2
Sutherland Road Barbados 13°16N 59°39W 323 r
Sutherlin U.S.A. 43°23N 123°19W 304 E2
Suthri India 23°3N 68°55E 242 H3
Sutjeska △ Bos.-H. 43°50N 18°32E 182 G3
Sutlej → Pakistan 29°23N 71°3E 242 E4
Sutter U.S.A. 39°10N 121°45W 306 F5
Sutter Buttes U.S.A. 39°12N 121°49W 306 F5
Sutter Creek U.S.A. 38°24N 120°48W 306 G6
Sutton Qué., Canada 45°6N 72°37W 313 A12
Sutton Dublin, Ireland 53°23N 6°7W 120 A3
Sutton N.Z. 45°34S 170°8E 285 F5
Sutton London, U.K. 51°21N 0°11W 125 B2
Sutton Nebr., U.S.A. 40°36N 97°52W 308 E5
Sutton W. Va., U.S.A. 38°40N 80°43W 309 F13
Sutton → Canada 55°15N 83°45W 298 A3
Sutton Coldfield U.K. 52°35N 1°49W 169 E6
Sutton in Ashfield U.K. 53°8N 1°16W 168 D6
Sutton L. Canada 54°15N 84°42W 298 B3
Suttor → Australia 21°36S 147°2E 280 C4
Suttsu Japan 42°48N 140°14E 220 C10
Sutwik I. U.S.A. 56°34N 157°12W 303 H8
Suva Fiji 18°6S 178°30E 287 B2
Suva Gora Macedonia 41°45N 21°3E 202 E5
Suva Planina Serbia 43°10N 22°5E 202 C6
Suva Reka Serbia 42°21N 20°50E 202 D4
Suvorov Russia 54°7N 36°30E 188 E9
Suvorov Is. = Suwarrow Is.
Cook Is. 13°15S 163°5W 289 J11
Suvorove Ukraine 45°35N 28°59E 183 E13
Suvorovo Bulgaria 43°20N 27°35E 203 C11
Suwa Japan 36°2N 138°8E 223 A10
Suwa-Ko Japan 36°3N 138°5E 223 A10
Suwałki Poland 54°8N 22°59E 184 D9
Suwana Indonesia 8°44S 115°36E 231 K18
Suwanee U.S.A. 34°3N 84°4W 316 A5
Suwannaphum Thailand 15°33N 103°47E 236 E4
Suwannee U.S.A. 29°20N 83°9W 317 F6
Suwannee → U.S.A. 29°17N 83°10W 317 F6
Suwannee Sd. U.S.A. 29°20N 83°15W 317 F6
Suwanose-Jima Japan 29°38N 129°43E 221 K4
Suwarrow Is. Cook Is. 13°15S 163°5W 289 J11
Suwayq aş Şuqban Iraq 31°32N 46°7E 246 D5
Suweis, Khalîg el Egypt 28°40N 33°0E 256 J8
Suweis, Qanâ es Egypt 31°0N 32°20E 256 H8
Suwon S. Korea 37°17N 127°1E 224 D3
Suyu S. Korea 37°37N 127°0E 137 B2
Suzaka Japan 36°39N 138°19E 223 A10
Suzdal Russia 56°29N 40°26E 188 D11
Suzhou Anhui, China 33°41N 116°59E 226 H9
Suzhou Jiangsu, China 31°19N 120°38E 229 B13
Suzu Japan 37°25N 137°17E 221 F8
Suzu-Misaki Japan 37°31N 137°21E 221 F8
Suzuka Japan 34°55N 136°36E 223 C8
Suzuka-Sammyaku
Japan 35°5N 136°30E 223 B8
Suzukishinden Japan 35°43N 139°31E 140 A2
Suzun Russia 53°47N 82°18E 217 B10
Suzzara Italy 44°59N 10°45E 198 D7
Svalbard Arctic 78°0N 17°0E 150 B8
Svalbard Radio = Longyearbyen
Svalbard 78°13N 15°40E 150 B8
Svalbarð Iceland 66°12N 15°43W 155 A11
Svalbarðseyri Iceland 65°45N 18°5W 155 B8
Svalöv Sweden 55°57N 13°8E 163 J7
Svalyava Ukraine 48°33N 22°59E 182 B7
Svaneke Denmark 55°8N 15°8E 163 J9
Svanemøllen Denmark 55°43N 12°34E 118 A3
Svängsta Sweden 56°16N 14°47E 163 H8
Svanskog Sweden 59°11N 12°33E 162 E6
Svappavaara Sweden 67°40N 21°3E 160 C19
Svärdsjö Sweden 60°45N 15°54E 162 D9
Svarstad Norway 59°27N 9°56E 164 E6
Svartå Sweden 59°8N 14°32E 162 E8
Svartårkot Iceland 65°20N 17°15W 155 B9
Svartevatn Norway 59°10N 6°56E 164 E3
Svartisen Norway 66°40N 13°59E 160 C15
Svartvik Sweden 62°19N 17°24E 162 B11
Svatove Ukraine 49°22N 38°15E 189 H10
Svatovo = Svatove
Ukraine 49°22N 38°15E 189 H10
Svatsum Norway 61°20N 9°50E 164 C6
Svay Chek Cambodia 13°48N 102°58E 236 F4
Svay Rieng Cambodia 11°9N 105°45E 237 G5
Sveaborg = Suomenlinna
Finland 60°9N 24°59E 121 C2
Svealand □ Sweden 60°20N 15°0E 162 D9
Svedala Sweden 55°30N 13°15E 163 J7
Sveg Sweden 62°2N 14°21E 162 B8
Sveindal Norway 58°29N 7°30E 164 F4
Sveinseyri Iceland 65°38N 23°51W 155 B3
Sveio Norway 59°33N 5°23E 164 E2
Svelgen Norway 61°46N 5°17E 164 C2
Svelvik Norway 59°37N 10°24E 164 E7
Svendborg Denmark 55°4N 10°35E 163 J4
Svene Norway 59°45N 9°31E 164 E6
Svenljunga Sweden 57°29N 13°5E 163 G7
Svenstavik Sweden 62°45N 14°26E 162 B8
Svenstrup Denmark 56°58N 9°50E 163 H3
Sverdlov Russia 55°46N 37°36E 129 B3
Sverdlovsk = Yekaterinburg
Russia 56°50N 60°30E 214 D7
Sverdlovsk Ukraine 48°5N 39°47E 189 H10
Sverdrup Chan. Canada 79°56N 96°25W 295 B10
Sverdrup Is. Canada 79°0N 97°0W 295 B10
Sverige = Sweden ■
Europe 57°0N 15°0E 161 H16
Svestad Norway 59°46N 10°36E 133 B2
Svetac Croatia 43°3N 15°43E 199 E12
Sveti Ivan = Zelina
Croatia 45°57N 16°16E 199 C13
Sveti Nikola, Prokhad
Europe 43°27N 22°6E 202 C6
Sveti Nikole Macedonia 41°51N 21°56E 202 E5
Sveti Rok Croatia 44°22N 15°39E 199 D12
Sveti Vrach = Sandanski
Bulgaria 41°35N 23°16E 202 E7
Svetlaya Russia 46°33N 138°18E 220 A9
Svetlogorsk = Svyetlahorsk
Belarus 52°38N 29°46E 177 B15
Svetlogorsk Russia 54°56N 20°10E 184 D7
Svetlograd Russia 45°25N 42°58E 191 H6
Svetlovodsk = Svitlovodsk
Ukraine 49°2N 33°13E 189 H7
Svetlyy Kaliningrad, Russia 54°41N 20°8E 184 D7
Svetlyy Orenburg, Russia 50°48N 60°51E 216 B6
Svidník Slovak Rep. 49°20N 21°37E 181 B14
Svignaskarð Iceland 64°40N 21°42W 155 C5
Svilaja Planina Croatia 43°49N 16°31E 199 E13
Svilajnac Serbia 44°15N 21°11E 202 B5
Svilengrad Bulgaria 41°49N 26°12E 203 E10
Svínafell Iceland 63°59N 16°51W 155 D10
Svinö Finland 60°7N 24°44E 121 C1
Svir → Russia 60°30N 32°48E 188 B7
Sviritsa Russia 60°29N 32°51E 188 B7
Svishtov Bulgaria 43°36N 25°23E 203 C9
Svislach Belarus 53°3N 24°2E 185 E11
Svitava → Czech Rep. 49°11N 16°37E 181 B9
Svitavy Czech Rep. 49°47N 16°28E 181 B9
Svitlovodsk Ukraine 49°2N 33°13E 189 H7
Svizzera = Switzerland ■
Europe 46°30N 8°0E 179 J4
Svobodnyy Russia 51°20N 128°0E 215 D13
Svoge Bulgaria 42°59N 23°23E 202 D7
Svolvær Norway 68°15N 14°34E 160 B16
Svorkmo Norway 63°9N 9°50E 164 A6
Svoronata Greece 38°7N 20°31E 207 C2
Svratka → Czech Rep. 49°11N 16°38E 181 B9
Svrljig Serbia 43°25N 22°6E 202 C6
Svyataya Nos, Mys Russia 60°25N 12°23E 164 D9
Svyatogorovsky Rudnik =
Dobropole Ukraine 48°25N 37°2E 189 H9
Svyetlahorsk Belarus 52°38N 29°46E 177 B15
Swa Burma 19°15N 96°17E 241 F6
Swa Tende
Dem. Rep. of the Congo 7°9S 17°7E 265 D3
Swabian Alps = Schwäbische Alb
Germany 48°20N 9°30E 179 G5
Swaffham U.K. 52°39N 0°42E 169 E8
Swains I. Amer. Samoa 11°11S 171°4W 289 J11
Swainsboro U.S.A. 32°36N 82°20W 316 C7
Swakop → Namibia 22°38S 14°36E 270 B2
Swakopmund Namibia 22°37S 14°30E 270 B1
Swale → U.K. 54°5N 1°20W 168 C6
Swamihalli India 14°52N 76°38E 245 G3
Swan → W. Austral.,
Australia 32°3S 115°45E 279 F2
Swan → Man., Canada 52°30N 100°45W 297 C8
Swan Hill Australia 35°20S 143°33E 282 C5
Swan Hills Canada 54°43N 115°24W 296 C5
Swan Is. = Santanilla, Is.
Honduras 17°22N 83°57W 320 C3
Swan L. Canada 52°30N 100°40W 297 C8
Swan Ra. U.S.A. 48°0N 113°45W 304 C7
Swan Reach Australia 34°35S 139°37E 282 C3
Swan River Canada 52°10N 101°16W 297 C8
Swanage U.K. 50°36N 1°58W 169 G6
Swanley U.K. 51°23N 0°11E 125 B4
Swansea N.S.W., Australia 33°3S 151°35E 283 B9
Swansea Tas., Australia 42°8S 148°4E 281 G4
Swansea Ont., Canada 43°38N 79°28W 141 B2
Swansea Swansea, U.K. 51°37N 3°57W 169 F4
Swansea S.C., U.S.A. 33°44N 81°6W 316 B8
Swansea □ U.K. 51°38N 4°3W 169 F3
Swanton U.S.A. 41°35N 83°53W 311 C13
Swar → Pakistan 34°40N 72°5E 243 B5
Swartberge S. Africa 33°20S 22°0E 270 D3
Swartmodder S. Africa 28°1S 20°32E 270 C3
Swartnossob → Namibia 23°8S 18°42E 270 B2
Swartruggens S. Africa 25°39S 26°42E 270 C4
Swarzędz Poland 52°25N 17°4E 185 F4
Swastika Canada 48°7N 80°6W 298 C3
Swatow = Shantou
China 23°18N 116°40E 229 F11
Swaziland ■ Africa 26°30S 31°30E 271 C5
Sweden ■ Europe 57°0N 15°0E 161 H16
Swedru Ghana 5°32N 0°41W 263 D4
Sweet Grass U.S.A. 48°59N 111°58W 304 B8
Sweet Home U.S.A. 44°24N 122°44W 304 D2
Sweet Springs U.S.A. 38°58N 93°25W 310 F3
Sweetwater Nev., U.S.A. 38°27N 119°9W 306 G7
Sweetwater Tenn.,
U.S.A. 35°36N 84°28W 315 D12
Sweetwater Tex., U.S.A. 32°28N 100°25W 314 E4
Sweetwater → U.S.A. 42°31N 107°2W 304 E10
Swellendam S. Africa 34°1S 20°26E 270 D3
Swider → Poland 52°6N 21°14E 185 F8
Świdnica Poland 50°50N 16°30E 185 H3
Świdnik Poland 51°13N 22°39E 185 G9
Świdwin Poland 53°47N 15°49E 184 E2
Świebodzice Poland 50°51N 16°20E 185 H3
Świebodzin Poland 52°15N 15°31E 185 F2
Świecie Poland 53°25N 18°30E 184 E5
Świerzawa Poland 51°1N 15°54E 185 G2
Świętokrzyski △ Poland 50°53N 20°59E 185 H7
Świętokrzyskie □ Poland 50°45N 20°45E 185 H7
Świętokrzyskie, Góry
Poland 51°0N 20°30E 185 H7
Swift Current Canada 50°20N 107°45W 297 C7
Swiftcurrent → Canada 50°38N 107°44W 297 C7
Swifts Creek Australia 37°17S 147°44E 283 D7
Swilly, L. Ireland 55°12N 7°33W 166 A4
Swinburne I. U.S.A. 40°33N 74°3W 132 C1
Swindon U.K. 51°34N 1°46W 169 F6
Swindon □ U.K. 51°34N 1°46W 169 F6
Swinemünde = Świnoujście
Poland 53°54N 14°16E 184 E1
Swinford Ireland 53°57N 8°58W 166 C3
Świnoujście Poland 53°54N 14°16E 184 E1
Switzerland ■ Europe 46°30N 8°0E 179 J4
Swords Ireland 53°28N 6°13W 120 A2
Swoyerville U.S.A. 41°18N 75°53W 313 E9
Syasstroy Russia 60°9N 32°33E 188 B7
Sycamore Ill., U.S.A. 41°59N 88°41W 311 C8
Sycamore Ohio, U.S.A. 40°57N 83°10W 311 D13
Sychevka Russia 55°59N 34°16E 188 E8
Syców Poland 51°19N 17°40E 185 G4
Syddanmark □ Denmark 55°30N 9°0E 163 J2
Sydenham S. Africa 29°6S 28°5E 123 A2
Sydenham → Canada 42°33N 82°25W 312 D2
Sydney N.S.W., Australia 33°52S 151°12E 139 B2
Sydney N.S., Canada 46°7N 60°7W 299 C7
Sydney, Univ. of
Australia 33°54S 151°11E 139 B2
Sydney Harbour Bridge
Australia 33°51S 151°12E 139 B2
Sydney Kingsford Smith ✕ (SYD)
Australia 33°57S 151°11E 139 B2
Sydney L. Canada 50°41N 94°25W 297 C10
Sydney Mines Canada 46°18N 60°15W 299 C7
Sydproven = Alluitsup Paa
Greenland 60°30N 45°35W 154 E6
Sydra, G. of = Surt, Khalīj
Libya 31°40N 18°30E 258 B3
Sydstranden Denmark 55°34N 12°38E 118 B3
Syeverodonetsk Ukraine 48°58N 38°35E 189 H10
Syfteland Norway 60°14N 5°27E 164 D2
Syke Germany 52°55N 8°50E 178 C4
Sykesville U.S.A. 41°3N 78°50W 312 E6
Sykkylven Norway 62°23N 6°35E 164 B3
Syktyvkar Russia 61°45N 50°40E 186 B9
Sylacauga U.S.A. 33°10N 86°15W 316 B3
Sylarna Sweden 63°2N 12°13E 164 A9
Sylhet Bangla. 24°54N 91°52E 241 C3
Sylhet □ Bangla. 24°50N 91°50E 241 C3
Sylt Germany 54°54N 8°22E 178 A4
Sylte Norway 62°18N 7°17E 164 B4
Sylvan Beach U.S.A. 43°12N 75°44W 313 C9
Sylvan Lake Canada 52°20N 114°3W 296 C6
Sylvania N.S.W., Australia 34°0S 151°7E 139 C1
Sylvania Ga., U.S.A. 32°45N 81°38W 316 C8
Sylvania Ohio, U.S.A. 41°43N 83°42W 311 C13
Sylvester U.S.A. 31°32N 83°50W 316 D6
Sym Russia 60°20N 88°18E 214 C9
Symphony Hall San Francisco, U.S.A. 136 c1
Synelnykove Ukraine 48°25N 35°30E 189 H8
Synevyr △ Ukraine 48°30N 23°40E 183 B8
Synevyrska Polyana
Ukraine 48°35N 23°41E 183 B8
Synnervika Norway 62°25N 11°54E 164 B8
Synnfjell Norway 61°5N 9°46E 164 C6
Synnot Ra. Australia 16°30S 125°20E 278 C4
Syntagma Square Athens, Greece 112 b3
Synyak Ukraine 48°33N 22°51E 182 B7
Syon Park U.K. 51°28N 0°18W 125 B2
Syowa Antarctica 68°50S 12°0E 151 C5
Syracuse = Siracusa Italy 37°4N 15°17E 201 E8
Syracuse Ind., U.S.A. 41°26N 85°45W 311 C11
Syracuse Kans., U.S.A. 37°59N 101°45W 308 G3
Syracuse N.Y., U.S.A. 43°3N 76°9W 313 C8
Syracuse Nebr., U.S.A. 40°39N 96°11W 308 E5
Syrdarya → Kazakhstan 46°3N 61°0E 216 C6
Syria ■ Asia 35°0N 38°0E 213 E8
Syriam Burma 16°44N 96°19E 241 G6
Syrian Desert = Shām, Bādiyat ash
Asia 32°0N 40°0E 246 C3

Syros Greece 37°28N 24°57E 204 D6
Sysslebäck Sweden 60°44N 12°52E 162 D6
Syvden Norway 62°5N 5°44E 164 B2
Syzran Russia 53°12N 48°30E 190 D9
Szabolcs-Szatmár-Bereg □ Hungary 48°2N 21°45E 182 B6
Szadek Poland 51°41N 18°59E 185 G5
Szamocin Poland 53°2N 17°7E 185 E4
Szamos → Hungary 48°7N 22°20E 182 B7
Szamotuły Poland 52°37N 16°33E 185 F3
Száraz → Hungary 46°10N 21°15E 182 D6
Szarvas Hungary 46°50N 20°38E 182 D5
Százhalombatta Hungary 47°20N 18°58E 182 C3
Szczawnica Poland 49°26N 20°30E 185 J7
Szczebrzeszyn Poland 50°42N 22°59E 185 H9
Szczecin Poland 53°27N 14°27E 184 E1
Szczecinek Poland 53°43N 16°41E 184 E3
Szczeciński, Zalew = Stettiner Haff Germany 53°47N 14°15E 178 B10
Szczekociny Poland 50°38N 19°48E 185 H6
Szczęśliwice Poland 52°12N 20°57E 142 B1
Szczucin Poland 50°18N 21°4E 185 H8
Szczuczyn Poland 53°36N 22°19E 184 E9
Szczyrk Poland 49°43N 19°2E 185 J6
Szczytna Poland 50°25N 16°28E 185 H3
Szczytno Poland 53°33N 21°0E 184 E7
Széchenyi-hegy Hungary 47°29N 18°57E 117 B1
Szechuan Basin = Sichuan Pendi China 31°0N 105°0E 228 B5
Szechwan = Sichuan □ China 30°30N 103°0E 228 B5
Szécsény Hungary 48°7N 19°30E 182 B4
Szeged Hungary 46°16N 20°10E 182 D5
Szeghalom Hungary 47°1N 21°10E 182 C6
Székesfehérvár Hungary 47°15N 18°25E 182 C3
Szekszárd Hungary 46°22N 18°42E 182 D3
Szendrő Hungary 48°24N 20°41E 182 B5
Szentendre Hungary 47°39N 19°4E 182 C4
Szentes Hungary 46°39N 20°21E 182 D5
Szentgotthárd Hungary 46°58N 16°19E 182 D1
Szentlőrinc Hungary 46°3N 18°1E 182 D3
Széphalom Hungary 47°34N 18°57E 117 A1
Szeping = Siping China 43°8N 124°21E 227 C13
Szerencs Hungary 48°10N 21°12E 182 B6
Szigetszentmiklós Hungary 47°21N 19°3E 182 C4
Szigetvár Hungary 46°3N 17°46E 182 D2
Szikszó Hungary 48°12N 20°56E 182 B5
Szklarska Poreba Poland 50°50N 15°33E 185 H2
Szkwa → Poland 53°11N 21°43E 185 E8
Szlichtyngowa Poland 51°42N 16°15E 185 G3
Szob Hungary 47°48N 18°53E 182 C3
Szolnok Hungary 47°10N 20°15E 182 C5
Szombathely Hungary 47°14N 16°38E 182 C1
Szprotawa Poland 51°33N 15°35E 185 G2
Sztálinváros = Dunaújváros Hungary 46°58N 18°57E 182 D3
Sztum Poland 53°55N 19°1E 184 E6
Sztutowo Poland 54°20N 19°15E 184 D6
Szubin Poland 53°1N 17°45E 185 E4
Szydłowiec Poland 51°15N 20°51E 185 G7
Szypliszki Poland 54°17N 23°2E 184 D10

T

Ta Khli Khok Thailand 15°18N 100°20E 236 E3
Ta Lai Vietnam 11°24N 107°23E 237 G6
Ta Pieh Shan = Dabie Shan China 31°20N 115°20E 229 B10
Taakoka Cook Is. 21°15S 159°43W 289 h
Taan Taiwan 24°22N 120°35E 225 B2
Taastrup Denmark 55°39N 12°18E 118 B1
Tab Hungary 46°44N 18°2E 182 D3
Tabacal Argentina 23°15S 64°15W 334 A3
Tabaco Phil. 13°22N 123°44E 232 E4
Tabagné Ivory C. 7°59N 3°4W 262 D4
Ţābah Si. Arabia 26°55N 42°38E 246 E4
Tabajara Brazil 8°56S 62°8W 331 B5
Tabalo Papua N. G. 1°24S 149°40E 286 A5
Tabalos Peru 6°26S 76°37W 330 B2
Tabanan Indonesia 8°32S 115°8E 231 K18
Tabankort Niger 17°44N 0°20E 263 B5
Tabaquite Trin. & Tob. 10°23N 61°18W 323 t
Tabar I. Papua N. G. 2°56S 152°0E 286 B7
Tabar Is. Papua N. G. 2°50S 152°0E 286 B7
Tabarka Tunisia 36°56N 8°46E 258 A1
Ţabas Khorāsān, Iran 32°48N 60°12E 247 C9
Ţabas Yazd, Iran 33°35N 56°55E 247 C8
Tabasará, Serranía de Panama 8°35N 81°40W 320 E3
Tabasco □ Mexico 18°0N 92°40W 319 D6
Tabāsīn Iran 31°12N 57°54E 247 D8
Tabata Japan 35°44N 139°46E 140 A3
Tabatinga Brazil 4°16S 69°56W 330 A4
Tabatinga, Serra da Brazil 10°30S 44°0W 332 D3
Tabayin Burma 22°42N 95°20E 241 D5
Tabelbala, Kahal de Algeria 28°47N 2°0W 261 C4
Tabelembila Algeria 24°43N 4°16E 261 D5
Taber Canada 49°47N 112°8W 296 D6
Taberg Sweden 57°40N 14°6E 163 G8
Taberg N.Y., U.S.A. 43°18N 75°37W 313 C9
Tabernacle St. Kitts & Nevis 17°23N 62°46W 322 d
Tabi Angola 8°10S 13°18E 265 D2
Tabira Brazil 7°35S 37°33W 332 C4
Tabiteuea Kiribati 1°25S 174°50E 277 A13
Tabla Niger 13°46N 3°1E 263 C5
Tablada Argentina 34°41S 58°32W 117 C1
Tablas Phil. 12°25N 122°2E 232 E4
Tablas de Daimiel △ Spain 39°9N 3°40W 195 F7
Tablas Strait Phil. 12°40N 121°48E 232 E3
Table, Pte. de la Réunion 21°14S 55°48E 272 f
Table B. Nfld. & L., Canada 53°40N 56°25W 299 B8
Table B. Western Cape, S. Africa 33°35S 18°25E 118 A1
Table C. N.Z. 39°6S 178°0E 284 F7
Table Grove U.S.A. 40°20N 90°27W 310 D6
Table I. Burma 14°12N 93°22E 245 G11
Table Mt. S. Africa 33°58S 18°26E 118 A1
Table Rock L. U.S.A. 36°36N 93°19W 308 G7
Tableland Trin. & Tob. 10°16N 61°16W 323 t
Tabletop, Mt. Australia 23°24S 147°11E 280 C4
Taboão da Serra Brazil 23°36S 46°45W 137 B1
Tabocal Brazil 2°42S 57°40W 329 D6
Tábor Czech Rep. 49°25N 14°39E 180 B7
Tabora Tanzania 5°2S 32°50E 268 D3
Tabora □ Tanzania 5°0S 33°0E 268 D3
Tabou Ivory C. 4°30N 7°20W 262 E3
Tabrīz Iran 38°7N 46°20E 213 C12
Tabuaeran Kiribati 3°51N 159°22W 289 G12
Tabubil Papua N. G. 5°20S 141°15E 286 C1
Tabuenca Spain 41°42N 1°33W 196 D3
Tabuk Phil. 17°24N 121°25E 232 C3
Tabūk Si. Arabia 28°23N 36°36E 251 K7
Tabūk □ Si. Arabia 27°40N 36°50E 248 B3
Tabunifi Micronesia 9°28N 138°4E 287 S16
Taburno-Camposauro △ Italy 41°8N 14°37E 201 A7
Tabwemasana, Mt. Vanuatu 15°20S 166°44E 287 E4
Täby Sweden 59°26N 18°2E 139 A2
Tacámbaro de Codallos Mexico 19°14N 101°28W 318 D4
Tacarigua Trin. & Tob. 10°38N 61°22W 323 t
Tacarigua, Laguna de Venezuela 10°15N 65°50W 328 A4
Tacheng Xinjiang Uygur, China 46°40N 82°58E 217 C10
Tacheng Taiwan 23°51N 120°19E 225 C2
Tach'i Taiwan 24°53N 121°17E 225 B3
Tachia Taiwan 24°25N 120°28E 225 B2
Tachia Hsi → Taiwan 24°20N 120°33E 225 B3
Tachibana-Wan Japan 32°45N 130°7E 222 E2
Tachikawa Japan 35°42N 139°25E 223 B11
Tach'ing Shan = Daqing Shan China 40°40N 111°0E 226 D6
Táchira □ Venezuela 8°7N 72°15W 328 B3
Tachoshui Taiwan 24°20N 121°44E 225 B3
Tachov Czech Rep. 49°47N 12°39E 180 B5
Tácina → Italy 38°57N 16°55E 201 D9
Tacloban Phil. 11°15N 124°58E 233 F5
Tacna Peru 18°0S 70°20W 330 D3
Tacna □ Peru 17°40S 70°20W 330 D3
Tacoma U.S.A. 47°14N 122°26W 306 C4
Tacopaya = Zudáñez Bolivia 19°6S 64°44W 331 D5
Tacuarembó Uruguay 31°45S 56°0W 335 C4
Tacuba Mexico 19°26N 99°11W 128 B1
Tacubaya Mexico 19°24N 99°10W 128 B1
Tacurong Phil. 6°40N 124°41E 233 H5
Tacutu → Brazil 3°1N 60°29W 329 C5
Tada-u Burma 21°49N 95°58E 241 E5
Tadahadi Solomon Is. 10°18S 161°35E 287 N11
Tademaït, Plateau du Algeria 28°30N 2°30E 261 C5
Tadéra Niger 20°29N 8°18E 261 D6
Tadine N. Cal. 21°33S 167°52E 288 d
Tadio, L. Ivory C. 5°10N 5°15W 262 D3
Tadjerdjeri, O. → Algeria 26°0N 8°0E 261 C6
Tadjerouna Algeria 33°31N 2°3E 261 B5
Tadjettaret, O. → Algeria 21°20N 7°22E 261 D6
Tadjmout Laghouat, Algeria 33°52N 2°30E 261 B5
Tadjmout Saoura, Algeria 25°37N 3°48E 261 C5
Tadjoura Djibouti 11°50N 42°55E 257 E5
Tadjoura, Golfe de Djibouti 11°50N 43°0E 257 E5
Tadmor N.Z. 41°27S 172°45E 285 B7
Tadoba △ India 20°30N 78°20E 244 D4
Tadotsu Japan 34°16N 133°45E 222 C5
Tadoule L. Canada 58°36N 98°20W 297 B9
Tadoussac Canada 48°11N 69°42W 299 C6
Tadpatri India 14°55N 78°1E 245 G4
Tadrés △ Niger 16°0N 7°10E 263 B6
Tadzhikistan = Tajikistan ■ Asia 38°30N 70°0E 217 E8
Tae-an S. Korea 36°45N 126°17E 224 D3
Tae-an Seashore National Park △ S. Korea 36°40N 126°0E 224 D3
Taebaek S. Korea 37°10N 128°59E 224 D4
Taebaeksan S. Korea 37°5N 128°54E 224 D4
T'aebaeksanmaek S. Korea 37°40N 128°50E 224 D4
Taedong-gang → N. Korea 38°41N 125°15E 224 C2
Taedong-man N. Korea 38°4N 125°7E 224 C2
Taegu = Daegu S. Korea 35°50N 128°37E 224 E4
Taegwan N. Korea 40°13N 125°12E 224 B2
Taehung N. Korea 40°5N 126°56E 224 B3
Taehwa-do N. Korea 39°26N 124°36E 224 C2
Taejŏn = Daejeon S. Korea 36°20N 127°28E 224 D3
Tælavåg Norway 60°15N 4°58E 164 D1
Taen, Ko Thailand 9°22N 99°57E 237 b
Tafalla Spain 42°30N 1°41W 196 C3
Tafar Sudan 6°52N 28°15E 257 F2
Tafassasset, O. → Algeria 22°0N 9°57E 261 D6
Tafelbaai = Table B. S. Africa 33°35S 18°25E 118 A1
Tafelberg Neth. Ant. 12°4N 68°50W 322 g
Tafelney, C. Morocco 31°3N 9°51W 260 B3
Tafermaar Indonesia 6°47S 134°10E 231 F8
Taffermit Morocco 29°37N 9°15W 260 C3
Tafí Viejo Argentina 26°43S 65°17W 334 B2
Tafihān Iran 29°25N 52°39E 247 D7
Tafilalet Morocco 31°20N 4°45W 260 B4
Tafiré Ivory C. 9°4N 5°4W 262 D3
Tafjord Norway 62°14N 7°24E 164 B4
Tafnidilt Morocco 28°47N 10°58W 260 C2
Tafo Ghana 6°15N 0°20W 263 D4
Tafraoute Morocco 29°50N 8°58W 260 C3
Tafresh Iran 34°45N 49°57E 247 C6
Taft Iran 31°45N 54°14E 247 D7
Taft Phil. 11°57N 125°30E 233 F5
Taft Calif., U.S.A. 35°8N 119°28W 307 K7
Taft Fla., U.S.A. 28°25N 81°21W 133 B2
Taftan Pakistan 29°0N 61°30E 240 C1
Taftān, Kūh-e Iran 28°40N 61°0E 247 D9
Tafu Taiwan 23°37N 121°23E 225 C3
Tafwap India 7°2N 93°43E 245 L11
Taga Samoa 13°46S 172°28W 287 V19
Taga Dzong Bhutan 27°5N 89°55E 241 B2
Tagana-an Phil. 9°42N 125°35E 233 G5
Taganrog Russia 47°12N 38°50E 189 J10
Taganrogskiy Zaliv Russia 47°0N 38°30E 189 J10
Tagânt □ Mauritania 19°0N 10°0W 260 E3
Tagap Ga Burma 26°56N 96°13E 241 B6
Tagatay Phil. 14°6N 120°56E 232 D3
Tagauayan I. Phil. 10°58N 121°13E 233 F3
Tagaung Burma 23°30N 96°2E 241 D6
Tagawa Japan 33°38N 130°51E 222 D2
Tagbilaran Phil. 9°39N 123°51E 233 G4
Tagdempt = Tiaret Algeria 35°20N 1°21E 261 A5
Tage Papua N. G. 6°19S 143°20E 286 D2
Tageren Canal Micronesia 9°33N 138°8E 287 R16
Tággia Italy 43°52N 7°51E 198 E4
Taghit Algeria 30°58N 2°0W 261 B4
Tagig → Phil. 14°31N 121°5E 127 B2
Tagish Canada 60°19N 134°16W 296 A2
Tagish L. Canada 60°10N 134°20W 296 A2
Tagkawayan Phil. 13°58N 122°32E 232 E4
Tagliacozzo Italy 42°4N 13°14E 199 F10
Tagliamento → Italy 45°38N 13°6E 199 C10
Táglio di Po Italy 45°0N 12°12E 199 D9
Tagna Colombia 2°24S 70°37W 328 D3
Tago Phil. 9°2N 126°13E 233 G6
Tago, Mt. Phil. 8°23N 125°5E 233 G5
Tagomago Spain 39°2N 1°39E 206 C2
Tagourãret Mauritania 17°45N 7°45W 262 B3
Tagpochau, Mt. N. Marianas 15°11N 145°44E 302 e
Taguatinga Distrito Federal, Brazil 16°12S 44°35W 333 E2
Taguatinga Tocantins, Brazil 12°27S 46°22W 333 D2
Tagudin Phil. 16°56N 120°27E 232 C3
Taguenout Haggueret Mali 21°14N 0°48W 261 D4
Taguig Phil. 14°31N 121°4E 127 B2
Tagula Papua N. G. 11°22S 153°15E 286 F7
Tagula I. Papua N. G. 11°30S 153°30E 286 F7
Tagum Phil. 7°33N 125°53E 233 H5
Tagus = Tejo → Europe 38°40N 9°24W 195 F2
Tahakopa N.Z. 46°30S 169°23E 285 G4
Tahala Morocco 34°0N 4°28W 260 B4
Tahan, Gunung Malaysia 4°34N 102°17E 237 K4
Tahānah-ye sūr Gol Afghan. 31°43N 67°35E 240 C2
Tahara Japan 34°40N 137°16E 223 C9
Tahat Algeria 23°18N 5°33E 261 D6
Tāherī Iran 27°43N 52°20E 247 E7
Tahgong Pt. N. Marianas 15°6N 145°39E 302 e
Tahiti French Polynesia 17°37S 149°27W 289 e
Tahlab → Pakistan 28°9N 62°45E 240 C1
Tahlequah U.S.A. 35°55N 94°58W 314 D7
Tahoe, L. U.S.A. 39°6N 120°2W 306 G6
Tahoe City U.S.A. 39°10N 120°9W 306 F6
Tahoka U.S.A. 33°10N 101°48W 314 E4
Taholah U.S.A. 47°21N 124°17W 306 C2
Tahora N.Z. 39°2S 174°49E 284 F3
Tahoua Niger 14°57N 5°16E 263 C6
Tahrūd Iran 29°26N 57°49E 247 D8
Tahsis Canada 49°55N 126°40W 296 D3
Tahta Egypt 26°44N 31°32E 256 B3
Tahtaköprü Turkey 39°57N 29°39E 203 G13
Tahtalı Dağları Turkey 38°20N 36°0E 212 C7
Tahu Taiwan 24°26N 120°52E 225 B2
Tahuamanu → Bolivia 11°6S 67°36W 330 C4
Tahuata, I. French Polynesia 9°57S 139°5W 289 f
Tahulandang Indonesia 2°27N 125°23E 231 D7
Tahuna Indonesia 3°38N 125°30E 231 D7
Taï Ivory C. 5°55N 7°30W 262 D3
Taï △ Ivory C. 5°25N 7°5W 262 D3
Tai Au Mun China 22°18N 114°17E 219 G11
Tai Hang China 22°16N 114°11E 122 B2
Tai Hu China 31°5N 120°10E 229 B12
Tai Lo Shan China 22°21N 114°13E 122 A2
Tai Mo Shan China 22°25N 114°7E 219 G11
Tai O China 22°15N 113°52E 219 G10
Tai Pang Wan China 22°33N 114°24E 219 F11
Tai Po China 22°27N 114°10E 219 G11
Tai Po Tsai China 22°20N 114°15E 122 A2
Tai Rom Yen △ Thailand 8°45N 99°30E 237 H2
Tai Seng Singapore 1°20N 103°53E 138 A3
Tai Shan China 36°25N 117°20E 227 F9
Tai Shui Hang China 22°24N 114°13E 122 A2
Tai Tam B. China 22°12N 114°13E 122 B2
Tai Tam Tuk Res. China 22°14N 114°13E 122 B2
Tai Wai China 22°22N 114°10E 122 A2
Tai Wan Tau China 22°17N 114°17E 122 B2
Tai Wo Hau China 22°21N 114°7E 122 A1
Tai Yue Shan = Lantau I. China 22°15N 113°56E 219 G10
Tai'an China 36°12N 117°8E 227 F9
Taiarapu, Presqu'île de Tahiti 17°47S 149°14W 289 e
Taibei = T'aipei Taiwan 25°4N 121°29E 225 A3
Taibique Canary Is. 27°42N 17°58W 153 e1
Taibus Qi China 41°54N 115°22E 226 D8
Taicang China 31°30N 121°5E 229 B13
Taichow = Taizhou China 32°28N 119°55E 229 A12
T'aichung Taiwan 24°9N 120°37E 225 B2
Taieri → N.Z. 46°3S 170°12E 285 G5
Taiga Madema Libya 23°46N 15°25E 258 D3
Taigu China 37°28N 112°30E 226 F7
Taihang Shan China 36°0N 113°30E 226 G7
Taihape N.Z. 39°41S 175°48E 284 F4
Taihe Anhui, China 33°20N 115°42E 226 H8
Taihe Jiangxi, China 26°47N 114°52E 229 D10
Taihoku = T'aipei Taiwan 25°4N 121°29E 225 A3
Taihsi Taiwan 23°51N 120°16E 225 C2
Taihu China 30°22N 116°20E 229 B11
Taijiang China 26°39N 108°21E 228 D7
Taikang China 34°5N 114°50E 226 G8
Taikkyi Burma 17°20N 96°0E 241 G6
Tailem Bend Australia 35°12S 139°29E 282 C3
Tailfingen Germany 48°15N 9°1E 179 G5
T'ailuko Taiwan 24°9N 121°37E 225 B3
T'aimali Taiwan 22°36N 121°0E 225 D3
Taimyr Peninsula = Taymyr, Poluostrov Russia 75°0N 100°0E 215 B11
Tain U.K. 57°49N 4°4W 167 D4
Tainaka Japan 34°36N 135°35E 133 B2
T'ainan Taiwan 23°0N 120°10E 225 D2
T'ainan □ Taiwan 23°15N 120°20E 225 C2
Tainggyo Burma 17°49N 94°29E 241 G5
Taining China 26°54N 117°9E 229 D11
Taiobeiras Brazil 15°49S 42°14W 333 E3
Taipa China 22°10N 113°35E 219 G10
T'aipei Taiwan 25°4N 121°29E 225 A3
T'aipei □ Taiwan 24°50N 121°35E 225 B3
Taiping Anhui, China 30°15N 118°6E 229 B12
Taiping Malaysia 4°51N 100°44E 237 K3
Taipingzhen China 33°35N 111°42E 226 H6
Taipu Brazil 5°37S 35°36W 332 C4
Tairbeart = Tarbert U.K. 57°54N 6°49W 167 D2
Tairenpokpi India 24°39N 93°40E 241 C4
Tairua N.Z. 37°0S 175°51E 284 D4
Taisha Japan 35°24N 132°40E 222 B4
Taishan China 22°14N 112°41E 229 F9
Taishō Japan 34°38N 135°27E 133 B1
Taishun China 27°30N 119°42E 229 D12
Taita N.Z. 41°12S 174°57E 143 B2
Taita Hills Kenya 3°25S 38°15E 268 C4
Taitao, C. Chile 45°53S 75°5W 336 C1
Taitao, Pen. de Chile 46°30S 75°0W 336 C2
T'aitung Taiwan 22°43N 121°4E 225 D3
T'aitung □ Taiwan 23°0N 121°0E 225 D3
Taivalkoski Finland 65°33N 28°12E 160 D23
Taiwan ■ Asia 23°30N 121°0E 225 C3
Taiwan Strait Asia 24°40N 120°0E 229 E12
Taixing China 32°11N 120°0E 229 A13
Taiyara Sudan 13°12N 30°47E 257 E3
Taiyiba Israel 32°36N 35°27E 250 F6
Taiyuan China 37°52N 112°33E 226 F7
Taizhong = T'aichung Taiwan 24°9N 120°37E 225 B2
Taizhou China 32°28N 119°55E 229 A12
Taizhou Liedao China 28°30N 121°55E 229 C13
Ta'izz Yemen 13°35N 44°2E 248 D4
Tājābād Iran 30°2N 54°24E 247 D7
Tajapuru, Furo do Brazil 1°50S 50°25W 332 B1
Tajarḥī Libya 24°21N 14°28E 258 D2
Tajen Taiwan 22°17N 120°53E 225 D2
Tajikistan ■ Asia 38°30N 70°0E 217 E8
Tajima Japan 37°12N 139°46E 221 F9
Tajimi Japan 35°19N 137°8E 223 B9
Tajo = Tejo → Europe 38°40N 9°24W 195 F2
Tajrīsh Iran 35°48N 51°25E 141 A2
Tājūrā Libya 32°51N 13°21E 258 B2
Tak Thailand 16°52N 99°8E 236 D2
Takāb Iran 36°24N 47°7E 213 D12
Takaba Kenya 3°21N 40°13E 267 D5
Takabanare-shima Japan 26°22N 127°59E 288 a
Takachiho Japan 32°42N 131°18E 222 E3
Takachu Botswana 22°37S 21°58E 270 B3
Takada Japan 37°7N 138°15E 221 F9
Takahagi Japan 36°43N 140°45E 221 F10
Takahashi Japan 34°51N 133°39E 222 C5
Takaido Japan 35°40N 139°37E 140 A2
Takaishi Japan 35°36N 139°31E 140 B2
Takaka N.Z. 40°51S 172°50E 285 A7
Takaki = Yamato Japan 35°27N 139°25E 223 B11
Takalous, O. → Algeria 22°36N 7°21E 261 D6
Takamaka Seychelles 4°50S 55°30E 272 c
Takamatsu Japan 34°20N 134°5E 222 C6
Takanabe Japan 32°8N 131°30E 222 E3
Takangkou Taiwan 23°28N 121°29E 225 C3
Takaoka Japan 36°47N 137°0E 223 A9
Takapau N.Z. 40°2S 176°21E 284 G5
Takapuna N.Z. 36°47S 174°47E 284 C3
Takarazuka Japan 34°47N 135°21E 133 A1
Takaroa French Polynesia 14°28S 144°58W 289 f
Takasago Japan 35°44N 139°52E 140 A4
Takasaki Japan 36°20N 139°0E 223 A11
Takatsu Japan 35°36N 139°37E 140 B2
Takatsuki Japan 34°51N 135°37E 223 C7
Takaungu Kenya 3°38S 39°52E 268 C4
Takayama Japan 36°18N 137°11E 223 A9
Takayama-Bonchi Japan 36°0N 137°18E 223 B9
Take-Shima Japan 30°49N 130°26E 221 J5
Takefu Japan 35°50N 136°10E 223 B8
Takehara Japan 34°21N 132°55E 222 C4
Takengon Indonesia 4°45N 96°50E 234 B1
Takeo Japan 33°12N 130°1E 222 D2
Tåkern Sweden 58°22N 14°45E 163 F8
Takeshima = Tok-do Asia 37°15N 131°52E 221 F5
Tākestān Iran 36°0N 49°40E 247 C6
Taketa Japan 32°58N 131°24E 222 E3
Takev Cambodia 10°59N 104°47E 237 G5
Takh India 33°6N 77°32E 243 C7
Takhār □ Afghan. 36°40N 70°0E 240 A3
Takht-Sulaiman Pakistan 31°40N 69°58E 242 D3
Taki Papua N. G. 6°29S 155°52E 286 D8
Takikawa Japan 43°33N 141°54E 220 C10
Takinegawa Japan 35°45N 139°44E 140 A3
Takla L. Canada 55°15N 125°45W 296 B3
Takla Landing Canada 55°30N 125°50W 296 B3
Takla Makan China 38°0N 83°0E 217 E10
Taklamakan Shamo = Takla Makan China 38°0N 83°0E 217 E10
Takoma Park U.S.A. 38°58N 77°0W 143 B3
Takotna U.S.A. 62°59N 156°4W 303 E8
Taksim Turkey 41°2N 28°58E 122 B1
Taku Japan 33°18N 130°3E 222 D2
Taku → Canada 58°30N 133°50W 296 B2
Takua Thung Thailand 8°24N 98°27E 237 a
Takum India 27°47N 93°37E 241 B4
Takum Nigeria 7°18N 9°36E 263 D6
Takume French Polynesia 15°49S 142°12W 289 f
Takundi Dem. Rep. of the Congo 4°45S 16°34E 265 C3
Takutu → Guyana 3°1N 60°29W 329 C5
Tal Halāl Iran 28°54N 55°1E 247 D7
Tala Uruguay 34°21S 55°46W 335 C4
Talachyn Belarus 54°25N 29°42E 188 E5
Talacogan Phil. 8°32N 125°39E 233 G5
Talagang Pakistan 32°55N 72°25E 242 C5
Talagante Chile 33°40S 70°50W 334 C1
Talahouhait Algeria 24°52N 1°5E 261 D5
Talaide Portugal 38°44N 9°18W 126 A1
Talaimannar Sri Lanka 9°6N 79°43E 245 K4
Talaïnt Morocco 29°41N 9°40W 260 C3
Talak Niger 18°0N 5°0E 263 B6
Talakag Phil. 8°16N 124°37E 233 G5
Talamanca, Cordillera de Cent. Amer. 9°20N 83°20W 320 E3
Talant France 47°19N 4°58E 173 E11
Talara Peru 4°38S 81°18W 330 A1
Talas Kyrgyzstan 42°30N 72°13E 217 D8
Talas Turkey 38°41N 35°33E 212 C6
Talas □ Kyrgyzstan 42°20N 72°0E 217 D8
Talas → Kazakhstan 44°0N 70°20E 217 D8
Talas Ala Too Kyrgyzstan 42°15N 72°0E 217 D8
Talasea Papua N. G. 5°20S 150°2E 286 C6
Talasskiy Alatau = Talas Ala Too Kyrgyzstan 42°15N 72°0E 217 D8
Talâta Egypt 30°36N 32°20E 251 H3
Talata Mafara Nigeria 12°38N 6°4E 263 C6
Talaud, Kepulauan Indonesia 4°30N 126°50E 231 D7
Talaud Is. = Talaud, Kepulauan Indonesia 4°30N 126°50E 231 D7
Talavera de la Reina Spain 39°55N 4°46W 194 F6
Talavera la Real Spain 38°53N 6°46W 195 G4
Talawgyi Burma 25°4N 97°19E 241 C6
Talayan Phil. 6°52N 124°24E 233 H5
Talayuela Spain 39°59N 5°36W 194 F5
Talbandh India 22°3N 86°20E 243 H12
Talbert, Sillon de France 48°53N 3°5W 172 D3
Talbot Australia 37°10S 143°44E 282 D5
Talbot, C. Australia 13°48S 126°43E 278 B4
Talbotton U.S.A. 32°41N 84°32W 316 C5
Talbragar → Australia 32°12S 148°37E 283 B8
Talca Chile 35°28S 71°40W 334 D1
Talcahuano Chile 36°40S 73°10W 334 D1
Talcher India 21°0N 85°18E 244 D7
Talcho Niger 14°44N 3°28E 263 C5
Taldy Kurgan = Taldyqorghan Kazakhstan 45°10N 78°45E 217 C9
Taldyqorghan Kazakhstan 45°10N 78°45E 217 C9
Tālesh Iran 37°58N 48°58E 213 D13
Tālesh, Kūhhā-ye Iran 37°42N 48°55E 213 D13
Talgar = Talghar Kazakhstan 43°19N 77°15E 217 D9
Talghar Kazakhstan 43°19N 77°15E 217 D9
Talguharai Sudan 18°19N 35°56E 256 D4
Talguppa India 14°13N 74°56E 245 G2
Tali Post Sudan 5°55N 30°44E 257 F3
Taliabu Indonesia 1°50S 125°0E 231 E6
Taliao Taiwan 22°36N 120°23E 225 D2
Talibon Phil. 10°9N 124°20E 233 F5
Talibong, Ko Thailand 7°15N 99°23E 237 J2
Talichien Taiwan 24°58N 121°55E 225 B3
Taliganga India 22°30N 88°22E 124 B2
Talihina U.S.A. 34°45N 95°3W 314 D7
Talikota India 16°29N 76°17E 245 F3
Talin Taiwan 23°36N 120°27E 225 C2
Talipao Phil. 5°59N 121°7E 233 J3
Talipapa Phil. 14°41N 121°1E 127 A2
Talisay Phil. 10°44N 122°58E 233 F4
Talisayan Phil. 9°0N 124°55E 233 G5
Taliwang Indonesia 8°50S 116°55E 235 D5
Talkeetna U.S.A. 62°20N 150°6W 303 E10
Talkha Egypt 31°3N 31°22E 251 G2
Tálknafjörður Iceland 65°34N 24°0W 155 B2
Tall 'Afar Iraq 36°22N 42°27E 213 D10
Tall Kalakh Syria 34°41N 36°15E 250 D7
Talla Egypt 28°5N 30°43E 256 B3
Talladega U.S.A. 33°26N 86°6W 316 B3
Tallaganda △ Australia 35°29S 149°37E 283 C8
Tallaght Ireland 53°17N 6°22W 120 B1
Tallahassee U.S.A. 30°27N 84°17W 316 E5
Tallangatta Australia 36°15S 147°19E 283 D7
Tallapoosa U.S.A. 33°45N 85°17W 316 B4
Tallapoosa → U.S.A. 32°30N 86°16W 316 C3
Tallard France 44°28N 6°3E 175 D10
Tallarook Australia 37°5S 145°6E 283 D6
Tallassee U.S.A. 32°32N 85°54W 316 C4
Tällberg Sweden 60°51N 15°2E 162 D9
Tallering Pk. Australia 28°6S 115°37E 279 E2
Talli Pakistan 29°32N 68°8E 242 E3
Tallinn Estonia 59°22N 24°48E 188 C3
Tallkrogen Sweden 59°16N 18°4E 139 B2
Tallmadge U.S.A. 41°6N 81°27W 312 E3
Tallulah U.S.A. 32°25N 91°11W 314 E9
Tălmaciu Romania 45°38N 24°19E 183 E9
Talmest Morocco 31°48N 9°21W 260 B3
Talmont-St-Hilaire France 46°27N 1°37W 174 B2
Talne Ukraine 48°50N 30°44E 189 H6
Talnoye = Talne Ukraine 48°50N 30°44E 189 H6
Taloda India 21°34N 74°11E 244 D2
Talodi Sudan 10°35N 30°22E 257 E3
Talofofo Guam 13°21N 144°45E 302 d
Tāloqān Afghan. 36°44N 69°33E 240 A3
Talovaya Russia 51°6N 40°45E 190 E5
Taloyoak Canada 69°32N 93°32W 294 C10
Talpa de Allende Mexico 20°23N 104°51W 318 C4
Talparo Trin. & Tob. 10°30N 61°17W 323 t
Talparo → Trin. & Tob. 10°34N 61°17W 323 t
Talquin, L. U.S.A. 30°23N 84°39W 316 E5
Talsi Latvia 57°10N 22°30E 184 A9
Talsi □ Latvia 57°20N 22°40E 184 A9
Talsinnt Morocco 32°33N 3°27W 261 B4
Taltal Chile 25°23S 70°33W 334 B1
Taltson → Canada 61°24N 112°46W 296 A6
Talwood Australia 28°29S 149°29E 281 D4
Talyawalka Cr. → Australia 32°28S 142°22E 282 B5
Tam Ky Vietnam 15°34N 108°29E 236 E7
Tam Quan Vietnam 14°35N 109°3E 236 E7
Tama Tōkyō, Japan 35°38N 139°26E 140 B1
Tama Iowa, U.S.A. 41°58N 92°35W 310 C4
Tama → Japan 35°32N 139°47E 140 B3
Tama △ Ethiopia 5°55N 36°5E 257 F4
Tama Kyūryō Japan 35°34N 139°30E 140 B2
Tamada Algeria 21°34N 3°20E 261 D5
Tamaden Japan 35°39N 139°38E 140 B2
Tamagawa-josui → Japan 35°41N 139°47E 140 A1
Tamakautoga Cook Is. 19°5S 169°55W 289 g
Tamalameque Colombia 8°52N 73°49W 328 B3
Tamale Ghana 9°22N 0°50W 263 D4
Taman Russia 45°14N 36°41E 189 K9
Taman Negara △ Malaysia 4°38N 102°26E 237 K4
Taman Sari Indonesia 6°8S 106°48E 122 A1
T'aman Shan Taiwan 24°42N 121°27E 225 B3
Tamana Japan 32°58N 130°32E 222 E2
Tamana Kiribati 2°30S 175°59E 277 A14
Tamana, Mt. Trin. & Tob. 10°28N 61°12W 323 t
Tamanar Morocco 31°1N 9°46W 260 B3
Tamanduateí → Brazil 23°37S 46°38W 137 B2
Tamanhint Libya 27°13N 14°37E 258 C2
Tamani Mali 13°20N 6°50W 262 C3
Tamano Japan 34°29N 133°59E 222 C5
Tamanrasset Algeria 22°50N 5°30E 261 D6
Tamanrasset □ Algeria 23°45N 4°30E 261 D5
Tamanrasset, O. → Algeria 22°0N 2°0E 261 D5
Tamanthi Burma 25°19N 95°17E 241 C5
Tamaqua U.S.A. 40°48N 75°58W 313 F9
Tamar → U.K. 50°27N 4°15W 169 G3
Támara Colombia 5°50N 72°10W 328 B3
Tamarac U.S.A. 26°12N 80°15W 317 J9
Tamarin Mauritius 20°19S 57°20E 272 e
Tamarinda Spain 39°55N 3°49E 206 B4
Tamarite de Litera Spain 41°52N 0°25E 196 D5
Tamaroa U.S.A. 38°8N 89°14W 310 F7
Tamashima Japan 34°32N 133°40E 221 G6
Tamási Hungary 46°40N 18°18E 182 D3
Tamaské Niger 14°49N 5°43E 263 C6
Tamatave = Toamasina Madag. 18°10S 49°25E 272 B2
Tamaulipas □ Mexico 24°0N 98°45W 319 C5
Tamaulipas, Sierra de Mexico 23°30N 98°20W 319 C5
Tamazula Mexico 24°57N 106°57W 318 C3
Tamazunchale Mexico 21°16N 98°47W 319 C5
Tamba-Dabatou Guinea 11°50N 10°40W 262 C2
Tambach Kenya 0°36N 35°31E 268 B4
Tambacounda Senegal 13°45N 13°40W 262 C2
Tambacounda □ Senegal 14°0N 13°0W 262 C2
Tambaram India 12°55N 80°7E 245 H5
Tambea Solomon Is. 9°16S 159°41E 287 M10
Tambelan, Kepulauan Indonesia 1°0N 107°30E 234 B3
Tambellup Australia 34°4S 117°37E 279 F2
Tambo Queens., Australia 24°54S 146°14E 280 C4
Tambo Peru 12°57S 74°1W 330 C3
Tambo → Peru 10°42S 73°47W 330 C3
Tambo de Mora Peru 13°30S 76°8W 330 C2
Tambobamba Peru 13°54S 72°8W 330 C3
Tamboerskloof S. Africa 33°56S 18°25E 118 A1
Tambohorano Madag. 17°30S 43°58E 272 B1
Tambopata → Peru 13°21S 69°36W 330 C4
Tambora Jakarta, Indonesia 6°8S 106°47E 122 A1
Tambora Nusa Tenggara Barat, Indonesia 8°12S 118°5E 235 D5
Tamboritha, Mt. Australia 37°31S 146°40E 283 D7
Tambov Russia 52°45N 41°28E 190 D5
Tambov □ Russia 52°50N 41°20E 190 D5
Tambre → Spain 42°49N 8°53W 194 C2
Tambuku Indonesia 7°8S 113°40E 235 D4
Tambul Papua N. G. 5°54S 143°54E 286 C2
Tamburâ Sudan 5°40N 27°25E 257 F2
Tambuyukan, Gunong Malaysia 6°13N 116°39E 235 A5
Tâmchekket Mauritania 17°25N 10°40W 262 B2
Tame Colombia 6°28N 71°44W 328 B3
Tâmega → Portugal 41°5N 8°21W 194 D2
Tamelelt Morocco 31°50N 7°32W 260 B3
Tamenglong India 25°0N 93°35E 241 C4
Tamerza Tunisia 34°23N 7°58E 258 B1
Tamgak, Mts. Niger 19°12N 8°35E 259
Tamgué, Massif du Guinea 12°0N 12°18W 262 C2
Tami Is. Papua N. G. 6°46S 147°55E 286 D4
Tamiahua, L. de Mexico 21°35N 97°35W 319 C5
Tamiami Canal U.S.A. 25°50N 81°0W 317 K8
Tamil Nadu □ India 11°0N 77°0E 245 J3
Tamis → Serbia 44°51N 20°39E 182 F5
Tamluk India 22°18N 87°58E 243 H12
Tammerfors = Tampere Finland 61°30N 23°50E 188 B2
Tammisaari Finland 60°0N 23°26E 188 B2
Tammisalo Finland 60°11N 25°5E 121 B3
Tammūh Egypt 29°55N 31°15E 117 B2
Tämnaren Sweden 60°10N 17°25E 162 D11
Tamo Abu, Banjaran Malaysia 3°10N 115°5E 235 B5
Tampa Angola 15°30S 13°27E 265 F2
Tampa Fla., U.S.A. 27°56N 82°27W 317 H7
Tampa, Tanjung Indonesia 8°55S 116°12E 231 K19
Tampa B. U.S.A. 27°50N 82°30W 317 H7
Tampa Int. ✈ (TPA) U.S.A. 27°59N 82°32W 317 H7
Tamparan Phil. 7°53N 124°20E 233 H5
Tampere Finland 61°30N 23°50E 188 B2
Tampico Tamaulipas, Mexico 22°13N 97°51W 319 C5
Tampico Ill., U.S.A. 41°38N 89°47W 310 C7
Tampin Malaysia 2°28N 102°13E 237 L4
Tampines Singapore 1°21N 103°56E 138 A3
Tampoi Malaysia 1°30N 103°39E 237 d
Tamrah Si. Arabia 20°24N 45°25E 248 B4
Tamri Morocco 30°49N 9°50W 260 B3
Tamrida = Qādub Yemen 12°37N 53°57E 249 D6
Tamsweg Austria 47°7N 13°49E 180 D6
Tamu Burma 24°13N 94°12E 241 C5
Tamuja → Spain 39°38N 6°29W 195 F4
Tamuning Guam 13°29N 144°47E 302 d
Tamworth N.S.W., Australia 31°7S 150°58E 283 A9
Tamworth Ont., Canada 44°29N 77°0W 312 B8
Tamworth Staffs., U.K. 52°39N 1°41W 169 E6
Tan An Vietnam 10°32N 106°25E 237 G6
Tan Chau Vietnam 10°48N 105°12E 237 G5
T'an-do N. Korea 39°30N 124°41E 224 C2
Tan Iddah Algeria 26°33N 9°42E 261 C6
Tan-Tan Morocco 28°29N 11°1W 260 C2
Tana → Coast, Kenya 2°32S 40°31E 268 C5
Tana → Finnmark, Norway 70°30N 28°14E 160 A23
Tana, L. Ethiopia 13°5N 37°30E 257 E4
Tana River Primate △ Kenya 1°55S 40°7E 268 C5
Tanabe Japan 33°44N 135°22E 223 D7
Tanabi Brazil 20°37S 49°37W 333 F2
Tanacross U.S.A. 63°23N 143°21W 303 E12
Tanafjorden Norway 70°45N 28°25E 160 A23
Tanaga I. U.S.A. 51°48N 177°53W 303 L3
Tanaga Volcano U.S.A. 51°53N 178°8W 303 L3
Tanah Abang Indonesia 6°12S 106°48E 122 B1
Tanah Kusir Indonesia 6°15S 106°46E 122 B1
Tanah Merah Malaysia 5°48N 102°9E 234 A2
Tanahbala Indonesia 0°30S 98°30E 234 C1
Tanahgrogot Indonesia 1°55S 116°15E 235 C5
Tanahjampea Indonesia 7°10S 120°35E 231 F6
Tanahmasa Indonesia 0°12S 98°39E 234 C1
Tanahmerah Indonesia 6°5S 140°16E 231 F10
Tanakpur India 29°5N 80°7E 243 E9
Tanakura Japan 37°10N 140°20E 221 F10
Tanamalwila Sri Lanka 6°26N 81°8E 245 L5
Tanami Desert Australia 18°50S 132°0E 278 C5
Tanami Mine Australia 19°59S 129°43E 278 C4
Tanana U.S.A. 65°10N 152°4W 303 D9
Tanana → U.S.A. 65°10N 151°58W 303 D10
Tananarive = Antananarivo Madag. 18°55S 47°31E 272 B2
Tananger Norway 58°57N 5°37E 164 F2
Tanannt Morocco 31°54N 6°56W 260 B3
Tanapag N. Marianas 15°14N 145°45E 302 e
Tánaro → Italy 44°55N 8°40E 198 D5
Tanauan Phil. 14°5N 121°10E 232 D3
Tanay Phil. 14°30N 121°17E 232 D3
Tanba-Sanchi Japan 35°7N 135°48E 223 B7
Tancheng China 34°25N 118°20E 227 G10
Tanch'ŏn N. Korea 40°27N 128°54E 224 B4
Tanda Ut. P., India 26°33N 82°35E 243 F10
Tanda Ut. P., India 28°57N 78°56E 243 E8
Tanda Ivory C. 7°48N 3°10W 262 D4
Tandag Phil. 9°4N 126°9E 233 G6
Tandaia Tanzania 9°25S 34°15E 269 D3
Tăndărei Romania 44°39N 27°40E 183 F12
Tandaué Angola 16°58S 18°5E 265 F3
Tandil Argentina 37°15S 59°6W 334 D4
Tandil, Sa. del Argentina 37°30S 59°0W 334 D4
Tandjilé □ Chad 9°30N 16°30E 259 G3
Tandjilé → Chad 9°45N 15°50E 259 G3
Tandlianwala Pakistan 31°3N 73°9E 242 D5
Tando Adam Pakistan 25°45N 68°40E 242 G3
Tando Allahyar Pakistan 25°28N 68°43E 242 G3
Tando Bago Pakistan 24°47N 68°58E 242 G3
Tando Mohommed Khan Pakistan 25°8N 68°32E 242 G3
Tando-Zinze Angola 5°22S 12°30E 265 D2
Tandou-Bengou Congo 3°50S 11°44E 264 C2
Tandou L. Australia 32°40S 142°5E 282 B5
Tandoureh △ Iran 37°50N 59°0E 246 B8
Tandragee U.K. 54°21N 6°24W 166 B5
Tandsjöborg Sweden 61°42N 14°43E 162 C8
Tandubas Phil. 5°8N 120°20E 233 J3
Tandula → India 21°6N 81°14E 244 D5
Tandula Tank India 20°40N 81°12E 244 D5
Tandur Andhra Pradesh, India 19°11N 79°30E 244 E4
Tandur Andhra Pradesh, India 17°14N 77°35E 244 F3
Tane-ga-Shima Japan 30°30N 131°0E 221 J5
Taneatua N.Z. 38°4S 177°1E 284 E6
Tanen Tong Dan = Dawna Ra. Burma 16°30N 98°30E 236 D2
Tanew → Poland 50°29N 22°16E 185 H9
Tanezrouft Algeria 23°9N 0°11E 261 D5
Tanezzuft, W. → Libya 25°51N 10°19E 258 C2
Tang, Koh Cambodia 10°16N 103°7E 237 G4
Tang, Ra's-e Iran 25°21N 59°52E 247 E8
Tang Krasang Cambodia 12°34N 105°3E 236 F5
Tanga Tanzania 5°5S 39°2E 268 D4
Tanga □ Tanzania 5°20S 38°0E 268 D4
Tanga Is. Papua N. G. 3°20S 153°15E 286 B7
Tanga Langua Grenada 12°14N 61°39W 323 q
Tangail Bangla. 24°15N 89°55E 241 C2
Tangalla Sri Lanka 6°1N 80°48E 245 L5
Tanganyika = Tanzania ■ Africa 6°0S 34°0E 268 D3
Tanganyika, L. Africa 6°40S 30°0E 268 D3
Tangarare Solomon Is. 9°36S 159°41E 287 M10
Tangasseri India 8°53N 76°35E 245 K3
Tangaza Nigeria 13°19N 4°55E 263 C5
Tangelo Park U.S.A. 28°27N 81°26W 133 B2
Tanger Morocco 35°50N 5°49W 260 A3
Tanger □ Morocco 35°43N 5°50W 260 A3
Tangerang Indonesia 6°11S 106°37E 234 D3
Tangerhütte Germany 52°26N 11°48E 178 C7
Tangermünde Germany 52°33N 11°58E 178 C7
Tanggu China 39°2N 117°40E 227 E9
Tanggula Shan China 32°40N 92°10E 218 C4
Tanggula Shankou China 32°42N 92°27E 218 C4
Tanghe China 32°47N 112°50E 226 H7
Tanghla Range = Tanggula Shan China 32°40N 92°10E 218 C4
Tangi India 19°56N 85°24E 244 E7
Tangier = Tanger Morocco 35°50N 5°49W 260 A3
Tangjia China 22°22N 113°35E 219 G10
Tangjia Wan China 22°21N 113°36E 219 G10
Tangorin Australia 21°47S 144°12E 280 C3
Tangorombohitr'i Makay Madag. 21°0S 45°15E 272 C2
Tangra Yumco China 31°0N 86°38E 218 C3
Tangshan China 39°38N 118°10E 227 E10
Tangtou China 35°28N 118°30E 227 G10
Tangub Phil. 8°3N 123°44E 233 G4
Tanguiéta Benin 10°35N 1°21E 263 C5
Tangxi China 29°3N 119°25E 229 C12
Tangyan He → China 28°54N 108°19E 228 C7
Taniao Taiwan 22°23N 120°53E 225 D2
Tanimbar, Kepulauan Indonesia 7°30S 131°30E 231 F8
Tanimbar Is. = Tanimbar, Kepulauan Indonesia 7°30S 131°30E 231 F8
Taninthari = Tenasserim Burma 12°6N 99°3E 237 F2
Tanis Egypt 31°0N 31°54E 251 H2
Tanjay Phil. 9°30N 123°5E 233 G4

Tanjong Malim Malaysia 3°42N 101°31E 237 L3
Tanjong Pelepas Malaysia 1°21N 103°33E 237 d
Tanjore = Thanjavur India 10°48N 79°12E 245 J4
Tanjung Bali, Indonesia 8°21S 116°9E 231 J19
Tanjung Kalimantan Selatan, Phil. 2°10S 115°25E 235 C5
Tanjung Duren Indonesia 6°10S 106°46E 122 B1
Tanjung Priok Indonesia 6°6S 106°52E 122 A2
Tanjung Putung △ Indonesia 2°54S 111°59E 235 C4
Tanjung Tokong Malaysia 5°28N 100°18E 237 c
Tanjungbalai Indonesia 2°55N 99°44E 234 B1
Tanjungbatu Indonesia 2°23N 118°3E 235 B5
Tanjungkarang Telukbetung Indonesia 5°20S 105°10E 234 D3
Tanjungpandan Indonesia 2°43S 107°38E 235 C3
Tanjungpinang Indonesia 1°5N 104°30E 234 B2
Tanjungpriok Indonesia 6°8S 106°55E 234 D3
Tanjungredeb Indonesia 2°9N 117°29E 235 B5
Tanjungselor Indonesia 2°55N 117°25E 235 B5
Tank Pakistan 32°14N 70°25E 242 C4
Tankhala India 21°58N 73°47E 242 J5
Tankwa-Karoo △ S. Africa 32°14S 19°50E 270 D2
Tanlu Taiwan 22°12N 120°44E 225 D2
Tanna Vanuatu 19°30S 169°20E 287 J7
Tännäs Sweden 62°26N 12°42E 162 B6
Tannersville U.S.A. 41°3N 75°18W 313 E9
Tannis Bugt Denmark 57°40N 10°15E 163 G4
Tannu Ola Asia 51°0N 94°0E 217 B12
Tannum Sands Australia 23°57S 151°22E 280 C5
Tano → Ghana 5°7N 2°56W 262 D4
Tanombella Algeria 25°30N 5°49E 261 C6
Tanon Str. Phil. 10°20N 123°30E 233 F4
Tanout Niger 14°50N 8°55E 259 F1
Tanquinho Brazil 11°58S 39°6W 333 D4
Tanshui Taiwan 25°10N 121°28E 225 A3
Tanshui Kang → Taiwan 25°10N 121°25E 225 A3
Tansilla Burkina Faso 12°23N 4°23W 262 C4
Tanta Egypt 30°45N 30°57E 256 H7
Tantabin Burma 17°1N 95°59E 241 G5
Tantoyuca Mexico 21°21N 98°14W 319 C5
Tantung = Dandong China 40°10N 124°20E 224 B2
Tantung Datu △ Malaysia 2°13N 109°3E 235 B3
T'antzu Taiwan 24°13N 120°42E 225 B2
Tanuku India 16°45N 81°44E 244 F5
Tanum Norway 59°53N 10°28E 133 A1
Tanūmah Si. Arabia 18°58N 42°10E 248 C3
Tanumshede Sweden 58°42N 11°20E 163 F5
Tanunda Australia 34°30S 139°0E 282 C3
Tanur India 11°1N 75°52E 245 J2
Tanus France 44°8N 2°19E 174 D6
Tanzania ■ Africa 6°0S 34°0E 268 D3
Tanzawa-Sanchi Japan 35°27N 139°0E 223 B11
Tanzhou China 22°16N 113°28E 219 G9
Tanzilla → Canada 58°8N 130°43W 296 B2
Tao, Ko Thailand 10°5N 99°52E 237 G2
Tao'an = Taonan China 45°22N 122°40E 227 B12
Tao'er He → China 45°45N 124°5E 227 B13
Taohua Dao China 29°50N 122°20E 229 C14
Taolanaro Madag. 25°2S 47°0E 272 D2
Taole China 38°48N 106°40E 226 E4
Taonan China 45°22N 122°40E 227 B12
Taora Solomon Is. 7°21S 157°30E 287 L9
Taoranting Park Beijing, China 114 c2
Taormina Italy 37°51N 15°17E 201 E8
Taos U.S.A. 36°24N 105°35W 305 H11
Taoudenni Mali 22°40N 3°55W 260 D4
Taoudrart, Adrar Algeria 24°25N 2°24E 261 D5
Taounate Morocco 34°25N 4°41W 260 B4
Taounate □ Morocco 34°30N 4°50W 260 B4
Taourirt Algeria 26°37N 0°20E 261 C5
Taourirt Morocco 34°25N 2°53W 261 B4
Taouz Morocco 30°53N 4°0W 260 B4
Taoyuan Hunan, China 28°55N 111°16E 229 C8
T'aoyüan Kaohsiung, Taiwan 23°9N 120°46E 225 C2
T'aoyüan Yünlin, Taiwan 25°0N 121°4E 225 B3
T'aoyüan □ Taiwan 24°55N 121°15E 225 B3
Tapa Estonia 59°15N 25°50E 188 C3
Tapa Shan = Daba Shan China 32°0N 109°0E 228 B7
Tapachula Mexico 14°54N 92°17W 319 E6
Tapada Portugal 38°49N 9°16W 126 A1
Tapah Malaysia 4°12N 101°15E 237 K3
Tapajós → Brazil 2°24S 54°41W 329 D7
Tapaktuan Indonesia 3°15N 97°10E 234 B1
Tapanahoni → Suriname 4°20N 54°25W 329 C7
Tapanila Finland 60°15N 25°2E 121 B3
Tapanui N.Z. 45°56S 169°18E 285 F4
Taparo Pt. Trin. & Tob. 10°3N 61°38W 323 t
Tapauá Brazil 5°40S 64°20W 331 B5
Tapauá → Brazil 5°40S 64°21W 331 B5
Tapaz Phil. 11°16N 122°32E 233 F4
Tapes Brazil 30°40S 51°23W 335 C5
Tapeta Liberia 6°29N 8°52W 262 D3
Taphan Hin Thailand 16°13N 100°26E 236 D3
Tapia de Casariego Spain 43°34N 6°56W 194 B4
Tapiales Argentina 34°42S 58°30W 117 C1
Tapiantana Group Phil. 6°20N 122°0E 233 H4
Tapiau = Gvardeysk Russia 54°39N 21°5E 184 D8
Tapilon = Daanbantayan Phil. 11°17N 124°2E 233 F5
Taping Taiwan 24°6N 120°53E 225 B2
Tapini Papua N. G. 8°19S 147°0E 286 E4
Tapiola Finland 60°10N 24°48E 121 B1
Tapiraí Brazil 19°52S 46°1W 333 E2
Tapirapé → Brazil 10°41S 50°38W 332 D1
Tapirapecó, Serra Venezuela 1°10N 65°0W 329 C5
Tapirapuã Brazil 14°51S 57°45W 331 C6
Taplan Australia 34°33S 140°52E 282 C4
Tapo-Capara △ Venezuela 7°55N 71°15W 328 B3
Tapoeripa Suriname 5°22N 56°34W 329 B6
Tapolca Hungary 46°53N 17°29E 182 D2
Tapsia India 22°32N 88°23E 124 B2
Tapti → India 21°8N 72°41E 244 D1
Tapu Taiwan 23°18N 120°35E 225 C2
Tapuae-o-Uenuku N.Z. 42°0S 173°39E 285 C8
Tapul Phil. 5°42N 120°55E 233 J3
Tapul Group Phil. 5°35N 120°50E 233 J3
Tapul I. Phil. 5°43N 120°55E 233 J3
Tapun India 27°35N 96°22E 241 B6
Tapurucuará Brazil 0°24S 65°2W 329 D4
Taputapu, C. Amer. Samoa 14°20S 170°51W 302 f
Taputimu Amer. Samoa 14°21S 170°46W 302 f
Taqṭaq Iraq 35°53N 44°35E 213 E11
Taquara Brazil 29°36S 50°46W 335 B5
Taquari → Brazil 19°15S 57°17W 331 D6
Taquaritinga Brazil 21°24S 48°30W 333 F2
Tara Queens., Australia 27°17S 150°31E 281 D5
Tara Ont., Canada 44°28N 81°9W 312 B3
Tara Maharashtra, India 19°5N 72°49E 130 A1
Tara Japan 33°2N 130°11E 222 D2
Tara Russia 56°55N 74°24E 214 D8
Tara Zambia 16°58S 26°45E 269 F2
Tara → Montenegro 43°21N 18°51E 202 C2
Tara △ Serbia 43°55N 19°30E 202 C3
Tara-Dake Japan 32°58N 130°6E 222 E2
Taraba □ Nigeria 8°0N 10°30E 263 D7
Taraba → Nigeria 8°30N 10°15E 263 D7
Tarabuco Bolivia 19°10S 64°57W 331 D5
Tarābulus Lebanon 34°31N 35°50E 250 D6
Tarābulus Libya 32°49N 13°7E 258 B2
Tarābulus □ Libya 32°53N 13°11E 261 B7
Tarabya Turkey 41°8N 29°3E 122 B2
Taraclia Taraclia, Moldova 45°54N 28°40E 183 E13
Taraclia Tighina, Moldova 46°34N 29°7E 183 D14
Taradale N.Z. 39°33S 176°53E 284 F5
Taradehi India 23°18N 79°21E 243 H8
Tarāghin Libya 26°0N 14°30E 258 C2
Taragi Japan 32°16N 130°56E 222 E2
Tarahouahout Algeria 22°41N 5°59E 261 D6
Tarajalejo Canary Is. 28°12N 14°7W 153 e2
Tarakan Indonesia 3°20N 117°35E 235 B5
Tarakit, Mt. Kenya 2°2N 35°10E 266 B4
Taralga Australia 34°26S 149°52E 283 C8
Tarama-Jima Japan 24°39N 124°42E 221 M2
Taramakau → N.Z. 42°34S 171°8E 285 C6
Taran, Mys Russia 54°56N 19°59E 184 D6
Taranagar India 28°43N 74°50E 242 E6
Taranaki □ N.Z. 39°25S 174°30E 284 F3
Taranaki, Mt. N.Z. 39°17S 174°5E 284 F3
Tarancón Spain 40°1N 3°1W 196 E1
Tarangire △ Tanzania 4°21S 36°7E 268 C4
Taransay U.K. 57°54N 7°0W 167 D1
Táranto Italy 40°28N 17°14E 201 B10
Táranto, G. di Italy 40°8N 17°20E 201 B10
Tarapacá Colombia 2°56S 69°46W 328 D4
Tarapacá □ Chile 20°45S 69°30W 334 A2
Tarapoto Peru 6°30S 76°20W 330 B2
Taraquá Brazil 0°6N 68°28W 328 C4
Tarare France 45°54N 4°26E 175 C8
Tararua Ra. N.Z. 40°45S 175°25E 284 G4
Tarasag Vanuatu 14°12S 167°36E 287 D5
Tarascon France 43°48N 4°39E 175 E8
Tarascon-sur-Ariège France 42°50N 1°36E 174 F5
Tarashcha Ukraine 49°30N 30°31E 177 D16
Tarata Peru 17°27S 70°2W 330 D3
Tarauacá Brazil 8°6S 70°48W 330 B3
Tarauacá → Brazil 6°42S 69°48W 330 B4
Taravao Tahiti 17°43S 149°18W 289 e
Taravao, Isthme de Tahiti 17°43S 149°19W 289 e
Taravo → France 41°42N 8°49E 175 G12
Tarawa Kiribati 1°30N 173°0E 288 G9
Tarawai I. Papua N. G. 3°13S 143°15E 286 B2
Tarawera N.Z. 39°2S 176°36E 284 F5
Tarawera, L. N.Z. 38°13S 176°27E 284 E5
Tarawera, Mt. N.Z. 38°14S 176°32E 284 E5
Taraz Kazakhstan 42°54N 71°22E 217 D8
Tarazona Spain 41°55N 1°43W 196 D3
Tarazona de la Mancha Spain 39°16N 1°55W 197 F3
Tarbæk Denmark 55°46N 12°35E 118 A3
Tarbagatay, Khrebet Kazakhstan 48°0N 83°0E 217 C10
Tarbaj Kenya 2°12N 40°8E 267 D5
Tarbat Ness U.K. 57°52N 3°47W 167 D5
Tarbela Dam Pakistan 34°8N 72°52E 242 B5
Tarbert Kerry, Ireland 52°34N 9°22W 166 D2
Tarbert Argyll & Bute, U.K. 55°52N 5°25W 167 F3
Tarbert W. Isles, U.K. 57°54N 6°49W 167 D2
Tarbes France 43°15N 0°3E 174 E4
Tarboro U.S.A. 35°54N 77°32W 315 D16
Tarbū Libya 26°0N 15°5E 258 C3
Tărcău, Munții Romania 46°39N 26°7E 183 D11
Tarcento Italy 46°13N 13°13E 199 B10
Tarchomin Poland 52°19N 20°58E 142 B1
Tarcoola Australia 30°44S 134°36E 281 E1
Tarcoon Australia 30°15S 146°43E 281 E4
Tarcutta Australia 35°16S 147°44E 283 C7
Tardeo India 18°57N 72°48E 130 B1
Tardets-Sorholus France 43°8N 0°52W 174 E3
Tardoire → France 45°52N 0°14E 174 C4
Taredjedja Algeria 25°12N 2°32E 261 C5
Taree Australia 31°50S 152°30E 283 A10
Tarella Australia 31°2S 143°2E 282 A5
Tarf, Ras Morocco 35°40N 5°11W 260 A3
Ṭarfā, Ra's aṭ Si. Arabia 17°2N 42°22E 248 C3
Tarfā, W. el → Egypt 28°25N 30°50E 256 B3
Tarfaya Morocco 27°55N 12°55W 260 C2
Târgoviște Romania 44°55N 25°27E 183 F10
Târgowek Poland 52°16N 21°3E 142 B2
Târgu Bujor Romania 45°52N 27°54E 183 E12
Târgu Cărbunești Romania 44°57N 23°31E 183 F8
Târgu Frumos Romania 47°12N 27°2E 183 C12
Târgu Jiu Romania 45°5N 23°19E 183 E8
Târgu Lăpuș Romania 47°27N 23°52E 183 C8
Târgu Mureș Romania 46°31N 24°38E 183 D9
Târgu Neamț Romania 47°12N 26°25E 183 C11
Târgu Ocna Romania 46°16N 26°39E 183 D11
Târgu Secuiesc Romania 46°0N 26°10E 183 E11
Targuist Morocco 34°59N 4°14W 260 B4
Târgușor Romania 44°27N 28°25E 183 F13
Tarhăus, Vf. Romania 46°40N 26°8E 183 D11
Tarhbalt Morocco 30°39N 5°20W 260 B3
Tarhūnah Libya 32°27N 13°36E 258 B2
Tari Papua N. G. 5°54S 142°59E 286 C2
Tariba Venezuela 7°49N 72°13W 328 B3
Ṭarīf U.A.E. 24°3N 53°46E 247 E7
Tarifa Spain 36°1N 5°36W 195 J5
Tarija Bolivia 21°30S 64°40W 334 A3
Tarija □ Bolivia 21°30S 63°30W 334 A3
Tarik I. Micronesia 7°20N 151°46E 287 T18
Tariku → Indonesia 2°55S 138°26E 231 E9
Tarīm Yemen 16°3N 49°0E 249 C5
Tarim Basin = Tarim Pendi China 40°0N 84°0E 217 E10
Tarim He → China 39°30N 88°30E 217 E11
Tarim Pendi China 40°0N 84°0E 217 E10
Tarime Tanzania 1°21S 34°22E 266 E3
Taritatu → Indonesia 2°54S 138°27E 231 E9
Tarka → S. Africa 32°10S 26°0E 270 D4
Tarka La Bhutan 27°12N 89°44E 243 F13
Tarkastad S. Africa 32°0S 26°16E 270 D4
Tarkhankut, Mys Ukraine 45°25N 32°30E 189 K7
Tarko Sale Russia 64°55N 77°50E 214 C8
Tarkwa Ghana 5°20N 2°0W 262 D4
Tarlac Phil. 15°29N 120°35E 232 D3
Tarlac □ Phil. 15°30N 120°30E 232 D3
Tarm Denmark 55°56N 8°31E 163 J2
Tarma Peru 11°25S 75°45W 330 C2
Tarn □ France 43°49N 2°8E 174 E6
Tarn → France 44°5N 1°6E 174 D5
Tarn-et-Garonne □ France 44°8N 1°20E 174 D5
Tarna → Hungary 47°31N 19°59E 182 C4
Târnava Mare → Romania 46°10N 23°43E 183 D8
Târnava Mică → Romania 46°9N 23°55E 183 D8
Târnăveni Romania 46°19N 24°13E 183 D9
Tårnby Denmark 55°37N 12°35E 118 B3
Tarnica Poland 49°4N 22°44E 185 J9
Tarnobrzeg Poland 50°35N 21°41E 185 H8
Tarnogród Poland 50°22N 22°45E 185 H9
Tarnopol = Ternopil Ukraine 49°30N 25°40E 177 D13
Tarnos France 43°32N 1°28W 174 E2
Târnova Moldova 48°10N 27°40E 183 B12
Târnova Romania 45°23N 21°59E 182 E6
Tarnów Poland 50°3N 21°0E 185 H8
Tarnowitz = Tarnowskie Góry Poland 50°27N 18°54E 185 H5
Tarnowskie Góry Poland 50°27N 18°54E 185 H5
Tärnsjö Sweden 60°9N 16°56E 162 D10
Táro → Italy 45°2N 10°15E 198 C7
Taroko △ Taiwan 24°10N 121°33E 225 B3
Ṭārom Iran 28°11N 55°46E 247 D7
Taroom Australia 25°36S 149°48E 281 D4
Taroudannt Morocco 30°30N 8°52W 260 B3
Taroudannt □ Morocco 30°30N 8°25W 260 B3
Taroume Cook Is. 21°15S 159°45W 289 h
Tarp Germany 54°39N 9°24E 178 A5
Tarpeena Australia 37°37S 140°47E 282 D4
Tarpon Springs U.S.A. 28°9N 82°45W 317 G7
Tarqua Bay Nigeria 6°24N 3°23E 124 B2
Tarquínia Italy 42°15N 11°45E 199 F8
Tarra Bulga △ Australia 38°27S 146°31E 283 E7
Tarrafal C. Verde Is. 15°18N 23°39W 153 j
Tarragona Spain 41°5N 1°17E 196 D6
Tarragona □ Spain 41°5N 1°0E 196 D6
Tarraleah Australia 42°17S 146°26E 281 G4
Tarrasa = Terrassa Spain 41°34N 2°1E 196 D7
Tàrrega Spain 41°39N 1°9E 196 D6
Tarri Somali Rep. 0°43N 41°38E 267 D5
Tarrytown Ga., U.S.A. 32°19N 82°34W 316 C7
Tarrytown N.Y., U.S.A. 41°4N 73°52W 313 E11
Târs Denmark 57°23N 10°7E 163 G4
Tarshiha = Me'ona Israel 33°1N 35°15E 250 E6
Tarsus Turkey 36°58N 34°55E 250 B5
Tarsus → Turkey 36°46N 34°52E 250 B5
Tartagal Argentina 22°30S 63°50W 334 A3
Tartane Martinique 14°45N 60°55W 322 j
Tärtär Azerbaijan 40°20N 46°58E 191 K8
Tärtär → Azerbaijan 40°26N 47°20E 191 K8
Tartas France 43°50N 0°49W 174 E3
Tartu Estonia 58°20N 26°44E 188 C4
Ṭarṭūs Syria 34°55N 35°55E 250 D6
Ṭarṭūs □ Syria 35°0N 36°0E 250 D7
Tarumirim Brazil 19°16S 41°59W 333 E3
Tarumizu Japan 31°29N 130°42E 222 F2
Tarussa Russia 54°44N 37°10E 188 E9
Tarutao = Ko Tarutao △ Thailand 6°31N 99°26E 237 J2
Tarutao, Ko Thailand 6°33N 99°40E 237 J2
Tarutung Indonesia 2°0N 98°54E 234 B1
Tarutyne Ukraine 46°12N 29°9E 183 D14
Tarvisio Italy 46°30N 13°35E 199 B10
Tarxien Malta 35°52N 14°31E 206 F8
Tarz Ulli Libya 25°32N 10°8E 258 C2
Taşağil Turkey 36°55N 31°14E 250 B2
Tasahku Burma 27°33N 97°52E 241 B6
Tasaret, O. → Algeria 26°25N 1°59E 261 C5
Tasāwah Libya 26°0N 13°30E 258 C2
Tasböget Kazakhstan 44°46N 65°33E 217 D7
Taschereau Canada 48°40N 78°40W 312 C4
Taseko → Canada 52°8N 123°45W 296 C4
Tasgaon India 17°2N 74°39E 244 F2
Tash-Kömür Kyrgyzstan 41°40N 72°10E 217 D8
Tash-Kumyr = Tash-Kömür Kyrgyzstan 41°40N 72°10E 217 D8
Tashauz = Dashoguz Turkmenistan 41°49N 59°58E 216 D5
Tashi Chho Dzong = Thimphu Bhutan 27°31N 89°45E 241 B2
Tashino = Pervomaysk Russia 54°56N 43°58E 190 C6
Ṭashk, Daryācheh-ye Iran 29°45N 53°35E 247 D7
Tashkent = Toshkent Uzbekistan 41°20N 69°10E 217 D7
Tashtagol Russia 52°47N 87°53E 217 B11
Tashu Taiwan 22°41N 120°25E 225 D2
Tasiilaq Greenland 65°40N 37°20W 154 D7
Tasik Kenyir Malaysia 5°5N 102°45E 237 K4
Tasikmalaya Indonesia 7°18S 108°12E 235 D3
Tåsinge Denmark 55°0N 10°36E 163 J4
Tåsjön Sweden 64°15N 15°40E 160 D16
Task Niger 14°56N 10°46E 259 F2
Taskan Russia 62°59N 150°20E 215 C16
Taşkent Turkey 36°55N 32°29E 250 B3
Tasker Niger 15°8N 10°40E 259 E2
Taşköprü Turkey 41°30N 34°15E 212 B6
Taskul Papua N. G. 2°32S 150°27E 286 B6
Taşlâc Moldova 47°4N 29°24E 183 C14
Tasman □ N.Z. 41°30S 172°40E 285 B7
Tasman → N.Z. 43°48S 170°8E 285 D5
Tasman, Mt. N.Z. 43°34S 170°12E 285 D5
Tasman Abyssal Plain Pac. Oc. 34°30S 153°15E 276 G9
Tasman B. N.Z. 40°59S 173°25E 285 A8
Tasman Basin Pac. Oc. 46°0S 158°0E 288 M7
Tasman Glacier N.Z. 43°37S 170°12E 285 D5
Tasman Mts. N.Z. 41°3S 172°25E 285 B7
Tasman Pen. Australia 43°10S 148°0E 281 G4
Tasman Sea Pac. Oc. 36°0S 160°0E 277 H10
Tasmania □ Australia 42°0S 146°30E 281 G4
Tasmanian Wilderness World Heritage Area △ Australia 43°0S 146°0E 281 G4
Tășnad Romania 47°30N 22°33E 182 C7
Tassili n'Ajjer Algeria 25°47N 8°1E 261 C6
Tassili n'Ajjer △ Algeria 26°5N 6°0E 258 C1
Tassili-Oua-n-Ahaggar Algeria 20°41N 5°30E 261 D6
Tassili Tin-Rerhoh Algeria 20°5N 3°55E 261 D5
Taşucu Turkey 36°19N 33°52E 250 B4
Taşucu Körfezi Turkey 36°16N 33°56E 250 B4
Tata Hungary 47°37N 18°19E 182 C3
Tata Morocco 29°46N 7°56W 260 C3
Tatabánya Hungary 47°32N 18°25E 182 C3
Tatakoto French Polynesia 17°20S 138°23W 289 f
Tatamba Solomon Is. 8°21S 159°51E 287 M10
Tatamá △ Colombia 5°5N 76°9W 328 B2
Tataouine Tunisia 32°57N 10°29E 258 B2
Tataouine □ Tunisia 32°0N 10°0E 261 B7
Tatar-Pazardzhik = Pazardzhik Bulgaria 42°12N 24°20E 203 D8
Tatar Republic = Tatarstan □ Russia 55°30N 51°30E 190 C10
Tatarbunary Ukraine 45°50N 29°39E 183 E14
Tatarovo Russia 55°45N 37°24E 129 B2
Tatarsk Russia 55°14N 76°0E 217 A9
Tatarstan □ Russia 55°30N 51°30E 190 C10
Tatatóváros = Tata Hungary 47°37N 18°19E 182 C3
Tatau, Pte. Tahiti 17°44S 149°8W 289 e
Tatau Malaysia 2°53N 112°51E 235 B4
Tatau I. Papua N. G. 2°48S 151°57E 286 B6
Tatebayashi Japan 36°15N 139°32E 223 A11
Tateshina-Yama Japan 36°8N 138°11E 223 A10
Tateyama Japan 35°0N 139°50E 223 C11
Tathlina L. Canada 60°33N 117°39W 296 A5
Tathlīth Si. Arabia 19°32N 43°30E 248 C3
Tathlīth, W. → Si. Arabia 20°35N 44°20E 248 B4
Tathong Channel China 22°15N 114°16E 122 B2
Tathong Pt. China 22°14N 114°17E 122 B2
Tathra Australia 36°44S 149°59E 283 D8
Tatinnai L. Canada 60°55N 97°40W 297 A9
Tatitlek U.S.A. 60°52N 146°41W 303 F11
Tatkon Burma 20°7N 96°13E 241 E6
Tatla Lake Canada 52°0N 124°20W 296 C4
Tatlısu Turkey 40°24N 27°55E 203 F11
Tatnam, C. Canada 57°16N 91°0W 297 B10
Tatra = Tatry Slovak Rep. 49°20N 20°0E 181 B13
Tatranský △ Slovak Rep. 49°10N 20°0E 181 B13
Tatry Slovak Rep. 49°20N 20°0E 181 B13
Tatshenshini → Canada 59°28N 137°45W 296 B1
Tatsuno Hyōgo, Japan 34°52N 134°33E 222 C6
Tatsuno Nagano, Japan 35°58N 138°0E 223 B10
Tatta Pakistan 24°42N 67°55E 242 G2
Tatuapé Brazil 23°31S 46°33W 137 B2
Tatuí Brazil 23°25S 47°53W 335 A6
Tatum U.S.A. 33°16N 103°19W 305 K12
Tat'ung = Datong China 40°6N 113°18E 226 D7
Tatura Australia 36°29S 145°16E 283 D6
Tatvan Turkey 38°31N 42°15E 213 C10
Ta'ū Amer. Samoa 14°15S 169°30W 302 g
Tau Rogaland, Norway 59°3N 5°55E 164 E2
Tauá Brazil 6°1S 40°26W 332 C3
Taubaté Brazil 23°0S 45°36W 335 A6
Tauberbischofsheim Germany 49°37N 9°39E 179 F5
Taucha Germany 51°23N 12°29E 178 D8
Tauern Austria 47°15N 12°40E 176 E7
Tauern-tunnel Austria 47°0N 13°12E 180 D6
Taufikia Sudan 9°24N 31°37E 257 F3
Taufkirchen Germany 48°2N 11°36E 131 B2
Taulé France 48°37N 3°55W 174 B2
Taumarunui N.Z. 38°53S 175°15E 284 E4
Taumaturgo Brazil 8°54S 72°51W 330 B3
Taung S. Africa 27°33S 24°47E 270 C3
Taungdwingyi Burma 20°1N 95°40E 241 E5
Taunggyi Burma 20°50N 97°0E 241 E6
Taungtha Burma 21°12N 95°25E 241 E5
Taungup Burma 18°51N 94°14E 241 F5
Taungup Pass Burma 18°40N 94°45E 241 F5
Taunsa Pakistan 30°42N 70°39E 242 D4
Taunsa Barrage Pakistan 30°42N 70°50E 242 D4
Taunton Somst., U.K. 51°1N 3°5W 169 F4
Taunton Mass., U.S.A. 41°54N 71°6W 313 E13
Taunus Germany 50°13N 8°34E 179 E4
Taupo N.Z. 38°41S 176°7E 284 E5
Taupo, L. N.Z. 38°46S 175°55E 284 E4
Tauragė Lithuania 55°14N 22°16E 184 C9
Tauragė □ Lithuania 55°15N 22°17E 184 C9
Tauranga N.Z. 37°42S 176°11E 284 D5
Tauranga Harb. N.Z. 37°30S 176°5E 284 D5
Taureau, Rés. Canada 46°46N 73°50W 298 C5
Taurianova Italy 38°21N 16°1E 201 D9
Tauri → Papua N. G. 8°8S 146°8E 286 E4
Tauroa Pt. N.Z. 35°10S 173°4E 284 B2
Taurus Mts. = Toros Dağları Turkey 37°0N 32°30E 250 B3
Taus = Domažlice Czech Rep. 49°28N 12°58E 180 B5
Tauste Spain 41°58N 1°18W 196 D3
Tautira Tahiti 17°44S 149°9W 289 e
Tauz = Tovuz Azerbaijan 41°0N 45°40E 191 K7
Tavaar Somali Rep. 3°6N 46°1E 267 D6
Tavan Bogd Uul Mongolia 49°10N 87°49E 217 C11
Tavares U.S.A. 28°48N 81°44W 317 G8
Tavares, I. dos Brazil 22°49S 43°6W 135 A2
Tavas Turkey 37°34N 29°4E 205 D11
Tavastehus = Hämeenlinna Finland 61°0N 24°28E 188 B3
Tavda Russia 58°7N 65°8E 214 D7
Tavda → Russia 57°47N 67°18E 214 D7
Tavernes de la Valldigna Spain 39°5N 0°13W 197 F4
Tavernier U.S.A. 25°1N 80°31W 317 K9
Taveta Kenya 3°23S 37°37E 268 C4
Taveuni Fiji 16°51S 179°58W 287 A3
Taviano Italy 39°59N 18°5E 201 C11
Tavignano → France 42°7N 9°33E 175 F13
Tavira Portugal 37°8N 7°40W 195 H3
Tavistock Ont., Canada 43°19N 80°50W 312 C4
Tavistock Devon, U.K. 50°33N 4°9W 169 G3
Távola Italy 40°54N 9°42E 200 B2
Tavora → Portugal 41°8N 7°35W 194 D3
Tavoy Burma 14°2N 98°12E 236 E2
Tavropos → Greece 39°10N 21°45E 204 B3
Tavros Greece 37°57N 23°43E 112 B2
Tavşanlı Turkey 39°32N 29°30E 205 B11
Tavua Fiji 17°37S 177°5E 287 A1
Tavuki Fiji 19°7S 178°8E 287 B2
Taw → U.K. 51°4N 4°4W 169 F3
Tawa N.Z. 41°10S 174°49E 143 A1
Tawa → India 22°48N 77°48E 242 H8
Tawa Tawa Mal Reef Papua N. G. 11°3S 152°55E 286 F7
Tawai India 27°48N 96°47E 241 B6
Tawas City U.S.A. 44°16N 83°31W 309 C12
Tawau Malaysia 4°20N 117°55E 235 B5
Tawau Hills △ Malaysia 4°20N 117°54E 235 B5
Taweisha Sudan 12°19N 26°40E 257 E2
Tawi-Tawi Phil. 5°10N 120°15E 233 J3
Tawi-tawi □ Phil. 5°0N 120°0E 233 J3
Tawngche Burma 26°34N 95°38E 241 B5
Tawu Taiwan 22°22N 120°54E 225 D2
Tāwurghā' Libya 32°1N 15°2E 258 B3
Tāwurghā', Sabkhat Libya 31°51N 15°15E 258 B3
Taxco Mexico 18°33N 99°36W 319 D5
Taxila Pakistan 33°42N 72°52E 242 C5
Taxkorgan Tajik Zizhixian China 37°49N 75°14E 217 E9
Tay → U.K. 56°37N 3°38W 167 E5
Tay, Firth of U.K. 56°25N 3°8W 167 E5
Tay, L. W. Austral., Australia 32°55S 120°48E 279 F3
Tay, L. Perth & Kinr., U.K. 56°32N 4°8W 167 E4
Tay △ U.K. 56°43N 3°59W 167 E5
Tay Ninh Vietnam 11°20N 106°5E 237 G6
Tayabamba Peru 8°15S 77°16W 330 B2
Tayabas = Quezon Phil. 9°15N 117°59E 233 G1
Tayabas Phil. 14°1N 121°35E 232 D3
Tayabas Bay Phil. 13°45N 121°45E 232 D3
Taygetos Oros Greece 37°0N 22°23E 204 D4
Taylakova Russia 59°13N 74°0E 214 D8
Taylakovy = Taylakova Russia 59°13N 74°0E 214 D8
Taylor B.C., Canada 56°13N 120°40W 296 B4
Taylor Fla., U.S.A. 30°26N 82°18W 316 E7
Taylor Mich., U.S.A. 42°14N 83°16W 311 B13
Taylor Nebr., U.S.A. 41°46N 99°23W 308 E4
Taylor Pa., U.S.A. 41°23N 75°43W 313 E9
Taylor Tex., U.S.A. 30°34N 97°25W 314 F6
Taylor, Mt. N.Z. 43°30S 171°20E 285 D6
Taylor, Mt. N. Mex., U.S.A. 35°14N 107°37W 305 J10
Taylorsville U.S.A. 38°2N 85°21W 311 F11
Taylorsville L. U.S.A. 38°0N 85°15W 311 G11
Taylorville U.S.A. 39°33N 89°18W 310 E7
Taymā Si. Arabia 27°35N 38°45E 246 E3
Taymyr, Oz. Russia 74°20N 102°0E 215 B11
Taymyr, Poluostrov Russia 75°0N 100°0E 215 B11
Tayport U.K. 56°27N 2°52W 167 E6
Tayrona △ Colombia 11°20N 74°2W 328 A3
Tayshet Russia 55°58N 98°1E 215 D10
Taytay Phil. 10°45N 119°30E 233 F2
Taytay Bay Phil. 10°55N 119°35E 233 F2
Tayuan Taiwan 25°3N 121°11E 225 A3
Tayug Phil. 16°2N 120°45E 232 C3
Tayūling Taiwan 24°11N 121°18E 225 B3
Tāyyebād Iran 34°45N 60°45E 247 C9
Tāyyebād □ Iran 34°44N 60°44E 247 C9
Tayynsha Kazakhstan 53°50N 69°45E 217 B7
Taz → Russia 67°32N 78°40E 214 C8
Taza Morocco 34°16N 4°6W 260 B4
Taza □ Morocco 34°15N 3°45W 260 B4
Tāza Khurmātū Iraq 35°18N 44°20E 213 E11
Tazawa-Ko Japan 39°43N 140°40E 220 E10
Taze Burma 22°57N 95°24E 241 D5
Tazenakht Morocco 30°35N 7°12W 260 B3
Tazerbo Libya 25°45N 21°0E 258 C4
Tazin → Canada 59°48N 109°55W 297 B7
Tazin L. Canada 59°44N 108°42W 297 B7
Tazlina U.S.A. 62°4N 146°27W 303 E11
Tazoult Algeria 35°29N 6°11E 261 A6
Tazovskiy Russia 67°30N 78°44E 214 C8
Tbilisi Georgia 41°43N 44°50E 191 K7
Tchad = Chad ■ Africa 15°0N 17°15E 259 F3
Tchad, L. Chad 13°30N 14°30E 259 F2
Tchaourou Benin 8°58N 2°40E 263 D5
Tch'eng-tou = Chengdu China 30°38N 104°2E 228 B5
Tchentlo L. Canada 55°15N 125°0W 296 B4
Tchetti Benin 7°50N 1°40E 263 D5
Tchibanga Gabon 2°45S 11°0E 264 C2
Tchien Liberia 5°59N 8°15W 262 D3
Tchin Tabaraden Niger 15°58N 5°56E 263 B6
Tcholliré Cameroon 8°24N 14°10E 264 A2
Tch'ong-k'ing = Chongqing China 29°35N 106°25E 228 C6
Tchoupitoulas Street New Orleans, U.S.A. 131 b2
Tczew Poland 54°8N 18°50E 184 D5
Te Anau N.Z. 45°25S 167°43E 285 F2
Te Anau, L. N.Z. 45°15S 167°45E 285 F2
Te Araroa N.Z. 37°39S 178°25E 284 D7
Te Aroha N.Z. 37°32S 175°44E 284 D4
Te Awamutu N.Z. 38°1S 175°20E 284 E4
Te Ika a Maui = North I. N.Z. 38°0S 175°0E 284 E4
Te Kaha N.Z. 37°44S 177°52E 284 D6
Te Karaka N.Z. 38°26S 177°53E 284 E6
Te Kauwhata N.Z. 37°25S 175°9E 284 D4
Te Kopuru N.Z. 36°2S 173°56E 284 C2
Te Kuiti N.Z. 38°20S 175°11E 284 E4
Te Manga Cook Is. 21°13S 159°45W 289 h
Te-n-Dghâmcha, Sebkhet Mauritania 18°30N 15°55W 262 B1
Te Papa Museum N.Z. 41°18S 174°47E 143 B1
Te Puke N.Z. 37°46S 176°22E 284 D5
Te Teko N.Z. 38°2S 176°48E 284 E5
Te Waewae B. N.Z. 46°13S 167°33E 285 G2
Te Wai Pounamu = South I. N.Z. 44°0S 170°0E 285 E5
Tea → Brazil 0°30S 65°9W 328 D4
Teaca Romania 46°55N 24°30E 183 D9
Teague U.S.A. 31°38N 96°17W 314 F6
Teahupoo Tahiti 17°50S 149°16W 289 e
Teaneck U.S.A. 40°53N 74°1W 132 A1
Teano Italy 41°15N 14°4E 201 A7
Teapa Mexico 17°33N 92°57W 319 D6
Teatro Municipal Rio de J., Brazil 135 c2
Teba Spain 36°59N 4°55W 195 J6
Tebakang Malaysia 1°6N 110°30E 235 B4
Teberau Malaysia 1°32N 103°45E 234 B2
Teberda Russia 43°30N 41°46E 191 J5
Teberu Malaysia 1°30N 103°42E 237 d
Tébessa Algeria 35°22N 8°8E 261 A6
Tébessa □ Algeria 35°0N 7°50E 261 B6
Tebet Indonesia 6°14S 106°50E 122 B2
Tebicuary → Paraguay 26°36S 58°16W 334 B4
Tebingtinggi Riau, Indonesia 1°0N 102°45E 234 B2
Tebingtinggi Sumatera Utara, Indonesia 3°20N 99°9E 234 B1
Tébourba Tunisia 36°49N 9°51E 258 A1
Téboursouk Tunisia 36°29N 9°10E 258 A1
Tebulos Georgia 42°36N 45°17E 191 J7
Tecamachalco Mexico 19°25N 99°14W 128 B1
Tecate Mexico 32°34N 116°38W 307 N10
Tecer Dağları Turkey 39°27N 37°27E 212 C7
Tech → France 42°36N 3°3E 174 F7
Techiman Ghana 7°35N 1°58W 262 D4
Techirghiol Romania 44°4N 28°32E 183 F13
Techou = Dezhou China 37°26N 116°18E 226 F9
Tecka Argentina 43°29S 70°48W 336 B2
Tecomán Mexico 18°55N 103°53W 318 D4
Tecopa U.S.A. 35°51N 116°13W 307 K10
Tecoripa Mexico 28°37N 109°57W 318 B3
Tecuala Mexico 22°23N 105°27W 318 C3
Tecuci Romania 45°51N 27°27E 183 E12
Tecumseh Ont., Canada 42°19N 82°54W 312 D2
Tecumseh Mich., U.S.A. 42°0N 83°57W 311 B13
Tecumseh Okla., U.S.A. 35°15N 96°56W 314 D6
Ted Somali Rep. 4°24N 43°55E 267 D5
Ted Williams Tunnel U.S.A. 42°21N 71°1W 116 A2
Teddington U.K. 51°25N 0°20W 125 B1
Tedjert Algeria 21°23N 6°25E 261 D6
Tedzhen = Tejen Turkmenistan 37°23N 60°31E 216 E6
Tees → U.K. 54°37N 1°10W 168 C6
Tees B. U.K. 54°40N 1°9W 168 C6
Teeswater Canada 43°59N 81°17W 312 C3
Tefé Brazil 3°25S 64°50W 329 D5
Tefé → Brazil 3°35S 64°47W 329 D5
Tefenni Turkey 37°18N 29°45E 205 D11
Tegal Indonesia 6°52S 109°8E 235 D3
Tegallalang Indonesia 8°27S 115°17E 231 J18
Tegalsari Indonesia 8°25S 114°8E 231 J17
Tegel Germany 52°34N 13°16E 115 A2
Tegel, Berlin ✕ (TXL) Germany 52°35N 13°14E 115 A2
Tegeler See Germany 52°34N 13°15E 115 A2
Tegelort Germany 52°34N 13°13E 115 A2
Tegernsee Germany 47°43N 11°46E 179 H7
Teggiano Italy 40°23N 15°32E 201 B8
Tegid, L. = Bala, L. U.K. 52°53N 3°37W 168 E4
Tegina Nigeria 10°5N 6°11E 263 C6
Tegua Vanuatu 13°15S 166°37E 287 C4
Tegucigalpa Honduras 14°5N 87°14W 320 D2
Teguidda i-n-Tessoum Niger 17°25N 6°37E 263 B6
Teguise Canary Is. 29°3N 13°33W 153 e2
Tehachapi U.S.A. 35°8N 118°27W 307 L8
Tehachapi Mts. U.S.A. 35°0N 118°30W 307 L8
Tehamiyam Sudan 18°20N 36°32E 256 D4
Teheran = Tehrān Iran 35°41N 51°25E 141 A2
Tehilla Sudan 17°42N 36°6E 256 D4
Téhini Ivory C. 9°39N 3°40W 262 D4
Tehoru Indonesia 3°23S 129°30E 231 E7
Tehrān Iran 35°41N 51°25E 141 A2
Tehrān □ Iran 35°30N 51°30E 247 C6
Tehrān Mehrābād ✕ (THR) Iran 35°41N 51°18E 141 A1
Tehrān Pārs Iran 35°44N 51°32E 141 A3
Tehri India 30°23N 78°29E 243 D8
Tehuacán Mexico 18°27N 97°23W 319 D5
Tehuantepec Mexico 16°21N 95°13W 319 D5
Tehuantepec, G. de Mexico 15°50N 95°12W 319 D5
Tehuantepec, Istmo de Mexico 17°15N 94°30W 319 D6
Tehuantepec Fracture Zone Pac. Oc. 13°0N 97°0W 289 F18
Tei Tong Tsui China 22°16N 114°17E 122 B2
Teide, Pico de Canary Is. 28°15N 16°38W 153 e1
Teifi → U.K. 52°5N 4°41W 169 E3
Teigebyen Norway 60°12N 11°0E 162 D5
Teign → U.K. 50°32N 3°32W 169 G4
Teignmouth U.K. 50°33N 3°31W 169 G4
Teiuș Romania 46°12N 23°40E 183 D8
Teixeira Brazil 7°13S 37°15W 332 C4
Teixeira Pinto Guinea-Biss. 12°3N 16°0W 262 C1
Tejakula Indonesia 8°8S 115°20E 231 J18
Tejam India 29°57N 80°11E 243 E9
Tejen Turkmenistan 37°23N 60°31E 216 E6
Tejen → Turkmenistan 37°24N 60°38E 247 B9
Tejo → Europe 38°40N 9°24W 195 F2
Tejo, Rio → Portugal 38°45N 9°3W 126 A2
Tejon Pass U.S.A. 34°49N 118°53W 307 L8
Tekamah U.S.A. 41°47N 96°13W 308 E5
Tekapo → N.Z. 44°13S 170°21E 285 E5
Tekapo, L. N.Z. 43°53S 170°33E 285 D5
Tekax Mexico 20°12N 89°17W 319 C7
Teke Turkey 41°4N 29°39E 203 E13
Tekeli Kazakhstan 44°50N 79°0E 217 D9
Tekeze → Ethiopia 14°20N 35°50E 257 E4
Tekija Serbia 44°42N 22°26E 202 B6
Tekirdağ Turkey 40°58N 27°30E 203 F11
Tekirdağ □ Turkey 41°0N 27°0E 203 E11
Tekirova Turkey 36°30N 30°32E 205 E12
Tekkali India 18°37N 84°15E 244 E7
Tekke Turkey 40°42N 36°12E 212 B7
Tekman Turkey 39°38N 41°29E 213 C9
Teknaf Bangla. 20°52N 92°18E 241 E4
Tekoa U.S.A. 47°14N 117°4W 304 C5
Tekokota French Polynesia 17°18S 142°34W 289 f
Tekong Besar, Pulau Singapore 1°25N 104°3E 237 d
Tekouiât, O. → Algeria 22°25N 2°35E 261 D5
Tekro Chad 19°32N 20°56E 259 E4
Tekstilyshchik Russia 55°42N 37°41E 129 B4
Tel → India 20°50N 83°54E 244 D6
Tel Aviv-Yafo Israel 32°4N 34°48E 251 F5
Tel Lakhish Israel 31°34N 34°51E 251 G5
Tel Megiddo Israel 32°35N 35°11E 250 F6
Tela Honduras 15°40N 87°28W 320 C2
Télagh Algeria 34°51N 0°32W 261 B4
Telanaipura = Jambi Indonesia 1°38S 103°30E 234 C2
Telašćica ⌂ Croatia 43°55N 15°10E 199 E12
Telavi Georgia 42°0N 45°30E 191 J7
Telč Czech Rep. 49°11N 15°28E 180 B8
Telciu Romania 47°25N 24°24E 183 C9
Telde Canary Is. 27°59N 15°25W 153 e1
Tele → Dem. Rep. of the Congo 2°48N 23°54E 264 B4
Telefomin Papua N. G. 5°10S 141°31E 286 C1
Telegraph Creek Canada 58°0N 131°10W 296 B2
Telegraph Hill San Francisco, U.S.A. 136 a2
Telekhany = Tsyelyakhany Belarus 52°30N 25°46E 177 B13
Telemark Norway 59°15N 7°40E 161 G12
Telemark □ Norway 59°25N 8°30E 164 E5
Telén Argentina 36°15S 65°31W 334 D2
Telen → Indonesia 0°10S 117°20E 235 C5
Teleneşti Moldova 47°30N 28°22E 183 C13
Teleng Iran 25°47N 61°3E 247 E9
Teleño Spain 42°23N 6°22W 194 C4
Teleorman □ Romania 44°0N 25°0E 183 G10
Teleorman → Romania 43°52N 25°26E 183 G10
Teles Pires → Brazil 7°21S 58°3W 331 B6
Telescope Pk. U.S.A. 36°10N 117°5W 307 J9
Telescope Pt. Grenada 12°7N 61°36W 323 q
Teletaye Mali 16°31N 1°30E 263 B5
Telfer Mine Australia 21°40S 122°12E 278 C3
Telford U.K. 52°40N 2°27W 169 E5
Telford and Wrekin □ U.K. 52°45N 2°27W 168 E5
Telfs Austria 47°19N 11°4E 180 D4
Telhal Portugal 38°48N 9°18W 126 A1
Telida U.S.A. 63°23N 153°16W 303 E9
Télimélé Guinea 10°54N 13°2W 262 C2
Teljo, J. Sudan 14°42N 25°26E 257 E2
Telkwa Canada 54°41N 127°5W 296 C3
Tell City U.S.A. 37°57N 86°46W 311 G10
Teller U.S.A. 65°16N 166°22W 303 D6
Tellicherry India 11°45N 75°30E 245 J2
Telluride U.S.A. 37°56N 107°49W 305 H10
Telok Blangah Singapore 1°17N 103°49E 138 B2
Telok Datok Malaysia 2°49N 101°31E 234 B2
Teloloapán Mexico 18°21N 99°51W 319 D5
Telpos Iz Russia 63°16N 59°13E 186 B10
Telsen Argentina 42°30S 66°50W 336 B3
Telšiai Lithuania 55°59N 22°14E 184 C9
Telšiai □ Lithuania 55°59N 22°15E 184 C9
Teltow Germany 52°23N 13°17E 115 B2
Teltow kanal Germany 52°26N 13°29E 115 B3
Teluk Anson = Teluk Intan Malaysia 4°3N 101°0E 237 K3
Teluk Bahang Malaysia 5°28N 100°13E 237 c
Teluk Betung = Tanjungkarang Telukbetung Indonesia 5°20S 105°10E 234 D3
Teluk Darvel Malaysia 4°45N 118°30E 233 J2
Teluk Intan Malaysia 4°3N 101°0E 237 K3
Teluk Kumbar Malaysia 5°18N 100°14E 237 c
Telukbutun Indonesia 4°13N 108°12E 235 B3
Telukdalem Indonesia 0°33N 97°50E 234 B1
Tema Ghana 5°41N 0°0 263 D5
Temagami, L. Canada 47°0N 80°10W 298 C3
Temanggung Indonesia 7°18S 110°10E 235 D4
Temassinine Algeria 23°18N 7°40E 261 D6
Tematangi French Polynesia 21°41S 140°40W 289 f
Temax Mexico 21°9N 88°56W 319 C7
Temba S. Africa 25°20S 28°17E 271 C4
Tembagapura Indonesia 4°20S 137°0E 231 E9
Tembe Dem. Rep. of the Congo 0°16S 28°14E 268 C2
Tembe ⌂ S. Africa 26°51S 32°24E 271 C5
Tembesi Indonesia 1°43S 103°6E 234 C2
Tembilahan Indonesia 0°19S 103°9E 234 C2
Temblador Venezuela 8°59N 62°44W 329 B5
Tembleque Spain 39°41N 3°30W 194 F7
Temblor Range U.S.A. 35°20N 119°50W 307 K7
Teme → U.K. 52°11N 2°13W 169 E5
Temecula U.S.A. 33°30N 117°9W 307 M9
Temerloh Malaysia 3°27N 102°25E 234 B2
Teminabuan Indonesia 1°26S 132°1E 231 E8
Temir Kazakhstan 49°1N 57°14E 187 E10
Temir-Khan-Shura = Buynaksk Russia 42°48N 47°7E 191 J8
Temirtau Kazakhstan 50°5N 72°56E 217 B8
Temirtau Russia 53°10N 87°30E 217 B11
Témiscamie → Canada 50°59N 73°5W 299 B5
Témiscaming Canada 46°44N 79°5W 298 C4
Témiscamingue, L. Canada 47°10N 79°25W 298 C4
Temnikov Russia 54°40N 43°11E 190 C6
Temnikovo Russia 55°43N 38°1E 129 B6
Temo → Italy 40°17N 8°28E 200 B1

Temora *Australia* 34°30S 147°30E **283** C7
Temosachic *Mexico* 28°57N 107°51W **318** B3
Tempe *U.S.A.* 33°24N 111°54W **305** K8
Tempelburg = Czaplinek
Poland 53°34N 16°14E **184** E3
Tempelhof *Germany* 52°27N 13°23E **115** B3
Tempelhof, Berlin ✈ (THF)
Germany 52°28N 13°27E **115** B3
Temperance *U.S.A.* 41°47N 83°34W **311** C13
Témpio Pausània *Italy* 40°54N 9°6E **200** B2
Tempiute *U.S.A.* 37°39N 115°38W **306** H11
Templar Bank *S. China Sea* 9°0N 117°30E **233** F1
Temple *U.S.A.* 31°6N 97°21W **314** F6
Temple B. *Australia* 12°15S 143°3E **286** G2
Temple City *U.S.A.* 34°6N 118°3W **126** B4
Temple Hills *U.S.A.* 38°48N 76°56W **143** C4
Temple Mount *Jerusalem* **123** b3
Temple Terrace *U.S.A.* 28°2N 82°23W **317** G7
Templemore *Ireland* 52°47N 7°51W **166** D4
Templeogue *Ireland* 53°18N 6°18W **120** B2
Templeton *U.S.A.* 35°33N 120°42W **306** K6
Templeton ➜ *Australia* 21°0S 138°40E **280** C2
Templin *Germany* 53°7N 13°28E **178** B9
Templo Mayor *Mexico City, Mexico* **128** b3
Tempoal de Sánchez
Mexico 21°31N 98°23W **319** C5
Tempapeliaukio Church
Finland 60°10N 24°56E **121** B2
Tempué *Angola* 13°27S 18°49E **265** E3
Temryuk *Russia* 45°15N 37°24E **189** K9
Temska ➜ *Serbia* 43°17N 22°33E **202** C6
Temuco *Chile* 38°45S 72°40W **336** A2
Temuka *N.Z.* 44°14S 171°17E **285** E6
Ten Degree Channel
India 10°0N 92°30E **245** K11
Ten Thousand Is. *U.S.A.* 25°55N 81°45W **317** K8
Tena *Ecuador* 0°59S 77°49W **328** D2
Tenabo *Mexico* 20°3N 90°14W **319** C6
Tenafly *U.S.A.* 40°54N 73°58W **132** A2
Tenaha *U.S.A.* 31°57N 94°15W **314** F7
Tenakee Springs *U.S.A.* 57°47N 135°13W **296** B1
Tenali *India* 16°15N 80°35E **245** F5
Tenancingo de Degollado
Mexico 18°58N 99°36W **319** D5
Tenango del Valle *Mexico* 19°7N 99°33W **319** D5
Tenaro, Akra *Greece* 36°22N 22°27E **204** E4
Tenasserim *Burma* 12°6N 99°3E **237** F2
Tenasserim □ *Burma* 14°0N 98°30E **236** F2
Tenayuca, Piramide de
Mexico 19°31N 99°10W **128** A1
Tenby *U.K.* 51°40N 4°42W **169** F3
Tenda, Colle di *France* 44°7N 7°36E **175** D11
Tendaho *Ethiopia* 11°48N 40°54E **257** E5
Tende *France* 44°5N 7°35E **175** D11
Tendelti *Sudan* 13°1N 31°55E **257** E3
Tendjedi, Adrar *Algeria* 23°41N 7°32E **261** D6
Tendrara *Morocco* 33°3N 1°58W **261** B4
Tendrovskaya Kosa
Ukraine 46°16N 31°35E **189** J6
Tendukhera *India* 23°24N 79°33E **243** H8
Teneguía, Volcanes de
Canary Is. 28°28N 17°51W **153** e1
Teneida *Egypt* 25°30N 29°19E **256** B2
Tenenkou *Mali* 14°28N 4°55W **262** C4
Tenente Marques ➜
Brazil 11°10S 59°56W **331** C6
Ténéré *Niger* 19°0N 10°30E **259** E2
Ténéré, Erg du *Niger* 17°35N 10°55E **259** E2
Tenerife *Canary Is.* 28°15N 16°35W **153** e1
Tenerife, Pico *Canary Is.* 27°43N 18°1W **153** e1
Tenerife Norte ✈ (TFN)
Canary Is. 28°28N 16°17W **153** e1
Tenerife Sur ✈ (TFS)
Canary Is. 28°3N 16°33W **153** e1
Ténès *Algeria* 36°31N 1°14E **261** A5
Teng Xian *Guangxi Zhuangzu,*
China 23°21N 110°56E **229** F8
Teng Xian *Shandong,*
China 35°5N 117°10E **227** G9
Tengah ➜ *Singapore* 1°23N 103°43E **138** A2
Tengah, Kepulauan
Indonesia 7°5S 118°15E **235** D5
Tengchong *China* 25°0N 98°28E **228** E2
Tengchowfu = Penglai
China 37°48N 120°42E **227** F11
Tenggarong *Indonesia* 0°24S 116°58E **235** C5
Tengger Feng *China* 43°12N 86°48E **217** D11
Tengger Shamo *China* 38°0N 104°0E **218** C5
Tenggol, Pulau *Malaysia* 4°48N 103°41E **237** K4
Tengiz Köli *Kazakhstan* 50°30N 69°0E **217** B7
Tenhult *Sweden* 57°41N 14°20E **163** G8
Teniente Enciso △
Paraguay 21°5S 61°8W **334** A3
Teniente Rodolfo Marsh
Antarctica 62°30S 58°0W **151** C18
Tenille *U.S.A.* 29°46N 83°19W **316** F6
Tenino *U.S.A.* 46°51N 122°51W **306** D4
Tenkasi *India* 8°55N 77°20E **245** K3
Tenke *Katanga,*
Dem. Rep. of the Congo 11°22S 26°40E **269** E2
Tenke *Katanga,*
Dem. Rep. of the Congo 10°32S 26°7E **269** E2
Tenkodogo *Burkina Faso* 11°54N 0°19W **263** C4
Tenna ➜ *Italy* 43°14N 13°47E **199** E10
Tennant Creek *Australia* 19°30S 134°15E **280** B1
Tennessee □ *U.S.A.* 36°0N 86°30W **315** D11
Tennessee ➜ *U.S.A.* 37°4N 88°34W **315** C10
Tennille *U.S.A.* 32°56N 82°48W **316** C7
Tennoji *Japan* 34°39N 135°30E **133** B2
Teno, Pta. de *Canary Is.* 28°21N 16°55W **153** e1
Tenom *Malaysia* 5°4N 115°57E **235** A5
Tenosique *Mexico* 17°29N 91°26W **319** D6
Tenri *Japan* 34°39N 135°49E **223** C7
Tenryū *Japan* 34°52N 137°49E **223** C9
Tenryū-Gawa ➜ *Japan* 35°39N 137°48E **223** B9
Tensift, Oued ➜ *Morocco* 32°3N 9°28W **260** B3
Tenterden *U.K.* 51°4N 0°42E **169** F8
Tenterfield *Australia* 29°0S 152°0E **281** D5
Tenuaiur, Uad ➜
W. Sahara 21°36N 16°0W **260** D1
Teo *Spain* 42°45N 8°30W **194** C2
Teófilo Otoni *Brazil* 17°50S 41°30W **333** E3
Tepa *Indonesia* 7°52S 129°31E **231** F7
Tepa Pt. *Cook Is.* 19°6S 169°55W **289** g
Tepalcatepec ➜
Mexico 18°35N 101°59W **318** D4
Tepalcates *Mexico* 19°23N 99°3W **128** B2
Tepecik *Bursa, Turkey* 40°7N 28°25E **203** F12
Tepecik *Kütahya, Turkey* 39°32N 29°28E **205** B11
Tepehuanes *Mexico* 25°21N 105°44W **318** B3
Tepelenë *Albania* 40°17N 20°2E **202** F4
Tepequem, Serra *Brazil* 3°45N 61°45W **329** C5
Tepetongo *Mexico* 22°28N 103°9W **318** C4
Tepeyac, Parque Nacional △
Mexico 19°30N 99°7W **128** B2
Tepic = Nayarit □ *Mexico* 22°0N 105°0W **318** C4
Tepic *Mexico* 21°30N 104°54W **318** C4
Teplá *Czech Rep.* 49°59N 12°52E **180** B5
Teplice *Czech Rep.* 50°40N 13°48E **180** A6
Teplitz = Teplice
Czech Rep. 50°40N 13°48E **180** A6
Teplyk *Ukraine* 48°40N 29°44E **183** B14
Tepoca, C. *Mexico* 30°20N 112°25W **318** A2
Tequila *Mexico* 20°54N 103°47W **318** C4
Ter ➜ *Spain* 42°2N 3°12E **196** C8
Ter Apel *Neths.* 52°53N 7°5E **170** B7
Téra *Niger* 14°0N 0°45E **263** C5
Tera ➜ *Spain* 41°54N 5°44W **194** D5
Tera Kora *Neth. Ant.* 12°11N 68°16W **322** h
Teraina *Kiribati* 4°43N 160°25W **289** G12
Terakeka *Sudan* 5°26N 31°45E **257** F3
Téramo *Italy* 42°39N 13°42E **199** F10
Terang *Australia* 38°15S 142°55E **282** E5
Terang, Teluk *Indonesia* 8°44S 116°0E **231** K19
Terawhiti, C. *N.Z.* 41°16S 174°38E **284** H3
Terazit, Massif de *Niger* 20°2N 8°30E **259** D1
Tercan *Turkey* 39°47N 40°23E **213** C9
Terceira *Azores* 38°43N 27°13W **153** d1
Tercero ➜ *Argentina* 32°58S 61°47W **334** C3
Terdal *India* 16°33N 75°3E **244** F2
Terebovlya *Ukraine* 49°18N 25°44E **177** D13
Teregova *Romania* 45°10N 22°16E **182** E7
Tereida *Sudan* 10°35N 31°17E **257** E3
Terek ➜ *Russia* 44°0N 47°30E **191** J8
Terengganu □ *Malaysia* 4°55N 103°0E **234** B2
Terenos *Brazil* 20°26S 54°50W **331** E7
Terepaima △ *Venezuela* 9°58N 69°17W **328** B4
Tereshka ➜ *Russia* 51°48N 46°26E **190** E8
Teresina *Brazil* 5°9S 42°45W **332** C3
Teresinha *Brazil* 0°58N 52°2W **329** C7
Terespol *Poland* 52°5N 23°37E **185** F10
Teressa *India* 8°15N 93°10E **245** K11
Teresva *Ukraine* 48°0N 23°42E **183** B8
Terewah, L. *Australia* 29°52S 147°35E **281** D4
Terges ➜ *Portugal* 37°49N 7°41W **195** H3
Tergnier *France* 49°40N 3°17E **173** C10
Terhazza *Mali* 23°38N 5°22W **260** D3
Teridgerie Cr. ➜
Australia 30°25S 148°50E **283** A8
Terijoki = Zelenogorsk
Russia 60°12N 29°43E **188** B5
Terlizzi *Italy* 41°8N 16°32E **201** A9
Terme *Turkey* 41°11N 37°0E **212** B7
Termez = Termiz
Uzbekistan 37°15N 67°15E **217** E7
Términi Imerese *Italy* 37°59N 13°42E **200** E6
Términos, L. de *Mexico* 18°37N 91°33W **319** D6
Termiz *Uzbekistan* 37°15N 67°15E **217** E7
Térmoli *Italy* 42°0N 15°0E **199** F12
Ternate *Indonesia* 0°45N 127°25E **231** D7
Terneuzen *Neths.* 51°20N 3°50E **170** C3
Terney *Russia* 45°3N 136°37E **220** B8
Terni *Italy* 42°34N 12°37E **199** F9
Ternitz *Austria* 47°43N 16°2E **180** D9
Ternivka *Ukraine* 48°32N 29°58E **183** B14
Ternopil *Ukraine* 49°30N 25°40E **177** D13
Ternopil □ *Ukraine* 48°10N 25°10E **189** H3
Ternopol = Ternopil
Ukraine 49°30N 25°40E **177** D13
Terowie *Australia* 33°8S 138°55E **282** B3
Terpni *Greece* 40°55N 23°26E **202** F7
Terra Bella *U.S.A.* 35°58N 119°3W **307** K7
Terra Nova △ *Canada* 48°33N 53°55W **299** C9
Terrace *Canada* 54°30N 128°35W **296** C3
Terrace Bay *Canada* 48°47N 87°5W **298** C2
Terracina *Italy* 41°17N 13°15E **200** A6
Terralba *Italy* 39°43N 8°39E **200** C1
Terranova di Sicilia = Gela
Italy 37°4N 14°15E **201** E7
Terranova Pausania = Ólbia
Italy 40°55N 9°31E **200** B2
Terrasini *Italy* 38°10N 13°4E **200** D6
Terrassa *Spain* 41°34N 2°1E **196** D7
Terrasson-la-Villedieu
France 45°8N 1°18E **174** C5
Terrazzano *Italy* 45°32N 9°4E **129** A1
Terre-de-Bas *Guadeloupe* 15°51N 61°38W **322** e
Terre-de-Bas *Guadeloupe* 16°10N 61°7W **322** e
Terre-de-Haut *Guadeloupe* 15°52N 61°34W **322** e
Terre des Hommes
Canada 45°31N 73°32W **130** A2
Terre Haute *U.S.A.* 39°28N 87°25W **311** E9
Terre Rouge *Mauritius* 20°7S 57°31E **272** e
Terrebonne B. *U.S.A.* 29°5N 90°35W **315** G9
Terrecht *Mali* 20°10N 0°10W **261** D4
Terrell *U.S.A.* 32°44N 96°17W **314** E6
Terrenceville *Canada* 47°40N 54°44W **299** C9
Terrick Terrick △
Australia 36°8S 144°13E **282** D6
Terrugem *Portugal* 38°41N 9°17W **126** A1
Terry *U.S.A.* 46°47N 105°19W **304** C11
Terrytown *U.S.A.* 29°54N 90°1W **131** B2
Terryville *U.S.A.* 41°41N 73°3W **313** E11
Terschelling *Neths.* 53°25N 5°20E **170** A5
Tersko-Kumskiy Kanal
Russia 44°32N 44°38E **191** H7
Tertenia *Italy* 39°42N 9°34E **200** C2
Terter = Tärtär ➜
Azerbaijan 40°26N 47°20E **191** K8
Teruel *Spain* 40°22N 1°8W **196** E3
Teruel □ *Spain* 40°48N 1°0W **196** E4
Tervel *Bulgaria* 43°45N 27°28E **203** C11
Tervola *Finland* 66°6N 24°49E **160** C21
Tervuren *Belgium* 50°49N 4°31E **116** B3
Tervuren, Park van
Belgium 50°49N 4°31E **116** B3
Teryaweynya L.
Australia 32°18S 143°22E **282** B5
Tešanj *Bos.-H.* 44°38N 18°1E **182** F3
Teschen = Cieszyn *Poland* 49°45N 18°35E **185** J5
Teseney *Eritrea* 15°5N 36°42E **257** D4
Tesha ➜ *Russia* 55°38N 42°9E **190** C6
Teshekpuk L. *U.S.A.* 70°35N 153°26W **303** A9
Teshio *Japan* 44°53N 141°44E **220** B10
Teshio-Gawa ➜ *Japan* 44°53N 141°45E **220** B10
Tesica *Serbia* 43°27N 21°45E **202** C5
Tesiyn Gol ➜ *Mongolia* 50°40N 93°20E **218** A4
Teslić *Bos.-H.* 44°37N 17°54E **182** F2
Teslin *Canada* 60°10N 132°43W **296** A2
Teslin ➜ *Canada* 61°34N 134°35W **296** A2
Teslin L. *Canada* 60°15N 132°57W **296** A2
Tesouro *Brazil* 16°4S 53°34W **331** D7
Tessalit *Mali* 20°12N 1°0E **261** D5
Tessaoua *Niger* 13°47N 7°56E **259** F1
Tessin *Germany* 54°2N 12°26E **178** A8
Tessit *Mali* 15°13N 0°18E **263** B5
Tessounfat *Mali* 22°53N 0°32E **261** D5
Test ➜ *U.K.* 50°56N 1°29W **169** G6
Testa del Gargano *Italy* 41°50N 16°10E **199** G13
Testigos, Is. Los *Venezuela* 11°23N 63°7W **321** D7
Tét *Hungary* 47°30N 17°33E **182** C2
Têt ➜ *France* 42°44N 3°2E **174** F7
Tetachuck L. *Canada* 53°18N 125°55W **296** C3
Tetas, Pta. *Chile* 23°31S 70°38W **336** A1
Tete *Mozam.* 16°13S 33°33E **269** F3
Tete □ *Mozam.* 15°15S 32°40E **269** F3
Tetenga, Caleta *Chile* 27°9S 109°19W **330** b
Tetepare *Solomon Is.* 8°45S 157°35E **287** M9
Teterev ➜ *Ukraine* 51°1N 30°5E **177** C16
Teterow *Germany* 53°46N 12°34E **178** B8
Teteven *Bulgaria* 42°58N 24°17E **203** D8
Tethul ➜ *Canada* 60°35N 112°12W **296** A6
Tetiyev *Ukraine* 49°22N 29°38E **177** D15
Tetlin *U.S.A.* 63°8N 142°31W **303** E12
Tetlin Junction *U.S.A.* 63°19N 142°36W **303** E12
Tetlin Nat. Wildlife Refuge △
U.S.A. 62°40N 141°50W **303** E12
Teton ➜ *U.S.A.* 47°56N 110°31W **304** C8
Tétouan *Morocco* 35°35N 5°21W **260** A3
Tétouan □ *Morocco* 35°35N 5°30W **260** A3
Tetovo *Macedonia* 42°1N 20°59E **202** D4
Tetschen = Děčín
Czech Rep. 50°47N 14°12E **180** A7
Tetuán *Spain* 40°27N 3°42W **127** B1
Tetufera, Mt. *Tahiti* 17°40S 149°26W **289** e
Tetyukhe = Dalnegorsk
Russia 44°32N 135°33E **220** B7
Tetyushi *Russia* 54°55N 48°49E **190** C9
Teuco ➜ *Argentina* 25°35S 60°11W **334** B3
Teufelsberg *Germany* 52°29N 13°14E **115** B2
Teulada *Italy* 38°58N 8°46E **200** D1
Teulon *Canada* 50°23N 97°16W **297** C9
Teun *Indonesia* 6°59S 129°8E **231** F7
Teuri-Tō *Japan* 44°26N 141°19E **220** B10
Teutoburger Wald
Germany 52°5N 8°22E **178** C4
Teutopolis *U.S.A.* 39°8N 88°29W **311** E8
Tevere ➜ *Italy* 41°44N 12°14E **199** G9
Tevere △ *Italy* 42°46N 12°14E **199** F9
Teverya *Israel* 32°47N 35°32E **250** F6
Teviot ➜ *U.K.* 55°29N 2°38W **167** F6
Tewantin *Australia* 26°27S 153°3E **281** D5
Tewkesbury *U.K.* 51°59N 2°9W **169** F5
Texada I. *Canada* 49°40N 124°25W **296** D4
Texarkana *Ark., U.S.A.* 33°26N 94°2W **314** E7
Texarkana *Tex., U.S.A.* 33°26N 94°3W **314** E7
Texas *Australia* 28°49S 151°9E **281** D5
Texas □ *U.S.A.* 31°40N 98°30W **314** F5
Texas City *U.S.A.* 29°24N 94°54W **314** G7
Texel *Neths.* 53°5N 4°50E **170** A4
Texline *U.S.A.* 36°23N 103°2W **314** C3
Texoma, L. *U.S.A.* 33°50N 96°34W **314** E6
Teykovo *Russia* 56°55N 40°30E **188** D11
Teyvareh *Afghan.* 33°30N 64°24E **240** B2
Teza ➜ *Russia* 56°32N 41°53E **190** B5
Tezin *Afghan.* 34°24N 69°30E **242** B3
Teziutlán *Mexico* 19°49N 97°21W **319** D5
Tezpur *India* 26°40N 92°45E **241** B4
Tezzeron L. *Canada* 54°43N 124°30W **296** C4
Tha-anne ➜ *Canada* 60°31N 94°37W **297** A10
Tha Deua *Laos* 17°57N 102°53E **236** D4
Tha Deua *Laos* 19°26N 101°50E **236** C3
Tha Pla *Thailand* 17°48N 100°32E **236** D3
Tha Rua *Thailand* 14°34N 100°44E **236** E3
Tha Sala *Thailand* 8°40N 99°56E **237** H2
Tha Song Yang *Thailand* 17°34N 97°55E **236** D1
Thaba Putsoa *Lesotho* 29°45S 28°0E **271** C4
Thabana Ntlenyana
Lesotho 29°30S 29°16E **271** C4
Thabaung *Burma* 17°2N 94°48E **241** G5
Thabazimbi *S. Africa* 24°40S 27°21E **271** B4
Thabeikkyin *Burma* 22°53N 95°59E **241** D5
Thabt, G. el *Egypt* 28°17N 34°1E **251** K5
Thādiq *Si. Arabia* 25°18N 45°52E **246** E5
Thai Binh *Vietnam* 20°35N 106°1E **228** G6
Thai Muang *Thailand* 8°24N 98°16E **237** H2
Thai Nguyen *Vietnam* 21°35N 105°55E **228** G5
Thailand ■ *Asia* 16°0N 102°0E **236** E4
Thailand, G. of *Asia* 11°30N 101°0E **237** G3
Thakhek *Laos* 17°25N 104°45E **236** D5
Thakurgaon *Bangla.* 26°2N 88°34E **241** B2
Thal *Pakistan* 33°28N 70°33E **242** C4
Thal Desert *Pakistan* 31°10N 71°30E **242** D4
Thala *Tunisia* 35°35N 8°40E **258** A1
Thala La = Hkakabo Razi
Burma 28°25N 97°23E **241** B6
Thalabarivat *Cambodia* 13°33N 105°57E **236** F5
Thalkirchen *Germany* 48°6N 11°32E **131** B2
Thallon *Australia* 28°39S 148°49E **281** D4
Thalu, Ko *Thailand* 9°26N 99°54E **237** b
Thalwil *Switz.* 47°17N 8°35E **179** H4
Thamarīt *Oman* 17°39N 54°2E **249** C6
Thames *N.Z.* 37°7S 175°34E **284** D4
Thames ➜ *Ont., Canada* 42°20N 82°25W **312** D2
Thames ➜ *U.K.* 51°29N 0°34E **169** F8
Thames ➜ *Conn., U.S.A.* 41°18N 72°5W **313** E12
Thames, Firth of *N.Z.* 37°0S 175°25E **284** D4
Thames Ditton *U.K.* 51°23N 0°20W **125** B1
Thames Estuary *U.K.* 51°29N 0°52E **169** F8
Thamesford *Canada* 43°4N 81°0W **312** C4
Thamesmead *U.K.* 51°30N 0°7E **125** A4
Thamesville *Canada* 42°33N 81°59W **312** D3
Thāmit, W. ➜ *Libya* 31°11N 16°8E **258** B3
Thamūd *Yemen* 17°18N 49°55E **249** C5
Than *India* 22°34N 71°11E **242** H4
Than Uyen *Vietnam* 22°0N 103°54E **236** B4
Thana Cr. ➜ *India* 19°4N 72°54E **130** c2
Thana Gazi *India* 27°25N 76°19E **242** F7
Thanbyuzayat *Burma* 15°58N 97°44E **241** G6
Thandaung *Burma* 19°4N 96°41E **241** F6
Thandla *India* 23°0N 74°34E **242** H6
Thandwe *Burma* 18°20N 94°30E **241** F5
Thane *India* 19°12N 72°59E **244** E1
Thanesar *India* 30°1N 76°52E **242** D7
Thanet, I. of *U.K.* 51°21N 1°20E **169** F9
Thangool *Australia* 24°38S 150°42E **280** C5
Thanh Hoa *Vietnam* 19°48N 105°46E **236** C5
Thanh Hung *Vietnam* 9°55N 105°43E **237** H5
Thanh Pho Ho Chi Minh
Vietnam 10°58N 106°40E **237** G6
Thanh Thuy *Vietnam* 22°55N 104°51E **236** A5
Thanjavur *India* 10°48N 79°12E **245** J4
Thann *France* 47°48N 7°5E **173** E14
Thano Bula Khan
Pakistan 25°22N 67°50E **242** G2
Thaolintoa L. *Canada* 61°30N 96°25W **297** A9
Thaon-les-Vosges *France* 48°15N 6°24E **173** D13
Thap Lan △ *Thailand* 14°15N 102°16E **236** E4
Thap Sakae *Thailand* 11°30N 99°37E **237** G2
Thap Than *Thailand* 15°27N 99°54E **236** E2
Thar Desert *India* 28°0N 72°0E **242** F5
Tharad *India* 24°30N 71°44E **242** G4
Thargomindah *Australia* 27°58S 143°46E **281** D3
Tharp Fracture Zone
S. Ocean 54°0S 135°0W **151** B14
Tharrawaddy *Burma* 17°38N 95°48E **241** G5
Tharrawaw *Burma* 17°41N 95°28E **241** G5
Tharthār, Buḩayrat ath
Iraq 34°0N 43°15E **213** E10
Tharthar, L. = Tharthār, Buḩayrat ath *Iraq* 34°0N 43°15E **213** E10
Tharthār, W. ath ➜ *Iraq* 33°59N 43°12E **213** E10
Thasopoula *Greece* 40°49N 24°45E **203** F8
Thasos *Greece* 40°40N 24°40E **203** F8
That Khe *Vietnam* 22°16N 106°28E **228** F6
Thatcher *Ariz., U.S.A.* 32°51N 109°46W **305** K9
Thatcher *Colo., U.S.A.* 37°33N 104°7W **305** H11
Thaton *Burma* 16°55N 97°22E **241** G6
Thau, Bassin de *France* 43°23N 3°36E **174** E7
Thaungdut *Burma* 24°30N 94°40E **241** C5
Thawatti *Burma* 19°32N 96°16E **241** F6
Thayer *U.S.A.* 36°31N 91°33W **308** G8
Thayetmyo *Burma* 19°20N 95°10E **241** F5
Thazi *Magwe, Burma* 19°59N 95°3E **241** F5
Thazi *Mandalay, Burma* 21°0N 96°5E **241** E6
The Broads *U.K.* 52°45N 1°30E **168** E9
The Everglades *U.S.A.* 25°50N 81°0W **317** K9
The Gulf = Persian Gulf
Asia 27°0N 50°0E **247** E6
The Hague = 's-Gravenhage
Neths. 52°7N 4°17E **170** B4
The Pas *Canada* 53°45N 101°15W **297** C8
The Wash *U.K.* 52°58N 0°20E **168** E8
The Weald *U.K.* 51°4N 0°20E **169** F8
Theater Carré *Amsterdam, Neths.* **112** b2
Thebes = Thiva *Greece* 38°19N 23°19E **204** C5
Thebes *Egypt* 25°40N 32°35E **256** B3
Thedaw *Burma* 21°2N 96°4E **241** E6
Thedford *U.S.A.* 41°59N 100°35W **308** E3
Theebine *Australia* 25°57S 152°34E **281** D5
Thègon *Burma* 18°39N 95°25E **241** F5
Thekulthili L. *Canada* 61°3N 110°0W **297** A7
Thelon ➜ *Canada* 64°16N 96°4W **297** A8
Thénezay *France* 46°44N 0°2W **172** F6
Thenon *France* 45°9N 1°4E **174** C5
Theodore *Queens.,*
Australia 24°55S 150°3E **280** C5
Theodore *Sask., Canada* 51°26N 102°55W **297** C8
Theodore *Ala., U.S.A.* 30°33N 88°10W **315** F10
Theodore Roosevelt △
U.S.A. 47°0N 103°25W **308** B2
Theodore Roosevelt L.
U.S.A. 33°40N 111°10W **305** K8
Thepha *Thailand* 6°52N 100°58E **237** J3
Thérain ➜ *France* 49°15N 2°27E **173** C9
Theresa *U.S.A.* 44°13N 75°48W **313** B9
Theressa I. *U.S.A.* 29°50N 82°4W **316** F7
Therma = Eagle Nest
U.S.A. 36°33N 105°16W **305** H11
Thermopolis *U.S.A.* 43°39N 108°13W **304** E9
Thermopylae *Greece* 38°48N 22°35E **204** C4
Thesprotia □ *Greece* 39°27N 20°22E **204** B2
Thessalon *Canada* 46°20N 83°30W **298** C3
Thessaloniki *Greece* 40°38N 22°58E **202** F6
Thessaloniki □ *Greece* 40°45N 23°0E **202** F7
Thessaloniki ✈ (SKG)
Greece 40°30N 23°0E **202** F7
Thessaloniki, Gulf of = Thessaloniki Kolpos
Greece 40°15N 22°45E **202** F6
Thessaloniki Kolpos
Greece 40°15N 22°45E **202** F6
Thessaly □ *Greece* 39°25N 22°0E **204** B4
Thetford *U.K.* 52°25N 0°45E **169** E8
Thetford Mines *Canada* 46°8N 71°18W **299** C5
Theun ➜ *Laos* 18°19N 104°0E **236** C5
Theunissen *S. Africa* 28°26S 26°43E **270** C4
Thevenard *Australia* 32°9S 133°38E **281** E1
Thiais *France* 48°46N 2°23E **134** B3
Thiamis ➜ *Greece* 39°15N 20°6E **204** B2
Thibodaux *U.S.A.* 29°48N 90°49W **315** G9
Thibaud *Dominica* 15°36N 61°24W **323** k
Thiberville *France* 49°8N 0°27E **172** C7
Thicket Portage *Canada* 55°19N 97°42W **297** B9
Thief River Falls *U.S.A.* 48°7N 96°10W **308** A5
Thiel Mts. *Antarctica* 85°15S 91°0W **151** E16
Thiene *Italy* 45°42N 11°29E **199** C8
Thiérache *France* 49°51N 3°45E **173** C10
Thiers *France* 45°52N 3°33E **174** C7
Thiès *Senegal* 14°50N 16°51W **262** C1
Thiès □ *Senegal* 14°45N 16°50W **262** C1
Thiesi *Italy* 40°31N 8°43E **200** B1
Thiet *Sudan* 7°37N 28°49E **257** F2
Thika *Kenya* 1°1S 37°5E **268** C4
Thille-Boubacar *Senegal* 16°31N 15°5W **262** B1
Thimân, W. ➜ *Egypt* 28°4N 33°45E **251** K4
Thimphu *Bhutan* 27°31N 89°45E **241** B2
Thina ➜ *S. Africa* 31°18S 29°13E **271** D4
Thinadhoo *Maldives* 0°32N 72°56E **272** d
Thingangyun *Burma* 16°49N 96°12E **241** G6
Þingeyjarsýsla □
Iceland 65°40N 16°30W **155** B10
Þingeyri *Iceland* 65°52N 23°30W **155** B3
Þingmúli *Iceland* 65°2N 14°37W **155** B12
Þingvallavatn *Iceland* 64°11N 21°9W **155** C5
Þingvellir *Iceland* 64°15N 21°7W **155** C5
Þingvellir △ *Iceland* 64°16N 21°5W **155** C5
Thio *N. Cal.* 21°37S 166°14E **288** d
Thionville *France* 49°20N 6°10E **173** C13
Thira = Santorini *Greece* 36°23N 25°27E **205** E7
Thirasia *Greece* 36°26N 25°21E **205** E7
Third Cataract *Sudan* 19°42N 30°20E **256** D3
Thirsk *U.K.* 54°14N 1°19W **168** C6
Thiruvananthapuram = Trivandrum *India* 8°41N 77°0E **245** K3
Thiruvarur *India* 10°46N 79°38E **245** J4
Thisio *Athens, Greece* **112** c1
Thisted *Denmark* 56°58N 8°40E **163** H2
Þistilfjörður *Iceland* 66°18N 15°24W **155** A11
Thistle I. *Australia* 35°0S 136°8E **282** C2
Thistletown *Canada* 43°44N 79°34W **141** A1
Thitgy *Burma* 18°15N 96°13E **241** F6
Thithia = Cicia *Fiji* 17°45S 179°18W **287** A3
Thitpokpin *Burma* 19°24N 95°58E **241** F5
Thiva *Greece* 38°19N 23°19E **204** C5
Thiviers *France* 45°25N 0°54E **174** C4
Thizy *France* 46°2N 4°18E **173** F11
Þjórsá ➜ *Iceland* 63°47N 20°48W **155** D6
Thlewiaza ➜ *Canada* 60°29N 94°40W **297** A10
Thnuak Pouk *Cambodia* 13°57N 103°4E **236** F4
Tho Vinh *Vietnam* 19°16N 105°42E **236** C5
Thoa ➜ *Canada* 60°31N 109°47W **297** A7
Thoen *Thailand* 17°43N 99°12E **236** D2
Thoeng *Thailand* 19°41N 100°12E **236** C3
Tholdi *Pakistan* 35°5N 76°6E **243** B7
Thomas *U.S.A.* 35°45N 98°45W **314** D5
Thomas, L. *Australia* 26°4S 137°58E **281** D2
Thomas Circle *Washington, D.C., U.S.A.* **143** a1
Thomas Hill Res. *U.S.A.* 39°34N 92°39W **310** E4
Thomaston *U.S.A.* 32°53N 84°20W **316** C5
Thomastown *Australia* 37°40S 145°2E **128** A2
Thomasville *Ala., U.S.A.* 31°55N 87°44W **315** F11
Thomasville *Ga., U.S.A.* 30°50N 83°59W **316** E6
Thomasville *N.C., U.S.A.* 35°53N 80°5W **315** D14
Thompson *Man., Canada* 55°45N 97°52W **297** B9
Thompson *Pa., U.S.A.* 41°52N 75°31W **313** E9
Thompson ➜ *B.C.,*
Canada 50°15N 121°24W **296** C4
Thompson ➜ *Mo.,*
U.S.A. 39°46N 93°37W **310** E3
Thompson Falls *U.S.A.* 47°36N 115°21W **304** C6
Thompson I. *U.S.A.* 42°19N 70°59W **116** B3
Thompson Pk. *U.S.A.* 41°0N 123°2W **304** F2
Thompson Sd. *N.Z.* 45°8S 166°46E **285** F1
Thompson Springs
U.S.A. 38°58N 109°43W **304** G9
Thompsontown *U.S.A.* 40°33N 77°14W **312** F7
Thomson *Ga., U.S.A.* 33°28N 82°30W **316** B7
Thomson *Ill., U.S.A.* 41°58N 90°6W **310** C6
Thomson ➜ *Australia* 25°11S 142°53E **280** C3
Thomson's Falls = Nyahururu
Kenya 0°2N 36°27E **268** B4
Thon Buri *Thailand* 13°45N 100°29E **138** C1
Thônes *France* 45°54N 6°18E **175** C10
Thong Yang *Thailand* 9°28N 99°56E **237** b
Thongwa *Burma* 16°45N 96°33E **241** G6
Thonon-les-Bains *France* 46°22N 6°29E **173** F13
Thonze *Burma* 17°38N 95°47E **241** G5
Thorez *Ukraine* 48°4N 38°34E **189** H10
Þórisjökull *Iceland* 64°32N 20°43W **155** C6
Þórisvatn *Iceland* 64°20N 18°55W **155** D8
Þórkötlustaðir *Iceland* 63°50N 22°24W **155** D4
Þorlákshöfn *Iceland* 63°51N 21°22W **155** D5
Thorn = Toruń *Poland* 53°2N 18°39E **185** E5
Thornaby on Tees *U.K.* 54°33N 1°18W **168** C6
Thornbury *Vic., Australia* 37°44S 145°1E **128** A2
Thornbury *Ont., Canada* 44°34N 80°26W **312** B4
Thornbury *N.Z.* 46°17S 168°9E **285** G3
Thorncliffe *Canada* 43°42N 79°20W **141** A2
Thorne *U.K.* 53°37N 0°57W **168** D7
Thornhill *Canada* 54°31N 128°32W **296** C3
Thornhill *Ont., Canada* 43°48N 79°25W **141** A2
Thornton *Western Cape,*
S. Africa 33°55S 18°32E **118** A2
Thornton *Colo., U.S.A.* 39°52N 104°58W **304** G11
Thornton *Iowa, U.S.A.* 42°57N 93°23W **310** B3
Thornton-Beresfield
Australia 32°50S 151°40E **283** B9
Thornton Heath *U.K.* 51°23N 0°6W **125** B3
Thorntown *U.S.A.* 40°8N 86°36W **311** D10
Thorold *Canada* 43°7N 79°12W **312** C5
Thorpes *Barbados* 13°9N 59°37W **323** r
Þórshöfn *Iceland* 66°12N 15°20W **155** A11
Thouarcé *France* 47°17N 0°30W **172** E6
Thouars *France* 47°0N 0°15W **172** F6
Thouet ➜ *France* 47°17N 0°6W **172** E6
Thouin, C. *Australia* 20°20S 118°10E **278** D2
Thousand Oaks *U.S.A.* 34°10N 118°50W **307** L8
Thrace *Turkey* 41°0N 27°0E **203** F10
Thrace, Sea of *Greece* 40°30N 25°0E **203** F8
Thredbo *Australia* 36°31S 148°20E **283** D8
Three Forks *U.S.A.* 45°54N 111°33W **304** D8
Three Gorges Dam
China 30°45N 111°15E **229** B8
Three Hills *Canada* 51°43N 113°15W **296** C6
Three Hummock I.
Australia 40°25S 144°55E **281** G3
Three Oaks *U.S.A.* 41°48N 86°36W **311** C10
Three Pagodas Pass *Asia* 15°20N 98°30E **236** E2
Three Points, C. *Ghana* 4°42N 2°6W **262** E4
Three Rivers *Calif.,*
U.S.A. 36°26N 118°54W **306** J8
Three Rivers *Mich.,*
U.S.A. 41°57N 85°38W **311** C11
Three Rivers *Tex., U.S.A.* 28°28N 98°11W **314** G5
Three Sisters Is.
Solomon Is. 10°10S 161°57E **287** N11
Three Springs *Australia* 29°32S 115°45E **279** E2
Threipmuir Res. *U.K.* 55°51N 3°19W **121** B2
Throgs Neck *U.S.A.* 40°48N 73°49W **132** B3
Throssell, L. *Australia* 27°33S 124°10E **279** E3
Throssell Ra. *Australia* 22°3S 121°43E **278** D3
Thrumshing △ *Bhutan* 27°25N 90°50E **241** B3
Thrushton △ *Australia* 27°47S 147°40E **281** D4
Thua ➜ *Kenya* 1°31S 39°30E **268** C4
Thuamal Rampur *India* 19°23N 82°56E **244** E6
Thuan Hoa *Vietnam* 8°58N 105°30E **237** H5
Thubun Lakes *Canada* 61°30N 112°0W **297** A6
Thueyts *France* 44°41N 4°9E **175** D8
Thuin *Belgium* 50°20N 4°17E **170** D4
Thuir *France* 42°38N 2°45E **174** F6
Thule = Qaanaaq
Greenland 77°40N 69°0W **154** B4
Thule Air Base = Uummannaq
Greenland 77°28N 69°13W **154** B4
Thun *Switz.* 46°45N 7°38E **179** J3
Thunder B. *U.S.A.* 45°0N 83°20W **312** B1
Thunder Bay *Canada* 48°20N 89°15W **298** C2
Thunderbolt *U.S.A.* 32°3N 81°4W **316** C8
Thunersee *Switz.* 46°43N 7°39E **179** J3
Thung Salaeng Luang △
Thailand 16°43N 100°50E **236** D3
Thung Song *Thailand* 8°10N 99°40E **237** H2
Thunkar *Bhutan* 27°55N 91°0E **241** B3
Thuong Tra *Vietnam* 16°2N 107°42E **236** D6
Thur ➜ *Switz.* 47°32N 9°10E **179** H5
Thurgau □ *Switz.* 47°34N 9°10E **179** H5
Thüringen □ *Germany* 51°0N 11°0E **178** D6
Thüringer Wald *Germany* 50°35N 11°0E **178** E6
Thurles *Ireland* 52°41N 7°49W **166** D4
Thurn P. *Austria* 47°20N 12°25E **180** D5
Thurrock □ *U.K.* 51°31N 0°23E **169** F8
Thursday I. *Australia* 10°30S 142°3E **286** F2
Thurso *Qué., Canada* 45°36N 75°15W **298** C4
Thurso *Highl., U.K.* 58°36N 3°32W **167** C5
Thurso ➜ *U.K.* 58°36N 3°32W **167** C5
Thurston I. *Antarctica* 72°0S 100°0W **151** D16
Thury-Harcourt *France* 48°59N 0°30W **172** D6
Thutade L. *Canada* 57°0N 126°55W **296** B3
Thy *Denmark* 56°52N 8°25E **163** H2
Thyborøn *Denmark* 56°42N 8°12E **163** H2
Þykkvabæjarklaustur
Iceland 63°30N 18°22W **155** D8
Þykkvibær *Iceland* 63°45N 20°37W **155** D6
Thyolo *Malawi* 16°7S 35°5E **269** F4
Thyssen-Bornemisza, Museo
Madrid, Spain **127** b3
Ti-n-Amzi ➜ *Niger* 18°20N 4°32E **263** B5
Ti-n-Barraouene, O. ➜
Africa 18°40N 4°5E **261** E5
Ti-n-Rerhoh *Algeria* 20°44N 4°2E **261** D5
Ti-n-Tanetfirt *Algeria* 24°49N 3°48E **261** D5
Ti-n-Tarabine, O. ➜
Algeria 21°16N 7°25E **261** D6
Ti-n-Toumma *Niger* 16°4N 12°40E **259** E2
Ti-n-Zaouatene *Algeria* 19°55N 2°55E **261** E5
Ti-Tree *Australia* 22°5S 133°22E **280** C1
Tiadiaye *Senegal* 14°25N 16°40W **262** C1
Tiahuanacu *Bolivia* 16°33S 68°42W **330** D4
Tian Shan *Asia* 40°30N 76°0E **217** D9
Tian'anmen Square
China 39°53N 116°21E **114** B2
Tianchang *China* 32°40N 119°0E **229** A12
Tiancun *China* 39°54N 116°12E **114** B1
Tiandeng *China* 23°6N 107°7E **228** F6
Tiandong *China* 23°36N 107°8E **228** F6
Tian'e *China* 25°1N 107°9E **228** E6
Tianguá *Brazil* 3°44S 40°59W **332** B3
Tianhe *China* 24°48N 108°40E **228** E7
Tianjin *China* 39°7N 117°12E **227** E9
Tiankoura *Burkina Faso* 10°47N 3°17W **262** C4
Tianlin *China* 24°21N 106°12E **228** E6
Tianmen *China* 30°39N 113°9E **229** B9
Tianquan *China* 30°7N 102°43E **228** B4
Tianshifu *China* 41°17N 124°22E **227** D13
Tianshui *China* 34°32N 105°40E **226** G3
Tiantai *China* 29°10N 121°2E **229** C13
Tiantan Park *Beijing, China* **114** c2
Tianyang *China* 23°42N 106°53E **228** F6
Tianyar *Indonesia* 8°12S 115°30E **231** J18
Tianzhen *China* 40°24N 114°5E **226** D8
Tianzhu *China* 26°54N 109°11E **228** D7
Tianzhuangtai *China* 40°43N 122°5E **227** D12
Tiarei *Tahiti* 17°32S 149°20W **289** e
Tiaret *Algeria* 35°20N 1°21E **261** A5
Tiaret □ *Algeria* 34°30N 1°30E **261** B5
Tias *Canary Is.* 28°57N 13°39W **153** e2
Tiassalé *Ivory C.* 5°58N 4°57W **262** D4
Tibagi *Brazil* 24°30S 50°24W **335** A5
Tibagi ➜ *Brazil* 22°47S 51°1W **335** A5
Tibasti, Sarir *Libya* 22°50N 18°30E **258** C3
Tibati *Cameroon* 6°22N 12°30E **263** D7
Tibe *Ethiopia* 9°2N 37°12E **257** F4
Tiber = Tevere ➜ *Italy* 41°44N 12°14E **199** G9
Tiber Res. *U.S.A.* 48°19N 111°6W **304** B8
Tiberias = Teverya *Israel* 32°47N 35°32E **250** F6
Tiberias, L. = Yam Kinneret
Israel 32°45N 35°35E **250** F6
Tibesti *Chad* 21°0N 17°30E **259** D3
Tibet = Xizang Zizhiqu □
China 32°0N 88°0E **217** F11
Tibet, L. *U.S.A.* 28°27N 81°31W **133** B1
Tibet, Plateau of *Asia* 32°0N 86°0E **210** E10
Tibiao *Phil.* 11°17N 122°2E **233** F4
Tibidabo *Spain* 41°25N 2°6E **114** A1
Tibiri *Niger* 13°34N 7°4E **263** C6
Țibleș, Vf. *Romania* 47°32N 24°15E **183** C9
Țibleșului, Munții
Romania 47°38N 24°5E **183** C9
Tibnī *Syria* 35°36N 39°50E **213** E8
Tibooburra *Australia* 29°26S 142°1E **281** D3
Tibradden Mt. *Ireland* 53°15N 6°16W **120** B2
Tibro *Sweden* 58°28N 14°10E **163** F8
Tibugá, G. de *Colombia* 5°45N 77°20W **328** B2
Tiburon *U.S.A.* 37°52N 122°27W **136** A2
Tiburón, I. *Mexico* 29°0N 112°25W **318** B2
Tiburtino *Italy* 41°53N 12°30E **136** B2
Ticao I. *Phil.* 12°31N 123°42E **232** E4
Tice *U.S.A.* 26°40N 81°49W **317** J8
Tichit *Mauritania* 18°21N 9°29W **262** B3
Tichla *Mauritania* 21°36N 14°58W **260** D2
Ticho *Ethiopia* 7°50N 39°32E **257** F4
Ticino □ *Switz.* 46°20N 8°45E **179** J4
Ticino ➜ *Italy* 45°9N 9°14E **179** J4
Ticleni *Romania* 44°53N 23°24E **183** F8
Ticomán *Mexico* 19°31N 99°8W **128** A2
Ticonderoga *U.S.A.* 43°51N 73°26W **313** C11
Ticul *Mexico* 20°24N 89°32W **319** C7
Tidaholm *Sweden* 58°12N 13°58E **163** F7
Tidal Basin *Washington, D.C., U.S.A.* **143** c1
Tidan *Sweden* 58°34N 14°1E **163** F8
Tiddim *Burma* 23°28N 93°45E **241** D4
Tiden *India* 7°15N 93°33E **245** L11
Tideridjaouine, Adrar
Algeria 23°0N 2°15E **261** D5
Tidikelt *Algeria* 26°58N 1°30E **261** C5
Tidioute *U.S.A.* 41°41N 79°24W **312** E5
Tidjikja *Mauritania* 18°29N 11°35W **262** B2
Tidmore = Seminole
U.S.A. 35°14N 96°41W **314** D6
Tidore *Indonesia* 0°40N 127°25E **231** D7
Tiébissou *Ivory C.* 7°9N 5°10W **262** D3
Tiéboro *Chad* 21°20N 17°7E **259** D3
Tiefa *China* 42°28N 123°26E **224** A1
Tiefersee *Germany* 52°24N 13°5E **115** B1
Tiegang Shuiku *China* 22°37N 113°53E **219** F10
Tiejiangyin *China* 39°49N 116°23E **114** C2
Tiel *Neths.* 51°53N 5°26E **170** C5
Tiel *Senegal* 14°55N 15°5W **262** C1
Tieling *China* 42°20N 123°55E **224** A1
Tielt *Belgium* 51°0N 3°20E **170** C3
Tien Shan = Tian Shan
Asia 40°30N 76°0E **217** D9
Tien-tsin = Tianjin *China* 39°7N 117°12E **227** E9
Tien Yen *Vietnam* 21°20N 107°24E **236** B6
T'ienching = Tianjin
China 39°7N 117°12E **227** E9
T'ienchung *Taiwan* 23°52N 120°35E **225** C2
Tienen *Belgium* 50°48N 4°57E **170** D4
Tiénigbé *Ivory C.* 8°11N 5°43W **262** D3
Tientsin = Tianjin *China* 39°7N 117°12E **227** E9
Tiergarten *Germany* 52°31N 13°21E **115** A3
Tieri *Australia* 23°2S 148°21E **280** C4
Tieroko, Tarso *Chad* 20°45N 17°52E **259** D3
Tierp *Sweden* 60°20N 17°30E **162** D11
Tierra Amarilla *Chile* 27°28S 70°18W **334** B1
Tierra Amarilla *N. Mex.,*
U.S.A. 36°42N 106°33W **305** H10
Tierra Colorada *Mexico* 17°11N 99°32W **319** D5
Tierra de Barros *Spain* 38°40N 6°30W **195** G4
Tierra de Campos *Spain* 42°10N 4°50W **194** C6
Tierra del Fuego □
Argentina 54°0S 67°45W **336** D3
Tierra del Fuego, I. Gr. de
Argentina 54°0S 69°0W **336** D3
Tierra del Fuego △
Argentina 54°50S 68°23W **336** D3
Tierralta *Colombia* 8°11N 76°4W **328** B2
Tiétar ➜ *Spain* 39°50N 6°1W **194** F4
Tieté ➜ *Brazil* 20°40S 51°35W **335** A5
Tifarati *W. Sahara* 26°9N 10°33W **260** C2
Tiffin *U.S.A.* 41°7N 83°11W **311** C13
Tiffin ➜ *U.S.A.* 41°17N 84°23W **311** C12
Tiflèt *Morocco* 33°54N 6°20W **260** B3
Tiflis = Tbilisi *Georgia* 41°43N 44°50E **191** K7
Tifton *U.S.A.* 31°27N 83°31W **316** D6
Tifu *Indonesia* 3°39S 126°24E **231** E7
Tiga, Î. *N. Cal.* 21°7S 167°49E **288** d
Tigalda I. *U.S.A.* 54°6N 165°5W **303** J6
Tigaon *Phil.* 13°38N 123°30E **232** E4
Tigbauan *Phil.* 10°41N 122°27E **233** F4
Tighina *Moldova* 46°50N 29°30E **183** D14
Tigil *Russia* 57°49N 158°40E **215** D16
Tigiria *India* 20°29N 85°31E **244** D7
Tignall *U.S.A.* 33°52N 82°44W **316** B7
Tignish *Canada* 46°58N 64°2W **299** C7
Tigray □ *Ethiopia* 13°35N 39°15E **257** E4
Tigre ➜ *Peru* 4°30S 74°10W **328** D3
Tigre ➜ *Venezuela* 9°20N 62°30W **329** B5
Tigris = Dijlah, Nahr ➜
Asia 31°0N 47°25E **246** D5
Tiguentourine *Algeria* 27°52N 9°8E **261** C6
Tigveni *Romania* 45°10N 24°31E **183** E9
Tigyaing *Burma* 23°45N 96°10E **241** D6
Tigzerte, O. ➜ *Morocco* 28°10N 9°37W **260** C3
Tih, Gebel el *Egypt* 29°32N 33°26E **256** B3
Tihodaine, Erg de *Algeria* 25°15N 7°15E **261** C6
Tihwa = Ürümqi *China* 43°45N 87°45E **217** D11
Tijara *India* 27°56N 76°31E **242** F7
Tijgerhof *S. Africa* 33°53S 18°30E **118** A2
Tiji *Libya* 32°0N 11°18E **258** B2
Tijuana *Mexico* 32°32N 117°1W **307** N9
Tijuca *Brazil* 22°56S 43°13W **135** B1
Tijuca, Pico da *Brazil* 22°56S 43°15W **135** B1
Tijuca △ *Brazil* 22°56S 43°15W **135** B1
Tikahau *French Polynesia* 15°0S 148°10W **289** f
Tikal *Guatemala* 17°13N 89°24W **320** C2
Tikamgarh *India* 24°44N 78°50E **243** G8
Tikaré *Burkina Faso* 13°15N 1°43W **263** C4
Tikchik Lakes *U.S.A.* 60°0N 159°0W **303** G8
Tikéi *French Polynesia* 14°58S 144°32W **289** f
Tikhonkaya = Birobidzhan
Russia 48°50N 132°50E **215** E14
Tikhoretsk *Russia* 45°56N 40°5E **191** H5
Tikhvin *Russia* 59°35N 33°30E **188** C7
Tikirarjuaq = Whale Cove
Canada 62°10N 92°34W **297** A10
Tikkadouine, Adrar
Algeria 24°28N 1°30E **261** D5
Tikkurila *Finland* 60°17N 25°2E **121** B3
Tiko *Cameroon* 4°4N 9°20E **263** E6
Tikopia *Pac. Oc.* 12°19S 168°49E **277** C12
Tikrit *Iraq* 34°35N 43°37E **213** E10
Tiksi *Russia* 71°40N 128°45E **215** B13
Tiladummati Atoll *Maldives* 7°0N 73°20E **272** d
Tilak Nagar *India* 28°38N 77°5E **120** B1
Tilamuta *Indonesia* 0°32N 122°23E **231** D6
Tilanqiao *China* 31°15N 121°29E **138** B1
Tilburg *Neths.* 51°31N 5°6E **170** C5
Tilbury *Ont., Canada* 42°17N 82°23W **312** D2
Tilbury *Essex, U.K.* 51°27N 0°22E **169** F8
Tilcara *Argentina* 23°36S 65°23W **334** A2
Tilden *U.S.A.* 42°3N 97°50W **308** D5
Tilemses *Niger* 15°37N 4°44E **263** B5
Tilemsi, Vallée du *Mali* 17°42N 0°15E **263** B5

Tilhar India 28°0N 79°45E 243 F8
Tilia, O. → Algeria 27°32N 0°55E 261 C5
Tilichiki Russia 60°27N 166°5E 215 C17
Tililane Algeria 27°49N 0°6W 261 C4
Tilin Burma 21°41N 94°6E 241 E5
Tilissos Greece 35°20N 25°1E 207 E6
Till → U.K. 55°41N 2°13W 168 B5
Tillabéri Niger 14°28N 1°28E 263 C5
Tillamook U.S.A. 45°27N 123°51W 304 D2
Tillanchong I. India 8°30N 93°37E 245 K11
Tillberga Sweden 59°40N 16°39E 162 E10
Tillia Niger 16°8N 4°47E 263 B5
Tillman U.S.A. 32°28N 81°6W 316 C8
Tillsonburg Canada 42°53N 80°44W 312 D4
Tillyeria Cyprus 35°6N 32°40E 207 E8
Tilogne Senegal 16°0N 13°40W 262 B2
Tilos Greece 36°27N 27°27E 205 E9
Tilpa Australia 30°57S 144°24E 282 A6
Tilrhemt Algeria 33°9N 3°22E 261 B5
Tilsit = Sovetsk Russia 55°6N 21°50E 184 C8
Tilt → U.K. 56°46N 3°51W 167 E5
Tilton U.S.A. 43°27N 71°36W 313 C13
Tiltonsville U.S.A. 40°10N 80°41W 312 F4
Tim Denmark 56°12N 8°19E 163 H2
Timah, Bukit Singapore 1°21N 103°46E 138 A2
Timanah Asia 19°0N 41°0E 248 C3
Timanfaya △ Canary Is. 29°0N 13°46W 153 e2
Timanskiy Kryazh Russia 65°58N 50°5E 186 A9
Timaru N.Z. 44°23S 171°14E 285 E6
Timashevo Russia 53°22N 51°9E 190 D10
Timashevsk Russia 45°35N 39°0E 191 H4
Timau Kenya 0°4N 37°15E 268 B4
Timbaki Greece 35°4N 24°45E 207 E5
Timbaúba Brazil 7°31S 35°19W 332 C4
Timbedgha Mauritania 16°17N 8°16W 262 B3
Timber Creek Australia 15°40S 130°29E 278 C5
Timber Lake U.S.A. 45°26N 101°5W 308 C3
Timber Mt. U.S.A. 37°6N 116°28W 306 H10
Timbio Colombia 2°20N 76°40W 328 C2
Timbiqui Colombia 2°46N 77°42W 328 C2
Timbo Guinea 10°35N 11°50W 262 C2
Timbo Liberia 5°35N 9°45W 262 D3
Timboon Australia 38°30S 142°58E 282 E5
Timbuktu = Tombouctou Mali 16°50N 3°0W 262 B4
Timdjaouine Algeria 21°37N 4°30E 261 D5
Timeiaouine Algeria 20°27N 1°50E 261 D5
Timellouline Algeria 29°22N 8°55E 261 C6
Times Square New York, U.S.A. 132 c2
Timétrine, Mts. Mali 19°25N 1°0W 261 E4
Timfi Oros Greece 39°59N 20°45E 204 B2
Timfristos, Oros Greece 38°57N 21°50E 204 C3
Timhadit Morocco 33°15N 5°4W 260 B3
Timi Cyprus 34°44N 32°31E 207 F8
Tîmia Niger 18°4N 8°40E 259 E1
Timimoun Algeria 29°14N 0°16E 261 C5
Timimoun, Sebkha de Algeria 28°50N 0°46E 261 C5
Timiris, Râs Mauritania 19°21N 16°30W 262 B1
Timiryazev Park Russia 55°49N 37°33E 129 B3
Timiș = Tamis → Serbia 44°51N 20°39E 182 F5
Timiș □ Romania 45°40N 21°30E 182 E6
Timiskaming, L. = Témiscamingue, L. Canada 47°10N 79°25W 298 C4
Timișoara Romania 45°43N 21°15E 182 E6
Timmersdala Sweden 58°32N 13°46E 163 F7
Timmins Canada 48°28N 81°25W 298 C3
Timmonsville U.S.A. 34°8N 79°57W 316 A10
Timok → Serbia 44°10N 22°40E 202 B6
Timoleague Ireland 51°39N 8°46W 166 E3
Timon Brazil 5°8S 42°52W 332 C3
Timor Asia 9°0S 125°0E 231 F7
Timor Leste = East Timor ■ Asia 8°50S 126°0E 231 F7
Timor Sea Ind. Oc. 12°0S 127°0E 278 B4
Timrå Sweden 62°29N 17°18E 162 B11
Timucuan ⌂ U.S.A. 30°28N 81°27W 316 E8
Tin, Ra's at Libya 32°37N 23°8E 258 B4
Tin Alkoum Algeria 24°42N 10°17E 261 D7
Tin Amzi, O. → Algeria 18°20N 4°32E 261 D6
Tin Atanai Algeria 25°52N 1°37E 261 C5
Tin Can Bay Australia 25°56S 153°0E 281 D5
Tin Ethisane Mali 19°3N 0°52W 263 B4
Tin Gornai Mali 16°38N 0°38W 263 B4
Tin Mt. U.S.A. 36°50N 117°10W 306 J9
Tina = Thina → S. Africa 31°18S 29°13E 271 D4
Tina, Khalîg el Egypt 31°10N 32°40E 251 G3
Tinaca Pt. Phil. 5°30N 125°25E 233 J5
Tinaco Venezuela 9°42N 68°26W 328 B4
Tinajo Canary Is. 29°4N 13°42W 153 e2
Tinca Romania 46°46N 21°58E 182 D6
Tindal Australia 14°31S 132°22E 278 B5
Tindivanam India 12°15N 79°41E 245 H4
Tindouf Algeria 27°42N 8°10W 260 C3
Tindouf □ Algeria 27°25N 5°50W 260 C3
Tinée → France 43°55N 7°11E 175 E11
Tineo Spain 43°21N 6°27W 194 B4
Tinerhir Morocco 31°29N 5°31W 260 B3
Tinfouchi Algeria 28°52N 5°49W 260 C3
Tinfunque △ Paraguay 23°55S 60°17W 334 A3
Ting Jiang → China 24°45N 116°35E 229 E11
Ting Kau China 22°22N 114°4E 122 A1
Tinggi, Pulau Malaysia 2°18N 104°7E 237 L5
Tingkan Taiwan 23°48N 120°52E 225 C2
Tingkawk Sakan Burma 26°4N 96°44E 241 B6
Tinglayan Phil. 17°15N 121°9E 232 C3
Tinglev Denmark 54°57N 9°13E 163 K3
Tingmerkpuk Mt. U.S.A. 68°34N 162°28W 303 B7
Tingo Maria Peru 9°10S 75°54W 330 B2
Tingrela Ivory C. 10°27N 6°25W 262 C3
Tingsryd Sweden 56°31N 15°0E 163 H9
Tingstäde Sweden 57°44N 18°37E 163 G12
Tingvoll Norway 62°55N 8°12E 164 B5
Tingwon Group Papua N. G. 2°37S 149°42E 286 B5
Tinh Bien Vietnam 10°36N 104°57E 237 G5
Tinharé, I. de Brazil 13°30S 38°58W 333 D4
Tinian N. Marianas 15°0N 145°38E 302 e
Tinian Channel N. Marianas 14°54N 145°36E 302 e
Tinigua △ Colombia 2°30N 74°8W 328 C3
Tiniguiban Phil. 11°22N 119°30E 233 F2
Tinjar → Malaysia 4°4N 114°18E 235 B4
Tinn = Atrå Norway 59°59N 8°45E 164 E5
Tinnevelly = Tirunelveli India 8°45N 77°45E 245 K3
Tinnoset Norway 59°43N 9°3E 164 E6
Tinnsjå Norway 59°55N 8°54E 164 E5
Tinogasta Argentina 28°5S 67°32W 334 B2
Tinos Greece 37°33N 25°8E 205 D7
Tiñoso, C. Spain 37°32N 1°6W 197 H3
Tinpahar India 25°0N 87°44E 243 G12
Tinputz Papua N. G. 5°33S 155°0E 286 C8
Tinrhert, Plateau du Algeria 29°30N 9°0E 261 C6
Tinsukia India 27°29N 95°20E 241 B5
Tinta Peru 14°3S 71°20W 330 C3
Tintamarre, Île St.-Martin 18°7N 63°2W 322 a
Tintina Argentina 27°2S 62°45W 334 B3
Tintinara Australia 35°48S 140°2E 282 C4
Tintioulé Guinea 10°13N 9°12W 262 C3
Tinto → Spain 37°12N 6°55W 195 H4
Tinui N.Z. 40°52S 176°5E 284 G5
Tinwald N.Z. 43°55S 171°43E 285 D6
Tioga N. Dak., U.S.A. 48°24N 102°56W 308 A2
Tioga Pa., U.S.A. 41°55N 77°8W 312 E7
Tioman, Pulau Malaysia 2°50N 104°10E 237 L5
Tione di Trento Italy 46°2N 10°43E 198 B7
Tionesta U.S.A. 41°30N 79°28W 312 E5
Tior Sudan 6°26N 31°11E 257 F3
Tioulilin Algeria 27°1N 0°2W 261 C4
Tipaza Algeria 36°35N 2°26E 261 A5
Tipaza □ Algeria 36°35N 2°25E 261 A5
Tipp City U.S.A. 39°58N 84°11W 311 E12
Tippecanoe → U.S.A. 40°30N 86°45W 311 D10
Tipperary Ireland 52°28N 8°10W 166 D3
Tipperary □ Ireland 52°37N 7°55W 166 D4
Tipton Calif., U.S.A. 36°4N 119°19W 306 J7
Tipton Ind., U.S.A. 40°17N 86°2W 311 D10
Tipton Iowa, U.S.A. 41°46N 91°8W 310 C5
Tipton Mo., U.S.A. 38°39N 92°47W 310 F4
Tipton Mt. U.S.A. 35°32N 114°12W 307 K12
Tiptonville U.S.A. 36°23N 89°29W 315 C10
Tiptur India 13°15N 76°26E 245 H3
Tiquié → Brazil 0°5N 68°25W 328 C4
Tira West Bank 31°52N 35°7E 123 A1
Tiracambu, Serra do Brazil 3°15S 46°30W 332 B2
Tirahart, O. → Algeria 23°45N 3°10E 261 D5
Tīrān Iran 32°45N 51°8E 247 C6
Tīrān Si. Arabia 27°57N 34°32E 251 L5
Tiranë Albania 41°18N 19°49E 202 E3
Tiranë ✈ (TIA) Albania 41°57N 19°42E 202 E3
Tirano Italy 46°13N 10°10E 198 B7
Tirari Desert Australia 28°22S 138°7E 281 D2
Tiraspol Moldova 46°55N 29°35E 183 D14
Tiratimine Algeria 25°56N 3°37E 261 C5
Tirau N.Z. 37°58S 175°46E 284 D4
Tirdout Mali 16°7N 1°5W 263 B4
Tire Turkey 38°5N 27°45E 205 C9
Tirebolu Turkey 40°58N 38°45E 213 B8
Tiree U.K. 56°31N 6°55W 167 E2
Tiree, Passage of U.K. 56°30N 6°30W 167 E2
Târgoviște = Târgoviște Romania 44°55N 25°27E 183 F10
Tîrgu Jiu = Târgu Jiu Romania 45°5N 23°19E 183 E8
Tîrgu Mureș = Târgu Mureș Romania 46°31N 24°38E 183 D9
Tirgua △ Venezuela 10°5N 68°48W 328 A4
Tirich Mir Pakistan 36°15N 71°55E 240 A3
Tiriolo Italy 38°57N 16°30E 201 D9
Tiririca, Serra da Brazil 17°6S 47°6W 333 E2
Tiriro Guinea 10°27N 8°40W 262 C3
Tiris W. Sahara 23°10N 13°20W 260 D2
Tiris Zemmour □ Mauritania 24°0N 9°0W 260 D3
Tiritiri o te Moana = Southern Alps N.Z. 43°41S 170°11E 285 D5
Tirna → India 18°4N 76°57E 244 E3
Tîrnavos Greece 39°45N 22°18E 204 B4
Tirodi India 21°40N 79°44E 244 D4
Tirol □ Austria 47°3N 10°43E 180 D3
Tiros Brazil 19°0S 45°58W 333 E2
Tirrukkovil Sri Lanka 7°7N 81°51E 245 L5
Tirsa Egypt 29°57N 31°12E 117 B2
Tirschenreuth Germany 49°53N 12°19E 179 F8
Tirschtiegel = Trzciel Poland 52°23N 15°50E 185 F2
Tirso → Italy 39°53N 8°32E 200 C1
Tirstrup Denmark 56°18N 10°42E 163 H4
Tirthahalli India 13°42N 75°14E 245 H2
Tirua Pt. N.Z. 38°25S 174°40E 284 E3
Tiruchchendur India 8°30N 78°11E 245 K4
Tiruchchirappalli India 10°45N 78°45E 245 J4
Tirukkoyilur India 11°57N 79°12E 245 J4
Tirumangalam India 9°49N 77°58E 245 K3
Tirumayam India 10°14N 78°45E 245 J4
Tirunelveli India 8°45N 77°45E 245 K3
Tirupati India 13°39N 79°25E 245 H4
Tiruppattur Tamil Nadu, India 10°8N 78°37E 245 J4
Tiruppattur Tamil Nadu, India 12°30N 78°30E 245 H4
Tiruppur India 11°5N 77°22E 245 J3
Tirur India 10°54N 75°55E 245 J2
Tiruttani India 13°11N 79°58E 245 H4
Tirutturaippundi India 10°32N 79°41E 245 J4
Tiruvadamarudur India 11°2N 79°27E 245 J4
Tiruvalla India 9°23N 76°34E 245 K3
Tiruvallar India 13°9N 79°57E 245 H4
Tiruvannamalai India 12°15N 79°5E 245 H4
Tiruvettipuram India 12°39N 79°33E 245 H4
Tiruvottiyur India 13°10N 80°22E 245 H5
Tisa India 32°50N 76°9E 242 C7
Tisa → Serbia 45°15N 20°17E 182 E5
Tisdale Canada 52°50N 104°0W 297 C8
Tishomingo U.S.A. 34°14N 96°41W 314 D6
Tishrīyaa Iraq 33°18N 44°24E 113 B2
Tisjön Sweden 60°56N 13°0E 162 D7
Tisnaren Sweden 58°58N 15°56E 163 F9
Tišnov Czech Rep. 49°21N 16°25E 181 B9
Tisovec Slovak Rep. 48°41N 19°56E 181 C12
Tissamaharama Sri Lanka 6°17N 81°17E 245 L5
Tissān, Ḥasy Libya 28°14N 12°26E 261 C7
Tissemsilt Algeria 35°35N 1°50E 261 A5
Tissemsilt □ Algeria 35°45N 1°45E 261 A5
Tissint Morocco 29°57N 7°16W 260 C3
Tista → India 25°23N 89°43E 241 C2
Tistedal Norway 59°8N 11°27E 164 E8
Tisza = Tisa → Serbia 45°15N 20°17E 182 E5
Tiszaföldvár Hungary 46°58N 20°14E 182 D5
Tiszafüred Hungary 47°38N 20°50E 182 C5
Tiszalök Hungary 48°1N 21°20E 182 B6
Tiszavasvári Hungary 47°58N 21°18E 182 C6
Tit Ahaggar, Algeria 23°0N 5°10E 261 D6
Tit Tademait, Algeria 27°0N 1°29E 261 C5
Tit-Ary Russia 71°55N 127°2E 215 B13
Titabar India 26°36N 94°12E 241 B5
Titaguas Spain 39°53N 1°6W 196 F3
Titao Burkina Faso 13°45N 2°5W 263 C4
Titel Serbia 45°10N 20°18E 182 E5
Tithwal Pakistan 34°21N 73°50E 243 B5
Titicaca, L. S. Amer. 15°30S 69°30W 330 D4
Titikaveka Cook Is. 21°16S 159°45W 289 h
Titisee Germany 47°54N 8°10E 179 H4
Titiwa Nigeria 12°14N 12°53E 263 C7
Titlagarh India 20°15N 83°11E 244 D6
Titisee ...
Tito Italy 40°35N 15°40E 201 B8
Titograd = Podgorica Montenegro 42°30N 19°19E 202 D3
Titova Korenica Croatia 44°45N 15°41E 199 D12
Titu Romania 44°39N 25°32E 183 F10
Titule Dem. Rep. of the Congo 3°15N 25°31E 268 B2
Titusville Fla., U.S.A. 28°37N 80°49W 317 G9
Titusville Pa., U.S.A. 41°38N 79°41W 312 E5
Tiu Keng Leng China 22°18N 114°15E 122 B2
Tivaouane Senegal 14°56N 16°45W 262 C1
Tivat Montenegro 42°28N 18°43E 202 D2
Tivedens △ Sweden 58°45N 14°35E 163 F8
Tiverton U.K. 50°54N 3°29W 168 G4
Tivoli Grenada 12°10N 61°37W 323 q
Tivoli Italy 41°58N 12°45E 199 G9
Tiwī Oman 22°45N 59°12E 249 B7
Tiyo Eritrea 14°41N 40°15E 257 E5
Tizapán Mexico 19°19N 99°13W 128 C1
Tizga Morocco 32°1N 5°9W 260 B3
Ti'zi N'Isli Morocco 32°28N 5°47W 260 B3
Tizi-Ouzou Algeria 36°42N 4°3E 261 A5
Tizi-Ouzou □ Algeria 36°35N 4°15E 261 A5
Tizimín Mexico 21°9N 88°9W 319 C7
Tiznados → Venezuela 8°16N 67°47W 328 B4
Tizhang He → China 38°21N 77°26E 217 E9
Tiznit Morocco 29°48N 9°45W 260 C3
Tiznit □ Morocco 29°35N 9°30W 260 C3
Tjæreborg Denmark 55°28N 8°36E 163 J2
Tjällmo Sweden 58°43N 15°21E 163 F9
Tjeggelvas Sweden 66°37N 17°45E 160 C17
Tjieggelvas = Tjeggelvas Sweden 66°37N 17°45E 160 C17
Tjirebon = Cirebon Indonesia 6°45S 108°32E 235 D3
Tjluring Indonesia 8°25S 114°13E 231 J17
Tjøme Norway 59°8N 10°26E 164 E7
Tjörn Sweden 58°0N 11°35E 163 F5
Tkibuli = Tqibuli Georgia 42°26N 43°0E 191 J6
Tkvarcheli = Tqvarcheli Georgia 42°47N 41°42E 191 J5
Tlachichilpan Mexico 18°37N 95°40W 319 D5
Tlahualilo de Zaragoza Mexico 26°7N 103°27W 318 B4
Tlalnepantla → Mexico 19°30N 99°18W 128 A1
Tlalpan Mexico 19°18N 99°10W 128 C2
Tlaquepaque Mexico 20°39N 103°19W 318 C4
Tlaxcala Mexico 19°19N 98°14W 319 D5
Tlaxcala □ Mexico 19°25N 98°10W 319 D5
Tlaxiaco Mexico 17°25N 97°35W 319 D5
Tlemcen Algeria 34°52N 1°21W 261 B4
Tlemcen □ Algeria 34°38N 1°30W 261 B4
Tleta Sidi Bouguedra Morocco 32°16N 9°59W 260 B3
Tlumach Ukraine 48°51N 25°0E 183 B10
Tłuszcz Poland 52°25N 21°25E 185 F8
Tlyarata Russia 42°9N 46°26E 191 J8
Tmassah Libya 26°19N 15°51E 258 C3
Tnine d'Anglou Morocco 29°50N 9°50W 260 C3
To Bong Vietnam 12°45N 109°16E 236 F7
To Kwai Wan China 22°18N 114°11E 122 B2
To-Shima Japan 34°31N 139°17E 223 C11
Toa Payoh Singapore 1°20N 103°51E 138 A3
Toad → Canada 59°25N 124°57W 296 B4
Toad River Canada 58°51N 125°14W 296 B3
Toamasina Madag. 18°10S 49°25E 272 B2
Toamasina □ Madag. 18°0S 49°0E 272 B2
Toay Argentina 36°43S 64°38W 334 D3
Toba China 31°19N 97°42E 228 B1
Toba Japan 34°30N 136°51E 223 C8
Toba, Danau Indonesia 2°30N 97°30E 234 B1
Toba Kakar Pakistan 31°30N 69°0E 242 D3
Toba Tek Singh Pakistan 30°55N 72°25E 242 D5
Tobago Trin. & Tob. 11°10N 60°30W 323 s
Tobarra Spain 38°37N 1°44W 197 G3
Tobelo Indonesia 1°45N 127°56E 231 D7
Tobermory Ont., Canada 45°12N 81°40W 312 A3
Tobermory Argyll & Bute, U.K. 56°38N 6°5W 167 E2
Tobi Pac. Oc. 2°40N 131°10E 231 D8
Tobi-Shima Japan 41°12N 139°34E 220 D9
Tobias Fornier Phil. 10°30N 121°57E 233 F3
Tobiishi Hana Iwo Jima 24°45N 141°17E 288 b
Tobin, L. Australia 21°45S 125°49E 278 D4
Tobin L. Canada 53°35N 103°30W 297 C8
Toblach = Dobbiaco Italy 46°44N 12°14E 199 B9
Toboali Indonesia 3°0S 106°25E 234 C3
Tobol → Russia 58°10N 68°12E 214 D7
Toboli Indonesia 0°38S 120°5E 231 E6
Tobolsk Russia 58°15N 68°10E 214 D7
Tobor Senegal 12°40N 16°15W 262 C1
Toboso Phil. 10°43N 123°31E 233 F4
Tobruk = Tubruq Libya 32°7N 23°55E 258 B4
Tobyhanna U.S.A. 41°11N 75°25W 313 E9
Tobyl = Tobol → Russia 58°10N 68°12E 214 D7
Tocache Nuevo Peru 8°9S 76°26W 330 B2
Tocantínia Brazil 9°33S 48°22W 332 C2
Tocantinópolis Brazil 6°20S 47°25W 332 C2
Tocantins □ Brazil 10°0S 48°0W 332 D2
Tocantins → Brazil 1°45S 49°10W 332 B2
Toccoa U.S.A. 34°35N 83°19W 315 D13
Toce → Italy 45°56N 8°29E 198 C5
Tochi → Pakistan 32°49N 70°41E 242 C4
Tochigi Japan 36°25N 139°45E 223 A11
Tochigi □ Japan 36°45N 139°45E 223 A11
Tocina Spain 37°37N 5°44W 195 H5
Töcksfors Sweden 59°31N 11°52E 162 E5
Točná Czech Rep. 49°58N 14°25E 135 C2
Toco Chile 22°5S 69°35W 330 E4
Toco Trin. & Tob. 10°49N 60°57W 323 t
Toco Hills U.S.A. 33°49N 84°20W 113 B2
Toconao Chile 23°11S 68°1W 334 A2
Tocopilla Chile 22°5S 70°10W 334 A1
Tocqueville = Rass el Oued Algeria 35°57N 5°2E 261 A6
Tocumwal Australia 35°51S 145°31E 283 C6
Tocuyo → Venezuela 11°3N 68°23W 328 A4
Tocuyo de la Costa Venezuela 11°2N 68°23W 328 A4
Todeli Indonesia 1°40S 124°29E 231 E6
Todenyang Kenya 4°35N 35°56E 268 B4
Todgarh India 25°42N 73°58E 242 G5
Todi Italy 42°47N 12°24E 199 F9
Todos os Santos, B. de Brazil 12°48S 38°38W 333 D4
Todos Santos Mexico 23°26N 110°13W 318 C2
Todt Hill U.S.A. 40°36N 74°6W 132 C1
Todtnau Germany 47°49N 7°56E 179 H3
Toe Hd. U.K. 57°50N 7°8W 167 D1
Toecé Burkina Faso 11°50N 1°16W 263 C4
Toetoes B. N.Z. 46°42S 168°41E 285 G3
Tofield Canada 53°25N 112°40W 296 C6
Tofino Canada 49°11N 125°55W 296 D3
Tofsingdalens △ Sweden 62°10N 12°28E 162 B6
Tofte Norway 59°33N 10°34E 164 E7
Tofua Tonga 19°45S 175°5W 287 P13
Toga Vanuatu 13°26S 166°42E 287 C10
Tōgane Japan 35°33N 140°22E 223 B12
Togba Mauritania 17°26N 10°12W 262 B2
Togbo C.A.R. 6°0N 17°27E 264 A3
Togiak U.S.A. 59°4N 160°24W 303 G7
Togiak Nat. Wildlife Refuge ⌂ U.S.A. 59°20N 160°15W 303 G7
Togian, Kepulauan Indonesia 0°20S 121°50E 231 E6
Togliatti Russia 53°32N 49°24E 190 D9
Togo ■ W. Afr. 8°30N 1°35E 263 D5
Togo Wichale Somali Rep. 9°22N 43°40E 267 C5
Togrōg Mongolia 47°25N 92°13E 217 C12
Togtoh China 40°15N 111°10E 226 D6
Tohiea, Mt. Moorea 17°33S 149°49W 289 e
Tohma → Turkey 38°29N 38°23E 212 C8
Tōhoku □ Japan 39°50N 141°45E 220 E10
Töhöm Mongolia 44°27N 108°2E 226 B5
Tohopekaliga, East L. U.S.A. 28°18N 81°15W 317 G8
Tohopekaliga, L. U.S.A. 28°12N 81°24W 317 G8
Toi Cook Is. 18°57S 169°51W 289 g
Toi Japan 34°54N 138°47E 223 C10
Toibalewe India 10°32N 92°30E 245 J11
Toiny St.-Martin 17°53N 62°47W 322 a
Toinya Sudan 6°17N 29°46E 257 F2
Toiyabe Range U.S.A. 39°30N 117°0W 304 G5
Tojikiston = Tajikistan ■ Asia 38°30N 70°0E 217 E8
Tojo Indonesia 1°20S 121°15E 231 E6
Tōjō Japan 34°53N 133°16E 222 C5
Tok U.S.A. 63°20N 142°59W 303 E12
Tok-do Asia 37°15N 131°52E 221 F5
Toka Guyana 3°58N 59°17W 329 C6
Tokaanu N.Z. 38°58S 175°46E 284 E4
Tokachi-Dake Japan 43°17N 142°5E 220 C11
Tokachi-Gawa → Japan 42°44N 143°42E 220 C11
Tōkagi Japan 35°42N 139°55E 140 A4
Tokai Japan 35°2N 136°55E 223 B8
Tokai Plantation S. Africa 34°3S 18°24E 118 B1
Tōkaichiba Japan 35°31N 139°30E 140 B2
Tokaj Hungary 48°8N 21°27E 182 B6
Tokala Indonesia 1°30S 121°40E 231 E6
Tōkamachi Japan 37°8N 138°43E 221 F9
Tokanui N.Z. 46°34S 168°56E 285 G3
Tokar Sudan 18°27N 37°56E 256 D4
Tokara-Rettō Japan 29°37N 129°43E 221 K4
Tokarahi N.Z. 44°56S 170°39E 285 E5
Tokarevo Russia 55°38N 37°54E 129 C5
Tokashiki-Shima Japan 26°11N 127°21E 221 L3
Tokat Turkey 40°22N 36°35E 212 B7
Tokat □ Turkey 40°15N 36°30E 212 B7
Tŏkch'ŏn N. Korea 39°45N 126°18E 224 C3
Tokeland U.S.A. 46°42N 123°59W 306 D3
Tokelau Is. Pac. Oc. 9°0S 171°45W 277 B16
Toki Japan 35°18N 137°8E 223 B9
Toki Pt. Wake I. 19°19N 166°35E 302 b
Tokmak Kyrgyzstan 42°49N 75°15E 217 D9
Tokmak Ukraine 47°16N 35°42E 189 J8
Toko Ra. Australia 23°5S 138°20E 280 C2
Tokomaru Bay N.Z. 38°8S 178°22E 284 E7
Tokoname Japan 34°53N 136°51E 223 C8
Tokoro-Gawa → Japan 44°7N 144°5E 220 B12
Tokoroa N.Z. 38°13S 175°50E 284 E4
Tokorozawa Japan 35°47N 139°28E 223 B11
Toksook Bay U.S.A. 60°32N 165°0W 303 F6
Toksun China 42°47N 88°38E 217 D11
Toktogul Kyrgyzstan 41°50N 72°50E 217 D8
Toku Tonga 18°10S 174°11W 287 P13
Tokuji Japan 34°11N 131°42E 222 C3
Tokuno-Shima Japan 27°56N 128°55E 221 L4
Tokushima Japan 34°4N 134°34E 222 C6
Tokushima □ Japan 33°55N 134°0E 222 D6
Tokuyama Japan 34°3N 131°50E 222 C3
Tōkyō Japan 35°43N 139°45E 140 B3
Tōkyō □ Japan 35°40N 139°30E 223 B11
Tōkyō B. = Tōkyō-Wan Japan 35°25N 139°50E 140 B4
Tōkyō Disneyland Japan 35°37N 139°53E 140 B4
Tōkyō Haneda ✈ (HND) Japan 35°33N 139°46E 140 B3
Tōkyō Harbour Japan 35°38N 139°46E 140 B3
Tōkyō Narita ✈ (NRT) Japan 35°45N 140°25E 223 B12
Tōkyō-Wan Japan 35°25N 139°50E 140 B4
Tolaga Bay N.Z. 38°21S 178°20E 284 E7
Tolbukhin = Dobrich Bulgaria 43°37N 27°49E 203 C11
Tolé C.A.R. 6°34N 16°1E 264 A3
Tole Bī Kazakhstan 43°42N 73°46E 217 D8
Toledo Brazil 24°44S 53°45W 335 A5
Toledo Phil. 10°23N 123°38E 233 F4
Toledo Spain 39°50N 4°2W 194 F6
Toledo Ill., U.S.A. 39°16N 88°15W 311 E8
Toledo Iowa, U.S.A. 42°0N 92°35W 310 C4
Toledo Ohio, U.S.A. 41°39N 83°33W 311 C13
Toledo Oreg., U.S.A. 44°37N 123°56W 304 D2
Toledo Wash., U.S.A. 46°26N 122°51W 304 C2
Toledo, Montes de Spain 39°33N 4°20W 195 F6
Toledo Bend Res. U.S.A. 31°11N 93°34W 314 F8
Tolentino Italy 43°12N 13°17E 199 E10
Tolfa Italy 42°9N 11°56E 199 F8
Tolga Algeria 34°40N 5°22E 261 B6
Tolga Queens., Australia 17°15S 145°29E 280 B4
Tolga Hedmark, Norway 62°26N 11°1E 164 B8
Tolhuaca △ Chile 38°15S 71°50W 336 A2
Toli China 45°57N 83°37E 217 C10
Toliara Madag. 23°21S 43°40E 272 C1
Toliara □ Madag. 21°0S 45°0E 272 C2
Tolima Colombia 4°40N 75°19W 328 C2
Tolima □ Colombia 3°45N 75°15W 328 C2
Tolitoli Indonesia 1°5N 120°50E 231 D6
Tolka → Ireland 53°21N 6°14W 120 A1
Tolkmicko Poland 54°19N 19°31E 184 D6
Tollarp Sweden 55°55N 13°58E 163 J7
Tollensesee Germany 53°30N 13°13E 178 B9
Tollhouse U.S.A. 37°1N 119°24W 306 H7
Tollygunge = Taliganga India 22°30N 88°22E 124 B2
Tolmachevo Russia 58°56N 29°51E 188 C5
Tolmezzo Italy 46°24N 13°1E 199 B10
Tolmin Slovenia 46°11N 13°45E 199 B10
Tolna Hungary 46°25N 18°48E 182 D3
Tolna □ Hungary 46°30N 18°30E 182 D3
Tolo Dem. Rep. of the Congo 2°55S 18°34E 264 C3
Tolo, Teluk Indonesia 2°20S 122°10E 231 E6
Tolo Harbour China 22°27N 114°12E 219 G11
Tolochin = Talachyn Belarus 54°25N 29°42E 188 E5
Tolokiwa I. Papua N. G. 5°19S 147°37E 286 C4
Tolong Bay Phil. 9°20N 122°49E 233 G4
Tolono U.S.A. 39°59N 88°16W 311 E8
Tolosa Spain 43°8N 2°5W 196 B2
Tolox Spain 36°41N 4°54W 195 J6
Toltén Chile 39°13S 74°14W 336 A2
Toluca México, Mexico 19°17N 99°40W 319 D5
Toluca Ill., U.S.A. 41°0N 89°8W 310 C7
Tolworth U.K. 51°22N 0°17W 125 B2
Tom Burke S. Africa 23°5S 28°0E 271 B4
Tom Price Australia 22°40S 117°48E 278 D2
Toma Burkina Faso 12°45N 2°53W 262 C4
Tomah U.S.A. 43°59N 90°30W 308 D8
Tomahawk U.S.A. 45°28N 89°44W 308 C9
Tomai Moldova 46°34N 28°19E 183 D13
Tomakomai Japan 42°38N 141°36E 220 C10
Tomales U.S.A. 38°15N 122°53W 306 G3
Tomales B. U.S.A. 38°15N 123°58W 306 G3
Tomanivi Fiji 17°37S 178°1E 287 A2
Tomar Portugal 39°36N 8°25W 195 F2
Tomaros, Oros Greece 39°29N 20°48E 204 B2
Tomarza Turkey 38°27N 35°48E 212 C6
Tomás Barrón Bolivia 17°35S 67°31W 330 D4
Tomashevka Belarus 51°33N 23°36E 185 G10
Tomashpil Ukraine 48°32N 28°31E 183 B13
Tomaszów Lubelski Poland 50°27N 23°25E 185 H10
Tomaszów Mazowiecki Poland 51°30N 20°2E 185 G7
Tomatlán Mexico 19°56N 105°15W 318 D3
Tomb of the Kings Jerusalem 123 a2
Tomba di Nerone Italy 41°58N 12°26E 136 B1
Tombadonkéa Guinea 11°0N 14°25W 262 C2
Tombador, Serra do Brazil 12°0S 58°0W 331 C6
Tombe Sudan 5°53N 31°40E 257 F3
Tombeau Bay Mauritius 20°6S 57°30E 272 e
Tombel Cameroon 4°45N 9°40E 264 B1
Tombigbee → U.S.A. 31°8N 87°57W 315 F11
Tombôco Angola 6°48S 13°18E 265 D2
Tombouctou Mali 16°50N 3°0W 262 B4
Tombouctou □ Mali 20°0N 3°0W 262 B4
Tombstone U.S.A. 31°43N 110°4W 305 L8
Tombua Angola 15°55S 11°55E 265 F2
Tomé Chile 36°36S 72°57W 334 D1
Tomé-Açu Brazil 2°25S 48°9W 332 B2
Tomelilla Sweden 55°33N 13°58E 163 J7
Tomelloso Spain 39°10N 3°2W 195 F7
Tomil Micronesia 9°31N 138°9E 287 R16
Tomil Harbor Pac. Oc. 9°30N 138°10E 287 R16
Tomilino Russia 55°39N 37°55E 129 C5
Tomingley Australia 32°26S 148°16E 283 B8
Tomini Indonesia 0°30N 120°30E 231 D6
Tomini, Teluk Indonesia 0°10S 121°0E 231 E6
Tominian Mali 13°17N 4°35W 262 C4
Tomiño Spain 41°59N 8°46W 194 D2
Tomintoul U.K. 57°15N 3°23W 167 D5
Tomioka Japan 36°15N 138°54E 223 A10
Tomislavgrad Bos.-H. 43°42N 17°13E 182 G2
Tomkinson Ranges Australia 26°11S 129°5E 279 E4
Tommot Russia 59°4N 126°20E 215 D13
Tommy Thompson Park Canada 43°38N 79°20W 141 B3
Tomnop Ta Suos Cambodia 11°20N 104°15E 237 G5
Tomo Colombia 2°38N 67°32W 328 C4
Tomo → Colombia 5°20N 67°48W 328 B4
Tomobe Japan 36°20N 140°20E 223 A12
Tomra Norway 62°34N 6°56E 164 B3
Toms Place U.S.A. 37°34N 118°41W 306 H8
Toms River U.S.A. 39°58N 74°12W 313 G10
Tomsk Russia 56°30N 85°5E 214 D9
Tomtabacken Sweden 57°30N 14°30E 163 G8
Tömük Turkey 36°42N 34°23E 250 B5
Tona Spain 41°51N 2°14E 196 D7
Tonalá Chiapas, Mexico 16°4N 93°45W 319 D6
Tonalá Jalisco, Mexico 20°37N 103°14W 318 C4
Tonale, Passo del Italy 46°16N 10°35E 198 B7
Tonami Japan 36°40N 136°58E 223 A8
Tonantins Brazil 2°45S 67°45W 328 D4
Tonasket U.S.A. 48°42N 119°26W 304 B4
Tonate Fr. Guiana 5°0N 52°28W 329 C7
Tonawanda U.S.A. 43°1N 78°53W 312 D6
Tonb Iran 26°15N 55°15E 247 E7
Tonbo Burma 18°31N 95°35E 241 F5
Tonbridge U.K. 51°11N 0°17E 169 F8
Tonda Papua N. G. 8°55S 141°34E 286 E1
Tondabayashi Japan 34°30N 135°36E 223 C7
Tondano Indonesia 1°35N 124°54E 231 D6
Tondela Portugal 40°31N 8°5W 194 E2
Tønder Denmark 54°58N 8°50E 163 K2
Tondern = Tønder Denmark 54°58N 8°50E 163 K2
Tondi India 9°45N 79°4E 245 K4
Tondi Kiwindi Niger 14°28N 2°2E 263 C5
Tondibi Mali 16°39N 0°14W 263 B4
Tondo Phil. 14°36N 120°57E 127 B1
Tondoro Namibia 17°45S 18°50E 270 A2
Tone → Australia 34°25S 116°25E 279 F2
Tone-Gawa → Japan 35°44N 140°51E 223 B12
Tonekābon Iran 36°45N 51°12E 247 B6
Tong I. Papua N. G. 2°2S 147°47E 286 B4
Tong Xian China 39°55N 116°35E 226 E9
Tong-Yeong S. Korea 34°50N 128°20E 224 E4
Tōngā Sudan 9°28N 31°3E 257 F3
Tonga ■ Pac. Oc. 19°50S 174°30W 287 P13
Tonga Trench Pac. Oc. 18°0S 173°0W 277 D16
Tongaat S. Africa 29°33S 31°9E 271 C5
Tongala Australia 36°14S 144°56E 283 D6
Tong'an China 24°37N 118°8E 229 E12
Tongareva = Penrhyn Cook Is. 9°0S 158°0W 289 H12
Tongariro, Mt. N.Z. 39°8S 175°38E 284 F4
Tongariro △ N.Z. 39°8S 175°33E 284 F4
Tongass Nat. Forest U.S.A. 54°45N 133°0W 303 J14
Tongatapu Tonga 21°10S 175°10W 287 Q13
Tongatapu Group Tonga 21°0S 175°0W 287 Q13
Tongbai China 32°20N 113°23E 229 A9
Tongbinggo S. Korea 37°31N 126°58E 137 B1
Tongcheng Anhui, China 31°4N 116°56E 229 B11
Tongcheng Hubei, China 29°15N 113°50E 229 C9
Tongchuan China 35°6N 109°3E 226 G5
Tongdao China 26°10N 109°42E 228 D7
Tongeren Belgium 50°47N 5°28E 170 D5
Tonggu China 28°31N 114°20E 229 C10
Tonggu Jiao China 22°22N 113°37E 219 G10
Tongguan China 34°40N 110°25E 226 G6
Tonghai China 24°10N 102°53E 228 E4
Tonghua China 41°42N 125°58E 224 B2
Tongjiang China 31°58N 107°11E 228 B6
Tongjosŏn Man N. Korea 39°30N 128°0E 224 C4
Tongkil Phil. 6°4N 121°48E 233 H3
Tongking, G. of = Tonkin, G. of Asia 20°0N 108°0E 236 C7
Tongliang China 29°50N 106°3E 228 C6
Tongliao China 43°38N 122°18E 227 C12
Tongling China 30°55N 117°48E 229 B11
Tonglu China 29°45N 119°37E 229 C12
Tongnan = Anyue China 30°9N 105°50E 228 B5
Tongoa Vanuatu 16°54S 168°34E 287 F6
Tongobory Madag. 23°32S 44°20E 272 C1
Tongoy Chile 30°16S 71°31W 334 C1
Tongqiao China 31°21N 121°22E 138 A1
Tongquil I. Phil. 6°2N 121°51E 233 H3
Tongren China 27°43N 109°11E 228 D7
Tongres = Tongeren Belgium 50°47N 5°28E 170 D5
Tongsa Dzong Bhutan 27°31N 90°31E 241 B3
Tongsha Tao Taiwan 26°12N 128°28E 225 b
Tongshi China 18°30N 109°20E 236 C7
Tongue U.K. 58°29N 4°25W 167 C4
Tongue → U.S.A. 46°25N 105°52W 304 C11
Tongwei China 35°0N 105°5E 226 G3
Tongxiang China 30°39N 120°34E 229 B13
Tongxin China 36°59N 105°58E 226 F3
Tongyang N. Korea 39°9N 126°53E 224 C3
Tongyu China 44°45N 123°4E 227 B12
Tongzi China 28°9N 106°49E 228 C6
Tonica U.S.A. 41°13N 89°4W 310 C7
Tonj Sudan 7°20N 28°44E 257 F2
Tonj → Sudan 7°31N 28°55E 257 F2
Tonk India 26°6N 75°54E 242 F6
Tonkawa U.S.A. 36°41N 97°18W 314 C6
Tonkin = Bac Phan Vietnam 22°0N 105°0E 236 B5
Tonkin, G. of Asia 20°0N 108°0E 236 C7
Tonle Sap Cambodia 13°0N 104°0E 237 F5
Tonnay-Charente France 45°56N 0°55W 174 C3
Tonneins France 44°23N 0°19E 174 D4
Tonnerre France 47°51N 3°59E 173 E10
Tönning Germany 54°19N 8°56E 178 A4
Tono Japan 39°19N 141°32E 220 E10
Tonoas I. Micronesia 7°22N 151°52E 287 T18
Tonopah U.S.A. 38°4N 117°14W 305 G5
Tonoshō Japan 34°29N 134°11E 222 C6
Tonosí Panama 7°20N 80°20W 320 E3
Tons → Haryana, India 30°30N 77°39E 242 D7
Tons → Ut. P., India 26°1N 83°33E 243 F10
Tønsberg Norway 59°19N 10°25E 164 E7
Tonsina U.S.A. 61°39N 145°11W 303 F11
Tonstad Norway 58°40N 6°45E 164 F3
Tonto △ U.S.A. 33°39N 111°7W 305 K8
Tonumea Tonga 20°30S 174°30W 287 Q13
Tonya Turkey 40°53N 39°16E 213 B8
Tonzang Burma 23°36N 93°42E 241 D4
Tonzi Burma 24°39N 94°57E 241 C5
Toobanna Australia 18°42S 146°9E 280 B4
Toodyay Australia 31°34S 116°28E 279 F2
Tooele U.S.A. 40°32N 112°18W 304 F7
Toompine Australia 27°15S 144°19E 281 D3
Toomsboro U.S.A. 32°50N 83°5W 316 C6
Toora Australia 38°39S 146°23E 283 E7
Toora-Khem Russia 52°28N 96°17E 217 B13
Toorak Australia 37°50S 145°1E 128 B2
Toowoomba Australia 27°32S 151°56E 281 D5
Top-ozero Russia 65°35N 32°0E 160 D25
Top Springs Australia 16°37S 131°51E 278 C5
Topalu Romania 44°31N 28°3E 183 F13
Topanga State Park ⌂ U.S.A. 34°7N 118°31W 126 B1
Topaz U.S.A. 38°41N 119°30W 306 G7
Topeka U.S.A. 39°3N 95°40W 308 F6
Topkapı Turkey 41°1N 28°55E 122 B1
Topkapı Palaca Turkey 41°1N 28°59E 122 B1
Topľa → Slovak Rep. 48°45N 21°45E 181 C14
Topley Canada 54°49N 126°18W 296 C3
Toplica → Serbia 43°15N 21°49E 202 C5
Toplița Romania 46°55N 25°20E 183 D10
Topo Azores 38°33N 27°45W 153 d1
Topo, Pta. do Azores 38°33N 27°46W 153 d1
Topocalma, Pta. Chile 34°10S 72°2W 334 C1
Topock U.S.A. 34°46N 114°29W 307 L12
Topola Serbia 44°17N 20°41E 202 B4
Topolčani Macedonia 41°14N 21°25E 202 E5
Topoľčany Slovak Rep. 48°35N 18°12E 181 C11
Topolnitsa → Bulgaria 42°11N 24°18E 203 D8
Topolobampo Mexico 25°36N 109°3W 318 B3
Topoloveni Romania 44°49N 25°5E 183 F10
Topolovgrad Bulgaria 42°5N 26°20E 203 D10
Topolvățu Mare Romania 45°46N 21°41E 182 E6
Toppenish U.S.A. 46°23N 120°19W 304 C3
Topraisar Romania 44°1N 28°27E 183 F13
Toprakkale Turkey 37°5N 36°8E 250 A7
Topusko Croatia 45°18N 15°59E 199 C12
Toquepala Peru 17°24S 70°25W 330 D3
Toqyraūyn → Kazakhstan 46°48N 75°24E 217 C9
Tor di Quinto Italy 41°56N 12°27E 136 B1
Tor Pignattara Italy 41°53N 12°31E 136 B2
Tor Sapienza Italy 41°53N 12°36E 136 B2
Torà Spain 41°49N 1°25E 196 D6
Tora Kit Sudan 11°2N 32°36E 257 E3
Toraka Vestale Madag. 16°20S 43°58E 272 B1
Toranomon Tokyo, Japan 140 c3
Torata Peru 17°23S 70°1W 330 D3
Torbalı Turkey 38°10N 27°21E 205 C9
Torbat-e Heydārīyeh Iran 35°15N 59°12E 247 C8
Torbat-e Jām Iran 35°16N 60°35E 247 C9
Torbay Canada 47°40N 52°42W 299 C9
Torbay □ U.K. 50°26N 3°31W 169 G4
Tørberget Norway 61°8N 12°7E 164 C9
Torbjörntorp Sweden 58°12N 13°36E 163 F7
Torcy France 48°51N 2°39E 134 A4
Tordesillas Spain 41°30N 5°0W 194 D6
Töreboda Sweden 58°41N 14°7E 163 F8
Torekov Sweden 56°26N 12°37E 163 H6
Torellò Spain 42°3N 2°16E 196 C7
Toreno Spain 42°42N 6°30W 194 C4
Torfaen □ U.K. 51°43N 3°3W 169 F4
Torfajökull Iceland 63°54N 19°0W 155 D7
Torgau Germany 51°34N 13°0E 178 D8
Torgelow Germany 53°37N 14°1E 178 B10
Torghay Kazakhstan 49°38N 63°29E 216 C6
Torghay → Kazakhstan 48°1N 62°45E 216 C6
Torghay Ustirti Asia 51°0N 63°0E 216 B6
Torghay Zhylghasy Kazakhstan 52°0N 64°30E 216 B6
Torgovaya = Salsk Russia 46°28N 41°30E 191 G5
Torhamn Sweden 56°6N 15°50E 163 H9
Torhout Belgium 51°5N 3°7E 170 C3
Torhovytsya Ukraine 48°36N 25°26E 183 B10
Tori Ethiopia 7°53N 33°35E 257 F3
Tori-Shima Japan 30°29N 140°19E 221 J10
Torigni-sur-Vire France 49°3N 0°58W 172 C6
Torija Spain 40°44N 3°2W 196 E1
Torino Italy 45°3N 7°40E 198 C4
Torit Sudan 4°27N 32°31E 257 G3
Torkamān Iran 37°35N 47°23E 213 D12
Torkovichi Russia 58°51N 30°21E 188 C6
Tormac Romania 45°30N 21°30E 182 E6
Tormes → Spain 41°18N 6°29W 194 D4
Tornado Mt. Canada 49°55N 114°40W 296 D6
Tornal'a Slovak Rep. 48°25N 20°20E 181 C13
Torneå = Tornio Finland 65°50N 24°12E 160 D21
Torneälven → Europe 65°50N 24°12E 160 D21
Torneträsk Sweden 68°24N 19°15E 160 B18
Tornio Finland 65°50N 24°12E 160 D21
Tornionjoki = Torneälven → Europe 65°50N 24°12E 160 D21
Tornquist Argentina 38°8S 62°15W 334 D3
Toro Baleares, Spain 39°59N 4°8E 206 B5
Toro Zamora, Spain 41°35N 5°24W 194 D5
Torö Sweden 58°48N 17°50E 163 F11
Toro, Cerro del Chile 29°10S 69°50W 334 B2
Toro □ Uganda 1°5N 30°22E 268 C3
Toro Pk. U.S.A. 33°34N 116°24W 307 M10
Torokina Papua N. G. 6°14S 155°3E 286 D8
Törökszentmiklós Hungary 47°11N 20°27E 182 C5
Toronto N.S.W., Australia 33°0S 151°30E 283 B9
Toronto Ont., Canada 43°39N 79°20W 141 B2
Toronto Ohio, U.S.A. 40°28N 80°36W 312 F4
Toronto, Univ. of Canada 43°39N 79°23W 141 B2
Toronto City Centre ✈ (YTZ) Canada 43°38N 79°24W 141 B2
Toronto Harbour Canada 43°38N 79°21W 141 B2
Toronto I. Canada 43°37N 79°23W 141 B2
Toronto Lester B. Pearson Int. ✈ (YYZ) Canada 43°46N 79°35W 141 A1
Toropets Russia 56°30N 31°40E 188 D6
Tororo Uganda 0°45N 34°12E 268 B3
Toros Dağları Turkey 37°0N 32°30E 250 B3
Toros Monumental, Templo de Barcelona, Spain 114 a3
Torotoro Bolivia 18°7S 65°46W 331 D4
Torotoro △ Bolivia 18°8S 65°46W 331 D4
Torpa India 22°57N 85°6E 243 H11
Torpo Norway 60°40N 8°43E 164 D5
Torquay Vic., Australia 38°20S 144°19E 282 E6
Torquay Torbay, U.K. 50°27N 3°32W 169 G4
Torquemada Spain 42°2N 4°19W 194 C6
Torrais, Pta. Azores 39°43N 31°7W 153 d2
Torrance U.S.A. 33°50N 118°20W 307 M8
Torrão Portugal 38°16N 8°11W 195 G2

Torre Annunziata *Italy* 40°45N 14°27E **201** B7
Torre de Moncorvo *Portugal* 41°12N 7°8W **194** D3
Torre del Campo *Spain* 37°46N 3°53W **195** H7
Torre del Greco *Italy* 40°47N 14°22E **201** B7
Torre del Mar *Spain* 36°44N 4°6W **195** J6
Torre Latino-americana *Mexico City, Mexico* **128** b2
Torre Lupara *Italy* 41°59N 12°39E **136** B2
Torre Nova *Italy* 41°51N 12°36E **136** B2
Torre-Pacheco *Spain* 37°44N 0°57W **197** H4
Torre Péllice *Italy* 44°49N 7°13E **198** D4
Torreblanca *Spain* 40°14N 0°12E **196** E5
Torrecampo *Spain* 38°29N 4°41W **195** G6
Torrecilla en Cameros *Spain* 42°15N 2°38W **196** C2
Torredembarra *Spain* 41°9N 1°24E **196** D6
Torredonjimeno *Spain* 37°46N 3°57W **195** H7
Torrejón de Ardoz *Spain* 40°27N 3°29W **194** E7
Torrejoncillo *Spain* 39°54N 6°28W **194** F4
Torrelaguna *Spain* 40°50N 3°38W **194** E7
Torrelavega *Spain* 43°20N 4°5W **194** B6
Torrellas ➔ *Spain* 41°23N 2°1E **114** A1
Torremaggiore *Italy* 41°41N 15°17E **199** G12
Torremolinos *Spain* 36°38N 4°30W **195** J6
Torrens, L. *Australia* 31°0S 137°50E **282** A2
Torrens Cr. ➔ *Australia* 22°23S 145°9E **280** C4
Torrens Creek *Australia* 20°48S 145°3E **280** C4
Torrent *Spain* 39°27N 0°28W **197** F4
Torrenueva *Spain* 38°38N 3°22W **195** G7
Torreón *Mexico* 25°33N 103°26W **318** B4
Torreperogil *Spain* 38°2N 3°17W **195** G7
Torres *Brazil* 29°21S 49°44W **335** B5
Torres *Mexico* 28°46N 110°47W **318** B2
Torres, Is. *Vanuatu* 13°15S 166°37E **287** C4
Torres del Paine △ *Chile* 51°3S 72°58W **336** D2
Torres Novas *Portugal* 39°27N 8°33W **195** F2
Torres Strait *Australia* 9°50S 142°20E **286** E2
Torres Vedras *Portugal* 39°5N 9°15W **195** F1
Torrevécchia *Italy* 41°55N 12°25E **136** B1
Torrevieja *Spain* 37°59N 0°42W **197** H4
Torrey *U.S.A.* 38°18N 111°25W **304** G8
Torricelli Mts. *Papua N. G.* 3°23S 142°15E **286** B2
Torridge ➔ *U.K.* 51°0N 4°13W **169** G3
Torridon, L. *U.K.* 57°35N 5°50W **167** D3
Torrijos *Phil.* 13°19N 122°5E **232** E4
Torrijos *Spain* 39°59N 4°18W **194** F6
Tørring *Denmark* 55°52N 9°29E **163** J3
Torrington *Conn., U.S.A.* 41°48N 73°7W **313** E11
Torrington *Wyo., U.S.A.* 42°4N 104°11W **304** E11
Torroella de Montgrì *Spain* 42°2N 3°8E **196** C8
Torrox *Spain* 36°46N 3°57W **195** J7
Torsås *Sweden* 56°24N 16°0E **163** H9
Torsby *Sweden* 60°7N 13°0E **162** D6
Torshälla *Sweden* 59°25N 16°28E **162** E10
Tórshavn *Færoe Is.* 62°5N 6°56W **160** E9
Torslanda *Sweden* 57°44N 11°45E **163** G5
Torsö *Sweden* 58°48N 13°45E **163** F7
Tortola *Br. Virgin Is.* 18°19N 64°45W **321** C7
Tórtoles de Esgueva *Spain* 41°49N 4°2W **194** D6
Tortoli *Italy* 39°55N 9°39E **200** C2
Tortona *Italy* 44°54N 8°52E **198** D5
Tortorici *Italy* 38°2N 14°49E **201** D7
Tortosa *Spain* 40°49N 0°31E **196** E5
Tortosa, C. *Spain* 40°41N 0°52E **196** E5
Tortosendo *Portugal* 40°15N 7°31W **194** E3
Tortue, Î. de la *Haiti* 20°5N 72°57W **321** B5
Tortuga *Trin. & Tob.* 10°22N 61°24W **323** t
Tortuguero △ *Costa Rica* 10°31N 83°29W **320** D3
Tortum *Turkey* 40°19N 41°35E **213** B9
Ţorūd *Iran* 35°25N 55°5E **247** C7
Torul *Turkey* 40°34N 39°18E **213** B8
Toruń *Poland* 53°2N 18°39E **185** E5
Torun *Ukraine* 48°40N 23°34E **183** B8
Tory I. *Ireland* 55°16N 8°14W **166** A3
Torysa ➔ *Slovak Rep.* 48°39N 21°21E **181** C14
Torzhok *Russia* 57°5N 34°55E **188** D8
Torzym *Poland* 52°19N 15°5E **185** F2
Tosa *Japan* 33°24N 133°23E **222** D5
Tosa-Shimizu *Japan* 32°52N 132°58E **222** E4
Tosa-Wan *Japan* 33°15N 133°30E **222** D5
Tosa-Yamada *Japan* 33°36N 133°38E **222** D5
Toscana □ *Italy* 43°25N 11°0E **198** E8
Toscanella = Tuscánia *Italy* 42°25N 11°52E **199** F8
Toscano, Arcipelago *Italy* 42°30N 10°30E **198** F7
Toshima *Japan* 35°43N 139°42E **140** A3
Toshimaen *Japan* 35°43N 139°38E **140** A2
Toshka *Egypt* 22°30N 31°53E **256** C3
Toshka Lakes *Egypt* 22°50N 31°0E **256** C3
Toshkent *Uzbekistan* 41°20N 69°10E **217** D7
Toshkent □ *Uzbekistan* 41°0N 69°40E **217** D7
Tosno *Russia* 59°38N 30°46E **188** C6
Tossa de Mar *Spain* 41°43N 2°56E **196** D7
Tösse *Sweden* 58°58N 12°39E **163** F6
Tostado *Argentina* 29°15S 61°50W **334** B3
Tostedt *Germany* 53°17N 9°42E **178** B5
Tostón, Pta. de *Canary Is.* 28°42N 14°2W **153** e2
Tosu *Japan* 33°22N 130°31E **222** D2
Tosya *Turkey* 41°1N 34°2E **212** B6
Toszek *Poland* 50°27N 18°32E **185** H5
Totak *Norway* 59°40N 8°0E **164** E5
Totana *Spain* 37°45N 1°30W **197** H3
Totebo *Sweden* 57°38N 16°12E **163** G10
Toteng *Botswana* 20°22S 22°58E **270** B3
Tôtes *France* 49°41N 1°2E **172** C8
Totias *Somali Rep.* 3°57N 43°57E **267** D5
Tótkomlós *Hungary* 46°24N 20°45E **182** D5
Totland *Norway* 61°56N 5°23E **164** C2
Totma *Russia* 60°0N 42°40E **186** C7
Totnes *U.K.* 50°26N 3°42W **169** G4
Totness *Suriname* 5°53N 56°19W **329** B6
Toto *Nigeria* 8°26N 7°5E **263** D6
Totonicapán *Guatemala* 14°58N 91°12W **320** D1
Totora *Bolivia* 17°42S 65°9W **331** D4
Totoya, I. *Fiji* 18°57S 179°50W **287** B3
Totten Glacier *Antarctica* 66°45S 116°10E **151** C8
Tottenham *N.S.W., Australia* 32°14S 147°21E **283** B7
Tottenham *Vic., Australia* 37°48S 144°51E **128** A1
Tottenham *Ont., Canada* 44°1N 79°49W **312** B5
Tottenham *London, U.K.* 51°35N 0°4W **125** A3
Tottori *Japan* 35°30N 134°15E **222** B6
Tottori □ *Japan* 35°30N 134°12E **222** B6
Touaret *Niger* 20°17N 7°8E **261** D6
Touat *Algeria* 27°27N 0°30E **260** C5
Touba *Ivory C.* 8°22N 7°40W **262** D3
Touba *Senegal* 14°50N 15°55W **262** C1
Toubkal, Djebel *Morocco* 31°0N 8°0W **260** B3
Toubkal △ *Morocco* 31°0N 8°2W **260** B3
T'ouch'eng *Taiwan* 24°52N 121°49E **225** B3
Toucy *France* 47°44N 3°15E **173** E10
T'oufen *Taiwan* 24°41N 120°54E **225** B2
Tougan *Burkina Faso* 13°11N 2°58W **262** C4
Touggourt *Algeria* 33°6N 6°4E **261** B6
Tougouri *Burkina Faso* 13°20N 0°30W **263** C4
Tougué *Guinea* 11°25N 11°50W **262** C2
Toukmatine *Algeria* 24°49N 7°11E **261** D6
Toukoto *Mali* 13°27N 9°52W **262** C3
Toul *France* 48°40N 5°53E **173** D12
Toulepleu *Ivory C.* 6°32N 8°24W **262** D3
Touliu *Taiwan* 23°42N 120°31E **225** C2
Toulon *Var, France* 43°10N 5°55E **175** E9
Toulon *Ill., U.S.A.* 41°6N 89°52W **310** C7
Toulouse *France* 43°37N 1°27E **174** E5
Toulouse Blagnac ✈ (TLS) *France* 43°37N 1°22E **174** E5
Toulouse Street *New Orleans, U.S.A.* **131** b2
Toumbo *Niger* 22°45N 14°8E **258** D2
Toumodi *Ivory C.* 6°32N 5°4W **262** D3
Tounan *Taiwan* 23°41N 120°28E **225** C2
Tounassine, Hamada *Algeria* 28°48N 5°0W **260** C4
Toungo *Nigeria* 8°20N 12°3E **263** D7
Toungoo *Burma* 19°0N 96°30E **241** F6
Touques ➔ *France* 49°22N 0°8E **172** C7
Touraine *France* 47°20N 0°30E **172** E7
Tourane = Da Nang *Vietnam* 16°4N 108°13E **236** D7
Tourcoing *France* 50°42N 3°10E **173** B10
Touriñán, C. *Spain* 43°3N 9°18W **194** B1
Tourîne *Mauritania* 22°23N 11°50W **260** D2
Tournai *Belgium* 50°35N 3°25E **170** D3
Tournan-en-Brie *France* 48°44N 2°46E **173** D9
Tournay *France* 43°13N 0°13E **174** E4
Tournon-St-Martin *France* 46°45N 0°58E **172** F7
Tournon-sur-Rhône *France* 45°4N 4°50E **175** C8
Tournus *France* 46°35N 4°54E **173** F11
Touros *Brazil* 5°12S 35°28W **332** C4
Tours *France* 47°22N 0°40E **172** E7
Touside, Pic *Chad* 21°1N 16°29E **259** D3
Toussoro, Mt. *C.A.R.* 9°7N 23°14E **264** A4
Toussus-le-Noble *France* 48°44N 2°6E **134** B1
Toussus-le-Noble ✈ *France* 48°44N 2°6E **134** B1
Touws ➔ *S. Africa* 33°45S 21°11E **270** D3
Touwsrivier *S. Africa* 33°20S 20°2E **270** D3
Tovar *Venezuela* 8°20N 71°46W **328** B3
Tovarkovskiy *Russia* 53°40N 38°14E **188** F10
Tovdal *Norway* 58°47N 8°10E **164** F5
Tovdalselva ➔ *Norway* 58°11N 8°7E **164** F5
Tovuz *Azerbaijan* 41°0N 45°40E **191** K7
Towada *Japan* 40°37N 141°13E **220** D10
Towada-Hachimantai △ *Japan* 40°20N 140°55E **220** D10
Towada-Ko *Japan* 40°28N 140°55E **220** D10
Towanda *Ill., U.S.A.* 40°36N 88°53W **311** D8
Towanda *Pa., U.S.A.* 41°46N 76°27W **313** E8
Towarri △ *Australia* 31°50S 150°37E **283** A9
Towchal Cable Car *Iran* 35°49N 51°24E **141** A2
Tower *U.S.A.* 47°48N 92°17W **308** B7
Tower, I. = Genovesa, I. *Ecuador* 0°20N 89°58W **330** a
Tower Bridge *London, U.K.* **125** b5
Tower Hamlets □ *U.K.* 51°32N 0°2W **125** A3
Tower of London *U.K.* 51°30N 0°4W **125** A3
Towerhill Cr. ➔ *Australia* 22°28S 144°35E **280** C3
Town Hall = Stadhuis *Amsterdam, Neths.* **112** b2
Towner *U.S.A.* 48°21N 100°25W **308** A3
Townsend *Ga., U.S.A.* 31°33N 81°31W **316** D8
Townsend *Mont., U.S.A.* 46°19N 111°31W **304** C8
Townshend I. *Australia* 22°10S 150°31E **280** C5
Townsville *Australia* 19°15S 146°45E **280** B4
Towra Pt. *Australia* 34°0S 151°10E **139** C2
Towraghondī *Afghan.* 35°13N 62°16E **240** B1
Towson *U.S.A.* 39°24N 76°36W **309** F15
Towuti, Danau *Indonesia* 2°45S 121°32E **231** E6
Toya-Ko *Japan* 42°35N 140°51E **220** C10
Toyama *Japan* 36°40N 137°15E **223** A9
Toyama □ *Japan* 36°45N 137°30E **223** A9
Toyama-Wan *Japan* 37°0N 137°30E **221** F8
Toyapakeh *Indonesia* 8°41S 115°29E **231** K18
Tøyen *Norway* 59°55N 10°47E **133** A3
Tōyo *Ehime, Japan* 33°56N 133°5E **222** D5
Tōyō *Kōchi, Japan* 33°26N 134°16E **222** D6
Toyohara = Yuzhno-Sakhalinsk *Russia* 46°58N 142°45E **215** E15
Toyohashi *Japan* 34°45N 137°25E **223** C9
Toyokawa *Japan* 34°48N 137°27E **223** C9
Toyonaka *Japan* 34°46N 135°28E **133** A1
Toyooka *Japan* 35°35N 134°48E **222** B6
Toyota *Japan* 35°3N 137°7E **223** B9
Toyoura *Japan* 34°6N 130°57E **222** C2
Tozeur *Tunisia* 33°56N 8°8E **258** B1
Tozeur □ *Tunisia* 34°0N 8°5E **261** B6
Tozkhurmato *Iraq* 34°56N 44°38E **213** E11
Tqibuli *Georgia* 42°26N 43°0E **191** J6
Tqvarcheli *Georgia* 42°47N 41°42E **191** J5
Trá Li = Tralee *Ireland* 52°16N 9°42W **166** D2
Tra On *Vietnam* 9°58N 105°55E **237** H5
Trabancos ➔ *Spain* 41°36N 5°15W **194** D5
Traben-Trarbach *Germany* 49°57N 7°7E **179** F3
Trabzon *Turkey* 41°0N 39°45E **213** B8
Trabzon □ *Turkey* 41°10N 39°45E **213** B8
Tracadie-Sheila *Canada* 47°30N 64°55W **299** C7
Trachenburg = Żmigród *Poland* 51°28N 16°53E **185** G3
Tracy *Calif., U.S.A.* 37°44N 121°26W **306** H5
Tracy *Minn., U.S.A.* 44°14N 95°37W **308** C6
Tradate *Italy* 45°43N 8°54E **198** C5
Trade Town *Liberia* 5°40N 9°50W **262** D3
Traer *U.S.A.* 42°12N 92°28W **310** B4
Trafalgar *Vic., Australia* 38°14S 146°12E **283** E7
Trafalgar *Dominica* 15°19N 61°21W **323** k
Trafalgar, C. *Spain* 36°10N 6°2W **195** J4
Trafalgar Square *London, U.K.* **125** b3
Trafaria *Portugal* 38°40N 9°13W **126** A1
Tragonhsi *Greece* 37°27N 25°29E **205** D7
Traiguén *Chile* 38°15S 72°41W **336** A2
Trail *Canada* 49°5N 117°40W **296** D5
Traill Ø *Greenland* 72°30N 23°0W **154** C8
Trainor L. *Canada* 60°24N 120°17W **296** A4
Traíra ➔ *Brazil* 1°4S 69°26W **328** D4
Trakai △ *Lithuania* 54°30N 25°10E **161** J21
Trákhonas *Cyprus* 35°12N 33°21E **207** E9
Tralee *Ireland* 52°16N 9°42W **166** D2
Tralee B. *Ireland* 52°17N 9°55W **166** D2
Tramore *Ireland* 52°10N 7°10W **166** D4
Tramore B. *Ireland* 52°9N 7°10W **166** D4
Tran Ninh, Cao Nguyen *Laos* 19°30N 103°10E **236** C4
Tranås *Sweden* 58°3N 14°59E **163** F8
Tranbjerg *Denmark* 56°6N 10°9E **163** H4
Tranby *Norway* 59°49N 10°15E **164** E7
Trancas *Argentina* 26°11S 65°20W **334** B2
Trancoso *Portugal* 40°49N 7°21W **194** E3
Tranebjerg *Denmark* 55°51N 10°36E **163** J4
Tranegilde *Denmark* 55°37N 12°20E **118** B2
Tranemo *Sweden* 57°30N 13°20E **163** G7
Trang *Thailand* 7°33N 99°38E **237** J2
Trangahy *Madag.* 19°7S 44°31E **272** B1
Trangan *Indonesia* 6°40S 134°20E **231** F8
Trangie *Australia* 32°4S 148°0E **283** B8
Trångsund *Sweden* 59°13N 18°8E **139** B2
Trångsviken *Sweden* 63°19N 13°59E **162** A7
Trani *Italy* 41°17N 16°25E **201** A9
Tranoroa *Madag.* 24°42S 45°4E **272** C2
Tranqueras *Uruguay* 31°13S 55°45W **335** C4
Trans-Alaska Pipeline *U.S.A.* 70°11N 148°27W **303** A10
Transamerica Pyramid *San Francisco, U.S.A.* **136** b2
Transantarctic Mts. *Antarctica* 85°0S 170°0W **151** E12
Transbay Terminal *San Francisco, U.S.A.* **136** b3
Transcarpathia = Zakarpattya □ *Ukraine* 48°20N 23°20E **183** B8
Transilvania *Romania* 46°30N 24°0E **183** D9
Transilvanian Alps = Carpaţii Meridionali *Romania* 45°30N 25°0E **183** E9
Transjordan = Jordan ■ *Asia* 31°0N 36°0E **251** H7
Transnistria = Stînga Nistrului □ *Moldova* 47°20N 29°15E **183** C14
Transtrand *Sweden* 61°6N 13°20E **162** C7
Transtrandsfjällen *Sweden* 61°8N 13°0E **162** C6
Transylvania = Transilvania *Romania* 46°30N 24°0E **183** D9
Trants Bay *Montserrat* 16°46N 62°9W **323** p
Trápani *Italy* 38°1N 12°29E **200** D5
Trappenfelde *Germany* 52°34N 13°39E **115** A4
Trapper Pk. *U.S.A.* 45°54N 114°18W **304** D6
Traralgon *Australia* 38°12S 146°34E **283** E7
Trarza □ *Mauritania* 18°0N 15°0W **260** E2
Trás-os-Montes = Cucumbi *Angola* 10°17S 19°5E **265** E3
Trasacco *Italy* 41°57N 13°32E **199** G10
Trăscău, Munţii *Romania* 46°14N 23°14E **183** D8
Trasimeno, L. *Italy* 43°8N 12°6E **199** E9
Träslövsläge *Sweden* 57°4N 12°16E **163** G6
Trastévere *Italy* 41°53N 12°28E **136** B1
Trasvase Tajo-Segura, Canal de *Spain* 40°15N 2°55W **196** E2
Trat *Thailand* 12°14N 102°33E **237** F4
Tratani ➔ *Pakistan* 29°19N 68°20E **242** E3
Traun *Austria* 48°14N 14°15E **180** C7
Traunreut *Germany* 47°57N 12°36E **179** H8
Traunsee *Austria* 47°55N 13°50E **180** D6
Traunstein *Germany* 47°52N 12°37E **179** H8
Travellers L. *Australia* 33°20S 142°0E **282** B5
Travemünde *Germany* 53°57N 10°52E **178** B6
Travers, Mt. *N.Z.* 42°1S 172°45E **285** C7
Traverse City *U.S.A.* 44°46N 85°38W **309** C11
Travis, L. *U.S.A.* 30°24N 97°55W **314** F6
Travnik *Bos.-H.* 44°17N 17°39E **182** F2
Trawbreaga B. *Ireland* 55°20N 7°25W **166** A4
Trbovlje *Slovenia* 46°12N 15°5E **199** B12
Treasure I. *U.S.A.* 37°49N 122°22W **136** B2
Treasure Island *U.S.A.* 27°46N 82°46W **317** H7
Treasury Is. *Solomon Is.* 7°22S 155°37E **287** L8
Trébbia ➔ *Italy* 45°4N 9°41E **198** C6
Trebel ➔ *Germany* 53°54N 13°2E **178** B9
Trebeurden *France* 48°46N 3°35W **172** D3
Trebević △ *Bos.-H.* 43°20N 18°45E **182** G3
Třebíč *Czech Rep.* 49°14N 15°55E **180** B8
Trebinje *Bos.-H.* 42°44N 18°22E **202** D2
Trebisacce *Italy* 39°52N 16°32E **201** C9
Trebišnjica ➔ *Bos.-H.* 42°47N 18°8E **202** D2
Trebišov *Slovak Rep.* 48°38N 21°41E **181** C14
Trebitsch = Třebíč *Czech Rep.* 49°14N 15°55E **180** B8
Trebižat ➔ *Bos.-H.* 43°15N 17°30E **199** E14
Trebnitz = Trzebnica *Poland* 51°20N 17°1E **185** G4
Trebnje *Slovenia* 45°54N 15°1E **199** C12
Třeboň *Czech Rep.* 49°1N 14°48E **180** B7
Trebonne *Australia* 18°37S 146°5E **280** B4
Treboñsko ⌓ *Czech Rep.* 49°1N 14°49E **180** B7
Trebujena *Spain* 36°52N 6°11W **195** J4
Trecate *Italy* 45°26N 8°44E **198** C5
Tregaron *U.K.* 52°14N 3°56W **169** E4
Tregnago *Italy* 45°31N 11°10E **199** C8
Tregrosse Is. *Australia* 17°41S 150°43E **280** B5
Tréguier *France* 48°47N 3°16W **172** D3
Trégunc *France* 47°51N 3°51W **172** E3
Treherne *Canada* 49°38N 98°42W **297** D9
Tréia *Italy* 43°19N 13°19E **199** E10
Treignac *France* 45°32N 1°48E **174** C5
Treinta y Tres *Uruguay* 33°16S 54°17W **335** C5
Treis-karden *Germany* 50°10N 7°18E **179** E3
Treklyano *Bulgaria* 42°33N 22°36E **202** D6
Trelawney *Zimbabwe* 17°30S 30°30E **271** A5
Trélazé *France* 47°26N 0°30W **172** E6
Trelew *Argentina* 43°10S 65°20W **336** B3
Trélissac *France* 45°11N 0°47E **174** C4
Trelleborg *Sweden* 55°20N 13°10E **163** J7
Tremadog Bay *U.K.* 52°51N 4°18W **168** E3
Tremblay-en-France *France* 48°56N 2°35E **134** A4
Tremblet *Réunion* 21°17S 55°48E **272** f
Trembowla = Terebovlya *Ukraine* 49°18N 25°44E **177** D13
Tremedal = Monte Azul *Brazil* 15°9S 42°53W **333** E3
Tremembe ➔ *Brazil* 23°27S 46°34W **137** A2
Trémiti *Italy* 42°8N 15°30E **199** F12
Tremont *U.S.A.* 40°50N 73°52W **132** A2
Tremonton *U.S.A.* 41°43N 112°10W **304** F7
Tremp *Spain* 42°10N 0°52E **196** C5
Trenche ➔ *Canada* 47°46N 72°53W **298** C5
Trenčiansky □ *Slovak Rep.* 48°45N 18°20E **181** C11
Trenčín *Slovak Rep.* 48°52N 18°4E **181** C11
Trengereid *Norway* 60°26N 5°37E **164** D2
Trenggalek *Indonesia* 8°3S 111°43E **235** D4
Trenno *Italy* 45°29N 9°6E **129** B1
Trenque Lauquen *Argentina* 36°5S 62°45W **334** D3
Trent ➔ *Ont., Canada* 44°6N 77°34W **312** B7
Trent ➔ *England, U.K.* 53°41N 0°42W **168** D7
Trentino-Alto Adige □ *Italy* 46°30N 11°20E **199** B8
Trento *Italy* 46°4N 11°8E **198** B8
Trento *Agusan del S., Phil.* 8°3N 126°2E **233** G6
Trenton = Quinte West *Canada* 44°10N 77°34W **312** B7
Trenton *Fla., U.S.A.* 29°37N 82°49W **317** F7
Trenton *Mich., U.S.A.* 42°8N 83°11W **311** B13
Trenton *Mo., U.S.A.* 40°5N 93°37W **310** D3
Trenton *N.J., U.S.A.* 40°14N 74°46W **313** F10
Trenton *Nebr., U.S.A.* 40°11N 101°1W **308** E3
Trenton *Ohio, U.S.A.* 39°29N 84°28W **311** E12
Trenton *S.C., U.S.A.* 33°45N 81°51W **316** B8
Trepassey *Canada* 46°43N 53°25W **299** C9
Treptow *Germany* 52°29N 13°27E **115** B3
Treptow an der Rega = Trzebiatów *Poland* 54°3N 15°18E **184** D2
Trepuzzi *Italy* 40°24N 18°4E **201** B11
Tres Arroyos *Argentina* 38°26S 60°20W **334** D3
Três Casas *Brazil* 6°59S 62°41W **331** B5
Três Corações *Brazil* 21°44S 45°15W **333** F2
Tres Equinas *Colombia* 0°43N 75°16W **328** C2
Três Lagoas *Brazil* 20°50S 51°43W **333** F1
Tres Lagos *Argentina* 49°35S 71°25W **336** C2
Tres Lomas *Argentina* 36°27S 62°51W **334** D3
Três Marias, Represa *Brazil* 18°12S 45°15W **333** E2
Tres Montes, C. *Chile* 46°50S 75°30W **336** C1
Tres Pinos *U.S.A.* 36°48N 121°19W **306** J5
Três Pontas *Brazil* 21°23S 45°29W **333** F2
Três Pontas, C. das *Angola* 10°28S 13°32E **265** E2
Tres Puentes *Chile* 27°50S 70°15W **334** B1
Tres Puntas, C. *Argentina* 47°0S 66°0W **336** C3
Três Rios *Brazil* 22°6S 43°15W **333** F3
Tres Ríos, Sa. dos *Brazil* 22°56S 43°17W **135** B1
Tres Valles *Mexico* 18°15N 96°8W **319** D5
Tresco *U.K.* 49°57N 6°20W **169** H1
Tresfjord *Norway* 62°31N 7°7E **164** B4
Treska ➔ *Macedonia* 42°0N 21°20E **202** E5
Treskavica *Bos.-H.* 43°40N 18°20E **182** G3
Trespaderne *Spain* 42°47N 3°24W **194** C7
Tresticklan △ *Sweden* 59°0N 11°42E **163** F5
Trets *France* 43°27N 5°41E **175** E9
Treuburg = Olecko *Poland* 54°2N 22°31E **184** D9
Treuchtlingen *Germany* 48°58N 10°54E **179** G6
Treuenbrietzen *Germany* 52°5N 12°52E **178** C8
Treungen *Norway* 59°1N 8°31E **164** E5
Trèves = Trier *Germany* 49°45N 6°38E **179** F2
Trevi *Italy* 42°52N 12°45E **199** F9
Trevi, Fontana di *Rome, Italy* **136** b3
Treviglio *Italy* 45°31N 9°35E **198** C6
Trevinca, Peña *Spain* 42°15N 6°46W **194** C4
Treviso *Italy* 45°40N 12°15E **199** C9
Trévoux *France* 45°57N 4°47E **175** C8
Trezzano sul Navíglio *Italy* 45°24N 9°4E **129** B1
Trgovište *Serbia* 42°20N 22°10E **202** D6
Triabunna *Australia* 42°30S 147°55E **281** G4
Triánda *Greece* 36°25N 28°10E **206** E12
Triangle *Zimbabwe* 21°2S 31°28E **271** B5
Triaucourt-en-Argonne *France* 48°59N 5°2E **173** D12
Tribal Areas □ *Pakistan* 33°0N 70°0E **242** C4
Tribly *U.S.A.* 28°28N 82°12W **317** G7
Tribsees *Germany* 54°5N 12°44E **178** A8
Tribulation, C. *Australia* 16°5S 145°29E **280** B4
Tribune *U.S.A.* 38°28N 101°45W **308** F3
Tribune Tower *Chicago, U.S.A.* **119** b2
Tricárico *Italy* 40°37N 16°9E **201** B9
Tricase *Italy* 39°56N 18°22E **201** C11
Trichinopoly = Tiruchchirappalli *India* 10°45N 78°45E **245** J4
Trichonida, L. *Greece* 38°34N 21°30E **204** C3
Trichur *India* 10°30N 76°18E **245** J3
Trida *Australia* 33°1S 145°1E **283** B6
Trier *Germany* 49°45N 6°38E **179** F2
Trieste *Italy* 45°40N 13°46E **199** C10
Trieste *Trieste, Italy* 45°40N 13°46E **199** C10
Trieste, G. di *Italy* 45°40N 13°35E **199** C10
Trieux ➔ *France* 48°43N 3°9W **172** D3
Triggiano *Italy* 41°4N 16°55E **201** A9
Triglav *Slovenia* 46°21N 13°50E **199** B10
Triglavski △ *Slovenia* 46°20N 13°50E **199** B10
Trigno ➔ *Italy* 42°4N 14°48E **199** F11
Trigo de Morais = Guijá *Mozam.* 24°27S 33°0E **271** B5
Trigueros *Spain* 37°24N 6°50W **195** H4
Trikala *Greece* 39°34N 21°47E **204** B3
Trikala □ *Greece* 39°41N 21°30E **204** B3
Trikeri *Greece* 39°6N 23°5E **204** B5
Trikomo *Cyprus* 35°17N 33°52E **207** E9
Trikora, Puncak *Indonesia* 4°15S 138°45E **231** E9
Trilj *Croatia* 43°38N 16°42E **199** E13
Trillo *Spain* 40°42N 2°35W **196** E2
Trim *Ireland* 53°33N 6°48W **166** C5
Trimbak *India* 19°56N 73°33E **244** E1
Trimmu Dam *Pakistan* 31°10N 72°8E **242** D5
Trincomalee *Sri Lanka* 8°38N 81°15E **245** K5
Trindade *Brazil* 16°40S 49°30W **333** E2
Trindade, I. *Atl. Oc.* 20°20S 29°50W **152** J9
Třinec *Czech Rep.* 49°41N 18°39E **181** B11
Trinidad = Jose Abad Santos *Phil.* 5°55N 125°39E **233** J5
Trinidad *Bolivia* 14°46S 64°50W **331** C5
Trinidad *Colombia* 5°25N 71°40W **328** B3
Trinidad *Cuba* 21°48N 80°0W **320** B4
Trinidad *Trin. & Tob.* 10°30N 61°15W **323** t
Trinidad *Uruguay* 33°30S 56°50W **334** C4
Trinidad *Colo., U.S.A.* 37°10N 104°31W **305** H11
Trinidad *D.C., U.S.A.* 38°54N 76°59W **143** B4
Trinidad ➔ *Mexico* 17°49N 95°9W **319** D5
Trinidad, G. *Chile* 49°55S 75°25W **336** C1
Trinidad, I. *Argentina* 39°10S 62°0W **336** A4
Trinidad & Tobago ■ *W. Indies* 10°30N 61°20W **323** t
Trinitápoli *Italy* 41°21N 16°5E **201** A9
Trinité, Havre de *Martinique* 14°44N 60°58W **322** j
Trinity *Nfld. & L., Canada* 48°59N 53°55W **299** C9
Trinity *Edinburgh, U.K.* 55°58N 3°12W **121** B2
Trinity *Tex., U.S.A.* 30°57N 95°22W **314** F7
Trinity ➔ *Calif., U.S.A.* 41°11N 123°42W **304** F2
Trinity ➔ *Tex., U.S.A.* 29°45N 94°43W **314** G7
Trinity B. *Canada* 48°20N 53°10W **299** C9
Trinity Church *New York, U.S.A.* **132** f1
Trinity College *Dublin, Ireland* **120** c3
Trinity Hills *Trin. & Tob.* 10°7N 61°7W **323** t
Trinity Is. *U.S.A.* 56°33N 154°25W **303** H9
Trinity Range *U.S.A.* 40°10N 118°40W **304** F4
Trinkat *India* 8°5N 93°30E **245** K11
Trinkitat *Sudan* 18°45N 37°51E **256** D4
Trino *Italy* 45°12N 8°18E **198** C5
Trinway *U.S.A.* 40°9N 82°1W **312** F2
Triolet *Mauritius* 20°4S 57°32E **272** e
Trionfale *Italy* 41°54N 12°26E **136** B1
Trionto, C. *Italy* 39°37N 16°43E **201** C9
Triora *Italy* 44°1N 7°46E **198** D4
Tripoli = Tarābulus *Lebanon* 34°31N 35°50E **250** D6
Tripoli = Tarābulus *Libya* 32°49N 13°7E **258** B2
Tripoli *Greece* 37°31N 22°25E **204** D4
Tripoli *Iowa, U.S.A.* 42°49N 92°16W **310** B4
Tripolitania *N. Afr.* 31°0N 13°0E **258** B2
Tripura □ *India* 24°0N 92°0E **241** D4
Tripylos *Cyprus* 34°59N 32°41E **207** F8
Trischen *Germany* 54°4N 8°40E **178** A4
Tristan da Cunha *Atl. Oc.* 37°6S 12°20W **255** K2
Trisul *India* 30°19N 79°47E **243** D8
Triulzo *Italy* 45°25N 9°16E **129** B2
Trivandrum *India* 8°41N 77°0E **245** K3
Trivento *Italy* 41°47N 14°33E **199** G11
Trizin *Greece* 37°25N 23°15E **204** D5
Trnava *Slovak Rep.* 48°23N 17°35E **181** C10
Trnavský □ *Slovak Rep.* 48°30N 17°45E **181** C10
Troarn *France* 49°11N 0°11W **172** C6
Trobriand Is. *Papua N. G.* 8°30S 151°0E **286** E6
Trocadero *Paris, France* **134** b1
Trochu *Canada* 51°50N 113°13W **296** C6
Trodely I. *Canada* 52°15N 79°26W **298** B4
Troebratskiy *Kazakhstan* 54°25N 66°4E **217** B7
Trogir *Croatia* 43°32N 16°15E **199** E13
Troglav *Croatia* 43°56N 16°36E **199** E13
Tróia *Italy* 41°22N 15°18E **201** A8
Troilus, L. *Canada* 50°50N 74°35W **298** B5
Troina *Italy* 37°47N 14°36E **201** E7
Trois Boutiques *Mauritius* 20°25S 57°58E **272** e
Trois Fourches, Cap des *Morocco* 35°26N 2°58W **261** A4
Trois-Pistoles *Canada* 48°5N 69°10W **299** C6
Trois Pitons, Morne *Dominica* 15°22N 61°20W **323** k
Trois-Rivières *Qué., Canada* 46°25N 72°34W **298** C5
Trois-Rivières *Guadeloupe* 15°57N 61°40W **322** e
Trois Rivières *Martinique* 14°28N 60°58W **322** j
Troisdorf *Germany* 50°48N 7°11E **178** E3
Troitse-Lykovo *Russia* 55°47N 37°23E **129** B2
Troitsk *Russia* 54°10N 61°35E **216** B6
Troitsko Pechorsk *Russia* 62°40N 56°10E **186** B10
Troitskosavsk = Kyakhta *Russia* 50°30N 106°25E **215** D11
Troitskoye *Russia* 46°26N 44°15E **191** G7
Troitskiy = Troitsk *Russia* 54°10N 61°35E **216** B6
Troja *Czech Rep.* 50°7N 14°25E **135** B2
Trölladyngja *Iceland* 64°54N 17°16W **155** C9
Trollbäcken *Sweden* 59°14N 18°12E **139** B3
Trollhättan *Sweden* 58°17N 12°20E **163** F6
Trollheimen *Norway* 62°46N 9°1E **164** B6
Trombay *India* 19°2N 72°56E **130** A2
Trombetas ➔ *Brazil* 1°55S 55°35W **329** D6
Tromelin I. *Ind. Oc.* 15°52S 54°25E **273** F4
Tromøy *Norway* 58°27N 8°51E **164** F5
Tromsø *Norway* 69°40N 18°56E **160** B18
Trona *U.S.A.* 35°46N 117°23W **307** K9
Tronador, Mte. *Argentina* 41°10S 71°50W **336** B2
Trøndelag *Norway* 64°17N 11°50E **160** D14
Trondheim *Norway* 63°36N 10°25E **164** A7
Trondheimsfjorden *Norway* 63°35N 10°30E **160** E14
Trondheimsleia *Norway* 63°25N 8°30E **164** A5
Trondhjem = Trondheim *Norway* 63°36N 10°25E **164** A7
Trönninge *Sweden* 56°37N 12°51E **163** H6
Tronto ➔ *Italy* 42°54N 13°55E **199** F10
Troodos *Cyprus* 34°55N 32°52E **207** F8
Troon *U.K.* 55°33N 4°39W **167** F4
Troparevo *Russia* 55°39N 37°29E **129** C2
Tropea *Italy* 38°41N 15°54E **201** D8
Tropenmuseum *Amsterdam, Neths.* **112** b3
Tropic *U.S.A.* 37°37N 112°5W **305** H7
Tropical Museum = Tropenmuseum *Amsterdam, Neths.* **112** b3
Tropojë *Albania* 42°23N 20°10E **202** D4
Troppau = Opava *Czech Rep.* 49°57N 17°58E **181** B10
Trosa *Sweden* 58°54N 17°33E **163** F11
Trostan *U.K.* 55°3N 6°10W **166** A5
Trostberg *Germany* 48°1N 12°33E **179** G8
Trostyanets *Sumy, Ukraine* 50°33N 34°59E **189** G8
Trostyanets *Vinnyts'ka, Ukraine* 48°31N 29°11E **183** B14
Trotsk = Chapayevsk *Russia* 53°0N 49°40E **190** D9
Trotsk = Gatchina *Russia* 59°35N 30°9E **188** C6
Trou Gras Pt. *St. Lucia* 13°51N 60°53W **323** m
Troumaka *St. Vincent* 13°18N 61°17W **323** n
Trout ➔ *Canada* 61°19N 119°51W **296** A5
Trout L. *N.W.T., Canada* 60°40N 121°14W **296** A4
Trout L. *Ont., Canada* 51°20N 93°15W **297** C10
Trout Lake *N.W.T., Canada* 56°30N 114°32W **296** B6
Trout Lake *Wash., U.S.A.* 46°0N 121°32W **306** E5
Trout River *Canada* 49°29N 58°8W **299** C8
Trout Run *U.S.A.* 41°23N 77°3W **312** E7
Trouville-sur-Mer *France* 49°21N 0°5E **172** C7
Trowbridge *U.K.* 51°18N 2°12W **169** F5
Troy *Turkey* 39°57N 26°12E **205** B8
Troy *Ala., U.S.A.* 31°48N 85°58W **316** D4
Troy *Ill., U.S.A.* 38°44N 89°54W **310** F7
Troy *Ind., U.S.A.* 37°59N 86°55W **311** G10
Troy *Kans., U.S.A.* 39°47N 95°5W **308** F6
Troy *Mich., U.S.A.* 42°37N 83°9W **311** B13
Troy *Mo., U.S.A.* 38°59N 90°59W **310** F6
Troy *Mont., U.S.A.* 48°28N 115°53W **304** B6
Troy *N.Y., U.S.A.* 42°44N 73°41W **313** D11
Troy *Ohio, U.S.A.* 40°2N 84°12W **311** D12
Troy *Pa., U.S.A.* 41°47N 76°47W **313** E8
Troyan *Bulgaria* 42°57N 24°43E **203** D8
Troyes *France* 48°19N 4°3E **173** D11
Trpanj *Croatia* 43°1N 17°15E **199** E14
Trstenik *Serbia* 43°36N 21°0E **202** C5
Trubchevsk *Russia* 52°33N 33°47E **189** F7
Truchas Pk. *U.S.A.* 35°58N 105°39W **305** J11
Trucial States = United Arab Emirates ■ *Asia* 23°50N 54°0E **247** F7
Truckee *U.S.A.* 39°20N 120°11W **306** F6
Trudeau, Montréal ✈ (YUL) *Canada* 45°28N 73°44W **130** B1
Trudfront *Russia* 45°56N 47°40E **191** H8
Trudovoye *Russia* 43°17N 132°5E **220** C6
Trudyashchikhsya, Ostrov *Russia* 59°58N 30°18E **137** B1
Trujillo *Colombia* 4°10N 76°19W **328** C2
Trujillo *Honduras* 16°0N 86°0W **320** C2
Trujillo *Peru* 8°6S 79°0W **330** B2
Trujillo *Spain* 39°28N 5°55W **195** F5
Trujillo *N. Mex., U.S.A.* 35°32N 104°42W **305** J11
Trujillo *Venezuela* 9°22N 70°38W **328** B3
Trujillo □ *Venezuela* 9°25N 70°30W **328** B3
Trujillo, Mte. = Duarte, Pico *Dom. Rep.* 19°2N 70°59W **321** C5
Trujillo Alto *Puerto Rico* 18°21N 66°1W **321** b
Truk *Micronesia* 7°25N 151°46E **287** T17
Trumann *U.S.A.* 35°41N 90°31W **315** D9
Trumansburg *U.S.A.* 42°33N 76°40W **313** D8
Trumbull, Mt. *U.S.A.* 36°25N 113°19W **305** H7
Trŭn *Bulgaria* 42°51N 22°38E **202** D6
Trun *Orne, France* 48°50N 0°2E **172** D7
Trundle *Australia* 32°53S 147°35E **283** B7
Trung-Phan = Annam *Vietnam* 16°0N 108°0E **236** E7
Truro *S. Austral., Australia* 34°24S 139°9E **282** C3
Truro *N.S., Canada* 45°21N 63°14W **299** C7
Truro *Corn., U.K.* 50°16N 5°4W **169** G2
Truskavets *Ukraine* 49°17N 23°30E **177** D12
Trŭstenik *Bulgaria* 43°31N 24°28E **203** C8
Trustrup *Denmark* 56°20N 10°46E **163** H4
Trutch *Canada* 57°44N 122°57W **296** B4
Truth or Consequences *U.S.A.* 33°8N 107°15W **305** K10
Trutnov *Czech Rep.* 50°37N 15°54E **180** A8
Truxton *U.S.A.* 42°45N 76°2W **313** D8
Truyère ➔ *France* 44°38N 2°34E **174** D6
Tryavna *Bulgaria* 42°54N 25°25E **203** D9
Tryonville *U.S.A.* 41°42N 79°48W **312** E5
Tryphena *N.Z.* 36°18S 175°28E **284** C4
Trysilelva ➔ *Norway* 61°2N 12°35E **164** D9
Tryvasshøgda *Norway* 59°59N 10°40E **133** A3
Trzcianka *Poland* 53°3N 16°25E **185** E3
Trzciel *Poland* 52°23N 15°50E **185** F2
Trzcińsko Zdrój *Poland* 52°58N 14°35E **185** F1
Trzebiatów *Poland* 54°3N 15°18E **184** D2
Trzebiez *Poland* 53°38N 14°31E **184** E1
Trzebnica *Poland* 51°20N 17°1E **185** G4
Trzemeszno *Poland* 52°33N 17°48E **185** F4
Tržič *Slovenia* 46°22N 14°18E **199** B11
Tsagaannur *Mongolia* 49°32N 89°42E **217** C11
Tsagan Aman *Russia* 47°34N 46°43E **191** G8
Tsala Apopka L. *U.S.A.* 28°53N 82°19W **317** G7
Tsamandas *Greece* 39°46N 20°21E **204** B2
Tsamkong = Zhanjiang *China* 21°15N 110°20E **229** G8
Tsandi *Namibia* 17°42S 14°50E **270** A1
Tsangpo = Brahmaputra ➔ *Asia* 23°40N 90°35E **241** D3
Tsaochiao *Taiwan* 24°39N 120°51E **225** B2
Ts'aot'un *Taiwan* 23°58N 120°41E **225** C2
Tsaratanana *Madag.* 16°47S 47°39E **272** B2
Tsaratanana, Mt. de = Maromokotro *Madag.* 14°0S 49°0E **272** A2
Tsaratanana ⌓ *Madag.* 13°57S 48°52E **272** A2
Tsarekonstantinovka = Kuybyshevo *Ukraine* 47°25N 36°40E **189** J9
Tsarevo = Michurin *Bulgaria* 42°9N 27°51E **203** D11
Tsarevo *Bulgaria* 42°28N 25°52E **203** D9
Tsaribrod = Dimitrovgrad *Serbia* 43°2N 22°48E **202** C6
Tsaritsani *Greece* 39°53N 22°14E **204** B4
Tsarkasianos *Greece* 38°10N 20°40E **207** C2
Tsarskoye Selo = Pushkin *Russia* 59°45N 30°25E **188** C6
Tsaryovokokshaysk = Yoshkar Ola *Russia* 56°38N 47°55E **190** B8
Tsau *Botswana* 20°8S 22°22E **270** B3
Tsavo *Kenya* 2°59S 38°28E **268** C4
Tsavo East △ *Kenya* 2°44S 38°47E **268** C4
Tsavo West △ *Kenya* 3°19S 37°57E **268** C4
Tsebrykove *Ukraine* 47°9N 30°10E **189** J6
Tselinograd = Astana *Kazakhstan* 51°10N 71°30E **217** B8
Tsementny = Fokino *Russia* 53°30N 34°22E **188** F8
Tseng Lan Shue *China* 22°20N 114°14E **122** A2
Tsengwen Hsi ➔ *Taiwan* 23°8N 120°19E **225** C2
Tsengwen Shuiku *Taiwan* 23°16N 120°34E **225** C2
Tsentralnyy □ *Russia* 52°0N 40°0E **190** D4
Tses *Namibia* 25°58S 18°8E **270** C2
Tsetserleg *Mongolia* 47°36N 101°32E **218** B5
Tseung Kwan *China* 22°20N 114°15E **122** B2
Tsévié *Togo* 6°25N 1°20E **263** D5
Tshabong *Botswana* 26°2S 22°29E **270** C3
Tshabuta *Dem. Rep. of the Congo* 7°42S 23°7E **265** D4
Tshane *Botswana* 24°5S 21°54E **270** B3
Tshela *Dem. Rep. of the Congo* 4°57S 13°4E **265** C2
Tshesebe *Botswana* 21°51S 27°32E **271** B4
Tshibeke *Dem. Rep. of the Congo* 2°40S 28°35E **268** C2
Tshibinda *Dem. Rep. of the Congo* 2°23S 28°43E **268** C2
Tshikapa *Dem. Rep. of the Congo* 6°28S 20°48E **265** D4
Tshilenge *Dem. Rep. of the Congo* 6°17S 23°48E **265** D4
Tshindjambo *Dem. Rep. of the Congo* 10°52S 22°43E **265** E4
Tshinota *Dem. Rep. of the Congo* 7°2S 20°58E **265** D4
Tshinsenda *Dem. Rep. of the Congo* 12°20S 28°0E **269** E2
Tshitadi *Dem. Rep. of the Congo* 6°46S 21°43E **265** D4
Tshofa *Dem. Rep. of the Congo* 5°13S 25°16E **265** D5
Tshuapa ➔ *Dem. Rep. of the Congo* 0°14S 20°42E **264** C4
Tshumbiri *Dem. Rep. of the Congo* 2°38S 16°18E **264** C3
Tshwane = Pretoria *S. Africa* 25°44S 28°12E **271** C4
Tshwane *Botswana* 22°24S 22°1E **270** B3
Tsiaotso = Jiaozuo *China* 35°16N 113°12E **226** G7
Tsibirihina ➔ *Madag.* 19°42S 44°31E **272** B1
Tsigara *Botswana* 20°22S 25°54E **270** B4
Tsihombe *Madag.* 25°10S 45°41E **272** D2
Tsiigehtchic *Canada* 67°15N 134°0W **294** C6
Ts'il-os ⌓ *Canada* 51°9N 123°59W **296** C4
Tsim Sha Tsui *China* 22°18N 114°10E **122** B2
Tsimlyansk *Russia* 47°40N 42°6E **191** G6
Tsimlyansk Res. = Tsimlyanskoye Vdkhr. *Russia* 48°0N 43°0E **191** F6
Tsimlyanskoye Vdkhr. *Russia* 48°0N 43°0E **191** F6
Tsinan = Jinan *China* 36°38N 117°1E **226** F9
Tsineng *S. Africa* 27°5S 23°5E **270** C3
Tsing Yi *China* 22°21N 114°6E **122** A1
Tsinghai = Qinghai □ *China* 36°0N 98°0E **218** C4
Tsingshih = Jinshi *China* 29°40N 111°50E **229** C8
Tsingtao = Qingdao *China* 36°5N 120°20E **227** F11
Tsingy de Bemaraha ⌓ *Madag.* 18°35S 45°25E **272** B2
Tsingy de Namoroka ⌓ *Madag.* 16°29S 45°25E **272** B2
Tsining = Jining *China* 35°22N 116°34E **226** G9
Tsinjoarivo *Madag.* 19°37S 47°40E **272** B2
Tsinjomitondraka *Madag.* 15°40S 47°8E **272** B2
Tsinling Shan = Qinling Shandi *China* 33°50N 108°10E **226** H5
Tsirigo = Kythira *Greece* 36°8N 23°0E **204** E5
Tsiroanomandidy *Madag.* 18°46S 46°2E **272** B2
Tsis I. *Micronesia* 7°17N 151°49E **287** U18
Tsiteli-Tsqaro *Georgia* 41°33N 46°0E **191** K8
Tsitondroina *Madag.* 21°19S 46°0E **272** C2
Tsitsihar = Qiqihar *China* 47°26N 124°0E **219** B7
Tsitsikamma △ *S. Africa* 34°3S 23°40E **270** D3
Tsivilsk *Russia* 55°50N 47°25E **190** C8
Tsivory *Madag.* 24°4S 46°5E **272** C2
Tskhinvali *Georgia* 42°14N 44°1E **191** J7
Tsna ➔ *Russia* 54°55N 41°58E **190** C6
Tsnori *Georgia* 41°40N 45°57E **191** K7
Tso Moriri, L. *India* 32°50N 78°20E **243** C8
Tsobis *Namibia* 19°27S 17°30E **270** A2
Tsodilo Hill *Botswana* 18°49S 21°43E **270** A3
Tsogni *Gabon* 2°48S 10°10E **264** C2
Tsogttsetsiy = Baruunsuu *Mongolia* 43°43N 105°35E **226** C3
Tsolo *S. Africa* 31°18S 28°37E **271** D4
Tsomo *S. Africa* 32°0S 27°42E **271** D4
Tsoukalades *Greece* 38°41N 20°47E **207** B2
Tsova *West Bank* 31°47N 35°6E **123** B1
Tsoying *Taiwan* 22°41N 120°17E **225** D2
Tsu *Japan* 34°45N 136°25E **223** C8
Tsu L. *Canada* 60°40N 111°52W **296** A6
Tsubata *Japan* 36°40N 136°44E **223** A8
Tsuchiura *Japan* 36°5N 140°15E **223** A12
Tsuen Wan *China* 22°22N 114°6E **122** A1
Tsugaru-Kaikyō *Japan* 41°35N 141°0E **220** D10
Tsuken-jima *Japan* 26°15N 127°56E **288** a
Tsukiji *Tokyo, Japan* **140** c5
Tsukuba *Japan* 36°2N 140°4E **223** A12
Tsukumi *Japan* 33°4N 131°52E **222** D3
Tsukushi-Sanchi *Japan* 33°25N 130°30E **222** D2
Tsumeb *Namibia* 19°9S 17°44E **270** A2
Tsumis *Namibia* 23°39S 17°29E **270** B2
Tsuna *Japan* 34°28N 134°56E **222** C6
Tsuno-Shima *Japan* 34°21N 130°52E **222** C2
Tsur Hadassa *Israel* 31°43N 35°6E **123** B1
Tsuru *Japan* 35°31N 138°57E **223** B10
Tsuruga *Japan* 35°45N 136°2E **223** B8
Tsuruga-Wan *Japan* 35°50N 136°3E **223** B8
Tsurugi *Japan* 36°29N 136°37E **223** A8

Tsurugi-San Japan 33°51N 134°6E 222 D6
Tsurumi → Japan 35°32N 139°40E 140 B3
Tsurumi-Saki Japan 32°56N 132°5E 222 E4
Tsuruoka Japan 38°44N 139°50E 220 E9
Tsurusaki Japan 33°14N 131°41E 222 D3
Tsushima Ehime, Japan 33°7N 132°32E 222 D4
Tsushima Gifu, Japan 35°10N 136°43E 223 B8
Tsushima Nagasaki, Japan 34°20N 129°20E 222 C1
Tsuyama Japan 35°3N 134°0E 222 B6
Tsvetkovo Ukraine 49°8N 31°33E 189 H6
Tsyelyakhany Belarus 52°30N 25°46E 177 B13
Tsz Wan Shan China 22°20N 114°11E 122 A2
Tu → Burma 21°50N 96°15E 241 E6
Tua Dem. Rep. of the Congo 3°38S 16°38E 264 C3
Tua → Papua N. G. 6°30S 144°28E 286 D3
Tua → Portugal 41°13N 7°26W 194 D3
Tuaheni Pt. N.Z. 38°43S 178°4E 284 E7
Tuai N.Z. 38°47S 177°10E 284 E6
Tuakau N.Z. 37°16S 174°59E 284 D3
Tual Indonesia 5°38S 132°44E 231 F8
Tualatin U.S.A. 45°23N 122°45W 306 E4
Tuam Ireland 53°31N 8°51W 166 C3
Tuamarina N.Z. 41°25S 173°59E 285 B8
Tuamotu, Îs. French Polynesia 17°0S 144°0W 289 f
Tuamotu Arch. = Tuamotu, Îs. French Polynesia 17°0S 144°0W 289 f
Tuamotu Ridge Pac. Oc. 20°0S 138°0W 289 K14
Tuanfeng China 30°38N 114°52E 229 B10
Tuanxi China 27°28N 107°8E 228 D6
Tuao Phil. 17°55N 121°22E 232 C3
Tuapa Cook Is. 18°57S 169°54W 289 g
Tuapse Russia 44°5N 39°10E 191 H4
Tuas Singapore 1°19N 103°39E 138 B1
Tuatapere N.Z. 46°8S 167°41E 285 G2
Tuba City U.S.A. 36°8N 111°14W 305 H8
Tuban Indonesia 6°54S 112°3E 235 D4
Tubani Botswana 24°46S 24°18E 270 B3
Tubarão Brazil 28°30S 49°0W 335 B6
Tūbās West Bank 32°20N 35°22E 251 F6
Tubas → Namibia 22°54S 14°35E 270 B2
Tubau Malaysia 3°10N 113°40E 235 B4
Tubbataha Reefs △ Phil. 8°53N 119°53E 233 G2
Tubigon Phil. 9°57N 123°58E 233 G4
Tübingen Germany 48°31N 9°4E 179 G5
Tubod Phil. 8°3N 123°48E 233 G4
Tubou Fiji 18°13S 178°48W 287 B3
Tubruq Libya 32°7N 23°55E 258 B4
Ţubruq □ Libya 30°0N 24°0E 258 B4
Tubuai French Polynesia 23°18S 149°30W 289 f
Tubuaï, Îs. French Polynesia 25°0S 150°0W 289 f
Tuburan Basilan, Phil. 6°39N 122°16E 233 H4
Tuburan Cebu, Phil. 10°44N 123°49E 233 F4
Tuc Trung Vietnam 11°1N 107°12E 237 G6
Tucacas Venezuela 10°48N 68°19W 328 A4
Tucano Brazil 10°58S 38°48W 332 D4
T'uch'ang Taiwan 24°35N 121°29E 225 B3
Tuchodi → Canada 58°17N 123°42W 296 B4
Tuchola Poland 53°33N 17°52E 184 E4
Tuchoměřice Czech Rep. 50°7N 14°16E 135 B1
Tuchów Poland 49°54N 21°1E 185 J8
Tuckahoe U.S.A. 40°56N 73°49W 132 A3
Tuckanarra Australia 27°7S 118°5E 279 E2
Tucker U.S.A. 33°51N 84°13W 316 B5
Tuckers Town Bermuda 32°20N 64°42W 153 a
Tucson U.S.A. 32°13N 110°58W 305 K8
Tucumán □ Argentina 26°48S 66°2W 334 B2
Tucumcari U.S.A. 35°10N 103°44W 305 J12
Tucunaré Brazil 5°18S 55°51W 331 B6
Tucupido Venezuela 9°17N 65°47W 328 B4
Tucupita Venezuela 9°2N 62°3W 329 B5
Tucuruí Brazil 3°42S 49°44W 332 B2
Tucuruí, Represa de Brazil 4°0S 49°30W 332 B2
Tucuruvi Brazil 23°28S 46°35W 137 A2
Tuczno Poland 53°13N 16°10E 185 E3
Tuddal Norway 59°46N 8°49E 164 E5
Tudela Spain 42°4N 1°39W 196 C3
Tudmur Syria 34°36N 38°15E 213 E8
Tudor, L. Canada 55°50N 65°25W 299 A6
Tudora Romania 47°31N 26°45E 183 C11
Tuella → Portugal 41°30N 7°12W 194 D3
Tuen Mun China 22°24N 113°59E 219 G10
Tueré → Brazil 2°48S 50°59W 332 B1
Tufello Italy 41°56N 12°32E 136 B2
Tüffer = Laško Slovenia 46°10N 15°16E 199 B12
Tufi Papua N. G. 9°8S 149°19E 286 E5
Tufnell Park U.K. 51°33N 0°8W 125 A3
Tufsingdal Norway 62°18N 11°44E 164 B8
Tufts Abyssal Plain Pac. Oc. 47°0N 140°0W 289 C14
Tufts University U.S.A. 42°24N 71°7W 116 A2
Tufu Pt. Amer. Samoa 14°13S 169°30W 302 g
Tugela → S. Africa 29°14S 31°30E 271 C5
Tughlakabad India 28°30N 77°16E 120 B2
Tugidak I. U.S.A. 56°30N 154°40W 303 H9
Tuguegarao Phil. 17°35N 121°42E 232 C3
Tugur Russia 53°44N 136°45E 215 D14
Tui Spain 42°3N 8°39W 194 C2
Tuileries, Jardin des Paris, France 134 b3
Tuindorp Neths. 52°25N 4°54E 112 A2
Tuineje Canary Is. 28°19N 14°3W 153 e2
Tukangbesi, Kepulauan Indonesia 6°0S 124°0E 231 F6
Tukarak I. Canada 56°15N 78°45W 298 A4
Tukayyid Iraq 29°47N 45°36E 246 D5
Tûkh Egypt 30°21N 31°12E 256 H7
Tukhlya Ukraine 48°55N 23°28E 183 B8
Tukituki → N.Z. 39°36S 176°56E 284 F5
Tukkae, Ao Thailand 7°51N 98°25E 237 a
Tukobo Ghana 5°1N 2°47W 262 D4
Tūkrah Libya 32°30N 20°37E 258 B4
Tuktoyaktuk Canada 69°27N 133°2W 294 C6
Tuku Taiwan 23°41N 120°23E 225 C2
Tukums Latvia 56°58N 23°10E 184 B10
Tukums □ Latvia 56°55N 23°0E 184 B10
Tukuran Phil. 7°51N 123°34E 233 H4
Tukuyu Tanzania 9°17S 33°35E 269 D3
Tula Amer. Samoa 14°15S 170°34W 302 f
Tula Hidalgo, Mexico 20°3N 99°21W 319 C5
Tula Tamaulipas, Mexico 23°0N 99°43W 319 C5
Tula Nigeria 9°51N 11°27E 263 D7
Tula Russia 54°13N 37°38E 188 E9
Tula □ Russia 53°45N 37°30E 188 F9
Tulagi Solomon Is. 9°5S 160°10E 287 M11
Tūlak Afghan. 33°55N 63°40E 240 B1
Tulan Taiwan 22°53N 121°13E 225 D3
Tulancingo Mexico 20°5N 98°22W 319 C5
Tulangbawang → Indonesia 4°24S 105°52E 234 C3
Tulare Serbia 42°48N 21°28E 202 D5
Tulare Calif., U.S.A. 36°13N 119°21W 306 J7
Tulare Lake Bed U.S.A. 36°0N 119°48W 306 K7
Tularosa U.S.A. 33°5N 106°1W 305 K10
Tulbagh S. Africa 33°16S 19°6E 270 D2
Tulcán Ecuador 0°48N 77°43W 328 C2
Tulcea Romania 45°13N 28°46E 183 E13
Tulcea □ Romania 45°0N 28°30E 183 E13
Tulchyn Ukraine 48°41N 28°49E 183 B13
Tüledi Araldary Kazakhstan 45°2N 50°16E 191 H10
Tūleh Iran 34°35N 52°33E 247 C7
Tulemalu L. Canada 62°58N 99°25W 297 A9
Tulgheş Romania 46°58N 25°45E 183 D10
Tuli Zimbabwe 21°58S 29°13E 269 G2
Tulia U.S.A. 34°32N 101°46W 314 D4
Tuliszków Poland 52°5N 18°18E 185 F5
Tulita Canada 64°57N 125°30W 294 C7
Ţūlkarm West Bank 32°19N 35°2E 251 F6
Tulla Ireland 52°53N 8°46W 166 D3
Tullahoma U.S.A. 35°22N 86°13W 315 D11
Tullamarine Australia 37°41S 144°50E 128 A1
Tullamore N.S.W., Australia 32°39S 147°36E 283 B7
Tullamore Offaly, Ireland 53°16N 7°31W 166 C4
Tulle France 45°16N 1°46E 174 C5
Tulln Austria 48°20N 16°4E 180 C9
Tullow Ireland 52°49N 6°45W 166 D5
Tullus Sudan 11°7N 24°31E 257 E1
Tully Queens., Australia 17°56S 145°55E 280 B4
Tully N.Y., U.S.A. 42°48N 76°7W 313 D8
Ţulmaythah Libya 32°40N 20°55E 258 B4
Tulnici Romania 45°51N 26°38E 183 E11
Tulovo Bulgaria 42°33N 25°32E 203 D9
Tulsa U.S.A. 36°10N 95°55W 314 C7
Tulse Hill U.K. 51°26N 0°6W 125 B3
Tulsequah Canada 58°39N 133°35W 296 B2
Tulu Milki Ethiopia 9°55N 38°20E 257 F4
Tulu Welel Ethiopia 8°56N 34°47E 257 F3
Tulua Colombia 4°6N 76°11W 328 C2
Tuluceşti Romania 45°34N 28°2E 183 E13
Tuluksak U.S.A. 61°6N 160°58W 303 F7
Tulun Russia 54°32N 100°35E 215 D11
Tulungagung Indonesia 8°5S 111°54E 235 D4
Tuma Russia 55°10N 40°30E 188 E11
Tuma → Nic. 13°6N 84°35W 320 D3
Tumacacori ⌂ U.S.A. 31°35N 111°6W 305 L8
Tumaco Colombia 1°50N 78°45W 328 C2
Tumaco, Ensenada Colombia 1°55N 78°45W 328 C2
Tumatumari Guyana 5°20N 58°55W 329 B6
Tumauini Phil. 17°17N 121°49E 232 C3
Tumba Dem. Rep. of the Congo 3°10S 23°36E 264 C4
Tumba Sweden 59°12N 17°48E 162 E11
Tumba, L. Dem. Rep. of the Congo 0°50S 18°0E 264 C3
Tumbarumba Australia 35°44S 148°0E 283 C8
Tumbaya Argentina 23°50S 65°26W 334 A2
Tumbes Peru 3°37S 80°27W 330 A1
Tumbes □ Peru 3°50S 80°30W 330 A1
Tumbler Ridge Canada 55°8N 121°0W 296 B4
Tumbur Sudan 4°20N 31°34E 257 G3
Tumbwe Dem. Rep. of the Congo 11°25S 27°15E 269 E2
Tumby Bay Australia 34°21S 136°8E 282 C2
Tumd Youqi China 40°30N 110°30E 226 D6
Tumen China 43°0N 129°50E 224 A4
Tumen Jiang → China 42°20N 130°35E 224 A5
Tumeremo Venezuela 7°18N 61°30W 329 B5
Tumiritinga Brazil 18°58S 41°38W 333 E3
Tumkur India 13°18N 77°6E 245 H3
Tumon B. Guam 13°31N 144°48E 302 d
Tump Pakistan 26°7N 62°16E 240 D1
Tumpat Malaysia 6°11N 102°10E 237 J4
Tumsar India 21°26N 79°45E 244 D4
Tumu Ghana 10°56N 1°56W 262 C4
Tumucumaque, Serra Brazil 2°0N 55°0W 329 C7
Tumupasa Bolivia 14°9S 67°55W 330 C4
Tumut Australia 35°16S 148°13E 283 C8
Tumwater U.S.A. 47°1N 122°54W 306 C4
Tuna India 22°59N 70°5E 242 H4
Tunadal Sweden 62°26N 17°22E 162 B11
Tunapuna Trin. & Tob. 10°38N 61°24W 323 t
Tunas de Zaza Cuba 21°39N 79°34W 320 B4
Tunbridge Wells = Royal Tunbridge Wells U.K. 51°7N 0°16E 169 F8
Tunçbilek Turkey 39°37N 29°29E 205 B11
Tunceli Turkey 39°6N 39°31E 213 C8
Tunceli □ Turkey 39°5N 39°35E 213 C8
Tuncurry Australia 32°17S 152°29E 283 B10
Tundla India 27°12N 78°17E 242 F8
Tundubai Sudan 18°36N 28°35E 256 D2
Tunduru Tanzania 11°8S 37°25E 269 E4
Tundzha → Bulgaria 41°40N 26°35E 203 E10
Tung Chung China 22°17N 113°57E 219 G10
Tung Lung Chau China 22°15N 114°17E 122 B2
Tung O China 22°11N 114°8E 122 B1
Tunga → India 15°0N 75°50E 245 G2
Tunga Pass India 29°0N 94°14E 241 A5
Tungabhadra → India 15°57N 78°15E 245 G4
Tungabhadra Dam India 15°0N 75°50E 245 G2
Tungao Taiwan 24°31N 121°50E 225 B3
Tungaru Sudan 10°9N 30°52E 257 E3
Tungawan Phil. 7°30N 122°20E 233 H4
Tungchi Yü Taiwan 23°15N 119°40E 225 C1
Tungch'uan = Dongchuan China 26°8N 103°1E 228 D4
Tungho Taiwan 22°58N 121°18E 225 D3
T'unghsiao Taiwan 24°29N 120°40E 225 B2
Tunghwa = Tonghua China 41°42N 125°58E 224 B2
Tungi Bangla. 23°53N 90°24E 241 D3
Tungkang Taiwan 22°27N 120°26E 225 D2
Tungla Nic. 13°24N 84°21W 320 D3
T'unglo Taiwan 24°30N 120°47E 225 B2
Tungnafellsjökull Iceland 64°45N 17°55W 155 C9
Tungsha Tao = Dongsha Dao China 20°45N 116°43E 229 G11
Tungshan Taiwan 24°38N 121°47E 225 B3
Tungshih Changhua, Taiwan 24°12N 120°43E 225 B2
Tungshih Chiai, Taiwan 23°27N 120°8E 225 C2
Tungsten Canada 61°57N 128°16W 296 A3
Tungufell Iceland 64°17N 20°10W 155 C6
Tungurahua □ Ecuador 1°15S 78°35W 328 D2
Tunguska, Nizhnyaya → Russia 65°48N 88°4E 215 C9
Tunguska, Podkamennaya → Russia 61°50N 90°13E 215 C10
Tungyin Tao Taiwan 26°22N 128°29E 225 b
Tuni India 17°22N 82°36E 244 F6
Tunia Colombia 2°41N 76°31W 328 C2
Tunica U.S.A. 34°41N 90°23W 315 D9
Tunis Baghdād, Iraq 33°23N 44°21E 113 A2
Tunis Tunisia 36°50N 10°11E 258 A2
Tunis □ Tunisia 36°46N 10°10E 261 A7
Tunis ✈ (TUN) Tunisia 36°52N 10°14E 200 F3
Tunis, Golfe de Tunisia 37°0N 10°30E 258 A2
Tunisia ■ Africa 33°30N 9°10E 258 B1
Tunja Colombia 5°33N 73°25W 328 B3
Tunkhannock U.S.A. 41°32N 75°57W 313 E9
Tunliu China 36°13N 112°52E 226 F7
Tunnel Creek △ Australia 17°41S 125°18E 278 C4
Tunnsjøen Norway 64°45N 13°25E 160 D15
Tunø Denmark 55°57N 10°27E 163 J4
Tuntutuliak U.S.A. 60°22N 162°38W 303 F7
Tunu □ Greenland 75°0N 30°0W 154 C7
Tununak U.S.A. 60°37N 165°15W 303 F6
Tunungayualok I. Canada 56°0N 61°0W 299 A7
Tunuyán Argentina 33°35S 69°0W 334 C2
Tunuyán → Argentina 33°33S 67°30W 334 C2
Tuo Jiang → China 28°50N 105°35E 228 C5
Tuolumne U.S.A. 37°58N 120°15W 306 H6
Tuolumne → U.S.A. 37°36N 121°13W 306 H5
Tuomarila Finland 60°11N 24°41E 121 B1
Tüp Kyrgyzstan 42°45N 78°20E 217 D9
Tūp Āghāj Iran 36°3N 47°50E 213 D12
Tupã Brazil 21°57S 50°28W 335 A5
Tupaciguara Brazil 18°35S 48°42W 333 E2
Tupelo U.S.A. 34°16N 88°43W 315 D10
Tupik Russia 55°42N 33°22E 188 E7
Tupinambaranas Brazil 3°0S 58°0W 329 D6
Tupirama Brazil 8°58S 48°12W 332 C2
Tupiratins Brazil 8°23S 48°8W 332 C2
Tupiza Bolivia 21°30S 65°40W 334 A2
Tupižnica Serbia 43°43N 22°10E 202 C6
Tupman U.S.A. 35°18N 119°21W 307 K7
Tupper Canada 55°32N 120°1W 296 B4
Tupper Lake U.S.A. 44°14N 74°28W 313 B10
Tüpqarghan Muyis Kazakhstan 44°40N 50°19E 191 H10
Tupungato, Cerro S. Amer. 33°15S 69°50W 334 C2
Tuquan China 45°18N 121°38E 227 B11
Túquerres Colombia 1°5N 77°37W 328 C2
Tura India 25°30N 90°16E 241 C3
Tura Russia 64°20N 100°17E 215 C11
Turabah Ḥā'il, Si. Arabia 28°20N 43°15E 246 D4
Turabah Makkah, Si. Arabia 21°15N 41°34E 248 B3
Turagua, Serranía Venezuela 7°20N 64°35W 329 B5
Turakina N.Z. 40°3S 175°16E 284 G4
Turakina → N.Z. 40°5S 175°8E 284 G4
Turakirae Hd. N.Z. 41°26S 174°56E 284 H3
Turama → Papua N. G. 7°40S 143°50E 286 D2
Tūrān Iran 35°39N 56°42E 247 C8
Turan Russia 51°55N 94°0E 217 B12
Turan Lowland Asia 43°30N 62°0E 216 D6
Turangi N.Z. 38°59S 175°48E 284 E4
Ţurayf Si. Arabia 31°41N 38°39E 246 D3
Turbaco Colombia 10°21N 75°25W 328 A2
Turbacz Poland 49°30N 20°8E 185 J7
Turbat Pakistan 25°59N 63°4E 240 D1
Turbe Bos.-H. 44°15N 17°35E 182 F2
Turbeville U.S.A. 33°54N 80°1W 316 B9
Turbo Colombia 8°6N 76°43W 328 B2
Turčianske Teplice Slovak Rep. 48°52N 18°52E 181 C11
Turco Bolivia 18°10S 68°11W 330 D4
Turcoaia Romania 45°7N 28°11E 183 E13
Turda Romania 46°34N 23°47E 183 D8
Tureberg Sweden 59°25N 17°55E 139 A1
Turéia French Polynesia 20°50S 138°32W 289 f
Turek Poland 52°3N 18°30E 185 F5
Turfan = Turpan China 43°58N 89°10E 217 D11
Turfan Basin = Turpan Pendi China 42°40N 89°25E 217 D11
Turfan Depression = Turpan Pendi China 42°40N 89°25E 217 D11
Turffontein S. Africa 26°14S 28°2E 123 B2
Turgayskaya Stolovaya Strana = Torghay Ustirti Asia 51°0N 63°0E 216 B6
Turgeon → Canada 50°0N 78°56W 298 C4
Tŭrgovishte Bulgaria 43°17N 26°38E 203 C10
Turgut Turkey 37°22N 28°4E 205 D10
Turgutlu Turkey 38°30N 27°43E 205 C9
Turgwe → Zimbabwe 21°31S 32°15E 271 B5
Turhal Turkey 40°24N 36°5E 212 B7
Turia → Spain 39°27N 0°19W 197 F4
Turiaçu Brazil 1°40S 45°19W 332 B2
Turiaçu → Brazil 1°36S 45°19W 332 B2
Turiec → Slovak Rep. 49°7N 18°55E 181 B11
Turin = Torino Italy 45°3N 7°40E 198 C4
Turinskaya Kultbaza = Tura Russia 64°20N 100°17E 215 C11
Turka Ukraine 49°10N 23°2E 185 J10
Turkana, L. Africa 3°30N 36°5E 268 B4
Turkayel Ethiopia 8°7N 45°21E 267 C6
Türkeli Turkey 40°30N 27°30E 203 F11
Turkestan = Türkistan Kazakhstan 43°17N 68°16E 217 D7
Turkestan Range Asia 39°35N 69°0E 217 E7
Túrkeve Hungary 47°6N 20°44E 182 C5
Turkey ■ Eurasia 39°0N 36°0E 212 C7
Turkey → U.S.A. 42°43N 91°2W 310 B5
Turkey Creek = Warmun Australia 17°2S 128°12E 278 C4
Turkey L. U.S.A. 28°30N 81°28W 133 A2
Turkey Lake Park U.S.A. 28°30N 81°28W 133 A2
Turki Russia 52°0N 43°15E 190 D6
Türkistan Kazakhstan 43°17N 68°16E 217 D7
Türkmenabat Turkmenistan 39°6N 63°34E 247 B9
Türkmenbashi Turkmenistan 40°5N 53°5E 247 A7
Turkmenistan ■ Asia 39°0N 59°0E 216 E5
Türkmenli Turkey 39°45N 26°30E 205 B8
Türkoğlu Turkey 37°23N 36°50E 212 D7
Turks & Caicos Is. ⧄ W. Indies 21°20N 71°20W 321 B5
Turks Island Passage W. Indies 21°30N 71°30W 321 B5
Turku Finland 60°30N 22°19E 188 B2
Turkwel → Kenya 3°6N 36°6E 268 B4
Turlock U.S.A. 37°30N 120°51W 306 H6
Turnagain → Canada 59°12N 127°35W 296 B3
Turnagain, C. N.Z. 40°28S 176°38E 284 G5
Turneffe Is. Belize 17°20N 87°50W 319 D7
Turner U.S.A. 48°51N 108°24W 304 B9
Turner Field U.S.A. 33°44N 84°23W 113 B2
Turner Pt. Australia 11°47S 133°32E 280 A1
Turner Valley Canada 50°40N 114°17W 296 C6
Turners Falls U.S.A. 42°36N 72°33W 313 D12
Turnham Green U.K. 51°29N 0°16W 125 B2
Turnhouse U.K. 55°57N 3°20W 121 B1
Turnhout Belgium 51°19N 4°57E 170 C4
Türnitz Austria 47°55N 15°29E 180 D8
Turnor L. Canada 56°35N 108°35W 297 B7
Turnov Czech Rep. 50°34N 15°10E 180 A8
Tŭrnovo = Veliko Tŭrnovo Bulgaria 43°5N 25°41E 203 C9
Turnu Măgurele Romania 43°46N 24°56E 183 G9
Turnu Roşu, P. Romania 45°33N 24°17E 183 E9
Turobin Poland 50°50N 22°44E 185 H9
Tuross Head Australia 36°3S 150°8E 283 D9
Turpan China 43°58N 89°10E 217 D11
Turpan Pendi China 42°40N 89°25E 217 D11
Turrawan Australia 30°28S 149°53E 283 A8
Turrës, Kala e Albania 41°10N 19°28E 202 E3
Turriff U.K. 57°32N 2°27W 167 D6
Tursāq Iraq 33°27N 45°47E 213 F11
Tursi Italy 40°15N 16°28E 201 B9
Turtle Head I. Australia 10°56S 142°37E 286 F2
Turtle Is. Phil. 6°7N 118°14E 233 H2
Turtle Is. S. Leone 7°40N 13°0E 262 D2
Turtle L. Canada 53°36N 108°38W 297 C7
Turtle Lake U.S.A. 47°31N 100°53W 308 B3
Turtleford Canada 53°23N 108°57W 297 C7
Turtucaia = Tutrakan Bulgaria 44°2N 26°40E 203 B10
Turua N.Z. 37°14S 175°35E 284 D4
Turukhansk Russia 65°21N 88°5E 215 C9
Turyinskiye Rudniki = Krasnoturinsk Russia 59°46N 60°12E 186 C11
Turzovka Slovak Rep. 49°25N 18°35E 181 B11
Tuscaloosa U.S.A. 33°12N 87°34W 315 E11
Tuscánia Italy 42°25N 11°52E 199 F8
Tuscany = Toscana □ Italy 43°25N 11°0E 198 E8
Tuscarawas → U.S.A. 40°24N 81°25W 312 F3
Tuscarora Mt. U.S.A. 40°55N 77°55W 312 F7
Tuscola Ill., U.S.A. 39°48N 88°17W 311 E8
Tuscola Tex., U.S.A. 32°12N 99°48W 314 E5
Tuscolana, Via Italy 41°52N 12°31E 136 B2
Tuscumbia Ala., U.S.A. 34°44N 87°42W 315 D11
Tuscumbia Mo., U.S.A. 38°14N 92°28W 310 F4
Tushino Russia 55°50N 37°24E 129 A2
Tuskegee U.S.A. 32°25N 85°42W 316 C4
Tusket Wedge = Wedgeport Canada 43°44N 65°59W 299 D6
Tustna Norway 63°10N 8°5E 164 A5
Tuszyn Poland 51°36N 19°33E 185 G6
Tutak Turkey 39°31N 42°46E 213 C10
Tutayev Russia 57°53N 39°32E 188 D10
Tuticorin India 8°50N 78°12E 245 K4
Tutin Serbia 42°58N 20°20E 202 D4
Tutóia Brazil 2°45S 42°20W 332 B3
Tutong Brunei 4°47N 114°40E 235 B4
Tutova → Romania 46°7N 27°30E 183 D12
Tutrakan Bulgaria 44°2N 26°40E 203 B10
Tuttle Creek L. U.S.A. 39°15N 96°36W 308 F5
Tuttlingen Germany 47°58N 8°48E 179 H4
Tutuala E. Timor 8°25S 127°15E 231 F7
Tutuba Vanuatu 15°33S 167°16E 287 E5
Tutubeia Papua N. G. 9°34S 150°40E 286 E6
Tutuila Amer. Samoa 14°19S 170°50W 302 f
Tutuko, Mt. N.Z. 44°35S 168°1E 285 E3
Tutun Egypt 29°9N 30°46E 256 J7
Tütz = Tuczno Poland 53°13N 16°10E 185 E3
Tuul Gol → Mongolia 48°30N 104°25E 218 B5
Tuva □ Russia 51°30N 95°0E 217 B12
Tuvalu ■ Pac. Oc. 8°0S 178°0E 277 B14
Tuvuca Fiji 17°40S 178°48W 287 A3
Tūwal Si. Arabia 22°17N 39°6E 248 B2
Tuxer Alpen Austria 47°10N 11°45E 180 D4
Tuxpan Mexico 20°57N 97°24W 319 C5
Tuxtla Gutiérrez Mexico 16°45N 93°7W 319 D6
Tuy = Tui Spain 42°3N 8°39W 194 C2
Tuy An Vietnam 13°17N 109°16E 236 F7
Tuy Duc Vietnam 12°15N 107°27E 237 F6
Tuy Hoa Vietnam 13°5N 109°10E 236 F7
Tuy Phong Vietnam 11°14N 108°43E 237 G7
Tuya L. Canada 59°7N 130°35W 296 B2
Tuyen Hoa Vietnam 17°50N 106°10E 236 D6
Tuyen Quang Vietnam 21°50N 105°10E 228 G5
Tuymazy Russia 54°36N 53°42E 216 B4
Tūysarkān Iran 34°33N 48°27E 213 E13
Tuyün = Duyun China 26°18N 107°29E 228 D6
Tuz Gölü Turkey 38°42N 33°18E 212 C5
Ţūz Khurmātū = Tozkhurmato Iraq 34°56N 44°38E 213 E11
Tuzi Montenegro 42°22N 19°20E 202 D3
Tuzigoot △ U.S.A. 34°46N 112°2W 305 J7
Tuzla Bos.-H. 44°34N 18°41E 182 F3
Tuzla Turkey 36°42N 35°6E 250 B6
Tuzlov → Russia 47°17N 39°57E 189 J10
Tuzluca Turkey 40°3N 43°39E 213 B10
Tuzly 45°54N 30°6E 183 E15
Tvååker Sweden 57°4N 12°25E 163 G6
Tvardiţa Moldova 46°9N 28°58E 183 D13
Tvedestrand Norway 58°38N 8°58E 164 F5
Tver Russia 56°55N 35°55E 188 D8
Tver □ Russia 56°50N 35°0E 188 D8
Tvrdošin Slovak Rep. 49°21N 19°35E 181 B12
Tvrdošovce Slovak Rep. 48°6N 18°4E 181 C11
Tvŭrditsa Bulgaria 42°42N 25°53E 203 D9
Twain U.S.A. 40°1N 121°3W 306 E5
Twain Harte U.S.A. 38°2N 120°14W 306 G6
Twardogóra Poland 51°23N 17°28E 185 G4
Tweed Canada 44°29N 77°19W 312 B7
Tweed → U.K. 55°45N 2°0W 167 F6
Tweed Heads Australia 28°10S 153°31E 281 D5
Tweedsmuir ⌂ Canada 53°0N 126°20W 296 C3
Twelve Apostles S. Africa 33°58S 18°23E 118 A1
Twentynine Palms U.S.A. 34°8N 116°3W 307 L10
Tweya Dem. Rep. of the Congo 0°54S 18°58E 264 C3
Twickenham U.K. 51°26N 0°20W 125 B1
Twickenham Rugby Ground U.K. 51°27N 0°20W 125 B1
Twillingate Canada 49°42N 54°45W 299 C9
Twin Bridges U.S.A. 45°33N 112°20W 304 D7
Twin City U.S.A. 32°35N 82°10W 316 C7
Twin Falls Canada 53°30N 64°32W 299 B7
Twin Falls Idaho, U.S.A. 42°34N 114°28W 304 E6
Twin Hills U.S.A. 59°23N 159°58W 303 G8
Twin Lakes U.S.A. 30°43N 83°13W 316 E6
Twin Peaks U.S.A. 37°45N 122°26W 136 B2
Twin Valley U.S.A. 47°16N 96°16W 308 B5
Twinnge Burma 23°10N 96°2E 241 D6
Twinsburg U.S.A. 41°19N 81°26W 312 E3
Twistringen Germany 52°48N 8°37E 178 C4
Twitchell Res. U.S.A. 34°59N 120°19W 307 L6
Two Boats Village Ascension I. 7°56S 14°22W 153 g
Two Harbors U.S.A. 47°2N 91°40W 308 B8
Two Hills Canada 53°43N 111°52W 296 C6
Two Rivers U.S.A. 44°9N 87°34W 308 C10
Two Rock Mt. Ireland 53°15N 6°14W 120 B2
Two Rocks Australia 31°30S 115°35E 279 F2
Two Thumb Ra. N.Z. 43°45S 170°44E 285 D5
Twofold B. Australia 37°8S 149°59E 283 D8
Ty Ty U.S.A. 31°28N 83°39W 316 D6
Tyachiv Ukraine 48°1N 23°35E 177 D12
Tybee Island U.S.A. 32°1N 80°51W 316 C9
Tychy Poland 50°9N 18°59E 185 H5
Tyczyn Poland 49°58N 22°2E 185 J9
Tydal Norway 63°4N 11°34E 164 A8
Tyin Norway 61°18N 8°15E 164 C5
Tykocin Poland 53°13N 22°46E 185 E9
Tyler Minn., U.S.A. 44°17N 96°8W 308 C5
Tyler Tex., U.S.A. 32°21N 95°18W 314 E7
Tyligul → Ukraine 47°4N 30°57E 189 J6
Tylldal Norway 62°8N 10°48E 164 B7
Tymanivka Ukraine 48°34N 28°50E 183 B13
Tymon North Ireland 53°18N 6°20W 120 B1
Týn nad Vltavou Czech Rep. 49°13N 14°26E 180 B7
Tynda Russia 55°10N 124°43E 215 D13
Tyndall U.S.A. 43°0N 97°50W 308 D5
Tyndinsky = Tynda Russia 55°10N 124°43E 215 D13
Tyne → U.K. 54°59N 1°32W 168 C6
Tyne & Wear □ U.K. 55°6N 1°17W 168 B6
Týnec nad Sázavou Czech Rep. 49°50N 14°36E 180 B7
Tynemouth U.K. 55°1N 1°26W 168 B6
Tynset Norway 62°17N 10°47E 164 B7
Tyonek U.S.A. 61°4N 151°8W 303 F10
Tyre = Sūr Lebanon 33°19N 35°16E 250 E6
Tyresta △ Sweden 59°12N 18°14E 162 E12
Tyrifjorden Norway 60°2N 10°8E 164 D7
Tyringe Sweden 56°9N 13°35E 163 H7
Tyristrand Norway 60°4N 10°6E 164 D7
Tyrnyauz Russia 43°21N 42°45E 191 J6
Tyrol = Tirol □ Austria 47°3N 10°43E 180 D3
Tyrone U.S.A. 40°40N 78°14W 312 F6
Tyrone □ U.K. 54°38N 7°11W 166 B4
Tyrrel Bay Grenada 12°27N 61°28W 323 q
Tyrrell → Australia 35°26S 142°51E 282 C5
Tyrrell, L. Australia 35°20S 142°50E 282 C5
Tyrrell L. Canada 63°7N 105°27W 297 A7
Tyrrhenian Sea Medit. S. 40°0N 12°30E 192 D6
Tysfjorden Norway 68°7N 16°25E 160 B17
Tysmenytsya Ukraine 48°54N 24°51E 183 B9
Tysnes Norway 60°1N 5°30E 164 D2
Tysnesøya Norway 60°0N 5°35E 164 D2
Tysons Corner U.S.A. 38°55N 77°13W 143 B2
Tysse Norway 60°23N 5°47E 164 D2
Tyssedal Norway 60°7N 6°35E 164 D3
Tystberga Sweden 58°51N 17°15E 163 F11
Tytuvėnai Lithuania 55°36N 23°12E 184 C10
Tyub Karagan, Mys = Tüpqarghan Muyis Kazakhstan 44°40N 50°19E 191 H10
Tyuleni, Ostrova = Tüledi Araldary Kazakhstan 45°2N 50°16E 191 H10
Tyuleniy Russia 44°28N 47°30E 191 H8
Tyuleniy, Mys Azerbaijan 40°12N 50°22E 191 K10
Tyulgan Russia 52°22N 56°12E 186 D10
Tyumen Russia 57°11N 65°29E 214 D7
Tyup = Tüp Kyrgyzstan 42°45N 78°20E 217 D9
Tywi → U.K. 51°48N 4°21W 169 F3
Tywyn U.K. 52°35N 4°5W 169 E3
Tzaneen S. Africa 23°47S 30°9E 271 B5
Tzermiado Greece 35°12N 25°29E 207 E6
Tzia = Kea Greece 37°35N 24°22E 204 D6
Tzoumérka, Óros = Athamanon Oros Greece 39°30N 21°26E 204 B3
Tzukong = Zigong China 29°15N 104°48E 228 C5
Tzukuan Taiwan 22°46N 120°16E 225 D2
Tzupo = Boshan China 36°28N 117°49E 227 F9
Tzutung Taiwan 23°45N 120°30E 225 C2

U

U Taphao Thailand 12°35N 101°0E 236 F3
U.S.A. = United States of America ■ N. Amer. 37°0N 96°0W 300 C7
U.S. Capitol Washington, D.C., U.S.A. 143 b3
U.S. Cellular Field U.S.A. 41°50N 87°37W 119 C3
U.S. Holocaust Museum Washington, D.C., U.S.A. 143 c1
U.S.S. Arizona ⌂ U.S.A. 21°22N 157°57W 302 K14
U.S.S. Constitution = Old Ironside Boston, U.S.A. 116 a3
U.S. Virgin Is. ⧄ W. Indies 18°20N 65°0W 321 C7
Ua Huka French Polynesia 8°55S 139°32W 289 f
Ua Pu French Polynesia 9°25S 140°0W 289 f
Uacalla Iero Somali Rep. 1°48N 42°38E 267 D5
Uachadi, Sierra = Uasadi-jidi Venezuela 4°54N 65°18W 329 C4
Uad Atui → W. Sahara 20°4N 15°59W 260 D2
Uad el Jat → W. Sahara 26°47N 13°3W 260 C2
Uainambi Colombia 1°43N 69°51W 328 C4
Uamba Angola 7°21S 16°10E 265 D3
Uanle Uen Somali Rep. 2°37N 44°54E 267 D5
Uargalò Somali Rep. 6°17N 47°31E 267 C6
Uarsciek Somali Rep. 2°28N 45°55E 267 D6
Uasadi-jidi Venezuela 4°54N 65°18W 329 C4
Uascen Somali Rep. 4°11N 43°13E 267 D5
Uatumã → Brazil 2°26S 57°37W 329 D6
Uauá Brazil 9°50S 39°28W 332 C4
Uaupés Brazil 0°8S 67°5W 328 D4
Uaupés → Brazil 0°2N 67°16W 328 C4
Uaxactún Guatemala 17°25N 89°29W 320 C2
Ub Serbia 44°28N 20°6E 202 B4
Ubá Brazil 21°8S 43°0W 333 F3
Uba Nigeria 10°29N 13°13E 263 C7
Ubai Papua N. G. 5°39S 150°38E 286 C6
Ubaitaba Brazil 14°18S 39°20W 333 D4
Ubajara △ Brazil 3°55S 40°50W 332 B3
Ubangi = Oubangi → Dem. Rep. of the Congo 0°30S 17°50E 264 C3
Ubaté Colombia 5°19N 73°49W 328 B3
Ubauro Pakistan 28°15N 69°45E 242 E3
Ubay Phil. 10°3N 124°28E 233 F5
Ubaye → France 44°28N 6°18E 175 D10
Ubayyiḍ, W. al → Iraq 32°34N 43°48E 213 F10
Ube Japan 33°56N 131°15E 222 D3
Úbeda Spain 38°3N 3°23W 195 G7
Ubeidiya West Bank 31°43N 35°17E 123 B2
Uberaba Brazil 19°50S 47°55W 333 E2
Uberaba → Brazil 23°35S 46°41W 137 B2
Uberaba, L. Brazil 17°30S 57°50W 331 D6
Uberlândia Minas Gerais, Brazil 19°0S 48°20W 333 E2
Uberlândia Roraïma, Brazil 0°48N 59°20W 329 C6
Überlingen Germany 47°46N 9°10E 179 H5
Ubiaja Nigeria 6°41N 6°22E 263 D6
Ubin, Pulau Singapore 1°24N 103°57E 138 A3
Ubolratna Res. Thailand 16°45N 102°30E 236 D4
Ubombo S. Africa 27°31S 32°4E 271 C5
Ubon Ratchathani Thailand 15°15N 104°50E 236 E5
Ubondo Dem. Rep. of the Congo 0°55S 25°42E 268 C2
Ubort → Belarus 52°6N 28°30E 177 B15
Ubrique Spain 36°41N 5°27W 195 J5
Ubud Indonesia 8°30S 115°16E 231 J18
Ubuna Solomon Is. 10°11S 161°24E 287 N11
Ubundu Dem. Rep. of the Congo 0°22S 25°30E 264 C5
Ucayali → Peru 4°30S 73°30W 330 A3
Uccle Belgium 50°48N 4°22E 116 B2
Uchab Namibia 19°47S 17°42E 270 A2
Uchiko Japan 33°33N 132°39E 222 D4
Uchiura-Wan Japan 42°25N 140°40E 220 C10
Uchiza Peru 8°25S 76°20W 330 B2
Uchquduq Uzbekistan 41°50N 62°50E 216 D6
Uchte Germany 52°30N 8°54E 178 C4
Uchur → Russia 58°48N 130°35E 215 D14
Uckermark Germany 53°5N 13°30E 178 B9
Ucluelet Canada 48°57N 125°32W 296 D3
Úcua Angola 8°43S 14°8E 265 D2
Uda → Russia 54°42N 135°14E 215 D14
Uda Walawe △ Sri Lanka 6°20N 81°0E 245 L5
Udagamandalam India 11°30N 76°44E 245 J3
Udainagar India 22°33N 76°13E 242 H7
Udaipur Raj., India 24°36N 73°44E 242 G5
Udaipur Tripura, India 23°32N 91°30E 241 D3
Udaipur Garhi Nepal 27°0N 86°35E 243 F12
Udala India 21°35N 86°34E 243 J12
Udalguri India 26°46N 92°8E 241 B4
Udayagiri Andhra Pradesh, India 14°52N 79°19E 245 G4
Udayagiri Orissa, India 20°8N 84°23E 244 D7
Udbina Croatia 44°31N 15°47E 199 D12
Uddeholm Sweden 60°1N 13°38E 162 D7
Uddevalla Sweden 58°21N 11°55E 163 F5
Uddjaure Sweden 65°56N 17°49E 160 D17
Udelnaya Russia 60°0N 30°21E 137 A2
Udelnoe Russia 59°58N 30°20E 137 B1
Uden Neths. 51°40N 5°37E 170 C5
Udgir India 18°25N 77°5E 244 E3
Udhampur India 33°0N 75°5E 243 C6
Udi Nigeria 6°17N 7°21E 263 D6
Údine Italy 46°3N 13°14E 199 B10
Udintsev Fracture Zone S. Ocean 57°0S 145°0W 151 B13
Udlding Germany 48°15N 11°25E 131 A1
Udmurtia □ Russia 57°30N 52°30E 186 C9
Udon Thani Thailand 17°29N 102°46E 236 D4
Udot I. Micronesia 7°22N 151°42E 287 T17
Udu Pt. Fiji 16°9S 179°57W 287 A3
Udumalaippettai India 10°35N 77°15E 245 J3
Udupi India 13°25N 74°42E 245 H2
Udva India 20°5N 73°0E 244 D1
Udvoy Balkan Bulgaria 42°50N 26°50E 203 D10
Udzungwa △ Tanzania 7°52S 36°35E 268 D4
Udzungwa Range Tanzania 9°30S 35°10E 269 D4
Ueckermünde Germany 53°44N 14°1E 178 B10
Ueda Japan 36°24N 138°16E 223 A10
Uedineniya, Os. Russia 78°0N 85°0E 150 B12
Uel Scimbirro Somali Rep. 2°23N 44°14E 267 D5
Uele → Dem. Rep. of the Congo 3°45N 24°45E 264 B4
Uelen Russia 66°10N 170°0W 215 C19
Uelzen Germany 52°57N 10°32E 178 C6
Ueno Mie, Japan 34°45N 136°8E 223 C8
Ueno Tōkyō, Japan 35°42N 139°46E 140 A3
Uetersen Germany 53°40N 9°40E 178 B5
Uetze Germany 52°28N 10°11E 178 C6
Ufa Russia 54°45N 55°55E 186 D10
Ufa → Russia 54°40N 56°0E 186 D10
Uffenheim Germany 49°33N 10°14E 179 F6
Ugab → Namibia 20°55S 13°30E 270 B1
Ugalla → Tanzania 5°8S 30°42E 268 D3
Ugalla River ⌂ Tanzania 5°50S 31°54E 268 D3
Uganda ■ Africa 2°0N 32°0E 268 B3
Ugento Italy 39°56N 18°10E 201 C11
Ugep Nigeria 5°53N 8°2E 263 D6
Ughelli Nigeria 5°33N 6°0E 263 D6
Ugie S. Africa 31°10S 28°13E 271 D4
Ugíjar Spain 36°58N 3°7W 195 J7
Ugine France 45°45N 6°25E 175 C10
Uglegorsk Russia 49°5N 142°2E 215 E15
Uglich Russia 57°33N 38°20E 188 D10
Ugljan Croatia 44°12N 15°10E 199 D12
Ugljane Croatia 43°35N 16°46E 199 E13
Ugolny = Beringovskiy Russia 63°3N 179°19E 215 C18
Ugolny = Karpinsk Russia 59°45N 60°1E 186 C11
Ugolnyye Kopi = Kopeysk Russia 55°7N 61°37E 216 A6
Ugoofaaru Maldives 5°40N 73°0E 272 d
Ugra → Russia 54°30N 36°7E 188 E9
Ugŭrchin Bulgaria 43°6N 24°26E 203 C8
Uh → Slovak Rep. 48°37N 22°0E 181 C15
Uherské Hradiště Czech Rep. 49°4N 17°30E 181 B10
Uherský Brod Czech Rep. 49°1N 17°40E 181 B10
Úhlava → Czech Rep. 49°45N 13°24E 180 B6
Uhlenhorst Namibia 23°45S 17°55E 270 B2
Uhniv Ukraine 50°22N 23°45E 185 H10
Üholičky Czech Rep. 50°9N 14°19E 135 B1
Uhrichsville U.S.A. 40°24N 81°21W 312 F3
Uhřiněves Czech Rep. 50°2N 14°35E 135 B3
Uibhist a Deas = South Uist U.K. 57°20N 7°15W 167 D1
Uibhist a Tuath = North Uist U.K. 57°40N 7°15W 167 D1
Uiche Angola 12°2S 20°51E 265 E4
Uido S. Korea 34°36N 125°50E 224 E2
Uig U.K. 57°35N 6°21W 167 D2
Uíge Angola 7°30S 14°40E 265 D2
Uíge □ Angola 7°0S 16°0E 265 D3
Uiha Tonga 19°54S 174°25W 287 P13
Uijeongbu S. Korea 37°44N 127°2E 224 D3
Ŭiju N. Korea 40°15N 124°35E 224 B2
Uinta Mts. U.S.A. 40°45N 110°30W 304 F8
Uiryeong S. Korea 35°19N 128°15E 224 E4
Uis Namibia 21°8S 14°49E 270 B1
Uiseong S. Korea 36°21N 128°45E 224 D4
Uitenhage S. Africa 33°40S 25°28E 270 D4
Uithoorn Neths. 52°14N 4°50E 112 B1
Uithuizen Neths. 53°24N 6°41E 170 A6
Ujazd Poland 50°23N 18°21E 185 H5
Ujazdów Poland 52°13N 21°1E 142 B2
Ujazdowski Castle Warsaw, Poland 142 c3
Újfehértó Hungary 47°49N 21°41E 182 C6
Ujh → India 32°10N 75°18E 242 C6
Ujhani India 28°0N 79°6E 243 F8
Uji Japan 34°53N 135°48E 223 C7
Uji-guntō Japan 31°15N 129°25E 221 J4
Ujiyamada = Ise Japan 34°25N 136°45E 223 C8
Ujjain India 23°9N 75°43E 242 H6
Újpalota Hungary 47°32N 19°8E 117 A2
Újpest Hungary 47°35N 19°4E 117 A2
Ujście Poland 53°3N 16°45E 185 E3
Újszász Hungary 47°19N 20°7E 182 C5
Ujung Kulon △ Indonesia 6°46S 105°19E 234 D3
Ujung Pandang Indonesia 5°10S 119°20E 231 F5
Uka Russia 57°50N 162°0E 215 D17
Ukara I. Tanzania 1°50S 33°0E 268 C3
Uke-Shima Japan 28°2N 129°14E 221 K4
Ukerewe I. Tanzania 2°0S 33°0E 268 C3
Ukholovo Russia 53°47N 40°30E 190 D5
Ukhrul India 25°10N 94°25E 241 C5
Ukhta Russia 63°34N 53°41E 186 B9
Uki Ni Masi Solomon Is. 10°15S 161°47E 287 N11
Ukiah U.S.A. 39°9N 123°13W 306 F3
Ukita Japan 35°40N 139°51E 140 A4
Ukmergė Lithuania 55°15N 24°45E 188 E3
Ukraine ■ Europe 49°0N 32°0E 189 H7
Uku Angola 11°24S 14°22E 265 E2
Ukwi Botswana 23°29S 20°30E 270 B3
Ulaan-Uul Mongolia 44°13N 111°10E 226 B6
Ulaanbaatar Mongolia 47°55N 106°53E 218 B5
Ulaangom Mongolia 50°5N 92°10E 217 B12
Ulaanjirem Mongolia 45°5N 105°30E 226 B3
Ulak I. U.S.A. 51°22N 178°57W 303 L3
Ulala = Gorno-Altaysk Russia 51°50N 86°5E 217 B11
Ulalu I. Micronesia 7°23N 151°41E 287 T17
Ulamambri Australia 31°19S 149°23E 283 A8
Ulamba Dem. Rep. of the Congo 9°3S 23°38E 265 D4
Ulamona Papua N. G. 5°0S 151°15E 286 C6
Ulan Bator = Ulaanbaatar Mongolia 47°55N 106°53E 218 B5
Ulan Erge Russia 46°19N 44°53E 191 G7
Ulan Khol Russia 45°18N 47°4E 191 H8
Ulan Ude Russia 51°45N 107°40E 215 D11
Ulanów Poland 50°30N 22°16E 185 H9
Ulaş Sivas, Turkey 39°26N 37°2E 212 C7
Ulaş Tekirdağ, Turkey 41°14N 27°42E 203 E11
Ulawa Solomon Is. 9°46S 161°57E 287 M11
Ulaya Morogoro, Tanzania 7°3S 36°55E 268 D4
Ulaya Tabora, Tanzania 4°25S 33°30E 268 C3
Ulcinj Montenegro 41°58N 19°10E 202 E3
Ulco S. Africa 28°21S 24°15E 270 C3
Ule älv = Oulujoki → Finland 65°1N 25°30E 160 D21
Ule träsk = Oulujärvi Finland 64°25N 27°15E 160 D22
Uleåborg = Oulu Finland 65°1N 25°29E 160 D21
Ulefoss Norway 59°17N 9°16E 164 E6
Ulëz Albania 41°46N 19°54E 202 E3
Ulfborg Denmark 56°16N 8°20E 163 H2

Ulhasnagar India 19°15N 73°10E 244 E1
Uliastay Mongolia 47°56N 97°28E 218 B4
Uljin S. Korea 36°59N 129°24E 224 D4
Uljma Serbia 45°2N 21°10E 182 E6
Ülken Kazakhstan 45°12N 73°58E 217 C8
Ülken Borsyq Qumy Kazakhstan 47°0N 59°11E 216 C5
Ulla → Spain 42°39N 8°44W 194 C2
Ulladulla Australia 35°21S 150°29E 283 C9
Ullapool U.K. 57°54N 5°9W 167 D3
Ullared Sweden 57°8N 12°42E 163 G6
Ulldecona Spain 40°36N 0°20E 196 E5
Ullerup Denmark 55°34N 12°36E 118 B3
Ulleungdo S. Korea 37°30N 130°30E 224 D5
Ullevål Norway 59°56N 10°46E 133 A3
Ullswater U.K. 54°34N 2°52W 168 C5
Ulm Germany 48°23N 9°58E 179 G5
Ulmarra Australia 29°37S 153°4E 281 D5
Ulmeni Buzău, Romania 45°4N 26°40E 183 E11
Ulmeni Maramureș, Romania 47°28N 23°18E 183 C8
Ulongué Mozam. 14°37S 34°19E 269 E3
Ulricehamn Sweden 57°46N 13°26E 163 G7
Ulrika Sweden 58°5N 15°23E 163 F9
Ulriksdal Sweden 59°23N 17°59E 139 A1
Ulsan S. Korea 35°20N 129°15E 224 E4
Ulsberg Norway 62°45N 10°0E 164 B6
Ulsta U.K. 60°30N 1°9W 167 A7
Ulsteinvik Norway 62°21N 5°53E 164 B2
Ulster □ U.K. 54°35N 6°30W 166 B5
Ulstrem Bulgaria 42°1N 26°27E 203 D10
Ultima Australia 35°30S 143°18E 282 C5
Ulubat Gölü Turkey 40°9N 28°35E 203 F12
Ulubey Turkey 38°25N 29°18E 205 C11
Uluborlu Turkey 38°4N 30°28E 205 C12
Uluçinar Turkey 36°24N 35°53E 250 B6
Uludağ Turkey 40°4N 29°13E 203 F13
Uludağ △ Turkey 40°5N 29°12E 203 F13
Uludere Turkey 37°28N 42°42E 213 D10
Ulugqat China 39°48N 74°15E 217 E8
Uluguru Mts. Tanzania 7°15S 37°40E 268 D4
Ulukışla Turkey 37°33N 34°28E 212 D6
Ulungur He → China 47°1N 87°24E 217 C11
Ulungur Hu China 47°20N 87°10E 217 C11
Ulupalakua Ranch U.S.A. 20°39N 156°24W 302 C5
Uluru Australia 25°23S 131°5E 279 E5
Uluru-Kata Tjuta △ Australia 25°19S 131°1E 279 E5
Ulutau Kazakhstan 48°39N 67°1E 217 C7
Uluwatu Indonesia 8°50S 115°5E 231 K18
Ulva U.K. 56°29N 6°13W 167 E2
Ulverston U.K. 54°13N 3°5W 168 C4
Ulverstone Australia 41°11S 146°11E 281 G4
Ulvik Norway 60°35N 6°54E 164 D3
Ulya Russia 59°10N 142°0E 215 D15
Ulyanka Russia 59°50N 30°14E 137 B1
Ulyanovo Russia 54°50N 22°6E 184 D9
Ulyanovsk = Simbirsk Russia 54°20N 48°25E 190 C9
Ulyanovsk □ Russia 54°5N 48°5E 190 C9
Ulyasutay = Uliastay Mongolia 47°56N 97°28E 218 B4
Ulysses U.S.A. 37°35N 101°22W 308 G3
Ulysses S. Grant Nat. Historic Site ⌂ U.S.A. 38°33N 90°28W 310 F6
Ulyzhylanshyq → Kazakhstan 48°51N 63°46E 216 C6
Um Al-Khanazir Island Iraq 33°17N 44°22E 113 B2
Umag Croatia 45°26N 13°31E 199 C10
Umala Bolivia 17°25S 68°5W 330 D4
'Umān = Oman ■ Asia 23°0N 58°0E 249 B7
Uman Ukraine 48°40N 30°12E 177 D16
Uman I. Micronesia 7°17N 151°52E 287 U18
Umaria India 23°35N 80°50E 243 H9
Umarkhed India 19°37N 77°46E 244 E3
Umarkot Pakistan 25°15N 69°40E 242 G3
Umarpada India 21°27N 73°30E 242 J5
Umatac Guam 13°18N 144°39E 302 d
Umatilla U.S.A. 45°55N 119°21W 304 D4
Umba Russia 66°42N 34°11E 186 A5
Umbagog L. U.S.A. 44°46N 71°3W 313 B13
Umbakumba Australia 13°47S 136°50E 280 A2
Umbértide Italy 43°18N 12°20E 199 E9
Umboi I. Papua N. G. 5°40S 148°0E 286 C5
Umbrella Mts. N.Z. 45°35S 169°5E 285 F4
Umbria □ Italy 42°53N 12°30E 199 F9
Umeå Sweden 63°45N 20°20E 160 E19
Umeälven → Sweden 63°45N 20°20E 160 E19
Umeda Japan 34°41N 135°29E 133 A1
Umera Indonesia 0°12S 129°37E 231 E7
Umerkhadi Mumbai, India 130 b2
Umfuli → Zimbabwe 17°30S 29°23E 269 F2
Umfurudzi ⌂ Zimbabwe 17°6S 31°40E 269 F3
Umgusa Zimbabwe 19°29S 27°52E 269 F2
Umgwenya → Mozam. 25°14S 32°18E 271 C5
Umiat U.S.A. 69°22N 152°8W 303 B9
Umim Urūmah Si. Arabia 25°43N 36°35E 256 B4
Umiujaq Canada 56°33N 76°33W 298 A4
Umka Serbia 44°40N 20°19E 202 B4
Umkomaas S. Africa 30°13S 30°48E 271 D5
Umm ad Daraj, J. Jordan 32°18N 35°48E 251 F6
Umm al Arānib Libya 26°10N 14°43E 258 C2
Umm al Qaywayn U.A.E. 25°30N 55°35E 247 E7
Umm al Qittayn Jordan 32°18N 36°40E 251 F7
Umm al' Abīd Libya 27°31N 15°2E 258 C3
Umm Arda Sudan 15°17N 32°31E 257 D3
Umm Bāb Qatar 25°12N 50°48E 247 E6
Umm Badr Sudan 14°13N 27°58E 257 E2
Umm Baiyud Sudan 12°5N 31°40E 257 E3
Umm Bel Sudan 13°35N 28°0E 257 E2
Umm Birkah Si. Arabia 27°44N 36°31E 256 B4
Umm Boim Sudan 11°43N 25°27E 257 E2
Umm Dam Sudan 13°45N 30°59E 257 E3
Umm Debi Sudan 14°37N 30°23E 257 E3
Umm Dubban Sudan 15°23N 32°52E 257 D3
Umm Durman = Omdurmān Sudan 15°40N 32°28E 257 D3
Umm el Fahm Israel 32°31N 35°9E 251 F6
Umm Gafala Sudan 13°22N 27°15E 257 E2
Umm Gimala Sudan 11°27N 28°12E 257 F2
Umm Inderaba Sudan 17°30N 33°13E 256 D3
Umm Isheirāt, G. Egypt 28°21N 34°18E 251 K5
Umm Keddada Sudan 13°33N 26°35E 257 E2
Umm Koweika Sudan 13°10N 32°16E 257 E3
Umm Lajj Si. Arabia 25°0N 37°23E 246 E3
Umm Merwa Sudan 18°4N 32°30E 256 D3
Umm Qantur Sudan 14°17N 31°22E 257 E3
Umm Qasr Iraq 30°1N 47°58E 246 D5
Umm Qurein Sudan 9°58N 28°55E 257 F2
Umm Ruwaba Sudan 12°50N 31°20E 257 E3
Umm Saiyala Sudan 14°25N 31°10E 257 E3
Umm Shanqa Sudan 13°14N 27°14E 257 E2
Umm Shugeira Sudan 13°34N 29°37E 266 B2
Umm Shutur Sudan 7°17N 33°14E 257 F3
Umm Sidr Sudan 14°29N 25°10E 257 E2
Umm Zehetir Egypt 28°48N 32°31E 256 J8
Umnak I. U.S.A. 53°15N 168°20W 303 K5
Umniati → Zimbabwe 16°49S 28°45E 269 F2
Umpqua → U.S.A. 43°40N 124°12W 304 E1
Umpulo Angola 12°38S 17°42E 265 E3
Ümraniye Turkey 41°1N 29°4E 122 B2
Umred India 20°51N 79°18E 244 D4
Umreth India 22°41N 73°4E 242 H5
Umri India 19°2N 77°39E 244 E3
Umtata = Mthatha S. Africa 31°36S 28°49E 271 D4
Umuahia Nigeria 5°31N 7°26E 263 D6
Umuarama Brazil 23°45S 53°20W 335 A5
Umuda I. Papua N. G. 8°29S 143°46E 286 E2
Umurbey Turkey 40°13N 26°36E 203 F10
Umvukwe Ra. Zimbabwe 16°45S 30°45E 269 F3
Umzimvubu S. Africa 31°38S 29°33E 271 D4
Umzingwane → Zimbabwe 22°12S 29°56E 269 G2
Umzinto = eMuziwezinto S. Africa 30°15S 30°45E 271 D5
Una India 20°46N 71°8E 242 J4
Una → Bos.-H. 45°0N 16°20E 199 D13
Unac → Bos.-H. 44°30N 16°9E 199 D13
Unaðsdalur Iceland 66°7N 22°36W 155 A4
Unadilla Ga., U.S.A. 32°16N 83°44W 316 C6
Unadilla N.Y., U.S.A. 42°20N 75°19W 313 D9
Unaí Brazil 16°23S 46°53W 333 E2
Unalakleet U.S.A. 63°52N 160°47W 303 E7
Unalaska U.S.A. 53°53N 166°32W 303 K6
Unalaska I. U.S.A. 53°35N 166°50W 303 K6
'Unayzah Si. Arabia 26°6N 43°58E 246 E4
'Unayzah, J. Asia 32°12N 39°18E 213 F8
Uncastillo Spain 42°21N 1°8W 196 C3
Uncía Bolivia 18°25S 66°40W 330 D4
Uncompahgre Peak U.S.A. 38°4N 107°28W 304 G10
Uncompahgre Plateau U.S.A. 38°20N 108°15W 304 G9
Undara Volcanic △ Australia 18°14S 144°41E 280 B3
Unden Sweden 58°45N 14°25E 163 F8
Underbool Australia 35°10S 141°51E 282 C4
Underground Atlanta U.S.A. 33°45N 84°24W 113 B2
Underhill, L. U.S.A. 28°32N 81°20W 133 A3
Undersaker Sweden 63°19N 13°21E 162 A7
Undredal Norway 60°57N 7°6E 164 D4
Unea I. Papua N. G. 4°53S 149°9E 286 C5
Unecha Russia 52°50N 32°37E 189 F7
Uneiuxi → Brazil 0°37S 65°34W 328 D4
Unětický potok → Czech Rep. 50°9N 14°24E 135 B2
Unga I. U.S.A. 55°15N 160°40W 303 J7
Ungarie Australia 33°38S 146°56E 283 B7
Ungarisch-Hradisch = Uherské Hradiště Czech Rep. 49°4N 17°30E 181 B10
Ungarisch-Ostra = Uherský Brod Czech Rep. 49°1N 17°40E 181 B10
Ungarra Australia 34°12S 136°2E 282 C2
Ungat Papua N. G. 2°40S 150°15E 286 B6
Ungava, Pén. d' Canada 60°0N 74°0W 295 D12
Ungava B. Canada 59°30N 67°30W 295 D13
Ungeny = Ungheni Moldova 47°11N 27°51E 183 C12
Unggi N. Korea 42°16N 130°28E 224 A5
Ungheni Moldova 47°11N 27°51E 183 C12
Unguala → Ethiopia 8°6N 41°9E 257 F5
Ungvár = Uzhhorod Ukraine 48°36N 22°18E 182 B7
Ungwana B. Kenya 2°45S 40°20E 268 C5
Ungwatiri Sudan 16°52N 36°10E 257 D4
Unhos Portugal 38°49N 9°7W 126 A2
Uni Russia 57°46N 51°31E 190 B10
União Brazil 4°35S 42°52W 332 B3
União da Vitória Brazil 26°13S 51°5W 335 B5
União dos Palmares Brazil 9°10S 36°2W 332 C4
Uničov Czech Rep. 49°46N 17°8E 181 B10
Unidad Santa Fe Mexico 19°23N 99°13W 128 B1
Uniejów Poland 51°59N 18°46E 185 G5
Unije Croatia 44°40N 14°15E 199 D11
Unimak I. U.S.A. 54°45N 164°0W 303 J7
Unimak Pass U.S.A. 54°15N 164°30W 303 J6
Unini → Brazil 1°41S 61°31W 329 D5
Union Miss., U.S.A. 32°34N 89°7W 315 E10
Union Mo., U.S.A. 38°27N 91°0W 310 F6
Union Ohio, U.S.A. 39°55N 84°12W 311 E12
Union S.C., U.S.A. 34°43N 81°37W 315 D14
Union City Calif., U.S.A. 37°36N 122°1W 306 H4
Union City Ga., U.S.A. 33°35N 84°33W 316 B5
Union City New York, U.S.A. 132 b1
Union City Ohio, U.S.A. 40°12N 84°48W 311 D12
Union City Pa., U.S.A. 41°54N 79°51W 312 E5
Union City Tenn., U.S.A. 36°26N 89°3W 315 C10
Union Gap U.S.A. 46°33N 120°28W 304 C3
Union Grove U.S.A. 42°41N 88°3W 311 B8
Union I. St. Vincent 12°36N 61°26W 323 n
Union Park U.S.A. 28°34N 81°17W 317 G8
Union Point U.S.A. 33°37N 83°4W 316 B6
Union Port U.S.A. 40°48N 73°51W 132 B2
Union Springs U.S.A. 32°9N 85°43W 316 C4
Union Square San Francisco, U.S.A. 136 b2
Union Star U.S.A. 39°59N 94°36W 310 E2
Union Station Toronto, Canada 141 c2
Union Station Chicago, U.S.A. 119 c1
Union Station Washington, D.C., U.S.A. 143 b3
Union Station Los Angeles, U.S.A. 127 b3
Union Station New Orleans, U.S.A. 131 b1
Union Station Plaza Washington, D.C., U.S.A. 143 b3
Uniondale S. Africa 33°39S 23°7E 270 D3
Uniontown Ky., U.S.A. 37°47N 87°56W 311 G9
Uniontown Pa., U.S.A. 39°54N 79°44W 309 F14
Unionville Ga., U.S.A. 31°26N 83°30W 316 D6
Unionville Mo., U.S.A. 40°29N 93°1W 310 D3
Unirea Romania 44°15N 27°35E 183 F12
United Arab Emirates ■ Asia 23°50N 54°0E 247 F7
United Arab Republic = Egypt ■ Africa 28°0N 31°0E 256 B3
United Center U.S.A. 41°53N 87°41W 119 B2
United Kingdom ■ Europe 53°0N 2°0W 165 E6
United Nations Headquarters New York, U.S.A. 132 c3
United Provinces = Uttar Pradesh □ India 27°0N 80°0E 243 F9
United States of America ■ N. Amer. 37°0N 96°0W 300 C7
Unity Canada 52°30N 109°5W 297 C7
Universal Studios U.S.A. 34°9N 118°21W 126 B2
Universales, Mtes. Spain 40°18N 1°33W 196 E3
Universidad Spain 40°27N 3°44W 127 B1
University City U.S.A. 38°39N 90°18W 310 F6
University Park Md., U.S.A. 38°58N 76°56W 143 B4
University Park N. Mex., U.S.A. 32°17N 106°45W 305 K10
University Place U.S.A. 47°14N 122°33W 306 C4
Unjha India 23°46N 72°24E 242 H5
Unmet Vanuatu 16°8S 167°15E 287 F5
Unna Germany 51°32N 7°42E 178 D3
Unnao India 26°35N 80°30E 243 F9
Uno, Ilha Guinea-Biss. 11°15N 16°13W 262 C1
Unpongkor Vanuatu 18°50S 168°59E 287 H6
Unruhstadt = Kargowa Poland 52°5N 15°51E 185 F2
Unsan N. Korea 40°6N 125°54E 224 B2
Unsengedsi → Zimbabwe 15°43S 31°14E 269 F3
Unst U.K. 60°44N 0°53W 167 A8
Unstrut → Germany 51°10N 11°48E 178 D7
Unter den Linden Berlin, Germany 115 a4
Unterbiberg Germany 48°6N 11°38E 131 B2
Unterdrauburg = Dravograd Slovenia 46°36N 15°5E 199 B12
Unterföhring Germany 48°11N 11°38E 131 A3
Unterfranken □ Germany 50°0N 10°0E 179 F5
Unterhaching Germany 48°3N 11°37E 131 B2
Unterlaa Austria 48°8N 16°24E 142 B2
Untermenzing Germany 48°10N 11°28E 131 A1
Unterschleissheim Germany 48°17N 11°34E 179 G7
Unuk → Canada 56°5N 131°3W 296 B2
Ünye Turkey 41°5N 37°15E 212 B7
Unzen-Amakusa △ Japan 32°15N 130°10E 222 E2
Unzen-Dake Japan 32°45N 130°17E 222 E2
Unzha Russia 58°0N 44°0E 190 A7
Unzha → Russia 57°49N 43°47E 190 B6
Uozu Japan 36°48N 137°24E 223 A9
Upata Venezuela 8°1N 62°24W 329 B5
Upatoi Cr. → U.S.A. 32°22N 84°58W 316 C5
Upemba, L. Dem. Rep. of the Congo 8°30S 26°20E 269 D2
Upemba △ Dem. Rep. of the Congo 9°0S 26°35E 269 D2
Upernavik Greenland 72°49N 56°20W 154 C5
Upington S. Africa 28°25S 21°15E 270 C3
Upleta India 21°46N 70°16E 242 J4
'Upolu Samoa 13°58S 172°0W 287 V20
Upolu Pt. U.S.A. 20°16N 155°52W 302 C6
Upper □ Ghana 10°30N 1°30W 263 C4
Upper Alkali L. U.S.A. 41°47N 120°8W 304 F3
Upper Arlington U.S.A. 40°0N 83°4W 311 E13
Upper Arrow L. Canada 50°30N 117°50W 296 C5
Upper Austria = Oberösterreich □ Austria 48°10N 14°0E 180 C7
Upper B. U.S.A. 40°40N 74°3W 132 C1
Upper Darby U.S.A. 39°55N 75°16W 309 F16
Upper East Side New York, U.S.A. 132 b3
Upper Elmers End U.K. 51°23N 0°1W 125 B3
Upper Foster L. Canada 56°47N 105°20W 297 B7
Upper Hutt N.Z. 41°8S 175°5E 284 H4
Upper Juba Somali Rep. 3°0N 43°0E 267 D5
Upper Klamath L. U.S.A. 42°25N 121°55W 304 E3
Upper Lake U.S.A. 39°10N 122°54W 306 F4
Upper Manilla Australia 30°38S 150°40E 283 A9
Upper Manzanilla Trin. & Tob. 10°31N 61°4W 323 t
Upper Missouri Breaks ⌂ U.S.A. 47°50N 109°55W 304 C9
Upper Musquodoboit Canada 45°10N 62°58W 299 C7
Upper New York B. = Upper B. U.S.A. 40°40N 74°3W 132 C1
Upper Norwood U.K. 51°24N 0°6W 125 B3
Upper Peirce Res. Singapore 1°22N 103°47E 138 A2
Upper Peoria L. U.S.A. 40°55N 89°27W 310 D7
Upper Red L. U.S.A. 48°8N 94°45W 308 A6
Upper Sandusky U.S.A. 40°50N 83°17W 311 D13
Upper Senegal & Niger = Mali ■ Africa 17°0N 3°0W 262 B4
Upper Sydenham U.K. 51°26N 0°4W 125 B3
Upper Tooting U.K. 51°25N 0°9W 125 B3
Upper Volta = Burkina Faso ■ Africa 12°0N 1°0W 262 C4
Upper West Side New York, U.S.A. 132 a2
Upphärad Sweden 58°9N 12°19E 163 F6
Uppland Sweden 59°59N 17°48E 162 E11
Upplands-Väsby Sweden 59°31N 17°54E 162 E11
Uppsala Sweden 59°53N 17°38E 162 E11
Uppsala län □ Sweden 60°0N 17°30E 162 D11
Upshi India 33°48N 77°52E 243 C7
Upstart, C. Australia 19°41S 147°45E 280 B4
Upton London, U.K. 51°32N 0°1E 125 A4
Upton Wyo., U.S.A. 44°6N 104°38W 304 D11
Uptown U.S.A. 41°58N 87°40W 119 B2
Uqsuqtuuq = Gjoa Haven Canada 68°38N 95°53W 294 C10
Ur Iraq 30°55N 46°25E 246 D5
Ura-Tyube = Uroteppa Tajikistan 39°55N 69°1E 217 E7
Urabá, G. de Colombia 8°25N 76°53W 328 B2
Urad Qianqi China 40°40N 108°30E 226 D5
Uraga-Suidō Japan 35°13N 139°45E 223 B11
Urakawa Japan 42°9N 142°47E 220 C11
Ural = Uralskiy □ Russia 64°0N 70°0E 214 C7
Ural = Zhayyq → Kazakhstan 47°0N 51°48E 187 E9
Ural Australia 33°21S 146°12E 283 B7
Ural Mts. = Uralskie Gory Eurasia 60°0N 59°0E 186 C10
Uralla Australia 30°37S 151°29E 283 A9
Uralmedstroy = Krasnouralsk Russia 58°21N 60°3E 186 C11
Uralsk = Oral Kazakhstan 51°20N 51°20E 190 E10
Uralskie Gory Eurasia 60°0N 59°0E 186 C10
Uralskiy □ Russia 64°0N 70°0E 214 C7
Urambo Tanzania 5°4S 32°0E 268 D3
Uran India 18°53N 72°56E 130 B2
Urana Australia 35°15S 146°21E 283 C7
Urana, L. Australia 35°16S 146°10E 283 C7
Urandangi Australia 21°32S 138°14E 280 C2
Uranga Australia 30°31S 153°1E 283 A10
Uranium City Canada 59°34N 108°37W 297 B7
Uraricaá → Brazil 3°20N 61°56W 329 C5
Uraricoera Brazil 3°27N 60°59W 329 C5
Uraricoera → Brazil 3°2N 60°30W 329 C5
Urasoe Japan 26°15N 127°43E 288 a
Uravakonda India 14°57N 77°12E 245 G3
Urawa = Saitama Japan 35°54N 139°38E 223 B11
Uray Russia 60°5N 65°15E 214 C7
Urayasu Japan 35°39N 139°53E 140 B4
'Uray'irah Si. Arabia 25°57N 48°53E 247 E6
Urbakh = Pushkino Russia 51°16N 47°0E 190 E8
Urbana Ill., U.S.A. 40°7N 88°12W 311 D8
Urbana Ohio, U.S.A. 40°7N 83°45W 311 D13
Urbandale U.S.A. 41°38N 93°43W 310 C3
Urbánia Italy 43°40N 12°31E 199 E9
Urbano Santos Brazil 3°12S 43°23W 332 B3
Urbe ✕ Italy 41°57N 12°30E 136 B2
Urbel → Spain 42°21N 3°40W 194 C7
Urbino Italy 43°43N 12°38E 199 E9
Urbión, Picos de Spain 42°1N 2°52W 196 C2
Urca Brazil 22°56S 43°9W 133 B2
Urcos Peru 13°40S 71°38W 330 C3
Urdaneta Phil. 15°59N 120°34E 232 D3
Urdinarrain Argentina 32°37S 58°52W 334 C4
Urdos France 42°51N 0°35W 174 F3
Ure → U.K. 54°5N 1°20W 168 C6
Uren Russia 57°35N 45°55E 190 B7
Ureparapara Vanuatu 13°32S 167°20E 287 C5
Ures Mexico 29°26N 110°24W 318 B2
Ureshino Japan 33°6N 129°59E 222 D1
Urewera △ N.Z. 38°29S 177°7E 284 E6
Urfa = Sanliurfa Turkey 37°12N 38°50E 213 D8
Urga = Ulaanbaatar Mongolia 47°55N 106°53E 218 B5
Urganch Uzbekistan 41°40N 60°41E 216 D6
Urgench = Urganch Uzbekistan 41°40N 60°41E 216 D6
Ürgüp Turkey 38°38N 34°56E 246 B2
Uri India 34°8N 74°2E 243 B6
Uri □ Switz. 46°43N 8°35E 179 J4
Uribante → Venezuela 7°25N 71°50W 328 B3
Uribe Colombia 3°13N 74°24W 328 C3
Uribia Colombia 11°43N 72°16W 328 A3
Uricani Romania 45°20N 23°9E 182 E8
Urimba Angola 10°56S 16°32E 265 E3
Uriondo Bolivia 21°41S 64°41W 334 A3
Urique Mexico 27°13N 107°55W 318 B3
Urique → Mexico 26°29N 107°58W 318 B3
Uritsk Russia 59°49N 30°10E 137 C1
Urk Neths. 52°39N 5°36E 170 B5
Urkiola ⌂ Spain 43°6N 1°2W 196 B3
Urla Turkey 38°20N 26°47E 205 C8
Urlaţi Romania 44°59N 26°15E 183 F11
Urmia = Orūmīyeh Iran 37°40N 45°0E 213 D11
Urmia, L. = Orūmīyeh, Daryācheh-ye Iran 37°50N 45°30E 213 D11
Üröm Hungary 47°35N 19°1E 117 A2
Uroševac Serbia 42°23N 21°10E 202 D5
Uroteppa Tajikistan 39°55N 69°1E 217 E7
Uroyan, Montanas de Puerto Rico 18°12N 67°0W 321 b
Urrao Colombia 6°20N 76°11W 328 B2
Urshult Sweden 56°31N 14°50E 163 H8
Ursus Poland 52°11N 20°52E 142 B1
Ursvik Sweden 59°23N 17°57E 139 A1
Uruaçu Brazil 14°30S 49°10W 333 D2
Uruana Brazil 15°30S 49°41W 333 E2
Uruapan Mexico 19°24N 102°3W 318 D4
Uruará Brazil 3°42S 53°51W 329 D7
Uruará → Brazil 2°6S 53°38W 329 D7
Urubamba Peru 13°20S 72°10W 330 C3
Urubamba → Peru 10°43S 73°48W 330 C3
Urubaxi → Brazil 0°31S 64°50W 329 D5
Urubu → Brazil 2°55S 58°25W 329 D6
Uruçara Brazil 2°32S 57°45W 329 D6
Uruçuí Brazil 7°20S 44°28W 332 C3
Uruçuí, Serra do Brazil 9°0S 44°45W 332 C3
Uruçuí Prêto → Brazil 7°20S 44°38W 332 C3
Urucuia → Brazil 16°8S 45°5W 333 E2
Urucurituba Brazil 2°41S 57°40W 329 D6
Uruguai → Brazil 26°0S 53°30W 335 B5
Uruguaiana Brazil 29°50S 57°0W 334 B4
Uruguay ■ S. Amer. 32°30S 56°30W 334 C4
Uruguay → S. Amer. 34°12S 58°18W 334 C4
Urukthapel I. Palau 7°17N 134°25E 288 c
Urumchi = Ürümqi China 43°45N 87°45E 217 D11
Ürümqi China 43°45N 87°45E 217 D11
Urundi = Burundi ■ Africa 3°15S 30°0E 268 C3
Urup → Russia 45°0N 41°10E 191 H5
Urup, Ostrov Russia 46°0N 151°0E 215 E16
Urutaí Brazil 17°28S 48°12W 333 E2
Uryupinsk Russia 50°45N 41°58E 190 E5
Urzhar Kazakhstan 47°5N 81°38E 217 C10
Urzhum Russia 57°10N 49°56E 190 B9
Urziceni Romania 44°40N 26°42E 183 F11
Usa Japan 33°31N 131°21E 222 D3
Usa → Russia 66°16N 59°49E 186 A10
Uşak Turkey 38°43N 29°28E 205 C11
Uşak □ Turkey 38°30N 29°0E 205 C11
Usakos Namibia 21°54S 15°31E 270 B2
Usborne, Mt. Falk. Is. 51°40S 59°55W 153 f
Ušće Serbia 43°30N 20°39E 202 C4
Usedom Germany 53°55N 14°2E 178 B10
Usedom ⌂ Germany 53°55N 14°0E 178 B10
Useless Loop Australia 26°8S 113°23E 279 E1
Usera Spain 40°22N 3°42W 127 B1
'Usfān Si. Arabia 21°58N 39°27E 248 B2
Ushakova, Ostrov Russia 82°0N 80°0E 150 A12
Ushakovo Russia 54°37N 20°16E 184 D7
Ushant = Ouessant, Î. d' France 48°28N 5°6W 172 D1
Üsharal Kazakhstan 46°10N 80°56E 217 C10
Ushashi Tanzania 1°59S 33°57E 268 C3
Ushat Sudan 7°59N 29°28E 257 F2
'Ushayrah Si. Arabia 21°46N 40°42E 256 C5
Ushibuka Japan 32°11N 130°1E 222 E2
Ushigome Japan 35°42N 139°44E 140 A3
Üshtöbe Kazakhstan 45°16N 78°0E 217 C9
Ushuaia Argentina 54°50S 68°23W 336 D3
Ushumun Russia 52°47N 126°32E 215 D13
Ushytsya → Ukraine 48°35N 27°8E 183 B12
Usina Brazil 22°57S 43°17W 135 B1
Usino Papua N. G. 5°32S 145°23E 286 C3
Usk Canada 54°38N 128°26W 296 C3
Usk → U.K. 51°33N 2°58W 169 F5
Uska India 27°12N 83°7E 243 F10
Uskedalen Norway 59°56N 5°53E 164 E2
Üsküb = Skopje Macedonia 42°1N 21°26E 202 D5
Üsküdar Turkey 41°1N 29°1E 122 B2
Uslar Germany 51°39N 9°38E 178 D5
Usman Russia 52°5N 39°48E 189 F10
Usoke Tanzania 5°8S 32°24E 268 D3
Usolye-Sibirskoye Russia 52°48N 103°40E 215 D11
Usolye-Solikamskoye = Berezniki Russia 59°24N 56°46E 186 C10
Usoro Nigeria 5°33N 6°11E 263 D6
Uspallata, P. de Argentina 32°37S 69°22W 334 C2
Uspenka = Kirovskiy Russia 45°7N 133°30E 220 B6
Ussel France 45°32N 2°18E 174 C6
Usson-du-Poitou France 46°16N 0°31E 174 B4
Ussuriysk Russia 43°48N 131°59E 220 C5
Ussurka Russia 45°12N 133°31E 220 B6
Ust-Aldan = Batamay Russia 63°30N 129°15E 215 C13
Ust-Amginskoye = Khandyga Russia 62°42N 135°35E 215 C14
Ust-Bolsheretsk Russia 52°50N 156°15E 215 D16
Ust-Buzulukskaya Russia 50°8N 42°11E 190 E6
Ust-Chaun Russia 68°47N 170°30E 215 C18
Ust-Chorna Ukraine 48°19N 23°56E 183 B8
Ust-Donetskiy Russia 47°35N 40°55E 191 G5
Ust-Ilimpeya = Yukta Russia 63°26N 105°42E 215 C11
Ust-Ilimsk Russia 58°3N 102°39E 215 D11
Ust-Ishim Russia 57°45N 71°10E 214 D8
Ust-Kamchatsk Russia 56°10N 162°28E 215 D17
Ust-Kamenogorsk = Öskemen Kazakhstan 50°0N 82°36E 217 C10
Ust-Khayryuzovo Russia 57°15N 156°45E 215 D16
Ust-Kut Russia 56°50N 105°42E 215 D11
Ust-Kuyga Russia 70°1N 135°43E 215 B14
Ust-Labinsk Russia 45°15N 39°41E 191 H4
Ust-Luga Russia 59°35N 28°20E 188 C5
Ust-Maya Russia 60°30N 134°28E 215 C14
Ust-Medveditskaya = Serafimovich Russia 49°36N 42°43E 190 F6
Ust-Mil Russia 59°40N 133°11E 215 D14
Ust-Nera Russia 64°35N 143°15E 215 C15
Ust-Nyukzha Russia 56°34N 121°37E 215 D13
Ust-Olenek Russia 73°0N 120°5E 215 B12
Ust-Omchug Russia 61°9N 149°38E 215 C15
Ust-Port Russia 69°40N 84°26E 214 C9
Ust-Slavyanka Russia 59°51N 30°32E 137 C3
Ust-Sysolsk = Syktyvkar Russia 61°45N 50°40E 186 B9
Ust-Tsilma Russia 65°28N 52°11E 186 A9
Ust-Urt = Ustyurt Plateau Asia 44°0N 55°0E 216 D5
Ust-Usa Russia 66°2N 56°57E 186 A10
Ust-Vorkuta Russia 67°24N 64°0E 186 A11
Ust-Zhuya = Chara Russia 56°54N 118°20E 215 D12
Ustaoset Norway 60°30N 8°2E 164 D5
Ustaritz France 43°24N 1°27W 174 E2
Ustecký □ Czech Rep. 50°30N 14°0E 180 A7
Uster Switz. 47°22N 8°43E 179 H4
Ústí nad Labem Czech Rep. 50°41N 14°3E 180 A7
Ústí nad Orlicí Czech Rep. 49°58N 16°24E 181 B9
Ústica Italy 38°42N 13°11E 200 D6
Ustinov = Izhevsk Russia 56°51N 53°14E 186 C9
Ustka Poland 54°35N 16°55E 184 D3
Ustroń Poland 49°43N 18°48E 185 J5
Ustrzyki Dolne Poland 49°27N 22°40E 185 J9
Ustupo Panama 9°27N 78°34W 328 B2
Ustyluh Ukraine 50°51N 24°10E 185 H11
Ustyurt Plateau Asia 44°0N 55°0E 216 D5
Ustyuzhna Russia 58°50N 36°32E 188 C9
Usu China 44°27N 84°40E 217 D10
Usuki Japan 33°8N 131°49E 222 D3
Usulután El Salv. 13°25N 88°28W 320 D2
Usumacinta → Mexico 18°24N 92°38W 319 D6
Usumbura = Bujumbura Burundi 3°16S 29°18E 268 C2
Usure Tanzania 4°40S 34°22E 268 C3
Usutuo → Mozam. 26°48S 32°7E 271 C5
Uta Indonesia 4°33S 136°0E 231 E9
Utah □ U.S.A. 39°20N 111°30W 304 G8
Utah L. U.S.A. 40°12N 111°48W 304 F8
Utansjö Sweden 62°46N 17°55E 162 B11
Utara, Selat Malaysia 5°28N 100°20E 237 c
Utarni India 26°5N 71°58E 242 F4
Utatlan Guatemala 15°2N 91°11W 320 C1
Ute Creek → U.S.A. 35°21N 103°50W 305 J12
Utebo Spain 41°43N 1°0W 196 D3
Utegi Tanzania 1°19S 34°13E 266 E3
Uteke Sweden 59°24N 18°15E 139 A3
Utena Lithuania 55°27N 25°40E 188 E3
Utete Tanzania 8°0S 38°45E 268 D4
Uthai Thani Thailand 15°22N 100°3E 236 E3
Uthal Pakistan 25°44N 66°40E 242 G2
Utiariti Brazil 13°0S 58°10W 331 C6
Utica N.Y., U.S.A. 43°6N 75°14W 313 C9
Utica Ohio, U.S.A. 40°14N 82°27W 312 F2
Utiel Spain 39°37N 1°11W 197 F3
Utikuma L. Canada 55°50N 115°30W 296 B5
Utinga Brazil 12°6S 41°5W 333 D3
Utkela India 20°6N 83°10E 244 D6
Utne Norway 60°25N 6°37E 164 D3
Utnur India 19°22N 78°46E 244 E4
Uto Japan 32°41N 130°40E 222 E2
Utö Sweden 58°56N 18°16E 162 F12
Utopia Australia 22°14S 134°33E 280 C1
Utrata Poland 52°15N 21°4E 142 B2
Utraula India 27°19N 82°25E 243 F10
Utrecht Neths. 52°5N 5°8E 170 B5
Utrecht KwaZulu Natal, S. Africa 27°38S 30°20E 271 C5
Utrecht □ Neths. 52°6N 5°7E 170 B5
Utrera Spain 37°12N 5°48W 195 H5
Utría △ Colombia 5°57N 77°21W 328 B2
Utsira Norway 59°19N 4°53E 164 E1
Utsjoki → Finland 69°51N 26°59E 160 B22
Utsunomiya Japan 36°30N 139°50E 223 A11
Uttar Pradesh □ India 27°0N 80°0E 243 F9
Uttaradit Thailand 17°36N 100°5E 236 D3
Uttaranchal □ India 30°0N 79°30E 243 D8
Uttarpara India 22°39N 88°21E 124 B1
Uttersler Mose Denmark 55°42N 12°29E 118 A2
Uttoxeter U.K. 52°54N 1°52W 168 E6
Utuado Puerto Rico 18°16N 66°42W 321 b
Uummannaq Greenland 70°58N 52°17W 150 B5
Uummannaq Greenland 77°28N 69°13W 154 B4
Uummannarsuaq = Nunap Isua Greenland 59°48N 43°55W 154 F6
Uusikaarlepyy Finland 63°32N 22°31E 160 E20
Uusikaupunki Finland 60°47N 21°25E 188 B1
Uva Russia 56°59N 52°13E 190 B11
Uvá → Colombia 3°41N 70°3W 328 C3
Uvac → Serbia 43°35N 19°30E 202 C3
Uvalda U.S.A. 32°2N 82°31W 316 C7
Uvalde U.S.A. 29°13N 99°47W 314 G5
Uvarovo Russia 51°59N 42°14E 190 E6
Uvat Russia 59°5N 68°50E 214 D7
Uvéa, I. Wall. & F. Is. 13°18S 176°10W 277 C15
Uvinza Tanzania 5°5S 30°24E 268 D3
Uvira Dem. Rep. of the Congo 3°22S 29°3E 268 C2
Uvs □ Mongolia 49°38N 93°0E 217 C12
Uvs Nuur Mongolia 50°20N 92°30E 217 B12
Uwa Japan 33°22N 132°31E 222 D4
'Uwairidh, Ḩarrat al Si. Arabia 26°50N 38°0E 246 E3
Uwajima Japan 33°10N 132°35E 222 D4
Uwanda △ Tanzania 7°46S 32°0E 268 D3
Uweinat, Jebel Sudan 21°54N 24°58E 256 C1
Uxbridge Canada 44°6N 79°7W 312 B5
Uxin Qi China 38°50N 109°5E 226 E5
Uxmal Mexico 20°22N 89°46W 319 C7
Uyak U.S.A. 57°38N 154°0W 303 H9
Üydzin Mongolia 44°9N 107°0E 226 B4
Uyo Nigeria 5°1N 7°53E 263 D6
Uyu → Burma 24°51N 94°57E 241 C5
Üyüklü Tepe Turkey 37°5N 27°21E 205 D9
Uyûn Mûsa Egypt 29°53N 32°40E 251 J3
Uyuni Bolivia 20°28S 66°47W 330 E4
Uzbekistan ■ Asia 41°30N 65°0E 217 D7
Uzboy → Turkmenistan 39°30N 55°0E 247 B7
Uzen Kazakhstan 43°29N 52°54E 187 F9
Uzen, Bolshoi = Uzen, Mal → Kazakhstan 49°4N 49°44E 191 F9
Uzen, Mal → Kazakhstan 49°4N 49°44E 191 F9
Uzerche France 45°25N 1°34E 174 C5
Uzès France 44°1N 4°26E 175 D8
Uzh → Ukraine 51°15N 30°12E 177 C16
Uzhgorod = Uzhhorod Ukraine 48°36N 22°18E 182 B7
Uzhhorod Ukraine 48°36N 22°18E 182 B7
Uzhok Ukraine 48°59N 22°52E 182 B7
Užice Serbia 43°55N 19°50E 202 C3
Uzlovaya Russia 54°0N 38°5E 188 F10
Üzümlü Turkey 36°44N 29°14E 205 E11
Uzuncaburç Turkey 36°35N 33°57E 250 B4
Uzunköprü Turkey 41°16N 26°43E 203 E10
Uzunkuyu Turkey 38°17N 26°33E 205 C8

V

V.C. Bird Int. ✕ (ANU) Antigua & B. 17°8N 61°47W 322 b
Vaal → S. Africa 29°4S 23°38E 270 C3
Vaal Dam S. Africa 27°0S 28°14E 271 C4
Vaalbos △ S. Africa 28°22S 24°20E 270 C3
Vaalwater S. Africa 24°15S 28°8E 271 B4
Vaasa Finland 63°6N 21°38E 160 E19
Vabre France 43°42N 2°24E 174 E6
Vác Hungary 47°49N 19°10E 182 C4
Vacaos, Mare aux Mauritius 20°22S 57°30E 272 e
Vacaria Brazil 28°31S 50°52W 335 B5
Vacata Fiji 17°15S 179°31W 287 A3
Vacaville U.S.A. 38°21N 121°59W 306 G5
Vaccarès, Étang de France 43°32N 4°34E 175 E8
Vach = Vakh → Russia 60°45N 76°45E 214 C8
Vache, Î. à Haiti 18°2N 73°35W 321 C5
Väckelsång Sweden 56°37N 14°58E 163 H8
Vaclavské náměstí Prague, Czech Rep. 135 b2
Vacoas Mauritius 20°18S 57°29E 272 e
Vada India 19°39N 73°8E 244 E1
Vadaul India 19°2N 72°55E 130 A2
Väddö Sweden 60°0N 18°50E 162 D12
Väderstad Sweden 58°19N 14°55E 163 F8
Vadheim Norway 61°13N 5°49E 164 C2
Vadnagar India 23°47N 72°40E 242 H5
Vado Ligure Italy 44°17N 8°26E 198 D5
Vadodara India 22°20N 73°10E 242 H5
Vadsø Norway 70°3N 29°50E 160 A23
Vadstena Sweden 58°28N 14°54E 163 F8
Vaduj India 17°36N 74°27E 244 F2
Vaduz Liech. 47°8N 9°31E 179 H5
Værlandet Norway 61°18N 4°44E 164 C1
Værøy Norway 67°40N 12°40E 160 C15
Vagalat Albania 39°44N 20°8E 206 B10
Vågåmo Norway 61°52N 9°6E 164 C6
Vágar Færoe Is. 62°5N 7°15W 160 E9
Vagarshapat = Yejmiadzin Armenia 40°12N 44°19E 191 K7
Vaggeryd Sweden 57°30N 14°10E 163 G8
Vaghena Solomon Is. 7°25S 157°45E 287 L9
Vaghia Greece 38°19N 23°11E 204 C5
Vagia, Akra Greece 36°15N 28°11E 206 E12
Vagney France 48°1N 6°43E 173 D13
Vagnhärad Sweden 58°57N 17°33E 163 F11
Vagos Portugal 40°33N 8°42W 194 E2
Vågsfjorden Norway 68°50N 16°50E 160 B17
Váh → Slovak Rep. 47°43N 18°7E 181 D11
Vahitahi French Polynesia 18°44S 138°52W 289 f
Vahsel B. Antarctica 75°0S 35°0W 151 D1
Váhtjer = Gällivare Sweden 67°9N 20°40E 160 C19
Vaï Greece 35°15N 26°18E 207 F7
Vaiea Cook Is. 19°6S 169°54W 289 g
Vaigach Russia 70°10N 59°0E 214 B6
Vaigai → India 9°15N 79°10E 245 K4
Vaiges France 48°2N 0°30W 172 D6
Vaihingen Germany 48°54N 8°57E 179 G4
Vaihiria, L. Tahiti 17°40S 149°25W 289 e
Vaijapur India 19°58N 74°45E 244 E2
Vaikam India 9°45N 76°25E 245 K3
Vail U.S.A. 39°40N 106°20W 300 C5
Vailala → Papua N. G. 7°57S 145°25E 286 D3
Vailhau, Récif Comoros Is. 11°48S 43°48E 272 a
Vailly-sur-Aisne France 49°24N 3°31E 173 C10
Vailoatai Amer. Samoa 14°21S 170°46W 302 f
Vaippar → India 9°0N 78°25E 245 K4
Vairaatea French Polynesia 19°19S 139°20W 289 f
Vairao Tahiti 17°47S 149°17W 289 e
Vaires-sur-Marne France 48°52N 2°38E 134 A4
Vaisali → India 26°28N 78°53E 243 F8
Vaison-la-Romaine France 44°14N 5°4E 175 D9
Vaitogi Amer. Samoa 14°24S 170°44W 302 f
Vaitupu Pac. Oc. 7°28S 178°41E 277 B14
Vajpur India 21°24N 73°17E 244 D1
Vakaga → C.A.R. 9°48N 21°32E 264 A4
Vakarai Sri Lanka 8°8N 81°26E 245 K5
Vakarel Bulgaria 42°35N 23°40E 202 D7
Vakfıkebir Turkey 41°2N 39°17E 213 B8
Vakh → Russia 60°45N 76°45E 214 C8
Vakhtan Russia 57°53N 46°47E 190 B8
Vaksdal Norway 60°29N 5°45E 164 D2
Vakuta I. Papua N. G. 8°51S 151°10E 286 E6
Val Hungary 47°22N 18°40E 182 C3
Val-de-Marne □ France 48°45N 2°28E 173 D9
Val-d'Isère France 45°27N 6°59E 175 C10
Val-d'Oise □ France 49°5N 2°10E 173 C9
Val-d'Or Canada 48°7N 77°47W 298 C4
Val Grande △ Italy 46°3N 8°25E 198 B5
Val Marie Canada 49°15N 107°45W 297 D7
Val Thorens France 45°20N 6°33E 175 C10
Valaam Russia 61°22N 30°57E 188 B6
Valadares Portugal 41°5N 8°38W 194 D2
Valahia Romania 44°35N 25°0E 183 F9
Valaichenai Sri Lanka 7°54N 81°32E 245 L5
Valais □ Switz. 46°12N 7°45E 179 J3
Valais, Alpes du Switz. 46°5N 7°35E 179 J3
Valandovo Macedonia 41°19N 22°34E 202 E6
Valašské Meziříčí Czech Rep. 49°29N 17°59E 181 B10
Valaxa Greece 38°50N 24°29E 204 C6
Vålberg Sweden 59°23N 13°11E 162 E7
Valbo Sweden 60°40N 17°0E 162 D10
Valbondione Italy 46°2N 10°1E 198 B7
Valby Denmark 55°39N 12°29E 118 B2
Vâlcani Romania 46°0N 20°26E 182 D5
Valcannuta Italy 41°52N 12°25E 136 B1
Vâlcea □ Romania 45°0N 24°10E 183 F9
Valcheta Argentina 40°40S 66°8W 336 B3
Valdagno Italy 45°39N 11°18E 199 C8
Valdahon France 47°8N 6°21E 173 E13
Valdai Hills = Valdayskaya Vozvyshennost Russia 57°0N 33°30E 188 D7
Valday Russia 57°58N 33°9E 188 D7
Valdayskaya Vozvyshennost Russia 57°0N 33°30E 188 D7
Valdeazogues → Spain 38°45N 4°55W 195 G6
Valdecañas, Embalse de Spain 39°45N 5°30W 194 F5
Valdelatas Spain 40°31N 3°42W 127 A1
Valdemarsvik Sweden 58°14N 16°40E 163 F10
Valdemoro Spain 40°12N 3°40W 194 E7
Valdepeñas Spain 38°43N 3°25W 195 G7
Valderaduey → Spain 41°31N 5°42W 194 D5
Valderice Italy 38°4N 12°37E 200 D5
Valderrobres Spain 40°53N 0°9E 196 E5
Valdés, Pen. Argentina 42°30S 63°45W 336 B4
Valdez Ecuador 1°15N 79°0W 328 C2
Valdez Alaska, U.S.A. 61°7N 146°16W 303 F11
Valdgeym = Dobropole Ukraine 48°25N 37°2E 189 H9
Valdivia Chile 39°50S 73°14W 336 A2
Valdivia Colombia 7°11N 75°27W 328 B2
Valdivia Abyssal Plain S. Ocean 62°30S 70°0E 151 C6
Valdobbiádene Italy 45°54N 12°0E 199 C8
Valdosta U.S.A. 30°50N 83°17W 316 E6
Valdoviño Spain 43°36N 8°8W 194 B2
Valdres Norway 61°5N 9°5E 164 C6
Vale Georgia 41°30N 42°58E 191 K6
Vale Oreg., U.S.A. 43°59N 117°15W 304 E5
Vale Va., U.S.A. 38°55N 77°20W 143 B1
Vale of Glamorgan □ U.K. 51°28N 3°25W 169 F4
Valea lui Mihai Romania 47°32N 22°11E 182 C7
Valea Mărului Romania 45°49N 27°42E 183 E12
Valemount Canada 52°50N 119°15W 296 C5
Valença = Valença do Piauí Brazil 6°20S 41°45W 332 C3
Valença Brazil 13°20S 39°5W 333 D4
Valença Portugal 42°1N 8°34W 194 C2
Valença do Piauí Brazil 6°20S 41°45W 332 C3
Valençay France 47°9N 1°34E 173 E8
Valence France 44°57N 4°54E 175 D8
Valence d'Agen France 44°6N 0°53E 174 D4

Valencia Phil. 7°57N 125°3E 233 H5
Valencia Spain 39°27N 0°23W 197 F4
Valencia Trin. & Tob. 10°39N 61°11W 323 t
Valencia N. Mex., U.S.A. 34°48N 106°43W 305 J10
Valencia Venezuela 10°11N 68°0W 328 A4
Valencia □ Spain 39°20N 0°40W 197 F4
Valencia ✕ (VLC) Spain 39°20N 0°26W 197 F4
Valencia, G. de Spain 39°30N 0°20E 197 F5
Valencia de Alcántara Spain 39°25N 7°14W 195 F3
Valencia de Don Juan Spain 42°17N 5°31W 194 C5
Valencia I. Ireland 51°54N 10°22W 166 E1
Valenciennes France 50°20N 3°34E 173 B10
Văleni Romania 44°15N 24°45E 183 F9
Vălenii de Munte Romania 45°11N 26°2E 183 E11
Valensole France 43°50N 5°59E 175 E9
Valentigney France 47°27N 6°51E 173 E13
Valentim, Sa. do Brazil 6°0S 43°30W 332 C3
Valentin Russia 43°8N 134°17E 220 C7
Valentine Nebr., U.S.A. 42°52N 100°33W 308 D3
Valentine Tex., U.S.A. 30°35N 104°30W 314 F2
Valenton France 48°44N 2°27E 134 B3
Valenza Italy 45°1N 8°38E 198 C5
Våler Hedmark, Norway 60°41N 11°50E 164 D8
Våler Østfold, Norway 59°29N 10°51E 164 E7
Valera Piemonte, Italy 45°33N 9°3E 129 A1
Valera Venezuela 9°19N 70°37W 328 B3
Valesdir Vanuatu 16°47S 168°10E 287 F6
Valestrand Norway 59°40N 5°26E 164 E2
Valga Estonia 57°47N 26°2E 188 D4
Valguarnera Caropepe Italy 37°30N 14°23E 201 E7
Valier U.S.A. 48°18N 112°16W 304 B7
Valinco, G. de France 41°40N 8°52E 175 G12
Valjevo Serbia 44°18N 19°53E 202 B3
Valka Latvia 57°46N 26°3E 188 D3
Valkeakoski Finland 61°16N 24°2E 188 B2
Valkenswaard Neths. 51°21N 5°29E 170 C5
Vall de Uxó = La Vall d'Uixó Spain 39°49N 0°15W 196 F4
Valla Sweden 59°2N 16°20E 162 E10
Valladolid Yucatán, Mexico 20°41N 88°12W 319 C7
Valladolid Spain 41°38N 4°43W 194 D6
Valladolid □ Spain 41°38N 4°43W 194 D6
Vallata Italy 41°2N 15°15E 201 A8
Vallcarca Spain 41°25N 2°9E 114 A1
Valldemossa Spain 39°43N 2°37E 206 B3
Valldoreix Spain 41°27N 2°3E 114 A1
Valle Norway 59°13N 7°33E 164 E4
Valle d'Aosta □ Italy 45°45N 7°15E 198 C4
Valle de Arán Spain 42°50N 0°55E 196 C5
Valle de la Pascua Venezuela 9°13N 66°0W 328 B4
Valle de las Palmas Mexico 32°20N 116°43W 307 N10
Valle de Santiago Mexico 20°23N 101°12W 318 C4
Valle de Zaragoza Mexico 27°25N 105°50W 318 B3
Valle del Cauca □ Colombia 3°45N 76°30W 328 C2
Valle del Ticino ⌂ Italy 45°22N 9°0E 198 C6
Valle Fértil, Sierra del Argentina 30°20S 68°0W 334 C2
Valle Gran Rey Canary Is. 28°5N 17°20W 153 e1
Valle Hermoso Mexico 25°35N 97°40W 319 B5
Valle Nacional Mexico 17°47N 96°18W 319 D5
Vallecas Spain 40°22N 3°37W 127 B2
Valledupar Colombia 10°29N 73°15W 328 A3
Vallehermoso Canary Is. 28°10N 17°15W 153 e1
Vallejo U.S.A. 38°7N 122°14W 306 G4
Vallenar Chile 28°30S 70°50W 334 B1
Vallensbæk Denmark 55°38N 12°21E 118 B2
Vallensbæk Strand Denmark 55°36N 12°23E 118 B2
Vallentuna Sweden 59°32N 18°5E 162 E12
Vallentunasjön Sweden 59°27N 18°1E 139 A2
Valleranello Italy 41°46N 12°29E 136 C1
Valleraugue France 44°6N 3°39E 174 D7
Vallet France 47°10N 1°15W 172 E5
Valletta Malta 35°54N 14°31E 206 F8
Valley, The Anguilla 18°13N 63°4W 322 a
Valley Center U.S.A. 33°13N 117°2W 307 M9
Valley City U.S.A. 46°55N 98°0W 308 B5
Valley Falls Oreg., U.S.A. 42°29N 120°17W 304 E3
Valley Falls R.I., U.S.A. 41°54N 71°24W 313 E13
Valley Junction = West Des Moines U.S.A. 41°35N 93°43W 310 C3
Valley of Flowers △ India 30°50N 79°40E 243 D8
Valley of the Kings Egypt 25°41N 32°34E 256 B3
Valley Springs U.S.A. 38°12N 120°50W 306 G6
Valley Station U.S.A. 38°6N 85°52W 311 F11
Valley View U.S.A. 40°39N 76°33W 313 F8
Valley Wells U.S.A. 35°27N 115°46W 307 K11
Valleyview Canada 55°5N 117°17W 296 B5
Valli di Comàcchio Italy 44°40N 12°15E 199 D9
Vallimanca, Arroyo Argentina 35°40S 59°10W 334 D4
Vallisaari Finland 60°7N 25°0E 121 C3
Vallo della Lucánia Italy 40°14N 15°16E 201 B8
Vallon-Pont-d'Arc France 44°24N 4°24E 175 D8
Vallorbe Switz. 46°42N 6°20E 179 J2
Valls Spain 41°18N 1°15E 196 D6
Vallvidrera Spain 41°24N 2°6E 114 A1
Valmaseda = Balmaseda Spain 43°11N 3°12W 196 B1
Valmeyer U.S.A. 38°18N 90°19W 310 F6
Valmiera Latvia 57°37N 25°29E 188 D3
Valnera Spain 43°9N 3°40W 194 B7
Valognes France 49°30N 1°28W 172 C5
Valona = Vlorë Albania 40°32N 19°28E 202 F3
Valongo Portugal 41°8N 8°30W 194 D2
Valozhyn Belarus 54°3N 26°30E 177 A14
Valpaços Portugal 41°36N 7°17W 194 D3
Valparai India 10°22N 76°58E 245 J3
Valparaíso Chile 33°2S 71°40W 334 C1
Valparaíso Zacatecas, Mexico 22°46N 103°34W 318 C4
Valparaiso Fla., U.S.A. 30°29N 86°30W 317 E3
Valparaiso Ind., U.S.A. 41°28N 87°4W 311 C9
Valparaíso □ Chile 33°2S 71°40W 334 C1
Valpovo Croatia 45°39N 18°25E 182 E3
Valpoy India 15°32N 74°8E 245 G2
Valréas France 44°24N 5°0E 175 D9
Vals Switz. 46°39N 9°11E 179 J5
Vals → S. Africa 27°23S 26°30E 270 C4
Vals, Tanjung Indonesia 8°26S 137°25E 231 F9
Vals-les-Bains France 44°42N 4°24E 175 D8
Valsad India 20°40N 72°58E 244 D1
Valsamata Greece 38°10N 20°36E 207 C2
Valtellina Italy 46°9N 9°55E 198 B6
Valþjófsstaður Iceland 65°1N 14°59W 155 B12
Valti Greece 38°27N 21°7E 207 C3
Valuyki Russia 50°10N 38°5E 189 G10
Valverde Canary Is. 27°48N 17°55W 153 e1
Valverde del Camino Spain 37°35N 6°47W 195 H4
Valverde del Fresno Spain 40°15N 6°51W 194 E4
Valvidrera → Spain 41°25N 2°0E 114 A1
Vama Romania 47°34N 25°42E 183 C10
Vambori India 19°17N 74°44E 244 E2
Vamdrup Denmark 55°25N 9°17E 163 J3
Vämhus Sweden 61°7N 14°29E 162 C8
Vammala Finland 61°20N 22°54E 188 B2
Vamos Greece 35°24N 24°13E 207 E5
Vamsadhara → India 18°21N 84°8E 244 E7
Van Turkey 38°30N 43°20E 213 C10
Van □ Turkey 38°30N 43°20E 213 C10
Van, L. = Van Gölü Turkey 38°30N 43°0E 213 C10
Van Alstyne U.S.A. 33°25N 96°35W 314 E6
Van Blommestein Meer Suriname 4°45N 55°5W 329 C6
Van Buren = Kettering U.S.A. 39°41N 84°10W 311 E12
Van Buren N.B., Canada 47°10N 67°55W 299 C6
Van Buren Ark., U.S.A. 35°26N 94°21W 314 D7
Van Buren Maine, U.S.A. 47°10N 67°58W 309 B20
Van Buren Mo., U.S.A. 37°0N 91°1W 308 G8
Van Canh Vietnam 13°37N 109°0E 236 F7
Van Diemen, C. N. Terr., Australia 11°9S 130°24E 278 B5
Van Diemen, C. Queens., Australia 16°30S 139°46E 280 B2
Van Diemen G. Australia 11°45S 132°0E 278 B5
Van Gogh-museum Amsterdam, Neths. 112 c1
Van Gölü Turkey 38°30N 43°0E 213 C10
Van Horn U.S.A. 31°3N 104°50W 314 F2
Van Horne U.S.A. 42°1N 92°5W 310 B4
Van Meter U.S.A. 41°32N 93°57W 310 C3
Van Ninh Vietnam 12°42N 109°14E 236 F7
Van Rees, Pegunungan Indonesia 2°35S 138°15E 231 E9
Van Tivu India 8°51N 78°15E 245 K4
Van Wert U.S.A. 40°52N 84°35W 311 D12
Van Yen Vietnam 21°4N 104°42E 228 G5
Vanadzor Armenia 40°48N 44°30E 191 K7
Vanak Iran 35°45N 51°23E 141 A2
Vanavana French Polynesia 20°47S 139°9W 289 f
Vanavara Russia 60°22N 102°16E 215 C11
Vanceburg U.S.A. 38°36N 83°19W 311 F13
Vancouver B.C., Canada 49°15N 123°7W 306 A3
Vancouver Wash., U.S.A. 45°38N 122°40W 306 E4
Vancouver, C. Australia 35°2S 118°11E 279 G2
Vancouver, Mt. U.S.A. 60°20N 139°41W 303 F13
Vancouver I. Canada 49°50N 126°0W 306 B2
Vancouver Int. ✕ (YVR) Canada 49°10N 123°10W 306 A3
Vanda = Vantaa Finland 60°18N 24°56E 121 B2
Vandalia Ill., U.S.A. 38°58N 89°6W 310 F7
Vandalia Mo., U.S.A. 39°19N 91°29W 310 E5
Vandalia Ohio, U.S.A. 39°54N 84°12W 311 E12
Vandavasi India 12°30N 79°30E 245 H4
Vandeloos B. Sri Lanka 8°0N 81°45E 245 L5
Vandenberg Village U.S.A. 34°43N 120°28W 307 L6
Vanderbijlpark S. Africa 26°42S 27°54E 271 C4
Vandergrift U.S.A. 40°36N 79°34W 312 F5
Vanderhoof Canada 54°0N 124°0W 296 C4
Vanderkloof Dam S. Africa 30°4S 24°40E 270 D3
Vanderlin I. Australia 15°44S 137°2E 280 B2
Vänern Sweden 58°47N 13°30E 163 F7
Vänersborg Sweden 58°26N 12°19E 163 F6
Vang Norway 61°7N 8°34E 164 C5
Vang Vieng Laos 18°58N 102°32E 236 C4
Vanga Kenya 4°35S 39°12E 268 C4
Vangaindrano Madag. 23°21S 47°36E 272 C2
Vangede Denmark 55°45N 12°30E 118 A2
Vangsnes Norway 61°9N 6°39E 164 C3
Vanguard Canada 49°55N 107°20W 297 D7
Vangunu Solomon Is. 8°40S 158°5E 287 M10
Vanikoro Pac. Oc. 11°39S 166°54E 277 C12
Vaniköy Turkey 41°3N 29°3E 122 B2
Vanimo Papua N. G. 2°42S 141°21E 286 B1
Vanino Russia 48°50N 140°5E 215 E15
Vanivilasa Sagara India 13°45N 76°30E 245 H3
Vaniyambadi India 12°46N 78°44E 245 H4
Vânju Mare Romania 44°25N 22°52E 182 F7
Vanløse Denmark 55°41N 12°28E 118 A2
Vännäs Sweden 63°58N 19°48E 160 E18
Vannes France 47°40N 2°47W 172 E4
Vannøya Norway 70°6N 19°50E 160 A18
Vanoise, Massif de la France 45°25N 6°40E 175 C10
Vanrhynsdorp S. Africa 31°36S 18°44E 270 D2
Vansada India 20°47N 73°25E 244 D1
Vansbro Sweden 60°32N 14°15E 162 D8
Vanse Norway 58°6N 6°41E 164 F3
Vansittart B. Australia 14°3S 126°17E 278 B4
Vantaa Finland 60°18N 24°56E 121 B2
Vantaankoski Finland 60°18N 24°50E 121 B2
Vantaanpuisto Finland 60°18N 24°53E 121 B2
Vanua Balavu Fiji 17°12S 178°55W 287 A3
Vanua Lava Vanuatu 13°50S 167°30E 287 C5
Vanua Levu Fiji 16°33S 179°15E 287 B3
Vanua Vatu Fiji 18°22S 179°15W 287 B3
Vanuatu ■ Pac. Oc. 15°0S 168°0E 287 E6
Vanves France 48°49N 2°17E 134 B2
Vanwyksvlei S. Africa 30°18S 21°49E 270 D3
Vanzylsrus S. Africa 26°52S 22°4E 270 C3
Vao N. Cal. 22°39S 167°32E 288 d
Vapnyarka Ukraine 48°32N 28°45E 183 B13
Var □ France 43°27N 6°18E 175 E10
Var → France 43°39N 7°12E 175 E11
Vara Sweden 58°16N 12°55E 163 F6
Vara, Pico da Azores 37°48N 25°13W 153 d3
Varada → India 15°0N 75°40E 245 G2
Varades France 47°25N 1°1W 172 E5
Varáita → Italy 44°9N 7°53E 198 D4
Varaldsøy Norway 60°6N 5°59E 164 D2
Varallo Italy 45°49N 8°15E 198 C5
Varāmīn Iran 35°20N 51°39E 247 C6
Varāmīn □ Iran 35°18N 51°35E 247 B6
Varanasi India 25°22N 83°0E 243 G10
Varangerfjorden Norway 70°3N 29°25E 160 A23
Varangerhalvøya Norway 70°25N 29°30E 160 A23
Varano, Lago di Italy 41°53N 15°45E 199 G12
Varaždin Croatia 46°20N 16°20E 199 B13
Varazze Italy 44°22N 8°34E 198 D5
Varberg Sweden 57°6N 12°20E 163 G6
Varcar Vakuf = Mrkonjić Grad Bos.-H. 44°26N 17°4E 182 F2
Vardak □ Afghan. 34°0N 68°0E 240 B3
Vardar = Axios → Greece 40°57N 22°35E 202 F6
Varde Denmark 55°38N 8°29E 163 J2
Varde Å → Denmark 55°35N 8°19E 163 J2
Vardø Norway 70°23N 31°5E 160 A24
Varedo Italy 45°35N 9°8E 129 A1
Varel Germany 53°23N 8°8E 178 B4
Varella, Mui Vietnam 12°54N 109°26E 236 F7
Varėna Lithuania 54°12N 24°30E 188 E3
Varennes-sur-Allier France 46°19N 3°24E 173 F10
Varennes-Vauzelles France 47°3N 3°9E 173 E10
Vareš Bos.-H. 44°12N 18°23E 182 F3
Varese Italy 45°48N 8°50E 198 C5
Vârfurile Romania 46°19N 22°31E 182 D7
Vårgårda Sweden 58°2N 12°49E 163 F6
Vargem Bonita Brazil 20°20S 46°22W 333 F2
Vargem Grande Brazil 3°33S 43°56W 332 B3
Varginha Brazil 21°33S 45°25W 335 A6
Vargön Sweden 58°22N 12°20E 163 F6
Varhaug Norway 58°37N 5°41E 164 F2
Vari Greece 38°24N 20°35E 207 C2
Varillas Chile 24°0S 70°10W 334 A1
Varkaus Finland 62°19N 27°50E 188 A4
Varkiza Greece 37°50N 23°49E 112 C2
Värmdölandet Sweden 59°20N 18°33E 162 E12
Värmeln Sweden 59°35N 12°54E 162 E6
Värmlands län □ Sweden 60°0N 13°20E 162 E6
Värmlandsbro Sweden 59°11N 13°0E 162 E7
Varna Bulgaria 43°13N 27°56E 203 C11
Varna □ Bulgaria 43°20N 27°30E 203 C11
Varna → India 16°48N 74°32E 244 F2
Värnamo Sweden 57°10N 14°3E 163 G8
Varnsdorf Czech Rep. 50°55N 14°35E 180 A7
Varnville U.S.A. 32°51N 81°5W 316 C8
Várpalota Hungary 47°12N 18°8E 182 C3
Vars Ont., Canada 45°21N 75°21W 313 A9
Vars Hautes-Alpes, France 44°37N 6°42E 175 D10
Vartdal Norway 62°20N 6°2E 164 B3
Vartiokylä Finland 60°13N 25°6E 121 B3
Vartiosaari Finland 60°11N 25°5E 121 B3
Varto Turkey 39°10N 41°27E 213 C9
Varvarin Serbia 43°43N 21°20E 202 C5
Varysburg U.S.A. 42°46N 78°19W 312 D6
Varzaneh Iran 32°25N 52°40E 247 C7
Várzea Alegre Brazil 6°47S 39°17W 332 C4
Várzea da Palma Brazil 17°36S 44°44W 333 E3
Várzea Grande Brazil 15°39S 56°8W 331 D6
Varzi Italy 44°49N 9°12E 198 D6
Varzo Italy 46°12N 8°15E 198 B5
Varzy France 47°22N 3°20E 173 E10
Vas □ Hungary 47°10N 16°55E 182 C1
Vasa = Vaasa Finland 63°6N 21°38E 160 E19
Vasa Barris → Brazil 11°10S 37°10W 332 D4
Vasamuseet Stockholm, Sweden 139 b3
Vásárosnamény Hungary 48°9N 22°19E 182 B7
Vascão → Portugal 37°31N 7°31W 195 H3
Vaşcău Romania 46°28N 22°30E 182 D7
Vasco S. Africa 33°54S 18°34E 118 A2
Vascongadas = País Vasco □ Spain 42°50N 2°45W 196 C2
Vasfanārd Iran 35°38N 51°20E 141 B2
Vashi India 19°4N 72°59E 130 A2
Vāshīr Afghan. 32°16N 63°51E 240 B1
Vashkivtsi Ukraine 48°23N 25°31E 183 B10
Vasht = Khāsh Iran 28°15N 61°15E 240 C1
Vasilevichi Belarus 52°15N 29°50E 177 B15
Vasiliki Greece 38°37N 20°36E 207 B2
Vasiliko = Michurin Bulgaria 42°9N 27°51E 203 D11
Vasiliko Greece 38°25N 23°40E 204 C5
Vasilikos Greece 37°43N 20°59E 207 D2
Vasilkov = Vasylkiv Ukraine 50°7N 30°15E 177 C16
Vasilyevskiy, Ostrov Russia 59°55N 30°16E 137 B1
Vasilyova Sloboda = Chkolovsk Russia 56°50N 43°10E 190 B6
Vasilyovo = Chkolovsk Russia 56°50N 43°10E 190 B6
Vaslui Romania 46°38N 27°42E 183 D12
Vaslui □ Romania 46°30N 27°45E 183 D12
Väsman Sweden 60°9N 15°5E 162 D9
Vassar Man., Canada 49°10N 95°55W 297 D9
Vassar Mich., U.S.A. 43°22N 83°35W 309 D12
Vassfaret Norway 60°38N 9°28E 164 D6
Västerås Sweden 59°37N 16°38E 162 E10
Västerbotten Sweden 64°36N 20°4E 160 D19
Västerdalälven → Sweden 60°30N 14°7E 162 D8
Västergötland Sweden 58°0N 13°10E 163 F7
Västerhaninge Sweden 59°7N 18°6E 162 E12
Västervik Sweden 57°43N 16°33E 163 G10
Västmanland Sweden 59°45N 16°20E 161 G17
Västmanlands län □ Sweden 59°45N 16°20E 162 E10
Vasto Italy 42°8N 14°40E 199 F11
Västra Götalands län □ Sweden 58°0N 13°0E 163 F6
Vasvár Hungary 47°3N 16°47E 182 C1
Vasylivka Ukraine 45°38N 28°50E 183 E13
Vasylkiv Ukraine 50°7N 30°15E 177 C16
Vatan France 47°4N 1°50E 173 E8
Vaté = Efate, I. Vanuatu 17°40S 168°25E 287 G6
Vatersay U.K. 56°55N 7°32W 167 E1
Vathi Greece 38°41N 20°47E 207 B2
Vathia Greece 36°29N 22°29E 204 E4
Vatia Amer. Samoa 14°15S 170°40W 302 f
Vatican City ■ Europe 41°54N 12°27E 136 B1
Vaticano, C. Italy 38°37N 15°50E 201 D8
Vatili Cyprus 35°6N 33°40E 207 E9
Vatin Serbia 45°12N 21°20E 182 E6
Vatiu = Atiu Cook Is. 20°0S 158°10W 289 J12
Vatnajökull Iceland 64°30N 16°48W 155 C10
Vatnås Norway 59°58N 9°37E 164 E6
Vatnsfjörður Iceland 65°56N 22°30W 155 B4
Vatolakkos Greece 35°27N 23°53E 207 E4
Vatoloha Madag. 17°52S 47°48E 272 B2
Vatomandry Madag. 19°20S 48°59E 272 B2
Vatra-Dornei Romania 47°22N 25°22E 183 C10
Vatrak → India 23°9N 73°2E 242 H5
Vattaru Atoll Maldives 3°16N 73°25E 272 d
Vättern Sweden 58°25N 14°30E 163 F8
Vatu Vara Fiji 17°26S 179°31W 287 A3
Vatulele Fiji 18°33S 177°37E 287 B1
Vauclin, Mt. du Martinique 14°33N 60°53W 322 j
Vauclin, Pte. de Martinique 14°34N 60°49W 322 j
Vaucluse Australia 33°51S 151°15E 139 B2
Vaucluse □ France 43°50N 5°20E 175 E9
Vaucouleurs France 48°37N 5°40E 173 D12
Vaucresson France 48°50N 2°9E 134 A1
Vaud □ Switz. 46°35N 6°30E 179 J2
Vaudreuil-Dorion Canada 45°23N 74°3W 313 A10
Vaughan Canada 43°50N 79°32W 141 A1
Vaughan Mont., U.S.A. 47°33N 111°33W 304 C8
Vaughn N. Mex., U.S.A. 34°36N 105°13W 305 J11
Vauhallan France 48°44N 2°12E 134 B2
Vaujours France 48°56N 2°34E 134 A4
Vaujours L. Canada 55°27N 74°15W 298 A5
Vaupés = Uaupés → Brazil 0°2N 67°16W 328 C4
Vaupes □ Colombia 1°0N 71°0W 328 C3
Vauvert France 43°42N 4°17E 175 E8
Vauxhall Alta., Canada 50°5N 112°9W 296 C6
Vauxhall London, U.K. 125 c4
Vav India 24°22N 71°31E 242 G4
Vavatenina Madag. 17°28S 49°12E 272 B2
Vava'u Tonga 18°36S 174°0W 287 P14
Vava'u Group Tonga 18°40S 174°0W 287 P14
Vavoua Ivory C. 7°23N 6°29W 262 D3
Vavuniya Sri Lanka 8°45N 80°30E 245 K5
Vawkavysk Belarus 53°9N 24°30E 177 B13
Vaxholm Sweden 59°25N 18°20E 162 E12
Växjö Sweden 56°52N 14°50E 163 H8
Våxtorp Sweden 56°25N 13°8E 163 H7
Vayalpad India 13°39N 78°38E 245 H4
Vayenga = Severomorsk Russia 69°5N 33°27E 160 B25
Vaygach, Ostrov Russia 70°0N 60°0E 214 C7
Veadeiros Brazil 14°7S 47°31W 333 D2
Veaikevárri = Svappavaara Sweden 67°40N 21°3E 160 C19
Vechelde Germany 52°16N 10°22E 178 C6
Vechta Germany 52°44N 8°17E 178 C4
Vechte → Neths. 52°34N 6°6E 170 B6
Vecsés Hungary 47°26N 19°19E 117 B3
Vedaranniyam India 10°25N 79°50E 245 J4
Vedavågen Norway 59°17N 5°12E 164 E2
Veddige Sweden 57°17N 12°20E 163 G6
Vedea → Romania 43°42N 25°41E 183 G10
Vedia Argentina 34°30S 61°31W 334 C3
Vedrette di Ries-Aurina ⌂ Italy 46°54N 12°5E 199 B9
Vedum Sweden 58°11N 13°0E 163 F7
Veedersburg U.S.A. 40°7N 87°16W 311 D9
Veendam Neths. 53°5N 6°52E 170 A6
Veenendaal Neths. 52°2N 5°34E 170 B5
Vefsna → Norway 65°48N 13°10E 160 D15
Vega Nordland, Norway 65°40N 11°55E 160 D14
Vega Tex., U.S.A. 35°15N 102°26W 314 D3
Vega Alta Puerto Rico 18°25N 66°20W 321 b
Vega Baja Puerto Rico 18°27N 66°23W 321 b
Vega de Ribadeo = Vegadeo Spain 43°27N 7°4W 194 B3
Vegadeo Spain 43°27N 7°4W 194 B3
Vegårshei Norway 58°44N 8°51E 164 F5
Vegas Verde = North Las Vegas U.S.A. 36°11N 115°7W 124 A1
Veggli Norway 60°3N 9°9E 164 D6
Veglia = Krk Croatia 45°8N 14°40E 199 C11
Vegoritida, L. Greece 40°45N 21°45E 202 F5
Vegreville Canada 53°30N 112°5W 296 C6
Veiholmen Norway 63°31N 7°58E 164 A4
Veimandu Channel Maldives 2°10N 73°20E 272 d
Veinge Sweden 56°33N 13°4E 163 H7
Veisiejai Lithuania 54°6N 23°42E 184 D10
Vejbystrand Sweden 56°19N 12°45E 163 H6
Vejen Denmark 55°30N 9°9E 163 J3
Vejer de la Frontera Spain 36°15N 5°59W 195 J5
Vejle Denmark 55°43N 9°30E 163 J3
Vejle Fjord Denmark 55°40N 9°50E 163 J3
Vela Luka Croatia 42°59N 16°44E 199 F13
Velachha India 21°26N 73°1E 244 D1
Velanai I. Sri Lanka 9°45N 79°45E 245 K4
Velas Azores 38°41N 28°13W 153 d1
Velas, C. Costa Rica 10°21N 85°52W 320 D2
Velasco, Sierra de Argentina 29°20S 67°10W 334 B2
Velay, Mts. du France 45°0N 3°40E 174 D7
Velbert Germany 51°20N 7°3E 178 D3
Velddrif S. Africa 32°42S 18°11E 270 D2
Velebit ⌂ Croatia 44°30N 15°15E 199 D12
Velebit Planina Croatia 44°50N 15°20E 199 D12
Velebitski Kanal Croatia 44°45N 14°55E 199 D11
Veleka → Bulgaria 42°4N 27°58E 203 D11
Veleň Czech Rep. 50°10N 14°33E 135 A3
Velencei-tó Hungary 47°13N 18°36E 182 C3
Velenje Slovenia 46°23N 15°8E 199 B12
Veles Macedonia 41°46N 21°47E 202 E5
Veleslavín Czech Rep. 50°5N 14°21E 135 B2
Velestino Greece 39°23N 22°43E 204 B4
Vélez Colombia 6°1N 73°41W 328 B3
Vélez-Málaga Spain 36°48N 4°5W 195 J6
Vélez Rubio Spain 37°41N 2°5W 197 H2
Velhas → Brazil 17°13S 44°49W 333 E3
Velika Croatia 45°27N 17°40E 182 E2
Velika Gorica Croatia 45°44N 16°5E 199 C13
Velika Kapela Croatia 45°10N 15°5E 199 C12
Velika Kikinda = Kikinda Serbia 45°50N 20°30E 182 E5
Velika Kladuša Bos.-H. 45°11N 15°48E 199 C12
Velika Kruša Serbia 42°19N 20°39E 202 D4
Velika Morava → Serbia 44°43N 21°3E 202 B5
Velika Plana Serbia 44°20N 21°4E 202 B5
Velikaya → Russia 57°48N 28°10E 188 D5
Velikaya Kema Russia 45°30N 137°12E 220 B8
Velikaya Lepetikha Ukraine 47°2N 33°58E 189 J7
Veliké Kapušany Slovak Rep. 48°34N 22°5E 181 C15
Velike Lašče Slovenia 45°49N 14°45E 199 C11
Veliki Jastrebac Serbia 43°25N 21°30E 202 C5
Veliki Kanal Serbia 45°45N 19°15E 182 E4
Veliki Popović Serbia 44°8N 21°18E 202 B5
Velikiy Ustyug Russia 60°47N 46°20E 186 B8
Velikiye Luki Russia 56°25N 30°32E 188 D6
Veliko Gradište Serbia 44°46N 21°29E 202 B5
Veliko Tŭrnovo Bulgaria 43°5N 25°41E 203 C9
Velikonda Range India 14°45N 79°10E 245 G4
Vélingara Kolda, Senegal 13°12N 14°5W 262 C2
Vélingara Louga, Senegal 15°0N 14°40W 262 B2
Velingrad Bulgaria 42°4N 23°58E 202 D7
Velino, Mte. Italy 42°9N 13°23E 199 F10
Velizh Russia 55°36N 31°11E 188 E6
Vélizy-Villacoublay France 48°47N 2°11E 134 B2
Velka-Chuchle Czech Rep. 50°1N 14°23E 135 B2
Velké Karlovice Czech Rep. 49°20N 18°17E 181 B11
Velké Meziříčí Czech Rep. 49°21N 16°1E 180 B9
Velké Přílepy Czech Rep. 50°9N 14°19E 135 B1
Veľký Javorník Slovak Rep. 49°19N 18°22E 181 B11
Veľký Krtíš Slovak Rep. 48°12N 19°21E 181 C12
Veľký Meder Slovak Rep. 47°52N 17°46E 181 D10
Veľký Tribeč Slovak Rep. 48°28N 18°15E 181 C11
Vella G. Solomon Is. 8°0S 156°50E 287 M9
Vella Lavella Solomon Is. 7°45S 156°40E 287 L9
Vellar → India 11°30N 79°36E 245 J4
Velletri Italy 41°41N 12°47E 200 A5
Vellinge Sweden 55°29N 13°2E 163 J6
Vellmar Germany 51°22N 9°28E 178 D5
Vellore India 12°57N 79°10E 245 H4
Velopoula Greece 36°55N 23°27E 204 E5
Velsk Russia 61°10N 42°5E 188 B11
Velten Germany 52°42N 13°10E 178 C9
Veluwezoom △ Neths. 52°5N 6°0E 170 B6
Velva U.S.A. 48°4N 100°56W 308 A3
Velvendos Greece 40°15N 22°6E 202 F6
Velyka Mykhaylivka Ukraine 47°4N 29°52E 183 C14
Velyki Luchky Ukraine 48°25N 22°34E 182 B7
Velykyy Bereznyy Ukraine 48°54N 22°28E 182 B7
Velykyy Bychkiv Ukraine 47°58N 24°1E 183 C9
Vemb Denmark 56°21N 8°21E 163 H2
Vembanad L. India 9°36N 76°15E 245 K3
Vemdalen Sweden 62°27N 13°51E 162 B7
Ven Sweden 55°55N 12°45E 163 J6
Venaco France 42°14N 9°11E 175 F13
Venado Mexico 22°56N 101°6W 318 C4
Venado Tuerto Argentina 33°50S 62°0W 334 C3
Venafro Italy 41°29N 14°2E 201 A7
Venarey-les-Laumes France 47°32N 4°26E 173 E11
Venaria Italy 45°8N 7°38E 198 C4
Venčane Serbia 44°24N 20°28E 202 B4
Vence France 43°43N 7°6E 175 E11
Venda Seca Portugal 38°46N 9°15W 126 A1
Vendas Novas Portugal 38°39N 8°27W 195 G2
Vendée □ France 46°50N 1°35W 172 F5
Vendée → France 46°20N 1°10W 172 F5
Vendéen, Bocage France 46°40N 1°20W 174 B2
Vendeuvre-sur-Barse France 48°14N 4°28E 173 D11
Vendôme France 47°47N 1°3E 172 E8
Vendrell = El Vendrell Spain 41°10N 1°30E 196 D6
Vendsyssel Denmark 57°22N 10°0E 163 G4
Vendychany Ukraine 48°38N 27°48E 183 B12
Venelles France 43°35N 5°28E 175 E9
Véneta, L. Italy 45°23N 12°25E 199 C9
Venetian Islands U.S.A. 25°47N 80°9W 128 B2
Venetie U.S.A. 67°1N 146°25W 303 C11
Véneto □ Italy 45°30N 12°0E 199 C9
Venev Russia 54°22N 38°17E 188 E10
Venézia Italy 45°27N 12°21E 199 C9
Venézia, G. di Italy 45°15N 13°0E 199 C10
Venézia, Palazzo Rome, Italy 136 c2
Venézia Tridentina = Trentino-Alto Adige □ Italy 46°30N 11°20E 199 B8
Venezuela ■ S. Amer. 8°0N 66°0W 328 B4
Venezuela, G. de Venezuela 11°30N 71°0W 328 A3
Venezuelan Basin Cent. Amer. 14°0N 68°0W 321 C6
Vengurla India 15°53N 73°45E 245 G1
Vengurla Rocks India 15°55N 73°22E 245 G1
Venice = Venézia Italy 45°27N 12°21E 199 C9
Venice Calif., U.S.A. 33°59N 118°27W 126 C2
Venice Fla., U.S.A. 27°6N 82°27W 317 H7
Vénissieux France 45°42N 4°53E 175 C8
Venjansjön Sweden 60°54N 14°0E 162 D8
Venkatagiri India 14°0N 79°35E 245 H4
Venkatapuram India 18°20N 80°30E 244 E5
Venlo Neths. 51°22N 6°11E 170 C6
Vennesla Norway 58°15N 7°59E 164 F4
Venosa Italy 40°58N 15°49E 201 B8
Venray Neths. 51°31N 6°0E 170 C6
Vent, Îs. du French Polynesia 17°30S 149°30W 289 f
Venta Lithuania 56°12N 22°42E 184 B9
Venta → Latvia 57°24N 21°33E 184 A8
Venta de Baños Spain 41°55N 4°30W 194 D6
Venta de Cardeña = Cardeña Spain 38°16N 4°20W 195 G6
Ventana, Punta de la Mexico 24°4N 109°48W 318 C3
Ventana, Sa. de la Argentina 38°0S 62°30W 334 D3
Ventas Spain 40°26N 3°40W 127 B1
Ventersburg S. Africa 28°7S 27°9E 270 C4
Ventersburgweg = Hennenman S. Africa 27°59S 27°1E 270 C4
Venterstad S. Africa 30°47S 25°48E 270 D4
Ventimíglia Italy 43°47N 7°36E 198 E4
Ventnor U.K. 50°36N 1°12W 169 G6
Ventorro del Cano Spain 40°23N 3°49W 127 B1
Ventoténe Italy 40°47N 13°25E 200 B6
Ventoux, Mt. France 44°10N 5°17E 175 D9
Ventspils Latvia 57°25N 21°32E 184 A8
Ventspils □ Latvia 57°20N 21°50E 184 A8
Ventuarí → Venezuela 3°58N 67°2W 328 C4
Ventucopa U.S.A. 34°50N 119°29W 307 L7
Ventura U.S.A. 34°17N 119°18W 307 L7
Venus U.S.A. 27°4N 81°22W 317 H8
Vénus, Pte. Tahiti 17°29S 149°29W 289 e
Venus B. Australia 38°40S 145°42E 283 E6
Venustiano Carranza Baja Calif., Mexico 30°25N 115°53W 318 A1
Venustiano Carranza Distrito Federal, Mexico 19°25N 99°5W 128 B2
Vera Argentina 29°30S 60°20W 334 B3
Vera Spain 37°15N 1°51W 197 H3
Veracruz Mexico 19°11N 96°8W 319 D5
Veracruz □ Mexico 19°0N 96°15W 319 D5
Veraval India 20°53N 70°27E 242 J4
Verbánia Italy 45°56N 8°33E 198 C5
Verbicaro Italy 39°45N 15°55E 201 C8
Verbier Switz. 46°6N 7°13E 179 J3
Vercelli Italy 45°19N 8°25E 198 C5
Verchovchevo Ukraine 48°32N 34°10E 189 H8
Vercors ⌂ France 45°0N 5°25E 175 D9
Verdalsøra Norway 63°48N 11°30E 160 E14
Verde → Argentina 41°56S 65°5W 336 B3
Verde → Goiás, Brazil 19°11S 50°44W 333 E1
Verde → Goiás, Brazil 18°1S 50°14W 333 E1
Verde → Mato Grosso, Brazil 11°54S 55°48W 331 C6
Verde → Mato Grosso do Sul, Brazil 21°25S 52°20W 331 E7
Verde → São Paulo, Brazil 23°9S 46°27W 137 A1
Verde → Chihuahua, Mexico 26°29N 107°58W 318 B3
Verde → Oaxaca, Mexico 15°59N 97°50W 319 D5
Verde → Veracruz, Mexico 21°10N 102°50W 318 C4
Verde → Paraguay 23°9S 57°37W 334 A4
Verde → Ariz., U.S.A. 33°33N 111°40W 300 D4
Verde, Cay Bahamas 23°0N 75°5W 321 B4
Verde Grande → Brazil 16°13S 43°49W 333 E3
Verde I. Phil. 13°33N 121°5E 232 E3
Verde Island Pass Phil. 13°34N 120°51E 232 E3
Verde Pequeno → Brazil 14°48S 43°31W 333 D3
Verden Germany 52°55N 9°14E 178 C5
Verdi Athina, Greece 38°2N 23°40E 112 A2
Verdi Nev., U.S.A. 39°31N 119°59W 306 F7
Verdikoussa Greece 39°47N 21°59E 204 B3
Verdon → France 43°43N 5°46E 175 E9
Verdon ⌂ France 43°50N 6°5E 175 E10
Verdugo Mts. U.S.A. 34°10N 118°16W 126 A2
Verdun Qué., Canada 45°27N 73°35W 130 B2
Verdun France 49°9N 5°24E 173 C12
Verdun-sur-le-Doubs France 46°54N 5°2E 173 F12
Vereeniging S. Africa 26°38S 27°57E 271 C4
Verga, C. Guinea 10°30N 14°10W 262 C2
Vergara Uruguay 32°56S 53°57W 335 C5
Vergato Italy 44°17N 11°7E 198 D8
Vergemont Cr. → Australia 24°16S 143°16E 280 C3
Vergennes U.S.A. 44°10N 73°15W 313 B11
Vergt France 45°2N 0°43E 174 C4
Verhalom Hungary 47°31N 19°1E 117 A2
Veria Greece 40°34N 22°12E 202 F6
Verín Spain 41°57N 7°27W 194 D3
Verkhnedvinsk = Vyerkhnyadzvinsk Belarus 55°45N 27°58E 188 E4
Verkhnetulomskoye Vdkhr. Russia 68°36N 31°12E 160 B24
Verkhnevilyuysk Russia 63°27N 120°18E 215 C13
Verkhniy Baskunchak Russia 48°14N 46°44E 191 F8
Verkhovye Russia 52°55N 37°15E 189 F9
Verkhovyna Ukraine 48°9N 24°47E 183 B9
Verkhoyansk Russia 67°35N 133°25E 215 C14
Verkhoyansk Ra. = Verkhoyanskiy Khrebet Russia 66°0N 129°0E 215 C13
Verkhoyanskiy Khrebet Russia 66°0N 129°0E 215 C13
Verma Norway 62°21N 8°3E 164 B5
Vermelho → Brazil 23°30S 46°46W 137 B1
Vermenton France 47°40N 3°42E 173 E10
Vermilion Alta., Canada 53°20N 110°50W 297 C6
Vermilion Ohio, U.S.A. 41°25N 82°22W 312 E2
Vermilion → Alta., Canada 53°22N 110°51W 297 C6
Vermilion → Ill., U.S.A. 41°19N 89°4W 310 C7
Vermilion B. U.S.A. 29°42N 92°0W 314 G9
Vermilion Bay Canada 49°51N 93°34W 297 D10
Vermilion L. U.S.A. 47°53N 92°26W 308 B7
Vermillion U.S.A. 42°47N 96°56W 308 D5
Vermillion → Canada 47°38N 72°56W 298 C5
Vermont U.S.A. 40°18N 90°26W 310 D6
Vermont □ U.S.A. 44°0N 73°0W 313 C12
Vermosh Albania 42°35N 19°42E 202 D3
Verna U.S.A. 27°23N 82°16W 317 H7
Vernadsky Antarctica 65°0S 64°0W 151 C17
Vernal U.S.A. 40°27N 109°32W 304 F9
Vernalis U.S.A. 37°36N 121°17W 306 H5
Vernazza Italy 44°10N 9°45E 198 D6
Verner Canada 46°25N 80°8W 298 C3
Verneuil-sur-Avre France 48°45N 0°55E 172 D7
Verneukpan S. Africa 30°0S 21°0E 270 D3
Vernier Switz. 46°11N 6°12E 179 J2
Vérnio Italy 44°3N 11°9E 198 D8
Vernon B.C., Canada 50°20N 119°15W 296 C5
Vernon Eure, France 49°5N 1°30E 172 C8
Vernon Calif., U.S.A. 34°0N 118°13W 126 B3
Vernon Ill., U.S.A. 38°48N 89°5W 310 F7
Vernon Ind., U.S.A. 38°59N 85°36W 311 F11
Vernon Tex., U.S.A. 34°9N 99°17W 314 D5
Vernonia U.S.A. 45°52N 123°11W 306 E3
Vernou Guadeloupe 16°11N 61°39W 322 e
Verny = Almaty Kazakhstan 43°15N 76°57E 217 D9
Vero Beach U.S.A. 27°38N 80°24W 317 H9
Véroia = Veria Greece 40°34N 22°12E 202 F6
Véroli Italy 41°41N 13°25E 199 G10
Verona Ont., Canada 44°29N 76°42W 313 B8
Verona Italy 45°27N 10°59E 198 C7
Verona Wis., U.S.A. 42°59N 89°32W 310 B7
Verrès Italy 45°40N 7°42E 198 C4
Verrières-le-Buisson France 48°44N 2°16E 134 B2
Verron Ra. Papua N. G. 4°21S 152°46E 286 C7
Versailles B. Aires, Argentina 34°38S 58°31W 117 B1
Versailles Yvelines, France 48°48N 2°7E 134 B1
Versailles Ill., U.S.A. 39°53N 90°39W 310 E6
Versailles Ind., U.S.A. 39°4N 85°15W 311 E11
Versailles Ky., U.S.A. 38°3N 84°44W 311 F12
Versailles Mo., U.S.A. 38°26N 92°51W 310 F4
Versailles Ohio, U.S.A. 40°13N 84°29W 311 D12
Versalles Bolivia 12°44S 63°18W 331 C5
Versmold Germany 52°2N 8°9E 178 C4
Vert, C. Senegal 14°45N 17°30W 262 C1
Vertou France 47°10N 1°28W 172 E5
Vertus France 48°54N 4°2E 173 D11
Verulam S. Africa 29°38S 31°2E 271 C5
Verviers Belgium 50°37N 5°52E 170 D5
Vervins France 49°50N 3°53E 173 C10
Veržej Slovenia 46°34N 16°13E 199 B13
Verzy France 49°9N 4°10E 173 C11
Vescovato France 42°30N 9°27E 175 F13
Veselí nad Lužnicí Czech Rep. 49°12N 14°43E 180 B7
Veselie Bulgaria 42°18N 27°38E 203 D11
Veselovskoye Vdkhr. Russia 46°58N 41°25E 191 G5
Veshenskaya Russia 49°35N 41°44E 190 F5
Veshnyaki Russia 55°43N 37°48E 129 B4
Vesle → France 49°23N 3°28E 173 C10
Vesolyy Posolok Russia 59°53N 30°28E 137 B2
Vesoul France 47°40N 6°11E 173 E13
Vessigebro Sweden 56°58N 12°40E 163 H6
Vest-Agder □ Norway 58°30N 7°15E 164 F4
Vestbygd Norway 58°6N 6°34E 164 F3
Vesterålen Norway 68°45N 15°0E 160 B16
Vestfjorden Norway 67°55N 14°0E 160 C16
Vestfold □ Norway 59°15N 10°0E 164 E7
Vestfossen Norway 59°44N 9°52E 164 E6
Vestgrønland = Kitaa □ Greenland 70°0N 47°0W 154 C6
Vestmannaeyjar Iceland 63°27N 20°15W 155 D6
Vestnes Norway 62°39N 7°5E 164 B4
Vestra Finland 60°19N 24°46E 121 B1
Vestre Gausdal Norway 61°12N 10°8E 164 C7
Vestskoven Denmark 55°41N 12°23E 118 A2
Vestspitsbergen Svalbard 78°40N 17°0E 150 B8
Vestur-skaftafellssýsla □ Iceland 63°50N 18°30W 155 D8
Vestvågøya Norway 68°18N 13°50E 160 B15
Vesuvio Italy 40°49N 14°26E 201 B7
Vesuvius, Mt. = Vesuvio Italy 40°49N 14°26E 201 B7
Vesyegonsk Russia 58°40N 37°16E 188 C9
Veszprém Hungary 47°8N 17°57E 182 C2
Veszprém □ Hungary 47°5N 17°55E 182 C2
Vésztő Hungary 46°55N 21°16E 182 D6
Vetapalem India 15°47N 80°18E 245 G5
Vetlanda Sweden 57°24N 15°3E 163 G9
Vetluga Russia 57°53N 45°45E 190 B7
Vetluga → Russia 56°36N 46°4E 190 B8
Vetluzhskiy Kostroma, Russia 58°23N 45°26E 190 A7
Vetluzhskiy Nizhniy Novgorod, Russia 57°17N 45°12E 190 B7
Vetovo Bulgaria 43°42N 26°16E 203 C10
Vetralla Italy 42°20N 12°2E 199 F9
Vetren Bulgaria 42°15N 24°3E 203 D8
Vettore, Mte. Italy 42°49N 13°16E 199 F10
Veurne Belgium 51°5N 2°40E 170 C2
Vevay U.S.A. 38°45N 85°4W 311 F11
Veveno → Sudan 6°40N 32°58E 257 F3
Vevey Switz. 46°28N 6°51E 179 J2
Vevi Greece 40°47N 21°38E 202 F5
Veynes France 44°32N 5°49E 175 D9
Veys Iran 31°30N 49°0E 247 D6
Vézelay France 47°27N 3°45E 173 E10
Vézelise France 48°30N 6°5E 173 D13
Vézère → France 44°53N 0°53E 174 D4
Vezhen Bulgaria 42°50N 24°20E 203 D8
Vezirköprü Turkey 41°8N 35°27E 212 B6
Vezzani France 42°10N 9°15E 175 F13
Vi Thanh Vietnam 9°42N 105°26E 237 H5
Viacha Bolivia 16°39S 68°18W 330 D4
Viadana Italy 44°56N 10°31E 198 D7
Vialar = Tissemsilt Algeria 35°35N 1°50E 261 A5
Viamão Brazil 30°5S 51°0W 335 C5
Viana Brazil 3°13S 44°55W 332 B3
Viana Spain 42°31N 2°22W 196 C2
Viana do Alentejo Portugal 38°17N 7°59W 195 G3
Viana do Bolo Spain 42°11N 7°6W 194 C3
Viana do Castelo Portugal 41°42N 8°50W 194 D2
Viana do Castelo □ Portugal 41°50N 8°30W 194 D2
Vianden Lux. 49°56N 6°12E 170 E6
Viangchan = Vientiane Laos 17°58N 102°36E 236 D4
Vianópolis Brazil 16°40S 48°35W 333 E2
Vianos Greece 35°2N 25°21E 207 F6
Viar → Spain 37°36N 5°50W 195 H5
Viaréggio Italy 43°52N 10°14E 198 E7
Viaur → France 44°8N 1°58E 174 D5

Vibble Sweden 57°37N 18°16E 163 G12
Vibo Valéntia Italy 38°40N 16°6E 201 D9
Viborg Denmark 56°27N 9°23E 163 H3
Vibraye France 48°3N 0°44E 172 D7
Vic Spain 41°58N 2°19E 196 D7
Vic, Étang de France 43°29N 3°50E 174 E7
Vic-en-Bigorre France 43°24N 0°3E 174 E4
Vic-Fezensac France 43°47N 0°19E 174 E4
Vic-le-Comte France 45°39N 3°14E 173 G10
Vic-sur-Cère France 44°59N 2°38E 174 D6
Vicálvaro Spain 40°24N 3°36W 127 B2
Vícar Spain 36°50N 2°38W 197 J2
Vicente Lopez Argentina 34°31S 58°30W 117 B2
Vicente Pérez Rosales △ Chile 41°11S 72°12W 336 B2
Vicenza Italy 45°33N 11°33E 199 C8
Vich = Vic Spain 41°58N 2°19E 196 D7
Vichada ☐ Colombia 5°0N 69°30W 328 C4
Vichada → Colombia 4°55N 67°50W 328 C4
Vichuga Russia 57°12N 41°55E 190 B5
Vichy France 46°9N 3°26E 173 F10
Vickan Sweden 57°25N 6°10E 164 G3
Vicksburg Ariz., U.S.A. 33°45N 113°45W 307 M13
Vicksburg Mich., U.S.A. 42°7N 85°32W 311 B11
Vico France 42°10N 8°49E 175 F12
Vico, L. di Italy 42°19N 12°10E 199 F9
Vico del Gargano Italy 41°54N 15°57E 199 G12
Viçosa Brazil 9°28S 36°14W 332 C4
Viçosa do Ceará Brazil 3°34S 41°5W 332 B3
Vicovu de Sus Romania 47°56N 25°41E 183 C10
Victor India 21°0N 71°30E 242 J4
Victor N.Y., U.S.A. 42°58N 77°24W 312 D7
Victor Emanuel Ra. Papua N. G. 5°20S 142°15E 286 C2
Victor Harbor Australia 35°30S 138°37E 282 C3
Victor Hugo = Hamadia Algeria 35°28N 1°57E 261 A5
Victoria = Labuan Malaysia 5°20N 115°14E 235 A5
Victoria Argentina 32°40S 60°10W 334 C3
Victoria B.C., Canada 48°30N 123°25W 306 B3
Victoria Chile 38°13S 72°20W 336 A2
Victoria Hong Kong, China 22°17N 114°9E 122 B2
Victoria Grenada 12°12N 61°42W 323 q
Victoria Guinea 10°50N 14°32W 262 C2
Victoria Gozo, Malta 36°3N 14°14E 206 E6
Victoria Mind. Or., Phil. 13°12N 121°12E 232 E3
Victoria Tarlac, Phil. 15°35N 120°41E 232 D3
Victoria Romania 45°44N 24°41E 183 E9
Victoria Seychelles 4°38S 55°28E 272 c
Victoria London, U.K. 125 c3
Victoria Kans., U.S.A. 38°52N 99°9W 308 F4
Victoria Tex., U.S.A. 28°48N 97°0W 314 G6
Victoria ☐ Australia 37°0S 144°0E 282 D6
Victoria ☐ Trin. & Tob. 10°15N 61°27W 323 t
Victoria → Australia 15°10S 129°40E 278 C4
Victoria, Grand L. Canada 47°31N 77°30W 298 C4
Victoria, L. Africa 1°0S 33°0E 268 C3
Victoria, L. N.S.W., Australia 33°57S 141°15E 282 B4
Victoria, Mt. = Tomanivi Fiji 17°37S 178°1E 287 A2
Victoria, Mt. Burma 21°14N 93°55E 241 E4
Victoria, Mt. Wellington, N.Z. 41°18S 174°48E 143 B1
Victoria, Mt. Papua N. G. 8°55S 147°32E 286 E4
Victoria, Pont Canada 45°29N 73°32W 130 B2
Victoria and Alfred Waterfront Cape Town, S. Africa 118 a1
Victoria Beach Canada 50°40N 96°35W 297 C9
Victoria de Durango = Durango Mexico 24°3N 104°39W 318 C4
Victoria de las Tunas = Las Tunas Cuba 20°58N 76°59W 320 B4
Victoria Falls Zimbabwe 17°58S 25°52E 269 F2
Victoria Gardens India 18°58N 72°50E 130 B2
Victoria Harbour Ont., Canada 44°45N 79°45W 312 B5
Victoria Harbour Hong Kong, China 22°17N 114°10E 122 B1
Victoria I. Canada 71°0N 111°0W 294 B8
Victoria Island Nigeria 6°25N 3°25E 124 B2
Victoria L. Nfld. & L., Canada 48°20N 57°27W 299 C8
Victoria L. Gauteng, S. Africa 26°13S 28°9E 123 B2
Victoria Lawn Tennis Courts Australia 37°50S 145°1E 128 B2
Victoria Ld. Antarctica 75°0S 160°0E 151 D11
Victoria Nile → Uganda 2°14N 31°26E 268 B3
Victoria Park Singapore 1°19N 103°49E 138 B2
Victoria Peak China 22°16N 114°8E 122 B1
Victoria Peaks Phil. 9°22N 118°20E 233 G2
Victoria Pk. Belize 16°48N 88°37W 319 D7
Victoria Ra. N.Z. 42°12S 172°7E 285 C7
Victoria River Australia 16°25S 131°0E 278 C5
Victoria Str. Canada 69°31N 100°30W 294 C9
Victoria West S. Africa 31°25S 23°4E 270 D3
Victoria Wharf Cape Town, S. Africa 118 a2
Victorias Phil. 10°54N 123°5E 233 F4
Victoriaville Canada 46°4N 71°56W 299 C5
Victorica Argentina 36°20S 65°30W 334 D2
Victorville U.S.A. 34°32N 117°18W 307 L9
Vicuña Chile 30°0S 70°50W 334 C1
Vicuña Mackenna Argentina 33°53S 64°25W 334 C3
Vidal U.S.A. 34°7N 114°31W 307 L12
Vidal Junction U.S.A. 34°11N 114°34W 307 L12
Vidalia U.S.A. 32°13N 82°25W 316 C7
Vidamlya Belarus 52°19N 23°47E 185 F10
Vidauban France 43°25N 6°27E 175 E10
Videbæk Denmark 56°6N 8°38E 163 H2
Videle Romania 44°17N 25°31E 183 F10
Videsæter Norway 61°57N 7°14E 164 C4
Vidette U.S.A. 33°2N 82°15W 316 B7
Vidigueira Portugal 38°12N 7°48W 195 G3
Vidin Bulgaria 43°59N 22°50E 202 C6
Vidio, C. Spain 43°35N 6°14W 194 B4
Vidisha India 23°28N 77°53E 242 H7
Vido Greece 39°38N 19°55E 206 B9
Vidra Romania 45°56N 26°55E 183 E11
Viduša Bos.-H. 42°55N 18°21E 202 D2
Vidzy Belarus 55°23N 26°37E 188 E4
Viechtach Germany 49°4N 12°53E 179 F8
Viedma Argentina 40°50S 63°0W 336 B4
Viedma, L. Argentina 49°30S 72°30W 336 C2
Vieille Case Dominica 15°36N 61°24W 323 k
Vieira do Minho Portugal 41°38N 8°8W 194 D2
Vielha Spain 42°43N 0°44E 196 C5
Viella = Vielha Spain 42°43N 0°44E 196 C5
Vielsalm Belgium 50°17N 5°54E 170 D5
Vienenburg Germany 51°57N 10°34E 178 D6
Vieng Pou Kha Laos 20°41N 101°4E 228 G3
Vienna = Wien Austria 48°12N 16°22E 142 A2
Vienna Ga., U.S.A. 32°6N 83°47W 316 C6
Vienna Ill., U.S.A. 37°25N 88°54W 308 G9
Vienna Mo., U.S.A. 38°11N 91°57W 310 F5
Vienna Va., U.S.A. 38°54N 77°16W 143 B2
Vienne France 45°31N 4°53E 175 C8
Vienne ☐ France 46°30N 0°42E 174 B4
Vienne → France 47°13N 0°5E 172 E7
Vientiane Laos 17°58N 102°36E 236 D4
Vientos, Paso de los Caribbean 20°0N 74°0W 321 C5
Vieques Puerto Rico 18°8N 65°25W 321 b
Vierge Pt. St. Lucia 13°49N 60°53W 323 m
Vierkant Pt. Neth. Ant. 12°7N 68°17W 322 h
Viernheim Germany 49°31N 8°35E 179 F4
Viersen Germany 51°15N 6°23E 178 D2
Vierwaldstättersee Switz. 47°0N 8°30E 179 J4
Vierzon France 47°13N 2°5E 173 E9
Vieste Italy 41°53N 16°10E 199 G13
Vietnam ■ Asia 19°0N 106°0E 236 C6
Vietnam Veterans Memorial U.S.A. 38°53N 77°2W 143 B3
Vietnam War Museum U.S.A. 41°58N 87°39W 119 B3
Vietz = Witnica Poland 52°40N 14°54E 185 F1
Vieux-Boucau-les-Bains France 43°48N 1°23W 174 E2
Vieux Bourg Guadeloupe 16°20N 61°36W 322 e
Vieux Carré = French Quarter New Orleans, U.S.A. 131 a2
Vieux Fort Guadeloupe 15°57N 61°41W 322 e
Vieux Fort Marie-Galante, Guadeloupe 15°59N 61°17W 322 e
Vieux Fort St. Lucia 13°46N 60°58W 323 m
Vieux Fort, Pte. du Guadeloupe 15°57N 61°42W 322 e
Vieux Fort, R. du → Guadeloupe 15°59N 61°17W 322 e
Vieux Grand Port Mauritius 20°22S 57°42E 272 e
Vieux-Habitants Guadeloupe 16°4N 61°46W 322 e
Vieux-Habitants, Rivière des → Guadeloupe 16°3N 61°46W 322 e
Vieux-Montréal Montréal, Canada 130 b3
View Park U.S.A. 34°0N 118°20W 126 B3
Vif France 45°5N 5°41E 175 C9
Viga Phil. 13°52N 124°18E 232 E5
Vigan Phil. 17°35N 120°28E 232 C3
Vigário Geral Brazil 22°48S 43°18W 135 A1
Vigeland Norway 58°5N 7°18E 164 F4
Vigentino Italy 45°26N 9°13E 129 B2
Vigévano Italy 45°19N 8°51E 198 C5
Viggbyholm Sweden 59°26N 18°7E 139 A2
Vighignolo Italy 45°29N 9°2E 129 B1
Vigia = Almenara Brazil 16°11S 40°42W 333 E3
Vigia Brazil 0°50S 48°5W 332 B2
Vigla Greece 39°7N 20°50E 207 A2
Viglas, Akra Greece 35°54N 27°51E 206 F11
Vignemalle France 42°47N 0°10W 174 F3
Vigneulles-lès-Hattonchâtel France 48°59N 5°43E 173 D12
Vignola Italy 44°29N 11°1E 198 D8
Vigo Spain 42°12N 8°41W 194 C2
Vigo, Ría de Spain 42°15N 8°45W 194 C2
Vigrestad Norway 58°34N 5°42E 164 F2
Vigsø Bugt Denmark 57°8N 8°47E 163 G2
Vihiers France 47°10N 0°30W 172 E6
Vihowa Pakistan 31°8N 70°30E 242 D4
Vihowa → Pakistan 31°8N 70°41E 242 D4
Viikki Finland 60°13N 25°1E 121 B3
Viipuri = Vyborg Russia 60°43N 28°47E 188 B5
Vijayadurg India 16°30N 73°25E 244 F1
Vijayawada India 16°31N 80°39E 244 F5
Vijosë → Albania 40°37N 19°24E 202 F3
Vík Iceland 63°25N 19°1W 155 D7
Vik Sogn og Fjordane, Norway 61°21N 6°6E 164 C3
Vika Sweden 60°57N 14°28E 162 D8
Vikarabad India 17°20N 77°54E 244 E3
Vikarbyn Sweden 60°55N 15°1E 162 D9
Vike Norway 60°42N 5°35E 164 D2
Vikedal Norway 59°30N 5°55E 164 E2
Vikeke = Viqueque E. Timor 8°52S 126°23E 231 F7
Vikeland = Vigeland Norway 58°5N 7°18E 164 F4
Viken Skåne, Sweden 56°9N 12°34E 163 H6
Viken Västra Götaland, Sweden 58°39N 14°20E 163 F8
Vikersund Norway 59°58N 9°59E 164 E6
Vikeså Norway 58°38N 6°3E 164 F3
Vikevåg Norway 59°5N 5°41E 164 E2
Vikhroli India 19°6N 72°55E 130 A2
Viking Canada 53°7N 111°50W 296 C6
Vikmanshyttan Sweden 60°18N 15°50E 162 D9
Vikna Norway 64°55N 10°58E 160 D14
Vikos-Aoos △ Greece 40°0N 20°45E 204 B2
Vikøyri Norway 61°4N 6°34E 164 C3
Vila Alferes Chamusca = Guijá Mozam. 24°27S 33°0E 271 B5
Vila António Enes = Angoche Mozam. 16°8S 39°55E 269 F4
Vila Bela da Santissima Trindade Brazil 15°0S 59°57W 331 C6
Vila Cabral = Lichinga Mozam. 13°13S 35°11E 269 E4
Vila Cabral = Niassa ☐ Mozam. 13°30S 36°0E 269 E4
Vila da Maganja Mozam. 17°18S 37°30E 269 F4
Vila da Ribeira Brava C. Verde Is. 16°32N 24°25W 153 j
Vila de Rei Portugal 39°41N 8°9W 194 F2
Vila do Bispo Portugal 37°5N 8°53W 195 H2
Vila do Conde Portugal 41°21N 8°45W 194 D2
Vila do Porto Azores 36°56N 25°9W 153 d4
Vila Franca de Xira Portugal 38°57N 8°59W 195 G2
Vila Franca do Campo Azores 37°43N 25°26W 153 d3
Vila Gamito Mozam. 14°12S 33°0E 269 E3
Vila Gomes da Costa Mozam. 24°20S 33°37E 271 B5
Vila Guilherme Brazil 23°30S 46°38W 137 B2
Vila Isabel Brazil 22°54S 43°15W 135 B1
Vila Jaguára Brazil 23°30S 46°45W 137 B1
Vila Machado Mozam. 19°15S 34°14E 269 F3
Vila Madalena Brazil 23°32S 46°41W 137 B1
Vila Maria Brazil 23°31S 46°36W 137 B2
Vila Mariana Brazil 23°34S 46°36W 137 B2
Vila Mouzinho Mozam. 14°48S 34°25E 269 E3
Vila Nova de Famalicão Portugal 41°25N 8°32W 194 D2
Vila Nova de Fos Côa Portugal 41°5N 7°9W 194 D3
Vila Nova de Gaia Portugal 41°8N 8°37W 194 D2
Vila Nova de Gaza = Xai-Xai Mozam. 25°6S 33°31E 271 C5
Vila Nova de Ourém Portugal 39°40N 8°35W 194 F2
Vila Nova do Corvo Azores 39°40N 31°8W 153 d2
Vila Pereira de Eça = Ondjiva Angola 16°48S 15°50E 265 F3
Vila Pery = Manica Mozam. 18°58S 32°59E 271 A5
Vila Pouca de Aguiar Portugal 41°30N 7°38W 194 D3
Vila Prudente Brazil 23°35S 46°33W 137 B2
Vila Real Portugal 41°17N 7°48W 194 D3
Vila Real ☐ Portugal 41°36N 7°35W 194 D3
Vila-real de los Infantes Spain 39°55N 0°3W 196 F4
Vila Real de Santo António Portugal 37°10N 7°28W 195 H3
Vila Texeira da Silva = Luau Angola 10°40S 22°10E 265 E4
Vila Vasco da Gama Mozam. 14°54S 32°14E 269 E3
Vila Velha Amapá, Brazil 3°13N 51°13W 329 C7
Vila Velha Espirito Santo, Brazil 20°20S 40°17W 333 F3
Vila Viçosa Portugal 38°45N 7°27W 195 G3
Viladecans Spain 41°18N 2°1E 114 B1
Vilafranca del Maestrat Spain 40°26N 0°16W 196 E4
Vilafranca del Penedès Spain 41°21N 1°40E 196 D6
Vilagarcía de Arousa Spain 42°34N 8°46W 194 C2
Vilaine → France 47°30N 2°27W 172 E4
Vilakalaka Vanuatu 15°25S 167°42E 287 E5
Vilanandro, Tanjona Madag. 16°11S 44°27E 272 B1
Vilanculos Mozam. 22°1S 35°17E 271 B6
Vilanova de Castelló Spain 39°5N 0°31W 197 F4
Vilanova i la Geltrú Spain 41°13N 1°40E 196 D6
Vilar Formosa Portugal 40°38N 6°45W 194 E4
Vilaseca Spain 41°7N 1°9E 196 D6
Vilaseca-Salou = Vilaseca Spain 41°7N 1°9E 196 D6
Vilbjerg Denmark 56°12N 8°46E 163 H2
Vilcabamba, Cordillera Peru 13°0S 73°0W 330 C3
Vilcanchos Peru 13°40S 74°25W 330 C3
Vilcheka, Zemlya Russia 80°30N 60°30E 150 A11
Vilches Spain 38°12N 3°30W 195 G7
Vile Parle India 19°6N 72°51E 130 A2
Vileyka Belarus 54°30N 26°53E 177 A14
Vilhelmina Sweden 64°35N 16°39E 160 D17
Vilhena Brazil 12°40S 60°5W 331 C5
Viliya = Neris → Lithuania 55°8N 24°16E 188 E3
Viljandi Estonia 58°28N 25°30E 188 C3
Viljoensdorp = Newcastle S. Africa 27°45S 29°58E 271 C4
Vilkaviškis Lithuania 54°39N 23°2E 184 D10
Vilkija Lithuania 55°3N 23°35E 184 C10
Vilkitskogo, Proliv Russia 78°0N 103°0E 215 B11
Vilkomir = Ukmergė Lithuania 55°15N 24°45E 188 E3
Vilkovo = Vylkove Ukraine 45°28N 29°32E 183 E14
Villa Abecia Bolivia 21°0S 68°18W 334 A2
Villa Adelina Argentina 34°31S 58°33W 117 B1
Villa Ana Argentina 28°28S 59°40W 334 B4
Villa Ángela Argentina 27°34S 60°45W 334 B3
Villa Ballester Argentina 34°33S 58°33W 117 B1
Villa Barilari Argentina 34°42S 58°20W 117 C2
Villa Bella = Serra Talhada Brazil 7°59S 38°18W 332 C4
Villa Bella Bolivia 10°25S 65°22W 331 C4
Villa Borghese Rome, Italy 136 a3
Villa Bosch Argentina 34°35S 58°33W 117 B1
Villa Bruzual Venezuela 9°20N 69°6W 328 C4
Villa C. Colon Argentina 34°41S 58°21W 117 C2
Villa Cañás Argentina 34°0S 61°35W 334 C3
Villa Cecilia = Ciudad Madero Mexico 22°19N 97°50W 319 C5
Villa Cisneros = Dakhla W. Sahara 23°50N 15°53W 260 D1
Villa Ciudadela Argentina 34°38S 58°33W 117 B1
Villa Colón Argentina 31°38S 68°20W 334 C2
Villa Constitución Argentina 33°15S 60°20W 334 C3
Villa de Arriaga Mexico 21°56N 101°20W 318 C4
Villa de Cura Venezuela 10°2N 67°29W 328 A4
Villa de Guadalupe Mexico 19°29N 99°6W 128 B2
Villa de María Argentina 29°55S 63°43W 334 B3
Villa de Méndez Mexico 25°7N 98°34W 319 B5
Villa del Nevoso = Ilirska-Bistrica Slovenia 45°34N 14°14E 199 C11
Villa del Rio Spain 37°59N 4°17W 195 H6
Villa del Rosario Venezuela 10°19N 72°19W 328 A3
Villa Devoto Argentina 34°36S 58°31W 117 B1
Villa Diamante Argentina 34°41S 58°25W 117 C2
Villa Dolores Argentina 31°58S 65°15W 334 C2
Villa Dominico Argentina 34°41S 58°19W 117 C3
Villa Frontera Mexico 26°56N 101°27W 318 B4
Villa Grove U.S.A. 39°52N 88°10W 311 E8
Villa Guillermina Argentina 28°15S 59°29W 334 B4
Villa Hayes Paraguay 25°5S 57°20W 334 B4
Villa Hidalgo Mexico 24°15N 99°26W 319 C5
Villa Iris Argentina 38°12S 63°12W 334 D3
Villa Lugano Argentina 34°41S 58°27W 117 C2
Villa Lynch Argentina 34°35S 58°31W 117 B1
Villa Madero Argentina 34°41S 58°30W 117 C1
Villa María Argentina 32°20S 63°10W 334 C3
Villa Mazán Argentina 28°40S 66°30W 334 B2
Villa Minozzo Italy 44°22N 10°28E 198 D7
Villa Montes Bolivia 21°10S 63°30W 334 A3
Villa Ocampo Argentina 28°30S 59°20W 334 B4
Villa Ocampo Durango, Mexico 26°27N 105°31W 318 B3
Villa Ojo de Agua Argentina 29°30S 63°44W 334 B3
Villa Rica U.S.A. 33°44N 84°55W 316 B5
Villa Sáenz Pena Argentina 34°37S 58°32W 117 B1
Villa San Giovanni Italy 38°13N 15°38E 201 D8
Villa San José Argentina 32°12S 58°15W 334 C4
Villa San Martín Argentina 28°15S 64°9W 334 B3
Villa Sanjurjo = Al Hoceïma Morocco 35°8N 3°58W 261 A4
Villa Santina Italy 46°24N 12°55E 199 B9
Villa Unión Mexico 23°12N 106°14W 318 C3
Villa Urquiza Argentina 34°34S 58°28W 117 B2
Villaba Phil. 11°13N 124°24E 233 F5
Villablino Spain 42°57N 6°19W 194 C4
Villacarlos Spain 39°53N 4°17E 206 B5
Villacarriedo Spain 43°14N 3°48W 194 B7
Villacarrillo Spain 38°7N 3°3W 195 G7
Villacastín Spain 40°46N 4°25W 194 E6
Villach Austria 46°37N 13°51E 180 E6
Villacidro Italy 39°27N 8°44E 200 C1
Villada Spain 42°15N 4°59W 194 C6
Villadiego Spain 42°31N 4°1W 194 C6
Villadóssola Italy 46°4N 8°16E 198 B5
Villafeliche Spain 41°10N 1°30W 196 D3
Villafranca Spain 42°17N 1°46W 196 C3
Villafranca de los Barros Spain 38°35N 6°18W 195 G4
Villafranca de los Caballeros Spain 39°26N 3°21W 195 F7
Villafranca del Cid = Vilafranca del Maestrat Spain 40°26N 0°16W 196 E4
Villafranca del Panadés = Vilafranca del Penedès Spain 41°21N 1°40E 196 D6
Villafranca di Verona Italy 45°21N 10°50E 198 C7
Villafranca Tirrena Italy 38°20N 15°25E 201 D8
Villagio Mussolini = Arboréa Italy 39°46N 8°35E 200 C1
Villagrán Mexico 24°29N 99°29W 319 C5
Villaguay Argentina 32°0S 59°0W 334 C4
Villaharta Spain 38°9N 4°54W 195 G6
Villahermosa Tabasco, Mexico 17°59N 92°55W 319 D6
Villahermosa Spain 38°46N 2°52W 197 G2
Villaines-la-Juhel France 48°21N 0°20W 172 D6
Villajoyosa Spain 38°30N 0°12W 197 G4
Villalba Puerto Rico 18°8N 66°30W 321 b
Villalba Spain 43°26N 7°40W 194 B3
Villalba de Guardo Spain 42°42N 4°49W 194 C6
Villalón de Campos Spain 42°5N 5°4W 194 C5
Villalpando Spain 41°51N 5°25W 194 D5
Villaluenga Spain 40°2N 3°54W 194 E7
Villamanán Spain 42°19N 5°35W 194 C5
Villamartín Spain 36°52N 5°38W 195 J5
Villamayor de Santiago Spain 39°50N 2°59W 196 F2
Villamblard France 45°2N 0°32E 174 C4
Villanova Monteleone Italy 40°30N 8°28E 200 B1
Villanueva Colombia 10°37N 72°59W 328 A3
Villanueva N. Mex., U.S.A. 35°16N 105°22W 305 J11
Villanueva de Castellón = Vilanova de Castelló Spain 39°5N 0°31W 197 F4
Villanueva de Córdoba Spain 38°20N 4°38W 195 G6
Villanueva de la Fuente Spain 38°42N 2°42W 197 G2
Villanueva de la Serena Spain 38°59N 5°50W 195 G5
Villanueva de la Sierra Spain 40°12N 6°24W 194 E4
Villanueva de los Castillejos Spain 37°30N 7°15W 195 H3
Villanueva de los Infantes Spain 38°43N 3°1W 195 G7
Villanueva del Arzobispo Spain 38°10N 3°0W 197 G2
Villanueva del Fresno Spain 38°23N 7°10W 195 G3
Villanueva y Geltrú = Vilanova i la Geltrú Spain 41°13N 1°40E 196 D6
Villaputzu Italy 39°26N 9°34E 200 C2
Villaquilambre Spain 42°39N 5°33W 194 C5
Villar del Arzobispo Spain 39°44N 0°50W 196 F4
Villar del Rey Spain 39°7N 6°50W 195 F4
Villard-de-Lans France 45°3N 5°33E 175 C9
Villarramiel Spain 42°2N 4°55W 194 C6
Villarreal = Vila-real de los Infantes Spain 39°55N 0°3W 196 F4
Villarrica Chile 39°15S 72°15W 336 A2
Villarrica Paraguay 25°40S 56°30W 334 B4
Villarrica △ Chile 39°24S 71°46W 336 A2
Villarrobledo Spain 39°18N 2°36W 197 F2
Villarroya de la Sierra Spain 41°27N 1°46W 196 D3
Villarrubia de los Ojos Spain 39°14N 3°36W 195 F7
Villars-les-Dombes France 46°0N 5°3E 173 F12
Villasayas Spain 41°24N 2°39W 196 D2
Villaseca de los Gamitos = Villaseco de los Gamitos Spain 41°2N 6°7W 194 D4
Villaseco de los Gamitos Spain 41°2N 6°7W 194 D4
Villasimíus Italy 39°8N 9°31E 200 C2
Villastar Spain 40°17N 1°9W 196 E3
Villatobas Spain 39°54N 3°20W 194 F7
Villaverde Spain 40°21N 3°42W 127 B1
Villaverde Bajo Spain 40°20N 3°40W 127 B1
Villavicencio Argentina 32°28S 69°0W 334 C2
Villavicencio Colombia 4°9N 73°37W 328 C3
Villaviciosa Spain 43°32N 5°27W 194 B5
Villazón Bolivia 22°0S 65°35W 334 A2
Ville-d'Avray France 48°49N 2°11E 134 B2
Ville-Marie Canada 47°20N 79°30W 298 C4
Ville Platte U.S.A. 30°41N 92°17W 314 F8
Villecresnes France 48°43N 2°31E 134 B4
Villedieu-les-Poêles France 48°50N 1°13W 172 D5
Villefort France 44°28N 3°56E 174 D7
Villefranche-de-Lauragais France 43°25N 1°44E 174 E5
Villefranche-de-Rouergue France 44°21N 2°2E 174 D6
Villefranche-du-Périgord France 44°38N 1°5E 174 D5
Villefranche-sur-Saône France 45°59N 4°43E 175 C8
Villegrande Bolivia 18°30S 64°10W 331 D5
Villejuif France 48°47N 2°21E 134 B3
Villel Spain 40°14N 1°12W 196 E3
Villemomble France 48°52N 2°30E 134 A4
Villemur-sur-Tarn France 43°51N 1°31E 174 E5
Villena Spain 38°39N 0°52W 197 G4
Villenauxe-la-Grande France 48°35N 3°33E 173 D10
Villenave-d'Ornon France 44°46N 0°33W 174 D3
Villeneuve-d'Ascq France 50°38N 3°9E 173 B10
Villeneuve-la-Garenne France 48°56N 2°19E 134 A2
Villeneuve-l'Archevêque France 48°14N 3°32E 173 D10
Villeneuve-le-Roi France 48°43N 2°24E 134 B3
Villeneuve-lès-Avignon France 43°58N 4°49E 175 E8
Villeneuve-St-Georges France 48°43N 2°27E 134 B3
Villeneuve-sur-Allier France 46°40N 3°13E 173 F10
Villeneuve-sur-Lot France 44°24N 0°42E 174 D4
Villeneuve-sur-Yonne France 48°5N 3°18E 173 D10
Villeparisis France 48°56N 2°36E 134 A4
Villeréal France 44°38N 0°45E 174 D4
Villers-Bocage France 49°3N 0°40W 172 C6
Villers-Cotterêts France 49°15N 3°4E 173 C10
Villers-sur-Mer France 49°21N 0°2W 172 C6
Villersexel France 47°33N 6°26E 173 E13
Villerupt France 49°28N 5°55E 173 C12
Villeurbanne France 45°46N 4°55E 175 C8
Villevaudé France 48°55N 2°39E 134 A4
Villiers S. Africa 27°2S 28°36E 271 C4
Villiers-le-Bâcle France 48°44N 2°8E 134 B1
Villiers-sur-Marne France 48°49N 2°32E 134 B4
Villingen-Schwenningen Germany 48°3N 8°26E 179 G4
Villinki Finland 60°9N 25°6E 121 C3
Villisca U.S.A. 40°56N 94°59W 310 D2
Villmanstrand = Lappeenranta Finland 61°3N 28°12E 188 B5
Villoresi, Canale Italy 45°33N 8°59E 129 A1
Villupuram India 11°59N 79°31E 245 J4
Vilna = Vilnius Lithuania 54°38N 25°19E 188 E3
Vilna Canada 54°7N 111°55W 296 C6
Vilnius Lithuania 54°38N 25°19E 188 E3
Vils Austria 47°33N 10°38E 180 D3
Vils → Bayern, Germany 48°37N 13°11E 179 G9
Vils → Bayern, Germany 49°10N 11°57E 179 F7
Vilsbiburg Germany 48°26N 12°22E 179 G8
Vilshofen Germany 48°37N 13°11E 179 G9
Vilusi Montenegro 42°44N 18°34E 202 D2
Vilvoorde Belgium 50°56N 4°26E 116 A2
Vilyuy → Russia 64°24N 126°26E 215 C13
Vilyuysk Russia 63°40N 121°35E 215 C13
Vimianzo Spain 43°7N 9°2W 194 B1
Vimioso Portugal 41°35N 6°31W 194 D4
Vimmerby Sweden 57°40N 15°55E 163 G9
Vimodrone Italy 45°30N 9°16E 129 A2
Vimont Canada 45°36N 73°43W 130 A1
Vimoutiers France 48°57N 0°10E 172 D7
Vimperk Czech Rep. 49°3N 13°46E 180 B6
Vina → Cameroon 7°45N 15°36E 264 A3
Viña del Mar Chile 33°0S 71°30W 334 C1
Vinanmek Palace Bangkok, Thailand 113 a2
Vinarós Spain 40°30N 0°27E 196 E5
Vincendo Réunion 21°21S 55°41E 272 f
Vincennes Val-de-Marne, France 48°51N 2°26E 134 A3
Vincennes Ind., U.S.A. 38°41N 87°32W 311 F9
Vincennes, Bois de France 48°49N 2°26E 134 B3
Vincent U.S.A. 34°33N 118°11W 307 L8
Vinces Ecuador 1°32S 79°45W 328 D2
Vinchina Argentina 28°45S 68°15W 334 B2
Vindava = Ventspils Latvia 57°25N 21°32E 184 A8
Vindelälven → Sweden 63°55N 19°50E 160 E18
Vindeln Sweden 64°12N 19°43E 160 D18
Vinderup Denmark 56°29N 8°45E 163 H2
Vindhya Ra. India 22°50N 77°0E 242 H7
Vine Grove U.S.A. 37°49N 85°59W 311 G11
Vineland Fla., U.S.A. 28°23N 81°30W 133 B1
Vineland N.J., U.S.A. 39°29N 75°2W 309 F16
Vineuil France 47°35N 1°22E 172 E8
Vinga Romania 46°1N 21°14E 182 D6
Vingåker Sweden 59°2N 15°52E 162 E9
Vingelen Norway 62°25N 10°52E 164 B7
Vingnes Norway 61°7N 10°26E 164 C7
Vinh Vietnam 18°45N 105°38E 236 C5
Vinh Linh Vietnam 17°4N 107°2E 236 D6
Vinh Loi = Bac Lieu Vietnam 9°17N 105°43E 237 H5
Vinh Long Vietnam 10°16N 105°57E 237 G5
Vinh Yen Vietnam 21°21N 105°35E 228 G5
Vinhais Portugal 41°50N 7°5W 194 D3
Vinica Croatia 46°20N 16°9E 199 B13
Vinica Macedonia 41°53N 22°30E 202 E6
Vinica Slovenia 45°28N 15°16E 199 C12
Vinings U.S.A. 33°53N 84°29W 113 A2
Vinita U.S.A. 36°39N 95°9W 314 C7
Vinje Sør-Trøndelag, Norway 63°12N 9°0E 164 A5
Vinje Telemark, Norway 59°37N 7°51E 164 E4
Vinjo Norway 60°48N 6°30E 164 D3
Vinkovci Croatia 45°19N 18°48E 182 E3
Vinnitsa = Vinnytsya Ukraine 49°15N 28°30E 177 D15
Vinnytsya Ukraine 49°15N 28°30E 177 D15
Vinnytsya ☐ Ukraine 49°20N 28°15E 189 H5
Vinodelnoye = Ipatovo Russia 45°45N 42°50E 191 H6
Vinohrady Prague, Czech Rep. 135 c3
Vinoř Czech Rep. 50°8N 14°34E 135 B3
Vinslöv Sweden 56°7N 13°55E 163 H7
Vinson Massif Antarctica 78°35S 85°25W 151 D16
Vinstra Norway 61°37N 9°44E 164 C6
Vinstra → Norway 61°37N 9°44E 164 C6
Vintar Phil. 18°14N 120°39E 232 B3
Vintjärn Sweden 60°50N 16°4E 162 D10
Vinton Calif., U.S.A. 39°48N 120°10W 306 F6
Vinton Iowa, U.S.A. 42°10N 92°1W 310 B4
Vinton La., U.S.A. 30°11N 93°35W 314 F8
Vinţu de Jos Romania 46°0N 23°30E 183 D8
Vinukonda India 16°4N 79°45E 245 F4
Viöl Germany 54°34N 9°11E 178 A5
Viola U.S.A. 41°12N 90°35W 310 C6
Violet Hill China 22°15N 114°11E 122 B2
Violet Town Australia 36°38S 145°42E 283 D6
Viotia ☐ Greece 38°20N 23°0E 204 C5
Vipacco = Vipava Slovenia 45°51N 13°58E 199 C10
Vipava Slovenia 45°51N 13°58E 199 C10
Vipiteno Italy 46°54N 11°26E 199 B8
Viqueque E. Timor 8°52S 126°23E 231 F7
Vir Croatia 44°17N 15°3E 199 D12
Virac Phil. 13°30N 124°20E 232 E5
Virachey Cambodia 13°59N 106°49E 236 F6
Virachey △ Cambodia 14°14N 106°55E 236 E6
Virago Sd. Canada 54°0N 132°30W 296 C2
Virajpet = Virarajendrapet India 12°10N 75°50E 245 H2
Viramgam India 23°5N 72°0E 242 H5
Viranşehir Turkey 37°13N 39°45E 213 D8
Virányos Hungary 47°31N 18°59E 117 A1
Virarajendrapet India 12°10N 75°50E 245 H2
Virawah Pakistan 24°31N 70°46E 242 G4
Virbalis Lithuania 54°39N 22°49E 184 D9
Virden Man., Canada 49°50N 100°56W 297 D8
Virden Ill., U.S.A. 39°30N 89°46W 310 E7
Vire France 48°50N 0°53W 172 D6
Vire → France 49°20N 1°7W 172 C5
Virei Angola 15°43S 12°52E 265 F2
Virgem da Lapa Brazil 16°49S 42°21W 333 E3
Vírgenes, C. Argentina 52°19S 68°21W 336 D3
Virgin → U.S.A. 36°28N 114°21W 305 H6
Virgin Gorda Br. Virgin Is. 18°30N 64°26W 321 C7
Virgin Is. (British) ⧄ W. Indies 18°30N 64°30W 321 C7
Virgin Is. (U.S.) ⧄ W. Indies 18°20N 65°0W 321 C7
Virgin Islands △ U.S. Virgin Is. 18°21N 64°43W 321 b
Virginia Free State, S. Africa 28°8S 26°55E 270 C4
Virginia Ill., U.S.A. 39°57N 90°13W 310 E6
Virginia Minn., U.S.A. 47°31N 92°32W 308 B7
Virginia ☐ U.S.A. 37°30N 78°45W 309 G14
Virginia, L. U.S.A. 28°35N 81°20W 133 A2
Virginia Beach U.S.A. 36°49N 76°9W 309 F16
Virginia City Mont., U.S.A. 45°18N 111°56W 304 D8
Virginia City Nev., U.S.A. 39°19N 119°39W 306 F7
Virginia Falls Canada 61°38N 125°42W 296 A3
Virginia Gardens U.S.A. 25°48N 80°18W 128 B1
Virginia Key U.S.A. 25°44N 80°8W 128 B2
Virginiatown Canada 48°9N 79°36W 298 C4
Virje Croatia 46°4N 16°59E 199 B13
Viroflay France 48°48N 2°10E 134 B2
Vironas Greece 37°55N 23°46E 112 B2
Viroqua U.S.A. 43°34N 90°53W 308 D8
Virovitica Croatia 45°51N 17°21E 182 E2
Virpazar Montenegro 42°14N 19°6E 202 D3
Virpur India 21°51N 70°42E 242 J4
Virserum Sweden 57°20N 15°35E 163 G9
Virton Belgium 49°35N 5°32E 170 E5
Virú Peru 8°25S 78°45W 330 B2
Virudunagar India 9°30N 77°58E 245 K3
Virum Denmark 55°47N 12°27E 118 A2
Virunga △ Dem. Rep. of the Congo 0°5N 29°38E 268 B2
Vis Croatia 43°4N 16°10E 199 E13
Visalia U.S.A. 36°20N 119°18W 306 J7
Visayan Sea Phil. 11°30N 123°30E 233 F4
Visby Sweden 57°37N 18°18E 163 G12
Viscount Melville Sd. Canada 74°10N 108°0W 295 B9
Visé Belgium 50°44N 5°41E 170 D5
Višegrad Bos.-H. 43°47N 19°17E 182 G4
Viseu Brazil 1°10S 46°5W 332 B2
Viseu Portugal 40°40N 7°55W 194 E3
Viseu ☐ Portugal 40°40N 7°55W 194 E3
Vişeu de Sus Romania 47°45N 24°25E 183 C9
Vishakhapatnam India 17°45N 83°20E 244 F6
Vishnyaki Russia 55°46N 37°53E 129 B5
Vişina Romania 43°52N 24°27E 183 G9
Vişineşti Moldova 46°20N 28°27E 183 D13
Visingsö Sweden 58°2N 14°20E 163 F8
Visitacion Valley U.S.A. 37°42N 122°23W 136 B2
Viskafors Sweden 57°37N 12°50E 163 G6
Viskan → Sweden 57°14N 12°12E 163 G6
Viški Kanal Croatia 43°4N 16°5E 199 E13
Vislanda Sweden 56°46N 14°30E 163 H8
Visnagar India 23°45N 72°32E 242 H5
Višnja Gora Slovenia 45°58N 14°45E 199 C11
Viso, Mte. Italy 44°38N 7°5E 198 D4
Viso del Marqués Spain 38°32N 3°34W 195 G7
Visoko Bos.-H. 43°58N 18°10E 182 G3
Visokoi I. Antarctica 56°43S 27°15W 151 B1
Visp Switz. 46°17N 7°52E 179 J3
Vissefjärda Sweden 56°32N 15°35E 163 H9
Visselhövede Germany 52°59N 9°34E 178 C5
Vissenbjerg Denmark 55°23N 10°7E 163 J4
Vista U.S.A. 33°12N 117°14W 307 M9
Vista Alegre Santiago, Chile 33°30S 70°43W 137 C1
Vista Alegre Lima, Peru 12°9S 76°59W 124 B3
Vista Bella Trin. & Tob. 10°17N 61°27W 323 t
Vista Grove U.S.A. 33°51N 84°16W 113 A3
Vistonida, L. Greece 41°0N 25°7E 203 E9
Vistonikos, Ormos = Vistonida, L. Greece 41°0N 25°7E 203 E9
Vistula = Wisła → Poland 54°22N 18°55E 184 D5
Vistula Lagoon = Zalew Wiślany Poland 54°20N 19°50E 184 D6
Vit → Bulgaria 43°30N 24°30E 203 C8
Vita India 17°17N 74°33E 244 F2
Vitacura Chile 33°23S 70°35W 137 B2
Vitanje Slovenia 46°25N 15°18E 199 B12
Vitebsk = Vitsyebsk Belarus 55°10N 30°15E 188 E6
Viterbo Italy 42°25N 12°6E 199 F9
Vitez Bos.-H. 44°10N 17°48E 182 F2
Viti Levu Fiji 17°30S 177°30E 287 A1
Vitiaz Str. Papua N. G. 5°40S 147°10E 286 C4
Vitiaz Trench Pac. Oc. 10°0S 170°0E 277 C13
Vitigudino Spain 41°1N 6°26W 194 D4
Vitim Russia 59°28N 112°35E 215 D12
Vitim → Russia 59°26N 112°34E 215 D12
Vitina Bos.-H. 43°17N 17°29E 199 E14
Vitina Greece 37°40N 22°10E 204 D4
Vitínia Italy 41°47N 12°24E 136 C1
Vítkov Czech Rep. 49°46N 17°45E 181 B10
Vitória = Vitória de São Antão Brazil 8°10S 35°20W 332 C4
Vitória Espirito Santo, Brazil 20°20S 40°22W 333 F3
Vitória Pará, Brazil 2°54S 52°1W 329 D7
Vitória da Conquista Brazil 14°51S 40°51W 333 D3
Vitória de São Antão Brazil 8°10S 35°20W 332 C4
Vitoria-Gasteiz Spain 42°50N 2°41W 196 C2
Vitória Seamount Atl. Oc. 20°0S 44°0W 152 J8
Vitorino Friere Brazil 4°4S 45°10W 332 B2
Vitosha △ Bulgaria 42°36N 23°18E 202 D7
Vitré France 48°8N 1°12W 172 D5
Vitry-le-François France 48°43N 4°33E 173 D11
Vitry-sur-Seine France 48°47N 2°23E 134 B3
Vitsand Sweden 60°20N 13°0E 162 D7
Vitsi, Oros Greece 40°40N 21°25E 202 F5
Vitsyebsk Belarus 55°10N 30°15E 188 E6
Vitsyebsk ☐ Belarus 55°10N 28°50E 188 E5
Vittaryd Sweden 56°58N 13°57E 163 H7
Vitteaux France 47°24N 4°30E 173 E11
Vittel France 48°12N 5°57E 173 D12
Vittória Italy 36°57N 14°32E 201 F7
Vittório = Vittório Véneto Italy 45°59N 12°18E 199 C9
Vittório Véneto Italy 45°59N 12°18E 199 C9
Vittoriosa Malta 35°54N 14°31E 206 F8
Vittsjö Sweden 56°20N 13°40E 163 H7
Viveiro Spain 43°39N 7°38W 194 B3
Vivian U.S.A. 32°53N 93°59W 314 E8
Viviers France 44°30N 4°40E 175 D8
Vivonne S. Austral., Australia 35°59S 137°9E 282 C2
Vivonne Vienne, France 46°25N 0°15E 174 B4
Vivonne B. Australia 35°59S 137°9E 282 C2
Viwa Fiji 17°10S 177°58E 287 A1
Vizagapatam = Vishakhapatnam India 17°45N 83°20E 244 F6
Vizandino, Moussio Athens, Greece 112 b3
Vizcaíno, Desierto de Mexico 27°30N 113°45W 318 B2
Vizcaíno, Sierra Mexico 27°30N 114°0W 318 B2
Vizcaya ☐ Spain 43°15N 2°45W 196 B2
Vizcaya Museum and Gardens U.S.A. 25°44N 80°13W 128 B2
Vize Turkey 41°34N 27°45E 203 E11
Vizianagaram India 18°6N 83°30E 244 E6
Vizille France 45°5N 5°46E 175 C9
Viziňada Croatia 45°20N 13°46E 199 C10
Viziru Romania 45°0N 27°43E 183 E12
Vizlinsky Zaliv = Zalew Wiślany Poland 54°20N 19°50E 184 D6
Vizzini Italy 37°10N 14°45E 201 E7
Vlaardingen Neths. 51°55N 4°21E 170 C4
Vlachiotis Greece 36°52N 22°42E 204 E4
Vlădeasa, Vf. Romania 46°47N 22°50E 182 D7
Vladičin Han Serbia 42°42N 22°1E 202 D6
Vladikavkaz Russia 43°0N 44°35E 191 J7
Vladimir Russia 56°15N 40°30E 188 D11
Vladimir ☐ Russia 56°5N 40°10E 190 B5
Vladimir Volynskiy = Volodymyr-Volynskyy Ukraine 50°50N 24°18E 177 C13
Vladimirci Serbia 44°36N 19°50E 202 B3
Vladimirovac Serbia 45°1N 20°53E 182 E5
Vladimirovka = Yuzhno-Sakhalinsk Russia 46°58N 142°45E 215 E15
Vladimirovka Russia 48°27N 46°10E 191 F8
Vladimirovo Bulgaria 43°32N 23°22E 202 C7
Vladimorvka Kazakhstan 50°51N 51°8E 190 E10
Vladislavovka Ukraine 45°12N 35°29E 189 K8
Vladivostok Russia 43°10N 131°53E 220 C5
Vladykino Russia 55°51N 37°35E 129 A3
Vlăhiţa Romania 46°21N 25°31E 183 D10
Vlasenica Bos.-H. 44°11N 18°59E 182 F3
Vlašić Bos.-H. 44°19N 17°37E 182 F2
Vlašim Czech Rep. 49°40N 14°53E 180 B7
Vlasinsko Jezero Serbia 42°44N 22°22E 202 D6
Vlasotince Serbia 42°59N 22°7E 202 D6
Vlezenbeek Belgium 50°48N 4°14E 116 B1
Vlieland Neths. 53°16N 4°55E 170 A4
Vlissingen Neths. 51°26N 3°34E 170 C3

Vlorë Albania 40°32N 19°28E 202 F3
Vlorës, Gjiri i Albania 40°29N 19°27E 202 F3
Vltava → Czech Rep. 50°21N 14°30E 180 A7
Vnukovo Russia 55°37N 37°17E 129 C1
Vo Dat Vietnam 11°9N 107°31E 237 G6
Vobarno Italy 45°39N 10°30E 198 C7
Voćin Croatia 45°37N 17°33E 182 E2
Vöcklabruck Austria 48°1N 13°39E 180 C6
Vodice Croatia 43°47N 15°47E 199 E12
Vodňany Czech Rep. 49°9N 14°11E 180 B7
Vodnjan Croatia 44°59N 13°52E 199 D10
Vodopyanovo = Donskoy Russia 53°55N 38°15E 188 F10
Voe U.K. 60°21N 1°16W 167 A7
Vogar Iceland 63°58N 22°22W 155 D4
Vogel Pk. Nigeria 8°24N 11°47E 263 D7
Vogelkop = Doberai, Jazirah Indonesia 1°25S 133°0E 231 E8
Vogelsberg Germany 50°31N 9°12E 178 E5
Voghera Italy 44°59N 9°1E 198 D6
Voh N. Cal. 20°58S 164°42E 288 d
Vohibinany Madag. 18°49S 49°4E 272 B2
Vohilava Madag. 21°4S 48°0E 272 C2
Vohimarina = Iharana Madag. 13°25S 50°0E 272 A3
Vohimena, Tanjon' i Madag. 25°36S 45°8E 272 D2
Vohipeno Madag. 22°22S 47°51E 272 C2
Voi Kenya 3°25S 38°32E 268 C4
Void-Vacon France 48°40N 5°36E 173 D12
Voineşti Iaşi, Romania 47°5N 27°27E 183 C12
Voineşti Prahova, Romania 45°5N 25°14E 183 E10
Voiron France 45°22N 5°35E 175 C9
Voisey B. Canada 56°15N 61°50W 299 A7
Voitsberg Austria 47°3N 15°9E 180 D8
Vojens Denmark 55°16N 9°18E 163 J3
Vojmsjön Sweden 65°0N 16°24E 160 D17
Vojnić Croatia 45°19N 15°43E 199 C12
Vojnik Italy 46°18N 15°19E 199 B12
Vojvodina □ Serbia 45°20N 20°0E 182 E5
Vokeo I. Papua N. G. 3°14S 144°2E 286 B3
Vokhtoga Russia 58°46N 41°8E 188 C11
Vokovice Czech Rep. 50°5N 14°21E 135 B2
Volary Czech Rep. 48°54N 13°52E 180 C6
Volborg U.S.A. 45°51N 105°41W 304 D11
Volcán de Colima △ Mexico 19°30N 103°40W 318 D4
Volcano U.S.A. 19°26N 155°14W 302 D6
Volcano Is. = Kazan-Rettō Pac. Oc. 25°0N 141°0E 288 E6
Volcans △ Rwanda 1°30S 29°26E 268 C2
Volcans d'Auvergne ⌓ France 45°20N 2°40E 174 C6
Volchansk = Vovchansk Ukraine 50°17N 36°58E 189 G9
Volchikha Russia 52°2N 80°23E 217 B10
Volchya → Ukraine 48°32N 36°0E 189 H8
Volda Norway 62°9N 6°5E 164 B3
Volga = Privolzhskiy □ Russia 56°0N 50°0E 190 B10
Volga Russia 57°58N 38°16E 188 C10
Volga → Russia 46°0N 48°30E 191 G9
Volga Hts. = Privolzhskaya Vozvyshennost Russia 51°0N 46°0E 190 E7
Volgelsdorf Germany 52°30N 13°44E 115 B5
Volgo-Baltiyskiy Kanal Russia 60°0N 38°0E 188 B9
Volgo-Donskoy Kanal Russia 48°40N 43°37E 191 F7
Volgodonsk Russia 47°33N 42°5E 191 G6
Volgograd Russia 48°40N 44°25E 191 F7
Volgograd □ Russia 49°40N 44°30E 190 F7
Volgogradskoye Vdkhr. Russia 50°0N 45°20E 190 E8
Volgorechensk Russia 57°28N 41°14E 190 B5
Volimes Greece 37°52N 20°39E 207 D2
Volintiri Moldova 46°26N 29°37E 183 D14
Volissos Greece 38°29N 25°54E 205 C7
Volkach Germany 49°52N 10°14E 179 F6
Völkermarkt Austria 46°39N 14°39E 180 E7
Volkhonka-Zil Russia 55°39N 37°37E 129 C3
Volkhov Russia 59°55N 32°15E 188 C7
Volkhov → Russia 60°8N 32°20E 188 B7
Volkhovstroy = Volkhov Russia 59°55N 32°15E 188 C7
Völklingen Germany 49°15N 6°50E 179 F2
Volkovysk = Vawkavysk Belarus 53°9N 24°30E 177 B13
Volksrust S. Africa 27°24S 29°53E 271 C4
Voll Norway 62°31N 7°27E 164 B4
Vollen Norway 59°48N 10°27E 133 B1
Volnansk Ukraine 48°2N 35°29E 189 H8
Volnovakha Ukraine 47°35N 37°30E 189 J9
Volochanka Russia 71°0N 94°28E 215 B10
Volodarsk Russia 56°12N 43°15E 190 B6
Volodarskoye Russia 59°54N 30°23E 137 B2
Volodymyr-Volynskyy Ukraine 50°50N 24°18E 177 C13
Vologda Russia 59°10N 39°45E 188 C10
Vologda □ Russia 60°15N 39°0E 188 B10
Volokolamsk Russia 56°5N 35°57E 188 D8
Volokonovka Russia 50°33N 37°52E 189 G9
Volos Greece 39°24N 22°59E 204 B4
Vološinovo = Novi Bečej Serbia 45°36N 20°10E 182 E5
Volosovo Russia 59°27N 29°32E 188 C5
Volovets Ukraine 48°43N 23°11E 183 B8
Volovo Russia 53°35N 38°1E 188 F10
Volozhin = Valozhyn Belarus 54°3N 26°30E 177 A14
Volsk Russia 52°5N 47°22E 190 D8
Volta □ Ghana 7°0N 0°30E 263 D5
Volta → Ghana 5°46N 0°41E 263 D5
Volta, L. Ghana 7°30N 0°0 263 D5
Volta Blanche = White Volta → Ghana 9°10N 1°15W 263 D4
Volta Redonda Brazil 22°31S 44°5W 333 F3
Voltaire, C. Australia 14°16S 125°35E 278 B4
Volterra Italy 43°24N 10°51E 198 E7
Voltri Italy 44°26N 8°45E 198 D5
Volturno → Italy 41°1N 13°55E 200 A6
Volubilis Morocco 34°2N 5°33W 260 B3
Volvi, L. Greece 40°40N 23°34E 202 F7
Volyn □ Ukraine 51°15N 24°30E 189 G3
Volyně Czech Rep. 49°10N 13°53E 180 B6
Volynkina-Derevnya Russia 59°53N 30°18E 137 B1
Volzhsk Russia 55°57N 48°23E 190 C9
Volzhskiy Russia 48°56N 44°46E 191 F7
Vomo Fiji 17°30S 177°15E 287 A1
Vonavona Solomon Is. 8°15S 157°5E 287 M9
Vondelpark Neths. 52°21N 4°52E 112 A2
Vondrozo Madag. 22°49S 47°20E 272 C2
Vonitsa Greece 38°55N 20°53E 207 B2
Vopnafjörður Iceland 65°45N 14°50W 155 B12
Vorarlberg □ Austria 47°20N 10°0E 180 D2
Voras Oros Greece 40°57N 21°45E 202 F5
Vorbasse Denmark 55°39N 9°6E 163 J3
Vorchdorf Austria 48°0N 13°55E 180 C6
Vorderrhein → Switz. 46°49N 9°25E 179 J5
Vordingborg Denmark 55°0N 11°54E 163 J5
Vorë Albania 41°23N 19°40E 202 E3
Voreio Aigaio □ Greece 38°50N 25°30E 205 C7
Voreppe France 45°18N 5°39E 175 C9
Vori Greece 35°4N 24°49E 207 E5
Vorios Evoikos Kolpos Greece 38°45N 23°15E 204 C5
Vorkuta Russia 67°48N 64°20E 186 A11
Vorma → Norway 60°9N 11°29E 164 D8
Vormsi Estonia 59°1N 23°13E 188 C2
Vorona → Russia 51°22N 42°3E 190 E6
Voronezh Russia 51°40N 39°10E 189 G10
Voronezh Ukraine 51°47N 33°28E 189 G7
Voronezh □ Russia 51°30N 39°30E 190 E4
Voronezh → Russia 51°32N 39°10E 189 G10
Vorontsovo-Aleksandrovskoye = Zelenokumsk Russia 44°24N 44°0E 191 H6
Voroshilov = Ussuriysk Russia 43°48N 131°59E 220 C5
Voroshilovgrad = Luhansk Ukraine 48°38N 39°15E 189 H10
Voroshilovsk = Alchevsk Ukraine 48°30N 38°45E 189 H10
Voroshilovsk = Stavropol Russia 45°5N 42°0E 191 H6
Vorpommersche Boddenlandschaft △ Germany 54°25N 12°32E 178 A8
Vorskla → Ukraine 48°50N 34°10E 189 H8
Võrts Järv Estonia 58°16N 26°3E 188 C4
Võru Estonia 57°48N 26°54E 188 D4
Vösendorf Austria 48°7N 16°20E 142 B2
Vosges France 48°20N 7°10E 173 D14
Vosges □ France 48°12N 6°20E 173 D13
Vosges du Nord ⌓ France 49°0N 7°30E 173 D14
Voskopojë Albania 40°35N 20°33E 202 F4
Voskresensk Russia 55°19N 38°43E 188 E10
Voskresenskoye Russia 56°51N 45°30E 190 B7
Voss Norway 60°38N 6°26E 164 D3
Vostochnyy Russia 55°49N 37°51E 129 B5
Vostok = Neftegorsk Russia 44°25N 39°45E 191 H4
Vostok Antarctica 78°30S 106°50E 151 D8
Vostok I. Kiribati 10°5S 152°23W 289 J12
Votice Czech Rep. 49°38N 14°39E 180 B7
Votkinsk Russia 57°0N 53°55E 186 C9
Votkinskoye Vdkhr. Russia 57°22N 55°12E 186 C10
Votsuri-Shima Japan 25°45N 123°29E 221 M1
Votuporanga Brazil 20°24S 49°59W 333 F2
Vouga → Portugal 40°41N 8°40W 194 E2
Vouillé France 46°38N 0°10E 172 F7
Voula Greece 37°49N 23°45E 112 C2
Vouliagmeni Greece 37°50N 23°46E 112 C2
Voulkaria, L. Greece 38°52N 20°50E 207 B2
Voulou C.A.R. 8°33N 22°36E 264 A4
Vouma → Cameroon 3°19N 14°9E 264 B2
Vouxa, Akra Greece 35°37N 23°32E 207 E4
Vouzela Portugal 40°43N 8°7W 194 E2
Vouziers France 49°22N 4°40E 173 C11
Vovchansk Ukraine 50°17N 36°58E 189 G9
Vovodo → C.A.R. 5°40N 24°21E 264 A4
Vowchyn Belarus 52°18N 23°18E 185 F10
Voyageurs △ U.S.A. 48°32N 93°0W 308 A7
Voynitsa Russia 65°10N 30°20E 160 D24
Vozhe, Ozero Russia 60°45N 39°0E 188 B10
Vozhega Russia 60°29N 40°12E 188 B11
Voznesensk Ukraine 47°35N 31°21E 189 J6
Voznesenye Russia 61°0N 35°28E 188 B8
Vrå Denmark 57°21N 9°56E 163 G3
Vráble Slovak Rep. 48°15N 18°16E 181 C11
Vraćevšnica Serbia 44°2N 20°34E 202 B4
Vrachneika Greece 38°10N 21°40E 204 C3
Vrådal Norway 59°20N 8°25E 164 E5
Vrancea □ Romania 45°50N 26°45E 183 E11
Vrancei, Munţii Romania 46°0N 26°30E 183 E11
Vrangelya, Ostrov Russia 71°0N 180°0E 215 B19
Vranica Bos.-H. 43°55N 17°50E 182 G2
Vranje Serbia 42°34N 21°54E 202 D5
Vranjska Banja Serbia 42°34N 22°1E 202 D6
Vranov nad Topl'ou Slovak Rep. 48°53N 21°40E 181 C14
Vransko Slovenia 46°17N 14°58E 199 B11
Vransko Jezero Croatia 43°53N 15°34E 199 E12
Vrapčište Macedonia 41°50N 20°53E 202 E4
Vratsa Bulgaria 43°15N 23°30E 202 C7
Vråvatn Norway 59°20N 8°8E 164 E5
Vrbas Serbia 45°40N 19°40E 182 E4
Vrbas → Bos.-H. 45°8N 17°29E 182 E2
Vrbnik Croatia 45°4N 14°40E 199 C11
Vrbovec Croatia 45°53N 16°28E 199 C13
Vrbovsko Croatia 45°24N 15°5E 199 C12
Vrchlabí Czech Rep. 50°38N 15°37E 180 A8
Vrede S. Africa 27°24S 29°6E 271 C4
Vredefort S. Africa 27°0S 27°22E 270 C4
Vredehoek S. Africa 33°57S 18°25E 118 A1
Vreden Germany 52°2N 6°50E 178 C2
Vredenburg S. Africa 32°56S 18°0E 270 D2
Vredendal S. Africa 31°41S 18°35E 270 D2
Vretstorp Sweden 59°1N 14°53E 162 E8
Vrgorac Croatia 43°12N 17°20E 199 E14
Vrhnika Slovenia 45°58N 14°15E 199 C11
Vriddhachalam India 11°30N 79°20E 245 J4
Vrïdi Ivory C. 5°15N 4°3W 262 D4
Vrigstad Sweden 57°22N 14°28E 163 G8
Vrindavan India 27°37N 77°40E 242 F7
Vrisses Greece 35°23N 24°13E 207 E5
Vrnograč Bos.-H. 45°10N 15°57E 199 C12
Vrondados Greece 38°25N 26°7E 205 C8
Vrpolje Croatia 45°13N 18°24E 182 E3
Vršac Serbia 45°8N 21°20E 182 E6
Vrsacki Kanal Serbia 45°15N 21°0E 182 E5
Vršovice Czech Rep. 50°4N 14°28E 135 B2
Vrútky Slovak Rep. 49°7N 18°55E 181 B11
Vryburg S. Africa 26°55S 24°45E 270 C3
Vryheid S. Africa 27°45S 30°47E 271 C5
Vsetín Czech Rep. 49°20N 18°0E 181 B11
Vu Liet Vietnam 18°43N 105°23E 236 C5
Vŭcha → Bulgaria 42°10N 24°26E 203 D8
Vučitrn Serbia 42°49N 20°59E 202 D4
Vukovar Croatia 45°21N 18°59E 182 E3
Vulcan Alta., Canada 50°25N 113°15W 296 C6
Vulcan Romania 45°23N 23°17E 183 E8
Vulcaneşti Moldova 45°41N 28°18E 183 E13
Vulcano Italy 38°24N 14°58E 201 D7
Vŭlchedruma Bulgaria 43°42N 23°27E 202 C7
Vulkaneshty = Vulcaneşti Moldova 45°41N 28°18E 183 E13
Vunduzi → Mozam. 18°56S 34°1E 269 F3
Vung Tau Vietnam 10°21N 107°4E 237 G6
Vunidawa Fiji 17°50S 178°21E 287 A2
Vunisea Fiji 19°3S 178°10E 287 B2
Vuranggo Solomon Is. 6°39S 156°38E 287 L9
Vŭrbitsa Bulgaria 42°59N 26°40E 203 D10
Vurshets Bulgaria 43°13N 23°23E 202 C7
Vutcani Romania 46°26N 27°59E 183 D12
Vuya Sudan 5°21N 29°40E 257 F2
Vuzlove Ukraine 48°22N 22°24E 182 B7
Vwaza ⌓ Malawi 10°58S 33°25E 269 E3
Vyara India 21°8N 73°28E 244 D1
Vyartsilya Russia 62°8N 30°45E 188 A6
Vyatka = Kirov Russia 58°35N 49°40E 186 C8
Vyatka → Russia 55°37N 51°28E 190 C10
Vyatskiye Polyany Russia 56°14N 51°5E 190 B10
Vyazemskiy Russia 47°32N 134°45E 215 E14
Vyazma Russia 55°10N 34°15E 188 E8
Vyazniki Russia 56°10N 42°10E 190 B6
Vyborg Russia 60°43N 28°47E 188 B5
Vyborgskaya Storona Russia 59°57N 30°22E 137 B2
Vychegda → Russia 61°18N 46°36E 186 B8
Vychodné Beskydy Europe 49°20N 22°0E 181 B15
Vyerkhnyadzvinsk Belarus 55°45N 27°58E 188 E4
Vyg-ozero Russia 63°47N 34°29E 186 B5
Vyhoda Ukraine 48°56N 23°55E 183 B8
Vykhino Russia 55°42N 37°48E 129 B4
Vyksa Russia 55°19N 42°11E 190 C6
Vylkove Ukraine 45°28N 29°32E 183 E14
Vylok Ukraine 48°6N 22°50E 182 B7
Vynohradiv Ukraine 48°9N 23°2E 182 B8
Vypin India 10°10N 76°15E 245 J3
Vyrnwy, L. U.K. 52°48N 3°31W 168 E4
Vyšehrad Czech Rep. 50°3N 14°25E 135 B2
Vyshkiv Ukraine 48°44N 23°39E 183 B8
Vyshkove Ukraine 48°3N 23°25E 183 B8
Vyshniy Volochek Russia 57°30N 34°30E 188 D8
Vyshzha = imeni 26 Bakinskikh Komissarov Turkmenistan 39°22N 54°10E 247 B7
Vyškov Czech Rep. 49°17N 17°0E 181 B9
Vysokaye Belarus 52°22N 23°22E 185 F10
Vysoké Mýto Czech Rep. 49°58N 16°10E 181 B9
Vysokovsk Russia 56°22N 36°30E 188 D9
Vyšší Brod Czech Rep. 48°37N 14°19E 180 C7
Vytegra Russia 61°0N 36°27E 188 B9
Vyzhnytsya Ukraine 48°15N 25°11E 183 B10
Vyzhnytsya ⌓ Ukraine 48°7N 25°15E 183 B10

W

W du Benin △ Benin 11°57N 2°43E 263 C5
W du Burkina Faso △ Burkina Faso 11°52N 2°50W 263 C4
W du Niger △ Niger 13°31N 2°28E 263 C5
W.A.C. Bennett Dam Canada 56°2N 122°6W 296 B4
Wa Ghana 10°7N 2°25W 262 C4
Waal → Neths. 51°37N 5°0E 170 C5
Waalwijk Neths. 51°42N 5°4E 170 C5
Waat Sudan 8°10N 32°7E 257 F3
Wabag Papua N. G. 5°32S 143°40E 286 C2
Wabakimi △ Canada 50°43N 89°29W 298 B2
Wabana Canada 47°40N 53°0W 299 C9
Wabasca → Canada 58°22N 115°20W 296 B5
Wabasca-Desmarais Canada 55°57N 113°56W 296 B6
Wabash U.S.A. 40°48N 85°49W 311 D11
Wabash → U.S.A. 37°48N 88°2W 311 G8
Wabasso U.S.A. 27°45N 80°26W 317 H9
Wabawng Burma 26°20N 97°25E 241 B6
Wabi → Ethiopia 7°45N 40°50E 257 F5
Wabigoon L. Canada 49°44N 92°44W 297 D10
Wabowden Canada 54°55N 98°38W 297 C9
Wąbrzeźno Poland 53°16N 18°57E 185 E5
Wabu Hu China 32°20N 116°50E 229 A11
Wabuda I. Papua N. G. 8°23S 143°37E 286 E2
Wabuk Pt. Canada 55°20N 85°5W 298 A2
Wabush Canada 52°55N 66°52W 299 B6
Waccasassa B. U.S.A. 29°10N 82°50W 317 F7
Wąchock Poland 51°4N 21°1E 185 G8
Wachterhof Germany 48°2N 11°42E 131 B3
Wächtersbach Germany 50°14N 9°17E 179 E5
Wacissa U.S.A. 30°22N 83°59W 316 E6
Waco U.S.A. 31°33N 97°9W 314 F6
Waconichi, L. Canada 50°8N 74°0W 298 B5
Wad Ban Naqa Sudan 16°32N 33°9E 257 D3
Wad Banda Sudan 13°10N 27°56E 257 E2
Wad el Haddad Sudan 13°50N 33°30E 257 E3
Wad en Nau Sudan 14°10N 33°34E 257 E3
Wad Hamid Sudan 16°30N 32°45E 257 D3
Wad Medanî Sudan 14°28N 33°30E 257 E3
Wad Thana Pakistan 27°22N 66°23E 242 F2
Wadai Africa 12°0N 19°0E 254 E5
Wadala India 19°1N 72°51E 130 A2
Wadayama Japan 35°19N 134°52E 222 B6
Wadbilliga △ Australia 36°25S 149°35E 283 D8
Waddān Libya 29°9N 16°10E 258 C3
Waddeneilanden Neths. 53°25N 5°10E 170 A5
Waddenzee Neths. 53°6N 5°10E 170 A5
Waddi, Chappal Nigeria 7°2N 11°43W 263 D7
Waddington U.S.A. 44°52N 75°12W 313 B9
Waddington, Mt. Canada 51°23N 125°15W 296 C3
Waddy Pt. Australia 24°58S 153°21E 281 C5
Wadebridge U.K. 50°31N 4°51W 169 G3
Wadena Sask., Canada 51°57N 103°47W 297 C8
Wadena Minn., U.S.A. 46°26N 95°8W 308 B6
Wädenswil Switz. 47°14N 8°40E 179 H4
Wadern Germany 49°32N 6°53E 179 F2
Wadestown N.Z. 41°16S 174°46E 143 B1
Wadeye Australia 14°28S 129°52E 278 B4
Wadgaon India 18°44N 73°39E 244 E1
Wadhams Canada 51°30N 127°30W 296 C3
Wadhwan = Surendranagar India 22°45N 71°40E 242 H4
Wadi India 17°4N 76°59E 244 F3
Wadi al-Arayis West Bank 31°43N 35°15E 123 B2
Wādī as Sīr Jordan 31°56N 35°49E 251 G6
Wādī Banī Walīd Libya 31°49N 14°0E 258 B2
Wâdi Feirân Egypt 28°42N 33°19E 251 K4
Wadi Fukin West Bank 31°42N 35°6E 123 B1
Wâdi Gemâl Egypt 24°35N 35°10E 256 C4
Wadi Halfa Sudan 21°53N 31°19E 256 C3
Wādī Mūsá Jordan 30°19N 35°29E 251 H6
Wadi Rum △ Jordan 29°30N 35°20E 251 J6
Wadian China 32°42N 112°29E 229 A9
Wadlew Poland 51°31N 19°23E 185 G6
Wadley Ala., U.S.A. 33°7N 85°34W 316 B4
Wadley Ga., U.S.A. 32°52N 82°24W 316 C7
Wadowice Poland 49°52N 19°30E 185 J6
Wadsworth Nev., U.S.A. 39°38N 119°17W 304 G4
Wadsworth Ohio, U.S.A. 41°2N 81°44W 312 E3
Waduk Pluit Indonesia 6°5S 106°46E 122 A1
Waegwan S. Korea 35°59N 128°23E 224 E4
Wafangdian China 39°38N 121°58E 227 E11
Wafania Dem. Rep. of the Congo 1°23S 20°22E 264 C4
Wafrah Si. Arabia 28°33N 47°56E 246 D5
Wagadugu = Ouagadougou Burkina Faso 12°25N 1°30W 263 C4
Wagener U.S.A. 33°39N 81°22W 316 B8
Wageningen Neths. 51°58N 5°40E 170 C5
Wageningen Suriname 5°50N 56°50W 329 B6
Wager B. Canada 65°26N 88°40W 295 C11
Wagga Wagga Australia 35°7S 147°24E 283 C7
Waggaman U.S.A. 29°55N 90°12W 131 B1
Waghai India 20°46N 73°29E 244 D1
Waghete Indonesia 4°10S 135°50E 231 E9
Wagin Australia 33°17S 117°25E 279 F2
Wagner U.S.A. 43°5N 98°18W 308 D4
Wagon Mound U.S.A. 36°1N 104°42W 305 H11
Wagoner U.S.A. 35°58N 95°22W 314 D7
Wagrowiec Poland 52°48N 17°11E 185 F4
Wah Pakistan 33°45N 72°40E 242 C5
Wah Fu China 22°15N 114°8E 122 B1
Wahai Indonesia 2°48S 129°35E 231 E7
Waharoa N.Z. 37°46S 175°45E 284 D4
Wahda Iraq 33°18N 44°26E 113 B2
Wahiawā U.S.A. 21°30N 158°2W 302 K13
Wahiawā District U.S.A. 21°31N 157°58W 302 J14
Wahiawā Res. U.S.A. 21°30N 158°3W 302 K13
Wâḥid Egypt 30°48N 32°21E 251 H3
Wahnai Afghan. 32°40N 65°50E 242 C1
Wahni Ethiopia 12°40N 36°39E 257 E4
Wahoo U.S.A. 41°13N 96°37W 308 E5
Wahpeton U.S.A. 46°16N 96°36W 308 B5
Währing Austria 48°14N 16°20E 142 A2
Wahx, Ras il- Malta 35°56N 14°20E 206 F7
Wai India 17°56N 73°57E 244 F1
Wai'ale'ale U.S.A. 22°4N 159°30W 302 A2
Waiale'e U.S.A. 21°41N 158°1W 302 J13
Waialua U.S.A. 21°34N 158°8W 302 J13
Waialua B. U.S.A. 21°35N 158°5W 302 J13
Waialua District U.S.A. 21°35N 158°5W 302 J13
Wai'anae U.S.A. 21°27N 158°11W 302 K13
Wai'anae Coast U.S.A. 21°26N 158°11W 302 K13
Wai'anae District U.S.A. 21°28N 158°10W 302 K13
Wai'anae Range U.S.A. 21°30N 158°10W 302 K13
Waiao Taiwan 24°54N 121°51E 225 B3
Waiapu → N.Z. 37°47S 178°29E 284 D7
Waiau N.Z. 42°39S 173°5E 285 C8
Waiau → Canterbury, N.Z. 42°47S 173°22E 285 C8
Waiau → Southland, N.Z. 46°12S 167°38E 285 G2
Waiawa → U.S.A. 21°23N 157°59W 302 K14
Waiawe Ganga → Sri Lanka 6°15N 81°0E 245 L5
Waibeem Indonesia 0°30S 132°59E 231 E8
Waiblingen Germany 48°49N 9°18E 179 G5
Waidhofen an der Thaya Austria 48°49N 15°17E 180 C8
Waidhofen an der Ybbs Austria 47°57N 14°46E 180 D7
Waidmannslust Germany 52°36N 13°20E 115 A3
Waigeo Indonesia 0°20S 130°40E 231 E8
Waihao → N.Z. 44°47S 171°10E 285 E6
Waihao Downs N.Z. 44°48S 170°55E 285 E5
Waihee-Waiehu U.S.A. 20°56N 156°31W 302 C5
Waiheke I. N.Z. 36°48S 175°6E 284 C4
Waihi N.Z. 37°23S 175°52E 284 D4
Waihi Beach N.Z. 37°25S 175°57E 284 D7
Waihola N.Z. 46°1S 170°8E 285 G5
Waihola L. N.Z. 45°59S 170°8E 285 F5
Waihou → N.Z. 37°15S 175°40E 284 D4
Waika Dem. Rep. of the Congo 2°22S 25°42E 264 C5
Waikabubak Indonesia 9°45S 119°25E 231 F5
Waikaia N.Z. 45°44S 168°51E 285 F3
Waikaka N.Z. 45°55S 169°1E 285 F4
Waikare, L. N.Z. 37°26S 175°13E 284 D4
Waikareiti, L. N.Z. 38°43S 177°10E 284 E6
Waikaremoana N.Z. 38°42S 177°12E 284 E6
Waikaremoana, L. N.Z. 38°49S 177°9E 284 E6
Waikari N.Z. 42°58S 172°41E 285 C7
Waikato → N.Z. 37°23S 174°43E 284 D3
Waikerie Australia 34°9S 140°0E 282 C4
Waikiekie N.Z. 35°57S 174°16E 284 B3
Waikīkī U.S.A. 21°17N 157°50W 302 K14
Waikokopu N.Z. 39°3S 177°52E 284 F6
Waikoloa Village U.S.A. 19°55N 155°49W 302 D6
Waikouaiti N.Z. 45°36S 170°41E 285 F5
Waikouaiti Downs N.Z. 45°30S 170°30E 285 F5
Wailea-Makena U.S.A. 20°40N 156°27W 302 C5
Wailing Wall = Western Wall Jerusalem 123 b3
Wailingding Dao China 22°6N 114°2E 219 G11
Wailua Hawai'i, U.S.A. 22°3N 159°20W 302 A2
Wailua Hawai'i, U.S.A. 20°51N 156°8W 302 C5
Wailuku U.S.A. 20°53N 156°30W 302 C5
Waimakariri → N.Z. 43°24S 172°42E 285 D7
Waimalu U.S.A. 21°24N 157°57W 302 K14
Waimānalo U.S.A. 21°21N 157°43W 302 K14
Waimānalo B. U.S.A. 21°20N 157°40W 302 K14
Waimānalo Beach U.S.A. 21°21N 157°42W 302 K14
Waimangaroa N.Z. 41°43S 171°46E 285 B6
Waimano → U.S.A. 21°25N 157°58W 302 K14
Waimarie N.Z. 41°35S 171°58E 285 B6
Waimate N.Z. 44°45S 171°3E 285 E6
Waimea Hawai'i, U.S.A. 21°58N 159°40W 302 B2
Waimea Hawai'i, U.S.A. 21°39N 158°3W 302 J13
Waimea B. U.S.A. 21°40N 158°5W 302 J13
Waimea Canyon U.S.A. 22°0N 159°39W 302 A2
Waimea Plain N.Z. 45°55S 168°35E 285 F3
Wainganga → India 18°50N 79°55E 244 E4
Waingapu Indonesia 9°35S 120°11E 231 F6
Waingmaw Burma 25°21N 97°26E 241 C6
Waini → Guyana 8°20N 59°50W 329 B6
Wainuiomata N.Z. 41°17S 174°56E 143 B2
Wainuiomata → N.Z. 41°20S 174°55E 143 B2
Wainwright Alta., Canada 52°50N 110°50W 297 C6
Wainwright Alaska, U.S.A. 70°38N 160°2W 303 A7
Waiotapu N.Z. 38°21S 176°25E 284 E5
Waiouru N.Z. 39°28S 175°41E 284 F4
Waipa → N.Z. 38°16S 175°21E 284 E4
Waipahi N.Z. 46°6S 169°15E 285 G4
Waipahu U.S.A. 21°23N 158°1W 302 K13
Waipapa Pt. N.Z. 46°40S 168°51E 285 G3
Waipara N.Z. 43°3S 172°46E 285 D7
Waipawa N.Z. 39°56S 176°38E 284 F5
Waipi'o U.S.A. 21°25N 158°0W 302 K14
Waipi'o Acres U.S.A. 21°28N 158°1W 302 K13
Waipi'o Peninsula U.S.A. 21°20N 158°0W 302 K14
Waipiro N.Z. 38°2S 178°22E 284 E7
Waipiro Bay N.Z. 38°1S 178°21E 284 E7
Waipoua Forest N.Z. 35°39S 173°33E 284 B2
Waipu N.Z. 35°59S 174°29E 284 B3
Waipukurau N.Z. 40°1S 176°33E 284 G5
Wairakei N.Z. 38°37S 176°6E 284 E5
Wairarapa, L. N.Z. 41°14S 175°15E 284 H4
Wairau → N.Z. 41°32S 174°7E 285 B9
Wairio N.Z. 45°59S 168°3E 285 F3
Wairoa N.Z. 39°3S 177°25E 284 F6
Wairoa → Hawke's Bay, N.Z. 39°4S 177°25E 284 F6
Wairoa → Northland, N.Z. 36°5S 173°59E 284 C2
Waisantiang Taiwan 23°29N 120°1E 225 C2
Waïsisi Vanuatu 19°32S 169°22E 287 J7
Waita Res. U.S.A. 21°55N 159°28W 302 B2
Waitaki → N.Z. 44°56S 171°7E 285 E6
Waitaki Plains N.Z. 44°22S 170°0E 285 E5
Waitangi N.Z. 35°16S 174°5E 284 B3
Waitara N.Z. 38°59S 174°15E 284 E3
Waitara → N.Z. 38°59S 174°14E 284 E3
Waitoa N.Z. 37°37S 175°35E 284 D4
Waitomo Caves N.Z. 38°16S 175°7E 284 E4
Waitotara N.Z. 39°49S 174°44E 284 F3
Waitotara → N.Z. 39°51S 174°41E 284 F3
Waitsburg U.S.A. 46°16N 118°9W 304 C4
Waitzen = Vác Hungary 47°49N 19°10E 182 C4
Waiuku N.Z. 37°15S 174°45E 284 D3
Wajima Japan 37°30N 137°0E 221 F8
Wajir Kenya 1°42N 40°5E 268 B5
Waka Dem. Rep. of the Congo 1°1N 20°13E 264 B4
Waka Ethiopia 7°2N 37°20E 257 F4
Wakai Suriname 5°18N 57°14W 329 B6
Wakarusa U.S.A. 41°32N 86°1W 311 C10
Wakasa Japan 35°20N 134°24E 222 B6
Wakasa-Wan Japan 35°40N 135°30E 223 B7
Wakatipu, L. N.Z. 45°5S 168°33E 285 F3
Wakaw Canada 52°39N 105°44W 297 C7
Wakaya Fiji 17°37S 179°0E 287 A2
Wakayama Japan 34°15N 135°15E 223 C7
Wakayama □ Japan 33°50N 135°30E 223 D7
Wake Japan 34°48N 134°8E 222 C6
Wake Forest U.S.A. 35°59N 78°30W 315 D15
Wake I. Pac. Oc. 19°18N 166°36E 302 b
WaKeeney U.S.A. 39°1N 99°53W 308 F4
Wakefield Jamaica 18°26N 77°42W 320 a
Wakefield N.Z. 41°24S 173°5E 285 B8
Wakefield W. Yorks., U.K. 53°41N 1°29W 168 D6
Wakefield Mass., U.S.A. 42°30N 71°5W 116 A2
Wakefield Mich., U.S.A. 46°29N 89°56W 308 B9
Wakema Burma 16°30N 95°11E 241 G5
Waki Japan 34°4N 134°9E 222 C6
Wakkanai Japan 45°28N 141°35E 220 B10
Wakkerstroom S. Africa 27°24S 30°10E 271 C5
Wakool Australia 35°28S 144°23E 282 C6
Wakool → Australia 35°5S 143°33E 282 C5
Wakre Indonesia 0°19S 131°5E 231 E8
Waku Papua N. G. 6°5S 149°9E 286 D5
Wakuach, L. Canada 55°34N 67°32W 299 A6
Wakulla U.S.A. 30°14N 84°14W 316 E5
Wakunai Papua N. G. 5°52S 155°13E 286 C8
Walamba Zambia 13°30S 28°42E 269 E2
Wałbrzych Poland 50°45N 16°18E 185 H3
Walbury Hill U.K. 51°21N 1°28W 169 F6
Walcha Australia 30°55S 151°31E 283 A9
Walcheren Neths. 51°30N 3°35E 170 C3
Walcott U.S.A. 41°46N 106°51W 304 F10
Wałcz Poland 53°17N 16°27E 185 E3
Waldbröl Germany 50°52N 7°37E 178 E3
Waldburg Ra. Australia 24°40S 117°35E 279 D2
Waldeck Germany 51°12N 9°4E 178 D5
Walden Colo., U.S.A. 40°44N 106°17W 304 F10
Walden N.Y., U.S.A. 41°34N 74°11W 313 E10
Waldenberg = Wałbrzych Poland 50°45N 16°18E 185 H3
Waldesruh Germany 52°28N 13°37E 115 B4
Waldkirch Germany 48°5N 7°58E 179 G3
Waldkirchen Germany 48°43N 13°36E 179 G9
Waldkraiburg Germany 48°11N 12°24E 179 G8
Waldo U.S.A. 29°48N 82°10W 316 F7
Waldperlach Germany 48°4N 11°40E 131 B3
Waldport U.S.A. 44°26N 124°4W 304 D1
Waldron U.S.A. 34°54N 94°5W 314 D7
Waldtrudering Germany 48°6N 11°42E 131 B3
Waldviertel Austria 48°30N 15°30E 180 C8
Walebing Australia 30°41S 116°13E 279 F2
Walembele Ghana 10°30N 1°58W 262 C4
Walensee Switz. 47°7N 9°13E 179 H5
Wales U.S.A. 65°37N 168°5W 303 D5
Wales □ U.K. 52°19N 4°43W 169 E3
Walewale Ghana 10°21N 0°50W 263 C4
Walgett Australia 30°0S 148°5E 281 E4
Walgreen Coast Antarctica 75°15S 105°0W 151 D15
Walhalla Australia 37°56S 146°29E 283 D7
Walis I. Papua N. G. 3°14S 143°18E 286 B2
Walker Mich., U.S.A. 42°58N 85°46W 311 B11
Walker Minn., U.S.A. 47°6N 94°35W 308 B6
Walker, L. Canada 50°20N 67°11W 299 B6
Walker L. Man., Canada 54°42N 95°57W 297 C9
Walker L. Nev., U.S.A. 38°42N 118°43W 304 G4
Walkerston Australia 21°11S 149°8E 280 K7
Walkerton Ont., Canada 44°10N 81°10W 312 B3
Walkerton Ind., U.S.A. 41°28N 86°29W 311 C10
Walkinstown Ireland 53°19N 6°20W 120 B1
Wall U.S.A. 44°0N 102°8W 308 C2
Wall Street New York, U.S.A. 132 f1
Walla Walla N.S.W., Australia 35°45S 146°54E 283 C7
Walla Walla Wash., U.S.A. 46°4N 118°20W 304 C4
Wallabout Bay New York, U.S.A. 132 f2
Wallace Idaho, U.S.A. 47°28N 115°56W 304 C6
Wallace N.C., U.S.A. 34°44N 77°59W 315 D16
Wallaceburg Canada 42°34N 82°23W 312 D2
Wallacetown N.Z. 46°21S 168°19E 285 G3
Wallachia = Valahia Romania 44°35N 25°0E 183 F9
Wallal Australia 26°32S 146°7E 281 D4
Wallam Cr. → Australia 28°40S 147°20E 281 D4
Wallambin, L. Australia 30°57S 117°35E 279 F2
Wallan Australia 37°26S 144°59E 283 D6
Wallangarra Australia 28°56S 151°58E 281 D5
Wallaroo Australia 33°56S 137°39E 282 B2
Walldürn Germany 49°34N 9°22E 179 F5
Wallenhorst Germany 52°21N 8°1E 178 C4
Wallenpaupack, L. U.S.A. 41°25N 75°15W 313 E9
Wallerawang Australia 33°25S 150°4E 283 B9
Wallingat △ Australia 32°14S 152°25E 283 B10
Wallingford U.S.A. 41°27N 72°50W 313 E12
Wallis & Futuna, Is. Pac. Oc. 13°18S 176°10W 277 C15
Wallowa U.S.A. 45°34N 117°32W 304 D5
Wallowa Mts. U.S.A. 45°20N 117°30W 304 D5
Walls U.K. 60°14N 1°33W 167 A7
Walls of Jerusalem △ Australia 41°56S 146°15E 281 G4
Wallsend Australia 32°55S 151°40E 283 B9
Wallula U.S.A. 46°5N 118°54W 304 C4
Wallumbilla Australia 26°33S 149°9E 281 D4
Walmsley L. Canada 63°25N 108°36W 297 A7
Walney, I. of U.K. 54°6N 3°15W 168 C4
Walnut U.S.A. 41°33N 89°36W 310 C7
Walnut Canyon ⌓ U.S.A. 35°15N 111°20W 305 J8
Walnut Creek U.S.A. 37°54N 122°4W 306 H4
Walnut Grove U.S.A. 34°4N 86°18W 316 A3
Walnut Hill U.S.A. 30°53N 87°30W 317 E2
Walpeup Australia 35°7S 142°2E 282 C5
Walpole W. Austral., Australia 34°58S 116°44E 279 F2
Walpole Mass., U.S.A. 42°9N 71°15W 313 D13
Walpole-Nornalup △ Australia 35°0S 116°45E 279 G2
Wals Austria 47°47N 12°58E 180 D5
Walsall U.K. 52°35N 1°58W 169 E6
Walsenburg U.S.A. 37°38N 104°47W 305 H11
Walsh U.S.A. 37°23N 102°17W 305 H12
Walsh → Australia 16°31S 143°42E 280 B3
Walsrode Germany 52°51N 9°35E 178 C5
Walt Disney Concert Hall Los Angeles, U.S.A. 127 b1
Walt Disney World U.S.A. 28°22N 81°33W 133 B1
Waltair India 17°44N 83°23E 244 F6
Walter D. Stone Memorial Zoo U.S.A. 42°28N 71°6W 116 A2
Walter F. George Res. U.S.A. 31°38N 85°4W 316 D4
Walterboro U.S.A. 32°55N 80°40W 316 C9
Walters U.S.A. 34°22N 98°19W 314 D5
Waltershausen Germany 50°54N 10°33E 178 E6
Waltham U.S.A. 42°23N 71°14W 116 A1
Waltham Forest □ U.K. 51°35N 0°0 125 A3
Walthamstow U.K. 51°34N 0°1W 125 A3
Waltman U.S.A. 43°4N 107°12W 304 E10
Walton Ky., U.S.A. 38°52N 84°37W 311 F12
Walton N.Y., U.S.A. 42°10N 75°8W 313 D9
Walton-on-Thames U.K. 51°23N 0°24W 125 B1
Walton-on-the-Naze U.K. 51°51N 1°17E 169 F9
Waltonville U.S.A. 38°13N 89°2W 310 F7
Walu Burma 26°28N 98°2E 241 B7
Walvis Bay Namibia 23°0S 14°28E 270 B1
Walvis Ridge Atl. Oc. 26°0S 5°0E 152 J12
Walvisbaai = Walvis Bay Namibia 23°0S 14°28E 270 B1
Walwa Australia 35°59S 147°44E 283 C7
Wamba Équateur, Dem. Rep. of the Congo 1°37S 22°30E 264 C4
Wamba Orientale, Dem. Rep. of the Congo 2°10N 27°57E 268 B2
Wamba Rift Valley, Kenya 0°58N 37°19E 268 B4
Wamba Nigeria 8°57N 8°42E 263 D6
Wamba → Dem. Rep. of the Congo 3°56S 17°12E 265 C3
Wambeek Belgium 50°55N 4°30E 116 A3
Wamego U.S.A. 39°12N 96°18W 308 F5
Wamena Indonesia 4°4S 138°57E 231 E9
Wamsutter U.S.A. 41°40N 107°58W 304 F10
Wamulan Indonesia 3°27S 126°7E 231 E7
Wan Chai China 22°16N 114°10E 122 B2
Wan Chai Lanes Hong Kong, China 122 c2
Wan Hat Burma 20°14N 97°53E 241 E6
Wan Kinghao Burma 21°34N 98°17E 241 E7
Wan Lai-kam Burma 21°21N 98°22E 241 E7
Wan Tup Burma 21°13N 98°42E 241 E7
Wan Xian China 38°47N 115°7E 226 E8
Wana Pakistan 32°20N 69°32E 242 C3
Wanaaring Australia 29°38S 144°9E 281 D3
Wanaka N.Z. 44°42S 169°9E 285 E4
Wanaka, L. N.Z. 44°33S 169°7E 285 E4
Wan'an China 26°26N 114°49E 229 D10
Wanani Comoros Is. 12°20S 43°47E 272 a
Wanapa Neth. Ant. 12°7N 68°14W 322 h
Wanapitei L. Canada 46°45N 80°40W 298 C3
Wanbi Australia 34°46S 140°17E 282 C4
Wandaik Guyana 4°27N 59°35W 329 C6
Wandel Sea = McKinley Sea Arctic 82°0N 0°0 154 A11
Wandérama Ivory C. 8°37N 4°25W 262 D4
Wanderer Zimbabwe 19°36S 30°1E 269 F3
Wandhari Pakistan 27°42N 66°48E 242 F2
Wanding China 24°5N 98°4E 228 E2
Wando S. Korea 34°21N 126°41E 224 E3
Wandoan Australia 26°5S 149°55E 281 D4
Wandsworth □ U.K. 51°27N 0°11W 125 B2
Wandur Marine △ India 11°30N 92°30E 245 J11
Wanfu China 40°8N 122°38E 224 B1
Wang → Thailand 17°8N 99°2E 236 D2
Wang Center, The Boston, U.S.A. 116 c2
Wang Kai Sudan 9°3N 29°23E 257 F2
Wang Noi Thailand 14°13N 100°44E 236 E3
Wang Saphung Thailand 17°18N 101°46E 236 D3
Wang Thong Thailand 16°50N 100°26E 236 D3
Wanga Dem. Rep. of the Congo 2°58N 29°12E 268 B2
Wangal Indonesia 6°8S 134°9E 231 F8
Wangan Taiwan 23°21N 119°29E 225 C1
Wanganella Australia 35°6S 144°49E 283 C6
Wanganui N.Z. 39°56S 175°3E 284 F4
Wanganui → W. Coast, N.Z. 43°3S 170°26E 285 D5
Wanganui → Wanganui-Manawatu, N.Z. 39°55S 175°4E 284 F4
Wangaratta Australia 36°21S 146°19E 283 D7
Wangary Australia 34°35S 135°29E 281 E2
Wangcang China 32°18N 106°20E 228 A6
Wangcheng China 28°22N 112°49E 229 C9
Wangdu China 38°40N 115°7E 226 E8
Wangdu Phodrang Bhutan 27°28N 89°54E 241 B2
Wangen Germany 47°41N 9°50E 179 H5
Wangerin = Węgorzyno Poland 53°32N 15°33E 184 E2
Wangerooge Germany 53°47N 7°54E 178 B3
Wangiwangi Indonesia 5°22S 123°37E 231 F6
Wangjiang China 30°10N 116°42E 229 B11
Wangkung Taiwan 23°57N 120°20E 225 C2
Wangmo China 25°11N 106°5E 228 E6
Wangolodougou Ivory C. 9°55N 5°10W 262 D3
Wangqing China 43°12N 129°42E 227 C15
Wani India 20°5N 78°55E 244 D4
Wanigela Papua N. G. 9°21S 149°9E 286 E5
Wanjung Taiwan 23°43N 121°25E 225 C3
Wankaner India 22°35N 71°0E 242 H4
Wankhede Stadium Mumbai, India 130 c2
Wanlaweyne = Uanle Uen Somali Rep. 2°37N 44°54E 267 D5
Wanless Canada 54°11N 101°21W 297 C8
Wanli Taiwan 25°10N 121°41E 225 A3
Wanluan Taiwan 22°34N 120°34E 225 D2
Wanneroo Australia 31°42S 115°46E 279 F2
Wannian China 28°42N 117°4E 229 C11
Wanning China 18°48N 110°22E 236 C8
Wannoo Billabong Roadhouse Australia 27°25S 115°49E 279 E2
Wannsee Germany 52°25N 13°9E 115 B1
Wanon Niwat Thailand 17°38N 103°46E 236 D4
Wanqinsha China 22°43N 113°33E 219 F10
Wanquan China 40°50N 114°40E 226 D8
Wanrong China 35°25N 110°50E 226 G6
Wansdorf Germany 52°38N 13°5E 115 A1
Wansen = Wiązów Poland 50°50N 17°10E 185 H4
Wanshan China 27°30N 109°12E 228 D7
Wanshan Qundao China 21°57N 113°45E 219 G10
Wanshengchang China 28°57N 106°53E 228 C6
Wanstead N.Z. 40°8S 176°30E 284 G5
Wanstead London, U.K. 51°34N 0°1E 125 A4
Wantage U.K. 51°35N 1°25W 169 F6
Wantan Taiwan 22°35N 120°29E 225 D2
Wantouliu Taiwan 24°1N 120°41E 225 B2
Wanxian China 30°42N 108°20E 228 B7
Wanyin Burma 20°23N 97°15E 241 E6
Wanyuan China 32°4N 108°3E 228 A7
Wanzai Guangdong, China 22°12N 113°31E 219 G10
Wanzai Jiangxi, China 28°7N 114°30E 229 C10
Wapakoneta U.S.A. 40°34N 84°12W 311 D12
Wapato U.S.A. 46°27N 120°25W 304 C3
Wapawekka L. Canada 54°55N 104°40W 297 C8
Wapello U.S.A. 41°11N 91°11W 310 C5
Wapikopa L. Canada 52°56N 87°53W 298 B2
Wapinda Dem. Rep. of the Congo 3°41N 22°48E 264 B4
Wapiti → Canada 55°5N 118°18W 296 B5
Wapping U.K. 51°30N 0°3W 125 A3
Wappingers Falls U.S.A. 41°36N 73°55W 313 E11

Wapsipinicon → U.S.A. 41°44N 90°19W **310** C6
Wapusk △ Canada 57°46N 93°22W **297** B10
War in the Pacific Nat. Hist. Park △
  Guam 13°24N 144°39E **302** d
Warab □ Sudan 7°30N 28°30E **257** F2
Warabi Japan 35°49N 139°41E **223** B11
Warangal India 17°58N 79°35E **244** F4
Waraseoni India 21°45N 80°2E **243** J9
Waratah Australia 41°30S 145°30E **283** G4
Waratah B. Australia 38°54S 146°5E **283** E7
Warburg Germany 51°28N 9°11E **178** D5
Warburton Vic.,
  Australia 37°47S 145°42E **283** D6
Warburton W. Austral.,
  Australia 26°8S 126°35E **279** E4
Warburton → Australia 28°4S 137°28E **281** D2
Warburton Ra. Australia 25°55S 126°28E **279** E4
Ward Dublin, Ireland 53°26N 6°20W **120** A1
Ward N.Z. 41°49S 174°11E **285** B9
Ward → Australia 26°28S 146°6E **281** D4
Ward Hunt, C. Papua N. G. 8°2S 148°10E **286** E5
Ward Hunt Str.
  Papua N. G. 9°30S 150°0E **286** E6
Ward I. N.Z. 41°18S 174°54E **143** B2
Ward Mt. U.S.A. 37°12N 118°54W **306** H8
Wardang I. Australia 34°30S 137°20E **282** C2
Warden S. Africa 27°50S 29°0E **271** C4
Wardha India 20°45N 78°39E **244** E4
Wardha → India 19°57N 79°11E **244** E4
Wardija Point Malta 36°2N 14°11E **206** D6
Wards I. U.S.A. 40°47N 73°55W **132** B2
Ware B.C., Canada 57°26N 125°41W **296** B3
Ware Herts., U.K. 51°49N 0°0 **169** F8
Ware Mass., U.S.A. 42°16N 72°14W **313** D12
Waregem Belgium 50°53N 3°27E **170** D3
Wareham U.K. 50°41N 2°7W **169** G5
Wareham Belgium 50°43N 5°15E **170** D5
Waren Germany 53°31N 12°40E **178** B8
Warendorf Germany 51°57N 8°1E **178** D4
Waresboro U.S.A. 31°15N 82°29W **316** D7
Waria → Papua N. G. 7°49S 147°41E **286** D4
Warialda Australia 29°29S 150°33E **281** D5
Wariap Indonesia 1°30S 134°5E **231** E8
Warin Chamrap
  Thailand 15°12N 104°53E **236** E5
Warka Poland 51°47N 21°12E **185** G8
Warkopi Indonesia 1°12S 134°9E **231** E8
Warkworth N.Z. 36°24S 174°41E **284** C3
Warm Baths = Bela Bela
  S. Africa 24°51S 28°19E **271** B4
Warm Springs Ga.,
  U.S.A. 32°53N 84°41W **316** C5
Warm Springs Nev.,
  U.S.A. 38°10N 116°20W **305** G5
Warman Canada 52°19N 106°30W **297** C7
Warmbad = Bela Bela
  S. Africa 24°51S 28°19E **271** B4
Warmbad Namibia 28°25S 18°42E **270** C2
Warmińsko-Mazurskie □
  Poland 54°0N 21°0E **184** D8
Warminster Wilts., U.K. 51°12N 2°10W **169** F5
Warminster Pa., U.S.A. 40°12N 75°6W **313** F9
Warmun Australia 17°2S 128°12E **278** C4
Warnberg Germany 48°11N 11°31E **181** B2
Warnemünde Germany 54°10N 12°4E **178** A8
Warner Brothers Studios
  U.S.A. 34°9N 118°20W **126** B2
Warner Mts. U.S.A. 41°40N 120°15W **304** F3
Warner Robins U.S.A. 32°37N 83°36W **316** C6
Warnes Bolivia 17°30S 63°10W **331** D5
Warnow → Germany 54°6N 12°9E **178** A8
Waroona Australia 32°50S 115°58E **279** F2
Warora India 20°14N 79°1E **244** D4
Warrabah △ Australia 30°31S 150°56E **283** A5
Warracknabeal Australia 36°9S 142°26E **282** D5
Warragul Australia 38°10S 145°58E **283** C6
Warrego → Australia 30°24S 145°21E **281** D4
Warrego Ra. Australia 24°58S 146°0E **280** C4
Warren N.S.W., Australia 31°42S 147°51E **283** A4
Warren Ark., U.S.A. 33°37N 92°4W **314** E8
Warren Ill., U.S.A. 42°29N 90°0W **310** B7
Warren Ind., U.S.A. 40°41N 85°26W **311** D11
Warren Mich., U.S.A. 42°28N 83°1W **311** B13
Warren Minn., U.S.A. 48°12N 96°46W **308** A5
Warren Ohio, U.S.A. 41°14N 80°49W **312** E4
Warren Pa., U.S.A. 41°51N 79°9W **312** E5
Warrenpoint U.K. 54°6N 6°15W **166** B5
Warrensburg Ill., U.S.A. 39°56N 89°4W **310** F7
Warrensburg Mo.,
  U.S.A. 38°46N 93°44W **310** F3
Warrenton Northern Cape,
  S. Africa 28°9S 24°47E **270** D3
Warrenton Ga., U.S.A. 33°24N 82°40W **316** C6
Warrenton Mo., U.S.A. 38°49N 91°9W **310** F5
Warrenton Oreg.,
  U.S.A. 46°10N 123°56W **306** D3
Warrenville U.S.A. 33°33N 81°48W **316** B8
Warri Nigeria 5°30N 5°41E **263** D6
Warrina Australia 28°12S 135°50E **281** D2
Warringal Park Australia 37°45S 145°4E **128** A2
Warrington N.Z. 45°43S 170°35E **285** F5
Warrington Warrington,
  U.K. 53°24N 2°35W **168** D5
Warrington Fla., U.S.A. 30°23N 87°17W **317** E2
Warrington □ U.K. 53°24N 2°35W **168** D5
Warriston U.K. 55°58N 3°11W **121** B2
Warrnambool Australia 38°25S 142°30E **282** E5
Warroad U.S.A. 48°54N 95°19W **308** A6
Warrumbungle △
  Australia 31°18S 149°1E **283** A8
Warruwi Australia 11°36S 133°20E **280** A1
Warsa Indonesia 0°47S 135°55E **231** E9
Warsak Dam Pakistan 34°11N 71°19E **242** B4
Warsaw = Warszawa
  Poland 52°14N 21°0E **142** B2
Warsaw Ill., U.S.A. 40°22N 91°26W **310** D5
Warsaw Ind., U.S.A. 41°14N 85°51W **311** C11
Warsaw Ky., U.S.A. 38°47N 84°54W **311** F12
Warsaw Mo., U.S.A. 38°15N 93°23W **310** F3
Warsaw N.Y., U.S.A. 42°45N 78°8W **312** D6
Warsaw Ohio, U.S.A. 40°20N 82°0W **312** F3
Warszawa Poland 52°14N 21°0E **142** B2
Warszawa ✈ (WAW)
  Poland 52°14N 21°0E **142** B2
Warta Poland 51°43N 18°38E **185** G5
Warta → Poland 52°35N 14°39E **185** F1
Wartenberg Germany 52°34N 13°31E **115** A4
Wartenburg = Barczewo
  Poland 53°50N 20°42E **184** E7
Warthbrücken = Kolo
  Poland 52°14N 18°40E **185** F5
Warthe = Warta →
  Poland 52°35N 14°39E **185** F1
Warthen U.S.A. 33°6N 82°48W **316** B7
Warthenau = Zawiercie
  Poland 50°30N 19°24E **185** H6
Waru Indonesia 3°30S 130°36E **231** E8
Warud India 21°30N 78°16E **244** D4
Warwick Queens.,
  Australia 28°10S 152°1E **281** D5

Warwick Warks., U.K. 52°18N 1°35W **169** E6
Warwick Ga., U.S.A. 31°50N 83°57W **316** D6
Warwick N.Y., U.S.A. 41°16N 74°22W **313** E10
Warwick R.I., U.S.A. 41°42N 71°28W **313** E13
Warwickshire □ U.K. 52°14N 1°38W **169** E6
Wasaga Beach Canada 44°31N 80°1W **312** B4
Wasagaming Canada 50°39N 99°58W **297** C9
Wasatch Ra. U.S.A. 40°0N 111°30W **304** F8
Wasbank S. Africa 28°15S 30°9E **271** C5
Wasco Calif., U.S.A. 35°36N 119°20W **307** K7
Wasco Oreg., U.S.A. 45°36N 120°42W **304** D3
Wase Nigeria 9°4N 9°54E **263** D6
Waseca U.S.A. 44°5N 93°30W **308** C7
Wasekamio L. Canada 56°45N 108°45W **297** B7
Wasgomura △ Sri Lanka 7°45N 81°0E **245** L5
Wash, The U.K. 52°58N 0°20E **168** E8
Washago Canada 44°45N 79°20W **312** B5
Washburn Ill., U.S.A. 40°55N 89°17W **310** D7
Washburn N. Dak.,
  U.S.A. 47°17N 101°2W **308** B3
Washburn Wis., U.S.A. 46°40N 90°54W **308** B6
Washim India 20°3N 77°0E **244** D3
Washington Neth. Ant. 12°17N 68°23W **322** h
Washington Tyne & W.,
  U.K. 54°55N 1°30W **168** C6
Washington D.C., U.S.A. 38°53N 77°2W **143** B3
Washington Ga., U.S.A. 33°44N 82°44W **316** B7
Washington Ill., U.S.A. 40°42N 89°24W **310** D7
Washington Ind., U.S.A. 38°40N 87°10W **311** F9
Washington Iowa, U.S.A. 41°18N 91°42W **310** C5
Washington Mo., U.S.A. 38°33N 91°1W **310** F5
Washington N.C., U.S.A. 35°33N 77°3W **315** D16
Washington N.J., U.S.A. 40°46N 74°59W **313** F10
Washington Pa., U.S.A. 40°10N 80°15W **312** F4
Washington Utah,
  U.S.A. 37°8N 113°31W **305** H7
Washington □ U.S.A. 47°30N 120°30W **304** C3
Washington, Mt.
  U.S.A. 44°16N 71°18W **313** B13
Washington Court House
  U.S.A. 39°32N 83°26W **311** E13
Washington Dulles ✈ (IAD)
  Washington, D.C., U.S.A. **143** B1
Washington Heights
  U.S.A. 40°51N 73°56W **132** A2
Washington I. U.S.A. 45°23N 86°54W **308** C10
Washington Land
  Greenland 80°30N 66°0W **154** A4
Washington Monument
  U.S.A. **143** b1
Washington Park
  U.S.A. 41°47N 87°36W **119** C3
Washington Ronald Reagan
  National ✈ (DCA)
  U.S.A. 38°51N 77°2W **143** B3
Washington Slagbaai Nat. Park △
  Neth. Ant. 12°16N 68°23W **322** h
Washougal U.S.A. 45°35N 122°21W **306** E4
Washpool △ Australia 29°22S 152°20E **281** D5
Washuk Pakistan 27°42N 64°45E **240** D2
Wasian Indonesia 1°47S 133°19E **231** E8
Wasilków Poland 53°12N 23°13E **185** E9
Wasilla U.S.A. 61°35N 149°26W **303** F10
Wasior Indonesia 2°43S 134°30E **231** E8
Wāsiţ □ Iraq 32°50N 45°50E **213** F11
Waskaganish Canada 51°30N 78°40W **298** B4
Waskaiowaka L. Canada 56°33N 96°23W **297** B9
Waskesiu Lake Canada 53°55N 106°5W **297** C7
Wassaw I. U.S.A. 31°53N 80°58W **316** D9
Wassaw Sd. U.S.A. 31°55N 80°59W **316** D9
Wasserburg Germany 48°3N 12°14E **179** G8
Wasserkuppe Germany 50°29N 9°55E **178** E5
Wassy France 48°30N 4°58E **173** D11
Wasu Papua N. G. 5°58S 147°12E **286** C4
Wasua Papua N. G. 8°18S 142°52E **286** E2
Waswanipi Canada 49°40N 76°29W **298** C4
Waswanipi, L. Canada 49°35N 76°40W **298** C4
Wat Bangkok, Thailand **113** b1
Wat Pho Bangkok, Thailand **113** b1
Wat Phra Keo Bangkok, Thailand **113** b1
Wat Traimit Bangkok, Thailand **113** c2
Watagans △ Australia 33°0S 151°28E **283** B9
Watam Papua N. G. 3°55S 144°33E **286** B3
Watampone Indonesia 4°29S 120°25E **231** E6
Watamu Kenya 3°23S 40°0E **268** C5
Watarrka △ Australia 24°10S 131°30E **280** C1
Watee Solomon Is. 10°30S 162°2E **287** N12
Watenstadt-Salzgitter = Salzgitter
  Germany 52°9N 10°19E **178** C6
Water of Leith U.K. 55°59N 3°10W **121** B1
Water Park Pt. Australia 22°56S 150°47E **280** C5
Water Tower Place Chicago, U.S.A. **119** a2
Water Valley U.S.A. 34°10N 89°38W **315** D10
Waterberg Plateau △
  Namibia 20°25S 17°18E **270** B2
Waterberge S. Africa 24°10S 28°0E **271** B4
Waterbury Conn., U.S.A. 41°33N 73°3W **313** E11
Waterbury Vt., U.S.A. 44°20N 72°46W **313** B12
Waterbury L. Canada 58°10N 104°22W **297** B8
Waterdown Canada 43°20N 79°53W **312** C5
Wateree → U.S.A. 33°45N 80°37W **316** B9
Waterford Ont., Canada 42°56N 80°17W **312** D4
Waterford Waterford,
  Ireland 52°15N 7°8W **166** D4
Waterford Calif., U.S.A. 37°38N 120°46W **306** H6
Waterford Mich., U.S.A. 42°45N 83°23W **311** B13
Waterford Pa., U.S.A. 41°57N 79°59W **312** E5
Waterford Wis., U.S.A. 42°46N 88°13W **311** B8
Waterford □ Ireland 52°10N 7°40W **166** D4
Waterford Harbour Ireland 52°8N 6°58W **166** D5
Watergraafsmeer Neths. 52°21N 4°56E **112** A2
Waterhen L. Canada 52°10N 99°40W **297** C9
Waterland Neths. 52°26N 4°58E **112** A2
Waterloo Belgium 50°43N 4°25E **116** B2
Waterloo Ont., Canada 43°30N 80°32W **312** C4
Waterloo Qué., Canada 45°22N 72°32W **313** A12
Waterloo S. Leone 8°22N 13°0W **262** G2
Waterloo Trin. & Tob. 10°28N 61°28W **323** t
Waterloo Ill., U.S.A. 38°20N 90°9W **310** F6
Waterloo Ind., U.S.A. 41°26N 85°1W **311** C11
Waterloo Iowa, U.S.A. 42°30N 92°21W **310** B4
Waterloo N.Y., U.S.A. 42°54N 76°52W **312** D8
Waterloo Wis., U.S.A. 43°11N 88°59W **311** A8
Waterval-Boven S. Africa 25°40S 30°18E **271** C5
Waterville Canada 45°16N 71°54W **313** A13
Waterville Maine,
  U.S.A. 44°33N 69°38W **309** C19
Waterville N.Y., U.S.A. 42°56N 75°23W **313** D9

Waterville Pa., U.S.A. 41°19N 77°21W **312** E7
Waterville Wash., U.S.A. 47°39N 120°4W **304** C4
Watervliet Mich., U.S.A. 42°11N 86°18W **311** B10
Watervliet N.Y., U.S.A. 42°44N 73°42W **313** D11
Wates Indonesia 7°51S 110°10E **235** D4
Watford Ont., Canada 42°57N 81°53W **312** D3
Watford Herts., U.K. 51°40N 0°24W **169** F7
Watford City U.S.A. 47°48N 103°17W **308** B2
Wathaman → Canada 57°16N 102°59W **297** B8
Wathaman L. Canada 56°58N 103°44W **297** B8
Watheroo Australia 30°15S 116°5E **279** F2
Watheroo △ Australia 30°19S 115°48E **279** F2
Watir, W. → Egypt 29°0N 34°40E **251** K5
Watkins Glen U.S.A. 42°23N 76°52W **312** D8
Watkinsville U.S.A. 33°52N 83°25W **316** B6
Watling I. = San Salvador I.
  Bahamas 24°0N 74°40W **321** B5
Watom I. Papua N. G. 4°7S 152°4E **286** C7
Watonga U.S.A. 35°51N 98°25W **314** D5
Watrous Sask., Canada 51°40N 105°25W **297** C7
Watrous N. Mex.,
  U.S.A. 35°48N 104°59W **305** J11
Watsa Dem. Rep. of the Congo 3°4N 29°30E **268** B2
Watseka U.S.A. 40°47N 87°44W **311** D9
Watsi Kenga
  Dem. Rep. of the Congo 0°49S 20°34E **264** C4
Watson Canada 52°10N 104°30W **297** C8
Watson Lake Canada 60°6N 128°49W **296** A3
Watsonia Australia 37°43S 145°6E **128** A2
Watsontown U.S.A. 41°5N 76°52W **312** E8
Watsonville U.S.A. 36°55N 121°45W **306** J5
Watt Mt. Dominica 15°19N 61°19W **323** k
Wattiwarriganna Cr. →
  Australia 28°57S 136°10E **281** D2
Wattwil Switz. 47°18N 9°6E **179** H5
Watu Dem. Rep. of the Congo 3°18S 20°3E **264** C4
Watuata = Batuata
  Indonesia 6°12S 122°42E **231** F6
Watubela, Kepulauan
  Indonesia 4°28S 131°35E **231** E8
Watubela Is. = Watubela,
  Kepulauan Indonesia 4°28S 131°35E **231** E8
Wau = Wâw Sudan 7°45N 28°1E **257** G5
Wau N. G. 7°21S 146°47E **286** D4
Waubamik Canada 45°27N 80°1W **312** A4
Waubay U.S.A. 45°20N 97°18W **308** C5
Waubra Australia 37°21S 143°39E **282** D5
Wauchope N.S.W.,
  Australia 31°28S 152°45E **283** A10
Wauchope N. Terr.,
  Australia 20°36S 134°15E **280** C1
Wauchula U.S.A. 27°33N 81°49W **317** H8
Waukarlycarly, L.
  Australia 21°18S 121°56E **278** D3
Waukeenah U.S.A. 30°25N 83°57W **316** E6
Waukegan U.S.A. 42°22N 87°50W **311** A9
Waukesha U.S.A. 43°1N 88°14W **311** B8
Waukon U.S.A. 43°16N 91°29W **308** D8
Waupaca U.S.A. 44°21N 89°5W **308** C9
Waupun U.S.A. 43°38N 88°44W **308** D9
Waurika U.S.A. 34°10N 98°0W **314** D6
Wausau Fla., U.S.A. 30°38N 85°35W **316** E4
Wausau Wis., U.S.A. 44°58N 89°38W **308** C9
Wauseon U.S.A. 41°33N 84°8W **311** C12
Wautoma U.S.A. 44°4N 89°18W **308** C9
Wauwatosa U.S.A. 43°2N 88°0W **311** A9
Waveland U.S.A. 39°53N 87°3W **319** E9
Waveney → U.K. 52°35N 1°39E **169** E9
Waverley N.S.W.,
  Australia 33°53S 151°15E **139** B2
Waverley N.Z. 39°46S 174°37E **284** F3
Waverley Gauteng, S. Africa 26°7S 28°14E **123** A2
Waverley Mass., U.S.A. 42°23N 71°10W **116** A1
Waverley Hall U.K. 32°41N 84°44W **316** B5
Waverley Station Edinburgh, U.K. **121** b3
Waverly Ala., U.S.A. 32°45N 85°35W **316** C5
Waverly Fla., U.S.A. 27°59N 81°37W **317** H8
Waverly Ill., U.S.A. 31°6N 81°43W **316** E8
Waverly Ill., U.S.A. 39°36N 89°57W **310** F7
Waverly Iowa, U.S.A. 42°44N 92°29W **310** B4
Waverly N.Y., U.S.A. 42°1N 76°32W **313** E8
Wavre Belgium 50°43N 4°38E **170** D4
Wavoi Burma 17°28N 96°41E **241** G6
Wâw Sudan 7°45N 28°1E **257** F2
Wāw al Kabīr Libya 25°20N 16°43E **258** C2
Wâw an Nāmūs Libya 24°55N 17°46E **258** D3
Wawa Ont., Canada 47°59N 84°47W **298** C3
Wawa Nigeria 9°54N 4°27E **263** D5
Wawa Sudan 20°30N 30°22E **257** D6
Wawanesa Canada 49°36N 99°40W **297** D9
Wawasee, L. U.S.A. 41°24N 85°42W **311** C11
Wawer Poland 52°15N 21°13E **142** B1
Wawona U.S.A. 37°32N 119°39W **306** H7
Wawoi → Papua N. G. 7°48S 143°16E **286** D2
Wawona Poland 52°17N 20°53E **142** B1
Waxahachie U.S.A. 32°24N 96°51W **314** E6
Waxxari China 38°42N 87°1E **217** E11
Way, L. Australia 26°45S 120°16E **278** E3
Way Kambas △ Indonesia 4°54S 105°43E **234** C3
Waya Fiji 17°19S 177°10E **287** A1
Waycross U.S.A. 31°13N 82°21W **316** D7
Wayi Sudan 5°8N 30°10E **257** F3
Wayland Mich., U.S.A. 42°40N 85°39W **311** B10
Wayland N.Y., U.S.A. 42°34N 77°35W **312** D7
Wayne W. Va., U.S.A. 38°13N 82°27W **309** F12
Wayne Nebr., U.S.A. 42°14N 97°1W **308** D6
Wayne County, Detroit ✈ (DTW)
  U.S.A. 42°13N 83°21W **311** B13
Wayne Lakes U.S.A. 40°1N 84°40W **311** E12
Waynesboro Ga., U.S.A. 33°6N 82°1W **316** B7
Waynesboro Miss.,
  U.S.A. 31°40N 88°39W **316** F3
Waynesboro Pa., U.S.A. 39°45N 77°35W **309** F15
Waynesboro Va., U.S.A. 38°4N 78°53W **309** F14
Waynesburg U.S.A. 39°54N 80°11W **309** F13
Waynesville Mo., U.S.A. 37°50N 92°12W **310** G4
Waynesville N.C.,
  U.S.A. 35°28N 82°58W **315** D13
Waynesville Ohio, U.S.A. 39°32N 84°5W **311** E12
Waynoka U.S.A. 36°35N 98°53W **314** C5
Wayside U.S.A. 33°4N 83°3W **316** B6
Waza Indonesia 5°51N 95°18E **234** A1
Waza △ Cameroon 11°15N 14°38E **259** F2
Wazikhwah Afghan. 32°53N 69°6E **240** B3
Wāzin Libya 31°58N 10°40E **258** B7
Wazirabad Delhi, India 28°43N 77°13E **242** E7
Wazirabad Pakistan 32°30N 74°8E **242** C6
Wazirpur India 28°41N 77°10E **120** A2
Wda → Poland 53°25N 18°29E **185** B5
We Indonesia 5°51N 95°18E **234** A1
Wé N. Cal. 20°55S 167°16E **287** d
Weald, The U.K. 51°4N 0°20E **169** F8
Wealdstone U.K. 51°35N 0°17W **125** A1
Weam Papua N. G. 8°37S 141°7E **286** E1
Wear → U.K. 54°55N 1°23W **168** C6
Weatherford Okla.,
  U.S.A. 35°32N 98°43W **314** D5
Weatherford Tex., U.S.A. 32°46N 97°48W **314** E6
Weau Papua N. G. 5°35S 152°8E **286** b
Weatherford Tex., U.S.A. 32°46N 97°48W **314** E6
Weaubleau U.S.A. 37°54N 93°32W **310** G3

Weaverville U.S.A. 40°44N 122°56W **304** F2
Webb City U.S.A. 37°9N 94°28W **308** G6
Webequie Canada 52°59N 87°21W **298** B2
Weber N.Z. 40°24S 176°20E **284** G5
Weber Basin Pac. Oc. 6°0S 131°0E **276** B5
Webo = Nyaake Liberia 4°52N 7°37W **262** E3
Webster Mass., U.S.A. 42°3N 71°53W **313** D13
Webster N.Y., U.S.A. 43°13N 77°26W **312** C7
Webster S. Dak., U.S.A. 45°20N 97°31W **308** C5
Webster City U.S.A. 42°28N 93°49W **310** B3
Webster Springs U.S.A. 38°29N 80°25W **309** F13
Weda Indonesia 0°21N 127°50E **231** D7
Weda, Teluk Indonesia 0°20N 128°0E **231** D7
Weddell Abyssal Plain
  S. Ocean 65°0S 20°0W **151** C2
Weddell I. Falk. Is. 51°50S 61°0W **153** f
Weddell Sea Antarctica 72°30S 40°0W **151** D1
Wedderburn Australia 36°26S 143°33E **282** D5
Weddin Mts. △ Australia 33°59S 148°0E **283** E3
Wedding Germany 52°32N 13°21E **115** A3
Wedel Germany 53°34N 9°42E **178** B5
Wedemark Germany 52°32N 9°43E **178** C5
Wedgeport Canada 43°44N 65°59W **299** D6
Wednesday I. Australia 10°31S 142°16E **286** E2
Wedowee U.S.A. 33°19N 85°29W **316** B4
Wedza Zimbabwe 18°40S 31°33E **269** F3
Wee Waa Australia 30°11S 149°26E **281** E4
Weed U.S.A. 41°25N 122°23W **304** F2
Weed Heights U.S.A. 38°59N 119°13W **306** G4
Weedsport U.S.A. 43°3N 76°34W **313** D8
Weedville U.S.A. 41°17N 78°30W **312** E6
Weemelah Australia 29°2S 149°15E **283** A8
Weenen S. Africa 28°48S 30°7E **271** C5
Weener Germany 53°9N 7°20E **178** B3
Weert Neths. 51°15N 5°43E **170** C5
Weesp Neths. 52°18N 5°2E **112** B3
Węgierska-Górka Poland 49°36N 19°7E **185** J6
Węgliniec Poland 51°18N 15°10E **185** G2
Węgorzewo Poland 54°13N 21°43E **184** D8
Węgorzyno Poland 53°32N 15°33E **184** E2
Węgrów Poland 52°24N 22°0E **185** F9
Wehda □ Sudan 8°30N 30°0E **257** F3
Wei He → Hebei, China 36°10N 115°45E **226** F8
Wei He → Shaanxi,
  China 34°38N 110°15E **226** G6
Weichang China 41°58N 117°49E **227** D9
Weichuan China 34°20N 113°59E **226** G7
Weida Germany 50°46N 12°2E **178** E8
Weiden Germany 49°41N 12°10E **179** F8
Weidling Austria 48°17N 16°18E **142** A1
Weidlingbach Austria 48°16N 16°15E **142** A1
Weifang China 36°44N 119°7E **227** F10
Weihai China 37°30N 122°6E **227** F12
Weil Germany 47°35N 7°37E **179** H3
Weilburg Germany 50°28N 8°17E **178** E4
Weilheim Germany 47°50N 11°9E **179** H7
Weimar Germany 50°58N 11°19E **178** E7
Weinan China 34°31N 109°29E **226** G5
Weingarten Germany 49°3N 8°31E **179** F4
Weinheim Germany 49°32N 8°39E **179** F4
Weining China 26°50N 104°17E **228** D5
Weipa Australia 12°40S 141°50E **280** A3
Weir → Australia 28°20S 149°50E **281** D4
Weir → Man., Canada 56°54N 93°21W **297** B10
Weir, L. U.S.A. 29°1N 81°56W **317** F8
Weir River Canada 56°49N 94°6W **297** B10
Weirsdale U.S.A. 28°59N 81°55W **317** G8
Weirton U.S.A. 40°24N 80°35W **312** F4
Weiser U.S.A. 44°15N 116°58W **306** D5
Weishan Shandong, China 34°47N 117°5E **227** G9
Weishan Yunnan, China 25°12N 100°20E **228** E3
Weissburg U.S.A. 49°2N 10°58E **179** F6
Weissenburg Germany 49°2N 10°58E **179** F6
Weissenfels Germany 51°11N 12°0E **178** D7
Weissensee Germany 52°33N 13°27E **115** A3
Weisskirchen = Hranice
  Czech Rep. 49°34N 17°45E **181** B10
Weisswasser Germany 51°30N 14°36E **178** D10
Weistrat □ = Bystrzyca →
  Dolnoślaskie, Poland 51°12N 16°55E **185** G3
Weistrat □ = Bystrzyca →
  Poland 37°54S 144°40E **282** D6
Wéitra Austria 48°41N 14°54E **180** C7
Weixi China 27°10N 99°10E **228** D2
Weixin China 27°48N 105°3E **228** D5
Weiyuan China 35°7N 104°10E **226** G3
Weiz Austria 47°13N 15°39E **180** D8
Weizhou Dao China 21°0N 109°5E **228** G7
Wejherowo Poland 54°35N 18°12E **184** D5
Wekusko L. Canada 54°40N 99°40W **297** C9
Welbourn Hill Australia 27°21S 134°6E **281** D1
Welch U.S.A. 37°26N 81°35W **309** G13
Welch □ □ Australia 31°15S 152°38E **283** A10
Welchman Hall Barbados 13°11N 59°34W **323** r
Weldya Ethiopia 11°50N 39°34E **257** E4
Welega □ Ethiopia 9°25N 34°20E **257** F3
Welford □ Sudan 25°5S 143°16E **280** D3
Weligama Sri Lanka 5°58N 80°25E **245** M5
Welkite Ethiopia 8°15N 37°42E **257** F4
Welkom S. Africa 28°0S 26°46E **270** D4
Welland Canada 43°0N 79°15W **312** D5
Welland → U.K. 52°51N 0°5W **169** E7
Wellawaya Sri Lanka 6°44N 81°6E **245** L5
Welles Harbor
  Midway Is. 28°13N 177°22W **302** d
Wellesley Hills U.S.A. 42°18N 71°16W **116** B3
Wellesley Is. Australia 16°42S 139°30E **280** B2
Welling U.K. 51°27N 0°6E **125** B5
Wellingborough U.K. 52°19N 0°41W **169** E7
Wellington N.S.W.,
  Australia 32°35S 148°59E **283** B8
Wellington Ont., Canada 43°57N 77°20W **312** C7
Wellington N.Z. 41°19S 174°46E **143** B1
Wellington Western Cape,
  S. Africa 33°38S 19°1E **270** D2
Wellington Somst., U.K. 50°58N 3°13W **169** G4
Wellington Telford & Wrekin,
  U.K. 52°42N 2°30W **169** E5
Wellington Colo., U.S.A. 40°42N 105°0W **304** F11
Wellington Kans., U.S.A. 37°16N 97°24W **308** G5
Wellington Nev., U.S.A. 38°45N 119°22W **306** G4
Wellington Ohio, U.S.A. 41°10N 82°13W **312** E2
Wellington Tex., U.S.A. 34°51N 100°13W **314** D4
Wellington, I. Chile 49°30S 75°0W **336** C2
Wellington, L. Australia 38°6S 147°20E **283** C7
Wellington Chan. Canada 75°0N 93°0W **295** B10
Wellington Int. ✈ (WLE)
  N.Z. 41°20S 174°50E **143** B1
Wellman U.S.A. 41°28N 91°50W **310** C5
Wells Somst., U.K. 51°13N 2°39W **169** F5
Wells Maine, U.S.A. 43°20N 70°35W **313** C14
Wells Nev., U.S.A. 41°7N 114°58W **304** F6
Wells, L. Australia 26°44S 123°15E **279** E3
Wells, Mt. Australia 17°25S 127°8E **278** C4
Wells Fargo Center Los Angeles, U.S.A. **127** b1
Wells Gray △ Canada 52°30N 120°15W **296** C4
Wells-next-the-Sea U.K. 52°57N 0°51E **168** E8
Wells River U.S.A. 44°9N 72°4W **313** B12

West Covina U.S.A. 34°4N 117°54W **307** L9
West Des Moines U.S.A. 41°35N 93°43W **310** C3
West Don → Canada 43°44N 79°24W **141** A2
West Drayton U.K. 51°30N 0°28W **125** A1
West Dunbartonshire □
  U.K. 55°59N 4°30W **167** E7
West End Bahamas 26°41N 78°58W **320** A4
West End Boston, U.S.A. **116** b1
West End Village Anguilla 18°10N 63°10W **322** a
West Falkland Falk. Is. 51°40S 60°0W **153** f
West Fargo U.S.A. 46°52N 96°54W **308** B5
West Farmington U.S.A. 41°23N 80°58W **312** E4
West Fiji Basin Pac. Oc. 17°0S 173°0E **288** J9
West Fjord = Vestfjorden
  Norway 67°55N 14°0E **160** C16
West Fork Trinity →
  U.S.A. 32°48N 96°54W **314** E6
West Frankfort U.S.A. 37°54N 88°55W **310** G8
West Grand L. U.S.A. 45°14N 67°59W **309** C20
West Green U.K. 31°37N 82°44W **316** D7
West Ham U.K. 51°31N 0°1E **125** A4
West Harrow U.K. 51°34N 0°21W **125** A1
West Hartford U.S.A. 41°45N 72°44W **313** E12
West Haven U.S.A. 41°17N 72°57W **313** E12
West Hazleton U.S.A. 40°58N 76°0W **312** E9
West Heath U.K. 51°29N 0°7E **125** B4
West Helena U.S.A. 34°33N 90°38W **315** D9
West Hill Canada 43°46N 79°10W **141** A3
West Hollywood U.S.A. 34°5N 118°21W **126** B2
West Hurley U.S.A. 41°59N 74°7W **313** E10
West I. India 13°35S 92°54E **245** H11
West Ice Shelf Antarctica 67°0S 85°0E **151** C7
West Indies Cent. Amer. 15°0N 65°0W **321** D7
West Jefferson U.S.A. 39°57N 83°17W **311** E13
West Jordan U.S.A. 40°36N 111°56W **304** F8
West Kensington London, U.K. **125** c1
West Kilburn London, U.K. **125** a1
West Lafayette U.S.A. 40°27N 86°55W **311** D10
West Lamma Channel
  China 22°14N 114°4E **122** B1
West Liberty Iowa,
  U.S.A. 41°34N 91°16W **310** C5
West Liberty Ky., U.S.A. 37°55N 83°16W **311** G13
West Liberty Ohio,
  U.S.A. 40°15N 83°45W **311** D13
West Linn U.S.A. 45°21N 122°36W **306** E4
West Lorne Canada 42°36N 81°36W **312** D3
West Los Angeles, University of
  U.S.A. 34°7N 118°23W **126** C2
West Lothian □ U.K. 55°54N 3°36W **167** F5
West Lunga → Zambia 13°6S 24°39E **265** E4
West Lunga △ Zambia 12°49S 24°47E **265** E4
West MacDonnell △
  Australia 23°38S 132°59E **278** D5
West Mariana Basin
  Pac. Oc. 15°0N 137°0E **288** F5
West Medford U.S.A. 42°25N 71°7W **116** A2
West Memphis U.S.A. 35°8N 90°10W **315** D9
West Miami U.S.A. 25°45N 80°17W **128** B1
West Midlands □ U.K. 52°26N 2°0W **169** E6
West Mifflin U.S.A. 40°21N 79°52W **312** F5
West Milford U.S.A. 41°8N 74°22W **313** E10
West Milton Ohio,
  U.S.A. 39°58N 84°20W **311** E12
West Milton Pa., U.S.A. 41°1N 76°50W **312** E8
West Molesey U.K. 51°24N 0°22W **125** B1
West Monroe U.S.A. 32°31N 92°9W **314** E8
West New Britain □
  Papua N. G. 5°0S 149°30E **286** C5
West New York New York, U.S.A. **132** a1
West Newton U.S.A. 40°14N 79°46W **312** F5
West Nicholson Zimbabwe 21°2S 29°20E **269** G2
West Odessa U.S.A. 31°50N 102°30W **314** F3
West of Twin Peaks
  U.S.A. 37°43N 122°27W **136** B2
West Palm Beach U.S.A. 26°43N 80°3W **317** J9
West Palm Beach Canal
  U.S.A. 26°40N 80°15W **317** J9
West Park S. Africa 26°9S 27°59E **123** A1
West Pensacola U.S.A. 30°25N 87°16W **317** E2
West Plains U.S.A. 36°44N 91°51W **308** G8
West Point Ga., U.S.A. 32°53N 85°11W **316** C4
West Point Iowa, U.S.A. 40°43N 91°27W **310** D5
West Point Miss., U.S.A. 33°36N 88°39W **316** E3
West Point N.Y., U.S.A. 41°24N 73°58W **313** E11
West Point Nebr., U.S.A. 41°51N 96°43W **308** E5
West Point Va., U.S.A. 37°32N 76°48W **309** G15
West Point L. U.S.A. 33°8N 85°0W **316** B4
West Pt. = Ouest, Pte. de l'
  Canada 49°52N 64°40W **299** C7
West Pt. Australia 35°1S 135°56E **282** C1
West Ra. Papua N. G. 4°15S 141°32E **286** C1
West Road → Canada 53°18N 122°53W **296** C4
West Rouge Canada 43°48N 79°7W **141** A4
West Roxbury U.S.A. 42°16N 71°9W **116** B2
West Rutland U.S.A. 43°36N 73°3W **313** C11
West Salem U.S.A. 38°31N 88°1W **311** F8
West Schelde = Westerschelde →
  Neths. 51°25N 3°25E **170** C3
West Seneca U.S.A. 42°51N 78°48W **312** D6
West Sepik □ Papua N. G. 3°30S 142°0E **286** C1
West Siberian Plain Russia 62°0N 75°0E **210** B9
West Springfield U.S.A. 38°47N 77°13W **143** C2
West Sussex □ U.K. 50°55N 0°30W **169** G7
West Terre Haute U.S.A. 39°28N 87°27W **311** E9
West Union Iowa, U.S.A. 42°57N 91°49W **310** B5
West Union Ohio, U.S.A. 38°48N 83°33W **311** F13
West Unity U.S.A. 41°35N 84°26W **311** C12
West Valley City U.S.A. 40°42N 111°58W **304** F8
West Virginia □ U.S.A. 38°45N 80°30W **309** F13
West Walker → U.S.A. 38°54N 119°9W **306** G4
West Wharf Pakistan 24°49N 66°58E **123** F1
West Wyalong Australia 33°56S 147°10E **283** B8
West Yellowstone
  U.S.A. 44°40N 111°6W **304** D8
West Yorkshire □ U.K. 53°45N 1°40W **168** D6
Westall, Pt. Australia 32°55S 134°4E **281** E1
Westbay U.S.A. 30°20N 85°49W **316** E4
Westbourne Green London, U.K. **125** a1
Westbrook U.S.A. 43°41N 70°22W **309** D18
Westbury Australia 41°30S 146°51E **283** G4
Westby U.S.A. 48°52N 104°3W **304** B12
Westchester Calif.,
  U.S.A. 33°57N 118°23W **126** C2
Westchester N.Y., U.S.A. 40°51N 73°51W **132** A2
Westcliff S. Africa 26°10S 28°1E **123** B2
Westdene S. Africa 26°10S 27°59E **123** B1
Westend Helsinki, Finland 60°9N 24°48E **141** C1
Westend Calif., U.S.A. 35°42N 117°24W **307** K9
Wester Hailes U.K. 55°55N 3°16W **121** B2
Westerland Germany 54°54N 8°17E **178** A4
Westerlo Belgium 51°6N 4°55W **170** C4
Westerly U.S.A. 41°22N 71°50W **313** E13
Western □ Ghana 5°30N 2°30W **262** D4
Western □ Kenya 0°30N 34°30E **268** B3
Western □ S. Leone 8°30N 13°0W **262** D2
Western □ Zambia 15°0S 24°4E **265** F4

Western Addition U.S.A. 37°47N 122°25W 136 B2
Western Australia □ Australia 25°0S 118°0E 279 E2
Western Cape □ S. Africa 34°0S 20°0E 270 D3
Western Dvina = Daugava → Latvia 57°4N 24°3E 188 D3
Western Ghats India 14°0N 75°0E 245 H2
Western Highlands □ Papua N. G. 5°45S 144°30E 286 C3
Western Isles □ U.K. 57°30N 7°10W 167 D1
Western Sahara ■ Africa 25°0N 13°0W 260 D2
Western Samoa = Samoa ■ Pac. Oc. 14°0S 172°0W 287 V20
Western Sierra Madre = Madre Occidental, Sierra Mexico 27°0N 107°0W 318 B3
Western Wall Jerusalem 123 b3
Westernport U.S.A. 39°29N 79°3W 309 F14
Westerschelde → Neths. 51°25N 3°25E 170 C3
Westerstede Germany 53°15N 7°55E 178 B3
Westerwald Germany 50°38N 7°56E 178 E3
Westfield Ill., U.S.A. 39°27N 88°0W 311 E8
Westfield Ind., U.S.A. 40°2N 86°8W 311 D10
Westfield Mass., U.S.A. 42°7N 72°45W 313 D12
Westfield N.Y., U.S.A. 42°20N 79°35W 312 D5
Westfield Pa., U.S.A. 41°55N 77°32W 312 E7
Westgate U.S.A. 38°57N 77°6W 143 B3
Westhill U.K. 57°9N 2°19W 167 D6
Westhope U.S.A. 48°55N 101°1W 308 A3
Westlake Western Cape, S. Africa 34°4S 18°26E 118 B1
Westlake Calif., U.S.A. 37°42N 122°29W 136 B2
Westland U.S.A. 42°15N 83°20W 311 B13
Westland △ N.Z. 43°16S 170°16E 285 D5
Westland Bight N.Z. 42°55S 170°5E 285 C5
Westlock Canada 54°9N 113°55W 296 C6
Westmar Australia 27°55S 149°44E 281 D4
Westmeath □ Ireland 53°33N 7°34W 166 C4
Westminster London, U.K. 51°30N 0°7W 125 A3
Westminster Calif., U.S.A. 33°45N 118°0W 307 M8
Westminster Colo., U.S.A. 39°50N 105°2W 304 G11
Westminster Md., U.S.A. 39°34N 76°59W 309 F15
Westmont U.S.A. 40°19N 78°58W 312 F6
Westmorland U.S.A. 33°2N 115°37W 307 M11
Westmount Canada 45°29N 73°35W 130 B2
Weston Ont., Canada 43°42N 79°30W 141 A1
Weston Malaysia 5°10N 115°35E 235 A5
Weston Ohio, U.S.A. 41°21N 83°47W 311 C13
Weston Oreg., U.S.A. 45°49N 118°26W 304 D4
Weston W. Va., U.S.A. 39°2N 80°28W 309 F13
Weston I. Canada 52°33N 79°36W 298 B4
Weston-super-Mare U.K. 51°21N 2°58W 169 F5
Westover U.S.A. 40°45N 78°40W 312 F6
Westphalia U.S.A. 38°26N 92°0W 310 F5
Westport Ont., Canada 44°40N 76°25W 313 B8
Westport Mayo, Ireland 53°48N 9°31W 166 C2
Westport N.Z. 41°46S 171°37E 285 B6
Westport Ind., U.S.A. 39°11N 85°34W 311 E11
Westport N.Y., U.S.A. 44°11N 73°26W 313 B11
Westport Oreg., U.S.A. 46°8N 123°23W 306 D3
Westport Wash., U.S.A. 46°53N 124°6W 306 D2
Westpunt Neth. Ant. 12°22N 69°10W 322 g
Westray Man., Canada 53°36N 101°24W 297 C8
Westray Orkney, U.K. 59°18N 3°0W 167 B5
Westree Canada 47°26N 81°34W 298 C3
Westville Calif., U.S.A. 39°8N 120°42W 306 F6
Westville Fla., U.S.A. 30°46N 85°51W 316 E4
Westville Ill., U.S.A. 40°2N 87°38W 311 D9
Westville Ind., U.S.A. 41°32N 86°54W 311 C10
Westwego U.S.A. 29°54N 90°8W 131 B2
Westwood U.S.A. 40°18N 121°0W 304 F3
Westwood Lakes U.S.A. 25°44N 80°23W 317 K9
Westwood Village U.S.A. 34°3N 118°26W 126 B2
Westzaan Neths. 52°28N 4°46E 112 A1
Wetar Indonesia 7°48S 126°30E 231 F7
Wetaskiwin Canada 52°55N 113°24W 296 C6
Wetherby U.K. 53°56N 1°23W 168 D6
Wethersfield U.S.A. 41°42N 72°40W 313 E12
Wetlet Burma 22°20N 95°53E 241 D5
Wetteren Belgium 51°0N 3°53E 170 D3
Wetton S. Africa 34°0S 18°31E 118 B2
Wetumpka U.S.A. 32°32N 86°13W 316 C3
Wetzlar Germany 50°32N 8°31E 178 E4
Wevok U.S.A. 68°53N 166°13W 303 B6
Wewahitchka U.S.A. 30°7N 85°12W 316 E4
Wewak Papua N. G. 3°38S 143°41E 286 B2
Wewoka U.S.A. 35°9N 96°30W 314 D6
Wexford Ont., Canada 43°45N 79°18W 141 A3
Wexford Wexford, Ireland 52°20N 6°28W 166 D5
Wexford □ Ireland 52°20N 6°25W 166 D5
Wexford Harbour Ireland 52°20N 6°25W 166 D5
Weybridge U.K. 51°22N 0°27W 125 B1
Weyburn Canada 49°40N 103°50W 297 D8
Weyer Markt Austria 47°51N 14°40E 180 D7
Weyhe Germany 52°58N 8°49E 178 C4
Weyib → Ethiopia 7°15N 40°15E 257 F5
Weymouth N.S., Canada 44°30N 66°1W 299 D6
Weymouth Dorset, U.K. 50°37N 2°28W 169 G5
Weymouth Mass., U.S.A. 42°13N 70°58W 313 D14
Weymouth, C. Australia 12°37S 143°27E 280 A3
Wezembeek-Oppem Belgium 50°51N 4°29E 116 A2
Wha Ti Canada 63°8N 117°16W 294 C8
Whakaari = White I. N.Z. 37°30S 177°13E 284 D6
Whakamaru N.Z. 38°23S 175°50E 284 E4
Whakatane N.Z. 37°57S 177°1E 284 D6
Whakatane → N.Z. 37°57S 177°1E 284 D6
Whale → Canada 58°15N 67°40W 299 A6
Whale Cove Canada 62°10N 92°34W 297 A10
Whale Pt. Ascension I. 7°57S 14°18W 153 g
Whales, B. of Antarctica 78°0S 160°0W 151 D12
Whalsay U.K. 60°22N 0°59W 167 A8
Whangaehu → N.Z. 40°3S 175°6E 284 G4
Whangamata N.Z. 37°12S 175°53E 284 D4
Whangamomona N.Z. 39°8S 174°44E 284 F3
Whanganui △ N.Z. 39°17S 174°53E 284 F3
Whangaparaoa Pen. N.Z. 36°40S 174°45E 284 C4
Whangarei N.Z. 35°43S 174°21E 284 B3
Whangarei Harb. N.Z. 35°45S 174°28E 284 B3
Whangaroa Harb. N.Z. 35°4S 173°46E 284 B2
Whangaruru Harb. N.Z. 35°24S 174°23E 284 B3
Wharanui N.Z. 41°55S 174°6E 285 B9
Wharekauri = Chatham Is. Pac. Oc. 44°0S 176°40W 285 a
Wharfe → U.K. 53°51N 1°9W 168 D6
Wharfedale U.K. 54°6N 2°1W 168 C5
Wharton N.J., U.S.A. 40°54N 74°35W 313 F10
Wharton Pa., U.S.A. 41°31N 78°1W 312 E6
Wharton Tex., U.S.A. 29°19N 96°6W 314 G6
Wharton Basin Ind. Oc. 22°0S 92°0E 273 F8
Whataroa N.Z. 43°18S 170°24E 285 D5
Whataroa → N.Z. 43°7S 170°16E 285 D5
Whatcom = Bellingham U.S.A. 48°46N 122°29W 306 B4
Wheatfield U.S.A. 41°13N 87°4W 311 C9
Wheatland Calif., U.S.A. 39°1N 121°25W 306 F5
Wheatland Ind., U.S.A. 38°40N 87°19W 311 F9
Wheatland Wyo., U.S.A. 42°3N 104°58W 304 E11
Wheatley Canada 42°6N 82°27W 312 D2
Wheaton Ill., U.S.A. 41°52N 88°6W 311 C8
Wheaton Md., U.S.A. 39°3N 77°3W 309 F15
Wheaton Minn., U.S.A. 45°48N 96°30W 308 C5
Wheelbarrow Pk. U.S.A. 37°26N 116°5W 306 H10
Wheeler Oreg., U.S.A. 45°41N 123°53W 304 D2
Wheeler Tex., U.S.A. 35°27N 100°16W 314 D4
Wheeler → Canada 57°2N 67°13W 299 A6
Wheeler L. U.S.A. 34°48N 87°23W 315 D11
Wheeler Pk. N. Mex., U.S.A. 36°34N 105°25W 305 H11
Wheeler Pk. Nev., U.S.A. 38°57N 114°15W 304 G6
Wheeler Ridge U.S.A. 35°0N 118°57W 307 L8
Wheelersburg U.S.A. 38°44N 82°51W 309 F12
Wheeling U.S.A. 40°4N 80°43W 312 F4
Whernside U.K. 54°14N 2°24W 168 C5
Whiddy I. Ireland 51°41N 9°31W 166 E2
Whirlwind Reef Papua N. G. 4°42S 148°16E 286 C5
Whiskey Jack L. Canada 58°23N 101°55W 297 B8
Whiskeytown-Shasta-Trinity ⌂ U.S.A. 40°45N 122°15W 304 F2
Whistleduck Cr. → Australia 20°15S 135°18E 280 C2
Whistler Canada 50°7N 122°58W 296 C4
Whitby Ont., Canada 43°52N 78°56W 312 C6
Whitby N. Yorks., U.K. 54°29N 0°37W 168 C7
Whitcombe Pass N.Z. 43°13S 170°55E 285 D5
White → Ark., U.S.A. 33°57N 91°5W 314 E9
White → Ind., U.S.A. 38°25N 87°45W 311 F9
White → S. Dak., U.S.A. 43°42N 99°27W 308 D4
White → Tex., U.S.A. 33°14N 100°56W 314 E4
White → Utah, U.S.A. 40°4N 109°41W 304 F9
White → Vt., U.S.A. 43°37N 72°20W 313 C12
White → Wash., U.S.A. 47°12N 122°15W 306 C4
White, L. Australia 21°9S 128°56E 278 D4
White B. Canada 50°0N 56°35W 299 C8
White Bird U.S.A. 45°46N 116°18W 304 D5
White Butte U.S.A. 46°23N 103°18W 308 B2
White City Fla., U.S.A. 29°53N 85°13W 316 F4
White City Oreg., U.S.A. 42°26N 122°51W 304 E2
White Cliffs Australia 30°50S 143°10E 282 A5
White Cloud Hill = Baiyun Hill China 23°8N 113°15E 121 B2
White Hall U.S.A. 39°26N 90°24W 310 E6
White Haven U.S.A. 41°4N 75°47W 313 E9
White Horse, Vale of U.K. 51°37N 1°30W 169 F6
White House, The Washington, D.C., U.S.A. 143 b1
White I. Grenada 12°26N 61°28W 323 q
White I. Bay of Plenty, N.Z. 37°30S 177°13E 284 D6
White L. Ont., Canada 45°18N 76°31W 313 A8
White L. La., U.S.A. 29°44N 92°30W 314 G8
White Mountain U.S.A. 64°41N 163°24W 303 D7
White Mountain Peak U.S.A. 37°38N 118°15W 305 H4
White Mountains Nat. Recr. Area ⌂ U.S.A. 65°30N 147°40W 303 D11
White Mts. Alaska, U.S.A. 65°30N 146°30W 303 D11
White Mts. Calif., U.S.A. 37°30N 118°15W 306 H8
White Mts. N.H., U.S.A. 44°15N 71°15W 313 B13
White Mts. △ Australia 20°43S 145°12E 280 C4
White Nile = Nîl el Abyad → Sudan 15°38N 32°31E 257 D3
White Nile Dam = Khazzân Jabal al Awliyâ Sudan 15°24N 32°20E 257 D3
White Oak U.S.A. 31°2N 81°43W 316 D8
White Otter L. Canada 49°5N 91°55W 298 C1
White Pass U.S.A. 46°38N 121°24W 306 D5
White Pigeon U.S.A. 41°48N 85°39W 311 C11
White Plains Ga., U.S.A. 33°28N 83°1W 316 B6
White Plains N.Y., U.S.A. 41°2N 73°46W 313 E11
White River Ont., Canada 48°35N 85°20W 298 C2
White River Mpumalanga, S. Africa 25°20S 31°0E 271 C5
White River S. Dak., U.S.A. 43°34N 100°45W 308 D3
White Rock B.C., Canada 49°2N 122°48W 306 A4
White Rock N. Mex., U.S.A. 35°50N 106°12W 305 J10
White Russia = Belarus ■ Europe 53°30N 27°0E 177 B14
White Sands ⌂ U.S.A. 32°46N 106°20W 305 K10
White Sea = Beloye More Russia 66°30N 38°0E 160 C25
White Springs U.S.A. 30°20N 82°45W 316 E7
White Sulphur Springs Mont., U.S.A. 46°33N 110°54W 304 C8
White Sulphur Springs W. Va., U.S.A. 37°48N 80°18W 309 G13
White Swan U.S.A. 46°23N 120°44W 306 D6
White Volta → Ghana 9°10N 1°15W 263 D4
Whitechapel U.K. 51°31N 0°3W 125 A3
Whitecliffs N.Z. 43°26S 171°55E 285 D6
Whitecourt Canada 54°10N 115°45W 296 C5
Whiteface Mt. U.S.A. 44°22N 73°54W 313 B11
Whitefield U.S.A. 44°23N 71°37W 313 B13
Whitefish U.S.A. 48°25N 114°20W 304 B6
Whitefish B. U.S.A. 46°40N 84°55W 298 C3
Whitefish Bay U.S.A. 43°6N 87°54W 311 A9
Whitefish L. Canada 62°41N 106°48W 297 A7
Whitefish Pt. U.S.A. 46°45N 84°59W 309 B11
Whitegull, L. = Goélands, L. aux Canada 55°27N 64°17W 299 A7
Whitehall Dublin, Ireland 53°22N 6°16W 120 A2
Whitehall London, U.K. 125 b3
Whitehall Mich., U.S.A. 43°24N 86°21W 308 D10
Whitehall Mont., U.S.A. 45°52N 112°6W 304 D7
Whitehall N.Y., U.S.A. 43°33N 73°24W 313 C11
Whitehall Wis., U.S.A. 44°22N 91°19W 308 C8
Whitehaven U.K. 54°33N 3°35W 168 C4
Whitehorse Canada 60°43N 135°3W 296 A1
Whiteman Ra. Papua N. G. 5°55S 150°0E 286 C6
Whitemark Australia 40°7S 148°3E 281 G4
Whiteplains Liberia 6°28N 10°40W 262 D2
Whiteriver U.S.A. 33°50N 109°58W 305 K9
Whitesand → Canada 60°9N 115°45W 296 A5
Whitesands S. Africa 34°23S 20°50E 270 D3
Whitesboro N.Y., U.S.A. 43°7N 75°18W 313 C9
Whitesboro Tex., U.S.A. 33°39N 96°54W 314 E6
Whiteshell ⌂ Canada 50°0N 95°40W 297 D9
Whiteside, Canal Chile 53°55S 70°15W 336 D2
Whitesville U.S.A. 42°2N 77°46W 312 D7
Whiteville U.S.A. 34°20N 78°42W 315 D15
Whitewater U.S.A. 42°50N 88°44W 311 B8
Whitewater B. U.S.A. 25°15N 81°0W 317 K8
Whitewater Baldy U.S.A. 33°20N 108°39W 305 K9
Whitewater L. Canada 50°50N 89°10W 298 B2
Whitewood Queens., Australia 21°28S 143°30E 280 C3
Whitewood Sask., Canada 50°20N 102°20W 297 C8
Whitfield Australia 36°42S 146°24E 283 D7
Whithorn U.K. 54°44N 4°26W 167 G4
Whitianga N.Z. 36°47S 175°41E 284 C4
Whiting U.S.A. 41°41N 87°30W 311 C9
Whitman U.S.A. 42°5N 70°56W 313 D14
Whitmore Village U.S.A. 21°31N 158°1W 302 J13
Whitney Ont., Canada 45°31N 78°14W 312 A6
Whitney Nev., U.S.A. 36°4N 115°5W 124 B2
Whitney, Mt. U.S.A. 36°35N 118°18W 306 J8
Whitney Point U.S.A. 42°20N 75°58W 313 D9
Whitstable U.K. 51°21N 1°3E 169 F9
Whitsunday I. Australia 20°15S 149°4E 280 J7
Whitsunday Islands △ Australia 20°15S 149°0E 280 J7
Whitsunday Passage Australia 20°16S 148°51E 280 J6
Whittemore U.S.A. 43°4N 94°26W 310 A2
Whittier Alaska, U.S.A. 60°47N 148°41W 303 F10
Whittier Calif., U.S.A. 33°58N 118°2W 126 C4
Whittlesea Australia 37°27S 145°9E 283 D6
Whitton U.K. 51°27N 0°21W 125 B1
Wholdaia L. Canada 60°43N 104°20W 297 A8
Whyalla Australia 33°2S 137°30E 282 B2
Wiang Kosai △ Thailand 17°54N 99°29E 236 D2
Wiarton Canada 44°40N 81°10W 312 B3
Wiawso Ghana 6°10N 2°25W 262 D4
Wiay U.K. 57°24N 7°13W 167 D1
Wiązów Poland 50°50N 17°10E 185 H4
Wibaux U.S.A. 46°59N 104°11W 304 C11
Wichabai Guyana 2°57N 59°35W 329 C6
Wichian Buri Thailand 15°39N 101°7E 236 E3
Wichita U.S.A. 37°42N 97°20W 308 G5
Wichita Falls U.S.A. 33°54N 98°30W 314 E5
Wick U.K. 58°26N 3°5W 167 C5
Wicked Pt. Canada 43°52N 77°15W 312 C7
Wickenburg U.S.A. 33°58N 112°44W 305 K7
Wickepin Australia 32°50S 117°30E 279 F2
Wickham Australia 20°42S 117°11E 278 D2
Wickham, C. Australia 39°35S 143°57E 281 F3
Wickliffe U.S.A. 41°36N 81°28W 312 E3
Wicklow Ireland 52°59N 6°3W 166 D5
Wicklow □ Ireland 52°57N 6°25W 166 D5
Wicklow Hd. Ireland 52°58N 6°0W 166 D6
Wicklow Mts. Ireland 52°58N 6°26W 166 C5
Wicklow Mts. △ Ireland 53°6N 6°21W 166 C5
Widawa Poland 51°27N 18°51E 185 G5
Widawka → Poland 51°27N 18°52E 185 G5
Wide B. Papua N. G. 5°5S 152°5E 286 C7
Widgeegoara Cr. → Australia 28°51S 146°34E 281 D4
Widgiemooltha Australia 31°30S 121°34E 279 F3
Widnes U.K. 53°23N 2°45W 168 D5
Wido S. Korea 35°35N 126°17E 224 E3
Więcbork Poland 53°21N 17°30E 185 E4
Wieden Austria 48°11N 16°22E 142 A2
Wiehengebirge = Nördlicher Teutoburger Wald-Wiehengebirge ⌂ Germany 52°18N 8°10E 178 C4
Wiehl Germany 50°56N 7°34E 178 E3
Wiek Germany 54°37N 13°17E 178 A9
Wielbark Poland 53°24N 20°55E 184 E7
Wieleń Poland 52°53N 16°9E 185 F3
Wielichowo Poland 52°7N 16°22E 185 F3
Wieliczka Poland 50°0N 20°5E 185 J7
Wielkopolski △ Poland 52°18N 16°45E 185 F3
Wielkopolskie □ Poland 52°10N 17°30E 185 F4
Wieluń Poland 51°15N 18°34E 185 G5
Wien Austria 48°12N 16°22E 142 A2
Wien-Schwechat ✕ (VIE) Austria 48°7N 16°35E 142 B3
Wiener Neustadt Austria 47°49N 16°16E 181 D9
Wienerberg Austria 48°9N 16°21E 142 B2
Wieprz → Poland 51°34N 21°49E 185 G8
Wieprza → Poland 54°26N 16°25E 184 D3
Wieruszów Poland 51°19N 18°9E 185 G5
Wierzbno Poland 52°11N 21°1E 142 B2
Wiesbaden Germany 50°4N 8°14E 179 E4
Wiesental Germany 49°13N 8°31E 179 F4
Wiesloch Germany 49°18N 8°41E 179 F4
Wiesmoor Germany 53°24N 7°47E 178 B3
Wieżyca Poland 54°14N 18°8E 184 D5
Wigan U.K. 53°33N 2°38W 168 D5
Wiggins Colo., U.S.A. 40°14N 104°4W 304 F11
Wiggins Miss., U.S.A. 30°51N 89°8W 315 F10
Wight, I. of U.K. 50°41N 1°17W 169 G6
Wigierski △ Poland 54°5N 23°5E 184 D10
Wigry, Jezioro Poland 54°2N 23°8E 184 D10
Wigston U.K. 52°35N 1°6W 169 E6
Wigton U.K. 54°50N 3°10W 168 C4
Wigtown U.K. 54°53N 4°27W 167 G4
Wigtown B. U.K. 54°46N 4°15W 167 G4
Wijde Wormer Neths. 52°28N 4°52E 112 A2
Wil Switz. 47°28N 9°3E 179 H5
Wilamowice Poland 49°55N 19°9E 185 J6
Wilanów Poland 52°10N 21°4E 142 B2
Wilanówka → Poland 52°13N 21°6E 142 C2
Wilber U.S.A. 40°29N 96°58W 308 E5
Wilberforce Canada 45°2N 78°13W 312 A6
Wilberforce, C. Australia 11°54S 136°35E 280 A2
Wilburton U.S.A. 34°55N 95°19W 314 D7
Wilcannia Australia 31°30S 143°26E 282 A5
Wilcox U.S.A. 41°35N 78°41W 312 E6
Wildbad Germany 48°44N 8°33E 179 G4
Wildcat Cr. → U.S.A. 40°28N 86°52W 311 D10
Wildenschwert = Ústí nad Orlicí Czech Rep. 49°58N 16°24E 181 B9
Wildeshausen Germany 52°54N 8°27E 178 C4
Wildeshauser Geest ⌂ Germany 52°54N 8°30E 178 C4
Wildon Austria 46°52N 15°31E 180 E8
Wildrose U.S.A. 36°14N 117°11W 307 J9
Wilds, The S. Africa 26°10S 28°2E 123 B2
Wildspitze Austria 46°53N 10°53E 180 E3
Wildwood U.S.A. 28°52N 82°2W 317 G7
Wilga Poland 51°52N 21°18E 185 G8
Wilge → S. Africa 27°3S 28°20E 271 C4
Wilhelm, Mt. Papua N. G. 5°50S 145°1E 286 C3
Wilhelm II Coast Antarctica 68°0S 90°0E 151 C7
Wilhelmina Geb. Suriname 3°50N 56°30W 329 C6
Wilhelmina Top = Trikora, Puncak Indonesia 4°15S 138°45E 231 E9
Wilhelmsburg Austria 48°6N 15°36E 180 C8
Wilhelmshagen Germany 52°26N 13°42E 115 B5
Wilhelmshaven Germany 53°31N 8°7E 178 B4
Wilhelmstal Namibia 21°58S 16°21E 270 B2
Wilkes-Barre U.S.A. 41°15N 75°53W 313 E9
Wilkes I. Wake I. 19°18N 166°34E 302 b
Wilkes Land Antarctica 69°0S 120°0E 151 D9
Wilket Creek Park Canada 43°43N 79°21W 141 A2
Wilkie Canada 52°27N 108°42W 297 C7
Wilkieston U.K. 55°54N 3°24W 121 B1
Wilkinsburg U.S.A. 40°26N 79°52W 312 F5
Wilkinson Lakes Australia 29°40S 132°39E 279 E5
Will Rogers State Historical Park ⌂ U.S.A. 34°2N 118°30W 126 B1
Willacoochee U.S.A. 31°20N 83°3W 316 D6
Willandra △ Australia 33°12S 145°0E 283 B6
Willandra Creek → Australia 33°22S 145°52E 282 B6
Willapa B. U.S.A. 46°40N 124°0W 304 C1
Willapa Hills U.S.A. 46°35N 123°25W 306 D3
Willard N.Y., U.S.A. 42°40N 76°50W 312 D8
Willard Ohio, U.S.A. 41°3N 82°44W 312 E2
Willaumez Pen. Papua N. G. 5°15S 150°2E 286 C6
Willbriggie Australia 34°28S 146°2E 283 C7
Willbrook Ireland 53°17N 6°16W 120 B2
Willcox U.S.A. 32°15N 109°50W 305 K9
Willemstad Neth. Ant. 12°5N 68°55W 322 g
Willenberg = Wielbark Poland 53°24N 20°55E 184 E7
Willesden U.K. 51°32N 0°15W 125 A2
Willesden Green U.K. 51°32N 0°13W 125 A2
Willet U.S.A. 42°28N 75°55W 313 D9
Willi Willi △ Australia 30°57S 152°27E 283 A10
William → Canada 59°8N 109°19W 297 B7
William, Mt. Australia 37°17S 142°35E 282 D5
William 'Bill' Dannelly Res. U.S.A. 32°6N 87°24W 315 E11
William Creek Australia 28°58S 136°22E 281 D2
Williams W. Austral., Australia 33°2S 116°52E 279 F2
Williams Ariz., U.S.A. 35°15N 112°11W 305 J7
Williams Calif., U.S.A. 39°9N 122°9W 306 F4
Williams Harbour Canada 52°33N 55°47W 299 B8
Williams Lake Canada 52°10N 122°10W 296 C4
Williamsbridge U.S.A. 40°52N 73°51W 132 A2
Williamsburg Fla., U.S.A. 28°24N 81°26W 133 B2
Williamsburg Iowa, U.S.A. 41°40N 92°1W 310 C4
Williamsburg Ky., U.S.A. 36°44N 84°10W 309 G11
Williamsburg New York, U.S.A. 132 f3
Williamsburg Pa., U.S.A. 40°28N 78°12W 312 F6
Williamsburg Va., U.S.A. 37°16N 76°43W 309 G15
Williamsburg Bridge New York, U.S.A. 132 e2
Williamsfield U.S.A. 40°55N 90°1W 310 D6
Williamson N.Y., U.S.A. 43°14N 77°11W 312 C7
Williamson W. Va., U.S.A. 37°41N 82°17W 309 G12
Williamsport Ind., U.S.A. 40°17N 87°17W 311 D9
Williamsport Pa., U.S.A. 41°15N 77°1W 312 E7
Williamston Mich., U.S.A. 42°41N 84°17W 311 B12
Williamston N.C., U.S.A. 35°51N 77°4W 315 D16
Williamstown Vic., Australia 37°51S 144°52E 128 B1
Williamstown Ky., U.S.A. 38°38N 84°34W 311 F12
Williamstown Mass., U.S.A. 42°43N 73°12W 313 D11
Williamstown N.Y., U.S.A. 43°26N 75°53W 313 C9
Williamsville U.S.A. 39°57N 89°33W 310 E7
Willikies Antigua & B. 17°3N 61°42W 322 b
Willimantic U.S.A. 41°43N 72°13W 313 E12
Willingboro U.S.A. 40°3N 74°54W 309 E16
Willis, L. U.S.A. 28°23N 81°28W 133 B2
Willisburg U.S.A. 37°49N 85°8W 311 G11
Williston Northern Cape, S. Africa 31°20S 20°53E 270 D3
Williston Fla., U.S.A. 29°23N 82°27W 317 F7
Williston N. Dak., U.S.A. 48°9N 103°37W 308 A2
Williston S.C., U.S.A. 33°24N 81°25W 316 B8
Williston L. Canada 56°0N 124°0W 296 B4
Willits U.S.A. 39°25N 123°21W 304 G2
Willmar U.S.A. 45°7N 95°3W 308 C6
Willmore Wilderness ⌂ Canada 53°45N 119°30W 296 C5
Willoughby N.S.W., Australia 33°48S 151°12E 139 A2
Willoughby Ohio, U.S.A. 41°39N 81°24W 312 E3
Willoughby B. Antigua & B. 17°2N 61°44W 322 b
Willow U.S.A. 61°45N 150°3W 303 F10
Willow Bunch Canada 49°20N 105°35W 297 D7
Willow L. Canada 62°10N 119°8W 296 A5
Willow Springs U.S.A. 41°44N 87°51W 119 C1
Willow Tree Australia 31°40S 150°45E 283 A9
Willow Wall, The China 42°10N 122°0E 227 C12
Willowdale Canada 43°46N 79°25W 141 A2
Willowick U.S.A. 41°38N 81°28W 312 E3
Willowlake → Canada 62°42N 123°8W 296 A4
Willowmore S. Africa 33°15S 23°30E 270 D3
Willows U.S.A. 39°31N 122°12W 306 F4
Willowvale = Gatyana S. Africa 32°16S 28°31E 271 D4
Wills, L. Australia 21°25S 128°51E 278 D4
Wills Cr. → Australia 22°43S 140°2E 280 C3
Willsboro U.S.A. 44°21N 73°24W 313 B11
Willunga Australia 35°15S 138°30E 282 C3
Wilma U.S.A. 30°9N 84°58W 316 E5
Wilmersdorf Berlin, Germany 115 c1
Wilmette U.S.A. 42°4N 87°42W 119 A2
Wilmington S. Austral., Australia 32°39S 138°7E 282 B3
Wilmington Kent, U.K. 51°25N 0°12E 125 B5
Wilmington Del., U.S.A. 39°45N 75°33W 309 F16
Wilmington Ill., U.S.A. 41°18N 88°9W 311 C8
Wilmington N.C., U.S.A. 34°14N 77°55W 315 D16
Wilmington Ohio, U.S.A. 39°27N 83°50W 311 E13
Wilmington Vt., U.S.A. 42°52N 72°52W 313 D12
Wilmslow U.K. 53°19N 2°13W 168 D5
Wilna = Vilnius Lithuania 54°38N 25°19E 188 E3
Wilpattu △ Sri Lanka 8°20N 79°50E 245 K4
Wilpena Australia 31°31S 138°37E 282 A3
Wilpena Cr. → Australia 31°25S 139°29E 282 A3
Wilsall U.S.A. 45°59N 110°38W 304 D8
Wilson N.C., U.S.A. 35°44N 77°55W 315 D16
Wilson N.Y., U.S.A. 43°19N 78°50W 312 C6
Wilson Pa., U.S.A. 40°41N 75°15W 313 F9
Wilson → Australia 16°48S 128°16E 278 C4
Wilson Bluff Australia 31°41S 129°0E 279 F4
Wilson Inlet Australia 35°0S 117°22E 279 G2
Wilson Str. Solomon Is. 8°0S 156°39E 287 M9
Wilsons Promontory Australia 38°59S 146°23E 283 E7
Wilsons Promontory △ Australia 38°59S 146°23E 283 D7
Wilster Germany 53°55N 9°23E 178 B5
Wilton Iowa, U.S.A. 41°35N 91°1W 310 C5
Wilton N. Dak., U.S.A. 47°10N 100°47W 308 B3
Wilton → Australia 14°45S 134°33E 280 A1
Wiltshire □ U.K. 51°18N 1°53W 169 F6
Wiltz Lux. 49°57N 5°55E 170 E5
Wiluna Australia 26°36S 120°14E 279 E3
Wimbledon U.K. 51°25N 0°13W 125 B2
Wimbledon Common U.K. 51°26N 0°14W 125 B2
Wimbledon Park U.K. 51°25N 0°11W 125 B2
Wimbledon Tennis Ground U.K. 51°25N 0°12W 125 B2
Wimborne Minster U.K. 50°48N 1°59W 169 G6
Wimereux France 50°45N 1°37E 173 B8
Wimmera → Australia 36°8S 141°56E 282 D4
Winam G. Kenya 0°20S 34°15E 268 C3
Winamac U.S.A. 41°3N 86°36W 311 C10
Winburg S. Africa 28°30S 27°2E 270 C4
Winchelsea Australia 38°10S 144°1E 282 E6
Winchendon U.S.A. 42°41N 72°3W 313 D12
Winchester N.Z. 44°11S 171°17E 285 E6
Winchester Hants., U.K. 51°4N 1°18W 169 F6
Winchester Conn., U.S.A. 41°53N 73°9W 313 E11
Winchester Idaho, U.S.A. 46°14N 116°38W 304 C5
Winchester Ill., U.S.A. 39°38N 90°27W 310 E6
Winchester Ind., U.S.A. 40°10N 84°59W 311 D12
Winchester Ky., U.S.A. 37°59N 84°11W 311 G12
Winchester Mass., U.S.A. 42°26N 71°8W 116 A2
Winchester N.H., U.S.A. 42°46N 72°23W 313 D12
Winchester Nev., U.S.A. 36°7N 115°7W 124 B2
Winchester Ohio, U.S.A. 38°56N 83°39W 311 F13
Winchester Tenn., U.S.A. 35°11N 86°7W 315 D11
Winchester Va., U.S.A. 39°11N 78°10W 309 F14
Wind → U.S.A. 43°12N 108°12W 304 E9
Wind Cave △ U.S.A. 43°32N 103°17W 308 D2
Wind Point U.S.A. 42°47N 87°46W 311 B9
Wind River Range U.S.A. 43°0N 109°30W 304 E9
Windamere Dam Australia 32°48S 149°51E 283 B8
Windau = Ventspils Latvia 57°25N 21°32E 184 A8
Windber U.S.A. 40°14N 78°50W 312 F6
Winder U.S.A. 34°0N 83°45W 316 A6
Windermere Western Cape, S. Africa 33°55S 18°30E 118 A2
Windermere Cumb., U.K. 54°23N 2°55W 168 C5
Windermere Fla., U.S.A. 28°29N 81°32W 133 B1
Windfall U.S.A. 40°22N 85°57W 311 D11
Windhoek Namibia 22°35S 17°4E 270 B2
Windisch-Feistritz = Slovenska Bistrica Slovenia 46°24N 15°35E 199 B12
Windischgarsten Austria 47°42N 14°21E 180 D7
Windischgratz = Slovenj Gradec Slovenia 46°31N 15°5E 199 B12
Windjana Gorge △ Australia 17°51S 125°0E 278 C3
Windom U.S.A. 43°52N 95°7W 308 D6
Windorah Australia 25°24S 142°36E 280 D3
Window Rock U.S.A. 35°41N 109°3W 305 J9
Windrush → U.K. 51°43N 1°24W 169 F6
Windsor N.S.W., Australia 33°37S 150°50E 283 B9
Windsor N.S., Canada 44°59N 64°5W 299 D7
Windsor Ont., Canada 42°18N 83°0W 312 D2
Windsor N.Z. 44°59S 170°49E 285 E5
Windsor Gauteng, S. Africa 26°7S 27°59E 123 A1
Windsor Windsor & Maidenhead, U.K. 51°29N 0°36W 169 F7
Windsor Calif., U.S.A. 38°33N 122°49W 304 G2
Windsor Colo., U.S.A. 40°29N 104°54W 304 F11
Windsor Conn., U.S.A. 41°50N 72°39W 313 E12
Windsor Ill., U.S.A. 39°26N 88°36W 311 E8
Windsor Mo., U.S.A. 38°32N 93°31W 310 F3
Windsor N.Y., U.S.A. 42°5N 75°37W 313 D9
Windsor Vt., U.S.A. 43°29N 72°24W 313 C12
Windsor, Gare Montréal, Canada 130 c2
Windsor & Maidenhead □ U.K. 51°29N 0°40W 169 F7
Windsor Caves Jamaica 18°21N 77°39W 320 a
Windsor Hills U.S.A. 33°59N 118°22W 126 C2
Windsorton S. Africa 28°16S 24°44E 270 C3
Windward Grenada 12°31N 61°26W 323 q
Windward Is. W. Indies 13°0N 61°0W 321 D7
Windward Passage = Vientos, Paso de los Caribbean 20°0N 74°0W 321 C5
Windward Side Neth. Ant. 17°38N 63°14W 322 a
Windy Arbour Ireland 53°18N 6°14W 120 B2
Winefred L. Canada 55°30N 110°30W 297 B6
Winejok Sudan 9°1N 27°30E 257 F2
Winfield Iowa, U.S.A. 41°7N 91°26W 310 C5
Winfield Kans., U.S.A. 37°15N 96°59W 308 G5
Winfield Mo., U.S.A. 39°0N 90°44W 310 F6
Wingate Mts. Australia 14°25S 130°40E 278 B5
Wingham N.S.W., Australia 31°48S 152°22E 283 A10
Wingham Ont., Canada 43°55N 81°20W 312 C3
Winisk Canada 55°20N 85°15W 298 A2
Winisk → Canada 55°17N 85°5W 298 A2
Winisk L. Canada 52°55N 87°22W 298 B2
Wink U.S.A. 31°45N 103°9W 314 F3
Winkler Canada 49°10N 97°56W 297 D9
Winklern Austria 46°52N 12°52E 180 E5
Winlock U.S.A. 46°30N 122°56W 306 D4
Winneba Ghana 5°25N 0°36W 263 D4
Winnebago U.S.A. 42°16N 89°15W 310 B7
Winnebago, L. U.S.A. 44°0N 88°26W 308 D9
Winnecke Cr. → Australia 18°35S 131°34E 278 C5
Winnemucca U.S.A. 40°58N 117°44W 304 F5
Winnemucca L. U.S.A. 40°7N 119°21W 304 F4
Winner U.S.A. 43°22N 99°52W 308 D4
Winnett U.S.A. 47°0N 108°21W 304 C9
Winnfield U.S.A. 31°56N 92°38W 314 F8
Winnibigoshish, L. U.S.A. 47°27N 94°13W 308 B6
Winning Germany 48°2N 11°37E 131 B2
Winnipeg Canada 49°54N 97°9W 297 D9
Winnipeg → Canada 50°38N 96°19W 297 C9
Winnipeg, L. Canada 52°0N 97°0W 297 C9
Winnipeg Beach Canada 50°30N 96°58W 297 C9
Winnipegosis Canada 51°39N 99°55W 297 C9
Winnipegosis L. Canada 52°30N 100°0W 297 C9
Winnipesaukee, L. U.S.A. 43°38N 71°21W 313 C13
Winnisquam L. U.S.A. 43°33N 71°31W 313 C13
Winnsboro La., U.S.A. 32°10N 91°43W 314 E9
Winnsboro S.C., U.S.A. 34°23N 81°5W 315 D14
Winnsboro Tex., U.S.A. 32°58N 95°17W 314 E7
Winokapau, L. Canada 53°15N 62°50W 299 B7
Winona Minn., U.S.A. 44°3N 91°39W 308 C8
Winona Miss., U.S.A. 33°29N 89°44W 315 E10
Winooski U.S.A. 44°29N 73°11W 313 B11
Winooski → U.S.A. 44°32N 73°17W 313 B11
Winschoten Neths. 53°9N 7°3E 170 A7
Winsen Germany 53°22N 10°13E 178 B6
Winsford U.K. 53°12N 2°31W 168 D5
Winslow = Bainbridge Island U.S.A. 47°38N 122°32W 306 C4
Winslow Ariz., U.S.A. 35°2N 110°42W 305 J8
Winslow Ind., U.S.A. 38°23N 87°13W 311 F9
Winslow Reef Kiribati 1°36S 174°57W 277 A16
Winsted U.S.A. 41°55N 73°4W 313 E11
Winston-Salem U.S.A. 36°6N 80°15W 315 C14
Winter Garden U.S.A. 28°34N 81°35W 317 G8
Winter Haven U.S.A. 28°1N 81°44W 317 G8
Winter Park U.S.A. 28°36N 81°20W 317 G8
Winterberg Germany 51°11N 8°33E 178 D4
Winterhaven U.S.A. 32°44N 114°38W 307 N12
Winters U.S.A. 38°32N 121°58W 306 G5
Winterset U.S.A. 41°20N 94°1W 310 C3
Wintersville U.S.A. 40°23N 80°42W 312 F4
Winterswijk Neths. 51°58N 6°43E 170 C6
Winterthur Switz. 47°30N 8°44E 179 H4
Winthrop U.S.A. 48°28N 120°10W 304 B3
Winton Queens., Australia 22°24S 143°3E 280 C3
Winton N.Z. 46°8S 168°20E 285 G3
Wintua Vanuatu 16°30S 167°26E 287 F5
Wipper → Germany 51°16N 11°12E 178 D7
Wirraminna Australia 31°12S 136°13E 282 A2
Wirrulla Australia 32°24S 134°31E 281 E1
Wisbech U.K. 52°41N 0°9E 169 E8
Wisconsin □ U.S.A. 44°45N 89°30W 310 B7
Wisconsin → U.S.A. 43°0N 91°15W 310 A5
Wisconsin Rapids U.S.A. 44°23N 89°49W 308 C9
Wisdom U.S.A. 45°37N 113°27W 304 D7
Wiseman U.S.A. 67°25N 150°6W 303 C10
Wishaw U.K. 55°46N 3°54W 167 F5
Wishek U.S.A. 46°16N 99°33W 308 B4
Wisła Poland 49°38N 18°53E 185 J5
Wisła → Poland 54°22N 18°55E 184 D5
Wisłok → Poland 50°13N 22°32E 185 H9
Wisłoka → Poland 50°27N 21°23E 185 H8
Wismar Mecklenburg-Vorpommern, Germany 53°54N 11°29E 178 B7
Wismar Guyana 5°59N 58°18W 329 B6
Wisner U.S.A. 41°59N 96°55W 308 E5
Wissant France 50°52N 1°40E 173 B8
Wissembourg France 49°2N 7°57E 173 C14
Wissous France 48°44N 2°19E 134 B2
Wisznice Poland 51°48N 23°13E 185 G10
Witbank = eMalahleni S. Africa 25°51S 29°14E 271 C4
Witdraai S. Africa 26°58S 20°48E 270 C3
Witham U.K. 51°48N 0°40E 169 F8
Witham → U.K. 52°59N 0°2W 168 E7
Withernsea U.K. 53°44N 0°1E 168 D8
Withlacoochee → Fla., U.S.A. 30°24N 83°10W 316 E6
Withlacoochee → Fla., U.S.A. 29°0N 82°45W 317 G7
Witjira △ Australia 26°22S 135°37E 281 D2
Witkowo Poland 52°26N 17°45E 185 F4
Witless Bay Canada 47°17N 52°50W 299 C9
Witney U.K. 51°48N 1°28W 169 F6
Witnica Poland 52°40N 14°54E 185 F1
Witnossob → Namibia 23°55S 18°45E 270 C3
Wittdün Germany 54°38N 8°23E 178 A4
Witte Pan Neth. Ant. 12°3N 68°17W 322 h
Witten Germany 51°26N 7°20E 178 D3
Wittenau Germany 52°35N 13°19E 115 A2
Wittenberge Germany 53°0N 11°45E 178 B7
Wittenburg Germany 53°31N 11°4E 178 B7
Wittenheim France 47°44N 7°20E 173 E14
Wittenoom Australia 22°15S 118°20E 278 D2
Witti, Banjaran Malaysia 5°11N 116°29E 235 A5
Wittingau = Třeboň Czech Rep. 49°1N 14°48E 180 B7
Wittingen Germany 52°44N 10°44E 178 C6
Wittlich Germany 49°59N 6°53E 179 F2
Wittmund Germany 53°34N 7°46E 178 B3
Wittow Germany 54°38N 13°20E 178 A9
Wittstock Germany 53°10N 12°28E 178 B8
Witu Kenya 2°23S 40°26E 268 C5
Witu Is. Papua N. G. 4°50S 149°25E 286 C5
Witvlei Namibia 22°23S 18°32E 270 B2
Witwatersrand, Univ. of S. Africa 26°11S 28°1E 123 B2
Witzenhausen Germany 51°20N 9°51E 178 D5
Wiwon N. Korea 40°54N 126°3E 224 B3
Wixom U.S.A. 42°32N 83°32W 311 B13
Wkra → Poland 52°27N 20°44E 185 F7
Władysławowo Poland 54°48N 18°25E 184 D5
Wleń Poland 51°2N 15°39E 185 G2
Wlingi Indonesia 8°5S 112°25E 235 D4
Włochy Poland 52°12N 20°54E 142 B1
Włocławek Poland 52°40N 19°3E 185 F6
Włodawa Poland 51°33N 23°31E 185 G10
Włoszczowa Poland 50°50N 19°55E 185 H6
Wo Mei China 22°21N 114°15E 122 A2
Wo Yi Hop China 22°23N 114°8E 122 A1
Woburn Ont., Canada 43°46N 79°12W 141 A3
Woburn Mass., U.S.A. 42°29N 71°9W 116 A2
Wodian China 32°50N 112°35E 226 H7
Wodonga Australia 36°5S 146°50E 283 D7
Wodzisław Śląski Poland 50°1N 18°26E 185 H5
Wœrth France 48°57N 7°45E 173 D14
Wohlau = Wołów Poland 51°20N 16°38E 185 G3
Woinbogoin China 32°51N 98°39E 228 A2
Woippy France 49°10N 6°8E 173 C13
Woitape Papua N. G. 8°33S 147°15E 286 E4
Wojcieszow Poland 50°58N 15°55E 185 H2
Wokam Indonesia 5°45S 134°28E 231 F8
Wokha India 26°6N 94°16E 241 B5
Woking U.K. 51°19N 0°34W 169 F7
Wokingham U.K. 51°24N 0°49W 169 F7
Wokingham □ U.K. 51°25N 0°51W 169 F7
Woko △ Australia 31°46S 151°49E 283 A9
Wola Poland 52°14N 20°57E 142 B1
Wolbrom Poland 50°24N 19°45E 185 H6
Wolcottville U.S.A. 41°32N 85°22W 311 C11
Wołczyn Poland 51°1N 18°3E 185 G5
Woldegk Germany 53°27N 13°34E 178 B9
Woldenberg = Dobiegniew Poland 52°59N 15°45E 185 F2
Woldenberg Park New Orleans, U.S.A. 131 b3
Wolf → Canada 60°17N 132°33W 296 A2
Wolf, Volcán Ecuador 0°2N 91°20W 330 a
Wolf Creek U.S.A. 47°0N 112°4W 304 C7
Wolf L. Canada 60°24N 131°40W 296 A2
Wolf Point U.S.A. 48°5N 105°39W 304 B11
Wolf Trap Farm Park U.S.A. 38°56N 77°17W 143 B2
Wolfe I. Canada 44°7N 76°20W 313 B8
Wolfeboro U.S.A. 43°35N 71°13W 313 C13
Wolfen Germany 51°39N 12°15E 178 D8
Wolfenbüttel Germany 52°10N 10°33E 178 C6
Wolfratshausen Germany 47°54N 11°24E 179 H7
Wolfsberg Austria 46°50N 14°52E 180 E7
Wolfsburg Germany 52°25N 10°48E 178 C6
Wolgast Germany 54°3N 13°44E 178 A9
Wolgok S. Korea 37°35N 127°1E 137 B2
Wolhusen Switz. 47°4N 8°4E 179 H4
Wolica Warszawa, Poland 52°9N 21°3E 142 C2
Wolica Warszawa, Poland 52°7N 20°51E 142 C1
Wolin Poland 53°50N 14°37E 184 E1
Woliński △ Poland 53°57N 14°28E 184 E1
Wólka Węglowa Poland 52°18N 20°52E 142 B1
Wollaston U.S.A. 42°15N 71°2W 116 B2
Wollaston, Is. Chile 55°40S 67°30W 336 E3
Wollaston Forland Greenland 74°25N 19°40W 154 C9
Wollaston L. Canada 58°7N 103°10W 297 B8
Wollaston Lake Canada 58°3N 103°33W 297 B8
Wollaston Pen. Canada 69°30N 115°0W 294 C8
Wollemi △ Australia 33°0S 150°30E 283 B9
Wollongong Australia 34°25S 150°54E 283 C9
Wolmar = Valmiera Latvia 57°37N 25°29E 188 D3
Wolmaransstad S. Africa 27°12S 25°59E 270 C4
Wolmirstedt Germany 52°14N 11°37E 178 C7
Wołomin Poland 52°19N 21°15E 185 F8
Wołów Poland 51°20N 16°38E 185 G3
Wolseley S. Austral., Australia 36°23S 140°54E 282 D4
Wolseley Western Cape, S. Africa 33°26S 19°7E 270 D2
Wolsey U.S.A. 44°25N 98°28W 308 C4
Wolstenholme, C. Canada 62°35N 77°30W 292 C12
Wolsztyn Poland 52°8N 16°5E 185 F3
Woltersdorf Germany 52°27N 13°44E 115 B5

446 Woluwe-St-Lambert
INDEX

Woluwe-St-Lambert *Belgium* 50°50N 4°24E **116** A2
Woluwe-St-Pierre *Belgium* 50°50N 4°25E **116** A2
Wolvega *Neths.* 52°52N 6°0E **170** B6
Wolverhampton *U.K.* 52°35N 2°7W **169** E5
Wondai *Australia* 26°20S 151°49E **281** D5
Wonenara *Papua N. G.* 6°48S 145°53E **286** D3
Wong Chuk Hang *China* 22°15N 114°10E **122** B2
Wong Chuk Wan *China* 22°23N 114°17E **122** A2
Wong Chuk Yeung *China* 22°24N 114°15E **122** A2
Wong Tai Sin *China* 22°20N 114°11E **122** A2
Wonga Wongué △ *Gabon* 0°29S 9°25E **264** C1
Wongalarroo L. *Australia* 31°32S 144°0E **282** A6
Wongan Hills *Australia* 30°51S 116°37E **279** F2
Wonju *S. Korea* 37°22N 127°58E **224** D3
Wonosari *Indonesia* 7°58S 110°36E **235** D4
Wonosobo *Indonesia* 7°22S 109°54E **235** D3
Wonowon *Canada* 56°44N 121°48W **296** B4
Wŏnsan *N. Korea* 39°11N 127°27E **224** C3
Wonthaggi *Australia* 38°37S 145°37E **283** E6
Wood Buffalo △ *Canada* 59°0N 113°41W **296** B6
Wood Green *U.K.* 51°36N 0°6W **125** A3
Wood Is. *Australia* 16°24S 123°19E **278** C3
Wood L. *Canada* 55°17N 103°17W **297** B8
Wood Ridge *U.S.A.* 40°50N 74°4W **132** A1
Wood River *U.S.A.* 38°52N 90°5W **310** F6
Woodah, I. *Australia* 13°27S 136°10E **280** A2
Woodbine *U.S.A.* 30°58N 81°44W **316** E8
Woodbine Race Track *Canada* 43°43N 79°36W **141** A1
Woodbourne *U.S.A.* 41°46N 74°36W **313** E10
Woodbridge *Ont., Canada* 43°47N 79°36W **141** A1
Woodbridge *Suffolk, U.K.* 52°6N 1°20E **169** E9
Woodbridge B. *Dominica* 15°19N 61°25W **323** k
Woodburn *U.S.A.* 45°9N 122°51W **304** D2
Woodbury *U.S.A.* 32°59N 84°35W **316** C5
Woodenbong *Australia* 28°24S 152°39E **281** D5
Woodend *Australia* 37°20S 144°33E **282** D6
Woodford *Queens., Australia* 26°58S 152°47E **281** D5
Woodford *London, U.K.* 51°36N 0°2E **125** A4
Woodford Bridge *U.K.* 51°36N 0°3E **125** A4
Woodford Green *U.K.* 51°36N 0°2E **125** A4
Woodfords *U.S.A.* 38°47N 119°50W **306** G7
Woodhaven *U.S.A.* 40°41N 73°51W **132** B2
Woodhouselee *U.K.* 55°52N 3°13W **121** B2
Woodlake *U.S.A.* 36°25N 119°6W **306** J7
Woodland *Calif., U.S.A.* 38°41N 121°46W **306** G5
Woodland *Maine, U.S.A.* 45°9N 67°25W **309** C20
Woodland *Pa., U.S.A.* 41°0N 78°21W **312** F6
Woodland *Wash., U.S.A.* 45°54N 122°45W **306** E4
Woodland Caribou ⌂ *Canada* 51°0N 94°45W **297** C10
Woodlands *Singapore* 1°26N 103°46E **138** A2
Woodlands, The *U.S.A.* 30°9N 95°29W **314** F7
Woodlark I. *Papua N. G.* 9°10S 152°50E **286** E7
Woodmont *U.S.A.* 38°59N 77°55W **143** B3
Woodonga *Australia* 36°10S 146°50E **281** F4
Woodridge *Canada* 49°20N 96°9W **297** D9
Woodroffe, Mt. *Australia* 26°20S 131°45E **279** E5
Woods, L. *Australia* 17°50S 133°30E **280** B1
Woods, L. of the *Canada* 49°15N 94°45W **297** D10
Woodside *S. Austral., Australia* 34°58S 138°52E **282** C3
Woodside *Vic., Australia* 38°31S 146°52E **283** E7
Woodside *London, U.K.* 51°23N 0°4W **125** B3
Woodside *N.Y., U.S.A.* 40°44N 73°54W **132** B2
Woodson *U.S.A.* 39°37N 90°14W **310** E6
Woodstock *N.S.W., Australia* 33°45S 148°53E **283** B8
Woodstock *Queens., Australia* 19°35S 146°50E **280** B4
Woodstock *N.B., Canada* 46°11N 67°37W **299** C6
Woodstock *Ont., Canada* 43°10N 80°45W **312** C4
Woodstock *Western Cape, S. Africa* 33°55S 18°27E **118** A1
Woodstock *Oxon., U.K.* 51°51N 1°20W **169** F6
Woodstock *Ga., U.S.A.* 34°6N 84°31W **316** A5
Woodstock *Ill., U.S.A.* 42°19N 88°27W **311** B8
Woodstock *Vt., U.S.A.* 43°37N 72°31W **313** C12
Woodsville *U.S.A.* 44°9N 72°2W **313** B13
Woodville *N.Z.* 40°20S 175°53E **284** G4
Woodville *Fla., U.S.A.* 30°19N 84°15W **316** E5
Woodville *Ga., U.S.A.* 33°40N 83°7W **316** B6
Woodville *Miss., U.S.A.* 31°6N 91°18W **314** F9
Woodville *Ohio, U.S.A.* 41°27N 83°22W **311** C13
Woodville *Tex., U.S.A.* 30°47N 94°25W **314** F7
Woodward *U.S.A.* 36°26N 99°24W **314** C5
Woody *U.S.A.* 35°42N 118°50W **307** K8
Woody → *Canada* 52°31N 100°51W **297** C8
Woolacombe *U.K.* 51°10N 4°13W **169** F3
Woolamai, C. *Australia* 38°30S 145°23E **283** E6
Woolbrook *Australia* 30°56S 151°25E **283** A9
Wooler *U.K.* 55°33N 2°1W **168** B5
Woolgoolga *Australia* 30°6S 153°11E **281** E5
Woollahra *Australia* 33°53S 151°15E **139** B2
Woolloomooloo *Sydney, Australia* **139** b2
Woolooware B. *Australia* 34°1S 151°8E **139** C1
Woolwich *U.K.* 51°29N 0°4E **125** B4
Woolworth Building *New York, U.S.A.* **132** e1
Woomargama △ *Australia* 35°50S 147°15E **283** C7
Woomera *Australia* 31°5S 136°50E **282** A2
Woonsocket *R.I., U.S.A.* 42°0N 71°31W **313** E13
Woonsocket *S. Dak., U.S.A.* 44°3N 98°17W **308** C4
Wooramel → *Australia* 25°47S 114°10E **279** E1
Wooramel Roadhouse *Australia* 25°45S 114°17E **279** E1
Wooroonooran △ *Australia* 16°25S 146°1E **280** B4
Wooster *U.S.A.* 40°48N 81°56W **312** F3
Woraksan △ *S. Korea* 36°50N 128°5E **224** D4
Worcester *Western Cape, S. Africa* 33°39S 19°27E **270** D2
Worcester *Worcs., U.K.* 52°11N 2°12W **169** E5
Worcester *Mass., U.S.A.* 42°16N 71°48W **313** D13
Worcester *N.Y., U.S.A.* 42°36N 74°45W **313** D10
Worcestershire □ *U.K.* 52°13N 2°10W **169** E5
Worden *U.S.A.* 38°56N 89°50W **310** F7
Wörgl *Austria* 47°29N 12°3E **180** D5
Workington *U.K.* 54°39N 3°33W **168** C4
Worksop *U.K.* 53°18N 1°7W **168** D6
Workum *Neths.* 52°59N 5°26E **170** B5
Worland *U.S.A.* 44°1N 107°57W **304** D10
World Bank *Washington, D.C., U.S.A.* **143** b1
World Financial Center *New York, U.S.A.* **132** e1
World Trade Center *Los Angeles, U.S.A.* **127** b1
World Trade Center *New Orleans, U.S.A.* **131** b3
World Trade Center, site of former *U.S.A.* 40°42N 74°0W **132** B1
World Trade Centre *Montréal, Canada* **130** c2
World War Two Memorial *Washington, D.C., U.S.A.* **143** b1
Worli *India* 19°1N 72°49E **130** A1
Wormhout *France* 50°52N 2°28E **173** B9
Worms *Germany* 49°37N 8°21E **179** F4
Worsley *Canada* 56°31N 119°8W **296** B5
Wörth *Bayern, Germany* 49°1N 12°24E **179** F8
Worth *Ill., U.S.A.* 41°41N 87°47W **119** C2
Wortham *U.S.A.* 31°47N 96°28W **314** F6
Wörther See *Austria* 46°37N 14°10E **180** E7
Worthing *U.K.* 50°49N 0°21W **169** G7
Worthington *Ind., U.S.A.* 39°7N 86°59W **311** E10
Worthington *Minn., U.S.A.* 43°37N 95°36W **308** D6
Worthington *Ohio, U.S.A.* 40°5N 83°1W **311** D13
Worthington *Pa., U.S.A.* 40°50N 79°38W **312** F5
Wosi *Indonesia* 0°15S 128°0E **231** F7
Wote *Kenya* 1°47S 37°38E **268** C4
Wou-han = Wuhan *China* 30°31N 114°18E **229** B10
Wour *Chad* 21°14N 16°0E **259** D3
Wousi = Wuxi *China* 31°33N 120°18E **229** B13
Wowoni *Indonesia* 4°5S 123°5E **231** E6
Woy Woy *Australia* 33°30S 151°19E **283** B9
Wrangel I. = Vrangelya, Ostrov *Russia* 71°0N 180°0E **215** B19
Wrangell *U.S.A.* 56°28N 132°23W **296** B2
Wrangell Mts. *U.S.A.* 61°30N 142°0W **303** F12
Wrangell-St. Elias △ *U.S.A.* 61°0N 142°0W **303** F12
Wrath, C. *U.K.* 58°38N 5°1W **167** C3
Wray *U.S.A.* 40°5N 102°13W **304** F12
Wrekin, The *U.K.* 52°41N 2°32W **169** E5
Wrens *U.S.A.* 33°12N 82°23W **316** B7
Wren's Nest *U.S.A.* 33°44N 84°25W **113** B2
Wrexham *U.K.* 53°3N 3°0W **168** D4
Wrexham □ *U.K.* 53°1N 2°58W **168** D5
Wriezen *Germany* 52°42N 14°7E **178** C10
Wright = Paranas *Phil.* 11°42N 125°2E **233** F5
Wright *Fla., U.S.A.* 30°27N 86°38W **317** E3
Wright *Wyo., U.S.A.* 43°45N 105°28W **304** E11
Wright Pt. *Canada* 43°48N 81°44W **312** C3
Wrightmyo *India* 11°47N 92°43E **245** J11
Wrightson, Mt. *U.S.A.* 31°42N 110°51W **305** L8
Wrightsville *U.S.A.* 32°44N 82°43W **316** C7
Wrightwood *U.S.A.* 34°22N 117°38W **307** L9
Wrigley *Canada* 63°16N 123°37W **294** C7
Wrigley Building *Chicago, U.S.A.* **119** b2
Wrigley Field *U.S.A.* 41°56N 87°39W **119** B3
Wrocław *Poland* 51°5N 17°5E **185** G4
Wronki *Poland* 52°41N 16°21E **185** F3
Września *Poland* 52°21N 17°36E **185** F4
Wschowa *Poland* 51°48N 16°20E **185** G3
Wu Hsi → *Taiwan* 24°9N 120°31E **225** B2
Wu Jiang → *China* 29°40N 107°20E **228** C6
Wu Kau Tang *China* 22°30N 114°14E **219** F11
Wu'an *China* 36°40N 114°15E **226** F8
Wubin *Australia* 30°6S 116°37E **279** F2
Wubu *China* 37°28N 110°42E **226** F6
Wuchang *China* 44°55N 127°5E **227** B14
Wucheng *China* 37°12N 116°20E **226** F9
Wuch'i *Taiwan* 24°16N 120°31E **225** B2
Wuchieh *Taiwan* 24°41N 121°47E **225** B3
Wuchow = Wuzhou *China* 23°30N 111°18E **229** F8
Wuchuan *Guangdong, China* 21°33N 110°43E **229** G8
Wuchuan *Guizhou, China* 28°25N 108°3E **228** C7
Wuchuan *Nei Monggol Zizhiqu, China* 41°5N 111°28E **226** D6
Wuday'ah *Si. Arabia* 17°2N 47°7E **248** C4
Wudi *China* 37°40N 117°35E **227** F9
Wuding *China* 25°24N 102°21E **228** E4
Wuding He → *China* 37°2N 110°23E **226** F6
Wudinna *Australia* 33°0S 135°22E **281** E2
Wudu *China* 33°22N 104°54E **226** H3
Wufeng *Henan, China* 30°12N 110°42E **229** B8
Wufeng *Taiwan* 24°4N 120°42E **225** B2
Wugang *China* 26°44N 110°35E **229** D8
Wugong Shan *China* 27°30N 114°0E **229** D9
Wuguishan *China* 22°25N 113°25E **219** G9
Wuhai *China* 39°47N 106°52E **218** C5
Wuhan *China* 30°31N 114°18E **229** B10
Wuhe *China* 33°10N 117°50E **227** H9
Wuhlgarten *Germany* 52°31N 13°34E **115** A4
Wuhsi = Wuxi *China* 31°33N 120°18E **229** B13
Wuhu *China* 31°22N 118°21E **229** B12
Wujiang *China* 31°10N 120°38E **229** B13
Wujiaochang *China* 31°18N 121°31E **138** B2
Wujih *Taiwan* 24°6N 120°38E **225** B2
Wukari *Nigeria* 7°51N 9°42E **263** D6
Wulai *Taiwan* 24°52N 121°33E **225** B3
Wulajie *China* 44°6N 126°33E **227** B14
Wulanbulang *China* 41°5N 110°55E **226** D6
Wular L. *India* 34°20N 74°30E **243** B6
Wulehe *Ghana* 8°39N 0°0 **263** D5
Wulff Land *Greenland* 82°0N 49°0W **154** A6
Wulian *China* 35°40N 119°12E **227** G10
Wuliang Shan *China* 24°30N 100°40E **228** E3
Wuliaru *Indonesia* 7°27S 131°0E **231** F8
Wulicheng *Taiwan* 23°47N 121°0E **225** C3
Wuling Shan *China* 30°0N 110°0E **228** C7
Wulong *China* 29°22N 107°43E **228** C6
Wulu *Taiwan* 23°10N 121°2E **225** C3
Wulumuchi = Ürümqi *China* 43°45N 87°45E **217** D11
Wum *Cameroon* 6°24N 10°2E **263** D7
Wuming *China* 23°12N 108°18E **228** F7
Wun Rog *Sudan* 9°0N 28°20E **257** F2
Wundanyi *Kenya* 3°24S 38°22E **268** C4
Wuning *China* 29°17N 115°5E **229** C10
Wunna → *India* 20°18N 78°48E **244** D4
Wunnummin L. *Canada* 52°55N 89°10W **298** B2
Wunsiedel *Germany* 50°2N 12°0E **179** E8
Wunstorf *Germany* 52°25N 9°26E **178** C5
Wuntho *Burma* 23°55N 95°45E **241** D5
Wupatki ⌂ *U.S.A.* 35°35N 111°20W **305** J8
Wuping *China* 25°5N 116°5E **229** E11
Wuppertal *Nordrhein-Westfalen, Germany* 51°16N 7°12E **178** D3
Wuppertal *Western Cape, S. Africa* 32°13S 19°12E **270** D2
Wuqia *China* 39°40N 75°7E **217** E9
Wuqing *China* 39°23N 117°4E **227** E9
Würm → *Germany* 48°8N 11°27E **131** B1
Würm-kanal *Germany* 48°13N 11°29E **131** A1
Wurtsboro *U.S.A.* 41°35N 74°29W **313** E10
Würzburg *Germany* 49°46N 9°55E **179** F5
Wurzen *Germany* 51°22N 12°44E **178** D8
Wushan *China* 34°43N 104°53E **226** G3
Wushi *China* 41°9N 79°13E **217** D9
Wushishi *Nigeria* 9°46N 6°7E **263** D6
Wusi *Vanuatu* 15°21S 166°40E **287** E4
Wusih = Wuxi *China* 31°33N 120°18E **229** B13
Wusong *China* 31°22N 121°29E **138** A1
Wutach → *Germany* 47°37N 8°15E **179** H4
Wutai *China* 38°40N 113°12E **226** E7
Wuting = Huimin *China* 37°27N 117°28E **227** F9
Wutong *China* 25°24N 110°4E **229** E8
Wutonghaolai *China* 42°50N 120°5E **227** C11
Wutongqiao *China* 29°22N 103°50E **228** C4
Wutung *Papua N. G.* 2°37S 141°1E **286** B1
Wuwei *Anhui, China* 31°18N 117°54E **229** B11
Wuwei *Gansu, China* 37°57N 102°34E **218** C5
Wuxi *Jiangsu, China* 31°33N 120°18E **229** B13
Wuxi *Sichuan, China* 31°23N 109°35E **228** B7
Wuxiang *China* 36°49N 112°50E **226** F7
Wuxuan *China* 23°34N 109°38E **228** F7
Wuxue *China* 29°52N 115°30E **229** C10
Wuyang *China* 33°25N 113°35E **226** H7
Wuyi *Hebei, China* 37°46N 115°56E **226** F8
Wuyi *Zhejiang, China* 28°52N 119°50E **229** C12
Wuyi Shan *China* 27°0N 117°0E **229** D11
Wuyishan *China* 27°45N 118°0E **229** D12
Wuyo *Nigeria* 10°23N 11°50E **263** C7
Wuyuan *Jiangxi, China* 29°15N 117°50E **229** C11
Wuyuan *Nei Monggol Zizhiqu, China* 41°2N 108°20E **226** D5
Wuzhai *China* 38°54N 111°48E **226** E6
Wuzhi Shan *China* 18°45N 109°45E **236** C7
Wuzhong *China* 38°2N 106°12E **226** E4
Wuzhou *China* 23°30N 111°18E **229** F8
Wyaaba Cr. → *Australia* 16°27S 141°35E **280** B3
Wyalkatchem *Australia* 31°8S 117°22E **279** F2
Wyalusing *U.S.A.* 41°40N 76°16W **313** E8
Wyandotte *U.S.A.* 42°12N 83°9W **311** B13
Wyandra *Australia* 27°12S 145°56E **281** D4
Wyangala, L. *Australia* 33°54S 149°0E **283** B8
Wyara, L. *Australia* 28°42S 144°14E **281** D3
Wycheproof *Australia* 36°5S 143°17E **282** D5
Wycliffe Well *Australia* 20°48S 134°14E **280** C1
Wyczółki *Poland* 52°9N 20°59E **142** C1
Wye → *U.K.* 51°38N 2°40W **169** F5
Wyemandoo *Australia* 28°28S 118°29E **279** E2
Wygoda *Poland* 52°15N 21°7E **142** B2
Wyk *Germany* 54°41N 8°33E **178** A4
Wymondham *U.K.* 52°35N 1°7E **169** E9
Wymore *U.S.A.* 40°7N 96°40W **308** E5
Wynberg *S. Africa* 34°2S 18°28E **118** B1
Wyndham *W. Austral., Australia* 15°33S 128°3E **278** C4
Wyndham *N.Z.* 46°20S 168°51E **285** G3
Wynyard *Tas., Australia* 41°5S 145°44E **281** G4
Wynyard *Sask., Canada* 51°45N 104°10W **297** C8
Wyola L. *Australia* 29°8S 130°17E **279** E5
Wyoming = Plympton-Wyoming *Canada* 42°57N 82°7W **312** D2
Wyoming *Ill., U.S.A.* 41°4N 89°47W **310** C7
Wyoming *Iowa, U.S.A.* 42°4N 91°0W **310** B6
Wyoming *Mich., U.S.A.* 42°54N 85°42W **311** B11
Wyoming □ *U.S.A.* 43°0N 107°30W **304** E10
Wyomissing *U.S.A.* 40°20N 75°59W **313** F9
Wyong *Australia* 33°14S 151°24E **283** B9
Wyperfeld △ *Australia* 35°35S 141°42E **282** C4
Wyrzysk *Poland* 53°10N 17°17E **185** E4
Wyśmierzyce *Poland* 51°37N 20°50E **185** G7
Wysoka *Poland* 53°13N 17°2E **185** E4
Wysokie *Poland* 50°55N 22°40E **185** H9
Wysokie Mazowieckie *Poland* 52°55N 22°30E **185** F9
Wyszków *Poland* 52°36N 21°25E **185** F8
Wyszogród *Poland* 52°23N 20°9E **185** F7
Wytheville *U.S.A.* 36°57N 81°5W **309** G13
Wyżyna Małopolska *Poland* 50°45N 20°0E **185** H7

X

Xa-Cassau *Angola* 9°5S 20°15E **265** D4
Xa-Muteba *Angola* 9°34S 17°50E **265** D3
Xaafuun *Somali Rep.* 10°25N 51°16E **267** B7
Xaafuun, Ras *Somali Rep.* 10°27N 51°24E **267** B7
Xabregas *Portugal* 38°43N 9°6W **126** A2
Xaçmaz *Azerbaijan* 41°31N 48°42E **191** K9
Xadded *Somali Rep.* 9°46N 48°2E **267** C6
Xaghra *Malta* 36°3N 14°16E **206** E7
Xai-Xai *Mozam.* 25°6S 33°31E **271** C5
Xaidulla *China* 36°28N 77°59E **217** E9
Xainza *China* 30°58N 88°35E **218** C3
Xalapa *Mexico* 19°32N 96°55W **319** D5
Xambioá *Brazil* 6°25S 48°40W **332** C2
Xangongo *Angola* 16°45S 15°5E **265** F3
Xankändi *Azerbaijan* 39°52N 46°49E **213** C12
Xanlar *Azerbaijan* 40°37N 46°12E **191** K8
Xanten *Germany* 51°39N 6°26E **178** D2
Xanthi *Greece* 41°10N 24°58E **203** E8
Xanthi □ *Greece* 41°10N 24°58E **203** E8
Xanthos *Turkey* 36°19N 29°18E **205** E11
Xanxerê *Brazil* 26°53S 52°23W **335** B5
Xapuri *Brazil* 10°35S 68°35W **330** C4
Xar Moron He → *China* 43°25N 120°35E **227** C11
Xarrë *Albania* 39°44N 20°3E **206** B10
Xátiva *Spain* 38°59N 0°32W **197** G4
Xau, L. *Botswana* 21°15S 24°44E **270** B3
Xavantina *Brazil* 21°15S 52°48W **335** A5
Xayar *China* 41°13N 82°48E **217** D10
Xenia *U.S.A.* 39°41N 83°56W **311** E13
Xeropotamos → *Cyprus* 34°42N 32°33E **207** F8
Xertigny *France* 48°3N 6°24E **173** D13
Xewkija *Malta* 36°2N 14°15E **206** E7
Xhora *S. Africa* 31°55S 28°38E **271** D4
Xhumo *Botswana* 21°7S 24°35E **270** B3
Xi Jiang → *China* 22°5N 113°20E **229** F9
Xi Xian *Henan, China* 32°20N 114°43E **229** A10
Xi Xian *Shanxi, China* 36°41N 110°58E **226** F6
Xia Xian *China* 35°8N 111°12E **226** G6
Xiachengzi *China* 44°40N 130°18E **227** B16
Xiachuan Dao *China* 21°40N 112°40E **229** G9
Xiaguan *China* 25°32N 100°16E **228** E3
Xiajiang *China* 27°30N 115°10E **229** D10
Xiajin *China* 36°56N 116°0E **226** F9
Xiamen *China* 24°25N 118°4E **229** E12
Xi'an *China* 34°15N 109°0E **226** G5
Xian Xian *China* 38°12N 116°6E **226** E9
Xianfeng *China* 29°40N 109°8E **228** C7
Xiang Jiang → *China* 28°55N 112°50E **229** C9
Xiangcheng *Henan, China* 33°29N 114°52E **226** H8
Xiangcheng *Henan, China* 33°50N 113°27E **226** H7
Xiangcheng *Sichuan, China* 28°53N 99°47E **228** C2
Xiangdu *China* 23°13N 106°58E **228** F6
Xiangfan *China* 32°2N 112°8E **229** A9
Xianggang = Hong Kong *China* 22°17N 114°11E **122** B1
Xianggang = Hong Kong □ *China* 22°11N 114°14E **219** G11
Xianghuang Qi *China* 42°2N 113°50E **226** C7
Xiangning *China* 35°58N 110°50E **226** G6
Xiangquan *China* 36°30N 113°1E **226** F7
Xiangquan He = Sutlej → *Pakistan* 29°23N 71°3E **242** E4
Xiangshan *China* 29°29N 121°51E **229** C13
Xiangshui *China* 34°12N 119°33E **227** G10
Xiangtan *China* 27°51N 112°54E **229** D9
Xiangxiang *China* 27°43N 112°28E **229** D9
Xiangyin *China* 28°38N 112°54E **229** C9
Xiangyun *China* 25°34N 100°35E **228** E3
Xiangzhou *China* 23°58N 109°40E **228** F7
Xianju *China* 28°51N 120°44E **229** C13
Xianning *China* 29°51N 114°16E **229** C10
Xianshui He → *China* 30°10N 100°59E **228** B3
Xiantao *China* 30°25N 113°25E **229** B9
Xianyang *China* 34°20N 108°40E **226** G5
Xianyou *China* 25°22N 118°38E **229** E12
Xiao Hinggan Ling *China* 49°0N 127°0E **219** B7
Xiao Xian *China* 34°15N 116°55E **226** G9
Xiaofeng *China* 30°35N 119°32E **229** B12
Xiaogan *China* 30°52N 113°55E **229** B9
Xiaogang Park *China* 23°6N 113°16E **121** B2
Xiaojin *China* 30°59N 102°21E **228** B4
Xiaolan *China* 22°38N 113°13E **229** F9
Xiaoping *China* 23°12N 113°13E **121** A2
Xiaoshan *China* 30°12N 120°18E **229** B13
Xiaoyi *China* 37°8N 111°48E **226** F6
Xiapu *China* 26°54N 119°59E **229** D12
Xiasha chong *China* 23°8N 113°9E **121** B1
Xiawa *China* 42°35N 120°38E **227** C11
Xiayi *China* 34°15N 116°10E **226** G9
Xichang *Guangdong, China* 23°9N 113°13E **121** B2
Xichang *Sichuan, China* 27°51N 102°19E **228** D4
Xicheng *China* 39°54N 116°19E **114** B1
Xicheng *China* 30°57N 105°54E **228** B5
Xichou *China* 23°25N 104°42E **228** E5
Xichuan *China* 33°0N 111°30E **226** H6
Xidan *China* 39°52N 116°20E **114** B2
Xide *China* 28°8N 102°19E **228** C4
Xiemahe *China* 31°38N 111°12E **229** B8
Xieng Khouang *Laos* 19°17N 103°25E **236** C4
Xifei He → *China* 32°45N 116°40E **226** H9
Xifeng *Gansu, China* 35°40N 107°40E **226** G4
Xifeng *Guizhou, China* 27°7N 106°42E **228** D6
Xifeng *Liaoning, China* 42°42N 124°45E **227** C13
Xifengzhen = Xifeng *China* 35°40N 107°40E **226** G4
Xigazê *China* 29°5N 88°45E **218** D3
Xihe *China* 34°2N 105°20E **226** G3
Xihua *China* 33°45N 114°30E **226** H8
Xilagani *Greece* 40°58N 25°28E **203** F9
Xili Shuiku *China* 22°36N 113°57E **219** F10
Xiliao He → *China* 43°32N 123°35E **227** C12
Xilin *China* 24°30N 105°6E **228** E5
Xilinhot *China* 43°52N 116°2E **226** C9
Xilokastro *Greece* 38°5N 22°38E **204** C4
Ximana *Mozam.* 19°24S 33°58E **269** F3
Xime *Guinea-Biss.* 11°59N 14°57W **262** C2
Ximeng *China* 22°50N 99°27E **228** F2
Xin Jiang → *China* 28°45N 116°35E **229** C11
Xin Xian = Xinzhou *China* 38°22N 112°46E **226** E7
Xinavane *Mozam.* 25°2S 32°47E **271** C5
Xinbin *China* 41°40N 125°2E **224** B2
Xincai *China* 32°43N 114°58E **229** A10
Xinchang *China* 29°28N 120°52E **229** C13
Xincheng *Guangxi Zhuangzu, China* 24°5N 108°39E **228** E7
Xincheng *Jiangxi, China* 26°48N 114°6E **229** D10
Xinchengzi *China* 42°2N 123°30E **224** A1
Xincun *China* 38°15N 117°45E **227** E9
Xindu *China* 30°50N 104°10E **228** B5
Xinfeng *Guangdong, China* 24°5N 114°16E **229** E10
Xinfeng *Jiangxi, China* 27°7N 116°11E **229** D11
Xinfeng *Jiangxi, China* 25°27N 114°58E **229** E10
Xinfengjiang Skuiku *China* 23°52N 114°30E **229** F10
Xing Xian *China* 38°27N 111°7E **226** E6
Xing'an *Guangxi Zhuangzu, China* 25°38N 110°40E **229** E8
Xingan *Jiangxi, China* 27°46N 115°20E **229** D10
Xingcheng *China* 40°40N 120°45E **227** D11
Xingguo *China* 26°21N 115°21E **229** D10
Xinghe *China* 40°55N 113°55E **226** D7
Xinghua *China* 32°58N 119°48E **227** H10
Xinghua Wan *China* 25°15N 119°20E **229** E12
Xinglong *China* 40°25N 117°30E **227** D9
Xingning *China* 24°3N 115°42E **229** E10
Xingping *China* 34°20N 108°28E **226** G5
Xingren *China* 25°24N 105°11E **228** E5
Xingshan *China* 31°15N 110°45E **229** B8
Xingtai *China* 37°3N 114°32E **226** F8
Xingu → *Brazil* 1°30S 51°53W **329** D7
Xingwen *China* 28°22N 104°50E **228** C5
Xingyang *China* 34°45N 112°52E **226** G7
Xinhe *China* 37°30N 115°15E **226** F8
Xinhua *China* 27°42N 111°13E **229** D8
Xinhuang *China* 27°21N 109°12E **228** D7
Xinhui *China* 22°25N 113°0E **229** F9
Xining *China* 36°34N 101°40E **218** C5
Xinjian *China* 28°37N 115°46E **229** C10
Xinjiang *China* 35°34N 111°11E **226** G6
Xinjiang Uygur Zizhiqu □ *China* 42°0N 86°0E **217** D11
Xinjie *China* 26°48N 101°15E **228** D3
Xinjin = Pulandian *China* 39°25N 121°58E **227** E11
Xinjin *China* 30°24N 103°47E **228** B4
Xinkai He → *China* 43°32N 123°35E **227** C12
Xinken *China* 22°39N 113°36E **219** F10
Xinle *China* 38°25N 114°40E **226** E8
Xinlitun *China* 42°0N 122°8E **227** D12
Xinlong *China* 30°57N 100°12E **228** B3
Xinmin *China* 41°59N 122°50E **224** B1
Xinning *China* 26°28N 110°50E **229** D8
Xinping *China* 24°5N 101°59E **228** E3
Xinshao *China* 27°21N 111°26E **229** D8
Xintai *China* 35°55N 117°45E **227** G9
Xintian *China* 25°55N 112°13E **229** E9
Xinwan *China* 22°47N 113°40E **219** F10
Xinxian *China* 31°36N 113°51E **229** B10
Xinxiang *China* 35°18N 113°50E **226** G7
Xinxing *China* 22°35N 112°15E **229** F9
Xinyang *China* 32°6N 114°3E **229** A10
Xinye *China* 32°30N 112°21E **229** A9
Xinyi *China* 22°25N 111°0E **229** F8
Xinyu *China* 27°49N 114°58E **229** D10
Xinzhan *China* 43°50N 127°18E **227** C14
Xinzheng *China* 34°20N 113°45E **226** G7
Xinzhou *Hainan, China* 19°43N 109°17E **236** C7
Xinzhou *Hubei, China* 30°50N 114°48E **229** B10
Xinzhou *Shanxi, China* 38°22N 112°46E **226** E7
Xinzo de Limia *Spain* 42°3N 7°47W **194** C3
Xiongyuecheng *China* 40°12N 122°5E **227** D12
Xiping *Henan, China* 33°22N 114°5E **226** H8
Xiping *Henan, China* 33°25N 111°8E **226** H6
Xiping *Zhejiang, China* 28°16N 119°29E **229** C12
Xique-Xique *Brazil* 10°50S 42°40W **332** D3
Xiruá → *Brazil* 6°3S 67°50W **330** B4
Xisha Qundao = Paracel Is. *S. China Sea* 15°50N 112°0E **230** A4
Xishui *Guizhou, China* 28°19N 106°9E **228** C6
Xishui *Hubei, China* 30°30N 115°15E **229** B10
Xitole *Guinea-Biss.* 11°43N 14°50W **262** C2
Xiu Shui → *China* 29°13N 116°0E **229** C10
Xiuning *China* 29°45N 118°10E **229** C12
Xiuren *China* 24°27N 110°12E **229** E8
Xiushan *China* 28°25N 108°57E **228** C7
Xiushui *China* 29°2N 114°33E **229** C10
Xiuwen *China* 26°49N 106°32E **228** D6
Xiuyan *China* 40°18N 123°11E **224** B1
Xixabangma Feng *China* 28°20N 85°40E **243** E11
Xixia *China* 33°25N 111°29E **226** H6
Xixiang *China* 33°0N 107°44E **219** F10
Xixón = Gijón *Spain* 43°32N 5°42W **194** B5
Xiyang *China* 37°38N 113°38E **226** F7
Xizang Zizhiqu □ *China* 32°0N 88°0E **217** F11
Xizhimen *China* 39°55N 116°19E **114** B1
Xlendi *Malta* 36°1N 14°12E **206** E6
Xochimilco, Parque Ecológico *Mexico* 19°18N 99°5W **128** C2
Xochob *Mexico* 19°21N 89°48W **319** D7
Xojayli = Khŭjayli *Uzbekistan* 42°29N 59°31E **216** D5
Xorasm = Khorazm □ *Uzbekistan* 43°0N 60°0E **216** D6
Xu Beihong Memorial Hall *Beijing, China* **114** a1
Xu Jiang → *China* 28°0N 116°25E **229** D11
Xuan Loc *Vietnam* 10°56N 107°14E **237** G6
Xuan'en *China* 30°0N 109°30E **228** C7
Xuanhan *China* 31°18N 107°38E **228** B6
Xuanhua *China* 40°40N 115°2E **226** D8
Xuanwei *China* 26°15N 103°59E **228** C5
Xuanwu *China* 39°52N 116°19E **114** B1
Xuanzhou *China* 30°56N 118°43E **229** B12
Xuchang *China* 34°2N 113°48E **226** G7
Xudat *Azerbaijan* 41°38N 48°41E **191** K9
Xuddur = Oddur *Somali Rep.* 4°11N 43°52E **267** D5
Xuefeng Shan *China* 27°5N 110°35E **229** D8
Xuejiaping *China* 31°39N 110°16E **229** B8
Xuhui *China* 31°11N 121°26E **138** B1
Xun Jiang → *China* 23°35N 111°30E **229** F8
Xun Xian *China* 35°42N 114°33E **226** G8
Xundian *China* 25°36N 103°15E **228** E4
Xunwu *China* 24°54N 115°37E **229** E10
Xunyang *China* 32°48N 109°22E **226** H5
Xunyi *China* 35°8N 108°20E **226** G5
Xupu *China* 27°53N 110°32E **229** D8
Xúquer → *Spain* 39°5N 0°10W **197** F4
Xushui *China* 39°2N 115°40E **226** E8
Xuwen *China* 20°20N 110°10E **229** G8
Xuyen Moc *Vietnam* 10°34N 107°25E **237** G6
Xuyong *China* 28°10N 105°22E **228** C5
Xuzhou *China* 34°18N 117°10E **227** G9
Xylophagou *Cyprus* 34°54N 33°51E **207** F9

Y

Y.S. Falls *Jamaica* 18°9N 77°49W **320** a
Ya Xian = Sanya *China* 18°14N 109°29E **236** C7
Yaamba *Australia* 23°8S 150°22E **280** C5
Ya'an *China* 29°58N 103°5E **228** C4
Yaapeet *Australia* 35°45S 142°3E **282** C5
Yaba *Nigeria* 6°30N 3°22E **124** A2
Yabassi *Cameroon* 4°30N 9°57E **263** E6
Yabelo *Ethiopia* 4°50N 38°8E **257** G4
Yabelo △ *Ethiopia* 6°0N 37°50E **257** F4
Yablanitsa *Bulgaria* 43°2N 24°5E **203** C8
Yablonovyy Khrebet *Russia* 53°0N 114°0E **215** D12
Yablonovyy Ra. = Yablonovyy Khrebet *Russia* 53°0N 114°0E **215** D12
Yabluniv *Ukraine* 48°24N 24°57E **183** B9
Yablunytsya *Ukraine* 48°19N 24°29E **183** B9
Yabrai Shan *China* 39°40N 103°0E **226** E2
Yabrūd *Syria* 33°58N 36°39E **250** E7
Yabucoa *Puerto Rico* 18°3N 65°53W **321** b
Yacheng *China* 18°22N 109°6E **236** C7
Yackandandah *Australia* 36°18S 146°52E **283** D7
Yacuiba *Bolivia* 22°0S 63°43W **334** A3
Yacuma → *Bolivia* 13°38S 65°23W **331** C4
Yadgir *India* 16°45N 77°5E **244** F3
Yadkin → *U.S.A.* 35°23N 80°4W **315** D14
Yadrin *Russia* 55°57N 46°12E **190** C8
Yadua *Fiji* 16°49S 178°18E **287** A2
Yaeyama-Rettō *Japan* 24°30N 123°40E **221** M1
Yafran *Libya* 32°4N 12°31E **258** B2
Yafran □ *Libya* 32°0N 12°20E **258** B2
Yaftābād *Iran* 35°37N 51°17E **141** B1
Yagaba *Ghana* 10°14N 1°20W **263** C4
Yagaji-shima *Japan* 26°39N 128°0E **288** a
Yagasa Cluster *Fiji* 18°57S 178°28W **287** B3
Yağcılar *Turkey* 39°25N 28°23E **205** B10
Yagodnoye *Russia* 62°33N 149°40E **215** C15
Yagoua *Cameroon* 10°20N 15°13E **259** F3
Yaguas → *Peru* 2°45S 70°10W **328** D3
Yahara *Japan* 35°44N 139°37E **140** A2
Yahila *Orientale, Dem. Rep. of the Congo* 0°13N 24°28E **264** B4
Yahila *Orientale, Dem. Rep. of the Congo* 1°48N 23°37E **264** B4
Yahk *Canada* 49°6N 116°10W **296** D5
Yaho *Japan* 35°40N 139°26E **140** A1
Yahotyn *Ukraine* 50°17N 31°46E **189** G6
Yahuma *Dem. Rep. of the Congo* 1°0N 23°10E **264** B4
Yahyalı *Turkey* 38°5N 35°2E **212** C6
Yaita *Japan* 36°48N 139°56E **221** F9
Yaiza *Canary Is.* 28°57N 13°46W **153** e2
Yaizu *Japan* 34°52N 138°20E **223** C10
Yajiang *China* 30°2N 100°57E **228** B3
Yajua *Nigeria* 11°27N 12°49E **263** C7
Yakacık *Turkey* 36°46N 36°11E **250** B7
Yakage *Japan* 34°37N 133°35E **222** C5
Yakamba *Dem. Rep. of the Congo* 2°42N 19°38E **264** B3
Yakapınar *Turkey* 36°57N 35°36E **250** B6
Yakima *U.S.A.* 46°36N 120°31W **304** C3
Yakima → *U.S.A.* 46°15N 119°14W **304** C4
Yakire *Japan* 35°45N 139°54E **140** A3
Yakishiri-Jima *Japan* 44°26N 141°25E **220** B10
Yako *Burkina Faso* 12°59N 2°15W **262** C4
Yakobi I. *U.S.A.* 58°0N 136°30W **296** B1
Yakoma *Dem. Rep. of the Congo* 4°5N 22°27E **264** B4
Yakoruda *Bulgaria* 42°1N 23°39E **202** D7
Yakossi *C.A.R.* 5°37N 23°19E **264** A4
Yakovlevka *Russia* 44°26N 133°28E **220** B6
Yakovlevskoye = Privolzhsk *Russia* 57°23N 41°16E **190** B5
Yaksu *S. Korea* 37°34N 127°1E **137** B2
Yaku-Shima *Japan* 30°20N 130°30E **221** J5
Yakumo *Japan* 42°15N 140°16E **220** C10
Yakutat *U.S.A.* 59°33N 139°44W **303** G13
Yakutat B. *U.S.A.* 59°45N 140°45W **303** G12
Yakutia = Sakha □ *Russia* 66°0N 130°0E **215** C14
Yakutsk *Russia* 62°5N 129°50E **215** C13
Yala *Thailand* 6°33N 101°18E **237** J3
Yala △ *Sri Lanka* 6°20N 81°30E **245** L5
Yaladağı *Turkey* 35°56N 36°3E **250** C7
Yalboroo *Australia* 20°50S 148°40E **280** J6
Yale *U.S.A.* 43°8N 82°48W **312** C2
Yalgoo *Australia* 28°16S 116°39E **279** E2
Yalgorup △ *Australia* 32°39S 115°38E **279** F2
Yali *Dem. Rep. of the Congo* 0°4N 21°3E **264** B4
Yaligimba *Dem. Rep. of the Congo* 2°13N 22°56E **264** B4
Yalikanda *Dem. Rep. of the Congo* 0°23N 24°47E **264** B4
Yalinga *C.A.R.* 6°33N 23°10E **264** A4
Yalkabul, Pta. *Mexico* 21°32N 88°37W **319** C7
Yallahs *Jamaica* 17°53N 76°35W **320** a
Yallahs Hill *Jamaica* 17°54N 76°30W **320** a
Yalleroi *Australia* 24°3S 145°42E **280** C4
Yalobusha → *U.S.A.* 33°33N 90°10W **315** E9
Yaloké *C.A.R.* 5°19N 17°5E **264** A3
Yalong Jiang → *China* 26°40N 101°55E **228** D3
Yalova *Turkey* 40°41N 29°15E **203** F13
Yalpuh, Ozero *Ukraine* 45°30N 28°41E **183** E13
Yalta *Ukraine* 44°30N 34°10E **189** K8
Yalu Jiang → *China* 39°55N 124°19E **224** C2
Yalvaç *Turkey* 38°17N 31°10E **212** C4
Yam Ha Melah = Dead Sea *Asia* 31°30N 35°30E **251** G6
Yam Kinneret *Israel* 32°45N 35°35E **250** F6
Yamada *Fukuoka, Japan* 33°33N 130°49E **222** D2
Yamada *Kanagawa, Japan* 35°33N 139°37E **140** B2
Yamada *Ōsaka, Japan* 34°47N 135°32E **133** A2
Yamaga *Japan* 33°1N 130°41E **222** D2
Yamagata *Japan* 38°15N 140°15E **220** E10
Yamagata □ *Japan* 38°30N 140°0E **220** E10
Yamagawa *Japan* 31°12N 130°39E **222** F2
Yamaguchi *Japan* 34°10N 131°32E **222** C3
Yamaguchi □ *Japan* 34°20N 131°40E **222** C3
Yamal, Poluostrov *Russia* 71°0N 70°0E **214** B8
Yamal Pen. = Yamal, Poluostrov *Russia* 71°0N 70°0E **214** B8
Yamanaka *Japan* 36°15N 136°22E **223** A8
Yamanashi *Japan* 35°41N 138°40E **223** B10
Yamanashi □ *Japan* 35°40N 138°40E **223** B10
Yamanie Falls △ *Australia* 18°29S 146°9E **280** B4
Yamantau, Gora *Russia* 54°15N 58°6E **186** D10
Yamasaki *Japan* 35°0N 134°32E **222** C6
Yamato *Japan* 35°27N 139°25E **223** B11
Yamato → *Japan* 34°36N 135°26E **133** B1
Yamato Ridge *Sea of Japan* 39°20N 135°0E **220** E7
Yamatotakada *Japan* 34°31N 135°45E **223** C7
Yamba *Australia* 29°26S 153°23E **281** D5
Yambarran Ra. *Australia* 15°10S 130°25E **278** C5
Yambata *Dem. Rep. of the Congo* 2°26N 21°58E **264** B4
Yambéring *Guinea* 11°50N 12°18E **262** C2
Yâmbiô *Sudan* 4°35N 28°16E **257** G2
Yambol *Bulgaria* 42°30N 26°30E **203** D10
Yamboyo *Dem. Rep. of the Congo* 0°40N 22°18E **264** B4
Yambuya *Dem. Rep. of the Congo* 1°17N 24°34E **264** B4
Yamdena *Indonesia* 7°45S 131°20E **231** F8
Yame *Japan* 33°13N 130°35E **222** D2
Yamethin *Burma* 20°29N 96°18E **241** E6
Yamma Yamma, L. *Australia* 26°16S 141°20E **281** D3
Yamoussoukro *Ivory C.* 6°49N 5°17W **262** D3
Yampa → *U.S.A.* 40°32N 108°59W **304** F9
Yampi Sd. *Australia* 16°8S 123°38E **278** C3
Yampil *Moldova* 48°15N 28°15E **177** D15
Yampol = Yampil *Moldova* 48°15N 28°15E **177** D15
Yamrat *Nigeria* 10°11N 9°55E **263** C6
Yamrukchal = Botev *Bulgaria* 42°44N 24°52E **203** D8
Yamuna → *India* 25°30N 81°53E **243** G9
Yamunanagar *India* 30°7N 77°17E **242** D7
Yamzho Yumco *China* 28°48N 90°35E **218** D4
Yan *Nigeria* 10°5N 12°11E **263** C7
Yan Kit *Singapore* 1°21N 103°58E **138** A3
Yan Oya → *Sri Lanka* 9°0N 81°10E **245** K5
Yana → *Russia* 71°30N 136°0E **215** B14
Yanagawa *Japan* 33°10N 130°24E **222** D2
Yanahara *Japan* 34°58N 134°2E **222** C6
Yanai *Japan* 33°58N 132°7E **222** D4
Yan'an *China* 36°35N 109°26E **226** F5
Yanaul *Russia* 56°25N 55°0E **186** C10
Yanbian *China* 26°47N 101°31E **228** D3
Yanbu *China* 23°5N 113°9E **121** B1
Yanbu 'al Baḩr *Si. Arabia* 24°0N 38°5E **246** F3
Yanchang *China* 36°43N 110°1E **226** F6
Yancheng *Henan, China* 33°35N 114°0E **226** H8
Yancheng *Jiangsu, China* 33°23N 120°8E **227** H11
Yanchep *Australia* 31°33S 115°37E **279** F2
Yanchi *China* 37°48N 107°20E **226** F4
Yanchuan *China* 36°51N 110°10E **226** F6
Yanco *Australia* 34°38S 146°27E **283** C7
Yanco Cr. → *Australia* 35°14S 145°35E **283** C6
Yandicoogina *Australia* 22°49S 119°12E **278** D2
Yandina *Solomon Is.* 9°7S 159°13E **287** M10
Yandja *Dem. Rep. of the Congo* 1°41S 17°43E **264** C3
Yandongi *Dem. Rep. of the Congo* 2°51N 22°16E **264** B4
Yandoon *Burma* 17°0N 95°40E **241** G5
Yanfeng *China* 25°52N 101°8E **228** E3
Yanfolila *Mali* 11°11N 8°9W **262** C3
Yang Xian *China* 33°15N 107°30E **226** H4
Yang-yang *S. Korea* 38°4N 128°38E **224** C4
Yang-Yang *Senegal* 15°30N 15°20W **262** B1
Yangambi *Dem. Rep. of the Congo* 0°47N 24°24E **264** B4
Yangbi *China* 25°41N 99°58E **228** E2
Yangcheng *China* 35°28N 112°22E **226** G7
Yangcheon *S. Korea* 37°30N 126°51E **137** B1
Yangchow = Yangzhou *China* 32°21N 119°26E **229** A12
Yangch'ü = Taiyuan *China* 37°52N 112°33E **226** F7
Yangchüan = Yangquan *China* 37°58N 113°31E **226** F7
Yangchun *China* 22°11N 111°48E **229** F8
Yangdok *N. Korea* 39°13N 126°38E **224** E3
Yanggang-do □ *N. Korea* 41°15N 128°0E **224** B4
Yanggao *China* 40°21N 113°55E **226** D7
Yanggu *China* 36°8N 115°43E **226** F8
Yanghuayuan *China* 39°49N 116°18E **114** C1
Yangiyul *Uzbekistan* 41°0N 69°3E **217** D7
Yangjae *S. Korea* 37°29N 127°2E **137** C2
Yangjiang *China* 21°50N 111°59E **229** G8
Yangjiazhuang *China* 31°22N 121°25E **138** A1
Yangjing *China* 31°15N 121°32E **138** B2
Yangju *S. Korea* 37°47N 127°7E **224** D3
Yangliuqing *China* 39°2N 117°5E **227** E9
Yangmei *Taiwan* 24°55N 121°8E **225** B3
Yangmingshan △ *Taiwan* 25°9N 121°32E **225** A3
Yangon = Rangoon *Burma* 16°45N 96°20E **241** G6
Yangonde *Dem. Rep. of the Congo* 0°3N 22°43E **264** B4
Yangping *China* 31°12N 111°25E **229** B8
Yangpingguan *China* 32°58N 106°5E **226** H4
Yangpu *China* 31°16N 121°32E **138** B2
Yangpu Park *China* 31°17N 121°31E **138** B2
Yangquan *China* 37°58N 113°31E **226** F7
Yangsan *S. Korea* 35°20N 129°2E **224** E4
Yangshan *China* 24°30N 112°40E **229** E9
Yangshuo *China* 24°48N 110°29E **229** E8
Yangtse = Chang Jiang → *China* 31°48N 121°10E **229** B13
Yangtze Kiang = Chang Jiang → *China* 31°48N 121°10E **229** B13
Yangudi Rassa △ *Ethiopia* 10°50N 40°42E **257** E5
Yangxin *China* 29°50N 115°12E **229** C10
Yangyuan *China* 40°1N 114°10E **226** D8
Yangzhong *China* 32°22N 119°52E **229** A12
Yangzhou *China* 32°21N 119°26E **229** A12
Yanhe *China* 28°31N 108°29E **228** C7
Yanji *China* 42°59N 129°30E **227** C15
Yanjin *China* 28°5N 104°18E **228** C5
Yanjing *China* 29°7N 98°33E **228** C2
Yankari △ *Nigeria* 9°50N 10°28E **263** D7

Yankton *U.S.A.* 42°53N 97°23W **308** D5
Yannawa *Thailand* 13°43N 100°32E **113** B2
Yanonge *Dem. Rep. of the Congo* 0°35N 24°38E **264** B4
Yanov = Ivanava *Belarus* 52°7N 25°29E **177** B13
Yanqi *China* 42°5N 86°35E **217** D11
Yanqing *China* 40°30N 115°58E **226** D8
Yanshan *Hebei, China* 38°4N 117°22E **227** E9
Yanshan *Jiangxi, China* 28°15N 117°41E **229** C11
Yanshan *Yunnan, China* 23°35N 104°20E **228** F5
Yanshou *China* 45°28N 128°22E **227** B15
Yantabulla *Australia* 29°21S 145°0E **281** D4
Yantai *China* 37°34N 121°22E **227** F11
Yantarnyy *Russia* 54°52N 19°57E **184** D6
Yantian *China* 22°35N 114°16E **219** F11
Yanting *China* 31°11N 105°24E **228** B5
Yantra → *Bulgaria* 43°40N 25°37E **203** C9
Yanuca *Fiji* 18°24S 178°0E **287** B1
Yanununbeyan △ *Australia* 35°29S 149°24E **283** C8
Yanwa *China* 27°35N 98°55E **228** D2
Yanyuan *China* 27°25N 101°30E **228** D3
Yanzhou *China* 35°35N 116°49E **226** G9
Yao *Chad* 12°56N 17°33E **259** F3
Yao *Japan* 34°37N 135°36E **223** C7
Yao Noi, Ko *Thailand* 8°7N 98°37E **237** a
Yao Xian *China* 34°55N 108°59E **226** G5
Yao Yai, Ko *Thailand* 8°0N 98°35E **237** a
Yao'an *China* 25°31N 101°18E **228** E3
Yaodu *China* 32°45N 105°22E **228** A5
Yaoundé *Cameroon* 3°50N 11°35E **263** E7
Yaowan *China* 34°15N 118°3E **227** G10
Yap *Pac. Oc.* 9°30N 138°10E **287** R16
Yapacana △ *Venezuela* 3°49N 66°44W **328** C4
Yapehe *Dem. Rep. of the Congo* 0°13S 24°28E **264** C4
Yapen *Indonesia* 1°50S 136°0E **231** E9
Yapen, Selat *Indonesia* 1°20S 136°10E **231** E9
Yapero *Indonesia* 4°59S 137°11E **231** E9
Yappar → *Australia* 18°22S 141°16E **280** B3
Yaqaga *Fiji* 16°35S 178°36E **287** A2
Yaqui → *Mexico* 27°37N 110°39W **318** B2
Yar-Sale *Russia* 66°50N 70°50E **214** C8
Yaracuy □ *Venezuela* 10°20N 68°45W **328** A4
Yaracuy → *Venezuela* 10°33N 68°15W **328** A4
Yaraka *Australia* 24°53S 144°3E **280** C3
Yaransk *Russia* 57°22N 47°49E **190** B8
Yarbasan *Turkey* 38°59N 28°49E **205** C10
Yardımcı Burnu *Turkey* 36°13N 30°25E **205** E12
Yare → *U.K.* 52°35N 1°38E **169** E9
Yaremcha *Ukraine* 48°27N 24°33E **183** B9
Yaren *Nauru* 0°33S 166°55E **288** H8
Yarensk *Russia* 62°11N 49°15E **186** B8
Yarfa *Si. Arabia* 24°37N 38°35E **256** C4
Yarí → *Colombia* 0°20S 72°20W **328** D3
Yarīm *Yemen* 14°20N 44°22E **248** D4
Yaritagua *Venezuela* 10°5N 69°8W **328** A4
Yarkand = Shache *China* 38°20N 77°10E **217** E9
Yarkant He → *China* 40°26N 80°59E **217** D10
Yarker *Canada* 44°23N 76°46W **313** B8
Yarkhun → *Pakistan* 36°17N 72°30E **243** A5
Yarlung Ziangbo Jiang = Brahmaputra → *Asia* 23°40N 90°35E **241** D3
Yarmouth *Canada* 43°50N 66°7W **299** D6
Yarmūk *Iraq* 33°18N 44°19E **113** B1
Yarmūk → *Syria* 32°42N 35°40E **250** F6
Yaroslavl *Russia* 57°35N 39°55E **188** D10
Yaroslavl □ *Russia* 59°20N 38°50E **188** C10
Yarra → *Trin. & Tob.* 10°48N 61°21W **323** t
Yarra Bend Park *Australia* 37°47S 145°0E **128** A2
Yarra Ranges △ *Australia* 37°40S 146°3E **283** D7
Yarra Yarra Lakes *Australia* 29°40S 115°45E **279** E2
Yarram *Australia* 38°29S 146°39E **283** E7
Yarraman *Australia* 26°50S 152°0E **281** D5
Yarras *Australia* 31°25S 152°20E **283** A10
Yarraville *Australia* 37°48S 144°53E **128** A1
Yarrawonga *Australia* 36°0S 146°0E **283** D7
Yartsevo *Sib., Russia* 60°20N 90°0E **215** C10
Yartsevo *Smolensk, Russia* 55°6N 32°43E **188** E7
Yarumal *Colombia* 6°58N 75°24W **328** B2
Yasa *Dem. Rep. of the Congo* 3°50S 21°25E **264** C4
Yasawa *Fiji* 16°47S 177°31E **287** A1
Yasawa Group *Fiji* 17°0S 177°23E **287** A1
Yaselda *Belarus* 52°7N 26°28E **177** B14
Yasen *Ukraine* 48°45N 24°10E **183** B9
Yashbum *Yemen* 14°19N 46°56E **248** D4
Yashi *Nigeria* 12°23N 7°54E **263** C6
Yashikera *Nigeria* 9°44N 3°29E **263** D5
Yashiro-Jima *Japan* 33°55N 132°15E **222** D4
Yashkul *Russia* 46°11N 45°21E **191** G7
Yasin *Pakistan* 36°24N 73°23E **243** A5
Yasinovataya *Ukraine* 48°7N 37°57E **189** H9
Yasinski, L. *Canada* 53°16N 77°35W **298** B4
Yasinya *Ukraine* 48°16N 24°21E **183** B9
Yasnyy *Russia* 51°1N 59°58E **216** B5
Yasothon *Thailand* 15°50N 104°10E **236** E5
Yass *Australia* 34°49S 148°54E **283** C8
Yasugi *Japan* 35°26N 133°15E **222** B5
Yāsūj *Iran* 30°31N 51°31E **247** D6
Yasuní △ *Ecuador* 1°19S 76°3W **328** D2
Yat *Niger* 20°28N 13°27E **259** D2
Yata → *Bolivia* 10°29S 65°26W **331** C4
Yata → *C.A.R.* 10°23N 22°45E **264** A4
Yata-Ngaya ⌓ *C.A.R.* 9°15N 23°25E **264** A4
Yatağan *Turkey* 37°20N 28°10E **205** D10
Yatakala *Niger* 14°50N 0°22E **263** C5
Yaté *N. Cal.* 22°9S 166°57E **288** d
Yates Center *U.S.A.* 37°53N 95°44W **308** G6
Yates Pt. *N.Z.* 44°29S 167°49E **285** E2
Yathkyed L. *Canada* 62°40N 98°0W **297** A9
Yathong *Australia* 32°37S 145°33E **283** B6
Yatolemu *Dem. Rep. of the Congo* 0°25N 24°35E **264** B4
Yatsuo *Japan* 36°34N 137°8E **223** A9
Yatsushiro *Japan* 32°30N 130°40E **222** E2
Yatsushiro-Kai *Japan* 32°30N 130°25E **222** E2
Yatta Plateau *Kenya* 2°0S 38°0E **268** C4
Yatua → *Venezuela* 1°30N 66°30W **328** C4
Yau Tong *China* 22°17N 114°14E **122** B2
Yauca *Peru* 15°39S 74°35W **330** D3
Yauco *Puerto Rico* 18°2N 66°51W **321** b
Yauri *Peru* 14°47S 71°25W **330** C3
Yauya *Peru* 8°59S 77°17W **330** B2
Yauyos *Peru* 12°19S 75°50W **330** C2
Yauza → *Russia* 55°54N 37°43E **129** B4
Yaval *India* 21°10N 75°42E **244** D2
Yavari → *Peru* 4°21S 70°2W **330** A3
Yávaros *Mexico* 26°42N 109°31W **318** B3
Yavatmal *India* 20°20N 78°15E **244** D4
Yavero → *Peru* 12°6S 72°57W **330** C3
Yavne *Israel* 31°52N 34°45E **251** G5
Yavoriv *Ukraine* 49°55N 23°20E **185** J10
Yavorov = Yavoriv *Ukraine* 49°55N 23°20E **185** J10
Yavuzeli *Turkey* 37°18N 37°24E **212** D7
Yawatahama *Japan* 33°27N 132°24E **222** D4
Yawnghwe *Burma* 20°39N 96°56E **241** E6
Yawri B. *S. Leone* 8°22N 13°0W **262** D2
Yaxi *China* 27°33N 106°41E **228** D6
Yaxian = Sanya *China* 18°14N 109°29E **236** C7
Yazagyo *Burma* 23°30N 94°6E **241** D5
Yazd *Iran* 31°55N 54°27E **247** D7
Yazd □ *Iran* 32°0N 55°0E **247** D7
Yazd-e Khvāst *Iran* 31°31N 52°7E **247** D7
Yazdān *Iran* 33°30N 60°50E **240** B1
Yazıköy *Turkey* 36°40N 27°20E **205** E9
Yazman *Pakistan* 29°8N 71°45E **242** E4
Yazoo City *U.S.A.* 32°51N 90°25W **315** E9
Ybbs *Austria* 48°12N 15°4E **180** C8
Ybycuí △ *Paraguay* 26°5S 56°46W **334** B4
Ybytyruzú △ *Paraguay* 25°51S 56°11W **335** B4
Ye *Burma* 15°15N 97°15E **236** E1
Ye-ngan *Burma* 21°9N 96°27E **241** E6
Ye-u *Burma* 22°46N 95°26E **241** D5
Ye Xian = Laizhou *China* 37°8N 119°57E **227** F10
Ye Xian *China* 33°35N 113°25E **226** H7
Yea *Australia* 37°14S 145°26E **283** D6
Yeading *U.K.* 51°31N 0°23W **125** A1
Yebawmi *Burma* 25°15N 95°45E **241** C5
Yebbi-Souma *Chad* 21°7N 17°54E **259** D3
Yebyu *Burma* 14°15N 98°13E **236** E2
Yecheng *China* 37°54N 77°26E **217** E9
Yecheon *S. Korea* 36°39N 128°27E **224** D4
Yecla *Spain* 38°35N 1°5W **197** G3
Yécora *Mexico* 28°20N 108°58W **318** B3
Yedashe *Burma* 19°10N 96°20E **241** F6
Yedebub Biheroch Bihereseboch na Hizboch □ *Ethiopia* 12°0N 36°0E **257** F4
Yedikule *Turkey* 40°59N 28°55E **122** C1
Yedintsy = Edineţ *Moldova* 48°9N 27°18E **183** B12
Yedri *Chad* 22°25N 17°30E **259** D3
Yedseram → *Nigeria* 12°30N 14°5E **263** C7
Yefremov *Russia* 53°8N 38°3E **188** F10
Yegguéba *Niger* 19°59N 12°52E **259** E2
Yeghegnadzor *Armenia* 39°44N 45°19E **213** C11
Yegorlyk → *Russia* 46°35N 41°57E **191** G5
Yegorlykskaya *Russia* 46°35N 40°35E **191** G5
Yegoryevsk *Russia* 55°27N 38°55E **188** E10
Yegri-Dere = Ardino *Bulgaria* 41°34N 25°9E **203** E9
Yegros *Paraguay* 26°20S 56°25W **334** B4
Yehbuah *Indonesia* 8°23S 114°45E **231** J17
Yehuda, Midbar *Israel* 31°35N 35°15E **251** G6
Yei *Sudan* 4°9N 30°40E **257** G3
Yei, Nahr → *Sudan* 6°15N 30°13E **257** F3
Yejmiadzin *Armenia* 40°12N 44°19E **191** K7
Yekaterinburg *Russia* 56°50N 60°30E **214** D7
Yekaterinenshtadt = Marks *Russia* 51°45N 46°50E **190** E8
Yekaterinodar = Krasnodar *Russia* 45°5N 39°0E **191** H4
Yekumbe *Dem. Rep. of the Congo* 1°2S 23°27E **264** C4
Yelabuga *Russia* 55°45N 52°4E **190** C11
Yelan *Russia* 50°55N 43°43E **190** E6
Yelandur *India* 12°6N 77°0E **245** H3
Yelarbon *Australia* 28°33S 150°38E **281** D5
Yelatma *Russia* 55°0N 41°45E **190** C5
Yelcho, L. *Chile* 43°18S 72°18W **336** B2
Yelenovka = Sevan *Armenia* 40°33N 44°56E **191** K7
Yelenovskiye Karyery = Dokuchayevsk *Ukraine* 47°44N 37°40E **189** J9
Yelets *Russia* 52°40N 38°30E **189** F10
Yélimané *Mali* 15°9N 10°34W **262** B2
Yelizavetgrad = Kirovohrad *Ukraine* 48°35N 32°20E **189** H7
Yell *U.K.* 60°35N 1°5W **167** A7
Yell Sd. *U.K.* 60°33N 1°15W **167** A7
Yellamanchilli = Elamanchili *India* 17°33N 82°50E **244** F6
Yellandu *India* 17°39N 80°23E **244** F5
Yellapur *India* 14°58N 74°43E **245** G2
Yellareddi *India* 18°12N 78°2E **244** E4
Yellow = Huang He → *China* 37°55N 118°50E **227** F10
Yellow → *U.S.A.* 30°30N 87°0W **317** E3
Yellow Sea *China* 35°0N 123°0E **227** G12
Yellowhead Pass *Canada* 52°53N 118°25W **296** C5
Yellowknife *Canada* 62°27N 114°29W **296** A6
Yellowknife → *Canada* 62°31N 114°19W **296** A6
Yellowstone → *U.S.A.* 47°59N 103°59W **304** C12
Yellowstone △ *U.S.A.* 44°40N 110°30W **304** D8
Yellowstone L. *U.S.A.* 44°27N 110°22W **304** D8
Yelnya *Russia* 54°35N 33°15E **188** E7
Yelsk *Belarus* 51°50N 29°10E **177** C15
Yelwa *Nigeria* 10°49N 4°41E **263** C5
Yemanzhelinsk *Russia* 54°58N 61°18E **216** B6
Yemassee *U.S.A.* 32°41N 80°51W **316** C9
Yembongo *Dem. Rep. of the Congo* 3°12N 19°2E **264** B3
Yemen ■ *Asia* 15°0N 44°0E **248** D4
Yemin Moshe *Jerusalem* **123** b2
Yemmiganur = Emmiganuru *India* 15°44N 77°29E **245** G3
Yen Bai *Vietnam* 21°42N 104°52E **228** G5
Yenagoa *Nigeria* 4°58N 6°16E **263** E6
Yenakiyeve *Ukraine* 48°15N 38°15E **189** H10
Yenakiyevo = Yenakiyeve *Ukraine* 48°15N 38°15E **189** H10
Yenangyat *Burma* 21°6N 94°48E **241** E5
Yenangyaung *Burma* 20°30N 95°0E **241** E5
Yenanma *Burma* 19°46N 94°49E **241** F5
Yenbo = Yanbu 'al Baḩr *Si. Arabia* 24°0N 38°5E **246** F3
Yenchao *Taiwan* 22°46N 120°21E **225** D2
Yenda *Australia* 34°13S 146°14E **283** C7
Yende Millimou *Guinea* 8°55N 10°10W **262** D2
Yendéré *Burkina Faso* 10°12N 4°59W **262** C4
Yendi *Ghana* 9°29N 0°1W **263** D4
Yengisar *China* 38°56N 76°9E **217** E9
Yengo *Congo* 0°22N 15°29E **264** B3
Yengo △ *Australia* 33°0S 150°55E **283** B9
Yéni *Niger* 13°30N 3°1E **263** C5
Yeni-Pazar = Novi Pazar *Serbia* 43°12N 20°28E **202** C4
Yenice *Ankara, Turkey* 39°14N 32°42E **212** C5
Yenice *Aydın, Turkey* 37°49N 28°35E **205** D10
Yenice *Çanakkale, Turkey* 39°55N 27°17E **205** B9
Yenice *Edirne, Turkey* 40°42N 26°9E **203** F10
Yenice *Kahramanmaraş, Turkey* 37°0N 35°4E **250** B6
Yenice → *Turkey* 37°37N 35°33E **212** D6
Yenifoça *Turkey* 38°44N 26°51E **205** C8
Yenihisar *Turkey* 37°22N 27°16E **205** D9
Yenikapı *Turkey* 41°0N 28°56E **122** B1
Yeniköy *Bursa, Turkey* 40°31N 29°22E **203** F13
Yeniköy *Çanakkale, Turkey* 39°55N 26°10E **205** B8
Yeniköy *İstanbul, Turkey* 41°6N 29°3E **122** B2
Yeniköy *Kütahya, Turkey* 38°52N 29°17E **205** C11
Yenipazar *Turkey* 37°49N 28°11E **205** D10
Yenişehir *Turkey* 40°16N 29°38E **203** F13
Yenisey → *Russia* 71°50N 82°40E **214** B9
Yeniseysk *Russia* 58°27N 92°13E **215** D10
Yeniseyskiy Zaliv *Russia* 72°20N 81°0E **214** B9
Yenki = Yanji *China* 42°59N 129°30E **227** C15
Yenne *France* 45°43N 5°44E **175** C9
Yenotayevka *Russia* 47°15N 47°0E **191** G8
Yenpu *Taiwan* 22°45N 120°35E **225** D2
Yenshui *Taiwan* 23°19N 120°16E **225** C2
Yenyuka *Russia* 57°57N 121°15E **215** D13
Yeo → *U.K.* 51°2N 2°49W **169** G5
Yeo, L. *Australia* 28°0S 124°30E **279** E3
Yeo I. *Canada* 45°24N 81°48W **312** A3
Yeoju *S. Korea* 37°20N 127°35E **224** D3
Yeola *India* 20°2N 74°30E **244** D2
Yeon-gi *S. Korea* 36°35N 127°15E **224** D3
Yeoncheon *S. Korea* 38°5N 127°4E **224** C3
Yeong-am *S. Korea* 34°47N 126°42E **224** E3
Yeong-ilman *S. Korea* 36°4N 129°28E **224** D4
Yeong-wol *S. Korea* 37°11N 128°28E **224** D4
Yeong-yang *S. Korea* 36°39N 129°7E **224** D4
Yeongcheon *S. Korea* 35°58N 128°56E **224** E4
Yeongdeok *S. Korea* 36°24N 129°22E **224** D4
Yeongdeungpo *S. Korea* 37°31N 126°54E **137** B1
Yeongdong *Chungcheongbuk-do, S. Korea* 36°10N 127°46E **224** D3
Yeongdong *Seoul, S. Korea* 37°30N 127°1E **137** B2
Yeonggwang *S. Korea* 35°16N 126°30E **224** E3
Yeongheungdo *S. Korea* 37°15N 126°27E **224** D3
Yeongju *S. Korea* 36°50N 128°40E **224** D4
Yeongju △ *S. Korea* 35°45N 129°20E **224** D4
Yeosu *S. Korea* 34°47N 127°45E **224** E3
Yeouido *S. Korea* 37°31N 126°55E **137** B1
Yeovil *U.K.* 50°57N 2°38W **169** G5
Yepes *Spain* 39°55N 3°39W **194** F7
Yeppoon *Australia* 23°5S 150°47E **280** C5
Yerba Buena I. *U.S.A.* 37°48N 122°21W **136** B2
Yerbent *Turkmenistan* 39°30N 58°50E **216** E5
Yerbogachen *Russia* 61°16N 108°0E **215** C11
Yerevan *Armenia* 40°10N 44°31E **191** K7
Yerington *U.S.A.* 38°59N 119°10W **304** G4
Yerkesik *Turkey* 37°7N 28°19E **205** D10
Yerköy *Turkey* 39°38N 34°28E **212** C6
Yerla → *India* 16°50N 74°30E **244** F2
Yermak *Kazakhstan* 52°2N 76°55E **214** D8
Yermo *U.S.A.* 34°54N 116°50W **307** L10
Yerólakkos *Cyprus* 35°11N 33°15E **207** E9
Yeropol *Russia* 65°15N 168°40E **215** C17
Yeroskipos *Cyprus* 34°46N 32°28E **207** F8
Yerres *France* 48°43N 2°30E **134** B4
Yershov *Russia* 51°23N 48°27E **190** E9
Yerupaja, Cerro *Peru* 10°16S 76°55W **330** C2
Yerushalayim = Jerusalem *Israel/West Bank* 31°47N 35°10E **123** B2
Yerville *France* 49°40N 0°53E **172** C7
Yes Tor *U.K.* 50°41N 4°0W **169** G4
Yesagyo *Burma* 21°38N 95°14E **241** E5
Yesan *S. Korea* 36°41N 126°51E **224** D3
Yeshin *Burma* 23°43N 95°6E **241** D5
Yeşikent = Erzin *Turkey* 36°57N 36°11E **250** B7
Yeşil → *Turkey* 37°20N 33°16E **250** A4
Yeşildere *Turkey* 37°9N 33°31E **250** A4
Yeşilhisar *Turkey* 38°20N 35°5E **212** C6
Yeşilırmak → *Turkey* 41°22N 36°37E **212** B7
Yeşilkent *Turkey* 36°57N 36°12E **212** D7
Yeşilköy *Turkey* 40°57N 28°49E **203** F12
Yeşilova *Turkey* 37°31N 29°46E **205** D11
Yeşilyurt *Manisa, Turkey* 38°22N 28°40E **205** C10
Yeşilyurt *Muğla, Turkey* 37°10N 28°20E **205** D10
Yeski Dzhumaya = Târgovişte *Romania* 44°55N 25°27E **183** F10
Yesnogorsk *Russia* 54°32N 37°38E **188** E9
Yeso *U.S.A.* 34°26N 104°37W **305** J11
Yessentuki *Russia* 44°5N 42°53E **191** H6
Yessey *Russia* 68°29N 102°10E **215** C11
Yeste *Spain* 38°22N 2°19W **197** G2
Yetman *Australia* 28°56S 150°48E **281** D5
Yetti *Mauritania* 26°10N 7°50W **260** C3
Yeu, Î. d' *France* 46°42N 2°20W **172** F4
Yevdokimovskoye = Krasnogvardeyskoye *Russia* 45°52N 41°33E **191** H5
Yevlakh = Yevlax *Azerbaijan* 40°39N 47°7E **191** K8
Yevlax *Azerbaijan* 40°39N 47°7E **191** K8
Yevpatoriya *Ukraine* 45°15N 33°20E **189** K7
Yeya → *Russia* 46°40N 38°40E **189** J10
Yeysk *Russia* 46°40N 38°12E **189** J10
Yezd = Yazd *Iran* 31°55N 54°27E **247** D7
Yezerishche *Belarus* 55°50N 29°59E **188** E5
Yhati *Paraguay* 25°45S 56°35W **334** B4
Yhú *Paraguay* 25°0S 56°0W **335** B4
Yi → *Uruguay* 33°7S 57°8W **334** C4
Yi 'Allaq, G. *Egypt* 30°21N 33°31E **251** H4
Yi He → *China* 34°10N 118°8E **227** G10
Yi Xian *Anhui, China* 29°55N 117°57E **229** C11
Yi Xian *Hebei, China* 39°20N 115°30E **226** E8
Yi Xian *Liaoning, China* 41°30N 121°22E **227** D11
Yialiás → *Cyprus* 35°9N 33°44E **207** E9
Yialousa *Cyprus* 35°32N 34°10E **207** E10
Yibin *China* 28°45N 104°32E **228** C5
Yichang *China* 30°40N 111°20E **229** B8
Yicheng *Henan, China* 31°41N 112°12E **229** B9
Yicheng *Shanxi, China* 35°42N 111°40E **226** G6
Yichuan *China* 36°2N 110°10E **226** F6
Yichun *Heilongjiang, China* 47°44N 128°52E **219** B7
Yichun *Jiangxi, China* 27°48N 114°22E **229** D10
Yidu *China* 36°43N 118°28E **227** F10
Yidun *China* 30°22N 99°21E **228** B2
Yifag *Ethiopia* 12°4N 37°46E **257** E4
Yifeng *China* 28°22N 114°45E **229** C10
Yigo *Guam* 13°32N 144°53E **302** d
Yiheyuan *China* 40°0N 116°14E **114** A1
Yihuang *China* 27°30N 116°12E **229** D11
Yijun *China* 35°28N 109°8E **226** G5
Yılanlıkale *Turkey* 36°59N 35°47E **250** B6
Yıldız Dağları *Turkey* 41°48N 27°36E **203** E11
Yıldız Park *Turkey* 41°2N 29°1E **122** B2
Yıldızeli *Turkey* 39°51N 36°36E **212** C7
Yilehuli Shan *China* 51°20N 124°20E **219** A7
Yiliang *Yunnan, China* 27°38N 104°2E **228** D5
Yiliang *Yunnan, China* 24°56N 103°11E **228** E4
Yilong *China* 31°34N 106°23E **228** B6
Yimen *China* 24°40N 102°10E **228** E4
Yimianpo *China* 45°7N 128°2E **227** B15
Yinchuan *China* 38°30N 106°15E **226** E4
Yindaik *Burma* 23°35N 95°22E **241** D5
Yindarlgooda, L. *Australia* 30°40S 121°52E **279** F3
Ying He → *China* 32°30N 116°30E **226** H9
Ying Xian *China* 39°32N 113°10E **226** E7
Yingcheng *China* 30°56N 113°35E **229** B9
Yingde *China* 24°10N 113°25E **229** E9
Yingjiang *China* 24°41N 97°55E **228** E1
Yingjing *China* 29°41N 102°52E **228** C4
Yingkou *China* 40°37N 122°18E **224** B1
Yingkow = Yingkou *China* 40°37N 122°18E **224** B1
Yingshan *Henan, China* 31°35N 113°50E **229** B9
Yingshan *Hubei, China* 30°41N 115°32E **229** B10
Yingshan *Sichuan, China* 31°4N 106°35E **228** B6
Yingshang *China* 32°38N 116°12E **229** A11
Yingtan *China* 28°12N 117°0E **229** C11
Yinhangzhen *China* 31°20N 121°31E **138** A2
Yining *China* 43°58N 81°10E **217** D10
Yinjiang *China* 28°1N 108°21E **228** C7
Yinmabin *Burma* 22°10N 94°55E **241** D5
Yioúra = Giaros *Greece* 37°32N 24°40E **204** D6
Yipinglang *China* 25°10N 101°52E **228** E3
Yirba Muda *Ethiopia* 6°12N 38°42E **257** F4
Yirga Alem *Ethiopia* 6°48N 38°22E **257** F4
Yirol *Sudan* 6°33N 30°30E **257** F3
Yirrkala *Australia* 12°14S 136°56E **280** A2
Yishan *China* 24°28N 108°38E **228** E7
Yishui *China* 35°47N 118°30E **227** G10
Yishun *Singapore* 1°26N 103°51E **138** A3
Yitong *China* 43°13N 125°20E **227** C13
Yiwu *China* 29°20N 120°3E **229** C13
Yixing *China* 31°21N 119°48E **229** B12
Yiyang *Henan, China* 34°27N 112°10E **226** G7
Yiyang *Hunan, China* 28°35N 112°18E **229** C9
Yiyang *Jiangxi, China* 28°22N 117°20E **229** C11
Yizhang *China* 25°27N 112°57E **229** E9
Yizheng *China* 32°18N 119°10E **229** A12
Ylästö *Finland* 60°17N 24°54E **121** B2
Yli-Kitka *Finland* 66°8N 28°30E **160** C23
Yliki, L. *Greece* 38°24N 23°15E **204** C5
Ylitornio *Finland* 66°19N 23°39E **160** C20
Ylivieska *Finland* 64°4N 24°28E **160** D21
Yngaren *Sweden* 58°50N 16°35E **163** F10
Yoakum *U.S.A.* 29°17N 97°9W **314** G6
Yob ⌓ *Eritrea* 17°15N 37°50E **257** D4
Yobe □ *Nigeria* 12°0N 11°30E **263** C7
Yobuko *Japan* 33°32N 129°54E **222** D1
Yodo → *Japan* 34°45N 135°35E **133** A2
Yog Pt. *Phil.* 14°6N 124°12E **232** D5
Yogan *Togo* 6°23N 1°30E **263** D5
Yoğuntaş *Turkey* 41°50N 27°4E **203** E11
Yogyakarta *Indonesia* 7°49S 110°22E **235** D4
Yogyakarta □ *Indonesia* 7°48S 110°22E **235** D4
Yoho △ *Canada* 51°25N 116°30W **296** C5
Yojoa, L. de *Honduras* 14°53N 88°0W **320** D2
Yok Don △ *Vietnam* 12°50N 107°40E **236** F6
Yokadouma *Cameroon* 3°26N 14°55E **264** B2
Yōkaichi *Japan* 35°6N 136°12E **223** B8
Yōkaichiba *Japan* 35°42N 140°33E **223** B12
Yokkaichi *Japan* 34°55N 136°38E **223** C8
Yoko *Cameroon* 5°32N 12°20E **263** D7
Yokohama *Japan* 35°27N 139°28E **223** B11
Yokosuka *Japan* 35°20N 139°40E **223** B11
Yokote *Japan* 39°20N 140°30E **220** E10
Yola *Nigeria* 9°10N 12°29E **263** D7
Yolaina, Cordillera de *Nic.* 11°30N 84°0W **320** D3
Yolombo *Dem. Rep. of the Congo* 1°36S 23°12E **264** C4
Ýolöten *Turkmenistan* 37°18N 62°21E **247** B9
Yom → *Thailand* 15°35N 100°1E **236** E3
Yombi *Gabon* 1°26S 10°37E **264** C2
Yona *Guam* 13°25N 144°46E **302** d
Yonago *Japan* 35°25N 133°19E **222** B5
Yonaguni-Jima *Japan* 24°27N 123°0E **221** M1
Yonaha-Dake *Japan* 26°43N 128°13E **288** a
Yŏnan *N. Korea* 37°55N 126°11E **224** D3
Yonezawa *Japan* 37°57N 140°4E **220** F10
Yong-in *S. Korea* 37°14N 127°12E **224** D3
Yong Peng *Malaysia* 2°0N 103°3E **237** M4
Yong Sata *Thailand* 7°8N 99°41E **237** J2
Yongama *Dem. Rep. of the Congo* 0°2N 24°35E **264** B4
Yongamp'o *N. Korea* 39°56N 124°23E **224** C2
Yong'an *China* 25°59N 117°25E **229** E11
Yongcheng *China* 33°55N 116°20E **226** H9
Yongchuan *China* 29°17N 105°55E **228** C5
Yongchun *China* 25°16N 118°20E **229** E12
Yongde *China* 24°5N 99°25E **228** E2
Yongdeng *China* 36°38N 103°25E **226** F2
Yongding *China* 24°43N 116°45E **229** E11
Yongdingman *China* 39°50N 116°20E **114** B2
Yonge Street *Toronto, Canada* **141** b3
Yongfeng *China* 27°20N 115°22E **229** D10
Yongfu *China* 24°59N 109°59E **228** E7
Yongfucun *China* 23°8N 113°17E **121** B2
Yonggyap Pass *India* 29°17N 95°37E **241** A5
Yonghe *China* 36°46N 110°38E **226** F6
Yonghong *India* 26°28N 94°58E **241** B5
Yŏnghŭng *N. Korea* 39°31N 127°18E **224** C3
Yŏnghŭng-man *N. Korea* 39°14N 127°30E **224** C3
Yongji *China* 34°52N 110°28E **226** G6
Yongjia *China* 28°10N 120°45E **229** C13
Yongkang *Yunnan, China* 24°9N 99°20E **228** E2
Yongkang *Zhejiang, China* 28°55N 120°2E **229** C13
Yongnian *China* 36°47N 114°29E **226** F8
Yongning *Guangxi Zhuangzu, China* 22°44N 108°28E **228** F7
Yongning *Ningxia Huizu, China* 38°15N 106°14E **226** E4
Yongping *China* 25°27N 99°38E **228** E2
Yongqing *China* 39°25N 116°28E **226** E9
Yongren *China* 26°4N 101°40E **228** D3
Yongsan *S. Korea* 37°32N 126°58E **137** B1
Yongshan *China* 28°11N 103°35E **228** C4
Yongsheng *China* 26°38N 100°46E **228** D3
Yongshun *China* 29°2N 109°51E **228** C7
Yongtai *China* 25°49N 118°58E **229** E12
Yongxin = Jinggangshan *China* 26°58N 114°15E **229** D10
Yongxing *China* 26°9N 113°8E **229** D9
Yongxiu *China* 29°2N 115°42E **229** C10
Yongzhou *China* 26°17N 111°37E **229** D8
Yonibana *S. Leone* 8°30N 12°19W **262** D2
Yonkers *U.S.A.* 40°56N 73°52W **132** A2
Yonne □ *France* 47°50N 3°40E **173** E10
Yonne → *France* 48°23N 2°58E **173** D9
Yopal *Colombia* 5°21N 72°23W **328** B3
York *W. Austral., Australia* 31°52S 116°47E **279** F2
York *Ont., Canada* 43°40N 79°26W **141** A2
York *York, U.K.* 53°58N 1°6W **168** D6
York *Ala., U.S.A.* 32°29N 88°18W **315** E10
York *Nebr., U.S.A.* 40°52N 97°36W **308** E5
York *Pa., U.S.A.* 39°58N 76°44W **309** F15
York, C. *Australia* 10°42S 142°31E **286** F2
York, City of □ *U.K.* 53°58N 1°6W **168** D6
York, Kap *Greenland* 75°55N 66°25W **154** B4
York, Vale of *U.K.* 54°15N 1°25W **168** C6
York I. *Antigua & B.* 17°2N 61°40W **322** b
York Mills *Canada* 43°45N 79°22W **141** A2
York Sd. *Australia* 15°0S 125°5E **278** C4
York University *Canada* 43°43N 79°22W **141** A1
Yorke Pen. *Australia* 34°50S 137°40E **282** C2
Yorketown *Australia* 35°0S 137°33E **282** C2
Yorkshire Dales △ *U.K.* 54°12N 2°10W **168** C5
Yorkshire Wolds *U.K.* 54°8N 0°31W **168** C7
Yorkton *Canada* 51°11N 102°28W **297** C8
Yorkville *Calif., U.S.A.* 38°52N 123°13W **306** G3
Yorkville *Ga., U.S.A.* 33°55N 84°58W **316** B5
Yorkville *Ill., U.S.A.* 41°38N 88°27W **311** C8
Yoro *Honduras* 15°9N 87°7W **320** C2
Yoron-Jima *Japan* 27°2N 128°26E **221** L4
Yorosso *Mali* 12°17N 4°55W **262** C4
Yos Sudarso, Pulau = Dolak, Pulau *Indonesia* 8°0S 138°30E **231** F9
Yosemite △ *U.S.A.* 37°45N 119°40W **306** H7
Yosemite Village *U.S.A.* 37°45N 119°35W **306** H7
Yoshida *Japan* 34°40N 132°42E **222** C4
Yoshimatsu *Japan* 32°0N 130°47E **222** F2
Yoshino-Kumano △ *Japan* 34°12N 135°55E **223** C7
Yoshkar Ola *Russia* 56°38N 47°55E **190** B8
Yotala *Bolivia* 19°10S 65°17W **331** D4
Yotsuya *Tokyo, Japan* **140** a2
Yotvata *Israel* 29°55N 35°2E **251** J6
You Jiang → *China* 22°50N 108°6E **228** F6
You Xian *China* 27°1N 113°17E **229** D9
You'anmen *China* 39°51N 116°19E **114** B1
Youbou *Canada* 48°53N 124°13W **306** B2
Youghal *Ireland* 51°56N 7°52W **166** E4
Youghal B. *Ireland* 51°55N 7°49W **166** E4
Youkounkoun *Guinea* 12°35N 13°11W **262** C2
Young *N.S.W., Australia* 34°19S 148°18E **283** C8
Young *Sask., Canada* 51°47N 105°45W **297** C7
Young *Uruguay* 32°44S 57°36W **334** C4
Young Ra. *N.Z.* 44°10S 169°30E **285** E4
Younghusband, L. *Australia* 30°50S 136°5E **282** A2
Younghusband Pen. *Australia* 36°0S 139°25E **282** D3
Youngsfield *S. Africa* 34°0S 18°30E **118** B1
Youngstown *Alta., Canada* 51°35N 111°10W **297** C6
Youngstown *Fla., U.S.A.* 30°22N 85°26W **316** E4
Youngstown *N.Y., U.S.A.* 43°15N 79°3W **312** C5
Youngstown *Ohio, U.S.A.* 41°6N 80°39W **312** E4
Youngsville *U.S.A.* 41°51N 79°19W **312** E5
Youngwood *U.S.A.* 40°14N 79°34W **312** F5
Youssoufia *Morocco* 32°16N 8°31W **260** B3
Youxi *China* 26°10N 118°13E **229** D12
Youyang *China* 28°47N 108°42E **228** C7
Youyu *China* 40°10N 112°20E **226** D7
Yozgat *Turkey* 39°51N 34°47E **212** C6
Yozgat □ *Turkey* 39°30N 35°0E **212** C6
Ypacaraí △ *Paraguay* 25°18S 57°19W **334** B4
Ypané → *Paraguay* 23°29S 57°19W **334** A4
Yport *France* 49°45N 0°15E **172** C7
Ypres = Ieper *Belgium* 50°51N 2°53E **170** D2
Ypsilanti *U.S.A.* 42°14N 83°37W **311** B13
Yreka *U.S.A.* 41°44N 122°38W **304** F2
Yrghyz *Kazakhstan* 48°37N 61°16E **216** C6
Yrghyz → *Kazakhstan* 48°6N 62°30E **216** C6
Ysabel Chan. *Papua N. G.* 2°0S 150°0E **286** B6
Yssingeaux *France* 45°9N 4°8E **175** C8
Ystabøhamn *Norway* 59°3N 5°23E **164** E2
Ystad *Sweden* 55°26N 13°50E **163** J7
Ysyk-Köl = Balykchy *Kyrgyzstan* 42°26N 76°12E **217** D9
Ysyk-Köl *Kyrgyzstan* 42°25N 77°15E **217** D9
Ysyk-Köl □ *Kyrgyzstan* 42°0N 78°0E **217** D9
Ythan → *U.K.* 57°19N 1°59W **167** D7
Ytre Arna *Norway* 60°27N 5°25E **164** D2
Ytre Enebakk *Norway* 59°44N 11°0E **164** E8
Ytre Rendal *Norway* 61°46N 11°8E **164** C8
Ytterhogdal *Sweden* 62°12N 14°56E **162** B8
Ytyk-Kyuyel *Russia* 62°30N 133°45E **215** C14
Yu Jiang → *China* 23°22N 110°3E **228** F7
Yü Shan *Taiwan* 23°25N 120°52E **225** C2
Yü Shan △ *Taiwan* 24°45N 121°12E **225** C3
Yu Xian = Yuzhou *China* 34°10N 113°28E **226** G7
Yu Xian *Hebei, China* 39°50N 114°35E **226** E8
Yu Xian *Shanxi, China* 38°5N 113°20E **226** E7
Yuan Jiang → *Hunan, China* 28°55N 111°50E **229** C8
Yuan Jiang → *Yunnan, China* 22°20N 103°59E **228** F4
Yuan'an *China* 31°3N 111°34E **229** B8
Yüanch'ang *Taiwan* 23°39N 120°18E **225** C2
Yuanjiang *Hunan, China* 28°47N 112°21E **229** C9
Yuanjiang *Yunnan, China* 23°32N 102°0E **228** F4
Yüanli *Taiwan* 24°27N 120°39E **225** B2
Yüanlin *Taiwan* 23°58N 120°30E **225** C2
Yuanling *China* 28°29N 110°22E **229** C8
Yuanmou *China* 25°42N 101°53E **228** E3
Yuanqu *China* 35°18N 111°40E **226** G6
Yuanshan *Taiwan* 24°45N 121°43E **225** B3
Yuanxiatian *China* 23°12N 113°17E **121** A2
Yuanyang *Henan, China* 35°3N 113°58E **226** G7
Yuanyang *Yunnan, China* 23°10N 102°43E **228** F4
Yuat → *Papua N. G.* 4°10S 143°52E **286** C2
Yuba → *U.S.A.* 39°8N 121°36W **306** F5
Yuba City *U.S.A.* 39°8N 121°37W **306** F5
Yūbari *Japan* 43°4N 141°59E **220** C10
Yubdo *Ethiopia* 8°58N 35°24E **257** F4
Yūbetsu *Japan* 44°13N 143°50E **220** B11
Yubo *Sudan* 5°23N 27°25E **257** F2
Yucatán □ *Mexico* 20°50N 89°0W **319** C7
Yucatán, Canal de *Caribbean* 22°0N 86°30W **320** B2
Yucatán, Península de *Mexico* 19°30N 89°0W **292** H11
Yucatan Basin *Cent. Amer.* 19°0N 86°0W **319** D7
Yucatan Channel = Yucatán, Canal de *Caribbean* 22°0N 86°30W **320** B2
Yucca *U.S.A.* 34°52N 114°9W **307** L12
Yucca Valley *U.S.A.* 34°8N 116°27W **307** L10
Yucheng *China* 36°55N 116°32E **226** F9
Yüch'ih *Taiwan* 23°54N 120°56E **225** C2
Yuching *Taiwan* 23°7N 120°27E **225** C2
Yuci *China* 37°42N 112°46E **226** F7
Yudu *China* 25°59N 115°30E **229** E10
Yuechi *China* 30°34N 106°25E **228** B6
Yuen Long *China* 22°26N 114°2E **219** G11
Yuendumu *Australia* 22°16S 131°49E **278** D5
Yueqing *China* 28°9N 120°59E **229** C13
Yueqing Wan *China* 28°5N 121°20E **229** D13
Yuexi *Anhui, China* 30°50N 116°20E **229** B11
Yuexi *Sichuan, China* 28°37N 102°26E **228** C4
Yuexiu Park *China* 23°8N 113°16E **121** B2
Yueyang *China* 29°21N 113°5E **229** C9
Yufu-Dake *Japan* 33°17N 131°33E **222** D3
Yugan *China* 28°43N 116°37E **229** C11
Yuğluk Dağı *Turkey* 36°59N 33°50E **250** B4
Yugo-Zarad *Russia* 55°40N 37°30E **129** B3
Yugoslavia = Serbia ■ *Europe* 43°20N 20°0E **202** C4
Yuhalixqui, Volcan *Mexico* 19°19N 99°4W **128** C2
Yuhuan *China* 28°9N 121°12E **229** C13
Yühuan Dao *China* 28°5N 121°15E **229** C13
Yujiang *China* 28°10N 116°43E **229** C11
Yukhnov *Russia* 54°44N 35°15E **188** E8
Yūki *Japan* 36°18N 139°53E **223** A11
Yukon *U.S.A.* 35°31N 97°45W **314** D6
Yukon → *U.S.A.* 62°32N 163°54W **303** E7
Yukon-Charley Rivers ⌓ *U.S.A.* 65°15N 144°0W **303** D12
Yukon Delta Nat. Wildlife Refuge ⌓ *U.S.A.* 61°0N 163°0W **303** F7
Yukon Flats *U.S.A.* 66°40N 145°45W **303** C11
Yukon Territory □ *Canada* 63°0N 135°0W **294** C6
Yüksekova *Turkey* 37°34N 44°16E **213** D11
Yukta *Russia* 63°26N 105°42E **215** C11
Yukuhashi *Japan* 33°44N 130°59E **222** D2
Yulara *Australia* 25°10S 130°55E **279** E5
Yule → *Australia* 20°41S 118°17E **278** D2
Yuleba *Australia* 26°37S 149°24E **281** D4
Yulee *U.S.A.* 30°38N 81°36W **316** E8
Yuli *China* 41°19N 86°15E **217** D11
Yuli *Nigeria* 9°44N 10°12E **263** D7
Yüli *Taiwan* 23°20N 121°18E **225** C3
Yulin *Guangxi Zhuangzu, China* 22°40N 110°8E **229** F8
Yulin *Hainan, China* 18°10N 109°31E **236** C7
Yulin *Shaanxi, China* 38°20N 109°30E **226** E5
Yuma *Ariz., U.S.A.* 32°43N 114°37W **307** N12
Yuma *Colo., U.S.A.* 40°8N 102°43W **304** F12
Yuma, B. de *Dom. Rep.* 18°20N 68°35W **321** C6
Yumali *Australia* 35°32S 139°45E **282** C3
Yumbe *Uganda* 3°28N 31°15E **268** B3
Yumbi *Équateur, Dem. Rep. of the Congo* 1°53S 16°34E **264** C3
Yumbi *Maniema, Dem. Rep. of the Congo* 1°12S 26°15E **268** C2
Yumbo *Colombia* 3°35N 76°28W **328** C2
Yumen *China* 39°50N 97°30E **218** C4
Yumurtalık *Turkey* 36°45N 35°48E **250** B6
Yun Gui Gaoyuan *China* 26°0N 104°0E **228** E3
Yun Ling *China* 27°0N 99°20E **228** D2
Yun Xian *Hubei, China* 32°50N 110°46E **229** A8
Yun Xian *Yunnan, China* 24°27N 100°8E **228** E3
Yuna *Australia* 28°20S 115°0E **279** E2
Yunak *Turkey* 38°49N 31°43E **212** C4
Yunan *China* 23°12N 111°30E **229** F8
Yunaska I. *U.S.A.* 52°38N 170°40W **303** K5
Yuncheng *Henan, China* 35°36N 115°57E **226** G8
Yuncheng *Shanxi, China* 35°2N 111°0E **226** G6
Yunfu *China* 22°50N 112°5E **229** F9
Yung Shue Wan *China* 22°13N 114°6E **122** B1
Yungan *Taiwan* 22°49N 120°12E **225** D2
Yungas *Bolivia* 17°0S 66°0W **331** D4
Yungay *Chile* 37°10S 72°5W **334** D1
Yungay *Peru* 9°2S 77°45W **330** B2
Yungk'ang *Taiwan* 23°2N 120°15E **225** C2
Yungki = Jilin *China* 43°44N 126°30E **227** C14
Yungning = Nanning *China* 22°48N 108°20E **228** F7
Yunhe *China* 28°8N 119°33E **229** C12
Yunkai Dashan *China* 22°30N 111°0E **229** F8
Yünlin □ *Taiwan* 23°40N 120°20E **225** C2
Yunlong *China* 25°57N 99°13E **228** E2
Yunmeng *China* 31°2N 113°43E **229** B9
Yunnan □ *China* 25°0N 102°0E **228** E4
Yunotsu *Japan* 35°5N 132°21E **222** B4
Yunquera de Henares *Spain* 40°47N 3°11W **196** E1
Yunshui *Taiwan* 23°23N 120°31E **225** C2
Yunt Dağı *Turkey* 38°56N 27°13E **205** C9
Yunta *Australia* 32°34S 139°36E **281** E2
Yunxi *China* 33°0N 110°22E **226** H6
Yunxiao *China* 23°59N 117°18E **229** F11
Yupanqui Basin *Pac. Oc.* 19°0S 101°0W **289** J17
Yuping *China* 27°13N 108°56E **228** D7
Yupukarri *Guyana* 3°45N 59°20W **329** C6
Yuqing *China* 27°13N 107°53E **228** D6
Yuraygir △ *Australia* 29°45S 153°15E **281** D5
Yurga *Russia* 55°42N 84°51E **214** D9
Yurimaguas *Peru* 5°55S 76°7W **330** B2
Yurkiyka *Ukraine* 48°42N 28°35E **183** B13
Yurungkax He → *China* 38°5N 80°34E **217** E10
Yuryev = Tartu *Estonia* 58°20N 26°44E **188** C4
Yuryev-Polskiy *Russia* 56°30N 39°40E **188** D10
Yuryevets *Russia* 57°25N 43°2E **190** B6
Yuscarán *Honduras* 13°58N 86°45W **320** D2
Yûsef, Bahr → *Egypt* 28°25N 30°35E **256** B3
Yushan *China* 28°42N 118°10E **229** C12
Yushanzhen *China* 29°28N 108°22E **228** C7
Yushe *China* 37°4N 112°58E **226** F7
Yushu *Jilin, China* 44°43N 126°38E **227** B14
Yushu *Qinghai, China* 33°5N 96°55E **218** C4
Yūsofābād *Iran* 35°43N 51°24E **141** A2
Yusufeli *Turkey* 40°50N 41°33E **213** B9
Yutai *China* 35°0N 116°45E **226** G9
Yutian *Hebei, China* 39°53N 117°45E **227** E9
Yutian *Sinkiang-Uigur, China* 36°52N 81°42E **217** E10
Yütze = Yuci *China* 37°42N 112°46E **226** F7
Yüweng Tao *Taiwan* 23°36N 119°30E **225** C1
Yuxarı Qarabağ = Nagorno-Karabakh □ *Azerbaijan* 39°55N 46°45E **213** C12
Yuxi *China* 24°30N 102°35E **228** E4
Yuyao *China* 30°3N 121°10E **229** B13
Yuyuantan Park *Beijing, China* **114** b2
Yuzawa *Japan* 39°10N 140°30E **220** E10
Yuzha *Russia* 56°34N 42°1E **190** B6
Yuzhno-Sakhalinsk *Russia* 46°58N 142°45E **215** E15
Yuzhnouralsk *Russia* 54°26N 61°15E **216** B6
Yuzhnyy □ *Russia* 44°0N 40°0E **191** H5
Yuzhou *China* 34°10N 113°28E **226** G7
Yuzovka = Donetsk *Ukraine* 48°0N 37°45E **189** J9
Yvelines □ *France* 48°40N 1°45E **173** D8
Yverdon-les-Bains *Switz.* 46°47N 6°39E **179** J2
Yvetot *France* 49°37N 0°44E **172** C7
Yzeure *France* 46°33N 3°22E **173** F10

Z

Zaandam *Neths.* 52°26N 4°49E **112** A1
Zaandijk *Neths.* 52°28N 4°49E **112** A1
Zaanstad *Neths.* 52°27N 4°50E **112** A1
Zab, Monts du *Algeria* 34°55N 5°0E **261** B6
Zāb al Kabīr → *Iraq* 36°1N 43°24E **213** D10
Zāb aş Şaghīr → *Iraq* 35°17N 43°29E **213** E10
Žabalj *Serbia* 45°21N 20°5E **182** E5
Žabari *Serbia* 44°22N 21°15E **202** B5
Zabarjad *Egypt* 23°40N 36°12E **256** C4
Zabaykalsk *Russia* 49°40N 117°25E **215** E12
Zabbar *Malta* 35°53N 14°32E **206** F8
Záběhlice *Czech Rep.* 50°3N 14°29E **135** B2
Zabīd *Yemen* 14°0N 43°10E **248** D3
Zabīd, W. → *Yemen* 14°7N 43°6E **248** D3
Zabki *Poland* 52°17N 21°6E **142** B2
Ząbkowice Śląskie *Poland* 50°35N 16°50E **185** H3
Žabljak *Montenegro* 43°18N 19°5E **202** C3
Zabłudów *Poland* 53°0N 23°19E **185** F9
Żabno *Poland* 50°9N 20°53E **185** H7
Zābol *Iran* 31°0N 61°32E **247** D9
Zābol □ *Afghan.* 32°0N 67°0E **240** C2
Zābolī *Iran* 27°10N 61°35E **247** E9
Zabolotiv *Ukraine* 48°28N 25°18E **183** B10
Zabolottya *Ukraine* 51°38N 24°16E **185** G11
Zabré *Burkina Faso* 11°12N 0°36W **263** C4
Zábřeh *Czech Rep.* 49°53N 16°52E **181** B9
Zabrze *Poland* 50°18N 18°50E **185** H5
Zabuzhzhya *Ukraine* 51°21N 23°42E **185** G10
Zabzuga *Ghana* 9°20N 0°30E **263** D5
Zacapa *Guatemala* 14°59N 89°31W **320** D2
Zacapu *Mexico* 19°50N 101°43W **318** D4
Zacatecas *Mexico* 22°47N 102°35W **318** C4
Zacatecas □ *Mexico* 23°0N 103°0W **318** C4
Zacatecoluca *El Salv.* 13°29N 88°51W **320** D2
Zacharo *Greece* 37°30N 21°39E **204** D3
Zachary *U.S.A.* 30°39N 91°9W **314** F9
Zachodnio-Pomorskie □ *Poland* 53°40N 15°50E **184** E2
Żacisze *Poland* 52°17N 21°4E **142** B2
Zacoalco de Torres *Mexico* 20°14N 103°35W **318** C4
Zacualtipán *Mexico* 20°39N 98°36W **319** C5
Zadar *Croatia* 44°8N 15°14E **199** D12
Zadawa *Nigeria* 11°33N 10°19E **263** C7

Zadetkyi Kyun *Burma* 10°0N 98°25E **237** G2
Zadonsk *Russia* 52°25N 38°56E **189** F10
Zafarqand *Iran* 33°11N 52°29E **247** C7
Zafra *Spain* 38°26N 6°30W **195** G4
Żagań *Poland* 51°39N 15°22E **185** G2
Zagaoua *Chad* 16°0N 21°10E **259** E4
Žagarė *Lithuania* 56°21N 23°15E **184** B10
Zagazig *Egypt* 30°40N 31°30E **256** H7
Zāgheh *Iran* 33°30N 48°42E **247** C6
Zaghouan *Tunisia* 36°23N 10°10E **258** A2
Zaghouan □ *Tunisia* 36°20N 10°0E **261** A7
Zaglou *Algeria* 27°17N 0°3W **261** C4
Zagnanado *Benin* 7°18N 2°28E **263** D5
Zagora *Greece* 39°27N 23°6E **204** B5
Zagora *Morocco* 30°22N 5°51W **260** B3
Zagorje *Slovenia* 46°8N 15°0E **199** B11
Zagórów *Poland* 52°10N 17°54E **185** F4
Zagorsk = Sergiyev Posad *Russia* 56°20N 38°10E **188** D10
Zagorsky = Krasnozavodsk *Russia* 56°27N 38°25E **188** D10
Zagórz *Poland* 49°30N 22°14E **185** J9
Zagreb *Croatia* 45°50N 15°58E **199** C12
Zagreb ✈ **(ZAG)** *Croatia* 45°45N 16°4E **199** C13
Zāgros, Kūhhā-ye *Iran* 33°45N 48°5E **247** C6
Zagros Mts. = Zāgros, Kūhhā-ye *Iran* 33°45N 48°5E **247** C6
Žagubica *Serbia* 44°15N 21°47E **202** B5
Zaguinaso *Ivory C.* 10°1N 6°14W **262** C3
Zagyva ➔ *Hungary* 47°5N 20°4E **182** C5
Zahamena ⌓ *Madag.* 17°37S 48°49E **272** B2
Zāhedān *Fārs, Iran* 28°46N 53°52E **247** D7
Zāhedān *Sīstān va Balūchestān, Iran* 29°30N 60°50E **247** D9
Zahirabad *India* 17°43N 77°37E **244** F3
Zahlah *Lebanon* 33°52N 35°50E **250** E6
Zahna *Germany* 51°55N 12°49E **178** D8
Záhony *Hungary* 48°25N 22°11E **182** B7
Zahrā *Iraq* 33°22N 44°19E **113** A1
Ẓahrān *Si. Arabia* 17°40N 43°30E **248** C3
Zainsk *Russia* 55°18N 52°4E **190** C11
Zaïre = Congo ➔ *Africa* 6°4S 12°24E **265** D2
Zaïre = Congo, Dem. Rep. of the ■ *Africa* 3°0S 23°0E **265** C4
Zaire □ *Angola* 7°0S 14°0E **265** D2
Zaječar *Serbia* 43°53N 22°18E **202** C6
Zaka *Zimbabwe* 20°20S 31°29E **271** B5
Zakamensk *Russia* 50°23N 103°17E **215** D11
Zakani *Dem. Rep. of the Congo* 2°33N 23°16E **264** B4
Zakarpattya □ *Ukraine* 48°20N 23°20E **183** B8
Zakataly = Zaqatala *Azerbaijan* 41°38N 46°35E **191** K8
Zakbayemé *Cameroon* 4°2N 10°34E **264** B2
Zakharkovo *Russia* 55°46N 37°18E **129** B1
Zakhodnaya Dzvina = Daugava ➔ *Latvia* 57°4N 24°3E **188** D3
Zākhū *Iraq* 37°10N 42°50E **213** D10
Zakinthos = Zakynthos *Greece* 37°47N 20°54E **207** D2
Zakinthos, Diavlos *Greece* 37°50N 21°0E **207** D2
Zakopane *Poland* 49°18N 19°57E **185** J6
Zakouma *Chad* 10°54N 19°49E **259** F3
Zakouma △ *Chad* 10°52N 19°45E **259** F3
Zakroczym *Poland* 52°26N 20°38E **185** F7
Zakros *Greece* 35°6N 26°10E **207** E7
Zakynthos *Greece* 37°47N 20°54E **207** D2
Zakynthos □ *Greece* 37°47N 20°57E **204** D2
Zakynthos ✈ **(ZTH)** *Greece* 37°45N 20°50E **207** D2
Zala *Angola* 7°52S 13°42E **265** D2
Zala *Ethiopia* 6°28N 37°13E **257** F4
Zala □ *Hungary* 46°42N 16°50E **182** D1
Zala ➔ *Hungary* 46°43N 17°16E **182** D2
Zalaegerszeg *Hungary* 46°53N 16°47E **182** D1
Zalakomár *Hungary* 46°33N 17°10E **182** D2
Zalalövő *Hungary* 46°51N 16°35E **182** D1
Zalamea de la Serena *Spain* 38°40N 5°38W **195** G5
Zalamea la Real *Spain* 37°41N 6°38W **195** H4
Zalău *Romania* 47°12N 23°3E **182** C8
Žalec *Slovenia* 46°16N 15°10E **199** B12
Zaleshchiki = Zalishchyky *Ukraine* 48°45N 25°45E **183** B10
Zalesye *Russia* 54°50N 21°31E **184** D8
Zalew Wiślany *Poland* 54°20N 19°50E **184** D6
Zalewo *Poland* 53°50N 19°41E **184** E6
Ẓalīm *Si. Arabia* 22°43N 42°10E **248** B3
Zalingei *Sudan* 12°51N 23°29E **259** F4
Zalishchyky *Ukraine* 48°45N 25°45E **183** B10
Žalov *Czech Rep.* 50°10N 14°22E **135** A2
Zalṭan *Ajdābiyā, Libya* 28°51N 19°52E **258** C3
Zalṭan *Zuwārah, Libya* 32°57N 11°52E **258** B2
Zalṭan, Jabal *Libya* 28°46N 19°45E **258** C3
Zalun *Burma* 17°29N 95°34E **241** G5
Załuski *Poland* 52°9N 20°55E **142** C1
Zama L. *Canada* 58°45N 119°5W **296** B5
Zambales □ *Phil.* 15°20N 120°10E **232** D3
Zambales Mts. *Phil.* 15°45N 120°5E **232** D3
Zambeke *Dem. Rep. of the Congo* 2°8N 25°17E **268** B2
Zambeze ➔ *Africa* 18°35S 36°20E **269** F4
Zambezi = Zambeze ➔ *Africa* 18°35S 36°20E **269** F4
Zambezi *Zambia* 13°30S 23°15E **265** E4
Zambezi △ *Zimbabwe* 17°54S 25°41E **269** F2
Zambezia □ *Mozam.* 16°15S 37°30E **269** F4
Zambia ■ *Africa* 15°0S 28°0E **269** F2
Zamboanga *Phil.* 6°59N 122°3E **233** H4
Zamboanga del Norte □ *Phil.* 8°0N 123°0E **233** H4
Zamboanga del Sur □ *Phil.* 7°40N 123°0E **233** H4
Zambrano *Colombia* 9°45N 74°49W **328** B3
Zambrów *Poland* 52°59N 22°14E **185** F9
Zamdorf *Germany* 48°8N 11°35E **131** B2
Zametchino *Russia* 53°30N 42°30E **190** D6
Zamfara □ *Nigeria* 12°10N 6°0E **263** C6
Zamfara ➔ *Nigeria* 12°5N 4°2E **263** C5
Zamora *Ecuador* 4°4S 78°58W **328** D2
Zamora *Michoacan, Mexico* 19°59N 102°16W **318** D4
Zamora *Spain* 41°30N 5°45W **194** D5
Zamora □ *Spain* 41°30N 5°46W **194** D5
Zamora ➔ *Ecuador* 2°59N 78°13W **328** D2
Zamora-Chinchipe □ *Ecuador* 4°15S 78°50W **328** D2
Zamość *Poland* 50°43N 23°15E **185** H10
Zamtang *China* 32°26N 101°6E **228** A3
Zam[illegible]ro, Sierra del *V[illegible]zuela* 4°0N 62°30W **329** C5
Zamzam, W. ➔ *Libya* 30°58N 14°48E **258** B2
Zan *Ghana* 9°26N 0°17W **263** D4
Zanaga *Congo* 2°48S 13°48E **264** C2
Záncara ➔ *Spain* 39°18N 3°18W **197** F1
Zanda *China* 31°32N 79°50E **218** C2
Zanderij *Suriname* 5°20N 55°16W **329** B6
Zandu *Dem. Rep. of the Congo* 5°11S 18°16E **265** D3
Zandvoort *Neths.* 52°22N 4°32E **170** B4
Zanesville *U.S.A.* 39°56N 82°1W **312** G2
Zanevka *Russia* 59°55N 30°31E **137** B3
Zangābād *Iran* 38°26N 46°44E **246** B5
Zangliveri *Greece* 40°36N 23°15E **202** F7
Zangue ➔ *Mozam.* 17°50S 35°21E **269** F4
Zanjān *Iran* 36°40N 48°35E **213** D13
Zanjān □ *Iran* 37°20N 49°30E **247** B6
Zanjān ➔ *Iran* 37°8N 47°47E **247** B6
Zannone *Italy* 40°58N 13°3E **200** B6
Zanow = Sianów *Poland* 54°13N 16°18E **184** D3
Zante = Zakynthos *Greece* 37°47N 20°54E **207** D2
Zanthus *Australia* 31°2S 123°34E **279** F3
Zanzibar *Tanzania* 6°12S 39°12E **268** D4
Zanzūr *Libya* 32°55N 13°1E **258** B2
Zaouatallaz *Algeria* 24°52N 8°30E **261** D6
Zaouiet El-Kala = Bordj Omar Driss *Algeria* 28°10N 6°40E **261** C6
Zaouiet Reggâne *Algeria* 26°32N 0°3E **261** C5
Zaoyang *China* 32°10N 112°45E **229** A9
Zaozernyy *Kazakhstan* 53°6N 71°9E **217** B8
Zaozhuang *China* 34°50N 117°35E **227** G9
Zap Suyu = Zāb al Kabīr ➔ *Iraq* 36°1N 43°24E **213** D10
Zapadna Morava ➔ *Serbia* 43°38N 21°30E **202** C5
Zapadnaya Dvina = Daugava ➔ *Latvia* 57°4N 24°3E **188** D3
Zapadnaya Dvina *Russia* 56°15N 32°3E **188** D7
Západné Beskydy *Europe* 49°30N 19°0E **181** B12
Zapadni Rodopi *Bulgaria* 41°50N 24°0E **202** E7
Západočeský □ *Czech Rep.* 49°35N 13°0E **180** B6
Zapala *Argentina* 39°0S 70°5W **336** A2
Zapaleri, Cerro *Bolivia* 22°49S 67°11W **334** A2
Zapata *U.S.A.* 26°55N 99°16W **314** H5
Zapatón ➔ *Spain* 39°0N 6°49W **195** F4
Zapiga *Chile* 19°40S 69°55W **330** D4
Zapolyarnyy *Russia* 69°26N 30°51E **160** B24
Zapopán *Mexico* 20°43N 103°24W **318** C4
Zaporizhzhya *Ukraine* 47°50N 35°10E **189** J8
Zaporizhzhya □ *Ukraine* 46°55N 35°50E **189** J8
Zaporozhye = Zaporizhzhya *Ukraine* 47°50N 35°10E **189** J8
Zapote *Phil.* 14°27N 120°56E **127** C1
Zappeion *Athens, Greece* **112** c2
Zaqatala *Azerbaijan* 41°38N 46°35E **191** K8
Zara *Turkey* 39°58N 37°43E **212** C7
Zarafshon *Uzbekistan* 41°34N 64°12E **216** D6
Zaragoza *Colombia* 7°30N 74°52W **328** B3
Zaragoza *Coahuila, Mexico* 28°29N 100°55W **318** B4
Zaragoza *Nuevo León, Mexico* 23°58N 99°46W **319** C5
Zaragoza *Spain* 41°39N 0°53W **196** D4
Zaragoza □ *Spain* 41°35N 1°0W **196** D4
Zarand *Kermān, Iran* 30°46N 56°34E **247** D8
Zarand *Markazī, Iran* 35°18N 50°25E **247** C6
Zărandului, Munţii *Romania* 46°14N 22°7E **182** D7
Zaranj *Afghan.* 30°55N 61°55E **240** C1
Zarasai *Lithuania* 55°40N 26°20E **188** E4
Zárate *Argentina* 34°7S 59°0W **334** C4
Zarautz *Spain* 43°17N 2°10W **196** B2
Zaraysk *Russia* 54°48N 38°53E **188** E10
Zaraza *Venezuela* 9°21N 65°19W **329** B4
Zard, Kūh-e *Iran* 32°22N 50°4E **247** C6
Zarechye *Russia* 55°41N 37°22E **129** B2
Zāreh *Iran* 35°7N 49°9E **247** C6
Zari *Nigeria* 13°4N 12°45E **263** C7
Zaria *Nigeria* 11°0N 7°40E **263** C6
Żarki *Poland* 50°38N 19°23E **185** H6
Zarko *Greece* 39°38N 22°6E **204** B4
Zarneh *Iran* 33°55N 46°10E **246** C5
Zărneşti *Romania* 45°33N 25°18E **183** E10
Zaros *Greece* 35°8N 24°54E **207** E5
Żarów *Poland* 50°56N 16°29E **185** H3
Zarqā', Nahr az ➔ *Jordan* 32°10N 35°37E **251** F6
Zarrīn *Iran* 32°46N 54°37E **247** C7
Zaruma *Ecuador* 3°40S 79°38W **328** D2
Żary *Poland* 51°37N 15°10E **185** G2
Zarza de Granadilla *Spain* 40°14N 6°3W **194** E4
Zarzaïtine *Algeria* 28°15N 9°34E **261** C6
Zarzal *Colombia* 4°24N 76°4W **328** C2
Zarzis *Tunisia* 33°31N 11°2E **258** B2
Zas *Spain* 43°4N 8°53W **194** B2
Zashaghan *Kazakhstan* 51°11N 51°20E **216** B4
Zaskar ➔ *India* 34°13N 77°20E **243** B7
Zaskar Mts. *India* 33°15N 77°30E **243** C7
Zastavna *Ukraine* 48°31N 25°51E **183** B10
Zastron *S. Africa* 30°18S 27°7E **270** D4
Żatec *Czech Rep.* 50°20N 13°32E **180** A6
Zaterechnyy *Russia* 44°48N 45°11E **191** H7
Zatishye = Elektrostal *Russia* 55°41N 38°32E **188** E10
Zator *Poland* 49°59N 19°28E **185** J6
Zatyshshya *Ukraine* 47°20N 29°51E **183** C14
Zavala *Bos.-H.* 42°50N 17°59E **202** D1
Zavāreh *Iran* 33°29N 52°28E **247** C7
Zave *Zimbabwe* 17°6S 30°1E **271** A5
Zaventem *Belgium* 50°53N 4°28E **116** A2
Zavetnoye *Russia* 47°13N 43°50E **191** G6
Zavidovići *Bos.-H.* 44°27N 18°10E **182** F3
Zavitaya = Zavitinsk *Russia* 50°10N 129°20E **215** D13
Zavitinsk *Russia* 50°10N 129°20E **215** D13
Zavodovski, I. *Antarctica* 56°0S 27°45W **151** B1
Zavodskoy = Komsomolskiy *Russia* 54°27N 45°33E **190** C7
Zavolzhsk *Russia* 57°30N 42°0E **190** B6
Zavolzhye = Zavolzhsk *Russia* 57°30N 42°0E **190** B6
Zavolzhye *Russia* 56°37N 43°26E **190** B6
Zawady *Poland* 52°10N 21°6E **142** B2
Zawadzkie *Poland* 50°37N 18°28E **185** H5
Zawichost *Poland* 50°48N 21°51E **185** H8
Zawidów *Poland* 51°1N 15°1E **185** G2
Zawiercie *Poland* 50°30N 19°24E **185** H6
Zāwīyah, J. az *Syria* 35°45N 36°35E **250** C7
Zāwiyat al Bayḍā = Al Bayḍā *Libya* 32°50N 21°44E **258** B4
Zāwiyat Masūs *Libya* 31°35N 21°1E **258** B4
Zâwiyet Abû Musallam *Egypt* 29°56N 31°9E **117** B1
Zawrā' Park *Iraq* 33°18N 44°23E **113** B2
Zâwyet Shammas *Egypt* 31°30N 26°37E **256** A2
Zâwyet Um el Rakham *Egypt* 31°18N 27°1E **256** A2
Zâwyet Ungeîla *Egypt* 31°23N 26°42E **256** A2
Zāyā *Iraq* 33°33N 44°13E **246** C5
Zāyandeh ➔ *Iran* 32°35N 52°0E **247** C7
Zaymah *Si. Arabia* 21°37N 40°6E **248** B3
Zaysan *Kazakhstan* 47°28N 84°52E **217** C10
Zaysan Köli *Kazakhstan* 48°0N 83°0E **217** C10
Zayü *China* 28°48N 97°27E **228** C1
Zazafotsy *Madag.* 21°11S 46°21E **272** C2
Zāzamt, W. ➔ *Libya* 30°29N 14°30E **258** B2
Zazir, O. ➔ *Algeria* 22°0N 5°40E **261** D6
Zázrivá *Slovak Rep.* 49°16N 19°7E **181** B12
Zbarazh *Ukraine* 49°43N 25°44E **177** D13
Zbąszyń *Poland* 52°14N 15°56E **185** F2
Zbąszynek *Poland* 52°16N 15°51E **185** F2
Zblewo *Poland* 53°56N 18°19E **184** E5
Zbraslav *Czech Rep.* 49°58N 14°23E **135** C2
Zbruch ➔ 48°32N 26°27E **183** B11
Zbuzany *Czech Rep.* 50°1N 14°17E **135** B1
Žďár nad Sázavou *Czech Rep.* 49°34N 15°57E **180** B8
Zdiby *Czech Rep.* 50°9N 14°27E **135** B2
Zdolbuniv *Ukraine* 50°30N 26°15E **177** C14
Ždrelo *Serbia* 44°16N 21°28E **202** B5
Zduńska Wola *Poland* 51°37N 18°59E **185** G5
Zduny *Poland* 51°39N 17°21E **185** G4
Zearing *U.S.A.* 42°10N 93°18W **310** B3
Zeballos *Canada* 49°59N 126°50W **296** D3
Zebbug *Malta* 35°52N 14°26E **206** F7
Zebbug *Gozo, Malta* 36°4N 14°14E **206** E6
Zebediela *S. Africa* 24°20S 29°17E **271** B4
Zebila *Ghana* 10°55N 0°30W **263** C4
Zebulon *U.S.A.* 33°6N 84°21W **316** B5
Zeebrugge *Belgium* 51°19N 3°12E **170** C3
Zeehan *Australia* 41°52S 145°25E **281** G4
Zeekoevlei *S. Africa* 34°4S 18°31E **118** B2
Zeeland *U.S.A.* 42°49N 86°1W **311** B10
Zeeland □ *Neths.* 51°30N 3°50E **170** C3
Zeelandia *Neth. Ant.* 17°30N 62°59W **322** a
Zeerust *S. Africa* 25°31S 26°4E **270** C4
Zefat *Israel* 32°58N 35°29E **250** F6
Zegdou *Algeria* 29°51N 4°45W **260** C4
Zege *Ethiopia* 11°43N 37°18E **257** E4
Zeggerene, Iracher *Mali* 16°49N 2°16E **263** B5
Zégoua *Mali* 10°32N 5°35W **262** C3
Zehden = Cedynia *Poland* 52°53N 14°12E **185** F1
Zehdenick *Germany* 52°58N 13°20E **178** C9
Zehlendorf *Germany* 52°26N 13°16E **115** B2
Zeigler *U.S.A.* 37°54N 89°3W **310** G7
Zeil, Mt. *Australia* 23°30S 132°23E **278** D5
Zeila *Somali Rep.* 11°21N 43°30E **267** B5
Zeist *Neths.* 52°5N 5°15E **170** B5
Zeitz *Germany* 51°2N 12°7E **178** D8
Zejtun *Malta* 35°51N 14°32E **206** F8
Żelechów *Poland* 51°49N 21°54E **185** G8
Zelena *Ukraine* 48°3N 24°45E **183** B9
Zelengora *Bos.-H.* 43°22N 18°30E **202** C2
Zelenodolsk *Russia* 55°55N 48°30E **190** C9
Zelenogorsk *Russia* 60°12N 29°43E **188** B5
Zelenograd *Russia* 56°1N 37°12E **188** D9
Zelenogradsk *Russia* 54°53N 20°29E **184** D7
Zelenokumsk *Russia* 44°24N 44°0E **191** H6
Zeleqa, W. ➔ *Egypt* 29°7N 34°31E **251** J5
Železná Ruda *Czech Rep.* 49°8N 13°15E **180** B6
Železnik *Serbia* 44°43N 20°23E **202** B4
Zelfana *Algeria* 32°27N 4°15E **261** B5
Zelienople *U.S.A.* 40°48N 80°8W **312** F4
Želiezovce *Slovak Rep.* 48°3N 18°40E **181** C11
Zelina *Croatia* 45°57N 16°16E **199** C13
Zell *Baden-W., Germany* 47°42N 7°52E **179** H3
Zell *Rhld-Pfz., Germany* 50°1N 7°10E **179** E3
Zell am See *Austria* 47°19N 12°47E **180** D5
Zella-Mehlis *Germany* 50°39N 10°40E **178** E6
Zelmen = Rovnoye *Russia* 50°52N 46°3E **190** E8
Zelów *Poland* 51°28N 19°14E **185** G6
Zeltweg *Austria* 47°11N 14°45E **180** D7
Zelyony Dol = Zelenodolsk *Russia* 55°55N 48°30E **190** C9
Žemaitijos △ *Lithuania* 56°2N 21°55E **184** B8
Zembra, I. *Tunisia* 37°5N 10°56E **258** A2
Zemgale = Jelgava *Latvia* 56°41N 23°49E **184** B10
Zémio *C.A.R.* 5°2N 25°5E **264** A5
Zemlya Imperatora Nikolaya II = Severnaya Zemlya *Russia* 79°0N 100°0E **215** B11
Zemmora *Algeria* 35°44N 0°51E **261** A5
Zemmur *W. Sahara* 25°5N 12°0W **260** C2
Zemongo ⌓ *C.A.R.* 6°45N 25°5E **264** A5
Zemoul, O. ➔ *Algeria* 29°15N 7°0W **260** C3
Zempelburg = Sępólno Krajeńskie *Poland* 53°26N 17°30E **184** E4
Zempléni-hegység *Hungary* 48°25N 21°25E **182** B6
Zemplínska šírava *Slovak Rep.* 48°48N 22°0E **181** C15
Zempoala *Mexico* 19°27N 96°23W **319** D5
Zemun *Serbia* 44°51N 20°25E **202** B4
Zendeh Jān *Afghan.* 34°21N 61°45E **240** B1
Zengbé *Cameroon* 5°46N 13°4E **263** D7
Zengcheng *China* 23°13N 113°52E **229** F9
Zenica *Bos.-H.* 44°10N 17°57E **182** F2
Zenne ➔ *Belgium* 51°4N 4°26E **116** A2
Zentsūji *Japan* 34°14N 133°47E **222** C5
Zenza ➔ *Angola* 8°45S 13°24E **265** D2
Zenza do Itombe *Angola* 9°16S 14°13E **265** D2
Žepče *Bos.-H.* 44°28N 18°2E **182** F3
Zephyr Field *U.S.A.* 30°1N 90°5W **131** B1
Zephyrhills *U.S.A.* 28°14N 82°11W **317** G7
Zepu *China* 38°11N 77°16E **217** E9
Zeraf, Bahr ez ➔ *Sudan* 9°42N 30°52E **257** F3
Żerań *Poland* 52°18N 20°58E **142** B1
Zerbst *Germany* 51°58N 12°5E **178** D8
Zerhamra *Algeria* 29°58N 2°30W **261** C4
Żerków *Poland* 52°4N 17°32E **185** F4
Zermatt *Switz.* 46°2N 7°46E **179** J3
Zernez *Switz.* 46°42N 10°7E **179** J6
Zernograd *Russia* 46°52N 40°19E **191** G5
Zernovoy = Zernograd *Russia* 46°52N 40°19E **191** G5
Zero Milestone *Washington, D.C., U.S.A.* **143** b1
Zerqan *Albania* 41°27N 20°20E **202** E4
Zerzeń *Poland* 52°12N 21°7E **142** B2
Zestaponi *Georgia* 42°6N 43°0E **191** J6
Zetel *Germany* 53°25N 7°58E **178** B3
Zetland = Shetland □ *U.K.* 60°30N 1°30W **167** A7
Zeulenroda *Germany* 50°39N 11°59E **178** E7
Zévallos *Guadeloupe* 16°18N 61°17W **322** e
Zeven *Germany* 53°17N 9°16E **178** B5
Zevenaar *Neths.* 51°56N 6°5E **170** C6
Zévio *Italy* 45°22N 11°8E **198** C8
Zeya *Russia* 53°48N 127°14E **215** D13
Zeya ➔ *Russia* 51°42N 128°53E **215** D13
Zeyne *Turkey* 36°25N 33°31E **250** B4
Zeytinbaği *Turkey* 40°24N 28°47E **203** F12
Zeytinburnu *Turkey* 40°58N 28°53E **122** C1
Zeytindağ *Turkey* 38°58N 27°4E **205** C9
Zghartā *Lebanon* 34°21N 35°53E **250** D6
Zgierz *Poland* 51°50N 19°27E **185** G6
Zgorzelec *Poland* 51°10N 15°0E **185** G2
Zguriţa *Moldova* 48°8N 28°1E **183** B13
Zhabei *China* 31°16N 121°26E **138** B1
Zhabinka *Belarus* 52°13N 24°2E **185** F11
Zhabokrych *Ukraine* 48°23N 28°59E **183** B13
Zhailma *Kazakhstan* 51°37N 61°33E **216** B6
Zhalaghash *Kazakhstan* 45°5N 64°40E **216** C6
Zhaltyr *Kazakhstan* 51°37N 69°49E **217** B7
Zhambyl = Taraz *Kazakhstan* 42°54N 71°22E **217** D8
Zhambyl □ *Kazakhstan* 44°0N 72°0E **217** D8
Zhanatas *Kazakhstan* 43°35N 69°35E **217** D7
Zhangaly *Kazakhstan* 47°1N 50°37E **191** G10
Zhangaözen *Kazakhstan* 43°18N 52°48E **216** D4
Zhangaqala *Kazakhstan* 48°56N 49°36E **191** F9
Zhangaqazaly *Kazakhstan* 45°48N 62°6E **216** C6
Zhangatas = Zhanatas *Kazakhstan* 43°35N 69°35E **217** D7
Zhangbei *China* 41°10N 114°45E **226** D8
Zhangguangcai Ling *China* 45°0N 129°0E **227** B15
Zhangjiabian *China* 22°33N 113°28E **219** F9
Zhangjiagang *China* 31°55N 120°30E **231** B13
Zhangjiakou *China* 40°48N 114°55E **226** D8
Zhangping *China* 25°17N 117°23E **229** E11
Zhangpu *China* 24°8N 117°35E **229** E11
Zhangshu *China* 28°4N 115°29E **229** C10
Zhangwu *China* 42°43N 123°52E **227** C12
Zhangye *China* 38°50N 100°23E **218** C5
Zhangzhou *China* 24°30N 117°35E **229** E11
Zhanhua *China* 37°40N 118°8E **227** F10
Zhänibek *Kazakhstan* 49°25N 46°50E **190** F8
Zhanjiang *China* 21°15N 110°20E **229** G8
Zhannetty, Ostrov *Russia* 76°43N 158°0E **215** B16
Zhanyi *China* 25°38N 103°48E **228** E4
Zhanyu *China* 44°30N 122°30E **227** B12
Zhao Xian *China* 37°43N 114°45E **226** F8
Zhao'an *China* 23°41N 117°10E **229** F11
Zhaocheng *China* 36°22N 111°38E **226** F6
Zhaojue *China* 28°1N 102°49E **228** C4
Zhaoping *China* 24°11N 110°48E **229** E8
Zhaoqing *China* 23°0N 112°20E **229** F9
Zhaotong *China* 27°20N 103°44E **228** D4
Zhaoyuan *Heilongjiang, China* 45°27N 125°0E **227** B13
Zhaoyuan *Shandong, China* 37°20N 120°23E **227** F11
Zhari Namco *China* 31°6N 85°36E **218** C3
Zharkent *Kazakhstan* 44°10N 80°0E **217** D10
Zharkovskiy *Russia* 55°56N 32°19E **188** E7
Zhashkiv *Ukraine* 49°15N 30°5E **177** D16
Zhashui *China* 33°40N 109°8E **226** H5
Zhaslyk *Uzbekistan* 43°58N 57°10E **216** D5
Zhayrang *Kazakhstan* 48°20N 70°10E **217** C8
Zhayyq ➔ *Kazakhstan* 47°0N 51°48E **187** E9
Zhdanov = Mariupol *Ukraine* 47°5N 37°31E **189** J9
Zhdanov *Russia* 55°44N 37°41E **129** B4
Zhecheng *China* 34°7N 115°20E **226** G8
Zhegao *China* 31°46N 117°45E **229** B11
Zhejiang □ *China* 29°0N 120°0E **229** C13
Zheleznodorozhnyy = Qŭnghirot *Uzbekistan* 43°2N 58°50E **216** D5
Zheleznodorozhnyy *Kaliningrad, Russia* 54°22N 21°19E **184** D8
Zheleznodorozhnyy *Komi, Russia* 62°35N 50°55E **186** B9
Zheleznodorozhnyy *Moskva, Russia* 55°45N 38°0E **129** B6
Zheleznogorsk *Russia* 52°22N 35°23E **189** F8
Zheleznogorsk-Ilimskiy *Russia* 56°34N 104°8E **215** D11
Zheltyye Vody = Zhovti Vody *Ukraine* 48°21N 33°31E **189** H7
Zhen'an *China* 33°27N 109°9E **226** H5
Zhenba *China* 32°34N 107°58E **228** A6
Zhenfeng *China* 25°22N 105°40E **228** E5
Zheng'an *China* 28°32N 107°27E **228** C6
Zhengding *China* 38°8N 114°32E **226** E8
Zhenghe *China* 27°20N 118°50E **229** D12
Zhengyang *China* 32°37N 114°22E **229** A10
Zhengyangguan *China* 32°30N 116°29E **229** A11
Zhengzhou *China* 34°45N 113°34E **226** G7
Zhenhai *China* 29°59N 121°42E **229** C13
Zhenjiang *China* 32°11N 119°26E **229** A12
Zhenkang *China* 23°58N 99°0E **228** F2
Zhenlai *China* 45°50N 123°5E **227** B12
Zhenning *China* 26°4N 105°45E **228** D5
Zhenping *Henan, China* 33°10N 112°16E **226** H7
Zhenping *Shaanxi, China* 31°59N 109°31E **228** B7
Zhenru *China* 31°16N 121°22E **138** B1
Zhenxiong *China* 27°27N 104°50E **228** D5
Zhenyuan *Gansu, China* 35°35N 107°30E **226** G4
Zhenyuan *Guizhou, China* 27°4N 108°21E **228** D7
Zherdevka *Russia* 51°56N 41°29E **190** E5
Zherebkove *Ukraine* 47°50N 29°52E **183** C14
Zhernovka *Russia* 59°56N 30°30E **137** B2
Zherong *China* 27°15N 119°52E **229** D12
Zhetiqara *Kazakhstan* 52°11N 61°12E **216** B6
Zhezdi *Kazakhstan* 48°3N 67°3E **217** C7
Zhezqazghan *Kazakhstan* 47°44N 67°40E **217** C7
Zhicheng *China* 30°25N 111°27E **229** B8
Zhicun *China* 23°0N 113°18E **121** B2
Zhidan *China* 36°48N 108°48E **226** F5
Zhigansk *Russia* 66°48N 123°27E **215** C13
Zhigulevsk *Russia* 53°28N 49°30E **190** D9
Zhijiang *Hubei, China* 30°28N 111°45E **229** B8
Zhijiang *Hunan, China* 27°27N 109°42E **228** D7
Zhijin *China* 26°37N 105°45E **228** D5
Zhilinda *Russia* 70°0N 114°20E **215** C12
Zhilino *Russia* 54°54N 21°54E **184** D8
Zhirnovsk *Russia* 50°57N 44°49E **190** E7
Zhirnovsky = Zhirnovsk *Russia* 50°57N 44°49E **190** E7
Zhirnoye = Zhirnovsk *Russia* 50°57N 44°49E **190** E7
Zhitomir = Zhytomyr *Ukraine* 50°20N 28°40E **177** C15
Zhizdra *Russia* 53°45N 34°40E **188** F8
Zhlobin *Belarus* 52°55N 30°0E **177** B16
Zhmerinka = Zhmerynka *Ukraine* 49°2N 28°2E **177** D15
Zhmerynka *Ukraine* 49°2N 28°2E **177** D15
Zhob *Pakistan* 31°20N 69°31E **242** D3
Zhob ➔ *Pakistan* 32°4N 69°50E **242** C3
Zhodino = Zhodzina *Belarus* 54°5N 28°17E **177** A15
Zhodzina *Belarus* 54°5N 28°17E **177** A15
Zhokhova, Ostrov *Russia* 76°4N 152°40E **215** B16
Zholkev = Nesterov *Ukraine* 50°4N 23°58E **177** C12
Zholkva = Nesterov *Ukraine* 50°4N 23°58E **177** C12
Zhongdian *China* 27°48N 99°42E **228** D2
Zhongdong *China* 22°48N 107°47E **228** F6
Zhongdu *China* 24°40N 109°40E **228** E7
Zhongning *China* 37°29N 105°40E **226** F3
Zhongshan *Antarctica* 69°0S 39°50E **151** C6
Zhongshan *Guangdong, China* 22°26N 113°20E **219** G9
Zhongshan *Guangxi Zhuangzu, China* 24°29N 111°18E **229** E8
Zhongshan Park *Beijing, China* **114** b2
Zhongshan Park *Shanghai, China* 31°13N 121°24E **138** B1
Zhongshankong *China* 22°35N 113°29E **219** F9
Zhongtiao Shan *China* 35°0N 111°10E **226** G6
Zhongwei *China* 37°30N 105°12E **226** F3
Zhongxiang *China* 31°12N 112°34E **229** B9
Zhongyang *China* 37°20N 111°11E **226** F6
Zhorany *Ukraine* 51°19N 23°58E **185** G10
Zhosaly *Kazakhstan* 45°29N 64°4E **216** C6
Zhoucun *Guangdong, China* 23°11N 113°11E **121** A2
Zhoucun *Shandong, China* 36°47N 117°48E **227** F9
Zhoujiadu *China* 31°11N 121°29E **138** B1
Zhoujiazhen *China* 31°16N 121°33E **138** B2
Zhouning *China* 27°12N 119°20E **229** D12
Zhoushan *China* 30°1N 122°6E **229** B14
Zhoushan Dao *China* 30°5N 122°10E **229** C14
Zhouzhi *China* 34°10N 108°12E **226** G5
Zhovti Vody *Ukraine* 48°21N 33°31E **189** H7
Zhovtneve *Lubelskie, Ukraine* 50°42N 24°12E **185** H11
Zhovtneve *Mykolayiv, Ukraine* 46°54N 32°3E **189** J7
Zhovtnevoye = Zhovtneve *Ukraine* 46°54N 32°3E **189** J7
Zhu Jiang ➔ *China* 22°45N 113°37E **229** F9
Zhuanghe *China* 39°40N 123°0E **224** C1
Zhucheng *China* 36°0N 119°27E **227** G10
Zhugqu *China* 33°40N 104°30E **226** H3
Zhuhai *China* 22°17N 113°34E **219** G10
Zhuji *China* 29°40N 120°10E **229** C13
Zhujiang Kou *China* 22°20N 113°45E **219** G10
Zhukovka *Russia* 53°35N 33°50E **188** F7
Zhulebino *Russia* 55°42N 37°50E **129** B5
Zhumadian *China* 32°59N 114°2E **226** H8
Zhuo Xian = Zhuozhou *China* 39°28N 115°58E **226** E8
Zhuolu *China* 40°20N 115°12E **226** D8
Zhuozhou *China* 39°28N 115°58E **226** E8
Zhuozi *China* 41°0N 112°25E **226** D7
Zhushadi *China* 23°11N 113°22E **121** A3
Zhushan *China* 32°15N 110°13E **229** A8
Zhuxi *China* 32°25N 109°40E **228** A7
Zhuzhou *China* 27°49N 113°12E **229** D9
Zhvanets *Ukraine* 48°33N 26°30E **183** B11
Zhympīty *Kazakhstan* 50°16N 52°35E **216** B4
Zhytomyr *Ukraine* 50°20N 28°40E **177** C15
Zhytomyr □ *Ukraine* 50°50N 28°10E **189** G5
Zi Shui ➔ *China* 28°40N 112°40E **229** C9
Žiar nad Hronom *Slovak Rep.* 48°35N 18°53E **181** C11
Zīārān *Iran* 36°7N 50°32E **247** B6
Ziarat *Pakistan* 30°25N 67°49E **242** D2
Zibo *China* 36°47N 118°3E **227** F10
Zichang *China* 37°18N 109°40E **226** F5
Zidarovo *Bulgaria* 42°20N 27°24E **203** D11
Zidi = Wandhari *Pakistan* 27°42N 66°48E **242** F2
Ziębice *Poland* 50°37N 17°2E **185** H4
Ziebingen = Cybinka *Poland* 52°12N 14°46E **185** F1
Ziegenhals = Głuchołazy *Poland* 50°19N 17°24E **185** H4
Zielenzig = Sulęcin *Poland* 52°26N 15°10E **185** F2
Zielona *Poland* 52°14N 21°11E **142** B3
Zielona Góra *Poland* 51°57N 15°31E **185** G2
Zielonka *Poland* 52°18N 21°9E **142** B2
Zierikzee *Neths.* 51°40N 3°55E **170** C3
Ziesar *Germany* 52°16N 12°17E **178** C8
Zifta *Egypt* 30°43N 31°14E **256** H7
Zigey *Chad* 14°43N 15°50E **259** F3
Zigon *Burma* 18°20N 95°37E **241** F5
Zigong *China* 29°15N 104°48E **228** C5
Ziguinchor *Senegal* 12°35N 16°20W **262** C1
Ziguinchor □ *Senegal* 12°45N 16°20W **262** C1
Zihuatanejo *Mexico* 17°39N 101°33W **318** D4
Zijin *China* 23°33N 115°8E **229** F10
Zile *Turkey* 40°15N 35°52E **212** B6
Žilina *Slovak Rep.* 49°12N 18°42E **181** B11
Žilinský □ *Slovak Rep.* 49°10N 19°0E **181** B12
Zillah *Libya* 28°30N 17°33E **258** C3
Zillertaler Alpen *Austria* 47°6N 11°45E **180** D4
Zima *Russia* 54°0N 102°5E **215** D11
Zimane, Adrar in *Algeria* 22°10N 4°30E **261** D5
Zimapán *Mexico* 20°45N 99°21W **319** C5
Zimba *Zambia* 17°20S 26°11E **269** F2
Zimbabwe *Zimbabwe* 20°16S 30°54E **269** G3
Zimbabwe ■ *Africa* 19°0S 30°0E **269** F3
Zimi *S. Leone* 7°20N 11°20W **262** D2
Zimnicea *Romania* 43°40N 25°22E **183** G10
Zimovniki *Russia* 47°10N 42°25E **191** G6
Zina *Cameroon* 11°19N 14°54E **259** F2
Zinave △ *Mozam.* 21°35S 33°40E **271** B5
Zinder *Niger* 13°48N 9°0E **259** F1
Zinder □ *Niger* 15°0N 10°30E **263** C7
Zinga *C.A.R.* 3°49N 18°34E **264** B3
Zinga *Tanzania* 9°16S 38°49E **269** D4
Zingaro ⌓ *Italy* 38°6N 12°53E **200** D5
Zingst *Germany* 54°26N 12°39E **178** A8
Ziniaré *Burkina Faso* 12°35N 1°18W **263** C4
Zinnowitz *Germany* 54°4N 13°54E **178** A9
Zinovyevsk = Kirovohrad *Ukraine* 48°35N 32°20E **189** H7
Zion *St. Kitts & Nevis* 17°8N 62°33W **322** d
Zion *Ill., U.S.A.* 42°27N 87°50W **311** B9
Zion △ *U.S.A.* 37°15N 113°5W **305** H7
Zionsville *U.S.A.* 39°57N 86°16W **311** E10
Zipaquirá *Colombia* 5°0N 74°0W **328** C3
Zirbitzkogel *Austria* 47°4N 14°34E **180** D7
Zirc *Hungary* 47°17N 17°52E **182** C2
Žiri *Slovenia* 46°5N 14°5E **199** B11
Žirje *Croatia* 43°39N 15°42E **199** E12
Zirke = Sieraków *Poland* 52°39N 16°2E **185** F3
Zirl *Austria* 47°17N 11°14E **180** D4
Zirndorf *Germany* 49°27N 10°57E **179** F6
Ziros *Greece* 35°5N 26°8E **207** E7
Zirreh, Gowd-e *Afghan.* 29°45N 62°0E **240** C1
Zisterdorf *Austria* 48°33N 16°45E **181** C9
Zitácuaro *Mexico* 19°24N 100°22W **318** D4
Žitava ➔ *Slovak Rep.* 48°14N 18°21E **181** C11
Žitište *Serbia* 45°30N 20°32E **182** E5
Zitong *China* 31°37N 105°10E **228** B5
Zitsa *Greece* 39°47N 20°40E **204** B2
Zittau *Germany* 50°53N 14°48E **178** E10
Zitundo *Mozam.* 26°48S 32°47E **271** C5
Živinice *Bos.-H.* 44°27N 18°36E **182** F3
Ziwa Maghariba = Kagera □ *Tanzania* 2°0S 31°30E **268** C3
Ziway, L. *Ethiopia* 8°0N 38°50E **257** F4
Zixi *China* 27°45N 117°4E **229** D11
Zixing *China* 25°59N 113°21E **229** E9
Ziyang *Shaanxi, China* 32°32N 108°31E **226** H5
Ziyang *Sichuan, China* 30°6N 104°40E **228** B5
Ziyuan *China* 26°2N 110°40E **229** D8
Ziyun *China* 25°45N 106°5E **228** E6
Ziz, Oued ➔ *Morocco* 31°40N 4°15W **260** B4
Zizhong *China* 29°48N 104°47E **228** C5
Žižkov *Czech Rep.* 50°5N 14°28E **135** B2
Zlarin *Croatia* 43°42N 15°49E **199** E12
Zlatar *Croatia* 46°5N 16°3E **199** B13
Zlatar *Serbia* 43°25N 19°47E **202** C3
Zlataritsa *Bulgaria* 43°2N 25°55E **203** C9
Zlaté Moravce *Slovak Rep.* 48°23N 18°24E **181** C11
Zlatibor *Serbia* 43°45N 19°43E **202** C3
Zlatitsa *Bulgaria* 42°41N 24°7E **203** D8
Zlatna *Romania* 46°8N 23°11E **183** D8
Zlatna Panega *Bulgaria* 43°5N 24°9E **203** C8
Zlatni Pyasŭtsi *Bulgaria* 43°17N 28°3E **203** C12
Zlatograd *Bulgaria* 41°22N 25°7E **203** E9
Zlatoust *Russia* 55°10N 59°40E **186** C10
Zletovo *Macedonia* 41°59N 22°17E **202** E6
Zličín *Czech Rep.* 50°3N 14°17E **135** B1
Zlín *Czech Rep.* 49°14N 17°40E **181** B10
Zlínský □ *Czech Rep.* 49°20N 17°40E **181** B10
Zlītan *Libya* 32°32N 14°35E **258** B2
Złocieniec *Poland* 53°30N 16°1E **184** E3
Złoczew *Poland* 51°24N 18°35E **185** G5
Zlot *Serbia* 44°1N 21°58E **202** B5
Złotoryja *Poland* 51°8N 15°55E **185** G2
Złotów *Poland* 53°22N 17°2E **184** E4
Zmeinogorsk *Kazakhstan* 51°10N 82°13E **217** B10
Żmigród *Poland* 51°28N 16°53E **185** G3
Zmiyev *Ukraine* 49°39N 36°27E **189** H9
Znamenka = Znamyanka *Ukraine* 48°45N 32°30E **189** H7
Znamensk *Russia* 54°36N 21°16E **184** D8
Znamyanka *Ukraine* 48°45N 32°30E **189** H7
Żnin *Poland* 52°51N 17°44E **185** F4
Znojmo *Czech Rep.* 48°50N 16°2E **180** C9
Zobeyrī *Iran* 34°10N 46°40E **246** C5
Zobia *Dem. Rep. of the Congo* 3°0N 25°59E **268** B2
Zobten = Sobótka *Poland* 50°54N 16°44E **185** H3
Zócalo *Mexico City, Mexico* **128** b3
Zoetermeer *Neths.* 52°3N 4°30E **170** B4
Zogang *China* 29°55N 97°42E **228** C1
Zogno *Italy* 45°48N 9°40E **198** C6
Zogqên *China* 32°13N 98°47E **228** A2
Zografou *Greece* 37°58N 23°47E **112** B2
Zolfo Springs *U.S.A.* 27°30N 81°48W **317** H8
Żoliborz *Poland* 52°16N 20°57E **142** B1
Zolochev = Zolochiv *Ukraine* 49°45N 24°51E **177** D13
Zolochiv *Ukraine* 49°45N 24°51E **177** D13
Zolotonosha *Ukraine* 49°39N 32°5E **189** H7
Zolotyy Potik *Ukraine* 48°54N 25°20E **183** B10
Zomba *Malawi* 15°22S 35°19E **269** F4
Zongo *Dem. Rep. of the Congo* 4°20N 18°35E **264** B3
Zonguldak *Turkey* 41°28N 31°50E **212** B4
Zonguldak □ *Turkey* 41°20N 31°45E **212** B4
Zongyang *China* 30°42N 117°12E **229** B11
Zonnebloem *S. Africa* 33°56S 18°26E **118** A1
Zonqor Pt. *Malta* 35°52N 14°34E **206** F8
Zonza *France* 41°45N 9°11E **175** G13
Zoo Baba *Niger* 18°13N 13°2E **259** E2
Zorgo *Burkina Faso* 12°15N 0°35W **263** C4
Zorita *Spain* 39°17N 5°39W **195** F5
Zorleni *Romania* 46°14N 27°44E **183** D12
Zornitsa *Bulgaria* 42°23N 26°58E **203** D10
Zorritos *Peru* 3°43S 80°40W **330** A1
Żory *Poland* 50°3N 18°44E **185** H5
Zorzor *Liberia* 7°46N 9°28W **262** D3
Zossen *Germany* 52°13N 13°27E **178** C9
Zou Xiang *China* 35°30N 116°58E **226** G9
Zouan-Hounien *Ivory C.* 6°55N 8°15W **262** D3
Zouar *Chad* 20°30N 16°32E **259** D3
Zouérate = Zouîrât *Mauritania* 22°44N 12°21W **260** D2
Zouîrât *Mauritania* 22°44N 12°21W **260** D2
Zouri *Gabon* 1°1S 8°53E **264** C1
Zourika *Niger* 19°16N 7°52E **259** E1
Zourma *Burkina Faso* 11°20N 0°50W **263** C4
Zousfana, O. ➔ *Algeria* 31°28N 2°17W **261** B4
Zoutkamp *Neths.* 53°20N 6°18E **170** A6
Zrenjanin *Serbia* 45°22N 20°23E **182** E5
Zuarungu *Ghana* 10°49N 0°46W **263** C4
Zuba *Nigeria* 9°11N 7°12E **263** D6
Zubayr *Yemen* 15°3N 42°10E **248** D3
Zubtsov *Russia* 56°10N 34°34E **188** D8
Zudáñez *Bolivia* 19°6S 64°44W **331** D5
Zuénoula *Ivory C.* 7°34N 6°3W **262** D3
Zuera *Spain* 41°51N 0°49W **196** D4
Zuetina = Az Zuwaytīnah *Libya* 30°58N 20°7E **258** B4
Ẓufār *Oman* 17°40N 54°0E **249** C6
Zug *Switz.* 47°10N 8°31E **179** H4
Zug *W. Sahara* 21°36N 14°9W **260** D2
Zugdidi *Georgia* 42°30N 41°55E **191** J5
Zugersee *Switz.* 47°7N 8°35E **179** H4
Zugliget *Hungary* 47°30N 18°59E **117** B1
Zugló *Hungary* 47°31N 19°8E **117** A2
Zugspitze *Germany* 47°25N 10°59E **179** H6
Zuhd, J. az *Si. Arabia* 28°20N 35°17E **251** K6
Zuid-Holland □ *Neths.* 52°0N 4°35E **170** C4
Zuidbeveland *Neths.* 51°30N 3°50E **170** C3
Zuiderwoude *Neths.* 52°26N 5°2E **112** A3
Zuidhorn *Neths.* 53°15N 6°23E **170** A6
Zújar *Spain* 37°34N 2°50W **195** H8
Zújar ➔ *Spain* 39°1N 5°47W **195** G5
Żukowo *Poland* 54°21N 18°22E **184** D5
Zula *Eritrea* 15°17N 39°40E **257** D4
Zulia □ *Venezuela* 10°0N 72°10W **328** B3
Züllichau = Sulechów *Poland* 52°5N 15°40E **185** F2
Zülpich *Germany* 50°41N 6°39E **178** E2
Zülz = Biała *Poland* 50°24N 17°40E **185** H4
Zumaia *Spain* 43°19N 2°15W **196** B2
Zumárraga *Spain* 43°5N 2°19W **196** B2
Zumbi *Brazil* 22°49S 43°10W **135** A1
Zumbo *Mozam.* 15°35S 30°26E **269** F3
Zummo *Nigeria* 9°51N 12°59E **263** D7
Zumpango *Mexico* 19°48N 99°6W **319** D5
Zunderdorp *Neths.* 52°24N 4°58E **112** A2
Zundi *Angola* 10°28S 16°48E **265** E3
Zungeru *Nigeria* 9°48N 6°8E **263** D6
Zunhua *China* 40°18N 117°58E **227** D9
Zuni Pueblo *U.S.A.* 35°4N 108°51W **305** J9
Zunyi *China* 27°42N 106°53E **228** D6
Zuo Jiang ➔ *China* 22°50N 108°6E **228** F6
Zuozhou *China* 22°42N 107°27E **228** F6
Županja *Croatia* 45°4N 18°43E **182** E3
Žur *Serbia* 42°13N 20°34E **202** D4
Zurbātīyah *Iraq* 33°9N 46°3E **213** F12
Zürich *Switz.* 47°22N 8°32E **179** H4
Zürich □ *Switz.* 47°26N 8°40E **179** H4
Zürichsee *Switz.* 47°18N 8°40E **179** H4
Żuromin *Poland* 53°4N 19°51E **185** E6
Zurrieq *Malta* 35°50N 14°28E **206** F7
Žut *Croatia* 43°52N 15°17E **199** E12
Zutphen *Neths.* 52°9N 6°12E **170** B6
Zuurberg △ *S. Africa* 33°12S 25°32E **270** D4
Zuvuvu ➔ *Brazil* 23°40S 46°42W **137** C1
Zuwārah *Libya* 32°58N 12°1E **258** B2
Zūzan *Iran* 34°22N 59°53E **247** C8
Žužemberk *Slovenia* 45°52N 14°56E **199** C11
Zvanka = Volkhov *Russia* 59°55N 32°15E **188** C7
Zvenigorodka = Zvenyhorodka *Ukraine* 49°4N 30°56E **189** H6
Zvenyhorodka *Ukraine* 49°4N 30°56E **189** H6
Zvezdets *Bulgaria* 42°6N 27°26E **203** D11
Zvishavane *Zimbabwe* 20°17S 30°2E **269** G3
Zvolen *Slovak Rep.* 48°33N 19°10E **181** C12
Zvonce *Serbia* 42°57N 22°34E **202** D6
Zvornik *Bos.-H.* 44°26N 19°5E **182** F4
Zwanenburg *Neths.* 52°23N 4°45E **112** A1
Zwedru = Tchien *Liberia* 5°59N 8°15W **262** D3
Zweibrücken *Germany* 49°15N 7°21E **179** F3
Zwenkau *Germany* 51°13N 12°20E **178** D8
Zwettl *Austria* 48°35N 15°9E **180** C8
Zwickau *Germany* 50°44N 12°30E **178** E8
Zwierzyniec *Poland* 50°36N 22°58E **185** H9
Zwiesel *Germany* 49°1N 13°13E **179** F9
Zwittau = Svitavy *Czech Rep.* 49°47N 16°28E **181** B9
Zwoleń *Poland* 51°21N 21°36E **185** G8
Zwölfaxing *Austria* 48°6N 16°28E **142** B2
Zwolle *Neths.* 52°31N 6°6E **170** B6
Zwolle *La., U.S.A.* 31°38N 93°39W **314** F8
Żychlin *Poland* 52°15N 19°37E **185** F6
Żyrardów *Poland* 52°3N 20°28E **185** F7
Zyryan *Kazakhstan* 49°43N 84°20E **217** C10
Zyryanka *Russia* 65°45N 150°51E **215** C16
Zyryanovsk = Zyryan *Kazakhstan* 49°43N 84°20E **217** C10
Zyuzino *Russia* 55°39N 37°34E **129** C3
Żywiec *Poland* 49°42N 19°10E **185** J6

WORLD: REGIONS IN THE NEWS

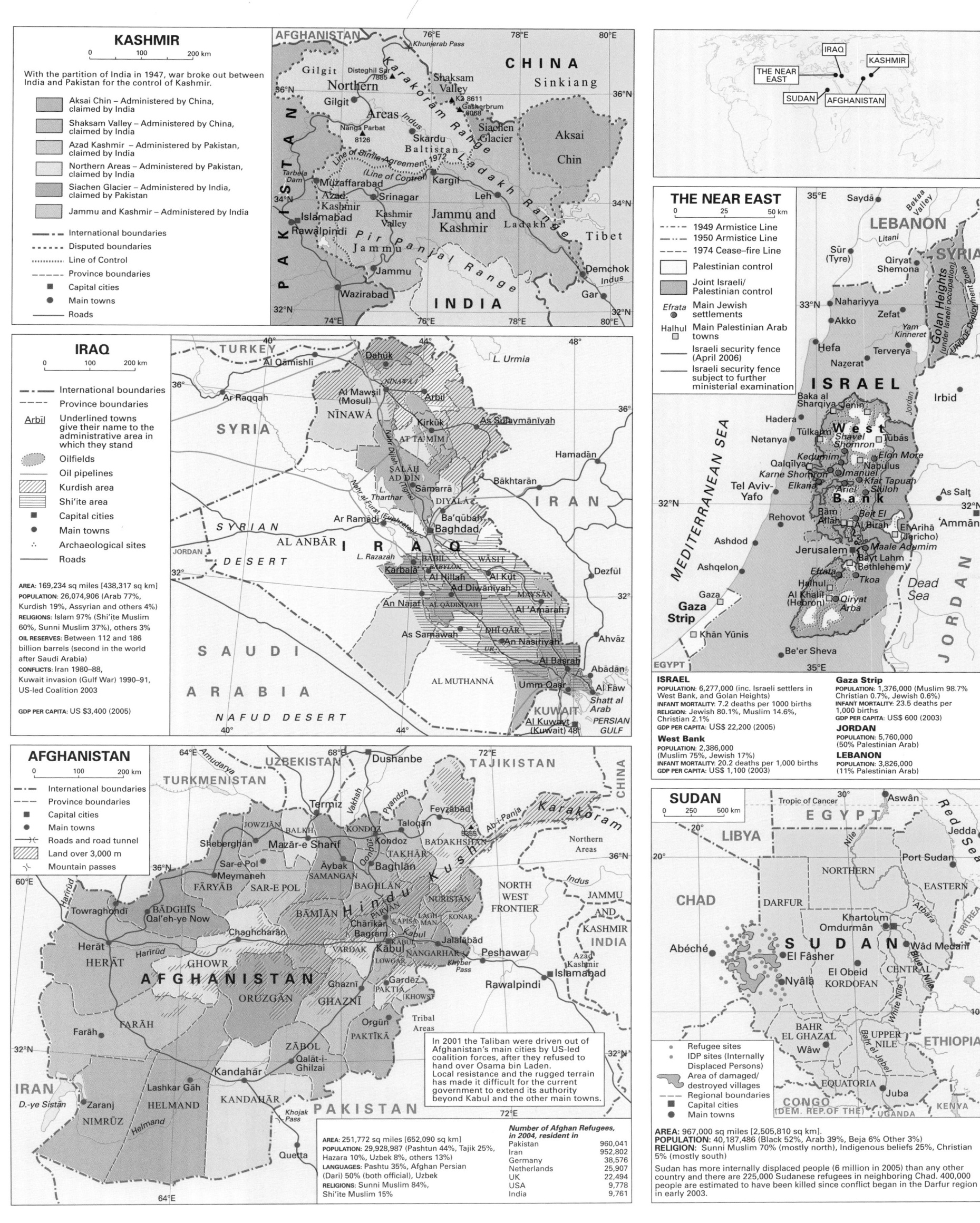

KASHMIR

0   100   200 km

With the partition of India in 1947, war broke out between India and Pakistan for the control of Kashmir.

- Aksai Chin – Administered by China, claimed by India
- Shaksam Valley – Administered by China, claimed by India
- Azad Kashmir – Administered by Pakistan, claimed by India
- Northern Areas – Administered by Pakistan, claimed by India
- Siachen Glacier – Administered by India, claimed by Pakistan
- Jammu and Kashmir – Administered by India

- — · — International boundaries
- — — — Disputed boundaries
- ········· Line of Control
- — — — Province boundaries
- ■ Capital cities
- ● Main towns
- —— Roads

IRAQ

0   100   200 km

- — · — International boundaries
- — — — Province boundaries
- Arbīl Underlined towns give their name to the administrative area in which they stand
- Oilfields
- Oil pipelines
- Kurdish area
- Shi'ite area
- ■ Capital cities
- ● Main towns
- ∴ Archaeological sites
- —— Roads

AREA: 169,234 sq miles [438,317 sq km]
POPULATION: 26,074,906 (Arab 77%, Kurdish 19%, Assyrian and others 4%)
RELIGIONS: Islam 97% (Shi'ite Muslim 60%, Sunni Muslim 37%), others 3%
OIL RESERVES: Between 112 and 186 billion barrels (second in the world after Saudi Arabia)
CONFLICTS: Iran 1980–88, Kuwait invasion (Gulf War) 1990–91, US-led Coalition 2003

GDP PER CAPITA: US $3,400 (2005)

AFGHANISTAN

0   100   200 km

- — · — International boundaries
- — — — Province boundaries
- ■ Capital cities
- ● Main towns
- —— Roads and road tunnel
- Land over 3,000 m
- ⋏ Mountain passes

In 2001 the Taliban were driven out of Afghanistan's main cities by US-led coalition forces, after they refused to hand over Osama bin Laden.
Local resistance and the rugged terrain has made it difficult for the current government to extend its authority beyond Kabul and the other main towns.

AREA: 251,772 sq miles [652,090 sq km]
POPULATION: 29,928,987 (Pashtun 44%, Tajik 25%, Hazara 10%, Uzbek 8%, others 13%)
LANGUAGES: Pashtu 35%, Afghan Persian (Dari) 50% (both official), Uzbek
RELIGIONS: Sunni Muslim 84%, Shi'ite Muslim 15%

Number of Afghan Refugees, in 2004, resident in

Pakistan	960,041
Iran	952,802
Germany	38,576
Netherlands	25,907
UK	22,494
USA	9,778
India	9,761

THE NEAR EAST

0   25   50 km

- — · — 1949 Armistice Line
- — — — 1950 Armistice Line
- — — — 1974 Cease-fire Line
- Palestinian control
- Joint Israeli/ Palestinian control
- *Efrata* Main Jewish settlements
- *Halhul* Main Palestinian Arab towns
- □ Israeli security fence (April 2006)
- — Israeli security fence subject to further ministerial examination

ISRAEL
POPULATION: 6,277,000 (inc. Israeli settlers in West Bank, and Golan Heights)
INFANT MORTALITY: 7.2 deaths per 1000 births
RELIGION: Jewish 80.1%, Muslim 14.6%, Christian 2.1%
GDP PER CAPITA: US$ 22,200 (2005)

West Bank
POPULATION: 2,386,000 (Muslim 75%, Jewish 17%)
INFANT MORTALITY: 20.2 deaths per 1,000 births
GDP PER CAPITA: US$ 1,100 (2003)

Gaza Strip
POPULATION: 1,376,000 (Muslim 98.7% Christian 0.7%, Jewish 0.6%)
INFANT MORTALITY: 23.5 deaths per 1,000 births
GDP PER CAPITA: US$ 600 (2003)

JORDAN
POPULATION: 5,760,000 (50% Palestinian Arab)

LEBANON
POPULATION: 3,826,000 (11% Palestinian Arab)

SUDAN

0   250   500 km

- ● Refugee sites
- ● IDP sites (Internally Displaced Persons)
- Area of damaged/ destroyed villages
- — — — Regional boundaries
- ■ Capital cities
- ● Main towns

AREA: 967,000 sq miles [2,505,810 sq km]
POPULATION: 40,187,486 (Black 52%, Arab 39%, Beja 6% Other 3%)
RELIGION: Sunni Muslim 70% (mostly north), Indigenous beliefs 25%, Christian 5% (mostly south)

Sudan has more internally displaced people (6 million in 2005) than any other country and there are 225,000 Sudanese refugees in neighboring Chad. 400,000 people are estimated to have been killed since conflict began in the Darfur region in early 2003.

KEY TO EUROPEAN MAP PAGES

 Large scale maps
(>1:3 900 000)

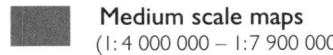 Medium scale maps
(1:4 000 000 – 1:7 900 000)

 Small scale maps
(<1:8 000 000)

● Paris p134   City maps

155 ICELAND

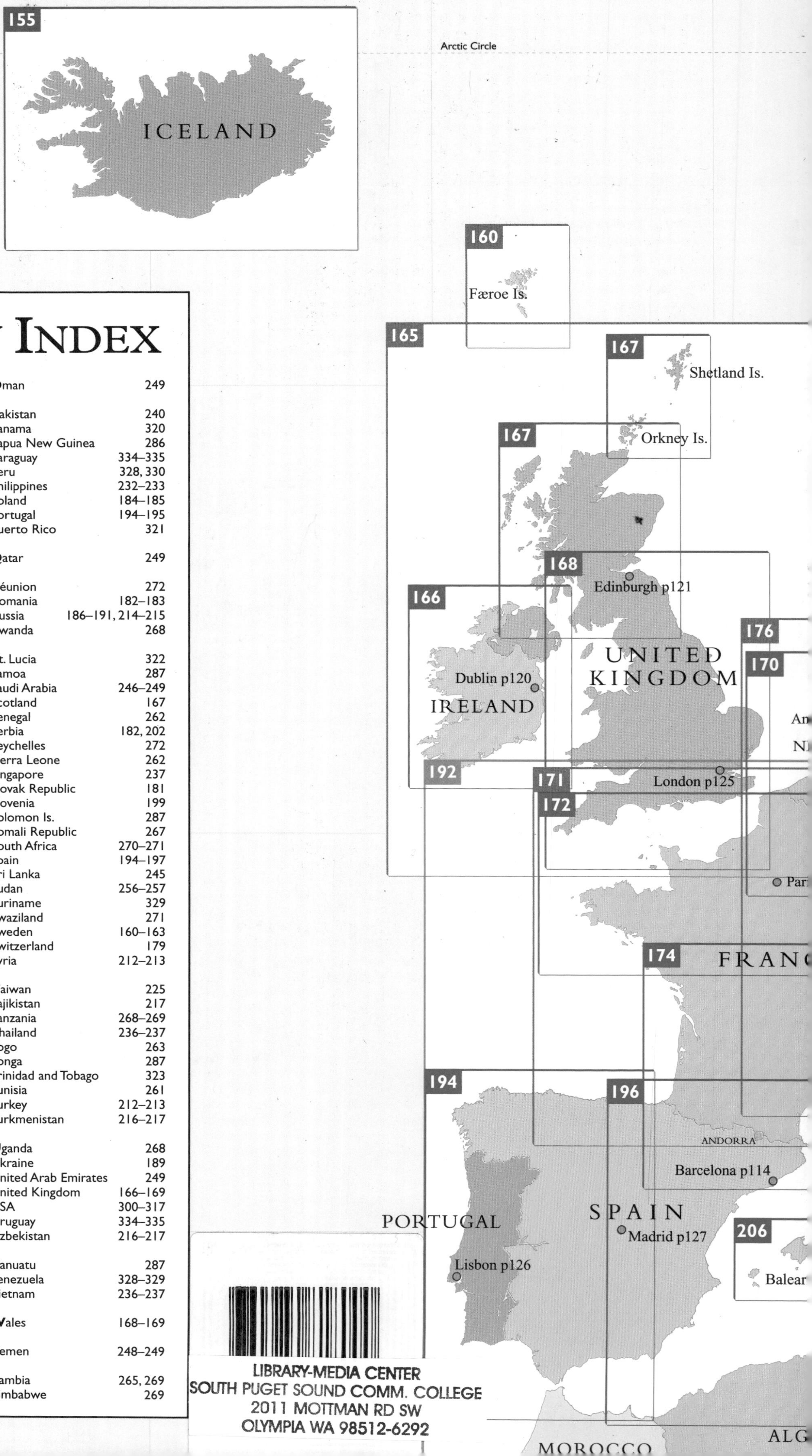

Arctic Circle

160 Færoe Is.

165

167 Shetland Is.

167 Orkney Is.

168 Edinburgh p121

166

176

170

UNITED KINGDOM

166 Dublin p120

IRELAND

192

171 London p125

172

174 FRANC

194

196

ANDORRA

Barcelona p114

PORTUGAL

SPAIN

Madrid p127

Lisbon p126

206 Balear

MOROCCO

ALG

An

N

Par

WORLD COUNTRY INDEX

Afghanistan 240
Albania 202
Algeria 260–261
Angola 265
Argentina 334, 336
Armenia 213
Australia 278–283
Austria 180–181
Azerbaijan 213
Azores 153

Bahamas 320–321
Bahrain 249
Bangladesh 241
Barbados 322
Belarus 188–189
Belgium 170
Belize 320
Benin 263
Bhutan 241
Bolivia 330–331
Bosnia-Herzegovina 198, 202
Botswana 270
Brazil 328–335
Brunei 235
Bulgaria 202–203
Burkina Faso 262–263
Burma (Myanmar) 236–237, 241
Burundi 268

Cambodia 236–237
Canary Is. 153
Cameroon 259, 264
Canada 294–299
Cape Verde Is. 153
Central African Republic 264
Chad 259
Chile 330, 334, 336
China 218–219, 226–229
Colombia 328
Comoros 272
Congo 264–265
Congo, Dem. Rep. of the 264–265, 268–269
Costa Rica 320
Croatia 182, 199
Cuba 320–321
Cyprus 207
Czech Republic 180–181

Denmark 163
Djibouti 267
Dominican Republic 321

Ecuador 328
Egypt 256
El Salvador 320
England 168–169
Equatorial Guinea 264
Eritrea 266–267
Estonia 188
Ethiopia 266–267

Fiji 287
Finland 160–161
France 172–175
French Guiana 329

Gabon 264
Gambia 262
Georgia 213

Germany 178–179
Ghana 262–263
Greece 202–205
Greenland 154
Guadeloupe 322
Guatemala 320
Guinea 262
Guinea-Bissau 262
Guyana 329

Haiti 321
Honduras 320
Hungary 182

Iceland 155
India 241, 242–245
Indonesia 230–231, 234–235
Iran 246–247
Iraq 246–247
Irish Republic 166
Israel 250–251
Italy 198–201
Ivory Coast 262

Jamaica 320
Japan 220–223
Jordan 251

Kazakhstan 216–217
Kenya 268
Korea, North 224
Korea, South 224
Kuwait 246–247
Kyrgyzstan 217

Laos 236
Latvia 188
Lebanon 250
Lesotho 271
Liberia 262
Libya 258
Lithuania 188
Luxembourg 170

Macedonia 202
Madagascar 272
Malawi 269
Malaysia 234–235
Mali 260–263
Malta 206
Martinique 322
Mauritania 260, 262
Mauritius 272
Mexico 318–319
Moldova 183
Mongolia 218–219
Montenegro 202
Morocco 260–261
Mozambique 269, 271

Namibia 270
Nepal 243
Netherlands 170
New Zealand 284–285
Nicaragua 320
Niger 259, 263
Nigeria 263
Northern Ireland 166
Norway 160–161, 164

Oman 249

Pakistan 240
Panama 320
Papua New Guinea 286
Paraguay 334–335
Peru 328, 330
Philippines 232–233
Poland 184–185
Portugal 194–195
Puerto Rico 321

Qatar 249

Réunion 272
Romania 182–183
Russia 186–191, 214–215
Rwanda 268

St. Lucia 322
Samoa 287
Saudi Arabia 246–249
Scotland 167
Senegal 262
Serbia 182, 202
Seychelles 272
Sierra Leone 262
Singapore 237
Slovak Republic 181
Slovenia 199
Solomon Is. 287
Somali Republic 267
South Africa 270–271
Spain 194–197
Sri Lanka 245
Sudan 256–257
Suriname 329
Swaziland 271
Sweden 160–163
Switzerland 179
Syria 212–213

Taiwan 225
Tajikistan 217
Tanzania 268–269
Thailand 236–237
Togo 263
Tonga 287
Trinidad and Tobago 323
Tunisia 261
Turkey 212–213
Turkmenistan 216–217

Uganda 268
Ukraine 189
United Arab Emirates 249
United Kingdom 166–169
USA 300–317
Uruguay 334–335
Uzbekistan 216–217

Vanuatu 287
Venezuela 328–329
Vietnam 236–237

Wales 168–169

Yemen 248–249

Zambia 265, 269
Zimbabwe 269